The **Columbia Gazetteer** of North America

The Columbia

Gazetteer of North America

Edited by SAUL B. COHEN

COLUMBIA UNIVERSITY PRESS New York

Columbia University Press

Publishers since 1893

New York   Chichester, West Sussex

Copyright © by Columbia University Press 2000

The Columbia Gazetteer of the World

Copyright © by Columbia University Press 1998

The Columbia Lippincott Gazetteer of the World

Copyright © by

Columbia University Press 1952, 1962

Maps copyright © by RMC, R.L. 00-S-10

www.randmcnally.com

Copyright under the Berne Convention

All rights reserved

Library of Congress

Cataloging-in-Publication Data

The Columbia gazetteer of North America /

edited by Saul B. Cohen

  p. cm.

Includes bibliographical references (p.).

ISBN 0-231-11990-9 (alk. paper)

1. North America—Gazetteers. I. Cohen, Saul Bernard.

E35 .C65 2000

917′.003—dc21

00-027512

∞

Casebound editions of

Columbia University Press

books are printed on permanent

and durable acid-free paper.

Printed in the United States

of America

Full-color map insert follows page 496.

Preface

With 50,000 entries, *The Columbia Gazetteer of North America* is far and away the most comprehensive encyclopedia of the geographical places and features of the region. The entries, drawn from the 1998 *Columbia Gazetteer of the World*, are designed to meet two goals—accuracy and maximum coverage of places and features. The information that is presented reflects the input of 58 geographical specialists intimately familiar with a wide variety of sources, and with personal knowledge of the places and data described in these sources.

The Gazetteer covers every incorporated place and county in the United States, along with several thousand unincorporated places, special-purpose sites, and physical features. The following categories indicate the scope, coverage, and sheer amount of information contained in the Gazetteer:

- The political world—regions, states, provinces, districts, counties, parishes, capitals, cities, towns, villages, neighborhoods, special districts.
- The physical world—continents, seas, gulfs, lakes, ponds, lagoons, rivers, bays, inlets, channels, streams, islands, archipelagoes, peninsulas, keys, sandbars, mountains, mountain ranges, plateaus, deserts, valleys, glaciers, volcanoes.
- Special places—national and state parks, forests, reserves and monuments, historic and archeological sites, resorts, theme parks, airports, ports, dams, nuclear plants, mines, canals, shopping malls, industrial zones, stadia, military bases, roads, highways, and expressways.

The Gazetteer is, in every sense, a guide to the profound changes that have taken place within North America and the Caribbean over the past half century, and thus has value to librarians; academic researchers; planners; students; writers; people in government, industry, and tourism; travelers; and all others for whom places hold fascination and who require accurate data about them.

The geography of the region has been altered by post-industrial, high-tech, financial service, resort, and tourist enterprises. Traditional manufacturing has weakened or disappeared from many parts of the United States, while holding its own in Canada, and increasing in parts of Mexico and the Caribbean. The number of family-owned farms in the U.S. continues to decline, as corporate farming exploits the benefits of scale. While grain and cattle producers worry about falling prices and declining export markets, those concentrating on specialized fruit, vegetable, and poultry output experience sustained growth.

The federal highway system of the U.S. has been extended to nearly every corner of the country, serving as the catalyst for urban and industrial development. Many of the military bases that proliferated during World War II have closed, while space-age–related centers have been developed. United States growth is reflected in such Gazetteer entries as those of San Jose, with its focus on the high technology of Silicon Valley, and Boston, with its Route 128–Yankee Division electronic highway. Charlotte, the third largest banking center in the United States; Cape Canaveral, with its John F. Kennedy Space Center; Miami's "Little Havana" created by the large influx of Cubans; and Vail, the nation's largest ski and summer recreation area—these all represent major developments that exemplify the post-World War II landscape.

Canada's main connection to the Pacific Rim, Vancouver, has flourished economically. Its largest metropolitan area, Toronto, which is the center for the country's manufacturing and service sectors, has benefited from the inflow of population and capital from Quebec.

In Mexico, cities within the "maquiladoras" duty-free border zone, such as Tiajuana, Juarez, and Matamoros, have attracted hundreds of thousands of manufacturing assembly jobs for the consumer products that are exported to the United States. Employment has also been stimulated by new, planned resorts along the Caribbean coast, such as Cancun and Cozumel. Bermuda has become a center for international financial services, including insurance and banking, which outstrip even its tourist industry as a source of income. The Cayman Islands, too, have emerged as an offshore banking center.

While there has been unprecedented economic expansion in much of North America and pockets of growth in the Caribbean, there has also been decline—in central cities throughout the United States; in the mill towns of the northeast; in the centers of the industrial "rustbelt" of the mid-west from Illinois, through Ohio, and also Pennsylvania. Major efforts at urban renewal have not wiped out the poverty of the ghettos. Economic recovery eludes Lowell, Massachusetts, new home to the second largest Cambodian population in the United States. The city had lost its textile mills and then saw the collapse of the computer industry that had replaced them. East St. Louis, once a transportation hub with nearby stockyards, remains depressed despite the introduction of river-boat gambling. The steel mills of Bethlehem, Pennsylvania, and Lackawanna, New York, are shuttered, as unemployment pervades these former centers of heavy industry.

Even the commercial nuclear power plants of the United

States are beginning to enter a period of decline. The number of plants skyrocketed from eighteen in the 1960s to 111 in 1990. However, no new stations have been authorized by the federal government since 1978. Yankee-Rowe in Franklin County, Massachusetts, the first nuclear power facility in the United States, was decommissioned in 1992, and other closings are scheduled.

Overpopulation, drought, and poor soils continue to plague rural Mexico, driving millions of peasants to migrate to Mexican cities or to the United States. Jamaica, too, remains mired in poverty; the sugar industry has declined, while new industries like bauxite mining, alumina, tourism, and apparel, cannot make up for the loss of agricultural jobs. In Cuba, the Castro government's efforts to diversify agriculture by decreasing the dependence upon sugar have failed, as sugar is still grown on two-thirds of all cropland. With the withdrawal of Russian economic and military aid, Cuba's economic difficulties have become endemic, as food and oil imports represent an increasingly heavy burden.

The foregoing are examples of the geographical changes represented in the North American Gazetteer's entries.

The spelling used in the Gazetteer takes into consideration that English-language spellings of foreign or native names vary considerably. While relying heavily on the spellings used by the U.S. Department of Interior's Board of Geographic Names, both for places within the United States and for foreign names, the editors have, at times, recommended alternative spellings. In general, the main headings of the entries are the names used by the official national agencies and transliterated into English.

The pronunciation of place-names in this Gazetteer follows the pronunciation guide found in Kenneth G. Wilson's *The Columbia Guide to Standard American English*, 1993. This guide is based on a rhyming scheme for words in the English language, and is commonly used by news broadcasters and newspapers.

I am deeply indebted to my editor colleagues—geographical scholars all—who gave unstintingly of their time and energies, and have helped bring this Gazetteer from concept to reality. I also wish to extend thanks and admiration to the Columbia University Press family, and especially to Lisa Hacken, Project Director of *The Columbia Gazetteer of the World*, Stephen Sterns, Managing Editor for the World Gazetteer and *The Columbia Gazetteer of North America*, James Raimes, Assistant Director of the Press for Reference Publishing, and William Strachan, Director of the Columbia University Press. Their commitment to the quality and integrity of the Gazetteer is in the highest scholarly traditions of an academic press.

Saul B. Cohen, Editor
University Professor Emeritus, Hunter College—CUNY

PUBLISHER
William B. Strachan

ASSISTANT DIRECTOR
OF THE PRESS FOR
REFERENCE PUBLISHING
James Raimes

CREATIVE DIRECTOR,
MANUFACTURING AND
TECHNOLOGY
Linda Secondari

BASED ON A DESIGN BY
Richard Hendel

PROJECT DIRECTOR
Lisa J. Hacken

MANAGING EDITOR
Stephen H. Sterns

ASSOCIATE EDITORS
Casper R. Grathwohl
Douglas M. Jacobs-Moore
Kathleen M. Kuntz
Susan H. McClung
Edward H. Morris
Paula J. Redes
Hua Shen

ASSISTANTS
Kathryn M. McGinley
Michael A. Olivo

FREELANCERS
Eric James Brestrup
Alex W. Costley
Christopher T. Fitzpatrick
Kathleen Luhrs
Matthew R. Rockwood

COPYEDITORS
Bruce I. Chadwick
Douglas Goertzen
Julia Kocich
Sonia Jaffe Robbins
David Robinson
Matthew R. Rockwood

PROOFREADERS
Sal Allocco
Jonathan G. Aretakis
Eve Minkoff Bayrock
Rachel Benzaquen
Joyce Brody
Mila Drumke
Mary Flower
Michael Goodman
Gretchen Gordon
Tessa Kale
David Lynch
Eleanor Mikucki
Michael A. Olivo
Patricia O'Neal
Paul F. State

Development of this project was initially undertaken by New England Publishing Associates (Ed Knappman, Vice-President; Larry Hand, Project Manager; Romanie Rout, Editor; Vicki Harlow, Researcher) and by the database consultants Carolyn Kuhn and Thomas Thackrey of Software Mart, Inc.

KANSAS
Paul T. Hellman
Washington, MO
Charles W. Martin
Kansas State University

KENTUCKY
Paul T. Hellman
Washington, MO
Dennis L. Spetz
University of Louisville

LOUISIANA
Paul T. Hellman
Washington, MO
Harley Jesse Walker
Louisiana State University

MAINE
Eldred Rolfe
University of Maine—Farmington

MARYLAND
James E. DiLisio
Towson University

MASSACHUSETTS
Robert P. Donnell
Framingham State College

MEXICO
Gary S. Elbow
Texas Tech University

MICHIGAN
Paul T. Hellman
Washington, MO
Eldor C. Quandt
Western Michigan University

MINNESOTA
Paul T. Hellman
Washington, MO
David A. Lanegran
Macalester College

MISSISSIPPI
Paul T. Hellman
Washington, MO
Robert W. Wales
University of Southern Mississippi

MISSOURI
Walter A. Schroeder
University of Missouri—Columbia

MONTANA
Jeffrey A. Gritzner
University of Montana

Paul T. Hellman
Washington, MO

NEBRASKA
Paul T. Hellman
Washington, MO
Leslie Hewes
University of Nebraska—Lincoln

NETHERLAND ANTILLES
Dennis Conway
Indiana University
Elizabeth J. Leppman
Miami University

NEVADA
Paul T. Hellman
Washington, MO
Paul F. Starrs
University of Nevada

NEW HAMPSHIRE
Paul T. Hellman
Washington, MO
William H. Wallace
University of New Hampshire

NEW JERSEY
Peter O. Wacker
Rutgers University

NEW MEXICO
Robert J. Czerniak
New Mexico State University
Paul T. Hellman
Washington, MO

NEW YORK
Thomas J. Gergel
SUNY at Oneonta

NORTH CAROLINA
John W. Florin
University of North Carolina, Chapel Hill
Paul T. Hellman
Washington, MO

NORTH DAKOTA
Douglas C. Munski
University of North Dakota

OHIO
Richard W. Janson
Canton, OH

OKLAHOMA
Paul T. Hellman
Washington, MO

Stephen J. Stadler
Oklahoma State University

OREGON
James G. Ashbaugh
Portland State University
Paul T. Hellman
Washington, MO

PENNSYLVANIA
Paul T. Hellman
Washington, MO
E. Willard Miller
The Pennsylvania State University

PUERTO RICO
Dennis Conway
Indiana University
Jose Molinelli
University of Puerto Rico

RHODE ISLAND
Robert J. Sullivan
Rhode Island College

SAINT KITTS AND NEVIS
Dennis Conway
Indiana University
Elizabeth J. Leppman
Miami University

SAINT LUCIA
Dennis Conway
Indiana University
Elizabeth J. Leppman
Miami University

SAINT VINCENT AND THE GRENADINES
Dennis Conway
Indiana University
Elizabeth J. Leppman
Miami University

SOUTH CAROLINA
Paul T. Hellman
Washington, MO
Charles Kovacik
University of South Carolina

SOUTH DAKOTA
Edward Patrick Hogan
South Dakota State University

TENNESSEE
Melvin C. Barber
University of Memphis

TEXAS

Paul T. Hellman
Washington, MO

James F. Petersen
Southwest Texas State University

TRINIDAD AND TOBAGO

Dennis Conway
Indiana University

Elizabeth J. Leppman
Miami University

TURKS AND CAICOS ISLANDS

Dennis Conway
Indiana University

Elizabeth J. Leppman
Miami University

U.S. VIRGIN ISLANDS

Dennis Conway
Indiana University

Elizabeth J. Leppman
Miami University

UTAH

Clifford Craig
Utah State University

Paul T. Hellman
Washington, MO

VERMONT

Harold A. Meeks
University of Vermont

VIRGINIA

James W. Fonseca
George Mason University

Paul T. Hellman
Washington, MO

WASHINGTON

William B. Beyers
University of Washington

Paul T. Hellman
Washington, MO

WEST VIRGINIA

Paul T. Hellman
Washington, MO

Kenneth C. Martis
West Virginia University

WISCONSIN

Paul T. Hellman
Washington, MO

Lutz Holzner
University of Wisconsin—Milwaukee

WYOMING

Paul T. Hellman
Washington, MO

Richard G. Reider
University of Wyoming

RESEARCHERS

Bruce P. Alexander
New York, NY

Michael J. Bennett
Washington, D.C.

Eugenie Bietry
Columbia University, NY

Rodney Carlisle
Rutgers University

Marjorie J. Davis
Mt. Juliet, TN

Jane Garry
New Haven, CT

Michael Golay
Exeter, NH

Margaret Heinrich Hand
Old Lyme, CT

George C. Hitt II
Montgomery, AL

Donna Hurst
University of Minnesota

Elizabeth Knappman
Chester, CT

Thomas Kolbe
Brimfield, MA

Michelle LaSeur
Austin, TX

Sylvia I. McKenzie
Bronx, NY

Anne J. Obee
San Diego, CA

Cristina Parsons
Northampton, MA

Romanie Rout
Chester, CT

Key to Population Figures

Recent population figures for many areas of the world are often difficult to obtain. Some countries have never taken a census; some only take partial censuses; some which do take censuses publish them completely only many years after the census is taken; some publish only part of the results of a census; and some have been known to suppress all results of a census. The population figures presented in this book are the best obtainable at the time of printing. The figures of the most recent complete census have been presented wherever possible. Recent official estimates have been used either when they were the result of careful annual corrections based on an earlier census or when there were no recent census figures. Unofficial estimates have been used only when no official figures of any kind were obtainable. Some population figures duplicate those in the fifth edition of the *Columbia Encyclopedia* (Anguilla, for instance), which were the best figures obtainable at the time of that book's printing in 1993.

Country	Population Source
Anguilla	*Columbia Encyclopedia (5th ed.)*
Antigua and Barbuda	*1991 census*
Bahamas	*1990 census*
Barbados	*unofficial estimates*
Bermuda	*unofficial estimates, Columbia Encyclopedia (5th ed.)*
Br. Virgin Isls.	*1991 census, unofficial esimates*
Canada	*1991 census, unofficial estimates*
Cayman Isls.	*1989 census*
Cuba	*unofficial estimates*
Dominica	*1991 census preliminary results*
Dominican Republic	*1993 census preliminary results, 1981 census*
Fr. West Indies	*Columbia Encyclopedia (5th ed.)*
Grenada	*Columbia Encyclopedia (5th ed.)*
Haiti	*1982 census, Columbia Encyclopedia (5th ed.)*
Jamaica	*1991 census*
Mexico	*1990 census*
Netherland Antilles	*Columbia Encyclopedia (5th ed.)*
Puerto Rico	*1990 U.S. census*
Saint Kitts and Nevis	*1997 official estimates, Columbia Encyclopedia (5th ed.)*
Saint Lucia	*1991 census*
St. Vincent/Grenadines	*1989 official estimates, unofficial estimates, Columbia Encyclopedia (5th ed.)*
Trinidad and Tobago	*1990 census, Columbia Encyclopedia (5th ed.)*
Turks and Caicos Isls.	*1990 census*
United States	*1995 official estimates, 1990 census*
U.S. Virgin Isls.	*Columbia Encyclopedia (5th ed.)*

Abbreviations

A.D. anno Domini [in the year of the Lord]
Acad., acad. Academy, academy
Afr. Africa, African
Afrik. Afrikaans
agr. agriculture; agricultural
Ala. Alabama
alt. altitude
Alta. Alberta
Amer. America; American
amp ampere(s)
amp-hr ampere-hour(s)
anc. ancient
Arab. Arabic
Ariz. Arizona
Ark. Arkansas
ASEAN Association of Southeast Asian Nations
Assn. Association
ASSR Autonomous Soviet Socialist Republic
Aug. August
Ave. Avenue
b. born
B.C. Before Christ; British Columbia
B.W.I. British West Indies
Belg. Belgian
bet. between
bldg., bldgs. building, buildings
Br. British
Btu British thermal units(s)
Bulg. Bulgarian
C Celsius (centigrade)
c. circa [about]
Calif. California
Can. Canadian
cc cubic centimeter(s)
cent., cents. century, centuries
Chin. Chinese
CIA Central Intelligence Agency
cm centimeter(s)
co. county; company
cos. counties
coed. coeducational
Col., col., cols. College, college(s)
Colo. Colorado
com. pop. commune population
Conn. Connecticut
Corp. Corporation
cu cubic
d. died
D.C. District of Columbia
Dan. Danish
Dec. December
Del. Delaware
dept., depts. department, departments
dist., dists. district, districts
div., divs. division, divisions
Dr. doctor
dr. dram(s)
Du. Dutch
E east; eastern; easterly
e.g. exempli gratia [for example]
EC European Community
ECSC European Coal and Steel Community
EDC European Defense Community
EFTA European Free Trade Association
elev. elevation
ENE east-northeast; east-northeastern; east-northeasterly
Eng. English
equip. equipment
ESE east-southeast; east-southeastern; east-southeasterly
esp. especially
est. estimated; established
et al. et alia [and others]
etc. et cetera
EV electron volts
EU European Union
Eur. European
F Fahrenheit
FBI Federal Bureau of Investigation
Feb. February

Finn. Finnish
fl oz fluid ounces(s)
Fla. Florida
Fr. French
ft foot; feet
ft-lb foot-pound(s)
Ga. Georgia
gal. gallon(s)
Gall. Gallery
GATT General Agreement on Tariffs and Trade
GDP gross domestic product
Gen. Genesis
Ger. German
GMT Greenwich mean time
GNP gross national product
Gov. Governor
govt. government
Gr. Greek
Grl. Greenlandic
hosp., hosps. hospital(s)
hp horsepower
hq. headquarters
hr, hrs hour(s)
ht. height
Hung. Hungarian
Hz hertz
i.e. id est [that is]
Icel. Icelandic
IGY International Geophysical Year
Ill. Illinois
in inch(es)
inc. incorporated
Ind. Indiana
Inst. Institute; Institution
Internatl., internatl. International, international
Isl., isl. Island, island
Isls., isls. Islands, islands
Ital. Italian
Jan. January
Jap. Japanese
Jr. Junior
kg kilograms
kgm kilogram meter(s)
kl kiloliter(s)
kph kilometers per hour
km kilometer(s)
kw kilowatt(s)
kwh kilowatt hour(s)
Ky. Kentucky
L. Lake
L.I. Long Island
La. Louisiana
Lab. Labrador
lat latitude
Lat. Latin
Lat. Amer. Latin America; Latin American
lb libra [pound]; librae [pounds]
Lib., lib., libs. Library, library, libraries
lim limit
Lith. Lithuanian
long. longitude
Lt. Lieutenant
Ltd. Limited
m meter(s)
M.E. Middle English
M.H.G. Middle High German
Man. Manitoba
Mass. Massachusetts
max. maximum
Md. Maryland
Mex. Mexican
mfg. manufacturing
mg milligram(s)
mi mile(s)
Mich. Michigan
min minute(s)
min. minimum
Minn. Minnesota

Miss. Mississippi
ml milliliter(s)
mm millimeter(s)
Mo. Missouri
Mont. Montana
mph miles per hour
Mt. mt. Mount, Mountain; mount, mountain
Mts., mts. Mountains, mountains
Mus., mus. Museum, museum
MW, megawatt(s)
Mwe megawatt(s) electric
N north; northern; northerly
N. Amer. North America; North American
N.B. New Brunswick
N.C. North Carolina
N.Dak. North Dakota
N.F. Newfoundland
N.H. New Hampshire
N.J. New Jersey
N.Mex. New Mexico
N.S. Nova Scotia
N.S.W. New South Wales
N.W.T. Northwest Territories
N.Y. New York
N.Z. New Zealand
NAFTA North American Free Trade Agreement
NASA National Aeronautics and Space Administration
Natl., natl. National, national
NATO North Atlantic Treaty Organization
naut. nautical
NE northeast, northeastern, northeasterly
Nebr. Nebraska
Neth. Netherlands
Nev. Nevada
NNE north-northeast; north-northeastern; north-northeasterly
NNW north-northwest; north-northwestern; north-northwesterly
No. numero [number]
Nor. Norwegian
Nov. November
NW northwest; northwestern; northwesterly
O.E. Old English
O.Fr. Old French
O.H.G. Old High German
O.N. Old Norse
OAS Organization of America States
Oct. October
Okla. Oklahoma
Ont. Ontario
oz ounce(s)
P.E.I. Prince Edward Island
P.I. Philippine Islands
P.R. Puerto Rico
Pa. Pennsylvania
PAU Pan American Union
Pers. Persian
pl. plural
Pol. Polish
pop. population
Port. Portuguese
prods. products
prov., provs. province(s)
pt pint(s)
qt quart(s)
Que. Quebec
R. River
R.C. Roman Catholic
R.I. Rhode Island
Rhode Isl. Rhode Island, the island
rpm revolution(s) per minute
RR railroad; railway; rail; rail line
RSFSR Russian Soviet Federated Socialist Republic
Rus. Russian
S south; southern; southerly
S. Amer. South America; South American
S.C. South Carolina
S.Dak. South Dakota

Sask. Saskatchewan
SE southeast; southeastern; southeasterly
SEATO Southeast Asia Treaty Organization
sec second(s); secant
sect. section
Sept. September
Skt. Sanskrit
Span. Spanish
sq square
SSE south-southeast; south-southeastern; south-southeasterly
SSR Soviet Socialist Republic
SSW south-southwest; south-southwestern; south-southwesterly
St. Saint; Street
Ste. *Sainte* [Saint, feminine]
STP Standard temperature and pressure
SW southwest; southwestern; southwesterly

Swed. Swedish
temp., temps. temperature, temperatures
Tenn. Tennessee
Turk. Turkish
TVA Tennessee Valley Authority
UAE United Arab Emirates
U.S. United States
U.K. United Kingdom
Ukr. Ukrainian
UN United Nations
UNRWA United Nations Relief and Works Agency
UNESCO United Nations Educational, Scientific, and Cultural Organization
uninc. unincorporated
Univ., univ., univs. University, university, universities
USBGN United States Board on Geographic Names
USSR Union of Soviet Socialist Republics
V volt(s)

V.I. Virgin Islands
Va. Virginia
vol. volume(s)
Vt. Vermont
W west; western; westerly
W.Va. West Virginia
Wash. Washington
WEU Western European Union
Wis. Wisconsin
WNW west-northwest; west-northwestern, west-northwesterly
WSW west-southwest; west-southwestern; west-southwesterly
wt. weight
WHO World Health Organization
WTO World Trade Organization
Wyo. Wyoming
yd yard(s)

Key to Pronunciation

Pronunciation of place names in *The Columbia Gazetteer of North America* appear in parentheses next to place-names. Generally, it has been our aim to "sound out" pronunciations in a way that approaches that of newspapers, and we believe that in the vast majority of cases our pronunciations are phonetically self-evident. However, we decided to avoid the ambiguity involved in showing, to take one instance, the pronunciation of the long "i" in "fight" as "eye" to produce "feyet." Instead, we adopted the scheme, shown below, which was used in Kenneth Wilson's *Columbia Guide to Standard American English*, showing the pronunciation of "fight" as "feit," and that of "fate" as "fait." Hyphens are used to separate syllables, and capital letters are used to indicate stressed syllables.

THE LIST OF SYMBOLS FOR THE PRONUNCIATIONS

Stressed Vowel Sounds

EE	(FEET)	feet
I	(FIT)	fit
E	(BED)	bed
A	(KAT) cat	(KAD) cad
AH	(FAH-thur) father	(PAHR) par
AH	(HAHT) hot	(TAH-dee) toddy
UH	(FUHJ) fudge	(FLUHD) flood
UH	(CHUHRCH) church	
AW	(FAWN) fawn	
U	(FUL) full	
OO	(FOOD) food	
OU	(FOUND) found	
O	(FO) foe	
EI	(FEIT) fight	
AI	(FAIT) fate	
OI	(FOIL) foil	
YOO	(FYOOR-ee-uhs) furious	

Unstressed Vowel Sounds

uh	(SO-fuh) sofa	
	(FING-guhr) finger	(SING-uhr) singer

Certain Vowel Sounds with R

AHR	(PAHR) par
ER	(PER) pair
IR	(PIR) peer
OR	(POR) pour
OOR	(POOR) poor
UHR	(PUHR) purr

Consonant Sounds

B	(BED)	bed
D	(DET)	debt
F	(FED)	fed
G	(GET)	get
H	(HED)	head
HW	(HWICH)	which
J	(JUHG)	jug
K	(KAD)	cad
L	(LAIM)	lame
M	(MAT)	mat
N	(NET)	net
NG	(SING-uhr)	singer
P	(PET)	pet
R	(RED)	red
S	(SET)	set
T	(TEN)	ten
V	(VET)	vet
Y	(YET)	yet
W	(WICH)	witch
CH	(CHUHRCH)	church
SH	(SHEEP)	sheep
TS	(ITS) its	(PITS-feeld) Pittsfield
TH	(THEI)	thigh
TH	(THEI)	thy
ZH	(A-zhuhr) azure	
	(VI-zhuhn) vision	(mi-RAHZH) mirage
Z	(GOODZ) goods	(HUH-buhz-tuhn) Hubbardston

A

Abaco and Cays, island group (□ c.780 sq mi/ 2,020 sq km; 1990 pop. 10,003), most N of the Bahamas; 26°28′N 77°05′W. It includes Great Abaco (the largest), Little Abaco, and the surrounding cays. The low isls., composed mainly of coral limestone, have native pine forests. Fishing, citrus, and vegetable production. Great Abaco was settled by Loyalists from N.Y. city in 1783.

Abajo Mountains (AH-buh-o), SE Utah, near Colo. state line, E of Colorado R., N of Blanding. Abajo Peak is the highest point (elev. 11,360 ft/3,463 m), 7 mi/ 11.3 km WSW of Monticello; Mt. Linnaeus (11,019 ft/ 3,359 m). Range lies within sect. of Manti-La Sal Natl. Forest.

Abalá (ah-bah-LAH), town (1990 pop. 1,480), ⊙ Abalá municipio, Yucatán, SE Mexico, 23 mi/37 km S of Mérida. Henequen, corn, tropical fruit.

Abasolo (ah-bah-SO-lo), city (1990 pop. 19,808), Guanajuato, central Mexico, on central plateau, 19 mi/ 31 km SW of Irapuato. Elev. 5,774 ft/1,760 m. Corn-growing center. Miguel Hidalgo y Costilla b. (1753) nearby. Also Cuitzeo de Abasolo and Cuitzeo de Hidalgo.

Abasolo 1 (ah-bah-SO-lo), town (1990 pop. 731), ⊙ Abasolo municipio, Coahuila, N Mexico, in E outliers of Sierra Madre Oriental, 20 mi/32 km N of Monclova; 27°10′N 101°28′W. Corn, wheat, fruit. Linked to Monclova by road and RR. **2** town (1990 pop. 1,276), ⊙ Abasolo municipio, Nuevo León, N Mexico and 19 mi/ 31 km NW of Monterrey; 25°55′N 100°25′W. On RR; grain, livestock. **3** town (1990 pop. 6,564), ⊙ Abasolo municipio,Tamaulipas, NE Mexico, 31 mi/50 km NE of Ciudad Victoria; 24°2′N 98°22′W. Elev. 262 ft/80 m. Cotton, maize, sugarcane; livestock.

Abbaye, Point, Mich.: see HURON BAY.

Abbeville (A-bee-vil), county (□ 511 sq mi/1,323 sq km; 1990 pop. 23,862), NW S.C.; ⊙ Abbeville; 34°13′N 82°27′W. Bounded SW by Savannah R., NE in part by the Saluda R. Includes part of Sumter Natl. Forest in SE. Piedmont agr. area (chickens, eggs, hogs, cattle; wheat, oats, soybeans, hay; dairying). Formed 1785.

Abbeville 1 (A-bee-vil), city (1990 pop. 3,173), ⊙ Henry co., SE Ala., 27 mi/43 km N of Dothan, near Chattahoochee R. In peanut and corn area; lumber milling, cotton ginning, textiles, egg and poultry processing. **2** city (1990 pop. 11,187), ⊙ Vermilion parish, S La., 17 mi/27 km SSW of Lafayette, on the Vermilion R., with access to the Intracoastal Waterway to S.; 29°58′N 92°07′W. Trade and processing center for a region of rice and sugarcane fields; fishing (crawfish, alligator, crab); mfg. (chemical prods., consumer goods). In the colorful Cajun country, Abbeville was settled (1843) by descendants of Acadians from N.S., Canada, and was laid out like a Fr. town. It grew around the St. Mary Magdalen R.C. church, built in 1845, and preserves much of the early atmosphere in its old bldgs. (historic district). Erath's Acadian History Mus., Abbey Players' Theater are here. Inc. 1850. **3** city (1990 pop. 5,778), ⊙ Abbeville co., NW S.C., 13 mi/21 km W of Greenwood, in Piedmont region; 34°10′N 82°22′W. Mfg. (apparel, metal prods., plastic). Agr. includes poultry, livestock, dairying; grains, soybeans. Secessionist meeting held here Nov. 1860. Referred to as "The Birthplace of the Confederacy." Also site of Jefferson Davis' last cabinet meeting in 1865.

Abbeville (A-bee-vil), town (1990 pop. 907), ⊙ Wilcox co., S central Ga., 27 mi/43 km E of Cordele, near Ocmulgee R.; 31°59′N 83°18′W. Agr. area that produces lumber and prefabricated buildings.

Abbeville (A-bee-vil), village (1990 pop. 399), Lafayette co., N Miss., 10 mi/16 km N of Oxford, near Tallahatchie R., forms Sardis Reservoir; 34°30′N 89°30′W. Mfg. (tool and die); agr. (corn, cotton, soybeans; cattle). Holly Springs Natl. Forest to E.

Abbot, town (1990 pop. 677), Piscataquis co., central Maine, on the Piscataquis, and 10 mi/16 km WNW of Dover-Foxcroft; 45°10′N 69°28′W.

Abbotsburg, village, Bladen co., S N.C., 18 mi/29 km SE of Lumberton; 34°31′N 78°44′W.

Abbotsford, dormitory town (1991 pop. 18,864), SW B.C., Canada, rural part of Vancouver urban area, 6 mi/10 km S of Mission, 5 mi/8 km S of Fraser R., and 2 mi/3 km N of U.S. border; 49°03′N 122°17′W. RR junction; elev. 90 ft/27 m. Dairying, mfg. (construction materials, plastic prods., food); sawmill, steelworks, logging, nonclay refractory, trout hatchery; fruit (strawberries, cranberries), hops.

Abbotsford, town (1990 pop. 1,916), on Clark-Marathon co. line, central Wis., 34 mi/55 km W of Wausau. In dairying region; dairy prods.. Mfg. (food prods., construction materials, accessories); feeds. Locally referred to as Abby or Abbyland.

Abbottstown, borough (1990 pop. 539), Adams co., S Pa., 14 mi/23 km WSW of York, on Beaver Creek; 39°52′N 76°59′W. Light mfg.; bakery prods. Agr. (grain, apples, cherries, potatoes; poultry, livestock, dairying).

Abbott, village (1990 pop. 314), Hill co., N central Texas, 10 mi/16 km S of Hillsboro; 31°52′N 97°04′W. Cotton. Aquilla L. reservoir to W.

Abbyville, village (1990 pop. 140), Reno co., S central Kansas, 16 mi/26 km WSW of Hutchinson; 37°58′N 98°12′W. Wheat.

Abejones (a-be-HO-nes), town (1990 pop. 1,402), in central Oaxaca, Mexico, 11 mi/17 km N of Ixtlán de Juárez, N of Oaxaca de Juarez; 17°24′N 96°35′W. Elev. 7,566 ft/2,306 m; 28 mi/45 km. Agr. (wheat, corn, beans) primarily for subsistence. Predominantly Zapotec population. Also known as San Miguel Abejones.

Abercorn (a-buhr-KORN), village (1991 pop. 321), S Que., on Missisquoi R. and 26 mi/42 km SSE of Granby, near Vt. border. Dairying.

Abercrombie (AB-uhr-krahm-bee), village (1990 pop. 252), Richland co., SE N.Dak., 14 mi/23 km NNW of Wahpeton, and on Red R., opposite Kent, Minn.; 46°27′N 96°43′W. Fort Abercrombie Historic Site is on site of U.S. post, est. 1857.

Aberdeen, town (1991 pop. 474), central Sask., Canada, 22 mi/35 km NE of Saskatoon; 52°19′N 106°17′W. Wheat.

Aberdeen 1 city (1990 pop. 24,927), ⊙ Brown co., NE S.Dak., c.100 mi/161km NE of Pierre; 150 mi/240 km NNW of Sioux Falls; 45°28′N 98°28′W. The trade and distributing center for a wheat and livestock region, it has grain elevators, soyoil, candy, and dairy-processing plants. Mfg. (machinery, electronic equip. chemicals, computers, printing, wood prods., ethanol, medical equip.). Northern State Univ. and the S.Dak. School for the Visually Handicapped are in the city. Municipal Airport to S. Richmond Lake State Rec. Area to NW; Mina State Rec. Area to W. Dakota Prairie Mus. Inc. 1882. **2** city (1990 pop. 16,565), Grays Harbor co., W Wash., 44 mi/71 km W of Olympia, a port of entry on Grays Harbor, at the mouth of the Chehalis and the Wishkah rivers; 46°59′N 123°49′W. RR junction. With its adjacent twin city, HOQUIAM, it has lumbering and shipping industries; other mfg. (seafood processing, steel foundry, copper foundry, printing and publishing, food and beverage prods., veneer, boatbuilding). The cities serve as a gateway to Olympic Natl. Park, to N. Home port of Washington's tall ship *Ambassador Lady Washington*. Grays Harbor Community Col. here. Inc. 1890

Aberdeen 1 town (1990 pop. 1,406), Bingham co., SE Idaho, 11 mi/18 km N of American Falls; 42°57′N 112°51′W. RR terminus (spur from Moreland); irrigated region (sheep, cattle, poultry; potatoes, sugar beets); mfg. (fertilizer). American Falls Dam to S, American Falls Reservoir (Snake R.) to SE. **2** town (1990 pop. 13,087), Harford co., NE Md.; 39°31′N 76°10′W. In a farm region. Just S, on Chesapeake Bay, is the U.S. Army's Aberdeen Proving Ground, a major research, development, and testing installation and site of the army ordnance center and school. The facility, opened in 1917, occupies 75,000 acres/30,353 ha. The U.S. Army Ordnance Mus. on the grounds is a comprehensive collection of arms and military vehicles dating from the Revolutionary War to the Vietnam era. Inc. 1892. **3** town (1990 pop. 6,837), ⊙ Monroe co., E. Miss., 24 mi/39 km NNW of Columbus, on Tombigbee R. at natural head of navigation; 33°49′N 88°32′W. RR junction to E. Mfg. (apparel, furniture), metal fabrication, chemical processing; agr. (cotton, wheat, corn, soybeans), dairying; timber. A number of fine antebellum homes are here, including The Magnolias (1850). Aberdeen Lock and Dam, on Tennessee-Tombigbee Waterway, forms Aberdeen L., to E. Inc. 1837. **4** town (1990 pop. 2,717), Moore co., central N.C., 30 mi/48 km W of Fayetteville, and 4 mi/6.4 km SW of Southern Pines; 35°08′N 79°25′W. RR junction. Trade center; shipping point for agr. area (tobacco, fruit, grain, poultry). Heavy and light mfg. World Golf Hall of Fame; Weymouth Woods State Park (Sandhills Nature Reserve) to NE. Fort Bragg Military Reserve to E. Inc. 1893.

Aberdeen, village (1990 pop. 1,329), Brown co., SW Ohio, on the Ohio R. (bridged), opposite Maysville, Ky.

Aberdeen Lake (□ 475), W central Keewatin dist., N.W.T., Canada; 50 mi/80 km long, 2 mi/3 km–18 mi/ 29 km wide; 64°30′N 99°00′W. Drained E by Thelon R.

Abernathy, town (1990 pop. 2,720), Hale and Lubbock cos., NW Texas, on the Llano Estacado, 17 mi/27 km N of Lubbock; 33°49′N 101°50′W. Agr. (soybeans, cotton, wheat); cattle, sheep. Near Blackwater Draw (creek).

Abernethy (a-buhr-NE-thee), village (1991 pop. 243), SE Sask., Canada, 30 mi/48 km WSW of Melville. Wheat, stock.

Abert, Lake (Al-buhrt), intermittently dry lake, Lake co., S Oregon, 30 mi/48 km N of Lakeview and N of Goose L., in the Great Basin; c.14 mi/23 km long, 5 mi/ 8 km wide. Elev. 4,255 ft/1,297 m. Crooked Creek runs from S; no outlet.

Abie (A-bee), village (1990 pop. 106), Butler co., E Nebr., 11 mi/18 km NE of David City, near Platte R.; 41°19′N 96°57′W.

Abilene 1 (AB-uh-leen), city (1990 pop. 6,242), ⊙ Dickinson co., central Kansas, on the Smoky Hill R.; 38°55′N 97°13′W. The city, a shipping point for a wheat and cattle region, has feed and flour mills. It was (1867–1871) a railhead for a large cattle-raising region extending SW into Texas. Millions of cattle followed the CHISHOLM TRAIL into Abilene's stockyards prior to shipment. A famous cowtown of the Old West, Abilene once had "Wild Bill" Hickok as its marshal. Abilene was the boyhood home of former President Dwight D. Eisenhower; the Eisenhower Center includes his old family homestead, a mus., the Eisenhower Lib., and his grave. Inc. 1869. **2** city (1990 pop. 106,654), ⊙ Taylor and Jones cos., W central Texas; 32°28′N 99°43′W. Elev. 1,738 ft/530 m. Metro Area is drained by several creeks, most important being Elm Creek, which feeds into Clear Fork of the Brazos R. to N. Buffalo hunters 1st settled here; the town, which was founded in 1881 with the coming of the RR, was named after Abilene, Kansas. Abilene grew as a shipping point for cattle ranches and has become the financial, commercial, and educational center of a large part of W Texas. RR junction. The city's diversified mfg. include electronic, aircraft, and missile components; oil-field and agr. equip.; food and dairy prods.; clothing; metals; and musical instruments. Livestock (cattle, sheep, and poultry); agr. (cotton, wheat, sorghum, hay); and minerals (oil, natural gas, caliche, sand, gravel, and clays) are important to the economy of the surrounding area. The hq. of regional petroleum interests are in Abilene. Hardin-Simmons Univ., Abilene Christian Univ., and McMurry Col. are in the city. Dyess Air Force Base on W end of city; Lytle and Kirby lakes are in S part of city, city limits extend N into Jones co., to include L. Fort Phantom Hill reservoir, L. Abilene and Abilene State Park to SW. Inc. 1882.

Abilene, Lake, reservoir, Taylor co., W central Texas, on Elm Creek (a S tributary of Clear Fork of Brazos R.), in Abilene State Park, 15 mi/24 km SW of Abilene; c.2.5 mi/4 km long; 32°45′N 99°52′W. Formed by dam built (1922) for Abilene water supply. Fishing.

Abingdon, city (1990 pop. 3,597), Knox co., W central Ill., 10 mi/16 km S of Galesburg; 40°47′N 90°24′W. Trade and shipping center in agr. area; cattle, hogs, poultry; corn, oats, barley, fruit, soybeans; dairy prods. Mfg. (fabricated metal prods., consumer goods). Inc. 1857.

Abingdon, town (1990 pop. 7,003), ⊙ Washington co., SW Va., in the Appalachians near Tenn. state line, 14 mi/23 km NE of Bristol; 36°42′N 81°58′W. Elev. c.2,000 ft/610 m. Trade center in agr. area (tobacco, corn, alfalfa; livestock, poultry, dairying). Mfg. (crushed rock, fabricated metal prods., machinery, consumer goods, food, apparel); machining, handicraft industries. Mt. resort. Jefferson Natl. Forest to NW; Mt. Rogers Natl. Recreation Area, Appalachian Trail to SE; S Holston Reservoir to S. Site of Va. Highlands Community Col., Barter Theatre. Settled c.1765; inc. 1778.

Abingdon, village, Harford co., NE Md., near Bush R., 21 mi/34 km ENE of Baltimore; 39°28′N 17°76′W. Makes clothing. Nearby are Aberdeen Proving Ground and Army Chemical Center. Founded in 1779 by William Paca, a signer of the Declaration of Independence.

Abington, town (1990 pop. 13,817), Plymouth co., E Mass., 18 mi/29 km SSE of Boston, just E of Brockton; 42°07′N 70°58′W. Mfg. (shoes, machinery, consumer goods). Includes North Abington. Settled 1668, inc. 1713.

Abington, village, Windham co., Conn., 16 mi/26 km NE of Willimantic. Has one of state's oldest churches (1751) and public libraries (1793).

Abington, township (1990 pop. 56,322), Montgomery co., SE Pa., a residential suburb 12 mi/19 km N of downtown Philadelphia; 40°07′N 75°07′W. Mfg. (abrasives, light mfg.). Penn State Univ. (Ogontz campus: 2-year) is here. Site of combat during the Revolutionary War. Includes Roslyn, Ardsley, Noble, part of Glenside. Pennypack Creek to E. Settled 1696, inc. 1906.

Abiquiu (A-bi-kee-oo), uninc. village (1990 pop. 500), Rio Arriba co., N N.Mex., on Rio Chama, in N foothills of Valle Grande Mts., and 44 mi/71 km SSE of Tierra Amarilla; 36°13′N 106°19′W. Elev. 6,063 ft/1,848 m. Cattle, sheep; alfalfa. Built on site of pueblo ruins. In area surrounded by Carson Natl. Forest (N) and Santa Fe Natl. Forest (S). Abiquiu Dam, Ghost Ranch Visitor Center and Echo Amphitheater to NW; Georgia O'Keeffe Natl. Historic Site, home and studio of renowned artist.

Abiquiu Reservoir (A-bi-kee-oo), Rio Arriba co., N N.Mex., on Rio Charma, 45 mi/72 km NNW of Santa Fe; 13 mi/21 km long; 36°13′N 106°24′W. Max. capacity 1,374,000 acre-ft. Intermittent. Formed by Abiquiu Dam (319 ft/97 m), built (1963) by the U.S. govt. for flood and debris control. Surrounded by, but not part of, Santa Fe Natl. Forest.

Abita Springs (uh-BEE-tuh), town (1994 pop. 1,674), St. Tammany parish, SE La., 4 mi/6 km E of Covington; 30°30′N 90°02′W. In agr. area; mfg. (beer, pharmaceuticals, concrete). Part of the "ozone belt" N of L. Pontchartrain. Noted for its spring water. Abita Springs State Park.

Abitibi (a-buh-TI-bee), county (□ 3,090 sq mi/ 8,003 sq km; 1991 pop. 25,334), W Que., on Ont. border, Canada; ⊙ Amos; 48°00′N 76°00′W.

Abitibi Lake (a-buh-TI-bee), irregularly shaped lake, c.60 mi/100 km long, SW Que. and E Ont., Canada; 48°40′N 79°45′W. A popular tourist area and the site of the Abitibi Game Reserve. The Abitibi R. drains the lake and flows W and N to the Moose R.

Abitibi River, 340 mi/547 km long, NE Ont., Canada; issues from L. Abitibi; flows N, past Iroquois Falls, through Abitibi Canyon (hydroelectric plant), to confluence with Moose R., which flows past Moosonee to James Bay.

Ableman, Wis.: see ROCK SPRINGS.

Above Rocks, town (1991 pop. 3,262), St. Catherine parish, E Jamaica, 10 mi/16 km NW of Kingston; 18°06′N 76°53′W.

Abraham Lincoln Birthplace National Historic Site, Larue co., central Ky., 3 mi/4.8 km S of Hodgenville. Abraham Lincoln was born in a log cabin in this area on Feb. 12, 1809. The exact location of the original cabin has not been conclusively established, but evidence seems to indicate that it was situated on top of the knoll where the memorial bldg. stands. Inside the bldg. is a log cabin representative of the type of cabin Lincoln was born in. Includes Sinking Spring, used by Lincoln, and forested area and hiking trails. Covers 117 acres/ 47 ha; est. 1916.

Abraham, Mount (4,049 ft/1,234 m), Franklin co., W central Maine, 23 mi/37 km NNW of Farmington.

Abraham, Plains of, fairly level field adjoining the upper part of the city of Quebec. Here, in 1759, the English, under Gen. James Wolfe, defeated the French, under Gen. Louis Montcalm. The battle decided the last of the Fr. and Indian Wars and led to Br. supremacy in Canada. Part of the battle site is now built over, but a part is preserved as a natl. park.

Abraham's Bay, town, SE Bahama Isls., on S central Mayaguana Isl., 330 mi/531 km SE of Nassau; 22°21′N 72°58′W. Sometimes Abraham Bay.

Abreus (ah-BRAI-oos), town, Cienfuegos prov., central Cuba, 11 mi/18 km NW of Cienfuegos; 22°17′N 80°35′W. In agr. region (sugarcane, cattle). The sugar center of Constancia is 3 mi/4.8 km S.

Abricots (ah-bree-KO), town (1982 pop. 891), Grande-Anse dept., Haiti, 7 mi/11.3 km W of Jérémie; 18°38′N 78°18′W. Coffee, sugarcane, cacao growing; fishing port. Sometimes called Les Abricots.

Abruzzi, Mount (10,700 ft/3,261 m), SE B.C., Canada, near Alta. border, in Rocky Mts., 55 mi/89 km SSE of Banff; 50°27′N 115°07′W.

Absaroka Range (ab-suh-RO-kuh), range of Rocky Mts. in S Mont. and NW Wyo., bet. Yellowstone R. (W and N) and Bighorn Basin (E); extends c.150 mi/241 km S from Yellowstone R. SW of Livingston, Mont., to Wind R. valley (Wyo.). BEARTOOTH RANGE, a NE spur, includes Granite Peak (12,799 ft/3,901 m), highest peak in Mont. The Absarokas are highest at Mt. Frances (13,136 ft/4,004 m; sometimes called Franks Peak), c.40 mi/64 km SSW of Cody, Wyo. Other summits over 12,000 ft/3,660 m include Washakie Needles (12,524 ft/ 3,817 m), Needle Mt. (12,106 ft/3,690 m), Fortress Mt. (12,085 ft/3,684 m), Dead Indian Peak (12,216 ft/ 3,723 m), Trout Peak (12,244 ft/3,732 m), Mt. Crosby (12,449 ft/3,794 m), all in Wyo.; and Cold Mt. (12,610 ft/ 3,844 m), in Mont. Range. The range divide forms E boundary of Yellowstone Natl. Park, and is the source of tributaries of the Bighorn and the Yellowstone rivers; it includes Absaroka Natl. Forest and part of Custer Natl. Forest in Mont., Shoshone Natl. Forest in Wyo. Sylvan Pass (8,559 ft/2,609 m), near E boundary of Yellowstone Natl. Park, and Ishawooa Pass (9,870 ft/ 3,008 m), 10 mi/16 km E of park, cross range in Wyo. Absaroka-Beartooth Wilderness Area covers most of Mont. part of range. Including Pinnacle Mt., Cutoff Mt., Haystack Park, and Livingston Park.

Absarokee (ab-suh-RO-kee), uninc. village (1990 pop. 1,067), Stillwater co., S Mont., 12 mi/19 km SW of Columbus and on Rosebud creek, near its confluence with the Stillwater R; 45°31′N 109°26′W. Hay, cattle. Cooney Reservoir State Park to SE; Custer Natl. Forest to SW, Gallatin Natl. Forest to W.

Absecon (ab-suh-KUHN), city (1990 pop. 7,298), Atlantic co., SE N.J., on W shore of Absecon Bay and 6 mi/ 9.7 km NW of Atlantic City; 39°25′N 74°30′W. Mfg. (concrete blocks, consumer goods); nursery prods., poultry. Settled c. 1780, inc. 1902.

Absecon Bay (ab-suh-KUHN), SE N.J., bet. Absecon and Atlantic City; 2.5 mi/4 km long. Absecon Inlet, N of Atlantic City, is principal entrance. Absecon Beach, a 10 mi/16 km sandbar bridged at several points to mainland, is SE of Absecon across Absecon Bay; on it are Atlantic City and other resorts. Lighthouse at N tip (1854–1932); no longer used. Lucy, "The Margate Elephant" (a six-story hollow pachyderm), is in S. It is a natl. historic landmark.

Abymes (ah-BEEM), town, W Grande-Terre, Guadeloupe, 2 mi/3.2 km NE of Pointe-à-Pitre. In sugar-growing region; mfg. of molasses. Sometimes called Les Abymes.

Acacoyagua (ah-kah-ko-YAH-gwah), town (1990 pop. 4,649), in SW of Chiapas, Mexico, 18 mi/29 km NW of Huixtla on Mexico Highway 200, at S base of Sierra Madre de Chiapas; 15°20′N 92°41′W. Agr. (corn, beans, sugarcane, rice, cacao).

Acadia (uh-KAI-dee-uh), region and former Fr. colony, E Canada, centered on N.S. but including also N.B., P.E.I., Canada, and the mainland coast from the Gulf of St. Lawrence S into Maine. The first and chief town, Port Royal (now Annapolis Royal, N.S.), was founded by the sieur de Monts in 1605 and was soon involved in the imperial struggle that was to end in Amer. with the Fr. and Indian Wars. The colony grew to be fairly prosperous with farmers on their dike-protected fields, fishermen on the shore, and fur traders in the forests. In 1755 the British took the Acadian farms and deported most of the Acadians to the more southerly Br. colonies, scattering them along the Atlantic coast from Maine to Ga. and sending some to the West Indies and Eur. A 2nd expulsion took place in 1758. Many exiles returned later. Today in Canada, Acadian (Fr. *Acadien*) means a Fr.-speaking inhabitant of the Maritime provs. Official language acts passed in 1969 and 1981 have given Fr. and Eng. equal status, which has weakened the Acadian community by integrating it more fully into the natl. culture. Many exiles who did not return found havens elsewhere, the most celebrated being the region around St. Martinville in S La., where the Cajuns — as they are called — still maintain a distinctive culture. The sufferings of the expulsion are described in Longfellow's "Evangeline."

Acadia (uh-KAI-dee-uh), parish (□ 662 sq mi/ 1,715 sq km; 1990 pop. 55,882), S La.; ⊙ Crowley; 30°13′N 92°23′W. Bounded W by Bayou Nezpique and Mermentau R., S by Bayou Queue de Tortue; drained by Bayou des Cannes. Mfg. (cotton ginning, rice milling, textiles, pipe fittings, sporting goods, lumber); logging; agr. (rice, corn, wheat, soybeans, vegetables, sweet potatoes; cattle, horses, poultry); aquaculture; oil and natural gas wells. The Blue Rose Mus. and Heritage Farm Village located here. Formed 1805.

Acadia (uh-KAI-dee-uh), a sect. of Conner township, Aroostook co., NE Maine, on Little Madawaska R., and 21 mi/34 km N of Presque Isle. In agr. region.

Acadia National Park (uh-KAI-dee-uh) (□ 65.5 sq mi/ 169.6 sq km), SE Maine, on the Atlantic coast; 44°14′N 68°12′W. The park occupies a major portion of Mount Desert Isl., Isle au Haut and several smaller isls., and the S tip of Schoodic Peninsula, covering a total of 41,888 acres/16,952 ha. Almost completely surrounded by the sea, the park is characterized by a rugged, glacier-scoured interior with numerous valleys, lakes, and peaks, and a wave-eroded coastline. A variety of land and sea life, both plant and animal, as well as several mus. and nature centers are found in Acadia. Est. 1919.

Acajete 1 (ah-kah-HAI-tai), town (1990 pop. 12,164), Puebla, central Mexico, ⊙ municipio, at SE foot of Malinche volcano, 17 mi/27 km ENE of Puebla; 19°08′N 97°56′W. Elev. 8,100 ft/2,469 m. On RR. Cereals, maguey; livestock. **2** town (1990 pop. 1,321) Veracruz, E Mexico, on RR and 6 mi/9.7 km NW of Xalapa Enríquez. Elev. 6,316 ft/1,925 m. Coffee, corn.

Acala (ah-KAH-lah), town (1990 pop. 11,064), Chiapas, S Mexico, on upper Grijalva R. and 23 mi/37 km ESE of Tuxtla Gutiérrez; 16°35′N 92°53′W. Elev. 1,631 ft/ 497 m. Agr. center (mangoes, sugarcane, fruit; livestock).

Acámbaro (ah-KAHM-bah-ro), city and township (1990 pop. 52,248), Guanajuato, central Mexico, on central plateau, on Lerma R., and 45 mi/72 km SSW of Querétaro; 20°02′N 100°43′W. Highway and RR junction. Agr. center (corn, wheat, sugar, vegetables, fruit; livestock); tanneries. Founded 1526.

Acambay (ah-KAM-bai), town (1990 pop. 3,600), Mexico state, central Mexico, 23 mi/37 km NE of El Oro de

Hidalgo; 19°57′N 99°50′W. Elev. 8,202 ft/2,500 m. Cereals; livestock. Formerly San Miguel Acambay.

Acampo (ah-KAHMP-o), uninc. village, San Joaquin co., central Calif., 3 mi/4.8 km N of Lodi. Fruit, nuts, vegetables, grapes; dairying; cattle; mfg. (flavorings and extracts, feeds, wine).

Acancéh (ah-kahn-SAI), town (1990 pop. 7,975), Yucatán, SE Mexico, 15 mi/24 km SE of Mérida; 20°49′N 89°29′W. RR junction in former henequen-growing region. Citrus fruit, livestock.

Acapetahua (ah-kah-pai-TAH-wah), town (1990 pop. 4,859), Chiapas, S Mexico, in Pacific lowlands, 16 mi/26 km NW of Huixtla; 15°7′N 92°40′W. Sugar, coffee, cacao, fruit; livestock. Formerly Acapetagua.

Acapetlahuaya (ah-kah-pait-lah-WAH-yah), town (1990 pop. 1,453), ⊙ General Canuto A. Neri municipio, in N central Guerrero, Mexico. A mountainous area near Nevado de Toluca. Hot climate. Balsas R. provides water; rich mineral deposits are not mined. Agr. (corn, beans, chili). On an unpaved road 2.5 mi/4 km from Mexico Highway 51 bet. Arcelia and Teloloapan.

Acaponeta (ah-kah-po-NAI-tah), city and township (1990 pop. 16,379), Nayarit, W Mexico, in coastal lowlands, on Acaponeta R., and 75 mi/121 km NNW of Tepic; 22°29′N 105°21′W. On RR. Mining (gold, silver, copper); processing; agr. center (corn, tobacco, beans, sugarcane, vegetables, fruit; cattle; mfg. (tobacco prods.).

Acaponeta River, c.120 mi/193 km long, W Mexico; rises in Durango in W outliers of Sierra Madre Occidental; flows S into Nayarit to Acaponeta, then turning W to lagoons and marshes which drain into the Pacific.

Acapulco de Juárez, city (1990 pop. 515,374) and township, Guerrero state, S Mexico, on Mexico Highways 95 and 200; 16°50′N 99°54′W. A fashionable resort, it has lavish hotels and facilities for deep-sea fishing and skin diving. Alvarez Internatl. Airport is to the E. Its natural harbor, surrounded by cliffs and promontories, served as a base for Spaniards exploring the Pacific and later played a key role in trade with the Philippines. The city was founded in 1550, and its importance led the Spanish to construct (18th cent.) the Fort of San Diego to protect the harbor from piracy. Today commercial activity in Acapulco is dominated by tourism and related industries. Acapulco has suffered frequent earthquake and hurricane damage.

Acateno, Mexico: see SAN JOSÉ ACATENO.

Acatic (ah-kah-TEEK), town (1990 pop. 8,798), Jalisco, central Mexico, on interior plateau, 30 mi/48 km ENE of Guadalajara; 20°50′N 102°58′W. Elev. 5,528 ft/1,685 m. Grain, fruit, vegetables, corn, beans, sugarcane, wheat; livestock.

Acatlán 1 (ah-kaht-LAHN), town (1990 pop. 549), Hidalgo, central Mexico, 20 mi/32 km E of Pachuca de Soto; 18°12′N 98°2′W. Elev. 6,955 ft/2,120 m. Corn, maguey; livestock. **2** town (1990 pop. 2,459), Veracruz, E Mexico, in Sierra Madre Oriental, 14 mi/23 km NNE of Xalapa Enríquez. Elev. 3,773 ft/1,150 m. Coffee, corn, fruit.

Acatlán de Juárez (ah-kaht-LAHN dai HWAH-rez), city (1990 pop. 6,850), Jalisco, W Mexico, on central plateau, 23 mi/37 km SW of Guadalajara. Elev. 4,570 ft/1,393 m. Sugarcane (sugar is main industry), wheat, alfalfa, beans, fruits, peanuts. Also called Santa Ana Acatlán.

Acatlán de Osorio (ah-kaht-LAHN dai o-SO-ree-o), city (1990 pop. 12,306) and township, ⊙ Acatlán municipio, Puebla, central Mexico, on central plateau, on Inter-Amer. Highway 190 and 60 mi/97 km SSE of Puebla; 18°12′N 98°3′W. Elev. 3,980 ft/1,213 m. Sugarcane, chilis, beans, corn, avocado, papaya. Noted for ceramics.

Acatlán de Pérez Figueroa (ah-kaht-LAHN dai PE-rez fee-ge-RO-ah), town (1990 pop. 5,050), in extreme N central Oaxaca, Mexico, borders the state of Veracruz, 47 mi/75 km NW of Tuxtepec; 18°31′N 96°38′W. Mountainous region in Papaloapan R. drainage. Agr. (corn, beans, rice, coffee, fruit, woods), cattle raising, dairy industry, poultry breeding. On paved road and RR.

Acatzingo de Hidalgo (ah-kat-SEEN-go dai ee-DAHL-go), town (1990 pop. 16,242), ⊙ Acatzingo municipio, Puebla, central Mexico, on central plateau, 27 mi/43 km ESE of Puebla; 18°59′N 97°49′W. Elev. 7,087 ft/2,160 m. Near highway junction. Agr. center (cereals, maguey, vegetables, fruit).

Acaxochitlán (ah-ka-sho-seet-LAHN), town (1990 pop. 3,018), Hidalgo, central Mexico, in Sierra Madre Oriental, 30 mi/48 km E of Pachuca de Soto; 20°11′N 98°11′W. Cattle and forestry are main industry; also avocados, peaches, apples.

Acaxtlahuacán de Albino Zertuche (ah-kasht-lah-wah-KAHN dai ahl-BEE-no sair-TOO-chai), town (1990 pop. 1,791), ⊙ Albino Zertuche municipio, Puebla, central Mexico, 40 mi/64 km S of Izúcar de Matamoros; 18°1′N 98°30′W. Elev. 1,543 ft/470 m. Corn, sugar, fruit; livestock. Also known as Albino Zertuche.

Acayucan (ah-kah-yoo-KAHN), city (1990 pop. 43,383) and township, Veracruz, SE Mexico, on Isthmus of Tehuantepec, 25 mi/40 km W of Minatitlán; 17°59′N 94°58′W. Agr. center (sugarcane, tobacco, tropical fruit; livestock).

Accident, town (1990 pop. 349), Garrett co., extreme NW Md., on the Allegheny Plateau, 30 mi/48 km W of Cumberland; 39°38′N 79°19′W. Named after a tract surveyed and claimed by 2 different individuals. The Texas Eastern Compressor here has a natural gas capacity of 63.5 billion ft/19.4 billion m. Nearby are Savage R. State Forest, Deep Creek L. State Park, and Garrett County Airport. Inc. 1916.

Accomac, county, Va.: see ACCOMACK.

Accomac (AK-o-mak), town (1990 pop. 466), ⊙ Accomack co., E Va., in Eastern Shore area, 24 mi/39 km S of Pocomoke City, Md., midway bet. Atlantic Ocean (E) and Chesapeake Bay (W); 37°43′N 75°40′W. Mfg. (lumber, food processing); agr. (grain, fruit, vegetables; poultry, livestock; timber. Ferry to Tangier Isl., from Onancock, to W; Natl. Aeronautics Space Administration Wallops Flight Center, Assateague Natl. Wildlife Refuge to NE; Kerr Place to W. Old debtors' prison, built in 1750s.

Accomack, county (□ 470 sq mi/1,217 sq km; 1990 pop 31,703), E Va., on Delmarva peninsula, bounded N by Md. state line, W by Chesapeake Bay, E by Atlantic Ocean; ⊙ Accomac; 37°45′N 75°45′W. Poultry processing. Coastal plain agr. area (potatoes, sweet potatoes, tomatoes, fruit, corn, barley, wheat, soybeans; poultry, hogs, cattle; fish, oysters, clams; pine timber). Ocean bathing, tourism, game fishing; many historic bldgs. (some dating from 17th cent.) remain. Off coast (E) lie barrier isls. (Chincoteague, Assateague, Assawoman, Metompkin, and Cedar). Co. includes Tangier Isl. and part of Smith Isl. group in Chesapeake Bay to W (ferry connection). Chincoteague Natl. Wildlife Refuge, part of Assateague Isl. Natl. Seashore in NE; NASA Wallops Flight Center in NE. Formed 1663.

Accord, village (1990 pop. 250), Ulster co., SE N.Y., on Rondout Creek, and 15 mi/24 km SW of Kingston in summer-resort area; 41°47′N 74°14′W. Mfg.

Accotink (AK-o-teenk), hamlet (1990 pop. 200), Fairfax co., N Va., near the Potomac, 9 mi/14.5 km SW of Alexandria, on Accotink Creek. George Washington's MOUNT VERNON home to E; Pohick Church (completed 1774), where Washington attended, to S; Ft. Belvoir Military Reservation to W.

Accoville (AI-ko-vil), uninc. town (1990 pop. 950), Logan co., SW W.Va., 10 mi/16 km SE of Logan, in coal-mining region. Mfg. (steel, machines).

Acequia (a-see-kwe-ah), village (1990 pop. 106), Minidoka co., S Idaho, 5 mi/8 km NE of Rupert, near Snake R.; 42°40′N 113°36′W. Irrigated agr. area. Minidoka Dam (Snake R.) to E.

Achille (ach-IL-ee), village (1990 pop. 491), Bryan co., S Okla., 11 mi/18 km S of Durant; 33°49′N 96°23′W. In agr. area.

Ackerman, town (1990 pop. 1,573), ⊙ Choctaw co., central Miss., 45 mi/72 km WSW of Columbus, on Yockanookany R.; 33°18′N 89°10′W. Agr. area (cotton; corn; cattle; timber); mfg. (shirts and sportswear, wood chips, industrial flanges, lumber processing).

Ackia Battleground National Monument (uh-KEE-uh), NE Miss., 7 mi/11.3 km NW of Tupelo. Marks site of battle of Ackia (May 1736), in which Chickasaw Indians, aided by English, defeated combined force of Fr. troops and Choctaw Indians. Result was opening of region to Eng. settlement. Absorbed by Natchez Trace Parkway (unit of natl. park system). Covers 49 acres/20 ha; est. 1938.

Ackley, town (1990 pop. 1,696), on Franklin-Hardin co. line, N central Iowa, near Beaver Creek, 15 mi/24 km SSE of Hampton; 42°32′N 93°02′W. Agr. (agr. trade center; vegetable cannery); RR junction. Inc. 1858.

Acklins Island, island (1990 pop. 405) and district (□ 120 sq mi/311 sq km), S Bahama Isls., just SE of Crooked Isl., c.250 mi/402 km SE of Nassau; 22°26′N 73°58′W. The isl. is 50 mi/80 km long and 1 mi/1.6 km–13 mi/21 km wide. Exports cascarilla, timber, and sponge. Main settlement, Snug Corner.

Ackworth, town (1990 pop. 66), Warren co., S central Iowa, 3 mi/4.8 km E of Indianola; 41°22′N 93°28′W.

Acme, village (1991 pop. 527), S Alta., Canada, 35 mi/56 km W of Drumheller; 51°30′N 113°30′W. Grain elevators, stock.

Acme 1 village, Columbus co., S N.C., 18 mi/29 km WNW of Wilmington, near Cape Fear R. Tobacco, cotton, sweet potatoes, livestock. **2** uninc. village (1990 pop. 14), Hardeman co., N Texas, 5 mi/8 km W of Quanah; 34°19′N 99°49′W. RR spur junction. Cotton; cattle; oil and gas.

Acme, locality, Kanawha co., W central W.Va., 23 mi/37 km SSE of Charleston.

Acmetonia (ak-mee-TON-ee-ah), uninc. town (1990 pop. 1,200), Harmar township, Allegheny co., W Pa., residential suburb 12 mi/19 km NE of downtown Pittsburgh, on Allegheny R.; 40°32′N 79°48′W. Agr. includes dairying, corn, hay. Lock and Dam No. 3 on Allegheny R.; Pennsylvania Turnpike crosses the river here.

Acoaxet, Mass.: see WESTPORT.

Acolman, Mexico: see ACOLMAN DE NEZAHUALCÓYOTL.

Acolman de Nezahualcóyoti (ah-KOL-mahn dai nai-sah-wahl-KO-yotl), town (1990 pop. 3,140), ⊙ Acolman municipio, Mexico state, central Mexico, 20 mi/32 km NE of Mexico city, and in the Zona Metropolitana de la Ciudad de México; 19°32′N 98°55′W. Elev. 7,513 ft/2,290 m. Maguey, cereals. Has church and monastery of San Agustín Acolman, built 1539–1560.

Acoma (A-kuh-muh) or **Ácoma**, pueblo (1990 pop. 2,590), Cibola co., W central N.Mex.; 34°52′N 107°40′W. Elev. c.7,000 ft/2,130 m. Founded c.1100–1250; in Acoma Indian Reservation. This "sky city" on top of a steep-sided sandstone mesa, 357 ft/109 m high and hard to access, is considered to be the oldest continuously inhabited community in the U.S. (since about 1150). The residents, who speak a Western Keresan language, are known for their fine Acoma pottery. Below the mesa are the cultivated fields and grazing grounds that help support the community. The pueblo's location has impressed visitors from Fray Marcos de Niza (1539) and Coronado's men (1540) to present-day tourists. Juan de Oñate was allowed entry in 1598, but the Native Americans resisted and were subdued only after intense fighting. The missionary Fray Juan Ramírez arrived in 1629. The Acoma people joined in the Pueblo revolt of 1680, were forced to submit to Diego de Vargas in 1692, joined in the later uprising of 1696, and were subdued again in 1699. They were later Christianized. Sheep, cattle; grain. Part of Laguna Indian Reservation to E and S.

Acomita (a-kuh-MEE-duh), uninc. village (1990 pop. 273), Cibola co., N.Mex., in Acoma Indian Reservation, 22 mi/35 km ESE of Grants on Rio San Jose; 35°04′N 107°36′W. Sheep, cattle; pottery, crafts.

Aconchi (ah-KON-chee), town (1990 pop. 1,579), Sonora, NW Mexico, on Sonora R. (irrigation), and 70 mi/113 km NE of Hermosillo; 29°50′N 110°12′W. Elev. 1,516 ft/462 m. Wheat, corn, beans, rice, soy, chilis, oranges, pineapples, watermelons, papayas, sugar; livestock.

Cross references are shown in SMALL CAPITALS. The pronunciation key is on page xv. The dates of population figures are on page xii.

Aconi Point, promontory on the Atlantic, NE N.S., Canada, at N end of Boularderie Isl., 7 mi/11 km NW of Sydney Mines; 46°19′N 60°17′W.

Acra, resort village (1990 pop. 575), Greene co., SE N.Y., in the Catskills, 12 mi/19 km WNW of Catskill; 42°19′N 74°03′W.

Acteopan (ahk-tee-O-pahn), town (1990 pop. 2,076), Puebla, central Mexico, 21 mi/34 km SW of Atlixco. Elev. 5,446 ft/1,660 m. Corn, sugar, fruit; wood; inactive mineral resources. Also called San Marcos Acteopan.

Actipán (ahk-tee-PAHN), officially Actipán de Morelos, village (1990 pop. 4,328), Acatzingo municipio, Puebla, central Mexico, 27 mi/43 km ESE of Puebla. Cereals, maguey, fruit.

Acton 1 uninc. town (1990 pop. 1,471), Los Angeles co., S Calif., 27 mi/43 km N of Los Angeles, on Santa Clara R.; 34°29′N 118°11′W. Cattle; dairying; poultry; fruit. Soledad Pass (3,225 ft/983 m) to NNE. San Gabriel Mts. to S. Pacific Coast Trail passes through town. **2** town (1990 pop. 1,727), York co., SW Maine, 12 mi/19 km NW of Alfred; 43°31′N 70°55′W. **3** town (1990 pop. 17,872), Middlesex co., E Mass., 21 mi/34 km WNW of Boston. Mfg. includes electrical machinery, chemicals, prefabricated houses, precision equip. and instruments. Points of interest include the Isaac Davis Home, residence of the 1st man to die at the battle of Concord during the Amer. Revolution. Includes villages of South Acton and West Acton. Settled c.1680, inc. 1735.

Acton, village, S Ont., Canada, 12 mi/19 km ENE of Guelph; 43°38′N 80°02′W. Light mfg.

Acton Vale, town (1991 pop. 4,468), S Que., Canada, 50 mi/80 km E of Montreal; 45°38′N 72°34′W. Woodworking; textile mfg.

Actopan (ahk-TO-pahn), city (1990 pop. 21,827), Hidalgo, central Mexico, on Inter-Amer. Highway 85, in central plateau, and 18 mi/29 km NW of Pachuca de Soto; 20°16′N 98°56′W. On RR. Agr. center (corn, wheat, wine, beans, fruit; livestock). Has 16th-cent. Augustinian monastery with anc. frescoes. Thermal springs nearby.

Actopan (ahk-TO-pahn), town (1990 pop. 3,899), ⊙ Actopan municipio, Veracruz, E Mexico, in Sierra Madre Oriental foothills, 20 mi/32 km E of Xalapa Enríquez; 20°19′N 98°59′W. Corn, coffee, fruit, sugarcane; tobacco.

Acuamanala (ah-kwah-mah-NAH-lah), town, Tlaxcala, central Mexico, 2 mi/4 km E of Zacateloco on W slope of Malinche volcano; 19°13′N 98°13′W. Agr. (corn, beans, maguey). Formerly Miguel Hidalgo y Costilla.

Acuitzio del Canje (ah-KWEET-see-o del KAHN-lai), town (1990 pop. 4,966), ⊙ Acuitzio, Michoacán, central Mexico, 16 mi/26 km SSW of Morelia. Cereals, wheat, corn, fruit; livestock; tanning; gold and copper sources.

Acula (ah-KOO-lah), town (1990 pop. 2,365), Veracruz, SE Mexico, in Sotavento lowlands, 19 mi/31 km S of Alvarado. Sugar, coffee, tropical fruit, corn, beans, rice; livestock; wood.

Aculco de Espinoza (ah-KOOL-ko dai es-pee-NO-sah), town (1990 pop. 1,487), ⊙ Aculco municipio, Mexico state, central Mexico, 22 mi/35 km SE of San Juan del Río; 19°56′N 00°32′W. Elev. 7,575 ft/2,309 m. Cereals; livestock.

Acul-du-Nord (ah-kyoo-dyoo–NOR), town (1982 pop. 2,348), Nord dept., N Haiti, 9 mi/14.5 km SW of Cap-Haïtien; 19°41′N 72°19′W. Rice, coffee, fruit; cattle. Fine harbor nearby.

Acul-Samedi (ah-kyool-sahm-DEE), village (1982 pop. 550), Nord-Est dept., NE Haiti, on the Plaine du Nord, 25 mi/40 km SE of Cap-Haïtien; 19°31′N 71°53′W. Fruit, coffee growing.

Acultzingo (ah-koolt-SEEN-go), town (1990 pop. 4,181), Veracruz, E Mexico, in Sierra Madre Oriental, 17 mi/27 km SW of Orizaba; 18°40′N 97°15′W. Elev. 5,512 ft/1,680 m. Coffee, sugar, fruit, corn.

Acuña (ah-KOON-yah), city (1990 pop. 52,983), ⊙ Acuña municipio, Coahuila, N Mexico, on the Rio Grande opposite Del Rio (Texas), 50 mi/80 km NW of Piedras Negras; 29°19′N 100°55′W. Elev. 656 ft/200 m. Stock-raising center (cattle, sheep); wheat, cereals, nuts, sugarcane. Also called Las Vacas and Ciudad Acuña.

Acushnet (a-KUHSH-net), town (1990 pop. 9,554), Bristol co., SE Mass., on estuary of Acushnet R., just N of New Bedford; 41°43′N 70°54′W. Electronic equipment. Settled c.1660, inc. 1860.

Acushnet River, c.15 mi/24 km long, SE Mass.; rises in SW Plymouth co.; flows S, past Acushnet, to Buzzards Bay bet. Fairhaven and New Bedford. Lower course is wide estuary.

Acworth 1 (AK-wuhrth), town (1990 pop. 4,519), Cobb co., NW central Ga., 27 mi/43 km NW of Atlanta; 34°04′N 84°41′W. Suburb of Atlanta on I-75. Mfg includes lumber, fabricated metal prods., furniture, automotive parts and supplies. Kennesaw Mt. Natl. Battlefield Park and Allatoona L. nearby. Inc. 1860. **2** town (1990 pop. 776), Sullivan co., SW N.H., 12 mi/19 km SW of Newport; 43°13′N 72°17′W. Drained by Cold N. (flows out of Crescent L. in NE corner). Apples, corn, maple; livestock; timber. Mfg. (lumber, maple prods.). Part of Honey Brook State Forest in SE. Has fine early church (1825).

Ada, county (☐ 1,060 sq mi/2,745 sq km; 1990 pop. 205,775), SW Idaho; ⊙ Boise; 43°27′N 116°14′W. Elev. 2,704 ft/824 m. Irrigated agr. area in Boise R. valley (N); bounded SW by the Snake. Dairying; hay, alfalfa; wheat, barley, oats, corn; sugar beets, fruit, vegetables; cattle, sheep. Mfg. at Boise. Bogus Basin Ski Area on N boundary; Lucky Peak Reservoir (Boise R.) and State Park in NE, Veterans Memorial State Park at Boise in N, Swan Falls, on Snake R., and Snake R. Bends of Pery Natural Area in S; part of Boise Natl. Forest on N boundary. Formed 1864.

Ada (AI-duh), city (1990 pop. 15,820), ⊙ Pontotoc co., S central Okla. It is a large cattle market and the center of a rich oil and ranch area. The city is also noted for horsebreeding, especially for the quarter horses that are raised. East Central State Univ. and the Sciences and Natural Resources Center of Okla. are here, and the Robert S. Kerr Water Research Center (a federal laboratory) is just S of the city. Inc. 1904.

Ada (AI-duh), town (1990 pop. 1,708), ⊙ Norman co., NW Minn., near Wild Rice R. and at source of Marsh R., 31 mi/50 km NNE of Fargo, N. Dak., in Red R. valley; 47°17′N 96°30′W. Elev. 907 ft/276 m. Trade and shipping point in grain, sugar beet area; mfg. (sunflower processing, printing and publishing, feeds). Founded 1874, inc. 1881.

Ada, village (1990 pop. 5,413), Hardin co., W central Ohio, 15 mi/24 km E of Lima, on Ottawa R.; 40°47′N 83°51′W. Trade center for farming area (corn, onions, wheat, dairy prods., poultry); lumber, sporting goods, machinery, rubber products. Seat of Ohio Northern Univ. Inc. 1861.

Adah, uninc. village, Fayette co., SW Pa., on the Monongahela, 10 mi/16 km W of Uniontown; 39°53′N 79°55′W. Agr. (corn, hay; dairying).

Adair 1 county (☐ 570 sq mi/1,476 sq km; 1990 pop. 8,409), SW Iowa; ⊙ Greenfield; 41°19′N 94°28′W. Drained by Middle, North, and Thompson rivers, and by Middle and East branches of the Nodaway. Rolling agr. area (corn; cattle, hogs, poultry); mfg. at Greenfield; bituminous-coal deposits. Site of first train robbery in the West, in NW corner of co. Henry Wallace Monument near Orient in S. Formed 1851. **2** county (☐ 412 sq mi/1,067 sq km; 1990 pop. 15,360), S Ky.; ⊙ Columbia; 37°06′N 85°16′W. Drained by Green R. and Russell Creek. Agr. area (hay, alfalfa, wheat, corn; hogs, cattle, poultry; dairying; burley tobacco); timber; some mfg. at Columbia. Part of Green River L. reservoir in NE. Central/Eastern time zone boundary follows N co. line (Adair is in central). Formed 1801. **3** county (☐ 574 sq mi/1,487 sq km; 1990 pop. 24,577), N Mo.; ⊙ Kirksville; 40°11′N 92°35′W. Drained by Chariton and Salt rivers. Corn, soybeans; hogs, sheep, cattle, mules, poultry; limestone; mfg. at Kirksville. Former coal mining center. Thousand Hills State Park W of Kirksville. Truman State Univ. and osteopathic college at Kirksville. Formed 1841. **4** county (☐ 577 sq mi/1,494 sq km; 1990 pop. 18,421), E Okla.; ⊙ Stilwell; 35°52′N 94°39′W. Bounded E by the Ark. state line, on W edge of Ozarks; drained by Illinois R. and Barre and Sallisaw creeks. Agr. (strawberries; fruits and vegetables; cattle, horses, poultry; dairying). Food processing and canning; some mfg. (electronic equip., industrial machinery, food prods.). Recreation. Adair State Park at center. Formed 1907.

Adair, town (1990 pop. 894), Guthrie and Adair cos., SW Iowa, 16 mi/26 km NW of Greenfield; 41°30′N 94°38′W. Agr. (corn, grain, poultry, cattle); feed milling; light mfg.

Adair (uh-DER), village (1990 pop. 685), Mayes co., NE Okla., 9 mi/14.5 km NNE of Pryor; 36°26′N 95°16′W. In rich stock-grazing and agr. region; mfg. (apparel, boating equip.).

Adair Bay, Span. *Bahia Adair*, inlet at head of Gulf of California, Sonora, NW Mexico, borders Altar Desert, SE of mouth of Colorado R.

Adair Village (uh-DER), village (1990 pop. 554), Benton co., W Oregon, residential community 8 mi/12.9 km NNE of Corvallis; 44°40′N 123°13′W. Agr. area (livestock, dairying, poultry; grain, vegetables, fruit, berries, nuts). McDonald State Forest to SW; Helmick State Park to N.

Adairsville (uh-DERZ-vil), town (1990 pop. 2,131), Bartow co., NW Ga., 14 mi/23 km ENE of Rome; 34°22′N 84°55′W. Mfg. includes consumer goods, chemicals, textiles, and quarry tile.

Adairville (uh-DER-vil), town (1994 pop. 906), Logan co., S Ky., at Tenn. state line, on South Fork of Red R., and 32 mi/51 km SW of Bowling Green; 36°40′N 86°50′W. Agr. (tobacco, grain; livestock; dairying); timber; mfg. (feeds, hoisery). Mineral springs.

Adak, Alaska: see ALEUTIAN ISLANDS.

Adak Island (AI-dak) (30 mi/48 km long, 3 mi/4.8 km–20 mi/32 km wide), Andreanof Isls., Aleutian Isls., SW Alaska, 50 mi/80 km WSW of Atka Isl., 9 mi/14.5 km E of Kanaga Isl.; 51°49′N 176°40′W. Rises to 3,900 ft/1,189 m on Mt. Moffett (N). Sweeper Cove (E) is main harbor. U.S. army, navy, and air bases, estab. here (1942) in World War II, were important in Aleutian campaign, and whose mission was to monitor Rus. submarines; closed 1995. Just E is Kagalaska Isl.

Adak Naval Air Station (AI-dak), on NE Adak Island, Andreanof Isls., Aleutian Isls., SW Alaska; 51°52′N 176°39′W. Closed 1995.

Adalberto Tejeda, Mexico: see VILLA ADALBERTO TEJEDA.

Adamant Mountain (10,980 ft/3,347 m), SE B.C., Canada, in Selkirk Mts. of the Rockies, 50 mi/80 km NNE of Revelstoke; 51°43′N 117°55′W.

Adams 1 (A-duhmz), county (☐ 1,197 sq mi/3,100 sq km; 1990 pop. 265,038), N central Colo.; ⊙ Brighton; 39°52′N 104°20′W. County is highly urbanized at W end, part of urbanized area of city of Denver, to S. Irrigated agr. area, with South Platte R. in W. Cattle, horses, wheat, hay, sunflowers, oats, barley, corn, sugar beets. Rocky Mt. Arsenal is in NW. Burr Lake State Park is in W. Problem-plagued Denver Internatl. Airport (1995) is located in W center of co., city of Denver has extended its limits out to it. This and other annexations of city of Denver that have accrued since 1990 will become part of Denver County in year 2000, decreasing the land areas of Adams and other cos. that surround it. This occurs every 10 years. Formed 1902. **2** county (☐ 1,370 sq mi/3,548 sq km; 1990 pop. 3,254), W Idaho; ⊙ Council; 44°54′N 116°27′W. Mt. area bounded W by Snake R. and Oregon, watered by headstreams of Weiser and Little Salmon rivers. Cattle grazing; agr. (apples, plums; alfalfa; oats, barley). Parts of Payette Natl. Forest scattered throughout co., especially NW and SE; part of Boise Natl. Forest in SE; parts of Hells Canyon Natl. Recreation Area in NW; Brundage Mt. and Payette Lakes ski areas in NE. Lost Valley Reservoir in center; Hells Canyon Dam (NW) and Oxbow Dam (W) are both on Snake R. Formed 1911. **3** county (☐ 871 sq mi/2,256 sq km; 1990 pop. 66,090), W Ill.; ⊙ Quincy; 39°59′N 91°11′W. Bounded W by the Mississippi; drained by Bear and McKee creeks. Agr. area (hogs, cattle, corn, wheat, soybeans, barley, sorghum; dairy prods.), with diversified mfg. (Quincy). Limestone quarries. Formed 1825. Part of Siloam Springs State Park in SE. **4** county (☐ 339 sq mi/878 sq km; 1990 pop. 31,095), E Ind., bounded E by Ohio state line; ⊙ Decatur; 40°45′N 84°56′W. Farming (cattle, hogs, poultry; soybeans, oats, wheat) and dairying area; timber. Diversified mfg., including the processing of dairy prods. and other foods. Drained by Wabash and St. Mary's rivers. Formed 1835. **5** county (☐ 425 sq mi/1,101 sq km; 1990 pop. 4,866), SW Iowa; ⊙ Corning; 41°01′N 94°42′W. Gently rolling prairie, drained by Middle and East branches of the Nodaway R., the Little Platte R., and One Hundred and Two R. Agr. (corn, hogs, cattle, poultry). Bituminous-coal deposits, clay, sand and gravel pits, limestone quarries. L. Icaria 4 mi/6.4 km N of Corning. Formed 1851. **6** county (☐ 486 sq km/33 sq mi; 1990 pop. 35,356), SW Miss.; ⊙ Natchez; 31°28′N 91°20′W. Bounded W by the Mississippi R. (La. state line), S by Homochitto R.; drained by St. Catherine Creek. Includes part of Homochitto Natl. Forest in SE. Agr. (cotton; corn, soybeans; timber); oil field; clay, limestone deposits; mfg. at Natchez. Natchez State Park in NE; Natchez Natl. Historical Park and Natchez Natl. Cemetery in W, at Natchez; Natchez Trace Natl. Parkway terminates at Natchez. Formed 1799. **7** county (☐ 564 sq mi/1,461 sq km; 1990 pop. 29,625), S Nebr.; ⊙ Hastings; 40°31′N 98°30′W. Agr. area drained by Little Blue R. and W Fork Big Blue R. Mfg. at Hastings; food processing, machinery; corn, soybeans, sorghum, cattle, dairying, hogs, poultry prods. Recreation area in E; Crystal L. State Recreation Area in SE. Formed 1871. **8** county (☐ 988 sq mi/2,559 sq km; 1990 pop. 3,174), SW N.Dak., borders S.Dak. on S.; ⊙ Hettinger; 46°05′N 102°31′W. Drained by Cedar Creek. Services, dairying, wheat, cattle, transportation, utilities. Small Mirror L. in S. Formed 1907. **9** county (☐ 588 sq mi/1,523 sq km; 1990 pop. 25,371), S Ohio; ⊙ West Union, 38°51′N 83°28′W. Bounded S by Ohio R., here forming Ky. state line; drained by small creeks. Part of Lexington Plain physiographic region. Includes Serpent Mound State Park. Agr. area (livestock, dairy prods., tobacco, corn); some mfg. at Manchester (lumber and wood products, industrial machinery, apparel). Formed 1799. **10** county (☐ 521 sq mi/1,349 sq km; 1990 pop. 78,274), S Pa.; ⊙ Gettysburg; 39°52′N 77°13′W. Rolling farmland with mts. in W, bounded S by Md. state line, W and NW by South Mts. Drained by Conewago Creek and its South Branch, and Rock Creek. Mfg. at Gettysburg. Agr. (apples, cherries, grapes, wheat, corn, oats, barley, hay, alfalfa, soybeans, potatoes; chickens, eggs, sheep, hogs, cattle, dairying); limestone. Gettysburg Natl. Military Park and Cemetery and Eisenhower Natl. Historical Site in S center; Appalachian Trail skirts W and NW co. line in adjacent Franklin and Cumberland cos.; Gettysburg RR, scenic RR in center; Ski Liberty ski resort in SW; part of Mont Alto State Forest in W; part of Michaux State Forest in NW; part of Caledonia State Park on W boundary; L. Meade reservoir in NE, L. Heritage reservoir in S center, both residential developments. Formed 1800. **11** county (☐ 1,895 sq mi/4,908 sq km; 1990 pop. 13,603), SE Wash.; ⊙ Ritzville; 47°00′N 118°34′W. In Columbia basin agr. region. Rolling prairies bounded SE by Palouse R. Drained in E by Cow Creek, forms Sprague L. in NE corner. Onions, asparagus, peppermint, potatoes, beans, alfalfa, hay, cattle, hogs, corn, wheat, barley, oats, fruit; dairying. Part of Columbia Natl. Wildlife Refuge in SW. Formed 1883. **12** county (☐ 1,929 sq mi/4,996 sq km; 1990 pop. 13,603), central Wis.; ⊙ Friendship; 46°59′N 118°33′W. Dairying, corn, soybeans, peas, beans, potatoes; timber; RR repair shops. Drained by tributaries of Wisconsin R., which bounds co. on W; part of the Dells of Wisconsin in SW. Borders Wisconsin R. (including Petenwell L. and Castle Rock L. reservoir) on W. Small lakes in SE, N, and center. Roche a Cri State Park near center. Formed 1848.

Adams 1 town (1990 pop. 9,445), Berkshire co., NW Mass., in the Berkshires, on the Hoosic R.; 42°38′N 73°07′W. Mfg. (chemicals, textiles, paper prods.). The Berkshire region attracts tourists year-round. A Society of Friends meeting house (built 1782) is the site of annual Quaker meetings. Susan B. Anthony b. here. Mount Greylock State Reservation; Savoy Mt. State Forest. Inc. 1778. **2** town (1990 pop. 756), Mower co., SE Minn., near Iowa state line, 15 mi/24 km SE of Austin, on Little Cedar R.; 43°33′N 92°43′W. Corn, oats, soybeans; cattle, sheep, hogs, poultry; dairying. Mfg. (printing and publishing, feeds, storage tanks). **3** town (1990 pop. 1,715), Adams co., central Wis., 30 mi/48 km S of Wisconsin Rapids; 43°57′N 89°49′W. Mfg. (shipping containers, modular housing). Founded before 1860; inc. 1926.

Adams 1 village (1990 pop. 472), Gage co., SE Nebr., 18 mi/29 km NE of Beatrice and on North Fork of Big Nemaha R.; 40°27′N 96°30′W. Grain. **2** village (☐ 1 sq mi/2.6 sq km; 1990 pop. 1,753), Jefferson co., N N.Y., 13 mi/21 km SSW of Watertown; 43°48′N 76°01′W. In dairy region. Mfg. (surgical equip., wood prods.). Inc. 1851. **3** village (1990 pop. 248), Walsh co., NE N.Dak., 35 mi/56 km W of Grafton, on Park R.; 48°25′N 98°04′W. Lake Zahl Natl. Wildlife Refuge to W. **4** village (1990 pop. 223), Umatilla co., NE Oregon, 13 mi/21 km NE of Pendleton on Wildhorse Creek; 45°46′N 118°33′W. Wheat, brans, peas, onions, apples, plums; cattle and sheep. Umatilla Indian Reservation to SE.

Adams Center, village (☐ 4 sq mi/10.4 sq km; 1990 pop. 1,675), Jefferson co., N N.Y., 9 mi/14.5 km SSW of Watertown; 43°51′N 76°00′W.

Adams, Fort, state park, R.I.: see NEWPORT, city.

Adams Historic Site, Quincy, E Mass., authorized 1946. Home of Presidents John Adams and John Quincy Adams and other members of the family.

Adams Lake (☐ 54), S B.C., Canada, 50 mi/80 km NNW of Vernon; 39 mi/63 km long, 1 mi/1.6 km–2 mi/3.2 km wide; 51°15′N 119°30′W. Drains SE into Shuswap L. by short Adams R.

Adams, Mount (12,276 ft/3,742 m), S Wash., in Cascade Range, 55 mi/89 km SW of Yakima. Snowcapped, in Mt. Adams Wilderness Area. Summit is on boundary of Gifford Pinchot Natl. Forest (W); Yakima Indian Reservation (E).

Adams, Mount, N.H.: see PRESIDENTIAL RANGE.

Adams Peak (8,197 ft/2,498 m), E Calif., in the High Sierras, 30 mi/48 km NNW of Reno, Nev.

Adams Peak,, Nev.: see OSGOOD MOUNTAINS.

Adamsburg (A-duhms-buhrg), borough (1990 pop. 257), Hempsfield township, Westmoreland co., SW Pa., 2 mi/3.2 km W of Jeanette; 40°18′N 79°39′W. Agr. (dairying).

Adams-Morgan, residential sect. in NW Washington D.C., N of Dupont Circle; 38°55′N 77°02′W. Known for its ethnic diversity and its many restaurants, shops, and night spots.

Adamstown (A-duhms-toun), borough (1990 pop. 1,108), Lancaster co., SE Pa., 10 mi/16 km SW of Reading; 40°14′N 76°03′W. Mfg. (apparel, food prods.). Agr. (grain, potatoes, apples; poultry, livestock; dairying). Settled 1739.

Adamsville (A-duhms-vil), city (1990 pop. 4,161), Jefferson co., N central Ala., 8 mi/12.9 km NW of downtown Birmingham.

Adamsville, town (1990 pop. 1,745), McNairy co., SW Tenn., 36 mi/58 km SE of Jackson; 35°14′N 88°23′W. Sawmills, cotton gins; mfg. includes plumbing prods., clothing, auto parts.

Adamsville, village, S Que., Canada, on Centre Yamaska R. and 8 mi/13 km SSW of Granby. Dairying.

Adamsville 1 village (1990 pop. 151), Muskingum co., central Ohio, 12 mi/19 km NE of Zanesville, in agr. area; 40°04′N 81°55′W. **2** village, Little Compton town, Newport co., R.I., 10 mi/16 km ENE of Newport, near Mass. border in a deep valley. Rhode Isl. Red chicken was developed on a farm nearby; 41°57′N 71°23′W.

Addieville, village (1990 pop. 257), Washington co., SW Ill., 5 mi/8 km W of Nashville; 38°23′N 89°29′W. In agr. area.

Addington, village (1990 pop. 100), Jefferson co., S Okla., 18 mi/29 km S of Duncan; 34°14′N 97°58′W. In agr. area. Wanrika L. reservoir (Beaver Creek) to W.

Addis (A-dis), town (1990 pop. 1,222), West Baton Rouge parish, SE La., on Mississippi R., 8 mi/13 km SSW of Baton Rouge; 30°21′N 91°16′W. RR junction; mfg. of rubber, fabricated sheet metal, resins, carbon black, conveyors. Formerly Baton Rouge Junction. Inc. 1915.

Addison, county (☐ 808 sq mi/2,093 sq km; 1990 pop. 32,953), W Vt., bounded W by L. Champlain and rising to Green Mts. in E; ⊙ Middlebury; 44°01′N 73°08′W. Agr. and resort region; dairying, fruit, wood prods., poultry. Lake and mt. resorts; winter sports. Includes part of Green Mt. Natl. Forest; drained by Otter Creek, New Haven, and White rivers. Organized 1787.

Addison 1 (A-di-suhn), town (1990 pop. 626), Winston co., NW Ala., 14 mi/23 km ENE of Double Springs. Center for mobile home mfg., furniture. **2** town (1990 pop. 1,114), Washington co., E Maine, at mouth of Pleasant R., 16 mi/26 km SW of Machias; 44°30′N 67°42′W. Fishing, lumbering, resorts. **3** town (1990 pop. 8,783), Dallas co., N Texas, suburb 12 mi/19 km N of downtown Dallas; elev. 643 ft/196 m; 32°57′N 96°50′W. Mfg. (electronic production and assembly, sheet metal fabrication, motor vehicle construction). Addison Municipal Airport is here. **4** town (1990 pop. 1,023), Addison co., W Vt., 8 mi/12.9 km NW of Middlebury and on L. Champlain; 44°04′N 73°20′W. Bridged here to Crown Point, N.Y., at Chimney Point, site of Fr. settlement (1730) near fort built by N.Y. expedition (1690). Daughters of the American Revolution State Park is here.

Addison 1 village (1990 pop. 32,058), Du Page co., NE Ill., 3 mi/4.8 km NE of Wheaton; 41°55′N 88°00′W. In addition to its foundries, industrial heating equip. is made in Addison. Inc. 1884. **2** village (1990 pop. 632), Lenawee co., SE Mich., 17 mi/27 km WNW of Adrian; 41°59′N 84°20′W. Grain, corn, wheat, soybeans, apples; dairy; poultry; concrete. Devils L. to E. **3** village (☐ 1 sq mi/2.6 sq km; 1990 pop. 1,842), Steuben co., S N.Y., on Canisteo R. and 9 mi/14.5 km WSW of Corning; 42°06′N 77°13′W. In dairying region. Inc. 1873.

Addison (A-dis-suhn), borough (1990 pop. 212), Somerset co., SW Pa., 23 mi/37 km SW of Somerset, near Md. state line; 39°44′N 79°20′W. Mfg. (lumber). Agr. (corn, hay, potatoes; livestock, dairying). Youghiogheny River L. reservoir to W.

Addison, W.Va.: see WEBSTER SPRINGS.

Addor (AD-or), village, Moore co., central N.C., 7 mi/11.3 km SE of Southern Pines near Drowning Creek. Tobacco, grain, livestock, poultry. Formerly Keyser.

Addy, uninc. village (1990 pop. 220), Stevens co., NE Wash., 8 mi/12.9 km NW of Chewelah, on Colville R. Wheat; dairying, hogs. Mfg. (magnesium ingots). Colville Natl. Forest to E.

Addyston (A-dees-tuhn), village (1990 pop. 1,198), Hamilton co., extreme SW Ohio, on Ohio R., and 10 mi/16 km W of Cincinnati; 39°08′N 84°41′W. Founded 1789. William Henry Harrison Memorial Park is nearby.

Adel 1 (AI-del), town (1990 pop. 5,093), ⊙ Cook co., S Ga., 23 mi/37 km NNW of Valdosta; 31°08′N 83°26′W. Mfg. includes metal prods., boats, automotive parts, metal finishing, wood prods., milling (veneer, lumber). Inc. 1889. **2** town (1990 pop. 3,304), ⊙ Dallas co., central Iowa, on Raccoon R., and 20 mi/32 km W of Des Moines; 41°36′N 94°01′W. Agr. (poultry hatchery, soybean processing); mfg. (brick and tile plant), brewery. Settled 1846, inc. 1887.

Adelaide Peninsula, NW Keewatin dist., N.W.T., Canada, extends 60 mi/97 km N into the Arctic Ocean, S of King William Isl.; 68°30′N 97°W. On N coast many relics of Franklin's expedition (1847–1848) have been found (Grant Point, Starvation Cove).

Adelanto, city (1990 pop. 8,517), San Bernardino co., S Calif., 32 mi/51 km N of San Bernardino, in SW part of Mojave Desert; 34°34′N 117°27′W. George Air Force Base to E; El Mirage L. (dry) to W. Cattle; alfalfa, fruit, grain; mfg. (industrial prods.).

Adeline, village (1990 pop. 141), Ogle co., N Ill., 12 mi/-

19 km NW of Oregon; 42°08′N 89°29′W. In rich agr. area (corn, oats, soybeans, hay; cattle, hogs); dairying.

Adell (ah-DEL), village (1990 pop. 510), Sheboygan co., E Wis., 15 mi/24 km SW of Sheboygan; 43°37′N 87°57′W. In dairy and grain area. Mfg. (food, wood prods.). Kettle Moraine Fish Hatchery to N.

Adelphi (uh-DEL-fei), village (1990 pop. 398), Ross co., S Ohio, 15 mi/24 km NE of Chillicothe and on small Salt Creek, in agr. area; 39°29′N 82°45′W.

Adena (uh-DEE-nuh), village (1990 pop. 842), Jefferson co., E Ohio, 15 mi/24 km SW of Steubenville; 40°13′N 80°54′W.

Adin, village, Modoc co., NE Calif., 27 mi/43 km SW of Alturas on Ash Creek. Trade center for agr. and lumbering region. Adin Pass (5,173 ft/1,577 m) to N; Modoc Natl. Forest to N, E, and S.

Adirondack, resort village (1990 pop. 200), Warren co., E N.Y., in the Adirondacks, on E shore of Schroon L., 18 mi/29 km WSW of Ticonderoga; 43°46′N 73°46′W.

Adirondack Mountains, mt. massif, N N.Y., bet. the St. Lawrence valley in the N, L. Champlain lowland in the E, the Mohawk valley in the S, and Block R. valley in the W. Rises to 5,344 ft/1,629 m at Mt. Marcy, the highest point in the state. Geologically a S extension of the Laurentian upland of Canada, the Adirondacks are sometimes mistakenly included in the Appalachian system. Composed chiefly of metamorphic rock, the Adirondacks were formed as pre-Cambrian igneous rocks (mainly granite) intruded upward, doming the earth's surface; subsequent faulting of the earth's crust and surface erosion have given the mts. a rugged topography. High Peaks sect. in NE part of S massif, largely in Clinton, Essex, and Warencos. The Pleistocene glaciers disrupted the earlier drainage patterns, creating numerous lakes. In the 1980s it was discovered that many of the region's lakes were unable to support life due to damage caused by acid rain. The Hudson, Ausable, and Black rivers, among many others, rise in the Adirondacks. The region is a year-round sports, recreation, and resort area; most of it has been set aside as Adirondack State Park. Within the boundaries of the park are 9,375 sq mi/24,281 sq km of public and private land, making it the largest park in the nation (larger than the combined area of the Grand Canyon, Yellowstone, and Glacier natl. parks). L. Placid and L. George are major resort centers. Lumbering declined after a forest preserve was established in 1892, but is still very important in the regional economy. Important mineral prods. include zinc, titanium, and talc.

Adjuntas (ahd-HOON-tahs), town (1990 pop. 19,451), W central P.R., in the Cordillera Central, 13 mi/21 km NNW of Ponce. Elev. 1,622 ft/494 m. Center for coffee production; also plantains, oranges, fruit. World's leading producer of citron. Light mfg. Garzas hydroelectric plant is 4 mi/6.4 km S. Manganese deposits nearby. The Alto de la Bandera resort and pass is 2.5 mi/4 km SE.

Admiralty Inlet, fjord, 230 mi/370 km long, NW Baffin Isl., N.W.T., Canada, of Lancaster Sound, bet. Brodeur and Borden peninsulas. One of the world's longest fjords, it is 2 mi/3 km–20 mi/32 km wide; shoreline is steep and abrupt, rising to c.1,000 ft/300 m–1,500 ft/460 m. Inlet has several arms. On NE shore of inlet is Arctic Bay trading post.

Admiralty Inlet, Wash.: see PUGET SOUND.

Admiralty Island (☐ 1,664 sq mi/4,310 sq km), SE Alaska, in the Alexander Archipelago, S of Juneau; 90 mi/145 km long, 35 mi/56 km wide; 57°44′N 134°20′W. Rises to 4,650 ft/1,417 m. Fishing (cannery at Angoon), lumbering.

Admire, village (1990 pop. 147), Lyon co., E central Kansas, 17 mi/27 km N of Emporia; 38°38′N 96°05′W. Livestock; grain.

Adobe Creek Reservoir, or **Blue Lake**, reservoir, Bent and Kiowa cos., SE Colo., on 3-mi/4.8-km channel draining W into Adobe Creek, 11 mi/18 km N of Las Animas; 5 mi/8 km long; 38°14′N 103°16′W. Max. storage capacity of 88,319 acre-ft. Formed by Adobe Creek Dam (14 ft/4 m high), built (1969) by Fort Lyon Canal Co. for irrigation.

Adolphustown (uh-DAHL-fuhs-toun), village (1991 pop. 886), SE Ont., on Adolphus Reach, inlet of L. Ontario, 20 mi/32 km ESE of Belleville; 44°05′N 77°02′W. Founded 1784 by United Empire Loyalists.

Adona (uh-DAHN-uh), village (1990 pop. 146), Perry co., central Ark., 40 mi/64 km NW of Little Rock, near Arkansas R.; 35°02′N 92°54′W. Petit Jean State Park to NW.

Adrian 1 (AI-dree-uhn), city (1990 pop. 22,097), ⊙ Lenawee co., SE Mich., on the R. Raisin, 41°53′N 84°02′W. RR junction. It is a mfg. (machinery, furniture, transportation equip., plastic prods., adhesives) and trading center for a fertile farm region. Airport. It is the seat of Adrian Col. and Siena Heights Col. Several lakes to NW. Inc. 1836. **2** agr. city (1990 pop. 1,582), Bates co., W Mo., near South Grand R., 10 mi/16 km N of Butler; 38°23′N 94°20′W. Corn, wheat, barley, sorghum; cattle, cows.

Adrian (AI-dree-uhn), town (1990 pop. 1,141), Nobles co., SW Minn., on Kanaranzi Creek, near Iowa state line, and 18 mi/29 km W of Worthington; 43°37′N 95°55′W. Corn, oats, soybeans; cattle, sheep, poultry; dairying. Mfg. (machinery, plastics, concrete).

Adrian 1 (AI-dree-uhn), village, (1990 pop. 615), Johnson and Emanuel cos., E central Ga., 16 mi/26 km WSW of Swainsboro; 32°32′N 82°35′W. Mfg. includes modular homes and cabinets. **2** village (1990 pop. 131), Malheur co., E Oregon, 20 mi/32 km SSW of Ontario and 3 mi/4.8 km W of Idaho boundry, on Snake R.; 43°44′N 117°04′W. Wheat, cattle, dairying, vegetables. Owyhee Dam and L. Owyhee State Park to SW; Succor Creek State Recreation Area to S. **3** village (1990 pop. 220), Oldham co., extreme N Texas, 47 mi/76 km WNW of Amarillo; 36°16′N 102°39′W. Cattle, wheat. Oil and natural gas.

Advance (AD-vants), city (1990 pop. 1,139), Stoddard co., SE Mo., 15 mi/24 km N of Bloomfield; 37°06′N 89°54′W. Mfg. (aluminum doors and windows). Rice, soybeans, corn.

Advance (AD-vants), town (1990 pop. 520), Boone co., central Ind., 8 mi/12.9 km SW of Lebanon; 40°00′N 86°37′W. Agr. area; steel fabricating.

Advance, uninc. village, Davie co., W central N.C., 14 mi/23 km SW of Winston-Salem near Yadkin R. Tobacco, grain; poultry, dairying, livestock. Mfg. (plastics, furniture, machine parts).

Advocate Harbour, village, N N.S., Canada, on Minas Channel, 20 mi/32 km W of Parrsboro; 45°20′N 64°47′W. Dairying, farming. Copper formerly mined here.

Adwolf, uninc. town, Smyth co., SW Va., 5 mi/8 km SW of Marion, near South Fork Holston R.; 36°47′N 81°35′W. Agr. area (tobacco, grain; livestock, dairying). Part of Jefferson Natl. Forest to S and SE, incl. Mt. Rogers Natl. Recreation Area to S.

Aeolus, Mount (ee-O-luhs) (8,672 ft/2,643 m), W Alta., 25 mi/40 km NE of B.C. border, Canada, in Rocky Mts., in Jasper Natl. Park, 27 mi/43 km N of Jasper; 53°16′N 118°04′W.

Affton, uninc. city (1990 pop. 21,106), St. Louis co., E Mo., a suburb of St. Louis, 10 mi/16 km SW of downtown St. Louis; 38°32′N 90°19′W. Mfg. (food, machinery, consumer goods, medical equip.). Grant's Farm tourist attraction in adjacent Grantwood Village.

Afognak (uh-FAHG-nak), village, S Alaska, on SE Afognak Isl., 20 mi/32 km NW of Kodiak. Est. in early 19th cent. by Russian settlers.

Afognak Island (uh-FAHG-nak) (43 mi/69 km long, 9 mi/14.5 km–23 mi/37 km wide), S Alaska, bet. Shelikof Strait (W) and Gulf of Alaska (E), N of Kodiak Isl.; 58°16′N 152°35′W. Rises to 2,546 ft/776 m (NE). Afognak village, SE. Some sheep farming.

Afton 1 town (1990 pop. 953), Union co., S Iowa, 9 mi/14.5 km E of Creston; 41°01′N 94°12′W. Mfg. (heating elements). **2** town (1990 pop. 2,645), Washington co., E Minn., residential suburb 11 mi/18 km E of St. Croix, on St. Croix R. at its exit from L. St. Croix; 44°53′N 92°49′W. Drained by Valley Branch Creek. Cattle, sheep soybeans, corn, oats. Afton State Park to S; Lower St. Croix Natl. Scenic Riverway on St. Croix R.; Afton Alps

Ski Area on St. Croix R.; L. Edith in N. **3** town (1990 pop. 915), Ottawa co., extreme NE Okla., 11 mi/18 km ENE of Vinita; 36°41′N 94°58′W. In rich farm area (grain, livestock, poultry, corn); mfg. (connecting rods, sawmill); RR junction to N. Grand L. of the Cherokees (Neosho R.) lies to E and S. Bernice State Park to SE. **4** town (1990 pop. 1,394), Lincoln co., W Wyo., near Idaho state line, just W of Salt R. Range, 70 mi/113 km NNW of Kemmerer; 42°43′N 110°55′W. Elev. 6,134 ft/1,870 m. Dairy and trade center for Star Valley (grain, flour, dairy prods., timber, furs; logging; printing). Nearby is Univ. of Wyoming agr. experiment station and coal mine. Bridger-Teton Nat. Forest to E. Settled c.1885, inc. 1902.

Afton 1 village (☐ 1 sq mi/2.6 sq km; 1990 pop. 838), Chenango co., S central N.Y., on the Susquehanna and 22 mi/35 km ENE of Binghamton; 42°13′N 75°31′W. In agr. area. Lumber, wood prods., livestock feed. **2** uninc. village, Nelson co., NW central Va., 3 mi/4.8 km SE of Waynesboro; 38°01′N 78°50′W. Mfg. (synthetic yarn, conveyors, wooden cabinets); timber. George Washington Natl. Forest to SW (incl. Wintergreen Ski Area), Shenandoah Natl. Park to NE, Appalachian Trail and Blue Ridge Parkway pass to W.

Agabama River (ah-gah-BAH-mah), c.73 mi/118 km long, central Cuba; rises in hills of Santa Clara (Villa Clara prov.); flows S to a delta on the Caribbean Sea, 12 mi/19 km SE of Trinidad (Sancti Spíritus prov.); 21°40′N 79°50′W. Drains 1,713 sq mi/4,437 sq km of land. Its lower course is called Manatí, which passes through the UNESCO-declared World Heritage site of the Iznaga valley (also known as "the valley of sugar mills"), the prime sugar-producing region of the world in the first 4 decades of the 19th cent., before mechanization. Only 1 sugar mill operates on its banks today.

Agar, town (1990 pop. 82), Sully co., central S.Dak., 10 mi/16 km N of Onida. Grain, poultry. Near Okobojo Creek.

Agassiz (A-guh-see), village, SW B.C., Canada, near Fraser R., 10 mi/16 km NE of Chilliwack, 49°14′N 121°46′W. Mixed farming, lumbering, fruit growing. Site of Agr. Canada experimental farm.

Agassiz, Lake (A-guh-see), glacial lake of the Pleistocene epoch; c.700 mi/1,127 km long, 250 mi/402 km wide. Formed by the melting of the continental ice sheet some 10,000 years ago; covered much of present-day NW Minn., NE N.D., S Manitoba, and SW Ont. The lake was named in 1879 in memory of Louis Agassiz for his contributions to the theory of the glacial epoch. L. Traverse, Big Stone L., and the Minnesota R. are in the channel of prehistoric R. Warren, L. Agassiz's original outlet to the S. As the ice melted, the water drained E into L. Superior; after the ice disappeared, N into Hudson Bay, it left lakes Winnipeg, Manitoba, and Winnipegosis, Red L., L. of the Woods, and other smaller lakes. The Red R. valley now occupies the lake bed and is an important crop-growing region due to its rich soil.

Agassiz, Mount (A-guh-see), peak (2,378 ft/725 m), Grafton co., NW N.H., 4 mi/6.4 km ESE of Bethlehem, in White Mts.

Agate Fossil Beds National Monument (A-gait) (4.8 sq mi/11.9 sq km), Sioux co., NW Nebr., 38 mi/61 km N of Scottsbluff. Renowned quarries containing numerous well-preserved Miocene mammal fossils. Includes both side of Niobrara R. Covers 3,055 acres/1,237 ha; authorized 1965.

Agattu Island (uh-GAH-too) (18 mi/29 km long, 4 mi/6.4 km–9 mi/14.5 km wide), Near Isls., Aleutian Isls., SW Alaska, 20 mi/32 km SE of Attu Isl.; 52°26′N 173°34′E. Rises to 2,075 ft/632 m. Uninhabited, mountainous, treeless.

Agawa River (A-guh-wuh), 60 mi/97 km long, central Ont., Canada; rises E of L. Superior; flows SW through Agawa Canyon, then S, and finally W, to L. Superior 60 mi/97 km NNW of Sault Ste Marie; 47°21′N 84°38′W. At its mouth uranium deposits were discovered, 1948; aboriginal pictographs found in 1959. Mouth and lower 8 mi/12.9 km on Agawa (sacred place) Bay are protected by Lake Superior Prov. Park (155,569 ha/384,633 ac).

Agawam (A-guh-wahm), town (1990 pop. 27,323), Hampden co., S Mass., on the Connecticut R.; includes village of Feeding Hills; 42°04′N 72°39′W. Largely residential, the town produces robotics, machinery, electronic equip., aircraft parts, dairy prods. Major amusement park. Rodinson State Park. Settled 1636, inc. 1855.

Agawam River, E Mass., small stream entering the Atlantic in Plymouth town; also former name of lower course of WESTFIELD RIVER in W Mass.

Agency 1 town (1990 pop. 616), Wapello co., SE Iowa, near Des Moines R., 6 mi/9.7 km E of Ottumwa; 41°00′N 92°18′W. In agr. area. Est. 1838 as Indian agency. **2** town (1990 pop. 642), Buchanan co., NW Mo., on Little Platte R. and 8 mi/12.9 km SE of St. Joseph; 39°39′N 94°45′W.

Agency Lake, Klamath co., S Oregon, N arm of Upper Klamath L., 23 mi/37 km NNW of Klamath Falls; bed is 6 mi/9.7 km long, 3 mi/4.8 km wide. Fed in N by Wood Creek. Part of Upper Klamath Natl. Wildlife Refuge on SW shore.

Agency Valley Dam, Oregon: see NORTH FORK.

Agenda, village (1990 pop. 81), Republic co., N Kansas, 13 mi/21 km SE of Belleville; 39°42′N 97°25′W. Corn, wheat.

Ages (AI-juhs), uninc. village (1990 pop. 500), Harlan co., SE Ky., in the Cumberland Mts., on Clover Fork of Cumberland R. and 4 mi/6.4 km E of Harlan. Bituminous coal; coal processing.

Agnew, uninc. village, Santa Clara co., W Calif., 3 mi/4.8 km N of Santa Clara. Branch of Hetch Hetchy Aqueduct runs E-W, to N. State mental hosp. Great American theme park to W.

Agnew Lake (AG-noo) (21 mi/34 km long, 1 mi/1.6 km wide), SE central Ont., Canada, on Spanish R. and 30 mi/48 km WSW of Sudbury; 46°22′N 81°45′W.

Agoura Hills, uninc. city (1990 pop. 20,390), Los Angeles co., S Calif., residential suburb 25 mi/40 km WNW of downtown Los Angeles, 8 mi/12.9 km N of the Pacific Ocean; 34°09′N 118°46′W. Santa Monica Mts. Natl. Recreation Area to S. Mfg. (electronic components, chemicals, printing and publishing).

Agra 1 (AG-ruh), village (1990 pop. 322), Phillips co., N Kansas, 11 mi/18 km E of Phillipsburg; 39°45′N 99°07′W. In corn belt; livestock. **2** village (1990 pop. 334), Lincoln co., central Okla., 8 mi/12.9 km SW of Cushing; 35°53′N 96°52′W. In agr. area; mfg. (leather prods.).

Agramonte 1 (ah-grah-MON-tai), town, Camagüey prov., E Cuba; 20°54′N 77°55′W. Sugar central (Ignacio Agramonte) just S of Florida and 23 mi/37 km WNW of Camagüey. **2** town, Matanzas prov., W Cuba, on RR and 38 mi/61 km SE of Matanzas; 22°40′N 81°06′W. In sugar- and citrus-growing region. It is surrounded by 7 sugar mills.

Agua Azul Natural Park (AH-gwah ah-ZOOL), a natl. park in central Chiapas, Mexico, 39 mi/62 km S of Palenque. The park is developed around a river with dozens of spectacular cascades and rapids, enhanced by the striking blue color of the water and green of the rainforest. Camping and hiking facilities.

Agua Blanca Iturbide (AH-gwah BLAHN-ka ee-toor-BEE-dai), town (1990 pop. 988), ⊙ Agua Blanca de Iturbide township, Hidalgo, central Mexico, 30 mi/48 km NE of Pachuca de Soto; 20°48′N 98°22′W. Corn, beans, sugar; livestock.

Agua Caliente, Mexico: see TIJUANA.

Agua Dulce (AH-gwah DOOL-sai), city (1990 pop. 38,490), SE Veracruz, Mexico, 9 mi/14 km NE of Minatitlán, located on the plains of the Tonalá R. Many roads built by PEMEX pass by this town. Hot climate. Important petroleum resources.

Agua Dulce, town (1990 pop. 794), Nueces co., S Texas, 32 mi/51 km W of Corpus Christi; 27°46′N 97°54′W. In agr. (sorghum, cattle, cotton), oil and gas producing area.

Agua Fria River, c.120 mi/193 km long, W Ariz., intermittent stream; rising 20 mi/32 km ENE of Prescott; flows generally S to join Gila R. 16 mi/26 km W of

Phoenix. New Waddell Dam (300 ft/91 m high, 4,800 ft/1,463 m long; built 1992) forms L. Pleasant, 30 mi/48 km NNW of Phoenix, used for irrigation and water storage from the Central Arizona Project. Hayden-Rhodes aqueduct crosses river 4 mi/6.4 km below (S of) dam.

Agua Prieta (AH-gwah pree-AI-tah), city (1990 pop. 37,664) and township, Sonora, NW Mexico, near U.S. border, 3 mi/4.8 km S of Douglas, Ariz., on RR, and highway; 31°18′N 109°33′W. Elev. 3,937 ft/1,200 m. Livestock; corn; copper smelter. Border crossing.

Aguacate (ah-gwah-KAH-tai), town, La Habana prov., W Cuba, on RR, and 36 mi/58 km ESE of Havana; 22°58′N 82°37′W. In agr. region (sugarcane, tobacco); stone quarrying. The sugar central R. Martínez Villena is just W.

Aguada (ah-GWAH-dah), town (1990 pop. 35,911), NW P.R., near the coast, 12 mi/19 km N of Mayagüez. The Coloso sugar mill is 1.5 mi/2.4 km E; light industry. At site of pre-Columbian village (where Columbus allegedly landed), considered to be founded 1506.

Aguada de Pasajeros (ah-GWAH-dah dai pah-sah-HAI-ros), town, Cienfuegos prov., central Cuba, on edge of the Ciénaga de Zapata, on RR, and 30 mi/48 km NW of Cienfuegos; 22°23′N 80°51′W. Produces sugar (Primero de Mayo sugar mill 5 mi/8 km SE), timber, charcoal, livestock. Lime pits.

Aguadilla (ah-gwah-DEE-yah), town (1990 pop. 59,335), NW P.R., a port on Mona Passage. Commercial and industrial area; mfg. (furniture, electric apparatus, chemical prods.), small factory mfg. airplanes. Fishing. Tourism. Home of island's tiny lace-making industry. Columbus reputedly landed at the site of Aguadilla in 1493. Has natural spring at El Parterre Park. Inter American Univ. has a campus here. Site of former Ramey Air Force Base, now used for commercial aviation.

Aguadores (a-gwah-DOR-ais), beach resort, Santiago de Cuba prov., E Cuba, 3.5 mi/5.6 km S of Santiago de Cuba, near 13,400-ft/4,084-m airstrip; 19°58′N 75°49′W.

Agualeguas (ah-gwah-LAI-gwahs), town (1990 pop. 2,648), ⊙ Agualeguas municipio, Nuevo León, N Mexico, 65 mi/105 km NE of Monterrey; 99°30′N 26°18′W. Cotton, corn, sugar, cactus fibers, cereals; cattle.

Aguanaval River (ah-gwah-nah-VAHL), c. 250 mi/402 km long, N central Mexico; rises in Sierra Madre Occidental 35 mi/56 km NW of Zacatecas; flows N, through Zacatecas, Durango, and Coahuila, past Río Grande, Nieves, and San Juan de Guadalupe, and along Durango-Coahuila border, to the Laguna de Viesca 9 mi/14.5 km NW of Viesca. Its lower course is used, together with Nazas R., to irrigate fertile Laguna dist. Its upper course is called Río Grande in Zacatecas.

Aguas Buenas (AH-gwahs BWAI-nahs), town (1990 pop. 25,424), E central P.R., in mts. 14 mi/23 km S of San Juan. Industrial and commercial area. Many residents commute to other cities. Horse raising. Tourism; ideal climate and panoramic views. Stone and sand mines nearby. Enormous caves are nearby.

Aguasabon River (a-gwuh-SAI-buhn), 45 mi/72 km long, NW Ont., Canada; rises 20 mi/32 km N of Schreiber, flows in a wide arc SE and S to L. Superior 45 mi/72 km45 mi/72 km ESE of Schreiber. Drainage of Long L. has been diverted to this river by channel and control dam, thus diverting waters of Long L. to L. Superior.

Aguascalientes (ah-gwahs-kah-lee-EN-tais), state (1990 pop. 719,659; 2,007 sq mi/5,198 sq km), central Mexico. ⊙ Aguascalientes; 22°27′N 101°53′W. Center of Mexican wine production, brandy-making, light industry. Cattle are raised on the wide plains and in the foothills; alfalfa, corn, wheat, chile, peaches; some mining in the mountainous areas, esp. silver and zinc; thermal waters. Aguascalientes is noted for its warm mineral springs and for its beautiful climate.

Aguascalientes (ah-gwahs-kah-lee-EN-tais), city (1990 pop. 455,234), ⊙ Aguascalientes state, central Mexico; 21°28′N 101°53′W. The city is a pleasant health resort, noted for its mineral waters and vineyards. Its industries include RR repair, motor vehicle assembly, and

the mfg. of textiles. Aguascalientes is built over an anc., intricate system of tunnels constructed by early, still unidentified, inhabitants. Founded in 1575, the city was long a Span. outpost; RR development in the late 19th cent. gave it commercial importance.

Aguathuna (a-gwuh-THOO-nuh), village, SW N.F., Canada, on Port au Port isthmus, 9 mi/14 km W of Stephenville; 48°33′N 58°45′W. Fishing. Port au Port peninsula is only Fr. community in NF.

Aguikchuk (uh-GWEEK-chuhk), Eskimo village, SW Alaska, on narrow channel separating Nelson Isl. from mainland, 90 mi/145 km WSW of Bethel.

Aguila, uninc. town (1990 pop. 900), Maricopa co., W central Ariz., 72 mi/116 km WNW of Phoenix. Elev. 2,160 ft/658 m. Cattle. Harquahala Mts. Wilderness Area to SW; Hummingbird Springs and Big Horn Mts. wilderness areas to S.

Aguilar, village (1990 pop. 520), Las Animas co., SE Colo., on Apishapa R., just E of Sangre de Cristo Mts., and 18 mi/29 km. NNW of Trinidad; 37°23′N 104°39′W. Elev. 6,400 ft/1,951 m. In agr. and grazing region, cattle, wheat, hay. Ludlow Massacre Monument to S. Inc. 1894.

Aguililla (ah-gee-LEE-yah), town (1990 pop. 7,578), ⊙ Agililla municipio, Michoacán, W Mexico, in Sierra Madre del Sur, 70 mi/113 km SW of Uruapan; 18°44′N 102°44′W. Elev. 3,199 ft/975 m. Cereals, sugar, fruit, tobacco; cheese; wood.

Aguirre (ah-GIR-rai), village, S P.R., on the coast, facing Puerto Jobos, 7 mi/11.3 km WSW of Guayama. Aguirre Forest Reserve nearby. Site of Aguirre Thermoelectric Complex.

Agujas, Point, Dominican Republic: see FALSO, CABO.

Ahmeek, village (1990 pop. 148), Keweenaw co., NW Upper Peninsula, Mich., 15 mi/24 km NNE of Houghton, on Keweenaw Peninsula; 47°17′N 88°24′W. Light mfg.

Ahome, Mexico: see LOS MOCHIS.

Ahoskie (uh-HAHS-kee), town (1990 pop. 4,391), Hertford co., NE N.C., 38 mi/61 km SE of Roanoke Rapids; 36°17′N 76°59′W. In agr. and timber area; peanuts, cotton, tobacco, sweet potatoes; chicken, hogs. Mfg. (apparel, fabricated metal, plastic, and wooden prods.; printing and publishing, sand and gravel processing).

Ahuacatlán (ah-wah-kaht-LAHN), city (1990 pop. 6,480) and township, Nayarit, W Mexico, on tributary of Ameca R., at S end of the Sierra Madre Occidental, 43 mi/69 km SE of Tepic, on RR; 21°5′N 104°28′W. Elev. 4,364 ft/1,330 m. Agr. center (corn, beans, sugar; cattle. Silver and gold deposits nearby.

Ahuacatlán (ah-wah-kaht-LAHN), town (1990 pop. 682), Puebla, central Mexico, in Sierra Madre Oriental, 8 mi/12.9 km NE of Zacatlán; 21°2′N 97°50′W. Elev. 4,364 ft/1,330 m. Corn, tobacco, sugar; fruit.

Ahuacuotzingo (ah-wah-kwot-SEEN-go), town (1990 pop. 2,220), Guerrero, SW Mexico, in Sierra Madre del Sur, 30 mi/48 km ENE of Chilpancingo de los Bravo; 17°30′N 98°55′W. Elev. 4,969 ft/1,515 m. Cereals, fruit, forest prods. (resin, rubber, vanilla).

Ahualulco de Mercado (ah-wah-LOOL-ko de mer-KAH-do), city (1990 pop. 11,696), Jalisco, W Mexico, on central plateau, 40 mi/64 km W of Guadalajara, on RR; 22°24′N 101°11′W. Agr. (corn, peanuts, beans, watermelons; goats, cattle).

Ahualulco del Sonido (ah-wah-LOOL-ko del so-NEE-do), town (1990 pop. 2,646), ⊙ Ahualulco municipio, San Luis Potosí, N central Mexico, on interior plateau, 20 mi/32 km NW of San Luis Potosí; 22°30′N 101°48′W. Elev. 6,240 ft/1,902 m. Thermal waters.

Ahuatempan, Mexico: see SANTA INÉS AHUATEMPAN.

Ahuatlán (ah-waht-LAHN), town (1990 pop. 1,044), Puebla, central Mexico, 12 mi/19 km E of Izúcar de Matamoros; 30°35′N 98°28′W. Elev. 4,127 ft/1,258 m. Corn, sugar; livestock. Also known as San Andrés Ahuatlán.

Ahuazotepec (ah-wah-so-TAI-pek), town (1990 pop. 1,216), Puebla, central Mexico, in Sierra Madre Oriental, 13 mi/21 km ESE of Tulancingo; 21°00′N 98°14′W. On RR.

Ahuehuetitla (ah-wai-wai-TEET-lah), town (1990 pop. 1,752), Puebla, central Mexico, 31 mi/50 km SE of Izúcar de Matamoros; 18°18'N 98°15'W. Cereals, sugarcane, tropical fruit; livestock.

Ahumada (ah-oo-MAH-dah), town (1990 pop. 7,241), ⊙ Ahumada municipio, Chihuahua, N Mexico, on RR, and 80 mi/129 km S of Juárez; 30°37'N 106°31'W. Elev. 3,875 ft/1,181 m. Agr. (cotton; livestock). Formerly called Villa González.

Aiaktalik (uh-ee-yak-TAH-lik), village, S Alaska, on Aiaktalik Isl. (5 mi/8 km long, 4 mi/6.4 km wide), in Sitkinak Strait, part of Trinity Isl., off S Kodiak Isl.; 56°42'N 154°7'W. Natives work in Kodiak Isl. canneries during summer. Has Russian Orthodox church.

Aibonito (ei-bo-NEE-to), town (1990 pop. 24,971), central P.R., in the Cordillera Central, 17 mi/27 km WSW of Caguas. In agr. region (vegetables, flowers; poultry). Poultry processing, light mfg.

Aiea (ah-YAI-ah), town (1990 pop. 8,906), Honolulu co., Oahu, Hawaii, a residential suburb 7 mi/11.3 km NW of downtown of Honolulu, on the E shore of Pearl Harbor, at mouth of Aiea stream; 21°23'N 157°55'W. Once a quiet sugarcane town with a sugar refinery, it is the site of numerous housing developments and a shopping center. Mfg. (chemicals, paper prods., food, publishing, transportation equip.). Many residents work at nearby military installations (U.S. Naval Reserve, Hickam Air Force Base, both to S). Bet. Aiea and Honolulu are the Tripler Army Medical Center and U.S. Fort Shafter, hq. of the Army's Pacific Ocean Division. Honolulu Interntl. Airport to SE. Ewa Forest Reserve to NE. Aloha Stadium to SE. U.S.S. *Bowfin* Submarine Mus. and passenger ferry to U.S.S. *Arizona* Natl. Memorial. Aliamanu Military Reserve and Aliamanu Crater to E. Keaiwa Heiau State Recreation Area to NE.

Aiken, county (□ 1,080 sq mi/2,797 sq km; 1990 pop. 120,940), SW S.C.; ⊙ Aiken; 33°32'N 81°38'W. At edge of Piedmont region, in Sand Hills belt; bounded SW by Savannah R., NE by North Fork of Edisto R.; drained by South Fork of the Edisto. Agr. includes chickens, eggs, hogs, cattle; corn, wheat, rye, oats, soybeans, sorghum, hay, cotton, peaches. Number of cotton-milling towns; kaolin deposits in W. Noted resort area around Aiken. Part of U.S. Dept. of Energy Savannah R. Nuclear Facility is in S. Formed 1871.

Aiken (AI-kuhn), city (1990 pop. 19,872), ⊙ Aiken co., SW S.C., 14 mi/23 km ENE of Augusta, Ga; 33°32'N 81°43'W. A resort and polo center, established by N industrialists at the turn of the century, Aiken is also an industrial city, Mfg. includes apparel, printing and publishing, drugs, chemicals, industrial prods. Agr. includes poultry, livestock; grain, peanuts, cotton, peaches. The mild climate and its location within the sandhills region have made it a prime training area for Thoroughbreds. Kaolin mines are nearby. The Univ. of S.C. at Aiken is located in the city. Nearby is the Dept. of Energy's Savannah R. Nuclear Plant, site of nuclear breeder reactor project which was abandoned in mid-1980s. Also nuclear weapons dismantling plant and a commercial nuclear waste disposal site, which caused controversy for accepting waste from outside the region. Inc. 1835.

Ailey (AI-lee), village (1990 pop. 579), Montgomery co., E central Ga., 11 mi/18 km W of Vidalia; 32°11'N 82°34'W. Mfg. (clothing, printing).

Ailsa Craig (AIL-suh), village (1991 pop. 857), S Ont., Canada, on Ausable R. and 18 mi/29 km NW of London. Dairying, mixed agr.

Ainslie, Lake (AINZ-lee) (12 mi/19 km long, 5 mi/8 km wide), NE N.S., Canada, on W Cape Breton Isl., 4 mi/6 km SE of Inverness; 46°8'N 61°11'W. Drained by Southwest Margaree R.

Ainsworth 1 (AINZ-wuhrth), town (1990 pop. 506), Washington co., SE Iowa, 7 mi/11.3 km E of Washington; 41°17'N 91°32'W. In agr. area. **2** town (1990 pop. 1,870), ⊙ Brown co., N Nebr., 45 mi/72 km SE of Valentine; 42°32'N 99°51'W. Trade center for livestock and grain. Long Pine State Recreation Area to E; Long L. State Recreation Area to SW. Inc. 1883.

Airdrie (AIR-dree), city (1991 pop. 12,456), S Alta., Canada, on Nose Creek, and 18 mi/29 km N of Calgary; 51°18'N 114°02'W. Bedroom community for Calgary; 500% pop. increase 1976–1981. Wheat, flax, cattle, mixed farming.

Airport Drive, town (1990 pop. 818), Jasper co., SW Mo. Residential suburb, 4 mi/6 km N of downtown Joplin, W of Joplin Airport; 37°08'N 94°31'W.

Airport Gardens, uninc. village (1990 pop. 300), Perry co., SE Ky., residential suburb 2 mi/3.2 km N of Hazard, on North Fork Kentucky R. Wendell H. Ford Airport to N.

Airway Heights, town (1990 pop. 1,971), Spokane co., E Wash., suburb 8 mi/12.9 km W of downtown Spokane; 47°38'N 117°35'W. Residential and commercial center for Fairchild Air Force Base to SW. Mfg. (conveyors, cranes and hoists; structural wood prods.). Spokane Internatl. Airport and Air Natl. Guard facility to SE; Spokane Raceway Park to NE. Spokane Polo Club to E. Spokane Plains Battlefield Monument to W.

Airy, Cape, SW extremity of Cornwallis Isl., E central Franklin dist., N.W.T., Canada, on Barrow Strait, at S entrance of McDougall Sound; 74°58'N 96°40'W.

Aishihik, village, SW Yukon, Canada, on Aishihik L., 100 mi/161 km NW of Whitehorse; 61°35'N 137°30'W.

Aishihik Lake, SW Yukon, Canada, 75 mi/121 km NW of Whitehorse; 40 mi/64 km long, 1–5 mi/8 km wide; 61°30'N 137°47'W. Drains S into Lewes R.

Aitkin (AI-kuhn), county (□ 1,995 sq mi/5,167 sq km; 1990 pop. 12,425), E central Minn.; ⊙ Aitkin; 46°36'N 93°24'W. Agr. area drained by Mississippi R., also by Willow, Rice, and Sandy rivers. Hay; timber; wild rice; deposits of marl and peat. Part of Mille Lacs L. in SW, Rice L. (center), Big Sandy L. reservoir (NE); Rice L. Natl. Wildlife Refuge in center; Savanna Portage State Park in NE; Solana State Forest in SE; Wealthwood State Forest in SW; Savannah State Forest to NE; Hill R. State Forest in NW. Sandy L. Indian Reservation in NE; East L. Indian Reservation in E center. Part of Cuyuna Range in W. County formed 1857.

Aitkin (AI-kuhn), town (1990 pop. 1,698), ⊙ Aitkin co., central Minn., on Mississippi R., 27 mi/43 km NE of Brainerd; 46°31'N 93°42'W. Elev. 1,213 ft/370 m. Timber; hay; wild rice. Mfg. (printing and publishing, concrete, wood containers). Rice L. Natl. Wildlife Refuge to E; Land O'Lakes State Forest to N; Wealthwood State Forest to S; Crow Wing State Forest to W; Cuyuna Iron Range to N; numerous natural lakes in vicinity, large Mille Lacs L. to S (resort area). Settled 1870.

Ajacuba (ah-hah-KOO-bah), town (1990 pop. 5,340), in S central part of Hidalgo, Mexico, 22 mi/35 km W of Pachuca de Soto; 20°24'N 99'W. Paved road to Tlaxcoapan.

Ajalpan (ah-HAL-pahn), town (1990 pop. 16,232), Puebla, central Mexico, 10 mi/16 km SE of Tehuacán; 18°17'N 97°19'W. Elev. 4,068 ft/1,240 m. Agr. center (corn, rice, sugar, fruit; livestock).

Ajax Mountain (AI-jaks) (10,900 ft/3,322 m), Idaho and Mont., in BITTERROOT RANGE, 14 mi/23 km NNE of Salmon. Summit is in Lemhi co., N Idaho, 1 mi/1.6 km SW of main ridge, which forms state line and Continental Divide. E slope in Beaverhead co., Mont.

Ajijic (ah-hee-HEEK), village (1990 pop. 7,572), Chapala municipio, Jalisco, central Mexico, on N shore of L. Chapala, 27 mi/43 km SSE of Guadalajara; 20°17'N 103°15'W. Resort; grain, fruit; livestock.

Ajo (AH-ho), uninc. town, (1990 pop. 2,919), Pima co., SW Ariz., 87 mi/140 km SW of Phoenix. Health resort; once a major copper mining and smelting town, but mine and smelter now closed; gold, silver, and lead mines nearby. Once a company town belonging to Phelps Dodge Corp. Terminus of RR spur from Gila Bend. Organ Pipe Cactus Natl. Monument is S. Tohono O'odham (Papago) Indian Reservation to E; Cabeza Prieta Natl. Wildlife Refuge to W (hq. in Ajo); Barry M. Goldwater Air Force Range (formerly Luke Air Force Range) to N and W.

Ajoupa-Bouillon (ah-zhoo-PAH–boo-YON), town, N Martinique, at E foot of Mont Pelée, 15 mi/24 km NNW of Fort-de-France. Sugar growing, rum distilling.

Ajuchitlán del Progreso (ah-hoo-chit-LAHN del pro-GRAI-so), town (1990 pop. 6,347), Guerrero, SW Mexico, on the Río Balsas, and 18 mi/29 km SE of Ciudad Altamirano; 18°10'N 10°28'W. Cereals, cotton, sugarcane, fruit.

Ajusco (ah-HOOS-ko), locality, Federal dist., central Mexico, at NE foot of Cerro Ajusco, 15 mi/24 km S of Mexico city and outside of the urbanized zone; 15°40'N 99°8'W. Cereals, vegetables, fruit; livestock.

Ajusco, Cerro (ah-HOOS-ko, SER-ro), extinct volcano (12,894 ft/3,930 m) in Federal dist., central Mexico, 19 mi/31 km SSW of Mexico city; 19°12'N 99°15'W. Its last eruption, believed to have taken place c.150 B.C., buried part of the anc. Cuicuilco pyramid near Tlalpan. Within Cumbres del Ajusco Natl. Park. Sometimes called Cruz del Marqués.

Aké (ah-KAI), Maya ruins in Yucatán, SE Mexico, 20 mi/32 km E of Mérida.

Akeley (AIK-lee), village (1990 pop. 393), Hubbard co., N central Minn., 10 mi/16 km SW of Walker; 47°00'N 94°43'W. Alfalfa, oats, barley, rye, beans; sheep. Mfg. (fixtures, wood prods.). Part of Paul Bunyan State Forest to N; Badoura State Forest to S; Eleventh Crow Wing L. to N.

Akhiok (UHK-hee-yok), village (1990 pop. 77), S Alaska, SW Kodiak Isl., on Alitak Bay (30 mi/48 km long, 9 mi/14.5 km wide at mouth), 90 mi/145 km SW of Kodiak; 56°56'N 154°10'W. Aleut fishing village; cannery. Has Rus. Orthodox church. Formerly also called Alitak.

Akiachak (AK-ee-ah-chak), Eskimo village (1990 pop. 481), SW Alaska, on Kuskokwim R., and 15 mi/24 km NE of Bethel; 60°52'N 161°24'W. Sometimes spelled Akiachok.

Akiak (AK-ee-ak), Eskimo village (1990 pop. 285), SW Alaska, on Kuskokwim R., and 22 mi/35 km ENE of Bethel; 60°53'N 161°11'W.

Akil (ah-KEEL), town (1990 pop. 7,304), Yucatán, SE Mexico, 17 mi/27 km SE of Ticul; 20°15'N 89°20'W. Henequen, sugar, fruit. Maya ruins nearby.

Aklavik (ak-LAH-vik), settlement (1991 pop. 801), Inuvik region, N.W.T., Canada, on the W channel of the Mackenzie R. The unsuitability of the land at the site led to the construction of INUVIK.

Akpatok Island (□ 551), SE Franklin dist., N.W.T., Canada, in Ungava Bay; 27 mi/43 km long, 15 mi/24 km wide; 60°25'N 68°02'W. Rises to 930 ft/283 m.

Akron (A-kruhn), city (1990 pop. 223,019), ⊙ Summit co., NE Ohio, on the Little Cuyahoga R.; 41°05'N 81°32'W. It is a port of entry and an important industrial and transportation center. Once the heart of the nation's rubber and tire mfg. industry, Akron still contains the hq. of some rubber corporations, and chemical and polymer corporations. Its other mfg. ranges from fishing tackle to plastics, rubber, missiles, and heavy machinery. The Ohio and Erie Canal (opened 1827) and later the RR spurred the city's growth. The first rubber plant was established in 1870. Focused on tire production, Akron's rubber industry followed the growth and decline of Detroit's automobile industry and by the mid-1980s virtually all the tire plants had shut down. Since then, the city has emphasized the production of polymer prods. such as coatings and engineered plastics. The city is the seat of the Univ. of Akron and the Inst. of Rubber Research. It has an art institute, a music center, and a symphony orchestra. Of note is a giant airdock for blimps, one of the world's largest bldgs. without inner supports. Polymer research is internationally recognized. Largest private employment sectors: automotive, chemicals, packaging, utilities, banks, transportation (aircraft systems). Inc. 1865.

Akron 1 (A-kruhn), town (1990 pop. 468), Hale co., W Ala., 15 mi/24 km NW of Greensboro, near Black Warrior R. **2** town (1990 pop. 1,599), ⊙ Washington co., NE Colo., 30 mi/48 km S of Sterling; 40°09'N 103°12'W. Elev. 4,300 ft/1,311 m. RR center in agr. area; cattle, wheat, sunflowers, beans, oats, corn, sugar beets. Mfg. (bird food, sunflower seeds). U.S. agr. experiment station nearby. Summit Springs Battlefield site to NE. Founded 1882, inc. 1887. **3** town (1990 pop. 1,001), Fulton co., N Ind., 9 mi/14.5 km ESE of Rochester; 41°02'N

86°01′W. In agr. area; hand tools, lumber, concrete prods., electric motors. **4** town (1990 pop. 1,450), Plymouth co., NW Iowa, near S.Dak. boundary (formed here by Big Sioux R.), 20 mi/32 km W of Le Mars; 42°49′N 96°33′W. Feed mill. Plotted 1871 as Portlandville; inc. 1882.

Akron 1 (A-kruhn), village, (1990 pop. 421), Tuscola co., E Mich., 18 mi/29 km E of Bay City; 43°34′N 83°30′W. In agr. area. **2** village (□ 1 sq mi/2.6 sq km; 1990 pop. 2,906), Erie co., W N.Y., 20 mi/32 km ENE of Buffalo, on Murder Creek; 43°01′N 78°30′W. Shipping center for dairying and farming region. Mfg. (metal fabricating, wood prods., transportation equip., food, computer parts). Agr. (wheat, hay, potatoes, cabbage, mushrooms). Nearby is Tonawanda Indian Reservation. Inc. 1849.

Akron (A-kruhn), borough (1990 pop. 3,869), Lancaster co., SE Pa., 10 mi/16 km NE of Lancaster, near Cocalico Creek; 40°09′N 76°12′W. Mfg. (industrial coatings, food, computer typesetting). Agr. (grain, soybeans, potatoes; livestock, poultry, dairying). Covered bridges in area. Inc. 1884.

Akulivik, village (1991 pop. 375), NW Que., Canada, on E shore of Hudson Bay, W side of Ungava Peninsula. Inhabited by Inuit people. Scheduled air service. Hunting, fishing, trapping.

Akulurak (uh-KOO-loo-rak), Inuit village, W Alaska, on Yukon R. delta, 9 mi/14.5 km E of mouth of Yukon R., 130 mi/209 km S of Nome; 62°34′N 164°33′W. Grew up around St. Mary's Jesuit Mission, Eskimo orphanage est. 1918. Catholic center for Lower Yukon.

Akun Island (AH-koon) (14 mi/23 km long, 2 mi/3.2 km–10 mi/16 km wide), in Krenitzin group, Fox Isls., E Aleutian Isls., SW Alaska, bet. Akutan Isl. (W) and Unimak Isl. (ENE); 54°12′N 165°32′W. Rises to 2,685 ft/818 m on Mt. Gilbert (N), extinct volcano.

Akutan (AK-oo-tan), village (1990 pop. 589), E Akutan Isl., Aleutian Isls., SW Alaska, 35 mi/56 km ENE of Dutch Harbor; 54°08′N 165°47′W. Fishing. Whaling station until 1938.

Akutan Island (AK-oo-tan), in Krenitzin group, Fox Isls., E Aleutian Isls., SW Alaska, 12 mi/19 km NE of Unalaska Isl.; 19 mi/31 km long, 15 mi/24 km wide; 54°08′N 165°53′W. Rises to 4,244 ft/1,294 m on Akutan Peak (center), active volcano (erupted 1946); earthquake in 1996.

Al Tahoe, village, El Dorado co., E Calif., near S shore of L. Tahoe, in the Sierra Nevada. Elev. 6,225 ft/1,897 m. By 1970, combined with Bijou and other S lake shore areas to form SOUTH LAKE TAHOE.

Alabama, state (□ 52,423 sq mi/135,775 sq km; 1995 est. pop. 4,252,928), SE U.S., admitted as the 22nd state of the Union in 1819; ⊙ MONTGOMERY. Ala.'s largest city is BIRMINGHAM, and the major seaport is MOBILE. Ala. is bounded on the N by Tenn., on the E by Ga., on the S by Fla. and the Gulf of Mexico, and on the W by Miss. Except for the mountainous sect. in the NE (the S end of the Cumberland Plateau), the state is a rolling plain with an average elev. of c.500 ft/152 m in 2 geologic regions—the Appalachian Piedmont above the fall line and the coastal plain below. These plains, drained by the ALABAMA and the TOMBIGBEE rivers and their tributaries, are primarily devoted to agr. The central BLACK BELT, formerly a principal cotton-growing area, is a center for raising cattle and poultry, Ala.'s most valuable agr. prods. Although about 28% of Ala.'s area is devoted to agr., mfg. accounts for a larger share of the state's income. Ala.'s major crops are peanuts, soybeans, and cotton. Forestry is also important to Ala. Where the Tennessee R. loops across the N, hydroelectric power from the Tennessee Valley Authority has been increasingly turning an agr. region into an industrial one. Major industries produce chemicals, textiles, paper prods., mobile homes, and processed foods. The state is rich in coal, oil, stone, and iron, further contributing to its industry. Agr. was practiced by groups such as the Creeks and Cherokee in the E, and the Choctaws and Chickasaws in the W when Span. explorers arrived. Cabeza de Vaca (and possibly Pánfilo de Narvaez) visited Ala. in 1528, and Hernando De Soto spent some time in the region in 1540. Eur. settlement was begun, however, not by the Spanish but in 1702 by the French in the Mobile area. The French and British contended for the furs gathered by the Native Americans. In 1763 the region passed to the British, who were victorious over France and Spain in the Fr. and Indian Wars. At the close of the Amer. Revolution, Great Britain ceded (1783) to the U.S. all land E of the Mississippi except Fla. The territory of Miss., which included parts of present-day Ala., was set up in 1798, but the land was largely a wilderness with a considerable fur trade and with only the beginnings of cotton cultivation. Both were interrupted during the War of 1812, when part of the Creek Confederacy began attacking under William Weatherford. Andrew Jackson defeated a group of Native Americans at Horseshoe Bend on March 27, 1814. That victory, coupled with the Br. demand for cotton, ushered in a period of heavy settlement. New settlers poured into the Ala. region, especially from Ga. and Tenn. The wealthy newcomers settled in the fertile bottomlands and established large plantations based on slave labor, which helped to produce cotton for the markets of Southern ports. Poorer newcomers took over less fertile uplands. The pop. grew to such an extent that the Territory of Ala., taking Saint Stephens as its capital, was set up in 1817 with William W. Bibb as governor; 2 years later it became a state. The slave-owning planters were dominant because of the prosperous cotton crop, and as the Civil War loomed closer, support of Southern rights and secession grew under the direction of "fire-eaters" such as William L. Yancey. Ala. broke away from the Union on Jan. 11, 1861, when its 2d constitutional convention passed the ordinance of secession. The govt. of the Confederacy was organized at Montgomery on Feb. 4, 1861, and Jefferson Davis was inaugurated as President of the Confederacy. Federal troops held the Tenn. valley after 1862. One of the principal naval battles of the war was won by Union Admiral D.G. Farragut in Mobile Bay in 1864, but most of the state was not occupied in force until 1865. Ala. ratified the 13th Amendment to the U.S. Constitution in 1865, but in 1867 it refused to ratify the 14th Amendment and was placed under military rule. That rule ended the following year when a new state legislature operating under a new constitution approved the 14th Amendment. However, Federal troops did not leave Ala. until 1876, and Afr. Americans continued to suffer enormous oppression for decades. In the Reconstruction era, Ala.'s govt. was filled with carpetbaggers and scalawags, and corruption was widespread. Few reforms emerged during this period; but the mining of coal and iron was expanded by Daniel Pratt and his successor, H.F. De Bardeleben, marking the rise of industry in Ala. RRs built during Reconstruction also encouraged industrialization. Birmingham was founded in 1871, and its first blast furnace began operations in 1880. The cotton textile industry developed in the 1880s. At that time farming was dominant, and the fortunes of the state rose and fell with the market price of cotton. Constant use and erosion, however, began to exhaust the land. Diversification of crops, much advocated in the 20th cent., was accelerated in 1915 when the boll weevil invaded and destroyed many cotton fields and the demand for food crops increased during World War I. The Great Depression and the agr. program of President Franklin D. Roosevelt's New Deal caused more farmers to produce subsistence crops and took more land away from the wasting cotton culture. After 1925, large numbers of Afr. Americans moved to mfg. centers in the N. Industrialization greatly increased during World War II; factories began producing machines, munitions, powder, and other war supplies. HUNTSVILLE became a center for rocket research, and its pop. more than quadrupled bet. 1950 and 1960. Industrialization and commerce increased throughout the state. During this period the state developed an ambitious inland waterways program to provide cheap water transportation, more hydroelectric power, and flood-control measures. An example is the TENNESSEE-TOMBIGBEE WATERWAY, a 254 mi/409 km canal that opened in 1985. In 1954 the U.S. Supreme Court handed down a decision ruling racial segregation in public elementary and secondary schools unconstitutional, and the decision was followed by an intensification of racial tension. Ala. has witnessed many civil rights protests, including a year-long Afr. Amer. boycott of public buses in Montgomery in 1955–1956 to protest segregated seating and a Freedom March from Montgomery to Selma led by Martin Luther King Jr. in 1965. Ala.'s constitution, adopted in 1901, provides for an elected governor and a bicameral legislature that is made up of a 35-member senate and a 105-member house of representatives. The state elects 2 Senators and 7 Representatives to the U.S. Congress and has 9 electoral votes. One of the most famous of Ala.'s political figures, George C. Wallace, a Democrat, was elected governor in 1962 and fought the federally ordered integration of schools in Ala. He was reelected 3 times: 1970, 1974, and 1982, the final time with substantial Afr. Amer. support. He entered the U.S. presidential race in 1968 as the candidate of the Amer. Independent party. He ran for the presidency twice more—in 1972 and 1976. Ala. has been the home of important natl. figures such as Hugo L. Black and Helen Keller. Places of interest in the state include RUSSELL CAVE National Monument, near Bridgeport, the site of caves that were inhabited almost continuously from 6000 B.C. to A.D. 1650, and Mound State Monument, near Tuscaloosa, the site of numerous early Native Amer. mounds. Among Ala.'s educational institutions are the Univ. of Ala., at Tuscaloosa, Birmingham, and Huntsville; Auburn Univ., at Auburn and at Montgomery; Birmingham Southern Col. and Howard Col., at Birmingham; Huntingdon Col., at Montgomery; the Univ. of Montevallo, at Montevallo; Tuskegee Institute, at Tuskegee; and Troy State Univ., at Troy, Montgomery, and Dothan. Ala. has 67 counties: AUTAUGA, BALDWIN, BARBOUR, BIBB, BLOUNT, BULLOCK, BUTLER, CALHOUN, CHAMBERS, CHEROKEE, CHILTON, CHOCTAW, CLARKE, CLAY, CLEBURNE, COFFEE, COLBERT, CONECUH, COOSA, COVINGTON, CRENSHAW, CULLMAN, DALE, DALLAS, DE KALB, ELMORE, ESCAMBIA, ETOWAH, FAYETTE, FRANKLIN, GENEVA, GREENE, HALE, HENRY, HOUSTON, JACKSON, JEFFERSON, LAMAR, LAUDERDALE, LAWRENCE, LEE, LIMESTONE, LOWNDES, MACON, MADISON, MARENGO, MARION, MARSHALL, MOBILE, MONROE, MONTGOMERY, MORGAN, PERRY, PICKENS, PIKE, RANDOLPH, RUSSELL, SAINT CLAIR, SHELBY, SUMTER, TALLADEGA, TALLAPOOSA, TUSCALOOSA, WALKER, WASHINGTON, WILCOX, and WINSTON.

Alabama River, 315 mi/507 km long, central Ala.; formed by the confluence of the Coosa and Tallapoosa rivers N of Montgomery; flows SW to Mobile, where it joins the Tombigbee R. to form the Mobile R.; drains c.22,600 sq mi/58,534 sq km. In the 1800s the river played an important role in the development of the region's economy as a transporter of goods. It remains an important transportation route of farm prods., lumber, and mfg. goods. The Cahaba R., its chief tributary, is the source of water for Birmingham.

Alabaster (a-luh-BA-stuhr), city (1990 pop. 14,732), Shelby co., N central Ala., 15 mi/24 km S of Birmingham; 33°13′N 86°49′W. Mfg. (rubber and plastic prods., machinery, concrete).

Alabaster, village, Iosco co., NE Mich., on Saginaw Bay, 6 mi/9.7 km SSW of Tawas City; 41°11′N 83°33′W. Gypsum quarrying.

Alachua (uh-LACH-choo-uh), county (□ 969 sq mi/2,510 sq km; 1990 pop. 181,596), N central Fla., bounded N by Santa Fe R.; ⊙ Gainesville; 29°40′N 82°21′W. Has many lakes (Orange, Newmans, Santa Fe). Produces hay, soybeans, corn, vegetables, peanuts, cotton, tobacco, citrus fruit, nuts (pecan, tung); livestock; lumber; and naval stores. Quarries limestone, phosphate, and flint in W. Named for a local ranch, Alachua means "the sink" from a combination of Span. and Seminole words, and is thought to refer to a chasm 2.5 mi/4 km SE of Gainesville. The Univ. of Fla. and Santa Fe Community Col. are located in Gainesville. Marjorie Kinnan Rawlings Historical Site in Hawthorne. Formed 1824 from a part of St. Johns co.

Cross references are shown in SMALL CAPITALS. The pronunciation key is on page xv. The dates of population figures are on page xii.

Alachua (ul-LACH-choo-uh), town (□ 25 sq mi/65 sq km; 1990 pop. 4,529), Alachua co., N central Fla., 15 mi/24 km NW of Gainesville; 29°46'N 82°28'W. Watermelon- and vegetable-shipping center. Founded 1884.

Alacrán (ah-la-KRAHN) or **Arrecife** (ahr-rai-SEE-fai), reef in Gulf of Mexico, 80 mi/129 km off N Yucatán coast; 13 mi/21 km long, c.7 mi/11.3 km wide; 22°00'N 88°50'W. Consists of numerous islets and rocks, among them Pérez Isl. (S), a narrow reef c.800 yd/732 m long, with fishing huts, good landing, and lighthouse.

Alacranes (a-luh-KRAHN-ais), town, Matanzas prov., W Cuba, on RR, and 19 mi/31 km S of Matanzas; 22°44'N 81°36'W. In agr. region (sugarcane, honey, cattle). For a time it was called Alfonso XII. The Puerto Rico Libre sugar mill is SE.

Aladdin, village, Crook co., NE Wyo., near S.Dak. state line and Black Hills, 19 mi/31 km NE of Sundance. Lowest elev. in Wyo. (3,125 ft/953 m) 10 mi/16 km to NE, on Belle Fourche R. at S.Dak. boundary. Bear Lodge unit of Black Hills Natl. Forest to W.

Alaganuck, Alaska: see ALAKANUK.

Alagnak Wild and Scenic River and Riverway (uh-LAG-nak) (□ 37 sq mi/96 sq km), Alaska. White water and salmon fishing. Authorized 1980.

Alakanuk (uh-LAK-ah-nuhk), village (1990 pop. 544), W Alaska, near Bering Sea, 10 mi/16 km NE of mouth of Yukon R., 120 mi/193 km S of Nome; 62°40'N 164°38'W. Sometimes spelled Alaganuck.

Alaktak (uh-LAK-tak), village, N Alaska, c.50 mi/80 km SE of Barrow, in delta of Ikpikpuk R., E of Dease Inlet, Arctic Ocean. Numerous small lakes in region. Hunting, fishing. Natural gas reserves in area.

Alalakeiki Strait (AH-lah-lah-kai-EE-kee), Pacific Ocean, bet. Kahoolawe (W) and Maui (E) isls., Maui co., Hawaii; 6 mi/11km wide; 20°36'N 156°29'W. Small Molokini Isl. near center.

Alamance (AL-uh-mans), county (□ 434 sq mi/1,124 sq km; 1990 pop. 108,213), N central N.C.; ⊙ Graham Junction; 36°02'N 79°24'W. Piedmont area; crossed by Haw R. (forms part of SE boundary). Tobacco, corn, hay, wheat, soybeans; dairying, hogs; timber; paper, machinery, electronics. Mfg. at Mebane, Graham, and Burlington. Formed 1849.

Alamance (AL-uh-mans), village (1990 pop. 258), N central N.C., 6 mi/9.7 km SW of Burlington; 36°01'N 79°29'W. Tobacco, grain; dairying. Mfg. (furniture fabrics). Alamance Battleground State Historic Site to SW. Alamance Municipal Airport to NE.

Alameda, county (□ 737 sq mi/1,909 sq km; 1990 pop. 1,279,182), W Calif.; ⊙ Oakland; 37°13'N 119°46'W. Extends from San Francisco Bay on W across Coast Ranges to San Joaquin Valley in NE corner; includes Livermore Valley (wines); includes part of Diablo Range in SE; drained by Alameda Creek; Coyote Creek forms part of S boundary. Cities of East Bay area include OAKLAND, ALAMEDA, BERKELEY, and Emeryville, which have port and industrial facilities and are linked to San Francisco (W) by San Francisco-Oakland Bay Bridge (toll); in S, bay is spanned by San Mateo Bridge (to N) near Hayward. Hetch Hetchy Aqueduct runs E-W through co., carries water from Sierra Nevada to San Francisco. Cattle; nursery prods., roses, grapes, honey, oats. Gypsum, limestone, sand gravel, clay quarrying; magnesite mining, stone quarrying. Calaveras Reservoir on S boundary. Del Valle State Recreation Area to NE, near Livermore. Redwood and Anthony Chabot Regional Park to N, near Oakland. Formed 1853.

Alameda, city (1990 pop. 76,459), Alameda co., W central Calif., suburb 3 mi/4.8 km S of downtown Oakland and 7 mi/11.3 km of downtown of San Francisco, on an island formed by Oakland harbor just off the E shore of San Francisco Bay; 37°45'N 122°17'W. Mfg. (printing and publishing, electronics, plastics prods., food, consumer goods, machinery). It is primarily residential and has excellent beaches, parks, and leisure-boating facilities. The Alameda Naval Air Station, a large U.S. carrier base to W, is scheduled by the Pentagon to be closed. An important Coast Guard base and Col. of Alameda (2-year) are also here. The city is connected with Oakland, Calif., on the mainland by 4 bridges and 2 tunnels. Metropolitan Oakland Internatl. Airport to SE. San Leandro Bay separates city from Bay Farm Isl. (bridged and now a peninsula) to S. Settled 1850, inc. as a city 1884

Alameda (al-uh-MEE-duh), town (1991 pop. 317), SE Sask., Canada, 34 mi/55 km ENE of Estevan. Grain elevators; livestock.

Alameda (AL-uh-mee-tuh), uninc. town, Bernalillo co., N central N.Mex., suburb 5 mi/8 km N of downtown Albuquerque, on Rio Grande. Site of Internatl. Balloon Fiesta.

Alamitos Bay, Los Angeles co., S Calif., in SE part of city of Long Beach, arm of Pacific Ocean, W of mouth of San Gabriel R., just E of Long Beach; circular channel surrounds reserve isls. of Naples section of Long Beach. Residential sand spit separates bay from ocean with Alamitos Beach on ocean side. NW arm called Marine Stadium, with Colorado Lagoon (lake) beyond its tip. Yacht clubs; Long Beach Marina and Boat Basin in SE, near ocean entrance. Los Cerritos Channel enters from NE. Pacific Coast Highway to E.

Álamo (AH-lah-mo), city (1990 pop. 20,908), ⊙ Temapache township, Veracruz, E Mexico, in Gulf lowlands, 17 mi/27 km NW of Tuxpam de Rodríguez Cano; 20°46'N 97°40'W. Corn, sugar, coffee, fruit. Oil wells nearby.

Alamo 1 uninc. city (1990 pop. 12,277), Contra Costa co., W Calif., residential suburb 10 mi/16 km E of downtown Oakland; 37°52'N 122°00'W. Light mfg. Mt. Diablo State Park to E. **2** city (1990 pop. 8,210), Hidalgo co., extreme S Texas, in the lower Rio Grande valley, 7 mi/11.3 km E of McAllen; 26°11'N 98°07'W. Elev. 99 ft/30 m. In rich irrigated vegetable, citrus, and cotton area; mfg. (fruit and fresh flower packaging, frozen vegetables). Santa Ana Natl. Wildlife Refuge 8 mi/12.9 km S, on Rio Grande (Mex. border). Inc. 1924.

Alamo 1 (AL-uh-mo), town (1990 pop. 855), Wheeler co., SE central Ga., 27 mi/43 km SSE of Dublin; 32°09'N 82°47'W. Mfg. includes shirts and cabinets. **2** town (1990 pop. 112), Montgomery co., W Ind., near Sugar Creek, 9 mi/14.5 km SW of Crawfordsville; 39°59'N 87°04'W. In agr. area. **3** town (1990 pop. 2,426), ⊙ Crockett co., W Tenn., 20 mi/32 km NW of Jackson; 35°47'N 89°09'W. Cotton, grain; livestock.

Alamo 1 (AL-uh-mo), uninc. village (1990 pop. 400), Lincoln co., SE Nev., 38 mi/61 km WSW of Caliente. Pahranagat Range to SE; Pahranagat Natl. Wildlife Refuge, including Upper and Lower Pahranagat lakes, to S; Key Pittman Wildlife Management Area to N; Desert Natl. Wildlife Range to S. Nellis Air Force Bombing and Gunnery Range to SW. **2** village (1990 pop. 69), Williams co., NW N.Dak., 33 mi/53 km NNE of Williston; 48°34'N 103°28'W.

Alamo Heights, city (1990 pop. 6,502), Bexar co., S central Texas; a residential suburb 4 mi/6.4 km NNE of downtown San Antonio on San Antonio R.; 29°28'N 98°28'W. City bounded by Terrell Hills on E, by San Antonio on all other sides. Fort Sam Houston to SE. Inc. 1926.

Alamo Reservoir, W Ariz., on Bill Williams R., on border of La Paz and Mojave cos., 45 mi/72 km ESE of Lake Havasu City; 34°13'N 113°35'W. Max. capacity 1,045,300 acre-ft. Formed by Alamo Dam (280 ft/85 m high) built (1968) by the Army Corps of Engineers for flood control. Alamo State Park on E shore.

Alamo, the [Span. = cottonwood], building located on Alamo Plaza, off Houston St., downtown San Antonio, Texas, "the cradle of Texas liberty." Built as a chapel after 1744, it is all that remains of the mission of San Antonio de Valero, which was founded in 1718 by the Franciscans and later converted into a fortress. In the Texas Revolution, San Antonio was taken by Texas revolutionaries in Dec. 1835, and was lightly garrisoned. Defying Santa Anna's demands for surrender, the Texans in the fort determined to fight against the hopeless odds. Feb. 24, 1836, Santa Anna's several thousand Mex. troops held about 189 Texans under siege in the Alamo. The seige ended March 6 with hand-to-hand combat, leaving the defenders dead, including heroes William B. Travis, James Bowie, Davy Crockett, and some 150 other defenders. The incident inspired the Texans, who 6 weeks later defeated the Mexicans at San Jacinto, crying, "Remember the Alamo!" The chapel-fort was bought by the state in 1883, the surrounding area was added in 1905, and the whole complex was restored and improved from 1936 to 1939. It remains the foremost symbol of the Lone Star State and one of the state's leading tourist attractions.

Alamogordo (al-uh-muh GOR-do), city (1990 pop. 27,596), ⊙ Otero co., S N.Mex., 68 mi/109 km NE of Las Cruces, on E side of Tularosa Valley, a wide dessert plain; 32°52'N 105°57'W. Elev. 4,335 ft/1,321 m. Holloman Air Force Base (1990 pop. 5,891), hq. of the 49th fighter wing and Ger. Tactical Training Center is 10 mi/16 km WSW, and the White Sands Missile Range (main entrance and facilities) is located 45 mi/72 km SW of Alamogordo. Trinity Site, where the first atomic bomb was exploded on July 16, 1945, is 55 mi/89 km NNW. The city was founded in 1898 with the arrival of the Southern Pacific RR. Mfg. (refrigerators, printing and publishing, wood molding, meat packing, concrete prods.). Cattle, sheep; pecans, pistachios, fruit, alfalfa, timber. N. Mex. State Univ. has a branch at Alamogordo. White Sands Natl. Monument is 18 mi/29 km WSW; White Sands Space Harbor, Space Shuttle Landing Site, 25 mi/40 km to W, in NE tip of Dona Ana co.; Internatl. Space Hall of Fame; the Mescalero Apache Indian Reservation to NE, and part of Lincoln Natl. Forest to E in Sacramento Mts.; Oliver Lee State Park to S; Cloudcraft Ski Area to E; Tombaugh Planetarium and Theater; Alameda Park Zoo; Sunspot Solar Observatory to SE near Mule Peak (8,097 ft/2,468 m); Alamagordo White Sands Regional Airport in SW of city. Inc. 1912.

Álamos (AH-lah-mos), city (1990 pop. 6,132) and township, Sonora, NW Mexico, in mt. valley, 31 mi/50 km E of Navojoa; 27°00'N 108°58'W. Elev. 1,345 ft/410 m. Mining center (silver, zinc, gold, copper). Iron deposits nearby. Lumbering.

Alamosa, county (□ 723 sq mi/1,873 sq km; 1990 pop. 13,617), S Colo.; ⊙ Alamosa; 37°34'N 105°46'W. Irrigated agr. area, watered by Rio Grande; bounded E by Sangre de Cristo Mts. Cattle, sheep, wheat, hay, oats, barley, vegetables, potatoes. San Luis Valley extends N-S between Sangra de Cristo and San Juan mts. Part of Great Sand Dunes Natl. Monument and San Isabel Natl. Forest in NE; San Luis Lakes State Park in NE; Alamosa Natl. Wildlife Reserve in SE; small part of Monte Vista Natl. Wildlife Reserve in SW. Formed 1913.

Alamosa, town (1990 pop. 7,579), ⊙ Alamosa co., S Colo., on Rio Grande, in San Luis Valley, and 90 mi/145 km SW of Pueblo; 37°28'N 105°52'W. Elev. 7,500 ft/2,286 m. RR junction. Shipping and processing center, with RR shops, for San Luis Valley; dairy and meat prods., potatoes; light mfg. Adams State Col. here. Nearby is state soldiers' and sailors' home. Rio Grande Natl. Forest to W; San Luis Lakes State Park and Great Sand Dunes Natl. Monument and part of San Isabel Natl. Forest in NE (including Blanca Peak, 14,345 ft/4,372 m); Alamosa Natl. Wildlife Refuge to SE; Monte Vista Natl. Wildlife Refuge. City founded and inc. 1878 with coming of RR.

Alanson, village (1990 pop. 677), Emmet co., NW Mich., 10 mi/16 km NE of Petoskey, bet. Burt (to E) and Crooked lakes (to S); 45°26'N 84°47'W. In resort area.

Alapaha (uh-la-puh-HAH), town (1990 pop. 812), Berrien co., S Ga., 18 mi/29 km ESE of Tifton, near Alapaha R.; 31°23'N 83°13'W. Mfg. includes greenhouses, aquaculture equip., lumber.

Alapaha River (uh-la-puh-HAH), 190 mi/306 km long, S Ga.; rises in SE corner of Dooly co.; flows SE, past Willacoochee and Statenville, into N Fla. to Suwannee R. 10 mi/16 km SW of Jasper.

Alaquines (ah-lah-KEE-nais), city (1990 pop. 1,012) and township, San Luis Potosí, N central Mexico, 30 mi/48 km NE of Río Verde; 22°10'N 99°35'W. Elev. 4,268 ft/1,301 m. Corn, wheat, cotton, maguey.

Alaska, state (□ 656,424 sq mi/1,700,135 sq km, including

86,051 sq mi/222,871 sq km of water surface; 1995 est. pop. 603,617), NW N. Amer., admitted 1959 as the 49th state; ⊙ JUNEAU; 65°17′N 151°39′W. Nearly ⅕ the size of the rest of the U.S., Alaska is the largest state in the Union, but ranks 49th in pop. The 1990 census marked the first time in Alaskan history it did not rank last in pop. ANCHORAGE is the largest city, with approximately ½ the state's pop. living in its metropolitan area (from Willow to Wasila); FAIRBANKS is 2d largest, along with Juneau. NOME was founded when gold was discovered (1898) in the sand on the beaches of the Seward Peninsula. Alaska is a large peninsula land at the NW extremity of N. Amer., bet. the Arctic Ocean and Beaufort Sea on the N and the Gulf of Alaska and the Pacific Ocean on the S. It is bounded on the E by Canada (Yukon and B.C.) and on the W by the Bering Sea, Bering Strait, and Chukchi Sea. The tip of the Seward Peninsula is only a few miles from Rus. Far East; the two are separated by the narrow Bering Strait. Seward Peninsula is chiefly tundra-covered and sparsely inhabited. The Bering Strait widens in the N to the Chukchi Sea, which slices into Alaska with Kotzebue Sound; in the S the strait widens to the Bering Sea, which cuts into Alaska with Norton Sound and Bristol Bay. The state again extends toward Russia in the Alaska Peninsula and the Aleutian Isls., reaching out a total of 1,200 mi/1,931 km toward the Komandorski Isls.; together they divide the Bering Sea from the Pacific. The Aleutian Range, which is the spine of the Alaska Peninsula, continues in the grass-covered, treeless Aleutian Isls., where the climate is foggy, damp, and cold in the winter and subject to violent winds (the williwaws). Once heavily populated by Aleuts and traversed by Rus. fur traders hunting sea otters, the Aleutians today are chiefly of strategic and fishing importance and constitute a wildlife refuge. The S shore of Alaska is deeply indented by 2 inlets of the wide Gulf of Alaska, Cook Inlet and Prince William Sound; the Kenai Peninsula bet. them extends SW toward Kodiak Isl. The narrow Alaska Panhandle dips SE along the coast from the Gulf of Alaska, cutting into B.C. It consists of the offshore isls. of the Alexander Archipelago and the narrow coast, which rises steeply to the mts. of the Boundary Range and the St. Elias Mts. Winters in the Panhandle are relatively mild, with heavy rainfall and, except on the upper slopes of the mts., comparatively little snow. The interior of Alaska, on the other hand, can have extremely cold winters and short, hot summers. In Arctic Alaska, N of the Brooks Range, the temp. in winter reaches −10°F/−23.3°C to −40°F/−40°C. The land here is mostly tundra, cut by many rivers, the longest being the Colville. Alaska's major river is the Yukon, which crosses the state from E to W for 1,200 mi/1,931 km, from the Can. border to the Bering Sea. The northernmost reach of Alaska is Point Barrow. Alaska's climate and terrain (rough coast and high mt. ranges) divide it into relatively isolated regions, and transportation relies heavily on airlines. Anchorage and S central Alaska is the most populous region. The Panhandle's connection with SEATTLE is by ships, which ply the INSIDE PASSAGE bet. the coast and the offshore isls. In S central Alaska, Anchorage is the center for the Alaskan RR and for airways; it is also connected with the Alaska Highway. The ports of Seward and Anchorage are the major terminus for the Alaska RR and highway system. Cordova and Kodiak depend on the ocean lanes and aircraft. In the N, the entire Arctic coast is icebound most of the year; the ground remains permanently frozen. Alaska has very little agr.; in number of farms and in the value of its farm prods., it ranks last in the nation. The state's best arable land is in its S central region, in the Matanuska Valley and the Tanana Valley and delta (the area around FAIRBANKS). Most of Alaska's farms are dairies and the state's most valuable farm commodities are dairy prods., potatoes, feed grains, beef cattle, and vegetables. Fishing is a leading industry. Alaska heads the nation in the value of its commercial catch—chiefly salmon, crab, shrimp, halibut, herring, and cod. Its largest mfg. enterprise is food processing, particularly the freezing and canning of fish. Lumbering and related industries are important. The state has many natl. parks, wildlife refuges, and 2 natl. forests. Mining, principally of petroleum, natural gas, sand, gravel, zinc, lead, coal, and other metals is the state's most valuable industry. Gold, which led to the opening of the area in the 19th cent., is still mined in quantity. Fur trapping, Alaska's oldest industry, endures, on a limited scale; pelts are obtained from a great variety of animals, but fur farming is now gone. The Kodiak bear of the Alaska Peninsula is a major attraction, as is sport fishing. The govt.—Federal, state, and local—is Alaska's major source of employment. The state's strategic location has generated considerable defense activity, including the establishment of permanent military bases. In 1968 vast reserves of oil and natural gas were discovered on the Arctic N Slope near PRUDHOE BAY. The petroleum reservoir was determined to be twice the size of any other field in N. Amer. In 1969 the lease sale of oil fields yielded over $900 million. The 800-mi/1,287-km-long Trans-Alaska pipeline (4 ft/1.2 m in diameter and raised on stilts), extending from the Arctic N Slope to the ice-free port of Valdez, opened in 1977 after bitter opposition from environmentalists, and oil has dominated the state economy ever since, although production has declined in the 1990s. Many of the state's exports to foreign countries are exported through Seattle. Trade with the Rus. Far East and Siberia is growing. The Alaska Permanent Fund was created in 1977, into which goes 25% of Alaska's oil royalty income. The fund, designed to provide the state with income after the oil reserves are depleted, pays dividends to all residents. Offshore oil drilling in the Beaufort Sea and onshore drilling on the coast of the Arctic Natl. Wildlife Refuge are opposed by environmentalists. Alaska's tourism has increased dramatically with the help of improvements in transportation; it ranks as one of the state's top industries. The state abounds in natural wonders, and many natl. parks and wildlife refuges were added when the Alaska Natl. Interest Lands Act was enacted to close most of the state to prospecting. In the Panhandle, the scenic beauty of the mts. and the rugged fjord-indented coast are augmented by such attractions as the MALASPINA Glacier and the acres of blue ice in GLACIER BAY NATIONAL PARK AND PRESERVE. In the Alaska Range of S central Alaska stands the highest point in N. Amer., Mt. McKinley (Denali) in DENALI NATIONAL PARK AND PRESERVE, while the Alaska Peninsula and the Aleutian Isls. have numerous volcanoes; KATMAI NATIONAL PARK AND PRESERVE contains the Valley of Ten Thousand Smokes, scene of a volcanic eruption in 1912. The 1,049-mi/1,688-km Iditarod sled dog race from Anchorage to Nome is a major attraction and a celebration of Alaskan heritage. The voyage of Vitus Bering and Aleksey Chirikov in 1741 climaxed the march of Rus. traders across Siberia. The survivors who returned with fur seal skins started a rush of fur hunters to the Aleutian Isls. Grigori Shelekhov in 1784 founded the 1st permanent settlement in Alaska on Kodiak Isl. and sent (1790) to Alaska the man who was to dominate the period of Rus. influence, Aleksandr Baranov. A monopoly was granted to the Rus. Amer. Company in 1799, and it was Baranov who directed its Alaskan activities. Baranov extended the Rus. trade far down the W coast of N. Amer. and even, after several unsuccessful attempts, founded (1812) a settlement in N Calif., Fort Ross. Rivalry for the NW coast was strong, and Br. and Amer. trading vessels began to threaten the Rus. monopoly. In 1821 the czar issued a ukase (imperial command) claiming the 51st parallel as the S boundary of Alaska and warning foreign vessels not to transgress beyond it. Br. and Amer. protests, the promulgation of the Monroe Doctrine, and Rus. embroilment elsewhere resulted (1825) in a negotiated settlement of the boundary at lat. 54°40′N (the present S boundary of Alaska). Rus. interests in Alaska gradually declined, and after the Crimean War, Russia sought to dispose of the territory altogether. In 1867, Alaska was sold to the U.S. for $7,200,000. The U.S. purchase was accomplished through the determined efforts of Secretary of State William H. Seward. Since Alaska appeared to offer no immediate financial return, it was neglected. The U.S. army officially controlled the area until 1876. After a small lapse, during which govt. was in the hands of customs men, the U.S. Navy was given charge (1879). It was not until after the discovery of gold in the Juneau region in 1880 that Alaska was given a governor and a feeble local administration (under the Organic Act of 1884). Missionaries, who had come to the region in the late 1870s, exercised considerable influence. Most influential was Sheldon Jackson, best known for his introduction of reindeer to help the Alaska Eskimo (Inuit). Sealing was the subject of a long internatl. controversy, which was not ended until the treaties of 1912. The KLONDIKE strike of 1896 brought a stampede, mainly of Americans, and most of them came through Alaska to Dawson, Yukon Territory. The big discoveries in Alaska itself followed—Nome in 1898–1899, Fairbanks in 1902. The miners and prospectors (the sourdoughs) took over Alaska, and the era of the mining camps reached its ht.; a criminal code was belatedly applied in 1899. Not until 1906 did Alaska get a territorial representative in Congress. The longstanding controversy concerning the boundary bet. the Alaska Panhandle and B.C. was aggravated by the large number of miners traveling the Inside Passage to the gold fields. The matter was finally settled in 1903 by a 6-man tribunal, composed of Amer., Can., and Br. representatives. The decision was generally favorable to the U.S., and a period of rapid bldg. and development began. Mining, requiring heavy financing, passed into the hands of Eastern capitalists, notably the monopolistic Alaska Syndicate. Opposition to the "interests" became the burning issue in Alaska and was catapulted into natl. politics; Gifford Pinchot and R. A. Ballinger were the chief antagonists, and this was a major issue on which Theodore Roosevelt split with President William Howard Taft. A new era began for Alaska when local govt. was established in 1912 and it became a U.S. territory (Juneau had officially replaced SITKA as the capital in 1900, although it did not begin to function as such until 1906). The building of the Alaska RR from Seward to Fairbanks was commenced with govt. funds in 1915. The commercial fishing industry, which started with canneries in 1879, spread rapidly and became a major industry by 1900. Alaska enjoyed an economic boom during World War II. The ALASKA HIGHWAY was built, supplying a weak but much-needed link with the U.S. After Jap. troops occupied the Aleutian isls. of Attu and Kiska, U.S. forces prepared for a counterattack. Attu was retaken in May 1943, after intense fighting, and the Japanese evacuated Kiska in Aug. after intensive U.S. bombardments. Dutch Harbor, Adak, Kodiak, and Sitka became major bases in World War II. The growth of air travel after the war, and the permanent military bases established in Alaska, particularly the DEW line, resulted in tremendous growth; bet. 1950 and 1960 the pop. nearly doubled. In 1958, Alaskans approved statehood by a 5-to-1 vote, and on Jan. 3, 1959, Alaska was officially admitted into the Union as a state, the first since Ariz. in 1912. On Mar. 27, 1964, the strongest earthquake ever recorded in N. Amer. occurred in Alaska, taking approximately 114 lives and causing extensive property damage, particularly in Valdez, Seward, and parts of Anchorage. The fishing industry was especially hard hit, with the loss of fleets, docks, and canneries from the resulting tidal waves. Reconstruction, with large-scale Federal aid, was speedily completed. In 1989 the tanker *Exxon Valdez* ran aground in Prince William Sound, releasing over 10 million gallons of oil into the water, resulting in the worst oil spill in U.S. history. Alaska operates under a constitution drawn up and ratified in 1956 (effective with statehood). Its executive branch is headed by a governor and a secretary of state, both elected (on the same ticket) for 4-year terms. Alaska's bicameral legislature has a senate with 20 members elected for 4-year terms and a house of representatives with 40 members elected for 2 years. The state sends 2 senators and 1 representative to the U.S. Congress and has 3 electoral votes.

Alaska has a state-wide system of vocational schools, cols., and graduate programs under the Univ. of Alaska with major campuses in Fairbanks, Anchorage, and Juneau. The Alaska natives (Inuit) are organized into 13 regional corporations under the Alaska Native Claims Settlement Act.

Alaska Current, branch of North Pacific drift, flowing counterclockwise in the Gulf of Alaska.

Alaska, Gulf of, broad N inlet of Pacific Ocean, on S coast of Alaska, bet. Alaska Peninsula (W) and Alexander Archipelago (E). Includes Kodiak Isl. Chief ports are Kodiak, Anchorage, Seward, and Valdez.

Alaska Highway, all weather graveled road, 1,523 mi/2,451 km long, extending NW from Dawson Creek, B.C., to Fairbanks, Alaska. An extension of an existing Can. road bet. Dawson Creek and Edmonton, Alta., the Alaska Highway was constructed (early 1940s) by 11,000 U.S. troops and 16,000 U.S. and Can. civilians, as a supply route to military forces in Alaska during World War II. It was a significant engineering feat because of the difficulties of terrain and weather. In the last stretch to Fairbanks the road used the previously built Richardson Highway. The Haines Cutoff connects the Alaska Highway with the Alaska Panhandle. In 1946 control of the Can. part of the road was transferred to Canada. In 1947 the entire highway was opened to unrestricted travel; it is one of the best routes to Alaska. The highway is open throughout the year, with roadside facilities along its length. It was formerly known as the Alaskan Internatl. Highway and the Alcan Highway.

Alaska North Slope, or **Arctic North Slope**, region (1990 pop. 5,979), N Alaska, bet. the Arctic Ocean and the Brooks Range. In 1968 large petroleum reserves were found in the PRUDHOE BAY area. In 1977 the 800-mi/1,287-km-long Trans-Alaska pipeline was completed to carry oil to the port of Valdez. Has significant oil, gas, and coal deposits. Shores frequented by bow head whales and polar bears, also a major caribou calving region. Contains North Slope Borough, Natl. Petroleum Reserve-Alaska; Artctic Natl. Wildlife Refuge. Commonly called North Slope.

Alaska Peninsula, SW Alaska, extends 500 mi/805 km SW from mainland, near 59°30′N 155°00′W, bet. Bristol Bay of Bering Sea (NW) and the Pacific (SE). Aleutian Range runs length of peninsula; includes many volcanoes, including those in Katmai Natl. Monument (NE). Native villages on both shores; fishing, brown bear watching and tourism. Weather is wet, cool, and foggy throughout year. Aleutian Isls. extend SW from tip of peninsula.

Alaska Range, S central Alaska, rising to the highest mt. in N. Amer., Mt. McKinley (20,320 ft/6,194 m). The range separates coastal Alaska from the interior and basins of the Yukon and Kuskokwin rivers.

Alatna (uh-LAT-nuh), village (1990 pop. 31), N central Alaska, on Koyukuk R., at mouth of Alatna R., and 100 mi/161 km N of Tanana, on Arctic Circle; 66°33′N 152°45′W. Airstrip. Gold in the area.

Alatna River (uh-LAT-nuh), c.200 mi/322 km long, N central Alaska; rises on S slope of Brooks Range near 67°51′N 155°10′W; flows SE to Koyukuk R. at Alatna.

Alava, Cape (ah-LAH-vah), Clallam co., NW Wash., westernmost point of lower 48 U.S. states, on the Pacific Ocean 15 mi/24 km S of Cape Flattery; 48°10′N 124°44′W. In coastal section of Olympia Natl. Park. Ozette Isl., part of Flattery Rock Natl. Wildlife Refuge, 1 mi/1.6 km off cape; Ozette Indian Reservation on N side of cape.

Alazan Bay, Texas: see BAFFIN BAY.

Alba (AL-buh), city (1990 pop. 465), Jasper co., SW Mo., on Spring R., and 12 mi/19 km NNE of Joplin; 37°14′N 94°25′W. Wheat, hay, soybeans; cattle.

Alba, village (1990 pop. 489), Wood co., NE Texas, near Sabine R., 35 mi/56 km NW of Tyler; 32°47′N 95°38′W. Dairying; cattle, poultry; vegetables; timber; mfg. (aluminum fabricating). Large L. Fork reservoir to NE, recreation area.

Alba (AL-bah), borough (1990 pop. 170), Bradford co., N Pa., 27 mi/43 km S of Elmira, on Alma Creek; 41°42′N 76°49′W. Agr. (corn, hay, livestock, dairying). Tioga State Forest on Armenia Mt., to W.

Albanel (al-buh-NEL), village (1991 pop. 2,496), S central Que., 9 mi/14 km W of Dolbeau; 48°52′N 72°25′W. Dairying.

Albanel, Lake, central Que., Canada, 5 mi/8 km SE of L. Mistassini, into which it drains; 50 mi/80 km long, 6 mi/10 km wide. Elev. 1,289 ft/393 m.

Albany 1 (AWL-buh-nee), county (□ 531 sq mi/1,375 sq km; 1990 pop. 292,594), E N.Y.; ⊙ Albany; 42°36′N 73°58′W. Bounded on E by the Hudson and partly on N by Mohawk R. and the N.Y. State Barge Canal. Includes the Helderbergs and part of the Catskills (resorts). Dairying, farming (hay, vegetables, horticultural crops); cattle and calves, lamb and sheep raising. Extensive mfg. at Albany, Watervliet, Cohoes (ranks 3rd in the state in numbers employed in mfg). Formed 1683; named in honor of James Stuart, Duke of York and Albany. **2** county (□ 4,309 sq mi/11,160 sq km; 1990 pop. 30,797), SE Wyo.; ⊙ Laramie; 41°38′N 105°44′W. Grain, livestock area bordering on Colo.; watered by Laramie R. (forms Wheatland Reservoir and L. Ione at center). Agr. (hay, alfalfa; cattle, sheep) timber; oil, natural gas. Parts of Medicine Bow Natl. Forest in SW and NE; part of Medicine Bow Mts. in SW; part of Laramie Mts. in NE and E. Snowy Range Ski Area in SW; Como Bluff, renowned dinosaur fossil bed, in NW. Hutton Lake Natl. Wildlife Refuge in S. Formed 1868.

Albany 1 (AWL-buh-nee), city (1990 pop. 16,327), Alameda co., W Calif., suburb 6 mi/9.7 km N of downtown Oakland, N of Berkeley, on Contra Coasta co. line, on the E shore of San Francisco Bay; 37°54′N 122°20′W. Mfg. (adhesives, fabricated metal prods., printing). Carlos Lee Tilden Regional Park and Berkeley Hills to E; Golden Gate Fields Race Track on bay side. Inc. 1908 **2** city (1990 pop. 78,122), ⊙ Dougherty co., SW Ga., on the Flint R.; 31°35′N 84°11′W. It is the industrial center of a pecan and peanut area. Airport. Among its many industries are agr. (peanut and pecan) processing, meat-packing, and cotton milling. Mfg. includes concrete, printing and publishing, fertilizer, millwork and lumber, construction materials, transportation equip., food, plastics and paper prods. Albany State Univ. and Darton Col. are units of the Univ. System of Ga. The Albany Naval Air Station, and a U.S. marine corps supply center are in the city. Scene of major rioting during civil rights struggle of the mid-1960s. A severe flood damaged the city in 1994. The Ga. Pecan Festival is held here annually. Nearby are Chehaw State Park and the popular resort, Radium Springs. Inc. 1841. **3** city (1990 pop. 1,958), ⊙ Gentry co., NW Mo., on East Fork of Grand R., and 43 mi/69 km NE of St. Joseph; 40°15′N 94°19′W. Corn, soybeans; cattle, hogs; mfg. (automatic controls). Founded c.1845. **4** city (□ 21 sq mi/54 sq km; 1990 pop. 101,082), ⊙ N.Y. state and of Albany co., E N.Y., on the W bank of the Hudson; 42°40′N 73°47′W. A deepwater port of entry, it handles much shipping, has major oil storage facilities, and is a transshipment point for turbines and generators. Airport (1st municipal airport in U.S., 1919). Though primarily a govt. and service center, the city still retains significant mfg., trucking, and warehousing functions. Mfg. (metal fabrication, machine tools for RR and transit vehicles, cardboard and paper prods., clothing and textiles, chemicals, plastics, cable and wire rope, petroleum prods.). In 1609, Henry Hudson visited the site, and 4 years later the Dutch built Fort Nassau, a fur-trading post on Castle Isl. In 1624 several Walloon families began permanent settlement at the Du. post of Fort Orange, later renamed Albany when the English took control (1664). Albany was long important as a fur-trading center and was involved in the Fr. and Indian Wars. In 1754 the Albany Congress met there, and after the Revolution the state capital was moved (1797) to Albany from N.Y. city. Albany's trade grew with the development of the state, particularly after the opening of the Champlain and Erie canals in the 1820s. It is the seat of the State Univ. of N.Y. at Albany, Union Univ. (Col. of Pharmacy, Albany Law School, and Albany Medical Col.), the Col. of St. Rose, Maria Col., and Russell Sage Jr. Col.; the State Univ. of N.Y. Regents Col. Degrees; and the Albany Inst. of History and Art. Siena Col. is in suburban Loudonville. Among the many old bldgs. are the Schuyler mansion (1762), where Gen. Philip Schuyler's daughter, Elizabeth, was married to Alexander Hamilton; Ten Broeck Mansion (1798); and Cherry Hill (1768), the home of Philip Van Rensselaer and his descendants until 1963. Since the decline in mfg. in the late 1950s, the city has undertaken several major revitalization efforts, including the Gov. Nelson A. Rockefeller Empire State Plaza, a 90 acres/36 ha complex of above- and underground shops and offices, administrative bldgs. (including the 44-story Corning Tower, offering panoramic views of surrounding countryside), convention facilities, parks, the largest and oldest state mus. in the nation, and the state lib.; the Knickerbocker Arena is S of the plaza. The plaza faces the lavish 19th-cent. capitol bldg. with impressive halls, stairways, and stonework built in the Fr. château style. The riverfront commercial dist. also enjoyed a revival in the 1980s, including a $120-million upgrade of its oil refinery. Site of Crossgates Mall, one of the largest shopping centers in U.S. An annual tulip festival is held in the city. Bret Harte was b. here, and Herman Melville, author of *Moby-Dick*, lived here. Inc. 1686. **5** city (1990 pop. 29,462), ⊙ Linn co., Ore., and extends into Benton co., 22 mi/35 km S of Salem, on the Willamette R. at the mouth of the Calapooia R.; 44°37′N 123°05′W. RR junction. Metals processing center for the Pacific Northwest (titanium, zirconium, columbium castings). Mfg. (food prods., furniture, prefabricated homes, construction materials, metal prods., printing and publishing). An annual world championship timber carnival is held here. Linn-Benton Community Col. Muncipal airport. Hemick State Park to NW; Ankeny Natl. Wildlife Refuge to N; McDonald State Forest to W. Inc. 1864.

Albany, town, St. Mary parish, N Jamaica, on RR, and 5 mi/8 km W of Annotto Bay; 18°17′N 76°51′W. Bananas.

Albany 1 (AWL-buh-nee), town (1990 pop. 2,357), Delaware co., E Ind., near Mississinewa R., 12 mi/19 km NE of Muncie; 40°18′N 85°14′W. Livestock, grain; tools, paper prods., paper boxes, aluminum die castings. **2** town (1990 pop. 2,062), ⊙ Clinton co., S Ky., in Cumberland foothills near Tenn. state line, 40 mi/64 km SW of Somerset; 36°41′N 85°08′W. Agr. (livestock, poultry, dairying); mfg. (concrete, apparel, consumer goods, feeds, charcoal); crushed stone, lumber. Fishing nearby. Wolf Creek Dam to N forms L. Cumberland on Cumberland R., Dale Hollow L. reservoir to SW, on Obey R. Area settled c.1800, est. 1838. **3** town (1994 pop. 903) named after the Natalbany R. in agr. and timber area of Livingston Parish, La., 8 mi/13 km W of Hammond; 30°30′N 90°35′W. **4** town (1990 pop. 1,548), Stearns co., central Minn., 20 mi/32 km WNW of St. Cloud, in area of small natural lakes; 45°37′N 94°34′W. RR junction. Dairying; poultry, hogs, sheep, cattle; grain; mfg. (food, consumer goods, machinery). Birch L. State Forest to NW. **5** town (1990 pop. 536), Carroll co., E central N.H., 32 mi/51 km NE of Laconia, in White Mt. Natl. Forest (except SE margin of town); 43°57′N 71°16′W. Drained by Swift R., source of Chocorua R. Agr. (livestock; some dairying; timber); mfg. (ostomy appliances). Nearby are Mt. Chocorua (3,475 acres/1,406 hat) and Mt. Paugus (3,201 ft/976 m). **6** town (1990 pop. 1,962), ⊙ Shackelford co., N central Texas, 31 mi/50 km NE of Abilene; 32°43′N 99°17′W. Elev. 1,429 ft/436 m. Cattle ranching (90% of income), horses, hogs, agr. (cotton, wheat, mesquite), oil and gas producing area; light mfg. Fort Griffin State Park is 14 mi/23 km NE. **7** rural town (1990 pop. 782), including Albany village, Orleans co., N Vt., on Black R., and 16 mi/26 km SW of Newport; 44°43′N 72°20′W. Granted 1782. **8** town (1990 pop. 1,140), Green co., S Wis., 13 mi/21 km NE of Monroe, and on Sugar R.; 42°42′N 89°26′W. In agr. area; mfg. (cheese, electric heating elements). On Sugar R. State Trail.

Albany 1 village (1990 pop. 835), Whiteside co., NW Ill., on the Mississippi, 14 mi/23 km WSW of Morrison, and 4 mi/6.4 km SSW of Clinton, Iowa; 41°47'N 90°13'W. In agr. area (corn, soybeans, oats, cattle, hogs). **2** village (1990 pop. 795), Athens co., SE Ohio, 9 mi/14 km SW of Athens; 39°14'N 82°12'W.

Albany, township, Oxford co., W Maine, on Crooked R., and c.30 mi/48 km WNW of Auburn, partly in White Mt. Natl. Forest. Includes Lynchville and Town House villages.

Albany, Fort, Canada: see FORT ALBANY.

Albany River, 610 mi/982 km long, W Ont., Canada; rising in L. St. Joseph; flowing generally E into James Bay, near Fort Albany. The Kenogami and Ogoki rivers are its chief tributaries. The river, named for the duke of York and Albany, later James II, was long an important fur-trading route.

Albee, village (1990 pop. 15), Grant co., E S.Dak., 12 mi/19 km SSE of Milbank.

Albemarle (AL-buh-marl), county (□ 739 sq mi/1,914 sq km; 1990 pop. 68,040), N central Va.; ⊙ CHARLOTTESVILLE (independent of co.); 38°01'N 78°33'W. W part is in the Piedmont and rises to the Blue Ridge (W); bounded SW in part by Rockfish R., S by James R.; drained by Rivanna R. and Hardware R. Agr. (wheat, apples, peaches, corn, hay, alfalfa); cattle, sheep, horses, poultry; dairying; timber. Limestone, soapstone. Includes part of Shenandoah Natl. Park in NW; Appalachian Trail, Blue Ridge (Natl.) Parkway follow W boundary, the latter becoming Skyline Drive in Shenandoah Park. Known for historic estates (notably Monticello and Ash Lawn); Univ. of Va. at Charlottesville. Formed 1774.

Albemarle (AL-buh-mahrl), city (□ 14 sq mi/36 sq km; 1990 pop. 14,939), ⊙ Stanly co., central N.C., in the Piedmont region; 35°21'N 80°11'W. RR junction. A marketing center in an agr. area (cotton, grain, soybeans; poultry, livestock). Mfg. (apparel, mobile homes, electrical equip., textiles, building materials, automobile components, printing and publishing). Pfeiffer Col. is to NW at Misenheimer. L. Tillery reservoir to E, Badin L. reservoir to NE, both on Yadkin R. Morrow Mt. State Park to E, on L. Tillery. Inc. 1857.

Albemarle and Chesapeake Canal, SE Va., a sect. (c.10 mi/16 km long) of Intracoastal Waterway; connects South Branch of Elizabeth R. (arm of Hampton Roads estuary) at Chesapeake in W, North Landing R. in E; channeled stream flows SSE to Currituck Sound, arm of Albermarle Sound, N.C. Atlantic Ocean to E.

Albemarle Sound (AL-buh-mahrl), large estuary of Atlantic Ocean, NE N.C., c.55 mi/89 km long, 3 mi/4.8 km–14 mi/23 km wide. Shallow and tideless, the sound is separated from the Atlantic Ocean by the Outer Banks sand barrier, branched through Oregeon Inlet from Pamlico Sound to SE. The Chowan R. (from N) and Roanoke R. (from W) are the main streams and enter the head of the sound. Intracoastal Waterway crosses Albermarle Sound near its mouth, from Alligator R. to Currituck Sound. Dismal Swamp Canal connects it with Chesapeake Bay to N. Fort Raleigh Natl. Historic Site on Roanoke Isl. and Wright Brothers Natl. Memorial at Kitty Hawk are at the E end of the sound on Outer Banks. Sound has several arms, including Currituck Sound (in behind Outer Banks), North R., Pasquotank R., Little R. and Perquimans R. estuaries, all on N side, and the Alligator R. estuary on S side. Elizabeth City and Edonton on N side.

Alberhill, uninc. village, Riverside co., S Calif., 19 mi/31 km S of Riverside on Temescal Wash; in Cleveland Natl. Forest. L. Elsinore reservoir to S; Santa Ana Mts. to SW, including Santiago Peak (5,686 ft/1,733 m) to W.

Alberni (al-BUHR-nee), city, S central Vancouver Isl., SW B.C., Canada, at head of Alberni Canal, just N of Port Alberni, 90 mi/145 km NW of Victoria; 49°16'N 124°48'W. In lumbering, fishing, and mining (gold, silver, copper, lead, zinc) area. Tourism and sport-fishing center.

Alberni Canal, fjord of Barkley Sound, SW B.C., Canada, in SW Vancouver Isl., extending NE and N to Port Alberni; 23 mi/37 km long, 1 mi/2 km wide. In lumbering, fishing, farming, and mining area. Navigable for ocean-going ships. Also called Alberni Inlet.

Albers, village (1990 pop. 700), Clinton co., SW Ill., 17 mi/27 km ESE of O'Fallon; 38°32'N 89°37'W. Agr. area (poultry, dairying); wood pallets. Coal-mining region.

Albert, county (□ 681 sq mi/1,764 sq km; 1991 pop. 25,640), SE N.B., Canada, on the Bay of Fundy, bounded N and E by Petitcodiac R. estuary; ⊙ Hopewell Cape.

Albert, village (1990 pop. 229), Barton co., central Kansas, on Walnut Creek, and 15 mi/24 km WNW of Great Bend; 38°27'N 99°00'W. Wheat. Oil and gas fields nearby.

Albert, Cape, E Ellesmere Isl., NE Franklin dist., N.W.T., Canada, E extremity of Bache Peninsula, on Kane Basin; 100 mi/161 km long, 25 mi/40 km wide; 79°2'N 74°15'W. Elev. 2,030 ft/619 m.

Albert City, town (1990 pop. 779), Buena Vista co., NW Iowa, 15 mi/24 km NE of Storm L.; 42°46'N 94°57'W. Mfg. (metal prods. and equip.).

Albert, Lake, lake, Hamlin and Kingsbury cos., E S.Dak., NE of Badger; 4 mi/6.4 km long, 2 mi/3.2 km wide. L. Poinsett to NE.

Albert Lea (LEE), city (1990 pop. 18,310), ⊙ Freeborn co., S Minn., near the Iowa state line; 43°39'N 93°22'W. Elev. 1,228 ft/374 m. RR junction and mfg. and marketing center in agr. area (poultry, cattle, sheep, hogs; dairying; corn, soybeans, potatoes). Mfg. (construction materials, printing and publishing, food prods., machinery, consumer goods). City is on W end of Albert Lea L.; Fountain L. at center of city, N of downtown. Municipal airport to N. Albert Lea Vocational Technical School here. Myre Big Island State Park to E; numerous natural lakes in area. Inc. 1878.

Albert Lea Lake (LEE), Freeborn co., S Minn., extends E from Albert Lea city; 7 mi/11.3 km long, 1 mi/1.6 km wide. Drains into Shellrock R. Myre Big Isl. State Park on W part of lake.

Albert Mines, locality, SE N.B., Canada, near Petitcodiac R., 16 mi/26 km SSE of Moncton; 45°49'N 64°34'W. In albertite, gypsum, oil-shale, manganese mining district.

Albert, Mount (3,550 ft/1,082 m), SE Que., Canada, on N side of Gaspé Peninsula, 60 mi/97 km E of Matane, in Shickshock Mts.

Albert Peak (10,008 ft/3,050 m), SE B.C., Canada, in Selkirk Mts., 15 mi/24 km E of Revelstoke; 51°02'N 117°51'W.

Albert Town, town, S Bahama Isls., on Long Cay or Fortune Isl., 250 mi/402 km SE of Nassau; 22°37'N 74°22'W. Sisal, stock, salt.

Albert Town, town (1991 pop. 3,389), Trelawny parish, W central Jamaica, 30 mi/48 km NW of May Pen; 18°17'N 77°33'W. Tropical fruit, spices.

Alberta (Al-bur-tuh), province (□ 255,285 sq mi/661,188 sq km, including 6,485 sq mi/16,796 sq km of water surface; 1991 pop. 2,545,553), W Canada, ⊙ EDMONTON, 2d-largest city; 55°00'N 115°00'W. The largest city is CALGARY; other important cities are LETHBRIDGE, Red Deer, Medicine Hat, St. Albert, and Fort McMurray. Alberta is bounded on the E by Sask.; on the N by Fort Smith Region, N.W.T.; on the W by B.C.; and on the S by Mont. Westernmost of the Prairie provs., it lies on a high plateau, rising on the W to the Continental Divide at the B.C. border. There are the foothills of the Rocky Mts. and the spectacular mountains themselves, with 3 noted natl. parks—Jasper, Banff, and Waterton Lakes (the Can. sect. of Waterton-Glacier Internatl. Peace Park). Although Alta. is known as a Prairie prov., only about ¼ of its area is actually treeless—chiefly the undulating prairie of S Alta. Central Alta. has parklike, partly wooded country, and the N stretches bear thousands of acres of virgin timberland. Endowed with many lakes, streams, and rivers, the prov. is drained by the Peace, the Athabasca, the N and S branches of the Sask., the Red Deer, the St. Mary, the Milk, and many other rivers. The pop. is concentrated in S and central Alta., and except for farm centers in the fertile valley of the Peace, the N portion is sparsely settled. Agr. remains an important part of Alta.'s economy. Grain, especially wheat, is the dominant crop. In the S, large irrigation developments, such as those around Lethbridge, have placed thousands of additional acres under cultivation. A variety of crops, such as sugar beets and potatoes, are grown in this area. The prov. is noted as well for the quality of its livestock. Meat-packing, flour milling, dairying, and food processing are important industries. But Alta.'s major industry, since the early 1960s, has been the exploitation of its vast petroleum and other mineral resources. Alta.'s coal beds contain about ½ of Canada's reserves, while the prov. leads the country in the production of oil; it is believed to have potentially the richest oil deposits in the world, most notably in the famous tar beds of the Athabasca R. Alta. provided 82% of Canada's crude petroleum output in 1988. Its sources of natural gas are also among the world's greatest. Pipelines radiate from Alta., carrying crude oil and natural gas to points in E and W Canada and into the United States. The production of crude oil decreased slightly in the 1980s, while the production of natural gas and coal increased. Construction, traditionally a booming industry in Alta., was severely weakened by the decline in oil production, leading to increased unemployment. Other industries include food and beverage production, lumbering, printing and publishing, and the mfg. of iron, steel, and clay prods. Tourism is the 3d-largest segment of Alta.'s industrial economy. Many visitors are drawn by the grand scale of Alta.'s landscape—its mt. scenery, rolling wheat fields, huge granaries, sprawling cattle ranches, and vast oil refineries. Annual festivals include the Indian Days Celebration at Banff, which attracts thousands of Native Americans from a wide area, and the famous Calgary Exhibition and Stampede. Other tourist attractions are Elk Island Natl. Park and the extensive Wood Buffalo Natl. Park, which shelters some 5,000 bison. In terms of special events, Edmonton hosted the Commonwealth Games (1978) and the World Univ. Games (1983), and Calgary hosted the 1988 Winter Olympics. Alta. was originally part of the territory granted to the Hudson's Bay Co. by King Charles II in 1670, and its early history was dominated by the fur trade. The first European known to have reached (1754) present-day Alta. was Anthony Hendon of the Hudson's Bay Co. There was also much exploration of the region by the Montreal-based North West Co., which merged with the Hudson's Bay Co. in 1821. Traders arrived from the upper Great Lakes before Sir Alexander Mackenzie crossed (1793) the region on his way to the Pacific. In 1794 a Hudson's Bay Co. fort was built at the site of present-day Edmonton. Destroyed by Native Americans in 1807, it was rebuilt 12 years later, and for 50 years it served traders and missionaries within a wide radius. The area remained under the control of the Hudson's Bay Co. until 1870 when it was sold, as part of the company's vast domain, to the newly created confederation of Canada. In 1874 the NW Mounted Police established Fort Macleod in S Alta., and the following year they built a log fort on the site of present-day Calgary. An act of 1882 created four administrative divisions from the N.W.T., and one was named Alta. in honor of Queen Victoria's daughter, Princess Louise Caroline Alberta, whose husband was then governor general of Canada. The RR came through in the mid-1880s, opening up the area to ranchers and homesteaders, but settlement was slow. In 1891 there were only 14,500 non-native settlers in the present prov. To settle the vast fertile land, the Can. govt. advertised for immigrants, offering many free acres as inducements. Within the next 5 years immigrants poured in due to the federal govt's vigorous immigration policy, the decrease of available arable land in the Amer. West, the introduction of a new strain of fast-maturing hard spring wheat, and the easing of the 22-year long depression endured by N. Amer. The city of Edmonton boomed during the 1898 Klondike gold rush, serving as a supply base, and its growth continued during the early 1900s as immigrants began settling the rich surrounding farmlands. Alta. became a prov. in 1905. The discovery (1914) of oil in quantity at Turner Valley, near Calgary, presaged a new era for the mineral-rich prov., but it was not until 1947, when oil was found in the Leduc fields near Edmonton, that the basic change in Alta.'s economy began. By then agr. had suffered extensively: the 1929 crash, followed by droughts, early frosts, grasshopper plagues, and dust storms, had triggered emigration from the area.

Alberta, town (1990 pop. 337), Brunswick co., S Va., 36 mi/58 km SW of Petersburg; 36°51′N 77°52′W. Agr. (cotton, peanuts, tobacco, grain; livestock, dairying); mfg. (lumber, draperies, clothing, mulch processing). Southside Va. Community Col. (Christianna Campus) to SW.

Alberta, village (1990 pop. 136), Stevens co., W Minn., 7 mi/11.3 km W of Morris; 45°34′N 96°02′W. Corn, oats, wheat, barley, sunflowers; hogs, cattle.

Alberta, Mount (11,874 ft/3,619 m), W Alta., Canada, near B.C. border, in Rocky Mts., in Jasper Natl. Park, 50 mi/80 km SE of Jasper; 52°17′N 117°29′W.

Alberton, town (1991 pop. 1,068), NW P.E.I., Canada, on Cascumpeque Bay, 30 mi/48 km NNW of Summerside. Fishing port.

Alberton (AL-buhr-tuhn), village (1990 pop. 354), Mineral co., W Mont., 25 mi/40 km WNW of Missoula, and on the Clark Fork R.; 47°00′N 114°29′W. Hay, irrigated agr.; cattle, timber. Nearly surrounded by Lolo Natl. Forest, Frenchtown Pond State Park to E.

Alberton, Md.: see DANIELS.

Albertson, village (1990 pop. 5,166), Nassau co., SE N.Y., on W L.I., 2 mi/3.2 km N of Mineola; 40°46′N 73°39′W. Mfg. (wire and cable).

Albertville, city (1990 pop. 14,507), Marshall co., NE Ala., 21 mi/34 km NW of Gadsden. In livestock and corn area; lumber milling, furniture, rubber, plastic bags, clothing, poultry processing.

Albertville, town (1990 pop. 1,251), Wright co., E Minn., near Crow R., 6 mi/9.7 km W of its confluence with Mississippi R., and 27 mi/43 km NW of Minneapolis; 45°14′N 93°39′W. Corn, oats, barley, soybeans, alfalfa; dairying; poultry; mfg. (concrete and steel prods., feeds, plastic molds, woodroof trusses). Crow Hassan Park Reserve to S; Mud L. and School L. in N part of town.

Albia, city (1990 pop. 3,870), ⊙ Monroe co., S Iowa, near Cedar R., 20 mi/32 km W of Ottumwa; 41°01′N 92°47′W. In bituminous-coal-mining area. Mfg. (machinery, apparel); agr. (corn, cattle, sheep); RR junction. Founded as Princeton; inc. 1859.

Albin (AL-bin), village (1990 pop. 120), Laramie co., SE Wyo., near Nebr. state line, 45 mi/72 km NE of Cheyenne; 41°25′N 104°05′W. Elev. 5,334 ft/1,626 m.

Albino Zertuche, Mexico: see ACAXTLAHUACÁN DE ALBINO ZERTUCHE.

Albion 1 (AL-bee-uhn), city (1990 pop. 2,116), ⊙ Edwards co., SE Ill., 16 mi/26 km W of Mount Carmel; 38°22′N 88°03′W. In agr. area (cattle, wheat, corn, soybeans, sorghum); feed processing, light mfg. Founded 1818 by Eng. settlers led by Morris Birkbeck and George Flower. Several early houses are preserved. Inc. 1869. **2** city (1990 pop. 10,066), Calhoun Co., S Mich., 18 mi/29 km W of Jackson, where the Kalamazoo R. is formed by its N and S branches; 42°15′N 84°45′W. Agr. area (corn, wheat, soybeans, onions, apples; hogs, cattle, poultry). Mfg. (construction materials, industrial prods.). Albion Col. is here. Several small lakes to N.

Albion 1 town (1990 pop. 1,823), ⊙ Noble co., NE Ind., 26 mi/42 km NNW of Fort Wayne; 41°24′N 85°25′W. In scenic lake region. Agr. (livestock, soybeans, grain, poultry, fruit; dairy prods.); mfg. (automobile parts, industrial supplies). Laid out 1847. **2** town (1990 pop. 585), Marshall co., central Iowa, 6 mi/9.7 km NNW of Marshalltown; 42°06′N 92°59′W. In agr. area. **3** town (1990 pop. 1,736), Kennebec co., S Maine, 22 mi/35 km NE of Augusta; 44°30′N 69°26′W. Elijah Lovejoy b. here. Inc. 1804. **4** town (1990 pop. 1,916), ⊙ Boone co., E central Nebr., 40 mi/64 km SW of Norfolk, and on Beaver Creek; 41°41′N 98°00′W. RR terminus. Dairy, livestock; grain. Inc. 1873.

Albion 1 village (1990 pop. 305), Cassia co., S Idaho, 15 mi/24 km SE of Burley; 42°25′N 113°35′W. Elev. 4,750 ft/1,448 m. Pomerelle Ski Area to S; part of Sawtooth Natl. Forest to S. **2** village (□ 2 sq mi/5.2 sq km; 1990 pop. 5,863), ⊙ Orleans co., W N.Y., on Barge Canal, and 30 mi/48 km W of Rochester; 43°15′N 78°11′W. Mfg. (precision and custom metal fabrication). Stone quarries. Inc. 1828. **3** village (1990 pop. 88), Pushmataha co., SE Okla., c.40 mi/64 km ESE of McAlester, on Kiamichi R., in Ouachita Mts; 34°39′N 95°05′W. Lumbering. Kiamichi Mts. to SE. **4** mill village in Lincoln town, Providence co., NE R.I., on Blackstone R. (bridged here), and 9 mi/14.5 km N of Providence; 41°57′N 71°12′W. **5** village (1990 pop. 632), Whitman co., SE Wash., 8 mi/12.9 km SE of Colfax and on South Fork of Palouse R., in the Palouse region; 46°48′N 117°15′W. Agr. (wheat, barley, oats; peas, alfalfa; sheep, hogs). Kamiak Butte (3,641 ft/1,110 m) to NE.

Albion, borough (1990 pop. 1,575), Erie co., NW Pa., 22 mi/35 km SW of Erie, on East Branch Conneaut Creek; 41°53′N 80°21′W. Mfg. (commercial printing, heavy duty trailers). Agr. (hay, corn, soybeans, potatoes, apples; livestock, dairying). Covered bridges to W. Settled 1815, inc. 1861.

Albright, village (1990 pop. 195), Preston co., N W.Va., on Cheat R., 3 mi/4.8 km NE of Kingwood; 39°29′N 79°38′W. RR terminus. Mfg. (inflatable boats). White water rafting, Alpine Lakes Ski Resort to SE.

Albuquerque (AL-buh-kuhr-kee), city (1990 pop. 384,736), ⊙ Bernalillo co., N central N.Mex., on the upper Rio Grande; 35°07′N 106°37′W. The largest city in the state, it is an important commercial, industrial, and transportation center that serves a rich timber, livestock, and farm area. Mfg. (electronics, consumer goods, furniture, food and beverage prods., fabricated metal prods., machinery, medical equip.). A major employer is the Sandia Laboratories. Sandia Military Reserve, to SE, has Atomic Mus. (SE of Kirtland Air Force Base) and is engaged in nuclear research, testing, and weapons development. Kirtland Air Force Base to SE, home of the air force special weapons center, is in Albuquerque. The city experienced rapid growth after World War II and continues to be one of the fastest growing cities in the U.S.; it attracts many high-technology industries, such as lasers, data processing, and solar energy. Span. settlers arrived in the mid-1600s but were repelled (1680) by Native Americans. The old town was founded in 1706 and named for the viceroy of New Spain, the duke of Alburquerque. The new town was plotted in 1880 in connection with the RR and grew rapidly, soon enveloping the old town. Albuquerque is a noted health resort with many hosps. It is the seat of the Univ. of N. Mex., the Univ. of Albuquerque, and Albuquerque Technical Vocational Inst. Tourist attractions in and about the city include the Church of San Felipe de Nerí (1706); the Old Town Plaza and Mus. of Natural History; numerous mus.; the Sandia mts. to E, with caves that contain remains of some of the oldest habitations in the Western Hemisphere; and many pueblos. Coronado State Monument and State Park to N, is an excavated pueblo near which Coronado camped in 1541. Isleta Indian Reservation to S. Albuquerque Internatl. Airport in S; State Fairgrounds and Race Track in SE; Petroglyph Natl. Monument to W; Indian Petroglyph State Park in NW part of city; Shooting Range State Park to W; Rio Grande Nature Center State Park and San Gabriel State Park, both on Rio Grande in city; part of Cibola National Forest to E, includes Sandia Crest (10,678 ft/3,255 m) to NE; Sandia Aerial Tram, Sandia Peak Ski Area, and Sandia Recreational Area, all NE; Indian Park in Cultural Center; Internatl. Balloon Fiesta (hot air balloon site) to N. Inc. 1890

Alburg, town (1990 pop. 1,362), including Alburg village, Grand Isle co., NW Vt., on peninsula jutting into L. Champlain from Que. border, 10 mi/16 km N of North Hero; 44°57′N 73°17′W. Port of entry; dairy prods. Fr. settlers before 1750, permanent settlers 1782. Bridge to Rouses Point, N.Y.

Alburnett, town (1990 pop. 456), Linn co., E Iowa, 12 mi/19 km N of Cedar Rapids; 42°08′N 91°37′W. Limestone quarries.

Alburtis (al-BUHR-tis), borough (1990 pop. 1,415), Lehigh co., E Pa., 9 mi/14.5 km SW of Allentown, on Swabia Creek; 40°30′N 75°35′W. RR junction. Mfg. (cryogenics). Agr. (potatoes, apples, grain, soybeans; livestock, poultry, dairying). Lock Ridge Furnace Mus.; Lehigh co. Velodrome, bicycle racing, to N.

Alcalde (al-KAHL-dai), uninc. village (1990 pop. 308), Rio Arriba co., N N.Mex., on Rio Grande, in San Juan Pueblo land grant, 28 mi/45 km NNW of Santa Fe; 36°04′N 106°03′W. Elev. 5,704 ft/1,739 m. Trading point. Cattle, sheep, chiles, alfalfa. Sangre de Cristo Mts. just E; parts of Santa Fe Natl. Forest to E and W; San Juan Pueblo and San Juan Indian Reservation to S.

Alcan Highway, Alaska: see ALASKA HIGHWAY.

Alcatraz, [Span. *Álcatraces*=pelicans], rocky island in San Francisco Bay, San Francisco co., W Calif., 3 mi/4.8 km NNW of downtown San Francisco and 1 mi/1.6 km N of mainland; part of city of San Francisco. First visited by the Spanish in 1769, it was named for its large pelican rookery. The Spanish fortified Alcatraz, which came under U.S. control in 1851. The isl. was used as a U.S. military prison from 1859 until 1933, when it became a Federal prison for criminals; it was closed in 1963. Nicknamed "The Rock," it was a symbol of the impregnable fortress prison with max. security and strict discipline. The isl. became part of Golden Gate Natl. Recreation Area in 1972, which includes mainland sections on both sides of Golden Gate Channel. Golden Gate Bridge 3 mi/4.8 km to W; Angel Isl. 2 mi/3.2 km N; Treasure Isl. 2 mi/3.2 km E.

Alcester (AWL-ses-tuhr), town (1990 pop. 843), Union co., SE S.Dak., 24 mi/38 km N of Elk Point. Dairy prods., corn; livestock, poultry; mfg. (pork processing, electronic components, sportswear). Union Co. State Park to SW.

Alcoa, industrial city (1990 pop. 6,400), Blount co., E Tenn., 15 mi/24 km S of Knoxville; 35°47′N 84°00′W. Mfg. (wood prods., large aluminum-reduction plants). Founded 1913 by Aluminum Co. of Amer., inc. 1919.

Alcolu (al-kuh-LOO), uninc. village, Clarendon co., E central S.C., 4 mi/6.4 km N of Manning, and 14 mi/23 km SSE of Sumter. Mfg. of hardwood for lumber.

Alcona (al-KO-nuh), county (□ 1,790 sq mi/4,636 sq km; 1990 pop. 10,145), NE Mich.; ⊙ Harrisville; 44°42′N 83°16′W. Bounded E by L. Huron, drained by Au Sable, Pine, and Little Wolf Creek rivers. Farm area (cattle, sheep, poultry; minor crops); fisheries, nurseries. Includes part of Huron Natl. Forest in SW ⅓ of co., separate small unit in NE (including Jewell L. campground). Hubbard L. (resort) is in N; Alacoma Dam Pond in SW (formerly Bamfield Pond) several other small lakes, especially SW; Negwegon State Park in NE corner; Harrisville State Park in E (both on L. Huron); Mt. Maria Ski Area S of Hubbard L. Organized 1869.

Alcorn, county (□ 401 sq mi/1,039 sq km; 1990 pop. 31,722), NE Miss., bordering N on Tenn.; ⊙ Corinth; 34°52′N 88°34′W. Farm-prods. processing center. Drained by Hatchie and Tuscumbia rivers. Agr. (corn, soybeans; cattle, hogs); lumbering; mfg. at Corinth. Formed 1870.

Alcorn, village, Claiborne co., SW Miss., near the Mississippi R., 25 mi/40 km NNE of Natchez. Agr. (cattle; corn, soybeans, cotton). Seat of Alcorn A&M Univ. (founded 1871).

Alcova Reservoir (al-KO-vuh), Natrona co., central Wyo., on North Platte R., 30 mi/48 km SW of Casper; 6 mi/9.7 km long; 42°33′N 106°42′W. Formed by Alcova Dam (earthfill; 265 ft/81 m high), built (1938) for flood control, irrigation, and water supply as unit in Kendrick project for land reclamation. Water diverted through Casper Canal to Casper area.

Alcovy River (al-KO-vee), c.50 mi/80 km long, N central Ga.; rises 5 mi/8 km NE of Lawrenceville; flows SE and S to JACKSON LAKE 13 mi/21 km NE of Jackson; 34°1′N 83°57′W.

Alcozauca de Guerrero (ahl-ko-sah-OO-ka de ge-RAI-ro), town (1990 pop. 1,670), Guerrero, SW Mexico, in Sierra Madre del Sur, near Oaxaca border, 15 mi/24 km SE of Tlapa de Comonfort; 17°30′N 98°23′W. Elev. 3,707 ft/1,130 m. Cereals, livestock.

Alda (AL-duh), village (1990 pop. 540), Hall co., SE central Nebr., 5 mi/8 km SW of Grand Island, near Wood R.; 40°51'N 98°28'W. Mfg. (farming equip., machinery, consumer goods). Stolley Recreational Area nearby.

Aldama (al-DAH-ma), city (1990 pop. 12,191), ⊙ Aldama municipio, Chihuahua, N Mexico, on Chuviscar R., and 18 mi/29 km NE of Chihuahua, on RR; 28°49'N 105°53'W. Elev. 4,140 ft/1,262 m. Silver, gold, and copper mining; corn, beans, cotton, potatoes; cattle.

Aldama, Villa, Mexico: see VILLA ALDAMA.

Aldamas, Los, Mexico: see LOS ALDAMAS.

Aldan (AL-duhn), borough (1990 pop. 4,549), Delaware co., SE Pa., residential suburb 7 mi/11.3 km SW of downtown Philadelphia; 39°55'N 75°17'W. Mfg.

Alden, town (1990 pop. 855), Hardin co., central Iowa, on Iowa R., and 17 mi/27 km NW of Eldora; 42°30'N 93°22'W. Livestock; grain. Limestone quarries nearby.

Alden 1 (AHL-duhn), village (1990 pop. 182), Rice co., central Kansas, 7 mi/11.3 km SSW of Lyons, near Arkansas R.; 38°14'N 98°18'W. Wheat. **2** (AWL-den), village (1990 pop. 623), Freeborn co., S Minn., near Iowa state line, 11 mi/18 km W of Albert Lea; 43°40'N 93°34'W. Livestock; grain, soybeans, alfalfa; dairying; mfg. (feeds, fertilizers). Freeborn L. to N. **3** village (□ 2 sq mi/5.2 sq km; 1990 pop. 2,457), Erie co., W N.Y., 18 mi/29 km E of Buffalo; 42°53'N 78°29'W. Mfg. includes machinery, fabricated metal prods., electronic goods; agr. Darien Lakes State Park 2 mi/3.2 km E; Darien L. Theme Park 5 mi/8 km E of village at Darien Center Crossroads. Inc. 1869.

Alder (Al-duhr), village (1990 pop. 125), Madison co., SW Mont., 50 mi/80 km SSE of Butte, and on Ruby R. at confluence of Alder Creek. RR terminus. Irrigated agr. crops (potatoes, vegetables, alfalfa; sheep, cattle). Brown's Gulch Mining Dist. to SE. Ruby Range to W, Ruby R. Reservoir to S. Parts of Beaverhead Natl. Forest to NE and SE. Laurin and Robbers Roost to NW.

Alder Dam, Wash.: see NISQUALLY RIVER.

Aldergrove, village, SW B.C., Canada, near Wash. border, in greater Vancouver urban expansion, 30 mi/48 km ESE of Vancouver; 49°04'N 122°28'W. Dairying; fruit, vegetables. Vancouver Game Farm is here.

Alderson, town (1990 pop. 1,152), Monroe and Greenbrier cos., SE W.Va., on Greenbrier R., 12 mi/19 km WSW of Lewisburg; 37°43'N 80°38'W. Agr. (grain, tobacco); livestock; dairying; poultry. Mfg. (printed circuit boards, commercial printing). Federal reformatory for women here. Settled 1777.

Alderson, village (1990 pop. 395), Pittsburg co., SE Okla., 5 mi/8 km SE of McAlester; 34°53'N 95°41'W. In farm area; mfg. (wooden craft items).

Alderwood Manor, uninc. town (1990 est. pop. 6,000), Snohomish co., NW Wash., residential suburb 18 mi/29 km N of downtown Seattle, and 10 mi/16 km S of Everett, E of Lynnwood. Puget Sound to W.

Aldie (AWL-dee), uninc. village (1990 pop. 250), Loudoun co., N Va., 10 mi/16 km SSW of Leesburg, on Little R. Light mfg., agr. (livestock; grain, apples). "Oak Hill" (1818), home of James Monroe; Oatlands, home of George Carter, to NE.

Aldine, uninc. city (1990 pop. 11,133), Harris co., extreme SE Texas, residential suburb 10 mi/16 km N of downtown Houston; 29°54'N 95°22'W. Houston Intercontinental Airport to NE; Natl. Veterans Administration Cemetery to W.

Aldora (al-DOR-uh), town (1990 pop. 127), Lamar co., W central Ga., 2 mi/3.2 km W of Barnesville; 33°03'N 84°10'W.

Aldrich (AWL-drich), town (1990 pop. 76), Polk co., SW central Mo., in the Ozarks, on Stockton Lake, and 9 mi/14.5 km SW of Bolivar; 37°32'N 93°32'W.

Aldrich 1 (AHL-drich), village, Shelby co., central Ala., 18 mi/29 km WSW of Columbiana. **2** (AWL-drich), village (1990 pop. 70), Wadena co., central Minn., 10 mi/16 km ESE of Wadena, on Partridge R., and 35 mi/56 km W of Brainerd; 46°22'N 94°56'W. Grain, beans; livestock, poultry; dairying; mfg. (trailers). Lyons State Forest to N. Inc. 1938.

Aldridge (AHL-drij), village, Walker co., N Ala., 28 mi/45 km NW of Birmingham.

Aledo (uh-LEDE-o), city (1990 pop. 3,681), ⊙ Mercer co., NW Ill., 23 mi/37 km SSW of Rock Island; 41°12'N 90°45'W. Trade and shipping center in agr. area; corn, oats, soybeans; cattle, hogs; dairy prods.; mfg. (plastic prods., meat processing).

Aledo, town (1990 pop. 1,169), Parker co., N central Texas, 15 mi/24 km W of Fort Worth, on Clear Fork Trinity R., a satellite community of Dallas–Fort Worth area; 32°42'N 97°35'W. Agr. (cattle, horses; horticulture; peaches, peanuts, pecans). Oil and natural gas.

Aleknagik (uh-LEK-nuh-gik), village (1990 pop. 185), SW Alaska, on Aleknagik L. (20 mi/32 km long), 16 mi/26 km NNW of Dillingham; 59°17'N 158°37'W. Fishing; cannery.

Alenuihaha Channel (AH-lai-NOO-ee-HAH-HAH), Pacific Ocean, bet. Maui and Hawaii isls., Hawaii; 26 mi/48 km wide.

Alert, abandoned settlement, on Ellesmere Isl., extreme N N.W.T., Canada, on the Arctic Ocean. The settlement has a meteorological station and a landing strip.

Alert Bay, village (1991 pop. 628), SW B.C., Canada, on Cormorant Isl., at entrance to Johnstone Strait just off N coast of Vancouver Isl., 100 mi/161 km NW of Courtenay, and 8 mi/13 km E of Port McNeill by ferry; 50°35'N 126°55'W. Elev. 380 ft/1,141 m. Lumber and fish-shipping port; fish canning, lumbering. Largest totem pole in the world (173 ft/53 m), Kwakintl Cultural Center here.

Alesk River, 160 mi/257 km long, SW Yukon and S Alaska; rises on E slope of St. Elias Mts. near 60°30'N 137°00'W; flows SSW in a winding course to Dry Bay of the Gulf of Alaska at 59°05'N 138°30'W.

Aleutian Islands (uh-LOO-shen), chain of rugged, volcanic islands curving c.1,200 mi/1,900 km W from the tip of the Alaska Peninsula and approaching the Komandorski Isls., Russia. A partially submerged continuation of the Aleutian Range, they separate the Bering Sea from the Pacific Ocean. Bounded S by the Aleutian trench, a deep chasm in the ocean floor known as a subduction zone. The Aleutians are composed of 4 main groups: Fox Isls., nearest to the mainland, including Unimak, Unalaska, Umnak, and Akutan; Andreanof Isls., including Amlia, Atka, Adak, Kanaga, and Tanaga; Rat Isls., including Amchitka and Kiska; and Near Isls., smallest and westernmost group, including Agattu and Attu. The Semichi Isls., of which Shemya Isl. is the largest, are nearby. The entire region is characterized by frequent earthquakes and volcanic eruptions. The Aleutians have few settlements and few good harbors, most are on the N sides of the isls. to obtain shelter from the N Pacific storms, the most important harbor is Dutch Harbor–Unalaska. The Aleutian low pressure system creates the frequent storms and rains and makes navigation difficult. Temperatures are relatively moderate with heavy rains and frequent fog. Almost completely treeless, the isls. have a luxuriant growth of grasses, bushes, and sedges. Hunting and fishing are the main occupations of the Aleuts. Contrasting ocean currents (from W-E on the N; from E-W on the S) create rich fishing grounds. The Aleutian Isls., which may have contained a pop. of 10,000 to 17,000 people, were visited in 1741 by Vitus Bering, a Dan. explorer employed by Russia. The indigenous Aleuts were exploited by the Rus. trappers and traders who, in search of fur seals, established settlements on the isls. in the late 18th and early 19th cent. The Aleutian Isls. were included in the Alaska purchase in 1867 and at that time became part of the U.S. By then there may have been only 1,400 people left, the result of disease and the impact of the Rus. fur trade in the 18th cent. After the purchase, the U.S. govt. forbade seal trapping off the Aleutians except by the Aleuts. Fishing and fur hunting are now controlled by the Federal govt. Dutch Harbor–Unalaska, one of the few good Aleutian harbors, became a transshipping point for NOME in 1900, after the discovery of gold turned Nome into a boom town. The Aleutian Isls. were important during World War II; in 1940, a U.S. naval base was established at Dutch Harbor. In 1942 the Japanese bombed the base and later occupied Attu, Kiska, and Agattu isls. From bases on Adak (closed 1995) and Amchitka, the U.S. launched a counterattack and regained the isls. in 1943. Research stations and military bases are located on the isls. Most of the isls. are incorporated in the Aleutian Natl. Wildlife Reserve. The Aleutians West Census Area has a (1990) pop. of 9,478. With the exception of Atka and the Unalaska area, the only people on the isls. are U.S. military and civilian personnel. The main settlements are on Unalaska isl. and Adak. Travel to the Aleutians is very difficult.

Aleutian Range (uh-LOO-shen), volcanic mountain chain, c.1,600 mi/2,600 km long, SW Alaska, extending W from L. Iliamna along the Alaska Peninsula, and continuing, partly submerged as the Aleutian Isls., to Attu isl. Mt. Redoubt (10,200 ft/3,109 m) is the highest peak. Part of the volcanic belt that rings the Pacific Ocean, the Aleutian Range has been active in recent years, notably at mts. of Augustine, Veniaminov, and Akutan.

Aleutians East, borough (□ 6,985 sq mi/18,091 sq km; 1990 pop. 2,646), SW Alaska. Includes c.170 mi/274 km of lower Alaska Peninsula, also E Aleutian Isls. (including Unimak Isl., Sanak Isls., and Izambek Isl.); bounded NW by Bering Sea, SE by Pacific Ocean. Izambek Natl. Wildlife Reserve in center. Part of Alaska Peninsula Natl. Wildlife Reserve in NE. Fishing. Seals; hides.

Alex, village (1990 pop. 639), Grady co., central Okla., 13 mi/21 km SE of Chickasha, and on Washita R.; 34°55'N 97°46'W. Mfg.

Alexander 1 county (□ 252 sq mi/653 sq km; 1990 pop. 10,626), extreme S Ill.; ⊙ Cairo; 37°11'N 89°20'W. Bounded W and S by Mississippi R. and SE by Ohio R.; drained by Cache R. Agr. area (livestock, corn, cotton), with some mfg. (lumber prods.; soybean processing; plastics prods.). Includes part of Shawnee Natl. Forest. One of 17 counties to retain the southern-style commission form of county government. Formed 1819. **2** county (□ 263 sq mi/681 sq km; 1990 pop. 27,544), W central N.C.; ⊙ Taylorsville.; 35°55'N 81°10'W. Piedmont area; bounded S by Catawba R. (forms Lookout Shoals reservoir in SE, L. Hickory reservoir in SW); drained by South Fork Yadkin R. (source). Farming (tobacco, corn, grain, hay, fruit); timber (pine). Textile, furniture, electronics mfg.; sawmilling. Mfg. at Taylorsville. Formed 1847 .

Alexander 1 town (1990 pop. 170), Franklin co., N central Iowa, 15 mi/24 km WNW of Hampton; 42°47'N 93°28'W. Livestock. **2** town (1990 pop. 478), Washington co., E Maine, in hunting, fishing area, 26 mi/42 km N of Machias; 45°05'N 67°28'W.

Alexander, village (1991 pop. 2,399), SW Man., Canada 15 mi/24 km W of Brandon; 49°49'N 100°18'W. Grain elevators; dairying.

Alexander 1 village (1990 pop. 201), on Pulaski-Saline co. line, central Ark., 12 mi/19 km SW of Little Rock; 34°37'N 92°26'W. Mfg. (machine prods., food prods., chemicals, concrete). **2** village (1990 pop. 85), Rush co., central Kansas, on Walnut Creek, and 8 mi/12.9 km SW of La Crosse; 38°28'N 99°32'W. Wheat, cattle. **3** village (1990 pop. 445), Genesee co., W N.Y., on Tonawanda Creek, and 7 mi/11.3 km SSW of Batavia; 42°53'N 78°15'W. **4** village (1990 pop. 216), McKenzie co., W N.Dak., 21 mi./34 km S of Williston; 47°50'N 103°38'W. Little Missouri Natl. Grassland is to S and SW.

Alexander Archipelago, island group off SE Alaska. The isls. are the exposed tops of the submerged coastal mts. that rise steeply from the Pacific Ocean. Deep, fjordlike channels separate the isls. and cut them off from the mainland; the N part of the INSIDE PASSAGE threads its way among the isls. The largest isls. are Chichagof, Admiralty, Baranof, WRANGELL, Revillagigedo, Kupreanof, Mitkoff, and PRINCE OF WALES. All the isls. are rugged, densely forested, and have an abundance of wildlife. The Tlingit and Haida are native to the area; the Tsimshian moved to Annette isl. from B.C. in 1887. Ketchikan (1990 pop. 8,263) on Revillagigedo isl., Sitka (1990 pop. 8,588) on Baranof isl., and Petersburg on Mitkof isl. are among the largest settlements.

Cross references are shown in SMALL CAPITALS. The pronunciation key is on page xv. The dates of population figures are on page xii.

Lumbering, trapping, fishing, and canning are the main industries. The archipelago was explored by Russia, Britain, Spain, France, and the U.S.

Alexander, Cape, NE Mackenzie dist., N.W.T., Canada, on Dease Strait, at N extremity of Kent Peninsula; 68°56′N 105°50′W.

Alexander City, city (1990 pop. 14,917), Tallapoosa co., E central Ala., 46 mi/74 km NE of Montogomery. In a piedmont farm area. Nearby Martin Dam supplies power for the city's textile mills; the dam also has created L. Martin, a recreational area. Clothing mfg. and iron foundries. Central Ala. Community Col. is here. Horseshoe Bend Natl. Military Park, site of a battle (1814) bet. the forces of the Native Amer. Creeks and Andrew Jackson. Inc. 1874.

Alexander, Lake, Morrison co., central Minn., 18 mi/29 km SW of Brainerd; 4.5 mi/7.2 km long, 1.5 mi/2.4 km wide; 46°12′N 94°32′W. Elev. 1,275 ft/389 m. Drains W through Fish Trap L. and Fish Trap Creek into Long Prairie R. Camp Ripley Military Reservation to E.

Alexander Mills, village (1990 pop. 662), Rutherford co., SW N.C., 2 mi/3.2 km SSE of Rutherfordton; 35°18′N 51°81′W. Grain, soybeans, poultry, livestock.

Alexandria 1 city (1990 pop. 5,709), Madison co., E central Ind., on small Pipe Creek, and 12 mi/19 km N of Anderson; 40°16′N 85°41′W. Agr. area; limestone quarries supply city's rock industry. Mfg. (electronic equip., mineral wool, wire prods., printing, furniture, machinery, tools, apparel, animal cages). Laid out 1836. **2** city (1990 pop. 49,188), ⊙ Rapides parish, central La., on Red R., 80 mi/129 km NW of Baton Rouge; 31°17′N 92°28′W. RR junction, river port. Trade, RR, and medical center for a rich agr. and timber area. Mfg. includes fabricated metal, wood panels, adhesives, fishing lures, crates, concrete, abrasives. During the Civil War the city was burned (May 1864) to the ground by Union troops. Alexandria is the hq. for Kisatchie Natl. Forest and the seat of a branch of La. State Univ. at Alexandria. La. Col. is in its neighboring twin city of Pineville. Home of Alexandria Natl. Cemetery. Bringhurst Park and zoo here. Alexander State Forest to S. Esler Regional Airport to NE. Inc. 1818. **3** independent city (16 sq mi/41 sq km; 1990 pop. 111,183), N Va., a suburb 6 mi/9.7 km S of Washington, D.C., a port of entry on the Potomac R. (crossed by Woodrow Wilson Memorial Bridge); 38°49′N 77°05′W. Bounded E by Potomac R. (D.C. boundary; SE corner touches Md. state line), S by Cameron Run creek, drained by Holmes Run creek (forms L. Barcroft reservoir to NW). A RR junction, it has extensive RR yards and repair shops, a deep-water port, and a large variety of mfg. (printing and publishing, fiber optics research, machinery, computer hardware, foods and beverages, pasteurizers, wood prods.). In the 1980s vast office developments such as Crystal City and Pentagon City have significantly changed Alexandria, making it one of the area's leading suburbs. A number of U.S. govt. bldgs. and scientific and engineering research firms are here. Its many historic bldgs. include Gadsby's Tavern (1752), frequented by Washington; Carlyle House (1752), where Washington received his commission as major; Christ Church (1767–1773), where Washington, and later Robert E. Lee, attended; and Ramsey House (1749–1751). The George Washington Masonic Natl. Memorial Temple (1923–1932), modeled after the anc. lighthouse at Alexandria, Egypt, houses Washington mementos. The *Alexandria Gazette,* among the nation's oldest daily newspapers, was first printed in 1784. Other points of interest: Alexandria Natl. Cemetery, Appomatox Confederate Monument, Torpedo Factory Arts Center, Ft. Ward Mus. George Washington's home of MOUNT VERNON and Woodlawn, one of the Washington family estates (made a natl. shrine in 1949) to S; an Episcopal seminary (1823); Ft. Belvoir Military Reservation to SW; and the U.S. Army Engineer Center, with an engineering school and research and development laboratories. Washington Natl. Airport to N (Arlington), George Washington Memorial Parkway follows Potomac R. to S. Seat of Northern Va. Community Col. (Alexandria campus). George Washington helped lay out the streets in 1749. The city was part of D.C. from 1789 to 1847, occupied by Federal troops throughout the Civil War. Permanently settled 1730s, inc. 1779.

Alexandria, town (1991 pop. 3,418), SE Ont., Canada, 20 mi/32 km NNE of Cornwall. Mfg.; agr. Seat of R.C. diocese, with cathedral.

Alexandria, town (1991 pop. 1,672), St. Ann parish, N central Jamaica, 10 mi/16 km SW of St. Ann's Bay; 18°17′N 21°77′W. In rich agr. region (citrus fruit, corn, pimento, coffee; cattle). Germans settled here 1836–1842.

Alexandria 1 town (1990 pop. 5,592), ⊙ Campbell co., N Ky., 14 mi/23 km SSE of downtown Cincinnati, Ohio; 38°57′N 84°22′W. Bet. Ohio R. (E) and Licking R. (W). Agr. (tobacco, corn, soybeans; cattle); mfg. (fishing floats, concrete, map printing, meat processing). Campbell County Historical Center, Log Cabin Mus. Est. 1834. **2** town (1990 pop. 7,838), ⊙ Douglas co., W Minn., 60 mi/97 km NW of St. Cloud; 45°52′N 95°22′W. Elev. 1,477 ft/450 m. RR junction. Resort; tourist and trade center; grain, soybeans, alfalfa; livestock, poultry; dairying; mfg. (dairy prods., concrete, machinery, electronics, furniture). Municipal airport to SW. Kensington Rune Stone is here. Andes Tower Hill Ski Area to W; L. Carlos State Park to N. Settled 1857, laid out 1865. **3** town (1990 pop. 341), Clark co., NE Mo., 14 mi/23 km E of Kahoka; 40°21′N 91°27′W. Heavily damaged by the flood of 1993. **4** town (1990 pop. 1,190), Grafton co., central N.H., 14 mi/23 km NNW of Franklin; 43°37′N 71°49′W. Drained by Fowler R. Agr. (vegetables, apples; cattle, poultry; dairying); mfg. (cabinets). Newfound L. in NE corner, Wellington State Park on W shore; Cardigan State Park, with Mt. Cardigan (3,121 ft/951 m), in W. **5** town (1990 pop. 518), ⊙ Hanson co., SE S.Dak., 15 mi/24 km ESE of Mitchell, near James R. Corn, wheat; dairy prods.; bldg. stone. **6** town (1990 pop. 730), De Kalb co., central Tenn., 17 mi/27 km SE of Lebanon; 36°05′N 86°02′W.

Alexandria 1 village (1990 pop. 224), Thayer co., SE Nebr., 10 mi/16 km ENE of Hebron and on branch of Little Blue R; 40°15′N 97°23′W. Livestock, grain. Alexandria Lakes State Recreational Area to E (Jefferson co.). **2** village (1990 pop. 468), Licking co., central Ohio, 11 mi/18 km W of Newark and on Raccoon Creek, in agr. area; 40°05′N 82°38′W.

Alexandria (A-leks-AN-dree-ah), borough (1990 pop. 411), Huntingdon co., central Pa., 6 mi/9.7 km NNW of Huntingdon, on Juniata R.; 40°33′N 78°05′W. Mfg. (stationery). Agr. (corn, hay, livestock, poultry, dairying). Rothrock State Forest to N; Indian Caverns to N at Spruce Creek.

Alexandria Bay, resort village (□ 1 sq mi/2.6 sq km; 1990 pop. 1,194), Jefferson co., N N.Y., on the St. Lawrence R. and 25 mi/40 km N of Watertown; 44°20′N 75°55′W. A gateway to the Thousand Isls; port of entry. Mfg. (clothing, wood prods., machinery, boats); dairying. Scenic, 5-span Thousand Isls. Internatl. Bridge (1938) spans the St. Lawrence nearby. Boldt Castle, on Heart Isl. in the St. Lawrence R., accessible by boat, is nearby. Inc. 1878.

Alexandrovsk, Alaska: see ENGLISH BAY.

Alexis, village (1990 pop. 908), in Mercer and Warren cos., NW Ill., near Henderson Creek, 11 mi/18 km NW of Galesburg; 41°03′N 90°32′W. In agr. area.

Alfajayucan (al-fa-ha-YOO-kahn), town (1990 pop. 988), Hidalgo, central Mexico, 45 mi/72 km NW of Pachuca de Soto; 20°24′N 98°16′W. Elev. 6,227 ft/1,898 m. Cereals, maguey, beans; livestock.

Alfalfa, county (□ 881 sq mi/2,282 sq km; 1990 pop. 6,416), N Okla.; ⊙ Cherokee; 36°43′N 98°19′W. Bounded N by Kansas state line. Intersected by Salt Fork of Arkansas R., impounded in co. by Great Salt Plains Dam, forming Great Salt Plains L.; and drained also by Medicine Lodge R. and Turkey and Eagle Chief creeks. Agr. (wheat, alfalfa, oats, hay; cattle, poultry); mfg. at Cherokee; oil. Includes Great Salt Plains Natl. Wildlife Refuge and Great Salt Plains State Park. Formed 1907.

Alfonso de Rojas (ahl-FON-zo dai RO-hahz), town, on Southern Alluvial Plain in S part of Pinar del Río prov., W Cuba; 22°20′N 83°25′W. Rice production.

Alfonso XII, Cuba: see ALACRANES.

Alford (AL-fuhd), town (1990 pop. 418), Berkshire co., W Mass., 17 mi/27 km SSW of Pittsfield, in the Berkshires, near N.Y. state line; 42°15′N 73°25′W. Resort.

Alford (AL-fuhrd), village (□ 1 sq mi/2.6 sq km; 1990 pop. 472), Jackson co., NW Fla., 10 mi/16 km WSW of Marianna; 30°41′N 85°24′W. Pecans.

Alfordsville, town (1990 pop. 74), Daviess co., SW Ind., 16 mi/26 km SE of Washington; 38°34′N 86°57′W. Near Glendale State Fish and Wildlife Area. Laid out 1845.

Alfred, town (1990 pop. 2,238), ⊙ York co., SW Maine, 12 mi/19 km W of Biddeford; 43°28′N 70°44′W. Settled 1764, inc. 1794.

Alfred, village (1991 pop. 1,130), SE Ont., 40 mi/64 km ENE of Ottawa, Canada; 45°33′N 74°52′W. Dairying.

Alfred, village (□ 1 sq mi/2.6 sq km; 1990 pop. 4,559), Allegany co., W N.Y., 8 mi/12.9 km SW of Hornell; 42°15′N 77°47′W. Agr. (dairy prods.; beef cattle; grain, potatoes). Mfg. of ceramics. Seat of Alfred Univ. (1857), State Univ. of N.Y. Col. of Technology, and N.Y. State Col. of Ceramics.

Alfred, Cape, SE extremity of Victoria Isl., S Franklin dist., N.W.T., Canada, on Victoria Strait, at entrance of Albert Edward Bay; 69°39′N 101°00′W.

Alfredo M. Terrazas, Mexico: see AXTLA DE TERRAZAS.

Alger (AL-gur), county (□ 5,044 sq mi/13,064 sq km; 1990 pop. 8,972), N Upper Peninsula, Mich.; ⊙ Munising. Bounded N by L. Superior; 47°09′N 86°28′W. Drained by Whitefish and small Sturgeon rivers, and by affluents of Manistique R. Includes Grand Isl. Part of Hiawatha Natl. Forest in center of co. Dairying, agr. (cattle, sheep; foraging); some mfg. at Munising; lumbering, paper mills, commercial fishing. Resorts. Contains Pictured Rocks Natl. Lakeshore in E; Wagner Falls State Park at center, Laughing Whitefish Falls State Park in W, and small lakes. Organized 1885.

Alger, village (1990 pop. 864), Hardin co., W central Ohio, 14 mi/23 km E of Lima, in agr. area; 40°44′N 83°52′W.

Algiers, section of NEW ORLEANS, La.: SE of downtown. Site of Algiers Naval Station. Phonetic spelling of the Arabic word meaning "the island."

Algoa (al-GO-uh), village, Jackson co., NE Ark., 11 mi/18 km SE of Newport on Cache R.

Algoma (al-GO-muh), district (□ 19,320; 1991 pop. 127,269), central Ont., Canada, on L. Superior; ⊙ Sault Ste. Marie; 48°00′N 84°00′W.

Algoma (al-GO-muh), town (1990 pop. 3,353), Kewaunee co., E Wis., on Door Peninsula, on L. Michigan, 27 mi/43 km ENE of Green Bay city, in lake-resort area; 44°36′N 87°27′W. RR terminus. Mfg. (lumber, furniture, industrial prods., consumer goods). S terminus of Ahnapee State Trail. Inc. 1879.

Algoma 1 (al-GO-muh), village (1990 pop. 420), Pontotoc co., N Miss., 5 mi/8 km S of Pontotoc; 34°10′N 89°02′W. Agr. area (cotton, corn, wheat, soybeans; cattle). **2** uninc. village (1990 pop. 60), McDowell co., S W.Va., 9 mi/14.5 km E of Welch, on Buzzard Branch creek. Semibituminous coal.

Algona, city (1990 pop. 6,015), ⊙ Kossuth co., N Iowa, on East Des Moines R., and 40 mi/64 km N of Fort Dodge; 43°04′N 94°13′W. Agr. (poultry packing, grain milling; rendering plants, meat prods.); mfg. (machine shops, concrete works, tool storage units); RR junction. Sand pits nearby. Ambrose A. Call State Park is SW. Settled 1854, inc. 1872.

Algona, inc. town (1990 pop. 1,694), King co., W Wash., suburb 25 mi/40 km S of Seattle, and 9 mi/14.5 km ENE of Tacoma; 47°17′N 122°15′W. General Services Administrative Center to E.

Algonac (al-GO-nak), town (1990 pop. 4,551), St. Clair co., E Mich., 25 mi/40 km SSW of Port Huron, and on St. Clair R. (Ont. boundary) just above its delta mouth on L. St. Clair; 42°37′N 82°31′W. Mfg. of nonferrous castings, machinery. Vegetable farming. Algonac State Park immediately N on river. Ferries to Wallaceburg, Ont., (E) and Harsens Isl., Mich. (S). Inc. 1867.

Algonquin, city (1990 pop. 11,663), McHenry co., NE Ill., on Fox R. and 8 mi/12.9 km N of Elgin; satellite community of Chicago; 42°09′N 88°17′W. In dairying area; corn, oats; mfg. (fabricated metal and plastic prods., dental instruments).

Algonquin Provincial Park (al-GAHNG-kin) (□ 2,741), SE Ont., W of Pembroke. It is hilly, with numerous lakes; Opeongo L. is largest. Camping, fishing, canoeing. Forms watershed bet. Ottawa R. and Georgian Bay. Est. 1893.

Algood (AL-guhd), town (1990 pop. 2,399), Putnam co., central Tenn., 5 mi/8 km NE of Cookeville; 36°12′N 85°28′W. Lumber, wood prods.

Alhambra, city (1990 pop. 82,106), Los Angeles co., S Calif., a suburb 6 mi/9.7 km E of downtown Los Angeles, and 4 mi/6.4 km S of Pasadena; 34°05′N 118°08′W. Mfg. (iron foundry, aluminum foundry, fabricated metal prods., corrugated boxes, electronic equip., food preparations, plastic prods.). San Gabriel Mts. and Angeles Natl. Forest to N; Mt. Wilson Observatory to NE. Inc. 1903.

Alhambra, village (1990 pop. 709), Madison co., SW Ill., 14 mi/23 km ENE of Edwardsville; 38°53′N 89°43′W. In agr. area (wheat, corn, soybeans; cattle); dairy.

Aliamanu (AH-LEE-ah-MAH-noo), town (1990 pop. 8,835), Oahu isl., Honolulu co., Hawaii, residential suburb 6 mi/9.7 km NW of downtown Honolulu, near Pearl Harbor; 21°21′N 157°54′W. Aliamanu Crater to N, Fort Shafter Military Reservation to NE, Honolulu Internatl. Airport to SE, Hickam Air Force Base to S.

Alibates Flint Quarries National Monument (□ 2.14 sq mi/5.54 sq km), Potter co., NW Texas, 30 mi/48 km NNE of Amarillo. Flint quarries, first worked by Native Americans c.10,000 years ago; rich archaeological and historic area. Formerly named Alibates Flint Quarries and Texas Panhandle Pueblo Cultural Natl. Monument; redesignated 1978; covers 1,371 acres/555 ha. Near SE shore of L. Meredith, adjoins L. Meredith Natl. Recreation Area. Authorized 1965.

Alice, city (1990 pop. 19,788), ⊙ Jim Wells co., S Texas, 40 mi/64 km W of Corpus Christi; 27°45′N 98°04′W. Elev. 205 ft/62 m. Long a cow town at a RR junction, Alice remains a cattle-shipping center. Oil and natural gas are also important to its economy. Mfg. (office equipment, fishing tools). Named for daughter of a King Ranch founder. Inc. 1910.

Alice, village (1990 pop. 62), Cass co., SE N.Dak., c.35 mi/56 km WSW of Fargo; 46°45′N 97°33′W.

Alice Arm, village, W B.C., Canada, near Alaska border, on Alice Arm, branch of Observatory Inlet of the Pacific, 90 mi/145 km NE of Prince Rupert; 55°29′N 129°29′W. Port; gold, silver, lead, and zinc mining; formerly mined copper and pyrites, formerly refined at Anyox.

Alice Town, town, NW Bahama Isls., on spit of North Bimini isl., 55 mi/89 km E of Miami, Fla., 130 mi/209 km WNW of Nassau. Resort; fishing, growing of sisal, coconuts, corn. Bailey Town is just N.

Aliceville, town (1990 pop. 3,009), Pickens co., W Ala., 10 mi/16 km SW of Carrollton, near Tombigbee R. Furniture, lumber.

Alicia (uh-LEESH-uh), town (1990 pop. 157), Lawrence co., NE Ark., 22 mi/35 km WNW of Jonesboro; 35°53′N 91°04′W. Lumber. Shirey Bay-Rainey Brake Wildlife Management Area to NW.

Aline (al-EEN), village (1990 pop. 295), Alfalfa co., N Okla., 33 mi/53 km WNW of Enid, near Eagle Chief Creek; 36°30′N 98°27′W. In agr. and livestock-raising area. Homesteaders Sod House Mus. to SE.

Aliquippa (A-li-KWI-pah), borough (1990 pop. 13,374), Beaver co., W Pa., 18 mi/29 km NNW of Pittsburgh, near Ohio R., in an industrialized region along the Ohio R. N of Pittsburgh; 40°37′N 80°15′W. Mfg. (printing and publishing, food, precious metals, chemicals). Aliquippa Hopewell Airport to SW. Ambridge Reservoir to W. Aliquippa grew after the expansion of steel mills in 1909. Inc. 1894.

Aliso Viejo, uninc. town (1990 pop. 7612), Orange co., S Calif., suburb 2 mi/3.2 km SE of Laguna Beach, on Pacific Ocean; 33°34′N 117°44′W. Mfg. (communications equip., cleaners and polishes, electronic and medical equip.).

Alitak, Alaska: see AKHIOK.

Alix, village (1991 pop. 782), S central Alta., Canada, on small Alix L., 28 mi/45 km ENE of Red Deer; 52°24′N 113°11′W. Lumbering, dairying, livestock raising.

Aljojuca (ahl-ho-HOO-kah), town (1990 pop. 3,765), Puebla, central Mexico, 10 mi/16 km NNW of Ciudad Serdán; 19°05′N 97°32′W. Elev. 8,202 ft/2,500 m. Cereals, maguey; livestock.

Alkali Lake (AL-kuh-lei), Kidder and Logan cos., S N.Dak.; hourglass shaped (3 mi/4.8 km long, 2 mi/3.2 km wide), connected by small creek and fed intermittently by short stream; 12 mi/19 km NE of Napoleon.

Alkali Lakes, Calif.: see SURPRISE VALLEY.

All Saints, village (1991 pop. 2,230), central Antigua, West Indies, Antigua and Barbuda Republic, 5 mi/8 km SE of St. John's.

Allaben, village (1990 pop. 250), Ulster co., SE N.Y., in the Catskills, on Esopus Creek, and 23 mi/37 km NW of Kingston; 42°07′N 74°23′W.

Allagash (AL-uh-gash), township (1990 pop. 359), Aroostook co., N Maine, at junction of St. John and Allagash rivers, 25 mi/40 km SW of Fort Kent; 47°04′N 69°05′W.

Allagash Lake (AL-uh-gash), Piscataquis co., N central Maine, c.70 mi/113 km N of Dover-Foxcraft, in wilderness recreational area; 4 mi/6.4 km long, 2 mi/3.2 km–3 mi/4.8 km wide. Connected by stream to Chamberlain L. to SE.

Allagash River (AL-uh-gash), c.80 mi/129 km long, N Maine; rises in Allagash L., N Piscataquis co.; flows NE, joining other lakes, through wilderness, to St. John R. at Allagash.

Allaire Village (ah-LER), historic site, Monmouth co., E central N.J. Operated as an iron foundry factory town from 1822 into the 1930s. Bought by James P. Allaire in 1822, 5,000 acres/2,025 ha. Allaire erected the Howell Furnace iron works and built a communal village, called Allaire Village, for the workers and their families. Allaire is now state-owned. Restoration projects have brought the village back to its original form.

Allais (uh-LAIS), uninc. village, Perry co., SE Ky., in Cumberland foothills, on North Fork Kentucky R. 1 mi/1.6 km N of Hazard. Bituminous coal.

Allakaket (al-la-KA-ket), native village (1990 pop. 170), N central Alaska, on Koyukuk R. at mouth of Alatna R., and 100 mi/161 km N of Tanana; 66°32′N 152°43′W.

Allamakee (AL-uh-mah-KEE), county (□ 658 sq mi/1,704 sq km; 1990 pop. 13,855), extreme NE Iowa, bounded by Minn. (N) and Wis. (E; state line here formed by the Mississippi); ⊙ Waukon; 43°16′N 91°22′W. Rolling prairie area drained by Upper Iowa R.; has hilly, forested "Little Switzerland" dist. in E. Rich dairying region, producing also hogs, poultry, cattle, corn; some mfg. Limestone quarries; lead, zinc, and iron deposits. Extensive local flooding along rivers in 1993. Lock and Dam No. 9 (Mississippi R.) above Harpers Ferry. Yellow River State Forest in SE. Effigy Mounds Natl. Monument in SE corner. Fish Farm Mounds State Preserve in NW. Luster Heights Correctional Camp in SE by Mississippi R. Formed 1847.

All-American Canal, 80 mi/129 km long, SE Calif., part of the federal irrigation system of the Hoover Dam. Built bet. 1934 and 1940 across the Colorado Desert, the canal is entirely within the U.S. and replaces the Inter-Calif. Canal, which passes through Mexico. Comes within 1 mi/1.6 km of Mex. border in 3 places. The Imperial Dam, NE of Yuma, Ariz., diverts water from the Colorado R. into the All-Amer. Canal, which runs W to Calexico, Calif. Smaller canals move water into the Imperial Valley; the Coachella Canal branches NW to the Coachella Valley; also Alamo R. branches N to Salton Sea; W of Calexico, canal and New R. branches N to Salton Sea and canal turns N becoming Westside Main Canal, also to Salton Sea. Canal and its branches entirely within Imperial co. This canal system irrigates more than 630,000 acres/254,961 ha and has greatly increased crop yield in the area; however, problems of drainage and salinity exist.

Allamore, village, Hudspeth co., extreme W Texas, 11 mi/18 km W of Van Horn. Elev. 4,619 ft/1,408 m. Shipping point for cattle; alfalfa, cotton, vegetables.

Allan, town (1991 pop. 765), S central Sask., Canada, 30 mi/48 km ESE of Saskatoon. Wheat; dairying.

Allard, Lake, E Que., Canada, 15 mi/24 km N of Havre St. Pierre; 50°31′N 63°31′W. Drains into the St. Lawrence. Here are world's largest ilmenite deposits.

Allatoona Lake (al-uh-TOO-nuh), reservoir (□ 32 sq mi/83 sq km), Bartow, Cherokee, and Cobb cos., NW Ga., on Etowah R., 34 mi/55 km NW of Atlanta and 4 mi/6.4 km E of Cartersville; 36 mi/58 km, with c.10-mi/16-km-long S arm; 34°09′N 84°45′W. Max. capacity 722,000 acre-ft. Little R. enters from E. Formed by Allatoona Dam (190 ft/58 m high, 1,250 ft/381 m long), built (1950) for flood control, power generation, recreation, and navigation. Dam was initial part in comprehensive plan for development of Alabama-Coosa river system. Red Top Mt. State Park is here.

Allegan (AL-uh-guhn), county (□ 1,833s q mi/4,747 sq km; 1990 pop. 90,509), SW Mich.; ⊙ Allegan. Bounded W by L. Michigan; 42°34′N 86°15′W. Drained by Kalamazoo and 2 Black rivers. Fruit growing (apples, peaches, cherries, grapes); dairying; agr. (onions, cucumbers, potatoes, soybeans, corn, grain, forage crops, hay; cattle, hogs, poultry). Mfg. at Allegan, Otsego, and Plainwell. Fisheries. Has resorts. Allegan State Forest; Saugatuck State Park in NW on L. Michigan; Yankee Springs State Recreation Area on E boundary, numerous lakes throughout co. Organized 1835.

Allegan (AL-uh-guhn), city (1990 pop. 4,547), ⊙ Allegan co., SW Mich., on Kalamazoo R., and 27 mi/43 km NW of Kalamazoo; 42°31′N 85°50′W. In farm area (livestock, dairy prods., poultry, oats, corn, fruit). Mfg. (pharmaceuticals, wood prods., furniture, electric prods., fabricated pipe, publishing). Resort. Airport to SE; L. Allegan to NW. Settled 1834; inc. as city 1907.

Allegany 1 (ala-GAI-NEE), county (□ 429 sq mi/1,111 sq km; 1990 pop. 74,946), W Md.; ⊙ Cumberland; 39°38′N 78°42′W. Bounded N by Pa. state line (Mason-Dixon Line), S by the Potomac and its North Branch (forms W.Va. state line here); drained by Evitts, Wills, and other creeks. The name comes from an Indian word meaning "beautiful stream," according to legend. A spectacular break in the mts. at Cumberland, known as the Narrows, opened the way W to early pioneers. The natl. road, cut through the gorge with its 1,000 ft/305 m high walls, was the first highway built with Federal funds. Cumberland also lies at the end of the Chesapeake and Ohio Canal. Preserved in what was Fort Cumberland, now Riverside Park, is the one-room cabin in which George Washington made his headquarters during the Fr. and Indian Wars of the 1750s. Appalachian ridge and valley county (E and central) includes Wills Mt.; the Alleghanies (W) include Dans Rock and Savage Mt. (NW corner). Bituminous-coal mines, lignite mines, clay pits, timber; glass, clay, stone mfg. at Cumberland. Agr. in fertile valleys, apples, peaches, maple syrup, dairy prods. Hunting, fishing. Co. includes Pratt Green Ridge State Forest (E) and Cumberland Narrows across Wills Mt. Mfg. enterprises are mainly food processing, apparel, and transportation equip. The basically rural county has a high level of unemployment due to declines in agr. and fishing. Formed 1789. **2** county (□ 1,980 sq mi/5,128 sq km; 1990 pop. 50,470), W N.Y., bounded S by Pa. border; ⊙ Belmont; 42°15′N 78°01′W. Dairying, oil (refineries), and natural-gas area; diversified mfg., especially at Wellsville. Also agr. (maple sugar, snap beans, corn); livestock, and poultry. Summer recreation and residences on small lakes. Includes part of Oil Spring Indian Reservation; Seneca Oil Spring, 1 mi/1.6 km W of Cuba (site of 1st Eur. discovery, in 1627, of petroleum in N. Amer.). Drained by Genesee and Canisteo rivers, Canaseraga Creek, and small Angelica Creek. Formed 1806.

Allegany, village (1990 pop. 1,980), Cattaraugus co., W N.Y., on Allegheny R., just W of Olean; 42°05′N 78°29′W. Mfg. (dairy prods., cutlery, lumber); sand and gravel pits. Agr. (hay, wheat, corn). St. Bonaventure

Univ. (1875) and Franciscan seminary. Allegany State Park and Allegany Indian Reservation are W. Inc. 1906.

Allegany Indian Reservation (1990 pop. 7,315), Cattaraugus co., SW N.Y., just E of Allegany, and 50 mi/80 km S of Buffalo. Largest of N.Y. state's 10 Native Amer. reservations (22,000 acres/8,903 ha), it belongs to the Seneca Nation, 1 of the 6 Nations of the Iroquois Confederacy. Noted for having the only U.S. city built on land leased from an Indian reservation (Salamanca). Beginning in mid-1800s with the extension of RRs through that part of the Allegheny R. valley running through the reservation, illegal but convenient leases bet. the Seneca and individuals or companies became common. Salamanca grew to be an important RR hub, and lobbying in Congress became so intense that a 5-year leasing agreement for the land was reached. After the 1st period of 5 years, Congress extended the lease for 12 more years, and then for another 99 years. The lease was due to expire in Feb. 1991, but in May 1990, after a prolonged controversy, it was extended for another 40 years, with the option of another 40-year extension after that.

Alleghany 1 (al-uh-GAI-nee), county (☐ 235 sq mi/609 sq km; 1990 pop. 9,590), NW N.C., bounded N by Va. state line; ⊙ Sparta; 36°29′N 81°7′W. In the Blue Ridge Mts.; drained by North Fork New R. Agr. area (corn, barley, hay, tobacco; poultry, dairying, cattle). Blue Ridge (Natl.) Parkway passes SW-NE, near S and E co. line. Stone Mt. State Park on S boundary. **2** county (☐ 446 sq mi/1,155 sq km; 1990 pop. 13,176), NW Va., ⊙ Covington (independent cities of Covington and Clifton Forge separate from co.); 37°46′N 80°00′W. In the Allegheny Mts.; bounded W by W.Va. state line; drained by Jackson R. and James R. Mfg. at Covington and Clifton Forge (esp. paper and rayon). Agr. (corn, hay, alfalfa, apples, peaches; cattle); iron and coal mining, limestone quarrying. Includes part of George Washington Natl. Forest (bounded S and SE by Jefferson Natl. Forest). Peters Mt. ridge on SE boundary; part of L. Moomaw reservoir (recreation area). Formed 1822.

Allegheny (A-luh-GAI-nee), county (☐ 744 sq mi/1,927 sq km; 1990 pop. 1,336,449), W Pa.; ⊙ Pittsburgh; 40°28′N 79°58′W. Industrial area drained by Ohio, Allegheny, and Monongahela rivers (which join to form Ohio R. in downtown Pittsburgh, referred to as the "three rivers") and by Youghiogheny R. Great steel center. Industrial development in late 1800s and early 1900s resulted from Pittsburgh's location at E end of vast Mississippi R. transportation system and building of RR systems; region benefited greatly from W expansion of U.S.; development also aided by bituminous-coal beds, to early settlement, and to early start in iron mfg. Metal prods., food, chemicals, paper, machinery, railroad supplies; bituminous coal, clay, limestone, sandstone, sand and gravel. With Pittsburgh at its center, the co.'s urban development has extended outward from it; agr. includes corn, wheat, oats, barley, hay, alfalfa, apples; sheep, cattle, some hogs; dairying. Several regional and county parks. Point State Park at center of Pittsburgh, at confluence of Allegheny and Monongahela rivers, site of Fort Pitt. Formed 1788.

Allegheny Mountains (A-luh-GAI-nee) or **Alleghenies**, E U.S., a part of the ALLEGHENY PLATEAU of the Appalachians, extending for more than 500 mi/805 km on E part of the plateau from N central Pa. into S W. Va. and SW Va. SW from West Branch of Susquehanna in Pa. an escarpment known in various sections as the Allegheny Front (in Pa. and again in W.Va.), Dans Mt. (in Md.), and Allegheny Mt. (in W.Va. and along W.Va.-Va. line) marks the E edge of the Alleghenies and overlooks the ridge-and-valley country of the Folded Appalachians to E; escarpment is highest (over 4,800 ft/1,463 m) in W.Va. On the W, the mt. belt merges with the rough country of the plateau region. The Alleghenies include several generally parallel NE-SW ridges (Laurel Hill, Chestnut Ridge, Rich, Cheat, and Shavers mts., Negro Mt.), and the highest points in Pa. (Mt. Davis, 3,213 ft/979 m) and W.Va. (Spruce Knob, 4,860 ft/1,481 m). Formed by folding of the E edge of the Paleozoic sedimentary rocks composing the plateau, the mts. are a rugged near-wilderness belt with large tracts of timber (mainly hardwoods) and deposits of bituminous coal, petroleum, natural gas, and clay. Parts (particularly in W.Va.) are noted for scenic beauty. North Branch of the Potomac and New R. have cut gorges through the Alleghenies. The name Alleghenies is also often applied to much of the adjoining plateau region (W). Formerly spelled Alleghany.

Allegheny Plateau (A-luh-GAI-nee), dissected plateau, W part of the Appalachian Mts., extending c.500 mi/805 km SW from N Pa. to SW Va., including W Md., rising to 4,860 ft/1,481 m at Spruce Knob, the highest peak in W.Va. The E Allegheny Plateau, known as the Allegheny Mts. or the Alleghenies, has a steep E-facing escarpment often called the Allegheny Front (c.1,500 ft/460 m–1,600 ft/490 m high) and is more rugged than the W portion. The plateau, consisting of flat-laying sedimentary rock, has been subsequently eroded to produce a rugged boundary. The mts. are rich in coal and timber, petroleum, and natural gas. Also Backbone Mt. (3,360 ft/1,024 m), highest point in Md.

Allegheny Portage Railroad National Historic Site (A-luh-GAI-nee) (1,247 acres/505 ha), Blair and Cambria cos., central Pa. Inclined-plane RR that lifted passengers and cargoes of boats on the Pa. Canal over the Allegheny Mts.; natl. park unit extends 7 mi/11.3 km through Blair Gap pass; covers 1,247 acres/505 ha; 40°21′N 78°51′W. Small section of historic site 5 mi/8 km NE of Johnstown. Authorized 1964.

Allegheny Reservoir, NW Pa. and SW N.Y., on Allegheny R., in Allegheny Natl. Forest, 7 mi/11.3 km E of Warren, Pa.; c.35 mi/56 km long; 41°50′N 79°00′W. Max. capacity 1,180,000 acre-ft. Kinzua (SE arm), Sugar (E arm), and Willow (E arm) bays. Salamanca, N.Y. at N tip. Formed by Kinzua Dam (169 ft/52 m high), built (1965) by the Army Corps of Engineers for power generation, flood control and navigation. In N.Y., Allegany State Park on E, Allegheny Indian Reservation on W and NE.

Allegheny River (A-luh-GAI-nee), 325 mi/523 km long, N.Y. and Pa.; rises in N central Potter co., N central Pa.; flows generally NW past Coudersport and Port Allegheny, Pa., Olean and Salamanca, N.Y., then SW, reentering Pa. through Allegheny Reservoir and flowing past Warren, Oil City, Franklin, Kittanning, and New Kensington, Pa., finally joining Monongahela R., from S, in downtown Pittsburgh to form Ohio R.; drains 11,580 sq mi/29,992 sq km; 41°52′N 77°52′W. Before the RR era, the river was an important commercial route and is still used to transport coal and other bulky freight. Kinzua Dam (completed 1965), a federal flood-control project on the river, forms Allegheny Reservoir; there are also dams on the river's tributaries. The Allegheny's basin has coal, oil, and natural gas. Navigable to East Brady through series of 9 locks and dams.

Allegre (uh-LEG-rai), uninc. village (1990 pop. 150), Todd co., S Ky., 15 mi/24 km ENE of Hopkinsville, near Pond R. Tobacco, grain, dairying, livestock. Mfg. (apparel).

Alleman (ALL-mun), village (1990 pop. 340), Polk co., central Iowa, 4 mi/6.4 km N of Ankeny; 41°49′N 93°36′W. Agr. (corn, oats, cattle). Big Creek State Park to W.

Allen 1 county (☐ 660 sq mi/1,709 sq km; 1990 pop. 300,836), NE Ind.; ⊙ Fort Wayne; 41°05′N 85°04′W. Bounded E by Ohio line; drained by Maumee, St. Joseph, and St. Mary's rivers. Wheat, oats, corn, soybeans; hogs; dairying; limestone. Major mfg. co. Formed 1823. **2** county (☐ 505 sq mi/1,308 sq km; 1990 pop. 14,638), SE Kansas; ⊙ Iola; 37°53′N 95°17′W. Rolling prairie area, drained by Neosho R. Cattle, wheat, soybeans, sorghum; dairying; rubber and plastics prods. Oil and gas fields. Formed 1855. **3** county (☐ 352 sq mi/912 sq km; 1990 pop. 14,628), S Ky.; ⊙ Scottsville; 36°45′N 86°11′W. Bounded S by Tenn., NE by Barren R. (forms Barren River L. reservoir); drained by Bays Fork and Trammel Fork rivers. Agr. area (cattle, poultry; dairying; hay, alfalfa, soybeans, wheat, corn, burley tobacco); oil wells, hardwood timber. Some mfg. at Scottsville. Formed 1815.

Allen, parish (☐ 755 sq mi/1,955 sq km; 1990 pop. 21,226), SW central La.; ⊙ Oberlin; 30°37′N 92°46′W. Bayou Nezpique forms SE boundary. Drained by Calcasieu R. and Bundick and Whisky Chitto creeks. Lumber milling, logging; mfg. (clothing, wood prods., plastics, resins); agr. (rice, corn, sweet potatoes, peaches, vegetables, soybeans, pecans; livestock; dairying); crawfish. Large West Bay State Wildlife Area in N center. Formed 1912.

Allen, county (☐ 410 sq mi/1,062 sq km; 1990 pop. 109,755), W Ohio; ⊙ Lima, 40°46′N 84°05′W. Intersected by Ottawa and Auglaize rivers. In the Till Plains physiographic region (an area of glacial till). Extensive mfg. at Lima. Diversified farming (livestock; corn, poultry, soybeans); mfg. (food prods., petroleum refining, chemicals, machinery, motor vehicle equip.). Limestone quarries. Formed 1831.

Allen, city (1990 pop. 18,309), Collin co., N Texas, suburb 20 mi/32 km NNE of downtown Dallas, on Cottonwood Creek; 33°06′N 96°40′W. Located in rapidly growing urban fringe with mixture of agr. (cotton, wheat; cattle, horses). Mfg. (electronic equip., medical equip., educational materials). L. Lavon to E.

Allen, town (1990 pop. 972), W of Pontotoc-Hughes co. line, S central Okla., 17 mi/27 km ENE of Ada, near Canadian R.; 34°52′N 96°24′W. Light mfg.

Allen 1 village (1990 pop. 191), Lyon co., E central Kansas, 15 mi/24 km N of Emporia; 38°39′N 96°10′W. In livestock and grain region. **2** or **Allen City**, village (1990 pop. 229), Floyd co., E Ky., 5 mi/8 km SSE of Prestonsburg, at confluence of Levisa Fork and Right Fork rivers, which form Big Sandy R., in the Cumberland Mts.; 37°36′N 82°43′W. Mfg. (motor vehicle parts, mining equip., steel fabrication, concrete blocks). **3** village (1990 pop. 331), Dixon co., NE Nebr., 12 mi/19 km SW of Ponca; 42°24′N 96°50′W.

Allen City, Ky.: see ALLEN.

Allen Park, city (1990 pop. 31,092), Wayne co., SE Mich., a suburb 8 mi/12.9 km WSW of downtown Detroit; 42°15′N 83°12′W. Drained by N and S branches of Ecorse R; touches R. Rouge on N. Mfg. includes motor vehicle and marine prototypes, liquor, sheet metal. Settled in the early 1800s and named after Lewis Allen, a settler from Detroit; inc. as a city 1957.

Allen, Port, Hawaii: see PORT ALLEN.

Allendale, county (☐ 412 sq mi/1,067 sq km; 1990 pop. 11,722), SW S.C.; ⊙ Allendale; 32°59′N 81°20′W. Bounded W by Savannah R.; drained SE by Coosawhatchie R. Agr. includes hogs and cattle; watermelons, corn, wheat, rye, oats, soybeans, peanuts, hay, cotton, peaches. Formed 1919.

Allendale 1 town (1990 pop. 6,950), Ottawa co., W Mich., 15 mi/24 km W of Grand Rapids, 14 mi/23 km E of L. Mich.; 42°59′N 85°57′W. Agr. area (corn, apples, vegetables; hogs, cattle, poultry). Mfg. (food prods., plastic extrusions). Site of Grand Valley State Univ. (formerly Grand Valley Community Col.). **2** town (1990 pop. 58), Worth co., NW Mo., 6 mi/9.7 km E of Grant City; 40°29′N 94°17′W. **3** town (1990 pop. 4,410), ⊙ Allendale co., SW S.C., 45 mi/72 km SSW of Orangeburg; 33°00′N 81°18′W. In agr. area noted for watermelons, lumber. Mfg. (yarns, apparel). Agr. includes livestock, grain, cotton, peaches.

Allendale, village (1990 pop. 476), Wabash co., SE Ill., 8 mi/12.9 km NNE of Mount Carmel; 38°31′N 87°42′W. In agr. area (mixed grain); oil, coal; sand, gravel.

Allendale, borough (1990 pop. 5,900), Bergen co., NE N.J., 12 mi/19 km NNW of Hackensack; 41°01′N 74°07′W. Settled 1740, inc. 1894.

Allende (ah-YEN-dai), city (1990 pop. 16,649) and township, Coahuila, N Mexico, 30 mi/48 km SW of Piedras Negras; 28°20′N 100°51′W. RR junction; agr. center (cereals, corn, beans, wheat, nuts; cotton; livestock); flour milling, cotton processing.

Allende (ei-EN-dai), town (1990 pop. 16,701), Nuevo León, N Mexico, on Inter-Amer. Highway, and 33 mi/53 km SE of Monterrey; 25°15′N 100°00′W. Oranges, sugar.

Allende 1 Mexico: see SAN MIGUEL DE ALLENDE. **2** Mexico: see VILLA DE ALLENDE. **3** Mexico: see VALLE DE ALLENDE.

Allenhurst, resort borough (1990 pop. 759), Monmouth co., E N.J., on the coast just N of Asbury Park, 14 mi/23 km E of Freehold; 40°14′N 74°00′W. Deal L. is near.

Allenport, uninc. town (1990 pop. 900), Shirley township, Huntingdon co., S central Pa., suburb 1 mi/1.6 km SE of Mount Union on Juniata R.; 40°22′N 77°52′W. Agr. includes dairying, livestock, poultry; grain.

Allenport, borough (1990 pop. 595), Washington co., SW Pa., 4 mi/6.4 km SE of Charleroi, on Monongahela R.; 40°05′N 79°51′W. Mfg. (rolled steel finishing). Agr. (corn, hay, dairying).

Allenstown, rural town (1990 pop. 4,649), Merrimack co., S central N.H., 7 mi/11.3 km SE of Concord, and 11 mi/18 km NNE of Manchester; 43°08′N 71°23′W. Drained by Suncook R. Agr. (apples, vegetables; poultry, livestock; dairying; nursery crops); mfg. (apparel). Part of Bear Brook State Park in SE. Settled before 1748, inc. 1831.

Allensville, village (1990 pop. 218), Todd co., S Ky., near Tenn. state line, 26 mi/42 km ESE of Hopkinsville, near Elk Fork Red R.; 36°43′N 87°04′W. Agr. (tobacco, grain; livestock); grain processing.

Allenton 1 village in North Kingstown municipality, Washington co., S central R.I., 20 mi/32 km S of Providence; 41°32′N 71°28′W. Woolens. **2** village (1990 pop. 645), Wash. co., E Wis., on tributary of Rock R. and 8 mi/12.9 km W of West Bend. Mfg. (metal prods. and equip.); dairy prods.

Allentown, city (1990 pop. 105,090), ⊙ Lehigh co., E Pa., 47 mi/76 km NNW of Philadelphia and 5 mi/8 km WSW of Bethlehem, its twin city, on the Lehigh R. at mouth of Little Lehigh Creek; 40°36′N 75°28′W. Allentown, situated in the agr. Lehigh valley and in the Pa. Dutch region, is an industrial and commercial city. Mfg. (food, printing and publishing, fabricated metal prods., chemicals, leather prods., electrical equip.; furniture, medical equip. and supplies). In the city are Muhlenberg Col., Cedar Crest Col., Allentown Col. of St. Francis de Sales (to S at Center Valley), United Wesleyan Col., Lehigh Co. Community Col. (7 mi/11.3 km NW at Schnecksville), and a campus of Penn State Univ. Allentown State Hos. in E. Allentown State Farm to E. Lehigh Valey Internatl. Airport to NE, Allentown Queen City Airport in S. Founded 1762 by William Allen, chief justice of the Commonwealth of Pa.; settled by representatives of various Ger. religious groups. First known as Northampton, it was renamed Allentown c.1836. The Liberty Bell was brought here (1777) for safekeeping during the Revolutionary War, and the city became a munitions center for the Continental Army. Points of interest include the Zion Reformed Church (where the Liberty Bell was kept); Malcolm Gross Memorial Rose Garden; Allentown Art Mus.; Haines Hill Mus.; Dorney Theme Park to SW; Lehigh Valley Velodrome, bicycle racing, to W; Mus. of Indian Culture. Allentown Symphony; Lehigh Valley Chamber Orchestra. Inc. as a borough 1811, as a city 1867.

Allentown, town (1990 pop. 273), Wilkinson co., central Ga., 34 mi/55 km SE of Macon; 32°35′N 83°14′W. Lumber and wood chips.

Allentown, borough (1990 pop. 1,828), Monmouth co., central N.J., 10 mi/16 km ESE of Trenton; 40°10′N 74°35′W. Produce. Imlay mansion (c.1790) here.

Allenville, village (1990 pop. 69), Moultrie co., central Ill., near Kaskaskia R., 7 mi/11.3 km SE of Sullivan; 39°33′N 88°32′W. In agr. area. Adjacent to Shelbyville Fish and Wildlife Area.

Allenwood, village, Monmouth co., E N.J., near Manasquan R., 7 mi/11.3 km SW of Asbury Park. Allaire State Park to NW.

Allerton, town (1990 pop. 599), Wayne co., S Iowa, 5 mi/8 km SW of Croydon; 40°42′N 93°22′W. Mfg. (food ingredients). Bob White State Park to W.

Allerton, village (1990 pop. 274), Vermilion co., E. Ill., 22 mi/35 km SW of Danville; 39°55′N 87°56′W. In agr. and bituminous-coal area.

Allerton, Mass.: see HULL.

Allerton Point, Mass.: see NANTASKET BEACH and HULL.

Alley, town, Clarendon parish, S Jamaica, on left bank of Minho R. near its mouth, and 11 mi/18 km S of May Pen; 17°48′N 77°16′W. In irrigated sugar region. Its church is allegedly oldest on the isl. Former capital of now dissolved Vere parish.

Alleyton, uninc. village, (1990 pop. 165), Colorado co., S Texas, on Colorado R., and 4 mi/6.4 km E of Columbus. Sand, gravel mining; agr.; timber; light mfg. Attwater Prairie Chicken Natl. Wildlife Refuge to E.

Alliance 1 (uh-LEI-ens), city (1990 pop. 9,765), ⊙ Box Butte co., NW Nebr., 45 mi/72 km NE of Scotts Bluff, in Great Plains region; 42°6′N 102°52′W. RR junction. RR repair shops; ships seed potatoes, grain, cattle. Mfg. (industrial hose, apparel). Municipal airport. Founded 1888. **2** city (1990 pop. 23,376), Mahoning and Stark cos., NE Ohio, on the Mahoning R.; 40°57′N 81°07′W. In a farm area. It is an industrial, distributing, and RR center. Mfg. includes steel, heavy machinery, electric tubing, chinaware, and industrial equip. It is the seat of Mount Union Col., where Clarke Observatory is located. Inc. 1854.

Alliance, village (1991 pop. 199), SE central Alta., Canada, 110 mi/177 km SE of Edmonton; 52°26′N 111°47′W. Mixed farming, dairying; grain elevators.

Alliance, village (1990 pop. 583), Pamlico co., E N.C., 16 mi/26 km E of New Bern; 35°08′N 48°76′W. Agr. area (cotton, peanuts, grain, hogs). Mfg. (fertilizer).

Alligator, village (1990 pop. 187), Bolivar co., NW Miss., 11 mi/18 km SW of Clarksdale; 34°05′N 90°43′W. In agr. area (corn, rice, cotton; cattle).

Alligator Alley, one of the 2 E-W highways (Tamiami Trail is the other) that crosses the Fla. Everglades from Miami–Fort Lauderdale on the Atlantic coast to Naples on the Gulf of Mexico coast. Originally a 2-lane parkway, it was incorporated into the interstate highway system as I-75 (and renamed accordingly) when rebuilt as a freeway during the 1990s.

Alligator Lake, Hyde co., E N.C., in Alligator Swamp, 13 mi/21 km NE of Bethaven, connected by channels to Alligator R. (NE) and Pungo R. (SW).

Alligator Pond, town (1991 pop. 1,542), Manchester parish, S Jamaica, on bay and beach, 10 mi/16 km S of Mandeville; 17°52′N 77°34′W. Fishing.

Alligator River, 25 mi/40 km long, NE N.C., S arm of Albemarle Sound extending S and E into Alligator Swamp; forms Dare-Tyrell co. line, also part of Tyrrell-Hyde co. line; 2 mi/3.2 km–5 mi/8 km wide. Its head is connected with Pungo R. (SW) by Alligator-Pungo R. Canal (c.20 mi/32 km long). Canal and Alligator R. form part of Intracoastal Waterway, bridged near entrance.

Alligator-Pungo River Canal, N.C.: see ALLIGATOR RIVER.

Alligerville, N.Y.: see KYSERIKE.

Allingtown, Conn.: see WEST HAVEN.

Allison 1 town (1990 pop. 1,000), ⊙ Butler co , N central Iowa, 29 mi/47 km NW of Waterloo; 42°45′N 92°47′W. Limestone quarry, sand and gravel pit nearby. Arnry Woods State Park to E. **2** uninc. town (1990 pop. 950), Fayette co., SW Pa., 10 mi/16 km NW of Uniontown, near Dunlap Creek; 39°59′N 79°51′W. Agr. (dairying). Bituminous-coal area.

Allison Gap, uninc. town (1990 pop. 900), Smyth co., SW Va., 14 mi/23 km WNW of Marion, on North Fork Holston R. Part of Jefferson Natl. Forest to NW. Sometimes Allisons Gap.

Allison Park, uninc. town (1990 pop. 5,600), Allegheny co., W Pa., suburb 8 mi/12.9 km NNE of downtown Pittsburgh, on Pine Creek; 40°33′N 79°57′W. Mfg. includes fabricated metals, chemicals, machinery, wood products. North Park L. Reservoir to NW.

Allisons Gap, Va.: see ALLISON GAP.

Allisonville, village, Marion co., central Ind., 9 mi/14.5 km NNE of downtown Indianapolis. Residential and shipping area. Retailing. Part of Indianapolis.

Alliston (A-lis-tuhn), town, S Ont., Canada, on Boyne R. near Nottawasaga R., and 40 mi/64 km NW of Toronto; mfg. of agr. machinery, motor vehicles; woodworking; agr.

Allock (AL-luhk), uninc. village, Perry co., SE Ky., in Cumberland foothills, 7 mi/11.3 km. ESE of Hazard. Bituminous coal.

Allons (AH-luhnz), village, Overton co., N Tenn., 4 mi/6 km N of Livingston; 36°27′N 85°21′W. Dale Hollow L. is nearby.

Allouez (al-o-EEZ), city (1990 pop. 14,431), Brown co., E Wis., a suburb 2 mi/3.2 km S of Green Bay on Fox R.; 44°28′N 88°01′W. Heritage Hill State Park is on river.

Allouez (ah-loo-ez), village, Keweenaw co., NW Upper Peninsula, Mich., 8 mi/12.9 km NE of Houghton; 47°17′N 88°24′W. In former copper mining region.

Allouez Bay, Wis.: see SUPERIOR BAY.

Alloway's Creek, c.25 mi/40 km long, SW N.J.; rises E of Salem; flows SW, past Quinton and Hancocks Bridge, to Delaware R. 6 mi/9.7 km SW of Salem. Navigable to Quinton.

Alloy (AL-oi), uninc. village, Fayette co., S central W.Va., 11 mi/18 km NW of Fayetteville, near Kanawha R. Livestock; corn. Coal. Mfg. (ferroalloys).

Allston, Mass.: see BOSTON.

Allumette Island (a-loo-MEHT) or Île aux Allumettes (EEL o-zah-luh-MEHT), SW Que., Canada, in an expansion of Ottawa R. called L. Allumette, opposite Pembroke; 16 mi/26 km long, 3 mi/5 km–7 mi/11 km wide.

Allyn, uninc. town (1990 pop. 8,001), Mason co., W Wash., 14 mi/23 km SW of Bremerton, on North Bay, extension of Case Inlet, Puget Sound, on isthmus of Kitsap Peninsula; end of Hood Canal inlet 3 mi/4.8 km to NW. Mfg. (dehydrated fruit). Stretch Point State Park to S; Coulter Creek Fish Hatchery to N.

Alma (ahl-MAH, AL-muh), city (1991 pop. 25,910), S central Que., Canada, on the Saguenay R.; 48°33′N 71°39′W. In 1954 its name was shortened from St. Joseph d'Alma. Pulp and paper, aluminum mfg.; granite quarries in region.

Alma 1 (AWL-muh), city (1990 pop. 9,034), Gratiot co., central Mich., on Pine R. and 36 mi/58 km W of Saginaw; 43°22′N 84°39′W. RR junction. In agr. area (beans, sugar beets, corn). Mfg. (fabricated metal prods., motor vehicle parts and components, plastics); oil refineries. Has Alma Col. Aiport to S. Settled 1853; inc. as village 1872, as city 1905. **2** (AL-muh), city (1990 pop. 446), Lafayette co., W central Mo., near Missouri R., 4 mi/6.4 km N of Concordia; 39°06′N 93°32′W. Corn, wheat, cattle, hogs; meat processing.

Alma 1 (AL-muh), town (1990 pop. 2,959), Crawford co., NW Ark., 13 mi/21 km NE of Fort Smith, on Frog Bayou; 35°29′N 94°13′W. Mfg. (canned vegetables, tool and die). **2** town (1990 pop. 3,663), ⊙ Bacon co., SE central Ga., 22 mi/35 km NNW of Waycross; 31°32′N 82°29′W. Mfg. includes food, motor vehicles, apparel, textiles, lumber. Inc. 1906. **3** town (1990 pop. 871), ⊙ Wabaunsee co., E central Kansas, on Mill Creek, branch of Kansas R. and 33 mi/53 km W of Topeka; 39°00′N 96°17′W. Wheat, grain. **4** town (1990 pop. 1,226), ⊙ Harlan co., S Nebr., 23 mi/37 km S of Holdrege, on S shore of Harlan Co. L.; 40°06′N 99°21′W. On reservoir and Republican R., near Kansas state line. Trade center for agr. region; grain; livestock. Mfg. (fur coats). Founded 1871. **5** town (1990 pop. 790), ⊙ Buffalo co., W Wis., on the Mississippi and 18 mi/29 km NW of Winona, Minn., at foot of bluffs; 44°19′N 91°55′W. Dairy prods., timber. Lock and Dam No. 4 completed here in 1935. Upper Mississippi R. Wildlife and Fish Refuge on both sides of river. Settled c.1852, inc. 1885.

Alma (AL-muh), village, S Ont., Canada, 18 mi/29 km NW of Guelph; 45°36′N 64°57′W. Dairying, mixed farming.

Alma 1 (AHL-muh), village (1990 pop. 148), Park co., central Colo., on South Platte R., in Rocky Mts., 12 mi/19 km N of Leadville, 13 mi/21 km S of Breckenridge; 39°17′N 106°03′W. Elev. 10,353 ft/3,156 m. Mines. Mt. Lincoln, Quandary Peak, Hoosier Pass, and Windy Ridge Bristlecone Pines nearby. **2** village (1990 pop. 388), Marion co., S central Ill., 7 mi/11.3 km NNE of Salem; 38°43′N 88°54′W. In agr. (wheat, soybeans, sorghum; cattle; dairying) and oil-producing area. **3** village (1990 pop. 205), Ellis co., N Texas, 4 mi/6.4 km

SE of Ennis; 32°17′N 96°32′W. Oil and natural gas. Cattle, dairying; cotton, corn, wheat. Bardwill L. to SW.

Alma Center, village (1990 pop. 416), Jackson co., W central Wis., 40 mi/64 km SE of Eau Claire; 44°26′N 90°54′W. In dairying region; construction; mfg. (cheese). Black R. State Forest to SE.

Alma Island, or **Île d'Alma** (EEL dahl-MAH), island, S central Que., at E end of L. St. John, bet. 2 outlets of the Saguenay, opposite Alma; 8 mi/13 km long, 3 mi/5 km wide; 48°35′N 71°42′W.

Almanor, Lake, Plumas co., NE Calif., in the Sierra Nevada, 5 mi/8 km SW of Westwood; c.10 mi/16 km long. Impounded by L. Almanor Dam (135 ft/41 m high, 1,250 ft/381 m long) on North Fork Feather R. Resort, noted for trout fishing; campgrounds; developed seasonal and year-round residential areas. Parts of Plumas Natl. Forest to SE; Lassen Natl. Forest to N and W; Mountain Meadows Reserve to NE; Lassen Volcanic Natl. Park to NW.

Almaville (AL-muh-vil), village, S Que., Canada, on St. Maurice R., opposite Shawinigan Falls; 46°31′N 72°45′W. In dairying, cattle- and pig-raising region.

Almedia (AL-mi-DEE-ah), uninc. town (1990 pop. 1,116), Columbia co., E central Pa., residential suburb 5 mi/8 km ENE of Bloomsburg on Susquehanna R.; 41°00′N 76°23′W. Agr. includes dairying.

Almena 1 (al-MEEN-uh), village (1990 pop. 423), Norton co., NW Kansas, on Prairie Dog Creek, and 10 mi/16 km ENE of Norton; 39°53′N 99°42′W. RR junction. Grain; livestock, poultry. **2** village (1990 pop. 625), Barron co., NW Wis., 16 mi/26 km WSW of Rice L., near Hay R.; 45°24′N 92°02′W. Dairy prods. Mfg. (cheese).

Almendares River (ahl-main-DAHR-ais), 27 mi/43 km long, Ciudad de La Habana prov., W Cuba; rises E of Tapaste; flows W and N to the Florida Straits, 3.5 mi/5.6 km W of Havana Harbor; 23°07′N 82°25′W. Serves as water supply and green area for Havana. Cascades (Husillo) along its course. Source for Albear Aqueduct, built in 1592 (which follows path of current Zanja Street in Havana), 1st in the New World of Eur. construction and which gave Havana its official city status.

Almira, village (1990 pop. 310), Lincoln co., E central Wash., 42 mi/68 km NNE of Moses L., 17 mi/27 km S of Grand Coulee Dam (forms Franklin D. Roosevelt L.); 47°43′N 118°57′W. In Columbia basin agr. region; ships wheat. Potatoes, barley, oats, alfalfa. Dry Falls Dam, (Columbia R.) forms Banks L., 18 mi/29 km SW.

Almoloya (ahl-mo-LO-yah), town (1990 pop. 3,316), Hidalgo, central Mexico, 38 mi/61 km SE of Pachuca de Soto; 19°60′N 98°28′W. Maguey.

Almoloya de Alquisiras (ahl-mo-LO-yah de ahl-kee-SEE-ras), town (1990 pop. 1,538), Mexico state, central Mexico, 31 mi/50 km SSW of Toluca de Lerdo; 18°52′N 99°52′W. Coffee, sugar, fruit.

Almoloya de Juárez (ahl-mo-LO-yah de HWAH-rais), town (1990 pop. 2,142), Mexico state, central Mexico, 31 mi/50 km SW of Mexico city; 19°21′N 00°35′W. Elev. 8,793 ft/2,680 m. Grain; livestock.

Almoloya del Río (ahl-mo-LO-yah del REE-o), town (1990 pop. 6,777), Mexico state, central Mexico, 13 mi/21 km SE of Toluca de Lerdo; 19°15′N 99°30′W. Elev. 8,494 ft/2,589 m. Agr. center (cereals, vegetables; livestock); dairying.

Almond 1 village (1990 pop. 458), on Allegany-Steuben co. line, W N.Y., 5 mi/8 km W of Hornell; 42°19′N 77°44′W. Agr. area. **2** village (1990 pop. 455), Portage co., central Wis., 19 mi/31 km SSE of Stevens Point; 44°15′N 89°24′W. In dairy and farm area.

Almont 1 (AWL-mahnt), village, Gunnison co., W central Colo., in Rocky Mts., 9 mi/14.5 km NNE of Gunnison, near head of Gunnison R. Elev. 8,018 ft/2,444 m. Gold medal fishing resort. In Gunnison Natl. Forest. **2** village (1990 pop. 2,354), Lapeer co., E Mich., 16 mi/26 km SE of Lapeer; 42°55′N 83°02′W. In farm area (fruit, grain, dairy prods.); mfg. of auto parts and metal tubing. Inc. 1885. **3** village (1990 pop. 117), Morton co., S central N.Dak., 30 mi/48 km WSW of Mandan, on Big Muddy Creek; 46°43′N 101°30′W.

Almonte (AL-mahnt), town (1991 pop. 4,382), SE Ont., Canada, on Mississippi R., and 26 mi/42 km WSW of Ottawa. Dairying; woodworking; light mfg.

Almyra (al-MEI-ruh), village (1990 pop. 311), Arkansas co., E central Ark., 10 mi/16 km SE of Stuttgart near Little La Grue Bayou; 34°24′N 91°24′W. In agr. area.

Alna (AHL-nuh), town (1990 pop. 571), Lincoln co., S Maine, on Sheepscot R., and 8 mi/12.9 km NNE of Wiscasset; 44°05′N 69°38′W. Meetinghouse built 1789. Includes Head Tide village.

Aloha (uh-LO-hah), uninc. city (1990 pop. 34,284), Washington co., NW Oregon, 7 mi/11.3 km E of Hillsboro; 45°29′N 122°52′W.

Alondra Park, uninc. city (1990 pop. 12,215), Los Angeles co., S Calif., residential suburb 9 mi/14.5 km SSW of downtown Los Angeles, 2 mi/3.2 km N of Gardena; 33°54′N 118°20′W.

Alorton (AL-or-ton), village (1990 pop. 2,960), St. Clair co., SW Ill., SE of East St. Louis, residential suburb of St. Louis, within St. Louis metropolitan area; 38°35′N 90°07′W. Agr. nearby (soybeans; dairying). Inc. 1944.

Alouette Lake (a-loo-EHT), SW B.C., Canada, 27 mi/43 km E of Vancouver; 11 mi/18 km long, 1 mi/2 km wide. Drained SW by Alouette R. (15 mi/24 km long; hydroelectric power) into Pitt R.

Alpatláhuac (ahl-paht-LA-wak), town (1990 pop. 1,110), Veracruz, E Mexico, at NE foot of the Pico de Orizaba, 8 mi/13 km WSW of Huatusco de Chicuellar; 19°07′N 97°00′W. Elev. 5,512 ft/1,680 m. Fruit.

Alpena (al-PEE-nuh), county (□ 1,695 sq mi/4,390 sq km; 1990 pop. 30,605), NE Mich.; ⊙ Alpena. Bounded E by L. Huron; 45°02′N 83°12′W; drained by Thunder Bay R. and its affluents. Dairy and farm area (cattle; beans, grain, raspberries). Mfg. at Alpena (hardboard, concrete blocks, paper, cement, limestone, iron foundry, printing and publishing). Limestone quarries; timber. Year-round resort area. Includes a state forest. Long L. in NE, large Fletcher Pond in W; Thunder Bay Underwater Preserve (est. 1981; 288 sq mi/746 sq km; has high density of shipwrecks); Mich. Isls. Natl. Wildlife Refuge in SE. Organized 1857.

Alpena (al-PEE-nuh), city (1990 pop. 11,354), ⊙ Alpena co., N Mich., 100 mi/161 km NNE of Bay City, on Thunder Bay, an arm of L. Huron; 45°04′N 83°26′W. RR junction. Limestone quarried nearby is used to make cement, Alpena's chief mfg. prod. Cement and limestone are transported on the Great Lakes by way of Alpena's harbor. Tourism; the city lies in a year-round resort area and has an annual winter carnival. Phelps-Collins Aiport to W. Alpena Community Col., Besser Mus. and Planetarium (on campus). Inc. 1871.

Alpena 1 (al-PEE-nuh), village (1990 pop. 319), Boone co., N Ark., 11 mi/18 km WNW of Harrison, in the Ozarks; 36°17′N 93°17′W. Also called Alpena Pass. **2** village (1990 pop. 251), Jerauld co., SE central S.Dak., 15 mi/24 km SW of Huron; near Sand Creek. Grain; dairy prods., livestock, poultry; meat prods.

Alpha 1 (AL-fa), village (1990 pop. 753), Henry co., NW Ill., 13 mi/21 km SW of Cambridge, and 16 mi/26 km N of Galesburg; 41°11′N 90°22′W. In agr. area (corn, oats, soybeans; cattle, hogs; dairying); mfg. of feed. **2** village (1990 pop. 219), Iron co., SW Upper Peninsula, Mich., 5 mi/8 km SW of Crystal Falls; 46°02′N 88°22′W. In dairying area. Crystella Ski Area nearby. **3** village (1990 pop. 105), Jackson co., SW Minn., 6 mi/9.7 km E of Jackson, near Iowa state line and East Fork Des Moines R.; 43°38′N 94°52′W. Agr. area (grain, soybeans, alfalfa; livestock).

Alpha, borough (1990 pop. 2,530), Warren co., W N.J., near Delaware R., 3 mi/4.8 km SE of Phillipsburg; 40°39′N 75°09′W. Mfg. (electronic equip., paper prods.). Inc. 1911.

Alpharetta (al-fuh-RET-uh), city (1990 pop. 13,002), Fulton co., NW central Ga., 22 mi/35 km NNE of Atlanta; 34°04′N 84°16′W. Mfg. includes fiber optic cable and circuit boards, concrete, packaging materials, tools, and medical prods. Rapidly expanding affluent suburban community on Atlanta's burgeoning N side. Regional mall, golf communities, and mixed-use office and commerical facilities rapidly transformed the former rural landscape in the 1980s and 1990s. Large concentration of executive housing near Chattahoochee R.

Alpine, county (□ 739 sq mi/1,914 sq km; 1990 pop. 1,113), E Calif.; ⊙ Markleeville; 38°35′N 119°48′W. Along crest of the Sierra Nevada S of L. Tahoe; most of co. in natl. forests: El Dorado (N), Toiyabe (E of Sierra divide) and Stanislaus (W of Sierra divide); bounded NE by Nev. state line. Includes Sonora Peak (11,429 ft/3,484 m) and Stanislaus Peak (11,202 ft/3,414 m). Pacific Crest Trail and divide of Sierra Nevada runs N-S through center of co. Mts. are crossed here by Kit Carson (or Carson) Pass and Ebbetts Pass (highways). Drained by North Fork Mokelumne R., Middle and Clark forks of the Stanislaus, and E and W forks of Carson R. (all of these have their sources in co.). Clark fork of Stanislaus forms S boundary. Hunting, fishing, camping; includes Alpine and Blue lakes, mineral springs. Alpine Village 5 mi/8 km N of Markleeville. Little agr., chiefly hay; some beef-cattle and sheep grazing. Some gold mining. Had silver boom from 1850s to 1870s; ruins of silver towns (Silver Mt., Silver King, Monitor) remain, west side of famous Comstock Lode (Virginia City, Yerington, Nev). Formed 1864. Grover Hot Springs State Park in N. Kirkwood Ski Resort in NW.

Alpine, uninc. city (1990 pop. 9,695), San Diego co., S Calif., residential suburb 25 mi/40 km ENE of downtown San Diego; 32°51′N 116°46′W. El Capitan L. Reservoir to NW; Capitan Grande Indian Reservation to N; Viejas Indian Reservation to E; Sequan Indian Reservation to SW; Cleveland Natl. Forest to N, E and S. Fruit, strawberries, flowers; dairying; poultry; mfg. (wiring devices, machinery parts).

Alpine 1 town (1990 pop. 5,637), ⊙ Brewster co., extreme W Texas, in mts. N of Big Bend of the Rio Grande; 30°21′N 103°39′W. Elev. 4,481 ft/1,366 m. RR junction; shipping point for cattle, sheep; light mfg. Resort, with dude ranches and state parks nearby. Big Bend Natl. Park is c.70 mi/113 km S. Sul Ross State Univ., with historical mus., is here. Founded 1882 with coming of RR. **2** town (1990 pop. 3,492), Utah co., N central Utah, suburb 24 mi/39 km SSE of Salt L. City, 16 mi/26 km NNW of Provo; 40°27′N 111°46′W. Dairying; cattle; mfg. (candy). Elev. c.5,000 ft/1,525 m; drained by Dry Creek. Timpanagos Cave Natl. Monument to SE; Uinta Natl. Forest and Lone Peak Wilderness Area to NE. Founded and named 1855 by Brigham Young.

Alpine, borough (1990 pop. 1,716), Bergen co., NE N.J., near Hudson R., 7 mi/11.3 km NE of Hackensack; 40°57′N 73°55′W. Upper income residential town. Includes part of Palisades Interstate Park.

Alpine, village (1990 pop. 200), Lincoln co., W Wyo., 24 mi/39 km SW of Jackson, near Idaho boundary, on Snake R., at head of Palisades Reservoir; 43°09′N 111°00′W. Timber; tourism. Grand Canyon of the Snake is upstream (E). Targhee Natl. Forest to N; Caribou Natl. Forest to W; Bridger Teton Natl. Forest to SE. Also called Alpine Junction.

Alpine, Lake, reservoir, Alpine co., E Calif., on Silver Creek, branch of North Fork Stanislaus R., in Eldorado Natl. Forest, 20 mi/32 km SW of Markleeville; 1 mi/1.6 km long; 38°28′N 120°00′W. Lake Alpine Village (summer resort) is on its N shore.

Alpine Peak (11,253 ft/3,430 m), Utah, 5 mi/8 km E of Draper in the Wasatch Range.

Alpine Village, village, Tulare co., E central Calif., 10 mi/16 km S of Sequoia Natl. Park boundary in Sequoia Natl. Forest, on Calif. 190 (highway).

Alpine Village 1 Calif.: see ALPINE, co. **2** Calif.: see SANTA ROSA MOUNTAINS.

Alplaus, village (1990 pop. including E. Glenville 6,518), Schenectady co., E N.Y., on Mohawk R. and the Barge Canal, and 4 mi/6.4 km N of Schenectady; 42°51′N 73°54′W.

Alpoca (al-PO-kuh), uninc. village (1990 pop. 350), Wyoming co., S W.Va., 14 mi/23 km ENE of Welch, in coal-mining region.

Alpoyeca (ahl-po-YE-kah), town (1990 pop. 2,665), Guerrero, SW Mexico, in Sierra Madre del Sur, 13 mi/21 km N of Tlapa de Comonfort; 17°40′N 98°30′W. Elev. 3,379 ft/1,030 m. Cereals, fruit.

Alquízar (ahl-KEE-zahr), town, La Habana prov., W Cuba, on RR, and 27 mi/43 km SSW of Havana;

22°48′N 82°35′W. Sugarcane, tomatoes, tobacco, potatoes, pineapples, vegetables. Charcoal burning and major textile mill.

Alright Island, in Gulf of St. Lawrence, E Que., Canada, one of Magdalen Isls., 65 mi/105 km NNE of Prince Edward Isl.; 8 mi/13 km long, 3 mi/5 km wide. House Harbour (SW) is chief settlement. Fisheries.

Alsask (al-SASK), town (1991 pop. 319), SW Sask., Canada, on Alta. border, 40 mi/64 km W of Kindersley. Sodium-sulphate mining; mfg. (grain elevators; dairying).

Alsea River (AHL-see), c.30 mi/48 km long, W Oregon; formed in Coast Range at confluence of North and South forks, 20 mi/32 km SW of Corvallis; flows W to the Pacific at Waldport.

Alsek River (AL-sek), 150 mi/241 km long, SE Alaska; rises in the Yukon near 60°50′N 137°40′W; flows S to the Pacific at Dry Bay 50 mi/80 km SE of Yakutak.

Alsen (AHL-suhn), village (1990 pop.113), Cavalier co., NE N.Dak., 20 mi/32 km SW of Langdon; 48°37′N 98°42′W. RR junction to W.

Alsey, village (1990 pop. 253), Scott co., W central Ill., 5 mi/8 km SSE of Winchester; 39°33′N 90°25′W. In agr. area.

Alsip, city (1990 pop. 18,227), Cook co., NE Ill., suburb 12 mi/19 km SSW of Chicago, just W of Blue Isl.; 41°40′N 87°44′W. Mfg. (fixtures, brick presses, metal prods., consumer goods, medical equip.).

Alstead (AWL-sted), town (1990 pop. 1,721), Cheshire co., SW N.H., 14 mi/23 km NNW of Keene; 43°07′N 72°18′W. Drained by Cold R. Agr. (sheep, poultry; corn, vegetables; nursery crops; sugar maples; timber; dairying); mfg. (textile machinery, computers). State's first paper mill built here (1793). L. Warren in E. Inc. 1772.

Alston, town (1990 pop. 160), Montgomery co., E central Ga., 10 mi/16 km SSW of Vidalia; 32°05′N 82°29′W.

Alta 1 town (1990 pop.1,820), Buena Vista co., NW Iowa, 6 mi/9.7 km NW of Storm L.; 42°40′N 95°17′W. Mfg. (fertilizers). Sand pits nearby. Municipal hosp. Inc. 1878. **2** town (1990 pop. 397), Salt Lake co., N central Utah, in Wasatch Mts., 20 mi/42 km SE of Salt L. City; 40°34′N 111°37′W. Elev. 8,650 ft/2,637 m. Winter resort bounded by Wasatch Natl. Forest (E, N, W), Uinta Natl. Forest (S); on Little Cottonwood Creek. Mining boomtown in 1860s and 1870s; reborn in 1937 with construction of Utah's first ski resort. Ski village of Brighton 3 mi/4.8 km NE, c.25 mi/40 km by road. Alta and Snowbird ski resorts; several small glacial lakes to E.

Alta, resort village, Placer co., E Calif., in the Sierra Nevada foothills, 25 mi/40 km NE of Auburn, near Bear R., on Boardman Canal. Tahoe Natl. Forest to N, E, and S.

Alta California, term used by the Spanish to refer to their possessions along the entire Pacific coast N of the Mex. state of Baja California. California was often represented on maps as an isl. some 3,000 mi/4,830 km long until the 18th-century explorations of the Jesuit father Eusebio Kino proved conclusively that the S part of the area was a peninsula and the rest of it mainland. Thereafter the peninsula came to be called Baja (Lower) to S and the mainland Alta (Upper) California to N.

Alta Loma, village, San Bernardino co., S Calif., 1 mi/1.6 km N of Cucamonga in S foothills of San Gabriel, suburb 38 mi/61 km E of downtown Los Angeles and 17 mi/27 km W of San Bernadino. Mfg. (furniture). Cucamonga Peak (7,447 ft/2,270 m) to N in Cucamonga Wilderness Area of Angeles Natl. Forest. John Rains Ranch House (1859) and oldest winery in Calif. to S at Cucamonga.

Alta Sierra, uninc. town (1990 pop. 5709), Nevada co., E central Calif., 4 mi/6.4 km NNW of Grass Valley; 39°07′N 121°03′W. Includes areas of Alta Hill, Glenbrook Heights, and Spring Hill.

Alta Sierra, village, Kern co., S central Calif., 5 mi/8 km W of Isabella L.

Alta Vista (AL-tuh VIS-tuh), town (1990 pop. 246), Chickasaw co., NE Iowa, 10 mi/16 km NNW of New Hampton; 43°12′N 92°25′W. In corn, hog, and dairy area.

Alta Vista, village (1990 pop. 477), Wabaunsee co., E central Kansas, 15 mi/24 km SW of Alma; 38°51′N 96°29′W. In livestock and grain region.

Altadena, uninc. city (1990 pop. 42,658), Los Angeles co., S Calif., residential suburb 11 mi/18 km NE of downtown Los Angeles and 2 mi/3.2 km N of Pasadena, on the S slopes of the San Gabriel Mts; 34°11′N 119°08′W. Light mfg. Angeles Natl. Forest to N; Mt. Wilson Observatory to NE. Founded 1887.

Altagracia (ahl-tuh-GRAH-see-uh), village, Camagüey prov., E Cuba, on RR, and 14 mi/23 km ENE of Camagüey; 21°27′N 77°45′W. In agr. region (fruit; cattle); manganese deposits. Also spelled Alta Gracia.

Altagracia, La, Dominican Republic: see LA ALTAGRACIA.

Altamaha River (AL-tuh-muh-hah), 137 mi/220 km long, SE Ga.; formed by confluence of Oconee and Ocmulgee rivers 7 mi/11.3 km NNE of Hazelhurst; flows SE, past Darien, to the Atlantic through Altamaha Sound (20 mi/3.2 km wide) at N end of St. Simon Isl.; 31°57′N 82°32′W. Dredged and navigable (for boats of light draft) with its branches for c.200 mi/322 km.

Altamahaw (al-tuh-MAH-haw), uninc. village, Alamance co., N central N.C., on Haw R., and 9 mi/14.5 km NNW of Burlington. Reported as Altamahaw-Ossipee by Census Bureau (1990 pop. 1,076); Ossipee 2 mi/3.2 km to S. Tobacco, grain; poultry, hogs.

Altamira (ahl-tah-MEE-rah), city (1990 pop. 24,122) and township, Tamaulipas, NE Mexico, on Gulf plain, 12 mi/19 km NNW of Tampico, on RR; 22°50′N 98°00′W. Agr. (henequen, citrus fruit, bananas, tomatoes). Saltworks.

Altamira (ahl-tah-MEE-rah), town (1993 pop. 4,124), Puerto Plata prov., N Dominican Republic, in Cordillera Septentrional, 13 mi/21 km SW of Puerto Plata; 19°42′N 70°50′W. Agr. region (coffee, cacao, fruit). Officially called San José de Altamira.

Altamirano (ahl-tah-mee-RAH-no), town (1990 pop. 4,148), Chiapas, S Mexico, on affluent of Jataté R., and 33 mi/53 km ENE of San Cristóbal de las Casas; 16°50′N 92°05′W. Elev. 3,346 ft/1,020 m. Corn, fruit. A Tzeltal-Maya community.

Altamirano, Mexico: see CIUDAD ALTAMIRANO.

Altamont 1 (AHL-ta-mout), city (1990 pop. 2,296), Effingham co., SE central Ill., 12 mi/19 km WSW of Effingham; 39°03′N 88°45′W. RR junction; wheat-shipping point. Agr. (wheat, soybeans, sorghum; dairy prods.; poultry, livestock); mfg. (plastic prods., furniture); oil field. Inc. as village in 1872, as city in 1901. **2** (AL-tuh-mahnt), uninc. city (1990 pop. 18,591), Klamath co., SW Oregon, residential suburb 2 mi/3.2 km SE of Klamath Falls, near Klamath R.; 42°12′N 121°43′W. Dairying; poultry, livestock; grain. Klamath County Fairgrounds; Kingsley Field Airport to N.

Altamont 1 (AL-tuh-mahnt), town (1990 pop. 1,048), Labette co., SE Kansas, 10 mi/16 km W of Oswego; 37°11′N 95°17′W. Trading and shipping point in livestock-raising, dairying, and agr. region. **2** town (1990 pop. 188), Daviess co., NW Mo., 7 mi/11 km W of Gallatin; 39°53′N 94°05′W. Cattle, hogs; dairy farms. **3** town (1990 pop. 679), ⊙ Grundy co., SE central Tenn., 35 mi/56 km NW of Chattanooga, in the Cumberlands; 35°28′N 85°42′W.

Altamont 1 (AL-tuh-mahnt), village (☐ 1 sq mi/2.6 sq km; 1990 pop. 1,519), Albany co., E N.Y., at base of the Helderbergs, 14 mi/23 km WNW of Albany; 42°42′N 74°02′W. Dairying; vegetable, apple, and grain area. Watervliet Reservoir and numerous small lakes with summer residences. **2** (AWL-tuh-mahnt), uninc. village, Schuylkill co., E central Pa., residential suburb 1 mi/1.6 km E of Frackville; 40°47′N 76°13′W. **3** (AL-tuh-mahnt), village (1990 pop. 48), Deuel co., E S.Dak., 6 mi/10 km N of Clear Lake. **4** village (1990 pop. 167), Duchesne co., NE Utah, 15 mi/24 km WNW of Roosevelt, near Lake Fork R., on Uintah and Ouray Indian Reservation, in S foothills of Uinta Mts.; 40°21′N 110°17′W. Elev. c. 6,400 ft/1,950 m. Sheep, cattle; oil and natural-gas refining.

Altamont Pass (elev. 486 ft/148 m), Alameda co., central Calif., 10 mi/16 km E of Livermore, on interstate highway. Connects Livermore Valley with Central Valley. One of 3 major windpower facilities in Calif., others at Tehachapi and San Gorgonio passes.

Altamonte Springs (AL-tuh-mawnt)[Span. = high hill], city (☐ 9 sq mi/23.3 sq km; 1990 pop. 34,879), Seminole co., central Fla., 8 mi/12.9 km N of Orlando.; 28°39′N 81°24′W. One of Orlando's major N suburbs, a growing residential and commercial center.

Altar (ahl-TAR), town (1990 pop. 4,914), Sonora, NW Mexico, on Altar R. affluent of Magdalena R., and 65 mi/105 km SW of Nogales on Mexico Highway 2; 30°40′N 111°50′W. Agr. (wheat, corn, cotton, beans); mining (copper).

Altata (ahl-TA-ta), village (1990 pop. 1,402) and port, Navolato municipio, Sinaloa, NW Mexico, minor port on shallow bay of Gulf of Calif., 35 mi/56 km WSW of Culiacán Rosales; 24°40′N 108°00′W. Oyster fishing.

Altavista, town (1990 pop. 3,686), Campbell co., S central Va., 21 mi/34 km S of Lynchburg, on Roanoke R., at mouth of Lynch Creek; 37°07′N 79°16′W. RR junction, in agr. area (tobacco, grain, soybeans; livestock; dairying); mfg. (apparel, textiles, fiberglass cloth, machinery, printing and publishing, furniture, construction materials, roller bearings, cedar chests). Leesville L. reservoir (Roanoke R.) to SW. Inc. 1910; rechartered 1936.

Altenburg (AWL-ten-buhrg), town (1990 pop. 307), Perry co., E Mo., near Mississippi R., 16 mi/26 km ESE of Perryville; 37°37′N 89°34′W. Mfg. (wood furniture, lumber). Historic Ger. settlement (1839) and original seminary of the Lutheran Church, Missouri Synod.

Altepexi (ahl-tai-PAI-he), town (1990 pop. 12,184), Puebla, central Mexico, 8 mi/12.9 km SE of Tehuacán, on RR; 18°15′N 97°15′W. Elev. 4,379 ft/1,335 m. Agr. (corn, sugar, fruit, wheat; livestock; fruit).

Altha (AL-thuh), village (☐ 1 sq mi/2.6 sq km; 1990 pop. 497), Calhoun co., NW Fla., 10 mi/16 km NNW of Blountstown; 30°34′N 85°07′W.

Altheimer (AHL-thei-muhr), town (1990 pop. 972), Jefferson co., central Ark., 11 mi/18 km NE of Pine Bluff, near Arkansas R.; 34°19′N 91°50′W.

Altmar, village (☐ 2 sq mi/5.2 sq km; 1990 pop. 336), Oswego co., N central N.Y., on Salmon R., and 25 mi/40 km E of Oswego; 43°30′N 76°00′W. State trout and salmon hatchery (for stocking various N U.S. rivers and streams). Prized coho salmon fishing in Salmon R.

Alto, town (1990 pop.1,027), Cherokee co., E Texas, 130 mi/209 km NW of Lufkin; 31°38′N 95°04′W. Elev. 433 ft/132 m. Vegetables, forage crops, peaches; cattle; timber; mfg. (fence posts; lumber). Caddoan Mounds State Historical Park to W, Stone Age Indian burial mounds; Davy Crockett Natl. Forest to SW. Inc. 1909.

Alto (AL-to), village (1990 pop. 651), Habersham and Banks cos., NE Ga., 17 mi/27 km NE of Gainesville; 34°28′N 83°34′W. Mfg. includes winemaking, fabrics, yarns, and pottery.

Alto Cedro (AHL-to SAID-ro), town, Holguín prov., E Cuba, 37 mi/60 km NNW of Santiago de Cuba; 20°31′N 75°58′W. RR junction picturesquely set in Sierra de Nipe foothills. The Alto Cedro sugar mill is 3 mi/4.8 km N.

Alto de la Bandera (AHL-to dai lah bahn-DER-ah), resort and pass (c.2,500 ft/760 m), W central P.R., in the Cordillera Central, 2.5 mi/4 km SE of Adjuntas. Sometimes Alto Bandera or El Alto de la Bandera.

Alto Lucero (ahl-to loo-SAI-ro), town (1990 pop. 4,094), Veracruz, E Mexico, in Sierra Madre Oriental, 14 mi/23 km NE of Xalapa Enríquez; 19°30′N 96°32′W. Corn, sugar, coffee, tobacco, fruit.

Alto Park (AL-to), village, Floyd co., NW Ga. 4 mi/6.4 km NW of Rome.

Alto Pass, village (1990 pop. 417), Union co., S Ill., 10 mi/16 km NNW of Jonesboro, 12 mi/19 km SW of Carbondale; 37°34′N 89°19′W. Agr. (cattle; sorghum, wheat; dairy prods.); mfg. (wine, jewelry). Located in Shawnee Natl. Forest; Pine Hills Recreational Area to W.

Alto Songo (AHL-to SON-o), town, Santiago de Cuba prov., E Cuba, on RR, and 13 mi/21 km NE of Santiago de Cuba; 20°10′N 75°42′W. Agr. center (tobacco, coffee, cacao, fruit); cattle raising. South Rosales sugar mill just S.

Alton (AHL-tuhn), city (1990 pop. 32,905), Madison co., SW Ill., suburb of St. Louis, on the Mississippi R. 5 mi/8 km above its confluence with the Missouri and 10 mi/16 km below its confluence with the Illinois; 38°53′N 90°09′W. Alton is a shipping and industrial center. Oil refineries to SE. Mfg. includes food prods., lime, crushed stone, lumber, crystal, paperboard, and steel. Agr. in outlying areas to N and E and across river in Mo. Of interest are a monument to abolitionist Elijah Lovejoy, who was killed by a mob in Alton (1837); a tablet marking the site of the last Lincoln-Douglas debate (1858); and a cemetery where many captured Confederate soldiers are buried. Extensive damage to downtown area in catastrophic flood (1993). New Lock and Dam No. 26R built in early 1990s 2 mi/3.2 km downstream from original downtown site. New suspension bridge (Clark Bridge) opened 1994. New Lewis Bridge spans Missouri R. 6 mi/9.7 km SW. Inc. 1837.

Alton 1 (AWL-tuhn), town (1990 pop. 57), Crawford co., S Ind., on Ohio R., and 15 mi/24 km SSE of English; 38°07′N 86°25′W. Agr. area; surrounded by Hoosier Natl. Forest. **2** town (1990 pop. 1,063), Sioux co., NW Iowa, on Floyd R., and just SW of Orange City. Cement and rendering works. Gravel pits nearby. Inc. 1883. **3** town (1990 pop. 771), Penobscot co., S central Maine, 16 mi/26 km N of Bangor; 45°02′N 68°46′W. Lumbering. **4** town (1990 pop. 692), ⊙ Oregon co., S Mo., 26 mi/42 km E of West Plains; 36°41′N 91°24′W. Apples, hay; cattle, hogs; timber; mfg. (airplane body parts); tourism. **5** town (1990 pop. 3,286), Belknap co., E central N.H., 13 mi/21 km SSE of Laconia; 43°29′N 71°15′W. Drained by Merrymeeting R., which flows into Alton Bay of L. Winnipesaukee. Agr. (vegetables; cattle, poultry; dairying; nursery crops; mfg. (textiles, machinery, computers). Long time resort. Part of L. Winnipesaukee in N. Mt. Major (1,780 ft/543 m) in NW. Settled 1770, inc. 1796. **6** town (1990 pop. 3,069), Hidalgo co., S Texas, residential suburb 7 mi/11.3 km NW of McAllen; 26°16′N 98°18′W. Irrigated agr. area (citrus, vegetables, cotton).

Alton (OL-tuhn), village, S Ont., Canada, on Credit R., and 5 mi/8 km SSE of Orangeville. Dairying; mixed farming.

Alton 1 (AHL-tuhn), village (1990 pop. 115), Osborne co., N Kansas, on South Fork Solomon R., and 14 mi/23 km W of Osborne; 39°28′N 98°57′W. Trading point for livestock and grain region. **2** village (1990 pop. 93), Kane co., S Utah, 27 mi/43 km N of Kanab, on Kanab Creek in scenic mt. region called the Pink Cliffs; 37°26′N 112°28′W. Elev. 6,875 ft/2,096 m. Situated bet. separate units of Dixie Natl. Forest to E and W. Cattle; timber. Cedar Breaks Natl. Monument to NW. Inc. 1935.

Alton Bay, N.H.: see ALTON, town.

Altona, town (1991 pop. 3,060), SE Man., Canada, 60 mi/97 km SSW of Winnipeg, near N.Dak. border. Grain, livestock; flour milling.

Altona, town (1990 pop. 156), DeKalb co., NE Ind., 6 mi/9.7 km W of Auburn; 41°21′N 85°09′W. In agr. area.

Altona, village (1990 pop. 559), Knox co., NW central Ill., 16 mi/26 km NE of Galesburg; 41°07′N 90°09′W. In agr. area (corn, wheat; dairying).

Altoona (awl-TOO-nah), city (1990 pop. 51,881), Blair co., central Pa., 80 mi/129 km E of Pittsburgh, on the E slopes of the Allegheny Mts., near the source of the Juniata R.; 40°30′N 78°24′W. RR center with construction and repair shops; mfg. (fabricated metal prods., food, machinery, electrical equip., chemicals; printing and publishing. Altoona Blair Co. Airport 14 mi/23 km to SE. Horseshoe Curve of the Pa. RR, an engineering feat (1854), made RR route through Allegheny Mts. possible; Wopsononock Mt. (2,580 ft/786 m) to NW. Penn State Univ. (Altoona campus: 2-year); Railroaders Memorial Mus.; Baker Mansion Mus.; Allegheny Ballet Co.; Altoona Symphony. Oak Spring Winery to N; Fort Robideau Natl. Historical Landmark (1778) to NE; Canoe Creek State Park to E; Prince Gallitzin State Park to NW; Allegheny Portage

RR Natl. Historical Site to SW. Settled c.1769, laid out (1849) by the Pa. RR as a switching point for locomotives preparing to mount the Allegheny Plateau. Inc. as a city 1868.

Altoona 1 (ahl-TOO-nuh), town (1990 pop. 960), Etowah co., NE central Ala., 18 mi/29 km W of Gadsden. Wood turnings, meat processing. **2** town (1990 pop. 7,191), Polk co., central Iowa suburb, 8 mi/12.9 km ENE of downtown Des Moines; 41°38′N 93°28′W. Mfg. (pasta); printing; agr. (corn cannery). Adventureland theme park to W. **3** town (1990 pop. 5,889), Eau Claire co., W central Wis., a suburb 3 mi/4.8 km E of Eau Claire, on Eau Claire R. (forms Altoona L.); 44°48′N 91°26′W. In mfg. and services area. Light mfg. Settled 1882, inc. 1887.

Altoona, village (1990 pop. 456), Wilson co., SE Kansas, on Verdigris R., and 10 mi/16 km E of Fredonia; 37°31′N 95°39′W. Trading and shipping point in livestock, dairy, and grain region. Wilson State Fishing L. to N.

Altos de Chavón (AHL-tos dai chah-VON), artists' community, Dominican Republic, E of La Romana. Constructed in the style of a Eur. village as a tourist attraction, near the resort (7,000 acres/2,830 ha) of Casa de Campo, overlooking Rio Chavón. Site of 2-year col. of the arts, a 5,000 seat outdoor theater, and regional archaeological mus.

Altotonga (ahl-to TON-gah), city (1990 pop. 12,305) and township, Veracruz, E Mexico, in Sierra Madre Oriental, 28 mi/45 km NW of Xalapa Enríquez; 19°46′N 97°14′W. Agr. center (corn, coffee, sugar, tobacco, fruit).

Altura (al-TOO-ruh), village (1990 pop. 349), Winona co., SE Minn., 15 mi/24 km W of Winona; 44°04′N 91°56′W. Dairying; poultry; livestock; grain. Part of Richard J. Dorer Hardwood State Forest to E and N; Whitewater Wildlife Area to W.

Alturas, town (1990 pop. 3,231), ⊙ Modoc co., NE Calif., on Pit R. at mouth of South Fork Pit R. and c.90 mi/145 km SE of Klamath Falls; 41°30′N 120°33′W. RR junction; shipping and trade center for stock-raising, farming, lumbering region. Potatoes, onions, horseradish, sugar beets; grain, cattle, sheep. Hq. of Modoc Natl. Forest. Hunting, fishing nearby. Warner Mts. are just E. XL Ranch Indian Reservation to NE; Big Sage Reservoir to NW; Modoc Natl. Wildlife Refuge to S; part of Modoc Natl. Forest to NW and E; South Warner Wilderness Area to SE; S end of Goose L. c.20 mi/32 km NNE. Inc. 1901.

Altus (AL-tuhs), city (1990 pop. 21,910), ⊙ Jackson co., 48 mi/77 km W of Lawton, near Salt Fork of Red R., SW Okla.; 34°38′N 99°18′W. Elev. 1,389 ft/423 m. Important RR junction. Agr. (cotton, wheat, sorghum; cattle); mfg. (consumer goods; printing and publishing; food processing). Altus Air Force Base (E), a large training facility, also contributes to the economy. Western Okla. State Col. (2-year); Mus. of the Western Prairie. Altus L. reservoir and Quartz Mt. State Park to N. The city was founded in 1892 as the town of Fraiser, but after floods forced the moving of the city to its present site it was renamed Altus [Lat. = high place]. Inc. 1907.

Altus, village (1990 pop. 433), Franklin co., NW Ark., 37 mi/60 km ENE of Fort Smith, near Arkansas R.; 35°26′N 93°45′W. Mfg. (graphite, electrodes, wines); wineries.

Altus Lake, reservoir, 12 mi/19 km long, on Green-Kiowa co. border, SW Okla., on North Fork Red R., 18 mi/29 km N of Altus; 34°53′N 99°17′W. Max. capacity 151,650 acre-ft. Formed by Altus Dam (c.100 ft/30 m high, 1,112 ft/339 m long), built (1941) for flood control and water supply on site of old Lugert Dam (1927) as chief unit of W.C. Austin project. Quartz Mt. State Resort Park on SW shore, at dam.

Altzayanca (ahlt-sah-YAHN-kah), town (1990 pop. 2,757), ⊙ Altzayanca municipio, Tlaxcala, central Mexico, 30 mi/48 km ENE of Tlaxcala; elev. 8,150 ft/2,484 m. Cereals, maguey, fruit; livestock; wood; textile mfg. Formerly called Atlzayanca; also known as Atlzayanca de Hidalgo.

Alum Creek (AL-uhm), uninc. town (1990 pop. 1,602), Kanawha co., W central W.Va., 10 mi/16 km W of Charlestown, on Big Coal R., at mouth of Alum Creek; 38°16′N 81°50′W. Mfg. (plastic prods., burial monuments); agr. (corn, tobacco; cattle; poultry). Kanawha State Forest to E, Fork Creek Wildlife Management Area to S.

Alum Creek Lake, reservoir (□ 5 sq mi/13 sq km), Del. co., central Ohio, on Alum Creek of Big Walnut Creek, 10 mi/16 km N of Columbus; 40°11′N 82°58′W. Max. capacity 134,800 acre-ft.; extends N-S. Formed by Alum Creek Dam (81 ft/25 m high) built (1974) by Army Corps of Engineers for flood control; also used for recreation, water supply, and as a fish and wildlife pond. Alum Creek State Park near dam.

Alum Rock, uninc. city (1990 pop. 16,890), Santa Clara co., W Calif., residential suburb 6 mi/9.7 km NE of downtown San Jose. Alum Rock Park to N. Reid Hillview Airport to S.

Alva 1 (AL-vuh), town (□ 2 sq mi/5.2 sq km; 1990 pop. 1,036), Lee co., SW Fla., 15 mi/24 km NE of Fort Myers, located on the Caloosahatchee River; 26°43′N 81°36′W. **2** town (1990 pop. 5,495), ⊙ Woods co., NW Okla., on Salt Fork of Arkansas R., and 50 mi/80 km NW of Enid; 36°47′N 98°40′W. Commercial and processing center for agr. area (esp. wheat and cattle); mfg. (aircraft parts, fishing lures). Cherokee Strip Mus. here. Northwestern State Univ. to S. Settled 1893.

Alva, village, Harlan co., SE Ky., in the Cumberland Mts., 10 mi/16 km SW of Harlan. Bituminous coal.

Alva B. Adams Tunnel, N Colo., in Rocky Mt. Natl. Park; 13 mi/21 km long; elev. 8,400 ft/2,560 m. Important unit in Colo.–Big Thompson project; conducts water ENE from Grand L. (supplied from L. Grandby reservoir), Grand co., through Front Range to point 6 mi/9.7 km SW of Estes Park, Larimer co.; 9.75 ft/3 m in diameter. Makes water available for irrigation and power on E slope of Continental Divide.

Alvarado (ahl-va-RAH-do), city (1990 pop. 23,411) and township, Veracruz, E Mexico, port on peninsula bet. Alvarado Lagoon and Gulf of Campeche, 38 mi/61 km SE of Veracruz; 18°46′N 95°45′W. RR terminus. Market center; fishing center (bass, turtles, crabs, oysters; pearls); agr. (rice, oranges, plantains, mangoes). Preserves character of 16th-cent. fishing village. Has old church (built 1779). Pedro de Alvarado, a lieutenant of Cortés, landed here in 1518.

Alvarado, town (1990 pop. 2,918), Johnson co., N central Texas, 24 mi/39 km S of Fort Worth; 32°24′N 97°12′W. Trade point in cotton; grain area; dairying; mfg. (tempered glass, concrete prods., oil and logging equip., mobile-home frames).

Alvarado 1 village, Alameda co., W Calif., 18 mi/29 km SE of Oakland on Alameda Creek. Beet-sugar, salt refining. Part of Union City. **2** (al-vuh-RAI-do), village (1990 pop. 356), Marshall co., NW Minn., on Snake R., in Red R. valley, 20 mi/32 km N of Grand Forks, N.Dak.; 48°11′N 97°00′W. Grain, beans, sugar beets, sunflowers, flax; cattle, sheep; mfg. (dry-bean processing).

Alvarado Lagoon, 20 mi/32 km long, up to 3 mi/4.8 km wide, Veracruz, SE Mexico, in Sotavento lowlands; 18°50′N 95°46′W. Port of Alvarado is at its opening on Gulf of Campeche. Receives united Papaloapan and San Juan rivers.

Álvarez, Villa de, Mexico: see VILLA DE ÁLVAREZ.

Álvaro Obregón, town (1990 pop. 7,719), Michoacán, central Mexico, 14 mi/23 km NE of Morelia; 19°40′N 101°10′W. Elev. 6,234 ft/1,900 m. Cereals, vegetables; livestock. Formerly called San Bartolo.

Álvaro Obregón (AHL-va-ro o-brai-GON), delegación (1990 pop. 642,753), Federal Dist., central Mexico, 9 mi/14.5 km SSW of Mexico city; a residential suburb of the capital (linked by subways); 21°01′N 100°23′W. Paper mill; mfg. of pencils, chemicals. Church and monastery of El Carmen (dating from 1615) is fine example of churrigueresque style. Monument to Álvaro Obregón is on site where he was killed. The home of Diego Rivera is opposite San Angel Inn, formerly a 17th-cent.

castle. Sometimes called Villa Álvaro Obregón; formerly called San Angel.

Álvaro Obregón 1 Guanajuato, Mexico: see SAN JOSÉ ITURBIDE. **2** Tabasco, Mexico: see FRONTERA.

Alvaton, town, Meriwether co., W Ga., 19 mi/31 km WSW of Griffin, near Flint R.; 33°10′N 84°34′W. Mfg. (freight-truck bodies).

Alverstone, Mount (OL-vuhr-stuhn) (14,500 ft/ 4,420 m), SW Yukon, on Alaska border, in St. Elias Mts; 60°21′N 139°04′W.

Alvin, city (1990 pop. 19,220), Brazoria co., SE Texas, suburb 22 mi/35 km SSE of Houston, 19 mi/31 km WNW of Texas City, on Mustang Bayou; 29°25′N 95°15′W. Elev. 51 ft/16 m. Rail junction. Urban fringe in agr. area (rice, cotton, soybeans, pecans); oil and natural gas; mfg. (concrete, rice milling, fabricated metal prods., electronic equip.). Seat of Alvin Community Col.

Alvin, village (1990 pop. 339), Vermilion co., E Ill., on North Fork of Vemilion R. and 10 mi/16 km N of Danville; 40°18′N 87°36′W. Corn, soybeans; cattle, poultry; dairying.

Alvinston (AL-vin-stuhn), village (1991 pop. 920), S Ont., Canada, on Sydenham R., and 30 mi/48 km ESE of Sarnia. Milling, fruit and vegetable canning.

Alviso, uninc. town, Santa Clara co., W Calif., suburb 5 mi/8 km N of Santa Clara; on Alviso Slough, branch of Guadalupe Slough. Duck hunting in marshes (N). Mfg. (aluminum foundry). S end of San Francisco Bay 4 mi/6.4 km to NW. Moffett Field Naval Air Station.

Alvo (AL-vo), village (1990 pop. 164), Cass co., SE Nebr., 28 mi/45 km SW of Plattsmouth; 40°52′N 96°23′W.

Alvon (al-VAHN), uninc. village (1990 pop. 100), Greenbrier co., SE W.Va., 9 mi/14.5 km NNE of White Sulphur Springs, in Monongahela Natl. Forest. Blue Bend Recreation Area to W.

Alvord 1 town (1990 pop. 204), Lyon co., NW Iowa, 9 mi/14.5 km SW of Rock Rapids; 43°20′N 96°17′W. In agr. area. **2** town (1990 pop. 865), Wise co., N Texas, c.45 mi/72 km NW of Fort Worth, near Big Sandy Creek, branch of West Fork of Trinity R.; 33°21′N 97°41′W. Agr. (peanuts, pecans, grain; cattle, sheep; dairying); gas and oil; mfg. (packaged ice).

Alvordton (AL-vuhr-tuhn), village (1990 pop. 298), Williams co., extreme NW Ohio, near Mich. state line, 14 mi/23 km NNE of Bryan; 41°41′N 84°27′W.

Amacueca (ah-mah-KWAI-kah), town (1990 pop. 2,685), Jalisco, W Mexico, on L. Sayula, 59 mi/95 km SSW of Guadalajara; 20°02′N 103°31′W. Agr. (grain, alfalfa, sugar, fruit); livestock.

Amacuzac (ah-ma-KOO-sak), town (1990 pop. 4,073), Morelos state, central Mexico, 24 mi/39 km SSW of Cuernavaca; 18°35′N 99°45′W. Elev. 3,547 ft/1,081 m. Rice, tropical fruit, vegetables. Hydroelectric plant, supplying Federal Dist., is on Amacuzac R. tributary of Río Balsas.

Amadjuak (uh-MA-joo-ak), Eskimo settlement, S Baffin Isl., SE Franklin dist., N.W.T., Canada, on Hudson Strait; 64°01′N 72°39′W.

Amadjuak Lake, SW Baffin Isl., SE Franklin Dist., N.W.T., Canada, borders W on the Great Plain of the Koukdjuak; 50 mi/80 km long, 28 mi/45 km wide; 65°00′N 71°00′W. Drains N into Nettilling L. by Amadjuak R. (c.50 mi/80 km long).

Amador, county (□ 604 sq mi/1,564 sq km; 1990 pop. 30,039), central and E Calif.; ⊙ Jackson; 38°27′N 120°40′W. Extends from Sacramento Valley (W) to the Sierra Nevada (E), where Mokelumne Peak rises to 9,332 ft/2,844 m. Narrows to 5 mi/8 km in E center. Bounded S in part by Mokelumne R. and its N fork; bounded N in part by Cosumnes R. and its S fork. Part of El Dorado Natl. Forest in E. Pardee and Camanche reservoirs (both on Mokelumne R.) on S boundary, in SW co. Agr. (barley, corn, oats, grapes, walnuts, cattle); timber; gold mining; quarrying (clay, sand, gravel). Gold Rush (1849) region made famous in the tales of Mark Twain and Bret Harte, centers around Jackson. Many old gold camps survive. Recreational region (trout fishing, lakes, winter sports). Formed 1854.

Amador City, city (1990 pop. 196), Amador co., central Calif., 37 mi/60 km ESE of Sacramento, near Sutter

Creek; 38°25′N 120°49′W. Gold; agr. (grapes, walnuts, grain; cattle); timber. In Calif. Gold Rush region (1849).

Amagansett, village and upscale summer community (1990 pop. 1,700), Suffolk co., SE N.Y., near S shore of E L.I., 14 mi/23 km ENE of Southampton; 40°58′N 72°09′W.

Amagon (AM-uh-gahn), village (1990 pop. 108), Jackson co., NE Ark., 11 mi/18 km ESE of Newport, near Cache R.; 35°33′N 91°06′W.

Amaknak Island (uh-MAK-nak), islet in Unalaska Bay, NE of Unalaska Isl., Fox Isls., Aleutian Isls., SW Alaska; site of Dutch Harbor. Also spelled Umaknak.

Amalga (uh-MAL-guh), village (1990 pop. 366), Cache co., NW Utah, 9 mi/14.5 km N of Logan on Bear R.; 41°51′N 111°54′W. Agr. (barley, wheat); dairying; cattle; mfg. (cheese).

Amana or **Amana Society**, collective name of 7 small communities, on both sides of Iowa R., c.20 mi/32 km WNW of Iowa City. Agr. (vegetable, fruit) and livestock (sheep, hogs, cattle, poultry); mfg. (woolen textiles, furniture, machinery, prepared foods, feed). The first village, Amana, was settled 1855 by members of the Community of True Inspiration, a Ger. religious sect. By 1861 they had laid out 5 more villages — East Amana, West Amana, High Amana, Middle Amana, South Amana — and had purchased Homestead. Settlers developed a successful communal way of life. Society was made a cooperative corporation, with separation of religious and economic administration, in 1932. The quaint villages, where craft culture has been preserved through the Amanite pattern of economic self-sufficiency, attract many visitors.

Amanalco de Becerra (ah-mah-NAHL-ko de bai-SER-rah), town (1990 pop. 793); ⊙ Amanalco municipio, Mexico state, central Mexico, 23 mi/37 km W of Toluca de Lerdo; 19°10′N 00°48′W. Elev. 7,546 ft/2,300 m. Agr. (cereals) and livestock.

Amanda, village (1990 pop. 729), Fairfield co., central Ohio, 9 mi/14 km WSW of Lancaster, in agr. area; 39°41′N 82°46′W.

Amanda Park, uninc. town (1990 pop. 800), Grays Harbor co., W Wash., 30 mi/48 km N of Hoquiam, at SW end of Quinault L., at outlet of Quinault R. Mfg. (cedar shakes). In NE corner of Quinault Indian Reservation. Parts of Olympic Natl. Park at opposite end of Quinault L., to NE; parts of Olympic Natl. Forest to N and E.

Amargosa, Calif.: see DEATH VALLEY JUNCTION.

Amargosa Desert (ah-mahr-GO-suh), Nye co., S Nev., parallel to Calif.-Nev. state line, NE of Death Valley, Calif.; extends SE c.40 mi/64 km from town of Beatty to Devil's Hole (small unit of Death Valley Natl. Monument); crossed by Amargosa R. Amargosa Sand Dunes.

Amargosa Range, Inyo co., E Calif., and Nye co., S Nev., barren mts. forming E wall of Death Valley (282 ft/86 m below sea level), lowest point in the Americas; extends N-S c.110 mi/177 km SSE from Grapevine Peak (8,738 ft/2,663 m), in Nevada, to Amargosa R. Funeral Peak (6,384 ft/1,946 m) is near center; includes Dante's View. Most of range in Death Valley Natl. Monument. E boundary of monument on E side of range. Sections of range are locally called Grapevine Mts., Funeral Mts., and Black Mts. Amargosa Desert is NE, in Nev., SE of Beatty.

Amargosa River (ah-mahr-GO-suh), intermittent stream; S Nev. and E Calif., rising in Pahute Mesa, Nev. c.40 mi/64 km N of Beatty, Nev.; flowing S; flows underground through Beatty then past Amargosa, Calif., E of Amargosa Range, then turns NNW to W side of range, to sink into Death Valley, Calif., meeting intermittent Salt Creek from N.

Amargosa Valley (ah-mahr-GO-suh), uninc. town, Nye co., S Nev., 70 mi/113 km NW of Las Vegas, 13 mi/21 km NE of Calif. boundary, near Forsythe, Wash. Cattle, sheep. Amargosa Desert extends to NW. Death Valley Natl. Monument to W; Devil's Hole, in small sect. of Death Valley Natl. Monument, to SE; Ash Meadows Wildlife Managment Area also to SE. Nevada Test Site to N. Formerly Lathrop Wells.

Amarillas (ah-muh-REE-yahz), town, Matanzas prov.,

W Cuba, on RR, 40 mi/64 km SE of Cárdenas; 22°28′N 80°54′W. Rice, sugarcane, citrus fruit; livestock. On edge of Zapata Swamps and in vicinity of Reynald García and Jesús Rabí sugar mills.

Amarillo, city (1990 pop. 157,615); ⊙ Potter and Randall cos., N Texas; 35°12′N 101°49′W. Elev. 3,676 ft/1,120 m. The commercial, banking, and industrial center of the Texas Panhandle, Amarillo grew after the coming of the RR in 1887, now a major RR junction and center. At the turn of the cent. it was a market for wheat farmers. After the discovery of gas (1918) and oil (1921), Amarillo developed into an industrial city. Its economy is also based on cattle ranching, meat-packing, flour milling, zinc and copper smelting, wood and fiberglass prods., as well as the production of helicopters, synthetic rubber, and farm and dairy items. Nearby Amarillo Air Force Base to E is closed. The city is the seat of Texas State Technical Col., Amarillo Col. (2 year), and Amarillo Vocational Col. It has civic and art centers. Amarillo Internatl. Airport in E, Tradewinds Airport in S. Nuclear weapons plant and plutonium storage. Close by is a U.S. govt. helium plant, and the 6-story stainless steel Helium Monument, next to Harrington Discovery Center, was dedicated to the helium industry in 1968. Palo Duro Canyon State Park to SE; Buffalo Lake Wildlife Refuge to SW; L. Meredith Natl. Recreation Area and Alibates Flint Quarries Natl. Monument to NE. Inc. 1899.

Amatán (ah-mah-TAHN), town (1990 pop. 2,768), Chiapas, S Mexico, near Tabasco border, in foothills of Sierra Madre, 13 mi/21 km NNW of Simojovel de Allende; 18°22′N 92°49′W. A Zoque Indian community.

Amatenango de la Frontera (ah-ma-tai-NAHN-go dai lah fron-TAI-rah), town (1990 pop. 589), Chiapas, S Mexico, in Sierra Madre, 3 mi/4.8 km NE of Motozintla de Mendoza; 15°30′N 92°15′W. Sugar.

Amatenango del Valle (ah-mah-tai-NAHN-go del VAI-ye), town (1990 pop. 2,537), Chiapas, S Mexico, in Sierra de Hueytepec, 20 mi/32 km SE of San Cristóbal de las Casas; 16°30′N 92°26′W. Corn, fruit. In Tzeltal-Maya Indian community.

Amatepec (ah-mah-tai-PEK), town (1990 pop. 1,751), Mexico state, central Mexico, 21 mi/34 km SW of Sultepec; 19°42′N 0°42′W. Elev. 7,546 ft/2,300 m. Agr. (sugar, coffee, fruit); silver and gold deposits nearby.

Amatitán (ah-mah-tee-TAHN), town (1990 pop. 6,777), Jalisco state, W Mexico, 25 mi/40 km NW of Guadalajara; 20°50′N 103°40′W. Elev. 4,236 ft/1,291 m. Grain, beans, sugar, tobacco, fruit.

Amatitlán (ah-mah-teet-LAHN), town (1990 pop. 1,484), Veracruz state, SE Mexico, on Papaloapan R., in Sotavento lowlands, and 25 mi/40 km W of San Andrés Tuxtla; 18°15′N 95°50′W. Sugarcane, tropical fruit. Amatlán until 1938.

Amatlán, Mexico: see AMATITLÁN.

Amatlán de Cañas (ah-mat-LAHN dai KAHN-yahs), town (1990 pop. 3,205), Nayarit state, W Mexico, near Ameca R. (Jalisco border), 55 mi/89 km SE of Tepic; 20°50′N 104°25′W. Agr. (corn, sugar) and livestock (cattle).

Amatlán de los Reyes (ah-mat-LAHN dai los RE-yes), town (1990 pop. 5,478), Veracruz state, E Mexico, in Sierra Madre Oriental, 3 mi/4.8 km S of Córdoba, on RR; 18°50′N 96°54′E. Anc. Indian settlement with Aztec remains. Picturesque market.

Amatlán Tuxpan, Mexico: see NARANJOS.

Amaxac de Guerrero (ah-MAH-hak dai ge-RER-o), town (1990 pop. 5,103), Tlaxcala state, central Mexico, 4 mi/6.4 km NE of Tlaxcala city. Grain, alfalfa, maguey; livestock.

Amazonia, town (1990 pop. 257), Andrew co., NW Mo., on Missouri R. and 5 mi/8 km SSW of Savannah; 39°53′N 94°53′W.

Amber, village (1990 pop. 418), Grady co., central Okla., 8 mi/12.9 km NNE of Chickasha; 35°09′N 97°52′W. Diversified agr. area.

Amberley, village (1990 pop. 3,108), Hamilton co., extreme SW Ohio, a NE suburb of Cincinnati; 39°12′N 84°27′W.

Ambia, town (1990 pop. 249), Benton co., W Ind., near

Ill. state line, 13 mi/21 km SW of Fowler; 40°29′N 87°31′W. In agr. area.

Ambler, borough (1990 pop. 6,609), Montgomery co., SE Pa., suburb 14 mi/23 km NNW of downtown Philadelphia, on Wissahickon Creek; 40°09′N 75°13′W. Mfg. (electronic imaging equipment, boilers, plastics, chemicals, printing and publishing); quarrying; some agr. Temple Univ. (Ambler Campus and Gardens). Fort Washington State Park to S. Inc. 1888.

Amboy, city (1990 pop. 2,377), Lee co., N Ill., on Green R., 11 mi/18 km SSE of Dixon; 41°43′N 89°19′W. In agr. area (corn, soybeans, cattle); RR shops; mfg. (dairy prods., crushed stone). Inc. 1857.

Amboy, town (1990 pop. 370), Miami co., N central Ind., 13 mi/21 km SE of Peru; 40°36′N 85°56′W. In agr. area. Doors.

Amboy 1 uninc. village, San Bernardino co., S Calif., c.72 mi/116 km ESE of Barstow on former U.S Highway 66. Interstate Highway 40 12 mi/19 km to N. Nearby is Amboy Crater, a volcanic cone. Devil's Playground to N (desert area). Twentynine Palms Marine Corps Base to SW; Bristol L. (dry) to S. **2** village (1990 pop. 517), Blue Earth co., S Minn., near Blue Earth R., 21 mi/34 km SSW of Mankato; 43°53′N 94°09′W. Agr. (grain, soybeans, alfalfa) and livestock; mfg. (fertilizers, horse stalls).

Ambridge, borough (1990 pop. 8,133), Beaver co., W Pa., 15 mi/24 km NW of downtown Pittsburgh, on the Ohio R. (bridged); 40°35′N 80°13′W. Founded by and named for the Amer. Bridge Co. in 1901. Mfg. (plastics, processed food, furniture fixtures, fabricated metal prods.). On the NW edge of town is Old Economy Village, 17 restored bldgs. of Ger. communal group (1824–1906). Inc. 1905.

Ambrose, town (1990 pop. 288), Coffee co., Ga., 12 mi/19 kmi SW of Douglas; 31°35′N 83°01′W. Mfg. includes apparel, motor vehicles, chemicals.

Ambrose (AM-broz), village (1990 pop. 48), Divide co., NW N.Dak., port of entry, 11 mi/18 km WNW of Crosby; 48°57′N 103°28′W. Near Can. border.

Amchitka Island (am-CHIT-kuh), 40 mi/64 km long, off W Alaska; one of the Aleutian Isls. It was selected in 1967 by the Atomic Energy Commission (AEC) as the site for underground tests of nuclear weapons, thus arousing much criticism, especially from environmental groups. The AEC financed the transplanting of much of the isl.'s animal life. In 1971 the use of Amchitka for the detonation of atomic devices without specific presidential approval was banned. Later that year, the first test was made, sanctioned by then President Richard Nixon.

Amchitka Pass, sea passage (60 mi/97 km wide), Aleutian Isls., SW Alaska, bet. Delarof Isls., at W end of Andreanof Isls. (E) and Rat Isls. (W); 51°45′N 179°25′W.

Amealco, Mexico: see AMEALCO DE BONFIL.

Amealco de Bonfil (ah-mai-AHL-ko de bon-FEEL), town (1990 pop. 46,358), Querétaro state, central Mexico, 33 mi/53 km SSE of Querétaro; 20°12′N 100°8′W. Elev. 6,775 ft/2,065 m. Agr. center (corn, wheat, beans, lentils, sugar, alfalfa; livestock). Formerly Amealco.

Ameca (ah-MAI-kah), city (1990 pop. 30,882) and township, Jalisco state, W Mexico, at W end of Transverse Volcanic Axis, on Ameca R., 45 mi/72 km WSW of Guadalajara; 20°34′N 104°03′W. Elev. 4,052 ft/1,235 m. Agr. center (grain, sugar, chickpeas, beans, alfalfa); tanning.

Ameca River, c.140 mi/225 km long, W Mexico; rises in Jalisco state 14 mi/23 km W of Guadalajara (20°34′N 104°03′W); flows W, past Ameca, along Nayarit-Jalisco border, to the Pacific at Banderas Bay 5 mi/8 km NW of Puerto Vallarta.

Amecameca de Juárez (ah-mai-kah-MAI-kah de HWAH-rais), city (1990 pop. 25,374), Mexico state, S central Mexico, at the foot of the Popocatépetl and Ixtacíhuatl volcanoes; 19°07′N 98°46′W. The sanctuary of El Sacromonte, the most venerated spot in Mexico after the shrine of Guadalupe, stands on a hill above Amecameca. The town's history dates back to 1200. Municipio is part of the Zona Metropolitana de la Ciudad de México.

Amelia (uh-MEEL-yuh), county (□ 358 sq mi/138 sq km; 1990 pop. 8,787), central Va.; ⊙ Amelia Court House; 37°20′N 77°58′W. Bounded N and NE by Appomattox R. (forms L. Chesdin in E corner of co.), SE by small Namozinc Creek. Agr. (mainly tobacco; also corn, barley, wheat, hay, alfalfa, soybeans; cattle; dairying); timber. Feldspar, mica, pegmatite deposits. Formed 1735.

Amelia, uninc. town (1990 pop. 2,447), St. Mary parish, S La., 6 mi/9.7 km ESE of Morgan City, on Intracoastal Waterway; 29°40′N 91°07′W. L. Palourde to N. Mfg. (aggregates, shipbuilding, offshore oil structures, oilfield equipment); heliport.

Amelia, village (1990 pop. 1,837), Clermont co., SW Ohio, 17 mi/27 km ESE of Cincinnati; 39°01′N 84°13′W. Mfg. (furniture).

Amelia Court House, uninc. town (1990 pop. 770); ⊙ Amelia co., central Va., 32 mi/51 km WSW of Richmond. Agr. (tobacco, grain, soybeans; cattle, dairying); mfg. (lumber, loose-leaf binders, furniture, clothing, concrete, wooden pallets); timber. Sailor's Creek Battlefield Historic Park to W. Also called Amelia.

Amelia Island (uh-MEEL-yuh), Nassau co., extreme NE Fla., one of the Sea Isls. in Atlantic Ocean, separated from the mainland by salt marshes (bridged by road and RR); extends 13.5 mi/21.7 km S from mouth of St. Marys R. and is c.2 mi/3.2 km wide; 30°40′N 81°27′W. Fernandina Beach resort, Fort Clinch State Park, and a lighthouse are located in the N part of isl.

Amenia 1 village (□ 2 sq mi/5.2 sq km; 1990 pop. 1,057), Dutchess co., SE N.Y., near Conn. border, 20 mi/32 km NE of Poughkeepsie; 41°51′N 73°32′W. Dairying area. Thomas L. Harris had his Brotherhood of the New Life sect here, 1863–1867. **2** (ah-MEN-ee-uh), village (1990 pop. 82), Cass co., E N.Dak., 8 mi/12.9 km N of Casselton, on Rush R.; 47°00′N 97°13′W. RR junction to N. Grain elevator.

América Libre (ah-MAI-ree-kah LEE-brai), sugar-mill village, Santiago de Cuba prov., E Cuba, 35 mi/56 km NW of Santiago de Cuba, near Maffo and Contramestre; 20°18′N 76°14′W.

American Canyon, city (1990 pop. 7706), Napa co., W Calif., residential suburb 4 mi/6.4 km N of Vallejo, on Amer. Canyon Creek, E of Napa R.; 38°10′N 122°16′W. Napa Co. Airport to N.

American Falls, city (1990 pop. 3,757); ⊙ Power co., SE Idaho, on Snake R., at S end of Amer. Falls Reservoir, 21 mi/34 km WSW of Pocatello; 42°47′N 112°51′W. Elev. 4,404 ft/1,342 m. Wheat-shipping center for irrigated agr. area (wheat, potatoes; cattle, sheep, poultry); potato processing; mfg. (farm machinery, concrete). Amer. Falls Dam (unit in Minidoka irrigation project) and large hydroelectric plant are here, American Falls Reservoir to NE. City grew after arrival of RR (1892). Moved to present site after construction (1927) of dam, reservoir of which inundated former site. Amer. Falls (c.50 ft/15 m high; in Snake R.) are nearby. S extension of Fort Hall Indian Reservation to E. Massacre Rocks State Park to SW.

American Falls Reservoir, Power, Bingham, and Bannock cos., SE Idaho, on Snake R. at town of American Falls; 21 mi/34 km long, max. width 9 mi/14.5 km; 42°47′N 112°51′W. Max. capacity 1.7 million acre-ft. Formed by Amer. Falls Dam (89 ft/27 m. high, 5,227 ft/1,593 m long), built (1927) as unit in Minidoka Project for power generation. Town relocated to higher ground with construction of dam. Bounded NE by Fort Hall Indian Reservation.

American Fork, city (1990 pop. 15,696), Utah co., N central Utah, just N of Utah L. (on Amer. Fork R.), 12 mi/19 km NNW of Provo and 28 mi/45 km SSE of Salt L. City; 40°22′N 111°47′W. Elev. 4,566 ft/1,392 m. Resort; mfg. (small arms and ammunition, software, wood prods., dairy prods., foods, chemicals); poultry. Location of Mormon Temple. Served by Provo R. irrigation project. Settled 1850, inc. 1853. Timpanogos Cave Natl. Monument in NE.

American River, c.30 mi/48 km long, formed in N central Calif., by joining of North Fork and South Fork Amer. rivers at Folsom L. reservoir, 20 mi/32 km NE

of Sacramento; flows SW through suburban Sacramento, enters Sacramento R. N of downtown Sacramento. North Fork Amer. R. (c.85 mi/137 km long) rises in E Placer co. in Sierra Nevada, near Squaw Peak, 9 mi/14.5 km WNW of Tahoe City, in Tahoe Natl. Forest; flows W, then SW, passes SE of Colfax and through North Fork Reservoir, receives Middle Fork from E 4 mi/6.4 km below dam, then continues past Auburn to Folsom L. reservoir. South Fork Amer. R. (c. 90 mi/145 km long) rises 10 mi/16 km SE of South L. Tahoe in E El Dorado co., in Sierra Nevada E of Pyramid Peak, in El Dorado Natl. Forest; flows W, receives Silver Creek from NE, flows past Coloma (Marshall Gold Discovery State Historical Park is here), turns SW and receives Weber Creek from E before re-entering Folsom L. reservoir. Middle Fork Amer. R. (c.65 mi/105 km) rises in E Placer co., in Sierra Nevada, 8 mi/12.9 km W of Tahoe City at Squaw Peak, about 1 mi/1.6 km S of source of North Fork Amer.; flows generally WSW through French Meadows Reservoir, receives Rubicon R. from SE, then continues, forming Placer-El Dorado co. line, to North Fork Amer. R. 3 mi/4.8 km NE of Auburn. The discovery of gold at Sutter's Mill along the river in 1848 led to the Calif. gold rush of 1849 and played an important part in U.S. history.

Americus, city (1990 pop. 16,512), seat of Sumter co., SW Ga.; inc. 1855; 32°04′N 84°14′W. Mfg. (polyurethane foam, furniture, fertilizer, clothing and fabrics, food, consumer prods., construction materials, and automotive trim); agr. includes a livestock market, crops (peanuts, corn, cotton), and minerals (kaolin and bauxite); 32°04′N 84°13′W. Charles Lindbergh made his first solo flight from Souther Field there. Georgia Southwestern Col. is in Americus. Nearby is Andersonville, as well as Plains, the home of Jimmy Carter.

Americus, village (1990 pop. 981), Lyon co., E central Kansas, near Neosho R., 8 mi/12.9 km NW of Emporia; 38°30′N 96°15′W. In cattle and grain region.

Amery, town (1990 pop. 2,657), Polk co., NW Wis., on Apple R., 30 mi/48 km NE of Hudson, in lake-resort area; 45°17′N 92°21′W. Dairy prods., poultry; mfg. (consumer goods, prepared food, stained glass, computer terminals, electronic assembly); grain elevators. Numerous small lakes in area. Settled 1884, inc. 1919.

Amery, Mount (AI-muh-ree) (10,940 ft/3,335 m), SW Alta., Canada, near B.C. border, in Rocky Mts., in Banff Natl. Park, 75 mi/121 km SE of Jasper; 52°02′N 116°59′W.

Ames, city (1990 pop. 47,198), Story co., central Iowa, on the Skunk R., 27 mi/43 km N of Des Moines; 42°01′N 93°37′W. Mfg. (electronic equip., water-analysis and water-treatment equip., motor vehicles, construction materials, machinery, printing). RR junction. Iowa State Univ. is located in Ames and contributes significantly to the economy. The Natl. Animal Disease Laboratory and the Iowa State Center, a large cultural, educational, and athletic complex, are also in the city. State Forest nursery. Inc. 1870.

Ames, town (1990 pop. 989), Liberty co., SE Texas, 43 mi/69 km NE of Houston; 30°03′N 94°44′W. Agr. (rice, soybeans, sorghum; cattle); oil, natural gas.

Ames 1 village (1990 pop. 166), Montgomery co., E central N.Y., 22 mi/35 km WSW of Amsterdam, near Canajoharie Creek; 42°50′N 74°35′W. **2** village (1990 pop. 268), Major co., NW Okla., 20 mi/32 km WSW of Enid; 36°15′N 98°11′W. In grain and livestock area.

Amesbury (AIMZ-be-ree), town (1990 pop. 14,997), Essex co., NE Mass., on the Merrimack R.; 42°51′N 70°57′W. Mfg. (electronic equip., machinery, metal prods., furniture). John Greenleaf Whittier lived here most of his life, and his house is preserved. Josiah Bartlett b. here. Inc. 1668.

Amesville, village (1990 pop. 250), Athens co., SE Ohio, 9 mi/14 km ENE of Athens, in livestock area; 39°25′N 81°59′W.

Amherst, county (□ 478 sq mi/185 sq km; 1990 pop. 28,578), W central Va.; ⊙ Amherst; 37°36′N 79°08′W. Mainly in the Piedmont region; rises NW to the Blue Ridge, here traversed by Blue Ridge Parkway and Appalachian Trail (both natl. park units), bounded SW, S, and SE by James R. Part of George Washington Natl. Forest in NW. Mfg. at Amherst; chiefly agr. (corn, hay, apples, peaches; cattle). Titanium ore deposits. Formed 1761.

Amherst, city (1990 pop. 10,332), Lorain co., N Ohio, 5 mi/8 km SW of Lorain, near L. Erie; 41°25′N 82°14′W. Settled c.1810.

Amherst, town (1991 pop. 9,742), N central N.S., Canada. Diverse light industries; service center for the surrounding agr. region. Salt beds nearby. Sir Charles Tupper, the Can. statesman, b. here. Across the border in N.B. is Fort Beausejour Natl. Historic Park.

Amherst 1 (AM-huhrst), town (1990 pop. 226), Hancock co., S Maine, 20 mi/32 km N of Ellsworth. **2** town (1990 pop. 35,228), Hampshire co., central Mass., in a fertile farm area; 42°22′N 72°31′W. Named for Lord Jeffrey Amherst, seat of the Univ. of Mass., Hampshire Col., and Amherst Col. Emily Dickinson b. here and lived here all her life. Other well-known individuals include: Helen Hunt Jackson (also b. here), Ray Stannard Baker, Eugene Field, Robert Frost, and Noah Webster all lived here. Inc. 1759. Includes town of North Amherst (1990 pop. 6239). **3** town (1990 pop. 9,068), Hillsborough co., S N.H., 12 mi/19 km SW of Manchester and 2 mi/3.2 km NE of Milford; 42°52′N 71°35′W. Drained by Beaver and Joe English brooks. Agr. (pumpkins, fruit, vegetables, nursery crops); livestock, poultry; dairying. Mfg. (sheet-metal fabrication, medical instruments, science education equip., fabrics, plastics molding, electronics). Horace Greeley b. here. Settled c.1733, inc. 1760. **4** town (1990 pop. 1,060), ⊙ Amherst co., central Va., in Blue Ridge foothills, 13 mi/21 km NNE of Lynchburg; 37°35′N 79°02′W. Agr. (fruit, tobacco, corn; cattle); mfg. (printing and publishing, lumber, heating and air-conditioning equip., apparel). Sweet Briar Col. to SW. George Washington Natl. Forest, Appalachian Trail to NW. **5** town (1990 pop. 792), Portage co., central Wis., on Waupeca R., 14 mi/23 km ESE of Stevens Point; 44°27′N 89°16′W. Trade center in dairy, timber, and farm area (poultry, truck). Standing Rock Ski Area to W.

Amherst 1 village (1990 pop. 231), Buffalo co., S central Nebr., 15 mi/24 km NW of Kearney; 40°50′N 99°16′W. **2** village (1990 pop. 742), Lamb co., NW Texas, on the Llano Estacado, c.45 mi/72 km NW of Lubbock; 34°00′N 102°24′W. Waterfowl hunting; fishing in nearby lakes. Muleshoe Wildlife Refuge to W.

Amherst, , suburb of Buffalo (□ 53 sq mi/137 sq km; 1990 pop. 45,800), Erie co., W N.Y., 8 mi/12.9 km NE of city center; 43°00′N 78°45′W. Mfg. (environmental pollution controls, sheet metal, plastic molding, industrial rubber supplies). Seat of Daemon College and State Univ. of N.Y. Graduate Center at Buffalo.

Amherst, Canada: see HAVRE AUBERT.

Amherst Island 1 (□ 22.8 sq mi/59.1 sq km), SE Ont., Canada, one of the Thousand Isls., at head of L. Ontario, near entrance to the St. Lawrence, 7 mi/11 km WSW of Kingston; 11 mi/18 km long, 5 mi/8 km wide; 44°08′N 76°43′W. Popular resort. Granted to La Salle by Louis XIV; originally called Île de Tonti. **2** island (10 mi/16 km long, 4 mi/6 km wide), in Gulf of St. Lawrence, E Que., Canada, southernmost of the Magdalen Isls., 50 mi/80 km N of Prince Edward Isl. and 5 mi/8 km S of Grindstone Isl.; 47°13′–47°17′N 60°46′–62°02′W. Havre Aubert (E) is chief town. Fisheries.

Amherst Junction, village (1990 pop. 269), Portage co., central Wis., 13 mi/21 km ESE of Stevens Point and 2 mi/3.2 km NW of Amherst; 44°28′N 89°19′W. RR junction. Standing Rock Ski Area to SW.

Amherstburg, town (1991 pop. 8,921), S Ont., on the Detroit R. It is the site of Fort Malden Natl. Historic Park. Fort Malden was built (1797–1799) to replace the post lost when Detroit was ceded to the U.S.

Amherstdale, uninc. town (1990 pop. 1,200), Logan co., SW W.Va., 11 mi/18 km ESE of Logan. RR junction. Coal mining.

Amicalola Falls (am-uh-kuh-LO-luh), in the Blue Ridge, Dawson co., N Ga., 15 mi/24 km W of Dahlonega, in Amicalola Falls State Park. Highest falls (729 ft/222 m) in the state, formed by 7 cascades of a mtn. stream; 34°33′N 84°14′W.

Amidon (AM-i-duhn), village (1990 pop. 24), ⊙ Slope co., SW N.Dak., 37 mi/60 km SW of Dickinson; 46°28′N 103°19′W. Lignite mine nearby. Highest point in N.Dak., White Butte (3,506 ft/1,069 m) to S. Burning Coal Vein and Columnar Cedars to NW, near Deep Creek. Little Mo. Natl. Grassland to W.

Amiktok Island (A-mik-tahk) 2 mi/3 km long, 1 mi/2 km wide, NE Lab., Canada, in Seven Islands Bay; 59°25′N 63°42′W. Just NE is Avigalik or Whale Isl.

Amish, village, Johnson co., E Iowa, 16 mi/26 km SW of Iowa City. Amish settlement.

Amisk Lake (□ 111 sq mi/287 sq km), NE Sask., Canada, on Man. border, 11 mi/18 km SW of Flin Flon; 23 mi/37 km long, 12 mi/19 km wide; 54°35′N 102°15′W. Contains Missi Isl. (7 mi/11 km long, 6 mi/10 km wide).

Amistad National Recreation Area (□ 90 sq mi/233 sq km), Val Verde co., S Texas. U.S. part of Internatl. Amistad Reservoir, on the Rio Grande (Mex. border), 5 mi/8 km NW of Del Rio. Boating, fishing, water sports. Mex. govt. has set aside a smaller recreational area on its side of the border. Authorized 1965.

Amite (uh-MIT), county (□ 731 sq mi/1,893 sq km; 1990 pop. 13,328), SW Miss.; ⊙ Liberty; 31°10′N 90°47′W. Borders S on state of La.; bounded in NW by Homochitto R.; drained by Tangipahoa and Tickfaw rivers, East and West forks Amite R. (join just S of state line). Agr. (cotton, corn; cattle, catfish; dairying; timber). Includes part of Homochitto Natl. Forest in NW. Formed 1809.

Amite (ai-MEET), town (1994 pop. 4,640), ⊙ Tangipahoa parish, SE La., 45 mi/72 km NE of Baton Rouge and on Tangipahoa R.; 30°44′N 90°31′W. Ships squash, jalapeño peppers, sweet potatoes, fruit, strawberries; dairy prods.; mfg. (lumber, signs), publishing and printing, oyster processing. Sandy Hollow State Wildlife Area to NE. Amite R. Diversion Canal. On the Delisle Map of 1718. Settled 1836, inc. 1861.

Amite River (uh-MIT), c.100 mi/161 km long, in SW Miss. and SE La., formed by joining of West and East forks, just S of La.-Miss. state line; flows S and E, past Denham Springs, La. (E of Baton Rouge), to L. Maurepas; navigable for c.37 mi/60 km of lower course, subject to frequent flooding. Petite Amite R. and Amite Diversion Canal connect lower course to Blind R., also flows to L. Maurepas. West Fork rises in N Atmico co., Mauritius Miss., flows S c.35 mi/56 km. East Fork rises in SW Lincoln co., Miss., flows SSW c.45 mi/72 km.

Amity 1 town (1990 pop. 99), De Kalb co., NW Mo., 5 mi/8 km SSW of Maysville; 39°52′N 94°25′W. **2** town (1990 pop. 1,175), Yamhill co., NW Oregon, 7 mi/11.3 km S of McMinnville; 45°07′N 123°12′W. Agr. area (berries, vegetables, grains; poultry, cattle, sheep, hogs); dairy prods. Wine production. Erratic Rock Wayside State Park to W; Maud Williamson State Park to E; Baskett Slough Natl. Wildlife Refuge to W.

Amity, village (1990 pop. 526), Clark co., S central Ark., 24 mi/39 km NW of Arkadelphia, near Caddo R.; 34°16′N 93°27′W.

Amity Gardens (A-mi-tee), uninc. town (1990 pop. 2,714), Berks co., SE central Pa., residential community 5 mi/8 km W of Pottstown on Schuylkill R.; 40°16′N 75°44′W.

Amityville, residential village (□ 2 sq mi/5.2 sq km; 1990 pop. 9,286), Suffolk co., SE N.Y., on S shore of W L.I., 9 mi/14.5 km E of Freeport; 40°40′N 73°25′W. Largely Afr.-Amer. community. Mfg. (aircraft and aerospace parts, electronic and computer equip., fiber optical systems, furniture, machinery, food service equip.). Settled 1780, inc. 1894.

Amixtlán (ah-misht-LAHN), town (1990 pop. 2,431), Puebla state, central Mexico, in SE foothills of Sierra Madre Oriental, 18 mi/29 km SE of Huauchinango; 20°10′N 97°47′W. Sugar, coffee, fruit.

Amlia Island (AM-lee-uh), Andreanof Isls., Aleutian Isls., SW Alaska, just E of Atka Isl.; 46 mi/74 km long, 3 mi/4.8 km—9 mi/14.5 km wide; 52°05′N 173°30′W. Rises to 2,020 ft/616 m.

Ammon, town (1990 pop. 5,002), Bonneville co., SE Idaho, 4 mi/6.4 km SE of Idaho Falls; 43°29′N 111°58′W. Elev. 4,710 ft/1,436 m. RR spur terminus; agr. (potatoes, grain, alfalfa); livestock (cattle, sheep); dairying; furniture mfg.

Ammonoosuc River (am-muh-NOO-sik) or **Lower Ammonoosuc River**, c.55 mi/89 km long, NW N.H.; rises in White Mts. at Mt. Washington in S Coos co.; flows generally W past Littleton, then SW past Lisbon to the Conn. R. at Woodsville. Wild Ammonoosuc R. rises in Kinsman Notch in N central Grafton co.; flows c.15 mi/24 km NW to the Ammonoosuc R. at Bath.

Amnicon River (AM-ni-kahn), c.30 mi/48 km long, Douglas co., extreme NW Wis.; rises in Bear L. c.23 mi/37 km S of Superior; flows generally NE, through Amnicon Falls State Park, to L. Superior 11 mi/18 km E of Superior. Waterfalls (highest: 35 ft/11 m) in park.

Amo, town (1990 pop. 380), Hendricks co., central Ind., on Mill Creek, 6 mi/9.7 km SW of Danville; 39°41′N 86°37′W. In agr. area.

Amole Peak, Ariz.: see TUCSON MOUNTAINS.

Amoles, Mexico: see PINAL DE AMOLES.

Amoret (a-mo-RET), town (1990 pop. 212), Bates co., W Mo., near Marais des Cygnes R., 14 mi/23 km W of Butler; 38°15′N 94°35′W.

Amorita (am-or-EET-uh), village (1990 pop. 56), Alfalfa co., N Okla., 22 mi/35 km ENE of Alva, near Kansas line; 36°55′N 98°17′W.

Amory (AIM-uh-ree), town (1990 pop. 7,093), Monroe co., NE Miss., 35 mi/56 km N of Columbus, near Tombigbee R.; 33°59′N 88°28′W. Trade and shipping center for agr. (cotton, corn, soybeans, wheat; dairying); timber; gas wells; mfg. (bldg. materials, transportation equip., metal and plastic prods., furniture, apparel); printing. Lock A, on Tennessee-Tombigbee Waterway is here. Amory Regional Mus. Aberdeen L. reservoir to SW. Founded 1887.

Amos (AI-muhs), town (1991 pop. 13,783), ⊙ Abitibi co., W Que., Canada, 50 mi/80 km ENE of Rouyn. Mining center (gold, copper, molybdenum, zinc, lead); lumbering. (wood prods., furniture). Inc. 1914.

Amoskeag Falls, N.H.: see MANCHESTER.

Amour Point, cape on Strait of Belle Isle, SE Lab., Canada, on NE side of entrance of Forteau Bay; 51°27′N 56°51′W. Lighthouse.

Amozoc, Mexico: see AMOZOC DE MOTA.

Amozoc de Mota (ah-mo-SOK dai MO-tah), town (1990 pop. 27,389), ⊙ Amozoc township, Puebla state, central Mexico, on central plateau, 10 mi/16 km E of Puebla city on Mexico Hwy 150; 19°02′N 98°2′W. Elev. 7,648 ft/2,331 m. RR junction. Sheep-grazing center; noted for woolen goods (serapes), silver inlaid spurs, and ceramics. Many colonial churches.

Ampersand Lake, Essex co., NE N.Y., in the Adirondacks, 12 mi/19 km WSW of L. Placid village; 44°13′N 74°12′W. The lake is c.1.25 mi/2.01 km long. Just N is Ampersand Mt. (3,365 ft/1,026 m), a peak in the High Peaks sect. of the Adirondacks, 16 mi/26 km NW of Mt. Marcy.

Amphitheater, suburb and school dist., 4 mi/6.4 km N of downtown Tucson, in N part of city, and N of city limits of Rillito R., Pima co., SE Ariz.

Amqui (AM-kwee) or **Saint Benoît Joseph Labre** (sain buh-NWAH zho-ZEHF LAH bruh), village (1991 pop. 4,339), ⊙ Matapedia co., E Que., Canada, at base of Gaspé Peninsula, on Matapedia R., near SE end of L. Matapedia, 50 mi/80 km E of Rimouski. Lumbering; dairying.

Amsterdam, city (□ 6 sq mi/15.5 sq km; 1990 pop. 20,714), Montgomery co., E central N.Y., on the Mohawk R.; 42°56′N 74°11′W. Historically famous for mfg. of carpets; mfg. now includes machinery, apparel, leather goods, furniture, transportation equip., consumer goods. The area was settled in 1783 and was named Amsterdam for its many early settlers from the Neth. Nearby stands Fort Johnson, home of the Br. colonial leader Sir William Johnson. Inc. 1885.

Amsterdam, town (1990 pop. 237), Bates co., W Mo., 14 mi/23 km WNW of Butler; 38°21′N 94°35′W. Sorghum, hay, corn; cattle.

Amsterdam, village (1990 pop. 669), Jefferson co., E

Ohio, 17 mi/27 km WNW of Steubenville, and on small Yellow Creek, in agr. and coal mining area; 40°29′N 80°57′W. Settled 1830, inc. 1904.

Amston, Conn.: see HEBRON.

Amund Ringnes Island (□ 1,764), Sverdrup Isls., N Franklin Dist., N.W.T., Canada, in the Arctic Ocean; 77°53′–78°49′N 95°30′–98°55′W. Separated from Ellef Ringnes Isl. (W) by Hassel Sound, from Meighen Isl. (N) and Axel Heiberg Isl. (E) by Good Friday Gulf, and from Cornwall Isl. (S) by Hendriksen Strait. Isl. is 70 mi/113 km long, 20 mi/32 km–45 mi/72 km wide; surface rises to over 2,000 ft/610 m.

Amundsen Gulf (AH-moon-suhn), N.W.T., Canada, arm (250 mi/402 km long) of the Arctic Ocean, opening off Beaufort Sea (W) bet. Mackenzie and Franklin dists; 70°N 120°W. Leading E is Dolphin and Union Strait (SE), which is continued E by Coronation Gulf, Dease Strait, and Queen Maud Gulf, eventually leading to Baffin Bay via several other straits. Separates Banks Isl. (N) and Mackenzie Dist. mainland (S), and washes W shore of Victoria Isl. Amundsen Gulf is westernmost sect. of the NW Passage through the Arctic Isls.; passage was first completed by Roald Amundsen's expedition, 1903–1906.

Ana María, Gulf of (AH-nah mah-REE-ah), Caribbean inlet of E Cuba, 40 mi/64 km W of Camagüey. Shallow sea, fringed by reefs (Ana María keys) and bounded by marshy coastland; c.20 mi/32 km N-S; 21°24′N 78°49′W.

Anacapa Island, Ventura co., S Calif., in Santa Barbara Isls., Pacific Ocean, 15 mi/24 km SW of Oxnard and 5 mi/8 km E of San Pedro Point, E end of Santa Cruz Isl., in Channel Isls. Natl. Park. It is the largest and westernmost of a subgroup of small isls. in this part of the Channels.

Anacoco (AN-uh-ko-ko), town (1990 pop. 823), Vernon parish, W La., 7 mi/11 km NNW of Leesville; 31°16′N 93°20′W. Agr. and livestock (cattle); timber. Dairying; mfg. (lumber, RR ties). L. Vernon reservoir and Anacoco L. reservoir, both in Anacoco Prairie State Game and Fish Preserve, to S. Peason Ridge State Wildlife Area to NE.

Anaconda (a-nuh-KAHN-duh), city (1990 pop. 10,278), ⊙ Deer Lodge co., 20 mi/32 km WNW of Butte on Warm Springs Creek, SW Mont. Continental Divide passes E-W 9 mi/14.5 km to S; 46°04′N 113°05′W. Cattle, hay; tourism. RR terminus to W of city. Discovery Basin Sky Area to NW; Georgetown L. reservoir to W; Lost Creek State Park to N; parts of Deerlodge Natl. Forest to NW and SE; part of Beaverhead Natl. Forest to SW; Anaconda-Pintler Wilderness Area to SW. Montana State Fish Hatchery at Washoe Park on N side of town. Marcus Daly chose this place (1883), first named "Copperopolis," to build the smelter and reduction plant for the Anaconda Copper Mining Co. and in the 1890s tried unsuccessfully to make it the state capital. The city's copper smelter, which was one of the largest in the world, was closed in the 1970s as the copper industry declined. High smokestack (535 ft/163 m) is now landmark and state park (Anaconda Stack State Park to SE). Anaconda Historic Dist.; Copper Village Mus. and Arts Center. Inc. 1887.

Anaconda Range (a-nuh-KAHN-duh), in SW Mont., extends W and SW to Idaho line from about Lost Trail Pass (SW) to Anaconda (NE) of Continental Divide in Rocky Mts. Continental Divide runs through center of range. Highest point, Mt. Evans (10,635 ft/3,242 m). Covered by Bitterroot and Deerlodge Natl. Forests, including all of Anaconda-Pintler Wilderness Area, NE branch of Bitterroot Range.

Anacortes (an-ah-KOR-tes), city (1990 pop. 11,451), Skagit co., NW Wash., on Fidalgo Isl. (bridged to mainland 7 mi/11 km SE), 20 mi/32 km SSW of Bellingham; 48°29′N 122°38′W. RR terminus. Port of entry. Ferry to Sydney, B.C., Canada; also ferries to San Juan Isl. (terminal 5 mi/8 km W); ferry to Huemes Isl., to N. Mfg. (printing and publishing, transportation equip., chemicals, food, petroleum refining). Oysters, vegetables, berries. On Guenes Channel, Rosario Strait to W. Anacortes Mus. here. Swinomish Indian Reservation to

SE. Saddlebag Isl. State Park (marina) to NE. Settled c.1860.

Anacostia, residential sect. encompassing part of SE Wash., D.C., across the Anacostia R. from downtown Washington, D.C.; 38°52′N 76°59′W. It was the 1st suburb of the city and contains Cedar Hill, the Victorian-era home of the abolitionist Frederick Douglass, as well as the Smithsonian Institution's Anacostia Mus., focusing on Afri.-Amer. history and culture.

Anacostia River (an-uh-CAHS-tee-uh), c.12 mi/19 km long, in central Md. and Wash., D.C., is formed by Sligo Creek, flowing into Northeast Branch, which converge at Hyattsville, Md. It flows SW, past Bladensburg, Cottage City, and Colmar Manor, Md., and through S part of Wash., D.C., to the Potomac. Part of Wash. harbor occupies lower part. A series of parks, including the Natl. Arboretum, Anacostia River Park, and Kenilworth Aquatic Gardens form part of the E bank within the D.C. boundaries. The river also borders Kingman L. and flows near Robert F. Kennedy (RFK) Stadium in Wash., D.C. The Whitney Young and Sousa bridges cross the river, and in Wash., D.C., a naval air station, a naval receiving station, and a naval yard are named after it. Before silting closed the port, Bladensburg was an important colonial shipping center. Once neglected and polluted, the river is now a focus of clean-up efforts.

Anadarko (an-uh-DAHR-ko), town (1990 pop. 6,586), ⊙ Caddo co., W central Okla., c.45/72 km mi. WSW of Okla. City, and on Washita R.; 35°04′N 98°14′W. Elev. 1,190 ft/363 m. Trade and processing center for rich agr. region (cotton, grain, alfalfa, livestock, poultry); mfg. (carpets, food). Apache, Delaware, and Wichita tribal hqs., and Natl. Hall of Fame for Famous Amer. Indians here. Seat of U.S. Riverside Indian School. Holds annual Amer. Indian Exposition. Indian City, U.S.A., tourist attraction, to S. Also regional center for Bureau of Indian Affairs Office. Founded 1901.

Anadarko Basin, W central Okla. including all parts of Caddo, Washita, Beckham, Roger Mills, Ellis, Woodward, Dewey, Blaine, Canadian, Custer, McCain, Garvin, Stephens, and Comanche cos. A subsurface basin just to the N of the Wichita Mtns. An area of significant oil and natural-gas reserves, up to 30,000ft/9,100 m deep.

Anaheim, city (1990 pop. 266,406), Orange co., S Calif., suburb 21 mi/34 km SE of downtown Los Angeles and 15 mi/24 km ENE of Long Beach; long NE annexation reaches Chino Hills; 33°51′N 117°52′W. Santa Ana reservoir drains E part of city, forms Prado Flood Control Basin (reservoir) to NE. Anaheim was founded by Germans in 1857 as an experiment in communal living. Lying in a former area of citrus fruit and walnut groves, the city is an important industrial center. RR junction. Mfg. (electronic equip., computer equip., transportation equip., plastic prods., prepared foods, fabricated metal prods., consumer goods, motor vehicles, molded rubber goods), metal fabrication. Anaheim is also one of the great tourist and convention centers in the U.S. World-famous tourist attractions include Disneyland (a gigantic amusement park and entertainment center; opened 1955) and the Anaheim Stadium (home of the Amer. League's Anaheim Angels baseball team and the Anaheim Convention Center); large Chino Hills State Park to NE. Inc. 1870.

Anaho Island, Nev.: see PYRAMID LAKE.

Anahola (AH-nah-HO-lah), town (1990 pop. 1,181), Kauai isl., Kauai co., Hawaii, 11 mi/18 km NNE of Lihue, ½ mi/⅕ km inland from Anahola Bay, E coast, at mouth of Anahola Stream; 22°08′N 159°19′W. Sugarcane; fish. Anahola Beach Park to N. Kealia and Moloaa forest reserves to NW.

Anáhuac (ah-NAH-wahk), city (1990 pop. 13,657) and township (1990 pop.), Nuevo León state, N Mexico, on Río Salado (irrigation area), 45 mi/72 km SW of Nuevo Laredo; 27°15′N 100°10′W. Cotton center, growing and ginning center.

Anahuac, town (1990 pop. 1,993), ⊙ Chambers co., SE Texas, on Trinity Bay (arm of Galveston Bay) at mouth of Trinity R., c.40 mi/64 km E of Houston; 29°45′N

94°40′W. Elev. 21 ft/6 m. Port, on channel connecting with Houston ship channel; fishing; tourist trade. Oil wells, agr. (rice, soybeans), cattle ranching in area. An important early port, it was the scene of clashes (1832, 1835) in which Anglo-Amer. settlers successfully opposed Mex. officials. Ruins of old Fort Anahuac (1830) are near. L. Anahuac to N; Anahuac Natl. Wildlife Refuge to SE. Inc. after 1940.

Anáhuac (ah-NAH-wahk) [Aztec = near the water], geographical term used variously in Mexico before the Span. Conquest. Today it commonly refers to that part of the central plateau of Mexico comprising the Pánuco and Lerma river systems and the lake basin of the Valley of Mexico.

Anaktuvuk Pass (a-nak-TOO-vuhk), village (1990 pop. 259), N Alaska, in pass of Brooks Range, near upper Anaktuvuk R.; 68°10′N 151°40′W. On major caribou migration route.

Anaktuvuk River (a-nak-TOO-vuhk), c.130 mi/209 km long, N Alaska; rises in N Brooks Range near 68°N 150°45′W; flows N to Colville R. at 69°31′N 151°30′W.

Anamoose, village (1990 pop. 277), McHenry co., N central N.Dak., 18 mi/29 km NW of Harvey; 47°52′N 100°14′W. Antelope L. to NE.

Anamosa, city (1990 pop. 5,100), ⊙ Jones co., E Iowa, on Wapsipinicon R., at mouth of Buffalo Creek, 21 mi/34 km ENE of Cedar Rapids; 42°06′N 91°16′W. Mfg. (apparel, bldg. materials, electronic equip.); agr. (packed poultry and eggs, dairy prods.). Limestone quarries nearby. Wapsipinicon State Park just S. Has state reformatory for men; mfg. at reformatory. Grant Wood b. near Anamosa. Extensive river and field flooding in 1993. First named Dartmouth, then Lexington; inc. 1856.

Añasco (ah-NYAHS-ko), town (1990 pop. 25,234), W P.R., near the coast, on Añasco R., 5 mi/8 km N of Mayagüez. Light mfg.; mangoes. Scene of last Indian rebellion (1511). Mayaguez airport is nearby.

Añasco River or **Río Grande de Añasco** (REE-o GRAN-deh deh ah-NYAS-koh), c.40 mi/64 km long, W P.R.; rises in the Cordillera Central W of Adjuntas; flows W to Mona Passage 4 mi/6.4 km NNW of Mayagüez. In its basin are new reservoirs and hydroelectric projects.

Anastasia Island (an-nah-STAI-zhuh), barrier beach in St. Johns co., NE Fla., on the Atlantic, sheltering Matanzas R. (W); 23 mi/23 km long, ½ mi/⅕ km–2.5 mi/4 km wide; N end connected with St. Augustine by bridge. Coquina quarries.

Anawalt (ahn-uh-WAHLT), village (1990 pop. 329), McDowell co., S W.Va., 11 mi/18 km SE of Welch; 37°19′N 81°26′W. Coal mining. Anawalt Wildlife Management Area to S.

Ancaster (ANG-kuhs-tuhr), residential town (1991 pop. 21,988), S Ont., Canada, 7 mi/11 km W of Hamilton; fruit growing, dairying.

Ancell (an-SEL), uninc. rural comunity, Scott co., SE Mo., near Mississippi R., 2 mi/3 km W of Scott City at Interstate 55 junction.

Ancho (AHN-cho), village, Lincoln co., central N.Mex., 22 mi/35 km NNE of Carrizozo. Trade center in cattle, sheep, alfalfa, grain. Jicarilla Mts. (elev. 6,127 ft/ 1,868 m) to SE; Gallinas Peak to N; both in sections of Lincoln Natl. Forest. Gran Quivira Unit, Salinas Natl. Monument, to NW.

Anchor Bay, Mich.: see SAINT CLAIR, LAKE.

Anchor Point, town, S Alaska, W Kenai Peninsula, on Cook Inlet, 12 mi/19 km NW of Homer, on Sterling Highway (Highway 1). Fishing. Anchor Point headland is at 59°46′N 151°52′W.

Anchorage (AIN-kuhr-uhj), city (1990 pop. 226,338), Anchorage census div., S central Alaska, a port at the head of Cook Inlet; 61°13′N 149°53′W. It is the largest city in the state, the administrative and commercial heart of S central and W Alaska; one of the nation's key defense centers, and a vital transportation hub. Glenn Highway connects the city to the Alaska Highway at Tok and Delta and the Parks Highway to Fairbanks. The internatl. airport is a regular stop on intercontinental and transpolar flights. The unified city and borough include two U.S. military bases, Fort Richardson and Elmendorf Air Force Base. Anchorage is also the hq. for the major oil and gas companies in Alaska. With oil discoveries in Cook Inlet in the late 1950's, and the discovery of massive petroleum and natural gas reserves in the PRUDHOE BAY region of N Alaska in 1968, the pop. has more than quadrupled. Tourism has also increased dramatically, due to improvements in transportation and the creation of numerous natl. parks. Anchorage was founded (1915) as construction hq. for the Alaska RR and grew as a RR town. The city was named for the anchorage at mouth of Ship Creek, the main port for construction materials and the engineering hq. for the RR. It also became a fishing center, a market and supply point for gold-mining regions to the N, and the metropolis for the farming of the Matanuska valley. World War II brought the establishment of the large military bases and the enormous growth of air and RR traffic. Its importance as a major refueling stop on the Great Circle Route has made it significant. The oil boom brought prosperity and growth in the 1970's and 1980's. The city suffered severe damage in the 1964 earthquake. Points of interest include Earthquake Park and several notable mus. A "Fur Rendezvous" winter carnival is held every Feb. in Anchorage. The city is the seat of Alaska Pacific Univ. Portage Glacier and L. Hood are nearby, and Mt. McKinley (Denali) is visible from the city. Anchorage Mus. of History and Art; Visual Arts Center. Historic Old Federal Building.; Ship Creek Salmon Viewing Platform; Potter Creek bird viewing area; Univ. of Alaska-Anchorage. Inc. 1920.

Anchorage, town (1990 pop. 2,082), Jefferson co., N Ky., residential suburb, 10 mi/16 km E of downtown Louisville; 38°16'N 85°32'W. RR junction. Mfg. (signs, crushed limestone). E.P. "Tom" Sawyer State Park to NW.

Anchorage, borough (□ 1,698 sq mi/4,398 sq km; 1990 pop. 226,338), S Alaska, coterminous with Anchorage city, bounded on W by Cook Inlet. Chugach State Park in center. Mfg. at Anchorage; agr. (vegetables, potatoes; dairying); tourism.

Anchorage Yacht Club, tourist complex, Union Isl., St. Vincent and the Grenadines, West Indies. Part of large tourism development project.

Anchorville, village (1990 pop. 3,202), St. Clair co., E Mich., on Anchor Bay of L. St. Clair, 12 mi/19 km NE of Mt. Clemens; 42°41'N 82°42'W. Mfg. of automation prods.

Anchovy, town (1991 pop. 3,633), St. James parish, NW Jamaica, on Jamaica RR, 3.5 mi/5.6 km S of Montego Bay; 18°24'N 77°56'W. Bananas, sugarcane.

Ancienne Lorette (ah-see-EHN lo-REHT), village, S central Que., Canada, on short Lorette R. (waterfalls), 7 mi/11 km W of Quebec. Shoe mfg.; agr., dairying; resort. Founded 1673 by Jesuits. Near by is Loretteville.

Ancient Oaks, uninc. town (1990 pop. 2,663), Lehigh co., E Pa., 7 mi/11.3 km SE of Allentown, on Little Lehigh Creek; 40°31'N 75°35'W. Agr. (grapes) and livestock; dairying. Lehigh Co. Velodrome (bicycle-racing circuit) to W; Clover Hill Winery to W; Trach Cellars Winery to NE.

Anclote Keys (ANK-klot), several small islands in Gulf of Mexico, W central Fla., opposite mouth of Anclote R., 6 mi/9.7 km WNW of Tarpon Springs; largest is 2.5 mi/4 km long. Natl. wildlife refuge.

Anclote River, c.17 mi/27 km long, W central Fla.; rises in SW Pasco co.; flows WSW past Tarpon Springs to Gulf of Mexico opposite Anclote Keys.

Anco (ANK-o), uninc. village (1990 pop. 360), Knott co., E Ky., in Cumberland foothills, 8 mi/12.9 km E of Hazard. RR terminus. Bituminous coal.

Andale, village (1990 pop. 566), Sedgwick co., S central Kansas, 18 mi/29 km WNW of Wichita; 37°47'N 97°37'W. In wheat region; feed, eggs. Cheney Reservoir and State Park to W.

Andalusia (an-duh-LOO-zhuh), city (1990 pop. 9,269), ⊙ Covington co., S Ala. In a farming and forestry area. Mfg. (food and meat prods., textiles, lumber, bldg. prods., and paper prods.). Lurleen B. Wallace State Jr. Col. Inc. 1844.

Andalusia 1 (an-duh-LOO-shah), town (1990 pop. 1,052), Rock Island co., NW Ill., on the Miss. R., 10 mi/16 km WSW of Rock Isl.; 41°26'N 90°43'W. Agr. (corn, soybeans, oats, cattle; dairying). Showstar ski area nearby. **2** (AN-duh-LOO-zuha), uninc. town (1990 pop. 3,400), Bucks co., SE Pa., suburb 11 mi/18 km NE of Philadelphia, on Delaware R. at mouth of Poquessing Creek; 40°04'N 74°58'W. Mfg.(book binding, fabricated metal prods., machinery). Meshaming State Park to E; airport to NW.

Anderson 1 county (□ 584 sq mi/1,513 sq km; 1990 pop. 7,803), E Kansas; ⊙ Garnett; 38°12'N 95°17'W. Gently rolling agr. area watered by Pottawatomie Creek. Cattle and grain raising, dairying, corn, soybeans, oats, wheat, sorghum. Formed 1855. **2** county (□ 204 sq mi/528 sq km; 1990 pop. 14,571), central Ky.; ⊙ Lawrenceburg, 38°00'N 84°58'W. Bounded E by Kentucky R., SW by Beech Fork; drained by Salt R. (enters upper end of Taylorsville L. reservoir in W end of co.). Gently rolling upland agr. area (burley tobacco; poultry, hogs, horses, cattle; hay, alfalfa, corn) in Bluegrass region. Mfg. at Lawrenceburg; stone quarrying. Beaver L. reservoir in center. Formed 1827. **3** county (□ 757 sq mi/1,961 sq km; 1990 pop. 145,196), NW S.C.; ⊙ Anderson; 34°31'N 82°38'W. Bounded SW by Tugaloo and Savannah rivers, NE by Saluda R.; drained by Seneca and Rocky rivers. Agr. (chickens, eggs, hogs, cattle; dairying; corn, wheat, oats, soybeans, sorghum, hay). Formed 1826. **4** county (□ 338; 1990 pop. 68,250), E Tenn.; ⊙ Clinton; 36°07'N 84°12'W. NW part is in the Cumberland, remainder of co. in ridge-traversed Great Appalachian Valley; drained by Clinch R. Includes Norris Lake (Norris Dam) and communities of Norris (a TVA center) and OAK RIDGE (center for nuclear research and atomic–materials production). Mineral-rich area with coal, clay, and oil and gas deposits. Lumbering, livestock raising, dairying, agr. (apples, tobacco, corn, hay). Mfg. at Clinton and Oak Ridge. Formed 1801. **5** county (□ 1,078 sq mi/2,792 sq km; 1990 pop. 48,024), E Texas; ⊙ PALESTINE; 31°48'N 95°39'W. Bounded W by Trinity R., E by Neches R. (L. Palestine formed by dam in NE corner). Transportation, processing center; partly wooded (extensive lumbering). Oil, natural gas. Diversified agr. (peaches, melons, vegetables, sorghum, grain, legumes), livestock area (cattle, hogs, poultry); forestry (Christmas trees). Hunting and fishing activities attract visitors. Rusk-Palestine and Texas State RR State Historical Park runs from Rusk (Cherokee co. to E) to Palestine. Formed 1846.

Anderson 1 city (1990 pop. 8,299), Shasta co., N Calif., near Sacramento R., 9 mi/14.5 km SSE of Redding; 40°27'N 122°17'W. Agr. (walnuts, olives, plums, prunes, grain, strawberries; cattle; dairy prods.); mfg. (paper prods., machinery); lumber. **2** city (1990 pop. 59,459), ⊙ Madison co., E central Ind., on the White R.; 40°05'N 85°41'W. It is a mfg. center in a fertile farm area; prods. include automotive parts, fabricated metal prods., furniture, light consumer goods, paper prods., electronic equip., and dairy prods. The city's industrial growth began with the discovery of natural gas in 1887. The automotive industry was est. in 1901. Anderson Col. is there. The city has a fine-arts center and a symphony orchestra. Nearby Mounds State Park has numerous prehistoric mounds. The Moravians operated a Native Amer. mission nearby (1801–1806). Inc. 1838. **3** city (1990 pop. 1,432), McDonald co., extreme SW Mo., in the Ozarks, on branch of Elk R., 16 mi/26 km S of Neosho; 36°38'N 94°27'W. Agr. (vegetables, apples, strawberries, grapes; livestock); timber; mfg. (mobile homes, livestock feed). **4** city (1990 pop. 26,184), ⊙ Anderson co., NW S.C.; 34°31'N 82°39'W. Commercial center for farming and livestock. Mfg. (electronic equip., machinery, paper prods., plastic prods., apparel, commercial printing, textiles, tool and die, crushed stone, prepared foods). Anderson Co. Col. is here. Settled in the 17th cent., inc. 1828.

Anderson 1 village (1990 pop 628), central Alaska, 13 mi/21 km SW of Nenana, on Nenana R.; 64°18'N 149°09'W. Terminus of spur road from George Parks Highway (Rt. 3). Denali Natl. Park and Preserve to S. Service center for Clear Air Force Base, ballastic missile early warning station, 6 mi/9.7 km SE. **2** uninc. village, ⊙ Grimes co., E central Texas, 9 mi/14.5 km NE of Navasota; 30°29'N 95°59'W. Elev. 368 ft/112 m. Trade, shipping point in agr. (dairying, cattle, fruit, honey, corn), timber area; mfg. (sheet-metal fabrication). Fanthorp Inn State Historic Site is here, log structure (1834) where many Texas notables are purported to have stayed. Gibbons Creek L. reservoir to N; Sam Houston Natl. Forest to E.

Anderson Lake (□ 52 sq mi/135 sq km), S central B.C., Canada, in Coast Mts., 16 mi/26 km W of Lillooet; 16 mi/26 km long, 1 mi/2 km–2 mi/3 km wide. Drains NE into Fraser R. through Seton L.

Anderson Ranch Reservoir, Elmore co., SW Idaho, on South Fork of Boise R., in Boise Natl. Forest, 40 mi/64 km SE of Boise; 18 mi/29 km long; 43°20'N 115°27'W. Formed by Anderson Ranch Dam (earth fill; 456 ft/139 m high, 1,350 ft/411 m long), built (1950) for power generation, irrigation, and flood control.

Anderson River, c.465 mi/750 km long, N.W.T., Canada; rising in several lakes in NE Inuvik Region; flows N and W before receiving the Carnwath R. and continues N to Liverpool Bay, an arm of the Arctic Ocean. The village of Stanton is at its mouth.

Anderson River, c.36 mi/58 km long, S Ind.; rises in W Crawford co.; flows SSW through the SE corner of Dubois co. and thence S along the boundary bet. Perry and Spencer cos. to join the Ohio R. near Troy.

Anderson Springs, Calif.: see LAKE, co.

Anderson Valley, Calif.: see BOONVILLE.

Andersonville, village, (1990 pop. 277), SW Ga., near Americus; 32°12'N 84°09'W. Mfg. (minerals, refractory prods.). Nearby is Andersonville Prison Historic Site (authorized 1970). During the Civil War, tens of thousands of Union soliders were confined in Andersonville, under conditions so bad that more than 12,000 soldiers died. Andersonville Natl. Cemetery contains more than 13,000 soldiers' graves. Inc. 1881.

Andes, village (□ 1 sq mi/2.6 sq km; 1990 pop. 292), Delaware co., S N.Y., 9 mi/14.5 km NNE of Pepacton reservoir, 22 mi/35 km SE of Oneonta; 42°11'N 74°46'W. In a resort area of the Catskills.

Andes, Lake, Charles Mix co., S S.Dak.; 14 mi/23 km long, c.2 mi/3.2 km wide. L. Andes Natl. Waterfowl Refuge and state fish hatchery. City of L. Andes on W end.

Andover, municipal borough (1991 pop. 1,094), N.B., Canada, on St. John R. (bridge), opposite mouth of Tobique R., 18 mi/29 km ENE of Presque Isle, Maine, in potato region; angling center. Formerly also called Tobique.

Andover, city (1990 pop. 15,216), Anoka co., E Minn., suburb 18 mi/29 km N of downtown Minneapolis, near Miss. R.; 45°15'N 93°19'W. Bounded by Rum R. on W. Mfg. (furniture, transportation equip., Christmas ornaments); agr. to N (alfalfa, rye). Carlos Avery Wildlife Area to E; part of Bunker Hills Park Reserve in SE.

Andover 1 (AND-o-vuhr), town (1990 pop. 2,540), Tolland co., E central Conn., on Hop R., 16 mi/26 km E of Hartford; 41°43'N 72°22'W. In agr. area. Light wood and machine industries. Small Andover L. is resort. Settled 1718, inc. 1848. **2** town (1990 pop. 99), Clinton co., E Iowa, 10 mi/16 km N of Clinton; 41°58'N 90°15'W. Limestone quarry nearby. **3** town (1990 pop. 4,047), Butler co., S central Kansas, suburb 11 mi/18 km ENE of Wichita; 37°41'N 97°08'W. Agr. area (cattle, corn, wheat). Oil and natural gas. Mfg. (refrigeration equip., paints). **4** town (1990 pop. 953), Oxford co., W Maine, 31 mi/50 km NNW of South Paris; 44°37'N 70°45'W. In resort area. Wood prods. **5** town (1990 pop. 29,151), Essex co., NE Mass; 42°39'N 71°10'W. Chiefly a textile producer in the 19th cent., Andover now makes toiletries, electronic equip., chemicals, medical instruments, computer equip., rubber prods., and shoes. Two preparatory schools (Phillips Andover Academy, 1778, for boys; and Abbot Academy, 1829, for girls) in Andover merged in 1973. The Addison Gallery of Amer. Art and the Robert S. Peabody Foundation archaeological mus. are on the Phillips Andover campus. In 1832, Samuel Francis Smith wrote the words for "America" in Andover. Harriet Beecher Stowe lived in the town and is buried here. Includes Shawsheen Village. Site of Harol Parkea State Forest. Inc. 1646. **6** town (1990 pop. 1,883), Merrimack co., S central N.H., 21 mi/34 km NW of Concord; 43°27′N 71°47′W. Drained by Blackwater R. Corn, apples, vegetables, nursery crops; cattle. Mfg. (machining, fencing, gas turbines). East Andover village, on Highland L., is resort. Bradley L. in S; Ragged Mt. (2,220 ft/677 m) on N boundary; Ragged Mt. Ski Area in NW; 2 covered bridges in W. Settled 1761, inc. 1779. **7** town (1990 pop. 373), Windsor co., S central Vt., 20 mi/32 km SW of Windsor, in Green Mts.; 43°16′N 72°43′W. Includes village of Simonsville.

Andover, township (1990 pop. 5,438), Sussex co., NW N.J., 5 mi/8 km S of Newton; 41°01′N 74°43′W. Ore deposit nearby furnished iron in Revolution.

Andover 1 village (1990 pop. 579), Henry co., NW Ill., 5 mi/8 km W of Cambridge; 41°17′N 90°17′W. In agr. area (corn, soybeans, oats; cattle, hogs; dairying). **2** village (□ 1 sq mi/2.6 sq km; 1990 pop. 1,125), Allegany co., W N.Y., 14 mi/23 km SSW of Hornell; 42°09′N 77°47′W. Oil wells; dairy prods.; field corn, hay. Inc. 1892. **3** village (1990 pop. 1,216), Ashtabula co., extreme NE Ohio, 21 mi/34 km SSE of Ashtabula, near Pa. state line, in agr. area; 41°37′N 80°35′W. Pymatuning Reservoir (recreation) is just E. **4** village (1990 pop. 106), Day co., NE S.Dak., 30 mi/48 km E of Aberdeen. Market town for rich farming region.

Andover Lake, Conn.: see HOP RIVER.

Andrade (ahn-DRAH-dai), village, Imperial co., S Calif., in Yuma Indian Reservation, near Colorado R., 6 mi/9.7 km W of Yuma, Ariz.; port of entry on Mexico border (Baja Calif. Norte state); on All-Amer. Canal.

Andreanof Islands (AN-dree-yah-nawf), group of Aleutian Isls., SW Alaska, bet. Pacific (S) and Bering Sea (N), extending c.275 mi/443 km bet. Rat Isls. (W) and Fox Isls. (E); near 52°N 172°57′–179°09′W. Largest isls. are Amlia, Atka, Adak, Kanaga, and Tanaga. Treeless and windswept isls. are usually fogbound. Named for Rus. navigator who explored them, 1760–1764. Isls. were site of several important U.S. bases during World War II; bases at Adak were enlarged and made permanent after 1943, but closed in 1995.

Andréville, Canada: see SAINT ANDRÉ DE KAMOURASKA.

Andrew, county (□ 430 sq mi/1114 sq km; 1990 pop. 14,632), NW Mo.; ⊙ Savannah; 39°59′N 94°47′W. Bounded W by Nodaway R., SW by the Missouri. Drained by One Hundred and Two R. and Platte R. Agr. region (corn, wheat; cattle, hogs); mfg. at Savannah. Urban growth in S from St. Joseph. Formed 1841.

Andrew, town (1990 pop. 319), Jackson co., E Iowa, 7 mi/11.3 km NE of Maquoketa; 42°08′N 90°35′W. In agr. area.

Andrew, village (1991 pop. 520), central Alta., Canada, near Whiteford L. (4 mi/6 km long), 50 mi/80 km ENE of Edmonton; 53°53′N 112°20′W. Mixed farming, dairying.

Andrew Johnson Historic Site, NE Tenn., authorized 1935, grave of Andrew Johnson; includes Andrew Johnson Natl. Cemetery. See GREENEVILLE, Tenn.

Andrews, county (□ 1,501 sq mi/3,888 sq km; 1990 pop. 14,338), W Texas; ⊙ Andrews; 32°17′N 102°38′W. On S Llano Estacado, bounded W by N.Mex. line; elev. 3,000 ft/914 m–5,000 ft/1,524 m. Drained in N by Seminole Draw and Monument Draw. Cattle ranching region; one of state's leading oil-producing cos.; also natural gas, minerals; some irrigated agr. (cotton, corn, sorghum, hay; cattle). Includes Shafter L., other shallow lakes (fishing); hunting. Formed 1876.

Andrews, city (1990 pop. 10,678), ⊙ Andrews co., W Texas, on S Llano Estacado, 33 mi/53 km NNW of Odessa; 32°19′N 102°32′W. Elev. 3,190 ft/972 m. Shipping, trading point for rich oil and natural gas; cattle ranching region with some agr. (corn, cotton, grain sorghum, hay). Shafter L. (fishing) is 7 mi/11.3 km NW.

Andrews 1 town (1990 pop. 1,118), Huntington co., NE central Ind., near Wabash R., 6 mi/9.7 km WSW of Huntington; 40°52′N 85°36′W. In agr. area. Sand and gravel, automotive parts, bronze castings. **2** town (1990 pop. 2,551), Cherokee co., extreme W N.C., 14 mi/23 km NE of Murphy, in Nantahala Natl. Forest; 35°12′N 83°49′W. Agr. (corn, soybean, tobacco, apples; cattle, chickens); mfg. (furniture, crushed stone, textiles, furniture, apparel). Nantahala Gorge is NE; Nantahala L. reservoir to E. **3** town (1990 pop. 3,050), Georgetown and Williamsburg cos., E S.C., 15 mi/24 km WNW of Georgetown; 33°27′N 79°34′W. Mfg. (fabricated metal prods., milled zircon, apparel); agr. (grain, tobacco; lumber) and livestock.

Andrews Air Force Base, U.S. military installation (4,279 acres/1,732 ha; 1990 pop. 10,228), central Md., 10 mi/16 km SE of Wash., D.C.; 38°48′N 76°52′W. It is the chief military airport of Wash., D.C., as well as the hq. for the air force's high-priority airlift command. Built originally as a pilot training base during World War II, it was enlarged in 1962 taking in the Anacostia Naval Air Station, and now employs more than 10,000 military personnel. First called Camp Springs Air Force Base after a nearby village, it was renamed in honor of Lt. Gen. Frank M. Andrews, commander of Eur. operations for the Army Air Corps after World War II. Est. 1943. Air Force I (President's airplane) is based here.

Andros, island (□ 2,300 sq mi/5,957 sq km; 1990 pop. 8,177), 30 mi/48 km SW of New Providence Isl., W Bahamas; 24°35′N 78°00′W. Considered to be one isl., it is actually a tightly grouped archipelago intersected by narrow, navigable channels. It possesses the largest land mass of the Bahamas and the only river in the country, the 15 mi/24 km Goose R. The isls. are largely wooded, and pine forests, creeks, and mangrove swamps predominate. Agr. (fruits, vegetables); timber. Most of the pop. lives in small settlements (includes Nicholl's Town, Kemp's Bay, and Andros Town) along the E coast. Called Espiritu Santo by the Spaniards, it was permanently settled in 1787.

Androscoggin (an-druh-SKAH-gin), county (□ 497 sq mi/1,287 sq km; 1990 pop. 105,259), SW Maine; ⊙ Auburn; 44°09′N 70°13′W. The "Twin Cities" of Lewiston and Auburn, on the Androscoggin, are centers of diversified industry; agr., dairying area; eggs; apples, vegetables. Androscoggin and Little Androscoggin rivers furnish power; several lakes are recreational centers. Formed 1854.

Androscoggin Lake, SW Maine, 16 mi/26 km NE of Lewiston on Androscoggin-Kennebec co. line; c.3 mi/4.8 km long, 1 mi/1.6 km to 2.5 mi/4 km wide. Drains through Dead R. into Androscoggin R.

Androscoggin River, c.175 mi/282 km long; rises in Umbagog L., on N.H.-Maine state boundary; flows S from lake at Errol, N.H., in Coos co., past Berlin, through White Mts., turns E at Gorham, and enters Maine; flows past Bethel, Rumford-Mexico, turns S at Livermore Falls; flows past Lewiston and Auburn, finally turns E at Brunswick before entering Merrymeeting Bay. Bay connected to Atlantic Ocean S through long channel; it also receives Kennebec R. from N.

Anegada, island (1991 pop. 162), Br. Virgin Isls., N of main group; 18°45′N 64°20′W. The only coral isl. (8 mi/20 km long by 1.5 mi/4 km wide) in this group (others are volcanic). It is called the "Sunken Island" because it has 300 wrecks on its reefs. It features 11 mi/18 km of beaches and is famous for its lobsters. Principal town: the Settlement.

Anegada: see VIRGIN ISLANDS.

Anegada Passage, channel (c.40 mi/64 km wide) in the West Indies, bet. the Atlantic and the Caribbean, separating Anegada and Virgin Gorda of Br. Virgin Isls. (W) from SE Leeward Isls. 18°30′N 63°40′W.

Aneroid, village (1991 pop. 98), S Sask., Canada, 45 mi/72 km SE of Swift Current; wheat, livestock.

Aneta (ah-NET-uh), village (1990 pop. 314), Nelson co., E central N.Dak., 19 mi/31 km NE of Cooperstown; 47°40′N 97°59′W.

Angamacutiro de la Unión (ahn-ga-ma-koo-TEE-ro de la oon-YON), town (1990 pop. 5,089), ⊙ Angamacutiro township, Michoacán, central Mexico, on affluent of Lerma R., 53 mi/85 km NW of Morelia; 20°08′N 101°40′W. Cereals, sugarcane, beans, melon; livestock. Also known as San Francisco.

Angangueo, Mexico: see MINERAL DE ANGANGUEO.

Ange Gardien (ahzh gahrd-YEH), village, S Que., Canada, on the St. Lawrence, 11 mi/18 km NE of Quebec; dairying.

Angel Albino Corzo, Mexico: see VILLA CORZO.

Angel de la Guarda Island (AHN-hel de la GWAR-da) (□ 330 sq mi/855 sq km), in Gulf of Calif., NW Mexico, 10 mi/16 km off coast of Lower Calif., across the strait Canal de las Ballenas; 50 mi/80 km long, 2 mi/3.2 km–10 mi/16 km wide; 28°15′N 114°00′W. Barren, uninhabited; rises to 3,281 ft./1,000 m; serves as seasonal fishing base (pearls, sharks, seals, whales). Site of Angel de la Guarda Natl. Park. Sometimes called Angel de la Guardia.

Angel Fire, village and retirement community (1990 pop. 98; 1996 pop c.500), Colfax co., NE N.Mex., 22 mi/35 km E of Taos, Sangre de Cristo Mts., E of main crest; source of Cimarron R. (smaller of 2 Cimarron rivers in area); 36°23′N 105°16′W. Tourism, fishing, recreation. Palo Flechado Pass (9,101 ft/2,774 m) and Vietnam Veterans Chapel to NW. Carson Natl. Forest to W. Angel Fire Mt. (11,060 ft/3,371 m) to E. Angel Fire Ski Area is here.

Angel Island, island in San Francisco Bay, Marin co., W Calif., 8 mi/12.9 km N of Alcatraz Isl. and 25 mi/40 km N of downtown San Francisco. Largest isl. in San Francisco Bay. Explored by the Spanish in 1775, it came under U.S. control in 1851. The U.S. army used the isl. as a base from 1863 to 1946; in 1952 a radar and missile site was established. During World War II, enemy prisoners of war were confined on Angel Isl. Angel Isl. State Park on entire isl. Passenger ferry from Tiburon to NW.

Angel R. Cabada (AHN-hel kah-BAH-dah), town (1990 pop. 11,082), SE Veracruz, Mexico, 24 mi/39 km from the port of Alvarado on Mexico Highway 180; 18°40′N 95°30′W. Tropical lowland (near sea level) near Papaloapan marshes. Formerly called El Mesión.

Angeles (AN-heh-les), village, W central P.R., in N hills of the Cordillera Central, 13 mi/21 km SSW of Arecibo.

Angelica, village (□ 2 sq mi/5.2 sq km; 1990 pop. 963), Allegany co., W N.Y., on small Angelica Creek and 19 mi/31 km W of Hornell; 42°17′N 78°01′W. Oldest village in co., founded in 1800 by Captain Philip Church, nephew of Alexander Hamilton. Church is buried with his wife 1 mi/1.6 km E at Until the Day Dawns Cemetery. Contingent of Fr. royalists settled here in 1806; 1 became Fr. ambassador to U.S., another was Victor Marie du Pont de Nemours. Co. fair held here.

Angelina, county (□ 864 sq mi/2,238 sq km; 1990 pop. 69,884), ⊙ LUFKIN E Texas; 31°15′N 94°36′W. Bounded N and NE by Angelina R. (forms large Sam Rayburn Reservoir), W and S by Neches R. Part of Angelina Natl. Forest is in E and Sam Rayburn Reservoir and Dam; Davy Crockett Natl. Forest is just beyond SW boundary. Heavily wooded, in heart of E Texas pine region; industries center on forest prods. (newsprint, lumber, creosoted wood, other wood prods.); commercial mfg. center. Also livestock (cattle, poultry, hogs); some agr. Hunting, fishing. Formed 1846.

Angelina River, c.200 mi/322 km long, E Texas; rises S of Tyler, at L. Tyler reservoir; flows generally SE to Neches R. 12 mi/19 km W of Jasper. Large Sam Rayburn Dam and Reservoir, a unit in Neches R. flood-control water-supply plan, occupies most of its lower course.

Angell Peak, Oregon: see ELKHORN RIDGE.

Angels Camp, city (1990 pop. 2,409), Calaveras co., central Calif., c.43 mi/69 km E of Stockton, in Sierra Nevada foothills, on Angels Creek. Mfg. (computer peripherals). Holds annual Jumping Frog Jubilee, honoring Mark Twain's story ("The Jumping Frog of Calaveras County"). Logging, gold mining, stone quarrying; cattle, grapes, walnuts, olives, honey, oats. Founded after gold was discovered here in 1848; inc. 1912.

Angers (ah-ZHAI), village, SW Que., Canada, on Ottawa R., 6 mi/10 km SW of Buckingham; lumbering, dairying.

Angie (AN-jee), village (1990 pop. 235), Wash. parish, SE La., 14 mi/23 km NNE of Bogalusa; 30°58'N 89°49'W. Miss. state line to N and E, Pearl R. to E. Sawmilling; timber; in agr. area (pumpkins, watermelons, cattle; dairying).

Angier (an-JIR), town (1990 pop. 2,235), Harnett co., central N.C., 21 mi/34 km SSW of Raleigh; 35°30'N 78°44'W. Agr. area (tobacco, cotton, grain, potatoes, sweet potatoes; poultry, livestock, catfish). Mfg. (firefighting equip., consumer goods, apparel, furniture). Coats Country Mus.

Anglais, Les (lai-zawng-GLE), village (1982 pop. 6,005), Sud dept., SW Haiti, on SW coast of Jacmel Peninsula, 33 mi/53 km W of Les Cayes; 18°19'N 74°13'W. Fruit, coffee, and tobacco growing.

Angle Inlet, village, L. of the Woods co., NW Minn., 31 mi/50 km NNE of Warroad, on Northwest Angle Inlet of L. of the Woods, opposite prov. of Ont., Canada; 49°20'N 95°03'W. Prov. of Man., Canada 5 mi/8 km to W. Surrounded by Northwest Angle State Forest and part of Red L. Indian Reservation. Fort St. Charles Historic Site to W.

Angleton, city (1990 pop. 17,140), ⊙ Brazoria co., SE Texas, c.40 mi/64 km. S of Houston; 29°10'N 95°25'W. Elev. 31 ft/9 m; RR junction; oil producing and agr. area (cotton, rice, pecans, sorghums); mfg. (medical supplies, rebuilt diesel engines). Co. fairgrounds, Brazoria co. airport to SW. Brazoria Natl. Wildlife Refuge to SE. Settled 1896, inc. 1912.

Angliers (alng-glee-AI), village (1991 pop. 307), W Que., Canada, on L. des Quinze, at head of Rapide des Quinze, short torrential stream, 20 mi/32 km ENE of Haileybury; 47°33'N 79°14'W. Hydroelectric power center, supplying Rouyn-Noranda mining region.

Angola, city (1990 pop. 5,824), ⊙ Steuben co., extreme NE Ind., 40 mi/64 km N of Fort Wayne, in hilly lake region; 41°38'N 85°00'W. Agr. and some mfg. (feed, brick, tile, automobile and boat parts, dock equip., wire baskets, sheet-metal fabrication, electrical equip., paint, needles). Resort area. Tri-State Col. is here. Pokagon State Park is nearby.

Angola (an-GO-luh), uninc. town (☐ 28.1 sq mi/72.8 sq km), West Feliciana parish, La., 18 mi/29 km NW of St. Francisville; 30°52'N 91°35'W. Covers 18,000 acres/7,285 ha; mostly sugarcane. Formerly Angola Plantation; Coroso erected on Lake Angola by d'Iberville in 1699. Location of the La. State (Angola) Prison, est. in 1890.

Angola, village (☐ 1 sq mi/2.6 sq km; 1990 pop. 2,231), Erie co., W N.Y., near L. Erie, 20 mi/32 km SSW of Buffalo; 42°38'N 79°01'W. On Norfolk and Western RR. Summer resort. Mfg. (water treatment and filtration equip., electrical equip.). Inc. 1873.

Angola Swamp, N.C.: see HOLLY SHELTER SWAMP.

Angoon (AN-goon), village (1990 pop. 638), SE Alaska, on W coast of Admiralty Isl., on Chatham Strait at mouth of Hood Bay, 65 mi/105 km S of Juneau; 57°28'N 134°31'W. Fishing; cannery.

Angostura (ahn-go-STOO-rah), city (1990 pop. 4,054) and township, Sinaloa state, NW Mexico, on Mocorito R., in Gulf of Calif. lowland, 60 mi/97 km NW of Culiacán Rosales; 25°22'N 108°11'W. Chickpeas, sugar, corn, tomatoes, fruit.

Angostura Reservoir (☐ 7 sq mi/18.1 sq km), Fall River co., SW S.Dak., on Cheyenne R., in Buffalo Gap Natl. Grassland, 50 mi/80 km S of Rapid City; 43°20'N 103°28'W. Max. capacity 197,100 acre-ft. Formed by Angostura Dam (193 ft/59 m high), built (1949) by the Bureau of Reclamation for irrigation; also used for flood control and recreation. Angostura State Recreational Area near dam.

Anguilla (an-GWIL-uh), town (1990 pop. 883), Sharkey co., W Miss., 33 mi/53 km SSE of Greenville, near Sunflower R.; 32°58'N 90°49'W. Agr. (cotton, corn, rice, soybeans; cattle; timber); mfg. (work gloves). Delta Natl. Forest to S.

Anguilla, island and British crown colony (☐ 35 sq mi/91 sq km; 1991 est. pop. 7,350), West Indies, northernmost of the Leeward Isls.; 18°13'N 63°03'W. Fishing, stock raising, and salt mining are the mainstays of the economy, which includes a growing tourist industry. In 1967 the Br. possessions of Anguilla, St. Kitts, and Nevis were united in the self-governing state of St. Kitts–Nevis-Anguilla, associated with Great Britain. Anguilla, claiming political and economic discrimination, seceded in 1967 and returned to Br. colonial rule in 1971. The isl. was officially separated from ST. KITTS AND NEVIS in 1980. A new constitution in 1982 gave Anguilla significant control over its internal affairs.

Anguille, Cape (ang-GWIL, ANG-GIL, ANG-gweil), westernmost point of N.F., Canada, 24 mi/39 km NW of Port aux Basques, 47°54'N 59°27'W.

Anguille Mountains, range in SW N.F., Canada, extending 40 mi/64 km NE from Cape Anguille along St. George Bay; rises to 1,759 ft/536 m; 47°55'N 59°10'W.

Angus (ANG-guhs), village, S Ont., Canada, near Nottawasaga R., 11 mi/18 km WSW of Barrie; 44°19'N 79°53'W. Dairying, mixed farming.

Angus (ANG-guhs), village, Nuckolls co., S Nebr., 20 mi/32 km NNE of Superior and on Little Blue R.

Angwin, uninc. town (1990 pop. 3,503), Napa co., W Calif., 15 mi/24 km NE of Santa Rosa; 38°35'N 122°27'W. L. Berryessa reservoir to E; Aetna Springs to N. Grapes, walnuts; nursery prods.; dairying; cattle. Seat of Pacific Union Col.

Aniak (uh-NEI-ak), village (1990 pop. 540), W Alaska, on Kuskokwim R. at mouth of Aniak R., 100 mi/161 km NE of Bethel; 61°45'N 159°40'W.

Aniak River (uh-NEI-ak), W Alaska; rises near 60°21'N 159°13'; flows 100 mi/161 km N to Kuskokwim R. at Aniak.

Aniakchak National Monument and Preserve (uh-nei-AK-chak), monument (☐ 214 sq mi/554 sq km) and preserve (☐ 728 sq mi/1,886 sq km) on the S side of Alaska Peninsula, SW Alaska, 440 mi/708 km NE of Anchorage; 56°55'N 158°02'W. This volcano (4,420 ft/1,347 m high) is part of the Aleutian Range. It and the surrounding area were designated as a U.S. natl. monument and preserve in 1973. The Aniakchak's crater (☐ 30 sq mi/78 sq km) is c.6 mi/9.7 km in diameter. It was thought to be extinct until it erupted in 1931, its last eruption to date. The surrounding preserve has many varieties of wildlife, incl. grizzly bears, wolf, moose, ptarmigan. Access is by chartered plane; no facilities. Est. 1978.

Animas River, c.110 mi/177 km long, SW Colo. and NW N.Mex.; rises in San Juan Mts. in N San Juan co., N of Silverton, Colo.; flows S past Silverton and Durango, Colo.; then SW past Aztec, N.Mex., to San Juan R. at Farmington, N.Mex. Hydroelectric plant 20 mi/32 km N of Durango. Haviland and Electra reservoirs, in side stream W of river. Whitewater kayaking.

Ánimas Trujano (AH-nee-mahs troo-HAH-no), town, (1990 pop. 2,006), central Oaxaca state, Mexico, on highway, 3.1 mi/5 km S of Oaxaca de Juárez; elev. 4,997 ft/1,523 m. On a branch of the Atoyac R. Temperate climate. Agr. (corn, beans, wheat, fruits) and some small-scale cattle raising; pottery. Also called San Juan Bautista Ánimas Trujano.

Anita, town (1990 pop. 1,068), Cass co., SW Iowa, 13 mi/21 km E of Atlantic; 41°26'N 94°46'W. Agr. (grain; livestock). Platted 1869, inc. 1875.

Aniwa (AN-i-wah), village (1990 pop. 249), Shawano co., E central Wis., 21 mi/34 km ENE of Wausau; 45°00'N 89°12'W. Dairying; maple syrup.

Anjou, residential suburb (1991 pop. 37,210) of Montreal, S central Que., Canada, 7 mi/11 km N of downtown, on Montreal Isl., midway bet. St. Lawrence and Prairies rivers; 45°36'N 73°32'W.

Ankeny, city (1990 pop. 18,482), Polk co., central Iowa suburb, 10 mi/16 km N of downtown Des Moines; 41°43'N 93°36'W. In agr. area; mfg. (food prods., farm machinery, tire chains). Des Moines Community Col. and Faith Baptist Bible Col. Big Creek State Park to NW. Saylorville Reservation to W.

Anmoore, town (1990 pop. 686), Harrison co., N W.Va., 4 mi/6.4 km ESE of Clarksburg; 39°15'N 80°17'W. Agr. (corn; cattle; poultry); mfg. (furniture); coal; petroleum.

Ann Arbor, city (1990 pop. 109,592), ⊙ Washtenaw co., S Mich., 35 mi/56 km W of downtown Detroit, satellite community about 15 mi/24 km beyond built-up area of Metro Detroit, on the Huron R.; 42°16'N 83°43'W. RR junction. It is a research and educational center, with a large number of govt. and industrial research and development firms, many in high-technology fields such as aerospace and nuclear research. Educational facilities include Univ. of Michigan, Concordia Col., and Washtenaw Community Col. Mfg. includes printing and publishing, electronic, medical, and transportation equip., and precision machinery. The city is also a medical center; in addition to the univ. hospitals and medical school, it has a community hospital and a neuropsychiatric hospital. Municipal Airport (S); Mus. of Art, Natural Science Mus., Kelsey Mus. of Archaeology, Matthaei Botanical Gardens, all associated with Univ. of Michigan. Cobblestone Farm, 19th-cent. farmhouse, 1837 cabin, gardens. Numerous lakes to N and NW. Inc. 1851.

Ann, Cape, NE Mass., N of Mass. Bay; 42°38'N 70°35'W. It includes Gloucester and Rockport with their fishing villages, resorts, and artists' colonies. Gloucester Harbor indents S shore; Annisquam Harbor N shore; Annisquam R., c.4 mi/6.4 km long, connects the harbors.

Anna, city (1990 pop. 4,805), Union co., S Ill., 2 mi/3.2 km E of Jonesboro; 37°27'N 89°14'W. Agr. (fruit, vegetables, sorghum, wheat; dairying); mfg. (shoes, construction materials, transportation equip.). Inc. 1865.

Anna, town (1990 pop. 904), Collin co., N Texas, 20 mi/32 km S of Sherman; 33°21'N 96°32'W. In agr. area (cotton, sorghum, wheat; cattle, horses).

Anna, village (1990 pop. 1,164), Shelby co., W Ohio, 8 mi/13 km N of Sidney, in agr. area; 40°24'N 84°11'W. Engine plant.

Anna, Lake, reservoir, Spotsylvania, Louisa, and Orange cos., NE Va., on North Anna R., 23 mi/37 km SW of Fredericksburg; c.17 mi/27 km long; 38°00'N 77°41'W. Max. capacity 373,000 acre-ft. Clear Creek arm extends NW. Formed by North Anna Dam (90 ft/27 m high), built (1971) for water supply and flood control. North Anna 1 and 2 Nuclear Power Plants on S shore, 7 mi/11.3 km NE of Mineral. Lake Anna State Park on N shore, in W.

Anna Maria (an-nah muh-REE-uh), resort city (1990 pop. 1,744), Manatee co., W central Fla., 13 mi/21 km W of Brandenton on Anna Maria Key (c.8 mi/12.9 km long), at mouths of Tampa and Sarasota bays; 27°31'N 82°43'W. Named after Queen Anna Maria, wife of King Charles II of Spain.

Annabella, village (1990 pop. 487), Sevier co., central Utah, 4 mi/6.4 km SSE of Richfield, near Sevier R.; 38°42'N 112°03'W. Barley, alfalfa; dairying; cattle. Parts of Fishlake Natl. Forest to NW and SE. Elev. 5,500 ft/1,676 m. Settled 1896.

Annabessacook, Lake (AN-uh-BES-uh-kuk), Kennebec co., S Maine, 12 mi/19 km WSW of Augusta and just S of Winthrop; 3.5 mi/5.6 km long; 44°15'N 69°59'W. Drains from S end to Cobbosseecontee L.

Annada (uh-NAI-duh), town (1990 pop. 70), Pike co., E Mo., near Miss. R., 21 mi/34 km ESE of Bowling Green; 39°15'N 90°49'W.

Annadale, a sect. of Staten Isl. borough of N.Y. city, in S Staten Isl., SE N.Y.; 40°33'N 74°11'W.

Annandale, uninc. city, Fairfax co., NE Va., 8 mi/12.9 km W of Alexandria and 9 mi/14.5 km SW of Wash., D.C.; 38°49'N 77°12'W. Diverse light mfg. North Va. Community Col. (Annandale campus).

Annandale, town (1990 pop. 2,054), Wright co., S central Minn., 20 mi/32 km S of St. Cloud; 45°15'N 94°07'W. Livestock; poultry; dairying; grain. Mfg. (publishing and printing, construction materials, agr. equip., industrial hand tools). Clearwater and Pleasant lakes to N; L. Maria State Park to NE; several natural lakes in area.

Annandale, village (1990 pop. 1,074), Hunterdon co., W N.J., 17 mi/27 km ESE of Phillipsburg, in farm area; 40°38'N 74°53'W. Several state parks in area.

Annandale-on-Hudson, village (1990 pop. 1,100), Dutchess co., SE N.Y., on E bank of the Hudson, 17 mi/27 km S of Hudson; 42°01′N 73°54′W. Seat of Bard Col.

Annapolis, county (□ 1,285 sq mi/3,328 sq km; 1990 est. pop. 23,641), W N.S., Canada, on Bay of Fundy; ⊙ Bridgetown.

Annapolis, city (1990 pop. 33,187), ⊙ Anne Arundel co., ⊙ Md. central Md., on the S bank of the Severn R.; 38°58′N 76°30′W. Annapolis is a port of entry on Cheasapeake Bay and the business and shipping center for the fruit and vegetable farmers of E Md. Local industries include the packaging of seafood and the manufacture of small boats and plastics and aerospace parts. The economy relies heavily on state and local govt., tourism, and pleasure boating. Annapolis was settled in 1649 by Puritans fleeing Va. Hostility bet. the Puritans and the R.C. governors of Md. resulted in the battle of the Severn R. in 1655, in which the Puritans successfully revolted, only to lose control after the Restoration in England. The settlement, originally called Providence, was later known as Anne Arundel Town, after the wife of the 2d Lord Baltimore. In 1694 it became the provincial capital of Md. and was renamed Annapolis for Princess (later Queen) Anne of England. On Oct. 19, 1774, Annapolis staged its own tea party when the owner of the *Peggy Stewart* was forced to burn the vessel at dockside. In 1783–1784, Annapolis served as the capital of the U.S. when the Congress met there. The city was the site of the Annapolis Convention (1786), which led to the Federal Constitutional Convention. George Washington resigned there as commander-in-chief of the Continental Army in 1783 and the treaty that ended the Revolutionary War was ratified in there in 1784. Other notable landmarks are the Old Treasury (c. 1695), the oldest original bldg. in Md.; the library (1737); St. John's Col. chartered in 1784; the Paca House (c. 1763), home of William Paca, signer of the Declaration of Independence and 3-time governor of Md.; and St. Anne's Church (1858–1859) and graveyard where the last royal governor of Annapolis, Sir Robert Eden (an ancestor of Prime Minister Anthony Eden) is buried. Much 18th cent. architecture is preserved in the city. Annapolis is the site of the U.S. Naval Acad., founded in 1845. Historic Annapolis, Inc., a powerful preservation organization, has helped retain the town's colonial atmosphere. The narrow streets from State Circle to City Dock house restaurants and shops and Market House on the dock offers fruits, vegetables, and seafood along with snacks to shoppers and tourists year round. The promenades and benches along the dock enable visitors to watch the comings and goings of both pleasure and work boats in the bay. At different times, Annapolis has been dubbed both the "Paris" and "Athens" of America.

Annapolis, town (1990 pop. 363), Iron co., SE central Mo., in the St. Francois Mts., 15 mi/24 km S of Ironton; 37°21′N 90°42′W. Rhyolite quarry; mfg (roofing granules plant).

Annapolis, village, Kitsap co., W Wash., adjacent to Port Orchard, on Sinclair Inlet. Ferry to Bremerton.

Annapolis Basin, tidal arm of Bay of Fundy, W N.S., Canada, extends 16 mi/26 km NE-SW bet. Digby and Annapolis Royal, where it receives Annapolis R.; up to 4 mi/6 km wide. Its entrance is narrow Digby Gut, bordered by cliffs (500 ft/152 m).

Annapolis River, c.75 mi/120 km long, N.S. Canada; rises in W; flows SW past Annapolis Royal to Annapolis Basin, an arm of the Bay of Fundy. The entrance to the basin, bordered by cliffs 500 ft/152 m high, is known as Digby Gut. Site of a prototype tidal power station. The Annapolis lowlands, an important agr. area, was the site of N.S.'s first successful farming colony.

Annapolis Royal, town (1991 pop. 633), W N.S., Canada, on the Annapolis R. Founded as Port Royal by the sieur de Monts in 1605, the settlement was destroyed (1613) by Eng. colonists under Samuel Argall but was rebuilt by the French. The fort changed hands bet. the French and the English 5 times from 1605 to 1710, when it capitulated to a force of New Englanders under Francis Nicholson. The name was then changed in honor of

Queen Anne. Annapolis Royal was the capital of N.S., 1713–1749. Fort Anne Historic Natl. Park includes the ruins of the fort. The officers' quarters (built 1797–1798) have been restored as a mus. Prototype tidal generator located here.

Annawan (AN-ah-wahn), village (1990 pop. 802), Henry co., NW Ill., 17 mi/27 km NE of Cambridge; 41°23′N 89°54′W. In agr area (corn, oats, soybeans; cattle, hogs; dairying); mfg. (wood-frame bldgs., log splitters, wheelchairs).

Anne Arundel (an-ah-RUN-del), county (□ 587 sq mi/1,520 sq km; 1990 pop. 427,239), central Md.; ⊙ Annapolis; 38°59′N 76°34′W. Bounded E by Chesapeake Bay, N and NE by Patapsco R., W by Patuxent R. Agr. economy includes vegetables, fruit, tobacco, poultry, livestock, dairy prods., seafood (fish, oysters, crabs). Industry includes search and navigational equip., and boatworks. Formed in 1650, it was named for the wife of Cecil Baltimore, the 2d Lord Baltimore. Chesapeake shores have many small resorts, especially in vicinity of Magothy, Severn, South rivers (tidal estuaries). Also recreational parks and beaches include Sandy Point State Park, Riviera Beach, Beverly Beach. U.S. Naval Research and Development Center here. In N are residential suburbs of Baltimore. Includes U.S. Naval Acad. at Annapolis, Fort George G. Meade (in W; c. 13,000 acres/5,261 ha; permanent Army post, est. 1917), Baltimore-Wash. Parkway. the 4.3 mi/6.9 km long Chesapeake Bay Bridge connecting Anne Arundel with the E shore of Md., Baltimore-Wash. Internatl. (B.W.I.) Airport, London Town Publik House and Gardens, William Paca House, St. John's Col., Victualling Warehouse Maritime Museum.

Anne, Cape, NW Somerset Isl., central Franklin Dist, N.W.T., Canada, on Barrow Strait, at N end of Peel Sound; 74°03′N 95°00′W.

Annette, village, SE Alaska, on SW Annette Isl., near former U.S. air base 55°03′N 131°34′W. Almost at U.S.-Canada border; 25 mi/40 km S of Ketchikan.

Annette Island, SE Alaska, Gravina Isls., Alexander Archipelago, 5 mi/8 km SSE of Ketchikan across Revillagigedo Channel; 20 mi/32 km long, 7 mi/11.3 km–10 mi/16 km wide; 55°08′N 131°27′W. Rises to 3,610 ft/1,100 m. Reserve of Tsimshian Indians; site of METLAKATLA town, est. 1887.

Annieopsquotch Mountains (a-nee-AHP-skwahch), range (40 mi/64 km long) in SW N.F., Canada, SW of Red Indian L.; rises to over 2,000 ft/610 m.

Annisquam (AN-nis-kwahm), village, Essex co., NE Mass., on Ipswich Bay, just S of Lanesville.

Annisquam Harbor, Mass.: see ANN, CAPE.

Annisquam River, Mass.: see ANN, CAPE.

Anniston (AN-nis-tuhn), city (1990 pop. 26,623), ⊙ Calhoun co., NE Ala., in a mining region of the Appalachian foothills. Diverse mfg. includes soil pipes, textiles, lumber, bricks, cabinets, and vaccines. Founded (1872) as an iron-manufacturing "company town," it was opened to the public in 1883. The Anniston Army Depot, located W of town, is a large ordnance depot and weapons incineration site. FORT MCCLELLAN, N of town, is former hq. of the U.S. Army Military Police and Chemical regiments and a research and development center for chemical and biological weapons, but its military functions were being moved in 1996. Harry M. Ayers State Technical Col. is here. Inc. 1873.

Anniston, town (1990 pop. 288), Mississippi co., extreme SE Mo., in Miss. Alluvial plain, near Miss. R., 8 mi/12.9 km S of Charleston; 36°49′N 89°19′W. Cotton, soybeans, corn.

Annona, village (1990 pop. 329), Red R. co., NE Texas, 38 mi/61 km E of Paris; 33°34′N 94°54′W. In agr. area (poultry, cattle; wheat); timber; mfg. (furniture).

Annotto Bay, town (1991 pop. 5,468), St. Mary parish, N Jamaica, banana port on right bank of Wag Water R. mouth, on RR to Port Antonio, 21 mi/34 km N of Kingston; 18°16′N 76°46′W. Trades also in coconuts, coffee, cacao, dyewood, sugarcane; sugar milling.

Annville (AN-vil), township (1990 pop. 4,294), Lebanon co., SE central Pa., 6 mi/9.7 km WSW of Lebanon;

40°19′N 76°30′W. Mfg. (apparel, printing and publishig, fabricated metal prods., machinery, crushed stone); agr. (grain; poultry, livestock, dairying). Seat of Lebanon Valley Col.; Indiantown Gap Military Reservation (est. 1935; scheduled to close) is 8 mi/12.9 km NW. Millard Airport to SW; Memorial L. State Park to NW; Pa. Natl. Race Course (horse racing). Settled c.1745, laid out 1765.

Annville, uninc. village (1990 pop. 470), Jackson co., SE central Ky., 15 mi/24 km NNE of London; 37°19′N 83°57′W. Burley tobacco, corn; cattle, dairying, poultry. Mfg. (rugs, asphalt, metal stampings).

Año Nuevo, Point (ahn-yo), promontory on coast of San Mateo co., W Calif., 20 mi/32 km NW of Santa Cruz. New Year's Point Lighthouse here. Named by Vizcaino, who sighted it soon after New Year's Day, 1603.

Anoka (uh-NO-kuh), county (□ 446 sq mi/1,155 sq km; 1990 pop. 243,641), E Minn.; ⊙ Anoka; 45°16′N 93°14′W. Agr. area bounded SW by Miss. R. and drained by Rum R. Alfalfa, rye; some dairying and poultry; deposits of marl and peat. Co. has become urbanized, mainly residential, part of growth from Minneapolis–St. Paul to S. Part of Carlos Avery Wildlife Area in E and NE; numerous small lakes in co., especially on center and SE. Formed 1857.

Anoka (uh-NO-kuh), city (1990 pop. 17,192), ⊙ Anoka co., E Minn., suburb 16 mi/26 km NNW of downtown Minneapolis, on the Miss. R. at its confluence with the Rum R.; 45°12′N 93°23′W. Originally a trading post and lumber town, it grew as a farm trade center. Mfg. (furniture, small-arms ammunition, electronic equip., light consumer goods, steel fabrication, industrial laundry machinery). Gateway North Industrial Airport to W. Anoka County Technical Col. and Anoka State Hosp. are here. Elm Creek Park Reserve to SW; Bunker Hill Park Reserve to E. Inc. 1878.

Anoka (uh-NO-kuh), village (1990 pop. 10), Boyd co., N Nebr., 2 mi/3.2 km N of Butte, near S.Dak. state line; 42°57′N 98°49′W.

Anse Amour, L', or **Lance Amour** (both: lans uh-MOOR), or **Anse aux Morts** (ahs o MOR), village, SE Lab., Canada, on Forteau Bay of Strait of Belle Isle, 45 mi/72 km WSW of Cape Norman, N.F.; 51°28′N 56°52′W.

Anse au Loup, L' (lans o LOO) or **Lance au Loup**, village (1991 pop. 630), SE Lab., Canada, on Anse au Loup, bay of Strait of Belle Isle, 40 mi/64 km WSW of Cape Norman, N.F.; 51°31′N 56°49′W. Fishing port.

Anse aux Morts, Canada: see ANSE AMOUR, L'.

Anse Chastenet (ANZ shahs-NEE), bay and beach, W St. Lucia, 10 mi/16 km SSW of Castries, near Soufrière. Scuba-diving center.

Anse-à-Foleur (awngs-ah-fo-LUHR), town, Nord-Ouest dept., N Haiti, on the coast, 14 mi/23 km E of Port-de-Paix; 19°54′N 72°37′W. Rice, cacao, fruit, coffee; bee-keeping.

Anse-à-Galets (awngs-ah-gah-LE), town, Haiti, N shore of Île de la Gonâve; 18°50′N 72°52′W. Banana, citrus fruit; fishing port.

Anse-à-Pitre (awngs-ah-PEE-truh), town (1982 pop. 1,362), Sud-Est dept., SE Haiti, on the coast, on Dominican Republic border opposite Pedernales, 50 mi/80 km SE of Port-au-Prince; 18°03′N 71°45′W. Timber; fishing port.

Anse-à-Veau (awngs-ah-VO), town (1982 pop. 1,239), Grande-Anse dept., SW Haiti, minor port on N coast of Jacmel Peninsula, 65 mi/105 km W of Port-au-Prince; 18°31′N 73°21′W. Agr. (oranges, limes, cotton, coffee, sugarcane); fishing port.

Anse-Bertrand (AWNGS–ber-TRAWNG), town, N Grande-Terre, Guadeloupe, 15 mi/24 km N of Pointe-à-Pitre. Sugar growing and milling; alcohol distilling.

Anse-d'Hainault (awngs–dang-NO), town (1982 pop. 5,220), Grande-Anse dept., SW Haiti, minor port on W tip of Jacmel Peninsula, 50 mi/80 km WNW of Les Cayes; 18°30′N 74°27′W. Coffee and cacao growing; fishing port. Manganese, bauxite deposits nearby.

Anse-la-Raye (ANS–lah–RAI), village (1991 pop. 1,476),

W St. Lucia, 5 mi/8 km SW of Castries; 13°55′N 61°01′W. Agr.; fishing.

Anselmo (an-SEL-mo), village (1990 pop. 189), Custer co., central Nebr., 20 mi/32 km NW of Broken Bow; 41°37′N 99°51′W. Livestock; grain. Victoria Springs State Recreational Area to E.

Anse-Rouge (awngs–ROOZH), village (1982 pop. 2,883), Artibonite dept., W Haiti, on Gulf of Gonaïves, 26 mi/42 km NW of Gonaïves; 19°38′N 73°03′W. Surrounded by salt marshes. Cotton growing and processing; beekeeping.

Anses-d'Arlets (AWNGS–dahr-LE), town, SW Martinique, 8 mi/12.9 km S of Fort-de-France. Coffee, cacao, sugarcane.

Ansley (ANZ-lee), village (1990 pop. 555), Custer co., central Nebr., 15 mi/24 km SE of Broken Bow; 41°17′N 99°22′W.

Anson, county (□ 537 sq mi/1,391 sq km; 1990 pop. 23,474), S N.C.; ⊙ Wadesboro; 34°58′N 80°05′W. Bounded S by S.C. state line, E by (Great) Pee Dee R. (Blewett Falls L. reservoir in NE), N by Rocky R. In Piedmont region; sand hills in SE. Agr. (cotton, corn, hay, fruit, soybeans, sorghum, oats, wheat, sweet potatoes, tobacco; poultry, turkeys, cattle, hogs); pine and oak timber. Dairy prods; cotton textiles; sawmilling. Sand and gravel. Cason Oil Field in S. Formed 1749.

Anson 1 residential town (1990 pop. 2,382), Somerset co., central Maine, on Kennebec R. opposite Madison, 9 mi/14.5 km W of Skowhegan; 44°48′N 69°56′W. Wood prods. Inc. 1798. **2** town (1990 pop. 2,644), ⊙ Jones co., W central Texas, 23 mi/37 km NNW of Abilene; 32°45′N 99°54′W. Trade, shipping center for cotton, cattle-ranching area; wheat, milo, watermelons, peanuts, sorghum, oats; mfg. (boat trailers, apparel); gas and oil wells near. Has annual Cowboys' Christmas Ball. Ruins of old Fort Phantom Hill and L. Fort Phantom Hill (fishing) are SE. Settled 1880, inc. 1904.

Ansonia, city (1990 pop. 18,403), New Haven co., SW Conn., on the Naugatuck R.; 41°20′N 73°04′W. Mfg. (brass and copper prods., iron castings, foundry prods., plastics, monuments, electronic devices, guns); printing; architectural woodworking. Settled in 1651 as part of Derby, Ansonia was founded (1844) as an industrial community by Anson G. Phelps, a metals merchant and philanthropist. Inc. as a city 1893.

Ansonia, village (1990 pop. 1,279), Darke co., W Ohio, 7 mi/11 km N of Greenville and on Stillwater R.; 40°13′N 84°39′W.

Ansonville, town, NE Ont., Canada, on Abitibi R., adjoining Iroquois Falls, 27 mi/43 km SE of Cochrane. Mfg. (pulp, paper, sulphite milling). Nearby are waterfalls and hydroelectric station.

Ansonville, village (1990 pop. 614), Anson co., S N.C., 9 mi/14.5 km N of Wadesboro; 35°06′N 80°06′W. Near (Great) Pee Dee R. Cotton, grain, tobacco, sweet potatoes, poultry, livestock. Mfg. (metal fabricating, nylon yarn).

Ansted, town (1990 pop. 1,643), Fayette co., S central W.Va., 30 mi/48 km ESE of Charleston; 38°8′N 81°05′W. Bituminous-coal-mining region. Agr. (grain, alfalfa); cattle. Has 18th-cent. tavern. Hawks Nest State Park to SW; Gauley R. Natl. Recreation Area to NE; New R. Gorge Natl. R. to S. Settled 1790.

Antassawamock Neck, Mass.: see MATTAPOISETT.

Antelope, county (□ 858 sq mi/2,222 sq km; 1990 pop. 7,965), NE Nebr.; ⊙ Neligh; 42°10′N 98°04′W. Agr. area drained by Elkhorn R. Rye, corn, soybeans, wildhay, alfalfa; cattle, dairying, hogs. Neligh Mills, historic water-powered mill, at Neligh, at center. Formed 1871.

Antelope 1 (AN-tuh-lop), village (1990 pop. 130), Sheridan co., NE Mont., 7 mi/11.3 km SE of Plentywood, on Antelope Creek, near Big Muddy Creek. Grain, sugar beets, alfalfa; livestock. Medicine L. Natl. Wildlife Refuge to S. **2** village (1990 pop. 34), Wasco co., N Oregon, 50 mi/80 km SSE of the Dalles, source of Antelope Creek; 44°54′N 120°43′W. Livestock. John Day Fossil Beds Natl. Monument and Clarno State Park to E.

Antelope Hills, Okla.: see ROGER MILLS.

Antelope Island (□ 36.2 sq mi/93.8 sq km; c. 15 mi/24 km long, 4 mi/6.4 km wide), Davis co., N Utah, largest isl. in Great Salt L., 20 mi/32 km NW of Salt Lake City. Cattle; grazing. Buffalo herd here. Antelope Isl. State Park (formerly part of Great Salt L. State Park) covers entire isl.; 4.5 mi from NE mainland shore. Causeway from Syracuse and Layton to N end.

Antelope Peak, Nev.: see MONITOR RANGE.

Antelope Range (AN-tuh-lop), Nye and Eureka cos., central Nev., c.35 mi/56 km SW of Eureka. Ninemile Peak (10,104 ft/3,080 m), highest point.

Antelope Wells, uninc. village, Hildago co., SW N.Mex., 75 mi/121 km SW of Deming, a remote port of entry on Mex. (Chihuahua state) border. Continental Divide passes N-S to W, through Animas Mts. (NW). Mountain/Central Time Zone boundary follows internatl. boundary; N.Mex. is in Mt. Time Zone.

Antequera, Mexico: see OAXACA DE JUÁREZ.

Antero, Mount (14,269 ft/4,349 m), in Sawatch Mts., Chaffee co., central Colo., 15 mi/24 km NW of Salida.

Antero Reservoir, SW Park co., central Colo., on small effluent Salt Creek of South Platte R., in Rocky Mts., c.70 mi/113 km SW of Denver; 4 mi/6.4 km long, 2.5 mi/4 km wide; elev. over 8,940 ft/2,725 m. Formed by earth-fill dam (35 ft/11 m high). Unit in water-supply system of Denver. Antero State Wildlife Area to NE.

Anthon (AN-thun), town (1990 pop. 638), Woodbury co., W Iowa, on Little Sioux R., 29 mi/47 km ESE of Sioux City; 42°23′N 95°52′W. In livestock and grain area.

Anthony 1 town (1990 pop. 2,516), ⊙ Harper co., S Kansas, 50 mi/80 km SW of Wichita; 37°08′N 98°01′W. Elev. 1,340 ft/408 m. RR junction. Trade center for grain and livestock area. Mfg. (rubber hoses and belts). **2** uninc. town (1990 pop. 5,160), Dona Ana co., S N.Mex., suburb 17 mi/27 km NNW of downtown El Paso, Texas, immediately N of Anthony, Texas, on E side of Rio Grande; 32°00′N 106°35′W. Irrigated agr. area. Mfg. (fabricated metal bldgs., dehydrated spices and herbs). **3** town (1990 pop 3,328), El Paso co., extreme W Texas, suburb 16 mi/26 km NNW of downtown El Paso; elev. 3,800 ft/1,158 m; 31°59′N 106°35′W. Cotton-growing area; mfg. (nuts and bolts, candy). Westernmost community in Texas. Inc. 1952. Bounded by N.Mex. on N and W. Federal penitentiary; Franklin Mts. State Park to E.

Anthony, village, in Coventry municipality, central R.I., 9 mi/14.5 km W of Warwick; 41°41′N 71°32′W. Nearby are Toigue L., Gen. Nathanael Green's home.

Anthony's Nose, promontory (910 ft/277 m), in Westchester co., SE N.Y., on E bank of the Hudson R., opposite Bear Mt., c.6 mi/9.7 km NNW of Peekskill; 41°19′N 73°58′W.

Anthracite, village, SW Alta., Canada, in Rocky Mts., in Banff Natl. Park, 4 mi/6 km E of Banff.

Anticosti (an-ti-KAHS-tee), low, flat island (1988 est. pop. 300), 135 mi/217 km long and 10 mi/16 km–30 mi/48 km wide, E Que., Canada, at the head of the Gulf of St. Lawrence; 49°30′N 63°00′W. The isl. was discovered by Cartier in 1534. Louis XIV granted it to Jolliet as a reward for his discovery of the Miss. R. Jolliet's heirs held it until 1763, when it was annexed to N.F. (then a separate colony). It was returned to Canada in 1774 and was privately owned (1895–1926) until it was sold to Consolidated Bathurst Inc., which promoted lumbering for pulpwood. Forest fires and transportation costs caused this enterprise to be shut down in 1972. Now known for its bountiful deer hunting.

Antietam (an-TEET-ham), village, Washington co., W Md., 7 mi/11.3 km N of Harpers Ferry, W.Va. and on the Potomac at mouth of Antietam Creek, which rises in S Franklin co., Pa., and flows c.40 mi/64 km S, through Hagerstown Valley, and feeds into Potomac R. On its banks just NE of Sharpsburg and c.3 mi/4.8 km N of Antietam is ANTIETAM NATL. BATTLEFIELD SITE. Antietam Natl. Cemetery (est. 1862) lies just outside Sharpsburg. The village of Antietam originally grew around a large iron works built by J. Chapline, the founder of Sharpsburg in 1765. Many Revolutionary War cannons were cast in the works. Only a kiln dating from 1845 remains. The Chesapeake and Ohio Canal crosses the Antietam R. over a picturesque multi-level acqueduct here.

Antietam National Battlefield Site, central Md. (□ 5 sq mi/13 sq km). Militarily, Antietam ended in a draw after the bloodiest conflict in a single day (Sept. 17, 1862) during the entire Civil War. The total forces numbered 41,000 under the command of Gen. Robert E. Lee of the Army of Northern Virginia and 87,000 under Gen. George B. McClellan of the Army of the Potomac. Diplomatically, the battle was a serious reversal for the South, which was trying to secure recognition from the English and French and their possible intervention. The repulse of the Confederates from Union soil also gave President Abraham Lincoln occasion to issue his famous Emancipation Proclamation on Sept. 20, 1862. The bloodiest fighting occured along the appropriately named Bloody Lane. Four divisions of Union troops led by Gen. Ambrose E. Burnside were held off for several hours by 400 Ga. riflemen at Burnside Bridge over Antietam Creek, one of a dozen stone bridges in the area built (c.1836) by immigrant workmen. The Dunker Church (c.1852–1853), rebuilt in 1963, was used both as a makeshift fort and a hosp. where wounded were nursed by Clara Barton, founder of the Amer. Red Cross. Antietam Natl. Cemetery (est. 1862) lies just outside of Sharpsburg. Authorized 1890.

Antietam National Cemetery, Md.: see ANTIETAM NATL. BATTLEFIELD SITE.

Antigo (ANT-i-go), town (1990 pop. 8,276), ⊙ Langlade co., NE Wis., on tributary of Eau Claire R., 26 mi/42 km NE of Wausau; 45°08′N 89°09′W. In potato growing area; mfg. (food and dairy prods., sand and gravel quarrying, transformers, lumber, plastic prods., wood prods., shoes). Has several cooperatives. The co. historical society has mus. here. Menominee Indian Reservation to SE. Settled 1876, inc. 1885.

Antigonish (an-ti-go-NISH), county (□ 541 sq mi/1,401 sq km; 1991 pop. 19,226) E central N.S., Canada, on Northumberland Strait and George Bay; ⊙ Antigonish; 45°37′N 61°58′W.

Antigonish (an-ti-go-NISH), town (1991 pop. 4,924), N central N.S., Canada, on an inlet of St. Georges Bay. The town was founded in 1784 by disbanded Brit. soldiers and later settled by Highland Scots. It is known for the Antigonish Movement, a cooperative movement promoted in the 1920s and 1930s by St. Francis Xavier Univ.

Antigua, island (□ 108 sq mi/280 sq km; 1991 pop. 58,114), Antigua and Barbuda Republic, Leeward Isls., 40 mi/64 km E of Nevis, 40 mi/64 km N of Guadelupe; 17°5N′ 61°50′W. Its chief city, St. John's, is capital of Antigua and Barbuda (□ 170.5 sq mi/441.6 sq km), and Redonda, a dependency. Antigua isl. (□ 108 sq mi/280 sq km; 13 mi/21 km long, 10 mi/16 km wide) is of volcanic origin in SW, of coral in N and E; rises to 1,329 ft/405 m. It is hilly with a heavily indented coast. Has dry, pleasant climate; water is scarce; occasional hurricanes in summer. Antigua's mainstay is tourism; also tropical fruit, vegetables, tobacco, livestock. There is a port for cruise ships in St. John's, and a yachting center at English Harbor. Processing industries: textile assembly, rum distilling, cotton ginning. Fishing for local consumption; offshore banking. Also a center for drugs and arms smuggling. The isl. was discovered 1493 by Columbus, who named it after a church in Seville. Colonized 1632 by the English from St. Kitts. Shortly thereafter occupied by the French, it was confirmed as Br. by Peace of Breda (1667). Nelson served (1784–1787) at historic dockyard of English Harbour. In 1941 a site on NE coast was leased to the U.S. for naval and military base, now aerospace tracking station and electronic listening base.

Antigua and Barbuda, republic (□ 171 sq mi/443 sq km; 1990 pop. 60,847), West Indies, in the Leeward Isls.; ⊙ SAINT JOHN'S; 17°03′N 61°48′W. It consists of the isl. of Antigua and 2 smaller isls., Barbuda and Redonda. Antigua is a hilly isl. with a heavily indented coast, while Barbuda is a flat coral isl. dominated by a large lagoon on its W side. Redonda is an uninhabited islet. Tourism is the dominant industry, although agr., fishing, and mfg. are also pursued. Antigua was sighted by Columbus in 1493 and named for a Sp. church in Seville. The isls. were successfully colonized in 1632, when the British introduced sugarcane from St. Kitts. Barbuda was colonized from Antigua in 1661. The abolition of slavery in 1834 hurt the sugar industry; sugar has not been commercially grown on Barbuda since 1985. Antigua and Barbuda, with Redonda as a dependency, became an associated state of the Commonwealth in 1967 and achieved full independence in 1981. Two sites are leased to the U.S. for use as tracking stations for space vehicles and missiles.

Antiguo Morelos (ahn-TEE-gwo moh-RAI-los), town (1990 pop. 3,017), Tamaulipas state, NE Mexico, on Inter-American Highway 85 and highway junction point with Mexico Highway 80, 12 mi/19 km S of Ciudad Mante; 22°35′N 99°08′W. Cereals, fruit; livestock.

Antilla (ahn-TEE-yah), town, Holguín prov., E Cuba, sugar port on N shore of landlocked Nipe Bay, 30 mi/48 km N of Holguín; 20°49′N 75°44′W. RR terminus, bulk sugar terminal, airfield. Has extensive docks; located in fertile agr. region (sugarcane, tropical fruit). Sawmilling. Nearby are iron mines and sugar mills.

Antilles: see WEST INDIES.

Antilles Current, ocean surface current flowing NW along N (Atlantic) side of the Greater Antilles, bet. 20°N and 30°N. It joins the current emerging from the Gulf of Mexico via the Straits of Fla. to form the Fla. Current, the last sect. of the GULF STREAM. Recent research suggests that the Antilles current is not identifiable as a permanent feature of the circulation.

Antimony, village (1990 pop. 83), Garfield co., S Utah, 15 mi/24 km SE of Junction, 43 mi/69 km S of Richfield, on East Fork of Sevier R.; 38°06′N 111°58′W. Elev. 6,050 ft/1,844 m. Separate units of Dixie Natl. Forest to E and W; Otter Creek Reservoir and Otter Creek State Park to N; antimony mine is here. Settled 1873.

Antioch, city (1990 pop. 62,195), Contra Costa co., W Calif., suburb 29 mi/47 km NE of downtown Oakland and 40 mi/64 km SSW of Sacramento, on the San Joaquin R.; 38°00′N 121°48′W. Opposite the mouth of the Sacramento (to N); elev. 25 ft/8 m. It is a growing, processing, and shipping center for agr. prods. of the fertile isls. in the delta area bet. the rivers. Calaveras Aqueduct runs E-W S of city. Mfg. (fabricated metal prods., printing and publishing, paper prods., concrete, gypsum products, industrial chemicals, sawmill machinery); agr. (asparagus, tomatoes, apples, walnuts, grain; nursery stock). Inc. 1872.

Antioch 1 village (1990 pop. 6,105), Lake co., extreme NE Ill., near Wis. line, 16 mi/26 km NW of Waukegan; 42°28′N 88°04′W. In farming and lake-resort area; food processing. Several lakes and Chain O'Lakes State Park are nearby. Settled 1836, inc. 1857. **2** village (1990 pop. 68), Monroe co., E Ohio, 7 mi/11 km SSE of Woodsfield, in agr. area; 39°41′N 81°04′W.

Antler, village (1990 pop. 74), Bottineau co., N N.Dak., port of entry 43 mi/69 km WNW of Bottineau; 48°58′N 101°16′W. Near Can. border.

Antler Peak, Nev.: see BATTLE MOUNTAIN.

Antlers, town (1990 pop. 2,524), ⊙ Pushmataha co., SE Okla., c.45 mi/72 km ENE of Durant, on Kiamichi R.; 34°13′N 95°37′W. N terminus of RR spur from Hugo. Lumber-milling town; also mfg. (textiles, lumber, apparel). McGee Creek State Park (W). Inc. 1903.

Antoine (AN-twahn), village (1990 pop. 160), Pike co., SW Ark., 25 mi/40 km WSW of Arkadelphia and on Antoine R.; 34°01′N 93°25′W. Mfg. (lumber, wood prods.).

Antoine, Lake (an-TWEIN), NE Grenada, West Indies, 12 mi/19 km NE of St. George's, in an extinct crater; 12°11′N 61°36′W.

Antoine River, c.30 mi/48 km long, SW Ark; rises in N Pike co.; flows SE, past Graysonia and Antoine, to Little Missouri R. 11 mi/18 km N of Prescott.

Anton, town (1990 pop. 1,212), Hockley co., NW Texas, on the Llano Estacado, 20 mi/32 km NW of Lubbock, on Yellow House Draw (creek); 33°48′N 102°09′W. Shipping and ginning point for agr. area (cotton, sorghum; cattle, hogs); oil and gas.

Anton Chico (AN-tuhn CHEE-ko), village (1990 pop. 400), Guadalupe co., E central N.Mex., on Pecos R., 27 mi/43 km S of Las Vegas; elev. 5,247 ft/1,599 m. Outfitting point in ranching; cattle, sheep. Sangre de Cristo Mts. are NW, in part of Santa Fe Natl. Forest.

Antón Lizardo Point (ahn-TON lee-SAHR-do), cape on Gulf coast of Veracruz state, E Mexico, 15 mi/24 km SE of Veracruz; 19°04′N 95°59′W.

Antonia, uninc. town, Jefferson co., E Mo., residential suburb 23 mi/37 km SSW of downtown St. Louis. Area served by Barnhart post office. Limestone quarry.

Antonio Carvajal, Mexico: see APETATITLÁN.

Antonio Escobedo (ahn-TO-nyo ehs-ko-BE-do), town (1990 pop. 4,582), Jalisco state, W Mexico, on E shore of L. Magdalena, 40 mi/64 km WNW of Guadalajara; 20°50′N 103°58′W. Grain, maguey, beans; livestock. Formerly San Juanito.

Antonito, town (1990 pop. 875), Conejos co., S Colo., or Rio De LaPinos, near Conejos R., in SE foothills of San Juan Mts., 28 mi/45 km SSW of Alamosa; 37°04′N 106°00′W. Elev. 7,888 ft/2,404 m. NE terminus of the Cumbres and Toltec Scenic RR to Chama, N.Mex. Shipping point in San Luis Valley; potatoes, wheat, cattle. Just 1 mi/1.6 km to NW is Conejos (founded 1854), one of oldest towns in Colo. Inc. 1889.

Antram (AN-tram), uninc. village, Fayette co., SW Pa., on the Monongahela, 10 mi/16 km W of Uniontown; 39°54′N 79°55′W. Some agr.; coal.

Antrim, county (□ 601 sq mi/1,557 sq km; 1990 pop. 18,185), NW Mich.; ⊙ Bellaire; 45°00′N 85°10′W; Bounded W by Grand Traverse Bay; drained by short Jordan R. Agr. (cattle, sheep, poultry; dairy prods.; cherries, apples, forage crops, grain); mfg. (food processing, industrial machinery). Tourism; resorts. Torch L., 17 mi/27 km long, dominates W part of co., roughly parallels Grand Traverse Bay; Intermediate and Bellaire lakes are in co., Skegmog and Elk L. forks part of SW boundary (in Grand Traverse co.), numerous smaller lakes, mostly in W; Shanty Creek and Schuss Mt. ski area in S, Maplehurst Ski area in SW. Organized 1863.

Antrim (AN-trim), town (1990 pop. 2,360), Hillsborough co., S N.H., 23 mi/37 km SW of Concord; 43°02′N 71°59′W. Drained by Contoocook R.; Gregg L. and Willard Pond in W. Agr. (hay, nursery crops, corn, beans, pumpkins; livestock, poultry; dairying); mfg. (furniture). Resorts. Bald Mt. (2,037 ft/621 m) in W. Settled 1741, inc. 1777.

Antrim, village, Antrim co., NW Mich., 28 mi/45 km NE of Traverse City and 1 mi/1.6 km SW of Mancelona; 44°53′N 85°04′W.

Antwerp 1 village (□ 1 sq mi/2.6 sq km; 1990 pop. 739), Jefferson co., N N.Y., on Indian R., 22 mi/35 km NE of Watertown; 44°12′N 75°36′W. **2** village (1990 pop. 1,677), Paulding co., NW Ohio, on Maumee R., near Ind. state line, 22 mi/35 km ENE of Fort Wayne, Ind.; 41°11′N 84°46′W. Dairy, livestock, grain; cheese making.

Anvik (AN-vik), village (1990 pop. 82), W Alaska, on Yukon R. at mouth of Anvik R., 35 mi/56 km NNW of Holy Cross; 62°39′N 160°12′W. Athapaskan Indian village.

Anvik River (AN-vik), c.125 mi/201 km long, W Alaska, SE of Norton Sound; rises near 63°39′N 160°8′W; flows generally S to Yukon R. at Anvik.

Anvil Island (□ 4 sq mi/10.4 sq km), SW B.C., Canada, in Howe Sound, 20 mi/32 km NNW of Vancouver; 3 mi/5 km long, 1 mi/2 km wide; rises to 2,475 ft/754 m.

Anyox (A-nee-ahks), village, W B.C., Canada, near Alaska border, on Observatory Inlet of the Pacific, 80 mi/129 km NNE of Prince Rupert. Former copper-mining and smelting center. Town shut down in 1935, after which salvage crews dismantled most of structures; ruins of brick bldgs. and smoke stacks remain. Port of Alice Arm is 25 km E.

Anza-Borrego Desert State Park (□ c. 639 sq mi/1,655 sq km), S Calif., occupying most of E San Diego co., and extending into Riverside and Imperial cos.; 557,825 acres/225,752 ha. A tract of the Colo. Desert, notable for its desert plants and colorful canyons, some of them containing palm groves. Drained by San Felipo R.; N part of park surrounds, but does not include, Borrego Springs resort area. Piñon pine, juniper woodlands. Vallecito Mts. in center, part of Santa Rose Mts in N; Salton Sea to NE. Est. 1933.

Apache, county (□ 11,219 sq mi/29,057 sq km; 1990 pop. 61,591), E and NE Ariz.; ⊙ St. Johns; 35°22′N 109°29′W. Mt. area bordering on N.Mex. to E and Utah to N, crossed by Zuni, Little Colo., and Puerco rivers; Black R. forms part of S boundary. Carrizo and Chuska Mts. in NE, White Mts. in SW, in Fort Apache Indian Reservation. Navajo Indian Reservation occupies N ½ of co. Canyon de Chelly Natl. Monument is in NE, SW of Chuska Mts., near N.Mex. line. Part of Petrified Forest Natl. Monument is in W, on Navajo co. line. NE corner of Apache co., called Four Corners, is only point in U.S. common to 4 states (Ariz., N.Mex., Colo., Utah). Small dam on Little Colo. R. near St. Johns provides water for irrigated area producing hay, alfalfa; cattle, sheep; grain, sorghum. Part of the Zuni Indian Reservation in SW corner; Lyman L. State Park in S center; part of Apache Sitgreaves Natl. Forest in S. 6th largest co. in U.S.; formed 1879.

Apache (ah-PACH-ee), town (1990 pop. 1,591), Caddo co., W central Okla., 14 mi/23 km SSW of Anadarko, and at head of L. Ellsworth reservoir; 34°53′N 98°21′W. In agr. area. Mfg. (apparel). Apache Historical Mus.; Fort Sill Apache Tribal Hq. here. Settled and inc. 1901.

Apache Junction, city (1990 pop. 18,100), Pinal co., central Ariz., residential suburb 29 mi/47 km E of downtown Phoenix; 33°24′N 111°32′W. Mfg. (printing and publishing, tool and die). Salt-Gila Aquaduct to SW; Usery Mt. Park to NW; Tonto Natl. Forest to N, including Tortilla Dam (Canyon L.); Lost Dutchman State Park to NE; Superstition Mts. to E.

Apache Lake, Maricopa co., central Ariz., on Salt R. and 43 mi/69 km ENE of Phoenix, in Tonto Natl. Forest; 17 mi/27 km long; 33°34′N 111°19′W. Max. capacity of 245,100 acre-ft. Formed by concrete-arched Horse Mesa Dam (300 ft/91 m high, 803 ft/245 m long; completed 1927), a unit in Salt R. irrigation project used for irrigation and power. Canyon L. reservoir below dam; headwaters border on Gila co.; Theodore Roosevelt Dam and reservoir 12 mi/19 km NE (upstream).

Apache Mountains, W Texas, NW-SE range in Culberson co., c.25 mi/40 km ENE of Van Horn; rises to 5,656 ft/1,724 m in Apache Peak.

Apache Pass (5,115 ft/1,559 m), Cochise co., SE Ariz., historic passage bet. Dos Cabezas Mts. and Chiricahua Mts., c.20 mi/32 km ESE of Willcox. On 19th cent. immigrant road to Calif. Co. maintains dirt road. Fort. Bowie Natl. Historic Site (c.3 acres/1.2 ha) S.

Apache Peak (7,711 ft/2,350 m), Cochise co., SE Ariz., in Whetstone Mts., c.20 mi/32 km N of Fort Huachuca.

Apalachee (ap-uh-LAICH-ee), town, Morgan co., N central Ga., 19 mi/31 km S of Athens, near Apalachee R.; 33°41′N 83°25′W.

Apalachee Bay (ap-pah-LACH-ee), a bight (c.30 mi/48 km wide) of the Gulf of Mexico, NW Fla., c.25 mi/40 km S of Tallahassee; receives Aucilla, Ochlockonee, and St. Marks rivers. Its marshy coast is a natl. wildlife refuge.

Apalachee River (ap-uh-LAICH-ee), c. 65 mi/105 km, N central Ga.; rises NE of Lawrenceville; flows SE, past High Shoals, to Oconee R. 6 mi/9.7 km WSW of Greensboro; 34°02′N 83°57′W.

Apalachicola (ap-pah-lach-i-KO-LAH), city (□ 2 sq mi/5.2 sq km; 1990 pop. 2,602), ⊙ Franklin co., NW Fla., c.65 mi/105 km SW of Tallahassee, on Apalachicola Bay (bridged here), at mouth of Apalachicola R.; 29°43′N 84°59′W. Port of entry and fishing center (oysters, shrimp); exports lumber, naval stores, crushed oyster shells; mfg. of fish meal and oil, seafood canning. Civil War blockade ended city's position as a leading cotton-shipping port after 1830. Monument here commemorates J. W. Gorrie, who invented ice-making process (1845). Founded c.1820, inc. 1838.

Apalachicola Bay (ap-pah-lach-i-KO-LAH), NW Fla., an arm of the Gulf of Mexico, bet. St. George (E) and St. Vincent (W) sounds, and sheltered by St. George Isl.; c.15 mi/24 km long, 7 mi/11.3 km wide; receives Apalachicola R. Connected with St. Andrew Bay by

Gulf Intracoastal Waterway, which extends c.6 mi/ 9.7 km up the mouth of Apalachicola R. and through L. Wimico.

Apalachicola River (ap-pah-lach-i-KO-LAH), 112 mi/ 180 km long, NW Fla.; formed at SW corner of Ga. on Fla. line by confluence of Flint and Chattahoochee rivers near town of Chattahoochee; flows S across NW Fla., into Apalachicola Bay at Apalachicola; has dredged channel. Except for area surrounding its mouth, R. forms boundary between Eastern and Central time zones in Fla. Receives Chipola R. From farthest headstream (N Ga.), 500 mi/805 km above mouth, drains 19,500 sq mi/50,505 sq km.

Apan (AH-pan), city (1990 pop. 22;934) and township, Hidalgo, central Mexico, on central plateau, on RR, and 34 mi/55 km SE of Pachuca de Soto; 19°42′N 98°27′W. Elev. 8,179 ft/2,493 m. Maguey-growing and pulque-distilling center.

Apango (ah-PAHN-go), town (1990 pop. 3,545), ☉ Mártir de Cuilapan township, Guerrero, SW Mexico, on N slopes of Sierra Madre del Sur, 18 mi/29 km NE of Chilpancingo de los Bravo; 17°50′N 99°15′W. Cereals, sugar, fruit, vanilla, forest prods. (resin).

Apaseo el Alto (ah-pah-SAI-o el AHL-to), city (1990 pop. 19,901) and township, Guanajuato, central Mexico, 12 mi/19 km ESE of Celaya; 20°27′N 100°38′W. Grain, alfalfa, fruit, vegetables; livestock.

Apaseo el Grande (ah-pah-SAI-o el GRAHN-dai), city (1990 pop. 17,542) and township, Guanajuato, central Mexico, on Apaseo R. and 7 mi/11.3 km E of Celaya, on RR; 20°32′N 100°41′W. Elev. 5,797 ft/1,767 m. Grain center.

Apaseo River (ah-pah-SAI-o), c.80 mi/129 km long, central Mexico; rises NW of Amealco (Querétaro); flows N and W, past Apaseo and Cortazar (Guanajuato), to Lerma R. 4 mi/6.4 km SE of Salamanca.

Apatzingán de la Constitución (ah-paht-seen-GAHN de la kon-stee-too-see-YON), city (1990 pop. 76,643) and township, ☉ Apatzingán township, Michoacán, W Mexico, 32 mi/51 km SW of Uruapan; 19°05′N 102°21′W. Rice, sugar, coffee, fruit.

Apaxco de Ocampo (ah-PASH-ko de o-KAHM-po), town (1990 pop. 10,681), ☉ Apaxco township, Mexico state, central Mexico, on RR, 38 mi/61 km N of Mexico city; 19°57′N 99°13′W. Cement milling.

Apaxtla de Castrejón (ah-PASHT-lah de kas-trai-HON), town (1990 pop. 7,458), Guerrero, ☉ Apaxtla township, SW Mexico, on S slope of central plateau, 30 mi/48 km SW of Iguala de la Independencia; 18°09′N 99°57′W. Cereals, sugar, coffee, tropical fruit.

Apazapan (ah-pah-SAH-pahn), town (1990 pop. 902), Veracruz, E Mexico, in Sierra Madre Oriental, 17 mi/ 27 km SE of Xalapa Enríquez; 19°20′N 96°30′W. Corn, coffee, fruit.

Apotatitlán (ah-pai-ta-teet-LAHN), town (1990 pop. 5,287), ☉ Apotatitlán de Antonio Carvajal township, Tlaxcala, central Mexico, 3 mi/4.8 km ENE of Tlaxcala; 19°14′N 98°16′W. Grain, maguey, alfalfa; livestock.

Apetatitlán de Antonio Carvajal, Mexico: see APETA-TITLÁN.

Apex (AI-peks), town (1990 pop. 4,968), Wake co., central N.C., suburb 12 mi/19 km WSW of Raleigh; 35°43′N 78°50′W. Agr. to S and W (tobacco, cotton, grain; poultry; livestock). Mfg. (medical prods.,lumber, signs, cosmetics, measuring devices). Jordan Lake State Recreation Area to W.

Apishapa River, 117 mi/188 km long, SE Colo.; rises in Sangre de Cristo Mts., in San Isabel Natl. Forest; flows NE, past Aguilar, to Arkansas R. 5 mi/8 km E of Fowler.

Apizaco (ah-pee-SAH-ko), city (1990 pop. 43,663) and township, Tlaxcala, central Mexico, in Tlaxcala Basin, 25 mi/40 km N of Puebla; 19°24′N 98°08′W. Elev. 7,900 ft/2,408 m. RR and highway junction. Agr. center (corn, wheat, barley, maguey, alfalfa, beans; livestock); pulque distilling, tanning, flour milling, mfg. of ceramics; iron foundry. Formerly Barrón Escandón.

Aplington, town (1990 pop. 1,034), Butler co., N central Iowa, on Beaver Creek, and 13 mi/21 km SSW of Allison; 42°34′N 92°52′W. Feed. Limestone quarries, sand and gravel pits nearby.

Apodaca (ah-po-DAH-kah), town (1990 pop. 103,364), Nuevo León, N Mexico, on RR, 10 mi/16 km NE of Monterrey; 25°48′N 100°05′W. Chickpeas, barley; livestock. Formerly Ciudad Apodaca.

Apollo (ah-PAH-lo), borough (1990 pop. 1,895), Armstrong co., W central Pa., 16 mi/26 km S of Kittanning, on Kiskiminetas R. opposite (SE of) Vandergrift; 40°34′N 79°33′W. Mfg. (machining, tool and die, food, apparel, concrete); bituminous coal, gas, clay, limestone in area; agr. (corn, hay; livestock; dairying). Laid out 1815, inc. 1848.

Apollo Beach (uh-PAH-LO), town (□ 5 sq mi/13 sq km; 1990 pop. 6,025), Hillsborough co., W central Fla., 16 mi/26 km S of Tampa; 27°46′N 82°24′W. Mfg. includes marine rescue equip.

Apopka (uh-POP-kuh), town (□ 9 sq mi/23.3 sq km; 1990 pop. 13,512), Orange co., central Fla., a suburb 12 mi/19 km NW of Orlando, near L. Apopka; 28°41′N 81°30′W. Shipping center for citrus fruit and other agr. prods.; box mfg. Settled 1856.

Apopka, Lake (uh-PAHP-kuh), central Fla., on the line bet. Orange and Lake cos.; nearly circular, and c.8 mi/ 12.9 km–9 mi/14.5 km in diameter; popular fishing area, with Winter Garden on SE shore. Connected by waterways with extensive central Fla. lake system, L. Apopka may be regarded as extreme head of Oklawaha R.

Aporo (ah-PO-ro), town (1990 pop. 1,544), Michoacán, central Mexico, on RR and 9 mi/14.5 km E of Hidalgo; 19°40′N 100°25′W. Corn, beans, sugar, fruit; livestock.

Apostle Islands, group of more than 20 wooded isls., in L. Superior, off N Wis. Madeline, 13 mi/21 km long, is the largest isl. and has the group's only settlement, La Pointe, at W end. Noted for wave-eroded sandstone cliffs and abundant wildlife, the isls. are visited by tourists and hunters. Of the isls., all but Madeline, along with an 11 mi/18 km strip of the adjacent shoreline, make up Apostle Isls. Natl. Lakeshore. Madeline Isl.: part of Bad River Indian Reservation at E end; Big Bay State Park on S shore. Airport at La Pointe. Ferry from Bayfield. Raspberry, Sand, and York isls. and Bayfield Peninsula in Bayfield co., other isls. in Ashland co.

Apostle Islands National Lakeshore, NW Wis., authorized 1970, 68,085 acres/27,554 ha, of which 16,322 acres/6,606 ha is land area. APOSTLE ISLANDS and an 11 mi/18 km strip of the Bayfield Peninsula, on the S shore of L. Superior.

Apozol (ah-PO-sol), town (1990 pop. 2,386), Zacatecas, N central Mexico, on Juchipila R., 55 mi/89 km NNE of Guadalajara; 21°30′N 103°5′W. Grain, fruit, vegetables; livestock.

Appalachia (ap-uh-LACH-uh), town (1990 pop. 1,994), Wise co., SW Va., 7 mi/11.3 km W of Norton, on Powell R., in the Cumberland Mts., near Ky. state line, in Jefferson Natl. Forest; 36°54′N 82°47′W. Mfg. (lumber); agr. (tobacco; hay; cattle); timber; coal. RR junction (coal mine RR spurs) Settled 1890; inc. 1906.

Appalachia Reservoir (ap-uh-LAI-chee-uh), Cherokee co., SW N.C., (c.10 mi/16 km long, c.2 mi/3.2 km) in Hiwassee R., 15 mi/24 km WNW of Murphy, at Tenn. state line, formed by Appalachia Dam (TVA completed 1943), 15 mi/24 km WNW of Murphy, for hydroelectric power and flood control.

Appalachian Mountains, mountain system of E N. Amer., extending in a broad belt (c.1,600 mi/2,570 km) SW from the Gaspé Peninsula in Que., Canada, to the Gulf coastal plain in Ala. Main sections in the system are the White Mts., Green Mts., Berkshire Hills, Catskill Mts., the Allegheny Plateau, Black Mts., Great Smoky Mts., the Blue Ridge, and the Cumberland Plateau. The Appalachian Mts., much-eroded remnants of a great mt. mass formed by folding, consist largely of sedimentary rocks. Mt. Mitchell (6,684 ft/2,037 m) in the Black Mts. is the highest peak. The Great Appalachian Valley is a chain of lowlands extending S and W from the Hudson Valley; its main segments are the Lehigh Valley, Lebanon Valley, Cumberland Valley, Shenandoah Valley, the Valley of Va., and the Valley of East Tenn. The Great Valley has long been an important N-S route and is one of the most fertile areas in the E U.S.

The Appalachians themselves are rich in coal; other mineral resources include iron, petroleum, and natural gas. The scenic ranges also abound in resorts and recreation areas; Shenandoah and Great Smoky Mts. natl. parks are in the region, and the APPALACHIAN NATIONAL SCENIC TRAIL winds 2,050 mi/3,299 km along the ridges of the Appalachians from Mt. Katahdin, Maine, to Springer Mt., Ga. Crossed by few passes, the Appalachians, esp. their central portion, were a barrier to early W expansion and played an important role in U.S. history; major E-W routes followed river valleys and gaps.

Appalachian National Scenic Trail, hiking path, 2,050 mi/3,299 km long, passing through 14 states, E U.S. Conceived in 1921 by Benton Mackaye, forester and regional planner, and completed in 1937, the trail extends along the ridges of the Appalachian Mts. from Mt. Katahdin, Maine, to Springer Mt., Ga. The largest part of the trail passes through 8 natl. forests and 2 natl. parks, but some of its length is still on private property. Hiking and trail clubs maintain shelters and campsites along the path. The trail was designated a natl. scenic trail in 1968.

Appanoose, county (□ 523 sq mi/1,355 sq km; 1990 pop. 13,743), S Iowa, on Mo. line; ☉ Centerville; 40°44′N 92°52′W. Prairie agr. region (sheep, hogs, cattle, poultry; corn, soybeans, hay) and bituminous-coal-mining area drained by Chariton R.; limestone quarries. Part of Stephens State Park in NE., Sharon Bluffs State Park SE of Centerville. Rathbun Dam and Lake in NW. Henry Creek State Park on N shore. Formed 1843.

Apperson, uninc. village, Osage co., N Okla., 25 mi/ 40 km WNW of Pawhuska. Kaw L. reservoir to W.

Apple Canyon Lake, reservoir (□ 1 sq mi/2.6 sq km), Jo Daviess co., NW Ill., on Hells Branch Creek, 27 mi/ 43 km ESE of Dubuque (Iowa); 42°25′N 90°10′W. Max. capacity 14,630 acre-ft. Formed by Apple Canyon L. Dam (78ft/24 m high), built (1978) for recreation.

Apple Creek, village (1990 pop. 860), Wayne co., N central Ohio, 6 mi/10 km SE of Wooster; 40°46′N 81°52′W. Grain prods.; lumber. Amish and Mennonite concentration.

Apple Creek, c.60 mi/97 km long, W Ill.; rises SW of Springfield; flows WSW, through Morgan and Greene cos., to Illinois R. c.12 mi/19 km NW of Carrollton; 39°33′N 89°54′W.

Apple Grove, uninc. village, Mason co., W W.Va., 13 mi/ 21 km S of Point Pleasant, on Ohio R. Agr. (grain, tobacco); livestock; light mfg. Chief Cornstalk Wildlife Management Area to NE.

Apple River, village (1990 pop. 414), Jo Daviess co., NW Ill., on Apple R., near Wis. line, and 18 mi/29 km ENE of Galena; 42°30′N 90°05′W. In agr. area. Apple R. Canyon State Park is nearby.

Apple River 1 c.40 mi/64 km long, in NW Ill.; rises just N of Jo Daviess co. in Wis.; flows generally SW and S, past Hanover (dammed here), to the Mississippi R. NW of Savanna; 46°26′N 89°56′W. Its upper canyon, near the site of Apple R. Canyon State Park (c.150 acres/61 ha). **2** c.50 mi/80 km long NW Wis.; rises in Staples L. on Barron-Polk co. line; flows SW through lake region, past Amery, to St. Croix R., 7 mi/ 11.3 km NE of Stillwater, Minn.

Apple Valley 1 city (1990 pop. 46,079), San Bernardino co., S Calif., 27 mi/43 km NNE of San Bernardino co., in SW part of Mojave Desert; 34°32′N 117°13′W. Lucerne L. (dry) to E. Cattle; fruit; grain, alfalfa; mfg. (fabricated metal, diversified light mfg.). **2** city (1990 pop. 34,598), Dakota co., SE Minn., residential suburb, 14 mi/23 km SSW of St. Paul, and 16 mi/26 km S of Minneapolis; 44°45′N 93°12′W. Mfg. (concrete, hand tools); agr. to S (grain, soybeans; livestock, dairying, poultry). Several small lakes in area, especially to NE and SW. Minn. Zoological Gardens (Zoo) in NE; part of Lebanon Hills Park in NE.

Appledore Island, Maine: see ISLES OF SHOALS.

Applegate, village (1990 pop. 297), Sanilac co., E Mich., on Black R., and 5 mi/8 km N of Croswell; 43°21′N 82°38′W. In agr. area.

Appleton, city (1990 pop. 65,695), Outagamie and Calumet cos., E Wis., ⊙ Outagamie co., on the Fox R. near its exit from the N end of L. Winnebago; 44°16′N 88°24′W. In a dairying and stock-raising region. RR junction. Waterfalls provide power for the city's industries, which produce paper, wood, metal, concrete, and dairy prods. Mfg. (crushing equip., foods, paper, paper prods., pipe fabrication, printing, concrete, machining, electronic controls). Appleton had the nation's 1st hydroelectric plant (1882) and the state's first electric streetcar (1886). The city is the seat of Lawrence Univ. Outagamie Airport to W. Inc. 1857.

Appleton 1 town (1990 pop. 1,069), Knox co., S Maine, 12 mi/19 km NW of Rockland; 44°17′N 69°15′W. **2** town (1990 pop. 1,552), Swift co., W central Minn., on Pomme de Terre R. near its mouth on Minnesota R., and 22 mi/35 km WSW of Benson; 45°12′N 96°01′W. RR junction and farm trade center (grain; livestock, poultry; dairying); mfg. (feeds, heat pumps, grain processing). Hydroelectric plant is here. Marsh L. (W) and Lac qui Parle (SE), both reservoirs of Minnesota R.; Shible L.; and other natural lakes to N. In Lac qui Parle Wildlife Area. Settled 1869, laid out 1870, inc. 1881.

Appleton, uninc. village, Allendale co., SW S.C., 4 mi/ 6.4 km NW of Allendale. Agr. and timber area.

Appleton City, city (1990 pop. 1,280), St. Clair co., W Mo., 18 mi/29 km SW of Clinton; 38°11′N 94°01′W. Agr. (corn, sorghum, sweet corn; cattle); mfg. (uniforms). Inc. 1871.

Appleton Mills, residential village, Anderson co., NW S.C., near Anderson.

Applewold (A-puhl-wuld), borough (1990 pop. 388), Armstrong co., W central Pa., suburb 1 mi/1.6 km S of Kittanning, on Allegheny R. (bridged to S); 40°48′N 79°31′W. Corn, hay; dairying.

Appleyard, village, Chelan co., central Wash., on the Columbia R. (Rock Isl. Reservoir) and 2 mi/3.2 km S of Wenatchee. Apples, pears; cattle, sheep.

Appling (AP-ling), county (☐ 514 sq mi/1,331 sq km; 1990 pop. 15,744), SE Ga., ⊙ Baxley; 31°45′N 82°17′W. Bounded NE by Altamaha R., SW by Little Satilla R. Coastal plain agr. (tobacco, corn, peanuts, soybeans, cotton; cattle, hogs, poultry); timber. Nuclear power plants: Hatch 1 (initial criticality Sept. 12, 1974; max. dependable capacity of 741 MWe) and Hatch 2 (initial criticality Sept. 22, 1978; max. dependable capacity of 761 MWe) are 11 mi/18 km N of Baxley. Use cooling water from the Altamaha R. Formed 1818.

Appling (AP-ling), village, ⊙ Columbia co., E Ga., 20 mi/32 km WNW of Augusta; 82°19′N 33°32′W. Mfg. includes printing equip. and lumber.

Appomattox (ap-uh-MA-tuks), county (☐ 335 sq mi/ 868 sq km; 1990 pop. 12,298), central Va.; ⊙ Appomattox; 37°22′N 78°48′W. Mfg. at Appomattox; agr. (esp. tobacco, hay, wheat, corn, soybeans; cattle; dairying); timber. Bounded NW by James R.; source of Appomattox R. in NE. Includes Appomattox Court House Natl. Historic Park. Holliday L. State Park, part of Buckingham Appomatox State Forest in NE. Formed 1845.

Appomattox, town (1990 pop. 1,707), ⊙ Appomattox co., central Va.; 37°21′N 78°49′W. Mfg. (agr. lime processing, lumber, clothing, furniture); agr. area (corn, tobacco, grain, soybeans; cattle). Holliday L. State Park, Buckingham Appomattox State Forest, and Appomattox Courthouse Natl. Historical Park. Inc. 1925.

Appomattox Court House National Historical Park (☐ 2 sq mi/5.2 sq km), Appomattox co., S central Va., 5 mi/8 km NE of Appomattox, 37°22′N 78°47′W. Site of surrender, April 9, 1865, of Confederate general Robert E. Lee to Union general Ulysses S. Grant. Authorized 1930.

Appomattox River, 137 mi/220 km long, central and E Va.; rises in NE Appomattox co., 10 mi/16 km NE of Appomattox; flows generally E past Farmville, through L. Chesdin reservoir and past Petersburg (head of navigation) to James R. at Hopewell.

Apponaug (AP-pon-awg), village, administrative center of Warwick city, Kent co., E R.I., on Greenwich Bay and Gorton Pond, 9 mi/14.5 km S of Providence.

Apponaug, R.I.: see WARWICK.

Aptos, uninc. town (1990 pop. 9,061), Santa Cruz co., W Calif., 7 mi/11.3 km E of Santa Cruz, on Monterey Bay, Pacific Ocean; 37°00′N 121°54′W. Berries, apples, flowers, nursery stock, vegetables. Resort area. Forest of Nisene Marks State Park to N.

Aptos Hills–Larkin Valley, uninc. town (1990 pop. 2,205), Santa Cruz co., W Calif., 8 mi/12.9 km E of Santa Cruz and 1 mi/1.6 km SE of Aptos, on Monterey Bay, Pacific Ocean; 36°58′N 121°50′W. Residential community; resort area.

Apulco (ah-POOL-ko), town (1990 pop. 1,325), Apulco municipio, Zacatecas, N central Mexico, 40 mi/64 km SW of Aguascalientes, 2 mi/3.2 km off Mexico Highway 125; 21°23′N 102°40′W. Elev. 5,906 ft/1,800 m. Grain, fruit, vegetables; livestock.

Aqua Fria (AH-gwuh FREE-uh), uninc. village (1990 pop. 3,717), Santa Fe co., N central N.Mex., suburb 4 mi/6.4 km WSW of Santa Fe, on Santa Fe R.; 35°38′N 106°01′W. Cattle, sheep; corn, chiles, grain. Rodeo Grounds to SE; Santa Fe Downs Racetrack to SW; Santa Fe Municipal Airport to W.

Aquarius Plateau, Garfield and Wayne cos., S central Utah. Largely in Dixie Natl. Forest. Includes several small lakes. Rises to 11,253 ft/3,430 m in BLUE BELL KNOLL.

Aquebogue, village (☐ 4 sq mi/10.4 sq km; 1990 pop. 2,060), Suffolk co., SE N.Y., on NE L.I., near Flanders Bay, 3 mi/4.8 km NE of Riverhead; 40°56′N 72°36′W. Summer-resort area.

Aqueduct Race Track, N.Y.: see OZONE PARK.

Aquia (uh-KWEI-yuh), uninc. village, Stafford co., NE Va., 12 mi/19 km NNE of Fredericksburg, on Aquia Creek. Aquia Church, here, built 1757. Quantico Marine Corps Base to N.

Aquia Creek, c.25 mi/40 km long, NE Va.; rises near Stafford-Fauquier co. line; flows E and SE to the Potomac 5 mi/8 km SE of Stafford. Navigable in lower reaches.

Aquia Harbor, uninc. town, Stafford co., NE Va., residential community 10 mi/16 km NNE of Fredericksburg, on Aquia Creek, 4 mi/4.8 km NW of mouth of Potomac R. estuary; 38°27′N 77°22′W.

Aquidneck, R.I.: see RHODE ISLAND, isl.

Aquila 1 (ah-KEE-lah), town (1990 pop. 1,515), in extreme SW part of Michoacán, Mexico, 33 mi/53 km SE of Tecoman; 18°35′N 103°31′W. Elev. 689 ft/210 m. Harsh terrain, small farming, mainly for subsistence. On gravel road S to Mexico Hwy. 200 (9 mi/15 km). **2** town (1990 pop. 729), Veracruz, E Mexico, in Sierra Madre Oriental, 15 mi/24 km WSW of Orizaba; 18°48′N 97°25′W. Fruit.

Aquiles Serdán (ah-KEE-lais ser-DAHN), mining settlement (1990 pop. 3,916), Chihuahua, N Mexico, 12 mi/19 km ESE of Chihuahua; 28°30′N 105°40′W. Elev. 4,560 ft/1,390 m. RR terminus; agr. and cattle raising. Historically a wealthy mining center. Formerly Santa Eulalia. The mining camp Francisco Portillo, formerly Santo Domingo, is nearby.

Aquilla, village (1990 pop. 360), Geauga co., NE Ohio, just S of Chardon; 41°34′N 81°11′W.

Aquin (ah-KANG), town (1982 pop. 3,820), Sud dept., SW Haiti, minor port on S coast of Jacmel Peninsula, 23 mi/37 km ENE of Les Cayes; 18°17′N 73°24′W. Agr. (tobacco, sugarcane, coffee, logwood, cotton); coffee processing; fishing port.

Aquismón (ah-kees-MON), town (1990 pop. 1,409), San Luis Potosí, E Mexico, 25 mi/40 km S of Ciudad Valles; 21°30′N 99°00′W. Cotton, sugar, cereals, fruit; livestock. Some Huastec-speaking pop.

Aquixtla (ah-KEESHT-lah), town (1990 pop. 557), Puebla, central Mexico, 9 mi/15 km SE of Zacatlán; 19°45′N 97°57′W. Corn, maguey.

Aquone Lake, N.C.: see NANTAHALA RIVER.

Arab (ER-uhb), city (1990 pop. 6,321), Marshall co., NE Ala., 11 mi/18 km W of Guntersville, near Guntersville Reservoir.

Arabi (A-ruh-bee), uninc. city (1990 pop. 8,787), St. Bernard parish, SE La., suburb 5 mi/8 km E of downtown New Orleans, on E bank of the Mississippi R.; 29°57′N 90°00′W. Mfg. of machinery; sugar refining.

Arabi (AR-uh-bee), town (1990 pop. 433), Crisp co., S central Ga., 9 mi/14.5 km SSE of Cordele; 31°50′N 83°44′W.

Arabos, Los, Cuba: see LOS ARABOS.

Arago, Cape (uh-RAH-go), Coos co., W Oregon, 10 mi/ 16 km WSW of city of Coos Bay, on Pacific Ocean. Cape Arago State Park is here.

Aragon (AR-uh-gahn), town (1990 pop. 902), Polk co., NW Ga., 11 mi/18 km E of Cedartown; 34°03′N 85°04′W. Mfg. of yarns.

Aragon (ah-rah-GON), village, Catron co., W N.Mex., on Tularosa R., at boundary of Apache-Sitgreaves (N) and Gila (S) Natl. Forests, 90 mi/145 km WSW of Socorro; elev. 6,679 ft/2,036 m. Pueblo ruins in vicinity. Continental Divide to E.

Aramberri (ah-rahm-BER-ee), city (1990 pop. 1,976), Nuevo León, N Mexico, 55 mi/89 km SSW of Linares; 24°5′N 99°50′W. Grain, fruit; livestock.

Arandas (ah-RAHN-dahs), city, (1990 pop. 30,889), Jalisco, central Mexico, 40 mi/64 km NE of Ocotlán; 20°44′N 03°04′W. Wheat- and bean-growing center.

Aranjuez (ah-RANG-wez), village, NW Trinidad, Trinidad and Tobago, 3.5 mi/5.6 km E of Port of Spain. In agr. region (coconuts, sugarcane).

Aransas, county (☐ 528 sq mi/1,368 sq km; 1990 pop. 17,892), S Texas; ⊙ Rockport; 28°06′N 96°59′W. On Gulf coast, much indented by Copano and St. Charles bays; Aransas Bay separates mainland from San Jose Isl., a Gulf barrier isl., and is traversed by Intracoastal Waterway. Wintering grounds of rare whooping cranes. Most of Aransas Natl. Wildlife Refuge is here. Cattle raising, cotton, sorghum, fisheries (shrimp, shellfish, fish), redfish hatchery; tourist trade (fishing, beaches); oyster shell. Some oil, natural gas. Rockport is a port (oil, seafood shipping). Goose Isl. State Park at center; Fulton Mansion State Historical Park; Copano Bay State Fishing Pier, at center, in and near Fulton. Formed 1871.

Aransas Bay, S Texas, inlet (c.25 mi/40 km long, c.5 mi/ 8 km wide) of Gulf of Mexico, bet. the mainland and St. Joseph Isl., part of an arc of sandy barrier isls. lining the Gulf Coast. Traversed by Gulf Intracoastal Waterway, which connects it with Corpus Christi Bay (via Redfish Bay) (SW), San Antonio Bay (NE). Principal ports are Rockport and Aransas Pass, with access to the Gulf through Aransas Pass channel. Copano Bay, NW arm of Aransas Bay, receives Aransas R. (c.50 mi/80 km long) and Mission R. from NW, Copano Creek (c.20 mi/32 km long) from N. St. Charles Bay (11 mi/ 18 km. long, 1 mi/1.6 km–3 mi/4.8 km wide) is NE arm. Aransas Natl. Wildlife Refuge is on NW shore; Goose Isl. is a State Park.

Aransas Pass, town (1990 pop. 7,180), San Patricio and Aransas cos., S Texas, on Redfish Bay, bet. Aransas Bay (NE), and Corpus Christi Bay (SW), and 17 mi/27 km NE of Corpus Christi; 27°53′N 97°06′W. Elev. 20 ft/6 m. A port on Intracoastal Waterway, passing through Bay. Causeway to Harbor Isl. (E) and ferry beyond it connect town with Port Aransas, at N end of Mustang Isl. Resort; fisheries; oil refineries (supplied by local fields and pipelines); mfg. (fishing equip., food processing, boat parts, steel fabricating). Aransas Municipal Airport. Ingleside Naval Station to SSW. Settled 1890, inc. 1910.

Aransas Pass, channel, Aransas and Nueces cos., S Texas, leading to man-made channel passes, natural channel is bet. Mustang and St. Joseph (San Jose) isls., through N end of Mustang Isl., a coastal sand barrier isl. Immediately behind the barrier isl., the pass splits into 2 branch channels, creating Harbor Isl. One channel leads directly N to Aransas bay; the other leads WSW to Corpus Christi Bay and is the main shipping channel. A free ferry crosses it, connecting Mustang and Harbor isls. at the town of Port Aransas. Redfish Bay separates Harbor Isl. from the mainland; a causeway connects Harbor Isl. with mainland town of Aransas Pass. Intracoastal Waterway passes through Redfish Bay against the mainland shore.

Aransas River, Texas: see ARANSAS BAY.

Arapaho (uh-RAP-uh-ho), town (1990 pop. 802), ⊙ Custer co., W Okla., 4 mi/6.4 km N of Clinton; 35°34′N 98°57′W. Elev. 1,669 ft/509 m. In agr. area (grain, alfalfa, cotton, peanuts, sorghum; cattle). Salt deposits nearby. Washita Wildlife Refuge to W.

Arapahoe, county (□ 805 sq mi/2,085 sq km; 1990 pop. 391,511), N central Colo., bordering Denver; ⊙ Littleton; 39°38′N 104°19′W. Agr. area, drained in W by South Platte R. Dairy prods.; wheat, sunflower, nursery co-ops; cattle. Buckley Air Natl. Guard Base at Aurora. Cherry Creek L. Reservoir and State Park are in W center. Located on W margin of Great Plains, W boundary of co. approaches Front Range of Rockies. W part of co. is highly urbanized, including cities of Aurora (port), Englewoods, and Littleton. E ¾ of co. is rural and sparsely populated. Plains Conservation Center SE of Aurora. Co. land area has been reduced by expansion of Denver co. in NW, which adjusts its boundary every decennial year to conform with expansions of city of Denver into neighboring counties. Formed 1861.

Arapahoe (uh-RAP-uh-ho), town (1990 pop. 1,001), Furnas co., S Nebr., 33 mi/53 km SSW of Lexington and near Republican R.; 40°18′N 99°54′W. Grain; livestock. Plotted 1871.

Arapahoe 1 (uh-RAP-uh-ho), village (1990 pop. 430), Pamlico co., E N.C., 13 mi/21 km SE of New Bern, near Neuse R. estuary; 05°01′N 76°49′W. Ferry 4 mi/6.4 km to S. Agr. (potatoes, grain, cotton, peanuts; hogs); mfg. (crab meat processing, aluminum pipe). **2** village (1990 pop. 393), Fremont co., W central Wyo., on Popo Agie R. at mouth of Beaver Creek, and 15 mi/24 km NE of Lander; 42°58′N 108°28′W. Elev. c.5,200 ft/1,585 m. Trading point in SE part of Wind River Indian Reservation.

Arapahoe Peak, mountain with twin peaks, N Colo., in Front Range, c.20 mi/32 km W of Boulder. Peaks are North Peak (13,502 ft/4,115 m) and South Peak (13,397 ft/4,083 m). Arapahoe glacier is on E face of South Peak. On Continental Divide, boundary bet. Roosevelt Natl. Forest (E) and Arapaho Natl. Forest (W). Also spelled Arapaho Peak.

Arborfield, town (1991 pop. 433), E Sask., Canada, 25 mi/40 km NE of Tisdale; dairying; wheat.

Arbuckle, uninc. city (1990 pop. 1,912), Colusa co., N central Calif., 13 mi/21 km S of Colusa; 39°01′N 122°04′W. Mfg. (nut processing); agr. (almonds, walnuts, wheat, oats, barley, fruit, rice, vegetables, sugar beets, tomatoes). On Tehema Colusa Canal; Sacramento R. to E; Colusa National Wildlife Refuge to N; Coast Ranges to W.

Arbuckle Mountains, range of low, rolling hills, rising c.700 ft/210 m above the prairie, S Okla.; remnant of mts. formed in the Precambrian era. Interesting folds and faults have resulted from the varying erosional rates of the different rock types found in the area. The Chicksaw Natl. Recreational Area (which includes the former Platt Natl. Park) contains many cold mineral springs and Arbuckle Reservoir, formed behind Arbuckle Dam.

Arbuckle Reservoir, Murray co., S Okla., on Rock Creek, in Chickasaw Natl. Recreation Area, 20 mi/32 km NNE of Ardmore; 9 mi/14.5 km long NW-SE; 34°25′N 97°01′W. Max. capacity 232,000 acre-ft. Formed by Arbuckle Dam (136 ft/41 m high), built (1966) by the U.S. govt. for flood control, water supply, and recreation. Also called L. of the Arbuckles.

Arbury Hills, uninc. village (1990 pop. 1,667), Will co., NE Ill., suburb 24 mi/39 km SSW of downtown Chicago, 3 mi/4.8 km SW of Tinley Park; 41°32′N 87°50′W. Residential.

Arbutus (ahr-BYUH-tus), suburban village (1990 pop. 19,750), Baltimore co., central Md., 5 mi/8 km SW of Baltimore; 39°14′N 76°42′W. Predominately an older suburb of individual houses, row houses, and apartments, Artubus is experiencing new development. Industries include motor manufacture, industrial gases, and metal prods.

Arbyrd (AHR-buhrd), city (1990 pop. 597), Dunklin co.,

extreme SE Mo., in the bootheel in Mississippi alluvial plain, 17 mi/27 km SW of Kennett; 36°02′N 90°14′W. Cotton, soybeans.

Arc Dome, Nev.: see TOIYABE RANGE.

Arcade 1 (ahr-KAID), uninc. city (1990 pop. 39,840), Sacramento co., S Calif., residential suburb 8 mi/12.9 km ENE of downtown Sacramento, near American R. McClellan A.F.B., which is scheduled for closing, to N. Statistically reported as Arden-Arcade; Arden is 3 mi/4.8 km SSW. **2** city (1990 pop. 697), Jackson co., NE central Ga., 12 mi/19 km NW of Athens; 34°05′N 83°34′W.

Arcade, village (□ 2 sq mi/5.2 sq km; 1990 pop. 2,081), Wyo. co., W N.Y., on Cattaraugus Creek and 35 mi/56 km SE of Buffalo; 42°31′N 78°25′W. Dairying region. Mfg. (wood prods., textiles). Settled c.1800, inc. 1871.

Arcadia, city (1990 pop. 48,290), Los Angeles co., S Calif., a residential suburb 12 mi/19 km NE of downtown Los Angeles, at the S foot of the San Gabriel Mts.; 34°08′N 118°02′W. Mfg. (electronic equip., fabricated metal prods., pharmaceuticals, furniture, motors, machinery). The Santa Anita racetrack and an arboretum are here. Angeles Natl. Forest to N. Inc. 1903.

Arcadia 1 (ahr-KAI-dee-uh), town (□ 4 sq mi/10.4 sq mi; 1990 pop. 6,488), ⊙ De Soto co., central Fla., on Peace R., and 30 mi/48 km E of Sarasota; 27°13′N 81°51′W. Trade and shipping center for extensive cattle and citrus-fruit area; citrus-fruit packing houses and canneries. Holds annual rodeos, cattle show. **2** town (1990 pop. 1,468), Hamilton co., central Ind., near Cicero Creek, 9 mi/14.5 km N of Noblesville; 40°10′N 86°01′W. In agr. area. **3** town (1990 pop. 485), Carroll co., W central Iowa, 9 mi/14.5 km W of Carroll; 42°05′N 95°02′W. In agr. area. **4** town (1990 pop. 3,079), ⊙ Bienville parish, NW La., 50 mi/80 km E of Shreveport; 32°33′N 92°55′W. In agr. area; poultry processing; lumber milling, wood prods.; mfg. (tubing, paper bags, and wrappers). Natural gas wells. **5** town (1990 pop. 609), Iron co., SE central Mo., in St. Francois Mts. just S of Ironton; 37°35′N 90°37′W. Mfg. (checkbook covers); resorts; tourism. Taum Sauk Mt., highest point in Mo., 5 mi/8 km W., Stouts Creek Shut-in, 4 mi/6.4 km, to E. **6** uninc. town (1990 pop. 2,000), Spartanburg co., NW S.C., 5 mi/8 km W of Spartanburg. Mfg. (apparel, textiles); agr. (grain, soybeans, peaches, apples; dairying; livestock). **7** (ahr-KAI-dee-ah), town (1990 pop. 2,166), Trempealeau co., W Wis., on Trempealeau R., and 17 mi/27 km NE of Winona, Minn.; 44°15′N 91°29′W. In dairy and livestock area; timber; mfg. (poultry processing, printing, meat prods.). Inc. 1925.

Arcadia 1 (ahr-KAI-dee-uh), village (1990 pop. 338), Crawford co., SE Kansas, at Mo. line, 16 mi/26 km NNE of Pittsburg; 37°38′N 94°37′W. In diversified agr. and coal-mining area. **2** (ahr-KAI-dee-ah), village, Manistee co., NW Michigan, on L. Michigan, and 17 mi/27 km N of Manistee; 44°29′N 86°13′W. In farm and resort area. Camp Arcadia, Lutheran retreat. **3** (ahr-KAI-dee-uh), village (1990 pop. 385), Valley co., central Nebr., 15 mi/24 km SW of Ord, and on Middle Loup R; 41°25′N 99°07′W. Livestock; grain. **4** village (1990 pop. 546), Hancock co., NW Ohio, 13 mi/21 km ENE of Findlay, and on South Branch of Portage R.; 41°07′N 83°32′W. **5** village (1990 pop. 320), Oklahoma co., central Okla., residential suburb 17 mi/27 km NE of downtown Oklahoma City, Arcadia L. to SW; 35°40′N 97°19′W. In oil-producing area. **6** village, Richmond town, R.I.; 41°33′N 71°42′W. Arcadia Management Area nearby.

Arcadia Lakes, town (1990 pop. 899), Richland co., central S.C., residential suburb 5 mi/8 km NE of downtown Columbia, on Garys L. reservoir. (Gills Creek); 34°02′N 80°57′W.

Arcahaie (arh-kah-AI), agr. town (1982 pop. 2,069), Ouest dept., W Haiti, on the Gulf of Gonaïves, 20 mi/32 km NW of Port-au-Prince; 19°49′N 72°55′W. Agr. (sugarcane, bananas, tobacco, coffee); lime essence distillery, sugar processing; fishing port. Sometimes L'Arcahaie.

Arcanum (ahr-KAI-nuhm), village (1990 pop. 1,953),

Darke co., W Ohio, 8 mi/13 km SSE of Greenville, in diversified farming area; 39°59′N 84°34′W.

Arcata, city (1990 pop. 15,197), Humboldt co., NW Calif., suburb 6 mi/9.7 km NE of Eureka, at N end of Humboldt Bay near Pacific Ocean; 40°52′N 124°05′W. RR junction; timber; mfg. (fertilizers, apparel, textile prods., paper mills, light consumer goods). Seat of Humboldt State Univ. Bret Harte lived here, 1857–1860. Arcata Airport to N; Azalia Reserve to N; Patrick's Point State Park and Trinidad State Beach to N; Hoopa Valley Indian Reservation to NE; Redwood Natl. Park to N; Six Rivers Natl. Forest to E. Founded 1850, inc. 1903.

Arcelia (ahr-SAI-lee-ah), town (1990 pop. 14,397), Guerrero, SW Mexico, in Río Balsas basin, 25 mi/40 km ESE of Ciudad Altamirano; 18°20′N 100°30′W. Corn, beans, chiles, fruits.

Archbald (ARCH-bawld), borough (1990 pop. 6,291), Lackawanna co., NE Pa., 9 mi/14.5 km NE of Scranton, on Lackawanna R.; 41°30′N 75°32′W. Mfg. (nuclear components, microcomputers); anthracite coal mining. Includes village of Eynon. Archbald Pothole State Park to NW. Settled 1831, inc. 1877.

Archbold (AHRCH-bold), village (1990 pop. 3,440), Fulton co., NW Ohio, 13 mi/21 km ENE of Bryan; 41°32′N 84°19′W. Agr. (hay, wheat); mfg. (agr. machinery, furniture, wood prods.); slaughterhouse.

Archdale (AHRCH-dail), town (1990 pop. 6,913), Randolph co., central N.C., suburb 4 mi/6.4 km SE of High Point, near source of Uwharrie R; 35°53′N 79°58′W. Agr. area (tobacco, grain, soybeans, poultry, dairying; livestock). Mfg. (furniture, fabricated metal prods., apparel). Founded 1773 by Quakers.

Archer, county (□ 925 sq mi/2,396 sq km; 1990 pop. 7,973), N Texas; ⊙ Archer City; 33°36′N 98°41′W. Drained by West Fork of Trinity R., Little Wichita and Wichita rivers; includes L. Kickapoo in W center, parts of Diversion (NW) and Wichita (E) lakes. Agr. (wheat), dairying; cattle ranching. Oil and natural gas fields. Formed 1858.

Archer 1 town (□ 2 sq mi/5.2 sq km; 1990 pop.1,372), Alachua co., N central Fla., 15 mi/24 km WSW of Gainesville; 29°31′N 82°31′W. RR junction; lumber milling; mfg. (mining machinery). **2** town (1990 pop. 131), O'Brien co., NW Iowa, 7 mi/11.3 km SE of Sheldon; 43°06′N 95°44′W. Livestock; grain.

Archer City, town (1990 pop. 1,748), ⊙ Archer co., N Texas, 22 mi/35 km S of Wichita Falls; 33°35′N 98°37′W. Elev. 1,045 ft/319 m. Trade center for oil-producing, cattle ranching, agr. area (wheat, dairying). L. Kickapoo reservoir to NW; L. Arrowhead reservoir to NE. Settled c.1880, inc. 1910.

Arches National Park (□ 114 sq mi/295 sq km), Grand co., E Utah, 4 mi/6.4 km N of Moab. Located in red-rock country and overlooking the gorge of the Colorado R., bounded on SE by Colorado R. Covers 73,379 acres/29,696 ha and contains a vast and unusual array of natural rock formations. Water, frost, and wind have carved 90 graceful and varicolored arches, windows, spires, and pinnacles. Features include Devils Garden, the Windows, and Delicate Arch, Fiery Furnace, and Klondike Bluffs. Landscape Arch, the longest stonospan in the world at 291 ft across and 188 ft high. There are also Anasazi petroglyphs in the park. Est. 1929 as a natl. monument; est. 1971 as a natl. park.

Archie, town (1990 pop. 799), Cass co., W Mo., on South Grand R., 12 mi/19 km S of Harrisonville; 38°28′N 94°20′W. Cattle; hay, wheat, sorghum.

Archuleta, county (□ 1,354 sq mi/3,507 sq km; 1990 pop. 5,345), SW Colo.; ⊙ Pagosa Springs; 37°11′N 107°02′W. Bounded S by N.Mex.; bounded E by San Juan Mts.; drained by San Juan, Piedra, and Navajo rivers. Agr.; sheep, cattle. Large part of co. is in San Juan Natl. Forest, especially N; small part of Rio Grande Natl. Forest, E of Continental Divide, is in SE corner. Chimney Rock Anasazi Ruins in W; Navajo State Park in SW, at head of Navajo Reservoir (San Juan R.) formed in N.Mex. Part of Southern Ute Indian Reservation in SW. Formed 1885.

Arco, town (1990 pop. 1,016), ⊙ Butte co., SE central

Idaho, 65 mi/105 km NW of Pocatello in mt. region, on Big Lost R.; 43°38′N 113°18′W. Elev. 5,318 ft/1,621 m. Trade center for agr. (grain; livestock) and mining area. Hq. for Craters of the Moon Natl. Monument. Idaho Natl. Engineering Laboratory (U.S. Department of Energy), large tract of land 10 mi/16 km E, including EBR-1 Natl. Historic landmark, 1st town electrified by nuclear reactor in world, begun 1949. Craters of the Moon Natl. Monument to SW; parts of Challis Natl. Forest to N and NW.

Arco, village (1990 pop. 104), Lincoln co., SW Minn., 6 mi/9.7 km SSE of Ivanhoe; 44°22′N 96°10′W. Agr. (grain; livestock; dairying); mfg. (feeds). L. Stay to NE.

Arco del Diablo, N.Mex.: see FLORIDA PEAK.

Arcola (arh-CO-lah), city (1990 pop. 2,678), Douglas co., E central Ill., 6 mi/9.7 km S of Tuscola; 39°40′N 88°17′W. Agr. (corn, soybeans, oats; dairying); mfg. (apparel, light consumer goods). Coal production in area. Platted 1855, inc. 1865.

Arcola (ahr-KO-luh), town (1991 pop. 496), SE Sask., Canada, 60 mi/97 km E of Weyburn. Grain elevators, lumber and flour mills; resort.

Arcola 1 (ahr-KO-luh), village (1990 pop. 564), Washington co., W Miss., 15 mi/24 km SE of Greenville, on Deer Creek, bet. Black Bayou (W) and Bogus Phalia R. (E); 33°16′N 90°52′W. Agr. (cotton, grain, soybeans, sorghum; cattle). **2** village (1990 pop. 666), Fort Bend co., SE Texas, suburb 17 mi/27 km SSW of downtown Houston, near Oyster Creek; 29°30′N 95°27′W. Oil and natural gas. Agr. (rice, cotton, vegetables). Houston Southwest Airport is here.

Arcos de Canasí, Cuba: see CANASÍ.

Arcosanti (ar-ko-SAHN-tee), locality, Yavapai co., W central Ariz., 55 mi/89 km N of Phoenix, near Cordes Junction, on Interstate Highway 17. Planned cliffside community designed by architect Paolo Soleri, being developed in mid-1990s with capacity for 5,000 residents. Billed as a prototype "arcology" experiment, combining architecture and ecology in urban planning. Site of seminars, workshops, and musical events. Prescott Natl. Forest to E and W.

Arctic Archipelago, group of more than 50 large isls., N.W.T., N Canada, in the Arctic Ocean. The S members of the group include Baffin (the archipelago's largest isl.), Victoria, Banks, Prince of Wales, and Somerset isls.; N of Viscount Melville and Lancaster sounds are the Queen Elizabeth Isls., of which Ellesmere is the largest. Tundra and permanent ice cover the isls., on which oil and coal have been discovered. After Greenland, the Archipelago is the world's largest high-arctic land area.

Arctic Bay, trading post (1991 pop. 543), N Baffin Isl., SE Franklin dist., N.W.T., Canada, on E side of Admiralty Inlet; 73°03′N 85°12′W. Meteorological station; site of R.C. mission. Fur-trading post was est. 1926, later abandoned, reestablished 1936. Seal, caribou, polar bear, fox furs. Oil exploration. Scheduled air service. Lead-zinc mine at Nanisivik, 10 mi/16 km E by road.

Arctic Current, Canada: see LABRADOR CURRENT.

Arctic North Slope, Alaska: see ALASKA NORTH SLOPE.

Arctic Red River, village (1991 pop. 144), Mackenzie dist., NW N.W.T., Canada, 80 mi/129 km S of Inuvik on W side of Mackenzie R., and S side of confluence of Arctic Red R.; 67°26′N 133°45′W. Est. 1868 as a mission. Connected by ferry to Dempster Highway, completed 1978. Furs, caribou meat.

Arctic Red River, c.310 mi/500 km long, W N.W.T., Canada; rising in the Mackenzie Mts. of Inuvik Region; flowing generally NW to the Mackenzie R. A post of the Royal Can. Mounted Police and the village of Arctic Red R. located at mouth of river.

Arctic Slope, Alaska: see ALASKA NORTH SLOPE.

Arctic Stream, Canada: see LABRADOR CURRENT.

Arctic Village, Indian village (1990 pop. 96), NE Alaska, on Chandalar R., and 110 mi/177 km N of Fort Yukon; 68°10′N 145°40′W. Formerly Arctic.

Arden, uninc. city (1990 pop. 52,200), Sacramento co., central Calif., residential suburb 6 mi/9.7 km E of downtown Sacramento, on Amer. R. McClellan Air

Force Base. to N; Sacramento Army Depot to S. Statistically reported as Arden-Arcade. Arcade 3 mi/4.8 km NNE.

Arden, town, Richland co., central S.C.; N residential section of Columbia.

Arden 1 village (1990 pop. 477), New Castle co., N Del., residential suburb 6 mi/9.7 km N of downtown Wilmington; 39°49′N 75°29′W. Drained by South Branch Naaman Creek. Post office name formerly Grubbs. Founded 1900 as single-tax colony. **2** uninc. village, Buncombe co., W N.C., industrial suburb 7 mi/11.3 km S of downtown Asheville. Mfg. (metal fabrication, printing, food and beverages processing; plastic prods., machinery, consumer goods). Asheville Municipal Airport to SW.

Arden Hills, town (1990 pop. 9,199) Ramsey co., E Minn., suburb 7 mi/11.3 km NW of downtown Minneapolis, and 8 mi/12.9 km NNW of downtown St. Paul; 45°04′N 93°10′W. Mfg. (feeds, printing ink, furniture, electronic and medical equip.). Numerous small lakes in area.

Ardencroft, village (1990 pop. 282), New Castle co., N Del., residential suburb 5 mi/8 km NE of downtown Wilmington; 39°48′N 75°29′W.

Ardentown, village (1990 pop. 325), New Castle co., N Del., residential suburb 5 mi/8 km NE of downtown Wilmington; 39°49′N 75°29′W.

Ardley, village, S central Alta., Canada, 25 mi/40 km E of Red Deer. Coal mining; oil and natural gas; agr. (wheat, barley; cattle).

Ardmore 1 (AHRD-mor), city (1990 pop. 23,079), ⊙ Carter co., S Okla., 85 mi/137 km SSE of Oklahoma City; 34°11′N 97°07′W. Elev. 886 ft/270 m. It is the commercial center of an oil and farm area. Industries include oil refining; tourism; mfg. (electronic and plastic prods., electronic equip., fabricated metal prods., feeds, construction materials, machinery, apparel, transportation equip.; publishing and printing); lumber. Adjacent L. Murray State Park and the nearby Arbuckle Mts. and Chickasaw Natl. Recreation Area (to N) offer recreation; Goddard Arts Center. Inc. 1898. **2** uninc. city (1990 pop. 12,646), Lower Merion township, Montgomery co., SE Pa., residential suburb 8 mi/12.9 km W of downtown Philadelphia; 40°00′N 75°17′W. Mfg. (printing and publishing, food). Settled c.1800.

Ardmore 1 (AHRD-moor), town (1990 pop. 1,090), Limestone co., N Ala., on Tenn. state line, 14 mi/23 km NNE of Athens. Mfg. of wire prods. **2** uninc. town (1990 pop. 2,250), St. Joseph co., N Ind., suburb 4 mi/6.4 km WNW of South Bend. South Bend Michiana Airport to N. **3** town (1990 pop. 866), Giles co., S Tenn., at Ala. state line, 11 mi/27 km SE of Pulaski; 35°01′N 86°50′W. Mfg. (clothing).

Ardmore, village, Fall R. co., SW S.Dak., 30 mi/48 km SSW of Hot Springs, and on Hat Creek, at Nebr. state line. In Buffalo Gap Natl. Grassland; Oglala Natl. Grasslands (Nebr.) to S.

Ardoch (AHR-dahk), village (1990 pop. 49), Walsh co., NE N.Dak., 25 mi/40 km NNW of Grand Forks; 48°12′N 97°20′W. RR junction. L. Ardoch and Ardoch Natl. Wildlife Refuge to NE.

Ardsley, residential village (☐ 1 sq mi/2.6 sq km; 1990 pop. 4,272), Westchester co., SE N.Y., just NE of Dobbs Ferry in N.Y. city suburban area; 41°00′N 73°50′W. Mfg. (earth-moving equip., electronics, transportation equip., medical apparatus). Several major corporations hq. here. Has large arboretum maintained by Columbia Univ. Ardsley-on-Hudson is c.1 mi/1.6 km. NW, on E bank of the Hudson.

Ardsley-on-Hudson, N.Y.: see ARDSLEY.

Area Metropolitana de la Ciudad de México, Mexico: see ZONA METROPOLITANA DE LA CIUDAD DE MÉXICO.

Arecibo (ah-re-SEE-boh), city (1990 pop. 93,385), N P.R., a port on the Atlantic Ocean, at the mouth of the Rio Grande de Arecibo. It has liquor distilleries and is the commercial and industrial center of a region mfg. (furniture, machinery, chemicals, apparel), food processing; cattle. Arecibo Observatory, largest radar/radio telescope in the world, is nearby. Arecibo was founded in 1616. Cambalache (E) and Río Abajo (S) forest reserves are nearby. Lighthouse mus.; airport.

Arecibo Observatory (ah-re-SEE-bo), radio-astronomy facility located at Arecibo, P.R. It was completed in 1963 and is operated by Cornell Univ. under contract with the U.S. Natl. Science Foundation. Largest radar/radio telescope in the world. The principal instrument is a fixed antenna of spherical sect., 1,000 ft/305 m in diameter, that is built into a natural limestone bowl. As a result of the resurfacing of the antenna, which was completed in 1974, observations are possible up to a frequency of 4,000 MHz. A 100 ft/30 m satellite antenna can be used in conjunction with the large antenna for interferometer observations. In addition there is a wide range of instrumentation for measuring ionospheric conditions. Principal research programs include studies of radio emissions from many types of objects, esp. the cores of supernovae called pulsars; radar studies of comets and asteroids; and ionospheric studies. Visitor center recently completed.

Arecibo River (ah-re-SEE-bo) or **Río Grande de Arecibo**, c.40 mi/64 km long, W central P.R.; rises in the Cordillera Central; flows N to the Atlantic just E of Arecibo. On its mid-course is the large Dos Bocas dam, reservoir, and hydroelectric plant (completed 1943). With the Dos Bocas project is now linked the Caonillas dam (230 ft/70 m high, 780 ft/238 m long) on the small Caonillas R., an affluent. Río Abajo Forest Reserve is W near L. Dos Bocas.

Aredale (AR-dail), town (1990 pop. 88), Butler co., N central Iowa, 12 mi/19 km NE of Alison; 42°49′N 93°00′W. Grain storage.

Arena (ah-REE-nah), village (1990 pop. 525), Iowa co., S Wis., near Wisconsin R., 27 mi/43 km WNW of Madison; 43°09′N 89°54′W. In dairying region; cheese. Tower Hill State Park is to W. Timberline Ski Area to SW.

Arena, Point, Calif.: see POINT ARENA.

Arenac (AHR-e-nak), county (☐ 680 sq mi/1,761 sq km; 1990 pop. 14,931), E Mich.; ⊙ Standish. Bounded SE by Saginaw Bay; 44°02′N 83°45′W; drained by Rifle, Pine, and Au Gres rivers. Dairy prods.; cattle, hogs, poultry; agr. (potatoes, corn, sugar beets, wheat, oats, soybeans, grain, beans, cucumbers). Metal prods., industrial machinery. Commercial fishing. Resorts. Arenac County Saginaw Project Indian Reservation is on S boundary. Formed 1831.

Arendtsville (A-rents-vil), borough (1990 pop. 693), Adams co., S Pa., 7 mi/11.3 km NNW of Gettysburg, on Conewago Creek; 39°55′N 77°17′W. Light mfg.; agr. (apples, cherries, grain, soybeans; livestock; dairying). Michaux State Forest to NW.

Arenzville (ARNZ-ville), village (1990 pop. 432), Cass co., W central Ill., 10 mi/16 km WSW of Virginia; 39°52′N 90°22′W. In agr. area (corn, soybeans, sorghum; cattle, hogs); corn seed processing, lumber, millwork.

Argenta (arh-JEN-tah), village (1990 pop. 940), Macon co., central Ill., 11 mi/34 km NE of Decatur; 39°58′N 88°49′W. Corn, wheat, soybeans.

Argenteuil (ahr-zhah-TUH-ee), county (☐ 783), SW Que., Canada, on Ont. border; ⊙ Lachute; 45°48′N 74°28′W.

Argentine Mountain (10,000 ft/3,048 m), SE B.C., Canada, in Selkirk Mts., on W edge of Hamber Provincial Park, 40 mi/64 km NNE of Revelstoke; 51°33′N 117°55′W.

Argentine Pass (13,207 ft/4,025 m), central Colo., in Front Range, bet. Clear Creek and Summit cos. One of Colo.'s highest passes, crosses Continental Divide. Once crossed by wagon road, 1st used 1872; now crossed by trail. Grays Peak nearby.

Argo, Ill.: see SUMMIT.

Argonia (ahr-GO-nee-uh), village (1990 pop. 529), Sumner co., S Kansas, on Chikaskia R. and 15 mi/24 km W of Wellington; 37°16′N 97°45′W. Grain; light mfg.

Argonne, Ill.: see LEMONT.

Argonne National Laboratory, nuclear research center, principal facilities located in DuPage co., Ill., 2 mi/3.2 km S of Darien and 27 mi/43 km SW of downtown Chicago, N of Des Plaines R.; 41°42′N 87°58′W. Surrounded by forest preserve. Associated with the Natl.

Reactor Testing Station, 50 mi/80 km W of Idaho Falls, Idaho. This atomic energy research and development establishment was founded in 1946 by the U.S. Atomic Energy Commission. Since 1966 the laboratory has operated under an agreement involving the U.S. Atomic Energy Commission, the Argonne Universities Association, and the Univ. of Chicago. The principal objectives of the laboratory are to carry out multidisciplinary basic research, much of which involves the use of radiation as a tool in the physical and life sciences, and to work on the design and development of nuclear reactors.

Argos, town (1990 pop. 1,642), Marshall co., N Ind., 8 mi/12.9 km SSE of Plymouth; 41°14′N 86°15′W. In agr. area. Mfg. (metal stampings, automobile parts, electric signs).

Arguello, Point (ar-gai-yo), SW Calif., coastal promontory and westernmost point of Santa Barbara co., 12 mi/19 km WSW of Lompoc. Lighthouse.

Argusville (AHR-guhs-vil), village (1990 pop. 161), Cass co., E N.Dak., 14 mi/23 km NNW of Fargo; 47°02′N 96°56′W.

Argyle 1 (AHR-geil), town (1990 pop. 206), Clinch co., S Ga., 20 mi/32 km WSW of Waycross; 31°04′N 82°39′W. **2** town (1990 pop. 178), Osage co., central Mo., 21 mi/34 km SSE of Jefferson City; 38°17′N 92°01′W. **3** town (1990 pop. 1,575), Denton co., N Texas, 9 mi/14.5 km S of Denton and 30 mi/48 km N of downtown Fort Worth, near Denton Creek; 33°06′N 97°10′W. Agr. area (cattle, horse; wheat, peanuts).

Argyle 1 village (1990 pop. 636), Marshall co., NW Minn., on Middle R., in Red R. valley, and 10 mi/16 km N of Warren; 48°20′N 96°49′W. Grain, alfalfa, beans, sugar beets, sunflowers; poultry, cattle, sheep; mfg. of livestock feeds. Old Mill State Park to E. **2** village (1990 pop. 295), Washington co., E N.Y., 9 mi/14.5 km SE of Glens Falls; 43°14′N 73°29′W. Dairying area. Lakes nearby. **3** village (1990 pop. 798), Lafayette co., S Wis., on East Branch of Pecatonica R. and 14 mi/23 km NW of Monroe; 42°42′N 89°52′W. In agr. area (cheese, sorghum); mfg. (water pumps, food processing). Yellowstone L. State Park to NW.

Argyle, township (1990 pop. 202), Penobscot co., S central Maine, on the Penobscot, 18 mi/29 km N of Bangor; 45°04′N 68°42′W. Agr.; lumbering.

Arial (AR-ee-uhl), uninc. town (1990 pop. 2,604), Pickens co., NW S.C., 3 mi/4.8 km NW of Easley; 34°51′N 82°38′W. Agr. includes poultry, hogs, dairying, corn.

Arichat (A-ruh-shaht), village, ⊙ Richmond co., E N.S., on S coast of Madame Isl., just S of Cape Breton Isl., 18 mi/29 km ESE of Port Hawkesbury; 45°31′N 61°01′W. Fishing port; lumbering. First settled by the French c.1730; raided by John Paul Jones during Amer. Revolution.

Ariguanabo, Lake (ahr-ee-gwah-NAH-bo), (5 mi/8 km long, 2.5 mi/4 km wide), Ciudad de La Habana prov., W Cuba, in Ariguanabo depression, 18 mi/29 km SW of Havana; 22°56′N 82°33′W. Largest inland body of water of the isl., with wells supplying a good share of Havana's drinking water. Large textile mill in nearby town of Ariguanabo.

Arikaree River, E Colo., NW Kansas, and SW Nebr., E central Colo.; South Fork rises near Limon; flows NE c.35 mi/56 km. North Fork rises N of Limon; flows ENE c.30 mi/48 km (both rise in N Lincoln co., E central Colo.); joins in S Washington co.; main stream flows ENE past Beecher Isl. Battleground site, through extreme NW corner of Kansas to Haigler, SW Nebr. joining North Fork Republican R.

Arima (ah-REE-mah), town (1990 pop. 44,147), N Trinidad, Trinidad and Tobago, on RR, and 16 mi/26 km E of Port of Spain, at head of extensive plain; 10°38′N 61°17′W. Once flourishing cacao center, the town has recovered as a regional market center, retail center. Originally a native Indian village and mission.

Arimao River (ah-ree-MOU), Villa Clara prov., central Cuba; flows c.50 mi/80 km WSW to the Caribbean Sea just E of Cienfuegos Bay; 22°01′N 80°24′W. Receives Hanabanilla R., noted for its waterfall.

Arimo, village (1990 pop. 311), Bannock co., SE Idaho, 25 mi/40 km SE of Pocatello; elev. 4,736 ft/1,444 m; 42°34′N 112°10′W. Wheat, oats, potatoes; cattle, sheep. Parts of Caribou Natl. Forest to N and SW.

Ario de Rayón (AH-ree-o dai rah-YON), village, Michoacán, central Mexico, on RR, and 5 mi/8 km NW of Zamora de Hidalgo. Cereals, sugarcane, vegetables; livestock. Sometimes Santa Mónica Ario.

Ario de Rosales (AH-ree-o dai ro-SAH-lais), city (1990 pop. 13,049) and township, ⊙ Ario municipio, Michoacán, central Mexico, on SW edge of central plateau, 20 mi/32 km SE of Uruapan; 19°12′N 101°42′W. Elev. 6,726 ft/2,050 m. Agr. center (cereals, coffee, tobacco, sugarcane, tropical fruit; cattle). Lumbering.

Arion, town (1990 pop. 148), Crawford co., W Iowa, on Boyer R., and 7 mi/11.3 km SW of Denison; 41°57′N 95°27′W.

Aripo, Mount (ah-REE-po), Span. *Cerro de Aripo*, peak (3,085 ft/940 m), N Trinidad, Trinidad and Tobago (highest peak of Trinidad and Tobago), 19 mi/31 km ENE of Port of Spain; 10°43′N 61°15′W.

Arispe, town (1990 pop. 92), Union co., S Iowa, on Grand R., and 10 mi/16 km SE of Creston; 40°57′N 94°13′W.

Arispe, Mexico: see ARIZPE.

Arista, Mexico: see VILLA DE ARISTA.

Aristazabal Island (A-ris-tah-zuh-BAHL), (□ 149 sq mi/386 sq km; 28 mi/45 km long, 10 mi/16 km wide), W B.C., Canada, in Hecate Strait, just W of Princess Royal Isl., across Laredo Channel; 52°40′N 128°08′W. Wooded surface is hilly, rises to 1,085 ft/331 m (S). Just N is small Rennison Isl.

Ariton (ER-uh-tuhn), farming town (1990 pop. 743), Dale co., SE Ala., 10 mi/16 km NNW of Ozark. Mfg. (farm equip., asphalt).

Arivechi (ah-ree-VE-chee), town (1990 pop. 926), Sonora, NW Mexico, on affluent of Yaqui R., and 110 mi/177 km E of Hermosillo; 28°55′N 109°10′W. Corn, beans; cattle.

Arizona, state (□ 114,006 sq mi/295,276 sq km; 1995 est. pop. 4,217,940), SW U.S., admitted as the 48th state of the Union in 1912; ⊙ (and largest city) PHOENIX; 34°36′N 112°32′S. Ariz. is bounded on the N by Utah; on the W by S Nev. and Calif. (Colorado R. forms all of Calif. and part of Nev. border); on the S by Mexico (Baja Calif. Norte and Sonora states); and on the E by N.Mex. NE corner (Four Corners) touches Colo., only point in U.S. common to 4 states. In N Ariz. is the Colorado Plateau, an area of dry plains more than 4,000 ft/1,219 m high, with deep canyons, including the famous GRAND CANYON carved by the Colorado R. Along the Little Colorado R., which runs NW through the plateau to join the Colorado, are the Painted Desert, where erosion has left colorful layers of sediment exposed, and the Petrified Forest Natl. Park, in NE, one of the world's most extensive areas of petrified wood. Lying S of the Grand Canyon are the San Francisco Peaks, including Humphreys Peak, the highest point (12,655 ft/3,857 m) in the state. The S edge of the Colo. Plateau is marked by an escarpment called Mogollon Rim. The S ½ of the state has desert basins broken up by mts. with rocky peaks and extending NW to SE across central Ariz. To the S, the Gila R., a major tributary of the Colorado, flows W across the entire S part of state. This area has desert plains separated by mt. chains running N and S; in the W the plains fall to the relatively low elev. of c.140 ft/43 m (lowest point in Ariz., 70 ft/21 m where Colorado R. enters Mexico) in the region around YUMA. Ariz. abounds in minerals, including copper, which has given it the name Copper State. Although some mt. peaks receive an annual rainfall of more than 30 in/76 cm, precipitation in most of the state is low, and much of the state's history has been shaped by the inadequate water supply. Since the early 20th cent., massive irrigation projects have been built in its valleys. Roosevelt, Horse Mesa, Mormon Flat, and Stewart Mt. dams, with reservoirs and storage lakes, irrigate the Salt R. valley. The Gillespie Dam (a private dam) on the Gila R., which helped irrigate the Gila Bend vicinity, was completely silted in and it was breached in the early 1990s. The Coolidge Dam, with its San Carlos reservoir, serves the area near CASA GRANDE in the SE. W Ariz. is irrigated by Colorado R. dams, which also serve Calif. These include Glen Canyon (L. Powell) in N and Hoover (L. Mead), Davis (L. Mohave), Parker (L. Havasu), Imperial (Imperial Reservoir), and Laguna dams in S. The lakes of Colorado R. in W are often referred to as Ariz.'s "West Coast." At the Parker dam, the Central Ariz. Project diverts water via canal to the cities of Phoenix and TUCSON. Ariz. also obtains water from groundwater pumping stations. The state's principal crops are cotton, hay, vegetables, fruit and sorghum. Cattle, sheep, hogs, poultry, and dairing are also important farm products. Agr. is centered in Phoenix and central Gila Valley (Casa Grand). Mfg. is the leading economic activity with aerospace, electronics, transportation equip., and construction materials, as the major prods. High-technology research and development, communications, and service industries are also extremely important. Copper is still the state's most valuable mineral; Ariz. is the nation's largest copper-producing state. Other leading mineral resources include molybdenum, sand, gravel, and cement. The mts. in the N and central regions have 3,180,000 acres/1,286,946 ha of commercial forests, chiefly ponderosa pines (the largest stand in the U.S.) and other firs, which support the state's lumber and bldg.-materials industries. The U.S. govt. owns about 95% of the commercial forests in the state. Natl. forests (Kaibab in N, Coconino and Prescott in S, Apache-Sitgreaves in E, Tonto in center, Coronado in SE) and state forests attract millions of tourists yearly. Tourism is bolstered in the N and NW by the Grand Canyon Natl. Park, the Painted Desert, the Petrified Forest Natl Park in E, Organ Pipe Natl Monument on Mex. border, Canyon de Chelly Natl. Monument in NE, meteor craters, anc. Native Amer. ruins, and the Navajo and Hopi reservations that cover nearly all of the state's NE quadrant. The SE region of the state has a warm, dry climate that also attracts a large tourist trade. Bet. 1940 and 1960 Arizona's pop. increased more than 100%, and bet. 1960 and 1970 it increased another 36%. The 35% pop. increase bet. 1980 and 1990 again ranked Ariz. among the fastest-growing states. Significant are the many communities that have grown or have been developed outside metro areas; retirees are moving here to escape the city as well as the cold. Other sites include Barry M. Goldwater (Luke) Air Force Range and Yuma Proving Ground (U.S.Army) in SW; Cabeza Prieta and Kofu Natl. Wildlife Refuges in SW. The mountainous N has not shared the pop. growth of the S sections of the state. There were 203,527 Native Americans in Ariz. in 1990, the 3d highest pop. in the U.S. In addition to the Navajo, the state's Native Americans include Mohave, Apache, Hopi, Paiute, Tahono O'odham (Papago), Pima, Maricopa, Yavapaí, Hualapai, Quechan, Mojave, Yaqui, and Havasupai pops. Part of large Navajo Indian Reservation in NE, also Hopi Indian Reservation, Fort Apache and San Carlos Indian Reservations in E, Tohono O'odham (Papago) and San Xavier Indian Reservation in S, Gila R. and Ak-Chin Indian Reservation in center, parts of Colorado River and Fort Mohave Indian Reservation in W, Havasupai, Hualapai and Kaibab Indian Reservation in NW. Agr. is the basis of their economy, but the lack of water makes farming difficult; thus there is much poverty. The gaming industry is very important on several reservations. Federal and state projects have sought to support Native Amer. education and to introduce modern farming methods on the reservations. The Native Amer. economy depends on production of handicrafts, including leather goods, woven items, pottery, and the famous silver and turquoise jewelry of the Navajos. Little is known of the earliest indigenous cultures in Ariz., but they probably lived in the region as early as 25,000 B.C. A later culture, the Hohokam (A.D. 500–1450) were pit dwellers who constructed extensive irrigation systems. The Pueblo flourished in Ariz. bet. the 11th and 14th cent. and built many of the elaborate cliff dwellings that still stand. The Apache and Navajo came to the area in c.1300 from Canada. Probably the

1st Span. explorer to enter Ariz. (c.1536) was Cabeza de Vaca. Franciscan friar Marcos de Niza reached the state in 1539; he was followed by Francisco Vasquez de Coronado, who led an expedition from Mexico in 1540 in search of the 7 legendary cities of gold. Despite extensive exploration, the region was neglected by the Spanish in favor of the more fruitful area of N.Mex. The 1st European to reach the Grand Canyon was Capt. García López de Cárdenas, who was sent by Coronado. Father Eusebio Kino, a Jesuit, founded the missions of Guevavi (1692) and Tumacacori (1696), near NOGALES, and San Xavier del Bac (1700), near Tucson. Jesuits, however, were expelled by the Hopi from the Span. Empire in 1767, and those in Ariz. subsequently lost their control. The Ariz. region came under Mex. control following the Mex. war of independence from Spain (1810–1821). In the early 1800s, U.S. mt. men, trappers and traders such as Kit Carson, trapped beaver in the area, but otherwise there were few settlers. In the Treaty of Guadalupe Hidalgo (1848), ending the Mexican War (1846–1848), Mexico relinquished control of the area N of the Gila R. to the U.S. This area became part of the U.S. Territory of N.Mex. in 1850. The U.S., wishing to build a RR through the area S of the Gila R., bought the area bet. the river and the S boundary of Ariz. from Mexico in the Gadsden Purchase (1853). Ariz.'s minerals, valued even by prehistoric miners, attracted most of the early explorers, and although the area remained a relatively obscure sect. of the Territory of N.Mex., mining continued sporadically. Small numbers of prospectors, crossing Ariz. to join the Calif. gold rush (1849), found gold, silver, and a neglected metal—copper. By the 1870s mining was flourishing, and by the following decade the Copper Queen Co. at Bisbee was exploiting one of the area's largest copper deposits. In 1877 silver was discovered at TOMBSTONE, setting off a boom that drew throngs of prospectors to Ariz. but lasted less than 10 years. Tombstone also became famous for its lawlessness; Wyatt Earp and his brothers gained their reputations during the famous gunfight (1881) at the O. K. Corral. In 1861, at the outbreak of the Civil War, conventions held at Tucson and Mesilla declared the area part of the Confederacy. In the only major battle in the Ariz. area, Confederate troops were defeated NW of Tucson in the battle of Picacho Pass. In 1863, Ariz. was organized as a separate territory, with its first, temporary capital at Fort Whipple. PRESCOTT became the capital in 1865. Charles D. Poston, who had worked to achieve the state's new status, was elected as the territory's 1st delegate to the U.S. Congress. The capital was moved to Tucson in 1867, back to Prescott in 1877, and finally to Phoenix in 1889. When Confederate troops were routed and Union soldiers went E to fight in the Civil War, settlement was abandoned. It was resumed after the war and encouraged by the Homestead Act (1862), the Desert Land Act (1877), and the Carey Act (1894)—all of which turned land over to settlers and required them to develop it. The region had been held precariously by U.S. soldiers during the intermittent warfare (1861–1886) with the Apaches, who were led by Cochise and later Geronimo. Gen. George Crook waged a successful campaign against the Apaches in 1882–1885, and in 1886 Geronimo finally surrendered to federal troops. Ranching began to thrive and sheep raising grew from solely a Navajo occupation to a major enterprise among white settlers. After 1897, the U.S. Forestry Bureau issued grazing permits to protect public land from depletion. By 1880 the Santa Fe and Southern Pacific RRs both extended into Ariz. In 1912, Ariz., still a frontier territory, attained statehood. Its constitution created a storm, with such "radical" political features as initiative, referendum, and judicial recall. Only after recall had been deleted did President Taft sign the statehood bill. Once admitted to the Union, Ariz. restored the recall provision. Irrigation, spurred by the Desert Land Act and by Mormon immigration, had promoted farming in the S part of the territory. By 1900, diverted streams were irrigating 200,000 acres/80,940 ha. With the opening of the Roosevelt Dam (1911), a federally financed project, massive irrigation projects transformed the new state's valleys. Although its mines were not unionized until the mid-1930s, strikes occurred at the copper mines of Clifton and Morenci in 1915, and at the Bisbee mines in 1917. During World War II, defense industries were est. in Ariz. Mfg., notably electronic industries, continued to develop after the war, especially around Phoenix and Tucson; in the 1960s, mfg. achieved economic supremacy over mining and agr. in Ariz. During the 1970s and 1980s the state experienced phenomenal economic growth as it and other SUNBELT states attracted high-technology industries with enormous growth potential. With the development of irrigation and hydroelectric projects along the Colo. R. and its tributaries, water rights became a subject of litigation bet. Ariz. and Calif. In 1963 the U.S. Supreme Court ruled that Calif.'s water rights on the Colorado pertained only to the main stream of the river. Ariz. was given rights to a share of the water from the river's main stream and sole water rights over its tributaries within Ariz.'s boundaries. In 1968, Congress passed legislation authorizing the Central Ariz. Project, a 335 mi/539 km canal system (Hayden-Rhodes and Salt-Gila aquaducts) to divert water from the Colorado R. to Gila and Santa Cruz river systems and to the booming metropolitan areas of Phoenix and Tucson. Construction began in 1974 for the canal, which uses a series of dams, tunnels, and pumps to raise the water 1,247 ft/380 m from the river valley to the desert plain. Attacked by environmentalists who feared that it would damage the fragile desert ecosystems, the project was finally completed in 1991 at a cost of more than $3.5 billion. The state's constitution provides for an elected governor and bicameral legislature, with a 30-member senate and a 60-member house of representatives. The governor and members of the legislature serve 2-year terms. The unit of local govt. is the co. The state elects 2 Senators and 6 Representatives to the U.S. Congress and has 8 electoral votes. Until the 1950s and 1960s the Democratic party predominated in Ariz. politics, but Republicans have since gained strength. In 1964, Senator Barry M. Goldwater of Ariz. was the unsuccessful Republican candidate for the U.S. presidency. Stewart L. Udall, an Ariz. Democrat, served as Secretary of the Interior under presidents Kennedy and Johnson. In 1988, Gov. Evan Meacham, a Republican, was convicted in his impeachment trial and removed from office. He was charged with obstructing justice and and financial improprieties. Educational institutions include the Univ. of Ariz., at Tucson; Ariz. State Univ., at Tempe; Northern Ariz. Univ., at FLAGSTAFF, many community colleges; and several private institutions. Ariz. has 15 cos.: APACHE, COCHISE, COCONINO, GILA, GRAHAM, GREENLEE, LA PAZ, MARICOPA, MOHAVE, NAVAJO, PIMA, PINAL, SANTA CRUZ, YAVAPAI, Yuma.

Arizona City, uninc. town (1990 pop. 1,940), Pinal co., S central Ariz., 9 mi/14.5 km SSE of Casa Grande. In irrigated agr. area (cotton, grain, fruit, vegetables; livestock); mfg. (transformers, plastics prods.). Tohomo O'odham (Papago) Indian Reservation to SW.

Arizpe (ah-REES-pai), city (1990 pop. 1,680) and township, ⊙ Arizpe municipio, Sonora, NW Mexico, on Sonora R., and 100 mi/161 km NNE of Hermosillo; 30°20′N 110°11′W. Agr. (wheat, corn, sugar; livestock). Anc. colonial capital of Sonora and Sinaloa. Sometimes spelled Arispe.

Arjay (AHR-jai), uninc. village (1990 pop. 700), Bell co., SE Ky., in the Cumberland Mts., 14 mi/23 km N of Middlesboro. In bituminous-coal mining area; mfg. (lumber); timber.

Arkabutla (ahrk-uh-BUHT-luh), village, Tate co., NW Miss., 10 mi/16 km NW of Senatobia. Agr. (cotton, grain; cattle). Arkabutla Reservoir to NE, on Coldwater R.

Arkadelphia (ahr-kuh-DEL-fee-uh), city (1990 pop. 10,014), ⊙ Clark co., S central Ark., 26 mi/42 km S of Hot Springs, and on Ouachita R. (head of navigation); 34°07′N 93°04′W. In timber, diversified farm area; mfg. (wood prods., apparel, furniture, transportation equip.; machining, printing, food processing). Seat of Ouachita Baptist Univ. and Henderson State Univ. First settled c.1807, inc. 1836.

Arkansas, state (□ 53,182 sq mi/137,741 sq km; 1995 est. pop. 2,483,769), S central U.S., admitted as the 25th state of the Union in 1836; 34°46′N 92°18′W. The ⊙ and largest city is LITTLE ROCK; other important cities are FORT SMITH, FAYETTEVILLE, NORTH LITTLE ROCK, PINE BLUFF, HOT SPRINGS, TEXARKANA, and WEST MEMPHIS. On the E, the Mississippi R. separates Ark. from Tenn. and Miss. The state is bounded on the N by Mo., on the W by Okla. and a part of Texas, and on the S by La. The Arkansas R. flows SE across the state bet. the Ozark plateau and the Ouachita Mts. and runs down to the S and E plains to empty into the Mississippi. The other rivers of the state also flow generally SE or S to the Mississippi; these include the St. Francis (which forms part of the E Mo. state line), the White R., the Ouachita, and the Red R. (which forms part of the Texas state line). The climate of Ark. is marked by long, hot summers and mild winters. The state's many lakes and streams and its abundant wildlife provide excellent hunting and fishing. Tourism is an important state industry. In particular, the mineral springs at Hot Springs attract many visitors. The state's transportation network is based on rivers as well as roads, RRs, and air travel. The 440 mi/708 km Arkansas R. Navigation System links Okla. and Ark. to the Mississippi R. A major cotton-producing state in the 19th cent., Ark. has since diversified its agr. production and overall economy. Soybeans and rice are of particular importance, however, cotton remains an important crop. Ark. has become a leading producer of poultry; other livestock and dairy prods. also contribute greatly to the farm economies. The state's most important mineral prods. are petroleum, bromine and bromine compounds, and natural gas, and it is the nation's leading bauxite producer. Principal mfg. includes food prods., chemicals, electrical equip., paper, lumber and wood prods., furniture, auto and airplane parts, and machinery. A people known as the Bluff Dwellers, who inhabited caves, probably lived in the Ark. area before 500. They were followed by the Mound Builders, who received their name from the mounds they constructed, apparently for ceremonial purposes. The first white men to arrive in Ark. (1541–1542) were probably members of the Span. expedition under Hernando De Soto. Later, the Fr. explorers Jacques Marquette and Louis Joliet came S along the Mississippi to the mouth of the Ark. R. A number of Native Amer. groups, such as the Osage, Quapaw, and Caddos, lived in the vicinity. In 1682, La Salle's lieutenant, Henri de Tonti, est. Ark. Post, the first white settlement in the Ark. area. La Salle claimed the Mississippi valley for France, and the region became part of the Fr. territory of La. The French ceded the La. territory to Spain in 1762 but regained it again before it passed to the U.S. under the La. Purchase (1803). Ark. became part of the Territory of Mo. in 1812. In 1819 it was made a separate entity, and the first territorial legislature met at Ark. Post. The capital was moved to Little Rock in 1821. Ark. achieved statehood in 1836. The cotton boom of 1818 brought the first large wave of settlers, and the Southern plantation system, moving W, fixed itself in the alluvial plains of S and E Ark. As the Civil War began, poorer farmers were generally indifferent to questions of slavery and states' rights. The slaveholding planters held the most political power, however, and after some hesitation, Ark. finally seceded (1861) from the Union. In the Civil War, Confederate defeats at Pea Ridge (March 1862), Prairie Grove (Dec. 1862), and Arkansas Post (Jan. 1863) led to Union occupation of N Ark., and Gen. Grant's Vicksburg campaign separated states W of the Mississippi from the rest of the Confederacy. In Sept. 1863, Federal troops entered Little Rock, where a Unionist convention in Jan. 1864 set up a govt. that repudiated secession and abolished slavery. Because the state refused at first to enfranchise blacks, Ark. was not readmitted to the Union until 1868, when a new constitution gave blacks the right to vote and hold office. Reconstruction in Ark.

reached a turbulent climax in the struggle (1874) of 2 Republican claimants to the governorship, Elisha Baxter and Joseph Brooks. Baxter's apparent success in the election was not accepted by Brooks, and followers of the 2 men resorted to violence in what became known as the Brooks-Baxter War. After President Ulysses S. Grant declared Baxter as governor, Baxter called a constituent assembly dominated by Democrats to frame a new state constitution. The convention adopted (1874) the constitution that, in amended form, still remains in force. During Reconstruction the regime of carpetbaggers and scalawags was detested by most Ark. whites, but it brought advances in education and (at exorbitant costs caused by corruption) RR construction. Because of high cotton prices and the failure to give the freed blacks any economic status, the broken plantation system was replaced by sharecropping and farm tenancy. The lives of the people of the Ozarks remained largely unchanged; they retained the customs, skills, and superstitions that have given the hill folk their distinctive regional characteristics. In the late 19th cent., as RR construction proceeded, Ark.'s pop. grew substantially, and bauxite and lumbering industries developed. Oil was discovered in Ark., near EL DORADO, in 1921. Disaster struck in 1927 when the Mississippi R. overflowed, flooding ⅕ of the state. With the fortunes of the state pegged to the price of cotton, the Depression of the early 1930s struck hard. Dispossessed tenants, black and white, formed (1939) the Southern Tenant Farmers Union; after trouble with the authorities, it moved its hq. to Memphis, Tenn. A strike called in 1936 spread to other regions before its strength waned. Other impoverished farmers migrated W to Calif. as "Arkies" — like the "Okies" from neighboring Okla. After World War I, Afr. Americans moved in a steady stream to the industrial N. World War II brought further loss of pop. as workers left Ark. for war factories elsewhere. The war, however, created a boom for new industries in the state, notably the processing of bauxite into aluminum. The decline of industrial output after the war was offset by the vigorous efforts of a state development commission formed in 1955 to attract new industry to Ark. In 1957, Gov. Orval Faubus of Ark. became a center of natl. and world attention when he resisted the attempted desegregation of public schools in Little Rock. In 1971, Ark. and landlocked Okla. joined in the Arkansas R. Navigation System, a project that developed the Arkansas R. basin to provide water transportation to the Mississippi. In the 1980s, the Ark.-based Wal-Mart merchandise chain became the largest retailer in the U.S. Started in 1962 as a small-town discount store, the chain would eventually make Ark. founder Sam Walton the wealthiest person in the U.S. Tyson's, also headquartered in Ark., became the largest poultry firm in the world. The state constitution (1874) provides for an elected governor and bicameral legislature, with a 35-member senate and a 100-member house of representatives. The representatives serve 2-year terms; governor and senators serve for 4 years. Ark. sends 2 senators and 4 representatives to the U.S. Congress and has 6 electoral votes. Ark. has long been dominated by the Democratic party, but in 1966 Winthrop Rockefeller was elected the state's first Republican governor since Reconstruction and was reelected in 1968. Bill Clinton was elected governor 5 times bet. 1978 and 1990. In 1992 Clinton was elected President of the U.S. Among the institutions of higher education in the state are the Univ. of Ark., at Fayetteville; Ark. State Univ., at Jonesboro; Hendrix Col. and the State Col. of Ark., at Conway; Ouachita Baptist Col. and Henderson State Col., at Arkadelphia; the Col. of the Ozarks, at Clarksville; Ark. Col., at Batesville; and Harding Col., at Searcy. Ark. has 75 cos.: ARKANSAS, ASHLEY, BAXTER, BENTON, BOONE, BRADLEY, CALHOUN, CARROLL, CHICOT, CLARK, CLEBURNE, CLEVELAND, COLUMBIA, CONWAY, CRAIGHEAD, CRAWFORD, CRITTENDEN, CROSS, DALLAS, DESHA, DREW, FAULKNER, FRANKLIN, FULTON, GARLAND, GRANT, GREENE, HEMPSTEAD, HOT SPRING, HOWARD, INDEPENDENCE, IZARD, JACKSON, JEFFERSON, JOHNSON, LAFAYETTE, LAWRENCE, LEE, LINCOLN, LITTLE RIVER, LOGAN, LONOKE, MADISON, MARION, MILLER, MISSISSIPPI, MONROE, MONTGOMERY, NEVADA, NEWTON, OUACHITA, PERRY, PHILLIPS, PIKE, POINSETT, POLK, POPE, PRAIRIE, PULASKI, RANDOLPH, SAINT FRANCIS, SALINE, SCOTT, SEARCY, SEBASTIAN, SEVIER, SHARP, STONE, UNION, VAN BUREN, WASHINGTON, WHITE, WOODRUFF, YELL.

Arkansas, county (□ 1,035 sq mi/2,681 sq km; 1990 pop. 21,653), E central Ark.; ⊙ Stuttgart and De Witt. Bounded S by Ark. R.; drained by White R. and small Bayou Meto; 34°17'N 91°22'W. Agr. (cotton, rice, corn, oats, soybeans, hay, lespedeza; livestock); lumbering, rice and cotton processing, commercial fishing; ships pecans. Has Ark. Post State Park (recreational area). Duck, quail hunting. Formed 1813.

Arkansas 1 and 2 Nuclear Power Plants, Ark.: see POPE CO.

Arkansas City (ahr-KAN-zez), city (1990 pop. 12,762), Cowley co., S Kansas, at the confluence of the Arkansas and the Walnut rivers, near the Okla. border, and 14 mi/23 km S of Winfield; 37°04'N 97°02'W. Elev. 1,120 ft/341 m. RR junction. Located in an agr. and oil region (rich oil fields were discovered in 1914). Mfg. (wheat milling, printing, transportation equip., mobile homes, petroleum refining). Ark. City was the starting point for the "run" (1893) of thousands of homesteaders into the Cherokee strip; a marker S of the city commemorates the event. Cowley County Community Col. and Vocational Tech. School in city. Cowley State Fishing L. to E. Cherokee Strip Living Mus. to S. Inc. 1872.

Arkansas City, village (1990 pop. 523), ⊙ Desha co., SE Ark., c.60 mi/97 km SE of Pine Bluff, and 15 mi/24 km NNW of Greenville, Miss., on the Mississippi R.; 33°36'N 91°12'W. Founded c.1873.

Arkansas Post, uninc. community (1990 est. pop. 20), on the Arkansas R., SE Ark. Founded by the French in 1686 as a trading post, it is the oldest white settlement in the state; it became the capital of the Ark. territory in 1819. Once an important port, Ark. Post was a Confederate stronghold during the Civil War until it was captured by Union troops in 1863. Ark. Post Natl. Memorial (formerly state park) is there.

Arkansas Post National Memorial (389 acres/157 ha), SE Ark. Authorized 1960. Site of the first permanent Fr. settlement in the lower Mississippi valley. Founded 1686. See ARKANSAS POST. Formerly Ark. Post State Park.

Arkansas River, c.1,450 mi/2,333 km long; rising in the Rocky Mts., N Lake co., central Colo., 8 mi/12.9 km WNW of Leadville; flows E through Turquoise L., and Leadville, then SE and E, past Cañon City, through Public Reservoir and city of Pueblo, past La Junta, through John Martin Reservoir, past Lamar, Colo., and past Kansas, continues past Dodge City, Great Bend, Hutchinson, through Wichita, SE into Okla., through Kaw and Keystone reservoirs, becoming a navigable stream at Tulsa due to the Ark. R. Navigation System. The river continues SE past Muskayes, through Webber Falls and Robert S. Kerr (joined here by Canadian R.) reservoirs. It enters state of Ark. at Fort Smith, flowing E and SE, through Ozark Reservoir and Dardanell L. Reservoir, through Little Rock and past Pine Bluff, entering Mississippi R. 25 mi/40 km ENE of McGeher, Ark. A series of dams from Tulsa to its mouth make the lower Arkansas navigable for barge traffic. A custom channel 30 mi/48 km N of McGeher to the White R. provides a more direct route to the Mississippi, flowing generally SE across the plains to the Mississippi. The Canadian and Cimarron rivers are its main tributaries. It is the chief waterway for the state of Ark., where it drains a broad valley. The upper course of the Arkansas R. has many rapids and flows through Royal Gorge, one of the deepest canyons in the U.S. More than 25 dams on the river provide flood control, power, and irrigation. During the warm months, because of its extensive use for irrigation, the middle course of the Arkansas is reduced to a trickle. The John Martin dam and reservoir in Colo. is one of the largest water-storage and flood-control units in the river basin. The Arkansas R. Navigation System, at Continental Divide, opened in 1971, makes the river navigable to Tulsa, Okla., 440 mi/708 km upstream. The Span. explorers Coronado and De Soto probably traveled along portions of the river in the 1540s. In 1806, Zebulon Pike, an American army officer, explored the river's upper reaches in Colorado. The Arkansas R. was an important trade and travel route in the 19th cent. Lake Fork rises in NW Lake co., flows 13 mi/21 km E through Turquiose L. Reservoir and SSE. East Fork rises in NE Lake and flows SW c. 20 mi/32 km past Landville, joining Lake Fork 4 mi/6.4 km SW of Leadville.

Arkinda (ahr-KIN-duh), village, Little River co., SW Ark., 35 mi/56 km NW of Texarkana, at Okla. line. A unit of Ouachita Natl. Forest to W (in Okla.).

Arkoe (AHR-ko), town (1990 pop. 64) Nodaway co., NW Mo., on One Hundred and Two R., and 6 mi/10 km SSE of Maryville; 40°15'N 94°49'W.

Arkoma (ahr-KO-muh), town (1990 pop. 2,393), Le Flore co., SE Okla., at Ark. state line 3 mi/4.8 km S of Fort Smith, Ark., on Poteau R., near its confluence with Ark. R.; 35°19'N 94°27'W.

Arkona (ahr-KO-nuh), village (1991 pop. 530), S Ont., Canada, 9 mi/14 km E of Forest. Dairying; mixed agr.

Arkport, village (1990 pop. 770), Steuben co., W N.Y., 18 mi/29 km WNW of Bath; 42°23'N 77°42'W. Mfg. (dairy prods.).

Arkwright 1 (ARK-wright), village, Coventry, R.I., 8 mi/12.9 km WNW of Warwick, on Pauxtent R.; 41°43'N 71°32'W. Nearby is J.L. Curran Park. **2** uninc. village (1990 pop. 670), Spartanburg co., NW S.C., a suburb 2 mi/3.2 km S of Spartanburg.

Arlee (AHR-lee), village (1990 pop. 484), Lake co., W Mont., near Jocko R., and 23 mi/37 km N of Missoula in S part of Flathead Indian Reservoir; 47°10'N 114°05'W. Mfg. (jelly supplements, bee pollen supplements, honey); agr. (cattle, sheep, hogs; corn, potatoes, oats, alfalfa). Mission Mts. Tribal Wilderness to NE; Lolo Natl. Forest to SW.

Arleta, suburban section of Los Angeles city, Los Angeles co., S Calif., 15 mi/24 km NW of downtown, S of intersection of Golden Gate Freeway and Van Nuys Avenue. Mfg. (luggage, electromedical apparatus).

Arlington, county (□ 26 sq. mi/67 sq. km.; 1990 pop. 170,936), N Va., ⊙ Arlington (uninc. city), across the Potomac R. from Wash., D.C, immediately N of Alexandria; 38°52'N 77°05'W. Co. and uninc. city of Arlington are coterminous. Arlington is a residential and commercial suburb of Washington, D.C., bounded NE, E by Potomac R. (D.C. boundary), N corner touches Md. state line. Major office and housing developments, especially in high-rise section, Rosslyn. Mfg. (printing and publishing, shipbuilding, apparel, bakery prods., radar systems). Ft. Myer Military Reservation, Office of Naval Research, ARLINGTON NATL. CEMETERY, ARLINGTON HOUSE NATL. MEMORIAL, and the Pentagon (Dept. of Defense) hq. are in East Federal Highway Administration Research Station, CIA hq. to N, on Potomac R. Marymount Univ., George Mason Univ. (Arlington Campus). Washington Natl. Airport in SE. Northern Va. Regional Park in N; Glen Carlyn Park in SW. Formerly called Alexandria, Arlington was ceded to the Federal govt. by Va. in 1790 and was part of D.C. until 1847, when it was returned to Va. It was named Arlington in 1920.

Arlington 1 city (1990 pop. 261,721), Tarrant co., N Texas, suburb 13 mi/21 km E of downtown Fort Worth, and 17 mi/27 km WSW of downtown Dallas; 32°41'N 97°07'W. Elev. 616 ft/188 m. Drained by West fork of the Trinity R in N, Village Creek forms L. Arlington in W. Part of the Dallas–Fort Worth metropolitan area in 1970s and 1980s, is now nearly landlocked by neighboring municipalities, Arlington was one of the fastest-growing U.S. cities, marked by a pop. increase of more than 64% bet. 1980 and 1990. It produces motor vehicles and parts, transportation equip., rubber and plastic prods., medical equip., electronic equip., oil-field equip. Arlington Municipal Airport in SE, Dallas–Fort Worth Internatl. Airport to NE. Six Flags Over Texas, a theme park, and Wet 'n' Wild water park are located there. The city is the home of the Amer. League's Texas

Rangers baseball team (the Ballpark at Arlington, formerly Arlington Stadium). It is also the seat of the Univ. of Texas at Arlington (Maverick Stadium); Arlington Convention Center. L. Joe Pool reservoir and Cedar Hill State Park to SE. Inc. 1896. **2** uninc. city, ⊙ Arlington co., NE Va., residential suburb 2 mi/3.2 km SW of Washington, D.C., on Potomac R., comprising entire co. of Arlington; 38°52′N 77°05′W.

Arlington 1 uninc. town (1990 pop. 950), Maricopa co., central Ariz., 40 mi/64 km W of Phoenix, near Gila R., and mouth of Hasayampa R. Irrigated agr. area (grain, cotton, alfalfa, sugar beets, citrus, vegetables; sheep, cattle, hogs). **2** town (1990 pop. 1,513), Calhoun and Early counties, SW Ga., 32 mi/51 km WSW of Albany; 31°26′N 84°44′W. Mfg. (food and beverage processing, veneer, apparel). Inc. as village 1881, as city 1923. **3** town (1990 pop. 465), Fayette co., NE Iowa, 18 mi/29 km SSW of West Union; 42°45′N 91°40′W. Dairy prods., livestock remedies. Limestone quarry (N). **4** town (1990 pop. 44,630), Middlesex co., E Mass., a residential suburb 5 mi/8 km NW of Boston; 42°25′N 71°10′W. Scene of fierce fighting after the Lexington and Concord battles in 1775. Some 17th-cent. bldgs. remain. Settled c.1630 as Menotomy, inc. as West Cambridge 1807, renamed Arlington 1867. **5** town (1990 pop. 1,886), Sibley co., S central Minn., on High Isl. Creek, 46 mi/74 km SW of Minneapolis; 44°36′N 94°04′W. Grain; livestock, poultry; dairying; mfg. (concrete prods., food processing, electronic wiring). In natural lakes region; Silver L. to NE, High Isl. L. to NW. **6** town (1990 pop. 1,178), Washington co., E Nebr., 8 mi/12.9 km E of Freemont; 41°27′N 96°21′W. Grain; alfalfa mill. **7** town (1990 pop. 795), Yadkin co., N N.C., 4 mi/6.4 km SSE of Elkin, near Yadkin R.; 36°13′N 80°49′W. Agr. area (tobacco, grain, soybeans; poultry, livestock; dairying). Inc. 1930. **8** town (1990 pop. 908), Kingsbury co., E S.Dak., 16 mi/26 km WNW of Brookings. In lake region. Agr. (grain; livestock; dairy prods.); mfg. of gun cases. L. Poinsett State Rec. Area to N; Oakwood Lakes State Park to NE. Founded 1880. **9** town (1990 pop. 1,541), Shelby co., SW Tenn., near Loosahatchie R., 23 mi/37 km NE of Memphis; 35°18′N 89°40′W. Mfg. (orthopedic implants). **10** town (1990 pop. 2,299), Bennington, co., SW Vt., on Batten Kill and 14 mi/23 km N of Bennington, in area of country estates and summer homes; 43°04′N 73°11′W. Scene on Vt. state seal is view from Thomas Chittenden home. Settled 1762. **11** town (1990 pop. 4,037), Snohomish co., NW Wash., on Stillaguamish R., at confluence of North and South forks, and 15 mi/24 km N of Everett; 48°11′N 122°08′W. RR junction. Timber, dairying, poultry; vegetables, berries. Mfg. (machinery, sheet metal prods., concrete prods., transportation equip., sawmills, wood prods., iron foundry, furniture, metal prods., light consumer goods). Wenberg State park to SW; Tulalip Indian Reservation to SW; Snoqualmie Natl. Forest, including Boulder R. Wilderness Area, to E.

Arlington 1 village (1990 pop. 200), Bureau co., N Ill., 13 mi/21 km NE of Princeton; 41°28′N 89°15′W. In agr. area (corn, soybeans; cattle, hogs). **2** village (1990 pop. 908), Rush co., E central Ind., 7 mi/11.3 km WNW of Rushville. Corn, wheat; hogs. **3** village (1990 pop. 457), Reno co., S central Kansas, 18 mi/29 km SW of Hutchinson; 37°53′N 98°10′W. In wheat area. **4** village (1990 pop. 449), S Carlisle co., SW Ky., 31 mi/50 km SW of Paducah; 36°47′N 89°00′W. Agr. area (tobacco, grain; livestock, poultry; dairying); mfg. (meat processing, lumber, RR ties). **5** village (□ 4 sq mi/10.4 sq km; 1990 pop. 11,948), Dutchess co., SE N.Y., adjoining Poughkeepsie (W); 41°42′N 73°52′W. Seat of Vassar Col. **6** village, Gaston co., S N.C., residential suburb 2 mi/3.2 km W of Gastonia. **7** village (1990 pop. 1,267), Hancock co., NW Ohio, 10 mi/16 km S of Findlay; 40°56′N 83°41′W. Limestone, concrete, plaster. **8** village (1990 pop. 425), Gilliam co., N Oregon, 50 mi/80 km E of the Dalles, and on Columbia R. (near Umatilla Indian Reservation) at mouth of China Creek; 45°43′N 120°11′W. RR junction. Wheat, oats, barley; cattle. Umatilla Natl. Wildlife Refuge to NE. Nearby Portland waste disposal site. **9** village, Spartanburg co., NW S.C., 16 mi/26 km W of Spartanburg. **10** village (1990 pop. 440), Columbia co., S central Wis., 19 mi/31 km N of Madison; 43°20′N 89°22′W. Mfg. (food processing). Agr. research station to S.

Arlington, urban area, Calif. Part of W Riverside (Arlington Ave). See RIVERSIDE.

Arlington Heights (AHR-ling-tuhn), uninc. town (1990 pop. 4,768), Monroe co., E Pa., residential suburb, 1 mi/1.6 km W of Stroudsburg, near Pocono Creek; 41°00′N 75°12′W.

Arlington Heights 1 village (1990 pop. 75,460), Cook co., NE Ill., a residential suburb of Chicago; 42°05′N 87°58′W. Its manufactures include machinery, drugs and medical equip., metal fabrication. Arlington Heights's pop. more than doubled during the 1960s as a result of large-scale residential construction. Arlington Park racetrack is located there. Founded 1836, inc. 1887. **2** village (1990 pop. 1,084), Hamilton co., extreme SW Ohio, a N suburb of Cincinnati; 39°13′N 84°28′W.

Arlington House National Memorial, Arlington co., NE Va., 2 mi/3.2 km SW of Washington, D.C., in Arlington Natl. Cemetery (authorized 1925, permanently est. by Congress 1955); covers 28 acres/11 ha. Antebellum home once belonging to Custis and Lee families, overlooks Potomac R. Memorial to Confederate Gen. Robert E. Lee. The home of Lee, inherited by his wife, the daughter of George Washington Parke Custis. Abandoned by the Lees early in the Civil War, it was later used as hq. for the Union army. The estate was confiscated for nonpayment of taxes, and c.200 acres/81 ha were set aside for a natl. cemetery in 1864.

Arlington Memorial Bridge, granite and concrete bridge across the Potomac R. connecting the Lincoln Monument in Wash., D.C., with Arlington Natl. Cemetery, N Va.; built 1926–1932.

Arlington National Cemetery (□ 1 sq mi/2.6 sq km), Arlington co., NE Va., across the Potomac R. from and 2 mi/3.2 km SE of Wash., D.C. More than 60,000 Amer. soldiers killed in battle, as well as other notable Americans including Presidents William Howard Taft and John F. Kennedy, Gen. John J. Pershing, and Admiral Robert E. Peary are interred here. Burial in Arlington is limited to active, retired, and former members of the armed forces, Medal of Honor recipients, high-ranking Federal govt. officials; and their dependents. Commemorative monuments include the Tomb of the Unknowns. The cemetery includes part of "Arlington," the former estate of the Custis and Lee families and the original tract set aside for the cemetery and Arlington House, now the Arlington House Natl. Memorial. Est. 1864.

Arma, town (1990 pop. 1,542), Crawford co., SE Kansas, near Mo. line, 10 mi/16 km N of Pittsburg; 37°32′N 94°42′W. Shipping point for coal-mining and agr. region. Crawford State Park to NW; Crawford State Fishing L. to S. Inc. 1909.

Armada (ahr-MAH-duh), town (1990 pop. 1,548), Macomb co., SE Mich., 16 mi/26 km N of Mt. Clemens; 42°50′N 82°52′W. In grain and fruit-growing area; mfg. (rubber prods., ball-bearing lead screws). Satellite community of Detroit.

Armadillo de los Infante (ahr-mah-DEE-yo dai los een-FAHN-tai), town (1990 pop. 5,906), San Luis Potosí, N Mexico, 22 mi/35 km NE of San Luis Potosí; 22°15′N 100°40′W. Small farming; livestock. Also known as Armadillo.

Armagh (AHR-muh), village (1991 pop. 840), S Que., Canada, 35 mi/56 km E of Quebec; 46°45′N 70°35′W. Lumbering; dairying; stock raising.

Armagh (AHR-mahg), borough (1990 pop. 104), Indiana co., SW central Pa., 10 mi/16 km NNW of Johnstown; 40°27′N 79°01′W. Corn, hay; livestock; dairying.

Armería (ahr-mai-REE-ah), city (1990 pop. 27,782), ⊙ Armería municipio, Colima, S Mexico, on Armería R., and 9 mi/15 km W of Tecoman; on RR; 18°55′N 104°00′W. Agr. (rice, corn, sugarcane, tropical fruits).

Armería River, c.140 mi/225 km long, W Mexico; rises in Jalisco S of Ameca; flows SE, past Ayutla, and S into Colima, past Armería, to the Pacific 7 mi/11.3 km SE of Cuyutlán. Called Ayutla in upper course (Jalisco), Ayuquila in middle course. Used for irrigation.

Armijo (ar-MEE-yo), uninc. town, Bernalillo co., N central N.Mex., residential suburb 3 mi/4.8 km S of downtown Albuquerque on Rio Grande. Albuquerque Internatl. Airport and Kirtland Air Force Base to E, across river.

Armington 1 village (1990 pop. 348), Tazewell co., central Ill., 19 mi/31 km SW of Bloomington; 40°20′N 89°18′W. In agr. area (corn, oats, soybeans; cattle, hogs). **2** village (1990 pop. 75), Cascade co., central Mont., on Belt Creek R., 20 mi/32 km SE of Great Falls. Grain, livestock; mining. Sluice Boxes State Park to S; part of Lewis and Clark Natl. Forest to E.

Armistead Seldon Lock and Dam, on Hale and Greene co. border, W central Ala., on Black Warrior R, 18 mi/29 km N of Demopolis; 71 ft/22 m high; 32°47′N 87°50′W. Built (1958) by Army Corps of Engineers for navigation. Forms Warrior Lake, reservoir (□ 12 sq mi/31 sq km) with max. capacity 58,650 acre-ft. Also known as Warrior Lake and A.I. Seldon.

Armona, town (1990 pop. 3,122), Kings co., S central Calif., 3 mi/4.8 km W of Hanford, near Mussel Slough; 36°19′N 119°43′W. Dairying; turkeys; grain (esp. barley), cantaloupes, pistachios, almonds; ships fruit.

Armonk, residential village (□ 6 sq mi/15.5 sq km; 1990 pop. 2,745), Westchester co., SE N.Y., 7 mi/11.3 km NNE of White Plains; 41°07′N 73°42′W. Mfg. (data processing equip., telecommunications systems, dental prods.). Affluent suburban community. Former long-time hq. of IBM Corp.

Armour, town (1990 pop. 854), ⊙ Douglas co., SE S.Dak., 57 mi/91 km NW of Yankton. Shipping center for grain, livestock, poultry; mfg. includes metal fabrication. L. Andes to SW. Founded 1886.

Armstrong 1 county (□ 664 sq mi/1,720 sq km; 1990 pop. 73,478), W Pa.; ⊙ Kittanning. Rolling timber area drained by Allegheny R. and Mahoning Creek; 40°48′N 79°27′W. Bounded SW by Kiskiminetas R., N by Allegheny R. and Red Bank Creek. Retail trade and services. Mfg. at Freeport, Kittanning, and Ford City. Agr. (corn, wheat, oats,, hay, alfalfa; sheep, hogs, cattle; dairying); bituminous coal; clay, limestone, sand. Formed 1800. **2** county (□ 913 sq mi/2,365 sq km; 1990 pop. 2,021), extreme N Texas; ⊙ Claude. In high plains of the Panhandle, with part of Caprock escarpment in E; elev. 2,400 ft/732 m–3,000 ft/914 m; 34°58′N 101°20′W. Co. is drained by Salt Fork of the Red R. (NE). Cattle ranching area, with some agr. (wheat, cotton, hay); sand and gravel. Duck hunting in small prairie lakes. Includes part of Palo Duro Canyon State Park (in SW) along Prairie Dog Town Fork of Red R. (extension of Red R.). Formed 1876.

Armstrong, city (1991 pop. 3,200), S B.C., Canada, 13 mi/21 km NNE of Vernon; 50°27′N 119°11′W. Fruit and vegetable growing, dairying; woodworking; alfalfa and flour milling.

Armstrong, city (1990 pop. 310), Howard co., central Mo., 9 mi/14 km N of Fayette; 39°16′N 92°42′W. Corn, soybeans; hogs, cattle.

Armstrong, town (1990 pop. 1,025), Emmet co., NW Iowa, on East Des Moines R. and 18 mi/29 km E of Estherville; 43°23′N 94°28′W. Feed mills, creamery. Gravel pit nearby.

Armstrong, Fort, U.S. army post, Honolulu, Hawaii, E side of Honolulu Harbor entrance, 1 mi/1.6 km S of downtown. Est. 1907 as U.S. Army post. Site is now U.S. Immigration Station.

Armstrong, Mount (9,161 ft/2,792 m), on Alta.–B.C. border, Canada, in Rocky Mts., 55 mi/89 km SW of Calgary.

Armstrong, Port, Alaska: see PORT ALEXANDER.

Armstrong Redwoods State Park, (□ 752 sq mi/1,948 sq km), Sonoma co., W Calif., near Russian R., 20 mi/32 km WNW of Santa Rosa, 10 mi/16 km NE of Pacific Ocean Coast, and 2 mi/3.2 km N of Guerneville. Est. in 1870s as a preserve by Colonel James Armstrong. Virgin redwood forest.

Armstrong Station, village, W Ont., Canada, near NW

end of L. Nipigon, 130 mi/209 km E of Sioux Lookout; 50°18′N 89°02′W. Gold mining; lumbering. Airport.

Armuchee (ahr-MOO-chee), village (1990 pop. 600), Floyd co., Ga., 10 mi/16 km SE of Summerville; 85°11′N 34°23′W. Wood prods., lumber, carpet.

Arnaudville (AHR-no-vil), town (1994 pop. 1,787), on St. Landry–St. Martin parish line, S central La., at head of navigation on Bayou Teche, 12 mi/19 km NE of Lafayette; 30°24′N 91°56′W. In agr. area (sugarcane, vegetables; cattle; dairying); catfish, crawfish; timber. Oil and gas field nearby. First known as La Junction.

Arnegard (AHRN-uh-gahrd), village (1990 pop. 122), McKenzie co., W N.Dak., 8 mi/12.9 km W of Watford City; 47°48′N 103°26′W.

Arnett (ahr-NET), town (1990 pop. 547), ⊙ Ellis co., NW Okla., 30 mi/48 km SW of Woodward; 36°08′N 99°46′W. Elev. 2,406 ft/733 m. In agr. area (barley, oats, sorghum; cattle; dairy prods.); mfg. (printing); oil and gas. Wildlife refuge to SW.

Arnold, city (1990 pop. 18,828), Jefferson co., central Mo., suburb 17 mi/27 km SSW of downtown St. Louis, on Meramec R. at its confluence with the Miss. R.; 38°25′N 90°22′W. Parts of city were damaged by a catastrophic flood in 1993. Mfg. (metal and glass prods., medical supplies, transportation equip., machinery, electronics).

Arnold, uninc. town (1990 pop. 3788), Calaveras co., central Calif., 55 mi/89 km ENE of Stockton, in Stanislaus Natl. Forest, near San Antonio Creek; 38°14′N 120°22′W. Timber; cattle; honey. Calaveras Big Trees State Park to E; Mt. Reba Ski Area to NE.

Arnold, village (1990 pop. 679), Custer co., central Nebr., 30 mi/48 km W of Broken Bow, and on South Loup R; 41°25′N 100°11′W. Livestock, grain. Arnold Lake State Recreational Area to SW.

Arnold, borough (1990 pop. 6,113), Westmoreland co., W central Pa., suburb 15 mi/24 km NE of downtown Pittsburgh, and 1 mi/1.6 km N of New Kensington, on Allegheny R.; 40°34′N 79°45′W. Mfg. (fabricated metal prods., food prods.); agr. (corn, hay; livestock; dairying). Inc. 1895.

Arnold City, uninc. village, Fayette co., SW Pa., 4 mi/6.4 km SE of Monessen, on Monogahela R.; 40°06′N 79°49′W.

Arnold Mills, village, Cumberland town, Providence co., NE R.I., 6 mi/9.7 km SE of Woonsocket, on Mass./R.I. border; 41°58′N 71°23′W. Nearby is Diamond Hill Reservoir and Pawtucket Reservoir.

Arnolds Park, town (1990 pop. 953), Dickinson co., NW Iowa, near West Okoboji L., 4 mi/6.4 km S of Spirit L.; 43°21′N 95°07′W. Mfg. (boxes, molds, castings). Sand and gravel pit nearby. Summer resort in vicinity of several state parks. Has monument commemorating Spirit L. Indian massacre (1857) of early settlers of region.

Arnoldsville, town (1990 pop. 275), Oglethorpe co., Ga., 9 mi/14.5 km SE of Athens; 33°55′N 83°13′W. Lumber.

Arnprior (ahrn-PREI-uhr), town (1991 pop. 6,679), SE Ont., Canada, on L. des Chats (widening of Ottawa R.), at mouth of Madawaska R., and 32 mi/51 km W of Ottawa. Pulp, and lumber milling; dairying; mfg. Resort.

Arntfield, village (1991 pop. 433), W Que., Canada, 11 mi/18 km WSW of Rouyn; 48°12′N 79°15′W. Mining (gold, copper, molybdenum, zinc, lead).

Aroma Park (a-RO-muh), village (1990 pop. 690), Kankakee co., NE Ill., at junction of Kankakee (bridged here) and Iroquois rivers, 3 mi/4.8 km SE of Kankakee; 41°04′N 87°48′W. In agr. area.

Aromas, uninc. town (1990 pop. 2273), Monterey co., W Calif., 10 mi/16 km N of Salinas, 8 mi/12.9 km E of Monterey Bay, Pacific Ocean, in Gabilan Range; 36°53′N 121°39′W. Cattle; dairying; vegetables, berries, grain.

Arona (ah-RO-nah), borough (1990 pop. 397), Westmoreland co., SW Pa., 6 mi/9.7 km WSW of Greensburg, on Little Sewickley Creek; 40°16′N 79°39′W. Dairying.

Aroostook (uh-ROO-stook), village (1991 pop. 409), W N.B., Canada, on St. John R. at mouth of Aroostook R., at Maine border, 16 mi/26 km NE of Presque Isle,

in potato region; 46°48′N 67°43′W. Site of hydroelectric power station.

Aroostook (uh-ROOS-tuk), largest county (□ 6,829 sq mi/17,687 sq km; 1990 pop. 86,936) in Maine, bordering on Que. and N.B., Canada; ⊙ Houlton; 46°38′N 68°35′W. One of nation's richest agr. areas, esp. for potatoes. Large tracts of lake-studded wilderness furnish lumber and offer hunting, fishing, canoeing; manganese deposits; mfg. (wood prods., farm machinery, food prods., fertilizers). Drained by Allagash, Aroostook, Fish, Little Madawaska, Machias, Mattawamkeag, Meduxnekeag, and St. John rivers. Formed 1839.

Aroostook River (uh-ROOS-tuk), c.140 mi/225 km long; rises in N Maine and winds E to the St. John R. in N.B., Canada; 46°20′N 68°48′W. The Aroostook War, caused by boundary disputes bet. Maine (U.S.) and N.B., took place in the Aroostook valley. The river gives its name to a county in the U.S. famous for potatoes.

Arouca (ah-ROO-kah), village, N Trinidad, Trinidad and Tobago, 12 mi/19 km E of Port of Spain. Sugarcane growing. Now a suburb of Port of Spain.

Arp, town (1990 pop. 812), Smith co., E Texas, 17 mi/27 km SE of Tyler; 32°13′N 95°03′W. Trade center in oil, agr., timber; mfg. (oil-field tanks, pressure vessels). Lakes Tyler and Tyler East to W.

Arpin, village (1990 pop. 312), Wood Co., central Wis., 10 mi/16 km SE of Marshfield; 44°32′N 90°01′W. Dairying, general farming; forests to S. Powers Bluff Ski Area to W.

Arriaga (ah-ree-AH-gah), city (1990 pop. 21,849) and township, ⊙ Arriaga municipio, Chiapas, S Mexico, in Pacific coastal lowland, on RR, and 13 mi/21 km NW of Tonalá; 16°13′N 93°54′W. Processing and agr. center (tropical fruit, sugarcane, tobacco, cereals; livestock); wood; tanning.

Arriaga, Mexico: see VILLA DE ARRIAGA.

Arriba, village (1990 pop. 220), Lincoln co., E Colo., 22 mi/35 km E of Limon; elev. 5,228 ft/1,593 m; 39°16′N 103°16′W. Cattle, wheat, sunflowers. Near South Fork Republican R. (source c.10 mi/16 km SW).

Arrochar, a sect. of Staten Isl. borough of N.Y. city, SE N.Y., in E Staten Isl., S of St. George; 40°36′N 74°05′W.

Arrow Lake (15 mi/24 km long, 2 mi/3 km wide), W Ont., on Minn. border, 40 mi/64 km WSW of Fort William; elev. 1,510 ft/460 m. Drains SE into L. Superior.

Arrow Lakes, 2 expansions of the Columbia R., S B.C. Both lie in narrow valleys bounded by mtn. ranges and are noted for their beauty; 50°00′N 118°00′W. Upper Arrow L. (□ 88 sq mi /228 sq km); Lower Arrow L. (□ 59 sq mi/153 sq km). Arrowhead is at the head of the upper lake.

Arrow Rock, town (1990 pop. 70), Saline co., central Mo., on Mo. R., and 14 mi/23 km WNW of Marshall; 39°04′N 92°57′W. Entire town is a natl. historical site; historical tavern and other buildings; state park adjacent; professional summer theatre; Mo. R. crossing of the Santa Fe Trail; platted 1829.

Arrow Rock Reservoir, on Boise R./Elmore co. border, SW Idaho, on Boise R., in Boise Natl. Forest, 14 mi/23 km E of Boise; 43°20′N 115°54′W. Middle Fork Boise and South Fork Boise rivers, both forming arms, meet near center. Max. capacity 286,500 acre-ft, used in irrigation of c.170,000 acres/68,799 ha. Formed by Arrow Rock Dam (concrete, arch-gravity; 350 ft/107 m high, 1,150 ft/351 m long), completed 1915 as unit in Boise irrigation project.

Arrowhead Hot Springs, Calif.: see SAN BERNARDINO, city.

Arrowhead Lake, uninc. town, Monroe co., E Pa., residential development 18 mi/29 km ESE of Wilkes-Barre in Pocono Mts.; 41°09′N 75°34′W. Arrowhead L. reservoir on Trout Creek to W; Lackawanna State Forest to NW.

Arrowhead, Lake, reservoir, San Bernardino co., S Calif., on Little Bear Creek, 11 mi/18 km NE of San Bernardino, in San Bernardino Mts. and San Bernardino Natl. Forest; 3 mi/4.8 km long; elev. 5,115 ft/1,559 m;

34°15′N 117°10′W. Surrounded by residential development, including towns of Blue Sky (W), Lake Arrowhead (S), and Cedar Glen (E; at dam).

Arrowhead Lake, reservoir (□ 25 sq mi/65 sq km), Clay and Archer cos., N central Texas, on Little Wichita R., 10 mi/16 km SE of Wichita Falls; 33°46′N 98°22′W. Max. capacity 685,000 acre-ft. Formed by Lake Arrowhead Dam (62 ft/19 m high), built (1966) for water supply. Lake Arrowhead State Park near dam.

Arrowhead Peak (4,237 ft/1,291 m), San Benardino co., S Calif., a W foothill summit of San Bernardino Mts., 5 mi/8 km NNE of San Bernardino; slope is marked by 7 acre/2.8 ha arrowhead-shaped rock outcrop. In San Bernadino Natl. Forest.

Arrowsic (uh-ROU-zik), farming and fishing town (1990 pop. 498), Sagadahoc co., SW Maine, on Arrowsic Isl., and across Kennebec R. from Bath; 43°51′N 69°47′W.

Arrowsmith, village (1990 pop. 313), McLean co., central Ill., 18 mi/29 km E of Bloomington; 40°27′N 88°37′W. In grain-growing area.

Arroyo (ah-ROI-yo), town (1990 pop. 18,910), SE P.R., 4 mi/6.4 km ESE of Guayama. Former sugar-milling center. Hosp. Tourism; mus. Hydroelectric plant on L. Carite just NW.

Arroyo Arenas (ah-RO-yo ah-RAI-nuhs), town, La Habana prov., W Cuba, 13 mi/21 km SW of Havana; 22°38′N 80°14′W. Tobacco, vegetables, fruit; livestock.

Arroyo City, uninc. village, (1990 pop. 496), Cameron co., extreme S Texas, 18 mi/29 km NE of Harlingen, on Arroyo Colorado. At W entrance to Laguna Atascosa Natl. Wildlife Refuge. Irrigated agr. area (sugarcane, cotton, vegetables, citrus).

Arroyo Grande, city (1990 pop. 14,378), San Luis Obispo co., SW Calif., 12 mi/19 km SSE of San Luis Obispo, and 3 mi/4.8 km E of Pacific Ocean coast, on Arroyo Grande Creek; 35°08′N 120°35′W. Grows flower and vegetable seeds; flowers, vegetables, strawberries, apples, avocados, grain, nursery prods.; cattle. Oil field nearby. Pismo State Beach to W; Los Padres Natl. Forest to E in Sierra Madre; Twitchell Reservoir to SE. Founded 1877, inc. 1911.

Arroyo Hondo (ah-RO-yo ON-do), village (1990 pop. 400), Taos co., N N.Mex., 10 mi/16 km NNW of Taos, near the Rio Grande. Cattle, sheep, wheat, hay, alfalfa. Parts of Pueblo de Taos Indian Reservation to E and S. Rio Grande Gorge and Bridge to SW.

Arroyo Naranjo (ah-RO-yo nah-RAHN-ho), town, La Habana prov., W Cuba, 7 mi/11.3 km S of Havana (linked by RR); 23°04′N 82°21′W. Dairying; fruit, vegetables.

Arroyo Seco, town (1990 pop. 1,239), Querétaro, central Mexico, 25 mi/40 km NNW of Jalpan de Serra; elev. 3,251 ft/991 m; 21°32′N 99°48′W. Cereals, sugar. Also known as Villa de Guadalupe.

Arroyos de Mantua (ah-RO-yos dai mahn-TOO-ah), town, Pinar del Río prov., W Cuba, on Gulf of Guanahacabibes, just E of Punta Ingleses; 22°22′N 84°23′W. In vegetable-producing area.

Arsenal, Ark.: see PINE BLUFF.

Arteaga 1 (ahr-tee-AH-gah), town (1990 pop. 3,996), Coahuila, N Mexico, in Sierra Madre Oriental, 8 mi/12.9 km ENE of Saltillo; 25°30′N 100°52′W. Elev. 3,957 ft/1,206 m. Corn, beans, istle fibers, candelilla wax, cattle; silver, lead deposits nearby. RR terminus. **2** (1990 pop. 10,909), Michoacán, W Mexico, in foothills, 70 mi/113 km SSW of Uruapan; 18°30′N 102°34′E. Elev. 3,957 ft/1,206 m. Cereals, coffee, sugar, fruit.

Artemisa (ahr-tai-MEES-ah), town (1994 est. pop. 41,000), La Habana prov., W Cuba, on Central Highway, on RR, and 35 mi/56 km SW of Havana; 22°49′N 82°46′W. Trading and processing center in agr. region (sugarcane, tobacco, fruit); mfg. (liquor, soap). Two sugar refineries nearby.

Artemus (AHRT-uh-muhs), village (1990 pop. 425), Knox co., SE Ky., in the Cumberland Mts., on Cumberland R., and 4 mi/6.4 km ESE of Barbourville. Agr. (tobacco, corn; cattle); timber.

Artesia 1 (ahr-TEE-zhuh), city (1990 pop. 15,464), Los

Angeles co., S Calif., suburb 15 mi/24 km SE of downtown Los Angeles, and 8 mi/12.9 km NE of Long Beach, near San Gabriel R.; 33°52′N 118°05′W. Mfg. (dairy prods., printing, photographic equip., machinery). Named for the many artesian wells in the vicinity. Now a suburb SE of Los Angeles. Founded 1875, inc. 1959; **2** city (1990 pop. 10,610), Eddy co., SE N.Mex., 40 mi/64 km S of Roswell, just W of the Pecos R.; 32°51′N 104°25′W. Elev. 3,380 ft/1,030 m. In an oil, gas, farm, and livestock area. Artesian wells, under tremendous pressure from confined acquifers extending from the nearby Sacramento and Guadalupe Mts., irrigate a large area. Mfg. (printing and publishing, plastic pipes). Lake McMillan Reservoir to S. Laid out in 1903, inc. 1939

Artesia (ahr-TEE-zhuh), village (1990 pop. 484), Lowndes co., E Miss., 14 mi/23 km WSW of Columbus; 33°25′N 88°38′W. RR junction. Agr. (cotton, grain, soybeans; cattle); ships hay; mfg. (portland cement). Golden Triangle Airport to E.

Artesian, village (1990 pop. 217), Sanborn co., SE central S.Dak., 18 mi/29 km ESE of Woonsocket; center of large artesian water basin. Trading point for farming region. Corn, wheat; dairy prods., livestock; honey.

Arthabaska (ahr-thuh-BA-skuh), county (□ 666 sq mi/1,725 sq km; 1991 pop. 60,257), S Que., Canada, on Nicolet R.; ⊙ Arthabaska; 46°00′N 72°00′W.

Arthabaska, town (1991 pop. 7,584), ⊙ Arthabaska co., S Que., Canada, on Nicolet R., and 45 mi/72 km N of Sherbrooke. Lumbering, dairying center; furniture mfg.

Arthur, county (□ 718 sq mi/1,860 sq km; 1990 pop. 462), W central Nebr.; ⊙ Arthur. Sandhills region devoted to cattle raising. Central/mountain time zone boundary follows E boundary. Several small natural lakes in NE, and at center, Industrial Three Mile and Swan lakes. Formed 1888.

Arthur, town (1990 pop. 272), Ida co., W Iowa, 7 mi/11.3 km E of Ida Grove; 42°20′N 95°20′W. In livestock and grain area.

Arthur, village (1991 pop. 2,123), S Ont., Canada, 24 mi/39 km NW of Guelph; 43°50′N 80°32′W. Milling, dairying; lumbering; light mfg.

Arthur 1 village (1990 pop. 2,112), in Douglas and Moultrie cos., E central Ill., 16 mi/26 km NNW of Mattoon; 39°43′N 88°28′W. In agr. area (corn, wheat, soybeans, broomcorn; dairy prods.; livestock). Mfg. (brooms, food prods.). Inc. 1877. Large Amish colony is nearby. **2** village (1990 pop. 128), ⊙ Arthur co., W central Nebr., 55 mi/89 km NW of North Platte; 41°34′N 101°41′W. Livestock. Several small lakes to SW and NE. **3** village (1990 pop. 400), Cass co., E N.Dak.,7 mi/11.3 km N of Casselton; 47°06′N 97°13′W.

Arthur Kill, narrow channel (c.14 mi/23 km long) connecting Raritan and Newark bays, SE N.Y. and NE N.J.; separates Staten Isl. from N.J. shore; bridged at Elizabeth (Goethals) and Perth Amboy, N.J. (Outerbridge Crossing).

Arthur, Lake, reservoir (□ 5 sq mi/13 sq km), Butler co., W central Pa., on Muddy Creek, 12 mi/19 km E of New Castle; 40°58′N 80°07′W. Max. capacity 98,000 acre-ft. Formed by Moraine State Park Dam (55 ft/17 m high), built (1968) for recreation. Moraine State Park near dam.

Arthur, Lake 1 La.: see MERMENTAU RIVER. **2** N.Dak.: see ALKALI LAKE.

Arthur V. Watkins Dam, Utah: see CUTLER RESERVOIR.

Arthur's Town, town, central Bahama Isls., on N Cat Isl., 115 mi/185 km ESE of Nassau; 24°38′N 75°42′W. Fruit, sisal.

Artibonite (ahr-tee-bo-NEET), department (1982 pop. 732,932), central Haiti; ⊙ Gonaïves. Bounded N by Nord-Ouest and Nord depts., E by Centre dept., S by Ouest dept. Agr. (bananas, rice, coffee, sugarcane, tobacco, fruit; cattle); copper and manganese deposits.

Artibonite Plain (ahr-tee-bo-NEET), fertile basin in W central Haiti, along lower Artibonite R., extending from the coast (Gulf of Gonaïves) 60 mi/97 km inland to Mirebalais. Main cities along the coast are Gonaïves

and Saint-Marc. Agr. (bananas, rice, coffee, cotton, sugarcane, tobacco, limes; cattle).

Artibonite River (ahr-tee-bo-NEE-tai), Span. *Artibonito*, largest stream of Hispaniola isl.; rises in Dominican Republic in Cordillera Central near Haiti line SW of Santiago; flows SW, W, and NW, partly along internatl. border, and into Haiti, through fertile Artibonite Plain, past Mirebalais and Petite-Rivière-de-l'Artibonite, to Gulf of Gonaïves 10 mi/16 km NNW of Saint-Marc; c.150 mi/241 km long. Navigable for small boats c.100 mi/161 km upstream. Used for irrigation. Principal affluent, Guayamouc R.

Artillery Lake, E Mackenzie dist., N.W.T., Canada, NE of Great Slave L.; 50 mi/80 km long, 1 mi/2 km–9 mi/14 km wide; 63°10′N 107°55′W. Drains SW into Great Slave L.

Arundel (A-ruhn-duhl), village (1991 pop. 555), SW Que., Canada, in the Laurentians, 30 mi/48 km WNW of St. Jérôme. Dairying; kaolin mined nearby. Skiing resort.

Arundel on the Bay, resort village, Anne Arundel co., central Md., on Chesapeake Bay, and 5 mi/8 km SE of Annapolis.

Arvada, city (1990 pop. 89,235), Jefferson and Adams cos., N central Colo., a suburb 6 mi/9.7 km NW of downtown Denver; 39°49′N 105°06′W. Elev. 5,337 ft/1,627 m. Primarily residential, drained by Ralston Creek. Arvada has some mfg. (machinery, paints, light industry). Arvada Center for the Arts and Humanities here. Colo. RR Mus. to SW. Rocky Flats Nuclear Plant to NW. Lake reservoir to N. Inc. 1904.

Arverne, neighborhood, SE N.Y., a residential and shore-resort sect. of S Queens borough of N.Y. city, on Rockaway Beach; 40°35′N 73°48′W.

Arviat or **Eskimo Point**, town (1991 pop. 1,323), S Keewatin Dist., N.W.T., Canada, on Hudson Bay; 61°07′N 94°04′W. Radio station, Royal Can. Mounted Police post. Furs, seals, caribou, fish; handicrafts. Hudson's Bay Co. trading post est. 1921. Became permanent settlement in 1970s. Scheduled air service. Inuit Cultural Inst., established to preserve Inuit culture is here.

Arvida, Canada: see JONQUIÈRE.

Arvin, town (1990 pop. 9,286), Kern co., S central Calif., 15 mi/24 km SE of Bakersfield; 35°12′N 118°50′W. RR terminus; trade, shipping, and processing center in agr. area (citrus fruit, apples, grapes, plums, vegetables, pistachios, almonds, cantaloupes, cotton, grain, sugar beets, beans; cattle; dairying). Tehachapi Mts. to S.

Arvonia (ar-VON-ee-uh), uninc. village (1990 pop. 720), Buckingham co., central Va., 24 mi/39 km SSE of Charlottesville, near junction of Slate R. and James R. Mfg. (slate aggregates and processing, rayon bags); agr. (tobacco, grain, apples; cattle); slate quarries. RR junction to N.

Asay Creek (AI-see), c.25 mi/40 km long, SW Utah; rises in Markagunt Plateau, NW Kane co., Dixie Natl. Forest; flows N, joining Panguitch Creek just N of Panguitch to form Sevier R.

Asbestos, town (1991 pop. 6,487), SE Que., Canada. Asbestos is mined in the area and asbestos prods. are made in the town. Other mfg. includes wood prods. and electrical equip.

Asbury 1 (AZ-bur-ee), town (1990 pop. 2,013), Dubuque co., E Iowa, 3 mi/4.8 km WNW of Dubuque; 42°30′N 90°45′W. **2** (AZ-ber-ree), town (1990 pop. 220), Jasper co., SW Mo., near Spring R., 15 mi/24 km NW of Carthage, near Kansas border; 37°16′N 94°35′W. Wheat, soybeans.

Asbury Park, city (1990 pop. 16,799), Monmouth co., E N.J., on the Atlantic coast; inc. 1897; 40°13′N 74°00′W. The city has a beach, boardwalk, and convention hall. Asbury Park was developed by James A. Bradley in the 1870s to be a Methodist campground, and named in honor of Bishop Francis Asbury. Asbury Park never attained campground status, but the area just to the S (Ocean Grove) did. Many places in Asbury Park named in honor of Bradley including 1 of the elementary schools. Mfg. of electronics, apparel, plastics, and candy. The steamship *Morro Castle*, which caught fire at sea in Sept. 1934, was grounded here and continued

to burn, with the loss of 125 lives. Bud Abbott b. here. Childhood home of Stephen Crane.

Ascension (uh-SIN-shuhn), parish (□ 300 sq mi/777 sq km; 1990 pop. 58,214), SE La.; ⊙ Donaldsonville; 30°16′N 91°00′W. Intersected by Miss. R. and Bayou Lafourche in SW; bounded on NE by Amite, Petite Amite, and Blind rivers, on N by Bayou Manchac. Agr. (strawberries, home gardening, nursery crops, sugarcane, pecans, peppers; cattle, horses, hogs, ostriches). Crawfish, alligators. Petrochemicals. Some mfg.; logging. Natural gas wells. Settled by Acadians bet. 1764 and 1772. Known for antebellum homes. Formed 1807.

Ascensión (ahs-sen-see-ON), town (1990 pop. 8,966), Chihuahua, N Mexico, on Casas Grandes R. (irrigation) and 100 mi/161 km SW of Juárez; 31°10′N 108°00′W. Elev. 4,222 ft/1,287 m. Cotton, cereals, fruit; cattle.

Ascensión Bay, Span. *Bahía la Ascensión*, Quintana Roo, SE Mexico, inlet of Caribbean Sea on E coast of Yucatán Peninsula, 10 mi/16 km N of Espíritu Santo Bay, E of Felipe Carrillo Puerto; 13 mi/21 km long N-S, 15 mi/24 km wide; 27°10′N 114°30′W. Vigía Chico is on NW shore.

Ascutney, Vt.: see WEATHERSFIELD.

Ascutney, Mount (UHZ-kut-nee), isolated peak (3,144 ft/958 m), SE Vt., near the Connecticut R., just S of Windsor. Ski resort and state park are here.

Ash Flat, village (1990 pop. 667), Sharp co., N Ark., 30 mi/48 km N of Batesville; 36°13′N 91°36′W. County govt., formerly at Evening Shade and Hardy, moved to this more centralized location. Tool and die. Harold W. Alexander Wildlife Management Area to E.

Ash Fork, uninc. village, Yavapai co., NW central Ariz., 47 mi/76 km W of Flagstaff; elev. 5,144 ft/1,568 m. In livestock area; timber. Onyx and sandstone quarries nearby; highway service center. From here, spur line from the Santa Fe RR heads S to Phoenix. Kaibab Natl. Forest to E.

Ash Grove, city (1990 pop. 1,128), Greene co., SW Mo., in the Ozarks, on Sac R. and 18 mi/29 km NW of downtown Springfield; 37°19′N 93°34′W. Agr. trading center; limestone quarry. Corn, wheat, soybeans; dairying; cattle; mfg. (caskets).

Asharoken, resort village (□ 6 sq mi/15.5 sq km; 1990 pop. 807), Suffolk co., SE N.Y. on N shore of W Long Isl., on Eatons Neck, 5 mi/8 km NE of Huntington; 40°56′N 73°23′W.

Ashaway, village (1990 pop. 1,624) in Hopkinton town, Washington co., SW R.I., 4 mi/6.4 km NE of Westerly, on Conn./R.I. border, near Pawcatuck R., Ashaway R.; 41°26′N 71°48′W. In agr. area; mfg.

Ashburn 1 town (1990 pop. 4,827), Turner co., S central Ga., 19 mi/31 km NNW of Tifton. Trade and processing for agr. and timber area; mfg. (cottonseed prods., furniture, textiles, transportation equip.; peanut shelling and processing, sawmilling; 31°43′N 83°39′W. Founded 1889. **2** town (1990 pop. 51), Pike co., E Mo., on Mississippi R., and 8 mi/12.9 km NW of Louisiana; wildlife area and wetlands on the Mississippi R.; 39°32′N 91°10′W. **3** uninc. town, Loudoun co., N Va., 5 mi/8 km ESE of Leesburg, on Goose Creek; 39°02′N 77°28′W. Agr. area (dairying; livestock; grain, soybeans, apples); mfg. (comsumer goods, food and beverage, commercial printing). George Washington Univ. (Va. campus); Dulles Intl. Airport to S.

Ashburnham (ASH-buhrn-ham), town (1990 pop. 5,433), Worcester co., N Mass., 7 mi/11.3 km NW of Fitchburg; 42°40′N 71°56′W. Furniture mfg.; dairying; fruit. State forest to N. Settled 1736, inc. 1765.

Ashby (ASH-bee), agr. town (1990 pop. 2,717), Middlesex co., N Mass., 7 mi/11.3 km N of Fitchburg, near N.H. line; 42°41′N 71°49′W. Settled c.1676, inc. 1767.

Ashby, village (1990 pop. 469), Grant co., W Minn., 18 mi/29 km SE of Fergus Falls; 46°05′N 95°49′W. Agr. area (grain, sugar beets, beans, sunflowers; livestock; dairying); mfg. (poultry processing, dairy prods.). L. Christina to E, Pelican L. to S, numerous other small lakes in area.

Ashcroft, village (1991 pop. 1,714), S B.C., Canada, on Thompson R., and 40 mi/64 km W of Kamloops;

50°43′N 121°16′W. Potatoes, tomatoes, livestock; distributing center for mining and agr. region. Cariboo Road (built 1862–1865, during Cariboo gold rush) leading to the Fraser R. gold mines, begins here.

Ashdown, town (1990 pop. 5,150), ⊙ Little River co., SW Ark., 18 mi/29 km N of Texarkana; 33°40′N 94°07′W. RR junction. In agr. area. Lumber milling. Mfg. (construction materials, paper, wooden prods., apparel). Large Millwood L. to NE; Millwood State Park to E. Founded 1892, inc. as city 1937.

Ashe (ASH), county (□ 426 sq mi/1,103 sq km; 1990 pop. 22,209), NW N.C.; ⊙ Jefferson; 36°25′N 81°30′W. In the Blue Ridge Mts.; bounded N by Va. state line, W by Tenn. state line and by Cherokee Natl. Forest. Drained by North Fork and South Fork of New R. Agr. area (tobacco, corn, hay; cattle, dairying). Mfg. at West Jefferson; timber, granite quarrying. Blue Ridge (Natl.) Parkway roughly parallels SE boundary. New River and Mt. Jefferson state parks in SE center. Formed 1799.

Asheboro, city (□ 11 sq mi/28 sq km; 1990 pop. 16,362), ⊙ Randolph co., central N.C., 28 mi/45 km S of Greensboro, near Deere R. in the Piedmont region; 35°43′N 79°48′W. Mfg. (transportation equip., furniture, small appliances, apparel, shoes; meat processing, printing and publishing; lumber, crushed stone). N.C. Zoological Park (1,400 acres) to S, specializes in Afr. animals; Unharrie Natl. Forest to SW. A prehistoric Keyauwee burial ground is nearby. Inc. 1796.

Ashepoo River, S S.C.; rises in Colleton co. S of Walterboro; flows SE and empties into Saint Helena Sound. River floodplain supported rice plantations during colonial and antebellum periods.

Asher, village (1990 pop. 449), Pottawatomie co., central Okla., 23 mi/37 km S of Shawnee, near Canadian R; 34°59′N 96°55′W. In agr. area.

Asherton, town (1990 pop. 1,608), Dimmit co., SW Texas, 65 mi/105 km N of Laredo; 28°26′N 99°45′W. A shipping point in irrigated agr. growing area (cattle; cotton, hay; pecans); oil and gas. Inc. 1925.

Asheville, city (1990 pop. 61,607), ⊙ Buncombe co., W N.C., 105 mi/169 km WNW of Charlotte on the Fr. Broad and the Swannanoa rivers, and on a plateau in the Blue Ridge Mts. Located near Great Smoky Mts. Natl. Park (to W) and sections of Pisgah Natl. Forest (NE and SW), Asheville is in the center of popular mt. area; 35°34′N 82°32′W. Tourism is a major business. The city is also a financial, distribution, transportation, and retail center for W N.C. Tobacco is processed and marketed; other mfg. includes textiles, electronic equip., paper, food, auto parts, and glass prods. Asheville's many points of interest include the Biltomore Estate, owned by Vanderbilts, to S, Colburn Mineral Mus.; and numerous recreational and scenic attractions. The writer Thomas Wolfe was born and lived here; his home is a public memorial. The Univ. of N.C. at Asheville is here, and the Natl. Climatic Data Center. Zebulon Vance Birthplace State Historical Site to NE. Asheville Buncombe Tech. Community Col. Randolph Community Col. Blue Ridge (Natl.) Parkway passes to E and SE; Municipal Airport to S. Inc. 1797.

Ashfield, agr. town (1990 pop. 1,715), Franklin co., W Mass., 10 mi/16 km WSW of Greenfield; 42°31′N 72°49′W. Seat of Sanderson Acad.

Ashford 1 town (1990 pop. 1,926), Houston co., extreme SE Ala., 10 mi/16 km ESE of Dothan in farming area. Mfg. (apparel, radiation monitoring equip.). **2** town (1990 pop. 3,765), Windham co., NE Conn., 11 mi/18 km N of Willimantic; 41°53′N 72°10′W. In agr. area. Includes villages of Warrenville (with 18th-cent. houses), Westford. State forests here.

Ashkum, village (1990 pop. 650), Iroquois co., E Ill., 13 mi/21 km NW of Watseka; 40°52′N 87°57′W. In rich agr. area.

Ashland 1 county (□ 426 sq mi/1,103 sq km; 1990 pop. 47,507), N central Ohio; ⊙ Ashland, 40°49′N 82°16′W. Drained by forks of Mohican R. Includes Mohican State Forest (recreation area), with a flood control dam. Agr. area (livestock; grain, hay; fruit); mfg. at Ashland and Loudonville; gravel pits. Formed 1846. **2** county (□ 2,290 sq mi/5,931 sq km; 1990 pop. 16,307), extreme N Wis., bounded N by L. Superior; ⊙ Ashland; 46°42′N 90°33′W. Includes Apostle Isls., just N of Chequamegon Bay. Part of Gogebic Range (source of iron ore) is in co. Drained by Bad R. Has sect. of Chequamegon Natl. Forest. The large Bad R. Indian Reservation is in N part; smaller unit is on E end of Madeline Isl. Agr. (barley); lumbering, iron mining. Copper Falls State Park is here. Large part of Chequamegon Natl. Forest in SW; Flambeau State Forest in SE; Big Bay State Park on Madeline Isl., in N; Most of Apostle Isls. Natl. Lakeshore (which excludes Madeline) in far N (L. Superior). Formed 1860.

Ashland 1 uninc. city (1990 pop. 16,590), Alameda co., W Calif., residential suburb 10 mi/16 km SE of downtown Oakland, 2 mi/3.2 km SE of San Leandro, on San Leandro R.; 37°42′N 122°07′W. L. Chabot reservoir and Anthony Chabot Reg. Park to N. **2** city (1990 pop. 23,622), Boyd co., E Ky., 12 mi/19 km WNW of Huntington, W.Va., on Ohio R. (Ohio state line, bridged); 38°27′N 82°38′W. Ashland lies in a region that yields chemicals, timber, steel, oil, and natural gas. Agr. (tobacco, alfalfa; cattle; dairy prods.); mfg. (cultured marble prods., paper prods., consumer goods, apparel, furniture, construction materials, refined oil; steel mills, printing and publishing). It is a river and RR shipping point with large repair yards. The city is part of a tri-state urbanized area, including Ironton, Ohio, and Huntington, W.Va. Ashland Community Col. Kentucky Highlands Mus., Ashland Area Art Gall., Paramount Arts Center. Federal prison. Settled 1786, inc. 1854. **3** city (1990 pop. 20,079), ⊙ Ashland co., N Ohio. In a farm area; inc. 1844; 40°54′N 82°19′W. Mfg. (machinery, steel, rubber prods.). Ashland Col. is here.

Ashland 1 town (1990 pop. 2,034), ⊙ Clay co., E Ala., 26 mi/42 km S of Anniston. Mfg. (apparel, furniture; poultry processing). **2** town (1990 pop. 1,032), ⊙ Clark co., SW Kansas, 40 mi/64 km SSE of Dodge City; 37°11′N 99°46′W. Elev. 1,970 ft/600 m. In grain and cattle region. Clark State Fishing L. to N. **3** town (1990 pop. 1,542), Aroostook co., NE Maine, on Aroostook R., and 45 mi/72 km NW of Houlton; 46°39′N 68°21′W. Ships potatoes, lumber. Gateway to NW Maine wilderness region. Settled c.1837, inc. 1862. **4** town (1990 pop. 12,066), Middlesex co., E central Mass., 3 mi/4.8 km SW of Framingham; 42°16′N 71°28′W. In rapidly developing suburban area. Mfg. (chemicals, medical equip., metal and electrical prods.). State Park nearby. Settled c.1750, inc. 1846. **5** town (1990 pop. 1,252), Boone co., central Mo., near Missouri R., 10 mi/16 km S of Columbia; 38°46′N 92°15′W. Mfg. (wood prods.). Unit of Mark Twain Natl. Forest to E. **6** town (1990 pop. 2,136), Saunders co., E Nebr., 23 mi/37 km NE of Lincoln, near Platte R; 41°02′N 96°22′W. RR junction. Grain. Mfg. (farm fences, shut-off valves, sand gravel). Memphis L. State Recreation Area to NW. Settled 1863, inc. 1886. **7** town (1990 pop. 1,915), Grafton co., central N.H., 16 mi/26 km N of Franklin; 43°43′N 71°37′W. Bounded W by Pemigewasset R.; drained Squam R. and by Owl Brook. Corn, nursery crops, vegetables, apples; poultry; dairying. Mfg. (textiles, rubber molding tools). Little Squam L. on E boundary. Separated from Holderness 1867. **8** town (1990 pop. 16,234), Jackson co., SW Oregon, on Bear Creek, 13 mi/21 km N of state border, and 11 mi/18 km SE of Medford; 42°11′N 122°42′W. Elev. 1,895 ft/578 m. Mfg. (lumber, millwork, jewelry); trade center for fruit, grain, timber. Gold mines nearby. Resort with mineral springs. Southern Oregon State Col. Annual Shakespearean Festival takes place in Aug. Mt. Ashland (7,523 ft/2,293 m) is 8 mi/12.9 km S in Siskiyou Mts. Siskiyou Summit pass (4,350 ft/1,326 m) to SE (I-5). Emigrant Reservoir to E. Parts of Rogue R. Natl. Forest to S and NE; Tub Springs State Wayside to SE; parts of Klamath Natl. Forest to S. Founded 1852, inc. 1874. **9** town (1990 pop. 5,864), Hanover co., E central Va., 16 mi/26 km N of Richmond; 37°45′N 77°28′W. Mfg. (transportation equip., wooden pallets, concrete prods., chemicals, electronic equip., machinery, printing and publishing, metal fabrication, apparel); diverse light mfg.; flour and lumber milling; in agr. area (dairying; cattle, poultry; grain, soybeans, tobacco, peanuts). Seat of Randolph-Macon Col. Patrick Henry and Henry Clay b. nearby. "Scotchtown," Patrick Henry's home (1771–1777) and later the home of Dolly Madison, is to NW. Settled 1848; inc. 1858. **10** town (1990 pop. 8,695) ⊙ Ashland co., extreme N Wis., port of entry on Chequamegon Bay of L. Superior, 60 mi/97 km E of Superior; 46°34′N 90°52′W. RR terminus with RR/ship transfer point; mfg. (apparel, consumer goods, construction materials, paper; printing); ironworks, woodworks. Agr. research station to W. Harbor is ice-bound Dec.-April; port ships iron ore (mined in Gogebic Range), coal, lumber. John F. Kennedy Airport. Northland Col. is here. Fr. explorers visited (17th cent.) the bay shore; and a Fr. mission was founded (1665) near Ashland by Father Allouez. Large Bad R. Indian Reservation to E; Chequamegon Natl. Forest to W and S. Apostle Isls. Natl. Lakeshore to N. Settled 1854, the city grew as an iron-mining and lumbering center, and as terminus for 1st RR in N Wisconsin (1877). Inc. in 1887.

Ashland 1 village (1990 pop. 1,257), Cass co., W central Ill., 20 mi/32 km WNW of Springfield; 39°53′N 90°00′W. Ships grain; agr. (cattle, hogs; sorghum, corn, soybeans). Inc. 1869. **2** village (1990 pop. 289), Natchitoches parish, NW central La., 24 mi/39 km N of Natchitoches; 32°07′N 93°07′W. Agr. and timber area. Kisatchie Natl. Forest to E. Mill Creek Reservoir to NE. Ashland oil field nearby. **3** village (1990 pop. 490), ⊙ Benton co., N Miss., 25 mi/40 km ENE of Holly Springs; 34°49′N 89°10′W. In agr. area (cotton, corn, soybeans; cattle; timber); mfg. (food prods., bulletin boards, auto parts). Holly Springs Natl. Forest to S and E. **4** (ASH-luhnd), village (1990 pop. 484), Rosebud co., SE Mont., 60 mi/97 km SSW of Miles City, and on Tongue R. at mouth of Otter Creek; 45°37′N 106°19′W. Mfg. (orthodontic supplies); cattle, sheep, frogs, sugar beets, beans, wheat, barley, oats. Div. hq. of Custer Natl. Forest, part of forest to E. Northern Cheyenne Indian Reservation to W. St. Labré Mission and School. Cheyenne Indian Mus., Indian artifacts gallery. Formerly called Birney and, before that, Strader. **5** village (1990 pop. 56), Pittsburg co., SE Okla., 21 mi/34 km WSW of McAlester; 34°46′N 96°04′W. In farm area. McAlester Army Ammunition Plant to E.

Ashland (ASH-luhnd), borough (1990 pop. 3,859), Schuylkill co., E central Pa., 10 mi/16 km NW of Pottsville, on Mahanoy Creek; 40°46′N 76°20′W. Mfg. (apparel; machining, printing); coal anthracite. Pioneer Tunnel Coal Mine tours; Anthracite Mus. Settled 1845, inc. 1857.

Ashland City, town (1990 pop. 2,552), ⊙ Cheatham co., N central Tenn., on Cumberland R., and 18 mi/29 km NW of Nashville; 36°17′N 87°04′W. In tobacco, grain, livestock area; mfg. (water heaters, concrete prods.).

Ashley, county (□ 939 sq mi/2,432 sq km; 1990 pop. 24,319), SE Ark.; ⊙ Hamburg; 33°11′N 91°46′W. Bounded S by La. line, W by Saline and Ouachita rivers (Felsenthal Lock and Dam, impounds L. Jack Lee); drained by Bayou Bartholomew. Agr. (cotton, rice, wheat, soybeans; hay; cattle). Mfg., processing industries at Crossett. Part of Felsenthal Natl. Wildlife Refuge in W; part of Lower Ouachita Wildlife Management Area; Overflow Natl. Wildlife Refuge in SE. Formed 1849.

Ashley, city (1990 pop. 583), Wash. co., SW Ill., 6 mi/9.7 km ESE of Nashville; 38°19′N 89°11′W. RR junction. In agr. and oil-producing area; soybeans, wheat, hogs; dairy prods.

Ashley 1 town (1990 pop. 767), in De Kalb and Steuben cos., NE Ind., 9 mi/14.5 km SSW of Angola; 41°32′N 85°04′W. Agr. area; mfg. (machinery, transportation equip., plastic prods., chemicals, septic tanks, utility manholes). **2** town (1990 pop. 1,052), ⊙ McIntosh co., S N.Dak., 90 mi/145 km SE of Bismarck; 46°01′N 99°22′W. Near S.Dak. state line. RR terminus. L. Hoskins to W. Moved from nearby lake to present location on RR in 1888.

Ashley 1 village (1990 pop. 518), Gratiot co., central

Mich., 31 mi/50 km SW of Saginaw; 43°11′N 84°28′W. RR junction in farm area. **2** village (1990 pop. 1,059), Delaware co., central Ohio, 15 mi/24 km SSE of Marion; 40°25′N 82°59′W. Makes furniture.

Ashley (ASH-lee), borough (1990 pop. 3,291), Luzerne co., NE central Pa., suburb 2 mi/3.2 km S of Wilkes-Barre, on Solomon Creek; 41°12′N 75°54′W. Mfg. (telecommunications equip.). Settled 1810, inc. 1870.

Ashley Falls, Mass.: see SHEFFIELD.

Ashley River, 40 mi/64 km long, SE S.C.; rises in Dorchester co. near Ridgeville; flows SE, joining Cooper R. at Charleston to form Charleston Harbor. Partly navigable.

Ashmore, village (1990 pop. 800), Coles co., E Ill., 9 mi/14.5 km ENE of Charleston; 39°31′N 88°01′W. In rich agr. area (corn, soybeans, sorghum); oil.

Ashokan (ah-SHO-kuhn), village (1990 pop. 300), Ulster co., SE N.Y., on N shore of Ashokan Reservoir, in resort area of the Catskills, 12 mi/19 km WNW of Kingston; 41°59′N 74°12′W.

Ashokan Dam, N Ulster co., SE N.Y., on Esopus Creek 1 mi/1.6 km N of Olivebridge, and 11.5 mi/18.5 km W of Kingston; 41°56′N 74°13′W. The 4,650-ft/1,417-m-long dam includes a 1,000 ft/305 m masonry sect. flanked at either end by earthen embankments with concrete-core walls. Spillway elev. 590 ft/180 m above sea level. Completed in 1912; impounds Ashokan Reservoir, a major component of N.Y. city water supply system. Capacity of 3 million acre-ft. Also known as the Olive Bridge or Olivebridge Dam.

Ashokan Reservoir (ah-SHO-kuhn) (□ 13 sq mi/34 sq km), SE N.Y.; 41°57′N 74°13′W. Completed 1912, it is approximately 10 mi/16 km long. It is supplied by the Esopus and Schoharie watersheds via the Shandaken Tunnel and provides part of N.Y. city's water supply. Water is carried to the city via the 92-mi/148 km-long Catskill Aqueduct. Completed in 1917, the aqueduct delivers water to Kensico Reservoir near White Plains and Hillview Reservoir in Yonkers, from where it is distributed to parts of N.Y. city through tunnels cut in solid rock. The aqueduct passes 1,114 ft/340 m under the Hudson R. at Storm King Mt. A steel pipe under The Narrows of N.Y. Bay carries water to Silver L., Staten Isl., 120 mi/193 km from Ashokan Reservoir.

Ashtabula (ASH-tuh-BYOO-luh), county (□ 706 sq mi/1,829 sq km; 1990 pop. 99,821), extreme NE Ohio; ⊙ Jefferson, 41°42′N 80°46′W. Bounded N by L. Erie; intersected by Grand and Ashtabula rivers and Conneaut and Pymatuning creeks. Includes part of Pymatuning Reservoir (recreation area). In the Glaciated Plain physiographic region. Agr. (livestock; dairy prods.; fruit, vegetables, corn); mfg. at Ashtabula and Conneaut (inorganic pigments, plastics, transportation equip.); greenhouses, apiaries, wineries. Lake resorts. State parks on L. Erie and near Pa. border. Formed 1811.

Ashtabula (ASH-tuh-BYOO-luh), city (1990 pop. 21,633), Ashtabula co., NE Ohio, on L. Erie at the mouth of the Ashtabula R.; 41°54′N 80°49′W. It is a port of entry on the St. Lawrence Seaway and receives large amounts of iron ore bound for Pittsburgh. Coal is also shipped. Mfg. includes transportation equip., chemicals, plastics, fiberglass prods.; tourism is a developing industry. Settled c.1801 by New Englanders, inc. as a village 1831, as a city 1891. A campus of Kent State Univ. is located there.

Ashtabula, Lake (ash-tuh-BYOO-luh), reservoir, Barnes and Griggs cos., E N.Dak., on Cheyenne R., 9 mi/14.5 km NNW of Valley City; c.20 mi/32 km long; 47°02′N 98°04′W. Max. capacity 176,000 acre-ft. Formed by Bald Hill Dam (33 ft/10 m), built by the Army Corps of Engineers for flood control and water supply. Valley City Federal Fish Hatchery below dam.

Ashtabula River, c.40 mi/64 km long, NE Ohio; rises in E Ashtabula co.; flows N and W into L. Erie at Ashtabula; 41°54′N 80°47′W.

Ashton 1 town (1990 pop. 1,114), Fremont co., E Idaho, near Henrys Fork, 14 mi/23 km NE of St Anthony; 44°04′N 111°27′W. Elev. 5,256 ft/1,602 m. Trading point

in irrigated agr. area (wheat, seed peas, potatoes); logging, lumbering; hydroelectric plant. Dude ranches nearby. Yellowstone Natl. Park (mainly in Wyo., partly in Mont. and Idaho to NE) and Grand Teton Natl. Park to SE. Isl. Park Reservoir with Harriman State Park on its shore; Targhee Natl. Forest to N and E. Upper Mesa Falls (114 ft/35 m) and Lower Mes Falls (65 ft/20 m), on Henry's Fork, to NE. Inc. 1906. **2** town (1990 pop. 462), Osceola co., NW Iowa, 7 mi/11.3 km S of Sibley; 43°18′N 95°47′W. In livestock and grain area.

Ashton 1 village (1990 pop. 1,042), Lee co., N Ill., 13 mi/21 km E of Dixon; 41°52′N 89°13′W. In rich agr. area (corn, oats, soybeans; cattle); ice cream and dairy prods. **2** village (1990 pop. 251), Sherman co., central Nebr., 10 mi/16 km E of Loup City, and on branch of Middle Loup R; 41°15′N 98°47′W. Sherman Reservoir and State Recreation Area to NW. **3** village, Cumberland town, Providence co., NE R.I., 6 mi/9.7 km SE of Woonsocket, on Blackstone R.; 41°56′N 71°25′W. **4** village (1990 pop. 148), Spink co., NE central S.Dak., 8 mi/13 km N of Redfield, on Snake Creek near James R.

Ashuanipi River, E Canada: see CHURCHILL RIVER, Labrador prov.

Ashuapmuchuan River (ash-wahp-moo-CHWAHN), 170 mi/274 km long, central Que., Canada; rises SSE of Chibougamau L.; flows SE in a winding course, through Ashuapmuchan L. (8 mi/13 km long), to L. St. John. Upper course is called Ducharme R.

Ashuelot (ash-WEE-luht), village, Cheshire co., SW N.H., 13 mi/21 km SW of Keene, 1 mi/1.6 km W of Winchester village, in town of Winchester, on Ashuelot R. Mfg. (screw machine prods., plastic fabricating). Covered bridge. Pisgah State Park to NW.

Ashuelot River (ash-WEE-luht), W N.H.; rises in Ashuelot Pond, S Sullivan co.; flows SW through Cheshire co. to the Conn. R. at Hinsdale, furnishing power at Keene, Swanzey, Winchester, Hinsdale, and other towns along its course (50 mi/80 km).

Ashville, town (1990 pop. 1,494), ⊙ St, Clair co., NE central Ala., on branch of Coosa R., and 18 mi/29 km SW of Gadsden. Mfg. (apparel).

Ashville 1 village (1990 pop. 800), Chautauqua co., extreme W N.Y., near Chautauqua L., 7 mi/11.3 km W of Jamestown; 42°06′N 79°22′W. **2** village (1990 pop. 2,254), Pickaway co., S central Ohio, 17 mi/27 km S of Columbus; 39°44′N 82°59′W. Food prods.

Ashville (ASH-vil), borough (1990 pop. 306), Cambria co., W central Pa., 11 mi/18 km ENE of Ebensburg, on Clearfield Creek; 40°33′N 78°32′W. Agr. (dairying). Glendale L. reservoir in Prince Gallitzin State Park to N.

Ashwaubenon (ash-WAW-be-nahn), city (1990 pop. 16,376), Brown Co., E Wis., residential suburb 3 mi/4.8 km SW of Green Bay city, on Fox R. Lambeau Football Field and County Arena in N; 44°29′N 88°04′W. Austin Straubel Airport to W. Oneida Indian Reservation to W. Heritage Hill State Park across river to E.

Asientos (ah-see-YEN-tos), town (1990 pop. 32,225), Aguascalientes, N central Mexico, 28 mi/45 km NNE of Aguascalientes; 22°30′N 102°03′W. Elev. 7,595 ft/2,315 m. Agr. (honey; cattle); hunting, fishing; mining (silver, gold, lead, copper, zinc, saltpeter, chalk; metals; coal).

Asile (ah-ZEEL), town (1982 pop. 557), Grande-Anse dept., SW Haiti, on Jacmel Peninsula, 22 mi/35 km NE of Les Cayes; 18°23′N 73°25′W. Agr. (sugarcane, tobacco, coffee, oranges); sugar processing. Lignite deposits nearby. Also called L'Asile.

Asilomar, Calif.: see MONTEREY PENINSULA.

Askewville (AS-kyoo-vil), village (1990 pop. 201), Bertie co., NE N.C., 8 mi/12.9 km N of Windsor; Agr. area (peanuts, cotton, tobacco, grain; poultry, livestock); 36°6′N 76°56′W.

Askov (AS-kahf), village (1990 pop. 343), Pine co., E Minn., 45 mi/72 km SW of Duluth on Bear Creek; 46°11′N 92°46′W. Rutabagas, oats, alfalfa; livestock; poultry; dairying; mfg. (dairy feeds). Banning State Park to SW; Sandstone Natl. Wildlife Refuge to S; state forest to NE.

Asotin (uh-SOT-in), county (□ 640 sq mi/1,658 sq km; 1990 pop. 17,605), extreme SE Wash.; ⊙ Asotin; 46°11′N 117°11′W. Plateau and rolling hill area rising to Blue Mts. in SW and bordering Oregon on S. Watered by Grande Ronde R. and by Joseph, Asotin, and George creeks. Bounded by Snake R. on E and part of N, forms Idaho state boundary on E. Agr. (alfalfa, hay, wheat, barley; timber. Part of Umatilla Natl. Forest, including small part of Wenaha-Tucannon Wilderness Area, in W; Chief Timothy State Park in N; Fields Spring State Park in S. Formed 1883.

Asotin (uh-SOT-in), town (1990 pop. 981), ⊙ Asotin co., SE Wash., in Palouse region; 28 mi/45 km SSE of Pullman and 6 mi/9.7 km SSW of Lewiston, Idaho, on Snake R. at mouth of Asotin Creek; 46°20′N 117°02′W. Wheat, barley, alfalfa; timber. Historical mus. Umatilla Natl. Forest to SW; Fields Spring State Park to S. Hells Canyon (Snake R.) to SE.

Aspen (AS-puhn), city (1990 pop. 5,049), ⊙ Pitkin co., central Colo., on the Roaring Fork R. at mouths of Hunter, Castle, and Maroon creeks; 39°11′N 106°49′W. Elev. 7,908 ft/2,410 m. Once a booming silver camp producing ⅓ of the nation's silver (there is still some mining), it was transformed from the private capital of a Chicago industrialist into a modern, cosmopolitan ski resort, one of most popular in the world. Mfg. (publishing, protective clothing, stucco-plaster, jewelry, skiwear). Area surrounded on all but NW by White River Natl. Forest. Independence Pass (and ghost town) 12,095 ft/3,687 m to SE. Four major ski areas: Aspen Mt. and Aspen Highlands to S, Buttermilk and Snowmass to W. Aspen Center for Enviromental Studies and the Aspen Music Festival at Whitier Opera House (which holds an annual festival) are here. Founded c. 1879 by silver prospectors from Leadville, inc. 1881.

Aspermont, town (1990 pop. 1,214), ⊙ Stonewall co., NW central Texas, 55 mi/89 km NW of Abilene; 33°08′N 100°13′W. Elev. 1,773 ft/540 m. Trade and shipping center for agr. and cattle ranching region; wheat, hay, peanuts; some oil, natural gas.

Aspers (AS-puhrs), uninc. village, Adams co., S Pa., 10 mi/16 km N of Gettysburg on Opossum Creek; 39°58′N 77°13′W. Mfg. (fruit processing, woodworking); agr. (dairying; livestock, poultry; potatoes, grain, apples).

Aspetuck River (AS-pe-tuhk), Fairfield co., SW Conn.; rises SE of Danbury; flows c.20 mi/32 km S to Saugatuck R. N of Westport. WEST ASPETUCK RIVER and EAST ASPETUCK RIVER, branches of Housatonic R., are N, in Litchfield co.

Aspinwall, town (1990 pop. 52), Crawford co., W Iowa, 15 mi/24 km SE of Denison; 41°54′N 95°07′W. Agr. area.

Aspinwall (AS-pin-wahl), borough (1990 pop. 2,880), Allegheny co., SW Pa., residential suburb 6 mi/9.7 km E of downtown Pittsburgh, on Allegheny R. (bridged); 40°29′N 79°54′W. Highland Park Zoo to S across river. Settled 1796; inc. 1893.

Asquam Lake, N.H.: see SQUAM LAKE.

Asquith, town (1991 pop. 525), S central Sask., Canada, 24 mi/39 km W of Saskatoon. Agr. (wheat; dairying).

Assabet River (A-suh-bet), in E Mass.; rises in E Worcester co.; flows c.30 mi/48 km NE, past Hudson and Maynard (water power), joining Sudbury R. to form Concord R. in Concord town.

Assaria (uh-SER-ee-uh), village (1990 pop. 387), Saline co., central Kansas, 11 mi/18 km S of Salina; 38°40′N 97°35′W. Agr. (wheat; livestock); mfg. (farm and landscape equip., concrete prods.).

Assateague Island (ASS-ah-teeg), narrow barrier island, c.35 mi/56 km long, off Atlantic shore (Delmarva Peninsula) of SE Md. and E Va.; bordered to the N by Sinepuxent Bay and to the S by Chincoteague Bay. Famous for wild ponies that roam free until they are rounded up annually for auction. The isl. is inhabited only by Coast Guard crews. Visitors are limited to hunters and fishermen. Surf fishing off the isl. yields catches of channel bass, bluefish, kingfish, and sea trout. Said to have been explored in 1524 by Giovanni Verrazano, nearly a cent. before the first Eur. settlers arrived in N. Amer. The only connection with the mainland are bridges from Lower Sinepuxent Neck to Md. and from the S end of the isl. to Virginia. Until 1933, Assateague and Fenwick isls. were one. In that year, a hurricane breached the isl., producing what is now called the Ocean City inlet. Due to the breach and subsequent construction of jetties, a massive erosion of the shoreface has resulted. In March 1962, another storm ripped through the isl. and decimated the N end.

Assateague Island National Seashore (□ 57 sq mi/148 sq km), Md. and Va., 37 mi/60 km barrier isl. Beaches; wildlife refuge for deer, fox, racoon, and birds as well as wild Chincoteague ponies rounded up for auction annually at Chincoteague, Va. The ponies, according to legend, are descended from horses which swam ashore from Span. galleons. A diet restricted to seaweed and shore grasses has stunted growth and produced a unique species of dwarf ponies. Recreational opportunities on the isl. include exhibits, guided tours, picnic areas, campsites, hiking trails, swimming, boating, fishing, hunting, off-road vehicle trails. Beach activities, including swimming and fishing, are considered among the best on the East Coast. Dune erosion due to tourist traffic. The area at the N end of the isl. (700 acres/283 ha) are administered by the Md. Dept. of Forests and Parks. The natl. park takes up a large area bet. the state park and Chincoteague Refuge, all of it in Md. Authorized 1965.

Assawoman Bay, tidal lagoon, Worcester co., SE Md., just S of Del. line; opens on the Atlantic through Ocean City Inlet; c.4 mi/6.4 km long, 2 mi/3.2 km wide.

Assawoman Island, Accomack co., E Va., barrier isl. off Atlantic shore, 8 mi/12.9 km NE of Accomac; c.4 mi/6.4 km long. Assawoman Inlet is at N, Gargathy Inlet at S end. Sometimes spelled Assawaman.

Assawompsett Pond (a-suh-WAWMP-set), reservoir, Plymouth co., SE Mass., on Newmarket R., 9 mi/14.5 km SE of Taunton; c.3 mi/4.8 km long; 41°50′N 70°55′W. Joined by streams to Long (SW) and Great Quittacas (SE) ponds. In lake region.

Assiniboia (uh-sin-uh-BOI-uh), town (1991 pop. 2,774), S Sask., Canada, 55 mi/89 km SSW of Moose Jaw; elev. 2,436 ft/742 m. Service center, grain elevators, lumber and flour mills; in coal-mining region.

Assiniboine, Mount (uh-SIN-uh-boin), (11,870 ft/3,618 m), on the B.C.-Alta. line, Canada, on the Continental Divide in the Rocky Mts. Focal point of Mt. Assiniboine Provincial Park (□ 20 sq mi/52 sq km; est. 1922).

Assiniboine River (uh-SIN-uh-boin), 590 mi/950 km long, Canada; rising in S Sask.; flowing SE into Man. then E to the Red R. at Winnipeg. Named for the local Native Americans, the Assiniboine. The Qu'Appelle and Souris rivers are its chief tributaries. The Assiniboine valley is one of Canada's leading wheat-growing areas. The river was explored by the Vérendrye family in 1736, and forts were built at its mouth and near the site of Portage la Prairie. Settlement spread W along the river from the Red R. valley to the plains.

Assonet, village, SE Mass.: see FREETOWN.

Assumption (uh-SUMP-shun), parish (□ 357 sq mi/925 sq km; 1990 pop. 22,753), SE La.; ⊙ Napoleonville; 29°57′N 91°02′W. Bounded W partly by Belle R.; intersected by Bayou Lafourche (navigable). Agr. (sugarcane, rice, corn, home gardens; cattle, horses); crawfish, crabs; sugar milling. Includes L. Verret in W (recreation). Has Madewood antebellum mansion, 1820. Formed 1807.

Assumption, city (1990 pop. 1,244), Christian co., central Ill., 13 mi/21 km E of Taylorville; 39°31′N 89°02′W. Bituminous coal mining; agr. (corn, wheat, soybeans, sorghum); mfg. grain storage structures. Inc. 1902.

Astacinga (ahs-tah-SEEN-gah), town (1990 pop. 645), Veracruz, E Mexico, 19 mi/31 km S of Orizaba; 18°30′N 97°10′W. Elev. 7,493 ft/2,284 m. Corn, beans, wheat; cattle; wood.

Astatula (as-tah-TOO-luh), village (□ 2 sq mi/5.2 sq km; 1990 pop. 981), Lake co., central Fla., 25 mi/40 km WNW of Orlando, near L. Harris; 28°42′N 81°43′W.

Asti, village, Sonoma co., W Calif., in Russian R. valley, 27 mi/43 km NW of Santa Rosa. Settled in 1880s as Ital.-Swiss colony.

Asticou, Maine: see MOUNT DESERT.

Aston (AS-tuhn), township (1990 pop. 15,080), Delaware co., SE Pa., suburb 13 mi/21 km SW of Philadelphia; 39°52′N 75°25′W. Includes the communities of Village Green and Green Ridge. Mfg. includes furniture, metal fabricated prods., plastic composites, transportation equip., machining, paper prods., printing and publishing.

Astor, town (□ 7 sq mi/18.1 sq km; 1990 pop. 1,273), Volusia co., E central Fla., 45 mi/72 km NNW of Orlando; 29°08′N 81°31′W.

Astoria, city (1990 pop. 10,069), ⊙ Clatsop co., NW Oregon, 70 mi/113 km NW of Portland on the Columbia R. estuary, and 5 mi/8 km E of the Pacific Ocean; 46°11′N 123°49′W. Elev. 19 ft/6 m. On peninsula (Smith Point) at NE side of Youngs Bay, which receives Youngs R. from the SE and Lewis and Clark R. from the S. Warrenton is at W side of the bay. A port of entry, Astoria is the trading center for the lower Columbia basin. The city's traditional industries (fishing, fish processing, and lumbering) have declined since the 1970s. Tourism and light mfg. are the principal economic activities. Astoria Bridge, 4 mi/6.4 km long, crosses the Columbia R. N to Point Ellice, Wash. Bridge and causeway, 2 mi/3.2 km long, cross Youngs Bay to the SW. Astoria Airport across bay. The Lewis and Clark expedition spent the winter of 1805–1806 at a nearby encampment, Fort Clatsop (to the SW; rebuilt in 1955 and now called Fort Clatsop Natl. Memorial). Fort Astoria, a fur-trading post est. 1811 by John Jacob Astor's Pacific Fur Co., was the first permanent U.S. settlement on the Pacific coast. Although the post was sold to the British in 1813, its vigorous activities helped to establish Amer. claims to the Oregon country and contributed much to the exploration of the continent. Fort Astoria was formally restored to the U.S. in 1818, but trade remained in Br. hands until the mid-1840s, when Amer. pioneers followed the Oregon Trail to the fort. In the late 18th cent., Astoria grew as a coastal and river port, later attracting Scandinavian settlers whose descendants make up most of its present-day pop. Points of interest include: the Astoria Column (125 ft/38 m high), built in 1926 with a pictorial frieze depicting the region's early history; the Columbia R. Maritime Mus.; and the Uppertown Firefighters Mus. Fish hatcheries to SE. Lighthouse and naval base at Tongue Point, 3 mi/4.8 km E. Clatsup State Forest to SE; Lewis and Clark Natl. Wildlife Refuge to E; Fort Stevens State Park on Pacific Ocean to W. Inc. 1876.

Astoria, town (1990 pop. 1,205), Fulton Co., W central Ill., 17 mi/27 km SSW of Lewiston; 40°13′N 90°21′W. Trade center in agr. (corn, wheat, soybeans, sorghum; cattle) and bituminous coal area. Inc. 1839.

Astoria, village (1990 pop. 155), Deuel co., E S.Dak., 15 mi/24 km SSE of Clear L., near Minn. line.

Astoria, commercial, industrial, and residential sect. of NW Queens, borough of N.Y. city, SE N.Y.; 40°46′N 73°57′W. Settled in the 17th cent. as Hallet's Cove. It was renamed for John Jacob Astor in 1839. Has the largest pop. of Gr.-Amer. in U.S. Several 18th-cent. houses remain.

Asunción Cacalotepec (ah-soon-see-ON kah-kah-LO-te-pek), town (1990 pop. 846), in central Oaxaca, Mexico, 52 mi/83 km E of Oaxaca de Juárez; 17°02′N 95°59′W. Elev. 6,890 ft/2,100 m. Mountainous region; mainly subsistence small farming. A Mixe-speaking community.

Asunción Cuyotepeji (ah-soon-see-ON koo-yo-te-PE-hee), town (1990 pop. 810), in NW Oaxaca, Mexico, 15 mi/24 km NNE of Huajuapam de León, on Mexico Hwy 125; 17°52′N 97°45′W. Elev. 6,004 ft/1,830 m. Agr. and woven straw textiles.

Asunción Donato Guerra, Mexico: see DONATA GUERRA.

Asunción Ixtaltepec (ah-soon-see-ON iks-TAHL-te-pek), town (1990 pop. 7,240), in SE Oaxaca, Mexico, 6 mi/10 km SE of Ciudad Ixtepec, and 6 mi/10 km NW of Juchitáh de Zaragoza; 16°30′N 95°09′W. Located on Isthmus of Tehuantepec on banks of Juchitan R. This road is one on the Isthmus that links Coazacoalcos and Salina Cruz. Agr. (corn; figs; cattle).

Asunción Nochixtlán (ah-soon-see-ON no-cheesh-TLAHN), town (1990 pop. 6,562), Oaxaca, S Mexico, on Inter-Amer. Highway 190, and 45 mi/72 km NW of Oaxaca de Juárez in the Mixteca Alta; 17°27′N 97°13′W. Elev. 6,726 ft/2,050 m. Agr. center (cereals, coffee, sugarcane, beans, fruit; goats). Sometimes called Nochistlán.

Asunción Ocotlán (ah-soon-see-ON o-kot-LAHN), town (1990 pop. 3,614), in S central Oaxaca, Mexico, 23 mi/37 km S of Oaxaca de Juárez, and 3 mi/5 km SW of Ocotlán de Morelos; elev. 4,921 ft/1,500 m. Agr. (corn, beans, fruits; livestock); woods; mezcal processing. A Zapotec community.

Asunción River, Mexico: see MAGDALENA RIVER.

Asunción Tlacolulita (ah-soon-see-ON tlah-ko-loo-LEE-tah), town (1990 pop. 664), in SE Oaxaca, Mexico, 37 mi/60 km W of Santo Domingo Tehuantepec; elev. 5,052 ft/1,540 m. Mountainous near Tehuantepec R. Pop. mainly Zapotec Indian. Small farming, mainly for subsistence.

Atalissa, town (1990 pop. 357), Muscatine co., SE Iowa, 11 mi/18 km NNW of Muscatine; 41°34′N 91°10′W.

Atanik (A-duh-nik), Eskimo village, NW Alaska, on Arctic Ocean, 20 mi/32 km NE of Wainwright.

Atarjea (ah-tar-HAI-ah), city (1990 pop. 286) and township, Guanajuato, central Mexico, 45 mi/72 km E of San Luis de la Paz; elev. 4,429 ft/1,350 m; 21°15′N 99°52′W. Grain, maguey, sugar; livestock.

Atascadero, city (1990 pop. 23,138), San Luis Obispo co., SW Calif., 15 mi/24 km N of San Luis Obispo, on the Salinas R.; 35°30′N 120°42′W. Residential and farming city. Cattle; grain, apples, avocadoes, tomatoes, strawberries, vegetables, flowers, nursery stock. A state mental hosp. is here. Founded 1913 as a model community.

Atascosa, county (□ 1,235 sq mi/3,199 sq km; 1990 pop. 30,533), SW Texas; ⊙ Jourdanton; 28°53′N 98°31′W. Drained by Atascosa R. Irrigated agr. area (esp. peanuts; also vegetables, strawberries, corn, grain sorghums, hay); cattle ranching; dairying. Oil, natural gas wells; clay, lignite, sand deposits. Formed 1856.

Atascosa River, c.90 mi/145 km long, S Texas; rises in SE Medina co. near Lytle; flows generally SE to Frio R. just above its mouth on the Nueces, S of Three Rivers.

Atchafalaya Bay (uh-CHA-fuh-lei-uh), arm of the Gulf of Mexico, S La., 15 mi/24 km S of Morgan City, at mouth of Atchafalaya R.; c.21 mi/34 km long NW-SE, 10 mi/16 km wide; 29°25′N 91°18′W. Point Chevreuil is at NW side of entrance; at SE side is Point Au Fer with shell reef extending c.10 mi/16 km NW. On the reef c.3 mi/5 km offshore is Eugene Isl., site of Point Au Fer Reef lighthouse. Four League Bay is an 11 mi/18 km-long SE extension of Atchafalaya Bay, with channel into gulf from SE end. Entire bay comprises the Atchafalaya Delta State Wildlife Area. A new delta is being formed in it by discharge through the Atchafalaya R. Salt mines in area.

Atchafalaya River (uh-CHA-fuh-lei-uh), navigable river, c.170 mi/270 km long, S central La.; 30°17′N 91°40′W; rises in N at confluence of Red and Miss. rivers; meanders S, in a former channel of the Mississippi, to Atchafalaya Bay in the Gulf of Mexico. A distributary of the Red and Mississippi rivers, the Atchafalaya flows to the gulf through an extensive system of guide levees and floodways. By law a set proportion of the water from the Mississippi R. is diverted into the Atchafalaya R. at the Old River Control Structure. The Atchafalaya Basin is filled with lakes, bayous, marshes, and cypress swamps. Because of the threat of flooding, the Basin is generally roadless and sparsely inhabited. The few roads follow tops of levees. Interstate Highway 10, which crosses the basin E-W, is a continuous bridge for most of the distance bet. Baton Rouge and Lafayette. Locally referred to as Tchafalaya.

Atchison 1 (ACH-i-suhn), county (□ 435 sq mi/1,127 sq km; 1990 pop. 16,932), NE Kansas; ⊙ Atchison; 39°31′N 95°18′W. Gently rolling agr. area, bounded E by Mo. (across Mo. R.); drained by Del. R. Livestock; corn, wheat, sorghum, soybeans, hay; grain milling.

Oil. Formed 1855. **2** county (□ 549 sq mi/1422 sq km; 1990 pop. 7,457), extreme NW Mo.; ⊙ Rockport; 40°25′N 95°25′W. On Missouri R. (W); drained by Tarkio and Nishnabotna rivers. Nebr. to W, Iowa to N. Severe flooding occurred along all rivers in 1993. Corn, wheat; hogs, cattle. Formed 1845.

Atchison (ACH-i-suhn), city (1990 pop. 10,656), ⊙ Atchison co., NE Kansas, on the Mo. R.; elev. 810 ft/247 m; 39°33′N 95°07′W. RR junction. Trade, shipping, and industrial center in a rich farm area. Mfg. (leather goods, consumer goods, feeds, steel pipe; metal casting, corn milling). Founded (1854) near a military post, est. 1818–1819 on Cow Isl. in the Mo. R. The Atchison, Topeka and Santa Fe RR was chartered here in 1859, and the city boomed as an important wagon-train, river, and RR terminal, one of the outfitting points for westward travel. Benedictine Col. and Amelia Earhart home are located here. Atchison State Fishing L. to N. Inc. as a city 1881.

Atco, village, Camden co., SW N.J., 16 mi/26 km SE of Camden. Rapidly suburbanizing area.

Atemajac de Brizuela (ah-tai-mah-HAHK dai bree-SWAI-lah), town (1990 pop. 3,790), Jalisco, W Mexico, 40 mi/64 km SW of Guadalajara; 20°10′N 103°45′W. Grain, beans, sugar, alfalfa.

Atempan (ah-TEM-pahn), town (1990 pop. 3,599), Puebla, central Mexico, 5 mi/8 km W of Teziutlán; 19°47′N 97°27′W. Corn, coffee, fruit.

Atenango del Río (ah-tai-NAHN-go del REE-o), town (1990 pop. 2,500), Guerrero, SW Mexico, on affluent of the Mezcala R.(Río Balsas system), and 34 mi/55 km ESE of Iguala de la Independencia; 18°05′N 99°05′W. Cereals, sugar, fruit.

Atenayuca (ah-tai-nah-YOO-kah), town (1990 pop. 1,973), ⊙ Juan N. Méndez municipio, Puebla, central Mexico, 45 mi/72 km SE of Puebla; 18°32′N 97°45′W. Corn, sugar; livestock.

Atenco 1 Mexico: see SAN MATEO ATENCO. **2** Mexico: see SAN JUAN ATENCO.

Atengo (ah-TEN-go), town (1990 pop. 1,533), Jalisco, W Mexico, 20 mi/32 km SW of Ameca; 20°20′N 104°13′W. Sugar, cotton, rice, tobacco.

Atenguillo (ah-ten-GWEE-yo), town (1990 pop. 1,496), Jalisco, W Mexico, 30 mi/48 km WSW of Ameca; elev. 4,452 ft/1,357 m; 20°26′N 104°30′W. Bananas, rice, sugarcane, tobacco, cotton.

Atenquique (ah-ten-KEE-kai), village, Jalisco, W Mexico, at E foot of the Colima peaks, 7 mi/11.3 km W of Tuxpan, on Mexico Highway; 54; 19°32′N 103°30′W. Lumbering center; soda, wood-pulp mills. Site of battle of Atenquique in 1858.

Atexcal, Mexico: see SAN MARTÍN ATEXCAL.

Atglen (AT-glen), borough (1990 pop. 825), Chester co., SE Pa., 8 mi/12.9 km WSW of Coatesville, near East Branch Octoraro Creek; 39°57′N 75°58′W. Mfg. (textiles; printing and publishing). Agr. area (grain, potatoes; poultry, livestock; dairying).

Athabasca (a-thuh-BA-skuh), town (1991 pop. 1,965), central Alta., W Canada, on Athabasca R., and 80 mi/129 km N of Edmonton. Grain elevators; lumbering; mixed farming, livestock raising. In area are oil, gas, silica-sand deposits. Home of Athabasca Univ. (est. 1972) for correspondence courses. Formerly Athabasca Landing.

Athabasca, Lake, 4th-largest lake (c.3,120 sq mi/8,100 sq km) of Canada, NE Alta. and SW Sask., W Canada, at the edge of the Can. Shield; c.200 mi/320 km long, 5 mi./8 km–35 mi/56 km wide; 59°10′N 109°30′W. A part of the Mackenzie R. system; receives the Athabasca R. from the S and drains N into Great Slave L. via the Slave R. Gold and uranium nearby. Fort Chipewyan was built (1788) at W end of the lake by Roderick McKenzie of the North West Co. and has been maintained. Steamers of the Hudson's Bay Co. ply the lake in summer bet. Chipewyan and Fond du Lac, from where the canoe route runs by way of Wollaston and Reindeer lakes to the Churchill R. Philip Turnor, the Br. surveyor, surveyed and mapped the lake 1790–1792.

Athabasca, Mount, 11,452 ft/3,491 m, W Alta., W Canada, in the Can. Rockies, at the headwaters of the Athabasca R. On the edge of the Columbia snowfield, and the Sask. and Athabasca glaciers flow around it.

Athabasca Pass, 5,736 ft/1,748 m high, W Alta. and E B.C., W Canada, leading from the headwaters of the Athabasca R. across the Continental Divide to the Columbia R. Discovered c.1811 by David Thompson, a Can. fur trader, or an agent of his, and for the next 50 years was the chief route of the Hudson's Bay men on their journeys to and from the Columbia R. country.

Athabasca River (ath-uh-BAS-kuh), 765 mi/1,231 km long, Alta., W Canada; rises in the Columbia snowfield of the Can. Rockies near the border of Alta. and B.C; flows N through Jasper Natl. Park, then NE and N across central Alta. to L. Athabasca. It is the southernmost headstream of the Mackenzie R. Its chief tributaries are the Pembina, Lesser Slave, and Clearwater rivers. The Athabasca R. has long been the main route to the Mackenzie valley. Extensive deposits of oil-bearing sand along the river near Fort McMurray.

Athabasca Sand Dunes, geological feature, NW Sask., W Canada; extend for 100 mi/161 km along S shore of L. Athabasca, from William R. (W) to MacFarlane R. (E). Has 6 sq mi/15.5 sq km of moving sand dunes from exposed delta sediments of receding lake. Feature is 8,000 years old. Athasbasca Sand Dunes Provincial Wilderness (□ 772 sq mi/2000 sq km).

Athabasca Tar Sands, geological feature, NE Alta. and NW Sask., W Canada, around Fort McMurray and McMurray R. basin. Development of oil-rich sands began in 1970s; extensive reserves. Road, RR, pipeline serve the area.

Athalia (uh-THAIL-yuh), village (1990 pop. 346), Lawrence co., S Ohio, on the Ohio R., and 10 mi/16 km NE of Huntington (W.Va.); 38°32′N 82°19′W.

Athalmer (uh-TAL-muhr) or **Lake Windermere** (WIN-duhr-meer), resort village, SE B.C., W Canada, on slope of Rocky Mts., on Columbia R., at N end of Windermere L., 50 mi/80 km SSW of Banff; elev. 2,624 ft/800 m.

Athapapuska Lake (a-thuh-puh-PUH-skuh) (□ 104 sq mi/269 sq km), NW Man., central Canada, on Sask. border, 12 mi/19 km SE of Flin Flon; 20 mi/32 km long, 20 mi/32 km wide; 54°32′N 101°40′W.

Athelstan, town (1990 pop. 31), Taylor co., SW Iowa, at Mo. state line, on Little Platte R., and 11 mi/18 km SE of Bedford; 40°34′N 94°32′W. In agr. area.

Athena (uh-THEEN-uh), town (1990 pop. 997), Umatilla co., NE Oregon, 18 mi/29 km NE of Pendelton, and 19 mi/31 km SSW of Walla Walla (Wash.); 45°48′N 118°29′W. Wheat, apples, plums, pears, onions; cattle. Umatilla Indian Reservation to S.

Athens, county (□ 504 sq mi/1,305 sq km; 1990 pop. 59,549), SE Ohio; ⊙ Athens; 39°21′N 82°03′W. Bounded SE by Ohio R., here forming W.Va. state line; intersected by Hocking R., small Shade R., and small Sunday and Federal creeks. In the Unglaciated Plain physiographic region. Agr. (livestock; fruit, corn); mfg. at Nelsonville and Athens (shoes, pens and mechanical pencils, paper prods.); limestone quarries. Formed 1805.

Athens 1 city (1990 pop. 16,901), ⊙ Limestone co., N Ala., 15 mi/24 km N of Decatur, near Tenn. state line. In cotton, corn, and dairying area; hosiery and lumber mills; bakery prods.; clothing, furniture, thermostats, wholesale farm supply, rubber gaskets; poultry processing. Has fine antebellum homes. Seat of Athens Col. (oldest in the state). Settled 1814, inc. 1818. Sacked and occupied by Federal troops 1862, recaptured 1864 by Gen. N.B. Forrest. **2** (ATH-uhnz), city (1990 pop. 45,734), ⊙ Clarke co., NE Ga., on the Oconee R., in a piedmont area; 33°58′N 83°23′W. Founded as the site of the Univ. of Ga.; its industries include poultry processing and mfg. (textiles, electronic goods, rope, industrial power supplies, pharmaceuticals, clocks and watches, clothing; printing and publishing, food packaging). Research and development facilities were added in the 1980s. Numerous Ga. statesmen have lived here, and some of their houses are among the city's fine examples of classic revival style—the Howell Cobb house (1850), the T. R. R. Cobb house (1830–1843), and the Joseph H. Lumpkin house (c.1845). Airport. Inc. 1806. The city and univ. hosted soccer events at Sanford Stadium during the 1996 Summer Olympic Games. **3** (A-thins), city (1990 pop. 1,404), Menard co., central Ill., near Sangamon R., 10 mi/16 km N of Springfield; 39°57′N 89°43′W. Ships grain; agr. (corn, wheat, soybeans); mfg. storage tanks. Inc. 1892. **4** city (1990 pop. 21,265), ⊙ Athens co., SE Ohio, on bluffs overlooking the Hocking R.; 39°20′N 82°06′W. In a coal-mining area of the Appalachian foothills. Printing and tool-making industries. Surveyed 1795–1796 by the Ohio Co. of Associates as the site of a univ. and was settled shortly thereafter. Seat of Ohio Univ. Wayne Natl. Forest lies to the N. Biotechnology research center. Inc. 1811. **5** city (1990 pop. 12,054), ⊙ McMinn co., SE Tenn., 50 mi/80 km NE of Chattanooga; 35°27′N 84°36′W. In timber and tobacco region; mfg. of clothing, furniture, textiles, machinery, electric motors, stoves, paper and wood prods. Seat of Tenn. Wesleyan Col. Laid out 1821. **6** city (1990 pop. 10,967), ⊙ Henderson co., E Texas, 34 mi/55 km WSW of Tyler; elev. 490 ft/149 m; 32°12′N 95°51′W. Shipping center of rich oil and gas; agr. area (melons, vegetables, nursery crops, black-eyed peas); ratites (emus, ostriches, rheas); mfg. (bldg. materials, medical equip.; printing, fabricated metal prods., bearing pads). Annual Old Fiddlers Contest. L. Athens reservoir to E; Cedar Creek Reservoir to W; Purtis Creek State Recreation Park to NW. Founded c.1850, inc. 1901.

Athens 1 (ATH-enz), town (1990 pop. 897), Somerset co., central Maine, 10 mi/16 km NNE of Skowhegan; 44°57′N 69°39′W. **2** town (1990 pop. 313), Windham co., SE Vt., 11 mi/18 km NNE of Newfane; 43°07′N 72°35′W. **3** town (1990 pop. 741), Mercer co., S W.Va., 6 mi/9.7 km NE of Princeton; 37°25′N 81°1′W. Coal-mining and agr. area. Mfg. (gears, shafts). Seat of Concord Col. **4** town (1990 pop. 951), Marathon co., central Wis., 22 mi/35 km WNW of Wausau; 45°01′N 90°04′W. In dairying, lumbering, and farming area; wood prods. Mfg. (sawmill; maple syrup).

Athens (A-thinz), village (1991 pop. 961), SE Ont., central Canada, 14 mi/23 km W of Brockville. Dairying; lumbering. Resort.

Athens 1 village, Howard co., SW Ark., 26 mi/42 km NNW of Nashville near Saline R. Ouachita Natl. Forest to N. **2** village (1990 pop. 278), Claiborne parish, N La., 45 mi/72 km ENE of Shreveport; 32°39′N 93°02′W. Agr. (cattle, poultry; dairying); timber. Athens gas field nearby. Claiborne State Park to NE. **3** village (1990 pop. 990), Calhoun co., S Mich., 15 mi/24 km S of Battle Creek; 42°05′N 85°14′W. In orchard and farm area. **4** village (□ 4 sq mi/10.4 sq km; 1990 pop. 1,708), Greene co., SE N.Y., on W bank of the Hudson R., and 27 mi/43 km S of Albany; 42°16′N 73°48′W. Summer resort. Settled 1686, inc. 1805.

Athens, borough (1990 pop. 3,468), Bradford Co., NE Pa., suburb 1 mi/1.6 km S of Sayre, on Susquehanna R., near mouth of Chemung R.; 41°57′N 76°31′W. Mfg. (machining; electronic equip.); agr. area (corn, hay; livestock; dairying). Yioga Point Mus. Originally the site of a Native Amer. village. Settled c.1778, inc. 1831.

Athens, suburban section of Los Angeles city, Los Angeles co., S Calif., residential suburb 8 mi/12.9 km S of downtown Los Angeles, 2 mi/3.2 km NE of Gardena. Willowbrook State Recreation Area to E.

Atherley, village, S Ont., central Canada, bet. L. Simcoe (S) and Couchiching L. (N), 3 mi/5 km E of Orillia; 44°36′N 79°22′W. Resort; dairying; mixed farming.

Atherton, town (1990 pop. 7,163), San Mateo co., W Calif., a residential suburb 25 mi/40 km SSE of San Francisco, bet. Redwood City (NW) and Menlo Park (SE), 3 mi/4.8 km SW of San Francisco Bay; 37°27′N 122°12′W. Inc. 1923. Hetch Hetchy Aqueduct passes to N.

Athol (A-thawl), town (1990 pop. 11,451), Worcester co., N Mass.; 42°35′N 72°13′W. Mfg. includes furniture, toys, lumber, textiles, and precision tools. The area was settled in 1735; inc. 1762.

Athol 1 (ATH-el), village (1990 pop. 346), Kootenai co., N Idaho, 20 mi/32 km N of Coeur d'Alene; 47°57′N

116°43′W. RR junction. Coeur d' Alene Natl. Forest to E; Farragut State Park at S end of L. Pend Oreille, to E; Silverwood Amusement Park is to S. **2** (ATH-uhl), village (1990 pop. 86), Smith co., N Kansas, 7 mi/11.3 km W of Smith Center; 39°46′N 98°55′W. In corn belt; grain; livestock. **3** summer-resort village (1990 pop. 250), Warren co., E N.Y., in the Adirondacks, near the Hudson R., 16 mi/26 km NW of Glens Falls; 43°29′N 73°51′W.

Atikameg Lake (uh-TI-kuh-meg) (□ 90 sq mi/233 sq km), NW Man., central Canada, near Sask. border, 10 mi/16 km NNE of The Pas; 19 mi/31 km long, 3 mi/5 km wide. Drains into Saskatchewan R.

Atikokan (a-ti-KO-kuhn), village (1991 pop. 4,047), W Ont., central Canada, on Atikokan R., near its mouth on Seine R., and 120 mi/193 km WNW of Fort William; elev. 1,284 ft/391 m; 48°45′N 91°37′W. Center of Steep Rock L. iron-mining region.

Atil (AH-teel), town (1990 pop. 754), Sonora, NW Mexico, on affluent of Magdalena R. (irrigation), and 50 mi/80 km SW of Nogales; 30°47′N 11°30′W. Wheat, corn, beans, cotton.

Atipac, Mexico: see TETLA.

Atitalaquia (ah-tee-tah-LAH-kee-ah), town (1990 pop. 5,959), Hidalgo, central Mexico, 32 mi/51 km W of Pachuca de Soto; 20°02′N 0°01′W. Corn, vegetables, fruit.

Atizapán, Mexico: see SANTA CRUZ ATIZAPÁN.

Atizapán de Zaragoza, Mexico: see CIUDAD ADOLFO LÓPEZ MATEOS.

Atka (AT-kuh), village (1990 pop. 73), SW Alaska, on Atka Isl., Aleutian Isls.; 52°12′N 174°12′W. Has Rus. Orthodox church. Sometimes called Nazan.

Atka Island (AT-kuh), Andreanof Isls., Aleutian Isls., SW Alaska, 50 mi/80 km ENE of Adak; 65 mi/ 105 km long, 2 mi/3.2 km–20 mi/32 km wide; 52°07′N 174°30′W. Rises to 4,852 ft/1,479 m on Korovin Volcano (NE). Atka village (E). Air base established during World War II, later expanded.

Atkins 1 town (1990 pop. 2,834), Pope co., N central Ark., 11 mi/18 km E of Russellville, near Ark. R.; 35°14′N 92°57′W. In diversified farm area. Mfg. (chicken feed; pickles and peppers; plastic prods.). Galla Co. Wildlife Management Area and Holla Bend Natl. Wildlife Refuge to SW. Settled 1840, inc. 1878. **2** town (1990 pop. 637), Benton co., E central Iowa, 14 mi/23 km SW of Cedar Rapids; 42°00′N 91°51′W. Feed milling. **3** uninc. town, Smyth co., SW Va., 5 mi/8 km E of Marion; 36°52′N 81°24′W. Mfg. (transportation equip., bldg. materials, wood prods.; steel fabricating, machining); agr. (dairying; livestock; corn, tobacco, fruit, vegetables); timber. Parts of Jefferson Natl. Forest to N and S; Appalachian Trail passes to E.

Atkinson, county (□ 318 sq mi/824 sq km; 1990 pop. 6,213), S Ga.; ⊙ Pearson; 31°17′N 82°52′W. Bounded W by Alapaha R.; drained by Satilla R. Coastal plain agr. includes cotton, corn, peanuts, tobacco; cattle, hogs, poultry; nursery prods.; timber. Formed 1917.

Atkinson 1 town (1990 pop. 950), Henry co., NW Ill., 12 mi/19 km NE of Cambridge; 41°25′N 90°00′W. In agr. area. **2** town (1990 pop. 1,380), Holt co., N Nebr., 18 mi/29 km WNW of O'Neill, and on Elkhorn R.; 42°31′N 98°58′W. Grain; dairy prods.; irrigation equip., sheet metal prods. Atkinson Lake State Recreation Area to S. Settled 1876, inc. 1884. **3** town (1990 pop. 5,188), Rockingham co., SE N.H., 4 mi/6.4 km NE of Salem, on Mass. state line (SE); 42°50′N 71°09′W. Nursery crops, apples, vegetables, beans; cattle, poultry; dairying. Mfg. (biotechnology chemicals, cyrogenic equip.).

Atkinson, village (1990 pop. 275), Pender co., SE N.C., 26 mi/42 km NNW of Wilmington; 34°31′N 78°10′W. Grain, peanuts, tobacco, sweet potatoes; turkeys, livestock. Moore's Creek Natl. Battlefield to SE.

Atkinson and Gilmanton Academy Grant, land grant, Coos co., N N.H., 37 mi/60 km NNE of Berlin. Bounded E by Maine state line. Wilderness area drained by Dead Diamond R.

Atkinson Mills, town (1990 pop. 332), Piscataquis co., central Maine, on Piscataquis R., and 8 mi/12.9 km ESE of Dover-Foxcroft; 45°09′N 69°03′W.

Atlacomulco de Fabela (aht-lah-ko-MOOL-ko dai fah-BAI-lah), town (1990 pop. 13,475), ⊙ Atlacomulco municipio, Mexico state, central Mexico, 22 mi/35 km ESE of El Oro de Hidalgo; 19°49′N 99°54′W. Grain, fruit; livestock.

Atlahuilco (aht-lah-WEEL-ko), town (1990 pop. 675), Veracruz, E Mexico, 10 mi/16 km S of Orizaba; 18°50′N 97°00′W. Coffee.

Atlamajalcingo del Monte (aht-lah-mah-hal-SEEN-go del MON-tai), town (1990 pop. 965), Guerrero, SW Mexico, in Sierra Madre del Sur, 20 mi/32 km SSW of Tlapa de Comonfort; 17°15′N 98°40′W.

Atlangatepec (aht-lahn-gah-TAI-pek), town (1990 pop. 455), Tlaxcala, central Mexico, 15 mi/24 km NNE of Tlaxcala; 19°35′N 98°12′W. Maguey.

Atlanta 1 city (□ 132 sq mi/342 sq km; 1990 pop. 394,017), ⊙ Ga. state and Fulton co., NW Ga., near the Appalachian foothills and the Chattahoochee R.; elev. 1,050 ft/320 m; 33°46′N 84°25′W. It is the largest metropolitan area in the state with a pop. in excess of 3.7 million in the late 1990s; the cultural, industrial, transportation, financial, and commercial center of the state; a port of entry; and one of the leading cities of the South. Major industries include textiles, furniture, food and beverages, telecommunications hardware, steel, paper, and chemicals. There are motor vehicle and aircraft assembly plants, insurance companies, and printing and publishing houses; and it is a major television broadcasting center. Atlanta is the home of numerous corporate hq., most notably Coca-Cola, which was founded here in 1892, United Parcel Service (UPS), Ga. Pacific, and Delta Airlines. Site of the 1996 Centennial Summer Olympics and the Paralympic games. Atlanta is a major warehouse and distribution center as well as the largest retail hub in the Southeast U.S. Also a major convention center with extensive facilities, including many large hotels. Hartsfield Internatl. Airport to S, one of the busiest in the world, and the subway system attest to Atlanta's continuing reputation as a transportation center. Hardy Ivy, the 1st settler, built (1833) a cabin on what had been Creek tribal land. The town, founded (1837) as Terminus, the end of a RR line, was inc. 1843 as Marthasville and renamed Atlanta in 1845. It became a RR and marketing hub and in the Civil War was an important communication and supply center; it fell to Gen. W.T. Sherman on Sept. 2, 1864. Most of the city was burned on Nov. 15, before Sherman began his march to the sea. The city was rapidly rebuilt and thrived as a commercial and industrial center. It was chosen temporary state capital in 1868 and became permanent capital following a popular vote in 1877. A number of conventions and expositions in the 19th and 20th cent. drew attention to Atlanta's strategic location. In 1973, Atlanta became the 1st major city in the South to elect an Afr.-Amer. mayor. The city has experienced rapid suburban growth, especially along the N I-285 perimeter highway; interstates 20, 75, and 85 pass through the city. I-285 serves as a 64 mile/103 km loop around Atlanta. The hq. of the Ga. Ports Authority, with its deepwater ports at Brunswick and Savannah, Ga., is here. Altanta is home to major TV affiliates and several cable television stations, such as TNT, WTBS, and CNN. Points of interest include the capitol (1889), housing the state lib.; the city hall (1929); the High Mus. of Art (1984), part of the Robert R. Woodruff Arts Center; the Coca-Cola mus.; Fernbank Mus. of Natural History, the state archives bldg., containing a historical mus. and lib.; the bldg. housing the huge *Cyclorama of the Battle of Atlanta*, which includes the reenactment of the battle bet. Generals Hood and Sherman and the burning of Atlanta made famous in Margaret Mitchell's book *Gone with the Wind*; Oakland Cemetery, containing Civil War dead; "Underground Atlanta," a 4-block tract covered for 50 years by a vast viaduct system, restored in the 1970s and again in the early 1990s; the Martin Luther King (MLK), Jr., Historic Site and the MLK Center for Nonviolent Social Change, which includes the Civil Rights leader's grave; Ebenezer Baptist Church, and the Sweet Auburn dist. of Atlanta, where King was born and lived (maintained by the Natl. Park Service); and Grant Park, with Zoo Atlanta and Confederate Fort Walker (restored). The Carter Presidential Center (1986) contains a mus. and lib. dedicated to former President Jimmy Carter as well as a forum (part of Emory Univ.) for the scholarly discussion of internatl. issues. The Federal penitentiary here (est. 1899) is one of the most widely known prisons in the U.S. Many depts. of the Federal govt. have branches here, including the Centers for Disease Control and Prevention; seat of natl. hq. of the Amer. Cancer Society, several univs., Fort McPherson, hq. of the U.S. Third Army, and a naval air station. The city's neighborhoods and parks are famous for their dogwood trees and azealeas. The annual fall arts festival of Atlanta attracts 1 million visitors each year. Nearby is Stone Mountain Park, with enormous relief carvings of Confederate figures and a 19th-cent. plantation, reminiscent of the Atlanta depicted in the film *Gone With the Wind* (1939). Also in the area are Kennesaw Mountain Natl. Battlefield Park and Six Flags Over Georgia, a large theme park, and Olympic City theme park. Seat of several private univs., including Emory, Agnes Scott, and Oglethorpe univs., the Atlanta Col. of Art, and the Atlanta Univ. center consisting of Spelman, Morehouse, Morros Brown, and Clark Atlanta cols., the Interdenominational Theological Center and Morehouse School of Medicine, the largest consortium of private Afr.-Amer. institutes of higher learning in the country with an annual enrollment in excess of 12,000 students. The several institutions representing the Univ. System of Ga. include 2 research univs., the Ga. Inst. of Technology, Ga. State Univ., Kennesaw State Univ., Clayton Col. and State Univ., S Polytechnic State Univ. and 2-year cols. including Dekalb and Atlanta Metropolitan cols. There is a symphony orchestra; Lenox Square (one of the largest shopping centers in the U.S.); the Georgia Dome, home for the city's professional football team (NFL Falcons); Turner Field (Natl. League Braves); a new coliseum (now under construction) for Atlanta's professional basketball team (NBA Hawks), and professional hockey team (the Thrashers) in 2000. Inc. as a city 1847. **2** city (1990 pop. 1,616), Logan co., central Ill., 9 mi/14.5 km NE of Lincoln, near Kickapoo Creek; 40°15′N 89°13′W. Agr. area (corn, soybeans).

Atlanta 1 town (1990 pop. 703), Hamilton co., central Ind., 5 mi/8 km S of Tipton, near Cicero Creek; 40°13′N 86°02′W. Corn, soybeans; hogs. **2** (et-LAN-uh), town (1990 pop. 118), Winn parish, La., 10 mi/16 km SW Winnfield; 31°48′N 92°44′W. In pine forest, lumber and agr. area. Early settlers from Ga. in 1858 **3** town (1990 pop. 6,118), Cass co., NE Texas, 21 mi/34 km SSW of Texarkana; elev. 264 ft/80 m; 33°07′N 94°09′W. Oil and natural gas. Agr. (fruit, vegetables; chickens, cattle). Timber. Mfg. (tool and die, lumber, apparel, ammunition containers, safety clothing and equip.). Atlanta State Park to NW, on S shore of Wright Patman L. reservoir.

Atlanta, village, ⊙ Montmorency co., N Mich., 33 mi/53 km W of Alpena, on Thunder Bay R.; 45°00′N 84°08′W. Cattle; forage crops, grain. Clear Lake State Park to N; Sheridan Valley Ski Area to SW.

Atlantic, county (□ 671 sq mi/1,738 sq km; 1990 pop. 224,327), SE N.J., on the Atlantic coast; ⊙ Mays Landing; 39°28′N 74°38′W. Many coast resorts (notably ATLANTIC CITY) along its isl.-dotted shore. Agr. includes vegetables, grain, fruit (esp. blueberries, strawberries); poultry; mfg. (textiles, glassware, clothing, furniture, bricks, boats, concrete blocks, food prods.); fishing. Includes part of pine barrens region (timber, cranberries). Drained by Great Egg Harbor and Mullica rivers. Formed 1837.

Atlantic, city (1990 pop. 7,432), ⊙ Cass co., SW Iowa, on East Nishnabotna R. (hydroelectric plant), and 45 mi/72 km ENE of Council Bluffs; 41°23′N 95°00′W. Trade and processing center; poultry-packing plants, corn and pumpkin canneries; mfg. of feed, beverages, foods, apparel, prefabricated steel bldgs., wood and sheet-metal prods., saws. Inc. 1869.

Atlantic, uninc. town (1990 pop. 900), Carteret co., E

N.C., 25 mi/40 km ENE of Morehead City, on Core Sound, opposite Core Banks, in Cape Lookout Natl. Seashore, across from Cape Lookout Natl. Seashore. Mfg. (fishing nets). Fish, crabs. Ferry to SW end of Portsmouth Isl. to NE. Cedar Island Natl. Wildlife Reserve to NE.

Atlantic, village, Accomack co., E Va., 7 mi/11.3 km WSW of Chincoteague, near Atlantic Ocean coast; 37°54′N 75°30′W. Mfg. (zinc anodes, boat components); agr. (livestock, poultry; grain, vegetables). NASA Wallops Flight Center is here.

Atlantic Beach 1 resort town (□ 7 sq mi/18.1 sq km; 1990 pop. 11,636), Duval co., NE Fla., on the Atlantic Ocean, adjacent to Neptune Beach, and 15 mi/24 km E of Jacksonville; 30°19′N 81°23′W. **2** town (1990 pop. 1,938), Carteret co., E N.C., on Bogue Isl., on Bogue Sound (Intracoastal Waterway to N; bridged), 2 mi/3.2 km SW of Morehead City; 34°42′N 76°44′W. Atlantic Ocean to S. Beach resort area. Just E is Fort Macon State Park, with fort built c.1826–1835, restored 1936. Theodore Roosevelt Natural Area State Park to W. Shackel Pond Banks (isl.), part of Cape Lookout Natl. Seashore, to E.

Atlantic Beach 1 resort and residential village (□ 1 sq mi/2.6 sq km; 1990 pop. 1,933), Nassau co., SE N.Y., on barrier beach off S shore of L.I., across Rockaway Channel (bridged) from Far Rockaway; 40°35′N 73°43′W. **2** village (1990 pop. 446), Horry co., E S.C., 11 mi/18 km NE of Myrtle Beach, on Atlantic Ocean, in Grand Strand Beach resort area; 33°47′N 78°43′W. Intracoastal Waterway passes to NW.

Atlantic City, city (1990 pop. 37,986), Atlantic co., SE N.J., an Atlantic resort and convention center; 39°22′N 74°27′W. Situated on Absecon Isl., a sandbar 10 mi/16 km long, Atlantic City was a fishing village until the construction of a RR in 1854, when it became a fashionable resort for Philadelphians and New Yorkers. The 1st boardwalk was built in 1870. Chief industry is tourism, with over 30 million visitors annually. In 1976 a N.J. state referendum legalized casino gambling for the city and in 1978, when the 1st casino opened, Atlantic City became the only U.S. city outside Nev. to offer such gambling. The industry grew rapidly, and the 14 casinos here put it on the same level as Las Vegas, Nev. The boardwalk, lined with casinos, hotels, shops, and amusements, is 6 mi/9.7 km long and 40 ft/12 m–60 ft/18 m wide. Urban blight, however, contrasts sharply with the prosperous hotels and casinos. Has a large convention hall where the Democratic natl. convention took place in 1964. The Miss Amer. Pageant is held here every Sept. Absecon Lighthouse, in operation 1854–1932, is a tourist attraction. The 1st Ferris wheel was built here in 1869. The board game Monopoly, which makes use of the city's street names, was invented here in 1930. Federal Aviation Administration (FAA) Research Center. Settled c.1790, inc. 1854.

Atlantic City, village, Fremont co., W central Wyo. on Rock Creek, in foothills of Wind River Range, 24 mi/39 km S of Lander; elev. 7,655 ft/2,333 m. Gold deposits; busy mining point in 1870. Shoshone Natl. Forest to NW.

Atlantic Highlands, resort borough (1990 pop. 4,629), Monmouth co., NE N.J., on Sandy Hook Bay, 8 mi/12.9 km NW of Long Branch; 40°25′N 74°01′W. Residential. Navesink Highlands (just E) are often called Atlantic Highlands. Settled before 1675, inc. 1887. Part of Gateway Natl. Recreation Area just NE.

Atlantic Mine, village, Houghton co., NW Upper Peninsula, Mich., 4 mi/6.4 km SW of Houghton; 47°05′N 88°37′W. Former copper-mining dist.

Atlantic Provinces, term used since 1949 to designate the Can. provs. of NEW BRUNSWICK, NEWFOUNDLAND AND LABRADOR, NOVA SCOTIA, and PRINCE EDWARD ISLAND.

Atlantis, town (□ 1 sq mi/2.6 sq km; 1990 pop. 1,653), Palm Beach co., SE Fla., 10 mi/16 km S of W. Palm Beach; 26°36′N 80°05′W. Mfg. of trophies and medical supplies. Heavily guarded community, fenced off from surrounding municipalities.

Atlapexco (aht-lah-PEKS-ko), agr. town (1990 pop. 1,434), Hidalgo, central Mexico, 9 mi/14.5 km SSE of Huejutla de Reyes; 20°01′N 98°21′W. Small farming.

Atlas, uninc. town (1990 pop. 1,182), Northumberland co., E central Pa., 7 mi/11.3 km E of Shamokin, and 1 mi/1.6 km NW of Mount Carmel, on North Branch Shamokin Creek; 40°47′N 76°25′W. Agr. (corn, hay, apples, potatoes; livestock, poultry; dairying).

Atlasburg (AT-luhs-buhrg), uninc. village (1990 pop. 706), Smith township, Washington co., SW Pa., 20 mi/32 km WSW of Pittsburgh, on Burgetts Fort Creek; 40°20′N 80°22′W. Mfg. (construction materials); agr. (corn, hay; dairying). Cross Creek Co. Park.

Atlatlahucan (aht-lah-tlah-WAH-kahn), town (1990 pop. 5,700), Morelos, central Mexico, 22 mi/35 km E of Cuernavaca; 182°55′N 98°50′W. Sugar, fruit, vegetables; livestock.

Atlautla de Victoria (aht-LOUT-lah de veek-TO-ree-ah), town (1990 pop. 6,999), ⊙ Atlautla municipio, Mexico state, central Mexico, at W foot of Popocatepetl, on RR, and 38 mi/61 km SE of Mexico City, within the Zona Metropolitana de la Ciudad de México; 19°01′N 98°45′W. Cereals, fruit; livestock. Also known as San Miguel Atlautla.

Atlequizayan (aht-lai-kee-SAH-yahn), town (1990 pop. 1,306), ⊙ Ignacio Allende municipio, Puebla, central Mexico, in SE foothills of Sierra Madre Oriental, 28 mi/45 km ESE of Huauchinango. Corn, sugar, fruit. In Totonac Indian area.

Atlin (AT-lin), village, NW B.C., W Canada, near U.S. (Alaska) border, on Atlin L., 90 mi/145 km NNE of Juneau (Alaska); 59°35′N 133°43′W. Lumbering; in mining (gold, silver, lead, zinc, coal) region. Resort.

Atlin Lake (AT-lin), long, irregular mountain lake (□ c.300 sq mi/780 sq km), NW B.C, W Canada, touching the Yukon Territory border; 59°30′N 133°45′W. Source of the Yukon R. The town of Atlin is on the E shore and is the hq. of the Atlin dist., a region in which there is both placer and quartz gold mining. In region noted for scenery and hunting.

Atlixco (aht-LEEKS-ko), city (1990 pop. 74,233) and township, Puebla, central Mexico, on central plateau, 18 mi/29 km SW of Puebla, on Inter-American Hwy 190; elev. 6,171 ft/1,881 m; 18°54′N 98°26′W. RR junction; processing and agr. center famous for grain (corn, wheat) and fruit (oranges, limes, mangoes); sugarcane and coffee. Tanneries, flour mills; mfg. of cotton yarn and fabrics, silverware, pharmaceuticals.

Atlixtac (aht-LEESH-tahk), town (1990 pop. 1,320), Guerrero, SW Mexico, in Sierra Madre del Sur, 20 mi/32 km E of Chilapa de Álvarez; elev. 3,281 ft/1,000 m; 17°32′N 98°57′W. Cereals; livestock.

Atlzayanca, Mexico: see ALTZAYANCA.

Atmore, city (1990 pop. 8,046), Escambia co., SW Ala., 25 mi/40 km WSW of Brewton. In agr. area (corn, cotton, strawberries); mfg. (lumber milling; fertilizer, carpet, clothing). Inc. 1907. State prison farm nearby.

Atoka (uh-TO-kuh), county (□ 990 sq mi/2,564 sq km; 1990 pop. 12,778), SE Okla.; ⊙ Atoka; 34°22′N 96°02′W. Drained by the Muddy Boggy and Clear Boggy creeks. Agr. (wheat, peanuts; sheep); timber; mfg. (furniture); coal mining; rock quarries. Boggy Depot State Park in W; Atoka Reservoir in N; McGee Creek L. and McGee Creek State Park in E. Formed 1907.

Atoka 1 (uh-TO-kuh), town (1990 pop. 3,298), ⊙ Atoka co., SE Okla., 31 mi/50 km NNE of Durant, and on Muddy Boggy Creek; 34°22′N 96°07′W. In agr. area (wheat, peanuts; sheep); mfg. (furniture, bulldozer attachments). Boggy Depot State Park to W; Atoka Reservoir to NE; McGee Creek L. reservoir and McGee Creek State Park to E. An agreement ending Choctaw and Chickasaw Native tribal govt. was signed here in 1897. East Shawnee Trail, a 19th-cent. cattle trail, passed through this area. Founded 1867. **2** town (1990 pop. 659), Tipton co., W Tenn., 25 mi/40 km NNE of Memphis; 35°26′N 89°47′W. In cotton-growing region.

Atoka Reservoir (uh-TO-kuh), Atoka co., SE Okla., on North Boggy Creek, 3 mi/4.8 km NNE of Atoka; 8 mi/12.9 km long; 34°26′N 96°03′W. Max. capacity 191,000 acre-ft. Formed by Atoka Dam (68 ft/21 m high), built (1964) by Oklahoma City (110 mi/177 km NW) for water supply.

Atolinga (ah-to-LEEN-gah), town (1990 pop. 1,756), Zacatecas, N central Mexico, near Jalisco border, 8 mi/12.9 km SW of Tlaltenango de Sánchez Román; elev. 4,659 ft/1,420 m. Grain, fruit; livestock.

Atomic City, village (1990 pop. 25), Bingham co., SE Idaho, c.20 mi/32 km NW of Blackfoot; 43°26′N 112°49′W. Grew after establishment (1949) of U.S. atomic-reactor testing station (just N); EBR-1 Natl. Historic Landmark to NW, on grounds of large Idaho Natl. Engineering Laboratory tract with the world's 1st nuclear reactor, Experimental Breeding Reactor #1. Big Southern Butte (7,550 ft/2,301 m) to SW. Inc. 1950.

Atotonilco, Mexico: see ATOTONILCO EL ALTO.

Atotonilco de Tula (ah-to-to-NEEL-ko de TOO-lah), town (1990 pop. 5,689), Hidalgo, central Mexico, 33 mi/53 km WSW of Pachuca de Soto; 20°04′N 99°13′W. Corn, fruit, vegetables.

Atotonilco el Alto (ah-to-to-NEEL-ko el AHL-to), city (1990 pop. 23,834) and township, Jalisco, central Mexico, on interior plateau, 55 mi/89 km ESE of Guadalajara, on Mexico Highway 90; elev. 5,171 ft/1,576 m; 20°35′N 102°30′W. RR terminus; agr. center (grain, cotton, chickpeas, oranges; livestock); flour milling, tanning, vegetable oil pressing, wine making. Also Atotonilco.

Atotonilco el Grande (ah-to-to-NEEL-ko el GRAHN-dai), town (1990 pop. 5,723), Hidalgo, central Mexico, on central plateau, 12 mi/19 km NNE of Pachuca de Soto, on Mexico Hwy 105; elev. 7,014 ft/2,138 m; 20°17′N 98°40′W. Corn, beans, fruit, maguey; livestock. Thermal springs nearby. Mineral del Chico, formerly called Atotonilco, is just S.

Atoyac 1 (ah-TO-yahk), town (1990 pop. 4,964), Jalisco, W Mexico, on E shore of L. Sayula, on central plateau, 45 mi/72 km SSW of Guadalajara; 29°40′N 103°31′W. Agr. center (alfalfa, grain, fruit; livestock). **2** town (1990 pop. 2,747), Veracruz, E Mexico, in Sierra Madre Oriental foothills, on RR, and 10 mi/16 km E of Córdoba; 19°54′N 96°35′W. Coffee, sugar, fruit. Notable waterfalls nearby.

Atoyac de Álvarez (ah-TO-yahk de AHL-vah-raiz), city (1990 pop. 18,561) and township, Guerrero, SW Mexico, in Pacific lowland, 40 mi/64 km NW of Acapulco de Juárez, on Mexico Highway 196; 17°12′N 100°28′W. Rice, sugar, fruit; livestock.

Atoyac River 1 c.200 mi/322 km long, central Mexico, upper course (largely in Puebla) of the Río Balsas; 18°25′N 97°11′W. **2** (ah-TO-yahk), in Oaxaca, S Mexico, rises in Sierra Madre del Sur, NW of Oaxaca de Juárez; flows S, W, and SW, to the Pacific Ocean 19 mi/31 km S of Jamiltepec; 18°10′N 98°31′W. Called Río Verde in lower course.

Atoyatempan (ah-to-yah-TEM-pahn), town (1990 pop. 4,448), Puebla, central Mexico, 25 mi/40 km SE of Puebla; 18°50′N 97°56′W. Cereals, vegetables; livestock.

Atrisco (uh-TREES-ko), uninc. town, Bernalillo co., central N.Mex., residential suburb of Albuquerque, 1.5 mi/2.4 km WSW of downtown on Rio Grande.

Attala (uh-TAL-uh), county (□ 737 sq mi/1,909 sq km; 1990 pop. 18,481), central Miss.; ⊙ Kosciusko; 33°05′N 89°34′W. Bounded W by Big Black R.; intersected by Yockanookany R. and Lobutcha Creek. Agr. (corn, cotton, hay, soybeans; cattle; timber; mfg. (paper prods., textiles). Natchez Trace Natl. Parkway crosses co. N-S. Formed 1833.

Attalla (uh-TAH-luh), city (1990 pop. 6,859), Etowah co., NE Ala., on branch of Coosa R., and just W of Gadsden. RR junction in iron-mining and agr. area; foundry prods. (chiefly screw machinery and cast-iron soil pipe), lumber, concrete, cranes, sausages, plastic tableware. Founded 1870, inc. 1872.

Attapulgus (at-uh-PUL-guhs), village (1990 pop. 380), Decatur co., SW Ga., 12 mi/19 km SSE of Bainbridge, near Fla. state line; 30°45′N 84°29′W. Mfg. includes mineral and clay production.

Attawapiskat River (at-uh-wuh-PIS-kat), c.465 mi/750 km long, N Ont., central Canada; flows E from Attawapiskat L., then N and E into James Bay. The trading posts of Attawapiskat and Lansdowne House are on the river.

Attean Mountain (AT-ee-uhn) (2,453 ft/748 m), Somerset co., W Maine, c.70 mi/113 km NNW of Skowhegan. In recreational area.

Attean Pond (AT-ee-uhn), Somerset co., W Maine, c.70 mi/113 km NNW of Skowhegan; 5 mi/8 km long, 2 mi/3.2 km wide. In hunting, fishing area.

Attica, city (1990 pop. 3,457), Fountain co., W Ind., on the Wabash R., and 21 mi/34 km WSW of Lafayette; 40°17′N 87°15′W. Trading center in agr. area; mfg. (cement prods., steel castings, primary metals, consumer goods, foods, machinery). Bear Creek Canyon and a natural stone arch are nearby. Settled 1825, inc. 1866.

Attica 1 (AT-i-kuh), village (1990 pop. 716), Harper co., S Kansas, 12 mi/19 km NW of Anthony; 37°14′N 98°13′W. RR junction. In wheat region; sheet metal. **2** village (□ 1 sq mi/2.6 sq km; 1990 pop. 2,630), Wyoming co., W N.Y., on Tonawanda Creek, and 10 mi/16 km SSW of Batavia; 42°52′N 78°16′W. In agr. area. Attica Correctional Facility (a maximum-security facility) is here, site of 1971 riots; also located here is the medium-security Wyoming Correctional Facility. Settled 1804, inc. 1837. **3** village (1990 pop. 944), Seneca co., N Ohio, 15 mi/24 km ESE of Tiffin; 41°04′N 82°55′W.

Attleboro (A-duhl-buh-ro), industrial city (1990 pop. 38,383), Bristol co., SE Mass., near the R.I. state line; 41°56′N 71°18′W. Its jewelry industry began in 1780; mfg. includes silverware, scientific instruments, chemicals, fabricated metal prods. Zoo. Settled 1634, inc. as a city 1914.

Attoyac Bayou, c.65 mi/105 km long, E Texas; rises in Rusk co.; flows generally SSE to Angelina R., 24 mi/39 km ESE of Lufkin. Lower c.15 mi/24 km arm of large Sam Rayburn Reservoir (in Angelina Natl. Forest).

Attu (AH-too), village, on NE Attu Isl., Aleutian Isls., SW Alaska, at head of Holtz Bay; 52°56′N 173°14′E. Natives evacuated by Jap. invaders in 1942, repatriated to mainland Alaska 1945. Has U.S. Coast Guard station.

Attu (AH-too), island, Alaska, Aleutian Isls., one of the farthest isls. from the mainland, 200 mi/322 km E of isl. of Ostrova (Russia), and 450 mi/724 km E of Russia's Kamchatka Peninsula, while it is 1,100 mi/1,770 km E (circle route is shorter) of the W tip of Alaska Peninsula. Part of the Near Isl. group. Highest point, 2,820 ft/860 m. Included in Aleutian Isls. Natl. Wildlife Refuge. In World War II occupied by Japanese.

Atwater, city (1990 pop. 22,282), Merced co., central Calif., suburb, 6 mi/9.7 km WNW of Merced, in the San Joaquin valley; 37°21′N 120°36′W. Processing and commercial center of an irrigated farming area. Mfg. (canned and frozen fruits and vegetables, wood prods.); tomatoes, sweet potatoes, cantaloupes, cotton, grain, alfalfa, sugar beets, almonds; dairying; cattle, poultry. Castle Air Force Base to NE; Merced Natl. Wildlife Refuge to S; San Luis Natl. Wildlife Refuge to SW. Inc. 1922.

Atwater, town (1990 pop. 1,053), Kandiyohi co., S central Minn., 14 mi/23 km E of Willmar; 45°08′N 94°46′W. Grain, sugar beets, peas, beans; livestock, poultry; dairying; mfg. (turkey feeds, agr. equip.). L. Elizabeth to S, Diamond L. to NW, numerous other small natural lakes in area.

Atwood, town (1990 pop. 1,388), ⊙ Rawlins co., NW Kansas, on Beaver Creek, and 27 mi/43 km N of Colby; elev. 2,843 ft/867 m; 39°48′N 101°02′W. Grain; livestock. Mfg. (small arms). Mus. Founded 1878, inc. 1885.

Atwood, village (1991 pop. 294), S Ont., central Canada, 22 mi/35 km N of Stratford. Dairying; mixed farming.

Atwood, village (1990 pop. 1,253), Piatt and Douglas cos., E central Ill., 26 mi/42 km E of Decatur; 39°47′N 88°27′W. Soybeans, corn, wheat.

Atwood, borough (1990 pop. 128), Armstrong co., W central Pa., 14 mi/23 km ESE of Kittanning, on E shore of Keystone L. reservoir (Plum Creek); 40°45′N 79°15′W. Agr. includes grain; livestock, dairying.

Atwood Cay, Bahama Isls.: see SAMANA ISLAND.

Atwood Keystone Lake, Pa.: see KEYSTONE LAKE.

Atwood Lake, reservoir, Tuscarawas and Carroll cos., E Ohio, on branch of Conotton R., 10 mi/16 km ENE of New Philadelphia; 6 mi/9.7 km long; 40°31′N 81°17′W. Max. capacity 49,700 acre-ft. Formed by Atwood Dam; built for flood control.

Atzacán (aht-sah-KAHN), town (1990 pop. 6,119), Veracruz, E Mexico, at SE foot of Pico de Orizaba, 4 mi/6.4 km NNE of Orizaba; 18°57′N 97°05′W. Coffee, fruit.

Atzala (aht-SAH-lah), town (1990 pop. 1,181), Puebla, central Mexico, 18 mi/29 km W of Puebla; 18°32′N 98°34′W. Cereals, beans, maguey.

Atzalán (aht-sah-LAHN), town (1990 pop. 1,493), Veracruz, E Mexico, 29 mi/47 km NW of Xalapa Enríquez; 19°40′N 72°15′W. Cereals, coffee, fruit.

Atzitzihuacán, Mexico: see SANTIAGO ATZITZIHUACÁN.

Atzizintla (aht-see-SEENT-lah), town (1990 pop. 2,786), Puebla, central Mexico, near Veracruz border, 15 mi/24 km WNW of Orizaba; 18°52′N 97°20′W. Cereals, maguey, fruit.

Atzompa 1 Mexico: see SOLEDAD ATZOMPA. **2** Mexico: see SAN GREGORIO ATZOMPA. **3** Mexico: see SAN JUAN ATZOMPA.

Au Fer, Point, La.: see ATCHAFALAYA BAY.

Au Gres (aw gres), village (1990 pop. 838), Arenac co., E Mich., on Au Gres R. near its mouth on Saginaw Bay, and 14 mi/23 km ENE of Standish; 44°02′N 83°41′W. Farming. Resort. Mfg. (light and heavy machinery, metal stampings, foundry equip.).

Au Gres River (OW grai), river, c.45 mi/72 km long, E Mich.; rises in lake in E Ogemaw co.; flows SE, past Au Gres, to Saginaw Bay; 44°21′N 83°57′W. Chief tributary is East Branch (c.30 mi/48 km long).

Au Sable Forks, village (1990 pop. 2,100), on border bet. Clinton and Essex cos., NE N.Y., at junction of East and West branches here forming Ausable R., 21 mi/34 km SSW of Plattsburg; 44°26′N 73°40′W. Timber area. Ausable Chasm of Ausable R. is NE.

Au Sable Point, Mich.: see SAGINAW BAY.

Au Sable River (aw SAI-bul), c.80 mi/129 km long, NE Mich.; formed by several branches near border bet. Crawford and Oscoda cos.; flows SE, past Mio, to L. Huron at Oscoda (Iosco co.); 44°48′N 83°57′W. Power dams in lower course, North Branch flows c.30 mi/48 km SE from Otsego co. Middle Branch (c.33 mi/53 km long) rises SW of Otsego L., flows S and E, past Grayling. South Branch rises in L. St. Helen, flows N, past Roscommon; c.37 mi/60 km long. Includes, Forest Dam Pond, Cooke Dam Pond, Loud Dam Pond, in Iosca co.

Au Train (aw TRAIN), village, Alger co., N Upper Peninsula, NW Mich., 8 mi/12.9 km WNW of Munising, on Au Train Bay of L. Superior, at mouth of Au Train R. (flows out of Cleveland Cliffs Power Basin reservoir 8 mi/12.9 km N through Au Train L. reservoir). Au Train Is. at W side of bay entrance; 46°25′N 86°50′W. Timber; fishing.

Auau Channel (OU-OU), Pacific Ocean, bet. Lanai and Maui isls., Hawaii, Maui co.; 8 mi/12.9 km wide.

Auberry, uninc. town (1990 pop. 1866), Fresno co., central Calif., 19 mi/31 km NW of Fresno, on Little Sandy Creek, near San Joaquin River Sierra Natl. Forest to NE; 37°05′N 119°30′W. Millerton Lake reservoir and State Recreational Area to SE. Cattle; dairying; timber.

Aubrey, town (1990 pop. 1,138), Denton co., N Texas, 38 mi/61 km N of Dallas; 33°17′N 96°58′W. In farm area; cotton, wheat; cattle; light mfg.

Aubry Lake (O-bree), NW Mackenzie dist., N.W.T., N Canada, NW of Great Bear L.; 40 mi/64 km long, 1 mi/2 km–13 mi/21 km wide; 67°25′N 126°28′W.

Auburn, village, SW Ont., central Canada, on Maitland R., and 10 mi/16 km E of Doderich. Dairying; mixed farming.

Auburn 1 (AW-buhrn), city (1990 pop. 33,830), Lee co., E Ala., just W of Opelika. The city's economy centers around Auburn Univ., the largest univ. in Ala. Auburn has received the nickname "the loveliest village on the Plains." Mfg. of hardware, wire, precision castings. Chewacla State Park just S of town. Inc. 1839 **2** city (1990 pop. 10, 592), ⊙ Placer co., central Calif., in Sierra Nevada foothills, 30 mi/48 km NE of Sacramento, and on North Fork of American R., which enters Folsom L. reservoir (state recreation area) to S; 38°54′N 121°05′W. Shipping center for orchard, and livestock region; mfg. (electronic equip., consumer goods, engines, optical instruments, bldg. materials; printing and publishing); rice, fruit, nuts, corn, apiary prods.; cattle, sheep. Resort. Old New Orleans Hotel here. Early mining camp (gold, discovered 1848, soon gave out). Inc. 1860. El Dorado Natl. Forest to E. **3** city (1990 pop. 3,724), Sangamon co., central Ill., 15 mi/24 km SSW of Springfield; 39°34′N 89°45′W. Agr. (corn, sorghum; cattle, hogs); mfg. (agr. machinery, sewer pipe). Inc. 1865. **4** city (1990 pop. 9,379), ⊙ DeKalb co., NE Ind., 21 mi/34 km N of Fort Wayne; 41°22′N 85°04′W. Trading center in agr. area (livestock; dairy prods.; soybeans, grain); mfg. (motor vehicles [an early auto-making center that gave its name to a line of pre–World War II automobiles], transportation equip., foundry prods., lumber, paper prods.). Settled 1836. **5** (AW-buhrn), city (1990 pop. 24,309), ⊙ Androscoggin co., SW Maine, on the Androscoggin R. (crossed by several bridges) opposite Lewiston; 44°04′N 70°15′W. Shoes have been manufactured here since c.1835; industry (also brick mfg.) is declining. Livestock. With Lewiston, Auburn forms one of the most important industrial complexes in Maine; abundant water power has spurred a large variety of mfg. Lost Valley Ski Resort is here; hotels nearby. Settled 1765 on the site of a Native Amer. village, inc. 1842. **6** city (□ 8 sq mi/20.7 sq km; 1990 pop. 31,258), ⊙ Cayuga co., W central N.Y., in the Finger Lakes region, on the outlet of Owasco L.; 42°56′N 76°34′W. Mfg. (transportation equip., machinery, rope, fiber optic instruments, bldg. machinery, leather specialty prods., steel and steel prods., fuel oil tanks, electronic parts, consumer goods). Site of Auburn State Prison (built 1816), in which Thomas Mott Osborne, the prison reformer (who was b. here), served a voluntary term, and which was the site of the 1st execution of a prisoner in the electric chair. The city's mus. has collections of historical documents and Native Amer. relics. The houses of William H. Seward and Harriet Tubman (who est. 1908 a home for elderly, indigent Afr.-Americans) are preserved. Seward practiced law here. Seat of Cayuga Co. Community Col. Settled 1793, inc. 1848. **7** city (1990 pop. 33,102), King co., W Wash., suburb 22 mi/35 km S of Seattle, and 10 mi/16 km ENE of Tacoma, on the Green (NE) and White (S) rivers; 47°18′N 122°13′W. It is a RR center and farm trade center. Large aircraft industry; site of a Federal Aviation Administration air traffic control center (est. 1962). Strawberries, vegetables; dairying; poultry, cattle; mfg. (lumber, dairy prods., aircraft parts, sheet metal prods., plastic prods., machinery and machinery parts, bldg. materials, furniture, wood prods., machinery parts; metal stamping). Large General Services Administration Center and Green River Community Col. here. Seattle Internatl. Raceway to NE. Kanaskat-Palmer and Nolte state parks to E; L. Tapps reservoir to S; Muckelshoot Indian Reservation to SE. Auburn Municipal Airport to N. Settled 1855, inc. 1914.

Auburn 1 (AW-buhrn), town (1990 pop. 3,139), Barrow co., NE central Ga., 8 mi/12.9 km WNW of Winder; 34°01′N 83°50′W. Mfg. includes crushed stone, plastic molds, clothing. **2** town (1990 pop. 283), Sac co., W Iowa, 13 mi/21 km SSW of Sac City; 42°15′N 94°52′W. Livestock; grain. **3** town (1990 pop. 1,273), Logan co., S Ky., 18 mi/29 km WSW of Bowling Green; 36°51′N 86°42′W. Agr. area (livestock; grain, tobacco); timber; mfg. (textiles, leather prods., gaskets and molds, furniture, cornmeal). **4** residential town (1990 pop. 15,005), Worcester co., S central Mass., 6 mi/9.7 km S of Worcester; 42°12′N 71°51′W. Paper, concrete and metal prods. Includes villages of West Auburn and Stoneville. First rocket launched here by Robert Goddard of Clark Univ., 1926. Settled 1714, inc. 1837. **5** town (1990 pop. 1,855), Bay co., E Mich., 9 mi/14.5 km W of Bay City, and 9 mi/14.5 km E of Midland, near Kawkawlin R.; 43°36′N 84°04′W. Commuter town for both cities and Saginaw. In agr. area. Mfg. (bean and grain processing, silicone production). Tri-Cities Airport to

S; Saginaw Valley State Univ. to SE. **6** (AW-buhrn), town (1990 pop. 3,443), ⊙ Nemaha co., SE Nebr., 55 mi/89 km SE of Lincoln, and on Little Nemaha R; 40°23′N 95°50′W. RR junction. Dairy prods.; grain; mfg. (apparel, furniture, construction equip.; bronze work). Sheridan (founded 1868) and Calvert (founded 1881) united as Auburn in 1882. Brownville State Recreation Area to E. **7** town (1990 pop. 4,085), Rockingham co., SE N.H., 5 mi/8 km E of Manchester; 43°00′N 71°20′W. Nursery crops, vegetables, apples; cattle, poultry; dairying; timber. Mfg. (sheet metal fabrication, wood prods.). Part of Massabesic L. in W.

Auburn 1 village (1990 pop. 89), Ritchie co., NW W.Va., 13 mi/21 km ESE of Harrisville; 39°06′N 80°51′W. **2** village, Lincoln co., W Wyo., bet. Idaho state line and Salt R., 6 mi/9.7 km NNW of Afton; elev. c.6,300 ft/1,920 m. Dairy prods.; grain; livestock. Hot springs, salt and sulphur deposits nearby. Salt R. range just E; Bridger-Teton Natl. Forest also to E.

Auburn (AW-buhrn), borough (1990 pop. 913), Schuylkill co., E central Pa., 8 mi/12.9 km SSE of Pottsville, on Schuylkill R.; 40°36′N 76°05′W. Mfg. (textiles, air filters, plastic and vinyl prods., apparel). Appalachian Trail passes to SE on Blue Mt. ridge; part of Weiser State Forest to S.

Auburn, neighborhood, Cranston city, Providence co., E central R.I., 4 mi/6.4 km SSW of Providence, near Pocasset R.; 41°46′N 71°25′W. Nearby are zoo, Mus. of Natural History and Planetarium of Providence's Roger Williams Park.

Auburn Heights, village, Oakland co., SE Mich., suburb 22 mi/35 km NW of downtown Detroit, and 3 mi/4.8 km ESE of Pontiac, on Clinton R.; 42°38′N 83°13′W. Area has been absorbed by Bloomfield township (S) and Auburn Hills (N).

Auburn Hills, city (1990 pop. 17,076), Oakland co., SE Mich., residential suburb 25 mi/40 km NNW of downtown Detroit, and 3 mi/4.8 km E and NE of Pontiac; 42°40′N 83°14′W. Oakland Univ. located on W border with Rochester Hills. Site of The Palace, the sports complex that is home to the Detroit Pistons Natl. Basketball Assn. team. Mfg. (industrial robotics, consumer goods, transportation equip., machinery, electronic equip., tilt tables, tooling and gauges, motor vehicles; machining).

Auburndale, town (□ 6 sq mi/15.5 sq km; 1990 pop. 8,858), Polk co., central Fla., 10 mi/16 km E of Lakeland, on several small lakes; 28°04′N 81°47′W. Citrus-fruit-shipping center, with large packing houses and canneries; also mfg. of boxes, asphalt, brick. Founded 1884, inc. 1911.

Auburndale, village (1990 pop. 665), Wood co., central Wis., 9 mi/14.5 km ESE of Marshfield; 44°37′N 90°00′W. In dairying and agr. area.

Auburndale, Mass.: see NEWTON.

Auburntown, town (1990 pop. 240), Cannon co., central Tenn., 9 mi/14.5 km N of Woodbury; 35°57′N 86°05′W.

Aucilla River (aw-SIL-LAH), c.75 mi/121 km long, S Ga. and NW Fla.; rises 5 mi/8 km NE of Thomasville (Ga.); flows SE into Fla., thence SSW into E end of Apalachee Bay (Gulf of Mexico), 25 mi/40 km WSW of Perry.

Audrain (AW-jrain), county (□ 692 sq mi/1792 sq km; 1990 pop. 23,599), NE central Mo.; ⊙ Mexico; 39°12′N 91°50′W. Drained by South Fork of Salt R. and West Fork of Cuivre R. Agr. (corn, wheat, soybeans, oats); cattle, hogs, saddle horses, sheep; mfg. at Mexico and Vandalia; fire-clay deposits, coal, lumber. Large Amish area in W. Formed 1836.

Audubon, county (□ 443 sq mi/1,147 sq km; 1990 pop. 7,334), W central Iowa; ⊙ Audubon; 41°40′N 94°54′W. Prairie agr. area (cattle, hogs, poultry; corn, hay, oats) drained by East Nishnabotna R. Coal deposits. Has Dan. villages of Kimballton and Elk Horn (Shelby co.). Formed 1851.

Audubon, city (1990 pop. 2,524), ⊙ Audubon co., W central Iowa, on East Nishnabotna R., 22 mi/35 km N of Atlantic; 41°43′N 94°55′W. Agr. (canned corn, hybrid seed corn, feed); mfg. (grocery store equip.; printing). RR terminus. Plotted 1878, inc. 1880.

Audubon (AW-duh-bahn), uninc. town (1990 pop. 6,328), Montgomery co., SE Pa., suburb 18 mi/29 km WNW of Philadelphia, on Schuylkill R., near mouth of Perkiomen Creek; 40°07′N 75°25′W. Mfg. includes medical equip.; agr. includes dairying and livestock; corn. Valley Forge Natl. Historical Park to S, state park nearby.

Audubon, village (1990 pop. 411), Becker co., W central Minn., 7 mi/11.3 km WNW of Detroit Lakes; 46°51′N 95°58′W. Dairying; poultry; sunflowers, grain, sugar beets, beans; mfg. (machining; cabinets). Numerous small lakes in area.

Audubon (UH-dau-bahn), borough (1990 pop. 9,205), Camden co., SW N.J., a suburb of Camden. Mostly residential. Named after John James Audubon, the ornithologist, who studied the birds of the area in 1829. Inc. 1905.

Audubon, Mount (13,223 ft/4,030 m), Boulder co., Colo., in the Front Range, in Roosevelt Natl. Forest, 18 mi/29 km NW of Boulder, S of Rocky Mt. Natl. Park, and just E of Continental Divide. Part of Indian Peaks Wilderness.

Audubon Park (AW-duh-buhn), town (1990 pop. 1,520), Jefferson co., N Ky., suburb 3 mi/4.8 km SSE of downtown Louisville; 38°12′N 85°43′W. Louisville Internatl. Airport, Standiford Field to S. Ky. Fair and Exposition Center to W.

Audubon Park (UH-dau-bahn), borough (1990 pop. 1,150), Camden co., SW N.J., just W of Audubon, and near Camden. Chiefly residential. Inc. after 1940.

Auglaize (o-GLAIZ), county (□ 400 sq mi/1,036 sq km; 1990 pop. 44,585), W Ohio; ⊙ Wapakoneta; 40°33′N 84°15′W. Drained by Auglaize and St. Marys rivers; part of Grand L. is in W. In the Till Plains physiographic region. Agr. area (livestock, poultry; corn, soybeans, wheat; dairying); mfg. at St. Marys, Wapakoneta, Minster, New Bremen (mechanical rubber goods, plastics, fabricated metal prods., machinery, consumer goods). Sand, gravel, and clay pits; hunting, fishing. Formed 1848.

Auglaize River, c.100 mi/161 km long, NW Ohio; rises SE of Lima; flows SW to Wapakoneta, then N, past Fort Jennings, joining the Maumee R. at Defiance; 41°17′N 84°21′W. Tributaries are Ottawa and Blanchard rivers (E), Little Auglaize R. (W).

August, uninc. town (1990 pop. 6,376), San Joaquin co., central Calif., residential suburb 2 mi/3.2 km SE of Stockton, near Mormon Slough; 37°59′N 121°16′W.

Augusta, county (□ 972 sq mi/2,517 sq km; 1990 pop. 54,677), NW Va.; ⊙ STAUNTON; 38°10′N 79°07′W. Agr. (apples, peaches, wheat, corn, hay, barley, soybeans, alfalfa); livestock raising (cattle, hogs, sheep, poultry); dairying; timber; manganese mining; rock quarrying. Mfg. at Staunton, Waynesboro (independent cities separate from co.). Mainly in S Shenandoah Valley; Shenandoah Mts. in W and NW, Blue Ridge in SE and E. Includes parts of Shenandoah Natl. Park, George Washington Natl. Forest, Appalachian Trail, Blue Ridge Parkway. Drained by Middle and South rivers (headstreams of the Shenandoah R.), Maury and Calfpasture rivers. Appalachian Trail, Blue Ridge Parkway follow SE boundary. Formed 1745.

Augusta 1 (aw-GUHST-uh), city (1990 pop. 44,639), ⊙ Richmond co., E Ga.; 33°28′N 81°59′W. At the head of navigation on the Savannah R. and protected by levees, Augusta is the trade center for a broad band of cos. in Ga. and S.C. known as the Central Savannah River Area. Also an important industrial center; mfg. (textiles, chemicals, bldg. materials, medical supplies, tools; wood, paper, metal, and plastic prods.). Hq. of the Natl. Golf Club, sponsor of the annual Masters Tournament. Augusta grew from an old river trading post existing as early as 1717 and was named by James Oglethorpe in 1735 after the mother of George III. In the Amer. Revolution, Augusta changed hands several times and was finally taken by Continental forces under Andrew Pickens and Light-Horse Harry Lee in 1781. It was state capital (1785–1795) and the U.S. Constitution was ratified here. Expanded rapidly after the Revolutionary War as a result of the tobacco and cotton industries. By 1820 the city was a trade terminus; mfg. began in 1828, when Augusta's 1st textile plant began operation with machinery brought from Philadelphia. During the Civil War, Augusta housed the largest Confederate powder works. Historical attractions include a boyhood home of President Woodrow Wilson, a U.S. arsenal (1815–1955), whose surviving bldgs. are part of Augusta State Univ., and old homes of Georgian and classic-revival styles. Paine Col. and Ga. Medical Col., a unit of the Univ. System of Ga., are also here. Nearby is Fort Gordon, with training schools for military police, the signal corps, and the corps of engineers. The waterfront facing the Savannah R. has been landscaped creating a riverwalk promenade along the levee with an amphitheater. The former Cotton Exchange bldg. now serves as a visitor's center and mus. Airport to S, E of Savannah R., on S.C. side. Inc. 1798. **2** (uh-GUHST-uh), city (1990 pop. 21,325), ⊙ Maine and Kennebec co., SW Maine, on the Kennebec R.; 44°19′N 69°43′W. Business center of a tourist region; mfg. (shoes, computers, electronic equip., paper prods.). Traders visited the site, long known as Cushnoc, even before 1628, when the Plymouth Co. established a trading post. Fort Western was built in 1754, and Benedict Arnold's expedition to Quebec gathered at the fort in 1775 (garrison house restored as a mus., 1921). The settlement around the fort developed with shipping and shipbuilding on the Kennebec; mfg. began in 1837, when a dam was built across the river. The capitol bldg. (1829) was designed by Charles Bulfinch but has been considerably enlarged and remodeled. James G. Blaine's early-19th-cent. home is the governor's mansion. Branch of the Univ. of Maine is here. Inc. as a town 1797, as a city 1849.

Augusta 1 (aw-GUHS-tuh), town (1990 pop. 2,759), ⊙ Woodruff co., E central Ark., c.65 mi/105 km NE of Little Rock, and on White R.; 35°17′N 91°21′W. In agr. area; sawmilling; commercial fishing; mfg. (fabricated metal prods., apparel). Henry Gray—Hurricane Lake Wildlife Management Area to SW. Settled 1846, inc. as city 1931. **2** (aw-GUHST-uh), town (1990 pop. 7,876), Butler co., S Kansas, on Walnut R., and 11 mi/18 km SW of El Dorado; 37°41′N 96°58′W. RR junction. Trading and shipping point for livestock, grain, oil, and gas region; mfg. (plastic prods., navigation equip.). Oil wells nearby. Mus. here. El Dorado State Park in vicinity. **3** town (1990 pop. 1,336), Bracken co., N Ky., 15 mi/24 km NW of Maysville, on the Ohio R. (ferry to Ohio); 38°46′N 84°00′W. Agr. (tobacco; poultry; dairying); mfg. (metal and plastic prods.). Was site of Augusta Col. (c.1800), one of 1st Methodist schools in U.S. Ferry landing in use since 1798; used in movie "Centennial." Captain Anthony Meldahl Lock and Dam, on Ohio R., to W. Founded 1792. **4** (uh-GUHS-tuh), town (1990 pop. 263), St. Charles co., E Mo., on Mo. R., 35 mi/56 km W of St. Louis; 38°34′N 90°52′W. Corn, grapes, soybeans; tourism; important winery area; art colony. Access to Katy Trail State Park. Area to S flooded in 1993; town was spared. **5** town (1990 pop. 1,510), Eau Claire co., W central Wis., on small tributary of Eau Claire R., and 20 mi/32 km SE of Eau Claire; 44°40′N 91°07′W. In dairying, stock-raising, and farming area (grain, cranberries); creameries, feed mill, cannery. Mfg. (fabricated metal prods., foods, wire harnesses). Inc. 1885.

Augusta 1 village (1990 pop. 614), Hancock co., W Ill., 17 mi/27 km SSE of Carthage; 40°13′N 90°57′W. Agr. (cattle, hogs; corn, wheat, soybeans, sorghum). **2** (uh-GUS-tuh), village, Kalamazoo co., SW Mich., 8 mi/12.9 km WNW of Battle Creek, on Kalamazoo R., and 12 mi/19 km ENE of Kalamazoo; 42°20′N 85°20′W. In farm area (corn, wheat, oats, fruit); mfg. wheat bran. **3** (aw-GUHS-tuh), village (1990 pop. 420), Lewis and Clark co., W central Mont., 43 mi/69 km W of Great Falls, and on Elk Creek. In agr. region. Cattle, sheep; wheat, barley, oats, alfalfa. Gibson Dam and Reservoir to NW and Willow Creek Reservoir to N, both on Sun R. Lewis and Clark Natl. Forest to W; Nilan Reservoir to W.

Augusta, Mount (14,070 ft/4,289 m), on Canada (Yukon)–U.S. (Alaska) border, in St. Elias Mts., 190 mi/

306 km W of Whitehorse (Yukon), on S edge of Seward Glacier; 60°18′N 140°00′W.

Augustine Island (AW-guhs-teen), S Alaska, in Kamishak Bay, at mouth of Cook Inlet, 60 mi/97 km W of Seldovia; 7 mi/11.3 km long, 7 mi/11.3 km wide; 59°22′N 153°26′W. Rises to 4,025 ft/1,227 m (active volcano).

Auke Bay (AWK), SE Alaska, small inlet on N shore of Stephens Passage, at NW end of Douglas Isl., 10 mi/16 km NW of Juneau; 58°22′N 134°40′W. Fishing. Campus of Univ. of Alaska Southeast. Marine Fisheries Center.

Aulander (AHL-and-uhr), town (1990 pop. 1,209), Bertie co., NE N.C., 18 mi/29 km N of Williamston; 36°13′N 77°06′W. Agr. area (peanuts, tobacco, cotton, grain; poultry; livestock). Mfg. (peanut processing). Ferry across Pamlico R. to N.

Aulatsivik Island, just off NE Lab., NE Canada; 12 mi/19 km long, 9 mi/14 km wide; 59°50′N 64°00W. Mainly mountainous, rising to 3,100 ft/945 m (S).

Aulavik National Park, NW N.W.T., N Canada, on N side of Banks Isl., on McClure Strait, 466 mi/750 km N of Inuvik. Bisected by Thomsen R. Former Banks Isl. #2 Bird Sanctuary along river. Landscape includes canyons, badlands. Large musk ox pop.; caribou, polar and grizzly bear; black brant, snow goose. Archaeological sites date to 3,400 years ago.

Aullville (AWL-vil), town (1990 pop. 72), Lafayette co., W central Mo., 16 mi/26 km SE of Lexington; 39°01′N 93°40′W.

Aulneau Peninsula (OL-no), W Ont., central Canada, on E shore of L. of the Woods, 20 mi/32 km S of Kenora; 30 mi/48 km long, 16 mi/26 km wide; 49°23′N 94°29′W.

Ault, town (1990 pop. 1,107), Weld co., N Colo., 10 mi/16 km N of Greeley; elev. 4,939 ft/1,505 m; 40°34′N 104°43′W. Sugar beets, grains, sunflowers; cattle; dairy. Pawnee Natl. Grassland to NE.

Aumsville (AHMZ-vil), town (1990 pop. 1,650), Marion co., NW Oregon, 10 mi/16 km SE of Salem; 44°51′N 122°52′W. RR junction to S. Fruits, nuts, vegetables; poultry; dairy prods. Silver Falls State Park to E.

Aupaluk, village (1991 pop. 131), N Que., E Canada, on W shore of Ungava Bay, E side of Ungava Peninsula, on Hopes Advance Bay. Populated by Inuit people. Hunting, fishing, trapping. Scheduled air service.

Auraria (aw-RAR-ee-uh), village, Lumpkin co., N Ga., 15 mi/24 km NW of Gainesville; 34°28′N 84°01′W.

Aurelia, town (1990 pop. 1,034), Cherokee co., NW Iowa, 6 mi/9.7 km ESE of Cherokee; 42°42′N 95°26′W. In livestock and grain area.

Auriesville, village (1990 pop. 65), Montgomery co., E central N.Y., on Mohawk R. and the Barge Canal, and 6 mi/9.7 km W of Amsterdam; 42°56′N 74°18′W. Here is R.C. Shrine of Our Lady of Martyrs, commemorating St. Isaac Jogues and other Fr. missionaries killed in 1640s by the Iroquois.

Auriol, Mount, peak (7,580 ft/2,310 m), S Yukon territory, NW Canada, overlooking Alaska Highway, SE of Kluane L.; 60°35′N 137°30′W. Named 1951 for president of France.

Aurora, county (☐ 712 sq mi/1,844 sq km; 1990 pop. 3,135), SE central S.Dak.; ⊙ Plankinton. Level farming area watered by Firesteel (NE) and Platte creeks. Corn, barley, soybeans, wheat; hogs, cattle; dairy prods. Stratosphere Balloon Landing site (1935) in SW. Formed 1879.

Aurora 1 city (1990 pop. 222,103), Adams and Arapahoe cos., N central Colo., a residential suburb, 5 mi/8 km from Denver; elev. 5,342 ft/1,628 m; 39°42′N 104°43′W. Founded during the silver boom of the 1890s, it is a business and technical center. Mfg. (furniture, aircraft fittings, electrical equip., precision measurement instruments, magnesium prods., computer software, paper prods., truck bed covers; printing and publishing). Tourism and construction are also important. Nearby are Lowry Air Force Base (to W in Denver), Fitzsimmons Army General Hosp., and Buckley Air Natl. Guard Base. Seat of Community Col. of Aurora. Cherry Creek State Park to S, Plaines Conservation Center to SE. Stapleton Internatl. Airport to NW

(closed in 1975); Denver Internatl. Airport to NE. Rocky Mt. Arsenal to N. Inc. 1903. **2** (aw-ROR-ah), city (1990 pop. 99,581), Kane and DuPage cos., NE Ill., on the Fox R.; 41°46′N 88°17′W. Satellite community of Chicago. It has large RR yards and a variety of manufactures, such as paper prods., plastic prods., rods and bearings, controls (thermostats), foods, and consumer goods. It was one of the 1st cities to use electricity for street lighting (1881). Seat of Aurora Univ. Has a notable historical mus. in a 20-room house built in 1857. Inc. 1837. **3** city (1990 pop. 3,825), Dearborn co., SE Ind., on Ohio R., and 4 mi/6.4 km SW of Lawrenceburg. In agr. area (livestock; tobacco, vegetables); sand and gravel; mfg. of coffins, burial vaults, and metal prods. Laid out 1819. Inundation by flood in 1937 caused much damage. **4** (uh-RO-ruh), city (1990 pop. 6,459), Lawrence co., SW Mo., in the Ozarks, 28 mi/45 km SW of Springfield; 36°58′N 93°43′W. Vegetables, fruit (apples, peaches); livestock; mfg. (shoes, grain prods., pet foods, wood prods., toys); timber. Laid out 1870. **5** city (1990 pop. 9,192), Portage co., NE Ohio, 22 mi/35 km SE of Cleveland, and on branch of Chagrin R.; 41°19′N 81°21′W. Sandstone quarry. Sea World and Geauga L. theme parks.

Aurora (uh-RO-ruh), town (1991 pop. 29,454), S Ont., central Canada, suburb 22 mi/35 km N of Toronto; 44°00′N 79°28′W. Mfg. (scales, transportation equip.; paperboard and paper prods.; plastics, wiring, electronic equip.; foods); flour prods.; poultry; eggs. School for boys.

Aurora 1 town (1990 pop. 196), Buchanan co., E Iowa, 13 mi/21 km NE of Independence; 42°37′N 91°43′W. **2** (uh-ROR-uh), town (1990 pop. 82), Hancock co., SE Maine, 22 mi/35 km N of Ellsworth; 44°52′N 68°15′W. In hunting, fishing area. **3** town (1990 pop. 1,965), St. Louis co., NE Minn., 14 mi/23 km E of Virginia, near St. Louis R., at E end of Mesabi Iron Range; 47°31′N 92°14′W. Open-pit iron mines nearby. Taconite plant; light mfg. Parts of Superior Natl. Forest to NW and E; Giants Ridge Ski Area to NW; Wynne L. to NW. Inc. 1903. **4** (uh-ROR-uh), town (1990 pop. 3,810), ⊙ Hamilton co., SE central Nebr., 20 mi/32 km E of Grand Island, and on Big Blue R; 40°52′N 98°00′W. RR junction. Livestock; grain; dairy prods. Mfg. (medical equip., fabricated homes, pet food). Inc. 1877. **5** town (1990 pop. 911), Sevier co., central Utah, near Sevier R., 4 mi/6.4 km SW of Salina; 38°55′N 111°55′W. Alfalfa, barley; dairying; cattle; salt, coal. Sect. of Fishlake Natl. Forest to E and W. Area settled 1863.

Aurora 1 (uh-ROR-uh), village (1990 pop. 101), Cloud co., N Kansas, 11 mi/18 km SE of Concordia; 39°27′N 97°31′W. In wheat region. **2** village (1990 pop. 687), Cayuga co., W central N.Y., in Finger Lakes region, on E shore of Cayuga L., 35 mi/56 km SW of Syracuse; 42°45′N 76°42′W. Agr. (grain); dairy prods.; poultry. Mfg. (toys). Summer residences and recreation on the lake. Seat of Wells Col. (1869). **3** village (1990 pop. 654), Beaufort co., E N.C., 19 mi/31 km NE of New Bern, at head of S arm of Pamlico R. estuary; 35°17′N 76°47′W. Agr. area (tobacco, cotton, peanuts, grain; cattle, hogs). Mfg. (phosphates); crab meat processing. Aurora Fossil Mus. **4** village (1990 pop. 567), Marion co., NW Oregon, 10 mi/16 km SW of Oregon City; 45°13′N 122°45′W. Mfg. (aluminum and steel doors, paints). Fruits, nuts, grains, vegetables. Dairy prods.; poultry. Founded 1855 as Christian communal colony. Champoeg State Park to W, on Pudding R. **5** village (1990 pop. 619), Brookings co., E S.Dak., 6 mi/9.7 km E of Brookings, near Deer Creek. Grain elevators. **6** village, Florence co., extreme NE Wis., 5 mi/8 km SW of Iron Mountain (Mich.), on Menominee R. (Mich. state line). Lumbering.

Aurora, Nev.: see HAWTHORNE.

Ausable Chasm, gorge, NE N.Y.; 2 mi/3.2 km long, 20 ft/6 m–50 ft/15 m wide, 100 ft/30 m–200 ft/61 m deep; 44°31′N 73°27′W. The chasm, with its rapids, waterfalls, and curious rock formations, is a popular tourist attraction; Rainbow Falls, 75 ft/23 m high, is at the S end. The Ausable R., rising in the Adirondack Mts.

and flowing NE to L. Champlain, continues to carve out the gorge as it passes over the sandstone bedrock.

Ausable Lakes, Essex co., NE N.Y., on East Branch Ausable R., in Adirondack Mts., in Adirondack Park, 22 mi/35 km SSE of Saranac Lake town. Consists of 2 lakes, Upper Ausable L. (c.1 mi/1.6 km long; 44°04′N 73°52′W) and Lower Ausable L. (c.2 mi/3.2 km long; 44°06′N 73°49′W). Mt. Marcy (5,344 ft/1,629 m), highest point in N.Y., to NW.

Ausable River, NE N.Y.; formed by East (c.30 mi/48 km long) and West (c.25 mi/40 km long) branches, both rising in the Adirondack Mts.; flow generally NE to their junction at Au Sable Forks village; thence the stream flows c.20 mi/32 km NE, through Ausable Chasm in its lower course, to L. Champlain, 10 mi/16 km S of Plattsburgh.

Austell (aw-STEL), town (1990 pop. 4,173), Cobb co., NW central Ga., 15 mi/24 km WNW of Atlanta; 33°49′N 84°38′W. Mfg. includes paper prods.; check printing. Inc. as town 1885, as city 1929.

Austin, county (☐ 656 sq mi/1,699 sq km; 1990 pop. 19,832), S Texas; ⊙ Bellville; 29°52′N 96°16′W. Bounded E by Brazos R.; bounded SW in part by San Bernard R. Agr. (cotton, peanuts, corn, hay, rice, sorghum); livestock (cattle, hogs, poultry); dairying. Timber; oil, natural-gas wells. Steven A. Austin State Park at San Felipe in E, founded 1823 as hq. of Stephen F. Austin's colony. Formed 1836.

Austin 1 city (1990 pop. 21,907), ⊙ Mower co., SE Minn., on the Cedar R., near the Iowa state line; elev. 1,198 ft/365 m; 43°40′N 92°58′W. RR junction and industrial and commercial center of a rich farm region (corn; dairying; poultry, cattle, hogs, sheep). Mfg. (foods, beverages, bldg. materials, linens, furniture, cremation urns, paper prods., compound containers; printing and publishing). Austin Community Col. and an arboretum and nature center here. Inc. 1868. **2** city (1990 pop. 465,622), ⊙ Travis co. and Texas, extends N into Williamson co., S central Texas, on the Colo. R. (Tom Miller Dam forms narrow L. Austin in city; Mansfield Dam forms L. Travis to NW); elev. 550 ft/168 m; 30°18′N 97°45′W. It is the commercial heart of a large ranching, poultry, dairy, cotton, and grain area, with a great variety of mfg. (jewelry, medical equip., consumer goods, computer equip., electronics, wood prods.). It is also a major convention city and an educational center, seat of the main campus of the Univ. of Texas, St. Edward's Univ., Huston-Tillotson Col., 2 theological seminaries, and Austin Community Col. The presence of the Univ. of Texas, a major research univ., has helped Austin attract and develop a large complex of high-technology mfg. and research and development firms and govt.-sponsored consortia. Defense and commercial trade industries are also important to the local economy. The site was selected in 1839 for the capital of the independent Texas republic and named by the legislature in honor of Stephen F. Austin. In 1870, following a referendum, Austin was made permanent capital. It remained a small commercial, governmental, and educational center until its industrial growth was spurred by the development of power and flood control projects on the Colo. R. (beginning in the 1930s) and by the urgencies of World War II. The massive capitol (completed 1888), set on a hill, is the most prominent of the many state bldgs.; on its grounds are the state lib., the old land office (1857), and 2 state historical mus. Also of interest are the governor's mansion (1856), the old Fr. embassy (1840; dating from the republic), the house of writer O. Henry, and the former studio of Elisabeth Ney. Univ. of Texas has Lyndon B. Johnson Lib., Memorial Stadium. Mueller Municipal Airport NE of downtown. A state mental hosp. is in Austin. Manor Downs, quarter horse racing at W edge of city; Natl. Wildflower Research Center in SW Austin, founded 1982 by Lady Bird Johnson. In the hills outside the city are many scenic and recreational areas, notably Barton Springs. Bergstrom Air Force Base (closed; will become the new city airport) adjoins the city on SE; Camp Mabry Military Reserve in W. Walter E. Long L. reservoir and Long Lake Metro Park to E; Lake Austin

Metro Park to E; McKinney Falls State Park adjoins city on SE. Inc. 1839.

Austin, town (1990 pop. 4,310), Scott co., SE Ind., 5 mi/8 km N of Scottsburg; 38°44′N 85°49′W. In agr. area; mfg. (canned foods, carbonated beverages; containers; hardwood lumber, pallets).

Austin 1 village (1990 pop. 235), Lonoke co., central Ark., 25 mi/40 km NE of Little Rock; 35°00′N 91°58′W. Mfg. (eggs; poultry processing). **2** village, Delta co., W Colo., on Gunnison R., and 7 mi/11.3 km ENE of Delta; elev. c.5,025 ft/1,532 m. Sheep. Shipping point for fruit prods. Fruit Growers Dam, 3 mi/4.8 km N on Surface Creek, is unit in Fruit Growers irrigation project. Black Canyon of the Gunnison Natl. Monument is to SE. **3** (AW-stuhn), village, Lander co., central Nev., in W foothills of Toiyabe Range, 60 mi/97 km W of Eureka; elev. 6,5277 ft/2,005 m. Distributing center; silver, gold; cattle; sand and gravel. Former co. seat, later moved to Battle Mt. Historic courthouse. Stokes Castle (1897), former home of mining millionaire, to W. Geographic center of Nevada, 25 mi/40 km to SE to Monitor Valley. Shoshone Range to W, Toiyabe Range to E. Bounded N, E, and S by Toiyabe Natl Forest. **4** village, Grant co., NE Oregon, 30 mi/48 km WSW of Baker on Middle Fork (John Day) R., near its source in Malheur Natl. Forest. Timber.

Austin (AW-stin), borough (1990 pop. 569), Potter co., N Pa., 11 mi/18 km SSW of Coudersport, on Freeman Run; 41°38′N 78°05′W. Mfg. (fabricated metal prods.); agr. (potatoes; dairying); timber. Prouty Place and Patterson state parks to NW; Sizeville State Park to SW; area surrounded by parts of state forest nearby.

Austin Lake, village, Kalamazoo co., SW Mich., 6 mi/9.7 km S of Kalamazoo; 42°09′N 85°32′W. Absorbed by city of Portage.

Austin, Lake, reservoir, Bexar co., S central Texas, on Colo. R., 3 mi/4.8 km WNW of downtown Austin; 24 mi/39 km long; 30°18′N 97°20′W. Max. capacity 21,500 acre-ft. Mansfield Dam at NW tip. Formed by Tom Miller Dam, built (1940) for power generation and flood control. Replaced earlier dam (built 1915) here made useless by floods. Lake Austin Metro Park on N shore.

Austinville, village (1990 pop. 700), Wythe co., SW Va., on New R., 10 mi/16 km SE of Wytheville. Mfg. (limestone processing; crushed stone); agr. (dairying; livestock; corn, cabbage); limestone quarrying in area. New River Trail State Park passes through town; Shot Tower State Historical Park to E; part of Jefferson Natl. Forest, including Mt. Rogers Natl. Recreation Area, to SW.

Austwell, village (1990 pop. 189), Refugio co., S Texas, 28 mi/45 km E of Refugio, and on Hynes Bay, an arm of San Antonio Bay; 28°23′N 96°50′W. Arkansas Natl. Wildlife Refuge to S.

Autauga (uh-TAW-guh), county (□ 604 sq mi/1,564 sq km; 1990 pop. 34,222), central Ala.; ⊙ Prattville. In the Black Belt, bounded S by Ala. R., W by Mulberry R. Farming area (cotton, hay, soybeans) with gently rolling land and forest. Formed 1818.

Autaugaville (uh-TAW-guh-vil), town (1990 pop. 681), Autauga co., central Ala., 10 mi/16 km WSW of Prattville. Wood prods.

Autlán de Navarro (out-LAHN dai nah-VAHR-ro), city (1990 pop. 34,073), Jalisco, W Mexico, in W outliers of Sierra Madre del Sur, 55 mi/89 km NW of Colima; 19°45′N 05°03′W. Agr. center (corn, wheat, sugar, cotton, fruit; livestock); tanneries.

Autryville (AW-tree-vil), village (1990 pop. 166), Sampson co., SE central N.C., on South R., and 15 mi/24 km ESE of Fayetteville; 35°00′N 78°38′W. Grain, tobacco, cotton, peanuts; livestock, poultry.

Aux Cayes, Haiti: see LES CAYES.

Auxier (AWKS-uhr), uninc. town (1990 pop. 900), Floyd co., E Ky., in Cumberland foothills, on Levisa Fork R., at mouth of Johns Creek (forms Dewey L. reservoir to SE), and 5 mi/8 km N of Prestonsburg. Mfg. (machining). Jeeny Wiley State Resort Park to S.

Auxvasse (o-VAHZ), town (1990 pop. 821), Callaway co., central Mo., 12 mi/19 km N of Fulton; 39°01′N 91°53′W. Soybeans, wheat, corn; cattle. Stone quarry (lime and crushed rock).

Auyuittuq National Park (□ c.8,290 sq mi/21,470 sq km), SE Baffin Region, N.W.T., N Canada, on E Baffin Isl., near Pangnirtung, on the Cumberland Peninsula. The 1st Can. natl. park to be created N of the Arctic Circle. Scenic fjords, glaciated mts., numerous glaciers, and the extensive Penny Ice Cap. Est. 1972.

Ava 1 (AI-vah), city (1990 pop. 674), Jackson co., SW Ill., 12 mi/19 km NW of Murphysboro; 37°53′N 89°30′W. In bituminous-coal-mining and agr. region (wheat, sorghum; cattle; dairying). **2** (AI-vuh), city (1990 pop. 2,938), ⊙ Douglas co., S Mo., in the Ozarks, 39 mi/63 km SE of Springfield; 36°57′N 92°40′W. Resort, timber, and agr. region; fruit; lumber; mfg. (electrical motors, apparel, sports protective gear). Cedarglade country to SW. Trappist monastery 20 mi/32 km SE. Founded 1864.

Avalon 1 town (1990 pop. 2,918), Los Angeles co., S Calif., on SE end of Santa Catalina Isl., overlooking Avalon Bay; 33°20′N 118°20′W. Ferry connections with Los Angeles and Long Beach harbors and Newport Beach; airport. Center of isl.'s resort and sport activities; has an Native Amer. mus., Bird Park, the Wrigley Estate, and a casino (no gambling), and theater. Founded 1888, inc. 1913. **2** (AV-uh-lahn), town (1990 pop. 159), Stephens co., NE Ga., 9 mi/14.5 km ESE of Toccoa, near S.C. state line; 34°30′N 83°11′W.

Avalon, village, Md., on Tilghman Isl. Built up from oyster shells, dumped over the docks by packing companies. The Tighlman Packing Co. here, started in 1900, closed in 1975.

Avalon 1 (a-VUH-luhn), resort borough (1990 pop. 1,809), Cape May co., S N.J., on Seven Mile Beach isl. (bridged to mainland), and 5 mi/8 km E of Cape May Courthouse, on the Atlantic Ocean; 39°05′N 74°44′W. Noted for its high sand dunes. **2** (A-vuh-lahn), borough (1990 pop. 5,784), Allegheny co., SW Pa., residential suburb, 6 mi/9.7 km NW of downtown Pittsburgh, on Ohio R.; 40°30′N 80°04′W. Settled 1802, inc. 1874.

Avalon Dam, N.Mex.: see PECOS.

Avalon Peninsula (□ 3,579 sq mi/9,270 sq km), SE N.F., E Canada; 47°00′N 53°15′W. Nearly divided at its center by Conception and St. Mary's bays. Most densely populated part of N.F.; St. John's is the chief city. A lighthouse and radio direction-finding station are at Cape Race, which is the easternmost point in N. Amer.

Avalon Wilderness Area, SE N.F., E Canada, at center of Avalon Peninsula, 40 mi/64 km SSW of St. John's. Numerous lakes and rivers in area; reserve protects unique flora and fauna, large caribou herd. No visitor facilities.

Ávalos or **Fundición de Ávalos** (AH-vah-los), industrial satellite area of Chihuahua, N Mexico, 4 mi/6.4 km SE of Chihuahua on Mexico Highway 45; 24°47′N 101°25′W. Lead and silver smelting center.

Avant (AI-vant), village (1990 pop. 369), Osage co., N Okla., 20 mi/32 km SE of Pawhuska, on Bird Creek; 36°29′N 96°03′W. Mfg. (titanium parts).

Avard (uh-VAHRD), village (1990 pop. 37), Woods co., NW Okla., 9 mi/14.5 km SW of Alva; 36°42′N 98°47′W. RR junction. In wheat-growing and livestock-raising area.

Avella (a-VE-lah), uninc. town (1990 pop. 1,200), Washington co., SW Pa., 27 mi/43 km WSW of Pittsburgh, on Cross Creek, near W.Va. state line; 40°16′N 80°27′W. Coal-mining region.

Avenal, town (1990 pop. 9,770), Kings co., S central Calif., c.52 mi/84 km SW of Fresno; 36°02′N 120°07′W. Supply center in Kettleman Hills oil field. Dairying; poultry; grain, fruit, nuts. Diablo Range to SW.

Aventura (av-ven-TOO-RAH), suburb (□ 3 sq mi/7.8 sq km; 1990 pop. 14,914), extreme NE Dade co., SE Fla., 12 mi/19 km N of Miami Beach; 25°57′N 80°07′W. Centered on Aventura Mall, NE Dade's largest regional shopping center. Inc. 1995, following secession from uninc. Dade co.

Avera (uh-VER-uh), village (1990 pop. 215), Jefferson co., E Ga., 36 mi/58 km SW of Augusta; 33°11′N 82°32′W. Mfg. includes camouflaged hunting clothing.

Averill Park, village (□ 3 sq mi/7.8 sq km; 1990 pop. 1,656), Rensselaer co., E N.Y., 9 mi/14.5 km. SE of Troy; 42°38′N 73°32′W. Mfg. (knit goods); fur dressing; wholesale trade.

Avery, county (□ 247 sq mi/640 sq km; 1990 pop. 14,867), NW N.C.; ⊙ Newland; 36°04′N 81°55′W. In the Blue Ridge mts.; bounded W by Tenn. state line; covers NW, N, and E Pisgah Natl. Forest; drained by Linville and North Toe rivers. Farming (corn, potatoes, hay, vegetables, apples), cattle raising; mining (mica, feldspar, kaolin). Appalachian Trail follows part of state line in W; Blue Ridge (Natl.) Parkway crosses co. in E. Ski resorts in N. Formed 1911.

Avery 1 village (1990 pop. 430), Shoshone co., N Idaho, 17 mi/27 km SSE of Wallace, on St Joe R. Timber. Built by RR as W transfer point on electrified sect. over mts. Surrounded by St. Joe Natl. Forest. **2** village (1990 pop. 430), Red River co., NE Texas, 41 mi/66 km WNW of Texarkana; 33°32′N 94°46′W. Agr. and timber area.

Avery Creek, uninc. town (1990 pop. 1,144), Buncombe co., W N.C., residential suburb, 7 mi/11.3 km S of downtown Asheville, on French Broad R.; 35°27′N 82°34′W. Pisgah Natl. Forest to W.

Avery Island, village, located on salt dome of same name, c.150 ft/46 m high and 2 mi/3 km in diameter, Iberia parish, S La., 9 mi/14 km SW of New Iberia, forming a low rise in an area of sea marshes and cypress swamps; 29°53′N 91°54′W. RR terminus. Mfg. of salt, sauces (tabasco). The isl.'s former owner, Edward Avery McIlhenny, author of *Bird City*, created Jungle Gardens and Bird Sanctuary, which contains many rare flora. Cayenne peppers are produced here. Salt mines in area since 1791. Intracoastal Waterway runs E-W bet. isl. and coast. Vermilion Bay extension of Gulf of Mexico 4 mi/6 km S. Also known as Petit Anse.

Avigalik Island or **Whale Island** (2 mi/3 km long, 2 mi/3 km wide), NE Lab., E Canada, in Seven Isls. Bay; 59°27′N 63°40′W. Just SW is Amiktok Isl.

Avilla 1 town (1990 pop. 1,366), Noble co., NE Ind., 5 mi/8 km SSE of Kendallville; 41°22′N 85°14′W. In agr. area. **2** (uh-VIL-luh), town (1990 pop. 99), Jasper co., SW Mo., 10 mi/16 km E of Carthage; 37°11′N 94°07′W.

Avinger, village (1990 pop. 478), Cass co., NE Texas, 26 mi/42 km NNW of Marshall; 32°53′N 94°32′W. In agr. area; mfg. (electrical conduit). L. o' the Pines reservoir to SW.

Avis (AI-vis), borough (1990 pop. 1,506), Clinton co., N central Pa., 8 mi/12.9 km ENE of Lock Haven bet. West Branch Susquehanna R. (S) and Pine Creek (E); 41°11′N 77°19′W. Mfg. (modular homes, wood prods.); Agr. (corn, hay; livestock; dairying). Ravensburg State Park to S; parts of Tiadaghton State Forest to N and SE; Bald Eagle State Forest to S.

Aviston (A-vis-ton), village (1990 pop. 924), Clinton co., S Ill., 7 mi/11.3 km W of Carlyle; 38°36′N 89°36′W. In agr. and oil-producing area.

Avoca, town (1990 pop. 1,497), Pottawattamie co., SW Iowa, 31 mi/50 km ENE of Council Bluffs; 41°28′N 95°20′W. Feed. Inc. 1875.

Avoca 1 (uh-VO-kuh), village (1990 pop. 150), Murray co., SW Minn., 6 mi/9.7 km ESE of Slayton, on Lime Creek; 43°57′N 95°39′W. Corn, oats, soybeans, alfalfa; livestock, poultry; dairying. Lime L. to W. **2** (A-vo-kuh), village (1990 pop. 254), Cass co., SE Nebr., 15 mi/24 km NW of Nebr. City; 40°47′N 96°07′W. **3** (ah-VO-kah), village (□ 1 sq mi/2.6 sq km; 1990 pop. 1,033), Steuben co., S N.Y., on Cohocton R., and 25 mi/40 km NW of Corning; 42°24′N 77°25′W. Agr. area. Settled 1843, inc. 1883. **4** (ah-VO-kah), village (1990 pop. 474), Iowa co., SW Wis., near Wis. R., 18 mi/29 km NNW of Dodgeville; 43°11′N 90°19′W. In dairying region.

Avoca (A-vuh-kah), borough (1990 pop. 2,897), Luzerne co., NE Pa., suburb, 6 mi/9.7 km SW of Scranton, and 10 mi/16 km NE of Wilkes-Barre, near Lackawanna R.; 41°20′N 75°44′W. Anthracite coal. Wilkes-Barre Scranton Internatl. Airport 1 mi/1.6 km to E. Inc. 1889.

Avocado Heights, uninc. city (1990 pop. 14,232), Los Angeles co., S Calif., residential suburb, 10 mi/16 km E of downtown Los Angeles, near San Gabriel R.; 34°02′N 118°00′W. Puerto Hills to S.

Avon (AI-VAHN), city (1990 pop. 7,337), Lorain co., N Ohio, 7 mi/11 km E of Lorain, near L. Erie; 41°28′N 82°01′W. In agr. area. Settled c.1814, inc. 1918.

Avon 1 town (1990 pop. 1,798), Eagle co., W central Colo., on Eagle R., 16 mi/26 km ESE of Eagle, and 8 mi/12.9 km W of Vail; elev. 7,430 ft/2,265 m; 39°38′N 106°31′W. Ski resort community; Arrowhead and Beaver Creek Ski Areas to SW. White River Natl. Forest to N, E, and S. **2** town (1990 pop. 13,937), Hartford co., central Conn., on Farmington R., and 8 mi/12.9 km WNW of Hartford; 41°47′N 72°51′W. Commercial center (insurance, printing); mfg. (fiber optics, electrical equip., aerospace equip. testing, concrete prods., chemicals, reflective types). Inc. 1830. **3** town, Hendricks co., central Ind., suburb 13 mi/21 km W of downtown Indianapolis. Large RR yard. Agr. area. Mfg. (bottled water, wood prods.). **4** town (1990 pop. 4,558), Norfolk co., E Mass., 14 mi/23 km S of Boston; 42°07′N 71°03′W. Residential and mfg. (dies, furniture, machinery, consumer goods). Settled c.1700, inc. 1888. **5** town (1990 pop. 970), Stearns co., central Minn., 14 mi/23 km WNW of St. Cloud, on Spunk Creek; 45°36′N 94°27′W. Dairying; livestock, poultry; grain, alfalfa, soybeans; mfg. (gears, metal fabrication, cabinets). Marl deposits in vicinity. Spunk L. to S. **6** (AI-vahn), uninc. town (1990 pop. 2,714), Lebanon co., SE Pa., residential suburb 1 mi/1.6 km E of Lebanon; 40°20′N 76°23′W. Includes the community of Avon Heights located 2 mi/3.2 km E of Lebanon. Agr. includes dairying; livestock, poultry; grain, soybeans.

Avon 1 (A-vahn), village (1990 pop. 957), Fulton co., W central Ill., 20 mi/32 km S of Galesburg; 40°39′N 90°26′W. Grain; dairy prods.; livestock. **2** (AI-vahn), village (1990 pop. 175), Powell co., W Mont., 27 mi/43 km W of Helena, and on Little Blackfoot R. Continental Divide to E. Cattle, sheep; potatoes, alfalfa; mining. Part of Helena Natl. Forest to NE and SE. **3** village (□ 2 sq mi/5.2 sq km; 1990 pop. 2,995), Livingston co., W central N.Y., on Genesee R., and 18 mi/29 km SSW of Rochester; 42°54′N 77°45′W. Mfg. (frozen foods, fabricated metal prods., thermoplastics, and injection moldings). Agr. (oats, wheat); sheep, hogs; dairying. Inc. 1867. **4** uninc. village, Dare co., NE N.C., 42 mi/68 km SSE of Manteo, in Cape Hatteras Natl. Seashore, Hatteras Isl., parts of N.C.'s Outer Banks, sand barrier bet. Pamlico Sound and the Atlantic Ocean. Cape Hatteras (lighthouse) 8 mi/12.9 km to S. Beach recreation area. **5** village (1990 pop. 576), Bon Homme co., SE S.Dak., 10 mi/16 km W of Tyndall. Corn, wheat; dairy prods.; livestock, poultry; mfg. (apparel).

Avon by the Sea (AI-vuhn), resort borough (1990 pop. 2,165), Monmouth co., E N.J., on the Atlantic coast, at mouth of Shark R., 14 mi/23 km ESE of Freehold; 40°11′N 74°01′W. Inc. 1900.

Avon Lake, city (1990 pop. 15,066), Lorain co., NE Ohio, on L. Erie; 41°49′N 82°01′W. Chiefly a residential suburb of the Cleveland–NE Ohio industrial area. Has an electric power plant, automotive assembly plant, plastics and aluminum castings plants. Several beaches. Inc. 1917.

Avon Park, town (□ 5 sq mi/13 sq km; 1990 pop. 8,042), Highlands co., central Fla., c.40 mi/64 km SE of Lakeland, in lake region near air force base; 27°35′N 81°30′W. Packing and shipping center for citrus fruit. Settled c.1885.

Avon River (AI-vuhn), 40 mi/64 km long, W central N.S., E Canada; rises in small lake 16 mi/26 km SW of Windsor; flows N, past Windsor, to the Minas Basin.

Avondale (A-vuhn-dail), city (1990 pop. 16,169), Maricopa co., S central Ariz., near Gila R., at mouth of Agua Fria R., suburb, 18 mi/29 km W of downtown Phoenix; 33°25′N 112°19′W. A service and retail center; agr. includes cotton, vegetables, and grain; mfg. (clothing; printing and publishing). Inc. 1946. Luke Air Force Base to N at Litchfield Park city; Gila River Indian Reservation to SE.

Avondale (A-vuhn-dail), uninc. town (1990 pop. 5,813), Jefferson parish, SE La., suburb, 5 mi/8 km W of downtown New Orleans, on Miss. R.; 29°54′N 90°11′W. Shipping facilities. Bayou Segnette State Park to SE.

Avondale 1 village (1990 pop. 550), Clay co., W Mo., suburb, 6 mi/10 km NE of downtown Kansas City; 39°08′N 94°32′W. **2** village, Westerly town, Washington co., SW R.I., 3 mi/4.8 km S of Westerly; 41°20′N 71°50′W. Nearby is Pawcatuck R., Block Isl. Sound, Little Narragansett Bay, and Westerly State Airport.

Avondale (A-vuhn-dail), borough (1990 pop. 954), Chester co., SE Pa., 13 mi/21 km NW of Wilmington (Del.), on East Branch White Clay Creek; 39°49′N 75°46′W. Mfg. (machining; mushroom processing; plastic molding, electrical equip.); agr. area (mushrooms, corn, hay, soybeans; livestock, poultry; dairying). New Garden Airport to E. White Clay Creek State Park (Pa./Del.) to S.

Avondale Estates (AV-uhn-dail), town (1990 pop. 2,209), De Kalb co., NW central Ga., residential suburb 9 mi/14.5 km E of Atlanta; 33°46′N 84°16′W. Light mfg. and market center. Houses RR yards of metropolitan Atlanta's Rapid Transit Authority (MARTA) system. Inc. 1927.

Avonia (a-VO-nee-ah), uninc. town (1990 pop. 1,336), Erie co., NW Pa., 9 mi/14.5 km WSW of Erie; 42°02′N 80°16′W. L. Erie 1 mi/1.6 km to NW, mouth of Walnut Creek to NE Fish hatchery on Trout Run to SW.

Avonlea (A-vuhn-LEE), village (1991 pop. 405), S Sask., W Canada, 35 mi/56 km SE of Moose Jaw; 50°01′N 105°04′W. Wheat.

Avonmore (A-vuhn-mor), borough (1990 pop. 1,089), Westmoreland co., SW central Pa., 27 mi/43 km E of Pittsburgh, on Kiskiminetas R.; 40°31′N 79°28′W. Mfg. (fabricated metal prods., glass prods.); subsurface bituminous coal. Inc. 1893.

Avoyelles (uh-VOILZ), parish (□ 826 sq mi/2,139 sq km; 1990 pop. 39,159), E central La.; ☉ Marksville; 31°08′N 92°04′W. Partly bounded N and E by Red R., SW by Bayou Boeuf, on E by Atchafalaya R., and Saline Bayou (with Saline L.) forms part of N boundary. Northernmost of the Acadian parishes of S La. Agr. (cotton, berries, corn, sorghum, hay, soybeans, sugarcane, sweet potatoes, vegetables; cattle, hogs, horses; honey); crawfish; mfg. (food prods., clothing); logging. Includes Eola oil and natural-gas field. Large casino on land owned by Tunica-Biloxi Native Americans. Has several lakes in NE. Marksville State Commemorative Area in W center, Grassy Lake State Wildlife Area in NE, Pomme de Terre and Spring Bayou State Wildlife Areas at center, part of Grand Cote Natl. Wildlife Refuge in W, Lake Ophelia Natl. Wildlife Refuge in N. Named after the Avoyelle Native tribe. Formed 1807.

Awendaw (AH-wen-daw), village, Charleston co., E S.C., 26 mi/42 km NE of Charleston. Ships oysters. Intracoastal Waterway canal passes bet. here and Bulls Bay to SE.

Axapusco (ah-shah-POOS-ko), town (1990 pop. 2,283), Mexico state, central Mexico, 32 mi/51 km NE of Mexico City, and part of the Zona Metropolitana de la Ciudad de México; 19°45′N 98°40′W. Maguey, corn; livestock.

Axel Heiberg Island (AK-suhl HEI-buhrg) (□ 13,583 sq mi/35,180 sq km), in the Arctic Ocean, N N.W.T., N Canada, W of Ellesmere Isl.; 79°30′N 90°00′W. Named by Nor. explorer Otto Sverdrup (who explored it 1898–1902) for one of his patrons. The isl.'s plateau surface (3,000 ft/915 m–6,000 ft/1,830 m high) is deeply indented by fjords.

Axial, former village (1960 pop. 5), now a ghost town, Moffat co., NW Colo., near Milk Creek, and 20 mi/32 km SW of Craig; elev. 6,440 ft/1,963 m. Former coalmining point; rich coal deposits nearby.

Axochiapan (ah-sho-chee-AH-pahn), town (1990 pop. 14,367), Morelos, central Mexico, 20 mi/32 km WSW of Izúcar de Matamoros; 18°30′N 98°45′W. Agr. center (sugar, rice, fruit, vegetables; livestock).

Axocuapan, Mexico: see TLALTETELA.

Axtell 1 (AKS-tuhl), village (1990 pop. 432), Marshall co., NE Kansas, 20 mi/32 km E of Marysville; 39°52′N 96°15′W. In corn and wheat area. **2** (AKS-tel), village (1990 pop. 707), Kearney co., S Nebr., 10 mi/16 km W of Minden; 40°28′N 99°07′W. Grain.

Axtla de Terrazas (AHSH-tlah dai ter-RAH-sahs), town (1990 pop. 29,331), San Luis Potosí, N central Mexico, 39 mi/63 km S of Ciudad Valles, 1 mi/1.6 km from Mexico Highway 85, on Axtla R.; elev. c.900 ft/274 m; 21°28′N 98°51′W. Phosphate mines nearby; cattle on lower slopes of Sierra Madre Oriental. Formerly Alfredo M. Terrazas.

Axton, uninc. village, Henry co., S Va., 10 mi/16 km ESE of Martinsville; 36°39′N 79°42′W. Mfg. (furniture, packaging materials).

Axutla (ah-HOOT-lah), town (1990 pop. 20 mi/32 km), Puebla, central Mexico, 30 mi/48 km S of Izúcar de Matamoros; 18°13′N 98°20′W. Corn, rice, sugar; livestock.

Ayahualulco (ah-yah-wah-LOOL-ko), town (1990 pop. 2,223), Veracruz, E Mexico, at S foot of Cofre de Perote, 20 mi/32 km SW of Xalapa Enríquez; 19°20′N 97°10′W. Corn, coffee, fruit.

Ayala (ah-YAH-lah), town (1990 pop. 12,692), Morelos, Ayala municipio, central Mexico, 3 mi/4.8 km SW of Cuautla; 18°45′N 98°58′W. Sugar, rice, fruit.

Ayapango de Gabriel Ramos Millán (ah-yah-PAHN-go de gahb-ree-EL RAH-mos meel-YAHN), town (1990 pop. 1,943), ☉ Ayapango municipio, Mexico state, central Mexico, on RR, 30 mi/48 km SE of Mexico City, and part of the Zona Metropolitana de la Ciudad de México; 19°07′N 98°48′W. Cereals; livestock.

Ayden (AI-duhn), town (1990 pop. 4,883), Pitt co., E N.C., 10 mi/16 km S of Greenville, near Swift Creek; 35°28′N 77°25′W. In agr. area (tobacco, grain, cotton, peanuts; chickens; livestock); mfg. (plastic prods., pine lumber, clothing, foods; machining, catfish processing).

Ayer (AI-yuhr), town (1990 pop. 6,871), including Ayer village, Middlesex co., N Mass., 11 mi/18 km ESE of Fitchburg; 42°34′N 71°34′W. Food prods., wood prods., machinery, knives, precision instruments, furniture; agr. (apples). Has Federal prison; state pheasant farm nearby. Former site of U.S. Fort Devens (military post decommissioned in 1996) now has new Deven's Commercial Center, which is being developed as an industrial service area with wholesaling, medical, and hosp. services. Settled before 1670, inc. 1871.

Ayers Cliff, village (1991 pop. 821), S Que., E Canada, on L. Massawippi, 17 mi/27 km SW of Sherbrooke; 45°10′N 72°02′W. Dairying; resort.

Aylesworth, Mount (EILZ-wuhrth) (9,310 ft/2,838 m), on U.S. (Alaska)-Canada (B.C.) border, in St. Elias Mts. 40 mi/64 km NE of Yakutat; 59°55′N 138°48′W.

Aylett, uninc. village, King William co., E Va., 27 mi/43 km NE of Richmond, on Mattaponi R.; 37°47′N 77°06′W. Mfg. (sand and gravel processing; lumber; coatings); agr. (grain, soybeans; cattle; dairying); timber.

Aylmer 1 (AIL-muhr), town (1991 pop. 6,244), S Ont., central Canada, 11 mi/18 km E of St. Thomas. Food canning, light mfg., woodworking, marble processing; lumbering; dairying. **2** residential town (1991 pop. 32,244), SW Que., E Canada, on Ottawa R., at NW end of L. Deschênes, 8 mi/13 km W of Ottawa.

Aylmer, Lake 1 (□ 340 sq mi/881 sq km; according to some sources □ 612 sq mi/1,585 sq km), E Mackenzie dist., N.W.T., N Canada, NE of Great Slave L.; c.40 mi/64 km long, 4 mi/6 km–40 mi/64 km wide; 64°05′N 108°30′W. Drained NE by Back R.; connected E with Clinton-Colden L. **2** S Que., E Canada, on St. Francis R., 27 mi/43 km NW of Megantic; 9 mi/14 km long, 4 mi/6 km wide. At N end of lake is Disraeli (Que.).

Aylmer, Mount (10,375 ft/3,162 m), SW Alta., W Canada, near B.C. border, in Rocky Mts., in Banff Natl. Park, 12 mi/19 km NE of Banff, overlooking L. Minnewanka.

Aylwin (AIL-win), village, SW Que., E Canada, on Gatineau R., and 40 mi/64 km NNW of Hull. Feldspar mining.

Aynor (AI-nuhr), agr. town (1990 pop. 470), Horry co., E S.C., 13 mi/21 km NW of Conway; 34°00′N 79°12′W. Mfg. includes clothing; lumber. Agr. includes livestock; grain, tobacco, soybeans.

Ayo el Chico, Mexico: see AYOTLÁN.

Ayoquezco de Aldama (ah-yo-KAIS-ko dai ahl-DAH-mah), town (1990 pop. 5,384), SW Oaxaca, Mexico,

34 mi/55 km SSW of Oaxaca de Juárez, on Mexico Highway 131; 16°41′N 96°50′W. Hot climate. Agr. (corn, beans, figs). Lead deposits. Zapotec pop. Formerly Santa María Ayoquezco.

Ayotlán (ah-yot-LAHN), town (1990 pop. 7,946), Jalisco, central Mexico, 10 mi/16 km E of Atotonilco el Alto; 20°33′N 102°20′W. Agr. center (wheat, corn, chickpeas, beans, fruit; livestock). Formerly Ayo el Chico.

Ayotoxco de Guerrero (ah-yo-TOSH-ko dai ge-RE-ro), town (1990 pop. 1,979), Puebla, E Mexico, in SE foothills of Sierra Madre Oriental, 25 mi/40 km S of Papantla de Olarte; 20°10′N 97°20′W. Sugar, fruit, coffee.

Ayotzintepec (ah-yot-ZIN-te-pek), town (1990 pop. 3,030), in NE Oaxaca, Mexico, 30 mi/48 km S of Tuxtepec; elev. 4,265 ft/1,300 m. Mountainous. Agr. (cereals, fruit, woods); mezcal processing and livestock. In Chinantec-speaking area.

Ayr, village, S Ont., central Canada, on Nith R. and 9 mi/14 km SE of Galt; 43°17′N 80°27′W. Dairying; mfg. of cereal foods, agr. implements.

Ayr 1 (ER), village (1990 pop. 101), Adams co., S Nebr., 10 mi/16 km S of Hastings, and on Little Blue R; 40°26′N 98°26′W. RR junction to N. Crystal Lake State Recreation Area to NE. **2** village (1990 pop. 19), Cass co., E N.Dak., c.18 mi/29 km NW of Casselton; 47°02′N 97°29′W.

Ayrshire, town (1990 pop. 195), Palo Alto co., NW Iowa, 10 mi/16 km SW of Emmetsburg; 43°02′N 94°49′W. In livestock and grain area.

Ayton (AI-tuhn), village, S Ont., central Canada, on South Saugeen R., and 35 mi/56 km S of Owen Sound; 44°03′N 80°56′W. Dairying; farming, fruit growing.

Ayutla (ai-OOT-lah), town (1990 pop. 6,625), Jalisco, W Mexico, 28 mi/45 km SSW of Ameca; 20°09′N 104°16′W. Agr. (cotton, sugarcane, tobacco, fruit, grain).

Ayutla de los Libres (ai-OOT-lah dai los LEE-brais), city (1990 pop. 6,214; 40,002 for entire municipio), Guerrero state, S Mexico, 53 mi/86 km E of Acapulco de Juárez; 16°58′N 99°04′W. It is the commercial center for an agr., cattle-raising, and lumbering area. Noted as site where the Plan of Ayutla was drawn up in 1854.

Azalea Park (uh-ZAI-lyuh), town (□ 3 sq mi/7.8 sq km;

1990 pop. 8,926), Orange co., central Fla., 6 mi/9.7 km E of Orlando; 28°33′N 81°17′W.

Azcapotzalco (ahs-kah-pot-SAHL-ko), delegación (1990 pop. 473,476), one of the N dists. of Mexico City, S Mexico, in the Federal Dist.; 19°22′N 99°12′W. Much industry interwoven with residential uses. An important RR center, with city's main RR yards, it is the terminus of mail and cargo traffic. Industries include motor vehicle assembling, oil refining, and the mfg. of textiles, paper, and records. Was a leading cultural center in the pre-Columbian period. Noted for its baroque colonial architecture and its 18th-cent. churches.

Aziscohos Lake (uh-ZIS-kuh-hahs), reservoir, Oxford co., W Maine, on Magalloway R., 45 mi/72 km NW of Rumsford, and 3 mi/4.8 km E of N.H. state line; c.14 mi/23 km long; 45°55′N 70°58′W. Formed by dam. Aziscohos Mt. (elev. 3,215 ft/980 m) to S. Sometimes spelled Aziscoos.

Azle, town (1990 pop. 8,868), Tarrant and Parker cos., N Texas, suburb, 15 mi/24 km NW of downtown Fort Worth urbanized area; 32°53′N 97°31′W. Agr. to W (dairying; cattle, poultry; eggs; cotton). Mfg. (machinery, bldg. materials, textiles, medical supplies, electronic equip.; machining). Eagle Mt. L. reservoir to E.

Azoyú (ah-so-YOO), town (1990 pop. 3,718), Guerrero, SW Mexico, in Pacific lowland, 19 mi/31 km W of Ometepec; 16°45′N 98°40′W. Sugar, coffee, fruit; livestock.

Aztalan State Park, Wis.: see LAKE MILLS.

Aztec (AZ-tek), town (1990 pop. 5,479), ⊙ San Juan co., NW N.Mex., 14 mi/23 km ENE of Farmington, on Animas R., near Colo. state line, in foothills of Rocky Mts.; elev. 5,623 ft/1,714 m.; 36°49′N 108°00′W. Trade center in fruit-growing region; grain, pumpkins, potatoes, blue corn; cattle, sheep. Aztec Ruins Natl. Monument is to NW; Navajo Lake Reservoir and State Park to E (San Juan R.); Southern Ute Indian Reservation to N (in Colo.).

Aztec Ruins National Monument (□ 319 acres/129 ha), San Juan co., NW N.Mex., 14 mi/23 km NE of Farmington, NW of Aztec. Ruins of a sophisticated 12th-cent. Pueblo settlement; has only restored kiva in U.S. Pueblo culture. Misnamed by early Eur. settlers. Est. 1923 by proclamation.

Aztla de Terrazas (AHST-lah dai tai-RAH-sahs), town

(1990 pop. 5,845), San Luis Potosí, E Mexico, on fertile gulf plain, 38 mi/61 km SSE of Ciudad Valles, and 3 mi/5 km off Inter-Amer. Highway 85; 21°28′N 98°60′W. Tobacco, sugar, coffee, fruit; livestock. Formerly Alfredo M. Terrazas.

Azua (AH-zoo-ah), province (□ 936 sq mi/2,424 sq km; 1993 pop. 194,209), S Dominican Republic, on the Caribbean Sea; ⊙ Azua. Mountainous, semiarid region, bounded N by the Cordillera Central (including Monte Tina, and crossed by the Sierra de Ocoa). Main crops (irrigation) coffee, tobacco, sugarcane, cereals, vegetables; lumbering. Est. 1845; formerly comprised larger area.

Azua (AH-zoo-ah), officially Azua de Compostela, city (1993 pop. 46,420), ⊙ Azua prov., SW Dominican Republic, 3 mi/4.8 km from its port on the Caribbean Sea (Ocoa Bay), at S foot of the Sierra de Ocoa, 55 mi/89 km W of Santo Domingo; 18°27′N 70°43′W. Leading town of the SW; trades in agr. prods. (sugarcane, coffee, rice, beans, corn, resin, fruit, medicinal plants; timber). Has internatl. airport. Ruins of anc. convent. Founded nearby in 1504; later destroyed by earthquake and moved to present site.

Azueta, Villa, Mexico: see VILLA AZUETA.

Azure Lake, E B.C., W Canada, in Cariboo Mts., in Wells Gray Provincial Park, 120 mi/193 km N of Kamloops, at foot of Azure Mt. (8,191 ft/2,497 m); 16 mi/26 km long, 1 mi/2 km–2 mi/3 km wide. Drains W into North Thompson R. through Clearwater L.

Azusa (ah-ZOO-sah), city (1990 pop. 41,333), Los Angeles co., S Calif., suburb 20 mi/32 km ENE of downtown Los Angeles, in the San Gabriel valley; 34°08′N 117°55′W. Drained by San Gabriel R, which forms Morris and San Gabriel reservoirs to NE. Residential and industrial city in a citrus-fruit-growing area. Mfg. (aerospace and aircraft navigation equip., baggage handling vehicles, industrial controls, electronic equip., fabricated metal prods., machinery, furniture, chemicals, optical instruments, lubricating oils, transportation equip., molded rubber goods, plastic prods., ordnance accessories, foods; aluminum foundry). Has a large Mex.-Amer. pop. Seat of Azusa Pacific Col. Angeles Natl. Forest, including San Gabriel Wilderness Area, to N. Inc. 1898.

B

B. Everett Jordan Lake, reservoir, Chatham, Durham, and Wake cos., central N.C., on New Hope R., 18 mi/29 km S of Chapel Hill; c.18 mi/29 km long, max. 3 mi/4.8 km wide; 35°38′N 79°03′W. Max. capacity 660,664 acre-ft. Haw R. arm c.5 mi/8 km long. Formed by B. Everett Jordan Dam (103 ft/31 m high), built (1974) by the Army Corps of Engineers for flood control and water supply. Jordan L. State Recreation Area on E shore. Also called Jordan L.

Babb, village (1990 pop. 45), Glacier co., N Mont. Port of Piegan on Canada (Alta.) border 10 mi/16 km N. In NW part of Blackfeet Indian Reservation, on St. Mary R., near its exit (N) from Lower St. Mary L. Tourism; cattle; wheat, honey. Many Glacier Road (dead end) leads W into Glacier Natl. Park and to L. Sherburne. Duck L. to E.

Babbitt, town (1990 pop. 1,562), St. Louis co., NE Minn., 12 mi/19 km S of Ely, at SW end of Birch L. reservoir; 47°38′N 91°56′W. Timber; dairying; cattle; alfalfa; recreation; mfg. (consumer goods); taconite plant. Terminus (to SE) of Reserve Mining Co. RR to Silver Bay iron ore–processing plant and loading facilities on L. Superior. In Vermilion Iron Range; Superior Natl. Forest to N, E, and S; Bear Head L. State Park to NW.

Babcock, town, Miller co., SW Ga., 8 mi/12.9 km SE of Colquitt; 31°06′N 84°38′W.

Babcock State Park (☐ 4,127 acres/1,670 ha), Fayette co., S central W.Va., in the Allegheny Mts., 20 mi/32 km NNE of Beckley. Borders on New R. to W, and New R. Gorge Natl. R.

Babine Lake (buh-BEEN) (☐ 249 sq mi/645 sq km), central B.C., Canada, 110 mi/177 km WNW of Prince George; 95 mi/153 km long, 1 mi/2 km–6 mi/10 km wide. Drained NW by Babine R. (c.60 mi/97 km long) into Skeena R.

Babine Mountains, range, central B.C., Canada, extends c.100 mi/161 km NW-SE bet. Babine R. (N), Babine L. (E), and Bulkley R. (S and W); rises to 7,827 ft/2,386 m on Cronin Mt., 16 mi/26 km NE of Smithers.

Baboosic Lake (buh-BOO-sik), reservoir, Hillsborough co., S N.H., on Amherst-Merrimack town border, 10 mi/16 km W of Merrimack; 1.5 mi/2.4 km long; 42°52′N 71°34′W. Drains N into Joe English Brook.

Baboquivari Mountains (BAH-bo-kee-VAH-ree), Pima co., S Ariz., extend c.40 mi/64 km N from Mex. line; rise to 7,730 ft/2,356 m in Baboquivari Peak, c.50 mi/80 km NW of Nogales; forms part of E boundary of Tohono O'odham (Papago) Indian Reservation; 31°46′N 111°35′W. Kitt Peak (6,875 ft/2,096 m) in N, site of Kitt Peak Natl. Observatory.

Babson Park, town (☐ 1 sq mi/2.6 sq km; 1990 pop. 1,125), Polk co., central Fla., 50 mi/80 km S of Orlando; 27°49′N 81°31′W. Numerous lakes are nearby.

Babylon, residential and resort village (☐ 2 sq mi/5.2 sq km; 1990 pop. 12,249), Suffolk co., SE N.Y., on L.I., on Great South Bay; 40°42′N 73°19′W. The 1st U.S. wireless station was built here by Marconi. Settled 1689, inc. as a village 1893.

Baca, county (☐ 2,557 sq mi/6,623 sq km; 1990 pop. 4,556), SE Colo.; ⊙ Springfield; 37°19′N 102°33′W. Grain and livestock region bordering on Okla. and N.Mex (S) and Kansas (E); drained by Cimarron R. in SE, also North Fork Simarron R. (source in S), Bear Creek, Two Buttes Creek, Garrizo Creek, and Sand Arroyo. Two Buttes Reservoir (State Fishing Area) in N; part of Comanche Natl. Grassland in S and SW. Formed 1889.

Baca (BAH-kah), town (1990 pop. 4,104), Yucatán, SE Mexico, 18 mi/29 km NE of Mérida; 26°49′N 108°28′W. Former henequen-growing area. Citrus fruit.

Bacadéhuachi (bah-kah-DAI-wah-chee), town (1990 pop. 1,482), Sonora, NW Mexico, in W outliers of Sierra Madre Occidental, 120 mi/193 km ENE of Hermosillo; 28°48′N 19°11′W. Livestock; wheat, corn.

Bacalar, Lake, Quintana Roo, SE Mexico, in E Yucatán Peninsula, 20 mi/32 km W of Chetumal; 30 mi/48 km long, 1 mi/1.6 km–4 mi/6.4 km wide. Connected with Río Honda by small river. Part of these waters flow into Río Honda via the Chac R.

Bacanora (bah-kah-NO-rah), town (1990 pop. 754), Sonora, NW Mexico, on affluent of Yaqui R., 95 mi/153 km E of Hermosillo; 28°59′N 109°23′W. Lead mining; wheat, corn; cattle.

Baccalieu Island (BA-kuh-loo), N.F., Canada, off NE Avalon Peninsula, at entrance of Conception Bay, 4 mi/6 km long, 1 mi/2 km wide; 48°08′N 52°48′W.

Baccaro Point (BA-kuh-ro), promotory on the Atlantic, SW N.S., Canada, southernmost point of N.S. mainland, 23 mi/37 km SSW of Shelburne; 43°27′N 65°28′W.

Bacchus, town, Salt Lake co., N Utah, 10 mi/16 km WSW of Salt Lake City. Absorbed by est. of West Valley City.

Bacerac (bah-SE-rak), town (1990 pop. 1,440), ⊙ Bacerac municipio, Sonora, NW Mexico, on Bavispe R., in W outliers of Sierra Madre Occidental, 85 mi/137 km SE of Douglas, Ariz.; 30°21′N 108°49′W. Elev. 3,760 ft/1,146 m. Gold mining; livestock; corn, wheat; forestry.

Bache Peninsula (baich), on E Ellesmere Isl., in N N.W.T., Canada. U.S. explorer Robert Peary proved this area was a peninsula when he explored (1898) the region. From 1926 to 1933 the Royal Can. Mounted Police had a post here, c.800 mi/1,287 km from the North Pole, which was the northernmost habitation in the world.

Bachelor, Mount (9,060 ft/2,761 m), W Deschutes co., central Oregon, peak in Cascade Range, just S of the Three Sisters, 18 mi/29 km W of Bend; 43°58′N 121°41′W. Mt. Bachelor Ski Resort is here.

Bachíniva (bah-CHEE-nee-vah), town (1990 pop. 2,306), Chihuahua, N Mexico, 70 mi/113 km W of Chihuahua; 30°02′N 107°20′W. Elev. 6,250 ft/1,905 m. Corn, beans, fruit; cattle; wood prods.

Back Bay, neighborhood, Mass., a residential and commercial sect. of Boston. Site of Boston Public Lib. and historic Trinity Church.

Back Bay, lagoon, Virginia Beach (independent city), SE Va., extending into Currituck co., N.C., N arm of Currituck Sound, N.C., sheltered from the Atlantic Ocean by barrier beach (including False Cape State Park) that continues S to Cape Hatteras; c.12 mi/19 km long, 5 mi/8 km wide. Back Bay Natl. Wildlife Refuge in N, Mackay Isl. Natl. Wildlife Refuge (Va./N.C.) to S.

Back River, industrial suburb, Baltimore co., central Md., 7 mi/11.3 km E of downtown Baltimore, on navigable Back R., a 12-mi/19-km arm of Chesapeake Bay. A large plant making stainless steel is located here, as well as a sewage disposal plant directly on the river.

Back River, c.600 mi/970 km long, N.W.T., Canada, flowing NE across the tundra to Chantry Inlet. Numerous lakes along its course. Named for Sir George Back, the 1st person to descend the river (1834).

Backbone Mountain, peak (3,360 ft/1,024 m), Garrett co., NW Md., in the Allegheny Mts., near W.Va. border. The highest spot in Md., Haynes Crest, is on the mt., and Table Rock, where Route 50 crosses the mt., is the highest elev. of any Md. highway. Backbone Mt. formed a geographic divide. Rivers on the E side flow into the Potomoc R. and Chesapeake Bay, and rivers on the W side flow to the Ohio R.

Backus, village (1990 pop. 240), Cass co., N central Minn., 20 mi/32 km S of Walker, on E shore of Pine Mountain L.; 46°49′N 94°30′W. Dairying; cattle, sheep; oats, alfalfa; mfg. (motor vehicles). Foothills State Forest to W.

Bacliff, residential suburb (1990 pop. 5,549), Galveston co., SE Texas, 9 mi/14.5 km NNW of Texas City, and 25 mi/40 km SE of Houston, on Galveston Bay; 29°30′N 94°59′W. Light mfg.

Bacoachi (bah-ko-AH-chee), town (1990 pop. 956), Sonora, NW Mexico, on plateau (elev. 3,500 ft/1,067 m), on Sonora R., and 75 mi/121 km SE of Nogales; 30°02′N 110°09′W. Wheat, corn; cattle. Silver, copper, gold deposits nearby.

Bacon, county (☐ 286 sq mi/741 sq km; pop. 9,566), SE central Ga. ⊙ Alma; 31°34′N 82°27′W. Bounded NE by Little Satilla R.; drained by affluents of Satilla R. Coastal plain agr. includes soybeans, blueberries, tobacco, cotton, corn, peanuts; in lumber area. Formed 1914.

Bacone (buh-KON), village, Muskogee co., E Okla., NE of downtown Muskogee. Part of city of Muskogee. Seat of Bacone Col., near Ark. R.

Bacons Castle, village, Surry co., SE Va., near James R., 12 mi/19 km S of Williamsburg. Agr. (peanuts, grain, melons; livestock). Chippoke's Plantation State Park to N; Hog Isl. Game Refuge to NE. Bacon's Castle, a Jacobean house built c.1655, was seized and held (1676) by followers in Bacon's Rebellion.

Baconton (1990 pop. 623), Mitchell co., SW Ga., 14 mi/23 km S of Albany, near Flint R.; 31°23′N 84°10′W. Mfg. includes dairy prods., clothing, yeast production.

Bácum (BAH-koom), town (1990 pop. 3,417), Sonora, NW Mexico, on Yaqui R. (irrigation), 55 mi/89 km ESE of Guaymas; 27°45′N 110°05′W. Rice, wheat, corn, fruit, vegetables; cattle.

Bacuranao (bah-koo-rah-NOU), town, La Habana prov., W Cuba, 7 mi/11.3 km E of Havana; 22°08′N 82°13′W. Dairying. Oil wells in area. Civilian airstrip adjacent.

Bad Axe, city (1990 pop. 3,484), ⊙ Huron co., E Mich., c.55 mi/89 km NE of Saginaw; 43°47′N 83°00′W. RR junction and trade center for agr. area (beans, sugar beets, grain; livestock); mfg. (machinery, plastic prods.). Municipal airport. Nearby is 19th-cent. Jewish agr. colony of Palestine, which failed. Settled c.1860; inc. as village 1885, as city 1905.

Bad Axe River, c.25 mi/40 km long, Vernon co., SW Wis., rises c.5 mi/8 km NW of Viroqua, flows SW to the Mississippi, nearly opposite Minn.-Iowa line, 20 mi/32 km S of La Crosse. Near its mouth Black Hawk was defeated in 1832.

Bad River 1 central Mich., with 2 branches; 43°06′N 84°21′W. The N branch rises S of Ithaca in Gratiot co., flows 25 mi/40 km E past St. Charles, to Shiawassee R., just SW of Saginaw. The S branch starts c.18 mi/29 km SW of Saginaw co.. The 2 branches meet at St. Charles and join Saginaw R. 5 mi/8 km farther E. 2 c.110 mi/177 km long, rises in SW central S.Dak., in W Jackson co. near Badlands Natl. Park; flows E to Missouri R. at Fort Pierre. Deposits of manganese and fuller's earth in basin. 3 c.65 mi/105 km long, rises in Iron co., N Wis., flows generally NW past Mellen, over Copper Falls and through Bad R. Indian Reservation. Receives Morengo, Potato, and White rivers, to L. Superior 12 mi/19 km E of Ashland.

Baddeck (ba-DEK), village, ⊙ Victoria co., NE N.S., Canada, central Cape Breton Isl., on Great Bras d'Or, at entrance to St. Patrick Channel, 27 mi/43 km W of Sydney; 46°06′N 60°45′W. Fishing port, summer resort. Alexander Graham Bell lived here, and organized 1st flight in Br. territory, made by J. A. D. McCurdy on Feb. 23, 1909.

Baden (BAI-duhn), village, S Ont., Canada, 10 mi/16 km WSW of Kitchener; 43°24′N 80°40′W. Dairying; mixed farming.

Baden (BAI-duhn), village, Prince Georges co., S Md., 22 mi/35 km SE of Washington, near Cedarville Natural Resources Management Area. St. Paul's Church, built in 1733, is still serving a Protestant Episcopal congregation. The E window is a memorial to the Reverend Thomas John Claggett (1743–1814), who was consecrated the 1st bishop of Md. in 1792.

Baden (BAH-duhn), borough (1990 pop. 5,074), Beaver co., W Pa., 17 mi/27 km NW of Pittsburgh, and 2 mi/3.2 km ENE of Aliquippa, on Ohio R.; 40°38′N 80°13′W. Mfg. (food). Agr. (corn, hay; dairying). Laid out c.1839, inc. 1868.

Baden-Powell, Mount (9,400 ft/2,865 m), Los Angeles co., S Calif., 33 mi/53 km NE of downtown Los Angeles, in San Gabriel Mts.; 34°21′N 117°45′W. Named for founder of Boy Scouts.

Badger, town (1990 pop. 569), Webster co., central Iowa,

8 mi/12.9 km N of Fort Dodge; 42°36′N 94°08′W. Livestock, grain.

Badger 1 village (1990 pop. 381), Roseau co., NW Minn., 13 mi/21 km SW of Roseau; 48°46′N 96°01′W. Grain, flax, alfalfa, sunflowers; dairying; livestock; mfg. (alfalfa pellets). Can. border (Man.) 14 mi/23 km to N. Rosean R. Wildlife Area to N. **2** village (1990 pop. 114), Kingsbury co., E S.Dak., 7 mi/11.3 km NNW of Arlington. L. Poinsett State Recreational Area to NE.

Badin (BAI-duhn), uninc. town (1990 pop. 1,481), Stanly co., central N.C., 6 mi/9.7 km NE of Albemarle, on Badin L., formed by Badin Dam in Yadkin R.; 35°24′N 80°06′W. Large aluminum reduction plant. Agr. area (cotton, grain, soybeans; livestock; dairying); mfg. (aluminum processing). Narrow Mt. State Park to SE.

Badin Lake, reservoir (□ 8 sq mi/20.7 sq km), on Montgomery (E)/Stanly (W) co. border, central N.C., on Yadkin R., 30 mi/48 km ESE of Kannapolis; 35°26′N 80°05′W. Max. capacity 142,800 acre-ft. Formed by Yadkin Narrows Dam (196 ft/60 m high), built (1917) for power generation. Uwharrie Natl. Forest to E. The reservoir is part of a large system including Tuckertown dam and reservoir upstream (N) and L. Tillary downsteam (S).

Badiraguato (bah-dee-rah-GWAH-to), city (1990 pop. 2,904) and township, Sinaloa, NW Mexico, 40 mi/64 km NNW of Culiacán Rosales; 25°28′N 107°33′W. Corn and sugar.

Badlands, SW S.Dak., E of Black Hills; arid plateau (150 ft/46 m–300 ft/91 m above surrounding countryside), c.120 mi/193 km long, 30 mi/48 km–50 mi/80 km wide, bounded S by White R., crossed by Bad R. Characterized by numerous ridges and mesas cut by erosion into colorful peaks, pinnacles, and valleys, with scant vegetation. Region's name has remained generic while lending the name to other areas of similar aspect. Rich in deposits of prehistoric fossils. Part of region (□ 192.2 sq mi/497.8 sq km) in Pennington and Jackson cos. was set aside (1939) as Badlands Natl. Park. Similarly eroded region is in SW N.Dak., extending N-S along right bank of Little Missouri R.

Badlands National Park, park (□ 380 sq mi/984 sq km), SW S.Dak., authorized 1929 as Badlands Natl. Monument, redesignated Badlands Natl. Park in 1978; 43°37′N 102°52′W. Land area more than doubled with S expansion (1968); 100 sq mi/259 sq km of the park has been designated wilderness. Cedar Pass Lodge at E entrance.

Báez (BEI-aiz), town, Villa Clara prov., central Cuba, on RR, and 9 mi/14.5 km SW of Placetas; 22°12′N 79°45′W. Tobacco, fruit; cattle. Copper and zinc deposits in vicinity.

Baffin, region (□ 392,905 sq mi/1,017,889 sq km; 1991 pop. 11,385), N.W.T., Canada; ⊙ Iqaluit. It extends N from the southernmost portion of the Hudson Bay to the N tip of Ellesmere Isl. and E from Prince Patrick Isl. to Baffin Isl. The region includes the isls. of Devon, Bathurst, Melville, Prince Patrick, and Somerset, in addition to the Melville Peninsula. Fishing, sealing, and craft making; mining. The region was created in the early 1970s by the territorial govt.

Baffin Bay, S Texas, inlet of Laguna Madre, 33 mi/53 km S of Corpus Christi; forms boundary of Kleberg and Kenedy cos.; c.15 mi/24 km long, 4 mi/6.4 km wide. Los Olmos Creek enters from W. Cayo Del Grullo (c.20 mi/32 km long, ½ mi/⅘ km–2 mi/3.2 km wide) is NW arm behind Padre Isl. Alazan Bay (c.12 mi/19 km long, 1 mi/1.6 km–3 mi/4.8 km wide) is NE arm.

Baffin Island (□ 183,810 sq mi/476,068 sq km), c.1,000 mi/1,610 km long and from 130 mi/210 km–450 mi/720 km wide, in the Arctic Ocean, E N.W.T., Canada; 68°30′N 70°00′W. It is the 5th-largest isl. in the world and the easternmost member of the Arctic Archipelago. Baffin Isl. is geographically and geologically a continuation of Lab., from which it is separated by Hudson Strait. The W side of the isl. is covered largely by tundra. There are many freshwater lakes, including Nettilling (1,956 sq mi/5,066 sq km) and Amadjuak. In the E, snow-covered mt. ranges rise more than 8,000 ft/2,440 m. Baffin Isl. has a deeply indented coastline with many fjords. Most of the isl.'s inhabitants are Eskimos who live mainly at coastal trading posts. Whaling, fur trading, and fishing are the chief occupations. The posts have stores, post offices, police stations, schools, and occasionally hosps. Martin Frobisher visited the isl. bet. 1576 and 1578, and Frobisher Bay, in the SE, is the principal town. The isl. is named for William Baffin, who explored the Arctic in 1616.

Bagdad 1 uninc. town (1990 pop. 1,858), Yavapai co., central Ariz., 41 mi/66 km W of Prescott, near Boulder Creek. Cattle, sheep; major copper-producing town. Bozarth Mesa to N, Prescott Natl. Forest to NE. **2** town (□ 4 sq mi/10.4 sq km; 1990 pop. 1,457), Santa Rosa co., NW Fla., 17 mi/27 km NE of Pensacola, near mouth of Blackwater R., on Blackwater Bay; 30°35′N 87°01′W. Lumbering.

Bagdad (BAG-dad), uninc. village (1990 pop. 225), Shelby co., N Ky., 10 mi/16 km NW of Frankfort. Guist Creek L. reservoir to SW. Tobacco, grain; livestock; dairying. Mfg. (animal feeds, consumer goods).

Baggs, village (1990 pop. 272), Carbon co., S Wyo., on Little Snake R., near Colo. border, 60 mi/97 km SSW of Rawlins; 41°02′N 107°39′W. Elev. 6,245 ft/1,903 m.

Bagley 1 town (1990 pop. 303), Guthrie co., W central Iowa, 13 mi/21 km NNE of Guthrie Center; 41°51′N 94°25′W. Feed milling. **2** (BAIG-lee), town (1990 pop. 1,388), ⊙ Clearwater co., NW Minn., 24 mi/39 km W of Bemidji, on Clearwater R.; 47°31′N 95°24′W. Elev. 1,441 ft/439 m. Dairying; poultry, eggs, cattle, sheep; grain, sunflowers, alfalfa; mfg. (hardwood prods., pulpwood, concrete products, wooden pallets). White Earth Indian Reservation and parts of White Earth State Forest to S; Miss. Headwaters State Forest and Itasca State Park to SE. Settled 1898, inc. 1900.

Bagley (BAG-lee), village (1990 pop. 306), Grant co., extreme SW Wis., on Mississippi R., and 9 mi/14.5 km S of Prairie du Chien; 42°53′N 91°05′W. In livestock and dairy region. Logs, lumber. Wyalusing State Park to NW at Wyalusing.

Bagnell (BAG-nuhl), town (1990 pop. 89), Miller co., central Mo., 8 mi/13 km S of Eldon; 38°13′N 92°36′W. River-fishing resort. Bagnell Dam nearby.

Bagnell Dam, Mo.: see LAKE OF THE OZARKS.

Bagot (BA-guht), county (□ 346 sq mi/896 sq km), S Que., Canada, on Richelieu R.; ⊙ St. Liboire; 45°35′N 72°45′W.

Bagotville, Canada: see LA BAIE.

Báguanos (BAH-gwuh-noz), town, Holguín prov., E Cuba, 15 mi/24 km SE of Holguín; 20°44′N 76°01′W. Site of López Peña sugar mill.

Bahama Banks, Bahamas: see GREAT BAHAMA BANK and LITTLE BAHAMA BANK.

Bahamas or **Commonwealth of the Bahamas**, country (□ 4,403 sq mi/11,404 sq km; 1990 pop. 255,056), in the Atlantic Ocean, consisting of some 700 isls. and islets and about 2,400 cays, beginning c.50 mi/80 km off SE Florida and extending c.600 mi/966 km SE almost to Haiti; 24°00′N 76°00′W. The country does not include the Turks and Caicos Isls., to the SE, which, although geographically part of the archipelago, have been separately administered by Great Britain since 1848. Until 1973, when they became independent, the Bahamas were administered as a Br. crown colony. The capital and principal city is NASSAU, on NEW PROVIDENCE ISLAND. Other chief isls., known as the "out islands" or "family islands," are Grand Bahama (1990 pop. 40,898), Great and Little Abaco (see ABACO AND CAYS), the BIMINIS, ANDROS, ELEUTHERA, Cat Isl., SAN SALVADOR, Great and Little Exuma (Exuma and Cays), Long Isl., CROOKED ISLAND, Acklins Isl., Mayaguana, Mariguana, and Great and Little INAGUA. The isls., composed mainly of limestone and coral, rise from a vast submarine plateau. Most of them are generally low, flat, and riverless, with many mangrove swamps, brackish lakes (connected with the ocean by underground passages), and coral reefs and shoals. Fresh water is obtained from rainfall and from desalinization. Navigation is hazardous, and many of the outer isls. are uninhabited and undeveloped, although steps have been taken to improve transportation facilities. Hurricanes occasionally cause severe damage, but the climate is generally excellent. The isls.' vivid subtropical atmosphere—brilliant sky and sea, lush vegetation, flocks of bright-feathered birds, and submarine gardens where multicolored fish swim among white, rose, yellow, and purple coral—as well as rich local color and folklore, has made the Bahamas one of the most popular resorts in the hemisphere. The isls.' many casinos are an additional attraction. Tourism, which has grown rapidly since the end of World War II, is by far the country's most important industry. Declining tourism in the late 1980s did serious damage to the country's economy. Offshore banking has also become important. Crawfish, rum, cement, salt, hormones, and aragonite are among the chief exports. The Bahamas also possesses facilities for petroleum transshipment. The country's pop. is primarily black and mulatto. English is the official language. The Bahamas have a relatively low illiteracy rate. The govt. provides free education through the secondary level; the Col. of the Bahamas was est. in 1974, although most Bahamans study in Jamaica or elsewhere. The Bahamas are governed by the constitution of 1973 and have a parliamentary form of govt. There is a bicameral legislature consisting of a Senate and a House of Assembly. The prime minister is the head of govt., and the monarch of the U.K., represented by an appointed governor-general, is the titular head of state. The Bahamas were inhabited by the Lucayos, a group of Arawaks, before the arrival of the Europeans. Christopher Columbus 1st set foot in the New World in the Bahamas (1492), presumably at San Salvador, and claimed the isls. for Spain. Although the Lucayos were not hostile, they were soon exterminated by the Spanish, who did not in fact colonize the isls. The 1st settlements were made in the mid–17th cent. by the English. In 1670 the isls. were granted to the lords proprietors of Carolina, who did not relinquish their claim until 1787, although Woodes Rogers, the 1st royal governor, was appointed in 1717. Under Rogers the pirates and buccaneers (notably Blackbeard) who frequented Bahamian waters were driven off. The Spanish attacked the isls. several times, and an Amer. force held Nassau for a short time in 1776. After the Amer. Revolution many Loyalists settled in the Bahamas, bringing with them slaves to labor on cotton plantations. In 1781 the Spanish captured Nassau and took possession of the whole colony, but under the terms of the Treaty of Paris (1783) the isls. were ceded to Great Britain. Plantation life gradually died out after the emancipation of slaves in 1834. Blockade-running into Southern ports in the U.S. Civil War enriched some of the islanders, and during the Prohibition era in the U.S. the Bahamas became a base for rum-running. The U.S. leased areas for bases in the Bahamas in World War II and in 1950 signed an agreement with Great Britain for the est. of a proving ground and a tracking station for guided missiles. In 1955 a free trade area was established at the town of Freeport. It proved enormously successful in stimulating tourism and has attracted offshore banking. In the 1950s black Bahamians, through the Progressive Liberal Party (PLP), began to oppose successfully the ruling white-controlled United Bahamian Party; but it was not until the 1967 elections that they were able to win control of the govt. The Bahamas were granted limited self-govt. in 1964, broadened (1969) through the efforts of Prime Minister Lynden O. Pindling, who served in office for 25 years. The PLP, campaigning on a platform of immediate independence, won an overwhelming victory in the 1972 elections and negotiations with Britain were begun. On July 10, 1973, the Bahamas became a sovereign state within the Commonwealth of Nations. Since the 1960s, the transport of illegal narcotic drugs has been a problem, as has an unprecedented flow of illegal refugees from other isls. The economy is weak, mostly due to a decrease in tourism and the poor management of state-owned industries. As part of a plan for structural reform for shaping future patterns of development, privatization was begun in the early- to mid-1990s with janitorial and messenger services; other hotel, transport, and telecommunications services were to follow.

Bahía de Banderas, Mexico: see VALLE DE BANDERAS.

Bahía Honda (bah-EE-ah ON-dah), town, Pinar del Río prov., W Cuba, on small bay of same name, 50 mi/ 80 km WSW of Havana; 22°58′N 83°10′W. Sugarcane, coffee, fruit, livestock.

Bahon (bah-ONG), town (1982 pop. 1,100), Nord dept., N Haiti, on Grande Rivière du Nord, 23 mi/37 km SSE of Cap-Haïtien; 19°28′N 72°07′W. Coffee growing and processing; oranges, limes.

Bahoruco (bah-ho-ROO-ko), province (□ 1,347 sq mi/ 3,489 sq km; 1993 pop. 101,742), SW Dominican Republic, on Haiti border; ⊙ Neiba; 18°30′N 71°21′W. Bounded by Sierra de Neiba (N) and Sierra de Bahoruco (S), watered by the Yaque del Sur. In its center is L. Enriquillo, a salt lake c.150 ft/46 m below sea level. In the fertile, irrigated depression are grown coffee, corn, rice, sugarcane, bananas, vegetables. Rich in fine tropical wood. Fishing and hunting at L. Enriquillo. Large salt deposits near Neiba. Formerly a part of Barahona prov., it was set up 1943.

Bahoruco, Sierra de (bah-ho-ROO-ko, see-ER-rah dai), range, SW Dominican Republic, parallel to the Cordillera Central and forming S watershed of L. Enriquillo; extends c.50 mi/80 km E from Haiti border to the Caribbean just S of Barahona. Rises to 5,348 ft/ 1,630 m.

Baidland (BAID-luhnd), uninc. town (1990 pop. 1,620), Washington co., SW Pa., residential suburb 2 mi/ 3.2 km W of Monongahela R; 40°11′N 79°57′W.

Baie Comeau (bai KO-mo), town (1991 pop. 26,012), E Que., Canada, on the St. Lawrence R. near the mouth of the Manicouagan R.; 49°13′N 68°09′W. A deepwater seaport, it has hydroelectric plants on the Outardes and Manicouagan rivers that supply the city of Quebec with electricity. Mfg. includes aluminum and paper prods. Brian Mulroney, former prime minister of Canada, b. here.

Baie d'Urfé (bai duhr-FAI), town (1991 pop. 3,849), S Que., Canada, on SW shore of Montreal Isl., on L. St. Louis, 18 mi/29 km WSW of Montreal; 45°24′N 73°55′W. Dairying, agr.; resort.

Baie, La (BAI, lah) or **Baieville** (BAI-vil), village (1991 pop. 20,995), S Que., Canada, 8 mi/13 km SW of Nicolet; dairying; pig raising.

Baie Saint Paul (bai saint POL), village (1991 pop. 3,733), ⊙ Charlevoix West co., SE central Que., Canada, on the St. Lawrence R., 55 mi/89 km NE of Quebec, opposite Île aux Coudres; 47°26′N 70°30′W. Lumbering, dairying; potatoes; poultry raising. Founded 1681. Iron mined nearby.

Baie Verte (bai VUHRT), inlet (15 mi/24 km long, 18 mi/29 km wide at mouth) of Northumberland Strait, bet. SE N.B. and N N.S., Canada, extending W from Cape Tormentine. At its head is Port Elgin. Smelt and lobster fisheries.

Baie-de-Henne (bai-duh–EN), town (1982 pop. 1,009), Nord-Ouest dept., NW Haiti, on Gulf of Gonaïves, 36 mi/58 km WNW of Gonaïves; 19°40′N 73°12′W. Fishing port. Bee-keeping.

Baie-Mahault (BE–mah-O), town, NE Basse-Terre, Guadeloupe, 5 mi/8 km NW of Pointe-à-Pitre. Agr. (sugar, cacao, coffee); distilling.

Baieville, Canada: see BAIE, LA.

Bailey, county (□ 827 sq mi/2,142 sq km; 1990 pop. 7,064), NW Texas; ⊙ Muleshoe; 34°04′N 102°49′W. Elev. 3,700 ft/1,128 m–4,060 ft/1,237 m. On the Llano Estacado and bounded W by N.Mex. line. Crossed by intermittent Blackwater Draw, extension of Double Mt. Fork of Brazos R. Diversified agr. (sorghum, cotton, wheat, corn, vegetables, potatoes; dairying); beef cattle. Has several lakes, Coyote L. in W center and Muleshoe Natl. Wildlife refuge to SE. Formed 1876.

Bailey 1 or **Baileys**, village (1990 pop. 553), Nash co., NE central N.C., 11 mi/18 km WNW of Wilson; 35°46′N 78°06′W. Agr. area (tobacco, cotton, peanuts, grain; livestock); mfg. (crushed stone, apparel). Country Doctor Mus. **2** village (1990 pop. 187), Fannin co., NE

Texas, 10 mi/16 km S of Bonham; 33°25′N 96°09′W. Agr. area.

Bailey Island, Maine: see HARPSWELL.

Bailey Town, town, NW Bahama Isls., on spit of North Bimini isl., just N of Alice Town, 55 mi/89 km E of Miami, Fla., and 130 mi/209 km WNW of Nassau. Resort; fishing. Just N is the Lerner Marine Laboratory (under auspices of Amer. Mus. of Natural History).

Baileys Crossroads, uninc. city, Fairfax co., NE Va., residential suburb, 5 mi/8 km NW of Alexandria, 6 mi/ 9.7 km SW of Washington, D.C.; 38°51′N 77°07′W. L. Barcroft reservoir to W.

Baileys Harbor, village, Door co., NE Wis., on Door Peninsula, on small inlet of L. Michigan, 20 mi/32 km NE of Sturgeon Bay, in resort and fishing area. Lumber. A coast guard station is here. Kangaroo L. (c.3 mi/ 4.8 km long) is to SW. Ridges Sanctuary is to NE.

Bailey's Prairie, village (1990 pop. 634), Brazoria co., SE Texas, residential suburb, 4 mi/6.4 km W of Angleton, on Oyster Creek, in Brazosport area; 29°08′N 95°29′W.

Baileyton, town (1990 pop. 309), Greene co., NE Tenn., 11 mi/18 km N of Greeneville; 36°20′N 82°50′W.

Baileyville, township (1990 pop. 2,031), Washington co., E Maine, on St. Croix R., along N.B. (Canada) border, W of Calais, and 30 mi/48 km N of Machias; 45°10′N 67°26′W. Includes village of Woodland. Inc. 1828.

Baillie, trading post, N Mackenzie dist., N.W.T., Canada, on Beaufort Sea of the Arctic Ocean; 70°32′N 128°25′W. Radio station. Just N is Cape Bathurst, northernmost point of Can. mainland; 4 mi/6 km WNW are the 2 Baillie Isls., larger of which is 10 mi/16 km long, 2 mi/ 3 km–7 mi/11 km wide.

Baillie Hamilton Island (17 mi/27 km long, 7 mi/11 km– 11 mi/18 km wide), N central Franklin dist., N.W.T., Canada, at N end of Wellington Channel, bet. Cornwallis (S), Devon (E and N), and Bathurst (W) Isls.; 75°50′N 94°45′W.

Baillif (bah-YEEF), town, SW Basse-Terre, Guadeloupe, 2.5 mi/4 km NNW of Basse-Terre. Vanilla. Sometimes called Le Baillif.

Bainbridge (BAIN-brij), city (1990 pop. 10,712), ⊙ Decatur co., SW Ga., on the Flint R.; 30°55′N 84°35′W. It grew up around a fort, used by Andrew Jackson, that was constructed during the Native Amer. Wars of 1817–1821. The city is a trade and industrial center as well as an inland port and barge terminal near the head of navigation on the Flint R. Mfg. includes carpets and yarns, printing and publishing, cotton. Harvesting equip., brooms and mops, outdoor lighting. Bainbridge Col. is a 2-year unit of the Univ. System of Ga. Nearby L. Seminole offers fishing, hunting, and boating. Inc. 1829.

Bainbridge 1 town (1990 pop. 682), Putnam co., W central Ind., 8 mi/12.9 km NNE of Greencastle; 39°46′N 86°49′W. In agr. area. **2** (BAIN-brij), uninc. town (1990 pop. 900), Lancaster co., SE Pa., 16 mi/26 km SE of Harrisburg, on Susquehanna R.; 40°05′N 76°40′W. Mfg. (fertilizers). Three Mile Isl. Nuclear Plant 5 mi/ 8 km to NNW. Nisley Vineyards to East York Haven Dam 4 mi/6.4 km NNW, at Conewago Falls.

Bainbridge 1 village (□ 1 sq mi/2.6 sq km; 1990 pop. 1,550), Chenango co., S central N.Y., on the Susquehanna, 25 mi/40 km NE of Binghamton; 42°17′N 75°28′W. Dairying and farming area. Mfg. (resin glues, sealants, adhesives). Settled before 1790, inc. 1829. **2** village (1990 pop. 968), Ross co., S Ohio, 17 mi/27 km WSW of Chillicothe, and on Paint Creek; 39°22′N 83°16′W. Trade center for farm area. Seip Mound State Park is nearby.

Bainbridge Island, town (1990 pop. 16,000), Kitsap co., W Wash., on Eagle Harbor, arm of Puget Sound, 8 mi/ 12.9 km W of Seattle; 47°38′N 122°31′W. Formed in 1991. Winery, art galleries; tourism. Direct ferry to downtown Seattle. Fay Bainbridge State Park to N; Fort Ward State Park to S.

Bainbridge Island 1 (15 mi/24 km long, 1 mi/1.6 km– 6 mi/9.7 km wide), S Alaska, in Gulf of Alaska, E of Kenai Peninsula, from which it is separated by Port Bainbridge, 40 mi/64 km E of Seward; 60°05′N 148°10′W. **2** NW Wash., in Puget Sound, W of Seattle;

11 mi/18 km long, 5 mi/8 km wide. Residential and resort isl., farms; berries, hothouse flowers; dairying. Bounded W by Port Orchard channel, S by Rich Passage. Includes villages of Port Madison, Winslow (major town on isl., directly opposite downtown Seattle), and Port Blakeley. Bridge across Agate Passage to Kitsap.

Bainbridge, Port, inlet (15 mi/24 km long, 3 mi/4.8 km wide) of Gulf of Alaska, on SE Kenai Peninsula, S Alaska, 35 mi/56 km E of Seward; 60°04′N 148°21′W.

Bainet (be-NE), town, Ouest dept., S Haiti, on the coast, 14 mi/23 km of Jacmel; 18°11′N 72°45′W. Coffee, fruit, sisal growing. Just S is Cape Bainet.

Bainoa (bei-NO-ah), town, La Habana prov., W Cuba, on RR, 28 mi/45 km ESE of Havana; 23°01′N 81°56′W. Sugarcane; cattle.

Bainville (BAIN-vil), village (1990 pop. 165), Roosevelt co., NE Mont., on Shotgun Creek, near Missouri R. and N.Dak. state line, 31 mi/50 km N of Sidney, and 26 mi/42 km W of Williston (N.Dak.); 48°08′N 104°13′W. Headwaters of L. Sakakawea (Garrison Reservoir, Mo.) and Fort Union Trading Post Natl. Historical Site (Mont./N.Dak.) to SE. Former army post and fur-trading point. RR junction to W.

Baird, city (1990 pop. 1,658), ⊙ Callahan co., N central Texas, 20 mi/32 km E of Abilene; 32°23′N 99°24′W. Elev. 1,708 ft/521 m. Trade, shipping point in cattle ranching, wheat, sorghum, peanuts; oil area; mfg. (feeds, candy). Clyde L. to SW. Settled 1880, inc. 1891.

Baird, Cape, NE Ellesmere Isl., NE Franklin dist., N.W.T., Canada, on Hall Basin, on S side of entrance of Lady Franklin Bay; 81°32′N 64°30′W. NE extremity of Judge Daly promontory.

Baird Glacier, in Coast Range of SE Alaska and NW B.C., Canada; 57°08′N 132°46′W. Drains into Frederick Sound, 17 mi/27 km N of Petersburg.

Baird Inlet (70 mi/113 km long, 1 mi/1.6 km–18 mi/ 29 km wide), W Alaska, bet. mouths of Yukon and Kuskokwim rivers, E of Nelson Isl.; 60°53′N 163°42′W. Opens out into Hazen Bay.

Baird Mountains, NW Alaska, bet. Kotzebue Sound and Kobuk R. (S) and Noatak R. (N and W); extend c.120 mi/193 km E-W; bet. 158° and 162°25′W 67°35′N. Rise to 5,100 ft/1,550 m.

Bairdford (BEIRD-fuhrd), uninc. town (1990 pop. 1,200), Allegheny co., W Pa., suburb 14 mi/23 km NNE of Pittsburgh; 40°37′N 79°52′W. Agr. includes dairying.

Bairdstown, village (1990 pop. 130), Wood co., NW Ohio, 9 mi/14 km NNE of Findlay; 41°11′N 83°37′W.

Baire (BEI-rai), town, Santiago de Cuba prov., E Cuba, on Central Highway, on RR, 40 mi/64 km WNW of Santiago de Cuba; 20°21′N 76°21′W. In citrus- and sugar-growing region. Scene (Feb. 24, 1895) of opening battle of Cuban war of independence.

Bairoil (BER-oil), village (1990 pop. 228), Sweetwater co., S central Wyo., 36 mi/58 km NNW of Rawlins; 42°14′N 107°33′W. Elev. 6,860 ft/2,091 m, at base of Green Mts. in Great Divide Basin. Natural gas-producing area.

Baja California (BAH-hah), state (□ 27,628 sq mi/ 71,557 sq km; 1990 pop. 1,660,855), NW Mexico, on the Baja California peninsula; ⊙ Mexicali; 28°32′N 112°45′W. A rapidly growing state, Baja California is a center of development for maquiladoras, foreign-owned assembly plants that produce finished goods for export to the U.S. The plants are centered around Mexicali and Tijuana. Mexicali also serves as the center of a rich cotton-producing area, while Tijuana is a noted tourist and industrial center and point of entry from the U.S. Ensenada is the state's most important port and is also a mfg., fishing, and tourist center. Baja California became a state in 1952.

Baja California (BAH-hah) or **Lower California**, peninsula, c.760 mi/1,223 km long and from 30 mi/48 km to 150 mi/241 km wide, NW Mexico, separating the Gulf of Calif. from the Pacific Ocean. The peninsula is divided at lat. 28°N into the state of Baja Calif. in the N, and the state of Baja Calif. Sur in the S. The land is generally desolate and arid. The only naturally cultivable areas are isolated mt. valleys. However, irrigation systems on the Colo. R. have made possible the development of a rich farming area around Mexicali, and the region is a leading natl. producer of cotton and wheat. The peninsula and surrounding waters are a paradise for naturalists and archaeologists, offering unparalleled opportunities for the study of marine life, plants and animals, and archaeological artifacts.

Baja California Sur (BAH-hah), state (□ 27,571 sq mi/71,409 sq km; 1990 pop. 317,764), NW Mexico, on the Baja California peninsula; ⊙ La Paz; 22°52′N 109°25′W. The state is lightly populated and has little arable land. There is some cotton grown commercially under irrigation and there is significant salt mining in the desert region in the N portion of the state. Tourism, the economic mainstay, is centered at Los Cabos, an internatl. beach resort area and sport-fishing destination. Baja California Sur was made a state in 1974.

Bajabonico, Dominican Republic: see IMBERT.

Bajío (bah-HEE-o), region, Mexico, in Quéretaro and Guanajuato states. This area is the most important agr. region in the country and is considered the breadbasket of the republic. It covers the Mex. high plateau N to the sierra of Guanajuato; S to the volcanic foothills; E to the heights separating the Celaya valley from Quéretaro. The Lerma R. has produced a series of lakes located at the foot of the central volcanic area. The soil is very fertile with water from the Lerma R. and its tributaries. Temperate and sub-humid climate.

Bajos de Haina, town (1993 pop. 68,261), on the Caribbean coast, 10 mi/16km W of Santo Domingo, San Cristóbal prov., S Dominican Republic; 18°25′N 70°02′W. Port and industrial center.

Baker 1 county (□ 585 sq mi/1,515 sq km; 1990 pop. 18,486) N central Fla., on Ga. line (N, E); ⊙ Macclenny; 30°19′N 82°16′W. Largely a flatwoods area; W part included in Okefenokee Swamp and Osceola Natl. Forest. Agr. (corn, vegetables, peanuts, cotton); forestry (lumber); naval stores. Formed 1861. **2** county (□ 355 sq mi/919 sq km; 1990 pop. 3,615), SW Ga.; ⊙ Newton; 32°25′N 84°27′W. Bounded SE by Flint R.; drained by Ichawaynochaway Creek. Coastal plain agr. (corn, peanuts, sugarcane, cotton, pecans) and lumber area; cattle, hogs, poultry. Formed 1825. **3** county (□ 3,088 sq mi/7,998 sq km; 1990 pop. 15,317), NE Oregon; ⊙ Baker City; 44°42′N 117°40′W. Bounded E by Snake R. (forms Idaho state boundary); Powder and North Powder rivers, Anthony Creek, and Burnt R. form part of N boundary. Drained by Powder R. Timber, gold, silver, copper. Barley, oats, potatoes; cattle, sheep; dairy prods. Blue Mts. in W; Wallowa Mts. in N; Oxbow and Brownlee dams on Snake R. in NE, S of Hells Canyon. Unity Lake State Park in SW; Farewell Bend State Park in SE corner; part of Hells Canyon Natl. Recreation Area in NE; part of Umatilla Natl. Forest in NE; parts of Wallowa-Whitman Natl. Forest in W and S; part of Malheur Natl. Forest in SW (including Monument Rock Wilderness Area). Formed 1862.

Baker, city (1990 pop.1,818), ⊙ Fallon co., E Mont., near N.Dak. line, 75 mi/121 km E of Miles City; 46°22′N 104°16′W. Farm trading point in large gas and oil field; gas and oil wells; cattle, hogs, sheep; wheat, oats, alfalfa. Medicine Rocks State Park to SW; Little Missouri Natl. Grassland to E (in N.Dak.). Settled as Lorraine, renamed Baker 1908, inc. 1914. O'Fallon Mus.; Baker L. recreation area located in town.

Baker 1 uninc. village (1990 pop. 650), San Bernardino co., SE Calif., 56 mi/90 km ENE of Barstow, in Mojave Desert. Silver L. to N, Soda L. to S (both dry). Soda Springs or Zzyzx (old resort, now desert research center) on W side of Soda L. Fort Irwin Mil. Reservation and Death Valley Natl. Monument to NW. Borax mining; mfg. of borates. **2** village, White Pine co., E Nev., 4 mi/6.4 km W of Utah line, 42 mi/68 km ESE of Ely. Hq. for Great Basin Natl Park, to W, includes Lehman Caves (former natl. momument) and Mt. Wheeler (13,063 ft/3,982 m). Parts of Humboldt Natl. Forest to N and S. Mt. Moriah (12,067 ft/3,678 m) to N. **3** uninc. village, Hardy co., NE W.Va., 12 mi/19 km E of Moorefield, on Lost R. (becomes underground stream to NE). Cattle, poultry; dairying; corn. Mfg. (photographic equipment, electronic assembly, mulch packaging). George Washington Natl. Forest to SE.

Baker, suburb (1990 pop. 13,233) of Baton Rouge, East Baton Rouge parish, SE central La., 10 mi/16 km N of downtown; 30°36′N 91°10′W. Mfg. of resins, dairy prods., mannequins for taxidermy; publishing and printing. Standard Oil Refinery built at turn of 20th cent. Was 1st known as Cottonville. Hard hit by boll weevil.

Baker City, town (1990 pop. 9,140), ⊙ Baker co., NE Oregon, 77 mi/124 km NE of Pendleton, on Powder R.; 44°46′N 117°49′W. Elev. 3,449 ft/1,051 m. Trade and shipping center for agr. prods. (potatoes, wheat, barley, oats), dairy prods., timber, gold, silver, copper, wood prods., printing and publishing. Cattle, sheep. Mines nearby laid out in 1865 after discovery of gold (1861–1862) in area. Elkhorn Ridge to W. Phillips and Powder rivers to SW. Anthony L. Ski Area to NW. Umatilla Natl. Forest to NE; parts of Wallowa-Whitman Natl. Forest to W and S. Known as Baker before 1989.

Baker Island, uninhabited island (□ 1 sq mi/2.6 sq km), central Pacific, near the equator, c.1,650 mi/2,655 km SW of Honolulu. The arid coral isl. was discovered in 1832 by Capt. Michael Baker, an American, and was claimed by the U.S. in 1856. Like Jarvis and Howland Isls., Baker was worked for guano by both Amer. and Br. companies during the 19th cent. In 1935 it was colonized by Americans from Hawaii in order to est. U.S. control against Br. claims. The colonists were removed during World War II. Baker Isl. is administered under the U.S. Dept. of the Interior.

Baker Island, Maine: see CRANBERRY ISLES.

Baker Lake (□ c.1,000 sq mi/2,590 sq km), Keewatin Region, N.W.T., Canada, W of Chesterfield Inlet of Hudson Bay. It has a post of the Royal Can. Mounted Police at its W end.

Baker Lake, reservoir, Whatcom co., NW Wash., on Baker R., in Cascade Range, in Mt. Baker–Snoqualmie Natl. Forest, 32 mi/51 km E of Bellingham, 10 mi/16 km SE of Mt. Baker summit; 10 mi/16 km long. 1 mi/1.6 km wide; 48°38′N 121°41′W. Formed by Upper Baker Dam Forest. Campgrounds. L. Shannon formed by (Lower) Baker Dam downstream, to SSW.

Baker, Mount (10,778 ft/3,285 m), Whatcom co., N Wash., in Cascade Range, 30 mi/48 km E of Bellingham, in Mt. Baker Natl. Forest; 48°48′N 121°54′W. Mt. Baker Natl. Recreation Area in S slopes; Mt. Baker Wilderness Area in all other directions. Mt. Baker Ski Area to NE; Baker R. and Baker L. reservoir to SE. 15 mi/24 km S of U.S.–Canada (B.C.) border; snowcapped extracted volcano clearly seen from Vancouver (B.C.) to NW.

Baker River, c.28 mi/45 km long, NW Wash., rises near Mt. Fury (8,292 ft/2,527 m), in N unit of North Cascades Natl. Park; flows generally SW through Baker L. (Upper Baker Dam) and L. Shannon (Lower Baker Dam), in Mt. Baker Natl. Forest to the Skagit R.

Bakers Island, NE Mass., in the Atlantic, c.6 mi/9.7 km E of Salem; c.½ mi/⅘ km long; 42°32′N 70°47′W. Has lighthouse.

Bakersfield, city (1990 pop. 174,820), seat of Kern co., S central Calif., 95 mi/153 km NNW of Los Angeles on Kern R., at the S end of the San Joaquin valley; 35°22′N 119°00′W. Elev. 406 ft/124 m. RR junction. It is an oil, mining, and agr. center. Mfg. (oil and gas, chemicals, printing and publishing, apparel, food and beverages, construction materials, fabricated metal prods., paper prods., petroleum refining, rubber goods, computers, machinery). Since the Kern R. oilfields were discovered in 1899, almost all of the major oil companies have established refineries in Bakersfield. Cotton, citrus fruits, potatoes, roses, beans, vegetables, sugar beets, nuts, apples, plums, melons, pumpkins; dairying; cattle. Bakersfield is one of the fastest growing U.S. cities, marked by a pop. increase of more than 65% 1980–1990. Gold was discovered in the region in 1855. Silver, borax, gypsum, and tungsten are mined in the vicinity. Oil and natural gas to SW. Calif. State Univ., Bakersfield and Bakersfield Community cols.; major aerospace facilities. Bakersfield Airport to N; Edwards Air Force Base 60 mi/97 km SE; Shirley Meadows Ski Area to NE; Buena Vista L. irrigation reservoir to SW; Sequoia Natl. Forest and S end of Sierra Nevada (Greenhorn Mts.) to NE; Isabella L. reservoir (Kern R.) to NE; Tule State Elk Reserve to W. Inc. 1898.

Bakersfield 1 town (1990 pop. 292), Ozark co., S Mo., in the Ozarks, near Norfork L., 22 mi/35 km SW of West Plains; 36°31′N 92°08′W. Cattle; timber, wood prods. **2** town (1990 pop. 977), Franklin co., NW Vt., 14 mi/23 km E of St. Albans; 44°47′N 72°47′W. Lumber, dairy, and maple prods.

Bakerstown (BAI-kuhrs-toun), uninc. suburb (1990 pop. 950) of Pittsburgh, Allegheny co., W Pa., 13 mi/21 km N of city center; 40°39′N 79°56′W. Mfg. includes commercial printing, fabricated metal products; agr. includes dairying.

Bakersville, ghost town, Cochise co., SE Ariz., near Warren, near Mex. border, 4 mi/6.4 km SE of Bisbee. Lavender Pit and Copper Queen mines nearby; tourist attraction.

Bakersville, village (1990 pop. 332), ⊙ Mitchell co., NW N.C., 8 mi/12.9 km NW of Spruce Pine near Toe R; 36°00′N 82°09′W. Mica mining, timber. Mfg. (apparel, wood-burning stoves, crushed stone, lumber). Appalachian Trail to N, on N.C.-Tenn. state line. Natural rhododendron gardens at Roan Mt.

Bal Harbour, resort suburb (1990 pop. 3,045), Dade co., SE Fla.; 25°53′N 80°07′W. Luxury resort community just N of Miami Beach. Upscale shopping and dining area, with many exclusive retailers.

Bala (BAH-luh), town, S Ont., Canada, on Muskoka R., on SW bay of Muskoka L., 15 mi/24 km W of Bracebridge; 45°01′N 79°37′W. Resort. Hydroelectric plant.

Balaclava, town (1991 pop. 2,837), St. Elizabeth parish, W Jamaica, on Jamaica RR, and 30 mi/48 km WNW of May Pen; 18°10′N 77°39′W. Cassava, tropical fruit and spices; livestock. Noted Oxford Caves are nearby.

Balancán (bah-lahn-KAN), city (1990 pop. 8,655) and township, Tabasco, SE Mexico, on Usumacinta R., 95 mi/153 km E of Villahermosa; 17°49′N 91°32′W. Rubber, rice, tobacco, fruit.

Balandra Bay (bah-LAHN-dra), small open bay, NE Trinidad, Trinidad and Tobago, 35 mi/56 km E of Port of Spain; 10°42′N 61°00′W. Known for its fine surf.

Balaton (BA-luh-tuhn), village (1990 pop. 737), Lyon co., SW Minn., near Cottonwood R., 15 mi/24 km S of Marshall; 44°13′N 95°52′W. Grain; livestock; dairying; mfg. (fertilizers). L. Yankton to NE.

Balboa, section of Newport Beach city, Orange co., S Calif., comprises peninsula bet. Balboa Isl., in Newport Bay, and the Pacific; both peninsula and isl. are residential; 6-mi/9.7-km-long sandy beach on ocean side of peninsula; yachting. Short bridge to island; ferry from isl. to peninsula; peninsula attached to mainland in NW (Balboa Boulevard).

Balcarres (bal-KA-ris), town (1991 pop. 661), SE Sask., Canada, near the Fishing Lakes, 19 mi/31 km N of Indian Head; 50°48′N 103°33′W. Grain elevators.

Balch Springs, city (1990 pop. 17,406), Dallas co., N Texas, residential suburb, 12 mi/19 km SE of downtown Dallas, and 3 mi/4.8 km S of Mesquite; 32°43′N 96°37′W. Mfg. (consumer goods).

Balcones Escarpment, dissected fault scarp, Texas, c.200 mi/322 km long, (E-W), c.100 mi/161 km wide), separating Edwards Plateau (SE extension of the Great Plains) from the Gulf Coastal plain; extends E and NE from near Uvalde to region NE of Austin; c.300 ft/91 m high near Austin.

Balcones Heights, town (1990 pop. 3,022), Bexar co., SW central Texas, residential suburb 5 mi/8 km NW of downtown San Antonio, surrounded by San Antonio; 29°29′N 98°32′W.

Balcony Falls, Va.: see JAMES RIVER.

Bald Eagle Creek, 50 mi/80 km long, central Pa.; rises in Allegheny Mts. in SW Centre co. at Blair co. line, 7 mi/11.3 km NE of Tyrone, and on NW side of Bald Eagle Mt. ridge; flows NE, along NW base of Bald Eagle Mt., past Millersburg, through Sayer (Blanchard) L. reservoir, in Bald Eagle State Park, to West Branch Susquehanna R., 2 mi/3.2 km E of Lock Haven at 40°44′N

78°07'W. Another Bald Eagle Creek rises immediately SW of the same source, 7 mi/11.3 km NE of Tyrone, on NW side of Bald Eagle Mt., and flows SW c.7 mi/11.3 km along base of Bald Eagle Mt., joining Little Juniata R. at Tyrone.

Bald Eagle Lake, Lake co., NE Minn., 12 mi/19 km ESE of Ely in Superior Natl. Forest; 4 mi/6.4 km long; max. width 2 mi/3.2 km; 47°49'N 91°33'W. Fed by small stream, drained by South Kawishiwi R. Connected NW by channel to Gabbro, or Gabro L. In Boundary Waters Canoe Area.

Bald Eagle Mountain, central Pa., NE-SW ridge (1,700 ft/518 m–2,000 ft/610 m), runs c.85 mi/137 km NE from just E of Tyrone, passes NW of State College and Bellafonte, SE of Lock Haven to W Branch of the Susquehanna R., opposite Muncy; 41°08'N 77°19'W–41°13'N 76°54'W. Sandstone, quartzite.

Bald Head, headland, York co., SW Maine, 3 mi/4.8 km SE of Ogunquit, 20 mi/32 km SSE of Alfred.

Bald Head Island, 4 mi/6.4 km long, 1 mi/1.6 km wide, Brunswick co., SE N.C., 5 mi/8 km SE of Southport. Mouth of Cape Fear R. estuary to W (Old Baldy Lighthouse), Atlantic Ocean to S and E, isl. separated from Smith Isl. to N by narrow channel. Cape Fear at SE end of isl. Village of Bald Head Isl. (1990 pop. 78) on Atlantic shore facing S.

Bald Hill Dam, N.Dak.: see ASHTABULA, LAKE.

Bald Knob, town (1990 pop. 2,653), White co., central Ark., c.55 mi/89 km NE of Little Rock; 35°18'N 91°34'W. RR junction. In agr. area famed for strawberry production. Mfg. (firearm accessories, electric motors, wood prods., lumber). Henry Gray–Hurricane L. Wildlife Management Area to SE.

Bald Knob, uninc. village, Boone co., W central W.Va., 15 mi/24 km SE of Madison. Mfg. (lumber, coal processing); bituminous coal, timber.

Bald Knob, W.Va.,: see SHAVERS MOUNTAIN.

Bald Mountain (2,080 ft/634 m), N central N.B., Canada, 32 mi/51 km ENE of Grand Falls.

Bald Mountain 1 peak (13,684 ft/4,171 m), in Rocky Mts., Summit Park co., N central Colo., on Continental Divide; 39°26'N 105°58'W. Prapah Natl. Forest to NW; Pike Natl. Forest to SE. **2** peak (2,443 ft/745 m), Franklin co., W Maine, 37 mi/60 km NW of Farmington, and just E of Mooselookmeguntic L.; 44°38'N 70°21'W. One of several Bald Mts. found in Maine.

Bald Mountain 1 Idaho: see SALMON RIVER MOUNTAINS. **2** Maine: see CAMDEN HILLS. **3** Nev.: see TOQUIMA RANGE.

Bald Mountains, range of the Appalachian Mts., along N.C.-Tenn. state line, NE of Great Smoky Mts. Natl. Park, c.20 mi/32 km SE of Greeneville, Tenn., and c.25 mi/40 km N of Asheville, N.C., bet. Nolichucky (N) and Pigeon (S) rivers. On state line is Big Bald Mt. (5,516 ft/1,681 m), 22 mi/35 km SE of Greeneville. SW portion sometimes called Max Patch Mts.; entire range sometimes considered part of Unaka Mts. Appalachian Trail passes through mts. on state line.

Baldoon, locality, S Ont., Canada, near the present Chatham. Lord Selkirk founded Scottish settlement here (1804); its failure prompted Selkirk to sponsor Scottish colonization of the W prairies.

Baldur (BOL-duhr), village, S Man., Canada, 45 mi/72 km SE of Brandon. Livestock center; grain elevators.

Baldwin 1 county (□ 2,027 sq mi/5,250 sq km; 1990 pop. 98,280), SW Ala., on Mobile Bay and Gulf of Mexico; ⊙ Bay Minette. Rich, level farmland; soybeans, subtropical fruits, potatoes, sugarcane, pecans, vegetables, gladiolus bulbs, timber. Crude oil and natural gas prods. Delta region affords good hunting and fishing. Drained by Alabama R. (NW), Little R. (N), Tensaw R. (W), and Perdido R. (E). Formed 1809. **2** county (□ 265 sq mi/686 sq km; 1990 pop. 39,530), central Ga.; ⊙ Milledgeville; 33°04'N 83°15'W. Piedmont agr. area (corn, pecans, fruit); cattle, poultry; timber. Drained by Oconee R. Formed 1803.

Baldwin, uninc. city (1990 pop. 22,719), Nassau co., SE N.Y., on the S shore of L.I., on Baldwin Bay; 40°39'N 73°37'W. Commuter pop. Varied mfg. Settled 1640s.

Baldwin 1 (bahld-win), town (□ 2 sq mi/5.2 sq km; 1990 pop. 1,450), Duval co., NE Fla.,19 mi/31 km W of Jacksonville; 30°18'N 81°58'W. RR junction in timber and livestock area. **2** town (1990 pop. 1,439), Habersham and Banks cos., NE Ga., 14 mi/23 km WSW of Toccoa; mfg. of clothing, janitorial supplies, and poultry feeds; 34°29'N 83°33'W. Nearby is the L. Russell Recreation Complex (in the Chattahoochee Natl. Forest), which offers recreation facilities. **3** town (1990 pop. 137), Jackson co., E Iowa, 9 mi/14.5 km W of Maquoketa; 42°04'N 90°50'W. Concrete blocks. **4** town (1990 pop. 2,379), St. Mary parish, S La., 36 mi/58 km SE of Lafayette, on Bayou Teche; 29°50'N 91°33'W. Elev. 14 ft/4 m. RR junction. Mfg. of concrete, pressure vessels; sugarcane; catfish, crawfish, oysters, crabs; natural gas and oil. Hunting, fishing. Cypremort Point State Park to SW. Also called La Teche. **5** town (1990 pop. 1,219), Cumberland co., SW Maine, on the Saco R., 26 mi/42 km WNW of Portland; 43°50'N 70°42'W. Includes villages of East Baldwin, West Baldwin, and North Baldwin. Saddleback Hills run E-W through the township. **6** town (1990 pop. 2,022), St. Croix co., W Wis., 23 mi/37 km WNW of Menomonie; 44°57'N 92°22'W. Dairy prods., poultry; mfg. (food prods., heavy mfg.). Au Galle Dam Recreational Area (Army Corps of Engineers) to SE.

Baldwin 1 village (1990 pop. 426), Randolph co., SW Ill., 18 mi/29 km N of Chester; 38°10'N 89°50'W. In agr. and bituminous coal mining area. Site of nuclear plant. **2** village (1990 pop. 821), ⊙ Lake co., W central Mich., 33 mi/53 km SW of Cadillac, on Baldwin R.; 43°53'N 85°50'W. Mfg. (fabricated metal prods., machinery). Resort area. Many lakes and streams (fishing) in region. Indian village sites and mounds nearby. Airport here. Shrine of the Pines log hunting lodge here, with over 200 log stumps and root carvings. Wald Hills Ski Area to NW; Manister Natl. Forest to W, S, and SE.

Baldwin, suburb (1990 pop. 21,923) of Pittsburgh, Allegheny co., SW Pa., 5 mi/8 km SE of downtown, near the Monongahela R.; 40°21'N 79°58'W. Bituminous coal region. Allegheny Co. Airport to S. Inc. 1952.

Baldwin City, town (1990 pop. 2,961), Douglas co., E Kansas, 13 mi/21 km S of Lawrence; 38°46'N 95°11'W. In livestock and grain area; dairy prods. Scene of battle (1856) bet. proslavery settlers and Free Staters. Baker Univ. (Methodist; est. 1858) is here. Douglas State Fishing L. to E. Laid out 1855, inc. 1870.

Baldwin Park, city (1990 pop. 69,330), Los Angeles co., S Calif., a residential suburb 16 mi/26 km E of downtown Los Angeles, bounded by San Gabriel R. in W and NW, in the fertile San Gabriel valley; 34°05'N 117°58'W. It has varied mfg. that has grown with the city's suburban development (fabricated metal prods., metal fabrication, printing, plastic prods.). Settled 1870, inc. 1956.

Baldwin Peninsula, NW Alaska, extends 45 mi/72 km NW bet. Kotzebue Sound (SW) and Hotham Inlet (NE), N of Seward Peninsula, 1 mi/1.6 km–12 mi/19 km wide; 66°33'N 161°55'W.

Baldwinsville, village (□ 3 sq mi/7.8 sq km; 1990 pop. 6,591), Onondaga co., central N.Y., on Seneca R., and 12 mi/19 km NW of Syracuse; 43°09'N 76°19'W. Resort and shipping center. Mfg. (consumer goods, paper prods., machinery, feed, flour). Timber. Agr. (potatoes, cabbage). Located 2 mi/3.2 km E is Lysander New Community, a planned community begun in 1970. Settled 1796, inc. 1847.

Baldwinsville, Mass.: see TEMPLETON.

Baldwyn, town (1990 pop. 3,204), Lee and Prentiss cos., NE Miss., 18 mi/29 km NNE of Tupelo; 34°30'N 88°37'W. In agr. area (cotton, grain, soybeans; cattle; dairying; timber); mfg. at Tupelo and Verona (apparel, furniture, plastics). Brices Cross Roads Natl. Battlefield Site to W.

Baldy Mountain (2,727 ft/831 m), W Man., Canada, 36 mi/58 km NW of Dauphin. Highest point of Duck Mt. range.

Baldy Peak 1 peak (11,403 ft/3,476 m), Apache co., E Ariz., in White Mts., 20 mi/32 km SW of Eager; 33°51'N 109°33'W. Sunrise Ski Area on N slopes; on boundary of Apache-Sitgreaves Natl. Forest (NE) and Fort Apache Indian Reservation (SW). **2** peak (12,441 ft/3,792 m), in E Sangre de Cristo Mts., W Colfax co., N N.Mex., 18 mi/29 km NW of Cimarron, on E boundary of Carson Natl. Forest.

Balfour, uninc. town (1990 pop. 1,118), Henderson co., SW N.C., 2 mi/3.2 km N of Hendersonville; 35°21'N 82°28'W.

Balfour (BAL-for), village (1990 pop. 33), McHenry co., central N.Dak., 25 mi/40 km ESE of Velva on Wintering R.; 47°57'N 100°31'W.

Balfour, Mount (10,741 ft/3,274 m), SW Alta., Canada, near B.C. border, in Rocky Mts., in Banff Natl. Park, 50 mi/80 km NW of Banff; 51°34'N 116°27'W.

Balgonie (bal-GO-nee), town (1991 pop. 1,096), S Sask., Canada, 16 mi/26 km E of Regina. Wheat.

Balise, delta, Plaquemines parish, La., 40 mi/64 km SE of Port Sulphur. This is the modern bird's foot delta, after a town est. in 1723 on an isl. at mouth of SE Pass. Name comes from the Fr. word for beacon. Formerly with the reputation of being "the wickedest spot in Louisiana," the town is now underwater.

Balkan (BAL-kuhn), village, Bell co., SE Ky., 7 mi/11.3 km E of Pinevillem, in the Cumberland Mts., near Cumberland R. Bituminous coal.

Ball, town (1990 pop. 3,305), Rapides parish, S La., 8 mi/13 km WNW of Alexandria; 31°25'N 92°25'W. Residential community in agr. and timber area (esp. longleaf pine). Unit of Kisatchie Natl. Forest to N. Camp Beauregard Military Reservation to SE.

Ball Club Lake, Itasca co., N central Minn., 18 mi/29 km WNW of Grand Rapids; 5.5 mi/8.9 km long, 1.5 mi/2.4 km wide. In Leech L. Indian Reservation and Chippewa Natl. Forest. Drains SE into Mississippi R. Has small resorts. Sometimes spelled Ballclub.

Ball Ground, town (1990 pop. 905), Cherokee co., NW Ga., 9 mi/14.5 km NE of Canton; 34°20'N 84°23'W. Mfg. of fire-truck equip., gravel and limestone processing, poultry processing.

Ball, Mount (10,865 ft/3,312 m), SW Alta., Canada, near B.C. border, in Rocky Mts., in Banff Natl. Park, 19 mi/31 km W of Banff; 51°09'N 116°00'W.

Ballantyne Strait, arm (80 mi/129 km long, 35 mi/56 km–60 mi/97 km wide) of the Arctic Ocean, W Franklin dist., N.W.T., Canada, bet. Prince Patrick Isl. (SW) and Brock and South Borden isls. (NE); 77°00'N 113°00'W–78°00'N–116°30'W.

Ballarat, ghost mining town, Inyo co., E Calif., in Panamint Valley, W of Death Valley.

Ballard (BAL-uhrd), county (□ 273 sq mi/707 sq km; 1990 pop. 7,902), W Ky., bounded SW by the Mississippi R. (Mo. state line), W, NW, and N by the Ohio R. (Ill. state line), S by Mayfield Creek; ⊙ Wickliffe; 37°03'N 89°00'W. Gently rolling upland rises above flood plains along river. Agr. (dark tobacco, burly tobacco, sorghum, hay, alfalfa, soybeans, wheat, corn; hogs, cattle, poultry; dairying); timber; clay pits. Ballard County Wildlife Management Area in N, Peal and Swan L. wildlife management areas in W; small lakes. Lock and Dam No. 7 in N, on Ohio R. Formed 1842.

Ballard, village (1990 pop. 644), Uintah co., NE Utah, 2 mi/3.2 km E of Roosevelt; 40°16'N 109°57'W. Wheat barley, alfalfa; cattle, sheep; dairying; oil and natural gas. Bottle Hollow Reservation to E. Area surrounded by sections of Uintah and Ouray Indian Reservation.

Ballard, Mount (7,370 ft/2,246 m), highest peak in Mule Mts., Cochise co., SE Ariz., 3 mi/4.8 km W of Bisbee; 31°26'N 109°57'W.

Ballenas, Canal Las (bah-YAI-nahs) [Span. = channel of whales], in Gulf of Calif., NW Mexico, bet. E coast of Lower Calif. and Angel de la Guarda Isl.; c.55 mi/89 km long, 10 mi/16 km–15 mi/24 km wide.

Balleza (bah-YAI-sah), town, Chihuahua, N Mexico, on Balleza R., and 40 mi/64 km W of Hidalgo del Parral; 26°58'N 106°20'N. Gold and silver mining. Formerly San Pablo Balleza.

Balleza River (bah-YAI-sah), c.75 mi/121 km long, Chihuahua, N Mexico, rises in Sierra Madre Occidental of Durango near Chihuahua border; flows N past San Pablo Balleza to Conchos R., 13 mi/21 km N of Valle de Olivos. Usually called San Juan R. in upper course.

Ballinger, town (1990 pop. 3,975), ⊙ Runnels co., W central Texas, at mouth of Elm Creek on Colorado R., 36 mi/58 km NE of San Angelo; 31°44′N 99°57′W. Elev. 1,637 ft/499 m. Trade, processing center in cattle, agr. area (dairying, hogs, sheep; cotton, wheat, sorghum); oil and gas; mfg. (fertilizers, fabricated metal prods., apparel, construction materials). Nearby reservoir (capacity 2,000 acre-ft.) on Elm Creek is unit of Colorado R. flood-control project. L. O.H. Ivie reservoir to SE. Laid out 1886, inc. 1892.

Ballston Lake, resort and residential village (1990 pop. 700), Saratoga co., E N.Y., on Ballston L. (c.2 mi/3.2 km long), 7 mi/11.3 km S of Ballston Spa; 42°55′N 73°52′W.

Ballston Spa, village (□ 1 sq mi/2.6 sq km; 1990 pop. 4,937), ⊙ Saratoga co., E N.Y., 6 mi/9.7 km SSW of Saratoga Springs; 43°00′N 73°50′W. Mfg. (medical equip., construction materials, paper prods., testing and measuring instruments). Mineral springs; formerly a popular resort. Settled 1771, inc. 1807.

Balltown, town (1990 pop. 64), Dubuque co., E Iowa, near Mississippi R., 12 mi/19 km NW of Dubuque; 42°38′N 90°52′W.

Ballville, uninc. village (1990 pop. 3,083), Sandusky co., N central Ohio, on Sandusky R., and just S of Fremont; 41°20′N 83°08′W. In agr. area; tomatoes.

Ballwin, suburb (1990 pop. 21,816) of St. Louis, St. Louis co., E Mo., 20 mi/32 km W of downtown; 38°35′N 90°32′W. It is mainly residential and commercial with some light industry; mfg. (machinery). Castlewood State Park to S.

Bally, borough (1990 pop. 973), Berks co., SE Pa., 16 mi/26 km SW of Allentown; 40°23′N 75°35′W. Mfg. (wood prods., refrigeration equipment, textiles, apparel). Agr. area (apples, grain, potatoes; livestock, dairying).

Balmat, mining village (1990 pop. 100), St. Lawrence co., N N.Y., 7 mi/11.3 km SSE of Gouverneur; 44°15′N 75°23′W. Zinc, lead, pyrites, talc, and wollastonite.

Balmorhea, town (1990 pop. 765), Reeves co., extreme W Texas, 34 mi/55 km SSW of Pecos, near Toyah Creek, and at NE base of Davis Mts.; 30°58′N 103°44′W. Elev. 3,205 ft/977 m. RR terminus to S at Toyahvale; center of Balmorhea irrigation project (water from creeks, San Solomon and Phantom L. springs). Cattle; cotton, hay, cantaloupes. Barilla Mts. to SE; Balmorhea State Park and Balmorhea L. to S, including historic San Solomon Springs.

Balneario de los Novillos (bahl-ne-AH-ree-o dai los no-VEE-yos), national park (□ 104 acres/42 ha), in N Coahuila, Mexico, 12 mi/19 km N of Acuña. The park is developed around a pool in the Arroyo de las Vacas. Desert landscapes.

Balsam Cone, N.C.: see BLACK MOUNTAINS.

Balsam Lake, town (1990 pop. 792), ⊙ Polk co., NW Wis., at W end of Balsam L., 35 mi/56 km W of Rice L.; 45°27′N 92°27′W. Dairying; farming. Resort. St. Croix Indian Reservation to NE.

Balsam Lake (□ 17 sq mi/44 sq km), Kawartha Lakes, S Ont., Canada, 65 mi/105 km NE of Toronto; 10 mi/16 km long, 1 mi/1.6 km–5 mi/8 km wide. Drains W into L. Simcoe through Trent canal. Coboconk village at N end.

Balsam Mountain, W N.C., ridge (an E extension of Great Smoky Mts.) extending c.40 mi/64 km SE from Tenn. state line, partly along Haywood-Swain co. line, NW end in Great Smoky Mts. Natl. Park and Eastern Cherokee Indian Reservation. Includes Richland Balsam (6,410 ft/1,954 m), 8 mi/12.9 km S of Waynesville, and Black Mt. (6,275 ft/1,913 m), 5 mi/8 km farther S.

Balsas, Río (BAHL-sahs), river, c.450 mi/724 km long, rising in the state of Puebla, E central Mexico. One of Mexico's longest rivers, flows in a curve from S to NW through Puebla and Guerrero states, where it waters a fertile valley, to Michoacán state, forming most of the boundary bet. the last 2 states. Then it turns SW, passing through a hot, dry region before emptying into the Pacific Ocean. Upper course is known as the Río Mescala. Lower course is dammed to form Infiernillo Reservoir (Presa Infiernillo).

Balta, village (1990 pop. 79), Pierce co., N central N.Dak., 17 mi/27 km SSW of Rugby; 48°10′N 100°02′W. Several mid-sized lakes in area. Unsuccessful claimant to title of geographical center of N. Amer.

Baltic 1 village, Houghton co., NW Upper Peninsula, Mich., 5 mi/8 km SW of Houghton, ½ mi/⅘ km SE of South Range; 47°04′N 88°38′W. **2** village (1990 pop. 659), Tuscarawas co., E Ohio, 14 mi/23 km WSW of New Philadelphia; 40°27′N 81°44′W. **3** village (1990 pop. 666), Minnehaha co., E S.Dak., 15 mi/24 km N of Sioux Falls, and on Big Sioux R. Corn, oats, barley; livestock, dairy prods.; stone quarry.

Baltic, Conn.: see SPRAGUE.

Baltimore, county (□ 682 sq mi/1,766 sq km; 1990 pop. 692,134), N Md.; ⊙ Towson; 39°26′N 76°37′W. Almost surrounds independent Baltimore city. Co. is bounded N by Pa. line, SE by Gunpowder R. and Chesapeake Bay, S and SW by Patapsco R.; also drained by Gunpowder Falls (stream), in which are Prettyboy and Loch Raven dams. The reservoir formed by the dams, along with Liberty Reservoir on the Patapasco R., provides the area's water. Co. contains suburbs of Baltimore; mfg. of steel and ships (Sparrows Point, Back R.), aircraft (Middle R.), communications equip., electric tools, scientific instruments. Fruit and dairy farms supply Baltimore market. Deeply indented bay shore (extreme SE) has summer resorts and industrial areas. In central part are estates (including Hampton Natl. Historic Site near Towson) in dist. known for horse racing (especially cross-country races), fox hunting, and jousting tournaments. Ballestone Mus. (c.1780) at the Rocky Point Golf Course was built by George Washington's grandfather. Co. includes part of Patapsco State Park and L. Roland. Formed in 1659, Baltimore co. and Baltimore city were separated 1851.

Baltimore, city (1990 pop. 736,014), N Md., surrounded by but politically independent of Baltimore co., on the Patapsco R. estuary, an arm of Chesapeake Bay; 39°18′N 76°37′W. The largest city in the state, it was named after George Calvert, the 1st Lord Baltimore, the royal proprietor of Md., whose title came from his estates in Ireland. It is a port of entry, a commercial and industrial center, an important RR point, and a seaport with extensive anchorages and dock and storage facilities. In 1991, in spite of serious decline from the 4th- to the 10th-busiest port in the nation, it still exported large amounts of coal and grain, iron, steel, and copper prods. Among Baltimore's leading industries are shipbuilding, sugar and food processing, oil refining, and the mfg. of chemicals, steel, copper, clothing, and aerospace equipment. The site was first surveyed in 1661, patented for settlement in 1691, and offically founded in 1729. The excellent harbor soon made Baltimore an important center for the shipping of tobacco and grain. Shipbuilding, an early industry, flourished during the Revolution and the War of 1812 with the fitting out of many privateers. The famous Baltimore clippers were built in the early 1800s. The nation's wars have played a large role in the city's history. When the British occupied Philadelphia in 1777, Baltimore became the meeting place of the Continental Congress. In the War of 1812, the gallant defense of Fort McHenry inspired Francis Scott Key to write "The Star-Spangled Banner." Baltimore experienced a phenomenal growth in the early 19th cent., largely because of the Natl. Road, connecting the port of entry to the West. When the Erie Canal (completed in 1825) endangered the city's hold on the trans-Allegheny traffic, Baltimore businessmen chartered (1827) the Baltimore and Ohio RR to meet the competition of N.Y. city as a new ocean outlet for the West. During the Civil War, Baltimore was strongly pro-Southern in sentiment; the 6th Mass. Regiment, passing through the city in April 1861, was attacked by a mob. In both World Wars, Baltimore was an important shipbuilding and supply-shipping center. A disastrous fire in 1904 destroyed almost the entire downtown sect. but enabled the emergence of a more beautiful and better planned city. During much of the 1960s and 1970s, Baltimore decayed rapidly, losing pop. (over 200,000 left the city bet. 1960 and 1990) and commerce, largely to neighboring suburbs, which boomed. The city engaged in vigorous urban development projects during the late 1970s and 1980s. These included the construction of Harborplace (a marketplace containing shops and restaurants) in the Inner Harbor area, along with an aquarium, hotels, a convention center, apartment bldgs., and condominiums. Several old neighborhoods were also restored, and in 1983 a rapid transit line to the suburbs was opened. The redevelopment, however, resulted in the displacement of many older, poorer residents. In 1984, the Colts, Baltimore's professional football team, abruptly moved to Indianapolis. In 1996 the Cleveland Browns professional football team relocated to Baltimore with a new name, the Baltimore Ravens. In 1992, the Orioles, Baltimore's professional baseball team, moved from Memorial Stadium (which had also housed the Colts) to Oriole Park at Camden Yards, which was built especially for baseball. Many of the city's famous residential streets of red brick houses with scrubbed white steps still exist, as do a variety of ethnic neighborhoods. An important cultural and educational center, Baltimore is the seat of the Johns Hopkins Univ. with its famous medical center; the Univ. of Baltimore; St. John's Seminary and Univ.; Loyola Col.; Col. of Notre Dame of Md.; Coppin State Col., a branch of the Univ. of Md. with schools of medicine, dentistry, pharmacy, nursing, law, and social work; and the Community Col. of Baltimore. The Natl. Assn. for the Advancement of Colored People (NAACP) moved its hq. from N.Y. city to Baltimore in 1986. Also in Baltimore are the Peabody Conservatory of Music, the Md. Col. of Art, the Md. Acad. of Sciences, the Walters Art Gall., and the Baltimore Mus. of Art. The Enoch Pratt Free Lib. and the municipal symphony orchestra are well known. The city's many historical attractions include Flag House (c.1793) where Mary Pickersgill made the huge Star Spangled Banner which flew over Fort McHenry and inspired Francis Scott Key; the Basilica of the Assumption, the 1st R.C. cathedral in the U.S. (1806–1821; designed by Benjamin H. Latrobe, who also superintended construction of the U.S. Capitol); the Edgar Allan Poe House (c.1830); Westminster Churchyard where Poe is buried; Fort McHenry Natl. Monument and Historic Shrine; the Baltimore and Ohio Transportation Mus.; and numerous colonial homes. The U.S.S. *Constellation*, a natl. historic shrine, is docked in Baltimore; it was the 1st U.S. Navy ship (1797) and is the oldest Navy ship still afloat. Other landmarks are the historic sq. Mt. Vernon Place, which contains the 1st national George Washington Monument (1815–1842; designed by Robert Mills, who also drew the plans for the better-known Washington Monument in D.C); Druid Hill Park, with a zoo and a natural history mus.; and Pimlico Race Course, site of the famous Preakness, held annually since 1873. Baltimore-Washington Internatl. Airport is nearby. H.L. Mencken and Babe Ruth were b. in Baltimore. Inc. 1745.

Baltimore, town (1990 pop. 201), Windsor co., SE Vt., 12 mi/19 km SW of Windsor.

Baltimore, village, S Ont., Canada, 5 mi/8 km N of Cobourg. Fruit; dairying; mixed farming.

Baltimore, village (1990 pop. 2,971), Fairfield co., S central Ohio, 9 mi/14 km N of Lancaster; 39°52′N 82°37′W. Small campground nearby.

Baltimore and Ohio Railroad or **B&O**, first U.S. public RR, chartered in 1827 by a group of Baltimore businessmen to regain trans-Allegheny traffic lost to the newly opened Erie Canal. Construction began in 1828, and the 1st division opened in May 1830, bet. Baltimore and Ellicott's Mills, Md. Horses were the 1st source of power, but the successful trial run of Peter Cooper's *Tom Thumb* in Aug. 1830, brought the change to steam locomotives. The B&O expanded steadily and reached St. Louis in 1857. During the Civil War the RR moved Union troops and supplies. By the end of the 19th cent. the B&O had achieved most of its present 5,800 mi/9,334 km of track and connected with Chicago, Philadelphia, and N.Y. city. By the mid-1900s it had become mainly a freight carrier. Faced with financial difficulties, the B&O merged with the Chesapeake and Ohio in 1965. The B&O was the 1st RR to publish a timetable, to use electric locomotives and specialty cars (e.g., dining and baggage), and to run fully air-conditioned trains.

Baltimore-Washington National Parkway, central Md. Approach to the nation's capital from the NE; includes Greenbelt Park, a natural woodland. Authorized 1950.

Bamberg, county (□ 395 sq mi/1,023 sq km; 1990 pop. 16,902), S central S.C.; ⊙ Bamberg; 33°13'N 81°02'W. Bounded N by South Fork of Edisto R. Agr. area includes hogs, cattle; dairying; corn, wheat, soybeans, sorghum, hay, cotton, watermelons. Formed 1897.

Bamberg, town (1990 pop. 3,843), ⊙ Bamberg co., S central S.C., 17 mi/27 km SSW of Orangeburg; 33°17'N 81°01'W. Site of Bamberg Job Corps Center. Mfg. includes machinery, commercial printing, textiles. Agr. area for soybeans, grains, cotton, watermelons; dairying.

Bamboo, town (1991 pop. 3,732), St. Ann parish, N central Jamaica, 10 mi/16 km W of Ocho Rios; 18°24'N 77°16'W. Road junction.

Bamfield, village, SW B.C., Canada, on SW Vancouver Isl., on Barkley Sound, 32 mi/51 km SSW of Port Alberni; 48°50'N 125°08'W. Commercial fishing (salmon, herring, crabs, shrimp) is mainstay; timber; tourism. Ferry to Port Alberni. Connected to rest of isl. by gravel logging road. W terminus of West Coast Trail from Port Renfrew; follows Pacific Coast through Pacific Rim Natl. Park. Bamfield Marine Center (1973).

Banagüises (bah-nah-GWEE-saiz), town, Matanzas prov., W Cuba, on RR, and 29 mi/47 km ESE of Cárdenas; 22°46'N 80°51'W. Sugarcane, fruit, vegetables; apiculture. Near Central México.

Banámichi (bah-NAH-mee-chee), town (1990 pop. 1,227), Sonora, NW Mexico, on Sonora R., 80 mi/129 km NE of Hermosillo; 30°00'N 110°14'W. Wheat, corn; cattle. Santa Elena gold mines nearby.

Banana River, shallow lagoon, 30 mi/48 km long, 3 mi/4.8 km wide, E central Fla., bet. Merritt Isl. and Cape Canaveral barrier beach, which separates it from the Atlantic. Connected by channels at N and S ends with Indian R. lagoon.

Bancroft 1 town (1990 pop. 857), Kossuth co., N Iowa, near East Des Moines R., 15 mi/24 km N of Algona; 43°17'N 94°13'W. In livestock and grain area. **2** town (1990 pop. 66), Aroostook co., E Maine, on Mattawamkeag R., and 33 mi/53 km SSW of Houlton; 45°41'N 67°58'W. In lumbering area.

Bancroft, village (1991 pop. 2,383), SE Ont., Canada, on the York R.; 45°03'N 77°51'W. Mining, milling, quarrying, dairying, lumbering, and tourism. The Bancroft Gemboree is an annual gathering of rock collectors.

Bancroft 1 (BAN-krawft), village (1990 pop. 393), Caribou co., SE Idaho, 30 mi/48 km ESE of Pocatello; 42°43'N 111°53'W. Elev. 5,423 ft/1,653 m. Grain; livestock; dairying. Portneuf Reservoir and Fort Hill Indian Reservation to NW; Caribou Natl. Forest to W. **2** village (1990 pop. 599), Shiawassee co., S central Mich., 9 mi/14.5 km SE of Owosso; 42°52'N 84°04'W. In farm area; light mfg. **3** village (1990 pop. 494), Cuming co., NE Nebr., 15 mi/24 km NNE of West Point, at SW boundary of Omaha Indian Reservation; 42°00'N 96°34'W. Grain; livestock. Nichardt Center, a mus., is here. **4** village (1990 pop. 30), Kingsbury co., E central S.Dak., 12 mi/19 km NW of De Smet. **5** uninc. village, Putnam co., W central W.Va., 16 mi/26 km NW of Charlestown, near Kanawha R. Livestock; grain.

Banded Peak (9,626 ft/2,934 m), SW Alta., Canada, near B.C. border, in Rocky Mts., 40 mi/64 km SE of Banff.

Banded Peak (12,778 ft/3,895 m.), in San Juan Mts., Archuleta co., SW Colo., near N.Mex. state line, 25 mi/40 km SE of Pagosa Springs, SE of Continental Divide; 37°06'N 106°37'W. In Rio Grande Natl. Forest.

Bandelier National Monument (ban-duh-LIR) (□ 51 sq mi/132 sq km), Sandoval co., extends into Los Alamos and Santa Fe cos., N N.Mex., 10 mi/16 km S of Los Alamos, proclaimed 1916. Ruins of 13th-cent. Pueblo cliff dwellings on slopes at edge of Pajarito Plateau. Rio Grande flows through E part into Cochito L. Reservoir.

Bandera, county (□ 797 sq mi/2,064 sq km; 1990 pop. 10,562), SW Texas; ⊙ Bandera; 29°44'N 99°13'W. Elev. 1,258 ft/383 m. On Edwards Plateau; elev. c.1,000 ft/305 m–2,000 ft/610 m; drained by Sabinal and Medina rivers; source of Cibola Creek in E. Medina L. (Medina R.; irrigation, recreation) forms part of boundary in SE. Hilly ranching area (cattle, sheep, goats), with guest (dude) ranches; some agr. (pecans, apples); hunting, fishing; some timber. Bandera Downs horse racing; Hill Country State Park in S center; Lost Maples State Park in W. Formed 1856.

Bandera, town (1990 pop. 877), ⊙ Bandera co., SW Texas, on Edwards Plateau, 40 mi/64 km NW of San Antonio, and on Medina R.; 29°43'N 99°04'W. In agr., ranching area; tourist trade (dude ranches); timber; diversified light mfg. Has mus. of pioneer relics. Medina L. (Medina R.; irrigation, recreation) is 7 mi/11.3 km SE. Hill Country State Park to SW. Founded 1854 by Mormons and later turned into a Pol. settlement.

Bandera, Alto, Dominican Republic: see TINA, MONTE.

Banderas Bay, Pacific inlet, in Nayarit and Jalisco, W Mexico, just N of Cape Corriente; 27 mi/43 km long, c.25 mi/40 km wide. Receives Ameca R. The tourist resort of Puerto Vallarta is at its head.

Banderilla (bahn-dai-REE-yah), town (1990 pop. 11,587), Veracruz, E Mexico, in Sierra Madre Oriental, on RR, 4 mi/6.4 km NNW of Xalapa Enríquez; 19°32'N 96°40'W. Corn, coffee, fruit. Noted for orchid gardens.

Bandon, town (1990 pop. 2,215), Coos co., SW Oregon, on Pacific Ocean, at mouth of Coquille R., 19 mi/31 km SSW of Coos Bay; 43°07'N 124°24'W. Timber; dairy prods.; poultry; cranberries. Mfg. (frozen fish, wood prods.). Fish hatchery to SE. Largely destroyed by forest fire in 1936; later replanned and rebuilt. Bandon Lighthouse and Historical Mus. South Bandon Ocean Wayside State Park and Bullards Bench State Park are here; Bandon State Park to S. Inc. 1891.

Banes (BAH-naiz), town, Holguín prov., E Cuba, 35 mi/56 km ENE of Holguín; 20°57'N 75°43'W. Agr. center trading in bananas and other tropical fruit as well as sugarcane, which are exported through its port Embarcadero de Banes, 3 mi/4.8 km SSE on Banes Bay. Sugar mill Nicaragua (formerly Boston) is 4 mi/6.4 km S. Airstrip (c.5,000 ft/1,524 m) just S.

Banes Bay (BAH-naiz), Holguín prov., E Cuba, 3 mi/4.8 km S of Banes, 35 mi/56 km E of Holguín; linked with sea by narrow channel; 20°53'N 75°43'W. Embarcadero de Banes, the port for Banes, is on its N shore, with facilities for bulk grain handling. Connects to Holguín city by road and to Central RR via Alto Cedro, 37 mi/60 km S.

Banff (bamf), town (1991 pop. 5,688), SW Alta., Canada, on the Bow R. in the Rocky Mts.; 51°10'N 115°34'W. A famous tourist center and a winter resort, it is the administrative hq. of Banff Natl. Park. The Banff Center for Continuing Education (formerly the Banff School of Fine Arts), a branch of the Univ. of Alta., has an intl. reputation for the depth and variety of its approach to continued learning.

Banff National Park (□ 2,564 sq mi/6,641 sq km), W Alta., Canada, in the Rocky Mts.. Noted for its mountain scenery and hot mineral springs, the park is a year-round resort area. Banff and L. Louise are the chief resort centers. Est. 1885.

Bangor (BANG-or), city (1990 pop. 33,181), ⊙ Penobscot co., SE Maine, at the confluence of the Penobscot and Kenduskeag rivers; 44°49'N 68°47'W. It is a port of entry, major commercial center for E and N Maine, and gateway to an extensive resort and lumber region; mfg. (shoes, pulp and paper, wood prods.). The city was settled in 1769 and was known as Sunbury. During the War of 1812 it was occupied by the British. In the 19th cent., Bangor was a shipbuilding center that carried on an extensive coastal and overseas trade in lumber, stone, and ice. The city has a theological seminary, a conservatory of music, and 3 cols. Its 400,000-volume public lib. is one of New England's largest. Bangor Internatl. Airport, part of which was once Dow Air Force Base, has one of the longest runways in the U.S. Inc. as a town 1791, as a city 1834.

Bangor 1 town (1990 pop. 1,922), Van Buren co., SW Mich., on Black R., 12 mi/19 km NW of Paw Paw, 22 mi/35 km NE of Benton Harbor; 42°18'N 86°06'W. In orchard and farm region. Mfg. (electronic equip., food). Bangor Train Factory, restored train depot where toy trains are manufactured. Settled c.1837; inc. 1877. **2** (BAN-gor), town (1990 pop. 1,076), La Crosse co., W Wis., near La Crosse R., 13 mi/21 km ENE of La Crosse, on La Crosse State Trail; 43°53'N 90°59'W. Butter, cheese; ships livestock. Mfg. (wood prods., lumber).

Bangor (BANG-gor), borough (1990 pop. 5,383), Northampton co., E Pa., 12 mi/19 km N of Easton on Martins Creek. Mfg. (machinery, apparel); slate quarrying. Agr. (grains, soybeans, potatoes; livestock; dairying). Appalachian Trail passes to N, on Kittatinny Mt. Founded 1773, inc. 1875.

Bangor, Wash.: see KITSAP, co.

Bangs, town (1990 pop. 1,555), Brown co., central Texas, 9 mi/14.5 km W of Brownwood; 31°42'N 99°07'W. Cattle, sheep, goats; peanuts, wheat, vegetables; oil and gas; mfg. (consumer goods).

Bangs Lake, Ill.: see WAUCONDA.

Baní (bah-NEE), city (1993 pop. 47,554), ⊙ Peravia prov., S Dominican Republic; 18°20'N 70°23'W. It is the commercial and mfg. center of the region. Agr. (bananas, coffee). Baní is linked to Santo Domingo by highway.

Bánica (BAH-nee-kah), town (1993 pop. 1,566), Elías Piña prov., W Dominican Republic, near Haiti border, on Artibonito R., 50 mi/80 km S of Monte Cristi; 19°02'N 71°37'W. In agr. region (rice, cotton; goats; timber). Founded 1503 as Real Villa de Bánica, rebuilt 1759. The ruined Haitian fort Biassou is nearby.

Banister River, S Va., c.65 mi/105 km long, rises in W Pittsylvania co. c.20 mi/32 km NW of Danville, flows NE and SE, past Halifax (hydroelectric dam), to Dan R., 6 mi/9.7 km E of South Boston, at Kerr Reservoir (Buggs Isl. L.); 36°50'N 79°34'W.

Bankhead Lake, Tuscaloosa co., W Ala., 32 mi/51 km WSW of Birmingham, on the Black Warrior R.; 33°26'N 87°15'W. Max. capacity 296,000 acre-ft. Formed by John Hollis Bankhead Lock and Dam (103 ft/31 m high), built by the Army Corps of Engineers for navigation and hydroelectric generation.

Banks, county (□ 231 sq mi/598 sq km; 1990 pop. 10,308), NE Ga.; ⊙ Homer; 34°21'N 83°30'W. Piedmont agr. area (hay, sweet potatoes, fruit; poultry, cattle; timber). Drained by headstreams of Broad R. Formed 1858.

Banks, town (1990 pop. 195), Pike co., SE Ala., 7 mi/11.3 km E of Troy. Farming.

Banks 1 village (1990 pop. 88), Bradley co., S Ark., 33 mi/53 km NE of El Dorado, near L'Aigle Creek (E) and Moro Bayon (W); 33°34'N 92°16'W. **2** village (1990 pop. 50), Boise co., SW Idaho, 30 mi/48 km N of Boise. Elev. 2,815 ft/858 m. North Fork Payette and South Fork Payette join here to form main stream. Inc. after 1950. **3** village (1990 pop. 563), Washington co., NW Oregon, 10 mi/16 km NW of Hillsboro, on fork of Dairy Creek; 45°37'N 123°06'W. Fruit, berries; cattle, sheep, hogs, poultry; dairy prods.; timber. Tillamook State Forest to W.

Banks Island 1 (□ c.26,000 sq mi/67,340 sq km), NW N.W.T., Canada, in the Arctic Ocean, in the Arctic Archipelago. It is the westernmost of the group and is separated from the mainland by Amundsen Gulf. Banks Isl., which has many lakes, is a hilly plateau rising to c.2,000 ft (610 m) in the S. Once inhabited by Inuit, it is now uninhabited except for occasional trappers. Br. explorer Sir Robert McClure discovered that it was an isl. in 1851. Can. explorer Vilhjalmur Stefansson spent much time (1914–1917) there and explored the interior. **2** island (□ 388 sq mi/1,005 sq km; 45 mi/72 km long, 6 mi/9.7 km–11 mi/18 km wide), W B.C., Canada, in Hecate Strait, separated from Pitt and McCauley isls. by Principe Channel; 53°N 130°W. Rises to 1,760 ft/536 m. Lumbering.

Banks Lake, reservoir (□ 42 sq mi/109 sq km), Grant co., E Wash., on Upper Grand Coulee R., 23 mi/37 km NE of Ephrata; 47°37'N 119°18'W. Max. capacity 1,275,000 acre-ft. Formed by Dry Falls Dam (123 ft/37 m high), built (1949) by the Bureau of Reclamation for flood control; also used for navigation, irrigation, and power generation. Site of Dry Falls of the Glacial Columbia R. just S.

Bankston, town (1990 pop. 35), Dubuque co., E Iowa, 15 mi/24 km W of Dubuque; 42°30′N 90°57′W.

Bannack (BAHN-nuhk), village (1990 pop. 50), Beaverhead co., SW Mont., 17 mi/27 km W of Dillon, on Grasshopper Creek (also known as Willard's Creek). Founded in 1862 with discovery of gold along creek, the 1st gold strike in Mont. Bannack became Mont.'s 1st territorial capital (1864–1865). It declined when many miners left the thin deposits for the richer gold fields near Virginia City, Mont. Bannack State Park now preserves the historic bldgs. of this virtual ghost town. Beaverhead Natl. Forest to W. Formerly spelled Bannock.

Banner, county (□ 746 sq mi/1,932 sq km; 1990 pop. 852), W Nebr.; ⊙ Harrisburg; 41°32′N 103°43′W. Agr. area in the Platte R. Valley bordering on Wyo.; drained by Pumpkin Creek. Cattle, hogs; wheat, potatoes, sunflower seeds. Wildcat Hills State Recreation Area on N boundary. Formed 1888.

Banner, village (1990 pop. 160), Fulton co., central Ill., 17 mi/27 km NE of Lewiston; 40°30′N 89°54′W. In agr. and bituminous coal area. Nearby are Rice, Big, and Goose lakes, bayou lakes near Illinois R.

Banner Elk, town (1990 pop. 933), Avery co., NW N.C., 11 mi/18 km WSW of Boone in Pisgah Natl. Forest; 36°09′N 81°52′W. Mt. resort. Livestock; corn, potatoes. Seat of Lees-McRae Col. Ski resorts in area, including Sugar Mt. and Hawksnest to SE. Grandfather Mt. (5,964 ft/1,818 m) to S.

Banner Hill, village, Unicoi co., NE Tenn., 1 mi/1.6 km SW of Erwin; 36°08′N 82°25′W.

Bannertown, uninc. village, Surry co., NW N.C., suburb 2 mi/3.2 km ESE of Mt. Airy.

Banning, city (1990 pop. 20,570), Riverside co., S Calif., 28 mi/45 km ESE of Riverside, in a fruit-growing area bet. Mt. San Jacinto and Mt. San Gorgonio; 33°57′N 116°54′W. Mfg. (consumer goods, electrical equip.). Colorado R. Aqueduct runs E–W to S. An annual stagecoach day festival is held, and the city has a stagecoach mus. Parts of San Bernardino Natl. Forest; Univ. of S Calif. art complex. Morongo Indian Reservation to N; Soboba Indian Reservation to S; Mt. San Jacinto Wilderness State Park to SE. Inc. 1913.

Bannock, county (□ 1,147 sq mi/2,971 sq km; 1990 pop. 66,026), SE Idaho; ⊙ Pocatello; 42°40′N 112°13′W. Mt. area drained by Bear and Portneuf rivers. Snake R. plain region in N. Bounded on NW corner by part of Amer. Falls Reservoir (Snake R.). Irrigated fields produce wheat, alfalfa, barley; sheep, cattle; dairying; mfg. at Pocatello. Manganese deposits. Co. is urbanized in NW around Pocatello. Parts of Caribou Natl. Forest in S, W and E; part of Fort Hill Indian Reservation in N. Formed 1893.

Bannock Creek, c.40 mi/64 km long, SE Power co., SE Idaho; rises in mt. region; flows N through Power co. and part of Fort Hall Indian Reservation, to American Falls Reservoir (Snake R.), NE of American Falls. Used for irrigation.

Bannockburn (BAN-ok-burn), suburb (1990 pop. 1,388) of Chicago, Lake co., extreme NE Ill., 25 mi/40 km NNW of city center; 42°11′N 87°52′W. Agr. (dairying to W); mfg. (metal fabrication, machinery). Trinity Col. and Divinity School.

Baños de Coamo, P.R.: see COAMO.

Banquete, uninc. village (1990 pop. 449), Nueces co., S Texas, 25 mi/40 km W of Corpus Christi. Oil, agr. area (sorghum, cotton; cattle).

Bantam, Conn.: see LITCHFIELD, town.

Bantam Lake, reservoir, in Litchfield and Morris towns, Litchfield co., W Conn., on Bantam R., 3 mi/4.8 km SW of Litchfield; 2.5 mi/4 km long; 41°42′N 73°13′W. River enters from NE, drains from N.

Bantam River, 22 mi/35 km long, NW Conn.; rises in 2 branches; flows S and SW from junction near Litchfield to Bantam L., thence NW and SW to Shepaug R. above Washington.

Bantry (BAN-tree), village (1990 pop. 16), McHenry co.,

N central N.Dak.,14 mi/23 km NW of Towner; 48°30′N 100°36′W.

Bar Harbor, town (1990 pop. 2,768), Hancock co., SE Maine, on Mt. Desert Isl. and on Frenchman Bay, and 15 mi/24 km SE of Ellsworth; 44°22′N 68°12′W. It was a famed New England resort for the wealthy during the 19th cent. Bar Harbor is a port of entry, with ferry connections to Yarmouth, N.S., during the summer. In Oct. 1947, a large part of the town was destroyed by a forest fire. Nearby Acadia Natl. Park is a major tourist attraction. Settled 1763, inc. 1796.

Bar Harbour Island (□ 5 sq mi/13 sq km), SE N.F., Canada, in Placentia Bay, 30 mi/48 km NNW of Argentia; 4 mi/6.4 km long, 2 mi/3.2 km wide. Fishing.

Bar Nunn, town (1990 pop. 835), Natrona co., E central Wyo., suburb 7 mi/11.3 km N of Casper; 42°55′N 106°20′W. RR junction to S; cattle, sheep; grain.

Baraboo (BER-ruh-boo), city (1990 pop. 9,203), ⊙ Sauk co., S central Wis., 32 mi/51 km NW of Madison, in hilly resort area of Baraboo Mts.; 43°28′N 89°44′W. Agr. and timber region; mfg. (construction materials, food and beverages, textiles, lumber, consumer goods, animal feed); rock quarries. Ringling Brothers' circus began here. Devils L. State Park to S, the Wisconsin Dells to N, and Indian mounds are nearby. Mirror L. State Park to NW.

Baraboo Mountains (BER-ruh-boo), in Columbia, Sauk, and Richland cos., S central Wis., an almost circular ridge of old crystalline rock (quartzite) just SW of Portage, bet. Baraboo and Wisconsin rivers; c.25 mi/40 mi in diameter. Highest point is 1,620 ft/494 m. Devils L., Mirror L., Wildcat Mt., Natural Bridge, and Rocky Harbor State Parks here; Wisconsin Dells in N, canyon formation on Wisconsin R.; part of Duxfloss Area of SW Wisc., which escaped Pleistocene glaciation.

Baraboo River (BER-ruh-boo), c.70 mi/113 km long, central Wis.; rising in Juneau co.; flows generally SE, past Reedsburg and Baraboo, to Wisconsin R. just S of Portage.

Barachois de Malbaie (bah-rah-SHWAH duh mahl-BAI), village, E Que., Canada, E Gaspé Peninsula, on Mal Bay of the Gulf of St. Lawrence, 18 mi/29 km SE of Gaspé. Fishing port, resort.

Baracoa (bah-rah-KO-uh), city (1996 est. pop. 50,000), Guantánamo prov., SE Cuba, a port near the E extremity of the isl.; 20°20′N 74°30′W. It is a processing and export center for a region producing banànas, coconuts, and cacao. Important commercial airport complements the single major highway into this remote and mountainous corner of the isl. New tourist facilities have opened in nearby beaches and inland locations. Founded c.1512 as a *villa* by the Span. explorer Diego de Velázquez, Baracoa is the oldest settlement in Cuba.

Barada (buhr-RAI-duh), village (1990 pop. 24), Richardson co., extreme SE Nebr., 10 mi/16 km N of Falls City, near Missouri R.; 40°13′N 95°34′W. Indian Cave State Park to N.

Baradères (bah-rah-DER), town (1982 pop. 1,192), Grande-Anse dept., SW Haiti, on Jacmel Peninsula, 34 mi/55 km ESE of Jérémie; 18°30′N 73°39′W. Agr. (bananas, limes, sugarcane, coffee, cotton); coffee and sugar processing.

Baraga (BAIR-uh-guh), county (□ 1,068 sq mi/2,766 sq km; 1990 pop. 7,954), NW Upper Peninsula, Mich.; partly bounded N by Keweenaw and Huron bays; ⊙ L'Anse; 46°43′N 88°20′W. Drained by Sturgeon R. and small Silver R. Dairy; cattle; forage crops; lumbering, industrial machinery, mineral wool mfg. Resorts. Contains L'Anse Indian Reservation; Craig Lake State Park in SE, Baraga State Park, w of L'Anse in NW; part of Ottawa Natl. Forest along W margin of co.; Mt. Arvon (1,979 ft/603 m), highest point in Mich., in Huron Mts., in NE part (moose range area), and many small lakes. S boundary is on Central/Eastern time zone (Barraga co. in Eastern). Region settled by Finnish immigrants. Formed 1875.

Baraga (BAIR-uh-guh), town (1990 pop. 1,231), Baraga co., NW Upper Peninsula, Mich., on Keweenaw Bay,

and 3 mi/4.8 km NW of L'Anse; 46°46′N 88°29′W. Mfg. (RR ties, materials-handling equip.). Resort; fishing. Native Amer. relics found in vicinity. Baraga State Park to S; W unit of L'Anse Indian Reservation N of town. Hanka Homestead, 1896 Finn. restored homestead.

Baraguá (bah-rah-GWUH), town, Ciego de Ávila prov., E Cuba; 21°38′N 78°38′W. Sugar mill 13 mi/21 km SE of Ciego de Ávila city.

Barahona (bah-rah-HO-nah), province (□ 1,340 sq mi/3,471 sq km; 1993 pop. 157,772), SW Dominican Republic; ⊙ Barahona; 18°10′N 71°15′W. Largely a peninsula jutting into the Caribbean S of Sierra de Bahoruco; includes mouth of the Yaque del Sur on Neiba Bay, and L. Rincón. Arid area, fertile in irrigated regions, where sugarcane and coffee are grown on large scale. Extensive forests yield fine hardwood. Rock salt, gypsum, and clay deposits. Set up 1888 as maritime dist.; Bahoruco prov. was separated from it in 1943.

Baranof (BER-uh-nof), village, SE Alaska, on Chatham Strait, NE Baranof Isl., 20 mi/32 km E of Sitka. Fish canning.

Baranof Island (BER-uh-nof) (□ 1,607 sq mi/4,162 sq km), SE Alaska, in Alexander Archipelago S of Chichagof Isl., bet. Chatham Strait (E) and Gulf of Alaska (W); center near 57°00′N 135°00′W. Isl. is 100 mi/161 km long, 30 mi/48 km wide; rises to 7,000 ft/2,134 m. Largest town, Sitka. Fishing, fish processing. Settled 1741 by Russians, Baranof Isl. was center of Rus. activity in N. Amer., 1804–1867, and hq. of Rus. fur-trading interest represented by Aleksandr Baranov. Famous for brown bears.

Barataria (ba-ruh-TAR-ee-uh), village (1990 pop. 1,160), Jefferson parish, extreme SE La., on Intracoastal Waterway, 13 mi/21 km S of New Orleans; 29°43′N 90°07′W. Shrimping port. Barataria Oil Field nearby.

Barataria (bah-rah-TAHR-ee-yah), residential suburb, NW Trinidad, Trinidad and Tobago, 2.5 mi/4 km E of Port of Spain. Agr. area (coconuts, fruit); lime-oil factory.

Barataria Bay (bar-uh-TER-ee-uh), SE La., separated from the Gulf of Mexico by Grand Isle and Grand Terre Isl., as well as other isls.; 29°22′N 89°56′W. Linked to Intracoastal Waterway to N by Bayou St. Denis. The bay is the major center of the La. shrimp industry and is trapped for muskrat furs. Oil and natural gas wells in area; bay region a major source of sulphur. In the early 19th cent. the bay was the hq. of Jean Laffite and his pirates.

Barbados (bahr-BAI-duhs), island state (□ 166 sq mi/430 sq km; 1990 est. pop. 260,000), in the West Indies; ⊙ Bridgetown; 13°10′N 59°33′W. The isl., E of St. Vincent, in the Windward Isls., is low and rises gradually toward its highest point at Mt. Hillaby (1,104 ft/340 m). Although there is ample rainfall from June to Dec., there are no rivers, and water must be pumped from subterranean caverns. The porous soil and moderate warmth are excellent for the cultivation of sugarcane, which was historically the isl.'s main occupation. The healthful and equable climate makes it a very popular tourist resort (tourism is the country's largest industry). Mfg. and banking are growing sectors of the economy. Although it was probably originally inhabited by Arawaks, it was uninhabited when Eng. expeditionaries 1st settled there in 1627 (1605, according to local tradition). Barbados remained a Br. colony until independence was granted in 1966. During the 19th cent. it was the administrative hq. of the Windward Isls., but in 1885 it became a separate colony. It was a member of the short-lived Federation of the West Indies (1958–1962). The isl. has a parliamentary form of govt. It is a member of the Commonwealth of Nations, the Organization of Amer. States, the Caribbean Community, and the UN.

Barbados Wildlife Reserve, St. Peter's parish, NE Barbados. Preserved mahogany forest run by Barbados Natl. Trust with flora and fauna, notably green Afr. monkeys brought to isl. in late 17th cent. Grenade Hall, a restored 19th-cent. semaphore signal station, and Farley Hill Park, with a partially ruined plantation house, are nearby.

Barbary Coast, waterfront area of San Francisco, Calif., on San Francisco Bay; extends S from downtown San Francisco. In the years after the 1849 gold rush, gamblers, gangsters, prostitutes, and confidence men flourished, and the brothels, saloons, and disreputable boardinghouses made the Barbary Coast — named after the pirate coast of N Afr. — notorious throughout the world.

Barber, county (□ 1,136 sq mi/2,942 sq km; 1990 pop. 5,874), S Kansas, Red Hills region, bordered S by Okla., drained by Medicine Lodge R. and Salt Fork Arkansas R.; ⊙ Medicine Lodge; 37°13′N 98°40′W. Cattle, wheat, sorghum. Gas, gypsum mines. Barber State Fishing L. in NE. Formed 1873.

Barbers Point, SW end of Oahu, Honolulu co., Hawaii, 8 mi/12.9 km W of Pearl Harbor, 13 mi/21 km W of Honolulu; 21°18′N 158°06′W. Barbers Point Naval Air Station 2 mi/3.2 km to E; oil refinery. Offshore mooring for oil tankers. Barbers Point Beach to E. Barbers Point Harbor to N.

Barberton, city (1990 pop. 27,623), Summit co., NE Ohio, an industrial suburb of Akron, on the Tuscarawas R.; 41°01′N 81°37′W. Rubber prods., metal and iron works, boilers, and insulation are mfg. L. Anna highlights the city's center. Inc. 1892.

Barbour 1 (BAHR-buhr), county (□ 904 sq mi/2,341 sq km; 1990 pop. 25,417), SE Ala., in Black Belt, bounded on E by Chattahoochee R. and Ga., on W by Pea R.; ⊙ Clayton and Eufala. Cotton, peanuts, corn; livestock; textiles. Founded 1832. **2** county (□ 343 sq mi/883 sq km; 1990 pop. 15,699), N W.Va.; ⊙ Philippi; 39°07′N 80°00′W. On Allegheny Plateau; includes part of Laurel Ridge; drained by Tygart R; includes part of Tygart R. Reservoir and Tygart L. State Park on N border. Coal mining. Agr. (honey, corn, alfalfa, hay); cattle, hogs, poultry, sheep; dairying. Timber; natural gas and oil wells. Some mfg. at Philippi. Part of Audra State Park on S border; Teten Creek Wildlife Management Area in E. Formed 1843.

Barbourmeade (BAHR-buhr-meed), residential suburb (1990 pop. 1,402) of Louisville, Jefferson co., N Ky., 9 mi/14.5 km ENE of downtown; 38°17′N 85°35′W.

Barboursville, town (1990 pop. 2,774), on Guyandotte R., at mouth of Mud R., 8 mi/12.9 km E of Huntington, W W.Va. Agr. (corn, tobacco); cattle; poultry. Mfg. (apparel, machinery). Coal, natural gas, and oil nearby. State hosp. Toll House log cabin (1837). Berch Fork State Park and Berch Fork L. Wildlife Management Area to SW. Chartered 1813.

Barboursville, uninc. village (1990 pop. 125), Orange co., N central Va., on RR, 15 mi/24 km NE of Charlottesville; 38°23′N 82°17′W. Mfg. (wine, lumber, furniture); in agr. region (livestock; dairying; grain, soybeans, grapes).

Barbourville (BAHR-buhr-vil), town (1990 pop. 3,658), ⊙ Knox co., SE Ky., in the Cumberland Mts., on Cumberland R., 21 mi/34 km NNW of Middlesboro; 36°52′N 83°52′W. In region producing bituminous coal; horses; tobacco; mfg. (wood prods., lumber, machinery, apparel, meat processing, coal processing, printing and publishing). Seat of Union Col. Dr. Thomas Walker State Historic Site to SW, containing replica of 1st cabin built by white settlers (1750) in Ky. Est. 1799.

Barbuda (bar-BEW-dah), island (□ 68 sq mi/176 sq km; 1991 pop. 1,241), dependency and parish of Antigua and Barbuda Republic, West Indies, 27 mi/43 km N of Antigua; 17°38′N 61°48′W. Codrington Lagoon is the habitat of frigate and other birds. Small-scale agr. production of cotton, bananas, coconuts, pineapple; wild sheep, deer, boar, ducks, guinea fowl, horses, donkeys. Tourism mainstay of economy; 2 full-service resorts, a 3d is planned. Sustained considerable damage from Hurricane Luis in Sept. 1995; ¾ of the buildings were affected.

Barca, La, Mexico: see LA BARCA.

Barcelona, village (1990 pop. 90), Chautauqua co., extreme W N.Y., on L. Erie, 16 mi/26 km SW of Dunkirk; 42°20′N 79°36′W.

Barceloneta (bahr-se-lo-NAI-tai), town (1990 pop. 20,947), N P.R., landing on Manatí R., near the coast,

27 mi/43 km W of San Juan. Important industrial area mfg. (clothing, chemical prods., electronics, pharmaceuticals, fruit juices). Tourism. W is Cambalache Forest Reserve. The village of Palmas Altas is 3 mi/4.8 km NW.

Barclay, town (1990 pop. 170), Queen Annes co., E Md., 18 mi/29 km W of Dover, Del.; 39°08′N 75°52′W. Inc. 1931.

Barden Reservoir, bet. Foster and Scituate municipalities, Providence co., R.I. Middle reservoir in a chain beginning in N with Ponaganset Reservoir. Then connected by Ponaganset R., which flows S to Barden Reservoir, which is then further connected to the Scituate Reservoir, largest reservoir in R.I. The valley now flooded was known as the Moswansicut R. Valley, which was paralleled by Indian trails, and, in the summer, covered with Indian cornfields.

Bardo (BAHRD-o), village, Harlan co., SE Ky., 5 mi/8 km S of Harlan, near Yellow R. Coal mining.

Bardolph, village (1990 pop. 301), McDonough co., W Ill., 5 mi/8 km ENE of Macomb; 40°30′N 90°33′W. In agr. area (corn, sorghum; cattle, hogs).

Bardstown, town (1990 pop. 6,801), ⊙ Nelson co., central Ky., SE of Louisville; 37°48′N 85°27′W. Elev. 647 ft/197 m. In a rich farm area (burley tobacco, grain, soybeans; livestock; dairying). The city is known for its distilleries, thus its nickname "Bourbon Capital of the World." RR spur terminus. Mfg. (consumer goods, beverages, furniture, bldg. materials, electrical equip., metal fabrication, plastics, printing and publishing). A monument to Amer. steamboat inventor (1791) John Fitch is in Bardstown. My Old Kentucky Home State Park., 1 mi/1.6 km to E, has "Federal Hill," home of Judge John Rowan (built c.1818), where his cousin Stephen Foster was inspired to write the song "My Old Kentucky Home" in 1952; Bernheim Arboretum and Research Forest to NW. Of note are the Cathedral of St. Joseph (1816–1819), whose paintings were given by Louis Philippe of France, and the Gethsemani Farms Trappist monastery (1848) to SW. The Barton Mus. of Whiskey History is a short distance away, distillery tours, to S. In the Civil War, Bardstown was occupied (Sept. 1862) by Gen. Braxton Bragg's Confederate army. Settled 1775, inc. 1780.

Bardwell, town (1990 pop. 819), ⊙ Carlisle co., SW Ky., 28 mi/45 km WSW of Paducah; 36°52′N 89°00′W. Trade center for agr. area (livestock; grain, dark and burley tobacco, apples; dairying); mfg. (ceramic lamps, light mfg.). Mississippi R. 5 mi/8 km to W.

Bardwell, village (1990 pop. 387), Ellis co., N Texas, 17 mi/27 km NW of Corsicana; 32°16′N 96°42′W. Agr. area. Bardwell L. (Waxahachie Creek) to NE.

Bardwell Lake, reservoir, Ellis co., NE central Texas, on Waxahachie Creek, 5 mi/8 km S of Ennis; 8 mi/12.9 km long; 32°15′N 96°38′W. Max. capacity 268,400 acre-ft. Formed by Bardwell Dam (78 ft/24 m high), built (1965) by the Army Corps of Engineers for flood control and water supply.

Bareville (BER-vil), uninc. town (1990 pop. 1,250), Lancaster co., SE Pa., residential suburb, 7 mi/11.3 km NE of Lancaster; 40°05′N 76°09′W. Mfg. includes burial vaults and caskets.

Barge Canal, N.Y.: see NEW YORK STATE BARGE CANAL.

Bargersville (BAHR-gers-vil), town (1990 pop. 1,681), Johnson co., central Ind., 7 mi/11.3 km NW of Franklin; 39°31′N 86°10′W. Agr. area; mfg. (wood furniture, robotics, machinery).

Baring (BER-ing), town (1990 pop. 182), Knox co., NE Mo., near South Fabius R., 6 mi/9.7 km N of Edina; 40°14′N 92°12′W.

Baring, Cape (BAI-ring), SW Victoria Isl., SW Franklin Dist., N.W.T., Canada, on Amundsen Gulf; W extremity of Wollaston Peninsula, at entrance of Prince Albert Sound; 70°01′N 116°58′W.

Bark River, c.55 mi/89 km long, SE Wis.; rises in SW Washington co.; flows SW through Nagawicka L., in small lake region, past Hartland, receives Scuppernong R. 4 mi/6.4 km N of Whitewater, continues W to Rock R., E of Fort Atkinson.

Barker, village (1990 pop. 569), Niagara co., W N.Y.,

35 mi/56 km NNE of Buffalo; 43°19′N 78°32′W. In fruit-growing area.

Barker Heights, town (1990 pop. 1,137), Henderson co., W N.C., residential suburb 2 mi/3.2 km SE of Hendersonville; 35°18′N 82°26′W.

Barker Point, N.Y.: see MANHASSET NECK.

Barker Ten Mile, uninc. town (1990 pop. 1,087), Robeson co., SE N.C., residential suburb 4 mi/6.4 km N of Lumberton; 34°40′N 78°59′W.

Barkerville, village, S central B.C., Canada, in Cariboo Mts., 80 mi/129 km SE of Prince George; 53°04′N 121°31′W. Tourism. Historic reconstruction. Former gold, silver mining. Gold rush 1858. Was terminal of Cariboo Wagon Road, built 1862–1865 from Ashcroft and Yale. Barkerville Prov. Historic Park here. Gateway to Bowron L. Prov. Park.

Barkeyville (BAHR-klee-vil), borough (1990 pop. 274), Venango co., NW Pa., 6 mi/9.7 km ENE of Grove City, at the source of North Branch Slippery Rock Creek; 41°12′N 79°58′W. Agr. includes dairying; livestock; corn, hay.

Barkhamsted, town (1990 pop. 3,369), Litchfield co., N Conn., 18 mi/29 km NW of Hartford, and on West and East branches of Farmington R.; 41°55′N 72°58′W. Dam on East Branch, here, forms Barkhamsted Reservoir (8 mi/12.9 km long). Includes villages of Pleasant Valley and Riverton (Hitchcock chairs made here after 1818). State forests. Inc. 1779.

Barkhamsted Reservoir (□ 4 sq mi/10.4 sq km), Litchfield co., E Conn., on East Branch of Farmington R., 11 mi/18 km NE of Torrington; 41°55′N 72°57′W. Max. capacity 113,000 acre-ft. Extends N to Mass. border. Formed by Sayville Dam (135 ft/41 m high), built for water supply.

Barkley, Lake, reservoir, SW Ky. and NW Tenn., on Cumberland R., formed by Barkley Dam (completed 1966), on Lyon/Livingston co. line, Ky., 23 mi/37 km E of Paducah, and 3 mi/4.8 km E of Kentucky Dam (Tennessee R.); c.60 mi/97 km long; 37°02′N 88°13′W. Lake extends E to Eddyville, then S through Lyon and Trigg cos., Ky., and Stewart co., Tenn., past Dover, Tenn. Max. capacity 2,082,000 acre-ft. Little R. forms 8-mi/12.9-km E arm. Lake parallels Kentucky L. reservoir (Tennesse R.) c.7 mi/11.3 km to W; land between the Lakes Recreation Area (managed by TVA) is bet. Short channel connects the lakes just above (S of) their respective dams. Cumberland City, Tenn., at S tip. Surrounded by natural reserves, including Cross Creeks Natl. Wildlife Refuge (S). Towns of Eddyville and Kuttawa, Ky., were moved (c. 1960) to allow for flooding of lake. Hydroelectricity, part of TVA system; recreation. Lake is c.60 mi/97 km long, 2 mi/3.2 km wide.

Barkley Sound, inlet (16 mi/26 km long, 15 mi/24 km wide) of the Pacific, in SW Vancouver Isl., SW B.C., Canada, in herring-fishing area; its head is near 49°00′N 125°00′W. Alberni Canal extends NE. Broken Group Isls. (includes Effingham Isls.) dot the sound; part of Pacific Rim Natl. Park. Fishing centers are Ucluelet and Bamfield, Port Alberni (at end of Alberni Inlet); there are fish-reduction plants at small settlements of Ecoole, Kildonan, Sarita River, Port Albion. Bamfield, transpacific cable terminal (1902-1959), is on S shore.

Barksdale 1 uninc. village (1990 pop. 617), Edwards co., SW Texas, on Edwards Plateau, on Nueces R., 38 mi/61 km NNW of Uvalde. Trading point in ranching area (Angora goats, sheep, cattle); oil and gas. **2** village (1990 pop. 756), Bayfield co., extreme N Wis., on SW shore of Chequamegon Bay, 4 mi/6.4 km NW of Ashland; 46°37′N 91°04′W. Produces chemicals and explosives.

Barksdale Air Force Base, La.: see SHREVEPORT.

Barlow 1 village (1990 pop. 706), Ballard co., W Ky., 25 mi/40 km W of Paducah; 37°02′N 89°02′W. Agr. area (tobacco, grain, soybeans; livestock; dairying); timber; mfg. (metal bipods). Ballard Co. Wildlife Management Area to N, Peal Wildlife Management Area to W; small lakes in area. Confluence of Ohio and Mississippi rivers 6 mi/9.7 km to SW. **2** village (1990 pop. 118), Clackamas co., NW Oregon, 9 mi/14.5 km SW of Oregon City; 45°15′N 122°43′W.

Barnabus, uninc. village (1990 pop. 500), Logan co., SW W.Va., 8 mi/12.9 km S of Logan, in coal-mining region.

Barnaby Island (3 mi/5 km long), E Que., Canada, in the St. Lawrence R., just off Rimouski.

Barnard 1 town (1990 pop. 234), Nodaway co., NW Mo., on One Hundred and Two R., and 12 mi/19 km S of Maryville; 40°10′N 94°49′W. **2** town (1990 pop. 872), Windsor co., central Vt., 9 mi/14.5 km NW of Woodstock; 43°43′N 72°37′W. Summer resort.

Barnard (BAHR-nahrd), village (1990 pop. 129), Lincoln co., N central Kansas, on Salt Creek of Solomon R., 11 mi/18 km NE of Lincoln; 39°11′N 98°02′W. Livestock; grain.

Barnard (BAHRN-uhrd), township, Piscataquis co., central Maine, 10 mi/16 km NE of Dover-Foxcroft. Includes village of Barnard.

Barnard, Mount (13,990 ft/4,264 m), E Calif., on Tulare/Inyo co. line, in the Sierra Nevada, c.4 mi/6.4 km NNW of Mt. Whitney, and on E boundary of Sequoia Natl. Park; 36°37′N 118°19′W.

Barnegat (BAHR-nuh-guht), township (1990 pop. 12,235), Ocean co., E N.J., 2 mi/3.2 km inland from Barnegat Bay, 13 mi/21 km S of Toms River; 39°46′N 74°16′W. Barnegat Lighthouse State Park to E.

Barnegat Bay (BAHR-nuh-guht), arm of the Atlantic Ocean, c.30 mi/50 km long, E N.J., entered through Barnegat Inlet bet. Long Beach Isl. and Isl. Beach Peninsula. A floating light 15 mi/24 km off the coast now alerts travelers since the lighthouse retired from service. The Barnegat Lighthouse is now part of a state park.

Barnegat Light (BAHR-nuh-guht), borough (1990 pop. 675), Ocean co., E N.J., at N end of Long Beach isl., on Barnegat Inlet (entrance to Barnegat Bay), and 14 mi/23 km SSE of Toms River; 39°45′N 74°06′W. Fishing. Site of abandoned Barnegat Lighthouse (1855), replaced (1930) by lightship, then replaced by a "Texas Tower," which was destroyed by a storm; 2 tower attendants died in the storm. A floating light 15 mi/24 km off the coast now serves as beacon. It is now a state park. Formerly Barnegat City.

Barnes, county (☐ 1,513 sq mi/3,919 sq km; 1990 pop. 12,545), SE N.Dak.; ⊙ Valley City; 46°55′N 98°04′W. Agr. area drained by Sheyenne R. Wheat, oats, barley, potatoes, soybeans, other grains; flax; livestock, hogs; flour milling, dairy prods. Metal stampings, electronic equip. L. Clausen Springs in S; L. Ashtabula Reservoir in N, formed by Bald Hill Dam NW of Valley City; Fox and Eckelson lakes in W. There are 2 fish hatcheries near Bald Hill Dam. Organized 1879.

Barnes, village (1990 pop. 167), Washington co., N Kansas, 13 mi/21 km SE of Washington; 39°42′N 96°52′W. Grain; dairying.

Barnes City, town (1990 pop. 221), on Mahaska-Poweshiek co. line, S central Iowa, near South Fork English R., 17 mi/27 km NNE of Oskaloosa; 41°30′N 92°28′W.

Barnesboro (BAHRNS-buhr-o), borough (1990 pop. 2,530), Cambria co., W central Pa., 25 mi/40 km NNE of Johnstown, 1 mi/1.6 km NW of Spangler, on West Branch of Susquehanna R.; 40°40′N 78°46′W. Mfg. (apparel, commercial printing, bottled water); bituminous coal; crushed stone. Laid out 1891, inc. 1893.

Barneston (BAHR-nez-tuhn), village (1990 pop. 122), Gage co., SE Nebr., 17 mi/27 km SSE of Beatrice, and on Big Blue R., near Kansas line; 40°02′N 96°34′W.

Barnesville, city (1990 pop. 4,747), ⊙ Lamar co., W central Ga., 13 mi/21 km SSE of Griffin; 33°03′N 84°10′W. Trade and processing center for agr. and timber area; mfg. of clothing, motor vehicle parts, furniture, lumber. Gordon Military Col., a unit of Univ. System of Ga., here. Settled c.1825, inc. 1854.

Barnesville 1 town (1990 pop. 170), Montgomery co., central Md., 25 mi/40 km NW of Washington, D.C.; 39°13′N 77°23′W. Nearby is the Al Marah Arabian horse farm and mus., reputedly the largest privately owned one in world. Named for William Barnes, a local landowner who later moved to Ohio and founded Barnesville in Belmont co. A mass grave of working men who died of cholera building the Chesapeake and Ohio Canal is in the yard of St. Mary's Church here. **2** town (1990 pop. 2,066), Clay co., W Minn., 24 mi/39 km SE of Fargo (N.Dak.), in Red R. valley; 46°38′N 96°25′W. Shipping point for agr. area (grain, potatoes; livestock; dairying); mfg. (concrete). RR shops. Barnesville Wildlife Area to NE.

Barnesville, village (1990 pop. 4,326), Belmont co., E Ohio, 26 mi/42 km WSW of Wheeling (W.Va.); 39°61′N 81°11′W. Mfg. (glass, machinery).

Barnet, town (1990 pop. 1,415), Caledonia co., NE Vt., on the Conn. R. (site of Comerford Dam, with large power plant; bridged to N.H.), 8 mi/12.9 km S of St. Johnsbury; 44°19′N 72°04′W. Includes villages of West Barnet (resort on Harvey Pond), East Barnet, and Passumpsic, on Passumpsic R. Light mfg.; wood prods., dairy. Settled 1770.

Barnet (BAHR-nit), village, SW B.C., Canada, on Burrard Inlet, 14 mi/23 km E of Vancouver, on Barnet Highway (Expressway); 49°18′N 122°57′W. Lumber-shipping port. Now part of city of Burnaby.

Barnett 1 (bahr-NET), town (1990 pop. 215), Morgan co., central Mo., near L. of the Ozarks, 10 mi/16 km ESE of Versailles; 38°22′N 92°40′W. **2** uninc. town (1990 pop. 3,052), Harris co., SE Texas, residential suburb 22 mi/35 km ENE of downtown Houston, near San Jacinto R.

Barneveld 1 (BAHR-nuh-veld), village (1990 pop. 272), Oneida co., N N.Y., 13 mi/21 km NNE of Utica; 43°17′N 75°11′W. Light mfg. Nearby, in Steuben Memorial Park, is the reconstructed log cabin and the grave of Baron von Steuben. **2** (BAHR-ne-veld), village (1990 pop. 660), Iowa co., S Wis., 26 mi/42 km WSW of Madison; 43°00′N 89°54′W. In dairying region. Blue Mound State Park is to NE. On Military Ridge State Trail. Lost River Cave to E.

Barney, town, Brooks co., S Ga., 18 mi/29 km NW of Valdosta; 31°00′N 83°30′W.

Barnhart, uninc. village (1990 pop. 135), Irion co., W Texas, 50 mi/80 km. SW of San Angelo. Livestock-shipping point.

Barnhart (BAHRN-hahrt), uninc. residential suburb (1990 pop. 4,911) of St. Louis, Jefferson co., E Mo., 24 mi/39 km S of downtown; 38°19′N 90°24′W. On Mississippi R. Mastodon State Park is to N. Mfg. (medical supplies).

Barnhart Island, St. Lawrence co., N N.Y., in the St. Lawrence R., at Ont. (Canada) line, 5 mi/8 km NE of Massena; 45°01′N 75°50′W. Isl. is c.3 mi/4.8 km long, ½ mi/⅘ km–1.5 mi/2.4 km wide.

Barnhill, village (1990 pop. 313), Tuscarawas co., E Ohio, 5 mi/8 km ESE of New Philadelphia; 40°27′N 81°22′W.

Barnsdall, town (1990 pop. 1,316), Osage co., N Okla., 12 mi/19 km SE of Pawhuska, on Bird Creek; 36°33′N 96°09′W. In livestock-raising area; mfg. (mircocrystalline waxes); oil and natural-gas deposits. Woolaroc Mus. to N; Birch L. reservoir to S. Called Bigheart until 1921.

Barnstable, county (☐ 1,305 sq mi/3,380 sq km; 1990 pop. 186,605), SE Mass., coextensive with Cape Cod; ⊙ Barnstable; 41°43′N 70°15′W. Co. airport in Hyannis. Summer resort area with many fine beaches; its small winter pop. is swelled by a great influx of summer visitors and residents. Plastic prods., concrete prods., machinery, navigation equip. Some agr., mostly in S; large quantities of cranberries are grown. Some fishing, particularly at Provincetown. In early 19th cent. a shipbuilding, shipping, and whaling center. Business center, Hyannis. Formed 1685.

Barnstable, town (1990 pop. 40,949), ⊙ Barnstable co., SE Mass., 26 mi/42 km SE of Plymouth; 41°40′N 70°21′W. Resort town on Cape Cod. Industries are tourism, fishing, and cranberry farming. Barnstable comprises 7 villages, including Hyannis. Points of interest include the home of the Revolutionary War patriot James Otis, in West Barnstable; the John F. Kennedy Memorial, in Hyannis; the Sturgis Lib., the oldest public lib. bldg. in the U.S. (1644); and several 18th-cent. bldgs. Sandy Neck Beach and lighthouse. From colonial times until the middle of the 19th cent., Barnstable had a prosperous coastal and overseas shipping trade. Includes villages of Centerville (1990 pop. 9,190); Cotuit (1990 pop. 2,364), resort town which used to have fishing and shellfishing industries; Cummington; Marston Mills (1990 pop. 8,017); Osterville (1990 pop. 2,911); Santuit; West Barnstable (1990 pop. 1,508), site of historic West Parish Meetinghouse; and Wianno, resort area. Inc. 1639.

Barnstead (BARN-sted), town (1990 pop. 3,100), Belknap co., E central N.H., 17 mi/27 km NE of Concord; 43°21′N 71°15′W. Drained by Suncook and Big rivers. Vegetables, corn, nursery crops, apples, berries; cattle, poultry; dairying; timber. Mfg. (machining, pine lumber). Upper and Lower Suncook L. in NW, Locke L. and Halfmoon L. in N.

Barnum, town (1990 pop. 174), Webster co., central Iowa, 9 mi/14.5 km W of Fort Dodge; 42°30′N 94°21′W. Livestock, grain.

Barnum 1 (BAHR-nuhm), village, SW Alaska, near Kuskokwim Bay, 20 mi/32 km NE of Platinum. Platinum mining. **2** village (1990 pop. 482), Carlton co., NE Minn., on Moose R., 33 mi/53 km SW of Duluth; 46°30′N 92°41′W. Dairying; poultry; oats, alfalfa; light mfg. Moose L. State Park to SW.

Barnwell, county (☐ 557 sq mi/1,443 sq km; 1990 pop. 20,293), SW S.C., bounded SW by Savannah R., NE by South Fork of Edisto R.; ⊙ Barnwell; 33°15′N 81°26′W. Includes most of U.S. Atomic Energy Commission installation along Savannah R. Agr. includes chickens, eggs, hogs, cattle; dairying; corn, wheat, rye, oats, soybeans, peanuts, hay, cotton, watermelons, asparagus, cucumbers, peaches. Naval stores. Formed 1785.

Barnwell, town (1990 pop. 5,255), ⊙ Barnwell co., W S.C., 33 mi/53 km SW of Orangeburg; 33°14′N 81°22′W. In agr. area that produces livestock; dairying; cotton, peanuts, peaches. Settled 1798, inc. 1842.

Baroda (buh-RO-duh), village (1990 pop. 657), Berrien co., extreme SW Mich., 10 mi/16 km S of St. Joseph, near L. Michigan; 41°57′N 86°29′W. In orchard and farm area. Mfg. (bldg. materials, fabricated metal prods.).

Baron, village, Adair co., E Okla., 8 mi/12.9 km N of Stilwell, near Ark. line.

Baron Bluff, headland on N St. Croix Isl., U.S. Virgin Isls., 5.5 mi/8.9 km NW of Christiansted; 17°47′N 64°47′W. Rises to 395 ft/120 m.

Barons, village (1991 pop. 262), S Alta., Canada, 24 mi/39 km NNW of Lethbridge; 49°59′N 113°05′W. Wheat; dairying.

Barr Lake, reservoir (☐ 3 sq mi/7.8 sq km), Adams co., N central Colo., on Beebe Draw, 13 mi/21 km NE of Denver, and N of Denver Internatl. Airport; 39°57′N 104°45′W. Max. capacity 41,800 acre-ft. Formed by Barr Dam (44 ft/13 m high), built (1893) for irrigation.

Barra Strait, narrow passage (3 mi/5 km long) bet. Bras d'Or L. and Great Bras d'Or, NE N.S., Canada, in central Cape Breton Isl., 10 mi/16 km SSW of Baddeck.

Barrackville, town (1990 pop. 1,443), Marion co., N W.Va., suburb 2 mi/3.2 km NW of Fairmont, on Buffalo Creek; 39°30′N 80°10′W. Agr. (corn, apples); livestock. Buffalo Creek Covered Bridge is here.

Barranca de Oblatos (bah-RAHN-ka de o-BLAHT-os), gorge of Santiago R., Jalisco, central Mexico, near Guadalajara; c.2,000 ft/610 m deep. Tourist site.

Barranquitas (bahr-rahn-KEE-tahs), town (1990 pop. 25,605), central P.R., summer hill-town resort in Cordillera Central, 18 mi/29 km WSW of Caguas. Elev. c.2,000 ft/610 m; has 500-ft/152-m-high cliffs. The San Cristobal Canyon or Cañón de San Cristobal (ka-NYON dai san chris-TOH-bal), with its spectacular cliffs and waterfalls, is a major attraction. Industrial and commercial area, light mfg. Agr. (plantains, coffee, citrus fruit). Tourism; mus. Burial place of Luis Muñoz Marín, the 1st elected governor of P.R.; and of his father, Louis Muñoz Rivera, one of the most influential politicians in P.R. at the beginning of the 20th cent.

Barraute (bah-ROT), village (1991 pop. 1,177), W Que., Canada, 24 mi/39 km ESE of Amos. Gold mining, lumbering, woodworking.

Barre (BER-ee), city (1990 pop. 9,482), Washington co., central Vt., SE of Montpelier; 44°12′N 72°30′W. Granite quarrying, which began in the region in the early 19th cent., is still important; city calls itself "granite capital of the world." Mfg. of RR equip., machines, and machine tools. Barre is a center for winter sports, hunting, and fishing. Settled late 18th cent., inc. 1894.

Barre (BAHR), town (1990 pop. 4,546), Worcester co., central Mass., near Ware R., 18 mi/29 km NW of Worcester; 42°25'N 72°07'W. Machine shop/tools; dairying. Has fine old houses. Includes villages of White Valley and South Barre. Settled c.1720, inc. 1774.

Barre Falls Reservoir, Worcester co., N central Mass., on Ware R., 16 mi/26 km NW of Worcester; 42°26'N 72°02'W. Max. capacity 63,000 acre-ft. Formed by Barre Falls Dam (64 ft/20 m high), built (1958) by Army Corps of Engineers for flood control.

Barren, county (☐ 499 sq mi/1,292 sq km; 1990 pop. 34,001), S Ky.; ⊙ Glasgow; 36°57'N 85°55'W. Bounded SW by Barren R.; drained by Beaver and Skaggs creeks. Agr. area (hogs, cattle, poultry; burley tobacco, hay, alfalfa, soybeans, wheat, corn); oil and gas wells, hardwood timber, stone quarries. Some mfg. (especially clothing) at Glasgow. Part of Mammoth Cave Natl. Park in NW corner; Diamond Caverns and Crystal Onyx Cave also in NW; other limestone caves in co., esp. in North Barren R. L. reservoir and State Resort Park on SW boundary. Formed 1798.

Barren Islands, group of 6 small islands, S Alaska, in NW part of Gulf of Alaska, bet. Kenai Peninsula (N) and Afognak Isl. (S), at mouth of Cook Inlet; 58°57'N 152°09'W. Largest is Ushagat Isl. (7 mi/11.3 km long); rises to 1,495 ft/456 m.

Barren Lands, Canada: see BARREN GROUNDS.

Barren Mountains, Calif.: see CHOCOLATE MOUNTAINS.

Barren River, 130 mi/209 km long, S Ky.; formed in Monroe co., SW of Tompkinsville by junction of East and West forks. Flows generally NW through Barren R. L. reservoir and Bowling Green to Green R., just E of Woodbury. East fork rises in NE Monroe co.; flows c.20 mi/32 km SW; West Fork rises in W Clay co., N Tenn.; flows c.15 mi/24 km NW.

Barren River Lake, reservoir, on Barren/Allen co. border, S Ky., on Barron R., 19 mi/31 km ESE of Bowling Green; c.18 mi/29 km long; 36°54'N 86°07'W. Arms extend into both cos.; Skaggs and Beaver creeks join to form E arms. Max. capacity 815,200 acre-ft. Formed by Barren R. L. Dam (118 ft/36 m high), built by the Army Corps of Engineers for flood control. Barren R. State Resort Park on E shore.

Barrett, village (1990 pop. 350), Grant co., W Minn., 7 mi/11.3 km SE of Elbow L. town, on W side of Barrett L.; 45°54'N 95°53'W. Dairying; livestock; grain, sugar beets, sunflowers; mfg. (machinery, silk screening).

Barrett Dam, Calif.: see COTTONWOOD CREEK.

Barrhead, town (1991 pop. 4,160), central Alta., Canada, on Paddle R., near its mouth on Pembina R., 50 mi/80 km NW of Edmonton; 54°07'N 114°24'W. Lumber and flour milling; dairying; mixed farming.

Barrie, city (1991 pop. 62,728), S Ont., Canada, on the W shore of L. Simcoe; 44°23'N 79°42'W. It is a commuter city in the Toronto metropolitan area. Diverse mfg. includes clothing, spirits, electronics, and leather goods. A large military base is nearby.

Barrie Island (8 mi/13 km long, 5 mi/8 km wide), S central Ont., Canada, one of the Manitoulin Isls., in North Channel of L. Huron, just off N shore of Manitoulin Isl., 5 mi/8 km W of Gore Bay; 45°55'N 82°40'W. Dairying; mixed farming.

Barrington 1 town (1990 pop. 6,164), Strafford co., SE N.H., 9 mi/14.5 km WNW of Dover; 43°13'N 71°02'W. Drained by Isinglass R.; Swains L., Menduns L. in S. Nursery crops, corn, apples; cattle; dairying. Mfg. (machinery). **2** town (1990 pop. 15,849), Bristol co., E R.I., on the Barrington R.; 41°45'N 71°19'W. Settled c.1670 and named for Lord Barrington, an Eng. theologian who advocated religious toleration, included in Mass. until 1746, inc. 1770. It is a residential and resort area. Barrington Col. is here.

Barrington, village (1990 pop. 9,504), Cook and Lake cos., NE Ill., suburb 32 mi/51 km NW of Chicago; 42°08'N 88°07'W. Mfg. (electric equip., machinery, paper prods.). Remnant agr. (grain). Sand, gravel pits. Inc. 1865.

Barrington (ba-RING-tuhn), borough (1990 pop. 6,774), Camden co., SW N.J., 4 mi/6.4 km SE of Camden; 39°52'N 75°02'W. Laid out c.1890, inc. 1917.

Barrington Hills, village (1990 pop. 4,202), Cook, McHenry, Lake, and Kane cos., NE Ill., sprawling residential suburb 34 mi/55 km NW of downtown Chicago, 8 mi/12.9 km NE of Elgin; 42°07'N 88°12'W. Several small lakes in city. Fox R. to NW.

Barrington River (BAR-reeng-tuhn), 15 mi/24 km long, Mass. and R.I.; rises in Seekonk town, SE Mass.; flows S and SSW, through East Providence, R.I., to Warren R., opposite Warren. Small-craft anchorage; boatyards near mouth.

Barrio La Perla (BAHR-ree-o lah PER-lah), neighborhood, NE P.R., N Old San Juan, on steep slope facing the Atlantic Ocean. Inner-city neighborhood made famous by Oscar Lewis's "La vida." Originally a squatter community. In spite of high unemployment and illegal drug trafficking, the community has significantly improved its living standards.

Barron, county (☐ 890 sq mi/2,305 sq km; 1990 pop. 40,750), NW Wis.; ⊙ Barron; 45°25'N 91°50'W. Drained by Red Cedar and Hay rivers. Contains many lakes; largest is Red Cedar L. in NE corner. Dairying (principal industry), cattle, hogs, sheep, hogs, poultry, especially turkey; agr. (potatoes, barley, oats, wheat, corn, peas, alfalfa). Hardscrabble Ski Area in E; W end of Tuscobin State Trail in NE. Formed 1859.

Barron, town (1990 pop. 2,986), ⊙ Barron co., NW Wis., near confluence of Yellow R. and small Vermillion R., 45 mi/72 km NNW of Eau Claire; 45°23'N 91°50'W. Commercial center for farming and dairying area; canning; mfg. (apparel, woodworking, machinery, food processing). Has poultry hatcheries and large cooperative creamery. Bldg. stone is quarried nearby. Founded before 1878; inc. 1887.

Barrón Escandón, Mexico: see APIZACO.

Barrouallie, town (1989 est. pop. 5,469), W St. Vincent, West Indies, 6 mi/9.7 km NW of Kingstown; 13°14'N 61°16'W. Arrowroot, bananas; fishing, whaling.

Barrow, county (☐ 171; 1990 pop. 29,721), NE central Ga.; ⊙ Winder; 33°59'N 83°43'W. Bounded S by Apalachee R. Piedmont agr. area (cotton, corn, hay, sweet potatoes, fruit); textile mfg. Formed 1914.

Barrow, town (1990 pop. 3,469), N Slope borough, N Alaska; 71°16'N 156°48'W. It is the northernmost U.S. settlement and the main trade center of N Alaska. Predominantly Inuit pop. Hunting of whales, employment with govt. agencies (esp. oil-rich North Slope borough), basketry, carving of ivory and bone, and tourism are important. Has a private col.; surrounded by Natl. Petroleum Reserve-Alaska, which extends S to Brooks Range and E to Colville R. Of interest are the nearby Will Rogers–Wiley Post monument and Birnirk, the site of an anc. Eskimo cultural and trade center. Oil fields were found in 1967 in the area of Prudhoe Bay, on the Arctic coast, from which Barrow receives substantial revenues. Inc. 1958.

Barrow, Point, northernmost point of Alaska, on Arctic Ocean, 9 mi/14.5 km NE of Barrow; 71°23'N 156°30'W. Discovered 1826 by F. W. Beechey and named for Sir John Barrow. Has played important part in Arctic exploration and aviation; starting point of Sir Hubert Wilkins's flight (1928) across North Pole. Naval base and research facility was est. 1944, 6 mi/9.7 km S of point, closed in 1970s. U.S. meteorological station set up here during 1st Internatl. Polar Year, 1882–1883.

Barry 1 county (☐ 576 sq mi/1,492 sq km; 1990 pop. 50,057), SW Mich.; ⊙ Hastings; 42°36'N 85°18'W. Drained by Thornapple R. Farm area; cattle, hogs, sheep, poultry; dairy prods.; oats, wheat, soybeans, beans, corn; mfg. electronic equip., industrial machinery, rubber and plastics prods. Mfg. at Hastings. L. resorts. Gun L. is W; Midville Ski area in NW, small lakes throughout co., largest is Gun L., in far W (Yankee Springs State Recreation Area on Gun L.). Organized 1839. **2** (BER-ri), county (☐ 800 sq mi/2,072 sq km; 1990 pop. 27,547), SW Mo., in the Ozarks; ☐ Cassville; 36°42'N 93°49'W. Drained by White R. Apples, grapes, peaches; cattle, turkeys, and broiler chickens, dairy prods., goats; hardwood timber; sport fishing; tourism. Mfg. at Monett and Cassville. Part of Mark Twain Natl. Forest in SE corner; Roaring R. State Park; caverns in area. Formed 1835.

Barry, city (1990 pop. 1,391), Pike co., W Ill., 15 mi/24 km WNW of Pittsfield; 39°42'N 91°02'W. Trade center of agr. area (corn, wheat, hay, apples, cattle, hogs); mfg. (blasting agents). Founded 1836, inc. 1859.

Barry, village (1990 pop. 40), Big Stone co., W Minn., near S.Dak. state line, 19 mi/31 km NNW of Ortonville; 45°33'N 96°33'W. Grain area. Big Stone L. State Park to S.

Barry's Bay, village (1991 pop. 1,088), SE Ont., Canada, at N end of Kamaniskeg L., 35 mi/56 km SW of Pembroke, in lumbering region. Supply center for E part of Algonquin Provincial Park.

Barryton, village (1990 pop. 393), Mecosta co., central Mich., on Chippewa R., 17 mi/27 km ENE of Big Rapids; 43°45'N 85°08'W. In agr. area; poultry hatchery; meat packing.

Barstow, city (1990 pop. 21,472), San Bernardino co., SE Calif., 55 mi/89 km NNE of San Bernardino, on the dry Mojave R. in Mojave Desert; 34°53'N 117°04'W. RR center and junction. Mfg. (aircraft, printing and publishing, consumer goods, medical equip.). RR shops, the Goldstone space tracking station are major employers. Edwards Air Force Base is c.50 mi/80 km W; Fort Irwin Military Reserve is c.35 mi/56 km NE; China L. Naval Weapons Center is c.60 mi/97 km NW; Twentynine Palms Marine Corps Base is c.50 mi/80 km SE. Barstow is an embarkation point for trips into Death Valley c.100 mi/161 km to N. Barstow Col. Calico Ghost Town to E. Founded in the 1880s as a silver-mining town. Inc. 1947.

Barstow, village (1990 pop. 535), Ward co., extreme W Texas, 7 mi/11.3 km E of Pecos, near Pecos R.; 31°27'N 103°23'W. Trading center in irrigated cotton, cattle area; oil and gas, natural-gas processing.

Bartelso (bar-TEL-so), village (1990 pop. 412), Clinton co., S Ill., 10 mi/16 km SW of Carlyle; 38°32'N 89°28'W. In agr., oil-producing area.

Barter Island (5 mi/8 km long, 3 mi/4.8 km wide), NE Alaska, in Arctic Ocean, just off mainland; 70°10'N 143°40'W. Weather station, limit settlement Kaktovik.

Barters Island, Lincoln co., S Maine, 3.5 mi/5.6 km long, in Sheepscot R., just E of Bath. Bridge to mainland.

Bartholomew, county (☐ 409 sq mi/1,059 sq km; 1990 pop. 63,657), S central Ind.; ⊙ Columbus; 39°13'N 85°54'W. Drained by East Fork of White R. and tributaries. Wheat, vegetables, soybeans, corn, tomatoes; hogs, cattle; timber. Mfg. at Columbus. Camp Atterbury in NW corner; Grouse Ridge State Fishing Area in SW; Driftwood State Fishing Area in NW. Formed 1821.

Bartholomew, Bayou, river in Ark. and La., c.300 mi/483 km long; rises S of Pine Bluff in Ark.; flows generally S, into Morehouse parish of La., to Ouachita R. 10 mi/16 km SW of Bastrop.

Bartles, Mount, peak (10,047 ft/3,062 m) in West Tavaputs Plateau, Carbon co., E Utah, 23 mi/37 km ENE of Price; 39°42'N 110°23'W.

Bartlesville, city (1990 pop. 34,256), ⊙ Washington co., 29 mi/47 km N of Tulsa, extends W into Osage Co.; NE Okla., on the Caney R.; 36°44'N 95°57'W. Elev. 715 ft/218 m. RR junction. It is a distribution center for a ranching and rich oil-producing area. Petroleum production, marketing, and research have been major enterprises since the 1st well was tapped in 1897. Mfg. (machinery, publishing and printing, consumer goods, petroleum prods, food, minerals). Of interest are the Price Tower, a concrete and glass bldg. with cantilevered floors, designed by Frank Lloyd Wright; and the Nellie Johnstone oil well, a replica of the 1st commercial oil well in the state. A U.S. Bureau of Mines energy research center is in the city. Woolaroc Mus., art collection, 14 mi/23 km SW; Tom Mix Mus. N at Dewey; Historic Phillips Mansion. Copan L. reservoir to N; Hulah L. reservoir and Wah-Sha-She State Park to NW. Osage Hills State Park to W. Inc. 1897.

Bartlett 1 (BAHRT-let), town (1990 pop. 2,290), Carroll co., E central N.H., on the Saco R., 26 mi/42 km S of Berlin; 44°04'N 71°14'W. Drained by Saco and Ellis rivers. Nursery crops; cattle; dairying; timber. Mfg. (wood prods., machining). Tourism. Town has 2 covered bridges. Story Land and Heritage N.H. theme parks on NE; in White Mts., parts of White Mt. Natl. Forest in N, S, and NE; Sawyer Rock State Picnic Area in W; Attitash-Bear Peak Ski Area and amusement park in S; Mt. Parker (3,015 ft/919 m) in N; Bear Mt. (3,320 ft/ 1,012 m) on S boundary. Settled after 1769, inc. 1790. **2** town (1990 pop. 26,989), Shelby co., SW Tenn., 8 mi/ 13 km NE of Memphis; 35°13'N 89°50'W. Mfg. of glass, medical supplies, computer and office equip. **3** town (1990 pop. 1,439), Williamson and Bell cos., central Texas, 40 mi/64 km NNE of Austin; 30°47'N 97°25'W. Elev. 599 ft/183 m. Trade center in cotton, corn, cattle, wheat. Settled 1882, inc. 1902.

Bartlett 1 village (1990 pop. 19,373), Cook, DuPage, and Kane cos., NE Ill., NW suburb of Chicago, 4 mi/6.4 km SE of Elgin; 41°58'N 88°12'W. **2** village (1990 pop. 107), Labette co., extreme SE Kansas, 20 mi/32 km E of Coffeyville, near Okla. line; 37°02'N 95°12'W. In dairying and agr. region. Mfg. (sorghum syrup). **3** village (1990 pop. 131), ⊙ Wheeler co., NE central Nebr., Sand Hills region, 60 mi/97 km WSW of Norfolk; 41°52'N 98°32'W. Livestock; grain. Pibel L. State Recreation Area to S. **4** village (1990 pop. 92), Ramsey co., NE central N. Dak., 20 mi/32 km ESE of Devils L.; 48°02'N 98°25'W. Stump L. to S.

Bartlett Reservoir, Maricopa co., central Ariz., on Verde R., in Tonto Natl. Forest, 35 mi/56 km NE of Phoenix; 33°49'N 111°36'W. Max. capacity of 1,060,605 acre-ft. Final unit in Salt R. valley-reclamation project. Formed by multiple-arched Bartlett Dam (287 ft/87 m high, 1,063 ft/324 m long; completed 1939); used for irrigation, flood control.

Bartlett Springs, village, Lake co., Calif., in Mendocino Natl. Forest, 10 mi/16 km NE of Clear Lake.

Bartlett Trough, broad-floored depression in Caribbean Sea, bet. Jamaica and Cayman Isls.; 22,788 ft/6,946 m deep; 18°00'N 81°00'W. Sometimes called Cayman Deep.

Bartlett's Ferry Dam, Ga. and Ala.: see CHATTAHOOCHEE RIVER.

Bartley 1 (BAHRT-lee), village (1990 pop. 339), Red Willow co., S Nebr., 15 mi/24 km ENE of McCook (Harry D. Strunk L.); 40°15'N 100°18'W. Livestock; grain. Medicine Creek Recreation Area to N (Frontier co.). **2** uninc. village (1990 pop. 500), McDowell co., S W.Va., on Dry Fork, 10 mi/16 km WSW of Welch, in coal-mining and agr. region.

Bartolomé Masó (bahr-tol-o-MAI mah-SO), sugar-mill town, Granma prov., E Cuba, 15 mi/24 km SE of Manzanillo; 22°10'N 76°55'W. Mill 2 mi/3.2 km S of Paso Malo dam. On Yara R., which forms part of larger Cauto R. valley, the largest hydrological basin in Cuba.

Barton 1 county (□ 900 sq mi/2,331 sq km; 1990 pop. 29,382), central Kansas; ⊙ Great Bend; 38°28'N 98°45'W. Sloping plain, drained (S) by Arkansas R. Wheat, alfalfa, corn; cattle, poultry; food processing. Extensive oil and natural-gas fields. Pawnee Rock State Monument in SW corner. Formed 1872. **2** county (□ 594 sq mi/1,538 sq km; 1990 pop. 11,312), SW Mo.; ⊙ Lamar; 37°30'N 94°20'W. Drained by a branch of Spring R. and by affluents of the Osage. Agr. (wheat, corn, hay, oats, soybeans; livestock; coal deposits. Mfg. at Lamar. Kansas border, Prairie State Park in W. Formed 1855.

Barton 1 town (1990 pop. 530), Allegany co., W Md., in the Alleghenies, and 17 mi/27 km WSW of Cumberland; 39°32'N 79°01'W. In bituminous-coal-mining area. Near Dans Mt. State Park. Named for Barton-on-Humber, the birthplace of the founder, Major Andrew Bruce Shaw. A heavy rainstorm in 1810 exposed "a mountain of coal" in the area known as Potomac Hollow. Mining didn't begin until 1854, though. Inc. 1900. **2** town (1990 pop. 908), including Barton village, Orleans co., N Vt., 13 mi/21 km S of Newport and on Barton R.; 44°45'N 72°10'W. Lumber, furniture; dairy

and maple prods. Winter sports. Includes Crystal Lake (resort) and village of Orleans. Granted 1781, settled 1795.

Barton 1 village (1990 pop. 24), Pierce co., N central N.Dak.,19 mi/31 km NW of Rugby; 48°30'N 100°10'W. Round L. to the SW. **2** village, Belmont co., E Ohio, 8 mi/13 km NW of Bellaire, on small Wheeling Creek.

Barton Hills Village, village (1990 pop. 320), Washtenaw co., SE Mich., residential suburb 2 mi/3.2 km NW of Ann Arbor, on Huron R.; 42°19'N 83°45'W. Agr. to N.

Barton Island, Knox co., S Maine, just W of and bridged to Vinalhaven Isl.; 0.75 mi/1.2 km long.

Barton River, c.15 mi/24 km long, N Vt.; rises in Crystal L. in Barton town; flows N into S Bay of L. Memphremagog at Newport.

Bartons, village, St. Catherine parish, S Jamaica, 12 mi/ 19 km W of Spanish Town; 18°02'N 77°08'W. Mfg. of cassava starch.

Bartonville, village (1990 pop. 5,643), Peoria co., central Ill., near junction of Illinois R. and Kickapoo Creek, just SSW of Peoria; 40°38'N 89°39'W. In agr. and bituminous-coal-mining area; steel-fabricating plant. Inc. 1903.

Bartow (BAHR-to), county (□ 476 sq mi/1,233 sq km; 1990 pop. 55,911), NW Ga.; ⊙ Cartersville; 34°07'N 84°44'W. Valley and ridge area drained by Etowah R., containing Allatoona Dam in E. Mining includes barite and limestone; mfg.of rugs, textiles, lumber). Agr. includes hay, sweet potatoes, fruit; cattle, hogs, and poultry. Formed 1832.

Bartow (BAR-to), town (□ 8 sq mi/20.7 sq km; 1990 pop. 14,716), ⊙ Polk co., central Fla.; 27°53'N 85°37'W. The economy is based on the production of phosphate and the raising of citrus fruit and cattle. Bartow was est. in 1853 on the site of a fort built in the Seminole War. Inc. 1882.

Bartow 1 (BAHR-to), village (1990 pop. 292), Jefferson co., E Ga., 9 mi/14.5 km SSW of Louisville, in farm area; 32°53'N 82°28'W. Mfg. includes cotton processing. **2** uninc. village, Pocahontas co., SE W.Va., 27 mi/43 km NNE of Marlinton, on Greenbriar R. Timber. Limestone. Mfg. (lumber, post and RR fencing). In Monongahela Natl. Forest.

Barwick, village (1990 pop. 385), Thomas and Brooks cos., S Ga., 16 mi/26 km ENE of Thomasville; 30°53'N 83°44'W. Mfg. of clothing.

Basalt, town (1990 pop. 1,128), Eagle co., W central Colo., on Roaring Fork R., just N of Elk Mts., 20 mi/ 32 km SE of Glenwood Springs; 39°22'N 107°01'W. Elev. 6,624 ft/2,019 m. Cattle; mfg. (cabinets, fabricated metal prods.), timber. Parts of White R. Natl. Forest to NE and SW at mouth of Fryingpan R.

Basalt, village (1990 pop. 407), Bingham co., SE Idaho, 10 mi/16 km SW of Idaho Falls, near Snake R.; 43°19'N 112°10'W. Elev. 4,572 ft/1,394 m. Potatoes, sugar beets, wheat, oats, barley; cattle, sheep; dairying. Fort Hall Indian Reservation to S.

Basaltic Peak, Colo.: see BLACK MOUNTAIN, Jackson co.

Basco, village (1990 pop. 99), Hancock co., W Ill., 6 mi/ 9.7 km SSW of Carthage; 40°19'N 91°12'W. In agr. area (corn, wheat, soybeans; cattle, hogs); limestone processing.

Base Station, N.H.: see MARSHFIELD.

Basehor (BAS-uhr), town (1990 pop. 1,591), Leavenworth co., NE Kansas, 16 mi/26 km WNW of Kansas City, 10 mi/16 km S of Leavenworth; 39°07'N 94°55'W. Satellite community of Kansas City. Agr. (corn, hogs).

Bash Bish Falls, SW Mass., scenic waterfall in Bash Bish State Forest, 26 mi/42 km SSW of Pittsfield. Recreation.

Bashaw (BA-sho), town (1991 pop. 807), S central Alta., Canada, on small Valley L., near Buffalo L., 40 mi/ 64 km NE of Red Deer; 52°35'N 112°58'W. Grain elevators, flour mills; dairying; mixed farming.

Basil (BAI-zuhl), former village, Fairfield co., central Ohio, annexed 1945 by Baltimore.

Basile (ba-ZEEL), town (1990 pop. 1,808), Evangeline parish, S central La., 36 mi/58 km NW of Lafayette, near Bayou Nezpique; 30°30'N 92°36'W. In agr. area (sugarcane, rice, sweet potatoes; cattle); crawfish, alligators. Founded 1905.

Basilica de Guadalupe, shrine, central Mexico, in the Federal Dist. The basilica of Guadalupe containing the shrine of Our Lady of Guadalupe (whose feast day is Dec. 12) is the focal point of the most famous pilgrimage in the Western Hemisphere. In 1531 a Native American, Juan Diego, reported to Archbishop Zumárraga a series of miraculous visions of the Virgin Mary on the hill of Tepeyacac. The Spanish prelate attempted to discredit the visions, but the spot was nevertheless renamed Guadalupe in honor of the shrine of Our Lady of Guadalupe, Spain. To this was added later the name of the revolutionary priest Hidalgo y Costilla, who adopted her banner as his standard (Guadalupe Hidalgo). She is the patroness of Mexico, especially beloved by Native Americans.

Basin, town (1990 pop. 1,180), ⊙ Big Horn co., N Wyo., on Big Horn R., just W of Bighorn Mts., 60 mi/97 km SW of Sheridan; 44°22'N 108°02'W. Elev. 3,870 ft/ 1,180 m. Beans, sugar beets; livestock. Medicine Lodge State Archaeological Site to E.

Basin, village (1990 pop. 200), Jefferson co., SW Mont., 20 mi/32 km NNE of Butte, on Boulder R., N of Basin Creek. Gold, silver mines; tourism based upon "Radon Health Mines." Deerlodge Natl. Forest to NW and S.

Basin Harbor, Vt.: see FERRISBURG.

Baskahegan Lake (bas-kuh-HEE-guhn), Washington co., E Maine, in hunting, fishing area near Brookton, c.55 mi/89 km NNW of Machias; 5 mi/8 km long. Source of Baskahegan Stream, flowing c.20 mi/32 km N and NW to Mattawamkeag R. near South Bancroft.

Baskatong Lake (BA-skuh-tahng) (27 mi/43 km long, 20 mi/32 km wide), SW Que., Canada, in the Laurentians, 90 mi/145 km N of Ottawa, at foot of Mt. Sir Wilfrid. Elev. 732 ft/223 m. Fed and drained by Gatineau R. At outlet of Gatineau R. is Mercier Dam.

Baskin (BAS-kin), village (1990 pop. 243), Franklin parish, NE La., 27 mi/43 km SE of Monroe, near Big Creek; 32°16'N 91°45'W. In agr. area.

Basking Ridge, village, Somerset co., N central N.J., 7 mi/11.3 km SW of Morristown, near Passaic R. At White's Tavern here, Gen. Charles Lee was captured by British (1776). Headquarters of AT&T. Settled early 18th cent.

Baskins, town (□ 1 sq mi/2.6 sq km; 1990 pop. 3,834), Pinellas co., W central Fla., 2 mi/3.2 km SE of Largo; 27°53'N 82°48'W.

Bass Islands, N Ohio, in L. Erie c.35 mi/56 km W of Toledo; 41°41'N 82°48'W. Group includes North Bass (c.1 mi/2 km long; site of Isle St. George village), Middle Bass (c.3 mi/5 km long; site of Middle Bass village), and South Bass (c.3 mi/5 km long), site of Put-in-Bay village and natl. monument commemorating Perry's victory in battle of L. Erie. Isls. are noted summer resorts, produce much wine, and have lake fisheries. With neighboring isls., sometimes called Wine Isls.

Bass Lake 1 Itasca co., N central Minn., 5 mi/8 km NW of Grand Rapids; 6.5 mi/10.5 km long, 1 mi/1.6 km wide. Drains into Mississippi R. from SE end. Deer L. to N. **2** SE Starke co., NW Ind. The 3d-largest natural lake in the state. Glacially formed. Average depth is 30 ft/9 m.

Bass Lake, reservoir, Madera co., central Calif., on North Fork Willow Creek, 35 mi/56 km NE of Madera, in the Sierra Nevadas, in Sierra Natl. Forest; 4 mi/ 6.4 km long; 37°15'N 119°32'W. Elev. 3,376 ft/1,029 m.

Bass River, c.10 mi/16 km long, SE N.J., rises in SE Burlington co., flows generally S, through Bass R. State Forest, to Mullica R. near its mouth on Great Bay.

Bass River, Mass.: see YARMOUTH.

Bass Rocks, Mass.: see GLOUCESTER.

Bassano (buh-SAH-no), town (1991 pop. 1,190), S Alta., Canada, near Bow R., 70 mi/113 km ESE of Calgary; 50°47'N 112°28'W. Coal mining, dairying; wheat, flax, barley, cattle. Nearby, on Bow R., is the Bassano irrigation dam (also called Horseshoe Bend).

Basse Terre (BAH-sei tahr), village, S Trinidad, Trinidad and Tobago, 15 mi/24 km SE of San Fernando.

Basse-Pointe (bahs–PWANGT), town, N Martinique, on the Atlantic, 13 mi/21 km NNW of Fort-de-France.

In sugar-growing region; sugar milling, rum distilling, mfg. of soap. Banana and pineapple plantation.

Basse-Terre (bahs–TER), town (1982 pop. 13,656), on SSW corner of Basse-Terre Isl., ⊙ Guadeloupe, in the West Indies; 16°00′N 61°43′W. Basse-Terre is a port that ships the prods. of the surrounding agr. area. Founded by the French in 1643, it retains its Fr. colonial atmosphere. Its commercial prosperity passed to Pointe-à-Pitre in the late 18th cent. The town was destroyed by a hurricane in 1979, setting back prospects for economic development.

Basseterre, town (1990 est. pop. 15,500), ⊙ St. Kitts and Nevis, on St. Kitts isl., West Indies; 17°18′N 62°43′W. Sugar refining is the leading industry; small-scale garment mfg., electronic assembly, and a brewery and bottling plant. Basseterre was founded by the French in 1627. Golden Rock Internatl. Airport is located here.

Basse-Terre (bahs–TER), island (□ 364 sq mi/943 sq km), the W half of Guadeloupe, is separated from Grande-Terre by narrow Rivière Salée channel; 16°10′N 61°40′W. It is rocky and mountainous; its highest point is active volcano Soufrière (4,869 ft/1,484 m). Chief prods. grown along the coast are cacao, coffee, vanilla, bananas, bay leaves, sugarcane. The isl. is sometimes referred to as Guadeloupe isl. proper.

Bassett 1 town (1990 pop. 74), Chickasaw co., NE Iowa, near Little Cedar R., 10 mi/16 km W of New Hampton; 43°03′N 92°31′W. **2** uninc. town (1990 pop. 1,579), Henry co., S Va., 8 mi/12.9 km NW of Martinsville, on Smith R. (forms Philipott Reservoir to NW); 36°45′N 79°59′W. Mfg. (plastic prods., furniture, fiberboard, printing, clothing, machining); in agr. area (tobacco; poultry, cattle). Fairy Stone State Park to W. Sometimes called Bassetts.

Bassett 1 village (1990 pop. 20), Allen co., SE Kansas, on Neosho R., 1 mi/1.6 km S of Iola; 37°54′N 95°24′W. **2** (BAS-et), village (1990 pop. 739), ⊙ Rock co., N Nebr., 115 mi/185 km WNW of Norfolk; 42°34′N 99°32′W. Trading, shipping point; grain. Mfg. (consumer goods, fertilizer).

Bassett Peak (7,663 ft/2,336 m), SW Graham co., SE Ariz., highest point in Galiuro Mts., c.45 mi/72 km NE of Tucson; 32°30′N 110°16′W. In Coronado Natl. Forest.

Bassfield, village (1990 pop. 249), Jefferson Davis co., S central Miss., 30 mi/48 km WNW of Hattiesburg, near source of Black Creek; 31°30′N 89°44′W. Mfg. (apparel). Jeff Davis State L. to NW.

Bassin-Bleu (bah-sang–BLUH), town (1982 pop. 720), Nord-Ouest dept., N Haiti, on Les Trois Rivières, 11 mi/18 km S of Port-de-Paix; 19°47′N 72°48′W. In fertile agr. region (coffee, tobacco, cotton); beekeeping.

Basswood Lake, in chain of lakes on Can./U.S. border bet. Lake co., NE Minn., and W Ont., Canada, 15 mi/24 km NE of Ely, Minn.; length, including W arm, 20 mi/32 km; max. width 4 mi/6.4 km; 48°04′N 91°34′W. Fed by short stream from E from Knife L.; drained to NW by Basswood R. to Crooked L., all on internatl. boundary. Includes several small isls. and long bays; Jackfish and Pipestone bays extend 10 mi/16 km SW into Minn. in Quetico Provincial Park (N) and Superior Natl. Forest including Boundary Water Canoe Area (S).

Bastian (BAS-tee-uhn), uninc. village, Bland co., SW Va., in the Allegheny Mts., 9 mi/14.5 km SE of Bluefield, in Jefferson Natl. Forest. Mfg. (apparel), agr. (tobacco, corn; livestock; dairying); timber. Appalachian Trail passes to SE.

Bastonnais River, Canada: see BOSTONNAIS RIVER.

Bastrop, county (□ 895 sq mi/2,318 sq km; 1990 pop. 38,263), S central Texas; ⊙ Bastrop; 30°06′N 97°18′W. Drained by Colorado R. Agr. (cotton, corn, alfalfa, wheat, grain, sorghum); livestock (cattle, emus, ostriches, hogs). Clay, lignite mining; oil, natural gas wells; some timber. L. Bastrop and Bastrop State Park near center of co.; Buescher State Park in E. Formed 1836.

Bastrop (BAS-truhp), city (1994 pop. 14,702), ⊙ Morehouse parish, NE La., 18 mi/29 km NNE of Monroe, near Bayou Bartholomew; 32°46′N 91°55′W. RR junction. An industrial city in a cattle, cotton, rice, and timber area. Bastrop is the center of the huge Monroe natural gas field (discovered 1916). Mfg. includes wood prods., insecticides, apparel, farm equip., paper, aluminum sulfate; printing and publishing; meat packing. Ga. Pacific State Wildlife Area to NW, Chemin-A-Haut State Park to N, Handy Brake Natl. Wildlife Refuge to NE. Founded c.1845.

Bastrop, town (1990 pop. 4,044), ⊙ Bastrop co., S central Texas, on Colorado R., 23 mi/37 km ESE of Austin; 30°06′N 97°18′W. Elev. 374 ft/114 m. Trade, shipping center of agr. (corn, sorghum, wheat, alfalfa, cotton); cattle, emus, ostriches; lignite, lumber area; mfg. (machinery, furniture). Univ. of Texas cancer research center. L. Bastrop and Bastrop State Park to NE; Buescher State Park to E. Was 1st called Mina, until 1837. Settled 1827, inc. 1837.

Batabanó (bah-tah-bah-NO), town, La Habana prov., W Cuba, on RR, and 29 mi/47 km S of Havana; 22°43′N 82°17′W. In agr. region (sugarcane, fruit, vegetables). Its port Surgidero de Batabanó (2.5 mi/4 km S), amidst thick mangroves, is point of embarkation for Isla de la Juventud. Settled in 1559.

Batabanó, Gulf of (bah-tah-bah-NO), inlet, SW Cuba, bounded S by Isla de la Juventud and NE by Zapata Peninsula (Matanzas prov.), 30 mi/48 km S of Havana; 22°15′N 82°30′W. Shallow sea (less than 200 ft/61 m deep) dotted by Los Canarreos Archipelago and numerous keys. Its NE sect. is also called Ensenada de la Broa. The original settlement of Havana was built on its shores before relocating to N coast.

Batavia 1 (ba-TAVE-ih-a), industrial city (1990 pop. 17,076), Kane co., NE Ill., on Fox R., satellite community, 34 mi/55 km W of Chicago; 41°51′N 88°17′W. In agr. area (corn, soybeans; dairying); mfg. (plastic prods., consumer goods, furniture, plumbing equip.). Limestone quarries. Bellevue Sanatorium is here. Nearby is Mooseheart, large residential and educational community supported by the Loyal Order of the Moose. Fermi Natl. Accelerator Laboratory immediately E (mostly in Cook co.). Founded 1834; inc. as village in 1856, as city in 1891. **2** city (□ 5 sq mi/13 sq km; 1990 pop. 16,310), ⊙ Genesee co., W N.Y.; 43°00′N 78°10′W. Batavia produces a variety of light mfg. It was laid out in 1801 by Joseph Ellicott, agent for the Holland Land Co. The city was a center of the Anti-Masonic movement in the 19th cent. Attica prison, site of the 1971 riots, is nearby. Inc. 1915.

Batavia, town (1990 pop. 520), Jefferson co., SE Iowa, 11 mi/18 km W of Fairfield; 40°59′N 92°10′W. Concrete blocks.

Batavia (buh-TAI-vee-uh), village (1990 pop. 1,700), ⊙ Clermont co., SW Ohio, 19 mi/31 km E of Cincinnati, on East Fork of Little Miami R., in agr. area; 39°04′N 84°11′W. Tools, machinery, grain prods. Mfg. (auto transmissions). Settled c.1797, laid out 1814, inc. 1842.

Batchawana, Mount (ba-chuh-WAH-nuh) (2,100 ft/640 m), central Ont., Canada, near L. Superior, 40 mi/64 km N of Sault Ste. Marie.

Batchtown, village (1990 pop. 225), Calhoun co., W Ill., near the Mississippi, 9 mi/14.5 km SSW of Hardin; 39°01′N 90°39′W. In apple-growing area.

Bates, county (□ 841 sq mi/2,178 sq km; 1990 pop. 15,025), W Mo.; ⊙ Butler; 38°15′N 94°20′W. Borders Kansas in W. Drained by Marais des Cygnes and South Grand rivers. Corn, wheat, sorghum, popcorn, pecans; cattle; coal, oil. Formed 1841.

Bates, village, Scott co., W Ark., 18 mi/29 km W of Waldron, near Okla. line, on Poteau R., in Ouachita Natl. Forest.

Bates City, town (1990 pop. 197), Lafayette co., W central Mo., near Missouri R., 6 mi/10 km W of Odessa; 39°00′N 94°04′W. Mfg. (consumer goods).

Batesburg, town (1990 pop. 6,107), Lexington and Saluda cos., W central S.C., 30 mi/48 km WSW of Columbia, L. Murray Reservoir to NE; 33°54′N 81°32′W. Mfg. includes poultry processing, electronic assembly, lumber, poles. Agr. includes grains; dairying; poultry; timber. Batesburg merged with the town of Leesville in the early 1990s.

Batesville 1 city (1990 pop. 9,187), ⊙ Independence co., NE central Ark., c.80 mi/129 km NNE of Little Rock, and on White R., in foothills of the Ozarks; 35°46′N 91°37′W. Processing center for agr. area (fruit, cotton, corn, hay; livestock). Mfg. (plastic prods., lime, limestone, printing, metal fabrication, wood prods., frozen foods, photographic chemicals, paper prods., cheese, bakery prods., motor vehicles, consumer goods, asphalt). Manganese mining; marble and limestone quarrying and processing. Seat of Ark. Col. Settled c.1810, inc. 1841. **2** city (1990 pop. 4,720), Ripley co., SE Ind., 16 mi/26 km N of Versailles; 39°18′N 85°13′W. In agr. area; meat packing, lumber milling; mfg. of caskets, furniture, metal prods., cutlery.

Batesville 1 town (1990 pop. 6,403), ⊙ Panola co. (along with Sardis), NW Miss., on Tallahatchie R., 55 mi/89 km S of Memphis, Tenn.; 34°19′N 89°56′W. Trade center for agr. (cotton, corn; poultry, cattle, hogs) and timber area; mfg. (bldg. materials, plastic, wood, and felt prods.; hospital furniture, concrete, sports equip.); sand and gravel. John W. Kyle State Park at Sardis L. reservoir to NE; Enid L. reservoir to SE. Founded 1855. **2** town (1990 pop. 1,313), Zavala co., SW Texas, 24 mi/39 km NE of Crystal City, on Leona R.; 28°56′N 99°36′W. Cattle ranching; cotton, vegetables, pecans; oil and gas.

Batesville, village (1990 pop. 95), Noble co., E Ohio, 17 mi/27 km ESE of Cambridge; 39°57′N 81°17′W.

Bath 1 county (□ 283 sq mi/733 sq km; 1990 pop. 9,692), NE Ky.; ⊙ Owingsville; 38°08′N 83°44′W. Bounded NE by Licking R., drained by Slate Creek. Rolling upland agr. area, in Bluegrass region (burley tobacco, corn, soybeans, hay, alfalfa; cattle, poultry; dairying); timber. Includes part of Daniel Boone Natl. Forest in SE. Has once-famous mineral baths (Olympia Springs, others) for which co. is named. Formed 1811. **2** county (□ 534 sq mi/1,383 sq km; 1990 pop 4,799), NW Va.; ⊙ Warm Springs; in the Allegheny Mts.; 38°03′N 79°44′W. Bounded W by W.Va. state line; drained by Jackson and Cowpasture rivers, almost entirely within George Washington Natl. Forest. Famous resort area, with noted mineral springs at Hot Springs, Warm Springs, Healing Spring, and Millboro Springs. Livestock raising (esp. sheep, cattle), horse breeding; agr. (hay); timber; hunting, fishing. Formed 1791.

Bath, city (1990 pop. 9,799), ⊙ Sagadahoc co., SW Maine, on the W bank of the Kennebec R., near its mouth on the Atlantic; 43°56′N 69°50′W. It is a port of entry with a good harbor. Once a great shipbuilding center, it still has active shipyards and marine mfg., but summer tourism is becoming increasingly important. Champlain and others visited or passed near this site when exploring the Kennebec R., and at nearby Popham Beach a short-lived colony was est. (1607) by George Popham. Shipbuilding began early; many clipper ships were constructed in the 19th cent., and the Bath Iron Works began to produce steel warships and commercial vessels in the 1880s. The city flourished, particularly during World Wars I and II, when a large number of destroyers were built. Marine mus. and many old mansions. Settled c.1670, inc. as a city 1847.

Bath, town (1991 pop. 2,151), St. Thomas parish, E Jamaica, on Plantain Garden R., and 30 mi/48 km E of Kingston; 17°57′N 76°21′W. Spa with sulphuric thermal springs. Trades in coconuts and copra.

Bath, town (1990 pop. 784), Grafton co., NW N.H., SW of Littleton; 44°10′N 71°59′W. Bounded by Connecticut R. (Vt. state line); drained by Ammonoosuc and Wild Ammonoosuc rivers. Agr. (cattle, poultry; vegetables, apples; dairying; nursery crops; timber); mfg. (lumber). Three covered bridges in S.

Bath 1 village (1991 pop. 653), W N.B., Canada, on St. John R., 25 mi/40 km N of Woodstock; 46°32′N 67°35′W. Potato growing, salmon fishing, logging. **2** village (1991 pop. 1,257), SE Ont., Canada, on North Channel of L. Ontario, opposite Amherst Isl., 14 mi/23 km W of Kingston. Dairying, fruit growing. Est. 1784 by United Empire Loyalists.

Bath 1 village (1990 pop. 388), Mason co., central Ill., on Illinois R., 7 mi/11.3 km SSW of Havana; 40°11′N 90°08′W. In irrigated agr. area (grain, vegetables). Near

Sand Prairie–Scrub Oak State Natl. Area. **2** village (□ 2 sq mi/5.2 sq km; 1990 pop. 5,801), ⊙ Steuben co., S N.Y., on Cohocton R., 30 mi/48 km NW of Elmira; 42°20′N 77°19′W. Mfg. (lighting fixtures; meat packing; aluminum and fiberglass prods., bldg. materials, fabricated metal prods.). In rich agr. area (dairy prods., potatoes); regional tourist center. Site of a U.S. Veterans' Administration Medical Center (opened 1878). State trout hatchery. Settled 1793, inc. 1816. **3** village (1990 pop. 154), Beaufort co., E N.C., on arm of Pamlico R. estuary, 14 mi/23 km ESE of Washington; 35°28′N 76°49′W. Goose Creek State Park to W. Bath State Historical Site. Oldest town in state; was capital of the prov. of N.C. The state's 1st public lib. started here in 1700. Settled c. 1690 on site of a Native Amer. village. Inc. 1705. **4** village, Aiken co., W S.C., 10 mi/16 km WSW of Aiken. Mfg. includes laolin, clay processing; agr. includes cotton, peanuts, grain; livestock.

Bath, borough (1990 pop. 2,358), Northampton co., E Pa., 8 mi/12.9 km N of Bethlehem, on Monocacy Creek. Mfg. (paving materials, chemicals, crushed stone, steel fabricating, apparel). Agr. (grain, soybeans, apples; livestock; dairying); slate, limestone. Allentown State Farm to SW. Laid out 1816, inc. 1856.

Bath, W.Va.: see BERKELEY SPRINGS.

Bath Beach, a residential and shore-resort section of SW Brooklyn borough of N.Y. city, SE N.Y., on Gravesend Bay; 40°36′N 74°00′W. U.S. Fort Hamilton is W.

Bathgate, village (1990 pop. 75), Pembina co., NE N.Dak.,11 mi/18 km NE of Cavalier; 48°52′N 97°28′W. On Tongue R. Former site of state school for the blind.

Bathsheba (bath-SHEE-buh), village, E Barbados, B.W.I., 9 mi/14.5 km NE of Bridgetown. Popular seaside resort. Flying-fish-catching fleet stationed here.

Bathurst, city (1991 pop. 14,409), N N.B., Canada, ⊙ Gloucester co., on Chaleur Bay, at the mouth of the Nepisiguit R.; 45°36′N 65°39′W. A popular beach resort, it also has 40% of Canada's reserves of lead, zinc, and silver. Largest zinc-producing mines in world. Its other industries include lumbering and shipbuilding, mixed farming, dairying; cod, oysters, clams; strawberries, blueberries. Settled mid–17th cent.

Bathurst, Cape, N Mackenzie dist., N.W.T., Canada, on Beaufort Sea of the Arctic Ocean; 70°32′N 128°25′W. Northermost point of Can. mainland. Just S is Baillie trading post; 4 mi/6 km WNW are the 2 Baillie Isls.

Bathurst Inlet, trading post (1991 pop. 18), NE Mackenzie dist., N.W.T., Canada, on Bathurst Inlet (150 mi/241 km long, 3 mi/5 km–65 mi/105 km wide) of Coronation Gulf; 66°51′N 108°01′W. Est. 1929 by prospectors, abandoned 1964. Site of R.C. mission; naturalist lodge est. 1969 revitalizing community. Scheduled air service.

Bathurst Island (□ 7,609 sq mi/19,707 sq km), in the Arctic Archipelago, Baffin Region, N.W.T., N Canada; 75°40′N 100°00′W. It is the present site of the North Magnetic Pole.

Batiscan (bah-tees-KAH), village (1991 pop. 869), ⊙ Champlain co., S central Que., Canada, on the St. Lawrence, at mouth of Batiscan R., 18 mi/29 km NE of Trois Rivières; 46°30′N 72°15′W. Lumbering; dairying.

Batiscan River, 110 mi/177 km long, S Que., Canada; issues from L. Batiscan (8 mi/13 km long), in Laurentides Park; flows W, then generally S, past Lac aux Sables, to the St. Lawrence at Batiscan.

Batoche (ba-TAHSH), historic site, central Sask., Canada, on the South Saskatchewan R. During Riel's Rebellion, Louis Riel made his hq. here, and the rebels were routed on May 12, 1885.

Baton Rouge (BAT-uhn ROOZH) [Fr. = red stick], city (1990 pop. 219,531), ⊙ La. and East Baton Rouge parish, SE La., on the E bank of the Mississippi R., 70 mi/113 km WNW of New Orleans; 30°27′N 91°08′W. The 2d-largest metropolitan area in La. Barge and RR transfer center; busy deepwater port of entry; important transportation, distribution, and commercial center for a large oil, natural-gas, and farm area; major oil-refining hub. The petrochemical and fuel corporation Exxon has large facilities and is one of Baton Rouge's major employers. Mfg. (concrete prods., pharmaceuticals, food and beverages, chemicals, plastics, resins); seafood, crawfish. Baton Rouge was founded in 1719 when the French built a fort on that strategic spot along the river. The settlement was ceded to Great Britain in 1762, captured by the Spanish in 1779, and acquired by the U.S. in 1815 (following a brief period when it was a part of Span. Fla). It became state capital in 1849. In the Civil War it was captured by David Farragut after the fall of New Orleans (May 1862); a Confederate attempt to recover it failed (Aug. 1862). It has notable antebellum houses. The old capitol (1882), built in the Gothic style of the original that was burned in the Civil War, still stands; a new 34-story capitol (tallest in U.S.) was completed in 1932. Also of interest are the gov.'s mansion, the old arsenal mus., and the Huey Long grave and memorial. The city has an arts and sciences center (with a planetarium), several museums (La. Naval War Mus., L.S.U. Rural Life Mus.), a zoo, and a symphony orchestra. The Mall of La. opened in 1997 (□ 7,628,000 sq ft/708,225 sq m), and the city is also the cite of Cortana Mall (one of the largest shopping centers in the U.S.). It is establishing itself as a city of fine restaurants. U.S.S. *Kidd*, World War II destroyer, docked near downtown. Seat of La. State Univ. and Agr. and Mechanical Col. and of Southern Univ. and Agr. and Mechanical Col. at Scotlandville. Port Hudson State Commemorative Area to NW. Port of Baton Rouge is S of downtown. Baton Rouge Harbor N of city on Mississippi R. Atchafalaya Basin to SW. Inc. 1817.

Batopilas (bah-to-PEE-las), town (1990 pop. 978) and township, Chihuahua, N Mexico, in Sierra Madre Occidental, on affluent of Río Verde, 145 mi/233 km SW of Chihuahua; 27°0′N 107°50′W. Elev. 1,873 ft/571 m. Mining settlement, gold, copper, silver mining; corn, wheat, cattle; lumber. Jesuit mission to Tarahumara Indians is here.

Batópilas (bah-TO-pee-lahs), village, Chihuahua state, Mexico. located in the Sierra Madre Occidental, c.115 mi/190 km NE of Los Mochis, 84 mi/135 km S of Creel. Founded in 1632, formerly an important gold- and silver-mining center, now noted as a minor tourist center and reputed to be a zone of marijuana production and drug trafficking. About half the pop. is Tarahumara Indian.

Batsto (BAT-sto), village, Burlington co., SE N.J., on small Batsto R. (dammed here), 27 mi/43 km SSE of Mount Holly, in pine-barrens area. Ironworks here (built 1765) made Revolutionary munitions. A state historic site is here.

Batsto River (BAT-sto), c.10 mi/16 km long, SE N.J.; rises in S Burlington co.; flows SSE through pine barrens to Mullica R. just below Batsto.

Batten Kill, river, c.60 mi/97 km long, Vt. and N.Y.; rises near Dorset, SW Vt.; flows SW and W, past Manchester, Vt., and Greenwich, N.Y., to the Hudson opposite Schuylerville. Famous for trout fishing.

Battery Park City, section of N.Y. city, SE N.Y., at SW tip of Lower Manhattan; 40°42′N 74°01′W. Constructed 1986–1988 on 92 acres/37 ha of landfill which came from the early 1980s excavation for the construction of the nearby World Trade Center. Extends along the Hudson R. side of Manhattan from Pier A on the S, to Chamber St. on the N, to West St. on the E; one of N.Y. city's most ambitious and successful commercial, residential, and urban–park development projects of the 1980s. The design team led by Vladimir Arsene created the development's unified style, distinguished by its masonry-clad bldgs. with punched windows and unarticulated, uniform facades, as well as its esplanades, marina, and public-art displays. A major tourist attraction and a choice commercial part of Manhattan; adjacent to the equally new World Trade and World Financial Centers.

Battery, the, park (□ 21 acres/8 ha), S tip of Manhattan isl., N.Y. city; 40°42′N 74°01′W. Site of former Du. and Eng. fortifications. Castle Clinton, a fort built in 1808 for the defense of N.Y. harbor, was ceded to the city in 1823 and renamed Castle Garden. It was remodeled and served as a noted amusement hall and opera house; Swed. soprano Jenny Lind made her U.S. debut on its stage in 1850. From 1855 to 1892 it served as the main immigration station for N.Y. city, and from 1896 to 1941 it housed an aquarium. After World War II the park was remodeled, and Castle Clinton became a natl. monument. The park also contains a war memorial and a statue of Giovanni da Verrazano, the 1st European to enter N.Y. harbor. Boats to Liberty Isl. and Ellis Isl. leave from the park. New residential communities, such as Battery Park City, have developed in the area N of the park.

Battie, Mount, Maine: see CAMDEN HILLS.

Battle Creek, city (1990 pop. 53,540), Calhoun co., S Mich., at the confluence of the Kalamazoo R. and Battle Creek stream; 42°17′N 85°13′W. RR junction. It is an agr. trade center known for its cereals. Other mfg. includes automotive parts and accessories, moldings, paper prods., and printing and publishing. W. K. Kellogg Regional Airport in W part of city. Battle Creek Sanitarium (founded by Dr. J. H. Kellogg in 1866 as the Health Reform Inst.), Kingman Natural History Mus., a bird sanctuary, Art Center of Battle Creek, Adventist Heritage Mus., Binder Park Zoo, a Natl. Cemetery, and Kellogg Community Col. are in or near the city. Fort Custer State Recrational Area in W part of city. Annual Cereal City Festival in June. Peanut butter invented here by J. H. Kellogg. Settled 1831, inc. as a city 1859.

Battle Creek 1 town (1990 pop. 818), Ida co., W Iowa, on Maple R., and 7 mi/11.3 km WSW of Ida Grove; 42°19′N 95°35′W. **2** town (1990 pop. 997), Madison co., NE central Nebr., 10 mi/16 km W of Norfolk; 42°00′N 97°35′W. Dairy; livestock; grain. Feeds.

Battle Creek or **Battle Creek River**, stream, c.50 mi/80 km long, S central Mich.; 42°26′N 84°46′W. Rises in small Duck L. (c.2 mi/3.2 km long) in NE Calhoun co. Flows N almost to Charlotte, then SW, past Bellevue, to Kalamazoo R. at Battle Creek city.

Battle Ground 1 town (1990 pop. 806), Tippecanoe co., W central Ind., 7 mi/11.3 km NNE of Lafayette; 40°31′N 86°50′W. In agr. area. A memorial park marks scene of the Battle of Tippecanoe (1811) bet. Native Americans and U.S. soldiers under Gen. W. H. Harrison. **2** town (1990 pop. 3,758), Clark co., SW Wash., 12 mi/19 km NE of Vancouver, near East Fork of Lewis R.; 45°47′N 122°32′W. RR terminus. Dairying; poultry, vegetables, berries, nuts, oats, barley. Mfg. (dairy prods., plastic prods., printing and publishing, furniture). Battle Ground L. State Park to NE.

Battle Harbour, village, ⊙ Lab., Canada, on small isl. just off SE coast, 25 mi/40 km NW of Misery Point, Belle Isle; 52°16′N 55°36′W. Fishing port. Has hosp. est. 1892 by Sir Wilfred Grenfell.

Battle Lake, village (1990 pop. 698), Otter Tail co., W Minn., 16 mi/26 km E of Fergus Falls, at W end of Battle L.; 46°17′N 95°43′W. Grain, sugar beets, beans, sunflowers; livestock; dairying; mfg. (printing and publishing, furniture). Battle here (1795) bet. Chippewa and Sioux Indians. Numerous small lakes in area.

Battle Lake (□ 9 sq mi/23.3 sq km), Otter Tail co., W Minn., 17 mi/27 km E of Fergus Falls; 6 mi/9.7 km long, 2 mi/3.2 km wide; 46°19′N 95°39′W. Elev. 1,332 ft/406 m. Fed by short streams from East Battle L. from E and Clitherall L. from S; drains N through chain of small lakes, including Blanche L., to Otter Tail L. Village of Battle Lake to SW. Sometimes referred to as West Battle L.

Battle Mountain, uninc. town (1990 pop. 3,542), ⊙ Lander co., N Nev., on Humboldt R., at mouth of Reese, c.65 mi/105 km WSW of Elko; 40°38′N 116°56′W. Elev. 4,510 ft/1,375 m. Chemical processing. Supply center for mining (gold, turquoise, silver) and cattle-ranching area. North Peak (8,550 ft/2,606 m) and Antler Peak (8,236 ft/2,510 m) to W. Shoshone Range to SE.

Battle Mountain, N Nev., Humboldt and Lander cos., S of Humboldt R., 10 mi/16 km W of Battle Mountain town. Antler Peak (8,236 ft/2,510 m) and North Peak (8,550 ft/2,606 m) are its summits.

Battleboro, village (1990 pop. 235), Nash and Edgecombe cos., NE central N.C., suburb 8 mi/12.9 km NNE of Rocky Mount; 36°02′N 77°45′W. Mfg. (consumer goods, commercial printing, metal fabrication, crushed stone). Agr. area (tobacco, peanuts, cotton, grain; chickens, cattle, hogs). N.C. Wesleyan Col. to S.

Battlefield, town (1990 pop. 1,526), Greene co., SW Mo., residential suburb, 8 mi/12.9 km SW of Springfield, near James R.; 37°07′N 93°22′W. Wilson's Creek Natl. Battlefield is to W. Light mfg.

Battleford, town (1991 pop. 4,107), N central Sask., Canada, at the confluence of the Battle and North Saskatchewan rivers. Battleford is one of the oldest towns in the central part of the prov. It served as capital (1876–1883) of the N.W.T. and figured prominently in Riel's Rebellion of 1885.

Battletown, uninc. village (1990 pop. 400), Meade co., N Ky., 7 mi/11.3 km NW of Brandenburg, on Ohio R. Tobacco, grain; livestock. Limestone quarrying. Mfg. (lime processing, crushed limestone).

Baudette (baw-DET), town (1990 pop. 1,146), ⊙ Lake of the Woods co., N Minn., on Rainy R. (Can. border), 55 mi/89 km WNW of International-Falls; 48°42′N 94°35′W. Elev. 1,083 ft/330 m. Summer resort area; port of entry; farm-trading point (wheat, oats, barley, potatoes, flax, sunflowers); timber; mfg. (pharmaceuticals). Hq. of U.S. forest and game reservation. L. of the Woods is 10 mi/16 km NW. Baudette Internatl. Airport and Seaplane Base to NW. Beltram Isl. State Forest to SW; parts of Red L. Indian Reservation to S and SW.

Bauld, Cape, Canada: see GREAT NORTHERN PENINSULA.

Bauta (BOU-tuh), town, La Habana prov., W Cuba, on Central Highway, on RR, 15 mi/24 km SW of Havana; 22°58′N 82°33′W. Cigar factories, cotton mill. Grows tobacco, sugarcane, pineapples, vegetables, and citrus.

Bauxite (BAHKS-eit), village (1990 pop. 412), Saline co., central Ark., near short Hurricane Creek, 3 mi/4.8 km E of Benton; 34°33′N 92°31′W. In major U.S. bauxite-mining area. Formerly a center of aluminum and aluminum production, the industry has largely left the state.

Baviácora (bah-vee-AH-ko-rah), town (1990 pop. 2,037), Sonora, NW Mexico, on Sonora R. (irrigation), 65 mi/105 km NE of Hermosillo; 29°20′N 110°05′W. Wheat, corn, beans, sugar; cattle.

Bavispe (bah-VEES-pe), town (1990 pop. 801), Sonora, NW Mexico, on Bavispe R., 80 mi/129 km SE of Douglas (Ariz.); 29°48′N 108°59′W. Corn, wheat, vegetables, sugar; livestock.

Bavispe River (bah-VEES-pe), c.200 mi/322 km long, Sonora, NW Mexico; 29°50′N 109°00′W. Rises in W outliers of Sierra Madre Occidental SW of Bacerac. Flows N, encircling a mt. mass, turns S, past Oputo, Huásabas, Granados, to the Yaqui (of which it is a principal headstream) 12 mi/19 km N of Sahuaripa. Also known as Río Batepito.

Bawlf, village (1991 pop. 327), central Alta., Canada, 17 mi/27 km ESE of Camrose. Dairying; mixed farming.

Baxley (BAKS-lee), town (1990 pop. 3,841) ⊙ Appling co., SE central Ga., 38 mi/61 km N of Waycross; 31°46′N 82°21′W. Market service center for surrounding agr. and forest area; tobacco market; mfg. of boxes, clothing, lumber and wood prods., steel fabrication, industrial and farm equip. Home of the only commercial turpentine distillery in the U.S. Inc. 1875.

Baxter, county (□ 586 sq mi/1,518 sq km; 1990 pop. 31,186), N Ark.; ⊙ Mountain Home; 36°17′N 92°20′W. Bounded N by Mo. line, S and SE by White R. (Bull Shoals Dam and Reservoir in NW); drained by the North Fork (Norfolk Dam and Reservoir and Fish Hatchery in E). Situated in Ozark region, the co. has emerged as a major retirement center. Agr. (hay, cattle, hogs). Resorts; fishing. Bull Shoals State Park on both sides of Bull Shoals Dam (White R.) in W; part of Ozark Natl. Forest in S, small part of Buffalo Natl. R. on SW boundary. Formed 1873.

Baxter 1 town (1990 pop. 938), Jasper co., central Iowa, 11 mi/18 km NW of Newton; 41°49′N 93°09′W. Livestock; grain. **2** town (1990 pop. 3,695), Crow Wing co., central Minn., near Mississippi R., 4 mi/6.4 km W of Brainerd; 46°20′N 94°16′W. Cattle, poultry; dairying; oats, alfalfa; mfg. (concrete). Camp Riley Military Reservation to SW; Gull L. reservoir and Pillsbury State Forest to NW. Inc. 1939. **3** town (1990 pop. 1,289), Putnam co., central Tenn., 5 mi/8 km W of Cookeville; 36°09′N 85°38′W. Sawmilling.

Baxter 1 village, Harlan co., SE Ky., 2 mi/3.2 km N of Harlan, in the Cumberland Mts., at joining of Poor and Clover forks of Cumberland R., form main stream. Bituminous coal; timber; mfg. (mining equip.). Pine Mt. Settlement School (boarding school est. 1913) to N, on 800 acres/324 ha. **2** uninc. village (1990 pop. 500), Marion co., N W.Va., 4 mi/6.4 km N of Fairmont, 2 mi/3.2 km NW of Rivesville. Bituminous coal.

Baxter Estates, residential village (1990 pop. 961), Nassau co., SE N.Y., on Manhasset Neck, W L.I., overlooking Manhasset Bay (W), and just N of Port Washington; 40°50′N 73°42′W.

Baxter Springs, town (1990 pop. 4,351), Cherokee co., extreme SE Kansas, on Spring R., near Okla. line, and 13 mi/21 km WSW of Joplin, Mo.; 37°01′N 94°44′W. RR junction. Mfg. (chemical equip., apparel, food processing, furniture, construction machinery). Grew as cattle town in 1860s and 1870s. Nearby monument commemorates Baxter Springs Massacre (1863), in which 87 Union soldiers were killed by guerrilla band under William Quantrill. Settled c. 1850, inc. 1868.

Bay 1 county (□ 1,033 sq mi/2,675 sq km; 1990 pop. 126,994), NW Fla., bounded on S by Gulf of Mexico; ⊙ Panama City; 30°14′N 85°37′W. Flatwoods area, with swampy coast indented by St. Andrew Bay. Cattle raising, forestry, paper prods., fishing, and some agr. (cotton, peanuts, sugarcane). Formed 1913. **2** county (□ 630 sq mi/1,632 sq km; 1990 pop. 111,723), E Mich.; ⊙ Bay City; 43°43′N 83°56′W. Bounded E by Saginaw Bay; drained by Saginaw R. and short Kawkawlin R. Agr. area (sugar beets, beans, soybeans, potatoes, cucumbers; dairy prods.; cattle, hogs, poultry). Mfg. at Bay City. Resorts. Saginaw Valley State Univ. SW of Bay City. State forests. Bay City State Park in E center on Saginaw Bay. Organized 1858.

Bay, town (1990 pop. 1,660), Craighead co., NE Ark., 10 mi/16 km SE of Jonesboro; 35°44′N 90°33′W.

Bay Center, village (1990 pop. 380), Pacific co., SW Wash., 8 mi/12.9 km WSW of South Bend, on Willaga Bay, arm of Pacific Ocean. Mfg. (fresh and frozen seafood).

Bay City 1 city (1990 pop. 38,936), ⊙ Bay co., S Mich., a port of entry on the Saginaw R. at its mouth on Saginaw Bay (an inlet of L. Huron); 43°35′N 83°53′W. Its harbor handles Great Lakes and ocean shipping; it is also a RR junction. Bay City is the industrial, marketing, and transportation center of a rich farm area that yields sugar beets, potatoes, and dairy prods. Shipbuilding is also important. The city grew as a large lumbering center, but when the forests were depleted (after 1890), it turned to diversified mfg. (metal fabrication, automobile parts, food prods., machinery, apparel). Saginaw Valley State Univ. at Univ. Center is to SW. County Mus. Bay City State Park to N on Saginaw Bay. Inc. 1859 with the consolidation of several settlements along the river. **2** city (1990 pop. 18,170), ⊙ Matagorda co., S Texas, 65 mi/105 km SW of Houston, near the Colorado R. and the Gulf of Mexico; 28°58′N 95°57′W. RR junction; shipping and industrial center for a region that produces oil, gas, salt, beef cattle, rice, cotton, grains; mfg. (plastics processing, chemicals); nuclear power plants. The co. mus. is here; Matagorda Bay and several Gulf beaches are within 25 mi/40 km (S and SE); Big Boggy Natl. Wildlife Refuge to SE. Inc. 1894.

Bay City, town (1990 pop. 1,027), Tillamook co., NW Oregon, 4 mi/6.4 km NNW of Tillamook, and on E side of Tillamook Bay, bet. mouths of Miami and Kilchis rivers; 45°31′N 123°53′W. Mfg. (meat prods.). Fish, crabs, shrimp. Dairy prods; cattle; tourism. Tillamook State Forest to E.

Bay City, village (1990 pop. 578), Pierce co., W Wis., 4 mi/6.4 km ENE of Red Wing, Minn., on L. Pepin, natural lake of Mississippi R.; 44°35′N 92°27′W.

Bay Farm Island, Calif.: see ALAMEDA, city.

Bay Harbor, town (1990 pop. 4,703), Bay co., NW Fla.; 25°53′N 80°07′W. Suburb of Panama City.

Bay Harbor Islands, town (1990 pop. 4,703), Dade co., SE Fla., in Biscayne Bay, just W of Bal Harbour; 25°53′N 80°08′W. Exclusive residential area.

Bay Head, resort borough (1990 pop. 1,226), Ocean co., E N.J., 11 mi/18 km NE of Toms R., at N end of Barnegat Bay, here entered by Point Pleasant Canal (part of Intracoastal Waterway; connects NW with Manasquan R.); 40°04′N 74°02′W. Noted for beautiful turn-of-the-century architecture.

Bay Hill, town (□ 4 sq mi/10.4 sq km; 1990 pop. 5,346), Sumter co., central Fla., c.8 mi/12.9 km SE of Inverness; 28°28′N 81°31′W.

Bay Meadows, Calif.: see SAN MATEO, city.

Bay Mills, village, Chippewa co., E Upper Pennisula, Mich., on St. Marys R., near Whitefish Bay, 12 mi/19 km WSW of Sault Ste. Marie; 46°26′N 84°35′W. Site of Bay Mills Indian Reservation (W unit); Hiawatha Natl. Forest to W.

Bay Minette, city (1990 pop. 7,168), ⊙ Baldwin co., SW Ala., 22 mi/35 km NE of Mobile, in farming, hunting, and fishing area. Furniture, clothing. James H. Faulkner State Community Col. is here. Founded c.1861.

Bay of Islands, Canada: see ISLANDS, BAY OF.

Bay of Pigs, Cuba: see COCHINOS BAY.

Bay Pines, town (□ 2 sq mi/5.2 sq km; 1990 pop. 4,171), W central Fla., 27 mi/43 km NE of Tampa; 27°49′N 82°46′W.

Bay Port, village, Huron co., E Mich., on Saginaw Bay, 22 mi/35 km W of Bad Axe; 43°50′N 83°22′W. Mfg. (steel tubing, crushed stone); resort.

Bay Ridge, a residential sect. of SW Brooklyn borough of N.Y. city, along the Narrows, N of Fort Hamilton; 40°38′N 74°02′W. Verrazano-Narrows Bridge connects the neighborhood to Staten Isl. In 19th cent., it was the center of a large Scandinavian immigrant community.

Bay Ridge, summer resort, Anne Arundel co., central Md., on Chesapeake Bay at S side of L. Ogleton, 4 mi/6.4 km SE of Annapolis. In the 1880s, Bay Ridge was advertised as a major resort. Today the once-public beach and pool are privately owned. The shorefront is the collective property of the owners of a few streets of houses facing the water.

Bay River, an irregular W inlet of Pamlico Sound, c.15 mi/24 km long, Pamlico co., E N.C., with Bayboro at its head. Intracoastal Waterway crosses its mouth and passes N through channel to Pamlico R. estuary.

Bay Roberts, town (1991 pop. 5,474), SE N.F., Canada, on Conception Bay, 8 mi/13 km S of Harbour Grace; 47°36′N 53°16′W. Woodworking, mfg. of furniture, hardware, bldg. materials. Formerly the base for a great fleet of schooners that fished the Lab. banks.

Bay Saint Louis, city (1990 pop. 8,063), ⊙ Hancock co., SE Miss., 15 mi/24 km WSW of Gulfport, on Miss. Sound, Gulf of Mexico, at entrance to St. Louis Bay (highway and RR bridges to Pass Christian); 30°18′N 89°19′W. Mfg. (communications equip., computer hardware, printing and publishing, robotic systems). Buccaneer State Park to SE; mouth of Jordan R. to NW. Inc. 1854.

Bay Shore, uninc. city (□ 6 sq mi/15.5 sq km; 1990 pop. 21,279), Suffolk co., SE N.Y., on S shore of L.I., at the widest point of Great South Bay; 40°43′N 73°15′W. It is noted as a fishing and duck-hunting center and has some light mfg. A ferry runs from there to Fire Isl. Founded 1708.

Bay Springs, town (1990 pop. 1,729), a ⊙ Jasper co. (seat shared with Paulding), E central Miss., 22 mi/35 km NNW of Laurel; 31°58′N 89°16′W. RR terminus. In agr. (cotton, corn; poultry, cattle; dairying) and timber area; mfg. (auto engine parts, lumber, meat prods., printing and publishing, apparel, household appliances). Bienville Natl. Forest to N. Settled 1896, inc. 1904.

Bay View, town, Emmet co., NW Mich., on Little Traverse Bay, 3 mi/4.8 km ENE of Petoskey; 42°47′N 78°51′W. Resort area. Petoskey State Park to N.

Cross references are shown in SMALL CAPITALS. The pronunciation key is on page xv. The dates of population figures are on page xii.

Bay View, village, Jefferson co., N central Ala., 10 mi/16 km NW of Birmingham.

Bay View, Mass.: see GLOUCESTER.

Bay View Garden, village (1990 pop. 418), Woodford co., central Ill., residential suburb, 7 mi/11.3 km NE of Peoria, on Illinois R. (upper Peoria L.); 40°48'N 89°31'W. Agr. area.

Bay Village, city (1990 pop. 17,000), Cuyahoga co., NE Ohio, a suburb of Cleveland. It is a residential community with some light industry. Inc. 1903.

Bayaguana (bah-yah-GWAH-nah), town (1993 pop. 12,470), Monte Plata prov., E central Dominican Republic, 25 mi/40 km NE of Santo Domingo; 18°47'N 69°36'W. Rice-growing center. Founded 1606.

Bayamo (bei-YAH-mo), city (1995 est. pop. 132,000), ⊙ and largest city of Granma prov., SE Cuba; 20°23'N 76°39'W. It is a mfg. and transportation center. Cattle raising, vegetable packing, and sugar refining are the main industries. Founded in 1513, Bayamo was an inland port until the 19th cent. A former center of revolutionary movements, it gave its name to the Cuban natl. anthem, *El Himno Bayamés.* Both the Ten Years War (1868–1878) and the successful revolt of 1895 began in Bayamo. Carlos Manual de Céspedes and Tomás Estrada Palma were born in the city.

Bayamón (bah-yah-MON), city (1990 pop. 220,262), NE P.R., W of San Juan. A residential, commercial, and industrial city; largest in pop. after San Juan. Mfg. includes clothing, medicines, plastics, cement prods., electric equip., and pharmaceuticals. Founded in 1772, it is one of the oldest settlements on the isl.

Bayamón River (bahyah-MON), c.25 mi/40 km long, E central and NE P.R., rises N of Cayey, flows N past Bayamón, to the Atlantic 2.5 mi/4 km WNW of Cataño. It has been channelized along the coastal plain.

Bayard 1 (BAI-uhrd), town (1990 pop. 511), Guthrie co., W central Iowa, 13 mi/21 km N of Guthrie Center; 41°51'N 94°33'W. In agr. area. **2** town (1990 pop. 1,196), Morrill co., W Nebr., 14 mi/23 km WNW of Bridgeport; 41°45'N 103°19'W. Grain, livestock; beet sugar refining. Mfg. Chimney Rock, landmark on Oregon Trail, to S. Founded c.1887. **3** town (1990 pop. 2,598), Grant co., SW N.Mex., 11 mi/18 km ESE of Silver City; 32°45'N 108°07'W. Silver City–Grant Co. Airport to S; Santa Rita Open Pit Copper Mine to NE; Bear Canyon Dam and Reservoir to NE; Gila Natl. Forest, including Black Peak and Continental Divide, to N.

Bayard 1 (BAI-uhrd), village (1990 pop. 400), Grant co., SW N.Mex., in foothills of Pinos Altos Mts., 11 mi/18 km E of Silver City, E of Central, in Gila Natl. Forest. Elev. 6,166 ft/1,879 m. Gold, silver, copper mines in vicinity. Veteran's Administration Hosp. is here. **2** village (1990 pop. 414), Grant co., W. Va., in Eastern Panhandle, on North Branch of Potomac R., 20 mi/32 km NW of Petersburg at the Md. state line; 39°16'N 79°22'W. Agr. (grain; livestock, poultry); mfg. (lumber, coal processing); coal mining. Mt. Storm L. and Stony R. reservoir to SE; Fairfax Stone State Monument to SW.

Bayboro, town (1990 pop. 733), ⊙ Pamlico co., E N.C., 18 mi/29 km E of New Bern, at head of Bay R. (inlet of Pamlico Sound); 35°08'N 76°46'W. Fishing. Agr. inland (cotton, peanuts, grain, potatoes, hogs); mfg. (feeds, food processing).

Baychester, residential section of NE Bronx borough of N.Y. city, SE N.Y., on Eastchester Bay; 40°22'N 73°51'W. Pelham Bay Park is here.

Bayfield, county (□ 2,041 sq mi/5,286 sq km; 1990 pop. 14,008), extreme N Wis., bounded N by L. Superior, E in N part by Chequamegon Bay; ⊙ Washburn; 46°37'N 91°10'W. A large portion of co. is on a wide peninsula. Drained by Namekagon R. and generally wooded, with some cutover farm land. There are several resort lakes. Barley; sheep, poultry; lumbering, fishing; some mfg. W end of Gogebic iron range is in co. Red Cliff Indian Reservation in N and a lage sect. of Chequamegon Natl. Forest runs from N center to SE (includes W Field Station). Tourism. East Branch of St. Croix Natl. Scenic Riverway on Namekagon R. in S; Port Mt. Ski Area in NE; Mt. Telemark Ski Area in S; mainland shore unit and 3 isls. of Apostle Isls. Natl. Lakeshore in extreme NE. Formed 1845.

Bayfield 1 town (1990 pop. 1,090), La Plata co., SW Colo., on Los Pinos R., in foothills of San Juan Mts., 15 mi/24 km ESE of Durango; 37°13'N 107°35'W. Elev. 6,892 ft/2,101 m. In cattle-raising area; hay, oats. Southern Ute Indian Reservation to S. San Juan Natl. Forest to E; Vallecito Reservoir and Lemon Reservoir to N. **2** town (1990 pop. 686), Bayfield co., extreme N Wis., on L. Superior, 16 mi/26 km N of Ashland; 46°48'N 90°49'W. Fishing resort, fruit-growing center (orchard-grown apples and raspberries); tourism. Apostle Isls. (Natl. Lakeshore), to NE and E, are reached from here. Ferry to Madeline Isl. Red Cliff Indian Reservation to N; Bayfield Fish Hatchery to SW; Port Mt. Ski Area to SW, near Mt. Ashwabay (1,316 ft/401 m). Settled 1856, inc. 1913.

Bayfield, village (1991 pop. 813), S Ont., Canada, on L. Huron, at mouth of Bayfield R., 12 mi/19 km S of Goderich; 43°34'N 81°42'W. Dairying, mixed farming.

Baylis, village (1990 pop. 257), Pike co., W Ill., 10 mi/16 km NNW of Pittsfield; 39°43'N 90°54'W. Grain; livestock.

Baylor, county (□ 901 sq mi/2,334 sq km; 1990 pop. 4,385), N Texas; ⊙ Seymour; 33°37'N 99°13'W. Prairie region, drained by Wichita R. (forms L. Kemp at N center of co. and Diversion L. in NE corner), Brazos R., and Millers Creek (forms Millers Creek Reservoir in SW corner). Livestock raising (beef cattle); agr. (cotton, wheat, hay). Oil, natural gas wells. Formed 1858.

Bayonet Point, city (□ 5 sq mi/13 sq km; 1990 pop. 21,860), Pasco co., W central Fla., 29 mi/47 km NNW of Tampa; 28°19'N 82°40'W. Mfg. (printing).

Bayonne (bai-YONE), city (1990 pop. 61,444), Hudson co., NE N.J., on a 3-mi-/4.8-km-wide peninsula; 40°39'N 74°06'W. It has textile, machinery, and oil and chemical industries. Its huge oil refineries (operating since 1875) are supplied by a branch of the oil pipeline from the Southwest. Bayonne provides the energy needs for the adjacent metropolitan area and the fuel for overseas aircraft and ships. On the city's 9-mi/14.5-km waterfront is a large U.S. naval engineering and supply depot. Early Du. traders came to this site c.1650; the British gained possession in 1664. Bayonne is connected to N.Y. city by Bayonne Bridge (1,675 ft/511 m long; opened 1931). Inc. 1869.

Bayou Bodcau Reservoir (BEI-yoo BAHD-ko), on Bossier/Webster parish border, NW La., on the Bayou Bodcau, 25 mi/40 km NE of Shreveport; c.20 mi/32 km long; 32°42'N 93°31'W. Max. capacity 1,197,700 acre-ft. Extends N to Ark. border and L. Etling reservoir (Ark.). Formed by Bayou Bodcau Dam (70 ft/21 m high; earth-construction), built (1949) flood control. Pool generally kept dry.

Bayou Cane (BEI-yoo KAIN), uninc. city (1990 pop. 15,876), Terrebonne parish, SE La., 4 mi/6 km NNW of Houma, on Bayou Cane, at confluence with Bayou Terrebonne; 29°37'N 90°45'W. Sugarcane, crawfish, catfish, alligators.

Bayou D'Arbonne Reservoir (□ 24 sq mi/62 sq km), Union Parish, N central La., on Bayou D'Arbonne R., 20 mi/32 km NW of Monroe; 32°43'N 92°20'W. Max. capacity 240,000 acre-ft. Formed by Bayou D'Arbonne Dam (51 ft/15 m high), built (1961) for recreation. D'Arbonne Natl. Wildlife Refuge just downstream. Also know as Bayou D'Arbonne L.

Bayou Goula (BEI-yoo GOO-luh), village, Iberville parish, SE central La., 16 mi/26 km S of Baton Rouge, on W bank of the Mississippi R.; 30°12'N 90°10'W. In sugarcane area.

Bayou La Batre (BAH-yoo lah BAH-truh), village (1990 pop. 2,456), Mobile co., extreme SW Ala., 21 mi/34 km SSW of Mobile, near Miss. Sound of Gulf of Mexico. Boatbuilding, petroleum, apparel; packing (chiefly seafood) and canning.

Bayou Vista (BEI-yoo VIS-tuh), uninc. village (1990 pop. 4,733), St. Mary parish, S. La., 4 mi/6 km WNW of Morgan City, on Bayou Teche; 29°42'N 91°16'W. Sugarcane; crawfish. Mfg. of tools, oil-field equipment.

Bayport, town (1990 pop. 3,200), Washington co., E Minn., at N end of L. St. Croix (in St. Croix R.), suburb 16 mi/26 km ENE of St. Paul and 3 mi/4.8 km SE of Stillwater; 45°01'N 92°46'W. Resort area; cattle, sheep; soybeans, corn, oats, alfalfa; mfg. (bldg. materials, printing). Minn. correctional facilities are here and in adjacent Oak Park Heights, to NW. Lower St. Croix Natl. Scenic Riverway on St. Croix R.

Bayport, village (□ 3 sq mi/7.8 sq km; 1990 pop. 7,702), Suffolk co., SE N.Y., on S L.I., on Great South Bay, just E of Sayville; 40°45'N 73°02'W. In shore-resort area.

Bays, Lake of (13 mi/21 km long, 6 mi/10 km wide), S Ont., Canada, in Muskoka lake region, 50 mi/80 km E of Parry Sound. Drained by Muskoka R.

Bays Mountain, NE Tenn., forested ridge in Great Appalachian Valley, E of Holston R.; from Knoxville area extends c.75 mi/121 km NE to vicinity of Va. line. Summit, 35°00'N 85°37'W.

Baysboro, uninc. town (1990 pop. 1,661), New Hanover co., SE N.C., 10 mi/16 km NE of Wilmington, on Intracoastal Waterway at Mason Inlet, short passage to Atlantic Ocean to SE; 34°17'N 77°47'W.

Bayshore Gardens, city (□ 3 sq mi/7.8 sq km; 1990 pop. 17,062), Manatee co., W central Fla., 4.5 mi/7.2 km S of Bradenton; 27°25'N 82°34'W.

Bayside 1 village, Humboldt co., Calif., 5 mi/8 km E of Arcata Bay, on Ca. Highway 255. **2** village (1990 pop. 400), Refugio co., S Texas, on Copano Bay, 23 mi/37 km NNE of Corpus Christi; 28°06'N 97°12'W. Resort area.

Bayside, section of NE Queens borough of N.Y. city, SE N.Y., on Little Neck Bay; 41°17'N 73°16'W. Mainly residential. Nearby Fort Totten was closed by the Defense Base Closure and Realization Commission in 1995.

Bayside, suburb (1990 pop. 4,789) of Milwaukee, Milwaukee and Ozaukee cos., SE Wis., 8 mi/12.9 km N of downtown, on L. Michigan; 43°10'N 87°54'W. Residential.

Baytown, suburb (1990 pop. 63,850) of Houston, Harris and Chambers cos., SE Texas, 20 mi/32 km E of downtown, at the head of Galveston Bay, on the Houston ship channel (crossed by bridge/tunnel to La Porte; 29°45'N 94°58'W. E of mouth of San Jacinto R. crossed by Lynchburg Ferry to San Jacinto Battleground State Historical Park. Large volumes of oil are produced in the area, refined in Baytown, and shipped throughout the world; mfg. (chemicals, steel pipe, medical supplies). Lee Col. is here. Houston Raceway Park, drag racing. Inc. 1948 after the consolidation of Goose Creek, Pelly, and Baytown.

Bayview, uninc. town (1990 pop. 1,318), Humboldt co., NW Calif., residential suburb 2 mi/3.2 km S of Eureka, on Humboldt Bay; 40°46'N 124°11'W. Eureka Municipal Airport is here. Humboldt Bay Natl. Wildlife Refuge to S.

Bayview 1 uninc. village, Beaufort co., E N.C., 17 mi/27 km ESE of Washington, on Pamlico R. estuary. Ferry to E crosses river. **2** village (1990 pop. 231), Cameron co., extreme S Texas, 17 mi/27 km NNE of Brownsville; 26°07'N 97°24'W. Residential community in irrigated agr. region. Laguna Atascosa Natl. Wildlife Refuge to N.

Bayview, Ala.: see BAY VIEW.

Bayview-Montalvin, uninc. town (1990 pop. 2988), Contra Costa co., W Calif., residential suburb, 13 mi/21 km NNW of downtown Oakland, and 4 mi/6.4 km N of Richmond, on San Pablo Bay; 38°00'N 122°19'W. Pinole Point to NW.

Bayville, village (□ 1 sq mi/2.6 sq km; 1990 pop. 7,193), Nassau co., SE N.Y., on N shore of W L.I., at base of Centre Isl. peninsula, c.3 mi/4.8 km NNW of Oyster Bay village; 40°54'N 73°33'W. Inc. 1919.

Baywood Park, uninc. town (1990 pop. c.4500), San Luis Obispo co., SW Calif., 10 mi/16 km WNW of San Luis Obispo, 1 mi/1.6 km NW of Osos, 1 mi/1.6 km E of Morro Bay on the Pacific Ocean. Statistically reported as Baywood–Los Osos (1990 pop. 14,733). Morro Bay State Park and Atascadero State Beach to W; Montana de Oro State Park to S. Flowers, nursery prods., strawberries, apples, avocados, vegetables, grain; cattle.

Bazile Mills (BAI-zil), village (1990 pop. 34), Knox co.,

NE Nebr., 3 mi/4.8 km N of Creighton, and on Bazile Creek; 42°30′N 97°54′W.

Bazine (buh-ZEEN), village (1990 pop. 373), Ness co., W central Kansas, on Walnut Creek, 12 mi/19 km E of Ness City; 38°27′N 99°41′W. Grain; livestock.

Beach 1 town, Ware co., SE Ga., 17 mi/27 km NNW of Waycross; 31°26′N 82°30′W. **2** town (1990 pop. 1,205), ⊙ Golden Valley co., W N.Dak., near Mont. border, 58 mi/93 km W of Dickinson; 46°54′N 104°00′W. Grain-shipping point (wheat, barley, oats). Little Mo. Grassland to E; Lamesteer Natl. Wildlife Refuge to SW, in Mont. Inc. 1908.

Beach Bluff, Mass.: see SWAMPSCOTT.

Beach City, village (1990 pop. 1,051), Stark co., E central Ohio, 14 mi/23 km SW of Canton and on Sugar Creek (a tributary of Tuscarawas R.); 40°41′N 81°36′W. Flood control dam (completed 1937) nearby.

Beach City, residential suburb (1990 pop. 852) of Houston, Chambers co., SE Texas, 28 mi/45 km ESE of downtown, on 10 mi/16 km of beachfront on Trinity Bay, arm of Galveston Bay, Gulf of Mexico; 29°43′N 94°50′W. Recreation.

Beach Haven, resort borough (1990 pop. 1,475), Ocean co., E N.J., on Long Beach isl., 17 mi/27 km NE of Atlantic City; 39°33′N 74°15′W. Fishing. Just S is Beach Haven Inlet, passage from the Atlantic leading into Intracoastal Waterway and channels to Little Egg Harbor (NW) and Great Bay (W).

Beach Park, city (1990 pop. 9,513), Lake co., NE Ill., residential suburb, 37 mi/60 km NNW of downtown Chicago, 3 mi/4.8 km N of Waukegan, near L. Michigan; 42°25′N 87°51′W. Ill. Beach State Park and Zion Nuclear Power Plant to E. City surrounds Waukegan Airport.

Beachburg, village (1991 pop. 766), SE Ont., Canada, 15 mi/24 km ESE of Pembroke; 45°44′N 76°51′W. Dairying; mixed farming.

Beachville, village, S Ont., Canada, on Thames R., 5 mi/8 km SW of Woodstock. Lime quarrying; dairying; mixed farming.

Beachwood, city (1990 pop. 10,677), Cuyahoga co., N Ohio, an E suburb of Cleveland; 41°29′N 81°31′W.

Beachwood, resort borough (1990 pop. 9,324), Ocean co., E N.J., on Toms R., opposite Toms River town; 39°55′N 74°12′W. Near Barnegat Bay.

Beacon, city (☐ 4 sq mi/10.4 sq km; 1990 pop. 13,243), Dutchess co., SE N.Y., on the E bank of the Hudson R., opposite Newburgh; 41°30′N 73°58′W. Beacon has textile and related industries, other varied mfg., and a large industrial research firm. The Newburgh-Beacon Bridge connects the city with Newburgh on the W bank. An incline RR ascends Mt. Beacon, site of a towering monument to Amer. Revolutionary soldiers who built signal fires there to warn of the coming of the British. The Beacon Correctional Facility is in the city. At Castle Point, 3 mi/4.8 km NNE, is Veteran's Hosp., occupying a prominent site overlooking the Hudson R. to the W. Beacon's historic bldgs. include the Madam Brett homestead (1709) and the Van Wyck homestead (1732). Settled 1663, inc. as a city in 1913 when Fishkill Landing and Matteawan villages were united.

Beacon, town (1990 pop. 509), Mahaska co., S central Iowa, 2 mi/3.2 km SW of Oskaloosa; 41°16′N 92°40′W. In coal-mining area.

Beacon Falls, town (1990 pop. 5,083), New Haven co., SW Conn., on Naugatuck R., 8 mi/12.9 km S of Waterbury; 41°26′N 73°03′W. Industry includes tools, agr., and paper and plastic prods. State forest here. Settled c.1678, inc. 1871.

Beacon Hill, neighborhood adjoining downtown Boston, Mass. Earliest of Boston's residential neighborhoods, with traditional homes of Boston aristocracy. 1st house built by William Slackstone c.1625. Fire beacon placed on hill 1634. Narrow town houses and mansions built in 18th and 19th cent., cobbled stone streets. Designed by Charles Bulfinch, the Mass. State House (built 1798, dome covered by gold leaf 1861) tops the hill. Hill was largely built up by early 18th cent. Present Beacon Hill is shaped by the shearing by 60 ft/18 m of 3 major hills (Mts. Vernon, Pemberton, and Beacon)

in 1st quarter of 18th cent. to facilitate the development of the neighborhood. Original name Treamount.

Beaconsfield (BEE-kuhnz-feeld), residential town (1991 pop. 19,616), S Que., Canada, on S shore of Montreal Isl., on L. St. Louis, 15 mi/24 km SW of Montreal; 45°26′N 73°50′W.

Beaconsfield, town (1990 pop. 27), Ringgold co., S Iowa, 11 mi/18 km ENE of Mount Ayr; 40°48′N 94°02′W. In agr. area.

Beadle, county (☐ 1,264 sq mi/3,274 sq km; 1990 pop. 18,253), E central S.Dak.; ⊙ Huron. Agr. area drained by James R. and Pearl, Foster, and Cain creeks. Corn, wheat; cattle, hogs, dairy prods.; poultry; honey; mfg. at Huron. James R. State Use Area in N. Formed 1873.

Bealeton, uninc. village, Fauquier co., N Va., 10 mi/16 km SSE of Warrenton; 38°34′N 77°45′W. Mfg. (millwork, wood prods., fabricated metal prods.); agr. (grain, soybeans, apples; livestock). Flying Circus Airport Mus. to SE.

Beallsville (BELZ-vil), village (1990 pop. 464), Monroe co., E Ohio, 12 mi/19 km SE of Barnesville, in agr. area; 39°52′N 81°02′W. Sawmilling.

Beallsville (BEELS-vil), borough (1990 pop. 530), Washington co., SW Pa., 13 mi/21 km SE of Washington; 40°03′N 80°01′W. Agr. (corn, hay; livestock; dairying).

Beals (BEELZ), town (1990 pop. 667), Washington co., E Maine, 15 mi/24 km SW of Machias; 44°27′N 67°36′W. Comprises Beals Isl. and village of Beals; summer resort, fishing port. Set off from Jonesport 1925.

Beals Creek, c.55 mi/89 km long, W Texas, formed W of Big Spring by headstreams rising on Llano Estacado, flows generally E to the Colorado 15 mi/24 km S of Colorado City.

Bealwood (BEEL-wud), Muscogee co., W Ga., residential suburb of Columbus.

Beaman, town (1990 pop. 183), Grundy co., central Iowa, on Wolf Creek, 9 mi/14.5 km S of Grundy Center; 42°13′N 92°49′W.

Beamsville, residential town, S Ont., Canada, near L. Ontario, 12 mi/19 km W of St. Catharines, and 18 mi/29 km E of Hamilton; 43°01′N 79°29′W. Now part of city of Lincoln; largely commuter pop. Fruit growing, fruit and vegetable canning, woodworking; poultry, dairy; mfg. (farm machinery, fabricated metal prods., chemicals, pottery, cement).

Beanblossom, village, Brown co., S central Ind., 4 mi/6.4 km N of Nashville. Crossroads community. Heavily forested. Hilly terrain.

Beans Grant, land grant, Coos co., N central N.H., 20 mi/32 km SW of Berlin, in White Mt. Natl. Forest. Eisenhower Memorial State Wayside is here.

Beans Purchase, land purchase, Coos co., NE N.H., 15 mi/24 km SSE of Berlin, in White Mt. Natl. Forest. Bounded on E by Maine state line; drained by Wild R.; crossed by Appalachian Trail. Wild R. Natl. Forest Campground in SE.

Bear, uninc. town, New Castle co., N Del., 9 mi/14.5 km SW of Wilmington, on Christina R; 39°46′N 75°39′W. Dairying; livestock; fruit, vegetables. Mfg. (electronic equip.).

Bear, Cape, at SE extremity of P.E.I., Canada, 13 mi/21 km SSE of Georgetown; 46°00′N 62°27′W.

Bear Creek, town (1990 pop. 913), Marion co., NW Ala., 19 mi/31 km NE of Hamilton.

Bear Creek, village (1990 pop. 418), Outagamie co., E Wis., 25 mi/40 km NW of Appleton; 44°31′N 88°43′W. Dairying; farming. Mfg. (food).

Bear Creek 1 c.55 mi/89 km long, in W Ill.; rises near Carthage in Hancock co.; flows SW and S to Mississippi R. N of Quincy; 40°24′N 91°09′W. **2** 40 mi/64 km long, in W central Ky.; rises in E Grayson co., near Clarkson; flows SSW to Green R. 9 mi/14.5 km W of Brownsville. Navigable for small crafts 8 mi/12.9 km above mouth. One of 17 streams so named in Ky.

Bear Creek Reservoir (☐ 1 sq mi/2.6 sq km), Franklin co., NW Ala., on Bear Creek, 13 mi/21 km SW of Russellville; 34°24′N 88°00′W. Max. capacity 39,700 acre-ft. Formed by Bear Creek Dam (1,385 ft/422 m long), built (1969) by TVA for flood control, recreation, and water storage.

Bear Grass, village (1990 pop. 77), Martin co., E N.C., 7 mi/11.3 km SSW of Williamston.

Bear Head, southernmost point of Cape Breton Isl., E N.S., Canada, on the Atlantic, at entrance to Canso Strait, 5 mi/8 km SE of Port Hawkesbury; 45°33′N 61°17′W.

Bear Island Lake, St. Louis co., NE Minn., on Bear Isl. R., 9 mi/14.5 km SSW of Ely; 3.5 mi/5.6 km long, 2 mi/3.2 km wide; 47°46′N 91°59′W. Drains to NE through One Pine and White Iron lakes. Bear Isl. (1 mi/1.6 km long) at center. Impounded by dam. On W boundary of Superior Natl. Forest and in Bear Isl. State Forest. Resorts.

Bear Lake, county (☐ 1,049 sq mi/2,717 sq km; 1990 pop. 6,084), SE Idaho; ⊙ Paris; 42°17′N 111°20′W. Mt. area bordering on Wyo. (E) and Utah (S). Agr. (hay, alfalfa, oats, barley, wheat; sheep, cattle, turkeys; dairying) near Bear L. on S boundary and in valley of Bear R. Includes most of Cache, in W, and part of Caribou, in NE, natl. forests. Bear L. State Park and Bear L. Natl. Wildlife Refuge at N end of lake. Formed 1875.

Bear Lake, village (1990 pop. 339), Manistee co., NW Mich., on Bear L. (c.2 mi/3.2 km long, 1 mi/1.6 km wide), 15 mi/24 km NNE of Manistee; 44°25′N 86°09′W. Trade and shipping center for resort and farm area (apples, cherries, berries); mfg. (food and beverages).

Bear Lake, borough (1990 pop. 193), Warren co., NW Pa., 8 mi/12.9 km NE of Corry, at N.Y. state line; 41°59′N 79°30′W. Mfg. (lumber); agr. (corn, hay; livestock, dairying).

Bear Lake (26 mi/42 km long, 4 mi/6 km wide), N central Man., Canada; 55°13′N 96°W; drains into Hayes R.

Bear Lake, lake (☐ 109 sq mi/282 sq km), Rich co., N Utah and SE Idaho, E of Bear River Range; c.20 mi/32 km long, 7 mi/11.3 km wide. Elev. 5,924 ft/1,806 m;. Used for irrigation, fishing, and recreation. Drains into Bear R. through canal completed 1915. Laketown, Utah, at S end; Garden City, Utah, on W side; St. Charles, Idaho, at NW end. Bear L. State Park, Idaho, at N end; Bear L. State Park, Utah, on W side. Rendezvous Branch State Park, Utah, at S end; Cisco Beach State Park, and Beach, Utah, on E side.

Bear, Mount (c.14,800 ft/4,511 m), S Alaska, in St. Elias Mts., 130 mi/209 km NNW of Yakutat; 61°18′N 141°08′W.

Bear Mountain 1 peak (1,284 ft/391 m high), SE N.Y., overlooking the Hudson R.; 41°19′N 74°01′W. The Bear Mt. sect. of the Palisades Interstate Park, with facilities for both summer and winter sports, is popular among N.Y. city residents. The remains of Fort Clinton, dating from the Amer. Revolution, are here. The Bear Mt. Bridge (2,257 ft/688 m long) crosses the Hudson R. near West Point. This suspension bridge was opened in 1924 and was acquired by N.Y. state in 1940. **2** peak (2,316 ft/706 m) in extreme NW Conn., in Taconic Mts., near Mass. and N.Y. state borders, NW of Salisbury village.

Bear Pond Mountains, NW Md. and S Pa., part of the Appalachians, in Franklin co., Pa., and Washington co., Md., on Mason-Dixon Line. Rise to 1,857 ft/566 m at their highest point; form NW boundary of Hagerstown Valley. Near Conococheague and West Branch rivers.

Bear River, village, NW N.S., Canada, on Bear R., near its mouth on Annapolis Basin 7 mi/11 km SE of Digby; 44°34′N 65°38′W. Cherry center; lumber, pulpwood.

Bear River, 25 mi/40 km long, in W N.S., Canada, flows NW to Annapolis Basin 4 mi/6 km E of Digby.

Bear River 1 c.75 mi/121 km long, in E central Calif.; rises in N Placer co., 23 mi/37 km WNW of Tahoe city, on Nev. line, fed by canal from L Spaulding reservoir (Yuba R.); flows SW and W through to Feather R. 15 mi/24 km S of Marysville. Rollins Dam on Camp Far West Reservoir. **2** 350 mi/563 km long; rising in the Uinta Mts., S Rich co., NE Utah; flowing in a U-shaped course NNE past Randolph into Wyo., past Cokeville, then NW into Idaho, to Soda Springs, then S past Preston, reentering Utah, passing Cornish, Elwood, Newton and Benson, and entering Bear L. Bay, Great Salt

L., 4 mi/6.4 km W of Brigham City. Natural Bear L. feeds into river through short tributary in SE Idaho. A perennial stream, the Bear played an important role in the development of the region by the Mormons in the mid-1800s. The Bear irrigates c.78 sq mi/202 sq km. At the river's mouth is Bear R. Migratory Bird Refuge. **3** c.12 mi/19 km long, in W Maine, rises in W Oxford co., flows SE to the Androscoggin at Newry. Screw Auger Falls in Grafton Notch is scenic feature.

Bear River City, village (1990 pop. 700), Box Elder co., N Utah, 10 mi/16 km NW of Brigham City and on Bear R. Alfalfa, grain; dairying; sheep, cattle. Elev. 4,253 ft/ 1,296 m. Salt Creek Waterfowl Management Area to W; Bear R. Bay of Great Salt L. to SW. Golden Spike Natl. Historical Site 25 mi/40 km to W. Dry farming in Utah began here 1863.

Bear Rocks, uninc. town, Fayette co., SW Pa., residential development 10 mi/16 km NE of Connellsville near Jacobs Creek; 40°07′N 79°27′W. Chestnut Ridge to SE.

Bear Town, uninc. town (1990 pop. 1,277), Pike co., S Miss., 2 mi/3.2 km S of McComb.

Bear Valley 1 village, Mariposa co., Calif., 2 mi/3.2 km S of Merced R. on Ca. Highway 49. **2** village, Alpine co., Calif., just W of Alpine-Calaveras co. line on Ca. Highway 4.

Bear Valley Springs, uninc. town (1990 pop. 1593), Kern co., S Calif., 18 mi/29 km SSE of Bakersfield, near Edison Canal; 35°10′N 118°38′W. Oil and natural gas. Grain, fruit, nuts, cotton; cattle.

Bearcamp River, 15 mi/24 km long, E central N.H.; rises in Sandwich Notch N of Squam L., in W Carroll co.; flows E to Ossipee L.

Bearcreek, village (1990 pop. 37), Carbon co., S Mont., near Wyo. line, 5 mi/8 km ESE of Red Lodge, on Bear Creek; 45°10′N 109°10′W. Coal mining; tourism.

Bearden 1 town (1990 pop. 1,021), Ouachita co., S Ark., 15 mi/24 km NE of Camden; 33°43′N 92°37′W. In agr. and timber area; mfg. (apparel, lumber). Founded 1882, inc. 1892. **2** (BIR-den), town, Knox co., E Tenn., residential suburb, just WSW of Knoxville, near the Tennessee R.

Beardmore (BEERD-mor), village (1991 pop. 454), W central Ont., Canada, 100 mi/161 km NE of Port Arthur, near L. Nipigon; 49°36′N 87°57′W. Elev. 1,009 ft/ 308 m. Gold mining.

Beardsley, village (1990 pop. 297), Big Stone co., W Minn., 22 mi/35 km NW of Ortonville, near Big Stone L. (on Minnesota R., forms S.Dak. boundary); 45°33′N 96°42′W. Grain, soybeans; livestock.

Beardstown, city (1990 pop. 5,270), Cass co., W central Ill., on Illinois R. (bridged) and 13 mi/21 km WNW of Virginia; 40°00′N 90°25′W. River port. Trade and shipping center in agr. area (corn, sorghum, soybeans; cattle, hogs); mfg. of apparel, concrete, lumber; RR shops. Treadway L. is just NE. Old city hall and courthouse (1845), in which Lincoln won the Armstrong murder case in the famous "Almanac Trial," is preserved. Indian mounds nearby. Settled 1819 as ferry crossing; inc. 1837. Home of Beardstown Ladies stock-market investment group.

Béarn (bai-AHRN), village (1991 pop. 1,014), W Que., Canada, near L. Timiskaming, 18 mi/29 km SE of Haileybury; 47°17′N 79°20′W. Gold mining.

Beartooth Highway, Park and Carbon cos., Mont., and Park co., Wyo., to the E and NE of Yellowstone Natl. Park. Scenic, 2-lane, switchback highway, built in 1932 at a cost of $2.5 million. Extends 66 mi/106 km between Cooke City and Red Lodge, Mont. It rises to 10,947 ft/ 3,337 m, affording a panoramic view of the alpine lakes and country below. Accessible lakes and trailheads are frequent. Open from June to September. An interpretive map is available at the Beartooth Ranger Dist., 3 mi/4.8 km S of Red Lodge.

Beartooth Range, S Mont. and NW Wyo., NE spur of Absaroka Range, bet. Stillwater R. (W) and Clarks Fork of the Yellowstone R. (E and S), NE of Yellowstone Natl. Park. In Park, Stillwater, Carbon cos., Mont. and Park co., Wyo. Includes Granite Peak (12,799 ft/ 3,901 m), highest point in Mont. Range includes parts of Custer (Mont.) and Shoshone (Wyo.) natl. forests.

NW extension is Granite Range, rising to 12,661 ft/ 3,859 m in Mt. Wood. Grasshopper Glacier 4 mi/ 6.4 km SW of Granite Peak. Beartooth Pass (10,947 ft/ 3,337 m), N Park co., Wyo., is crossed by Beartooth Scenic Highway.

Beartown Mountain (1,865 ft/568 m), SW Mass., in Beartown State Forest (□ 13 sq mi/34 sq km), 5 mi/ 8 km NE of Great Barrington, in the Berkshires; 42°16′N 73°15′W. Year-round recreation area.

Beasley, town (1990 pop. 485), Fort Bend co., SE Texas, 38 mi/61 km SW of Houston; 29°30′N 95°55′W. Agr. area (rice, cotton, vegetables, soybeans, nurseries). Oil and natural gas.

Beata, Cape (bai-AH-tah), Caribbean headland of SW Dominican Republic, southernmost point of Hispaniola isl., 45 mi/72 km SSW of Barahona; 17°36′N 71°27′W. Beata Isl. is 3 mi/4.8 km SW. Lighthouse.

Beata Island (bai-AH-tah) (c.5 mi/8 km long, 5 mi/ 8 km wide), in the Caribbean, just off SW coast of Dominican Republic, 50 mi/80 km SW of Barahona; 17°35′N 71°30′W.

Beatrice (BEE-tris), city (1990 pop. 12,354), ⊙ Gage co., SE Nebr., on the Big Blue R; 40°16′N 96°45′W. RR junction. The old Oregon Trail is 20 mi/32 km to SW and is the trading and industrial center for a grain, dairy, and livestock area. Mfg. (tools, concrete prods., printing, machinery, metal prods., food, animal feed, wood prods.). A campus of Southeast Community Col. here. Homestead Natl. Monument to W; Rockford L. State Recreation Area to E. Inc. as a city 1873.

Beatrice (BEE-uh-tris), town (1990 pop. 454), Monroe co., SW central Ala., 16 mi/26 km NNE of Monroeville. Lumber.

Beattie (BEE-tee), village (1990 pop. 221), Marshall co., NE Kansas, 12 mi/19 km E of Marysville; 39°51′N 96°25′W. In grain area; feeds.

Beatty, uninc. town (1990 pop. 1,623), Nye co., S Nev., 100 mi/161 km NW of Las Vegas, 12 mi/19 km NE of Calif. boundary; 36°56′N 116°42′W. Light mfg.; cattle; tourism. Amargosa R. flows underground through town. Gateway to Death Valley Natl. Monument (Nev./ Calif.), to SW. Nellis Air Force Bombing and Gunnery Range to NE; Nev. Test Site to E. Amargosa Desert extends to SE. Rhyolite, ghost town, and historical silver mining dist., to W.

Beattyville (BAI-tee-vil), town (1990 pop. 1,131), ⊙ Lee co., E central Ky., 33 mi/53 km ESE of Richmond, in the Cumberland Mts., on Kentucky R., at joining of North and South Forks, which form main stream; 37°34′N 83°42′W. Agr. (tobacco; livestock); mfg. (concrete, wood prods., apparel); limestone, coal, oil, hardwood timber region. At E edge of Daniel Boone Natl. Forest. Est. 1842

Beau Lake (BO), Aroostook co., Maine and Que., Canada, narrow lake on internatl. line, and 23 mi/37 km NW of Fort Kent, Maine; 5 mi/8 km long.

Beauce (bos), county (□ 1,128 sq mi/2,922 sq km; pop.), S Que., Canada, on Maine border and on Chaudière R.; ⊙ Beauceville East; 46°00′N 70°45′W.

Beauceville (BOS-vil), town (1991 pop. 3,869), S Que., Canada, on Chaudière R., 50 mi/80 km SSE of Quebec, opposite Beauceville East; 46°12′N 70°46′W. Lumbering; light mfg.; in dairying region.

Beauceville East, town, ⊙ Beauce co., S Que., Canada, on Chaudière R., 50 mi/80 km SSE of Quebec, opposite Beauceville; 46°12′N 70°46′W. Lumbering; market in dairying region.

Beaucoup Creek (BUCK-up), c.65 mi/105 km long, S Ill., rises SW of Nashville, flows SE and S past Pinckneyville, to Big Muddy R., E of Murphysboro; 38°21′N 89°17′W.

Beaufort 1 (BO-fuhrt), county (□ 957 sq mi/ 2,479 sq km; 1990 pop. 42,283), E N.C., near the Atlantic coast; ⊙ Washington; 35°28′N 76°50′W. Bounded E in part by Pungo R. estuary. Fishing; timber; agr. area (wheat, barley, oats, soybeans, sorghum, sweet potatoes, cotton, peanuts; cattle, hogs). Mfg. at Washington. Resorts along coast. Goose Creek State Park in center on N side of Pamlico R. Tidal Pamlico R. and Tar R. divide co. E-W through middle. Formed 1705. **2-**

(BYOO-fuhrt), county (□ 922 sq mi/2,388 sq km; 1990 pop. 86,425), extreme S S.C.; ⊙ Beaufort; 32°21′N 80°41′W. Extends along Atlantic coast from New R. (S) to St. Helena Sound (NE) bounded by Combahee R. (NE) and New R. SW. Includes several of Sea Isls., notably Port Royal Isl. (site of Beaufort), Parris Isl., St. Helena Isl., Hilton Head Isl. Intracoastal Waterway passes along coast. Includes Hunting Isl. State Park in E section. Formerly a region of great plantations; now a year-round resort area, with fishing, canning, agr. (corn, soybeans, tomatoes; cattle, hogs), lumbering. Formed 1785.

Beaufort, city (1990 pop. 9,576), ⊙ Beaufort co., S S.C., 50 mi/80 km SW of Charleston, on Port Royal Isl., one of Sea Isls.; 32°25′N 80°41′W. Located on the Intracoastal Waterway with a bridge crossing to St. Helena Isl. Year-round resort and tourist center; canning, processing, and shipping point for truck, shrimping, oystering, and lumbering area, with good harbor. Mfg. includes consumer goods, plastic prods., apparel, machinery, fabricated metal prods. Is the 2d-oldest town in S.C.; founded 1711. Held by Union forces from Nov. 1861, to end of Civil War. Has many fine old bldgs., including Episcopal church (built 1724; remodeled), natl. cemetery, arsenal (1795).

Beaufort (BO-fuhrt), town (1990 pop. 3,808), ⊙ Carteret co., E N.C., 35 mi/56 km SE of New Bern, opposite Morehead City, at mouth of Beaufort Harbor (bridged to Morehead City, connected with the Atlantic by Beaufort Inlet); here entered by short Newport R; 34°43′N 76°39′W. Fishing center; resort; port of entry; mfg. (wood prods., food processing, apparel). Fort Macon State Park to S, on Bogue Isl. Intracoastal Waterway, turns N from Bogue Sound, through Beaufort Harbor and canal, to Nuese R. (N). Core Sound to E, Bogue Sound to W, both behind Outer Banks. Historic Beaufort includes Josiah Bell House (1767); N.C. Maritime Mus. Laid out 1722.

Beaufort Sea (BO-fuhrt), U.S. and Canada; part of Arctic Ocean, bounded by N.W.T. (E and SE), Yukon Territory (S), Alaska (SW), Banks Isl. (E); Mackenzie R. and its delta enter from S. Flurry of oil and natural gas exploration began in mid-1970s and continues into the 1990s amid environmental concerns. Oil and gas production occurs offshore and onshore, esp. around Tuktoyaktuk, N.W.T. Inuvik, E of delta, is primary staging and service center for operation. It was 1st visited by the Can. explorer Vilhjalmur Stefansson in 1914.

Beauharnois (bo-HAHR-nwah), county (□ 147 sq mi/ 381 sq km), SW Que., Canada, on the St. Lawrence R.; ⊙ Beauharnois; 45°14′N 74°03′W.

Beauharnois (bo-HAHR-nwah), city (1991 pop. 6,449), S Que., Canada, on L. St. Louis, a broadening of the St. Lawrence R.; 45°19′N 73°52′W. Steel, aluminum, metal alloys, paper, chemicals, and furniture are produced. Beauharnois is at the E outlet of the Beauharnois Canal, part of the St. Lawrence Seaway System, and is the site of a large hydroelectric development.

Beauharnois Canal, SW Que., Canada, extends 15 mi/ 24 km bet. L. St. Francis (W) and L. St. Louis (NE), on S side of the St. Lawrence, bypassing rapids. The 1st canal, opened 1843, soon became obsolete and was superseded (1899) by Soulanges Canal, on N side of the St. Lawrence. New Beauharnois Canal was begun 1930, has fall of 83 ft/25 m, and has important hydroelectric power station. Project was subject of political scandal.

Beaulieu, Canada: see SAINTE PÉTRONILLE.

Beaumont 1 city (1990 pop. 9,685), Riverside co., S Calif., suburb 22 mi/35 km ESE of Riverside, at summit of San Gorgonio Pass; 33°56′N 116°59′W. Fruit growing (mainly cherries); mfg. (concrete, printing and publishing, plastic pipe, metal fabrication). Settled in mid-19th cent.; inc. 1912. Part of San Bernadino Natl. Forest to N; Morango Indian Reservation to NE. **2** city (1990 pop. 114,323), ⊙ Jefferson co., SE Texas, 75 mi/121 km ENE of Houston; 30°05′N 94°08′W. A port of entry on the Sabine-Neches Waterway. Twin city to Port Arthur, 18 mi/29 km SE. Bounded by Neches R at E, and Pine Isl. Bayou on N. A ship channel (completed 1916, reconstructed 1927) provides the facilities of a modern deepwater port, with shipyards and large storage tanks, also a RR junction. Beaumont is an important industrial and shipping center and a major oil city. With Port Arthur and Orange, it forms the "Golden Triangle," a vast petrochemical and industrial complex. Other industries are based on the forests and vast farmlands of the area. There are rice mills, granaries, lumber and paper plants, meat-packing houses, huge metalworks, and an alligator farm. The lush pine forests were the base of the lumbering that began here before the Civil War. Shipbuilding followed, and, as livestock raising and rice farming spread in the surrounding area, Beaumont became a significant processing and transportation center. Its city life was revolutionized in 1901 when the world's 1st principal oil gusher came in at nearby Spindletop; a 58 ft/18 m granite shaft marks the spot, which is a natl. historic site. Beaumont Municipal Airport to W. Beaumont has a pioneer mus., an oil mus., an art center, S Texas State Fairgrounds, and the Parkdale Mall (one of the largest shopping centers in the U.S.). It is the seat of Lamar Univ. (main campus). Annual events include a horse show, a river festival, and a rodeo. Village Creek State Park to N; part of Big Thicket Natl. Preserve N of city. Inc. 1838.

Beaumont (BO-mahnt), town (1990 pop. 1,054), Perry co., SE Miss., 24 mi/39 km ESE of Hattiesburg, on Leaf R.; 31°10′N 88°55′W. Timber; cotton, corn; poultry. Mfg. (plywood). De Soto Natl. Forest to S; L. Perry State L. to S.

Beaumont–Port Arthur Canal, Texas: see SABINE-NECHES WATERWAY.

Beauport (bo-POR), city (1991 pop. 69,158), S Que., Canada, on the St. Lawrence R.; 46°51′N 71°11′W. It is a suburb of Quebec city. Settled in 1634, it is one of the oldest communities in Canada.

Beauregard (BO-ri-gahrd), parish (□ 1,184 sq mi/3,067 sq km; 1990 pop. 30,083), W La.; ⊙ De Ridder; 30°51′N 93°17′W. Bounded W by Sabine R., here forming Texas line, drained by Bear Head, Bundick, and Whisky Chitto rivers. Diversified lumber and agr. area (blueberries, feed grains, hay, nursery crops, rice, soybeans, squash, watermelons; cattle, exotic fowl); dairying. Mfg. of clothing, chemicals, plastics, resins; logging, paper mills. Sand and gravel pits. Bundicks Fish and Game Preserve at Bundick L. in NE. Named after Gen. Beauregard. Formed 1912.

Beauregard (BO-ruh-gahrd), village (1990 pop. 206), Copiah co., SW Miss., 40 mi/64 km SSW of Jackson; 31°43′N 90°23′W. Agr. (cotton, corn; cattle).

Beaurivage (bo-ree-VAHZH), village, S. Que., Canada, 28 mi/45 km S of Quebec. Dairying; pigs, cattle.

Beauséjour (BO-sai-ZHOOR), town (1991 pop. 2,633), SE Man., Canada, near Brokenhead R., 30 mi/48 km ENE of Winnipeg; 50°04′N 96°31′W. Lumber and flour milling, dairying. Glass-sand quarries nearby.

Beauséjour, Fort, Canada: see FORT BEAUSÉJOUR.

Beauty, uninc. village (1990 pop. 500), Martin co., E Ky., 16 mi/26 km NW of Williamson (W.Va.), near Tug Fork Big Sandy R. (W.Va. state boundary). Bituminous coal.

Beaux Arts Village, residential suburb (1990 pop. 303) of Seattle, King co., W Wash., 6 mi/9.7 km ESE of downtown, on E shore of L. Washington, on East Channel separating Mercer Isl. from mainland and N of E end of Mercer Isl. (Morrow) Bridge, at mouth of Mercer Slough; 47°35′N 122°12′W.

Beaver 1 county (□ 1,817 sq mi/4,706 sq km; 1990 pop. 6,023), W Okla. Panhandle; ⊙ Beaver; 36°45′N 100°28′W. High plains (elev. c.2,500 ft/762 m); bounded N by Kansas, S by Texas; intersected by Beaver R. (continuation of North Canadian R.), Cimarron R., and Kiowa Creek. Easternmost of 3 Panhandle cos. Wheat, sorghum, corn; cattle. Natural-gas and salt deposits; oil. Includes Beaver State Park in N center. Formed 1890. **2** county (□ 443 sq mi/1,147 sq km), W Pa.; ⊙ Beaver; 40°41′N 80°20′W. Mining, agr., and mfg. area; drained by Ohio and Beaver rivers, and also drained by Connoquenessing and Raccoon creeks. Urbanized and industrialized along river margins; bounded W by Ohio state line. Gen. Anthony Wayne est. (1792–1793) one of 1st army training camps here. Mfg. at Beaver Falls, Beaver, Aliquippa, Ambridge, and their suburbs; iron and steel plants, assorted heavy industry; bituminous coal, sandstone, clay, sand and gravel. Agr. (corn, wheat, hay, alfalfa, apples; sheep, cattle; dairying). Nuclear power plants: Beaver Valley 1 (initial criticality May 10, 1976; max. dependable capacity of 810 MWe) and Beaver Valley 2 (initial criticality August 4, 1987; max. dependable capacity of 820 MWe) are 17 mi/27 km W of McCandless, and both use cooling water from the Ohio R. Ambridge Reservoir in S center; Raccoon Creek State Park in SW. Formed 1800. **3** county (□ 2,592 sq mi/6,713 sq km; 1990 pop. 4,765), SW Utah; ⊙ Beaver; 38°20′N 113°13′W. Mt. area drained by Beaver R., and bordering on Nev. on W. Some agr. and ranching in valleys; alfalfa, barley, potatoes; dairying; cattle; lead, sulphur. Part of Fishlake Natl. Forest in W. Elk Meadows Ski Area in E; Minersville Reservoir and State Park in SE. Most of co.'s pop. is in E. Formed 1856.

Beaver 1 town (1990 pop. 46), Boone co., central Iowa, on Beaver Creek, and 13 mi/21 km W of Boone; 42°02′N 94°08′W. **2** or **Beaver City**, town (1990 pop. 1,584), ⊙ Beaver co., E Okla. Panhandle, on high plains, on North Canadian (Beaver) R., c.70 mi/113 km NW of Woodward; 36°48′N 100°31′W. Elev. 2,500 ft/762 m. Shipping center for wheat and cattle area; oil- and natural-gas-producing region; dairy prods.; poultry. Trail Mus. here. Beaver State Park to N. Was first settled by squatters c.1880; in 1887 became capital of the short-lived Territory of Cimarron. **3** town (1990 pop. 1998), ⊙ Beaver co., SW Utah, on Beaver R., c.45 mi/72 km NE of Cedar City, W of Tushar Mts.; 38°16′N 112°38′W. Resort and processing point for livestock and irrigated agr. area; alfalfa, potatoes; cattle; mfg. (dairy prods.). Minersville Reservoir and State Park to W; Fishlake Natl. Forest, including Elk Meadows Ski Area, to East Beaver Fish Hatchery to E. Historic dist.; elev. 5,970 ft/1,820 m. Settled 1856 by Mormons. Had mining boom in 19th cent. **4** uninc. town (1990 pop. 930), Clallam co., NW Wash., 42 mi/68 km WSW of Port Angeles, at SW end of L. Pleasant, near Sol Duc (Soleduck) R. Timber; mfg. (wood prods.). Olympic Natl. Forest to E. Also called Tyee. **5** uninc. town (1990 pop. 1,244), Raleigh co., S W.Va., suburb 4 mi/6.4 km SE of Beckley; 37°44′N 81°09′W. Little Beaver State Park to E.

Beaver 1 village (1990 pop. 103), N central Alaska, on Yukon R., and 110 mi/177 km N of Fairbanks, near Arctic Circle; 66°19′N 147°18′W. **2** village (1990 pop. 336), Pike co., S Ohio, 20 mi/32 km NNE of Portsmouth, and on small Beaver Creek; 39°02′N 82°51′W. Sawmills.

Beaver, borough (1990 pop. 5,028), ⊙ Beaver co., W Pa., on Ohio R., near mouth of Beaver R., 24 mi/39 km NW of Pittsburgh; 40°41′N 80°18′W. Mineral region. Light mfg.; agr. area (corn, alfalfa; livestock; dairying). Site of Fort McIntosh (1778); Pa. State Univ., Beaver campus, to S, near Monaca; Nuclear Power Plant at Shippingport, 7 mi/11.3 km WSW on Ohio R.; Montgomery Dam on Ohio R., 5 mi/8 km WSW. Laid out 1791, inc. 1802.

Beaver Bay, village (1990 pop. 147), Lake co., NE Minn., 49 mi/79 km. NE of Duluth, 24 mi/39 km NE of Two Harbors, on L. Superior ("North Shore"), at mouth of Beaver R.; 47°15′N 91°17′W. Resort area. Superior Natl. Forest to NW; Split Rock Lighthouse State Park and Gooseberry Falls State Park to SW.

Beaver City, village (1990 pop. 707), ⊙ Furnas co., S Nebr., 40 mi/64 km S of Lexington, on Beaver Creek, near Kansas line; 40°08′N 99°49′W. Grain.

Beaver City, Okla.: see BEAVER, town.

Beaver Creek, district, Washington co., W Md., on small Beaver Creek, 6 mi/9.7 km SE of Hagerstown. Cannery, grain mills. Nearby are Mt. Aetna Caverns, Appalachian Trail, Greenbrier State Park, M. Powell State Fish Hatchery near Wagners Crossroads. The village school is preserved as a small mus. and also contains a farm tool collection and a millinery center. The Beaver Creek Fish Hatchery supplies trout to area streams and is fed by a warm spring.

Beaver Creek, village (1991 pop. 104), SW Y.T., Canada, on Alaska Hwy., 160 mi/257 km NW of Haines Junction, 5 mi/8 km E of Alaska border, 19 mi/31 km SE of highway border crossing. This was the meeting point of highway construction crews working from E and W, Sept. 25, 1942. It is Canada's westernmost municipality. Travel services.

Beaver Creek, village (1990 pop. 249), Rock co., extreme SW Minn., 19 mi/31 km ENE of Sioux Falls, S.Dak., on Beaver Creek; 43°36′N 96°21′W. Corn, oats, soybeans; hogs, cattle, poultry; dairying; mfg. (motor vehicle parts). RR junction to SW.

Beaver Creek 1 152 mi/245 km long, in Colo., Kansas, and Nebr.; rises in SE Kit Carson co., E Colo.; flows ENE into Kansas, past Kanorudo, NW Kansas past Atwood, into S Nebr., past Beaver City, to Republican R. near Orleans, just above Karlan County L. reservoir. Receives Sappa Creek c.20 mi/32 km above its mouth. **2** c.65 mi/105 km long, central Iowa; rises 20 mi/32 km S of Fort Dodge; flows S and SE to Des Moines R. (Saylorville Reservoir), just N of Des Moines. **3** c.100 mi/161 km long, in E Mont.; rises in NE Fallon co.; flows N past Wibaux, then NE to Little Missouri R. in W N.Dak., in Little Missouri Natl. Grassland. **4** 84 mi/135 km long, in NE central Nebr.; rises in Wheeler co.; flows SE past Albion and St. Edward, to Loup R. near Genoa. **5** c.65 mi/105 km long, SW Okla.; rises in NE Comanche co.; flows generally S, through oil-producing area, past Waurika, Sugden, and Ryan, to Red R. just S of Ryan. Dammed 5 mi/8 km N of Waurika to form Waurika L. **6** stream in central Colo., rising in Holy Cross Wilderness; flowing N to Eagle R. Site of Beaver Creek Ski Resort 2 mi/3.2 km S of Eagle R. (Avon, Colo.)

Beaver Creek Reservoir, Rio Grande co., S Colo., on Beaver Creek, 16 mi/26 km WSW of Del Norte, in Rio Grande Natl. Forest; 1.5 mi/2.4 km long; 37°35′N 107°37′W. Max. capacity of 5,702 acre-ft. Formed by Beaver Park Dam (96 ft/29 m high), built (1970) by the Colo. Dept. of Natural Resources for irrigation.

Beaver Crossing, village (1990 pop. 448), Seward co., SE Nebr., 13 mi/21 km SW of Seward, on West Fork of Big Blue R.; 40°46′N 97°16′W. Grain.

Beaver Dam, city (1990 pop. 14,196), Dodge co., SE Wis., 37 mi/60 km NE of Madison, on Beaver Dam L.; 43°27′N 88°50′W. RR junction in a productive farm and dairy area. There is a foundry here. Mfg. (food processing, metal fabrication, machinery, printing, metal prods.). Horicon Natl. Wildlife Refuge and Horicon Marsh State Wildlife Area to NE. Inc. 1856.

Beaver Dam, town (1990 pop. 2,904), Ohio co., W Ky., 29 mi/47 km SSE of Owensboro; 37°24′N 86°52′W. Trade and mining center; bituminous coal; agr. (grain, burley tobacco, hay, strawberries; cattle, hogs); timber; mfg. (textiles, apparel, millwork, motor-vehicle parts, rough-cut lumber). "Twin city" of Hartford 4 mi/6.4 km to NNW.

Beaver Dam, locality, S Ont., Canada, 7 mi/11 km S of St. Catharines, battle (June 24, 1813) in War of 1812.

Beaver Dam Creek, Va.: see MECHANICSVILLE.

Beaver Dam Lake, Barron co., NW Wis., 13 mi/21 km WNW of Rice L.; 4 mi/6.4 km long, c.½ mi/⅘ km wide; drained by Hay R. Cumberland is on SE end, on what was formerly an isl.

Beaver Dam Lake, Wis.: see BEAVER DAM.

Beaver Falls, city (1990 pop. 10,687), Beaver co., W Pa., 27 mi/43 km NW of Pittsburgh, on falls of the Beaver R., 4 mi/6.4 km N of its junction with the Ohio; 40°45′N 80°19′W. A steel center in an area of coal mines, natural-gas deposits, and clay pits, it is known for its cold-drawn steel. Mfg. (food prods., primary metals, clay prods., fabricated metal prods., chinaware). Agr. (alfalfa; livestock; dairying).The plates for U.S. currency are made here. The city was founded on a Native Amer. trail that later became a pioneer road. Geneva Col. is here; Beaver Co. Airport to NW; Beaver Falls Historical Society Mus. Settled c.1793, inc. 1868.

Beaver Falls, village (1990 pop. 700), Lewis co., N central N.Y., on Beaver R., 25 mi/40 km ESE of Watertown; 43°53′N 75°25′W. Mfg. (machinery).

Beaver Island, 14 mi/23 km long, from 3 mi/4.8 km–6 mi/9.7 km wide, off N Mich., Charlevoix co., in

L. Michigan; 45°39′N 85°33′W. It is the largest of the Beaver Isls. and has forests, Front L. at N end, Genesareth L. at S end, beaches, and a harbor at St. James village, Mormon settlement (1847–1856). Historic Mormon print shop is the only surviving original structure. A popular resort with seasonal cabins. Small road system serves entire isl. Maritime Mus.; Beaver Head Lighthouse at S end.

Beaver Islands, archipelago (c.70 mi/113 km long) in NE L. Michigan, Mich.; extends SW-E, from 20 mi/32 km W of Leelanau peninsula to c.30 mi/48 km W of Straits of Mackinac. Part of Charlevoix co. Includes Manitou Isls., Fox Isls., Beaver Isl. (c.13 mi/21 km long, largest of group). NW and N of Beaver Isl. are Garden Isl. (5 mi/8 km long, 2.5 mi/4 km wide; Indian burial grounds); High Isl. (3.5 mi/5.6 km long,2 mi/3.2 km wide); Hog Isl. (3 mi/4.8 km long, 1.5 mi/2.4 km. wide; bass fishing); and Gull Isl. (1.5 mi/2.4 km long, ½ mi/⅘ km wide). N Manitou and S Manitou isls. are part of Sleeping Bear Dunes Natl. Lakeshore (remainder on mainland); Garden Isl. and Hog Isl. comprise the Michigan Isls. Natl. Wildlife Refuge.

Beaver Kill, stream, c.35 mi/56 km long, SE N.Y., rises in the Catskills in W Ulster co., flows generally W to East Branch of Delaware R. 8 mi/12.9 km E of Hancock. Trout fishing; state park on upper course.

Beaver Lake, Carroll co., NW Ark., on the White R., 12 mi/19 km ENE of Rogers; c.50 mi/80 km long; 36°25′N 93°50′W. Extends SW into Benton and Washington cos. Max. capacity of 1,952,000 acre-ft. Formed by Beaver Dam (218 ft/66 m high), built (1963) by the Army Corps of Engineers for flood control and the generation of hydroelectric power.

Beaver Meadows, borough (1990 pop. 985), Carbon co., E Pa., 3 mi/4.8 km SE of Hazleton. Former anthracite coal area; 40°55′N 75°54′W. Light mfg. (signs); agr. (potatoes, hay; livestock; dairying). Settled 1787.

Beaver River, resort village (1990 pop. 200), Herkimer co., N central N.Y., in the Adirondacks, c.60 mi/97 km NNE of Utica; 43°54′N 74°55′W. Many lakes nearby.

Beaver River 1 305 mi/491 km long, in Alta. and Sask., Canada; issues from Beaver L. (11 mi/18 km long) in Alta. just S of Lac la Biche; flows E into Sask. and near Doré L. turns N to Churchill R. at W end of Lac la Plonge. **2** c.150 mi/241 km long, in the SE Yukon, Canada; flowing SE to the Liard in B.C. W of Nelson Forks.

Beaver River 1 c.50 mi/80 km long, in N central N.Y.; rises in small lakes in Hamilton co.; flows W to Black R. 7 mi/11.3 km N of Lowville. In upper course, it widens into Beaver R. (c.9 mi/14.5 km long, c.1 mi/1.6 km wide). **2** 21 mi/34 km long, W Pa.; formed by junction of Mahoning and Shenango rivers 3 mi/4.8 km SW of New Castle in Lawrence co.; 40°57′N 80°22′W. It flows S, past West Pittsburgh, Beaver Falls, and New Brighton, to Ohio R. at Rochester **3** c.80 mi/129 km long, in Utah; in Great Basin; rises in Tushar Mts., SE Beaver co., SW Utah, flows W past Beaver, through Minersville Reservoir and past Minersville, then N past Milford, terminating in E central Black Rock Desert in SE corner of Millard co.; intermittent. Dammed 5 mi/8 km E of Minersville. NE of Sevier L. and SW of Delta.

Beaver Springs, uninc. village (1990 pop. 725), Snyder co., central Pa., 22 mi/35 km WSW of Sunbury on Beaver Creek; 40°44′N 77°12′W. Mfg. includes apparel, wood prods.; agr. includes dairying; livestock; corn. A reservoir and state park are nearby.

Beaver Valley 1 and 2 Nuclear Power Plants, Pa.: see BEAVER CO.

Beaverdale (BEE-vuhr-dail), uninc. town (1990 pop. 1,278), Adams township, Cambria co., W central Pa., 11 mi/18 km E of Johnstown, South Fork Little Conemaugh R.; 40°19′N 78°41′W. Mfg. of apparel; agr. (corn; livestock; dairying). Beaverdam Run reservoir to E. Reported as Beaverdale-Lloydell by U.S. Census Bureau.

Beaverdam, village (1990 pop. 467), Allen co., W Ohio, 10 mi/16 km NE of Lima, in stock-raising area; 40°52′N 83°59′W.

Beaverdam Lake, village, Orange co., SE N.Y., 6 mi/9.7 km km SW of Newburgh; 41°27′N 74°07′W.

Beaverdell, village, S B.C., Canada, on West Kettle R., 23 mi/37 km E of Penticton; 49°26′N 119°05′W. Beaverdell Hotel, oldest operating hotel in B.C., is here.

Beaverhead, county (□ 5,572 sq mi/14,431 sq km; 1990 pop. 8,424), SW Mont.; ⊙ Dillon; 45°07′N 112°54′W. Mt. region bounded by Idaho and Continental Divide on W and S. Crossed by Big Hole (forms part of N boundary), Beaverhead, and Red Rock rivers. Talc mining; sheep, cattle; alfalfa, hay, barley, potatoes. Upper and Lower Red Rock lakes formed by Red Rock R., in Red Rock L. Natl. Wildlife Refuge in SE, a trumpeter swan nesting area. Maverick Mt. ski area in N center; Bannack State Park in center; Beaverhead Rock State Park on NE boundary; sections of Beaverhead Natl. Forest and Bitterroot Range in W; widely scattered section of Beaverhead Natl. Forest in W, N, S, and SE, including part of Anaconda-Pintler Wilderness Area in extreme NW. Big Hole Natl. Battlefield-Nez Percé Natl. Historic Park in NW near Wisdom. Formed 1865.

Beaverhead Mountains, Idaho and Mont.: see BITTERROOT RANGE.

Beaverhead River, Mont.: see JEFFERSON RIVER.

Beaverhill Lake (□ 80 sq mi/207 sq km), central Alta., Canada, 35 mi/56 km E of Edmonton. Drains N into North Saskatchewan R., through Beaverhill Creek.

Beaverlodge, town (1991 pop. 1,779), W Alta., Canada, near B.C. border, and near Beaverlodge R., 26 mi/42 km W of Grande Prairie; 55°12′N 119°27′W. Lumbering; mixed farming, wheat.

Beaverlodge Lake or **Beaver Lodge Lake**, in northernmost Sask., Canada, N of L. Athabaska; 59°46′N 108°18′E; 8 mi/13 km long, 1 mi/2 km wide. Development of uranium deposits begun here in 1951. Airfield on N shore.

Beaverton, city (1990 pop. 1,150), Gladwin co., E central Mich., on Tobacco R., 21 mi/34 km NW of Midland; 43°52′N 84°29′W. In farm area (livestock; grain); mfg. (rubber prods., insulation). Gladwin State Park to N.

Beaverton, suburb (1990 pop. 53,310) of Portland, Washington co., NW Oregon, 6 mi/9.7 km WSW of downtown; 45°28′N 122°49′W. Beaverton has become the heart of the Silicon Forest high-technology mfg. complex. Principal hq. for electronic companies have been est. here. Hq. of Nike shoes. Agr. (berries, grapes, vegetables; poultry, cattle). Mfg. (food processing, wines, furniture, millwork, paper prods., sheet metal work, electronic equip., computer software). Bald Peak State Park to SW. Inc. 1893.

Beaverton (BEE-vuhr-tuhn), town (1990 pop. 317), Lamar co., W Ala., c.15 mi/24 km NNE of Vernon.

Beaverton, village, S Ont., Canada, on L. Simcoe, at mouth of Beaverton R., 22 mi/35 km W of Lindsay; 44°26′N 79°09′W. Mfg. of toys, bricks; lumbering. Resort.

Beavertown, borough (1990 pop. 877), Snyder co., central Pa., 20 mi/32 km WSW of Sunbury; 40°45′N 77°10′W. Mfg. (textiles); agr. (hay, apples; livestock; dairying). Snyder-Middleswarth State Park to NW; Walker L. reservoir to N; Faylor L. reservoir to W; parts of Bald Eagle State Forest to N and S.

Beaverville, village (1990 pop. 278), Iroquois co., E Ill., 14 mi/23 km NE of Watseka; 40°57′N 87°39′W. In rich agr. area (corn, soybeans; cattle, hogs). Iroquois Co. Conservation Area to NE.

Becal (BE-kal), village (1990 pop. 5,910), Calkiní municipio, Campeche, SE Mexico, in W Yucatán peninsula, 45 mi/72 km SW of Mérida; 20°26′N 90°01′W. Corn, sugar, henequen, chicle, fruit; livestock.

Becán (be-KAN), historic site, N Campeche state, Mexico, accessible by dirt road 4.3 mi/7 km W of Xpujil on Mex. Highway 186. An example of Rio Bec–style architecture. Most of the bldgs. are covered with dense vegetation, but part of the staircases and many of the rooms are visible.

Bécancour (bai-kah-KOOR), village (1991 pop. 10,911), ⊙ Nicolet co., S Que., Canada, on Bécancour R., near its mouth on the St. Lawrence, and 5 mi/8 km E of Trois Rivières; 46°20′N 72°26′W. Dairying; pig raising.

Becancour River or **Bécancour River**, 75 mi/121 km long, S Que., Canada; rises near Thetford Mines; flows WSW, then NW past Daveyluyville and Bécancour, to the St. Lawrence 5 mi/8 km ENE of Trois Rivières.

Becharof Lake (be-SHAH-rawf) (40 mi/64 km long, 12 mi/19 km wide), SW Alaska, 130 mi/209 km W of Kodiak; 57°55′N 156°21′W.

Bechtelsville (BEK-tuhls-vil), borough (1990 pop. 884), Berks co., SE Pa., 16 mi/26 km ENE of Reading on Swamp Creek; 40°22′N 75°37′W. Mfg. (machinery, fabricated metal prods.). Agr. area (grain, apples; livestock, dairying). Founded 1852, inc. 1890.

Beckemeyer (BECK-mei-er), village (1990 pop. 1,070), Clinton co., S Ill., 3 mi/4.8 km W of Carlyle; 38°36′N 89°25′W. In agr. area (corn, wheat, sorghum); mfg. (metal prods., wooden pallets, zinc smelting).

Becker, county (□ 1,445 sq mi/3,743 sq km; 1990 pop. 27,881), W Minn.; ⊙ Detroit Lakes; 46°55′N 95°40′W. Agr. area (oats, barley, wheat, hay, alfalfa, soybeans, sunflowers, sugar beets, wild rice, beans; hogs, cattle, sheep, poultry; dairying); timber watered by numerous lakes, including White Earth L., in N, and Detroit L. and Cormorant L., in SW. Deposits of marl and peat. Part of White Earth Indian Reservation in N; Tamarac Natl. Wildlife Refuge and Hubbel Pond Wildlife Area in center; Two Inlets and Smokey Hills state forests in E; part of White Earth State Forest in NE; small part of Itasca State Park in NE. Co. formed 1858.

Becker, town (1990 pop. 902), Sherburne co., central Minn., 18 mi/29 km SE of St. Cloud, bet. Mississippi (SW) and Elk (NE) rivers; 45°22′N 93°52′W. Grain, alfalfa, soybeans, potatoes; hogs; mfg. (wood prods., plastics). Sand Dunes State Forest and Sherburne Natl. Wildlife Refuge to NE.

Becket, town (1990 pop. 1,481), Berkshire co., W Mass., on West Branch of Westfield R., 12 mi/19 km SE of Pittsfield; 42°17′N 73°05′W. The Jacob's Pillow Dance festival, the country's oldest such festival, is celebrated here. Highest point on the Mass. Turnpike 1,724 ft/525 m. October Mt. State Forest.

Beckham (BEK-uhm), county (□ 904 sq mi/2,341 sq km; 1990 pop. 18,812), W Okla.; ⊙ Sayre; 35°15′N 99°41′W. Rolling plains, bounded W by Texas line; intersected by North Fork of Red R., and by Elk Creek. Agr. (cotton, wheat, sorghum, oats, peanuts; cattle, horses); honey. Mfg. at Elk City. Oil and natural gas wells. Salt deposits. Formed 1907.

Beckley, city (1990 pop. 18,296), ⊙ Raleigh co., S W.Va.; 43 mi/69 km SSE of Charlestown; 37°47′N 81°11′W. Beckley's major industries include tourism, agr. (livestock; grain, cotton, nursery crops), and mfg. (machinery, printing and publishing, machinery, furniture, electrical equipment, glass, lumber, beverages). Once prominent, coal production has declined. The city holds an annual Appalachian Arts and Crafts Festival. Raleigh Co. Memorial Airport to E. Beckley Exhibition Coal Mine includes tours, and mining demonstrations. In New R. City Park is Youth Mus. of S W.Va./Mountain Homestead; plays about W. Va.'s fight for statehood and the Hatfield-McCoy feud are presented. Tamarack State Craft Center, I-77 South at Milepost 44, W.Va. Turnpike. Little Beaver State Recreation Area 10 mi/16 km to SE; L. Stephens reservoir 9 mi/14.5 km to W; New R. Gorge Natl. R. to NE (including Grandview Visitor Center); Plum Orchard Wildlife Management Area to N; Winterplace Ski Resort to S. Inc. 1927.

Beckville, town (1990 pop. 783), Panola co., E Texas, near the Sabine, 22 mi/35 km SSW of Marshall, near Martin Creek; 32°14′N 94°27′W. In agr. (poultry, cattle, hogs); lumber area. Martin Creek L. State Park to W.

Beckwourth Pass, mt. pass (c.5,212 ft/1,589 m), extreme SE Lassen co., E of Plumas co. line, NE Calif., across the Sierra Nevada E of Sierra Valley, c.25 mi/40 km NW of Reno, Nev. Was route of an emigrant trail in 1850s. Beckwourth village (10 mi/16 km W of Pass) and Beckwourth Peak (7,250 ft/2,210 m) are W. Formerly spelled Beckwith. State Highway 70 passes through.

Beddington, town (1990 pop. 43), Washington co., E Maine, on Beddington L., 32 mi/51 km WNW of Machias; 44°49′N 68°00′W. Diatomaceous earth.

Bede, Point, S Alaska, SW tip of Kenai Peninsula, at E side of entrance to Cook Inlet; 59°19′N 152°00′W.

Bedeque Bay (buh-DEHK), inlet (8 mi/13 km long, 12 mi/19 km wide at entrance) of Northumberland Strait, SW P.E.I., Canada. At head of bay is Summerside.

Bedford 1 county (□ 1,017 sq mi/2,634 sq km), S Pa., ⊙ Bedford, 40°00'N 78°30'W. Highland agr. and mineral-producing area; drained by Raystown Branch of Juniata R.; bounded S by Md. state line, E by Rays Hill ridge; part of Allegheny Mts. in NW, Wills Mt. ridge is in SW part. Agr. (corn, oats, barley, hay, alfalfa, apples; sheep, hogs, cattle; dairying). Bituminous coal, limestone, sand; timber. Warriors Path State Park in NE; part of Gallitzin State Forest in NW; Shawnee L. reservoir and Shawnee State Park in W; Koon and Gordon reservoirs (both Evans Creek) in SW; Pine Ridge Natural Area in SE. Formed 1771. **2** county (□ 482; 1990 pop. 30,411), central Tenn.; ⊙ Shelbyville; 35°30'N 86°28'W. In state's central basin; drained by Duck R.; livestock raising (especially the noted Tennessee Walking Horse); dairying; agr. (hay, corn, grain). Mfg. at Shelbyville. Formed 1807. **3** county (□ 769 sq mi/1,899 sq km; 1990 pop. 46,656), SW central Va.; ⊙ Bedford; 37°18'N 79°31'W. Center, SE part in the Piedmont region, with Blue Ridge in NW; Peaks of Otter are in NW, part of Jefferson Natl. Forest in NW. Bounded SW by Roanoke R. (forms Leesville L., Smith Mt. L. reservoirs in S), NE by James R.; drained by short Otter R. Agr. (tobacco, barley, corn, wheat, tomatoes, peaches, apples; cattle, sheep; dairying); timber; feldspar mining. Appalachian Trail, Blue Ridge Parkway follow parts of NW boundary. Smith Mt. L. State Park in S. Formed 1754.

Bedford 1 city (1990 pop. 13,817), ⊙ Lawrence co., S Ind.; 38°52'N 86°29'W. Bedford limestone, quarried here and shipped all over the world, was used in the construction of the Empire State Bldg. and the Pentagon. The city also has several small industrial plants and a foundry. Carvings and the many old stone bldgs. and houses are notable. Laid out 1825. Inc. 1889. **2** city (1990 pop. 1,528), ⊙ Taylor co., SW Iowa, near Mo. line, 33 mi/53 km SW of Creston; 40°40'N 94°43'W. Dairy prods., packed poultry; stoneworks. L. of Three Fires State Park, with fish hatchery and small lake to NE. Inc. 1885. **3** city (1990 pop. 14,822), Cuyahoga co., NE Ohio, a suburb of Cleveland; 41°24'N 81°33'W. Although chiefly residential, it has plants that manufacture furniture, china, rubber goods, auto parts, processed foods, and tools. Settled c.1813 on the site of a Moravian settlement (1786), inc. as a city 1931. **4** city (1990 pop. 6,073), ⊙ Bedford co., SW central Va., separate from surrounding Bedford co., in the Piedmont region, 20 mi/32 km W of Lynchburg, near Otter R; 37°20'N 79°31'W. Mfg. (printing and publishing, furniture, rubber prods., foods, paper prods., meat processing, steel, textiles); flour milling, feldspar mining and processing; in agr. area (important tobacco market, grain, apples; livestock; dairying); timber. Elks Natl. Home here. "Poplar Forest" (1806–1809), country home of Thomas Jefferson, is 12 mi/19 km E; Peaks of Otter are to NW, in Jefferson Natl. Forest. Smith Mt. L. State Park to S. Inc. 1890; reinc. 1912.

Bedford, town (1991 pop. 2,665), ⊙ Missisquoi co., S Que., Canada, near N.Y. border, on Pike R., 18 mi/29 km SW of St. Jean. In oats, hay, cattle region.

Bedford, town (1990 pop. 761), ⊙ Trimble co., N Ky., 35 mi/56 km NE of Louisville, 10 mi/16 km S of Madison (Ind.), in N part of Bluegrass region; 38°35'N 85°19'W. Agr. (tobacco, grain; livestock, poultry; dairying); mfg. (brass prods., firearms, machinery).

Bedford, village (1991 pop. 11,618), S N.S., Canada, on Bedford Basin, N part of Halifax Harbour, 7 mi/11 km NNW of Halifax. Site of ND firing range.

Bedford 1 village (□ 3 sq mi/7.8 sq km; 1990 pop. 1,828) in Bedford town (1990 pop. 16,906), Westchester co., SE N.Y., suburban area E of Mt. Kisco; 41°12'N 73°39'W. Caramoor Art and Music Center. Maximum-security Tacoma Correctional Facility for Women is at nearby Bedford Hills village. Also known as Bedford Village. **2** village, Lincoln co., W Wyo., near Salt R. and Idaho line, 12 mi/19 km N of Afton. Elev. 5,620 ft/1,713 m. Grain; livestock. Salt R. Range just E; Bridger-Teton Natl. Forest to E.

Bedford, borough (1990 pop. 3,137), ⊙ Bedford co., S Pa., 32 mi/51 km S of Altoona, on Raystown Branch of Juniata R.; 40°00'N 78°30'W. Mfg. (wood and fiberglass prods., bicycles, printing and publishing, fabricated metal prods., electrical insulation); agr. (apples, grain, soybeans; livestock; dairying); timber. Old Bedford Village period resoration, to N; Shawnee L. reservoir and Shawnee State Park to W; Coral Caverns to W; Fort Bedford Park and Mus., scale model of Old Fort Bedford. Settled c.1750, laid out 1766, inc. 1795.

Bedford 1 residential suburb (1990 pop. 12,996) of Boston, Middlesex co., E Mass., 14 mi/23 km NW of city center; 42°30'N 71°17'W. Mfg. (machinery, consumer goods, communications equip.). Several pre-Revolutionary houses remain. Site of Hanscom Field, air force research laboratory. Settled c.1637, inc. 1729. **2** suburb (1990 pop. 12,563) of Manchester, Hillsborough co., S N.H., 4 mi/6.4 km SW of city center; 42°56'N 71°31'W. Drained by Riddle Brook. Nursery crops, fruit, vegetables; livestock; dairying. Mfg. (auto parts, plastics, paper prods., beverages, computer software, leather prods., medical instruments). Uncanoonuc Mts. (1,329 ft/405 m) in N. Settled 1737, inc. 1750. **3** suburb (1990 pop. 43,762) of Fort Worth, Tarrant co., N Texas, 10 mi/16 km NE of downtown; 32°51'N 97°07'W. Mfg. (plastic molds, printing, telecommunications equip.). The city has grown since the 1970s along with the N Dallas–Fort Worth area. Dallas–Fort Worth Internatl. Airport to NE. Settled c.1843, inc. 1954.

Bedford Basin, Canada: see HALIFAX HARBOUR.

Bedford Heights, city (1990 pop. 12,131), Cuyahoga co., N Ohio, a residential suburb of Cleveland; 41°25'N 81°31'W. Inc. 1951.

Bedford Hills, N.Y.: see BEDFORD.

Bedford Institute of Oceanography, Dartmouth, N.S., Canada, opposite Halifax, on N side of E end of MacKay Bridge. Situated on Bedford Basin at entrance to The Narrows. The facility was greatly expanded during the 1970s. It has been the base for oceanographic research in the Can. waters of the Atlantic Ocean, Hudson Bay, and waters surrounding the Arctic isls., with special emphasis during 1980s and 1990s on development of Grand and George's Banks oil and natural gas fields, oil exploration along Lab. coast and fluctuations in fish catches, esp. the cod industry collapse in mid-1990s.

Bedford Park, suburb (1990 pop. 566) of Chicago, Cook co., NE Ill., 9 mi/14.5 km SW of downtown; 41°46'N 87°47'W. Industrial area; mfg. (electronic equip., paper prods., fabricated metal, furniture, bookbinding, film processing, lubricants and oils, machinery, chemicals, cosmetics, commercial printing). Chicago Midway Airport to NE.

Bedford Springs, village, Bedford co., S Pa., 1 mi/1.6 km S of Bedford, on Shobers Run; 39°59'N 78°30'W. Mineral springs.

Bedford Village, N.Y.: see BEDFORD.

Bedford-Stuyvesant, residential section of N Brooklyn borough of N.Y. city, SE N.Y. Settled 1662 by Dutch. Center of the largest Afr.-Amer. community in N.Y. (2d-largest in U.S.). Concord Baptist Church here has the largest Afr.-Amer. congregation in U.S. The Bedford-Stuyvesant Restoration Corp. has been spearheading several successful projects that are helping to revive the economy here. Colloquially known as Bed-Stuy.

Bedloe's Island, N.Y.: see STATUE OF LIBERTY NATIONAL MONUMENT.

Bedminster, township (1990 pop. 7,086), Somerset co., N central N.J., on North Branch of Raritan R., 8 mi/12.9 km N of Somerville, opposite Far Hills, in rapidly suburbanizing area; 40°40'N 74°40'W. A telecommunications center. Peapack Ski Area to NW.

Bee, county (□ 880 sq mi/2,279 sq km; 1990 pop. 25,135), S Texas; ⊙ Beeville; 28°25'N 97°44'W. Bounded on NE by Blanco Creek; drained by Aransas R. (source) and Medio Creek (part of N boundary). Oil, natural gas wells; agr. (corn, grain sorghum, cotton, wheat); cattle and horse ranching; sand and gravel. Formed 1857.

Bee, village (1990 pop. 209), Seward co., SE Nebr., 7 mi/11.3 km NNW of Seward; 41°00'N 97°03'W.

Bee Branch, town, Van Buren co., N central Ark., 25 mi/40 km N of Conway. Large Greers Ferry L. Reservoir to N.

Bee Cave, residential suburb (1990 pop. 241) of Austin, Travis co., S Texas, 11 mi/18 km W of downtown, near Colorado R; 30°18'N 97°57'W. L. Travis reservoir to N.

Bee Ridge, town (□ 3 sq mi/7.8 sq km; 1990 pop. 6,406), W central Fla., Sarasota co., 5 mi/8 km SE of Sarasota; 27°17'N 82°28'W.

Beebe (BEE-bee), town (1990 pop. 4,455), White co., central Ark., 32 mi/51 km NE of Little Rock; 35°04'N 91°53'W. In agr. area. Mfg. (fabricated steel prods., feeds, concrete prods., apparel). Ark. State Univ.–Beebe Branch (2-year).

Beebe Plain (BEE-bee), village (1991 pop. 975), S Que., Canada, near L. Memphremagog, 32 mi/51 km SSW of Sherbrooke, at Vt. boundary. Dairying.

Beech Bottom, village (1990 pop. 415), Brooke co., N W.Va., in Northern Panhandle, on Ohio R., 10 mi/16 km N of Wheeling; 40°13'N 80°39'W. Coal mining. Mfg. (steel fabricating).

Beech Creek, village, Muhlenberg co., W central Ky., 7 mi/11.3 km ESE of Greenville. Bituminous coal.

Beech Creek, borough (1990 pop. 716), Clinton co., central Pa., 8 mi/12.9 km SW of Lock Haven, on Beech Creek; 41°04'N 77°35'W. Mfg. (fabricated metal prods., wood prods.); agr. (grain; livestock; dairying); timber. Sproul State Forest to NW; Sayer (Blanchard) L. reservoir in Bald Eagle State Park, to SW.

Beech Fork, river, c.125 mi/201 km long, central Ky.; rises in W Boyle co.; flows NW, then NE of Springfield, then generally W, to S of Bardstown to Rolling Fork 10 mi/16 km NE of Elizabethtown, which continues NE to Salt R.

Beech Grove, city (1990 pop. 13,383), Marion co., central Ind. Inc. 1906. Primarily residential, it has some mfg. (flour and wheat milling, RR repair, chemicals).

Beech Grove, village (1990 pop. 233), McLean co., W Ky., 18 mi/29 km SE of Henderson. Agr. (tobacco, soybeans, grain; livestock). One of 7 places so named in Ky.

Beech Island, uninc. town, Aiken co., SW S.C., residential suburb 5 mi/8 km SE of Augusta, Ga. Mfg. includes plastic and paper prods. Agr. includes cotton, peanuts, grain; livestock. Redcliffe Plantation State Park is here. Savannah R. Nuclear Plant to SE.

Beech Mountain, village (1990 pop. 239), Watauga co., NW N.C., 11 mi/18 km W of Boone, in Pisgah Natl. Forest; 36°12'N 81°53'W. Ski resort area.

Beecher, village (1990 pop. 2,032), Will co., NE Ill., near Ind. line, 35 mi/56 km S of Chicago; 41°21'N 87°36'W. Agr. (corn, oats, soybeans; dairying); mfg. (machinery, wood prods.).

Beecher City, village (1990 pop. 437), Effingham co., SE central Ill., 14 mi/23 km WNW of Effingham; 39°11'N 88°47'W. Agr. (wheat, soybeans; cattle, hogs).

Beecher Falls, Vt.: see CANAAN.

Beechey, Cape, NE Ellesmere Isl., NE Franklin dist., N.W.T., Canada, on Robeson Channel, near N entrance of Lady Franklin Bay; 81°52'N 63°00'W.

Beechey Island, islet, E central Franklin dist., N.W.T., Canada, in Erebus Bay, inlet of Barrow Strait, at S end of Wellington Channel, just off SW Devon Isl.; 74°43'N 92°56'W. Rises to c.650 ft/198 m. Br. explorer Sir John Franklin wintered here 1845–1846; later isl. was base of Arctic explorers and searchers for Franklin's expedition.

Beechey Point (BEE-chee), Inuit village, N Alaska, on Arctic Ocean, 20 mi/32 km WNW of Prudhoe Bay, W of mouth of Kuparuk R., 185 mi/298 km ESE of Barrow; 70°28'N 149°02'W. Trading post. Airfield.

Beechmont, uninc. village (1990 pop. 500), Muhlenberg co., W Ky., 8 mi/12.9 km ESE of Greenville. Bituminous coal. Tobacco. Grain; livestock.

Beechwood, uninc. town (1990 pop. 2,676), Ottawa co., SW Mich., suburb, 1 mi/1.6 km NW of Holland; 42°47'N 86°07'W. Holland State Park to W.

Beechwood, village, Iron co., NW Mich., 6 mi/9.7 km

NW of Iron River, in Ottawa Natl. Forest; 46°09′N 88°46′W. Timber; hunting, fishing.

Beechwood Village, residential suburb (1990 pop. 1,263) of Louisville, Jefferson co., N Ky., 7 mi/11.3 km E of downtown; 38°15′N 85°37′W.

Beef Island, islet (c.2.5 mi/4 km long), Br. Virgin Isls., just E of Tortola isl., on Sir Francis Drake's Channel; 18°27′N 64°31′W. Beef Isl. Internatl. Airport here.

Beemer, village (1990 pop. 672), Cuming co., NE Nebr., 8 mi/12.9 km W of West Point, on Elkhorn R; 41°55′N 96°48′W. Livestock; grain, feeds. Mfg.

Beersheba Springs, town (1990 pop. 596), Grundy co., SE central Tenn., 35 mi/56 km NNW of Chattanooga, in the Cumberlands; 35°28′N 85°39′W. Chalybeate spring.

Beeton, village, S Ont., Canada, 35 mi/56 km NW of Toronto, in agr. region.

Beeville, city (1990 pop. 13,547), ⊙ Bee co., S Texas, 50 mi/80 km NW of Corpus Christi, on Poesta Creek; 28°24′N 97°45′W. Beeville is the trade center of an agr. co. (cattle, horses; cotton, corn, wheat, sorghum); oil and gas. It has Bee Co. Community Col. Chase Field Air station to S; McConnell Corrections Unit. Settled in the 1830s, inc. 1908.

Beggs, town (1990 pop. 1,150), Okmulgee co., E central Okla., 10 mi/16 km NW of Okmulgee; 35°46′N 96°01′W. Supply center for oil and natural gas area. Mfg. (refining heaters). Inc. 1902.

Behm Canal (BEEM), natural channel, 120 mi/193 km long, SE Alaska, almost circling Revillagigedo Isl., which it separates from the mainland (E) and from Cleveland Peninsula (N and NW). In it is Bell Isl.; forms W boundary of Misty Fiords Natl. Monument.

Beiseker (BEI-suh-kuhr), village (1991 pop. 605), S Alta., Canada, 35 mi/56 km NE of Calgary; 51°23′N 113°32′W. Wheat.

Bejou (be-ZHOO), village (1990 pop. 110), Mahnomen co., NW Minn., 9 mi/14.5 km N of Mahnomen, on Marsh Creek; 47°26′N 95°58′W. Grain, wild rice, alfalfa; livestock. In NW part of White Earth Indian Reservation.

Bejucal (bai-hu-KAHL), town, La Habana prov., W Cuba, on RR, 13 mi/21 km S of Havana; 22°55′N 82°23′W. Cigar factories. Grows tobacco, sugarcane, fruit; cattle raising. Important vegetable producer for metropolitan Havana area. Terminal of 1st RR line in Cuba (to Havana).

Bejucal de Ocampo (beh-HOO-kal de oh-KAM-po), town (1990 pop. 241), Chiapas, S Mexico, in Sierra Madre, 7 mi/11.3 km NE of Motozintla de Mendoza; 15°45′N 92°05′W. Fruit.

Bel Air 1 town (1990 pop. 8,860), ⊙ Hartford co., NE Md., 22 mi/35 km NE of Baltimore; 39°32′N 76°21′W. Capital and trading center (since 1782) for horse-breeding and agr. area (dairy prods., poultry, grain); vegetable cannery, clothing factory. Tudor Hall (built 1822 by Junius Brutus Booth), birthplace of Edwin and John Wilkes Booth, is nearby. Theatrical tradition carried on by Hartford Community Col. Drama Society. Several large housing developments provide housing for commuters to Edgewood Arsenal. Settled c. 1782. Inc. 1874. **2** uninc. town, Fairfax co., NE Va., residential suburb, 8 mi/12.9 km WSW of Wash., D.C.; 38°51′N 77°10′W. L. Barcroft reservoir to SE.

Bel Air, suburban section of Los Angeles city, Los Angeles co., S Calif., 12 mi/19 km W of downtown, in foothill canyons of Santa Monica Mts. Natl. Recreation Area, just W of Beverly Hills. The Los Angeles campus of the Univ. of Calif. is to S.

Bel Aire (bel ER), residential suburb (1990 pop. 3,695) of Wichita, Sedgwick co., Kansas, 6 mi/9.7 km NE of downtown; 37°45′N 97°16′W. Sometimes spelled Belleaire.

Bel Alton (BELL AWL-ton), village, Charles co., S Md., 30 mi/48 km S of Wash., D.C. St. Ignatius Church (c.1790; open to public) and St. Thomas Manor (closed) are bldgs. of a Jesuit mission established on the Port Tobacco River to "Christianize" Indians. Lord Baltimore, anxious to avoid the appearance of establishing an R.C. state, used the old (c.1279) Statute of Mortmain to keep the Jesuits from buying land as a religious order. The society circumvented the law by registering the land as individuals. The manor house "palace" was begun in 1741, burned by the British in 1781, and rebuilt. The view here of the Tobacco and Potomac rivers was described in 1784 as "the most majestic, grand and elegant in the whole world." When the Jesuit order was suppressed by the Catholic Church in 1773, a "Corporation of Roman Catholic Gentlemen" took possession of the property. The Jesuits obtained title again in 1805. After assassinating Lincoln in 1865, John Wilkes Booth hid in the woods here before fleeing to Virginia. Experienced growth in 1890s after Pope Creek RR was built. Nearby are Zekiah Swamp and Charles County Fairgrounds.

Belcamp (BALL-camp), village, Harford co., NE Md., on Bush R., 23 mi/37 km ENE of Baltimore. Model industrial town, developed around the Bata Shoe Co., which now has over 100 plants worldwide. The Belcamp site is the hq. Factory est. here 1939 by Czech refugees.

Belcher 1 uninc. village (1990 pop. 500), Pike co., E Ky., in the Cumberland Mts., on Russell Fork R., 12 mi/19 km SE of Pikeville. In bituminous-coal area. Belcher Interstate Park and Jefferson Natl. Forest to SE, both on Va. state boundary. **2** village (1990 pop. 249), Caddo parish, NW La., 15 mi/24 km N of Shreveport, on Red R.; 32°45′N 93°56′W. Agr. (cotton; livestock) and timber area; oil and natural gas; heavy mfg.; gasoline refining.

Belcher Islands (□ c.1,110 sq mi/2,870 sq km), in E Hudson Bay, Baffin region, N.W.T., Canada, off W Que.; 56°20′N 79°30′W. Flaherty Isl. is the largest of the tundra-covered group.

Belchertown (BEL-chuhr-toun), town (1990 pop. 10,579), Hampshire co., W central Mass., 15 mi/24 km NE of Springfield, near Quabbin Reservoir; 42°17′N 72°24′W. Poultry; dairying; apples. Includes village of Dwight. Old Stone mus. here. Settled 1731, inc. 1761.

Belcherville, uninc. village (1990 pop. 34), Montague co., N Texas, near Red R., 38 mi/61 km E of Wichita Falls. In agr. area.

Belcourt, town (1990 pop. 2,458), Rolette co., N N.Dak., 7 mi/11.3 km W of Rolla, at SE end of Turtle Mts.; 48°50′N 99°45′W. Mfg. (cargo trailers). Located in and hq. for Turtle Mt. Indian Reservation; tribal community col., tribal-operated casino.

Belden, village (1990 pop. 149), Cedar co., NE Nebr., 15 mi/24 km S of Hartington; 42°24′N 97°12′W.

Beldenville, village, Pierce co., W Wis., 9 mi/14.5 km SE of River Falls. Dairying; stock raising.

Belding (BEL-ding), city (1990 pop. 5,969), Ionia co., S central Mich., on Flat R., 12 mi/19 km NW of Ionia; 43°06′N 85°13′W. In agr. area (apples, beans, potatoes). The city is the site of the Gus Macker 3 on 3 basketball competition, a nationally known event. Mfg. (beverages, brass items, sheet metal, metal fabrication). Settled c.1855; inc. 1893.

Belen (buh-LIN), town (1990 pop. 6,547), Valencia co., W central N.Mex., on Rio Grande, 30 mi/48 km S of Albuquerque; 34°39′N 106°46′W. Elev. 4,808 ft/1,465 m. Rail junction. Trade and shipping point in irrigated grain, livestock, fruit region. Mfg. (concrete, printing and publishing). Senator Willie M. Chavez State Park to N; part of Cibola Natl. Forest to E.

Belen (BEL-uhn), village, Quitman co., NW Miss., 5 mi/8 km W of Marks. Agr. (soybeans).

Belews Lake (buh-LOOZ), in Rockingham co. and along Forsyth co. border, N N.C., on Belews Creek, 1 mi/1.6 km S of its confluence with Dan R., 20 mi/32 km NE of Winston-Salem; c.10 mi/16 km long; 36°19′N 80°01′W. Max. capacity 306,240 acre-ft. Formed by Belews Dam (147 ft/45 m high), built (1972) by the Duke Power Co. for power generation.

Belfair, uninc. town (1990 pop. 750), Mason co., W Wash., 12 mi/19 km SW of Bremerton, on Union R., 1 mi/1.6 km NE of end of Hood Canal inlet. Dairying; poultry. Belfair State Park to SW. Kitsap Co. Airport and Bremerton Raceways to NE.

Belfast, city (1990 pop. 6,355), ⊙ Waldo co., S Maine; resort on Penobscot Bay, opposite Castine, 30 mi/48 km SSE of Bangor; 44°25′N 69°01′W. Mfg. (food processing, clothing, wood prods.); financial services; tourism. Port of entry. Shipping and shipbuilding center in mid–19th cent. Settled 1770; sacked twice by British (1779, 1814); inc. town 1773, city 1853.

Belfast (BEL-fast), uninc. town (1990 pop. 1,102), Northampton co., E Pa., residential community 7 mi/11.3 km NNW of Easton near Bushkill Creek; 40°46′N 75°16′W. Jacobsburg State Park and Environmental Education Center to N.

Belfast, village (□ 36 sq mi/93 sq km; 1990 pop. 1,100), Allegany co., W N.Y., on Genesee R., and 10 mi/16 km NNW of Belmont; 42°17′N 78°07′W. In dairying and poultry area.

Belfield, town (1990 pop. 887), Stark co., W N.Dak., 20 mi/32 km W of Dickinson, on tributary of Heart R.; 46°53′N 103°12′W. Oil fields. At E edge of Little Missouri Natl. Grassland and N.Dak. Badlands. Theodore Roosevelt Natl. Park (south unit) is to S.

Belford, village, Monmouth co., E N.J., near Sandy Hook Bay, 15 mi/24 km NE of Freehold. Largely residential.

Belford, Mount (14,197 ft/4,327 m), in Rocky Mts., Chaffee co., central Colo., in the San Isabel Natl. Forest, E of Contintental Divide; 38°57′N 106°21′E.

Belfry, uninc. town (1990 pop. 800), Pike co., E Ky., in the Cumberland Mts., 5 mi/8 km S of Williamson (W.Va.). Bituminous coal; coal processing.

Belfry (BEL-free), village (1990 pop. 270), Carbon co., S Mont., 12 mi/19 km ESE of Red Lodge, on Bear Creek, near its entrance to Clarks Fork of the Yellowstone R. Cattle, sheep; barley, oats, sugar beets, and alfalfa.

Belgique (bel-JEEK), uninc. community, Perry co., E Mo., near Mississippi R., 9 mi/14 km NNE of Perryville. Severely damaged by flood of 1993.

Belgium, town (1990 pop. 928), Ozaukee co., E Wis., 8 mi/12.9 km N of Port Washington; 43°30′N 87°50′W. Mfg. (consumer goods, sheepskin); cheese. Harrington Beach State Park to E, on L. Michigan.

Belgium, village (1990 pop. 511), Vermilion co., E Ill., 3 mi/4.8 km S of Danville; 40°03′N 87°37′W. In agr. (corn, soybeans; cattle) and bituminous coal–mining area.

Belgrade 1 (BEL-graid), resort town (1990 pop. 2,375), Kennebec co., S Maine, 10 mi/16 km NNW of Augusta; 44°29′N 69°50′W. Includes Belgrade Lakes and North Belgrade villages. Hq. for Belgrade Lakes resort area. Settled 1774, inc. 1796. **2** town (1990 pop. 3,411), Gallatin co., SW Mont., near Gallatin R., 10 mi/16 km NW of Bozeman; 45°47′N 111°11′W. Timber; cattle, sheep, hogs, poultry; wheat, barley, oats, potatoes; dairying. Mfg. (wood prods., bldg. materials, meat, machinery).

Belgrade 1 (BEL-graid), village (1990 pop. 700), Stearns co., central Minn., 40 mi/64 km WSW of St. Cloud; 45°27′N 95°00′W. Grain, soybeans, alfalfa; poultry, cattle, sheep, hogs; dairying; mfg. (bldg. materials, steel tanks, crafts). **2** village (1990 pop. 157), Nance co., E central Nebr., 10 mi/16 km NW of Fullerton; 41°28′N 98°04′W. Dairy prods., grain; livestock.

Belgrade Lakes, S Maine, group of stream-linked lakes in NW Kennebec co., at center of recreational area noted for canoeing, fishing. Include Great Pond (6 mi/9.7 km long, 2 mi/3.2 km–4 mi/6.4 km wide), Long Pond (7 mi/11.3 km long, c.1 mi/1.6 km wide), Messalonskee L. (10 mi/16 km long, c.1 mi/1.6 km wide), and smaller East, North, Ellis, and McGrath ponds.

Belhaven, town (1990 pop. 2,269), Beaufort co., E N.C., 24 mi/39 km E of Washington, on NW shore of Pungo R. estuary; 35°32′N 76°37′W. Agr. inland (sweet potatoes, cotton, peanuts, tobacco, grain; livestock). Mfg. (food processing, apparel, boats).

Belington, town (1990 pop. 1,850), Barbour co., N W.Va., on Tygart R., 8 mi/12.9 km NNW of Elkins; 39°01′N 79°56′W. Agr. (corn); livestock. Mfg. (lumber). Coal-mining; timber. Civil War battle was fought on Laurel Ridge to East Audra State Park to W; Teter Creek Wildlife Management Area. Inc. 1905.

Belize (be-LEEZ), Span. *Belice* (be-LEE-say), republic (□ 8,867 sq mi/22,965 sq km; 1991 est. pop. 184,340), Central Amer., on the Caribbean Sea; ⊙ Belmopan.

Bounded on N by Mexico, S and W by Guatemala, and E by the Caribbean. The main port, Belize City, was capital until 1970. The country is divided into 6 dists.: BELIZE, CAYO, COROZAL, ORANGE WALK, STANN CREEK, and TOLEDO. The land is generally low, with mangrove swamps and cays along the coast, but in the S rises to Victoria Peak (c.3,700 ft/1,128 m). The climate is tropical. Although most of the area is heavily forested, yielding mahogany, cedar, and logwood, there are regions of fertile savannas and barren pine ridges. Only a small fraction of the land is cultivated. In addition to woods, the chief prods. are sugar, clothing, bananas, citrus fruits, and fish. The majority of people are of Afr., Maya, or Span.-Amer. descent. Eng. is the official language, but Span. is widely spoken, as are Gari'funa (black Carib) and Mayan languages. Once part of the Mayan civilization, the region was probably traversed by Cortés on his way to Honduras, but the Spanish made no attempt at colonization. Br. buccaneers, who used the cays to prey on Span. shipping, founded Belize (early 17th cent.). Br. settlers from Jamaica began the exploitation of timber. Spain contested Br. possession several times until defeated at the last battle of St. Georges Cay (1798). From 1862 to 1884 the colony, known as Br. Honduras, was administered by the governor of Jamaica. Since 1821, Guatemala has claimed the territory as part of its inheritance from Spain. Upon gaining independence in 1821, Mexico also made a claim on Belize, but the country renounced it in an 1893 treaty. As Belize progressed toward independence, the tension bet. Britain and Guatemala over the issue increased. In 1964 the colony gained complete internal self-govt., in 1971 the name Belize was adopted, and in 1981 Belize achieved independence, a development that prompted Guatemala to threaten war. Relations improved, however, and in Sept. 1991 Guatemala officially recognized Belize's independence and sovereignty.

Belknap (BEL-nap), county (□ 468 sq mi/1,212 sq km; 1990 pop. 49,216), central N.H.; ⊙ Laconia; 43°31'N 71°25'W. Bounded in NE by large L. Winnipesaukee, extreme N by Squam L., W by Pemigewasset R. Recreational and agr. area, with resort area on L. Winnipesaukee. Nursery crops, apples, corn, sugar maples, berries; cattle, poultry; dairying. Mfg. at Laconia, Meredith, and Tilton. Drained by Winnipesaukee, Merrymeeting, and Suncook rivers. Tourism, recreation. L. Waukewan in NW; Winnisquam L. in NW center; Crystal L. and Upper and Lower Suncook lakes in SE; Ellacoya State Beach in NE; Gunstock Ski Area, Belknap State Forest in center. Formed 1840.

Belknap, village (1990 pop. 125), Johnson co., S Ill., 7 mi/11.3 km SSW of Vienna; 37°19'N 88°56'W. Near Cache R. State Natl. Area.

Belknap, Fort, Texas: see NEWCASTLE.

Belknap, Mount (BEL-nap), peak (12,139 ft/3,700 m) in Tushar Mts., on Piute-Beaver co. line, SW central Utah, 30 mi/48 km SW of Richfield. In Fishlake Natl. Forest.

Belknap Mountains, small mountain range, Belknap co., central N.H., in recreational area SW of L. Winnipesaukee; Belknap Mt. (2,384 ft/727 m) is highest peak in Belknap Mt. State Forest. Also Mt. Major (1,780 ft/543 m) to E. Gunstock Ski Area on N side.

Belkofski, village, SW Alaska, near tip of Alaska Peninsula; 55°05'N 162°00'W. Fur farming and trapping. Natives work at nearby fish canneries during the summer.

Bell 1 county (□ 361 sq mi/935 sq km; 1990 pop. 31,506), extreme SE Ky., in the Cumberland Mts.; ⊙ Pineville; 36°44'N 83°40'W. Bounded S by Tenn., SE by Va.; drained by Cumberland R. and its tributaries. Bituminous coal-mining area, with limestone quarries, iron deposits, and some farms (dairy prods.; livestock; burley tobacco, fruit); some mfg. (chiefly at Middlesboro). Includes Pine Mt. State Park in center, Ky. Ridge Forest in SW, part of Daniel Boone Natl. Forest in N, part of Cumberland Gap Natl. Historical Park along SE boundary. Formed 1867 as Josh Bell co.; renamed bet. 1870 and 1880. **2** county (□ 1,087 sq mi/2,815 sq km; 1990 pop. 191,088), central Texas; ⊙ Belton; 31°02'N 97°28'W. Co.'s 2 populated centers, Temple (E central) and Killeen (W), are 21 mi/34 km apart. Drained by Leon and Lampasas rivers, which join at center of co. to form Little R. Rich blacklands agr. area (cotton, corn, sorghum, soybeans, alfalfa, wheat); cattle, exotic fowl (emus, ostriches). Hunting, fishing. Oil and gas, clay, lignite, limestone. Mfg. at Temple, Belton. Part of large Fort Hood Military Reserve on NW boundary; part of large Belton L. reservoir in N; Stillhouse Hollow L. reservoir in W center. Formed 1850.

Bell, suburb (1990 pop. 34,365) of Los Angeles, Los Angeles co., S Calif., 6 mi/9.7 km SE of downtown, drained by Los Angeles R.; 33°59'N 118°11'W. It is chiefly residential; mfg. (printing, industrial machinery, lighting fixtures, metal fabrication). Inc. 1927.

Bell Acres (BEL-AI-kuhrs), borough (1990 pop. 1,436), Allegheny co., W Pa., residential suburb 13 mi/21 km WNW of Pittsburgh; 40°35'N 80°10'W. Agr. area includes dairying. Big Sewickley Creek to NW.

Bell Arthur, uninc. village, Pitt co., E N.C., 6 mi/9.7 km W of Greenville. Formerly Arthur.

Bell Buckle, town (1990 pop. 326), Bedford co., central Tenn., 10 mi/16 km NE of Shelbyville; 35°35'N 86°21'W. In rich farm area. Seat of Webb School.

Bell Center, village (1990 pop. 127), Crawford co., SW Wis., near Kickapoo R., 23 mi/37 km NE of Prairie du Chien; 43°17'N 90°49'W. Stock raising; dairying. Hunting. Snow Bowl Ski Area nearby.

Bell City, city (1990 pop. 469), Stoddard co., SE Mo., in Mississippi R. alluvial plain, 6 mi/10 km SE of Advance; 37°01'N 89°49'W. Rice, cotton, soybeans.

Bell Gardens, suburb (1990 pop. 42,355) of Los Angeles, Los Angeles co., S Calif., 7 mi/11.3 km SE of downtown, E of Los Angeles R.; 33°58'N 118°09'W. Mfg. (tools, motor vehicle parts, fabricated wire prods., coffee, paper prods., electronic equip.). Inc. 1961.

Bell Island, island, SE N.F., Canada, in Conception Bay; 50°44'N 55°35'W. The isl. is 6 mi/10 km long and 3 mi/5 km wide. Its famous undersea iron mines were closed in 1966 after having been worked for 72 years.

Bell Island (8 mi/12.9 km long, 2 mi/3.2 km–3 mi/4.8 km wide), SE Alaska, in Alexander Archipelago, in Behm Canal, N of Revillagigedo Isl., 40 mi/64 km N of Ketchikan; 55°57'N 131°29'W. Has hot springs.

Bella Bella, village (1991 pop. 1,104), W B.C., Canada, on NW Denny Isl., on inlet of Hecate Strait, 170 mi/274 km SSE of Prince Rupert; 52°09'N 128°07'W. Fish canning, logging. Helicopter logging in area allows harvest without roads and floating; is also unregulated (does not require permits). Trees are airlifted directly to barges. Access by air and B.C. ferries. Heiltsuk band of people inhabit area. Waglisla Indian Village here. Ellerslie Lake area to NE is proposed as World Heritage Area.

Bella Coola, village, W central B.C., Canada, in Coast Mts., at mouth of Bella Coola R., at head of North Bentinck Arm of Burke Channel; 52°22'N 126°45'W. W terminus of 400-mi/644-km Route 20, the "Freedom Road," from Williams L. Opened in 1953, the highway remained mostly unpaved until 1990s. Ferry service from coastal ports has ceased. Seaplane service. Fishing; timber; mixed farming in Bella Coola Valley.

Bella Villa, residential suburb (1990 pop. 708) of St. Louis, St. Louis co., E Mo., 8 mi/13 km SSW of downtown; 38°32'N 90°17'W. Surrounded by uninc. city of Lemay.

Bella Vista (BE-ya VEES-tah), town (1990 pop 884), Chiapas, S Mexico, in Sierra Madre, 19 mi/31 km N of Motozintla de Mendoza; 15°30'N 92°08'W. Sugar, fruit. Called San Pedro Remate until 1934.

Bella Vista, village (1990 pop. 9,083), Benton co., extreme NW Ark., 4 mi/6.4 km N of Bentonville on Mo. boundary, on Sugar Creek., in the Ozarks; 36°28'N 94°17'W. Mineral springs. Resort and retirement community.

Belladère (bel-ah-DER), town, Ouest dept., E Haiti, near Dominican Republic border and Dominican town of Elías Piña, 11 mi/18 km ENE of Lascahobas; 18°51'N 71°47'W. Tobacco, sugarcane, log-wood, coffee; cattle; coffee processing.

Bellaire (BEL-er), city (1990 pop. 6,028), Belmont co., E Ohio, 6 mi/10 km SSW of Wheeling (W.Va.), across Ohio R. (bridged); 40°01'N 80°46'W. Mfg. (glass prods., enamelware, stoves, clay prods., food); coal mining. Settled c.1802.

Bellaire, village (1990 pop. 1,104), ⊙ Antrim co., NW Mich., 25 mi/40 km NE of Traverse City, near L. Bellaire (c.4 mi/6.4 km long, 1.5 mi/2.4 km wide); 44°58'N 85°12'W. In farm area (apples, potatoes); mfg. (furniture, fishing gear, motors); resort. Airport here. Shanty Creek Ski Area to SE; Torch L. 3 mi/4.8 km W.

Bellaire, residential section of E Queens borough of N.Y. city, SE N.Y.; 40°43'N 73°45'W. Belmont Park Race Track is nearby.

Bellaire, residential suburb (1990 pop. 13,842) of Houston, Harris co., SE Texas, SW 7 mi/11.3 km SW of downtown, near Brays Bayou, surrounded by city of Houston; 29°41'N 95°27'W. Mfg. (food, light mfg.).

Bellamy (BE-la-mee), village, Sumter co., W Ala., 10 mi/16 km SSE of Livingston. Lumber.

Bellamy River, c.15 mi/24 km long, Strafford co., SE N.H.; rises in Swains L. 9 mi/14.5 km W of Dover; flows E through Bellamy Reservoir and past Dover, through SE as tidal stream to Little Bay, channel connecting Great Bay to Atlantic Ocean.

Bellavista (be-ya-VEES-tah), processing center (1990 pop. 21), Nayarit, Compostela municipio, W Mexico, N suburb of Tepic; 27°37'N 104°50'W. In rich agr. region.

Bellbrook, city (1990 pop. 6,511), Greene co., SW Ohio, 10 mi/16 km SE of Dayton, near Little Miami R.; 39°02'N 84°05'W.

Belle 1 (BEL), town (1990 pop. 1,218), Maries co., central Mo., in the Ozarks, near Gasconade R., 12 mi/19 km NE of Vienna; 38°17'N 91°43'W. Agr., cattle; dairying; timber; light mfg. **2** town (1990 pop. 1,421), Kanawha co., W central W.Va., on Kanawha R., 10 mi/16 km SE of Charleston; 38°13'N 81°32'W. Mfg. (chemicals). Shrewsburg Home (1800).

Belle Ayr Mountain, peak (c.3,300 ft/1,006 m) of the Catskills, Ulster co., SE N.Y., near Pine Hill, NW of Kingston; 42°07'N 74°30'W. Skiing center.

Belle Bay, Canada: see FORTUNE BAY.

Belle Center, village (1990 pop. 796), Logan co., W central Ohio, 10 mi/16 km N of Bellefontaine; 40°31'N 83°46'W. Butter, cheese; limestone.

Belle Chasse (bel CHAIS), residential and industrial suburb (1990 pop. 8,512) of New Orleans, Plaquemines parish, SE La., 6 mi/10 km SSE of downtown, on W bank of Mississippi R.; 29°51'N 90°00'W. Free ferry to Braithwaite. New Orleans Naval Air Station to SW. Mfg. includes fabricated sheet metal, shipbuilding, electric equip. Orange Festival.

Belle Fourche (BELL-foosh), town (1990 pop. 4,335), ⊙ Butte co., W S.Dak., 52 mi/84 km NW of Rapid City, at confluence of Redwater Creek and Belle Fourche R., near Orman (Belle Fourche Reservoir) dam to NE. Shipping center for cattle and sheep. Wheat, flour, alfalfa, beet sugar; wool; dairy prods.; mfg. (bldg. materials, apparel, bentonite, clay processing). Black Hills Round-up takes place here annually. Mud Buttes (3295 ft/1004 m) to N; Black Hills (Natl. Forest) to S. U.S. Geographical Center (50 states) 25 mi/40 km NE. Settled 1878, inc. 1903.

Belle Fourche Reservoir (□ 15 sq mi/39 sq km), Butte co, W S.D., on Owl Creek, 50 mi/80 km NNW of Rapid City; 44°44'N 103°40'W. Max. capacity 278,216 acre-ft. Formed by Belle Fourche Dam (also known as Orman Dam; 122 ft/37 m high), built (1911) by the Bureau of Reclamation for irrigation; also used for flood control and recreation.

Belle Fourche River (bel FYOOSH), c.290 mi/467 km long, rises in NE Wyo. near Wright, in S Campbell co., flows NE past Moorcroft, through Keyhole Reservoir and past Devils Tower (Natl. Monument) and Hulett, then E into S.Dak., past town of Belle Fourche (N of Black Hills), joining Cheyenne R. 50 mi/80 km ENE of Rapid City. The Belle Fourche project provides flood control and recreation facilities as well as irrigating c.57,000 acres/23,068 ha in South Dakota.

Belle Glade, city (□ 4 sq mi/10.4 sq km; 1990 pop.

16,177), NW Palm Beach co., SE Fla., just E of S tip of L. Okeechobee; 26°41′N 80°40′W. Trade and processing center for a vegetable-farming, sugarcane, and cattle area. The city has a large, impoverished migrant-worker pop. Agr. experiment station located nearby. Inc. 1928.

Belle Harbor, residential section of S Queens borough of N.Y. city, SE N.Y., on Rockaway Peninsula; 40°35′N 73°52′W. In shore-resort area.

Belle Haven 1 town (1990 pop. 526), Accomack co. and Worthampton co., E Va., 11 mi/18 km S of Onancock, in Eastern Shore area, on arm of Chesapeake Bay; 37°32′N 75°49′W. Mfg. (fertilizer); agr. area (vegetables, grain; livestock). **2** uninc. town, Fairfax co., NE Va., residential suburb 1 mi/1.6 km SW of Alexandria, 8 mi/12.9 km S of Washington, D.C., on Potomac R., at mouth of Cameron Run creek; 38°46′N 77°03′W. Woodrow Wilson Bridge to NE.

Belle Isle, town (□ 4 sq mi/10.4 sq km; 1990 pop. 5,272), Orange co., central Fla., 7 mi/11.3 km S of Orlando, adjacent to Orlando Intl. Airport; 28°28′N 81°20′W.

Belle Isle 1 one of the 5 Isls., in St. Mary parish, S La., salt dome rising above sea marshes on N shore of Atchafalaya Bay, c.40 mi/64 km SE of New Iberia; 29°31′N 91°23′W. Elev. c.130 ft/40 m. Salt mine; oil and natural gas wells nearby. **2** (□ 1.6 sq mi/4.1 sq km), SE Mich., in Detroit R., 2.5 mi/4 km E of downtown Detroit, 1 mi/1.6 km downstream (W) of L. St. Clair outflow; c.2 mi/3.2 km long, 1 mi/1.6 km wide. Connected to mainland by Douglas MacArthur bridge. City park (swimming, boating, horseback riding); symphony shell, zoological gardens, aquarium, rose gardens, golf course, nature center. Dossin Great Lakes Mus.; Can./U.S. border in channel to S.

Belle Isle (beh-LEIL) (□ 20 sq mi/52 sq km), off N N.F., Canada, at NE entrance of the Strait of Belle Isle, 30 mi/48 km ENE of Cape Norman; 10 mi/16 km long, 3 mi/5 km wide. Rises to 680 ft/207 m. At N extremity is Misery Point lighthouse (52°01′N 55°17′W); another lighthouse is at S end. Inhabited in fishing season only.

Belle Isle, Va.: see JAMES RIVER.

Belle Isle, Strait of (beh-LEIL), c.35 mi/60 km long, 10 mi/16 km–15 mi/24 km wide, bet. the isl. of Newfoundland and Lab. The N entrance to the Gulf of St. Lawrence, it is deep and free of rocks and shoals; ice blocks it from Nov. to June. Strong tidal current. The tiny rock isl. Belle Isle (700 ft/213 m high), at the Atlantic entrance, has a lighthouse and is the 1st land sighted by ships from Europe.

Belle Meade, city (1990 pop. 2,839), Davidson co., central Tenn., residential suburb 7 mi/11 km S of Nashville; 36°06′N 86°51′W. Belle Meade, a restored antebellum mansion and estate open to the public, was famous for its race horses. Inc. 1938.

Belle Plaine, city (1990 pop. 2,834), Benton co., E central Iowa, near Iowa R., 22 mi/35 km SW of Vinton; 41°53′N 92°16′W. RR division point; corn seed processing, cement-block mfg. Platted 1861, inc. 1863.

Belle Plaine 1 (bel PLAIN), town (1990 pop. 1,649), Sumner co., S Kansas, near Arkansas R., 16 mi/26 km NE of Wellington; 37°23′N 97°16′W. RR junction. In wheat region. Bartlett Arboretum to W. **2** town (1990 pop. 3,149), Scott co., S Minn., on Minnesota R., 35 mi/56 km SW of Minneapolis; 44°37′N 93°45′W. Livestock; grain; dairying; mfg. (fertilizers, printing and publishing, pharmaceuticals). Bell Plain Airport to N. Minnesota Valley State Park to NE. Platted 1853.

Belle Prairie City, town (1990 pop. 64), Hamilton co., SE Ill., 9 mi/14.5 km N of McLeansboro; 38°13′N 88°32′W. In rich agr. area.

Belle Rive, village (1990 pop. 396), Jefferson co., S Ill., 10 mi/16 km SE of Mount Vernon; 38°13′N 88°44′W. In agr. area (wheat, sorghum, cattle); mfg.

Belle River, town (1991 pop. 4,298), S Ont., Canada, on S shore of L. St. Clair, 15 mi/24 km E of Windsor; 42°18′N 82°43′W. Dairying; mixed farming.

Belle River, c.65 mi/105 km long, E Mich., rises W of Imlay City in Lapeer co. at 42°53′N 83°07′W; flows out of Lang L. SE, past Memphis, to St. Clair R. at Marine City.

Belle Terre, summer-resort village (1990 pop. 839), Suffolk co., SE N.Y., on N shore of L.I., overlooking Port Jefferson Harbor, just N of Port Jefferson; 40°57′N 73°04′W.

Belle Valley, village (1990 pop. 267), Noble co., E Ohio, 17 mi/27 km S of Cambridge, and on small Duck Creek, in livestock area; 39°49′N 81°34′W. Coal mining.

Belle Vernon or **Bellevernon** (both: BEL VUHR-nuhn), borough (1990 pop. 1,213), Fayette co., SW Pa., 23 mi/37 km S of Pittsburgh, 2 mi/3.2 km SSE of Monessen, on Monongahela R. (bridged); 40°07′N 79°52′W. Mfg. (machinery, commercial printing); bituminous coal. Agr. (corn, hay, alfalfa; livestock; dairying). Laid out 1813, inc. 1863.

Belle View, uninc. town, Fairfax co., NE Va., residential suburb 11 mi/18 km NW of Washington, D.C., near Potomac R.; 38°46′N 77°03′W. Wolf Trap Farm Park for the Performing Arts to SW.

Belleair (bell-ER) (□ 2 sq mi/5.2 sq km; 1990 pop. 3,968), Pinellas co., W central Fla., just SW of Clearwater; 27°56′N 82°48′W.

Belleaire Beach (bel-ER), town (□ 1 sq mi/2.6 sq km; 1990 pop. 2,070), Pinellas co., W central Fla., 16 mi/26 km NW of St. Petersburg on the Gulf of Mexico; 27°55′N 82°50′W.

Belleaire Bluffs (bel-ER), town (1990 pop. 2,128), Pinellas co., W central Fla., 22 mi/35 km W of Tampa; 27°54′N 82°51′W. Mfg. includes commercial printing.

Belle-Anse, Haiti: see SALTROU.

Bellechasse (behl-SHAS), county (□ 653 sq mi/1,691 sq km; 1991 pop. 29,475), SE Que., Canada, on Maine border, on the St. Lawrence R.; ⊙ St. Raphael; 46°40′N 70°30′W.

Bellefontaine (bel-FOUN-tin), city (1990 pop. 12,142), ⊙ Logan co., W central Ohio; 40°22′N 83°47′W. It is a trade and RR center for a farm area. Mfg. includes electrical equip., motors, and tools. East of the city is Campbell Hill, the highest point in Ohio (1,549 ft/472 km). Settled 1818, inc. 1835.

Bellefontaine (bel-fahnt-AIN), village, Webster co., central Miss., 30 mi/48 km WNW of Starksville. Agr. area; mfg. (leather prods.).

Bellefontaine Neighbors (bel-FOUN-tuhn NAI-buhrz), residential suburb (1990 pop. 10,922) of St. Louis, St. Louis co., E Mo., 10 mi/16 km NNW of downtown; 38°45′N 90°13′W. St. Louis State Hosp.; veterans' home here. Founded c.1819, inc. 1950.

Bellefonte (BEL-font), town (1990 pop. 1,243), New Castle co., N Del., residential suburb 3 mi/4.8 km NE of downtown Wilmington on Delaware R; 39°46′N 75°30′W. Bellevue State Park to NW. Inc. 1915.

Bellefonte (be-lah-FAHN-tai), borough (1990 pop. 6,358), ⊙ Centre co., central Pa., 44 mi/71 km SW of Williamsport, on Spring Creek; 40°54′N 77°46′W. Mt. resort. Mfg. (lime processing, brass forgings, commercial printing, machinery); limestone quarries; agr. in area (dairying). Bald Eagle Mt. ridge passes to NW; Howard State Nursery, in Bald Eagle State Park, to NE; Centre County Lib. and Historical Mus.; Rockview State Correctional Center to S; Bellefonte Skypark to W. Laid out 1775, inc. 1806.

Bellemeade (BEL-meed), residential suburb (1990 pop. 927) of Louisville, Jefferson co., N Ky., 9 mi/14.5 km E of downtown; 38°15′N 85°35′W.

Bellerive (bel-REEV), residential suburb (1990 pop. 238) of St. Louis, St. Louis co., E Mo., 10 mi/16 km NW of downtown; 38°42′N 90°18′W. Site of Univ. of Mo.–St. Louis (UMSL).

Bellerose, village (1990 pop. 1,101), Nassau co., SE N.Y., on W L.I., just W of Floral Park; 40°43′N 73°43′W. Mfg. (machinery). Belmont Park Race Track is nearby. Settled 1908, inc. 1924.

Belleview (BEL-vyoo), town (□ 1 sq mi/2.6 sq km; 1990 pop. 2,666), Marion co., N central Fla., 10 mi/16 km SSE of Ocala; 29°03′N 82°02′W. Packing houses (citrus fruit), citrus-fruit cannery.

Belleville, city (1991 pop. 37,243), SE Ont., Canada, on L. Ont.; 44°10′N 77°23′W. Machinery, automotive accessories, optical lenses, cheddar cheese. Seat of Albert Col. and the Ont. School for the Deaf.

Belleville, city (1990 pop. 42,785), ⊙ St. Clair co., SW Ill.; 38°31′N 90°00′W. Coal-mining area. Belleville also has farm-related industries and a large variety of mfg., including mining equip., printing, shoes, iron prods., food prods., and bldg. materials. Belleville Area Community Col. is here. Scott Air Force Base (est. 1917 for flight instruction) is hq. of the Military Air Transport Service; it lies 6 mi/9.7 km ENE. Apple orchards to SE. Inc. 1819.

Belleville 1 (BEL-vil), town (1990 pop. 2,517), ⊙ Republic co., N Kansas, 18 mi/29 km N of Concordia; 39°49′N 97°37′W. RR junction. Trade center for corn, wheat, and livestock area; mfg. (medical equip.). Founded 1869, inc. 1878. **2** town (1990 pop. 3,270), Wayne co., SE Mich., on Huron R., suburb 24 mi/39 km WSW of Detroit; 42°12′N 83°28′W. In diversified agr. area; mfg. (automotive parts, horticulture equip., consumer goods, furniture, asphalt); resort. Willow Run Airport to NW. Belleville L. to W. Settled 1826; inc. as village 1905, as city 1946.

Belleville, township (1990 pop. 34,213), Essex co., NE N.J., on the Passaic R., just N of Newark; 40°47′N 74°09′W. Electrical equip., optical equip., gloves, and precision instruments are among its mfg. John Stevens's boat, built here in 1798 for the run to N.Y., contained one of the country's 1st steam engines. Settled c.1680, set off from Newark 1839, inc. 1910.

Belleville 1 uninc. town (1990 pop. 1,589), Union township, Mifflin co., central Pa., 8 mi/12.9 km W of Lewistown, on Kishacoquillas Creek; 40°36′N 77°43′W. Mfg. (wine, food, agr. machinery). Rich agr. area (soybeans, grain; livestock; dairying). Rothrock State Forest to N; Stone Mt. ridge to NW; Jacks Mt. ridge to SE; Brookmere Winery to NE; Greenwood Furnace State Park to N. **2** town (1990 pop. 1,456), Dane and Green cos., S Wis., on Sugar R., 17 mi/27 km SSW of Madison; 42°51′N 89°32′W. In farm area; processes dairy prods., poultry; mfg. (food; machinery).

Belleville 1 (BEL-vil), village (1990 pop. 390), Yell co., W central Ark., 22 mi/35 km SW of Russellville, near Petit Jean R.; 35°05′N 93°27′W. Ozark Natl. Forest to N; Ouachita Natl. Forest to SW. **2** village, in North Kingstown town, R.I.; 41°33′N 71°27′W.

Bellevue 1 (BEL-vyoo), city (1990 pop. 8,146), on Huron-Sandusky co. line, N Ohio, 13 mi/21 km SW of Sandusky; 41°17′N 82°52′W. RR junction (with repair shops) in agr. area (cherries, grain; livestock); electrical prods., machinery, food prods. Limestone quarries. Seneca Caverns are nearby. Named Bellevue in 1839. **2** city (1990 pop. 86,874), King co., W Wash., suburb 6 mi/9.7 km E of Seattle, on E shore of L. Washington, opposite city of Seattle, connected by Evergreen Point Bridge; inc. 1953; 47°36′N 122°10′W. Mfg. (computers, machinery, electrical equip., aircraft parts, printing and publishing, food, bldg. materials, medical equip., chemicals, fertilizers, paper prods.). It grew as a major suburban city in the 1980s and has one of the most extensive networks of office complexes in the Pacific Northwest. In the city, Bellevue Sq. serves as the state's largest shopping center. Bellevue is connected with Seattle by 2 floating bridges. Bellevue Community Col. is here. L. Sammamish is E of city; L. Sammamish State Park to SE.

Bellevue 1 (BEL-vyoo), town (1990 pop. 1,275), Blaine co., S central Idaho, 5 mi/8 km SE of Hailey, on Big Wood R (forms Magic Reservoir); 43°28′N 114°16′W. Elev. 5,190 ft/1,582 m. Agr. (cattle, sheep); mfg. (log homes); logging. Blaine County Historical Mus. **2** town (1990 pop. 2,239), Jackson co., E Iowa, on Mississippi R. (lock and dam here), 19 mi/31 km NE of Maquoketa; 42°15′N 90°25′W. Mfg. (machinery). Clay pits and limestone quarry nearby. Bellevue State Park and U.S. fish hatchery are here. Settled 1830s, inc. 1844. **3** town (1990 pop. 6,997), Campbell co., N Ky., suburb 2 mi/3.2 km E of downtown Cincinnati (Ohio), on the Ohio R., 1 mi/1.6 km NE of Newport; 39°06′N 84°28′W. Mfg. (machining, printing and publishing, production molds, diversified light mfg.).

Bellevue 1 (BEL-vyoo), village (1990 pop. 1,491), Peoria co., N central Ill., suburb 6 mi/9.7 km W of downtown

Peoria; 40°41′N 89°40′W. Agr. (corn, oats, vegetables; cattle). Greater Peoria Airport to SW. Inc. 1941. **2** fishing village, Talbot co., E Md., 11 mi/18 km NNW of Cambridge, and on Tred Avon R. Bellevue-Oxford ferry was est. 1683 by Richard Royston. Vegetable, fruit cannery; crabs. In the coves and up the creeks are sites of many 17th- and 18th-cent. shipyards. **3** village (1990 pop. 1,401), Eaton co., S central Mich., on Battle Creek, 12 mi/19 km NE of Battle Creek city; 42°26′N 85°01′W. In farm area (grain, corn, beans); cement mfg., crushed limestone. Settled 1830; inc. 1867. **4** village (1990 pop. 333), Clay co., N Texas, 33 mi/53 km SE of Wichita Falls; 33°37′N 98°01′W. Market, in agr. area (cotton, wheat, pecans; peaches; cattle); oil and gas.

Bellevue (BEL-vyoo), borough (1990 pop. 9,126), Allegheny co., SW Pa., residential suburb 4 mi/6.4 km NNW of downtown Pittsburgh, on Ohio R.; 40°29′N 80°03′W. Light mfg. Settled 1802, inc. 1867.

Bellevue (BEL-vyoo), suburb (1990 pop. 30,982) of Omaha, Sarpy co., E Nebr., 7 mi/11.3 km S of downtown, on the Missouri R.; highway bridge to Omaha; 41°09′N 95°55′W. RR junction. Mfg. (fertilizers, printing, computer and communication equip., food, apparel, concrete prods., whirlpool baths, feed); also has telecommunications services. The oldest city in the state, Bellevue was a trading post in the early 1800s and the site of a Presbyterian Native Amer. mission in the 1840s and 1850s. The Strategic Air Command Mus. is here. Bellevue Univ. (est. 1965) here. Offutt Air Force Base to S. Inc. 1855.

Bellevue Manor, uninc. village (1990 pop. 660), New Castle co., NE Del., 4 mi/6.4 km NE of Wilmington, on Delaware R. Bellevue State Park to W.

Bellevue Mountain, peak (12,519 ft/3,816 m) in Rocky Mts., Gunnison and Pitkin cos., W central Colo., 14 mi/23 km SSW of Aspen, in the Elk Mts. Also spelled Belleview.

Bellflower, city (1990 pop. 61,815), Los Angeles co., S Calif.; 33°54′N 118°08′W. It is mainly residential with some basic industries (fabricated metal prods., steel foundry, rubber goods). Bounded on E by San Gabriel R. Inc. 1957.

Bellflower, town (1990 pop. 413), Montgomery co., E central Mo., near West Fork of Cuivre R., 8 mi/13 km E of Montgomery City; 39°00′N 91°20′W. Cattle; corn, soybeans.

Bellflower, village, McLean co., E central Ill., 25 mi/40 km ESE of Bloomington; 40°20′N 88°31′W. In rich agr. area (corn, soybeans; cattle).

Bellingham, city (1990 pop. 52,179), ⊙ Whatcom co., NW Wash., 78 mi/126 km N of Seattle, 43 mi/69 km SE of Vancouver (B.C.); 48°45′N 122°28′W. A port of entry on Bellingham Bay, arm of Rosario Strait (to SW) and Strait of Ga. (to NW), one of the best landlocked harbors on the Pacific coast, 17 mi/27 km S of Canada (B.C.) border. Ferry service to Alaska. Vegetables, berries, grain, alfalfa; dairying; cattle; mfg. (machinery, electrical equip., printing and publishing, concrete prods., food processing, wood prods., apparel, aircraft parts, beverages, plastic prods., shipbuilding, vehicle parts). It is an important shipping point for lumber, pulp, paper, and canned and frozen fruit. Settled in 1852 as Whatcom, it merged with 3 adjoining towns to form Bellingham in 1903. Western Wash. Univ., Whatcom Community Col., and Whatcom Mus. of History and Art are in the city, which has many notable scenic parks. Lummi Indian Reservation to W. Moran State Park is on Orcas Isl. in Bellingham Bay. Inc. 1904.

Bellingham, town (1990 pop. 14,877), Norfolk co., S Mass., 20 mi/32 km SE of Worcester; 42°05′N 71°28′W. Woolens, medical equip., furniture, consumer goods. Includes South Bellingham village. Settled c. 1713, inc. 1719.

Bellingham, village (1990 pop. 247), Lac qui Parle co., SW Minn., near S.Dak. border, 10 mi/16 km NNW of Madison; 45°08′N 96°16′W. Corn, soybeans, oats, wheat; hogs, cattle, sheep; mfg. (concrete, fertilizers). Marsh L. reservoir on Minnesota R. and Lac qui Parle Wildlife Refuge Area to NE.

Bellmawr (BEL-mor), residential borough (1990 pop. 12,603), Camden co., SW N.J.; 39°52′N 75°05′W. Site of industrial park with mfg. (machinery, aircraft parts). Inc. 1926.

Bellmead, town (1990 pop. 8,336), McLennan co., E central Texas, residential suburb 4 mi/6.4 km NE of downtown Waco, near Brazos R.; 31°36′N 97°05′W. Texas State Technical Col. and T.S.T.C. Airport to N.

Bellmont, village (1990 pop. 271), Wabash co., SE Ill., 8 mi/12.9 km W of Mount Carmel; 38°22′N 87°54′W. In agr. area (grain); oil, natural gas, coal.

Bellmore, residential village (□ 3 sq mi/7.8 sq km; 1990 pop. 16,438), Nassau co., SE N.Y., near S shore of L.I., 8 mi/12.9 km SE of Mineola; 40°39′N 73°31′W.

Bellot Strait, Arctic channel (30 mi/48 km long, 2 mi/3 km–8 mi/13 km wide), S Franklin dist., N.W.T., Canada, bet. Boothia Peninsula (S) and Somerset Isl. (N); 72°00′N 94°30′W. Connects Gulf of Boothia and Prince Regent Inlet (E) with Peel Sound and Franklin Strait (W). N shore rises steeply to c.1,500 ft/457 m, S shore to c.2,500 ft/762 m. Fort Ross trading post, on N shore, was est. 1937. Bellot Strait is keystone of the NW Passage; it was discovered (1852) by Lt. Joseph René Bellot while searching for the Franklin expedition. Was 1st crossed from W by Hudson's Bay Co. ship *Aklavik* in 1937.

Bellows Falls, industrial village (1990 pop. 3,313) of Rockingham town, Windham co., SE Vt., on terraces above the Connecticut R. (2 bridges), and 20 mi/32 km N of Brattleboro; 43°08′N 72°27′W. Makes paper (industry begun 1802), wood prods., furniture, and precision instruments; ships dairy prods. Navigation canal and lock, said to have been begun (1792) in U.S., was completed 1802 around 50-ft/15-m falls (once called "Great Falls") here; used for some time after arrival of RR (1849; 1st in Vt.) and rebuilt (1926–1928) as part of hydroelectric power development. The 1st bridge over Connecticut R. was built here (1785). Steel Arch bridge, longest single arch in the country when built in 1905, dismantled in 1982.

Bellport, summer-resort village (□ 1 sq mi/2.6 sq km; 1990 pop. 2,572), Suffolk co., SE N.Y., on S shore of L.I., on Bellport Bay (inlet of Great South Bay), 4 mi/6.4 km ESE of Patchogue; 40°45′N 72°56′W.

Bells 1 town (1990 pop. 1,643), Crockett co., W Tenn., on South Fork of Forked Deer R., 16 mi/26 km WNW of Jackson; 35°43′N 89°05′W. **2** town (1990 pop. 962), Grayson co., N Texas, 11 mi/18 km E of Sherman; 33°37′N 96°24′W. In agr. area (cattle, horses, poultry; wheat, peanuts); oil and gas.

Bellton, town, Hall and Banks cos., NE Ga., 12 mi/19 km NE of Gainesville; 34°23′N 83°39′W.

Bellville, city (1990 pop. 3,378), ⊙ Austin co., S Texas, 52 mi/84 km WNW of Houston; 29°56′N 96°15′W. Trade, shipping point in farm area (cotton, peanuts, rice; poultry; livestock). Oil and gas field nearby. Mfg. (paper prods., fabricated metal prods., concrete prods., furniture). Settled 1847, inc. 1927.

Bellville, village (1990 pop. 1,568), Richland co., N central Ohio, 10 mi/16 km S of Mansfield, on Clear Fork of Mohican R.; 40°39′N 82°32′W. In agr. area (grain, potatoes, dairy prods.); greenhouses. Settled 1809, plotted 1815, inc. 1841.

Bellwood 1 town, Geneva co., SE Ala., near Choctawhatchee R., 11 mi/18 km NNE of Geneva. **2** uninc. town, Chesterfield co., E central Va., residential suburb 7 mi/11.3 km S of downtown Richmond, near James R.; 37°24′N 77°26′W.

Bellwood 1 village (1990 pop. 20,241), Cook co., NE Ill., suburb 14 mi/23 km WNW of downtown Chicago; 41°52′N 87°52′W. Inc. 1900. Bellwood's mfg. includes consumer goods, brass items, printing, paper prods., adhesives, and concrete prods. **2** village (1990 pop. 395), Butler co., E Nebr., 9 mi/14.5 km SE of Columbus, near Platte R; 41°20′N 97°14′W.

Bellwood, borough (1990 pop. 1,976), Blair co., central Pa., 8 mi/12.9 km NNE of Altoona, on Little Juniata R.; 40°36′N 78°19′W. Food processing; printing and publishing; some agr.; bituminous coal in area.

Belly River, 150 mi/241 km long, N Mont. and S Alta., Canada, rises in Mont.; flows NNE at Continental Divide, NW Glacier co., in Glacier Natl. Park, SE of Mt. Merritt; watered by Chaney, Ahern, and Shepard Glaciers; flows NNE through several small lakes, then crosses into Alta., Canada; continues NE through SE edge of Waterton Lakes Natl. Park and past Blood Indian Reserve (forms W boundary), to Oldman R. 10 mi/16 km NW of Lethbridge.

Belmar (BEL-mahr), resort borough (1990 pop. 5,877), Monmouth co., E N.J., on the coast, on S side of Shark R. mouth, and 14 mi/23 km ESE of Freehold; 40°10′N 74°01′W. Fishing; boating. Inc. 1890.

Belmond, town (1990 pop. 2,500), Wright co., N central Iowa, near Iowa R., 10 mi/16 km NNE of Clarion; 42°51′N 93°36′W. RR junction. Agr. (soybean-processing plant; dairy prods., feed, hybrid seed corn; mfg. (engine parts, printing). Extensive damage in floods of 1993. (The damage to Iowa was as much with "field" flooding as it was river flooding.) Inc. 1881.

Belmont, county (□ 539 sq mi/1,396 sq km; 1990 pop. 71,074), E Ohio; ⊙ St. Clairsville, 40°00′N 80°58′W. Bounded E by Ohio R., here forming W.Va. line; also drained by small Captina, Wheeling, and McMahon creeks. Includes Piedmont Reservoir. In the Unglaciated Plain physiographic region. Coal mining; mfg. at Bellaire, Martins Ferry, and Bridgeport (apparel, food, industrial machinery); agr. (fruit, corn; dairy prods.); limestone quarries, coal mines. Formed 1801.

Belmont, city (1990 pop. 24,127), San Mateo co., W Calif., residential suburb 18 mi/29 km SSE of San Francisco, 3 mi/4.8 km SW of San Francisco Bay. Mfg. (plastics, construction materials, publishing and printing, electronic equip., biological prods., pottery). The Col. of Notre Dame (est. 1851) is here. Bay Meadows Race track to N. San Francisco State Fish and Game Refuge to W, including Upper and Lower Crystal Springs reservoir on San Andreas fault. Laid out 1851, inc. 1926

Belmont 1 (BEL-mahnt), town (1990 pop. 24,720), Middlesex co., E Mass., a residential suburb of Boston; 42°24′N 71°11′W. Includes Waverley and McLean hosps. Bottled water. Settled 1636, inc. 1859. **2** town (1990 pop. 1,554), Tishomingo co., extreme NE Miss., near Ala., 34 mi/55 km ENE of Tupelo; 34°30′N 88°12′W. In timber and agr. area; mfg. (bldg. equip., furniture, apparel). **3** town (1990 pop. 5,796), Belknap co., central N.H., 6 mi/9.7 km S of Laconia; 43°28′N 71°28′W. Bounded on NW by Silver L., Hutkins Pond, and lower end of Winnisquam L. Vegetables, nursery crops, apples; poultry, cattle; dairying. Mfg. (machining, fabricated metal prods., food). Includes village of Winnisquam 3 mi/4.8 km SW of Laconia, mfg. (sheet metal, concrete, machinery). Berenson's Belmont Greyhound Race Track in SE. Inc. as Upper Gilmanton 1859, renamed 1869. **4** town (1990 pop. 8,434), Gaston co., S N.C., 8 mi/12.9 km E of Gastonia, 12 mi/19 km W of Charlotte, near Catawba R. (L. Wylie reservoir); 35°15′N 81°02′W. Mfg. (textiles, apparel). Seat of Belmont Abbey Col. Monastery and Cathedral (completed 1894). **5** uninc. town (1990 pop. 3,184), Cambria co., W central Pa., residential suburb 3 mi/4.8 km SSE of Johnstown, on Stonycreek R.; 40°16′N 78°53′W. **6** town (1990 pop. 912), Pleasants co., NW W.Va., on Ohio R., 4 mi/6.4 km W of St. Marys; 39°22′N 81°15′W. **7** town (1990 pop. 823), Lafayette co., SW Wis., 7 mi/11.3 km E of Platteville; 42°44′N 90°19′W. Makes cheese. First Capitol State Park to N; Platte Mounds are nearby.

Belmont, village (1991 pop. 1,364), S Ont., Canada, on Kettle Creek, 10 mi/16 km SE of London. Dairying; mixed farming.

Belmont 1 village (□ 1 sq mi/2.6 sq km; 1990 pop. 1,006), ⊙ Allegany co., W N.Y., on Genesee R., 21 mi/34 km WSW of Hornell; 42°13′N 78°01′W. In dairying area; metal fabrication, machinery. Inc. 1871. **2** village (1990 pop. 471), Belmont co., E Ohio, 15 mi/24 km W of Bellaire; 41°09′N 81°02′W. In coal-mining area.

Belmont (BEL-mahnt), locality, Nye co., central Nev., 40 mi/64 km NNE of Tonopah. Mining ghost town; silver mines discovered 1863 yielded until 1885. Belmont Courthouse is a State Historical Monument.

Belmont, NE residential suburb of Port of Spain, NW Trinidad, Trinidad and Tobago.

Belmont Corner, town, Waldo co., S Maine, just SW of Belfast. Has resorts on Tilden Pond.

Belmont Junction, N.C.: see NORTH BELMONT.

Belmont Lake, on S L.I., SE N.Y., just NW of Babylon; 40°44′N 73°20′W. State park (□ 348 acres/141 ha) here: water sports, picnicking; hiking and bridle paths.

Belmont Park, N.Y.: see NASSAU, co.

Belmore, village (1990 pop. 161), Putnam co., NW Ohio, 17 mi/27 km WNW of Findlay, in agr. region; 41°09′N 83°59′W.

Bel-Nor (bel-NOR), residential suburb (1990 pop. 2,935) of St. Louis, St. Louis co., E Mo., 10 mi/16 km NW of downtown; 38°42′N 90°19′W. Inc. 1937.

Beloeil (buh-LUH-ee), suburban town (1991 pop. 18,516), S Que., Canada, on Richelieu R., 18 mi/29 km ENE of Montreal; 45°34′N 73°12′W. Center of most prosperous dairy and produce areas of Que.; mfg. (prefabricated bldgs.); market in agr. region.

Beloit 1 (bel-OIT), city (1990 pop. 4,066), ⊙ Mitchell co., N Kansas, on Solomon R., 50 mi/80 km NNW of Salina; 39°28′N 98°06′W. RR junction. In corn, wheat, rye, cattle, sheep area; mfg. farm machinery; flour milling. Inc. 1872. **2** (be-LOIT), city (1990 pop. 35,573), Rock co., S Wis., on Ill. boundary, 38 mi/61 km SSE of Madison, 15 mi/24 km N of Rockford (Ill.), on the Rock R.; 42°31′N 89°01′W. Elev. 750 ft/229 m. Twin city with Vanesville, 13 mi/21 km N; South Beloit (Ill.) adjoins it. RR junction in an agr. area. Beloit's mfg. includes pulp- and paper-making machinery, engines, food, knives. A trading post was established on the site in 1824 for trade with the Winnebagos, and in 1837 the 1st permanent settlers arrived from New England. Beloit Col., founded in 1846, is in the city. Blackhawk Technical. Col. to N. Inc. 1846.

Beloit, village (1990 pop. 1,037), Mahoning co., NE Ohio, 22 mi/35 km SW of Youngstown; 40°57′N 81°00′W. Fire-clay mines.

Belpre (BEL-prai), city (1990 pop. 6,796), Washington co., SE Ohio, on the Ohio R. (bridged), opposite Parkersburg (W.Va.); 39°17′N 81°36′W. In fruit- and vegetable-growing area. Settled 1789, inc. 1902. Nearby is Blennerhassett Isl.

Belpre (BEL-prai), village (1990 pop. 116), Edwards co., S central Kansas, 17 mi/27 km E of Kinsley; 37°57′N 99°05′W. Wheat.

Bel-Ridge, residential suburb (1990 pop. 3,199) of St. Louis, St. Louis co., E Mo., 10 mi/16 km NW of downtown; 38°42′N 90°19′W.

Belt, village (1990 pop. 571), Cascade co., central Mont., on Belt Creek, 18 mi/29 km SE of Great Falls; 47°23′N 110°56′W. Dairying; poultry, cattle, sheep, hogs; wheat, barley, oats, alfalfa; mfg. (marble, consumer goods); coal mining. Part of Lewis and Clark Natl. Forest to E. Originally named Castner.

Belton 1 city (1990 pop. 18,150), Cass co., W Mo., residential suburb 20 mi/32 km S of Kansas City; 38°49′N 31°94′W. Mfg. (metal fabrication, transformers). Richards-Gebaur Airport to W (former air-force base). **2** city (1990 pop. 12,476), ⊙ Bell co., central Texas, suburb 7 mi/11.3 km WSW of Temple, on Leon R. (forms large Belton L. reservoir in NW part of city) at mouth of Nolan Creek; 31°04′N 97°27′W. Elev. 511 ft/156 m. Market center in rich agr. area (cotton, corn, grain; cattle); mfg. (furniture, machinery, paper prods., fabricated metal prods., apparel). Seat of Univ. of Mary Hardin-Baylor. Large Fort Hood Military Reserve to W; Lampasas R. to S (forms Stillhouse Hollow L. reservoir to SW). Founded 1850, renamed 1851, inc. 1884.

Belton, town (1990 pop. 4,646), Anderson co., NW S.C., 10 mi/16 km E of Anderson; 34°31′N 82°30′W. Mfg. includes textiles, clothing, paint. Agr. includes dairying; livestock, poultry; soybeans, sorghum. Inc. 1855.

Belton, Mont.: see WEST GLACIER.

Belton Lake, reservoir, Bell and Coryell cos., central Texas, on Leon R., 9 mi/14.5 km W of Temple; c.25 mi/40 km long, with c.15-mi/24-km-long W arm; 31°06′N 97°28′W. Max. capacity 1,876,700 acre-ft. Formed by Belton Dam (187 ft/57 m high), built (1954) by the Army Corps of Engineers for flood control and water supply. W arm extends into Ft. Hood Military Base; Mother Neff State Park on E shore.

Beltrami (bel-TRA-mee), county (□ 3,055 sq mi/7,912 sq km; 1990 pop. 34,384), NW Minn.; ⊙ Bemidji; 48°01′N 94°55′W. Drained by headwaters of Mississippi R. in S (source is to SW in Clearwater co.). Agr. (oats, barley, wheat, wild rice, hay, alfalfa, sunflowers; sheep, cattle, poultry; dairying); freshwater fish; resort area. Includes large part of Red L. Indian Reservation; part of Leech L. Indian Reservation in SE; L. Bemidji State Park in S; large Upper Red and Lower Red lakes in N center; part of Chippewa Natl. Forest in SE; Red L. State Forest in NE; Buena Vista State Forest and part of Mississippi Headwaters State Forest in S; parts of Beltrami Isl. State Forest and Red L. Wildlife Area in N. Formed 1866.

Beltrami (bel-TRA-mee), village (1990 pop. 137), Polk co., NW Minn., 16 mi/26 km SSE of Crookston, on Sand Hill R.; 47°32′N 96°31′W. Grain, potatoes; dairying; mfg. (fertilizers).

Beltsville, village (1990 pop. 14,476), Prince Georges co., central Md., 12 mi/19 km NNE of Wash., D.C.; 39°02′N 76°55′W. Has airport. Named for a local land owner, Truman Belt. Its proximity to the Wash. Beltway, built with federal funds in the 1950s and 1960s, is coincidental. Nearby are Patuxent wildlife research center of Dept. of the Interior and the U.S. Dept. of Agr. research center (16 sq mi/41 sq km).

Beltzville Lake (BELTS-vil), reservoir, Carbon co., E Pa., on Pohopoco Creek, in Beltzville State Park, 4 mi/6.4 km E of Leighton; 7 mi/11.3 km long; 40°20′N 75°38′W. Max. capacity 93,220 acre-ft. Formed by Beltzville Dam (150 ft/46 m high), built (1972) by the Army Corps of Engineers.

Belvedere 1 uninc. town, Los Angeles co., S Calif., residential suburb 3 mi/4.8 km E of downtown Los Angeles, and 2 mi/3.2 km W of Monterey Park. **2** town (1990 pop. 2,147), Marin co., W Calif., on W side of Tiburon Peninsula, on E shore of Richardson Bay (inlet of San Francisco Bay), 7 mi/11.3 km N of downtown San Francisco; 37°52′N 122°28′W. Mfg. (furniture). Angel Isl. State Park to SE; Mt. Tamalpais Game Refuge, in Richardson Bay, to NW; Golden Gate straits to S. **3** uninc. town (1990 pop. 6,133), Aiken co., SW S.C. , residential suburb 3 mi/4.8 km NNE of Augusta (Ga.); 33°32′N 81°56′W. Mfg. of laboratory glassware. Agr. includes cotton, peanuts, grain; livestock, poultry. Kaolin clay mining. **4** uninc. town, Fairfax co., NE Va., residential suburb 8 mi/12.9 km SW of Wash., D.C., 6 mi/9.7 km WNW of Alexandria. L.; 38°50′N 77°09′W. Barcroft reservoir to NE.

Belvedere Gardens, Calif.: see BELVEDERE.

Belvidere (BEL-vi-dir), city (1990 pop. 15,958), ⊙ Boone co., N Ill., on the Kishwaukee R.; 42°15′N 88°50′W. Farm trade center (corn, oats; dairying); mfg. (insulating parts, salon equip., ice cream, fabricated metal prods.). Inc. 1847.

Belvidere 1 (BEL-vi-DIR), town (1990 pop. 2,669), ⊙ Warren co., NW N.J., on Delaware R., at mouth of Pequest R., and 11 mi/18 km NNE of Phillipsburg; 40°49′N 75°04′W. Mfg. includes vitamins, transportation equip.; dairy prods. Settled 1759, laid out 1799, inc. 1845. **2** (BEL-vuh-dir), town (1990 pop. 228), Lamoille co., N Vt., on North Branch Lamoille R., and 12 mi/19 km NNW of Hyde Park, in Green Mts.; 44°45′N 72°40′W. Includes villages of Belvidere Junction and Belvidere Corners.

Belvidere 1 (BEL-vi-dir), village (1990 pop. 117), Thayer co., SE Nebr., 5 mi/8 km N of Hebron, and on branch of Little Blue R; 40°15′N 97°33′W. RR junction. Dairy prods.; livestock; grain. **2** village (1990 pop. 63), Jackson co., S central S.Dak., 11 mi/18 km E of Kadoka, on White R. Wheat, oats; livestock. Pine Ridge Indian Reservation to S.

Belview, village (1990 pop. 383), Redwood co., SW Minn., near Minnesota R., 11 mi/18 km WNW of Redwood Falls; 44°36′N 95°19′W. Livestock, poultry; grain, soybeans; dairying; granite. Joseph R. Brown State Wayside to N.

Belville, village (1990 pop. 66), Brunswick co., SE N.C., 4 mi/6.4 km W of Wilmington, on Cape Fear R. (bridged to Wilmington); 34°13′N 77°59′W.

Belvoir, Fort, U.S. Army military reservation, Fairfax co., E Va., on peninsula extending into Potomac R., 18 mi/29 km SSW of Wash., D.C.; Gunston Cove to SW. A permanent post of Corps of Engineers. Ruins of "Belvoir" (1741), Lord Fairfax's estate, here. U.S. fish hatchery nearby. Formerly Fort Humphreys.

Belvue (BEL-vyoo), village (1990 pop. 207), Pottawatomie co., NE Kansas, on Kansas R., and 27 mi/43 km WNW of Topeka; 39°13′N 96°10′W.

Belwood, village (1990 pop. 631), Cleveland co., S N.C., 15 mi/24 km N of Shelby. Agr. area (cotton, grain; poultry, livestock); 35°28′N 81°31′W.

Belzoni (bel-ZO-nee), town (1990 pop. 2,536), ⊙ Humphreys co., W Miss., on Yazoo R., and 29 mi/47 km SW of Greenwood; 33°10′N 90°29′W. Agr. (cotton, corn, soybeans; cattle; timber); mfg. (catfish processing; consumer goods, apparel). "Catfish Capital of World." Wister Gardens. Prehistoric Native Amer. artifacts found near here, 1951. Founded c.1827.

Bement (be-MENT), village (1990 pop. 1,668), Piatt co., central Ill., 8 mi/12.9 km S of Monticello; 39°55′N 88°34′W. In corn and soybean area; mfg. wood cabinets. Inc. 1874. Bryant Cottage State Historical Site.

Bemidji (buh-MID-jee), city (1990 pop. 11,245), ⊙ Beltrami co., N central Minn., 140 mi/225 km WNW of Duluth, at S end of L. Bemidji; 47°28′N 94°52′W. Elev. 1,361 ft/415 m. Resort area; tourism is the major industry. Also a trade and marketing center for the dairy farms of the region; grain, sunflowers; livestock, poultry; timber; mfg. (printing and publishing; bldg. materials, textiles, trusses, beverages, consumer goods, lumber, wire harnesses, computer equip., garage doors, crating materials). On the lakeshore stands an 18-ft/5-m statue of legendary Paul Bunyan and his blue ox. Bemidji Beltrami Airport to NW. Seat of Bemidji State Univ. Mississippi Headwaters State Forest to W; Paul Bunyan State Forest to S; Chippewa Natl. Forest and Leech L. Indian Reservation to E; Buena Vista Ski Area to N; L. Itasca, in Itasca State Park, source of Mississippi R., 24 mi/39 km to SW; L. Irving to S. Inc. 1896.

Bemidji, Lake (buh-MID-jee) (□ 11 sq mi/28 sq km), Beltrami co., NW central Minn., 14 mi/23 km WNW of Duluth; 5 mi/8 km long, c.2 mi/3.2 km wide; 47°30′N 94°51′W. Elev. 1,340 ft/408 m. Fed and drained (to E) by Mississippi R. Resort area. City of Bemidji at S end with downtown on SW shore; narrow isthmus at S end separates L. Bemidji from L. Irving. L. Bemidji State Park is at N end.

Bemis (BE-mis), village, Madison co., W Tenn., 3 mi/5 km S of Jackson. Mfg. includes textiles.

Bemis Heights, village (1990 pop. 115), Saratoga co., E N.Y., on the Hudson R., and 11 mi/18 km SE of Saratoga Springs; 42°58′N 73°38′W. Amer. Revolution battles (Sept. 19, and Oct. 7, 1777) fought near here are commemorated by natl. historical park 9 mi/14.5 km SE of Saratoga Springs.

Bemus Point, resort village (1990 pop. 383), Chautauqua co., extreme W N.Y., on Chautauqua L., 9 mi/14.5 km WNW of Jamestown; 42°09′N 79°23′W.

Ben Avon (BEN AI-vahn), borough (1990 pop. 2,096), Allegheny co., SW Pa., residential suburb 6 mi/9.7 km NW of downtown Pittsburgh, on Ohio R.; 40°30′N 80°04′W. Emsworth Dam, on Ohio R., is here. Inc. 1891.

Ben Avon Heights (BEN AI-vahn), borough (1990 pop. 373), Allegheny co., SW Pa., residential suburb 6 mi/9.7 km NW of downtown Pittsburgh, 1 mi/1.6 km E of Ben Avon, near Ohio R.; 40°30′N 80°04′W.

Ben Davis, village, Marion co., central Ind., suburb 7 mi/11.3 km W of downtown Indianapolis. Became part of Indianapolis Jan. 1, 1970. Indianapolis Internatl. Airport to SW.

Ben Hill, county (□ 255 sq mi/660 sq km; 1990 pop. 16,245), S central Ga.; ⊙ Fitzgerald; 31°46′N 83°13′W. Bounded NE by Ocmulgee R., W by Alapaha R. Coastal plain agr. that includes cotton, corn, tobacco, peanuts; cattle and hogs; and timber area. Formed 1906.

Ben Lomond, uninc. town (1990 pop. 7,884), Santa Cruz

co., W Calif., in Santa Cruz Mts., 9 mi/14.5 km NNW of Santa Cruz; 37°06′N 122°05′W. Redwood groves nearby.

Ben Lomond, village (1990 pop. 157), Sevier co., SW Ark., 20 mi/32 km SE of De Queen, near Little R.; 33°49′N 94°06′W.

Bena (BEE-nuh), village (1990 pop. 147), Cass co., N central Minn., 33 mi/53 km ESE of Bemidji, on S shore of L. Winnibigoshish reservoir; 47°20′N 94°12′W. Cattle; dairying; alfalfa, oats. In Leech L. Indian Reservation and Bowstring State Forest and part of Chippewa Natl. Forest. Mud Goose Wildlife Area to SE; Leech L. reservoir to SW.

Benavides, town (1990 pop. 1,788), Duval co., S Texas, c.60 mi/97 km WSW of Corpus Christi; 27°36′N 98°24′W. In area producing oil, salt (piped as brine to Corpus Christi chemical works), cotton, vegetables; cattle. Inc. 1936.

Benbow, village, Humboldt co., NW Calif., on South Fork Eel R., and c.53 mi/85 km SSE of Eureka, in the redwood country. Timber; cattle, sheep. Resort area; Benbow L. State Recreation Area is here.

Benbrook, city (1990 pop. 19,564), Tarrant co., N Texas, a residential suburb 9 mi/14.5 km SW of downtown Fort Worth; 32°40′N 97°27′W. On Clear Fork Trinity R., and c.6 mi/10 km to S.; drained by Walnut and Marys creeks. Area to S and W, urban-growth area.

Bend, city (1990 pop. 20,469), ⊙ Deschutes co., W central Oregon, 12 mi/19 km SE of Portland, on the Deschutes R., at the E foot of the Cascade Range; 44°04′N 121°18′W. Lumbering is the primary industry. Tourism. Seat of Central Oregon Community Col. Mfg. (beverages, lumber, millwork, bldg. materials, ordnance; medical equip.; printing and publishing). Agr. (potatoes, alfalfa, wheat, oats, barley; sheep, cattle); dairy prods. Points of interest are Deschutes Historical Center, Newberry Natl. Volcanic Monument to S, and the High Desert Mus. Hq. for Deschutes Natl. Forest, including the Three Sisters Wilderness Area, to W. Arnold Ice Cave to SE, Lava Coast Forest to S, Lava beds to SE. In area are Pilot Butte (E) and Tumalo (N) state parks. LaPine State Recreation Area to S; Marys Peak. Inc. 1904.

Bendersville (BEN-duhrz-vil), borough (1990 pop. 560), Adams co., S Pa., 10 mi/16 km N of Gettysburg, near Opossum Creek; 39°58′N 77°15′W. Mfg. (ceramic prods.; apple cider and apple butter); agr. (potatoes, grain, apples; livestock; poultry). Michaux State Forest to N; Appalachian Trail passes to N.

Benedict 1 village (1990 pop. 16), Wilson co., SE Kansas, on Verdigris R., and 16 mi/26 km WSW of Chanute; 37°37′N 95°44′W. RR junction. Livestock; grain; dairying. **2** summer resort and fishing village, Charles co., S Md., opposite Hallowing Point, on Patuxent R. (bridged), and 33 mi/53 km SE of Wash., D.C. It has a boatbuilding industry and a small seafood industry. **3** village (1990 pop. 230), York co., SE central Nebr., 11 mi/18 km N of York; 41°00′N 97°36′W. Feeds. **4** village (1990 pop. 52), McLean co., N Dak., 30 mi/48 km SSE of Minot; 47°49′N 101°04′W. **5** uninc. village (1990 pop.), Lee co., extreme SW Va., 25 mi/40 km W of Norton, at Ky. state line. In bituminous-coal region.

Benedicta (be-nuh-DIK-tuh), town, Aroostook co., E central Maine, 35 mi/56 km SW of Houlton. In lumbering, recreational area.

Benevolence (be-NE-vo-lens), town, Randolph co., SW Ga., 8 mi/12.9 km NNE of Cuthbert; 31°52′N 84°44′W.

Benewah, county (□ 784 sq mi/2,031 sq km; 1990 pop. 7,937), N Idaho, on Wash. state line; ⊙ St. Maries; 47°13′N 116°40′W. Rolling, hilly area drained by St. Joe and St. Maries rivers. Lumber; lentils; wheat, oats, barley; cattle. Palouse region in the W. Heyburn State Park in N, at S tip of Coeur d'Alene L.; part of St. Joe Natl. Forest in S; Coeur d'Alene Indian Reservation in W half of co. Formed 1915.

Bengies (BEN-jeez), suburban village, Baltimore co., central Md., 12 mi/19 km ENE of downtown Baltimore.

Bengough (behn-GAHF), town (1991 pop. 527), S Sask.,

W Canada, 40 mi/64 km ESE of Assiniboia; 49°24′N 105°07′W. Wheat; in coal-mining region.

Benham (BEN-ham), village (1990 pop. 717), Harlan co., SE Ky., 2 mi/3.2 km ESE of Cumberland, in the Cumberland Mts., near Poor Fork of Cumberland R.; 36°57′N 82°57′W. Bituminous coal; timber. Black Mt. to SE, highest point in Ky. (4,139 ft/1,262 m). Ky. Coal Mining Mus. Jefferson Natl. Forest to E.

Benicia, city (1990 pop. 24,437), Solano co., W Calif., port on Carquinez Strait, suburb 24 mi/39 km NE of downtown San Francisco, and 18 mi/29 km NNE of Oakland, SE of Vallejo; 38°04′N 122°09′W. At NW end of Benicia-Martinez Bridge. Mfg. (plastics, beer, cutting tools, conveyors, machinery; structural metal work). U.S. arsenal here est. 1849 as army post. Has many mid-19th-cent. landmarks. Founded 1847, inc. 1850. Nearby Suisun (E) and San Pablo (W) bays are both N extensions of San Francisco Bay.

Benito (buh-NEE-to), village (1991 pop. 427), W Man., central Canada, 18 mi/29 km SW of Swan R. Mixed farming; wheat.

Benito Juárez 1 (be-NEE-to HWAH-rez), town (1990 pop. 2,549), ⊙ Juárez municipio, Michoacán, central Mexico, 13 mi/21 km SSW of Zitácuaro; 19°12′N 100°28′W. Cereals; livestock. Also Laureles. **2** town (1990 pop. 1,088), Veracruz, E Mexico, 50 mi/80 km WNW of Túxpam de Rodríguez Cano; 20°52′N 98°11′W. Corn, fruit. **3** town (1990 pop. 2,279), N Zacatecas, Mexico, 5 mi/8 km NW of Sain Alto. Formerly Florencia de Benito Juárez.

Benito Juárez (be-NEE-to HWAH-rez), delegación (1990 pop. 407,811), in the S central part of Distrito Federal, Mexico, 6 mi/10 km N of Tlalpan. New delegation created in 1970. One of 4 delegacións that make up the core of Mexico city.

Benito Juárez, Mexico: see SAN JERÓNIMO.

Benito Juárez, Mexico: see CANCÚN.

Benjamin, village (1990 pop. 225), ⊙ Knox co., N Texas, c.75 mi/121 km WSW of Wichita Falls; 33°34′N 99°47′W. Elev. 1,456 ft/444 m. In grain, cotton, vegetable, and cattle area.

Benjamin Franklin National Memorial, downtown Philadelphia, SE Pa., at 20th and Race Streets, on W side of Logan Circle park. Colossal seated statue of Benjamin Franklin by James Earle Fraser in rotunda of Franklin Inst.

Benjamin Harrison, Fort,, Ind.: see INDIANAPOLIS.

Benjamín Hill, town (1990 pop. 5,561), N Sonora, Mexico, in the Magdalena R. basin on the W slope of the Sierra Madre Occidental, 11 mi/18 km N of Hermosillo. Water from the tributary of the Concepción R. Important RR center. Hot dry climate. Agr. (wheat, cotton); cattle.

Benkelman (BEN-ki-men), town (1990 pop. 1,193), ⊙ Dundy co., S Nebr., 50 mi/80 km WSW of McCook, and on Republican R., near Kansas state line; 40°02′N 101°31′W. Farm trade center in Great Plains region; livestock; grain; poultry prods. Fish hatchery N of town, also fish hatchery at Rock Creek State Recreation Area, 15 mi/24 km NW. Settled 1880.

Benld (ben-ELD), city (1990 pop. 1,604), Macoupin co., SW Ill., 13 mi/21 km SSE of Carlinville; 39°05′N 89°47′W. In agr. and bituminous-coal-mining area; mfg. tool and die. Inc. 1904; reincorporated 1930 as city.

Bennet, village (1990 pop. 544), Lancaster co., SE Nebr., 10 mi/16 km SE of Lincoln; 40°40′N 96°30′W. Livestock, poultry; dairy; grain.

Bennett, county (□ 1,190 sq mi/3,082 sq km; 1990 pop. 3,206), S S.Dak., on Nebr. state line; ⊙ Martin. Farming area drained by South Fork White R. and Bear-in-the-Lodge and Pass creeks. Wheat, flax, soybeans; hogs; honey. La Creek Lake and La Creek Natl. Wildlife Refuge in S. Pine Ridge Indian Reservation to N (Jackson Co.) and W (Shannon Co.); Rosebud Indian Reservation to E (Todd Co.). Formed 1909.

Bennett 1 town (1990 pop.1,757), Adams co., N central Colo., 30 mi/48 km E of Denver, near Kiowa Creek; 39°45′N 104°25′W. Elev. 5,483 ft/1,671 m. Wheat, sunflowers, sugar beets; cattle, horses. **2** town (1990 pop.

395), Cedar co., E Iowa, 8 mi/12.9 km ESE of Tipton; 41°44′N 90°58′W. In agr. area. Machine shop.

Bennett, uninc. village, Chatham co., central N.C., 18 mi/29 km WSW of Asheboro, and c.25 mi/40 km WSW of Pittsboro, near Deep R. Mfg. (signs). Tobacco, grain; poultry, livestock.

Bennettsville, town (1990 pop. 9,345), ⊙ Marlboro co., NE S.C., 30 mi/48 km N of Florence; 34°37′N 79°41′W. Mfg. includes beverages, machinery, paper prods., transportation equip., wood prods.; bldg. materials, foods; sand and gravel processing, printing and publishing. Timber; soybeans, grain, cotton; hogs. Laid out 1818.

Benning, Fort, Ga.: see FORT BENNING MILITARY RESERVATION.

Bennington, county (□ 677 sq mi/1,753 sq km; 1990 pop. 35,845), SW Vt., on Mass. and N.Y. state lines, in Green Mts.; ⊙ Bennington and Manchester; 43°01′N 73°06′W. Mfg. (paper and wood prods.); dairying; major winter and summer resorts. Includes Mt. Equinox, part of Green Mt. Natl. Forest. Drained by Batten Kill and Deerfield, Hoosic, Walloomsac, and Mettawee rivers. Organized 1779.

Bennington, city (1990 pop. 568), Ottawa co., N central Kansas, near Solomon R., 8 mi/12.9 km SE of Minneapolis; 39°01′N 97°35′W. In livestock and grain region. Ottawa State Fishing L. to N.

Bennington 1 town (1990 pop. 866), Douglas co., E Nebr., 10 mi/16 km NW of Omaha, near Missouri R; 41°22′N 96°09′W. Lies beyond urban fringe. **2** town (1990 pop. 1,236), Hillsboro co., S N.H., 22 mi/35 km W of Manchester; 43°00′N 71°54′W. Drained by the Contoocook R. (forms Powder Mill Pond on S boundary). Agr. (poultry, livestock; vegetables, apples; dairying; timber); mfg. (specialty papers). Crotched Mt. (2,055 ft/626 m) in E. **3** town (1990 pop. 16,451), ⊙ Bennington co. (along with Manchester), SW Vt.; 42°53′N 73°12′W. It includes the villages of North and Old Bennington. Major mfg. includes transportation equip., paper prods., electronic products, clothing, plastic prods., and pottery. The surrounding area has dairy farms and several ski areas. Points of interest include a monument (300 ft/91 m) commemorating the Revolutionary War battle of Bennington; Bennington Mus. (paintings, furniture, decorative arts); the site of the 1st schoolhouse in Vt.; Catamount Tavern, meeting place of the Green Mt. Boys; the site of abolitionist William Lloyd Garrison's printing shop; the Old First Church (1805); and the Walloomsac Inn, opened in 1763. Seat of Bennington Col. Chartered 1749, settled 1761.

Bennington, village (1990 pop. 251), Bryan co., S Okla., 20 mi/32 km E of Durant; 34°00′N 96°02′W. Trade center for rich agr. and livestock-raising area.

Bennington Battlefield, Rensselaer co., E N.Y., near Vt. state line, just NW of Bennington (Vt.); 42°56′N 73°18′W. State park here (171 acres/69 ha) is on field of Amer. Revolution battle of Bennington (Aug. 16, 1777), in which Continentals defeated Br. forces.

Benns Church, uninc. village, Isle of Wight co., SE Va., 10 mi/16 km SW of Newport News; James R. Bridge to Newport News 7 mi/11.3 km to NE. Agr. (cotton, peanuts, grain, soybeans; livestock. St. Lukes Church (or Old Brick Church), one of oldest Protestant churches in Amer., now restored, said to have been built in 1632.

Benoit (ben-OIT), village (1990 pop. 641), Bolivar co., NW Miss., 18 mi/29 km N of Greenville; 33°38′N 91°00′W. Agr. (cotton, corn, soybeans, rice; cattle). L. Benoit to S, result of dam on Deer R.; L. Whittington, oxbow lake of Mississippi R., to W; Dahomy Natl. Wildlife Refuge to NE.

Bensalem (ben-SAI-luhm), uninc. city (1990 pop. 52,399), Bucks co., SE Pa., suburb 15 mi/24 km NW of downtown Philadelphia, on Poquessing Creek; 40°06′N 74°57′W. Includes the communities of Nottingham, Eddington Gardens, and Newportville Terrace. Mfg. includes awnings, bldg. materials, paper prods., machinery, plastic prods., leather prods., food, fabricated metal prods., consumer goods, chemicals, electronic equip., tranportation equip., labels; printing.

Philadelphia Park Race Track is here. Neshaminy State Park to SE.

Bensenville (BEN-sin-vil), village (1990 pop. 17,767), Cook and Du Page cos., NE Ill., a suburb of Chicago; 41°57′N 87°56′W. Has varied light manufactures. O'Hare Internatl. Airport is nearby. Inc. 1894.

Bensley, uninc. town, Chesterfield co., E central Va., residential suburb 6 mi/9.7 km S of downtown Richmond, on James R.; 37°27′N 77°26′W. Falling Creek Reservoir to NW, Pocahontas State Forest and Park to SW.

Benson, county (□ 1,439 sq mi/3,727 sq km; 1990 pop. 7,198), N central N.Dak.; ⊙ Minnewaukan; 48°04′N 99°21′W. Agr. area watered by Sheyenne R. in S. Dairy prods., wheat, barley, rye; livestock, poultry. Textile prods. Located in Prairie Pothole Country. Devils L. on E border; Buffalo L. Natl. Wildlife Refuge on W border. L. Ibsen in N; Pleasant L. in NW; Cranberry and Long lakes in W; Devils L. Sioux Indian Reservation in SE, including Fort Totten Historic Site, and Sully Hill Natl. Game Preserve. Organized 1884.

Benson 1 town (1990 pop. 3,824), Cochise co., SE Ariz., on San Pedro R., and 44 mi/71 km SE of Tucson; 31°57′N 110°17′W. RR junction. Cattle, hogs; grain, alfafa. Little Dragoon Mts. (6,727 ft/2,050 m) NE. Parts of Coronado Natl. Forest to E, NW and SW; San Pedro Riparian Natl. Conservation Area to S. **2** town (1990 pop. 3,235), ⊙ Swift co., W Minn., 30 mi/48 km NW of Willmar, on Chippewa R; 45°19′N 95°36′W. Elev. 944 ft/288 m. RR junction and shipping point; grain, sugar beets, beans; dairying; livestock; mfg. (apparel, machinery, fertilizers). Hassel L. and L. Moose to N; Monson L. State Park to E. Plotted 1870, inc. as village 1877, as city 1908. **3** town (1990 pop. 2,810), Johnston co., central N.C., 30 mi/48 km S of Raleigh; 35°22′N 78°32′W. In agr. area (cotton, tobacco, grain, peanuts; poultry, livestock); mfg. (printing and publishing; veneers, textiles, apparel). Settled 1779; inc. 1887. **4** town (1990 pop. 847), Rutland co., W Vt., on L. Champlain, and 18 mi/29 km WNW of Rutland; 43°42′N 73°18′W.

Benson, village (1990 pop. 410), Woodford co., central Ill., 13 mi/21 km NE of Eureka; 40°51′N 89°07′W. In agr. area.

Benson (BEN-suhn), borough (1990 pop. 277), Somerset co., SW Pa., 6 mi/9.7 km S of Johnstown, on Stonycreek R.; 40°12′N 78°55′W. Agr. (hay, corn; dairying). Quemahoning Reservoir to SW.

Benson, W suburb of Omaha, Douglas co., E Nebr. 3 mi/4.8 km NW of downtown; part of city of Omaha.

Bensonhurst, residential sect. of SW Brooklyn borough of N.Y. city, SE N.Y.; 40°36′N 73°59′W. Has an ethnic mix of residents, esp. Italians, Jews, and Chinese, with a growing pop. of E Europeans and Hispanics.

Bent, county (□ 1,541 sq mi/3,991 sq km; 1990 pop. 5,048), SE Colo.; ⊙ Las Animas; 37°57′N 103°04′W. Irrigated agr. area, drained by Purgatoire and Arkansas rivers, forms John Martin Reservoir in N center. Cattle; wheat, hay, sorghum, barley, corn, vegetables. L. Hasty State Park in NE.

Bent Creek, uninc. town (1990 pop. 1,487), Buncombe co., W N.C., residential suburb 5 mi/8 km SE of downtown Asheville; 35°30′N 82°36′W. Pisgah Natl. Forest to SW.

Bentley, town (1990 pop. 36), Hancock co., W Ill., 6 mi/9.7 km SSE of Carthage; 40°20′N 91°06′W. In agr. area (corn, wheat, soybeans).

Bentley, village (1991 pop. 840), S central Alta., W Canada, near Gull L., on Blindman R., and 18 mi/29 km NW of Red Deer; 52°28′N 114°03′W. Dairying; mixed farming.

Bentleyville, village (1990 pop. 674), Cuyahoga co., N Ohio, a SE suburb of Cleveland; 41°26′N 81°26′W.

Bentleyville (BENT-lee-vil), borough (1990 pop. 2,673), Washington co., SW Pa., 13 mi/21 km ESE of Washington, on Pigeon Creek; 40°07′N 80°00′W. Mfg. (machinery, monuments). Agr. (corn, hay; dairying). Bentleyville Reservoir to N. Laid out 1816, inc. 1868.

Benton 1 county (□ 876 sq mi/2,269 sq km; 1990 pop. 97,499), extreme NW Ark.; ⊙ Bentonville; 36°22′N 94°48′W. Bounded W by Okla. state line, N by Mo. state line; drained by White (Beaver L. in E) and Illinois (SW) rivers; situated in Ozark region. Agr., chicken, turkeys, cattle, hogs; dairy prods.; timber. Mfg. at Bentonville, Siloam Springs, and Rogers. Poultry hatcheries, nurseries. Mineral springs (resorts). Pea Ridge Natl. Military Park in NE. Formed 1830. **2** county (□ 406 sq mi/1,052 sq km; 1990 pop. 9,441), W Ind., bounded W by Ill. state line; ⊙ Fowler; 40°37′N 87°19′W. Corn, wheat, oats, rye, hay, soybeans; hogs, poultry; limestone. Drained by small Sugar and Big Pine creeks. Formed 1840. **3** county (□ 718 sq mi/1,860 sq km; 1990 pop. 22,429), E central Iowa; ⊙ Vinton; 42°04′N 92°04′W. Prairie agr. area (hogs, cattle, poultry; corn, oats) drained by Cedar R.; limestone quarries. Extensive flooding of rivers and fields, 1993. Formed 1837. **4** county (□ 413 sq mi/1,070 sq km; 1990 pop. 30,185), central Minn.; ⊙ Foley; 45°42′N 94°00′W. Bounded W by Mississippi R. Agr. area (dairying; livestock, poultry; grain, soybeans); deposits of marl in NW. Little Rock L. in W, near Mississippi R. Formed 1849. **5** county (□ 408 sq mi/1,057 sq km; 1990 pop. 8,046), N Miss., bounded N by Tenn. state line; ⊙ Ashland; 34°49′N 89°11′W. Drained by Wolf R. and Tippah Creek. Agr. (cotton, corn, hay, sweet potatoes, soybeans; cattle; timber). Includes part of Holly Springs Natl. Forest in E and S, about ⅔ of co. Formed 1870. **6** county (□ 742 sq mi/1922 sq km; 1990 pop. 13,859), central Mo., in Ozark region; ⊙ Warsaw; 38°18′N 93°18′W. Drained by Osage, South Grand, and Pomme de Terre rivers; crossed by Truman L. and L. of the Ozarks. Corn; cattle, poultry; lake fishing; resorts, tourism, and recreation; lumber; hydroelectricity. Harry S. Truman State Park, 2 mi/3 km W of Warsaw; Truman Dam at Warsaw. Port of L. of the Ozarks in E. Formed 1835. **7** county (□ 679 sq mi/1,759 sq km; 1990 pop. 70,811), W Oregon; ⊙ Corvallis; 44°30′N 123°25′W. Agr. (corn, beans, blueberries, wheat, oats, barley, apples, cherries, pears, plums, grapes; poultry, sheep, cattle); dairy prods.; wineries. Coast Range is in W. Willamette R. Valley in E. William L. Finley Natl. Wildlife Refuge in S; Washburne Wayside State Park in SE; McDonald State Forest in NE; part of Siuslaw Natl. Forest in W. Formed in 1847. **8** county (□ 430 sq mi/1,114 sq km; 1990 pop. 14,524), W Tenn.; ⊙ Camden; 36°04′N 88°04′W. Bounded E and NW by arms of Kentucky Reservoir (Tennessee R.); traversed by Big Sandy R., here entering an arm of reservoir. Dairying; livestock and poultry raising; agr. (corn, soybeans, sorghum). Gravel pits. Area includes several wildlife refuges and state parks, including Nathan Bedford Forest historic area. Formed 1835. **9** county (□ 1,760 sq mi/4,558 sq km; 1990 pop. 112,560), S Wash., on Oregon state line; ⊙ Prosser; 46°15′N 119°30′W. In Columbia Basin region. Bisected by Yakima R., which joins Columbia R. above Kennewick. Apples, pears, peaches, grapes, hops, corn, onions, carrots, asparagus, potatoes, alfalfa, hay, wheat; cattle, sheep. Wash. Nuclear 2 nuclear power plant, 12 mi/19 km NW of Richland, uses cooling water from mechanical towers, and has a max. dependable capacity of 1085 MWe. Large U.S. Dept. of Energy Hanford Site in N, extends into Grant and Franklin cos. Columbia R. forms co. boundary on S (Oregon state), E, and N; W boundary is surveyed line. Horse Heaven Hills run E-W through S center. Columbia R. forms L. Umatilla reservoir in SW; McNary Dam, in S forms L. Wallula in SE, E, and N. Umatilla Natl. Wildlife Refuge and Crow Butte State Park in SW. Formed 1905.

Benton 1 city (1990 pop. 18,177), ⊙ Saline co., central Ark. on Saline R.; 34°34′N 92°34′W. The once major aluminum industry has largely abandoned the area. Mfg. (fabricated metal prods., wood prods., veneers, advertising stands, ceramic seal faces, machinery; apparel finishing, tooling, sheet metal fabrication). Founded 1836. **2** city (1990 pop. 7,216), ⊙ Franklin co., S Ill., 22 mi/35 km S of Mount Vernon; 38°00′N 88°55′W. Trade center for coal-mining, oil, and natural gas and agr. area; mfg. (chemicals, consumer goods). Livestock, poultry; dairy prods.; sorghum. Rend L. reservoir to NNW, fishing, hunting, golf. Rend L. Community Col. 8 mi/12.9 km N. Inc. 1841.

Benton 1 town (1990 pop. 39), 15 mi/24 km SW of Boone; 40°42′N 94°21′W. In livestock and grain area. **2** town (1990 pop. 3,899), ⊙ Marshall co., W Ky., 21 mi/34 km SE of Paducah, near East Fork Clarks R. and Ky. Reservoir; 36°51′N 88°21′W. Ships strawberries; agr. (tobacco, soybeans, grain; livestock); timber; mfg. (bldg. materials, wood prods., truck covers, mobile homes; aluminum fabrication, meat processing, lumber processing). Annual (May) Southern Harmony Singing Festival (since 1884). Ky. Dam Village State Resort Park to N; Kenlake State Resort Park, on Ky. L., to SE; Ky. L. reservoir on Tennessee R., to NE. **3** (bin-tuhn), town (1990 pop. 2,047), ⊙ Bossier parish, NW La., near Red R., 12 mi/19 km N of Shreveport; 32°42′N 93°45′W. In agr. area (cotton, soybeans, pecans; cattle, horses; dairying); mfg. of wood and paper prods. Black Bayou Reserve to SE, Cypress Bayou Reserve to E. **4** town (1990 pop. 2,312), Kennebec co., S Maine, 12 mi/19 km NNE of Augusta, bet. the Kennebec and the Sebasticook rivers; 44°35′N 69°31′W. Fiberboard mfg. Settled c.1775, inc. 1842 as Sebasticook, renamed 1850. **5** town (1990 pop. 575), ⊙ Scott co., SE Mo., near Mississippi R.,14 mi/23 km S of Cape Girardeau; 37°06′N 89°33′W. Cotton, corn, soybeans, melons, wheat; wood prods. **6** town (1990 pop. 330), Grafton co., NW N.H., 15 mi/24 km SSW of Littleton, in White Mt. Natl. Forest; 44°02′N 71°53′W. Black Mt. (2,836 ft/864 m) in W; Long Pond Natl. Forest Campground in S, Wildwood State Campground in E. **7** town (1990 pop. 992), ⊙ Polk co., SE Tenn., near Hiwassee R., 38 mi/61 km ENE of Chattanooga; 35°10′N 84°39′W. In timber and farm area; furniture mfg. **8** town (1990 pop. 898), Lafayette co., SW Wis., on Galena R., and 15 mi/24 km ENE of Dubuque; 42°34′N 90°22′W. In dairy and livestock area. Formerly a lead- and zinc-mining center.

Benton 1 uninc. village, Mono co., E Calif., 32 mi/51 km N of Bishop; elev. 5,377 ft/1,639 m. Mining; cattle raising. Benton Hot Springs 4 mi/6.4 km to W. White Mt., to E, includes White Mt. Peak (14,246 ft/4,342 m), to SE, and Boundary Peak, highest point in Nev. (13,140 ft/4,005 m) to NE, on state line. Parts of Inyo Natl. Forest to E and W; parts of Toiyabi Natl. Forest (Nev.) to N and NE. **2** village (1990 pop. 669), Butler co., S Kansas, 14 mi/23 km W of El Dorado; 37°47′N 97°06′W. In grain and livestock area.

Benton (BEN-tuhn), borough (1990 pop. 958), Columbia co., NE central Pa., 25 mi/40 km W of Wilkes-Barre, on Fishing Creek; 41°11′N 76°23′W. Mfg. (iron castings, lumber, apparel). Agr. (grain, potatoes, apples; livestock, poultry; dairying).

Benton City 1 town (1990 pop. 139), Audrain co., NE central Mo., 7 mi/11 km SE of Mexico; 39°07′N 91°45′W. **2** town (1990 pop. 1,806), Benton co., S Wash., on Yakima R., and 10 mi/16 km W of Richland; 46°16′N 119°29′W. Apples, peaches, pears, grapes, wheat, potatoes, vegetables; mfg. (petroleum refining; wineries). Horse Heaven Hills to S. U.S. Dept. of Energy Hanford Site (large tract) to N.

Benton Harbor, city (1990 pop. 12,818), Berrien co., SW Mich., 2 mi/3.2 km NE of St. Joseph, on L. Michigan, at the mouth of the St. Joseph R.; 42°07′N 86°27′W. Mfg. (transportation equip., wood prods., canned fruits and vegetables, computer equip., electronic equip., socket assemblies; printing). Once the center of Michigan's fruit industry and a popular tourist spot, the city has gone into economic decline. Many of its businesses have closed, and it has experienced severe pop. loss. Municipal Airport is here. Seat of L. Michigan Col. (2-year). Race riots occured in 1968 after the assassination of Dr. Martin Luther King, Jr. Boxer Muhammad Ali (Cassius Clay) b. here. Inc. 1869.

Benton Heights, town, Union co., S N.C., just NW of Monroe.

Benton Heights, uninc. village (1990 pop. 5,465), Berrien co., SW Mich., 2 mi/3.2 km E of Benton Harbor, adjacent to St. Joseph; 42°07′N 86°25′W.

Benton, Lake, Lincoln co., SW Minn., 10 mi/16 km S of Ivanhoe; 5 mi/8 km long, 1 mi/1.6 km wide; 44°17′N 96°14′W. Fed from NW by Norwegian Creek; drained

NE through Coon Creek; small dam at outflow. Lake Benton village at SW end.

Benton Ridge, village (1990 pop. 351), Hancock co., NW Ohio, 7 mi/11 km WSW of Findlay; 41°00′N 83°49′W.

Bentonia (ben-TO-nee-uh), village (1990 pop. 390), Yazoo co., W central Miss., 15 mi/24 km S of Yazoo City, near Big Black R.; 32°38′N 90°22′W. Agr. (cotton, grain; cattle; timber); mfg. (lumber).

Bentonville, city (1990 pop. 11,257), ⊙ Benton co., extreme NW Ark., 5 mi/8 km NW of Rogers, near Sugar co., in the Ozark Mts.; 36°22′N 94°12′W. Mfg. (fabricated metal prods., plastic molding, electronic equip., textiles, cutting tools, modular homes, cheese; poultry processing). Fish hatchery. Mineral springs and Bella Vista (resort) to N. Seat of Northwest Ark. Community Col. Wal-Mart, Inc., corporate hq.; Wal-Mart Visitors Center located in original 5-and-10 variety store on Main St. once operated by Sam (b. here) and Helen Walton. (the 1st Wal-Mart was built in Rogers, 6 mi/9.7 km E). Named for Mo. Senator Thomas Hart Benton. Settled 1837.

Bentonville, Battlefield State Historic Site (□ 5 acres/2 ha), Johnston co., central N.C., 15 mi/24 km S of Smithfield. Near here Union army under Sherman defeated (March 1865) Joseph E. Johnston's Army of Tenn. in one of last major engagements of Civil War. Battlefield has been preserved; Confederate monument here. Includes restored bldgs. and field hosp. exhibit.

Bent's Fort, trading post of the American West, on the Arkansas R., in present-day Otero co., SE Colo., 5 mi/8 km ENE of La Junta, and c.15 mi/24 km above the mouth of the Purgatoire R. The trading company headed by Charles Bent and Ceran St. Vrain, one of the most successful in the West, also included William Bent and 2 other Bent brothers. They had their 1st post in the area in 1826 and in 1833 moved to the completed fort, often called Bent's Old Fort. Because William Bent was the manager and chief trader in all the years of its prosperity, it is also sometimes called Fort William. Within its adobe walls came all the famous mt. men of the later period, as the fort on the mt. branch of the Santa Fe Trail came to dominate the trade of all the Native Americans S of the Black Hills as well as that of the Mexicans and the arriving Americans. Kit Carson was a hunter here 1831–1842. S. W. Kearny and Sterling Price each briefly used the fort for their troops in the Mex. War. According to the generally accepted story, the Native Amer. trade fell off and William Bent attempted to sell the fort to the U.S. govt.; he reached no satisfactory conclusion and in anger abandoned the fort and set the powder in it on fire, partially destroying it. In any case the fort was abandoned by 1852. William Bent erected a new establishment farther down the Arkansas in 1853. That post (Bent's New Fort) he leased to the govt. in 1860. Fort Lyon was afterward built around it.

Bent's Old Fort National Historic Site (800 acres/324 ha), Otero co., near Arkansas R., SE Colo., 5 mi/8 km ENE of La Junta. Fur-trading post and rest station on the Santa Fe Trail; originally built c.1830 by Charles and William Bent. Current fort is a reconstruction. Authorized 1960. See BENT'S FORT.

Benwood, town (1990 pop. 1,669), Marshall co., N W.Va., in N Panhandle, on the Ohio R., 5 mi/8 km S of Wheeling; 40°0′N 80°43′W. Mfg. (steel fabricating; industrial machinery mfg.; limestone processing). Agr. (corn); livestock, poultry. Bituminous-coal mining. Chartered 1853.

Benzie (BEN-zee), county (□ 859 sq mi/2,225 sq km; 1990 pop. 12,200), NW Mich., on L. Michigan (W); ⊙ Beulah; 44°37′N 86°15′W. Drained by Betsie R. and small Platte R. Agr. (fruit [esp. apples], cherries, grapes, plums; also forage crops). Resorts. Includes the larger Crystal and Platte lakes in W, and other smaller lakes; part of Sleeping Bear Dunes Natl. Lakeshore (including the former Benzie State Park) in NW. Organized 1869.

Benzonia (ben-ZO-nee-uh), village (1990 pop. 449), Benzie co. NW Mich., on SE end of Crystal L., 7 mi/11.3 km E of Frankfurt; 44°37′N 86°05′W. In agr. area (corn, beans); mfg. (motor vehicle parts).

Bequia (BEK-wai), island (□ 7 sq mi/18.1 sq km; 1994 est. pop. 4,900), St. Vincent and the Grenadines, West Indies, 9 mi/14.5 km S of St. Vincent; 13°00′N 61°15′W. Largest of the Grenadines. New airport opened in 1992 for inter-isl. aircraft. Fishing, boatbuilding, and tourism; former whaling center.

Berea (buh-REE-uh), city (1990 pop. 19,051), Cuyahoga co., NE Ohio, a suburb of Cleveland; 41°22′N 81°54′W. Residential community with a number of industries, such as plastics, alloy, and light engineering. Seat of Baldwin-Wallace Col. Settled 1809, inc. as a city 1930.

Berea 1 (buh-RAI-uh), town (1990 pop. 9,126), Madison co., central Ky., near the Cumberland Mts., 36 mi/58 km SSE of Lexington, near Silver Creek; 37°34′N 84°17′W. Agr. (tobacco; livestock, poultry; dairying); mfg. (crafts, recycled aluminum cans, jams and jellies, woven accessories, fire extinguishing gauges, candles and promotional items, fabricated metal prods., machinery, transportation equip.). Madison Airport to N. Seat of Berea Col. (1855). Lexington-Bluegrass Army Depot to N. Daniel Boone Natl. Forest to SE. Anc. Native Amer. fortifications at Indian Fort Mt. to E. **2** uninc. town, (1990 pop. 13,535), Greenville co., NW S.C., residential suburb 4 mi/6.4 km NW of downtown Greenville, near Saluda R.; 34°52′N 82°28′W.

Beresford, town (1990 pop. 1,849), Union and Lincoln cos., SE S.Dak., 30 mi/48 km S of Sioux Falls. Trade center for corn-raising region; farm implements; dairy prods.; livestock; mfg. (paper prods., machinery). Children's home and Lutheran home for aged and infirm are here.

Bergen (BUHR-guhn), county (□ 246 sq mi/637 sq km; 1990 pop. 825,380), extreme NE N.J., bounded E by Palisades of Hudson R. and N by N.Y. line; ⊙ Hackensack; 40°57′N 74°04′W. Industrial and residential area; varied mfg. (fabricated metal prods., textiles, chemicals, food prods., paper goods, concrete prods.). Major retail shopping and residential area. Includes part of Palisades Interstate Park and Oradell Reservoir. Drained by Ramapo, Saddle, Passaic, and Hackensack rivers. Formed 1675.

Bergen 1 (BUHR-jen), village (1990 pop. 1,103), Genesee co., W N.Y., 15 mi/24 km WSW of Rochester; 43°04′N 77°56′W. Bergen Swamps nearby. **2** village (1990 pop. 12), McHenry co., central N.Dak., 10 mi/16 km ESE of Velva; 48°00′N 100°43′W.

Bergen, N.J.: see JERSEY CITY.

Bergenfield (BUHR-guhn-FEELD), borough (1990 pop. 24,458), Bergen co., NE N.J.; 40°55′N 74°00′W. It is mainly residential with some light industry. Its Old South Church was built in 1799. Inc. 1894.

Berger (BUHR-juhr), town (1990 pop. 247), Franklin co., E central Mo., on Missouri R., 20 mi/32 km WNW of Washington; 38°40′N 91°20′W. Dairying; corn, wheat, soybeans, grapes; cattle; light mfg.; wineries.

Bergerville (BUHR-guhr-vil), SW suburb of Quebec, Que., Canada, on the St. Lawrence R.; airport.

Bergholz (BUHR-golz), village (1990 pop. 713), Jefferson co., E Ohio, 17 mi/27 km NW of Steubenville, and on small Yellow Creek, in coal-mining area; 40°32′N 80°55′W. Lumber, metal stampings. Settled 1885, inc. 1906.

Bergstrom Air Force Base, Texas: see AUSTIN.

Bering Glacier, S Alaska, in St. Elias Range glacier system, W and NW of Cape Yakataga; c.45 mi/72 km long, 20 mi/32 km wide; 60°15′N 143°30′W. Drains into Gulf of Alaska, just N of Kayak Isl.

Bering Land Bridge Preserve (□ 4,351 sq mi/11,269 sq km), NW Alaska, Seward Peninsula; authorized 1978. Remnant of land bridge that connected Alaska with Asia.

Bering Sea (□ c.878,000 sq mi/2,274,020 sq km), N extension of the Pacific Ocean bet. Siberia and Alaska. It is screened from the Pacific proper by the Aleutian Isls. The Bering Strait connects it with the Arctic Ocean. The sea's largest embayments are the Gulf of Anadyr, Norton Sound, and Bristol Bay. The Anadyr R. enters the sea from the W and the Yukon R. from the E. The warm Japan Current has little influence on the Bering Sea, which has much ice; it can usually be traversed by ship only June–Oct. The sea has many isls., notably Nunivak, St. Lawrence, Hall, St. Matthew, and the Pribilof Isls. (all owned by the U.S.), and the Komandorski Isls. (Russia). The sea was explored by the Rus. Dezhnev in the 17th cent., but not until after the voyages of Vitus Bering (1728, 1741) was its fur-seal wealth made widely known. The whole region was under the control of the Rus.-Amer. Co., but it proved impossible to prevent mariners from other nations from getting the skins of the seals and the sea otters. The question of protecting the seals became (1886) the subject of a bitter internatl. incident called the Bering Sea Fur-Seal Controversy. The seal herd that summered in the Pribilof Isls. wintered farther S; when returning N in the spring they could be taken in the open sea. The pelagic (open-sea) sealing, practiced by Can. and other sealing vessels, greatly reduced the herd and threatened it with extinction. The Alaska Commercial Co., which had a U.S. monopoly on the sealing, protested to the U.S. govt., and in 1886 several Can. vessels were seized and were condemned by a court at Sitka, Alaska. The legal basis for such action was the claim that Russia had controlled all the Bering Sea and that the control had passed to the U.S. with the purchase of Alaska in 1867; by claiming to exercise jurisdiction beyond the 3-mi/4.8-km limit the U.S. had invoked the doctrine of mare clausum (closed sea) for the 1st time. The British refused to accept this action, and a move to settle the matter of protection by internatl. agreement was blocked by the Canadians. The matter was referred to an internatl. court of arbitration, which, meeting in Paris, declared in 1893 against the U.S. claim and awarded U.S. $473,151 in damages to the owners of the seized vessels. It also imposed some restrictions on pelagic sealing, but these were ineffective. In 1911, Great Britain, Russia, Japan, and the U.S. agreed to prohibit pelagic sealing; sealing in the Pribilofs was put completely under U.S. supervision. For several years sealing was stopped completely, and then it was resumed but only under careful restrictions. In 1941, Japan withdrew from the agreement, but a new agreement was signed in 1956.

Berkeley 1 county (□ 1,229 sq mi/3,183 sq km; 1990 pop. 128,776), SE S.C.; ⊙ Moncks Corner; 33°12′N 79°57′W. Bounded N by Santee R.; Santee-Cooper irrigation, power and barge transport development with Santee dam on Santee R. Pinopolis Dam on Cooper R forming L. Moultrie. Includes part of Francis Marion Natl. Forest. Mfg. of limestone, sand, gravel, clay. Agr. includes dairy prods.; timber; poultry (eggs), hogs, sheep, cattle; cotton, corn, wheat, oats soybeans, tobacco, and hay. Formed 1882. **2** county (□ 322 sq mi/834 sq km; 1990 pop. 59,253), NE W.Va., in Eastern Panhandle; ⊙ Martinsburg; 39°28′N 78°01′W. Bounded NE by Potomac R. (Md. state line) and SW by Va. Mt. ridges; partly in Great Appalachian Valley; drained by Opequon and Back creeks, short tributaries of the Potomac R. Agr. (grains, soybeans, hay, alfalfa, sorghum, vegetables, fruits); livestock, poultry; dairying. Limestone quarrying. Mfg. at Martinsburg. Berkeley Springs known for mineral waters. Part of Sleepy Creek Wildlife Management Area to W. Formed 1772.

Berkeley 1 city (1990 pop. 102,724), Alameda co., W Calif., suburb 4 mi/6.4 km N of downtown Oakland, adjoins Oakland, on the E shore of San Francisco Bay; 37°52′N 122°18′W. Mfg. (lab instruments, fabricated metal prods., construction materials, machinery, chemicals, consumer goods, printing ink, vitreous china, electronic equip., biological prods., copper artwork, foods, medical instruments; printing and publishing, metal smelting, electroplating; iron foundry, winery [sake]). Originally part of the Rancho San Antonio granted to the Peralta family in 1820 by the Span. crown, the site was purchased by Americans in 1853. The settlement, at first called Oceanview, was named Berkeley in 1866. The city's pop. increased significantly after the San Francisco earthquake of 1906. Seat of a campus of the Univ. of Calif. at Berkeley and several divinity schools. The campus of the former was a center for student unrest and the "counterculture" movement throughout the 1960s and early 1970s. Points of interest in Berkeley include a marina; Tilden Park; Univ. Mus.; Lawrence Hall of Science; Berkeley Aquatic Park; and Armstrong Col. (1918). Lawrence Radiation Laboratory, an atomic research center, is nearby. Berkeley Hills to NE; Charles L. Tilden Regional Park to N. Inc. 1878. **2** city (1990 pop. 12,450), St. Louis co., E Mo., a suburb 12 mi/19 km WNW of downtown St. Louis; E of Lambert–St. Louis Airport; 38°44′N 90°20′W. Mfg. (pharmaceuticals, truck lifts, plastic prods., airplanes; outdoor advertising; steel fabrication). Inc. 1937.

Berkeley 1 village (1990 pop. 5,137), Cook co., NE Ill., W suburb of Chicago; 41°53′N 87°54′W. **2** (BUHRK-lee), village, Cumberland town, Providence co., NE R.I., 7 mi/11.3 km SE of Woonsocket, on Blackstone R.; 41°55′N 71°25′W. Nearby is Our Lady of Atonement Novitiate.

Berkeley, N.J.: see SEASIDE PARK.

Berkeley, Cape, N extremity of Prince of Wales Isl., central Franklin dist., N.W.T., N Canada, on Barrow Strait and Viscount Melville Sound; 73°59′N 100°25′W.

Berkeley Heights, village (1990 pop. 11,980), Union co., NE N.J., on Passaic R., and 14 mi/23 km W of Newark; 40°40′N 74°25′W. Mfg. (chemicals, metal prods., electronics). Suburb.

Berkeley Hills, W Calif., Contra Costa co.; SW foothills extend into Alameda co.; NW-SE range (c.1,000–2,000 ft.) rising 5 mi/8 km E of S San Francisco Bay; Berkeley and Oakland are on W slopes, Orinda to NE. Univ. of Calif. at Berkeley on W.

Berkeley Lake (BUHRK-lee), town (1990 pop. 791), Gwinnett co., Ga., 5 mi/8 km NNE of Norcross. Suburban bedroom community of Atlanta.

Berkeley Point, W extremity of Victoria Isl., SW Franklin dist., N.W.T., N Canada, on Prince of Wales Strait; 70°39′N 119°05′W.

Berkeley Springs, town (1990 pop. 735), ⊙ Morgan co., NE W.Va., in Eastern Panhandle, 18 mi/29 km NW of Martinsburg. Health resort (since colonial days) with mineral springs, within Berkeley Springs State Park. RR-spur terminus. Agr. (grain, apples); cattle; poultry. Mfg. (furniture, sporting goods, bottled water; printing and publishing, silica processing). Glass-sand pits; lumbering. Cacapon State Park to SW; Widmeyer Wildlife Management Area to W; Sleepy Creek Wildlife Management Area to E; state fish hatchery at Ridge to S. Chartered 1776 by George Washington as Bath, still its official name.

Berkey (BUHR-kee), village (1990 pop. 264), Lucas co., NW Ohio, 15 mi/24 km WNW of Toledo, near Mich. state line; 41°44′N 83°52′W.

Berkley (BUHR-klee), city (1990 pop. 16,960), Oakland co., SE Mich., a residential suburb 13 mi/21 km NW of Detroit; 42°30′N 83°11′W. Light mfg. Inc. 1932.

Berkley 1 town (1990 pop. 39), Boone co., central Iowa, on Beaver Creek, and 15 mi/24 km SW of Boone; 41°57′N 94°06′W. In livestock and grain area. **2** town (1990 pop. 4,237), Bristol co., SE Mass., at mouth of Taunton R., 4 mi/6.4 km S of Taunton. Includes Assonet Neck. Settled 1638, inc. 1755.

Berks (BUHRKS), county (□ 865 sq mi/2,240 sq km; 1990 pop. 336,523), SE central Pa.; ⊙ Reading; 40°25′N 75°55′W. Rolling agr. and industrial area with Blue Mt. ridge on NW boundary. Drained by Schuylkill R. and Maiden and Tulpehocken creeks; bounded NW by Blue Mt. Mfg. at Reading, Boyertown, Sinking Spring, Shoemakersville, Hamburg, and Kutztown. Agr. (corn, wheat, oats, mushrooms, hay, alfalfa, soybeans, potatoes, plums, apples; chickens, sheep, hogs, cattle; dairying). Co. urbanized in S center around Reading and in SE center. In Pa. Du. region. Pa. Du. Folk Culture Center in N and Lenhartsville. First settled by Swedes. Daniel Boone b. near Reading. RR shops. L. Ontelaunee reservoir in N center; Blue Marsh L. State Recreational Area in W center; Onyx and Crystal caves in N; parts of French Creek State park, Hopewell Furnace Natl. Historical Site in S; part of Weisser State Forest in NW; Appalachian Trail (natl. scenic) closely follows NW boundary. Formed 1752.

Berkshire (BUHRK-shir), county (□ 946 sq mi/2,450 sq km; 1990 pop. 139,352), W Mass., bordering Vt., N.Y., and Conn.; ⊙ Pittsfield; 42°22′N 73°13′W. Embraces most of the Berkshire Hills; popular summer and winter resort area, with mfg. towns. Textile prods., paper mills, plastics prods., metal prods., industrial machinery, search and navigation equip., electronic capacitors. Livestock; hay, fruit, nursery prods.; dairying. Mt. Greylock (3,491 ft/1,064 m), highest point in Mass., is near North Adams. Rivers include Housatonic, Hoosic, and Farmington. In N, Hoosac RR Tunnel pierces the Hoosac Range. Appalachian Trail traverses co. (N-S). Formed 1761.

Berkshire (BUHRK-shir), town (1990 pop. 1,190), Franklin co., N Vt., 19 mi/31 km NE of St. Albans, and on Missisquoi R., at Canada (Que.) border; 44°58′N 72°46′W. Dairy prods. Settled 1792, inc. 1795 or 1796.

Berkshire, Mass.: see LANESBORO.

Berkshire, village (1990 pop. 350), Tioga co., S N.Y., on Owego Creek, and 20 mi/32 km NW of Binghamton; 42°17′N 76°10′W.

Berkshire Hills (BUHRK-shir), mountainous region of wooded hills with many small lakes and streams, W Mass. The Berkshires are a S extension of the Green Mts., but the name is generally applied to all highlands in W Mass. Mt. Greylock, 3,491 ft/1,064 m, is the highest point in the hills and in the state. Tourism is a principal industry. The Berkshire Hills have numerous resorts, state parks, and forests. The Housatonic, Hoosic, and Westfield rivers drain the region. Pittsfield, North Adams, Great Barrington, and Lenox are the largest towns in the Berkshires. Site of Mt. Greylock State Park and War Memorial Monument.

Berlin (BUHR-lin), city (1990 pop. 11,824), Coos co., NE N.H., 85 mi/137 km NNE of Concord, and N of the White Mts., at falls of the Androscoggin R.; 44°29′N 71°15′W. Boundaries extend W into White Mt. Natl. Forest. Nursery crops, vegetables, apples; cattle, poultry; dairying; timber. Mfg. (steel fabrication; fabricated metal prods., bottled water, bldg. materials, electronics, lumber, pulp, paper). In a heavily forested region, it early became the site of pulp and paper mills. Seat of N.H. Technical Col. (Berlin campus). Center of Nor. settlement. Has the 1st ski club organized (1872) in the U.S. Milan Hill State Park to NW; Moose Brook State Park to S; Berlin Fish Hatchery 8 mi/12.9 km to W; Mahoosuc Range to SE; Nansen Wayside State Park at N end of city. Inc. 1829.

Berlin 1 (BUHR-lin), industrial town (1990 pop.16,787), Hartford co., central Conn., 10 mi/16 km SSW of Hartford; 41°36′N 72°46′W. Home to over 100 small-to-medium-sized mfg. industries, including metal prods., machinery, tools, lacquer, fishing tackle, bricks, wood and paper prods.; dairying. Includes mfg. villages of East Berlin and Kensington (1990 pop. 8,306). Corporate hq. of Northeast Utilities. Hanging Hills are S. Settled 1686, inc. 1785. **2** (buhr-LIN), town (1990 pop. 480), Colquitt co., Ga., 11 mi/18 km SE of Moultrie; 31°04′N 83°37′W. **3** (BUHR-lin), town (1990 pop. 2,616), Worcester co., SE Md., 21 mi/34 km E of Salisbury; 38°20′N 75°13′W. In agr. and timber area. Poultry packing; mfg. of clothing, wood prods., flour; vegetable canneries, large fruit-tree nurseries. Steven Decatur Park is S of town, and Decatur memorabilia are in the mus. at Snow Hill, 17 mi/27 km SE. In town are Burley Cottage (c.1834) and Burley Manor, or Hammond House (c.1814). Birthplace of Stephen Decatur, naval hero. **4** (buhr-LIN), town (1990 pop. 2,293), Worcester co., E central Mass., 12 mi/19 km NE of Worcester, near Wachusett Reservoir; 42°23′N 71°38′W. Fruit; dairying. Settled 1665, inc. 1784. **5** town (1990 pop. 2,561), Washington co., central Vt., just S of Montpelier; 44°12′N 72°37′W. **6** (BUHR-lin), town (1990 pop. 5,371), Green Lake and Waushara cos., central Wis., on Fox R., and 20 mi/32 km WSW of Oshkosh; 43°58′N 88°57′W. In dairy, livestock, and farm area; mfg. (shoes, apparel, tallow and bonemeal, fabricated metal prods., machinery). Inc. 1857.

Berlin 1 (BUHR-lin), village (1990 pop. 180), Sangamon co., central Ill., 14 mi/23 km W of Springfield; 39°45′N 89°54′W. In agr. area. **2** village (1990 pop. 1,200), Rensselaer co., E N.Y., on Hoosic R., and 16 mi/26 km E of Troy; 42°40′N 73°22′W. Woodworking. **3** (buhr-LIN), village (1990 pop. 32), La Moure co., SE central N.Dak., 10 mi/16 km W of La Moure, near Cottonwood Creek; 46°22′N 98°29′W.

Berlin 1 borough (1990 pop. 5,672), Camden co., SW N.J., 15 mi/24 km SE of Camden; 39°47′N 74°56′W. Mfg. (plastics, machine parts, glass prods.; metal fabrication); vegetable farming. Inc. 1927. **2** (BUHR-lin), borough (1990 pop. 2,064), Somerset co., SW Pa., 9 mi/14.5 km SE of Somerset; highest borough (elev. 2,322 ft/708 m) in Pa.; 39°55′N 78°57′W. Mfg. (snack foods, wood prods., maple sugar); surface bituminous coal; agr. (grain; livestock; dairying); timber. Settled c.1769 by Germans, laid out 1784, inc. 1833.

Berlin, Ont.: see KITCHENER.

Berlin Heights (BUHR-lin), village (1990 pop. 691), Erie co., N Ohio, 14 mi/23 km SE of Sandusky; 41°20′N 82°31′W.

Bermuda, British crown colony (□ 21 sq mi/54 sq km; 1991 pop. 58,460), comprising some 150 coral rocks, islets, and isls. (of which some 20 are inhabited), in the Atlantic Ocean, c.570 mi/917 km SE of Cape Hatteras, N.C.; ⊙ HAMILTON, on Bermuda, or Great Bermuda, the largest isl.; 32°18′N 64°45′W. Smaller isls. are Somerset, Ireland, and St. George. Bermuda, with its fine beaches, excellent climate, picturesque sites, and easy access from the U.S. East Coast, is a fashionable and popular year-round resort. Three main harbors are at Hamilton, St. George, and West End. Its coral reefs are the northernmost in the world. The colony's economic mainstays are tourism, internatl. financial services (including insurance and banking), and expenditures by U.S. military personnel stationed here. Insurance and reinsurance surpassed tourism as the isl.'s main industry in 1997. Sales of fuel to aircraft and ships, and pharmaceuticals are major exports, though both are minor in comparison to tourism and financial services. Reputedly the 1st person to set foot here was the Span. navigator Juan de Bermúdez (1503–1511), but they remained uninhabited, despite visits by Spaniards and Englishmen, until Sir George Somers and a group of colonists on their way to Va. were shipwrecked here in 1609. This incident was known to Shakespeare when he wrote *The Tempest.* Long called Somers Isls., the Bermudas were 1st governed by chartered companies but were acquired by the crown in 1684. The harbor of St. George was a base for privateers during the War of 1812, and the isl. was a center for Confederate blockade runners during the Amer. Civil War. Onions became a main crop during the early 20th cent. During World War II the isls. played an important strategic role. The U.S., under a 99-year lease, operates a naval and air force base. Internal self-govt. was granted in 1968. In the 1970s, Bermuda experienced significant unrest due to racial tensions and the question of political independence. Tensions eased during the 1980s and 1990s. In 1995, the voters rejected an independence referendum. Most of the isl.'s elected officials are of Afr. ancestry, reflecting the pop. mix, which is c.70% Afro-Caribbean. Four foreign-held military bases used to track Soviet submarines in the North Atlantic were closed in the mid-1990's and returned to the govt. of Bermuda. Southside, the former U.S. Naval air station adjoining Bermuda's airport, is to be developed as a port, relocating Hamilton's container terminal. The Can. base at Daniel's Head is to be converted to ecotourism. The Br. bases at Morgan's Point and Tudor Hill will be converted into residences and tourist facilities.

Bermuda Dunes, uninc. town (1990 pop. 4,571), Riverside co., S Calif., residential suburb 3 mi/4.8 km SSW of Palm Desert, in E foothills of Santa Rosa Mts.; 33°45′N 116°17′W.

Bermuda Hundred, uninc. village, Chesterfield co., E central Va., 12 mi/19 km NE of Petersburg, on James R., near mouth of Appomattox R. During the Civil War the Union Army was trapped here after its defeat at Drewrys Bluff. Founded 1613.

Bermuda Triangle, a roughly triangular area in the North Atlantic Ocean, bet. Bermuda, Fla., and P.R.;

Area in square miles is shown by the symbol □ capital city or county seat by ⊙

c.18°00′N–32°00′N. A number of planes and ships have unaccountably disappeared here.

Bern, village (1990 pop. 190), Nemaha co., NE Kansas, near Nebr. state line, 10 mi/16 km NNE of Seneca; 39°57′N 95°58′W. In livestock and grain region. Mfg. (pet food; meat processing).

Bernalillo (buhr-nuh-LEE-o), county (□ 1,168 sq mi/3,025 sq km; 1990 pop. 480,577), N central N.Mex.; ⊙ Albuquerque; 35°02′N 106°40′W. Cattle, some sheep; dairying; chiles, corn, hay, alfalfa, oats, barley, grapes. Limestone. Coal. Drained by Rio Grande and Rio Puerco. Part of Cibola Natl. Forest in E, Sandia Mts. and Manzano Range in E. Isleta Indian Reservation, including Isleta Pueblo, in S; parts of Laguna and Cañoncito Indian Reservation in W; Indian Petroglyoph State Park in NW center; Petroglyph Natl. Monument and Shooting Range State Park in W center; San Gabriel and Rio Gabriel Nature Center state parks, in Albuquerque, at center of co.; Sandia State Recreational Area and Sandia Park Ski Area, at Sandia Crest peak, in NE. Formed 1852.

Bernalillo (buhr-nuh-LEE-o), town (1990 pop. 5,960), ⊙ Sandoval co., N central N.Mex., on Rio Grande, just NW of Sandia Mts., 18 mi/29 km NNE of Albuquerque; 35°19′N 106°33′W. Elev. 5,052 ft/1,540 m. Livestock; fruit; chiles; dairying; timber. Mfg. (power tool accessories, treated wood prods.). Located in N part of Sandia Pueblo land grant. Part of Cibola Natl. Forest to SE. Coronado State Monument and State Park, to N, includes ruins of pueblos once used (1540–1542) by Coronado as hq. Village settled 1698 by Spaniards. Sandia Crest Recreational Area and Sandia Peak Ski Area to SE; San Felipe Indian Reservation to NE, Zia and Santa Ana Indian Pueblos to NW.

Bernard, town (1990 pop. 123), Dubuque co., E Iowa, 15 mi/24 km SSW of Dubuque; 42°18′N 90°49′W. In agr. area.

Bernards (buhr-NAHRDZ), township (1990 pop. 17,199), Somerset co., N N.J., 7 mi/11.3 km SW of Morristown; 40°40′N 74°34′W. Inc. 1798.

Bernardston (BUHR-nuhrdz-tuhn), agr. town (1990 pop. 2,048), Franklin co., N Mass., on short Falls R., and 6 mi/9.7 km N of Greenfield, near Vt. state line; 42°42′N 72°33′W. Dairying. Recreation area. Permanently settled 1738, inc. 1762.

Bernardsville (BUHR-nahrdz-vil), residential borough (1990 pop. 6,597), Somerset co., N central N.J., 7 mi/11.3 km SW of Morristown; 40°43′N 74°35′W. In agr., resort area; engineering; laminated materials. Settled early 18th cent., inc. 1924.

Berne, city (1990 pop. 3,559), Adams co., E Ind., 12 mi/19 km S of Decatur; 40°40′N 84°57′W. In agr. area; poultry hatcheries. Mfg. of dairy prods., transportation equip., boxes, furniture, apparel; printing and publishing. Settled 1852 by Swiss; inc. 1887.

Berne, village (1990 pop. 600), Albany co., E N.Y., 19 mi/31 km W of Albany; 42°35′N 74°07′W. Small lakes nearby with summer residences.

Bernhards Bay, resort village (1990 pop. 400), Oswego co., N central N.Y., on N shore of Oneida L., 22 mi/35 km W of Rome; 43°15′N 75°54′W.

Bernice (buhr-NEES), town (1990 pop. 1,543), Union parish, N La., 20 mi/32 km N of Ruston; 32°50′N 92°40′W. Logging; mfg. (furniture parts, wood chips, lumber, uniforms); in agr. area (dairying; hogs; cattle; vegetables). Bernice oil and gas field nearby. Unit of Kisatchie Natl. Forest to NW. Bayou D'Arbonne L. reservoir to E (state park). Settled 1841, inc. 1889. Formerly known as Big Woods.

Bernice, village (1990 pop. 330), Delaware co., NE Okla., 15 mi/24 km NW of Jay, near Grand L. of the Cherokees, to SE (Neosho R.); 36°37′N 94°54′W. Bernice State Park to E.

Bernie, city (1990 pop. 1,847), Stoddard co., SE Mo., in Mississippi alluvial plain, 9 mi/14 km S of Dexter; 36°40′N 89°58′W. Cotton, soybeans; mfg. (wood tool handles, headwear). Inc. 1908.

Bernierville, Que.: see SAINT FERDINAND.

Bernstadt (BUHRN-stat), uninc. village (1990 pop. 400), Laurel co., SE central Ky., in Cumberland foothills, 7 mi/11.3 km W of Condon. Agr. (tobacco; cattle; dairying); makes cheese. Site of mass immigration by Swiss. Wood Creek L. reservoir to N; Daniel Boone Natl. Forest to W. Settled 1881.

Bernville (BUHRN-vil), borough (1990 pop. 789), Berks co., SE central Pa., 12 mi/19 km NW of Reading, on Northkill Creek, at its entrance to Tulpehocken Creek; 40°25′N 76°02′W. Light mfg. (grapes; grain; poultry, livestock; dairying). Calvaresi Winery to N. Blue Marsh L. reservoir and State Recreational Area to SE. Founded 1819, inc. 1851.

Berrien 1 (BER-ree-uhn), county (□ 466; 1990 pop. 14,153), S Ga.; ⊙ Nashville; 31°16′N 83°14′W. Coastal plain agr. includes cotton, corn, tobacco, peanuts; cattle and hogs; fish farming; forestry. Area drained by Alapaha and Withlacoochee rivers. Formed 1856. **2** (BER-ee-en), county (□ 1,580 sq mi/4,092 sq km; 1990 pop. 161,378), extreme SW Mich.; ⊙ St. Joseph. Bounded S by Ind. state line, W by L. Michigan; 41°56′N 86°35′W. Drained by St. Joseph and Paw Paw rivers and small Galien R. Fruit-growing region (peaches, apples, pears, plums, grapes, cherries, strawberries, melons); also corn, soybeans; hogs; cattle; dairy prods. Mfg. at Niles and St. Joseph. Resorts. Western Dunes State Park in SW; Paw Paw L. in far N. Organized 1831. Nuclear power plants: Cook 1 and Cook 2 are 11 mi/18 km S of Benton Harbor; use cooling water from L. Michigan.

Berrien Springs (BER-ree-en), village (1990 pop. 1,927), Berrien co., extreme SW Mich., on St. Joseph R., 12 mi/19 km SE of Benton Harbor; 41°57′N 86°20′W. In fruit and dairy area. Mfg. zinc and aluminum die castings, furniture, and fruit prods. Has resorts. Airport to W. Seat of Andrews Univ. Plotted 1830, inc. 1867.

Berriozábal (bai-ree-o-SAH-bahl), town (1990 pop. 14,110), Chiapas, S Mexico, in Chiapas Valley, 10 mi/16 km W of Tuxtla Gutiérrez; 16°52′N 93°15′W. Cereals, sugar, tobacco, fruit; livestock. A Zoque Indian community.

Berry, town (1990 pop. 1,218), Fayette co., W Ala., 13 mi/21 km E of Fayette. Pine and hardwood lumber.

Berry, uninc. village (1990 pop. 240), Harrison co., N Ky., on South Fork of Licking R., and 10 mi/16 km NNW of Cynthiana, in Bluegrass region; 38°31′N 84°22′W. Agr. (burley tobacco; grain; livestock).

Berry Hill, city (1990 pop. 802), Davidson co., N Tenn., suburb 3 mi/5 km S of Nashville; 36°07′N 86°46′W.

Berry Islands, archipelago and district (□ 14 sq mi/36 sq km; 1990 pop. 628), NW Bahama Isls.; group of numerous cays on NE edge of the Great Bahama Bank, N of Andros Isl., 140 mi/225 km E of Miami (Fla.), and 35 mi/56 km NW of Nassau, extending in large curve c.50 mi/80 km bet. 25°20′N and 25°50′N. Some agr. (coconuts; sisal; livestock). Surrounding waters teem with fish.

Berryessa Lake, reservoir (□ 328 sq mi/850 sq km), Napa co., central Calif., Putah Creek, just W of Berryessa Peak (3,057 ft/932 m), 19 mi/31 km W of Davis; 38°31′N 122°06′W. Max. capacity 1,902,086 acre-ft. Extends N-S. Formed by Monticello Dam (304 ft/93 m high), built (1957) by the Bureau of Reclamation for irrigation, water supply, flood control, and recreation.

Berrys Chapel, town (1990 pop. 3,000), Williamson co., central Tenn., 4 mi/6 km N of Franklin.

Berrysburg (BER-reez-buhrg), borough (1990 pop. 376), Dauphin co., S central Pa., 18 mi/29 km S of Sunbury; 40°36′N 76°48′W. Grain; livestock, poultry; dairying. Mahantango Mt. ridge to W.

Berryville 1 town (1990 pop. 3,212), ⊙ Carroll co. (along with Eureka Springs), Carroll co., NW Ark., 39 mi/63 km NE of Fayetteville, on Osage Creek, in the Ozark Mts.; 36°22′N 93°34′W. In fruit, dairy, and vegetable area; lumber milling. Mfg. (machinery, electrical cable harnesses; poultry slaughtering). Resort area (fishing). Madison Co. Wildlife Management Area to SW. Laid out 1850. **2** town (1990 pop. 3,097), ⊙ Clarke co., N Va., in Shenandoah Valley, 10 mi/16 km E of Winchester, near W.Va. state line; 39°08′N 77°58′W. Mfg. (furniture, honey, wood prods.); printing and publishing. Agr. (apples, peaches, grain; horse breeding;

timber. Annual horse show. State Arboretum of Va. to S, near Boyce. Laid out 1798; inc. 1870.

Bersimis River, Canada: see BETSIAMITES RIVER.

Bertha, village (1990 pop. 507), Todd co., central Minn., 13 mi/21 km SSE of Wadena, near Little Partridge R.; 46°16′N 95°03′W. Grain, potatoes, beans; livestock; poultry; dairying; mfg. (plastic molds, bedding, agr. trailers).

Bertha, Mount (10,204 ft/3,110 m), SE Alaska, in Fairweather Range, 4 mi/6.4 km ENE of Mt. Crillon, 100 mi/161 km WNW of Juneau, in Glacier Bay Natl. Monument; 58°41′N 137°01′W. Surrounded by Brady Icefield.

Berthier (ber-TYAI), county (□ 1,816 sq mi/4,703 sq km), S Que., E Canada, extending NW from the St. Lawrence R.; ⊙ Berthierville; 46°15′N 73°25′W.

Berthierville (BER-tyai-vil) or **Berthier** (ber-TYAI), town (1991 pop. 3,854), ⊙ Berthier co., S Que., E Canada, on the St. Lawrence R., 45 mi/72 km NNE of Montreal; 46°05′N 73°10′W. Milling, distilling, mfg.; market in agr. region. Site of ruins of 1st Protestant church built (1786) after Br. conquest of Canada.

Berthold (BUHR-thold), village (1990 pop. 409), Ward co., N central N.Dak., 20 mi/32 km NNW of Minot; 48°19′N 101°44W. RR terminus. Wheat; cattle.

Berthoud, town (1990 pop. 2,990), Larimer co., N Colo., 7 mi/11.3 km S of Loveland, on Little Thompson R.; 40°18′N 105°04′W. Elev. c.5,030 ft/1,533 m. Sugar beets, potatoes, grain; cattle, livestock. Mfg. (plastic forming; mobile homes). Oil field nearby. Agr. research. Carter L. to W.

Berthoud Pass (11,314 ft/3,449 m), on Continental Divide, passes N-S, in Front Range, in Clear Creek and Grand cos., N central Colo., c.40 mi/64 km W of Denver. Crossed by U.S. Highway 40. Winter Park Ski Area to N. Nearby are Arphaho (N) and Pike (S) natl. forests.

Bertie (BUHR-tee), county (□ 741 sq mi/1,919 sq km; 1990 pop. 20,388), NE N.C.; ⊙ Windsor; 36°03′N 76°57′W. On Atlantic coastal plain; bounded S and SW by Roanoke R., E by Chowan R. and Albermarle Sound; drained by Cashie R. Agr. (peanuts, tobacco, corn, cotton, wheat, oats, soybeans, sorghum; chickens, cattle, hogs); fishing. Timber (gum, pine). Formed 1722.

Bertie (BUHR tee), town, Bertie co., NE N.C., adjacent to Windsor, on Cashie R. Residential.

Bertram 1 town (1990 pop. 201), Linn co., E Iowa, 7 mi/11.3 km E of Cedar Rapids; 41°57′N 91°32′W. Limestone quarries nearby. **2** town (1990 pop. 849), Burnet co. central Texas, 38 mi/61 km NNE of Austin; 30°44′N 98°03′W. Cattle, sheep, goats; clay; mfg. (cultured granite and marble, tile).

Bertrand (BUHR-chrand), town (1990 pop. 692), Mississippi co., extreme SE Mo., in Mississippi alluvial plain, 6 mi/10 km W of Charleston; 36°54′N 89°27′W.

Bertrand (BUHR-trend), village (1990 pop. 708), Phelps co., S Nebr., 15 mi/24 km WNW of Holdrege; 40°31′N 99°37′W. Livestock; grain.

Berwick, town (1991 pop. 2,150), NW N.S., E Canada, near Cornwallis R., 12 mi/19 km W of Kentville; 45°02′N 64°44′W. Fruit-growing and -packing center.

Berwick 1 (BUHR-wik), town (1990 pop. 4,375), St. Mary parish, S La., on Berwick Bay of Atchafalaya R., opposite Morgan City (1 mi/2 km E; connected by bridge), 48 mi/77 km S of Baton Rouge; 29°42′N 91°14′W. Port town; Berwick lock. Sugarcane; mfg. of seafood prods. (shrimp, crawfish), concrete, and wheelchair elevators; boatyards. Townsite laid out by Thomas Berwick in 1797. **2** town (1990 pop. 5,995), including Berwick village, York co., SW Maine, on Salmon Falls R., opposite Somersworth (N.H.), and 15 mi/24 km SSW of Sanford; 43°18′N 70°50′W. Textiles. Settled c.1627. South and North Berwick were set off from Berwick in early 19th cent.

Berwick (BUHR-wik), village, (1990 pop. 93), McHenry co., N central N.Dak., 12 mi/19 km W of Rugby; 48°21′N 100°14′W.

Berwick (BUHR-wik), borough (1990 pop. 10,976), Columbia co., E central Pa., on Susquehanna R. (bridged), 23 mi/37 km SW of Wilkes-Barre; 41°03′N 76°15′W.

Mfg. (paper prods., florist prods., apparel, electrical prods., textiles, fabricated metal prods., plastic prods., modular homes, transportation equip., food). Agr. (apples, potatoes, grain; livestock, poultry; dairying). Settled 1783, inc. 1818. Site of Susquehanna 1 and 2 Nuclear Power Plants.

Berwind (BUHR-wind), uninc. village (1990 pop. 500), McDowell co., S W.Va., on Dry Fork, 11 mi/18 km SSW of Welch. In semibituminous-coal field. Berwind L. Wildlife Management Area to S.

Berwyn, city (1990 pop. 45,426), Cook co., NE Ill., a residential suburb of Chicago, near the Chicago Sanitary and Ship Canal; 41°50′N 87°47′W. Varied light industry and manufactures. Inc. 1891.

Berwyn (BUHR-win), uninc. town (1990 pop. 8,150), Chester co., SE Pa., residential suburb 15 mi/24 km WNW of downtown Philadelphia; 40°2′N 75°26′W. Mfg. (printing and publishing; inorganic chemicals). Devon 1 mi/1.6 km E.

Berwyn, village (1991 pop. 581), W Alta., W Canada, near Peace R., 19 mi/31 km WSW of Peace R.; 56°09′N 117°45′W. Lumbering; mixed farming; wheat.

Berwyn 1 (BUHR-win), village, Prince Georges co., central Md., a NE suburb of Wash., D.C. adjacent to Berwyn Heights. Laid out on the W side of the Baltimore and Ohio RR tracks in the 1890s. **2** village (1990 pop. 122), Custer co., central Nebr., 8 mi/12.9 km SE of Broken Bow, on Mud Creek; 41°21′N 99°30′W.

Berwyn, Okla.: see GENE AUTRY.

Berwyn Heights, town (1990 pop. 2,952), Prince Georges co., central Md., NE suburb of Washington, adjacent to Berwyn (W); 38°59′N 76°55′W.

Besnard Lake (BEHZ-nahrd), N central Sask., W Canada, 150 mi/241 km N of Prince Albert; 28 mi/45 km long, 6 mi/10 km wide. Drains NE into Churchill R.

Bess, Mount (10,550 ft/3,216 m), on Alta.-B.C. border, in Rocky Mts. at NW edge of Jasper Natl. Park, 65 mi/105 km WNW of Jasper; 53°22′N 119°22′W.

Bessemer (BES-se-muhr), city (1990 pop. 33,497), Jefferson co., N central Ala., just SW of Birmingham. Founded as a mining town, it was named after Sir Henry Bessemer, inventor of the Bessemer Process. The surrounding area is rich in minerals. Once predominant, iron and steel mfg. here has declined. Mfg. now includes fabricated metal prods., construction equip., RR equip., and foundry prods. Seat of Bessemer State Technical Col. Inc. 1887.

Bessemer (BE-suh-mur), town (1990 pop. 2,272), ⊙ Gogebic co., W Upper Peninsula, Mich., 6 mi/9.7 km NE of Ironwood; 46°28′N 90°02′W. Cattle; lumber milling, mfg. wood prods. Ottawa Natl. Forest to N and E; Porcupine Mts. State Park to NE; Big Powderhorn Ski Area to W. Inc. as village 1887, as city 1889.

Bessemer (BE-suh-muhr), borough (1990 pop. 1,196), Lawrence co., W Pa., 8 mi/12.9 km WSW of New Castle, near Ohio state line, on Hickory Run; 40°58′N 80°29′W. Mfg. (bulk cement, crushed limestone, rubber prods.); strip mines (coal) in area; agr. (grain; livestock; dairying). Inc. c.1910.

Bessemer (BE-suh-muhr), locality, Guilford co., N central N.C., in E part of Greensboro, 3 mi/4.8 km ENE of downtown, on East Bessemer Ave.

Bessemer City (BE-suh-muhr), town (1990 pop. 4,698), Gaston co., SW N.C., suburb 6 mi/9.7 km WNW of Gastonia; 35°16′N 81°17′W. Mfg. (textiles and textile printing, apparel, machine parts and machining, crushed stone; foundry prods.).

Bessie, village (1990 pop. 248), Washita co., W Okla., 7 mi/11.3 km N of Cordell; 35°22′N 98°59′W. In agr. area; mfg. (calcium sulfate).

Bessmay, village, Jasper co., E Texas, 28 mi/45 km NNE of Beaumont. Lumber milling.

Bethalto (be-THAL-to), village (1990 pop. 9,507), Madison co., SW Ill., 8 mi/12.9 km E of Alton; 38°53′N 90°02′W. In agr. area (corn, wheat; poultry, livestock; dairy prods.). Inc. 1869.

Bethany 1 city (1990 pop. 3,005), ⊙ Harrison co., NW Mo., 55 mi/89 km NE of St. Joseph; 40°16′N 94°01′W. Corn, wheat; cattle; mfg. (caps and gloves); limestone quarry. Founded 1845, inc. 1858. **2** city (1990 pop. 20,075), Oklahoma co., central Okla., suburb 8 mi/12.9 km WNW of downtown Oklahoma City; 35°30′N 97°38′W. Mfg. includes small airplanes and tires. Settled in 1906 by members of the Nazarene church. Seat of Southern Nazarene Univ. Wiley Post Airport to N; L. Overholsen reservoir (North Canadian R.) to W. Inc. 1910.

Bethany 1 town (1990 pop. 4,608), New Haven co., S Conn., 9 mi/14.5 km NW of New Haven; 41°25′N 72°59′W. In hilly agr. and light industry. Primarily a suburban residential area. Has fine Episcopal church (1809) and Beecher House. **2** town, Morgan co., central Ind., 7 mi/11.3 km NNW of Martinsville. **3** town (1990 pop. 1,139), Brooke co., N W.Va., in N Panhandle, 12 mi/19 km NE of Wheeling, on Buffalo Creek, near Pa. state line; 40°12′N 80°33′W. Agr. (grain, apples); cattle; dairying. Seat of Bethany Col. (coed.), includes Bethany Leadership Center. Brooke Co. Historical Society Mus. Castleman Run Wildlife Management Area to SE.

Bethany (BE-thuh-NEE), village, S Ont., central Canada, 15 mi/24 km SW of Peterborough; 44°11′N 78°34′W. Dairying; mixed farming.

Bethany 1 village (1990 pop. 1,369), Moultrie co., central Ill., 16 mi/26 km SE of Decatur; 39°38′N 88°44′W. Corn, wheat, soybeans; livestock, poultry; dairy prods. **2** uninc. village (1990 pop. 399), Caddo parish, extreme NW La., on Texas state line, 19 mi/31 km SW of Shreveport; 32°22′N 94°02′W. In natural-gas area; wood prods. (timber); agr. (vegetables, cotton; dairying). Also called Lickskillet.

Bethany (BE-thuh-nee), borough (1990 pop. 238), Wayne co., NE Pa., 3 mi/4.8 km NW of Honesdale, on the Jadwin Reservoir; 41°36′N 75°17′W.

Bethany Beach, village (1990 pop. 326), Sussex co., SE Del., on Atlantic Ocean, 20 mi/32 km SE of Georgetown, 14 mi/23 km N of Ocean City (Md.); 38°32′N 75°04′W. Fishing; mfg. (printing and publishing); beach resort area; tourism. Del. Seashore State Park to N; Fenwick Isl. State Park to S; Assawoman Wildlife Area to SW, Assawoman Canal passes 2 mi/3.2 km to W.

Bethel 1 (BE-thuhl), town (1990 pop. 17,541), Fairfield co., SW Conn.; 41°22′N 73°24′W. Mfg. (wire, textiles, fabricated metal prods., chemicals, electronic components, diamond jewelry prods., batteries, dental and optical components, and tool and die prods.; aluminum and steel fabrication, comercial printing). P. T. Barnum b. here. Founded c.1800, inc. 1855. **2** town (1990 pop. 2,329), including Bethel village, Oxford co., W Maine, 20 mi/32 km NW of South Paris, on Androscoggin R.; 44°25′N 70°46′W. In resort area of at foot of White Mts. Sunday River Ski Resort is here; lodge on mt. and hotels nearby. Passenger RR service to Portland. **3** town (1990 pop. 117), Shelby co., NE Mo., on North R., 5 mi/8 km N of Shelbyville; 39°52′N 92°01′W. Corn, soybeans; hogs, cattle; crushed stone. Founded 1844 by Prussian immigrant William Keil as a communistic, utopian enterprise; historic site; restored bldgs. **4** town (1990 pop. 1,842), Pitt co., E central N.C., 15 mi/24 km N of Greenville; 35°48′N 77°22′W. Tobacco, cotton, peanuts, grain; sweet potatoes, chickens, hogs, cattle. Mfg. (corrugated boxes, fertilizer). **5** town (1990 pop. 1,866), Windsor co., central Vt., on White R., 16 mi/26 km NNW of Woodstock; 43°51′N 72°40′W. Sports equip.; dairy and maple prods. Granite quarries. Chartered 1778.

Bethel 1 (BE-thel), village (1990 pop. 4,674), SW Alaska, on lower Kuskokwim R., 270 mi/435 km SSE of Nome; 60°48′N 161°45′W. Supply point for miners and trappers. Airport. Hosp. Univ. of Alaska col. Main city for lower Yukon and Kuskokwim rivers. Est. 1885 as Moravian mission. **2** village (1990 pop. 178), Sussex co., SW Del., 3 mi/4.8 km WNW of Laurel, on Broad Creek; 38°34′N 75°37′W. Agr. area; oyster beds on creek. Robert L. Graham Wildlife Area to W. Ferry across Nanticoke R. to NW. **3** village (1990 pop. 394), Anoka co., E Minn., 27 mi/43 km N of Minneapolis; 45°23′N 93°16′W. Agr. area (dairying; poultry; rye, alfalfa); mfg. (machining parts, trophies) **4** resort village (1990 pop. 350), Sullivan co., SE N.Y., 9 mi/14.5 km WNW of Monticello, near White L. (E); 41°41′N 74°50′W. Site of the 3-day Woodstock rock festival, July 1969. **5** village (1990 pop. 2,407), Clermont co., SW Ohio, 25 mi/40 km ESE of Cincinnati; 38°59′N 84°05′W. In agr. area; nurseries. Settled 1797. **6** (BE-thuhl), uninc. village (1990 pop. 600), Berks co., SE Pa., 11 mi/18 km NE of Lebanon; 40°28′N 76°17′W. Mfg. includes concrete highway prods.; steel fabricating; lumber. Agr. includes dairying; livestock, poultry; soybeans, grain; timber. Appalachian Trail on Blue Ridge Mt. passes to N.

Bethel Acres, town (1990 pop. 2,505), Pottawatomie co., central Okla., residential suburb 4 mi/6.4 km W of Shawnee, 28 mi/45 km ESE of Oklahoma City, near North Canadian R.; 35°18′N 97°02′W. Shawnee Reservoir, in E extremity of Oklahoma City, to W.

Bethel Island, uninc. town (1990 pop. 2115), Contra Costa co., W Calif., 10 mi/16 km ENE of Antioch, in delta region of San Joaquin R., on Bethel Isl. (marsh isl.); 38°02′N 121°39′W. Asparagus, tomatoes, nursery stock, grain, walnuts, almonds.

Bethel Park (BE-thuhl PAHRK), borough (1990 pop. 33,823), Allegheny co., SW Pa., suburb 8 mi/12.9 km S of downtown Pittsburgh; 40°19′N 80°02′W. RR junction. Mfg. (tool and die, ventilation materials, machinery; diverse light mfg.). U.S. Bureau of Mines Experimental Mine to E; South Regional Park to E. Inc. 1949.

Bethel Springs, town (1990 pop. 755), McNairy co., SW Tenn., 29 mi/47 km SSE of Jackson; 35°14′N 88°36′W. In pine-timber and cotton region.

Bethel Town, town (1991 pop. 2,768), Westmoreland parish, W Jamaica, 33 mi/53 km S of Montego Bay. Marketing center in agr. region (sugarcane, rice, coffee, cacao, spices, breadfruit); livestock.

Bethesda (be-THEZ-dah), uninc. city (1990 pop. 62,936), Montgomery co., W central Md., a residential suburb of Wash., D.C. Residential area settled in the late 17th cent. by the Scottish, English, and Irish. Natl. Inst. of Health, the U.S. Naval Hosp., the Natl. Cancer Inst., the Food and Drug Administration, and the U.S. Inst. of Standards and Technology. Affiliated health care concerns and other businesses fill the large office centers which have transformd the city's downtown.

Bethesda, village (1990 pop. 1,161), Belmont co., E Ohio, 17 mi/27 km W of Bellaire; 40°01′N 81°04′W. Lumber mills.

Bethlehem (BETH-luh-hem), city (1990 pop. 71,428), Northampton and Lehigh cos., E Pa., 48 mi/77 km NNW of Philadelphia, 5 mi/8 km ENE of Allentown, its twin city, on the Lehigh R.; 40°37′N 75°22′W. The steel industry, which began in 1873 and was once dominated by the giant Bethlehem Steel Corp., has been replaced by a mixture of more diversified production. Last blast furnace closed in 1995. Mfg. (fabricated metal prods., machinery, textiles, chemicals, medical supplies and equip.; printing and publsihing, food processing). Settled 1740–1741 by Moravians. During the Revolutionary War a community bldg. was used as a hosp. for Continental soldiers. Tourist center; points of interest include the Central Moravian Church (c.1803), the Schnitz House (1749), and other early Moravian bldgs.; historic 18th-cent. industrial area. America's oldest Bach Choir performs 3 times annually. Seat of Lehigh Univ., Moravian Col., and Northampton Co. Area Community Col. Allentown State Farm to NW; Lost River Caverns to S at Hellertown; Public Rose Garden; Kemerer Mus. of Decorative Arts; Moravian Mus.; Allentown State Hosp. on W boundary; Lehigh Valley Internatl. Airport to NW. Inc. 1845 as a borough, as a city 1917.

Bethlehem 1 town (1990 pop. 3,071), Litchfield co., W Conn., on Pomperaug R., 10 mi/16 km NW of Waterbury; 41°38′N 73°12′W. In hilly agr. region. One of country's 1st theological seminaries conducted here by Rev. Joseph Bellamy in mid-18th cent. Inc. 1787. **2** town (1990 pop. 2,033), Grafton co., NW N.H., 5 mi/8 km ESE of Littleton; 44°15′N 71°35′W. Drained by Ammonoosuc R.; E ½ in White Mt. Natl. Forest. One of state's highest towns (elev. 1,440 ft/439 m). Sugar maples; cattle; dairying; timber. Mfg. (printing and publishing; apparel). Beaver Brook Natl. Forest Wayside

Area in center. Sugarloaf and Zealand Natl. Forest campgrounds in E. Mt. Cleveland (2,397 ft/731 m) and Mt. Agassiz (2,378 ft/725 m) in S. Includes Maplewood and Pierce Bridge villages. **3** uninc. town (1990 pop. 3,186), Alexander co., W central N.C., 7 mi/11.3 km N of Hickory; 35°48'N 81°17'W. L. Hickory reservoir (Catawba R.) to S. Tobacco, grain; poultry, livestock; dairying. Mfg. (cutting dies). **4** town (1990 pop. 2,694), Ohio co., N W.Va., in the N. Panhandle, suburb 4 mi/6.4 km SE of Wheeling, near Ohio R.; 40°02'N 80°41'W. Burchers Run Wildlife Management Area to SE; Ogleby Park to SW. Inc. after 1940.

Bethlehem 1 (BETH-luh-hem), village (1990 pop. 348), Barrow co., NE central Ga., 20 mi/32 km W of Athens; 33°56'N 83°43'W. Mfg. includes poultry processing. **2** village, Caroline co., E Md., 15 mi/24 km NNE of Cambridge. Choptank wetlands preserve is nearby. **3** village, central St. Croix Isl., U.S.V.I., 5 mi/8 km W of Christiansted. Fredensborg Pond, isl.'s largest freshwater marsh, nearby.

Bethpage, uninc. village (□ 3 sq mi/7.8 sq km; 1990 pop. 15,761, including Old Bethpage), Nassau co., SE N.Y., on W L.I.; 40°45'N 73°29'W. Aerospace research. Mfg. of upholstering fabrics here, as well. A village restoration in Old Bethpage features 20 pre-Civil War bldgs. A state park lies to the E.

Bethune 1 (be-THOON), village (1990 pop. 173), Kit Carson co., E Colo., 8 mi/12.9 km W of Burlington, on Landsman Creek; 39°17'N 102°25'W. Elev. 4,257 ft/1,298 m. Wheat and corn area. Sunflowers, beans, sorghum. **2** village (1990 pop. 405), Kershaw co., N central S.C., 20 mi/32 km NE of Camden, near Lynches R; 34°24'N 80°20'W. Mfg. of fabrics and egg processing. Agr. includes poultry, cattle; corn, cotton.

Betsiamites River or **Bersimis**, Que., E Canada, c.240 mi/390 km long; rises in the highlands of E Que.; flows SE into the St. Lawrence R. at Betsiamites. Two hydroelectric plants provide power; Bersimis Dam (1,050,000-kw capacity; completed 1956) impounds L. Pipmuacan.

Betsie River, c.35 mi/56 km long, NW Mich.; rises in small Grass L. in SE Benzie co.; flows SW, past Thompsonville, then NW through Manistee co., back into Benzie co., to L. Michigan at Frankfort; 44°35'N 85°47'W.

Betsy Layne, town (1990 pop. 975), Floyd co., E Ky., in Cumberland foothills, on Levisa Fork R., and 9 mi/14.5 km NW of Pikeville. Bituminous coal, gas, and oil; mfg. (oil processing). Also spelled Betsey Lane.

Bettendorf, city (1990 pop. 28,132), Scott co., E Iowa, Quad Cities area, suburb, 3 mi/4.8 km E of downtown Davenport, on the Mississippi R.; 41°33'N 90°28'W. Has surpassed East Moline (Ill.) in pop. to become 4th member of the Quad Cities. Mfg. (transportation equip., asphalt prods., pools and spas, electronic prods.; metal processing). Scott Community Col. in adjacent Riverdale. Extensive flooding in area, 1993. Settled c.1840, inc. 1903.

Betteravia, uninc. village, Santa Barbara co., SW Calif., 5 mi/8 km WSW of Santa Maria, 5 mi/8 km NE of Pacificcoast. Vegetables, fruit (esp. strawberries), flowers, grain; cattle.

Betterton (BE-tuhr-tuhn), fishing and resort town (1990 pop. 360), Kent co., E Md., 13 mi/21 km S of Havre de Grace, and on Sassafras R.; 39°22'N 76°04'W. Popular beach resort; peaches, apples, and pears grown nearby.

Bettles, village (1990 pop. 36), N central Alaska, on upper Koyukuk R., and 120 mi/193 km N of Tanana; 66°54'N 151°50'W. Supply center. Hunting; mining. Airstrip.

Bettsville, village (1990 pop. 752), Seneca co., N Ohio, 9 mi/14 km NNW of Tiffin; 41°15'N 83°14'W. In agr. area; dolomite prods.

Between, town (1990 pop. 82), Walton co., N central Ga., 6 mi/9.7 km WNW of Monroe; 33°49'N 83°49'W.

Beulah (BYOO-luh), village (1990 pop. 460), Bolivar co., NW Miss., 5 mi/8 km SSE of Rosedale, on L. Beulah (c.6 mi/9.7 km long), an oxbow lake of the Mississippi R.; 33°47'N 90°58'W. Agr. (cotton, corn, rice, soybeans; cattle). Dahomey Natl. Wildlife Refuge to SE.

Beulah, town (1990 pop. 3,363), Mercer co., W central N.Dak., 60 mi/97 km NW of Bismarck, on Knife R.; 47°16'N 101°46'W. Lignite mines; coal-gasification plant. Livestock; dairy prods.; wheat, corn. L. Sakakawea to N.

Beulah 1 (BYOO-luh), village, Pueblo co., S central Colo., in E foothills of Wet Mts., 25 mi/40 km SW of Pueblo; elev. 6,205 ft/1,891 m. Soda springs here. Large marble deposits nearby. San Isabel Natl. Forest to W. L. San Isabel, near source of St. Charles R. to SW. **2** resort village, ⊙ Benzie co., NW Mich., on E end of Crystal L., 8 mi/12.9 km ENE of Frankfort; 44°37'N 86°05'W. Cherries, apples; light mfg. Annual smelt run festival held on small Cold Creek here. Sleeping Bear Dunes Natl. Lakeshore to NW; Platte L. 3 mi/4.8 km to N. **3** village, Crook co., NE Wyo., just N of Black Hills, near S.Dak. state line, 17 mi/27 km NE of Sundance; elev. 3,510 ft/1,070 m. Farm trading point. Parts of Black Hills Natl. Forest to W and S.

Beulah, Lake, Wis.: see LAKE BEULAH.

Beulah Reservoir, Oregon: see NORTH FORK.

Beulaville (BYOO-luh-vil), town (1990 pop. 933), Duplin co., SE N.C., 25 mi/40 km SSW of Kinston, 12 mi/19 km E of Kenansville; 34°55'N 77°46'W. In farm area; tobacco, cotton, grain; poultry, livestock. Mfg. (apparel, textiles, hydraulic cylinders).

Beverley Beach, resort, Anne Arundel co., central Md., on Chesapeake Bay, 7 mi/11.3 km S of Annapolis. Once a public resort, the beach is now owned privately by the community.

Beverly 1 city (1990 pop. 38,195), Essex co., NE Mass., on Mass. Bay; 42°34'N 70°51'W. Its chief manufactures are research, electronic and scientific equip.; consumer goods, and chemicals. Settled in 1626 by Roger Conant, 1 of the founders of Mass. In 1775 the schooner *Hannah*, the 1st ship of the U.S. navy, was outfitted here and commissioned by Gen. George Washington at Glover's Wharf. In 1787, Beverly became the site of the 1st cotton mill in the U.S. Points of interest include Balch house (1636), believed to be the oldest house in the U.S.; the John Cabot house (1781), which is preserved as a mus.; the John Hale house (1694); and several other Colonial bldgs. Beverly Farms, a residential and resort sect. of the city, was the summer home of Oliver Wendell Holmes. Seat of Endicott and North Shore Community cols. Includes Pride's Crossing, an estate area with RR station. Inc. as a city 1894. **2** city (1990 pop. 2,973), Burlington co., W N.J., on Delaware R., and 4 mi/6.4 km W of Burlington; 40°03'N 74°55'W. Mfg. (jet engine parts, adhesive labels); vegetables, fruit. Site of Civil War camp and hosp., and of a natl. cemetery. Inc. 1857.

Beverly, town, Elbert co., NE Ga., 8 mi/12.9 km E of Elberton; 34°05'N 82°43'W.

Beverly 1 village (1990 pop. 131), Lincoln co., N central Kansas, on Saline R., and 9 mi/14.5 km E of Lincoln; 39°00'N 97°58'W. Livestock; grain. **2** village (1990 pop. 1,444), Washington co., SE Ohio, on Muskingum R., and 13 mi/21 km NW of Marietta; 39°34'N 81°39'W. Large nursery; timber. Summer camps. **3** village (1990 pop. 696), Randolph co., E central W.Va., on Tygart R., 6 mi/9.7 km S of Elkins; 38°50'N 79°52'W. Mfg. (wood prods.). Monongahela Natl. Forest to SE. Civil War battle of Rich Mt. (1861), a Union victory, was fought nearby.

Beverly Beach, village (1990 pop. 312), Flagler co., NE Fla., 21 mi/34 km N of Daytona Beach; 29°31'N 81°09'W.

Beverly Hills 1 city (1990 pop. 31,971), Los Angeles co., S Calif., a suburb 8 mi/12.9 km WNW of downtown Los Angeles; 34°05'N 118°24'W. The largely residential city is home to many motion-picture and television personalities. Some light mfg. (printing and publishing; electric and electronic prods., apparel, consumer goods, fabricated metal prods.). Rodeo Drive, the exclusive central shopping area, is known worldwide. The city of Beverly Hills has become synonymous with wealth, luxury, and fame. Twentieth Cent. Fox studios

(Century City) to SW; Farmer's Market in SE; Santa Monica Natl. Recreation Area to NW; Coldwater Canyon in N; Cedars-Sinai Medical Center to E. Inc. 1914. **2** city (1990 pop. 10,610), Oakland Co., SE Mich., on R. Rouge, residential suburb 15 mi/24 km NW of downtown Detroit, and 9 mi/14.5 km SSE of Pontiac; 42°31'N 83°14'W.

Beverly Hills 1 town (□ 2 sq mi/5.2 sq km; 1990 pop. 6,163), Citrus co., W central Fla., 10 mi/16 km NW of Inverness, and 7 mi/11.3 km E of Crystal River; 28°54'N 82°27'W. **2** town (1990 pop. 2,048), McLennan co., E central Texas, residential suburb 4 mi/6.4 km S of downtown Waco.

Beverly Hills, village (1990 pop. 660), St. Louis co., E Mo., residential suburb 10 mi/16 km NW of downtown St. Louis; 38°42'N 90°17'W.

Beverly Park, village, Snohomish co., NW Wash., suburb 5 mi/8 km S of Everett, 23 mi/37 km NNE of Seattle, and S of Pinehurst.

Beverly Shores, town (1990 pop. 622), Porter co., NW Ind., on L. Michigan, 16 mi/26 km NNE of Valparaiso; 41°41'N 86°59'W. Developed as a resort village and residential community.

Bevier (buh-VEER), city (1990 pop. 643), Macon co., N central Mo., in valley of Chariton R., 5 mi/8 km W of Macon; 39°45'N 92°33'W. Former coal-mining community. Long Branch L. to NE.

Bevier (BEE-vuhr), village, Muhlenberg co., W Ky., 5 mi/8 km SSE of Central City, and 5 mi/8 km ENE of Greenville. Bituminous coal.

Bevil Oaks, town (1990 pop. 1,350), Jefferson co., SE Texas, residential suburb 11 mi/18 km NW of downtown Beaumont, on Pine Island Bayou; 30°09'N 94°16'W. Oil and natural gas. Agr. (cattle; rice, soybeans). Main unit of Big Thicket Natl. Preserve to N.

Bevington, town (1990 pop. 67), Warren co., S central Iowa, 12 mi/19 km W of Indianola; 41°21'N 93°47'W.

Bexar (BAI-hahr), county (□ 1,256 sq mi/3,253 sq km; 1990 pop. 1,185,394), SW central Texas; ⊙ SAN ANTONIO; 29°26'N 98°31'W. Balcones Escarpment crosses N of co. SW-NE, dividing hills (in NW) from prairies; co. elev. c.600 ft/183 m–1,200 ft/366 m. Drained by Medina and San Antonio rivers. Heavily urbanized at center in San Antonio area; rapidly growing commercial, industrial and residential area. Agr. around perimeter of co. (corn, grain sorghum, wheat, nursery crops, vegetables); beef and dairy cattle. Oil, natural-gas wells; also limestone, gravel. Tourism. Calaveras, Braunig, Blue Wing, and Mitchell reservoirs in SE part of co.; San Antonio Missions Natl. Historical Park, J. A. Navarro State Historic Park, and San Jose State Historic Site are in San Antonio; numerous military bases in San Antonio area. Formed 1836.

Bexley, city (1990 pop. 13,088), Franklin co., central Ohio; 39°59'N 82°58'W. Residential community completely within the confines of Columbus. Inc. 1908.

Bibb 1 county (□ 625 sq mi/1,619 sq km; 1990 pop. 16,576), central Ala.; ⊙ Centreville. Mining and agr. area crossed (N-S) by Cahaba R. and (SE-NW) by fall line. Coal deposits in N, hog raising in plateau region (SE), cotton and peanuts in Black Belt (SW), and beef cattle. Formed 1818. Part of Talladega Natl. Forest in S. **2** county (□ 251 sq mi/650 sq km; 1990 pop. 149,967), central Ga.; ⊙ Macon; 32°48'N 84°59'W. Mfg. area (textiles, clay and wood prods.) drained by Ocmulgee R. and intersected by the fall line; agr. includes hogs, poultry, cattle; dairying; clay mining. Contains Ocmulgee Natl. Monument. Formed 1822.

Bibb City, town (1990 pop. 597), Muscogee co., W Ga., N suburb of Columbus; 32°30'N 84°59'W. Mfg. (textiles, yarns, tire cord).

Bic (BEEK), village, SE Que., E Canada, on the St. Lawrence R., and 10 mi/16 km SW of Rimouski; 48°22'N 68°42'W. Resort; woodworking. Nearby is Bic Isl.

Bic Island (BIK) or **Île de Bic** (EEL duh BEEK), island, in the St. Lawrence R., SE Que., E Canada, 15 mi/24 km WSW of Rimouski; 3 mi/5 km long; 48°24'N 68°51'W. Formerly a St. Lawrence pilot station, now a resort.

Cross references are shown in SMALL CAPITALS. The pronunciation key is on page xv. The dates of population figures are on page xii.

Biche, Lac la (BEESH, LAHK lah), lake, E Alta., W Canada, 40 mi/64 km ENE of Athabasca; 20 mi/32 km long, 10 mi/16 km wide. On S shore is Lac la Biche village. Drained W by La Biche R. into Athabasca R.

Bickett Knob (3,328 ft/1,014 m), a summit of the Allegheny Mts., Monroe co., S W.Va., 7 mi/11.3 km SSE of Alderson.

Bicknell, city (1990 pop. 3,357), Knox co., SW Ind., 13 mi/21 km NE of Vincennes; 38°47'N 87°19'W. In bituminous-coal area; makes electric coils; grain, fruit farms. Laid out 1869. City grew after opening of 1st coal mine, in 1875.

Bicknell (BIK-nuhl), village (1990 pop. 327), Wayne co., S central Utah, 7 mi/11.3 km SE of Loa, near Fremont R.; 38°20'N 111°32'W. Elev. 7,125 ft/2,172 m. Settled 1875 as Thurber Town; renamed 1916, when Thomas Bicknell donated a lib. to town. Bicknell Bottoms Waterfowl Management Area and Fish Hatchery to SW.

Biddeford (BI-duh-fuhrd), city (1990 pop. 20,710), York co., SW Maine, on the Saco R.; 43°28'N 70°26'W. Has an industrial park; mfg. (textiles, shoes, clothing, and electrical appliances); Biddeford Pool is a resort at the mouth of the Saco R. The 1st permanent settlement est. 1630. During the 17th cent. the town exported lumber and fish, and in 1840 the 1st cotton mill was built. Seat of St. Francis Col. Inc. as a town 1718, as a city 1855.

Bieber, uninc. village, Lassen co., NE Calif., on Pit R., and 60 mi/97 km NE of Redding. Trade center; timber; cattle; grain, potatoes, strawberries. Nearby are Modoc (N) and Lassen (SE) natl. forests. Ahjumawi Lava Springs State Park and Big L. reservoir to W.

Bienfait (BEEN-fait), town (1991 pop. 799), SE Sask., W Canada, 9 mi/14 km E of Estevan, near U.S. (N.Dak.) border; 49°09'N 102°48'W.

Bienvenido (byen-ve-NEE-do), town (1990 pop. 1,386), ⊙ Hermenegildo Galeana municipio, Puebla, central Mexico, 22 mi/35 km E of Huauchinango. Sugar, coffee, fruit. In Totonac area.

Bienville (bee-IN-vil), parish (□ 826 sq mi/2,139 sq km; 1990 pop. 15,979), NW La., ⊙ Arcadia; 32°31'N 92°55'W. Bounded partly W by L. Bistineau; drained by several tributaries of Red R. Driskill Mt. (NE) is highest point (535 ft/163 m) in state, 5 mi/8 km ESE of Bryceland. Agr. (cotton, berries, peaches, hay, sweet potatoes, squash, watermelons; horses, cattle, poultry; dairying). Logging. Part of Jackson-Bienville State Wildlife Area in E, Kepler Creek L. reservoir in W center, Mill Creek Reservoir in S. Named for Jean Baptiste Sieur de Bienville, founder of New Orleans. Formed 1848.

Bienville (bee-IN-vil), village (1990 pop. 316), Bienville parish, NW La., 13 mi/21 km S of Arcadia; 32°22'N 92°59'W. In agr. area; natural-gas fields nearby. Driskill Mt. (535 ft/163 m), 7 mi/11 km NE, is highest point in La.

Bienville, Lake (byen-VEEL), lake (□ 392 sq mi/1,015 sq km), N Que., E Canada; 54 mi/87 km long, 12 mi/19 km wide; 55°25'N 72°30'W. Drained by Great Whale R.

Bierstadt, Mount (14,060 ft/4,285 m), Clear Creek co., N central Colo., in Front Range, 1 mi/1.6 km W of Mt. Evans, in Pike Natl. Forest, 9 mi/14.5 km S of Georgetown.

Big Annemessex River (a-nah-ME-seks), c.15 mi/24 km long, SE Md., tidal estuary entering Tangier Sound of Chesapeake Bay, c.4 mi/6.4 km S of Fairmont. Fishing, oystering.

Big Bald, N.C. and Tenn.: see BALD MOUNTAINS.

Big Basin, uninc. village, Santa Cruz co., W Calif., c.15 mi/24 km NW of Santa Cruz, 18 mi/29 km WSW of San Jose and 5 mi/8 km NE of Pacific Ocean coast, in Big Basin Valley of Santa Cruz Mts., on Scott Creek. Lies at SE edge of Big Basin State Park (□ over 28 sq mi/73 sq km, in Santa Cruz and San Mateo cos.), which has groves of giant redwoods, some 330 ft/101 m high and millennia old. Campgrounds, lodgings; sports facilities.

Big Bay, village, Marquette co., NW Mich., on Upper Peninsula, 23 mi/37 km NW of Marquette, on Big Bay of L. Superior, and NW end of L. Independence; 46°48'N 87°43'W. The Huron Mt. Club, 5 mi/8 km–10 mi/16 km to NW, beyond end of public road, large

private colony of summer residences, constructed of natural materials, owned by such prominent business families as the Fords and Armours from Detroit, Chicago, and Milwaukee. Club dates to early 1900s. Area centered around lakes Howe, Rush, Mountain, Pine, Ives, and Conway, bet. Huron Mts. and L. Superior. Tourism area.

Big Bay De Noc (duh NAHK), a N arm of Green Bay, Upper Peninsula, N Mich., penetrating c.20 mi/32 km into Delta co.; 45°47'N 86°42'W. Separated from L. Michigan (E) by Garden Peninsula, from Little Bay De Noc (W) by peninsula terminating in Peninsula Point.

Big Bear City, uninc. town (1990 pop. 4,920), San Bernardino co., S Calif., 27 mi/43 km ENE of San Bernardino, at E end of Big Bear L. reservoir; 34°16'N 116°51'W. Area surrounded by San Bernardino Natl. Forest. Goldmine Ski Area and Heart Bar State Park to SE.

Big Bear Lake, city (1990 pop. 5,351), San Bernardino co., S Calif., 22 mi/35 km ENE of San Bernardino, on shore of Big Bear L. reservoir; 34°14'N 116°54'W. Mfg. (printing and publishing; bldg. materials, navigation systems, lumber). San Bernardino Mts. to S. Area surrounded by San Bernardino Natl. Forest. Snow Summit Ski Area to SE; Bear Creek Lodge to W.

Big Bear Lake, reservoir, San Bernardino co., S Calif., on Bear Creek, 18 mi/29 km ENE of San Bernardino, in San Bernardino Mts.; 7 mi/11.3 km long; 34°13'N 116°58'W. Elev. 6,754 ft/2,059 m. Resort area. Towns of Big Bear Lake and Moonridge on S shore, Big Bear City at E end. This area was center of earthquake activity in the early 1990s.

Big Beaver, village, Oakland co., SE Mich., 9 mi/14.5 km SE of Pontiac; 42°33'N 83°07'W. Absorbed by city of Troy.

Big Beaver, borough (1990 pop. 2,298), Beaver co., W Pa., 4 mi/6.4 km NW of Beaver Falls, covers 18 sq mi/47 sq km of mostly rural land; 40°49'N 80°21'W. Beaver R. is E boundary. Agr. includes dairying. North Fork Little Beaver Creek to W.

Big Belt Mountains, range of Rocky Mts., mainly Broadwater and Meagher cos., W central Mont., E of Missouri R., partially covered by Helena Natl. Forest; extend c.80 mi/129 km N-S. Rise to elev. of 9,480 ft/2,890 m at Mt. Edith at center of range.

Big Bend, town (1990 pop. 1,299), Waukesha co., SE Wis., suburb 9 mi/14.5 km S of Waukesha, and 19 mi/31 km SW of Milwaukee, on Fox R.; 42°52'N 88°12'W. In farm and lake area; light mfg.

Big Bend, former village, McLean co., central N.Dak., near Missouri R., 20 mi/32 km NW of Washburn, and 2 mi/3.2 km E of Riverdale. Site inundated by L. Sakakawea.

Big Bend National Park (□ 1,252 sq mi/3,243 sq km), Brewster co., W Texas; formed by the Rio Grande along the U.S.–Mex. border, running SE then NE in a big bend, notably through deep canyons such as the Santa Elena. The river, the desert plains, and the Chisos Mts. offer sharp contrasts in wilderness scenery. The park has archaeological treasures, petrified trees, vestiges of prehistoric Native Amer. cultures, and rare forms of animal (deer, fox, coyote, javelina, black bear, mt. lion; jay, hummingbird, roadrunner) and plant life (1,100 plant variations). Road access 79 mi/127 km S of Marathon (E) and 108 mi/174 km S of Alpine (W). Lodge and visitors center at Chisos Basin; hq. at Panther Junction. Est. 1944; designated Biosphere Reserve 1976.

Big Black Mountain, peak (4,139 ft/1,262 m), E Ky., in the Cumberland Mts., 23 mi/37 km E of Harlan, near Va. state line. Highest point in Ky.

Big Black River, c.330 mi/531 km long, central and W Miss.; rises in E Webster co., N of Mathiston; flows SW past Valden, Durant, and Edwards to the Mississippi R. 23 mi/37 km SSW of Vicksburg.

Big Blue River 1 c.75 mi/121 km long, central Ind.; rises in Henry co.; flows generally SW, past New Castle and Shelbyville, to East Fork of White R. near Edinburgh. **2** c.250 mi/402 km long, in Nebr. and Kansas; main branch rises in W Hamilton co. (SE Nebr.), less than 5 mi/8 km from Platte R., SSE of Grand Island; flows

S, past Seward and Beatrice (Nebr.), and Marysville (Kansas), through Tuttle Creek Reservoir (45 mi/72 km long, 2 mi/3.2 km wide), to Kansas R. near Manhattan. Receives Little Blue R. at Blue Rapids (Kansas). W branch rises in N Adams co. (Nebr.), NW of Hastings, flows E c.100 mi/161 km to Big Blue R. N of Crete.

Big Bone Lick, Ky.: see BURLINGTON.

Big Bromley, Vt.: see MANCHESTER.

Big Cabin, village (1990 pop. 271), Craig co., NE Okla., 8 mi/12.9 km SSW of Vinita; 36°32'N 95°13'W. In agr. area; mfg. (construction materials).

Big Cedar Lake, Wis.: see SLINGER.

Big Cedar River, c.60 mi/97 km long, SW Upper Peninsula, N Mich.; rises in NW Menominee co.; flows SSE, past Powers, to Green Bay c.25 mi/40 km NE of Menominee.

Big Coal River, c.55 mi/89 km long, W central W.Va.; formed in NW Raleigh co., 20 mi/32 km W of Beckley, by joining of Marsh and Clear forks (both c.35 mi/56 km long); flows NW to Kanawha R. at St. Albans. Bituminous-coal mining in its valley. Also called Coal R.

Big Coppitt Key (KAHP-it), island (□ 1 sq mi/2.6 sq km; 1990 pop. 2,388), Monroe co., Fla. Keys, 10 mi/16 km NE of Key West; 24°36'N 81°39'W.

Big Cormorant Lake, Minn.: see CORMORANT LAKE.

Big Costilla Peak (ko-STEE-uh) (12,739 ft/3,883 m), Taos co., N N.Mex., in Sangre de Cristo Mts., near Colo. state line, 20 mi/32 km SE of Costilla village. Also called Costilla Peak.

Big Creek, village (1990 pop. 123), Calhoun co., N central Miss., 23 mi/37 km ENE of Grenada, near Yalobusha R.; 33°50'N 89°25'W. Grenada Waterfowl Refuge to SW.

Big Creek 1 c.40 mi/64 km long, SW Ala. and SE Miss.; rises in NW Mobile co. (Ala.); flows S, joining Escatawpa R. in SE Jackson co. (Miss.), 13 mi/21 km NE of Pascagoula. **2** c.40 mi/64 km long, SE Ind.; rises in Ripley co.; flows generally SW, joining small Graham Creek to form Muscatatuck R. in W Jefferson co. **3** c.40 mi/64 km long, SW Ind.; rises N of Evansville in Vanderburgh co.; flows NW and SW to the Wabash R. c.6 mi/9.7 km NW of Mount Vernon. **4** 124 mi/200 km long. W central Kansas; rises in NW corner of Gove co.; flows ESE, past Ellis and Hays, to Smoky Hill R. 7 mi/11.3 km SSW of Russell. **5** c.75 mi/121 km long, NE La.; rises in West Carroll parish; flows SW to Boeuf R. 10 mi/16 km W of Winnsboro; 31°19'N 92°05'W.

Big Creek Lake, reservoir, Polk Co., central Iowa, on Big Creek, in Big Creek State Park, 1 mi/1.6 km S of and parallel to Saylorville Reservoir, and 13 mi/21 km NNW of Des Moines; 3 mi/4.8 km long; 41°47'N 93°43'W. Max. capacity 35,500 acre-ft. Formed by Big Creek Dam (66 ft/20 m high), built (1972) by the Army Corps of Engineers for flood control.

Big Cypress Creek, c.120 mi/193 km long, in NE Texas and NW La.; formed by headstreams rising E of Winnsboro, in NW Wood co., Texas; flows NE through Lakes Cypress Springs and Bob Sandlin, then generally SE, through L. O' the Pines, past Jefferson, through Caddo L., into La., joins Black Bayou in E Caddo L. in Caddo parish, 18 mi/29 km NNW of Shreveport. Little Cypress Bayou enters W end of Caddo L. from SW. Also called Cypress Creek, Big Cypress Bayou, or Cypress Bayou.

Big Cypress Lake, Indian River co., E central Fla., 31 mi/50 km NW of Fort Pierce; c.5 mi/8 km long, 2 mi/3.2 km wide; 27°44'N 80°44'W.

Big Cypress Preserve (□ 1,118 sq mi/2,896 sq km), SW Fla. Subtropical plant and animal life; ancestral home of Seminole and Miccosukee peoples. Authorized 1974.

Big Cypress Swamp, large forested wetland mainly in Collier co., SW Fla.; borders on the Everglades (E). Lumbering; oil wells at Sunniland. Contains Seminole Indian Reservation.

Big Cypress Swamp, Del. and Md.: see CYPRESS SWAMP.

Big Darby Creek, Ohio: see DARBY CREEK.

Big Delta, village, E Alaska, on Tanana R., at mouth of Delta R., 9 mi/14.5 km NNW of Delta Junction, and 75 mi/121 km SE of Fairbanks, on Alaska Highway; 64°09'N 145°50'W. Big Delta State Historical Park;

Alaska Pipeline roadhouse suspended over Tanana R. here, viewing area for tourists.

Big Eau Pleine Reservoir, Wis.: see BIG EAU PLEINE RIVER.

Big Eau Pleine River (o PLAIN), c.40 mi/64 km long, central Wis.; rises in Marathon co.; flows SE to Wisconsin R. 17 mi/27 km SSW of Wausau. Near its mouth, the river widens to form Big Eau Pleine Reservoir (9 mi/14.5 km long, ½mi/⁹⁄₁₀ km–2 mi/3.2 km wide). Dam is on W arm of Du Bay Reservoir.

Big Falls, village (1990 pop. 341), Koochiching co., N Minn., 35 mi/56 km SW of International Falls, on Big Fork R.; 48°11′N 93°48′W. Timber; pulpwood, lumber. In Pine Island State Forest; Koochiching State Forest to E.

Big Falls, hamlet (1990 pop. 75), Waupaca co., central Wis., on Little Wolf R. (tributary of the Wolf R.), and 18 mi/29 km NNE of Waupaca; 44°37′N 89°01′W. In dairy, poultry, and farm area.

Big Flat, town (1990 pop. 93), Stone co., N Ark., c.22 mi/35 km NW of Mountain View; 36°00′N 92°24′W. Ozark Natl. Forest to N, E, and SE.

Big Flats, village (□ 3 sq mi/7.8 sq km; 1990 pop. 2,658), Chemung co., S N.Y., near Chemung R., 7 mi/11.3 km WNW of Elmira; 42°08′N 76°55′W.

Big Fork River, 160 mi/257 km long, N Minn.; formed by confluence of Popple and Bowstring rivers in Dura L., 45 mi/72 km NE of Bemidji, in N central Itasca co.; 47°45′N 94°02′W; flows E past Bigfork, then gradually N, in very serpentine course, through Koochiching and Pine Island state forests, past Big Falls, to Rainy R., Can. (Ont.) border, 16 mi/26 km WSW of International Falls.

Big Hole National Battlefield (656 acres/265 ha), Beaverhead co., SW Mont., on North Fork Big Hole R., and the Nez Percé Natl. Historical Trail, at edge of Beaverhead Natl. Forest, 48 mi/77 km SW of Anaconda. Authorized 1910 as a natl. monument, designation changed 1963. Scene of 1877 battle between U.S. troops led by Col. John Gibbons and Nez Percé Native Americans led by Chief Joseph, as part of effort to confine the latter to reservation.

Big Hole River, 142 mi/229 km long, SW Mont.; rises in W Beaverhead co., in Skinner L., in Beaverhead Mts. of Bitterroot Range, 3 mi/4.8 km E of Continental Divide and Idaho state line; flows N, around Pioneer Mts. then SE, finally NE, joining Jefferson R. just N of Twin Bridges. Drains livestock region.

Big Horn 1 county (□ 5,014 sq mi/12,986 sq km; 1990 pop. 11,337), S Mont.; ⊙ Hardin; 45°26′N 107°29′W. Irrigated region bordering on Wyo.; drained by Bighorn and Little Bighorn rivers. Wheat, barley, oats, hay, beans, sugar beets; cattle. Part of Crow Indian Reservation in S; W part of Northern Cheyenne Indian Reservation in E. Pryor, Bighorn, and Rosebud mts. in S. Bighorn Reservoir, in center and SW of co., formed on Bighorn R. in Bighorn Canyon Natl. Recreation Area (includes Yellowtail Dam). Little Bighorn Battlefield Natl. Monument and Reno-Benteen Battlefield Memorial in center; Rosebud Battlefield and Tongue River (on Tongue R. reservoir) state parks, in SE. Chief Plenty Coups State Park in W. Formed 1913. **2** county (□ 3,159 sq mi/8,182 sq km; 1990 pop. 10,525), N Wyo.; ⊙ Basin; 44°31′N 107°59′W. Irrigated agr., natural-gas, oil, and coal region bordering Mont. on N; watered by Bighorn R. Agr. (sugar beets, oats, barley, beans, hay, alfalfa; cattle, sheep). Mfg. at Greybull and Lovell. Bighorn Mts. dominate E part of co.; part of Bighorn Natl. Forest located along E margin of co. Bighorn L. (formed by Bighorn R.) and Bighorn Canyon Natl. Recreation Area in N, both extend into Mont. Medicine Lodge State Archaeological Site in SE; Medicine Wheel Natl. Historic Landmark in NE; Pryor Mountain Wild Horse Range in N. Ski area. Formed 1890.

Big Horn 1 village (1990 pop. 20), Treasure co., S central Mont., on Yellowstone R., near mouth of Bighorn R., and 59 mi/95 km NE of Billings. **2** village, Sheridan co., N Wyo., on Little Goose Creek, just E of Bighorn Mts., and 9 mi/14.5 km S of Sheridan; elev. 4,059 ft/-

1,237 m. Livestock. Bighorn Mts. and Bighorn Natl. Forest to W.

Big Horn Mountains, Maricopa co., W Ariz., E of Harquahala Mts., 15 mi/24 km NW of Tonopah, W of Hassayampa R.; rise to c.3,000 ft/914 m in NW. Big Horn Mountains Wilderness Area.

Big Indian, resort village (1990 pop. 350), Ulster co., SE N.Y., in the Catskill Mts., on Esopus Creek, and 25 mi/40 km WNW of Kingston; 42°06′N 74°27′W. Big Indian Mt. (elev. 3,721 ft/1,134 m) is 5 mi/8 km S.

Big Indian River, Mich.: see INDIAN RIVER.

Big Island, uninc. village, Bedford co., SW central Va., on James R., 13 mi/21 km NW of Lynchburg. Mfg. (paper processing; lumber); timber. In area are George Washington (N) and Jefferson (NW) natl. forests.

Big Island 1 SE Franklin dist., N.W.T., N Canada, in Hudson Strait, off S Baffin Isl.; 36 mi/58 km long, 3 mi/5 km–16 mi/26 km wide; 62°40′N 70°45′W. **2** W Ont., central Canada, in S part of L. of the Woods, bet. Aulneau Peninsula and U.S. (Minn.) border, 40 mi/64 km S of Kenora, and just N of Bigsby Isl.; 12 mi/19 km long, 7 mi/11 km wide.

Big Island, the: see HAWAII.

Big Kandiyohi Lake (kan-dee-YO-hei), Kandiyohi co., S central Minn., 9 mi/14.5 km SSE of Willmar; 3.5 mi/5.6 km long, 2 mi/3.2 km wide; 45°00′N 94°59′W. Fed and drained (S) by South Fork Crow R. Also known as Kandiyohi L.

Big Lake 1 town (1990 pop. 3,113), Sherburne co., S central Minn., 7 mi/11.3 km NW of Elk River city, bet. Mississippi (S) and Elk (N) rivers; 45°20′N 93°45′W. Grain, soybeans, potatoes, alfalfa; hogs; mfg. (computer parts, oil filters, rubber stamps, ice augers). Sand Dunes Natl. Forest and Sherburne Natl. Wildlife Refuge to N. **2** town (1990 pop. 3,672), ⊙ Reagan co., W Texas, in rough prairie, c.60 mi/97 km WSW of San Angelo, on N side of Big L.; 31°11′N 101°27′W. Elev. 2,678 ft/816 m. Market, shipping point for oil and ranching area (sheep, goats, cattle; cotton, grains).

Big Lake 1 lake, Washington co., E Maine, 30 mi/48 km NNW of Machias; 8 mi/12.9 km long. Resorts. **2** intermittent lakes, S Mont., in Stillwater co., 25 mi/40 km WNW of Billings; 5 mi/8 km long; average width 1 mi/1.6 km. Eastlick Pond–Big Lake Wildlife Management area at N end.

Big Lake, Ill.: see BANNER.

Big Lake National Wildlife Refuge, NE Ark., 11 mi/18 km W of Blytheville; c.10 mi/16 km long, 1 mi/1.6 km wide, on Right Hand Chute (Little R.). Also Big Lake Wildlife Management Area parallels refuge on E. Migratory birds.

Big Lost River, c.120 mi/193 km long, central Idaho; rises in Pioneer Mts. of S Caster co., N of Hyndman Peak (Challis Natl. Forest); flows NE then SE through Mackay Reservoir, past Mackay and Arco, past EBR-1 nuclear reactor (Natl. Historic Landmark), and into a depression in E part of Butte co. in tract of Idaho Natl. Engineering Laboratory. Dam in upper course (4 mi/6.4 km NW of Mackay) forms Mackay Reservoir. Big Lost and Little Lost rivers center into the subterranean Snake River Plain Aquifer and reemerge at Thousand Springs, on Snake R., c.100 mi/161 km to SW, 20 mi/32 km WNW of Twin Falls.

Big Manitou Falls, Wis.: see BLACK RIVER.

Big Monon Creek, c.35 mi/56 km long, NW Ind.; rises in NW Pulaski co.; flows generally SSE to L. Shafer.

Big Moose, resort village (1990 pop. 75), Herkimer co., N central N.Y., in the Adirondack Mts., c.50 mi/80 km NNE of Utica; 43°49′N 74°55′W. Big Moose L. (□ c.2 sq mi/5.2 sq km) is just E.

Big Muddy Creek, 191 mi/307 km long, in W Canada (Sask.) and NW U.S. (Mont.); rises in Sask., just across internatl. border; flows S, past Plentywood (Mont.) and Medicine Lake, to Missouri R. just W of Culbertson.

Big Muddy River, c.135 mi/217 km long, S Ill.; rises in Jefferson co.; flows S and SW, past Murphysboro, to the Mississippi R. S of Grand Tower; 38°28′N 89°05′W.

Big Nemaha River (nee-MAH-hah), 40 mi/64 km long, SE Nebr.; formed by confluence of North and South

forks near Falls City; flows E to Missouri R. near Rulo. North Fork rises 15 mi/24 km S of Lincoln, flows 95 mi/153 km SE, past Tecumseh and Humboldt; South Fork rises in NE Kansas, near Seneca, flows 68 mi/109 km N and E.

Big Oak Flat, uninc. village, Tuolumne co., central Calif., in mining and resort region of the Sierra Nevada, c.56 mi/90 km ESE of Stockton, on Hetch Hetchy Aqueduct. Apples, hay; timber; cattle. Yosemite Natl. Park is E; Stanislaus Natl. Forest to E. Groveland–Big Oak Flat area had a combined 1990 pop. of 2,753.

Big Pine, town (1990 pop. 1,158), Inyo co., E Calif., in Owens Valley, 15 mi/24 km S of Bishop, on Owens R.; 37°10′N 118°18′W. Cattle. Big Pine Indian Reservation is here; Kings Canyon Natl. Park to W and S; John Muir Wilderness in the Sierra Nevada is W; Inyo Mts. to E; parts of Inyo Natl. Forest to E and W.

Big Pine Key, island (1990 pop. 4,206), Monroe co., lower Fla. Keys, 30 mi/48 km NE of Key West; 24°41′N 81°22′W. Mfg. includes concrete, grated horseradish, and diving compressors.

Big Pine Lake, lake, Otter Tail co., W Minn., 35 mi/56 km NE of Fergus Falls; 5 mi/8 km long, 2 mi/3.2 km wide; 46°37′N 95°30′W. Has fishing, boating, and swimming resorts. Fed from Little Pine L. (circular, 2 mi/3.2 km wide) to NW, drains S past dam to Rush L.; both drained by Otter Tail R.; also fed from N by Todd R. Perham town to W. Sometimes known as Pine L.

Big Pine Mountain, Calif.: see SAN RAFAEL MOUNTAINS.

Big Piney, village (1990 pop. 454), Sublette co., W Wyo. at confluence of North Piney and Middle Piney creeks, near Green R., 26 mi/42 km SW of Pinedale, and 1 mi/1.6 km S of Marbleton; 42°32′N 110°07′W. Elev. 6,798 ft/2,072 m. Livestock; lumber; logging.

Big Port Walter, Alaska: see PORT WALTER.

Big Raccoon Creek, Ind.: see RACCOON CREEK.

Big Rapids, city (1990 pop. 12,603), ⊙ Mecosta co., W central Mich., 47 mi/76 km NNE of Grand Rapids, at the falls of the Muskegon R.; 43°42′N 85°29′W. Elev. 920 ft/280 m. Agr. and light mfg. (fabricated metal prods., transportation equip., tools, footwear, bldg. materials; publishing) predominate, and Big Rapids serves as a shipping point for the region's grains. Extensive natural gas wells are nearby. Airport here. Seat of Ferris State Univ., part of the Univ. of Mich. system. Manistee Natl. Forest to W. Inc. 1869.

Big Rice Lake, Minn.: see RICE LAKE.

Big River, uninc. town (1990 pop. 702), San Bernardino co., SE Calif., 35 mi/56 km NNE of Blythe, and 5 mi/8 km W of Parker (Ariz.); 34°08′N 114°22′W. Planned residential community on Colorado R., in Colorado River Indian Reservation.

Big River, village (1991 pop. 809), central Sask., W Canada, on Cowan L., 70 mi/113 km NW of Prince Albert; 53°50′N 107°02′W. Lumbering; mixed farming. Resort.

Big River 1 c.40 mi/64 km long, NW Calif.; rises in SE Mendocino co., c.10 mi/16 km W of Ukiah; flows W to the Pacific Ocean at Mendocino. **2** c.130 mi/209 km long, E central Mo.; rises in Washington co.; meanders N through Jefferson co., to the Meramec R. 25 mi/40 km WSW of St. Louis. Subject to frequent flooding, esp. 1993, and to contamination from lead mines.

Big Rock, uninc. village, Buchanan co., SW Va., 35 mi/56 km NW of Norton, near Ky. state line, in Cumberland Mts.; 37°21′N 82°11′W. Bituminous coal. Mfg. (mining equip., mine supports; machining). Breaks Interstate Park on Ky. state line to SW.

Big Rock Point Nuclear Power Plant, Mich.: see CHARLEVOIX.

Big Run, borough (1990 pop. 699), Jefferson co., W central Pa., 5 mi/8 km ENE of Punxsutawney, on Canoe Creek; 40°58′N 78°52′W. Mfg. (drilling equip., apparel); agr. (alfalfa, corn; dairying). Punxsatawney Municipal Airport to W.

Big Sable River, c.30 mi/48 km long, W Mich.; rises in W Lake co.; flows W, widening into Hamlin L. (behind Ludington Dunes; c.10 mi/16 km long, 2 mi/3.2 km wide) before entering L. Michigan just N of Ludington;

Cross references are shown in SMALL CAPITALS. The pronunciation key is on page xv. The dates of population figures are on page xii.

44°03′N 85°56′W. Ludington State Park is bet. Hamlin L. and L. Michigan.

Big Saline Bayou (suh-LEEN BEI-yo), river, c.30 mi/48 km long, in E central La.; flows SE from its source in Catahoula L., through Saline L. (c.5 mi/8 km long), to Red R. 10 mi/16 km NNE of Marksville; 31°20′N 92°05′W. Saline State Wildlife Area is E of its upper course.

Big Sandy 1 town (1990 pop. 740), Chouteau co., N Mont., on Big Sandy Creek, and 35 mi/56 km SW of Havre; 48°11′N 110°07′W. Ferry crosses Missouri R. 11 mi/18 km SSW. Coal, natural gas; cattle, hogs; wheat, rye, barley, oats, alfalfa. Rocky Boy's Indian Reservation to NE. Upper Missouri Natl. Wild and Scenic R. and Coal Banks Landing State Recreation Area to S. **2** town (1990 pop. 505), Benton co., NW Tenn., on arm of Kentucky Reservoir, near mouth of Big Sandy R., and 14 mi/23 km ESE of Paris; 36°14′N 88°05′W. **3** town (1990 pop. 1,185), Upshur co., NE Texas, 14 mi/23 km SW of Gilmer, on Sabina R., at mouth of Big Sandy Creek; 32°35′N 95°06′W. Elev. 333 ft/101 m. RR junction. Dairying; cattle, poultry; vegetables, peaches; oil, lumber area.

Big Sandy Creek, 193 mi/311 km long, central and E Colo.; rises in NE El Paso co.; flows ENE through Ramah Reservoir to Limon, then SE, past Hugo, to Arkansas R. 8 mi/12.9 km E of Lamar.

Big Sandy Lake (□ 17 sq mi/44 sq km; □ 8 sq mi/20.7 sq km in natural state), Aitkin co., central Minn., 26 mi/42 km NE of Aitkin, in Savanna State Forest; 6 mi/9.7 km long, max. width 4 mi/6.4 km; elev. 1,218 ft/371 m. Fishing resorts. Natural lake expanded by dam at NE end on Prairie R. Sandy Lake Indian Reservation to NE. Sandy Lake Fur Post (1794), a historic site, is on W shore. Sometimes called Sandy L.

Big Sandy River 1 c.80 mi/129 km long, Ariz.; formed by confluence of Cottonwood Wash and Trout Creek, at small sect. of Hualapi Indian Reservation near Hualapai Peak, Mohave co., W Ariz.; flows S, past Wikieup, joining Santa Maria R. 43 mi/69 km ENE of Parker to form Bill Williams R.; intermittent. Hualapai Mts. to W. **2** 27 mi/43 km long, NE Ky. and W W.Va.; formed at Louisa (Ky.) near dam by joining of Tug and Levisa forks; flows generally N forming part of Ky.–W.Va. state line, to Ohio R. at Catlettsburg (Ky.), and Kenova (W.Va.), 8 mi/12.9 km W of Huntington (W.Va.), where Ky., W.Va., and Ohio meet. Navigable by small crafts. **3** c.65 mi/105 km long, in W Tenn.; rises N of Lexington in Henderson co.; flows N, past Bruceton, to Kentucky Reservoir (Tennessee R.) c.15 mi/24 km N of Big Sandy, near Ky. state line; 36°24′N 88°04′W. Lower course, chiefly below Big Sandy town, forms arm of reservoir.

Big Savage Mountains, NW Md. and SW Pa., ridge of the Alleghenies, rising to 2,850 ft/869 m W of Barton (Md.); runs c.30 mi/48 km NE from Savage R. W of La Vale to point WNW of Hyndman (Pa.). Named for an early surveyor, John Savage.

Big Sioux River (SOO), 295 mi/470 km long, S.Dak. and Iowa; rises in E Day Co., near Waubay, in NE S.Dak.; flows S past Watertown and Sioux Falls; receives Pipestone Creek from NE, then forms Iowa–S.Dak. state line (last 85 mi/137 km), continuing S past Canton (S.Dak.) and Akron (Iowa), to join the Missouri R. at Sioux City (Iowa). Passes through an agr. region that produces corn, soybeans, oats; hogs, beef cattle.

Big Sky, village (1990 pop. 500), Gallatin co., SW Mont., 31 mi/50 km SSW of Bozeman, resort area in Gallatin Natl. Forest, on the West Fork of the Gallatin R. Separate units of Lee Metcalf Wilderness Area to N and S; Big Sky Ski Resort to W; Yellowstone Natl. Park to SE.

Big Slide Mountain (4,255 ft/1,297 m), Essex co., NE N.Y., in the Adirondack Mts., c.4 mi/6.4 km NE of Mt. Marcy, and 9 mi/14.5 km SSE of Lake Placid village; 44°11′N 73°53′W.

Big South Fork, Tenn. and Ky.: see SOUTH FORK CUMBERLAND RIVER, and BIG SOUTH FORK NATIONAL RIVER AND RECREATION AREA.

Big South Fork National River and Recreation Area (□ 192 sq mi/497 sq km), on Tenn.-Ky. state line, includes parts of Scott, Fentress, and Pickett cos. in N Tenn. and McReary co. in SE Ky. Scenic gorges and valleys of Big South Fork of the Cumberland R. Recreation includes boating, hiking, camping, fishing. Includes restored coal-mining community (Ky.). Authorized 1974, Natl. Park Service assumed managemet 1976.

Big Spencer Mountain (3,230 ft/985 m), Piscataquis co., central Maine, E of Moosehead L., 23 mi/37 km NNE of Greenville. In recreational area.

Big Spirit Lake, NW Iowa, largest glacial lake (4 mi/6.4 km long, 3 mi/4.8 km wide) in state, almost at Minn. state line, just N of Spirit Lake town. Resort area with Mini-Waken State Park on N shore and Marble Beach State Park and fish hatchery on S shore. Region was scene of Native Amer. massacre (1857), commemorated by monument at nearby Arnolds Park.

Big Spring, city (1990 pop. 23,093), ⊙ Howard co., 100 mi/161 km WSW of Abilene, W central Texas, on Beals Creek; 32°14′N 101°28′W. Elev.2,397 ft/731 m. The spring for which it was named once fed a branch of the Colorado R. but has become dry. The city is the trade center for a farm (sesame, vegetables, cotton) and cattle region. A variety of oil- and gas-related industries have been developed since the discovery of oil in 1928. Mfg. (printing, sheet metal fabricating; lightning protection equip., wooden prods., carbon black, clothing, plastic prods.). Of interest are a historical mus., the Comanche Trail Park, and Big Spring State Park on Sulphur Draw, S of city. Seat of Howard Col. (2-year), Webb Air Force Base (closed) to SW, and a veterans' hosp. are also here. Inc. 1907

Big Springs, village (1990 pop. 495), Deuel co., W Nebr., near Colo. state line, 20 mi/32 km E of Chappell, and on South Platte R.; 41°03′N 102°04′W. Grain.

Big Spruce Knob, mountain peak (4,673 ft/1,424 m), Pocahontas co., E W.Va., 7 mi/11.3 km NW of Marlinton, in Monongahela Natl. Forest; highest summit of Gauley Mt., a N-S ridge (14 mi/23 km long) of the Allegheny Mts. Sometimes called Spruce Mt. Spruce Knob, c.45 mi/72 km NE, is highest point in state. Highland Scenic Highway passes to N and W.

Big Squaw Mountain (3,196 ft/974 m), Piscataquis co., central Maine, W of Moosehead L., 31 mi/50 km NW of Dover-Foxcroft. Big Squaw ski resort.

Big Stone, county (□ 527 sq mi/1,365 sq km; 1990 pop. 6,285), W Minn.; ⊙ Ortonville; 45°25′N 96°24′W. Bounded W and SW by Big Stone L. (S.Dak. state line), on S by Minnesota R. (flows out of Big Stone L.). Agr. area (alfalfa, wheat, corn, oats, barley, soybeans; hogs). Surrounded by part of Lac qui Parle Wildlife Area. Artichoke L. in E, Marsh L. (formed by Minnesota R.) in SE, several small lakes in center of co.; Big Stone Lake State Park in SW. Formed 1862.

Big Stone City, town (1990 pop. 669), Grant co., NE S.Dak., 10 mi/16 km NE of Milbank and on Big Stone L., at Minn. state line, opposite Ortonville (Minn.); at mouth of North Fork Whetstone R. Dairy prods., grain; granite and monuments; mfg. (cheese, bricks); tourism. Big Stone Lake State Park to N.

Big Stone Gap, town (1990 pop. 4,748), Wise co., SW Va., 8 mi/12.9 km WSW of Norton, on Powell R. (at mouth of South Fork Powell R.) at its gap through the Cumberland Mts., near Ky. state line; 36°51′N 82°46′W. Elev. c.1,400 ft/427 m. RR junction; Mfg. (lumber, mining machinery, concrete; printing); agr. (tobacco; cattle); timber; bituminous coal mines. Mt. resort; Southwest Va. Mus. (founded 1935), with regional historical and cultural collections. Natural Tunnel State Park is 12 mi/19 km S. Mountain Empire Community Col. Parts of Jefferson Natl. Forest to NW, SE. Inc. 1888.

Big Stone Lake, reservoir, at Ortonville (Minn.), on Minn./S.Dak. state line, on Minnesota R.; c.25 mi/40 km long, 1 mi/1.6 km wide; 45°18′N 96°28′W. Located in the outlet channel of prehistoric L. Agassiz, it is the source of the Minnesota R., which exits lake on SE end through dam and crosses S Minn., and serves as a storage reservoir for the Minnesota Valley. Little Minnesota R. enters N end. Formed by Big Stone Dam. Big Stone Lake State Park (Minn.) on SE shore and Hartford Beach State Park (S.Dak.) on W shore.

Big Sunflower River, Miss.: see SUNFLOWER RIVER.

Big Sur (SUHR), village, Monterey co., W Calif., 25 mi/40 km S of Monterey, 2 mi/3.2 km NE from Pacific Ocean coast, and on Big Sur R., a short stream in Santa Lucia Range. Pfeiffer Big Sur State Park (843 acres/341 ha) to SE, with recreational facilities. Point Sur 8 mi/12.9 km NW (Andrew Molero State Park); Julia Pfeiffer Burns State Park to SE. Scenic Big Sur coastal drive (State Highway 1); Los Padres Natl. Forest to E and SE.

Big Thicket Preserve (□ 134 sq mi/347 sq km), SE Texas, N of Beaumont. Large number of plant and animal species in "biological crossroads" of N. Amer. Impenetrable woods, streams, marshes. Main Unit follows course of Neches R., from Steinhagen reservoir S to Beaumont, and part of Pine Isl. Bayou. Five smaller units are generally W of Main Unit. Big Thicket Mus. at Saratoga has logging and pioneer artifacts; Visitor Information Station 7 mi/11.3 km N of Kountze; nature and canoe trails. Authorized 1974.

Big Thompson River, 78 mi/126 km long, in Larimer co., N Colo.; rises at Continental Divide N of Longs Peak in Rocky Mt. Natl. Park; flows E, past Estes Park and Loveland, to South Platte R. 6 mi/9.7 km SE of Greeley. Receives Little Thompson R. 4 mi/6.4 km above its mouth. Receives water from Colorado R. (via ALVA B. ADAMS TUNNEL and temporary pipeline). Olympus Dam (60 ft/18 m high, 1,880 ft/573 m long; constructed 1947–1949 as unit in Colorado–Big Thompson project) is just E of Estes Park; forms small reservoir; hydroelectric power. Flash flood through Big Thompson Canyon, July 31, 1976, killed 139. Little Thomson R., c. 50 mi/80 km long; rises near Longs Peak, Rocky Mts., in NW Boulder co.; flows ENE past Berthound, joining Big Thompson R. at Milliken.

Big Timber, town (1990 pop. 1,557), ⊙ Sweet Grass co., S Mont., on Yellowstone R., at mouth of Boulder R., and 53 mi/85 km E of Bozeman; 45°50′N 109°57′W. Livestock-shipping point. Sheep, cattle, hogs; hay. Crazy Mts. to NW. Greycliff Prairie Dog Town State Park to SE; parts of Gallatin Natl. Forest to NW and S. Yellowstone River Trout Hatchery. Dude ranches nearby. Inc. 1902.

Big Timber Creek, c.20 mi/32 km long, SW N.J.; rises NE of Glassboro; flows generally NNW, forming part of Gloucester-Camden co. line, to Delaware R. at Westville. Lower 8 mi/12.9 km navigable.

Big Trout Lake, NW Ont., central Canada, in NW Patricia dist.; 28 mi/45 km long, 20 mi/32 km wide; elev. 770 ft/235 m; 53°45′N 90°W. Drains N into Severn R.

Big Tujunga Canyon; Big Tujunga Creek; Big Tujunga No. 1 Dam, Calif.: see TUJUNGA CREEK.

Big Tupper Lake, N.Y.: see TUPPER LAKE.

Big Valley, village (1991 pop. 303), S central Alta., W Canada, on Big Valley Creek, and 40 mi/64 km N of Drumheller; 52°02′N 112°45′W. Oil and gas; coal mining; mixed farming, wheat, barley, flax; cattle.

Big Water, village (1990 pop. 326), Kane co., S Utah, 16 mi/26 km NW of Page (Ariz.), near Wahweap Creek; elev. c.4,200 ft/1,280 m; 37°04′N 111°39′W. Cattle. Formerly known as Glen Canyon Dam City. Paria Canyon–Vermilion Cliffs Wilderness Area to S; L. Powell (Colorado R.) to E. Est. late 1950s with construction of Glen Canyon Dam; inc. 1983.

Big Wells, town (1990 pop. 756), Dimmit co., SW Texas, 17 mi/27 km SE of Crystal City, near the Nueces R.; 28°34′N 99°34′W. In irrigated vegetable-growing area. Natural gas and oil. Inc. 1933.

Big Wichita River, Texas: see WICHITA RIVER.

Big Wood River, c.120 mi/193 km long, Idaho; rises in Sawtooth Mts., S central Idaho, in NW Blaine co.; flows S, past Ketchum and Hailey, and through Magic Reservoir, then W to Snake R. 10 mi/16 km SW of Gooding, receives Little Wood R. at Gooding. Magic Dam (129 ft/39 m high, 700 ft/213 m long; completed 1907) is 19 mi/31 km S of Hailey; forms Magic Reservoir (11 mi/18 km long, 2 mi/3.2 km wide). Used for irrigation.

Area in square miles is shown by the symbol □ capital city or county seat by ⊙

Bigelow (BI-guh-lo), town (1990 pop. 32), Holt co., NW Mo., near Missouri R., 3 mi/5 km SW of Mound City; 40°06′N 95°17′W. Squaw Creek Natl. Wildlife Refuge and Big Lake State Park nearby.

Bigelow 1 (BI-guh-lo), village (1990 pop. 340), Perry co., central Ark., 27 mi/43 km NW of Little Rock, near Arkansas R., near mouth of Fourche La Fave R.; 35°00′N 92°37′W. **2** village (1990 pop. 232), Nobles co., SW Minn., on Iowa state line, 9 mi/14.5 km SW of Worthington; 43°30′N 95°41′W. Grain, corn, soybeans; livestock, poultry; dairying; mfg. (feeds). Ocheda L. to NE.

Bigelow Mountain (BI-guh-lo), (4,150 ft/1,265 m), on border bet. Franklin and Somerset cos., W Maine, c.35 mi/56 km NNW of Farmington.

Bigfork, town (1990 est. pop. 1,000), Flathead co., NW Mont., 17 mi/27 km SE of Kalispell, at NE of Flathead L., at mouth of Swan R.; lake mouth of Flathead R. to W. Logging; tourism; cherries, berries. Mfg. (wild berry preserves). Wayfarers Unit of Flathead Lake State Park to S; Flathead Natl. Forest to E.

Bigfork, village (1990 pop. 384), Itasca co., N Minn., 35 mi/56 km N of Grand Rapids, on Big Fork R., at mouth of River R.; 47°45′N 93°39′W. Timber, lumber; alfalfa; cattle. Scenic State Park and George Washington State Forest to E; Big Fork State Forest to W.

Biggar, town (1991 pop. 2,322), W Sask., W Canada, 50 mi/80 km SSE of North Battleford; 52°03′N 107°59′W. RR junction. Grain elevators; lumbering.

Biggers, village (1990 pop. 337), Randolph co., NE Ark., 11 mi/18 km NE of Pocahontas, on Current R.; 36°19′N 90°48′W. Mfg. (wooden components). Dave Donaldson–Black River Wildlife Management Area to SE.

Biggs, city (1990 pop. 1,581), Butte co., N central Calif., 20 mi/32 km N of Yuba City; 39°25′N 121°43′W. Ships prunes, peaches, olives, kiwi; almond, walnuts, nursery stock, rice. Feather R. to E.

Biggs Army Air Field, Texas: see EL PASO.

Biggsville, village (1990 pop. 349), Henderson co., W Ill., 7 mi/11.3 km SE of Oquawka; 40°51′N 90°51′W. In agr. area.

Bigheart, Okla.: see BARNSDALL.

Bighorn Basin, Wyo. and Mont.: see BIGHORN RIVER.

Bighorn Canyon National Recreation Area (☐ 188 sq mi/487 sq km), Big Horn and Carbon cos., S Mont., and Big Horn co., N Wyo. Yellowstone Reservoir formed by Yellowtail Dam, 42 mi/68 km SE of Billings (Mont.), and spectacular Bighorn Canyon, both on the Bighorn R. Authorized 1964.

Bighorn Lake, S Mont. and N Wyo., on Yellowstone R., in Bighorn Canyon Natl. Recreation Area, 40 mi/64 km SSE of Billings; c.40 mi/64 km long; 45°17′N 107°59′W. Max. capacity 1,428,000 acre-ft. Formed by Yellowtail Dam (arch construction; 494 ft/151 m high), built (1966) by the Bureau of Reclamation for flood control and recreation.

Bighorn Mountains, range of the Rocky Mts., mostly in N central Wyo., extends into S Mont., c.120 mi/193 km in length, located E of the Bighorn R. Cloud Peak (Wyo.), 13,167 ft/4,013 m, is the highest point. The glaciated mt. range contains Bighorn Natl. Forest, and includes Cloud Peak Wilderness Area. Also spelled Big Horn.

Bighorn River, 461 mi/742 km long, Wyo. and Mont.; formed in W central Wyo. by the confluence of the Wind and Popo Agie rivers at Riverton; flows N through Boysen Reservoir (Boysen Dam), past Thermopolis and Greybull, through Big Horn Lake Reservoir (Wyo.-Mont. state line), Yellowtail Dam in Mont., through Crow Indian Reservation and past Hardin (Mont.), joining the Yellowstone R. in S Mont. 30 mi/ 48 km NNE of Hardin. The Bighorn Basin, part of the Missouri R. basin project, has several dams that provide for flood control, irrigation, hydroelectricity, and recreation. Boysen and Yellowtail are the principal dams; Bighorn L. behind Yellowtail Dam is the nucleus of Bighorn Canyon Natl. Recreation Area. In 1807 a U.S. trading post was established at the mouth of the Bighorn. The battle bet. the forces of Col. George Custer and the Sioux took place (1876) near the junction of

the Bighorn and the Little Bighorn rivers. Also spelled Big Horn.

Biglerville (BIG-luhr-vil), borough (1990 pop. 993), Adams co., S Pa., 7 mi/11.3 km N of Gettysburg, near Conewago Creek; 39°55′N 77°15′W. Mfg. (machinery, paper prods., foods, wood prods.; commercial printing); limestone quarrying. Agr. (grain, soybeans, potatoes, apples, cherries; poultry, livestock; dairying). N terminus of Gettysburg RR, scenic RR. Natl. Apple Mus.

Bigsby Island, W Ont., central Canada, in S part of L. of the Woods, bet. Big Isl. and U.S. (Minn.) border, 50 mi/80 km S of Kenora; 7 mi/11 km long, 6 mi/10 km wide; 49°03′N 94°34′W.

Bijou, Calif.: see AL TAHOE.

Bijou Creek, c.45 mi/72 km long, NE central Colo.; formed by confluence of 2 headstreams, South and West Bijou creeks, which rise on border bet. El Paso and Elbert cos.; West Bijou flows NNE c.70 mi/113 km, South Bijou flows c.75 mi/121 km NE, then N past Deer Trail, joining West Bijou in Adams co.; larger creek flows NNE to South Platte R. 5 mi/8 km W of Fort Morgan. Flow is intermittent.

Bill Williams Mountain (9,265 ft/2,824 m), Coconino co., N central Ariz., 3 mi/4.8 km S of Williams, in Kaibab Natl. Forest. Williams Ski Area is here.

Bill Williams River, c.40 mi/64 km long, W Ariz.; formed by confluence of Big Sandy and Santa Maria rivers near S tip of Hualpai Mts.; flows W through Alamo Lake Reservoir to Havasu L. in Colorado R. on Calif. state line, just NE of Parker Dam. Forms boundary of La Paz (S) and Mohave (N) cos.

Billerica (bil-RI-kuh), town (☐ 26 sq mi/67 sq km; 1990 pop. 37,609), Middlesex co., NE Mass., on the Concord R.; 42°34′N 71°16′W. Important high-tech center. Mfg. includes computer hardware and software, precision instruments and machinery, wood and metal prods., and chemicals. The town's historical attractions include several 17th–19th-cent. homes and a Native Amer. site and burial ground dating back to 1,000 B.C. Includes village of Pinehurst (1990 pop. 6,614). Settled 1637, inc. 1655.

Billings, county (☐ 1,153 sq mi/2,986 sq km; 1990 pop. 1,108), W N.Dak.; ⊙ Medora; 47°02′N 103°22′W. Oil and agr. area watered by Little Missouri R. and headwaters of Green and Knife rivers. In N.Dak. Badlands and Little Missouri Natl. Grasslands; Theodore Roosevelt Natl. Park, S unit in center of co., Elkhorn Ranch unit in NW; Chateau de Mores Historic Site and Sully Creek State Primitive Park in W. Formed 1879; organized 1886.

Billings 1 city (1990 pop. 989), Christian co., SW Mo., in the Ozark Mts., 18 mi/29 km SW of Springfield; 37°03′N 93°33′W. Dairying; fruit; poultry. **2** city (1990 pop. 81,151), ⊙ Yellowstone co., S Mont., on the Yellowstone R., in a valley surrounded by low mt. ranges, 45°48′N 108°32′W. Mont.'s largest city. Medical, mfg., and trade center for the S Mont. and N Wyo. region. Mfg. (printing and publishing; paper and wood prods.; dairy prods., processed foods, computer equip., apparel, fabricated steel, machinery, petroleum prods.). Wheat, sugar beets, cattle, sheep, and wool are traded. Tourism has become important to the city's economy. Founded in 1882 by the Minn. and Mont. Improvement Co., Billings quickly became an important shipping point and fur-trading center. Inc. as a city 1885, largest city in Mont. Seat of Rocky Mt. Col. and Mont. State Univ. at Billings. Moss Mansion, the Peter Yegen Jr. Mus., Western Heritage Center, Yellowstone Art Center, ZooMontana are here. Billings-Logan Intl. Airport to N. Pryor Mts. to S, Bull Mt. to N. Lake Elmo State Park to N; Pictograph State Park to E; Crow Indian Reservation to SE.

Billings, town (1990 pop. 555), Noble co., N Okla., 18 mi/ 29 km NNW of Perry, on Red Rock Creek; 36°31′N 97°26′W. In grain and livestock area; mfg. (collectible dolls, industrial machinery, powdered metal parts). Oil and gas wells.

Billingsley, town (1990 pop. 150), Autauga co., central Ala., 20 mi/32 km NW of Prattville. Lumber.

Billy Chinook, Lake (shuh-NUK), reservoir, Jefferson co., N central Oregon, on Deschutes R., 7 mi/11.3 km WSW of Madras; c.16 mi/26 km long; 44°37′N 122°17′W. Max. capacity 535,000 acre-ft. Metolius R. forms W arm (13 mi/21 km long), Crooked R. forms S arm (6 mi/9.7 km long). Formed by Round Butte Dam (430 ft/131 m high), built (1964) by Portland General Electric Co. for power generation. Warm Springs Indian Reservation to NW.

Biloxi (bi-LUHK-see), city (1990 pop. 46,319), ⊙ Harrison co. (seat shared with Gulfport), SE Miss., 54 mi/ 87 km WSW of Mobile (Ala.), 77 mi/124 km ENE of New Orleans, 12 mi/19 km E of Gulfport, on a small peninsula bet. Biloxi Bay and Mississippi Sound, arm of the Gulf of Mexico; 30°25′N 88°55′W. Biloxi R. enters bay from NW. Highway and RR bridges cross entrance of Biloxi Bay to Ocean Springs (E); highway bridge crosses back bay to D'Iberville (N). The warm, coastal climate has made Biloxi a popular resort dating back to before the Civil War. Mfg. (fishing fleet and shrimp trawls; seafood, fish, and shrimp processing; bakery prods., marble prods.; printing and publishing). The 1st Eur. settlement in the lower Mississippi valley was est. 1699 across the bay at Old Biloxi (now Ocean Springs) by the French. New Biloxi was founded in 1719 and was the capital of the Fr. colony of Louisiana until 1722, when New Orleans replaced it. Scene of civil rights unrest and violence in the 1960s. In the city are Keesler Air Force Base, a U.S. coast guard air station, and a Veterans Administration medical center. Gulfport-Biloxi Regional Airport to W, at Gulfport. Seat of Miss. Gulf Coast Community Col.-Jefferson Davis Campus; has a symphony, and a theater group. In W is "Beauvoir" (built 1852–1854), the last home of Jefferson Davis; the Biloxi Light House (built 1848); Ft. Maurepas (1699) to NE; on coast, passenger ferry to Ship Isl., part of Gulf Isls. Natl. Seashore, large gambling casino complex on gulf; Maritime and Seafood Industry Mus.; Gulf Coast Coliseum; Arts and Cultural Center. De Soto Natl. Forest to N, Deer Isl. to SE. Inc. as a town 1838, as a city 1896.

Biloxi Bay (bi-LUHK-see), S Miss., arm of Miss. Sound, Gulf of Mexico, separated from gulf by narrow peninsula occupied by city of Biloxi; c.17 mi/27 km long, 1 mi/1.6 km–3 mi/4.8 km wide. Bridged bet. Biloxi and Ocean Springs (at entrance). Receives Biloxi R. (45 mi/ 72 km long) from NW, through Big L. and Back Bay of Biloxi; also Tchoutacabouffa R. from NE, Bernard Bayou from W.

Biltmore Forest, uninc. town (1990 pop. 1,327), Buncombe co., W N.C., residential suburb 3 mi/4.8 km S of Asheville; 35°31′N 82°32′W. Vanderbilt country estate (☐ 13 sq mi/34 sq km) here. Biltmore Homespun Shops (est. 1901 by Mrs. Vanderbilt) keep alive the arts of dyeing, spinning, and hand-weaving wool into cloth. Biltmore Mansion and Estate on French Bound R. to W.

Bim, uninc. village (1990 pop. 400), Boone co., W central W.Va., 12 mi/19 km SE of Madison.

Biminis, island group in the Straits of Florida (1990 pop. 1,639), forming the NW sect. of the Bahamas. Includes North and South Bimini and surrounding cays. Exceptionally good fishing attracts many tourists. According to legend, the Biminis are the location of the fountain of youth sought by Juan Ponce de León.

Binford, village (1990 pop. 233), Griggs co., E central N.Dak., 13 mi/21 km NW of Cooperstown; 47°33′N 98°20′W. RR terminus. Red Willow L. to N.

Bingen (BEENG-gen), village (1990 pop. 645), Klickitat co., S Wash., 3 mi/4.8 km NE of Hood R. (Oregon), across Columbia R. (Bonneville Reservoir), 59 mi/ 95 km E of Vancouver; 45°43′N 121°28′W. Sawmills; grapes, wheat; dairying; cattle; timber. Bridge.

Binger (BING-guhr), village (1990 pop. 724), in Caddo co., W central Okla., 18 mi/29 km NNW of Anadarko, on Sugar Creek; 35°18′N 98°20′W. In agr. area (wheat, cotton, corn, peanuts); oil wells; cotton ginning, peanut processing.

Bingham, county (☐ 2,120 sq mi/5,491 sq km; 1990 pop. 37,583), SE Idaho; ⊙ Blackfoot; 43°13′N 112°24′W. Irrigated agr. area drained by Snake and Blackfoot rivers and Amer. Falls Reservoir. Potatoes, sugar beets; barley, wheat, oats; alfalfa; sheep, cattle; dairying. Part of Snake R. Plain in W and Fort Hall Indian Reservation in S. Amer. Falls Reservoir on S boundary. Part of Idaho Natl. Engineering Laboratory (U.S. Dept. of Energy) in NW. Formed 1885.

Bingham (BING-guhm), town (1990 pop. 1,230), Somerset co., central Maine, on the Kennebec R., 22 mi/35 km NNW of Skowhegan; 45°02′N 69°49′W. In resort area; wood prods. Wyman Dam (for hydroelectric power) impounds Wyman L. here. Settled 1780, inc. 1812.

Bingham 1 village (1990 pop. 98), Fayette co., S central Ill., 11 mi/18 km NNW of Vandalia; 39°06′N 89°12′W. In agr. area. **2** village, Dillon co., NE S.C., 10 mi/16 km W of Dillon. Agr. includes livestock; cotton, soybeans.

Bingham Canyon or **Bingham**, uninc. village, Salt Lake co., N central Utah, 22 mi/35 km SW of Salt Lake City, in a canyon of the Oquirrh Mts.; elev. 6,400 ft/1,951 m. At first (1848) a farm of the Mormons Thomas and Sanford Bingham, it became (1860s) a booming mining town, dealing in gold, then silver and lead, and in the 20th cent., copper. Tourism; gold mining. The world's largest open-pit mine, Kennecott Corp. Bingham Mine, is located in nearby Upper Bingham; major tourist attraction. The town's single street, squeezed into a mt. gulch, is 6 mi/9.7 km long.

Bingham Farms (BING-guhm), village (1990 pop. 1,001), Oakland Co., SE Mich., residential suburb 16 mi/26 km NW of downtown Detroit, 9 mi/14.5 km S of Pontiac; 42°30′N 83°16′W. Mfg. (advertising displays, transportation equip.).

Bingham Lake, village (1990 pop. 155), Cottonwood co., SW Minn., 4 mi/6.4 km NW of Windom, at S end of Bingham L.; 43°54′N 95°02′W. Livestock; grain, soybeans; mfg. (medical equip.). Small lakes in area.

Binghamton, industrial city (□ 10 sq mi/26 sq km; 1990 pop. 53,008), ⊙ Broome co., S central N.Y., at the confluence of the Chenango and the Susquehanna rivers; 42°06′N 75°54′W. Largest of the Triple Cities (Binghamton, Endicott, and Johnson City), formerly famous for shoes. Diverse industries include marking devices, foods, fabricated metal prods., machinery, aerospace control systems, electronic equip., photographic materials, and computers; precision machining. Grew mainly after the Chenango Canal connected it with Utica in 1837. The 1st RR service began in 1869. Broome Co. Community Col. and the State Univ. of N.Y. at Binghamton are in the vicinity. The city's Roberson Center and Mus. Complex has a planetarium, theater, and holdings in art, science, and history. Chenango Valley State Park lies 9 mi/14.5 km to the NE. Settled 1787, inc. as a city 1867.

Binscarth, village (1991 pop. 469), W Man., central Canada, on Silver Creek, 65 mi/105 km NW of Brandon; 50°37′N 101°17′W. Wheat.

Biola, uninc. village, Fresno co., central Calif., 7 mi/11.3 km NW of Fresno, on San Joaquin R. Irrigated agr.; dairying.

Biorka (bee-YOR-kah), village, SW Alaska, on Sedanka Isl. (10 mi/16 km long, 4 mi/6.4 km wide), Aleutian Isls., 15 mi/24 km E of Unalaska; 53°50′N 166°13′W.

Birch Bay, town (1990 pop. 2,656), Whatcom co., NW Wash., on Birch arm of Strait of Georgia; 48°55′N 122°45′W. Dairying; vegetables, stawberries, blueberries, flowers; fish, crabs, prawns, oysters. Petroleum tank farms to S. Birch Bay State Park to SW.

Birch Hills, town (1991 pop. 939), central Sask., W Canada, 20 mi/32 km SE of Prince Albert; 52°59′N 105°26′W. Flour milling.

Birch Island, resort island, Cumberland co., SW Maine, in Casco Bay, just W of Harpswell; c.1.5 mi/2.4 km long.

Birch Lake (□ 9 sq mi/23.3 sq km), St. Louis and Lake cos., NE Minn., 12 mi/19 km S of Ely, in Superior Natl. Forest and Bear Isl. State Forest; 15 mi/24 km long, 1 mi/1.6 km wide; 47°44′N 92°37′W. Fishing resorts. Formed by dam on South Fork Kawishiwi R. (river splits and returns to itself in area NE of lake), enters NE end of lake from NE (forms 4 mi/6.4 km NE arm),

exits N through dam from same end. Lake also receives small Birch R. from W and Dunka R. from S.

Birch Mountains, NE Alta., W Canada, W of Athabaska R., near S edge of Wood Buffalo Natl. Park; extend c.150 mi/241 km NE-SW; rise to 2,689 ft/820 m at 57°23′N 112°39′W.

Birch Run, village (1990 pop. 992), Saginaw co., E central Mich., 14 mi/23 km SSE of Saginaw; 43°15′N 83°47′W. In agr. area; steel fabricating.

Birch Tree, city (1990 pop. 599), Shannon co., S Mo., in the Ozark Mts., 27 mi/43 km NE of West Plains. Sawmills; mfg. (shoes, lumber, flooring). Mark Twain Natl. Forest to E and S.

Birchwood, hamlet (1990 pop. 443), Washburn co., NW Wis., 13 mi/21 km NE of town of Rice Lake; 45°39′N 91°32′W. In lake resort area; wood prods., canoes, lumber. On Tuscobia State Trail, on short sect. of Red Cedar R., bet. L. Chetak (NE) and Red Cedar L. (SW).

Birchwood Park, town (1990 pop. 2,250), New Castle co., N Del., residential suburb 8 mi/12.9 km SW of downtown Wilmington, 3 mi/4.8 km E of Newark; 39°41′N 75°41′W.

Birchwood Village, village (1990 pop. 1,042), Washington co., E Minn., and 9 mi/14.5 km NE of downtown St. Paul, on S shore of White Bear L.; 45°03′N 92°58′W.

Bird, Cape, S extremity of Somerset Isl., S Franklin dist., N.W.T., N Canada; 72°00′N 95°10′W.

Bird City, village (1990 pop. 467), Cheyenne co., extreme NW Kansas, 30 mi/48 km NNE of Goodland; 39°45′N 101°31′W. In agr. area (grain; cattle).

Bird Creek, river, c.100 mi/161 km long, in NE Okla.; rises in Osage co.; flows SE, past Pawhuska, Barnsdall, Avant, Skiatook, and N part of Tulsa to Verdigris R. just N of Catoosa.

Bird in Hand, uninc. village, Lancaster co., SE Pa., 7 mi/11.3 km E of Lancaster, near Mill Creek, in Pa. Dutch region; 40°02′N 76°10′W. Mfg. includes metal fabricating, diversified light mfg. Agr. includes dairying; livestock, poultry; grain. Tourism. Bird in Hand Farmers Market and Weavertown One Room School are here.

Bird Island, town (1990 pop. 1,326), Renville co., S central Minn., 5 mi/8 km E of Olivia; 44°45′N 94°53′W. Agr. area; mfg. (fertilizers).

Bird Island, Hawaii: see NIHOA.

Bird of Paradise Island, Trinidad and Tobago: see LITTLE TOBAGO ISLAND.

Bird Rocks, islet in the Gulf of St. Lawrence, E Que., E Canada, NE of the Magdalen Isls.; 47°50′N 61°09′W. Lighthouse.

Birds, village (1990 pop. 160), Lawrence co., SE Ill., 8 mi/12.9 km N of Lawrenceville; 38°50′N 87°40′W. In agr. area.

Birdsboro (BUHRDS-buhr-o), borough (1990 pop. 4,222), Berks co., SE Pa., 8 mi/12.9 km SE of Reading, on Schuylkill R., at mouth of Hay Creek; 40°15′N 75°48′W. Mfg. (paper prods., feeds, bldg. materials, aluminum sand castings, RR track ballast, nylon resins and adhesives; apparel). Agr. area (grain, apples, potatoes, soybeans; livestock, poultry; dairying). HOPEWELL FURNACE NATIONAL HISTORIC SITE is here. Daniel Boone Homestead, 18th-cent. farmhouse built on foundation of Daniel Boone's birthplace. French Creek State Park to SE. Settled 1740, inc. 1872.

Birdseye, town (1990 pop. 472), Dubois co., SW Ind., 14 mi/23 km ESE of Jasper; 38°19′N 86°42′W. In agr. area. Near Ferdinand State Forest. Laid out 1880.

Birdwood, Mount (10,160 ft/3,097 m), on Alta.-B.C. border, W Canada, in Rocky Mts., near S edge of Banff Natl. Park, 30 mi/48 km SSE of Banff; 50°47′N 115°21′W.

Birmingham 1 (BUHR-ming-ham), city (1990 pop. 265,968), ⊙ Jefferson co., N central Ala., in the Jones Valley, near the S end of the Appalachian system. Largest city in the state and once the leading iron and steel center in the South. Industry has diversified to include textiles, chemicals, automotive parts, and aircraft production. Health-care services are also important. Commerce, banking, insurance, research, and govt. add to

the economy. Founded and inc. 1871, Birmingham developed rapidly with the expansion of the RR. The city, connected with the Gulf of Mexico by canal, became a port of entry and an important trade and communications center. Educational institutions in the city include the expansive Univ. of Ala. at Birmingham, Birmingham-Southern Col., Miles Col., Samford Univ., Jefferson State Community Col., and Lawson State Community Col. Birmingham supports a football and track stadium, botanical and Jap. gardens, a symphony, ballet group, theater, planetarium, sports hall of fame, horse and dog racing track, zoo, and an art mus.; a festival of arts is held annually. Overlooking the city, on nearby Red Mt., is a huge iron statue of Vulcan, the mythical god of the forge. Inc. 1871. **2** city (1990 pop. 19,997), Oakland co., SE Mich., suburb 21 mi/34 km NW of downtown Detroit, and 7 mi/11.3 km SE of Pontiac, on the R. Rouge; 42°32′N 83°13′W. Largely residential. Mfg. (publishing; blower housings, industrial lumber, gauges and tools, paper prods.). Oakland Troy Airport to E. Settled 1819, inc. as a village 1864, as a city 1933.

Birmingham 1 town (1990 pop. 386), Van Buren co., SE Iowa, 10 mi/16 km N of Keosauqua; 40°52′N 91°57′W. In agr. area. **2** town (1990 pop. 222), Clay co., W Mo., suburb 8 mi/13 km NE of downtown Kansas City; 39°10′N 94°27′W.

Birmingham (BUHR-ming-ham), borough (1990 pop. 109), Huntingdon co., central Pa., 2 mi/3.2 km SE of Tyrone, on Little Juniata R.; 40°38′N 78°12′W. Agr. (corn, hay; dairying). Rothrock State Forest to SE.

Birnamwood, village (1990 pop. 693), Shawano co., E central Wis., 21 mi/34 km E of Wausau; 44°55′N 89°12′W. Lumber.

Biron (BEI-ruhn), village (1990 pop. 794), Wood co., central Wis., on Wisconsin R., 3 mi/4.8 km NE of Wisconsin Rapids; 44°25′N 89°45′W. Cranberries; paper, pulp, and sulfite milling.

Birta (BUHRT-uh), village, Yell co., W central Ark., 18 mi/29 km S of Russellville. Petit Jean Wildlife Management Area to N.

Birtle, town (1991 pop. 802), SW Man., Canada, on Birdtail R., 50 mi/80 km NW of Brandon; 50°26′N 101°03′W. Mixed farming. Training school for Native peoples.

Bisbee, city (1990 pop. 6,288), ⊙ Cochise co., SE Ariz., 20 mi/32 km ESE of Sierra Vista, 7 mi/11.3 km N of the Mex. border; elev. 5,490 ft/1,673 m; 31°23′N 109°55′W. Formerly a great copper-producing center, but mining has declined significantly. Mfg. (printing, publishing; electronic resistors, window blinds). After the rich copper deposits were discovered (c.1876), the city was built in 2 steep-sided canyons, Mule Pass Gulch and Brewery Gulch. Inc. 1900. Nearby is Coronado Natl. Memorial to SW, which commemorates the visit (1540) of Francisco Coronado. Historic town of Tombstone 20 mi/32 km NNW; Lavender Pit (open-pit copper mine) and Copper Queen underground mine to SE and NW, tourist attraction; several ghost towns in area.

Bisbee (BIZ-bee), village (1990 pop. 227), Towner co., N.Dak., 12 mi/19 km NW of Cando; 48°37′N 99°22′W. RR terminus.

Biscay (BIS-kee), village (1990 pop. 113), McLeod co., S central Minn., 6 mi/9.7 km SE of Hutchinson, on South Fork Crow R.; 44°49′N 94°16′W. Dairying; livestock; grain.

Biscayne Bay (biss-KAIN), c.40 mi/60 km long, shallow inlet of the Atlantic Ocean, SE Fla. Main body of water in Dade Co., surrounded by many cities and suburbs, including the port of Miami. Crossed by several causeways to Miami Beach and 1 to Key Biscayne. Famous resort center to NE in Miami Beach. Tourism is the economic mainstay. Biscayne Natl. Park, originally Biscayne Natl. Monument (est. 1968), is at the S end.

Biscayne National Park (biss-KAIN), aquatic park (□ 271 sq mi/702 sq km) encompassing 25 isls., SE Fla. Example of a living coral reef; includes part of Biscayne Bay. Authorized 1968; enlarged in 1980.

Biscayne Park (biss-KAIN), town (1990 pop. 3,068),

Dade co., SE Fla., 5 mi/8 km N of Miami; 25°52′N 80°10′W. Inc. 1932.

Biscoe, town (1990 pop. 1,484), Montgomery co., central N.C., 24 mi/39 km S of Asheboro; 35°21′N 79°46′W. Mfg. (apparel, textiles, fabricated metal prods., furniture frames; foam fabrication). Uwharris Natl. Forest to SW.

Biscoe (BIS-ko), village (1990 pop. 484), Prairie co., E central Ark., 12 mi/19 km WSW of Brinkley.

Bishop 1 town (1990 pop. 3,475), Inyo co., E Calif., 83 mi/134 km ENE of Fresno, in Owens Valley, at E base of the Sierra Nevada, c.50 mi/80 km SE of Mono L.; elev. 4,147 ft/1,264 m; 37°22′N 118°24′W. Mfg. (plastics, treated minerals; printing and publishing; tungsten mining). Resort in stock-raising and mining region (tungsten, gold, silver). Bishop Airport to E. Hq. of Inyo Natl. Forest. In Bishop Creek Canyon (SW) is a power plant. Paiute Indian reservation nearby. Settled 1861, inc. 1903. Laws RR Mus. and Historical Site. Bishop Indian Reservation. Kings Canyon Natl. Park to SW; parts of Inyo Natl. Forest to E and W; Inyo Mts to E, Sierra Nevada to W. **2** town (1990 pop. 158), Oconee co., NE central Ga., 10 mi/16 km SSW of Athens; 33°49′N 83°26′W. **3** town (1990 pop. 3,337), Nueces co., S Texas, 29 mi/47 km SW of Corpus Christi, and 8 mi/12.9 km NE of Kingsville; 27°34′N 97°47′W. Trade, processing center in oil, cotton area; grain, sorghum; large plant nearby produces chemicals from natural gas; mfg. (industrial chemicals and plastics, natural-gas processing).

Bishop Hill, village (1990 pop. 131), Henry co., NW Ill., 8 mi/12.9 km SSE of Cambridge; 41°12′N 90°07′W. In agr. and bituminous-coal area. Founded 1846 as a religious communal venture by Swed. immigrants led by Erik Janson, who is buried here. Restored blds. part of Bishop Hill State Historic Site.

Bishopric, village, S Sask., W Canada, on Johnstone L., SE end of Old Wives L., 28 mi/45 km SSW of Moose Jaw. Sodium-sulfate production.

Bishop's Falls, town (1991 pop. 4,232), central N.F., E Canada, on Exploits R., 8 mi/13 km NE of Grand Falls; 49°01′N 55°31′W. Pulp milling and lumbering center. Pulp is pumped to Grand Falls paper mills.

Bishops Head, fishing village, Dorchester co., E Md., on the Eastern Shore, 22 mi/35 km S of Cambridge, on Honga R.

Bishopville, town (1990 pop. 3,560), ⊙ Lee co., NE central S.C., 20 mi/32 km NNE of Sumter; 34°13′N 80°15′W. Mfg. includes beverages and beverage containers, textiles, apparel; fabric finishing. Agr. includes timber, cotton, grains, peanuts, soybeans. Lee State Park is E, on Lynches R. State penitentiary nearby.

Biskotasi Lake (BI sko-ta-see), SE central Ont., Canada, 75 mi/121 km NW of Sudbury; drained S by Spanish R. Lake is 27 mi/43 km long and 2 mi/3 km wide.

Bismarck 1 (BIS-mahrk), city (1990 pop. 1,579), St. Francois co., E Mo., in the St. Francois Mts., 8 mi/13 km SE of Park Hills; 37°46′N 90°37′W. Agr., cattle; mfg. (machinery); lumber prods.; former important iron and lead mining. RR junction. Laid out 1868. **2** city (1990 pop. 49,256), ⊙ N.Dak. and Burleigh co., S central N.Dak., on the Missouri R.; 46°48′N 100°46′W. RR junction. A trade and distribution point for a large spring wheat, livestock, and dairy region. Mfg. (construction materials, printing and publishing, beverages, wood prods., fabricated metal prods., steel fabrication, furniture). Bismarck has grown to become a business and finance center, as well as the principal area for development of the oil reserves in nearby Williston Basin. Lewis and Clark camped nearby 1804–1805. Menoken Historic Site to E. L. Oahe Reservoir 15 mi/24 km SE. With the beginning of the river traffic in the 1830s, a steamboat port called the "Crossing on the Missouri" emerged here. In 1872, Camp Greeley (later Camp Hancock) was erected to protect those who were building the Northern Pacific RR. When the RR reached the fort the next year, a town was laid out; it was subsequently named Bismarck (for Germany's chancellor) in the hope of attracting Ger. investment in the RR. Bismarck boomed as a river port and RR center and as a supply point for the Black Hills gold mines (1874). It became the territorial capital in 1883. Of interest are the state capitol (1932), a skyscraper; the state historical mus.; Camp Hancock mus.; United Tribes Education Center; and the Heritage Center. Univ. of Mary (1959) to S and Bismarck State Col. (1939, 2 yr.) are here. Fort Lincoln State Park to SW, as is the state penitentiary. Inc. 1873.

Bison 1 (BEI-suhn), village (1990 pop. 252), Rush co., central Kansas, 6 mi/9.7 km E of La Crosse; 38°31′N 99°12′W. In wheat and cattle area. **2** village (1990 pop. 451), ⊙ Perkins co., NW S.Dak., 110 mi/177 km NNE of Rapid City. Grain; cattle; lignite mines. Grand R. Natl. Grassland to N; Llewellyn John's Memorial and Shadehill State Rec. Areas to NE.

Bison Peak (12,431 ft/3,789 m.), in Tarryall Mts., in E Park co., central Colo., c.40 mi/64 km SSW of Denver.

Bisonó (bee-so-NO), town (1993 pop. 21,894), 14 mi/22 km NW of Santiago de los Caballeros, Santiago prov., N Dominican Republic; 19°34′N 70°52′W. Market town in rice-producing region.

Bistineau, Lake (BIS-tin-o), reservoir, ½ in Webster parish and ½ on Bienville-Bossier parish border, NW La., on Bayou Dorcheat, c.20 mi/32 km SE of Shreveport; c.20 mi/32 km long; 32°20′N 93°25′W. Drains S through Loggy Bayou to Red R. Three state parks and reserves nearby.

Bithlo, town (□ 10 sq mi/26 sq km; 1990 pop. 4,834), Orange co., central Fla., 17 mi/27 km E of Orlando; 28°34′N 81°06′W. Derived from Native Amer. word for "canoe."

Bitter Creek, c.80 mi/129 km long, SW Wyo.; rises in Rocky Mts. in SE Sweetwater co.; flows NW and W, past Rock Springs, to Green R. (Flaming Gorge Reservoir) near Green River town.

Bitter Lake, lake, Day co., NE S.Dak., 10 mi/16 km ESE of Webster; 4 mi/6.4 km long, 2 mi/3.2 km wide.

Bittern Lake, village (1991 pop. 161), central Alta., W Canada, on S end of Bittern L. (8 mi/13 km long, 5 mi/8 km wide), 10 mi/16 km W of Camrose; 53°00′N 113°03′W. Coal mining; oil and gas; wheat; barley, cattle.

Bitterroot Range, part of the Rocky Mts., forms most of Idaho-Mont. state line; extends from Snake R. Plain in S NNW to L. Pend Oreille. S part, N to Lost Trail Pass (7,014 ft/2,138 m), forms Continental Divide and is also called Beaverhead Mts. N part of the range forms border bet. Pacific (W) and Mountain (E) time zones. The main range, running NW-SE, includes Trapper Peak (10,157 ft/3,096 m). Mt. Ajax, Idaho (10,900 ft/3,322 m), in an E-running spur to the S, is the highest peak. Salmon and Clearwater drainage basins to W, Missouri and Clarks Fork drainage basins to E. Discovered in the 1804–1805 expedition of Lewis and Clark, the rugged mt. range has long been one of the most impenetrable in the U.S.; except for its foothills, it remains almost completely unexploited.

Bitterroot River, c.97 mi/156 km long, SW Mont.; rises in S Ravalli co.; flows N past Hamilton to join the Clark Fork R. 5 mi/8 km W of Missoula. A R.C. mission was built in the river valley in 1841, and the missionaries are credited with establishing farming in the area. The **Bitter Root project** irrigates c.27 sq mi/70 sq km. The W fork of the Bitterroot R, rises in far S Ravalli co., surrounded on 3 sides by Idaho state line and crest of Bitterroot Range, flows N through Painted Rocks L. The E fork of the Bitterroot R. rises at Continental Divide, SE Ravalli co., and flows W, both forks c.40 mi/64 km long.

Bivalve 1 (bei-VALV), village, Wicomico co., SE Md., 17 mi/27 km WSW of Salisbury, on Nanticoke R. Fishing, oystering; muskrat trapping. Known as Waltersville until 1877, when it was renamed in honor of the oyster with the opening of a new post office by J. E. Willing, the postmaster. The Bivalve Oyster Packing Co. had a shucking house here. Old expressions of speech of the original settlers—having a "slip-hitch" on the tongue when affected by whiskey, for example—are still heard here. **2** village, Cumberland co., S N.J., on Maurice R., near Delaware Bay, 17 mi/27 km SE of Bridgeton. Once a major port for oystering region.

Biwabik (bi-WAW-bik), town (1990 pop. 1,097), St. Louis co., NE Minn., 7 mi/11.3 km E of Virginia, in Mesabi Iron Range, near St. Louis R.; 47°31′N 92°20′W. Iron mines. Part of Superior Natl. Forest to N; Giant Ridge Ski Area to NE; numerous small lakes in region, including Wynne L. to NE.

Bixby, city (1990 pop. 9,502), Tulsa co., NE Okla., on Arkansas R., suburb 16 mi/26 km SSE of downtown Tulsa; 35°56′N 95°52′W. In agr. area (soybeans, grain; livestock); mfg. (fabricated metal prods., tranportation equip., consumer goods; publishing and printing); oil wells. Founded 1893, inc. 1907.

Bizard, Ile (bee-ZAHR, EEL), island, S Que., E Canada, in L. of the Two Mountains, just W of Montreal Isl.; 4 mi/6 km long, 3 mi/5 km wide; 45°29′N 73°54′W.

Black, town (1990 pop. 174), Geneva co., SE Ala., 7 mi/11.3 km E of Geneva, near Fla. state line.

Black, native village, W Alaska, on Bering Sea, 25 mi/40 km SW of Yukon R. mouth and delta; 62°20′N 165°19′W.

Black Bay, inlet of L. Superior, W central Ont., central Canada, 24 mi/39 km E of Port Arthur, adjoining Thunder Bay; 40 mi/64 km long, 11 mi/18 km wide. Receives Black Sturgeon R.

Black Bayou 1 (BEI-yo) or **Bayou Black**, SE La., waterway extending c.45 mi/72 km generally W from vicinity of Houma, past Houma, and through marshy coastal region, to Atchafalya R. near Morgan City. Partly followed by Intracoastal Waterway. **2** c.70 mi/113 km long, NE Texas and NW La.; rises in Cass co., Texas, S of L. Texarkana and N of Atlanta; flows SSE past Atlanta into Caddo parish, La., past Rodessa, into and through E end of Caddo L. reservoir, to Red R. 6 mi/10 km N of Shreveport; 32°42′N 93°54′W.

Black Bear Creek, c.100 mi/161 km long, N Okla.; rises E of Enid, in Garfield co.; flows E, through Noble and Pawnee cos., past town of Pawnee, to Arkansas R. c.40 mi/64 km NW of Tulsa.

Black Belt, term applied to several areas of Miss. and Ala., the heart of the Old South, which are characterized by black soil and excellent cotton-growing conditions. The Black Belt area was historically important as the nation's main cotton producer in the mid-1800s. Soil depletion, erosion, the boll weevil, and economic conditions combined to eliminate the region's lead as a cotton producer (W Texas and Calif. are now major producers). Livestock, poultry; peanuts and soybeans have become important crops in area.

Black Bottom, village, Harlan co., SE Ky., ENE of Harlan, near Louellen and Closplint, on Clover Fork R. Bituminous coal.

Black Butte, summit (7,448 ft/2,270 m) of the Coast Ranges, NW Glenn co., N central Calif., 35 mi/56 km W of Orland, in Mendocino Natl. Forest. Black Butte L. reservoir 8 mi/12.9 km W of Orland.

Black Butte, Mont.: see GRAVELLY RANGE.

Black Butte Reservoir, Calif.: see STONY CREEK.

Black Canyon, gorge cut by Colorado R. bet. Mohave co., NW Ariz. and Clark co., SE Nev.; extends 21 mi/34 km S from Hoover Dam, in Lake Mead Natl. Recreation Area.

Black Canyon City, uninc. town (1990 pop. 1,811), Yavapai co., central Ariz., 44 mi/71 km N of Phoenix, on Aqua Fria R., at mouth of Turkey Creek. Cattle; alfalfa, wheat. In area are Tonto (E) and Prescott (NW) natl. forests.

Black Canyon Dam, Gem co., SW Idaho, on Payette R., 5 mi/8 km NE of Emmett. Concrete gravity dam (c.180 ft/55 m high, over 1,000 ft/305 m long) completed 1924. Unit in Payette div. of Boise irrigation project. Power plant supplies electricity to Minidoka and Owyhee projects.

Black Canyon of the Gunnison National Monument (□ 32 sq mi/83 sq km), Montrose co., W Colo. Deep, narrow canyon of the Gunnison R., named for its dark-colored walls, which are always in shadow. The natl. monument includes 12 mi/19 km of the deepest sect. of the gorge. Main entrance from S, from Montrose; N entrance from Crawford, roads not connected. Wilderness designation, 1976. Authorized 1933.

Cross references are shown in SMALL CAPITALS. The pronunciation key is on page xv. The dates of population figures are on page xii.

Black, Cape, NE extremity of Ellesmere Isl., NE Franklin dist., N.W.T., N Canada, on Lincoln Sea of the Arctic Ocean, at N entrance of Robeson Channel; 82°23′N 61°00′W. Peary landed a supply cache here, 1908.

Black Creek, town (1990 pop. 1,152), Outagamie co., E Wis., 15 mi/24 km N of Appleton; 44°28′N 88°27′W. RR junction. Dairying; farming; cheese; livestock; mfg. (concrete, shipping containers).

Black Creek, village (1990 pop. 669), Wilson co., E central N.C., 7 mi/11.3 km S of Wilson; 35°38′N 77°55′W. Tobacco, grain, peanuts, cotton, sweet potatoes; chickens, cattle, hogs. Mfg. (boats).

Black Creek 1 c.120 mi/193 km long, in S Miss.; rises in S Jefferson Davis co., 25 mi/40 km WNW of Hattiesburg; flows SE through De Soto Natl. Forest, to Pascagoula R. in N Jackson co., 20 mi/32 km NNW of Pascagoula. **2** c.80 mi/129 km long, in NE S.C.; rises in Western Chesterfield co. near N.C. state line; flows generally S through L. Robinson reservoir, then SE, past Hartsville, to Pee Dee R. 11 mi/18 km NE of Florence.

Black Diamond, town (1991 pop. 1,623), S Alta., W Canada, at foot of Rocky Mts., on Sheep R., 25 mi/40 km SSW of Calgary, on E edge of Turner Valley oil field; 50°42′N 114°14′W. Coal mining; wheat, flax; cattle. Ski resort.

Black Diamond, town (1990 pop. 1,422), King co., W central Wash., 30 mi/48 km SE of Seattle, near Green R.; 47°19′N 122°01′W. RR terminus. Logging; coal mining. Kanaskat-Palmer and Nolte state parks to E; Howard Hanson Dam and Reservoir to E.

Black Dome, peak (3,990 ft/1,216 m) of the Catskill Mts., in Greene co., SE N.Y., 13 mi/21 km WNW of Catskill; 42°16′N 74°08′W.

Black Eagle, town (1990 pop. 850), Cascade co., W central Mont., suburb 1 mi/1.6 km N, and across Missouri R. from, downtown Great Falls. Black Eagle Dam to SE on Missouri R. Electrolytic refining of copper and zinc.

Black Earth, town (1990 pop. 1,248), Dane co., S Wis., 19 mi/31 km W of Madison; 43°08′N 89°45′W. In agr. area; cheesemaking.

Black Hawk, county (□ 571 sq mi/1,479 sq km; 1990 pop. 123,798), E central Iowa; ⊙ Waterloo; 42°28′N 92°18′W. Prairie agr. area (hogs, cattle, poultry; corn, oats, soybeans) drained by Cedar R.; limestone quarries, sand pits. Mfg. at Waterloo and Cedar Falls. George Wyth State Park located in Waterloo and Cedar Falls. Extensive flooding in 1993. Formed 1853.

Black Hawk 1 village (1990 pop. 227), Gilpin co., N central Colo., on North Fork of Clear Creek, in Front Range, 2 mi/3.2 km E of Central City, 25 mi/40 km W of Denver; 39°47′N 105°29′W. Elev. 8,056 ft/2,455 m. Gold mines. Mfg. (jewelry). Legalized gambling. Part of the Central City–Black Hawk Natl. Historic Dist. Nearby is site of 1st gold lode discovery (1859) in Colo. In vicinity are Pike (SW) and Roosevelt (NW) natl. forests. **2** village, Pennington Co., SW S.Dak., 6 mi/9.7 km NW of Rapid City, at E edge of the Black Hills; elev. 3,493 ft/1,065 m. Mfg. (marble prods.).

Black Hawk Lake, Sac co., W central Iowa, 8 mi/12.9 km S of Sac City. Black Hawk L.; 2 mi/3.2 km long. State park.

Black Hawk State Historic Site, Ill.: see ROCK ISLAND.

Black Hills 1 range, in Yavapai co., central Ariz., NE of Prescott; rises 7,743 ft/2,360 m in Mingus Mt., in Prescott Natl. Forest. Former copper-mining dist. **2** rugged mountain range (□ c.6,000 sq mi/15,540 sq km), enclosed by the Belle Fourche (N) and Cheyenne (S and E) rivers, SW S.Dak. and NE Wyo., rising c.2,500 ft/762 m above the surrounding Great Plains; Harney Peak, 7,242 ft/2,207 m above sea level, is the highest point bet. the Rocky and the Applachian mts. Geologically, Black Hills formation is an outlier of the Rockies, a remnant of a once-larger mt. range. The mts. received their name from the heavily forested slopes that appear black from afar. Native Americans, pioneer settlers, and RR companies depended on its wood for fuel and bldg. materials. Gold was discovered here in 1874 by an expedition led by Gen. George Custer, and the resulting gold rush drove out the indigenous pop. Towns (esp. mining settlements) grew rapidly after 1876, chiefly Custer, Deadwood, Lead, Spearfish, and Hot Springs (all in S.Dak.). Gold is still mined in the area; Homestake Mine is one of the largest gold mines in the U.S. Other important minerals found here are uranium, feldspar, mica, and silver. Also a major recreational area of the N plains and a principal tourist spot. Black Hills Natl. Forest covers most of area, mostly in S.Dak. and small part in Wyo. Wind Cave Natl. Park, Jewel Cave Natl. Monument, and Custer State Park are attractions; numerous waterfalls, caves; several ski areas. The 6,000-ft/1,829-m Mt. Rushmore, with its gigantic mt. sculpture of Presidents Washington, Jefferson, Lincoln, and T. Roosevelt, is famous throughout the world (see MOUNT RUSHMORE NATIONAL MEMORIAL). Crazy Horse Monument 5 mi/8 km N of Custer has sculpture of a legendary warrior, and is considered the Native Amer. version of Mt. Rushmore. Fauna include bison, pronghorn antelope, beaver, deer, elk, prairie dog, and a wide range of birds.

Black Island, E N.F., E Canada, in E part of Notre Dame Bay, 3 mi/5 km W of New World Isl. and 6 mi/10 km SSE of Twillingate; 2 mi/3 km long, 1 mi/2 km wide. On E coast is settlement of Black Isl.

Black Island, Maine: see LONG ISLAND.

Black Jack, town (1990 pop.6,131), St. Louis co., E Mo., residential suburb 12 mi/19 km NNW of downtown St. Louis, 3 mi/4.8 km E of Florrisant, near Missouri R. Bounded by Coldwater Creek on N. Named for early Afr.-Amer. resident whose simple gravemarker is in cemetery to W.

Black Lake, town (1991 pop. 4,449), S Que., E Canada, on Black L. (2 mi/3 km long), 5 mi/8 km SW of Thetford Mines; 46°03′N 71°21′W. Asbestos-mining center; mfg. (fabricated structural metal, machinery).

Black Lake, N Sask., W Canada, E of L. Athabasca; 35 mi/56 km long, 2 mi/3 km–11 mi/18 km wide; 59°10′N 105°20′W. Drained through Wollaston L. into Churchill R. by Fond du Lac R.

Black Lake 1 in Cheboygan and Presque Isle cos., N Mich., on Black R., SE of Cheboygan; c.6 mi/9.7 km long, 3 mi/4.8 km wide; 45°28′N 84°10′W. Onaway State Park at E end. **2** in Ottawa co., SW Mich., on Black R., W of Holland; c.8 mi/12.9 km long; 43°07′N 86°14′W. Also known as L. Macatawa.

Black Lake, reservoir, St. Lawrence co., N N.Y., on Indian R., c.5 mi/8 km S of Ogdensburg; c.16 mi/26 km long; 44°36′N 75°28′W. Black Creek enters from SW. Parallel to St. Lawrence R. (7 mi/11.3 km NW). Formed by Eel Weir. Eel Weir State Park at N end.

Black Lake Bayou (BEI-yoo), c.60 mi/97 km long, NW La.; rises S of Homer, Claiborne parish; flows S into Black L. (c.50 mi/80 km SE of Shreveport); 31°51′N, 92°56′W.

Black Lake Bayou Reservoir (□ 22 sq mi/57 sq km), Natchitoches co., NW La., on Black Lake Bayou, 15 mi/24 km NNE of Natchitoches; 31°50′N 92°57′W. Max. capacity 320,000 acre-ft. Formed by Black Lake Bayou Dam (44 ft/13 m high), built (1990) for recreation.

Black Lick, uninc. town (1990 pop. 1,100), Indiana co., W central Pa., 14 mi/23 km NE of Latrobe, on Blacklick Creek; 40°27′N 11°79′W. Agr. includes dairying; livestock.

Black Mesa, tableland, 7,000 ft/2,134 m, Apache and Navajo cos., NE Ariz., in Navajo and Hopi Indian Reservation. Forms NE-facing escarpment. Bituminous coal deposits. Ruins of anc. Pueblo Indian fort found here. Hopi Indian pueblos in SW. Yale Point (8,050 ft/2,454 m), on E flank, is highest elev.

Black Mesa, tableland in Yavapai co., NW central Ariz., N of Prescott, in Prescott Natl. Forest; rises to 6,800 ft/2,073 m.

Black Mesa, Cimarron co., extreme NW Okla., volcanic plateau (elev. 4,973 ft/1,516 m) in the Panhandle, 27 mi/43 km NW of Boise City, near N.Mex. and Colo. state lines. Highest point in state.

Black Mountain, town (1990 pop. 5,533), Buncombe co., W N.C., in the Blue Ridge, suburb 13 mi/21 km E of Asheville; 35°36′N 82°19′W. Mfg. (transportation equip., electrical prods., machinery and machine parts, furniture, textiles, fabricated metal prods., machine parts). Seat of Montreal-Anderson Col. (2-year). Pisgah Natl. Forest to NE.

Black Mountain 1 (9303 ft/2836 m), S Catron co., W N.Mex., 40 mi/64 km N of Silver City, in Gila Natl. Forest. Black Range and source of Gila R. to E; Black Peak, 30 mi/48 km S. Gila Cliff Dwellings Natl. Monument to SW. **2** peak (10,583 ft/3,226 m), in Rocky Mts., Jackson co., N Colo., in the Routt Natl. Forest. Also known as Basaltic Peak. **3** peak (11,654 ft/3,552 m), in Rocky Mts., S Park co., central Colo., 20 mi/32 km NE of Salida, S part of Park Range, in Pike Natl. Forest.

Black Mountain, N.C.: see BALSAM MOUNTAIN.

Black Mountains 1 Mohave co., W Ariz., extend c.90 mi/145 km along Colorado R., S from L. Mead. Hoover Dam is in Black Canyon. Mt. Wilson (5,445 ft/1,660 m) is highest point in range. Mt. Nutt and Warm Springs Wilderness Areas in S. **2** W N.C., highest range in the Appalachian Mts. and a spur of the Blue Ridge, in Yancey and Buncombe cos. NE of Asheville, extends N 20 mi/32 km to Burnsville; rises to 6,684 ft/2,037 m at Mt. Mitchell, highest point in N. Amer. E of Rocky Mts. Other peaks include Balsam Cone (6,645 ft/2,025 m) and Cattail Peak (6,593 ft/2,010 m). Mostly in Pisgah Natl. Forest.

Black Mountains, Calif.: see AMARGOSA RANGE.

Black Oak, village (1990 pop. 277), Craighead co., NE Ark., 27 mi/43 km WSW of Blytheville; 35°50′N 90°22′W. St. Francis Sunken Lands Wildlife Management Area to W and SW.

Black Pond, Piscataquis co., N central Maine, narrow lake (6 mi/9.7 km long) NW of Chesuncook L., c.65 mi/105 km N of Dover-Foxcroft. In wilderness recreational area.

Black Range, SW N.Mex., extends N-S through Grant, Catron, and Sierra cos.; lies largely within Gila Natl. Forest. Prominent point, Reeds Peak (10,011 ft/3,051 m). Continental Divide runs N-S through N part of range.

Black Rapids Glacier, E Alaska, Alaska Range, at foot of Mt. Hayes; 25 mi/40 km long, 2 mi/3.2 km wide; 63°28′N 146°W. Elev. 400 ft/122 m at face. In 1936, due to undetermined disturbance, glacier moved forward 5 mi/8 km in 6 months; it is a surge glacier.

Black River, town (1991 pop. 3,590), ⊙ St. Elizabeth parish, SW Jamaica, port at mouth of Black R., 70 mi/113 km W of Kingston; 18°02′N 77°51′W. Exports logwood, coffee, sugar, ginger, citrus fruit, honey, tobacco, watermelons, corn (maize). Base for river and deep-sea fishing.

Black River, village (□ 1 sq mi/2.6 sq km; 1990 pop. 1,349), Jefferson co., N N.Y., on Black R., 6 mi/9.7 km ENE of Watertown; 44°00′N 75°47′W.

Black River, 33 mi/53 km long, St. Elizabeth parish, SW Jamaica, longest river of the isl.; rises in S outliers of the Cockpit Country just W of Balaclava; flows SW to coast at town of Black River; 17°54′N–18°11′N 76°16′N–77°51′W. Navigable for small vessels for c.25 mi/40 km. Used for irrigation.

Black River 1 c.200 mi/322 km long, E Alaska; rises in 2 headstreams in the Yukon; flows W to Porcupine R. 12 mi/19 km E of Fort Yukon. **2** c.130 mi/209 km long, E Ariz.; rises SE of White Mts. in S part of Apache co., c.15 mi/24 km S of Eager, in Apache-Sitgreaves Natl. Forest; flows SW then NW to White R., forming Salt R. c.40 mi/64 km NE of Globe. Black and Salt rivers form boundary bet. Fort Apache (N) and San Carlos (S) Indian reservations. **3** E central La., name given to sect. (57 mi/92 km long) of OUACHITA RIVER bet. influx of Tensas R. and its mouth, c.35 mi/56 km E of Alexandria. River has large meanders. **4** SW Mich.; rises in N Allegan co.; flows c.10 mi/16 km NW into Ottawa co., then c.10 mi/16 km W to Holland, widening into Black L. W of Holland, then W through short passage into L. Michigan; 42°25′N 86°14′W. **5** c.25 mi/40 km long, SW Mich.; South Fork rises in N Van Buren co.; flows W, past Bloomingdale, Breedsville, and Bangor, to L. Michigan at South Haven; 42°10′N 86°00′W. Receives North Fork (c.15 mi/24 km long), Middle Fork (c.20 mi/32 km long), just before entering L. Michigan. **6** c.65 mi/105 km long, N Mich.; formed in NE Otsego co.; flows N through forested region to Black L., then

NW to Cheboygan R. c.4 mi/6.4 km above its mouth; 45°02′N 84°22′W. **7** c.60 mi/97 km long, E Mich.; rises N of Sandusky in NE Sanilac co.; flows SSE, past Applegate and Croswell, to St. Clair R. at Port Huron; 43°41′N 82°48′W. **8** c.50 mi/80 km long, SE N.C.; formed by joining Great Coharin and Six Run creeks in Sampson co., 15 mi/24 km S of Clinton; flows SSE to Cape Fear R. 10 mi/16 km NW of Wilmington. Receives South R. from NW 30 mi/48 km S of Clinton. **9** c.12 mi/19 km long, N Ohio; formed by East and West branches at Elyria; flows N to L. Erie at Lorain, where navigable lower sect. (c.4 mi/6 km long) is part of harbor of Lorain. East Branch rises in Medina co., flows generally N, past Lodi and Grafton. West Branch rises near New London, flows NE c.30 mi/48 km, past Rochester. **10** 135 mi/217 km long, E S.C.; rises in central Lee co.; flows SE, past Kingstree, to Great Pee Dee R. just above its mouth on Winyah Bay, near Georgetown. Important rice plantations situated along this waterway in antebellum period; many plantations still exist. Partly navigable. **11** c.30 mi/48 km long, N Vt.; rises near Craftsbury; flows N to L. Memphremagog at Newport. **12** c.40 mi/64 km long, S central Vt.; rises near Plymouth; flows S and SE, through small Amherst, Echo, and Rescue lakes, past Proctorsville and Cavendish. Dammed at N Springfield to form reservoir. Flows into Connecticut R. S of Springfield. **13** c.25 mi/40 km long, in extreme NW Wis.; rises in Douglas co., in small lake near Minn. state line; flows generally NNE, through Pattison State Park, to Nemadji R. 9 mi/14.5 km S of Superior. Big Manitou Falls, 165 ft/50 m high, in Pattison State Park, 12 mi/19 km S of Superior, are highest in Wis. **14** c.300 mi/480 km long, in Mo. and Ark.; rises in the Ozarks of SE Mo.; flows SE, then SW to the White R. near Newport (Ark.). Partly navigable. Clearwater Dam is on the river near Piedmont (Mo.). Canoeing and fishing in the Ozarks. **15** c.120 mi/193 km long, N N.Y.; rises in the Adirondack Mts.; flows mainly N and W to Black River Bay, an inlet of L. Ontario. Its falls provide hydroelectric power for factories and mills. **16** c.160 mi/257 km long, central Wis.; rises in E Taylor co., NE of Medford; flows winding course SW past Neillsville and Black River Falls to the Mississippi R. NW of La Crosse. Lower 10 mi/16 km of channel have been absorbed by impoundment of Mississippi R. by Lock and Dam No. 7 at La Crosse. It has been used to transport lumber, coal, and petroleum prods.

Black River Bay, N.Y.: see BLACK RIVER.

Black River Falls, town (1990 pop. 3,490), ⊙ Jackson co., W central Wis., on both banks of Black R., c.45 mi/72 km SE of Eau Claire; 44°17′N 90°50′W. Trade center in timber and farm area; lumber; mfg. (machinery, frozen foods, transportation equip.). Winnebago Indian Reservation to E. Black River State Forest to E and S. Settled before 1840; inc. 1883.

Black Rock, town (1990 pop. 736), Lawrence co., NE Ark., 27 mi/43 km NW of Jonesboro, on Black R., near mouth of Strawberry R.; 36°06′N 91°06′W. Mfg. (lime prods.). Old Davidsonville State Park to N.

Black Rock Desert, arid region of lava beds and alkali flats, Humboldt and Pershing cos., NW Nev., in Toiyabe Natl. Forest, stretching c.70 mi/113 km NE from Gerlach. Jackson Mts. to E, Black Rock Range to W, site of Burning Man rituals. The Quinn R. sinks into the desert from NE. The sect. in NW corner of Pershing co. is sometimes known as Granite Creek Desert. SW extension is Smoke Creek Desert.

Black Springs, village (1990 pop. 97), Montgomery co., W Ark., 38 mi/61 km W of Hot Springs, in Ouachita Natl. Forest.; 34°27′N 93°42′W.

Black Squirrel Creek, c.60 mi/97 km, E central Colo.; rises in N El Paso co.; flows S to Arkansas R. 13 mi/21 km E of Pueblo. West Fork (c.20 mi/32 km long, rises NE of Colorado Springs) joins it 25 mi/40 km ESE of Colorado Springs.

Black Sturgeon Lake, W central Ont., central Canada, 60 mi/97 km NNE of Port Arthur, S of L. Nipigon; elev. 829 ft/253 m; 12 mi/19 km long, 3 mi/5 km wide. Drained S into Black Bay of L. Superior by Black Sturgeon R., 45 mi/72 km long.

Black Tom, part of Jersey City, N.J. In July 1916, Ger. saboteurs demolished U.S. munitions stores here; in Jan. 1917, they destroyed the Kingsland, N.J., munitions plant. Sued by the U.S. govt. in 1922 but vindicated in 1930 by an internatl. claims commission, the Ger. govt., upon hearings in 1939, was ultimately ordered to pay $50 million in damages. Also called Black Tom Isl.

Black Warrior River, navigable river, 178 mi/286 km long; rises in N central Ala.; flows generally SW to join the Tombigbee R. at Demopolis.

Blackburn, town (1990 pop. 308), Saline co., central Mo., 15 mi/24 km W of Marshall; 39°06′N 93°29′W. Corn, soybeans; livestock.

Blackburn, village (1990 pop. 110), Pawnee co., N Okla., 28 mi/45 km NE of Stillwater, on Arkansas R.; 36°22′N 96°35′W.

Blackburn Crossing Dam, Texas: see PALESTINE, LAKE.

Blackburn, Mount (16,390 ft/4,996 m), S Alaska, in Wrangell Mts., 100 mi/161 km ENE of Valdez; 61°44′N 143°27′W.

Blackduck, village (1990 pop. 718), Beltrami co., N Minn., 23 mi/37 km NE of Bemidji; 47°43′N 94°32′W. Mfg. (draperies and bedspreads); sawmill. Blackduck L. to W. Chippewa Natl. Forest to S, Buena Vista State Forest to W; Upper and Lower Red lakes to NW.

Blackduck Lake, Beltrami co., N Minn., 22 mi/35 km NE of Bemidji, 3 mi/4.8 km long, 2 mi/3.2 km wide; 47°44′N 94°36′W. Drained N by Blackduck R. Fishing resorts. Site of prehistoric village on S shore. Village of Blackduck to E. Chippewa Natl. Forest and Blackduck State Forest to S.

Blackey (BLAK-ee), village (1990 pop. 200), Letcher co., SE Ky., in the Cumberland Mts., on North Fork Kentucky R., 15 mi/24 km ESE of Hazard. RR junction. Timber; coal mining.

Blackfalds, town (1991 pop. 1,769), S central Alta., W Canada, near Red Deer R., 8 mi/13 km N of Red Deer; 52°23′N 113°48′W. Mixed farming; dairying; wheat.

Blackfoot, city (1990 pop. 9,646), ⊙ Bingham co., SE Idaho, on Blackfoot R. at its confluence with the Snake R., 22 mi/35 km N of Pocatello; 43°11′N 112°20′W. Elev. 4,508 ft/1,374 m. RR junction in irrigated agr. area (sugar beets, potatoes, grain); mfg. (foods, fertilizers, apparel, farm equip., concrete). Eastern Idaho Fair takes place here annually; World Potato Exposition. Fort Hill Indian Reservation to E and S. Originally called Grove City. Founded 1878, inc. 1907.

Blackfoot, reservoir, mainly in Caribou co., SE Idaho, on Blackfoot R., 32 mi/51 km E of Pocatello; 43°01′N 111°43′W. Max. capacity 410,000 acre-ft. Formed by Blackfoot Dam (44 ft/13 m high), built (1911) by the Bureau of Reclamation for flood control; also used for recreation. Caribou Natl. Forest to E.

Blackfoot River 1 100 mi/161 km long, SE Idaho; formed by confluence of 2 forks in Caribou co.; flows NW, through Blackfoot Reservoir (14 mi/23 km long; stores water for irrigation), and W, past Blackfoot, to Snake R. 2 mi/3.2 km W of Blackfoot. **2** c.120 mi/193 km long, W Mont.; rises in central Lewis and Clark co. at Continental Divide; flows W to the Clark Fork, 4 mi/6.4 km E of Missoula.

Blackford, county (□ 165 sq mi/427 sq km; 1990 pop. 14,067), E Ind.; ⊙ Hartford City; 40°28′N 85°19′W. Livestock; corn, soybeans, oats. Gas and oil wells; stone quarries. Mfg. at Hartford City and Montpelier. Drained by Salamonie R. and small Lick Creek. Formed 1838.

Blackford, uninc. village (1990 pop. 150), Webster co., W Ky., on Tradewater R., near mouth of Slover Creek, and 26 mi/42 km WNW of Madisonville. RR junction. Agr. (tobacco, grain; livestock).

Blackfork, village, Lawrence co., S Ohio, 15 mi/24 km S of Jackson. Clay prods.

Blackhawk, uninc. town (1990 pop. 6199), Contra Costa co., W Calif., residential suburb 15 mi/24 km E of downtown Oakland; 37°49′N 121°55′W. Diablo State Park to N. Apples, walnuts, nursery stock.

Blackhead Peak (12,500 ft/3,810 m), in San Juan Mts., Archuleta co., SW Colo., 13 mi/21 km ENE of Pagosa Springs, in Rio Grande Natl. Forest, W of Continental Divide.

Blackie, village (1991 pop. 303), S Alta., W Canada, 35 mi/56 km SSE of Calgary; 50°36′N 113°37′W. Wheat.

Blacklead Island, islet, SE Franklin dist., N.W.T., N Canada, in Cumberland Sound, off Baffin Isl.; 64°59′N 66°11′W. Former Hudson's Bay Co. post and Br. whaling station.

Blacklog Mountain, central Pa., NE-SW ridge (1,800 ft/549 m–2,000 ft/610 m), runs from NE Fulton co. c.35 mi/56 km NE; forms part of border bet. Juniata and Mifflin cos.; 40°14′N 77°52′W–40°30′N 77°35′W. Parallels Shade Mt. Ridge to E.

Blackmore, Mount, Mont.: see GALLATIN.

Blackomb Mountain, SW B.C., W Canada, 7,503 ft/2,287 m, in Coast Range, 60 mi/97 km N of Vancouver and 6 mi/10 km ESE of Whistler, in Garibaldi Prov. Park. Popular ski facility; Horstman Glacier, only public glacier-skiing in N. Amer. Seventh Heaven Express Chairlift.

Blacks Fork, c.120 mi/193 km long, NE Utah and SW Wyo.; rises near Tokewanna Peak in Uinta Mts., central Summit co., Utah; flows NE through Meeks Cabin reservoir (on Utah-Wyo. state line), past Fort Bridger and Granger (Wyo.), and SE to Green R. 20 mi/32 km N of Utah state line. Lower 7 mi/11.3 km is arm of Flaming Gorge reservoir, and is in Flaming Gorge Natl. Recreation Area.

Blacks Harbour, village (1991 pop. 1,139), SW N.B., E Canada, on the Bay of Fundy, 38 mi/61 km WSW of St. John. Hake, cod, sardine, lobster fishing; sardine- and lobster-canning center.

Blacksburg, city (1990 pop. 34,590), Montgomery co., SW Va., 26 mi/42 km W of Roanoke, 7 mi/11.3 km N of Christiansburg, drained by Stroublers Creek; 37°13′N 80°25′W. Mfg. (transportation equip., machinery, fiber-optic components, fabricated metal prods., reptile food and supplies, gutters; coffee processing, machining, printing); agr. (corn, apples; livestock; dairying). Mus. of Geological Sciences. Appalachian Trail passes to N; part of Jefferson Natl. Forest to NW; Mountain L. is NW. Seat of Va. Polytechnic Inst. and State Univ. Settled 1745; inc. 1871.

Blacksburg, town (1990 pop. 1,907), Cherokee co., N S.C., 8 mi/12.9 km ENE of Gaffney, near N.C. state line, NE of Broad R.; 35°07′N 81°31′W. Mfg. includes textiles, construction materials, industrial chemicals, crushed stone, limestone, woven cane. Agr. includes turkeys, hogs; wheat, soybeans, peaches.

Blackshear, city (1990 pop. 3,263), ⊙ Pierce co., SE Ga., 9 mi/14.5 km NE of Waycross; 31°18′N 82°14′W. Tobacco market; mfg. includes lumber, machinery parts, clothing, and shoes. Egg processing. Agr. includes corn and soybeans. Inc. 1859.

Blackstock, village, Chester and Fairfield cos., N S.C., 11 mi/18 km S of Chester. Producer of timber.

Blackstone 1 residential town (1990 pop. 8,023), including Blackstone village, Worcester co., S Mass., on Blackstone R., 22 mi/35 km SSE of Worcester, at R.I. state line; 42°02′N 71°32′W. Settled 1662, inc. 1845. **2** town (1990 pop. 3,497), Nottoway co., central Va., 34 mi/55 km WSW of Petersburg; 37°04′N 78°00′W. Mfg. (lumber; RR ties; concrete, rubber, and plastic prods.; textiles; fertilizer); tobacco market; trade center for agr. area (tobacco, grain, soybeans; livestock, poultry; dairying); timber. Fort Pickett Military Reservation to SE. Blackstone Municipal Airport to E. Inc. 1888; reinc. 1914.

Blackstone River, c.50 mi/80 km long, Mass. and R.I.; rises near Worcester, Mass.; flows SE to Narragansett Bay at Providence, R.I. Drops 438 ft/134 m from Worcester co. (Mass.) to the river's mouth. The river's clean water and water power were major factors in the early development of the area's textile industry. In 1828, a canal and lock system was built along its entire length, and by the 1830s, there was a mill dam for every mile of the river. Made obsolete by the construction of the Worcester and Providence RR in 1847. Called Seekong R. below Pawtucket.

Cross references are shown in SMALL CAPITALS. The pronunciation key is on page xv. The dates of population figures are on page xii.

Blackstone River Valley National Heritage Corridor (□ 412 sq mi/1,067 sq km), Mass. Important site of the Amer. Industrial Revolution, textile industry and old Blackstone Canal. Authorized 1986.

Blacksville, village (1990 pop. 168), Monongalia co., N W.Va., at Pa. state line, 16 mi/26 km NW of Morgantown, on Dunkard Creek; 39°43′N 80°13′W. Coal mining.

Blackville, town (1990 pop. 2,688), Barnwell co., W S.C., 25 mi/40 km WSW of Orangeburg; 33°21′N 81°16′W. Mfg. includes plastics, transportation equip., furnaces, consumer goods, apparel. Agr. includes melons, grains, peanuts, cotton; poultry, livestock; dairying. Nearby is experiment station of Clemson Agr. Col.

Blackwater, town (1990 pop. 221), Cooper co., central Mo., on Blackwater R., near the Missouri R., 13 mi/21 km W of Boonville; 38°58′N 92°59′W.

Blackwater Bay, NE arm of Pensacola Bay, opening S into the East Bay arm, NW Fla.; receives Blackwater and Yellow rivers.

Blackwater Falls State Park (□ c.3 sq mi/7.8 sq km), NE W.Va., 10 mi/16 km E of Parsons, in the Allegheny Mts. Scenic area surrounds Blackwater Falls (63-ft/19-m drop) in Blackwater R., an E tributary of Laurel Fork R.; below falls is Blackwater Canyon, a gorge with 1,000-ft/305-m walls. Lodge. Surrounded by Monongahela Natl. Forest.

Blackwater Lake, W Mackenzie dist., N.W.T., N Canada, E of Franklin Mts.; 30 mi/48 km long, 2 mi/3 km–8 mi/13 km wide; 64°N 123°05′W. Drains W into Mackenzie R. by short Blackwater R.

Blackwater National Wildlife Refuge (□ c.14 sq mi/36 sq km), Md., on Blackwater R. Set up for research on fur-bearing animals and for waterfowl preservation. Part of a chain of resting places for ducks and geese following the annual fall flyaway from Canada. Canada geese, mallards, blue-winged teal, and black ducks are raised here and hundreds of thousands of muskrats live in the marches. The bald eagle is also found here. Est. 1931.

Blackwater River, 140 mi/225 km, S central B.C., W Canada; rises in Coast Mts. W of Quesnel; flows E to Fraser R. 25 mi/40 km NW of Quesnel. Sometimes called West Road R.

Blackwater River 1 c.55 mi/89 km long, in Ala. and Fla.; rises 15 mi/24 km SW of Andalusia, S Ala.; flows SW, across NW Fla., into Pensacola Bay near Bagdad. **2** c.35 mi/56 km long, E Md., on the Eastern Shore; rises in W Dorchester co.; winds SE through marshes (muskrat trapping) to Fishing Bay. Bordered by Blackwater Natl. Wildlife Refuge. **3** c.55 mi/89 km long, W Mo.; rises in Johnson co.; flows NE to Lamine R. in Cooper co. Channelized in upper ½. **4** c.35 mi/56 km long, S central N.H.; rises SW of Andover near Mt. Kearsarge, in W central Merrimack co.; flows N then SE past Andover, through Blackwater Reservoir SW of Salisbury, to the Contoocook R. 8 mi/12.9 km NW of Concord. **5** 80 mi/129 km long, E Va.; rises in central Prince George co., SE of Petersburg; flows SE and S, past Franklin (head of 12-ft/4-m navigation channel), joins Nottoway R. at N.C. state line to form Chowan R. **6** c.50 mi/80 km, S Va.; rises in the Blue Ridge SW of Roanoke; flows SE and E, across Franklin co., passes N of Rocky Mount to Roanoke R. 25 mi/40 km SE of Roanoke, where it forms W arm of Smith Mt. L. reservoir.

Blackwell, town (1990 pop. 7,538), Kay co., N Okla., 12 mi/19 km WNW of Ponca City, and on Chikaskia R.; 36°47′N 97°17′W. Market and shipping center for agr. (wheat, grain; livestock, poultry) and oil-producing area. Oil refining; mfg. (machinery, metal prods., flour milling, steel processing). Top of Okla. Historical Mus. Founded and inc. 1893.

Blackwell, village (1990 pop. 339), Nolan co., W Texas, 26 mi/42 km S of Sweetwater; 32°04′N 100°19′W. In farm and cattle-ranching area; sheep, goats; cotton. Oil and gas. Oak Creek Reservoir to SE..

Blackwell's Island, N.Y.: see ROOSEVELT ISLAND.

Blackwood, village (1990 pop. 5,120), Camden co., SW N.J., on Big Timber Creek, 10 mi/16 km S of Camden; 39°47′N 75°03′W. Clothing mfg. In rapidly suburbanizing area. Seat of Camden Co. Col. Settled 1701.

Bladen (BLAI-duhn), county (□ 887 sq mi/2,297 sq km; 1990 pop. 28,663), SE N.C.; ⊙ Elizabethtown; 34°37′N 78°33′W. On coastal plain; bounded E by South and Black rivers, W by Big Swamp R.; crossed by Cape Fear R.; source of Waccamaw R. in SE; several small lakes in N and NE, including White, Singletarey, Horseshoe, Bay Tree, and Bakers. Agr. (tobacco, corn, peanuts, wheat, oats, soybeans, hay, sweet potatoes, cotton; turkeys, cattle, hogs); timber (pine, gum, cypress); sawmilling. Singletary Lake State Park in SE center, Jones Lake State park in N center, Turn Bull Educational State Forest and Bladen Lakes State Forest in center. Formed 1734.

Bladen (BLAI-den), village (1990 pop. 280), Webster co., S Nebr., 20 mi/32 km SSW of Hastings, on Little Blue R; 40°19′N 98°35′W.

Bladenboro (BLAI-duhn-buhr-o), town (1990 pop. 1,821), Bladen co., SE N.C., 14 mi/23 km SE of Lumberton, near Big Swamp R; 34°32′N 78°47′W. Tobacco, cotton, corn, peanuts, soybeans; livestock, poultry. Mfg. (steel drums, cotton yarns, apparel).

Bladensburg (BLAI-denz-buhrg), town (1990 pop. 8,064), Prince Georges co., S central Md., a residential suburb of Washington, D.C., on the Anacostia R.; 38°57′N 76°56′W. Originally called Garrison's Landing, it was renamed in honor of Thomas Bladen, governor of Md. 1742–1747. The defeat (August 24, 1814) here of Amer. troops under Gen. W. H. Winder permitted the British under Gen. Robert Ross to march on Wash., D.C., and burn many of the public bldgs. Despite the outlawing of dueling 4 years before, the town was also the scene of the historic duel in which Stephen Decatur, the naval hero, was mortally wounded in 1820 by James Barron. Was a busy port shipping out flour and tobacco, until the river silted up by 1800. Site of Bostwick House (c.1746) and Indian Anne Tavern also known as George Washington House (c.1755–1765). Home of William Wirt, anti-Masonic candidate for president in 1832. Chartered 1742, inc. 1854.

Blades, town (1990 pop. 834), Sussex co., SW Del., on Nanticoke R., 2 mi/3.2 km S of Seaford; 38°38′N 75°36′W. Primarily agr. area.

Blain, borough (1990 pop. 266), Perry co., S central Pa., 35 mi/56 km W of Harrisburg, on Sherman Creek; 40°20′N 77°30′W. Agr. (livestock; dairying). Covered bridges in area. Big Spring and Fowlers Hollow state parks to SW; parts of Tuscarora State Forest to N and S.

Blaine 1 county (□ 2,661 sq mi/6,892 sq km; 1990 pop. 13,552), S central Idaho; ⊙ Hailey; 43°23′N 113°59′W. Drained by Big Wood R. Winter resort area at Sun Valley in N. Livestock grazing (sheep, cattle); agr. (potatoes, sugar beets; alfalfa, hay; wheat, barley, oats). Mining of silver, lead, gold, zinc, copper. Irregular-shaped co. has 40-mi/64-km S extension in E to Snake R. (L. Walcott reservoir) and part of Minidoka Natl. Wildlife Refuge; Sawtooth Natl. Forest, in N and NW, part of Sawtooth Natl. Recreation Area in NW and source of Salmon R., part of Craters of the Moon Natl. Monument in E; includes parts of Pioneer and Sawtooth mts.; Snake R. Plain in S; Magic Reservoir on SW boundary. Formed 1895. **2** county (□ 4,238 sq mi/10,976 sq km; 1990 pop. 6,728), N Mont., on Can. (Sask.) border; ⊙ Chinook; 48°26′N 108°58′W. Agr. region, bounded by Missouri R. on S (and part of Upper Missouri Natl. Wild and Scenic R.). Drained by Milk R. and Peoples, Cow, Battle, and Lodge creeks. Wheat, barley, oats, hay, beans; cattle, sheep, hogs; oil and natural gas. Part of Fort Belknap Indian Reservation in SE. Formed 1912. Chief Joseph Bear's Paw Field 15 mi/24 km S of Chinook; Black Coulee Natl. Wildlife Refuge 10 mi/16 km S of Turner. **3** county (□ 714 sq mi/1,849 sq km; 1990 pop. 675), central Nebr., in Sand Hills region; ⊙ Brewster; 41°55′N 99°58′W. Ranching region drained by North Loup, Middle Loup, and Dismal rivers. Cattle, hogs; grain. Part of Nebr. Natl. Forest (man-made; mainly ponderosa pine and red cedar; cedar plantation) in W. Formed 1885. **4** county (□ 938 sq mi/2,429 sq km; 1990 pop. 11,470), W central Okla.; ⊙ Watonga; 35°52′N 98°25′W. Elev. 1,515 ft/462 m. Intersected by North Canadian, Canadian, and Cimarron (in NE corner) rivers. RR junction. Agr. (wheat, oats; cattle; dairy prods.). Shipping, processing of farm prods. at Watonga. Gypsum mining and processing; oil and natural gas; salt deposits. Roman Nose State Park to N. Formed 1891.

Blaine, city (1990 pop. 38,975), Anoka co., SE Minn., a suburb 12 mi/19 km N of downtown Minneapolis, near Mississippi R.; 45°10′N 93°12′W. Mfg. (medical equip., gun parts, optical components, beauty prods., fabricated metal prods., bldg. materials, furniture, prototype models, apparel, countertops, machinery, consumer goods). The area was organized as a township in 1877 and was named in honor of James G. Blaine, then senator from Maine. Anoka Co. Airport in S. Olympic Ice Arena. Small natural lakes to E. Settled 1862, inc. 1964.

Blaine 1 agr. town (1990 pop. 784), Aroostook co., NE Maine, 27 mi/43 km N of Houlton, near Can. (N.B.) border; 46°28′N 67°50′W. Inc. 1874. **2** town (1990 pop. 2,489), Whatcom co., NW Wash., on Semiahmoo Bay, arm of Strait of Georgia, at Can. (B.C.) border, opposite White Rock (B.C.), 20 mi/32 km NW of Bellingham; 49°00′N 122°46′W. Port of entry; RR junction. In agr. region; fish, oysters; mfg. (fishing nets, wine prods., medical supplies, paper prods., petroleum refining, seafood processing). Tourist and farm trade center. Birch Bay State Park to S. The Peace Arch (state park) is on internatl. border. Plotted c.1884.

Blaine 1 village (1990 pop. 271), Lawrence co., NE Ky., 34 mi/55 km SSW of Ashland, on Blaine Creek, forms Yatesville L. reservoir to NE; 38°01′N 82°50′W. In mountainous agr. (burley tobacco, alfalfa, corn; cattle) and coal area. **2** village, Belmont co., E Ohio, 4 mi/6 km ESE of St. Clairsville.

Blaine Lake, town (1991 pop. 575), central Sask., W Canada, 50 mi/80 km N of Saskatoon, near 2 small Blaine Lakes; 52°50′N 106°53′W. Grain elevators, flour mills.

Blair (BLER), county (□ 527 sq mi/1,365 sq km; 1990 pop. 130,542), central Pa.; ⊙ Hollidaysburg; 40°28′N 78°20′W. Mfg. at Tyrone, Altoona, and Hollidaysburg; limestone, sand, clay, shale, bituminous coal; agr. (corn, wheat, hay, alfalfa, appes; sheep, hogs, cattle; dairying). Mountainous agr. and industrial area; drained by Frankstown Branch of Juniata and Little Juniata rivers. Allegheny Mts. in W, Tussey Mt. ridge on SE boundary; Bald Eagle Mt. ridge on NE boundary. Most of lead used by George Washington's armies in Amer. Revolution was mined here. Canoe Creek State Park in E; part of Allegheny Portage RR Natl. Historical Site in W. Dunning, Loop, Lock and Brush mt. ridges in SE center. Formed 1846.

Blair 1 town (1990 pop. 6,860), ⊙ Washington co., E Nebr., 20 mi/32 km NNW of Omaha, on Missouri R.; 41°32′N 96°08′W. Farm trade center; livestock, grain, and dairy prods. Mfg. (plastic prods., concrete bins and hoppers, belt conveyors, corn prods., printing, meat processing). Seat of Dana Col. Nuclear power plant to N. De Soto Natl. Wildlife Refuge to SE has barge dock on Missouri R. Founded 1869. **2** town (1990 pop. 922), Jackson co., SW Okla., 10 mi/16 km N of Altus; 34°46′N 99°19′W. In agr. and stock-raising area; textiles. Quartz Mt. State Park and Altus L. reservoir to N. **3** town (1990 pop. 1,126), Trempealeau co., W Wis., on Trempealeau R. (water power), and 33 mi/53 km N of La Crosse; 44°17′N 91°13′W. Cheese production.

Blairmore, town, S Alta., W Canada, near B.C. border, in Rocky Mts., on Crowsnest R., 100 mi/161 km SSW of Calgary; 49°36′N 114°26′W. Elev. 4,235 ft/1,291 m. Distributing center for Crowsnest coal-mining region. Logging; sheep; tourism.

Blairs, uninc. village, Pittsylvania co., S Va., suburb 7 mi/11.3 km NNE of Danville; 36°40′N 79°22′W. Mfg. (lumber, asphalt, linens); agr. (dairying; cattle; tobacco, grain, soybeans).

Blairsburg, town (1990 pop. 269), Hamilton co., central Iowa, 10 mi/16 km E of Webster City; 42°28′N 93°38′W.

Blairsden, uninc. village, Plumas co., NE Calif., in the Sierra Nevada, on Middle Fork Feather R., 21 mi/34 km

SE of Quincy. Alfalfa, hay; cattle; timber. Mohawk Valley (W; Plumas-Eureka State Park; hot springs), Gold L. (S), and winter-sports areas are nearby. Parts of Plumas Natl. Forest to W and S.

Blairstown 1 town (1990 pop. 672), Benton co., E central Iowa, 16 mi/26 km S of Vinton; 41°54′N 92°04′W. Feed milling. **2** town (1990 pop. 185), Henry co., W central Mo., on Big Creek of South Grand R., 16 mi/26 km NW of Clinton; 38°33′N 93°57′W. Agr.

Blairstown, resort village and township (1990 pop. 5,331), Warren co., NW N.J., on Paulins Kill, 13 mi/21 km NNE of Belvidere; 40°58′N 75°00′W. In hilly region. Fruit, vegetables; dairy. Blair Acad. for boys (1848) here. Summer camp nearby.

Blairsville (BLERZ-vil), village (1990 pop. 564), ⊙ Union co, N Ga., 24 mi/6.4 km N of Dahlonega, in the Blue Ridge, near Nottely Reservoir, in Chattahoochee Natl. Forest; 34°52′N 83°57′W. Mfg. includes poultry processing; apparel. Near Brasstown Bald, L. Notley, and Vogel State Park. Growing recreation and retirement area.

Blairsville (BLERS-vil), borough (1990 pop. 3,595), Indiana co., SW central Pa., 10 mi/16 km NNE of Latrobe, on Conemaugh R. (bridged); 40°25′N 79°15′W. Mfg. (fertilizer, electronic prods., fasteners, seamless tubing for nuclear reactors, machinery); mining (bituminous coal); stone quarries; agr. (corn, hay; livestock, poultry; dairying). Canal and turnpike center (c.1830). Blacklick Creek 2 mi/3.2 km W. Keystone State Park to SW; Chestnut Ridge to E. Settled c.1792, laid out c.1819, inc. 1825.

Blakely (BLAIK-lcc), town (1990 pop. 5,595), ⊙ Early co., SW Ga., 37 mi/60 km NW of Bainbridge, near Ala. state line; 31°23′N 84°56′W. Mfg. includes a peanut market and processing center; mfg. of apparel, wood and paper prods. Agr. includes corn and cotton. Native Amer. burial mounds nearby. Founded 1821.

Blakely (BLAIK-lee), borough (1990 pop. 7,222), Lackawanna co., NE Pa., a residential suburb 6 mi/9.7 km NNE of downtown Scranton, on Lackawanna R.; 41°29′N 75°35′W. Mfg. (machinery). Archbald Pothole State Park to NE. Inc. 1867.

Blakely Mountain Dam, Ark.: see HAMILTON, LAKE; OUACHITA, LAKE; and OUACHITA RIVER.

Blakesburg, town (1990 pop. 333), Wapello co., SE Iowa, 12 mi/19 km WSW of Ottumwa; 40°57′N 92°38′W. In agr. and coal-mining area.

Blakeslee, village (1990 pop. 128), Williams co., extreme NW Ohio, 10 mi/16 km WNW of Bryan; 41°32′N 84°46′W.

Blakiston Island or **St. Clement's Island**, St. Marys co., S Md., in Potomac R., 8 mi/12.9 km SW of Leonardtown; less than 1 mi/1.6 km long. Large cross (c.1934) here commemorates 1st mass celebrated (1643) by colonists off the ships *Ark* and *Dove*. St. Clements Island State Park is here. Sometimes spelled Blackiston.

Blanca, village (1990 pop. 272), Costilla co., S Colo., in San Luis Valley just W of Sangre de Cristo Mts., 10 mi/16 km S of Blanca Peak, 19 mi/31 km E of Alamosa; elev. 7,746 ft/2,361 m; 37°26′N 105°30′W. Vegetables. Great Sand Dunes Natl. Monument to N; San Isabel and Rio Grande natl. forests to N; Smith Reservoir to SE.

Blanca Peak (14,345 ft/4,372 m), S Colo., in Sangre de Cristo Mts., just SW of Old Baldy, 22 mi/35 km ENE of Alamosa. Highest peak in range. Boundaries of Huerfano, Costilla, and Alamosa cos. converge at peak. Great Sand Dunes Natl. Monument 6 mi/9.7 km N. In area San Isabel (NE) and Rio Grande (W) natl. forests.

Blanchard 1 (BLAN-chuhrd), town (1990 pop. 67), Page co., SW Iowa, on Mo. state line, near Tarkio R., 15 mi/24 km SW of Clarinda; 40°34′N 95°13′W. In agr. area. **2** town (1994 pop. 1480), Caddo parish, NW La., suburb 7 mi/11 km NW of downtown Shreveport; 32°36′N 93°54′W. RR junction; in agr. and timber area; oil and natural gas; machining. Cross L. reservoir to S; Soda L. State Wildlife Area to N. Named after former senator and governor. **3** town (1990 pop. 78), Piscataquis co., central Maine, on the Piscataquis R., 19 mi/31 km WNW of Dover-Foxcroft; 45°15′N 69°38′W. **4** town

(1990 pop. 1,922), McClain co., central Okla., 17 mi/27 km ENE of Chickasha, 23 mi/37 km SSW of Okla. City; 35°08′N 97°39′W. In agr. area; mfg. (frozen food, porcelain dolls, grain elevators). Settled 1906, inc. 1907.

Blanchard, village (1990 pop. 120), Bonner co., N Idaho, 25 mi/40 km NNW of Coeur d'Alene, near Wash. state line; elev. 2,442 ft/744 m. Timber. Mfg. (decorative bark).

Blanchard Dam, Morrison co., central Minn., on Mississippi R., 9 mi/14 km S of Litttle Falls; 46 ft/14 m high; 45°52′N 94°22′W. Built (1925) for power generation; also used for recreation. Forms reservoir (□ 2 sq mi/5.2 sq km); max. capacity 16,358 acre-ft.

Blanchard River, c.95 mi/153 km long, NW Ohio; rises N of Kenton in Hardin co.; flows N, past Mount Blanchard, then W, past Findlay and Ottawa, to Auglaize R. at Dupont; 41°02′N 84°17′W.

Blanchardville, town (1990 pop. 802), Lafayette co., S Wis., on East Branch of Pecatonica R., 30 mi/48 km SW of Madison; 42°48′N 89°51′W. Cheese factories.

Blanche, village (1990 pop. 225), Bell co., SE Ky., in the Cumberland Mts., 4 mi/6.4 km NNE of Pineville. Bituminous-coal mining.

Blanchester (BLAN-CHE-stuhr), village (1990 pop. 4,206), Clinton co., SW Ohio, 31 mi/50 km ENE of Cincinnati; 39°17′N 83°59′W. In livestock-raising and farming area; mfg. of pumps, clothing, canned foods.

Blanchisseuse (BLAHN-chee-shers), village (1990 pop. 2472), on N Trinidad coast, Trinidad and Tobago, 17 mi/27 km NE of Port of Spain. Coconuts, coffee, cacao. Situated on fine bay with noted surf. Fishing. Beach resort with swimming lagoon on 28 acres/11 ha of rain forest.

Blanco (BLAINK-o), county (□ 713 sq mi/1,847 sq km; 1990 pop. 5,972), S central Texas in hill country of Edwards Plateau; ⊙ Johnson City; elev. c.950 ft/290 m–1,800 ft/549 m; 30°16′N 98°24′W. Drained by Pedernales and Blanco rivers. Ranching (cattle, sheep, goats, turkey); mohair, wool marketed; agr. (hay, peaches, wheat). Hunting, fishing. Blanco State Park in S; part of Lyndon B. Johnson Natl. Historical Park at center of co., NW of Johnson City; Pedernales Falls State Park in E. Formed 1858.

Blanco (BLAINK-o), town (1990 pop. 1,238), Blanco co., S central Texas, c.45 mi/72 km N of San Antonio, on Blanco R; elev. 1,350 ft/411 m; 30°06′N 98°25′W. In cattle- and sheep-ranching and farm (wheat, peaches, pecans) area. Blanco State Park to SW (camping, bathing, fishing). Was co. seat 1858–1891.

Blanco, Dominican Republic: see LUPERÓN.

Blanco, Cape (BLAINK-o), promontory, westernmost point of Oregon, 40 mi/64 km SSW of Coos Bay, 8 mi/12.9 km NNW of Port Orford; 42°50′N 124°34′W. Cape Blanco State Park is here. Lighthouse.

Blanco, Río (BLAHN-ko, REE-o), small river, c.10 mi/16 km long, in E P.R.; flows to the Vieques Passage. Near its source are waterfalls and the Río Blanco hydroelectric plant.

Blanco River (BLAINK-o), c.70 mi/113 km long, S central Texas; rises in springs on Edwards Plateau in Kendall co.; flows E and SE to the San Marcos R. just S of San Marcos, 1 mi/1.6 km downstream from San Marcos Springs, source of San Marcos R. Blanco State Park at Blanco, in Blanco co., is recreation area (camping, fishing, swimming, boating).

Bland, county (□ 358 sq mi/927 sq km; 1990 pop. 6,514), SW Va.; ⊙ Bland; 37°07′N 81°07′W. Scenic region of the Allegheny Mts., bounded N by W.Va. state line. Most of co. lies within Jefferson Natl. Forest. Drained by Wolf, Walker creeks. Agr. (corn, hay, alfalfa, tobacco; cattle, sheep; dairying); timber; limestone quarrying, manganese deposits. Appalachian Trail passes E-W through middle of co. Formed 1861.

Bland, town (1990 pop. 651), Gasconade co., E central Mo., in the Ozarks, 32 mi/51 km SW of Hermann; 38°17′N 91°37′W. Mfg. (pool tables).

Bland, uninc. village, ⊙ Bland co., SW Va., 12 mi/19 km SSE of Bluefield, near Walker Creek. Mfg. (dry type transformers and switches, clothing, lumber); agr.

(dairying; livestock; corn, tobacco); timber. Big Walker Lookout (elev. 3,405 ft/1,038 m) to W.

Blandburg (BLAND-buhrg), uninc. village (1990 pop. 700), Reade township, Cambria co., central Pa., 12 mi/19 km N of Altoona; 40°41′N 78°24′W.

Blandford, agr. town (1990 pop. 1,187), Hampden co., SW Mass., 19 mi/31 km WNW of Springfield; 42°11′N 72°57′W.

Blanding, town (1990 pop. 3,162), San Juan co., SE Utah, just S of Abajo Mts., 19 mi/31 km SW of Monticello; elev. 6,105 ft/1,861 m; 37°37′N 109°28′W. Irrigated livestock-raising area; also wheat. Mfg. (uranium processing; pottery; circuit boards); oil and natural gas, uranium mine. Settled 1905 as Grayson, renamed 1915. Hovenweep Natl. Monument to SE; Natural Bridges Natl. Monument 25 mi/40 km W. Recapture Reservoir to NE; large Navajo Indian reservation to S. Edge of the Cedars State Park to W; Devils Canyon to NE. Manti–La Sal Natl. Forest to NNW.

Blandinsville, village (1990 pop. 762), McDonough co., W Ill., 12 mi/19 km WNW of Macomb; 40°32′N 90°52′W. Corn, wheat; livestock.

Blandon (BLAN-duhn), uninc. town (1990 pop. 1,100), Berks co., SE central Pa., 8 mi/12.9 km NNE of Reading, near Willow Creek; 40°26′N 75°53′W. Mfg. includes lumber prods., metal prods., machined parts, food prods. Agr. includes dairying; livestock, poultry; grain, soybeans. L. Ontelaunee reservoir to NW.

Blandville, village, Ballard co., SW Ky., near Mayfield Creek, 7 mi/11.3 km ESE of Wickliffe; 36°56′N 88°57′W. Agr. (tobacco, grain; livestock).

Blaney Park (BLAI-nee), village, Schoolcraft co., S Upper Peninsula, Mich., 19 mi/31 km NE of Manistique; 46°06′N 85°55′W. Fishing. Has lumbering mus. Seney Natl. Wildlife Refuge to NW.

Blanford, village (1990 pop. 500), Vermillion co., W Ind., 15 mi/24 km NNW of Terre Haute, near Ill. state line. Wheat, corn; hogs.

Blanket, village (1990 pop. 381), Brown co., central Texas, 14 mi/23 km NE of Brownwood; 31°49′N 98°47′W. In farm area. Mfg. (rebuilt campers).

Blasdell (BLAIZ-del), village (□ 1 sq mi/2.6 sq km; 1990 pop. 2,900), Erie co., W N.Y., near L. Erie, 6 mi/9.7 km S of Buffalo; 42°47′N 78°49′W. Metal prods., abrasives, chemicals; farming. Inc. 1898.

Blauvelt (BLOU-velt), village (□ 4 sq mi/10.4 sq km; 1990 pop. 4,838), Rockland co., SE N.Y., near W bank of the Hudson R., 3 mi/4.8 km SW of Nyack; 41°04′N 73°57′W. Blauvelt sect. of Palisades Interstate Park is here.

Blawnox (BLAW-nuhks), borough (1990 pop. 1,626), Allegheny co., SW Pa., suburb 8 mi/12.9 km NE of downtown Pittsburgh, on Allegheny R.; 40°29′N 79°51′W. Mfg. (metal fabricating, construction equip., cold-drawn steel, protective coatings). Settled 1867.

Bleckley (BLEK-lee), county (□ 219 sq mi/567 sq km; 1990 pop. 10,430), central Ga.; ⊙ Cochran; 32°26′N 83°20′W. Bounded W by Ocmulgee R.; drained by Little Ocmulgee R. Coastal-plain agr. (corn, peanuts, cotton, wheat, fruit); cattle and hogs. Formed 1912.

Bledsoe (BLED-so), county (□ 404 sq mi/1,046 sq km; 1990 pop. 9,669), central Tenn.; ⊙ Pikeville; 35°36′N 85°13′W. On Cumberland Plateau, here cut by fertile Sequatchie R. valley. Fall Creek Falls (256 ft/78 m), highest waterfall in E U.S., is here. Timber; dairying; livestock raising; tomatoes, fruit. Coal mining. Formed 1807.

Blencoe, town (1990 pop. 250), Monona co., W Iowa, near Missouri R., 7 mi/11.3 km S of Onawa; 41°55′N 96°04′W. Farm trade center.

Blenheim (BLE-nuhm), town (1991 pop. 4,679), S Ont., central Canada, 10 mi/16 km ESE of Chatham; 42°20′N 82°00′W. Light mfg.; resort; corn, vegetables, fruit.

Blenheim (BLEN-uhm), village (1990 pop. 191), Marlboro co., NE S.C., 22 mi/35 km N of Florence; 34°30′N 79°39′W. Mfg. of plywood. Agr. includes timber, cotton.

Blenheim Lower Dam, N.Y.: see SCHOHARIE RESERVOIR.

Blenky Islands, group of islets, S Franklin dist., N.W.T., N Canada, in James Ross Strait, bet. Boothia Peninsula

(NE) and King William and Matty isls. (SW); 69°33′N 95°17′W.

Blennerhassett (blen-uhr-HAS-uht), uninc. town (1990 pop. 2,924), Wood co., NW W.Va., residential suburb 5 mi/8 km W of Parkersburg, on Ohio R.; 39°15′N 81°37′W. Blennerhassett Isl. Historic State Park to N. Tourism.

Blennerhassett Island, in the Ohio R., 4 mi/6.4 km W of Parkersburg, Wood co., NW W.Va., coterminous with Blennerhassett Isl. Historic State Park; 3 mi/4.8 km long. Has a reconstructed mansion (early 1800s) of aristocrat Harman Blennerhassett. The isl. was ransacked by the local militia when Aaron Burr's scheme to establish a SW empire (with which Blennerhassett was connected) was declared traitorous by President Thomas Jefferson. Access by sternwheeler from Point Park. Guided tours of park and gardens and horse-drawn wagon rides available. Blennerhassett Mus.

Blessing, uninc. town (1990 pop. 571), Matagorda co., S Texas, 16 mi/26 km WSW of Bay City. RR junction. Oil and natural gas, salt. Rice, cotton; cattle.

Blevins, village (1990 pop. 253), Hempstead co., SW Ark., 14 mi/23 km N of Hope; 33°52′N 93°34′W. Mfg. (egg processing).

Blewett, uninc. village (1990 pop. 25), Uvalde co., SW Texas, 14 mi/23 km W of Uvalde. Cattle, sheep, goats.

Blewett Falls Lake (BLOO-et), reservoir, on border bet. Richmond and Anson cos., S N.C., on Pee Dee (on Great Pee Dee) R., at confluence of Yadkin (N) and Rock (W) rivers forming Pee Dee R., 6 mi/9.7 km WNW of Rockingham; c.25 mi/40 km long; 34°57′N 79°51′W. Tillery Dam, on Yadkin R. at N tip. Receives Little R. from N in upper reach. Formed by Blewett Falls Dam.

Blind River, town (1991 pop. 3,355), S Ont., central Canada, on North Channel of L. Huron; 46°10′N 82°58′W. Center of Algoma uranium fields. Logging, lumber; resort area. Just to the E is Ont.'s 1st uranium mine (1955).

Bliss 1 village (1990 pop. 185), Gooding co., S Idaho, on Snake R., 35 mi/56 km NW of Twin Falls; 42°56′N 114°57′W. RR junction; logging; mfg. (poles). Malad Gorge State Park to SE; Bray L. reservoir to NE. Bliss Dam (Snake R.) is upstream (S). **2** village, Wyoming co., W N.Y., 13 mi/21 km SSW of Warsaw; 42°35′N 78°15′W. Farming; dairying.

Blissfield, village (1990 pop. 3,172), Lenawee co., SE Mich., on R. Raisin, 9 mi/14.5 km SE of Adrian; 41°49′N 83°51′W. RR junction 4 mi/6.4 km SE. In agr. area (corn, wheat, sugar beets; livestock); mfg. (tomato processing; machinery, wood-burning stoves, construction materials, plastic prods.).

Block Island, off S R.I. near the E entrance to L.I. Sound; 7 mi/11.2 km long, 3.5 mi/5.6 km wide; 41°08′N 71°35′W. New Shoreham (1990 pop. 821; inc. 1672) is municipality designated as Block Isl., with the center being Old Harbor. Visited by Du. navigator Adriaen Block in 1614, it was settled in 1661. The murder (1636) here of John Oldham, an Eng. trader, was the direct cause of the Pequot War. The Native Amer. Manisses lived here. Sachem and Little Sachem ponds recall that era. It is estimated that there were 1,000 Native Americans on the isl. when New Shoreham was incorporated. Current topographic maps indicate a Native cemetery here. Characterized by numerous small ponds, low hills, and a mild climate, the isl. has long been a favorite sport fishing and resort area. The Federal govt. built the isl.'s main harbor, known as Old Harbor (1870–1876). Ferry services to Point Judith and Newport (R.I.) and New London (Conn.). Its 2 harbors accommodate local fishing boats and summer leisure craft. There are 2 lighthouses, 1 at Sandy Point, the other at South East Point. Airport.

Block Island Sound, R.I., arm of the Atlantic Ocean, bet. Block Isl. and R.I. mainland, E of L.I. Sound and NE of Montauk Point (L.I.), W of R.I. Sound; c.10 mi/16 km wide.

Blockton, town (1990 pop. 213), Taylor co., SW Iowa, near Mo. state line, on Little Platte R., 14 mi/23 km ESE of Bedford; 40°37′N 94°28′W.

Blodgett (BLAH-juht), town (1990 pop. 202), Scott co., SE Mo., in Mississippi alluvial plain, 7 mi/11 km SSE of Benton; 37°00′N 89°31′W. Cotton, corn, soybeans.

Bloedel (blo-DEL), village, SW B.C., W Canada, on E central Vancouver Isl., on Discovery Passage, 35 mi/56 km NNW of Courtenay; 50°07′N 125°22′W. Lumbering.

Blomidon, Cape (BLAH-mi-duhn), promontory (elev. 670 ft/204 m), on N coast of N.S., E Canada, S of Parrsboro, on E side of peninsula separating Minas Channel and Minas Basin, and at NE end of North Mts.; 45°18′N 64°19′W.

Blomidon Range, coast range in W N.F., E Canada, on S shore of the Bay of Isls.; part of the Lewis Hills; rises to 2,502 ft/763 m 18 mi/29 km W of Corner Brook.

Blomkest (BLAWM-kest), village (1990 pop. 183), Kandiyohi co., S central Minn., 11 mi/18 km S of Willmar; 44°56′N 95°01′W. Mfg. (machinery); agr. (grains; livestock, poultry; dairying). Big Kandiyohi L. to NE.

Bloodsworth Island, low marshy isl. (c.5 mi/8 km long, 4 mi/6.4 km wide), Dorchester co., E Md., in Chesapeake Bay, on Tangier Sound (E) and Hooper Strait (N), and just N of South Marsh Isl. Once home to a dozen families, since 1942 it has only been used as a naval shelling range. Like the other isls. of the bay and the Eastern Shore itself, it has been eroding at the rate of 8 ft/2.4 m annually since the 1800s.

Bloomburg, village (1990 pop. 376), Cass co., NE Texas, 20 mi/32 km S of Texarkana, near Ark. state line; 33°08′N 94°03′W. In agr. and timber area; wood and pulp processing.

Bloomdale, village (1990 pop. 632), Wood co., NW Ohio, on South Branch of Portage R., 7 mi/11 km W of Fostoria; 41°11′N 83°34′W. Food prods.

Bloomer, town (1990 pop. 3,085), Chippewa co., W central Wis., on tributary of Chippewa R., 13 mi/21 km NNW of Chippewa Falls; 45°06′N 91°29′W. Mfg. (construction materials, polyethelene film, foods). Settled before 1850; inc. 1920.

Bloomfield 1 city (1990 pop. 2,580), ⊙ Davis co., SE Iowa, near Fox R., 18 mi/29 km S of Ottumwa; 40°45′N 92°25′W. In sheep-raising area; mfg. (wood prods., machinery, propane tanks, iron castings); agr. (soybeans, corn). Has James B. Weaver homestead. Lake Wapello State Park to NW. Inc. 1863. **2** city (1990 pop. 1,800), ⊙ Stoddard co., SE Mo., on Crowley's Ridge, 19 mi/31 km W of Sikeston; 36°53′N 89°55′W. Farm and lumber center. Rice, corn, cotton, soybeans, wheat; mfg. (absorbent clay prods., plastic prods.). Settled 1824. **3** city (1990 pop. 45,061), Essex co., NE N.J., an industrial and residential suburb of Newark; 40°48′N 74°11′W. Electrical equip., adhesives, paints, plastics, rubber prods., and semiconductor gaskets. Seat of Bloomfield Col. (1868). Named for the Revolutionary War general Joseph Bloomfield, who later became governor of N.J., the town was a supply point for both sides during the war. In the 19th cent. it was a trade and transportation hub. The Presbyterian church here dates from 1796. Settled c.1660, inc. as a town 1812, as a city 1900.

Bloomfield 1 town (1990 pop. 19,483), Hartford co., N Conn., a suburb of Hartford; 41°50′N 72°44′W. Shade wrapper tobacco leaf and dairy region; mfg. of helicopter parts. Settled c.1642, inc. 1835. **2** town (1990 pop. 2,592), ⊙ Greene co., SW Ind., near West Fork of White R., c.40 mi/64 km SE of Terre Haute; 39°02′N 86°56′W. Agr. area mfg. (hydraulic jacks, ceramic tile, medical supplies, limestone prods., concrete). **3** town (1990 pop. 845), Nelson co., central Ky., 10 mi/16 km NE of Bardstown, in Bluegrass region; 37°54′N 85°19′W. Agr. (tobacco, grain; livestock; dairying); mfg. (flour, dessert mixes). Taylorsville L. State Park and reservoir to NE. **4** town (1990 pop. 1,181), Knox co., NE Nebr., 17 mi/27 km NE of Creighton; 42°36′N 97°39′W. Livestock; dairy prods.; grain. Santee Indian Reservation to NW. Settled 1890. **5** town (1990 pop. 5,214), San Juan co., NW N.Mex., on San Juan R., 13 mi/21 km E of Farmington; 36°42′N 107°58′W. Elev. 5,453 ft/1,662 m. Trade center for irrigated grain and bean region; mfg. (gasoline refining). Aztec Ruins Natl. Monument is 9 mi/14.5 km N, boundary of Navajo Indian Reservation 15 mi/24 km W. Chaco Canyon Natl. Historical Park c.40 mi/64 km S; Angel Peak (6,988 ft/2,130 m) Natl. Recreation Area to SE; Salmon Ruins to W. **6** town (1990 pop. 253), Essex co., NE Vt., on Connecticut R., at mouth of Nulhegan R., 14 mi/23 km N of Guildhall; 44°49′N 71°37′W. Record state cold temperature.

Bloomfield 1 village (1991 pop. 689), SE Ont., central Canada, near L. Ontario, 15 mi/24 km SSE of Belleville; 43°59′N 77°14′W. Lumber; mixed farming, fruit (apples). **2** village (1990 pop. 1,331), Ontario co., W N.Y., 22 mi/35 km SE of Rochester; 42°54′N 77°26′W. Pop. figure includes East Bloomfield and Holcomb.

Bloomfield, borough (1990 pop. 1,092), ⊙ Perry co., central Pa., 20 mi/32 km NW of Harrisburg; 40°25′N 77°11′W. Printing and publishing. Agr. area (dairying). Appalachian Trail passes to SE; Little Buffalo State Park to N. Laid out c.1824. Post office is New Bloomfield.

Bloomfield, Ohio: see BLOOMINGDALE.

Bloomfield Hills, city (1990 pop. 4,288), Oakland co., SE Mich., suburb 25 mi/40 km NW of downtown Detroit, 4 mi/6.4 km SE of Pontiac; 42°34′N 83°15′W. Drained by R. Rouge. Mfg. (paper prods., transportation equip., carbide cutting tools). Seat of the Cranbrook Acad. of Arts and Sciences and Oakland Community Col. Settled c.1819; inc. as village 1926, as city 1932.

Bloomfield Township, city (1990 pop. 42,137), Oakland co., SE Mich., suburb of Detroit, 3 mi/4.8 km S of Pontiac; 42°34′N 83°16′W. Numerous lakes within city and to W. Drained by R. Rouge.

Blooming Grove, town (1990 pop. 847), Navarro co., E central Texas, 14 mi/23 km W of Corsicana; 32°05′N 96°43′W. Market point in agr. area (cattle, emus; dairying; cotton, corn, wheat); steel fabrication.

Blooming Prairie, town (1990 pop. 2,043), Steele co., SE Minn., 17 mi/27 km SSE of Owatonna; 43°52′N 93°02′W. Agr. area (grain, soybeans, peas; livestock, poultry; dairying); mfg. (hog and chicken feed, soybean oil). Cedar R. to E.

Blooming Valley, borough (1990 pop. 391), Crawford co., NW Pa., 6 mi/9.7 km ENE of Meadville, near Woodcock Creek; 41°40′N 80°02′W. Agr. (potatoes, grain; livestock; dairying). Woodcock Creek L. reservoir to NW.

Bloomingburg 1 village (1990 pop. 316), Sullivan co., SE N.Y., at base of the Shawangunk range, on Shawangunk Kill, 10 mi/16 km N of Middletown; 41°33′N 74°26′W. In resort area. Also spelled Bloomingburgh. **2** village (1990 pop. 769), Fayette co., S central Ohio, 5 mi/8 km NNE of Washington Court House; 39°37′N 83°24′W.

Bloomingdale 1 town (1990 pop. 2,271), Chatham co., Ga., 13 mi/21 km W of Savannah; 32°07′N 81°19′W. Steel fabrication. **2** town (1990 pop. 341), Parke co., W Ind., 6 mi/9.7 km N of Rockville; 39°50′N 87°15′W. In agr. area. Mfg. (plastic prods. and hardwood lumber). **3** uninc. town (1990 pop. 2,070), Lancaster co., SE Pa., residential suburb 3 mi/4.8 km N of Lancaster; 40°04′N 76°18′W. Pa. Farm Mus. to NE.

Bloomingdale 1 village (1990 pop. 16,614), Du Page co., NE Ill., suburb WNW of Chicago, 11 mi/18 km SE of Elgin; 41°57′N 88°05′W. Mfg. (plastics, industrial equip., computers, hinges, containers). Remnant agr. (corn, oats; dairying). **2** village (1990 pop. 503), Van Buren co., SW Mich., on Black R., 20 mi/32 km WNW of Kalamazoo; 42°22′N 85°57′W. Mfg. of motor vehicle stampings. **3** village (1990 pop. 600), Essex co., NE N.Y., in the Adirondacks, 6 mi/9.7 km NNE of Saranac L. village; 44°24′N 74°06′W. **4** village (1990 pop. 227), Jefferson co., E Ohio, 10 mi/16 km W of Steubenville; 40°21′N 80°51′W. Laid out 1816. Also called Bloomfield.

Bloomingdale, borough (1990 pop. 7,530), Passaic co., N N.J., on Pequannock R., 10 mi/16 km NW of Paterson; 41°01′N 74°19′W. Residential. Inc. 1918. Many lakes in vicinity.

Bloomington 1 uninc. city (1990 pop. 15,116), San Bernardino co., S Calif., suburb 50 mi/80 km E of downtown Los Angeles, 6 mi/9.7 km SW of San Bernardino; 34°04′N 117°24′W. RR center; citrus-growing area being replaced by urban development. Vegetables. Mfg.

(metal smelting, metal plate work; fabricated metal prods., mobile homes). Rialto Municipal Airport to N; Colton Airport to E. **2** city (1990 pop. 51,972), ⊙ McLean co., central Ill., one of Bloomington-Normal twin cities; 40°28′N 88°58′W. Agr. (corn, wheat, soybeans; cattle; dairying). Mfg. includes food processing (candy, meat and dairy prods., seeds), consumer goods, electric equip., fiberboard; offset printing. In 1856 the state Republican party was organized here, at which time Lincoln delivered his famous "lost speech" (no copy of it is known to exist). Seat of Illinois Wesleyan Univ. Illinois State Univ. is in adjacent Normal (formerly North Bloomington). Of interest are the burial place of Adlai E. Stevenson and the David Davis Mansion, a State Historic site. Inc. 1839. **3** city (1990 pop. 60,633), ⊙ Monroe co., S central Ind.; 39°10′N 86°31′W. In a densely forested region. Mfg. includes electric and electronic equip., furniture, and elevators. Quarrying and marketing of the limestone abundant in the area has sustained the city's economy for many years. Seat of Indiana Univ., and its growth is closely related to the development of that institution. In the area are 2 state parks, a state forest, Hoosier Natl. Forest, and lakes Monroe (Ind.'s largest) and Lemon. Settled 1816, inc. 1878. **4** city (1990 pop. 86,335), Hennepin co., SE Minn., a suburb 9 mi/14.5 km S of downtown Minneapolis; 44°49′N 93°19′W. Bounded on S and E by Minnesota R.; Long Meadow L. in E (Minn. Valley Natl. Wildlife Refuge). RR junction. Mfg. (machinery, bakery and dairy prods., signs, medical prods., fiberglass tanks, computer software, electronic equip., coin meters, fabricated metal prods., trailer hitches, lawn and garden equipment). Minneapolis–St. Paul Internatl. Airport to NE. Seat of Normandale Community Col. Bloomington Art Center and the Mall of America (one of the largest malls in the U.S.) are here. Hyland Park Reserve in W, including Richardson Nature Center; Fort Snelling Natl. Cemetery and Fort Snelling State Park to NE. Inc. 1953.

Bloomington, town (1990 pop. 1,888), Victoria co., S Texas, near Guadalupe R., 13 mi/21 km SSE of Victoria; 28°38′N 96°54′W. RR junction, in oil-producing, agr. (cattle; dairying; cotton, rice, corn) area.

Bloomington 1 village (1990 pop. 197), Bear Lake co., SE Idaho, near Bear L., 5 mi/8 km S of Paris; 42°11′N 111°24′W. Elev. 5,969 ft/1,819 m. Agr.; cattle, sheep; dairying. Cache Natl. Forest to W; Bear Lake State Park and Natl. Wildlife Refuge to SE. **2** village (1990 pop. 129), Franklin co., S. Nebr., 5 mi/8 km W of Franklin, on Republican R., near Kansas state line; 40°05′N 99°02′W. Livestock; grain; poultry prods. **3** village (1990 pop. 800), Ulster co., SE N.Y., on Rondout Creek, 4 mi/6.4 km SW of Kingston; 41°53′N 74°03′W. **4** village (1990 pop. 776), Grant co., extreme SW Wis., on branch of small Grant R., 16 mi/26 km SE of Prairie du Chien; 42°53′N 90°55′W. In farm area; meat processing.

Bloomsburg, industrial town (1990 pop. 12,439), ⊙ Columbia co., E Pa., 32 mi/51 km SE of Williamsport, on the Susquehanna R., 1 mi/1.6 km NE of mouth of Fishing Creek; 40°00′N 76°27′W. Mfg. (textiles, furniture, asphalt, foods, plastic prods., solariums and greenhouses, commercial printing, aluminum fabrication). Agr. (livestock, poultry; corn, hay, apples; dairying). Seat of Bloomsburg Univ. of Pa. Bloomsburg Municipal Airport in E by river. Settled 1772, inc. 1870.

Bloomsbury, borough (1990 pop. 890), Hunterdon co., W N.J., on Musconetcong R., 6 mi/9.7 km ESE of Phillipsburg; 40°38′N 75°05′W. Gravel pit and fish hatchery nearby.

Bloomville, village (1990 pop. 949), Seneca co., N Ohio, 9 mi/14 km ESE of Tiffin; 41°03′N 83°01′W. In agr. area; limestone quarry.

Blossburg (BLAWS-buhrg), borough (1990 pop. 1,571), Tioga co., N Pa., 30 mi/48 km N of Williamsport, on Tioga R.; 41°40′N 77°04′W. Mfg. (lumber; fabricated metal prods.; printing and publishing). Agr. (livestock; grain; dairying; timber). Parts of Tioga State Forest E, S, and W. Settled c.1802.

Blossom, town (1990 pop. 1,440), Lamar co., NE Texas, 10 mi/16 km E of Paris; 33°39′N 95°22′W. In agr. area (cotton, corn, soybeans). Mfg. (candy, aircraft parts).

Blount 1 (BLOUNT), county (□ 650 sq mi/1,684 sq km; 1990 pop. 39,248), N central Ala.; ⊙ Oneonta; 33°58′N 86°35′W. Hilly region drained by Mulberry and Locust forks of Black Warrior R. Soybeans, wheat, corn; poultry; coal, iron, limestone. Formed 1818. **2** (BLUHNT), county (□ 584 sq mi/1,513 sq km; 1990 pop. 85,969), E Tenn.; ⊙ Maryville; 35°42′N 83°56′W. Bounded SE by N.C., SW by Little Tennessee R., NW by Fort Loudoun Reservoir (Holston R.). Great Smoky Mts. in E and SE. Includes part of Great Smoky Mountains Natl. Park. Lumbering; marble quarrying; livestock raising; dairying; agr. (apples, strawberries, corn, tobacco, hay). Industry at Alcoa (aluminum reduction), Maryville. Formed 1795.

Blountstown, city (□ 3 sq mi/7.8 sq km; 1990 pop. 2,404), ⊙ Calhoun co., NW Fla., 45 mi/72 km W of Tallahassee, near Apalachicola R.; 30°26′N 85°02′W. Lumber and naval-stores center. Named after Native Amer. chief. Founded c.1823, inc. 1925.

Blountsville 1 (BLOUNTS-vil), town (1990 pop. 1,527), Blount co., N central Ala., 15 mi/24 km SE of Cullman, 11 mi/18 km NW of Oneonta. Meat processing; lumber; clothing; furniture. **2** town (1990 pop. 155), Henry co., E Ind., 11 mi/18 km NNE of New Castle; 40°04′N 85°14′W. In agr. area.

Blountville (BLUHNT-vil), village, ⊙ Sullivan co., NE Tenn., in Great Appalachian Valley, 15 mi/24 km N of Johnson City; 36°32′N 82°19′W.

Blowing Rock, town (1990 pop. 1,257), Watauga and Caldwell cos., NW N.C., in the Blue Ridge Mts, 16 mi/26 km NNW of Lenoir, near Yadkin R., on NE edge of Pisgah Natl. Forest; 36°07′N 81°40′W. Tobacco, corn; cattle; timber; mfg. (ice cream, tool and die). Cone Memorial Park to N, former estate (□ 5 sq mi/13 sq km) of industrialist Moses Cone. Resort area; ski resorts. Named for rock formation in Johns River Gorge where air currents return objects tossed from cliff. Blue Ridge Parkway passes to N.

Bloxom, village, Accomack co., E Va., 8 mi/12.9 km N of Accomac, in Eastern Shore area; 37°49′N 75°37′W. Agr. (poultry, livestock; grain, vegetables). Chesapeake Bay to W, Atlantic Ocean to E.

Blubber Bay, village, SW B.C., W Canada, at N tip of Texada Isl., on the Strait of Georgia, 80 mi/129 km NW of Vancouver; 49°48′N 124°37′W. Lime-shipping port; limestone quarrying, copper mining; lumbering.

Blue Ash, city (1990 pop. 11,860), Hamilton co., extreme SW Ohio, 11 mi/18 km NE of Cincinnati; 39°15′N 84°24′E.

Blue Ball, uninc. village, Boggs township, Clearfield co., central Pa., 10 mi/16 km SE of Clearfield; 40°55′N 78°16′W. Post office called West Decatur.

Blue Bank, resort village, Lake co., extreme NW Tenn., on S shore of Reelfoot L., 20 mi/32 km N of Dyersburg. Fishing; eagle-watching center. State park nearby.

Blue Basin, waterfalls, N Trinidad, Trinidad and Tobago, 5 mi/8 km N of Port of Spain, in valley of small Diego Martin R. Tourist site.

Blue Bell, uninc. town (1990 pop. 6,091), Montgomery co., SE Pa., suburb 14 mi/23 km NNW of Philadelphia, 4 mi/6.4 km NE of Norristown, near Wissahickon Creek; 40°08′N 75°16′W. Mfg. includes machinery, transportation equip., crushed stone, electrical equip., textiles, computer mfg. and systems; machining. Wings Field airport in S; Fort Washington State Park to SE; seat of Montgomery Co. Community Col.

Blue Bell Knoll, highest peak (11,253 ft/3,430 m) in Aquarius Plateau, Garfield co., S central Utah, 27 mi/43 km NNE of Escalante.

Blue Diamond, village, Perry co., SE Ky., in Cumberland foothills, 4 mi/6.4 km NNW of Hazard. Bituminous coal.

Blue Earth, county (□ 765 sq mi/1,981 sq km; 1990 pop. 54,044), S Minn.; ⊙ Mankato; 44°01′N 94°03′W. Bounded N in part by Minnesota R., drained by Blue Earth, Watonwan, Maple, Big Cobb, and Le Sueur rivers. Agr. area (corn, oats, soybeans, alfalfa, peas; hogs, cattle, sheep). Food processing and mfg. at Mankato. Minneopa State Park in N; several small natural lakes in co., esp. in NE corner, including Madison and Eagle lakes. Formed 1853.

Blue Earth, city (1990 pop. 3,745), ⊙ Faribault co., S Minn., 37 mi/60 km S of Mankato, at confluence of East and West branches Blue Earth R., which form main stream (flows N), near Iowa state line; elev. 1,084 ft/330 m; 43°38′N 94°05′W. Trade center for diversified-farming area (grain, soybeans, alfalfa; livestock); mfg. (canned foods, grain-based prods., meal [feather, bone]; stainless steel fabrication; printing and publishing). Municipal Airport to S. Plotted 1856, inc. 1874.

Blue Earth River, 130 mi/209 km long; rises in Kossuth co., N Iowa; flows generally N into S Minn., past Blue Earth city, to Minnesota R. at Mankato. Tributaries are Watonwan and Le Sueur rivers.

Blue Grass, town (1990 pop. 1,214), Scott co., E Iowa, 10 mi/16 km W of Davenport; 41°30′N 90°45′W. Livestock; grain.

Blue Hill, resort town (1990 pop. 1,941), Hancock co., S Maine, on W shore of Blue Hill Bay, 13 mi/21 km SW of Ellsworth; 44°23′N 68°34′W. Pottery made here. Hill for which it is named is 940 ft/287 m high (tram to summit). Copper and granite have been unearthed here. Summer music festival. Seat of George Stevens Acad. (1803). Holt House (1815) is home of the Blue Hill Historical Society. Settled 1762, inc. 1789.

Blue Hill, village (1990 pop. 810), Webster co., S Nebr., 20 mi/32 km S of Hastings; 40°19′N 98°27′W. RR junction. Shipping point for grain, livestock.

Blue Hill Bay, Hancock co., S Maine, inlet of the Atlantic Ocean, extending inland 20 mi/32 km from entrance W of Mt. Desert Isl.

Blue Hills (bloo HILZ), E Mass., low wooded hills S of Boston, just S of Milton. Recreation, bridle trails. On Great Blue Hill (635 ft/194 m) is Blue Hill Observatory, forerunner of Mt. Washington Observatory (N.H.).

Blue Hills or **Providenciales**, island (□ 41.6 sq mi/107.7 sq km; 1990 pop. 4,821), Turks and Caicos Isls., crown colony of U.K., bet. North Caicos (NE) and West Caicos (SSW) isls., on Caicos Passage; 17 mi/27 km long, 12 mi/19 km wide; 21°45′N 72°15′W. Luxury resorts, including one of the 1st Club Med resorts, and scuba-diving centers. The most developed isl. in Turks and Caicos. Site of Ludington Internatl. Airport. Formerly famous for salt pans.

Blue Hole Spring, Ohio: see CASTALIA.

Blue Island, city (1990 pop. 21,203), Cook co., NE Ill., a residential and industrial suburb 15 mi/24 km SSW of downtown Chicago, on the Calumet Sag channel; 41°39′N 87°40′W. It has oil refineries, RR yards and shops, canneries, and plants mfg. plastics, foods, fluorescent ballasts, electronic equip., chemicals; steel fabricating. Inc. 1843.

Blue Lagoon, on S coast of St. Vincent, St. Vincent and the Grenadines, West Indies. Caribbean Sailing Yacht Marina.

Blue Lake, city (1990 pop. 1,235), Humboldt co., NW Calif., 12 mi/19 km NE of Eureka, near Mad R.; 40°53′N 124°00′W. Dairying; cattle, sheep, lambs; timber. Mfg. (beer, wood prods.). Six Rivers Natl. Forest to E.

Blue Lake 1 oxbow lake (c.8 mi/12.9 km long) in Monona co., W Iowa, near Mo. R., 1 mi/1.6 km W of Onawa. Lewis and Clark State Park here. **2** Greater Sitka Borough, SE Alaska, on Sawmill Creek, on Baranof isl., 5 mi/8 km SE of Sitka; 57°01′N 135°08′W. Max. capacity 208,000 acre-ft. Formed by Blue Lake Dam (141 ft/43 m high), built (1961) by the City of Sitka for its water supply.

Blue Lake, Colo.: see ADOBE CREEK RESERVOIR.

Blue Lakes 1 pair of lakes, Alpine co., E Calif., on Blue Creek, in Sierra Nevada mts., 12 mi/19 km SW of Markleeville; 38°35′N 119°56′W. Known as Upper Blue and Lower Blue lakes. **2** reservoirs, Lake co., NW Calif., in Coast Range, 9 mi/14.5 km NNW of Lakeport; 39°09′N 122°58′W. Drained by Cold Creek; diversion channel feeds into Scotts Creek. Consists of Blue (1.5 mi/2.4 km long) and Lower Blue (⁹⁄₁₀ mi/1 km long) lakes. Blue L. village bet. the lakes.

Blue Licks Springs, village, Nicholas co., N Ky., on Licking R., 40 mi/64 km NE of Lexington, in Bluegrass region. Former resort with mineral springs. Salt lick once used by bison. Blue Licks Battlefield State Park, commemorating 1 of the last battles of the Revolutionary War (August 19, 1782), is here. A mus. houses fossil mammals found in vicinity. Also spelled Blue Lick Springs.

Blue Mesa Reservoir, Gunnison co., W central Colo., on Gunnison R., 22 mi/35 km WSW of Gunnison, in Curecanti Natl. Recreation Area; 16 mi/26 km long; 38°27′N 107°20′W. Max. capacity 941,000 acre-ft. Formed by Blue Mesa Dam (333 ft/101 m high), built (1966) by the Bureau of Reclamation for power generation, flood control, and irrigation. Lake Fork Gunnison R. enters from S 1 mi/1.6 km above dam; Morrow Point Reservoir below dam.

Blue Mound, town (1990 pop. 2,133), Tarrant co., N Texas, residential suburb 7 mi/11.3 km N of downtown Fort Worth; 32°51′N 97°20′W. Saginaw is to W. Mecham Field airport is to SW.

Blue Mound 1 village (1990 pop. 1,161), Macon co., central Ill., 12 mi/19 km SW of Decatur; 39°42′N 89°07′W. Wheat, corn, soybeans. **2** village (1990 pop. 251), Linn co., E Kansas, 10 mi/16 km WSW of Mound City; 38°05′N 95°00′W. In agr. area.

Blue Mounds, village (1990 pop. 446), Dane co., S Wis., 23 mi/37 km W of Madison; 43°01′N 89°49′W. Blue Mounds (elev. 1,261 ft/384 m) State Park to NW. Cheese making. On Military Ridge State Trail.

Blue, Mount 1 peak (3,187 ft/971 m), Franklin co., W central Maine, center of Mt. Blue State Park, 20 mi/32 km WNW of Farmington. Well-traveled road part of the way to summit. Scenic views. **2** peak (4,530 ft/1,381 m) of White Mts., Grafton co., NW N.H., SW of Franconia Notch.

Blue Mountain, town (1990 pop. 221), Calhoun co., E. Ala., N of Anniston. Twine and yarn mfg. Fort McClellan is nearby.

Blue Mountain 1 village (1990 pop. 146), Logan co., W Ark., 11 mi/18 km E of Booneville; 35°07′N 93°43′W. Ozark Natl. Forest to N; Blue Mountain L. reservoir (Petit Jean R.) to S and Ouachita Natl. Forest beyond it. **2** village (1990 pop. 667), Tippah co., N Miss., 25 mi/40 km ESE of Holly Springs; 34°40′N 89°01′W. Agr. (cotton, corn, soybeans; cattle; dairying); mfg. (furniture, cat litter and clay prods., foam rubber prods.). Seat of Blue Mountain Col. (Baptist; for women; 1873, includes Doll Collection Exhibit). Holly Spring Natl. Forest to W and N.

Blue Mountain, 2,085 ft/636 m, in Long Range Mts., NW N.F., E Canada, 24 mi/39 km SE of Point Riche.

Blue Mountain, ridge, E central Pa., NE-SW ridge (1,300 ft/396 m–2,000 ft/610 m) of the Appalachian Mts.; runs from N Franklin co., NW of Shippensburg, c.150 mi/241 km NE, past Harrisburg on N, to Northampton co., where it joins Kittatinny Mt., near N.J. Traversed by Appalachian Trail from NE end to NW of Harrisburg; 40°22′N 76°48′W. Slate, limestone. A 2d Blue Mt. Ridge is c.15 mi/24 km NW of the SW portion of the other, extends c.25 mi/40 km from NE Northumberland to Juniata R. in NW Juniata co., closely parallels Shade Mt. ridge to SE.

Blue Mountain, c.2,621 ft/799 m, W Ark., 13 mi/21 km NE of Mena on border bet. Polk and Scott cos., in Ouachita Mts., Ouachita Natl. Forest.

Blue Mountain, N.Y.: see BLUE MOUNTAIN LAKE.

Blue Mountain Dam, Ark.: see PETIT JEAN RIVER.

Blue Mountain Lake, resort village (1990 pop. 220), Hamilton co., NE central N.Y., in the Adirondacks, at E end of Blue Mountain L. (c.2.5 mi/4 km long, c.1 mi/1.6 km wide), 26 mi/42 km S of Tupper L. village; 43°52′N 74°26′W. In summer- and winter-resort area. Comprehensive Adirondack Mus. Blue Mt. (elev. 3,759 ft/1,146 m) is just N. At junction of State Routes 28 and 30.

Blue Mountain Peak, 7,520 ft/2,292 m, E Jamaica, in the Blue Mts., highest peak of the isl., 15 mi/24 km ENE of Kingston; 18°03′N 76°35′W. Hostel near its summit. Known for its views. Coffee grown on slopes.

Blue Mountains, mountain range in E Jamaica, sinuous central ridge running some 30 mi/48 km from NW to SE along the parish boundaries of Portland (N), with St. Andrew and St. Thomas (S), branching N and S into long spurs; 18°02′N 76°35′W. From Stony Hill (8 mi/12.9 km N of Kingston), a chain of high peaks exceeding 6,000 ft/1,829 m for 10 mi/16 km attains a summit elev. of 7,402 ft/2,256 m. Popular tourist area known for its dense vegetation and fine scenery. High-quality coffee, grown on mt. slopes, is exported worldwide. High, John Crow, Blue Mountain, and Silver Hill peaks are outstanding markers above 4,000 ft/1,219 m.

Blue Mountains, uplifted, eroded part of the Columbia Plateau, c. 6,500 ft/1,981 m high, NE Oregon and SE Wash.; runs generally E of John Day and Pendleton (Oregon) and Walla Walla (Wash.). Lava flows cover much of the surface. The upper, wooded slopes support logging activities. Recreation and livestock grazing are the mts.' principal economic uses. Rock Creek Butte, 9,097 ft/2,773 m high, in Elkhorn Ridge, W of Baker (Oregon), is the highest point in the Blue Mts. The Blue Mts. were a major physical obstacle for those who once traveled the Oregon Trail.

Blue Point, shore-resort village (□ 1 sq mi/2.6 sq km; 1990 pop. 4,230), Suffolk co., SE N.Y., near S shore of L.I., near Great South Bay, 2 mi/3.2 km WSW of Patchogue; 40°45′N 73°02′W. Bldg. materials. Bluepoint oysters take their name from here.

Blue Range, Greenlee co., E Ariz., W of Blue R., N of Elifton, in sect. of Apache-Sitgreaves Natl. Forest. Chief peaks are Mitchell (7,951 ft/2,423 m) and Rose (8,786 ft/2,678 m; range's highest point) peaks.

Blue Rapids, town (1990 pop. 1,131), Marshall co., NE Kansas, on Big Blue R. near mouth of Little Blue R., 11 mi/18 km S of Marysville; 39°40′N 96°39′W. Gypsum processing; stone quarries, sandpits. Alcove Springs Park. Inc. 1872.

Blue Ridge 1 town (1990 pop. 1,336), ⊙ Fannin co., N Ga., 38 mi/61 km ENE of Dalton, in the Blue Ridge and Chattahoochee Natl. Forest; 34°52′N 84°20′W. Mfg. includes textiles, clothing; printing and publishing. Blue Ridge dam and lake nearby. Scenic outdoor recreation area. Inc. 1887. **2** uninc. town (1990 pop. 2,840), Botetourt co., W central Va., in the Blue Ridge Mts., suburb 11 mi/18 km NNE of Roanoke; 37°22′N 79°49′W. Mfg. (crushed stone, bldg. materials). Blue Ridge Parkway passes to W; Appalachian Trail passes to NW.

Blue Ridge 1 resort village, Essex co., NE N.Y., in the Adirondacks, 19 mi/31 km NW of Ticonderoga; 43°57′N 73°47′W. Post office in North Hudson. **2** village (1990 pop. 521), Collin co., N Texas, 25 mi/40 km SSE of Sherman; 33°17′N 96°24′W. In agr. area (cotton, wheat, sorghum; cattle, horses).

Blue Ridge, E range of the Appalachian Mts., extending S from S Pa. to N Ga.; highest mts. in the E U.S. Mt. Mitchell, 6,684 ft/2,037 m high, is the tallest peak. Beginning with a narrow ridge in the N, c.10 mi/16 km wide, the range broadens toward the S, reaching a max. width of 70 mi/113 km in N.C. Receiving much rain, the region is heavily forested; wood is the area's chief resource. The Blue Ridge was a barrier to the pioneers' W movement. Numerous gaps cross the ridge; the gap at Harpers Ferry (W.Va.) was an important RR traverse. Most of the people of the Blue Ridge live on small farms in sheltered valleys and retain traditional lifestyles and speech. Principal economic activities here include livestock raising, farming, tobacco growing, and lumber production. Commercial apple orchards are found in Va., Md., and Pa. The Blue Ridge is a major East Coast recreation area noted for its resorts and scenery. The APPALACHIAN TRAIL winds atop the range. Skyline Drive (Va.), following the crest of the Blue Ridge in Shenandoah Natl. Park, has many roadside lookouts. The BLUE RIDGE PARKWAY, designed especially for motor-vehicle pleasure driving, links the Shenandoah and Great Smoky Mountains natl. parks.

Blue Ridge Dam, Ga.: see BLUE RIDGE LAKE.

Blue Ridge Lake, reservoir (□ 5 sq mi/13 sq km), Fannin co., N Ga., on Toccoa R. (called Ocoee R. in Tenn., to N), in Chattahoochee Natl. Forest, 3 mi/4.8 km ENE of Blue Ridge town; 10 mi/16 km long; 34°52′N 84°16′W. Max. capacity 200,800 acre-ft. Formed by Blue Ridge L. (167 ft/51 m high, 1,000 ft/305 m long), built (1931) by private interests for power generation, now owned by TVA. Red Top Mountain State Park is here. Also called L. Toccoa.

Blue Ridge Manor, village (1990 pop. 550), Jefferson co., N Ky., residential suburb 8 mi/12.9 km E of downtown Louisville; 38°14′N 85°33′W.

Blue Ridge Parkway, limited-access highway, 469 mi/755 km long, in Va. and N.C., bet. Front Royal (Va.) and Balsam (N.C.), unit of natl. park system; average elev. 3,000 ft/914 m. Scenic route in the Blue Ridge mts. between Shenandoah (to N) and Great Smoky Mountains (to S) natl. parks; many roadside parks, lookouts, and trails; the 1st natl. parkway. Continues as Skyline Drive in Shenandoah Natl. Park. Passes Waynesboro, Roanoke (Va.), and Asheville (N.C.). Authorized 1936.

Blue Ridge Summit, uninc. town (1990 pop. 1,800), Franklin co., S Pa., 6 mi/9.7 km ESE of Waynesboro, at Md. state line; 39°43′N 77°28′W. Mfg. (bldg. equip.; book publishing); resort area. Fort Ritchie Military Reservation (Md.) to SW; Victor Cullen State Hosp. (Md.) to SE. South Mountain Ridge and Appalachian Trail to W.

Blue River, village, SE B.C., W Canada, at foot of Rocky Mts., on North Thompson R., 75 mi/121 km SW of Jasper; 52°06′N 119°18′W. Lumbering.

Blue River 1 village (1990 pop. 440), Summit co., central Colo., 3 mi/4.8 km S of Breckenridge, on Blue R.; elev. c.10,000 ft/3,048 m; 39°25′N 106°02′W. Area surrounded by Arapaho Natl. Forest; Continental Divide to S and SE. Timber; tourism. **2** village (1990 pop. 438), Grant co., SW Wis., on Wis. R. at mouth of Blue R., 30 mi/48 km E of Prairie du Chien; 43°11′N 90°34′W. Makes cheese; mfg. (cattle butchering); lumber.

Blue River 1 c.65 mi/105 km long, Greenlee co., E Ariz.; rises near N.Mex. state line c.28 mi/45 km SSE of Eager; flows generally S through Apache-Sitgreaves Natl. Forest to San Francisco R. 12 mi/19 km NE of Clifton. **2** c.75 mi/121 km long, N central Colo.; rises at Continental Divide, in Park Range near Quandary Peak; flows N past Breckenridge and Frisco, through Dillon Reservoir, then NNW past Silverthorne, past Gore Range (W), through Green Mountain Reservoir to Colo. R. at Kremmling. Green Mountain Dam (309 ft/94 m high, 1,060 ft/323 m long; completed 1943 as unit in Colorado–Big Thompson project) is 13 mi/21 km SSE of Kremmling. Green Mountain Reservoir 4 mi/6.4 km long, 1 mi/1.6 km wide at dam, formed by dam, has capacity of 154,645 acres/62,585 ha; stores water for generation of power and irrigation. **3** c.50 mi/80 km long, S Ind.; rises in NE Washington co.; flows SW and S, past Salem, to Ohio R. just SE of Leavenworth. **4** c.95 mi/153 km long, S Okla.; rises in SW Pontotoc co.; flows SE, past Milburn, to Red R. 23 mi/37 km WSW of Hugo.

Blue River Lake, reservoir, Lane co., W central Oregon, on Blue R., 37 mi/60 km ENE of Eugene; 5 mi/8 km long; 44°10′N 122°19′W. Max. capacity 89,000 acre-ft. Formed by Blue River Dam (278 ft/85 m high), built (1968) by the Army Corps of Engineers for flood control.

Blue River Peak, Colo.: see GORE RANGE.

Blue Springs, city (1990 pop. 40,153), Jackson co., W Mo., commuter suburb 18 mi/29 km E of Kansas City; 39°01′N 94°16′W. Agr. to E, wheat, corn; dairy farms. Mfg. (fabricated metal prods., tool and die, apparel, transportation equip., paper prods.).

Blue Springs, town (1990 pop. 108), Barbour co., SE Ala., 27 mi/43 km SW of Eufaula. Bottled spring water. Blue Springs State Park nearby.

Blue Springs 1 village (1990 pop. 140), Union co., N Miss., 10 mi/16 km SE of New Albany; 34°23′N 88°52′W. In agr. and dairying area; mfg. (machining; wood prods.). **2** village (1990 pop. 431), Gage co., SE Nebr., 10 mi/16 km SSE of Beatrice, on Big Blue R; 40°08′N 96°39′W. RR junction. Poultry prods.; grain.

Bluefield, city (1990 pop. 12,756), Mercer co., extreme S

W.Va., on Va. state line, in the Allegheny Mts., 75 mi/121 km SSE of Charlestown and adjacent to Bluefield (Va.) to SW; 37°15′N 81°13′W. Mfg. (printing and publishing, baked goods, transportation equip., machinery); lumber; quarries, coal mines. RR center, airport. Seat of Bluefield State Col. Pinnacle State Park to NW; Camp Creek State Forest to N. Settled 1777, inc. 1889.

Bluefield, town (1990 pop. 5,363), Tazewell co., SW Va., 70 mi/113 km W of Roanoke, on W.Va. state line, adjoining Bluefield (W.Va.), to NE; 37°14′N 81°16′W. Mfg. (transportation equip., machinery, pulverized limestone, construction materials, laminated veneers, commercial printing, machining, coal processing); agr. (dairying; livestock; tobacco, grain); bituminous coal, limestone.

Bluefields, town and minor port (1991 pop. 2,564), Westmoreland parish, SW Jamaica, 7 mi/11.3 km ESE of Savanna-la-Mar; 18°10′N 78°02′W. Ships logwood.

Bluegrass Region, the, N and central Ky., physiographic region (□ c.8,000 sq mi/20,720 sq km) with Lexington at its heart; bounded NW, N, and NE by Ohio R., on other sides by semicircle of low hills (the Knobs) extending SE from vicinity of Louisville in curve enclosing Bardstown, Danville, and Richmond, then NE to the Ohio near Maysville. A gently rolling plain (elev. c.1,000 ft/305 m) of exceptionally rich phosphatic limestone soil; watered by Kentucky and Licking rivers and their forks. Inner Bluegrass (□ c.2,400 sq mi/6,216 sq km), the richest part, centers on Lexington; region is known for its thoroughbred horse farms which provide contenders for famed Kentucky racetracks. Around it a less fertile shale belt, in turn surrounded by the Outer Bluegrass, with soils similar to the inner region. Besides saddle and race horses, cattle, mules, sheep, and other livestock, region produces bluegrass seed, burley tobacco, forage crops, corn, grains.

Bluejacket, village (1990 pop. 175), Craig co., NE Okla., 11 mi/18 km NNE of Vinita; 36°47′N 95°04′W. In farm area.

Bluestone, Natl. Wild and Scenic River and Riverway (□ 7 sq mi/18.1 sq km), Summers and Mercer cos., S W.Va., c.18 mi/29 km SSE of Beckley; consists of c.10 mi/16 km of the lower Bluestone R. immediately above its entrance to Bluestone L. reservoir (SW); 37°37′N 80°56′W. Fishing, hiking, boating; known for its scenery. Authorized 1988.

Bluestone Lake, reservoir, S W.Va. and S Va., on New R., 2 mi/3.2 km SSW of Hinton; c.36 mi/58 km long; 80°54′N 31°37′W. Max. capacity 631,000 acre-ft. Bluestone R. enters from SW to form a c.8-mi/12.9-km W arm. Formed by Bluestone Dam (165 ft/50 m high) built (1948) for flood control and power generation. Bluestone State Park in N, near dam; Bluestone Wildlife Management Area surrounds most of lake.

Bluestone River, 77 mi/124 km long, in Va. and W.Va.; rises near Va.-W.Va. state line in N Tazewell co., SW Va., 10 mi/16 km W of Bluefield; flows generally NE into W.Va., NW of Bluefield and Princeton (W.Va.), to New R. (Bluestone Reservoir) 4 mi/6.4 km S of Hinton. Lower c.10 mi/16 km flows through Natl. Wild and Scenic River and Riverway, Pipestone and Bluestone State Parks.

Bluewater 1 uninc. village (1990 pop. 217), San Bernardino co., SE Calif., 3 mi/4.8 km ENE of Parker (Ariz.), on Colorado River Indian Reservation; 34°10′N 114°16′W. Residential community. **2** uninc. village (1990 pop. 300), Cibola co., N.Mex., 10 mi/16 km NW of Grants, on Rio San Jose R., just E of Zuni Mts.; elev. 6,627 ft/2,020 m. Bluewater Lake Reservoir and State Park to W and parts of Cibola Natl. Forest to E and SW.

Bluewater Lake, reservoir, Cibola and McKinley cos., NW N.Mex., on Bluewater Creek, in Bluewater Lake State Park, 37 mi/60 km ESE of Gallup; 8 mi/12.9 km long; 35°15′N 108°04′W. Max. capacity 52,775 acre-ft. Formed by Bluewater Dam (arch dam; 75 ft/23 m high), built by Bluewater Toltec Irrigation Dept. for irrigation.

Bluff City, city (1990 pop. 1,390), Sullivan co., NE Tenn., on South Fork of Holston R., 12 mi/19 km NNE of Johnson City; 36°28′N 82°16′W. In hilly agr. area. Cherokee Natl. Forest nearby.

Bluff City, village (1990 pop. 69), Harper co., S Kansas, on Bluff Creek of Chikaskia R., 10 mi/16 km SE of Anthony, near Okla. state line; 37°04′N 97°52′W. Grain; livestock.

Bluff Dale, uninc. village (1990 pop. 123), Erath co., N central Texas, c.45 mi/72 km SW of Fort Worth. In agr. area.

Bluffdale, town (1990 pop. 2,152), Salt Lake co., N central Utah, suburb 19 mi/31 km S of Salt Lake City, on Jordan R. Utah L.; 40°28′N 111°57′W. Cattle; dairying. At entrance to Camp Williams Military Reservation, to SW.

Bluffs, village (1990 pop. 774), Scott co., W central Ill., near Ill. R., 9 mi/14.5 km NNW of Winchester; 39°45′N 90°31′W. In agr. area (corn, soybeans, sorghum; cattle, hogs).

Bluffton, city (1990 pop. 9,020), ⊙ Wells co., E Ind., on the Wabash R., 24 mi/39 km S of Fort Wayne; 40°44′N 85°10′W. Farming and dairying center; mfg. (food processing, machinery, fabricated metal prods., fiberglass prods., foods, rubber prods., transportation equip.); limestone quarrying. RR junction. Has a large arboretum. Ouabache State Park to E. Laid out 1838, inc. 1858.

Bluffton 1 town (1990 pop. 138), Clay co., SW Ga., 17 mi/27 km SSW of Cuthbert; 31°31′N 84°52′W. **2** town (1990 pop. 738), Beaufort co., S S.C., on May R., 17 mi/27 km NE of Savannah (Ga.); 32°14′N 80°51′W. Fishing; oysters. Resort; Hilton Head resort area to SE. Mfg. includes consumer goods, linens. Agr. includes livestock; tomatoes, vegetables.

Bluffton 1 village (1990 pop. 187), Otter Tail co., W Minn., 5 mi/8 km WNW of Wadena, on Leaf R.; 46°28′N 95°13′W. In agr. area; dairying; grain; mfg. (chemical fertilizers). **2** village (1990 pop. 3,367), Allen co., W Ohio, 15 mi/24 km NE of Lima; 40°56′N 83°55′W. RR junction; limestone quarrying and crushing; mfg. of electrical apparatus, clothing, food and dairy prods. Seat of Bluffton Col., a Mennonite institution. Founded 1833, inc. 1861.

Bluford, village (1990 pop. 747), Jefferson co., S Ill., 8 mi/12.9 km E of Mount Vernon; 38°19′N 88°44′W. In agr. area.

Blum, village (1990 pop. 358), Hill co., N central Texas, 13 mi/21 km NW of Hillsboro, on Nolan Creek; 32°08′N 97°24′W. In farm area.

Blunt, village (1990 pop. 342), Hughes co., central S.Dak., 20 mi/32 km NE of Pierre, on Medicine Knoll Creek. In agr. area; RR junction.

Blying Sound (BLEI-yeeng), S Alaska, NW arm of Gulf of Alaska; washes Kenai Peninsula S of Seward.

Blyth (BLITH), village (1991 pop. 955), S Ont., central Canada, 15 mi/24 km E of Goderich. Lumbering; dairying.

Blythe 1 town (1990 pop. 8,428), Riverside co., SE Calif., in irrigated Palo Verde Valley, near Colorado R. (5 mi/8 km E), c.60 mi/97 km N of Yuma (Ariz.), and c.90 mi/145 km E of Indio (Calif.); 33°37′N 114°36′W. Cotton, alfalfa, melons, grain. Mfg. (concrete); gypsum mining. RR spur terminus to SW at Ripley. Seat of Palo Verde Col. (2-year); Blythe Airport to W; Colorado River Indian Reservation (Calif. and Ariz.) to NE; fish hatchery to N; Big Maria Mts. to N. Laid out 1910, inc. 1916. **2** (BLEITH), town (1990 pop. 300), Richmond and Burke cos., E Ga., 16 mi/26 km SW of Augusta; 33°17′N 82°12′W.

Blythedale (BLEI-dail), town (1990 pop. 130), Harrison co., NW Mo., 16 mi/26 km NNE of Bethany; 40°28′N 93°55′W.

Blytheville (BLEITH-vil), city (1990 pop. 22,906), ⊙ Miss. co. (shares functions with Osceola), NE Ark., near the Mississippi R., near Mo. state line; 35°55′N 89°55′W. Trading center for a cotton area; soybeans and feed crops are grown in the region. Mfg. (transportation equip., plastic prods., canned foods, discharge ballasts, machinery, fluid valves, fabricated metal prods., bldg. materials, agr. chemicals). Seat of Miss. Co. Community Col. Big Lake Wildlife Management Area and Natl. Wildlife Refuge are located in area. Inc. 1891.

Blythewood, village (1990 pop. 164), Richland co., central S.C., 15 mi/24 km NNE of Columbia; 34°13′N 80°58′W. Mfg. includes machining; laminated paper prods., specialty chemicals. Agr. includes poultry, livestock; grain.

Boalsburg (BOLS-buhrg), uninc. town (1990 pop. 2,206), Centre co., central Pa., 4 mi/6.4 km E of State College; 40°46′N 77°47′W. Mfg. (electric and electronic equipment). Agr. area (vegetables, grain; livestock, poultry; dairying). Columbus Chapel; Boal Mansion and Mus., Pa. Military Mus. Rothrock State Forest to S; Tussey Mt. Ski Area to E. Was important stagecoach stop. Laid out 1810. Birthplace of Memorial Day.

Boar Island, Canada: see BURGEO ISLANDS.

Boardman, town (1990 pop. 1,387), Morrow co., N Oregon, 19 mi/31 km W of Herniston, on Columbia R and L. Umatilla reservoir; 45°50′N 119°42′W. Food processing. Umatilla Natl. Wildlife Refuge (Wash. and Oregon) to N and W. Umatilla Ordnance Depot to E.

Boardman River, c.45 mi/72 km long, NW Mich.; rises NE of Kalkaska in Kalkaska co., flows SW and N, past Kalkaska and through forest region, to West Arm of Grand Traverse Bay at Traverse City; 44°40′N 85°23′W. Trout fishing.

Boat Basin, village, SW B.C., Canada, on W central Vancouver Isl., on Clayoquot Sound, 32 mi/51 km NW of Tofino; 49°29′N 126°25′W. Gold mining; fishing, logging.

Boaz 1 (BO-az), town (1990 pop. 6,928), Marshall co., NE Ala., 14 mi/23 km SE of Guntersville; 34°12′N 86°09′W. Mobile homes, furniture, textiles. Snead State Junior Col. Major factory-outlet center is here. Settled 1878, inc. 1891. **2** uninc. town (1990 pop. 1,137), Wood co., NW W.Va., 7 mi/11.3 km NNE of Parkersburg and 4 mi/6.4 km SSW of Marietta (Ohio), on Ohio R.; 39°22′N 81°29′W. Agr. (grain, soybeans); livestock, poultry. Wood Co. Airport to SE. Early Americana Mus. and Henderson Hall mansion (1836) are here.

Boaz, village (1990 pop. 131), Richland co., S central Wis., on Mill Creek (tributary of the Wisconsin R.), 7 mi/11.3 km W of Richland Center; 43°19′N 90°31′W. In dairy and livestock region. Eagle Cave to SW.

Boaz Island, small island of W Bermuda, just NE of Somerset Isl., 4.5 mi/7.2 km W of Hamilton; ½ mi/⁹⁄₁₀ km long, ⅓ mi/³⁄₁₀ km wide; 32°18′N 64°51′W. Inhabited. Road connects SW with Somerset Isl., NE with Ireland Isl.

Bobcaygeon (bawb-KAI-juhn), village (1991 pop. 2,562), S Ont., Canada, on small isl. bet. Sturgeon (W) and Pigeon (E) lakes, 20 mi/32 km NW of Peterborough; 44°32′N 78°33′W. Center for Kawartha lakes resorts; boatbuilding, dairying. Former lumber center.

Bobtown, uninc. town (1990 pop. 1,008), Greene co., SW Pa., 8 mi/12.9 km N of Morgantown (W.Va.) and 14 mi/23 km SE of Waynesburg (Pa.), near W.Va. state line; 39°45′N 79°58′W. Dairying.

Boca Chica (BO-kah CHEE-kah), town and beach resort community (1981 pop. 25,831), on S coast of Dominican Republic, on a small Caribbean bay, 19 mi/31 km E of Santo Domingo and just E of Santo Domingo airport. Sugar milling and refining.

Boca Chica, Texas: see BRAZOS ISLAND.

Boca Dam, Calif.: see LITTLE TRUCKEE RIVER.

Boca de Cangrejos (BO-kah day kahn-GRAI-hos), locality, NE P.R., 4 mi/6.4 km E of San Juan. Fishing.

Boca del Río (BO-kah del REE-o), town (1990 pop. 8,381), Veracruz state, E Mexico, on Gulf of Mexico, 6 mi/9.7 km S of Veracruz; 19°08′N 96°08′W. Beach resort, with adjoining Mocambo beaches.

Boca Grande, Fla.: see GASPARILLA ISLAND.

Boca Raton (BO-kuh ruh-TAWN), city (□ 29 sq mi/75 sq km; 1990 pop. 61,492), extreme SE Palm Beach co., SE Fla., on the Atlantic; 26°22′N 80°06′W. Popular resort city that experienced significant industrial and residential (including retirement) development in the 1970s and 1980s. A major retailing industry and high-tech mfg. made it the 2d-most important urban center in Palm Beach co. after West Palm Beach. Mfg. includes computers, plastics, electrical equip., furniture, jewelry, paint, and hovercrafts. Fla. Atlantic Univ. and Marymount Col.; internatl. mus. of cartoon art. Inc. 1925.

Boca West (BO-kuh), suburban residential community (□ 2 sq mi/5.2 sq km; 1990 pop. 2,874) adjoining Boca Raton, Palm Beach co., SE Fla.; 26°22′N 80°09′W.

Bochil (bo-CHEEL), town (1990 pop. 6,579), Chiapas state, S Mexico, in N spur of Sierra Madre, 23 mi/37 km NE of Tuxtla Gutiérrez; elev. 4,173 ft/1,272 m. Cereals, tobacco, sugar, fruit. In Tzotzil Maya–speaking area.

Bock (BAWK), village (1990 pop. 115), Mille Lacs co., E Minn., 5 mi/8 km NE of Milaca, near Bogus Brook; 45°46′N 93°32′W. Agr. area (grain; livestock, poultry; dairying). Part of Rum R. State Forest to N.

Bocoyna (bo-KOI-nah), town (1990 pop. 961), Chihuahua state, N Mexico, in Sierra Madre Occidental, on Chihuahua-Pacific Railroad, 110 mi/177 km WSW of Chihuahua; 27°50′N 107°32′W. Grain, beans, fruit; cattle.

Bodcau Bayou and Creek (BOD-kaw), river, c.125 mi/ 201 km, in Ark. and La.; rises as Bodeau Creek S of Hope in Hempstead co., SW Ark., flows generally S, past Stamps through L. Erling Reservoir, into NW La., through Bodcau State Wildlife Area to Red R. just S of L. Bistineau. Dam 35 mi/56 km NE of L. Erling. Lafayette Wildlife Management Area to W of L. Erling. Called Bodeau Creek, above L. Erling, in Ark.

Bodden Town, town (1989 pop. 3,407), in Cayman Isls., on S central coast of Grand Cayman isl., 8 mi/12.9 km E of Georgetown.

Bode, town (1990 pop. 335), Humboldt co., N central Iowa, 11 mi/18 km NW of Dakota City; 42°52′N 94°17′W.

Bodega Bay (bo-DAI-gah), uninc. town (1990 pop. 1,127), Sonoma co., W Calif., 18 mi/29 km W of Santa Rosa, at N end of Bodega Bay, Pacific Ocean; 38°19′N 123°02′W. Sonoma Coast State Beach to N. Dairying, sheep, poultry, fruit, nursery products, grain; fish, urchins. Alfred Hitchcock's movie *The Birds* was filmed here (1963).

Bodega Bay, Sonoma co., W Calif., shallow, sandchoked inlet of Pacific Ocean, 20 mi/32 km W of Santa Rosa; sheltered on W by peninsula terminating at Bodega Head. On E shore is Bodega Bay village (fishing), formerly called Bay. A Rus. fur post was est. here c.1811. Was an active harbor until 1870s.

Bodfish, uninc. town (1990 pop. 1283), Kern co., S central Calif., 30 mi/48 km NE of Bakersfield, on Kern R. (Isabella Dam and Lake to NE), in Sierra Nevada; 35°35′N 118°30′W. Parts of Sequoia Natl. Forest to E and W; Miracle Hot Springs to SW; Shirley Meadows Ski Area to NE. Resort area. Tourism. Cattle; grain; timber.

Bodie, uninc. village, Mono co., E Calif., in the Sierra Nevada, c.11 mi/18 km ESE of Bridgeport. Gold mining. In 1870s, was gold boom town, with pop. of c.12,000. Bodie State Historical Park; Mono L. 8 mi/12.9 km to S; Nevada state line 5 mi/8 km to NE.

Bodie Island (BO-dee), Dare co., E N.C., name given to section of the Outer Banks N of Oregon Inlet (bridged to Hatteras Isl.), Atlantic Ocean to E, Roanoke Sound to W and just E of Roanoke Isl.; lighthouse at S end on Oregon Inlet.

Bodkin Point, low headland, Anne Arundel co., central Md., at S side of mouth of Patapsco R. on Chesapeake Bay, 15 mi/24 km SE of downtown Baltimore.

Boelus (BO-luhs) or **Howard City**, village (1990 pop. 203), Howard co., SE central Nebr., on Middle Loup R., 16 mi/26 km SW of St. Paul. Nearby dam, on Loup R., is part of power project. Inc. as Howard City.

Boerne (BUHR-nee), town (1990 pop. 4,274), ⊙ Kendall co., S central Texas, on Edwards Plateau, 30 mi/48 km NNW of San Antonio, near Cibolo Creek; 29°48′N 98°44′W. Elev. 1,403 ft/428 m. Trade center, vacation and health resort in hilly region; sheep, Angora goats, and cattle. Mfg. (printing, diversified light and consumer goods mfg.). Guadalupe R. State Park to E; Cascade Caverns nearby. Founded c.1850 by Germans, inc. 1909.

Boerum Hill, section of W central borough of Brooklyn, N.Y. city, SE N.Y., residential brownstone precinct just S of Brooklyn Heights. In the mid-19th cent. this was

a fashionable dist. of fine row houses. Today it is an ethnically mixed community that after years of neglect has been partly designated as the Boerum Hill Historic Dist., which has preserved several architecturally distinctive row and single houses, particularly in the vicinity of Pacific, Dean, and Hoyt Sts. In the mid-1970s, Atlantic Ave. developed as a mile-long magnet for antique shops and restaurants extending from the Middle Eastern–flavored Cobble Hill area (W of Court St.) to 3d Ave.

Boeuf River (BEF), c.230 mi/370 km long, in Ark. and La.; rises in Chicot co., SE Ark. SE of Dermott, flows S and SW, into NE La., past Rayville and Hebert to Ouachita R. c.6 mi/9.7 km NNE of Harrisonburg. Navigable by small craft..

Bog Walk, town (1991 pop. 8,794), St. Catherine parish, central Jamaica, on gorge of Cobre R. (irrigation), on RR, 9 mi/14.5 km NNW of Spanish Town; 18°06′N 77°01′W. Coconuts and bananas; milk processing. Hydroelectric station.

Bogachiel River (BO-guh-sheel), c.50 mi/80 km long, Clallan and Jefferson cos., NW Wash.; rises NW of Mt. Olympus, in Olympic Natl. Park, flows NW through park and part of Olympic Natl. Forest to junction with Soleduck (Sol Duc) R., forming Quillayute R. E of La Push.

Bogalusa (bo-guh-LOO-suh), city (1994 pop. 14,915), Washington parish, SE La., 53 mi/85 km NNE of New Orleans, near Pearl R.; elev. 105 ft/32 m.; 30°47′N 89°52′W. Mfg. and trading center of the Pearl R. valley. Its name derives from the Bogue Lusa [Native Amer. = smoky or dark waters] creek that flows through the city. Founded in 1906 when the lumber industry established operations in the extensive pine area. Mfg. includes textiles, fabricated metal prods., food, machinery, furniture, wood prods., printing and publishing. Timber; agr. (watermelons, pumpkins; cattle, exotic fowl; dairying). Seat of La. State Univ. Forestry School. George R. Carr Memorial Airfield nearby. Annual Watermelon Festival. Ben's Creek State Wildlife Area to W, Bogue Chitto Natl. Wildlife Refuge to S. Inc. 1914.

Bogard (BO-gahrd), town (1990 pop. 228), Carroll co., NW central Mo., 7 mi/11 km N of Carrollton; 39°27′N 93°31′W. Corn; hogs, cattle.

Bogart (BO-gahrt), town (1990 pop. 1,018), Oconee and Clarke cos., NE central Ga., 9 mi/14.5 km W of Athens; 33°57′N 83°32′W. Mfg. includes textiles, signs, foods, transportation equip.; light mfg.

Bogart, Mount (10,315 ft/3,144 m), SW Alta., Canada, near B.C. border, near SE edge of Banff Natl. Park, 23 mi/37 km SE of Banff.

Bogata (bo-GO-tuh), town (1990 pop. 1,421), Red R. co., NE Texas, 24 mi/39 km SE of Paris, near Sulphur R.; 33°28′N 95°12′W. In agr. and timber area; mfg. (concrete).

Boger City (BO-guhr), uninc. town (1990 pop. 1,373), Lincoln co., W central N.C., 2 mi/3.2 km ENE of Lincolnton; 35°28′N 81°12′W. Cotton, grain; chickens, cattle, hogs; dairying.

Boggstown, village, Shelby co., central Ind., 8 mi/ 12.9 km WNW of Shelbyville. In agr. area. Mfg. (meat processing, fertilizer blending).

Boggy Creek, Okla.: see CLEAR BOGGY CREEK.

Boggy Peak (1,329 ft/405 m), SW Antigua, Antigua and Barbuda Republic, West Indies, 5 mi/8 km S of St. John's; 17°03′N 61°51′W.

Bogoslof Island (BO-guh-slawv), volcanic islet, SW Alaska, Aleutian Isls., in Bering Sea, 27 mi/43 km N of Umnak Isl.; 53°56′N 168°02′W. Of recent formation, its recorded eruptions (each changing isl.'s shape), were in 1796 (when it 1st appeared), 1883, 1906, 1910, and 1923–1927. Useful landfall for navigators to Bering Sea.

Bogota (buh-GO-tuh), residential borough (1990 pop. 7,824), Bergen co., NE N.J., on Hackensack R., just SE of Hackensack; 40°52′N 74°01′W. Mfg. (machinery). Inc. 1894.

Bogue (BOG), village (1990 pop. 150), Graham co., NW Kansas, on South Fork Solomon R., 8 mi/12.9 km E of Hill City; 39°21′N 99°41′W. Grain.

Bogue Chitto (bo-guh CHIT-uh), uninc. village (1990

pop. 689), Lincoln co., SW Miss., 10 mi/16 km S of Brookhaven, on the Bogue Chitto; 32°50′N 88°55′W. Mfg. (wood chips).

Bogue Chitto (bo-guh CHIT-uh), river, c.105 mi/169 km long, in SW Miss.; and SE La.; rises near Brookhaven, Lincoln co., SW Miss.; flows SE, past Bogue Chitto village (Miss.) and Franklinton (La.), to Pearl R. c.24 mi/ 39 km S of Bogalusa, in Bogue Chitto Natl. Wildlife Refuge.

Bogue Falaya (bog fuh-LEI-uh), stream, c.23 mi/37 km long, in SE La.; rises in Washington parish; flows generally SSE, past Covington, to Tchefuncte R. c.10 mi/ 16 km above its mouth; 30°26′N 90°06′W. Also called Long R.

Bogue Island (BOG) or **Bogue Banks**, narrow sand barrier (c.25 mi/40 km long), Carteret co., E N.C., bet. Atlantic Ocean (Onslow Bay, S) and Bogue Sound (N). On E end are town of Atlantic Beach and Fort Macon State Park (□ ½ sq mi/1.3 sq km; recreational facilities; town of Emerald Isles in W part; old fort begun in 1820s, restored 1936). Bridges to mainland at both ends. Intracoastal Waterway passes to N in Bogue Sound.

Bogue Islands, St. James parish, merged with Montego Bay to form Montego Bay Freeport, Jamaica; 18°28′N 77°57′W. An important tanker berth center for cruise ships. Known for oyster beds and marine gardens.

Bogue Sound (BOG), Carteret co., E N.C., waterway sheltered from the Atlantic Ocean by Bogue Isl. sand barrier; c.30 mi/48 km long E-W, 2 mi/3.2 km wide; connected with ocean by Bogue Inlet at W end, Beaufort Inlet at E end. Bridged in E bet. Morehead City and Atlantic Beach and in W to Cedar Point. Intracoastal Waterway passes through length of sound.

Bohemia, village (□ 8 sq mi/20.7 sq km; 1990 pop. 9,556), Suffolk co., SE N.Y., in central L.I., 26 mi/42 km WSW of Riverhead; 40°46′N 73°07′W. Light mfg.

Bohom, Mexico: see CHAMULA.

Boiceville (BOIS-vil), village, Ulster co., SE N.Y., in the Catskills, on Esopus Creek, 15 mi/24 km WNW of Kingston, near Ashokan Reservoir; 42°00′N 74°16′W. Summer recreational residences and tourist area. Lumber milling.

Boiestown (BOIZ-toun), village, central N.B., Canada, on Southwest Miramichi R., 40 mi/64 km NNW of Fredericton; 46°27′N 66°24′W. Lumbering; salmon fishing.

Boiling Lake, S Dominica, 6 mi/9.7 km ENE of Roseau. Actually a geyser of boiling sulphur, about 300 ft/91 m by 200 ft/61 m.

Boiling Spring Lakes, town (1990 pop. 1,650), Brunswick co., SE N.C., 18 mi/29 km SSW of Wilmington; 34°01′N 78°04′W. Orton Pond, inlet of Cape Fear R. estuary, to NE. Sunny Point Army Base to E; Orton Plantation Gardens and Brunswick Town State Historic Site to NE.

Boiling Springs 1 town (1990 pop. 2,445), Cleveland co., S N.C., 7 mi/11.3 km WSW of Shelby near Broad R; 35°15′N 81°40′W. Cotton, grain, soybeans, sorghum; poultry, livestock. Wood prods., construction materials, textiles, transportation equip. Seat of Gardner-Webb Univ. **2** uninc. town (1990 pop. 1,978), South Middleton township, Cumberland co., S Pa., 15 mi/ 24 km WSW of Harrisburg, on Yellow Breeches Creek; 40°09′N 77°08′W. Mfg. (handmade violins). Agr. area (grain; livestock, poultry; dairying). Appalachian Trail passes to S and E. **3** uninc. town (1990 pop. 3,522), Spartanburg co., NW S.C., 7 mi/11.3 km NNW of Spartanburg; 35°02′N 81°58′W. Agr. area that produces livestock, poultry; grain, soybeans, sorghum, peaches, apples; dairying.

Bois Blanc Island (bwah BLAH) (2 mi/3 km long), S Ont., Canada, in Detroit R., opposite Amherstburg, at U.S. border (Mich. state line), just E of Grosse Île; 45°45′N 84°28′W. Lighthouse.

Bois Blanc Island (BO BLAHNK), Mackinac co., N Mich., in the Straits of Mackinac, 6 mi/9.7 km N of Cheboygan; c.12 mi/19 km long, 4 mi/6.4 km wide; 45°46′N 84°30′W. Hunting, fishing; resort. Village of Pointe Aux Pins on S side, ferry from Cheboygan.

Round, and Mackinac isls. to NW. Lakes on isl. include L. Mary and Thompson, Echo, and Duncan lakes.

Bois Brule River (BWAH BROOL), c.35 mi/56 km, NW Wis., rises in central Douglas co., flows NE and N, through Brule R. State Forest, to L. Superior 23 mi/37 km E of Superior. Trout fishing. Fish hatchery. Sometimes called Brule R.

Bois de Sioux River (BWAH da soo), river, 30 mi/48 km, in N. and S.Dak. and Minn.; rises in L. Traverse, NE S.Dak., flows N and joins Otter Tail R. at Wahpeton, N.Dak. (opposite Breckenridge, Minn.), to form Red R. of the North. Forms S.Dak-Minn. and N.Dak.-Minn. state lines.

Bois Island (BWAH), S N.F., Canada, in Bay d'Espoir; 9 mi/14 km long, 3 mi/5 km wide; 47°45′N 55°57′W.

Bois, Lac des (BWAH, lahk dai), lake, NW Mackenzie dist., N.W.T., Canada, NW of Great Bear L.; 30 mi/48 km long, 12 mi/19 km wide; 66°50′N 125°10′W. Drains N into Anderson R.

Boise, county (□ 1,906 sq mi/4,937 sq km; 1990 pop. 3,509), W Idaho; ⊙ Idaho City; 44°01′N 115°45′W. Mt. area cut by canyons of Payette R. and its Middle and South forks. Arrow Rock Dam and Reservoir and part of Lucky Peak Reservoir, both on Boise R., and Middle Fork Boise R. form S boundary; SE boundary formed by North Fork Boise R. Gold, silver, lead; lumber; cattle. Boise Natl. Forest extends throughout co. except for W margin. Part of Sawtooth Wilderness Area in E, in Sawtooth Range. Formed 1864.

Boise (BOI-see), city (1990 pop. 125,738), ⊙ Idaho and Ada co., SW Idaho, on the Boise R.; 43°37′N 116°14′W. The largest city in Idaho, with one of the fastest growing metropolitan areas in the U.S., Boise is a RR junction and an important trade and transportation center. Mfg. (food processing, paper and wood prods., computer hardware and software, specialty semiconductors and electronics). Has many state and Federal govt. offices. A gold rush in the Boise valley and the establishment of a military post in 1863 led to the founding of Boise City, which grew as a distributing center for miners and became the capital of Idaho Territory in 1864. Later, particularly with the building of Arrow Rock (1911–1915) and Lucky Peak dams, both on SF, the region was developed for farming, and Boise drew wealth from orchards and fields rather than mines. Increased irrigation, hydroelectric power, and flood-control projects associated with the Boise R. have increased the area's agr. yield. In the city are Boise State Univ., Idaho State Historical Mus., an art mus., zoo, and Old Idaho Penitentiary and Mus. in E part of city; Botanical Gardens adjacent. Boise Municipal Airport in S. Snake River Birds of Prey Natural Area 30 mi/48 km S, at Swan Falls, Morrison-Knudsen Nature Center; Lucky Peak Reservoir (Boise R.) and State Park to SE, Veterans Memorial State Park in N part of city, on Snake R.; Boise Natl. Forest to NE; Bogus Basin Ski Area to N. Inc. 1864.

Boise City (BOI-zee), city (1990 pop. 1,509), ⊙ Cimarron co., extreme NW Okla., on high plains of the Panhandle, 50 mi/80 km W of Guymon, c.110 mi/177 km NW of Amarillo (Texas), near North Canadian (Beaver) R.; elev. 4,165 ft/1,269 m. RR junction. In wheat area; cattle, sheep; mfg. (flour milling, plastic parts). Has grain elevator. Black Mesa (4,973 ft/1,516 m), highest point in Okla., 27 mi/43 km to NW; Black Mesa State Park, 18 mi/29 km NW. Old Santa Fe Trail runs SW-NE of town. Rita Blanca Natl. Grassland to SW. Accidentally bombed in 1943 by U.S. servicemen from Dalhart Army Base. Inc. 1925.

Boise Project, in the Boise, Payette, and Snake river valleys, SW Idaho and E Oregon. Developed in 1905 by the U.S. Bureau of Reclamation for irrigation, hydroelectricity, flood control, and recreation. The project has turned the area into a major U.S. grain-producing and dairying region. Anderson Ranch, Arrow Rock, Lucky Peak, and Boise dams are the principal facilities of the project's Arrow Rock div., located bet. the Snake and Boise rivers. The Payette div., bet. the Payette and Boise rivers, includes Black Canyon, Cascade, and Deadwood dams.

Boise River, c.75 mi/121 km long, Idaho and Oregon; rising in SW Idaho, Middle and South forks join at Arrow Rock Reservoir, on the boundary of Boise and Elmore cos., 20 mi/32 km E of Boise, and flowing W through Lucky Peak Reservoir, through city of Boise, past Middleton and Parma, joining the Snake R., 2 mi/3.2 km S of Nyssa (Oregon), at the Oregon state line. South Fork Boise R., rises in N Camac co., 60 mi/97 km E of Boise, flows c.100 mi/161 km generally SW through Anderson Ranch Reservoir then NW to Arrow Rock Reservoir; Middle Fork Boise R., rises in NW Elmore co., Sawtooth Range, 60 mi/97 km ENE of Boise, flows c.70 mi/113 km SW, joining South Fork at Arrow Rock Reservoir. North Fork Boise R. rises in E Boise co., in Sawtooth Range, 60 mi/97 km NE of Boise, flows c.50 mi/80 km SW, joining Middle Fork 15 mi/24 km ENE of Arrow Rock Dam, forms most of boundary bet. Boise and Elmore cos. In 1811 the Boise R., originally called Reed's R., was explored by an expedition financed by John Jacob Astor (1763–1848), an Amer. merchant. Irrigation, hydroelectric power, public water consumption and flood control are part of the Boise Project.

Boissevain (BOI-suh-VAIN), town (1991 pop. 1,484), SW Man., Canada, 45 mi/72 km S of Brandon; 49°14′N 100°03′W. Wheat. Internatl. Peace Gardens are 15 mi/24 km S, on U.S. border.

Boissevain (BOUZ-uh-vain), uninc. village, Tazewell co., SW Va., 5 mi/8 km NW of Bluefield, Va., near W.Va. state line. Livestock; coal mining.

Bokchito (bok-CHEET-uh), village (1990 pop. 576), Bryan co., S Okla., 14 mi/23 km E of Durant, near Blue R.; 34°01′N 96°08′W. In agr. area (corn, peanuts); cattle.

Bokobá (bo-ko-BAH), town (1990 pop. 1,939), Yucatán state, SE Mexico, 29 mi/47 km E of Mérida. Henequen.

Bokoshe (buh-KO-shuh), village (1990 pop. 403), Le Flore co., E Okla., 13 mi/21 km NW of Poteau; 35°11′N 94°47′W. RR junction. In farm area.

Bolaños (bo-LAHN-yos), town (1990 pop. 1,112), Jalisco state, W Mexico, on affluent of Santiago R., 75 mi/121 km NNW of Guadalajara; 21°41′N 103°46′W. Grain, vegetables; livestock. The region nearby was formerly known for silver mines.

Bolaños River (bo-LAHN-yos), c.80 mi/129 km long, Jalisco state, W Mexico; formed by Mezquitic and Colotlán rivers 40 mi/64 km W of Colotlán near Zacatecas border. Flows NNE-SSW, past Bolaños and San Martín de Bolaños, to Santiago R. Merges with Lerma-Santiago S of Sierra Bolaños.

Bolans, village (1991 pop. 1,447), SW Antigua, Antigua and Barbuda Republic, West Indies, 5 mi/8 km SSW of St. John's.

Bolckow (BAWL-ko), town (1990 pop. 253), Andrew co., NW Mo., on One Hundred and Two R., 25 mi/40 km N of St. Joseph; 40°07′N 94°49′W.

Boley (BO-lee), town (1990 pop. 908), Okfuskee co., E central Okla., 20 mi/32 km NE of Seminole, near Canadian R.; 35°29′N 96°28′W. In farming area; mfg. (electronic equip.).

Boligee (BO-luh-gee), town (1990 pop. 268), Greene co., W Ala., 10 mi/16 km SW of Eutaw, near Tombigbee R.; 32°45′N 88°01′W.

Bolinas (bo-leen-ahs), uninc. town (1990 pop. 1,098), Marin co., W Calif., suburb 15 mi/24 km NW of downtown San Francisco and 10 mi/16 km WSW of San Rafael, on Bolinas Bay at entrance to Bolinas Lagoon (c.3.5 mi/5.6 km long); lagoon and bay lie within NW extension of San Andreas Fault; 37°55′N 122°42′W. Resort; fishing. Coast guard lifesaving station here. At SE end of Point Reyes Natl. Seashore.

Boling, town (1990 pop. 1,119), Wharton co., S Texas, c.45 mi/72 km SW of Houston; 29°15′N 95°57′W. RR junction, in irrigated agr. (rice, cotton); sulfur-producing area.

Bolingbroke (BO-leeng-bruk), town, Monroe co., central Ga., 12 mi/19 km NW of Macon; 32°56′N 83°48′W. Mfg. includes crushed stone and asphalt.

Bolingbrook, village (1990 pop. 40,843), Will and Du Page cos., NE Ill., suburb 24 mi/39 km SW of downtown Chicago, 12 mi/19 km NNE of Joliet, near Des Plaines R.; 41°42′N 88°04′W. Agr. (corn; livestock) to W. Trade show exhibits held here. Mfg. (medical instruments and supplies, electric and electronic equip.). Argonne Natl. Laboratory to E. Clow Airport to W.

Bolivar (BAH-liv-uhr), county (□ 905 sq mi/2,344 sq km; 1990 pop. 41,875), W Miss., bounded W by the Mississippi R. (Ark. state line); ⊙ Rosedale and Cleveland; 33°47′N 90°52′W. Drained by Sunflower R. In rich agr. region (soybeans, corn, wheat, sorghum, rice, alfalfa; cattle; timber). Great River Road State Park in W; L. Bolivar State Lake at center; lakes Beulah and Whittington, oxbow lakes of Mississippi R., in W, form part of state line. Formed 1836.

Bolivar 1 (BAH-li-vuhr), city (1990 pop. 6,845), ⊙ Polk co., SW central Mo., in the Ozarks, bet. Pomme de Terre R. and Stockton Lake, 29 mi/47 km N of Springfield; 37°36′N 93°24′W. Cattle; grain center. Light mfg., transportation equip. Seat of Southwest Baptist Col. Statue of Simón Bolívar dedicated here (1948) by president of Venezuela. **2** (BAH-li-VAHR, BAH-li-vuhr), city (1990 pop. 5,969), ⊙ Hardeman co., SW Tenn., 27 mi/43 km SSW of Jackson; 35°15′N 89°00′W. In agr. area (cotton, corn; livestock); lumbering; gravel and clay mining. State mental health hosp. nearby. Founded 1824.

Bolivar (BOL-uh-vuhr), town (1990 pop. 1,013), Jefferson co., W.Va., in E Panhandle, 1 mi/1.6 km SW of Harpers Ferry and 6 mi/9.7 km NE of Charlestown; 39°19′N 77°45′W. Agr. (grain, apples); livestock, poultry; dairying. Harpers Ferry Natl. Historic Park to E; Appalachian Trail passes through town.

Bolivar 1 (BAH-lah-vuhr), village (1990 pop. 1,261), Allegany co., W N.Y., 14 mi/23 km SW of Belmont; 42°04′N 78°10′W. Mfg. of barber and industrial scissors; dairy farming. Surrounding region was prominent early petroleum-producing area from late 19th to early 20th cent. Inc. 1882. **2** village (1990 pop. 914), Tuscarawas co., E Ohio, 11 mi/18 km N of New Philadelphia and on Tuscarawas R.; 40°40′N 81°28′W. Near here on a tributary (Sandy Creek) is Bolivar Dam (6,300 ft/1,920 m long, 87 ft/27 m high; completed 1937 for flood control), impounding reservoir of 149,600 acre-ft. capacity. Fort Laurens State Park is nearby. Site of important Delaware Indian village of Tuscarora in early 1700s.

Bolivar (BO-li-vahr), borough (1990 pop. 544), Westmoreland co., SW central Pa., 14 mi/23 km NW of Johnstown, on Conemaugh R. (bridged), at mouth of Hendricks Creek; 40°23′N 79°09′W. Chestnut Ridge to W. Mfg. (fabricated metal prods.). Agr. (grain, soybeans; livestock; dairying);

Bolivar Peninsula, S Texas, NE of Galveston, extends to SW bet. Galveston and East bays (NW) and the Gulf (SE); c.23 mi/37 km long. Port Bolivar, on Galveston Bay entrance (ferry to Galveston), is at tip; High Isl. oil field is near base; resort beaches along Gulf shore. Gulf Intracoastal Waterway follows land cut extending full length of peninsula on inland side.

Bolivia, sugar-mill town, Ciego de Ávila prov., E Cuba, on RR line, in swampy coastlands, about 7 mi/11.3 km S of N coast and 19 mi/31 km E of Morón; 22°11′N 78°22′W. RR terminus, airfield.

Bolivia, village (1990 pop. 228), Brunswick co., SE N.C., 18 mi/29 km SW of Wilmington. Tobacco, sweet potatoes, grain; cattle, hogs.

Bolling Air Force Base, D.C.: see WASHINGTON, D.C.

Bollinger (bo-lin-guhr), county (□ 621 sq mi/1608 sq km; 1990 pop. 10,619), SE Mo.; ⊙ Marble Hill; 37°19′N 90°01′W. Crossed by Castor and Whitewater rivers; drainage channels in SE. Corn, soybeans, wheat; livestock; timber. Part of Mark Twain Natl. Forest in NW; Duck Creek Conservation Area in SW. Formed 1851.

Bolonchén de Rejón (bo-lon-CHEN de re-HON), village (1990 pop. 3,110), Hopelchen municipio, Campeche state, SE Mexico, on Yucatán Peninsula, 50 mi/80 km ENE of Campeche; 20°05′N 89°55′W. Timber; sugarcane, henequen, chicle, tropical fruit. La Gruta de

Xtucumbi-Xunan, famous water caves with a number of picturesque caverns and pools and an archaeological site are nearby. Also known as Bolonchenticul.

Bolonchenticul, Mexico: see BOLONCHÉN DE REJÓN.

Bolondrón (bo-lon-DRON), town, Matanzas prov., W Cuba, on RR, 20 mi/32 km SSE of Matanzas; 22°45′N 81°26′W. Agr. center (sugarcane, fruit, honey); bet. Juan Avila and Cuba Libre sugar mills. Stone quarrying, lumbering.

Bolsón de los Lipanos, Mexico: see LIPANOS, BOLSÓN DE LOS.

Bolsón de Mapimí, Mexico: see MAPIMÍ, BOLSÓN DE.

Bolton, town, within city of Caledon, S Ont., central Canada, on Humber R., 22 mi/35 km NW of Toronto; 43°53′N 79°44′W. Residential satellite for Toronto. Mfg. (construction materials, pet food, foods), milling, meatpacking; mixed farming, dairying; steel mill. Resort.

Bolton 1 (BOL-tuhn), town (1990 pop. 4,575), Tolland co., central Conn., 13 mi/21 km E of Hartford; 41°45′N 72°26′W. Has state park and small lakes at scenic Bolton Notch State Park. Settled 1718, inc. 1720. **2** town (1990 pop. 3,134), Worcester co., E central Mass., 15 mi/24 km NNE of Worcester, in suburban area; 42°26′N 71°37′W. Fruit; dairying; pigs. Mfg. of electronic and precision instruments. **3** town (1990 pop. 971), Chittenden co., NW Vt., on Winooski R., 18 mi/29 km E of Burlington, in Green Mts.; 44°24′N 72°51′W. Winter sports (Bolton Valley ski area).

Bolton 1 village (1990 pop. 637), Hinds co., W Miss., 25 mi/40 km E of Vicksburg and 15 mi/24 km WNW of Jackson; 32°21′N 90°27′W. Agr. (cotton, corn, soybeans; cattle, poultry); mfg. (lumber, plastic prods.). Natchez Trace (Natl.) Parkway passes to SE. **2** village (1990 pop. 531), Columbus co., SE N.C., 26 mi/42 km WNW of Wilmington; 34°19′N 78°24′W. Peanuts, tobacco, grain; livestock; mfg. (plastic fabricating). L. Waccamaw (State Park) to SW.

Bolton Landing, summer-resort village, Warren co., E N.Y., on W shore of L. George, 17 mi/27 km N of Glens Falls; 43°33′N 73°39′W.

Bolton Valley, ski area, Chittenden co., NW Vt., in town of Bolton, 18 mi/29 km E of Burlington.

Bomarton, uninc. village (1990 pop. 23), Baylor co., N Texas, 11 mi/18 km SW of Seymour. In cattle area.

Bombardopolis (bong-bahr-do-po-LEE), agr. town (1982 pop. 1,200), Nord-Ouest dept., NW Haiti, 38 mi/61 km WSW of Port-de-Paix; 19°42′N 73°20′W. Cotton growing and mfg.

Bombay Hook Island, Kent co., E Del., in Delaware Bay, at entrance to Delaware R., 6 mi/9.7 km E of Smyrna, marshy area separated from mainland by slough (W) and Leipsic R. (S); 8.5 mi/13.7 km long; 39°17′N 75°26′W. Resort of Woodland Beach, near N end, connected by bridge to mainland. S part is Bombay Hook Natl. Wildlife Refuge.

Bomoseen, Lake (BO-mo-zeen), in towns of Castleton and Hubbardton, Rutland co., W Vt., 12 mi/19 km W of Rutland; 7.5 mi/12.1 km long, 1.5 mi/2.4 km wide; 43°37′N 73°13′W. Largest lake wholly within Vt. Surrounded by wooded hills, it is a popular summer resort. Bomoseen and Half Moon state parks here.

Bon Accord (boh nah-KOR), village (1991 pop. 1,460), central Alta., W Canada, 20 mi/32 km N of Edmonton. Oil production.

Bon Air, uninc. city, Chesterfield co., E central Va., residential suburb 9 mi/14.5 km W of downtown Richmond, near James R.; 37°31′N 77°34′W. John Tyler Community Col. (Midlothian Campus) to W.

Bon Air, town (1990 pop. 91), Talladega co., E central Ala., 18 mi/29 km SW of Talladega, near Coosa R. Yarn.

Bon Air, village, White co., central Tenn., 5 mi/8 km E of Sparta; 35°57′N 85°22′W. Surveying camp of Vanderbilt Univ. School of Engineering nearby.

Bon Aqua (bahn A-kwuh), resort village, Hickman co., Tenn., 33 mi/53 km SW of Nashville. Mineral springs.

Bon Homme (BON-hom), county (☐ 581 sq mi/ 1,505 sq km; 1990 pop. 7,089), SE S.Dak., on Neb. state line; ⊙ Tyndall. Bordered S by Missouri R. and W by

Choteau Creek. Diversified farming: corn, wheat, soybeans; dairy prods.; hogs, sheep. Springfield State Recreation and Tabor and Sand Creek State Lakeside Use areas in SE; all on Lewis & Clark L. Formed 1862.

Bon Secour (BON suh-KUHR), village and fishing resort, Baldwin co., SW Ala., on inlet (crossed by Intracoastal Waterway) of Bon Secour Bay (SE arm of Mobile Bay), 40 mi/64 km S of Bay Minette. Fishing; aluminum prods. mfg.

Bon Secours, Canada: see L'ISLET.

Bon Wier, uninc. village (1990 pop. 475), Newton co., E Texas, 55 mi/89 km NE of Beaumont, on Sabine R. (La. state line). Timber area. Mfg. (plywood processing).

Bona, Mount (c.16,420 ft/5,005 m), S Alaska, in St. Elias Mts., 150 mi/241 km ENE of Cordova; 61°23′N 141°45′W.

Bonadelle Ranchos–Madera Ranchos, uninc. town (1990 pop. 5705), Madera co., S central Calif., residential community 8 mi/12.9 km E of Madera; 36°58′N 119°54′W.

Bonaire (bawn-ER), island (☐ 112 sq mi/290 sq km/1990 est. pop. 11,000), in the Neth. Antilles, West Indies, in Caribbean Sea; 12°12′N 68°15′W. Kralendijk is the chief town. Tourism is the economic mainstay, though salt mining is also a significant industry. Known for its fine beaches, skin diving, and pink flamingos.

Bonampak (bo-NAHM-pak), ruined city of the Late Classic period of the Maya, 84 mi/135 km SE of Palenque, in Chiapas state, S Mexico. Discovered in 1946, it consists of a group of temples, one of which is remarkable for a number of very well-preserved frescoes, painted in bright, flat colors, depicting scenes of Maya life in considerable detail.

Bonanza 1 village (1990 pop. 520), Sebastian co., W Ark., 10 mi/16 km S of Fort Smith, near Okla. state line; 35°13′N 94°25′W. **2** village (1990 pop. 16), Saguache co., S central Colo., in S part of Sawatch Mts., 5 mi/8 km SE of Ouray Peak and 14 mi/23 km N of Saguache; elev. 9,465 ft/2,885 m; 38°17′N 106°08′W. Gold mining. Surrounded by Rio Grande Natl. Forest, Continental Divide to NW. **3** (bo-NAN-zuh), village (1990 pop. 323), Klamath co., S Oregon, on Lost R., 17 mi/27 km E of Klamath Falls; 42°12′N 121°24′W. Agr. (barley, potatoes; poultry, cattle); dairy prods. Fremont Natl. Forest to NE. Gerber Reservoir to E. **4** uninc. village, Uintah co., NE Utah, 32 mi/51 km SSE of Vernal, near Colo. state line, near White R. Cattle; gilsonite mining. Hill Creek Extension of Uintah and Ouray Indian Reservation to W.

Bonanza Creek, stream, c.20 mi/30 km long, W Yukon Territory, NW Canada; flows NW to the Klondike R. near Dawson. The 1st gold strike in the Yukon occurred here in 1896.

Bonao (bo-NOU), city (1993 pop. 61,147), central Dominican Republic, ⊙ Monseñor Nouel prov., 22 mi/35 km SSE of La Vega; 18°55′N 70°28′W. Agr. center (coffee, cacao, fruit); nickel deposits. Named for a fort built here by Christopher Columbus.

Bonaparte, town (1990 pop. 465), Van Buren co., SE Iowa, on Des Moines R., 9 mi/14.5 km E of Keosauqua; 40°42′N 91°47′W. Mfg. (gloves, feed, plastic prods.).

Bonaparte, Lake, Lewis co., N N.Y., 28 mi/45 km ENE of Watertown, in W foothills of the Adirondacks; c.2 mi/3.2 km long; 44°09′N 75°23′W. Bonaparte or L. Bonaparte, a resort community, is on S shore. Named for Joseph Bonaparte, king of Spain and Napoleon's brother, who owned land in what is now Lewis co. following the Fr. Revolution.

Bonasse (BO-nahs-se), village, SW Trinidad, Trinidad and Tobago, on Cedros Bay, 45 mi/72 km SW of Port of Spain.

Bonaventure (bah-nuh-VEHN-chur), county (☐ 3,464 sq mi/8,972 sq km), E Que., E Canada, in S part of Gaspé Peninsula, on Chaleur Bay; ⊙ New Carlisle; 48°20′N 66°00′W.

Bonaventure, village (1991 pop. 2,844), E Que., E Canada, on SE Gaspé Peninsula, on Chaleur Bay, at mouth of Bonaventure R., 7 mi/11 km WNW of New Carlisle; 48°03′N 65°28′W. Lumbering; dairying.

Bonaventure Island, in the Gulf of St. Lawrence, off E

Que., E Canada, c.3 mi/5 km N of Perce Rock; 3 mi/5 km long, 1 mi/2 km wide; 48°30′N 64°10′W. Largest bird sanctuary on the North Atlantic coast here.

Bonaventure River, 75 mi/121 km long, E Que., E Canada, on Gaspé Peninsula; rises in the Shickshock Mts., flows S to Chaleur Bay at Bonaventure. Trout, salmon.

Bonavista (BAH-nuh-vi-stuh), town (1991 pop. 4,597), E N.F., E Canada, on E shore of Bonavista Bay, near Cape Bonavista, on RR, 80 mi/129 km NNW of St. John's; 48°38′N 53°07′W. Fishing center, with fish-filleting, cold-storage plants. Site of govt. facilities.

Bonavista Bay, arm of the Atlantic Ocean, c.40 mi/60 km long and 40 mi/60 km wide, E N.F., E Canada. Irregular and filled with isls. Cape Bonavista, the headland of the Bonavista Peninsula, marks the S entrance to the bay and is the reputed landfall (1497) of John Cabot, the discoverer of N.F. Bonavista is the chief fishing town.

Bonavista, Cape, promontory, E N.F., E Canada, at SE limit of Bonavista Bay, 4 mi/6 km NNE of Bonavista; 48°41′N 53°05′W. Reputed landfall of John Cabot, discoverer of N.F., in 1497.

Bonbon (BONG-BONG), town (1982 pop. 652), Sud dept., SW Haiti, on NW tip of Jacmel Peninsula, 17 mi/27 km W of Jérémie. Coffee, cacao, sugarcane. Fishing port.

Bonclarken, N.C.: see FLAT ROCK.

Bond, county (☐ 382 sq mi/989 sq km; 1990 pop. 14,991), SW central Ill.; ⊙ Greenville; 38°52′N 89°26′W. Drained by Kaskaskia R. and Shoal Creek. Agr. area (corn, wheat; dairy; livestock), with bituminous coal mines, natural gas wells. Mfg. (clothing, rubber prods.). Formed 1817.

Bonduel (bah-doo-EL), town (1990 pop. 1,210), Shawano co., NE Wis., 26 mi/42 km NW of Green Bay; 44°44′N 88°27′W. Mfg. (pickles, signs, lumber).

Bondurant, town (1990 pop. 1,584), Polk co., central Iowa, suburb 10 mi/16 km NE of downtown Des Moines; 41°41′N 93°27′W. In agr. area (corn, oats); mfg. (dairying machinery).

Bondville, village (1990 pop. 354), Champaign co., E central Ill., 6 mi/9.7 km W of Champaign, near source of Kaskaskia R.; 40°06′N 88°22′W. Corn, soybeans.

Bondville, Vt.: see WINHALL.

Bone Gap, village (1990 pop. 271), Edwards co., SE Ill., 7 mi/11.3 km NE of Albion; 38°26′N 88°00′W. In agr. area.

Bonesteel, village (1990 pop. 297), Gregory co., S S.Dak., 20 mi/32 km ESE of Burke. Corn, rye, oats.

Bonfield, town (1991 pop. 1,937), SE central Ont., central Canada, on L. Nosbonsing, 16 mi/26 km ESE of North Bay. In dairying, mica-mining region.

Bonfield, village (1990 pop. 299), Kankakee co., NE Ill., 10 mi/16 km W of Kankakee; 41°08′N 88°03′W. In agr. area.

Bonham, town (1990 pop. 6,686), ⊙ Fannin co., NE Texas, near Red R., 25 mi/40 km E of Sherman; 33°35′N 96°10′W. Elev. 568 ft/173 m. Beef cattle; cotton, peanuts, soybeans, corn, wheat; winery (to N end at Ivanhoe); mfg. (textiles, machinery, fertilizers, concrete, furniture). Caddo Natl. Grassland to NE; Bonham State Park to SE; L. Bonham reservoir to N, and a replica of old Fort Inglish are nearby. Plotted 1837.

Boniface, Canada: see SAINT BONIFACE DE SHAWINIGAN.

Bonifay (BAH-NAH-FAI), town (1990 pop. 2,612), Holmes co., NW Fla., in the Fla. Panhandle, 25 mi/40 km W of Marianna; 30°46′N 85°40′W. Mfg. includes apparel, concrete, lumber, machinery; metal fabrication.

Bonita, uninc. city (1990 pop. 12,542), San Diego co., S Calif., residential suburb 9 mi/14.5 km SE of downtown San Diego, 4 mi/6.4 km E of San Diego Bay, on Sweetwater R.; 32°40′N 117°02′W. Sweetwater Reservoir to NE; Upper and Lower Otay reservoirs to E.

Bonita (buh-NEE-tuh), village (1990 pop. 265), Morehouse parish, NE La., 18 mi/29 km NE of Bastrop, near Bayou Bonne Idee and Ark. state line; 32°55′N 91°40′W. In agr. area (rice, cotton); timber; catfish. Handy Brake Natl. Wildlife Reserve to SW.

Bonita, Point, promontory, Marin co., W Calif., on N

shore of the Golden Gate strait at its Pacific entrance, 7 mi/11.3 km WNW of downtown San Francisco; radio beacon station, lighthouse (est. 1855). In part of Golden Gate Natl. Recreation Area (formerly part of Fort Barry Military Reserve).

Bonita Springs (bo-NEE-tuh), suburb (□ 11 sq mi/ 28 sq km; 1990 pop. 13,600), of Naples, Lee co., SW Fla., 12 mi/19 km N of Naples; 26°20′N 81°47′W. Mfg. of shell novelties; fishing.

Bonne Bay (bahn), inlet (15 mi/24 km long, 4 mi/6 km wide at mouth) of Gulf of St. Lawrence, W N.F., E Canada, 40 mi/64 km N of Corner Brook, at foot of Gros Morne Mt. (2,645 ft/806 m); 49°33′N 57°55′W. On shores are numerous fishing settlements. Main village is Rocky Harbour. Sheep. Gros Morne Natl. Park, a UNESCO World Heritage Area, is here.

Bonne Terre (bon TER), city (1990 pop. 3,871), St. Francois co., E Mo., in the St. Francois Mts. near Big R., 5 mi/8 km N of Flat R.; 37°55′N 90°32′W. RR-shipping center. Corn, wheat; livestock; mfg. (aluminum foundry; concrete, toys, crushed rock); limestone quarrying. Historic lead-mining and milling center and a former "company town" of St. Joseph Lead Co., natl. historic site; deep mines now open to the public. Inc. 1864.

Bonneau (BAHN-o), village (1990 pop. 374), Berkeley co., E S.C., 37 mi/60 km N of Charleston. L. Moultrie reservoir to W; 33°18′N 79°57′W.

Bonneauville (BAH-nuh-vil), borough (1990 pop. 1,282), Adams co., S Pa., 5 mi/8 km ESE of Gettysburg; 39°48′N 77°08′W. Agr. includes dairying; livestock; poultry; grain, soybeans, apples.

Bonnechère River (bon-SHER), 120 mi/193 km long, SE Ont., central Canada; rises in Algonquin Provincial Park, flows E, through several lakes, past Renfrew, to Ottawa R. 10 mi/16 km ENE of Renfrew.

Bonner, county (□ 1,919 sq mi/4,970 sq km; 1990 pop. 26,622), N Idaho; ⊙ Sandpoint; 48°17′N 116°36′W. Mt. area bordering on Mont. (E) and Wash. (W), located in Idaho panhandle, and drained by Priest and Pend Oreille rivers and Clark Fork. Silver, lead, copper; lumber; cattle; alfalfa, hay; oats, grains. Mont. state line forms Mountain/Pacific time zone boundary, co. is in Pacific time zone; NW extension of co. comes within 10 mi/16 km of Can. border. Priest L., Priest L. State Park and Upper Priest L. Scenic Area in NW arm of co., Round L. State Park in SW center; part of Kaniksu Natl. Forest in NW, part of Kootenai Natl. Forest in NE; large Pend Oreille L. in S and SE, extends into Kootenai co.; Albeni Falls Dam (Pend Oreille R.) in SW, Cabinet Gorge Dam on Clark Fork, in SE; Schweitzer Basin Ski Area in N center. Formed 1907.

Bonner (BAHN-nuhr), village (1990 pop. 200), Missoula co., W Mont., on Blackfoot R. near its mouth, on the Clark Fork and 7 mi/11.3 km E of Missoula. Timber; cattle; alfalfa; lumber mill. Lolo Natl. Forest to N and S.

Bonner Springs, city (1990 pop. 6,413), Wyandotte co., NE Kansas, on Kansas R., and 14 mi/23 km W of Kansas City (Kansas); 39°04′N 94°52′W. RR junction. In wheat, potato, and livestock region; mfg. (cement, milling equipment); food processing. Small gas wells nearby. Inc. 1898.

Bonners Ferry, town (1990 pop. 2,193), ⊙ Boundary co., N Idaho, on Kootenai R., and 20 mi/32 km S of Can. border, 30 mi/48 km NNE of Sandpoint; 48°42′N 116°19′W. RR junction and trade center for irrigated agr. area; logging, lumbering; mfg. (sawmill prods., light mfg.). Floods on the Kootenai caused much damage May 1948. Kootenai Co. Mus. Kootenai Natl. Wildlife Refuge to W; Kaniksu Natl. Forest to W, NE and SE. Inc. 1894. Ruby Ridge, site of 1992 shootout bet. Federal agents and white supremacists, is nearby.

Bonnet Carre Spillway (BO-nuh KER-ree), St. Charles parish, SE La., emergency flood-control spillway bet. E bank of the Mississippi R., c.25 mi/40 km above New Orleans, at Norco, and L. Pontchartrain; c.7 mi/11 km long, 1 mi/2 km–2 mi/3 km wide; 30°01′N, 90°25′W. Mississippi floodwaters are diverted into the lake, averting damage to New Orleans and other downstream communities. Completed 1935. Also Bonné Carre.

Bonnet, Lac du (bo-NAI, lahk duh), lake (20 mi/32 km long, 1 mi/2 km–4 mi/6 km wide), SE Man., central Canada, 55 mi/89 km NE of Winnipeg; expansion of Winnipeg R. At N end are McArthur and Great Falls, hydroelectric stations and dam; at S end is town of Lac du Bonnet.

Bonnet Mountain (10,615 ft/3,235 m), SW Alta., W Canada, near B.C. border, in Rocky Mts., in Banff Natl. Park, 24 mi/39 km NW of Banff; 51°26′N 115°53′W.

Bonneville, county (□ 1,900 sq mi/4,921 sq km; 1990 pop. 72,207), SE Idaho; ⊙ Idaho Falls; 43°23′N 111°36′W. Mt. area bordering on Wyo. (E). Drained by Snake R. NW and NE; also by Willow Creek. Irrigated Snake R. valley extends through NW. Agr. (wheat, barley, oats, rye; alfalfa; potatoes; sheep, cattle; dairying). Parts of Targhee and Caribou natl. forests are in E; parts of Grays L. (dry) Natl. Wildlife Refuge in S. Palisades Reservoir in E, Ririe Reservoir, on Willow Creek, in N center. Formed 1911.

Bonneville (BAHN-uh-vil), uninc. village (1990 pop. 80), Multnomah co., NW Oregon, 35 mi/56 km ENE of Portland, on Columbia R., at Bonneville Dam. Fish hatchery. Sternwheeler Mus. here. John B. Yeon State Park to SW; Mt. Hood Natl. Forest, including Columbia Wilderness Area, to S.

Bonneville Dam (BAHN-uh-vil), one of the major dams on the Columbia R. where it passes through the Cascade Mts., on state line of Oregon and Wash.; 2,690 ft/ 820 m long, 197 ft/60 m high. Built (1933–1943) by the U.S. Corps of Engineers; one of the largest hydroelectric projects undertaken under the New Deal. Its reservoir extends c.40 mi/64 km to the Dalles Dam, 1 mi/ 1.6 km wide. Used for navigation, flood control, and power production. Locks permit barges to pass around the dam. Bonneville Power Administration contracted for power from 5 nuclear plants, to be built by Wash. Public Power Supply System (WPPSS), which were never finished. New larger locks (1994) improve passage of barges. Fish (salmon) passage problems going downstream.

Bonneville, Lake (BON-ih-vil), anc. lake, once covering c.20,000 sq mi/51,800 sq km, in what is now NW Utah, near Nev. state line. The lake expanded during the period of heavy precipitation brought on by the advancing glaciers of the late Cenozoic era and melting of stationary and retreating glaciers. At the end of the Pleistocene epoch, the lake's area shrank rapidly. Its 6 terraces still exist and locate the different lake levels. Great Salt and Utah lakes and L. Sevier are remnants of L. Bonneville, which was named for U.S. explorer Benjamin de Bonneville. A large part of the salt flats and desert is used for weapons testing, military vehicle-proving grounds, and high-tech hazardous waste disposal. Bonneville Speedway (Bureau of Land Management-B.L.M.) is 15 mi/24 km ENE of Wendover. Newfoundland Evaporation Basin in N part of Great Salt Lake Desert captures overflow from Great Salt L., filled since 1989 when lake rose to record levels due to heavy snowfall in Wasatch and Uinta ranges.

Bonneville Salt Flats, Utah: see GREAT SALT LAKE DESERT.

Bonney, village (1990 pop. 339), Brazoria co., SE Texas, residential suburb 10 mi/16 km N of Angleton, in Brazosport Area; 29°18′N 95°27′W. Agr. (rice, sorghum, cotton, pecans).

Bonney Lake, town (1990 pop. 7,494), Pierce co., W central Wash., residential suburb 8 mi/24 km ESE of Tacoma, near Carbon R.; 47°11′N 122°10′W. Agr. area; flower bulbs, vegetables, berries; dairying; poultry. L. Tapps reservoir to NE.

Bonney, Mount (10,194 ft/3,107 m), SE B.C., W Canada, in Selkirk Mts., in Glacier Natl. Park, 30 mi/48 km ENE of Revelstoke; 51°12′N 117°32′W.

Bonnie, village (1990 pop. 411), Jefferson co., S Ill., 7 mi/ 11.3 km S of Mount Vernon; 38°12′N 88°54′W. In agr. area (wheat, corn, soybeans; cattle). Rend L. Game Management Area to SW. Rend L. Community Col. 5 mi/8 km S.

Bonnie Doone, uninc. town (1990 pop. 3,893), Cumberland co., S central N.C., residential suburb 7 mi/11.3 km WNW of downtown Fayetteville; 35°06′N 78°57′W. Fort Bragg Military Reserve and Pope Air Force Base to N.

Bonnieville (BAHN-ee-vil), uninc. village (1990 pop. 300), Hart co., central Ky., 8 mi/12.9 km N of Munfordville, on Bacon Creek; 37°22′N 85°54′W. Agr. area (tobacco, grain; livestock; dairying). Mfg. (metal forming, textile mfg.).

Bonny Blue, uninc. village, Lee co., SW Va., in the Cumberland Mts., at Ky. state line, 25 mi/40 km W of Norton. Bituminous coal.

Bonny Reservoir, Yuma co., E Colo., on South Fork Republican R., in Bonny State Recreation Area, 23 mi/ 37 km NNE of Burlington, and 6 mi/9.7 km W of Kansas state line; 3 mi/4.8 km long; 39°36′N 102°08′W. Max. capacity 349,000 acre-ft. Formed by Bonny Dam (119 ft/36 m high), built by the Bureau of Reclamation for irrigation and flood control. Bonny Dam Airport is here.

Bonnyman (BAHN-ee-muhn), uninc. town (1990 pop. 800), Perry co., SE Ky., in Cumberland foothills, 4 mi/ 6.4 km NW of Hazard. Bituminous coal; coal processing, mfg. (concrete).

Bonnyville, town (1991 pop. 5,132), E Alta., W Canada, near Sask. border, on small lake, 65 mi/105 km N of Vermilion; 54°16′N 110°45′W. Lumber and flour milling, dairying.

Bono (BO-no), town (1990 pop. 1,220), Craighead co., NE Ark., 8 mi/12.9 km NW of Jonesboro; 35°54′N 90°47′W. Mfg. (lamps, food).

Bonpas Creek, c.40 mi/64 km long, SE Ill.; rises E of Olney, flows S to Wabash R. at Grayville; 38°44′N 87°58′W.

Bonsall, uninc. town (1990 pop. 1,881), San Diego co., S Calif., suburb 38 mi/61 km N of downtown San Diego, on San Luis Rey R.; 33°17′N 117°13′W. Fruit, avocados, flowers, ornamentals; poultry. Camp Pendleton Marine Corps Base to W; Pala Indian Reservation to NE.

Book Cliffs, rugged U-shaped escarpment (c.1,500 ft/ 457 m high), N of Colorado R., E Utah, and W Colo., extending through parts of Garfield, Carbon, and Grand cos., Utah, and Mesa and Garfield cos., Colo. E part roughly parallels Colo. R. 18 mi/29 km to NW of it, at edge of Grand Valley; W part roughly parallels Price R. to NE of it. Form S limit of East Tavaputs Plateau in E Utah and of Roan Plateau in W Colo. Remnants of Basket-Maker culture have been found near cliffs in Carbon co. Roan Cliffs are parallel escarpment to NW extending NE into Colo.

Booker, town (1990 pop. 1,236), on border of Lipscomb and Ochiltree cos., extreme N Texas, in high plains of the Panhandle, c.70 mi/113 km W of Woodward, Okla.; 36°27′N 100°32′W. Meat processing.

Booker T. Washington, Natl. Monument (□ 224 acres/ 91 ha), Franklin co., S Va., 12 mi/19 km NE of Rocky Mount, authorized 1956. Birthplace (1856) and childhood home of Booker T. Washington, early Afr.-Amer. leader, educator, founder of Tuskegee Inst., author of *Up From Slavery*.

Boomer, uninc. town (1990 pop. 1,051), Fayette co., S central W.Va., on Kanawha R.,13 mi/21 km NW of Fayetteville. Coal-mining and industrial area. Cattle; grain.

Boone 1 county (□ 601 sq mi/1,557 sq km; 1990 pop. 28,297), N Ark.; ⊙ Harrison; 36°18′N 93°05′W. Bounded N by Mo. state line; drained by White R. and Crooked Creek; situated in Ozark region. Agr., cattle, hogs, poultry, timber. Mfg. at Harrison. Lead and zinc mines, marble deposits, glass sand. Recreation, growing retirement pop. Parts of large Bull Shoals Reservoir in NE corner; arm of Table Rock Reservoir in NW corner (both on White R.). Formed 1869. **2** county (□ 281 sq mi/728 sq km; 1990 pop. 30,806), N Ill., on Wis. line (N); ⊙ Belvidere; 42°19′N 88°48′W. Drained by Kishwaukee R. Agr. (livestock; corn, oats, vegetables; dairying). Mfg. (machine parts, paper and metal prods., motor vehicles). Formed 1837. **3** county (□ 423 sq mi/1,096 sq km; 1990 pop. 38,147), central Ind.; ⊙ Lebanon; part of Indianapolis metropolitan area; 40°03′N 86°28′W. Diversified mfg. at Lebanon. Corn, soybeans, vegetables; hogs, cattle; dairy prods.. Drained by Sugar, Raccoon, and Eagle creeks and Eel R. Boone's Pond State Fishing Area in SE. Formed 1830. **4** county (□ 573 sq mi/1,484 sq km; 1990 pop. 25,186), central Iowa; ⊙ Boone; 42°02′N 93°55′W. Prairie agr. area (hogs, cattle, poultry; corn, oats, soybeans) drained by Des Moines R. and Beaver Creek; bituminous-coal deposits. Ski Valley Ski Area SW of Boone. Holst State Forest in N; Ledges State Park and Iowa Arboretum S of Boone. Widespread flooding in 1993. Formed 1846. **5** county (□ 256 sq mi/663 sq km; 1990 pop. 57,589), N Ky.; ⊙ Burlington; 38°58′N 84°43′W. Bounded N and W by Ohio R., forms Ohio (N) and Ind. (W) state lines; drained by Gunpowder Creek. Gently rolling agr. area (burley tobacco, corn, soybeans, alfalfa, hay; cattle, poultry; dairying) in N part of Bluegrass region; mfg. at Florence, Burlington, and Hebron. NE part of co. is within urbanized area of Cincinnati (Ohio), to NE. Cincinnati-Northern Ky. Internatl. Airport in NE corner. Big Bone Lick State Park in S; Bullock Pen L. reservoir in S (on Ten Mile Creek). Formed 1798. **6** county (□ 683 sq mi/1769 sq km; 1990 pop. 112,379), central Mo., borders Missouri R. in SW; ⊙ Columbia; 38°59′N 92°18′W. Corn, wheat, soybeans, hay; pumpkins; cattle, sheep; lumber; limestone; mfg. at Columbia and Centralia. Main campus Univ. of Mo. at Columbia. Rock Bridge State Park S of Columbia; Finger Lakes State Park (reclaimed strip mine) N of Columbia. Parts of Mark Twain Natl. Forest in SE. Flooding occured in S part of co. in 1993, esp. around Hartsburg. Formed 1820. **7** county (□ 687 sq mi/1,779 sq km; 1990 pop. 6,667), E central Nebr.; ⊙ Albion; 41°42′N 98°03′W. Agr. region drained by Cedar R. and Beaver Creek. Cattle, hogs, corn, alfalfa, sorghum; dairying. Formed 1875. **8** county (□ 503 sq mi/1,303 sq km; 1990 pop. 25,870), W central W.Va.; ⊙ Madison; 38°01′N 81°43′W. On Allegheny Plateau; drained by Big Coal and Little Coal rivers and Cabin Creek. Bituminous-coal-mining region; natural-gas and oil fields; some agr. (honey, tobacco); timber. Fork Creek Wildlife Management Area. Formed 1847.

Boone 1 city (1990 pop. 12,392), ⊙ Boone co., central Iowa, on the Des Moines R.; 42°02′N 93°52′W. RR and industrial center with plants making machinery, fabricated metal prods., plastic signs, dust filters, foods, paper prods. Laid out (1865) by the RR, which built a long, high double-track bridge here. In 1887 it annexed the nearby rival town of Boonesboro (founded 1851). Seat of Des Moines Area Community Col. Ski Valley Ski Area to SW; Holst State Forest and Barkley Memorial State Park to NW; Ledges State Park to S; Iowa Arboretum to SE. Inc. 1865. **2** city (1990 pop. 12,915), ⊙ Watauga co., NW N.C., 22 mi/35 km NNW of Lenoir, near the Blue Ridge Parkway; 36°12′N 81°40′W. Tobacco market and cattle center; mt. resort (skiing); mfg. (textiles, apparel, log homes, furniture, lumber, electrical equip., consumer goods, shoes, construction equip., catnip), consumer goods. Blue Ridge Parkway passes to S and E. Pisgah Natl. Forest to SW. Cone Memorial Park (□ 3,500 acres/1,416 ha), former estate of industrialist Moses Cone, to S. Seat of Appalachian State Univ. Appalachian Cultural Mus., Appalachian Heritage Mus., Daniel Boone Native Gardens.

Boone, village (1990 pop. 341), Pueblo co., S central Colo., 19 mi/31 km E of Pueblo, on Arkansas R., at mouth of Haynes Creek: 38°15′N 104°15′W. Elev. 4,500 ft/1,372 m. Cattle; wheat, hay, beans, sorghum, corn. Pueblo Army Depot to W.

Boone Heights, uninc. town (1990 pop. 750), Knox co., SE Ky., residential suburb 2 mi/3.2 km E of Barbourville, near Cumberland R. Coal-mining region. Tobacco.

Boone River, 100 mi/161 km, N central Iowa; rises in Hancock co., flows S, past Webster City, to Des Moines R. 17 mi/27 km N of Boone.

Boones Mill, village (1990 pop. 239), Franklin co., S Va., in Blue Ridge foothills, 10 mi/16 km S of Roanoke; 37°07′N 79°57′W. Mfg. (modular homes, wood prods.); agr. (tobacco, grain, apples; cattle).

Boonesboro, former settlement, Clark co., central Ky., 10 mi/16 km N of Richmond, on the Kentucky R. Named for Daniel Boone, who in 1775 built a small fort here. The seat of the govt. of then Transylvania co. for several years, Boonesborough was later abandoned because of repeated attacks by Native Americans. The restored fort is within Fort Boonesborough State Park. Boones Station State Park to NW. Also spelled Boonesborough.

Booneville 1 town (1990 pop. 3,804), shares ⊙ functions with Paris, Logan co., W Ark., 32 mi/51 km SE of Fort Smith, on Petit Jean R.; 35°08′N 93°55′W. Market for agr. area (fruit; livestock, poultry); dairy prods.; sawmilling, cotton ginning; RR yards. Mfg (consumer goods, furniture, foods, fabricated metal prods., lumber). Hq. for fishermen and hunters. A unit of Ozark Natl. Forest to E; Ouachita Natl. Forest to S; Blue Mt. L. reservoir to SE; Fort Chaffee Military Reservation to NW. **2** town (1990 pop. 7,955), ⊙ Prentiss co., NE Miss., 20 mi/32 km S of Corinth; 34°39′N 88°34′W. In agr. (soybeans, cotton, corn, hay; cattle; dairying; timber) area; mfg. (furniture, paper and vinyl prods., cheese, machinery, apparel, office supplies, fabricated metal prods.), meat and lumber processing. In Civil War, scene of a Union victory won by Gen. P. H. Sheridan (1862). Seat of Northeast Miss. Community Col. Bay Springs L. reservoir to E. Settled 1859, inc. 1869.

Booneville, village (1990 pop. 232), ⊙ Owsley co., E central Ky., on South Fork Kentucky R., and 32 mi/51 km WNW of Hazard, in the Cumberland Mts.; 37°28′N 83°40′W. Agr. (burley tobacco; livestock); coal; timber. Parts of Daniel Boone Natl. Forest to NW and S. Est. 1843.

Boonsboro, town (1990 pop. 2,445), Washington co., W Md., at W base of South Mt., and 11 mi/18 km SSE of Hagerstown; 39°31′N 77°40′W. Settled in 1788 by George and William Boone who were related to the famous Daniel, according to legend. By the 1830s, it was a major outfitting point W on the NATIONAL ROAD. Gen. Thomas J. "Stonewall" Jackson was surprised, unmounted, by charging Federal calvarymen near here on Sept. 11, 1862, and nearly captured. A Confederate patrol being driven out of the town by other Federals wheeled back and rescued him. An early Washington Monument, built by the citizens of Boonesboro in 1 day (July 4, 1827) here was reconstructed by the Civilian Conservation Corps and dedicated on July 4, 1936. Site of the Salem Union Church, notable because of a conflict bet. Lutheran and Reformed members over the shape of its windows. A cannon from the War of 1812, cast by a local foundry, on Main Street is the focal point of political gatherings.

Boonton (BOON-tuhn), town (1990 pop. 8,343), Morris co., N N.J., on Rockaway R., 9 mi/14.5 km NNE of Morristown; 40°55′N 74°25′W. Mfg. (plastics, electrical and radio equip., apparel), agr. (dairy prods.; livestock; vegetables). Parsippany Reservoir (just S) is impounded by Boonton Dam (114 ft/35 m high, 3,100 ft/945 m long; completed 1905) in Rockaway R. Was iron center in mid–19th cent. First Bakelite factory here. Settled 1760, inc. 1867.

Boonville 1 city (1990 pop. 6,724), ⊙ Warrick co., SW Ind., 16 mi/26 km ENE of Evansville; 38°03′N 87°16′W. Trade center for bituminous-coal-mining and agr. area (grain, soybeans, fruit, tomatoes); mfg. (transportation equip., concrete prods., machinery, pallets, plastic parts). Scales L. State Forest is nearby. Platted 1818. **2** city (1990 pop. 7,095), ⊙ Cooper co., central Mo., on Missouri R., and 23 mi/37 km W of Columbia; 38°57′N 92°45′W. Agr., service center; mfg. (foods, rubber prods., apparel, mobile and modular homes, construction materials, machinery, corncob pipes, shoes, dairy prods.). Kemper Military School (a junior col.); state correctional center for boys. Platted 1817. Union forces won a Civil War battle nearby in 1861. Annual music festivals.

Boonville, town (1990 pop. 1,009), Yadkin co., N N.C. 8 mi/12.9 km E of Elkin, near Yadkin R; 36°13′N 80°42′W. Agr. area (tobacco, soybeans, grain; poultry, livestock; dairying); mfg. (apparel, textiles).

Boonville 1 uninc. village, Mendocino co., NW Calif., in Anderson Valley (apples, nursery stock, hops, grapes, apples, pears; cattle), in the Coast Ranges, 12 mi/19 km SW of Ukiah. Mfg. (beer). Hendy Woods State Park to NW. **2** village (□ 1 sq mi/2.6 sq km; 1990 pop. 2,220), Oneida co., central N.Y., 20 mi/32 km NNE of Rome; 43°28′N 75°19′W. Trade center for dairying region; mfg. (dairy prods., furniture, lumber, wood prods.); timber; maple syrup. Author and critic Walter D. Edmonds b. here and lived in nearby Talcottville. Settled c.1791, inc. 1855.

Booth Point, S King William Isl., Franklin dist., N.W.T., NW Canada, on Simpson Strait, opposite Adelaide Peninsula; 68°29′N 96°28′W.

Boothbay, town (1990 pop. 2,648), Lincoln co., S Maine, on peninsula, 10 mi/16 km S of Wiscasset; 43°50′N 69°36′W. Resort, boatbuilding, fishing, and cruise center. Settled as Newagen 1630, inc. 1764. Boothbay Harbor, town, also a resort, was set off in 1889. Has gallery and arts center, U.S. fish hatchery (1903).

Boothia, Gulf of (BOO-thee-uh), N.W.T., NW Canada, inlet (250 mi/402 km long) of the Arctic Ocean, bet. Boothia Peninsula (W) and Baffin Isl. and Melville Peninsula (E); 67°10′–70°00′N 85°30′–92°00′W. Up to 130 mi/209 km wide.

Boothia Peninsula (BOO-thee-uh), (□ 12,483 sq mi/32,331 sq km), Kitikmeot Region, N.W.T., NW Canada; the northernmost (71°58′N) tip of the N. Amer. mainland. Almost an isl., being connected with the mainland only by the narrow Isthmus of Boothia. Topographically and in climate it is like the isls. of the Arctic Archipelago. A narrow strait separates it in the N from Somerset Isl. To the E the Gulf of Boothia separates it from Baffin Isl. Virtually uninhabited except for a few hundred settlers at Spence Bay and Thom Bay. Discovered and explored (1829–1833) by Br. explorer John Ross and named for a patron of the expedition, Sir Felix Booth. Near the SW end the expedition of Br. explorer Sir John Franklin ended in tragedy. Roald Amundsen, a Nor., explored the peninsula in 1903–1905.

Boothville, uninc. village (1990 pop. with Venice 2,743), Plaquemines parish, extreme SE La., on W bank (levee) of the Mississippi R., and 50 mi/80 km SE of New Orleans; 29°19′N 89°24′W. Fishing; oysters; citrus (esp. oranges), tomatoes.

Boothwyn (BOOTH-win), uninc. town (1990 pop. 5,069), Delaware co., SE Pa., residential suburb 16 mi/26 km SW of Philadelphia, near Del. state line; 39°50′N 75°27′W. Light mfg.

Bootjack, uninc. town (1990 pop. 1,295), Mariposa co., central Calif., 4 mi/6.4 km ESE of Mariposa, on Snow Creek; 37°28′N 119°53′W. Timber; cattle. Sierra Natl. Forest to E.

Boquerón (bo-kai-RON), village, SW P.R., facing Mona Passage, 12 mi/19 km S of Mayagüez. Fishing. Beach resort; tourism. Hq. of U.S. Fish and Wildlife Caribbean Refuge. Cabo Rojo Wildlife Refuge is S. Saltworks c.5 mi/8 km SSW.

Boquerón (bo-KAI-ron), minor port of Guantánamo, Guantánamo prov., E Cuba, on Guantánamo Bay, opposite Caimanera, and just N of U.S. naval reserve; 19°59′N 75°07′W.

Bor Peak (9,073 ft/2,765 m), SE B.C., W Canada, in Selkirk Mts., 30 mi/48 km NW of Nelson; 49°50′N 117°45′W.

Borah Peak, peak, 12,662 ft/3,859 m high, Custer co., central Idaho, 105 mi/169 km NW of Pocatello in the Lost R. Mts., in Challis Natl. Forest; highest point in the state; 44°08′N 113°46′W. Named for William E. Borah.

Bord-de-Mer-Jean-Rabel, Haiti: see JEAN-RABEL.

Bordeaux Mountain (bor-DO) (elev. 1,277 ft/389 m), St. John isl., U.S. Virgin Isls., West Indies, in VIRGIN ISLANDS NATIONAL PARK.

Borden, county (□ 906 sq mi/2,347 sq km; 1990 pop. 799), NW Texas; ⊙ Gail; 32°44′N 101°25′W. E-facing Cap Rock escarpment of Llano Estacado runs N-S through center; elev. 1,200 ft/366 m–3,000 ft/914 m. Drained by Colorado R. Cattle and horse ranching, some agr. (cotton, wheat, milo, oats, soybeans, pecans);

limestone. Part of L. J.B. Thomas in SE corner. Formed 1876.

Borden, town (1991 pop. 436), S P.E.I., E Canada, on Northumberland Strait, 27 mi/43 km W of Charlottetown; 46°15′N 63°42′W. Fishing port, terminal of train ferry from Cape Tormentine, N.B.

Borden, village (1991 pop. 215), S central Sask., central Canada, near North Saskatchewan R., 30 mi/48 km NW of Saskatoon. Wheat; mixed farming.

Borden Islands, 2 isls. (□ c.4,000 sq mi/10,360 sq km), formerly thought to be a single isl., NW Franklin dist., N.W.T., N Canada, in the Arctic Ocean; 77°21′N–78°39′N 108°40′W–113°10′W; separated from Prince Patrick Isl. (SW) by Ballantyne Strait, from Melville Isl. (S) by Hazen Strait, and from Ellef Ringnes and Lougheed isls. (E) by Prince Gustav Adolph Sea. Consists of North Borden Isl. (65 mi/105 km long, 30 mi/48 km wide) and South Borden Isl. (55 mi/89 km long, 40 mi/64 km wide; plateau rises to over 1,000 ft/305 m), separated by Wilkins Sound. Off South Borden Isl. is Brock Isl.

Borden Peninsula, N Baffin Isl., SE Franklin dist., N.W.T., N Canada, extends 140 mi/225 km N into Lancaster Sound; 71°52′N–73°50′N 80°40′W–85°40′W; 40 mi/64 km–105 mi/169 km wide. Coastal cliffs rise to c.1,500 ft/457 m (NE); interior of peninsula consists of mountainous country rising to over 3,000 ft/914 m.

Bordentown, city (1990 pop. 4,341), Burlington co., W N.J., on Delaware R., and 5 mi/8 km S of Trenton; 40°08′N 74°42′W. Mfg. (animal feed, pre-cast concrete, beverages, electrical equip.), printing; grain, dairy prods. Damaged by British in Amer. Revolution. Clara Barton's school (built 1739; now a Red Cross memorial) and youth correctional facilities here. Joseph Bonaparte lived here 1816–1839. Settled 1682; inc. as borough 1825, as city 1867.

Boreas Mountain (elev. 3,776 ft/1,151 m), Essex co., NE N.Y., in the High Peaks sect. of the Adirondacks, 9 mi/14.5 km SSE of Mt. Marcy, and 13 mi/21 km NW of Schroon L. village; 44°00′N 73°53′W.

Borger, city (1990 pop. 15,675), Hutchinson co., 40 mi/64 km NE of Amarillo, extreme N Texas, in the Panhandle; 35°39′N 101°24′W. Elev. 3,116 ft/950 m. After the discovery of oil in 1925, Borger grew as the industrial center of a vast natural-gas and oil field. In the area are many refineries and factories, mfg. (construction materials, chemicals, machinery). Irrigated agr. and livestock raising also add to the city's economy. Frank Phillips Col. is in Borger, as is a monument to Native Amer. flint quarries. Inc. 1930.

Borgne, Lake (BORN), saltwater bay (c.27 mi/43 km long) in SE La., 15 mi/24 km E of downtown New Orleans; 30°01′N 89°37′W. Bounded by Orleans parish and city of New Orleans on NW, L. Borgne is a W arm of the Mississippi Sound and a link bet. the Gulf of Mexico (through Mississippi Sound) and L. Pontchartrain (NW), to which it is connected by navigable Rigolets and Chef Menteur passes. Biloxi State Wildlife Area on SE shore. Intracoastal Waterway parallels NW shore; branch of it, Mississippi R. Gulf Outlet canal, parallels SW shore.

Borgne, Le (luh BOR-nyuh), town (1982 pop. 2,915), Nord dept., N Haiti, on the Atlantic, 21 mi/34 km WNW of Cap-Haïtien; 19°51′N 72°32′W. Agr. (oranges, limes, bananas, coffee, cacao, cotton). Fishing port.

Borinquen (bo-reen-KAIN), locality, P.R., site of airport N of Aguadilla. Named for derived from Boriquén, the pre-Columbian Taíno name for P.R.

Boriquén: see PUERTO RICO.

Boron, uninc. town (1990 pop. 2,101), Kern co., S central Calif., near Rogers Dry L., 46 mi/74 km W of Barstow, in Mojave Desert; 35°00′N 117°39′W. Borax works. On N boundary of Edwards Air Force Base. Highway service center (State Highway 58).

Borough (Boro) Park, neighborhood, SW Brooklyn, N.Y. city (□ 1.5 sq mi/3.9 sq km), SE N.Y. Bounded by 8th Ave. on N, 60th St. on W, 36–37th Sts., on E, and 20th and MacDonald Aves. on S and SE. Began as a residential development during the Brooklyn real estate boom of the 1920s. The majority of the pop. is Jewish (90% Orthodox), having moved here from the Williamsburg and Crown Heights sects. of Brooklyn (many have since moved on to Kiryas Joel, Monseng, and New Square, N.Y.). Since 1990 there has been a significant influx of orthodox Muslims from Southwest Asia, who now comprise 5–10% of the pop. Borough Park offers upscale shopping for Manhattanites, particularly for children's "dress-up" clothes. Seat of 70 yeshivas, as compared to 16 public schools.

Borrego Desert State Park, Calif.: see ANZA-BORREGO DESERT STATE PARK.

Borrego Springs (bow-ray-go), uninc. town (1990 pop. 2,244), San Diego co., S Calif., 58 mi/93 km NE of San Diego, and 30 mi/48 km NE of Palm Desert, near San Felipe R., located in pocket of land surrounded by Anza-Borrego Desert State Park; 33°14′N 116°21′W. Hot springs; resort; cattle. Santa Rosa Mts. to N. Los Coyotes Indian Reservation to W.

Boscawen (BAWS-kuh-wen), town (1990 pop. 3,586), Merrimack co., S central N.H., 9 mi/14.5 km NNW of Concord; 43°19′N 71°39′W. Bounded E by Merrimack R., W in part by Beaverdam Brook. Agr. (livestock, poultry; apples, vegetables, nursery crops; dairying); mfg. (lumber and wood prods., construction materials), sand and gravel processing. Part of N.H. State Forest Nursery in N; Hannah Dustin Memorial State Historic Site in E. Site of Daniel Webster's 1st law office (1805). Merrimack County Farm. W. P. Fessenden b. here. Settled 1734, inc. 1760.

Boscobel, town (1990 pop. 2,706), Grant co., extreme SW Wis., on Wisconsin R., 23 mi/37 km ENE of Prairie du Chien; 43°08′N 90°42′W. Mfg. (electrical prods.; dairy prods., feed). Gideons Bible Society founded here, 1898. Bull Run Ski Area to SW. Inc. 1873.

Bosencheve National Park (bo-sen-CHE-ve), national park (59 sq mi/153 sq km), in the central part of the state of Mexico, Mexico, 12 mi/19 km E of Zitácuaro, Michoacán, and 99 mi/160 km W of Mexico City. Mountainous terrain with pine and fir forests. Includes the Laguna del Carmen where migrating birds congregate.

Bosque, county (□ 1,002 sq mi/2,595 sq km; 1990 pop. 15,125), central Texas; ⊙ Meridian; 31°53′N 97°37′W. Hilly in W, bounded NE and E by Brazos R., drained by Bosque R. Agr. (oats, corn, grain sorghums, wheat, pecans, peaches); livestock (cattle, sheep; dairying) marketed. Limestone quarrying; timber (mainly cedar). Meridan State Park near co. center; L. Whitney reservoir on E boundary (Brazos R.). Formed 1854.

Bosque, El, Mexico: see EL BOSQUE.

Bosque Farms (BAHS-ke), or **Bosque**, town (1990 pop. 3,791), Valencia co., central N.Mex., 15 mi/24 km S of Albuquerque, on Rio Grande; 34°51′N 106°42′W. Dairying; cattle, sheep; grain, grapes. Winery. Isleta Indian Reservation adjoins town on N and E. Manzano Mts. to E.

Bosque River, c.100 mi/161 km long, central Texas; rises as intermittent stream (sometimes called North Bosque R.) in Erath co., flows generally SE, past Stephenville, to the Brazos R. just NW of Waco. Near mouth, dam (1923) impounds L. Waco (39,000 acre-ft.; recreational area). Lake receives Middle Bosque R. (c.35 mi/56 km long) from W, South Bosque R. (c.20 mi/32 km long) from S.

Bossier (BO-zhuhr), parish (□ 841 sq mi/2,178 sq km; 1990 pop. 86,088), NW La.; ⊙ Benton; 32°42′N 93°45′W. Situated on Ark. state line (N); bounded W by Red R., SE by Loggy Bayou and L. Bistineau, NE by Bodcau Bayou; drained by the Bodcau and Red Chute bayous. Agr. area (cotton, corn, sorghum, blueberries, pecans, soybeans, home gardens, wheat; cattle, horses, rabbits; honey; dairying), with oil and natural-gas fields, refineries, pipelines; timber. Mfg. at Bossier City; also logging; petroleum refining; mfg. (clothing, wood and paper prods., plastics, construction materials, and metal prods.) in parish. Shipping on Red R. Formed 1843. Barksdale Air Force Base at center of parish. Cypress Bayou and Black Bayou reservoirs in W center, Loggy Bayou State Wildlife Area in SE, part of Bodcau State Wildlife Area in NE.

Bossier City (BO-zhuhr), city (1990 pop. 52,721), Bossier parish, NW La., on the Red R., twin city across from (1 mi/2 km E of) Shreveport, with which it is connected by several bridges. RR junction. Barksdale Air Force Base in SE part of city, home of the 2nd U.S. Air Force, is the major employer. Agr. (cotton, soybeans, pecans; cattle, horses; dairying); mfg. (cultured marble, signs, labels, plastic parts, fabricated metal prods., construction materials, lighting fixtures); printing and publishing. Bossier Parish Community Col.; Barnwell Cultural Center. La. Down thoroughbred race track in E. Black Bayou and Cypress Bayou reservoirs to N. Red Chute Bayou flows through E part of city. Inc. 1907.

Bostic, village (1990 pop. 371), Rutherford co., SW N.C., 17 mi/27 km WNW of Shelby; 35°21′N 81°50′W. RR junction to W. Grain, soybeans; poultry, livestock; dairying; mfg. (yarn, pallets).

Boston, city (1990 pop. 574,283), ⊙ Mass. and Suffolk co., E Mass., at the head of Boston Bay; 42°20′N 71°01′W. The largest city in New England, and known as the "Hub," Boston is a major financial and retailing center, a leading port, and a market for fish, wool, and gypsum. Its industries include publishing, food processing, and the mfg. of pharmaceuticals, shoes, textiles, and machinery. High-technology research and development as well as computer and electronic mfg. industries have flourished in the Boston area, especially the corridor along the Yankee Division Highway (formerly Route 128). Tourism has become increasingly important to Boston's economy. Est. 1638 by the elder John Winthrop as the main colony of the Massachusetts Bay Co., Boston was an early center of Amer. Puritanism, with notable ministers and theocratic-minded statesmen contributing to the vigorous intellectual life. The nation's oldest public school, Boston Public Latin, was opened in 1635; Harvard Univ., the nation's oldest col., was founded at nearby Cambridge in 1636; 1st public lib. was started in 1653, 1st public park (Boston Common), 1634, and the 1st newspaper in the 13 colonies, the *Newsletter*, appeared in 1704. With its excellent port, Boston soon gained commercial ascendancy over the other towns of colonial Mass. As the Amer. Revolution approached, it became a center of opposition to the British. The Battle of Bunker Hill, fought on Breed's Hill on June 17, 1775, was one of the 1st battles of the Revolution, and Boston was under siege until the British withdrew in March 1776. After a short postwar depression, Boston entered a period of prosperity that lasted until the mid–19th cent. Ships built here made Boston known around the world. Prominent families built substantial houses on Beacon Hill and in the Back Bay sects. and patronized the arts and letters, making Boston "the Athens of America." Despite the generally conservative tone of their culture, upper-class Bostonians backed reformers, notably the abolitionists. The growth of industry brought many immigrants (at 1st mostly Irish), and Boston changed from a commercial city surrounded by farms to an industrial center. The city's neighborhoods include the North End, South End, West End (all parts of the original area of the city), Roxbury (annexed 1868) and West Roxbury (with the Roxbury Latin School, Forest Hills Cemetery, and BROOK FARM), Dorchester (annexed 1874) and Mattapan (where Richard Mather had been the minister), East Boston, Charlestown (annexed 1874), Brighton (annexed 1874), and Allston, Jamaica Plain (annexed 1874; site of Jamaica Pond and Olmstead Park, and the famous Arnold Arboretum), and Hyde Park, Readville, Roslindale, South Boston (site of annual St. Patrick's Day parade), and Back Bay–Beacon Hill (Back Bay's Kenmore Square is terminal point for Boston Marathon). Revitalization projects in the city include the Faneuil Hall Marketplace and the construction of new skyscrapers, including the John Hancock Tower (740 ft/226 m; 1976). Observatory is the tallest bldg. in New England. In spite of downtown developments, Boston grows increasingly suburban; in 1990, less than ⅕ of the metropolitan area's residents lived in the central city. The city, with its broad avenues running into the crooked narrow streets of colonial Boston, cherishes the landmarks of the past: the 17th-cent.

house in which Paul Revere lived; Old North Church, famous for its part in Revere's story; Old South Meetinghouse, a rallying place for patriots during the Revolution; the old statehouse (1713), now a mus., in front of which the Boston Massacre took place; the Boston Common and the Public Garden; Faneuil Hall, the "Cradle of Liberty"; the golden-domed statehouse, with its facade designed by Charles Bulfinch; and the red-brick houses of Louisburg Square. Among notable Boston churches are King's Chapel, the birthplace of Amer. Unitarianism (1785); the Mother Church of Christian Science (founded by Mary Baker Eddy in 1866); and Trinity Church (1872–1877), designed by H. H. Richardson and decorated by John LaFarge. Boston Light (1716), at the entrance to Boston Harbor, is the oldest lighthouse in the U.S. Boston is one of the great cultural centers of the nation. In the city are the Mass. Historical Society (founded 1791); the Boston Athenaeum (1807); the Boston Public Lib.; the New England Conservatory of Music; the Boston Symphony Orchestra; the Mus. of Fine Arts; the Inst. of Contemporary Art; the Isabella Stewart Gardner Mus.; the John F. Kennedy Lib.; the Arnold Arboretum; and the offices of the *Christian Science Monitor.* Harvard Medical School is in Boston proper, as are the New England Medical Center, Mass. General Hosp., Brigham and Women's Hosp., Children's Hosp. Medical Center, and Angel Memorial Children's Hosp. Other educational institutions include Boston Univ., Simmons Col., Emerson Col., Emmanuel Col., Suffolk Univ., and Northeastern Univ., Wentworth Inst., Mass. Col. of Pharmacy, Berklee School of Music. The Boston Naval Shipyard (est. 1800, closed 1973) was the berth of the restored U.S.S. *Constitution,* which was originally launched (1797) a short distance away. USS Constitution Natl. Park is located in Charlestown. Served by Logan Internatl. Airport situated across Boston Harbor and connected across an arm of the harbor from downtown Boston to East Boston by the Sumner and Callahan tunnels, and a 3d tunnel, opened in 1996, named for baseball great Ted Williams. The city is connected northward via Charlestown and Chelsea by the Mystic River bridge. The American League's Red Sox play baseball in Fenway Park; the Natl. Hockey League's Bruins and the Natl. Basketball Assn. Celtics play in the Fleet Center (1995). Other key attractions include the Boston Mus. of Science, the Franklin Park Zoo, the Children's Mus., the New England Aquarium, the Mus. of Afro-Amer. Artists, the Mus. of Transportation, and the Computer Mus. Boston Harbor Isls. State Park and Thompson Isl. Education Center. Inc. 1822

Boston 1 (BAW-stuhn), town (1990 pop. 1,395), Thomas co., S Ga., 12 mi/19 km ESE of Thomasville; 30°47'N 83°47'W. Mfg. of candy and clothing. Inc. 1870. **2** town (1990 pop. 159), Wayne co., E Ind., near Ohio state line, 7 mi/11.3 km S of Richmond; 39°44'N 84°51'W. **3** uninc. town (1990 pop. 1,300), Allegheny co., SW Pa., residential suburb 4 mi/6.4 km SE of McKeesport, on Youghiogheny R. (bridged); 40°18'N 79°49'W.

Boston 1 uninc. village (1990 pop. 400), Nelson co., central Ky., 10 mi/16 km WSW of Bardstown, near Beech Fork river. Tobacco, grain; livestock; dairying. Timber. Mfg. (lumber and wood prods., bourbon whiskey). Fort Knox Military Reservation to NW; Bernheim Forest to NE. One of 5 places so named in Ky. **2** village (1990 pop. 500), Erie co., W N.Y., 20 mi/32 km SSE of Buffalo; 42°39'N 78°45'W. **3** uninc. village (1990 pop. 200), ⊙ Bowie co., NE Texas, 20 mi/32 km W of Texarkana. Elev. 390 ft/119 m. Cattle; dairying; grains.

Boston African American Historic Site, E Mass., authorized 1980. Site features oldest Afr.-Amer. church in the U.S. and the Black Heritage Trail.

Boston Bay, Mass., inner portion (13 mi/21 km long NW-SE) of Massachusetts Bay of the Atlantic Ocean; its entrance is bet. S tip of Deer Isl. (N) and Allerton Point (S). Boston is at head of N arm (Boston Harbor), which is entered by Mystic and Charles rivers in N and by Neponset R. in S (Dorchester Bay); Quincy Bay is the portion lying off Quincy (on SW shore); SE arm, sheltered on E by Nantasket Peninsula, is called Hingham Bay. Has deepwater anchorages, dredged channels, and extensive port facilities in its bordering cities. Boston Harbor Isls. State Park. Largest of its isls. are Thompson, Spectacle, Long, and Peddocks. Name Boston Harbor is sometimes applied to entire bay.

Boston Heights, village (1990 pop. 733), Summit co., NE Ohio, 11 mi/18 km N of Akron; 41°16'N 81°31'W.

Boston Historical Park, E Mass. Many sites include Old South Meeting House, the home of Paul Revere, obelisk commemorating the Battle of Bunker Hill, and part of the Charlestown Navy Yard. USS *Constitution* is currently moored and is an active ship in the U.S. Navy maintained by the Natl. Park Service. Authorized 1974.

Boston Mountains, most rugged part of the Ozarks, mostly in NW Ark., with parts in NE Okla.; highest parts are Pilot Knob (2,345 ft/715 m) and Sherman Mt. (2,171 ft/662 m). Run E-W from E of Muskogee (Okla.) to W of Clinton (Ark.). Arkansas R. is to S; Buffalo R. to NE. Isolated because of its geographical makeup, the region developed its own lifestyle; mt. people occupied small farms, cultivating the narrow valleys and living on the ridges. The Boston Mts., along with the rest of the highlands, have become a popular recreation center in Ark. Part of this range is included in the Ozark Natl. Forest. Timber; poultry, livestock.

Bostonia, uninc. city (1990 pop. 13,670), San Diego co., S Calif., residential suburb 16 mi/26 km ENE of downtown San Diego, 2 mi/3.2 km NE of El Cajon, in vineyard and orchard region (citrus fruit, avocados); 32°49'N 116°57'W. Dairying; poultry; ornamental plants.

Bostonnais River (bahs-to-NAI), 70 mi/113 km, S central Que., E Canada; issues from Grand Lac Bostonnais (8 mi/13 km long), 40 mi/64 km S of L. St. John, flows SW to St. Maurice R. just N of La Tuque. There are several falls. Also called Bastonnais R.

Bostwick, town (1990 pop. 307), Morgan co., N central Ga., 17 mi/27 km SSW of Athens; 33°44'N 83°31'W.

Boswell, town (1990 pop. 767), Benton co., W Ind., 8 mi/12.9 km SSW of Fowler; 40°31'N 87°23'W. In grain area; sawmill. Mfg. (pallets, planters).

Boswell, village (1990 pop. 643), Choctaw co., SE Okla., 21 mi/34 km W of Hugo; 34°01'N 95°52'W. In agr. area (corn, soybeans, cotton; cattle); mfg. (millwork, post setters).

Boswell (BAWS-wel), borough (1990 pop. 1,485), Somerset co., SW Pa., 12 mi/19 km SW of Johnstown, on Quemahoning Creek; 40°09'N 79°01'W. Mfg. (lumber, crushed stone), coal processing. Agr. (grain, potatoes; livestock; dairying); subsurface bituminous coal. Laurel Mt. Resort to W; Laurel Ridge State Park to NW; Quemahoning Reservoir to E. Inc. 1904.

Bosworth, city (1990 pop. 334), Carroll co., NW central Mo., near Grand R., 13 mi/21 km NE of Carrollton; 39°28'N 93°20'W. Wheat, corn, soybeans; hogs; mfg. (apparel).

Botetourt (baw-dee-TAWT), county (☐ 545 sq mi/1,412 sq km; 1990 pop. 24,992), W central Va.; ⊙ Fincastle; 37°32'N 79°47'W. Mainly in Great Appalachian Valley, traversed by ridges; Blue Ridge is along SE boundary. Drained by James R. and Craig Creek. Includes parts of Jefferson Natl. Forest in W and E and George Washington Natl. Forest in N. Agr. (esp. tomatoes, wheat, corn, hay, alfalfa, soybeans, potatoes, apples, peaches; cattle, sheep; dairying); timber; limestone quarrying. Mt. resorts. Formed 1770.

Botha (BAH-thuh), village (1991 pop. 174), S central Alta., W Canada, 8 mi/13 km E of Stettler. Dairying; wheat.

Bothell (BAH-thuhl), city (1990 pop. 12,345), King co., W central Wash., 12 mi/19 km NNE of Seattle, on Sammamish R., 3 mi/4.8 km E of N end of L. Washington; 47°46'N 122°12'W. Agr. area, to N and E (vegetables, berries; dairying; poultry); mfg. (machinery, medical instruments and supplies, fabricated metal prods., electronic and computer equip., chemicals, navigation instruments). Bothell Landing, historical park and mus.

Bothwell, town (1991 pop. 955), S Ont., near Thames R., 23 mi/37 km NE of Chatham; 42°38'N 81°52'W. In dairying, mixed-farming region; formerly oil production.

Bothwell, uninc. village, Box Elder co., N Utah, 18 mi/29 km NW of Brigham City. Alfalfa, grain; dairying; cattle, sheep.

Botkins, village (1990 pop. 1,340), Shelby co., W Ohio, 13 mi/21 km N of Sidney; 40°29'N 84°11'W. Grain prods.

Bottineau (bah-tuh-NO), county (☐ 1,677 sq mi/4,343 sq km; 1990 pop. 8,011), N N.Dak., borders Man. and Sask. (Canada) on N; ⊙ Bottineau; 48°47'N 100°50'W. Agr. area watered by Souris and Cut Bank rivers. Oil and natural-gas deposits; diversified farming, dairy produce, livestock; wheat. Turtle Mts. in NE; part of J. Clark Salyer Natl. Wildlife Refuge along Souris R.; L. Metigoshe State Park, state forest and Bottineau Ski Area in NE. Formed 1873; organized 1884.

Bottineau (bah-tuh-NO), town (1990 pop. 2,598), ⊙ Bottineau co., N N.Dak., 61 mi/98 km NE of Minot, and on branch of Souris R.; 48°49'N 100°26'W. Diversified farming; dairy prods.; wheat, barley; cattle. Near Turtle Mts.; L. Metigoshe State Park to N; Lords L. to SE. Seat of N.Dak. State Univ., Bottineau campus. Inc. as village in 1888 and as city in 1904.

Bottom, principal settlement of Saba, Du. West Indies, in the Leewards, 30 mi/48 km NW of St. Kitts; 17°38'N 63°15'W. Built within extinct crater, and reached from ocean through steps ("the Ladder") cut into rock. Inhabitants engage in fishing, shipbuilding, lace making.

Botwood, town (1991 pop. 3,663), NE central N.F., E Canada, at head of the Bay of Exploits, near mouth of Exploits R., 160 mi/257 km NW of St. John's; 49°09'N 55°21'W. Port for Grand Falls newsprint mills and Buchans copper, lead, zinc, gold, silver output; fish-smoking plant. Lumbering in region. Port is closed during winter months. Experimental trans-Atlantic transport flights were made from here, 1937–1938.

Boucherville (BOO-shuhr-vil), city (1991 pop. 33,796), suburb of Montreal, S Que., E Canada, on SE shore of the St. Lawrence R., and 10 mi/16 km NE of Montreal; 45°37'N 73°27'W. Mfg. (printing presses, paper and paperboard prods., pharmaceuticals, hardware, plastic prods., crushed stone). La Fontaine Bridge/tunnel to Montreal Isl. is S. Îles des Boucherville opposite city. Founded 1668 by Pierre Boucher; manor house built by him still stands nearby, now owned by Jesuits.

Bouctouche (buhk-TOOSH), village (1991 pop. 2,364), E N.B., E Canada, on Northumberland Strait, at mouth of Buctouche R. (30 mi/48 km long), 20 mi/32 km NNW of Shediac. Fishing (oysters, cod, lobster, herring, smelt) and lumber port. Service center for coastal region. Area settled by Acadians.

Bouillante (boo-YAWNGT), town, W Basse-Terre, Guadeloupe, 10 mi/16 km NNW of Basse-Terre. Mfg. of alcohol; trading. Thermal springs nearby.

Boularderie Island (boo-lahr-duh-REE) (25 mi/40 km long, 2 mi/3 km–6 mi/10 km wide), NE N.S., E Canada, off Cape Breton Isl., bet. Great Bras d'Or and St. Andrew Channel, NW of Sydney; 46°13'N 60°27'W. Coal is mined in N.

Boulder (BOL-duhr), county (☐ 751 sq mi/1,945 sq km; 1990 pop. 225,339), N central Colo.; ⊙ Boulder; 40°05'N 105°21'W. Irrigated agr. and cattle region. Fruit, vegetables, wheat, hay, beans, barley, corn, sugar beets; poultry; dairying. Mining (coal, gold). Part of Rocky Mt. Natl. Park in NW and of Front Range in W; part of Roosevelt Natl. Forest in W; Eldorado Canyon State Park in S. Eldora Ski Area in SW. Formed 1861.

Boulder, city (1990 pop. 83,312), ⊙ Boulder co., N central Colo., on Boulder Creek, suburb 22 mi/35 km NW of Denver; 40°01'N 105°15'W. Situated c.5,363 ft/1,635 m above sea level, it is a major resort at edge of the Rocky Mts. Mfg. (machinery, consumer goods, foods, bioresearch, printing and publishing, electric and electronic equip., computer equip., apparel, printing ribbons, paper prods., fabricated metal prods., transportation equip., aerospace research, furniture, telephone apparatus, medical supplies). Principally a scientific research and education center; the Univ. of Colo., the Natl. Center for Atmospheric Research, the World Data Center, and Henderson Mus. are here. Boulder Municipal Airport to NE. Roosevelt Natl. Forest to W;

Rocky Mt. Natl. Park to NW; El Dorado Canyon State Park to S. Inc. 1871.

Boulder, town (1990 pop. 1,316), ⊙ Jefferson co., SW central Mont., on Boulder R., and 27 mi/43 km S of Helena; 46°14′N 122°07′W. Resort, "radon health mines"; gold, silver, lead, zinc mines; livestock; alfalfa, oats. Elkhorn Ghost Town to S; Boulder Hot Springs to S; sections of Deerlodge Natl. Forest to S, W, and E; part of Helena Natl. Forest to NE and N. Originally named Boulder Valley. Inc. 1865.

Boulder, village (1990 pop. 126), Garfield co., S Utah, 55 mi/89 km E of Panguitch; 37°55′N 111°25′W. Cattle. Dixie Natl. Forest to N. Anasazi Indian Village State Historic Park is here. Calf Creek Recreation Area to S. In 1942, this was last town in U.S. to receive mail by mule. Settled 1889.

Boulder City, city (1990 pop. 12,567), Clark co., SE Nev., suburb 20 mi/32 km SE of Las Vegas and Ariz. boundary, 6 mi/9.7 km WSW of HOOVER DAM forms L. Mead (to NE), on Colorado R.; 35°58′N 114°50′W. Elev. c.2,500 ft/762 m. Mfg. (paper prods., construction materials). Artist colony. Year-round tourist center; hq. of L. Mead Natl. Recreation Area to N and E. Highland Range (crucial bighorn habitat area) to S. Built (1932) by the Federal govt. as hq. during the dam's construction; it became a self-governing municipality by act of Congress in 1958. Only city in Nev. in which casino gambling is prohibited. Inc. 1959.

Boulder Creek, uninc. town (1990 pop. 6,725), Santa Cruz co., W Calif., in Santa Cruz Mts., 13 mi/21 km NNW of Santa Cruz on San Lorenzo R.; 37°08′N 122°08′W. Berries, artichokes, vegetables, flowers, nursery prods. Gateway to Big Basin Redwoods State Park (NW).

Boulder Creek, 55 mi/89 km long, N central Colo.; rises at Continental Divide in N Front Range, SE Boulder co., near Rollins Pass (11,671 ft/3,557 m); flows E and NE, past Eldora, Nederland, and Boulder, to St. Vrain Creek 4 mi/6.4 km E of Longmont. Near Nederland is hydroelectric plant, at L. Edora.

Boulder Dam, Nev.: see HOOVER DAM.

Boulder Hill, uninc. city (1990 pop. 8,894), Kendall co., NE Ill., suburb 4 mi/6.4 km S of Aurora, on Fox R.; 41°42′N 88°20′W. RR junction.

Boulder Lake, reservoir (⊔ 6 sq mi/15.5 sq km), St. Louis co., NE Minn., on Otter R., at S edge of Cloquet Valley State Forest, 20 mi/32 km N of Duluth; 47°03′N 92°12′W. Max. capacity 30,300 acre-ft. Formed by Boulder Lake Dam (20 ft/6 m high), built for power generation; also used for recreation.

Boulder Reservoir, Boulder co., N central Colo., on Dry Creek, 5 mi/8 km NNE of Boulder; 1 mi/1.6 km long; 40°05′N 105°13′W. Max. capacity 61,576 acre-ft. Formed by dam (44 ft/13 m high), built by the City of Boulder for water supply and irrigation. Sixmile Reservoir immediately to S.

Boulder River, 71 mi/114 km, Jefferson co., SW Mont.; rises in W Jefferson co. at Continental Divide, in Deerlodge Natl. Forest, flows SE past Boulder, then S to Jefferson R. 7 mi/11.3 km E of Whitehall.

Bound Brook, borough (1990 pop. 9,487), Somerset co., N central N.J., on the Raritan R.; 40°34′N 74°32′W. Largely residential, it produces chemicals, pharmaceuticals, and dyes. During the Amer. Revolution, George Washington maintained an outpost here, and Amer. forces were defeated (April 1777) by those of Br. Gen. Cornwallis. Local attractions include Washington's campgrounds and several 18th-cent. houses. Settled 1681, inc. 1891.

Boundary, county (⊔ 1,278 sq mi/3,310 sq km; 1990 pop. 8,332), N Idaho, in Panhandle region; ⊙ Bonners Ferry; 48°48′N 116°27′W. Mt. area drained by Kootenai, Moyie, Pack, and Upper Priest rivers and bordering on Wash. (W), B.C. (Canada; N) and Mont. (E). Livestock (cattle) raising; alfalfa, hay; hops, oats, barley, wheat; timber; silver, lead, thorium. E boundary is Pacific/Mountain time zone boundary. Kaniksu Natl. Forest extends throughout most of co., part of Kootenai Natl. Forest in SE corner; Kootenai Natl. Wildlife Refuge at center. Formed 1884.

Boundary Peak, 13,140 ft/4,005 m high, Esmeralda co., SW Nev., and Mono co., SE Calif., in the White Mts. in Inyo Natl Forest, 60 mi/97 km WSW of Tonopah (Nev.) and 32 mi/51 km NNE of Bishop (Calif); 37°50′N 118°21′W. Highest point in Nev.

Boundary Waters, loosely defined area of numerous lakes and rivers 50–75 mi/81–121 km to either side of the U.S. (N Minn.)–Canada (SW Ont.) border, bounded E by L. Superior and W by Rainy L. Most of area protected by Quetico Provincial Park (Ont.), Voyageurs Natl. Park, Superior Natl. Forest (which includes the Boundary Waters Canoe Area) and several state forests in Minn. on the U.S. side. Boating, canoeing, fishing, hiking, cross-country skiing, snowmobiling.

Bountiful, city (1990 pop. 36,659), Davis co., N central Utah, residential suburb 7 mi/11.3 km N of Salt Lake City; 40°52′N 111°52′W. Some farming and floral nurseries. Mormon Temple located here. Fruit; dairying; mfg. (machinery, motor vehicles, printing and publishing, metal prods.). Drained by Holbrook and Mill creeks; near Great Salt L. Bountiful Peak (9,259 ft/2,822 m) 6 mi/9.7 km to NNE; Wasatch Range and Natl. Forest to E. The Perrigrine Sessions, a Mormon group, settled here, 1847; called Sessions Settlement until 1855.

Bouquet River, c.40 mi/64 km long, NE N.Y., rises in the Adirondacks, E central Essex co., flows NE and N, past Elizabethtown, to L. Champlain 2 mi/3.2 km below Willsboro. Receives North Branch above Willsboro.

Bourbeuse River, 138 mi/222 km long, E central Mo.; rises NE of Rolla in Phelps co., meanders NE through the N Ozarks to Meramec R. in Franklin co.

Bourbon 1 (BUHR-buhn), county (⊔ 638 sq mi/1,652 sq km; 1990 pop. 14,966), SE Kansas; ⊙ Fort Scott; 37°51′N 94°50′W. In Prairie region, bordered E by Mo.; watered by Marmaton and Little Osage rivers. Cattle, hogs; corn, oats, wheat, soybeans, hay, general agr.; metal prods. Bourbon State Fishing L. in W; Fort Scott Natl. Historical Site and Natl. Cemetery at Fort Scott. Formed 1855. **2** county (⊔ 291 sq mi/754 sq km; 1990 pop. 19,236), N central Ky.; ⊙ PARIS; 38°12′N 84°12′W. Drained by South Fork of Licking R. and Houston, Stoner, and Hinkston (forms part of E boundary) creeks; Silas Creek forms part of N boundary. Gently rolling agr. area (burley tobacco, soybeans, wheat, corn, hay, alfalfa; hogs, cattle, horses, poultry; dairying), in Bluegrass region; limestone quarries. Some mfg. at Paris. Formed 1785.

Bourbon 1 (BUHR-buhn), town (1990 pop. 1,672), Marshall co., N Ind., 10 mi/16 km SE of Plymouth; 41°18′N 86°07′W. In agr. area (livestock, poultry; grain); feed milling, meat processing; mfg. (plastic prods.; hardwood lumber, windows, transportation prods., wire); foundry. **2** town (1990 pop 1,188), Crawford co., E central Mo., in the Ozarks, near Meramec R., 15 mi/24 km NNE of Steelville; 38°08′N 91°15′W. Grain; livestock. Onondaga Cave State Park to S.

Bourbonnais (bur-bahn-A), village (1990 pop. 13,934), Kankakee co., NE Ill., near Kankakee R., 3 mi/4.8 km NNW of Kankakee; 41°09′N 87°52′W. In agr. area. Settled by Fr. Canadians. Seat of Olivet Nazarene Univ.

Bourlamaque (boor-luh-MAHK), town, W Que., E Canada, 60 mi/97 km ESE of Rouyn, just S of Val d'Or; 48°05′N 77°47′W. Mining and agr. center.

Bourne (BORN), town (1990 pop. 16,064), Barnstable co., SE Mass., crossed by Cape Cod Canal, 15 mi/24 km W of Barnstable; 41°43′N 70°35′W. The canal was bridged in 1935. Summer resort town. Tourism is the chief industry, followed by fishing and farming. Of note are the Mass. Maritime Acad., a replica (built 1926) of the Aptucxet Trading Post (1627), Sacrifice Rock, and Wishing Rock. Site of Cape Cod Canal Administration. Includes villages of Bournedale, Cataumet, Monument Beach (1990 pop. 1,842), Pocasset (1990 pop. 2,756), Sagamore (1990 pop. 2,589; site of 1 of 2 bridges across Cape Cod Canal to Cape Cod; Cape Cod electric power plant on Cape Cod Canal; also site

of state beach), and Buzzards Bay (1990 pop. 3,250). Settled 1627, inc. 1884.

Bourne (BORN), village (1990 pop. 19), Baker co., NE Oregon, 18 mi/29 km W of Baker, on Powder R., near its source SW of Elkhorn Ridge, in Wallowa-Whitman Natl. Forest.

Bournedale, Mass.: see BOURNE.

Bournemouth Bath, Jamaica: see ROCK FORT.

Bouton (BOW-tuhn), town (1990 pop. 149), Dallas co., central Iowa, on Beaver Creek, 5 mi/8 km E of Perry; 41°51′N 94°00′W. In agr. area.

Boutte (boo-TAI), town (1990 pop. 2,702), St. Charles parish, La., 5 mi/8 km S of Hahnville; 29°54′N 92°31′W. Noted for Alligator Festival.

Bovey (BO-vee), village (1990 pop. 662), Itasca co., N central Minn., 7 mi/11.3 km NE of Grand Rapids, near N end of Trout L., in W end of Mesabi Iron Range; 47°17′N 93°24′W. Iron mines in vicinity; light mfg. Ore-washing plant nearby on Trout L. Inc. 1921.

Bovill, village (1990 pop. 256), Latah co., N Idaho, 30 mi/48 km ENE of Moscow, on Potlatch R.; 46°52′N 116°23′W. RR terminus; lumber; cattle, sheep; alfalfa, oats, barley. Part of St. Joe Natl. Forest to NW; Dworshak Reservoir and State Park to SE.

Bovina, town (1990 pop. 1,549), Parmer co., W Texas, 75 mi/121 km SW of Amarillo, near Running Water Draw creek; 34°31′N 102°53′W.

Bow (BO), town (1990 pop. 5,500), Merrimack co., S central N.H., 5 mi/8 km S of Concord; 43°07′N 71°31′W. Bounded E by Merrimack R. Agr. (vegetables, apples; poultry, livestock; dairying; nursery crops; timber); mfg. (feeds, Christmas decorations, cabinets, zirconium dioxide), machining. Mary Baker Eddy b. here. Bow Mills village has state's oldest sawmill (c.1800).

Bow Island, town (1991 pop. 1,484), SE Alta., W Canada, near South Saskatchewan R., 35 mi/56 km WSW of Medicine Hat. Oil and natural gas; coal mining. Cattle; wheat, flax.

Bow Lake, N.H.: see STRAFFORD.

Bow Mar, town (1990 pop. 854), Arapahoe and Jefferson cos., N central Colo., residential suburb 9 mi/14.5 km SSW of downtown Denver, near South Platte R.; 39°37′N 105°02′W. Elev. c.5,500 ft/1,676 m. Marston L. reservoir to W; Centennial Race Track to E.

Bow River (BO), 315 mi/507 km long, Alta., W Canada; rises in the Rocky Mts., S Alta., W Canada; flows SE through Banff Natl. Park., emerging from the mts. in the Bow R. Pass and continues past Calgary SE across the plains to its junction with the Belly R. to form the South Saskatchewan R. at Medicine Hat. Several irrigation, or diversion, dams have been built along the Bow, most notably the Bassano or Horseshoe Bend Dam (built 1912).

Bowbells (BO-belz), village (1990 pop. 498), ⊙ Burke co., NW N.Dak., 60 mi/97 km NW of Minot; 48°47′N 102°15′W. RR junction. Lignite mines; dairy farms; livestock; grain (esp. wheat), flax. Upper Des Lacs L. and Des Lacs Natl. Wildlife Refuge to E; Lostwood Natl. Wildlife Refuge to SW.

Bowden (BO-duhn), town (1991 pop. 923), S central Alta., W Canada, 25 mi/40 km SSW of Red Deer; 51°55′N 114°02′W. Oil and natural gas; large oil refinery. Mixed farming, dairying; wheat, barley, oats; cattle, hogs.

Bowden, town, St. Thomas parish, SE Jamaica, just E of Port Morant, 32 mi/51 km ESE of Kingston; 17°53′N 76°19′W. Ships bananas. Served by narrow-gauge RR.

Bowden Point, SW Devon Isl., E central Franklin dist., N.W.T., W Canada, on Wellington Channel; 75°02′N 92°15′W.

Bowdens (BOU-duhns), uninc. village, Duplin co., E central N.C., 10 mi/16 km SSW of Mt. Olive. Cucumbers, peppers, tobacco, grain; poultry, livestock.

Bowdle, village (1990 pop. 589), Edmunds co., N central S.Dak., 38 mi/61 km ESE of Mobridge. Grain; dairy prods.; livestock, poultry.

Bowdoin Center (BO-duhn), town center, Sagadahoc co., SW Maine, 12 mi/19 km NW of Bath.

Bowdoin, Lake (BOU-doin), NE Mont., Phillips co., 8 mi/12.9 km ENE of Malta; 7 mi/11.3 km long, max.

width 2 mi/3.2 km. Drains into Beaver Creek to E, Milk R. is to W and N, fed by Milk R. Bowden Natl. Wildlife Refuge surrounds lake.

Bowdoinham (BO-duhn-ham), town (1990 pop. 2,192), Sagadahoc co., SW Maine, on the Kennebec R., 8 mi/12.9 km NW of Bath; 44°01'N 69°52'W.

Bowdon (BOU-duhn), town (1990 pop. 1,981), Carroll co., W Ga., 10 mi/16 km WSW of Carrollton, and 5 mi/8 km E of the Ala. state line; 33°32'N 85°15'W. Mfg. of clothing, textile prods.. Settled 1830, inc. 1859.

Bowdon, village (1990 pop. 196), Wells co., central N.Dak., 13 mi/21 km SSW of Fessenden; 47°28'N 99°42'W.

Bowen (BO-WIN), village (1990 pop. 462), Hancock co., W Ill., 14 mi/23 km SSE of Carthage; 40°13'N 91°03'W. In agr. area.

Bowen Island (□ 10 sq mi/26 sq km), SW B.C., W Canada, in Howe Sound, NW of Vancouver; 3 mi/5 km wide, max. elev. 2,479 ft/756 m; 49°23'N 123°23'W. Resort; lumbering; residential.

Bowerbank, resort town (1990 pop. 72), Piscataquis co., central Maine, on Sebec L. and 6 mi/9.7 km N of Dover-Foxcroft; 45°18'N 69°15'W.

Bowers, village (1990 pop. 179), Kent co., E Del., 10 mi/16 km SE of Dover, on Delaware Bay bet. mouth of Murderkill R. (S) and mouth of St. Jones R. (N); 39°03'N 75°24'W. Fishing; oysters; beach resort. Harvey Conservation Area to N. Also called Bowers Beach.

Bowerston, village (1990 pop. 343), Harrison co., E Ohio, 14 mi/23 km NW of Cadiz.

Bowersville, town (1990 pop. 311), Hart co., NE Ga., 8 mi/12.9 km W of Hartwell; 34°22'N 83°05'W. Light mfg.; clothing.

Bowersville, village (1990 pop. 225), Greene co., S central Ohio, 27 mi/43 km ESE of Dayton. In agr. area.

Bowie, county (□ 922 sq mi/2,388 sq km; 1990 pop. 81,665), in extreme NE corner of Texas; ⊙ Boston; 33°27'N 94°25'W. Bounded N by Red R. (here, the Okla. and Ark. state lines), E by Ark. state line, S by Sulphur R. (forms Wright Patman L. in center of boundary). Partly forested (pine, oak, gum); timber; agr. (cotton, corn, wheat, milo, rice, corn, vegetables, blueberries); cattle; dairying. Oil and gas; sand and gravel. Mfg., processing at Texarkana (partly in Ark.). Formed 1840.

Bowie, city (1990 pop. 37,589), Prince Georges co., W central Md.; 38°58'N 76°45'W. Mainly a residential community. Principal points of interest are Bowie Race Track, the Woodward Mansion (c.1743), which serves as city hall, and Belair Stables, a house and mus. (c.1746). Originally founded in 1870 under the name Huntington City, it was renamed in 1874 for Oda Bowie, governor of Md. Bowie State Col. here was 1st est. 1867 in Baltimore as the Baltimore Normal School, a private training school for teachers. Inc. 1916.

Bowie, town (1990 pop. 4,990), Montague co., N Texas, c.45 mi/72 km SE of Wichita Falls; 33°33'N 97°50'W. In agr. region (watermelons, cantaloupes, peanuts, grain; cattle; dairying). Mfg. (machinery; diversified light mfg.). Founded 1882, inc. 1892.

Bowlegs, village (1990 pop. 398), Seminole co., central Okla., 5 mi/8 km S of Seminole, near Little R.; 35°08'N 96°40'W. Livestock; grain.

Bowler (BOU-ler), hamlet (1990 pop. 279), Shawano co., E central Wis., 33 mi/53 km ESE of Wausau; 44°51'N 88°58'W. Lumbering. Stockbridge Indian Reservation to NE, Menominee Indian Reservation to NNE.

Bowling Green 1 city (1990 pop. 40,641), ⊙ Warren co., S Ky., on the Barren R.; 36°58'N 86°26'W. Elev. 496 ft/151 m. RR junction to SW. Shipping and marketing center for agr. (tobacco, corn; livestock; dairying) and Mfg. (apparel, consumer goods, plastic prods., tranportation equip., beverages, pet food, store fixtures, construction materials, packaging materials, crushed limestone; printing and publishing; motor vehicle assembly). Occupied by the Confederates at the beginning of the Civil War until the Federal advance forced them to retreat in 1862. Bowling Green/Warren County Airport. Seat of Western Kentucky Univ. (including Ky. Mus. and Lib.). Natl. Corvette Mus. Mammoth Cave Natl. Park, a popular tourist attraction to NE; Lost River Caves to S. To the SW lie the ruins of a Shaker settlement est. 1798. Inc. 1812. **2** city (1990 pop. 2,976), ⊙ Pike co., E Mo., near Mississippi R., 26 mi/42 km SSE of Hannibal; 39°20'N 91°12'W. Wheat, corn, soybeans, fruit; light mfg.; limestone. Settled 1819. **3** city (1990 pop. 28,176), ⊙ Wood co., NW Ohio; 41°23'N 83°39'W. In a farm area. Mfg. includes tomato products, machinery, trailers, rubber, and plastics. Seat of Bowling Green State Univ. Inc. 1855.

Bowling Green, town (□ 1 sq mi/2.6 sq km; 1990 pop. 1,836), Hardee co., central Fla., 6 mi/9.7 km N of Wauchula; 27°38'N 81°49'W. Ships strawberries.

Bowling Green 1 village, Clay co., W Ind., on Eel R., 15 mi/24 km SE of Brazil. Agr. area. Hogs; soybeans. Original county seat of Clay co. Est. 1825. **2** uninc. village, York co., N S.C., at N.C. state line, 11 mi/18 km N of York, and 7 mi/11.3 km S of Gastonia, N.C. Mfg. includes cotton yarns; agr. includes cotton, peaches; livestock. **3** village (1990 pop. 727), ⊙ Caroline co., NE Va., 19 mi/31 km SSE of Fredericksburg, near Mattaponi R.; 38°2'N 77°20'W. Mfg. (lumber, wood prods.); in agr. area (potatoes, corn, soybeans; cattle); timber. Fort A.P. Hill Military Reservation is to NE.

Bowlus (BO-luhs), village (1990 pop. 260), Morrison co., central Minn., 10 mi/16 km S of Little Falls; 45°49'N 94°24'W. N of confluence of North Branch and South Branch Two Rivers; main stream Two Rivers flows ENE 3 mi/4.8 km to Mississippi R. Grain, potatoes, sunflowers; livestock, poultry; dairying; mfg. (feeds).

Bowman (BO-muhn), county (□ 1,169 sq mi/3,028 sq km; 1990 pop. 3,596), extreme SW N.Dak.; ⊙ Bowman; 46°06'N 103°31'W. Agr. area watered by Little Missouri R., Cedar Creek, and N Fork of Grand R. Lignite coal abundant. Cattle; wheat, flax. Bowman Haley Dam and L. in SE; Butte View State Campground in NE; Fort Dilts on N boundary; Little Missouri Natl. Grasslands beyond N boundary. Formed 1883; eliminated 1903 due to lack of settlement and reorganized 1907.

Bowman, city (1990 pop. 791), Elbert co., NE Ga., 11 mi/18 km NW of Elberton; 34°12'N 83°02'W. Mfg. of clothing.

Bowman, town (1990 pop. 1,063), Orangeburg co., S central S.C., 15 mi/24 km SE of Orangeburg; 33°21'N 80°40'W. Mfg. of lumber. Agr. includes poultry, livestock; grain, cotton, tobacco, peanuts, pecans, peaches; timber.

Bowman (BO-muhn), village (1990 pop. 1,741), ⊙ Bowman co., extreme SW N.Dak., 56 mi/90 km SSW of Dickinson; 46°10'N 103°24'W. Lignite mines; livestock raising; dairying; grain, wheat, flax. Inc. 1907.

Bowmanstown (BO-muhns-toun), borough (1990 pop. 888), Carbon co., E Pa., on Lehigh R. 3 mi/4.8 km W of Palmerton; 40°47'N 75°39'W. Mfg. (feeds, inorganic pigments). Appalachian Trail passes to S, on Blue Mt. Ridge. Beltzville L. reservoir and Beltzville State Park to NE.

Bowmansville, village (1990 pop. 600), Erie co., W N.Y., 10 mi/16 km ENE of Buffalo; 42°56'N 78°41'W. Stone quarrying.

Bowmanville (BO-muhnz-vil), town, S Ont., on L. Ontario, 9 mi/14 km E of Oshawa; 43°55'N 78°41'W. Commuter suburb of Toronto. Main community within Regional Municipality of Newcastle. Port, with good natural harbor; mfg. of transportation equip., rubber prods., publishing, machinery; publishing. Mixed farming; apples. Resort. Bowmanville Zoo here.

Bowstring Lake (□ 15 sq mi/39 sq km), Itasca co., N Minn., 25 mi/40 km NW of Grand Rapids; 5.5 mi/8.9 km long, 3.5 mi/5.6 km wide; 47°32'N 93°54'W. Elev. 1,320 ft/402 m. Fishing resorts. Fed from E (at Muskrat Bay) and drained to NW (to Sand L.) by Bowstring R. In Bowstring State Forest (overlaps natl. forest boundary) surrounded by Chippewa Natl. Forest and by Leech L. Indian Reservation, except in NE. Sometimes written Bow String.

Bowstring River, c.60 mi/97 km long, Itasca co., N Minn.; rises in Grave L., 19 mi/31 km NNW of Grand Rapids; 47°29'N 93°44'W. Flows first through Little Bowstring L., NW through Bowstring L., Sand, Little Sand, and Rice lakes, joins Popple R. (from SW) at head of Dora L. to form Big Fork R.

Box Butte, county (□ 1,077 sq mi/2,789 sq km; 1990 pop. 13,130), NW Nebr.; ⊙ Alliance; drained in N by Niobrara R; 42°12'N 103°04'W. Agr. area; cattle, hogs, poultry prods.; wheat, beans, alfalfa, corn, potatoes, including seed potatoes, and sugar beets. Several small natural lakes in SE; Kilpatrick L. in SW. Formed 1886.

Box Elder, county (□ 6,729 sq mi/17,428 sq km; 1990 pop. 36,485), NW Utah; ⊙ Brigham City; 41°30'N 113°05'W. Agr. area bordering on Nev. (W) and Idaho (N). Great Salt L. (SE) is entered by Bear R. Great Salt L. Desert is in SW. Mfg. at Brigham City; sugar beets, peaches, cherries, wheat, barley, alfalfa; cattle, sheep; salt, magnesium. N part of Newfoundland Evaporation Basin (receives flood overflow from Great Salt L. to E) in SW; most of N ½ of Great Salt L. in SE part of co. W 90% of co,. nearly uninhabited. Willard Bay State Park in SE, on Great Salt L.; Golden Spike Natl. Historical Site in E center, N of Great Salt L. Part of Hill Air Force Base Firing Range in S; small part of Caribou Natl. Forest in NE corner. Formed 1856.

Box Elder, village (1990 pop. 250), Hill co., N Mont., on Boxelder Creek, 23 mi/37 km SW of Havre; 48°19'N 110°01'W. In livestock region. Hq. located in W part of Rocky Boy's Indian Reservation.

Boxboro (BAWKS-buh-ro), town (1990 pop. 3,343), Middlesex co., NE central Mass., 21 mi/34 km NE of Worcester; 42°29'N 71°31'W. Fruit; dairying; telecommunications. Also spelled Boxborough.

Boxford, rural town (1990 pop. 6,266), Essex co., NE Mass., 9 mi/14.5 km ESE of Lawrence, in suburban area; 42°41'N 71°01'W. State forest just S and N.

Boxholm, town (1990 pop. 214), Boone co., central Iowa, 14 mi/23 km NW of Boone; 42°10'N 94°06'W.

Boy Lake, Cass co., N central Minn., 29 mi/47 km WSW of Grand Rapids; 4 mi/6.4 km long, 1.5 mi/2.4 km wide; 47°05'N 94°09'W. Fed from S and drained to W by Boy R. into Leech L; mid-sect. of lake has large W arm. Resorts. On E boundary of Leech L. Indian Reservation, in Chippewa Natl. Forest.

Boy River, village (1990 pop. 43), Cass co., N central Minn., 22 mi/35 km ENE of Walker, on Boy R. Dairying; oats. Leech L. to W, Boy L. to S; Leech L. Indian Reservation to SW and N; 47°10'N 94°07'W.

Boy River, c.60 mi/97 km long, in N central Minn.; rises in central Cass co., in Ten Mile L., 7 mi/11.3 km S of Walker; flows generally E through Birch, Paquet, Mud, Pleasant, Deep, Child, Woman, and Girl lakes, receives short stream from Little Boy L. to S, turns N in Inguadona L., enters and exits through E end of Boy L., passes through Skelly L., then turns W to enter Boy Bay at E end of Leech L.; 46°58'N 94°31'E.

Boyce (BOIS), town (1990 pop. 1,361), Rapides parish, central La., 15 mi/24 km WNW of Alexandria, near Red R.; 31°23'N 92°40'W. In agr. area (cotton, rice, vegetables); timber; catfish, crawfish. Units of Kisatchie Natl. Forest to NE and S, L. Rodemacher to W, Cotile L. and Hotwells Health Resort to SW.

Boyce, village (1990 pop. 520), Clarke co., N Va., in Shenandoah Valley, 9 mi/14.5 km SE of Winchester; 39°05'N 78°03'W. Agr. (grain, apples, soybeans; horses). Va. State Arboretum to S.

Boyceville, town (1990 pop. 913), Dunn co., W Wis., 12 mi/19 km NNW of Menomonie; 45°02'N 92°02'W. In dairy and grain area; mfg. (fabrics, dairy food ingredients).

Boyd 1 county (□ 161 sq mi/417 sq km; 1990 pop. 51,150), NE Ky.; ⊙ Catlettsburg; 38°21'N 82°41'W. Bounded NE by the Ohio R. (Ohio state line), E by Big Sandy R. (W.Va. state line); drained by East Fork Little Sandy R. Hilly industrial and mineral region, partially urbanized in N part of co., continuation of Huntington (W.Va.) urban area to E. Mfg. in Ashland and Cablettsburg. Bituminous-coal mines, oil and gas wells, clay pits, limestone and sandstone quarries, iron deposits; hardwood timber tracts; some agr. (burley tobacco, hay, alfalfa; cattle). Formed 1860. **2** county (□ 544 sq mi/1,409 sq km; 1990 pop. 2,835), N Nebr.; ⊙ Butte; 42°53'N 98°46'W. Agr. area bounded N by S.Dak., S by

Niobrara R., NE by Missouri R.; drained by Keya Paha R. and Ponca Creek. Cattle, hogs; dairying; corn, sorghum, alfalfa. Formed 1891.

Boyd, town (1990 pop. 1,041), Wise co., N Texas, 27 mi/43 km NW of Fort Worth, near West Fork of Trinity R.; 33°04′N 97°33′W. In agr. area (dairying; livestock; peanuts, pecans); mfg. (aircraft components, gas and oil tanks). Eagle Mt. L. reservoir to S.

Boyd 1 village (1990 pop. 251), Lac qui Parle co., SW Minn., 10 mi/16 km SW of Montevideo, on Ten Mile Creek; 44°51′N 95°54′W. Livestock; poultry; grain; dairying; mfg. (fertilizers). **2** village (1990 pop. 40), Carbon co., S Mont., at the confluence of Stanley and Cow creeks, 35 mi/56 km SW of Billings; 45°28′N 109°04′W. Cattle, sheep; barley, oats, and sugar beets. **3** village (1990 pop. 683), Chippewa co., W central Wis., 17 mi/27 km E of Chippewa Falls; 44°57′N 91°02′W. Mfg. (wood prods.).

Boyden, town (1990 pop. 651), Sioux co., NW Iowa, near source of West Branch Floyd R., 15 mi/24 km NNE of Orange City; 43°11′N 96°00′W. Feed.

Boydton, town (1990 pop. 453), ⊙ Mecklenburg co., S Va., 30 mi/48 km E of South Boston; 36°40′N 78°23′W. Mfg. (high-carbon wire), in agr. area (grain, soybeans, tobacco; livestock; poultry; dairying). Former seat of Randolph-Macon Col. 1832–1868; later moved to Ashland. Mecklenburg Correctional Center to SE. Occoneechee State Park to SW; Kerr Reservoir (Buggs Isl. L.) on Roanoke R. to S.

Boyer River, 139 mi/224 km long, W Iowa; rises near Storm Lake; flows S and SW, past Denison, Logan, and Missouri Valley, to Missouri R. 13 mi/21 km N of Council Bluffs.

Boyertown (BOI-uhr-toun), borough (1990 pop. 3,759), Berks co., SE Pa., 15 mi/24 km E of Reading; 40°19′N 75°38′W. Mfg. (wood, metal, electronic, plastic, and paper prods.; machinery, medical supplies, transportation equip.; printing and publishing). Agr. area (grain, apples, soybeans, potatoes; livestock, poultry; dairying). Boyertown Area Historical Society, Boyertown Mus. of Historic Vehicles. Founded c.1835, inc. 1866.

Boyes Hot Springs, uninc. town (1990 pop. 5,973), Sonoma co., W Calif., 16 mi/26 km SE of Santa Rosa, 10 mi/16 km N of San Pablo Bay, on Sonoma Creek; 38°19′N 122°30′W. Fruit, grain; cattle, sheep, poultry; dairying. Sonoma Mts. to W.

Boykin (BOI-kin), town, Miller co., SW Ga., 16 mi/26 km NNW of Bainbridge; 31°06′N 84°41′W.

Boykin, village, Sumter co., central S.C., 10 mi/16 km S of Camden. Well known for sport hunting; home of Boykin spaniel dog.

Boykins, town (1990 pop. 658), Southampton co., SE Va., 16 mi/26 km SW of Franklin, near N.C. state line; 36°34′N 77°12′W. RR junction; agr. (peanuts, cotton, grain, melons; livestock); timber. Raids of Nat Turner's slave insurrection (1831) began here.

Boyle, county (□ 182 sq mi/471 sq km; 1990 pop. 25,641), central Ky.; ⊙ Danville; 37°37′N 84°52′W. Bounded E by Dix R. (Herrington L. reservoir); drained by Salt, Beech Fork and North Rolling Fork rivers. Gently rolling and partly hilly upland, partly in outer Bluegrass agr. area (burley tobacco, hay, alfalfa, soybeans, wheat, corn, berries; hogs, cattle, poultry; dairying) stone quarries. Mfg. at Danville. Includes Perryville Natl. Cemetery and Perryville Battlefield State Historic Site in NW, near Perryville, Danville Natl. Cemetery and Constitution Square Historic Site in E at Danville. Formed 1842.

Boyle, village (1991 pop. 665), central Alta., W Canada, 20 mi/32 km ESE of Athabaska. Wheat; livestock.

Boyle, village (1990 pop. 651), Bolivar co., NW Miss., 3 mi/4.8 km S of Cleveland; 33°42′N 90°43′W. In agr. area (cotton, corn, rice, soybeans; cattle); mfg. (pharmaceutical needles).

Boylston (BOILS-tuhn), residential town (1990 pop. 3,517), Worcester co., central Mass., just E of Wachusett Reservoir, 7 mi/11.3 km NNE of Worcester; 42°22′N 71°43′W. Includes village of Morningdale. Settled 1705, inc. 1786.

Boyne City (BOIN), town (1990 pop. 3,478), Charlevoix

co., NW Mich., on L. Charlevoix at mouth of small Boyne R., 12 mi/19 km SSW of Petoskey; 45°12′N 85°00′W. In area producing cherries, apples, potatoes; mfg. (transportation equip., gun cases, electrical prods., magnets, plastic prods.). Resort. Airport here. Smelt festival held here each spring. Young State Park to NW. Inc. as village 1885, as city 1907.

Boyne Falls (BOIN), village (1990 pop. 369), Charlevoix co., NW Mich., on Boyne R., 14 mi/23 km S of Petoskey; 45°10′N 84°54′W. Lumber; wood siding; resort. Airport here. Boyne Mt. Ski Area to S; Thunder Mt. Ski Area to W.

Boynton, village (1990 pop. 391), Muskogee co., E Okla., 18 mi/29 km WSW of Muskogee; 35°38′N 95°39′W. In agr. area.

Boynton Beach (BOIN-tuhn), city (□ 15 sq mi/39 sq km; 1990 pop. 46,194), Palm Beach co., SE Fla., on the Atlantic coast, 13 mi/21 km S of West Palm Beach; 26°31′N 80°04′W. Major suburban area, including mfg. and retirement communities. Resort; vegetable-shipping point. Inc. 1920 as Boynton.

Boys Town, town (1990 pop. 794), Douglas co., residential suburb 9 mi/14.5 km W of downtown Omaha, E Nebr.; 41°15′N 96°07′W. Founded 1917 by Father Edward J. Flanagan (1886–1948) for homeless or abandoned boys. The village is governed by the boys themselves and maintained by voluntary contributions. Girls were admitted for the 1st time in 1979. Also called "The City of Little Men." Inc. 1936.

Boysen Reservoir, Fremont co., central Wyo., on Bighorn R., 15 mi/24 km S of Thermopolis; c.20 mi/32 km long; 43°24′N 108°09′W. Max. capacity 1,473,000 acreft. Formed by Boysen Dam (144 ft/44 m high), built by the Bureau of Reclamation for irrigation, flood control, and power generation. Wind River Indian Reservation to N; Boysen State Park on E shore.

Bozeman (BOZ-muhn), city (1990 pop. 22,660), ⊙ Gallatin co., SW Mont., 112 mi/180 km W of Billings and 72 mi/116 km ESE of Butte; 45°41′N 111°02′W. Center of a farming and livestock-raising area. Tourism and lumber are also important industries. Mfg. (printing and publishing, bronze casting; apparel, dairy prods., furniture, consumer goods, soft drinks, hand tools, silicon crystals, alfalfa pellets, construction materials, fabricated metal prods., electronic parts). Named after John M. Bozeman, a pioneer who led the 1st Eur. settlers here in 1864. Hq. of Gallatin Natl. Forest, units of forest to NE and S and Yellowstone Natl. Park is 45 mi/72 km S. Seat of Montana State Univ. Mus. of the Rockies, Gallatin Co. Pioneer Mus., Amer. Computer Mus., Bozeman Fish Technology Center, Emerson Cultural Center. Bridger Bowl Ski Area to NE, Bozeman Hot Springs to W. Inc. 1883 (formerly called Missouri).

Bozeman Trail, a pioneer and miners' trail E of Bighorn Mts. linking the goldfields of Colo. and Mont. Scouted by John Bozeman in 1864.

Bozrah (BAH-zhrah), town (1990 pop. 2,297), New London co., SE Conn., on Yantic R., 5 mi/8 km W of Norwich; 41°32′N 72°10′W. Mfg. (textiles, bedding; plastics, sports equip., insulation, aerospace padding goods, cement). Includes villages of Gilman and Fitchville; agr. Resorts on Gardner L. (S). Settled in late 17th cent., inc. 1786.

B. P. Steinhagen Lake, reservoir (□ 23 sq mi/60 sq km), Tyler co., E Texas, on Neches R., at N end of Big Thicket Natl. Preserve, 50 mi/80 km SE of Lufkin; 33°47′N 94°10′W. Max. capacity 306,400 acre-ft. Formed by Town Bluff Dam (45 ft/14 m high, 6,698 ft/2,042 m long), built (1951) by Army Corps of Engineers for power generation, water supply, and recreation. Martin Dies Jr. State Park at N end of reservoir.

Bracebridge, town (1991 pop. 12,308), ⊙ Muskoka dist., S Ont., central Canada, on Muskoka R., near L. Muskoka, and 70 mi/113 km NW of Peterborough; 45°02′N 79°18′W. Lumber milling, boatbuilding, light mfg. Tourist center for Muskoka dist. Airport.

Bracken (BRAK-uhn), county (□ 208 sq mi/539 sq km; 1990 pop. 7,766), N Ky.; ⊙ Brooksville; 38°41′N 84°04′W. Bounded N by Ohio R. (Ohio state line), S

in part by North Fork of Licking R. Gently rolling upland agr. area (burley tobacco, corn, hay, alfalfa; cattle, poultry; dairying), in N part of Bluegrass region; shipping, some mfg. at Augusta. Formed 1796.

Brackenridge, borough (1990 pop. 3,784), Allegheny co., W central Pa., suburb 17 mi/27 km NE of downtown Pittsburgh, on Allegheny R. (bridged); 40°36′N 79°44′W. Mfg. of glass prods. and specialty steel; steel testing. Agr. to N (hay; dairying); bituminous coal. Deer L. Regional Park to NW. Inc. 1901.

Brackettville, town (1990 pop. 1,740), ⊙ Kinney co., SW Texas, 29 mi/47 km E of Del Rio; elev. 1,110 ft/338 m; 29°19′N 100°24′W. Ranching region (sheep, cattle, goats); agr. (cotton, oats, sorghum). Here are large Las Moras Springs and old U.S. Fort Clark (founded 1852, deactivated 1944) to SW; replica of Alamo at Alamo Village; Kickapoo Caverns State Park to N (Edwards co.). Inc. 1928.

Bradbury, city (1990 pop. 829), Los Angeles co., S Calif., residential suburb 17 mi/27 km NE of downtown Los Angeles, SE Monrovia; 34°09′N 117°58′W. Angeles Natl. Forest and San Gabriel Mts. to N.

Bradbury Heights, village, Prince Georges co., central Md., suburb just SE of Washington. Nearby are Washington and Lincoln natl. cemeteries, U.S. Naval Photo Interpretation Center, and U.S. Census Bureau.

Bradbury Park, village, Prince Georges co., central Md., suburb SE of Washington, D.C.

Braddock, village (1990 pop. 56), Emmons co., S N.Dak., 39 mi/63 km ESE of Bismarck; 46°33′N 100°05′W. Goose L. to SE; Long L. Natl. Wildlife Refuge to NW.

Braddock, borough (1990 pop. 4,682), Allegheny co., W Pa., suburb 8 mi/12.9 km ESE of downtown Pittsburgh, on the Monongahela R.; 40°23′N 79°52′W. Light mfg. (motors). Once a steel-mfg. center, the pop. has decreased with the decline of the industry. In 1755, Gen. Edward Braddock was defeated here by Fr. and Native Amer. forces. Settled 1742, inc. 1867.

Braddock Heights, summer resort (1990 pop. 4,778), Frederick co., W Md., on crest of Catoctin Mt. (elev. here c.1,000 ft/305 m) and 5 mi/8 km W of Frederick; 39°25′N 77°31′W. Braddock's Springs here was used by the troops of Gen. Edward Braddock and Colonel George Washington during the French and Indian Wars. A marker for the NATIONAL ROAD is near the spring, which is now covered and provides water through a pump. A summer resort since 1896, the ridge is only 250 ft/76 m wide here. A ski center was established in recent years. Nearby are Gambrill and Gathland state parks.

Braddock Hills, borough (1990 pop. 2,026), Allegheny co., SW Pa., residential suburb 6 mi/9.7 km E of downtown Pittsburgh, 2 mi/3.2 km NNE of Braddock, near Monongahela R.; 40°25′N 79°51′W. Inc. 1946.

Braddyville, town (1990 pop. 219), Page co., SW Iowa, on Mo. state line, on Nodaway R., 10 mi/16 km S of Clarinda; 40°34′N 95°02′W.

Bradenton (BRAI-duhn-tuhn), city (□ 13 sq mi/34 sq km; 1990 pop. 43,779), ⊙ Manatee co., W central Fla., on Tampa Bay at the mouths of the Braden and the Manatee rivers; 27°29′N 82°34′W. A popular winter resort with excellent fishing in the rivers, bay, and the Gulf of Mexico. Shipping center for area citrus fruit and other crops. Hernando DeSoto is believed to have landed nearby in 1539; the DeSoto Natl. Memorial is to the W. Area was settled (1850s) by Joseph Braden, whose castle-like home is a local landmark. S. Fla. Mus. and Bishop Planetarium are here. Inc. 1903.

Bradenton Beach (BRAI-duhn-tuhn), town (□ 1 sq mi/2.6 sq km; 1990 pop. 1,657), Manatee co., W central Fla., on Anna Maria Key, 8 mi/12.9 km WSW of Bradenton; 27°27′N 82°42′W. Mfg. includes industrial prototypes.

Bradenville (BRAI-den-vil), uninc. town (1990 pop. 1,100), Derry township, Westmoreland co., SW Pa., 2 mi/3.2 km E of Latrobe; 40°19′N 79°20′W. Mfg. includes tool and die. Agr. (dairying).

Bradford 1 county (□ 293 sq mi/759 sq km; 1990 pop. 22,515), N central Fla., bounded S by Santa Fe R.; ⊙ Starke; 29°56′N 82°10′W. Flatwoods area dotted with lakes. Agr. (corn, strawberries, vegetables, tobacco, pecans), livestock raising, forestry. Formed 1858. **2** county (□ 1,161 sq mi/3,007 sq km; 1990 pop. 60,967), NE Pa.; ⊙ Towanda; 41°47′N 76°31′W. Bounded N by N.Y. state line; drained by Susquehanna R. and Towanda and Sugar creeks. Hilly agr. region. Mfg. at Towanda and Sayre. Agr. (corn, hay, alfalfa, soybeans, apples, honey; hogs, cattle, dairying). Refuge for Fr. nobles founded 1793 at Asylum (Fr. *Azilum*) in E center; flourished until Napoleon's grant of amnesty 1802. Sections of Tioga State Forest in W and S center; Mt. Pisgah State Park in W center. Settled 1763 by Moravian missionaries; formed 1812.

Bradford, city (1990 pop. 9,625), McKean co., NW Pa., in the Alleghenies, 85 mi/137 km NNW of State College, 30 mi/48 km ESE of Jamestown (N.Y.), at joining of East and West Branches Tunungant Creek, which form main stream, near the N.Y. state line; 41°57′N 78°38′W. The growth of the city was initiated by the discovery of oil (c.1871), which has been eclipsed by diverse mfg. (cigarette lighters, petroleum prods., machinery, lumber prods., fabricated metal prods., paper prods., plastic prods.; oil refining). Seat of Univ. of Pittsburgh-Bradford Campus (4-year); Zippo Municipal Bradford Regional Airport 10 mi/16 km to S. Allegheny Natl. Forest (includes Allegheny Reservoir) and Allegany State Park (N.Y.) to NW; the area is popular for hunting and fishing. Settled c.1823, inc. as a city 1879.

Bradford 1 town (1990 pop. 1,103), Penobscot co., central Maine, 20 mi/32 km NNW of Bangor; 45°05′N 68°54′W. Wood prods. **2** town (1990 pop. 1,405), Merrimack co., S central N.H., 20 mi/32 km W of Concord; 43°14′N 71°58′W. Drained by Warner R., Hoyt Brook. Agr. (livestock; poultry; apples, vegetables; dairying; nursery crops; timber). Mfg. (construction materials, wood prods.). L. Massasecum in E; part of Low State Forest in S; covered bridge in NE. **3** town (1990 pop. 1,154), Gibson co., NW Tenn., 10 mi/16 km NE of Trenton; 36°05′N 88°49′W. In farm area. **4** town (1990 pop. 2,522), including Bradford village (1990 pop. 725), Orange co., E Vt., on the Connecticut R., 17 mi/27 km E of Chelsea, at mouth of Waits R.; 44°00′N 72°09′W. Wood and dairy prods., maple sugar. Winter sports. C.E. Clark b. here. First geographical globes in U.S. said to have been made here (c.1814) by James Wilson. Settled 1765.

Bradford, village, S Ont., central Canada, on Schomberg R., 35 mi/56 km NNW of Toronto; 44°07′N 79°34′W. Vegetable farming, woodworking.

Bradford 1 village (1990 pop. 874), White co., central Ark., 26 mi/42 km SW of Newport near Departee Creek; 35°25′N 91°27′W. Agr. area (pecans, strawberries, honey). **2** village (1990 pop. 678), Stark co., N central Ill., 12 mi/19 km NE of Toulon; 41°10′N 89°39′W. In agr. and bituminous-coal area. **3** village, Chickasaw co., NE Iowa, 12 mi/19 km SW of New Hampton. Site of "The Little Brown Church in the Vale" (erected 1862), familiarized in the song by W.S. Pitts. **4** village (1990 pop. 2,005), on Miami-Darke co. line, W Ohio, 10 mi/16 km W of Piqua; 40°08′N 84°26′W. In agr. area. Baskets; canned tomatoes. **5** village (1990 pop. 1,469), in Westerly town, Washington co., SW R.I., on Pawcatuck R. (bridged here), 4 mi/6.4 km ENE of Westerly town; 41°23′N 71°45′W. Nearby is Woody Hill Management Area, Burlingame State Park, and Indian Cedar Swamp.

Bradford Woods, borough (1990 pop. 1,329), Allegheny co., W Pa., residential suburb 14 mi/23 km NNW of Pittsburgh; 40°38′N 80°04′W. Agr. area on urban fringe (grain; livestock; poultry; dairying).

Bradgate, town (1990 pop. 124), Humboldt co., N central Iowa, on Des Moines R., 14 mi/23 km NW of Dakota City; 42°47′N 94°25′W. Livestock; grain.

Bradley 1 county (□ 654 sq mi/1,694 sq km; 1990 pop. 11,793), S Ark.; ⊙ Warren; 33°26′N 92°10′W. Bounded W by Moro Bayou, SW by Ouachita R., and E in part by Saline R. Drained by Saline R. in NE and L'Aigle Creek in center. Agr. (potatoes, vegetables; cattle); timber. Mfg. of apparel and wood prods. at Warren. Moro Bay State Park in SW; part of Felsenthal Natl. Wildlife Reservoir in S; includes N end of L. Jack Lee (Ouachita/

Saline rivers). Formed 1840. **2** county (□ 338 sq mi/875 sq km; 1990 pop. 73,712), SE Tenn., ⊙ Cleveland; 35°09′N 84°52′W. Bounded S by Ga., N by Hiwassee R. Timber; corn, hay, fruit; livestock. Mfg. at Cleveland. Includes part of Cherokee Natl. Forest. Formed 1836.

Bradley 1 town (1990 pop. 1,136), Penobscot co., S central Maine, on the Penobscot R., 10 mi/16 km NE of Bangor; 44°53′N 68°35′W. **2** uninc. town (1990 pop. 2,144), Raleigh co., S W.Va., suburb 5 mi/8 km N of Beckley; 37°51′N 81°12′W. Mfg. (coal processing); agr. (cattle; grain); bituminous coal. New River Gorge Natl. R. to E; Plum Orchard Wildlife Management Area to N.

Bradley 1 village (1990 pop. 585), Lafayette co., SW Ark., 26 mi/42 km WSW of Magnolia, near La. state line; 33°06′N 93°39′W. Conway Cemetery State Park to W; Lafayette Wildlife Management Area to E and L. Erling reservoir beyond it. **2** village (1990 pop. 10,792), Kankakee co., NE Ill., near Kankakee R., suburb just N of Kankakee; 41°08′N 87°51′W. In agr. area (corn, soybeans; dairying); mfg. (wood prods., pharmaceuticals, beverage cans, machinery). Organized as North Kankakee in 1892; inc. and renamed in 1896. **3** village (1990 pop. 166), Grady co., central Okla., 18 mi/29 km SE of Chickasha, near Washita R.; 34°52′N 97°42′W. Inc. 1938. **4** village (1990 pop. 117), Clark co., NE S.Dak., 17 mi/27 km SSW of Webster.

Bradley Beach, resort borough (1990 pop. 4,475), Monmouth co., E N.J., on the Atlantic coast, 2 mi/3.2 km S of Asbury Park; 40°12′N 74°00′W. Fisheries. Developed in the 1870s by James A. Bradley, a brush manufacturer from N.Y. city. Settled c.1858, inc. 1893.

Bradleyville, uninc. town, Taney co., S Mo., in the Ozarks, in Mark Twain Natl. Forest, 20 mi/32 km NE of Branson. Cattle; hay, timber. Charcoal.

Bradner, village (1990 pop. 1,093), Wood co., NW Ohio, 12 mi/19 km ESE of Bowling Green; 41°20′N 83°27′W. In agr. area. Mfg. of oil well machinery, feed milling; stone quarries; poultry hatcheries.

Bradshaw 1 village, Baltimore co., central Md., 15 mi/24 km ENE of downtown Baltimore. The Marquis de Lafayette ordered 4 local men arrested here in 1781 for guiding raiding parties of Br. soldiers from a fleet anchored in Gunpowder Creek. One, Walter Pickett (or Pigot), a miller, was hanged; the 3 others apparently escaped. One, John Paul, a wealthy landowner, reportedly had the aid of a lady who hid him under her hoop skirts. Site of a jousting competition attracting riders from all over the state who spear metal rings of various sizes for "womanhood and Christianity." The winner of a race among women riders chooses the "King of Love and Beauty." Gunpowder Falls State Park is nearby. **2** village (1990 pop. 330), York co., SE central Nebr., 10 mi/16 km W of York; 40°52′N 97°45′W. Livestock. **3** village (1990 pop. 394), McDowell co., S W.Va., on Dry Fork, 12 mi/19 km WSW of Welch; 37°21′N 81°47′W. Mfg. (apparel); semibituminous coal. Panther State Forest to NW; Berwind L. Wildlife Management Area to SE.

Bradshaw Mountains, Yavapai co., central Ariz., S of Prescott. Rises to 7,694 ft/2,345 m at Spruce Mt., in Prescott Natl. Forest. Much gold formerly mined here.

Brady, town (1990 pop. 5,946), ⊙ McCulloch co., central Texas, on Brady Creek, c.70 mi/113 km ESE of San Angelo; 31°07′N 99°22′W. (Elev. 1,670 ft/509 m). RR junction; trade, shipping, processing center of agr., in cattle-ranching region. Ships cotton, wool, mohair, peanuts, wheat. Mfg. (combed mohair and wool, oil rigs, foundry sand, and silica flour). Brady Reservoir to W. Settled c.1876, inc. 1906.

Brady 1 village (1990 pop. 200), Pondera co., NW Mont., 10 mi/16 km SSE of Conrad. In irrigated agr region; wheat, barley, oats; sheep, cattle. **2** village (1990 pop. 331), Lincoln co., S central Nebr., 22 mi/35 km ESE of North Platte city, on Platte R; 41°01′N 100°22′W. Jeffery Reservoir to S (on Tri-County Supply Canal).

Brady Creek, c.60 mi/97 km long, W central Texas; rises near Eden, Concho co., on edge of Edwards Plateau; flows generally E through Brady Reservoir, past Brady, to the San Saba R. 21 mi/34 km E of Brady.

Brady, Fort, Mich.: see SAULT SAINTE MARIE.

Brady Glacier, SE Alaska, in Fairweather Range; 58°38′N 136°50′W; flows in 2 branches, 1 to Glacier Bay (N), the other 40 mi/64 km S to Cross Sound.

Brady Lake, village (1990 pop. 490), Portage co., NE Ohio, 12 mi/19 km NE of Akron, on Brady L. (c.4 mi/6 km long), a reservoir supplying water to Akron; 41°10′N 81°19′W.

Brady Mountains, Texas: see MCCULLOCH.

Brady Reservoir, McCulloch co., central Texas, on Brady Creek, 4 mi/6.4 km W of Brady; 8 mi/12.9 km long; 31°08′N 99°21′W. Max. capacity 208,000 acre-ft. Formed by Brady Dam (104 ft/32 m high), built (1963) by the City of Brady for water supply and flood control.

Braeside (BRAI-seid), village (1991 pop. 562), SE Ont., central Canada, on L. des Chats, 3 mi/5 km NW of Arnprior; 45°28′N 76°24′W. Lumbering.

Bragg City, town (1990 pop. 117), Pemiscot co., in the bootheel of extreme SE Mo., in Mississippi alluvial plain, 15 mi/24 km WNW of Caruthersville; 36°16′N 89°54′W. Rice, cotton, broom corn, soybeans.

Braggs, village (1990 pop. 308), Muskogee co., E Okla., 11 mi/18 km SE of Muskogee; 35°39′N 95°12′W. In agr. area.

Braham (BRAI-yuhm), town (1990 pop. 1,139), Isanti co., E Minn., 11 mi/18 km NNE of Cambridge; 45°43′N 93°10′W. Livestock, poultry; dairying; grain, soybeans; mfg. (machinery, consumer goods, construction materials, pontoon boats, molded rubber). Rush L. to E.

Braidwood, city (1990 pop. 3,584), Will co., NE Ill., 19 mi/31 km SSW of Joliet; 41°16′N 88°13′W. Trade center in agr. area (corn, soybeans; dairying). Nuclear-power plant nearby. Inc. 1873. John Mitchell b. here.

Braidwood 1 and 2 Nuclear Power Plants, Illinois: see WILL.

Brainard (BRAI-nahrd), village (1990 pop. 326), Butler co., E Nebr., 8 mi/12.9 km SE of David City; 41°10′N 97°00′W. Dairy and poultry prods.; livestock; grain.

Brainerd, city (1990 pop. 12,353), ⊙ Crow Wing co., central Minn., 55 mi/89 km N of St. Cloud, on the Mississippi R.; 46°21′N 94°11′W. Elev. 1,212 ft/369 m. In a pine-forested and lake region. Agr. (dairying; poultry; oats, wild rice, alfalfa); mfg. (fabricated metal and metal prods., construction materials, lumber and wood prods., plastic prods., foods and beverages, fishing tackle; printing and publishing). Founded (1870) by the Northern Pacific RR, it is still a RR center with repair shops. Brainerd Community Col., Brainerd State School and Hosp. to E. Paul Bunyan Amusement Center here. Cuyuna Iron Range to NE; Crow Wing State Park and Camp Ripley Military Reservation to SW; Pillsbury State Forest to W; Crow Wing State Forest to NE. Inc. 1881.

Braintree 1 (BRAIN-tree), town (1990 pop. 33,836), E Mass., a suburb 4 mi/6.4 km SE of Boston; 42°12′N 71°00′W. Metal, rubber, and paper mfg., electric and medical machinery, shoes, books, building materials. Included Quincy (birthplace of John Adams and John Quincy Adams) until 1792 and Randolph until 1793. John Hancock and Gen. Sylvanus Thayer, superintendent of West Point (1817–1833), were b. here. The Thayer Acad. here was founded by the general. Includes villages of East and South Braintree. Inc. 1640 **2** town (1990 pop. 1,174), Orange co., central Vt., 16 mi/26 km W of Chelsea, on Third Branch of White R.; 43°58′N 72°43′W. Includes hamlet of East Braintree.

Braircliffe Acres, village (1990 pop. 552), Horry co., E S.C., 9 mi/14.5 km NE of Myrtle Beach, on Atlantic Ocean, in Grand Strand Beach resort area. Intracoastal Waterway passes to NW.

Bralorne (BRAI-lorn), village, SW B.C., W Canada, in Coast Mts., 110 mi/177 km N of Vancouver; 50°47′N 122°49′W. Gold and silver mining; logging; cattle.

Braman, village (1990 pop. 251), Kay co., N Okla., near Kansas state line, 8 mi/12.9 km NNW of Blackwell, on Chikaskia R.; 36°55′N 97°19′W. In agr. area.

Brampton, city (1991 pop. 234,445), S Ont., central Canada, NW of Toronto; 43°41′N 79°46′W. Noted for its greenhouses and flowers. Motor vehicles, shoes, lumber, optical goods. Inc. 1852 as a village, 1873 as a town, and 1976 as a city.

Bramwell, village (1990 pop. 620), Mercer co., S W.Va., on Bluestone R., at Va. state line, 6 mi/9.7 km NW of Bluefield; 37°19′N 81°18′W. Coal-mining area. Livestock; corn; potatoes. Pinnacle Rock State Park to S. Inc. 1888.

Branch, county (□ 519 sq mi/1,344 sq km; 1990 pop. 41,502), S Mich.; ☉ Coldwater. Bounded S by Ind. state line; 41°55′N 85°02′W; drained by St. Joseph and Coldwater rivers. Agr. (forage crops, wheat, corn, soybeans, tomatoes, apples, cherries, grapes; cattle, hogs, sheep, poultry); dairy prods. Mfg. at Coldwater. Marl and clay deposits. Many small lakes (resorts), esp. on Coldwater R. in E. Organized 1833.

Branch, town (1990 pop. 2,400), Chicago co., E Minn., 38 mi/61 km N of St. Paul, drained by North Branch Sunrise R.; 45°30′N 92°57′W. Municipality includes all of surveyed township, excluding town of North Branch. Agr. (dairying; poultry; cattle; grain, alfalfa).

Branch, village (1990 pop. 299), Franklin co., W Ark., 25 mi/40 km ESE of Fort Smith; 35°18′N 93°57′W.

Branch Lake, reservoir, Hancock co., S Maine, on small stream, 5 mi/8 km NW of Ellsworth; 5.5 mi/8.9 km long; 44°34′N 68°31′W. Drains SE into Union R. Also called Branch Pond.

Branch River, 10 mi/16 km long, N R.I.; formed near Oakland by junction of Pascoag and Clear rivers; flows NE, furnishing water power at Oakland, Glendale, Nasonville, Slatersville, and Forestdale, to Blackstone R. at Mass. state line, just NW of Woonsocket. Dam at Slatersville forms Slatersville Reservoir (c.3 mi/4.8 km long).

Branched Oak Lake, reservoir, Lancaster co., SE Nebr., on Branched Oak Creek, tributary of Oak Creek, in Branched Oak Lake State Recreation Area, 15 mi/24 km NW of Lincoln; 4 mi/6.4 km long; 40°58′N 96°44′W. Max. capacity 115,000 acre-ft. Formed by Branched Oak Dam (82 ft/25 m high), built by the Army Corps of Engineers for flood control and recreation.

Branchville, town (1990 pop. 1,107), Orangeburg co., S central S.C., 17 mi/27 km S of Orangeburg, near Edisto R; 33°15′N 80°49′W. Animal-prod. processing. Named for its importance as a RR junction.

Branchville, village (1990 pop. 55), Southampton co., SE Va., near N.C. state line, 19 mi/31 km SW of Franklin, near Meherrin R; 36°34′N 77°15′W. Agr. (peanuts, cotton, grain; livestock; timber.

Branchville, borough (1990 pop. 851), Sussex co., NW N.J., near Paulins Kill, 6 mi/9.7 km N of Newton, in hilly agr. region; 41°08′N 74°45′W. Appalachian Trail to NW.

Brandenburg, town (1990 pop. 1,857), ☉ Meade co., NW Ky., 28 mi/45 km SW of Louisville, on Ohio R. (bridged to W); 38°00′N 86°10′W. In agr. area (barley tobacco, soybeans, grain; livestock); mfg. (utility trailers, signs, organic chemicals). Otter Creek Park and Fort Knox Military Reservation to SE; Doe Valley L. to E. Doe Run Inn (1825) still in use. Est. 1825.

Brandon, city (1991 pop. 38,567), SW Man., central Canada, on the Assiniboine R.; 49°50′N 99°57′W. The business center of the wheat-raising area of SW Man., Brandon has an extensive trade in farm prods. and machinery. Also grain; hogs, cattle; fertilizer. Publishing. Seat of the annual provincial exhibition and of the Man. Winter Fair. A govt. experimental farm adjoins the city. Seat of Brandon Univ. Named for the old Hudson's Bay Co. post, Brandon House, built in 1793.

Brandon 1 uninc. city (□ 29 sq mi/75 sq km; 1990 pop. 57,985), Hillsborough co., W central Fla., 10 mi/16 km E of Tampa; 27°55′N 82°17′W. Chiefly a residential suburb, it is also a retail and service center. Experienced significant developmental and pop. growth, particularly due to the construction of new highways connecting it to other Fla. urban centers. Citrus fruits and vegetables are grown in the area, which also has cattle and dairy farms. **2** city (1990 pop. 11,077), ☉ Rankin co., central Miss., suburb 13 mi/21 km E of Jackson; 32°16′N 90°00′W. In agr. (cotton, soybeans, corn, sweet potatoes, vegetables, potatoes) and timber area; mfg. (fabricated metal and plastic prods., carbon dioxide, hydrogen sulfide, wood prods., transportation equip.;

machining). Natural-gas field in vicinity. Allen C. Thompson Airport to W. Ross Barnett Reservoir, on Pearl R., to N.

Brandon 1 town (1990 pop. 320), Buchanan co., E Iowa, 10 mi/16 km SW of Independence; 42°18′N 92°00′W. Limestone quarries. **2** town (1990 pop. 3,543), Minnehaha co., SE S.Dak., 5 mi/8 km ENE of Sioux Falls (suburb). Mfg. (feeds, transportation equip., hydraulic fittings). Great Bear Valley Ski Area to SW. RR junction. **3** town (1990 pop. 4,223), including Brandon village, Rutland co., W Vt., on Otter Creek, 15 mi/24 km NNW of Rutland, in resort area; 43°47′N 73°04′W. Wood and dairy prods., fertilizers, electronic supplies. Stephen A. Douglas' birthplace is preserved. From bog iron discovered here (1810), John Conant made stoves after 1820. Town chartered 1761 as Neshobe, renamed 1784. **4** town (1990 pop. 872), Fond du Lac co., E central Wis., 16 mi/26 km WSW of Fond du Lac; 43°44′N 88°46′W. RR junction in agr. area (dairy prods.); meat processing.

Brandon 1 village (1990 pop. 441), Douglas co., W Minn., 13 mi/21 km WNW of Alexandria; 45°58′N 95°35′W. Grain; livestock, poultry; dairying (butter); mfg. (fertilizer, pontoons). Numerous natural lakes in area; Chippewa L. to NE. **2** residential village, Greenville co., NW S.C., just SW of Greenville. Also known as Branwood. **3** village (1990 pop. 80), Hill co., N central Texas, 9 mi/14.5 km E of Hillsboro. In farm area.

Brandon, locality, Prince George co., E Va., on James R., 15 mi/24 km E of Hopewell. Nearby are historic Brandon and Upper Brandon estates, with 18th-cent. houses and famous gardens.

Brandonville, village (1990 pop. 73), Preston co., N W.Va., 16 mi/26 km E of Morgantown; 39°40′N 79°37′W.

Brandsville, city (1990 pop. 167), Howell co., S Mo., in the Ozarks, 10 mi/16 km SE of West Plains; 36°38′N 91°42′W. Apples; livestock; timber; mfg. (wood prods.); tourism.

Brandt, village (1990 pop. 123), Deuel co., E S.Dak., 7 mi/11.3 km SSE of Clear L. Cochrane Lake State Rec. Area to NE.

Brandy Station, uninc. village, Culpeper co., N Va., 5 mi/8 km ENE of Culpeper. Agr. (dairying; livestock; grain, apples, peaches). Scene of the greatest Civil War cavalry engagement (also called the battle of Fleetwood Hill) which preceded the Gettysburg Campaign.

Brandypot, group of 3 islets, E Que., E Canada, in the St. Lawrence R., just E of Hare Isl., opposite Rivière du Loup.

Brandywine Creek (BRAN-dee-wein), c.20 mi/32 km long, in SE Pa. and N Del.; rises in small E and W branches in Chester co., Pa., which join 10 mi/16 km SE of Coatesville; flows SE, past Chadds Ford, enters N Del., through Brandywine State Park, to Christina R. 1 mi/1.6 km WNW of its mouth on the Del. R. at Wilmington; 39°55′N 75°38′W.

Brandywood, uninc. town (1990 pop. 900), New Castle co., NE Del., residential suburb 6 mi/9.7 km NNE of downtown Wilmington, at Pa. state line; 39°49′N 75°30′W. Highest point in Del. (442 ft/135 m), 1 mi/1.6 km NW, on Ebright Road.

Branford, town (1990 pop. 27,603), New Haven co., S Conn., on L.I. Sound, 7 mi/11.3 km ESE of New Haven; 41°16′N 72°47′W. Mainly residential, with a busy retail shopping area. Tourism and mfg. of electrical prods. and marine equipment are central to the economy. Settled 1644, inc. 1930 as a town.

Branford, village (1990 pop. 670), Suwannee co., N central Fla., 30 mi/48 km NW of Gainesville; 29°57′N 82°55′W. Mfg. includes limestone, survey stakes; some agr.

Branson, city (1990 pop. 3,706), Taney co., SW Mo.; 36°38′N 93°15′W. Primarily residential and commercial, the city's economic mainstay is its country-music industry, which began rapid growth in the 1970s. With over 30 entertainment theaters, Branson draws millions of tourists annually. Fishing, boating, swimming on adjacent L Taneycomo and Table Rock L. Mfg. (meat processing; printing; sand and gravel). Nearby is the Col.

of the Ozarks. Silver Dollar City theme park to N. Shepherd of the Hills Mus. Inc. 1904.

Branson, village (1990 pop. 58), Las Animas co., S Colo., on RR, 36 mi/58 km ESE of Trinidad, near N.Mex. state line; 37°00′N 103°52′W. Elev. 6,299 ft/1,920 m. Cattle; wheat, hay, sorghum.

Brant, county (□ 421 sq mi/1,090 sq km; 1991 pop. 110,806), S Ont., central Canada, on Grand R.; ☉ Brantford; 43°05′N 80°15′W.

Brant Lake, summer-resort village (1990 pop. 850), Warren co., E N.Y., in the Adirondacks, at S end of Brant L. (c.5 mi/8 km long), 26 mi/42 km N of Glens Falls; 43°41′N 73°46′W. Sometimes called Horicon.

Brant Park, Mass.: see MARSHFIELD.

Brantford, city (1991 pop. 81,997), S Ont., central Canada, on the Grand R.; 43°08′N 80°16′W. Leading mfg. city, noted esp. for its large farm implement factories. Named for the Mohawk chieftain Joseph Brant, who led the Six Nations of the Iroquois to the region after the Amer. Revolution and who is buried in the old Mohawk Church nearby. The Mohawk Inst., a Native Amer. residential school, is nearby. Alexander Graham Bell was living here in 1876 when he made his 1st successful experiment in the transmission of sound by electric wire. A mus., formerly his home, exhibits the 1st telephone.

Brantingham, summer resort village (1990 pop. 500), Lewis co., N central N.Y., 40 mi/64 km N of Utica, on Brantingham L. (c.1.5 mi/2.4 km long); 43°42′N 75°16′W. Est. 1873 as hunting resort. Methodist summer recreation center (Aldersgate) on Pleasant L., adjacent to Brantingham L.

Brantley, county (□ 447 sq mi/1,158 sq km; 1990 pop. 11,077), SE Ga.; ☉ Nahunta, 31°12′N 81°59′W. Bounded N and E by Satilla R. Coastal plain agr., tobacco; cattle and hogs; timber. Mfg. of lumber and millwork prods. Formed 1920.

Brantley, town (1990 pop. 1,015), Crenshaw co., S Ala., on Conecuh R., 10 mi/16 km S of Luverne. Lumber, clothing. Inc. 1895.

Brantley Reservoir (□ 13 sq mi/34 sq km), Eddy co., SE N.Mex., on Pecos R., 10 mi/16 km NW of Carlsbad; 32°35′N 104°20′W. Max. capacity 966,300 acre-ft. Formed by Brantley Dam (103 ft/31 m high), built (1988) by the Bureau of Reclamation for flood control; also used for irrigation and recreation. Brantley Lake State Park at S end of reservoir.

Branwood, S.C.: see BRANDON.

Bras d'Or Lake (brah dor) (□ c.360 sq mi/930 sq km), arm of the Atlantic Ocean, indenting deeply into Cape Breton Isl., N.S., SE Canada, and occupying much of the interior. A narrow channel links it with the sea. The region was the scene of important experiments in the early history of aviation. In 1907, Alexander Graham Bell founded at Baddeck the Aerial Experiment Assn., and on Feb. 23, 1909, J. A. D. McCurdy piloted his airplane, the *Silver Dart*, for ½ mi/⁸⁄₁₀ km.

Braselton (BRAS-uhl-tuhn), town (1990 pop. 418), Jackson co., NE central Ga., 11 mi/18 km W of Jefferson; 34°06′N 83°47′W. Winemaking (wineries open to the public); chicken processing; cellular-telephone and tool-and-die mfg. Has 2 major road-racing tracks. Town went bankrupt in 1994 after being purchased by private investors in 1989.

Brashear (bruh-SHIR), town (1990 pop. 318), Adair co., N Mo., on North Fork of Salt R., 10 mi/16 km ESE of Kirksville; 40°08′N 92°22′W.

Brasher Falls, village (1990 pop. 750), St. Lawrence co., N N.Y., on St. Regis R., 10 mi/16 km SSE of Massena; 44°49′N 74°47′W.

Brasil, sugar mill, Camagüey prov., N central Cuba, one of Cuba's largest sugar mills; formerly called Jaronú, as is current nearby town.

Brass Islands, two uninhabited islets known as Outer Brass (108 acres/44 ha) and Inner Brass (128 acres/52 ha), NW U.S. Virgin Isls., just off N coast of St. Thomas Isl., 4 mi/6.4 km NW of Charlotte Amalie; 18°23′N 64°57′W.

Brasstown Bald, peak, 4,784 ft/1,458 m, N Ga., in the

Blue Ridge of the Appalachian Mts., near the N.C. state line; 34°52′N 83°48′W. The highest point in Georgia.

Brassua Lake (BRAS-oo-uh), Somerset co., W central Maine, c.60 mi/97 km NNW of Skowhegan and just W of Moosehead L.; irregularly shaped, 6 mi/9.7 km max. width. In hunting, fishing area.

Braswell, town (1990 pop. 247), Paulding co., NW Ga., 37 mi/60 km NW of Atlanta; 33°59′N 84°58′W.

Bratenahl (BRA-tuh-nol), village (1990 pop. 1,356), Cuyahoga co., N Ohio, NE suburb surrounded on 3 sides by Cleveland, bordered N by L. Erie; 41°34′N 81°37′W.

Brattleboro (BRA-tuhl-buhr-o), town (1990 pop. 12,241), Windham co., SE Vt., on the Connecticut R.; 42°51′N 72°37′W. Once an artists' colony, Brattleboro has become a sports center and resort town. Brattleboro Mus. and Art Center and several medical and psychiatric institutions are here. Printing, mfg. (books, furniture, wood prods., aircraft parts). Chartered 1753.

Bravo del Norte, Río, U.S. and Mexico: see RIO GRANDE.

Bravo, Río, U.S. and Mexico: see RIO GRANDE.

Brawley, city (1990 pop. 18,923), Imperial co., SE Calif., in the irrigated Imperial Valley, 11 mi/18 km SE of the Salton Sea and 13 mi/21 km N of El Centro; 32°59′N 115°32′W. Vegetables, tomatoes, melons, cotton, alfalfa; cattle, sheep; corn, sugar beets. Mfg. (farm machinery and parts). The Imperial Valley Rodeo and Brawley Cattle Call is an important city event. Natl. Parachute Test Range to W. Inc. 1908

Braxton, county (□ 516 sq mi/1,336 sq km; 1990 pop. 12,998), central W.Va.; ⊙ Sutton; 38°42′N 80°43′W. On Allegheny Plateau; drained by Elk, Little Kanawha, and Birch rivers. Agr. (honey, corn, alfalfa, fruit); livestock; poultry. Mfg. (glass, fabricated metal prods., rebuilt aircraft engines, aircraft ground-support equip., military systems; machining, meat processing). Oil and natural-gas wells; coal mines; timber. Burnsville L. reservoir (Little Kanawha R.), in Burnsville Lake Wildlife Management Area in N; Sutton L. reservoir (Elk R.), in Elk River Wildlife Management Area in E. Formed 1836.

Braxton (BRAKS-tuhn), village (1990 pop. 141), Simpson co., S central Miss., 22 mi/35 km SSE of Jackson; 32°01′N 89°58′W. Agr. (cotton, corn; cattle, poultry; timber).

Braymer (BRAI-muhr), city (1990 pop. 886), Caldwell co., NW Mo.,19 mi/31 km SW of Chillicothe; 39°35′N 93°47′W. Agr., feed mill; sheep, cattle, hogs.

Brayton, town (1990 pop. 148), Audubon co., W central Iowa, near East Nishnabotna R., 13 mi/21 km S of Audubon; 41°32′N 94°55′W. Concrete prods. Sand pit nearby.

Brazeau, Mount (BRA-zo) (11,386 ft/3,470 m), W Alta., W Canada, near B.C. border, in Rocky Mts., in Jasper Natl. Park, 40 mi/64 km SE of Jasper; 52°33′N 117°21′W.

Brazil, city (1990 pop. 7,640), ⊙ Clay co., W Ind., on small Birch Creek, 16 mi/26 km ENE of Terre Haute; 39°31′N 87°07′W. Agr. area (livestock; grain); mfg. (aircraft parts, truck trailers, plastic prods., labels, fabricated metal prods., consumer goods, construction materials). Clay pits, bituminous-coal mines.

Brazoria, county (□ 1,597 sq mi/4,136 sq km; 1990 pop. 191,707), S Texas; ⊙ Angleton; 29°10′N 95°26′W. On Gulf of Mexico. Bounded on SW by Linville Bayou and Cedar L. Creek, on far N by Clear Creek; drained by Brazos and San Bernard rivers; Gulf Intracoastal Waterway passes along coast. Freeport (center of BRAZOSPORT industrial area) is deepwater port (ships sulphur, chemicals). Large oil, sulphur, natural gas, salt, sand and gravel production; magnesium extracted from sea water; extensive chemical industry. Irrigated agr. (rice, sorghum, corn, cotton, hay, soybeans, pecans); beef cattle. Fishing, swimming on coast. Bryan Beach (formerly Velasco) State Park in S; Brazoria Natl. Wildlife Refuge in S; Varner-Hogg State Historical Park in W, at W Columbia. Formed 1836.

Brazoria, town (1990 pop. 2,717), Brazoria co., 15 mi/24 km NW of Freeport, in Brazosport area, S Texas, near Brazos R., c.50 mi/80 km SSW of Houston; 29°03′N 95°34′W. In agr. area, bet. Brazos (NE) and San Bernard (SW) rivers. Original town (Old Brazoria, c.½mi/⁸⁄₁₀ km away), founded in 1820s, was a port for Austin's colony, later a cotton and rice center; it was abandoned when town moved to site on RR. Mfg. (sheet metal, cultural marble). San Bernard Natl. Wildlife Refuge to S.

Brazos, county (□ 590 sq mi/1,528 sq km; 1990 pop. 121,862), E central Texas; ⊙ Bryan; 30°39′N 96°17′W. Bounded E by Navasota R., W, and SW by Brazos R. Rich agr. area (cotton, corn, wheat, oats, sorghum, pecans); extensive dairying, livestock ranching (cattle, hogs). Sand and gravel, lignite, gas and oil. Mfg., processing at Bryan. Formed 1841.

Brazos (BRAH-zos), river, 870 mi/1,400 km long, N.Mex. and Texas; rises in N N.Mex. near the Colo. state line; flows into El Vado L. at El Vado L. State Park, then into Rio Chama then into Rio Grande, N of Espanola, then flows SE across Texas to enter the Gulf of Mexico at Freeport. Flows through a fertile farming area of N Texas, where cotton is produced in the irrigated river's valley. Supplies water to nearby cities; several dams provide flood control and hydroelectric power. Navigable upstream.

Brazos Island, extreme S Texas, 3 mi/4.8 km SE of Port Isabel; a barrier beach c.4 mi/6.4 km long, bet. Laguna Madre and Gulf of Mexico; bridged to mainland. Here is Boca Chica (resort) beach region (swimming, fishing), of which isl. is a part, extending c.8 mi/12.9 km S from Brazos Santiago Pass separated Brazos Isl. from Padre Isl. (to N) to mouth of the Rio Grande. In Mexican War, Gen. Zachary Taylor established a supply base at port of Brazos Santiago (since destroyed) on Brazos Isl. Undeveloped Brazos Island State Park is here.

Brazos Santiago Pass, extreme S Texas, channel connecting Gulf of Mexico and Laguna Madre; passes bet. Padre and Brazos isls., 3 mi/4.8 km E of Port Isabel; its deepwater channel connects with Gulf Intracoastal Waterway near Port Isabel and continues SW through land cut to port of Brownsville (S terminus of Intracoastal Waterway).

Brazosport, Brazoria co., S Texas, industrial area and shipping port at mouth of Brazos R. of Gulf of Mexico, on Gulf Intracoastal Waterway; centered on Freeport (deepwater port), it also includes Lake Jackson, Clute, Angleton, and other communities. Sulphur production, processing, shipping; chemical mfg. (esp. extraction of magnesium and bromine from seawater). Old port of Velasco now part of Surfride Beach.

Brea, city (1990 pop. 32,873), Orange co., S Calif., suburb 22 mi/35 km SE of downtown Los Angeles; 33°55′N 117°52′W. Industrial, commercial, and residential suburb in the Orange County Metro Area. Industry is centered on oil; most industries related to its production and processing. Mfg. (electronic equip., protective coatings, plastic prods., transportation equip., aircraft and aircraft parts, furniture, circuit boards, machinery, rubber prods., electroplating, printing and publishing). Developed during an oil boom in the early 1900s. Of note is the campsite of Span. explorer Don Gaspar de Portolá, the 1st European to visit the area. Carbon Canyon Dam, on Carbon Canyon Creek, in E. Puente Hills to N; Chino Hills State Park to E. Inc. 1917

Breaks Interstate Park, Ky. and Va.: see ELKHORN CITY.

Breathitt (BRETH-it), county (□ 495 sq mi/1,282 sq km; 1990 pop. 15,703), E central Ky., in the Cumberland Mts.; ⊙ Jackson; 37°31′N 83°19′W. Drained by N and Middle forks of Kentucky R., small Troublesome Creek, and several other creeks. Mt. agr. area (cattle; honey, apples, sweet and Irish potatoes, burley tobacco, hay); bituminous-coal mines; timber. Has been called "Bloody Breathitt" because of feuds among family clans which occurred here. Parts of Robinson Forest, Univ. of Ky. experimental forest, in SE. Formed 1839.

Breaux Bridge (BRO brij), city (1994 pop. 7,058), St. Martin parish, S central La., 8 mi/13 km NE of Lafayette, and on navigable Bayou Teche; RR terminus; 30°17′N 91°54′W. In agr. area (rice, sugarcane, vegetables; cattle); timber; crawfish, catfish, alligators; mfg. (raw sugar, salt). Inc. 1871.

Breckenridge, city (1990 pop. 418), Caldwell co., NW Mo., 13 mi/21 km W of Chillicothe; 39°45′N 93°47′W. Corn, wheat; sheep, cattle, hogs. Mormon massacre site to S.

Breckenridge 1 (BREK-en-rij), town (1990 pop. 1,285), ⊙ Summit co., central Colo., on Blue R., just S of Gore Range, 60 mi/97 km WSW of Denver; 39°30′N 106°02′W. Elev. 9,602 ft/2,927 m; Gold and silver mines; livestock. Tourism. Music festivals. Once a mining and trade center, with pop. of c.8,000, for group of gold-mining camps. Now a Natl. Historic Dist. (dates to 1860s) with Breckenridge ski area nearby. Quandary Peak and Mt. Lincoln are in the vicinity. Area surrounded by Arapaho Natl. Forest, Dillon Reservoir (on Blue R.) to N. Popular ski and summer resort. Continental Divide passes to S and SE. **2** town (1990 pop. 1,301), Gratiot co., central Mich., 27 mi/43 km W of Saginaw; 43°24′N 84°28′W. In farm area (livestock; dairy prods.; grain, beans); grain elevator; grain processing. **3** town (1990 pop. 3,708), ⊙ Wilkin co., W Minn., 43 mi/69 km S of Fargo (N. Dak.) and opposite (E of) Wahpeton (N. Dak.), at point where Otter Tail and Bois de Sioux rivers join to form Red R. of the North; 46°16′N 96°35′W. Elev. 965 ft/294 m; RR center, trade and shipping point for agr. area (grain, sunflowers, sugar beets, potatoes; hogs, poultry); mfg. (agr. chemicals, sunflower seeds). Breckenridge-Wahpeton Interstate Airport to SW, in N.Dak. Bois de Sioux and Red rivers form Minn.–N.Dak. state line. Small Breckenridge L. reservoir, on Otter Tail R., to E. Laid out 1857, inc. 1908. **4** town (1990 pop. 5,665), ⊙ Stephens co., N central Texas, c.90 mi/145 km W of Fort Worth, on small Gonzales Creek; 32°45′N 98°54′W. Elev. 1,220 ft/372 m. Cattle; agr. and oil-producing area; mfg. (aircraft components, filter elements). Possum Kingdom State Park to NE; Hubbard Creek Reservoir to NW; L. Daniel reservoir to S. Settled 1876, inc. 1919.

Breckenridge, village (1990 pop. 251), Garfield co., N Okla., 8 mi/12.9 km ENE of Enid; 36°27′N 97°43′W. In agr. area.

Breckenridge Hills, village (1990 pop. 5,404), St. Louis co., E Mo., a residential suburb of St. Louis, 12 mi/19 km NW of downtown St. Louis; 38°43′N 90°22′W.

Breckinridge (BREK-in-rij), county (□ 585 sq mi/1,515 sq km; 1990 pop. 16,312), NW Ky.; ⊙ Hardinsburg; 37°46′N 86°25′W. Bounded NW by the Ohio (Ind. state line), S by Rough R. (forms Rough River L. reservoir); drained by South Fork Panther Creek and Sinking Creek. Rolling agr. area (burley tobacco, corn, soybeans, wheat, hay, alfalfa; cattle); timber tracts; limestone quarries; some mfg. at Hardinsburg. Rough River Dam State Park on S border; Yellowbank Wildlife Management Area in N, on Ohio R. Formed 1799.

Breckinridge, Camp, Ky.: see MORGANFIELD.

Brecksville, city (1990 pop. 11,818), Cuyahoga co., N Ohio, 12 mi/19 km SSE of downtown Cleveland; 41°19′N 81°38′W. Settled c.1811, inc. 1921.

Breda, town (1990 pop. 467), Carroll co., W central Iowa, 10 mi/16 km NNW of Carroll; 42°10′N 94°58′W. Dairy prods.; feed.

Bredenbury, agr. town (1991 pop. 390), SE Sask., central Canada, near Man. prov. line, 26 mi/42 km SE of Yorkton; 50°56′N 102°02′W.

Breed's Hill, Mass.: see CHARLESTOWN.

Breedsville, village (1990 pop. 213), Van Buren co., SW Mich., on Black R. and 25 mi/40 km NE of St. Joseph; 42°21′N 86°04′W. Mfg. (wood prods., conveyor systems).

Breese (BREZ), city (1990 pop. 3,567), Clinton co., SW Ill., 8 mi/12.9 km E of Carlyle; 38°36′N 89°31′W. In agr. area (corn, wheat, fruit; poultry, livestock; dairy prods.); mfg. (steel storage bldgs., floor tresses). Inc. 1876.

Breezy Point, village (1990 pop. 432), Crow Wing co., central Minn., 16 mi/26 km N of Brainerd, on W shore of Pelican L.; 46°37′N 94°13′W. Agr. (dairying; poultry; oats, alfalfa). Formerly called Pelican Lakes. Crow Wing State Forest to NW.

Breezy Point, neighborhood of Brooklyn, N.Y. city, SE N.Y., at far W tip of Breezy Point peninsula ending at Rockaway Point, S of Jamaica Bay; 40°33′N 73°56′W. Opposite Coney Isl.–Brighton Beach; site of private shorefront community. In 1963, reacting to public sentiment, local-govt. efforts led to preservation of the area from high-rise beachfront development.

Bremen 1 (BREE-muhn), town (1990 pop. 4,356), Haralson co., NW Ga., c.45 mi/72 km W of Atlanta, near Ala. state line; 33°43′N 85°09′W. Agr. area; mfg includes apparel, service packaging, steel hose, medical supplies. Inc. 1883. **2** town (1990 pop. 4,725), Marshall co., N Ind., 12 mi/19 km NE of Plymouth; 41°27′N 86°09′W. Mfg. (tool and die, feed, bldg. materials, fabricated metal prods., transportation equip., fiberglass prods., paper prods., consumer goods, motor vehicles, machinery, medical goods, electronic parts, peppermint and spearmint processing).

Bremen 1 (BREE-muhn), village (1990 pop. 267), Muhlenberg co., W Ky., 6 mi/9.7 km NNW of Central City; 37°21′N 87°13′W. Bituminous-coal mining; agr. (tobacco, grain; livestock); mfg. (lumber, cured meats). **2** village (1990 pop. 1,386), Fairfield co., central Ohio, 9 mi/14 km E of Lancaster, on small Rush Creek and Raccoon Run; 39°44′N 82°27′W. In agr. area; mfg. of glass prods., building materials, cheese; lumber milling. Oil wells, molding sand pits; timber.

Bremen (BREM-uhn), township (1990 pop. 674), Lincoln co., S Maine, on Muscongus Bay, c.8 mi/12.9 km E of Damariscotta; 43°58′N 69°25′W. Includes village of Medomak.

Bremer, county (□ 439 sq mi/1,137 sq km; 1990 pop. 22,813), NE Iowa; ⊙ Waverly; 42°46′N 92°18′W. Rolling prairie agr. area (hogs, cattle, poultry; corn, oats; dairying) drained by Cedar, Wapsipinicon, and Shell Rock rivers. Mfg. at Waverly. Limestone quarries, sand and gravel pits. Ski Villa Ski Area in W. General flooding in 1993. Formed 1851.

Bremerton (BRE-muhr-tuhn), city (1990 pop. 38,142), Kitsap co., NW Wash., on W side of Puget Sound, on Sinclair Inlet, at entrance to Port Washington, channel which leads to Dyes Inlet; on Kitsap Peninsula, 13 mi/21 km W of Seattle (linked by ferry); 47°33′N 122°42′W. Terminus of RR spur. Est. 1891 when the area was selected as the site for the U.S. Puget Sound Naval Shipyard. Economy centered around the naval installation, where many types of U.S. vessels (including Polaris submarines) are built and repaired in its 6 drydocks. The navy's Polaris Missile Facility is also here. Although the majority of residents are employed by the U.S. govt., some logging and wood-product enterprises exist, and tourism is important; mfg. (textile bags), printing and publishing. Gateway to the Olympic Peninsula, with easy access to the Cascade and Olympic mts. The U.S.S. *Missouri*, docked here, is a natl. shrine; it was the scene of the official Jap. surrender at the end of World War II. Bremerton Col. (2-year); Naval Mus., U.S.S. *Turner Joy* (tours). Illahee State Park to N; Scenic Beach State Park to NW; Belfair State Park to SW. Inc. 1901.

Bremo Bluff (BREEM-o BLUHF), uninc. village, Fluvanna co., central Va., on James R. (bridged), 25 mi/40 km SSE of Charlottesville. RR junction; hydroelectric plant; agr. (tobacco, grain, alfalfa; cattle); sand, gravel; slate quarrying nearby. "Bremo" estate, with mansion (begun 1815) designed by Thomas Jefferson, to W.

Bremond, town (1990 pop. 1,110), Robertson co., E central Texas, c.40 mi/64 km SE of Waco; 31°10′N 96°40′W. In cotton, corn, watermelon area. Twin Oak Reservoir to E. Inc. 1938.

Brenham, city (1990 pop. 11,952), ⊙ Washington co., S central Texas, c.70 mi/113 km WNW of Houston; 30°09′N 96°24′W. Elev. 350 ft/107 m. Trade, shipping, and processing center in rich Brazos valley agr. area; mfg. (textiles, power supplies, wire hangers; food processing, printing). Oil and natural-gas wells nearby. Seat of Blinn Col. (2-year). Somerville Lake reservoir and State Park to NW. Founded in 1844.

Brent, town (1990 pop. 2,776), Bibb co., central Ala., near Cahaba R., opposite Centerville. Lumber; toys.

Brent, suburb (□ 10 sq mi/26 sq km; 1990 pop. 21,624), Escambia co., extreme NW Fla., 2 mi/3.2 km NW of Pensacola; 30°28′N 87°15′W.

Brentford, village (1990 pop. 69), Spink co., NE central S.Dak., 22 mi/35 km SSE of Aberdeen.

Brentford Bay, N Boothia Peninsula, SE Franklin dist., N.W.T., W Canada, small inlet of Prince Regent Inlet, opposite Fort Ross; 71°55′N 94°20′W.

Brentwood 1 city (1990 pop. 7,563), Contra Costa co., W Calif., a suburb 28 mi/45 km ENE of downtown Oakland and 8 mi/12.9 km SE of Antioch; 37°56′N 121°43′W. Shipping center for irrigated agr. area (fruit, nuts, vegetables, esp. asparagus). Inc. 1948. Calaveras Aqueduct runs E-W to N of town. **2** city (1990 pop. 8,150), St. Louis co., E Mo., residential, commercial, and industrial suburb W of St. Louis, 9 mi/14.5 km W of downtown; 38°37′N 90°20′W. Mfg. (machining, silk screening; construction materials, protective coatings, consumer goods, gauges, aluminum prods., paper prods., foods, machinery, furniture, medical supplies). Inc. 1929. **3** city (1990 pop. 16,392), Williamson co., central Tenn., 12 mi/19 km S of Nashville, 35°56′N 84°05′W. In fertile farming region (livestock; tobacco; dairying). Many businesses and insurance companies have their offices here, but there is some mfg., including automotive parts and pens and pencils. Inc. 1969.

Brentwood 1 town (1990 pop. 3,005), Prince Georges co., central Md., suburb just NE of Washington, D.C., near Anacostia R., and just E of Mt. Rainer; 38°57′N 76°58′W. Originally called Highlands, it changed its name after the Civil War. Inc. 1912. **2** town (1990 pop. 2,590), Rockingham co., SE N.H., 6 mi/9.7 km W of Exeter; 42°59′N 71°02′W. Drained by Exeter R. Agr. (cattle, poultry; vegetables; dairying; nursery crops); mfg. (construction materials). **3** uninc. town (□ 10 sq mi/26 sq km; 1990 pop. 45,218), Suffolk co., SE N.Y., on central L.I., in the town of Islip; 40°46′N 73°15′W. Mainly residential, with various light industry. Josiah Warren led (1851) an experiment in communal living in Brentwood. In the 1980s, Brentwood built the Heartland Industrial Park, which has spurred the town's growth. Former site of Pilgrim Psychiatric Center is now a campus of N.Y. Inst. of Technology.

Brentwood, uninc. village (1990 pop. 3,568), Hamilton co., extreme SW Ohio, N suburb of Cincinnati, c.8 mi/13 km from downtown Cincinnati; 40°22′N 80°46′W.

Brentwood (BRENT-wud), borough (1990 pop. 10,823), Allegheny co., W Pa., a residential suburb 5 mi/8 km S of downtown Pittsburgh; 40°22′N 79°58′W. Allegheny Co. Airport to SE. Inc. 1915.

Brentwood, suburban section of Los Angeles city, Los Angeles co., S Calif., affluent residential area 13 mi/21 km W of downtown Los Angeles, extending into foothills of Santa Monica Mts., just NE of Santa Monica. Includes Brentwood Heights and Brentwood Park.

Bressler (BRES-luhr), uninc. town (1990 pop. 1,100), Dauphin co., S Pa., residential suburb 4 mi/6.4 km SE of downtown Harrisburg, and 1 mi/1.6 km SW of Enhart, near Susquehanna R.; 40°13′N 76°49′W. Light mfg.

Breton (BRE-tuhn), village (1991 pop. 484), S central Alta., W Canada, 50 mi/80 km SW of Edmonton; 53°07′N 114°29′W. Mixed farming, dairying.

Breton, Cape (BRE-tuhn), E extremity of Cape Breton Isl., E N.S., E Canada, 23 mi/37 km SE of Sydney; 45°56′N 59°48′W.

Breton Island (BREE-tuhn) (c.20 mi/32 km wide), SE La., hook-shaped isl. (c.6 mi/10 km long) in Gulf of Mexico, E of Mississippi R. delta, c.60 mi/97 km SE of New Orleans; with nearby isls. comprises Breton Isl. bird reservation; 29°27′N 89°11′W. To NW is **Breton Sound** (c.20 mi/32 km wide), an arm of the Gulf of Mexico lying bet. La. coast (W) and Breton Isl. (SE); Chandeleur Sound adjoins on E.

Breton Woods (BRE-tuhn), village, Ocean co., E N.J., 8 mi/12.9 km NE of Toms River.

Bretton Woods, N.H.: see CARROLL.

Brevard (bre-VAHRD), county (□ 1,557 sq mi/4,033 sq km; 1990 pop. 398,978), E central Fla., on the Atlantic Ocean (E); ⊙ Titusville; 28°18′N 80°42′W. Lowland region bordered by barrier beaches enclosing Indian R. and Banana R. lagoons, and Merritt Isl.; W part is a marshy peat area drained by St. Johns R., which forms several lakes here. Included in Indian R. dist., which is noted for its citrus fruit (esp. oranges). Currently a booming growth area undergoing urbanization. Also vegetable farming, tourism, and fishing industry. Formed 1844.

Brevard (bruh-VAHRD), town (1990 pop. 5,388), ⊙ Transylvania co., SW N.C., near French Broad R., 27 mi/43 km SSW of Asheville, in the Blue Ridge Mts; 35°14′N 82°43′W. Agr. trade center (tobacco, corn; cattle, poultry). Mfg. (cabinets, threads, fine paper, ceramics, sensors). Seat of Brevard Col. (junior; coed.). Many picturesque waterfalls (Connester Falls to S, 110 ft/34 m) in vicinity. Pisgah Natl. Forest to NW; including Cradle of Forestry Historic Site and Looking Glass Falls to N; Brevard Music Center is here. Inc. 1867.

Brevoort Island 1 SE Franklin dist., N.W.T., N Canada, in the Atlantic Ocean, off Hall Peninsula, SE Baffin Isl.; 25 mi/40 km long, 5 mi/8 km wide; 63°30′N 64°20′W. **2** islet, NE Franklin dist., N.W.T., W Canada, off E Ellesmere Isl., in Smith Sound, just S of Cape Sabine (Pim Isl.); 78°48′N 74°50′W.

Brevoort Lake (bruh-VORT), Mackinac co., SE Upper Peninsula, Mich., 12 mi/19 km NW of St. Ignace and 2 mi/3.2 km NE of L. Michigan shore, in Hiawatha Natl. Forest; c.5 mi/8 km long, 2 mi/3.2 km wide; 46°00′N 84°56′W. Fishing, camping. Little Brevoort L. beyond NW end.

Brewer, industrial city (1990 pop. 9,021), Penobscot co., S Maine, on E bank of the Penobscot R. opposite Bangor (linked by bridge); 44°46′N 68°43′W. Pulp and paper mills, brickworks, fabrics. Settled 1770, town inc. 1812, city 1889.

Brewer, Mount, peak (13,570 ft/4,136 m) of the Sierra Nevada, Tulare co., E Calif., in Kings Canyon Natl. Park, 17 mi/27 km WSW of Independence; 36°42′N 118°29′W. .

Brewerton, village (□ 3 sq mi/7.8 sq km; 1990 pop. 2,954), Onondaga co., central N.Y., at W end of Oneida L., 13 mi/21 km N of Syracuse; 43°14′N 76°08′W. Here are remains of Fort Brewerton (1759), now in state reservation.

Brewster, county (□ 6,193 sq mi/16,040 sq km; 1990 pop. 8,681), extreme W Texas; ⊙ Alpine; 29°48′N 103°15′W. State's largest co. (larger than state of Conn.). Rugged mt. area (elev. c.1,700 ft/518 m–7,000 ft/2,134 m) within Big Bend of the Rio Grande (here forming Mex. border, on SE and SW); much of most scenic wild area in S (including Chisos Mts. and Santa Elena, Mariscal, and Boquillas canyons) is included in Big Bend Natl. Park. Santiago Mts. are in central part, Glass Mts. partly in NE. Large-scale cattle, sheep, goat, horse ranching; tourist trade, dude ranches; some irrigated agr. (pecans, apples); beekeeping. Mercury mines (now inactive); copper, sulphur deposits, bentonite, perlite, fluorspar. Part of Rio Grande Wild and Scenic River (Natl. Park System) in SE. Formed 1887.

Brewster 1 town (1990 pop. 8,440), Barnstable co., SE Mass., 12 mi/19 km ENE of Barnstable, on Cape Cod Bay; 41°45′N 70°04′W. Mfg. includes cable industry prods.; summer resort. Cape Cod Natural History Mus. is here. Was shipping center in sailing-ship days. Includes villages of East and West Brewster. Site of Nickerson State Park. Settled 1656, inc. 1803. **2** town (1990 pop. 1,633), Okanogan co., N Wash., 20 mi/32 km SSW of Okanogan, on Columbia R. (L. Pateros reservoir), confluence of Okanogan to E; 48°06′N 119°47′W. Timber; apples, wheat; cattle, sheep. Fort Okanogan State Park to E.

Brewster 1 village (1990 pop. 296), Thomas co., NW Kansas, 18 mi/29 km W of Colby; elev. 3,411 ft/1,040 m; 39°21′N 101°22′W. In grain region. Mfg. (hand tools); sunflower seeds and their processing. **2** village (1990 pop. 532), Nobles co., SW Minn., 9 mi/14.5 km NE of Worthington, near Okabena Creek; 43°42′N 95°27′W. Corn, oats, soybeans; cattle, sheep, hogs, poultry; dairying; mfg. (feeds). **3** village (1990 pop. 22), ⊙ Blaine co., central Nebr., 100 mi/161 km NW of Grand Island, on North Loup R; 41°56′N 99°52′W. Livestock; grain. **4** village (1990 pop. 1,566), Putnam co., SE N.Y., 9 mi/14.5 km W of Danbury (Conn); 41°23′N 73°37′W. Trade

Cross references are shown in SMALL CAPITALS. The pronunciation key is on page xv. The dates of population figures are on page xii.

center for farming, dairying, summer-resort area. Mfg. (reflective films and papers, high-voltage electronic equip.; plastic assemblies, metal fabrication). Peach L. (resort) and several N.Y. city water-supply reservoirs are nearby. Jurist James Kent b. nearby, 1763. Settled 1850, inc. 1894. **5** village (1990 pop. 2,307), Stark co., E central Ohio, 13 mi/21 km WSW of Canton, on Beach City L.; 40°44′N 81°37′W. Dairy prods.

Brewster Islands, E Mass., group of islands, in the outer harbor, lying at entrance to Boston Bay from Massachusetts Bay, N of Point Allerton. Boston Light (oldest lighthouse in N. Amer., erected in 1716; 102 ft/31 m above water) is on Little Brewster Isl. (site of Boston Light, the oldest manned lighhouse in the U.S.; on Natl. Register of Historic Places). Part of Boston Harbor Islands State Park. Others in group include Great Brewster (largest drumlin in Boston Harbor), Middle Brewster, Outer Brewster, and Calf isls.

Brewton, city (1990 pop. 5,885), ⊙ Escambia co., S Ala., near Fla. state line and Conecuh R., 25 mi/40 km ENE of Atmore. In agr. and livestock area; lumber and lumber prods., textiles, clothing, RR car maintenance; oil and gas. Jefferson Davis Community Col. here. Fort Crawford est. here, 1818.

Brewton, town, Laurens co., central Ga., 7 mi/11.3 km NE of Dublin; 32°35′N 82°47′W.

Brian Head, village (1990 pop. 109), Iron co., SW Utah, 13 mi/21 km E of Cedar City. Dixie Natl. Forest and Cedar Breaks Natl. Monument to S; Brian Head Peak to E. Brian Head Ski Resort is here; 37°42′N 112°50′W. Called Monument Peak until 1890; ski resort developed 1964. Inc. 1975.

Brian Head Peak, peak (11,307 ft/3,446 m.), on W rim of Markagunt Plateau, Iron co., SW Utah, 13 mi/21 km E of Cedar City; 37°40′N 112°49′W. Dixie Natl. Forest; just N of Cedar Breaks Natl. Monument. Brian Head Ski Area to W. Called Monument Peak until 1890.

Briar Creek (BREI-uhr), borough (1990 pop. 616), Columbia co., E central Pa., suburb 2 mi/3.2 km WSW of Berwick, on Susquehanna R., at mouth of Briar Creek; 41°02′N 76°17′W. Briar Creek Park L. reservoir to N.

Briarcliff Manor, upper-income residential village (□ 6 sq mi/15.5 sq km; 1990 pop. 7,070, including Scarborough), Westchester co., SE N.Y., 2 mi/3.2 km SE of Ossining; 41°08′N 73°50′W. Settled 1896, inc. 1902.

Bricelyn, village (1990 pop. 426), Faribault co., S Minn., 16 mi/26 km ESE of Blue Earth, near East Fork Blue Earth R., and near Iowa state line; 43°33′N 93°48′W. RR junction. Corn, oats, soybeans; livestock. Walnut Lake Wildlife Area to N.

Brices Cross Roads (BREI-ses), National Battlefield Site (□ 1 acre/⅖ ha), Lee co., NE Miss., 15 mi/24 km N of Tupelo. Site (June 10, 1864) of a rout of Union troops by Confederate cavalry under Gen. N.B. Forrest. Authorized 1929.

Briceville, village, Anderson co., E Tenn., 20 mi/32 km NW of Knoxville, at foot of Cross Mt.; 36°11′N 84°11′W. Coal mining.

Brick, township (1990 pop. 66,473), Ocean co., E central N.J., 3 mi/4.8 km SE of Lakewood, on S branch Metedeconk R.; 40°03′N 74°06′W. Residential and resort area with some light industry, commercial development. Inc. 1850.

Brickerville (BRI-kuhr-vil), uninc. town (1990 pop. 1,268), Lancaster co., SE Pa., 13 mi/21 km N of Lancaster; 40°13′N 76°17′W. Agr. includes dairying; livestock, poultry and eggs; grain, soybeans. Speedwell Forge L. reservoir to SW.

Brickeys, village, Lee co., E Ark., 12 mi/19 km ENE of Marianna, near (old channel) St. Francis R..

Bridalveil Fall, Calif.: see YOSEMITE NATIONAL PARK.

Bridge City 1 uninc. town (1990 pop. 8,327), Jefferson parish, SE La., suburb 4 mi/6 km W of downtown New Orleans, on Mississippi R., at S end of Huey P. Long Bridge; 29°56′N 90°10′W. Elev. 5 ft/2 m. Bayou Segnette State Park to SE. **2** town (1990 pop. 8,034), Orange co., SE Texas, suburb 8 mi/12.9 km SW of Orange and 10 mi/16 km NE of Port Arthur; 30°01′N 93°50′W. Oil and natural gas. Cattle; rice. Mfg. (steel and metal processing).

Bridgehampton, shore-resort village (□ 9 sq mi/23.3 sq km; 1990 pop. 1,997), Suffolk co., SE N.Y., on SE L.I., 6 mi/9.7 km ENE of Southampton; 40°56′N 72°17′W. In dairying, farming, and potato-growing area.

Bridgeport 1 (BRIJ-poort), city (1990 pop. 2,936), Jackson co., extreme NE Ala., on Tenn. R., near Tenn. line, and 25 mi/40 km NE of Scottsboro. Yarn, clothing, shoes. Settled in early 19th cent. **2** city (1990 pop. 141,686), Fairfield co., SW Conn., on L.I. Sound; 41°11′N 73°12′W. Port of entry and chief industrial city in Conn. Mfg. includes electrical appliances, transportation equip., clothing, ammunition, fabricated metal prods., wiring devices, machinery, helicopters, motor vehicles, and building materials. Settled in 1639 and grew as a fishing community. The Barnum Inst. of Science and History commemorates the showman P.T. Barnum, who lived here. Seat of the Univ. of Bridgeport and a community col. Inc. 1836. **3** city (1990 pop. 2,118), Lawrence co., SE Ill., 4 mi/6.4 km W of Lawrenceville; 38°42′N 87°45′W. In oil, natural gas, and agr. area (wheat, sorghum; dairying); oil refineries (oil processing), pumping station; makes electronic equip. Inc. 1865.

Bridgeport 1 town (1990 pop. 8,569), Saginaw co., E central Mich., on Cass R., 5 mi/8 km SSE of Saginaw; 43°22′N 83°52′W. In farm area. Mfg. (machinery, battery-operated vehicles, medical supplies, pickles and sauerkraut, gauges and dies). **2** town (1990 pop.1,581), ⊙ Morrill co., W Nebr., 30 mi/48 km ESE of Scotts Bluff and on North Platte R.; 41°40′N 103°05′W. Trade center for irrigated grazing, alfalfa beans, sugar-beet area. Nearby buttes, Courthouse Rock and Jail Rock, points of interest area to S. RR junction across river (N). Chimney Rock Natl. Historical Site to W; Bridgeport State Recreation Area to W. Reilly Hill to NE (4,409 ft/1,344 m). **3** town (1990 pop. 3,581), Wise co., N Texas, c.40 mi/64 km NW of Fort Worth and on West Fork of Trinity R., dammed just W to form L. Bridgeport; 33°12′N 97°45′W. Agr. (grain, cotton, corn; dairying); mfg. (bricks, crushed limestone); clay; oil and gas. Former coal-mining center. Settled 1873, inc. 1913. **4** town (1990 pop. 1,498), Douglas co., central Wash., 50 mi/80 km NE of Wenatchee and on Columbia R., at mouth of Forter Creek, here crossed by bridge below (W) Chief Joseph Dam; 48°01′N 119°40′W. Alfalfa, wheat, barley, oats; cattle, sheep. Fort Okanogan State Park near mouth of Okanogan R., 7 mi/11.3 km N. Colville Indian Reservation across river, to N. Bridgeport State Park across river, to NE. **5** town (1990 pop. 6,739), Harrison co., N W.Va., 5 mi/8 km E of Clarksburg; 39°17′N 80°15′W. Agr. (grain, nursery crops); cattle, poultry; dairying. Benedum Airport to NE. Simpson Creek Covered Bridge to NW. Chartered 1816.

Bridgeport, village, NE N.S., E Canada, on NE coast of Cape Breton Isl., 10 mi/16 km NE of Sydney; 43°29′N 80°29′W. Coal mining. Mine shafts extend under the sea.

Bridgeport 1 uninc. village (1990 pop. 525), ⊙ Mono co., E Calif., 75 mi/121 km NW of Bishop, near Nev. state line (to NE). Mining; cattle; resort area. Bridgeport Reservoir is to N. Bodie State Historic Park to E; Toiyabe Natl. Forest to N and W; Sierra Nevada to W; Yosemite Natl. Park to SW; Mono L. 17 mi/27 km SSE. **2** village (1990 pop. 2,318), Belmont co., E Ohio, on the Ohio R. (bridged), opposite Wheeling (W.Va.); 40°04′N 80°46′W. Laid out 1806. **3** village (1990 pop. 137), Caddo co., W central Okla., on Canadian R. and 16 mi/26 km E of Weatherford; 35°32′N 98°22′W. In agr. area.

Bridgeport, borough (1990 pop. 4,292), Montgomery co., SE Pa., on Schuylkill R., suburb 15 mi/24 km NW of downtown Philadelphia, 1 mi/1.6 km S of Norristown; 40°06′N 75°20′W. Mfg. (food prods., paper prods., fabricated metal prods., metal prods., grinding wheels). Settled 1829, inc. 1851.

Bridgeport Dam, Texas: see BRIDGEPORT LAKE.

Bridgeport Lake, reservoir, Wise co., N Texas, on West Fork Trinity R., 40 mi/64 km NW of Fort Worth; c.10 mi/16 km long; 33°13′N 97°50′W. Max. capacity 923,814 acre-ft. Formed by Bridgeport Dam (122 ft/37 m high), built (1972) for water supply and irrigation.

Bridgeport Reservoir, Calif.: see EAST WALKER RIVER.

Bridger (BRI-juhr), village (1990 pop. 692), Carbon co., S Mont., on Clarks Fork Yellowstone R., downstream (N) from mouth of Bridger Creek and 40 mi/64 km SW of Billings; 45°17′N 108°55′W. Mfg (upholstered furniture); sugar beets, corn, barley, oats; cattle, sheep; coal. Pryor Mts. to E, Crow Indian Reservation to E, sect. of Custer Natl. Forest and Pryor Mts. Natl. Wild Horse Range to SE. Formerly called Bridger's Crossing.

Bridger, Fort, Wyo.: see FORT BRIDGER STATE HISTORIC SITE.

Bridger Peak (11,007 ft/3,355 m), in Sierra Madre, Carbon co., S Wyo., 12 mi/19 km WSW of Encampment; 41°11′N 107°01′W. In Medicine Bow Natl. Forest; Battle Pass 9,955 ft/3,034 m to SE.

Bridger Range (BRI-juhr), in Rocky Mts., S Mont., mainly Gallatin co., extends SE to Park co., rises NE of Bozeman; length c.25 mi/40 km N-S. Sacagawea Peak, near center of range, 9,665 ft/2,946 m, highest point.

Bridger's Pass (c.7,500 ft/2,286 m), in Sierra Madre of Continental Divide, Carbon co., S Wyo., c.25 mi/40 km SSE of Rawlins. Discovered by Jim Bridger, famous Native Amer. scout and guide; used in 1860s by Pony Express; was part of Overland Route.

Bridgeton 1 city (1990 pop. 17,779), St. Louis co., E Mo., suburb 13 mi/21 km NW of downtown St. Louis, W of Lambert–St. Louis Airport; 38°46′N 90°25′W. Mfg. (consumer goods, food mill equip., fabricated metal prods., syrups and drink mixes, vending machines, battery chargers, wheel balancers, pharmaceuticals, medical instruments, graphite prods.). Settled c.1765, inc. 1843. **2** city (1990 pop. 18,942), ⊙ Cumberland co., S N.J., on the Cohansey R.; 39°25′N 75°13′W. Once a rural farm center (peach and apple orchards still important), it has become highly industrialized, with glassworks, printing, food-processing, textile, and clothing industries. Downtown is highly Victorian, but with several 18th-cent. bldgs., including the restored Potter's Tavern, a Revolutionary center in colonial days; and a Presbyterian church (1792). The city's liberty bell, in the co. courthouse lobby, rang on July 7, 1776, for the reading of the Declaration of Independence. Has zoo. Settled 1686, inc. 1865.

Bridgeton 1 village, Parke co., W Ind., 9 mi/14.5 km SSE of Rockville, on Big Raccoon Creek. Agr. area (corn; hogs). Covered bridge here and many others in the surrounding area. Seasonal tourist site, esp. in autumn. Laid out 1857. **2** village (1990 pop. 453), Craven co., E N.C., 2 mi/3.2 km ENE of and opposite New Bern, on Neuse R. (bridged); 35°07′N 77°01′W. Agr. area (tobacco, cotton, peanuts, grain; poultry, livestock). Mfg. (machining, metal plating).

Bridgetown, city (1980 pop. 7,552), ⊙ Barbados, West Indies. The isl.'s commercial center and chief port; important financial center and transshipment point. Tourist and health resort. Sugar, rum, and molasses are the leading exports. Founded by the British in 1628. Grantley Adams Internatl. Airport nearby.

Bridgetown, town (1991 pop. 1,021), ⊙ Annapolis co., W N.S., E Canada, on Annapolis R. and 12 mi/19 km ENE of Annapolis Royal; 44°51′N 65°09′W. Woodworking, lumbering. First settled c.1650 by the French.

Bridgetown, town, Caroline co., E Md., near headwaters of Tuckahoe R. and 21 mi/34 km WSW of Dover (Del.). The post office changed names in 1841 from Nine Bridges to Bridgetown. There were once 9 small bridges here, subsequently reduced to 1 single, concrete bridge.

Bridgeview, city (1990 pop. 14,402), Cook co., NE Ill., SW suburb of Chicago; 41°44′N 87°48′W. Inc. 1947.

Bridgeville, town (1990 pop. 1,210), Sussex co., SW Del., 8 mi/12.9 km N of Seaford, near Nanticoke R; 38°44′N 75°35′W. Shipping center in fruit- and vegetable-growing agr. region; mfg. (frozen foods). Inc. 1871.

Bridgeville, borough (1990 pop. 5,445), Allegheny co., SW Pa., industrial suburb 8 mi/12.9 km SW of downtown Pittsburgh, on Chartiers Creek; 40°21′N 80°06′W.

Area in square miles is shown by the symbol □ capital city or county seat by ⊙

Mfg. (glass and wood prods., fabricated metal, polyester resins, ammunition, apparel, gaskets). Woodville State Hosp. to N. Inc. 1901.

Bridgewater, town (1991 pop. 7,248), SW N.S., E Canada, on Lahave R. and 50 mi/80 km WSW of Halifax; 44°22′N 64°31′W. Lumber-shipping port; sawmilling. Founded 1810.

Bridgewater 1 resort town (1990 pop.1,654), Litchfield co., W Conn., on Housatonic R., 11 mi/18 km NNE of Danbury; 41°31′N 73°21′W. In hilly agr. region. Early 19th-cent. church and houses. **2** town (1990 pop. 209), Adair co., SW Iowa, 12 mi/19 km WSW of Greenfield. Livestock shipping. **3** rural town (1990 pop. 647), Aroostook co., E Maine, 21 mi/34 km N of Houlton, near Can. (N.B.) border; 46°25′N 67°50′W. Ships potatoes; lumber. Port of entry. Inc. 1858. **4** town (1990 pop. 21,249), Plymouth co., E Mass.; 41°58′N 70°59′W. Mfg. includes shoes and metal prods. Its iron foundry industry dates from colonial times. Bridgewater State Col. and a state prison are here. Inc. 1656. **5** town (1990 pop. 796), Grafton co., central N.H., 14 mi/23 km N of Franklin; 43°40′N 71°41′W. Bounded E by Pemigewasset R., W by Newfound L. Agr. (cattle, poultry; vegetables, apples; dairying; nursery crops). Resort; winter sports. **6** town (1990 pop. 32,509), Somerset co., N N.J., 10 mi/16 km W of Piscataway; 40°35′N 74°36′W. Industrial with mfg. (telecommunications and office equip., clothing). Rapidly expanding suburb. Inc. 1798. **7** town (1990 pop. 895), Windsor co., S central Vt., on Ottauquechee R., 6 mi/9.7 km WSW of Woodstock; 43°37′N 72°39′W. Wood prods. Includes village of Bridgewater Corners. **8** town (1990 pop. 3,198), Rockingham co., NW Va., 7 mi/11.3 km SW of Harrisonburg, on North R., in Shenandoah Valley; 38°22′N 78°58′W. Mfg. (furniture, clothing, rayon textiles, aircraft training aids; printing, machining, poultry processing); agr. area (dairying; livestock, poultry; grain, soybeans, apples, peaches); timber. Seat of Bridgewater Col. Natural Chimneys Regional Park to W; part of George Washington Natl. Forest, including Hone Quarry Recreation Area, to NW. Inc. 1835.

Bridgewater 1 village (1990 pop. 537), Oneida co., central N.Y., 15 mi/24 km S of Utica; 42°52′N 75°15′W. **2** village (1990 pop. 533), McCook co., SE S.Dak., 28 mi/45 km ESE of Mitchell and 37 mi/60 km W of Sioux Falls. Trade center for diversified farming region; dairy prods.; livestock, poultry; corn, wheat, rye.

Bridgewater, borough (1990 pop. 751), Beaver co., W Pa., residential suburb 1 mi/1.6 km N of Beaver, on Beaver R., at its mouth on Ohio R.; 40°42′N 80°17′W. Was 19th-cent. river port. Inc. 1835.

Bridgman, village (1990 pop. 2,140), Berrien co., extreme SW Mich., on L. Michigan and 12 mi/19 km SW of St. Joseph; 41°56′N 86°33′W. In fruit-growing and vegetable-farming area; nurseries. Mfg. of fabricated metal prods., machinery, paper prods.; sand processing). Resort. Warren Dunes State Park nearby.

Bridgton, town (1990 pop. 4,307), including Bridgton village, Cumberland co., SW Maine, bet. Highland and Long lakes, 35 mi/56 km NW of Portland; 44°02′N 70°44′W. Mfg. and resort center. At North Bridgton village is Bridgton Acad. Settled 1770, inc. 1794.

Bridport, town (1990 pop. 1,137), Addison co., W Vt., on L. Champlain, 7 mi/11.3 km W of Middlebury; 43°58′N 73°19′W. Agr.; sheep.

Bridwell Heights, village (1990 pop. 2,700), Sullivan co., NE Tenn., 5 mi/8 km E of Kingsport.

Brielle (bre-EL), borough (1990 pop. 4,406), Monmouth co., E N.J., near mouth of Manasquan R., 16 mi/26 km SE of Freehold; 40°06′N 74°03′W. Sports-fishing and recreational-boating center. Named after Brielle, Neth., because of the many windmills once used here. Most of the town (the Salt Works and 50 homes and bldgs.) was burned (April 1778) by the British. Only the home of Dirck (or Derrick) Longstreet, a loyal Br. subject, escaped the flames; now known as "The Boxwood Cottage" (built 1760) and still used as a residence.

Brier Creek (BREI-uhr), c.75 mi/121 km long, E Ga.; rises near Warrenton; flows SE, past Keysville, to Savannah R. 12 mi/19 km E of Sylvania; 31°58′N 84°49′W. Sometimes written Briar Creek.

Brier Island (BREI-uhr) (4 mi/6 km long, 2 mi/3 km wide), W N.S., E Canada, at entrance to Bay of Fundy, 30 mi/48 km NNW of Yarmouth and just SW of Long Isl.; 44°15′N 66°22′W. On W coast is fishing village of Westport.

Brigantine (BRI-guhn-teen), resort city (1990 pop. 11,354), Atlantic co., SE N.J., on Brigantine Isl. and 3 mi/4.8 km NE of Atlantic City; 39°24′N 74°22′W.

Brigantine Island (BRI-guhn-teen), island (6 mi/9.7 km long), off N.J. coast, just NE of Atlantic City, with which it is connected by bridge across Absecon Inlet. Brigantine, resort city, is here.

Brigden, village, S Ont., central Canada, on Bear Creek and 12 mi/19 km SSE of Sarnia. Dairying; fruit growing; in former oil-producing region.

Briggsdale, village, Weld co., N Colo., on Crow Creek and 24 mi/39 km NE of Greeley; elev. 4,840 ft/1,475 m. Trading point; wheat, sunflowers, sugar beets, beans; cattle. Pawnee Natl. Grassland to NW and E.

Briggsville, Mass.: see CLARKSBURG.

Brigham City (BRIG-uhm), city (1990 pop. 15,644), ⊙ Box Elder co., N Utah, 20 mi/32 km N of Ogden; 41°30′N 112°00′W. Center of a large farm area served by the Ogden R. project. Sheep, cattle; wheat, sugar beets, and orchard fruit, especially cherries and peaches, are raised. Mfg. (propulsion systems, space shuttle rocket boosters, construction materials, flour, fabricated metal prods.), petroleum refining. Founded as Box Elder in 1851; name was changed to honor Brigham Young in 1856. Golden Spike Natl. Historic Site, marking the spot where the last RR spike was driven in 1869, is 30 mi/48 km to the W. Great Salt Lake and mouth of Bear R. to W; Wasatch Range and Natl. Forest to E. RR junction. Inc. 1869.

Bright, village (1990 pop. 3,945), Dearborn co., SE Ind., 8 mi/12.9 km N of Lawrenceburg and 18 mi/29 km WNW of downtown Cincinnati (Ohio); 39°12′N 84°52′W. Satellite community of Cincinnati. Cattle; wheat.

Brighton, plantation (1990 pop. 94), Somerset co., W central Maine, 18 mi/29 km N of Skowhegan; 45°02′N 69°41′W. Includes hamlet of Brighton.

Brighton 1 (BREIT-uhn), city (1990 pop. 4,518), Jefferson co., central Ala., W of Birmingham. **2** city (1990 pop. 14,203), ⊙ Adams co., extends into Morgan co., N central Colo., on South Platte R., suburb 20 mi/32 km NNE of downtown Denver; 39°57′N 104°47′W. Elev. 4,983 ft/1,519 m. Shipping and processing point in grain and sugar-beet region; mfg. (chemicals, sealing tape, fabricated metal prods., construction materials). Barr Lake State Park to SE. Denver Internatl. Airport 8 mi/12.9 km to SE. Inc. 1887.

Brighton, town (1991 pop. 4,366), S Ont., central Canada, near L. Ontario, 20 mi/32 km WSW of Belleville; 44°02′N 77°44′W. Fruit and vegetable canning, light mfg.; corn, vegetable, fruit market. E is L. Ontario end of Murray Canal.

Brighton 1 town (1990 pop. 684), Washington co., SE Iowa, 10 mi/16 km SW of Washington; 41°10′N 91°49′W. Food cannery. **2** town (1990 pop. 5,686) and satellite community of Detroit, in Livingston co., SE Mich., 18 mi/29 km N of Ann Arbor; 42°31′N 83°46′W. In rich agr. area; timber; mfg. (transportation equip., fences, chemicals, wood prods., thermoplastics). Summer resort. Island Lake State Recreation Area to SE; Huron Meadows Metro park to S; Mt. Brighton Ski Area to NW; Brighton State Recreation Area to W, numerous lakes in area. Settled 1832; inc. 1867 as village and 1928 as city. **3** town (1990 pop. 717), Tipton co., W Tenn., 28 mi/45 km NE of Memphis; 35°29′N 89°44′W. In cotton area. **4** town (1990 pop. 1,562), Essex co., NE Vt., 20 mi/32 km SE of Newport, on Nulhegan R.; its center is Island Pond village, on scenic Island Pond; 44°47′N 71°52′W. Brighton State Park is here. Lumber; dairy prods.. Chartered 1781, settled 1820.

Brighton 1 village (1990 pop. 2,270), Macoupin co., W Ill., 10 mi/16 km N of Alton; 39°02′N 90°08′W. Agr., bituminous-coal mining. **2** uninc. village, Salt L. co., N central Utah, in a basin of Wasatch Mts. near Alta and c. 25 mi/40 km SE of Salt Lake City, on Big Cottonwood Creek in Wasatch Natl. Forest; elev. 8,750 ft/2,667 m. Year-round resort (skiing at Solitude and Brighton ski resorts, skating, hiking, fishing, swimming). Small Silver L. is here; several small glacial lakes to SW. Ski Village of Alta 3 mi/4.8 km to SW, road access c.25 mi/40 km.

Brighton, Mass.: BOSTON.

Brighton Beach, neighborhood, S sect. of borough of Brooklyn, N.Y. city, SE N.Y., just E of Coney Isl., at the Lower Bay entrance to N.Y. Harbor; 40°35′N 73°57′W. Contains N.Y city's largest concentration of Jews from the former Soviet Union, many of whom are from Black Sea towns such as Odessa (hence the area's nickname, "Little Odessa"). The 20,000 Soviet immigrants (largest concentration in U.S.) come from Leningrad, Moscow, and central Asia as well. The Brooklyn real-estate boom of the 1920s led to the radical transformation of a little seaside village into a thriving residential suburb of Jewish immigrants beginning in 1925; the pop. increased during the Depression and again after World War II, with an influx of Holocaust refugees from E Europe. Overcrowding led to an outflow of Amer.-born children of immigrants that lasted through the mid-1960s. Then, in the late 1960s and early 1970s, a 2d influx of immigrant Soviet Jews were joined by residents from the older immigrant neighborhoods of East Flatbush (Brooklyn) and the Grand Concourse (Bronx). Attitudinally the newer Soviet Jews are often at odds with the older residents.

Brightwaters, village (□ 1 sq mi/2.6 sq km; 1990 pop. 3,265), Suffolk co., SE N.Y., on S shore of W L.I., on Great South Bay, just W of Bay Shore; 40°43′N 73°16′W. Laid out 1907, inc. 1916.

Brigus (BRI-guhs), town (1991 pop. 929), SE N.F., E Canada, on N coast of Avalon Peninsula, at head of Conception Bay, on RR and 25 mi/40 km W of St. John's; 47°32′N 53°13′W. Fishing port; sawmilling; farming; dairying; vegetables.

Brilliant, village, S B.C., W Canada, on Columbia R., at mouth of Kootenay R., 16 mi/26 km NNE of Trail; 49°19′N 117°38′W. In mining (gold, silver, lead, zinc) and lumbering region.

Brilliant, village (1990 pop. 1,672), Jefferson co., E Ohio, 6 mi/10 km S of Steubenville and near the Ohio R.; 40°16′N 80°39′W.

Brillion (BRIL-ee-ahn), town (1990 pop. 2,840), Calumet co., E Wis., 17 mi/27 km ESE of Appleton; 44°10′N 88°04′W. Trade center for agr. area (oats, clover seeds; dairy); mfg. (lawn mowers, fabricated metal prods., zinc electroplating). Settled 1850; inc. 1885 as village, 1944 as city.

Brimfield, town (1990 pop. 3,001), Hampden co., S Mass., 19 mi/31 km E of Springfield; 42°08′N 72°13′W. Medical instruments; fruit orchards. Brimfield State Forest is nearby. Largest flea market in the NE held here 3 times annually. Settled c.1706, inc. 1731.

Brimfield 1 village (1990 pop. 797), Peoria co., central Ill., 17 mi/27 km WNW of Peoria; 40°50′N 89°52′W. In agr. and bituminous-coal area. Jubilee College State Park is nearby. **2** village, Noble co., NE Ind., 6 mi/9.7 km W of Kendallville. Agr. area. Mfg. (kiln-dried hardwood, plastic molds). **3** uninc. village (1990 pop. 3,223), Portage co., NE Ohio, 9 mi/14 km E of Akron, just N of Mogadore Reservoir (recreation); 41°06′N 81°22′W.

Brimley, village, Chippewa co., E Upper Peninsula, Mich., on Whitefish Bay, 12 mi/19 km SW of Sault Ste. Marie; 46°24′N 84°34′W. Agr.; lumbering. Brimley State Park to NE on L. Superior; Hiawatha Natl. Forest to W; Bay Mills Indian Reservation (W unit) to NW.

Brimson (BRIMP-suhn), town (1990 pop. 72), Grundy co., N Mo., on Thompson R., 8 mi/12.9 km NW of Trenton; 40°08′N 93°44′W.

Brimstone Hill, volcanic cone, on W coast of St. Kitts, Federation of Saint Kitts and Nevis, West Indies; 17°21′N 65°50′W. Elev. 751 ft/229 m. Site of fortress built by British in 18th cent. partially restored, dedicated as 32-acre/13-ha natl. park in 1985. Citadel houses mus. of colonial history.

Brinkley, town (1990 pop. 4,234), Monroe co., E central Ark., c.60 mi/97 km ENE of Little Rock near Cache R.; 34°52′N 91°11′W. RR junction. Mfg. (apparel), rice processing. Dagmar Wildlife Management Area to W. Laid out c.1872.

Brinkman, village, Greer co., SW Okla., 9 mi/14.5 km N of Mangum. Ships wheat.

Brinsmade (BRINZ-maid), village (1990 pop. 21), Benson co., NE central N.Dak., 22 mi/35 km WNW of Devils L.; 48°10′N 99°19′W.

Brinson, village (1990 pop. 238), Decatur co., SW Ga., 11 mi/18 km WNW of Bainbridge, on Atlantic coast RR line; 30°59′N 84°44′W. In farm area.

Briny Breezes, village (1990 pop. 400), Palm Beach co., SE Fla., just SE of Boynton Beach; 26°30′N 80°02′W.

Brion Island (bree-OH), in the Gulf of St. Lawrence, E Que., E Canada, northermost of the Magdalen Isls., 30 mi/48 km NE of Grindstone Isl.; 4 mi/6 km long, 1 mi/2 km wide; 47°48′N 61°28′W.

Briones Reservoir, Contra Costa co., W central Calif., on Bear Creek, 9 mi/14.5 km N of downtown Oakland; c.15 mi/24 km long; 37°56′N 122°10′W. Extends NE and E; max. capacity 67,500 acre-ft. Formed by Briones Dam (261 ft/80 m high), built (1964) for Bay Area water supply.

Brisbane, city (1990 pop. 2,952), San Mateo co., W Calif., suburb 7 mi/11.3 km S of downtown San Francisco, on S San Francisco Bay; 37°42′N 122°24′W. Mfg. (carbon prods., foods, consumer goods, machinery, fabricated metal prods., computers), publishing and printing. Port facilities. Cow Palace Arena (Daly City) and Candlestick Park baseball stadium (San Francisco) to N; San Bruno Mts. to W.

Brisbin, borough (1990 pop. 369), Clearfield co., central Pa., 14 mi/23 km SSE of Clearfield and 1 mi/1.6 km N of Hontzdale; 40°50′N 78°20′W. Grain; livestock.

Briscoe, county (□ 901 sq mi/2,334 sq km; 1990 pop. 1,971), NW Texas; ⊙ Silverton; 34°31′N 101°12′W. SW part in Llano Estacado, bounded by E-facing Caprock escarpment; elev. 2,100 ft/640 m–3,300 ft/1,006 m. Drained by Tule Creek (forms MacKenzie Reservoir on W border) and Prairie Dog Town Fork of Red R. Irrigated agr. (cattle ranching; wheat, grain sorghum, vegetables, melons, cotton). Clay prods., fuller's earth. Formed 1876.

Briseñas de Matamoros (bree-SEN-yahs de mah-tah-MO-ros), town (1990 pop. 3,711), ⊙ the municipality of Briseñas, in extreme NW Michoacán, Mexico, 33 mi/53 km NW of Zamoro de Hidalgo; 20°18′N 102°35′W.

Bristol 1 county (□ 691 sq mi/1,790 sq km; 1990 pop. 506,325), SE Mass., on Buzzards Bay and the Atlantic Ocean; ⊙ Fall River; 41°48′N 71°06′W. Intersected by Taunton R. Its early activities of whaling and shipping gave way to textile milling after mid–19th cent., with centers at Fall River, New Bedford, and Taunton. Varied mfg.; pottery; agr. (hay; livestock, poultry; fruit, vegetables). Resort activities on coast. Formed 1685. **2** county (□ 44 sq mi/114 sq km; 1990 pop. 48,859), E R.I., bounded by Narragansett Bay (SW), Mass. state line (NE), and Mt. Hope Bay (SE); ⊙ Bristol; 41°42′N 71°17′W. Resorts; fishing; mfg. (textiles, plastic goods, food prods., machinery); shipbuilding and boatbuilding; agr. (dairy prods.; poultry; vegetables). Drained by Barrington, Warren, and Kickamuit rivers. Inc. 1747.

Bristol 1 industrial city (1990 pop. 60,640), Hartford co., central Conn., on the Pequabuck R.; 41°40′N 72°56′W. Its clock-making industry dates from 1790. Mfg. includes machinery, electric equip., fabricated metal prods., wire forms, paper punches, jewelry; metal stamping. ESPN, a nationally televised all-sports network, is located here. The Amer. Clock and Watch Mus. A chrysanthemum festival is held annually. Settled 1727, inc. 1785. **2** industrial city (1990 pop. 23,421), Sullivan co., extreme NE Tenn., on Va. state line, adjoining Bristol (Va.) and 21 mi/34 km NNE of Johnson City; 36°35′N 82°12′W. The two border cities, although separate municipalities, are economically a unit that is the transportation and processing center of a mountainous region. Livestock is raised; electronic equip., fabricated metal prods., and hardwood caskets are produced here. Shelby's Fort (built 1771) was frequented by Daniel Boone. Two hundred years of controversy preceded the location of the state line down the middle of State St. Seat of King Col. In the area are Bristol Caverns and an internatl. car raceway. Settled 1749 as Sapling Grove; inc. 1856 as separate town, 1890 as city. **3** independent city (1990 pop. 18,426), SW Va., 138 mi/222 km SW of Roanoke, on Beaver Creek, on Tenn. state line, adjoining Bristol (Tenn.) to S; 36°36′N 82°10′W. RR junction. Mfg. (mining equip., fabricated metal prods., clothing, machinery, construction materials, universal joints, consumer goods, foods, transportation equip.). Seat of Va. Intermont Coll. S Holston Reservoir and Cherokee Natl. Forest (both in Tenn.) to SE.

Bristol 1 town, Pierce co., SE Ga., 18 mi/29 km NNE of Waycross; 31°26′N 82°12′W. **2** town (1990 pop. 1,133), Elkhart co., N Ind., on St. Joseph R., and 9 mi/14.5 km N of Goshen, near Mich. state line; 41°43′N 85°49′W. Mfg. (fabricated metal prods., construction materials, plastic prods., transportation equip., machinery, textiles, wood prods., fiberglass parts), meat processing. **3** resort and fishing town (1990 pop. 2,326), Lincoln co., S Maine, 7 mi/11.3 km E of Wiscasset, on the Atlantic coast and Damariscotta R.; 43°55′N 69°29′W. This area, Pemaquid, was visited by early explorers and traders; settled c.1626; became a well-known trading post. Several forts were built here, and area was subject to Native Amer. and Fr. attacks in 17th and 18th cents. Includes villages of Round Pond and New Harbor. Monhegan Isl. is off the coast. **4** town (1990 pop. 2,537), Grafton co., central N.H., 10 mi/16 km NNW of Franklin; 43°37′N 71°43′W. Bounded S and E by Pemigewasset R. (forms Franklin Falls Reservoir in S); drained by Newfound R. Agr. (cattle, poultry; vegetables, apples; nursery crops; timber); mfg. (medical supplies, concrete, oil seals), machining. Surrounded by hills and lakes; part of Newfound L. in NW corner. Inc. 1819. **5** town (1990 pop. 21,625), ⊙ Bristol co., E R.I., a port on Narragansett Bay; 41°41′N 71°16′W. Inc. 1681 as a Plymouth Colony town, ceded to Rhode Island 1746. An early center of commercial trade, the port was (18th–19th cent.) a base for whaling and shipbuilding. The Herreshoff boatyard, where many winners of the America's Cup were built, was in operation until 1945. Mfg. includes wire and cable, cotton thread, and fiberglass boats. King Philip's War (1675–1676) began and ended on the site of the town, and a monument on Mt. Hope (221 ft/67 m) marks the spot where King Philip fell. Bristol Art Mus. has paintings and sculptures. On Hope St. is a row of preserved colonial homes. Colt State Park is former summer estate farm of Samuel Pomeray Colt. Seat of Roger Williams Col. and the R.I. Soldiers' Home. Mt. Hope Bridge connects Bristol with Portsmouth. **6** town (1990 pop. 3,762), Addison co., W Vt., 10 mi/16 km NNE of Middlebury and on New Haven R., in Green Mts.; 44°07′N 73°04′W. Winter and summer resort area. Lumber; dairy prods.. Chartered 1762, settled 1786. Includes Bristol village. **7** town, Kenosha co., extreme SE Wis., suburb 11 mi/18 km W of Kenosha. In dairy and livestock region; cheese; mfg. (electrical and electronic equip., woven wood shades, machining tools).

Bristol 1 village (□ 2 sq mi/5.2 sq km; 1990 pop. 937), ⊙ Liberty co., NW Fla., on Apalachicola R., and c.40 mi/64 km W of Tallahassee; 30°25′N 84°58′W. Lumber; naval stores. **2** village, Kendall co., NE Ill., near Fox R. and 7 mi/11.3 km SW of Aurora; 41°41′N 88°25′W. In agr. area. **3** village (1990 pop. 419), Day co., NE S.Dak., 11 mi/18 km W of Webster. Dairy prods.; livestock, poultry; grain. Amsden Dam State Lakeside Use Area to W.

Bristol (BRIS-tuhl), borough (1990 pop. 10,405), Bucks co., SE Pa., suburb 18 mi/29 km NE of downtown Philadelphia and 9 mi/14.5 km SSW of Trenton (N.J.), on the Delaware R. (bridged) opposite (N of) Burlington (N.J.); 46°06′N 74°50′W. Mfg. (plastics prods., paper prods., medical supplies, electronic equip.), commercial printing. The state's 3d-oldest borough, it was once a busy river port with important shipbuilding activities. Among its historic structures is the Friends Meetinghouse, built c.1710. Historic Fallsington, a restoration of 17th- and 18th-cent. bldgs. is to the N, and Pennsburg Manor State Park, a replica of William Penn's country manor is to the NE. Neshaminy State Park to W. Settled 1697, inc. 1720.

Bristol Bay, borough (□ 519 sq mi/1,344 sq km; 1990 pop. 1,410), SW Alaska, at the base of the Alaska Peninsula, bounded on W by Kyichak Bay, arm of Bristol Bay, Bering Sea. Part of Naknek Lake and Katmai Natl. Park and Preserve in E. Fishing. Seals; hides.

Bristol Bay, arm (250 mi/402 km long, 180 mi/290 km wide at mouth) of Bering Sea, bet. SW Alaskan mainland (N) and Alaska Peninsula (S and E); 57°00′–59°00′N 157°20′–162°00′W. Receives Togiak, Nushagak, and Kvichak rivers. World's largest salmon fishery with many cannery villages. Shallow; navigation hazardous for larger vessels. Main city is Dillingham. Sports fishing, hunting; tourism.

Bristol Ferry, hamlet in Portsmouth municipality, Newport co., E R.I., at N end of Rhode Isl., 10 mi/16 km N of Newport and 3 mi/4.8 km S of Bristol; 41°37′N 71°15′W. Mt. Hope Bridge (1929) leads to Bristol, on mainland.

Bristol Lake, S San Bernardino co., S Calif., intermittently dry bed (c.10 mi/16 km long) in Mojave Desert, just S of Amboy. Twentynine Palms Marine Corps Base to W.

Bristow 1 town (1990 pop. 197), Butler co., N central Iowa, 5 mi/8 km E of Alison; 42°46′N 92°54′W. In agr. area. **2** (BRIS-to), town (1990 pop. 4,062), Creek co., central Okla., 32 mi/51 km SW of Tulsa; 35°49′N 96°23′W. In diversified agr. (peanuts; dairying) and oil-producing area. Mfg. (apparel, machinery, lock sets, foods). Settled c.1898.

Bristow (BRIS-tou), village (1990 pop. 107), Boyd co., N Nebr., 15 mi/24 km ESE of Butte bet. the Niobrara and the Missouri rivers; 42°50′N 98°34′W.

British Columbia, province (□ 366,255 sq mi/948,600 sq km, including 6,976 sq mi/18,068 sq km of water surface; 1991 pop. 3,282,061), westernmost prov. of Canada, ⊙ VICTORIA; 55°00′N 125°00′W. The largest city and chief port is VANCOUVER, followed by Victoria and NANAIMOother centers include NEW WESTMINSTER, NORTH VANCOUVER, WEST VANCOUVER, BURNABY, RICHMOND, SURREY, PORT COQUITLAM, KAMLOOPS, , and PRINCE GEORGE. Bounded E by Alta., S by Mont., Idaho, and Wash., W by the Pacific Ocean, NW by Alaska, and N by the Yukon and by the Fort Smith Region of the N.W.T. Off its deeply indented Pacific coast lie many isls., notably Vancouver Isl. (c.280 mi/450 km long) and the sparsely inhabited Queen Charlotte Isls. The prov. is almost wholly mountainous, with the Rocky Mts. in the SE, the Coast Mts. along the Pacific, and the Stikine Mts. in the NW. Chief of the many rivers is the Fraser, which, with its tributaries, drains much of central and S B.C. as it flows to the Pacific. Other rivers in that region include the upper Columbia and the Kootenay. In the N are the Peace, the Stikine, the Nass, and the Skeena. Hydroelectric power is highly developed; large plants along the rivers operate pulp and paper mills. The largest station, at Kemano on the Nechako R., serves one of the biggest aluminum plants in the world, at Kitimat. Innumerable long, narrow lakes are found throughout the interior, supplying vast backwaters for dams. Large areas of central and N B.C. are sparsely settled, almost 75% of the pop. crowding the SW coastal tip in the Georgia Strait region. Less than 10% of the prov. can be used for grazing or cultivation, since nearly 75% of the land is covered with forests. B.C.'s evergreens make up about 50% of all of Can. timber. Lumbering and related enterprises (such as pulp and paper mfg.) are the prov.'s major industries. Next in importance is mining; B.C. is rich in mineral resources, and geologists, technicians, and adventurers are continually searching for new deposits. Copper, mined principally at Kamloops, Princeton, and Brittania, and coal are the prov.'s 2 largest mineral resources. Also important are natural gas, oil, zinc, gold, silver, nickel, and iron. The mine at Kimberley, one of the world's largest, is known for its silver, lead, and zinc. B.C. ranks 1st among the provs. in fishing; the most important catches are salmon, halibut, and herring. Beef is also an important product, especially along the Fraser R., which is known for its sprawling ranches. Other industries include food processing and the mfg. of transportation equip., machinery, chemicals, furniture, and electrical items. Tourism is one of the prov.'s most important industries; B.C. attracts millions of visitors annually, and the land is a hunting and fishing paradise. There are 4 natl. parks—Glacier, Mt. Revelstoke, Yoho, and Kootenay—and hundreds of provincial parks and camping grounds. The climate along the W coast, tempered by the warm Japan Current, has made that area, especially Vancouver and Victoria, very attractive to tourists. Vancouver grew rapidly throughout the 1980s, experiencing a real-estate boom and heavy immigration and capital inflow from China and Hong Kong. Migrants from within Canada were attracted by the region's mild climate, recreation facilities, and prosperity. Continually inhabited for 6,000–8,000 years by Kwakiutl, Haida, Tsimshian, and other coastal native groups (known especially for their totem poles and potlatches). Spaniard Juan Peréz was probably the 1st European to sail (1774) along the coast, but he did not make a landing. In 1778, Capt. James Cook, on his last voyage, explored the coast in his search of the Northwest Passage and claimed the area for Great Britain. Rival Br. and Span. claims for the area were resolved by the Nootka Conventions of 1790–1792, which gave both equal trading rights but did not resolve ownership. From 1792 to 1794, George Vancouver explored and mapped the coast from Oregon to Alaska. In 1793, Sir Alexander Mackenzie reached the Pacific overland; followed by early-19th-cent. fur traders and explorers of the North West Co. who established posts in what was then the colony of New Caledonia. Hudson's Bay Co. absorbed the North West Co. in 1821; in 1843, Fort Victoria was established by James Douglas as a trading post for the company. Rival Br. and Amer. claims to the area were settled when the boundary was set at the 49th parallel by the Oregon Treaty of 1846. Amer. settlers and Western congressmen had pressed for "54°40′ or fight," while Br. claims sought a border at the 42° parallel; 54°40′ had been the Rus.-Amer. line of 1824, and the 42d parallel had marked the Span. Mex. possessions' N reach (the Adams-Onis line of 1819). The Oregon crisis of 1845–1846 focused on the "Oregon triangle," the region bet. the Columbia R. of the 49th parallel—an area originally settled by Br. pioneers and later penetrated by Amer. settlers. The final agreement gave the 49th parallel, whose E anchor, Lake of the Woods (fixed by the Treaty of Utrecht in 1713 by Britain and France) gave about ½ of all Oregon to each claimant and effective outlets to the Pacific. Further controversy resulted in the San Juan Boundary Dispute. Partly as protection against further Amer. expansion, Vancouver Isl. was ceded (1849) by the Hudson's Bay Co. and became a crown colony. In 1858 gold was discovered in the sandbars of the Fraser R. and additional deposits were found on many of its tributaries. The great gold rushes that resulted brought profound changes. Fort Victoria boomed as a supply base for the miners, and the town of Victoria quickly sprang up around it. Officials of the crown came to keep order, and to supervise govt. projects and the building of roads. Some 30,000 miners moved into what was then unorganized territory; this led to the creation (1858) of a new colony on the mainland, called B.C., and the end of the Hudson's Bay Co.'s supremacy. In 1863 the newly settled territory about the Stikine R. was added. In 1866, Vancouver Isl. and B.C. were combined, and in 1871 voted to join the new Can. confederation. The Canadian Pacific Railway finally reached Vancouver in 1885, providing access to new markets, furthering agr., mining, and lumbering; steamship service with the East Asia was inaugurated, and Vancouver grew as a busy port. The opening (1914) of the Panama Canal was a further boost to trade and commerce. A long dispute with the U.S over the Alaska border was finally settled by the Alaska Boundary Commission in 1903. B.C. sends 6 senators (appointed) and 32 representatives (elected) to the natl. parliament. Environmental pollution due to the exploitation of its raw-resource industries is a major issue. The Univ. of B.C. is at Vancouver, the Univ. of Victoria is at Victoria, and Simon Fraser Univ. is at Burnaby. The new Univ. of Northern B.C. has been established in the interior at Prince George.

British Virgin Islands, B.W.I.: see VIRGIN ISLANDS.

British West Indies: see WEST INDIES.

Britt, town (1990 pop. 2,133), Hancock co., N Iowa, near West Branch Iowa R., 10 mi/16 km E of Garner; 43°06′N 93°47′W. Processing of dairy prods.; tankage; mfg. of cabinets. A state park is NE. Inc. 1887.

Brittania Beach, town, SW B.C., W Canada, on E shore of Howe Sound, 26 mi/42 km N of Vancouver. Former copper-mining center (Br. Empire's largest copper producer, closed in 1974). Hydroelectric plant. Tourism; B.C. Mus. of Mining (mus. village).

Brittany Farms-Highlands (BRI-tuh-nee), uninc. town (1990 pop. 2,747), Bucks co., SE Pa., residential suburb 22 mi/35 km N of Philadelphia, on West Branch Neshaminy Creek; 40°16′N 75°12′W. Agr. area on urban fringe.

Britton, town (1990 pop. 1,394), ⊙ Marshall co., NE S.Dak., 42 mi/68 km NE of Aberdeen. Farming and cattle center; dairy prods.; livestock, poultry; wheat, corn; mfg. (transportation equip.). Fort Sisseton and Roy Lake State Parks to SE. Municipal hosp.

Britton (BRIT-uhn), village (1990 pop. 694), Lenawee co., SE Mich., 12 mi/19 km NE of Adrian; 41°59′N 83°49′W. In agr. area.

Broa, Ensenada de la, Cuba: see ENSENADA DE LA BROA.

Broad Brook, Conn.: see EAST WINDSOR.

Broad Creek, navigable tidal stream, c.7 mi/11.3 km long, SW Del.; formed 2 mi/3.2 km E of Laurel by junction of Beaverdam and James creeks; flows W to Nanticoke R. near Md. state line. Sometimes called Laurel R.

Broad Pass, pass, on Parks Highway, S central Alaska, bet. Fairbanks and Anchorage; elev. 2,300 ft/701 m. Crossed by Alaska RR. Also known as Windy Pass.

Broad Ripple, neighborhood, Marion co., central Ind., 7 mi/11.3 km N of downtown Indianapolis, on the Central Canal. Residential, shopping, and entertainment area.

Broad River, tidal channel, c.18 mi/29 km long, in both Beaufort and Jasper cos., S S.C., bet. mainland (W) and Port Royal and Parris isls. (E). Receives Coosawhatchie R. at N head; joins Coosaw R. channel on NE; continues SE to Atlantic Ocean as Port Royal Sound.

Broad River 1 c.90 mi/145 km long, NE Ga.; rises in the Blue Ridge, near Toccoa; flows SE to Savannah R. 21 mi/34 km SE of Elberton; 34°17′N 83°10′W. **2** in N.C. and S.C.; rises in N.C. on E slopes of the Blue Ridge Mts. in E Buncombe co., SE of Asheville; flows SE through Hickory Nut Gorge and L. Lure reservoir, receives Green R. 8 mi/12.9 km SW of Forest City, also receives First Broad R. (c.60 mi/97 km long, rises in NE Rutherford co., flows past Shelby) from N, flows S into S.C., through part of Sunter Natl. Forest and Parr Reservoir, joined by Saluda R. from NW at Columbia to form Congaree R.

Broad Top City, borough (1990 pop. 331), Huntingdon co., S central Pa., 21 mi/34 km SSW of Huntingdon, on Broad Top Mt.; 40°12′N 78°08′W. Agr. (livestock; timber); bituminous coal. Trough Creek State Park to N; Buchanan State Forest to SE; Raystown Reservoir to NW.

Broad Top Mountain, S Huntingdon co., S Pa., at Broad Top City, plateau-like mt. (c.2,000 ft/610 m) of the Appalachian system, c.30 mi/48 km SE of Altoona. Rich bituminous-coal beds.

Broadalbin, village (□ 1 sq mi/2.6 sq km; 1990 pop. 1,397), Fulton co., E central N.Y., 8 mi/12.9 km N of Amsterdam, on Sacandaga Reservoir; 43°03′N 74°12′W. Summer recreational area. Fiber conversion; spray cleaners and soaps; furniture. Settled 1770, inc. 1924.

Broaddus, village (1990 pop. 212), San Augustine co., E Texas, 26 mi/42 km E of Lufkin, in Angelina Natl. Forest; 31°18′N 94°16′W. Timber. Recreation. Sam Rayburn Reservoir to W, S, and SE.

Broadfields, village (1990 pop. 273), Jefferson co., N Ky., residential suburb 7 mi/11.3 km E of downtown Louisville.

Broadkill River, c.15 mi/24 km long, SE Del.; rises 4 mi/6.4 km N of Georgetown, N central Sussex co.; flows E, past Milton (head of navigation), to Del. Bay c.4 mi/6.4 km NW of Lewes. Receives Lewes and Rehoboth Canal 1 mi/1.6 km inland of its mouth.

Broadland, village (1990 pop. 40), Beadle co., E central S.Dak., 10 mi/16 km NNW of Huron.

Broadlands, village (1990 pop. 340), Champaign co., E Ill., 19 mi/31 km SE of Champaign; 39°54′N 88°00′W. In agr. area.

Broadmoor, uninc. town (1990 pop. 3,739), San Mateo co., W Calif., residential suburb 7 mi/11.3 km SW of downtown San Francisco, near Pacific Ocean; 37°42′N 122°29′W. Thornton State Beach to NW; part of Golden Gate Natl. Recreation Area to SE.

Broadmoor, SW suburb of Colorado Springs, El Paso co., on Cheyenne Creek, central Colo.; elev. c.6,200 ft/1,890 m. Absorbed by city of Colorado Springs.

Broadus (BRAH-duhs), village (1990 pop. 572), ⊙ Powder River co., SE Mont., on Powder R. near mouth of Little Powder R., and 70 mi/113 km SSE of Miles City; 45°26′N 105°25′W. Trading point for agr. region; coal mines; cattle, sheep; wheat, oats. Belle Creek Oil Fields to SE. Custer Natl. Forest to W. Powder R. Historical Mus.

Broadview, town (1991 pop. 797), SE Sask., Canada, 90 mi/145 km E of Regina; 50°23′N 102°34′W. Grain elevators; lumbering.

Broadview 1 village (1990 pop. 8,713), Cook co., NE Ill., suburb 8 mi/12.9 km W of downtown Chicago; 41°51′N 87°51′W. Mfg. (bldg. materials, fabricated metal prods., medical equip., glassware, consumer goods, paper prods.), printing. Veterans hosp. nearby. Inc. 1913. **2** village (1990 pop.133), Yellowstone co., S Mont., 27 mi/43 km NW of Billings; 46°06′N 108°53′W. Agr. area (cattle, sheep; grain, sugar beets, beans).

Broadview Heights, city (1990 pop. 12,219), Cuyahoga co., N Ohio, a suburb 13 mi/21 km S of downtown Cleveland; 41°19′N 81°42′W. Inc. 1926.

Broadwater, county (□ 1,238 sq mi/3,206 sq km; 1990 pop. 3,318), W central Mont.; ⊙ Townsend; 46°20′N 111°30′W. Agr. and mining region, drained by Missouri R. (upper part of Canyon Ferry Lake and State Park in N). Missouri R. forms part of SE boundary. Wheat, barley, hay; hogs, sheep; gold. Sections of Helena Natl. Forest in W, N, and E. Formed 1897.

Broadwater, village (1990 pop. 160), Morrill co., W Nebr., 15 mi/24 km ESE of Bridgeport and on North Platte R; 41°36′N 102°50′W. Trout fishing; grain. Remains of prehistoric man nearby.

Broadway 1 town (1990 pop. 973), Lee co., central N.C., 7 mi/11.3 km ESE of Sanford; 35°27′N 79°02′W. Tobacco, cotton, grain; chickens, cattle, hogs; mfg. (tool and die; feeds; printing). Raven Rock State Park to E. **2** town (1990 pop. 1,209), Rockingham co., NW Va., in Shenandoah Valley, 12 mi/19 km NNE of Harrisonburg; 38°36′N 78°47′W. Mfg. (pottery, clothing, crushed stone, lumber), printing, metal fabrication; poultry-packing center; agr. area (dairying; livestock, poultry; grain, soybeans, apples, peaches); timber; limestone.

Broadway, famous thoroughfare in N.Y. city. It extends from Bowling Green near the foot of Manhattan isl. N to 262d St. in the Bronx. Throughout its length Broadway is chiefly a commercial street. In lower Manhattan it runs through the financial center of the country, Chinatown, and Soho; N of Union Sq. (14th St.) it passes a merchandising sect.; further N, Herald Sq., once a focus for major department stores, remains a major retail center; finally around Times Sq. (42d St.), which has undergone significant redevelopment, it enters the theater dist., or the "Great White Way," the most storied portion of Broadway. Further N, it passes Columbus Circle and the Upper West Side, West Harlem,

Washington Heights, and Inwood sects. of Manhattan. Points of interest along Broadway include Trinity Church (Wall St.); St. Paul's Chapel, built 1766 (near City Hall); the Woolworth Bldg. (at Barclay St.); the Lincoln Center for the Performing Arts (64th–66th streets); Columbia Univ. (113th–121st streets); the Columbia-Presbyterian Medical Center (168th St.); and Van Cortlandt Park (at the N end of the city). Broadway was laid out by the Dutch and was the principal street of New Amsterdam; its N stretches in Manhattan were formerly called Bloomingdale Road.

Broadwell, village (1990 pop. 146), Logan co., central Ill., 9 mi/14.5 km SSW of Lincoln; 40°04′N 89°26′W. In agr. area (corn, soybeans; cattle, hogs); bituminous coal.

Brock, village (1990 pop. 143), Nemaha co., SE Nebr., 10 mi/16 km NW of Auburn, on Little Nemaha R; 40°28′N 95°57′W. Dairy and poultry prods.; grain.

Brock Island (□ 414 sq mi/1,072 sq km), NW Franklin dist., N.W.T., N Canada, in Arctic Ocean, off Borden Isls.; 25 mi/40 km long, 20 mi/32 km wide; 77°55′N 114°00′W.

Brocket, village (1990 pop. 81), Ramsey co., NE central N.Dak., 24 mi/39 km ENE of Devils L.; 48°12′N 098°21′W. RR junction to S.

Brockport, village (□ 2 sq mi/5.2 sq km; 1990 pop. 8,749), Monroe co., W N.Y., on the Barge Canal, 15 mi/24 km W of Rochester; 43°12′N 77°56′W. In agr. area; mfg. of glass containers, cleaning materials; nurseries. Seat of State Univ. of N.Y. Col. at Brockport. Inc. 1829.

Brockton (BRAWK-tuhn), industrial city (1990 pop. 92,788), Plymouth co., E Mass.; 42°05′N 71°02′W. Formerly a large shoe and leather-prods. center, it now makes textiles, clothing, machinery and machine tools, plastics, and electrical and electronic equip.; food processing. Has col., art center, and historic mus. State park nearby. Settled c.1700, set off from Bridgewater 1821, inc. as a city 1881.

Brockton, village (1990 pop. 365), Roosevelt co., NE Mont., on Missouri R., 32 mi/51 km E of Wolf Point, in SE part of Fort Peck Indian Reservation; 48°09′N 104°55′W. Wheat, barley, oats, alfalfa; sheep, hogs.

Brockville, city (1991 pop. 21,582), SE Ont., central Canada, on the St. Lawrence R., in rich dairy region; 44°35′N 75°41′W. Mfg. includes telecommunications equip., power tools, pharmaceuticals, and baby foods. Summer resort.

Brockway, village (1990 pop. 60), McCone co., E Mont., on Redwater R., 55 mi/89 km WNW of Glendive. In grain and livestock region.

Brockway, borough (1990 pop. 2,207), Jefferson co., W central Pa., 8 mi/12.9 km N of Du Bois; 41°15′N 78°47′W. Mfg. (glass prods,. lumber, machinery). Agr. area (livestock; corn, hay; dairying); surface bituminous coal. Settled 1822, inc. 1883.

Brocton 1 village (1990 pop. 322), Edgar co., E Ill., 14 mi/23 km WNW of Paris; 39°43′N 87°55′W. Agr. (corn, soybeans, sorghum; cattle, hogs). **2** village (□ 1 sq mi/2.6 sq km; 1990 pop. 1,387), Chautauqua co., extreme W N.Y., near L. Erie, 9 mi/14.5 km SW of Dunkirk; 42°23′N 79°26′W. In grape-growing area; mfg. (machinery for ceramic and woodworking industries); agr. (poultry). A short-lived community of the Brotherhood of the New Life was founded here in 1867 by Thomas L. Harris. Inc. 1894.

Broderick, village, Yolo co., central Calif., on Sacramento R., suburb ½ mi/⁹⁄₁₀ km W of downtown Sacramento and N of West Sacramento. River port in fruit-growing area.

Brodeur Peninsula (bro-DUHR), NW Baffin Isl., N.W.T., N Canada, extends 200 mi/322 km N into Lancaster Sound, bet. Prince Regent Inlet and the Gulf of Boothia (W) and Admiralty Inlet (E); 45 mi/72 km–90 mi/145 km wide; 71°00′–73°52′N 83°58′–90°10′W. Connected with rest of Baffin Isl. by narrow isthmus. Coastal cliffs rise to c.1,000 ft/305 m.

Brodhead 1 (BRAWD-hed), town (1990 pop. 1,140), Rockcastle co., central Ky., on Dix R., 26 mi/42 km SE of Danville; 37°23′N 84°25′W. In agr. area (burley tobacco, corn; livestock; dairying); mfg. (mining equip.).

2 town (1990 pop. 3,165), Green co., S Wis., 20 mi/32 km NW of Beloit, near Sugar R.; 42°37′N 89°22′W. In dairying area; mfg. (agr. and transportation equip.). S terminus of Sugar River State Trail. Inc. 1891.

Brodheadsville (BRAWD-heds-vil), uninc. town (1990 pop. 1,389), Monroe co., E Pa., 11 mi/18 km SW of Stroudsburg; 40°55′N 75°24′W. Mfg. (transportation equip.). Agr. (grain, soybeans; livestock; dairying); resort area. Peasant Valley Airport. Appalachian Trail passes to S on Blue Mt. ridge.

Brodnax (BRAWD-naks), town (1990 pop. 388), Brunswick and Mecklenburg cos., S Va., 5 mi/8 km E of South Hill; 36°42′N 78°01′W. Mfg. (lumber; yarns and textiles, clothing); agr. area (tobacco, cotton, grain, peanuts; livestock); timber.

Brogden, uninc. town (1990 pop. 3,246), Wayne co., E central N.C., residential suburb 3 mi/4.8 km SSW of downtown Goldsboro, on Neuse R; 35°17′N 78°01′W.

Brokaw, village (1990 pop. 224), Marathon co., central Wis., on Wisconsin R., and 4 mi/6.4 km N of Wausau; 45°01′N 89°39′W. Paper milling.

Broken Arrow, city (1990 pop. 58,043), Tulsa and Wagoner cos., NE Okla., suburb 13 mi/21 km SE of Tulsa; 36°02′N 95°47′W. Agr. area to S and E. Mfg. (medical equip., construction materials, machinery, transportation equip., aviation-simulation equip., mining and drilling equip., industrial tapes, decals, molded shapes, stretch film, aircraft-engine parts, fabricated metal prods.). Coal reserves in area. Country Club Airport to N. Founded 1903.

Broken Bow 1 town (1990 pop. 3,778), ⊙ Custer co., central Nebr., 34 mi/55 km N of Lexington and on Mud Creek; 41°24′N 99°38′W. Shipping point for livestock and grain. Mfg. (fabricated metal prods., medical supplies, machinery). Settled 1880, inc. as city 1888. **2** town (1990 pop. 3,961), McCurtain co., extreme SE Okla., 9 mi/14.5 km NNE of Idabel; 34°01′N 94°44′W. In agr. (vegetables and fruit; poultry) and timber area. Lumber milling, cotton ginning; mfg. (wood prods., machine-shop prods., timber, pilings and poles, consumer goods), poultry processing. Broken Arrow L. reservoir, Hochatown and Beavers Bend state parks, and McCurtain Co. Wilderness Area to N, in Ouachian Mts. Settled 1910, inc. 1912.

Broken Bow Lake, reservoir, McCurtain co., SE Okla., on Mountain Fork R., 20 mi/32 km NNE of Idabel; c.20 mi/32 km long; 34°08′N 94°41′W. Max. capacity 1,368,800 acre-ft. Formed by Broken Bow Lake Dam (208 ft/63 m high), built (1968) by the Army Corps of Engineers for flood control, water supply and power generation. McCurtain Co. Wilderness Area on N shore, Beavers Bend State Resort park on SE shore, and Hoochatown State Park on W shore.

Brome, county (□ 488 sq mi/1,264 sq km; pop.), S Que., E Canada, on U.S. (Vt.) border; ⊙ Knowlton; 45°10′N 72°30′W.

Brome, village (1991 pop. 290), S Que., E Canada, 16 mi/26 km SE of Granby. Dairying; resort.

Bromide (BROM-eid), village (1990 pop. 162), on border bet. Coal and Johnston cos., S Okla., 27 mi/43 km SSE of Ada; 34°25′N 96°29′W. In farm area.

Bromley, town (1990 pop. 1,137), Kenton co., N Ky., residential suburb 3 mi/4.8 km WSW of Cincinnati (Ohio), and 2 mi/3.2 km W of Covington (Ky.), on the Ohio R. (Anderson Ferry 6 mi/9.7 km to W); 39°04′N 84°33′W. Mfg. (signs; machining, printing and publishing).

Bromley Mountain, ski resort, Manchester town, Bennington co., SW Vt., in the Green Mts.

Bromont, village (1991 pop. 3,408), S central Que., E Canada, 6 mi/10 km SSE of Granby, on Yamaska R. Mt. Bromont, site of downhill skiing events, 1976 Montreal Winter Olympics. Popular recreation area for Montrealers.

Bromptonville, town (1991 pop. 3,190), S Que., E Canada, on St. Francis R., and 5 mi/8 km NNW of Sherbrooke; 45°28′N 71°56′W. Lumbering; metalworking. Hydroelectric plant.

Bronaugh (BRO-naw), town (1990 pop. 211), Vernon co.,

W Mo., 12 mi/19 km SSW of Nevada; 37°41′N 94°28′W. Agr. (sorgum, wheat; cattle); coal in area.

Bronson, town (1990 pop. 2,342), Branch co., S Mich., 11 mi/18 km SW of Coldwater; 41°52′N 85°11′W. Shipping point for agr. area; mfg. of metal prods., steering systems, trailer hitches. Inc. as village 1866, as city 1934.

Bronson 1 village (□ 4 sq mi/10.4 sq km; 1990 pop. 875), ⊙ Levy co., N central Fla., 23 mi/37 km SW of Gainesville; 29°26′N 82°38′W. Lumber; naval stores. **2** village (1990 pop. 209), Woodbury co., NW Iowa, 13 mi/21 km SE of Iowa City; 42°24′N 96°12′W. Agr. area (corn; cattle, hogs). **3** village (1990 pop. 343), Bourbon co., SE Kansas, 18 mi/29 km W of Fort Scott; 37°53′N 95°04′W. Grain; livestock; dairying. Bourbon State Fishing L. to S. **4** village (1990 pop. 259), Sabine co., E Texas, 40 mi/64 km E of Lufkin; 31°21′N 94°00′W. Cattle; timber. Sabine Natl. Forest to E; Angelina Natl. Forest to W; Sam Rayburn Reservoir to SW.

Bronson, Minn.: see LAKE BRONSON.

Bronston, uninc. village (1990 pop. 400), Pulaski co., S Ky., 8 mi/12.9 km SSW of Somerset, on Cumberland R., on upper reach of L. Cumberland reservoir. Recreation area. Burley tobacco, grain; livestock; dairying. Mfg. (lumber; meat processing).

Bronte, town (1990 pop. 962), Coke co., W Texas, 30 mi/48 km N of San Angelo; elev. 1,893 ft/577 m; 31°53′N 100°17′W. Old Fort Chadbourne is c.7 mi/11.3 km N. Oil and gas; cattle, sheep; cotton; mfg. (natural-gas-collecting equip., apparel). Oak Creek Reservoir to N.

Bronwood, town (1990 pop. 513), Terrell co., SW Ga., 6 mi/9.7 km NE of Dawson; 31°50′N 84°22′W.

Bronx River, c.20 mi/32 km long, SE N.Y.; issues from Kensico Reservoir; flows SW through the Bronx, past the Bronx Zoo and Bronx Botanical Gardens, into the East R. The Bronx River Parkway, completed in 1924 as the 1st limited-access parkway in the U.S., parallels a portion of the river.

Bronx, the (BRAWNKS), borough (□ 57 sq mi/148 sq km; 1990 pop. 1,203,789) of N.Y. city, coextensive with Bronx co., SE N.Y.; 40°51′N 73°53′W. The name comes from Jonas Bronck, who purchased the land from Native Americans in 1639. N.Y. city acquired the Bronx, which had been the lower portion of Westchester co., in 2 stages in 1875 and 1895. With the consolidation of N.Y. city in 1898 it became a separate borough; the co. was not organized until 1912. The only mainland borough of N.Y. city, it comprises the S part of a peninsula bordered W by the Hudson R., SW by the Harlem R. (which separates it from Manhattan), S by the East R., and E by L.I. Sound. Among the many bridges linking the borough to Manhattan and Queens are the Henry Hudson, the Triborough, the Bronx-Whitestone, and the Throgs Neck. The borough is also connected to Manhattan by subway and commuter RR lines. With the extension of mass transit to the Bronx in the early 20th cent., the pop. of the sparsely settled area rapidly increased. The Bronx became home to many immigrants from E and S Europe; pop. has become more ethnically diverse since World War II and now has a majority of Hispanic and Afr.-Amer. residents, with growing Afr. and Caribbean communities. The declining local economy led to a deterioration of housing, and the term "South Bronx" became synonymous with urban blight. Attempts at renovation have been successful in many neighborhoods characterized by housing abandonment for much of the 1970s and 1980s. Although the Bronx is no longer an extensive shipping, warehouse, and factory center, the Hunts Point Terminal Market is the major wholesale produce center for N.Y. city. Areas of interest in the borough include Riverdale, Co-op City, Parkchester, Grand Concourse, City Isl., Fort Schuyler, and Mott Haven. Large areas of the borough are set aside for parks, notably Bronx Park, with the N.Y. Zoological Park (Bronx Zoo) and the N.Y. Botanical Garden; Van Cortlandt Park, and Pelham Bay Park, with Orchard Beach on L.I. Sound. Among the institutions of higher learning in the Bronx are Fordham Univ., Manhattan Col., Albert Einstein Col. of Medicine (of Yeshiva Univ.), the N.Y. State Maritime Col., Herbert H. Lehman Col. and

Hostos Community Col. of the City Univ. of N.Y. Other points of interest are Yankee Stadium (1923) and the Edgar Allan Poe cottage (1812).

Bronxville, upper-income suburb (1990 pop. 6,028) N of N.Y. city, Westchester co., SE N.Y., bet. Mount Vernon (S) and Tuckahoe (N); part of Eastchester town; 40°56′N 73°49′W. Seat of Sarah Lawrence Col., Concordia Col. Inst., and a school for girls. Settled 1664, inc. 1898.

Bronx-Whitestone Bridge, vehicular suspension bridge across East R. bet. SE Bronx borough and Whitestone sect. of Queens borough of N.Y. city, SE N.Y.; 40°48′N 73°50′W. Link bet. New England and L.I. highways. Completed 1939; 3,770 ft/1,149 m long, with 2,300-ft/701-m center span 135 ft/41 m above water.

Brook, town (1990 pop. 899), Newton co., NW Ind., near Iroquois R., 8 mi/12.9 km NNE of Kentland; 40°52′N 87°22′W. In agr. area. Meat processing; transportation equip., plastic prods. Settled 1832.

Brook Farm (bruk FAHRM), an experimental utopian farm, 1841–1847, at West Roxbury (now part of Boston), Mass., based on cooperative living. Founded by George Ripley, a Unitarian minister, the farm was initially financed by a joint-stock company with 24 shares of stock at $500 per share. Each member was to take part in the manual labor in an attempt to make the group self-sufficient. Intellectual life was stimulating, with such members as Nathaniel Hawthorne, John S. Dwight, Charles A. Dana, and Isaac Hecker, and such visitors as Ralph Waldo Emerson, W. E. Channing, Margaret Fuller, Horace Greeley, and Orestes Brownson. Brook Farm was mainly an outgrowth of Unitarianism, although most of the members had left that church and were advocates of the literary and philosophical movement known as Transcendentalism. Economically, the community's excellent school was the most successful part of the venture (anticipating John Dewey's progressive-education ideas of learning from experience); agr. showed little profit because of the sandy soil and the inexperience of the farmers. The popularity of the doctrines of Charles Fourier led, especially through the efforts of Albert Brisbane, to Brook Farm's conversion to a phalanx in 1844. The group, however, did not long survive the financial disaster of the burning (1846) of the uncompleted central bldg. The *Harbinger* (1845–1849), printed at Brook Farm and edited by Ripley, was rather a Fourierist weekly newspaper and was continued in N.Y. city with Parke Godwin as editor after 1847.

Brook Park, city (1990 pop. 22,865), Cuyahoga co., NE Ohio, a SW suburb of Cleveland; 41°25′N 81°49′W. Major office complex here; Cleveland municipal airport. Major transportation equip. and casting plants. Inc. 1914.

Brook Park, village (1990 pop. 125), Pine co., E Minn., 9 mi/14.5 km NNW of Pine City; 45°56′N 93°04′W. RR junction; agr. (dairying; livestock; oats).

Brookdale, uninc. town (1990 pop. 5,339), Orangeburg co., S central S.C., residential suburb 2 mi/3.2 km NNE of Orangeburg; 33°31′N 80°50′W.

Brookdale, uninc. village, Santa Cruz co., W Calif., in Santa Cruz Mts., 12 mi/19 km NNW of Santa Cruz, on San Lorenza R. Big Basin Redwoods State Park to NW.

Brooke, county (□ 92 sq mi/238 sq km; 1990 pop. 26,992), N W.Va., in N Panhandle; ☉ Wellsburg; 40°16′N 80°34′W. Bounded W by Ohio R. (Ohio state line), E by Pa. Mfg. at Wellsburg, Follansbee, and Weirton. Coal mines, natural-gas and oil wells. Some agr. (grain, alfalfa, hay, apples); cattle; dairying. Drained by Cross and Buffalo creeks. Includes part of city of Weirton in N. Part of Castleman Run Wildlife Management Area in SE. Formed 1797.

Brooker, village (1990 pop. 312), Bradford co., N central Fla., 15 mi/24 km N of Gainesville; 29°53′N 82°19′W.

Brookeville, town (1990 pop. 54), Montgomery co., central Md., 20 mi/32 km N of Washington, D.C.; 39°11′N 77°04′W. Founded in 1780, it was an addition to Brooke Grove, surveyed (1762) by James Brooke, a member of the "Court Circle" of St. Mary's, the original settlement

in Md. The Brookes were among the prominent early Catholic families of the colony.

Brookfield 1 city (1990 pop. 4,888), Linn co., N central Mo., 40 mi/64 km SW of Kirksville; 39°47′N 93°04′W. Corn, wheat, soybeans; cattle; mfg. (plastic prods., fabricated metal prods., ductwork, brake cables, apparel, pharmaceuticals). Pershing State Park at nearby Laclede. Founded 1859. **2** city (1990 pop. 35,184), Waukesha co., SE Wis., a suburb 10 mi/16 km W of downtown Milwaukee; 43°03′N 88°07′W. Although principally a residential community, Brookfield has undergone suburban expansion since 1975 with its iron foundries and mfg. (electronic equip., fabricated metal prods., safety ladders, water-softener components, polishes and detergents, burial vaults; plastic fabrication). Also a center for retailing and business. Inc. 1954.

Brookfield 1 resort town (1990 pop. 14,113), Fairfield co., SW Conn., bet. L. Candlewood and the Housatonic R., on Still R., and 6 mi/9.7 km NNE of Danbury; 41°28′N 73°23′W. Lithography; mfg. of connectors, fabricated metal prods.; machine and tool-making shops; electronic-equip. assembly; handicraft center. Inc. 1788. **2** town (1990 pop. 2,968), including Brookfield village, Worcester co., S central Mass., 15 mi/24 km WSW of Worcester; 42°12′N 72°06′W. Recreation (Quaboag Pond); mfg. (wire, cables); dairying. Settled 1664, inc. 1718. **3** town (1990 pop. 518), Carroll co., SE N.H., 17 mi/27 km NNW of Rochester; 43°33′N 71°05′W. Drained by Branch R., Pike Brook. Agr. (poultry, eggs; vegetables, apples; dairying; nursery crops); mfg. (circuit boards). **4** town (1990 pop. 1,089), Orange co., central Vt., in Green Mts., 10 mi/16 km NW of Chelsea and on Second Branch of White R.; 44°01′N 72°35′W. Allis State Park nearby. Cross-country ski center is here.

Brookfield, village (1990 pop. 18,876), Cook co., NE Ill., a residential suburb 8 mi/12.9 km WSW of downtown Chicago; 41°49′N 87°51′W. Mfg. of fabricated metal (esp. aluminum) prods. The noted Chicago Zoological Park (Brookfield Zoo) is here. Inc. 1893.

Brookford, village (1990 pop. 451), Catawba co., W central N.C., residential suburb 2 mi/3.2 km S of Hickory, on Henry Fork R.; 35°42′N 81°20′W. Mfg. (textiles).

Brookgreen, former plantation, Georgetown co., E S.C., bet. Waccamaw R. (W) and the Atlantic Ocean (E), 15 mi/24 km NE of Georgetown. Brookgreen Gardens (□ 6 sq mi/15.5 sq km), created from parts of 4 old estates, gardens and sculpture attract tourists.

Brookhaven, city (1990 pop. 10,243), ☉ Lincoln co., SW Miss., 50 mi/80 km SSW of Jackson; 31°34′N 90°27′W. RR junction. In a dairy, timber, and agr. area (cotton, corn; poultry, cattle); mfg. (wood prods., apparel, lumber, wire cloth, asphalt; machining). Oil and gas fields are nearby. Homochitto Natl. Forest to W. Inc. 1859.

Brookhaven, uninc. town (1990 pop. 3,836), Monongalia co., N W.Va., residential suburb 3 mi/4.8 km SE of Morgantown, on Deckers Creek; 39°36′N 79°52′W.

Brookhaven, village (□ 6 sq mi/15.5 sq km; 1990 pop. 3,118), Suffolk co., SE N.Y., on S shore of L.I., on Bellport Bay (inlet of Great South Bay), 5 mi/8 km ENE of Patchogue; 40°46′N 72°54′W. Brookhaven Natl. Laboratory for atomic research is c.7 mi/11.3 km N.

Brookhaven (BRUK-HA-ven), borough (1990 pop. 8,567), Delaware co., SE Pa., residential suburb 13 mi/21 km SW of downtown Philadelphia and 2 mi/3.2 km NW of Chester, near Ridley Creek; 39°52′N 75°23′W. Light mfg. Inc. 1945.

Brookhaven National Laboratory, scientific research center, Upton, L.I., SE N.Y.; 40°52′N 72°53′W. Founded 1947 by Associated Universities Inc., which is a management corporation sponsored by 9 E U.S. univs. This corporation runs the laboratory under a contract with the U.S. Atomic Energy Commission. At Brookhaven an internatl. staff conducts multidisciplinary scientific work, e.g., fundamental studies of atomic nuclei, investigations of the effects and uses of nuclear radiation, and research and development in nuclear technology. Among the laboratory's equip. are a number of highly sophisticated nuclear reactors, particle accelerators, and electronic computers. The facilities also include a medical-research center for work in nuclear medicine.

Science students are drawn from univs. throughout the world to work at the laboratory as part of their training. In 1997 its contract with the Atomic Energy Commission was withdrawn, and new sponsors are being sought.

Brookings, county (□ 804 sq mi/2,082 sq km; 1990 pop. 25,207), E S.Dak., on Minn. state line; ☉ Brookings. Agr. area drained by Big Sioux R. and Deer Creek. Corn, wheat, soybeans, flax; dairy prods.; cattle, hogs, poultry; honey; gravel and concrete. Formed 1862.

Brookings, town (1990 pop. 4,440), Curry co., SW Oregon, on the Pacific Ocean, 53 mi/85 km SW of Grants Pass, 6 mi/9.7 km NW of Calif. state line, at mouth of Chetco R.; 42°03′N 124°17′W. Lumber. Printing and publishing. Poultry, fish; sheep, cattle. Azalea State Park NE of town; Loeb State Park to NE; Winchuck State Wayside to SE; Harris Bench and Samuel H. Boardman state parks to NW; Siskiyou Natl. Forest to E.

Brookland, town (1990 pop. 919), Craighead co., NE Ark., 8 mi/12.9 km NE of Jonesboro; 35°53′N 90°34′W.

Brookland, residential sect. in NE Washington, D.C., E of Catholic Univ. Begun in 1887 on the old Brooks Estate, the area attracted many Ital. and Irish Catholics. Catholic Univ. opened in 1889. Now largely a middle-class Afr.-Amer. neighborhood.

Brookland, S.C.: see WEST COLUMBIA.

Brookland Terrace, village, New Castle co., N Del., residential suburb 4 mi/6.4 km W of downtown Wilmington, SW of Willow Run.

Brooklawn, residential borough (1990 pop. 1,805), Camden co., SW N.J., on Delaware R. just below Camden; 39°52′N 75°07′W. Built in World War I to house shipyard workers; inc. 1924.

Brooklet, town (1990 pop. 1,013), Bulloch co., E Ga., 8 mi/12.9 km SE of Statesboro; 32°23′N 81°40′W. Mfg. includes plastic prods.; millwork.

Brooklin, town (1990 pop. 785), Hancock co., S Maine, on Eggemoggin Beach and opposite Deer Isle, 20 mi/32 km SSW of Ellsworth; 44°15′N 68°32′W. In agr., recreational area.

Brookline 1 town (1990 pop. 54,718), Norfolk co., E Mass., suburb adjacent to (W of) Boston; 42°19′N 71°08′W. Settled 1630s, set off from Boston and inc. 1705, it was known as "Muddy River" until separating from Boston. The town is known for its affluent pop., and the 1st U.S. country club was opened here. Small businesses. The birthplace of President John F. Kennedy here is a natl. historic site. Other points of interest are the poet Amy Lowell's home and an antique auto mus. Site of Pine Manor Junior, Hebrew, and Hellenic cols. Lars Anderson Park; Frederic Law Olmsted Natl. Historic Site. **2** town (1990 pop. 2,410), Hillsborough co., S N.H., 10 mi/16 km WSW of Nashua; 42°44′N 71°40′W. Bounded S by Mass. state line; drained by Nissitissit R. and Spaulding Brook. Pumpkins, fruit, vegetables, nursery prods., corn; livestock, poultry; dairying. Mfg. (sewn prods., parachute equip., consumer goods, lumber, tool and die). **3** town (1990 pop. 403), Windham co., SE Vt., 4 mi/6.4 km NE of Newfane; 43°00′N 72°36′W.

Brookline, uninc. village, Jackson co., S Mich., suburb 2 mi/3.2 km SW of Jackson.

Brookline, Pa.: see HAVERFORD.

Brooklyn, city (1990 pop. 11,706), Cuyahoga co., N Ohio, a S suburb of Cleveland; 41°27′N 81°46′W. Inc. 1927.

Brooklyn 1 town (1990 pop. 6,681), Windham co., E Conn., on Quinebaug R., 15 mi/24 km ENE of Willimantic; 41°47′N 71°57′W. In agr. area; electrical prods. Includes East Brooklyn village (1990 pop. 1,481). Has 18th-cent. houses, monument to Gen. Israel Putnam, whose farm and tavern are here. Settled c.1703, inc. 1786. **2** town (1990 pop. 1,162), Morgan co., central Ind., on Whitelick Creek, 9 mi/14.5 km NNE of Martinsville; 39°32′N 86°22′W. In agr. area; brick, tile. **3** town (1990 pop. 1,439), Poweshiek co., central Iowa, 10 mi/16 km NNE of Montezuma; 41°43′N 92°26′W. In livestock and grain area. Inc. 1869. **4** town (1990 pop. 789), on border bet. Green and Dane cos., S Wis., 15 mi/24 km S of

Madison; 42°51'N 89°22'W. Dairy; livestock, poultry farms; makes condensed milk.

Brooklyn, village, SW N.S., E Canada, on Liverpool Harbour, at mouth of Mersey R., opposite Liverpool. Paper milling.

Brooklyn 1 village (1990 pop. 1,144), suburb within St. Louis metropolitan dist., St. Clair co., SW Ill., on the Mississippi R., 1 mi/1.6 km N of East St. Louis; 38°38'N 90°10'W. Also called Lovejoy (P.O.). Inc. 1873. **2** village (1990 pop. 1,027), Jackson co., S Mich., 13 mi/21 km SE of Jackson; 42°06'N 84°15'W. Mfg. (machinery, construction materials, fabricated metal prods.). W.S. Hays State Park to SE; Michigan Internatl. Speedway to SE on Vineyard L.

Brooklyn, borough of N.Y. city (☐ 71 sq mi/184 sq km; 1990 pop. 2,300,664), coextensive with Kings co., SE N.Y., at the W extremity of L.I.; became a borough of N.Y. city in 1898; 40°38'N 73°57'W. Residential and industrial region, with the largest pop. of the city's 5 boroughs; among its mfg. are machinery, apparel, paper prods., and chemicals. Center of important foreign and domestic commerce; has extensive waterfront facilities. The Brooklyn, Manhattan, and Williamsburg bridges span the East R., linking the borough to Manhattan; beneath the river are the Brooklyn-Battery Tunnel (for vehicular traffic) and subway tunnels. The Verrazano-Narrows Bridge connects the borough with Staten Isl. The Dutch and English settled the area in 1636 and 1637; about 9 years later Du. farmers established the hamlet of Brueckelen, near the present Borough Hall. By 1664, 6 towns had been established: Breuckelen (the name was later anglicized to Brooklyn), Bushwick, Flatbush, Gravesend, and New Utrecht. Kings co. was est. 1683; Brooklyn was inc. 1816 as a village (Brooklyn Ferry) and was chartered as a city in 1834. In the 1830s Brooklyn Heights became one of the 1st suburbs accessible to N.Y. city by ferry. Brooklyn absorbed many settlements and villages, such as Flatbush, New Utrecht, and Gravesend (all in the 17th cent.). After annexing Williamsburg and Bushwick in 1855, Brooklyn became the 3d-largest city in the U.S. and continued to absorb other local villages until it became coextensive with Kings co. in 1896. In 1898, when it became a borough of N.Y. city, its pop. was 830,000. Immigration doubled its pop. over the next 20 years. Brooklyn remains a borough of many well-defined neighborhoods, from the gentrified brownstone communities of Park Slope and Cobble Hill to Bedford-Stuyvesant, the largest Afr.-Amer. neighborhood in the city (and one the largest in the U.S.). Brighton Beach and Manhattan Beach have a large community of Rus. Jews, and there are also neighborhoods of Hispanics, Italians, Poles, Hasidic Jews, Russians, Chinese, W. Indians, and other ethnic groups. Among the numerous educational institutions in the borough are Brooklyn Col. of the City Univ. of N.Y., Polytechnic Inst. of N.Y., Pratt Inst., St. Joseph's Col., L.I. Univ., and Brooklyn Law School. The N.Y. Naval Shipyard (popularly known as the Brooklyn Navy Yard) was located on the East R. from 1801 until its closing in the late 1960s. It has been converted to an industrial and commercial park. Its closing coincided with the decline of Brooklyn as a port. Fort Hamilton (built 1831 as a harbor defense) overlooks the Narrows of N.Y. Bay. Near beautiful Prospect Park, the scene of fierce fighting in the Amer. Revolution, is the main bldg. of the Brooklyn Public Lib. Also in that area are the Brooklyn Mus., the Brooklyn Botanic Garden, and the innovative Brooklyn Acad. of Music. The Brooklyn Children's Mus. is in Crown Heights. Ebbets Field in the borough was home to the Brooklyn Dodgers baseball team until 1958, when the team moved to Los Angeles. Among the many structures that give the borough its appellation "City of Churches" are the Plymouth Church of the Pilgrims, where Henry Ward Beecher preached. Other points of interest in the borough include Coney Isl., with its beach and amusement park; the Brooklyn Historical Society; the N.Y. Aquarium (at Coney Isl.); and the Lefferts Homestead (1777). Marine Park and parts of Jamaica Bay are included in Gateway Natl. Recreation Area. Walt Whitman worked as an editor for the *Daily Eagle*, a noted newspaper published in Brooklyn from 1841 until 1955.

Brooklyn Bridge, vehicular suspension bridge, N.Y. city, SE N.Y., southernmost of the bridges across the East R., bet. lower Manhattan and Brooklyn; 40°42'N 73°59'W. Built 1869–1883. The achievement of J. A. Roebling and his son W. A. Roebling, it has a span of 1,595 ft/486 m. It was the 1st steel-wire suspension bridge in the world and was the world's longest suspension bridge at the time of its completion.

Brooklyn Center, city (1990 pop. 28,887), Hennepin co., SE Minn., a suburb 7 mi/11.3 km NNW of downtown Minneapolis, on Mississippi R.; 45°04'N 93°19'W. Drained by Shingle Creek. Area has been marked by suburban and economic growth since the 1970s. Mfg. (grinding wheels, custom banners, electrical equip., construction materials, laboratory equip., batteries, apparel), printing, packaging. Inc. 1911.

Brooklyn Heights, village (1990 pop. 1,450), Cuyahoga co., N Ohio, a S suburb of Cleveland, adjacent to Brooklyn; 41°26'N 81°41'W.

Brooklyn Heights, a residential sect. of NW Brooklyn borough of N.Y. city, SE N.Y.; 40°42'N 73°59'W. Overlooks harbor and Manhattan skyline. World hq. of Jehovah's Witnesses is here. Seat of St. Francis Col. Plymouth Church of the Pilgrims (1849) was an important center of the abolitionist movement and the Underground RR.

Brooklyn Park, city (1990 pop. 56,381), Hennepin co., SE Minn., a suburb 9 mi/14.5 km NNW of downtown Minneapolis, on Mississippi R.; 45°06'N 93°20'W. Drained by Shingle Creek. Brooklyn Park has been marked by significant industrial and pop. growth. Mfg. (machinery, wood prods., bakers prods., fabricated metal prods., tools, feeders, medical supplies, pharmaceutical prods.), printing and publishing. Seat of North Hennepin Community Col. and Suburban Hennepin Technical Col. Coon Rapids Dam (Regional Park) in NE, on Mississippi R. Chartered as a city 1969.

Brooklyn-Battery Tunnel, vehicular tunnel, N.Y. city, SE N.Y., bet. the Battery at S tip of Manhattan and NW Brooklyn at Hamilton Ave. and then to the 33-mi/53-km-long Belt Parkway system of highways encircling Brooklyn and Queens; 40°42'N 74°00'W. Under SW entrance to East R. just NE of Governors Isl.; its 1.7-mi/2.7-km length required construction of ventilation shaft which appears at the surface as a small mid-channel isl. in the East R. Longest auto tunnel in N. Amer. The construction of 2 parallel tunnels was begun in 1941, halted during World War II, and completed in 1950 at a total cost of $80 million. The major link bet. Manhattan and Staten Isl., the tunnel is used by 60,000 vehicles per day.

Brooklyn-Queens Expressway (BQE), SE N.Y., Brooklyn and Queens boroughs of N.Y. city, extreme W end of L.I. Short but vital 11-mi/18 km highway; Interstate Route 278 (I-278); partly elevated, partly depressed; from Verrazano-Narrows Bridge N to Astoria Park near La Guardia Airport and Triborough Bridge. When roadbed was being built in Brooklyn Heights in 1951, BQE was placed below grade, permitting construction of a wide, straight cantilevered esplanade, called the Promenade, over 3 levels of traffic and allowing pedestrians onto the E side, offering impressive views of the Manhattan skyline and harbor to the W.

Brookneal, town (1990 pop. 1,344), Campbell co., SW central Va., 27 mi/43 km SE of Lynchburg, on Falling R., 2 mi/3.2 km N of its mouth on Roanoke R.; 37°02'N 78°57'W. RR junction; mfg. (lumber, fleecewear, textiles, hardwood flooring, furniture); tobacco market; agr. area (tobacco, grain, soybeans; cattle; dairying). Grave and former estate ("Red Hill") of Patrick Henry to E. Brookneal Fish Hatchery is here.

Brookport, city (1990 pop. 1,070), Massac co., extreme S Ill., on Ohio R. (bridged here), 4 mi/6.4 km NW of Paducah (Ky.), 5 mi/8 km ESE of Metropolis; 37°07'N 88°37'W. Trade center for agr. area. Inc. 1888.

Brookridge, town (1990 pop. 2,805), Hernando co., W central Fla., 6 mi/9.7 km W of Brooksville.

Brooks 1 county (☐ 492; 1990 pop. 15,398), S Ga.; ⊙ Quitman; 30°51'N 83°35'W. Bounded S by Fla. state line, E by Little and Withlacoochee rivers. Coastal plain agr. prods. include tobacco, cotton, corn, peanuts; cattle, hogs. Mfg. includes apparel and other textile prods. Formed 1858. **2** county (☐ 943 sq mi/2,442 sq km; 1990 pop. 8,204), S Texas; ⊙ Falfurrias; 27°02'N 98°12'W. Drained in NE by Los Olmos Creek, in center by Palo Blanco and Baluarte creeks. Diversified irrigated agr. (watermelons, sorghum, corn; beef cattle; dairying). Exotic fowl (ostriches, emus) raised. Oil and natural-gas fields. Formed 1911.

Brooks, town (1991 pop. 9,433), S Alta., W Canada, near L. Newell (10 mi/16 km long, 5 mi/8 km wide), 65 mi/105 km NNW of Medicine Hat, in irrigated region; 50°34'N 111°54'W. Natural-gas production; alfalfa-seed processing, ranching.

Brooks 1 town (1990 pop. 328), Fayette co., W central Ga., 12 mi/19 km WNW of Griffin; 33°17'N 84°28'W. **2** town (1990 pop. 2,464), Bullitt co., NW Ky., suburb 13 mi/21 km S of downtown Louisville; 38°04'N 85°43'W. Burley tobacco, grain; livestock; dairying. Mfg. (candle holders, machinery, construction materials, wood prods., plastic prods.). **3** town (1990 pop. 900), Waldo co., S Maine, 10 mi/16 km NNW of Belfast; 44°32'N 69°07'W. In recreational area.

Brooks 1 village (1990 pop. 158), Lake co., NW Minn., 11 mi/18 km ESE of Red Lake Falls, on Brooks Creek; 47°48'N 96°00'W. Agr. (grain, sunflowers, sugar beets, alfalfa, potatoes; cattle). **2** uninc. village (1990 pop. 490), Marion co., NW Oregon, 7 mi/11.3 km NNE of Salem. Dairying; poultry; fruit, vegetables, berries, nurseries. Mfg. (frozen fruits and vegetables).

Brooks Mount (11,940 ft/3,639 m), S central Alaska, in Alaska Range, in Mt. McKinley Natl. Park, 140 mi/225 km N of Anchorage; 63°11'N 150°39'W.

Brooks Peninsula, SW B.C., W Canada, on NW Vancouver Isl., forming Brooks (NW) and Checleset (SE) bays; 12 mi/19 km long, 6 mi/10 km wide. W extremity is Cape Cook (50°07'N 127°55'W).

Brooks Range, mountain chain, northernmost part of the Rocky Mts., extending about 600 mi/970 km E-W across N Alaska. Mt. Chamberlin (9,020 ft/2,749 m), near the Can. border, is the highest peak. While physiographically part of the Rockies, its origins are believed to be quite different, having its beginnings in Arctic Canada, then moving SW into Alaska and undergoing uplift in the Eastern Brooks Range (Romanzoff Uplift). Rugged, barren, snow-covered, and uninhabited, Brooks Range separates the oil-rich Arctic coastal plain from the Yukon R. basin. An oil pipeline was built across the range in 1977; it begins at Prudhoe Bay in the N and extends to the port of Valdez, in S Alaska. Source of numerous minerals including gold.

Brooksburg, town (1990 pop. 79), Jefferson co., SE Ind., near Ohio R., 8 mi/12.9 km E of Madison; 38°44'N 85°14'W. In agr. area.

Brookshire, town (1990 pop. 2,922), Waller co., SE Texas, 35 mi/56 km W of Houston; elev. 168 ft/51 m; 29°46'N 95°57'W. Cotton, rice; cattle; mfg. (machinery, foods). Inc. after 1940.

Brookside, uninc. city (1990 pop. 15,307), New Castle co., N Del., residential suburb 10 mi/16 km WSW of downtown Wilmington and 3 mi/4.8 km SE of Newark; 39°40'N 75°44'W. Small industrial park and shopping centers.

Brookside 1 town (1990 pop. 1,365), Jefferson co., N central Ala., 11 mi/18 km NW of Birmingham. Coal mines in vicinity. **2** (BRUK-seid), uninc. town (1990 pop. 2,200), Erie co., NW Pa., residential suburb 5 mi/8 km E of Erie and 1 mi/1.6 km SE of Lake Erie (Great Lakes); 42°08'N 79°59'W. Pa. State Univ.–Behrend Campus to S.

Brookside 1 village (1990 pop. 183), Fremont co., S central Colo., near Arkansas R., suburb 2 mi/3.2 km SE of Cañon City; elev. c. 5,240 ft/1,597 m; 38°24'N 105°11'W. **2** village, Harlan co., SE Ky., in the Cumberland Mts., on Clover Fork of Cumberland R. and 3 mi/4.8 km E of Harlan. Bituminous coal. **3** village (1990 pop. 703), Belmont co., E Ohio, 4 mi/6 km N of Bellaire, on small Wheeling Creek; 40°04'N 80°47'W.

Brookside Village, village (1990 pop. 1,470), Brazoria co., SE Texas, residential suburb 11 mi/18 km S of downtown Houston, adjacent to its S city limits, on Clear Creek; 29°35′N 95°19′W.

Brookston, town (1990 pop. 1,804), White co., NW central Ind., 11 mi/18 km SW of Monticello; 40°36′N 86°52′W. In agr. area. Mfg. (machinery, paper prods.).

Brookston, village (1990 pop. 107), St. Louis co., E Minn., 23 mi/37 km W of Duluth, on St. Louis R. near mouth of Cloquet R.; 46°52′N 92°35′W. RR junction to W. Potatoes, oats, alfalfa; livestock; dairying. At N end of Fond du Lac Indian Reservation.

Brooksville 1 town (□ 4 sq mi/10.4 sq km; 1990 pop. 7,440), ⊙ Hernando co., W central Fla., c.40 mi/64 km N of Tampa; 28°33′N 82°23′W. RR junction; shipping center for citrus-fruit and limestone area; packing houses, cannery, concrete plant, sawmill. Nearby are Devil's Punch Bowl, an arid sink, and Weekiwachee Spring, which forms a river flowing 12 mi/19 km to Gulf of Mexico. Inc. 1925. **2** town (1990 pop. 760), Hancock co., S Maine, 20 mi/32 km SW of Ellsworth; 44°21′N 68°45′W. In recreational area. **3** town (1990 pop. 1,098), Noxubee co., E Miss., 20 mi/32 km SSW of Columbus; 33°13′N 88°34′W. In agr. (cotton, grain, soybeans; cattle; dairying) and timber area. Post office name formerly Brookville. Aliceville L. reservoir (Miss.-Ala. state line) to E; Noxubee Natl. Wildlife Refuge to W.

Brooksville, village (1990 pop. 670), ⊙ Bracken co., N Ky., 24 mi/39 km NNE of Cynthiana; 38°40′N 84°04′W. In agr. area (burley tobacco, corn; dairying; poultry); light mfg. Walcott Covered Bridge to N.

Brookton, township, Washington co., E Maine, Brookton village, on Baskahegan L., and c.55 mi/89 km NNW of Machias. In hunting, fishing area.

Brookville, town (1990 pop. 2,529), ⊙ Franklin co., SE Ind., on Whitewater R. at influx of its East Fork (at the S end of Brookville Reservoir), and 29 mi/47 km SSW of Richmond; 39°25′N 85°01′W. Trading center in agr. area (grain; hogs); mfg. (construction materials, rubber washers, plastic prods., hardwood; meat processing). Laid out 1808. Lew Wallace b. here.

Brookville 1 village (1990 pop. 226), Saline co., central Kansas, 15 mi/24 km WSW of Salina; 38°46′N 97°51′W. In wheat and cattle region. **2** village (□ 4 sq mi/10.4 sq km; 1990 pop. 3,716), Nassau co., SE N.Y., on W L.I., 7 mi/11.3 km NE of Mineola; 40°48′N 73°34′W. **3** village (1990 pop. 4,621), Montgomery co., W Ohio, 14 mi/23 km WNW of Dayton, on small Wolf Creek; 39°52′N 84°26′W. Furniture, transportation equip.

Brookville (BRUK-vil), borough (1990 pop. 4,184), ⊙ Jefferson co., W central Pa., 15 mi/24 km NNW of Punxsutawney, at confluence of West Fork and Sandy Lick creeks, which form Red Bank Creek; 41°09′N 79°04′W. Light mfg. (lumber, plastic prods., fabricated metal prods., premium graphite). Agr. area (livestock; corn, hay, alfalfa; dairying); bituminous coal, oil, gas. Cook Forest State Park to NW, Clear Creek State Park and State Forest to N. Settled 1801, laid out 1830, inc. 1843.

Brookville, Miss.: see BROOKSVILLE.

Brookville Lake, reservoir, Franklin and Union cos., SE Ind., on East Fork Whitewater R., 1 mi/1.6 km N of Brookville; 15 mi/24 km long; 39°26′N 85°00′W. Formed by Brookville Dam, built (1974) by the Army Corps of Engineers for water supply and flood control. Mounds and Quakertown state recreation areas located here.

Broomall (BROO-mahl), uninc. city (1990 pop. 10,930), Maple township, Delaware co., SE Pa., a residential suburb 10 mi/16 km W of downtown Philadelphia; 39°58′N 75°20′W. Bounded E by Darby Creek. Mfg. (fabricated metal prods., glass prods., chemicals).

Broome, co. (□ 710 sq mi/1,852 sq km; 1990 pop. 212,160), S N.Y., bounded by Pa. border (S); ⊙ Binghamton; 42°09′N 75°49′W. Drained by Susquehanna, Chenango, Tioughnioga, West Branch of the Delaware, and Otselic rivers. Includes Chenango Valley State Park. Dairying area, with extensive high-tech mfg., esp. at centers of Binghamton, Johnson City, and the Broome Co. Industrial Park E of Binghamton; agr. (grain; poultry, livestock); produces maple sugar and syrup. Formed 1806.

Broomes Island, village, Calvert co., S Md., on narrow point in Patuxent R., and 9 mi/14.5 km SSW of Prince Frederick. A waterfront community of oystermen and fishermen some of whom serve as guides to sportsmen. The "island," actually a narrow point jutting into the Patuxent, has a view far along the river in either direction.

Broomfield, city (1990 pop. 24,638), Boulder co., Jefferson and Adams cos., N central Colo., residential and industrial suburb 13 mi/21 km NNW of downtown Denver, and 10 mi/16 km SE of Boulder; elev. 5,420 ft/1,652 m; 39°56′N 105°03′W. City grew rapidly in 1970s–1990s. Mfg. (spring-energized seals, space-vehicle equip., fabricated metal prods., epitaxial wafers, flame-retardant clothing, motor vehicles, furniture, medical supplies and equip., machinery, networking prods., electronic equip., consumer goods, accoustical prods., riboflavin), printing.

Brooten (BROO-tuhn), village (1990 pop. 589), Stearns co., central Minn., 44 mi/71 km W of St. Cloud; 45°30′N 95°07′W. RR junction. Agr. area (dairying; sheep, hogs, cattle, poultry; grain, soybeans); mfg. (medical supplies; light mfg.). In area of small natural lakes; Tamarack L. to SE, L. Johanna to W.

Bross, Mount (14,172 ft/4,320 m), Park co., central Colo., in Park Range, 12 mi/19 km NE of Leadville. Surrounded by Pike Natl. Forest.

Brossard, city (1991 pop. 64,793), S central Que., E Canada, residential suburb 5 mi/8km SE of downtown Montreal, on SE shore of St. Lawrence R., N of Champlain Bridge; 42°27′N 73°29′W. Mfg. (furniture, electronic prods., explosives).

Brothertown, village, Calumet co., E Wis., on E shore of L. Winnebago and 15 mi/24 km NNE of Fond du Lac. In agr. region. Settled 1832 by Brothertown Indians.

Broughton 1 village (1990 pop. 218), Hamilton co., SE Ill., 12 mi/19 km SSE of McLeansboro; 37°55′N 88°27′W. In agr. area. **2** village (1990 pop. 151), Paulding co., NW Ohio, 16 mi/26 km SW of Defiance; 41°05′N 84°33′W.

Broughton Island, village (1991 pop. 461), Franklin dist., E N.W.T., N Canada, on Broughton Isl., off E coast of Baffin Isl.; 67°33′N 64°02′W. Settled in 1956 with establishment of D.E.W. Line station (Crystal III). Handicrafts; fishing, hunting, sealing. Outfitting post for Auyuittuq Natl. Park. Scheduled air service.

Broughton Island (□ 49 sq mi/127 sq km), SW B.C., W Canada, in NE Queen Charlotte Strait, 15 mi/24 km NNE of Alert Bay; 17 mi/27 km long, 1 mi/2 km–5 mi/8 km wide. Just off NW coast is North Broughton Isl. (□ 16 sq mi/41 sq km), 8 mi/13 km long, 1 mi/2 km–3 mi/5 km wide.

Broussard (BROO-sahrd), town (1994 pop. 3,833), Lafayette parish, S La., 6 mi/10 km SE of Lafayette; 30°09′N 91°56′W. In agr. area (sugarcane, rice, vegetables, sweet potatoes; cattle; dairying); mfg. (oil field equip., machinery, fabricated metal prods.); oil and natural gas. Longfellow Evangeline State Commemorative Area to E.

Broward, county (□ 1,319 sq mi/3,416 sq km; 1990 pop. 1,255,488), SE Fla., on the Atlantic coast; ⊙ Fort Lauderdale; 26°08′N 80°27′W. This is one of Fla.'s most urbanized cos., experiencing much of its growth since 1970. Major business and retail centers, and several large planned retirement communities. Beaches on coastal margin lined with resorts. Port Everglades in Dania is one of largest in SE U.S. Interior lies in the Everglades, which are underlaid by peat deposits and here crossed by drainage canals bet. L. Okeechobee (NW) and coast. Contains Seminole Indian reservations. Formed 1915.

Browder, village (1990 pop. 500), Muhlenberg co., W Ky., 8 mi/12.9 km E of Greenville. Bituminous coal and agr. (tobacco, grain; livestock).

Brower, Inuit trading village, N Alaska, 55 mi/89 km SE of Barrow, SW of Smith Bay.

Browerville (BROU-wuhr-vil), town (1990 pop. 782), Todd co., central Minn., 8 mi/12.9 km N of Long Prairie, on Long Prairie R., at mouth of Eagle Creek; 46°05′N 94°52′W. Livestock, poultry; dairying; grain, potatoes, beans; mfg. (dairy prods.).

Brown 1 county (□ 307 sq mi/795 sq km; 1990 pop. 5,836), W Ill.; ⊙ Mount Sterling; 39°57′N 90°45′W. Bounded by Illinois R. (SE) and La Moine R. (NE); drained by small McKee Creek. Agr. (cattle, hogs; corn, sorghum, soybeans). Bituminous coal. Formed 1839. Part of Siloam Springs State Park in SW. **2** county (□ 316 sq mi/818 sq km; 1990 pop. 14,080), S central Ind.; ⊙ Nashville; 39°12′N 86°14′W. Drained by small Bean Blossom Creek and by Salt Creek and its N fork. Heavily forested. Agr. (fruit, vegetables; hogs, livestock); timber. Brown County State Park in SW (Weed Patch Hill, one of highest points in Ind., 1,058 ft/322 m); Hoosier Natl. Forest in extreme S. Yellowwood State Forest in W; part of Morgan-Monroe State Forest in NW corner. Formed 1836. **3** county (□ 572 sq mi/1,481 sq km; 1990 pop. 11,128), NE Kansas; ⊙ Hiawatha; 39°49′N 95°33′W. Gently rolling corn-belt region bordered N by Nebr., in the Loess Hills region; watered by headstreams of Delaware R. Wheat, sorghum, corn, soybeans, hay; cattle, hogs. Kickapoo Indian Reservation is in SW; Iowa Sac and Fox Indian Reservation is in NE. Formed 1855. **4** county (□ 618 sq mi/1,601 sq km; 1990 pop. 26,984), S Minn.; ⊙ New Ulm; 44°13′N 94°43′W. Bounded N by Minnesota R. and drained by Cottonwood and Little Cottonwood rivers. Agr. area (corn, oats, hay, alfalfa, soybeans, peas; hogs, sheep, cattle, poultry; dairying); quartzite, silica. L. Hanska reservoir in S; Flandran State Park in NE at New Ulm. County formed 1855. **5** county (□ 1,225 sq mi/3,173 sq km; 1990 pop. 3,657), N Nebr.; ⊙ Ainsworth, in Sand Hills region; 42°26′N 99°55′W. Cattle grazing region with some irrigation bounded N by Niobrara R.: drained in S by Calamus R. Cattle, hogs; dairying; corn. Several small natural lakes, including Hagan in SE and Moon, Pine, and Willow in SW. Long Pine State Recreation Area in NE; Long L. State Recreation Area in SW. Formed 1883. **6** county (□ 491 sq mi/1,272 sq km; 1990 pop. 34,966), SW Ohio; ⊙ Georgetown, 38°56′N 83°52′W. Bounded S by Ohio R., here forming Ky. state line; drained by Little Miami R. and small White Oak Creek. In the Till Plains physiographic region, except for the SE corner which is in the Lexington Plain region. Agr. (livestock, poultry; tobacco, corn, soybeans; dairy prods.); mfg. at Georgetown (leather prods., machinery, medical equip. and supplies). Includes Grant Memorial State Park. Formed 1817. **7** county (□ 1,731 sq mi/4,483 sq km; 1990 pop. 35,580), NE S.Dak., on N.Dak. state line; ⊙ Aberdeen. Agr. area drained by James R. and Elm, Maple, Mud, and Foot creeks. Mfg. at Aberdeen. Wheat, corn, flax, soybeans, vegetables; cattle, hogs. Richmond Lake State Rec. Area in W. Elm Lake reservoir in NW. Includes Mud Lakes Reservoir and Columbia Road Reservoir. Sand Lake Natl. Wildlife Refuge in NE. Formed 1879. **8** county (□ 957 sq mi/2,479 sq km; 1990 pop. 43,371), central Texas; ⊙ BROWNWOOD; 31°46′N 99°00′W. Bounded S by Colorado R.; drained by Pecan Bayou (dam impounds L. Brownwood) and Jim Ned Creek. Agr. (peanuts, oats, sorghum, wheat, pecans, vegetables; hay), livestock (beef and dairy cattle, sheep, Angora goats, hogs). Oil, natural gas, clay, glass sand. Fishing in L. Brownwood State Park. Formed 1856. **9** county (□ 615 sq mi/1,593 sq km; 1990 pop. 194,594), E Wis., bounded N by Green Bay of L. Michigan; ⊙ Green Bay; 44°28′N 87°59′W. NE part on Door Peninsula; drained by Fox R. Primarily a dairying, farming (barley, oats, wheat, corn, peas, beans, alfalfa; hay; cattle, sheep), and lumbering region, with mfg. at Green Bay and De Pere. Center of co. urbanized by Green Bay and its suburbs. Heritage Hill State Park at Alloez, in center; part of Oneida Indian Reservation in W. Formed 1818.

Brown City, village (1990 pop. 1,244), Sanilac co., E Mich., 14 mi/23 km NE of Imlay City; 43°12′N 82°59′W. In agr. area (grain, sugar beets, beans); mfg. (machinery, transportation equip.).

Brown County State Park, S of Nashville in S Brown

co., Ind. Heavily forested; hilly terrain. State's largest state park. Seasonal tourist site, especially in autumn.

Brown Deer, city (1990 pop. 12,236), Milwaukee co., SE Wis., on the Milwaukee R.; 43°10′N 87°58′W. It is a residential suburb 7 mi/11.3 km NNW of downtown Milwaukee. Mfg. (consumer goods, machinery). Inc. 1955.

Brown, Fort, Texas: see BROWNSVILLE.

Brownell (broun-EL), village (1990 pop. 44), Ness co., W central Kansas, 16 mi/26 km NE of Ness City; 38°38′N 99°44′W. Grain; livestock.

Brownfield 1 town (1990 pop. 1,034), Oxford co., W Maine, on the Saco and 27 mi/43 km SW of South Paris; 43°56′N 70°55′W. Wood prods. Severely damaged (1947) by forest fire. **2** town (1990 pop. 9,560), ⊙ Terry co., NW Texas, on Llano Estacado, 35 mi/56 km SW of Lubbock, near Sulphur Draw (intermittent stream); 33°10′N 102°16′W. Elev. 3,312 ft/1,009 m. Cattle, mineral, agr. (cotton, wheat, peanuts, vegetables) region. Mfg. (sodium sulfate, cottonseed oil, feed, mattresses, ice). Oil and gas. Inc. 1926.

Browning, city (1990 pop. 331), Linn and Sullivan cos., N Mo., on Locust Cr. 18 mi/29 km NNW of Brookfield; 40°01′N 93°09′W. Corn, wheat, soybeans; sheep, cattle, hogs; feed.

Browning, town (1990 pop. 1,170), Glacier co., N Mont., on Willow Creek and 32 mi/51 km WSW of Cut Bank; 48°34′N 113°01′W. Trade point and hq. for Blackfeet Indian Reservation located near center of reservation; hogs; mfg. (textile prods.). Glacier Natl. Park to W. Mus. of the Plains Indian. Inc. 1920.

Browning, village, (1990 pop. 193) Schuyler co., W central Ill., on Illinois R., and 10 mi/16 km E of Rushville; 40°07′N 90°22′W. In agr. area. Sanghois Conservation Area nearby.

Brownington 1 town (1990 pop. 84), Henry co., W central Mo., 9 mi/14.5 km S of Clinton; on S side of S Grand Arm of Truman L.; 38°15′N 93°43′W. Coal in area; corn, sorghum; cattle. **2** town (1990 pop. 705), Oreleans co., N Vt., on Willoughby R., and 8 mi/12.9 km S of Newport; 44°49′N 72°07′W. "Old Stone House" is here.

Brownlee Park, village (1990 pop. 2,536), Calhoun co., S Mich., suburb 3 mi/4.8 km ESE of Battle Creek; 42°19′N 85°07′W.

Brownlee Reservoir, NE Oregon and W Idaho, on Snake R., 43 mi/69 km E of Baker City, Oregon; c.90 mi/145 km long; 44°22′N 117°13′W. Max. capacity 1,426,700 acre-ft. Powder R. enters from W, forming 8-mi/12.9-km arm. Formed by Brownlee Dam (310 ft/94 m high), built (1959) by the Idaho Power Co. for power generation.

Brownlow Point, NE Alaska, cape on Beaufort Sea, on W side of Camden Bay; 70°09′N 145°50′W.

Browns, village (1990 pop. 207), Edwards co., SE Ill., on Bonpas Creek and 4 mi/6.4 km E of Albion; 38°22′N 87°58′W. RR junction. Agr.; oil.

Browns Ferry 1, 2, and 3 Nuclear Power Plants, Ala.: see LIMESTONE CO.

Browns Mills, village, Burlington co., central N.J., on Rancocas Creek, and 11 mi/18 km E of Mt. Holly. Mirror L. (c.2 mi/3.2 km long) just E. Service and residential center for Fort Dix Military Reservation just N.

Browns Point, uninc. town (1990 pop. 1,950), Pierce co., W Wash., residential suburb 4 mi/6.4 km N of downtown Tacoma, at Browns Pt., on Dalco Passage of Puget Sound, at entrance to Commencement Bay, Tacoma's harbor. Lighthouse. Dash Point State Park to NE.

Brown's Point, Trinidad and Tobago: see CROWN POINT.

Browns River, c.30 mi/48 km, NW Vt.; rises near Mt. Mansfield; flows W and N to Lamoille R. at Fairfax.

Brown's Town, town (1991 pop. 6,762), St. Ann parish, N Jamaica, 10 mi/16 km WSW of St. Ann's Bay; 18°24′N 77°22′W. Road and market center in agr. region (fruit, grain; livestock). Germans settled here 1836–1842.

Browns Valley, town (1990 pop. 804), Traverse co., W Minn., 22 mi/35 km SW of Wheaton, on Little Minnesota R. and S.Dak. state line; 45°35′N 96°49′W. Grain, soybeans, sunflowers, sugar beets; livestock, poultry; dairying; mfg. (fertilizer). Remains of Browns Valley

man, associated by some anthropologists with Folsom culture, found here 1934. L. Traverse (on Minn.-S.Dak. boundary) to N.

Brownsboro, village (1990 pop. 545), Henderson co., E Texas, 19 mi/31 km W of Tyler; 32°17′N 95°36′W. Agr. area.

Brownsboro Farm, village (1990 pop. 670), Jefferson co., N Ky., residential suburb 10 mi/16 km ENE of downtown Louisville; 38°17′N 85°35′W. E. P. "Tom" Sawyer State Park to SE.

Brownsboro Village, village (1990 pop. 361), Jefferson co., N Ky., residential suburb 4 mi/6.4 km E of downtown Louisville; 38°15′N 85°40′W.

Brownsburg, town (1990 pop. 7,628), Hendricks co., central Ind., satellite community, 11 mi/18 km W of downtown Indianapolis; 39°50′N 86°23′W. Mfg. (aircraft sheet metal, consumer goods).

Brownsburg, village (1991 pop. 2,480), S Que., Canada, 4 mi/6 km WNW of Lachute; 45°41′N 74°24′W. Mfg.; dairying center.

Brownsdale, village (1990 pop. 695), Mower co., SE Minn., 8 mi/12.9 km NE of Austin; 43°44′N 92°52′W. In agr. area (dairying; poultry, livestock; corn, soybeans); mfg. (tunneling equip., printing, feeds).

Brownstown 1 town (1990 pop. 2,872), ⊙ Jackson co., S Ind., near East Fork of White R., 24 mi/39 km E of Bedford; 38°53′N 86°03′W. In agr. area (vegetables, grain; poultry); mfg. (machinery, consumer goods, paper milling, canned goods). A state forest and state beach are nearby. Laid out 1816. **2** uninc. town (1990 pop. 900), Lancaster co., SE Pa., 9 mi/14.5 km NE of Lancaster on Conestoga R.; 40°07′N 76°12′W. Agr. includes dairying; livestock; grain. Covered bridges in area.

Brownstown 1 village (1990 pop. 668), Fayette co., S central Ill., 8 mi/12.9 km E of Vandalia; 39°00′N 88°57′W. In agr. (corn, wheat, sorghum, soybeans; cattle; dairying) and oil-producing area. **2** uninc. village (1990 pop. 50), Yakima co., S Wash., 14 mi/23 km SW of Yakima, in NE part of Yakima Indian Reservation. Irrigated agr. area (fruit, grain; livestock). Mfg. (conveyors).

Brownstown, borough (1990 pop. 937), Cambria co., W central Pa., suburb 1 mi/1.6 km NW of Johnstown, near confluence of Stonycreek and Little Conemaugh rivers, which form Conemaugh R.; 40°19′N 78°56′W. Mfg. (machinery, trailers, printing and publishing, race-car trailers, apparel).

Brownsville 1 city (1990 pop. 10,019), ⊙ Haywood co., W Tenn., 24 mi/39 km W of Jackson; 35°36′N 89°16′W. In timber and cotton area; lawn and garden equip., rubber and plastic prods. Settled c.1810; inc. 1823. **2** city (1990 pop. 98,962), ⊙ Cameron co., extreme S Texas, on the Rio Grande c.17 mi/27 km from its mouth at the Gulf of Mex.; 25°55′N 97°28′W. Elev. 57 ft/17 m. It is an important port of entry across the river from Matamoros, Mex.; a deepwater channel (completed 1936) accommodates ocean vessels; a land cut NE to Brazos Santiago Pass, bypassing Rio Grande shipping channel, is S terminus of Intracoastal Waterway. Brownsville is a trade, processing, and distributing point for the rich, irrigated lower Rio Grande valley; it has many industries connected with oil and natural gas. Other prods. include shrimp, electronic equip., and aircraft and auto parts. The establishment of Fort Texas there by Gen. Zachary Taylor in 1846 invited a Mex. attack that precipitated the Mex. War. The fort was renamed (1846) for Major Jacob Brown, killed while commanding its defense. Active until 1944, Fort Brown was held briefly by Union forces in the Civil War. The town of Brownsville grew around the fort and was a cattle-shipping point in the late 19th cent. In 1906 a group of Afr.-Amer. soldiers stationed at Fort Brown were blamed for a night gun raid on the town that resulted in an innocent civilian's death. President Theodore Roosevelt, in a highly controversial directive, ordered the dishonorable discharge of 167 of the Afr.-Amer. soldiers. In 1972 the secretary of the army reversed that order. Brownsville has Texas Southmost Col. (2-year); occupies bldgs. in former Fort Brown;

Brownsville Internatl. Airport in E side of city, and a zoo. Nearby recreational areas include South Padre Isl., Padre Isl. Natl. Seashore 50 mi/80 km to NE, road access only from Corpus Christi (N); Palo Alto Battlefield Natl. Historic Site to N; Laguna Atascosa Natl. Wildlife Refuge to NNE; Brazos Isl. State Park to E. Inc. 1850.

Brownsville 1 town (□ 2 sq mi/5.2 sq km; 1990 pop. 15,607), Escambia co., NW Fla.; 25°49′N 80°14′W. **2** town (1990 pop. 897), ⊙ Edmonson co., central Ky., 18 mi/29 km NE of Bowling Green, on Green R.; 37°11′N 86°15′W. Elev. 1,826 ft/557 m. Agr. (burley tobacco, grain; livestock; dairying); mfg. (apparel). Mammoth Cave Natl. Park is immediately to E; Nolin River Lake reservoir to NE. **3** town (1990 pop. 1,281), Linn co., W Oregon,17 mi/27 km SSE of Albany and on Calapooia R.; 44°23′N 122°58′W. Timber. Fruit, vegetables.

Brownsville 1 (BROUNS-vil), uninc. village (1990 pop. 7,897), Ouachita Parish, N La., 2 mi/3 km SW of Monroe, at E end of Cheniere Brake reservoir (State Fish Preserve); 32°29′N 92°10′W. Pop. figure includes Bawcomville. **2** village (1990 pop. 415), Houston co., extreme SE Minn., 8 mi/12.9 km SSW of La Crosse, Wis., on Mississippi R., on pool of Lock and Dam No. 8; 43°42′N 91°16′W. Corn, oats. Richard J. Dorer Memorial Hardwood State Forest to W; Wildcat Bluff to SW, rises c.400 ft/122 m above Mississippi R.; numerous isls. in river to NE (Upper Mississippi R. Natl. Wildlife Refuge). **3** village (1990 pop. 415), Dodge Co., E Wis., 11 mi/18 km SSW of Fond du Lac; 43°37′N 88°29′W. Dairying; general farming. Horicon Natl. Wildlife Refuge to W.

Brownsville, borough (1990 pop. 3,164), Fayette co., SW Pa., 29 mi/47 km S of Pittsburgh, on Monongahela R. (bridged to West Brownsville, 1 mi/1.6 km NW); 40°01′N 79°53′W. Mfg. (scrap-iron processing, plastic glass, barges). Agr. area (grain, alfalfa, soybeans; livestock; dairying). Pioneers on Cumberland Road transferred here to water travel on Mississippi R. system. Laid out 1785, inc. 1815; consolidated 1933 with South Brownsville.

Brownsville, a largely residential sect. of E Brooklyn borough of N.Y. city; 40°40′N 73°50′W. Most of its pop. is Afr.-Amer.

Brownton, village (1990 pop. 781), McLeod co., S Minn., 20 mi/32 km WSW of Glencoe, near Buffalo Creek; 44°43′N 94°20′W. Agr. area (dairying; poultry; grain, peas, soybeans); light mfg.

Browntown 1 uninc. town (1990 pop. 960), Luzerne co., NE central Pa., residential suburb 7 mi/11.3 km ENE of Wilkes-Barre, and 9 mi/14.5 km SW of Scranton; 41°18′N 75°47′W. **2** town (1990 pop. 256), Green co., S Wis., 8 mi/12.9 km W of Monroe, and on Pecatonica R.; 42°34′N 89°47′W. Dairy prods. (cheese); mfg. iron castings. Hunting and recreation area nearby. Browntown-Cadiz State Recreation Area to E (former Cadiz Springs State Park).

Brownvale, village, W Alta., Canada, 25 mi/40 km WSW of Peace R.; 56°07′N 117°54′W. Lumbering; mixed farming, wheat.

Brownville, town (1990 pop. 1,506), including Brownville Junction village, Piscataquis co., central Maine, on Pleasant R., and 13 mi/21 km NE of Dover-Foxcroft, bet. Sebec and Schoodic lakes; 45°21′N 69°00′W. Wood prods. Old slate quarries here. Airport at Brownville Junction. Inc. 1824.

Brownville 1 village (1990 pop. 148), Nemaha co., SE Nebr., 10 mi/16 km E of Auburn, and on Missouri R; 40°23′N 95°39′W. Trade center in fruit region. Was busy river port in 1850s; hoped to become state capital; still has cruises and Merriweather Lewis steamboat mus. Cooper Station Nuclear Power Plant. Brownville State Recreation Area here. **2** village (1990 pop. 1,138), Jefferson co., N N.Y., on Black R., and 4 mi/6.4 km NW of Watertown; 44°00′N 75°58′W.

Brownwood, city (1990 pop. 18,387), ⊙ Brown co., 62 mi/100 km SW of Abilene, on Pecan Bayou, central Texas; 31°43′N 98°58′W. Elev. 1,342 ft/409 m. RR junction; industrial community (printing, fabricated metal prods., furniture, beverages, electronic equip.); processes and ships cattle, wool, poultry, sheep, Angora goats, wheat, vegetables, nuts, and meat from the surrounding agr. area. Nearby L. Brownwood is a large reservoir used for irrigation as well as for fishing and boating. Oil and gas. Howard Payne Univ. is there; the Douglas MacArthur Acad. of Freedom is on its campus. Inc. 1876

Brownwood, Lake, reservoir (□ 11 sq mi/28 sq km), Brown co., central Texas, on Pecan Bayou, 60 mi/96 km SE of Abilene; 31°50′N 99°00′W. Max. capacity 448,200 acre-ft. Formed by Lake Brownwood Dam (120 ft/37 m high), built (1933) for water supply; also used for recreation. Lake Brownwood State Park on W bank.

Broxton (BRAHKS-tuhn), city (1990 pop. 1,211), Coffee co., S central Ga.,7 mi/11.3 km NNW of Douglas; 31°37′N 82°53′W. Mfg. of mobile homes and clothing.

Broyhill Park, uninc. town, Fairfax co., NE Va., residential suburb 10 mi/16 km W of Wash., D.C.; 38°51′N 77°11′W.

Bruce, county (□ 1,650 sq mi/4,274 sq km; 1991 pop. 65,268), S Ont., Canada, on L. Huron; ⊙ Walkerton; 44°30′N 81°15′W. Site of Bruce nuclear facility; in 1997, 3 units here were shut down until at least 2003.

Bruce, town (1990 pop. 2,127), Calhoun co., N central Miss., 30 mi/48 km ENE of Grenada, and on Skuna R.; 33°59′N 89°20′W. RR terminus. Agr. (cotton, corn, soybeans, sorghum; cattle; timber); mfg. (furniture, apparel; lumber). Inc. 1927.

Bruce 1 village (1990 pop. 235), Brookings co., E S.Dak., 10 mi/16 km NNW of Brookings, and on Big Sioux R. Honey. Oakwood Lakes State Park to W. **2** village (1990 pop. 844), Rusk co., NW Wis., 45 mi/72 km N of Eau Claire; 45°27′N 91°16′W. Dairy prods.; livestock; lumber. Christie Mt. Ski Area to W.

Bruce Mines, town (1991 pop. 684), S central Ont., Canada, on L. Huron, 30 mi/48 km SE of Sault Ste. Marie; 46°17′N 83°47′W. Copper and traprock mining; dairying.

Bruce Peninsula National Park (□ 106 sq mi/275 sq km), SW Ont., Canada, occupies both sides of Bruce Peninsula and isl. group N and W of Tobermory (excluding W end of peninsula and properties on either side of Highway 6). Niagara Escaprment follows Georgian Bay shore. Opposite side borders L. Huron. Major isls. are Cove, Echo, North Otter, Russel, Bears Rump, and Flowerpot; Flowerpot was formerly part of Georgian Bay Isls. Natl. Park. Waters surrounding isls. designated as Fathom Five Natl. Marine Park. Hiking, camping, swimming, cross-country skiing. Est. 1986.

Bruceton, town (1990 pop. 1,586), Carroll co., NW Tenn., on Big Sandy R., and 10 mi/16 km E of Huntingdon; 36°03′N 88°15′W. In agr. area. Settled 1920; inc. 1925.

Bruceton Mills, or **Bruceton**, village (1990 pop. 132), Preston co., N W.Va., 15 mi/24 km E of Morgantown; 39°39′N 79°38′W. Mfg. (coal processing). Chestnut Ridge Park and Coopers Rock State Forest to W.

Bruceville 1 town (1990 pop. 471), Knox co., SW Ind., 8 mi/12.9 km NE of Vincennes; 38°46′N 87°25′W. In agr. area; bituminous-coal mines nearby. Laid out 1829. **2** town (1990 pop. 1,075), McLennan co., E central Texas, 15 mi/24 km SSW of Waco; 31°18′N 97°15′W. Cattle; grain, cotton; dairying.

Bruderheim (BROO-duhr-heim), town (1991 pop. 1,208), central Alta., Canada, 30 mi/48 km NE of Edmonton; 53°48′N 112°55′W. Mixed farming; dairying.

Bruin, borough (1990 pop. 646), Butler co., W Pa., 15 mi/24 km NE of Butler; 41°03′N79°43′W. Located on Beaver Creek (its mouth on Allegheny R., 3 mi/4.8 km to NE).

Bruin, Lake (BROOIN), natural oxbow lake, Tensas parish, E La., 3 mi/5 km N of St. Joseph; c.12 mi/19 km long; 32°00′N 91°13′W. Horseshoe-shaped with land opening on S end; formed by a cutoff of the Mississippi R. L. Bruin State Park in S.

Bruin Peak (10,285 ft/3,135 m), in West Tavaputs Plateau, E Carbon co., E Utah, 25 mi/40 km E of Price.

Brule (BROOL), county (□ 846 sq mi/2,191 sq km; 1990 pop. 5,485), S central S.Dak., ⊙ Chamberlain. Agr. area bounded W by Missouri R. (L. Francis Case reservoir).

Drained by Smith Creek in N; Red L. is in W. Diversified farming; corn, wheat; cattle, hogs. Formed 1875.

Brule 1 village (1990 pop. 411), Keith co., SW central Nebr., 10 mi/16 km W of Ogallala and on South Platte R.; 41°06′N 101°53′W. **2** (BROOL), village, Douglas co., NW Wis., on Bois Brule R. and 26 mi/42 km ESE of Superior. Fishing. Bule River State Rearing Station. In Brule R. State Forest.

Brûlé Lake, expansion of Athabaska R., W Alta., W Canada, in Rocky Mts., on E edge of Jasper Natl. Park, 26 mi/42 km NNE of Jasper; 8 mi/13 km long, 1 mi/1.6 km wide; elev. 3,228 ft/984 m. Jasper House, Hudson's Bay Co. trading post, was est. 1799 at outlet of lake; moved 1801 to Jasper L. and abandoned 1875.

Brule Lake (BROOL), Cook co., NE Minn., in Superior Natl. Forest, 20 mi/32 km NW of Grand Marais; 7 mi/11.3 km long, 2 mi/3.2 km wide; 47°56′N 90°41′W. Drained E by Brule R. Mainly in Boundary Waters Canoe Area. Misquah Hills to NE; Eagle Mt., highest point in Minn. (2,301 ft/701 m) to SE; several isls. in lake.

Brule River 1 (BROOL), c.50 mi/80 km long, SW Upper Peninsula, Mich.; rises in Boule L. in SW Iron co.; flows SE, forming part of Mich.-Wis. state line, in nearly its entire length, to the Michigamme in SE Iron co., forming Menominee R.; 46°02′N 88°50′W. **2** c.40 mi/64 km long, Wis.; rises in Brule Lake, in Iron co., Michigan. Enters the Menominee R. NW of Iron Mt., Mich. Forms Wis.-Mich. state boundary its entire length, from its exit from L. Brule to its confluence with Paint R. 3 mi/4.8 km N of Florence to form the Menominee R., which continues SE to Green Bay of L. Michigan, also forming state boundary. Ottawa Natl. Forest to N, Nicolet Natl. Forest to S.

Brumley (BRUHM-lee), town (1990 pop. 81), Miller co., in the Ozarks central Mo., near Osage R.; 10 mi/16 km SE of Osage Beach; 38°05′N 92°29′W. Hay, cattle. Lake of the Ozarks State Park 5 mi/8 km NW.

Brundidge (BRUHN-dij), town (1990 pop. 2,472), Pike co., SE Ala., 10 mi/16 km SE of Troy. Mfg. (apparel, consumer goods, lumber prods.); lumber.

Bruneau River, NE Nev. and SW Idaho; rises in E Elko co., Nev., 35 mi/56 km NW of Wells; flows generally N through Humboldt Natl. Forest, into Owyhee co., Idaho; receives Jarbidge R., from SSE, and Clover Creek (East Fork), then NNW past Bruneau to Snake R. (C.J. Strike Reservoir) 16 mi/26 km SW of Mountain Home. Used for irrigation.

Brunette Island (□ 9 sq mi/23 sq km), S N.F., Canada, in Fortune Bay, 12 mi/19 km NW of Grand Bank; 5 mi/8 km long, 3 mi/5 km wide; 47°17′N 55°55′W. Has lighthouse and radio station. Fishing.

Bruni, uninc. village (1990 pop. 698), Webb co., S Texas, 40 mi/64 km ESE of Laredo. Cattle. Oil and natural gas; uranium. Mfg. (uranium processing).

Bruning (BROON-ing), village (1990 pop. 332), Thayer co., SE Nebr., 10 mi/16 km N of Hebron; 40°20′N 97°33′W. Dairy.

Bruno, town (1991 pop. 656), S central Sask., Canada, 18 mi/29 km WNW of Humboldt; 52°16′N 105°31′W. Grain elevators; dairying, brick making.

Bruno 1 village (1990 pop. 89), Pine co., E Minn., 42 mi/68 km SW of Duluth; 46°16′N 92°40′W. Agr. area (dairying). **2** village (1990 pop. 141), Butler co., E Nebr., 9 mi/14.5 km ENE of David City, S of Platte R.; 41°16′N 96°57′W.

Brunson, village (1990 pop. 587), Hampton co., SW S.C., 11 mi/18 km SE of Allendale; 32°55′N 81°11′W. Mfg. of machining; agr. (livestock; grain, soybeans, cotton, peanuts, watermelons).

Brunsville, town (1990 pop. 137), Plymouth co., NW Iowa, 5 mi/8 km W of Le Mars; 42°48′N 96°16′W. Livestock; grain.

Brunswick 1 county (□ 1,050 sq mi/2,720 sq km, 1990 pop. 50,985), SE N.C.; ⊙ Southport; 34°2′N 78°13′W. Bounded E and NE by Cape Fear R., S by the Atlantic Ocean, SW by S.C. state line, W by Waccamaw R. Drained by Town Creek, Green Swamp in N center. Forested and swampy tidewater area; includes Smith and Bald Head isls. (Cape Fear). Farming (tobacco, corn, sweet potatoes; cattle, hogs); fishing, timber.

Beach resorts along coast. Intracoastal Waterway canal parallels coast and passes through Cape Fear R. estuary to Carolina Beach Inlet. Mfg. at Leland. Brunswick 1 and 2 Nuclear Power Plants located at Southport. Town burned by British (1776), 60 excavated bldg. sites, Brunswick Town State Historical Site. Sunny Point Army Base in E. Orton Pond, arm of Cape Fear R., in E, including Orton Plantation and Gardens. Formed 1764. **2** county (□ 569 sq mi/1,474 sq km; 1990 pop. 15,987), S Va., ⊙ Lawrenceville; 36°45′N 77°51′W. Bounded S by N.C. state line, N by Nottoway R.; drained by Meherrin R. and short Fontaine Creek. Agr. (esp. tobacco; also wheat, corn, soybeans, cotton, hay, sweet potatoes, peanuts); some dairying; livestock (cattle, hogs, poultry). Mfg. at Lawrenceville. Part of Ft. Pickett Military Resevation in NW. N arms of L. Gaston reservoir (Roanoke R.) in S. Formed 1732.

Brunswick 1 (BRUHNZ-wik), city (1990 pop. 16,433), ⊙ Glynn co., SE Ga., on St. Simon's Sound, near the Atlantic coast; 31°08′N 81°28′W. Ga.'s 2d leading port city, after Savannah. Container docks and motor vehicles. Import terminals dominate, with 3 berthing and storage ports: Mayor's Port terminal, Colonels Isl. port terminal, and Marine port terminal are the largest; sheltered harbor is used by coastal freighters and fishing and shrimping fleets. Sunny Point Military Ocean Terminal is used for shipping radioactive waste. The gateway to offshore resort isls. (see SEA ISLANDS), Brunswick has a large seafood harvesting and processing industry (primarily shrimp and crab) and a large pulp-paper milling capacity. Coastal Ga. Community Col. is a unit of the Univ. System of Ga. Brunswick Col., part of the state univ. system, is here. The Federal Law Enforcement Training Center and the Brunswick Job Corps Center, occupying the former Glynco Naval Air Station are just to the N. The old town dist., with its many beautiful Victorian homes, is listed on the Natl. Register. Airport. Laid out 1771–1772; inc. 1856. **2** city (1990 pop. 1,074), Chariton co., N central Mo., at junction of Grand R. with the Missouri, and 25 mi/40 km S of Brookfield; 39°25′N 93°07′W. Pecans, soybeans, wheat, corn; hogs; mfg. (gloves). Site of Fr. Fort Orléans (1723) is nearby. Laid out c.1837. **3** city (1990 pop. 28,230), Medina co., N Ohio, a suburb of Cleveland; 41°15′N 81°51′W. Small farm community for many years; pop. burgeoned with the housing boom after World War II. Light industrial plants. Settled 1815 as part of the Conn. Western Reserve, inc. 1960.

Brunswick 1 town (1990 pop. 20,906), Cumberland co., S Maine, on the Androscoggin R. and Casco Bay, and 24 mi/39 km NE of Portland; 43°53′N 69°58′W. In a resort area. It is a growing commercial center for S Maine; prods. include shoes and clothing. Bowdoin Col. (1794) and a U.S. naval air station are in Brunswick. Maine Statehouse Theatre operates in summer. Nathaniel Hawthorne and Henry Wadsworth Longfellow were students at Bowdoin Col. during the 1820s. Longfellow later taught there; a house dating from 1808 was once his home. Hawthorne's first novel, *Fanshawe* (1828), was printed in the town. In 1851, Harriet Beecher Stowe wrote *Uncle Tom's Cabin* here; her house (now an inn) is a natl. landmark. Bowdoin Pines are 125 years old and 90 ft/27 m tall. After the Civil War, textiles became Brunswick's chief industry, but the industry declined after World War II. Settled as a trading post in 1628, inc. 1738. **2** town (1990 pop. 5,117), Frederick co., W Md., on the Potomac (bridged here to Va.) in Middletown Valley, and 15 mi/24 km WSW of Frederick; 39°19′N 77°37′W. Town is on a large tract patented as "Hawkins Merry Peep o'Day" by John Hawkins in 1753. Tract was laid out as Berlin in 1787 but its name was changed to Brunswick, when repair shops were est. here by the Baltimore and Ohio RR, to avoid confusion with Berlin on the Eastern Shore in 1890. RR and Chesapeake and Ohio Canal (now abandoned) arrived here c.1834. **3** town (1990 pop. 92), Essex co., NE Vt., on the Connecticut R., and 32 mi/51 km SE of Newport; 44°43′N 71°39′W. Former Mineral Springs resort here.

Brunswick 1 village (1990 pop. 182), Antelope co., NE

Nebr., 15 mi/24 km N of Neligh; 42°20′N 97°58′W. **2** village (1990 pop. 302), Columbus co., S N.C., 4 mi/6.4 km S of Whiteville; 34°17′N 78°42′W. Timber, tobacco, grain; livestock.

Brunswick 1 and 2 Nuclear Power Plants, N.C.: see BRUNSWICK, CO.

Brush, town (1990 pop. 4,165), Morgan co., NE Colo., on Beaver Creek, near South Platte R., 9 mi/14.5 km E of Fort Morgan; elev. 4,231 ft/1,290 m; 40°15′N 103°37′W. RR junction. Shipping point in sugar-beet, cattle, sunflowers, wheat, barley, corn, beans region; mfg. (feeds). Annual rodeo and fiesta here. Inc. 1884.

Brush Prairie, uninc. town (1990 pop. 2,650), Clark co., SW Wash., 9 mi/14.5 km NE of Vancouver (Wash.), on Salmon Creek; 45°44′N 122°33′W. Fruit, nuts, vegetables; poultry; dairying.

Brushton, village (1990 pop. 522), Franklin co., N N.Y., on small Little Salmon R. and 11 mi/18 km W of Malone; 44°49′N 74°30′W. In farming and dairying area.

Brusly (BROO-lee), town (1990 pop. 1,824), West Baton Rouge parish, SE central La., 6 mi/10 km SSW of Baton Rouge, and on W bank of the Mississippi R.; 30°23′N 91°15′W. In sugarcane area (sugar plant); mfg. (machinery, shipbuilding); oil and natural-gas fields in vicinity. Named for *brule* [Fr. = burnt] after practice of annually burning cane.

Brussels, village (1991 pop. 1,196), S Ont., central Canada, on Middle Maitland R. and 23 mi/37 km E of Goderich. Dairying; lumbering.

Brussels 1 village (1990 pop. 125), Calhoun co., W Ill., near the Mississippi and Illinois rivers, 15 mi/24 km S of Hardin; 38°57′N 90°35′W. In apple-growing area. **2** village, Door co., NE Wis., on Door Peninsula, 14 mi/23 km SW of Sturgeon Bay. Dairying; farming. Settled 1854 by Belgians.

Bryan 1 (BREI-uhn), county (□ 439; 1990 pop. 15,438), SE Ga.; ⊙ Pembroke; 32°01′N 81°26′W. Bounded SE by the Atlantic Ocean, NE by Ogeechee R.; drained by Canoochee R. Includes Ossabaw Isl. coastal plain. Agr. (peanuts, tobacco; cattle), forestry, and fishing area. Formed 1793. **2** county (□ 943 sq mi/2,442 sq km; 1990 pop. 32,089), S Okla.; ⊙ Durant; 33°58′N 96°15′W. Bounded S by Red R., and W by Washita Arm of L. Texoma (Washita R.), impounded by Denison Dam (in SW); drained by Blue R. Agr. (corn, hay, soybeans, peanuts; cattle; dairy prods.). Mfg. at Durant. Lumbering. Historic Fort Washita in NW. Formed 1907.

Bryan 1 city (1990 pop. 8,348), ⊙ Williams co., extreme NW Ohio, 16 mi/26 km NW of Defiance; 41°29′N 84°34′W. Trade center for agr. area; mfg. (toys, furniture, lubricating equip., transportation equip., wood and metal prods.). Laid out 1840; inc. as village in 1841, as city in 1941. **2** city (1990 pop. 55,002), ⊙ Brazos co., 85 mi/137 km NW of Houston, E central Texas; elev. 367 ft/112 m; 30°40′N 96°22′W. Settled in the early 19th cent. in an area of large plantations, Bryan was long a cotton center. Farms still produce agr. goods, and mfg. includes bldg. materials, furniture, and electronic, office, and laboratory equip. The economy, however, is primarily tied to education and research. Texas A&M Univ. straddles corporate limits bet. Bryan and adjacent city of College Station (SE). Inc. 1872.

Bryan, Lake, reservoir, on border bet. Whitman and Columbia cos., SE Wash., on Snake R., 40 mi/64 km NNE of Walla Walla; 28 mi/45 km long; elev. 640 ft/195 m; 46°35′N 118°01′W. Max. capacity 556,000 acre-ft. Formed by Little Goose Lock and Dam (98 ft/30 m high), built (1970) by the Army Corps of Engineers for power generation. Central Ferry State Park on N shore. Extends into Garfield co.

Bryan Station, locality, Fayette co., central Ky., 5 mi/8 km NE of Lexington. Bryan Station Memorial site of historic fort. Unsuccessful Br. and Native Amer. attack made here (Aug. 1782) immediately preceded Revolutionary battle of Blue Licks at BLUE LICKS SPRINGS.

Bryant 1 town (1990 pop. 5,269), Saline co., central Ark., 15 mi/24 km SW of Little Rock and 16 mi/9.7 km E of Benton; 34°36′N 92°29′W. In bauxite-mining region. Mfg. (furniture, cat litter). **2** town (1990 pop. 273), Jay

co., E Ind., 6 mi/9.7 km N of Portland; 40°32′N 84°58′W. In agr. area.

Bryant 1 village (1990 pop. 273), Fulton co., central Ill., 5 mi/8 km NNE of Lewiston; 40°28′N 90°05′W. In agr. area. Bituminous coal. **2** village, Okmulgee co., E central Okla., 5 mi/8 km SW of Henryetta.

Bryant Mountain (3,040 ft/927 m), Greenville co., NW S.C., in the Blue Ridge, c.20 mi/32 km NNE of Greenville.

Bryant Pond, Maine: see WOODSTOCK.

Bryce Canyon National Park (BREIS) (56 sq mi/145 sq km), Garfield and Kane cos., SW Utah. The Pink Cliffs of the Paunsaugunt Plateau, c.2,000 ft/610 m high, were formed by water, frost, and wind action on alternate strata of softer and harder limestone; the result is colorful and unique erosional forms. Bounded W, S, and NE by Dixie Natl. Forest. Anasazi were probably the 1st Native Americans to inhabit the area, and many of their artifacts are exhibited. Est. 1923 as Bryce Canyon Natl. Monument, authorized as Utah Natl. Park, 1924; name changed 1928. State Highway 12 crosses N end of park, park road extends S nearly length of park.

Bryce, Mount (11,507 ft/3,507 m), SE B.C., W Canada, near Alta. prov. border, in Rocky Mts., in Hamber Provincial Park, 65 mi/105 km SSE of Jasper; 52°02′N 117°20′W.

Bryceland (BREIS-luhnd), village (1990 pop. 103), Bienville parish, NW La., 45 mi/72 km E of Shreveport, in farming area; 32°27′N 93°00′W. Driskill Mt. (535 ft/163 m), highest point in La., is 5 mi/8 km ESE.

Bryn Athyn (BREN A-thin), borough (1990 pop. 1,081), Montgomery co., SE Pa., residential suburb 14 mi/23 km N of downtown Philadelphia, on Pennypack Creek; 40°08′N 75°04′W. Swedenborgian cathedral located here.

Bryn Mawr 1 (BREN MAHR), uninc. town (1990 pop. 3,271), Lower Merion township, Montgomery co., SE Pa., a residential suburb 10 mi/16 km WNW of downtown Philadelphia; 40°01′N 75°19′W. Drained by Mill Creek. Light mfg. (powdered metals; printing and publishing). Seat of Bryn Mawr Col., opened in 1885 by the Society of Friends; Ellen Cushing Col., Harcun Col. **2** (brin MAHR), uninc. town (1990 pop. 3,200), King co., W Wash., residential suburb 7 mi/11.3 km SSE of downtown Seattle, NW of Renton, at S end of L. Washington. Renton Municipal Airport to SE.

Bryson, village (1991 pop. 763), SW Que., E Canada, on Ottawa R., and 60 mi/97 km NW of Ottawa; 45°41′N 76°37′W. Dairying; cattle, pigs.

Bryson, village (1990 pop. 520), Jack co., N Texas, 12 mi/19 km E of Graham; 33°09′N 98°23′W. Agr. (cattle; wheat, peanuts); oil-producing area; oil refining; mfg. (metal coating and plating).

Bryson City (BREI-suhn), town (1990 pop. 1,145), ⊙ Swain co., W N.C., 50 mi/80 km WSW of Asheville, on Tuckasegee R., which enters Little Tenn. (a.k.a. 14.5 km to W in arm of Fontana L. reservoir; 35°25′N 83°27′W. Mt. resort center bet. Great Smoky Mts. Natl. Park (to N) and Nantahala Natl. Forest (to W and S). Eastern Cherokee Indian Reservation to E (Qually boundary). Timber; corn, oats, tobacco; livestock; mfg. (wooden prods., textiles). Deep Creek Campground (natl. park) to N. Oconoluftee Indian Village and Mus. of the Cherokee Indian at Cherokee Reservation. Great Smoky Mts. to N, Cowee Mts. to S.

Bryte, town, Yolo co., central Calif., suburb 3 mi/4.8 km WNW of downtown Sacramento, on Sacramento R. Fruit, nuts, sugar beets; rice, wheat; tomatoes, melons, sunflowers. Natomas Airport to NE.

Bucatunna Creek (buhk-uh-TAHN-uh), c.90 mi/145 km, E Miss.; rises SE of Meridian near Ala. state line; flows generally S to Chickasawhay R., 13 mi/21 km. SE of Waynesboro.

Buccoo Reef (boo-KOO), undersea garden, Tobago, Rep. of Trinidad and Tobago, 6 mi/9.7 km E of Scarborough, extends bet. Buccoo and Pigeon Point on SW coast of isl. Has Nylon Pool, an offshore shallow sandy lagoon.

Buchanan 1 county (□ 573 sq mi/1,484 sq km; 1990 pop.

20,844), E Iowa, ⊙ Independence; 42°28′N 91°50′W. Prairie agr. area (cattle, hogs, poultry; corn, oats) drained by Wapsipinicon R. and Buffalo Creek. Many sand and gravel pits, some limestone quarries. Widespread flooding in 1993. Formed 1837. **2** county (□ 411 sq mi/1,064 sq km; 1990 pop. 83,083), NW Mo.; ⊙ St. Joseph; 39°40′N 94°48′W. Bounded W by Missouri R.; drained by the Little Platte. Stock raising (cattle, hogs); agr. (corn, wheat, hay, apples, tobacco); limestone; mfg. centered at St. Joseph. Formed 1838. **3** county (□ 503 sq mi/1,303 sq km; 1990 pop.31,333), SW Va., in the Allegheny Mts.; ⊙ Grundy; 37°16′N 82°02′W. Bounded NW by Ky. state line, NE by W.Va. state line (reaches Tug Fork R. in far N); drained by Levisa Fork of the Big Sandy R. Agr. (hay, potatoes, sweet potatoes, tobacco; poultry; cattle); timber; bituminous-coal mining. Formed 1858.

Buchanan 1 (byoo-KAN-uhn), city (1990 pop. 1,009), ⊙ Haralson co., NW Ga., 15 mi/24 km NNW of Carrollton, near Ala. state line; 33°48′N 85°11′W. Apparel and textile mfg. Former Queen Anne–style courthouse now owned by historical society. **2** city (1990 pop. 4,992), Berrien co., extreme SW Mich., on St. Joseph R. and 6 mi/9.7 km W of Niles; 41°49′N 86°22′W. Mfg. (transportation equip., flagpoles, furniture, construction equip., electronic equip., vending machine foods). Native Amer. village sites and mounds nearby. Ski resort in vicinity. Platted 1837; inc. as village 1863, as city 1929.

Buchanan, town (1990 pop. 1,222), Botetourt co., W central Va., 22 mi/35 km NNE of Roanoke, on James R., in the Blue Ridge; W terminus of James R. and Kanawha Canal (1851); 37°31′N 79°41′W. Mfg. (contract sewing; limestone prods., rubber prods., buttons); agr. (livestock; dairying; grain, apples, vegetables); limestone quarrying. Peaks of Otter are SE. Inc. 1833 and 1892.

Buchanan (boo-KA-nuhn), village (1991 pop. 338), SE Sask., central Canada, 15 mi/24 km WNW of Canora; 51°42′N 102°45′W. Mixed farming.

Buchanan, village (□ 1 sq mi/2.6 sq km; 1990 pop. 1,970), Westchester co., SE N.Y., just S of Peekskill, near E bank of the Hudson R.; 41°15′N 73°56′W. Mfg. of textiles and apparel. Indian Point nuclear plants are here. Inc. 1928.

Buchanan Bay, E Ellesmere Isl., NE Franklin dist., N.W.T., N Canada, arm (40 mi/64 km long, 12 mi/19 km–20 mi/32 km wide) of Kane Basin, on S side of Bache Peninsula; 78°40′–79°03′N 74°30′–77°30′W. On N shore of bay was site of Bache Peninsula post and meteorological station.

Buchanan Dam, Calif.: see CHOWCHILLA RIVER.

Buchanan, Lake, reservoir (□ 32 sq mi/83 sq km), on border bet. Llano and Burnet cos., S central Texas, on Colorado R., 12 mi/19 km W of Burnet; c.20 mi/32 km long; 30°35′N 97°21′W. Max. capacity 1,000,000 acre-ft. Formed by Buchanan Dam, built 1937. Town of Buchanan Dam on S shore, on E side of dam.

Buchans, town (1991 pop. 1,164), central N.F., E Canada, on Red Indian L.; 48°51′N 56°52′W. Large mine yields lead, silver, zinc, and copper.

Buchon, Point, San Luis Obispo co., SW Calif., coastal promontory at SW extremity of Estero Bay, Pacific Ocean, just S of Morro Bay. Site of Montana de Oro State Park.

Buchtel (BUK-tuhl), village (1990 pop. 640), Athens co., SE Ohio, 10 mi/16 km NNW of Athens; 39°29′N 82°11′W.

Buck Grove, town (1990 pop. 20), Crawford co., W Iowa, 7 mi/11.3 km SSW of Denison; 41°55′N 95°24′W.

Buck Hill Falls, uninc. town (1990 pop. 950), Barrett township, Monroe co., NE Pa., in Pocono Mts., 14 mi/23 km NNW of Stroudsburg, on Buck Hill Creek; 41°11′N 75°15′W. Summer and winter sports; hunting, fishing.

Buck Island 1 islet (41.55 acres/16.82 ha), U.S. Virgin Isls., off SE St. Thomas Isl., 5 mi/8 km SSE of Charlotte Amalie; 18°16′N 64°54′W. Lighthouse. **2** islet (17.64 acres/7.14 ha), U.S. Virgin Isls., off NE St. Croix Isl., 6 mi/9.7 km NE of Christiansted; 17°48′N 64°37′W.

Buckeye 1 town (1990 pop. 5,038), Maricopa co., SW

central Ariz., near Gila R., 30 mi/48 km W of Phoenix; 33°24′N 112°35′W. Agr. area (cotton, grain, vegetables, fruit), mfg. (apparel, construction materials, chemicals). Inc. 1929. **2** town (1990 pop. 105), Hardin co., central Iowa, 9 mi/14.5 km SW of Iowa Falls; 42°25′N 93°22′W. In agr. area (fertilizer).

Buckeye Lake, village (1990 pop. 2,986), Licking co., central Ohio, 9 mi/14 km SSW of Newark, and on Buckeye L. (c.7 mi/11 km long); 39°58′N 82°29′W. State park (□ c.6 sq mi/15.5 sq km) here; camping, recreational facilities. Beside lake created for Ohio Canal c.1827.

Buckeye Lake, reservoir (□ 4 sq mi/10.4 sq km), Licking co., central Ohio, on tributary of South Fork Licking R., 11 mi/18 km S of Newark; 39°56′N 82°29′W. Max. capacity 20.000 acre-ft. Formed by Buckeye Lake Dam (12 ft/4 m high), built (1832) for recreation. Buckeye Lake State Park on S shore.

Buckeystown (BUHK-EIZ-town), village, Frederick co., W Md., near Monocacy R., 6 mi/9.7 km SSW of Frederick. Originally settled at the time of Revolutionary War by Ger. families. George and Michael Buckey established the Buckey Tannery here in 1775.

Buckfield, town (1990 pop. 1,566), Oxford co., W Maine, on Nezinscot R., 10 mi/16 km NE of South Paris; 44°17′N 70°22′W. In farming, recreational area; wood prods.

Buckhannon (buhk-HAN-uhn), town (1990 pop. 5,909), ⊙ Upshur co., central W.Va., on Buckhannon R., 21 mi/34 km SSE of Clarksburg; 38°59′N 80°13′W. Region known for its agr. (apples, wine); livestock; poultry. Mfg. (building materials, plastic prods., clothing; lumber milling, coal processing). Coal mines, gas wells. Timber. Seat of W.Va. Wesleyan Col. Audra State Park to NE; Stonecoal L. reservoir and Wildlife Management Area to W. Settled 1770.

Buckhannon River (buhk-HAN-uhn), c.45 mi/72 km long, central W.Va.; formed in SW Randolph co. by junction of short Right and Left forks; flows generally N, past Buckhannon, to Tygart R. 6 mi/9.7 km SSW of Philippi.

Buckhead, suburban downtown, N Atlanta, Fulton co., Ga. This former independent community was annexed to the city of Atlanta in 1952. Beginning in the 1920s, Buckhead began emerging as a desirable location for the mansions of prominent Atlantans and soon became the most exclusive residential dist. of the city. Known for its large, heavily wooded, and lavishly landscaped lots filled with azaleas and dogwood trees. Antique stores and art gal. cluster here. Nearby is Lenox Square, built in 1959. That mall has evolved into the largest retail shopping center in the Southeast U.S. High-rise housing, office bldgs., and hotels now make this area a leading mixed-use suburban downtown in the Atlanta region.

Buckhead, town (1990 pop. 176), Morgan co., N central Ga., 7 mi/11.3 km ESE of Madison; 33°34′N 83°22′W.

Buckholts, village (1990 pop. 335), Milam co., central Texas, c.55 mi/89 km NE of Austin; 30°52′N 97°07′W. Cotton, corn, and cattle area.

Buckhorn Island, N.Y.: see GRAND ISLAND.

Buckhorn Lake, Kawartha Lakes, S Ont., central Canada, 11 mi/18 km NNW of Peterborough; 9 mi/14 km long, 1 mi/2 km–3 mi/5 km wide. Drained E by Trent Canal.

Buckingham, county (□ 583 sq mi/1,510 sq km; 1990 pop. 12,873), central Va.; ⊙ Buckingham; 37°34′N 78°31′W. Bounded NW and N by James R., S by Appomattox R.; drained by small Slate and Willis rivers. Agr. (mainly tobacco; also hay, wheat, corn, apples, peaches; cattle); extensive lumbering, slate quarrying; sand, kyanite. Power plant on James R. Part of Buckingham-Appomattox State Forest in SW. Formed 1761.

Buckingham, town (1991 pop. 10,548), SW Que., E Canada, on Lièvre R. near its mouth on Ottawa R., and 17 mi/27 km NE of Ottawa; 45°35′N 75°25′W. Paper milling, lumbering; mining (feldspar, silica, phosphate rock); mfg. of chemicals; dairying.

Buckingham (BUH-keeng-ham), uninc. town (1990

pop. 2,000), Bucks co., SE Pa., 4 mi/6.4 km E of Doylestown, near Mill Creek; 40°19′N 79°03′W. Light mfg. (wines); agr. includes dairying; livestock; poultry; grain, apples, grapes. Wineries to E and SE.

Buckingham 1 village (1990 pop. 340), Kankakee co., NE Ill., 16 mi/26 km WSW of Kankakee; 41°02′N 88°10′W. In agr. area. **2** village (1990 pop. 102), Dallas co., N Texas, residential suburb 11 mi/18 km NNE of downtown Dallas, surrounded by city of Richardson; 32°55′N 96°43′W. **3** uninc. village, ⊙ Buckingham co., central Va., 34 mi/55 km ENE of Lynchburg, on Slate R. Mfg. (wood prods.); agr. (tobacco, grain, fruit; cattle); timber; slate. Holliday Lake State Park, Buckingham-Appomattox State Forest to SW. Also called Buckingham Court House.

Buckingham Court House, Va.: see BUCKINGHAM.

Buckland, town (1990 pop. 1,928), Franklin co., NW Mass., in hills, 10 mi/16 km W of Greenfield; 42°35′N 72°48′W. Apple orchards; dairying. Recreation; growing tourist trade (SHELBURNE FALLS village). Deerfield R. bounds township on N. Inc. 1779.

Buckland 1 village (1990 pop. 318), NW Alaska, on NE Seward Peninsula, on Buckland R., and 10 mi/16 km SE of Kotzebue Bay; 65°58′N 161°07′W. **2** village (1990 pop. 239), Auglaize co., W Ohio, 12 mi/19 km SW of Lima, and on Auglaize R., in agr. area; 40°39′N 84°16′W.

Buckland River, 120 mi/193 km long, NW Alaska, at base of Seward Peninsula; rises near 65°25′N 159°30′W; flows NW, past Buckland, to Eschscholtz Bay, 15 mi/24 km N of Buckland.

Buckley, town (1990 pop. 3,516), Pierce co., W central Wash., 20 mi/32 km ESE of Tacoma, on White R., near foothills of Cascade Range; 47°10′N 122°01′W. Vegetables, berries; mfg. (metal stampings); timber; mining, logging in region. Mad Mountain Dam to E, on White R., Carbon River entrance to Mount Rainier Natl. Park to SE. Part of Snoqualmie Natl. Forest, including Clearwater Wilderness Area, to SE. Settled 1888, inc. 1890.

Buckley 1 village (1990 pop. 557), Iroquois co., E Ill., 37 mi/60 km SSW of Kankakee; 40°36′N 88°02′W. In agr. area. **2** village (1990 pop. 402), Wexford co., NW Mich., 18 mi/29 km S of Traverse City; 44°30′N 85°40′W. In agr. area. Mfg. boats.

Bucklin, city (1990 pop. 616), Linn co., N central Mo., 10 mi/16 km E of Brookfield; 39°46′N 92°53′W. Corn, wheat, soybeans; sheep; cattle; RR junction.

Bucklin (BUHK-lin), village (1990 pop. 710), Ford co., SW Kansas, 25 mi/40 km SE of Dodge City; 37°32′N 99°37′W. RR junction. Wheat; cattle.

Buckman, village (1990 pop. 201), Morrison co., central Minn., 15 mi/24 km ESE of Little Falls, on Buckman Creek; 45°53′N 94°05′W. Agr. area (dairying; poultry; potatoes, grain).

Bucknell Manor, uninc. town, Fairfax co., NE Va., residential suburb 2 mi/3.2 km S of Alexandria, 9 mi/14.5 km S of Wash., D.C., near Potomac R.; 38°46′N 77°04′W.

Buckner, city (1990 pop. 2,873), Jackson co., W Mo., 22 mi/35 km E of Kansas City; satellite community of Kansas City; 39°07′N 94°12′W. Wheat, corn, sorghum; dairying; cattle, hogs; mfg. (zinc and aluminum castings).

Buckner 1 village (1990 pop. 325), Lafayette co., SW Ark., 34 mi/55 km E of Texarkana, near Dorchant Bayou, and NW of L. Columbia reservoir; 33°21′N 93°26′W. **2** village (1990 pop. 478), Franklin co., S Ill., 12 mi/19 km N of Herrin; 37°58′N 89°01′W. In bituminous-coal-mining and agr. area. **3** uninc. village (1990 pop. 400), Oldham co., N Ky., industrial suburb 18 mi/29 km NE of Louisville and 4 mi/6.4 km SW of La Grange. In agr. area (tobacco, grain; livestock; dairying). Mfg. (merchandise displays, tool and die, swimming pool kits, construction materials, lumber, chemicals, foods); printing and publishing.

Buckroe Beach, uninc. town, Hampton City, SE Va., residential suburb 2 mi/3.2 km N of Fort Monroe.

Bucks, county (□ 622 sq mi/1,611 sq km; 1990 pop. 541,174), SE Pa.; ⊙ Doylestown; 40°20′N 75°06′W. Bounded E and SE by Del. R. SE part of co. lies in

corridor bet. Philadelphia and Trenton (N.J.), and is highly urbanized. Residential and agr. area. Mfg. at Bristol, Croydon, Ivyland, Langhorne, Warminster, Newtown, Fairless Hills, Chalfont, and Perkasie. Agr. (corn, wheat, alfalfa, soybeans, apples; poultry, hogs, cattle; dairying); limestone, sandstone, granite quarrying. George Washington crossed the Del. R. at WASHINGTON CROSSING. Nishaminy and Pennbury Manor state parks in SE, Tyler State Park in SE center, Washington Crossing State Park and Washington Crossing State Historical Park in NE; Ralph Stover State Park in NE, L. Nockamixon reservoir and Nockamixon State Park in N center, Roosevelt State Park in N. Formed 1682.

Buckskin, Mount, Colo.: see PARK RANGE.

Bucksport 1 town (1990 pop. 4,825), including Bucksport village, Hancock co., S Maine, on the Penobscot R., and 18 mi/29 km WNW of Ellsworth; 44°38′N 68°45′W. Paper mill built 1930. Site of Jed Prouty Tavern (1804) and Waldo-Hancock bridge. Old Fort Knox (1846) is across river. Settled 1762, inc. 1792. **2** uninc. town (1990 pop. 1,022), Horry co., E S.C., 13 mi/21 km W of Myrtle Beach, on Waccamaw R. (Intracoastal Waterway); 33°40′N 79°06′W. Tourism and the fishing industry that harvests oysters, clams, crabs, shrimp, and fish are the main industries.

Bucoda, village (1990 pop. 536), Thurston co., W Wash., 18 mi/29 km S of Olympia, on Skookumchuck R.; 46°48′N 122°52′W. In agr. region (vegetables, blueberries, hay; poultry). Skookumchuck Dam and Reservoir to E.

Buctouche, [Micmac = big bay], village (1986 pop. 2,420), N.B., E Canada, 25 mi/40 km N of Moncton, port on Northumberland Strait; 46°28′N 64°44′W. Acadians settled here 1784, Eng. after 1800. Fishing, lumbering, shipbuilding remain important. Future in high-technology development. Birthplace of Acadian author Antonine Maillet and industrialist billionaire K.C. Irving.

Buctzotz (BOOK-tsots), town (1990 pop. 5,817), Yucatán, SE Mexico, 23 mi/37 km NNE of Izamal. Henequen, corn, beans, tropical fruit.

Bucyrus (byoo-SEI-ruhs), city (1990 pop. 13,496), ⊙ Crawford co., N central Ohio, on the Sandusky R.; 40°50′N 82°59′W. In a farm area. Trade and industrial center. Mfg. includes machinery, electronic prods., fabricated metal prods. Settled 1818, inc. 1886.

Bucyrus (boo-SEI-ruhs), village (1990 pop. 22), Adams co., SW N.Dak., 8 mi/12.9 km NW of Hettinger; 46°03′N 102°47′W.

Bud, uninc. village (1990 pop. 500), Wyoming co., S W.Va., 8 mi/12.9 km SE of Pineville. Coal.

Buda (BYOO-dah), town (1990 pop. 1,795), Hays co., S central Texas, 15 mi/24 km SSW of Austin; 30°05′N 97°50′W. Agr. (cattle; cotton; fruits, vegetables); mfg. (consumer goods, crushed limestone, cement; diversified light mfg.).

Buda (BYOO-dah), village (1990 pop. 563), Bureau co., N Ill., 13 mi/21 km ENE of Kewanee; 41°19′N 89°40′W. Grain; livestock.

Budd Lake, resort village (1990 pop. 7,272), Morris co., N N.J., on Budd L. (c.2 mi/3.2 km long), and 14 mi/23 km WNW of Morristown; 40°52′N 74°44′W.

Bude (BYOOD), town (1990 pop. 969), Franklin co., SW Miss., 32 mi/51 kmE of Natchez, on Homochitto R., and in Homochitto Natl. Forest; 31°27′N 90°50′W. In agr. (cotton, corn) and timber area; mfg. (apparel). Inc. 1912.

Buechel (BYOO-chuhl), town (1990 pop. 7,081), Jefferson co., NW Ky., residential suburb 7 mi/11.3 km SE of downtown Louisville; 38°11′N 85°38′W. Industrial park (electronic prods.) to S.

Buellton, city (1990 pop. 3,506), Santa Barbara co., SW Calif., 30 mi/48 km WNW of Santa Barbara, on Santa Ynez R.; 34°38′N 120°12′W. Los Padres Natl. Forest to NE. Fruit, grapes, grain, vegetables, avocados; cattle. Mfg. (machine parts, adhesives and sealants, hand tools, gaskets); winery.

Buena (BOO-nah), town, Atlantic co., S N.J., 12 mi/19 km WNW of Mays Landing. Inc. after 1940.

Buena Esperanza, Gran Banco de, Cuba: see GRAN BANCO DE BUENA ESPERANZA.

Buena Park, city (1990 pop. 68,784), Orange co., S Calif., a suburb 20 mi/32 km SE of downtown Los Angeles and 3 mi/4.8 km W of Anaheim; 33°52′N 118°00′W. Food processing, mfg. (aircraft parts, musical instruments, electronic equip.) and tourism are important to the city's economy. Large warehouse center for retail and wholesale groceries and dry goods. Fullerton Municipal Airport in NE. Knott's Berry Farm, a re-created gold rush town theme park; Movieland Wax Mus.; a civic light opera and community playhouse; a Jap. village surrounding a deer compound; and a transportation mus. are here. Inc. 1953.

Buena Vista (BYOO-nuh VIS-tuh), county (□ 580 sq mi/1,502 sq km; 1990 pop. 19,965), NW Iowa; ⊙ Storm Lake; 42°44′N 95°09′W. Prairie agr. area (hogs, cattle, poultry; corn, oats, soybeans) drained by Little Sioux R. and by headstreams of Raccoon, Boyer, and Maple rivers; includes reclaimed swampland and has system of drainage ditches. Sand and gravel pits. Wanata State Park in NW corner. Storm L. in S has several local parks along its shores. Pickerel L. in NE corner (glacial origin). Formed 1851.

Buena Vista (BYOO-nah VIS-tah), independent city (□ 7 sq mi/18.1 sq km; 1990 pop. 6,406), W Va., separate from surrounding Rockbridge co., in the Blue Ridge, on North R., 25 mi/40 km NNW of Lynchburg, on W edge of part of George Washington Natl. Forest; 37°43′N 79°21′W. Mfg. (plastic prods., construction materials, clothing, transportation equip., electrical prods., lumber, machinery, paper, silk textiles, bricks, leather goods), printing and publishing, yarn dyeing. Agr. area (dairying; livestock; grain, apples, soybeans); timber. Southern Va. Col. (2-year). Natural Bridge is 12 mi/19 km SW. Founded 1889; inc. 1891.

Buena Vista 1 (BYOO-nah VIS-tah), town (1990 pop. 1,752), ⊙ Chaffee co., central Colo., on Arkansas R., at mouth of Cottonwood Creek, in foothills of Sawatch Mts., and 22 mi/35 km NNW of Salida; 38°49′N 106°08′W. Elev. 7,954 ft/2,424 m. Resort; trade and shipping point in agr. and silver-mining region; some agr. in valley (lettuce, potatoes, grain; livestock); light mfg. Mt. Yale 9 mi/14.5 km W. Parts of San Isabel Natl. Forest to E and W; Ark. Headwaters State Park to S. **2** town (1990 pop. 1,472), ⊙ Marion co., W Ga., 29 mi/47 km ESE of Columbus; 32°19′N 84°31′W. Mfg. of furniture; poultry processing; lumber. Settled 1830. **3** (BOO-nah VIS-tah), town (1990 pop. 7,655), Atlantic co., S N.J., 5 mi/8 km NE of Vineland; 39°30′N 74°53′W. Inc. 1867.

Buena Vista, village, Coahuila, N Mexico, 5 mi/8 km SSW of Saltillo. A Mexican War battle (Feb. 22–23, 1847) bet. U.S. forces under Zachary Taylor and Mexicans under Santa Anna took place nearby; after fierce fighting, Santa Anna withdrew.

Buena Vista, Bahía de (BWAIN-uh VEE-stuh, bah-EE-uh dai), shallow inlet off N coast of Sancti Spíritus prov., central Cuba, separated by keys from Old Bahama Channel, 10 mi/16 km E of Caibarién; c.30 mi/48 km E-W, 6 mi/9.7 km wide; 22°30′N 79°08′W.

Buena Vista Lake, Calif.: see KERN RIVER.

Buenaventura (boo-ee-nah-ven-TOO-rah), town (1990 pop. 4,559), Chihuahua, N Mexico, in Sierra Madre Occidental, on Santa María R., and 120 mi/193 km NW of Chihuahua; 29°50′N 107°30′W. Agr. center (cotton, corn, wheat, beans, tobacco; cattle). Also known as El Valle.

Buenavista de Cuéllar (boo-ee-nah-VEES-tah DAI koo-AI-ar), town (1990 pop. 5,723), ⊙ municipio, Guerrero, SW Mexico, on RR and 12 mi/19 km NE of Iguala de la Independencia, just off Mexico Hwy 95; 18°30′N 99°22′W. Elev. 3,596 ft/1,096 m. Cereals, sugar, fruit, beans, peanuts; forest prods. (resin, vanilla, rubber); marble and iron mining.

Buenavista Tomatlán (boo-ee-nah-VEES-tah to-maht-LAHN), town (1990 pop. 7,464), ⊙ Buenavista municipio, Michoacán, W Mexico, 16 mi/26 km W of Apatzingán de la Constitución, on Mexico Hwy 120; 19°08′N 102°37′W. Rice, fruit, sugarcane. Sometimes Tomatlán.

Buey River (BOO-WAI), 56 mi/90 km long, Granma prov., E Cuba. Runs through prov., draining area of 205 sq mi/531 sq km.

Buff Bay, town (1991 pop. 2,596), Portland parish, NE Jamaica, on coast, on RR, and 15 mi/24 km WNW of Port Antonio; 18°14′N 76°40′W. Bananas, coconuts, cacao.

Buffalo 1 county (□ 975 sq mi/2,525 sq km; 1990 pop. 37,447), S central Nebr.; ⊙ Kearney; 40°51′N 99°04′W. Agr. area drained by South Loup and Wood rivers; bounded S by Platte R. Mfg. at Kearney. Dairying; cattle, hogs, potatoes; wheat, soybeans, corn, sorghum, alfalfa. Ravenna Lake State Recreation Area in NE; Windmill State Wayside Area in SE; Union Pacific State Wayside Area in SW. Formed 1870. **2** county (□ 487 sq mi/1,261 sq km; 1990 pop. 1,759), central S.Dak.; ⊙ Gann Valley; 44°03′N 99°10′W. Agr. area with Crow Creek Indian Reservation in W; bounded W by Missouri R. Diversified farming; wheat. Formed 1864. **3** county (□ 709 sq mi/1,836 sq km; 1990 pop. 13,584), W Wis.; ⊙ Alma; 44°22′N 91°45′W. Bounded NW by Chippewa R., W and SW by the Miss. R., SE by Trempealeau R.; drained by Buffalo R. Hilly dairy and in S livestock area; also produces alfalfa, hay; cattle, hogs, sheep; timber; dairying. Part of Miss. River Wildlife and Fish Refuge on Miss. R. W part of Buffalo River State Trail in NE. Includes Merrick State Park. Formed 1853.

Buffalo 1 city (1990 pop. 2,414), ⊙ Dallas co., SW central Mo., in the Ozarks, near Niangua R., 32 mi/51 km NNE of Springfield; 37°38′N 93°05′W. Wheat, corn, sorghum; poultry; dairying; mfg. (apparel), poultry processing. Recreation on Niangua R. Settled 1839, inc. 1854. **2** city (□ 52 sq mi/135 sq km; 1990 pop. 328,123), ⊙ Erie co., W N.Y., on L. Erie and the Niagara and Buffalo rivers; 42°53′N 78°51′W. With over 37 mi/60 km of waterfront, it is an important port of entry and a commercial port (called Gateway Metroport). However, improvements in the St. Lawrence Seaway in the late 1950s, creation of a natl. system of superhighways (and subsequent rise of trucking), and improvements in the Welland Canal in the early 1990s have all contributed to a substantial decline in Buffalo's port and break-in-bulk functions. Buffalo remains, however, a major RR hub. Diversified mfg. and financial center, with many banks. A village laid out (1803) here by Joseph Ellicott for the Holland Land Co. was almost completely destroyed by fire (1813) in the War of 1812 and recovered slowly until the opening of the Erie Canal in 1825. Transportation was a primary factor in the city's growth, and Buffalo became a major Great Lakes port. The city developed as a major flour-milling center and thrived on heavy industry such as steel milling and automobile and locomotive mfg., as well as tanneries and breweries. However, these industries all fell into serious decline and by the 1980s, Buffalo had lost its traditional economic base. The Buffalo area has since benefited greatly from the Free Trade Agreement (1988) bet. the U.S. and Canada, attracting a great deal of Can. investment in real estate and mfg. Its educational institutions include the State Univ. of N.Y., with campuses at Buffalo and suburban Amherst, Canisius Col., D'Youville Col., Villa Maria Col., Sisters of Charity Hosp. School of Nursing, Trocaire Col., Bryant and Stratton Business Inst., Erie Community Col. (City Campus), Houghton Col. (Buffalo Campus), Medgille Col., as well as a large number of non-degree vocational and technical institutes. Of interest are the Albright-Knox Art Gall., the Buffalo Mus. of Science, the Buffalo and Erie Co. Historical Societys mus., the Walden Galleria (one of the largest shopping centers in U.S.), and the Buffalo Zoological Gardens. Notable bldgs. include the city hall (1932) and the Prudential Bldg. (1895–1896), designed by Louis Sullivan. Has a music hall and a philharmonic orchestra. The Buffalo Bills of the Natl. Football League play in Rich Stadium (located in nearby Orchard Park, N.Y.), and Memorial Auditorium is home to the Natl. Hockey League's Sabres. Roswell Park Cancer Inst., founded in 1898, and one of the world's oldest and largest cancer centers, is located here. The Peace Bridge (1927) connects Buffalo with Fort Erie (Ont.). Has an internatl. airport. Grover Cleveland became mayor of Buffalo in 1882. It was here in 1901, at the Pan-American Exposition, that President McKinley was assassinated and where Theodore Roosevelt subsequently took the presidential oath. The McKinley monument and the Theodore Roosevelt Inaugural Natl. Historic Site commemorate the 2 events. Millard Fillmore's home was here. Inc. 1832.

Buffalo 1 town (1990 pop. 1,260), Scott co., E Iowa, on the Mississippi R., 8 mi/12.9 km WSW of Davenport; 41°27′N 90°43′W. Concrete blocks, clay prods., pearl buttons. **2** town (1990 pop. 6,856), ⊙ Wright co., E Minn., 34 mi/55 km WNW of Minneapolis; 45°10′N 93°52′W. Livestock, poultry; grain; dairying; mfg. (construction materials, feeds, cellulose insulation, machinery, plastic prods., printing and publishing). L. Maria State Park to NW; several small natural lakes in area. Settled c.1855, inc. 1887. **3** town (1990 pop. 1,312), ⊙ Harper co., NW Okla., 30 mi/48 km NNW of Woodward, on Buffalo Creek; 36°49′N 99°37′W. Elev. 1,791 ft/546 m. Wheat; cattle; mfg. (feeds). Oil and gas wells. Founded 1907, inc. 1908. **4** uninc. town (1990 pop. 1,569), Union co., N S.C., 3 mi/4.8 km W of Union; 34°43′N 81°40′W. Mfg. of apparel fabrics; agr. includes poultry, livestock; dairying; grain, peaches. **5** town (1990 pop. 488), ⊙ Harding co., NW S.Dak., 105 mi/169 km N of Rapid City, on S fork of Grand R. near its headwaters. Trade center for oil, sheep and cattle region. **6** town (1990 pop. 1,555), Leon co., E central Texas, 65 mi/105 km E of Waco; 31°27′N 96°03′W. Vegetables, watermelons, grains; timber; oil and natural gas; light mfg. **7** town (1990 pop. 969), Putnam co., W central W.Va., near the Kanawha, 25 mi/40 km NW of Charleston and 7.5 mi/12.1 km NNW of Winnfield; 38°36′N 81°58′W. Agr. (corn, tobacco); cattle; poultry. Chief Cornstalk Wildlife Management Area to NW. **8** town (1990 pop. 915), Buffalo co., W Wis., on the Mississippi R. and 14 mi/23 km NNW of Winona (Minn.); 44°13′N 91°52′W. Lock and Dam No. 5 and Merrick State Park to SE. **9** town (1990 pop. 3,302), ⊙ Johnson co., N Wyo., on Clear Creek and 37 mi/60 km SSE of Sheridan, just E of Bighorn Mts. and Bighorn Natl. Forest (includes Cloud Peak Wilderness); 44°20′N 106°43′W. Elev. 4,645 ft/1,416 m. Resort; shipping point in sheep and cattle region; agr. (sugar beets, grain). To S is site of Fort McKinney; L. De Smet 7 mi/11.3 km N. Founded c.1880, inc. 1884.

Buffalo 1 village (1990 pop. 503), Sangamon co., central Ill., 12 mi/19 km ENE of Springfield; 39°51′N 89°24′W. In agr. area. **2** village (1990 pop. 500), White co., NW Ind., 9 mi/14.5 km N of Monticello, on Tippecanoe R., at head of L. Shafer. Soybeans, grain; cattle. **3** village (1990 pop. 293), Wilson co., SE Kansas, 14 mi/23 km NE of Fredonia; 37°42′N 95°42′W. Livestock; grain; dairying. Wilson State Fishing L. to E. **4** uninc. village (1990 pop. 500), Larue co., central Ky., 16 mi/26 km SE of Elizabethtown. Agr. area (tobacco; livestock; dairying). One of 6 places so named in Ky. **5** village (1990 pop. 204), Cass co., E N.Dak., 7 mi/11.3 km W of Casselton; 46°55′N 97°32′W.

Buffalo Bayou, c.45 mi/72 km long, S Texas, rises in creeks W of Houston, flows E, through Houston, to San Jacinto R. near its mouth. Turning basin in bayou is port of Houston; deepwater Houston Ship Channel to Gulf of Mexico is in bayou's lower 15-mi/24-km course.

Buffalo Bill Dam, Wyo.: see SHOSHONE RIVER.

Buffalo Bill Reservoir (□ 15 sq mi/39 sq km), Park co., NW Wyo., on South Fork Shoshone R., 3 mi/5 km SW of Cody; 44°30′N 109°15′W. Max. capacity 644,540 acre-ft. Formed by Buffalo Bill Dam (350 ft/107 m high), built (1910) by the Bureau of Reclamation for power generation; also used for irrigation, water supply, recreation, and as a fish and wildlife pond. Shosone Natl. Forest to W.

Buffalo Center, town (1990 pop. 1,081), Winnebago co., N Iowa, 17 mi/27 km NW of Forest City; 43°23′N 93°56′W. In agr. area.

Buffalo Creek 1 c.50 mi/80 km long, E Iowa; rises E of Oelwein; flows SE to Wapsipinicon R. at Anamosa.

2 70 mi/113 km long, S central Minn.; rises at S edge of Kandiyohi co.; flows generally E, in very serpentine course, past Browntown and Glencoe and E of Lester Prairie, to South Fork Crow R. 4 mi/6.4 km SW of Watertown. **3** 17 mi/27 km long, SW W.Va.; rises in Logan co.; flows SW joining Guyandotte R. Coal camps and settlements (including Accoville, Amherstdale, Kistler, Lorado, Lundale, Robinette) were built along creek after the completion of the Chesapeake and Ohio RR spur line in 1912. In Feb. 1972, coal refuse dam broke, killing 125 people.

Buffalo Gap 1 village (1990 pop. 173), Custer co., SW S.Dak., 7 mi/11.3 km ENE of Hot Springs and on branch of Cheyenne R. Trade center for ranching region. Part of Buffalo Gap Natl. Grassland to E; Wind Cave Natl. Park to NW. **2** village (1990 pop. 499), Taylor co., W central Texas, 12 mi/19 km SSW of Abilene, on Elm Creek; 32°16′N 99°49′W. Elev. 1,926 ft/587 m. Old frontier town. Agr. (cotton, sorghum, hay; cattle). L. Abilene and Abilene State Park to SW.

Buffalo Grove, city (1990 pop. 36,427), Lake and Cook cos., NE Ill., residential suburb 26 mi/42 km NW of downtown Chicago, near Des Plaines R.; 42°10′N 87°57′W. Mfg. (paper prods., transportation equip., amusement games, machinery, chemicals, foods, electronic equip.).

Buffalo Lake, village (1990 pop. 734), Renville co., S Minn., 18 mi/29 km E of Olivia; 44°44′N 94°37′W. Agr. area (dairying; poultry, livestock; grain, sugar beets, soybeans); mfg. (feeds, nylon ropes), beef processing. Buffalo Creek passes to NE.

Buffalo Lake (□ 55 sq mi/142 sq km), S central Alta., W Canada, 35 mi/56 km ENE of Red Deer. Drains S into Red Deer R.

Buffalo Lake, an expansion of Fox R., in Marquette co., S central Wis., 11 mi/18 km N of Portage; c.16 mi/26 km long. Montello is at E end; Endeavor at W end.

Buffalo Lake, Texas: see TIERRA BLANCA CREEK.

Buffalo Lithia Springs, Va.: see BUFFALO SPRINGS.

Buffalo Mineral Springs, Va.: see BUFFALO SPRINGS.

Buffalo Narrows, town (1991 pop. 1,060), NW Sask., W Canada, on W end of Churchill L. on strip of land bet. Peter Pond and Churchill lakes, 200 mi/322 km NW of Saskatoon; 55°51′N 108°29′W. Sport fishing and hunting area. Timber; furs. Airstrip; highway access from S.

Buffalo National River (□ 147 sq mi/381 sq km; wilderness □ 16 sq mi/41 sq km), Newton, Searcy, Marion and Baxter cos., N Ark., includes all but upper 10 mi/16 km of Buffalo R., one of few free-flowing rivers in lower 48 U.S. states. Has numerous springs, caves. Includes former Buffalo River State Park in E part. Unit of U.S. natl. park system; canoeing, rafting, fishing, swimming, hiking. Est. 1972; designated wilderness 1978.

Buffalo Peak, Colo.: see TARRYALL MOUNTAINS.

Buffalo Peaks, in Park Range, in Rocky Mts., on border bet. Chaffee and Park cos., central Colo., in Pike (E) and San Isabel (W) natl. forests. Includes East Peak (13,301 ft/4,054 m) and West Peak (13,327 ft/4,062 m).

Buffalo River 1 c.150 mi/241 km, in N Ark.; rises in SW Ozark Natl. Forest, Newton co.; flows ENE, through the Ozarks, past Gilbert, to White R. 14 mi/23 km SE of Yellville. All but the upper 10 mi/16 km is within Buffalo Natl. River (Natl. Park). **2** 80 mi/129 km long, in W Minn.; rises in central Becker co., in Tamarack L.; flows generally WNW through Rock, Rice, and Buffalo lakes, past Hawley, through Buffalo River State Park, and past Glyndon, to Red R. of the North near Georgetown, 15 mi/24 km N of Fargo (N.Dak.). **3** c.72 mi/116 km long, in W central Tenn.; rises in N Lawrence co.; flows W and N past Linden, to Duck R. 7 mi/11 km SSW of Waverly; 35°21′N 87°22′W. **4** c.55 mi/89 km long, in W Wis.; rises in NW Jackson co.; flows W, past Osseo and Mondovi (hydroelectric plant), then turns SW, reaching the Miss. R. 2 mi/3.2 km NW of Alma.

Buffalo Springs, uninc. village, Mecklenburg co., S Va., 13 mi/21 km ESE of South Boston, on Kerr Reservoir (Buggs Isl. L.), formed in Roanoke R. Mineral springs; resort area. Staunton River State Park to N. Also called Buffalo Lithia Springs, Buffalo Mineral Springs.

Buffington (BUH-feeng-tuhn), village (1990 pop. 800), Fayette co., SW Pa., 6 mi/9.7 km W of Uniontown, near Dunlap Creek; 39°55′N 79°50′W. Agr. (corn, hay; dairying).

Buford (BYOO-fuhrd), town (1990 pop. 8,771), Gwinnett co., N central Ga., 33 mi/53 km NE of Atlanta; 34°07′N 84°00′W. Rapidly growing suburb of Atlanta near L. Lanier. Mfg. of chemicals, wood prods., crushed stone, quartz glass tubing, clothing, tools, sheet metal fabrication. Growing reputation as an arts community. Lanier Mus. of Natural History.

Buford Dam, on the Chattahoochee R., on the border of Gwinnett and Forsyth cos., Ga., NE of Atlanta. Built (1950s) by the U.S. Army Corps of Engineers. Impounds the 59-sq-mi/153-sq-km L. Lanier, the most popular recreational lake in the state.

Buhl 1 town (1990 pop. 3,516), Twin Falls co., S Idaho, near the Snake R. (bridged 5 mi/8 km N), 15 mi/24 km W of Twin Falls; 42°36′N 114°46′W. RR terminus and shipping center for irrigated agr. area (beans, potatoes, sugar beets); dairy prods.; mfg. (food packaging, esp. rainbow trout); tourism. Has U.S. fish hatchery; the rainbow trout capital of the world. Thousand Springs to N, across Snake R.; Hagerman Fossil Beds Natl. Monument to NW; Balanced Rock to W. Founded 1906, inc. 1909. **2** (BYOOL), town (1990 pop. 915), Saint Louis co., NE Minn., in Mesabi Iron Range, 9 mi/14.5 km ENE of Hibbing; 47°30′N 92°46′W. Mining; timber; agr. (dairying; poultry; oats, alfalfa); mfg. (marble countertops). Open-pit and underground iron mines in vicinity. Superior Natl. Forest to N.

Buhler (BYOO-luhr), town (1990 pop. 1,277), Reno co., S central Kansas, on Little Arkansas R., and 10 mi/16 km NE of Hutchinson; 38°08′N 97°46′W. Wheat; mfg. (egg processing).

Buie (BOO-ee), uninc. village, Robeson co., S N.C., 11 mi/18 km NW of Lumberton. Grain, tobacco; livestock. Sometimes spelled Buies.

Buies Creek (BOO-eez), uninc. town (1990 pop. 2,085), Harnett co., central N.C., near Cape Fear R., 26 mi/42 km NNE of Fayetteville; 35°24′N 78°44′W. Cotton, tobacco, sweet potatoes, grain; poultry, livestock. Seat of Campbell Univ. Settled 1746.

Bulan (BOO-luhn), uninc. town (1990 pop. 800), Perry co., SE Ky., in Cumberland foothills, 4 mi/6.4 km NNE of Hazard. Bituminous coal.

Bulkley River, 120 mi/193 km long, W central B.C., Canada; rises in Coast Mts. near W side of Babine L.; flows a short distance W, then NW, past Telkwa and Smithers, to Skeena R. at Hazelton.

Bull Run, uninc. town, Prince William co., NE Va., residential suburb 5 mi/8 km NW of Manassas; 38°46′N 77°31′W. Bull Run Natl. Battlefield Park to NE.

Bull Run, small stream, NE Va., forms Fairfax–Prince William co. line; rises c.13 mi/21 km NW of Manassas; flows SE, past Occoquan, to Potomac R. at Woodbridge. Important Civil War battles, the 1st and 2d battles of Bull Run, were fought NW of Manassas on July 21, 1861, and Aug. 29–30, 1862. The 1st battle of Bull Run (or 1st battle of Manassas) was the 1st major engagement of the war. Both battles were victories for the Confederacy. Both battlefields are included in Manassas Natl. Battlefield Park (est. 1940).

Bull Run River, c.30 mi/48 km long, NW Oregon; rises in Cascade Range in E Multnomah co.; flows WSW through Bull Run Reservoirs 1 and 2 to Little Sandy R., 3 mi/4.8 km NE of Sandy. Bull Run Dam (200 ft/61 m high, 935 ft/285 m long; completed 1929 by city of Portland) is in lower course c.10 mi/16 km upstream. Major source of Portland's water supply.

Bull Savanna/Junction, town (1991 pop. 6,888), St. Elizabeth parish, SW Jamaica, 12 mi/19 km SW of Mandeville; 17°54′N 77°36′W. Adjoining road junction towns which form one urban community.

Bull Shoals Lake, reservoir (□ 716 sq mi/1,854 sq km), N central Ark., on Ark.-Mo. border, on White R., 6 mi/9.7 km WSW of Mountain Home; 36°22′N 92°34′W. Max. capacity 5,408,000 acre-ft. Extends mainly E-W, into Baxter, Marion, and Boone cos. (Ark.) and Ozark and Taney cos. (Mo.). Formed by Bull Shoals Dam (256 ft/78 m high), built (1951) by Army Corps of Engineers for power generation, recreation, and as a fish and wildlife pond. Bull Shoals State Park on SE shore next to town of Bull Shoals

Bull Valley, village (1990 pop. 574), McHenry co., NE Ill., residential suburb, 5 mi/8 km E of Woodstock; 42°18′N 88°20′W.

Bullard, town (1990 pop. 890), Smith co., E Texas, 15 mi/24 km S of Tyler, near the Neches; 32°08′N 95°19′W. Agr. and timber area. Mfg. (transport vehicles, lumber). L. Palestine reservoir to W.

Bullards Bar Dam, Calif.: see YUBA RIVER.

Bullen Bay, inlet of W Curaçao, Neth. Antilles, 10 mi/16 km NW of Willemstad, with which it is linked by pipe lines. Petroleum prods. are shipped from here.

Bullen, Cape (BOO-luhn), S extremity of Devon Isl., E Franklin Dist., N.W.T., Canada, on Lancaster Sound; 74°22′N 85°12′W.

Bullhead City, city (1990 pop. 21,951), Mohave co., NW Ariz., 30 mi/48 km W of Kingman and 20 mi/32 km N of Needles, Calif., 4 mi/6.4 km S of Davis Dam, opposite Laughlin, Nev.; 35°06′N 114°33′W. Elev. 675 ft/206 m. Highway crosses dam. Mfg. (structural wood products, boatbuilding). S end of L. Mead Natl. Recreation Area ajoins city on N; Mt. Nutt Wilderness Area to E; Fort Mohave Indian Reservation (Ariz.-Calif.-Nev.) to S. Laughlin–Bullhead City Airport to N. Planned retirement community, includes community of Riveira 3 mi/4.8 km to SW. First developed in 1970s; doubled pop. in 1980s.

Bullitt (BUL-it), county (□ 300 sq mi/777 sq km; 1990 pop. 47,567), NW Ky.; ⊙ Shepherdsville; 37°58′N 85°42′W. Bounded in NW corner by Ohio R., W by Salt R., SW by Rolling Fork; drained by Floyds Fork. Rolling agr. area (cattle, poultry; burley tobacco, hay, alfalfa, soybeans, corn; dairying). Mfg. at Brooks and Shepherdsville. Whiskey distillery at Clement in SE (since 1795). Part of Fort Knox Military Reservation in W; part of Bernheim Forest and Arboretum in SE. Formed 1796.

Bulloch (BUL-uhk), county (□ 684; 1990 pop. 43,125), E Ga.; ⊙ Statesboro; 32°23′N 81°44′W. Bounded NE by Ogeechee R. Coastal plain agr. includes cotton, tobacco, corn, peanuts, cattle, hogs, and forestry prods.. Formed 1796.

Bullock, county (□ 626 sq mi/1,621 sq km; 1990 pop. 11,042), SE Ala.; ⊙ Union Springs. Rolling agr. area watered by headstreams of Conecuh and Pea rivers. Livestock, pecans, peanuts. Formed 1866.

Bullock Creek, village, Midland co., central Mich., suburb 2 mi/3.2 km S of Midland; 43°35′N 84°14′W.

Bullpasture River, river, c.25 mi/40 km long, NW Va.; rises in NE Highland co.; flows SSW, paralleling Cowpasture R. to E, turning SE to enter Cowpasture R. at Williamsville; 38°27′N 79°28′W.

Bulls Bay, E S.C., Charleston co., inlet on coast, c.25 mi/40 km NE of Charleston, bet. Bull Isl. (SW) and Raccoon Key (NE); c.9 mi/14.5 km long, 4 mi/6.4 km wide. Intracoastal Waterway canal passes immediately inland from W shore. Sometimes called Bull Bay.

Bulls Gap, town (1990 pop. 659), Hawkins co., NE Tenn., 11 mi/18 km SW of Rogersville; 36°15′N 83°04′W.

Bulls Island, Charleston co., E S.C., on coast, c.20 mi/32 km ENE of Charleston, just SW of Bulls Bay; c.6 mi/9.7 km long. Sometimes called Bull Isl.

Bulpitt, village (1990 pop. 206), Christian co., central Ill., 18 mi/29 km SE of Springfield; 39°35′N 89°25′W. In agr. area. Near Sangchris Lake and State Park. Bituminous coal.

Bumpkin Island, island, E Mass., part of Hull, Mass., SE of downtown, in Hinham Bay. Part of Boston Harbor Islands State Park.

Buna, town (1990 pop. 2,127), Jasper co., SE Texas, 27 mi/43 km NNE of Beaumont; 30°26′N 93°57′W. RR junction. Timber; cattle, vegetables. Oil and gas. Mfg. (steel tanks). Big Thicket Natl. Preserve is to the W.

Bunavista, uninc. village (1990 pop. 410), Hutchinson co., extreme N Texas, 37 mi/60 km NE of Amarillo and

3 mi/4.8 km W of Borger. Cattle, wheat, corn. Oil and natural gas.

Bunceton, city (1990 pop. 341), Cooper co., central Mo., 13 mi/21 km S of Boonville; 38°47′N 92°47′W. Wheat, corn; cattle.

Buncombe (BUHN-kuhm), county (□ 660 sq mi/ 1,709 sq km; 1990 pop. 174,821), W N.C.; ⊙ Asheville; 35°36′N 82°31′W. In the Blue Ridge Mts.; Black Mts. in E, parts of Pisgah Natl. Forest in NE and SW; crossed by French Broad and Swannanoa rivers. Agr. (tobacco, corn, hay, chickens, dairying, cattle), timber, sand and gravel, tourism. Mfg. at Asheville, Arden, Weaverville, Swannanoa. Zebulon Vance Birthplace State Historical Site in N. Blue Ridge (Natl.) Parkway, crosses co. SW-NE. Formed 1791.

Buncombe, village (1990 pop. 208), Johnson co., S Ill., 7 mi/11.3 km NW of Vienna; 37°28′N 88°58′W. In agr. area.

Bunker Hill, city (1990 pop. 1,722), Macoupin co., SW central Ill., 15 mi/24 km NE of Alton; 39°02′N 89°57′W. In agr. area; bituminous coal mining; ships grain; food processing. Inc. 1857.

Bunker Hill 1 town (1990 pop. 1,010), Miami co., N central Ind., 8 mi/12.9 km S of Peru; 40°40′N 86°06′W. In livestock and grain area; dairy prods. Limestone. **2** uninc. town (1990 pop. 800), Berkeley co., NE W.Va., 11 mi/18 km SSW of Martinsburg; 39°20′N 78°3′W. Agr. (grain, apples); livestock; poultry; dairying. Mfg. (corrugated boxes, wooden pallets). Bunker Hill Mill (1888). Settled c.1729, the oldest recorded settlement in the state.

Bunker Hill 1 or **Bunkerhill**, village (1990 pop. 111), Russell co., central Kansas, 8 mi/12.9 km E of Russell, near Smoky Hill R.; 38°52′N 98°42′W. In livestock and grain region. Oil fields in vicinity. **2** uninc. village (1990 pop. 1,242), Coos co., SW Oregon, on Isthmus Slough, near Coos Bay, and suburb 2 mi/3.2 km SE of Coos Bay City; 43°21′N 124°12′W.

Bunker Hill, Mass.: see CHARLESTOWN.

Bunker Hill Village, town (1990 pop. 3,391), Harris co., SE Texas, residential suburb 10 mi/16 km W of downtown Houston, near Buffalo Bayou; 29°45′N 95°31′W. Surrounded by city of Houston.

Bunkie (BUHNK-ee), city (1990 pop. 5,044), Avoyelles parish, E central La., 28 mi/45 km SE of Alexandria; 30°57′N 92°11′W. In agr. area (cotton, sugarcane, corn); mfg. of wood prods.; signs. RR junction is SE. Annual Corn Festival. Grand Cote Natl. Wildlife Refuge is N, Chicot State Park is SW. Founded 1882.

Bunn (BUHN), village (1990 pop. 364), Franklin co., N central N.C., 25 mi/40 km ENE of Raleigh, near Tar R.; 35°57′N 78°15′W. Tobacco, grain, sweet potatoes, poultry, livestock. Mfg. (lumber, roof and floor trusses). Perry's Pond to SW.

Bunnell (buh-NEL), town (□ 2 sq mi/5.2 sq km; 1990 pop. 1,873), ⊙ Flagler co., NE Fla., 30 mi/48 km S of St. Augustine; 29°28′N 81°15′W. Ships vegetables, citrus fruit. In the heart of a major growth area N of Daytona known as Palm Coast.

Bunnlevel, uninc. village, Harnett co., central N.C., 17 mi/27 km NNE of Fayetteville. Mfg. (sportswear and jackets, crushed stone).

Buras (BYU-ruhs), uninc. town (1990 pop. with Triumph 3,072), Plaquemines parish, extreme SE La., 55 mi/89 km SE of New Orleans, and on W bank (levee) of the Mississippi R., in the delta; 29°20′N 89°30′W. Citrus-fruit-growing center (esp. oranges); vegetables, tomatoes; fish and shellfish; boatyard. Hunting, fur trapping nearby.

Burbank 1 city (1990 pop. 93,643), Los Angeles co., S Calif., 9 mi NNW of downtown Los Angeles; 34°11′N 118°20′W. Bounded N, W, and S by city of Los Angeles; Glendale to E. Former aircraft mfg. center, now making of aerospace controls, motion pictures, studio equip., including facilities owned by Lockheed, and tourism dominate the local economy. Several motion-picture studios, such as Walt Disney, Warner Bros., and National Broadcasting Corp. (NBC) hq. are in or near Burbank. Hollywood-Burbank Airport is in W. Universal Studios, Hollywood district of Los Angeles, including

Griffith Park, Los Angeles to S; Wildwood Canyon Park in NE; Angeles Natl. Forest and San Gabriel Mts. to N. Inc. 1911. **2** city (1990 pop. 27,600), Cook co., NE Ill., suburb 12 mi/19 km SW of downtown Chicago, S of Midway Airport; 41°44′N 87°46′W. Mfg. of packaging control systems; printing.

Burbank, uninc. town (1990 pop. 4902), Santa Clara co., W Calif., residential suburb 3 mi/4.8 km SW of downtown San Jose, surounded by city of San Jose; 37°19′N 121°56′W.

Burbank 1 village (1990 pop. 289), Wayne co., N central Ohio, 13 mi/21 km NNW of Wooster, on Wayne-Medina county line, in agr. area; 40°59′N 81°59′W. **2** village (1990 pop. 165), Osage co., N Okla., 22 mi/ 35 km W of Pawhuska, on Salt Creek; 36°42′N 96°43′W. In oil-producing area. Kaw L. reservoir to NW.

Burchard (BUHR-chuhrd), village (1990 pop. 105), Pawnee co., SE Nebr., 10 mi/16 km W of Pawnee City; 40°08′N 96°20′W. Burchard L. to NE.

Burden, village (1990 pop. 518), Cowley co., SE Kansas, 13 mi/21 km ENE of Winfield; 37°18′N 96°45′W. In grain, cattle area; oil.

Burdett (buhr-DEHT), village (1991 pop. 239), SE Alta., Canada, near South Saskatchewan R., 40 mi/64 km WSW of Medicine Hat. Ranching.

Burdett, village (1990 pop. 372), Schuyler co., W central N.Y., in Finger Lakes region, near Seneca L., 3 mi/ 4.8 km NE of Watkins Glen; 42°25′N 76°50′W.

Burdette (buhr-DET), village (1990 pop. 148), Mississippi co., NE Ark., 7 mi/11.3 km S of Blytheville; 35°48′N 89°57′W.

Burdickville, village, Hopkinton town, R.I.; 41°25′N 71°44′W.

Bureau, county (□ 873 sq mi/2,261 sq km; 1990 pop. 35,688), N Ill.; ⊙ Princeton; 41°24′N 89°31′W. Bounded SE by Illinois R.; drained by Green and Spoon rivers and Bureau Creek; includes L. Depue, a bayou of Illinois R. Crossed by old Ill. and Miss. Canal. Agr. (corn, soybeans; cattle, hogs; dairying). Sand and gravel pits. Mfg. (industrial machinery, hardware, jewelry, environmental controls). Formed 1837.

Bureau, village (1990 pop. 350), Bureau co., N Ill., on Bureau Creek, near Illinois R., 14 mi/23 km W of La Salle; 41°17′N 89°21′W. In agr. area (corn, soybeans; cattle, hogs). Also called Bureau Junction.

Bureau Creek or **Big Bureau Creek**, c.65 mi/105 km long, N Ill.; rises in Lee co.; flows SW and S to Tiskilwa, then generally E, past Bureau, to Ill. R. 3 mi/4.8 km SW of Depue; 41°42′N 89°04′W.

Bureau Junction, Ill.: see BUREAU.

Burford, town (1991 pop. 5,733), S Ont., central Canada, 9 mi/14 km WSW of Brantford. Dairying, mixed farming.

Burfordville, uninc. place, Cape Girardeau co., SE Mo., on Whitewater R., and 8 mi/12.9 km W of Jackson. Historic Bollinger Mill and Covered Bridge (both on Natl. Historic Register) to SW, on Whitewater R.

Burgaw (BUHR-gaw), town (1990 pop. 1,807), ⊙ Pender co., SE N.C., 22 mi/35 km N of Wilmington; 34°32′N 77°55′W. In strawberry-growing area, also grain, soybeans, sweet potatoes, peanuts, tobacco; turkeys, cattle, hogs; mfg. (meat processing, safety equip., wood and paper prods., polyurethane foam, apparel, electrical equip.). Moores Creek Natl. Battlefield to SW.

Burgeo (BUHR-gee-o), coast town (1991 pop. 2,400), SW N.F., E Canada, 70 mi/113 km E of Port aux Basques; 47°37′N 57°39′W. Fishing port, with fish-filleting, freezing, cold-storage plants. Just SE are Burgeo Isls.

Burgeo Islands, group of 12 islets just off S N.F., E Canada, 2 mi/3 km SE of Burgeo. Principal isl. is Boar Isl., 2 mi/3 km E of Burgeo; lighthouse; 47°47′N 57°36′W.

Burgess (BUHR-jes), town (1990 pop. 97), Barton co., SW Mo., 18 mi/29 km WNW of Lamar, near Kansas state line; 37°33′N 94°36′W. Prairie State Park to S.

Burgess, uninc. village, Northumberland co., E Va., 70 mi/113 km SE of Fredericksburg, near Chesapeake Bay; 37°52′N 76°20′W. Mfg. (fabric joints, yachts; oyster processing); agr. (grain, soybeans; poultry, cattle); fish, oysters, crabs.

Burgettstown (BUHR-zhets-toun), borough (1990 pop. 1,634), Washington co., SW Pa., 22 mi/35 km WSW of Pittsburgh, on Burgetts Fork Creek; 40°22′N 80°23′W. Mfg. (food prods., wood prods.). Agr. (corn, hay; dairying); surface bituminous coal. Hillman State Park to N. Laid out 1795, inc. 1881.

Burgin (BUHR-gin), town (1990 pop. 1,009), Mercer co., central Ky., 4 mi/6.4 km E of Harrodsburg, in Bluegrass region; 37°45′N 84°46′W. Mfg. (machinery, chemicals). Dix Dam to E, on Dix R., forms Herrington L. reservoir.

Burgoon (buhr-GOON), village (1990 pop. 224), Sandusky co., N Ohio, 9 mi/14 km SW of Fremont; 41°16′N 83°15′W. In agr. area.

Burgos (BOOR-gos), town (1990 pop. 975), Tamaulipas NE Mexico, 50 mi/80 km ENE of Linares; 24°55′N 99°50′W. Cereals, sugar, onions; cattle. Unmined sulphur here.

Burien (BYOOR-ee-en), city (1990 pop. 25,089), King co., W Wash., residential suburb 9 mi/14.5 km S of downtown Seattle, on Puget Sound; 47°28′N 122°21′W. Retail shopping center. Seattle-Tacoma (SeaTac) Internatl. Airport to SE.

Burin (BYOOR-in), town (1991 pop. 2,940), S N.F., E Canada, on inlet of Placentia Bay, on E coast of Burin Peninsula, 28 mi/45 km E of Grand Bank; 47°03′N 55°11′W. Fishing port, with cold-storage plants.

Burin Peninsula, S N.F., E Canada, bet. Fortune and Placentia bays; 85 mi/137 km long, 20 mi/32 km wide. Mainly hilly, rising to 995 ft/303 m. Chief towns on peninsula are Grand Bank, Burin, Fortune. Lumbering.

Burkburnett (buhrk-buhr-NET), city (1990 pop. 10,145), Wichita co., N Texas, suburb 12 mi/19 km NNW of Wichita Falls, on Red R. (Okla. state line); 34°04′N 98°33′W. Elev. 1,040 ft/317 m. A shipping center for cattle, horses; cotton, wheat; it also produces many oil wells and refineries. Mfg. (fiberglass reinforced pipes, wood prods.; juice processing). The area's 1st big gusher (1918) brought a boom that transformed the small community into a central oil town with a pop. that exceeded 30,000. Inc. 1913

Burke 1 county (□ 832; 1990 pop. 20,579), E Ga.; ⊙ Waynesboro; 33°04′N 82°00′W. Bounded NE by S.C. state line, formed here by Savannah R.; drained by Brier Creek. Mfg. of lumber and wood prods. Coastal plain cotton region; also produces corn, soybeans, oats, peanuts, wheat, cotton; cattle, hogs; timber. Formed 1777. Nuclear power plants, Vogtle 1 (initial criticality March 9, 1987; max. dependable capacity of 1,100 MWe) and Vogtle 2 (initial criticality March 28, 1989; max. dependable capacity of 1,096 MWe) are 26 mi/42 km SE of Augusta. The plants use cooling water from the Savannah R. **2** county (□ 514 sq mi/1,331 sq km; 1990 pop. 75,744), W central N.C.; ⊙ Morganton; 35°45′N 81°42′W. In Piedmont region; part of Pisgah Natl. Forest in NW; drained by Catawba R. (forms L. James reservoir in W, Rhodhiss L. reservoir in E; hydroelectric plants. Agr. area (oats, soybeans; chickens, hogs; hay, corn, wheat); timber. Mfg. at Morganton. South Mts. State Park in S. Sources of Henrys Fork and Jacobi Fork rivers in E. Formed 1777. **3** county (□ 1,118 sq mi/ 2,896 sq km; 1990 pop. 3,002), NW N.Dak.; ⊙ Bowbells; 48°47′N 102°31′W. Borders Canada (Sask.) on N. Rich agr. area. Cattle raising; mining. Wheat, barley, flax. Upper Des Lacs L. and part of Des Lacs Natl. Wildlife Refuge in E; Upper Lostwood L. and Lostwood Natl. Wildlife Refuge in S. Formed 1910.

Burke, uninc. city, Fairfax co., NE Va., residential suburb 14 mi/23 km SW of Wash., D.C., 4 mi/6.4 km S of Fairfax, on Pohick Creek; 38°46′N 77°16′W. Mfg. (signs, binders).

Burke 1 town (1990 pop. 756), ⊙ Gregory co., S S.Dak., 45 mi/72 km S of Chamberlain. Trade center for farming and ranching region; livestock; dairy prods.; grain. Burke Lake State Recreation Area to E. **2** town (1990 pop. 1,406), Caledonia co., NE Vt., on Passumpsic R. and 12 mi/19 km N of St. Johnsbury; 44°36′N 71°55′W. Includes villages of West and East Burke; site of historical mus. Burke Mt. (3,267 ft/996 m), with ski area, is here.

Burke 1 village (1990 pop. 80), Shoshone co., N Idaho, near Mont. state line, 7 mi/11.3 km NE of Wallace. Terminus of RR spur from Wallace. Lead, zinc, silver, copper mines. St. Joe Natl. Forest to N, Lolo Natl. Forest (Mont.) to E, Coeur d'Alene Natl. Forest to S. **2** village (1990 pop. 209), Franklin co., NE N.Y., on Lake Trout R., and near Canada (Que.) border, 8 mi/12.9 km NE of Malone; 44°53′N 74°10′W. In dairying area. **3** village (1990 pop. 314), Angelina co., E Texas, 6 mi/9.7 km S of Lufkin; 31°13′N 94°46′W. Timber area; cattle. Davy Crockett Natl. Forest to W; Angelina Natl. Forest to E.

Burke Mountain, ski area, in town of Burke, Caledonia co., NE Vt., 12 mi/19 km N of St. Johnsbury.

Burkes Garden, uninc. village, Tazewell co., SW Va., 12 mi/19 km SSW of Bluefield, in Burkes Garden, a fertile mt. basin (c.8 mi/12.9 km long, 4.5 mi/7.2 km wide; elev. c.3,000 ft/914 m) of the Allegheny Mts. Livestock raising.

Burkesville, town (1990 pop. 1,815), ⊙ Cumberland co., S Ky., in Cumberland foothills, on Cumberland R. and 34 mi/55 km ESE of Glasgow; 36°47′N 85°22′W. Summer resort in agr. area (livestock, poultry; fruit, corn, hay, burley tobacco); mfg. (apparel, machinery; lumber processing). One of earliest U.S. oil wells, accidentally tapped in 1829, was nearby. Dale Hollow State Park, on Dale Hollow Lake reservoir to SE. Inc. as town 1810, as city 1926.

Burket, town (1990 pop. 200), Kosciusko co., N Ind., 8 mi/12.9 km SW of Warsaw; 41°09′N 85°58′W. In agr. area (eggs; poultry). Glacial lakes.

Burkett, Mount (9,730 ft/2,966 m), on U.S. (Alaska)–Canada (B.C.) border, in Coast Range, 40 mi/64 km NE of Petersburg; 57°13′N 132°15′W.

Burkettsville (BUHR-kits-vil), village (1990 pop. 268), on border bet. Mercer and Darke cos., W Ohio, 17 mi/27 km N of Greenville; 40°22′N 84°38′W.

Burkeville 1 uninc. village (1990 pop. 515), Newton co., E Texas, 67 mi/108 km NNE of Beaumont. Highway crossroads. Timber area. Sabine Natl. Forest to N; Toledo Bend Reservoir (Sabine R.) to NE. **2** village (1990 pop. 535), Nottoway co., central Va., 13 mi/21 km SE of Farmville; 37°11′N 78°12′W. RR junction; mfg. (veneer sheets, crushed granite); agr. (grain, soybeans, tobacco; livestock; dairying); granite. Twin Lakes State Park to W; Gallion State Forest to SW.

Burkittsville (BUHR-kits-vil), town (1990 pop. 194), Frederick co., W Md., at E base of South Mt. and 12 mi/19 km W of Frederick; 39°23′N 77°38′W. Laid out as a town and named for a settler, Henry Burkitt, in 1829. Site of War Correspondents Memorial (1896), an elaborate structure with both a Moorish arch and firehouse tower, designed and built by George Alfred Townsend, a Civil War correspondent and later a successful novelist who wrote under the name of Gath.

Burk's Falls, village (1991 pop. 977), SE central Ont., central Canada, 45 mi/72 km S of North Bay; 45°37′N 79°25′W. Lumbering. Also Burks Falls.

Burleigh (BUHR-lee), county (□ 1,625 sq mi/4,209 sq km; 1990 pop. 60,131), central N.Dak.; ⊙ Bismarck; 46°58′N 100°28′W. Agr. area drained by Apple Creek and bounded W by Missouri R. Lignite mines; agr. prods. Lake Oahe Reservoir in SW; Florence Lake and Canfield Lake natl. wildlife refuges in N; Chaska Historic Site in E; Menoken Historic Site in center; parts of Long L. and Long Lake Natl. Wildlife Refuge in SE. Harriet, Pelican, Salt, New Jonas, and other small lakes in N. Formed 1873.

Burleson, county (□ 677 sq mi/1,753 sq km; 1990 pop. 13,625), S central Texas; ⊙ Caldwell; 30°29′N 96°37′W. Bounded NE by Brazos R., S by Yegua Creek (forms Somerville L.), SW by E Yegua Creek. Diversified agr. (cotton, corn, grain sorghum, peanuts, pecans, wheat, oats, soybeans), livestock (cattle, hogs, horses). Farm prods. processed at Caldwell, Somerville. Lake Somerville State Park in S. Formed 1846.

Burleson, city (1990 pop. 16,113), Johnson and Tarrant cos., N central Texas, 15 mi/24 km S of Fort Worth; 32°31′N 97°19′W. Trade point in cotton, corn, grain, dairying area. Mfg. (wood prods, machinery, construction materials; steel fabrication). Satellite community of Fort Worth.

Burley, city (1990 pop. 8,702), ⊙ Cassia co., S Idaho, on Snake R. and 35 mi/56 km E of Twin Falls; 42°32′N 113°48′W. Elev. 4,165 ft/1,269 m. RR junction and shipping point for irrigated agr.; dairying; sugar beets, alfalfa, grain; cattle, sheep; mfg. (wood prods., canned vegetables, machinery, feeds; printing). Hq. Sawtooth Natl. Forest to S and SW. Milner Dam to W (Snake R.). Founded 1905, inc. 1906.

Burlingame, city (1990 pop. 26,801), San Mateo co., W Calif., suburb 14 mi/23 km S of downtown San Francisco and 2 mi/3.2 km NW of San Mateo, on San Francisco Bay; 37°36′N 122°22′W. Mainly residential, with some commercial and diversified light mfg. (plastic and metal prods., furniture, computers, book bindings). Named for U.S. diplomat Anson Burlingame. San Francisco State Fish and Game Refuge to SW, including San Andreas Fault. Founded 1868, inc. 1908.

Burlingame, town (1990 pop. 1,074), Osage co., E Kansas, 12 mi/19 km NW of Lyndon; 38°45′N 95°50′W. Trading and shipping point in livestock and grain region. Founded 1855, inc. 1861.

Burlington, county (□ 819 sq mi/2,121 sq km; 1990 pop. 395,066), W and central N.J., bounded NW by Del. R.; ⊙ Mount Holly; 39°52′N 74°40′W. Mfg. (textiles, shoes, clothing; metal, leather, paper, and concrete prods.; food prods., canned goods; lumber, bricks; chemicals, dyes; metal industries and prods., industrial machinery, electronic equip.; shipbuilding). Agr. (vegetables, fruit, grain; livestock; dairy prods.). E and SE parts of co. are in pine barrens region, producing cranberries; several state forests here. Drained by Rancocas Creek and Bass, Wading, and Batsto rivers. Formed 1681.

Burlington 1 city (1990 pop. 27,208), ⊙ Des Moines co., SE Iowa, on 4 hills overlooking the Miss. R. (spanned here by RR and highway bridges); 40°48′N 91°07′W. Farm, shipping, and mfg. center with a RR junction and RR shops and docks. The site was selected for a fort in 1805. A Native Amer. village, Sho-quo-quon ("Flint Hills") was here. Grave of Chief Tama to NE. Eur. settlement began in 1833. Was the temporary capital of Wis. Territory (1837) and of Iowa Territory (1838–1840). Mfg. (basket prods., construction materials, transportation equip., furniture, electrical equip., agr. equip., foods, machinery, storage bins, tempered glass; printing). One of the oldest newspapers in the state, the Burlington *Hawk-Eye*, is still published. SE Community Col. is in West Burlington and there are several parks along the Miss. Inc. 1836. **2** city (1990 pop. 9,835), Burlington co., W N.J., on the Del. R. (bridged here to Bristol, Pa.) bet. Trenton and Camden, in a rich farm area; 40°04′N 74°50′W. A shipping point for farm and dairy prods. Mfg. includes. metals, textiles, and clothing. Grew mainly as a port; was also on a Philadelphia–New York coach line, and RR tracks were laid down Broad St. in 1834. The 1st colonial money was printed here by Benjamin Franklin in 1726; the 1st newspaper in N.J. appeared in 1777. St. Mary's Church (built 1703) and The Friends' school (1792) still stand. The birthplaces of James Fenimore Cooper and of James Lawrence are preserved. Settled 1677 by Friends, inc. 1733. **3** city (1990 pop. 39,498), Alamance co., N N.C., 33 mi/53 km WNW of Durham and 22 mi/35 km E of Greensboro, on the Haw R. (passes to N and E); 36°4′N 79°27′W. Mfg. (plastic, paper, and cardboard prods., apparel, signs, textiles, machinery, computer equip., motors; printing and publishing, pork processing). In May 1771, 2,000 colonial "Regulators" clashed with Br. troops c.5 mi/8 km SW; the site is in Alamance Battleground State Historical Site. In the city are a notable wildlife mus. and the Technical Inst. of Alamance. Burlington Reservoir to N. Alamance Municipal Airport to SW. Elon Col. to W; Alamance Community Col. to SE at Graham. Settled c.1700, inc. 1866. **4** city (1990 pop. 39,127), ⊙ Chittenden co., NW Vt., on L. Champlain; 44°29′N 73°13′W. The largest city in the state, it is a port of entry, a year-round resort, and a major industrial center. Mfg. (electronics and computer parts, furniture, machinery); dairy; maple sugar and other food prods. Battery Park was the scene of an abortive Br. naval attack (Aug. 3, 1813) during the War of 1812. Seat of the Univ. of Vt. and Trinity and Champlain cols. Burlington Internatl. Airport is in S Burlington. Amer. Revolutionary hero Ethan Allen spent his last years near Burlington village (part of his farm is included in Ethan Allen Park) and is buried nearby. The Burlington *Free Press* (founded 1827) became Vt.'s 1st daily newspaper in 1848. Philosopher John Dewey b. here. Settled 1773, inc. 1865. **5** city (1990 pop. 8,855), Racine co., SE Wis., on Fox R. at mouth of small White R., and 31 mi/50 km SSW of Milwaukee; 42°40′N 88°16′W. In farm area; mfg. (iron, steel; meat prods.); lake resort. Seat of St. Francis Col. Site of Mormon colony (1844–1849) nearby. Settled 1835; inc. as village 1896, as city 1900.

Burlington, town (1991 pop. 129,575), SE Ont., central Canada, on L. Ontario. First settled (1798) by Mohawk Loyalist Joseph Brant, Burlington's economy was built on the shipment of wheat, lumber, and quarried rock by waterway. A suburb of Hamilton and a beach resort, it produces metal tubing, brushes, chemicals, and other manufactured items.

Burlington 1 town (1990 pop. 2,941), ⊙ Kit Carson co., E Colo., c.150 mi/241 km ESE of Denver, near Sand Creek, near Kansas state line; 39°18′N 102°16′W. Elev. 4,165 ft/1,269 m. Grain-shipping point. Cattle; wheat, oats, sunflowers, sorghum, hay. Mfg. (printing and publishing). Bonny State Park to N. Inc. 1888. **2** town (1990 pop. 7,026), Hartford co., central Conn., on Farmington R. and 16 mi/26 km W of Hartford; 41°45′N 72°57′W. State fish hatchery, Nassahegan State Forest here. Settled 1740, inc. 1806. **3** town (1990 pop. 568), Carroll co., central Ind., 12 mi/19 km W of Kokomo, near Wildcat Creek; 40°29′N 86°23′W. Corn, soybeans; hogs. Aluminum awnings, signs. **4** town (1990 pop. 2,735), ⊙ Coffey co., E Kansas, on Neosho R., and 27 mi/43 km SE of Emporia; elev. 1,030 ft/314 m; 38°11′N 95°44′W. Trade center for diversified-farming region; dairy prods. Mfg. (puppets; plush prods.). John Redmond Reservoir to NW (Flat Hills Natl. Wildlife Refuge). Wolf Creek Nuclear Power Plant nearby. Inc. 1870. **5** town (1990 pop. 6,070), ⊙ Boone co., N Ky., suburb 14 mi/23 km SW of Cincinnati (Ohio), and 12 mi/19 km WSW of Covington (Ky.); 39°01′N 84°43′W. Farm trade center in N fringe of Bluegrass region (burley tobacco, corn; livestock; dairying); mfg. (plastic prods., construction materials, signs, consumer goods, statues, safety boxes; sheet-metal fabrication). Cincinnati/Northern Ky. Internatl. Airport 3 mi/4.8 km to NE. Big Bone Lick State Park, where many bones of prehistoric mammals have been found, is to S; Dinsmore Homestead (1842) to W. Est. 1824. **6** town (1990 pop. 360), Penobscot co., E central Maine, 35 mi/56 km NE of Bangor; 45°16′N 68°22′W. In hunting, fishing area. **7** town (1990 pop. 23,302), Middlesex co., E Mass., a residential suburb NW of Boston; 42°30′N 71°12′W. Important high-tech area. Mfg. includes electronic components, precision instruments, computer and communications software, and other prods. Its pre-Revolutionary meetinghouse, remodeled, still stands. Major retail shopping mall. Site of Lahry Medical Clinic. Settled 1641, inc. 1799. **8** town (1990 pop. 995), Ward co., N central N.Dak., 5 mi/8 km NW of Minot, on Souris (Mouse) R; 48°16′N 101°25′W. **9** town (1990 pop. 4,349), Skagit co., NW Wash., 20 mi/32 km SSE of Bellingham, and 4 mi/6.4 km N of Mt. Vernon, near Skagit R.; 48°28′N 122°20′W. RR junction. Trade center for agr. region; strawberries, raspberries, vegetables, grain, tulips; mfg. (abrasive wheels, plastic prods., aircraft parts, tugboats, feeds, construction materials, dairy prods.; vegetable processing,). Bay View State Park to W; Larrabee State Park to NW. Settled 1882, inc. 1902.

Burlington 1 village (1990 pop. 400), Kane co., NE Ill., 17 mi/27 km NW of Geneva; 42°02′N 88°32′W. In dairying and livestock area. **2** village (1990 pop. 294), Calhoun co., S Mich., on St. Joseph R. and 15 mi/24 km SE of Battle Creek city; 42°06′N 85°04′W. In agr. area. **3** uninc. village (1990 pop. 3,003), Fulton co., NW Ohio, 8 mi/13 km WNW of Wauseon, and just off the Ohio Turnpike; 38°25′N 82°31′W. **4** village (1990 pop.

169), Alfalfa co., N Okla., 15 mi/24 km WNW of Cherokee; 36°53′N 98°25′W. In grain-growing and livestock-raising area. **5** uninc. village (1990 pop. 150), Mineral co., W.Va., in E Panhandle, on Patterson Creek, 7 mi/11.3 km. SSE of Keyser. Has restored tavern dating from c.1785. Williamsport Grist Mill (1882). **6** village (1990 pop. 184), Big Horn co., N Wyo., near Greybull R., 20 mi/32 km WNW of Basin; 44°27′N 108°25′W. Elev. c.4,300 ft/1,311 m. In elevated grain-growing area known as Emblem Bench.

Burlington (BUHR-leeng-tuhn), borough (1990 pop. 479), Bradford co., NE Pa., 8 mi/12.9 km W of Towanda. Agr. (corn, hay, soybeans; dairying). Mt. Pisgah State Park to NW.

Burlington Junction, city (1990 pop. 634), Nodaway co., NW Mo., on Nodaway R. and 12 mi/19 km NW of Maryville; 40°27′N 95°04′W. Corn, soybeans, wheat; cattle, hogs.

Burnaby, city (1991 pop. 158,858), E suburb of Vancouver, SW B.C., W Canada; 49°18′N 122°57′W. A transportation, industrial, and distribution center, its prods. include steel, trucks, telecommunications and electronic equip., lumber, and processed fish. Named for local businessman Robert Burnaby (1828–1878); began as a residential community for Vancouver. Seat of Simon Fraser Univ.

Burnet (BUHR-nit), county (☐ 1,020 sq mi/2,642 sq km; 1990 pop. 22,677), central Texas; ☉ Burnet; 30°46′N 98°10′W. Bounded W by Colorado R., drained by it in S, forms L. Travis (headwaters in co. in SE), Lake Marble Falls, L. Lyndon B. Johnson, Inks L. and L. Buchanan (last 3 on W boundary). Also drained by Lampasas R. (NE); source of San Gabriel R., center of co. Mts. in W rise to c.1,600 ft/488 m. Ranching (goats, sheep, cattle); agr. (pecans, fruit); cedar timber. Noted for granite, limestone quarries; sand and gravel; clay. Tourist trade (guest ranches; hunting, fishing); Longhorn Cavern State Park and Inks Lake State Park in W are near Burnet. Formed 1852.

Burnet (BUHR-nit), town (1990 pop. 3,423), ☉ Burnet co., central Texas, near Colorado R., c.45 mi/72 km NW of Austin; elev. 1,319 ft/402 m; 30°45′N 98°13′W. In agr. (pecans, fruit; cattle, sheep, goats) region; cedar timber; limestone quarrying. Mfg. (semiconductor chemicals, crushed stone, steel castings). Tourist trade attracted by Longhorn Cavern State Park 9 mi/14.5 km SW and Inks Lake State Park 6 mi/9.7 km W; L. Buchanan to NW. U.S. fish hatchery here. Grew around Fort Croghan (est. 1849); inc. 1885.

Burnett, county (☐ 880 sq mi/2,279 sq km; 1990 pop. 13,084), NW Wis.; ☉ Grantsburg; 45°52′N 92°02′W. St. Croix R. here (N) forms Minn. state line, except in N; also drained by Namekagon R. Wooded terrain with numerous lakes throughout co. Sheep; lumbering. St. Croix Natl. Scenic Riverway follows St. Croix and Namokagon rivers. Gov. Knowles (St. Croix) State Forest in W; St. Croix Indian Reservation on Big Sand L. in SE. Formed 1856.

Burnettown, village (1990 pop. 493), Aiken co., SW S.C., 8 mi/12.9 km WSW of Aiken; 33°30′N 81°50′W. Mfg. includes kaolin clay; agr. includes cotton, peanuts, grain; livestock, poultry.

Burnettsville, town (1990 pop. 401), White co., NW central Ind., 8 mi/12.9 km E of Monticello; 40°46′N 86°35′W.

Burney, uninc. town (1990 pop. 3,423), Shasta co., N Calif., in an agr. valley of Cascade Range, c.45 mi/72 km NE of Redding, on Barney Creek; 40°53′N 121°40′W. Timber; grain, potatoes; mfg. (printing and publishing). McArthur-Burney Falls State Park (120 ft/37 m waterfall; recreational, camping facilities) is North Shasta Natl. Forest to N, Lassen Natl. Forest to SE; Lassen Volcanic Natl. Park to SE.

Burnham (BUHR-nuhm), town (1990 pop. 961), Waldo co., S Maine, on the Sebasticook R., c. 20 mi/32 km NE of Waterville; 44°40′N 69°22′W. Includes Winnecook, resort village near Unity Pond.

Burnham (BUHRN-am), village (1990 pop. 3,916), Cook co., NE Ill., suburb 17 mi/27 km SSE of downtown Chicago, bounded by Hammond (Ind.) to E, Calumet City (S), and Chicago (N); 41°38′N 87°32′W. Oil refining, mfg. lubrication oils.

Burnham (BUHRN-huhm), borough (1990 pop. 2,147), Mifflin co., central Pa., suburb 3 mi/4.8 km N of Lewistown on Kishacoquillas Creek; 40°38′N 77°33′W. Mfg. (concrete, glass prods., steel forgings). Agr. area (corn, hay; poultry, livestock; dairying). Settled 1795, inc. 1911.

Burns, town (1990 pop. 2,913), ☉ Harney co., E central Oregon, on Silvies R., 20 mi/32 km NW of Malheur L. and N of Harney L.; 43°35′N 119°03′W. Elev. 4,148 ft/1,264 m. Timber. Sheep, cattle. Burns Indian Reservation to NW. Ochoco Natl. Forest to NW; Malheur Natl. Forest to N; Malheur Natl. Wildlife Refuge to S. Inc. 1899.

Burns 1 village (1990 pop. 226), Marion co., SE central Kansas, 19 mi/31 km SSE of Marion; 38°05′N 96°53′W. In grain and livestock area. **2** village (1990 pop. 254), Laramie co., SE Wyo., near Lodgepole Creek, 24 mi/39 km E of Cheyenne; 41°11′N 104°21′W. Elev. 5,455 ft/1,663 m.

Burns Flat, town (1990 pop. 1,027), Washita co., W Okla., 16 mi/26 km SW of Clinton; 35°21′N 99°10′W. Agr. and oil-production area. Mfg. (transportation equip., machinery).

Burns Harbor, town (1990 pop. 788), Porter co., NW Ind., suburb 9 mi/14.5 km E of Gary, on L. Michigan; 41°37′N 87°08′W. Ind. Dunes Natl. Lakeshore and State Park to NE. Steel and steel prods.

Burns Lake, village (1991 pop. 1,682), central B.C., W Canada, on Burns L. (16 mi/26 km long), 130 mi/209 km WNW of Prince George; 54°14′N 125°46′W. Cattle-raising and logging center; gold, silver, copper, and lead mining. Fishing resorts. Gateway to Tweedsmuir Provincial Park. Begun in 1911 as construction camp for Grand Trunk Pacific RR.

Burnside, village (1990 pop. 695), Pulaski co., S Ky., 8 mi/12.9 km S of Somerset, in Cumberland foothills, on Cumberland R. (upper reach of L. Cumberland reservoir); 36°59′N 84°35′W. Mfg. (charcoal briquettes, asphalt, crushed stone); timber. Daniel Boone Natl. Forest immediately to S; General Burnside State Park to S.

Burnside, borough (1990 pop. 350), Clearfield co., central Pa., 10 mi/16 km N of Barnesboro, on West Branch of Susquehanna R.; 40°48′N 78°47′W. Agr. (dairying; livestock); lumber mfg.

Burnsville, city (1990 pop. 51,288), Dakota co., SE Minn., suburb 14 mi/23 km S of downtown Minneapolis and 14 mi/23 km SW of downtown St. Paul, on Minn. R.; 44°45′N 93°16′W. Mfg. (machinery, labels, electronic equip., pharmaceutical supplies, security cards and keys, computer equip., bird food, machinery, aerospace parts, cigarettes, trade show displays, furniture; printing and publishing). Several small lakes in S, including Crystal L.

Burnsville 1 town (1990 pop. 949), Tishomingo co., extreme NE Miss., 13 mi/21 km ESE of Corinth, on Tennessee-Tombigbee Waterway; 34°50′N 88°19′W. In timber and agr. area (corn, wheat, soybeans; hogs); mfg. (chemical protection suits, electrical goods). **2** town (1990 pop. 1,482), ☉ Yancey co., W N.C., at N end of Black Mts., 26 mi/42 km NNE of Asheville; 35°55′N 82°17′W. Mfg. (textiles, apparel, lumber, industrial sand, transportation equip.; sand and gravel processing). **3** town (1990 pop. 495), Braxton co., central W.Va.; 15 mi/24 km SW of Weston, on Little Kanawha R.; 38°51′N 80°39′W. Agr. (grain, apples); livestock, poultry. Burnsville L. reservoir (Wildlife Management Area) to SE.

Burnt Creek Camp, iron-mining center in W Lab., E Canada, on Que. border; 54°50′N 67°35′W.

Burnt Island, E N.F., Canada, on W side of Bonavista Bay, 35 mi/56 km WNW of Cape Bonavista; 1 mi/1.6 km long, 1 mi/1.6 km wide; 48°50′N 53°50′W. Fishing.

Burnt River, c.75 mi/121 km, NE Oregon; rises in Blue Mts., in W Baker co.; flows 1st SE to Unity Reservoir, where it receives South Fork (c.15 mi/24 km long) from SW, then generally E to Snake R. 3 mi/4.8 km E of Huntington. Unity Dam (83 ft/25 m high, 675 ft/206 m long; completed 1938) in upper course forms small reservoir.

Burntside Lake (☐ 11 sq mi/28 sq km), St. Louis co., NE Minn., 4 mi/6.4 km NW of Ely; 9 mi/14.5 km long, 3 mi/4.8 km wide; 47°55′N 91°59′W. Elev. 1371 ft/113 m. Drained through Burntside R. (small dam raises lake level); river parallels S shore for 5 mi/8 km to Shagawa L. Resort area. In Superior Natl. Forest; many small isls.

Burr, village (1990 pop. 75), Otoe co., SE Nebr., 11 mi/18 km SW of Syracuse; 40°32′N 96°17′W.

Burr Oak 1 village, Winneshiek co., NE Iowa, near Minn. state line, 12 mi/19 km NNW of Decorah. Limestone quarries nearby. **2** village (1990 pop. 278), Jewell co., N Kansas, on tributary of Republican R., 8 mi/12.9 km NW of Mankato; 39°52′N 98°17′W. In corn and wheat area. **3** village (1990 pop. 882), St. Joseph co., SW Mich., on Prairie R., and 5 mi/8 km NE of Sturgis; 41°51′N 85°19′W. In diversified agr. area (wheat, potatoes, corn); mfg. of plastics.

Burr Ridge, village (1990 pop. 7,669), Cook and Du Page cos., NE Ill., suburb 16 mi/26 km SW of downtown Chicago, near Des Plaines R.; 41°45′N 87°55′W. Mfg. (machinery, decals and labels, electric and electronic equip., paper prods., laboratory supplies, horticultural chemical prods., foods, mechanical shaft seals; printing and publishing). Argonne Natl. Laboratory to SW.

Burrard Inlet (buh-RAHRD), SW B.C., W Canada, arm (extends 23 mi/37 km E) of Strait of Georgia; 1 mi/1.6 km–4 mi/6.4 km wide. On S shore is Vancouver city, and, opposite, North Vancouver. Near head are Ioco and Port Moody. Indian Arm (13 mi/21 km long) extends N.

Burrillville (BUHR-ril-vil), town (1990 pop. 16,230) and municipality, Burrillville municipality, Providence co., NW R.I.; 41°58′N 71°42′W. Named for James Burrill, Jr., attorney general of the state who later became a chief justice and U.S. senator. Major communities in municipality include Pascoag (1990 pop. 4,995) and Harrisville (1990 pop. 1,670). Wilson and Pascoag reservoirs; Black Hut, Buck Hill, and George Washington management areas. Inc. 1806

Burro Mountains (BOO-ro), SW N.Mex., extend N-S in Grant co., within part of Gila Natl. Forest. Highest point at Burro Peak (8,035 ft/2,449 m), 6 mi/9.7 km SW of Tyrone.

Burrton, village (1990 pop. 866), Harvey co., S central Kansas, 18 mi/29 km W of Newton; 38°01′N 97°40′W. RR junction. In wheat, livestock, and dairying region; mfg. (metal fabricating). Oil wells nearby.

Burrwood (BUHR-wud), village, Plaquemines parish, extreme SE La., on Southwest Pass (1 of 3 mouths of the Miss. R.), near SW extremity of the delta, 80 mi/129 km SE of New Orleans; elev. 2 ft/1 m. Hq. for channel maintenance engineers. Southernmost town in La. Helioport. Southwest Pass lighthouse (28°58′N 89°23′W) is on opposite bank of pass. Oil wells and natural-gas fields in vicinity.

Burt, county (☐ 497 sq mi/1,287 sq km; 1990 pop. 7,868), E Nebr.; ☉ Tekamah; 41°51′N 96°19′W. Agr. area bounded E by Missouri R. forms Iowa state line; drained by Logan Creek. Corn, soghum, cattle, hogs; dairying. Small part of Omaha Indian Reservation in extreme N. Pelican Point State Recreation Area in E, on Missouri R. Formed 1854; annexed part of Monona co. (Iowa) in 1943.

Burt, town (1990 pop. 575), Kossuth co., N Iowa, near East Des Moines R., 9 mi/14.5 km N of Algona; 43°12′N 94°13′W.

Burt, village (1990 pop. 400), Niagara co., W N.Y., 30 mi/48 km NNE of Buffalo, near L. Ontario; 43°19′N 78°43′W. Mfg. of chemicals, catalysts and additives; fruit and vegetables.

Burt Lake, Cheboygan co., N Mich., 11 mi/18 km SW of Cheboygan; c.10 mi/16 km long, 4.5 mi/7.2 km wide; joined by streams to Mullett (E) and Crooked (W) lakes. W arm touches Emmitt co. boundary. Forested resort lake. Burt Lake State Park at S end.

Burton, city (1990 pop. 27,617), Genessee co., SE Mich., suburb 3 mi/4.8 km SE of Flint; 43°00′N 83°37′W. Mfg.

(dairy prods., machinery, tool and die, paper prods.); diverse light mfg.

Burton, uninc. town (1990 pop. 6,917), Beaufort co., S S.C., 2 mi/3.2 km W of Beaufort. Mfg. of nails, wastebaskets.

Burton, village (1991 pop. 3,833), ⊙ Sunbury co., central N.B., E Canada, on St. John R., and 14 mi/23 km ESE of Fredericton. In fruit-growing and lumbering region.

Burton 1 uninc. village, Floyd co., E Ky., 13 mi/21 km SW of Pikeville, on Beaver Creek. Bituminous coal. **2** village (1990 pop. 9), Keya Paha co., N Nebr., 10 mi/16 km NE of Springview, near Keya Paha R. and S.Dak. state line; 42°54′N 99°35′W. **3** village (1990 pop. 1,349), Geauga co., NE Ohio, 28 mi/45 km E of Cleveland, on Cuyahoga R.; 41°29′N 81°08′W. **4** village (1990 pop. 311), Washington co., S central Texas, 13 mi/21 km W of Brenham; 30°10′N 96°35′W. Agr. (cattle; cotton); mfg. (meat processing).

Burton Camp, camp village, Tulare co., S central Calif.

Burton Lake, reservoir, Rabun co., NE Ga., on Tallulah R., in Chattahoochee Natl. Forest, 18 mi/29 km NNW of Toccoa; c.7 mi/11.3 km long; 34°47′N 83°31′W. Formed by power dam. Seed L. reservoir below dam (S). Moccasin Creek State Park at N end of lake.

Burtrum (BUHR-truhm), village (1990 pop. 172), Todd co., central Minn., 11 mi/18 km SE of Long Prairie; 45°52′N 94°41′W. In lake region. Grain, potatoes, beans; livestock; dairying. Big Swan L. to W, Mound L. to S.

Burwash Landing, trading post (1991 pop. 77), SW Yukon, W Canada, near U.S. (Alaska) border, on Kluane L. at foot of St. Elias Mts., 140 mi/225 km WNW of Whitehorse, and on Alaska Highway; 61°22′N 139°W. Gold, discovered (1903) nearby, resulted in a small rush.

Burwell, town (1990 pop. 1,278), ⊙ Garfield co., central Nebr., 70 mi/113 km NNW of Grand Island, at junction of North Loup and Calamus rivers; 41°46′N 99°07′W. Trade center for cattle area; grain. Mfg. (alfalfa and feeds processing, hydraulic rakes). Annual rodeo. Ft. Hartsuff State Historical Park to SE (Valley co.). Plotted 1883.

Busby, village (1990 pop. 409), Big Horn co., S Mont., 34 mi/55 km ESE of Hardin, on Rosebud Creek, in W part of Northern Cheyenne Indian Reservation; 45°32′N 106°58′W. Cattle; grain, beans, alfalfa. Rosebud Battlefield State Park to S.

Bush, village (1990 pop. 351), Williamson co., S Ill., 6 mi/9.7 km WNW of Herrin; 37°50′N 89°07′W. In bituminous-coal-mining and agr. area.

Bush River, NE Md., estuary (c.12 mi/19 km long) entering Chesapeake Bay in S Hartford co.; traverses Aberdeen Proving Ground.

Bushkill, uninc. town (1990 pop. 900), Lehman turnpike, Pike co., NE Pa., 13 mi/21 km NE of Stroudsburg, on Bushkill Creek, W of its mouth on Del. R.; 41°05′N 75°00′W. Resort area. Bushkill Falls, on Little Bushkill Creek to N; Forest Park and Saw Creek ski areas to N; Del. State Forest to N; part of Del. Gap Natl. Recreation Area to SE.

Bushnell (BUHSH-nuhl), city (1990 pop. 3,288), McDonough co., W Ill., 12 mi/19 km NE of Macomb; 40°32′N 90°30′W. RR and industrial center in agr. area; corn, wheat; livestock; stockyards; mfg. (food prods., handtools). Inc. 1865.

Bushnell (buhsh-NEL), town (☐ 2 sq mi/5.2 sq km; 1990 pop. 1,998), ⊙ Sumter co., central Fla., 12 mi/19 km NE of Brooksville; 28°39′N 82°06′W. Agr. shipping point. Dade Memorial Park nearby commemorates massacre of Major Francis L. Dade and his men by Native Americans in 1835.

Bushnell 1 village (1990 pop. 119), Kimball co., W Nebr., 10 mi/16 km W of Kimball, and on Lodgepole Creek, near Wyo. and Colo. state lines; 41°13′N 103°53′W. Grain. Lodgepole State Wayside Area and Oliver Reservoir to E. **2** village (1990 pop. 81), Brookings co., E S.Dak., 7 mi/11.3 km E of Brookings, on Deer Creek. Arts and crafts center; home to several nationally known artists.

Bushnellsville, village (1990 pop. 200), Ulster co., SE N.Y., in the Catskills, near Esopus Creek and 25 mi/40 km NW of Kingston; 42°09′N 74°25′W.

Bushong (BUHSH-ahng), village (1990 pop. 57), Lyon co., E central Kansas, 17 mi/27 km N of Emporia; 38°38′N 96°15′W. In cattle-grazing region.

Bushton, village (1990 pop. 341), Rice co., central Kansas, 21 mi/34 km NE of Great Bend; 38°30′N 98°23′W. In wheat area. Natural-gas processing. Oil wells nearby.

Bushwick, a residential section of N Brooklyn borough of N.Y. city, SE N.Y., on the border of Queens, and on Newtown Creek; 40°42′N 73°56′W. Populated largely by Ger. immigrants from the 1840s, it is now mostly Hispanic and Afr.-Amer. Brewers' Row, one the nation's major collection of breweries, was located here, along with a flourishing theater dist., both of which fell victim to Prohibition and the Depression. Sustained heavy property damage by rioters during the blackout of 1977.

Bussey, town (1990 pop. 494), Marion co., S central Iowa, near Cedar Creek, 14 mi/23 km SE of Knoxville; 41°12′N 92°52′W. In livestock-raising area.

Bustamante 1 (boos-tah-MAHN-te), town (1990 pop. 2,782), ⊙ Bustamante municipio, Nuevo León, NNW Mexico, in N outliers of Sierra Madre Oriental, on RR, and 60 mi/97 km N of Monterrey; 26°30′N 100°20′W. Grain; livestock. **2** town (1990 pop. 1,293), Tamaulipas, NE Mexico, in Sierra Madre Oriental, 45 mi/72 km WSW of Ciudad Victoria; elev. 5,636 ft/1,718 m; 23°55′N 99°50′W. Cereals; livestock.

Bute Inlet (boot), SW B.C., W Canada, arm (50 mi/80 km long, 1 mi/2 km–3 mi/5 km wide) of Strait of Georgia, a fjord receiving Homathko R. Inlet was proposed (1862) as terminal of transcontinental RR.

Butler 1 county (☐ 777 sq mi/2,012 sq km; 1990 pop. 21,892) S Ala.; ⊙ Greenville. Coastal plain drained by branches of Sepulga R. Soybeans, corn, peanuts; livestock (esp. poultry); lumber milling. Formed 1819. **2** county (☐ 581 sq mi/1,505 sq km; 1990 pop. 15,731), N central Iowa; ⊙ Allison; 42°43′N 92°47′W. Rolling prairie agr. area (hogs, cattle, poultry; corn, oats, soybeans) drained by Shell Rock R. Limestone quarries, sand and gravel pits. Henry Woods State Park in E. Widespread local flooding in 1993. Formed 1851. **3** county (☐ 1,446 sq mi/3,745 sq km; 1990 pop. 50,580), SE Kansas; ⊙ El Dorado; 37°46′N 96°49′W. Located in Flint Hills Region, drained by Walnut R. Cattle, hogs, poultry; sorghum, soybeans, alfalfa, hay. Butler Co. Fishing L. in SE. (El Dorado L. at center of co.). Formed 1855. **4** county (☐ 431 sq mi/1,116 sq km; 1990 pop. 11,245), W central Ky.; ⊙ Morgantown; 37°12′N 86°40′W. Drained by Green (forms part of E and W borders) and Barren rivers; bounded SW by Mud R. Rolling agr. area (burley tobacco, dark tobacco, hay, soybeans, wheat, corn; hogs, cattle); catfish; coal mines, stone quarries; timber. Formed 1810. **5** county (☐ 716 sq mi/1,854 sq km; 1990 pop. 38,765), SE Mo.; ⊙ Poplar Bluff; 36°43′N 90°24′W. Ozarks in the NW and the Mississippi alluvial lowland in SE; bounded E by St. Francis R.; drained by Black R. Resort, agr. area. Cotton, corn, soybeans, and rice in SE; apples; livestock; lumber; mfg. at Poplar Bluff. Parts of Mark Twain Natl. Forest in N and L. Wappapello in NE. Formed 1849. **6** county (☐ 584 sq mi/1,513 sq km; 1990 pop. 8,601), E Nebr.; ⊙ David City; 41°13′N 97°07′W. Agr. area, part of Loess Plain, bounded N by Platte R.; drained in SW by Big Blue R. Cattle, hogs, poultry; corn, soybeans, sorghum, alfalfa, dairy prods. Formed 1868. **7** county (☐ 471 sq mi/1,220 sq km; 1990 pop. 291,479), extreme SW Ohio; ⊙ HAMILTON, 39°27′N 84°34′W. Bounded W by Ind. state line; intersected by Great Miami R. and its small tributaries. Includes site of Fort Hamilton. In the Till Plains physiographic region. Agr. area (cattle, hogs, sheep, poultry; dairy prods.; corn); mfg. at Hamilton and Middletown (millwork, furniture, paper prods., plastic prods., construction materials, electronic equip.; electric furnaces and steel mills); limestone quarries. Formed 1803. **8** county (☐ 794 sq mi/2,056 sq km; 1990 pop. 152,013), W Pa.; ⊙ Butler; 40°54′N 79°54′W. SE and NE corners touch Allegheny R; drained by Connoquenessing and Slippery Rock creeks. Mfg. at Butler and Zelienople. Agr. (corn, wheat, oat, hay, alfalfa, potatoes, apples; sheep, hogs, cattle; dairying); bituminous coal, limestone; L. Arthur reservoir (on Muddy Creek), in Moraine State Park, in W. Formed 1800.

Butler 1 city (1990 pop. 1,872), ⊙ Choctaw co., SW Ala., 35 mi/56 km SE of Meridian, Miss., near the Missippi state line. Lumber, oil, minerals are located in this area. Mfg. includes paper, plywood; agr. includes peanut farming and cotton. **2** city (1990 pop. 2,601), DeKalb co., NE Ind., 10 mi/16 km NE of Auburn, near Ohio state line; 41°26′N 84°52′W. Trading center in agr. area (poultry, livestock; grain, soybeans; dairy prods.); mfg. (foundry prods., plastics, suspension components, construction materials, containers, transportation equip.). **3** city (1990 pop. 4,099), ⊙ Bates co., W Mo., near Marais des Cygnes R., 58 mi/93 km S of Kansas City; 38°15′N 94°20′W. Corn, wheat, sorghum; cattle; coal, oil; mfg. (crushed stone, pet food, store displays, paper prods.). Founded 1850s. **4** city (1990 pop. 15,714), ⊙ Butler co., W Pa., 28 mi/45 km NNE of Pittsburgh, on Connoquenessing Creek; 40°51′N 79°54′W. RR junction. Mfg. (glass prods., plastic prods., machinery, abrasives, construction materials, fabricated metal prods., transportation equip., electronic equip.; printing and publishing); bituminous coal, natural gas, oil, and limestone. Butler Co. Airport 6 mi/9.7 km to SSW. Moraine State Park, including L. Arthur reservoir to NW. Inc. as a borough 1817, as a city 1917. **5** city (1990 pop. 2,079), Waukesha co., SE Wis., on Menomonee R. and a suburb 10 mi/16 km NW of downtown Milwaukee; 43°06′N 88°04′W. Mfg. (machinery, rubber prods., paper prods.; metal spinning, meat processing). Until 1930, called New Butler.

Butler, town (1990 pop. 1,673), ⊙ Taylor co., W central Ga., 40 mi/64 km SW of Macon; 32°34′N 84°14′W. Mfg. includes electrical prods.; textile finishing, and machining; agr. and timber region; sawmilling center; clay pits nearby. Inc. 1854.

Butler 1 village (1990 pop. 156), Montgomery co., S central Ill., 4 mi/6.4 km NNW of Hillsboro; 39°12′N 89°31′W. In agr. and bituminous-coal-mining area. **2** village (1990 pop. 625), Pendleton co., N Ky., on Licking R., and 23 mi/37 km SSE of Covington; 38°47′N 84°22′W. Mfg. (transportation equip., lime, crushed limestone, machinery). **3** village (1990 pop. 968), Richland co., N central Ohio, 12 mi/19 km SSE of Mansfield, and on Clear Fork of Mohican R.; 40°36′N 82°25′W. Ski resort nearby. **4** village (1990 pop. 341), Custer co., W Okla., 16 mi/26 km WNW of Clinton; 35°38′N 99°11′W. In wheat-, livestock-, and cotton-producing area. Foss L. reservoir to SW; Foss State Park to S; Washita Natl. Wildlife Refuge to W. **5** village (1990 pop. 17), Day co., NE S.Dak., 10 mi/16 km WSW of Webster. Agr. trade center.

Butler, borough (1990 pop. 7,392), Morris co., N N.J., 10 mi/16 km NW of Paterson; 41°00′N 74°20′W. Mfg. (plastics, paper, and concrete prods.). Residential area. St. Anthony's Monastery (Franciscan) here. Settled 1695, inc. 1901.

Butler, Lake, Pinellas co., W central Fla., near Tarpon Springs; c.5 mi/8 km long, 1 mi/1.6 km wide.

Butlerville 1 village, Jennings co., SE Ind., 6 mi/9.7 km ENE of North Vernon. Agr. area. Mfg. (boxes, pallets). **2** village (1990 pop. 188), Warren co., SW Ohio, 26 mi/42 km ENE of Cincinnati; 39°19′N 84°05′W. In agr. area.

Butlin, resort village, NW Bahama Isls., on Grand Bahama Isl., E of West End. Opened 1950, closed in 1990.

Butner, uninc. town (1990 pop. 4,679), Granville co., N N.C., 15 mi/24 km NE of Durham, at entrance to Camp Butner Natl. Guard Base, to W; 36°08′N 78°46′W. Site of Federal prison. Mfg. (synthetic fabrics and bldg. materials, agr. machinery, electronic equip., wooden prods., paper prods.). Falls Lake Reservoir to S.

Buttahatchee River (buh-duh-HA-chee), c.75 mi/121 km long, in NW Ala. and NE Miss.; rises in Winston co., Ala.; flows generally SW to Monroe co., Miss., joining Tombigbee R. 12 mi/19 km NNW of Columbus (Miss.).

Butte 1 (BYOOT), county (☐ 1,640 sq mi/4,248 sq km; 1990 pop. 181,120), N central Calif.; ⊙ Oroville; 39°40′N

121°36′W. Flatlands of the Sacramento Valley in W, rise to c.6,600 ft/2,012 m in the Sierra Nevada in E. Drained by Feather R. (and its forks) and the Butte R. Parts of W border formed by Sacramento R. (NW) and Butte Creek (SW), part of S border formed by South Honcut Creek. Agr. (rice, nuts, kiwi fruit, olives, prunes, peaches; barley, corn, oats, wheat, beans; cattle); timber. Gold, silver, platinum. Extensive logging (pine, fir, cedar). Processing industries (lumber and rice milling, olive oil extracting, fruit canning). Parts of Lassen (NE) and Plumas (E) natl. forests; L. Oroville reservoir and State Recreation Area (Feather R.) in E center; Thermalito Afterbays Reservoir W of Oroville, in S center, for irrigation. Formed 1850. **2** county (□ 2,233 sq mi/ 5,783 sq km; 1990 pop. 2,918), SE central Idaho; ⊙ Arco; 43°43′N 113°10′W. Watered by Big Lost R. Agr. (sheep, cattle; alfalfa, hay; oats, barley, some wheat); mineral resources include silver, lead, manganese. Includes Craters of the Moon Natl. Monument in SW (extends S into Blaine co.); part of Lost R. Range and Challis Natl. Forest in NW and W, part of Salmon Natl. Forest in N, part of Targhee Natl. Forest in NE. Large part of Idaho Natl. Engineering Laboratory dominates E part of co., EBR-1 (Experimental Breeding Reactor), Natl. Historic Landmark, is within laboratory tract, in SE. Formed 1917. **3** county (□ 2,266 sq mi/5,869 sq km; 1990 pop. 7,914), W S.Dak.; ⊙ Belle Fourche. Agr. area, bounded W by Wyo. and Mont.; drained by Belle Fourche R. and North and South Forks Moreau R. (NE) and Owl, Indian and Sulphur creeks. Diversified farming; mfg. at Belle Fourche. Corn, hay, sugar beets; dairy prods.; cattle, sheep; wool. Belle Fourche Reservoir on Owl Creek, Geographical Center of U.S. (50 states) at co. center, 5 mi/8 km W of Castle Rock. Formed 1881.

Butte (BYOOT), city (1990 pop. 33,336), ⊙ Silver Bow co., SW Mont., 45 mi/72 km SSW of Helena. Continental Divide to E and S, Deerlodge Natl. Forest surrounds area. Trade, distribution, and industrial center. The mining industry has dominated the city's economy since its establishment in 1862, with copper the major product. Berkeley pit copper mine closed 1983 and the city's economy has declined since then; limited copper mining resumed late 1980s, and zinc, silver, manganese, gold, lead, and arsenic are also extracted from the numerous mines in the region. First a gold-mining camp, then a silver center, Butte gained importance when copper was discovered (c.1880), and Marcus Daly with his Anaconda Copper Mining Co. began to exploit the "richest hill on earth." The expansion of the open-pit copper mine within the city limits has forced sects. of the city to relocate. Butte's reputation as a "wide-open" town peaked during the "War of the Copper Kings." Seat of Mont. Tech of the Univ. of Mont. Local attractions include Anselmo Mine, Berkeley Pit, World Mus. of Mining, Mineral Mus., Art Chateau, Our Lady of The Rockies; and Copper King Mansion, 32-room former home of "copper king" and politician William A. Clark (1880s). Hq. of Deerlodge Natl. Forest. Butte and Silver Bow cos. merged in 1977 (except for village of Walkerville). Inc. 1879.

Butte 1 (BYOOT), village (1990 pop. 452), ⊙ Boyd co., N Nebr., 32 mi/51 km NNW of O'Neill, near S.Dak. state line, bet. Niobrara R. and Ponca Creek; 42°54′N 98°50′W. **2** village (1990 pop.129), McLean co., central N.Dak., 42 mi/68 km SE of Minot; 47°50′N 100°40′W.

Butte City, uninc. village, Glenn co., N central Calif., 19 mi/31 km W of Chico, on Sacramento R. Prunes, citrus; nuts, rice.

Butte Creek, N central Calif., c.110 mi/177 km long; rises in Butte co., 23 mi/37 km NE of Paradise; flows SSW, passes W of Paradise and SE of Chico, continues S to Sacramento R. 4 mi/6.4 km ESE of Colusa. Butte Sink marsh is 8 mi/12.9 km above creek's mouth.

Butte des Morts (BYOOT dah MOR), village, Winnebago co., E central Wis., 7 mi/11.3 km NW of Oshkosh, on N shore of L. Butte des Morts (c.6 mi/9.7 km long, 2 mi/3.2 km wide; a widening of Fox R.).

Butte Falls (BYOOT), village (1990 pop. 252), Jackson co., SW Oregon, 22 mi/35 km NE of Medford; 42°32′N

122°34′W. Fish hatchery. Crater Lake Natl. Park to NE; part of Rogue River Natl. Forest to E.

Butte La Rose (BYOOT lah roz), town, St. Martin parish, La., 14 mi/23 km NE of St. Martinville; 30°16′N 91°14′W. In Atchafalaya Swamp inside Atchafalaya Basin levees; a fort during the Civil War. Now a recreation area with many hunting camps.

Butterfield, town (1990 pop. 248), Barry co., SW Mo., in Ozark region, 5 mi/8 km NNW of Cassville; 36°45′N 93°54′W.

Butterfield, village (1990 pop. 509), Watonwan co., S Minn., 8 mi/12.9 km W of St. James; 43°57′N 94°47′W. RR junction. Grain, soybeans; livestock; mfg. (fowl processing).

Butterfield Lake, Jefferson co., N N.Y., 7 mi/11.3 km E of Alexandria Bay; c.4 mi/6.4 km long, ½ mi/⁸⁄₁₀ km– 1 mi/1.6 km wide; 44°19′N 75°47′W. Resort; fishing.

Buttermilk Channel, N.Y.: see NEW YORK HARBOR.

Buttermilk Falls State Park, W central N.Y., near Cayuga L., c.2 mi/3.2 km S of Ithaca, along gorge of small Buttermilk Creek; 42°25′N 76°30′W. Has scenic glens, many waterfalls and rapids; camping, hiking, swimming.

Butternut, village (1990 pop. 416), Ashland co., N Wis., to S Butternut L., 43 mi/69 km SSE of Ashland; 46°00′N 90°30′W. Lumbering; dairying, poultry raising; woodworking. Large Turtle Flambeau Flowage reservoir 15 mi/24 km to E; units of Chequamagon Natl. Forest to W and SE; Flambeau State Forest to E.

Buttle Lake (□ 11 sq mi/28 sq km), long narrow lake (18 mi/29 km long, 1 mi/1.6 km wide) in mts. of central Vancouver Isl., B.C., W Canada, 24 mi/39 km W of Courtenay. Lumbering area. Drained N by Campbell R. S part is in Strathcona Park.

Button Rock Reservoir, Boulder co., N central Colo., on North St. Vrain R., in Roosevelt Natl. Forest, 14 mi/ 23 km NNW of Boulder; 2 mi/3.2 km long; 40°13′N 105°21′W. Max. capacity 21,493 acre-ft. Formed by Button Rock Dam (210 ft/64 m high), built (1967) by the City of Longmont for water supply.

Buttonwillow, uninc. town (1990 pop. 1,301), Kern co., S central Calif., 23 mi/37 km W of Bakersfield; 35°24′N 119°28′W. Oil and natural-gas field, with pipelines. Cattle; grain, cotton; vegetables, sugar beets, fruit, nuts. Calif. Aqueduct passes to SW; Tule State Elk Reserve and Buena Vista L. irrigation reservoir to SE.

Buttonwoods, neighborhood, Warwick municipality, Kent co., E central R.I., on Greenwich Bay, 2 mi/3.2 km W of Warwick, town; 41°41′N 71°25′W.

Butts, county (□ 185 sq mi/479 sq km; 1990 pop. 15,326), central Ga.; ⊙ Jackson; 33°17′N 83°58′W. Bounded E by Ocmulgee R. (here forming Lloyd Shoals Reservoir). Piedmont agr. area that produces cattle and hogs. Formed 1825.

Buttzville, village, Warren co., NW N.J., on Pequest R., 3 mi/4.8 km E of Belvidere. In hilly region; trout fishing.

Butztown (BUHTS-toun), uninc. town (1990 pop. 1,500), Northampton co., E Pa., residential suburb 3 mi/4.8 km NE of Bethlehem; 40°39′N 75°19′W.

Buxton (BUHK-stuhn), town (1990 pop. 6,494), York co., SW Maine, near the Saco R., 13 mi/21 km W of Portland; 43°38′N 70°32′W. Settled 1740, inc. 1772.

Buxton 1 (BUHKS-tuhn), uninc. village, Dare co., E N.C., 41 mi/76 km S of Manteo on Pamlico Sound, on Hatteras Isl. sand barrier in Outer Banks, in Cape Hatteras Natl. Seashore. Cape Hatteras (lighthouse) 3 mi/ 4.8 km to S; Atlantic Ocean to E and S. Fishing, swimming. **2** village (1990 pop. 343), Traill co., E N.Dak., 23 mi/37 km S of Grand Forks; 47°36′N 97°05′W. Baked pinto beans.

Buzzard Roost Dam, S.C.: see GREENWOOD, LAKE, .

Buzzards Bay, inlet of the Atlantic Ocean, 30 mi/48 km long and 5 mi/8 km–10 mi/16 km wide, SE Mass., connected with Cape Cod Bay by the Cape Cod Canal and bounded on the SE by the Elizabeth Isls. Its shores are very irregular. The village of Buzzards Bay (1990 pop. 3,250), seat of Cape Cod Canal administration, is in the town of Bourne on the shore of the bay; 41°46′N 70°37′W.

Byam Martin Channel (BEI-uhm), N central Franklin dist., N.W.T., N Canada, arm (150 mi/241 km long, 30 mi/48 km–65 mi/105 km wide) of the Arctic Ocean, bet. Melville (W) and Bathurst (E) isls.; 76°00′N 105°00′W. Connects Prince Gustav Adolph Sea (N) with Viscount Melville Sound (S).

Byam Martin Island (BEI-uhm), central Franklin dist., N.W.T., N Canada, in Byam Martin Channel; 30 mi/ 48 km long, 20 mi/32 km wide; 75°10′N 104°10′W.

Byars (BEI-uhrs), village (1990 pop. 263), McClain co., central Okla., 22 mi/35 km WNW of Ada; 34°52′N 97°02′W. In agr. area. Canadian R. to N.

Byers 1 (BEI-uhrs), village (1990 pop. 46), Pratt co., S Kansas, 12 mi/19 km NNW of Pratt; 37°47′N 98°52′W. In wheat area. **2** village (1990 pop. 510), Clay co., N Texas, near Red R., 20 mi/32 km NE of Wichita Falls, on Wichita R., near its mouth on Red R.; 34°04′N 98°11′W. Cotton; cattle; wheat, pecans, peaches. Oil and gas.

Byers Peak, Colo.: see VASQUEZ MOUNTAINS.

Byesville (BEIZ-vil), village (1990 pop. 2,435), Guernsey co., E Ohio, 5 mi/8 km SSE of Cambridge, and on Wills Creek; 39°59′N 81°32′W. In agr. area; mfg. (plastics, pottery, toys).

Byfield, Mass.: see NEWBURY.

Byhalia (bi-HAIL-ee-uh), town (1990 pop. 955), Marshall co., N Miss., 12 mi/19 km NW of Holly Springs; 34°51′N 89°41′W. In soybean-growing area; mfg. (wood prods., foods, motor vehicles, construction materials; metal stamping).

Bylas, uninc. town, Graham co., SE Ariz., 80 mi/129 km NE of Tucson, on Gila R., in S part of San Carlos Indian Reservation. Agr. trade center; cattle; wheat, corn, cotton. Mt. Turnbull (8,280 ft/2,524 m) to SW; San Carlos Reservoir to W.

Bylot Island (□ 4,968 sq mi/12,867 sq km), E Franklin dist., N.W.T., N Canada, in the Arctic Ocean, off N Baffin Isl.; 90 mi/145 km long, 60 mi/97 km–70 mi/ 113 km wide; 72°49′–73°53′N 76°20′–81°00′W; bounded E by Baffin Bay, separated from Baffin Isl. by Pond Inlet, Eclipse Sound, and Navy Board Inlet, and from Devon Isl. (NW) by Lancaster Sound. Mainly an ice-covered plateau, rising to c.2,000 ft/610 m; Mt. Thule (S) rises to c.6,600 ft/2,012 m. On S coast are several spring and summer Eskimo camps.

Byng (BEENG), town (1990 pop. 755), Pontotoc co., central Okla., on Canadian R; 34°52′N 96°39′W. Agr. area; oil; mfg. (Christmas-tree stands).

Byng Inlet, village, S central Ont., central Canada, on Byng Inlet of Georgian Bay, at mouth of Magnetawan R., 40 mi/64 km NW of Parry Sound; 45°46′N 80°33′W. Fishing; lumbering.

Bynum 1 (BEI-nuhm), village (1990 pop. 1,917), Calhoun co., NE Ala., 8 mi/12.9 km W of Anniston; 33°36′N 85°51′W. **2** village (1990 pop. 40), Teton co., NW Mont., 13 mi/21 km NNW of Choteau, and on Muddy Creek. In irrigated wheat region; oil and natural gas. Bynum Reservoir to SW.

Bypro (BEI-pro), uninc. village, Floyd co., SE Ky., in the Cumberland Mts., on Beaver Creek, 13 mi/21 km SW of Pikeville and 1 mi/1.6 km SE of Burton. In bituminous-coal, oil, gas area.

Byram (BEI-ruhm), township (1990 pop. 8,048), Sussex co., NW N.J., 8 mi/12.9 km SE of Newton; 40°57′N 74°42′W. Mfg. (glass, pharmaceuticals). Inc. 1798.

Byram River, c.20 mi/32 km long, in N.Y. and Conn.; rises in Byram L. S of Mt. Kisco (N.Y.); flows S, through Conn., forming 1.5 mi/2.4 km of S state line, to L.I. Sound at Port Chester, N.Y. Diversion dam directs part of its flow into Kensico Reservoir.

Byrdstown, town (1990 pop. 998), □ Pickett co., N Tenn., near Ky. state line and Dale Hollow Reservoir, 35 mi/56 km NNE of Cookeville; 36°34′N 85°08′W.

Byrnes Mill, village (1990 pop. 1,578), Jefferson co., E Mo., residential suburb 26 mi/42 km SW of downtown St. Louis, on Big R.; 38°26′N 90°34′W.

Byromville (BEI-ruhm-vil), agr. town (1990 pop. 452), Dooly co., central Ga., 10 mi/16 km NW of Vienna; 32°12′N 83°55′W.

Byron, city (1990 pop. 2,284), Ogle co., N Ill., on Rock R. (bridged here), and 12 mi/19 km SW of Rockford; 42°07′N 89°15′W. In rich agr. area. Founded 1835 by New Englanders. Site of nuclear power plant. Inc. 1878. **Byron 1** (BEI-ruhn), town (1990 pop. 2,276), Peach co., central Ga., 13 mi/21 km SSW of Macon; 32°39′N 83°46′W. Mfg. includes chemicals, explosive devices, insulation adhesives; light mfg. **2** town (1990 pop. 111), Oxford co., W Maine, on Swift R., and 35 mi/56 km N of South Paris; 44°43′N 70°39′W. In resort area. **3** town (1990 pop. 2,441), Olmsted co., SE Minn., 10 mi/16 km W of Rochester; 44°01′N 92°39′W. Grain, soybeans; livestock, poultry; dairying; mfg. (elevators, agr. machinery; printing). Part of Richard J. Dorer Memorial Hardwood State Forest to N.

Byron 1 uninc. village (1990 pop. 900), Contra Costa co., W Calif., 13 mi/21 km SE of Antioch. Clifton Court Forebay, irrigation reservoir on Old R. (old channel San Joaquin R.) to SE. Fruit, nuts, vegetables, grain, nursery stock. Mfg. (canned-food specialties). **2** village (1990 pop. 573), Shiawassee co., S central Mich., on Shiawassee R., and 18 mi/29 km SW of Flint; 42°49′N 83°57′W. Mfg. of metal prods. **3** (BEI-ruhn), village (1990 pop. 140), Thayer co., S Nebr., 15 mi/24 km SW of Hebron, at Kansas state line; 40°00′N 97°46′W. **4** village (1990 pop. 57), Alfalfa co., N Okla., 22 mi/35 km NNE of Alva, near Kansas state line; 36°53′N 98°17′W. In grain and livestock area. **5** village (1990 pop. 470), Big Horn co., N Wyo., on Shoshone R., near Mont. state line, and 7 mi/11.3 km WSW of Lovell; 44°47′N 108°30′W. Elev. 4,020 ft/1,225 m. In irrigated sugar-beet region. Gas wells nearby.

Byron 1 and 2 Nuclear Power Plants, Illinois: see OGLE.

Bytown, Canada: see OTTAWA.

Bywood, Pa.: see UPPER DARBY.

C

Cabaiguán (kah-bei-GWAHN), town (pop. 31,000), Sancti Spíritus prov., central Cuba, on Central Highway, on RR, and 37 mi/60 km SE of Santa Clara; 22°07′N 79°30′W. Agr. center (tobacco, sugarcane, fruit, livestock); sugar mills. Remberto Abad and Melanio Hernández are 4 mi/6.4 km and 7 mi/11.3 km SE, respectively.

Caballo Reservoir (kuh-BEI-yo), Sierra co., SW central N.Mex., on Rio Grande, 18 mi/29 km S of Truth or Consequences (town at N end); 14 mi/23 km long, 1 mi/1.6 km wide; 32°53′N 107°17′W. Max. capacity 346,000 acre-ft. Formed by Caballo Dam (earthfill; 97 ft/30 m high, 4,590 ft/1,399 m long), built (1938) for irrigation and flood control. Caballo L. State Park on E shore at S end.

Caballones, Canal de (kah-bah-YON-ais, kah-NAHL dai), shallow channel (c.2 mi/3.2 km long) through the Doce Leguas (Span. = twelve leagues) keys, off Caribbean coast of E Cuba, 75 mi/121 km WSW of Camagüey; 20°50′N 78°57′W. Links Gulf of Ana María to NW with Gulf of Guacanayabo in SE.

Cabañas (kah-BAHN-yahs), town, La Habana prov., W Cuba, minor internatl. port on sheltered Cabañas Bay, 38 mi/61 km WSW of Havana; 22°58′N 82°55′W. In agr. region (sugarcane, fruit, livestock); fishing, lumbering. Sugar mills of Pablo de la Torriente and Harlem 1 mi/1.6 km and 14 mi/23 km WSW, respectively.

Cabano (ka-ba-NO), village (1991 pop. 3,145), SE Que., Canada, on L. Temiscouata, 32 mi/51 km ESE of Rivière du Loup; 47°41′N 68°53′W. Lumbering, dairying, truck gardening.

Cabaret (kah-bah-RAI), town (1982 pop. 1,985), Ouest dept., W Haiti, on Gulf of Gonaïves, 13 mi/21 km NNW of Port-au-Prince; 18°44′N 72°25′W. Sisal, fruit. Fishing port. Also called Duvalierville.

Cabaritta River, c.25 mi/40 km long, Westmoreland parish, W Jamaica, flows S, W, and S, to coast just W of Savanna-la-Mar; 18°18′N 78°07′W.

Cabarrus (kuh-BAHR-uhs), county (□ 365 sq mi/945 sq km; 1990 pop. 98,935), S central N.C.; ⊙ Concord; 35°23′N 80°32′W. In Piedmont region; drained by Rocky R. Agr. area (corn, soybeans, sorghum, wheat, hay; cattle, hogs, dairying, poultry); timber (pine, oak). Mfg. cigarettes at Concord and Harrisburg. Formed 1792.

Cabazon, uninc. town (1990 pop. 1,588), Riverside co., S Calif., suburb 35 mi/56 km E of Riverside, on floor of San Gorgonio Pass; 33°55′N 116°46′W. Cabazon Tunnel carries Colorado R. Aqueduct, which passes to SE through San Jacinto Mts., here to Los Angeles. Parts of San Bernardino Natl. Forest to N and S. Morongo Indian Reservation to N; Mt. San Jacinto Wilderness State Park to SE.

Cabell (KAB-uhl), county (□ 288 sq mi/746 sq km; 1990 pop. 96,827), W W.Va.; ⊙ Huntington, state's second largest city (since 1980); 38°25′N 82°14′W. Bounded NW by Ohio R. (Ohio state line); drained by Guyandotte and Mud rivers. Agr. (corn, tobacco, alfalfa, nursery crops, hay); cattle; poultry. Natural gas and oil wells, bituminous-coal mining. Mfg. at Huntington, Culloden, Milton, and Barboursville. Part of Beech Fork State Park in SW; Greenbottom Wildlife Management Area. Formed 1809.

Cabery (KA-buh-ree), village (1990 pop. 268), in Ford and Kankakee cos., E Ill., 20 mi/32 km WSW of Kankakee; 40°59′N 88°12′W. Rich agr. area.

Cabezas de San Juan (KAH-bo RO-ho), cape, P.R.: see SAN JUAN, CAPE. Northeastern-most corner of P.R.

Cabin Creek, uninc. town (1990 pop. 1,300), Kanawha co., W central W.Va., at mouth of small Cabin Creek on Kanawha R. (bridged), 16 mi/26 km SE of Charleston. RR junction. Power plant; oil refining; mfg. (lumber). Known for its Cabin Creek quilts. Also called Cabin Creek Junction.

Cabin John, village (1990 pop. 5,341), Montgomery co., central Md., on the Potomac c.10 mi/16 km above Wash., D.C.; 38°58′N 77°09′W. Site of Cabin John Bridge on McArthur Blvd., a single masonry arch built in 1857–1863 to carry water from the Great Falls of the Potomac to Wash. The conduit, 100 ft/30 m high and 220 ft/67 m long, still carries 20% of the D.C. water supply as vehicular traffic moves over the bridge. Nearby is the Naval Research and Development Center, started in 1936, which contains a towing tank, the aquatic equivalent of a wind tunnel to test scale models. A biological observation station is on Plummer Island.

Cabinet Gorge Reservoir (□ 12 sq mi/31 sq km), Sanders co., NW Mont., on Clark Fork and Thompson Fork of Pend Oreiller R., in Kaniksu Natl. Forest bet. Cabinet Mts. and Bitterroot Range, 28 mi/45 km SSW of Libby; 47°58′N 115°44′W. Max. capacity 400,000 acre-ft. Formed by Noxon Rapids Dam (170 ft/52 m high), built (1960) by U.S. Forest Service for power generation; also used for recreation.

Cabinet Mountains, range of Rocky Mts. in NW Mont. Lincoln and Sanders cos., extend NW into Bonner co., Idaho, rise just W of Libby, extend c.65 mi/105 km S along the Clark Fork to Thompson Falls. Kootenai Natl. Forest (N), Lolo Natl. Forest (S). Cabinet Mts. wilderness. Highest point, Snowshoe Peak (8,712 ft/2,655 m). Lead and silver mines.

Cable, village (1990 pop. 817), Bayfield co., N Wis., on small Cable L., 32 mi/51 km SW of Ashland; 46°12′N 91°17′W. Mfg. (wooden trusses, lumber). Skiing; tourism. Chequamegon Natl. Forest to N and E.

Cabo Corrientes, Mexico: see EL TUITO.

Cabo Cruz (KAH-bo KROOS) or **Cape Cruz**, village, Granma prov., E Cuba, on the Caribbean Sea, 95 mi/153 km W of Santiago de Cuba, 17 mi/27 km E of the Cape Cruz; 19°51′N 77°44′W. Important lighthouse for mariners.

Cabo Rojo, town (1990 pop. 38,521), SW P.R., near the coast, 7 mi/11.3 km S of Mayagüez. Processing center in agr. region (sugarcane, plantains, watermelons, livestock); light mfg.; tourism. Nearby on the ocean are saltworks. Cape Rojo, Span. *Cabo Rojo*, is 11 mi/18 km SSW. Lighthouse.

Cabo San Lucas (KAH-bo sahn LOO-kahs), resort (1990 pop. 16,059), Baja California Sur, NW Mexico, at S tip of peninsula, 90 mi/145 km SSE of La Paz, at S highway terminus; 22°50′N 109°52′W. Has developed as an exclusive tourist resort. Lead deposits nearby. Cape San Lucas, at W gate of Gulf of California, is 2 mi. S.

Cabo San Lucas, Mexico: see SAN LUCAS, CAPE.

Cabool (kuh-BOOL), city (1990 pop. 2,006), Texas co., S central Mo., in the Ozarks, 31 mi/50 km NNW of West Plains; 37°07′N 92°05′W. Elev. 1,264 ft/385 m. Dairy, lumber prods.; livestock; mfg. (food prods., fixtures). Inc. 1906.

Caborca, Mexico: see HEROICA CABORCA.

Cabot 1 town (1990 pop. 8,319), Lonoke co., central Ark., 22 mi/35 km NE of Little Rock; 34°58′N 92°01′W. In agr. area; mfg. (apparel, furniture). **2** town (1990 pop. 1,043), including Cabot village, Washington co., N central Vt., 15 mi/24 km NE of Montpelier; 44°23′N 72°17′W. Cheese mfg. Chartered 1781.

Cabot (KA-buht), uninc. village, Butler co., W Pa., 9 mi/14.5 km SE of Butler on Little Buffalo Creek; 40°45′N 79°46′W. Mfg. (construction materials, industrial oils), sheet metal fabricating. Agr. includes dairying, livestock; corn, hay.

Cabot, Mount (4,160 ft/1,268 m), in White Mts., Coos co., N central N.H., 10 mi/16 km W of Berlin, in White Mt. Natl. Forest.

Cabral (kah-BRAHL), town (1993 pop. 10,961), Barahona prov., SW Dominican Republic, on the Yaque del Sur, and 6 mi/9.7 km W of Barahona; 18°18′N 71°10′W. Coffee-growing center.

Cabrera (kah-BRE-rah), town (1993 pop. 3,049), Samaná prov., NE Dominican Republic, on the Atlantic Ocean, 50 mi/80 km E of Puerto Plata; 19°35′N 69°58′W. In agr. region (coffee, cacao, bananas). Until 1891 called Tres Amarras.

Cabri, town (1991 pop. 561), SW Sask., Canada, 40 mi/64 km NW of Swift Current; 50°37′N 108°27′W. Grain elevators.

Cabrillo (□ 144 acres/58 ha), natl. monument, S Calif., in city of San Diego, San Diego co., at Point Loma, W of entrance to San Diego Bay, 5 mi/8 km WSW of downtown San Diego, on Pacific Ocean. Memorial to Juan Rodríguez Cabrillo, Port. explorer who claimed U.S. West Coast for Spain, 1542. Old Point Loma Lighthouse (1880s). Tidal pools have marine life. Authorized 1913.

Cabrillo Beach, Calif.: see SAN PEDRO.

Cabrón, Cape (kah-BRON), NE headland of Dominican Republic, NE of Samaná.

Cacahoatán (kah-kah-wah-TAHN), town (1990 pop. 10,598), Chiapas, S Mexico, at S foot of Tacaná volcano, near Guatemala border, 8 mi/12.9 km NE of Tapachula; 14°59′N 92°09′W. Coffee growing.

Cacahuamilpa (kah-kah-wah-MEEL-pah), large caves in Guerrero, SW Mexico, 10 mi/16 km NE of Taxco de Alarcón; 18°10′N 99°30′W. Discovered 1835.

Cacahuatepec, Mexico: see SAN JUAN CACAHUATEPEC.

Cacalchén (kah-kahl-CHEN), town (1990 pop. 5,857), Yucatán, SE Mexico, 25 mi/40 km E of Mérida; 21°01′N 89°10′W. RR junction in former henequen-growing region. Citrus fruit.

Cacapon Mountain (kuh-KAI-puhn), ridge (c.2,000 ft/610 m), Hampshire and Morgan cos., NE W.Va., in Appalachian Mts. and E. Panhandle of W.Va. From point 8 mi/12.9 km NNE of Capon Bridge, extends c.16 mi/26 km NNE to the Potomac R. SE of Great Cacapon. Rises to 2,650 ft/808 m near S end, at Va. state line; Cacapon R. runs along W foot. Most of mt. in Cacapon State Park (c.6,115 acres/2,475 ha), with bridle and foot trails; observation points; and facilities for swimming, fishing, camping, and sports.

Cacapon River (kuh-KAI-puhn), c.115 mi/185 km long; rises in S Hardy co., NE W.Va., as Lost R., flows c.25 mi/40 km NNE, submerged as an underground stream for c.5 mi/8 km, then emerges just W of Wardensville as Cacapon R., then flows c.85 mi/137 km NNE to the Potomac R. at Great Cacapon village; 39°04′N 78°38′W. Lost R. State Park (c.3,712 acres/1,502 ha) is 2 mi/3.2 km W of the upper Lost R., with camping, picnicking, and recreational facilities and mineral springs.

Cache (KASH), county (□1,173 sq mi/3,038 sq km; 1990 pop. 70,183), N Utah; ⊙ Logan; 41°41′N 111°45′W. Irrigated agr. area bordering on Idaho and drained by Bear R. Includes fertile Cache Valley (extending N-S) in NW part of co. and part of Cache Natl. Forest and Wasatch Range in E. Wheat, barley, alfalfa, hay, sugar beets, vegetables, raspberries; cattle. Mfg. at Logan. Hardware Ranch Game Management Area in SE; Mt. Naomi Wilderness Area in E. Part of Wellsville Mt. Wilderness Area in SW; Hyrum State Park in SW. Beaver Mt. Ski Area in NE corner; Powder Mt. Ski Area on S boundary. Wasatch Natl. Forest in all of E ½, also S and SW. Small part of Caribou Natl. Forest in NW. Formed 1856.

Cache (KASH), town (1990 pop. 2,251), Comanche co., SW Okla., 12 mi/21 km W of Lawton, just S of the Wichita Mts.; 34°37′N 98°37′W. The large Fort Sill Military Reservation is to N (W entrance).

Cache Bay (KASH), town (1991 pop. 712), SE central Ont., Canada, on NW shore of L. Nipissing, 26 mi/42 km W of North Bay. Lumbering, fishing center.

Cache Creek 1 c.85 mi/137 km long, in NW Calif.; rises in Lake co., in Coast Range, flows SE through Clear L. reservoir, past Esparta and N of Woodland to Sacramento R. in Yolo co., 12 mi/19 km NW of Sacramento. **2** c.100 mi/161 km long, SW Okla.; rises in SE Caddo co., flows NE, then S past Apache, where it enters L. Ellsworth reservoir, through Fort Sill Military Reservation, city of Lawton and Walters, to Red R. c.17 mi/27 km S of Walters. West Cache Creek, its main branch, enters 10 mi/16 km S of Walters.

Cache la Poudre River (KASH lah POO-druh), 126 mi/203 km long, N Colo.; rises at Continental Divide in NW corner of Rocky Mt. Natl. Park, Larimer co., flows N through Roosevelt Natl. Forest, E past Poudro Park,

---

and SE past Fort Collins, Windsor, and Greely, to South Platte R. 5 mi/8 km E of Greeley. Waters sugar beet, livestock region. Receives water from Laramie R. through Laramie-Poudre (or Greeley-Poudre) Tunnel (c.2 mi/3.2 km long; finished 1911), used to irrigate 125,000 acres/50,588 ha in Larimer and Weld cos. Also called Poudre R.

Cache River 1 (KASH), c.55 mi/89 km long, in S Ill.; rises in E Union co., flows SE, W, and S, through rich agr. area, to Ohio R. c.5 mi/8 km above Cairo; 37°27′N 89°14′W. Focus of Cache R. State Natural Area and Cypress Creek Natl. Wildlife Refuge. **2** c.213 mi/343 km long, in Mo. and Ark.; rises in Butler co., SE Mo., flows SW into Ark., past Grubbs, to White R. at Clarendon;.

Cachuma Dam, Calif.: see SANTA YNEZ RIVER.

Cacocúm (kah-ko-KUM), agr. town, Holguín prov., E Cuba, on central RR line, 12 mi/19 km SW of Holguín; 20°44′N 76°20′W. Cristino Naranjo sugar mill is 4 mi/6.4 km E.

Cacouna (kuh-KOO-nuh), village, SE Que., Canada, on the St. Lawrence, and 6 mi/10 km NNE of Riviére du Loup. Dairying, lumbering; resort. Just N, in the St. Lawrence, is Cacouna Isl. (2 mi/3 km long).

Cactus, town (1990 pop. 1,529), Moore co., extreme N Texas, 15 mi/24 km N of Dumas; 36°02′N 102°00′W. Agr. area (cattle, sorghum, wheat). Mfg. (leather tanning, meat processing [Monfort]).

Caddo (KA-do), county (□ 1,290 sq mi/3,341 sq km; 1990 pop. 29,550), W central Okla.; ⊙ Anadarko; 35°10′N 98°22′W. Intersected by Washita R.; drained by Fort Cobb and Sugar creeks. Hilly agr. area (cotton, wheat, sorghum, fruits and vegetables, hay, corn, peanuts; cattle). Mfg. and farm-products processing at Anadarko, Apache, and Cement; sand and gravel. Red Rock Canyon State Park to N; Fort Cobb State Park and Fort Cobb L. reservoir in NW. Formed 1907.

Caddo (KA-do), parish (□ 900 sq mi/2,331 sq km; 1990 pop. 248,253), extreme NW La., situated on Texas-Ark. border (W), bounded E by Red R., S by Bayou Pierre; ⊙ Shreveport; 32°25′N 93°48′W. Includes Cross L. (resort), now part of Shreveport, and part of Caddo L. on Texas boundary in NW. Large oil production, esp. in N; natural gas wells, oil and gas refineries, pipelines. Agr. (chiefly cotton; also berries, peaches, corn, sorghum, hay, home gardens, nursery crops, vegetables, rice; cattle, horses, hogs, poultry, exotic fowl; dairying); timber; logging. Varied mfg. (chemicals, paper, glass prods., metal prods., industrial machinery, motor vehicles). Milling of cotton, cottonseed. Shipping on Red R. Soda L. State Wildlife Area in N center, Black Bayou L. in N, Wallace L. on S boundary. Named after the Caddo Indian tribe. Formed 1838.

Caddo 1 (KA-do), village (1990 pop. 918), Bryan co., S Okla., 11 mi/18 km NE of Durant; 34°07′N 96°16′W. In farm area (grain, cotton, peanuts); mfg. (candy, portable boats, plastic gaskets). **2** uninc. village (1990 pop. c.40), Stephens co., N central Texas, 14 mi/23 km E of Breckenridge. Elev. 1,250 ft/381 m. In agr. area (cotton; wheat; cattle). Oil and gas; mfg. (natural gas processing).

Caddo Gap (KA-do), village, Montgomery co., W Ark., 5 mi/8 km SE of Norman and on Caddo R. in Ouachita Natl. Forest.

Caddo Lake (KA-do), extreme NW La. and NE Texas, on Cypress Bayou (Cypress R. in Texas), 15 mi/24 km NNW of Shreveport, La.; c.15 mi/24 km long; 32°42′N 93°55′W. Max. capacity 755,000 acre-ft. Extends W into Texas, forming part of Marion/Harrison co. border. Formed by Caddo Dam (47 ft/14 m high; earth-construction), built (1971) for flood control. Callo L. State Park (Texas) at W end.

Caddo Mills (KA-do), town (1990 pop. 1,068), Hunt co., NE Texas, 9 mi/14.5 km SW of Greenville; 33°04′N 96°13′W. Agr. (dairying; nursery crops; cotton; wheat; cattle, horses).

Caddo River (KA-do), c.80 mi/129 km long, SW Ark.; rises W of Norman about 8 mi/12.9 km SSW of Mt. Ida, Montgomery co., flows ESE past Glenwood, through DeGray L. Reservoir (state park) to Ouachita R. 4 mi/6.4 km N of Arkadelphia.

Caddoa Reservoir, Colo.: see JOHN MARTIN RESERVOIR.

Cadereyta de Montes (ka-dai-RAI-tah de MON-tes), city (1990 pop. 6,680) and township, Querétaro, central Mexico, on central plateau, 38 mi/61 km ENE of Querétaro on Mexico Hwy 120; 20°37′N 0°38′W. Elev. 6,791 ft/2,070 m. Agr. center (corn, wheat, sugar, vegetables, alfalfa, livestock).

Cadereyta Jiménez (ka-dai-RAI-tah hee-MAI-nes), city (1990 pop. 34,293) and township, Nuevo León, N Mexico, on RR, and 20 mi/32 km ESE of Monterrey on Mexico Hwy 40; 25°38′N 99°59′W. Agr. center (grain, chickpeas, cotton, stock). Large oil refinery.

Cadillac, city (1990 pop. 10,104), ⊙ Wexford co., NW Mich., on E shore of L. Cadillac (c.3 mi/4.8 km long, 1 mi/1.6 km wide) and 37 mi/60 km SSE of Traverse City; 44°15′N 85°25′W. Elev. 1,328 ft/405 m. RR junction and trade center for resort and agr. area (livestock, poultry; dairy prods.; grain). Mfg. (automotive parts, air cargo containers and pallets, tool and die prods., iron castings, rubber and plastic products, fiberglass boats, fans, vacuum cleaners, hardware, concrete prods.). Hq. for Manistee and Huron natl. forests. Year-round resort with recreational facilities. Caberfae Ski Area to W, Lost Pines Ski Area to NW; L. Mitchell (3 mi/4.8 km long, 3 mi/4.8 km wide) W, with William Mitchell State Park; Manistee Natl. Forest to W; Huron Natl. Forest 50 mi/80 km to NE. Settled c.1871; inc. as village 1875, as city 1877.

Cadillac 1 (KA-di-lak), village (1991 pop. 977), W Que., Canada, 14 mi/23 km WNW of Malartic. Gold mining. **2** village (1991 pop. 134), S Sask., Canada, 40 mi/64 km S of Swift Current. Wheat.

Cadillac, Lake, Mich.: see CADILLAC, city.

Cadillac Mountain, Maine: see MOUNT DESERT ISLAND.

Cadiz 1 (1990 pop. 202), Henry co., E central Ind., 7 mi/11.3 km WNW of New Castle; 39°57′N 85°29′W. In agr. area. **2** (KAI-diz), town (1990 pop. 2,148), ⊙ Trigg co., W Ky., 21 mi/34 km W of Hopkinsville, on Little R., at head of Little R. Arm at L. Barkley; 36°52′N 87°49′W. Trade, shipping center for agr. area (tobacco, wheat, corn; livestock), with timber; mfg. (transportation equipment, lumber, food, apparel, machining, plastics). Fort Campbell Military Reservation to SE. County museum here. Woods and Wetlands Wildlife Center to SW; L. Barkley (including airport) State Resort Park and Land Between the Lakes Recreation Area (Tennessee Valley Authority) to SW. Est. 1820.

Cadiz (KAI-diz), village (1990 pop. 3,439), ⊙ Harrison co., E Ohio, 20 mi/32 km WSW of Steubenville; 40°16′N 80°59′W. Coal mining center. Inc. 1818.

Cadiz Lake, San Bernardino co., SE Calif., intermittently dry bed (c.12 mi/19 km long) in Mojave Desert, 35 mi/56 km ENE of Twentynine Palms. Old Woman Mts. to NE, Sheep Hole Mts. to SW; Colorado R. Aqueduct to SE.

Cadomin (KA-do min), village, W Alta., Canada, in Rocky Mts., near E side of Jasper Natl. Park, at foot of Luscar Mt. (8,534 ft/2,601 m), 33 mi/53 km ENE of Jasper. Coal mining; cattle, sheep.

Cadosia (kuh-DO-zhuh), village (1990 pop. 300), Delaware co., S N.Y., 33 mi/53 km ESE of Binghamton, near junction of E and W branches forming Delaware R.; 41°58′N 75°16′W.

Cadott (kuh-DAHT), town (1990 pop. 1,328), Chippewa co., W central Wis., near Yellow R., 12 mi/19 km E of Chippewa Falls; 44°57′N 91°09′W. Lumbering, dairying, and stock-raising area. Mfg. (vinyl profiles, light mfg.). L. Wissota State Park to W. Annual Rock and Country Music Festival (since 1994).

Cadwell, town (1990 pop. 458), Laurens co., central Ga., 17 mi/27 km SSW of Dublin; 32°20′N 83°02′W. Mfg. wooden cabinets.

Cadyville, village (1990 pop. 900), Clinton co., extreme NE N.Y., on Saranac R., and 9 mi/14.5 km W of Plattsburgh; 44°42′N 73°36′W. In Adirondack Park.

Caesar Creek Lake, reservoir (□ 4 sq mi/10.4 sq km), Warren co., SW Ohio, on Caesar Creek, 15 mi/24 km E of Middletown; 39°28′N 83°58′W. Max. capacity 242,200 acre-ft. Formed by Caesar Lake Dam (168 ft/51 m high), built (1976) by Army Corps of Engineers for flood control; also used for recreation and water supply. Little Miami State Park near dam; Caeser Creek State Park on E shore.

Caesars Head, summit (3,208 ft/978 m) in the Blue Ridge Mts., on N.C.-S.C. state line, c.25 mi/40 km NNW of Greenville, Transylvania co., N.C., Greenville co., S.C. Its S face is a precipice c.1,500 ft/457 m high, with fine view. Resort village of Caesars Head , S.C., to SE. Caesars Head State Park, S.C.

Cagles Mill Lake, reservoir, on Owen-Putney co. border, W central Ind., on small branch of Deer Creek, 10 mi/16 km SSW of Greenville; 4 mi/6.4 km long; 39°29′N 86°54′W. Formed by Cataract Dam, built (1953) by Army Corps of Engineers for flood control. Lieber State Recreation Area on NE shore; Cataract Falls to SE.

Caguas (KAH-gwahs), city (1990 pop. 133,447), E central P.R. Largest of P.R.'s inland cities, Caguas is an industrial and commercial center. Tobacco; varied mfg. includes diamond cutting; plastic and leather goods. Historical Mus. of Caguas.

Cahaba (kuh-HAH-buh), village, Dallas co., W central Ala., at junction of Cahaba and Alabama rivers, 10 mi/16 km SSW of Selma. Site of 1st state capital, 1819–1826.

Cahaba Heights (kuh-HAH-buh), residential suburb (1990 pop. 4,778), Jefferson co., N. central Ala., just SE of Birmingham; 33°27′N 86°43′W.

Cahaba River (kuh-HAH-buh), c.200 mi/322 km long, central Ala.; rises NE of Birmingham, flows SW, past Centreville, then S to Alabama R. 8 mi/12.9 km SSW of Selma. Used in upper course as water source for Birmingham.

Cahokia, village (1990 pop. 17,550), St. Clair co., SW Ill., a residential suburb of St. Louis, Mo. on the Mississippi R.; 38°33′N 90°10′W. Inc. 1927. The first permanent settlement in Ill., Cahokia's name is derived from a local Native Amer. group. The French established a mission in 1699 and a fur-trading post later. Cahokia was occupied by the British in 1765 and captured by the Americans under George Rogers Clark in 1778. It has several bldgs. dating from the 18th cent. Parks Col. of Aeronautical Technology, part of St. Louis Univ., is here. Nearby is Cahokia Mounds State Park.

Cahokia Creek, c.55 mi/89 km long, central and SW Ill.; rises in Macoupin co., flows generally SW, past Edwardsville, to the Mississippi above East St. Louis; 39°11′N 89°41′W.

Cahokia Mounds Historic Site, approximately 85 Native Amer. earthworks in Cahokia Mounds Historic Site, SW Ill., near East St. Louis; 38°39′N 90°03′W. Largest group of mounds N of Mexico. Monks Mound, a rectangular, flat-topped earthwork, 100 ft/30.5 m high with a 17 acres/7 ha base, is named for Trappist monks who settled there in the early 19th cent. The people who constructed the mounds were village dwellers who lived in a fertile river-bottom area; their culture flourished c.1300-c.1700. The mounds constitute a natl. historic landmark.

Caibarién (kei-bah-ree-AIN), city (1994 est. pop. 37,000), Villa Clara prov., central Cuba, 32 mi/51 km ENE of Santa Clara; 22°31′N 79°28′W. Distributing and shipping point for agr. region (sugarcane, tobacco, fruit). Its port is served by natl. and internatl. lines. Also an important sponge-fishing center. Sawmilling, sugar refining (at Central Reforma, SW), fish canning.

Caicos Islands: see TURKS AND CAICOS ISLANDS.

Caicos Passage, channel (c.40 mi/64 km wide) in the Caribbean, separates Mayaguana isl. in SE Bahama Isls. (W) from Caicos Isls., dependency of Jamaica (E); 22°20′N 72°20′W.

Caillou Bay (KEI-yoo), SE La., arm of the Gulf of Mexico bet. marshy coast and Isles Dernieres, 35 mi/56 km SSW of Houma; c.10 mi/16 km long NW-SE, 2 mi/3 km–6 mi/10 km wide; 29°06′N 90°56′W. Channel to E connects bay with L. Pelto, W extension of Terrebonne Bay. Connected by navigable waterways with tidal Caillou Lake (c.5 mi/8 km long, 3 mi/5 km wide) in marshy coastal area, c.3 mi/5 km NE (inland) from Caillou Bay. Small Caillou Island is c.20 mi/32 km E of

Caillou Bay, bet. Terrebonne Bay and Timbalier Bay. Oil and natural gas in vicinity.

Caimanera (kai-muh-NER-uh), town, Guantánamo prov., E Cuba, port for Guantánamo (11 mi/18 km N; linked by RR), on W shore of sheltered Guantánamo Bay, just N of the U.S. naval reserve; 19°59′N 75°09′W. Ships chiefly sugarcane and coffee.

Caimito (kei-MEE-to), town, La Habana prov., W Cuba, on Central Highway, on RR, 19 mi/31 km SW of Havana; 22°53′N 82°27′W. Tobacco, vegetables, citrus fruit. Sugar milled at the central Habana Libre (4 mi/6.4 km NNW). Asphalt deposits and sulphurous springs nearby.

Cains River, c.70 mi/113 km long, in central N.B., Canada; rises 30 mi/48 km NE of Fredericton, flows NE to the Southwest Miramichi R. 30 mi/48 km SW of Newcastle.

Cainsville, city (1990 pop. 387), Harrison co., NW Mo., 18 mi/29 km NE of Bethany; 40°26′N 93°46′W. Corn, soybeans, wheat; cattle; limestone, rock quarries. Sometimes spelled Cainesville.

Cainsville, village, S Ont., Canada, on Grand R., and 3 mi/5 km E of Brantford. Dairying; fruit, vegetables.

Cairnbrook (KERN-bruk), uninc. town (1990 pop. 1,081), Somerset co., SW Pa., 15 mi/24 km SSE of Johnstown; 40°07′N 78°49′W. Mfg. (lumber, sandstone processing); coal. Agr. (livestock; timber);

Cairo 1 (KAI-ro), city (1990 pop. 9,035), ⊙ Grady co., SW Ga., 13 mi/21 km WNW of Thomasville; 30°53′N 84°13′W. Major market and shipping center for cane syrup; processes sugarcane, nuts; mills (lumber, veneer, pulp), and food canneries; agr. center and light mfg. region. Settled 1866, inc. 1870. **2** city (1990 pop. 4,846), ⊙ Alexander co., extreme S Ill., on a levee-protected tongue of land adjacent to the confluence of the Mississippi and Ohio rivers (spanned by 2 bridges); 37°00′N 89°10′W. It is a center for shipping by river, RR, and highway, and processing and distributing point for a large and fertile farm area. Mfg. (grain and soybean processing, polyurethene prods., lumber, cleaning prods.). Agr. (cotton and grain). The city and surrounding area are popularly called "Little Egypt" because of the deltalike geographical similarity. Permanent settlement began in 1837. Cairo was a strategic point in the Civil War; it was a crowded military camp, a depot for Union supplies, and General Grant's hq. during much of his Western campaign. Town was scene of riots and racial tensions during late 1960s. The city has been endangered by floods, but Federal flood control projects have decreased this potentiality. Fort Defiance State Park, the site of a Civil War fort, offers a magnificent view of the convergence of the Ohio and Mississippi rivers and of 2 bridges. Inc. 1818, followed by unsuccessful settlement; reincorporated in 1837.

Cairo (KAI-ro), town (1990 pop. 282), Randolph co., N central Mo., 6 mi/9.7 km N of Moberly; 39°30′N 92°26′W. Soybeans, corn; hogs, cattle; coal in area.

Cairo 1 (KAI-ro), village (1990 pop. 733), Hall co., S central Nebr., 15 mi/24 km WNW of Grand Island and 5 mi/8 km S of Loup R; 41°00′N 98°36′W. Shipping point for grain and livestock; potatoes. Mfg. (livestock chutes and panels, fire trucks, printing). **2** village (1990 pop. 290), Ritchie co., NW W.Va., 20 mi/32 km ESE of Parkersburg, on N fork Hughes R.; 39°12′N 81°09′W. Mfg. (lumber); agr. (grain; cattle). North Bend State Park to E, North Bend Trail passes E-W through village.

Caja de Muertos (KAH-hah MWER-tos) or **Muertos Island**, small island (c.1.5 mi/2.4 km long, ½ mi/⁸⁄₁₀ km wide), off S coast of P.R., 10 mi/16 km SE of Ponce. Beaches. Nature reserve. Lighthouse. Ferry from Ponce on weekends.

Cajahs Mountain (KAI-juhs), town (1990 pop. 2,429), Caldwell co., W central N.C., residential suburb 5 mi/8 km S of Lenoir; 35°51′N 81°32′W. Agr. area (tobacco, grain, poultry, livestock).

Cajalco Reservoir, Calif.: see MATHEWS, LAKE.

Cajeme, Mexico: see CIUDAD OBREGÓN.

Cajon Pass (kah-HON) or Cajon Summit (4,257 ft/ 1,298 m), San Bernadino co., S Calif., bet. E end of San Gabriel Mts. and NW end of San Bernardino Mts., NW of San Bernardino; connects Mojave Desert (N) with Los Angeles basin. Santa Fe Trail 1849 Monument S of pass.

Calabasas (KAL-uh-BAS-uhs), city, Los Angeles co., S Calif., 26 mi/42 km WNW of downtown Los Angeles, in upper (W) end of San Fernando Valley. Residential area. Mfg. (printing and publishing, rubber goods, draperies, electric and electronic equipment). Santa Monica Mts. Natl. Recreation Area to S. Motion Picture Country Home and Hospital is here.

Calabash, town (1990 pop. 1,210), Brunswick co., SE N.C., 46 mi/74 km SW of Wilmington, at S.C. state line; 33°53′N 78°34′W. Atlantic Ocean 3 mi/4.8 km to SE; Intracoastal Waterway canal passes 2 mi/3.2 km to SE. Agr. area (tobacco, grain, sweet potatoes, soybeans, livestock). Mfg. (screen printing; major seafood restaurant center for surrounding tourist region).

Calabazar 1 (kahl-uh-buh-ZAHR), town, La Habana prov., W Cuba, on Almendares R., on RR, and 7 mi/ 11.3 km S of Havana; 23°01′N 82°22′W. Dairying, mfg. of cigars. **2** or **Calabazar de Sagua**, town, Villa Clara prov., central Cuba, on RR, and 16 mi/26 km N of Santa Clara; 22°38′N 79°54′W. Sugar-growing center with several centrals (sugar mills) in vicinity: Unidad Proletaria (NW), El Vaquerito (W), Perucho Figueredo (NNE), B. Coroneaux (SW).

Calabogie (ka-luh-BO-gee), village, SE Ont., Canada, on Madawaska R. and on Calabogie L. (4 mi/6 km long), 50 mi/80 km E of Ottawa; 45°18′N 76°43′W. Dairying, mixed farming; in lead-mining region. Ski resort.

Calais (KAL-is), city (1990 pop. 3,963), Washington co., E Maine, on St. Croix R. (here crossed by Internatl. Bridge) opposite St. Stephen, N.B., Canada; 45°07′N 67°12′W. Port of entry. Mfg. (wood prods., bldg. materials); blueberries canned. Milltown (W) is a suburb. Moosehorn Natl. Wildlife Refuge nearby. Champlain and Sieur de Monts planted settlement (1604) on St. Croix Isl. in the St. Croix here. Calais settled 1779, town inc. 1809, city 1850.

Calais (KAL-is), town (1990 pop. 1,521), Washington co., central Vt., 9 mi/14.5 km NNE of Montpelier; 44°22′N 72°28′W.

Calamus, town (1990 pop. 379), Clinton co., E Iowa, 29 mi/47 km W of Clinton; 41°49′N 90°45′W. In agr. area.

Calamus, reservoir (□ 8 sq mi/20.7 sq km), Loop and Garfield cos., central Nebr., on Calamus R., 75 mi/ 120 km NW of Grand Island; 41°50′N 99°12′W. Max. capacity of 177,623 acre-ft. Formed by Virginia Smith Dam (91 ft/28 m high), built (1986) by the Bureau of Reclamation for irrigation. Calamus Reservoir State Recreational Area near dam.

Calamus River, 76 mi/122 km long, N Nebr.; source of Moon L. in Brown co., flows through Sand Hills, SE to North Loup R. at Burwell. Canoeing on river.

Calapooia River (kal-uh-POO-yuh), c. 70 mi/113 km long, W Oregon; rises in Cascade Range c. 35 mi/56 km ENE of Eugene, flows WNW, past Brownsville, to Willamette R. at Albany.

Calaveras, county (□ 1,020 sq mi/2,642 sq km; 1990 pop. 31,998), central Calif., in the Sierra Nevada; ⊙ San Andreas; 38°13′N 120°33′W. Mokelumne R. and its N fork form the N boundary, and Stanislaus R. and its N fork form the S boundary. County is drained by Calaveras R. and its N fork, and by South Fork Mokelumne R. Stanislaus Natl. Forest and part of Calaveras Big Trees State Park (redwoods) on SE boundary. Dams store water for power, water supply, and irrigation. Winter sports area; also camping, hunting, fishing. Gold mining; timber; cement production. Cattle; walnuts, olives; honey, oats, grapes. Angels Camp, the scene of one of Mark Twain's stories, and other old Calif. gold rush (1849) towns survive. Pardee and Camanche reservoirs (Mokelumne R.) on N boundary, in NW; New Melones and Tulloch reservoirs (Stanislaus R.) on SE boundary; New Hogan L. reservoir (Calaveras R.) in W. Ski Area in E. Formed 1850.

Calaveras Big Trees State Park (□ c.5,996 acres/ 2,427 ha), Calaveras and Tuolumne cos., on both sides of North Fork Stanislaus R., E central Calif., on W slope of the Sierra Nevada, c.60 mi/97 km ENE of Stockton. In 1852, the 1st grove of *Sequoia gigantea* discovered in the sierras was found here by a hunter. Includes many of the finest sequoias (some almost 300 ft/ 91 m tall) in Calif. Recreational area; summer and winter sports, camping. Park surrounded by Stanislaus Natl. Forest.

Calaveras Dam, Calif.: see CALAVERAS RIVER.

Calaveras Reservoir, water supply reservoir (c.2 mi/ 3.2 km long) for San Francisco, in Santa Clara and Alameda cos., W Calif., formed by dam on Alameda Creek, 8 mi/12.9 km NNE of San Jose. Arroyo Hondo enters from SE.

Calaveras River, c.80 mi/129 km long, central Calif.; rises in NE Calaveras co. 28 mi/45 km E of Jackson, near Stanislaus R.; flows SW, past Arnold, through New Hogan Reservoir, where it receives North Fork from NE, to San Joaquin R. just W of Stockton. North Fork Calaveras R. rises in N central Calaveras co., c.18 mi/ 29 km E of Jackson, flows W then S to New Hogan Reservoir, c.20 mi/32 km. In W Calaveras co. is Calaveras Dam (220 ft/67 m high, 1,200 ft/366 m long) impounding New Hogan Reservoir (c.8 mi/12.9 km long). The Calaveras is also site of projected New Hogan Reservoir of Central Valley project.

Calcahualco (kahl-kah-WAHL-ko), town (1990 pop. 872), Veracruz, E Mexico, in Sierra Madre Oriental, at NE foot of the Pico de Orizaba, 8 mi/12.9 km WSW of Huatusco. Fruit.

Calcasieu (KAL-kuh-shoo), parish (□ 1,104 sq mi/ 2,859 sq km; 1990 pop. 168,134), extreme SW La.; 30°13′N, 93°12′W; ⊙ Lake Charles. Bounded W by Sabine R., here forming Texas state line, bounded in far E by Bayou Lacassine. Lake Charles city is deepwater port on Calcasieu R. Agr. (rice, sorghum, home gardens, soybeans, honey; cattle, horses, sheep, hogs); crawfish, shrimp, crabs; sulphur mines; oil and natural gas wells; coal; logging. Diversified mfg. and processing of farm, lumber, and petroleum prods.. Has small lakes (resorts; fishing). Intracoastal Waterway crosses parish in SW, just N of parish boundary. Sam Houston Jones State Park in N center, Nibletts Bluff Park in W, Sabine Isl. State Wildlife Area on Sabine R. in W, Nature's Nest Swamp and L. Bienvenu in SW. Formed 1840.

Calcasieu Lake, La.: see CALCASIEU RIVER.

Calcasieu River (KAL-kuh-shoo), c. 200 mi/320 km long, W central La.; rising in Vernon parish and flowing SE into Rapides parish, then SW into Allen parish, past Oakdale, through small part of Jefferson Davis parish, into Calcasieu parish, and the city of Lake Charles; 30°03′N, 93°17′W. From Lake Charles the river is paralleled on W by the Calcasieu Ship Channel, which affords ship access to the city from Gulf of Mexico 30 mi/48 km S, and barge access to Intracoastal Waterway 10 mi/16 km S. River enters large natural Calcasieu Lake and Cameron parish before exiting into Gulf through 5 mi/8 km channel. Sabine Natl. Wildlife Refuge on both sides of Calcasieu L.

Calderas Bay (kahl-DAI-rahs), small inlet of the Caribbean, S Dominican Republic, just SE of Ocoa Bay, 45 mi/72 km WSW of Santo Domingo. Saltworks.

Calderwood Island (KAHL-duhr-wud), Knox co., S Maine, in Penobscot Bay just SE of North Haven Isl.; ¾ mi/1.2 km long.

Calderwood Reservoir, E Tenn. and N.C., on Little Tennessee R., 35 mi/56 km S of Knoxville; 5 mi/8 km long; 35°29′N 83°55′W. Formed by Calderwood Dam (concrete, arch, overflow type; 230 ft/70 m high), built (1930) for power supply.

Caldwell 1 county (□ 348 sq mi/901 sq km; 1990 pop. 13,232), W Ky., 37°08′N 87°52′W; ⊙ Princeton. Bounded NE by Tradewater R. Rolling agr. area (tobacco, hay, alfalfa, soybeans, wheat, corn; hogs, cattle, poultry; dairying). Coal, timber; limestone quarries; mfg. at Princeton. Includes part of Pennyrile Forest State Park and L. Beshear reservoir on E boundary; Jones-Keeney Wildlife Management Area in E. Formed 1809. **2** county (□ 430 sq mi/1,114 sq km; 1990 pop. 8,380), NW Mo.; 39°39′N 93°58′W.; ⊙ Kingston. Corn, wheat, oats, soybeans; cattle, hogs; some mfg. at Hamilton. Formed 1836 specifically for Mormon settlement. **3** county (□ 474 sq mi/1,228 sq km; 1990 pop. 70,709), W central N.C.; ☉ Lenoir; 35°57′N 81°32′W. The Blue Ridge Mts. in NW; bounded in S by Catawba R. (forms Hickory L. and Rhodhiss L. reservoirs); drained by Yadkin R. Agr. area (potatoes, cattle, hogs, chickens, tobacco, corn, wheat, hay, dairy prods.); timber. Mfg. at Lenoir, Hudson, and Granite Falls. Part of Pisgah Natl. Forest in W; Tuttle Educational State Forest in SW. Formed 1841. **4** county (□ 547 sq mi/1,417 sq km; 1990 pop. 26,392), S central Texas; 29°50′N 97°36′W; ☉ Lockhart. Bounded SW by San Marcos R. Agr. (cotton, corn, grain, sorghum, vegetables); livestock (cattle, poultry, esp. turkeys). Oil, natural-gas fields. Mfg. farm-products processing at Lockhart and Luling. Lockhart State Park at center of co. Formed 1848.

Caldwell (KAWLD-wel), parish (□ 550 sq mi/1,425 sq km; 1990 pop. 9,810), NE central La.; 32°06′N 92°05′W; ☉ Columbia. Bounded E by Boeuf R.; intersected by Ouachita R. and Castor Creek. Agr. (cotton, hay, soybeans; cattle, horses); aquaculture; logging; oil and natural gas wells. Large Boeuf State Wildlife Area in E. Formed 1838.

Caldwell, city (1990 pop. 18,400), ☉ Canyon co., SW Idaho, 23 mi/37 km WNW of Boise, on the Boise R.; 43°40′N 116°40′W. Elev. 2,369 ft/722 m. Junction of RR spur to Wilder and on the site of an Oregon Trail camping ground, the city is a major processing and distribution center for an agr. and livestock area. Mfg. transportation equipment, wood prods., concrete, water filters. Caldwell is the seat of an agr. experiment station and Albertson's Col. Deer Flat Natl. Wildlife Refuge and L. Lowell to S. Inc. 1890.

Caldwell 1 town (1990 pop. 1,351), Sumner co., S Kansas, near Okla. state line, 19 mi/31 km SSW of Wellington; 37°02′N 97°36′W. In wheat and livestock region. City grew as trading point on Chisholm Trail. Laid out 1871, inc. 1879. **2** town (1990 pop. 3,181), ☉ Burleson co., S central Texas, c.65 mi/105 km ENE of Austin; 30°31′N 96°42′W. Elev. 406 ft/124 m. Trade, processing center for cotton, corn area. Mfg. (metal fabrication, wire prods.). Somerville L. and L. Somerville State Park to S.

Caldwell, village (1990 pop. 1,786), ☉ Noble co., E Ohio, 20 mi/32 km SSE of Cambridge, and on small Duck Creek; 39°46′N 81°31′W. Oil wells. Laid out 1857.

Caldwell (KAWLD-wuhl), borough (1990 pop. 7,549), Essex co., in NE N.J., 8 mi/12.9 km NW of Newark; 40°50′N 74°16′W. Mfg. (clothing, plastic prods., drugs). Residential. Seat of Caldwell Col. Grover Cleveland's birthplace, now a mus., here. Settled before 1785, inc. 1892.

Caledonia (KA-li-DO-nee-uh), county (□ 657 sq mi/1,702 sq km; 1990 pop. 27,846), NE Vt., partly bounded E by Connecticut R.; 44°27′N 72°05′W; ☉ St. Johnsbury. Mfg. (scales, machinery, paper); dairying; lumber, granite. Winter and summer resorts. Drained by Passumpsic, Moose, Lamoille, and Wells rivers. Organized 1792.

Caledonia, town (1991 pop. 1,390), S Ont., Canada, on Grand R. and 14 mi/23 km SSE of Hamilton. Dairying. Gypsum mining, natural-gas production; hydroelectric station.

Caledonia 1 (KA-li-DO-nee-uh), town (1990 pop. 2,846), ☉ Houston co., extreme SE Minn., Iowa state line, 17 mi/27 km SW of La Crosse, Wis.; 43°37′N 91°30′W. Elev. 1,188 ft/362 m. Grain, soybeans; livestock, poultry; dairying. Mfg. (tubing, frozen food, software, sandpaper); lumber. Beaver Valley Creek State Park to W; Richard J. Dorer Memorial Hardwood State Forest to W, N, and E. Settled c.1855. **2** town (1990 pop. 821), Lowndes co., E Miss., 14 mi/23 km NNE of Columbus, near Buttahatchie R.; 33°40′N 88°19′W. Agr. (cotton, grain, soybeans; cattle; timber. Mfg. (RR ties, apparel, oil and gas equipment). **3** town (1990 pop. 142), Washington co., E central Mo., in the St. Francois Mts., near Big R. 13 mi/21 km S of Potosi; 37°45′N 90°46′W. Mixed farming; historic lead and iron mining region. Plotted 1818.

Caledonia 1 (KA-li-DO-nee-uh), village (1990 pop. 885), Kent co., SW Mich., 14 mi/23 km SE of Grand Rapids; 42°47′N 85°30′W.Agr.; dairying. Mfg. (paint, motor vehicle parts, thermoplastic materials). Middleville Ski Area to SE. **2** village (□ 2 sq mi/5.2 sq km; 1990 pop. 2,262), Livingston co., W central N.Y., 18 mi/29 km SW of Rochester; 42°58′N 77°51′W. Mfg. (electrical equipment; dairy and farm supplies); limestone quarries. Agr. (dairy prods.; grain). Site of state trout hatchery. Inc. 1887. **3** village (1990 pop.154), Traill co., E N.Dak., 10 mi/16 km ENE of Hillsboro, near junction of Goose R. with Red R. of the North; 47°27′N 53°96′W. **4** village (1990 pop. 644), Marion co., central Ohio, 9 mi/14 km ENE of Marion, and on Olentangy R.; 40°39′N 82°58′W. Agr. area.

Caledonia Mines, village, NE N.S., Canada, near NE coast of Cape Breton Isl., just SW of Glace Bay. Coal-mining center.

Caledonia Springs, village, SE Ont., Canada, 45 mi/72 km E of Ottawa. Resort, with medicinal springs.

Calera 1 (kuh-LER-ruh), town (1990 pop. 2,136), Shelby co., central Ala., 10 mi/16 km SW of Columbiana; 33°06′N 86°45′W. Lumber, lime prods. Settled in mid-19th cent. **2** town (1990 pop. 1,536), Bryan co., S Okla., 5 mi/8 km SW of Durant; 33°55′N 96°25′W. Agr. (oats, peanuts, corn).

Calera, Mexico: see VICTOR ROSALES.

Calexico, city (1990 pop. 18,633), Imperial co., S Calif., 10 mi/16 km S of El Centro, at the Mexican border (Baja California Norte state); 32°41′N 115°30′W. RR terminus and port of entry from its adjacent sister city of Mexicali, Mexico, it is also a trade center in the southern part of the irrigated Imperial Valley (vegetables, tomatoes, melons, dates; cotton; wheat, corn, alfalfa; cattle, sheep). Tourism is central to the city's economy. Mfg. (electronic components). On All-American Canal. Inc. 1908.

Calf Island, Mass.: see BREWSTER ISLANDS.

Calfpasture River, c.40 mi/64 km long, NW Va.; rises in the Allegheny Mts. in W Augusta co., in George Washington Natl. Forest, flows SSW, past Goshen, joining Maury R. 2 mi/3.2 km SE of Goshen. Cowpasture R. to W.

Calgary (KAL-guh-ree), city (1991 pop. 710,677), S Alta., at the confluence of the Bow and Elbow rivers; 51°05′N 114°05′W. The 2d-largest metropolitan area in Alta. after EDMONTON, Calgary is a transportation and financial center for Canada's oil and natural-gas industries. Other industries include flour milling, meat packing, brewing, and lumbering. Calgary is a wholesale and processing center for a large agr. and stock-raising area. The city began (1875) as the 2d post of the NW Mounted Police and expanded with the arrival (1883) of the Can. Pacific RR. Calgary's early economic growth was based on the burgeoning open-range cattle industry and the opening of S Alta. to cash-crop farming. The discovery (1914) of oil at Turner Valley began an expansion that has made Calgary one of Canada's fastest-growing cities. It is the site of the Univ. of Calgary, the Glenbow Mus., and the 2d-largest zoo in Canada. The Calgary Stampede, inaugurated (1912) by Guy Weadick, an Amer. trick roper, is an annual rodeo and agr. fair. Calgary hosted the 1988 Winter Olympics. Gateway to Rocky Mts. and Banff and Waterton Lakes Natl. Parks, ski resorts.

Calhan, village (1990 pop. 562), El Paso co., central Colo., 30 mi/48 km NE of Colorado Springs; 39°01′N 104°17′W. Elev. 6,507 ft/1,983 m. Cattle, wheat, oats. Ramah State Wildlife Area to NE.

Calhoun 1 (kal-HOON), county (□ 612 sq mi/1,585 sq km; 1990 pop. 116,034), NE Ala.; 33°46′N 85°49′W; ☉ Anniston. Agr. area bounded on W by Coosa R. Agr. (hay, soybeans, wheat; poultry, cattle). Textiles. Deposits of iron ore, limestone, bauxite, barites. Part of Talladega Natl. Forest in E. Formed 1832. **2** county (□ 632 sq mi/1,637 sq km; 1990 pop. 5,826), S Ark.; 33°32′N 92°30′W; ☉ Hampton. Bounded E by Moro Bayou, S by Ouachita R., NW by Two Bayou; drained by Champagnolle Creek. H. K. Thatcher Lock and Dam on Ouachita R. on S boundary. Cattle.

Formed 1852. **3** county (□ 574 sq mi/1,487 sq km; 1990 pop. 11,011), NW Fla.; 30°24′N 85°12′W; ☉ Blountstown. Lowland area drained by Chipola R. and bounded E by Apalachicola R.; contains N end of Dead L. Agr. (corn, peanuts, sugarcane, vegetables), stock raising (hogs, cattle), and forestry (lumber, naval stores); clay pits in E. Formed 1838. **4** county (□ 289 sq mi/749 sq km; 1990 pop. 5,013), SW Ga.; 31°32′N 84°39′W; ☉ Morgan. Intersected by Ichawaynochaway Creek. Coastal plain agr. (cotton, corn, truck, peanuts, pecans; cattle, hogs, poultry); timber area. Formed 1854. **5** county (□ 283 sq mi/733 sq km; 1990 pop. 5,322), W Ill., on hilly peninsula, bounded by Mississippi (W, S) and Illinois (E) rivers, which join at co.'s SE tip; 39°09′N 90°40′W; ☉ Hardin. Apple-growing region; producing also hogs, vinegar. Several wildlife-management areas on both rivers. One of 17 Ill. cos. to retain southern-style commission form of government Formed 1825. **6** county (□ 572 sq mi/1,481 sq km; 1990 pop. 11,508), central Iowa; 42°23′N 94°38′W; ☉ Rockwell City. Prairie agr. area (corn, oats, soybeans; hogs, cattle, poultry) drained by Raccoon R. Bituminous-coal deposits, sand and gravel pits. Twin Lakes State Park in N. General flooding in 1993. Formed 1851. **7** county (□ 718 sq mi/1,860 sq km; 1990 pop. 135,982), S Mich.; 42°15′N 85°00′W; ☉ Marshall. Drained by Kalamazoo and St. Joseph rivers, and by Battle Creek. Agr. (cattle, hogs, sheep, poultry; oats, wheat, soybeans, hay, onions, corn, apples; dairy prods.). Mfg. at Battle Creek city, Albion, and Marshall. Kellogg Bird Sanctuary is in co.; Fort Custer State Recreation Area, Natl. Cemetery, and W.K. Kellogg Regional Airport in W at Battle Creek; Duck L. in NE, several smaller lakes in NW. Formed 1833. **8** county (□ 588 sq mi/1,523 sq km; 1990 pop. 14,908), N central Miss.; 33°56′N 89°20′W; ☉ Pittsboro. Drained by Skuna and Yalobusha rivers. Agr. (cotton, corn, sorghum, soybeans; cattle; timber) Bauxite, lignite, clay deposits. Grenada Waterfowl Refuge in SW. Formed 1852. **9** county (□ 392 sq mi/1,015 sq km; 1990 pop. 12,753), central S.C.; 33°40′N 80°46′W; ☉ St. Matthews. Bounded by Congaree R. (N) and L. Marion reservoir (SE). Mfg. (sand, clay, kaolin). Agr. (cattle, hogs; corn, wheat, rye, oats, soybeans, hay; cotton; pecans, vegetables). Formed 1908. **10** county (□ 1,032 sq mi/2,673 sq km; 1990 pop. 19,053), S Texas; 28°26′N 96°36′W; ☉ Port Lavaca. On Gulf of Mexico coast, here indented by San Antonio Bay (SW) and Lavaca Bay (arm of Matagorda Bay) splits co. in N center, and Matagorda bays, and protected by Matagorda Isl. Includes Green L. in W. Fisheries; seafood packing; irrigated agr. (cotton, corn, sorghums, rice); livestock raising; crabs, shrimp, crayfish farming. Oil, natural gas wells; refineries. Coast resorts. Port Lavaca Causeway State Recreation Area at Port Lavaca; Matagorda Isl. State Park in SE, at NE end of isl. Espiritu Santo Bay connects the two bays behind Matagorda Isl., sand barrier isl. paralleling Gulf Coast and part of co. Formed 1846. **11** county (□ 281 sq mi/728 sq km; 1990 pop. 7,885), central W.Va.; on Allegheny Plateau, drained by Little Kanawha R.; 38°50′N 81°07′W; ☉ Grantsville. Agr. (corn, potatoes, alfalfa, hay); cattle; poultry. Oil and natural gas wells. Formed 1856.

Calhoun 1 city (1990 pop. 7,135), ☉ Gordon co., NW Ga., 21 mi/34 km NNE of Rome, near Oostanaula R.; 34°29′N 84°56′W. Textile mfg. center; concrete, silica prods., ball bearings; pulpwood, lumber, sawmilling. Inc. 1852. New Echota Natl. Historic Landmark commemorating the capital of the Cherokee Nation is nearby. **2** city (1990 pop. 450), Henry co., W central Mo., 11 mi/18 km NE of Clinton; 38°28′N 93°37′W. Soybeans, corn, wheat; cattle. Former coal-mining center.

Calhoun (kal-HOON), town (1990 pop. 854), ☉ McLean co., W Ky., 17 mi/27 km SW of Owensboro, on Green R. (bridged); 37°32′N 87°15′W. Agr. (tobacco, grain, soybeans, tomatoes; livestock). Mfg. (burial vaults, apparel, tomato canning). Est. 1784.

Calhoun 1 (kal-HOON), village (1990 pop. 232), Richland co., SE Ill., 6 mi/9.7 km SSE of Olney; 38°38′N 88°02′W. Agr. (sorghum, apples; dairying); oil. **2** uninc. village (1990 pop. 4,082), Ouachita parish, NE central

La., 14 mi/23 km W of Monroe; 32°30′N 92°21′W. Cotton, soybeans, cattle; lumbering. Cheniere Brake L. and Fish Preserve to SE.

Calhoun, S.C.: see CLEMSON.

Calhoun City (kal-HOON), town (1990 pop. 1,838), Calhoun co., N central Miss., on Yalobusha R., 28 mi/45 km ENE of Grenada; 33°51′N 89°18′W. Agr. (cotton, corn, soybeans, sorghum; cattle). Mfg. (apparel, wood prods., leather material, furniture, machining, concrete). Grenada Waterfowl Refuge to SW. Inc. 1905.

Calhoun Falls, town (1990 pop. 2,328), Abbeville co., NW S.C., 26 mi/42 km WSW of Anderson, near Savannah R.; 34°05′N 82°35′W. Textile mfg. Agr. (poultry, livestock, dairying, grain, soybeans).

Calhoun, Lake, Ill.: see GALVA.

Calibogue Sound (kal-uh-BO-gee), Beaufort co., S S.C., inlet of the Atlantic Ocean, entrance on S 15 mi/24 km E of Savannah, Ga., to Hilton Head Isl. to E.; connected by channel to Port Royal Sound (N). Traversed by Intracoastal Waterway.

Calico Mountains (c.3,000 ft/914 m), San Bernardino co., S Calif., small range in Mojave Desert, 8 mi/12.9 km E of Barstow. Noted for brilliantly colored strata. Calico, a ghost silver mining town of 1880s, is here.

Calico Rock, town (1990 pop. 938), Izard co., N Ark., 19 mi/31 km SE of Mountain Home, and on White R.; 36°07′N 92°07′W. In agr. area. Mfg. (lumber; farm supplies). Ozark Natl. Forest to SW. North Central Unit Correctional Inst. to NE at Pineville.

Caliente (kah-lee-EN-tai), town (1990 pop. 1,111), Lincoln co., SE Nev., on Meadow Valley Wash, at mouth of Clover Creek, and 110 mi/177 km SSE of Ely; 37°37′N 114°30′W. Elev. c.4,395 ft/1,340 m. Perlite, zinc, sand, and gravel; cattle farms. Cathedral Gorge State Park to NE; Beaver Dam State Park to E, Kershaw-Ryan State Park to S. Delmar Mts. to SW. Mission-style train station (1923).

Califon (KA-li-fawn), borough (1990 pop. 1,073), Hunterdon co., W N.J., on South Branch of Raritan R., and 19 mi/31 km WSW of Morristown; 40°43′N 74°50′W. Fruit, truck, wheat.

California, state (□ 163,707 sq mi/424,001 sq km; 1995 est. pop. 31,589,153), W U.S., admitted as the 31st state of the Union in 1850; ⊙ SACRAMENTO. The largest cities are LOS ANGELES, SAN DIEGO, SAN JOSE, SAN FRANCISCO, LONG BEACH, OAKLAND, and SACRAMENTO. Calif. is bounded on the N by Oregon, on the E by Nev. and Ariz. (from which it is separated by the Colorado R.), on the S by Mexico (Baja Calif. Norte state), and on the W by the Pacific Ocean. Ranking 1st among the U.S. states in pop. and 3d in area, Calif. has a diverse topography and climate. A series of low mts. known as the Coast Ranges extends along the 1,200 mi/1,931 km coast. Most of coastal areas and mts. immediately inland, from Eureka in N to Los Angeles in S, are subject to frequent and often severe earthquakes from the San Andreas and other geological faults; also, some areas in NE, esp. around Lassen Peak, are volcanically active. The Coast Ranges receive heavy rainfall in the N, but the climate of these mts. is considerably drier in S Calif., and S of the Golden Gate no major rivers reach the ocean. The entire coastline is subject to fog, formed by clash of cool ocean currents from N and warm land surface; fog adds to region's beauty, but is also the contributor to infamous multicar pileups on Calif.'s freeways. Behind the coastal ranges in central Calif. lies the great Central Valley, a long alluvial valley drained by the Sacramento and San Joaquin rivers. In the SE lie vast deserts, notably the Mojave Desert, site of Joshua Tree Natl. Monument. Rising as an almost impenetrable granite barrier E of the Central Valley is the Sierra Nevada range, which includes Mt. Whitney (highest point in U.S. outside Alaska, 14,494 ft/4,418 m), Kings Canyon Natl. Park, Sequoia Natl. Park, and Yosemite Natl. Park (all in S part of Sierras, SE Calif.). The Cascade Range, the northern continuation of the Sierra Nevada, includes Lassen Volcanic Natl. Park. Death Valley Natl. Monument is E of the S Sierra Nevada. Calif. has an enormously productive and diverse economy. Although agr. is 2d to industry as the basis of the state's economy, Calif. is the leading state in the production of fruits and vegetables, including tomatoes, carrots, asparagus, broccoli, spinach, broccoli, citrus, and artichokes. The state's most valuable crops are grapes, nursery prods., cotton, flowers, almonds, lettuce, strawberries, and oranges. Cattle, poultry and dairy prods. also contribute a major share of farm income. The state produces the major share of U.S.-produced wine, esp. Sonoma and Napa cos., N of San Francisco. Calif.'s farms are highly productive as a result of good soil, a long growing season, and the use of modern agr. methods. Irrigation is widely used in almost every agr. district. The gathering and packing of crops is done largely by seasonal migrant labor, including thousands of Mexicans. Fishing remains an important industry in NW. Much of the state's mfg. depends on the processing of farm produce and upon such local natural resources as mineral deposits and forests. Petroleum is the state's most valuable mineral, although reserves are being depleted rapidly. Other important prods. are natural gas, cement, and sand and gravel. Since World War II heavy industry in the state has increased enormously, notably in the manufacture of transportation equip., electronic equip., machinery, and metal prods. Major reductions in the defense industry in the late 1980s and in the 1990s have had a severe negative impact on region. The "Silicon Valley," bet. Palo Alto and San Jose, earns its nickname as the nation's leading producer of semiconductors. Calif. continues to be a major U.S. center for motion-picture and television production, although Hollywood's luster has faded since the 1950s and the industry has dispersed to adjacent areas (Burbank, Studio City, Beverly Hills). Tourism is an important source of income. Disneyland, Sea World, and other theme parks draw many visitors each year, as does San Francisco with its numerous attractions, including the Golden Gate Bridge. Calif. also abounds in natural beauty, including the giant sequoia trees (among the oldest living things on earth), Redwood Natl. Park in NW, Lassen Volcanic Natl. Park in NE, Channel Islands Natl. Park off SW coast; Point Reyes Natl. Seashore and Golden Gate Natl. Recreation Area in W; Whiskeytown-Shasta-Trinity Natl. Recreation Area in N; and Santa Monica Mts. Natl. Recreation Area in SW. Several natl. forests include Six Rivers, Trinity, and Mendocino (NW); Klamath and Shasta (N); Modoc and Lassen (NE); Plumas, Tahoe, Eldorado, Stanislaus, Tuolumne, Sierra, Sequoia, and Inyo (E); Cleveland, San Bernardino, San Gabriel, and Los Padres (S). The Sierras contain many natl. parks and forests, and there are miles of beautiful beaches, especially in Southern Calif. One of the state's most acute problems is an inadequate water supply. The once fertile Owens valley is now arid, its waters tapped by Los Angeles 175 mi/282 km away. In the lush, fruit-growing Imperial Valley, irrigation is controlled by the All-American Canal, which draws from the Colorado R. To the N, the Central Valley receives its water supply mainly from streams descending out of the Sierra Nevada. After a cutback in federally funded water projects in the late 1970s and 1980s, many Calif. cities began to buy their water from areas with a surplus. In addition to irrigation water supply, drinking water for major cities is carried by long concrete aqueducts, including Hath Hatchy in center, Los Angeles and Colorado rivers aqueducts in S. The first voyage (1542) to Alta Calif. (Upper Calif.), as the region N of Baja Calif. (Lower Calif.) came to be known, was commanded by the Span. explorer Juan Rodríguez Cabrillo, who explored San Diego Bay and the area farther N along the coast. In 1579 an Eng. expedition headed by Sir Francis Drake landed near Point Reyes, N of San Francisco, and claimed the region for Queen Elizabeth I. In 1602, Sebastián Vizcaíno, another Spaniard, explored the coast and Monterey Bay. Colonization was slow, but finally in 1769 Gaspar de Portolá, governor of the Californias, led an expedition up the Pacific coast and established a colony on San Diego Bay. The following year he explored the area around Monterey Bay and later returned to establish a presidio there. Soon afterward, Monterey became the capital of Alta Calif. Accompanying Portolá's expedition was Father Junipero Serra, a Franciscan missionary who founded a mission at San Diego. Franciscans later founded several missions that extended as far N as Sonoma, N of San Francisco. The missionaries sought to Christianize the Native Americans, but also forced them to work as manual laborers, helping to build the missions into vital agr. communities. Cattle raising was of primary importance, and hides and tallow were exported. The missions have been preserved and are now open to visitors. In 1776, Juan Bautista de Anza founded San Francisco, where he established a military outpost. The early colonists, called the Californios, lived a pastoral life and for the most part were not interfered with by the central govt. of New Spain (as the Span. empire in the Americas was called) or later (1820s) by that of Mexico. The Californios did, however, become involved in local politics, as when Juan Bautista Alvarado led a revolt (1836) and made himself governor of Alta Calif., a position he later persuaded the Mexicans to let him keep. Under Mex. rule the missions were secularized (1833–1834) and the Native Americans released from their servitude. The degradation of Native American peoples, which continued under Mex. rule and culminated after U.S. settlers came to the area, was described by Helen Hunt Jackson in her novel *Ramona* (1884). Many mission lands were subsequently given to Californios, who established the great ranchos, vast cattle-raising estates. Colonization of Calif. remained largely Mex. until the 1840s. Rus. fur traders had penetrated S to the Calif. coast and established Fort Ross, N of San Francisco, in 1812. Jedediah Strong Smith and other trappers made the first U.S. overland trip to the area in 1826, but U.S. settlement did not become significant until the 1840s. In 1839, Swiss-born John Augustus Sutter arrived and established his "kingdom" of New Helvetia on a vast tract in the Sacramento valley. He did much for the overland Amer. immigrants, who began to arrive in large numbers in 1841. Some newcomers met with tragedy, including the Donner Party, which was stranded in the Sierra Nevada after a heavy snowstorm. Political events in the territory moved swiftly in the next few years. After having briefly asserted the independence of Calif. in 1836, the Californios drove out the last Mex. governor in 1845. Under the influence of the Amer. explorer John C. Frémont, U.S. settlers set up (1846) a republic at Sonoma under their home-styled Bear Flag. The news of war bet. the U.S. and Mexico (1846–1848) reached Calif. soon afterward. On July 7, 1846, Commodore John D. Sloat captured Monterey, the capital, and claimed Calif. for the U.S. The Californios in the N worked with U.S. soldiers, but those in the S resisted U.S. martial law. In 1847, however, U.S. Gen. Stephen W. Kearny defeated the southern Californios. By the Treaty of Guadalupe Hidalgo (1848), Mexico formally ceded the territory to the U.S. In the same year a major event in Calif.'s history occurred: while establishing a sawmill for John Sutter near Coloma, James W. Marshall discovered gold and touched off the Calif. gold rush. The forty-niners, as the gold-rush miners were called, came in droves, spurred by the promise of fabulous riches from the mother lode. San Francisco rapidly became a boom city, and its bawdy, lawless coastal area, which became known as the Barbary Coast, gave rise to the vigilantes, extralegal community groups formed to suppress civil disorder. Amer. writers such as Bret Harte and Mark Twain recorded the local color as well as the violence and human tragedies of the roaring mining camps. With the gold rush came a huge increase in pop. and a pressing need for civil govt. In 1849, Californians sought statehood and, after heated debate in the U.S. Congress arising out of the slavery issue, Calif. entered the Union as a free, nonslavery state by the Compromise of 1850. San Jose became the capital. Monterey, Vallejo, and Benicia each served as the capital before it was finally moved to Sacramento in 1854. In 1853, Congress authorized the survey of a RR route to link Calif. with the eastern seaboard, but the transcontinental RR was not completed until 1869.

Area in square miles is shown by the symbol □ capital city or county seat by ⊙

In the meantime communication and transportation depended upon ships, the stage coach, the pony express, and the telegraph. Chin. laborers were imported in great numbers to work on RR construction. The Burlingame Treaty of 1868 provided, among other things, for unrestricted Chin. immigration. That was at first enthusiastically endorsed by Californians, but after a slump in the state's shaky economy, the white settlers viewed the influx of the lower-paid Chin. laborers as an economic threat. Ensuing bitterness and friction led to the Chin. Exclusion Act of 1882. A RR-rate war (1884) and a boom in real estate (1885) fostered a new wave of overland immigration. Cattle raising on the ranchos gave way to increased grain production. Vineyards were planted by 1861, and the first trainload of oranges was shipped from Los Angeles in 1886. By the turn of the cent. the discovery of oil, industrialization resulting from the increase of hydroelectric power, and expanding agr. development attracted more settlers. Los Angeles grew rapidly in this period and, in pop., soon surpassed San Francisco, which suffered greatly after the great earthquake and fire of 1906. Improvements in urban transportation stimulated the growth of both Los Angeles and San Francisco; the advent of the cable car and the electric RR made possible the development of previously inaccessible areas. As industrious Jap. farmers acquired valuable land and a virtual monopoly of Calif.'s vegetable farming operations, the issue of Asian immigration again arose. The bitter struggle for the exclusion of Asians plagued internatl. relations, and in 1913 the Calif. Alien Land Act was passed despite President Woodrow Wilson's attempts to block it. The act provided that persons ineligible for U.S. citizenship could not own agr. land in Calif. Successive waves of settlers arrived in Calif., attracted by a new real-estate boom in the 1920s and by the promise of work in the 1930s. The influx during the 1930s of displaced farm workers, depicted by John Steinbeck in his novel *The Grapes of Wrath*, caused profound dislocation in the state's economy. During World War II the Jap. immigrants and Jap.-Americans in Calif. were removed from their homes and placed in relocation centers after a Jap. submarine was sighted off the coast. Industry in Calif. expanded rapidly during the war; the production of ships and aircraft attracted many workers who later settled in the state. Prosperity and rapid pop. growth continued after the war. Many Afr. Americans who came during World War II to work in the war industries settled in Calif. By the 1960s they constituted a sizable minority in the state, and racial tensions reached a climax. In 1964, Calif. voters approved an initiative measure, Proposition 14, allowing racial discrimination in the sale or rental of housing in the state, a measure later declared unconstitutional by the U.S. Supreme Court. In 1965 riots broke out in Watts, a predominantly Afr.-Amer. sect. of Los Angeles, touching off a wave of riots across the U.S. Also in the 1960s migrant farm workers in Calif. formed a union and struck many growers to obtain better pay and working conditions. Unrest also occurred in the state's universities, especially the Univ. of Calif. at Berkeley, where students demonstrated and protested in 1964. In 1970, S Calif. was struck by the worst brush fire in state history, and in 1971 a severe earthquake hit S Calif. along the San Andreas fault. In the late 1970s, Californians staged a "tax revolt," passing legislation to cut property taxes. During the 1970s and 1980s Calif. continued to grow rapidly, with a major shift of pop. to the state's interior. The metropolitan areas of Riverside-San Bernardino, Modesto, Stockton, Bakersfield, and Sacramento were among the fastest growing in the nation during the 1980s. In 1989, a major earthquake hit N Calif., killing 60 and injuring thousands. The cities of San Francisco, Oakland, and Santa Cruz were especially hard hit, suffering extensive damage from the earthquake itself and the resulting fires. Another devastating earthquake hit Northridge (just outside of downtown Los Angeles) in Jan. 1994. Cuts in Federal defense spending and natl. recession hurt the state economy in the late 1980s and early 1990s. In April 1992, 4 white Los Angeles police officers were acquitted of police brutality after they had been videotaped beating a Afri.-Amer. motorist. The acquittal touched off race riots in South-Central Los Angeles and a number of other neighborhoods and resulted in 58 deaths, thousands of arrests, and approximately $1 billion in property damage. The state's first constitution was adopted in 1849. The present constitution dates from 1879 and provides for initiative, referendum, and recall of public officials. The state's executive branch is headed by a governor elected for a 4-year term. Calif.'s bicameral legislature has a senate with 40 members elected for 4-year terms and an assembly with 80 members elected for 2 years. Local govt. is carried out on the co. and city level. The state elects 2 Senators and 52 Representatives to the U.S. Congress and has 54 electoral votes. Republicans have played a more dominant role than Democrats in Calif. politics during the 20th cent. Ronald Reagan, a former movie actor and leading conservative Republican, was elected governor in 1966 and reelected in 1970. Reagan tried unsuccessfully to gain the Republican presidential nomination in 1976 before being elected President in 1980 and reelected in 1984. Among the state's more prominent institutions of higher learning are the Univ. of Calif., with 9 campuses; Calif. State Univ., with 12 campuses; Occidental Col. and the Univ. of Southern Calif., at Los Angeles; Stanford Univ., at Palo Alto; the Calif. Inst. of Technology, at Pasadena; Mills Col., at Oakland; and the Claremont Colleges, at Claremont. Calif. has 58 cos.: ALAMEDA, ALPINE, AMADOR, BUTTE, CALAVERAS, COLUSA, CONTRA COSTA, DEL NORTE, EL DORADO, FRESNO, GLENN, HUMBOLDT, IMPERIAL, INYO, KERN, KINGS, LAKE, LASSEN, LOS ANGELES, MADERA, MARIN, MARIPOSA, MENDOCINO, MERCED, MODOC, MONO, MONTEREY, NAPA, NEVADA, ORANGE, PLACER, PLUMAS, RIVERSIDE, SACRAMENTO, SAN BENITO, SAN BERNARDINO, SAN DIEGO, SAN FRANCISCO, SAN JOAQUIN, SAN LUIS OBISPO, SAN MATEO, SANTA BARBARA, SANTA CLARA, SANTA CRUZ, SHASTA, SIERRA, SISKIYOU, SOLANO, SONOMA, STANISLAUS, SUTTER, TEHAMA, TRINITY, TULARE, TUOLUMNE, VENTURA, YOLO, and YUBA.

California, city (1990 pop. 3,465), ⊙ Moniteau co., central Mo., 21 mi/34 km W of Jefferson City; 38°37′N 92°34′W. Wheat, soybeans, corn; dairying; stock raising. Mfg. (feather processing, food, apparel, wood prods.). Founded 1845, inc. 1857.

California, town, ⊙ California municipio, Santander dept., N central Colombia, 15 mi/24 km NE of Bucaramanga. Coffee, sugarcane, livestock.

California, village, W Trinidad, Trinidad and Tobago, on RR, and 17 mi/27 km SSE of Port of Spain. Sugarcane, coconuts.

California, village (1990 pop. 130), Campbell co., N Ky., 21 mi/34 km SE of downtown Cincinnati, Ohio, on the Ohio R.; 38°55′N 84°15′W.

California, borough (1990 pop. 5,748), Washington co., SW Pa., 26 mi/42 km S of Pittsburgh, on Monongahela R., at mouth of Pike Run; 40°04′N 79°54′W. Light mfg. Agr. (livestock; corn, hay; dairying); bituminous coal. Seat of California Univ. of Pa. Laid out c. 1850, inc. c.1863.

California City, city (1990 pop. 5,955), Kern co., S central Calif., 55 mi/89 km ESE of Bakersfield, on Cache Creek, in Fremont Valley, Mojave Desert; 35°11′N 117°49′W. Cattle; mfg. (printing and publishing). Los Angeles Aqueduct passes to W; Red Rock Canyon State Recreation Area to N; Edwards A.F.B. to S.

California, Gulf of, arm of the Pacific Ocean, c.700 mi/1,127 km long and 50 mi/80 km to 130 mi/209 km wide, NW Mexico; separates Baja Calif. from the Mex. mainland. The gulf is part of a depression that extends inland to the Coachella Valley, S Calif. The Imperial Valley and the Salton Sea, once part of the gulf, have been cut off from it by the growth of the Colorado R. delta. The gulf deepens from N to S; its greatest depth is c.8,500 ft/2,591 m. The coastline is irregular, with numerous isls.; Tiburón, inhabited by aboriginal tribes, is the largest. Storms and tidal currents hinder navigation in the gulf. Commercial and sport fishing thrive; pearl, sponge, and oyster beds are harvested. The region is a developing tourist center; La Paz, Guaymas, and Mazatlán are major cities. The area was first explored in 1538 by the Spaniard Francisco de Ulloa. Also known as Sea of Cortés (Span. *Mar de Cortés*).

California Hollow, village, Columbiana co., E Ohio, 15 mi/24 km S of Youngstown.

California, Lower, peninsula: see BAJA CALIFORNIA.

Calihualá (kah-lee-wah-LAH), town (1990 pop. 704), in W Oaxaca, Mexico, 9 mi/14 km WNW of Silacayoapan; in the Mixteca Baja and mountainous. Elev. 3,215 ft/980 m. Agr. (corn and beans); woven straw textiles, livestock; liquor. Unpaved roads.

Calimaya de Díaz González (ka-lee-MAH-yah dai DEE-az gon-SAHL-eez), town (1990 pop. 6,726), Mexico state, central Mexico, 10 mi/16 km SSE of Toluca de Lerdo; 19°12′N 100°29′W. Agr. center (cereals, vegetables, livestock); dairying.

Calimesa (KAL-i-MAI-sah), city (1990 pop. 4647), Riverside co., S Calif., residential suburb 17 mi/27 km E of Riverside; 34°00′N 117°03′W. Cattle, dairying, poultry; grain, alfalfa, nursery prods.. Mfg. (concrete products).

Calimete (kahl-ee-MAI-tai), town, Matanzas prov., W Cuba, on RR and 40 mi/64 km SSE of Cárdenas; 22°31′N 80°54′W. Sugarcane, fruit, cattle. Sugar mills Reynold García to NW and Jesús Rabí to E.

Calio (KAL-ee-o), village (1990 pop. 43), Cavalier co., NE N.Dak., 16 mi/26 km NE of Cando; 48°37′N 98°56′W.

Calion (KAL-ee-yuhn), village (1990 pop. 558), Union co., S Ark., 10 mi/16 km NE of El Dorado, on Ouachita R. (E) and Calion L. (S); 33°19′N 92°32′W. Mfg. (furniture).

Calipatria (ka-li-PA-tree-ah), city (1990 pop. 2,690), Imperial co., S Calif., 11 mi/18 km N of Brawley, 7 mi/11.3 km SE of Salton Sea, in Imperial Valley; 33°08′N 115°31′W. Mfg. (biological prods.); irrigated agr. (vegetables, tomatoes, sugar beets, melons, cotton, wheat, alfalfa). Salton Sea Natl. Wildlife Refuge to NW (in S part of lake). Inc. 1919.

Calistoga (ka-li-STO-gah), city (1990 pop. 4,468), Napa co., W Calif., 13 mi/21 km NE of Santa Rosa, near head of Napa R. valley; 38°35′N 122°35′W. Geysers and hot springs (health resorts); wineries in area. Wine grapes, prunes, walnuts. Mt. St. Helena to N, and a petrified forest to SW. Bothe-Napa Valley State Park to SW, Robert Louis Stevenson Memorial State Park to N. Founded 1859; inc. as town in 1886, as city in 1937.

Calixtlahuaca (ka-leesh-tlah-WAH-kah), historic site, Mexico state, central Mexico, 4 mi/6.4 km NW of Toluca de Lerdo. Has archaeological remains of various pre-Columbian cultures, including temple of Quetzalcoatl, pyramid of Tlaloc, Tzompantli (House of Skulls).

Calkiní (kal-kee-NEE), city (1990 pop. 11,657) and township, Campeche, SE Mexico, in NW Yucatán Peninsula, on RR, 50 mi/80 km SW of Mérida on Mexico Highway 180; 20°21′N 90°03′W. Lumbering and agr. center (corn, rice, sugar, henequen, chicle, fruit).

Call, uninc. village (1990 pop. 170), Newton and Jasper cos., E Texas, 40 mi/64 km NNE of Beaumont, near the Sabine R. In lumbering area.

Callahan, county (□ 901 sq mi/2,334 sq km; 1990 pop. 11,859), central Texas; ⊙ Baird; 32°17′N 99°22′W. Drained by Pecan Bayou and Jim Ned, Battle, Deep, and Hubbard creeks. Ranching (cattle), agr. (grain, sorghum, peanuts, wheat). Oil, natural-gas production and processing. Clyde L. in W center. Formed 1858.

Callahan, village (□ 1 sq mi/2.6 sq km; 1990 pop. 946), Nassau co., NE Fla., 19 mi/31 km NW of Jacksonville; 30°33′N 81°49′W. Lumbering; farming.

Callahan, Mount, Nev.: see TOIYABE RANGE.

Callander (KA-luhn-duhr), village, SE central Ont., Canada, on Southeast Bay of L. Nipissing, 8 mi/13 km SE of North Bay; 46°13′N 79°22′W. Dairying; lumbering.

Callao (KA-lee-o), city (1990 pop. 332), Macon co., N central Mo., near Chariton R., 8 mi/12.9 km W of Macon; 39°45′N 92°37′W. Corn, wheat, soybeans; cattle, hogs. Platted 1858.

Callaway, county (□ 847 sq mi/2,194 sq km; 1990 pop. 32,809), central Mo.; ⊙ Fulton; 38°50′N 91°55′W.

Bounded S by Missouri R. Urban growth in S from Jefferson City around Holts Summit (Jefferson City has been annexed into Callaway co.). Corn, wheat, oats, soybeans; livestock (cattle, hogs, and saddle horses); fire clay, coal, limestone; mfg. at Fulton and Jefferson City. During the Civil War the co. seceded from the U.S. and by treaty with the state militia formed the "Kingdom of Callaway." Unit of Mark Twain Natl. Forest in W. Serious flooding in 1993 damaged highways, Jefferson City Airport, residences, and industries; the Renz Correctional Facility permanently closed as a result. Callaway Nuclear Power Plant (Union Electric Co.), located 10 mi/16 km SE of Fulton, began service 1984, uses cooling water from the Missouri R., and has a max. dependable capacity of 1125 MWe. Formed 1820.

Callaway, town (□ 5 sq mi/13 sq km; 1990 pop. 12,253), Bay co., NW Fla., located in the Fla. Panhandle 6 mi/ 9.7 km E of Panama City.

Callaway 1 (KA-luh-wai), village (1990 pop. 212), Becker co., W Minn., 12 mi/19 km NNW of Detroit Lakes town, near Buffalo R., at S edge of White Earth Indian Reservation; 46°58′N 95°54′W. Grain, wild rice, alfalfa; livestock; dairying; mfg. (wild rice milling); timber. Numerous small lakes to E. **2** village (1990 pop. 539), Custer co., central Nebr., 17 mi/27 km SW of Broken Bow, and on South Loup R; 41°17′N 99°55′W. Dairy prods., grain; cattle. Mfg. (fertilizer).

Callaway Nuclear Power Plant, Mo.: see CALLAWAY.

Callender, town (1990 pop. 384), Webster co., central Iowa, 11 mi/18 km SW of Fort Dodge; 42°21′N 94°17′W. Livestock; grain.

Callensburg (KA-lins-buhrg), borough (1990 pop. 205), Clarion co., W central Pa., 10 mi/16 km SW of Clarion, on Clarion R., at mouth of Cherry Run; 41°07′N 79°33′W. Agr. (grain; dairying; livestock).

Callery (KA-li-ree), borough (1990 pop. 420), Butler co., W Pa., 21 mi/34 km N of Pittsburgh, on Breakneck Creek; 40°44′N 80°02′W. Agr. (corn, hay; livestock; dairying).

Calliaqua, town (1989 est. pop. 20,282), S St. Vincent, West Indies, 2 mi/3.2 km SE of Kingstown; 13°07′N 61°11′W. Cotton, arrowroot, bananas.

Callicoon, resort village (1990 pop. 500), Sullivan co., SE N.Y., on the Delaware R. (here forming Pa. line), 21 mi/ 34 km WNW of Monticello; 41°49′N 74°55′W. Seat of St. Joseph Seraphic Seminary.

Calliham, uninc. village (1990 pop. 25), McMullen co., S Texas, near Frio R., 10 mi/16 km W of Three Rivers. Cattle; oil field area. Choke Canyon State Park is here, Choke Canyon L. (Frio R.) to N.

Callimont (KA-li-mahnt), borough (1990 pop. 55), Somerset co., SW Pa., 17 mi/27 km SSE of Somerset bet. Wills Creek (N) and Flaugherty Creek (S); 39°47′N 78°55′W. Agr. includes dairying; livestock; corn, oats.

Callisburg, village (1990 pop. 344), Cooke co., N Texas, 22 mi/35 km WNW of Sherman, near Red R. (Okla. boundary); 33°42′N 97°01′W. Dairying, sheep, peanuts. L. Texoma to NE; L. Kiowa to S.

Calloway, county (□ 410 sq mi/1,062 sq km; 1990 pop. 30,735), W Ky.; 36°37′N 88°16′W; ⊙ Murray. Bounded S by state of Tenn., by Tennessee L. (Kentucky L. reservoir); drained by East and West forks of Clarks R. and by Mayfield Creek. Gently rolling agr. area (tobacco, hay, alfalfa, soybeans, wheat, corn; hogs, cattle, poultry; dairying). Some mfg. at Murray. Part of Kenlake State Resort Park in NE corner. Formed 1821.

Calmar (KAL-mahr), town (1991 pop. 1,225), central Alta., Canada, near North Saskatchewan R., 25 mi/ 40 km SW of Edmonton; 53°15′N 113°47′W. Oil and gas; mixed farming, dairying.

Calmar, town (1990 pop. 1,026), Winneshiek co., NE Iowa, 9 mi/14.5 km SSW of Decorah; 43°10′N 91°52′W. Ships hay, grain, flax; mfg. of wood prods..

Calnali (kal-NAH-lee), town (1990 pop. 3,154), Hidalgo, central Mexico, in Sierra Madre Oriental, 20 mi/32 km SW of Huejutla de Reyes; 20°54′N 98°26′W. Corn, rice, sugar, tobacco, fruit, livestock.

Caloosahatchee River (kuh-loo-sah-HACH-ee), c.75 mi/121 km long, S Fla.; rises in L. Hicpochee near Moore Haven; flows WSW past Fort Myers into Gulf

of Mexico through San Carlos Bay (an inlet sheltered by Sanibel Isl.). Tidal below La Belle, river is c.1 mi/ 1.6 km wide in lower 20 mi/32 km. L. Hicpochee (c.4 mi/6.4 km long) is connected with L. Okeechobee (just NE) by short Caloosahatchee Canal, thus joining river to E part of Okeechobee Waterway system.

Calotmul (ka-lot-MOOL), town (1990 pop. 2,623), Yucatán, SE Mexico, 23 mi/37 km N of Valladolid on Mexico Hwy 295; 21°01′N 88°10′W. Henequen, sugar, corn. RR terminus.

Calpan, Mexico: see SAN ANDRÉS CALPAN.

Calpet, village, Sublette co., W Wyo., near Green R., 75 mi/121 km NW of Rock Springs. Bridger-Teton Natl. Forest to W.

Calpulálpan (kal-poo-LAHL-pahn), city (1990 pop. 21,551) and township, Tlaxcala, central Mexico, on RR, and 38 mi/61 km NE of Mexico City, on Mexico Hwy 136; 19°35′N 98°34′W. Elev.8,458 ft/2,578 m. Maguey-growing and -processing center; cattle; wheat.

Caltepec (kal-TE-pek), town (1990 pop. 434), Puebla, central Mexico, 20 mi/32 km SSW of Tehuacán; 18°10′N 97°28′W. Corn; livestock. In the Popoloca Indian area.

Calumet, industrialized region of NW Ind. and NE Ill., along the S shore of L. Michigan. A heavy industry and steel mfg. region, the area has become increasingly residential. Chief cities of the region are Gary, East Chicago, and Hammond (all in Ind.).

Calumet (kal-yoo-MET), county (□ 397 sq mi/ 1,028 sq km; 1990 pop. 34,291), E Wis.; 44°04′N 88°13′W; ⊙ Chilton. Bounded W by L. Winnebago; drained by Manitowoc R. Dairying, farming (barley, oats, corn, peas, hay); cattle, sheep. Varied mfg. at Chilton, New Holstein, and Brillion. High Cliff State Park in NW, on L. Winnebago. Formed 1836.

Calumet 1 (1990 pop. 160), O'Brien co., NW Iowa, 10 mi/16 km SSE of Primghar; 42°56′N 95°32′W. In agr. area. **2** (KAL-yoo-met), uninc. town (1990 pop. 800), Mount Pleasant township, Westmoreland co., SW Pa., 7 mi/11.3 km SSE of Greensburg; 40°12′N 79°29′W.

Calumet (ka-loo-MET), village (1991 pop. 650), SW Que., Canada, on Ottawa R., and 15 mi/24 km W of Lachute. Dairying.

Calumet 1 (kal-yoo-MET), village (1990 pop. 818), Houghton co., NW Upper Peninsula, Mich., 10 mi/ 16 km NNE of Houghton, on Keweenaw Peninsula; 47°15′N 88°27′W. Dairy; cattle farming; lumbering. Mfg. (printed circuit boards). Resort. Village grew after development of Calumet and Hecla copper mine here in 1860s. F.J. McLain State Park to W on L. Superior. Inc. 1875 as Red Jacket, renamed 1929. **2** village (1990 pop. 382), Itasca co., N central Minn., 14 mi/23 km ENE of Grand Rapids in Mesabi Iron Range; 47°19′N 93°16′W. Iron-mining dist. Swan L. to E; Hill Annex Mine State Park to N. **3** (KAL-yoo-met), village (1990 pop. 560), Canadian co., central Okla., 10 mi/16 km NW of El Reno, on North Canadian R. Agr. area (wheat, cattle); mfg. (dog food).

Calumet City (1990 pop. 37,840), Cook co., NE Ill., a suburb 18 mi/29 km SSE of downtown Chicago, in the greater Chicago metropolitan area, near Ind.; 41°36′N 87°32′W. Grand Calumet and Little Calumet rivers flow through city. Mfg. (chemicals, electronics, gelatins, plastics, adhesives). Once heavily industrial, the city is primarily residential with some light mfg. Formerly called West Hammond, it grew as a suburb of Hammond, Ind. Settled 1868, inc. 1911.

Calumet Harbor, artificial harbor on L. Michigan, at the mouth of the Calumet R., Cook co., NE Ill., in S Chicago; 41°43′N 87°31′W. The harbor, dredged to 27 ft/ 8 m, is formed behind a breakwater extending c.2 mi/ 3.2 km into L. Michigan. It is a unit of the Port of Chicago and a principal terminal for shipping on the Great Lakes and the St. Lawrence Seaway. The chief prods. handled there were raw materials for steelmaking and iron prods., but the industry has fundamentally declined. Calumet R. (c.8 mi/13 km long) connects the harbor with L. Calumet (c.2 sq mi/5 sq km) in S Chicago. Once a shallow body of water with marshy shores,

the lake has been transformed into a modern deep-water port. Some heavy industry, grain-storage bins, and warehouses surround it. Canals connect the lake with the Calumet region of Indiana and with the Chicago Sanitary and Ship Canal.

Calumet Island (ka-loo-MET), village, SW Que., Canada, on Ottawa R. and 25 mi/40 km ESE of Pembroke. Lead, zinc mining.

Calumet Park, village (1990 pop. 8,418), Cook co., NE Ill., suburb 14 mi/23 km SSW of downtown Chicago, E of Blue Isl.; 41°39′N 87°39′W. Mfg. (belts, fasteners, rope, metal stampings). Inc. 1912; name changed from Burr Oak in 1925. CALUMET CITY is 7 mi/11.3 km SE.

Calumet River, c.8 mi/12.9 km long; NE Ill., short stream entirely within industrial S Chicago; an important unit of Calumet (South Chicago) Harbor, which serves Chicago and the heavily industrialized Calumet region of NW Ind., and part of ILLINOIS WATERWAY system; 41°38′N 87°33′W. Formed just SE of L. Calumet by Little Calumet and Grand Calumet rivers; flows N, through dredged and dock-lined channel, to L. Michigan at Calumet Harbor. Little Calumet and Grand Calumet rivers, rising generally E of Gary, Ind., flows generally W, in dredged channels; handles much shipping at Gary. Little Calumet R. is linked to Calumet Sag Channel, and thence with Chicago Sanitary and Ship Canal. Grand Calumet R. is connected by ship canal to Indiana Harbor at East Chicago, Ind. Large landfill "mountains" dominate area along Chicago's extreme S end.

Calumet Sag Channel, NE Ill., federally operated navigation and drainage canal (c.16 mi/26 km long) leading generally W from Little Calumet R. near Calumet Park to Chicago Sanitary and Ship Canal near Lemont; part of ILLINOIS WATERWAY system; 41°41′N 87°50′W. Has a lock at Blue Isl.

Calvert (KAL-vert), county (□ 345 sq mi/894 sq km; 1990 pop. 51,372), S Md.; 38°32′N 76°32′W; ⊙ Prince Frederick. Narrow tidewater peninsula bounded E by Chesapeake Bay, S and W by Patuxent R.; drained by many small creeks. Agr. area (tobacco, grain, truck, livestock); fisheries (oysters, crabs, fish); timber; some boat bldg. Resort area (fishing, hunting, and water sports, especially at Solomons, Broomes Isl., Chesapeake Beach). Nuclear power plants: Calvert Cliffs 1 (initial criticality Oct. 7, 1974) and Calvert Cliffs 2 (initial criticality Nov. 30, 1976) are 40 mi/64 km S of Annapolis; use cooling water from Chesapeake Bay and each has max. dependable capacity of 825 MWe. Named for the first Lord Baltimore and is the state's smallest county. Attractions include Battle Creek Cypress Swamp Sanctuary, Calvert Cliffs State Park, Calvert Marine Mus., Chesapeake Beach RR Mus., Cove Point Light Station, and Jefferson Patterson Park and Mus. Formed in 1650.

Calvert, town (1990 pop. 1,536), Robertson co., E central Texas, c.50 mi/80 km SSE of Waco, near the Brazos; 30°58′N 96°40′W. Elev. 335 ft/102 m. Trade (cotton, grain, watermelons, dairying); cattle, poultry area. Mfg. (candles). Settled nearby as Sterling, c.1840; moved to present site on RR and renamed 1869; inc. 1896.

Calvert, village, Mobile and Washington cos., SW Ala., 33 mi/53 km N of Mobile, near Alabama R.; lumber.

Calvert, historic hamlet, Cecil co., NE Md., 24 mi/39 km W of Wilmington, Del. Friends' meeting house, built 1724, is still used. Originally called Brick Meeting House. A suburb begun in 1961, almost all the 1,500 homes were built by one developer. Founded 1701.

Calvert City, town (1990 pop. 2,531), Marshall co., W Ky., near Tennessee R., 15 mi/24 km ESE of Paducah; 37°01′N 88°20′W. Agr. area (tobacco, grain; livestock). Mfg. (industrial chemicals, roof trusses, automotive catalysts, security screens, structural steel); chemical processing. Kentucky Dam (forms Kentucky L., on Tenn. R.) and Kentucky Dam Village State Resort Park to SE; airport at Kentucky Dam.

Calvert Cliffs 1 and 2 Nuclear Power Plants, Maryland: see CALVERT CO.

Calvert Cliffs, highlands (c.100 ft/30 m–150 ft/46 m

high), S Md., along W shore of Chesapeake Bay; extending c.30 mi/48 km S from Chesapeake Beach to vicinity of Patuxent R. mouth. The cliffs, first described by John Smith in 1608, are a geological microcosm of the entire Atlantic coast. The exposed clays protected in the state park are rich in marine fossils. A drawing of a shell from the cliffs in Martin Lister's *Historia Synopsis Methodica Conchyliarum* (1685) was the first illustration of an American fossil published. Near the S end is Calvert Cliffs Nuclear Power Plant.

Calvert Island (□ 100 sq mi/161 sq km), SW B.C., Canada, in Queen Charlotte Sound; 20 mi/32 km long, 2 mi/3 km–10 mi/16 km wide; 51°35′N 128°00′W. Rises to 3,430 ft/1,045 m on Mt. Buxton (N); S and W coasts are thickly wooded. Just N is Hecate Isl. (□ 17 sq mi/44 sq km), 5 mi/8 km long, 5 mi/8 km wide.

Calverton 1 village (□ 28 sq mi/73 sq km; 1990 pop. 4,759), Suffolk co., SE N.Y., on E L.I., on Peconic R., and 4 mi/6.4 km W of Riverhead; 40°55′N 72°45′W. **2** uninc. village, Fauquier co., N Va., 8 mi/12.9 km SE of Warrenton; 38°37′N 77°40′W. Mfg. (water analysis kits, wood prods.); agr. (grain, soybeans, apples; livestock).

Calverton Park, town (1990 pop. 1,404), St. Louis co., E Mo., residential suburb 12 mi/19 km NW of downtown St. Louis; 38°46′N 90°18′W.

Calvillo (kahl-VEE-yo), city (1990 pop. 16,624) and township, Aguascalientes, N central Mexico, on Calvillo R., and 28 mi/45 km W of Aguascalientes on Mexico Hwy 70; 21°53′N 102°41′W. Agr. center (cereals, beans, chickpeas, tobacco, sugar, wine, fruit, livestock).

Calvillo River, c.50 mi/80 km long, N central Mexico; rises in mts. of Aguascalientes near Zacatecas border, flows SW, past Calvillo, to Juchipila R. at Jalpa. Irrigates fertile fruit-growing area.

Calvin 1 village (1990 pop. 207), Winn parish, N central La., 7 mi/11 km NNW of Winnfield; 31°58′N 92°47′W. Located in Kisatchie Natl. Forest. Timber; gas field nearby; recreation. **2** village (1990 pop. 27), Cavalier co., NE N.Dak., 28 mi/45 km WNW of Langdon; 48°51′N 98°56′W. **3** village (1990 pop. 251), Hughes co., central Okla., 11 mi/18 km SE of Holdenville, and on Canadian R.; 34°58′N 96°15′W. In stock raising (cattle and hogs) and agr. (peanuts) area.

Calwa, uninc. town (1990 pop. 6640), Fresno co., central Calif., residential suburb 3 mi/4.8 km SSE of downtown Fresno, in irrigated agr. area (fruit, avocados, vegetables, grain, dairying, poultry). Rail center and junction.

Calypso, village (1990 pop. 481), Duplin co., E central N.C., 17 mi/27 km SSW of Goldsboro; 35°08′N 78°06′W. Tobacco, grain, cotton, poultry, livestock. Mfg. (apparel, furniture, meat processing).

Calzones, Cerro (kal-SO-nes, SER-ro), peak (9,186 ft/2,800 m) in Guanajuato, central Mexico, 15 mi/24 km N of Guanajuato; 21°10′N 101°15′W.

Camagüey (kah-muh-GWAI), province, (1995 est. pop. 840,000), E central Cuba; 22°21′N 77°51′W; ⊙ Camagüey. Holds 12.8% of Cuba's territory and 7.6% of the pop. The area is a vast prairie, of which 72% is suited for agr. Produces 12% of Cuba's sugar. The major economic activities are cattle raising (practiced here since the early colonial period, using ½ of the arable land, and earning the prov. the nickname "the Texas of Cuba"), the cultivation of sugarcane (667,000 acres/269,935 ha) and rice (55,000 acres/22,259 ha), and the production of chromite. Meatpacking, pineapple canning, and other agr. processing; 14 sugar mills. Isl. keys off N shore, recently connected by elevated road over water, provide 40 mi/64 km of shoreline for internatl. tourist development.

Camagüey (kah-muh-GWAI), city (1995 est. pop. 295,000), ⊙ Camagüey prov., E Cuba; 21°23′N 77°54′W. Cuba's 3d most populous city; a leading hub of RR, road, and air transport as well as an important commercial center. The economy is based on agr., cattle raising, and mining. Industries (mainly meatpacking and dairy processing) are mostly related to processing and transport. Founded in 1514 as Santa Maria del Puerto Principe, the city was moved to its present site in 1528 and renamed for the Native Amer. village that previously occupied that site. During the colonial period Camagüey produced salted beef for the Span. fleets and was often sacked by Eng., Fr., and Du. pirates. The city, which has retained much of its Span. colonial atmosphere, is noted for its churches, mansions, narrow twisting streets, and colonial historic district in the city core. Since 1959, the city has established several hospitals, incl. a tertiary care facility, and a univ.

Camagüey Archipelago (kah-muh-GWAI), coral reefs off N coast of E Cuba, E of the Sabana Archipelago, and forming S flank of Old Bahama Channel; extend c.150 mi/241 km NW-SE; 22°18′N 78°00′W. Among the hundreds of keys are the larger keys of Coco, Romano, and Guillermo Sabinal. Sometimes called Jardines del Rey. Recently linked to mainland by causeways to promote tourism. Key Coco has 4,600 ft/1,402 m airstrip.

Camajuaní (kah-mah-wahn-EE) or **Cayaguani**, town, Villa Clara prov., central Cuba, on RR, and 14 mi/23 km E of Santa Clara; 22°29′N 79°45′W. Agr. center (sugarcane, tobacco, cattle) with processing industries; mfg. (food and beverages, cigars, agr. implements). The sugar central of José Perez is SE.

Camak (KAI-muhk), village (1990 pop. 220), Warren co., E Ga., 37 mi/60 km W of Augusta; 33°27′N 82°39′W. Granite quarrying.

Camanche (kuh-MANCH), town (1990 pop. 4,436), Clinton co., E Iowa, on the Mississippi R. (forms Ill. state line here), and 6 mi/9.7 km SW of Clinton; 41°47′N 90°16′W.

Camanche Reservoir (□ 12 sq mi/31 sq km), San Joaquin co., central Calif., on Mokelumne R., near Mokelumne Aqueduct, 31 mi/50 km NE of Stockton; 38°14′N 121°01′W. Max. capacity 450,000 acre-ft. Formed by Camanche Dam (171 ft/52 m high), built (1964) for irrigation; also used for power generation, flood control, water supply, recreation, and as a fish and wildlife pond. Pardee Reservoir upstream.

Camano Island (kuh-MAIN-o), Island co., NW Wash., isl. (15 mi/24 km long) in Puget Sound, E of Whidbey Isl. (remainder of co., no connections), and 13 mi/21 km NW of Everett. Bridged to mainland; summer and fishing resorts. Separated from mainland by Davis and other sloughs, at NE end; Port Susan Bay, E; bounded by Saratoga Passage, W; and Skagit Bay, N. Vegetables, berries; dairying; poultry. Mfg. (machinery). Villages include Utsalady (N), Camano (W), and Madrona Beach. Camano Isl. State Park on SW shore.

Camargo (kah-MAHR-go), city (1990 pop. 33,582) and township, Chihuahua, N Mexico, near confluence of Conchos and Florido rivers, 85 mi/137 km SE of Chihuahua on Mexico Hwy 45; 27°41′N 105°10′W. Elev. 5,423 ft/1,653 m. RR junction; health resort; mining (silver, gold, lead, copper) and agr. center (cotton, wheat, corn, tobacco; cattle); cotton and wheat milling, lumbering. Ojo Caliente spas are 3 mi/4.8 km SW.

Camargo (kuh-MAHR-go), town (1990 pop. 1,022), Montgomery co., NE central Ky., 4 mi/6.4 km SE of Mt. Sterling; 38°00′N 83°53′W. Agr. area (tobacco, corn, soybeans; cattle, poultry, dairying).

Camargo 1 (kah-MAHR-go), village (1990 pop. 372), Douglas co., E central Ill., on Embarras R., and 5 mi/8 km E of Tuscola; 39°47′N 88°10′W. In agr. area. **2** village (1990 pop. 185), Dewey co., W Okla., 18 mi/29 km W of Taloga, near Canadian R.; 36°01′N 99°17′W. In grain-growing and stock-raising area.

Camargo, Mexico: see CIUDAD CAMARGO, Tamaulipas.

Camarillo, city (1990 pop. 52,303), Ventura co., S Calif., 8 mi/12.9 km ENE of Oxnard, 8 mi/12.9 km N of Pacific Ocean and 47 mi/76 km WNW of Los Angeles, near Arroyo Simi; 34°13′N 119°02′W. It is the center of a fertile farm area where citrus fruits, avocados, vegetables, nursery prods., apiary prods., and flowers are grown. Camarillo also has electronic and aerospace industries as well as mfg. plants (telephone apparatus, cosmetics, perfumes, solar panels, dental and medical equip.). The city has grown significantly since the 1970s along with the S California area. St. John's Col. is located there. Oxnard Air Force Base to W. Santa Monica Natl. Recreation Area to S. Inc. 1964.

Camarón de Tejeda, Mexico: see VILLA ADALBERTO TEJEDA.

Camas, county (□ 1,079 sq mi/2,795 sq km; 1990 pop. 727), S central Idaho; 43°28′N 114°49′W; ⊙ Fairfield. Drained by Camas Creek in S; source of South Fork Boise R. in N. Big Woods R. (Magic Reservoir) forms part of SE boundary. Cattle; alfalfa, hay, barley; dry-farming area; timber. Deposits of lead, silver, zinc, gold, copper. Part of Sawtooth Mts. are in N. Sawtooth Natl. Forest covers N ½ of co.; Soldier Mt. Ski Area at center; Mormon Reservoir in S. Formed 1917.

Camas (KA-mahs), town (1990 pop. 6,442), Clark co., SW Wash., 13 mi/21 km E of Vancouver, and on Columbia R.; 45°35′N 122°25′W. Timber, paper mills; fruit; salmon, poultry. Mfg. (concrete, sawmill, computer equip., printing and publishing, tools). Inc. 1908.

Camas (KA-mahs), village, Sanders co., NW Mont., 60 mi/97 km NW of Missoula, 22 mi/35 km W of Polson, in W part of Flathead Indian Reservation. Lolo Natl. Forest to W.

Cambria (KAIM-bree-uh), county (□ 693 sq mi/1,795 sq km; 1990 pop. 163,029), W central Pa.; ⊙ Ebensburg; 40°29′N 78°43′W. Bounded S in part by Stonycreek R., SW by Laurel Hill ridge; Allegheny Mts. are in E part; drained by Conemaugh, Little Conemaugh, and Stonycreek rivers; West Branch of Susquehanna R. rises in N. Urbanized in SW corner, around Johnstown. Settled by Welsh. Mfg. at Johnstown and Edensburg. Agr. (corn, wheat, hay, alfalfa, potatoes; sheep, hogs, cattle, dairying); bituminous coal, clay, limestone. Parts of Allegheny Portage RR Natl. Historic Site in E and SW corner; part of Gallitzin State Forest in SW; Glendale L. reservoir, in Prince Gallitzen State Park, in NE. Formed 1804.

Cambria (KAM-bree-uh), uninc. town (1990 pop. 5,382), San Luis Obispo co., SW Calif., on Santa Cruz Creek, 2 mi/3.2 km NE of Pacific Ocean, 30 mi/48 km NW of San Luis Obispo; 35°33′N 121°05′W. Cattle; grain; apples, avocados; nursery stock, flowers. San Simeon State Beach to NW; Santa Lucia Range to NE.

Cambria 1 (KAIM-bree-uh), village (1990 pop. 1,230), Williamson co., S Ill., 12 mi/19 km WNW of Marion; 37°46′N 89°06′W. In bituminous-coal mining and agr. area. **2** village (1990 pop. 768), Columbia co., S central Wis., 18 mi/29 km E of Portage; 43°32′N 89°06′W. In agr. area; makes butter, cheeses.

Cambrian Park, uninc. town (1990 pop. 2,998), Santa Clara co., W Calif., residential suburb 6 mi/9.7 km SSW of downtown San Jose, surrounded by city of San Jose; 37°16′N 121°56′W. Los Gatos Creek to W.

Cambridge, city (1991 pop. 92,772), S Ont., Can., on the Grand R., NW of Hamilton; 43°23′N 80°19′W. It was formed in 1973 with the amalgamation of Galt, Hespeler, and Preston, and parts of Waterloo and North Dumfries townships. Galt was a Scot. settlement founded in 1817, while Hespeler and Preston were founded in the early 1800s by Mennonites from Pa. Cambridge is a heavily industrialized area with mfg. (textiles, chemicals, wood prods., plastics). Hespeler was a quarrying center and Preston had a well-known health resort.

Cambridge 1 (KAIM-brij), city (1990 pop. 11,514), ⊙ Dorchester co., E Md., Eastern Shore, a port of entry on the Choptank R. at its mouth on Chesapeake Bay; 38°34′N 76°05′W. It was founded 1684 and named after the univ. town in England. A prosperous canning and fishpacking area for many years, the closing of a major company in 1962 put 1,200 out of work and exacerbated racial tensions. In June 1963, demonstrations against restaurants that refused to serve blacks triggered civil disorders, and caused the governor, Spiro Agnew, later vice president of the U.S., to send in the Natl. Guard. The guard remained for almost a year. A federal job-training program, in addition to a governor's committee and the passage of the Civil Rights Act in the summer of 1964, reduced tensions. Still a fishing and yachting center, Cambridge now has a printing plant as well as electronics firms. Five Md. governors are buried in the graveyard of Christ Protestant Episcopal Church (c.1882), built after the original bldg. dating from the 1690s was burned. Inc. 1745. **2** city (1990 pop. 95,802), ⊙ Middlesex co., E Mass., across the Charles R. from Boston; 42°23′N 71°07′W. Seat of Middlesex County Court. A famous educational and research center, it is the seat of Harvard Univ. (founded 1636), Radcliffe Col., Massachusetts Inst. of Technology, Lesley Col., and several theological seminaries. Its printing and publishing industry dates from about 1639, when Stephen Daye established the 1st printing press in Amer. Functions as an important high-tech research center. Manufactures include computers, electronic and medical equip., candy, chemicals, pharmaceuticals, bldg. materials, cameras, and elevators. Computer and biotech industries. Cambridge was a gathering place for colonial troops; here, on July 3, 1775, Washington took command. It was the 1st seat of the Mass. constitutional convention of 1780. Craigie House (1759) served as Washington's hq. (1775–1776). Other historic structures are Elmwood (1767), the birthplace and home of James Russell Lowell; the Cooper-Frost-Austin house (c.1657); and the Episcopal church (1761). Lowell, Longfellow, Mary Baker Eddy, and other notable people are buried in Mt. Auburn Cemetery. Many mus. are in the city. Cambridge's principal center and tourist attraction, Harvard Square, has undergone considerable urban renewal in the past 2 decades. Its transit system has been expanded and the number of shops and businesses has multiplied. Includes village of Mt. Auburn. Settled 1630 as New Towne, inc. as a city 1846. **3** city (1990 pop. 11,748), ⊙ Guernsey co., E central Ohio; 40°01′N 81°35′W. Settled 1798 by immigrants from the Isle of Guernsey. It is the trade and mfg. center for a dairy and livestock area. Lakes and parks surround the city. The large Salt Fork State Park is nearby. Inc. 1837.

Cambridge, town (1991 pop. 3,384), St. James parish, NW Jamaica, in fertile interior valley, on Kingston-Montego Bay RR, and 11 mi/18 km S of Montego Bay; 18°19′N 77°54′W. Banana growing. Caves nearby.

Cambridge 1 town (1990 pop. 714), Story co., central Iowa, on Skunk R., and 10 mi/16 km SSW of Nevada; 41°53′N 93°31′W. Cannery. **2** town (1990 pop. 490), Somerset co., central Maine, 22 mi/35 km NE of Skowhegan; 45°01′N 69°27′W. **3** town (1990 pop. 5,094), ⊙ Isanti co., E Minn., 42 mi/68 km N of Minneapolis, on Rum R.; 45°33′N 93°13′W. Elev. 965 ft/294 m. Agr. area (dairying; poultry, livestock; grain, soybeans); mfg. (machinery and instruments, fabricated metal, prepared foods, chemicals, printing and publishing). Numerous small lakes in area; Fannie L., on Isanti Brook, to SE. **4** (KAIM-brij), town (1990 pop. 1,107), Furnas co., S Nebr., 25 mi/40 km ENE of McCook and where Medicine Creek joins the Republican R; 40°16′N 100°10′W. In agr. (grain) and cattle-raising region; metal fabrication. Medicine Creek Reservoir and State Recreation Area (Harry D. Strunk L.) to NW (in Frontier co.). Founded 1874. **5** town, Coos co., N N.H., 15 mi/24 km NNE of Berlin. Bounded E by Maine state line; drained in NW by Androscoggin R. Timber. Mountainous wilderness area. Cambridge Black Mt. (2,711 ft/826 m) in center; S end of Umbagog L. in NE corner. **6** town (1990 pop. 2,667), including Cambridge village, Lamoille co., NW Vt., on Lamoille R., and 13 mi/21 km WNW of Hyde Park, in Green Mts. foothills, just NW of Mt. Mansfield; 44°37′N 72°49′W. Maple sugar. Includes Jeffersonville village. Settled 1783. **7** town (1990 pop. 963), Dane co., S Wis., on small Koshkonong Creek, and 19 mi/31 km ESE of Madison; 43°00′N 89°01′W. In agr. and lake-resort area; candy, dairy prods.. Mfg. (hand-glazed stoneware, candy, machinery). Mink ranch here.

Cambridge 1 village (1990 pop. 374), Washington co., W Idaho, 17 mi/27 km SW of Council, and on Weiser R, near mouth of Little Weiser R.; 44°34′N 116°41′W. Agr. (cattle, sheep; potatoes, sugar beets); dairying; lumber; mfg. (fertilizers). Hitt Mt. Ski Area to W; parts of Payette Natl. Forest to N and W. **2** village (1990 pop. 2,124), ⊙ Henry co., NW Ill., 21 mi/34 km SE of Moline; 41°17′N 90°11′W. In agr. and bituminous-coal area. Inc. 1861. **3** village (1990 pop. 74), Cowley co., SE Kansas, 18 mi/29 km ENE of Winfield; 37°19′N 96°40′W. In livestock and grain area. **4** village (□ 1 sq mi/2.6 sq km; 1990 pop. 1,906), Washington co., E N.Y., near Vt. border, 27 mi/43 km NE of Troy; 43°01′N 73°22′W. Farm trade center. Cambridge Historical Dist. within the village. Small lakes nearby. Its weekly, *Washington County Post,* was founded in 1787. Settled c.1761, inc. 1866.

Cambridge Bay, hamlet (1991 pop. 1,116), on the SE shore of Victoria Island, Kitikmeot Region, N.W.T., Canada; 69°07′N 105°02′W. Can. govt. post and weather station; hq. of the Kitikmeot Region.

Cambridge City, town (1990 pop. 2,091), Wayne co., E Ind., on Whitewater R., and 15 mi/24 km W of Richmond; 39°49′N 85°10′W. In grain and livestock area; mfg. (metal prods., caskets, fixtures, food prods., agr. machinery, paint); timber. Prehistoric earthworks have been found here.

Cambridge Junction, village, Lenawee co., SE Mich., 20 mi/32 km NW of Adrian; 42°03′N 84°13′W. In agr. area. The Walker Tavern (built 1832) is now a pioneer mus. Located in Irish Hills. Michigan Internatl. Speedway to N; Walter J. Hayes State Park on Wamplers L. to E; Vineyard L. to N.

Cambridge Springs, borough (1990 pop. 1,837), Crawford co., NW Pa., 22 mi/35 km S of Erie, near French Creek; 41°47′N 80°03′W. Mfg. (pottery, plastics prods., metal prods., feeds). Agr. (corn, hay, potatoes; livestock, dairying). Seat of Alliance Col. Mt. Pleasant Ski Area to NW.

Camden 1 (KAM-duhn), county (□ 656; 1990 pop. 30,167), extreme SE Ga.; ⊙ Woodbine; 30°55′N 81°38′W. Bounded S by St. Marys R. at Fla. line, E by the Atlantic, N by Little Satilla R.; intersected by Satilla R.; includes Cumberland Isl. Coastal plain lumbering, fishing, and farming; cattle. Formed 1772. **2** county (□ 655 sq mi/1,696 sq km; 1990 pop. 27,495), central Mo.; ⊙ Camdenton; 38°01′N 92°46′W. In the Ozarks, crossed by L. of the Ozarks; drained by Niangua R. Agr. (corn, wheat; dairying; turkeys, cattle). Oak, cedar, pine timber; mfg. at Camdenton. Major resort, recreation, and tourism area since the 1930s. L. of the Ozarks State Park in NE; Ha Ha Tonka State Park in S. Caves and springs. Large increase in seasonal and permanent residences on lake during 1970s and 1980s.Formed 1841. **3** county (□ 227 sq mi/588 sq km; 1990 pop. 502,824), SW N.J., bounded NW by Delaware R.; ⊙ Camden; 39°47′N 74°57′W. Shipbuilding, food processing, mfg. (food prods., radio and television equip., textiles, leather, clothing, pens, lumber; metal, rubber, plastic, and paper prods.; chemicals); RR shops, marine terminals; agr. (fruit, truck, soybeans, corn). Drained by Great Egg Harbor, Mullica River, and Big Timber Creek. W largely residential. Formed 1844. **4** county (□ 305 sq mi/790 sq km; 1990 pop. 5,904), NE N.C.; ⊙ Camden; 36°20′N 76°09′W. Bounded N by Va. state line, SE by North R. estuary, S by Albemarle Sound, SW by Pasquotank R. estuary. Tidewater area, partly in Dismal Swamp (N). Timber (pine, gum), agr. (corn, soybeans, cotton, wheat, peanuts, potatoes, cattle). Duck hunting, fishing. Dismal Swamp canal crosses co. in NW, to Chesapeake Bay (branch of Intracoastal Waterway). Canal Welcome Center in N, on U.S. Highway 17. Formed 1777.

Camden 1 (KAM-duhn), city (1990 pop. 14,380), ⊙ Ouachita co., S Ark., 28 mi/45 km NNW of El Dorado, and on Ouachita R.; 33°34′N 92°50′W. RR junction. Mfg. (paper milling, printing presses, paper prods., construction materials, apparel). Southern Ark. Univ. Tech (2 years). Poison Spring Battleground State Historical Monument to NW. Settled 1824, inc. 1847. **2** city (1990 pop. 238), Ray co., W central Mo., on a former channel of the Missouri R., and 6 mi/9.7 km S of Richmond; 39°12′N 94°01′W. Soybeans, wheat; hogs, cattle. Plotted 1838. **3** city (1990 pop. 87,492), ⊙ Camden co., W N.J., a port of entry on the Delaware R. opposite Philadelphia; 39°56′N 75°06′W. The arrival of the Camden and Amboy RR in 1834 spurred the city's growth as a commercial, shipbuilding, and mfg. center. In 1858, Richard Esterbrook opened a steel-pen factory, and the Campbell canned-foods company originated in 1869. Still hq. for Campbell's, but food processing facilities have closed. Many of the city's largest industries, such as steel, chemicals, aerospace, electronics, and oil, have declined significantly or left. The weakened industries left Camden with great amounts of air pollution, high unemployment, and urban decay that has led to widespread poverty and crime. Majority of the population is African-, Hispanic-, and Asian- Americans. Of interest are Walt Whitman's home, the Campbell Mus., and the county historical society's mus. in Charles S. Boyer Memorial Hall (formerly the Joseph Cooper house; built 1726). Access to Philadelphia is via the Walt Whitman Bridge (1957) and the Benjamin Franklin Bridge (1926). Camden campus of Rutgers, the N.J. state univ., and the N.J. State Aquarium are here. Settled 1681, inc. 1828. **4** city (1990 pop. 6,696), ⊙ Kershaw co., N central S.C., near Wateree R., 28 mi/45 km NE of Columbia, in the sandhills; 34°15′N 80°36′W. Popular winter resort established by northern industrialists at the turn of the cent., known for polo, steeplechase races, and hunting. Trade and processing center. Mfg. (apparel, printing and publishing, lumber, medical supplies, fabricated metal prods., concrete). In agr. (poultry, cattle; cotton, corn) and timber area. Location of Kershaw co. fine arts center. In Revolutionary War the battles of Camden (Aug. 16, 1780) and Hobkirks Hill (April 25, 1781) were fought nearby. City burned May 8, 1781, by evacuating British. In Civil War it again was burned (Feb. 1865). Settled c. 1735, inc. 1791.

Camden 1 (KAM-duhn), town (1990 pop. 2,414), ⊙ Wilcox co., SW central Ala., near Alabama R., 33 mi/53 km SW of Selma; 32 °00′N 87°17′W. Lumber, apparel. **2** town (1990 pop. 1,899), Kent co., central Del., 3 mi/4.8 km SSW of Dover; 39°06′N 75°32′W. Fruit-growing area to W. Part of N.G. Wilder Wildlife Area to W. Suburb of Dover. **3** town (1990 pop. 607), Carroll co., W central Ind., on Deer Creek, and 7 mi/11.3 km NE of Delphi; 40°37′N 86°32′W. In agr. area. **4** town (1990 pop. 5,060), Knox co., S Maine, resort center in Camden Hills, on W shore of Penobscot Bay, and 7 mi/11.3 km N of Rockland; 44°13′N 69°04′W. Summer-stock productions in garden theater; arts; picturesque yacht harbor; winter sports. Textiles, yarns, boatbuilding; financial services. Poet Edna St. Vincent Millay is a native of the region. Settled 1769, inc. 1791. **5** town (1990 pop. 3,643), ⊙ Benton co., NW Tenn., 19 mi/31 km E of Huntingdon; 36°04′N 88°06′W. In agr. area (sorghum, corn, cotton); sawmill; sand and gravel pits. Freshwater pearls are cultivated in the nearby Kentucky Reservoir (Tenn. R.). Nathan Bedford Forrest Park, with mus. of Civil War relics, is near. Laid out 1836. **6** uninc. town (1990 pop. 1,200), Polk co., E Texas, 29 mi/47 km S of Lufkin. Elev. 322 ft/98 m. Lumbering; mfg. (plywood prods.).

Camden 1 village (1990 pop. 115), Schuyler co., W Ill., 12 mi/19 km WNW of Rushville; 40°08′N 90°46′W. In agr. area. **2** village (1990 pop. 482), Hillsdale co., S Mich., 13 mi/21 km SSW of Hillsdale, near NE corner Ind. state line (2 mi/3.2 km W) and Ohio state line (4 mi/6.4 km S); 41°45′N 84°45′W. In dairying and agr. area. **3** village (□ 2 sq mi/5.2 sq km; 1990 pop. 2,552), Oneida co., central N.Y., 17 mi/27 km NW of Rome; 43°20′N 75°45′W. In farming and dairying area; mfg. (metal prods.). Inc. 1834. **4** uninc. village, ⊙ Camden co., NE N.C., near Pasquotank R., 3 mi/4.8 km ENE of Elizabeth City (bridged across head of Pasquotauk estuary). Dismal Swamp Canal enters river from NW. Grain, cotton, peanuts, potatoes, cattle. **5** village (1990 pop. 2,210), Preble co., W Ohio, 25 mi/40 km WSW of Dayton, and on small Seven Mile Creek; 39°39′N 84°38′W.

Camden Bay, shallow indentation, 45 mi/72 km wide, NE Alaska, on Beaufort Sea, bet. Brownlow Point (W) and Barter Isl. (E); 70°02′N 144°40′W. Receives Canning R.

Camden Hills, Knox co., S Maine, in semicircle around Camden, include Mt. Battie, Mt. Megunticook (1,385 ft/422 m.), Bald Mt. (also called Bald Rock Mt.), and Ragged Mt. Center of Camden Hills State Park (4,962 acres/2,008 ha). Has hiking trails, cross-country and downhill skiing, snowmobiling. Views from Mt. Battie.

Camden on Gauley (GAW-lee), village (1990 pop. 171), Webster co., central W.Va., 14 mi/23 km NE of Summersville, on Gauley R. Monongahela Natl. Forest to SE; Big Ditch Wildlife Management Area to NE.

Camden Point, town (1990 pop. 373), Platte co., W Mo., near Platte R., 10 mi/16 km NE of Platte City; 39°27′N 94°45′W.

Camdenton, town (1990 pop. 2,561), ⊙ Camden co., central Mo., in the Ozarks, near L. of the Ozarks, 50 mi/80 km SW of Jefferson City; 38°00′N 92°45′W. Major resort and tourism center. Calcite mines. Mfg. (transportation equip., wood prods., soldering equipment, steel fabrication, concrete). Plotted and inc. 1931 as a planned town after the L. of the Ozarks submerged the earlier county seat.

Camelback Mountain (2,704 ft/824 m), Maricopa co., central Ariz., in SE spur of Phoenix Mts., 5 mi/8 km NE of downtown Phoenix, within the city of Phoenix city limits. Recreation area for metro Phoenix; resort area.

Camelberg, peak (1,192 ft/363 m), in Virgin Islands Natl. Park, St. John Isl., U.S. Virgin Isls.; 18°20′N 64°45′W.

Camels Hump, peak (4,083 ft/1,244 m), N central Vt., one of highest in Green Mts., 20 mi/32 km SE of Burlington. State forest here.

Camerino Z. Mendoza, Mexico: see CIUDAD MENDOZA.

Cameron (KAM-ruhn), parish (□ 1,444 sq mi/3,740 sq km: 1990 pop. 9,260), extreme SW La.; ⊙ Cameron; 29°48′N 93°18′W. Largest parish in the state. In marshy coastal area, bounded W by Sabine L. and Sabine R., S by Gulf of Mexico. Beach area along Gulf referred to as the Cajun Riviera (incl. Holly Beach). Cattle, horses; crawfish, oysters, shrimp, crabs, finfish (esp. menhaden), alligators; fur trapping (nutria). Agr. (hay, rice, soybeans). Oil and natural gas deposits. Navigable waterways include Calcasieu, Mermentau, Tau, and Sabine rivers, and Intracoastal Waterway. Calcasieu L. at center, Grand L. in E, and numerous other lakes in parish. Sabine Natl. Wildlife Refuge crosses parish from Sabine L. E to E side of Calcasieu L. Cameron Prairie and Lacassine Natl. Wildlife refuges in NE, part of Rockefeller Natl. Wildlife Refuge in SE. Formed 1820.

Cameron 1 (KAM-ruhn), county (□ 398 sq mi/1,031 sq km; 1990 pop. 5,913), N central Pa.; ⊙ Emporium; 41°26′N 78°12′W. Mountainous area, once important for logging; drained by Sinnemahoning Creek and its Driftwood Branch, Bennett Branch, and First Fork. Recreation region; mfg. at Emporium; bituminous coal, sandstone, shale, natural gas. Agr. (oats, hay, alfalfa; cattle, some dairying; timber); sects. of Elk State Forest throughout co., especially S and E, and part of Sinnemahoning State Park in E; part of Bucktail State Park follows Sinnemahoning Creek and its Driftwood Branch to Emporium. Formed 1860. **2** county (□ 1,276 sq mi/3,305 sq km; 1990 pop. 260,120), extreme S Texas; ⊙ Brownsville; 26°08′N 97°27′W. Metropolis of lower Rio Grande valley. Bounded S by the Rio Grande (Mex. border), E by Gulf of Mexico; Laguna Madre separates S end of Padre Isl. from mainland. Drained by Arroyo Colorado. Willacy Canal (W) and North Floodway control water supply to irrigated region. Rich irrigated year-round agr. area, processing and shipping citrus, vegetables, sugarcane, nursery crops, sorghum, cotton. Warm winter climate, nearness to Mexico, and Gulf beaches and fishing attract tourists. Ocean shipping from Brownsville (on 15 mi/24 km deepwater channel to Gulf and the Intracoastal Waterway) and Port Isabel. Oil, natural gas production and refining, clay mining. Major resort area at South Isl. and Boca Chica Isl.; Las Palmas State Wildlife Management Area in NW; Laguna Atascosa Natl. Wildlife Refuge in NE; Palo Alto Battlefield Historic Site in S, N of Brownsville; Brazos Isl. State Park and Port Isabel Lighthouse State Historic Site in SE. Formed 1848.

Cameron (KAM-ruhn), city (1990 pop. 4,831), De Kalb and Clinton cos., NW Mo., 32 mi/51 km E of St. Joseph; 39°44′N 94°14′W. Trade center for agr. area (corn, oats, hay; livestock). Mfg. (concrete). Wallace State Park nearby. Plotted 1855. Western Missouri State Correctional Center (penitentiary).

Cameron 1 town (1990 pop. 5,580), ⊙ Milam co., central Texas, on Little R., and c.45 mi/72 km SSE of Waco; 30°51′N 96°58′W. Elev. 402 ft/123 m. Market, shipping, processing center in agr. area (cotton, sorghum, wheat, corn; cattle, poultry). Mfg. (steel fabrication, plastic prods., furniture, construction materials). Founded 1846, inc. 1888. **2** town (1990 pop. 1,177), Marshall co., N W.Va., in Northern Panhandle, 11 mi/18 km SE of Moundsville, near Pa. state line, on Grave Creek; 39°49′N 80°34′W. Agr. (corn, potatoes; livestock; poultry). Timber. Coal fields in region. Light mfg. Settled 1788. **3** town (1990 pop. 1,273), Barron co., NW Wis., 7 mi/11.3 km S of Rice L.; 45°23′N 91°44′W. RR junction. In lake resort area. Mfg. (industrial packaging veneer, maintenance equip.). Agr. (dairying, potatoes). Prairie L. to SE; large L. Chetok to SE.

Cameron 1 (KAM-ruhn), uninc. village (1990 pop. 2,041), ⊙ Cameron parish, extreme SW La., on Calcasieu R. bet. L. Calcasieu and mouth of river on Gulf of Mexico, and 31 mi/50 km S of Lake Charles; 29°48′N 93°18′W. Elev. 8 ft/3 m. Toll ferry across Calcasieu R. Mfg. (machinery, metal prods., fish meal); shrimp, crabs, oysters, fish. Hunting nearby. Oil and natural gas fields in vicinity. Sabine Natl. Wildlife Refuge to N and NW. **2** village (1990 pop. 215), Moore co., central N.C., 12 mi/19 km SSW of Sanford; 35°19′N 79°15′W. Tobacco, grain; poultry, livestock. Antique furniture sold. **3** village (1990 pop. 327), Le Flore co., SE Okla., 8 mi/12.9 km NE of Poteau, and 17 mi/27 km SSW of Fort Smith (Ark.); 35°07′N 94°32′W. In farm area. **4** village (1990 pop. 504), Calhoun co., central S.C. 10 mi/16 km NE of Orangeburg; 33°33′N 80°42′W. Mfg. (furniture, shelled pecans, timber, agr. chemicals). Agr. (livestock; grains, cotton, soybeans, pecans).

Cameron Cone (10,707 ft/3,263 m), in Rocky Mts., El Paso co., central Colo., in Pike Natl. Forest, 7 mi/11.3 km W of Colorado Springs, and 4 mi/6.4 km E of Pikes Peak.

Cameron Falls, village, W central Ont., Canada, on Nipigon R. (falls), and 65 mi/105 km NE of Port Arthur; 49°08′N 88°20′W. Hydroelectric-power center in lumbering, gold-mining region.

Cameron, Mount (14,239 ft/4,340 m), in Park Range, Lake and Park cos., central Colo., 11 mi/18 km NE of Leadville, S of Continental Divide.

Cameron Park, uninc. city (1990 pop. 11,897), El Dorado co., E central Calif., planned residential community 27 mi/43 km ENE of downtown Sacramento, on Deer Creek; 38°41′N 121°00′W. Cattle, lamb, poultry; apples; timber. Mfg. (plastic prods.). Folsom L. reservoir and State Recreation Area to NW; Shingle Springs Indian Reservation to W.

Cameron Pass (10,276 ft/3,132 m), State Highway 14, in S tip of Medicine Bow Mts., N Colo., bet. Larimer and Jackson cos., NW of Rocky Mt. Natl. Park and Neota Wilderness, set aside to be preserved in natural state. Just S are the dramatic Nokhu Crags. Continental Divide to S. Colo. State Forest (W); Roosevelt Natl. Forest (E). State Highway 14 is closed in winter.

Camilla (kuh-MIL-uh), town (1990 pop. 5,008), ⊙ Mitchell co., SW Ga., 24 mi/39 km S of Albany; 31°14′N 84°13′W. In farm and timber area; peanut, pecan, and poultry processing. Mfg. (apparel, cottonseed oil; plastic and wood prods.; lumbering). Laid out 1857, inc. 1858.

Camillus, village (1990 pop. 1,150), Onondaga co., central N.Y., 8 mi/12.9 km W of Syracuse; 43°02′N 76°18′W. In dairy and grain area. Once a major cutlery mfg. center. Inc. 1852.

Camilo Cienfuegos (kah-MEE-lo see-en-FWAI-goz), sugar-milling town, La Habana prov., W Cuba, on RR, and 26 mi/42 km E of Havana; 23°10′N 81°56′W. Formerly Hershey. Currently named after anti-Batista guerrilla fighter and ally of Fidel Castro, who died in early year of revolution in an airplane crash.

Caminada Bay (KAM-i-nahd-uh), shallow bay (c.10 mi/16 km long NW-SE, 6 mi/10 km wide), Lafourche parish, SE La., c.45 mi/72 km S of New Orleans; adjoins Barataria Bay (E); connected with Timbalier Bay (W) by Southwestern Louisiana Canal; 29°15′N 90°03′W. Grand Isle (Jefferson parish) to SE. Wisner State Wildlife Area on SW shore.

Camino (kah-MEE-no), uninc. village, El Dorado co., E central Calif., 7 mi/11.3 km E of Placerville, in Sierra Nevada foothills, near Weber Creek. Timber; mfg. (paper mill); cattle, lamb, poultry; apples. Sly Park Reservoir to E; Union Valley Reservoir to NE, on Silver Creek; Eldorado Natl. Forest to N and E.

Camlaren (kam-LAI-rin), village, S central Mackenzie Dist., N.W.T., Canada, on Gordon L. (28 mi/45 km long, 2 mi/3 km–5 mi/8 km wide), 50 mi/80 km NE of Yellowknife; 62°59′N 113°12′W. Gold mining.

Cammack Village (KAM-mak), town (1990 pop. 828), Pulaski co., central Ark., residential suburb 3 mi/4.8 km NW of downtown Little Rock, near Arkansas R.; 34°46′N 92°20′W. Murray Lock and Dam to NW.

Camocuautla (kah-mo-KWOUT-lah), town (1990 pop. 1,179), Puebla, central Mexico, in Sierra Madre Oriental, 20 mi/32 km SE of Huauchinango. Corn, sugar, fruit. Also known as San Pedro. In Totonac Indian area.

Camp, county (□ 203 sq mi/526 sq km; 1990 pop. 9,904), NE Texas; ⊙ Pittsburg; 32°58′N 94°58′W. Agr. area (hay, peaches, blueberries; cattle, poultry; dairying). Extensive timber, lumber milling; oil and natural gas wells; coal; clay. Founded 1874.

Camp Atterbury, old military base, Ind., 8 mi/12.9 km NW of Columbus; 8 mi/12.9 km N-S, 4 mi/6.4 km E-W, mainly in Bartholomew co., extends $\frac{1}{2}$ mi/$\frac{8}{10}$ km into Johnson co.

Camp Borden, large military training establishment (31 sq mi/81 sq km), S Ont., Can., NW of Toronto. Includes an armored-vehicle range at Meaford, to the NW.

Camp Connell, uninc. village, Calaveras co., E central Calif., in the Sierra Nevada, c.60 mi/97 km ENE of Stockton. Winter sports. Calaveras Big Trees State Park to SW.

Camp Crook, village (1990 pop. 146), Harding co., NW S.Dak., 20 mi/32 km W of Buffalo, on Little Missouri R., near Mont. state line; 45°32′N 103°58′W. Trade center for ranching area. Unit of Custer Natl. Forest to W (in Mont.), smaller unit to S.

Camp David, U.S. presidential retreat, Frederick co., Md., near Thurmont, and 60 mi/97 km NNW of Wash., D.C., in the middle of Catoctin Mt. Natl. Park. Fort Ritchie, 3 mi/4.8 km NW on Pa. border, major center for intelligence training in World War II, scheduled to close. This 10,000 acres/4,047 ha tract of land was built in 1939 by the Civilian Conservation Corps and the Works Progress Administration and called "Hi-Catoctin." Franklin Roosevelt later dubbed it "Shangri-La," and Dwight Eisenhower renamed it Camp David, for his grandson. Scene of the Camp David Accords (1978), negotiated by President Jimmy Carter, which made peace between Egypt and Israel. Barred to public, but maximum security fencing can be glimpsed from Park Central Road, N of the visitor center.

Camp Douglas, village (1990 pop. 512), Juneau co., central Wis., 46 mi/74 km ENE of La Crosse; 43°55′N 90°16′W. Wood prods.. U.S. Camp Williams military reservation is here. Mill Bluff State Park to NW. Central Wis. Conservation Area and Necedah Natl. Wildlife Area to N.

Camp Gagetown, military camp, S central N.B. Can. Largest (436 sq mi/1,129 sq km) military camp in Canada. Est. 1952.

Camp Hill, town (1990 pop. 1,415), Tallapoosa co., E Ala., 20 mi/32 km ESE of Alexander City; 32°47′N 85°39′W. Lumber, cotton prods.. Inc. 1907.

Camp Hill, borough (1990 pop. 7,831), Cumberland co., S Pa., suburb 3 mi/4.8 km SW of downtown Harrisburg, near the Susquehanna R.; 40°14′N 76°55′W. Mfg. (crushed stone, coal processing equip., food, electronic equip., microfilm, fabricated metal prods.). Capital City Airport to SE; Navy Ships Parts Control Center to W; Camp Hill State Correctional Inst. to S. Founded 1756.

Camp LeJeune (luh-JOON), U.S. marine corps base (□

130 sq mi/336 sq km), Onslow co., SE N.C., SE of Jacksonville, on both sides of New R. estuary. Bounded SE by Atlantic Ocean, Intracoastal Waterway canal parallels coast. It is the major E coast training center and support base for the Atlantic Fleet Marine Force, includes Amphibians Training Complex. Est. 1941.

Camp Nelson, village, Jessamine co., central Ky., 7 mi/11.3 km SSW of Nicholasville, on Kentucky R., in bluegrass region. In Civil War, site of important Federal military camp (Camp Nelson). Natl. Cemetery (est. 1866) is to N. Chimney Rock, a 125 ft/38 m-high limestone formation to NW, on bend of Kentucky R., in Jim Beam Nature Preserve to W; Daniel Boone's Cave.

Camp Parole, Md.: see PAROLE.

Camp Point, village (1990 pop. 1,230), Adams co., W Ill., 18 mi/29 km ENE of Quincy; 40°02′N 91°04′W. In agr. area; feed mill. Inc. 1857.

Camp Richardson, uninc. village, El Dorado co., E Calif., in the Sierra Nevada, on S shore of L. Tahoe, 3 mi/4.8 km W of South Lake Tahoe. Resort Area. Eldorado Natl. Forest to W; Emerald Bay State Park to N.

Camp Springs, village (1990 pop. 16,392), Prince Georges co., central Md., SE suburb of Wash., D.C.; 38°48′N 76°55′W. A base for Union forces during the Civil War, much of Camp Springs has been absorbed by Andrews Air Force Base. The World Weather Center is here.

Camp Upton, N.Y.: see YAPHANK.

Camp Verde, town (1990 pop. 6,243), Yavapai co., central Ariz., on Verde R., and 35 mi/56 km E of Prescott; 34°34′N 111°51′W. Mfg. (machinery). Montezuma Castle Natl. Monument is just NE; Camp Verde Indian Reservation to NW; surrounded by Prescott Natl. Fores. Fort Verde State Historic Park is here.

Camp Verde, uninc. village (1990 pop. 41), Kerr co., SW Texas, c.50 mi/80 km NW of San Antonio. Elev. 1,800 ft/549 m. On site of old U.S. fort, est. July 8, 1855, where pre–Civil War experimental camel corps was organized.

Camp Wood, village (1990 pop. 595), Real co., SW Texas, on Edwards Plateau 34 mi/55 km NNW of Uvalde, and on Nueces R; 29°40′N 100°00′W. Elev. 1,450 ft/442 m. Shipping point for wool, mohair, timber; in ranching area (cattle, sheep, goats). Mfg. (leather goods).

Campania Island (kam-PAN-yuh) (□ 49 sq mi/127 sq km; 18 mi/29 km long. 2 mi/3 km–5 mi/8 km wide), W B.C., Canada, in Hecate Strait just S of Pitt Isl. and W of Princess Royal Isl.; 53°05′N 129°35′W.

Campbell 1 county (□ 159 sq mi/412 sq km; 1990 pop. 83,866), N Ky.; ⊙ Alexandria; 38°57′N 84°22′W. Bounded N and E by Ohio R. (Ohio state line), W by Licking R. Gently rolling uplands in N part of bluegrass region. N part is in Cincinnati, Ohio, urbanized area. Mfg. at Newport and Bellevue. Some agr. (vegetables, tobacco, hay, alfalfa, soybeans, corn; cattle). Formed 1794. **2** county (□ 771 sq mi/1,997 sq km; 1990 pop. 1,965), N S.Dak., borders N.Dak. on N; ⊙ Mound City; 45°45′N 100°02′W. Agr. area, with state game refuge extending along Missouri R., the W boundary. Mountain/Central time zone coincides with Missouri R. channel. Pocasse Natl. Wildlife Refuge on L. Pocasse in NW; L. Hiddenwood in SE. Dairy prods.; cattle, hogs; wheat, corn, barley. Formed 1873. **3** county (□ 447 sq mi/1,158 sq km; 1990 pop. 35,079), NE Tenn.; ⊙ Jacksboro; 36°25′N 84°09′W. Partly (NW) in the Cumberlands; bounded N by Ky., SE by Clinch R. Includes part of Norris Reservoir. Bituminous-coal mining, lumbering (hardwoods), some agr. (livestock, tobacco, corn, hay). Formed 1806. **4** county (□ 507 sq mi/1,313 sq km; 1990 pop. 47,572), SW central Va.; ⊙ Rustburg; 37°12′N 79°05′W. Bounded N by James R., S by Roanoke R., drained by Falling and Otter rivers. Co. excludes independent city of Lynchburg to N. Mfg. at Altavista. Agr. (tobacco, corn, hay, wheat, alfalfa, barley, soybeans; cattle, poultry; dairying); timber. Formed 1782. **5** county (□ 4,801 sq mi/12,435 sq km; 1990 pop. 29,370), NE Wyo.; ⊙ Gillette; 44°14′N 105°32′W. Grain and livestock area (wheat, oats; sheep, cattle) bordering Mont.; watered by Little Powder and Belle Fourche rivers. Coal, natural gas, and uranium found here. Small

unit of Thunder Basin Natl. Grassland in NE, with part of large main unit in SE. Pumpkin Buttes in SW. Formed 1911.

Campbell 1 (KAM-buhl), city (1990 pop. 36,048), Santa Clara co., W Calif., suburb 5 mi SW of San Jose in Silicon Valley area; 37°17′N 121°57′W. Drained by Los Gatos Creek. Computer-based economy; former orchard area. Mfg. (computer equipment). Phillips Jr. Col.-Condie Campus. Founded 1885, inc. 1952. **2** city (1990 pop. 2,165), Dunklin co., extreme SE Mo., near St. Francis R., 18 mi/29 km N of Kennett; 36°29′N 90°04′W. Cotton, rice, soybeans, peaches. Inc. 1900. **3** city (1990 pop. 10,038), Mahoning co., E Ohio, just SE of Youngstown, and on Mahoning R.; 41°04′N 80°35′W. Until 1926, called East Youngstown.

Campbell, town (□ 2 sq mi/5.2 sq km; 1990 pop. 3,884), Osceola co., central Fla., 20 mi/32 km S of Orlando; 28°15′N 81°27′W. Numerous lakes nearby.

Campbell 1 village (1990 pop. 233), Wilkin co., W Minn., 14 mi/23 km SE of Breckenridge on Rabbit R; 46°06′N 96°24′W. Grain, sunflowers, sugar beets. Mfg. (fertilizers). **2** village (1990 pop. 432), Franklin co., S Nebr., 25 mi/40 km SW of Hastings, and on Little Blue R; 40°17′N 98°43′W. Livestock, poultry; grain. **3** village (1990 pop. 683), Hunt co., NE Texas, 9 mi/14.5 km E of Greenville; 33°08′N 95°57′W. Agr. area (cattle; dairying; cotton, nursery crops).

Campbell, Fort, Ky.: see HOPKINSVILLE.

Campbell Hill, village (1990 pop. 351), Jackson co., SW Ill., 17 mi/27 km NW of Murphysboro; 37°55′N 89°32′W. In agr. region.

Campbell Hill (1,549 ft/472 m), Logan co., W central Ohio, just E of Bellefontaine; 40°22′N 83°43′W. Highest point in state.

Campbell Island (□ 64 sq mi/166 sq km; 14 mi/23 km long, 2 mi/3 km–6 mi/10 km wide), SW B.C., Canada, in NE Queen Charlotte Sound, just W of Bella Bella; 52°08′N 128°12′W. Rises to 1,160 ft/354 m. Campbell Isl. village on NE coast.

Campbell River, village (1991 pop. 21,175), SW B.C., Canada, E central Vancouver Isl., on Discovery Passage at mouth of Campbell R. (40 mi/64 km long), 26 mi/42 km NNW of Courtenay; 50°01′N 125°15′W. Lumbering, fishing port; resort, salmon sport-fishing center. Site of John Hart hydroelectric project.

Campbellford, town (1991 pop. 3,528), S Ont., Canada, on Trent R., and 25 mi/40 km E of Peterborough; 44°18′N 77°48′W. Milling; dairying; lumbering; resort.

Campbell's Bay, village (1991 pop. 912), SW Que., Canada, on Ottawa R., and 26 mi/42 km ESE of Pembroke; 45°44′N 76°36′W. Dairying; cattle, pigs.

Campbellsburg, town (1990 pop. 606), Washington co., S Ind., 10 mi/16 km WNW of Salem; 38°38′N 86°15′W. In agr. area.

Campbellsburg (KA-muhls-buhrg), village (1990 pop. 604), Henry co., N Ky., 12 mi/19 km S of Carrollton, in bluegrass region; 38°31′N 85°12′W. Agr. (tobacco, soybeans, grain; livestock; dairying. Mfg. (wire harness assembly).

Campbellsport, town (1990 pop. 1,732), Fond du Lac co., E Wis., near branch of Milwaukee R., 14 mi/23 km SE of Fond du Lac; 43°36′N 88°16′W. In farm area (dairy prods.; grain). Mfg. (construction materials). Kettle Moraine State Forest (N Unit) to E. Inc. 1902.

Campbellsville (KA-muhls-vil), city (1990 pop. 9,577), ⊙ Taylor co., central Ky., 65 mi/105 km SSE of Louisville; 37°21′N 85°20′W. Agr. area (tobacco, corn, oats, hay, wheat; dairying); oak, cherry, and walnut timber; limestone quarries. Mfg. (wood prods., furniture, food and beverages, metal prods., printing and publishing). Taylor Co. Airport to E. Campbellsville Col. (2-year Baptist) here. Green River L. reservoir and State Park to S. Est. 1817.

Campbellton, city (1991 pop. 8,699), N N.B., Can., on the Restigouche R., near the head of Chaleur Bay; 49°17′N 54°56′W. Large sawmills; shipping port for pulpwood. Starting point for canoe, fishing (salmon and trout), and hunting trips into the forested interior.

Campbellton, uninc. town (1990 pop. 275), Atascosa co.,

SW Texas, 45 mi/72 km SSE of San Antonio, on Atascosa R.

Campbellton (KA-muhl-tuhn), village (1990 pop. 202), Jackson co., NW Fla., near Ala. line, 16 mi/26 km NW of Marianna; 30°56′N 85°24′W. Lumber- and gristmills.

Campbelltown (KAM-buhl-toun), uninc. town (1990 pop. 1,609), Lebanon co., SE central Pa., residential community 2 mi/3.2 km S of Palmyra; 40°16′N 76°34′W. Reigle Field airport is here.

Campeche (kahm-PAI-chai), state (□ 21,924 sq mi/56,783 sq km; 1990 pop. 535,185), SE Mexico, on the Gulf of Campeche; ⊙ Campeche; 17°48′N 89°25′W. Comprising most of the W ½ of the YUCATÁN peninsula, the state lies in hot, humid lowlands. Rainfall in the SW sector is heavy. Much of the state was extensively forested, and logwood (called *campeche* in Span.) has been one of the chief exports. Agr. and stock raising are important in the more arid NE sector. Using Campeche as a base, the Span. explorer Francisco de Montejo led (1531–1535) expeditions against the Maya Indians. The coast was a haunt of pirates from the 17th cent. to the 19th cent. The principal ports are Campeche and Carmen, a small town on an island at the entrance to the Laguna de Términos.

Campeche (kahm-PAI-chai), city (1990 pop. 150,518) and township; ⊙ Campeche state, SE Mexico, on the Yucatán peninsula; 19°50′N 90°30′W. It was fortified and is still partly surrounded by 18th-cent. walls. Although it remains an export center for the surrounding region, Campeche's economy is increasingly linked to the offshore oil fields in the Bay of Campeche. The city, once the site of the pre-Columbian town called Kimpech (whose remains are still observable), was founded in 1540 by the son of the Span. conquistador Francisco de Montejo. It was sacked frequently by English buccaneers. From 1862 to 1864, Fr. forces blockaded the city. The city has a 16th-cent. cathedral.

Campeche, Gulf of, inlet of the Gulf of Mexico, SE Mexico, bounded by Yucatán Peninsula (E), Isthmus of Tehuantepec (S), and S sect. of Veracruz state (W); roughly bet. 18°10′N and 21°00′N. Into it flows Papaloapan, Coatzacoalcos, Grijalva, and Candelaria (through Laguna de Términos) rivers. Main ports are Veracruz, Coatzacoalcos, Carmen, and Campeche. The shoal N of Yucatán Peninsula and NW of Gulf of Campeche is called Campeche Bank.

Campechuela (kahm-paich-oo-AI-luh), town (1994 est. pop. 20,000), Granma prov., E Cuba, on E shore of the Gulf of Guacanayabo, 13 mi/21 km SW of Manzanillo; 20°14′N 77°16′W. In agr. region (sugarcane, pineapples, coffee). Large bulk sugar terminal that handled 5.7% of natl. sugar exports in 1993.

Campgaw, N.J.: see FRANKLIN LAKES.

Campo 1 (KAM-po), uninc. village, San Diego co., S Calif., near Mex. border, 40 mi/64 km ESE of San Diego. Cattle. South terminus of Pacific Crest Natl. Scenic Trail 9 mi/14.5 km to WSW. Campo Indian Reservation to E, Manzanita Indian Reservation to NE. Cleveland Natl. Forest to W. **2** village (1990 pop. 121), Baca co., SE Colo., near Okla. line, 24 mi/35 km S of Springfield; 37°06′N 102°34′W. Elev. 4,339 ft/1,323 m. Wheat, sorghum; cattle. Source of North Fork Cimmaron R. to NW. Surrounded by units of Comanche Natl. Grassland.

Campo Florido (KAHM-po flo-REE-do), town, Ciudad de La Habana prov., W Cuba, on RR, and 14 mi/23 km E of Havana; 23°04′N 81°16′W. Vegetables, livestock.

Campobello, village (1990 pop. 465), Spartanburg co., NW S.C., 17 mi/27 km NW of Spartanburg; 35°07′N 82°09′W. Mfg. (contract embroidery, canvas production, construction materials, fixtures).

Campobello (KAM-po-BE-lo), island, 9 mi/15 km long and 3 mi/5 km wide, in Passamaquoddy Bay, N.B., Can., just off the coast of Maine; 44°53′N 66°57′W. The island passed to Canada by the Convention of 1817. President Franklin Delano Roosevelt had a summer home in Welchport, the main settlement, for many years. It is now preserved in Roosevelt-Campobello Intl. Park.

Campos Point (KAHM-pos), on Pacific coast of Colima, W Mexico, at SE gate of Manzanillo Bay, just S of Manzanillo; 19°05′N 104°22′W.

Camp-Perrin (kawng–pe-RANG), city (1982 pop. 704), Sud dept., SW Haiti, on Jacmel Peninsula, 13 mi/21 km NW of Les Cayes; 18°19′N 73°52′W. Agr. (cacao, limes, bananas, coffee, sugarcane); cattle; coffee processing. Lignite deposits nearby.

Campti (KAMP-tee), town (1990 pop. 929), Natchitoches parish, NW central La., on Red R., 14 mi/23 km N of Natchitoches; 31°54′N 93°07′W. Cotton; lumber; mfg. (portable bldgs., wood chips, kraft linerboard). Clear L., part of NW La. State Wildlife Area, to NE. Inc. 1903.

Campton 1 town (1990 pop.), Walton co., N central Ga., 5 mi/8 km N of Monroe; 33°52′N 83°43′W. **2** town (1990 pop. 2,377), Grafton co., central N.H., 24 mi/39 km NNW of Laconia, in White Mts.; 43°49′N 71°39′W. Drained by Pemigewasset R., Mad R. Fruit, vegetables; poultry, cattle; dairying; timber. Mfg. (printing, asphalt, apparel, aggregate and gravel processing, caskets). Three covered bridges. Parts of White Mt. Natl. Forest in NE and W. Campton Natl. Forest Campground in N. Settled c. 1765.

Campton (KAMP-tuhn), village (1990 pop. 484), ⊙ Wolfe co., E central Ky., in the Cumberland Mts., 40 mi/64 km ESE of Winchester; 37°44′N 83°32′W. Wolfe County Mus. here. Daniel Boone Natl. Forest is to NW; Natural Bridge State Park to W; Red River Gorge, in Red River Natl. Geological Area to N.

Campus, village (1990 pop. 137), Livingston co., NE central Ill., 20 mi/32 km NE of Pontiac; 41°01′N 88°18′W. In agr. area.

Camrose, city (1991 pop. 13,420), central Alta., Canada; 53°01′N 112°49′W. In a mixed farming area; RR center. Camrose Lutheran Col. is here.

Camú River (kah-MOO), c.50 mi/80 km long, central Dominican Republic; rises in the Cordillera Central S of La Vega city, flows N and E, past La Vega, and through fertile La Vega Real valley, to Yuna R. just SE of Pimentel.

Camuy (kahm-WEE), town (1990 pop. 28,917), NW P.R., on the coast, 8 mi/12.9 km W of Arecibo. Dairying center, one of principal milk producers on isl. Light mfg. Deep caves nearby situated above large underground streams.

Cana Point (KAH-nah), E headland of E Saona Isl., Dominican Republic, off SE Hispaniola isl., at SW gate of Mona Passage; 18°07′N 68°34′W.

Canaan 1 (KAI-nuhn), town (1990 pop. 1,057), Litchfield co., NW Conn., on the Housatonic, and 19 mi/31 km NW of Torrington, in Taconic Mts.; 41°57′N 73°18′W. Includes villages of South Canaan and Falls Village (gypsum, limestone prods., agr., and construction materials). State forests. CANAAN village is in North Canaan town (N). Canaan Mts. surround. **2** rural town (1990 pop. 1,636), Somerset co., central Maine, 8 mi/12.9 km E of Skowhegan; 44°46′N 69°32′W. Wood prods.. **3** town (1990 pop. 3,045), Grafton co., W central N.H., 11 mi/18 km E of Lebanon; 43°40′N 72°02′W. Drained by Mascoma R. Agr. (cattle, poultry; vegetables, apples; dairying; nursery crops; timber). Mfg. (lumber, machinery, canoe paddles). Canaan Street L. in center. Goose Pond in NW. Canaan Street, historic village, in center. Settled 1766, inc. 1770. **4** town (1990 pop. 1,121), Essex co., extreme NE Vt., on the Connecticut and 30 mi/48 km N of Guildhall; 44°58′N 71°34′W. Includes Beecher Falls village, port of entry on Que. line.

Canaan (KA-non), village, Tobago, Republic of Trinidad and Tobago. Hotel area near Crown Point, SW Tobago.

Canaan 1 (KAI-nuhn), village in North Canaan town, Litchfield co., NW Conn., in Taconic Mts., 17 mi/27 km NW of Torrington. Trade center. Tourist railroad. Canaan town is S. **2** village (1990 pop. 450), Columbia co., E N.Y., near Mass. state line, 28 mi/45 km SE of Albany; 42°23′N 73°27′W. Commercial activities include pet food processing. Berkshire Industrial School for boys is nearby.

Canaan Street, N.H.: see CANAAN.

Canada, country (□ 3,851,787 sq mi/9,976,128 sq km;1991 pop. 27,296,859), N N. Amer., ⊙ OTTAWA; 45°15′N 75°45′W. It is a federation of 10 provinces — NEWFOUNDLAND AND LABRADOR, NOVA SCOTIA, NEW BRUNSWICK, PRINCE EDWARD ISLAND, QUEBEC, ONTARIO, MANITOBA, SASKATCHEWAN, ALBERTA, and BRITISH COLUMBIA — and the YUKON TERRITORY and the NORTHWEST TERRITORIES. A new Inuit-controlled territory of NUNAVUT, made up from the E portion of the N.W.T., came into effect Apr. 1, 1999. Canada occupies all of N. Amer. N of the U.S. (and E of Alaska) except for the Fr. isls. of St. Pierre and Miquelon. It is bounded on the E by the Atlantic Ocean, on the N by the Arctic Ocean, and on the W by the Pacific Ocean and Alaska. A transcontinental border, formed in part by the Great Lakes, divides Canada from the U.S.; Nares and Davis straits separate Canada from Greenland. The ARCTIC ARCHIPELAGO extends far into the Arctic Ocean. Canada has a very long and irregular coastline; Hudson Bay and the Gulf of St. Lawrence indent the E coast and the Inside Passage extends along the W coast. The ice-clogged straits bet. the isls. of N Canada form the Northwest Passage. During the Ice Age all of Canada was covered by a continental ice sheet that scoured and depressed the land surface, leaving a covering of glacial drift, depositional landforms, and innumerable lakes and rivers. Aside from the Great Lakes, which are only partly in the country, the largest lakes of N. Amer. — Great Bear, Great Slave, and Winnipeg — are entirely in Canada. The St. Lawrence is the chief river of E Canada. The Saskatchewan, Nelson, Churchill, and Mackenzie river systems drain central Canada, and the Columbia, Fraser, and Yukon rivers drain the W part of the country. Canada has a bowl-shaped geologic structure rimmed by highlands, with Hudson Bay at the lowest point. The country has 8 major physiographic regions — the Canadian Shield, the Hudson Bay Lowlands, the Western Cordillera, the Interior Lowlands, the Great Lakes–St. Lawrence Lowlands, the Appalachians, the Arctic Lowlands, and the Innuitians. The exposed portions of the Can. Shield cover more than half of Canada. This once-mountainous region, which contains the continent's oldest rocks, has been worn low by erosion over the millennia. Its upturned E edge is indented by fjords. The Shield is rich in minerals, especially iron and nickel, and in potential sources of hydroelectric power. In the center of the Shield are the Hudson Bay Lowlands, encompassing Hudson Bay and the surrounding marshy land. The Western Cordillera, a geologically young mt. system parallel to the Pacific coast, is composed of a series of N-S trending ranges and valleys that form the highest and most rugged sect. of the country; Mt. Logan (19,850 ft/6,050 m) is the highest point in Canada Part of this region is made up of the Rocky Mts. and the Coast Mts., which are separated by plateaus and basins. The isls. off W Canada are partially submerged portions of the Coast Mts. The Western Cordillera is also rich in minerals, timber, and potential sources of hydroelectric power. Bet. the Rocky Mts. and the Canadian Shield are the Interior Lowlands, a vast region filled with sediment from the flanking higher lands. The Lowlands are divided into the prairies, the plains, and the Mackenzie Lowlands. The prairies are Canada's granary, while grazing is important on the plains. The smallest and southernmost region is the Great Lakes–St. Lawrence Lowlands, Canada's heartland. Dominated by the St. Lawrence R. and the Great Lakes, the region provides a natural corridor into central Canada, and the St. Lawrence Seaway gives the interior cities access to the Atlantic. This sect., which is composed of gently rolling surface on sedimentary rocks, is the location of extensive farmlands, large industrial centers, and most of Canada's population. In SE Canada and on N.F. is the N end of the Appalachian Mt. system, an old and geologically complex region with a generally low and rounded relief. The Arctic Lowlands and the Innuitians are the most isolated areas of Canada and are barren and snow covered for most of the year. The Arctic Lowlands comprise much of the Arctic Archipelago and contain sedimentary rocks that may have oil-bearing strata. In the extreme N, mainly on Ellesmere Isl., is the Innuitian Mt. system, which rises to c.10,000 ft/3,050 m. Canada's climate is influenced by latitude and topography. The Interior Lowlands make it possible for polar air masses to move S and for subtropical air masses to move N into Canada. Hudson Bay and the Great Lakes act to modify the climate locally. The Western Cordillera serves as a climatic barrier that prevents polar air masses from reaching the Pacific coast and blocks the moist Pacific winds from reaching into the interior. The Cordillera has a typical highland climate that varies with altitude; the W slopes receive abundant rainfall, and the whole region is forested. The Interior Lowlands are in the rain shadow of the Cordillera; the S portion has a steppe climate in which grasses predominate. S Canada has a temperate climate, with snow in the winter (especially in the E) and cool summers. Farther to the N, extending to the timberline, is the humid subarctic climate characterized by short summers and a snow cover for about ½ the year. On the Arctic Archipelago and the N mainland is the tundra, with its mosses and lichen, permafrost, near year-round snow cover, and ice fields. A noted phenomenon off the coast of E Canada is the persistence of dense fog, which is formed when the warm air over the Gulf Stream passes over the cold Lab. Current as the 2 currents meet off Newfoundland. Mfg. is Canada's most important economic activity, engaging 15% of the work force. The remainder are employed in service (3⁄7%) and public administration (7%), industries and trade (18%), finance (7%), construction (6%), transportation (8%), agr. (1%), and mining (1%). Mfg. accounts for 20% of Canada's GDP, while service industries rank a close second at 19%. The leading prods. are transportation equipment, pulp and paper, processed foods, chemicals, primary and fabricated metals, petroleum, electrical and electronic prods., wood prods., printed materials, machinery, clothing, and nonmetallic minerals. Industries are centered in Ont., Que., and, to a lesser extent, B.C. and Alta. Canada's industries depend on the country's rich energy resources, which include hydroelectric power, petroleum, natural gas, coal, and uranium. Service industries, including tourism, are the next-largest segment of the GDP, followed by financial services. Canada is a leading mineral producer, although much of its mineral resources are difficult to reach due to permafrost. It is the world's largest source of nickel, zinc, and uranium, and a major source of lead, asbestos, gypsum, potash, tantalum, and cobalt. Other important mineral resources are petroleum, natural gas, copper, gold, iron ore, coal, silver, molybdenum, and sulphur. The mineral wealth is located in many areas; some of the most productive regions are Sudbury, Ont. (copper and nickel); Timmins, Ont. (lead, zinc, and silver); and Kimberley, B.C. (lead, zinc, and silver). Petroleum and natural gas are found in Alta. and Sask. Agr. contributes about 4% of the GDP. The sources of the greatest farm income are livestock and dairy prods. Among the biggest income-earning crops are wheat, oats, barley, corn, and canola. Canada is one of the world's leading agr. exporters, especially of wheat. Man., Sask., and Alta. are the great grain-growing provinces, and, with Ont., are also the leading sources of beef cattle. The main fruit-growing regions are found in Ont., B.C., Que., and N.S. Apples and peaches are the principal fruits grown in Canada. More than ⅓ of the total land area is classified as forest and Can. timber production ranks among the highest in the world. Fishing is an important economic activity in Canada. Cod and lobster from the Atlantic and salmon from the Pacific have been the principal catches, but cod industry was halted in mid-1990s, due to overfishing. About ¾ of the take is exported. The fur industry, once so important but no longer dominant in the nation's economy, is centered in Que. and Ont. The U.S. is by far Canada's leading trading partner, followed by Japan and Great Britain. Mfg. goods make up the bulk of the imports;

motor vehicles and parts are both the largest import and export. Other important exports are newsprint, lumber, pulp, crude petroleum, wheat, machinery, aluminum, natural gas, and hydroelectric power. The James Bay Project was an issue for Can. and U.S. environmentalists and led to 1993 decision by Que. govt. to shelve Phase 2 of project. A major problem for Canada is that large segments of its economy—notably in mfg., petroleum, and mining—are controlled by foreign, especially U.S. interests. This deprives the nation of much of the profits of its industries and makes the economy vulnerable to developments outside Canada. This situation is mitigated somewhat by the fact that Canada itself is a large foreign investor. In June 1993, Canada was 1st N. Amer. country to ratify NAFTA. Since the free-trade agreement, Can. investment in U.S. border cities, such as Buffalo, N.Y., has increased dramatically. More than 34% of the Can. pop. are of Br. descent, and some 25% are of Fr. origin. The influx of many Eur., Asian, and Indian immigrants has steadily diversified the country's ethnic composition, especially in major cities. Over 75% of the total pop. live in cities, the largest of which are TORONTO, MONTREAL, VANCOUVER, OTTAWA, EDMONTON, CALGARY, WINNIPEG, QUEBEC, and HAMILTON. Canada has complete religious liberty, though its growing multiculturalism has at times caused tensions among ethnic and religious groups. The country is almost equally divided bet. Roman Catholics (46%) and Protestants (41%). The largest Protestant denominations are United Church of Canada, Anglican Church of Canada, and Presbyterian. Eng. and Fr. are the official languages, and federal documents are published in both languages. In 1991, 60.57% of Canadians cited Eng. as their first language, 23.83% were Fr. speaking. Prior to the arrival of Europeans in Canada, the area was inhabited by Native Americans and Inuits who came from Asia via the Bering Strait more than 10,000 years ago. The Vikings landed in Canada A.D. c.1000. Their arrival is described in Icelandic sagas and confirmed by archaeological discoveries in N.F. John Cabot, sailing under Eng. auspices, touched the E coast in 1497. In 1534, the Frenchman Jacques Cartier planted a cross on the Gaspé Peninsula. These and many other voyages to the Can. coast were in search of a NW passage to Asia. Subsequently, Fr.-Eng. rivalry dominated Can. history until 1763. The first permanent white settlement in Canada was founded in 1605 by the sieur de Monts and Samuel de Champlain at Port Royal (now ANNAPOLIS ROYAL, N.S.) in ACADIA. A trading post was est. 1608 in Que. Meanwhile the English, moving to support their claims under Cabot's discoveries, attacked Port Royal (1614) and captured Que. (1629). However, the French regained Que. (1632), and through the Co. of New France (Co. of 100 Associates), began to exploit the fur trade and establish new settlements. The French were primarily interested in fur trading. Bet. 1608 and 1640, fewer than 300 settlers arrived. The sparse Fr. settlements sharply contrasted with the relatively dense Eng. settlements along the Atlantic coast to the S. Meanwhile, both missionaries, such as Jacques Marquette, and traders, such as Pierre Radisson and Médard Chouart des Groseilliers, were extending Fr. knowledge and influence. The greatest of all the empire builders in the W was Robert Cavelier, sieur de La Salle, who descended the Mississippi R. to its mouth and who envisioned the vast colony in the W that was made a reality by men like Duluth, Bienville, Iberville, and Cadillac. The French, however, did not go unchallenged. The English had claims on Acadia, and the Hudson's Bay Co. in 1670 began to vie for the lucrative fur trade of the W. When the long series of wars bet. Britain and France broke out in Europe, they were paralleled in N. Amer. by the Fr. and Indian Wars. The Peace of Utrecht (1713) gave Britain Acadia, the Hudson Bay area, and N.F. To strengthen their position the French built additional forts in the W (among them Detroit and Niagara). The decisive battle of the entire struggle took place in 1759, when Wolfe defeated Montcalm on the Plains of Abraham, bringing about the fall of Que. to the British. Montreal

fell in 1760. By the Treaty of Paris in 1763, France ceded all its N. Amer. possessions E of the Mississippi to Britain, while La. went to Spain. The Fr. residents of Que. strongly resented the Royal Proclamation of 1763, which imposed Br. institutions on them. Many of its provisions, however, were reversed by the Quebec Act (1774), which granted important concessions to the French and extended Que.'s borders W and S to include all the inland territory to the Ohio and the Mississippi. This act infuriated the residents of the 13 colonies (the future U.S.). In 1775 the Amer. Continental Congress had as its first act not a declaration of independence but the invasion of Canada. In the Amer. Revolution the Canadians remained passively loyal to the Br. crown, and the effort of the Americans to take Canada failed dismally. Loyalists from the colonies in revolt fled to Canada and settled in large numbers in N.S. and Que. In 1784, the prov. of N.B. was carved out of N.S. for the loyalists. The result, in Que., was sharp antagonism bet. the deeply rooted, Catholic French Canadians and the newly arrived, Protestant British. To deal with the problem the British passed the Constitutional Act (1791). It divided Que. into Upper Canada (present-day Ont.), predominantly Br. and Protestant, and Lower Canada (present-day Que.), predominantly Fr. and Catholic. Each new prov. had its own legislature and institutions. This period was one of further exploration. Alexander Mackenzie made voyages in 1789 to the Arctic Ocean and in 1793 to the Pacific, searching for the NW Passage. Mariners also reached the Pacific NW, and such men as Capt. James Cook, John Meares, and George Vancouver secured for Britain a firm hold on what is now B.C. During the War of 1812, Can. and Br. soldiers repulsed several Amer. invasions. The N.B. boundary and the boundary W of the Great Lakes was disputed with the U.S. for a time, but since the War of 1812 the long border has generally been peaceful. Rivalry bet. the Northwest Company and the Hudson's Bay Co. erupted into bloodshed in the Red River Settlement and was resolved by amalgamation of the companies in 1821. The new Hudson's Bay Co. then held undisputed sway over Rupert's Land and the Pacific West until U.S. immigrants challenged Br. possession of Ore. and obtained the present boundary (1846). After 1815 thousands of immigrants came to Canada from Scotland and Ireland. Movements for political reform arose. In Upper Canada, William Lyon Mackenzie struggled against the Family Compact. In Lower Canada, Louis J. Papineau led the Fr. Can. Reform party. There were rebellions in both provs. The British sent Lord Durham as governor general to study the situation, and his famous report (1839) recommended the union of Upper and Lower Canada under responsible govt. The 2 Canadas were made 1 prov. by the Act of Union (1841) and became known as Canada West and Canada East. Responsible govt. was achieved in 1849 (it had been granted to the MARITIME PROVINCES in 1847), largely as a result of the efforts of Robert Baldwin and Louis H. La Fontaine. The movement for federation of all the Can. provinces was given impetus in the 1860s by a need for common defense, the desire for some central authority to press RR construction, and the necessity for a solution to the problem posed by Canada West and Canada East, where the Br. majority and Fr. minority were in conflict. When the Maritime Provs., which sought union among themselves, met at the Charlottetown Conference of 1864, delegates from the other provs. of Canada attended. Two more conferences were held—the Que. Conference later in 1864 and the London Conference in 1866 in England—before the Br. N. Amer. Act in 1867 made federation a fact. In 1982 this act was renamed the Constitutional Act of 1867. The four original provs. were Ont. (Canada West), Que. (Canada East), N.S., and N.B. The new federation acquired the vast possessions of the Hudson's Bay Co. in 1869. The Red River Settlement became the prov. of Man. in 1870. In 1873, P.E.I. joined the federation, and Alta. and Sask. were admitted in 1905. N.F. joined in 1949. Bet. 1891 and 1914, more than

3 million people came to Canada, largely from continental Europe, following the path of the newly constructed continental RR. In the same period, mining operations were begun in the Klondike and the Canadian Shield. Large-scale development of hydroelectric resources helped foster industrialization and urbanization. Canada played a vital role on the Allied side in World War II. Despite economic strain, Canada emerged from the war with enhanced prestige and took an active role in the UN. Canada joined NATO in 1949. Since the war, uranium, iron, and petroleum resources have been exploited; uses of atomic energy have been developed; and hydroelectric and thermal plants have been built to produce electricity for new and expanded industries. The St. Lawrence Seaway was opened in 1959. The Montreal internatl. exposition, Expo '67, opened in 1967 and was applauded for displaying a degree of taste and interest far superior to that of most such exhibitions. Canada hosted the 1976 Summer Olympics at Montreal and the 1988 Winter Olympics at Calgary. Canada is an independent constitutional monarchy and a member of the Commonwealth of Nations. The nominal Br. monarchy is represented in the country by the office of governor general. The basic constitutional document is the Canada Act of 1982, which replaced the Br. N. Amer. Act of 1867 and gave Canada the right to amend its own constitution. The Canada Act, passed by Great Britain, made possible the Constitution Act of 1982, which was passed in Canada and included a Charter of Rights and Freedoms guaranteeing the rights of women and native peoples and protecting other civil liberties. Que.'s provincial govt. did not accept the new constitution. The Meech Lake Accord, a set of constitutional reforms designed to induce Que. to accept the constitution, failed on June 22, 1990, when N.F. and Man. did not approve it. In Oct. 1992, Can. voters rejected a complex package of constitutional changes intended to discourage the separatist movement in Que. The Can. federal govt. has authority in all matters not specifically reserved to the provincial govts. The provincial govts. have power in the fields of property, civil rights, education, and local govt. They may levy only direct taxes. The federal govt. may veto any provincial law. Power on the federal level is exercised by the Can. Parliament and the cabinet of ministers, headed by the prime minister. The Parliament has 2 houses: the Senate and the House of Commons. There are 104 senators, apportioned among the provinces and appointed by the governor general on the advice of the prime minister. Senators are appointed for life. Members of the House of Commons are elected, largely from single-member constituencies. Elections must be held at least every 5 years. The Commons may be dissolved and new elections held at the request of the prime minister. Canada has an independent judiciary; the highest court is the Supreme Court, with 9 members.

Canada, village (1990 pop. 540), Pike co., E Ky., in the Cumberland Mts., 5 mi/8 km SW of Williamson, W.Va. Bituminous-coal mining and timber area.

Cañada, La, Mexico: see LA CAÑADA.

Canada Lake, resort village, Fulton co., E central N.Y., on Canada L. (c.3 mi/4.8 km long), in the Adirondacks, 12 mi/19 km NW of Gloversville; 43°10′N 74°31′W.

Canada, Lower: see QUEBEC, city.

Cañada Morelos, Mexico: see MORELOS CAÑADA.

Canada, Upper: see ONTARIO, prov.

Canadarago Lake (kan-uhn-dah-RAI-go), one of the Finger Lakes, Otsego co., central N.Y., 23 mi/37 km SSE of Utica; 4 mi/6.4 km long, c.1 mi/1.6 km wide; 42°49′N 75°01′W. Drains S through outlet to Susquehanna R. Once heavily polluted, lake is now pristine, with numerous summer and year-round residences.

Cañadas de Obregón (kan-YAH-dahs de oh-bre-GON), town (1990 pop. 2,374), Cañadas de Obregón municipio, Jalisco, central Mexico, 50 mi/80 km NE of Guadalajara; 21°12′N 102°40′W. Corn, beans, livestock. Formerly Villa Obregón.

Canada's Wonderland (370 acres/148 ha), theme park and recreation area, S central Ont., Can., 19 mi/31 km

NNW of downtown Toronto, E of Hwy. 400 at Rutherford Rd. interchange in Vaughan. Rides, historical theme areas, shops, entertainment.

Canadensis (KA-nah-DEN-sis), uninc. town (1990 pop. 1,200), Barrett township, Monroe co., NE Pa., in Pocono Mts., 14 mi/23 km N of Stroudsburg, on Brodhead Creek; 41°11′N 75°15′W. Mfg. (machining, metal fabricating). Part of Delaware State Forest to E.

Canadian, county (□ 905 sq mi/2,344 sq km; 1990 pop. 74,409), central Okla., ⊙ El Reno. Drained by Canadian R. (forms E pt. of S boundary) and North Canadian R. Oklahoma City has annexed into the co. in E and SE. Co. is urbanized in E and center. Mfg. at El Reno and Oklahoma City. Agr. area (cattle, sheep, hogs, dairying; wheat, barley, oats, corn, hay). Historic Ft. Reno near center of co.

Canadian, town (1990 pop. 2,417), ⊙ Hemphill co., extreme N Texas, in high plains of the Panhandle, c.45 mi/72 km NE of Pampa, and on Canadian R.; 35°54′N 100°22′W. Elev. 2,339 ft/713 m; Wheat and cattle region. Oil and gas. Black Kettle Natl. Grassland, including L. Marion, to E. Settled 1887 as RR town. Inc. 1908.

Canadian, village (1990 pop. 261), Pittsburg co., SE Okla., 18 mi/29 km NNE of McAlester, near Eufaula L.; Canadian R. to N; 35°10′N 95°39′W. In agr. area. L. Arrowhead reservoir (S arm of Eufaula L.) and Arrowhead State Park and Lodge to E.

Canadian, river, c.850 mi/1,368 km long; begins at N.M.-Colo. border in the Sangre de Cristo Mts., flows SE to Raton and then S past Springer, and through Conchas Lake Reservoir, then E through Ute Lake Reservoir, then into N Texas (Texas Panhandle), passes N of Amarillo, flows through Lake Meredith Reservoir (Natl. Recreation Area); it continues into Okla. where it passes Taloga, Oklahoma City (to SW), Norman, Purcell, and N of Ala., through large Eufaula L. Reservoir, where it is joined from W by North Canadian R., then joins Arkansas R. (Kern McClellan Navigation System) in headwaters of Robert S. Kern L. Reservoir, c.25 mi/40 km SE of Muskogee. In the mid-1800s, the Canadian R. valley was followed by pioneers going W along the Fort Smith-Santa Fe Trail. Eufaula Reservoir stores the water of the Canadian and North Canadian rivers; its dam generates electricity. Sanford Dam impounds L. Meredith, which lies over one of the world's largest natural gas fields. The lake is part of L. Meredith Natl. Recreation Area.

Canadice Lake (kan-uh-DEES), Ontario co., W central N.Y., smallest of the Finger Lakes, bet. Hemlock L. (W) and Honeoye L. (E); c.3 mi/4.8 km long; 42°43′N 77°31′W.

Canadohta Lake (KA-nah-DO-tah), uninc. town (1990 pop. 950), Crawford co., NW Pa., residential, 20 mi/32 km NE of Meadville on Canadohta L.; 41°48′N 79°46′W.

Canajoharie (kan-uh-jo-HER-ee), village (□ 1 sq mi/2.6 sq km; 1990 pop. 2,278), Montgomery co., E central N.Y., on Mohawk R. and the Barge Canal, and 20 mi/32 km WSW of Amsterdam; 42°53′N 74°34′W. Electroplating, plastic prods., food. Here are Van Alstyne House (1749), with historical collections, and a lib. and art gallery. Settled c.1730 by Dutch and Germans; inc. 1829.

Canal Fulton (FUL-tuhn), village (1990 pop. 4,157), Stark co., E central Ohio, 13 mi/21 km WNW of Canton, and on Tuscarawas R.; 40°54′N 81°35′W. Canoeing. Annual Canal Days festival, canal-boat replica.

Canal Winchester, village (1990 pop. 2,617), on Fairfield-Franklin co. line, central Ohio, 13 mi/21 km SE of Columbus; 39°51′N 82°49′W. Glass prods..

Canalou (kuh-NAL-oo), city (1990 pop. 319), New Madrid co., extreme SE Mo., in Mississippi alluvial plain, 15 mi/24 km NW of New Madrid; 36°45′N 89°41′W. Cotton, rice, soybeans.

Canandaigua (kan-uhn-DAI-gwuh), city (□ 4 sq mi/10.4 sq km; 1990 pop. 10,725), ⊙ Ontario co., W central N.Y., at the N end of Canandaigua L.; 42°53′N 77°16′W. It is a resort, summer-recreation, and farm-trade center; electronics components mfg. The courthouse was the scene of Susan B.

Anthony's trial (1873) for voting illegally. Vineyards and winery are in Naples Valley 18 mi S, at S end of Canandaigua L. Seat of Community Col. of the Finger Lakes and Performing Arts Center, summer home of Rochester Philharmonic Orchestra. Settled 1789, inc. 1913.

Canandaigua Lake (kan-uhn-DAI-gwuh), one of the Finger Lakes, W central N.Y., with Canandaigua city at N end and Naples Valley at S end; 16 mi/25 km long, 1 mi/1.6 km–1.5 mi/2.4 km wide. Drains N to Clyde R. Vineyards in Naples Valley; summer resort; grape-growing and wine-producing region.

Cananea (kah-nah-NAI-ah), city (1990 pop. 24,967) and township, ⊙ Cananea municipio, Sonora, NW Mexico, in spur of Sierra Madre Occidental, on RR, and 45 mi/72 km ESE of Nogales, Ariz., on Mexico Hwy 2; 30°58′N 110°18′W. Elev. 4,885 ft/1,489 m. One of the world's leading copper-mining centers; copper smelting. Also silver, lead, zinc, and gold deposits. Cattle raising. Has large U.S.-origin pop.

Canaries, village (1991 pop. 1,024), W St. Lucia, 8 mi/12.9 km SW of Castries. Bananas, coconuts, agr. prods..

Canarreos, Los (kah-NAHR-rai-os, los), archipelago along N and E shores of the Isla de Juventud (formerly Isle of Pines), off SW Cuba, in the Gulf of Batabanó, extending for c.60 mi/97 km; 21°38′N 82°14′W. A chain of numerous semideserted keys, with fine ecological reserves.

Canarsie (kuh-NAHR-see), a sect. of E Brooklyn borough of N.Y. city, SE N.Y., on Jamaica Bay; 40°38′N 73°55′W. Pop. is racially mixed, with predominantly Hispanic and Afr.-Amer. residents in the N.

Cañas (KAH-nyahs), town, La Habana prov., W Cuba, on RR, 3 mi/4.8 km E of Artemisa; 22°48′N 82°42′W. Tobacco, sugarcane, fruit. Also Las Cañas.

Canaseraga (kan-uh-suhr-AI-guh), village (□ 1 sq mi/2.6 sq km; 1990 pop. 684), Allegany co., W N.Y., on Canaseraga Creek, and 11 mi/18 km NNW of Hornell; 42°27′N 77°46′W.

Canaseraga Creek (kan-uh-suhr-AI-guh), c.45 mi/72 km long, W central N.Y.; rises SE of Nunda, flows generally SE, past Canaseraga, then generally N, past Dansville, to the Genesee R. NE of Mt. Morris.

Canasí (kahn-uh-SEE), town, Matanzas prov., W Cuba, near coast, on RR, and 14 mi/23 km W of Matanzas; 23°06′N 81°46′W. In sugar- and fruit-growing region.

Canastota (kan-uh-STO-tuh), village (□ 3 sq mi/7.8 sq km; 1990 pop. 4,673), Madison co., central N.Y., 21 mi/34 km E of Syracuse; 43°04′N 75°45′W. Mfg. (medical prods., plastic prods., machinery, limestone products). In potato-, bean-, onion-, and sweet corn-growing area. International Boxing Hall of Fame is here. Inc. 1835.

Canatlán de las Manzanas (kah-naht-LAHN dai lahs mahn-SAH-nahs), city (1990 pop. 8,356) and township, ⊙ Canatlan municipio, Durango, N Mexico, on interior plateau, on RR, and 35 mi/56 km NNW of Victoria de Durango; 24°15′N 104°45′W. Elev. 6,398 ft/1,950 m. Stock-raising and agr. center (cereals, alfalfa, fruit).

Canby 1 town (1990 pop. 1,826), Yellow Medicine co., SW Minn., 28 mi/45 km NW of Marshall, near S. Dak. state line, on Canby Creek; 44°42′N 96°16′W. Agr. area (grain, soybeans, alfalfa, sugar beets; livestock); trade center for farm cooperatives. Mfg. (fertilizers, steel and aluminum fabrication, machinery). Lac qui Parle R. to SE. Inc. as township 1879, as city 1905. **2** town (1990 pop. 8,983), Clackamas co., NW Oregon, 8 mi/12.9 km SW of Oregon City, and on Molalla R., near its confluence with Willamette R. to N; 45°16′N 122°41′W. RR junction. Mfg. (printing and publishing, sheet metal work, lumber). Wineries. Agr. (berries, grapes, nuts, grain; poultry); dairy prods.. Canby Depot Mus. Mollala R. State Park to W.

Canby Mountain (13,478 ft/4,108 m), in San Juan Mts., San Juan co., SW Colo., 6 mi/9.7 km E of Silverton. In coal-mining district.

Cancún (kahn-KOON), city (1990 pop. 167,730) and township, ⊙ Benito Juárez municipio, Quintana Roo state, SE Mexico; 21°10′N 86°49′W. An internatl. resort, and Mexico's most popular, Cancún is known for its

beautiful beaches, agreeable climate, and luxurious hotels and facilities. Built in the early 1970s at a location selected with the assistance of a computer, Cancún is an entirely new, planned city and resort area. Its success has been rapid, but not without problems, foremost among which are providing adequate living conditions for the resort's workers and controlling development impacts in environmentally sensitive zones. Internatl. airport to E.

Candela (kahn-DAI-lah), town (1990 pop. 1,493), Coahuila, N Mexico, in E foothills of Sierra Madre Oriental, 16 mi/26 km SW of Lampazos (Nuevo León). Cereals, livestock.

Candelaria (kahn-dai-LAH-ree-ah), town, Pinar del Río prov., W Cuba, on Central Highway, on RR, and 45 mi/72 km SW of Havana; 22°57′N 83°06′W. In agr. region (sugarcane, tobacco, coffee, corn, pineapples, cattle). Mfg. (cigars).

Candelaria Loxicha (kahn-dai-LAH-ree-ah lok-SEE-chah), town (1990 pop. 1,633), in S Oaxaca, Mexico, 14 mi/22 km N of San Pedro Pochutla, on Mexico Hwy 175; 16°03′N 96°41′W. Elev. 1,475 ft/450 m. Near the Pacific Ocean. Agr. (coffee, beans, corn, sugarcane, mezcal, tropical fruits). Steep terrain with climate varying with elev. A coastal Zapotec community.

Candelaria River, c.130 mi/209 km long, Campeche, SE Mexico; rises in Guatemala near internatl. border, flows NW and N through tropical forest country, to the Laguna de Términos 38 mi/61 km E of Carmen. Navigable for c.45 mi/72 km. Used for logging.

Candia (KAN-dee-yuh), town (1990 pop. 3,557), Rockingham co., SE N.H., 10 mi/16 km ENE of Manchester; 43°02′N 71°18′W. Drained by North Branch R. Agr. (cattle, poultry; dairying; vegetables, nursery crops); light mfg. Part of Bear Brook State Park in NW; Charmingfair Ski Area in center. Settled c.1743, inc. 1763.

Candle, village, NW Alaska, on N side of Seward Peninsula, on Kiwalik R., near its mouth on Kotzebue Sound, 70 mi/113 km SSE of Kotzebue. Gold in area; center of game-fishing and hunting region. Has airfield, radio station, school. Scene of gold rushes, 1901 and 1906.

Candle Lake (□ 150 sq mi/389 sq km), central Sask., Canada, 45 mi/72 km NNE of Prince Albert; 12 mi/19 km long, 7 mi/11 km wide. Adjoined S by Torch L. (5 mi/8 km long, 2 mi/3 km wide). Drains E into Saskatchewan R.

Candler (KAND-luhr), county (□ 251; 1990 pop. 7,744), E central Ga.; ⊙ Metter; 32°24′N 82°04′W. Coastal plain agr. (cotton, corn, tobacco, soybeans, pecans, peanuts; cattle, hogs); timber area. Drained by Canoochee R. Formed 1914.

Candler (KAND-luhr), uninc. village, Buncombe co., W N.C., in the Blue Ridge Mts., 8 mi/12.9 km WSW of Asheville. Mfg. (machinery, chemicals, furniture, wood prods.). Pisgah Natl. Forest to S.

Candlewood, Lake, reservoir (□ 8.4 sq mi/21.8 sq km), Litchfield and Fairfield cos., W Conn., on Rocky R., 1 mi/1.6 km S of its junction with Housatonic R., extending 10 mi/16 km N of Danbury (at S end), 10 mi/16 km long, with 2 parallel arms extending 5 mi/8 km, shoreline c.65 mi/105 km long; 41°34′N 73°26′W. Formed by Candlewood Dam. Recreation. Candlewood Shores on SE shore, W shore developments are Candlewood Isle, Candlewood Knolls, and Knollcrest.

Cando (KAN-doo), town (1990 pop. 1,564), ⊙ Towner co., N N.Dak., 31 mi/50 km NNW of Devils L.; 48°29′N 99°12′W. Grain elevator, creamery, livestock, poultry. Mfg. (concrete). Named 1884, inc. 1901.

Candor (KAN-dor), town (1990 pop. 748), Montgomery co., central N.C., 26 mi/42 km ESE of Albemarle, near Drowning Creek; 35°17′N 79°44′W. Mfg. (textiles, furniture, knit prods.).

Candor, village (1990 pop. 869), Tioga co., S N.Y., on Catatonk Creek, and 18 mi/29 km SE of Ithaca; 42°13′N 76°20′W. Agr. (dairy prods.; poultry; grain).

Cane River Falls, St. Andrew parish, SE Jamaica, scenic spot on small Cane R., and 6 mi/9.7 km E of Kingston; 17°56′N 76°42′W. Formerly a hideout of notorious bandits.

Caneadea (kan-uh-DEE-uh), resort village (1990 pop. 500), Allegany co., W N.Y., on Genesee R. at mouth of small Caneadea Creek, and 22 mi/35 km NNW of Wellsville; 42°23′N 78°07′W. About 2 mi/3.2 km W, dam on creek impounds L. Rushford (c.2 mi/3.2 km long).

Canelas (kah-NAI-lahs), town (1990 pop. 716), Durango, N Mexico, in Sierra Madre Occidental, 55 mi/89 km ENE of Culiacán Rosales(Sinaloa); 25°10′N 106°30′W. Silver, gold, lead mining.

Caney (kah-NAI), town, Santiago de Cuba prov., E Cuba, 4 mi/6.4 km NE of Santiago de Cuba; 20°03′N 75°46′W. Has iron mines and textile factory. Site of fort stormed (1898) by Amer. forces during Span.-Amer. War. San Juan Hill is just S. Also El Caney.

Caney (KAIN-ee), town (1990 pop. 2,062), Montgomery co., SE Kansas, on affluent of Caney R., and 17 mi/27 km W of Coffeyville, at Okla. state line; 37°00′N 95°55′W. Small mfg. center (printing, farm machinery) in grain and livestock area. Oil and gas wells nearby. Founded 1871, inc. 1887.

Caney (KAIN-ee), village (1990 pop. 184), Atoka co., SE Okla., 20 mi/32 km NNE of Durant, on Clear Boggy Creek; 34°13′N 96°12′W. In agr. area; mfg. (wine, grape juice).

Caney Fork, river, 144 mi/232 km long, central Tenn.; flowing NW to the Cumberland R. On Caney Fork, part of the TVA, are Great Falls Dam and Center Hill Dam, which provide flood control and power for the surrounding area.

Caney River (KAIN-ee), c.165 mi/266 km long, in Kansas and Okla.; rises in SE Kansas; flows S and SE into Osage co. in Okla., past Bartlesville, to Verdigris R., just NE of Tulsa. Hulah Dam (94 ft/29 m high, 6,315 ft/1,925 m long, including dikes; begun 1946 for flood control, water supply) is c.13 mi/21 km NNW of Bartlesville; impounds Hulah Reservoir (capacity 295,000 acres-ft.).

Caneyville, village (1990 pop. 549), Grayson co., W central Ky., 31 mi/50 km N of Bowling Green, on Caney Creek; 37°25′N 86°29′W. Agr. area (tobacco, grain; livestock, poultry; dairying; timber). Mfg. (feeds, chemicals, apparel, food processing). Rough River L. reservoir and Rough River Dam State Resort Park to N..

Canfield, city (1990 pop. 5,409), Mahoning co., E Ohio, 7 mi/11 km SW of Youngstown; 41°01′N 80°46′W. In timber, sandstone, and fruit area. Surveyed 1798.

Canfield, village, S Ont., Canada, 20 mi/32 km SSE of Hamilton; 42°58′N 79°45′W. Fruit. Just SE is RR junction of Canfield Junction.

Caniapiscau (kan-yuh-PIS-ko), river, c.575 mi/930 km long, NE Que., Canada; issuing from Caniapiscau L.; flows generally NW past Fort Mackenzie, and joins the Mélèzes to form the Koksoak R., which then flows NE to Ungava Bay at Kuujjuaq. The river's lower course drains part of the iron belt of N Que.

Canisteo (kan-uh-STEE-o), village (1990 pop. 2,421), Steuben co., S N.Y., on Canisteo R. at mouth of small Bennett Creek, and 5 mi/8 km SE of Hornell; 42°16′N 77°36′W. Mfg. (printing, cheese); dairy prods., poultry; timber. Settled before 1790, inc. 1873.

Canisteo River, c.55 mi/89 km long, S N.Y.; rises in W central N.Y. in area NW of Hornell; flows generally S and SE, past Hornell, to Tioga R. 5 mi/8 km SW of Corning.

Canistota, village (1990 pop. 608), McCook co., SE S.Dak., 10 mi/16 km SSE of Salem; 43°36′N 97°17′W. Livestock, grain; mfg. (power supplies, electronic equipment). Clinic for bone diseases is here. L. Vermillion State Rec. Area to E.

Cañitas de Felipe Pescador (kahn-YEE-tahs dai fe-LEE-pai pes-KAH-dor), town (1990 pop. 5,752), NE Zacatecas, Mexico, 7 mi/12 km SE of Benito Juárez, 58 mi/93 km N of the city of Zacatecas; 23°35′N 102°45′W. Elev. 6,631 ft/2,021 m. Temperate dry climate. Agr. (corn, beans, wheat, chiles), cattle.

Canjilon (kah-nee-LON), uninc. village, Rio Arriba co., N N.Mex., in foothills of San Juan Mts., 16 mi/26 km SSE of Tierra Amarilla. Elev. 7,787 ft/2,373 m. Trading point in sheep and agr. region. In Carson Natl. Forest.

Canjilon Mt. (10,913 ft/3,326 m) and Canjilon Lakes to NE.

Canmore (KAN-mor), town (1991 pop. 5,681), SW Alta., Canada, near B.C. border, in Rocky Mts., on Bow R., and 12 mi/19 km SE of Banff; 51°06′N 115°21′W. Elev. 4,296 ft/1,309 m. Coal mining; cattle, sheep. Tourist services, ski resorts. Oil and natural-gas deposits nearby.

Cannel City, uninc. village (1990 pop. 600), Morgan co., E Ky., 40 mi/64 km ESE of Mt. Sterling city. In coal mining and agr. area.

Cannelburg, town (1990 pop. 97), Daviess co., SW Ind., 8 mi/12.9 km E of Washington; 38°40′N 87°00′W. In agr. area.

Cannelton, city (1990 pop. 1,786), Perry co., S Ind., on Ohio R., and c.45 mi/72 km E of Evansville; 37°55′N 86°44′W. Shipping, mining, and mfg. center, in agr., coal, and clay area. Mfg. (clay prods., furniture, wood prods.). Sandstone quarrying. Founded 1837.

Cannelton (KAN-uhl-tuhn), uninc. village, Kanawha co., S central W.Va., c.19 mi/31 km SE of Charleston, on Kanawha R.

Cannifton (KA-nif-tuhn), village, SE Ont., Canada, on Moira R., N suburb of Belleville.

Canning, village, W central N.S., Canada, near SW shore of Minas Basin, 9 mi/14 km NE of Kentville. Fruit-growing and dairying center.

Canning River, c.130 mi/209 km long, NE Alaska; rises in N Brooks Range near 68°37′N 146°37′W; flows N to Camden Bay of Arctic Ocean at 70°03′N 145°35′W.

Cannington, village, S Ont., Canada, on Beaverton R., and 15 mi/24 km W of Lindsay; 44°21′N 79°02′W. Dairying, lumber.

Cannon, county (☐ 270 sq mi/699 sq km; 1990 pop. 10,467), central Tenn.; ☉ Woodbury; 35°49′N 86°04′W. Drained by small affluents of Cumberland and Stones rivers. Livestock raising, dairying, lumbering; truck farming. Formed 1836.

Cannon Air Force Base, Curry co., N.Mex., 3 mi/4.8 km W of Clovis. It is the home of 522d, 523d, and 524th fighter squadrons, as well as the 429th electronic combat squadron. Est. 1942.

Cannon Beach, town (1990 pop. 1,221), Clatsop co., NW Oregon, 22 mi/35 km SSW of Astoria, on Pacific Ocean; 45°53′N 123°57′W. Timber, fish, tourism. Mfg. (seafood processing). Tillamook State Forest to SE; Saddle Mt. State Park to NE; Ecola State Park to N; Hug Point State Park and Tolovana Beach State Wayside to S.

Cannon Creek Lake, reservoir, Bell co., SE Ky., on Cannon Creek, 5 mi/8 km NNE of Middleboro; 2 mi/3.2 km long; 36°39′N 83°39′W. Max. capacity 16,700 acre-ft. Formed by Cannon Dam (125 ft/38 m high), built (1972) by the Commonwealth of Kentucky for water supply.

Cannon Falls, town (1990 pop. 3,232), Goodhue co., SE Minn., on Cannon R., and 30 mi/48 km S of St. Paul; 44°31′N 92°54′W. Farm trading point (grain, soybeans; livestock, poultry; dairying). Mfg. (construction materials, machinery, apparel, printing and publishing). Hydroelectric plant. Part of Richard J. Dorer State Forest to NE.

Cannon Mountain (4,007 ft/1,221 m), in White Mts., Grafton co., NW N.H., W of Franconia Notch, from which is visible the Old Man of the Mt. (also called Great Stone Face), rock formation 48 ft/15 m high, on S side of mt. resembling profile of a man's face. Aerial tramway built 1938; ski trails. Also known as Profile Mt.

Cannon River, c.100 mi/161 km long, SE Minn.; rises in lake region of SW Rice co.; flows generally NE, through Cannon L. reservoir, past Faribault and Northfield, and past Cannon Falls, to Mississippi R., 2 mi/3.2 km NW of Red Wing; 44°35′N 92°33′W. Flows through part of Richard J. Dorer Memorial State Forest in lower course. Little Cannon R. (c.20 mi/32 km long) joins it from S just W of Cannon Falls.

Cannonball River, 135 mi/217 km long, SW N.Dak.; rises in E Slope co. near Amidon; flows ESE past Mott and Elgin, receives Cedar Creek, and turns NE to the Missouri, forming N boundary at Sioux co. and Standing Rock Indian Reservation; 46°28′N 103°12′W.

Cannondale, Conn.: see WILTON.

Cannonsburg, uninc. village (1990 pop. 750), Boyd co., NE Ky., residential suburb 7 mi/11.3 km SW of Ashland. Tobacco, cattle. Coal.

Cannonville, village (1990 pop. 131), Garfield co., S Utah, 28 mi/45 km SE of Panguitch, and on Paria R.; 37°34′N 112°02′W. Elev. 6,000 ft/1,830 m. Alfalfa, barley; cattle.; irrigation to surrounding farms. Bryce Canyon Natl. Park to W; Kodachrome Basin State Park to SE.

Cano (KAH-no), town, Ciudad de la Habana prov., W Cuba, on RR, and 8 mi/12.9 km SW of Havana; 23°02′N 82°28′W. Sugarcane, vegetables, livestock. Also El Cano.

Canobie Lake (KAN-uh-bee), reservoir and resort lake, Rockingham co., SE N.H., on Policy Brook, 2 mi/3.2 km W of Salem; 1.5 mi/2.4 km long; 42°47′N 71°15′W. Amusement park (Canobie Lake Park).

Canoe Lake, W Sask., Canada, 170 mi/274 km N of North Battleford, 13 mi/21 km long, 10 mi/16 km wide; 55°10′N 108°15′W. Drains into Churchill R.

Canoga Park, suburban sect. of LOS ANGELES city, Los Angeles co., S Calif., in San Fernando Valley, 22 mi/35 km NW of downtown Los Angeles; residential. Drained by Los Angeles R. Mfg. (dental and medical supplies, rubber prods., metal prods.). Santa Monica Mts. to S, Santa Susana Mts. to N; Chatsworth Reservoir to N.

Canon, city (1990 pop. 737), Franklin and Hart cos., NE Ga., 9 mi/14.5 km W of Hartwell; 34°21′N 83°07′W. Mfg. (apparel).

Cañon City (KAHN-yon), city (1990 pop. 12,687), ☉ Fremont co., S central Colo., at the entrance of the Grand Canyon of the Arkansas R. (see ROYAL GORGE), 35 mi/56 km WNW of Pueblo; 38°26′N 105°13′W. It is a health and tourist resort in a scenic area with mineral springs. Marble and limestone are quarried, and a variety of other minerals are found in the region. Mfg. (tools, cement, printing and publishing, computer cable, pressed flowers, belt conveyors). Royal Gorge suspension bridge to W. San Isable Natl. Forest to S. State prison is here. Laid out 1859 on the site of a blockhouse built (1807) by Zebulon M. Pike, inc. 1872.

Cañon del Río Blanco National Park (kahn-YON del REE-o BLAHN-ko), (☐ 218 sq mi/563 sq km), in central Veracruz, Mexico, 3.1 mi/5 km S of the city of Orizaba. This park extends from the Cumbres de Acultzingo incline to the town of Fortín de las Flores 5.6 mi/9 km W of Orizaba. The vertical canyon walls are impressive at an elev. of 4,300 ft/1,311 m. The vegetation is different on each level of elev. with pines and fir trees to ash, walnut, cacao, guava, avocado, giant ferns, and other species. A RR line completed in 1873 crosses the park.

Cañon del Sumidero National Park (kahn-YON del soo-mee-DE-ro), in central Chiapas, Mexico, 15 mi/24 km N of Chiapa de Corzo and N of Tuxtla Gutiérrez. The sheer walls of the canyon end in the Grijalva R. below. There are 5 lookout sites with spectacular views of the canyon. What was once roiling rapids is now calm since the construction of the Chicoasén Dam. Legend says that, during the Span. conquest, Indians would jump off the cliffs of this canyon rather than be captured.

Canonchet (ka-NON-chet), village, Hopkinton town, Washington co., SW R.I., 30 mi/48 km SW of Providence; 41°27′N 71°45′W.

Canoncito (kah-nuhn-SEE-to), uninc. town (1990 pop. 1,189), Santa Fe co., N central N.Mex., 11 mi/18 km SSE of Santa Fe; 35°07′N 107°05′W. Timber. Cattle, sheep, grain, alfalfa. Glorieta Mesa to SE; Sangre de Cristo Mts. to NE.

Canonsburg (KA-nuhns-buhrg), borough (1990 pop. 9,200), Washington co., SW Pa., 16 mi/26 km SW of Pittsburgh and 7 mi/11.3 km NE of Washington, on Chartiers Creek; 40°15′N 80°11′W. Though its steel and coal industries have declined, it remains an important mfg. center (fabricated metal prods., machinery, printing and publishing, food, plastic prods.). State Training School in NE. A gram of radium produced here was presented to Marie Curie in 1921 when she visited the town. The Log Cabin School (est. 1777; the 1st school W of the Allegheny Mts.) is preserved. The Black Horse

Tavern was a famous gathering place for leaders of the Whiskey Rebellion (1794). Roberts House (1804) is an example of W Pa. manor architecture. Inc. 1802.

Canoochee (kuh-NOO-chee), town, Emanuel co., E central Ga., 9 mi. ENE of Swainsboro; 32°40′N 82°10′W.

Canoochee River (kuh-NOO-chee), c.100 mi/161 km long, SE Ga.; rises N of Swainsboro; flows SE to Ogeechee R. 15 mi/24 km WSW of Savannah; 32°30′N 82°12′W.

Canora (ka-NO-ruh), town (1991 pop. 2,381), E Sask., Canada, near Whitesand R., 30 mi/48 km N of Yorkton; 51°38′N 102°26′W. Lumber and flour milling, dairying.

Canouan (KAN-oo-an), island (1994 est. pop. 700), dependency of St. Vincent, St. Vincent and the Grenadines, 24 mi/39 km off Beguia, bet. Mustique and Mayreau; 13°43′N 61°19′W. Tourist facilities, resort development being planned.

Canova, village (1990 pop. 172), Miner co., E S.Dak., 9 mi/14.5 km S of Howard, West Fork Vermillion R; 43°52′N 97°30′W. Dairy prods., livestock; grain.

Canóvanas, town (1990 pop. 36,816), NE P.R., just S of Loiza. Industrial and commercial center; mfg. (electronics, machinery, petroleum prods.). El Comandante horse racing track is here.

Cansahcab (kahn-SAH-kahb), town (1990 pop. 4,437), Yucatán, SE Mexico, on RR, and 35 mi/56 km ENE of Mérida; 21°10′N 89°06′W. Henequen, corn, beans, tropical fruit.

Canso, town (1991 pop. 1,228), S central N.S., Canada, on the Atlantic Ocean, near Cape Canso, the easternmost point of N.S. peninsula proper; 45°21′N 61°00′W. The harbor was much used by fishing fleets in colonial times and was fortified by the British in 1720. The Gut, or Strait, of Canso, scarcely 1 mi/1.6 km wide in places, separates N.S. peninsula from Cape Breton Isl.

Canso, Cape, promontory on islet of Andrew, just off E extremity of N.S. peninsula, Canada, 5 mi/8 km ESE of Canso; 45°18′N 60°56′W.

Canso Causeway, E N.S., Canada, 28 mi/45 km E of Antigonish. Connects Cape Breton Isl. with mainland, takes Trans-Canada Highway across 2 mi/3.2 km-wide Strait of Canso. Port Hastings is at E end; gap and low-level bridge near E end allows boat passage. Toll crossing. Constructed in 1955 from rock gouged from large hill at W end.

Canso, Strait of or **Gut of Canso**, channel (17 mi/27 km long, 2 mi/3 km wide), N.S., Canada, separating Cape Breton Isl. from N.S. mainland and leading from the Atlantic to Northumberland Strait. Port Hawkesbury and Mulgrave are chief towns on it.

Cantamayec (kahn-tah-MAH-yek), town (1990 pop. 1,212), Yucatán, SE Mexico, 9 mi/14.5 km SW of Sotuta. Henequen, sugarcane, fruit.

Canterbury 1 town (1990 pop. 4,467), Windham co., E Conn., bet. Little and Quinebaug rivers, 14 mi/23 km NNE of Norwich; 41°42′N 72°00′W. Agr. area; dairy prods.. Has early 19th-cent. house in which Prudence Crandall had school attended by Afr. Amer. girls, 1833–1834. Site of Moses Cleaveland's birthplace is marked. Settled c.1690, inc. 1703. **2** town (1990 pop. 1,687), Merrimack co., S central N.H., 9 mi/14.5 km N of Concord; 43°21′N 71°32′W. Bounded W by Merrimack R.; drained by Soucook R. Agr. (vegetables, apples; poultry; dairying; nursery crops). Mfg. (smoked cheese). Shaker Village in E center.

Canton 1 (KAN-tuhn), city (1990 pop. 13,922), Fulton co., W central Ill., 13 mi/21 km NNE of Lewiston, satellite community 23 mi/37 km WSW of downtown Peoria; 40°33′N 90°02′W. In the corn belt, it is a trade and industrial center for a coal and agr. area (corn, wheat, soybeans, sorghum @ttle). Spoon River Community Col. is here. Inc. 1849. **2** city (1990 pop. 10,062), ⊙ Madison co., central Miss., 23 mi/37 km NNE of Jackson; 32°36′N 90°01′W. Trade and processing center in agr. (vegetables, potatoes, cotton, corn, soybeans; poultry; dairying) and timber area. Mfg. (poultry processing, dairy prods., furniture, metal prods., light mfg.). Has fine antebellum homes. Telda Bogue, restored log home, built in 1830s. Ross Barnett Reservoir, on Pearl R., to SE; Natchez Trace (Natl.) Parkway passes to SE. Inc. 1836. **3** city (1990 pop. 2,623), Lewis co., NE Mo., on Mississippi R., and 30 mi/48 km N of Hannibal; 40°07′N 91°31′W. Agr. (grain; hogs, cattle). Mfg. (telephone parts). Culver-Stockton Col. Lock and Dam No. 20. Settled 1827. **4** city (1990 pop. 84,161), ⊙ Stark co., NE Ohio, at the junction of 3 branches of Nimishillen Creek; 40°49′N 81°22′W. It is a steel-processing center in an iron and steel area (stainless steel). Other manufactures include machinery, automated-teller machines, wood prods. Canton has a community theater, an opera company, and a symphony. In the city are Malone Col. and the Professional Football Hall of Fame. Walsh Col. is in suburban North Canton. Stark County Branch of Kent State Univ., Stark Technical Col., and Malone Col. are located in the vicinity. William McKinley lived in Canton; his grave, monument, and a museum are in the McKinley State Memorial. Inc. 1822.

Canton 1 (KAN-tuhn), town (1990 pop. 8,268), Hartford co., NW central Conn., on Farmington R., and 14 mi/23 km NW of Hartford; 41°51′N 72°54′W. Agr. (tobacco, dairy prods.). Mfg. (chemicals, wrought iron, brass, transportation equip., machinery). Mfg. at Collinsville village (1990 pop. 2,591), whose edge-tool and metal-prods. industry began 1826. Settled 1737, inc. 1806. **2** town (1990 pop. 4,817), ⊙ Cherokee co., NW Ga., 33 mi/53 km N of Atlanta, and on Etowah R., at end of Allatoona Reservoir; 34°15′N 84°29′W. Mfg. (machinery, concrete, cat toys, metal prods., apparel, plastics, food processing; electrical equip.). Emerging suburban community N of Atlanta. Inc. 1833. **3** town (1990 pop. 951), Oxford co., W Maine, on the Androscoggin R., and 19 mi/31 km NNE of South Paris; 44°28′N 70°17′W. Farming, recreational area; wood prods.. **4** town (☐ 19 sq mi/49 sq km; 1990 pop. 18,530), Norfolk co., E Mass., 42°11′N 71°08′W. A residential and industrial suburb of Boston. Mfg. (rubber goods, textiles, plastics, metal, paper, transportation equipment, pharmaceutical prods.). Paul Revere operated a copper-rolling mill here. The town has a state hosp. for the physically handicapped. Blue Hills Reservation State Park, skiing nearby. Settled 1630, inc. 1797. **5** town (1990 pop. 3,790), Haywood co., W N.C., 16 mi/26 km WSW of Asheville, and on Pigeon R; 35°32′N 82°50′W. Agr.. (tobacco, corn, potatoes; dairying, hogs, cattle). Mfg. (lumber, paper prods., textiles). Parts of Pisgah Natl. Forest to S and NW. **6** town (1990 pop. 2,787), ⊙ Lincoln co., SE S.Dak., 18 mi/29 km S of Sioux Falls and on Big Sioux R. (Iowa state line); 43°17′N 96°34′W. Agr. (grain; dairy prods., livestock, poultry). Mfg. (construction materials, machinery). Newton Hills State Park to S. Annual winter sports tournament. RR junction. Founded 1860. **7** town (1990 pop. 2,949), ⊙ Van Zandt co., NE Texas, 35 mi/56 km WNW of Tyler; 32°32′N 95°51′W. Elev. 540 ft/165 m. Agr. (cattle; dairying; hay, sweet potatoes, vegetables, grains, cotton); timber. Mfg. (furniture, light mfg.).

Canton 1 (KAN-tuhn), village (1990 pop. 794), McPherson co., central Kansas, 13 mi/21 km E of McPherson; 38°23′N 97°25′W. RR junction. In wheat, livestock, and oil area. McPherson State Fishing L. and Maxwell Game Preserve to N. **2** village (1990 pop. 362), Fillmore co., SE Minn., near Iowa state line, 12 mi/19 km SE of Preston; 43°31′N 91°55′W. Agr. (corn, oats, soybeans; livestock, poultry; dairying). Richard J. Dorer Memorial Hardwood State Forest to NE. **3** village (☐ 2 sq mi/5.2 sq km; 1990 pop. 6,379), ⊙ St. Lawrence co., N N.Y., on Grass R., and 16 mi/26 km SE of Ogdensburg; 44°36′N 75°10′W. Food processing. In agr. area (dairy prods.; corn, hay). Seat of St. Lawrence Univ. and the State Univ. of N.Y. Col. of Technology. Frederic Remington b. here. Irving Bacheller born in nearby Pierrepont. Settled 1799, inc. 1845. **4** village (1990 pop. 632), Blaine co., W central Okla., 17 mi/27 km NW of Watonga; 36°03′N 98°35′W. In agr. area (grain, livestock); dairying. Mfg. (solar water pumps). To N is Canton Reservoir on North Canadian R.

Canton (KAN-tuhn), borough (1990 pop. 1,966), Bradford co., N Pa., 31 mi/50 km NNE of Williamsport, on Towanda Creek; 41°39′N 76°50′W. Mfg. (plastic prods., machinery, valves, feeds). Agr. (corn, hay, apples; livestock, dairying). Tiadaghton State Forest to S, Tioga State Forest, on Armenia Mt., to NW. Settled c.1796, inc. 1864.

Canton, N.Dak.: see HENSEL.

Canton Lake, reservoir, Blaine co., W central Okla., on N. Canadian R., 42 mi/68 km SW of Enid; 6 mi/9.7 km long; 36°05′N 98°35′W. Max. capacity 390,000 acre-ft. Formed by Canton Dam (earth-fill; 68 ft/21 m high), built for flood control and irrigation.

Canton Township, suburb, Wayne Co., SE Mich., 23 mi/37 km W of downtown Detroit; borders Washtenaw co. on W. Drained by Lower R. Rouge and its tributaries. Has remnant agr. Mfg. (industrial gases, machinery, transportation equip., magnetic prods., business forms).

Cantrall (KAN-trul), village (1990 pop. 123), Sangamon co., central Ill., 9 mi/14.5 km N of Springfield; 39°55′N 89°40′W. Agr. (corn, soybeans; cattle, hogs).

Cantril, town (1990 pop. 262), Van Buren co., SE Iowa, near Mo. line, 9 mi/14.5 km SE of Keosauqua; 40°38′N 92°04′W.

Cantwell, village (1990 pop. 147), S central Alaska, E of Mt. McKinley Natl. Park, 30 mi/48 km S of Nenana, on Alaska RR junction at Parks Highway, Denali Highway connecting to Paxson on Richardson Highway; 63°22′N 148°55′W. Hunting.

Canute (kuh-NOOT), village (1990 pop. 538), Washita co., W Okla., 6 mi/9.7 km E of Elk City; 35°25′N 99°16′W. In agr. area; cotton.

Canutillo, uninc. town (1990 pop. 4,442), El Paso co., extreme W Texas, on the Rio Grande, and suburb 12 mi/19 km NNW of downtown El Paso; 31°55′N 106°35′W. Old channel Rio Grande (N.Mex state boundary to W). In irrigated agr. area. Mfg. (steel fabrication, electrical equip.). Franklin Mts. State Park to E.

Canwood, village (1991 pop. 367), central Sask., Canada, 35 mi/56 km WNW of Prince Albert; 53°22′N 106°36′W. Grain elevators.

Canyon, county (☐ 603 sq mi/1,562 sq km; 1990 pop. 90,076), SW Idaho, bounded S by Snake R., and drained by Boise R.; ⊙ Caldwell; 43°38′N 116°43′W. Agr. area bordering on Oregon. Agr. (dairying; sheep, cattle; alfalfa, hay, oats, barley, wheat, corn, sugar beets, potatoes, vegetables; tree fruits). L. Lowell (Deer Flat Reservoir), 5 mi/8 km W of Nampa, is unit in Boise irrigation project, which includes most of co. Deer Flat Natl. Wildlife Refuge. Formed 1891.

Canyon, city (1990 pop. 11,365), ⊙ Randall co., extreme N Texas, in high plains of the Panhandle, near junction of Palo Duro Creek and Tierra Blanca Creek to form Prairie Dog Town Fork of Red R., and 18 mi/29 km SSW of Amarillo; 34°58′N 101°55′W. Elev. 3,566 ft/1,087 m. RR junction; market, shipping center for cattle and wheat area. Light mfg. Seat of West Texas A&M Univ. and Panhandle-Plains Historical Society Mus. Palo Duro Canyon State Park attracts tourists. Buffalo L. Natl. Wildlife Refuge is SW. Settled 1892, inc. 1906.

Canyon City, village (1990 pop. 648), ⊙ Grant co., NE central Oregon, 55 mi/89 km N of Burns, on Canyon Creek near its confluence with John Day R. 2 mi/3.2 km N; 44°23′N 118°57′W. Elev. 3,194 ft/974 m. Poultry, sheep, cattle. Strawberry Mt. Range to SE, with Strawberry Mt. Wilderness Area. Parts of Malheur Natl. Forest to N and S.

Canyon de Chelly National Monument (duh SHAI) [De Chelly, Span. corruption of Navajo *Tsegi* = rock canyon] (☐ 131 sq mi/339 sq km), Apache co., NE Ariz. The area contains the ruins of several hundred prehistoric Native Amer. villages, most of them built A.D. 350–1300. The spectacular cliff dwellings include Mummy Cave, with a 3-story tower house. Artifacts have been found, and there are numerous pictographs in rock shelters and on cliff faces. The earliest people living in the region were the Basket Makers, predecessors of the Pueblo. The Navajo came to the canyon c.1700, and it became their chief stronghold. In 1805 a

Span. expedition fought the Navajo in a rock shelter (dubbed Massacre Cave) in Canyon del Muerto (site of a prehistoric burial ground). In 1864 a U.S. cavalry force under Kit Carson engaged the Navajo in Canyon de Chelly. Park is within Navajo Indian Reservation; modern dwellers continue to live and graze livestock within boundaries. Est. 1931.

Canyon Diablo, gorge, Cocnino co., NE central Ariz., 30 mi/48 km SE of Flagstaff; 225 ft/69 m deep, 500 ft/152 m wide; formed by tributary of Little Colorado R. Settlement of same name in N, at S edge of Navajo Indian Reservation.

Canyon Ferry Dam, Mont.: see MISSOURI RIVER.

Canyon Lake, city (1990 pop. 7,938), Riverside co., S Calif., surrounding Railroad Canyon Reservoir (San Jacinto R.) 20 mi/32 km SSE of Riverside; 33°41′N 117°15′W. Privately inc. gated community, closed to general public. L. Elsinore State Park to W.

Canyon Lake 1 reservoir, Comal co., S central Texas, on Guadalupe R., 35 mi/56 km NNE of San Antonio; 15 mi/24 km long; 29°52′N 98°11′W. Max. capacity 1,129,300 acre-ft. Formed by Canyon Dam (219 ft/67 m high), built (1964) by the Army Corps of Engineers for flood control and water supply. **2** reservoir, S central Ariz., on Salt R., and c.35 mi/56 km ENE of Phoenix, in Tonto Natl. Forest; 33°34′N 111°26′W. Max. capacity of 57,900 acre-ft. Formed by Mormon Flat Dam (224 ft/68 m high, 505 ft/154 m long; completed 1925), unit in Salt R. irrigation project; concrete-arch dam used for irrigation and power.

Canyonlands National Park, (☐ 527 sq mi/1,365 sq km), mainly in San Juan co., also Wayne and Garfield cos., SE Utah. Est. 1964. Green R. joins Colorado R. at center of park. Located in a desert region, the park contains a maze of deep canyons and many unusual features carved by wind and water, including spires, pinnacles, and arches; surrounding mesas rise more than 7,800 ft/2,377 m. Cataract Canyon, through which the raging waters of the Colorado and Green rivers flow, contains one of the world's largest exposures of red sandstone. Island in the Sky, a plateau overlooking the junction of the Green and Colorado rivers, has walls that drop in giant steps 2,200 ft/671 m to the canyon floor. Upheaval Dome, pushed upward by the pressure of surrounding rock on underground salt deposits, contains a crater 1 mi/1.6 km wide and 1,500 ft/457 m deep. Also found in the park are many Native Amer. petroglyphs drawn on rocks c.1,000 years ago. Bighorn sheep, mule deer, and beaver live in the park.

Canyonville, town (1990 pop. 1,219), Douglas co., SW Oregon, 20 mi/32 km S of Roseburg, on Canyon Creek near its confluence with South Umpqua R.; 42°55′N 123°16′W. Timber. Umpqua Natl. Forest to E.

Caonao River (kah-o-NOU), Camagüey prov., Cuba; flows N-NW through central part of prov., through rich pasture and sugarcane region; forms boundary between Camagüey and Ciego de Ávila provs; empties into Jigüey Bay, just S of Cayo Romano.

Caonillas River (kah-o-NEE-yahs), c.25 mi/40 km long, W central P.R.; small affluent of the Arecibo, rises in the Cordillera Central. On it are L. Caonillas (artificial) and hydroelectric plant, adjoined NW by Dos Bocas reservoir and hydroelectric project. Caonillas Dam was dedicated Jan. 3, 1949.

Cap à l'Aigle (kahp ah LE-gluh), village (1991 pop. 761), ⊙ Charlevoix East co., SE central Que., Canada, on the St. Lawrence R., and 2 mi/3 km ENE of La Malbaie. Resort.

Cap Chat (kahp SHAH), village (1991 pop. 2,926), E Que., Canada, on N Gaspé Peninsula, on the St. Lawrence R., and 40 mi/64 km ENE of Matane; 49°05′N 66°41′W. Lumbering, dairying.

Cap de la Madeleine (kahp duh lah mahd-LEN), city (1991 pop. 33,716), S Que., Canada, at the confluence of the St. Maurice and St. Lawrence rivers; 46°22′N 72°30′W. Mfg. (paper prods., plywood, aluminum prods., apparel). The shrine and sanctuary of Nôtre Dame du Cap is here.

Cap Estate, resort (1991 pop. 387), N St. Lucia, 7 mi/11.3 km NNE of Castries. Area of luxury homes and expensive hotels.

Cap, Le, Haiti: see CAP-HAÏTIEN.

Cap Saint Ignace (kahp se-tee-NYAHS), village (1991 pop. 2,990), SE Que., Canada, on the St. Lawrence R., and 6 mi/10 km ENE of Montmagny, opposite the Île aux Grues. Dairying, lumbering.

Cap Santé (kap sah-TAI), village (1991 pop. 2,563), ⊙ Portneuf co., S central Que., Canada, on the St. Lawrence R., and 30 mi/48 km W of Quebec. Agr.

Capac (KA-pak), town (1990 pop. 1,583), St. Clair co., E Mich., 25 mi/40 km W of Port Huron; 43°00′N 82°55′W. In farm area (livestock; vegetables, sugar beets, grain); dairying. Mfg. (transportation equipment). Inc. 1873.

Caparra (kah-PAH-rah), ruins in N P.R., adjoining Fort Buchanan, 4 mi/6.4 km S of San Juan. First Eur. settlement in P.R., founded 1508 by Ponce de León, abandoned 1521.

Capco No. 1 Dam, Calif. and Oregon: see KLAMATH RIVER.

Cape Bald, lobster-fishing village, SE N.B., Canada, on Northumberland Strait, 12 mi/19 km E of Shediac.

Cape Breton (BRE-tuhn), county (☐ 972 sq mi/2,517 sq km; 1991 pop. 120,098), E N.S., Canada, on E part of Cape Breton Isl.; ⊙ Sydney. Coal mining.

Cape Breton Highlands National Park (BRE-tuhn), 367 sq mi/951 sq km, N Cape Breton Island, N. S., Canada. Covers a large tableland and includes sections of the rugged Atlantic coastline. Est. 1936.

Cape Breton Island, (☐ 3,970 sq mi/10,282 sq km), forming the NE part of N.S., and separated from the mainland by the narrow Gut, or Strait, of Canso, Canada; 46°10′N 60°45′W. The easternmost point is called Cape Breton. The center of the isl. is occupied by the Bras d'Or salt lakes. Gently sloping in the S, the isl. rises to rugged hills in the wilder N part. The inhabitants are mainly of Scottish Highlander descent. There are many summer resorts on the lakes and fishing villages on the coast. In the NE are steelworks dependent on the extensive Sydney coal fields. The Cabot Trail, a scenic road through Cape Breton Highlands Natl. Park, commemorates the discovery of Cape Breton Isl. in 1497 by John Cabot. The island was a Fr. possession from 1632 to 1763. After the Peace of Utrecht (1713), many Acadians migrated here from mainland N.S., which was ceded to the English. They renamed the isl. Île Royale and established the fortress at Louisburg. With the final cession of Canada to the British (1763), Cape Breton was attached to N.S. It was made a separate colony in 1784, with Sydney as its capital, but was rejoined to N.S. in 1820.

Cape Canaveral (kuh-NA-vah-rul), town (☐ 7 sq mi/18.1 sq km; 1990 pop. 8,014), Brevard co., E central Fla., 7 mi/11.3 km N of Cocoa Beach, and just S of the John F. Kennedy Space Center; 28°23′N 80°36′W. Mfg. (metal prods., fishing boats, machining, space shuttle components).

Cape Canaveral (kuh-NA-vah-rul), low, sandy promontory extending E into the Atlantic Ocean from a barrier isl., E central Fla., separated from Merritt Isl. by the Banana R., a lagoon; 28°23′N 80°36′W. Named (1963) Cape Kennedy in memory of President John F. Kennedy, it reverted to its original name in 1973. The John F. Kennedy Manned Space Flight Center of NASA is located here. Since 1947 the cape has been the principal U.S. launching site for long-range missiles, earth satellites, and manned space flights. The 1st U.S. space satellite (Explorer I; 1958); John Glenn, the 1st American to orbit Earth (1962); and Neil Armstrong, the 1st man on the moon (1969) were launched into space from the cape. In Nov. 1982, operational flights of space shuttles began, marked by the loss of the space shuttle Challenger and its crew above the cape in 1986. The region around Cape Canaveral has attracted many rocket and guided-missile–related industries. Patrick Air Force Base is nearby to the S.

Cape Carteret (kahr-tuh-RET), town (1990 pop. 1,008), Carteret co., E N.C., 20 mi/32 km E of Jacksonville, and 20 mi/32 km W of Morehead City, on Bogue Sound (Intracoastal Waterway; bridged); 34°41′N 77°03′W. Bogue Isl. and Atlantic Ocean to S; Croatan Natl. Forest to N. Mfg. (veneers).

Cape Charles, town (1990 pop. 1,398), Northampton co., E Va., 33 mi/53 km NE of Norfolk, in Eastern Shore area; Cape Charles, S tip of Delmarva Peninsula 8 mi. to SSE; 37°16′N 76°00′W. On harbor on Chesapeake Bay; Chesapeake Bay Bridge-Tunnel to SSE. RR terminus; RR barge ferry to Norfolk. Mfg. (concrete prods., fertilizer). Agr. (grain, vegetables, livestock, poultry). Limestone. Resort (fishing, bathing). Inc. 1886.

Cape Charles, village, SE Lab., Canada, on the Atlantic, on Cape St. Charles, 22 mi/35 km NW of Misery Point, Belle Isle; 52°13′N 55°40′W. Fishing; lumber.

Cape Cod, narrow peninsula of glacial origin (☐ 399 sq mi/1,033 sq km), SE Mass., extending 65 mi/105 km E and N into the Atlantic Ocean. It is generally flat, with sand dunes, low hills, and numerous lakes. The cape's familiar hook shape is a result of the action of winds and ocean currents on the sand and gravel of different glacial deposits. Bartholomew Gosnold, an Eng. explorer, visited the cape in 1602 and named it for the abundant codfish once found in surrounding waters. It is accessed by RR, road, and air. Fishing, whaling, shipping, and salt making were important until the late 1800s. Tourism and cranberry growing (Cape Cod is the nation's largest producer of cranberries) are the economic mainstays. Suburban development and pops. (particularly retirement communities) have gradually increased. Major retirement area. Towns on Cape Cod include Barnstable; Provincetown, site of the Pilgrim's 1st landing (1620); Falmouth, location of Woods Hole, an oceanographic center; and Bourne, through which the Cape Cod Canal passes. This lockless canal, 17.5 mi/28.2 km long, 32 ft/10 m deep, was built (1910–1914) from private funds and purchased by the U.S. govt. in 1927. The canal accommodates oceangoing vessels and cuts the distance bet. New York City and Boston by 75 mi/121 km. Parts of Cape Cod constitute Cape Cod Natl. Seashore (27,000 acres/10,927 ha; est. 1961; visitor center at Eastham). It contains beaches, sand dunes, heathlands, marshes, fresh-water ponds, and historic sites, including the first Marconi Wireless Station in the U.S. First transatlantic message sent Jan. 19, 1903; also famous lighthouses: Nauset Light and Highland Light.

Cape Cod Bay, S arm of Massachusetts Bay on Atlantic coast, E Mass.; enclosed by Cape Cod peninsula; c.25 mi/40 km wide.

Cape Cod National Seashore, SE Mass., see CAPE COD.

Cape Coral, city (☐ 117 sq mi/303 sq km; 1990 pop. 74,991), Lee co., SW coastal Fla., located on an estuary of the Caloosahatchee R.; 26°38′N 82°00′W. It is the major suburb of Ft. Myers, and is mostly a residential city that has grown rapidly along with the SW Fla. area. There are 2 industrial parks in the vicinity, and boatbuilding is an industry. A branch of the Univ. of S. Fla. is located in nearby Ft. Myers. Cape Coral has a cultural center and a historical mus. The city's pop. more than doubled bet. 1980 and 1990, and it was the fastest-growing city in the U.S. during that decade. Inc. 1970.

Cape Cruz, Cuba: see CABO CRUZ.

Cape Dorset, trading post (1991 pop. 961), SW Baffin Isl., SE Franklin Dist., N.W.T., Canada, on small isl. at S extremity of Foxe Peninsula, on Hudson Strait; 64°14′N 76°33′W. Radio station. Hunting, fishing, trapping. Major native settlement, native arts center; site of R.C. mission. Scheduled air service. Cape Dorset Wildlife Sanctuaries here.

Cape Elizabeth, residential and resort town (1990 pop. 8,854), Cumberland co., SW Maine, just S of Portland, and on S shore of Casco Bay; 43°33′N 70°12′W. Portland Head Light (1791) at tip of Cape Elizabeth peninsula. Two Lights and Crescent Beach State Park are here. Settled c.1630, set off from Falmouth 1765.

Cape Fear River, 202 mi/325 km long, E central N.C.; formed by the junction of the Deep and Haw rivers at Haywood (Lee and Chatham co. line); flows SE past Lillington, Fayetteville, Elizabethtown, and Wilmington, where it turns S as an estuary, enters Atlantic

Ocean 3 mi/4.8 km W of Cape Fear. Carolina Beach and Corncake inlets form E outlets to Atlantic Ocean. Longest river entirely within N.C. Dams and locks make the river navigable to Fayetteville, N.C.; its estuary forms part of the Intracoastal Waterway. During the colonial period the river was a main route to the interior. Receives Northeast Cape Fear R. from N at Wilmington; receives Black R. from NW 10 mi/16 km NW of Wilmington.

Cape Florida, Dade co., SE Fla., 5 mi/8 km SE of Miami. At the SE end of Key Biscayne islet, it contains Bill Baggs State Park and Beach and a historic lighthouse.

Cape Girardeau (juh-RAHR-do), county (□ 586 sq mi/1,518 sq km; 1990 pop. 61,633), SE Mo.; ⊙ Jackson; 37°22′N 89°40′W. Bounded E by Mississippi R., crossed by Whitewater R.; drainage channels in S. Agr. (corn, soybeans, hay, peaches; cattle); lumber; dairy prods.. Mfg. at Cape Girardeau city and Jackson. Trail of Tears State Park in NE. One of 5 original counties of Mo. Formed 1812.

Cape Girardeau, city (1990 pop. 34,438), Cape Girardeau co., SE Mo., overlooking the Mississippi R., and 100 mi/161 km SSE of St. Louis; 37°18′N 89°32′W. It is a transportation, trade, and distribution center with factories that manufacture a variety of prods.. Mfg. (plastic prods., feed, textiles, printing, shoes, rubber prods., electronic equip., cement, paper prods., transportation equip., apparel). Its position on the river, near the confluence with the Ohio R., spurred its early growth. It lies in the New Madrid earthquake region. During the Civil War the city was occupied by Union forces. Known for its roses. Southeast Mo. State Univ. is here. Mo. Veterans' Home. The city is connected with Ill. by a highway bridge. Founded 1793, inc. as a city 1843.

Cape Halkett, Alaska: see HALKETT, CAPE.

Cape Harrison, promontory, NE Lab., Canada, coast of Labrador Sea, 150 mi/241 km NE of Goose Bay; 18 mi/29 km long, 10 mi/16 km wide.

Cape Hatteras, N.C.: see HATTERAS, CAPE.

Cape Hatteras National Seashore (HAT-uh-ruhs), Dare and Hyde cos., E N.C. The first natl. seashore. Includes 3 barrier isls. in Outer Banks: Ocracoke in SE, Hatteras in E, and Bodie Isl. in NE. Cape Hatteras Lighthouse in SE. Extends from Ocracoke Inlet NE to Cape Hatteras, then N to Oregon Inlet. State Highway 12 extends length of park, connected by ferry to Cedar Isl. and mainland in SW. Pamlico Sound to W, Atlantic Ocean to E and SE; Pea Isl. Natl. Wildlife Reserve in N. Ferry bet. Ocracoke and Hatteras isls., bridge across Oregon Inlet in N; Pea Isl. and Hatteras Isl. connected by land. Authorized 1937.

Cape Henry, Va.: see HENRY, CAPE.

Cape Island, S.C.: see ROMAIN, CAPE.

Cape Krusenstern (KROO-zuhn-stuhrn), trading post, N Mackenzie Dist., N.W.T., Canada, on Cape Krusenstern, on Coronation Gulf, at E end of Dolphin and Union Strait; 68°23′N 113°55′W.

Cape Krusenstern Monument (KROO-zuhn-stuhrn) (□ 1,030 sq mi/2,668 sq km), Alaska; authorized 1978. Archaeological sites of indigenous communities dating back 4,000 years. Site of Red Dog Zinc Mine.

Cape Lookout, N.C.: see LOOKOUT, CAPE.

Cape Lookout National Seashore (55 mi/89 km long; □ 44 sq mi /114 sq km), Carteret co., E N.C. Three barrier isls. in Outer Banks, Core Sound inside barrier (W), Atlantic Ocean to E and S. Historic Portsmouth Village in Ocracoke Inlet. Shackleford Banks (S), Core Banks (SE), Portsmouth Isl. (NE) extends from Beaufort Inlet, S of Beauford, SE to Cape Lookout then NE to Ocracoke Inlet, passenger ferries to Core Banks from Williston, Cape Lookout lighthouse from Harkers Isl. and to Portsmouth Isl. from Atlantic (town) with beaches, sand dunes, and salt marshes; Cape Lookout Lighthouse. Authorized 1966.

Cape May, county (□ 620 sq mi/1,606 sq km; 1990 pop. 95,089), S N.J.; ⊙ Cape May Courthouse; 39°04′N 74°51′W. Essentially a peninsula. Bounded on the N by Tuckahoe R. and Great Cedar Swamp, on the E by the Atlantic Ocean, and on the W by Delaware Bay; drained by Dennis Creek to the W and Great Cedar Swamp Creek to NE. Southernmost co. of N.J., settled in the 17th cent., with a long heritage of fishing, oystering, seafaring, and farming. Beach resorts at Cape May city, and along Atlantic Ocean barrier isls. at Wildwood, Avalon, and Sea Isle City each have distinctive character.

Cape May, city (1990 pop. 4,668), Cape May co., S N.J., at the end of Cape May peninsula, on the Atlantic Ocean; 38°56′N 74°54′W. One of the nation's oldest beach resorts, it became popular in the mid–19th cent., when it was known as the "President's Playground"; Lincoln, Grant, Arthur, Buchanan, Hayes, and Benjamin Harrison vacationed here. There are various mansions and Victorian hotels that display 19th-cent. architecture. The city is connected by ferry to Del., and a coast guard base is nearby. Settled in the 1600s, inc. 1857.

Cape May, peninsula, Cape May co., S N.J., on the Atlantic Ocean, at the S extremity of N.J. Has a lighthouse on Cape May Point at the entrance to Delaware Bay. Beach resort community of Cape May is located at the end of the cape.The cape is bisected by a canal, c.3 mi/4.8 km above the point, which was constructed by the Federal govt. in 1942–1943 as a war emergency measure to provide an alternative to the longer, more hazardous route around the cape. The canal is part of the New Jersey Intracoastal Waterway. In the past few decades erosion has washed away nearly ⅒ mi/³⁄₁₀ km of the cape at Cape May Point.

Cape May Court House, village (1990 pop. 4,426), ⊙ Cape May co., S N.J., 13 mi/21 km NE of Cape May, and 27 mi/43 km S of Mays Landing; 39°05′N 74°49′W. Agr. (dairy, sweet potatoes, poultry, vegetables) food processing. Historical mus. here. Laid out 1703.

Cape May Harbor, S N.J., artifically enlarged bay (3 mi/4.8 km long, .34 mi/.53 km wide) on Atlantic coast of Cape May Peninsula, just NE of Cape May city. Intracoastal Waterway channel enters from Jarvis Sound (N), connects WNW with Delaware Bay through Cape May Canal (1942–1943) across S tip of peninsula.

Cape May Point, resort borough (1990 pop. 248), Cape May co., S N.J., at tip of Cape May Peninsula, W of Cape May city; 38°56′N 74°58′W. Nearby is a lighthouse. Cape May Point State Park, a popular birdwatching area, is nearby.

Cape Negro Island, islet, SW N.S., Canada, at entrance of small Negro Harbour, 18 mi/29 km S of Shelburne; 43°31′N 65°21′W.

Cape Sable Island, SW N.S., Canada; 7 mi/11 km long, 3 mi/5 km wide; 43°28′N 65°36′W. Connected to the mainland by a causeway over Barrington Passage. Clark's Harbour (1991 pop. 1,076), a fishing port, is on the W coast.

Cape San Antonio, Cuba: see SAN ANTONIO, CAPE.

Cape Smith, abandoned trading post, SW Smith Isl. (13 mi/21 km long, 1 mi/2 km–3 mi/5 km wide), E Keewatin Dist., N.W.T., Canada, in Hudson Bay, off NW Ungava Peninsula, 10 mi. W of Akulivik, Que.; 60°44′N 78°28′W.

Cape Tormentine, N.B.: see TORMENTINE, CAPE.

Cape Vincent, village (1990 pop. 683), Jefferson co., N N.Y., on L. Ontario at its outlet via St. Lawrence R., 23 mi/37 km NW of Watertown; 44°07′N 76°19′W. A center for the Thousand Isls. resort, tourism, and recreation area. Has ferry connections to Wolfe Isl., Ont., and thence to Kingston, Ont. Port of entry. U.S. fish hatchery.

Capels (KAI-pulz), uninc. village, McDowell co., S W.Va., 3 mi/4.8 km NNW of Welch, on Tug Fork R. Semibituminous coal.

Capens, Maine: see DEER ISLE, Piscataquis co.

Capers Island 1 Beaufort co., S S.C., near NE entrance to Port Royal Sound, S of St. Helena Isl., 11 mi/18 km SE of Beaufort; c.2 mi/3.2 km long. Separated by narrow channels from Pritchard Isl. (NE), and Phillips Isl. (NW). **2** Charleston co., SE S.C., just SW of Bulls Isl., 15 mi/24 km ENE of Charleston; c.3 mi/4.8 km long. Separated from mainland to NW by Intracoastal Waterway.

Capesterre (kahp-STER), town, SE Basse-Terre isl., Guadeloupe, 11 mi/18 km ENE of Basse-Terre. Trading; liquor distilling. Sometimes called La Capesterre.

Cap-Francais, Haiti: see CAP-HAÏTIEN.

Cap-Haïtien (kahp–ah-ee-SYANG), city (1986 est. pop. 72,500), ⊙ Nord dept., N Haiti, on the Atlantic Ocean; 19°45′N 72°12′W. Haiti's 2d largest city, it is a seaport, commercial center, and tourist attraction. It has an internatl. airport. Agr. dominates the regional economy, with tobacco, sugar, coffee, cacao, bananas, essential oils, and pineapples as the major commercial crops; also sugar processing. Founded by the French in 1670, the city was the capital of colonial Haiti for a century. In 1791, Cap-Haïtien was captured by Toussaint L'Ouverture, leader of a slave rebellion. From 1811 to 1820 it served as capital of the kingdom of Henri Christophe, whose Sans Souci Palace and famous citadel, La Ferrière, still stand. Despite earthquakes (notably in 1842), bombings, and civil strife, Cap-Haïtien retains some picturesque colonial charm. It is also known as Le Cap and Cap-Francais.

Capilano River, 18 mi/29 km long, SW B.C., Canada; flows out of Coast Range, from Capilano Mt., S to entrance of First Narrows of Burrard Inlet. Mouth is W of Lions Gate Bridge. Capilano L. formed by Cleveland Dam. Suspension foot bridge 450 ft/137 m high, 230 ft/70 m long, above Capilano Canyon. Salmon hatchery.

Capistrano, Calif.: see SAN JUAN CAPISTRANO.

Capital View, uninc. town (1990 pop. c. 4,000), Richland co., central S.C., residential suburb 7 mi/11.3 km E of downtown Columbia, at SW edge of Fort Jackson Military Reservation.

Capitan (kah-pee-TAHN), town (1990 pop. 842), Lincoln co., S central N.Mex., 18 mi/29 km ESE of Carrizozo; 33°32′N 105°35′W. Elev. 6,351 ft/1,936 m. Health resort; trading point in agr. (cattle, sheep); mining region. Capitan Mts. to ENE; El Capitan Mts. to E (10,083 ft/3,073 m); area surrounded by Lincoln Natl. Forest; site of Smokey Bear Capitan Historical State Park (gravesite of Smokey the Bear).

Capitol Heights, town (1990 pop. 3,633), Prince Georges co., central Md., E suburb of Wash., D.C.; 38°53′N 76°55′W. A somewhat elevated older residential area not far from the Capitol near Fairview Heights, District Heights, and Forest Heights.

Capitol Hill, residential sect. in SE and NE Wash., D.C., and location of U.S. Capitol, Lib. of Congress, and other govt. offices; 38°53′N 77°00′W. The area S and E of the Capitol contains blocks of refurbished town houses, apartments, cafés, and shops.

Capitol Peak, Colo.: see ELK MOUNTAINS.

Capitol Reef, national park (□ 377 sq mi/976 sq km), S Utah, Wayne co., extends S deep into Garfield co., also Sevier and Emery cos. Highly colored sandstone cliffs bisected by gorges; named for a white, dome-shaped rock. Originally called Capitol Reef Natl. Monument, changed to Capitol Reef Natl. Park in 1971, when its boundary was greatly expanded to include entire 70-mi/113-km uplifted sandstone cliff. N part of park crossed by Fremont R. and State Highway 26; unimproved roads give access to isolated parts of park. Authorized 1937.

Capitol, U.S., building in which the Congress of the U.S. holds session. Located between Constitution and Independence avenues at 1st Street on Capitol Hill in Wash., D.C. The West Front overlooks the city; the impressive Capitol dome is visible from Va. The bldg. stretches from N to S more than 751 ft/229 m, and E to W 350 ft/107 m. There were 9 architects of the Capitol and construction began in 1793, with George Washington laying the cornerstone. The 1st wing was completed in 1800, and the S wing was completed in 1807. The British burned the Capitol in Aug. 1814. The present dome, made of cast iron, was not completed until 1863, during the presidency of Abraham Lincoln. The most impressive interior of the Capitol is the Rotunda. Beneath the bldg. is a subway linking the Capitol with the Senate and House office bldgs.

Capitola, city (1990 pop. 10,171), Santa Cruz co., W Calif., on N shore of Monterey Bay, a suburb 4 mi/6.4 km E of Santa Cruz, at mouth of Soquel Creek; 36°59′N

121°57′W. Flower growing. Forest of Nisene Marks State Park; New Brighton State Beach to SW. Inc. 1949.

Capon Bridge (KAI-pahn), village (1990 pop. 192), Hampshire co., NE W.Va., in E Panhandle, 17 mi/27 km ESE of Romney, on Cacapon R.; 39°17′N 78°26′W. Buffalo Camp for the Cultural Arts is here. Edwards Run Wildlife Management Area to N.

Capon Springs (KAI-pahn), uninc. village, Hampshire co., NE W.Va., in E Panhandle near Va. state line, 15 mi/24 km W of Winchester, Va. At N edge of George Washington Natl. Forest (includes Hawk Recreation Area to S). Mineral springs (waters shipped). Mfg. (wooden furniture). Was once a noted resort area.

Capreol (KAI-pree-ol), town (1991 pop. 3,809), S central Ont., Canada, near Wapitei L., 16 mi/26 km NNW of Sudbury; 46°42′N 80°55′W. Distributing center in mining (nickel, copper) and lumbering region.

Caprock, Texas: see LLANO ESTACADO.

Capron 1 (KAI-prawn), village (1990 pop. 144), Southampton co., SE Va., 15 mi/24 km W of Franklin; 36°42′N 77°12′W. In agr. area (cotton, peanuts, grain; livestock). **2** (KAP-rahn), village (1990 pop. 682), Boone co., N Ill., 12 mi/19 km NNE of Belvidere; 42°23′N 88°44′W. In agr. area (corn; dairying). Mfg. (filters, consumer goods). **3** village (1990 pop. 38), Woods co., NW Okla., 8 mi/12.9 km NNE of Alva; 36°53′N 98°34′W. In wheat and cattle area.

Cap-Rouge, village (1991 pop. 14,105), S central Que., Canada, suburb SW of Quebec City, on NW shore of St. Lawrence R., at mouth of Cap Rouge R.; 46°45′N 71°21′W. Campus of St-Augustin-et-Notre-Dame-de-Foy seminary.

Captain Cook, town (1990 pop. 2,595), W Hawaii isl., Hawaii, co., Hawaii, 52 mi/84 km WSW of Hilo, 1.5 mi/2.4 km inland from Kona (W) Coast; 19°30′N 155°54′W. Cattle, coffee, fruit. Tourism. Cook's Heiau (Temple), Captain Cook Monument, and Cook Point Lighthouse to W; Kealakekua Bay State Underwater Park to SW; Hikiau Heiau to SW; Honaunau Forest Reserve to NE.

Captiva Island (kap-TEE-vuh), SW Fla., narrow barrier island (c.7 mi/11.3 km long) in Gulf of Mexico N of Sanibel Isl.; partly shelters Pine Isl. Sound (E); 26°28′N 82°07′W. Site of Captiva, a fishing village and resort. Captiva Pass is an inlet c.5 mi/8 km N of Captiva village and at S end of Lacosta Isl.

Capulalpam de Mendéz (kah-POO-lahl-pahm), town (1990 pop. 1,427), E Oaxaca, Mexico, 3 mi/5 km ESE of Ixtlán de Juárez; 17°15′N 96°29′W. Elev. 6,496 ft/1,980 m. In the Sierra de Juárez. Temperate climate to cold at higher elevs. Agr. (cereals, fruits), and active mining. Road connects with Ixtlán de Juárez.

Capulhuac de Mirafuentes (kah-POOL-wak dai mee-rah-FWEN-tes), town (1990 pop. 13,187), ⊙ Capulhuac municipio, Mexico state, central Mexico, 28 mi/45 km W of Mexico city. Elev. 8,527 ft/2,599 m. Cereals, livestock.

Capulin Volcano (KA-pyoo-lin), national monument, NW Union co., NE N.Mex., 793 acres/321 ha, 25 mi/40 km ESE of Raton, N of Capulin. Large symmetrical cinder cone of inactive volcano, of geologically recent occurrence. Authorized 1916.

Caraballo (kah-rah-BAH-yo), town, La Habana prov., W Cuba, on RR, and 28 mi/45 km E of Havana; 23°03′N 81°55′W. Sugarcane, vegetables.

Caracas Bay (kuh-RA-kus), inlet of SW Curacao, Neth. Antilles, 5 mi/8 km SE of Willemstad. Noted for its scenery and old Span. fortress, it is now a petroleum-bunkering station, exporting fuel and diesel oil. Has 3 wharves, which accommodate large vessels. Formerly a quarantine station.

Caracol (kah-rah-KOL), agr. town (1982 pop. 1,114), Nord-Est dept., N Haiti, on the Atlantic, 11 mi/18 km ESE of Cap-Haïtien; 19°42′N 72°01′W. Sugarcane, fruit; sugar processing.

Carácuaro de Morelos (kah-RAH-kwah-ro), town (1990 pop. 2,454), in E central Michoacán, Mexico, 47 mi/75 km SE of Pátzcuaro; 18°48′N 101°00′W. Elev. 3,281 ft/1,000 m. Mountainous region near the Balsas R. Poor roads.

Carapichaima (KAH-rah-pee-CHEI-mah), village, W Trinidad, Trinidad and Tobago, 12 mi/19 km SE of Port of Spain.

Caraquet (KA-ruh-ket), town (1991 pop. 4,556), NE N.B., Canada, on Caraquet Bay, inlet of Chaleur Bay, near mouth of Caraquet R. (18 mi/29 km long), 36 mi/58 km ENE of Bathurst; 47°48′N 64°57′W. Fishing center (oysters, lobster, clams, smelt, mackerel). Acadian Historic Village, recreating period 1780–1890, is nearby. Founded 1758 by Breton fishermen.

Caraquet Island (2 mi/3 km long), NE N.B., in Chaleur Bay, at entrance of Caraquet Bay (6 mi/10 km long, 3 mi/5 km wide), 4 mi/6 km NE of Caraquet; 47°49′N 64°54′W.

Caratunk (KAHR-uh-tuhnk), township (1990 pop. 98), Somerset co., central Maine, on the Kennebec R. and Appalachian Trail, and c.33 mi/53 km above Madison; 45°12′N 69°52′W. In hunting, fishing area.

Caraway, town (1990 pop. 1,178), Craighead co., NE Ark., 22 mi/35 km ESE of Jonesboro; 35°45′N 90°19′W. Mfg. (electronic equipment, apparel). St. Francis Sunken Lands Wildlife Management Area to W.

Carberry, town (1991 pop. 1,481), SW Man., Canada, 26 mi/42 km E of Brandon; 49°52′N 99°21′W. Mixed farming, stock raising.

Carbet (kahr-BE), town, NW Martinique, at W foot of the Pitons du Carbet (3,960 ft/1,207 m; 3 pinnacles), 10 mi/16 km NW of Fort-de-France. Trading center; cacao growing, rum distilling. Sometimes called Le Carbet.

Carbó (kahr-BO), town (1990 pop. 3,941), N Sonora, Mexico, 7 mi/11 km N of Hermosillo; 29°42′N 110°57′W. Elev. 1,463 ft/446 m. Dry desert climate. On the Zanjón R., a tributary of the San Miguel R. On RR, 6 mi/10 km NE of Mexico Hwy 15.

Carbon 1 (KAHR-buhn), county (☐ 2,062 sq mi/5,341 sq km; 1990 pop. 8,080), S Mont.; ⊙ Red Lodge; 45°14′N 109°01′W. Irrigated agr. and mining region bordering on Wyo. on S; drained by Clark's Fork Yellowstone R. and Rock Creek; bounded on SE by Bighorn R. (Bighorn L. reservoir) and on N by Yellowstone R. Cattle, sheep, barley, oats, hay, corn, sugar beets, beans; coal, natural gas. Cooney Reservoir and State Park on W. Numerous small lakes in SW, mostly glacial. Sects. of Custer Natl. Forest in SE and SW; both forests include parts of Absaroka-Beartooth Wilderness Area, also part of Gallatin Natl. Forest in SW corner. Pryor Mts. Natl. Wild Horse Range in SE corner. Formed 1895. **2** county (☐ 388 sq mi/1,005 sq km; 1990 pop. 56,846), E Pa.; ⊙ Jim Thorpe; 40°55′N 75°42′W. Mt. region drained by Lehigh R., which forms part of N and NW boundary and flows S through co.; Blue Mt. ridge on S boundary; E part on Pocono plateau, part of NE boundary formed by Tobyhanna and Tunkhannock creeks. Some mfg. at Lehighton, Palmerton, and Nesquehoning. Former anthracite-coal-mining region. Agr. (corn, wheat, oats, alfalfa, hay, soybeans, potatoes; sheep, hogs, cattle, dairying). Appalachian Trail follows S boundary; Hickory Run State Park in N, Lehigh Gorge State Park in NW; Beltzville L. reservoir and Beltzville State Park in SE. Settled 1746 by Moravian missionaries; formed 1843. **3** county (☐ 1,484 sq mi/3,844 sq km; 1990 pop. 20,228), central Utah; ⊙ Price; 39°33′N 110°34′W. Mining and ranching region drained by Price R., bounded on E by Green R. Coal fields at Wattis (SW) and Sunnyside (SE); hay; cattle. Includes much of West Tavaputs Plateau. Scofield Reservoir and State Park and Price Canyon Recreation Area in NW. Part of Manti–La Sal Natl. Forest length of W boundary. Formed 1894. **4** county (☐ 7,964 sq mi/20,627 sq km; 1990 pop. 16,659), S Wyo.; ⊙ Rawlins; 41°41′N 106°55′W. Grain and livestock area bordering Colo. on S; watered by North Platte, Little Snake, and Medicine Bow rivers. Agr. (alfalfa, hay; cattle, sheep). Coal, oil, natural gas, uranium found here. Pathfinder Reservoir in N; part of Pathfinder Natl. Wildlife Refuge in N; Pathfinder Bird Refuge in N; large Seminoe Reservoir in N; Seminoe State Park in N center. Continental Divide runs N-S in W; part of Great Divide Basin in NW. Parts of Medicine Bow Forest in

SE and S; Sierra Madre (mts.) in S; Medicine Bow Mts. in SE. Formed 1868.

Carbon 1 town (1990 pop. 350), Clay co., W Ind., 6 mi/9.7 km NNE of Brazil; 39°36′N 87°07′W. In agr. and bituminous-coal area. Sawmill. **2** town (1990 pop. 60), Adams co., SW Iowa, near Middle Nodaway R., 6 mi/9.7 km NW of Corning; 41°02′N 94°49′W.

Carbon, village (1991 pop. 416), S Alta., Canada, on Kneehill R., and 19 mi/31 km W of Drumheller. Coal mining; wheat, barley, flax.

Carbon, village (1990 pop. 255), Eastland co., N central Texas, 38 mi/61 km N of Brownwood; 32°16′N 98°49′W. Agr. (peanuts, vegetables). Mfg. (livestock handling equipment). L. Leon to NE.

Carbon Cliff, village (1990 pop. 1,492), Rock Island co., NW Ill., near Rock R. (bridged), and 8 mi/12.9 km E of Moline; residential suburb of Rock Isl./Moline; 41°30′N 90°23′W. Agr. (cattle, corn, soybeans; dairying). Woods Airport to NE.

Carbon Hill, city (1990 pop. 2,115), Walker co., NW central Ala., 15 mi/24 km W of Jasper. Coal mining; lumber, boats, apparel. Inc. 1891.

Carbon Hill, village (1990 pop. 362), Grundy co., NE Ill., 20 mi/32 km SSW of Joliet and 2 mi/3.2 km NW of Coal City; 41°17′N 88°17′W. In agr. (corn, soybeans; dairying) and bituminous-coal area.

Carbon, Mount, Colo.: see CASTLE PEAK.

Carbonado (kahr-buhn-AH-do), village (1990 pop. 495), Pierce co., W central Wash., 23 mi/37 km SE of Tacoma, on Carbon R.; 47°05′N 122°03′W. Carbon R. Entrance to Mt. Rainier Natl. Park to SE. Snoqualmie Natl. Forest, including Clearwater Wilderness Area, to E.

Carbondale 1 (KAHR-buhn-dail), city (1990 pop. 27,033), Jackson co., S Ill.; 37°43′N 89°13′W. RR, division point and retail center of a coal-mining and farming area. Southern Ill. Univ. is a major employer. Memorial Day was inaugurated (1868) in Carbondale by Gen. John Logan. Giant City State Park and a wildlife refuge are nearby. Inc. 1869. **2** city (1990 pop. 10,664), Lackawanna co., NE Pa., 14 mi/23 km NE of Scranton, on the Lackawanna R.; 41°34′N 75°30′W. Former anthracite coal–mining center now has diversified mfg. (glass prods., construction material, apparel, lumber). Carbondale Clifford Airport 7 mi/11.3 km to NW. Fairview State Hosp. 3 mi/4.8 km to E (Wayne co.). Merli Sarnoski Park to NW, Archbald Pothole State Park to SW. Terence Powderly, the labor leader, was b. here. Inc. 1851.

Carbondale 1 town (1990 pop. 3,004), Garfield co., W central Colo., on Roaring Fork R., at mouth of Crystal R., just N of Elk Mts., and 11 mi/18 km SSE of Glenwood Springs; 39°23′N 107°12′W. Elev. 6,181 ft/1,884 m. In irrigated region producing livestock and grain; light mfg. Parts of White River Natl. Forest to N, E, and S. Ski Sunrise ski resort to NW. **2** town (1990 pop. 1,526), Osage co., E Kansas, 15 mi/24 km N of Lyndon; 38°49′N 95°41′W. In livestock and grain region. Osage State Fishing L. to S.

Carbonear (kahr-buh-NIR), town (1991 pop. 5,259), SE N.F., Canada, on Avalon Peninsula, on W shore of Conception Bay, 28 mi/45 km WNW of St. John's; 47°44′N 53°15′W. Commercial center and fishing port. Just N, at Victoria, is hydroelectric station.

Carbonera, Mexico: see VILLA JUÁREZ, town.

Carbury, village, Bottineau co., N N.Dak., port of entry near Can. border, 5 mi/8 km NW of Bottineau; 48°53′N 100°32′W. L. Metigoshe State Park, Turtle Mt. State Forest to NE.

Carcross, village (1991 pop. 183), S Yukon, Canada, on L. Bennett, 40 mi/64 km SSE of Whitehorse; 60°11′N 134°43′W. On RR; coal, gold mining; tourist center.

Cardale (KAHR-dail), uninc. village, Fayette co., SW Pa., 8 mi/12.9 km WNW of Uniontown, near Dunlap Creek; 39°57′N 79°51′W. Agr. (dairying).

Cárdenas (KAHR-dai-nahs), city (1994 est. pop. 63,000), N central Cuba, Matanzas prov., a port on Cárdenas Bay; 22°51′N 82°15′W. Industrial center; prefab housing plant, electric power substation, offshore oil fields; exports sugar and sisal. Mfg. includes tobacco, beer, and soap. A fishing fleet is based here.

Founded in 1828 as a shipping point for the sugar industry of the surrounding area. Provides work force for hotel resorts of nearby Varadero.

Cárdenas 1 (KAHR-dai-nahs), city (1990 pop. 14,582) and township, San Luis Potosí, N central Mexico, on interior plateau, on RR, and 85 mi/137 km E of San Luis Potosí; 22°00′N 99°41′W. Agr. center (grain, cotton, fruit; livestock). **2** city (1990 pop. 61,017) and township, Tabasco, SE Mexico, near Grijalva R. and Chiapas border, 30 mi/48 km W of Villahermosa on Mexico Highway 180; 17°59′N 93°21′W. Agr. center (bananas, tobacco, coffee, rice).

Carderview, village, Johnson co., extreme NE Tenn., on Watauga Reservoir, 13 mi/21 km E of Elizabethton. Est. 1947–1948 following evacuation of former town of Butler, 3 mi/5 km E.

Cardiff, town (1990 pop. 72), Jefferson co., N central Ala., 12 mi/19 km NW of Birmingham; 33°38′N 86°55′W.

Cardiff, village (1990 est. pop. 500), Harford co., NE Md., 33 mi/53 km NNE of Baltimore. It is a heavily Welsh community near Pa. border. Slate quarries in Cardiff attracted Welsh miners starting in 1733. Whiteford, Md., and Delta, Pa., combined with Cardiff to form one community. The quarries are now abandoned.

Cardiff-by-the-Sea, uninc. village, San Diego co., S Calif., on the Pacific Ocean, 21 mi/34 km N of San Diego. Flowers, citrus fruit, vegetables, avocados. Resort area.

Cardigan (KAHR-di-guhn), village (1991 pop. 359), E P.E.I., Canada, on Cardigan R., near its mouth on the Gulf of St. Lawrence, 24 mi/39 km E of Charlottetown; 46°14′N 62°37′W. Mixed farming, dairying, potatoes.

Cardigan Bay, inlet (10 mi/16 km long, 7 mi/11 km wide at entrance) of Gulf of St. Lawrence, E P.E.I., Canada. On it is Georgetown.

Cardigan, Mount, N.H.: see ORANGE.

Cardin (KAHRD-in), village (1990 pop. 165), Ottawa co., extreme NE Okla., 6 mi/9.7 km NNE of Miami, near Kansas line; 36°58′N 94°50′W. In lead- and zinc-mining region.

Cardinal, village (1991 pop. 1,552), SE Ont., Canada, on the St. Lawrence, and 8 mi/13 km NE of Prescott, opposite Galop Isl., and at foot of the Galops Rapids; 44°47′N 75°23′W. Dairying, starch mfg.

Cardington, village (1990 pop. 1,770), Morrow co., central Ohio, 14 mi/23 km ESE of Marion; 40°29′N 82°54′W. In agr. area. Founded 1822.

Cardonal (kahr-do-NAHL), town (1990 pop. 766), in central part of Hidalgo, Mexico, 22 mi/35 km NW of Octopan; 20°36′N 99°80′W. Elev. 6,857 ft/2,090 m.

Cardston, town (1991 pop. 3,480), SW Alta., Canada, near the U.S. border; 49°12′N 113°19′W. It was founded in 1887 by Mormons from Utah under the leadership of Charles Ora Card, son-in-law of Brigham Young. The chief Mormon temple of Canada is here. It is a ranch and irrigation agr. center. Nearby is the Blood Reserve, the largest reserve for Native Americans in Canada.

Cardwell, city (1990 pop. 792), Dunklin co., in the bootheel of extreme SE Mo., near St. Francis R., 19 mi/31 km SW of Kennett; 36°02′N 90°17′W. Cotton, rice, soybeans, broom corn; mfg. (wood prods.).

Careenage (kuh-REE-naig), shallow inner harbor of Bridgetown, Barbados, where wooden boats were once careened and scraped. Now landing site for local tour boats and small pleasure boats.

Carefree 1 town (1990 pop. 1,666), Maricopa co., central Ariz., residential suburb, 27 mi/43 km E of downtown Phoenix, 2 mi/3.2 km E of Cave Creek; 33°49′N 111°55′W. Adjoins Scottsdale to S; Tonto Natl. Forest to E; Bartlett Resevoir to E and Horseshoe Lake Resevoir to NE, both on Verde R. **2** town, Crawford co., S Ind., 4 mi/6.4 km N of Leavenworth. Near Wyandotte Caves.

Carenage (ka-REN-ahzh), village, NW Trinidad, Trinidad and Tobago, just outside old U.S. naval base (W; now govt. bldgs.) and 3 mi/4.8 km WNW of Port of Spain. Coconuts; fishing.

Carencro (KER-in-kro), city (1990 pop. 5,429), Lafayette parish, S La., suburb 6 mi/10 km N of Lafayette; 30°19′N 92°02′W. In agr. area (cotton, rice, sugarcane; cattle; dairying); timber; mfg. (wood millwork, rubber pipe seals, fiberglass buildings, meat packing). Lafayette Reggae Festival. New Evangeline Downs thoroughbred race track to SE. Also known as La Chapelle.

Caretta (kuh-RET-uh), uninc. town (1990 pop. 850), McDowell co., S W.Va., 12 mi/19 km SSW of Welch.

Carey 1 uninc. village (1990 pop. 300), Blaine co., S central Idaho, 50 mi/80 km NE of Twin Falls, on Little Wood R. Timber; millwork. Cattle, sheep. Carey L. to NE; Lava Crater to SE. **2** village (1990 pop. 3,684), Wyandot co., N central Ohio, 15 mi/24 km ESE of Findlay; 40°57′N 83°23′W. Trade, shipping center for truck farming and dairying area; porcelain prods., rubber goods; limestone quarries. Shrine of Our Lady of Consolation is here. Plotted 1843, inc. 1858.

Cargo Muchacho Mountains (moo-CHA-CHO), Imperial co., SE Calif., small range in Colorado Desert near Colorado R., c.10 mi/16 km NW of Yuma, Ariz. Max. elev. 2,225 ft/678 m. Gold mines.

Caribbean National Forest (□ 44 sq mi/114 sq km), natl. reserves in P.R., consisting of the Toro Negro unit (center), 25 mi/40 km SW of San Juan, and Luquillo unit (NE), 10 mi/16 km SE of San Juan. Contains El YUNQUE peak. It is only tropical forest in U.S. Natl. Forest System. Over 100 billion gal/379 billion liters of annual rainfall, c.240 tree species, and 4 forest types. Highest interior mt. regions of the Cordillera Central, with wild game and tropical biota. Highest peak in forest is Cerro de Punta (4,389 ft/1,338 m). Reforestation program. Several hydroelectric projects. Summer resort area. Endangered native species, such as the P.R. parrot, are protected. Est. 1935.

Caribbean Sea, tropical sea (□ c.970,000 sq mi/2,512,300 sq km), arm of the Atlantic Ocean, Central America; 15°00′N 75°00′W. It is bordered on the N and E by the West Indies archipelago, on the S by S. Amer., and on the W by the Central Amer. isthmus. The Caribbean is linked to the Gulf of Mexico by the Yucatán Channel; to the Atlantic by many straits, of which the Windward Channel and Mona Passage are the most important; and to the Pacific Ocean by the Panama Canal. The Magdalena is the largest river entering the sea; L. Maracaibo is its largest embayment. Geologically, the Caribbean Sea consists of 2 main basins separated by a broad, submarine plateau. Cayman Trench, a trench bet. Cuba and Jamaica, contains the Caribbean's deepest point (24,721 ft/7,535 m below sea level). The Caribbean's water is clear, warm (75°F/24°C), and less salty than the Atlantic; the basin has a very low tidal range (c.1 ft/0.3 m). The Caribbean Sea has a counterclockwise current; water enters through the Lesser Antilles, is warmed, and exits via the Yucatán Channel, where it forms the Gulf Stream. Volcanic activity and earthquakes are common in the Caribbean, as are destructive hurricanes that originate over the sea or in the Atlantic. After the Caribbean was visited by Christopher Columbus in 1493, Spain claimed the area, and its ships searched for treasure. With the Span. discovery of the Pacific Ocean in 1513 the Caribbean became the main route of their expeditions and, later, of convoys. Pirates and warships of rival powers preyed on Span. ships in the Caribbean. Although Spain controlled most of the sea, Britain, France, Holland, and Denmark established colonies on the isls. along the E fringe. The 1800s brought U.S. ships into the Caribbean, especially after 1848, when many gold-seekers crossed the sea to reach Calif. via Panama. After unsuccessful Fr. attempts in the late 19th cent. to build a canal across Panama, the U.S., in 1903, assumed control of the project. The 1914 opening of the Panama Canal paved the way for increased U.S. interest and involvement in this strategic sea, sometimes called the "American Mediterranean." Several Caribbean isls. have U.S. military bases, many of which were established during World War II as support bases to protect the Panama Canal. The naval base at Guantanamo Bay in Cuba (est. 1899) is the oldest U.S. Caribbean base. U.S. policy since the Monroe Doctrine of 1823 has been to exclude foreign powers from the Caribbean; however, in 1959, Cuba became the first country to come under strong foreign (Soviet) influence. U.S. intervention in the affairs of Caribbean countries, such as the Cuban missile crisis of 1962, the landing of U.S. marines at Santo Domingo in 1965 and at Grenada in 1983, and the U.S. invasion of Panama in 1990, reflects the region's importance in U.S. eyes. This influence has disappeared with Soviet collapse and breakup of USSR. U.S. military bases are limited to Roosevelt Roads in P.R., Guantanamo Bay in Cuba, and the Panama Canal. Petroleum, iron ore, bauxite, sugar, coffee, and bananas are the main local prods. moved on the sea. Economically, the region is dependent on U.S. and Eur. patronage and a large tourism industry. The Caribbean Sea has also acted as a barrier, isolating the isls. and preventing the mingling of peoples on the scale characteristic of Latin America. In the 1990s, however, the increased need for labor due to the growth of tourism attracted immigrants to some of the isls. in the sea.

Cariboo Mountains (KAR-i-boo), range, c.200 mi/320 km long, E B.C., Canada, rising to 11,750 ft/3,582 m at Mt. Sir Wilfrid Laurier. It runs roughly parallel with the main Rocky Mt. range to the NE, from which it is separated by the Rocky Mt. Trench, occupied by the Fraser R. In the foothills to the W is the Cariboo dist., scene of the famous Cariboo gold rush of 1860. Many camps sprang up in the region, and much gold was taken out, but after 1866 the diggings declined. Many gold seekers stayed on in the region, and today several thousand make their living by a combination of mining, hunting, and farming. The Cariboo wagon road, built (1862–1865) by the govt., facilitated the settlement of the interior of the prov. It started from Yale, at the head of navigation on the Fraser R., and ended in the Cariboo dist. nearly 400 mi/640 km to the N. Bowron L. and Wells Gray provincial parks are in the Cariboo Mts.

Caribou, county (□ 1,798 sq mi/4,657 sq km; 1990 pop. 6,963), SE Idaho; ⊙ Soda Springs; 42°46′N 111°33′W. Mt. area bordering Wyo. (E) and crossed by Blackfoot R., passing through Blackfoot Reservoir in NW. Elev. 5,779 ft/1,761 m. Wheat, barley; alfalfa; cattle, sheep, hogs; dairying. Phosphate mines near Conda; large chemical mfg. and processing activities at Soda Springs. Part of Caribou Natl. Forest in E and NW. Small part of Cache Natl. Forest in S; part of Fort Hall Indian Reservation in NW corner; part of Grays L. Natl. Wildlife Refuge on N boundary. Formed 1919.

Caribou (KAR-uh-boo), city (1990 pop. 9,415), Aroostook co., NE Maine, on the Aroostook R., and c.50 mi/80 km N of Houlton; 46°52′N 67°59′W. A processing and shipping hub for a potato-growing region, it is also a winter sports center. Site of former Loring Air Force Base. Dairy prods., fertilizer and starch are also important. Inc. 1859.

Caribou Gold Mines (KA-ri-boo), locality, central N.S., Canada, 27 mi/43 km SE of Truro; 45°03′N 62°57′W. Gold reserves in area.

Caribou Island (KA-ri-boo), in Northumberland Strait, N N.S., Canada, 5 mi/8 km N of Pictou; 3 mi/5 km long, 1 mi/2 km wide; 45°45′N 62°44′W.

Caribou Lake (KAR-uh-boo), Piscataquis co., central Maine, 30 mi/48 km NW of Millinocket; 8 mi/12.9 km long, 1 mi/1.6 km wide; 45°52′N 69°18′W. Joined to Chesuncook L. (N) by channel; Pine R., the former outlet, submerged by lake's raised level.

Carice (kah-REES), village (1982 pop. 1,513), Nord-Est dept., NE Haiti, in the Massif du Nord, 25 mi/40 km SE of Cap-Haïtien; 19°23′N 71°50′W. Citrus fruit, coffeegrowing.

Carichi (ka-REE-chee), town (1990 pop. 1,540), in central Chihuahua, Mexico, 37 mi/60 km SW of Cuauhtemoc. Elev. 7,185 ft/2,190 m. Mountainous region (Sierra Tarahumara). In Tarahumara Indian area. Agr. (corn, wheat, beans, potatoes, wood prods., fruit); livestock and horse raising. Cold climate. Jesuit mission to Tarahumara Indians here.

Carichic, Mexico: see CARICHI.

Carillon (kah-ree-YOH), village (1991 pop. 193), SW Que., Canada, on Ottawa R. and 7 mi/11 km SSW of Lachute. Dairying.

Cross references are shown in SMALL CAPITALS. The pronunciation key is on page xv. The dates of population figures are on page xii.

Carite Forest Reserve, Puerto Rico: see GUAVATE.

Carite, Lake (kah-REE-te), reservoir, SE P.R., in the Sierra de Cayey, on headstream of the La Plata, and 6 mi/9.7 km N of Guayama. Water from the lake, diverted into small Guamaní R., operates 3 hydroelectric plants and, after traversing a 3,060-ft/933-m tunnel, reaches S coast. Carite Forest Reserve to NE.

Carl, town (1990 pop. 263), Barrow co., NE central Ga., 5 mi/8 km W of Winder; 34°00′N 83°49′W.

Carl Junction, city (1990 pop. 4,123), Jasper co., SW Mo., near Spring R., residential suburb of Joplin, 7 mi/11.3 km N of Joplin; 37°09′N 94°32′W. Dairying; wheat, soybeans, corn; light mfg.

Carl Sandburg Home, National Historic Site, Henderson co., SW N.C., at Flat Rock, 4 mi/6.4 km S of Hendersonville; "Connemara" Farm, home of author Carl Sandburg during his last 22 yrs. (1945–1967). Authorized 1968.

Carle Place, residential village (1990 pop. 5,107), Nassau co., SE N.Y., on W L.I., just E of Mineola; 40°45′N 73°36′W. Several shopping centers in the area.

Carleton 1 county (□ 1,300 sq mi/3,367 sq km; 1991 pop. 26,026), W N.B., Canada, on Maine border, intersected by St. John R.; ⊙ Woodstock. **2** county (□ 947 sq mi/2,453 sq km), SE Ont., Canada, on Ottawa R. and on Que. border; ⊙ Ottawa; 45°15′N 75°45′W. Includes municipalities of Napean, Kanata, Gloucester, and Vanier. Ottawa-Carleton regional govt. supersedes county administration. Dairying, mixed farming; cattle, maple syrup.

Carleton (KAHRL-tuhn), town (1990 pop. 2,770), Monroe co., extreme SE Mich., 10 mi/16 km N of Monroe; 42°03′N 83°23′W. Satellite community of Detroit, 25 mi/40 km SW of downtown. RR junction in farm area (wheat, corn; livestock); mfg. (glass prods.). Inc. 1911.

Carleton, village (1991 pop. 2,749), E Que., Canada, S Gaspé Peninsula, on Chaleur Bay, 13 mi/21 km ENE of Dalhousie; 46°15′N 63°40′W. Fishing port, resort.

Carleton, village (1990 pop. 144), Thayer co., SE Nebr., 10 mi/16 km NNW of Hebron, and on branch of Little Blue R; 40°17′N 97°40′W.

Carleton Island, Jefferson co., N N.Y., 1 of the Thousand Isls., in the St. Lawrence R., at Ont. line, 3 mi/4.8 km NE of Cape Vincent; 44°11′N 76°17′W. Isl. is 2.3 mi/3.7 km long.

Carleton, Mount (2,690 ft/820 m), N N.B., Canada, 50 mi/80 km SW of Dalhousie; 47°22′N 66°52′W. Highest in prov.

Carleton Place, town (1991 pop. 7,432), SE Ont., Canada, on Mississippi R., at N end of Mississippi L., and 28 mi/45 km SW of Ottawa; 45°08′N 76°09′W. Commuter suburb. RR shops; mfg., dairying, lumbering.

Carlin, town (1990 pop. 2,220), Elko co., N central Nev., on Humboldt R., near mouth of Maggie Creek, and 20 mi/32 km WSW of Elko; 40°43′N 116°06′W. Elev. 4,950 ft/1,509 m. RR center. Cattle, sheep; gold mining. Emigrant Pass to W (6,114 ft/1,864 m), U.S. Highway 80 pass bet. Tuscarora Mts. (N) and Cortez Mts. (S). South Fork State Recreational Area and part of Humboldt Natl. Forest to E. Settled 1868, inc. 1927.

Carlinville, city (1990 pop. 5,416), ⊙ Macoupin co., SW central Ill., near Macoupin Creek, 37 mi/60 km SSW of Springfield; 39°16′N 89°52′W. Bituminous coal mines, natural-gas wells; agr. (corn, wheat, livestock, poultry); nursery. Inc. 1837. Elaborate co. courthouse (built 1867–1870), and Blackburn Col. are here. Noted for its large concentration of Sears-catalog-purchased homes from early ½ of 20th cent.

Carlisle (KAHR-leil), county (□ 199 sq mi/515 sq km; 1990 pop. 5,238), W Ky.; ⊙ Bardwell; 36°51′N 88°58′W. Bounded W by the Mississippi R. (Mo. state line), N by Mayfield Creek; drained by Obion and West Fork Mayfield creeks. Gently rolling agr. area, W part in Mississippi flood plain (dark and burley tobacco, corn, hay, alfalfa, soybeans, wheat, sorghum; hogs, cattle, poultry; dairying; timber). Clay Wildlife Management Area to NE. Formed 1886.

Carlisle 1 (KAHR-leil), town (1990 pop. 2,253), Lonoke co., central Ark., 30 mi/48 km E of Little Rock, on Two Prairie Bayou; 34°47′N 91°45′W. Trade center for agr. area; rice milling; mfg. (land levelers, rice prods.). Founded 1871. **2** town (1990 pop. 613), Sullivan co., SW Ind., 10 mi/16 km S of Sullivan; 38°58′N 87°24′W. Bituminous-coal mining. Wabash Valley Correctional Inst. nearby. **3** town (1990 pop. 3,241), Warren co., S central Iowa, near Des Moines R., satellite community, 9 mi/14.5 km SE of Des Moines; 41°30′N 93°29′W. Brick and tile plant. RR junction. **4** (KAHR-leil), town (1990 pop. 1,639), ⊙ Nicholas co., N Ky., 15 mi/24 km ENE of Paris, in Bluegrass region; 38°18′N 84°02′W. Mfg. (pet foods, underwear). Est. 1816. **5** (KAHR-leil), town (1990 pop. 4,333), Middlesex co., NE central Mass., residential suburb 8 mi/12.9 km S of Lowell, near Concord R.; 42°32′N 71°21′W. Great Brook Farm State Park.

Carlisle 1 village (1990 pop. 4,872), Warren co., SW Ohio, 6 mi/10 km NE of Middletown; 39°34′N 84°19′W. **2** (KAHR-leil), village (1990 pop. 470), Union co., N S.C., 12 mi/19 km SE of Union in Sumter Natl. Forest; 34°35′N 81°27′W. RR junction. Industries include timber, livestock, and poultry.

Carlisle (KAHR-lil), borough (1990 pop. 18,419), ⊙ Cumberland co., S Pa., 17 mi/27 km WSW of Harrisburg, on Conodoguinet Creek; 40°12′N 77°12′W. Mfg. (electronics; paper, rubber, wood, food, and leather prods.; lumber; printing and publishing, machinery). In the last conflict (1754–1763) of the Fr. and Indian Wars, the Forbes (1758) and the Bouquet (1763) expeditions were organized here. A munitions depot during the Revolution, Carlisle was hq. for George Washington during the Whiskey Rebellion in 1794. Molly Pitcher is buried in the Old Graveyard. The borough was a stop on the Underground RR and was attacked during the Civil War by Gen. Fitzhugh Lee. Carlisle is the seat of the U.S. Army War Col. and Dickinson Col. Carlisle Barracks military reservation to E; Carlisle Regional Performing Arts Center, Carlisle Fairgrounds, Co. Historical Society; Kings Gap Environmental Education center to SW. Hessian Powder Magazine Historic Site is here; Appalachian Trail passes to E and SE. Inc. 1782.

Carlisle Bay (kahr-LEI), open roadstead (½ mi/⁸⁄₁₀ km long, ½ mi/⁸⁄₁₀ km wide), SW Barbados, B.W.I., on which Bridgetown is located; 13°05′N 59°37′W. Some larger vessels anchor here, while ships up to 14 ft/4 m draft can dock alongside the inner Careenage harbor in the city. Now a deep-water harbor accommodates most shipping.

Carlock, village (1990 pop. 418), McLean co., central Ill., 9 mi/14.5 km NW of Bloomington; 40°34′N 89°07′W. Evergreen L. reservoir to NE. Agr. (corn, soybeans; cattle).

Carlos (KAHR-luhs), village (1990 pop. 361), Douglas co., W Minn., 8 mi/12.9 km NNE of Alexandria; 45°58′N 95°17′W. Agr. area (dairying; poultry, livestock; grain). L. Carlos State Park to W.

Carlos A. Carillo (KAR-los ah kah-REE-yo), village (1990 pop. 19,221), Cosamaloapan municipio, Veracruz, SE Mexico, on Papaloapan R., and 5 mi/8 km E of Cosamaloapan; 18°30′N 95°40′W. Sugar refinery; alcohol prods. Formerly San Cristóbal.

Carlos, Lake (KAHR-luhs), Douglas co., W Minn., 4 mi/6.4 km N of Alexandria; 5 mi/8 km long (N-S), 1 mi/1.6 km wide; 45°57′N 95°21′W. Resorts. Drained to E by Long Prairie R. from N side of lake. Village of Carlos to E. L. Ida to W, L. Miltona to N; L. Carlos State Park at N end.

Carlos Rojas (KAHR-los RO-hahz), town, Matanzas prov., W Cuba, on RR and 12 mi/19 km S of Cárdenas; 22°51′N 81°11′W. In agr. region (sugarcane, fruit, sisal). The refineries and sugar centrals of Granma and Victoria de Yaguajay are 6 mi/9.7 km NW.

Carlow Island, Washington co., E Maine, just NW of Eastport and bet. Cobscook and Passamaquoddy bays. Linked to mainland and Moose Isl. by causeways.

Carlsbad 1 city (1990 pop. 63,126), San Diego co., S Calif., suburb 32 mi/51 km NNW of San Diego, and 4 mi/6.4 km SSE of Oceanside, on the Pacific coast; 33°07′N 117°17′W. Carlsbad's pop. more than tripled from 1970 to 1990. It has electronic and aircraft industries, machine shops, and a crystal silica quarry. Major agr. prods. are tomatoes, fruit, avocados; cattle, dairying; and flowers; the flower fields in bloom are a tourist attraction. Mfg. (computer parts, medical and dental equip., electronic equip., plastic and medicinal prods., machine tools). Mineral springs, 2 lagoons (1 freshwater and 1 tidewater), and many water sports facilities here. La Costa resort spa. Carlsbad and South Carlsbad state beaches. Settled in the 1880s, inc. 1952. **2** city (1990 pop. 24,952), ⊙ Eddy co., SE N.Mex., 76 mi/122 km SSE of Roswell, on the Pecos R.; 32°23′N 104°14′W. In a grazing and irrigated farm area. Elev. 3,550 ft/1,082 m. Terminus of RR spur to potash mines. Mfg. (concrete prods., printing and publishing, potash processing, steel fabrication, mining vehicles and equip., salt processing). Potash and salt mines to E. Other industries include agr., ranching, and tourism. The climate is mild, and, on Pecos R., Avalon Reservoir and Lake McMillan Reservoir, both to N, provide water recreation. The Carlsbad reclamation project, begun in 1906, serves more than 20,000 acres/8,094 ha. A 2-year branch of N.Mex. State Univ. is located in Carlsbad. A state zoological and botanical park is on the city's outskirts. CARLSBAD CAVERNS NATIONAL PARK to SW; Living Desert State Park is here; Brantley L. State Park to NW; Lincoln Natl. Forest, in Guadalupe Mts., to SW, include Sitting Bull Falls. Settled 1888. Inc. 1918.

Carlsbad, uninc. village (1990 pop. 100), Tom Green co., W Texas, 25 mi/40 km NW of San Angelo and on North Concho R. Cattle; cotton.

Carlsbad Caverns National Park (□ 73 sq mi/189 sq km), Eddy co., SE N.Mex., in the Guadalupe Mts., 5 mi/8 km N of Texas state boundary. Entrance (E end) 18 mi/29 km SSW of Carlsbad. Originally established as Carlsbad Cave Natl. Monument 1923; est. as a natl. park 1930. These connecting limestone caves in desert region, with remarkable stalactite and stalagmite formations and huge chambers, began forming c.5 million years ago as groundwater started dissolving the rock. The caverns, among the largest in the world, were discovered c.1900. The temp. of the caves remains constant at 56°F/13.3°C. Interior trail is electrically lighted for c.7 mi/11.3 km. The Big Room, 754 ft/230 m below the surface, is the most majestic of the many chambers; its perimeter is c.1.25 mi/2 km long. Each evening during the spring, summer, and fall, the countless bats that inhabit the cave swarm out to feed on insects. The park also contains 76 other caves (including Lechuguilla Cave and New Cave). Bounded by Lincoln Natl. Forest (Guadalupe Mts.) on W.

Carlstadt (KAHRL-stat), industrial borough (1990 pop. 5,510), Bergen co., NE N.J., 8 mi/12.9 km NNE of Newark; 40°49′N 74°03′W. Mfg. (chemicals, clothing, plastics, shoes, textiles, brushes, paints, food prods., and aluminum prods.). Inc. 1894.

Carlton, county (□ 875 sq mi/2,266 sq km; 1990 pop. 29,259), E Minn.; ⊙ Carlton; 46°35′N 92°40′W. Bordered on E in part by Wis.; drained in NE by St. Louis R., also by Kettle, Moose, and Nemadji rivers. Agr. area (dairying; poultry; alfalfa, hay, oats). Includes part of Fond du Lac Indian Reservation in N; part of Fod du Lac State Forest in N. part of Nemadji State Forest in SE corner; Jay Cooke State Park in NE. Moose L. State Park in S. County formed 1857.

Carlton 1 town (1990 pop. 282), Madison co., NE Ga., 10 mi/16 km WSW of Elberton; 34°02′N 83°02′W. Granite quarrying. **2** town (1990 pop. 923), ⊙ Carlton co., E Minn., 17 mi/27 km WSW of Duluth and 5 mi/8 km SE of Cloquet, on St. Louis R., 6 mi/9.7 km W of Wis. state line; 46°39′N 92°25′W. Elev. 1,089 ft/332 m. Agr. area (dairying; poultry; oats, alfalfa); mfg. (feeds, printing, rainwear). Jay Cook State Park to E; Fond du Lac Indian Reservation to NW. **3** town (1990 pop. 1,289), Yamhill co., NW Oregon, on North Yamhill R., and 30 mi/48 km SW of Portland; 45°17′N 123°10′W. Mfg. (processed meats, gloves, aprons). Agr. (berries, grapes, apples, pears, plums, peaches, cherries; poultry); dairy prods. Wineries. Siuslaw Natl. Forest to W; Tillamook State Forest to NW.

Carlton, village, S central Sask., Canada, near North Saskatchewan R., 40 mi/64 km SW of Prince Albert;

52°49′N 106°30′W. Dairying, mixed farming. Indian Treaty Diamond Jubilee celebrated here (Aug., 1936).

Carlton, village (1990 pop. 39), Dickinson co., central Kansas, 16 mi/26 km S of Abilene; 38°41′N 97°17′W. In wheat area.

Carlton Hill, N.J.: see EAST RUTHERFORD.

Carlyle (KAHR-leil), city (1990 pop. 3,474), ⊙ Clinton co., S Ill., on Kaskaskia R., and 13 mi/21 km WNW of Centralia; 38°37′N 89°22′W. Trade center of agr. area (corn, wheat, sorghum). Mfg. (boat seats, pallets, tablecloths). L. Carlyle to NE, popular fishing and boating area. Carlyle Dam and Fish Hatchery on E end of town. State fish hatchery is nearby. Eldon Hazlet and South Shore State Parks nearby. Laid out 1818, inc. 1837.

Carlyle, town (1991 pop. 1,181), SE Sask., Canada, at foot of Moose Mt., 50 mi/80 km NE of Estevan; 49°38′N 102°16′W. Grain elevators, lumbering, dairying.

Carlyle Lake, reservoir (□ 38 sq mi/98 sq km), Clinton co., S central Ill., on Kaskaskia R., 40 mi/64 km E of E. St. Louis; 38°37′N 89°21′W. Max. capacity 1,273,734 acre-ft. Formed by Carlyle L. Dam (62 ft/21 m high), built (1967) by Army Corp of Engineers for flood control; also used for recreation, water supply, and navigation. State parks on S shore.

Carlyss (KAHR-lis), town (1990 pop. 3,305), Calcasieu parish, La., 5 mi/8 km S of Sulphur; 30°10′N 93°22′W. In agr. area (sorghum, rice); crawfish ponds.

Carmacks (KAHR-maks), Indian village (1991 pop. 243), S Yukon, Canada, on Yukon R. and 100 mi/161 km NNW of Whitehorse; 62°06′N 136°19′W. Elev. 1,770 ft/ 539 m. River port. Only bridge crossing on Yukon bet. Whitehorse and Dawson. Coal mined.

Carman (KAHR-muhn), town (1991 pop. 2,567), S Man., Canada, on Boyne R. and 50 mi/80 km SW of Winnipeg; 49°30′N 98°00′W. Grain elevators, dairying, woodworking; hydroelectric power.

Carmangay (KAHR-muhn-gai), village (1991 pop. 251), S Alta., Canada, 35 mi/56 km NNW of Lethbridge; coal mining; grain elevators, dairying.

Carmans River, c.11 mi/18 km long, Suffolk co., SE N.Y.; rises in small lake in E central L.I.; flows generally S, past Yaphank, to Bellport Bay (inlet of Great South Bay) just E of Brookhaven.

Carmel (KAHR-muhl), city (1990 pop. 25,380), Hamilton co., central Ind., satellite community of Indianapolis, 6 mi/9.7 km SW of Noblesville; 39°58′N 86°07′W. Agr. area; mfg. (electronics and machinery, construction materials, printing, consumer goods, publishing, fabricated metal prods.).

Carmel (kahr-MEL), town (1990 pop. 1,906), Penobscot co., S Maine, 13 mi/21 km W of Bangor; 44°47′N 69°02′W.

Carmel, Calif.: see CARMEL-BY-THE-SEA.

Carmel Bay, Monterey co., W Calif., arm of Pacific Ocean S of Monterey Peninsula, 4 mi/6.4 km SW of Monterey, 3 mi/4.8 km long and ½ mi/⁹⁄₁₀ km wide. Carmel R. enters from E. Town of Carmel-by-the-Sea on E shore. Pebble Beach Golf Course on NE. Pescado Point on N, Point Lobos State Reserve on S.

Carmel Hamlet, village (1990 pop. 4,800), ⊙ Putnam co., SE N.Y., 13 mi/21 km W of Danbury (Conn.), and on L. Glenida (c. 1 mi/1.6 km long; part of N.Y. city water-supply system); 41°23′N 73°43′W. Trade center for dairying and summer-resort area. Part of Metropolitan N.Y. exurbia. L. Carmel and many reservoirs nearby.

Carmel, Lake, reservoir and resort lake, Putnam co., SE N.Y., 1.5 mi/2.4 km N of Carmel; 2 mi/3.2 km long; 41°26′N 73°40′W. Town of Lake Carmel on E shore.

Carmel, Mount (4,417 ft/1,346 m), Monterey co., W Calif., in Santa Lucia Range, 12 mi/19 km S of Monterey, 7 mi/11.3 km E of Pacific Ocean.

Carmel, Mount, Conn.: see HAMDEN.

Carmel Point, uninc. village, Monterey co., W Calif.,2 mi/3.2 km SSW of Carmel-by-the-Sea, on Monterey Bay of Pacific Ocean. Point Lobos State Reserve to W.

Carmel River, c.40 mi/64 km long, Monterey co., W Calif.; rises c.25 mi/40 km SE of Monterey, at S Ventana Cone, peak in Coast Ranges; flows generally, NNW,

past town of Carmel Valley to Carmel Bay at Carmel-by-the-Sea, 5 mi/8 km SSW of Monterey.

Carmel Valley, uninc. town (1990 pop. 4,407), Monterey co., W Calif., 11 mi/18 km SSE of Monterey, on Carmel R.; 36°30′N 121°43′W. Grapes; vegetables; dairying; cattle; mfg. (men's clothing, winery). Sierra de Salinas to NE, Santa Lucia Range to SW.

Carmel Woods, uninc. village, Monterey co., W Calif., 3 mi/4.8 km S of Monterey, near Carmel Bay. N of Carmel-by-the-Sea.

Carmel-by-the-Sea, city (1990 pop. 4,239), Monterey co., S Calif., 5 mi/8 km SSW of Monterey, S of Monterey Peninsula on Carmel Bay, at mouth of Carmel R.; 36°33′N 121°55′W. Agr. (grapes, strawberries, vegetables; dairying); mfg. (printing and publishing); winery; tourism, recreation. It is a tourist spot as well as an artists' and writers' community. Art shows and an annual Bach festival are held in the village. The bay, named in 1602 by Carmelite friars in Vizcaíno's expedition, is famed for its beauty. Mission San Carlos Borromeo, site of burial place of Father Junípero Serra. World-famous Pebble Beach golf course to N. Also called Carmel. Inc. 1916.

Carmen, town (1990 pop. 4,188), Nuevo León, N Mexico, on Salinas R., and 19 mi/31 km NNW of Monterrey; 25°50′N 100°20′W. Elev. 1,522 ft/464 m. On RR. Irrigated agr. region (cotton, corn, sugar; livestock).

Carmen, village (1990 pop. 459), Alfalfa co., N Okla., 35 mi/56 km WNW of Enid, on Eagle Chief Creek; 36°34′N 98°27′W. In agr. area (grain, livestock, poultry; dairy prods.).

Carmen 1 Mexico: see CIUDAD DEL CARMEN. **2** Mexico: see TEQUEXQUITLA.

Carmen Island 1 in Campeche, SE Mexico; 23 mi/37 km long, c. 2 mi/3.2 km wide. Forms narrow bar bet. the Laguna de Términos (S) and the Gulf of Campeche (N); 18°38′N 91°49′W. **2** (□ 59 sq mi/153 sq km), in Lower California, NW Mexico, in Gulf of California, off the peninsula's SE coast, 10 mi/16 km E of Loreto; 10 mi/16 km long, 2 mi/3.2 km–6 mi/9.7 km wide; 26°0′N 111°0′W. Elev. 1,575 ft/480 m. Barren, uninhabited. Salt on coasts.

Carmen Mountains, Texas: see CARMEN, SIERRA DEL.

Carmen River, c.150 mi/241 km long, Chihuahua, N Mexico; rises in Sierra Madre Occidental as Santa Clara R. 45 mi/72 km NE of Guerrero; flows N to lagoon 5 mi/8 km NNE of Ahumada. Often dry.

Carmen, Sierra del, N spur of the Sierra Madre Oriental in Coahuila, N Mexico, extends c. 80 mi/129 km NW from c.28°30′N 102°00′W to the Rio Grande (Texas border) at Big Bend Natl. Park; continued by its U.S. sect. Sierra del Carmen or Carmen Mts. Rises to over 8,924 ft/2,720 m.

Carmen, Sierra del, or **Carmen Mountains**, Brewster co., extreme W Texas, in the Big Bend; a NW extension of Sierra del Carmen (part of the Sierra Madre Oriental) of Coahuila, Mex., range is a group of ridges extending c.30 mi/48 km SE from point c.55 mi/89 km SE of Alpine, through BIG BEND NATIONAL PARK, to the Rio Grande (U.S.-Mex. border), where river's gorge (Boquillas Canyon) is a scenic feature. Sue Peaks (5,857 ft/1,785 m) have highest elev. of U.S. portion. One of main ridges is Sierra del Caballo Muerto or Dead Horse Mts. (c.22 mi/35 km long).

Carmi (KAHR-mei), city (1990 pop. 5,564), ⊙ White co., SE Ill., on Little Wabash R., and 32 mi/51 km NE of Harrisburg; 38°05′N 88°10′W. RR junction. Trade and shipping center in agr. area (wheat, corn, sorghum, cattle); mfg. (coal processing, rubber mixing, rubber prods., clothing). Coal, oil, natural gas in area. Inc. 1819.

Carmi, Lake, NW Vt., in Franklin town, 14 mi/23 km NE of St. Albans; 3 mi/4.8 km long.

Carmichael (KAHR-mei-kuhl), uninc. residential suburb (1990 pop. 48,702), Sacramento co., N central Calif., 9 mi/14.5 km ENE of downtown Sacramento, on the American R.; 38°38′N 121°19′W. Mfg. (ornamental metal work, printing and publishing, draperies); agr to SE (dairying; poultry; nursery stocks; corn, sugar beets).

Carmichaels (KAHR-mei-kuhls), borough (1990 pop. 532), Greene co., SW Pa., 11 mi/18 km E of Waynesburg;

near Muddy Creek; 39°53′N 79°58′W. Mfg. (conveyor belts, machinery); subsurface bituminous coal. Agr. (dairying, livestock).

Carnation, town (1990 pop. 1,243), King co., W Wash., suburb 19 mi/31 km E of downtown Seattle, on Snoqualmie R., at mouth of Tolt R.; 47°39′N 121°55′W. Timber; dairying, strawberries, poultry. Mfg. (tool and die, signs). Retail shopping center. Snoqualmie Natl. Forest to E; Tolt Reservoir to E.

Carnduff, town (1991 pop. 1,062), SE Sask., Canada, 55 mi/89 km E of Estevan, near N.Dak. border; 49°10′N 101°47′W. Grain elevators, dairying.

Carnegie 1 (KAHR-nuh-gee), town, Randolph co., SW Ga., 9 mi/14.5 km S of Cuthbert; 31°38′N 84°46′W. **2** town (1990 pop. 1,593), Caddo co., W central Okla., 20 mi/32 km W of Anadarko, and on Washita R.; 35°06′N 98°35′W. In agr. area (cotton, wheat, peanuts, corn); mfg. (concrete, furniture). Kiowa Headquarters and Tribal Mus.

Carnegie (KAHR-nai-gee), borough (1990 pop. 9,278), Allegheny co., SW Pa., an industrial suburb 5 mi/8 km SW of downtown Pittsburgh, on Chartiers Creek; 40°24′N 80°05′W. A steel town, it has coal mines and plants that make chemicals and electrical equip. Heavy Mfg. The Neville House was the home of Gen. John Neville, an officer in the Fr. and Indian Wars and the Amer. Revolution. The borough was named for Andrew Carnegie. Inc. 1894.

Carnes Mountain (10,000 ft/3,048 m), SE B.C., Canada, in Selkirk Mts., E of Glacier Park, 24 mi/39 km N of Revelstoke; 51°21′N 118°07′W.

Carnesville (KAHRNZ-vil), village (1990 pop. 514), ⊙ Franklin co., NE Ga., 15 mi/24 km SSE of Toccoa; 34°22′N 83°14′W. Light mfg. and clothing.

Carney 1 village (1990 pop. 25,578), Baltimore co., N Md., a suburb 8 mi/12.9 km NE of downtown Baltimore; 39°24′N 76°31′W. **2** village (1990 pop. 558), Lincoln co., central Okla., 21 mi/34 km S of Stillwater; 35°48′N 97°01′W. In agr. area.

Carneys Point, village (1990 pop. 7,686), Salem co., SW N.J., on Delaware R., 10 mi/16 km N of Salem; 39°42′N 75°28′W. Increasingly suburbanized area. Location of Salem Community Col.

Carnifex Ferry State Park, W.Va.: see GAULEY RIVER.

Carnot-Moon (kahr-NO), uninc. city (1990 pop. 10,187), Allegheny co., W Pa., a residential suburb 13 mi/21 km WNW of Pittsburgh, near Ohio R.; 40°31′N 80°12′W. Includes communities of Carnot and Moon, each with a pop. of c.5,000. Pittsburgh Internatl. Airport to SW.

Caro (KAHR-o), town (1990 pop. 4,054), ⊙ Tuscola, co., E Mich., on Cass R. and 28 mi/45 km ENE of Saginaw; 43°29′N 83°24′W. In farm area (livestock; sugar beets, beans, potatoes, grain); dairying, beet sugar refining; mfg. (plastics, carbide and ceramic tools, business forms, thermoplastic parts, electrical fuel pumps). Settled 1867; inc. 1871.

Caroga Lake (kah-RO guh), resort village (1990 pop. 800), Fulton co., E central N.Y., in the Adirondacks, 10 mi/16 km NW of Gloversville; 43°08′N 74°29′W. Small East Caroga and West Caroga lakes are here.

Carol City, uninc. residential city (□ 7 sq mi/18.1 sq km; 1990 pop. 53,331), Dade co., SE Fla., betw. Miami and Fort Lauderdale; 25°56′N 80°16′W. The city has become a growing middle-class suburb. Pro Player Stadium, home of the Miami Dolphins football team and the Fla. Marlins baseball team, and site of the New Year's Day Orange Bowl football game, is here.

Carol Stream, village (1990 pop. 31,716), Du Page co., NE Ill., suburb 24 mi/39 km W of downtown Chicago, 3 mi/4.8 km N of Wheaton; 41°55′N 88°07′W. Mfg. (steel prods., printing, electronic equip., consumer goods).

Caroleen (kar-o-LEEN), uninc. village, Rutherford co., SW N.C., near Broad R., and 15 mi/24 km W of Shelby. Grain, soybeans, poultry, livestock. Mfg. (rugs).

Carolina (kah-ro-LEE-nah), town (1990 pop. 177,806), NE P.R., 12 mi/19 km ESE of San Juan. Commercial and industrial center; mfg. (pharmaceuticals, chemical prods., electronics). Many banking institutions here; Univ. of P.R.–Carolina, Universidad del Caribe, and

Colegio Universitario del Este. Louis Muñoz Marín internatl. airport is located here.

Carolina, village, in Charlestown and Richmond towns, Washington co., SW R.I., on Pawcatuck R., and 32 mi/ 51 km SSW of Providence.

Carolina Beach, town (1990 pop. 3,630), New Hanover co., SE N.C., 14 mi/23 km S of Wilmington, bet. Cape Fear R. and the Atlantic Ocean to E, on Pleasant Isl., Cape Fear R. estuary to W, Carolina Beach Inlet (Intracoastal Waterway; bridged) to N; 34°2′N 77°54′W. Mfg. (machine parts). Carolina Beach State Park is here.

Caroline 1 county (□ 326 sq mi/844 sq km; 1990 pop. 27,035), E Md.; ☉ Denton; 38°52′N 75°50′W. On the Eastern Shore; bounded E by Del. state line, W by Choptank R. and Tuckahoe Creek. Agr. area (produce, esp. tomatoes; fruit, dairy prods., corn, soybeans, barley, poultry; livestock), with some timber (hardwoods, evergreens); vegetable canneries, poultry-dressing plants; mfg. paper prods. Formed 1774, the town took its name from Caroline Eden, the wife of Sir Robert Eden, the last royal governor of Maryland. **2** county (□ 538 sq mi/1,393 sq km; 1990 pop. 19,217), NE Va.; ☉ Bowling Green. Bounded NE by Rappahannock R., SW by North Anna R., S by Pamunkey R.; drained by the Mattaponi R.; 38°01′N 77°20′W. Ft. A. P. Hill Military Reservation in N. Agr. (hay, barley, wheat, corn, soybeans, tobacco, sweet and white potatoes; cattle); timber; stone quarrying. Formed 1728.

Caron, town, S Sask., Canada, 15 mi/24 km WNW of Moose Jaw. Wheat.

Caroni (KA-ro-nee), county (□ 214 sq mi/554 sq km; 1990 pop. 182,096), W Trinidad, Trinidad and Tobago, on the Gulf of Paria; 10°30′N 61°22′W.

Caroni (KA-ro-nee), village, NW Trinidad, Trinidad and Tobago, on Caroni R., 8 mi/12.9 km ESE of Port of Spain. Sugarcane growing and milling. Has new housing development.

Caroni River, c.25 mi/40 km long, NW Trinidad, Trinidad and Tobago; flows W to the Gulf of Paria just S of Port of Spain (Caroni Swamp). Partly navigable for flat-boats.

Caroni Swamp (KA-ro-nee), swamp, Trinidad, Trinidad and Tobago, SSE of Port of Spain, 10 mi/16 km E of Caroni, 5 mi/8 km bordering Gulf of Paria, W coast. Low area stretching from San Juan in the N to Waterloo in the S. Extensive mangrove forests, nesting place of white ibis and scarlet ibis, the natl. bird. Experiencing effects of development.

Carp Lake, village, Emmet co., N Mich., 5 mi/8 km SW of Mackinaw City, at W end of L. Paradise; 45°41′N 84°45′W. Resort Area.

Carp River, c.25 mi/40 km long, SE Upper Peninsula, Mich.; rises in Carp L. in SW Chippewa co.; flows SE to St. Martin Bay of L. Huron; 46°10′N 85°01′W.

Carpenter, town (1990 pop. 102), Mitchell and Worth cos., N Iowa, near Cedar R., 15 mi/24 km NW of Osage; 43°24′N 93°01′W. Limestone quarries, sand and gravel pits nearby.

Carpenter Dam, Ark.: see HAMILTON, LAKE and OUACHITA RIVER.

Carpentersville, village (1990 pop. 23,049), Kane co., NE Ill., on Fox R., satellite community 38 mi/61 km WNW of Chicago; 42°07′N 88°16′W. In agr. area (corn, soybeans, livestock, dairy prods.); mfg. (machine parts, paints, switches, metal fabrications, valves, steel forging, resins, fans). Settled 1834, platted 1851, inc. 1887.

Carpinteria, city (1990 pop. 13,747), Santa Barbara co., SW Calif., on the Pacific Ocean, 15 mi/24 km E of Santa Barbara; 34°23′N 119°31′W. Asphalt pits; ships citrus fruit (lemons), avocados, vegetables; flowers; cattle; mfg. (medical supplies, footwear, aerospace parts, fans and blowers, broadcasting equip.). Site of Carpinteria State Beach; Los Padres Natl. Forest to E. Estab. 1863 on site of Indian village visited by Portolá in 1769.

Carpio, village (1990 pop. 178), Ward co., NW central N.Dak., 24 mi/39 km NW of Minot, and on Des Lacs R.; 48°26′N 101°43′W. Upper Souris Wildlife Refuge to E.

Carquinez Strait (KAR-KEE-nez), W Calif.; 8 mi/- 12.9 km long, c.1 mi/1.6 km wide at narrowest point. Swift tidal strait connecting SUISUN BAY with N part (San Pablo Bay) of SAN FRANCISCO BAY. Part of deep water shipping channel to Sacramento. Contra Costa co. (S), Solano co. (N). Just SE of Vallejo is Carquinez Bridge, also RR highway bridges at Martinez.

Carrabassett River (kar-uh-BAS-et), c.40 mi/64 km long, W central Maine; rises in Franklin co. E of Rangeley L.; flows NE then SE, past Kingfield to the Kennebec above Madison.

Carrabassett Valley (kar-uh-BAS-et), township (1990 pop. 325) Franklin co., W Maine, on the Carrabassett R. and 27 mi/43 km N of Farmington; 45°04′N 70°16′W. Winter sports at Sugarloaf Ski Resort; condominium and lodge on mt.; seasonal homes and hotels nearby.

Carrabelle (KA-rah-bel), town (□ 4 sq mi/10.4 sq km; 1990 pop. 1,200), Franklin co., NW Fla., c.45 mi/72 km SSW of Tallahassee; 29°51′N 84°40′W. Port of entry on St. George Sound; resort and fishing center; exports lumber. Inc. as city in 1931.

Carrboro, city (1990 pop. 11,553), Orange co., N central N.C., suburb 11 mi/18 km SW of Durham and 1 mi/ 1.6 km W of Chapel Hill; 35°55′N 79°4′W. RR terminus. Mfg. (machinery, wooden cabinets, medical equip., electric motors). Agr. area (tobacco, grain, soybeans, poultry, livestock, dairying). Univ. L. reservoir to SW.

Carrcroft, uninc. village (1990 pop. 720), New Castle co., NE Del., residential suburb 4 mi/6.4 km NE of downtown Wilmington. Bellevue State Park to S.

Carrcroft Crest, uninc. town (1990 pop. 825), New Castle co., NE Del., residential suburb 5 mi/8 km NE of downtown Wilmington. Bellevue State Park to S.

Carrefour (kahr-FOOR), village (1982 pop. 129,470), Ouest dept., S Haiti, 5 mi/8 km W of Port-au-Prince; 18°32′N 72°25′W. Middle- and upper-class suburb of Port-au-Prince.

Carrera Island (KA-rer-ah), islet (□ 20 acres/8 ha), off NW Trinidad, Trinidad and Tobago, in the Gulf of Paria, 6 mi/9.7 km W of Port of Spain; 10°39′N 61°37′W. Convict depot. Sometimes called, together with small adjoining Cronstadt Isl., the Diego Isls.

Carriacou (KA-ruh-KOO), island (□ 13 sq mi/34 sq km; 1991 pop. 4,595), S Grenadines, largest isl. of the group, dependency of Grenada in West Indies, 30 mi/48 km NE of St. George's, Grenada; 7 mi/11.3 km long, up to 3 mi/4.8 km wide; 12°30′N 61°27′W. Hilly, indented isl. Rises to 980 ft/299 m. Grows cotton and limes. Main settlement is Hillsborough, on W coast.

Carrick's Ford, W.Va.: see PARSONS.

Carrier (KAR-ee-uhr), village (1990 pop. 171), Garfield Co., N central Okla., 8 mi/12.9 km NW of Enid; 36°28′N 98°00′W. Agr. and oil-production region.

Carrier Mills, village (1990 pop. 1,991), Saline co., SE Ill., 6 mi/9.7 km SW of Harrisburg; 37°41′N 88°37′W. In bituminous-coal region; agr. (sorghum, cattle). Inc. 1894. Near Shawnee Nat'l Forest.

Carriere (kar-ee-YAI), uninc. village (1990 pop. 700), Pearl River co., S Miss., 7 mi/11.3 km NNE of Picayune. Agr. area (cotton, corn, berries; cattle; dairying). Mfg. (beef processing, cabinets).

Carrigain, Mount (KER-uh-guhn) or **Carrigan**, peak (4,647 ft/1,416 m) of White Mts., Grafton co., N central N.H., 10 mi/16 km ENE of North Woodstock, in White Mt. Natl. Forest.

Carrington, town (1990 pop. 2,267), ☉ Foster co., central N.Dak., 43 mi/69 km NNW of Jamestown; 47°27′N 99°07′W. Services, livestock, wheat. RR junction. Arrowwood Natl. Wildlife Refuge to SE. Plotted 1882, inc. 1900.

Carrizal Point (kah-REE-sal), headland on Pacific coast of Colima, W Mexico, 9 mi/14.5 km W of Manzanillo; 19°05′N 104°27′W.

Carrizo Gorge, E San Diego co., S Calif., 60 mi/97 km E of San Diego, in Anza-Borrego Desert State Park. Spectacular canyon (c.11 mi/18 km long, more than 1,000 ft/305 m deep), at SE end of Laguna Mts., just N of Jacumba. Carrizo Creek (intermittent) flows E through canyon.

Carrizo Mountains, in Apache co., NE corner of Ariz., in Navajo Indian Reservation; Pastora Peak (9,412 ft/ 2,869 m) is highest point.

Carrizo Peak (kah-REE-zo), (9,650 ft/2,941 m), in Sacramento Mts., S central N.Mex., 9 mi/14.5 km ENE of Carrizozo.

Carrizo Springs, town (1990 pop. 5,745), ☉ Dimmit co., SW Texas, 11 mi/18 km S of Crystal City, near Nueces R; 28°31′N 99°51′W. Elev. 602 ft/183 m. RR-spur terminus, shipping and trade center of irrigated vegetable-growing area; also cattle; pecans, cotton, hay. Mfg. (blue jeans). Settled 1862, inc. 1910.

Carrizozo (kahr-i-ZO-zo), town (1990 pop. 1,075), ☉ Lincoln co., S central N.Mex., 20 mi/32 km NNW of the Sierra Blanca, 59 mi/95 km NNE of Alamogordo.; 33°38′N 105°52′W. Elev. 5,426 ft/1,654 m. Trade and cattle and sheep-shipping center. Carrizo Peak is 9 mi/ 14.5 km ENE; Valley of Fires Natl. Recreation Area, in the Malpais volcanic flow area, to W. Town laid out 1899 with coming of RR. Trinity Site, location of 1st atomic bomb test (July 16, 1945), is 33 mi/53 km to W; only open to public once each year. Jicarilla Mts. to NE.

Carro, El, Mexico: see VILLA GONZÁLES ORTEGA.

Carroll, plantation (1990 pop. 185), Penobscot co., E central Maine, 38 mi/61 km SE of Millinocket; 45°24′N 68°03′W. In hunting, fishing area.

Carroll 1 county (□ 642 sq mi/1,663 sq km; 1990 pop. 18,654), NW Ark.; ☉ Eureka Springs and Berryville; 36°20′N 93°31′W. Bounded N by Mo. line; drained by White and Kings rivers and small Osage Creek; situated in Ozark region. Agr. (cattle hogs, chickens, turkeys), dairy prods., pine and oak timber. Mfg. at Berryville. Mineral springs, health resorts. Tourism. Beaver L. Dam (White R.) in W; arm of Table Rock L. in NE corner; small part of Hobbs Wildlife Management Area in SW corner. Formed 1833. **2** county (□ 495 sq mi/ 1,282 sq km; 1990 pop. 71,422), W Ga.; ☉ Carrollton, 33°35′N 85°05′W. Bounded W by Ala. state line and SE by Chattahoochee R. Poultry-production and textile-mfg. area that is drained by Little Tallapoosa R.; cattle, hogs, poultry; lumbering and light mfg. Formed 1826. **3** county (□ 465 sq mi/1,204 sq km; 1990 pop. 16,805), NW Ill.; ☉ Mount Carroll; 42°04′N 89°55′W. Bounded W by the Mississippi; drained by Plum R. and Elkhorn Creek. Includes Mississippi Palisades State Park. Livestock, corn, hay, wheat, oats, produce; dairy prods.; mfg. refrigeration equip. Formed 1839. **4** county (□ 375 sq mi/971 sq km; 1990 pop. 18,809), NW central Ind.; ☉ Delphi; 40°35′N 86°34′W. Intersected by Wabash R.; drained by Tippecanoe R. (L. Freeman reservoir) in NW corner, and Wildcat and Deer creeks. Farming and dairying (rye, oats, corn, soybeans; hogs); mfg. (furniture, crushed limestone; meat and poultry packing, lumber milling, other mfg.); timber. Includes part of L. Freeman. Knob Lake Fishing Area in SW corner. Formed 1828. **5** county (□ 570 sq mi/ 1,476 sq km; 1990 pop. 21,423), W central Iowa; ☉ Carroll, 42°02′N 94°53′W. Prairie agr. area (cattle, hogs, poultry, corn, oats) drained by Raccoon, Middle Raccoon, East and West Nishnabotna rivers. Mfg. at Carroll. Bituminous-coal deposits. Swan L. State Park at center. Widespread flooding in 1993. Formed 1851. **6** county (□ 137 sq mi/355 sq km; 1990 pop. 9,292), N Ky.; ☉ Carrollton, 38°40′N 85°07′W. Bounded N by Ohio R. (Ind. state line), SE by Eagle Creek; drained by Kentucky and Little Kentucky rivers. Gently rolling upland agr. area in outer Bluegrass region (burley tobacco, hay, alfalfa, soybeans, corn; hogs, cattle, horses). Sand and gravel pits. Some mfg. at Carrollton. General Butler State Resort Park in center. Formed 1838. **7** county (□ 452 sq mi/1,171 sq km; 1990 pop. 123,372), N Md.; ☉ Westminster; 39°34′N 77°01′W. Bounded NW by Monocacy R., N by Pa. state line; drained by branches of Patapsco R. Piedmont region; dairying, stock and poultry raising; agr. (corn, wheat, potatoes, vegetables, apples); stone quarries; some mfg. (machinery, electronic equip.); lumbering. Formed in 1836. Takes its name from Charles Carroll of Carrollton, signer of the Declaration of Independence. Birthplace of Francis Scott Key, composer of the "Star Spangled

Banner." Western Md. Col., a private liberal-arts col. since 1867, is just NW of Westminster. Other points of interest are the farm of Whittaker Chambers where he buried the "Pumpkin Papers," evidence in the trial of Alger Hiss; the Carroll County Farm Mus.; Shriver Homestead (c.1797); Carroll County Courthouse (c.1838); Shellman House (c.1807).; the Uniontown Historic District and Western Md. RR Mus. Formed 1836. **8** county (☐ 634 sq mi/1,642 sq km; 1990 pop. 9,237), central Miss.; ⊙ Carrollton and Vaiden; 33°27′N 89°55′W. Drained by Big Black R. (forms part of SE boundary) and Yalobusha R. (extreme NW boundary). Agr. (soybeans, corn, wheat; cattle; timber). Formed 1833. **9** (KER-uhl), county (☐ 702 sq mi/1,818 sq km; 1990 pop. 10,748), NW central Mo.; ⊙ Carrollton; 39°25′N 93°30′W. Missouri R. on S, Grand R. on E. Wheat, corn, soybeans, pecans; hogs, cattle; mfg. at Carrollton and Bosworth. Formed 1833. **10** county (☐ 992 sq mi/2,569 sq km; 1990 pop. 35,410), E N.H.; ⊙ Ossipee; 43°52′N 71°13′W. Bounded E by Maine state line; SW by L. Winnipesaukee; Squam L. on W boundary. Agr. and recreational region; summer and winter resorts in L. Winnipesaukee area and White Mountains in S. Agr. in center and S (vegetables, nursery crops, corn, apples; cattle, hogs, poultry; dairying). Granite quarrying; some mfg. at Conway and Wolfeboro. Drained by Saco, Ellis, Bearcamp, and Ossipee rivers. Ossippe L. in E center; Squam L. in W; L. Wentworth in S, with Wentworth State Park on N shore; Ossippee Mts. in center; Pinkham Notch pass (2,032 ft/619 m) on N boundary; Crawford Notch pass (1,773 ft/540 m) and Crawford Notch State Park in extreme NW; Hemenway State Forest in center; part of White Mt. Natl. Forest in N and W; General John Wentworth State Historical Site in S; Several ski areas, especially in N; Pine River State Forest in SE; White Lake State Park in center; Echo Lake State Park in N. Formed 1840. **11** county (☐ 396 sq mi/1,026 sq km; 1990 pop. 26,521), E Ohio; ⊙ Carrollton, 40°34′N 81°05′W. Drained by small Sandy, Conotton, and Yellow creeks. Includes Atwood Reservoir. In the Unglaciated Plain physiographic region. Agr. area (livestock, dairy prods., corn); mfg. at Carrollton and Malvern (textiles, printing and publishing, fabricated metal prods., ceramic wall and floor tile); fire-clay quarries. Formed 1832. **12** county (☐ 596 sq mi/1,544 sq km; 1990 pop. 27,514), NW Tenn.; ⊙ Huntingdon; 35°59′N 88°27′W. Drained by Big Sandy R. and headstreams of the Obion. Hardwood lumber; clay; agr. area (cotton, corn, soybeans, sorghum, livestock, truck). Mfg. in McKenzie. Formed 1821. **13** county (☐ 477 sq mi/1,235 sq km; 1990 pop. 26,594), SW Va.; ⊙ Hillsville; 36°43′N 80°43′W. Independent city of Galax, on W boundary, separate from co. Drained by New R. In the Blue Ridge; bounded S by N.C. state line. Mfg. at Hillsville; agr. (hay, alfalfa, corn, clover, cabbage, apples, peaches; cattle; dairying); timber; limestone quarrying. Includes part of Jefferson Natl. Forest (including part of Mt. Rogers Natl. Recreation Area), New River Trail State Park in NW; Blue Ridge Parkway passes through SE, S. Formed 1842.

Carroll, city (1990 pop. 9,579), ⊙ Carroll co., W central Iowa, on Middle Raccoon R., and 50 mi/80 km W of Boone; 42°04′N 94°51′W. RR junction; mfg. (prefabricated bldgs.; refrigeration units; meat processing; casement windows and doors; feed). Has Franciscan hosp. Swan L. State Park to SE. Inc. 1869.

Carroll, town (1990 pop. 528), Coos co., N central N.H., 12 mi/19 km E of Littleton; 44°18′N 71°29′W. Drained by Carroll Stream and Ammonoosuc R. Agr. (livestock, poultry; nursery crops; timber); mfg. (asphalt). Became a well-known resort for the wealthy with opening of Mt. Washington Hotel in 1902. Includes resorts of Twin Mountain, Fabyan House, and Bretton Woods (scene in 1944 of UN monetary conference), Bretton Woods Ski Area. Part of White Mt. Natl. Forest in E Sugarloaf and Zealand Natl. Forest campgounds to S; Site of Twin Mt. Fish Hatchery. Mt. Washington Cog RR 6 mi/9.7 km to NW and then 6 mi/9.7 km to NE.

Carroll 1 village (1990 pop. 237), Wayne co., NE Nebr., 10 mi/16 km WNW of Wayne; 42°16′N 97°11′W. **2** village (1990 pop. 558), Fairfield co., central Ohio, 19 mi/31 km SE of Columbus, in agr. area; 39°47′N 82°42′W.

Carroll Gardens, W central section of borough of Brooklyn, N.Y. city, SE N.Y. Cobble Hill neighborhood to N. Known as Red Hook until present name coined in 1960s. An unusual plan for housing lots and row houses, developed in 1896 by Richard Butts, has given the community a special flavor, little changed by time: 11 broad allées lined with row houses but with lush, green front lawns and tree-lined streets that give the dist. its name. The pop. is dominated by Italians, originally coming mainly from S Italy and Sicily in late 19th cent. Carroll Gardens Historic Dist. encloses a small quiet residential enclave of row houses (late 1860s to early 1880s) built for middle-class merchants. Named after Charles Carroll of Md., a signer of the Declaration of Independence.

Carroll Valley (KER-uhl), borough (1990 Pop. 1,457), Adams co., S Pa., residential community 9 mi/14.5 km SW of Gettysburg, near Md. state line, on Toms Creek; 39°45′N 77°22′W. Location of ski resorts, covered bridges, Mont Alto State Forest. Appalachian Trail to W.

Carrollton 1 (KER-uhl-tuhn), city (1990 pop. 16,029), ⊙ Carroll co., W Ga., on the Little Tallapoosa R.; 33°35′N 85°05′W. Mfg. includes fiber-optic cable, ropes, yarns, stainless steel pipe, food processing, concrete, apparel, textile finishing, prefabricated homes, electrical wire, machinery, lumber, printing and publishing. State Univ. of W Ga. is here. Inc. 1897. **2** city (1990 pop. 2,507), ⊙ Greene co., W Ill., 30 mi/48 km NNW of Alton; 39°17′N 90°24′W. Trade center of agr. area; ships grain, livestock, dairy prods. Settled 1818, inc. 1861. **3** city (1990 pop. 6,521), Saginaw co., E central Mich., on Saginaw R., suburb 1 mi/1.6 km N of Saginaw; 43°27′N 83°56′W. Beet sugar refining; mfg. of asphalt mixes. **4** city (1990 pop. 4,406), ⊙ Carroll co., NW central Mo., near Missouri R.,30 mi/48 km S of Chillicothe; 39°21′N 93°30′W. Corn, wheat, soybeans; hogs; mfg. (paper prods., uniforms, concrete, sealants and adhesives). Settled 1818, inc. 1833. **5** city (1990 pop. 82,169), Dallas, Collin, and Denton cos., N Texas, a suburb 14 mi/23 km NNW of downtown Dallas; 32°59′N 96°54′W. Elev. 470 ft/143 m. Bounded on W by Elm Fork Trinity R. In a rapidly growing commercial and industrialized area. The city, whose pop. nearly quadrupled from 1970 to 1990, is near fringe of Dallas–Fort Worth Metroplex, nearly enveloped by new municipalities to N. Dallas–Fort Worth Internatl. Airport to SW. Mfg. (metal, plastic and paper prods., aircraft and auto parts, electronic equip., household items). Lewisville L. reservoir and State Park to NW. Founded by settlers from Carrollton, Ill. 1844; est. 1872.

Carrollton 1 (KER-rol-tuhn), town (1990 pop. 1,170), ⊙ Pickens co., W Ala., 30 mi/48 km W of Tuscaloosa. Lumber milling. **2** town (1990 pop. 3,715), ⊙ Carroll co., N Ky., 42 mi/68 km NE of Louisville, on the Ohio R., at mouth of Kentucky R.; 38°40′N 85°09′W. Agr. area (horses, cattle, hogs; corn, burley tobacco); mfg. (roll-form metals, children's rocking horses, speaker cabinets, concrete prods., metal tubes, asphalt, printing and publishing). General Butler State Resort Park is to SE, includes Ski Butler Ski Area. Inc. 1799 as Port William; renamed Carrollton 1838.

Carrollton 1 village (1990 pop. 221), a ⊙ Carroll co. (shared with Vaiden), Miss., 15 mi/24 km E of Greenwood; 33°30′N 89°55′W. In agr. (cotton, grain, soybeans; cattle; timber) area. **2** village (1990 pop. 100), Cattaraugus co., W N.Y., on Allegheny R., and 10 mi/16 km WNW of Olean, in Allegany Indian Reservation; 41°07′N 78°39′W. **3** village (1990 pop. 3,042), ⊙ Carroll co., E Ohio, 21 mi/34 km SE of Canton; 40°34′N 81°05′W. In agr. area (grain, wool); rubber goods, chinaware, brick. Laid out 1815.

Carrolltown (KER-uhl-toun), borough (1990 pop. 1,286), Cambria co., W central Pa., 23 mi/37 km NNE of Johnstown; 40°36′N 78°42′W. Mfg. (wooden furniture); strip coal (bituminous) mining. Agr. area (corn, hay; dairying). Laid out 1840, inc. 1858.

Carrollville, village, Milwaukee co., SE Wis., near L. Michigan, suburb 12 mi/19 km S of Milwaukee; mfg. Now part of City of Oak Creek.

Carrot River, town (1991 pop. 1,027), E Sask., Canada, 35 mi/56 km NE of Tisdale; 53°17′N 103°35′W. Dairying, wheat.

Carrot River, 250 mi/402 km long, E Sask. and W Man., Canada; issues from Wakaw L. (12 mi/19 km long, 1 mi/2 km wide), 35 mi/56 km SSE of Prince Albert; flows ENE, parallel to Saskatchewan R., crossing into Man. to Saskatchewan R. 6 mi/10 km W of The Pas. Valley is one of richest agr. regions of prov.; here the Chevalier de la Corne introduced (1754) 1st grain in the Prairies.

Carrsville, village (1990 pop. 98), Livingston co., W Ky., 16 mi/26 km NW of Marion, on the Ohio R.; 37°23′N 88°22′W. Agr. (burley tobacco, soybeans, grain; livestock). Mantle Rock Nature Preserve to S.

Carrville, town, Tallapoosa co., E central Ala., on Tallapoosa R. and 21 mi/34 km SSW of Dadeville. Yates Dam is just NW.

Carry Ponds, Somerset co., W central Maine, 35 mi/56 km NNW of Skowhegan; 3 lakes ranging from 1 mi/1.6 km to 2 mi/3.2 km in length.

Carson, county (☐ 924 sq mi/2,393 sq km; 1990 pop. 6,576), extreme N Texas; ⊙ Panhandle; 35°24′N 101°20′W. In high plains of the Panhandle; elev. 3,300 ft/1,006 m–3,500 ft/1,067 m. Drained by McClellan Creek (source), and small tributaries of Red and Canadian rivers. Cattle ranching and wheat, corn, hay region, underlaid by Panhandle natural gas and oil field, one of world's largest, with gas pipelines to several U.S. cities. L. Meredith Natl. Recreation Area and Alibates Flint Quarries Natl. Monument 1 mi/1.6 km beyond NW corner of co. Formed 1876.

Carson, city (1990 pop. 83,995), Los Angeles co., S Calif., an industrial and residential suburb of Los Angeles, 7 mi/11.3 km S of downtown; 33°51′N 118°16′W. Drained by Dominguez Channel. Oil refining is the major industry, but there is mfg. of fabricated metals, paper, and many other prods. Calif. State Univ. (Dominguez Hills which also has educational software industry). Nearly surrounded by city of Los Angeles; bounded by Compton on NE. Los Angeles R. to E.

Carson 1 town (1990 pop. 705), Pottawattamie co., SW Iowa, 23 mi/37 km E of Council Bluffs; 41°14′N 95°25′W. Shipping point for livestock and farm produce. **2** uninc. town (1990 pop. 990), Skamania co., SW Wash., 4 mi/6.4 km NE of Steveson, on Columbia R. (Bonneville reservoir), near mouth of Wind R. Timber; mfg. (machinery, sawmill).

Carson, village (1990 pop. 383), ⊙ Grant co., S N.Dak., 45 mi/72 km SW of Bismarck; 46°25′N 101°34′W. Dairy farms; poultry, wheat, corn. L. Tschida to NW.

Carson City, city (1990 pop. 40,443), ⊙ Nev., independent city, W Nev., 23 mi/37 km S of Reno in the Carson valley, drained in E by Carson R.; 39°08′N 119°44′W. Elev. 4,687 ft/1,429 m. Inc. 1875. Former seat of Ormsby co. In July 1969, the limits of Carson City were extended to coincide with the Ormsby co. boundary. Ormsby co. was put out of existence, making Carson City an independent city, not part of any co. and statistically having county equivalent status. Western Nevada Community Col. is located here.The city is a trade center for a mining and agr. area; mfg. (machine prods. and machinery, construction materials, agr. speciality prods., medical instruments, microelectronic components, molded rubber parts, printing and publishing); sand and gravel, agr. (cattle, poultry, vegetables, hay; dairying); gaming. The state govt. is a major employer, and tourism is economically important. The city was laid out in 1858 on the site of Eagle Station, a trading post established (1851) on the immigrant trail from Salt L. City to Calif. It served as a supply station for miners in the valley, achieved importance with the discovery (1859) of the COMSTOCK LODE, and later became the terminus of the RR carrying ore. In 1861, when the Territory of Nevada was created, the city was made the capital, and in 1864 it became the state capital. A U.S. mint, which closed in 1893, is occupied by the Nevada State Mus. Carson City Airport to NE of city center.

Parts of Toiyabe Natl. Forest and L. Tahoe Nevada State Park. Bounded W by L. Tahoe, extends to Calif. co. boundary near center of lake; Carson Range in W; Pine Nut Mts. in E.

Carson City, town (1990 pop. 1,158), Montcalm co., central Mich., on Fish Creek and 35 mi/56 km NNW of Lansing; 43°10′N 84°50′W. In agr. area (grain, beans, apples; livestock, poultry; dairy prods.); mfg. (plastic moldings, feeds). Settled 1854; inc. 1887.

Carson Lake, Churchill co., W Nev., intermittent body of water S of Carson Sink, 10 mi/16 km SSE of Fallon; 9 mi/14.5 km long, 6 mi/9.7 km wide. Surrounded by sections of Fallon Naval Air Station.

Carson Pass, E Calif., highway pass (elev. 8,650 ft/2,637 m) across the Sierra Nevada, in Alpine co., 17 mi/27 km SSW of S Lake Tahoe. State Highway 88 passes through. In Eldorado Natl. Forest. Discovered by Kit Carson when he guided Frémont's expedition into Calif. in 1843–1844; it was later crossed by an emigrant trail. Kirkwood Ski Area to W. Also called Kit Carson Pass.

Carson Range, W Nev., E spur of Sierra Nevada, extending N-S along E shore of L. Tahoe. Rises to 10,776 ft/3,285 m in Mt. Rose, 14 mi/23 km SSW of Reno. Much of it is in Toiyabe Natl. Forest; includes Mt. Rose ski areas and resorts.

Carson River (c.150 mi/241 km long), c. 35 mi/56 km long; Calif. and Nev.; west fork rises in Sierra Nevada near Carson Pass (8,573 ft/2,613 m), Calif.; flows NE past Woodfords, then N into Nev.; E fork rises in Sierra Nevada range, in SE Alpine co., E Calif, c.20 mi/32 km SSE of Marklerville; flows N past Marlerrville and into Nevada, past Minden; joins W fork 4 mi/6.4 km NW of Minden; main stream continues through Carson City, then NE past Dayton, through Lahontan Reservoir into Silver Springs, and past Fallon, flowing into Carson Sink; there is no outlet. Fed by melted snow. The river's course was followed by Calif.-bound travelers in the 1850s and 1860s. Lahontan Dam, part of the Newlands project, impounds river water for irrigation and produces electricity.

Carson Sink, swampy area (□ c.100 sq mi/259 sq km), part of larger playa, over 1,000 sq mi/2,590 sq km, Churchill co., W Nev. A remnant of Pleistocene L. Lahontan. Fallon Natl. Wildlife Refuge, Stillwater Natl. Wildlife Refuge, and Stillwater Wildlife Management Area are in S part; section of Fallon Naval Area in NE. Carson R. flows into sink.

Carsonville 1 village (1990 pop. 583), Sanilac co., E Mich., 8 mi/12.9 km E of Sandusky, near Black R.; 43°25′N 82°40′W. In agr. area (wheat, corn, sugar beets). **2** uninc. village, St. Louis co., Mo., residential suburb 8 mi/12.9 km NW of downtown St. Louis. Univ. of Mo. St. Louis campus to E.

Carstairs, town (1991 pop. 1,645), S central Alta., 35 mi/56 km N of Calgary; 51°32′N 114°06′W. Grain elevators, lumbering, clay mining, mixed farming.

Carswell, uninc. village (1990 pop. 500), McDowell co., S W.Va., 3 mi/4.8 km E of Welch.

Carswell Air Force Base, Texas: see FORT WORTH.

Cartagena (kahr-tuh-HAIN-uh), town, Cienfuegos prov., central Cuba, 19 mi/31 km N of Cienfuegos, on Natl. Highway; 22°26′N 80°26′W. Sugarcane, cattle.

Cartago, village, Inyo co., E central Calif., 20 mi/32 km S of Lone Pine on US 395, on W side of Owens L.

Carter 1 county (□ 412 sq mi/1,067 sq km; 1990 pop. 24,340), NE Ky.; ⊙ Grayson; 38°19′N 83°02′W. Drained by Little Sandy R. and Tygarts Creek. Hilly agr. area (burley tobacco, corn, hay, alfalfa; cattle); clay, sand, gravel, limestone; coal, iron and asphalt; timber. Mfg. at Grayson and Olive Hill. Tyarts State Forest, Cascade Caverns State Nature Preserve, and Carter Caves State Resort Park in W; Grays L. State Park and part of Grayson L. reservoir in S; also several caves and natural bridges in co., especially in W part. Formed 1838. **2** county (□ 506 sq mi/1,311 sq km; 1990 pop. 5,515), S Mo.; ⊙ Van Buren; 36°57′N 90°56′W. In the Ozarks; drained by Current R. Livestock; lumber, timber; tourism. Mark Twain Natl. Forest in E and SW; Ozark Natl. Scenic Riverways follows Current R. N-S through center of co.; Big Spring (former state park) S of Van Buren. More than ⅔ of co. is natl. forest, natl. park, or state forest. Formed 1859. **3** county (□ 3,348 sq mi/8,671 sq km; 1990 pop. 1,053), SE Mont.; ⊙ Ekalaka; 45°30′N 104°32′W. Plains area bordering on S.Dak. (E) and Wyo. (S); drained by Little Missouri R. and Boxelder Creek. Wheat, oats, hay; cattle, sheep. Source of O'Fallon Creek in NW. Medicine Rocks State Park in N; 2 sections of Custer Natl. Forest there, one in N center and the other in E. Formed 1917. **4** county (□ 833 sq mi/2,157 sq km; 1990 pop. 42,919), S Okla.; ⊙ Ardmore; 34°15′N 97°17′W. Drained by Washita R. and by small Walnut and Caddo creeks. Includes a sect. of the Arbuckle Mts. (recreation area) in far N, and part of L. Murray (state park; recreation). Stock raising (horses, cattle, sheep). Oil and natural-gas wells. Some agr. (wheat, hay, vegetables, corn, peanuts; dairying). Mfg. at Ardmore. Part of L. Murray reservoir and L. Murray State Park and Lodge on S boundary. Formed 1907. **5** county (□ 355 sq mi/919 sq km; 1990 pop. 51,505), NE Tenn.; ⊙ Elizabethton; 36°18′N 82°08′W. Borders S and SE on N.C.; Unaka Mts. lie along boundary; Roan Mt. in S; drained by Watauga and Doe rivers. Includes parts of Cherokee Natl. Forest and Watauga L. reservoir. Timber, agr. (tobacco, grain; livestock; fruit); iron-ore deposits, limestone quarries. Mfg. at Elizabethton. Formed 1796.

Carter 1 uninc. village, Carter co., NE Ky., 27 mi/43 km W of Ashland. Mfg. (crushed limestone); tobacco. Carter Caves State Resort Park to S. **2** village (1990 pop. 286), Beckham co., W Okla., 14 mi/23 km SSW of Elk City; near N Fork Red R.; 35°13′N 99°30′W. In agr. area; light mfg. **3** village, Tripp co., S S.Dak., 17 mi/27 km W of Winner; 43°23′N 100°12′W. Rosebud Indian Reservation (Todd co.) to W (co. line is also Mountain/Central time zone boundary).

Carter Caves State Resort Park, Ky.: see OLIVE HILL.

Carter Dome, N.H.: see CARTER-MORIAH RANGE.

Carter Lake, town (1990 pop. 3,200), Pottawattamie co., SW Iowa, located bet. Oxbow L. (also called Carter L.) on N and Missouri R. on S, suburb just NE of Omaha (Nebr.); 41°17′N 95°55′W. Nearly surrounded by city of Omaha on Nebr. side of river; separated from remainder of Iowa by change in river course. Mfg. (steel prods.).

Carter Lake Reservoir, Larimer co., N central Colo., on small sidestream of Dry Creek, 8 mi/12.9 km SW of Loveland; 3 mi/4.8 km long; 40°19′N 105°13′W. Max. capacity of 116,800 acre-ft. Formed by Carter L. Dam (184 ft/56 m high), built by the Bureau of Reclamation for irrigation and power generation.

Carteret (kahr-tuh-RET), county (□ 1,351 sq mi/3,499 sq km; 1990 pop. 52,556), E N.C., on the Atlantic Ocean; ⊙ Beaufort; 34°52′N 76°30′W. Bounded S and E by Atlantic Ocean (Onslow Bay, E by Raleigh Bay), NE by Pamlico Sound N in part by Neuse R. estuary. Bounded W by White Oak R., Bogue Sound in S, Core Sound in E. Tidewater area bordered by Bogue and Portsmouth isls. and other sand barriers includes part of Croatan Natl. Forest in W. Mfg. at Beaufort and Morehead City; fishing. Agr. area (corn, wheat, oats, soybeans, sorghum, potatoes, cotton). Resorts along coast. Intracoastal Waterway follows coast through Bogue Sound, then crosses co. N-S through Beaufort Harbor and canal. Cedar Isl. Natl. Wildlife Reserve in NE, Cape Lookout Natl. Seashore, on Core and Shackleford banks, in SE, including Cape Lookout (lighthouse). Fort Macon State Park in S. Formed 1722.

Carteret (kah-tuh-RAHT), borough (1990 pop. 19,025), Middlesex co., NE N.J., on Arthur Kill, opposite Staten Isl.; 40°34′N 74°13′W. It has oil and copper refineries and industries that produce steel and chemicals. Inc. 1906.

Carter-Moriah Range (KAR-duhr–mo-REI-yuh), Coos co., E N.H., range of White Mts. lying S of the Androscoggin R., E of Presidential Range, in White Mt. Natl. Forest. Carter Dome (4,843 ft/1,476 m) is the highest peak; other major peaks are Mt. Hight (4,690 ft/1,430 m); South Carter Mt. (4,458 ft/1,359 m); Middle Carter Mt. (4,645 ft/1,416 m); North Carter Mt. (4,539 ft/1,383 m); Imp Mt. (3,708 ft/1,130 m), site of Imp Face, a striking rock profile; Mt. Moriah (4,041 ft/1,232 m); Middle Moriah Mt. (3,775 ft/1,151 m); and Shelburne Moriah Mt. (3,748 ft/1,142 m). Appalachian Trail follows crest of range.

Carters Lake, Murray co., NW Ga., on the Coosawattee R.; 463 ft/141 m high, impounding Carters L. (6 mi/9.7 km long, max. capacity of 472,800 acre-ft.). Built in 1974 by the Army Corps of Engineers for flood control and hydroelectric-power generation.

Cartersburg, village, Hendricks co., central Ind., 4 mi/6.4 km W of Plainfield. Agr. area. Residential.

Cartersville, city (1990 pop. 12,035), ⊙ Bartow co., NW Ga., on Etowah R., 37 mi/60 km NW of Atlanta; 34°10′N 84°48′W. Mfg. includes beverages, steel, concrete blocks, motor vehicles, yarn dyeing, printing and publishing, clothing, furniture, textile printing, consumer goods, plastics. Mining (barite, ochre, manganese, limestone, marble). Allatoona Dam and Etowah Mounds State Park (featuring Indian mounds) nearby. Mississippian culture. Rapidly growing area due to its location near the I-75 corridor N of Atlanta. Founded 1832, inc. 1850.

Carterville 1 city (1990 pop. 3,630), Williamson co., S Ill., 7 mi/11.3 km W of Marion, 8 mi/12.9 km E of Carbondale; 37°45′N 89°04′W. Area of urban growth bet. Marion and Carbondale. In bituminous-coal-mining and agr. (sorghum, dairy prods., fruit) area. Mfg. (electrical equip., consumer goods, light mfg.). Site of John A. Logan Community Col. and School of Technical Careers. Crab Orchard L. and Natl. Wildlife Refuge are S. Inc. 1892. **2** city (1990 pop. 2,013), Jasper co., SW Mo., near Spring R., suburb just N of Joplin; 37°08′N 94°26′W. Former lead- and zinc-mining town. Mfg. (wood and concrete prods.). Laid out 1875.

Carthage 1 (KAHR-thij), city (1990 pop. 2,657), ⊙ Hancock co., W Ill., near the Mississippi, 14 mi/23 km E of Keokuk, Iowa; 40°24′N 91°08′W. Trade center in agr. area (corn, wheat, soybeans, cattle, hogs; dairy prods.); mfg. (cigars, electronic switches). At one time the seat of Carthage Col. Inc. 1837. In 1844, Joseph Smith, Mormon leader, and his brother were killed in the city jail by a mob; the old jail is now property of the Mormon Church. **2** city (1990 pop. 10,747), ⊙ Jasper co., twin city to Joplin, SW Mo., on the Spring R.; 37°10′N 94°18′W. Its limestone quarries are some of the largest of their kind, and Carthage marble (by which the limestone is marketed) is a major prod. Mfg. (food processing, machinery, construction materials, electronics, furniture). A Civil War battle was fought here July 5, 1861; the city was burned and rebuilt after the war. Inc. 1873.

Carthage 1 (KAHR-thij), town (1990 pop. 887), Rush co., E central Ind., on Big Blue R., and 10 mi/16 km NNW of Rushville; 39°44′N 85°34′W. Agr. area (corn; hogs, poultry); lumber, paperboard. **2** town (1990 pop. 458), Franklin co., W Maine, 16 mi/26 km WSW of Farmington; 44°37′N 70°25′W. Settled 1803, inc. 1826. **3** town (1990 pop. 3,819), ⊙ Leake co., central Miss., 48 mi/77 km NE of Jackson, near Pearl R.; 32°44′N 89°31′W. In agr. (cotton, corn; cattle, poultry; dairying) and timber area; mfg. (clothing, wire harnesses, lumber, poultry processing, rebuilt forklifts). Small Indian reservations (Choctaw) to N and SE. Natchez Trace (Natl.) Parkway passes to W. **4** town (1990 pop. 976), ⊙ Moore co., central N.C., 12 mi/19 km N of Southern Pines; 35°21′N 79°25′W. Tobacco, grain, soybeans, poultry, cattle, hogs; mfg. (textile fabrics, sweatshirts, concrete). House in the Horseshoe State Historic Site to N, scene of Revolutionary War conflict (1781). **5** town (1990 pop. 2,386), ⊙ Smith co., N central Tenn., on Cumberland R. (here crossed by Cordell Hull Bridge), near mouth of Caney Fork, and 20 mi/32 km E of Lebanon; 36°15′N 85°57′W. Tobacco market; plastic parts. Center Hill Dam near by. Founded 1804. **6** town (1990 pop. 6,496), ⊙ Panola co., E Texas, near Sabine R., 27 mi/43 km S of Marshall; elev. 302 ft/92 m; 32°08′N 94°20′W. Trade center for oil, natural gas, timber; poultry, cattle; mfg. (plastic cups, sheet metal fabrication, poultry processing). L. Murvaul to SW; Jim

Reeves Memorial, Tex Ritter Mus., both country singers from Carthage. Seat of Panola Col. (2-year); County Heritage Mus. Founded 1848.

Carthage 1 (KAHR-thij), village (1990 pop. 452), Dallas co., S central Ark., 29 mi/47 km E of Arkadelphia; 34°04′N 92°33′W. **2** village (□ 2 sq mi/5.2 sq km; 1990 pop. 4,344), Jefferson co., N N.Y., on Black R., and 15 mi/24 km E of Watertown; 43°58′N 75°35′W. In agr. area; mfg. (paper, machinery, concrete, tile, cheese). Small lakes (with summer residences and winter sports) nearby. As with the rest of the greater Watertown region, village has economically benefited from the rapid growth of nearby Fort Drum, although the social impact has been mixed. Settled before 1801, inc. 1841. **3** village (1990 pop. 221), Miner co., E central S.Dak.,15 mi/24 km NW of Howard, and on branch of James R. Poultry, livestock, grain. L. Carthage State Lakeside Use Area to NE.

Cartwright 1 village (1991 pop. 611), SE Lab., Canada, on S side of entrance of Sandwich Bay; 53°42′N 57°W. Lumbering. **2** village (1991 pop. 329), S Man., Canada, on Badger Creek and 60 mi/97 km SSE of Brandon, near N.Dak. border. Grain, mixed farming.

Caruthers, uninc. town (1990 pop. 1,603), Fresno co., central Calif., 12 mi/19 km SSW of Fresno; 36°33′N 119°51′W. Dairying, cattle, grapes, figs, olives, cotton, nectarines, vegetables, grain, sugar beets, almonds.

Caruthersville (kuh-RUH-thurz-vil), city (1990 pop. 7,389), ⊙ Pemiscot co., in the boot heel of extreme SE Mo., on Mississippi R., from which it is protected by high levees, and 19 mi/31 km NW of Dyersburg, Tenn.; 36°10′N 89°40′W. Agr. center. Cotton, rice, soybeans; mfg. (materials handling equipment, brake pads, wire-bound boxes, barges). In New Madrid earthquake region. Laid out 1857.

Carver, county (□ 376 sq mi/974 sq km; 1990 pop. 47,915), S central Minn.; ⊙ Chaska; 44°49′N 93°47′W. Bounded SE by Minnesota R.; drained in NW by South Crow R. Agr. area with fringe of Minneapolis/St. Paul urbanized area in NE (dairying; cattle, poultry, hogs; wheat, corn, soybeans, oats, hay, alfalfa). Numerous small natural lakes, especially in NE, including L. Waconia (in N center) and S extremity of L. Minnetonka (NE). Formed 1855.

Carver, town (1990 pop. 10,590), Plymouth co., SE Mass., 7 mi/11.3 km SW of Plymouth; 41°53′N 70°46′W. Cranberry-picking equip.; cranberry bogs. Includes North Carver village. Settled c.1660, inc. 1790. Myles Standish State Forest is just E.

Carver, village (1990 pop. 744), Carver co., S Minn., suburb 23 mi/37 km SW of downtown Minneapolis, on Minnesota R.; 44°45′N 93°37′W. Agr. area (dairying, poultry); mfg. (wood prods., furniture). Minn. Valley State Trail across river, to SE.

Carville (KAHR-vil), uninc. village (1990 pop. 1,108), Iberville parish, SE central La., on E bank (levee) of the Mississippi R., and 16 mi/26 km S of Baton Rouge; 30°13′N 91°06′W. Mfg. (hydraulic acid, styrene prod., polystyrene resin pallets). Hansen's Disease Center, once a leper colony and now a research and rehabilitation center for the disease, 2 mi/3 km W. Toll ferry across Mississippi R. to White Castle.

Carway, village, SW Alta., Canada, on Mont. border, 55 mi/89 km SSW of Lethbridge; 49°01′N 113°23′W. Coal mining; cattle, sheep, flax, sugar beets.

Cary, plantation (1990 pop. 235), Aroostook co., E Maine, 9 mi/14.5 km S of Houlton, on N.B. border (Canada); 45°59′N 67°50′W. In agr., lumbering area.

Cary, city (1990 pop. 43,858), Wake co., central N.C., rapidly growing suburb 8 mi/12.9 km W of downtown Raleigh; 35°46′N 78°47′W. Planned unit development; dramatic pop. increase in 25 years. Mfg. (industrial equip., printing, machinery, stone processing). State fairgrounds to NE. William B. Umstead State Park to N, Research Triangle Park to NW. Raleigh-Durham Internatl. Airport to N. Walter Hines Page b. here. Founded 1852; inc. 1870.

Cary 1 village (1990 pop. 10,043), McHenry co., NE Ill., adjacent to Fox R., 12 mi/19 km N of Elgin, satellite community of Chicago; 42°12′N 88°15′W. Mfg. (saws, circuit boards, heaters, seals, drill bits, valves, stripping machines). **2** village (1990 pop. 392), Sharkey co., W Miss., 32 mi/51 km N of Vicksburg on Deer Creek; 32°47′N 90°55′W. Agr. (cotton, corn, rice, soybeans; cattle; timber). Delta Natl. Forest to E.

Caryville 1 (KA-ree-vil), town (□ 3 sq mi/7.8 sq km; 1990 pop. 631), Washington co., NW Fla., on Choctawhatchee R., and 7 mi/11.3 km W of Bonifay; 30°46′N 85°48′W. Farming, lumbering. **2** town (1990 pop. 1,751), Campbell co., NE Tenn., 28 mi/45 km NW of Knoxville; 36°18′N 84°13′W. In coal, iron ore, tobacco region.

Casa (KAS-uh), village (1990 pop. 200), Perry co., central Ark., c.50 mi/80 km NW of Little Rock; 35°01′N 93°02′W.

Casa Blanca (KAH-suh BLAHN-kuh), town, La Habana prov., W Cuba, on E shore of Havana Harbor, just opposite Havana (connected by ferry); 23°09′N 82°20′W. Coaling station and oil depot. Site of Natl. Observatory of Meteorology, La Cabaña Fort (N), and the Cuban Navy Yard.

Casa Conejo (kah-sah KOH-NAY-ho), uninc. town (1990 pop. 3,286), Ventura co., S Calif., residential suburb, 13 mi/21 km E of Oxnard and 4 mi/6.4 km WSW of Thousand Oaks; 34°11′N 118°57′W. Santa Monica Mts. Natl. Recreational Area to S. Citrus, vegetables, nursery stock.

Casa de Oro-Mount Helix (kah-sah day oh-row), uninc. city (1990 pop. 30,727), San Diego co., S Calif., residential suburb 12 mi/19 km E of downtown San Diego; 32°46′N 116°57′W. Mt. Helix in N; Sweetwater Reservoir to S.

Casa Grande, city (1990 pop. 19,082), Pinal co., 43 mi/69 km SSE of Phoenix, S Ariz.; inc. 1915; 32°53′N 111°44′W. It lies in an irrigated farm area near the Casa Grande Mts. Cotton, sugar beets, alfalfa, cantaloupe, wheat, poultry, cattle. The city was named after an excavated pueblo that is included in Casa Grande Natl. Monument to NE. Casa Grande is a retail trade center of S central Ariz. Picacho Reservoir to E; Gila R. Indian Reservation to N; Tohono O'odham (Papago) Indian Reservation to S; Ak-Chin Indian Reservation to NW; Table Top Wilderness Area to W.

Casa Grande National Monument (□ 7/10 sq mi/2 sq km), Pinal co., S Ariz., N of Coolidge, c.40 mi/64 km SE of Phoenix. Built c.1350 by Hohokam Indians, is only prehistoric structure of its type still standing. Here are also ruins of villages and a mus. of Indian artifacts. Ruins of massive 4-story structure built from desert soil. Proclaimed 1892; est. 1918

Casar (KAI-suhr), village (1990 pop. 328), Clevand co., S N.C., 16 mi/26 km NNW of Shelby; 35°30′N 81°37′W. Cotton, grain, soybeans, poutlry, livestock; timber. Mfg. (wooden skids, furniture frames).

Casas (KAH-sas), town (1990 pop. 441), Tamaulipas, NE Mexico, 25 mi/40 km E of Ciudad Victoria. In agr. region (sugarcane, cereals, fruit).

Casas Grandes (KAH-sas GRAHN-dais), town (1990 pop. 2,834), Chihuahua, N Mexico, on interior plateau, on Casas Grandes R., and 130 mi/209 km SW of Juárez; 30°22′N 108°00′W. Cotton, cereals, livestock. Nuevo Casas Grandes is 2.5 mi/4 km NE. Also known as Pueblo Viejo.

Casas Grandes (KAH-sas GRAHN-dais), historical site, in NW Chihuahua, Mexico, 3.1 mi/5 km W of Nuevo Casas Grandes. It is a vast historical area near the town of Casas Grandes. Archaeological explorations have uncovered many different monuments and structures. Also known as Paquimé (pah-kee-MAI).

Casas Grandes River, c.250 mi/402 km long, Chihuahua, N Mexico; rises in Sierra Madre Occidental S of Buenaventura; flows N, past Casas Grandes and Nuevo Casas Grandes, and, as it approaches U.S. border, curves E to L. Guzmán. Used for irrigation.

Casas, Las, Mexico: see SAN CRISTÓBAL DE LAS CASAS.

Cascada de Basaseachic (kahs-KAH-dah dai bah-sah-se-AH-cheek), a natl. park, in W Chihuahua, Mexico, 174 mi/280 km W of the city of Chihuahua and 112 mi/180 km W of Cuauhtémoc, on a paved road [Mexico 16]. The park is on the N part of the Sierra Tarahumara. It has the tallest waterfall in Mexico and the 4th-highest waterfall in N. Amer. The water falls through an arch in the rock from a height of 1,017 ft/310 m into open rock columns. Found in La Candameña Canyon, it is surrounded by vertical walls 1,640 ft/500 m tall and dense pine and evergreen vegetation.

Cascade, county (□ 2,711 sq mi/7,021 sq km; 1990 pop. 77,691), W central Mont.; ⊙ Great Falls; 47°19′N 111°21′W. Agr. and mining region drained by Missouri, Sun, and Smith rivers. Wheat, barley oats, hay, some corn, potatoes, cattle, sheep, hogs, dairying, timber. Part of Lewis and Clark Natl. Forest in E and SE and part of Little Belt Mts. in SE. Giant Springs State Park in N near Great Falls; Sluice Boxes State Park in SE; most of Benton L. Natl. Wildlife Refuge in N; Sulphur Springs in NE; Ulm Pishkun State Park in NW, seat of large buffalo jump, or pishkun. Formed 1887.

Cascade, town (1991 pop. 1,220), Hanover parish, NW Jamaica, 6 mi/9.7 km ESE of Lucea; 18°24′N 78°06′W. Rice, yams, fruit.

Cascade 1 town (1990 pop. 877), ⊙ Valley co., W central Idaho, 65 mi/105 km N of Boise and on North Fork of Payette R., at Cascade Dam; 44°31′N 116°02′W. Elev. 4,800 ft/1,463 m. RR terminus and trade center for lumber, agr., cattle; oats area; dairying, lumber milling; mfg. (sourdough cultures). Gold, silver, lead mines, mercury in area. Cascade Reservoir formed by Cascade Dam. Parts of Boise Natl. Forest to E and W, Payette Natl. Forest to NE and NW. Founded 1912–1913 when Van Wyck, Crawford, and Thunder City joined; inc. 1917. **2** town (1990 pop. 1,812), Dubuque and Jones cos., E Iowa, on North Fork Maquoketa R., and 22 mi/35 km SW of Dubuque. Dairy prods. Settled 1834, platted 1842, inc. 1881.

Cascade, village, S B.C., Canada, on Wash. border, on Kettle R., and 12 mi/19 km E of Grand Forks; 49°01′N 118°13′W. Fruit, vegetables.

Cascade 1 village (1990 pop. 729), Cascade co., W central Mont., on Missouri R., and 25 mi/40 km SW of Great Falls; 47°16′N 111°42′W. Dairying; catttle, sheep, hogs, wheat, oats, barley, alfalfa. Originally called Dodge. **2** village (1990 pop. 620), Sheboygan co., E Wis., on branch of Milwaukee R. at N end of Ellen L., and 15 mi/24 km WSW of Sheboygan; 43°39′N 88°00′W. Dairy and grain area. Cheese.

Cascade Caverns, Texas: see BOERNE.

Cascade Caves, Ky.: see OLIVE HILL.

Cascade Locks, town (1990 pop. 930), Hood R. co., N Oregon, 37 mi/60 km ENE of Portland, on Columbia R., 3 mi/4.8 km upstream (E) of Bonneville Dam; 45°40′N 121°52′W. Mfg. (lumber, cedar fencing). Agr. (cherries, apples, pears). U.S. Corps of Engineers constructed (1896) a series of locks around rapids near here. Highway toll bridge across river. Mt. Hood Natl. Forest, including the Columbia Wilderness Area, to S; John Yeon State Park to SW; Lang Viento and Starvation Creek State Parks to E.

Cascade Range, mountain chain, c.700 mi/1,130 km long, extending S from B.C. (Canada) to N Calif., where it becomes the Sierra Nevada; it parallels the Coast Ranges, 100 mi/161 km–150 mi/241 km inland from the Pacific Ocean. Many of the range's highest peaks are volcanic cones, covered with snowfields and glaciers; Lassen Peak, 10,457 ft/3,187 m high, in Lassen Volcanic Natl. Park, is still active. Mt. St. Helens erupted in 1980 in one of the greatest volcanic explosions in U.S. history. Mt. Rainier (14,410 ft/4,392 m), in Mount Rainier Natl. Park, is the highest point in the Cascades; Mt. Shasta and Mt. Hood are other prominent peaks. The Columbia R. flows from E to W across the range. Of the many lakes in the Cascades, Crater L., in Crater L. Natl. Park, and L. Chelan, in L. Chelan Natl. Recreation Area, are the most famous. Other federal lands in this popular recreation area are North Cascades Natl. Park, Ross L. Natl. Recreation Area, and Lava Beds Natl. Monument; natl. forests cover an extensive area. Receiving more than 100 in/254 cm of precipitation annually, the Cascades are a major source of water in the NW of the U.S. Hydroelectricity is generated on the W slope; irrigation is used in the fertile

E side valleys. Timber is the region's chief resource, but a growing concern for ecology and the environment has developed into a major political debate surrounding the forests. The CASCADE TUNNEL, 8 mi /13 km, is the longest RR tunnel in N. Amer.

Cascade Reservoir, Valley co., W Idaho, on N. Fork Payette R. at town of Cascade; 21 mi/34 km long; 44°31′N 116°01′W. Upper part bridged at Donnelly. Formed by earth-fill dam (90 ft/27 m high, 700 ft/213 m long; completed 1949), used for power generation and for irrigation of c.110,000 acres/44,517 ha in Boise project. Boise Natl. Forest on SW shore.

Cascade River, 20 mi/32 km long, NE Minn.; rises in Cascade L. in Cook co., SW of Eagle Mt. (in Superior Natl. Forest); flows S, to L. Superior in Cascade R. State Park, 18 mi/29 km WSW of Grand Marais, where it passes through Cascade Falls before entering lake. Recreational area extending along lake front.

Cascade Tunnel, Chelan and King cos., central Wash., RR tunnel c.8 mi/12.9 km long, through the crest of the Cascade Range c.45 mi/72 km E of Seattle. Completed 1929 to replace earlier tunnel (1897), it is one of longest in world. Runs beneath Stevens Pass (4,061 ft/ 1,238 m).

Cascajal (kahs-kah-HAHL), town, Villa Clara prov., central Cuba, on Central Highway, on RR, and 38 mi/ 61 km NW of Santa Clara; 22°37′N 80°04′W. Sugarcane, tobacco, livestock.

Cascapedia, Canada: see GRAND CASCAPEDIA.

Cascapedia River (ka-skuh-PEE-dee-uh) or **Cascapédia River** (kahs-kah-pai-dee-AH), 75 mi/121 km long, E Que., Canada, on Gaspé Peninsula; rises in the Shickshock Mts.; flows SSE, past Grand Cascapedia, to Chaleur Bay 24 mi/39 km ENE of Dalhousie. Noted salmon stream.

Casco 1 (KAS-ko), resort town (1990 pop. 3,018), Cumberland co., SW Maine, on Sebago L., and 25 mi/40 km NNW of Portland; 43°58′N 70°30′W. Includes part of Sebago L. State Park. Near South Casco village is Nathaniel Hawthorne's boyhood home, in Raymond town. **2** town (1990 pop. 544), Kewaunee co., E Wis., on Door Peninsula, 20 mi/32 km E of Green Bay city; 44°32′N 87°37′W. In dairying and farming area. RR junction to SW. Fruit (cherries, apples, strawberries, pears, plums).

Casco Bay (KAS-ko), deep inlet of the Atlantic Ocean, 200 sq mi/518 sq km, SW Maine; 43°38′N 70°03′W. The bay, with its more than 200 wooded, hilly isls., has many summer estates and resorts. Portland, Maine, is the principal harbor.

Cascorro (KAHS-kor-ro), town, Camagüey prov., E Cuba, on Central Highway and 32 mi/51 km ESE of Camagüey; 21°11′N 77°27′W. Cattle raising, dairying.

Cascumpeque Bay (KA-skuhm-pehk), inlet of the Gulf of St. Lawrence, NW P.E.I., Canada; 7 mi/11 km long, 10 mi/16 km wide at entrance. At head of bay is Alberton.

Case-Pilote (kahz–pee-LAWT), town, W Martinique, Fr. West Indies, 3 mi/4.8 km NW of Fort-de-France. Distilleries; fishing.

Caseville, village (1990 pop. 857), Huron co., E Mich., at mouth of small Pigeon R., on Saginaw Bay, and 16 mi/26 km NW of Bad Axe; 43°56′N 83°16′W. Resort. Albert E. Sleeper State Park to NE.

Casey, county (□ 445 sq mi/1,153 sq km; 1990 pop. 14,211), central Ky.; ⊙ Liberty; 37°19′N 84°55′W. Bounded E corner by Fishing Creek; drained by Green R., South Fork Rolling River, and Casey Creek. Hilly agr. area (corn, hay, alfalfa, burley tobacco, soybeans; hogs, cattle, poultry; dairying); timber; limestone quarries. Mfg. at Liberty. Formed 1806.

Casey (KAI-see), city (1990 pop. 2,914), Clark co., E Ill., 17 mi/27 km WSW of Marshall; 39°17′N 87°59′W. Oil, natural gas; agr. (corn, wheat, soybeans, cattle, hogs; dairy prods.); mfg. (circuit boards, toll and machining). Inc. 1896. Had oil boom in early 20th cent.

Casey, town (1990 pop. 441), Guthrie co., SW Iowa, 11 mi/18 km S of Guthrie Center, near Middle R.; 41°30′N 94°31′W. In agr. region (corn, hogs, poultry); mfg. (concrete).

Casey, Fort, Wash.: see PORT TOWNSEND.

Caseyville 1 village (1990 pop. 4,419), St. Clair co., SW Ill., 7 mi/11.3 km E of East St. Louis, and residential suburb within St. Louis metropolitan area; 38°37′N 90°01′W. Some agr. **2** village (1990 pop. 43), Union co., W Ky., 14 mi/23 km SW of Morganfield, on the Ohio R. just N of mouth of Tradewater R. Agr. area.

Cash, village (1990 pop. 214), Craighead co., NE Ark., 14 mi/23 km WSW of Jonesboro, near Cache R.; 35°47′N 90°55′W.

Cashie River (kash-EE), c.50 mi/80 km long, NE N.C.; rises in NW Bertie co.; flows SE past Windsor (head of navigation), and ESE to Albemarle Sound 5 mi/8 km N of Plymouth; immediately N of mouth of Roanoke R. In lower course, connected with Roanoke R. by short passage.

Cashiers, uninc. village, Jackson co., W N.C., 20 mi/ 32 km SSE of Sylva, in Nantahala Natl. Forest. Cattle, corn, tobacco; timber. Center of tourist and second-home area. Thorpe L. reservoir to N.

Cashion, uninc. town (1990 pop. 3,014), Maricopa co., central Ariz., residential suburb 14 mi/23 km W of downtown Phoenix, on Gila R., at confluence of Salt River. Gila R. Indian Reservation to S.

Cashion (KASH-uhn), village (1990 pop. 430), Kingfisher co., central Okla., 24 mi/39 km NNW of Oklahoma City; 35°47′N 97°40′W. In agr. area.

Cashmere, town (1990 pop. 2,544), Chelan co., central Wash., on Wenatchee R., and 10 mi/16 km N of Wenatchee; 47°31′N 120°28′W. Apples, pears; mfg. (concrete prods., aircraft parts, candy, small arms ammunition); timber, wood prods. Chelan County Historical Society Mus. Leavenworth Ski Area to NW; Wenatchee Natl. Forest to N, W, and S; Alpine Lakes Wilderness Area to W. Cashmere Mt. (8,501 ft/2,591 m) to W; Swank Pass (4,102 ft/1,250 m) to S (U.S. Highway 97). Settled 1889, inc. 1904.

Cashton, village (1990 pop. 780), Monroe co., S central Wis., 23 mi/37 km ESE of La Crosse; 43°44′N 90°46′W. In timber and dairy region (butter, cheese).

Casilda (kah-SEEL-duh), town, Sancti Spíritus prov., central Cuba, port for Trinidad (3 mi/4.8 km N; linked by RR), on sheltered bay, 45 mi/72 km S of Santa Clara; 21°45′N 80°00′W. Fishing and seaside resort.

Casimiro Castillo (kah-see-MEE-ro kah-STEE-yo), settlement (1990 pop. 21,738), ⊙ Casimiro Castillo municipio, Jalapa, Mexico, 22 mi/35 km SSW of Autlán, 2 mi/3 km E of Mexico Hwy. 80; 19°36′N 104°26′W. Elev. 2,021 ft/616 m. In upper valley of Purificación R. Small-farmer agr.; corn, manioc, tropical fruits, livestock. Also called La Resolana.

Casnovia (kas-NO-vee-uh), village (1990 pop. 376), Muskegon and Kent cos., SW Mich., 20 mi/32 km NNW of Grand Rapids, and 21 mi/34 km E of Muskegon; 43°13′N 85°47′W. In fruit growing and dairying area; mfg.

Caspar, uninc. village, Mendocino co., NW Calif., on the Pacific Ocean, 6 mi/9.7 km S of Fort Bragg. Fruit; dairying; cattle. Russian Gulch State Park to S.

Casper, city (1990 pop. 46,742), ⊙ Natrona co., E central Wyo., on the North Platte R., 150 mi/241 km NW of Cheyenne, at N end of Laramie Mts.; 42°49′N 106°19′W. Elev. 5,123 ft/1,561 m. It is the 2d-largest city in Wyo. and is a rail, distributing, processing, and trade center in a farming, ranching, and mineral-rich area. An oil boom town since the 1st well was tapped in 1890, it has many oil-affiliated industries. Open-pit uranium mining nearby; also gas and coal production. The city has wool and livestock markets, meat-packing plants, and a growing tourist industry. Mfg. (soft drinks; canvas tents; log homes; countertops; printing and publishing; intravenous medications; insulated glass; concrete pipes; ready-mix concrete; sandpaper; fabricated structural steel; steel pipe; metal buildings; pipe valves; vehicle springs; gates; mining equipment; oil field units and skids; fiberglass tanks; woodworking devices; rubber prods.; fire trucks; temperature controls; trophies; aerosol defense prods.). At this fording place on the Oregon Trail, the Mormons in 1847 established a ferry, which was in the 1850s superseded by Platte Bridge. The city was founded (1888) with the coming of the RR and expanded with the discovery of oil at Salt Creek, followed by the Teapot Dome and Big Muddy finds. In 1948 wells in the Lost Soldier field of Sweetwater co. brought another boom. Casper has Casper Col. (2-year) and Wyo. Univ. at Casper. Nearby at Mills, to W, are the Central Wyoming Fairgrounds; the restored Old Fort Caspar Mus. (a clerk's error accounts for the later spelling of the name); and Casper Mt. (c.8,000 ft/2,438 m high). Tourist attractions in the surrounding area include Hell's Half Acre, a spectacular eroded area; Independence Rock; and a petrified forest. Oregon Trail Veterans' Cemetery to NE of town; Natrona County International Airport to NW; Edness Kimball Wilkins State Park to E; Hogadon Ski Area to S. Inc. 1889.

Caspian (KAS-peen), town (1990 pop. 1,031), Iron co., SW Upper Peninsula, Mich., on Iron R., and 2 mi/ 3.2 km S of Iron R.; 46°04′N 88°37′W. Resort, in area of small lakes; mfg. (sawdust shavings). Inc. 1918.

Caspian Lake, NE Vt., resort lake in Greensboro town, 18 mi/29 km NW of St. Johnsbury; c.2 mi/3.2 km long.

Cass 1 county (□ 383 sq mi/992 sq km; 1990 pop. 13,437), W central Ill., bounded N by Sangamon R. and W by Illinois R.; ⊙ Virginia; 39°58′N 90°15′W. Agr. (corn, soybeans, sorghum, sweet potatoes, cattle, hogs). Mfg. (gloves); river, RR shipping. Includes Treadway L. Formed 1837. Dominant town is Beardstown on Illinois R. Beardstown was once the county seat. Site M State Fish and Wildlife Area is near Chandlerville. **2** county (□ 415 sq mi/1,075 sq km; 1990 pop. 38,413), N central Ind.; ⊙ Logansport; 40°46′N 86°21′W. Intersected by the Wabash. Drained by Eel R. and Deer Creek. Agr. area (hogs, poultry; corn, fruit, produce); nurseries, timber. Mfg. and shipping at Logansport. Formed 1828. **3** county (□ 565 sq mi/1,463 sq km; 1990 pop. 15,128), SW Iowa; ⊙ Atlantic; 41°19′N 94°55′W. Prairie agr. area (cattle, hogs, poultry, corn) drained by East Nishnabotna and West Nodaway rivers; coal deposits. Mfg. at Atlantic. Anita State Park in NE; Cold Springs State Park in W. General flooding of rivers and fields in 1993. Formed 1851. **4** county (□ 508 sq mi/1,316 sq km; 1990 pop. 49,477), SW Mich.; ⊙ Cassopolis. Bounded S by Ind. state line; 41°54′N 85°59′W. Drained by St. Joseph R. and short Dowagiac Creek. A lake and farm region (grain, vegetables, peppermint, apples, cherries, grapes; hogs, cattle, sheep; dairy prods.); mfg. (wood and plastic prods., transportation equip.) at Dowagiac. Resorts. Site along underground RR chosen by emancipated slaves. Part of urbanized area of South Bend, Ind./ Niles, Mich., in SW corner; Swiss Valley Ski Area in E. Formed 1829. **5** county (□ 2,414 sq mi/6,252 sq km; 1990 pop. 21,791), N central Minn.; ⊙ Walker; 46°57′N 94°19′W. Bounded S by Crow Wing R., N by Mississippi R. Agr. area (dairying; cattle, sheep, poultry; wild rice, hay, alfalfa, oats); timber. Leech L. is in NW, part of Winnibigoshish L. in N and of Cass L. in NW, part of Gull L. reservoir in S; much of Leech L. Indian Reservation and Chippewa Natl. Forest in N; Schoolcraft State Park in NE; Mud Goose Wildlife Area in NE; part of Bowstring State Forest in N, other state forests include: Remer and Land O'Lakes (E), Foothills and Welsh L. (W), Battleground (center), Pillsbury (S). Formed 1851. **6** county (□ 698 sq mi/1,808 sq km; 1990 pop. 63,808), W Mo.; ⊙ Harrisonville; 38°38′N 94°20′W. Drained by South Grand R. Corn, wheat, sorghum, sweet corn; cattle, horses, poultry; oil and gas wells; limestone. Kansas City urban growth in N around Belton and Raymore. Formed 1849. **7** county (□ 566 sq mi/1,466 sq km; 1990 pop. 21,318), SE Nebr.; ⊙ Plattsmouth; 40°54′N 96°08′W. Agr. region bounded E by Missouri R. and Iowa, N by Platte R. Cattle, dairying, hogs, corn, sorghum, alfalfa. Flooding occured along river in 1993. Lousville Lakes State Recreation Area and Platte R. State Park in N. Formed 1868. **8** county (□ 1,767 sq mi/4,577 sq km; 1990 pop. 102,874), E N.Dak.; ⊙ Fargo; 46°55′N 97°15′W. Rich agr. area bounded E by Red R. of the North (Minn. boundary); drained by Maple, Sheyenne, and Rush rivers. Largest urbanized area in N. Dak. around Fargo, in E central part. Mfg. (farm equip., computer software, food processing). Cattle, hogs, wheat, soybeans, barley, flax. Maple Creek Historic Site in S. Formed 1873. **9** county (□ 960 sq mi/2,486 sq km; 1990 pop. 29,982), NE Texas; ⊙ Linden; 33°04′N 94°20′W. Bounded E by Ark. and La., N by Sulphur R. (forms Wright Patman L. reservoir). Rolling, partly forested area; timber; agr. (fruit, forage crops, vegetables; cattle, chickens). Oil, natural-gas wells; iron ore. Mfg. at Linden, Atlanta. Atlanta State Park in N. Formed 1846.

Cass, uninc. village (1990 pop. 150), Pocahontas co., E W.Va., on Greenbrier R., 15 mi/24 km NE of Marlinton, in Monongahela Natl. Forest. Agr. region. N terminus of Greenbriar R. State Trail to S; Cass Scenic RR is here (State Park to N); Seneca State Forest to S; Elk R., Silver Creek, and Snowshoe Mt. ski resorts to N; Natl. Radio Astronomy Observatory to NE.

Cass City, town (1990 pop. 2,276), Tuscola co., E Mich., on Cass R., and 13 mi/21 km NE of Caro; 43°36′N 83°10′W. Trade center for agr. area (livestock, poultry; grain; dairy prods.); heavy mfg. Settled 1866; inc. 1883.

Cass Lake, town (1990 pop. 923), Cass co., N central Minn., 15 mi/24 km ESE of Bemidji; 47°22′N 94°35′W. Sawmill; light mfg.; timber; cattle, sheep, poultry; oats, alfalfa, wild rice; dairying. Consolidated Chippewa Agency here; forest experiment station and tree nursery nearby. In Chippewa Natl. Forest and Greater Leech L. Indian Reservation; Bowstring State Forest to E; Welsh L. State Forest to S; Cass L. reservoir to NE; Pike Bay (S extension of Cass L.) to SE. Inc. 1899.

Cass Lake 1 Oakland co., SE Mich., 3 mi/4.8 km SW of Pontiac; c 3 mi/4.8 km long, 1 mi/1.6 km wide. Bathing, boating, fishing. Lake is bounded by municipalities of Kings Harbor (E), Orchard Lake (S), Waterford township (N), West Bloomfield township (W). Dodge Brothers No. 4 State Park on N side. **2** (□ 25 sq mi/65 sq km) Cass and Beltrami cos., N central Minn., 13 mi/21 km E of Bemidji; 10 mi/16 km long, 7 mi/11.3 km wide; 47°27′N 94°28′W. Elev. 1,303 ft/397 m. Fed and drained (E) by Mississippi R.; water control dam increases lake level and area. Fishing, boating, and bathing resorts. In Leech L. Indian Reservation and Chippewa Natl. Forest. Cass Lake town to SW. Star Isl. (2.5 mi/4 km long, 1 mi/1.6 km wide; narrow channel connects lake to Pike Bay to S, virtually a separate lake 4 mi/6.4 km wide) in W center.

Cass River, c.80 mi/129 km long, E central Mich.; formed near Cass City by branches rising to E; flows W and SW past Caro, Vassar, and Frankenmuth, to Saginaw R. just S of Saginaw city; 43°35′N 83°10′W.

Cassadaga (kas-uh-DAI-ga), resort village (□ 1 sq mi/2.6 sq km; 1990 pop. 768), Chautauqua co., extreme W N.Y., on Cassadaga Lakes, 10 mi/16 km S of Dunkirk; 42°20′N 79°19′W. Mfg. (wood prods.).

Cassadaga Creek, N.Y.: see CASSADAGA LAKES.

Cassadaga Lakes, 3 small lakes (Upper, Middle, and Lower Cassadaga lakes), Chautauqua co., extreme W N.Y., 17 mi/27 km N of Jamestown; 42°21′N 79°19′W. Resorts. Connected and drained by Cassadaga Creek, which flows c.30 mi/48 km generally SE to Conewango Creek 5 mi/8 km E of Jamestown.

Cassandra (kuh-SAN-druh), borough (1990 pop. 192), Cambria co., W central Pa., 16 mi/26 km ENE of Johnstown, on Little Conemaugh R.; 40°24′N 78°38′W.

Casselberry, suburb (□ 6 sq mi/15.5 sq km; 1990 pop. 18,911) of Orlando, Seminole co., central Fla., 10 mi/16 km N of city center; 28°39′N 81°19′W.

Casselman, village (1991 pop. 2,434), S Ont., Canada, on South Nation R., and 30 mi/48 km ESE of Ottawa; 45°19′N 75°05′W. Dairying, mixed farming.

Casselman (KA-suhl-man), borough (1990 pop. 89), Somerset co., SW Pa., 11 mi/18 km SW of Somerset, on Casselman R.; 39°53′N 79°12′W. Corn, oats, hay; livestock, dairying.

Casselman River, c.60 mi/97 km long, NW Md. and SW Pa.; formed by branches joining in N Garrett co., Md.; flows (NE past Salisbury and Meyersdale, Pa., NW to Rockwood, thence SW) to Youghiogheny R. at Confluence, Pa.

Casselton, town (1990 pop. 1,601), Cass co., E N.Dak.,

20 mi/32 km W of Fargo; 46°53′N 97°12′W. RR junction; grain, dairy prods. Maple Creek Historic Site to S. Inc. 1883.

Cassia, county (□ 2,580 sq mi/6,682 sq km; 1990 pop. 19,532), S Idaho; ⊙ Burley; 42°16′N 113°37′W. Agr. area bordering on Utah and Nev. (both on S) (Nev. is in Pacific time zone, co. is in Mountain time zone), bounded N by Snake R.; drained by Raft R. and Goose Creek. Irrigated regions are in N, along Snake R., and in W, along Goose Creek, around Oakley. Potatoes, sugar beets, dry beans; wheat, barley, oats, corn; alfalfa, hay; cattle; dairying. Parts of Sawtooth Natl. Forest in SW, center and E; Pomerelle Ski Area in center; City of Rocks Natl. Historic Landmark in S, granite columns (c.600 ft/183 m). Formed 1879.

Cassiar Mountains (ka-see-AHR), small range, N B.C., Canada, near head of Stikine R., NE of Dease L. Gives its name to surrounding district.

Cassidy, village, SW B.C., Canada, on SE Vancouver Isl., 7 mi/11 km SSE of Nanaimo; 49°04′N 123°53′W. Coal mining; vegetables, mixed farming. Fish hatchery on nanaimo R. Nanaimo Airport here. Nearby Cedar-on-Sea was site of religious commune, 1927–1933.

Cassopolis (kas-AH-po-lis), town (1990 pop. 1,822), ⊙ Cass co., SW Mich., on a small lake 22 mi/35 km NE of South Bend, Ind.; 41°54′N 86°00′W. In agr. area (livestock, poultry; fruit, grain, vegetables, peppermint); dairy prods.; timber; mfg. (plastics, heavy machinery, mobile office trailers). Diamond L. to SE. Summer resort. Settled 1831; inc. 1863.

Casstown, village (1990 pop. 246), Miami co., W Ohio, 4 mi/6 km E of Troy, in agr. area; 40°03′N 84°07′W.

Cassumit Lake, village, NW Ont., Canada, in Patricia dist., on Richardson L. (4 mi/6 km long), 100 mi/161 km NNW of Sioux Lookout; 51°28′N 92°21′W. Gold mining.

Cassville, city (1990 pop. 2,371), ⊙ Barry co., SW Mo., in the Ozarks, 45 mi/72 km SE of Joplin; 36°40′N 93°52′W. Ships livestock, poultry, dairy prods., fruit. Mfg. (consumer goods, machinery, poultry processing, metal prods.). Crystal Caverns to N; sport fishing, tourism. Roaring River State Park and trout hatchery nearby. Platted 1845.

Cassville 1 town (1990 pop.1458), Monongalia co., N W.Va., 6 mi/9.7 km WNW of Morgantown, on Scotts Run Creek; 39°39′N 80°3′W. In coal-mining region. Livestock; poultry; grain. **2** town (1990 pop. 1,144), Grant co., extreme SW Wis., on Mississippi R., and 22 mi/35 km NW of Dubuque, Iowa and 24 mi/39 km SSE of Prairie du Chien; 42°43′N 90°59′W. In agr. area; mfg. (speaker cones). Nelson Dewey State Park and Stonefield State Historical Site in NW. Lock and Dam No. 10 to NW (upstream).

Cassville (KAS-vil), borough (1990 pop. 183), Huntingdon co., S Pa., 14 mi/23 km S of Huntingdon; 40°1′N 78°01′W. Corn, hay, livestock, dairying. Sideling Hill ridge to E.

Castaic, village, Los Angeles co., Calif., 15 mi/24 km N of San Fernando Valley on interstate highway, near S end of Castaic Damand L.

Castaic Lake, Los Angeles Co., S Calif., on Castaic Creek, 7 mi/11.3 km NNW of Santa Clarita; 34°30′N 117°36′W. Elev. 1,516 ft/462 m. NW arm is 5 mi/8 km long, NE arm (in Angeles Natl. Forest) 3 mi/4.8 km long; max. capacity 350,000 acre-ft. Elderberry Forebay, enclosed sect. of NW arm, receives water from Pyramid L. reservoir (NW) via West Branch Calif. Aqueduct. Formed by Castaic Dam (320 ft/98 m high), built (1973) by the Calif. Dept. of Water Resources for irrigation and water storage. Castaic L, State Recreation Area at dam.

Castalia, town (1990 pop. 177), Winneshiek co., NE Iowa, 15 mi/24 km SSE of Decorah; 43°06′N 91°40′W. Milk receiving and shipping point. Limestone quarries nearby.

Castalia 1 (kuh-STAL-yuh), village (1990 pop. 261), Nash co., NE central N.C., 17 mi/27 km WNW of Rocky Mount; 36°4′N 78°3′W. Tobacco, grain, livestock. Mfg. (apparel). **2** village (1990 pop. 915), Erie co.,

N Ohio, 7 mi/11 km SW of Sandusky; 41°24′N 82°48′W. Blue Hole Spring here attracts tourists.

Castana, town (1990 pop. 159), Monona co., W Iowa, on Maple R. and 10 mi/16 km E of Onawa; 42°04′N 95°54′W. In livestock and grain area.

Castanea (KAS-TAI-nee-uh), uninc. town (1990 pop. 1,123), Clinton co., N central Pa., residential suburb 1 mi/1.6 km S of Lock Haven, on Bald Eagle Creek, 2 mi/3.2 km W of its mouth on West Branch Susquehanna R.; 41°07′N 77°25′W. Light Mfg. Agr. includes corn, hay, dairying, livestock. Bald Eagle State Forest to S.

Castaños (kas-TAH-nyos), city (1990 pop. 18,368) and township, ⊙ Castaños municipio, Coahuila, N Mexico, in NE foothills of Sierra Madre Oriental, on RR, and 8 mi/12.9 km S of Monclova, on Mexico Highway 53-57; 26°47′N 101°26′W. In agr. region (wheat). Mineral resources in area.

Castile (KAS-steil), village (□ 1 sq mi/2.6 sq km; 1990 pop. 1,078), Wyoming co., W N.Y., 11 mi/18 km SSE of Warsaw; 42°37′N 78°02′W. Food processing and dairying. Summer recreation area, largely due to presence of nearby Letchworth State Park.

Castillo (kah-STEE-yo), town (1993 pop. 5,682), Duarte prov., E central Dominican Republic, in La Vega Real valley, 16 mi/26 km ESE of San Francisco de Macorís; 19°15′N 70°00′W. Agr. (cacao, coffee, rice, corn).

Castillo de San Marcos (kuh-STEE-yo duh san MAHR-kos), monument, St. Augustine, NE Fla. Old Span. masonry fort, authorized as monument 1924.

Castillo de Teayo (kas-TEE yo de teh-AH-yo), town (1990 pop. 3,945), Veracruz, E Mexico, 20 mi/32 km SW of Túxpam de Rodríguez de Cano; 20°50′N 97°40′W. In agr. region (corn, sugarcane, tropical fruit, fiber plants).

Castine (kas-TEEN), resort town (1990 pop. 1,161), Hancock co., S Maine, on peninsula in Penobscot Bay, and 22 mi/35 km SW of Ellsworth; 44°24′N 68°49′W. Has a mus., Fort Madison (1811; rebuilt in Civil War), Fort George (1779; Br.-built), Maine Maritime Acad. Plymouth Colony trading post nearby, 1626; early Fr. mission here; town changed hands several times among French, British, Dutch, and Americans. British held it in Revolution and in War of 1812. Named for Baron St. Castin or Castine, who settled here 1667; inc. 1796.

Castine, village (1990 pop. 163), Darke co., W Ohio, 12 mi/19 km S of Greenville, in agr. area; 39°56′N 84°37′W.

Castle, village (1990 pop. 94), Okfuskee co., central Okla., 25 mi/40 km WSW of Okmulgee, near North Canadian R.; 35°28′N 96°22′W. Mfg. (pipeline-padding machines).

Castle Air Force Base, Calif.: see MERCED, city.

Castle Clinton, N.Y.: see BATTERY, THE.

Castle Crags, Shasta/Siskiyou cos., N Calif., group of granite pinnacles (up to 6,000 ft/1,829 m) in Klamath Mts., 4 mi/6.4 km SW of Dunsmuir. Castle Crags State Park here (4,382 acres/1,773 ha; campgrounds) is traversed by Sacramento R.

Castle Creek, creek, 14 mi/23 km, Pennington Co., SW S.Dak.; rises out of Deerfield Reservoir 15 mi/24 km NNW of Custer in Black Hills; flows N and E to join Rapid Creek 4 mi/6.4 km W of Silver City.

Castle Dale, town (1990 pop. 1,704), ⊙ Emery co., central Utah, on Cottonwood Creek, which joins Ferron and Huntington creeks 5 mi/8 km E to form San Rafael R., 30 mi/48 km SSW of Price; 39°13′N 111°01′W. Agr. area (alfalfa, cattle); elev. 5,771 ft/1,759 m. Coal mines in vicinity. Deposits of radioactive ores nearby. Manti–La Sal Natl. Forest to W. Settled 1880s.

Castle Dome Mountains, Yuma co., SW Ariz., extend c.30 mi/48 km S from Kofa Mts.; rise to 3,788 ft/1,155 m in Castle Dome Peak, c.40 mi/64 km NE of Yuma. Mostly in Kofa Natl. Wildlife Refuge.

Castle Gap, Texas: see CASTLE MOUNTAIN.

Castle Gate, uninc. town, Carbon co., central Utah, 4 mi/6.4 km N of Helper, 10 mi/16 km NNW of Price and on Price R. Coal mines. Highway crossroad, no longer viable. Moved from Spring Creek Canyon to Helper Canyon.

Castle Harbour, sheltered inlet of E Bermuda, bet. St. David's Isl. and Bermuda Isl., which are joined by causeway (N); 2.5 mi/4 km long, 2 mi/3.2 km wide. Entrance in S.

Castle Hayne, uninc. town (1990 pop. 1,182), New Hanover co., SE N.C., 9 mi/14.5 km NNE of Wilmington, near Northeast Cape Fear R.; 34°21′N 77°54′W. Mfg. (concrete, steel fabricating, cleaning prods., crushed stone). Sweet potatoes, peanuts, tobacco, corn.

Castle Hill, town (1990 pop. 449), Aroostook co., N Maine, 9 mi/14.5 km W of Presque Isle; 46°42′N 68°13′W. In agr., lumbering area.

Castle Hills 1 uninc. town (1990 pop. 1,475), New Castle co., N Del., residential suburb 4 mi/6.4 km S of downtown Wilmington. Delaware Memorial Bridge 2 mi/3.2 km E; New Castle County Airport 2 mi/3.2 km W. **2** town (1990 pop. 4,198), Bexar co., S central Texas, residential suburb 6 mi/9.7 km N of downtown San Antonio, on Olmos Creek; 29°31′N 98°31′W. San Antonio Internatl. Airport to E.

Castle Island, E Mass., tip of a peninsula extending into Dorchester Bay section of Boston Harbor in South Boston. Recreational park; site of old Fort Independence, pre-Revolutionary and Civil War fortification.

Castle Mountain 1 (7,329 ft/2,234 m), on Alaska-Canada (B.C.) border, in Coast Range, 30 mi/48 km E of Petersburg; 56°52′N 132°7′W. **2** (c.3,154 ft/961 m), Upton co., W Texas, near Pecos R., 6 mi/9.7 km SSE of Crane. Gave its name to Castle Gap, adjacent pass used by westbound pioneers, which was scene of Indian and outlaw attacks.

Castle Peak 1 (14,265 ft/4,348 m), Pitkin and Gunnison cos., W central Colo., highest point in Elk Mts., 12 mi/ 19 km NNE of Crested Butte. Also known as Mt. Carbon. White River/Gunnison Natl. Forests here. **2** (10,190 ft/3,106 m), S Alaska, in Wrangell Mts., 100 mi/161 km ENE of Valdez; 61°35′N 143°26′W. **3** (9,103 ft/2,775 m) in Nevada co., E Calif., a summit of the Sierra Nevada, 10 mi/16 km WNW of Trukee, near Donner Pass. In Tahoe Natl. Forest. **4** peak (11,820 ft/3,603 m) in Sawtooth Mts., Custer co., S central Idaho, c.40 mi/64 km NNW of Hailey. In Sawtooth Natl. Recreation Area.

Castle Pinckney National Monument, Charleston co., SE S.C., on Shutes Folly Isl., in Charleston Harbor, 1 mi/1.6 km E of the Battery, S tip of city of Charleston, and 1 mi/1.6 km S of Patricots Point, city of Mount Pleasant. Undeveloped.

Castle Point, N.Y.: see BEACON.

Castle Rock 1 town (1990 pop. 8,708), ⊙ Douglas co., central Colo., on Plum Creek, and 25 mi/40 km SSE of Denver; 39°22′N 104°50′W. Elev. 6,202 ft/1,890 m. Dairying, fruit, cattle, wheat, oats. Mfg. (magnetic pulleys, asphalt). Named for stone formation that once served as pioneer landmark. Castlewood Canyon State Park to SE. **2** town (1990 pop. 2,067), Cowlitz co., SW Wash., 10 mi/16 km N of Kelso and on Cowlitz R., 3 mi/ 4.8 km to N; 46°16′N 122°54′W. Mouth of Toutle R; source of mud flows from Mt. Saint Helens. Trade center for agr. region; vegetables; cattle; dairying; logging. Mt. Saint Helens Natl. Volcanic Monument to E; Seaquest State Park and Silver L. reservoir to E. Inc. 1890.

Castle Rock Reservoir (□ 26 sq mi/67 sq km), Adams co., central Wis., on Wisconsin R., 30 mi/48 km NW of Portage; 43°52′N 89°58′W. Max. capacity 195,000 acre-ft. Formed by Castle Rock Dam (38 ft/ 12 m high), built (1950) for power generation; also used for recreation. Petenwell L. upstream. Buckhorn State Park on W shore.

Castle Shannon (KA-suhl SHA-nuhn), borough (1990 pop. 9,135), Allegheny co., SW Pa., suburb 5 mi/8 km S of downtown Pittsburgh; 40°22′N 80°01′W. Mfg. (printing). Inc. 1919.

Castle Valley, village (1990 pop. 211), Grand co., E Utah, 11 mi/18 km ENE of Moab, 2 mi/3.2 km SE of Colorado R., on Castle Creek; 38°37′N 109°24′W. Oil and natural gas. Manti–La Sal Natl. Forest to SE.

Castleberry, town (1990 pop. 669), Conecuh co., S Ala., 11 mi/18 km SSW of Evergreen.

Castleberry, Texas: see RIVER OAKS.

Castleford, village (1990 pop. 179), Twin Falls co., S Idaho, 5 mi/8 km SW of Buhl, on Deep Creek; 42°31′N 114°52′W. Irrigated agr. area. Balanced Rock to W.

Castlegar, city (1991 pop. 6,579), S B.C., Canada, on Columbia R., near mouth of Kootenay R., and 16 mi/ 26 km N of Trail; 49°19′N 117°40′E. In mining (gold, silver, lead, zinc) and lumbering region.

Castleton, town (1990 pop. 4,278), Rutland co., W Vt., 10 mi/16 km W of Rutland, in L. Bomoseen summer resort area; 43°37′N 73°10′W. Fruit; slate quarries at Hydeville village. Castleton State Col. Ethan Allen and Seth Warner met here (1775) to plan Ticonderoga attack. Chartered 1761, settled 1770.

Castleton, village, SE Ont., Canada, 28 mi/45 km W of Belleville. Dairying, fruitgrowing.

Castleton, village (1990 pop. 37), Marion co., central Ind., 10 mi/16 km NE of Indianapolis; 39°54′N 86°03′W. Became part of Indianapolis on Jan. 1, 1970. Major shopping area, retailing.

Castleton, botanical gardens and resort in St. Mary parish, E central Jamaica, 15 mi/24 km N of Kingston; 18°12′N 77°26′W. Known for its tropical vegetation and lily pond. Also called Castleton Gardens.

Castleton Corners, a sect. of Staten Isl. borough of N.Y. city, SE N.Y., on N Staten Isl.; 40°32′N 74°07′W.

Castleton River, c.20 mi/32 km long, W Vt.; rises W of Proctor; flows S and W to Poultney R. near Fair Haven.

Castleton-on-Hudson, village (1990 pop. 1,491), Rensselaer co., E N.Y., on E bank of the Hudson R., and 9 mi/14.5 km S of Albany; 42°31′S 73°45′W. Settled by the Dutch c.1630; inc. 1827.

Castlewood 1 town (1990 pop. 549), Hamlin co., E S.Dak., 13 mi/21 km S of Watertown and on Big Sioux R. Mfg. (picture frames). Pelican State Rec. Area to NW. **2** uninc. town, Russell co., SW Va., 21 mi/34 km ESE of Norton, near Clinch R.; 36°53′N 82°16′W. Mfg. (apparel, machining); in agr. area (tobacco, corn, alfalfa; cattle, sheep, dairying).

Castor, town (1991 pop. 933), SE Alta., 115 mi/185 km SE of Edmonton; 52°13′N 111°54′W. Coal mining; oil and natural gas; flour milling, dairying, wheat, barley, oats, flax.

Castor (KAS-tuhr), village (1990 pop. 196), Bienville parish, NW La., near Black L. Bayou, and 37 mi/60 km SE of Shreveport; 32°15′N 93°10′W. In agr. and timber area; mfg. (lumber, wood prods.). Kepler Creek L. reservoir to N.

Castor Creek, c.65 mi/105 km long, N central La.; rises in Jackson parish; flows SE and S, joining Dugdemona R. to form Little R. just above Rochelle; 31°47′N 92°21′W.

Castor River (KAS-tuhr), c.70 mi/113 km long, SE Mo.; rises in St. Francois co.; flows S and SE to South Bollinger co. where its water is diverted to the Mississippi R. by the Headwaters Diversion Channel. The lower course of the Castor R. flows through Stoddard co. to join the drainage channels of the Little River Drainage District.

Castorland, village (1990 pop. 292), Lewis co., N central N.Y., on Black R., and 21 mi/34 km ESE of Watertown; 43°52′N 75°31′W.

Castries (KAH-strees), town (1991 pop. 1,991; 1991 metropolitan area pop. 51,994), ⊙ and commercial center of SAINT LUCIA. Its excellent landlocked harbor is one of the best in the West Indies and a cruise ship port of call. Castries was founded by the French in 1650, and was an important coaling station under Br. rule in 19th and early 20th cents. Heavily damaged by fire several times (most recently in 1948), it has few old bldgs. Regional airport at Vigie Bay, 1 mi/1.6 km N.

Castro, county (□ 899 sq mi/2,328 sq km; 1990 pop. 9,070), NW Texas, ⊙ Dimmitt. On Llano Estacado; 34°31′N 102°15′W. Elev. 3,500 ft/1,067 m–4,000 ft/ 1,219 m. Drained by Running Water Draw. Cattle, sheep, hogs; wheat; also irrigated agr. (cotton, corn). Organized 1891.

Castro Valley, uninc. city (1990 pop. 48,619), Alameda co., W Calif., residential suburb 13 mi/21 km SE of downtown Oakland, E of San Francisco Bay; 37°43′N 122°04′W. Chiefly residential, it also has light industries. San Lorenzo Creek to S; L. Chabot reservoir and Anthony Chabot Regional Park to N.

Castroville 1 uninc. town (1990 pop. 5,272), Monterey co., W Calif., 2 mi/3.2 km NE of Monterey Bay, 8 mi/ 12.9 km NW of Salinas; 36°46′N 121°45′W. On Tembladero Slough. "Artichoke Center of the World"; annual Artichoke Festival. Artichokes, vegetables, fruits, strawberries; dairying, cattle; mfg. (electronic components). Moss Landing State Park to N. Noted for artichoke production. **2** town (1990 pop. 2,159), Medina co., SW Texas, on Medina R., and 24 mi/39 km W of San Antonio; 29°21′N 98°52′W. Elev. 760 ft/232 m. Market point in irrigated farm area (cotton, vegetables, peanuts; livestock). Light mfg. Landmark Inn State Historic Site former stagecoach stop restored to 1840s era. Settled 1844 by Alsatians and others, under Henry Castro; Eur. influence is still evident in buildings and customs.

Caswell (KAZ-wel), county (□ 428 sq mi/1,109 sq km; 1990 pop. 20,693), N N.C.; ⊙ Yanceyville; 36°23′N 79°19′W. In Piedmont region; bounded N by Va. state line; drained by Dan and Hyde rivers; part of Hyde reservoir in NE. Agr. (tobacco, corn, wheat, oats, soybeans, sorghum, potatoes, cattle, hogs, hay); timber (pine, oak). City of Danville, Va. on N boundary. Formed 1777.

Caswell (KAZ-wel), township (1990 pop. 408), Aroostook co., NE Maine, 9 mi/14.5 km NE of Caribou, on Can. border (N.B); 47°01′N 67°52′W. Produces limestone.

Caswell Beach, village (1990 pop. 175), Brunswick co., SE N.C., 2 mi/3.2 km SSW of Southport, on Atlantic Ocean, at entrance to Cape Fear R. estuary. Intracoastal Waterway passes to N. Lighthouse; 33°53′N 78°2′W. Beach resort area. Formerly Fort Caswell.

Cat Cays, string of islets, NW Bahama Isls., adjoining South Bimini isl., and administratively a part of the Biminis; 60 mi/97 km long (N-S). Gun Cay has lighthouse at 25°34′N 79°18′W.

Cat Island, Harrison co., SE Miss. Wooded anchorshaped sand isl. in the Gulf of Mexico, one of chain of isls. lying bet. Mississippi Sound (N) and Chandeleur Sound (S), 10 mi/16 km S of Gulfport; c.5 mi/8 km long E-W. Intracoastal Waterway passes to N.

Catacombs Mountain (10,800 ft/3,292 m), W Alta., Canada, near B.C. border, in Rocky Mts., in Jasper Natl. Park, 35 mi/56 km SSE of Jasper; 52°26′N 117°45′W.

Catadupa, town, St. James parish, W Jamaica, on Jamaica RR and 15 mi/24 km SSE of Montego Bay; 18°17′N 77°52′W. Banana growing. Significant as a name 1st given to the waterfalls of the River Nile (Egypt).

Catahoula (kat-uh-HOO-luh), parish (□ 732 sq mi/ 1,896 sq km; 1990 pop. 11,065), E La.; ⊙ Harrisonburg; 31°46′N 91°49′W. Bounded E by Black (Ouachita) and Tensas rivers, S by Red R. and Big Saline Bayou, N by Boeuf R. and Deer Creek; intersected by Ouachita and Little rivers, Bushley Creek. Includes L. Larto in S. Agr. (cotton, corn, soybeans, sorghum, hay, sweet potatoes, peas, cattle, horses); turtles; catfish; sand and gravel pits; logging. Catahoula Natl. Wildlife Refuge beyond its W boundary in La Salle parish, Sicily Isl. Hills State Wildlife Area in N, part of Saline State Wildlife Area in SW. Named after Indian words for big clear lake. Formed 1808.

Catahoula Lake (kat-uh-HOO-luh), La Salle parish, central La., 16 mi/26 km NE of Alexandria; c.13 mi/ 21 km long; 31°30′N 92°06′W. Inlet: Little R. (SW end); outlets: Little R. (NE), Big Saline Bayou (SE). Recreation area; fishing. Catahoula Natl. Wildlife Refuge on E end, Saline State Wildlife Area to SE.

Cataldo (cat-al-do), uninc. village (1990 pop. 100), Bonner co., N Idaho, 21 mi/34 km ESE of Coeur d'Alene, on Coeur d'Alene R. Lumber and timbers. Coeur d'Alene Natl. Forest to N. Old Mission (at Cataldo) State Park to SW, built 1853.

Catalina, uninc. town (1990 pop. 4,864), Pima co., S Ariz., suburb 18 mi/29 km N of Tucson. Cattle, sheep. Part of Coronado Natl. Forest to E; Catalina State Park to S; Mt. Lemmon (9157 ft/2791m) 6 mi/9.7 km SE, site of Biosphere 2 environmental experiment (1995) on N side of mt. Residential community.

Catalina (kah-tah-LEE-nah), island, Dominican Republic, off the SE coast in La Romana prov., 3.5 mi/9 km SW of La Romana. Cruise port.

Catalina Channel, Calif.: see SAN PEDRO CHANNEL.

Catalina de Güines (kah-tah-LEE-nuh dai GWEE-naiz), town, La Habana prov., W Cuba, on Central Highway, on RR, and 28 mi/45 km SE of Havana; 22°55′N 81°58′W. Potatoes, tomatoes, tobacco, sugarcane (and mills), and cattle.

Catalina Island, Calif.: see SANTA CATALINA.

Cataño (kah-TAH-no), town (1990 pop. 34,587), N P.R., facing San Juan Bay, opposite Old San Juan. Mfg. Bacardi rum plant, one of the world's largest, is here. Tourism. Busy ferry port carrying passengers to Old San Juan and Hato Rey.

Cataouatche, Lake (kat-uh-HOO-chee), SE La., 8 mi/13 km SW of New Orleans, in marshy region; c.7 mi/11 km long, 3 mi/5 km wide; 29°50′N 90°14′W. Joined by passage to the Mississippi (N) and 2 passages to L. Salvador (S). Salvador State Wildlife Area on W shore.

Cataract Dam, Ind., see CAGLES MILL LAKE.

Cataraqui River (ka-tuh-RA-kwee), 70 mi/113 km long, S Ont., Canada, issues from Rideau L.; flows in a winding course SW to E end of L. Ontario at Kingston. Forms SW part of Rideau Canal.

Catarina, uninc. city (1990 pop. 45), Dimmit co., SW Texas, 25 mi/40 km SSE of Crystal City. In irrigated vegetable growing area.

Catasauqua (KA-tuh-SAW-kwah), borough (1990 pop. 6,662), Lehigh co., E Pa., residential suburb 3 mi/4.8 km NNE of Allentown, on Lehigh R.; 40°38′N 75°27′W. Mfg. (industrial fans, iron and steel forgings). Lehigh Valley Internatl. Airport in center of borough. Allentown State Farm to N. Inc. c.1853.

Catatonk Creek (KA-tuh-tunk), c.25 mi/40 km long, S N.Y.; drains Spencer L. N of Spencer; flows S, E, and SE to Owego Creek just N of Owego.

Cataumet, Mass.: see BOURNE.

Catawba (kuh-TAW-buh), county (□ 413 sq mi/1,070 sq km; 1990 pop. 118,412), W central N.C.; ⊙ Newton; 35°39′N 81°12′W. In Piedmont area; bounded E and N by Catawba R. (forms Hickory and Lookout Shoals reservoirs in N, part of L. Norman reservoir in E); drained by South Fork Catawba R. and it branches, Jacobs Fork and Henrys Fork rivers; hydroelectric plants. Agr. area (corn, wheat, hay, sorghum, dairying, oats, soybeans, cattle, chickens, hogs); timber (pine, oak). Mfg. at Hickory, Newton and Conover. Formed 1842.

Catawba 1 (kuh-TAW-buh), village (1990 pop. 467), Catawba co., W central N.C., on Catawba R., and 16 mi/26 km E of Hickory; 35°42′N 81°4′W. Grain, soybeans, dairying, cattle, poultry, hogs. Mfg. (industrial gloves, aluminum tubing, concrete culverts, wooden furniture frames, socks). L. Norman reservoir to SE, Lookout Shoals L. reservoir to N, both on Catawba R. Murrays Mill Historic District. **2** village (1990 pop. 268), Clark co., W central Ohio, 11 mi/18 km ENE of Springfield, in agr. area; 39°59′N 83°37′W. **3** uninc. village, York co., N S.C., 7 mi/11.3 km SE of Rock Hill, near Catawba R. Landsford Canal State Park to S. RR junction. Mfg. includes paper, steel processing and fabrication, hardboard. Agr. includes cotton, grain, livestock, poultry. **4** uninc. village, Roanoke co., SW Va., in Jefferson Natl. Forest, 11 mi/18 km NW of Roanoke. Livestock; timber. Appalachian Trail passes to S. **5** (kah-TAH-buh), village (1990 pop. 178), Price co., N Wis., 28 mi/45 km SSW of Park Falls; 45°32′N 90°31′W. In wooded area; dairying. Flambeau R. State Forest to NW; Unit of Chequamegon Natl. Forest to S.

Catawba 1 and 2 Nuclear Power Plants, S.C.: see YORK.

Catawba Island, resort village, Ottawa co., N Ohio, on N shore of Marblehead Peninsula on L. Erie, 12 mi/19 km NW of Sandusky. Vineyards, peach orchards; tourism.

Catawba River (kuh-TAW-buh), c. 220 mi/354 km long, in N.C. and S.C.; rises in W McDowell co., W N.C. in the Blue Ridge Mts. S of Mt. Mitchell, c.20 mi/32 km E of Asheville; flows E through L. James reservoir, past Morganton, through L. Rhodhiss reservoir, past Hickory and through L. Hickory reservoir, turns S in Lookout Shoals reservoir, then through L. Norman reservoir to W of Mooresville (formed by Cowans Ford Dam), through Mountain Island L. reservoir, then flows bet. Charlotte and Gastonia, N.C., and through L. Wylie reservoir where it forms N.C.-S.C. state line for 7 mi/11.3 km, continues into S.C., then flows past rock Hill and through Fishing Creek reservoir, turns SE as it enters L. Waters reservoir and becomes Water R. Receives South Fork Catawba R. from NE in L. Wylie reservoir. South Fork Catawba R., W central N.C. formed by joining of Henrys Fork (c.25 mi/40 km long) and Jacobs Fork (c.20 mi/32 km long) rivers (both rise in E Burke co.), flows c.45 mi/72 km SE past Bogeu City and NE of Gastonia to Catawba R. in L. Wylie reservoir, 10 mi/16 km SE of Gastonia; forms 5 mi/8 km arm of L. Wylie.

Catawissa (KA-tuh-WIS-ah), borough (1990 pop. 1,683), Columbia co., E central Pa., 3 mi/4.8 km S of Bloomsburg, on Susquehanna R. at mouth of Catawissa Creek; 40°57′N 76°27′W. Mfg. (soft drinks, furniture). Agr. area (grain, apples, potatoes; poultry, livestock, dairying). Several covered bridges to S on Roaring Creek and its South Branch. Catawissa Mt. to E. Laid out 1787, inc. 1892.

Catazajá (ka-ta-sa-HAH), town (1990 pop. 2,809), Chiapas, SE Mexico, in lowlands, on affluent of the Usumacinta and 17 mi/27 km W of Emiliano Zapata (Tabasco). Rubber, rice, tropical fruit, timber.

Cateechee (KAT-uh-chee), village, Pickens co., NW S.C., 22 mi/35 km WSW of Greenville, and 1 mi/1.6 km NW of Norris. Cotton mill.

Catemaco (ka-te-MA-ko), city (1990 pop. 21,260), Veracruz, SE Mexico, on L. Catemaco, at SE foot of Tuxtla Volcano, 8 mi/12.9 km E of San Andrés Tuxtla; 18°28′N 95°10′W. Agr. center (fruit, high-grade tobacco). Weekend resort center.

Catemaco, Lake, Mexico: see LAGUNA DE CATAMACO NATIONAL PARK.

Catfish River, Wis.: see YAHARA RIVER.

Cathay (kath-AI), village (1990 pop. 54), Wells co., central N.Dak., 12 mi/19 km SE of Fessenden; 47°32′N 99°24′W.

Cathcart, uninc. town (1990 pop. 950), Snohomish co., NW Wash., suburb 13 mi/21 km NE of downtown Seattle, 5 mi/8 km S of Snohomish, on Skykomish R. Dairying, poultry, berries, vegetables.

Cathedral City, city (1990 pop. 30,085), Riverside co., S Calif., in Coachella Valley, suburb 6 mi/9.7 km SE of Palm Springs, on Whitestone R.; 33°50′N 116°27′W. Resort and retirement community. Pop. nearly tripled 1980–1990. San Bernardino Natl. Forest to SW; Agua Caliente Indian Reservation to N and W.

Cathedral Peak, mountain (10,940 ft/3,335 m) of the Sierra Nevada, Tuolomne/Mariposa line, in E Calif., 15 mi/24 km WSW of Mono L., in Yosemite Natl. Park.

Cathedral Pines, Conn.: see CORNWALL.

Cathedral Rocks, Calif.: see YOSEMITE NATIONAL PARK.

Catherine Hall, township and sugar mill, St. James parish, NW Jamaica, just SE of Montego Bay; 18°28′N 77°56′W. Sugar estate.

Catherine, Lake, Garland and Hot Spring cos., W central Ark., on Ouachita R., 11 mi/18 km ESE of Hot Springs; c.12 mi/19 km long; 34°25′N 92°53′W. Extends W to Carpenter Dam (and L. Hamilton). Formed by Remmel Dam. Lake Catherine State Park on S shore.

Catherine, Mount, peak (10,020 ft/3,054 m) in Pavant Mts., central Utah, c.10 mi/16 km ENE of Fillmore.

Cathlamet (kath-LAM-it), village (1990 pop. 508), Wahkiakum co., SW Wash., 22 mi/35 km W of Longview and on Cathlamet Channel of Columbia R., at mouth of Elochoman R. (has 2 salmon hatcheries to NE); 46°12′N 123°23′W. Timber, logging. Bridge S to Puget Isl., highway continues S to ferry across main channel Columbia R. to Westport, Oregon. Columbian White-tailed Deer Natl. Wildlife Refuge. County Historical Mus. Covered bridge on Grays R., to NW.

Catlettsburg (KAT-lits-buhrg), town (1990 pop. 2,231), ⊙ Boyd co., NE Ky., 4 mi/6.4 km SSE of Ashland, Ky., and 9 mi/14.5 km W of Hunbtington, W.Va., on Ohio R., at mouth of Big Sandy R. (Ky., Ohio, and W.Va. meet at confluence); 38°25′N 82°35′W. Mfg. (oil processing, coal processing, asphalt, boats). Settled as trading post 1808.

Catlin, village (1990 pop. 2,173), Vermillion co., E Ill., 6 mi/9.7 km SW of Danville; 40°04′N 87°42′W. Bituminous-coal mines; agr. (corn, wheat, soybeans, livestock, poultry; dairying).

Cato (KA-to), village (□ 1 sq mi/2.6 sq km; 1990 pop. 581), Cayuga co., W central N.Y., 16 mi/26 km N of Auburn; 43°10′N 76°34′W.

Catoctin (ka-TAHK-tin), village, Frederick co., N Md., at E base of Catoctin Mt., and 11 mi/18 km N of Frederick.

Catoctin Creek, c.35 mi/56 km long, Frederick co., NW Md.; rises in the Blue Ridge; flows S, through Middletown Valley, to the Potomac R. 3 mi/4.8 km E of Brunswick.

Catoctin Mountain, E prong of the Blue Ridge in Md.; extends c.37 mi/60 km SSW from Pa. line in W Frederick co., Md., into Loudoun co., Va. Elev. 1,740 ft/530 m. Separated from W prong of Blue Ridge (South Mt.) in Md. by Middletown Valley. Catoctin Recreational Demonstration Area (10,126 acres/4,098 ha), just W of Thurmont, Md., is under jurisdiction of Natl. Capital Parks system; it includes Camp David, a presidential retreat.

Catoctin Mountain Park (□ 9 sq mi/23.3 sq km), Frederick co., NW Md.; campgrounds, trails, and scenic drive located in the Catoctin Mts.; includes Camp David, the presidential retreat. The 6,000 acres/2,428 ha have been allowed to develop into a climax hardwood forest, populated by deer, foxes, and raccoons. Authorized 1936.

Catonsville, uninc. city (1990 pop. 35,233), Baltimore co., N Md., a suburb of Baltimore. Named in honor of Richard Caton, a son-in-law of Charles Carroll of Carrollton. The Baltimore Co. campus of the Univ. of Md. is located here, as well as Catonsville Community Col.

Catoosa (kuh-TOO-suh), county (□ 167 sq mi/433 sq km; 1990 pop. 42,464), NW Ga.; ⊙ Ringgold; 34°54′N 85°08′W. Bounded N by Tenn. state line. Cotton, potatoes, corn, fruit, cattle, poultry; timber; textile mfg. Includes parts of Chickamauga and Chattanooga Natl. Military Park and Chattahoochee Natl. Forest. Formed 1853.

Catoosa, town (1990 pop. 2,954), Rogers co., NE Okla., suburb 15 mi/24 km E of downtown Tulsa, on Verdigris R. at mouth of Bird Creek; 36°10′N 95°46′W. Agr. and coal mining; mfg. (machinery and heavy mfg.) Largest port on Kerr McClellan Ark. Navigational System; Port of Catoosa on Verdigris R.

Catorce, Mexico: see REAL DE CATORCE.

Catron (kuh-TRON), county (□ 6,929 sq mi/17,946 sq km; 1990 pop. 2,563), W N.Mex.; ⊙ Reserve; 33°55′N 108°25′W. Cattle, goats, sheep; hay, alfalfa, wheat, oats, barley; mining (gold and silver); timber and quarrying region. Watered by Gila, San Francisco, and Tularosa rivers; bounded W by Ariz. Includes parts of Gila (S), Apache-Sitgreaves (NW), and Cibola (NE) natl. forests. Tularosa and Mogollon mts. in SW; Datil Mts. in NE; serpentine Continental Divide runs N-S through county's E center. Gila Cliff Dwellings Natl. Monument in S boundary; co. formed 1921. Datil Well Natl. Recreation Site in NE; Plains of San Agustin in E center. 28th largest co. in U.S.

Catron (KA-truhn), city (1990 pop. 81), New Madrid co., extreme SE Mo., near Mississippi R., 10 mi/16 km W of New Madrid; 36°36′N 89°42′W. Rice, cotton, soybeans.

Catskill, village (□ 2 sq mi/5.2 sq km; 1990 pop. 4,690), ⊙ Greene co., SE N.Y., on the Hudson R.; 42°12′N 73°52′W. Connected with the mfg. town of Hudson, N.Y. by the Rip Van Winkle Bridge (completed 1935), it is a gateway to resorts in the Catskill Mts. The Catskill Game Farm is nearby. Thomas Cole lived and painted in the village. Settled 17th cent. by Dutch, inc. 1806.

Catskill Aqueduct, N.Y., see ASHOKAN RESERVOIR.

Catskill Creek, SE N.Y., rises in the Catskills in E Schoharie co., flows c.40 mi/64 km generally SE, joining Kaaterskill Creek just as it broadens W of Catskill before joining the Hudson R.

Catskill Mountains, dissected plateau of the Appalachian Mt. system, SE N.Y., W of the Hudson R. This glaciated region, which is well wooded and rolling, with deep gorges and many beautiful waterfalls, is drained by the headwaters of the Delaware R. and by Esopus, Schoharie, Rondout, and Catskill creeks. The topography bet. the N and S portions of the Catskills differs noticeably: the S Catskills of Delaware, Sullivan, and Ulster cos., with higher summits, deeper, narrower valleys and more blocky, subalpine character contrast with the more rounded, yet elevated hills and flatter skyline of the Catskills S of the Helderberg Escarpment in Schoharie co. and W of the Helderberg Escarpment in Greene co. Most of the summits are c.3,000 ft/914 m above sea level; Slide Mt. (elev. 4,180 ft/1,274 m) and Hunter Mt. (elev. 4,040 ft/1,231 m) are the highest. Close to N.Y. city, the area has long been a popular resort, esp. in the summer, but in recent years has declined, especially with closing of most of its hotels. Of the 19 reservoirs that are N.Y. city's sole source of pure, untreated drinking water (c.1,000,000,000 gals/3,785,300,000 liters per day), all of the large ones are found within the Catskill Mts. The Ashokan, Pepacton and Cannonville reservoirs are the 3 largest of this system. Protection of this water supply is a major political and economic issue involving N.Y. city and the residents of the Catskills. Catskill Forest Preserve embraces some of the most impressive scenery of the Catskills, including the region of the Rip Van Winkle legend.

Cattail Peak, N.C.: see BLACK MOUNTAINS.

Cattaraugus (ka-tuh-RAW-guhs), county (□ 1,322 sq mi/3,424 sq km; 1990 84,234), W N.Y., bounded S by Pa. border; ⊙ Little Valley; 42°14′N 78°40′W. Intersected by Allegheny R.; drained by Cattaraugus, Conewango, and Ischua creeks. Dairying; farming (fruit, hay, potatoes), stock-raising area. Diversified mfg., esp. at Olean, Salamanca. Natural gas and oil wells; sand and gravel pits. Includes Allegany State Park, Allegany Indian Reservation, and part of Cattaraugus Indian Reservation. Name derived from Seneca word meaning "bad-smelling banks," referring to natural gas leaks. With adjacent Allegany and Chatauqua cos., prominent in the late-19th and early-20th-cent. petroleum industry, based on the "Pennsylvania" oil fields, which were played out by the late 1930s. Formed 1808.

Cattaraugus (ka-tuh-RAW-guhs), village (1990 pop. 1,100), Cattaraugus co., W N.Y., 29 mi/47 km NW of Olean; 42°19′N 78°52′W. Mfg. of wood prods., custom laminates, RR car and trailer-truck interiors; lumber milling. Agr. (dairy prods.; poultry; hay; sweet corn, potatoes). Cattaraugus Indian Reservation is NW. Settled 1851 during construction of Erie RR; inc. 1882.

Cattaraugus Creek (ka-tuh-RAW-guhs), c.70 mi/113 km long, W N.Y.; rises in Wyoming co.; flows SW and W, through Cattaraugus Indian Reservation, to L. Erie 12 mi/19 km NE of Dunkirk. Receives S. Branch near Gowanda.

Caucel (KOU-sel), village (1990 pop. 4,861), Merída municipio, Yucatán, SE Mexico, on RR and 6 mi/9.7 km NW of Mérida. Henequen.

Caucomgomoc Lake (kawk-muh-GAHM-uhk), Piscataquis co., N central Maine, 50 mi/80 km N of Greenville, in wilderness recreational area; 6 mi/9.7 km long, 2 mi/3.2 km wide.

Caunao (koun-OU), town, Cienfuegos prov., central Cuba, on RR and 3.5 mi/5.6 km NE of Cienfuegos; 22°12′N 79°18′W. In agr. region (sugarcane, coffee, tobacco, fruit).

Caunao River (koun-OU), c.70 mi/113 km long, Camagüey prov., E Cuba; rises NW of Camagüey city; flows N to Jigüey Bay 15 mi/24 km E of Cunagua; 22°06′N 80°24′W.

Caura Valley (KO-rah), N Trinidad, Trinidad and Tobago, along small Caura R. and 8 mi/12.9 km E of Port of Spain. Has luxuriant tropical vegetation. Once secluded picnic ground, now site of water reservoir.

Causapscal (ko-sahp-SKAHL), village (1991 pop. 2,160), E Que., on Matapédia R., and 35 mi/56 km NW of Campbellton; 48°21′N 67°13′W. Dairying, lumbering.

Causey (KAW-see), uninc. village, (1990 pop. 57), Roosevelt co., E N.Mex., 33 mi/53 km SSE of Portales, near Texas state boundary; 33°52′N 103°07′W. Livestock; grain, cotton.

Cauto (KOU-to), river, c. 213 mi./343 km long, Cuba; rising in the Sierra Maestra, Santiago de Cuba prov.; 20°33′N 77°14′W. It flows NW and W to the Caribbean Sea just N of Manzanillo. Longest river in Cuba.

Cauto Cristo (KOU-to KREE-sto), agr. town, NE Granma prov., near Holguín prov. line, SE Cuba, on Cauto R., and in middle of Cauto R. valley; 20°33′N 76°28′W. Surrounded by dense network of canals.

Cavaillon (kah-vei-YONG), agr. town (1982 pop. 745), Sud dept., SW Haiti, on Jacmel Peninsula, near the coast, 6 mi/9.7 km NE of Les Cayes; 18°18′N 73°39′W. Agr. (coffee, limes, tobacco, bananas, sugarcane); essential oils distilling.

Cavalier, county (□ 1,511 sq mi/3,913 sq km; 1990 pop. 6,064), NE N.Dak., bordering Man., Canada, on N; ⊙ Langdon Drift; 48°46′N 98°27′Wt. Prairie area, drained by Pembina, Tongue and Park rivers. Durum wheat, barley, dairy prods., cattle. Agr. experiment station at Langdon; Frostfire Mt. Ski Area to NE; Rush L. in NW. Formed 1873.

Cavalier, town (1990 pop. 1,508), ⊙ Pembina co., NE N.Dak., 70 mi/113 km NNW of Grand Forks, and on Tongue R.; 48°47′N 97°37′W. Spring wheat, dairy produce, livestock, potatoes; mfg. (farm equip.). Icelandic State Park to W. Founded 1875, inc. 1885.

Cavallo Pass, Texas: see MATAGORDA ISLAND.

Cave City 1 town (1990 pop. 1,503), Sharp co., N Ark., 13 mi/21 km NNE of Batesville; 35°57′N 91°32′W. Mfg. (tool and die). **2** town (1990 pop. 1,953), Barren co., S Ky., 10 mi/16 km NNW of Glasgow; 37°08′N 85°57′W. Agr. (burley tobacco, grain; livestock, poultry; dairying); mfg. (sportswear, kitchen cabinets, boat trailers, conveyor systems). Tourist center for limestone cave region of Ky. MAMMOTH CAVE NATIONAL PARK to W; Onyx and Crystal Onyx caves to SW, Mammoth Onyx and Horse caves to N. Ky. Action Park and Guntown Mt. Amusement Park to W.

Cave Creek, town (1990 pop. 2,925), Maricopa co., central Ariz., residential suburb 27 mi/43 km NNE of downtown Phoenix, 2 mi/3.2 km W of Carefree; 33°49′N 111°58′W. Tonto Natl. Forest to E and N; Cave Creek Dam, on Cave Creek, to SW. Pioneer Ariz. Mus. to W.

Cave Creek Dam, Ariz.: see SALT RIVER.

Cave in Rock, village, Hardin co., extreme SE Ill., on Ohio R. (ferry here), and 8 mi/12.9 km E of Elizabethtown; 37°28′N 88°09′W. In agr. area. Cave in Rock State Park is nearby.

Cave Junction, town (1990 pop. 1,126), Josephine co., SW Oregon, 25 mi/40 km SW of Grants Pass on Illinois R., at mouth of West Fork Illinois; 42°10′N 123°38′W. Timber. Wineries. Dairy prods. Pears, grapes. L. Selmac Reservoir to NE. Illinois R. State Park to SW. Gateway to Oregon Caves Natl. Monument to SE. Parts of Siskiyou Natl. Forest to W and SE.

Cave Run Lake, reservoir (□ 13 sq mi/34 sq km), Bath, Rowan, Menifee, and Morgan cos., E Ky., on Licking R., in Daniel Boone Natl. State Forest, 7 mi/11 km SW of Morehead; 38°07′N 83°32′W. Max. capacity 614,100acre-ft. Formed by Cave Run Lake Dam (139 ft/42 m high), built (1974) by Army Corps of Engineers for flood control: also used for recreation. Twin Knobs Campsite near dam.

Cave Spring, uninc. city, Roanoke co., SW Va., residential suburb 4 mi/6.4 km SW of downtown Roanoke; 37°13′N 80°00′W. Blue Ridge Parkway passes to S and SE. Roanoke Mtn. Rec. Area to E.

Cave Spring, town (1990 pop. 950), Floyd co., NW Ga., 14 mi/23 km SW of Rome, near Ala. state line; 34°07′N 85°20′W. Mfg. includes polystyrene packaging, meat processing. Nearly 100 old blds. are listed on the Natl. Register of Historic Places, now typically occupied by antique and craft shops.

Cave Springs, town (1990 pop. 465), Benton co., extreme NW Ark., 8 mi/12.9 km SW of Rogers, and 8 mi/12.9 km NW of Springdale on Osage Creek, in the Ozarks.

Cave Valley, town (1991 pop. 1,777), St. Ann parish, central Jamaica, 18 mi/29 km SW of St. Ann's Bay; 18°16′N 77°22′W. In rich agr. region (citrus fruit, corn, pimento, coffee; cattle). Site of ruins of military barracks.

Cavendish, town (1990 pop. 1,323), Windsor co., S central Vt., 20 mi/32 km SSW of Woodstock, and on Black R.; 43°24′N 72°35′W. Winter sports. Includes Proctorsville village and Proctor-Piper state forest. Settled 1769.

Cavetown, village, Washington co., W Md., 7 mi/11.3 km E of Hagerstown. Elev. 750 ft/229 m.

Cavour (KUH-vor), village (1990 pop. 166), Beadle co., E central S.Dak., 10 mi/16 km E of Huron.

Cawker City (KAWK-uhr), village (1990 pop. 588), Mitchell co., N Kansas, 17 mi/27 km W of Beloit; 39°30′N 98°25′W. In grain and livestock area; mfg. of farm machinery. Solomon R. formed just S by confluence of South Fork and North Fork. Located on N side of Waconda L. Reservoir.

Cawood (KAI-see), town (1990 pop. 800), Harlan co., SE Ky., 7 mi/11.3 km SE of Harlan, in Cumberland Mts. Bituminous coal. Martin's Fork L. reservoir to SW; Cranks Creek Wildlife Management Area to SE.

Caxhuacán (kash-wah-KAN), town (1990 pop. 3,187), Puebla, central Mexico, in SE foothills of Sierra Madre Oriental, 29 mi/47 km ESE of Huauchinango; 20°04′N 97°36′W. Sugarcane, coffee, tobacco, fruit. In Totonac Indian area.

Cay Lobos, or **Lobos Cay**, islet and district (including Cay Sal, □ 7 sq mi/18.1 sq km), S Bahama Isls., on S fringe of the Great Bahama Bank, separated from Cuba by 20-mi/32-km-wide Old Bahama Channel, 185 mi/298 km S of Nassau; 22°24′N 77°37′W. Lighthouse.

Cay Sal, [Span. = salt key], uninhabited islet, Bahama Isls., on SW fringe of Cay Sal Bank, on 45 mi/72 km–wide Nicholas Channel, separating the bank from Cuba, and 100 mi/161 km SE of Key West, Fla. Belongs with Cay Lobos (200 mi/322 km ESE) to Cay Lobos dist.

Cay Sal Bank, shoal (c.70 mi/113 km long, up to 45 mi/72 km wide) in the West Indies, bet. Florida (W) and Cuba (S), 100 mi/161 km S of Miami; bounded by Straits of Florida (NW), Santaren Channel (E), and Nicholas Channel (S). Cay Sal reef is on its W fringe.

Cayajabos (kei-yuh-HO-boz), town, La Habana prov., W Cuba, 38 mi/61 km SW of Havana; 22°51′N 82°51′W. Tobacco, sugarcane, fruit.

Cayamas, Cayería Las (kei-YAH-mahz, kei-yah-REE-uh lahs), small keys off SW Cuba, in the Gulf of Batabanó, about 2.5 mi/4 km from SW shore of La Habana prov., and 35 mi/56 km SSW of Havana; chain is c.10 mi/16 km long (N-S); 22°35′N 82°31′W. Also, Las Cayamas Keys.

Cayce (KAI-see), city (1990 pop. 11,163), Lexington co., central S.C., on Congaree R., 2 mi/3.2 km S of downtown Columbia; 33°57′N 81°03′W. Mfg. includes steel fabrication, burial vaults, pizza dough, structural framing, steel reinforcing bars, paints, commercial water heaters; Agr. includes dairying, poultry, hogs, corn. Cayce Historical Mus. is here.

Cayce, village (1990 pop. 200), Fulton co., extreme W Ky., 28 mi/45 km WSW of Mayfield. Agr. area (tobacco, grain; livestock). Boyhood home of "Casey" Jones, RR engineer famed in balladry; nearby is monument to him.

Cayemites Islands (kai-MEET), 2 islets (□ 17 sq mi/44 sq km), W Haiti, in Gulf of Gonaïves, just off N Jacmel Peninsula, 90 mi/145 km W of Port-au-Prince; 18°40′N 73°40′W. Just W of the larger, Grande Cayemite, is Petite Cayemite. Cotton growing; bauxite deposits.

Cayería Diego Pérez (kei-yah-REE-uh dee-AI-go PAI-raiz), group of islets off S coast of Matanzas prov., W central Cuba, S of Zapata Peninsula, bet. Batabanó and Cazone gulfs of Caribbean Sea; 22°09′N 81°40′W.

Cayes, Haiti: see LES CAYES.

Cayes-de-Jacmel (kai–duh–ZHAK-MEL) or **Cayes-Jacmel**, town (1982 pop. 1,262), Sud-Est dept., S Haiti, on the coast, 10 mi/16 km E of Jacmel; 18°14′N 72°24′W. Coffee, citrus growing; bauxite deposits nearby. Fishing port.

Cayetano Rubio (ka-ye-TAH-no ROO-bee-yo), town, Querétaro, central Mexico, on interior plateau, 2 mi/3.2 km E of Querétaro. Cotton milling. Formerly called Hércules.

Cayey (kei-AI), town (1990 pop. 46,553), SE P.R., in the Sierra de Cayey mts. Industrial and commercial area; mfg. (furniture, electric prods., clothing, carbonated beverages). The Univ. of P.R.-Cayey is located on site of former U.S. military barracks.

Cayey, Sierra de (kei-AI, see-ER-reh-dai), mountain range, SE P.R., just N of Guayama, extending c.20 mi/32 km W-E. Rises to 2,963 ft/903 m (Cerro La Santa). In the region are L. Carite reservoir and hydroelectric plants.

Cayley, village (1991 pop. 229), S Alta., Canada, 40 mi/64 km S of Calgary; 50°27′N 113°51′W. Wheat, dairying.

Cayman Brac, island (□ 12.85 sq mi/33.28 sq km; 1989 pop. 1,441) of Cayman Isls., Br. crown colony, West Indies, easternmost of the group, separated by narrow channel from Little Cayman isl. (W), and 75 mi/121 km ENE of Grand Cayman isl.; 19°45′N 79°50′W; c.11 mi/18 km long, 1 mi/1.6 km wide, rising to 130 ft/40 m. Resorts at Tiara Beach and Brac Reef Beach. Large caves in the limestone cliff running down the center of the isl. are open to visitors and are still used as hurricane shelters.

Cayman Deep, Caribbean Sea: see BARTLETT TROUGH.

Cayman Islands (□ 100 sq mi/259 sq km; 1989 pop. 25,355), Br. crown colony, comprising 3 isls. in the West Indies. George Town, the ⊙ and chief port, is on Grand Cayman; the other isls. are Little Cayman and Cayman Brac; 19°30′N 80°40′W. Finance and tourism are the economic mainstays of the Cayman Islands. The isls. are notable as an offshore banking center; since the 1970s tourism has increased substantially. The isls. were sighted by Christopher Columbus in 1503.

Cayman Trench, submarine trench in the Caribbean Sea Basin extending along the S slope of the Cayman Ridge, S of Cuba, with maximum depth reaching 23,179 ft/7,065 m at c. 14°N.

Cayo Cantiles (KEI-yo kahn-TEE-lais), one of largest keys W of Isla de la Juventud, S coast of Cuba; 21°42′N 82°30′W. Part of Los Canarreos Archipelago.

Cayo Cruz (KEI-yo KRUZ), small key just N of Cayo Romano, in Camagüey Archipelago, off N coast of Camagüey prov., E central Cuba; 22°15′N 77°46′W. Fast becoming a major tourist and beach resort.

Cayo Cruz del Padre (KEI-yo KRUZ DAIL PAH-drai), largest and northernmost key of Sabana Archipelago, off coast of Matanzas prov., N Cuba; 23°15′N 80°55′W.

Cayo Guá (KEI-yo GWAH), small key off point with same name, Granma prov., SE Cuba, in Gulf of Guacanayabo; 20°21′N 77°15′W.

Cayo Largo, Cuba: see LARGO, CAYO.

Cayo Mambí (KAI-yo mahm-BEE), town, Holguín prov., E Cuba, on landlocked inlet, 5 mi/8 km NNW of Sagua de Tánamo, just offshore from Frank País sugar mill; 20°40′N 75°16′W. Sugarcane, fruit.

Cayo Piedra (KAI-yo pee-AI-druh), town, in S central Isla de la Juventud, off S coast of Cuba, in the middle of Lanier Swamp; 21°40′N 82°46′W. Bird-watching.

Cayo San Juan (KAI-yo sahn hwahn), several small keys W of Isla de la Juventud, in Los Canarreos Archipelago, off S shore of Cuba; 21°43′N 82°33′W.

Cayon, village, E St. Kitts, West Indies, 4 mi/6.4 km N of Basseterre.

Cayos Balandras (KAI-yos bah-LAHN-drahz), small keys N of Niquero Bay, Granma prov., SE Cuba, in S part of Gulf of Guacanayabo; 20°05′N 77°37′W.

Cayos de Ana María (KAI-yos dai AH-nah mah-REE-uh), N-S alignment of small keys about 18 mi/29 km long in gulf of same name, off S shore of Ciego de Ávila prov., central Cuba; 21°30′N 78°47′W.

Cayos de San Felipe, Cuba: see SAN FELIPE, CAYOS DE.

Cayos los Guzmanes (KAI-yos los guz-MAHN-aiz), small keys in Gulf of Batabanó, 6 mi/9.7 km S of town of Guarimar, SW La Habana prov., W Cuba; 22°37′N 82°42′W. Aligned N-S.

Cayucos, uninc. town (1990 pop. 2,960), San Luis Obispo co., Calif., on Pacific Ocean; 35°27′N 120°53′W. Small section of Los Padres Natl. Forest to E; Santa Lucia Range to N. Flowers, nursery stock, apples, avocados, strawberries, vegetables, beans, grain, cattle.

Cayuga (kai-YOO-guh), county (□ 778 sq mi/2,015 sq km; 1990 pop. 82,313), W central N.Y.; ⊙ Auburn; 42°56′N 76°33′W. Bounded N by L. Ontario and extending S into Finger Lakes region; crossed by N.Y. State Barge Canal; drained by Seneca R. Dairying and farming (hay, corn, grain) area, with diversified mfg. mainly at Auburn. Summer residences on scenic Cayuga, Skaneateles, and Owasco lakes. Named for the 4th tribe of the Iroquois Confederacy. Formed 1799.

Cayuga, town (1990 pop. 1,083), Vermillion co., W Ind., near Wabash R., 15 mi/24 km SE of Danville, Ill.; 39°57′N 87°28′W. Agr. and bituminous-coal area; mfg. (canned goods, brick, corrugated shipping containers, feeds, ice cream). Electric power plant nearby.

Cayuga (kai-YOO-guh), village, ⊙ Haldimand co., S Ont., Canada, on Grand R., and 20 mi/32 km S of Hamilton. Natural-gas production, light mfg., dairying; limestone, gypsum, and sandstone quarries.

Cayuga 1 (kai-YOO-guh), village (□ 1 sq mi/2.6 sq km; 1990 pop. 556), Cayuga co., W central N.Y., on Cayuga L. near N end, 7 mi/11.3 km W of Auburn; 42°55′N 76°43′W. **2** (kah-YOO-guh), village (1990 pop. 60), Sargent co., SE N.Dak.,11 mi/18 km W of Lidgerwood, on Wild Rice R.; 46°04′N 97°22′W. RR junction to E at Geneseo.

Cayuga and Seneca Canal, N.Y.: see SENECA RIVER.

Cayuga Heights (kai-YOO-guh), residential village (□ 1 sq mi/2.6 sq km; 1990 pop. 3,457), Tompkins co., W central N.Y., on Cayuga L., just N of Ithaca, in Finger Lakes region; 42°28′N 76°29′W.

Cayuga Lake (kai-YOO-guh), W central N.Y.; 38 mi/61 km long, 1 mi/1.6 km–3.5 mi/5.6 km wide; 42°45′N 76°44′W. Longest of the Finger Lakes. It is connected by canal and by the Seneca R. with the Barge Canal to the N. Cornell Univ. and Wells Col. overlook Cayuga's steep banks. Near the S end of the lake are Taughannock Falls, 215 ft/66 m high.

Cayuta Creek (kuh-YOO-tuh), c.35 mi/56 km long, N.Y. and Pa.; rises in Cayuta L. (c.2 mi/3.2 km long) SW of Ithaca, W central N.Y.; flows generally SE to Susquehanna R. at Sayre, Pa.

Cazadero, uninc. village, Sonoma co., NW Calif., 13 mi/21 km SW of Healdsburg, on Austin Creek. Timber, cattle, lambs. Mfg. (concrete). Austin Creek State Recreation Area to NE.

Cazenovia 1 (kaz-uh-NO-vee-uh), village (□ 1 sq mi/2.6 sq km; 1990 pop. 3,007), Madison co., central N.Y., at S end of Cazenovia L., 18 mi/29 km SE of Syracuse; 42°55′N 75°50′W. In dairy farming area; dielectrics, electronics circuitry. Seat of Cazenovia Col. Settled 1793, inc. 1810. **2** village (1990 pop. 288), Richland co., S central Wis., 10 mi/16 km W of Reedsburg; 43°31′N 90°12′W. In dairy and livestock region.

Cazenovia Lake (kaz-uh-NO-vee-uh), Madison co., central N.Y., 15 mi/24 km SE of Syracuse; 4 mi/6.4 km long; 42°57′N 75°53′W. Resort area.

Cazones, Mexico: see CAZONES DE HERRERA.

Cazones de Herrera (ka-SO-nais de er-RER-rah), town (1990 pop. 4,285), Veracruz, Mexico, on small Cazones R., near Gulf of Mexico, 18 mi/29 km SSE of Túxpam de Rodríguez Cano. Fruit, fiber plants, rubber.

Cazones, Gulf of (kuh-ZON-aiz), off Matanzas prov., S Cuba, bet. Zapata Peninsula (N) and Jardines Bank (S), 45 mi/72 km WSW of Cienfuegos; c.30 mi/48 km long, up to 10 mi/16 km wide; 22°00′N 81°20′W. Fringed by keys. Its NW extension is called Ensenada de Cazones.

Cebolleta (se-bo-YET-uh), uninc. village, Cibola co., W N.Mex., on branch of San Jose R., 27 mi/43 km E of Grants. Shrine of Our Lady of Lourdes nearby. Parts of Laguna Pueblo Indian village and Cañoncito Indian Reservation is to S. San Mateo Mts. and part of Cibola Natl. Forest, including Mt. Taylor, to NW. Also spelled Seboyeta.

Cebolleta Mountains, N.Mex.: see SAN MATEO MOUNTAINS.

Ceboruco Volcano (sai-bo-ROO-ko), twin peak (7,100 ft/2,164 m), Nayarit, W Mexico, in Sierra Madre Occidental, 6 mi/9.7 km NW of Ahuacatlán; 21°3′N 104°30′W. Active.

Cecil (SEE-sill), county (□ 417 sq mi/1,080 sq km; 1990 pop. 71,347), extreme NE Md.; ⊙ Elkton; 39°34′N 75°57′W. At head of Chesapeake Bay and at base of Eastern Shore, it is bounded S by Sassafras R., E by Del. state line, N by Pa. state line, W by the Susquehanna. Drained by Elk R. (receives Chesapeake and Delaware Canal W of Chesapeake City), Northeast R., Bohemia R., and Octoraro Creek. Livestock raising, dairying, agr. (wheat, corn, vegetables, fruit); granite quarries, sand and gravel pits; mfg. (transportation equip., medical instruments, rubber goods); commercial fisheries. Includes Elk Neck (state park and state forest) and Susquehanna Flats (waterfowl hunting). The co. was created by proclamation in 1674, and takes its name from Cecil Calvert, the 2d Lord Baltimore. A boundary dispute in the N part of the co. bet. Lord Baltimore and William Penn was resolved only by the drawing of the Mason-Dixon line in 1765.

Cecil 1 (SEE-suhl), town (1990 pop. 376), Cook co., S Ga., 16 mi/26 km NNW of Valdosta; 31°03′N 83°23′W. **2** (SE-sil), uninc. town (1990 pop. 750), Washington co., SW Pa., suburb 13 mi/21 km SW of downtown Pittsburgh; 40°19′N 80°10′W. Mfg. (paints, nonferrous castings). Agr. (dairying).

Cecil 1 (SEE-suhl), village (1990 pop. 249), Paulding co., NW Ohio, near Maumee R., 12 mi/19 km WSW of Defiance; 41°13′N 84°36′W. **2** (SEE-sil), village (1990 pop. 373), Shawano co., NE Wis., at E end of Shawano L., 30 mi/48 km NW of Green Bay city; 44°48′N 88°27′W. Lumbering.

Cecilia, town (1990 pop. 1,374), St. Martin parish, La. 5 mi/8 km NE of Breaux Bridge; 30°20′N 91°51′W. Oil field nearby. Crawfish on E bank of Bayou Teche.

Cecilia, uninc. village (1990 pop. 300), Hardin co., N Ky., 5 mi/8 km W of Elizabethtown. RR junction. Tobacco, grain, livestock, dairying. Mfg. (agr. fertilizers, hams and bacon, bulk materials handling equip.). Addington Field Airport to E.

Cecilton (SEE-sill-ton), town (1990 pop. 489), Cecil co., NE Md., 16 mi/26 km SE of Havre de Grace; 39°24′N 75°52′W. Nearby are historic estates.

Cedar 1 county (□ 582 sq mi/1,507 sq km; 1990 pop. 17,381), E Iowa; ⊙ Tipton; 41°46′N 91°07′W. Prairie agr. area (hogs, cattle, corn, oats, soybeans) drained by Cedar R.; limestone quarries. Local flooding occured in 1993. Formed 1837. **2** county (□ 496 sq mi/1285 sq km; 1990 pop. 12,093), W Mo., in Ozark region; ⊙ Stockton; 37°43′N 93°51′W. Drained by Sac R. Corn, wheat, hay, soybeans; cattle; hardwood timber. Mfg. at El Dorado Springs and Stockton. Stockton Dam and Lake SE of Stockton. Stockton State Park occupies peninsula at center of lake. Formed 1843. **3** county (□ 745 sq mi/1,930 sq km; 1990 pop. 10,131), NE Nebr.; ⊙ Hartington; 42°36′N 97°15′W. Agr. region bounded N by Missouri R. and S.Dak.; drained by Logan R. Cattle, dairying, hogs, corn, barley, alfalfa. Formed 1857.

Cedar 1 village (1990 pop. 25), Smith co., N Kansas, on North Fork Solomon R., and 10 mi/16 km SW of Smith Center; 39°39′N 98°56′W. Grain, livestock. **2** town, Leelanau co., NW Mich., 10 mi/16 km NW of Traverse City; 44°50′N 85°47′W. In fruit-growing, farming, and resort area. S end of Lower Leelanau L. to E.

Cedar Bluff 1 town (1990 pop. 1,174), Cherokee co., NE Ala., on Coosa R., and 6 mi/9.7 km NE of Centre. Farming, lumber, women's apparel. **2** town (1990 pop. 1,290), Tazewell co., SW Va., in the Allegheny Mts., on Clinch R., 29 mi/47 km WSW of Bluefield; 37°05′N 81°45′W. Mfg. (steel fabrication, electronic and coal-mining equip., mine-roof supports); agr. (livestock; dairying; corn, tobacco).

Cedar Bluff, reservoir (□ 17 sq mi/44 sq km), Trego co., NE Kansas, on Smoky Hill R., 23 mi/37 km WSW of Hayes; 38°47′N 99°44′W. Max. capacity 730,180 acre-ft. Formed by Cedar Bluff Dam (202 ft/62 m high), built (1952) by the Bureau of Reclamation for irrigation; also used for flood control, recreation, water supply, and as a fish and wildlife pond. Cedar Bluff State Park on S shore.

Cedar Bluffs, village (1990 pop. 591), Saunders co., E Nebr., 6 mi/9.7 km SW of Fremont, near Platte R; 41°23′N 96°36′W. Livestock, grain.

Cedar Breaks Monument (□ 9 sq mi/23.3 sq km), SE Iron co., SW Utah, 14 mi/23 km ESE of Cedar City. Authorized 1933. Natural amphitheater (sandstone formation, 2,000 ft/610 m deep) in Pink Cliffs formed by erosion. Multi-colored pinnacles, arctic-alpine life zones. Bounded on all sides by Dixie Natl. Forest; Ashdown Gorge Wilderness Area on W.

Cedar City, city (1990 pop. 13,443), Iron co., SW Utah, just W of Markagunt Plateau and Cedar Canyon, just NE of Kolob Terrace, 45 mi/72 km NE of St. George, 220 mi/354 km SSW of Salt Lake City; 37°41′N 113°04′W. Elev. 5,834 ft/1,778 m. Home of Southern Utah Univ. and trade center for livestock and agr. area; barley, alfalfa; dairying; sheep, cattle; mfg. (plaster, wool prods., fuel, consumer goods, lumber). Sawmill and coal and iron mines, are nearby. RR terminus; junction of RR spur to Iron Mountain to NW. Sections of Dixie Natl. Forest (hunting and fishing) are E and SW, including Ashdown Gorge Wilderness Area (E); Cedar Breaks Natl. Monument (E). Columbia Iron Mine to W; Iron Mission State Historical Park to N. Settled 1851, 1st iron smelter W of Miss. R.; inc. 1868.

Cedar Creek 1 c.35 mi/56 km long, N Va.; rises 15 mi/24 km SW of Strasburg, in NW Shenandoah co.; flows NE, then SE, joining North Fork Shenandoah R. 1 mi/1.6 km E of Strasburg. Civil War battlesite (Oct. 19, 1864). **2** c.50 mi/80 km long, S Iowa; rises in Lucas co.; flows E and generally N to Des Moines R., 9 mi/14.5 km WSW of Oskaloosa. **3** c.75 mi/121 km long, SE Iowa; rises in Mahaska co.; flows generally SE to Skunk R. in Henry co. **4** c.125 mi/201 km long, N.Dak.; rises in Slope co., SW N.Dak.; flows E to Cannonball R.; 46°22′N 103°17′W.

Cedar Creek Reservoir 1 Franklin co., NW Ala., on Cedar Creek, 25 mi/40 km SW of Florence; 34°31′N 87°59′W. Max. capacity 111,500 acre-ft. Formed by Cedar Creek Dam (83 ft/25 m high) built in 1974 by the TVA for flood control, recreational, and water supply purposes. **2** Henderson and Kaufman cos., NE Texas, on Cedar Creek, 12 mi/19 km W of Athens; c.25 mi/40 km long; 32°12′N 96°03′W. Max. capacity 1,085,000 acre-ft. Formed by Joe B. Hoggsett Dam (73 ft/22 m high), built (1965) for water supply.

Cedar Falls, city (1990 pop. 34,298), Black Hawk co., N Iowa, on the Cedar R., adjoins Waterloo on E; 42°31′N 92°27′W. It developed as a milling center in the late 19th cent. after the coming of the RR; its name is derived from the cedar tree. The town of North Cedar merged with Cedar Falls. Largely residential, the city has light mfg. (machining, agr. equip., printing). Cedar Falls is the seat of the Univ. of Northern Iowa and of the Evangelical Campgrounds, scene of the annual Interdenominational Bible Conference. It has a Historical Society Mus. and George Wyth State Park is in the E part of the city, on the boundary with Waterloo. Inc. 1854.

Cedar Fort, village (1990 pop. 248), Utah co., N central Utah, 33 mi/53 km SSW of Salt Lake City, between Cedar Valley (SE) and Oquirrh Mts. (NW). Sheep, cattle. Stagecoach Inn and Camp Floyd state historic parks to S at Fairfield, on old Pony Express Route. Camp Williams Military Reservation to N.

Cedar Gap, uninc. locality, Wright co., S central Mo., in the Ozarks, 14 mi/23 km W of Hartville. Elev. 1,694 ft/516 m. Highest point on cross-state highway and RR in the Missouri Ozarks.

Cedar Grove, town (1991 pop. 697), 3 mi/4.8 km NE of Saint John's, near N shore, Saint John Parish, N Antigua Isl., Antigua and Barbuda Republic; 17°10′N 61°49′W.

Cedar Grove 1 town (□ 1 sq mi/2.6 sq km; 1990 pop. 1,479), Bay co., located in NW Fla., just E of Panama City; 30°10′N 85°37′W. **2** town (1990 pop. 246), Franklin co., SE Ind., 5 mi/8 km SSE of Brookville; 39°22′N 84°56′W. Agr. area. **3** town (1990 pop. 1,213), Kanawha co., W central W.Va., on Kanawha R., 14 mi/23 km SE of Charleston; 38°13′N 81°25′W. Bituminous coal, gas, and oil region. Site of Booker T. Washington's boyhood home is nearby. Settled 1773. **4** town (1990 pop. 1,521), Sheboygan co., E Wis., 12 mi/19 km SSW of Sheboygan; 43°34′N 87°49′W. In dairy and grain area. Mfg. (iron castings, vegetable packing: peas, corn, lima beans). Harrington Beach State Park to SE.

Cedar Grove, township (1990 pop. 12,053), Essex co., NE N.J., in Watchung Mts., 8 mi/12.9 km NNW of Newark; 40°51′N 74°13′W. Mfg. (gauges, brushes). Largely residential. Overbrook state mental hospital here.

Cedar Heights 1 village, Prince Georges co., central Md., E suburb of Wash., D.C. **2** uninc. village, Whitemarsh township, Montgomery co., SE Pa., residential suburb 1 mi/1.6 km NE of Conshohocken; 40°5′N 75°17′W.

Cedar Hill, city (1990 pop. 19,976), Dallas and Ellis cos., N Texas, suburb 18 mi/29 km SW of Dallas; 32°34′N 96°57′W. Agr. to S (cattle; dairying; cotton); mfg. (prod. samples, concrete pipes, diversified light mfg.). On S fringe of rapidly growing urban area. L. Joe Pool reservoir to NW, Cedar Hill State Park is on SE shore.

Cedar Hills 1 uninc. town (1990 pop. 9,294), Washington co., NW Oregon, residential suburb 5 mi/8 km W of downtown Portland; 45°30′N 122°48′W. **2** town (1990 pop. 769), Utah co., N central Utah, residential suburb 12 mi/19 km NNW of Provo and 28 mi/45 km SSE of Salt Lake City; 40°23′N 111°45′W. Agr. area. Uinta Natl. Forest to E; Timpanogos Cave Natl. Monument to NE.

Cedar Island 1 in St. Lawrence co., N N.Y., one of the Thousand Isls., in the St. Lawrence R., near Ont. line, just W of Chippewa Bay; c.1 mi/1.6 km long; 44°27′N 75°47′W. Site of Cedar Isl. State Park (recreational area). **2** Accomack co., E Va., barrier island just off Atlantic shore, 5 mi/8 km SE of Accomac; 6 mi/9.7 km long. Metompkin Inlet, Metompkin Isl. to N; Wachapreague Inlet, Parramore Isl. to S. **3** Carteret co., E N.C., in Pamlico Sound, arm of Atlantic Ocean, 30 mi/48 km NE of Morehead City, separated from mainland to SW by narrow channel (bridged), Core Sound to SE, West Bay to W; 9 mi/14.5 km long, 3 mi/4.8 km wide. Cedar Island Natl. Wildlife Reserve covers island. Ferry from NE tip of isl. to Ocracoke village, Ocracoke Isl., in Outer Banks, to NE.

Cedar Island, Maine: see ISLES OF SHOALS.

Cedar Key, city (□ 1 sq mi/2.6 sq km; 1990 pop. 668), Levy co., N central Fla., 55 mi/89 km SW of Gainesville, on small isl. connected by causeway with the Gulf coast; 29°08′N 83°02′W. Fishing; mfg. of palmetto brushes. Also is major resort.

Cedar Lake, town (1990 pop. 8,885), Lake co., NW Ind., on a small lake, 5 mi/8 km WSW of Crown Point; 41°22′N 87°26′W.

Cedar Lake (□ 537 sq mi/1,391 sq km), W Man., Canada, 50 mi/80 km SE of the Pas and 4 mi/6.4 km N of L. Winnipegosis; 40 mi/64 km long, 32 mi/51 km wide. Drained E into L. Winnipeg by Saskatchewan R.

Cedar Lake, reservoir, Jackson co., S Ill., on Cedar Creek, mostly in Shawnee Natl. Forest, 4 mi/6.4 km SW of Carbondale; 6 mi/9.7 km long; 37°39′N 89°17′W. Max. capacity of 41,500 acre-ft. Formed by Cedar Creek Dam (52 ft/16 m high), built (1973) for water supply.

Cedar Lake, Minn.: see KORONIS, LAKE.

Cedar Mill, uninc. town (1990 pop. 9,697), Washington co., NW Oregon, residential suburb 6 mi/9.7 km W of downtown Portland, on Cedar Mill Creek; 45°32′N 122°47′W. Tualatin Mts. to N. Agr. area on urban fringe. Dairying, poultry, fruit, vegetation, nurseries, fur farms.

Cedar Mills, village (1990 pop. 80), Meeker co., S central Minn., 11 mi/18 km S of Litchfield, on South Fork Crow R.; 44°57′N 94°31′W. Grain; livestock; dairying. Cedar L. to NE.

Cedar Park, town (1990 pop. 5,161), Williamson co., central Texas, 18 mi/29 km NNW of downtown Austin; 30°30′N 97°49′W. Ships cedar; limestone quarries; mfg. (precast concrete, drilling rig instruments). Large L. Travis reservoir to SW.

Cedar Park, suburb of Annapolis, Anne Arundel co., central Md.

Cedar Point 1 village (1990 pop. 275), La Salle co., N Ill., 5 mi/8 km S of La Salle; 41°15′N 89°07′W. In agr. area. **2** village (1990 pop. 39), Chase co., E central Kansas, on Cottonwood R., and 17 mi/27 km SW of Cottonwood Falls; 38°15′N 96°49′W. Livestock, grain. **3** village (1990 pop. 628), Carteret co., E N.C., 19 mi/31 km ESE of Jacksonville, at Cedar Pt., at entrance to Bogue Sound and mouth of White Oak R. (both bridged); 34°40′N 77°4′W. Atlantic Ocean to S.

Cedar Point, low peninsula, St. Marys co., S Md., on S side of Patuxent R. entrance from Chesapeake Bay and 18 mi/29 km N of Point Lookout. Site of Patuxent Naval Air Test Center. Cedar Point Lighthouse, built by the coast guard in 1894, was sited at the mouth of the Patuxent R. 15 mi/24 km E of Leonardtown. The lighthouse became a isl. when cut off from the mainland; it was abandoned in 1928.

Cedar Point, Ohio: see SANDUSKY BAY.

Cedar Rapids, city (1990 pop. 108,751), □ Linn co., E central Iowa, on the Cedar R., city of Marion adjoins it on NE; 41°58′N 91°40′W. Named for the surging rapids in the river; 2d-largest city in Iowa. It is a commercial and industrial city as well as a distribution and RR center for an extensive agr. area. Mfg. (food and beverages, electrical equip., machinery, printing, fabricated metal prods., consumer goods, plastics). Coe Col., Mt. Mercy Col., and Kirkwood Community Col. are there. Of note are the city's Masonic Library (1884); an art mus. with a collection by the artist Grant Wood; and Municipal Island, a strip of land in the main channel of the Cedar R., on which the municipal bldg. and a neoclassical war memorial are located. The Duane Arnold Energy Center, the 1st nuclear powered generator in Iowa, is in Cedar Rapids. Inc. as a city 1856.

Cedar Rapids, village (1990 pop. 396), Boone co., E central Nebr., 11 mi/18 km SW of Albion; 41°33′N 98°09′W. Dairy and poultry prods., livestock, grain, cattle feeding, fertilizer.

Cedar Reservoir (□ 40 sq mi/104 sq km), Navarro, Kaufman, and Henderson cos., NE Texas, on Cedar Creek, 60 mi/96 km SE of Dallas; 32°11′N 96°04′W. Max. capacity 1,085,000 acre-ft. Formed by Joe B. Hogsett Dam (59 ft/29 m high), built (1966) for water supply.

Cedar River, village, Menominee co., SW Upper Peninsula, Mich., at mouth of Big Cedar R. on Green Bay of L. Michigan, 23 mi/37 km NNE of Menominee; 45°24′N 87°21′W. J. W. Wells State Park on nearby lakeshore.

Cedar River 1 300 mi/483 km long, Minn. and Iowa; rises in SW Dodge co., SE Minn., in 3 short forks (West Fork, c.5 mi/8 km; Middle Fork, c.10 mi/16 km; East Fork, c.15 mi/24 km); flows S, past Austin, Minn., and into NE Iowa then generally SE through E Iowa, past Charles City, Nashua, Cedar Falls, Waterloo and Cedar Rapids, passes 10 mi/16 km W of Muscatine and Mississippi R., before joining Iowa R. at Columbus Junction, SE Iowa. Not navigable. Sometimes known as Red Cedar R. Recreation. Receives Shell Rock and West Fork Cedar rivers N of Cedar Falls, receives Little Cedar R. at Nashua. **2** 120 mi/193 km long, N central Nebr.; rises in Holt and Garfield cos.; flows SE, past Belgrade, to Loup R. at Fullerton. **3** 45 mi/72 km long, W central Wash.; rises in Cascade Range E of Tacoma, in SE King co.; flows NW through Chester Morse L. (Masonry Dam) to S end of L. Washington at Renton.

Cedar Springs, town (1990 pop. 2,600), Kent co., SW Mich., on small Cedar Creek, and 18 mi/29 km NNE of Grand Rapids; 43°13′N 85°32′W. In resort and agr. area (livestock; grain, potatoes, corn); dairy prods.; feed mill; lumber; mfg. (tool and die, snack foods, plastic moldings). Jordan Col. (2-year). Settled 1859; inc. 1871.

Cedar Springs (SEE-duhr), village, Early co., Ga., 15 mi/

24 km SSW of Blakely. Mfg. of corrugated paperboard, conduit tubing.

Cedar Vale, village (1990 pop. 760), Chautauqua co., SE Kansas, on Caney R. and 18 mi/29 km WNW of Chautauqua; 37°06′N 96°30′W. In grazing and grain region. Mfg. (crushed limestone, feeds).

Cedarbluff, village, Clay co., E Miss., 11 mi/18 km W of West Point. Agr. (cotton, corn; cattle).

Cedarburg, city (1990 pop. 9,895), Ozaukee co., E Wis., on tributary of Milwaukee R., and a suburb 17 mi/27 km N of Milwaukee; 43°17′N 87°59′W. Trade center in dairying and farming area; light and heavy mfg.; limestone quarries. Settled 1842, inc. 1885. Hamilton historic district, covered bridge. Winery.

Cedaredge, town (1990 pop. 1,380), Delta co., W Colo., on Surface Creek and 14 mi/23 km NE of Delta; 38°53′N 107°55′W. Elev. 6,264 ft/1,909 m. Orchards. Light mfg. Grand Mesa Lakes to NW; Grand Mesa Natl. Forest to N.

Cedarhurst 1 village, Carroll co., N Md., 8 mi/12.9 km SE of Westminster. The Congoleum plant here has been mfg. dry felt since 1913; at that time the station on the RR serving it was called Asbestos. **2** residential village (1990 pop. 5,716), Nassau co., SE N.Y., 1 of "5 Towns of L.I." on W L.I., near E shore of Jamaica Bay, 7 mi/11.3 km SE of Jamaica; 40°37′N 73°43′W. Mfg. of tension meters, tachometers, and dental alloys. Inc. 1910.

Cedarpines Park, village, San Bernardino co., S Calif., in San Bernardino Mts. c.10 mi/16 km NNW of San Bernardino. Resort Area. In San Bernardino Natl. Forest.

Cedartown (SEE-duhr-toun), town (1990 pop. 7,978), ⊙ Polk co., NW Ga., 17 mi/27 km SSW of Rome and on small Cedar Creek; 34°01′N 85°16′W. Mfg. includes apparel, metal office furniture, plastics, paper and paperboard, graphic-arts film, steel prods., and fishing boats. Iron mines near by. Springs here furnish city water supply. Settled on site of Cherokee village. Town name derived from abundance of cedar trees growing on limestone-rich soil in the area.

Cedarville 1 village, Crawford co., NW Ark., 13 mi/21 km N of Fort Smith. Mfg. (cabinets). Ozark Natl. Forest to N. **2** uninc. village, Modoc co., NE Calif., in Surprise Valley, 18 mi/29 km NE of Alturas. Farming, stock raising. Gateway to Warner Mts. (W; hunting). South Warner Wilderness Area to SW. **3** village (1990 pop. 751), Stephenson co., N Ill., 5 mi/8 km N of Freeport; 42°22′N 89°38′W. In agr. area. Birthplace of Jane Addams; her grave is here. **4** village, Mackinac co., SE Upper Peninsula, Mich., on L. Huron, and 20 mi/32 km NE of St. Ignace; 45°59′N 84°21′W. Mfg. (floating docks, limestone). De Tour State Park to E; Hiawatha Natl. Forest to W; Les Cheneaux Isls. to S. **5** village, Cumberland co., S N.J., 7 mi/11.3 km S of Bridgeton. Market center for vegetable-growing region; canned vegetables. **6** village (1990 pop. 3,210), Greene co., S central Ohio, 11 mi/18 km S of Springfield; 39°45′N 83°49′W. Seat of Cedarville Col. Settled 1805.

Cedral (sai-DRAHL), city (1990 pop. 7,261) and township, ⊙ Cedral municipio, San Luis Potosí, N central Mexico, on RR, and 13 mi/21 km NW of Matehuala; 23°50′N 100°40′W. Agr.; cattle; silver mining.

Cedros (SEE-druhs), village, SW Trinidad, Trinidad and Tobago, on N shore of SW peninsula (Cedros Bay), on the Serpent's Mouth, 45 mi/72 km SW of Port of Spain, adjoined by Bonasse (E); 10°06′N 61°48′W. Coconut processing.

Cedros Bay (SEE-druhs), inlet of Gulf of Paria, SW Trinidad, Trinidad and Tobago, at SW peninsula, 45 mi/72 km SW of Port of Spain; 10°06′N 61°52′W. At its head is Bonasse. Bathing.

Cedros Island (SAI-dros) (□ 134 sq mi/347 sq km), on Pacific coast of Lower California, NW Mexico, bordering on Sebastián Vizcaíno Bay (E), 15 mi/24 km NW of Eugenia Point; extends 23 mi/37 km N-S bet. 28°03′–28°22′N, up to 11 mi/18 km wide. Rises to 3,487 ft/1,063 m. Sparsely inhabited; has wild life (deer, reptiles, sea lions).

Ceepeecee, village, W Vancouver Isl., SW B.C., Canada, on Hecate Channel, 20 mi/32 km N of Nootka; 49°52′N

126°42′W. Fishing port; fish-reduction plant, fueling station.

Ceiba (sai-EE-bah), town (1990 pop. 17,145), E P.R., near the coast, 33 mi/53 km ESE of San Juan. Livestock (dairying); light mfg. Fishing. Adjoining E is Roosevelt Roads U.S. naval reservation.

Ceiba del Agua (SAI-bah dail AH-gwuh), town, La Habana prov., W Cuba, on Central Highway, on RR, and 25 mi/40 km SW of Havana; 22°52′N 82°40′W. Tobacco, fruit, vegetables.

Ceiba, La, Dominican Republic: see HOSTOS.

Ceiba Mocha (SAI-bah MO-chah), town, Matanzas prov., W Cuba, and RR, on Central Highway, and 10 mi/16 km WSW of Matanzas; 22°59′N 81°43′W. Sugarcane, fruit, livestock.

Celaya (sai-LAH-ya), city (1990 pop. 214,856) and township, Guanajuato state, W central Mexico on Mexico Highway 45; 20°32′N 100°48′W. In a region watered by the Lerma irrigation works, Celaya is the center of a prosperous corn, cereal, and bean growing area in the Bajío region. Cattle raising and the associated dairy industry are also important. Founded in 1571, Celaya was frequently involved in Mexican wars. It was the first city to be captured (Sept. 28, 1810) by Hidalgo y Costilla. In 1915, Álvaro Obregón decisively defeated Pancho Villa at Celaya.

Celebration, planned town, extreme NW Osceola co., Fla., at main entrance to Walt Disney World. A major residential development (49,000 acres/19,830 ha) and architectural showcase built by the Disney corporation. Founded and opened in 1995 and will accomodate a pop. of 20,000 when completed by 2010.

Celeste, village (1990 pop. 733), Hunt co., NE Texas, 12 mi/19 km NNW of Greenville; 33°17′N 96°11′W. In agr. area (cattle, horses; dairying; cotton, wheat).

Celestine (SEL-uhs-teen), village, Dubois co., SW Ind., 8 mi/12.9 km E of Jasper. Agr. area. Mfg. (wooden cabinets).

Celestún (sai-les-TOON), town (1990 pop. 4,293), Yucatán, SE Mexico, minor port on narrow bar off NW Yucatán Peninsula, 50 mi/80 km W of Mérida; 20°50′N 90°22′W. Henequen growing, fishing.

Celilo, Lake (suh-LEI-lo), reservoir (□ 18 sq mi/47 sq km), on N central Oregon (Wasco co.) and S central Wash. (Klickitat co.) border, on Columbia R., 3 mi/4.8 km E of the Dalles, Oregon; 25 mi/40 km long; 45°31′N 121°08′W. Elev. 161 ft/49 m. Max. capacity 330,000 acre-ft. John Day Lock and Dam at NE tip. Deschutes R. enters from S. Formed by the Dalles Dam (260 ft/79 m high), built (1952–1957) by the U.S. Army Corps of Engineers for navigation and power generation.

Celina (suh-LEI-nuh), city (1990 pop. 9,650), ⊙ Mercer co., W Ohio, on Grand L., 27 mi/43 km WSW of Lima; 40°33′N 84°34′W. Furniture mfg. L. resort; fishing, hunting. Settled 1834.

Celina 1 (suh-LEE-nuh), town (1990 pop. 1,493), ⊙ Clay co., N Tenn., on Cumberland R., at Obey R. mouth, and 28 mi/45 km N of Cookeville, near Ky. line; 36°33′N 85°30′W. Dale Hollow Reservoir is just E. **2** town (1990 pop. 1,737), Collin co., N Texas, 37 mi/60 km N of Dallas; 33°19′N 96°46′W. Trade point in agr. area (cotton, grains, livestock); mfg. (liquid ferric sulfate, water treatment chemicals).

Celoron (SEL-uhr-rahn), village (1990 pop. 1,232), Chautauqua co., extreme W N.Y., on Chautauqua L., 3 mi/4.8 km W of Jamestown; 42°06′N 79°16′W. Summer recreational area. Inc. 1896.

Cement, village (1990 pop. 642), Caddo co., W central Okla., 12 mi/19 km SW of Chickasha; 34°56′N 98°08′W. In agr. area.

Cement City, village (1990 pop. 493), Lenawee co., SE Mich., 13 mi/21 km SSE of Jackson; 42°04′N 84°19′W. In agr. area; cement mfg.

Cementon (se-MEN-tuhn), uninc. town (1990 pop. 1,050), Whitehall township, Lehigh co., E Pa., suburb 6 mi/9.7 km NNW of Allentown, on Lehigh R., opposite (W of) Northampton; 40°41′N 75°30′W. Agr. area (grain, apples; livestock, dairying).

Cemetery Ridge, Pa.: see GETTYSBURG.

Cempoala, Mexico: see ZEMPOALA.

Cempoaltépetl 1 Mexico: see ZEMPOALTÉPETL. **2** Mexico: see ZEMPOALTEPETL.

Cenotillo (sai-no-TEE-yo), town (1990 pop. 3,042), Yucatán, SE Mexico, 26 mi/42 km E of Izamal. Henequen.

Centennial, village, Albany co., S central Wyo., in Snowy Range of Medicine Bow Mts., 28 mi/45 km W of Laramie. Elev. 8,076 ft/2,462 m. Former gold-mining area. Snowy Range Ski Area and Snowy Range Pass to NW. Mus. Medicine Bow Natl. Forest to W and SE.

Center, city (1990 pop. 552), Ralls co., NE Mo., 16 mi/26 km SW of Hannibal; 39°30′N 91°31′W. Corn, soybeans; hogs. Clarence Cannon Dam and Mark Twain L. 6 mi/9.7 km W.

Center 1 town (1990 pop. 1,963), Saguache and Alamosa cos., S Colo., near Rio Grande, W of Sangre de Cristo Mts., 23 mi/37 km S of Saguache, in San Luis Valley; 37°45′N 106°06′W. Elev. 7,645 ft/2,330 m. Terminus of RR spur from Monte Vista. Barley, wheat, oats, sheep, cattle, vegetables, potatoes. Inc. 1907. **2** town (1990 pop.), Jackson co., NE central Ga., 7 mi/11.3 km NNW of Athens; 34°3′N 83°25′W. **3** town (1990 pop. 4,950), ⊙ Shelby co., E Texas, c.55 mi/89 km S of Marshall; 31°47′N 94°10′W. Elev. 345 ft/105 m. Pine timber, watermelons, vegetables; cattle, poultry, eggs; lumber milling; mfg. (hardwood flooring). Large Toledo Bend Reservoir to E; Sabine Natl. Forest to E. Founded 1866, inc. 1903.

Center 1 village (1990 pop. 112), ⊙ Knox co., NE Nebr., 10 mi/16 km N of Creighton on S edge of Santee Indian Reservation and on Bazile Creek; 42°36′N 97°52′W. **2** village (1990 pop. 826), ⊙ Oliver co., central N. Dak., 37 mi/60 km NW of Bismarck, and on Square Butte Creek; 47°06′N 101°17′W. Lignite mines, livestock, wheat, corn. Fort Clark Historic Site to N; Nelson L. to SE; Cross Ranch State Park to NE.

Center City, village (1990 pop. 451), ⊙ Chisago co., E Minn., 33 mi/53 km NNE of St. Paul and 1 mi/1.6 km E of Lindstrom, at SE end of North Center L.; 45°23′N 92°49′W. Elev. 907 ft/276 m. In region of resorts and lakes; grain; cattle, poultry; dairying; mfg. (cheese). Important Swed. settlement. Interstate State Park, on St. Croix R., to E; St. Croix Wild River State Park to N.

Center Conway, village, Carroll co., E N.H., 36 mi/58 km NE of Laconia, 3 mi/4.8 km E of Conway village, in town of Conway, near Maine state line, bet. Saco R. (N) and Conway L. (S). Mfg. (ceramic components, rifle barrels, software, ski hats, rainwear, tool and die). Resort area.

Center Harbor, town (1990 pop. 996), Belknap co., central N.H., 11 mi/18 km N of Laconia; 43°42′N 71°30′W. Bounded in E corner by Center Harbor of L. Winnipesaukee, in extreme N by Squam L., in SW by Winona L. and L. Waukewan. Agr. (cattle, poultry; dairying; nursery crops); mfg. (software, computer-aided design). Resort area. Children's Mus. is here.

Center Hill, city (□ 1 sq mi/2.6 sq km; 1990 pop. 735), Sumter co., central Fla., 13 mi/21 km SW of Leesburg; 28°38′N 82°00′W. Agr. shipping point.

Center Hill Lake, reservoir, central Tenn., on Caney Fork R., 18 mi/29 km WSW of Cookeville; 64 mi/103 km long; 36°05′N 85°49′W. Max. capacity 2,092,000 acre-ft. Falling Water R. forms 8-mi/12.9-km E arm. Formed by Center Hill Dam (concrete, straight gravity, earthfill-wings construction; 246 ft/75 m high), built by U.S. Army Corps of Engineers for flood control and power generation.

Center Junction, town (1990 pop. 166), Jones co., E Iowa, 10 mi/16 km E of Anamosa; 42°06′N 91°05′W.

Center Line, city (1990 pop. 9,026), Macomb co., SE Mich., suburb 10 mi/16 km N of downtown Detroit; 42°28′N 83°01′W. Surrounded by city of Warren. Mfg. (metals and machinery). U.S. arsenal here. Inc. as village 1925, as city 1935.

Center Montville, town, Waldo co., S Maine, 11 mi/18 km W of Belfast. Agr., recreational area.

Center Moriches, village (□ 5 sq mi/13 sq km; 1990 pop. 5,987), Suffolk co., SE N.Y., on S L.I., on Moriches Bay, 11 mi/18 km E of Patchogue; 40°47′N 72°47′W.

Center Ossipee, N.H.: see OSSIPEE.

Center Point 1 town (1990 pop. 278), Clay co., W Ind., 8 mi/12.9 km SSE of Brazil; 39°25′N 87°04′W. In agr. and bituminous-coal area. Old-surface coal mines. **2** town (1990 pop. 1,693), Linn co., E Iowa, near Cedar R., 16 mi/26 km NNW of Cedar Rapids; 42°10′N 91°46′W. Feed. Limestone quarries nearby.

Center Point 1 village (1990 pop. 22,658), Jefferson co., N. central Ala., 11 mi/18 km NE suburb of Birmingham; 33°39′N 86°40′W. **2** village, Howard co., SW Ark., 8 mi/12.9 km NW of Nashville. **3** uninc. village (1990 pop. 566), Kerr co., SW Texas, 9 mi/14.5 km SE of Kerrville and on Guadalupe R. In resort and ranching (cattle, sheep, goats; wheat, pecans, apples) region. Mfg. (aircraft parts, heating equip.).

Center Rutland, Vt.: see RUTLAND, city.

Center Valley, uninc. town (1990 pop. 900), Lehigh co., E Pa., 6 mi/9.7 km SSE of Allentown and 1 mi/1.6 km N of Coopersburg; 40°31′N 75°23′W. Light Mfg. Agr. (apples, grain; livestock, dairying, poultry).

Centerbrook, Conn.: see ESSEX.

Centerburg, village (1990 pop. 1,323), Knox co., central Ohio, 13 mi/21 km WSW of Mount Vernon, and on North Fork of Licking R.; 40°18′N 82°42′W.

Centerdale, neighborhood, NW North Providence, NE R.I.

Centerfield, town (1990 pop. 766), Sanpete co., central Utah, on San Pitch R., just E of its confluence with Sevier R., 15 mi/24 km SW of Manti; 39°07′N 111°49′W. Elev. 5,125 ft/1,562 m. Alfalfa, barley, wheat; dairying; cattle, sheep; mfg. (asphalt). Parts of Fishlake Natl. Forest to W and SE; Manti-La Sal Natl. Forest to E. Sevier Bridge Reservoir to NW.

Centerport, village (□ 3 sq mi/7.8 sq km; 1990 pop. 5,333), Nassau co., SE N.Y., on Centerport Harbor (SE arm of Huntington Bay) on N shore of W L.I., 3 mi/4.8 km NE of Huntington; 40°53′N 73°22′W.

Centerport, borough (1990 pop. 284), Berks co., E central Pa., 11 mi/18 km NNW of Reading, on Irish Creek; 40°29′N 76°00′W. Grain; livestock, dairying.

Centerport Harbor, N.Y.: see CENTERPORT.

Centerton, village (1990 pop. 491), Benton co., extreme NW Ark., 9 mi/14.5 km W of Rogers, in the Ozarks; 36°21′N 94°16′W. Mfg. (air and fuel ducting). Location of new regional airport.

Centertown, town (1990 pop. 356), Cole co., central Mo., near Missouri R.,13 mi/21 km W of Jefferson City; 38°37′N 92°24′W.

Centertown, village (1990 pop. 383), Ohio co., W Ky., 5 mi/8 km WSW of Hartford; 37°25′N 87°00′W. RR spur terminus. Coal and agr. (tobacco, grain; livestock).

Centerview, town (1990 pop. 214), Johnson co., W central Mo., near Blackwater R., 5 mi/8 km W of Warrensburg; 38°45′N 93°50′W.

Centerville 1 city (1990 pop. 5,936), ⊙ Appanoose co., S Iowa, 32 mi/51 km SW of Ottumwa; 40°43′N 92°52′W. In agr. and coal-mining area; mfg. center (concrete mesh and wire prods., rubber prods., auto-ignition parts, heat-transfer prods.); limestone quarrying. Sharon Bluffs State Park is SE. Has Indian Hills Community Col. Rathbun Dam and Reservoir to N. Plotted 1846, inc. 1855. **2** city (1990 pop. 21,082), Montgomery co., SW Ohio, a residential suburb of Dayton; 39°38′N 84°08′W. Inc. 1879. **3** city (1990 pop. 11,500), Davis co., N Utah, 13 mi/21 km N of downtown Salt Lake City; 40°55′N 111°53′W. Elev. 4,246 ft/1,294 m. Suburb of Salt Lake City. Wheat, barley, vegetables; dairying; cattle, sheep; mfg. (highway safety prods., steel mills). Drained by Centerville Creek. Farmington Bay Waterfowl Management Area in W; Wasatch Range and Natl. Forest to E. Settled 1848, inc. 1915. **4** uninc. city, Fairfax co., NE Va., residential suburb 20 mi/32 km W of Washington, D.C. Mfg. (mulch processing, security cameras, commercial printing); some agr. (nursery stock). Bull Run Regional Park to S, Manassas Natl. Battlefield Park to W. Dulles Intl. Airport to N.

Centerville 1 uninc. town, New Castle co., N Del., near Pa. state line, 5 mi/8 km NNW of Wilmington; 39°49′N 75°37′W. Elev. 440 ft/134 m. Brandywine Creek State Park to SE; Mus. of Natural History and Winterthur Mus. and gardens to S. **2** town (1990 pop, 3,251), Houston co., Ga., 16 mi/26 km S of Macon; 32°38′N 83°41′W. Mfg. includes profile extrusions, aircraft parts. **3** town (1990 pop. 2,398), Wayne co., E Ind., near a fork of Whitewater R., 6 mi/9.7 km W of Richmond; 39°49′N 85°00′W. In livestock, grain, poultry, and dairying area; mfg. (masonry waterproofing materials). Town was previously the county seat. **4** town (1990 pop. 30), Washington co., E Maine, 11 mi/18 km W of Machias; 44°45′N 67°37′W. **5** town, Frederick co., Md., 7 mi/11.3 km SE of Frederick. **6** town (1990 pop. 1,633), Anoka co., E Minn., suburb 14 mi/23 km N of downtown St. Paul and 16 mi/26 km NE of downtown Minneapolis; 45°09′N 93°02′W. Grain; mfg. (machining). In region of small natural lakes; parts of Centerville and Peltier lakes in W (including part of Chain of Lakes–Rice Creek Regional Park). **7** uninc. town (1990 pop. 4,866), Anderson co., NW S.C., residential suburb 4 mi/6.4 km W of downtown Anderson; 34°31′N 82°43′W. Anderson Co. Airport is here. Hartwell L. reservoir to W. **8** town (1990 pop. 887), Turner co., SE S.Dak., 26 mi/42 km NE of Yankton, on Vermillion R. In agr. and livestock area; corn; poultry. Founded 1883. **9** town (1990 pop. 3,616), ⊙ Hickman co., central Tenn., on Duck R. and 45 mi/72 km SW of Nashville; 35°47′N 87°28′W. Trade center in fertile agr., lumbering, phosphate-mining area; mfg. of shoes, clothing, wood prods. **10** town (1990 pop. 812), ⊙ Leon co., E central Texas, c.70 mi/113 km ESE of Waco; 31°15′N 95°58′W. Elev. 410 ft/125 m. Agr. and timber area. Oil and gas; light mfg.

Centerville 1 village (1990 pop. 89), ⊙ Reynolds co., SE Mo., in the Ozarks, 34 mi/55 km SE of Salem; 37°26′N 90°57′W. Timber; tourist and recreation area. Surrounded by Mark Twain Natl. Forest. **2** village (1990 pop. 30), Cascade co., W central Mont. on Sand Coulee Creek, 10 mi/16 km SE of Great Falls. Cattle, grain, potatoes. **3** village (1990 pop. 115), Franklin co., N central N.C., 13 mi/21 km NE of Louisburg, near Fishing Creek; 36°11′N 78°6′W. Tobacco, grain, livestock, poultry.

Centerville 1 borough (1990 pop. 249), Crawford co., NW Pa., 9 mi/14.5 km NW of Titusville, on Oil Creek; 41°44′N 79°45′W. Mfg. (lumber). Agr. (corn, hay; livestock, dairying). **2** borough (1990 pop. 3,842), Washington co., SW Pa., 28 mi/45 km S of Pittsburgh, on Monongahela R.; 40°01′N 79°57′W. Agr. (corn, hay, apples; livestock, dairying). Includes village of Richeyville in NW. Settled 1766, laid out 1821, inc. 1895.

Centerville 1 Ala.: see CENTREVILLE. **2** Mass.: see BARNSTABLE, town.

Centla, Mexico: see FRONTERA.

Centrahoma (sen-truh-HOM-uh), village (1990 pop. 106), Coal co., S central Okla., 20 mi/32 km SE of Ada; 34°36′N 96°20′W. Agr. area in dormant coal-mining region.

Central 1 town (1990 pop. 1,835), Grant co., SW N.Mex., in foothills of Pinos Altos Mts., 7 mi/11.3 km E of Silver City; 32°46′N 108°09′W. Elev. 5,980 ft/1,823 m. Copper, zinc, lead mining to NE. Cattle, grain, alfalfa. Part of Gila Natl. Forest to N. Bear Canyon Dam and Reservoir to NE. **2** town (1990 pop. 2,438), Pickens co., NW S.C., 23 mi/37 km WSW of Greenville; 34°43′N 82°46′W. Mfg. includes yarns; agr. includes dairying, poultry, hogs, corn. **3** town (1990 pop. 2,635), Carter co., extreme NE Tenn., 3 mi/5 km E of Johnson City.

Central 1 or **Central House**, village, E central Alaska, on Steese Highway and 25 mi/40 km SW of Circle. Junction for Circle Hot Springs. **2** village, Washington co., SW Utah, 23 mi/37 km N of St. George, on Santa Clara R. Elev. 5,500 ft/1,676 m. Cattle. Dixie Natl. Forest to W, N, and E.

Central Bridge, village (1990 pop. 800), Schoharie co., E central N.Y., on Schoharie Creek at mouth of small Cobleskill Creek, and 30 mi/48 km W of Albany; 42°42′N 74°20′W. George Westinghouse b. here. Nearby are the Howe and Secret caverns.

Central Butte, town (1991 pop. 562), S Sask., Canada, 50 mi/80 km NW of Moose Jaw. RR junction; wheat.

Central Catorce de Julio (sen-TRAHL kah-TOR-sai dai HOO-lee-o), sugar-mill village, Cienfuegos prov., central Cuba, 9 mi/14.5 km NW of Cienfuegos; 22°15′N 80°33′W.

Central City 1 town (1990 pop. 1,063), Linn co., E Iowa, on Wapsipinicon R., and 17 mi/27 km NNE of Cedar Rapids; 42°12′N 91°31′W. **2** town (1990 pop. 4,979), Muhlenberg co., W Ky., 33 mi/53 km S of Owensboro, and 8 mi/12.9 km NNE of Greenville; 37°17′N 87°07′W. Elev. 415 ft/126 m. RR junction. Trade center in bituminous coal mining and agr. (livestock; corn, tobacco, hay) area; mfg. (machinery, apparel, metal prods., lumber); oil wells, hardwood timber. Paradise Fossil Plants, power plant, to E. Everly Brothers Monument here. Settled as Morehead's Horse Mill; renamed after 1870 with arrival of RR; est. 1871. **3** town (1990 pop. 2,868), ⊙ Merrick co., E central Nebr., 20 mi/32 km NE of Grand Island and near Platte R; 41°06′N 98°00′W. RR junction. Livestock; dairy prods., grain. Mfg. (mobile homes, fertilizer, electronic farm scales, concrete). Hord Lake State Recreation Area at river. Plotted 1864.

Central City 1 village (1990 pop. 335), ⊙ Gilpin co., N central Colo., on N fork of Clear Creek, in Front Range, and 27 mi/43 km W of Denver; 39°47′N 105°30′W. Elev. 8,496 ft/2,590 m. Gold, silver, lead, copper, zinc, uranium mines. Nearby, in Quartz Hill, is Glory Hole, huge mining pit c.1,000 ft/305 m long, 300 ft/91 m deep. Casino gambling. Play and music festival takes place annually (July) in old Central City Opera House (1878) now owned by Univ. of Denver. Next door is Teller House (1872), famous frontier hotel. City settled 1859, at time of Gregory gold strike; inc. 1886. Decline set in as gold production fell off, but there was increase of mining activity during World War II. **2** village, Grundy co., NE Ill., 24 mi/39 km SSW of Joliet; 38°32′N 89°07′W. In agr. and bituminous-coal area. **3** village, (1990 pop. 1,340), Marion co., S Ill., on Crooked Creek and just N of Centralia and 11 mi/18 km ESE of Carlyle; 38°32′N 89°07′W. In agr. and oil-producing area; large nurseries. Inc. 1857. **4** village (1990 pop. 185), Lawrence co., W S.Dak., 2 mi/3.2 km W of Deadwood, near Whitewood Creek. Surrounded by Black Hills Natl. Forest, in Black Hills mining region.

Central City, borough (1990 pop. 1,246), Somerset co., SW Pa., 16 mi/26 km SSE of Johnstown, on Dark Shade Creek; 40°06′N 78°48′W. Timber; coal-mining area. Gallitzin State Forest to NE. Inc. 1918.

Central, Cordillera (sen-TRAHL, kor-dee-YE-rah), mountain chain of P.R., extending c.80 mi/129 km W-E through almost the entire length of the isl. Rises to 4,389 ft/1,338 m in the Cerro de Punta. Subsidiary branches are the Sierra de Luquillo (NE) and Sierra de Cayey (SE). Known for its pleasant summer climate and scenery. There are several water reservoirs and hydroelectric plants. Coffee, plantains, bananas, tobacco and fruit are grown.

Central, Cordillera (sen-TRAHL, kor-dee-YER-rah), main interior range of the Dominican Republic, extends E c.220 mi/354 km from Haiti border to Mona Passage; 18°45′N 70°30′W. Densely wooded. Highest peaks: Monte Tina and Pico Duarte, highest in the West Indies. Sometimes called Cibao Mts.

Central Falls, industrial city (1990 pop. 17,637), Providence co., NE R.I., on Blackstone R. (bridged here), adjoining Pawtucket, and 6 mi/9.7 km N of Providence in area the smallest city in the state; 41°54′N 71°23′W. Declining textiles and thread, glass, glass fabrics, food prods., beverages, plastics, toys, chemicals, machinery; printing. Privately-owned prison for federal prisoners. Once called Chocolate Hill after a chocolate works est. there in 1790. Inc. 1895.

Central Heights, town, Cerro Gordo co., N Iowa, just W of Mason City.

Central Islip (EIS-lip), village (□ 5 sq mi/13 sq km; 1990 pop. 26,028), Suffolk co., SE N.Y., on central L.I., 5 mi/8 km NNE of Bay Shore; 40°47′N 73°12′W. In poultry-raising and dairying area. Central Islip Psychiatric Center is here on former site of state-operated psychiatric center. Seat of N.Y. Inst. of Technology.

Central Lake, village (1990 pop. 954), Antrim co., NW Mich., 17 mi/27 km S of Charlevoix, and on short river bet. N end of Intermediate L. (c.8 mi/12.9 km long, 1 mi/1.6 km wide) and Hanley L.; 45°04′N 85°15′W. In agr. area (corn, potatoes). Mfg. (steel stampings, bullet proof vests, electrical motor protectors).

Central Pacolet (PAK-o-let), village (1990 pop. 257), Spartanburg co., NW S.C., 10 mi/16 km E of Spartanburg and 2 mi/3.2 km NNE of Pacolet, near Pacolet R; 34°54′N 81°45′W. Agr. includes poultry, livestock, grain, peaches.

Central Park, uninc. town (1990 pop. 2,669), Grays Harbor co., W Wash., 5 mi/8 km E of Aberdeen, on Chehalis R.; 46°58′N 123°42′W. Timber; peas, hay. Aberdeen Fish Hatchery to W.

Central Park, village, Vermilion co., E Ill., residential suburb 2 mi/3.2 km S of Danville. Coal region.

Central Park (1.3 sq mi/3.4 sq km), the largest park in Manhattan, N.Y. city; bordered by 59th St. on the S, Fifth Ave. on the E, 110th St. on the N, and Central Park W. on the W; 40°47′N 73°57′W. The land, acquired by the city in 1856, was improved according to the plans of U.S. landscape architects Frederick L. Olmsted and Calvert Vaux, which took 20 years to implement. The park has rolling terrain with lakes and ponds, greeneries, bridle paths, walks, and park drives. There are many playgrounds and other recreational facilities, including the Wollman Skating Rink. The Metropolitan Mus. of Art stands in the park on Fifth Ave.; other points of interest include a formal garden, a zoo, an Egyptian obelisk popularly called "Cleopatra's Needle," a N.Y. city reservoir, and the Mall. In the open-air Delacorte Theater, Shakespearian dramas and other plays are presented free of charge during the summer. The private Central Park Conservancy works with N.Y. city to preserve and improve the park.

Central Patricia, village, NW Ont., Canada, in Patricia dist., on Kawinogans R., 2 mi/3 km NE of Pickle L., and 120 mi/193 km NE of Sioux Lookout; 51°29′N 90°09′W. Gold mining.

Central Point, town (1990 pop. 7,509), Jackson co., SW Oregon, 5 mi/8 km NW of Medford near Bear Creek; 42°22′N 122°54′W. Mfg. (lumber prods., aluminum boats). Agr. (hops, pears, apples, wheat, cherries, peaches; poultry, cattle); dairy prods. TouVelle State Park to NE.

Central Square, village (□ 1 sq mi/2.6 sq km; 1990 pop. 1,671), Oswego co., N central N.Y., 15 mi/24 km N of Syracuse; 43°17′N 76°08′W. In dairying area.

Central Utah Project, N central Utah. Begun 1959 near Vernal, Utah, by the U.S. Bureau of Reclamation in conjunction with the Colorado River storage project. Water, collected from streams in the Uinta Mts., is carried across the Wasatch Range to the densely populated Salt Lake City region by a system of dams, reservoirs, tunnels, aqueducts, and canals. Includes Soldier Creek, Strawberry Dam and Reservoir, 25 mi/40 km E of Provo, plus Deer Creek Reservoir and Jordanelle Reservoir; provides water for domestic and industrial use, irrigation, hydroelectricity, fish and wildlife preservation, and flood control through the Provo River Drainage.

Central Valley, uninc. town (1990 pop. 4,340), Shasta co., N Calif., 8 mi/12.9 km NE of Redding, just S of Shasta Dam and Reservoir; 40°41′N 122°22′W. Paper mill; timber; cattle; walnuts; grain.

Central Valley, village (□ 2 mi/3.2 km; 1990 pop. 1,929), Orange co., SE N.Y., on Ramapo R.,8 mi/12.9 km WSW of Highland Falls; 41°19′N 74°07′W. Location of Woodbury Common, major retail shopping mall, at intersection of N.Y. State Thruway and Route 17.

Central Valley, great valley of central Calif., c.450 mi/ 724 km long and c.50 mi/80 km wide, bet. the Sierra Nevada (E) and the Coast Ranges (W). The Sacramento (N) and San Joaquin (S) rivers drain most of the valley before converging in a large delta and flowing W into San Francisco Bay. Neither river is navigable, but 2 deep water channels have been dug, one c.20 mi/ 32 km E of San Joaquin to Terminus, W of Lodi, and the Sacramento Deep Water Channel (43 mi/69 km), N to Sacramento. Sacramento (N center) is largest city in valley; also important are Fresno and Bakersfield (S)

and Stockton and Modesto (center). The valley and its delta is Calif.'s leading agricultural and horticultural region, generally irrigated throughout. The valley is located with canals that distribute water from rivers and reservoirs to fields. The Hetch Hetchy in center, and California Aqueduct is S, deliver drinking water from mt. areas to metropolitan areas in concrete channels which keep the water relatively clean; 430 mi/692 km long N-S, from 70 mi/113 km NW of Los Angeles to N of Redding, 80 mi/129 km S of Oregon boundary; 40 mi/64 km–50 mi/80 km wide. With its long growing season and fertile soil, the valley has the largest single concentration of fruits, vegetables, and general farming in the U.S.; cotton, grain, sugar beets and other crops are also grown, grapes grown, especially in the S, generally for raisins and table grapes (popular Sonoma co. and Napa co. wine-producing area are W of valley). Precipitation ranges from 30 in/76 cm in the north to 6 in/15.2 cm in the south. ⅔ of the valley's agr. land is located in the south, while ⅔ of the water is in the north. The Central Valley project attempts to remedy this problem by bringing water from the Sacramento basin in the N into the San Joaquin Valley in the S. The Tulare L. basin in the extreme S part of the valley is very dry and has alkaline conditions that make it almost totally unsuitable for irrigation. The Central Valley supported a large Native Amer. pop., but it declined rapidly when ranching and agr. were introduced in the 19th cent. In 1848, gold was discovered nearby. Irrigation was introduced in the 1880s. Regional mfg. (petrochemical prods.). Oil and natural gas are found along SW margin.

Central Village 1 Conn.: see PLAINFIELD. **2** Mass.: see WESTPORT.

Centralhatchee (sen-truhl-HACH-ee), town (1990 pop. 301), Heard co., W Ga., 22 mi/35 km N of La Grange, near Chattahoochee R.; 33°22′N 85°06′W.

Centralia 1 (sin-TRAIL-yah), city (1990 pop. 14,274), Clinton and Marion cos., S Ill., 11 mi/18 km ESE of Carlyle; 38°31′N 89°07′W. Major RR junction. In an oil, natural gas, coal, and agr. (wheat, corn, sorghum, fruit, cattle) region. Inc. 1859. Founded in 1853 by the Illinois Central RR and named accordingly, it is the shipping center for the prods. of the area. Its RR yards are still the major industry, but other mfg. includes plastic automobile bodies, barbecue sauces, crates and pallets, RR car wheels, fuses, hoses, bathroom fixtures, and plastic bottles. Kaskaskia Community Col. and Centralia Correctional Center to W. **2** city (1990 pop. 3,414), Boone co., central Mo., 20 mi/32 km NNE of Columbia; 39°12′N 92°07′W. Corn, wheat, oats, soybeans; cattle, sheep, hogs. Mfg. (metal fabrication; plastics; lumber prods.). Laid out 1857. A massacre occurred here in 1864 during the Civil War. **3** city (1990 pop. 12,101), Lewis co., SW Wash., 23 mi/37 km S of Olympia, at the confluence of the Skookumchuck R.; 46°43′N 122°58′W. Elev. 189 ft/58 m. Inc. 1889. It is a RR junction and a farm trade center, with a significant timber industry; vegetables; dairying; poultry; mfg. (cabinets, apparel, printing and publishing, motor vehicles, food, furinature, and metal prods.). A coal-fired electric steam plant and 2 nearby dams generate electricity. Centralia Col. (2-year) and the co. fairgrounds are here. Skookumchuck Reservoir and Fish Hatchery to NE. Chehalis Indian Reservation to NW. Chehalis Centralia Airport to S.

Centralia, town (1990 pop. 123), Dubuque co., E Iowa, 8 mi/12.9 km W of Dubuque; 42°28′N 90°50′W.

Centralia 1 (sen-TRAIL-yuh), village (1990 pop. 452), Nemaha co., NE Kansas, 8 mi/12.9 km SSW of Seneca; 39°43′N 96°07′W. In livestock and grain region: dairying. **2** village, Craig co., NE Okla., 15 mi/24 km NW of Vinita.

Centralia (SEN-trai-lee-ah), borough (1990 pop. 63), Columbia co., E central Pa., 2 mi/3.2 km N of Ashland; 40°47′N 76°20′W. Livestock. Former anthracite-coal center. All houses in Centralia were condemned in 1992, because of a slow-burning underground fire feeding on coal veins beneath the town. Most of the c.1,100 residents here in 1980 had moved away by 1995 as a

result of the fire and a federal home-buyout program. However, more than 40 residents were still disputing the condemnation and fighting through courts to hold onto their homes. The fire had been burning since the early 1960s, and geologists said it could burn for 500–1,000 years longer, until the coal is consumed. Inc. 1866.

Centre (SAWNG-truh), department (1982 pop. 361,470), E central Haiti. Bounded on N by Nord and Nord-Est depts., E by Dominican Republic, W by Artibonite dept., S by Ouest dept.; ☉ Hinche. Agr. (coffee, cotton, sugarcane, sisal, fruit); cattle. Lignite deposits.

Centre, county (□ 1,111 sq mi/2,877 sq km), central Pa.; ☉ Bellefonte; 40°54′N 77°49′W. Mt. region, bounded NW by West Branch Susquehanna R. and by Moshannon Creek; drained by Bald Eagle Creek. Allegheny Mts. across NW part, paralleled by Bald Eagle Mt. ridge in central part and by Tussey and Long mts. along S boundary. Agr. (corn, wheat, oats, hay, alfalfa, soybeans, vegetables, apples; eggs, sheep, hogs, cattle, dairying); mfg. at Bellefonte and State Col. Limestone, bituminous coal, clay, sandstone. Part of Rothrock State Forest in SE; part of Sproul State Forest in N; Moshannon State Forest and Black Moshannon State Park in SW; Bald Eagle State Park, including Howard State Nursery and Sayer Reservoir, in NE; McCall Dam State Park in NE corner; Penn Roosevelt State Park in S; Poe Valley State Park in SE. Formed 1800.

Centre, town (1990 pop. 2,893), ☉ Cherokee co., NE Ala., near Coosa R., 22 mi/35 km NE of Gadsden. Apparel mfg., cottonseed processing, poultry feed, egg processing, wood prods. Settled c.1840. Inc. 1937.

Centre Hall, borough (1990 pop. 1,203), Centre co., central Pa., 6 mi/9.7 km SE of Bellefonte; 40°50′N 77°40′W. In hunting, fishing region. Mfg. (feeds, amusement rides, frozen and canned vegetables). Agr. (corn, hay, wheat, vegetables; poultry, livestock, dairying). Nittany Mt. ridge passes to NW; Colyer Lake Recreational Area to S; Centre Airport to SE; part of Bald Eagle State Forest to N; Penn's Cave is to NE.

Centre Island, peninsula on N shore of W L.I., SE N.Y., enclosing part of Oyster Bay, N of Oyster Bay village; c.5 mi/8 km long; 40°54′N 73°31′W. Site of Bayville and Centre Isl. villages.

Centreville, city (1990, pop. 7,489), St. Clair co., SW Ill., residential suburb 5 mi/8 km ESE of St. Louis, Mo.; 38°34′N 90°05′W. RR yards. City is noted for its serpentine corporated limits. Surroundes Frank Holton State Park.

Centreville 1 town (1990 pop. 2,508), ☉ Bibb co., central Ala., on Cahaba R., and 30 mi/48 km SE of Tuscaloosa; lumber, children's clothing, cabinets. Sometime spelled Centerville. **2** town (1990 pop. 2,097), ☉ Queen Annes co., E Md., on the Eastern Shore 19 mi/31 km N of Easton, and on Corsica R.; 39°02′N 76°04′W. In agr. area. Name was changed from Chester Mills to Centreville in 1797 The town has 1 of the 2 18th-cent. courthouses in Md., among other notable 18th- and 19th-cent. bldgs. Nuclear research facility here. Sometimes spelled Centerville. **3** town (1990 pop. 1,771), on Wilkinson and Amite cos., SW Miss., near La. state line, 37 mi/60 km SSE of Natchez; 31°05′N 91°04′W. Agr. (cotton, corn; cattle; dairying; timber); mfg. (hardwood chips, children's clothing). Source of Buffalo R. to N. Inc. 1880.

Centreville, village (1991 pop. 529), W N.B., Canada, near Maine border, 20 mi/32 km NNW of Woodstock. Lumbering; potatoes.

Centreville 1 village (1990 pop. 1,516), ☉ St. Joseph co., SW Mich., on Prairie R., and 25 mi/40 km S of Kalamazoo; 41°55′N 85°31′W. In agr. area (grain, corn, mint); mfg. (molded plastic parts, recreational vehicles). Settled 1826. **2** industrial village in West Warwick town, Kent co., central R.I., on Pawtuxet R., and 11 mi/18 km SSW of Providence. Textile mfg. and finishing.

Centro, Mexico: see VILLAHERMOSA.

Centuria (sen-TUHR-ee-ah), town (1990 pop. 790), Polk co., NW Wis., near Balsam L., 35 mi/56 km NNE of Hudson; 45°27′N 92°33′W. Dairying.

Century, town (□ 3 sq mi/7.8 sq km; 1990 pop. 1,989), Escambia co., extreme NW Fla., near Ala. state line and

Escambia R., 40 mi/64 km N of Pensacola; 30°58′N 87°15′W. Lumber milling. Grew around sawmill est. in 1900.

Century, Okla.: see DOUTHAT.

Century Village, name given to 4 retirement communities, Broward and Palm Beach cos., SE Fla. During the 1970s and 1980s communities were constructed at 4 separate locations: Deerfield Beach and Pembroke Pines in Broward co., and West Palm Beach and Boca Raton in Palm Beach co. Together these 4 communities contain housing for 54,00 residents, but vacancy rates steadily rose in the 1990s as the migration of retirees into SE Fla. slowed. Successful marketing by the developer, Cenvill Corp., created a nationwide demand for such communities, not only in Fla., Ariz., and other Sunbelt states, but also in the outer fringes of major metropolitan areas in the Northeast and Midwest.

Cerbat Mountains (cer-bot), Mohave co., NW Ariz., just E of Black Mts.; extend c.25 mi/40 km N from Kingman. Rise to 6,900 ft/2,103 m in Mt. TIPTON, at N end.

Cercado, El, Dominican Republic: see EL CERCADO.

Cerca-la-Source (ser-kah–lah–SOORS), agr. town (1982 pop. 1,874), Centre dept., E Haiti, 14 mi/23 km E of Hinche; 19°10′N 71°47′W. Coffee, limes, sugarcane; cattle; bee-keeping; timber; gold deposits.

Cereal, village (1991 pop. 200), SE Alta., 50 mi/80 km ESE of Hanna; 51°25′N 110°48′W. Mixed farming.

Ceredo (suhr-EE-do), town (1990 pop. 1,916), Wayne co., W W.Va., suburb 6 mi/9.7 km W of downtown Huntington, near the Ohio R. at mouth of Twelvepole Creek; 38°23′N 82°32′W. In agr. and bituminous-coal region. Tri-State Airport (Walker Long Field) to S; Ramsdell House (1858); Camden Park (turn-of-century amusement park) is here. Founded 1857.

Ceres, city (1990 pop. 26,314), Stanislaus co., central Calif., in San Joaquin Valley, a suburb 4 mi/6.4 km SE of Modesto; 37°36′N 120°58′W. Grapes, peaches, figs, dates; vegetables; grain; dairying; poultry, cattle; mfg. (canvas prods., food and beverage machinery, fabricated rubber goods, lumber, metal doors, furniture, printing). Inc. 1918.

Ceres (SEER-eez), village (1990 pop. 400), Allegany co., N.Y., and McKean co., Pa., 9 mi/14.5 km SE of Olean, N.Y.; 42°00′N 78°16′W. Post office is in N.Y.

Ceresco (suh-RES-ko), village (1990 pop. 825), Saunders co., E Nebr., 8 mi/12.9 km N of Lincoln; 41°03′N 96°39′W. Livestock, grain. Pioneer State Wayside Area to N.

Ceresville (SEERZ-vill), hamlet, Frederick co., N Md., on Monocacy R. and 3 mi/4.8 km NE of Frederick. A 4-story grain mill, built here about 1745, still dominates the community.

Cerralvo (se-RAHL-vo), town (1990 pop. 7,653), Nuevo León, N Mexico, 43 mi/69 km NE of Monterrey on Mexico Highway 57; 26°06′N 99°37′W. Elev 656 ft/ 200 m. Agr. (cotton, grain), livestock, tourism. Originally Ciudad de León, founded in 1557 as a mining center, the oldest settlement in Nuevo León.

Cerralvo Island (☐ 60 sq mi/155 sq km), off SE Lower California, NW Mexico, in Gulf of California, 28 mi/ 45 km E of La Paz; 19 mi/31 km long and up to 5 mi/ 8 km wide; 24°08′N 109°40′W. Mountains here are rich in minerals, especially copper and silver. Originally a volcano. In its center a peak rises 2,493 ft/760 m. Uninhabited.

Cerritos (ser-EE-tos), city (1990 pop. 13,176) and township, ⊙ Cerritos municipio, San Luis Potosí, N central Mexico, on interior plateau, on RR, and 50 mi/80 km ENE of San Luis Potosí; 22°25′N 100°16′W. Elev. 3,783 ft/1,153 m. Agr. center (grain, cotton, fruit, livestock).

Cerritos, city (1990 pop. 53,240), Los Angeles co., S Calif., suburb 14 mi/23 km SE of downtown Los Angeles and 7 mi/11.3 km NE of Long Beach, bounded on W by San Gabriel R.; 33°52′N 118°04′W. Mfg. (furniture, sheet metal, machinery, heavy industrial goods, printing and publishing, consumer goods).

Cerro Azul (SER-ro ah-ZOOL), town (1990 pop. 24,503),

N Veracruz, Mexico, 8 mi/13 km NW of Túxpam de Rodríguez Cano.

Cerro de Garnica (SE-ro dai gar-NEE-kah), a national park, in W Michoacán, Mexico, 15 mi/24 km E of the city of Morelia and W of Ciudad Hidalgo. This park has 2 observation points overlooking the Thousand Peaks (Mil Cumbres) landscape. Formed in 1936, this park remains largely undeveloped.

Cerro de la Estrella (SE-ro dai lah es-TRE-yah), a national park, in SE Mexico City, Distrito Federal, Mexico, in Ixtapalapa. Cerro de la Estrella was where the Aztecs lit their fires to celebrate the beginning of each 52-year cycle. This was called the New Fire Ceremony and was the most important ritual in all Aztec Mexico. The priests would light kindling on the chest of a sacrificed person and if it continued to burn, this meant that the world would continue. Runners would then carry flames to temples throughout the Aztec empire. Today, this park is the scene of an annual Easter week pilgrimage during which thousands of Mexicans take part in a passion drama. Beautiful views of the twin volcanoes Popocatépetl and Iztaccihuatl can be seen from this hill.

Cerro de San Pedro or **San Pedro**, town (1990 pop. 129), San Luis Potosí, N central Mexico, on interior plateau, 12 mi/19 km ENE of San Luis Potosí; 22°15′N 100°40′W. Elev. 6,719 ft/2,048 m. Silver, gold, lead mining.

Cerro Gordo (SAIR-o GORE-do), county (☐ 575 sq mi/ 1,489 sq km; 1990 pop. 46,733), N Iowa; ⊙ Mason City; 43°04′N 93°15′W. Rolling prairie agr. area (cattle, hogs, poultry; corn, oats, soybeans) drained by Shell Rock R. and Lime Creek. Limestone quarries, sand and gravel pits. Clear L. Reservoir in W; Clear Lake State Park on S shore; McIntosh Woods State Park on N shore. Formed 1851.

Cerro Gordo 1 (SER-o GOR-do), village (1990 pop. 1,436), Piatt co., central Ill., 12 mi/19 km ENE of Decatur; 39°53′N 88°43′W. In rich agr. area; ships grain. Inc. 1873. **2** village (1990 pop. 227), Columbus co., SE N.C., 13 mi/21 km W of Whiteville, near S.C. state line; 34°19′N 78°55′W. Tobacco, peanuts, grain, livestock.

Cerro Gordo, mountain pass, E Mexico, on Mexico Highway 140 bet. Veracruz and Xalapa Enríquez, site of a decisive battle (April 17–18, 1847) of the Mexican War; 19°45′N 98°49′W. Elev. 10,039 ft/3,060 m; elev. at San Juan Teotihuacán: 2,490 ft/759 m.

Cerro Pelado, N.Mex.: see VALLE GRANDE MOUNTAINS.

Cerro Vista (se-ro), peak (11,939 ft/3,639 m), Taos/Mora co. line, N N.Mex., in Sangre de Cristo Mts., 15 mi/ 24 km SE of Taos in Carson Natl. Forest.

Cerros Island, Mexico: see CEDROS ISLAND.

Cerulean (suhr-IL-uhn), uninc. village, Trigg co., SW Ky., 15 mi/24 km WNW of Hopkinsville, on Muddy Fork Little R. Agr. area. Also known as Cerulean Springs.

Céspedes (SAIS-pai-daiz), town, Camagüey prov., E Cuba, on Central Highway, on RR, and 4 mi/6.4 km NW of Florida; 21°34′N 78°17′W. Site of Carlos Manuel de Céspedes sugar mill, named after famous officer of Cuba's 19th-cent. independence wars.

Cetronia (se-TRO-nee-ah), uninc. town (1990 pop. 950), Lehigh co., E Pa., residential suburb 4 mi/6.4 km W of Allentown; 40°35′N 75°31′W.

Cevicos (SAI-vee-kos), village (1993 pop. 1,958), Duarte prov., E central Dominican Republic, on NE slopes of the Cordillera Central, 38 mi/61 km ESE of La Vega; 19°00′N 69°58′W. Agr. (tobacco growing).

Ceylon, village (1991 pop. 163), S Sask., Canada, 40 mi/ 64 km WSW of Weyburn; 36°50′N 40°02′E. Wheat.

Ceylon (SEE-lawn), village (1990 pop. 461), Martin co., S Minn., 13 mi/21 km SW of Fairmont, near Iowa state line; 43°31′N 94°37′W. Grain, soybeans; livestock; mfg. (fertilizer, awnings). Tuttle L. to NE, Okamanpedan L. to E, both on East Fork Des Moines R., Clear L. to W.

Chaba Peak (10,540 ft/3,213 m), on Alta.-B.C. border, Canada, in Rocky Mts., 50 mi/80 km SSE of Jasper, in Columbia Icefield; 52°12′N 117°40′W.

Chabot, Lake, reservoir (☐ 1 sq mi/2.6 sq km), Alameda co., central Calif., on San Leandro Creek, 3 mi/4.8 km

E of San Leandro, at S end of Redwood Regional Park; 37°44′N 122°07′W. Max. capacity 20,050 acre-ft. Formed by Chabot Dam (142 ft/43 m high), built (1892) for water supply; owned by East Bay Municipal dist.

Chacachacare (sha-KAH-shah-kah-ree), islet, off NW Trinidad, Trinidad and Tobago, in the Dragon's Mouth, 13 mi/21 km W of Port of Spain; 10°41′N 61°45′W. Covers 151 acres/61 ha; 2 mi/3.2 km long, 2 mi/3.2 km wide. Chacachacare village (center), once a whaling establishment, was turned into a leper settlement, since evacuated.

Chacaltianguis (chah-kal-tee-AHN-gwees), town (1990 pop. 4,268), Veracruz state, SE Mexico, on Papaloapan R., 4 mi/6.4 km SSW of Cosamaloapan. Sugar, bananas; livestock.

Chackbay (SHAK-bai), uninc. town (1990 pop. 2,276), Lafourche parish; 7 mi/11 km N of Thibodeaux; 29°53′N 90°47′W. Hosts Gumbo Festival with Cajun band. Also known as Chegby.

Chaco Culture (CHAH-ko) Natl. Historical Park (☐ 53 sq mi/137 sq km), San Juan co., NW N.Mex., proclaimed 1907, 66 mi/106 km SSE of Farmington. Pre-Columbian ruins (13) of the Anasazi. Hundreds of small ruins representing the highest peak period of Pueblo prehistoric civilization (A.D. 900–1000). Includes Pueblo Bonito Ruins. Bounded N by Escabada Wash, which becomes Chaco R. here.

Chacon (chuh-KON), uninc. village (1990 pop. 300), Mora co., N central N.Mex., 20 mi/32 km SSE of Taos, in Sangre de Cristo Mts. Cattle, sheep; mfg. (apparel). Carson Natl. Forest to W; Cerro Vista peak (11,939 ft/ 3639 m) to NW.

Chadbourn (CHAD-buhrn), town (1990 pop. 2,005), Columbus co., SE N.C., 25 mi/40 km SSE of Lumberton. RR junction. Tobacco, peanuts, grain; livestock. Mfg. (apparel, machinery, lumber).

Chadds Ford, uninc. village (1990 pop. 250), Birmingham township, Delaware co., SE Pa., 9 mi/14.5 km NNW of Wilmington, Del., on Brandywine Creek; 39°52′N 75°35′W. Mfg. (winery, prefabricated aluminum bldgs., spherical projection domes and screens). Howe defeated Washington here on Brandywine Creek, Sept. 11, 1777. Brandywine R. Mus. and Wildflower Garden; Chadds Ford Winery to W; Brandywine Battlefield State Historical Site to E.

Chadron, town (1990 pop. 5,588), ⊙ Dawes co., NW Nebr., 50 mi/80 km N of Alliance, near White R. and S.Dak. line, in Great Plains region; 42°49′N 103°00′W. Trading point; seed potatoes, dairy and poultry prods., livestock, grain; lumber, timber. Chadron State Col. here. Pine Ridge Unit of Nebr. Natl. Forest (and campground) and Chadron State Park to S. RR junction to W. Founded 1885.

Chadwick, village (1990 pop. 557), Carroll co., NW Ill., 7 mi/11.3 km SSE of Mount Carroll; 42°00′N 89°53′W. In rich agr. area.

Chadwicks 1 resort village, Ocean co., E N.J., on peninsula bet. Barnegat Bay and the Atlantic, 8 mi/12.9 km ENE of Toms River. Fisheries. **2** village (1990 pop. 2,100), Oneida co., central N.Y., 6 mi/9.7 km S of Utica; 43°02′N 75°16′W.

Chaffee, county (☐ 1,015 sq mi/2,629 sq km; 1990 pop. 12,684), central Colo.; ⊙ Buena Vista, 38°44′N 106°10′W. Continental Divide forms W boundary. Cattle area, drained by Arkansas R., valley runs N-S through center. Some wheat, vegetables. Includes parts of San Isabel Natl Forest in all but river margins. Part of Sawatch Mts. in W. Monarch Ski Area in SW. Arkansas Headwaters State Park in S center. Formed 1879.

Chaffee (CHAF-fee), city (1990 pop. 3,059), Scott co., SE Mo., in Mississippi alluvial plain, 11 mi/18 km SW of Cape Girardeau; 37°10′N 89°39′W. Corn, wheat, soybeans; mfg. (apparel). Laid out 1837, inc. 1906.

Chaffee, Fort, Ark.: see FORT SMITH.

Chagrin Falls (shuh-GRIN), village (1990 pop. 4,146), Cuyahoga co., N Ohio, 16 mi/26 km ESE of Cleveland, on Chagrin R.; 41°26′N 81°23′W.

Chagrin River, c.45 mi/72 km long, NE Ohio; rises S of Chardon; flows SW to Chagrin Falls, then N, through suburbs of Cleveland, to L. Erie just N of Willoughby; 41°40′N 81°26′W.

Chaguanas (shah-GWAH-nahs), village, W Trinidad, Trinidad and Tobago, on RR, 11 mi/18 km SE of Port of Spain; 10°30′N 61°23′W. Sugarcane growing and milling.

Chaguaramas Bay (shah-gah-RAH-mas), inlet in NW Trinidad, Trinidad and Tobago, on the Gulf of Paria, 8 mi/12.9 km WNW of Port of Spain; 10°40′N 61°38′W. In area leased 1940 to U.S. as naval base. Serves as transfer point for bauxite from the Guianas to Mobile, Ala. Here Span. admiral Apadoca scuttled his fleet in 1797 on approach of the British. Former U.S. base now govt. office center.

Chagvan, Indian fishing village, SW Alaska, on SE shore of Kuskokwim Bay, S of Goodnews Bay; 58°48′N 161°38′W.

Chahuites (chah-WEE-tes), town (1990 pop. 8,846), Oaxaca state, Mexico. Off Mexico Higway 200 (Inter-Amer. Highway), 71 mi/114 km E of Juchitáh de Zaragoza. Agr. Has coasts on Mar Muerto and connections with RR.

Chain O' Lakes, NE Ill., several lakes near Wis. line and NNW of Chicago, joined to each other by Fox R. Many popular resorts. Included are Fox (the largest), Grass, Nippersink, Pistakee lakes. Chain O' Lakes State Park is along shores of Fox and Grass lakes.

Chain of Lakes, Martin co., S Minn.: see MIDDLE CHAIN OF LAKES.

Chain of Ponds, W Maine, series (5 mi/8 km long) of narrow linked lakes in N Franklin co., near Que. (Canada) border.

Chain-O-Lakes, village (1990 pop. 111), Barry co., Mo., SW 13 mi/21 km SE of Cassville, on Table Rock L. (White R.). Surrounded by Mark Twain Natl. Forest, Roaring R. State Park to NW. Recreational area. Residential.

Chakachamna Lake (cha-kuh-CHAM-nuh), S Alaska, 80 mi/129 km W of Anchorage; 17 mi/27 km long, 2 mi/3.2 km wide; 61°12′N 152°35′W. Fed by surrounding glaciers; drained E by Chakachatna R.

Chakachatna River (cha-kuh-CHAT-nuh), 40 mi/64 km long, S Alaska; issues from Chakachamna L. at 61°13′N 152°25′W; flows SE to Cook Inlet at Trading Bay.

Chaksinkín (chak-seen-KEEN), town (1990 pop. 1,567), Yucatán state, SE Mexico, 7 mi/11.3 km E of Tekax. Agr. (henequen, fruit).

Chalcatongo de Hidalgo (chahl-kah-TON-go de hee-DAHL-go), town (1990 pop. 1,565), in Oaxaca state, Mexico, 60 mi/90 km W of Oaxaca, and 60 mi/90 km S of Huajuapam de León; elev. 8,200 ft/2,500 m. Mountainous with temperate climate. Agr. (corn, beans, wheat, coffee, sugarcane, fruits; woods; livestock and poultry); unmined minerals. Also known as Villa Chalcatongo.

Chalchicomula de Sesma, Mexico: see CIUDAD SERDÁN.

Chalchihuitán (chal-chee-wee-TAHN), town (1990 pop. 633), Chiapas state, S Mexico, in N spur of Sierra Madre del Sur, 35 mi/56 km NE of Tuxtla Gutiérrez; 17°00′N 92°40′W. Elev. 4,167 ft/1,270 m. Beans, coffee, tobacco, sugarcane, fruit; cattle; lumber and fine woods. In Tzotzil Maya–speaking area. Formerly San Pablo.

Chalchihuites (chal-chee-WEE-tes), town (1990 pop. 4,286), ⊙ Chalchihuites, Zacatecas state, N central Mexico, on interior plateau, near Durango border, 95 mi/153 km NW of Zacatecas; 23°28′N 103°53′W. Elev. 7,615 ft/2,321 m. Agr. (corn, wheat, fruit; cattle); mining. Anc. ruins nearby at Suchil.

Chalco de Díaz Covarrubias (CHAL-ko dai DEE-as ko-va-ROO-bee-as), town (1990 pop. 224,190), ⊙ Chalco municipio, Mexico state, central Mexico, 20 mi/32 km SE of Mexico city, at edge of dry L. Chalco (a basin of Anáhuac region); in the Zona Metropolitana de la Ciudad de México; 19°15′N 98°54′W. Elev. 7,448 ft/2,270 m. Mfg. center (paper milling, coffee processing, iron and steel founding). Anc. Aztec town, with archaeological remains nearby.

Chalco, Lake (CHAHL-ko), lake, central Mexico, the southernmost of 5 shallow, interconnected lakes that occupied the Valley of México in pre-Columbian times. Along with neighboring L. Xochimilco, it is a freshwater lake. A system of canals and tunnels constructed at various times since the Span. colonial period has drained all but a small remnant of the original lake.

Chaleur Bay (shuh-LOOR), inlet of the Gulf of St. Lawrence, c.85 mi/140 km long and from 15 mi/24 km to 25 mi/40 km wide, bet. N N.B. and the Gaspé Peninsula, E Que., Canada. It is the submerged valley of the Restigouche R., which enters at its head. Chaleur Bay is a famous fishing ground for cod, herring, mackerel, and salmon, and many Acadian fishing villages line both coasts. The bay was discovered and named by Jacques Cartier in 1534.

Chalfant (CHAWL-fant), borough (1990 pop. 959), Allegheny co., SW Pa., residential suburb 8 mi/12.9 km E of downtown Pittsburgh; 40°24′N 79°50′W.

Chalfont (CHAWL-fuhnt), borough (1990 pop. 3,069), Bucks co., SE Pa., suburb 23 mi/37 km N of downtown Philadelphia and 4 mi/6.4 km SW of Doylestown, on Neshaminy Creek at joining of its North and West branches; 40°17′N 75°12′W. Mfg. (chemicals, crushed stone, conveyors, flexible packaging, amusement games). Agr. (grain, soybeans, apples; livestock, poultry; dairying). L. Galena reservoir to N.

Chalfonte, uninc. town (1990 pop. 1,740), New Castle co., NE Del., residential suburb 5 mi/8 km N of downtown Wilmington. Highest point in Del. (442 ft/135 m; unnamed), 1 mi/1.6 km N at Pa. state line, on Ebright Road.

Chalk River, village (1991 pop. 874), SE Ont., Canada, on Chalk R., near its mouth on Ottawa R., 95 mi/153 km WNW of Ottawa; 46°01′N 77°27′W. It is a govt. research establishment, operated by Natl. Research Council of Canada for Atomic Energy Control Board; its chief feature, a large heavy-water atomic pile, was operational in 1947.

Chalkyitsik, Indian village (1990 pop. 90), E Alaska, on Black R., 40 mi/64 km E of Fort Yukon, on Arctic Circle; 66°36′N 143°44′W. Formerly called Fishhook.

Challenge-Brownsville, uninc. town (1990 pop. 1096), Yuba co., N central Calif.; 39°28′N 121°16′W. Although statistically reported as one by Census Bureau, these villages have separate post offices: Brownsville is 14 mi/23 km ESE of Oroville, Challenge is 18 mi/29 km E of Oroville. Bullards Bar Reservoir to SE. Plumas and Tahoe Natl. forests to E. Timber; cattle; dairying; fruit, grain.

Challis, town (1990 pop. 1,073), ⊙ Custer co., central Idaho, 50 mi/80 km SSW of Salmon; 44°31′N 114°13′W. Elev. 5,288 ft/1,612 m. Agr. (hay, alfalfa; grain, barley, oats; cattle); lumber. Parts of Challis Natl. Forest to E and W. Land of the Yankee Fork State Park and Natl. Forest Historic Area to S; ghost towns and gold mining dredge. Molybdenum mining nearby.

Chalma (CHAL mah), town (1990 pop. 2,362), Veracruz state, E Mexico, 5 mi/8 km N of Huejutla de Reyes. Corn, fruit.

Chalmers, town (1990 pop. 525), White co., NW central Ind., 7 mi/11.3 km SW of Monticello; 40°40′N 86°52′W. In agr. area.

Chalmette (shal-MET), uninc. city (1990 pop. 31,860), ⊙ St. Bernard parish, extreme SE La., suburb 7 mi/11 km SE of downtown New Orleans, on E bank (levee) of the Mississippi R.; 29°57′N 89°58′W. Mfg. of furniture, paper prods., gasoline and diesel petroleum. Jean Lafitte Natl. Historical Park, Chalmette Unit (70 acres/28 ha; est. 1939) is here; it contains battlefield where Andrew Jackson defeated the British in 1815, just before ratification of Treaty of Ghent. Site of Elaine R. Nuñez Community Col. Also known as Port Chalmette.

Chalybeate (kuh-LEE-bee-uht), village, Tippah co., N Miss., 20 mi/32 km W of Corinth and 2 mi/3.2 km ESE of Walnut, near Tenn. state line.

Chalybeate Springs (kuh-LEE-bee-uht), town, Meriwether co., W Ga., 15 mi/24 km W of Thomaston; 32°51′N 84°34′W.

Chama (CHAH-muh), town (1990 pop. 1,048), Rio Arriba co., N N.Mex., on Rio Chama, near Colo. state line, and 75 mi/121 km S of Alamosa, Colo.; 36°53′N 106°34′W. Elev. 7,875 ft/2,400 m. RR terminus; shipping point for Colo. oil fields to N. Azotea Tunnel (water) through Continental Divide to W. Logging.

Chama, village, Costilla co., S Colo., in W foothills of Sangre de Cristo Mts., 5 mi/8 km SE of San Luis. Elev. 6,420 ft/1,957 m. Vegetables, potatoes, wheat; sheep, cattle. Sanchez Reservoir to S.

Chamacuero de Comonfort, Mexico: see COMONFORT.

Chambas (CHAHM-buhz), town, Ciego de Ávila prov., E Cuba, on RR, and 17 mi/27 km W of Morón; 22°12′N 78°55′W. Cattle raising.

Chambellan (shawng-be-LAWNG), village (1982 pop. 1,000), Grande-Anse dept., Haiti, 9 mi/14.5 km SW of Jérémie; 18°34′N 74°19′W. Coffee, cocoa growing.

Chamberino (chahm-buhr-EE-no), uninc. town (1990 pop. 700), Dona Ana co., S N.Mex., suburb 22 mi/35 km NNW of downtown El Paso, Texas, on Rio Grande. In irrigated agr. area; vineyards and winery.

Chamberlain, town (1990 pop. 2,347), ⊙ Brule co., S S.Dak., 65 mi/105 km W of Mitchell, on Missouri R. (Highway I-90 crosses here). Resort; livestock-shipping center; dairy prods. Large deposits of low-grade manganese nearby. Crow Creek Indian Reservation to N (Buffalo co.); Lower Brule Indian Reservation to NW (Lyman co.); Fort Kiowa (1822) to NW. Red L. to SE; RR terminus. Inc. 1881.

Chamberlain Lake (CHAIM-buhr-lin), Piscataquis co., N central Maine, 70 mi/113 km N of Dover-Foxcroft, in wilderness recreation area; 13 mi/21 km long, 1 mi/1.6 km–2.5 mi/4 km wide. Connected by streams to Allagash and Eagle lakes and Round Pond. Part of Allagash Wilderness Waterway.

Chamberlayne, uninc. town, Henrico co., E central Va., residential suburb 5 mi/8 km N of downtown Richmond, on Chamberlayne Avenue, near Chickahominy R.; 37°37′N 77°25′W.

Chamberlin, Mount (9,020 ft/2,749 m), NE Alaska, highest peak in Brooks Range; 69°17′N 144°52′W.

Chambers 1 (CHAIM-buhrs), county (☐ 603 sq mi/1,562 sq km; 1990 pop. 36,876), E Ala.; ⊙ Lafayette. Drained (NW) by Tallapoosa R., bounded on E by Chattahoochee R. and Ga. Agr. (livestock, hay); textile milling. Formed 1832. **2** county (☐ 868 sq mi/2,248 sq km; 1990 pop. 20,088), SE Texas; ⊙ Anahuac; 29°41′N 94°40′W. On Gulf coastal plains, and bounded S by East Bay; indented by Trinity Bay, extension of Galveston Bay, here receiving Trinity R. Bounded SE by Gulf Intracoastal Waterway. A leading Texas oil-producing co.; irrigated agr. (esp. rice, soybeans); cattle. Natural gas, sulphur; salt, clay, sand, and gravel. Anahuac Natl. Wildlife Refuge in SE. Formed 1858.

Chambers, village (1990 pop. 341), Holt co., N central Nebr., 20 mi/32 km SSW of O'Neill; 42°12′N 98°45′W. Meat and cold-storage prods.; cattle.

Chambers Island, Door co., NE Wis., in Green Bay, 12 mi/19 km NE of Menominee, Mich.; 3 mi/4.8 km long, 2 mi/3.2 km wide. Mackaysee L. on N part of isl.

Chambersburg, village, Gallia co., S Ohio, on the Ohio (locks and dam here), and 9 mi/14 km S of Gallipolis. Also called Eureka.

Chambersburg (CHAM-buhrs-buhrg), borough (1990 pop. 16,647), ⊙ Franklin co., S Pa., 45 mi/72 km SW of Harrisburg, on Conococheague Creek; 39°55′N 77°39′W. Mfg. (apparel, construction materials, transportation equip., electronic equip., machinery, feeds, primary metals, paper, food, and plastic prods.; printing, publishing). Agr. area (grain, potatoes, soybeans, apples; livestock, poultry; dairying). Chambersburg was hq. of abolitionist John Brown in 1859 and of Confederate Gen. Robert E. Lee before the battle of Gettysburg. The town was raided by Confederate cavalry in July 1864, when it was burned after refusing to pay an indemnity of $100,000 in gold. Seat of Wilson Col. Appalachian Trail passes to E; Michaux State Forest to NE; Buchanan State Forest to W; Caledonia State Park to E; Mont Alto State Park to SE; Letterkenny Army Depot to N. Settled 1730, inc. 1803.

Chamblee (SHAM-blee), city (1990 pop. 7,668), DeKalb co., NW central Ga., 10 mi/16 km NNE of Atlanta;

33°53′N 84°18′W. Blue-collar suburb of Atlanta; recent expansion of Asian and Hispanic pop. Booming Asian retail complex. Location of DeKalb-Peachtree airport, a major general aviation airport. Mfg. (furniture, electronics, machinery; printing and publishing). Many antique shops in old storefront and warehouses. Inc. as city 1922.

Chambly (shah-BLEE), county (□ 138 sq mi/357 sq km), S Que., Canada, on St. Lawrence and Richelieu rivers; ⊙ Longueuil; 45°30′N 73°20′W.

Chambly (shahn-BLEE), city (1991 pop. 15,893), S Que., Canada, on the Richelieu R., E of Montreal; 45°27′N 73°18′W. Chambly Fort was built in 1665 and was a strategic point in the defense of New France against the British and the Iroquois. The British captured it in 1760. It was seized by the invading Americans in 1775 and burned when they withdrew in 1776. The partially restored fort is a natl. historic site.

Chambord (shah-BOR), village (1991 pop. 1,739), S central Que., Canada, on S shore of L. St. John, 10 mi/16 km SE of Roberval; 48°26′N 72°03′W. Lumbering; agr. (dairying; pig raising).

Chamela (chah-ME-lah), village, in SW Jalisco, Mexico, on the Pacific coast N of the 19°30′N parallel, bet. the Chamela and Rivas land points. A small, little-known beach resort. On Chamela Bay.

Chamita (chuh-MEE-tuh), village, Rio Arriba co., N N.Mex., on W bank of Rio Grande, near confluence of Rio Chama and Rio Grande, and 26 mi/42 km NNW of Santa Fe. Elev. 5,719 ft/1,743 m. Fruit, chiles, grain, beans; livestock. Settled 1595 as San Gabriel. Once capital of N.Mex. under Span. rule. Valle Grande Mts. are W.

Chamizal National Memorial (KAM-ee-zahl), El Paso co., in downtown El Paso, W Texas. Memorializes the peaceful settlement (1963) of the 99-year border dispute between the U.S. and Mexico, in which a strip of land N of Rio Grande, lost to U.S. when river shifted its channel, was returned to Mexico. Covers 55 acres/22 ha. Ampitheatre and auditorium also here. Authorized 1966.

Chamois (shuh-MOI), city (1990 pop. 449), Osage co., central Mo., on Missouri R., and 24 mi/39 km ENE of Jefferson City; 38°40′N 91°46′W. Agr. (grain; dairying; livestock); mfg. (uniforms). Large coal-fueled electric power plant. Area damaged in flood of 1993.

Champ, village (1990 pop. 11), St. Louis co., E Mo., suburb 15 mi/24 km NW of downtown St. Louis, W of city of Bridgeton; 38°44′N 90°27′W. Est. here in early 1960s with the aspiration of attracting the Olympic Games and major industries; neither succeeded.

Champagne (sham-PAIN), Indian village, SW Yukon, Canada, 50 mi/80 km W of Whitehorse, on Alaska Highway and on bend of Dezadensh R.; 60°47′N 136°29′W. Historical mile 974.6 of Alaska Hwy. Roadhouse built 1902; became supply center in 1904 gold rush.

Champaign 1 (sham-PAIN), county (□ 997 sq mi/2,582 sq km; 1990 pop. 173,025), E Ill.; ⊙ Urbana; 40°08′N 88°12′W. Prairie agr. region, with its mfg., commercial, and industrial center at twin cities of Champaign-Urbana. Agr. (corn, wheat, soybeans, alfalfa; livestock; dairying); mfg. (machinery, dairy prods., apparel, consumer goods, concrete, edible oils, computer software; book publishing). Drained by Sangamon, Kaskaskia, and Embarras rivers, and by South Fork of Vermilion R. Univ. of Illinois at Champaign-Urbana. Parkland Community Col. in Champaign. Formed 1833. **2** county (□ 433 sq mi/1,121 sq km; 1990 pop. 36,019), W central Ohio; ⊙ Urbana, 40°08′N 83°46′W. Intersected by Mad R., Darby Creek, and small Buck and Little Darby creeks. In the Till Plains physiographic region. Agr. area (sheep, cattle, poultry; soybeans; honey; dairy prods.); mfg. at Urbana (paper prods., chemicals, transportation equip., motor vehicle parts and accessories); sand and gravel pits. Includes Ohio Caverns and a state game farm. Formed 1805.

Champaign, city (1990 pop. 63,502), Champaign co., E central Ill.; 40°06′N 88°15′W. It adjoins the city of Urbana and is a commercial and industrial center in a fertile farm area. The Univ. of Illinois at Champaign-Urbana and Parkland Col. are here. The city's economic mainstays are agr. and the univ. resources. Founded in 1855 with the arrival of the Illinois Central RR, Champaign was first called West Urbana. Inc. 1861.

Champion, village (1991 pop. 351), S Alta., Canada, 70 mi/113 km SE of Calgary; 50°13′N 113°09′W. In coal-mining region; cereal-foods mfg.; wheat growing.

Champion, village, Marquette co., NW Upper Peninsula, Mich., 27 mi/43 km W of Marquette; 46°30′N 87°57′W. RR junction; ships potatoes. Van Riper State Park to W on L. Mich.

Champion's Hill, Miss.: see EDWARDS.

Champlain (sham-PLAIN), county (□ 8,586 sq mi/22,238 sq km), central Que., Canada, extending N from the St. Lawrence; ⊙ Batiscan; 47°30′N 73°15′W.

Champlain, village (1991 pop. 1,610), S Que., Canada, on the St. Lawrence, and 12 mi/19 km NE of Trois Rivières; 46°26′N 72°21′W. Dairying; lumbering.

Champlain, village (□ 1 sq mi/2.6 sq km; 1990 pop. 1,273), Clinton co., extreme NE N.Y., on Great Chazy R., near L. Champlain and Que. border, 20 mi/32 km N of Plattsburg; 44°59′N 73°26′W. Port of entry. Mfg. (knitting mills, textiles). Settled 1789, inc. 1873.

Champlain Canal, N.Y.: see CHAMPLAIN, LAKE.

Champlain, Lake, 125 mi/201 km long, and ½ mi/8/10 km–14 mi/23 km wide, forming part of N.Y.-Vt. border and extending into Quebec; 44°26′N 73°20′W. The 4th-largest freshwater lake in U.S. (□ 490 sq mi/1,269 sq km), L. Champlain lies in an elongated plain bet. Adirondacks and Green Mts. Link in Hudson–St. Lawrence waterway; connected with Hudson (at Fort Edward) by Champlain div. of the Barge Canal (Champlain Canal), a manmade channel running 8 mi/12.9 km N to Whitehall, following a natural lowland representing a higher level of the lake after Pleistocene deglaciation. Richelieu R. connects the lake with St. Lawrence. L. George drains into it through a narrow channel, and many isls. dot its surface, including Grand Isle, Isle La Motte, and Valcour Isl. Region noted for its scenery; many resorts. Burlington (Vt.) and Plattsburgh (N.Y.) are the largest lakeshore cities. Named for explorer Samuel de Champlain; scene of battles in Fr. and Indian Wars. Amer. Revolution battles at Crown Point and Ticonderoga; naval engagement 1776. Amer. victory of Thomas Macdonough in War of 1812.

Champlin (CHAM-plin), city (1990 pop. 16,849), Hennepin co., E Minn., residential suburb 15 mi/24 km NNW of downtown Minneapolis, on Mississippi R., opposite Anoka (N); 45°10′N 93°23′W. Light mfg. Part of Elm Creek Park Reserve in W, including Leman's L.

Champoeg Memorial State Park (sham-POO-ee) (□ 615 acres/249 ha), NW Oregon, Marion co., on the Willamette R., and 7 mi/11.3 km SE of Newberg. Commemorates 1st settlement of Willamette valley (early 19th cent.) and establisment (1843) of 1st Amer. provisional territorial govt. on Pacific coast. Points of interest are Robert Newell House Mus., Log Cabin Mus., Pioneer Mothers Memorial.

Champotón (cham-po-TON), city (1990 pop. 18,505) and township, Campeche, SE Mexico, on SW Yucatán Peninsula, minor port on Gulf of Campeche, 37 mi/60 km SSW of Campeche; 19°20′N 90°43′W. Agr. (sugar, henequen, corn, tobacco, fruit; livestock); fishing. Pre-Columbian ruins nearby.

Chamula (chah-MOO-lah), town (1990 pop. 1,989), Chiapas, S Mexico, in Sierra de Hueytepec, 5 mi/8 km NW of San Cristóbal de las Casas. Elev. 7,546 ft/2,300 m. Cereals, fruit. Indian village with market, picturesque fiestas. In Tzotzil Maya–speaking area. Also known as Bohom.

Chanal (CHAH-nal), town (1990 pop. 4,198), Chiapas, S Mexico, in Sierra de Hueytepec, 32 mi/51 km E of San Cristóbal de las Casas; 16°45′N 92°25′W. Agr. center (wheat, corn, sugar, tobacco, coffee, fruit; livestock). A Tzeltal-Maya town.

Chance, village, Somerset co., SE Md., on tidewater on the Eastern Shore, 23 mi/37 km SW of Salisbury; bridge to Deal Isl. (just S). A dozen or so skipjacks, a portion of the 50 or so traditional sailing ships that dredge oysters from Chesapeake Bay, are usually moored at a narrows here called Upper Thorofare. Deal Isl. Wildlife Management Area is nearby.

Chancellor, village (1990 pop. 276), Turner co., SE S.Dak., 18 mi/29 km SW of Sioux Falls. Corn, oats, potatoes.

Chancellorsville, uninc. village, Spotsylvania co., NE Va., near Rappahannock R., 10 mi/16 km W of Fredericksburg. Site of Civil War battle of Chancellorsville (Apr. 27–May 6, 1863; sometimes called battle of Salem Church), in which a Confederate victory led to invasion of Pa. and battle of Gettysburg. Battleground is now a unit in Fredericksburg and Spotsylvania Co. Battlefields Memorial Natl. Military Park. Stonewall Jackson Memorial Shrine, 16 mi/26 km to SE at Guinea, commemorates Confederate leader mortally wounded at Chancellorsville.

Chance's Peak, mountain, Montserrat, 2.25 mi/4.3 km E of Plymouth; 16°43′N 62°10′W. Volcanic, erupted July 18, 1995.

Chandalar, village, N central Alaska, 183 mi/295 km N of Fairbanks, on Chandalar L., Chandalar R., in S foothills of Philip Smith Mts. of Brooks Range. Trans-Alaska Pipeline and service road 50 mi/80 km to W. No road access. Air field.

Chandalar River, 280 mi/451 km long, N central Alaska; rises in 3 headstreams in Brooks Range, the longest headstream rises as East Chandalar R. (69°N 144°10′W); flows SW to Venetie, where it is joined by combined Middle Fork and North Fork, and here becomes Chandalar R. proper, flowing SE to Yukon R. 20 mi/32 km W of Fort Yukon.

Chandeleur Islands (shan-duh-LUHR), SE La., crescent-shaped archipelago (c.26 mi/42 km long) in the Gulf of Mexico, c.40 mi/64 km N of mouth of the Mississippi R., and 75 mi/121 km E of New Orleans; 29°50′N 88°50′W. Mostly in St. Bernard parish, S part in Plaquemines parish. Lighthouse at N end of chain (30°3′N 80°52′W). Breton Natl. Wildlife Refuge here. Boat access. W of isls. is Chandeleur Sound (c.20 mi/32 km wide), an arm of the Gulf of Mexico, bet. marshy La. coast (W) and Chandeleur Isls. (E). Adjoins Miss. Sound (N), Breton Sound (SW), numerous openings to Gulf (E). Also called Islas de la Chandeleur.

Chandeleur Sound, La.: see CHANDELEUR ISLANDS.

Chandler, city (1990 pop. 90,533), Maricopa co., S central Ariz., suburb 13 mi/21 km SE of downtown Phoenix, in the Salt R. valley; 33°17′N 111°52′W. Elev. 1,213 ft/370 m. Bounded by Western Canal on N. It is primarily a residential community, and is noted for its modern developments in technology, research, and agr. Mfg. (machinery, bldg. materials, metal, rubber, and plastic prods., chemicals). The city's pop. has expanded greatly due to its new industrial advancements. Tourism is also important, and the San Marcos Golf Resort is in Chandler. Williams Air Force Base is nearby, but closed in early 1990s. Many of Chandler's citizens work in nearby Phoenix, which has also undergone extensive technological development. Adjoins Gila R. Indian Reservation; Chandler Municipal Airport to SE. Inc. 1920.

Chandler 1 town (1990 pop. 3,099), Warrick co., SW Ind., 5 mi/8 km WSW of Boonville; 38°02′N 87°22′W. In agr. and bituminous-coal area. Mfg. (electronics, hardwoods, kiln dried lumber). **2** town (1990 pop. 2,596), ⊙ Lincoln co., central Okla., 40 mi/64 km ENE of Oklahoma City, near Deep Fork of the Canadian R.; 35°42′N 96°52′W. Elev. 865 ft/264 m. Trade, processing, shipping center for agr. area noted for pecans; dairying. Mfg. (metal prods., apparel, expanded metal, transportation equip.). Settled 1891. **3** town (1990 pop. 1,630), Henderson co., E Texas, near Neches R. (at headwaters of L. Palestine reservoir), 11 mi/18 km W of Tyler; 32°18′N 95°28′W. Agr. area (cattle, horses; vegetables, melons); timber.

Chandler, village (1991 pop. 3,382), E Que., Canada, on E Gaspé Peninsula, on the Gulf of St. Lawrence, at mouth of Grand Pabos R., 35 mi/56 km SSW of Gaspé; 48°20′N 64°40′W. Pulp-milling center.

Chandler, village (1990 pop. 316), Murray co., SW Minn.,

11 mi/18 km WSW of Slayton; 43°55′N 95°57′W. Agr. (corn, oats, soybeans; livestock, poultry; dairying); mfg. (fertilizer, meat processing, concrete prods.).

Chandler Bay, Maine: see WOHOA BAY.

Chandler Heights, uninc. town (1990 pop. 2,791), Maricopa co., central Ariz., residential suburb 27 mi/43 km SE of downtown Phoenix and 9 mi/14.5 km SE of Chandler. Irrigated agr. region (fruit, vegetables, grain, cotton; livestock). Gila River Indian Reservation to SW.

Chandler Purchase, land purchase, Coos co., N central N.H., 14 mi/23 km SW of Berlin, in White Mt. Natl. Forest. Drained by Saco R. Recreation and timber area.

Chandlerville, village (1990 pop. 689), Cass co., W central Ill., near Sangamon R., 8 mi/12.9 km NNE of Va.; 40°02′N 90°09′W. In agr. area (corn, soybeans, sorghum; cattle, hogs). Panther Creek Conservation Area, and Site M Fish and Wildlife Area to SE.

Chanega, Alaska: see CHENEGA.

Chanenga, Alaska: see CHENEGA.

Change Island (□ 9 sq mi/23 sq km), E N.F., Canada, in Notre Dame Bay, 16 mi/26 km E of Twillingate and 3 mi/5 km W of Fogo Isl.; 49°37′N 54°27′W; 7 mi/11 km long,2 mi/3 km wide. At N end is fishing village. With nearby islets, makes up group of Change Isles.

Chanhassen (CHAN-ha-sen), city (1990 pop. 11,732), Carver co., central Minn., near L. Minnetonka, suburb 15 mi/24 km W of downtown Minneapolis; 44°51′N 93°33′W. Bounded by Minnesota R. on S. Mfg. (millwork, furniture, machinery, medical equip., consumer goods, electronics; printing). Univ. of Minn. Landscape Arboretum is here. Numerous lakes in area; L. Minnetonka to N, L. Minnewashta in NW.

Chankom (chan-KOM), town (1990 pop. 625), Yucatán, SE Mexico, 20 mi/32 km WSW of Valladolid, in tropical forest. Town made famous in classic ethnographic study. Formerly Chan-Kom.

Channahon (SHAN-uh-hahn), village (1990, pop. 4,266), Will co., NE Ill., suburb 10 mi/16 km SW of Joliet, on Des Plaines R. at mouth of Du Page R., Ill. and Mich.; 41°25′N 88°13′W. Canal passes to W. Mfg. (chemicals, steel processing). Channahon State Trail Access is here. Des Plaines Conservation Area to S.

Channel Islands, National Park (□ 390 sq mi/ 1,010 sq km), Santa Barbara and Ventura cos., SW Calif. Comprises Anacapa, Santa Barbara, San Miguel, Santa Cruz, and Santa Rosa isls. of Channel Isls. off S Calif. coast, Pacific Ocean. Santa Barbara is privately owned, San Miguel jointly owned by Park Services and U.S. Navy. Santa Barbara Isl. (c.47 mi/76 km S of Oxnard), part of Ventura co., all others in Santa Barbara co., c.25 mi/ 40 km S of coast, across Santa Barbara Channel. Originally a natl. monument, it was redesignated a natl. park in 1980. Authorized 1938. Also known as Santa Barbara Islands.

Channel Islands Beach, uninc. town (1990 pop. 3,317), Ventura co., S Calif., residential suburb 2 mi/3.2 km SW of Oxnard, on Pacific Ocean; 34°10′N 119°13′W. Includes areas of Silver Strand and Oxnard Beach.

Channel Lake, uninc. village (1990 pop. 1,660), Lake co., NE Ill., suburb 49 mi/79 km NW of downtown Chicago, 2 mi/3.2 km W of Antioch, 1 mi/1.6 km S of Wis. boundary; 42°28′N 88°09′W. Situated on neck of land bet. Channel L. (N) and L. Marie (S). Chain O' Lakes State Park to SW.

Channel Lake, NE Ill., W of Antioch; c.2 mi/3.2 km long; 42°29′N 88°08′W. Connected by stream to Chain O' Lakes.

Channel–Port Aux Basques, town (1986 pop. 5,901), SW coast of isl. of N.F., Canada. Main W point of entry, E terminal for marine ferry service to Sydney, N.S.; 47°34′N 59°09′W. Incorporates Channel, Port aux Basques, Grand Bay E and W, and Mouse Isl. RR terminus. Administrative and service center. Fishing

Channelview, uninc. city (1990 pop. 25,564), Harris co., SE Texas, suburb 13 mi/21 km E of downtown Houston, near Buffalo Bayou and Houston Ship Channel; 29°47′N 95°07′W. Drained by Carpenter Bayou. Mfg. (chemicals, refinery, machinery, printing, transportation equip., asphalts, metal prods.). Major chemical

plant explosion 1990. Sheldon Wildlife Management Area to N.

Channing 1 village, Dickinson co., SW Upper Peninsula, Mich., 22 mi/35 km N of Iron Mountain; 46°08′N 88°57′W. RR junction in forest and farm area. Large Michigamme Reservoir to W. **2** village (1990 pop. 277), ⊙ Hartley co., extreme N Texas, in high plains of the Panhandle, 45 mi/72 km NW of Amarillo; 35°40′N 102°19′W. Elev. 3,817 ft/1,163 m. Irrigated area; market, shipping point for cattle, grain.

Chantal (shawng-TAHL), town (1982 pop. 1,346), Sud dept., SW Haiti, on Jacmel Peninsula, 10 mi/16 km W of Les Cayes; 18°12′N 73°53′W. Coffee, limes, bananas, sugarcane.

Chantilly, uninc. city, Fairfax co., NE Va., suburb, 22 mi/ 35 km W of Wash., D.C., 6 mi/9.7 km SSW of Reston; 38°52′N 77°24′W. Mfg. (printing, computer equip., electronics, medical equip., bakery prods., construction materials, fabricated metal prods.); agr. to W (nursery prods.; dairying); limestone quarrying. Chantilly Battlefield Civil War battle (Sept. 1862) site is here. Dulles Internatl. Airport to N.

Chantrey Inlet, N Keewatin dist., N.W.T., Canada, bay of the Arctic Ocean, on E side of Adelaide Peninsula, sheltered by King William Isl.; 100 mi/161 km long, 50 mi/80 km wide at mouth; 67°N 95°W. Receives Back R. at head; contains Montreal Isl.

Chantry Island, islet, SW Ont., in L. Huron, Canada, just W of Southampton; lighthouse; 44°28′N 81°23′W.

Chanute (shuh-NOOT), city (1990 pop. 9,488), Neosho co., SE Kansas, on the Neosho R., 63 mi/101 km SE of Empora; 37°40′N 95°27′W. RR junction. It is a processing and trade center for an agr. region. Mfg. (prefabricated wood bldgs., construction materials, fabricated metal prods., apparel, transportation equip., electronics, metalwork). Oil and natural gas deposits in vicinity. Neosho County Community Col. and the Safari Mus. are here. Nearby is the site of the first mission in Kansas. Inc. 1873 following the consolidation of four contiguous towns.

Chapa de Mota (CHAH-pa de MO-ta), town (1990 pop. 756), Mexico state, central Mexico, 30 mi/48 km NW of Mexico city; 19°45′N 99°47′W. Grain, maguey; livestock.

Chapab (cha-PAHB), town (1990 pop. 1,894), Yucatán, SE Mexico, 10 mi/16 km NE of Ticul. Henequen, sugar, fruit.

Chapala (chah-PAH-lah), city (1990 pop. 15,664), Jalisco, central Mexico, on N shore of L. Chapala, 28 mi/45 km SSE of Guadalajara, on Mexico Highway 44; 20°20′N 103°10′W. Tourist resort; fishing. Hydroelectric plant.

Chapala, lake, W Mexico, in Jalisco and Michoacán states; c.50 mi/80 km long, 8 mi/12.9 km wide; 20°04′N 102°35′W. It is the largest lake in Mexico. Set in a depression on the central plateau, L. Chapala is fed by the Lerma R., which flows into it from the E, and is drained by the Río Grande de Santiago, which flows out by the NE corner. It is a popular scenic resort. Fishing is a local occupation. Since the early 1950s the waters have been receding at an alarming rate and the lake is rapidly becoming choked with water hyacinths; studies have been initiated to determine an effective conservation program.

Chapantongo (chah-po-TON-go), town (1990 pop. 1,707), Hidalgo, central Mexico, 45 mi/72 km WNW of Pachuca de Soto; 20°17′N 99°24′W. Corn, beans, maguey; livestock.

Chaparra, Cuba: see JESÚS MENÉNDEZ.

Chaparral (sha-pah-RAHL), uninc. town (1990 pop. 2,962), Dona Ana co., S N.Mex., suburb 16 mi/26 km NNE of downtown El Paso, Texas, in area formerly included in Ft. Bliss Military Reservation (N.Mex. and Texas); 32°01′N 106°24′W.

Chapeau (shah-PO), village (1991 pop. 445), SW Que., Canada, on Allumette Isl., in Ottawa R., 7 mi/11 km NNE of Pembroke. Dairying; cattle, pigs.

Chapel Acres, uninc. town, Fairfax co., NE Va., residential suburb 16 mi/26 km SW of Washington, D.C.; 38°44′N 77°14′W. Burke L. reservoir and park to NW.

Chapel Hill 1 town (1990 pop. 38,719), Orange co., central N.C., 9 mi/14.5 km SW of Durham at the edge of the Piedmont region; 35°55′N 79°02′W. Primarily residential, the town's economy is based on research and education. Research Triangle Park 10 mi/16 km to E, business park developed by Duke Univ., N.C. State Univ. and Univ. of N.C. Chapel Hill is the seat of the Univ. of N.C. (first public univ. in U.S., est. 1795). Ackland Art Mus., Morehead Planatarium, N.C. Botanical Gardens, Coker Arboretum are here. Univ. L. reservoir to SW. Horace Williams Airport to NW. Founded 1792, inc. 1851. **2** town (1990 pop. 833), Marshall co., central Tenn., 20 mi/32 km E of Columbia, in farm region; 35°37′N 86°42′W. Nathan Bedford Forrest b. here.

Chapel Island, E N.F., Canada, in Notre Dame Bay, 14 mi/23 km S of Twillingate; 7 mi/11 km long, 4 mi/ 6 km wide; 49°27′N 54°45′W.

Chapelle, La (shah-PEL, lah), agr. town (1982 pop. 1,271), Artibonite dept., central Haiti, 20 mi/32 km SE of Saint-Marc; 19°25′N 72°33′W. On fertile plain (fruit).

Chapelton, town (1991 pop. 3,930), Clarendon parish, central Jamaica, on affluent of Minho R., on RR, and 8 mi/12.9 km NNW of May Pen; 18°05′N 77°16′W. Trades in bananas. Tavanore estate house, a historical site.

Chapin 1 (CHAI-pin), village (1990 pop. 632), Morgan co., W central Ill., 5 mi/8 km NNE of Winchester; 39°46′N 90°24′W. In agr. area (corn, wheat, sorghum, soybeans; cattle, hogs). **2** village, Franklin co., N central Iowa, 12 mi/19 km N of Hampton. **3** village (1990 pop. 282), Lexington co., central S.C., 20 mi/32 km WNW of Columbia; 34°10′N 81°20′W. Mfg. of boats, concrete, decals.

Chapin, Mount, Colo.: see MUMMY RANGE.

Chapingo (chah-PEEN-go), village, Mexico state, central Mexico, 2 mi/3.2 km S of Texcoco de Mora. Seat of natl. agr. col.; murals by Diego Rivera adorn main bldg. and chapel.

Chapleau (shah-PLO), town (1991 pop. 3,077), central Ont., Canada, 100 mi/161 km NNE of Sault Ste. Marie; 47°50′N 83°24′W. RR division point. Market for surrounding gold-mining region; lumber mills.

Chaplin, agr. town (1990 pop. 2,048), Windham co., E central Conn., on Natchaug R., 7 mi/11.3 km NNE of Willimantic; 41°47′N 72°07′W. Has 19th-cent. bldgs., state park, state forest.

Chaplin, village (1991 pop. 332), S Sask., Canada, on N side of Chaplin L. (□ 66 sq mi/171 sq km), 50 mi/80 km W of Moose Jaw; 50°28′N 106°40′W. Sodium-sulphate production. Largest known natural supply of sodium sulphate; wheat, rye.

Chapman 1 town, Butler co., S Ala., 12 mi/19 km SW of Greenville. Lumber and lumber prods. **2** town (1990 pop. 1,264), Dickinson co., E central Kansas, on Smoky Hill R., 11 mi/18 km E of Abilene; 38°58′N 97°01′W. Trade center for livestock, grain, and dairy region. Mfg. (crushed stone, agr. lime). **3** town (1990 pop. 422), Aroostook co., NE Maine, 40 mi/64 km NNW of Houlton; 46°37′N 68°06′W. In agr. area.

Chapman, village (1990 pop. 292), Merrick co., SE central Nebr., 10 mi/16 km NE of Grand Isl., and near Platte R; 41°01′N 98°09′W. Popcorn.

Chapman, borough (1990 pop. 254), Northampton co., E Pa., 10 mi/16 km N of Bethlehem, on Monocacy Creek; 40°45′N 75°24′W. Grain; livestock; dairying. Slate quarries.

Chapman Camp, village, SE B.C., Canada, on St. Mary R., 2 mi/3 km SE of Kimberley; 49°39′N 115°58′W. Timber; tourism.

Chapman, Mount (10,150 ft/3,094 m), SE B.C., Canada, in Selkirk Mts., near W side of Hamber Provincial Park, 65 mi/105 km N of Revelstoke; 51°56′N 118°19′W.

Chapmanville, town (1990 pop. 1,110), Logan co., SW W.Va., on Guyandotte R., 9 mi/14.5 km N of Logan; 38°23′N 82°32′W. Agr. (tobacco). Mfg. (coal mining, construction equip., apparel). Chief Logan State Park to S.

Chapopotla, Mexico: see IXHUATLÁN DEL SURESTE, Veracruz.

Chappaqua (chuh-PAH-guh), upper-income residential

village (1990 pop. 6,400), Westchester co., SE N.Y., in N.Y. city suburban area, 5 mi/8 km E of Ossining; 41°09′N 73°45′W. Mfg. (photographic equip. and supplies). Originally a Quaker community; later estate area. Horace Greeley lived here.

Chappaquiddick Island (CHAP-uh-KWID-dik), part of EDGARTOWN, Dukes co., SE Mass., off E Martha's Vineyard, from which a narrow channel separates it; c.5 mi/8 km long. Resort area. Cape Poge (lighthouse here), at N tip, extends N into Nantucket Sound. Wasque Point at S tip; has lighthouse (41°25′N 70°27′W); site of famous Dyke Bridge.

Chappell, town (1990 pop. 979), ⊙ Deuel co., W Nebr., 80 mi/129 km SE of Scotts Bluff, on Lodgepole Creek, in Great Plains; 41°05′N 102°28′W. Agr. (wheat, grain, sunflower seeds; livestock; dairy prods.). Near Colo. border; on old Oregon Trail. Plotted 1884.

Chappell Hill, uninc. village (1990 pop. 310), Washington co., S central Texas, 9 mi/14.5 km E of Brenham, near the Brazos; elev. 317 ft/97 m. Agr. area; mfg. (metal coatings). Washington-on-the-Brazos State Park to NE.

Chappells (CHAP-uhls), village (1990 pop. 45), Newberry co., W central S.C., on Saluda R., 18 mi/29 km E of Greenwood; 34°10′N 81°52′W. L. Greenwood reservoir and state park to W.

Chaptico (chap-TEE-ko), village, St. Marys co., S Md., 10 mi/16 km NW of Leonardtown. Named for an Indian tribe that lived in the area, it was the hqs. of a revolution against Lord Baltimore led by John Goode in 1689. Christ Church (c.1737) was one of original churches of Md.

Chapulco (chah-POOL-ko), town (1990 pop. 3,539), Puebla, central Mexico, 11 mi/18 km N of Tehuacán, on Mexico Highway 150; elev. 6,726 ft/2,050 m. Corn, sugar, fruit; livestock.

Chapulhuacán (chah-pool-wah-KAHN), town (1990 pop. 2,472), Hidalgo, central Mexico, in foothills of Sierra Madre Oriental, on Inter-Amer. Highway 85, and 21 mi/34 km NE of Jacala; 20°59′N 95°54′W. Corn, rice, sugar, tobacco, fruit. Picturesque Indian settlement.

Chapultenango (chah-pool-te-NAN-go), town (1990 pop. 1,908), Chiapas, S Mexico, in N spur of Sierra Madre, 40 mi/64 km N of Tuxtla Gutiérrez. Orange growing. A Zoque Indian community.

Chapultepec (chah-POOL-te-pek), town (1990 pop. 3,798), Mexico state, central Mexico, 10 mi/16 km SE of Toluca de Lerdo; 19°12′N 99°18′W. Cereals; livestock.

Chapultepec (chah-POOL-te-pek), [Aztec = grasshopper hill], park (□ 2.5 sq mi/6.5 sq km) in Mexico City. It was originally developed as a residence for Aztec rulers. A castle built on a hill there in the late 18th cent. as a summer home for the Span. viceroys later became the traditional home of the rulers of Mexico. It is now the National Mus. of History. Chapultepec, heavily fortified, was the scene of spectacular fighting during the Mex. War.

Charapan (cha-RAH-pan), town (1990 pop. 3,536), ⊙ Charapan municipio, Michoacán, central Mexico, 23 mi/37 km S of Zamora de Hidalgo; elev. 8,858 ft/2,700 m. Wheat is principal crop. A Tarascan community.

Charcas, city (1990 pop. 10,155) and township, San Luis Potosí, N central Mexico, on the Meseta Central, 70 mi/113 km N of San Luis Potosí; 23°07′N 101°06′W. Elev. 6,748 ft/2,057 m. Important commercial mining (lead, copper, silver, zinc).

Charcas, Mexico: see DOCTOR MORA.

Charco Redondo, Mexico: see MELCHOR OCAMPO, Nuevo León.

Chardon (SHAHR-duhn), village (1990 pop. 4,446), ⊙ Geauga co., NE Ohio, 25 mi/40 km ENE of Cleveland; 41°34′N 81°12′W. Maple-sugar festival annual event. Laid out c.1808.

Chardonnières (shahr-do-NYER), town (1982 pop. 2,862), Sud dept., SW Haiti, on SW coast of Jacmel Peninsula, 28 mi/45 km W of Les Cayes; 18°16′N 74°10′W. Coffee, limes, tobacco. Fishing port.

Charenton (SHER-in-tuhn), uninc. village (1990 pop. 1,534), St. Mary parish, La., 7 mi/11 km NW of Franklin; 29°52′N 91°31′W. Drainage and navigation canal; oil

and gas field nearby. Chitimachae (the only Indian tribe native to S La.) Reservation. Originally known as Indian Bend, it was named for Charenton, France.

Chariton (SHER-uh-tuhn), county (□ 759 sq mi/1966 sq km; 1990 pop. 9,202), N central Mo.; ⊙ Keytesville; 39°31′N 92°57′W. Bounded by Missouri R. (S) and Grand R. (W); drained by Chariton R. Agr. (corn, wheat, soybeans; hogs, cattle, sheep); bituminous coal in area. Some mfg. at Salisbury and Brunswick. Swan L. Wildlife Refuge in NW. Major flooding occurred in 1993. Formed 1820.

Chariton, city (1990 pop. 4,616), ⊙ Lucas co., S Iowa, on Chariton R., c.45 mi/72 km SSE of Des Moines; 41°01′N 93°18′W. Agr. trade and coal-mining center; mfg. of structural steel fabric. RR shops and Haw L. State Park to S. Founded by Mormons in 1849; inc. in 1857.

Chariton River, c.280 mi/451 km long, N Mo. and S Iowa; rises in S central Iowa; flows SE and S to Missouri R. above Glasgow; mostly channelized in Missouri with a new mouth on the Missouri R. 10 miles above its natural mouth. Before channelization, it received East Chariton R. (or East Fork), rising S of Kirksville, Mo., and flowing c.90 mi/145 km S and SW. East Fork now has its own mouth on Missouri R. East Fork has Long Branch Lake reservoir; Thomas Hill Lake (reservoir) on Middle Fork, a tributary of East Fork.

Charlack (SHAHR-lak), town (1990 pop. 1,388), St. Louis co., E Mo., residential suburb 11 mi/18 km NW of downtown St. Louis; 38°42′N 90°20′W.

Charlemagne (shahr-luh-MAH-nyuh), village (1991 pop. 5,598), S Que., Canada, on L'Assomption R., just N of its mouth on the St. Lawrence, 16 mi/26 km NNE of Montreal; 45°43′N 73°29′W. Tobacco growing; dairying.

Charlemont, agr. town (1990 pop. 1,249), Franklin co., NW Mass., in hilly country, on Deerfield R., 14 mi/23 km W of Greenfield; 42°38′N 72°52′W. Dairying; woodworking.

Charleroi (SHAHR-luh-roi), borough (1990 pop. 5,014), Washington co., SW Pa., on Monongahela R., opposite (SW of) Monessen; 40°08′N 79°54′W. Lock No. 4 is here. Mfg. (sheet-metal fabricating, apparel, glass prods., concrete prods., plastic prods., paper prods.; commercial printing); bituminous coal; agr. (corn, hay; dairying). Laid out 1890, inc. 1892.

Charles, county (□ 643 sq mi/1,665 sq km; 1990 pop. 101,154), S Md.; ⊙ La Plata; 38°29′N 77°01′W. On SW shore (Potomac R.; bridged here to Va.) of the Md. peninsula; co. is partly bounded SE by Wicomico R., E by Patuxent R., N by Mattawoman Creek. Tidewater agr. area (chiefly tobacco), with some lumbering, commercial fishing and oystering; tobacco markets at La Plata and Hughesville. Swamps along streams (notably Wicomico R.) contain stands of timber and provide hunting. A proclamation by Gov. Josias Fendall created this co. out of St. Mary's County in 1658 named for Charles Calvert, Lord Baltimore. Tobacco auctions, open to the public, are conducted every spring in La Plata, Hughesville, and Waldurf as they have been since 1895 when La Plata replaced Port Tobacco as the co. seat. St. Catharine, a mid-19th-cent. house owned by the Mudd family, was where Dr. Samuel Mudd set the leg of John Wilkes Booth, broken as he fled the assassination of Abraham Lincoln. The cornerstone of St. Ignatius Church was set in 1798 and the entire church rebuilt after a fire in 1866, according to the original specifications. It is the oldest active Jesuit parish in the U.S. Charles Co. Community Col. here.

Charles, city, Toombs co., E central Ga., 6 mi/9.7 km NNW of Lyons; 32°13′N 82°25′W.

Charles, river, c.60 mi/97 km long; rising in E Mass. and flowing generally NE to Boston Bay; it separates Boston from Cambridge. Extensive development to the riverfront includes the Esplanade, a series of fishing sites, playgrounds, and walking paths; and the Hatch Shell, where free, open-air concerts are held by the Boston Pops Orchestra. Recreational sailing and canoeing, col. rowing, and boat races are common on the river; the Charles R. Regatta is held on the last Sunday in Oct.

Site of 1st water-powered textile mill in Waltham, 1810. Impounded by Charles R. Dam and Lock at Boston's Inner Harbor.

Charles, Cape, E Va., S tip of Eastern Shore peninsula (Delmarva Peninsula), on N side of entrance to Chesapeake Bay, at N end of Chesapeake Bay Bridge-Tunnel, opposite Cape Henry; 37°07′N 75°57′W. Cape Charles lighthouse is on Smith Isl. to SE. Town of Cape Charles 8 mi/12.9 km NNW, on Chesapeake Bay, terminus of RR barge ferry from Norfolk. Kiptopeke State Park. Fishermans Isl. Natl. Wildlife Refuge to S.

Charles City, county (□ 203 sq mi/526 sq km; 1990 pop. 6,282), E Va.; ⊙ Charles City; 37°21′N 77°03′W. In Tidewater region, bounded S by James R., and E by Chickahominy R., which enters James R. in SE corner. Agr. (hay, barley, wheat, corn, soybeans; poultry, cattle); timber. Harrison L. Natl. Fish Hatchery in SW. Many historic estates, including Westover, Berkeley (birthplace of Benjamin Harrison and William Henry Harrison), Evelynton, and Shirley. Formed 1634 as one of 1st cos. of Va.

Charles City, city (1990 pop. 7,878), ⊙ Floyd co., N Iowa, on Cedar R., 28 mi/45 km ESE of Mason City; 43°04′N 92°40′W. RR junction. Mfg. (wood prods., food processing, animal vaccines and pharmaceuticals, machinery, ladders, bldg. materials). Limestone quarries nearby. Settled 1850, inc. 1869.

Charles City, uninc. village, ⊙ Charles City co., E Va., 26 mi/42 km SE of Richmond, near James R. Mfg. (paper goods, funiture, hot tubs). Many fine historic estates in area, including Evelynton, Edgewood, and Berkeley to W.

Charles Island, SE Franklin Dist., N.W.T., Canada, in Hudson Strait, off N Ungava Peninsula; 26 mi/42 km long, 1 mi/2 km wide; 62°38′N 74°10′W.

Charles, Lake, La.: see CALCASIEU RIVER.

Charles Mill Reservoir, Ohio: see MIFFLIN.

Charles Mix, county (□ 1,150 sq mi/2,979 sq km; 1990 pop. 9,131), S S.Dak., on Nebr. line; ⊙ Lake Andes. Agr. area watered by Choteau and Platte creeks and bounded SW by Missouri R. Part of Choteau Creek and branch form E boundary in Bon Homme co. L. Frances Case Reservoir forms Nebr. boundary in S. Corn, wheat, soybeans, sorghum, hay; cattle, hogs, poultry; dairy prods. L. Andes Reservoir and Natl. Wildlife Refuge in E center. Yankton Indian Reservation in all of SE ½ of county (hq. at Marty in S); Yankton Treaty Monument in SE. Formed 1862.

Charles Mound, hill (1,235 ft/376 m) in NW Ill., near Wis. state line, 10 mi/16 km NE of Galena; 42°30′N 90°14′W. Highest point in state. Several similar mounds in vicinity.

Charles Pinckney National Historic Site, Charleston co., SE S.C., 9 mi/14.5 km NE of downtown Charleston. Authorized 1988; home and estate of Amer. diplomat and one of the framers of the U.S. Constitution.

Charles River, in R.I.: see PAWCATUCK RIVER.

Charles Town, town (1990 pop. 3,122), ⊙ Jefferson co., NE W.Va., in East Panhandle, 16 mi/26 km SSE of Martinsburg; 39°17′N 77°51′W. RR junction. Agr. (grain, soybeans, apples; livestock; horse-breeding; dairying); mfg. (printing and publishing, asphalt prods.). Limestone and dolomite quarrying. Resort. Charles Town Racetrack (thoroughbred racing), Summit Point Raceway are here. Harpers Ferry Natl. Historic Park to NE; Shannondale Springs Wildlife Management Area to SE; Appalachian Trail passes to E; Leetown Natl. Fish Hatchery to NW. John Brown was tried (1859) and hanged here. Harewood, where Dolly Madison was married, is nearby. Town laid out 1786.

Charlesbourg (SHAHRL-boorg), city (1991 pop. 70,788), S Que., Canada; 46°52′N 71°16′W. Northern suburb of Quebec city, and 1 of the oldest parishes in the prov. Includes part of the seigniory 1st granted to the Jesuits in 1626 and settled in 1659. Formerly known as Bourg Royal.

Charleston, county (□ 1,357 sq mi/3,515 sq km; 1990 pop. 295,039), SE S.C.; ⊙ Charleston; 32°49′N 79°54′W. Extends along Atlantic Coast, from mouth of South Edisto R. (SW) to mouth of Santee R. (NE). Much of

Intracoastal Waterway passes inland parallel to coast. SEA ISLANDS here (notably Edisto, Wadmalaw, Johns, James, Kiawah, Seabrook, Folly isls.). Has many popular coast resorts (notably Kiawah, Seabrook, Folly Beach, and Isle of Palms); Fort Sumter Natl. Monument, Fort Moultrie, Castle Pinckney Natl. Monument are in Charleston Harbor. Part of Francis Marion Natl. Forest in NE. County was a rich plantation region in antebellum days; now has chief mfg. and shipping center of the state (Charleston), some agr. (sweet potatoes, corn, vegetables; hogs, cattle); fisheries, hunting. Formed 1785.

Charleston 1 city (1990 pop. 20,398), ⊙ Coles co., E Ill.; 39°28′N 88°10′W. Charleston is an industrial, RR, and trade center located in an agr. area; shoes are also made. Eastern Illinois Univ. is here. A Lincoln-Douglas debate was held in Charleston on Sept. 8, 1858. Inc. 1835. Local attractions include an enormous statue of Lincoln and nearby Lincoln Log Cabin State Park and Fox Ridge State Park. Near Embaras R. **2** city (1990 pop. 2,328), ⊙ Tallahatchie co. (seat shared with Sumner), NW central Miss., 35 mi/56 km N of Greenwood; 34°00′N 90°03′W. Agr. (cotton, corn, wheat, soybeans; cattle; timber); mfg. (paper prods., apparel, furniture; textiles); clay, sand, fuller's-earth pits. Lumber milling. Tallahatchie Natl. Wildlife Refuge to NW. **3** city (1990 pop. 5,085), ⊙ Mississippi co., extreme SE Mo., near Mississippi R., 11 mi/18 km SW of Cairo, Ill.; 36°55′N 89°20′W. Cotton, corn, soybeans, popcorn, potatoes, melons; mfg. (transportation equip., machinery). Laid out 1837. **4** city (1990 pop. 80,414), ⊙ Charleston co., SE S.C., 85 mi/137 km NE of Savannah, Ga., on low, narrow peninsula in Charleston Harbor, formed by the confluence of the Ashley and Cooper rivers, 32°47′N 79°56′W. Founded in 1680 and inc. as a city in 1783, Charleston is the oldest city in the state and one of the chief ports of entry in the SE U.S. Charleston Internatl. Airport to NW. In the bay, or bordering on it, are Sullivans Isl., site of Fort Moultrie; James Isl.; Morris Isl., with a lighthouse; Fort Sumter; and Castle Pinckney. Many transportation routes converge at Charleston, and through its excellent, sheltered harbor off the Atlantic Ocean, an extensive coastal and foreign trade is conducted. Diverse mfg. includes chemicals, steel, motor vehicle parts, pulp and paper, textiles, bottling machinery, and clothing. Charleston is hq. for the 6th U.S. naval dist. and for the U.S. Air Force defense command. Extensive mil. facilities include a Polaris submarine base and a huge navy yard (est. 1901); Charleston Airforce Base. The English settled at Albemarle Point (1670), on the W bank of Ashley R., c. 7mi/11km from modern Charleston. They later moved to Oyster Point, where their capital, Charles Town (the city's original name), had been laid out. The city became the most important seaport in the Southern colonies and the leading center of wealth and culture in the South. Non Eng. immigrants, among whom the Fr. Huguenots were most prominent, added a cosmopolitan touch. Charleston's Dock Street Theatre (1736) was one of the first theaters to be established in the U.S. In the Revolutionary War, Charleston was defended successfully against the British in 1776 and 1779; however, the city was surrendered in 1780 to the British, who held it until 1782. The capital of S.C. was moved from Charleston to Columbia in 1788, but Charleston remained a regional economic and social center. The city was the scene of the first hostile act of the Civil War, the firing on Fort Sumter (April 12, 1861), not long after a S.C. convention had met here in Dec. 1860 and voted to secede from the Union. The city had its harbor blockaded by Union forces and was under seige for more than 2 years before it fell in Feb. 1865. A violent earthquake, Aug. 31, 1886, and periodic tornadoes and hurricanes, such as Hurricane Hugo in 1989, have caused much damage to the city and surrounding area; however, many outstanding colonial bldgs. and historic sites survive. Of note are St. Michael's Episcopal Church, Miles Brewton house, Old Slave Mart Mus. and Gallery, and Charleston Mus. (1773), one of oldest mus. in U.S. The waterfront, called the Battery, and the Grace Memorial Bridge over the Cooper R., are famous landmarks. Tourists are attracted by the city's unique charm, mild climate, nearby beaches, and gardens. Annual events include an azalea festival and Spoleto. Educational institutions include the Citadel, the Medical Univ. of S.C., Charleston Southern Univ., and the Col. of Charleston, the first municipal col. in the country. Nearby is Isle of Palms, a noted resort. **5** city (1990 pop. 653), Bradley co., SE Tenn., on Hiwassee R., and 35 mi/56 km NE of Chattanooga; 35°17′N 84°45′W. **6** (CHAHRLZ-tuhn), city (1990 pop. 57,287), ⊙ W.Va. and Kanawha co., W central W.Va., on the Kanawha R., where it is joined by the Elk R.; 38°21′N 81°37′W. The largest city in W.Va., Charleston is an important transportation and trading center for the highly industrialized Kanawha valley. Mfg. (chemicals, pipe and sheet-metal fabricating, printing and publishing, machinery, food and beverages, concrete, RR ties). The city grew around the site of Fort Lee (1788). Daniel Boone lived there from 1788 to 1795. The capital was transferred there from Wheeling in 1870, moved back to Wheeling in 1875, then returned to Charleston in 1885. The state capital bldg. (completed 1932) has a dome higher than the U.S. capital. Yeager Airport to NE. Univ. of Charlestown is here; W. Va. State Col. to W, at Institute. The Cultural Center at State Capital Complex contains an art gallery, mus., planetarium, and notable gardens. Tri-State Greyhound Park at Cross Lanes to W; Coonskin Park to NE; Kanawha State Forest to SW. Charlestown Ordnance Center to W. Inc. 1794.

Charleston 1 (CHAHRLZ-tuhn), town (1990 pop. 2,128), NW Ark., 21 mi/34 km ESE of Fort Smith; 35°17′N 94°02′W. Shares the capital functions with Ozark, Franklin co. Ships livestock, poultry, eggs; mfg. (bookcases, computer furniture, apparel, food processing, plywood). Fort Chaffee Military Reservation to SW. **2** town (1990 pop. 1,187), Penobscot co., central Maine, 25 mi/40 km NW of Bangor; 45°04′N 69°02′W. **3** uninc. town (1990 pop. 500), Coos co., W Oregon, 6 mi/9.7 km WSW of downtown Coos Bay, at entrance to South Slough, arm of Coos Bay; entrance to Coos Bay 1 mi/1.6 km W. Fishing port. Mfg. (canned seafood, fish processing). Coos Head U.S. Naval Facility to W. Cape Arago and Sunset Bay State Park 3 mi/4.8 km to W. **4** town (1990 pop. 844), Orleans co., N Vt., on Clyde R., 8 mi/12.9 km SE of Newport; 44°50′N 72°00′W. Lumber. Includes village of West Charleston.

Charleston, village (1990 pop. 336), Wasatch co., N central Utah, at N end of Deer Creek Reservoir on Provo R., 18 mi/29 km NE of Provo; 40°28′N 111°28′W. Elev. 5,600 ft/1,707 m. Barley, alfalfa; dairying; cattle, sheep, horses. Sundance Ski Resort to SW; part of Uinta Natl. Forest to W. Midway State Fish Hatchery to NW; Deer Creek State Park in S. Large Wasatch Mountain State Park to NW.

Charleston, sect. of Staten Isl. borough of N.Y. city, SE N.Y., on SW Staten Isl.; 40°32′N 74°14′W.

Charleston Harbor, inlet (☐ 8 sq mi/20.7 sq km) of the Atlantic Ocean at Charleston, S.C.; formed by junction of Ashley and Cooper rivers. Morris and Moultrie isls. shelter the entrance. Charleston Harbor is part of the Intracoastal Waterway. U.S. Navy Yard is on Cooper R., 8 mi/12.9 km above Charleston.

Charleston Peak, Nev.: see SPRING MOUNTAINS.

Charlestown 1 city (1990 pop. 5,889), Clark co., SE Ind., near Ohio R., 15 mi/24 km NE of New Albany; 38°27′N 85°40′W. Chemical mfg.; U.S. arsenal here (ammunition for U.S. govt.). Printing. **2** (CHAHRLZ-toun), former city, now part of Boston, Middlesex co., E Mass., on Boston Harbor, bet. the Mystic and the Charles rivers. Mfg. (metals, electronics, bookbinding, printing). The oldest part of Boston, it was the site of the U.S. navy yard (est. 1801, closed 1973) where the U.S.S. *Constitution* is moored. The battle of Bunker Hill was fought in the vicinity (on Breed's Hill) on June 17, 1775; site of Bunker Hill Monument. Samuel Morse was b. in Charlestown. The Navy Yard is now the site of residential and commercial developments and is maintained by Natl. Park Service as a Natl. Historical Park. Settled 1629, included in Boston 1874.

Charlestown, town (1980 pop. 1,771) on the isl. of Nevis, St. Kitts and Nevis, West Indies. Charlestown is the chief town and port of the isl. Alexander Hamilton b. here. It was a fashionable center in the 17th cent.

Charlestown 1 town (1990 pop. 578), Cecil co., NE Md., on Northeast R., 26 mi/42 km WSW of Wilmington, Del.; 39°35′N 75°59′W. An 18th-cent. port, it has been designated a Natl. Historic Dist. and preserves fourteen 18th-cent. homes. In 1786 the co. seat was moved from Charlestown to Elkton. Inc. 1786. **2** town (1990 pop. 4,630), Sullivan co., SW N.H., 10 mi/16 km SSW of Claremont; 43°15′N 72°23′W. Bounded W by Connecticut R. (Vt. state line). Agr. (cattle, poultry; apples, corn; nursery crops); mfg. (marine hardware, concrete, transportation equip.). Hubbard Hill State Forest in N. Cory Number Four restoration. Settled 1740 as Township No. 4 and defended by Phineas Stevens against French and Indians, inc. 1753 **3** (CHARLES-town), town (1990 pop. 6,478), Washington co., SW R.I., on Block Isl. Sound, 32 mi/51 km SSW of Providence; 41°22′N 71°41′W. Includes Quonochontaug village and parts of Carolina, Shannock, and part of Kenyon villages. Agr. (potatoes). Resorts; Charlestown Beach (summer colony) is on sandbar separated from mainland by Ninigret Pond (c.5 mi/8 km long). Town has Narragansett Indian Reservation with granite church (1859) and Indian burial ground; bird and game sanctuary. Inc. 1738. The 1938 hurricane caused great damage here. Formerly called Cross's Mills.

Charlevoix (SHAHR-luh-voi), county (☐ 1,390 sq mi/3,600 sq km; 1990 pop. 21,468), NW Mich.; ⊙ Charlevoix. Bounded NW by L. Michigan; 45°28′N 85°27′W; drained by short Boyne and Jordan rivers. Includes BEAVER ISLANDS group. Dairying; agr. (cattle, poultry; potatoes, cherries, apples, seed); iron foundries, plastics prods. Some mfg. at Charlevoix, Boyne City, and East Jordan. Flour, lumber mills; fisheries. Resorts. Charlevoix, dominant feature in W half of co., and Walloon, in N forms part of boundary, W Emmet co., lakes (fishing, boating, winter sports) nearby; Fisherman's Isl. State Park in W on L. Michigan; Young State Park at co. center near Boyne City. Organized 1869. Big Rock Point nuclear power plant (initial criticality September 27, 1962) is 4 mi/6.4 km NE of Charlevoix. Uses cooling water from L. Michigan and has a max. dependable capacity of 67 MWe. It has the lowest capacity of any nuclear power plant in operation in the U.S. today.

Charlevoix (SHAHR-luh-voi), town (1990 pop. 3,116), ⊙ Charlevoix co., NW Mich., on narrow isthmus bet. L. Charlevoix (SE) and L. Michigan (NW), 44 mi/71 km N NE of Traverse City; 45°18′N 85°15′W. In agr. area (potatoes, seed); mfg. (candles, transportation equip., store display racks, pollution control systems). Resort. Has Coast Guard station and U.S. fish hatchery. Ferry service to Beaver Isl. (St. James) from here. Airport to SW. Fisherman's Isl. State Park to SW. Settled 1852; inc. as village 1879, as city 1905.

Charlevoix East (shahr-luh-VWAH), county (☐ 719 sq mi/1,862 sq km; 1991 pop. 17,413), E central Que., Canada, on the St. Lawrence; ⊙ à l' Aigle; 47°50′N 70°15′W.

Charlevoix, Lake (SHAHR-luh-voi), NW Mich., extends 14 mi/23 km SE from Charlevoix city, which is on its short outlet to L. Michigan, to Boyne City; 2 mi/3.2 km wide; 45°16′N 85°08′W. Resort; fishing. Receives short Boyne R. in SE. Short Jordan R. in narrow South Arm (extends to East Jordan; c.8 mi/12.9 km long).

Charlevoix West, county (☐ 1,496 sq mi/3,875 sq km), E central Que., Canada, on the St. Lawrence R.; ⊙ Baie St. Paul; 47°45′N 70°45′W. Fishing, logging, mixed farming. NW half of co. is in Laurentides Reserve. Ferry to Île aux Coudres in St. Lawrence, site of Cartier's landing, 1535.

Charlo, village (1990 pop. 358), Lake co., W Mont., 18 mi/29 km S of Polson, in Flathead Indian Reservation; 47°26′N 114°10′W. Cattle, sheep, hogs; potatoes, corn, oats. Ninepipe Reservoir and Natl. Wildlife Refuge to E; Natl. Bison Range to S. Formerly called Big Flat, then Charlotte.

Charlotte, county (☐ 1,243 sq mi/3,219 sq km; 1991

pop.26,607), SW N.B., Canada, on the Bay of Fundy and on Maine border (St. Croix R.); ⊙ St. Andrews. Includes Grand Manan, Deer, and Campobello isls.

Charlotte 1 county (□ 859 sq mi/2,225 sq km; 1990 pop. 110,975), SW Fla., on Gulf of Mexico; ⊙ Punta Gorda; 26°53′N 81°57′W. Lowland area with Charlotte Harbor in W. Cattle raising; vegetable growing; fishing. Formed 1921. Major retirement center, and the average age of the pop. is among the highest of all Fla.'s cos. **2** county (□ 477 sq mi/1,235 sq km; 1990 pop. 11,688), S Va.; ⊙ Charlotte Court House; 37°00′N 78°39′W. Rolling region, bounded W and S by Roanoke (Staunton) R. Agr. (esp. tobacco; also corn, hay, wheat, soybeans; beef cattle; dairying); timber. Formed 1765.

Charlotte, city (1990 pop. 395,934), ⊙ Mecklenburg co., S N.C., 140 mi/225 km WSW of Raleigh, near S.C. state line; 35°12′N 80°49′W. The largest city of the state and the foremost commercial banking and industrial center of the Piedmont region; 3d largest banking center in the U.S.; site for many foreign firms (Ger., Jap., Can.). Charlotte is an air and transportation hub as well as a distribution point for the Carolina mfg. belt. Hydroelectric power from the Catawba R. (to W) where L. Wylie dam forms L. Wylie reservoir to W; Mountain Isl. and L. Norman reservoir to NW, serves the city's industries. The city (settled c.1750) was named for Queen Charlotte, wife of King George III of England. The citizens there were among the most outspoken in their opposition to the Br. govt., and it was at Charlotte that the Mecklenburg Declaration of Independence was signed in May 1775. In his brief occupation of the city (Sept.–Oct. 1780), Br. Gen. Charles Cornwallis called it a "hornet's nest of rebellion." In the economic, social, and political realms, Charlotte has become a rather progressive Southern city. The Univ. of N.C. (to NE) at Charlotte, Queens Col., Johnson C. Smith Univ., and Central Piedmont Community Col. are here. The Mint Mus. of Art is a reproduction of the U.S. Mint, located in the city from 1837 until 1913. The Charlotte Coliseum, to W (home of NFL and NBA teams), has one of the largest steel, aluminum, and precast concrete domes in the world. President James K. Polk was born in Charlotte. James R. Polk Memorial State Historical Site to S, at Pineville. Charlotte Mus. of History, Nature Mus., Univ. Research Park to NE. Charlotte-Douglass Internatl. Airport to W. Independence Arena in SE. Charlotte Motor Speedway, to NE, in Concord, can seat over 16,000. Kelly Space Voyager Planetarium. Inc. 1768.

Charlotte 1 (SHAHR-luht), town (1990 pop. 359), Clinton co., E Iowa, 16 mi/26 km WNW of Clinton; 41°57′N 90°28′W. Dairy prods. **2** town (1990 pop. 271), Washington co., E Maine, c.10 mi/16 km S of Calais; 45°00′N 67°16′W. In hunting, fishing area. **3** town (1990 pop. 8,083), ⊙ Eaton co., S central Mich., 18 mi/29 km SW of Lansing; 42°33′N 84°49′W. Satellite community of Detroit. In agr. area (grain, beans, corn). Maple-sugar distribution point. Mfg. (concrete, furniture, timber, transportation equip., glass containers, polyester compounds). The Kellogg Foundation's company unit is here. Settled before 1840; inc. as village 1863, as city 1871. **4** town (1990 pop. 854), ⊙ Dickson co., N central Tenn., 33 mi/53 km W of Nashville; 36°11′N 87°21′W. Lumbering. **5** town (1990 pop. 1,475), Atascosa co., SW Texas, 42 mi/68 km SSW of San Antonio; 28°51′N 98°42′W. Vegetables, strawberries, peanuts; dairying; cattle. Inc. after 1940. **6** town (1990 pop. 3,148), Chittenden co., NW Vt., 12 mi/19 km S of Burlington, on L. Champlain; 44°19′N 73°13′W. Summer resort; dairy prods. Ferry to Essex, N.Y. Mt. Philo state park here. Chartered 1762, settled 1784.

Charlotte Court House, town (1990 pop. 531), ⊙ Charlotte co., S Va., 37 mi/60 km SE of Lynchburg; 37°02′N 78°38′W. Mfg. (computer assembly); agr. (grain, soybeans, tobacco; cattle; dairying); trade point in tobacco, timber area.

Charlotte Hall, village (1990 pop. 1,992), St. Marys co., S Md., 32 mi/51 km SSE of Washington; 38°29′N 76°48′W. Est. 1698. The Charlotte Hall School here.

Charlotte Harbor, town (□ 2 sq mi/5.2 sq km; 1990 pop. 3,327), Charlotte co., SW Fla., 25 mi/40 km NW of Fort Myers; 26°57′N 82°03′W. Mfg. includes printing and publishing, and furniture.

Charlotte Harbor, SW Fla., shallow inlet of the Gulf of Mexico, sheltered by the barrier isls. Gasparilla and Lacosta (W) and opening into Pine Isl. Sound (S) and Gasparilla Sound (N); c.25 mi/40 km long, 5 mi/8 km wide; 26°45′N 82°10′W. Channel dredged from S end of Gasparilla Isl. to Punta Gorda, the chief port. Receives Peace and Myakka rivers in N.

Charlotte Park, town (□ 1 sq mi/2.6 sq km; 1990 pop. 2,225), Charlotte co., SW Fla., c.30 mi/48 km NW of Fort Myers; 26°53′N 82°02′W.

Charlotte River, c.30 mi/48 km long, E central N.Y.; rises in W Schoharie co.; flows SW to Susquehanna just E of Oneonta.

Charlotte Town, Dominica: see ROSEAU.

Charlotte Town, Grenada: see GOUYAVE.

Charlottesville, independent city (□ 10 sq mi/26 sq km; 1990 pop. 40,341), ⊙ Albemarle co., separate from co., central Va., 70 mi/113 km NW of Richmond, on Rivanna R., in Piedmont region; 38°02′N 78°29′W. RR junction. Mfg. (bldg. materials, electronic equip., furniture, computer circuit boards, consumer goods, printing and publishing); agr. (grain; livestock, poultry; dairying. Br. Gen. John Burgoyne's captured army was quartered nearby in 1779–1780, and in 1781 Sir Banastre Tarleton raided the city. To SE are MONTICELLO, home of Thomas Jefferson; Ash Lawn, home of James Monroe. Michie Tavern Mus. and the birthplaces of Meriwether Lewis and George Rogers Clark are here. Seat of Univ. of Va., founded 1819 by Thomas Jefferson; the Inst. of Textile Technology is to W; Piedmont Va. Community Col. is to S. Charlottesville-Albemarle Airport to N. L. Monticello reservoir to SE. Founded 1762, chartered as a city 1888.

Charlottetown, city (1991 pop. 15,396), ⊙ and chief port of P.E.I., Canada, on the S coast; 46°14′N 63°08′W. Agr. (dairying); food processing, tourism, fishing (lobster, scallops, clams, cod, haddock, mackerel), farming, and mfg. (wool and cotton knitwear). The French est. (c.1720) a fort and settlement across the harbor, known as Port la Joie. Charlottetown was laid out by the British in 1768 and named for Queen Charlotte, consort of George III. Its growth was slow until the middle of the 19th cent., when it became noted for the sailing vessels it built for fishing and lumber transport. The Charlottetown Conference of the Maritime Provs. (1864) was the first step toward Can. confederation. Univ. of P.E.I. and Confederation Centre of the Arts are here. Harness racing at Charlottetown Driving Park.

Charlotteville, village, Tobago, Rep. of Trinidad and Tobago, overlooking Man of War Bay, NE Tobago, 16 mi/26 km NE of Scarborough. Fishing.

Charlton, county (□ 799 sq mi/2,069 sq km; 1990 pop. 8,496), SE Ga.; ⊙ Folkston; 30°47′N 82°08′W. Bounded S and SE by Fla. state line (formed here by St. Marys R.) and NE by Satilla R.; W part included in Okefenokee Swamp. Flatwoods area drained by Suwanee R. (W); sugarcane, tobacco; lumber, logging, sawmilling, wood prods.; cattle. Formed 1854.

Charlton, town (1991 pop. 279), E Ont., Canada, 25 mi/40 km S of Kirkland L.; 47°49′N 80°00′W. In silver-mining, farming region.

Charlton, agr. town (□ 43 sq mi/111 sq km; 1990 pop. 9,576), Worcester co., S central Mass., 12 mi/19 km SW of Worcester; 42°08′N 71°58′W. Woolen goods, fiber optics; dairy prods. Settled c.1735, inc. 1755. Includes village of Dodge.

Charlton Heights (CHAHRL-tuhn), locality, Fayette co., S central W.Va., on Kanawha R., 26 mi/42 km SE of Charleston. Part of Gauley Bridge.

Charlton Island (□ 113 sq mi/293 sq km), SE Keewatin Dist., N.W.T., Canada, at head of James Bay; 19 mi/31 km long, 9 mi/14 km wide; 51°58′N 79°25′W. Game sanctuary.

Charnisay, Fort (CHAHR-ni-SAI), S N.B., Canada, on the Bay of Fundy, at mouth of St. John R., opposite St. John; built 1645 by Fr. governor Charnisay, abandoned in mid–18th cent. Rebuilt 1758 by General Monckton and named Fort Frederick, it was burned 1775 by the Americans; rebuilt 1778 and named Fort Howe; abandoned 1821.

Charny (shahr-NEE), village (1991 pop. 10,239), S Que., Canada, on Chaudiére R., near its mouth on the St. Lawrence, and 8 mi/13 km SSW of Quebec; 46°43′N 71°16′W. RR center.

Charo (CHAH-ro), town (1990 pop. 3,943), Michoacán, central Mexico, 10 mi/16 km E of Morelia. Cereals, fruit; livestock.

Charter Oak 1 uninc. town (1990 pop. 8858), Los Angeles co., S Calif., residential suburb 20 mi/32 km E of downtown Los Angeles; 34°06′N 117°51′W. Pacific Coast Baptist Col. is here; Bonelli Reg. Park to SE. **2** town (1990 pop. 497), Crawford co., W Iowa, 13 mi/21 km WNW of Denison; 42°04′N 95°35′W. In agr. area.

Chase 1 county (□ 778 sq mi/2,015 sq km; 1990 pop. 3,021), E central Kansas; ⊙ Cottonwood Falls; 38°17′N 96°35′W. Located in Flint Hills region, drained by Cottonwood R. Cattle; wheat, soybeans, hay; hogs, poultry. Cast State Fishing Lake at co. center. Formed 1859. **2** county (□ 897 sq mi/2,323 sq km; 1990 pop. 4,381), SW Nebr.; ⊙ Imperial; 40°31′N 101°41′W. Agr. area bounded W by Colo. and drained by Frenchman Creek. Cattle, hogs; corn, wheat, popcorn, beans, potatoes. Central-Mountain time-zone boundary follows E boundary. Enders Reservoir State Recreation Area in SE; Champion Mill State Historical Park and Champion L. State Recreation Area in S center. Historic flour mill on Frenchman Creek. Formed 1886.

Chase, town (1990 pop. 577), Rice co., central Kansas, 8 mi/12.9 km W of Lyons; 38°21′N 98°20′W. In wheat and livestock area.

Chase, village (1991 pop. 2,083), S B.C., Canada, on South Thompson R., 30 mi/48 km ENE of Kamloops; 50°49′N 119°41′W. Lumbering; irrigated farming, fruit growing.

Chase, village, Lake co., W central Mich., 6 mi/9.7 km E of Reed City; 43°53′N 85°38′W. Manister Natl. Forest to SW.

Chase City, town (1990 pop. 2,442), Mecklenburg co., S Va., 25 mi/40 km ENE of South Boston; 36°47′N 78°27′W. Mfg. (furniture, apparel, wooden pallets, medical equip., footwear, food prods.); agr. area (tobacco, peanuts, cotton, grain; livestock, poultry; dairying); timber. Inc. 1873.

Chaseburg, village (1990 pop. 365), Vernon co., SW Wis., on small Coon Creek, 13 mi/21 km SSE of La Crosse; 43°38′N 91°05′W. In dairying and stock-raising region. Cheese.

Chaska (CHAS-kuh), city (1990 pop. 11,339), ⊙ Carver co., S central Minn., suburb 21 mi/34 km SW of Minneapolis; 44°49′N 93°36′W. Drained by Chaska Creek. Trade and shipping point in agr. area; mfg. (electronic equip., chemicals, food processing, furniture, feeds, paper prods.). Minnesota Valley State Trail across river, to SE; small natural lakes in area; prehistoric Native Amer. mounds in city park. Settled 1853, inc. as village 1871, as city 1891.

Chassell, village, Houghton co., NW Upper Peninsula, Mich., on Portage L., 7 mi/11.3 km SSE of Houghton; 47°01′N 88°31′W. Trade center for farm and resort area.

Chat, Cape (shah), on Gulf of St. Lawrence, E Que., Canada, on N Gaspé Peninsula, at S side of mouth of the St. Lawrence, 2 mi/3 km W of Cap Chat village; 49°05′N 66°45′W. Lighthouse.

Chataingier (SHAT-e-NIR), village (1990 pop. 281), Evangeline parish, S central La., 27 mi/43 km NNW of Lafayette, near Bayou des Cannes; 30°34′N 92°19′W. In agr. area (cotton, sugarcane, rice, sweet potatoes; cattle).

Chatanika (cha-tuh-NEE-kuh), village, central Alaska, 20 mi/32 km NNE of Fairbanks. On Steese Highway. Gold in area; tourism, sports fishing.

Châtard (shah-TAHR), village, Nord dept., N Haiti, 22 mi/35 km SW of Cap-Haïtien, just S of Plaisance; 19°35′N 72°28′W. Coffee, cacao, oranges, limes.

Chateaubelair, town (1989 est. pop. 7,064), W St. Vincent, West Indies, 8 mi/12.9 km N of Kingstown; 13°17′N 61°15′W. Cotton, coconuts.

Chateaugay (sha-to-GAI), village (☐ 1 sq mi/2.6 sq km; 1990 pop. 845), Franklin co., NE N.Y., on Chateaugay R., near Que. (Canada) border, 12 mi/19 km NE of Malone; 44°55′N 74°04′W. Port of entry. Mfg. (cheese). State trout hatchery. Settled 1796, inc. 1869.

Chateaugay (sha-to-GAI), river, c.50 mi/80 km long; rising in Chateaugay L. in Adirondacks, NE N.Y., and flowing through Que. (Canada) to empty into St. Lawrence R. 10 mi/16 km below Montreal, opposite Ottawa R. mouth. Site of Amer. defeat in War of 1812 battle of Chateaugay (1813); Can. and Native Amer. force turned back Amer. attack on Montreal.

Chateaugay Lakes, N.Y.: see UPPER CHATEAUGAY LAKE.

Châteauguay (shah-to-GAI), county (☐ 265 sq mi/686 sq km.), S Que., Canada, on the St. Lawrence, near N.Y. border; ⊙ Ste. Martine; 45°10′N 73°45′W.

Châteauguay, suburban town, S Que., Canada, on Châteauguay R., near its mouth on L. St. Louis, 14 mi/23 km SW of Montreal; 44°56′N 73°45′W. Market in dairying region; mfg. (plastic prods.).

Château-Richer (shah-TO ree-SHAI), village (1991 pop. 3,690), ⊙ Montmorency No. 1 co., S central Que., Canada, on the St. Lawrence R., and 15 mi/24 km NE of Quebec; 47°00′N 71°01′W. Stone quarrying; sawmill; resort.

Chatfield, town (1990 pop. 2,226), Fillmore and Olmsted cos., SE Minn., 18 mi/29 km SE of Rochester, on North Branch Root R.; 43°50′N 92°11′W. Grain, soybeans; livestock, poultry; dairying; mfg. (fiberglass farm equip., beef hides, furniture). Parts of Richard J. Dorer Memorial Hardwood State Forest to SW and SE. Founded before 1856.

Chatfield, village (1990 pop. 206), Crawford co., N central Ohio, 10 mi/16 km N of Bucyrus; 40°57′N 82°57′W.

Chatfield Lake, reservoir, N central Colo., on Douglas-Jefferson co. border, on the S. Platte R., in Chatfield State Recreation Area, 13 mi/21 km SSW of downtown Denver; 3 mi/4.8 km long; 39°33′N 105°02′W. Max. capacity of 355,000 acre-ft. Formed by Chatfield Dam (124 ft/38 m high), built (1973) by the Army Corps of Engineers for flood control.

Chatham 1 (CHA-tuhm), county (☐ 441 sq mi/1,142 sq km; 1990 pop. 216,935), E Ga.; ⊙ Savannah; 31°58′N 81°05′W. Bounded N by S.C. line (formed here by Savannah R.), E by the Atlantic, and S by Ogeechee R.; includes Tybee and Skidaway isls. Mfg. and shipping at Savannah, a port of entry. Dairy farming; fishing. Formed 1777. **2** county (☐ 707 sq mi/1,831 sq km; 1990 pop. 38,759), central N.C.; ⊙ Pittsboro; 35°42′N 79°15′W. In Piedmont area bounded S in part, by Cape Fear and Deep rivers; also drained by Haw R. (joins Deep R. on S boundary to form Cape Fear R.) and New Hope R. Agr. area (tobacco, corn, wheat, soybeans, sorghum, hay; chickens, cattle, hogs, turkeys; dairying); timber. Mfg. at Siler City. Jordan L. State Recreation Area, on Jordan L. reservoir, in E. Part of Harris L. reservoir in SE. Formed 1770.

Chatham, city (1991 pop. 43,557), S Ont., Canada, E of Detroit, Mich., on the Thames R.; 42°24′N 82°11′W. Industrial center in a rich mixed-farming and fruit-raising region. It was a N terminus for the Underground RR prior to the Amer. Civil War.

Chatham (CHA-tuhm), town (1991 pop. 6,544), NE N.B., Canada, on Miramichi R. 12 mi/19 km from its mouth, and 75 mi/121 km NNW of Moncton; 47°02′N 65°28′W. Port, shipping lumber, fish, pulp. Lumber, pulp, paper mills. Has R.C. cathedral. Airfield.

Chatham 1 (CHA-tuhm), town (1990 pop. 617), Jackson parish, N central La., on Castor Creek, 24 mi/39 km SW of Monroe; 32°19′N 92°27′W. In agr. area; mfg. of wooden pallets. Gas field nearby. Caney Creek reservoir to SW. **2** town (1990 pop. 6,579), including Chatham village, Barnstable co., SE Mass., on Atlantic shore of Cape Cod, 17 mi/27 km E of Hyannis; 41°40′N 69°59′W. Summer resort; fishing; cranberries. Champlain landed here 1606. Has 18th-cent. bldgs. Includes villages of North Chatham, South Chatham, West Chatham (1990 pop. 1,504). Monomoy Isl., a sandspit extending 10 mi/16 km S, is a Natl. Wildlife Refuge and site of a lighthouse. Settled 1665, inc. 1712. **3** town (1990 pop. 268), Carroll co., E N.H., in White Mts., 23 mi/37 km SSE of Berlin; 44°09′N 71°02′W. Bounded E by Maine state boundary. All of town, except SE corner, in White Mt. Natl. Forest. Mfg. (outdoor apparel). Chandler Mt. (3,329 ft/1,015 m) in W; West Royce Mt. (3,020 ft/920 m) in NE corner; Robbins Ridge crosses town E-W. Upper Kimball Pond in SE; Basin Pond and Cold River Natl. Forest Campgrounds in NE. **4** town (1990 pop. 1,354), ⊙ Pittsylvania co., S Va., 15 mi/24 km N of Danville, on Cherrystone Creek; 36°49′N 79°24′W. Mfg. (apparel, metal die castings, lumber and plywood, cable, wine; printing and publishing); trading center in rich agr. area (dairying; cattle; tobacco, grain, soybeans); timber. Chatham Correctional unit to SW. Inc. 1852.

Chatham 1 (CHA-tuhm), fishing village, SE Alaska near S end of Chichagof Isl., on Chatham Strait 35 mi/56 km NNE of Sitka; 57°31′N 134°56′W. **2** village (1990 pop. 6,074), Sangamon co., central Ill., 9 mi/14.5 km SSW of Springfield; 39°40′N 89°42′W. In agr. area. **3** village (1990 pop. 268), Alger co., N Upper Peninsula, Mich., 14 mi/23 km SW of Munising; 46°20′N 86°55′W. In agr. area. Mich. State Univ. maintains an agr. experiment station here. Hiawatha Natl. Forest to N and E; Laughing Whitefish Falls State Park to NW.

Chatham (CHA-tuhm), residential borough (1990 pop. 8,007), Morris co., NE N.J., on Passaic R., and 11 mi/18 km W of Newark; 40°44′N 74°22′W. Hothouse flowers. Mfg. (metal prods., plastic resins, thermostats, sponge and rubber prods.). Has pre-Revolutionary inn. Settled 1749, inc. 1897.

Chatham, village (☐ 1 sq mi/2.6 sq km; 1990 pop. 1,920), Columbia co., SE N.Y., 22 mi/35 km SE of Albany; 42°21′N 73°35′W. RR junction in diversified farm area; mfg. (boxboard, plastic moldings). Summer residences and recreation on small lakes nearby. Inc. 1869.

Chatham Sound, W B.C., Canada, channel of Dixon Entrance, extends N from Porcher Isl. to mouth of Portland Inlet, separating Dundas Isls. from Tsimpsean Peninsula; 40 mi/64 km long, 8 mi/13 km–15 mi/24 km wide.

Chatham Strait, SE Alaska, navigable channel extending 210 mi/338 km N-S through NW portion of Alexander Archipelago, separating Admiralty Isl. from Chichagof and Baranof isls.; 7 mi/11.3 km–8 mi/12.9 km wide; 134°50′W 56°10′–59°10′N. Continued N by Lynn Canal and NW by Icy Strait. Named 1794 by Vancouver after Lord Chatham.

Chatmoss-Laurel Park, uninc. town, Henry co., S Va., residential suburb 4 mi/6.4 km E of Martinsville; 36°40′N 79°48′W.

Chatom (CHA-tuhm), town (1990 pop. 1,094), ⊙ Washington co., SW Ala., 55 mi/89 km NNW of Mobile. Raincoat mfg., petroleum processing.

Chatooga River, 40 mi/64 km long, portion of NW boundary bet. S.C. and Ga., designated a Natl. Wild and Scenic R.; rises in Blue Ridge Mts. in SW N.C.; forms portion of boundary bet. S.C. and Ga., joins with Tallulah R. to form Tugaloo R.

Chats, Lac des (SHAH, lahk dai), expansion of Ottawa R., SE Ont., Canada, 30 mi/48 km E of Ottawa; 24 mi/39 km long. Receives Madawaska and Mississippi rivers.

Chatsworth 1 town (1990 pop. 2,865), ⊙ Murray co., NW Ga., 11 mi/18 km E of Dalton; 34°47′N 84°47′W. Talc-mining center; mfg. of yarns, industrial coatings, textiles, chemicals, metal prods.. Nearby Chohutta Wilderness Area lies at the S end of the Appalachian Mts. Chattahochee Natl. Forest. Moravian mission (1802-1833). **2** town (1990 pop. 1,186), Livingston co., E central Ill., 20 mi/32 km ESE of Pontiac; 40°45′N 88°17′W. In agr., clay area. Laid out 1858, inc. 1867. **3** town (1990 pop. 103), Sioux co., NW Iowa, near S.Dak. line, 24 mi/39 km W of Orange City; 42°55′N 96°30′W.

Chatsworth, village (1991 pop. 521), S Ont., Canada, 8 mi/13 km SSE of Owen Sound; 44°27′N 80°53′W. Dairying; lumbering; mixed farming.

Chatsworth, suburb of Los Angeles, Los Angeles co., S Calif., in extreme NW corner of city, in San Fernando Valley, 23 mi/37 km NW of downtown. Mfg. (electronics, medical supplies, transportation equip., plastic prods.). Santa Susana Mts. to N; Simi Hills to W; Chatsworth Reservoir to S.

Chattahoochee (chat-uh-HOO-chee), county (☐ 253; 1990 pop. 16,934), W Ga.; ⊙ Cusseta; 32°21′N 84°47′W. Bounded W by Ala. state line (formed here by Chattahoochee R.); W part included in Fort Benning Military Reservation. Poultry. Formed 1854.

Chattahoochee (chat-tah-HOO-chee), town (☐ 5 sq mi/13 sq km; 1990 pop. 4,382), Gadsden co., NW Fla., near Ga. line, on Apalachicola R. (formed just N by junction of Chattahoochee and Flint rivers), and 37 mi/60 km WNW of Tallahassee; 30°41′N 84°50′W. Mfg. (furniture; lumber). Dam (power, navigation) nearby in Flint R.

Chattahoochee River (chat-uh-HOO-chee), 436 mi/702 km long, Ga. and Fla.; rises in N Ga., near Helen; flows generally S to join the Flint R. in L. Seminole on the Ga.-Fla. state line; the combined waters form the Apalachicola R., c.90 mi/145 km long, which flows S, along the city of Atlanta, to Apalachicola Bay, NW Fla., and the Gulf of Mexico; 34°48′N 83°47′W. The Jim Woodruff Dam impounds L. Seminole and provides hydroelectricity. The Columbia, Walter F. George, Bartlett's Ferry, and Goat Rock dams produce power and regulate navigation on the lower Chattahoochee. Buford Dam forms L. Sidney Lanier (used for recreation) and is the source of Atlanta's water supply. The Flint R., 330 mi/531 km long, rising in W central Georgia, is navigable to Bainbridge, Ga., and is a valuable source of power in W Georgia.

Chattahoochee River National Recreation Area (chat-uh-HOO-chee) (☐ 14 sq mi/36 sq km), Ga. This series of 13 park sites along the Chattahoochee R. in the Atlanta area is administered by the Natl. Park Service as a part of its urban parks program. Authorized 1978.

Chattanooga (chat-uh-NOO-guh), city (1990 pop. 152,466), ⊙ Hamilton co., E Tenn., on both sides of the Tennessee R. near Ga. state line, 100 mi/161 km NNW of Atlanta; 35°02′N 85°18′W. Elev. 1,000 ft/305 m. An important mfg. and marketing center for a widespread area. Foremost mfg. includes textiles, metal and wood prods., chemicals, machinery, and primary metals. Also a resort center, Chattanooga is almost entirely surrounded by mts., with many historical and tourist attractions on or near Lookout Mt., Missionary Ridge, Tennessee Cave, and Signal Mt. To the W of the city, the Tennessee R. cuts through the Cumberland Plateau in a magnificent gorge, c.1,000 ft/305 m deep. A trading post was est. in 1810; by 1835, regular steamship service began there. A center first of salt- and then cotton-shipping, the city expanded with the arrival of the RR in the 1840s and 1850s. It was of strategic importance in the Civil War. Northern industrialists developed the iron industry during the 1870s. Electric power, augmented by the TVA project after 1933, has played an important role in the city's development. Chickamauga Dam is nearby. SE and SW of the city lies Chickamauga and Chattanooga Natl. Military Park (est. 1890), part of which lies in Ga. Also of interest are Rock City Gardens, a wildlife sanctuary, a freshwater aquarium, historic cemeteries, and many old bldgs. Cultural institutions include an opera, symphony orchestra, community theater, and art gallery. A U.S. coast guard station is on L. Chickamauga, and the city is the seat of the Univ. of Tenn. at Chattanooga. Inc. 1839.

Chattanooga (chat-uh-NOO-guh), village (1990 pop. 437), Comanche co., SW Okla., 19 mi/31 km SW of Lawton; 34°25′N 98°39′W. In agr. area.

Chattaroy (CHAT-uh-roi), town (1990 pop. 1,182), Mingo co., SW W.Va., on Tug Fork R., 2 mi/3.2 km N of Williamson; 37°42′N 82°16′W. Bituminous-coal region. Mfg. (mining equip.).

Chattooga (chuh-TOO-guh), county (☐ 317; 1990 pop. 22,242), NW Ga., on Ala. state line; ⊙ Summerville; 34°29′N 85°21′W. Hilly area, including part of Chattahoochee Natl. Forest (E). Agr. includes cotton, corn,

Cross references are shown in SMALL CAPITALS. The pronunciation key is on page xv. The dates of population figures are on page xii.

hay, sweet potatoes, fruit; cattle, hogs, poultry; textile mfg., sawmilling. Formed 1838.

Chattooga River 1 c.50 mi/80 km long, Ga. and Ala.; formed by confluence of several headstreams in Chattooga co., NW Ga.; flows SW, past Summerville, Ga., into Cherokee co., NE Ala., where it enters Coosa R. 3 mi/4.8 km NNE of Centre. Little R. is tributary. **2** 40 mi/64 km long, Ga., N.C., and S.C.; rises in the Blue Ridge in SW N.C.; flows SW, mostly along Ga.-S.C. state line, to a point just SE of Tallulah Falls, S.C., joining Tallulah R. to form Tugaloo R. Designated as a natl. wild and scenic river; popular white-water rafting venue. The movie *Deliverance* filmed here.

Chatuge Lake (chuh-TOO-guh), reservoir, SW N.C. and NE Ga., on Hiwassee R., 3 mi/4.8 km SE of Hayesville, N.C.; 35°01′N 83°47′W. Formed by Chatuge Dam, built (1942) for flood control. Partly bounded by Nantahala (N.C.) and Chattahoochee (Ga.) natl. forests.

Chatwood, uninc. town (1990 est. pop. 1,000), West Goshen township, Chester co., SE Pa., residential suburb 1 mi/1.6 km E of West Chester; 39°57′N 75°35′W. West Chester Airport to NE.

Chaubunagungamaug, Lake (chaw-BUH-nuh-GUHNG-guh-mawg), reservoir, Worcester co., S Mass., on Conn. border, 15 mi/24 km S of Worcester; c.3 mi/4.8 km long; 42°01′N 71°49′W. Resort. Also called Chargagogmanchogagog.

Chaudière (sho-DYEHR), river, 115 mi/185 km long; rising in Lac Mégantic, SE Que., Canada, near the Maine-Que. boundary; flowing generally N to the St. Lawrence R. opposite the city of Que. A hydroelectric power plant at Chaudière Falls (130 ft/40 m high) supplies electricity to the Que. city region.

Chaudière Falls, in the Ottawa R. in the heart of the city of Ottawa, Ont., Canada. The river is narrowed by rocky cliffs to a width of c.200 ft/60 m and drops 50 ft/15 m in a series of cascades. Several bridges cross the river here, passing over the falls.

Chaumont (shuh-MO), village and fishing center (1990 pop. 593), Jefferson co., N N.Y., on Chaumont Bay (inlet of L. Ontario) at mouth of small Chaumont R., 13 mi/21 km NW of Watertown; 44°04′N 76°07′W. Regional recreation center: Long Point State Park, SW across Chaumont Bay, on Point Peninsula.

Chauncey (CHAWN-see), town (1990 pop. 312), Dodge co., S central Ga., 10 mi/16 km SE of Eastman, near Little Ocmulgee R.; 32°07′N 83°04′W. Mfg. includes wooden utility poles.

Chauncey, village (1990 pop. 980), Athens co., SE Ohio, 5 mi/8 km NNW of Athens, and on Hocking R.; 39°23′N 82°07′W.

Chautauqua 1 (shuh-TAH-kwah), county (□ 644 sq mi/1,668 sq km; 1990 pop. 4,407), SE Kansas; ⊙ Sedan; 37°08′N 96°15′W. In Osage Questas region, bordered S by Okla.; drained by Caney R. in W. Cattle; hay, oats, wheat. Oil and natural gas fields. Formed 1875. **2** (shuh-TAW-kwah), co. (□ 1,062 sq mi/2,751 sq km; 1990 pop. 141,895), extreme W N.Y., bounded NW by L. Erie; ⊙ Mayville; 42°17′N 79°24′W. Mfg. at Jamestown and Dunkirk; 1 of N.Y.'s leading agr. regions (poultry; seeds, fruit; dairying). State fish hatchery. Resorts on L. Erie and on Chautauqua L. Site of Chautauqua Inst. Formed 1808.

Chautauqua (shuh-TAH-kwah), town (1990 pop. 132), Chautauqua co., SE Kansas, 30 mi/48 km W of Coffeyville, near Okla. state line; 37°01′N 96°10′W. In livestock and grain area. Mus.

Chautauqua (shuh-TAW-kwuh), resort village (1990 pop. 500), Chautauqua co., extreme W N.Y., 15 mi/24 km NW of Jamestown; 42°14′N 79°30′W. Self-contained Victorian community on shore of scenic L. Chautauqua; originally founded as meeting place for Methodist ministers and laity. Summer center for arts, education, religion, and recreation. Cars may not be used in the village. Chautauqua Inst., founded in 1864, is located here; received N.Y. charter as nonprofit corporation in 1902. Famous people connected with the school include U.S. Presidents Garfield, Grant, McKinley, Harding, and both Roosevelts; explorers Admiral Richard Byrd and Amelia Earhart; inventors Henry

Ford and Thomas Edison; Senator Robert Kennedy, William Jennings Bryan, Jane Addams, Carrie Chapman Catt, Ida Tarbell, Frances Willard, and N.Y. governor Al Smith. Village formerly known as Fair Point.

Chautauqua Lake (shuh-TAW-kwuh), W N.Y., 18 mi/29 km long and ranging from 1,000 ft/305 m to over 2 mi/3.2 km wide; 42°12′N 79°26′W. At an elev. of 1,308 ft/399 m, lake is 735 ft/224 m higher than L. Erie. A high ridge between Mayville and Westfield causes the lake to drain SE via Chadakoin Creek, then to the Allegheny-Ohio R. on to the Gulf of Mexico, rather than to L. Erie and the St. Lawrence R. The lake averages 24 ft/7 m deep; max. depth 77 ft/23 m. From 1874 until 1925 a fleet of steamboats plied the lake serving summer residents and visitors who crowded the many hotels and resorts dotting its shores; a few of the boats continued to operate into the 1950s. Fruit-growing region. Chautauqua Festival, an annual summer event, features music, plays, and lectures.

Chauvin (SHO-van), uninc. town (1990 pop. 3,375), Terrebonne parish, La., 13 mi/21 km SE of Houma; 29°26′N 90°35′W. The primary industry is shrimping, has annual blessing of the shrimp fleet; nearby are oil fields. Also known as Little Caillou.

Chauvin (SHO-vin), village (1991 pop. 360), E Alta., Canada, near Sask. border, 30 mi/48 km ESE of Wainwright; 52°41′N 110°08′W. Grain elevators; dairying.

Chaves (CHAH-ves), county (□ 6,075 sq mi/15,734 sq km; 1990 pop. 57,849), SE N.Mex.; ⊙ Roswell; 33°21′N 104°28′W. Formed 1889. Livestock and irrigated agr. area; watered by Pecos R. and Rio Hondo. Cattle, sheep, rye; alfalfa, hay, chiles, some sorghum, melons, pecans, cotton, corn, some wheat, millet; dairying. Bitter L. Natl. Wildlife Refuge, Bottomless Lakes State Park, and Dexter Natl. Fish Hatchery in S center; small parts of Lincoln Natl. Forest, and N end of Guadalupe Mts., in SW; Mescalero Sands in E.

Chavéz, Mexico: see TEPATEPEC.

Chavies (CHAI-veez), uninc. village (1990 pop. 500), Perry co., SE Ky., in Cumberland foothills, on North Fork Kentucky R., and 11 mi/18 km NW of Hazard. Agr. (tobacco; livestock). Buckhorn L. State Resort Park to SW; part of Daniel Boone Natl. Forest to S.

Chavinda (cha-VIN-dah), town (1990 pop. 7,437), ⊙ Chavinda municipio, Michoacán, central Mexico, on RR, and 35 mi/56 km SW of La Piedad de Cabadas; elev. 5,043 ft/1,537 m. Agr. center (grain, beans, sugar, fruit; livestock); flour milling.

Chazy (shai-ZEE), village (1990 pop. 100), Clinton co., extreme NE N.Y., on Little Chazy R., near L. Champlain, 14 mi/23 km N of Plattsburg; 44°51′N 73°27′W. In agr. area. Miner Inst., agr. and environmental research center, founded by William Miner, 19th-cent. RR industrialist and philanthropist.

Chazy Lake (shai-ZEE) (□ c.2 sq mi/5.2 sq km), Clinton co., extreme NE N.Y., in Adirondacks, 18 mi/29 km W of Plattsburg; 4 mi/6.4 km long; 44°45′N 73°50′W. Drained by Great Chazy R.

Cheaha (CHEE-huh), peak (2,407 ft/734 m high), E Ala., 12 mi/19 km S of Anniston, in the Talladega Mts.; highest point in Alabama. It is included in Talladega Natl. Forest.

Cheat Lake, uninc. town (1990 pop.3,992), Monongalia co., N W.Va., residential suburb 6 mi/9.7 km NE of Morgantown, on Cheat L. reservoir (Cheat R.), near Pa. state line; 39°40′N 79°50′W. Chestnut Ridge Park to NE, Coopers Rock State Forest to E.

Cheat Mountain, ridge (c.3,000 ft/914 m), E W.Va., in the Allegheny Mts.; extends c.45 mi/72 km from N central Pocahontas co., near head of Shavers Fork R. (which parallels ridge on E and cuts across it in N) NNE to Tucker-Randolph co. line NE of Elkins, in Monongahela Natl. Forest. Rises to 4,830 ft/1,472 m near S end, above 4,000 ft/1,219 m in other summits. Civil War battle of Cheat Mtn. (a Union victory) was fought in Sept. 1861.

Cheat River, c.75 mi/121 km long, E W.Va. and SW Pa.; formed by junction of Shavers Fork and Laurel Fork rivers at Parsons, W.Va., in Monongahela Natl. Forest; flows N past Rowlesburg and NW through Cheat R.

reservoir (dam just S of state line), to Monongahela R. at Point Marion, Pa. Lower river's gorge is 1,000 ft/305 m deep. White-water rafting. Civil War battle of Corrick's Ford fought at Parsons.

Cheatham (CHEE-tuhm), county (□ 305 sq mi/790 sq km; 1990 pop. 27,140), N central Tenn.; ⊙ Ashland City; 36°16′N 87°05′W. Drained by Cumberland and Harpeth rivers. Agr. (apples, grain, hay, tobacco; livestock). Cheatham reservoir and state wildlife management area are here. Formed 1856.

Cheatham Lake, reservoir (□ 12 sq mi/31 sq km), on Dixon (SW)–Cheatham (NE) co. border, N central Tenn., on Cumberland R., 16 mi/26 km SSE of Clarksville; 36°14′N 87°19′W. Max. capacity 104,000 acre-ft. Fed by Harpeth R. Formed by Cheatham Dam (75 ft/23 m high), built (1957) by U.S. Army Corps of Engineers for power generation, navigation, and recreation.

Chebanse, village (1990 pop. 1,082), in Iroquois and Kankakee cos., E Ill., 8 mi/12.9 km SSW of Kankakee; 41°00′N 87°54′W. Ships grain.

Chebeague Island, Maine: see GREAT CHEBEAGUE ISLAND.

Cheboygan (shuh-BOI-guhn), county (□ 885 sq mi/2,292 sq km; 1990 pop. 21,398), N Mich.; ⊙ Cheboygan. Bounded N by Straits of Mackinac; 45°28′N 84°30′W. Drained by Cheboygan, Black, and Sturgeon rivers. Cattle, dairy prods.; potatoes, forage crops. Mfg. at Cheboygan. Limestone quarrying, sawmilling, metal industries. Includes Mullett (center), Black (on E boundary), and Douglas and Burt (both W) lakes (resorts; fishing, boating); Cheboygan State Park in N, Aloha State Park in center, on E shore of Mullett L., Burt L. State Park on S end of Burt L. in W; Old Mill State Historical Park, 18th-cent. watermill, in NW. Univ. of Mich. biological station is on Douglas L. Organized 1853.

Cheboygan (shuh-BOI-guhn), town (1990 pop. 4,999), ⊙ Cheboygan co., N Mich., at mouth of Cheboygan R., on South Channel of the Straits of Mackinac, c.65 km/105 km NW of Alpena, and 55 mi/89 km S of Sault Ste. Marie; 45°38′N 84°28′W. RR terminus, port of entry and trade center for agr. (cattle; dairy prods.) and resort area. Mfg. (concrete, thread mill cutters, faucets; limestone quarrying). On Douglas L. (SW) is Univ. of Mich. Biological Station. Cheboygan State Park to E. Important lumber center in late 19th cent. Settled 1857; inc. as village 1871, as city 1889.

Cheboygan River (shuh-BOI-guhn), c.6 mi/9.7 km long, N Mich.; drains Mullett L.; flows N, past Cheboygan, into South Channel of the Straits of Mackinac; 45°34′N 84°29′W. Receives Black R. from SE, 2 mi/3.2 km N of Mullett L.

Checotah (chi-KO-tuh), town (1990 pop. 3,290), McIntosh co., E Okla., 21 mi/34 km SSW of Muskogee; 35°28′N 95°31′W. Trade center for cattle and timber area. Fountainhead State Park and Eufala L. reservoir (Canadian and North Canadian rivers) to SW. Settled 1872.

Chedabucto Bay (sheh-duh-BUHK-to), inlet of the Atlantic, E N.S., Canada, opposite S end of Cape Breton Isl., at S entrance to Strait of Canso; 15 mi/24 km long, 10 mi/16 km wide at entrance; 45°23′N 61°10′W. At head of bay is Guysborough.

Cheeching (CHEE-cheng), village, SW Alaska; 60°03′N 164°12′N.

Cheektowaga, town (1990 pop. 84,387), Erie co., W. N.Y., E of Buffalo; 42°53′N 78°45′W. Pop. grew significantly after World War II. Buffalo Internatl. Airport nearby. Settled 1809; inc. 1834.

Cheenik, Alaska: see GOLOVIN.

Cheesman Lake, central Colo., on Douglas-Jefferson co. border, on South Platte R., in Pike Natl. Forest, 40 mi/64 km SSW of Denver; 4 mi/6.4 km long; 39°13′N 105°15′W. Formed by Cheesman Dam (200 ft/61 m high, 710 ft/216 m long), built (1904) by the City of Denver for water supply.

Chef Menteur Pass (SHEHF muhn-TUHR), navigable waterway in city of New Orleans, Orleans parish, SE La., 20 mi/32 km ENE of downtown New Orleans, connecting L. Borgne (SE) and L. Pontchartrain (NW);

c.7 mi/11 km long; 30°04′N 89°48′W. Fort Macomb State Commemorative Area is on W bank. Also known as Chef Liar Pass.

Chefornak, village (1990 pop. 320), SW Alaska, 85 mi/137 km WSW of Bethel, W end at Dall L.; 60°13′N 164°16′W.

Chefuncte River, La.: see TCHEFUNCTA RIVER.

Chegoggin Point (shuh-GAH-gin), cape on the Atlantic, SW N.S., Canada, 3 mi/5 km NW of Yarmouth; 43°51′N 66°9′W. Silica is mined.

Chehalis (shuh-HAI-lis), town (1990 pop. 6,527), ⊙ Lewis co., SW Wash., on Chehalis R., 27 mi/43 km S of Olympia and 4 mi/6.4 km S of Centralia; 46°40′N 122°58′W. Vegetables; dairying; poultry; mfg (metal doors, flavorings, flooring, prefabricated wood bldgs., sawmills, frozen vegetables, steel foundry, food processing); logging; oil and gas drilling. County Historical Mus. Lewis and Clark State Park to SE; Rainbow Falls State Park to W. Chehalis Centralia Airport to N. Settled 1873, inc. 1890.

Chehalis River (shuh-HAI-lis), c.115 mi/185 km long, SW Wash.; rises in SW Lewis co.; flows N, past Chehalis and Centralia, receives Skookmachuck N, then NW past Chehalis Indian Reservation, to Grays Harbor at Aberdeen.

Chelan (shuh-LAN), county (□ 2,993 sq mi/7,752 sq km; 1990 pop. 52,250), central Wash.; ⊙ Wenatchee; 47°53′N 120°39′W. Mt. area on E side of Cascade Range region, including L. Chelan reservoir in N ⊙ Wenatchee Natl. Forest covers most of co., except for Columbia R. margin and lower river valley. Irrigated fruit-growing region; apples, pears, alfalfa, hay, wheat, barley; livestock; lumber; gold. Parts of Alpine Lakes and Henry M. Jackson Wilderness areas in W; parts of Glacier Peak and L. Chelan–Sawtooth Wilderness areas in NW; Lincoln Rock and Wenatchee Confluence state parks in E; L. Chelan Natl. Recreation Area and part of S unit of North Cascades Natl. Park in NW; Squilchuck state park in S; L. Wenatchee reservoir and State Park in W center; small part of Okanogan Natl. Forest in N. Ski areas at Chelan, Leavenworth, and S of Wenatchee. Formed 1899.

Chelan (shuh-LAN), town (1990 pop. 2,969), Chelan co., central Wash., 15 mi/24 km N of Wenatdill, at L. Chelan Dam, 2 mi/3.2 km W of Columbia R. (L. Entiat reservoir), on Stehekin R.; 47°51′N 120°02′W. Trade center for recreational agr. area. Apples, pears; timber. Passenger ferry to NW end of L. Chelan, 55 mi/89 km (L. Chelan Natl. Recreational Area). L. Chelan State Park to W, and Twenty-five Mile Creek State Park to NW, both on SW shore of L. Chelan. Wells Dam, Columbia R., 9 mi/14.5 km to NE. Echo Valley Ski Area to N. Wenatchee Natl. Forest to W and NW; Okanogan Natl. Forest to N. Ice Caves to N. Settled 1892, inc. 1902.

Chelan, Lake (shuh-LAN), reservoir, at Chelan, Chelan co., N central Wash., on Chelan R., in Cascade Range; 47 mi/76 km long, max. 2 mi/3.2 km wide; 47°50′N 120°01′W. Fed by streams from the Cascade Range; flows into Columbia R. via Chelan R. L. Chelan Dam, built at the lake's outlet, generates electricity. The N part of the lake is part of the L. Chelan Natl. Recreation Area; partly in Wenatchee Natl. Forest. State parks on S shore. Lake traversed by passenger ferry.

Chelmsford, town, S central Ont., Canada, 12 mi/19 km NW of Sudbury; 46°35′N 81°12′W. Dairying center; nickel and copper mining.

Chelmsford (CHELMZ-ford), town (1990 pop. 32,388), Middlesex co., NE Mass., 21 mi/34 km NW of Boston; inc. 1655; 42°36′N 71°22′W. Once a lumber and textile town, Chelmsford is largely residential. Industries include granite and plastic prods., and precision instruments. Includes village of North Chelmsford.

Chelsea, city (□ 2 sq mi/5.2 sq km; 1990 pop. 28,710), Suffolk co., E Mass., a suburb of Boston; 42°24′N 71°02′W. Its industries include printing and the mfg. of rubber, plastics, electrical machines, shoes, chemicals, and consumer goods; also dairy company hq. Oil storage tanks line Chelsea's docks, which connect with the Atlantic by way of the Chelsea R. Large Cambodian immigrant pop. From 1624 to 1739, Chelsea was part of Boston and was called Winnisimmet. At the battle of Chelsea Creek (1775), Revolutionary forces made one of their first captures of a Br. ship. During the siege of Boston (1775–1776), part of Washington's army was stationed in Chelsea. George Washington slept at the surviving Cary-Bellingham House, built in 1659. Site of 2 conflagrations, 1908 and 1973. Settled 1624, inc. as a town 1739, as a city 1857.

Chelsea 1 (CHEL-see), town (1990 pop. 336), Tama co., central Iowa, 10 mi/16 km ESE of Toledo; 41°55′N 92°24′W. Oat processing. **2** town (1990 pop. 2,497), Kennebec co., S Maine, 5 mi/8 km SE of Augusta; 44°15′N 69°43′W. In agr., resort, lumbering area. Togus village is site of U.S. soldiers' home. Inc. 1850. **3** town (1990 pop. 3,772), Washtenaw co., SE Mich., 14 mi/23 km WNW of Ann Arbor; 42°18′N 84°01′W. In agr. area (livestock, poultry; grain, potatoes): dairying. Mfg. (auto parts, flour, paper, metal prods., medical implants, meat processing; printing). Waterlou State Recreation Area to W; Pinckney State Recreation Area to NE. Many small lakes nearby. Settled c.1850; inc. before 1870, reincorporated 1889. **4** town (1990 pop. 1,620), Rogers co., NE Okla., 17 mi/27 km WSW of Vinita; 36°31′N 95°26′W. In agr. area (soybeans, dairying; feed milling; mfg. (contract sewing, detergents, feeds). Coal and shale mines. Oologah L. reservoir (Verdigris R.) to W. **5** town (1990 pop. 1,166), ⊙ Orange co., E central Vt., 20 mi/32 km SSE of Montpelier, and on First Branch of White R.; 43°59′N 72°27′W. Agr.; lumber. Settled 1784.

Chelsea, village (1991 pop. 5,091), SW Que., Canada, on Gatineau R., 8 mi/13 km NW of Ottawa. Dairying, lumbering; resort.

Chelsea, village (1990 pop. 33), Faulk co., NE central S.Dak., 25 mi/40 km SSW of Aberdeen.

Chelsea 1 section of Manhattan borough of N.Y. city, SE N.Y., mainly bet. 14th and 28th Sts., W of Ave. of the Americas; 40°44′N 73°59′W. Mostly residential. Decayed piers along Hudson R. have been redeveloped commercially as a sporting and entertainment center. Site of General Theological Seminary and several pre–Civil War churches. **2** section of Staten Isl. borough of N.Y. city, SE N.Y., on W Staten Isl. just NE of Carteret, N.J., across Arthur Kill; 40°36′N 74°11′W.

Cheltenham (CHEL-tuhn-HAM), township (1990 pop. 35,509), Montgomery co., SE Pa., residential suburb 8 mi/12.9 km N of downtown Philadelphia; 40°03′N 75°05′W. Includes communities of Cheltenham, WYNCOTE, ELKINS PARK, Edge Hill, Melrose Park, La Mott, Chelten Hills, and part of GLENSIDE. Mfg. (jewelry, laboratory devices). Seat of Tyler School of Art (Temple Univ.).

Cheltenham (CHELL-tenam), village, Prince Georges co., central Md., 15 mi/24 km SE of Washington, D.C. U.S. Naval Communications Station (1938) is nearby. It maintains round-the-clock communication with both ships at sea and other shore stations. The 1,200-acre/486-ha Boys Village, also near here, has been a refuge for teenage boys since 1872, first privately, then as a state facility since 1937. Rosaryville State Park nearby.

Chelyan (SHEL-yuhn), uninc. town (1990 pop. 950), Kanawha co., W central W.Va., on the Kanawha R., 14 mi/23 km SE of Charleston, in coal-mining and industrial region.

Chemainus (chuh-MAI-nuhs), town (1991 pop. 562), SW B.C., Canada, on Vancouver Isl., on Stuart Channel of Strait of Georgia, 40 mi/64 km NNW of Victoria; 48°55′N 123°43′W. Lumber-milling center, pulp mill, lumber-shipping port. Dairying, fruit growing, vegetables. Retirement town. Ferries to Thetis and Kuper Isls.

Chemax (che-MASH), town (1990 pop. 6,315), Yucatán, SE Mexico, 18 mi/29 km E of Valladolid; 20°38′N 87°55′W. Henequen, sugar, corn, fruit.

Chemung (shuh-MUHNG), county (□ 412 sq mi/1,067 sq km; 1990 pop. 95,195), S N.Y.; ⊙ Elmira. Rolling hilly area, bounded S by Pa. border, cut by Chemung R. valley; drained by Cayuta Creek and small Newtown and Wynkoop's creeks; 42°08′N 76°45′W. Mfg., esp. at Elmira; agr. (dairy prods.; poultry); sand and gravel pits. After exterminating Susquehannas, Senecas controlled area, which was then settled by refugee tribes from SE. U.S. Gen. Sullivan defeated Native Amer. and Tory forces in Battle of Newtown (1779), clearing way for Eur. settlement of region. Formed 1836.

Chemung (shuh-MUHNG), river, c.45 mi/72 km long, formed in S central N.Y. by junction of Cohocton and Tioga rivers near Corning, N.Y.; flows SE past Elmira to Susquehanna R. near Sayre, Pa. Amer. Revolution Battle of Newtown near what is now Elmira (1779).

Chena Hot Springs (CHEE-nuh), village, central Alaska, 40 mi/64 km E of Fairbanks. Dog mushing, cross-country skiing; hot-springs resort.

Chenaga, Alaska: see CHENEGA.

Chenalhó (chen-ahl-O), town (1990 pop. 1,564), Chiapas, S Mexico, in Sierra de Hueytepec, 12 mi/19 km NNE of San Cristóbal de las Casas. Wheat, fruit. In Tzotzil Maya–speaking area. Also known as San Pedro.

Chenango (shuh-NAIN-go), county (□ 908 sq mi/2,352 sq km; 1990 pop. 51,768), central N.Y.; ⊙ Norwich; 42°30′N 75°37′W. Bounded E by Unadilla R.; drained by Susquehanna, Otselic, and Chenango rivers. Mfg. at Norwich, Bainbridge, Greene, Sherburne; agr. (dairying; maple sugar; general farm crops; poultry); timber. Mfg. began at South Otselic (1816), 18 mi/29 km E of Cortland, with Gladding, oldest fish-line factory in U.S. Pharmaceuticals began at Norwich (1885). By 1833, Chenango Canal, running bet. Binghamton and Utica with connections to Erie Canal, brought prosperity to the area. Gail Borden, who pioneered the process of condensing milk in 1856, b. here. Formed 1798.

Chonango Bridge, village (1990 pop. 2,890), Broome co., S N.Y., on Chenango R., 5 mi/8 km N of Binghamton; 42°11′N 75°52′W. Agr. (dairying area).

Chenango Forks (shuh-NAIN-go), village (1990 pop. 500), Broome co., S N.Y., at junction of Tioughnioga and Chenango rivers, 11 mi/18 km N of Binghamton; 42°14′N 75°51′W.

Chenango River (shuh-NAIN-go), c.90 mi/145 km long, central N.Y.; rises SW of Utica; flows S and SW, through dairying and vegetable-growing valley, to Susquehanna R. at Binghamton. Receives Tioughnioga R. at Chenango Forks. Chenango Valley State Park covers 928 acres/376 ha. S of Chenango Forks is recreational area (camping, summer and winter sports). Chenango Canal, built 1836–1837 as link in Erie Canal system, joined Utica and Binghamton; abandoned 1878.

Chenango Valley State Park (shuh-NAIN-go) (□ 2 sq mi/5.2 sq km), N.Y., 8 mi/12.9 km NE of Binghamton, in Chenango R. valley; 42°12′N 75°50′W. There are 2 natural glacially formed lakes; full 18-hole golf course; ecological and cultural environments include rivers, bogs, and the Chenango Canal.

Chenega (che-NAI-guh), Indian fishing village (1990 pop. 94), S Alaska, on S Chenega Isl., on Prince William Sound, 50 mi/80 km ENE of Seward; 60°17′N 148°05′W. Formerly also called Chanega, Chanenga, or Chenaga.

Chenega Island (che-NAI-guh), S Alaska, in W Prince William Sound, bet. Kenai Peninsula (W) and Knight Isl. (E), 50 mi/80 km ENE of Seward; 7 mi/11.3 km long, 4 mi/6.4 km wide; 60°20′N 148°4′W. Indian village in S by same name.

Chenequa (chen-AW-kwuh), village (1990 pop. 601), Waukesha co., SE Wis., on Chenequa L., 11 mi/18 km NW of Waukesha; 43°07′N 88°22′W. In farm and lake-resort region.

Chénéville (SHAI-nai-vil), village (1991 pop. 635), SW Que., Canada, 28 mi/45 km NE of Buckingham. Lumbering; dairying; cattle, pigs.

Cheney 1 (CHEE-nee), town (1990 pop. 1,560), Sedgwick co., S Kansas, 25 mi/40 km W of Wichita; 37°37′N 97°46′W. In grain, livestock, and dairy area. Mfg. (aircraft components). Cheney Reservoir and Cheney State Park nearby. **2** town (1990 pop. 7,723), Spokane co., E Wash., 11 mi/18 km SSW of Spokane; 47°29′N 117°35′W. RR junction. Wheat, barley, oats, alfalfa, vegetables; dairying; mfg. (flour milling, communications equip.).

Four Lakes Battle Monument to N; Turnbull Natl. Wildlife Refuge to S; numerous lakes. Site of Eastern Wash. Univ. Mus. of Anthropology and Gall. of Art. Founded 1880, inc. 1883.

Cheney, reservoir (□ 19 sq mi/49 sq km), Sedgwick, Reno, and Kingman cos., S central Kansas, on N. Fork Ninnescah R., 30 mi/48 km W of Wichita; 37°44′N 97°47′W. Max. capacity 566,275 acre-ft. Formed by Cheney Dam (80 ft/24 m high), built (1964) for water supply; also used for flood control and recreation. Cheney State Park on NE shore.

Cheneyville (CHAI-nee-vil), town (1990 pop. 1,005), Rapides parish, central La., on small Bayou Boeuf, and 22 mi/35 km SE of Alexandria; 31°01′N 92°17′W. Oil and natural-gas field; cotton and vegetable farms; other agr. includes sugarcane and cattle. Grand Cote Natl. Wildlife Refuge to NE.

Chenier Perdue (shin-YAI puhr-doo), ridge, Cameron parish, La.; 29°49′N 92°56′W. One of the Cheniers (oak tree–covered ridge) that parallels the Gulf Coast of SW La.

Chenoa (shin-NO-ah), city (1990 pop. 1,732), McLean co., central Ill., 23 mi/37 km NE of Bloomington; 40°44′N 88°43′W. In rich agr. and livestock area; machine-shop prods. Limestone quarry. Laid out 1856, inc. 1865.

Cheoah Dam (CHEE-uh-wuh), Graham and Swain cos., W N.C., on Little Tennessee R., E of Tapoco, and 1 mi/1.6 km E of Tenn. border; 230 ft/70 m high, 770 ft/235 m long; 35°27′N 83°48′W. Built 1919 for power generation; concrete, arch, overflow type. For hydroelectric power. L. Cheoah, minor reservoir, extends 5 mi/8 km E, to Fontana Dam.

Cheoah River, c.20 mi/32 km long, Graham co., W N.C.; rises in the Appalachian Mts. NE of Andrews; flows NW past Robbinsville, through Santeetlah L., to Little Tennessee R. just below (W of) Cheoah Dam, near Tenn. state line.

Chepachet, R.I.: see GLOCESTER.

Chepachet River (che-PACH-et), c.8 mi/12.9 km long, NW R.I.; rises in ponds in Glocester town; flows generally NE, joining Pascoag R. near Oakland to form Branch R. Dammed S of Chepachet town to form Smith and Sayles Reservoir (c.1.5 mi/2.4 km long).

Chephren, Mount (10,715 ft/3,266 m), SW Alta., near B.C. border, Canada, in Rocky Mts., in Banff Natl. Park, 70 mi/113 km NW of Banff (town); 51°51′N 116°43′W.

Chequaga Falls, N.Y.: see MONTOUR FALLS.

Chequamegon Bay (shi-KWAH-muh-guhn), SW arm of L. Superior, N Wis., forming the harbor for Ashland (on SE shore); 12 mi/19 km long, 1 mi/1.6 km–5 mi/8 km wide. Bay is sheltered by small narrow isl. (Long Isl.) and Chequamegon Point on E side just S of Apostle Isls. Fr. explorers visited (17th cent.) the bay shores. Bad River Indian Reservation on SE shore.

Cherán (che-RAN), town (1990 pop. 11,846), Michoacán, central Mexico, on central plateau, 23 mi/37 km N of Uruapan; 19°40′N 101°58′W. Corn, sugar, tobacco, fruit; livestock. A Tarascan community.

Cheraw (chi-RAW), town (1990 pop. 5,505), Chesterfield co., NE S.C., on Pee Dee R., and 40 mi/64 km N of Florence; 34°42′N 79°54′W. Mfg. (food and beverage processing, textiles, plastic prods., fabricated metal prods., machinery, screwdrivers, furniture, bldg. materials); agr. area (lumber; cotton, grain, tobacco, watermelons, peaches; poultry, livestock). Ships farm produce. Settled in mid–18th cent. by Welsh. Has fine old bldgs., notably St. David's Episcopal church (1770–1773). Cheraw State Park (c.7,400 acres/2,995 ha; recreational facilities) is S.

Cheraw, village (1990 pop. 265), Otero co., SE central Colo., on Arkansas R., 6 mi/9.7 km SE, 9 mi/14.5 km N of La Junta; 38°06′N 103°30′W. Elev. 4,130 ft/1,259 m. Horse Creek Reservoir to NE; L. Meredith Reservoir to NW; Bent's Old Fort Natl. Historic Site to S.

Cheriton (CHER-i-tun), village (1990 pop. 515), Northampton co., E Va., 5 mi/8 km NE of Cape Charles town, in Eastern Shore area, Chesapeake Bay to W, Altantic Ocean to E; 37°17′N 75°58′W. Mfg. (seafood processing); agr. (grain, vegetables; livestock, poultry); seafood.

Cherokee 1 (CHER-uh-kee), county (□ 599 sq mi/1,551 sq km; 1990 pop. 19,543), NE Ala.; ⊙ Centre. Agr. area bordering on Ga., drained by Coosa, Chattooga, and Little rivers. Agr. (soybeans, cotton, corn; livestock); lumber milling, iron mining. Deposits of coal and limestone. Formed 1836. **2** county (□ 428 sq mi/1,109 sq km; 1990 pop. 90,204), NW Ga.; ⊙ Canton; 34°14′N 84°28′W. Drained by Etowah R. (forms Allatoona Reservoir here); mfg. of textiles; agr. (poultry, eggs, cattle, hogs). Rapidly suburbanizing bedroom community on Atlanta's N side. Formed 1831. **3** county (□ 577 sq mi/1,494 sq km; 1990 pop. 14,098), NW Iowa; ⊙ Cherokee; 42°44′N 95°37′W. Prairie agr. area (hogs, cattle, sheep, poultry; corn, oats, soybeans) drained by Little Sioux and Maple rivers. Local flooding in 1993. Formed 1851. **4** county (□ 591 sq mi/1,531 sq km; 1990 pop. 21,374), extreme SE Kansas; ⊙ Columbus; 37°10′N 94°50′W. Agr. area located in Cherokee Lowlands region, bordered S by Okla. and E by Mo.; drained by Spring R. in SE; by Nasho R. and Lighting Creek in W. Agr. (cattle, hogs; wheat, soybeans, apples, sorghum); textiles. Coal, lead, zinc deposits. Formed 1866. **5** county (□ 466 sq mi/1,207 sq km; 1990 pop. 20,170), extreme W N.C.; ⊙ Murphy; 35°8′N 84°03′W. Partly in the Blue Ridge Mts.; bounded S by Ga. state line, W and NW by Tenn. state line; Unicoi and Snowbird mts. in N; drained by Hiwassee R. (Apalachia and Hiwassee reservoirs in center) and Nottely R. All except SW corner in Nantahala Natl. Forest. Largely forested (oak, pine); agr. (corn, hay, tobacco, apples; cattle, chickens; timber); marble quarrying. Some mfg. at Murphy. Formed 1839. **6** county (□ 776 sq mi/2,010 sq km; 1990 pop. 34,049), E Okla.; ⊙ Tahlequah; 35°54′N 95°00′W. Bounded W by Fort Gibson L.; intersected by Illinois R. (forms Temkiller L. reservoir in SE). Agr. (fruit, vegetables, corn, grain), dairying; cattle. Mfg. at Tahlequah. Rocky Ford State Park in NE; Sequoyah State Park in W (including Western Hills Lodge); Cherokee Landing State Park in S. Formed 1907. **7** county (□ 397 sq mi/1,028 sq km; 1990 pop. 44,506), N S.C.; ⊙ Gaffney; 35°02′N 81°37′W. Bounded N by N.C. line, S by Pacolet R.; drained by Broad R. Mfg. of limestone, shale, clay. Agr., esp. cotton (grain, wheat, soybeans, hay, peaches; livestock, turkeys, hogs; dairying). Includes Cowpens Natl. Battlefield Site in NW, and part of Kings Mt. Natl. Military Park in NE. Formed 1798. **8** county (□ 1,062 sq mi/2,751 sq km; 1990 pop. 41,049), E Texas; ⊙ Rusk; 31°50′N 95°10′W. Bounded W by Neches R. (forms L. Palestine in NW corner), partly E by Angelina R. Partly wooded (extensive lumbering). Agr. (esp. tomatoes; also vegetables, forage crops, peaches; cattle); greenhouses; timber, Christmas trees. Oil, natural gas wells; minerals (iron ore). Mfg. processing at Rusk, Jacksonville. Jacksonville L. is in W center. Strike L. is on E boundary; Caddoan Mounds State Historical Park is in W; Jim Hogg State Historical Park and Rusk-Palestine and Texas State RR State Historical Park runs from Rusk W to Palestine (Anderson co.). Formed 1846.

Cherokee, city (1990 pop. 6,026), ⊙ Cherokee co., NW Iowa, on Little Sioux R., and 45 mi/72 km ENE of Sioux City; 42°45′N 95°32′W. Trade center; mfg. (feeds, concrete, machinery, agr. equip., pork prods.). Has Mental Health Inst. and Sanford Mus. and Planetarium. Founded 1870, inc. 1873.

Cherokee 1 (CHER-uh-kee), town (1990 pop. 1,479), Colbert co., NW Ala., 16 mi/26 km W of Tuscumbia, near Tennessee R.; cotton goods. Sulfur wells, asphalt mines, marble quarries in vicinity. **2** town (1990 pop. 651), Crawford co., extreme SE Kansas, 8 mi/12.9 km SW of Pittsburg; 37°20′N 94°49′W. RR junction. In agr. and coal-mining region. **3** town (1990 pop. 1,787), ⊙ Alfalfa co., N Okla., 37 mi/60 km NW of Enid; 36°45′N 98°20′W. Elev. 1,181 ft/360 m. Trade, milling, shipping center for rich agr. area (wheat, corn, oats, alfalfa; dairying). Oil and natural gas. The Great Salt Plains L. reservoir, including Great Salt Plains State Park, Natl. Wildlife Refuge, and Fish Hatchery to E.

Cherokee, uninc. village, Swain co., W N.C., 18 mi/29 km W of Waynesville, S gateway to Great Smoky Mts. Natl. Park. Mfg. (textiles, seafood processing, leather moccasins and novelties; printing). Hq. of Eastern Cherokee (Qualla) Indian Reservation to N and W.

Cherokee Falls, village, Cherokee co., N S.C., on Broad R., and 6 mi/9.7 km E of Gaffney. Agr. includes poultry, grain, soybeans.

Cherokee Lake, on Grainger-Jefferson co. border and in Hamblen and Hawkins cos., NE Tenn., on Holston R., 26 mi/42 km NE of Knoxville and 5 mi/8 km NNW of Jefferson City; c.60 mi/97 km long; 36°10′N 83°32′W. Max. capacity 1,565,400 acre-ft. Formed by Cherokee Dam (175 ft/53 m high), built (1942) by TVA for flood control and power generation. Panther Creek State park on SE shore.

Cherokee Sound, town, N Bahama Isls., on E shore of Great Abaco Isl., 18 mi/29 km SSW of Hope Town; 26°16′N 77°03′W. Fishing.

Cherokee Strip, part of former Indian Territory of U.S., now part of OKLAHOMA; bounded N by Kansas line, it was a strip (50 mi/80 km) extending more than 200 mi/322 km E from E end of Okla. Panhandle. Opened 1893 to white settlement, it became part of Okla. Territory and, later, part of state. Also called Cherokee Outlet.

Cherokees, Lake of the, Okla.: see LAKE OF THE CHEROKEES.

Cherry, county (□ 6,009 sq mi/15,563 sq km; 1990 pop. 6,307), N Nebr.; ⊙ Valentine; 42°32′N 101°07′W. Sand Hill grazing region drained by Niobrara, Snake, North Loup and Middle Loup rivers; bounded N by S.Dak. Agr. (cattle, hogs; dairying; alfalfa, wild hay). Largest co. in state (land area; 43rd in U.S). Central/Mountain time zone boundary runs N-S through co. center. Merritt State Recreation Area at center; Cottonwood L. State Recreation Area in W; Bowrig Ranch State Historical Park in NW, Ft. Niobrara Natl. Wildlife Refuge in NE; Samuel R. McKelvic Natl. Forest in the NE; Valentine Natl. Migratory Waterfowl Refuge, with numerous natural lakes in and around it in E. Numerous small lakes also in SW ¼ and NW corner of co. Natural lakes among the Sand Hills formed in low pockets where local water table breaks the surface. Snake R. Falls, SW of Valentine. Home to waterfowl and beavers. Formed 1877.

Cherry 1 village (1990 pop. 487), Bureau co., N Ill., 14 mi/23 km ENE of Princeton; 41°25′N 89°12′W. Scene of mine disaster (1909) that killed 270 men. **2** uninc. village, Washington co., E N.C., 18 mi/29 km E of Plymouth, N of Phelps L. Agr. (peanuts, tobacco, cotton, grain; poultry, livestock). Pettigrew State Park and Somerset Place State Historical Site, rice manor built 1830s, to S on Phelps L.

Cherry Creek, village (□ 1 sq mi/2.6 sq km; 1990 pop. 539), Chautauqua co., extreme W N.Y., 15 mi/24 km NNE of Jamestown; 42°17′N 79°05′W. Agr. (fruit and vineyards; dairy prods.); timber.

Cherry Creek, 64 mi/103 km long, central Colo.; rises in high plateau in NW El Paso co.; flows N to South Platte R. in Denver. Cherry Creek Dam, 6 mi/9.7 km SE of Denver, completed 1950, is 140 ft/43 m high, 14,300 ft/4,359 m long. Flood control, irrigation. Forms Cherry Creek L. (Cherry Creek State Park). At midstream is Castlewood Canyon State Park 5 mi/8 km SE of Castle Rock.

Cherry Creek Lake, Arapahoe co., N central Colo. on Cherry Creek, in Cherry Creek State Park 9 mi/14.5 km SE of downtown Denver; 3 mi/4.8 km long; 39°45′N 104°49′W. Max. storage capacity of 193,600 acre-ft. Formed by Cherry Creek Dam (103 ft/31 m high), built by the Army Corps of Engineers for flood control.

Cherry Creek Range, (c.8,000 ft/2,438 m), NE Nev., in Elko and White Pine cos. Copper, gold, lead, and zinc have been mined here. Highest point is High Peak, 9,662 ft/2,945 m.

Cherry Fork, village (1990 pop. 178), Adams co., S Ohio, 34 mi/55 km WNW of Portsmouth; 38°53′N 83°37′W.

Cherry Grove, uninc. village (1990 pop. 4,972), Hamilton co., extreme SW Ohio, an E suburb of Cincinnati, c.10 mi/16 km from downtown, near Clermont co. line; 39°04′N 84°19′W.

Cherry Grove, N.Y.: see FIRE ISLAND.

Cherry Grove Beach, uninc. village, Horry co., E S.C. 18 mi/29 km NE of Myrtle Beach on Atlantic Ocean in Grand Strand beach resort area.

Cherry Hill, township (1990 pop. 69,319), Camden co., W central N.J.; 39°53′N 75°00′W. Largely residential, Cherry Hill has been marked by great development and housing growth, esp. since the 1970s. Local industries include corrugating machinery, engineering, electronics, and service and retailing. Site of major racetrack; also early-19th-cent. Barclay Farmstead. Formerly called Delaware township (until 1961).

Cherry Hills Village, town (1990 pop. 5,245), Arapahoe co., N central Colo., a residential suburb 8 mi/12.9 km S of downtown Denver, bounded N and E by Denver, S by Greenwood Village, W by Englewood; 39°38′N 104°57′W. Elev. c.5,480 ft/1,670 m.

Cherry Lake, reservoir (□ 2 sq mi/5.2 sq km), Tuolumne Co., E Calif., on Cherry Creek, in Stanislaus Natl. Forest adjacent to Yosemite Natl. Park, 23 mi/37 km NW of Yosemite Village; 8 mi/12.9 km long; 37°54′N 119°55′W. Elev. 4,701 ft/1,433 m. Max. capacity 268,000 acre-ft. Formed by Cherry Valley Dam (300 ft/91 m high), built (1956) by the City of San Francisco for hydroelectricity and water supply. Emigrant Basin Wilderness Area just NE.

Cherry Mountain (3,050 ft/930 m), in White Mts., Coos co., N central N.H., 14 mi/23 km E of Littleton, in White Mt. Natl. Forest, in town of Carroll.

Cherry Tree, borough (1990 pop. 431), Indiana co., W central Pa., 5 mi/8 km NNW of Barnesboro, on West Branch Susquehanna R., at mouth of Cush Cushion Creek; 40°43′N 78°48′W.

Cherry Valley, uninc. town (1990 pop. 5,945), Riverside co., S Calif., suburb 28 mi/45 km ESE of Riverside, 2 mi/3.2 km N of Beaumont, in Jacinto Valley; 33°58′N 116°58′W. Part of San Bernardino Natl. Forest to NE; Morongo Indian Reservation to E. Agr. (grain, alfalfa; cattle; dairying). Edward Dean Mus. of Decorative Arts is here.

Cherry Valley, village, S Ont., Canada, on Spence L. (4 mi/6 km long), near L. Ontario, 5 mi/8 km SSW of Picton; 46°10′N 62°55′W. Fruit.

Cherry Valley 1 village (1990 pop. 659), Cross co., E Ark., 12 mi/19 km N of Wynne; 35°23′N 90°45′W. Mfg. (fertilizer, aeration equip.). **2** village (1990 pop. 1,615), Winnebago co., N Ill., on Kishwaukee R. (bridged here), and 7 mi/11.3 km ESE of Rockford; 42°14′N 88°57′W. In agr. area. **3** village (1990 pop. 617), Otsego co., central N.Y., 11 mi/18 km NE of Cooperstown; 42°47′N 74°45′W. Burned (Nov. 11, 1778) during Amer. Revolution by Native Amer. and Tory forces; over 40 people killed. Settled c.1740.

Cherry Valley, borough (1990 pop. 96), Butler co., W Pa., 21 mi/34 km NNE of Butler, on South Fork Scrubgrass Creek; 41°09′N 79°47′W. Corn, hay; dairying.

Cherry Valley, Mass.: see LEICESTER.

Cherryfield, town (1990 pop. 1,183), Washington co., E Maine, 25 mi/40 km ENE of Ellsworth, and on Narraguagus R.; 44°37′N 67°57′W. Agr. (blueberries); lumbering. Settled c.1757, inc. 1816.

Cherryland, uninc. city (1990 pop. 11,088), Alameda co., W Calif., residential suburb 12 mi/19 km SE of downtown Oakland and 3 mi/4.8 km NNE of Hayward; 37°41′N 122°06′W. Jap. gardens are here.

Cherrytree, uninc. village, Cherrytree township, Venango co., NW Pa., 7 mi/11.3 km SSW of Titusville, on Cherrytree Run; 41°31′N 79°43′W.

Cherryvale 1 town (1990 pop. 2,464), Montgomery co., SE Kansas, 10 mi/16 km ENE of Independence; 37°16′N 95°32′W. RR junction. In agr. area (grain; livestock, poultry; dairying); grain milling. Mfg. (fiberglass boats, wood prods., paper prods.). Oil and gas wells in vicinity. Tri-City Airport to NE. Big Hill L. Reservoir to E. Established by RR company in 1871, inc. 1880. **2** uninc. town (1990 pop. 3,061), Sumter co., central S.C., residential suburb 6 mi/9.7 km WNW of downtown Sumter, at S entrance to Shaw Air Force Base; 33°57′N 80°27′W. Manchester State Forest to S.

Cherryville, town (1990 pop. 4,756), Gaston co., SW N.C., 11 mi/18 km NE of Shelby; 35°22′N 81°22′W. Agr. area (cotton, grain, tobacco; poultry, livestock; dairying). Mfg. (chemicals, textiles, powdered metal parts, apparel, and furniture). Inc. 1889.

Cherryville, uninc. community, Crawford co., E central Mo., in the Ozarks, 10 mi/16 km SSE of Steelville. Former iron mines.

Cherrywood Village, village (1990 pop. 340), Jefferson co., N Ky., residential suburb 5 mi/8 km E of downtown Louisville; 38°15′N 85°39′W.

Chesaning, town (1990 pop. 2,567), Saginaw co., E central Mich., on Shiawassee R., and 19 mi/31 km SW of Saginaw; 43°10′N 84°07′W. In agr. area (sugar beets, corn, grain; livestock); meat packing; mfg. (wood, plastic, and glass prods.; transportation equip.). Inc. 1869. Area formerly (1819–1837) an Indian reservation.

Chesapeake, independent city (□ 353 sq mi/914 sq km; 1990 pop. 151,976), SE Va., 7 mi SSE of downtown Portsmouth, on South Branch of Elizabeth R. (arm of Chesapeake Bay); 36°40′N 76°18′W. Bounded S by N.C. state line and by cities of Suffolk (W), Portsmouth and Norfolk (N), Virginia Beach (E). RR junction. Within its vast area are residential sects.; much farmland, with related agr. industries; and a large part of the Great Dismal Swamp (Natl. Wildlife Refuge). Mfg. (machinery, feeds, dairy prods., chemicals, furniture, construction materials, computer equip.); agr. (hay, wheat, corn, soybeans, peanuts; cattle, hogs). Site of Tidewater Community Col. (Chesapeake campus). Battle of Great Bridge was fought here (1775). Hampton Roads Airport in NW. Dismal Swamp Canal in W (completed 1822), Albemarle and Chesapeake Canal in NE, both branches of Intracoastal Waterway. U.S. Navy Fentress Field (airfield) in SE. Inc. 1963 with merger of Norfolk co. and South Norfolk independent city.

Chesapeake (CHES-uh-peek), town (1990 pop. 1,896), Kanawha co., W central W.Va., on the Kanawha R., 10 mi/16 km SSE of Charleston; 38°13′N 81°32′W. Mfg. (sand and gravel processing, metal fabricating).

Chesapeake (CHE-suh-peek), village (1990 pop. 1,073), Lawrence co., S Ohio, on the Ohio (bridged), opposite Huntington, W.Va.; 38°26′N 82°27′W. Inc. 1908.

Chesapeake and Ohio Canal, former waterway, c.185 mi/298 km long, from Wash., D.C., to Cumberland, Md., running along the N bank of the Potomac R. A successor to the Potomac Company's (1784–1828) navigation improvement project, the Chesapeake and Ohio Canal was planned to extend W to Pittsburgh. Work was begun in 1828, but financial and labor problems (leading in 1834 to the first use of Federal troops to settle a labor dispute), as well as opposition from the rival Baltimore and Ohio RR, delayed completion to Cumberland until 1850. Although extension to Pittsburgh proved impractical, the canal experienced a busy period in the 1870s carrying coal from the Cumberland mines. The canal was used until it was damaged by floods in 1924. It was sold in 1938 to the U.S. govt. The canal, partially restored, was made a natl. monument in 1961. In 1971 it became a natl. historic park (D.C., Md., W.Va.; 30 sq mi/78 sq km). The paths along the canal are now popular with hikers and bicyclists.

Chesapeake Bay, inlet of the Atlantic Ocean (□ 3,237 sq mi/8,384 sq km), separating the Delmarva Peninsula from the mainland, E Md. and E Va; c.200 mi/320 km long and 3 mi/4.8 km–30 mi/48 km wide. The bay is the drowned estuary of the Susquehanna R. and is fed by many rivers including the Potomac, Rappahannock, and James. Chesapeake Bay is entered from the Atlantic Ocean through a 12-mi/19-km wide gap bet. capes Henry and Charles, Va. The Chesapeake Bay Bridge-Tunnel runs across the mouth of the bay. An important part of the Intracoastal Waterway, the bay is linked with the Delaware R. by the Chesapeake and Delaware Canal. Baltimore, Md., is the largest city and main port on the bay; Norfolk, Va., is an important port and naval base. The bay's uses for commercial fishing (oysters and crabs) and recreation have declined as area development grew. Projects in the 1980s, however, were undertaken to reverse this trend. The Eng. colonist John Smith explored and charted Chesapeake Bay in 1608.

Chesapeake Bay Bridge-Tunnel, E Va., across the mouth of Chesapeake Bay, SE Va., connecting Cape Charles and Northampton co. (N) with Virginia Beach and Norfolk (S); 17.6 mi/28.3 km long. Opened in 1964, replacing car ferries (RR barge ferry continues to operate), the complex consists of a chain of low trestle bridges, 2 high bridges, and 2 tunnels (each 1 mi/1.6 km long) under the shipping channels. The tunnels are anchored on 4 artificial isls.

Chesapeake Beach (CHES-a-peek), resort town (1990 pop. 2,403), Calvert co., S Md., on Chesapeake Bay, 30 mi/48 km SE of Wash., D.C.; 38°42′N 76°32′W. Sport fishing. Development started in 1900 when Otto Mears, a Colo. builder, began the Chesapeake Beach RR Co. Billed as "Washington's Only Salt Water Resort," it boasted a 1.5 mi/2.4 km boardwalk, but went bankrupt during the Depression. Now a residential bedroom community for upscale Washington D.C. commuters.

Chesapeake City, town (1990 pop. 735), Cecil co., NE Md., near terminus of Chesapeake and Delaware Canal, and 21 mi/34 km SW of Wilmington, Del.; 39°32′N 75°49′W. The town developed around a canal started in 1801 and opened in 1829, cutting the water route between Philadelphia and Baltimore by 296 mi/476 km. The city's fortunes have remained tied to the canal, which is used mainly by pleasure craft. Canal mus. here. Nearby are Port Herman and Hollywood Beach, summer resorts.

Chesdin, Lake, E central Va., on Chesterfield-Dinwiddie co. line, extending into Amelia co., formed in Appomattox R. by George F. Brasefield Dam 10 mi/16 km W of Petersburg; c.13 mi/21 km long; 37°13′N 77°31′W. Dam is 57 ft/17 m high; built in 1968 by the Appomattox R. Water Authority for water-supply purposes. Max. reservoir capacity of 37,000 acre-ft. Recreation.

Cheshire (CHE-shuhr), county (□ 729 sq mi/1,888 sq km; 1990 pop. 70,121), SW N.H.; ⊙ Keene; 42°55′N 72°15′W. Bounded W by Connecticut R. (Vt. state line); S by Mass. state line. Mfg. at Keene, also at Jaffrey, Troy, West Jaffrey, and Fitzwilliam. Mica and feldspar mining and processing, granite quarries; timber; agr. (apples, vegetables, corn, nursery crops, hay; cattle, sheep, poultry; dairying). Numerous lakes and ponds including Highland L. in NE and Spofford L. in W; resorts on lakes. Drained by Ashuelot R. and headwaters of the Contoocook R. Chesterfield Gorge State Park in W; Pisgah State Park and Wantastiquet Natural Area in SW; Rhododendron and Monandnock state parks in SE, including Monadnock Mt. (3,165 ft/965 m); part of Annett State Forest in SE; part of Honey Brook State Forest on N boundary. Formed 1769.

Cheshire 1 (CHE-shuhr), town (1990 pop. 25,684), New Haven co., S central Conn.; 41°30′N 72°54′W. In a farm area. It is chiefly residential, with some light industry in the manufacture of brass and heavy machinery. The painter John Frederick Kensett b. here. Settled 1695, inc. 1780. **2** resort town (1990 pop. 3,479), Berkshire co., NW Mass., on Hoosic R., and 9 mi/14.5 km NNE of Pittsfield; 42°34′N 73°09′W. Agr. Includes state park and village of Farnams and Cheshire Harbor. Appalachian Trail in vicinity. Settled 1766, inc. 1793.

Cheshire Harbor, Mass.: see CHESHIRE.

Chesilhurst (CHE-zuhl-huhrst), borough (1990 pop. 1,526), Camden co., S N.J., 20 mi/32 km SE of Camden; 39°43′N 74°52′W. Vegetable-farming center. Wharton State Forest to E.

Chesley (CHEHS-lee), town (1991 pop. 1,852), S Ont., Canada, on North Saugeen R., and 20 mi/32 km SSE of Owen Sound; 44°18′N 81°06′W. Light mfg.

Chesnee (CHEZ-nee), town (1990 pop. 1,280), Spartanburg co., NW S.C., 15 mi/24 km N of Spartanburg near N.C. state line; 35°08′N 81°51′W. Mfg. includes machine parts, textiles. Agr. includes dairying; grain, soybeans, peaches, apples. In 1781 British lost battle of Cowpens; Cowpens Natl. Battlefield located to the E.

Chest Springs, borough (1990 pop. 166), Cambria co., SW central Pa., 9 mi/14.5 km NE of Ebensburg; 40°34′N 78°36′W. Corn, hay; livestock; dairying.

Cross references are shown in SMALL CAPITALS. The pronunciation key is on page xv. The dates of population figures are on page xii.

Chestatee River (CHEST-uh-tee), c.50 mi/80 km long, NE Ga.; rises in the Blue Ridge, in N Lumpkin co., flows S to Chattahoochee R. 7 mi/11.3 km W of Gainesville; 34°40′N 83°54′W.

Chester 1 county (□ 759 sq mi/1,966 sq km; 1990 pop. 376,396), SE Pa.; ⊙ West Chester; 39°58′N 75°45′W. Bounded NE (in part) by Schuylkill R.; bounded S by Md. and Del. state lines; W by Octoraro and East Octoraro creeks. Industrial and agr. area, drained by Schuylkill R. (N) and Brandywine Creek. Chester Valley (35 mi/56 km long, ½ mi/⁸⁄₁₀km–2 mi/3.2 km wide) extends WSW from Schuylkill R. below Valley Forge. Agr. (corn, wheat, oats, mushrooms, barley, hay, alfalfa, soybeans, potatoes, apples; poultry, eggs, sheep, hogs, cattle; dairying). Mfg. at Malvern, Downingtown, Coatesville, and West Chester; granite, limestone. Hopewell Furnace Natl. Historical Site and part of Fr. Creek State Park in N; Marsh Creek Reservoir and State Park in N center; White Clay Creek State Park in S (adjacent to White Clay Creek State Park, Del.). Formed 1682. **2** county (□ 586 sq mi/1,518 sq km; 1990 pop. 32,170), N S.C.; ⊙ Chester; 34°41′N 81°09′W. Bounded W by Broad R., E by Catawba R. Includes part of Sumter Natl. Forest in W. Mainly agr. area, with mfg. of textiles. Agr. includes chickens, eggs, turkeys, hogs, cattle; dairying; corn, wheat, sorghum, hay. Great Falls is electric power generating center. Formed 1785. **3** county (□ 285 sq mi/738 sq km; 1990 pop. 12,819), SW Tenn.; ⊙ Henderson; 35°26′N 88°37′W. Drained by South Fork of Forked Deer R. Timber, cotton, sorghum; livestock. Contains part of Chickasaw State Park and State Forest. Indian mounds at Pinson Mounds State Park, NW of Henderson. Formed 1879.

Chester 1 city (1990 pop. 8,194), ⊙ Randolph co., SW Ill., on the Mississippi (bridged here) near mouth of Kaskaskia R., and c.50 mi/80 km SSE of St. Louis; 37°55′N 89°49′W. Trade and shipping center in agr., livestock-raising, and dairying area; mfg. (clothing, food prods.). Bituminous-coal mines, stone quarries. Menard Correctional Center and Menard Psychiatric Hosp. are here. Nearby are Fort Kaskaskia (near old site of Kaskaskia) and Pierre Menard Home State Historic Site. Founded 1819, inc. 1835. **2** city (1990 pop. 41,856), Delaware co., SE Pa., suburb 13 mi/21 km SW of downtown Philadelphia, on the Delaware R. (bridged to N.J.); 39°51′N 75°22′W. The sect. of the Delaware R., bet. Philadelphia and Del., is Pa.'s only seaport and is intensely developed for that reason. It is a port of entry and has a shipbuilding industry that dates from before the Civil War. Mfg. (metal prods., marine anchors, food prods., machinery, communications equip., paper prods., consumer goods). Area has large storage facilities (tank farms) and ship transfer facilities. The oldest city in the state, Chester (est. as Upland) was the site of William Penn's 1st landing (1682) in Amer. Penn renamed the settlement and convened (1682) the 1st assembly of the prov. here. Seat of Widener Univ. Historic attractions include the foundations of the original settlement, in Gov. Printz Park; the Morton Homestead (1654); the Caleb Pusey House, at Landingford Plantation (1683); the old courthouse (1724); and the Wash. House (1747). Settled c.1644 by Swedes, inc. as a city 1866. **3** city (1990 pop. 7,158), ⊙ Chester co., N S.C., 50 mi/80 km NNW of Columbia; 34°42′N 81°12′W. RR junction. Mfg. of textiles, prepared foods, fabricated metal prods., electronic equip., consumer goods, construction materials, chemicals, barges. Agr. includes poultry, livestock; dairying; grain, sorghum. Settled in late 18th cent., inc. as town 1849, as city 1893. Hydroelectric power, developed on nearby rivers in early 20th cent., stimulated textile industry. **4** uninc. city (1990 pop. 14,986), Chesterfield co., E central Va., near James R., 14 mi/23 km S of Richmond; 37°21′N 77°26′W. RR junction. Mfg. (printing, computer equip., furniture, plastic prods., paper prods., tobacco processing, oil refining, lumber milling); agr. (tobacco, grain, soybeans; cattle). Seat of John Tyler Community Col. (Chester campus). Henricus Historical Park to E.

Chester, town (1991 pop. 10,762), S N.S., Canada, at head of Mahone Bay, 30 mi/48 km WSW of Halifax; 44°32′N 64°14′W. Seaside resort, tuna-fishing center; mfg. of marine engines, furniture. Settled c.1760.

Chester 1 uninc. town (1990 pop. 2,082), Plumas co., NE Calif., in the Sierra Nevada, on NW shore of L. Almanor, 30 mi/48 km NW of Quincy; 40°18′N 121°14′W. RR terminus. Resort. Timber; sawmill; cattle; hay; tourism. Lassen Volcanic Natl. Park to NW. Lassen Natl. Forest surrounds area; Caribou Peak Wilderness Area to N. **2** town (1990 pop. 3,417), including Chester village, Middlesex co., S Conn., on the Connecticut, and 15 mi/24 km SE of Middletown; 41°23′N 72°28′W. Business-downtown area consists of retail art and antique shops; agr.; mfg. (fabricated metal prods., construction materials, wood prods.). State forest here. Settled 1692, inc. 1836. Seasonal ferry to Hadlyme. **3** town (1990 pop. 1,072), Dodge co., S central Ga., 17 mi/27 km SW of Dublin; 32°23′N 83°09′W. Contract sewing. **4** town (1990 pop. 158), Howard co., NE Iowa, near Minn. border, on Upper Iowa R., and 15 mi/24 km NW of Cresco; 43°29′N 92°21′W. Wood prods.; sand and gravel pits nearby. **5** town (1990 pop. 442), Penobscot co., central Maine, on the Penobscot, and 43 mi/69 km NNE of Bangor; 45°26′N 68°29′W. Lumbering, recreational camps. **6** town (1990 pop. 1,280), Hampden co., W Mass., in the Berkshires, on West Branch of Westfield R., and 18 mi/29 km SE of Pittsfield; 42°18′N 72°57′W. Abrasives, mica, emery, granite. Settled 1760, inc. 1765. **7** town (1990 pop. 942), ⊙ Liberty co., N Mont., on Cottonwood Creek, and 70 mi/113 km NNE of Great Falls, 57 mi/92 km W of Havre; 48°31′N 110°58′W. Grain. L. Elwell reservoir and Tiber Dam, on Marias R., to SW. East Butte to N (6,958 ft/2,121 m). Mfg. Co. mus.; Village Arts Center. Post office est. 1895. Inc. 1910. **8** town (1990 pop. 2,691), Rockingham co., SE N.H., 11 mi/18 km E of Manchester; 42°58′N 71°15′W. Source of Exeter R. Mfg. (wood prods., machining, printing and publishing); agr. (nursery crops, vegetables; cattle, poultry; dairying); timber. **9** resort town (1990 pop. 2,832), including Chester village, Windsor co., SE Vt., on Williams R., 26 mi/42 km S of Woodstock; 43°17′N 72°37′W. Wood prods.; talc; printing. Winter sports. **10** town (1990 pop. 2,905), Hancock co., N W.Va., in Northern Panhandle, 30 mi/48 km WNW of Pittsburgh, Pa., on Ohio R., opposite (1 mi/1.6 km SW of) East Liverpool, Ohio (bridged); 40°36′N 80°33′W. Mfg. (furniture, chemicals, construction materials, church supplies). Agr. (grain, nursery crops). Tomlinson Run State Park (c.1,398 acres/566 ha) is 4 mi/6.4 km S. Hillcrest Wildlife Management Area to SE. Laid out 1896.

Chester 1 village (1990 pop. 125), Crawford co., NW Ark., 24 mi/39 km NNE of Fort Smith; 35°40′N 94°10′W. Mfg. L. Fort Smith State Park to SE; separate units of Ozark Natl. Forest to E and W. **2** village (1990 pop. 351), Thayer co., SE Nebr., 10 mi/16 km S of Hebron, at Kansas border; 40°00′N 97°37′W. Vegetables, grain; livestock; dairy and poulty prods. **3** village (1990 pop. 3,270), Orange co., SE N.Y., 16 mi/26 km SW of Newburgh; 41°19′N 74°16′W. Agr. area (dairying; horse breeding). Summer resort. Hambletonian, famous trotter, foaled and buried here. Inc. 1892. **4** village (1990 pop. 285), Tyler co., E Texas, 30 mi/48 km SSE of Lufkin; 30°55′N 94°35′W. Agr. and timber area. Oil and natural gas.

Chester, borough (1990 pop. 1,214), Morris co., N central N.J., 11 mi/18 km W of Morristown; 40°47′N 74°41′W. In agr. area.

Chester, Md.: see KENT ISLAND.

Chester Heights, borough (1990 pop. 2,273), Delaware co., SE Pa., residential suburb 17 mi/27 km SW of downtown Philadelphia and 5 mi/8 km NW of Chester, on Chester Creek; 39°53′N 75°28′W. Mfg. (fabricated metal prods.). Franklin Mint and Mus. to NE. Inc. 1946.

Chester Hill, borough (1990 pop. 945), Clearfield co., central Pa., residential suburb 1 mi/1.6 km SW of Philipsburg, on Moshannon Creek; 40°53′N 78°13′W.

Chester River, c.40 mi/64 km long, E Md.; formed by joining of Cypress Creek and Unicorn Brook, at Millington (head of navigation), flows SW, past Crumpton and Chestertown, to Chesapeake Bay; lower portion is wide estuary, 4 mi/6.4 km wide at mouth. Eastern Neck Isl. Natl. Wildlife Refuge to NE of mouth; Kent Isl. to SW of mouth. Kent Narrows joins lower estuary to Eastern Bay, to S. Forms Kent–Queen Annes co. line entire length.

Chesterbrook 1 uninc. town (1990 pop. 4,561), Chester co., SE Pa., residential suburb 15 mi/24 km W of Philadelphia near Valley Creek; 40°04′N 75°27′W. **2** uninc. town, Fairfax co., NE Va., residential suburb, 6 mi/9.7 km WNW of Wash., D.C.; 38°55′N 77°09′W. Little Falls Dam on Potomac R., to NE. Federal Highway Administration Research Station and CIA hq. to N.

Chesterfield 1 county (□ 805 sq mi/2,085 sq km; 1990 pop. 38,577), N S.C., ⊙ Chesterfield; 34°38′N 80°09′W. Bounded E by Pee Dee R., W by Lynches R., N by N.C.; in the Sand Hills, Cheraw is mfg. center. Mfg. includes mining of gold, silver, shale, granite, sand and gravel, and clay. Mainly agr. including chickens, eggs, turkeys, hogs, cattle; corn, wheat, rye, tobacco, hay, watermelons, peaches. In S is Carolina Sand Hills Natl. Wildlife Refuge and the Sand Hills State Forest for reforestation and game preservation. Formed 1798. **2** county (□ 438 sq mi/1,134 sq km; 1990 pop. 209,274), E central Va.; ⊙ Chesterfield; 37°22′N 77°35′W. Co. excludes independent cities of Richmond, Colonial Heights. Bounded S by Appomattox R. (forms L. Chesdin reservoir in S), N and NE by James R. Agr. (wheat, corn, tobacco, hay, soybeans; cattle, poultry). Pocahontas State Forest and Park in center; Presquile Natl. Wildlife Reserve in E on Turkey Isl., in James R.; Swift Creek Reservoir in W. Civil War battlesites at villages of Bermuda Hundred in SE, Drewry's Bluff in NE. Formed 1749.

Chesterfield, city (1990 pop. 37,991), St. Louis co., E Mo., suburb 19 mi/31 km W of downtown St. Louis, on Missouri R.; 38°38′N 90°34′W. Babler State Park to SW. Mfg. (apparel, fabricated metal prods., paper prods., construction materials, plastic prods.). Chesterfield Airport and industrial area located in W part of city known as Chesterfield Valley or Gumbo Bottoms. Though protected by levee, this area was inundated by 1993 flood, causing extensive damage to the airport and businesses. The levee and airport have been rebuilt and businesses have returned. Major shopping mall. Est. 1988.

Chesterfield 1 town (1990 pop. 2,730), Madison co., E central Ind., 5 mi/8 km E of downtown Anderson; 40°07′N 85°35′W. Mfg. (fabricated metal prods.). **2** town (1990 pop. 1,048), Hampshire co., W Mass., on Westfield R., and 12 mi/19 km WNW of Northampton; 42°23′N 72°51′W. Agr. **3** town (1990 pop. 3,112), Cheshire co., SW N.H., 10 mi/16 km WSW of Keene; 42°53′N 72°27′W. Bounded W by Connecticut R. (Vt. state line). Agr. (cattle, poultry; vegetables, apples, nursery crops; dairying); mfg. (lumber). Spofford L. in center Chesterfield Gorge State Park in N, part of Wantastiquet Mt. State Forest in SW corner; part of Pisgah State Park in SE; Road's End Farm Ski Area in center. Granted 1752 by Mass. Bay Colony as Township No. 1 in the Conn. valley, chartered and settled 1761. **4** town (1990 pop. 5,152), Burlington co., S N.J., 8 mi/12.9 km SE of Trenton; 40°07′N 74°39′W. Inc. 1798. **5** town (1990 pop. 1,373), ⊙ Chesterfield co., N S.C., 42 mi/68 km NNW of Florence, near N.C. border; 34°43′N 80°04′W. Mfg. includes textiles, apparel; agr. area for timber, grain, peaches, watermelons.

Chesterfield 1 village, Macoupin co., SW Ill., 10 mi/16 km WSW of Carlinville; 39°14′N 90°03′W. In agr. and bituminous-coal area. **2** uninc. village, ⊙ Chesterfield co., E central Va., 13 mi/21 km SSW of Richmond. Mfg. (primary metals, lumber); agr. (grain, soybeans, tobacco; cattle). Chesterfield Mus., Magnolia Grange. Chesterfield Airport to N. Pocahontas State Forest and Park to W. Sometimes called Chesterfield Court House.

Chesterfield Court House, Va.: see CHESTERFIELD, village.

Chesterfield Inlet, town (1991 pop. 316), Can. govt. post in the Keewatin Region, N.W.T., at the mouth of Chesterfield Inlet of Hudson Bay; 63°20′N 90°42′W. Hunting, fishing. Est. 1912 as Hudson's Bay Co. post and R.C. mission. Has R.C. Mission Hosp., radio station. Scheduled air service.

Chesterfield Inlet, E Keewatin Dist., N.W.T., Canada, fjord of Hudson Bay; extends WNW from Chesterfield Inlet trading post to Baker L.; 140 mi/225 km long, 1 mi/2 km–10 mi/16 km wide; with Baker L. it is over 200 mi/322 km long.

Chesterfield Township, suburb, Macomb co., SE Mich., 27 mi/43 km NE of downtown Detroit, on Anchor Bay of L. St. Clair. Selfridge Air Natl. Guard Base to S. Mfg. (automotive parts, fabricated metal and plastic prods., consumer goods, machining, electronic equip.).

Chesterhill, village (1990 pop. 309), Morgan co., E central Ohio, 22 mi/35 km WNW of Marietta; 39°29′N 81°52′W.

Chesterton, town (1990 pop. 9,124), Porter co., NW Ind., 10 mi/16 km N of Valparaiso, satellite community of Chicago and Gary; 41°36′N 87°04′W. Agr. area (fruit; poultry; dairy prods.); diversified mfg. Indiana Dunes State Park and Natl. Lakeshore to N.

Chestertown, town (1990 pop. 4,005), ⊙ Kent co. (since 1696), E Md., on the Eastern Shore, on Chester R., and 30 mi/48 km E of Baltimore; 39°13′N 76°04′W. Trade center for resort and agr. area; mfg.; vegetable and fish canneries. Filled with 18th-cent. homes. William Peale, the Md. artist, b. here. Notable bldgs. include: Emmanuel Episcopal Church (c.1768); Ship Ballast House (early 18th cent.); Geddes-Piper House (c.1730–1754); Barroll House (c.1735); the Abbey (c.1735), official home of the president of Wash. Col.; Chestertown Customhouse (c.1760); River House (c.1740). At 201 Water St. (c.1785), a collection of ship models is housed. Laid out 1706.

Chestertown, village (1990 pop. 900), Warren co., E N.Y., in Adirondack Mts., 25 mi/40 km NNW of Glens Falls; 41°21′N 74°16′W. Mfg. (log homes).

Chesterville, town (1990 pop. 1,012), Franklin co., W central Maine, 11 mi/18 km SSE of Farmington; 44°32′N 70°05′W. In agr. area.

Chesterville, village (1991 pop. 1,559), SE Ont., Canada, on South Nation R., and 30 mi/48 km SE of Ottawa. Dairying, lumbering.

Chesterville, village (1990 pop. 286), Morrow co., central Ohio, 12 mi/19 km WNW of Mt. Vernon, and on Kokosing R.; 40°29′N 82°41′W.

Chestnut Hill, NW residential section of city of Philadelphia, Pa.; 40°04′N 75°12′W. Drained by Wissahickon Creek.

Chestnut Hill (CHEST-nuht HIL), beautiful residential suburb of Boston, E Mass.; also partly in Newton and partly in Brookline. Main seat of Boston Col. Retail malls. Hammond Pond Recreational Park.

Chestnut Hill, Conn.: see COLUMBIA.

Chestnut Ridge, village (□ 4.4 sq mi/10.4 sq km; 1990 pop. 7,517), Rockland co., SE N.Y., 7 mi/11.3 km NW of Nyack; 41°04′N 74°02′W. Mfg. (computer and electronic equip.).

Chestnut Ridge (2,200 ft /671 m–2,700 ft/823 m), a ridge of the Allegheny Mts., SW Pa. and N W.Va., runs 80 mi/129 km NNE from Preston and Monongalia cos., W.Va., to just E of Indiana, Pa. Cut by Youghiogheny R. just SE of Connellsville and by Conemaugh R. E of Blairsville.

Chestochina, Alaska: see CHISTOCHINA.

Chesuncook (chuh-SUHN-kuk), township, Piscataquis co., N central Maine, on Chesuncook L. 43 mi/69 km NE of Greenville. In hunting, fishing area.

Chesuncook Lake (chuh-SUHN-kuk), reservoir, at Ripogenus Dam village, Piscataquis co., N central Maine, on West Branch of Penobscot R., 28 mi/45 km NW of Millinocket; 22 mi/35 km long, max. 4 mi/6.4 km wide; 45°53′N 69°06′W. Elev. 942 ft/287 m. Lake joined by channel to Caribou L. (S). Formed by Ripogenus Dam. Chesuncook village on NW shore, opposite Gero Isl. (2 mi/3.2 km long).

Cheswick (CHES-wik), borough (1990 pop. 1,971), Allegheny co., SW central Pa., suburb 12 mi/19 km NE of

downtown Pittsburgh, on Allegheny R.; 40°32′N 79°47′W. Mfg. (plastic prods., paper prods., tanks machinery, fabricated metal prods.). Lock and Dam No. 3, on Allegheny, here. Inc. 1902.

Cheswold (CHEZ-wold), village (1990 pop. 321), Kent co., central Del., 5 mi/8 km NNW of Dover, bet. Leipsic R. (N) and St. Jones R. (S); 39°13′N 75°34′W. Fruit-growing area.

Chetek (che-TEK), town (1990 pop. 1,953), Barron co., NW Wis., on small Chetek L. and Chetek R. (tributary of the Red Cedar), and 36 mi/58 km NNW of Eau Claire; 45°19′N 91°39′W. In dairying and poultry-raising area; mfg. Summer resort. Settled 1863, inc. 1891.

Cheticamp (SHEH-ti-kamp), village, NE N.S., Canada, on NW Cape Breton Isl., on the Gulf of St. Lawrence, 30 mi/48 km NNE of Inverness; 46°37′N 61°01′W. Fishing port; gypsum quarrying, rug making. Acadian center. Just offshore is Cheticamp Isl.

Cheticamp Island, NE N.S., Canada, in the Gulf of St. Lawrence, off NW Cape Breton Isl., opposite Cheticamp; 3 mi/5 km long, 1 mi/2 km wide; 46°38′N 61°02′W. Freestone quarrying.

Chetopa (chuh-TO-puh), town (1990 pop. 1,357), Labette co., SE Kansas, near Okla. state line, on Neosho R., and 26 mi/42 km E of Coffeyville; 37°02′N 95°05′W. RR junction. In agr. (cattle, sheep; oats, soybeans, other agr. prods.) area; mfg. (clothing). Coal in vicinity. Settled 1857, laid out 1868, inc. 1870.

Chetumal (che-too-MAL), city (1990 pop. 94,158) and township, ⊙ Quintana Roo State, E Mexico, on Mexico Highways 186 and 307; 18°30′N 88°17′W. Chetumal is a major import center and free port as well as an export point for the hardwoods of the region, including cedar and mahogany. The city is almost entirely modern, as it was destroyed by hurricane in 1955. Also Ciudad Chetumal.

Chetumal Bay, inlet of Caribbean Sea, on E coast of Yucatán Peninsula, on border of Mexico and Belize; 35 mi/56 km long N-S, 3 mi/4.8 km–20 mi/32 km wide; 18°30′N 88°18′W. Ports of Corozal (Belize) and Chetumal (Mexico) are on W shore. Receives the Río Hondo.

Chetwynd, district municipality (1986 pop. 2,774), NE corner B.C., Canada, Pine R. valley, 193 mi/311 km N of Prince George. Originally Little Prairie, it developed after World War II as service center for oil and gas, forestry, and coal fields. Village 1962, changed to municipality 1983.

Chevak (CHEE-vak), village (1990 pop. 598), W Alaska, near Yukon R. delta, on Hooper Bay; 61°31′N 165°35′W.

Cheverie (sheh-vuh-REE), village, N central N.S., Canada, on Minas Basin, 6 mi/10 km N of Hantsport; 45°09′N 64°10′W. Gypsum quarrying, lumbering.

Cheverly (SHEV-early), town (1990 pop. 6,023), Prince Georges co., central Md., E suburb of Wash., D.C.; 38°56′N 76°55′W. Inc. 1931.

Cheviot (SHIV-ee-uht, SHEV-), city (1990 pop. 9,616), Hamilton co., extreme SW Ohio, a residential W suburb of Cincinnati, c.7 mi/11 km from downtown; 39°09′N 84°37′W. Diverse light mfg. Settled early 1800s; inc. 1904.

Chevreuil, Point, La.: see ATCHAFALAYA BAY.

Chevrolet (shev-ruh-LAI), village (1990 pop. 272), Harlan co., SE Ky., in the Cumberland Mts., 3 mi/4.8 km SE of Harlan. In bituminous-coal region.

Chevy Chase (SHEH-VEE chase), town (1990 pop. 8,559), Montgomery co., W central Md., an expanding residential suburb of Wash., D.C.; 38°59′N 77°04′W. The name comes from an old English ballad containing the French word chevauchee, meaning border raid. The Audubon Naturalists Society maintains a mansion here with 40 acres/16 ha of garden and wildlife sanctuary open year-round. Founded as a village, inc. 1910.

Chevy Chase, residential sect. in NW Wash., D.C., near Conn. Ave. at the Md. state line; 38°58′N 77°05′W. An exclusive neighborhood of fine homes and tree-lined streets, extending across the D.C. line into Montgomery Co., Md.

Chevy Chase Heights, uninc. town (1990 pop. 1,535),

White township, Indiana co., W central Pa.; 40°38′N 79°08′W. Residential suburb 1 mi/1.6 km N of Indiana.

Chewelah (choo-EL-ah), town (1990 pop. 1,945), Stevens co., NE Wash., 21 mi/34 km SSE of Colville and on Colville R., at mouth of Chewelah Creek; 48°17′N 117°44′W. Wheat, barley, oats; dairying; hogs; timber; mfg. (clothing, concrete, lumber). Gifford Ferry, crosses Roosevelt L. reservoir, 20 mi/32 km to W. Colville Natl. Forest to N and E; 49 Degrees North Ski Area to E at Chewelah Mt. (5,775 ft/1,760 m); Kaniksa Natl. Forest to W, beyond Chewelah Mt. Inc. 1903.

Chewton (CHOO-tuhn), uninc. town (1990 pop. 800), Lawrence co., W Pa., 7 mi/11.3 km S of New Castle on Beaver R.; 40°53′N 80°19′W. Agr. includes dairying, livestock; corn, hay.

Cheyenne 1 (shei-AN), county (□ 1,781 sq mi/ 4,613 sq km; 1990 pop. 2,397), E Colo.; ⊙ Cheyenne Wells; 38°49′N 102°35′W. Agr. area bordering on Kansas; drained by Big Sandy Creek, source of North Fork of Smoky Hill R. in center. Wheat, sunflowers, sorghum, corn; cattle. Formed 1889. **2** county (□ 1,020 sq mi/2,642 sq km; 1990 pop. 3,243), extreme NW Kansas; ⊙ St. Francis; 39°46′N 101°43′W. Agr. region, bordered N by Nebr. and W by Colo.; drained by South Fork of Republican R. Barley, wheat; sheep, cattle, hogs. Formed 1886. **3** (SHEI-an), county (□ 1,196 sq mi/ 3,098 sq km; 1990 pop. 9,494), W Nebr.; ⊙ Sidney; 41°13′N 102°59′W. Agr. area in Platte River valley bounded S by Colo.; drained by Lodgepole Creek. Cattle, hogs; wheat, sunflower seeds, sugar beets; oil and gas. Oregon Trail goes from SE corner to N central part of co. Formed 1870.

Cheyenne (shei-AN), city (1990 pop. 50,008), ⊙ of state and of Laramie co., SE Wyo., on Crow Creek, near the Colo. and Nebr. state lines, 90 mi/145 km N of Denver, Colo.; 41°08′N 104°47′W. Elev. 6,062 ft/1,848 m. Major RR junction and center. The largest city in Wyo., it is a market for sheep and cattle ranches and a shipping center with good transportation facilities. Mfg. (dairy prods.; feeds; lumber; wood prods.; printing and publishing; machinery; petroleum prods.; construction materials; fabricated metal prods.). The city was established after the Union Pacific RR selected this site for a division point in 1867. It was made territorial capital in 1869. In the 1870s the development of the area as a cattle-ranching sect. and the opening of the Black Hills gold fields stimulated the city's growth. Cheyenne revives its past annually with a Frontier Days celebration, first held in 1897. Landmarks include the state capitol and the supreme court bldg., which houses the state historical mus. and lib.; civic center. It is the seat of Laramie Co. Community Col. Airport on N side; to W are Francis E. Warren Air Force Base and Curt Gowdy State Park. Inc. 1868.

Cheyenne (shei-AN), town (1990 pop. 948), Roger Mills co., W Okla., on Washita R., near Texas border, and 20 mi/32 km NW of Elk City; 35°36′N 99°40′W. Elev. 1,933 ft/589 m. In cattle, grain, and dairying area; mfg. (feeds). Battle of the Washita (1868), bet. troops under Gen. Custer and the Cheyenne Indians, took place nearby; now a memorial. Black Kettle Mus. here. Antelope Hills to NW; Sandstone Creek, to SE, world's first Upstream Flood Prevention Project. Located in Black Kettle Natl. Grassland. Founded c.1892.

Cheyenne, river, c.295 mi/475 km long, NE Wyoming and W S.Dak.; rises in NE Converse co., Wyo., by convergence of Dry Fork and Antelope creeks in Thunder Bay Natl. Grassland (43°25′N 105°03′W); flows E c.65 mi/105 km before entering S.Dak, in Fall River co., then passes around S end of Black Hills, past Edgemont, through Buffalo Gap Natl. Grassland and Black Hills Natl. Forest, through Angostura Reservoir, then NE past Hot Springs, Badlands Natl. Park, and Wasta, and then ENE, forming S boundary of Cheyenne River Indian Reservation. Enters Missouri R. (L. Oahe reservoir) 32 mi/51 km NNW of Pierre. The lower 35 mi/ 56 km of river is an arm of L. Oahe.

Cheyenne Agency, former village, Dewey co., N central S.Dak., 45 mi/72 km N of Pierre, and on Missouri R.

Once the hq. for Cheyenne R. Indian Reservation. Site now covered by L. Oahe Reservoir.

Cheyenne Mountain (c.9,565 ft/2,915 m), in Front Range, El Paso co., central Colo., 11 mi/18 km SW of Colorado Springs. Halfway up mt. is Shrine of the Sun Memorial, located in North Cheyenne Park, erected in memory of Will Rogers; consists of 100 ft/30 m tower. Interior decorated with frescoes; has bust of Rogers sculptured by Jo Davidson. Mt. interior holds hq. of N. Amer. Air Defense Command (NORAD).

Cheyenne Wells, town (1990 pop. 1,028), ⊙ Cheyenne co., E Colo., 160 mi/257 km SE of Denver, near Smoky Hill R., near Kansas state line; 38°49′N 102°20′W. Elev. 4,296 ft/1,309 m. Cattle, wheat, sunflowers, corn, sorghum; mfg. (oil production). Eastern Colo. Historical Society Mus.

Cheyney (CHAI-nee), uninc. village, Thornburg township, Delaware co., SE Pa., suburb 18 mi/29 km W of downtown Philadelphia on Chester Creek; 39°55′N 75°31′W. Agr. (alfalfa, nursery prods.; cattle; dairying). Cheyney Correctional Inst. to SE; Ridley Creek State Park to NE; seat of Cheyney Univ. of Pa., to NW.

Chiapa, Mexico: see SAN JOSÉ CHIAPA.

Chiapa de Corzo (chee-AH-pah dai KOR-so), city (1990 pop.3,953), Chiapas, S Mexico, on the Grijalva R., and 8 mi/12.9 km SE of Tuxtla Gutiérrez; 16°42′N 92°59′W. Agr. center (mangoes, corn, cotton, sugar, coffee, fruit; livestock; timber). Picturesque city; has old cathedral, 16th-cent. fountain. Was an anc. Native Amer. capital.

Chiapas, state (□ 28,732 sq mi/74,416 sq km; 1990 pop. 3,210,496), SE Mexico, on the Pacific Ocean bet. Guatemala and the Isthmus of Tehuantepec; ⊙ Tuxtla Gutiérrez; 14°32′N 90°23′W. Chiapas is crossed by mt. ranges rising from the isthmus and extending SE into Guatemala. They are separated by low, subtropical valleys. Paralleling the coastal plain is the Sierra Madre de Chiapas. The state's principal river valley is the Grijalva, NE of which are the central highlands. Farther to the NE are lower ranges, lakes, and valleys, falling away toward the Usumacinta R. and the rainforested plains of Tabasco. This sparsely inhabited region contains valuable forests of dyewoods and hardwoods and is also the site of ruined Mayan cities (notably Palenque). The area is also the retreat of the Lacandones, a gradually disappearing indigenous Maya people. The climate of Chiapas, except for the highlands, is hot. Rainfall is heavy from June to Nov. Subsistence crops are grown, and coffee (of which Chiapas is a leading natl. producer), rubber, and cacao are economically important, as is livestock breeding. The state's rich mineral resources, esp. silver, gold, and copper, remain mostly unexploited, although petroleum production has become significant. The state is also a major producer of hydroelectric power from dams on the Grijalva R. In general, economic development has been hindered by remoteness and inadequate communication; but RRs, airlines, and the Inter-Amer. Highway link Tuxtla Gutiérrez with the highland towns and are opening up the interior. Conquered with difficulty by the Spanish, Chiapa, as it was then called, was attached to the captain generalcy of Guatemala. Never ethnologically, geographically, nor politically a part of colonial Mexico, Chiapas maintained a quasi-independence during the political anarchy that followed the collapse in 1823 of the empire of Agustín de Iturbide. This status separated Chiapas from the Central Amer. states and oriented it toward Mexico. Interesting archaeological sites have been discovered near the village of Chiapa de Corzo. In 1982 a severe eruption by the volcano El Chichónal resulted in thousands of deaths and released an enormous cloud of volcanic ash into the upper atmosphere. Scene of Zapatista Liberation Army uprising Jan. 1994.

Chiapas, Rio Grande de, Mexico and Guatemala: see GRIJALVA RIVER.

Chiapas Valley, Chiapas, S Mexico, comprises N lowland of Sierra Madre along upper Grijalva R. (here sometimes called Chiapa R.); bounded SE by Sierra de Hueytepec. The most densely populated area of the state, with Tuxtla Gutiérrez as its center; it is extremely fertile (sugar, coffee, tobacco, cotton, cereals, vegetables, fruit; livestock).

Chiapilla (chee-ah-PEE-yah), town (1990 pop. 3,380), Chiapas, S Mexico, on affluent of upper Grijalva R., and 29 mi/47 km ESE of Tuxtla Gutiérrez. Corn, fruit; livestock. In Tzotzal Maya–speaking area.

Chiautempan (chee-ah-wah-TEM-pahn), city (1990 pop. 35,498), Tlaxcala, central Mexico, on RR, and 3 mi/4.8 km E of Tlaxcala. Agr. center (corn, wheat, barley, alfalfa, beans, pulque; livestock). Mfg. (wood, textile industry with fine cashmere sweaters). Also Santa Ana Chiautempan.

Chiautla 1 Mexico: see SAN ANDRÉS CHIAUTLA. **2** Mexico: see CHIAUTLA DE TAPIA.

Chiautla de Tapia (chee-OUT-lah dai TAH-pee-ah), town (1990 pop. 9,078), ⊙ Chiautla municipio, Puebla, central Mexico, 24 mi/39 km SSW of Izúcar de Matamoros. 18°17′N 98°35′W. Elev. 3,363 ft/1,025 m. Agr. center (rice, sugar, fruit; livestock); cheese, cream, milk; honey bees. Has resources of gold, silver, lead, iron mining.

Chiautzingo, Mexico: see SAN LORENZO CHIAUTZINGO.

Chibougamau (shi-BOO-guh-moo), town (1991 pop. 8,855), central Que., E Canada, on L. Doré, 140 mi/225 km NW of Roberval; 49°52′N 74°21′W. In lumbering and mining region.

Chibougamau Lake, N Que., E Canada, S of L. Mistassini, 160 mi/257 km NW of Roberval; 30 mi/48 km long, 15 mi/24 km wide; 49°50′N 74°15′W. Drained W by Chibougamau R. (130 mi/209 km long) into Waswanipi R.

Chicago, city (□ 200 sq mi/520 sq km; 1990 pop. 2,783,726), ⊙ Cook co., NE Ill., on L. Michigan; 41°50′N 40°87′W. The 3d-largest city in the U.S. and the heart of a metropolitan area of over 8 million people, it is the commercial, financial, industrial, and cultural center for a vast region and a midcontinental shipping point. It is a port of entry, a major Great Lakes port, and an important RR and highway hub. O'Hare Internatl. Airport is the busiest passenger airport in the world. Nicknames: "Second City" refers to its traditional status as 2d to N.Y. city; "Chicagoland" is popular today with local media; and "Chi-Town" (SHEI-toun). An enormous variety of goods are manufactured in the area and shipped all over the world. Despite an overall decline in industry, the Chicago metropolitan area has retained large grain mills and elevators, iron and steel works, steel-fabrication plants, stockyards, meatpacking establishments, and printing and publishing houses. Among its many other prods. are steel drums, food prods., fabricated metal prods., motors, electronic equip., wood prods., boxes, paper prods., consumer goods, office prods., tools, laboratory equip., chemicals, packaging materials, foundry equip., microfilm equip., apparel, paint cans, candy, machinery, leather prods. Extends more than 20 mi/32 km along the lakefront, then sprawls inland to the W. Its metropolitan area stretches N to the Wis. border and in the S to industrial suburbs on the border of Ind. and beyond. The city's arteries are its expressways, boulevards, and a system of elevated RR (part of it a subway). The elevated lines extend into the heart of the city, making a huge rectangle, the celebrated Loop, which gives its name to the downtown sect. "The El" serves city and its inner suburbs. Supplemented by the Metra commuter RR system. In or near the center of the city are the Merchandise Mart, the world's largest commercial bldg.; the Chicago Public Lib., which has neighborhood and traveling branches; the Chicago Board of Trade bldg.; Orchestra Hall, home of the world-famous Chicago Symphony Orchestra; and the Chicago Civic Opera. La Salle St. is the financial center. On the lakefront, which has many beaches, are Grant Park, with the Art Inst. of Chicago, the Field Natural History Mus., the Adler Planetarium, the Buckingham Memorial Fountain, and the John G. Shedd Aquarium. Nearby is the stadium of Soldier Field, home of the Chicago Bears, the city's Natl. Football League team. To the N along Michigan Ave. lies the "Magnificent Mile," Chicago's famous shopping dist. In the residential dist. to the N lies Lincoln Park, with the Chicago Historical Society, the Chicago Acad. of Sciences, a zoological garden, and a conservatory; sculpture in the park includes the noted standing figure of Abraham Lincoln (1887) by Augustus Saint-Gaudens and the John P. Altgeld memorial monument (1915) by Gutzon Borglum. The N side is also the site of Wrigley Field, the home of the Natl. League Cubs, 1 of Chicago's 2 major league baseball teams. The Amer. League's White Sox, play on the S side at Comiskey Park. The new Comiskey Park opened in 1994 across the street from the old one (which was torn down). The S side of Chicago is the seat of the Univ. of Chicago, with its imposing Gothic bldgs. and attractive spaciousness. On S side is Jackson Park, with the Mus. of Science and Industry and Washington Park, with the Du Sable Mus. of Afr.-Amer. History. Traditionally known for its ethnic diversity with separate neighborhoods, much of the S-and W-side ethnic groups have been dispersed to the suburbs, while Afr.-Amer. and Hispanic (esp. Mex.) communities have expanded into these areas. Here, also, were the Union Stock Yards (founded 1865 and closed in the 1970s) and, at the S edge of the city, are the once-enormous iron and steel works (large, mountainous landfills around Calumet R.). The W side extends over a vast area and is usually spoken of as a region of nationalities because the many groups living here, though crowded next to each other physically, are more or less separate culturally. These neighborhoods grew up rapidly in the late 19th and early 20th cent. In the W side and the suburbs to the W are large industrial areas and 2 well-known parks—Garfield Park, with its noted conservatory, and Humboldt Park. The W is famous for Hull House, the settlement house founded (1889) by Jane Addams. In 1961, the Hull House location, part of an urban renewal project, was selected as the site of a branch of the Univ. of Ill. in Chicago. The W stretches out to a series of suburbs. Other points of interest are McCormick Place, the mammoth convention and exhibition center on the lakefront; the Auditorium, designed by Louis H. Sullivan; St. Patrick's Church (dedicated 1856); and the beloved Water Tower that survived the great fire. Notable as dividing lines in the city are the 2 branches of the Chicago R. In early days the river was valuable because the narrow watershed bet. it and the Des Plaines R. (draining into the Mississippi R. through the Illinois R.) offered an easy portage that led explorers, fur traders, and missionaries to the great central plains. Father Marquette and Louis Jolliet arrived here in 1673, and the spot was well known for a cent. before Jean Baptiste Point Sable (or Point du Sable) set up a trading post at the mouth of the river. John Kinzie, who succeeded him as a trader, is usually called the father of Chicago. The military post, FORT DEARBORN, was est. 1803. In the War of 1812, its garrison perished and it was rebuilt in 1816. The construction of the Erie Canal in the next decade speeded the settling of the Midwest and the growth of Chicago. Harbor improvements, lake traffic, and the peopling of the prairie farmlands brought prosperity to the city. The Illinois and Michigan Canal, authorized by Congress in 1827 and completed in 1848, was soon rendered virtually obsolete by the RRs. By 1860, a number of lines connected Chicago with the rest of the nation, and the city was launched on its career as the great midcontinental shipping center. Gurdon S. Hubbard had already contributed to the establishment of the meatpacking industry, with its large stockyards. In 1871, the shambling city built of wood was almost entirely destroyed by a great fire (which legend says was started when Mrs. O'Leary's cow kicked over a lantern). The fire, one of the most famous disasters of U.S. history, killed several hundred people, rendered 90,000 homeless, and destroyed some $200 million worth of property. Chicago was rebuilt as a city of stone and steel. Debris from the fire is now fill in a lake adjacent to the Chicago R. Grant Park occupies much of fill area. Industries sprang up, attracting thousands of immigrants, and many ethnic groups have contributed to the modern city. With industry came labor troubles, highlighted by the Haymarket Square riot of 1886 and the great strikes at Pullman in 1894. Upton Sinclair's novel of the Chicago stockyards, *The Jungle*, aroused public indignation and led to investigations and subsequent improvements. The city, although proud of its reputation for brawling lustiness, was also the center of Midwestern culture. Theodore Thomas and the Chicago Symphony Orchestra founded a great musical tradition. Chicago's literary reputation was established in the early 20th cent. by such men as Carl Sandburg, Theodore Dreiser, Eugene Field, Edgar Lee Masters, and James T. Farrell. Saul Bellow and Studs Terkel would continue this tradition later in the cent. Most notable in the development of Amer. thought and taste in art was the World's Columbian Exposition of 1893. One of the architects at the fair was Louis H. Sullivan who, together with D. H. Burnham, John W. Root, Frank Lloyd Wright, and others, made Chicago a leading architectural center. In 1909, D. H. Burnham and Edward Bennett devised their famous Plan of Chicago, later known as the "Burnham Plan," a forward-looking piece of city planning containing many features which were implemented later. It was here that one of the distinctive U.S. contributions to architecture, the skyscraper, came into being. Chicago's continuing interest in this type of structure is seen in the John Hancock Center (1968), the Amoco bldg. (1973), and the Sears Tower (1974), then the world's tallest (and still the nation's tallest). The city has long been an important printing and publishing center, and the circulation of the Chicago *Tribune* is among the largest in the country. Seat of many cols. and univs. besides the Univ. of Chicago, including De Paul Univ., Northeastern Ill. Univ., Ill. Inst. of Technology, Loyola Univ. of Chicago, Mundelein Col., Roosevelt Univ., St. Xavier Col., Chicago State Univ., Columbia Col., North Park Col., parts of Northwestern Univ., and a branch of the Univ. of Ill. There are a number of theological seminaries, schools of music, art, and law, and numerous community cols. The noted Newberry Lib. and the Lib. of Internatl. Relations are here. The 1st decade of the 20th cent. saw the development of many agencies concerned with civic improvement, among them the City Club (1903), the Chicago Assn. of Commerce (1908), and the City Plan Commission (1909), which directs the development of the city. However, bet. World War I and 1933, Chicago earned unenviable renown as the home ground of gangsters—Al Capone being perhaps the most notorious—and its reputation for gangster warfare persisted long after that violent era had passed. Despite the worldwide depression of the 1930s, Chicago's world's fair, the Cent. of Progress Exposition (1933–1934), proved how greatly the city had prospered and advanced. Perhaps the single most significant event in World War II occurred (Dec. 2, 1942) under the W stand of the Univ. of Chicago's Stagg Field, when a group of scientists working on the govt.'s atomic bomb project achieved the world's 1st nuclear chain reaction. With the war came a considerable growth of the Chicago metropolitan area, especially the outlying suburbs. The city itself has declined 23% in pop. bet. 1950 and 1990, although it has avoided the worst of the economic decay of other large Midwestern cities, due to a diverse economic base. Chicago's many cultural attractions and points of interest help make it a popular convention city. Among the many political conventions held here were the Republican natl. conventions of 1952 and 1960, and the Democratic natl. conventions of 1952, 1956, 1968, and 1996. The 1968 Democratic Natl. Convention was plagued by violent clashes bet. demonstrators and city police and the Natl. Guard. Mayor Richard J. Daley was criticized by the natl. media for his role in putting down the demonstrators, but Chicagoans supported him and he was one of the city's most popular mayors. His son served as mayor during the 1990s. Construction of 130-mi/209-km "Deep Tunnel" began in the 1980s, designed to collect sewage and stormwater overflow. Inc. 1837.

Chicago Harbor, NE Ill., former commercial port of Chicago, now used mainly by pleasure boats, on L. Michigan at one-time mouth (now intake) of Chicago R.; some shipping enters river through locks here; 41°52′N 87°36′W. Bulk of city's lake commerce is now handled by Calumet (South Chicago) Harbor, to S. Meigs Field (closed), Chicago's original airport, is located on breakwater that forms boat marina. Water filtration plant and Navy Pier is located 1 mi/1.6 km N of Chicago R. lock. Navy Pier was opened to the public in 1916. In World Wars I and II, it served as a naval training center. Now it is an entertainment, recreation and exposition center.

Chicago Heights, city (1990 pop. 33,072), Cook co., NE Ill., S of Chicago; 41°30′N 87°38′W. Settled in the 1830s, inc. as a city 1892. Industrial community where steel, transportation equip., fabricated metal prods., tiles, and chemicals are manufactured. Seat of Prairie State Col.

Chicago Portage National Historic Site, Affiliated Area, Lyons, NE Ill. Portion of a portage discovered (1673) by Marquette and Jolliet; later used as a link between the Great Lakes and the Mississippi R. Authorized 1952.

Chicago Ridge, village (1990 pop. 13,643), Cook co., NE Ill., SW suburb of Chicago; 41°42′N 87°46′W.

Chicago River, NE Ill.; formed in Chicago by the junction of its North (24 mi/39 km long) and South (10 mi/16 km long) branches; flows SE via a canal into the Des Plaines R. at Lockport; 41°53′N 87°36′W. The river formerly flowed E, then NE via a channel, into L. Michigan. Its course was reversed by the Chicago Sanitary and Ship Canal. The use of L. Michigan's water to flush the canal was a heated political issue finally settled in 1930 when the U.S. Supreme Court ordered a reduction in the amount of water being diverted from the lake. This decision forced Chicago to build sewage treatment plants. The channels of the Chicago R. and the North Branch have been improved to aid deep-draft vessels and barges.

Chicago Sanitary and Ship Canal, 30 mi/48 km long, NE Ill., federally operated navigable waterway and drainage canal, linking South Branch of Chicago R. in Chicago with Des Plaines R. (locks) at Lockport; part of ILLINOIS WATERWAY; 22 ft/6.7 m deep, 162 ft/49 m–290 ft/88 m wide; 41°42′N 87°56′W. Built 1892–1900; opened 1900 as Chicago Drainage Canal, later improved and renamed. Carries the reversed flow of Chicago R. (originally into L. Michigan), which disposes of city's treated sewage; and replaces old Illinois and Michigan Canal, part of whose course it parallels, as a shipping artery. Locks prevent the river from entering the lake.

Chicamacomico River (CHI-kah-mah-KAW-mee-ko) [Algonquin = dwelling place by the Big Water], c.25 mi/40 km long, Dorchester co., E Md., on the Eastern Shore; rises just E of East New Market; flows S and W to Transquaking R.

Chichagof (CHI-chuh-gawf), village, SE Alaska, on W coast of Chichagof Isl., 50 mi/80 km NW of Sitka.

Chichagof Harbor (CHI-chuh-gawf), abandoned settlement, SW Alaska, on NE Attu Isl., Aleutian Isls., on Bering Sea, at entrance of Holtz Bay, across bay from Attu village; 52°56′N 173°15′E.

Chichagof Island (CHI-chuh-gawf) (□ 2,104 sq mi/5,449 sq km), SE Alaska, in Alexander Archipelago N of Baranof Isl., bounded by Chatham Strait (E), Icy Strait (NE), Cross Sound (NW), Gulf of Alaska (W), and Peril Strait (S); 75 mi/121 km long, 50 mi/80 km wide; rises to c. 4,000 ft/1,219 m (N); center near 57°51′N 135°34′W. Hoonah village, NE. Fishing, fish processing and canning, lumbering, subsistence hunting and fishing. Tungsten and nickel deposits. Named for Admiral Vasili Chichagov. Ferry service to Juneau and other points.

Chichén Itzá (chee-CHEN eet-SAH), city of the anc. Maya, one of the largest Maya sites in Yucatán, central Yucatán, Mexico; 20°40′N 88°32′W. Founded around 2 large cenotes, or natural wells. Spanning 2 great periods of Maya civilization, Chichén Itzá shows both Classic and Post-Classic architectural styles. Much of the site

has been reconstructed and is open to tourists. There is a mus. at the park and tourist facilities nearby.

Chichester (CHEI-ches-tuhr), town (1990 pop. 1,942), Merrimack co., S central N.H., 7 mi/11.3 km ENE of Concord; 43°15′N 71°24′W. Drained by Suncook R. Agr. (livestock; apples, corn, vegetables; dairying; nursery crops; timber); mfg. (lumber).

Chichester, resort village (1990 pop. 270), Ulster co., SE N.Y., in Catskill Mts., near Esopus Creek, 20 mi/32 km NW of Kingston; 42°06′N 74°18′W. Skiing nearby.

Chichihualco (chee-chee-WAHL-ko), town (1990 pop. 8,880), ⊙ Leonardo Bravo municipio, Guerrero, SW Mexico, on N slopes of Sierra Madre del Sur, 14 mi/23 km NW of Chilpancingo de los Bravo, and near Mexico Highway 196; 17°40′N 99°40′W. Cereals, sugar, tobacco, fruit; forest prods. (resin, rubber, vanilla).

Chichimilá (chee-chee-mee-LAH), town (1990 pop. 3,743), Yucatán, SE Mexico, 5 mi/8 km SSW of Valladolid. Henequen, sugar, fruit; timber.

Chichiquila (chee-chee-KEE-lah), town (1990 pop. 1,947), Puebla, central Mexico, 7 mi/11.3 km NW of Huatusco. Cereals, fruit.

Chick Springs, S.C.: see TAYLORS.

Chickahominy (CHI-kah-HAW-mi-nee), river, c.90 mi/145 km long, Va.; rises 12 mi/19 km NW of Richmond; flows SE past Mechanicsville and Roxbury to James R. 10 mi/16 km W of Williamsburg. Major Civil War battles fought in area.

Chickaloon (CHI-kah-loon), village, S Alaska, on Matanuska R., 25 mi/40 km ENE of Palmer, and on Glenn Highway, in Talkeetna Mts. Significant coal deposits.

Chickamauga (chi-kuh-MAW-guh), city (1990 pop. 2,149), Walker co., NW Ga., 12 mi/19 km S of Chattanooga (Tenn.); 34°52′N 85°17′W. In agr. area. Mfg. includes carpeting materials and telecommunication equip. Nearby are Fort Oglethorpe (1903; U.S. Army post) and field of Civil War battle (1863) of Chickamauga, which preceded Union retreat to Chattanooga. Battlefield is now part of Chickamauga and Chattanooga Natl. Military Park. City inc. 1891.

Chickamauga and Chattanooga National Military Park (chi-kuh-MAW-guh, cha-tuh-NOO-guh) (□ 12 sq mi/31 sq km), Ga. (9.8 sq mi/25.4 sq km) and Tenn. (2.9 sq mi/7.5 sq km), SW and SE of Chattanooga (Tenn.). Commemorates some of the bloodiest Civil War battles, including one in which Confederate army under Gen. Bragg defeated Union forces under Gen. Rosencrans. Authorized 1890.

Chickamauga Lake (CHI-kah-MAW-guh), reservoir (□ 54 sq mi/140 sq km), Hamilton, Meigs, and Rhea cos., SE Tenn., on Tennessee R., 5 mi/8 km NE of downtown Chattanooga; c.60 mi/97 km long; 35°06′N 85°12′W. Max. capacity 705,300 acre-ft. Hiwassee R. forms 20-mi/32-km SE arm. Formed by Chickamauga Dam (129 ft/39 m high), built (1940) by TVA for navigation, flood control, and power generation. State parks on SE shore.

Chickamaw Beach (CHI-kuh-maw), village (1990 pop. 132), Cass co., N central Minn., 28 mi/45 km NNW of Brainerd, and 1 mi/1.6 km NE of Pine River, on Norway Brook, at S end of Norway L. Resort area.

Chickasaw 1 (CHI-kuh-saw), county (□ 505 sq mi/1,308 sq km; 1990 pop. 13,295), NE Iowa; ⊙ New Hampton; 43°03′N 92°19′W. Rolling prairie; dairying and agr. area (hogs, cattle; corn, soybeans), with limestone quarries, sand and gravel pits. Drained by Cedar, Wapsipinicon, and Little Cedar rivers. Historic Little Brown Church in SW. General flooding in 1993. Formed 1851. **2** county (□ 504 sq mi/1,305 sq km; 1990 pop. 18,085), NE central Miss.; ⊙ Houston and Okolona; 33°55′N 88°57′W. Drained by Yalobusha R. and Chookatonchee Creek. Agr. (cotton, corn, soybeans, wheat; cattle; dairying). Timber; clay deposits. Mfg. at Okolona, Houston, and New Houlka (upholstered furniture major industry in all 3 towns). Natchez Trace (Natl.) Parkway passes N-S through center of co.; part of Tombigbee Natl. Forest in N. Formed 1836.

Chickasaw (CHI-kuh-saw), city (1990 pop. 6,649), Mobile co., SW Ala., 5 mi/8 km N of Mobile. Petroleum refining.

Chickasaw, village (1990 pop. 378), Mercer co., W Ohio, 9 mi/14 km SSE of Celina; 40°26′N 84°29′W.

Chickasaw Bogue (CHI-kuh-saw BAWG), stream, c.25 mi/40 km long, SW Ala.; rises in Marengo co.; flows W to Tombigbee R. 8 mi/12.9 km W of Linden.

Chickasaw Creek (CHI-kuh-saw), c.40 mi/64 km long, extreme SW Ala.; rises in Mobile co.; flows through co. S to Mobile Bay near Mobile.

Chickasaw National Recreation Area, park (□ 15 sq mi/39 sq km), S Okla., just SW of Sulpher. Mineral springs, including bromide waters, streams, and lakes. Name honors Chickasaw Nation; authorized 1976, after combination of Platt Natl. Park (est. 1906) and Arbuckle Natl. Recreation Area, after creation of Arbuckle Reservoir.

Chickasawhay River (chi-kuh-suh-HAI), c.210 mi/ 338 km long, SE Miss.; formed by Okatibbee and Chunky creeks at Enterprise; flows SE, S, and SW, past Quitman, Waynesboro, and Leakesville, joins Leaf R. to form Pascagoula R. in N George co., 9 mi/14.5 km NW of Lucedale.

Chickasha, city (1990 pop. 14,988), ⊙ Grady co., S central Okla., on the Washita R.; elev. 1,095 ft/334 m; 35°02′N 97°57′W. E. Important RR junction; in agr. area; industrial park; mfg. (furniture, medical equip. and supplies, house trailers, fabricated metal prods., animal feeds, magnetic switches, fiberglass, prepared foods), machining. Seat of the Univ. of Science and Arts of Okla. Inc. 1898.

Chicken, village, E Alaska, near Canada (Yukon) border, on Taylor Highway to Eagle and Dawson (Yukon), 75 mi/121 km W of Dawson. Placer gold mining; tourism; hunting. Airfield.

Chico (CHEE-ko), city (1990 pop. 40,079), Butte co., N Calif., 80 mi/129 km NNW of Sacramento; 39°45′N 121°49′W. In a region noted for its almond and walnut production; olives, kiwi fruit; grain; cattle; nursery stock. Mfg. (canned fruits and vegetables, aircraft parts, beer, consumer goods, machinery). Seat of Calif. State Univ. at Chico, a U.S. botanical experiment station; a community col. is in nearby Durham. Lassen Volcanic Natl. Park lies 55 mi/89 km NE; Plumas Natl. Forest to NE; site of Bidwell Mansion State Historical Park. Inc. 1872.

Chico, town (1990 pop. 800), Wise co., N Texas, c.45 mi/ 72 km NW of Fort Worth; 33°17′N 97°47′W. Ships crushed stone; limestone processing; oil and gas. L. Bridgeport and Wise Co. State Park (recreation area) is just SW.

Chico, unincorporated village (1990 pop. 420), Kitsap co., W Wash., on Chico Bay, Dyes Inlet, arm of Puget Sound, and 5 mi/8 km NW of Bremerton. U.S. Naval Reservation to S.

Chico, El, Mexico: see MINERAL DEL CHICO.

Chicoasén (chee-ko-ah-SEN), town (1990 pop. 2,520), in N central Chiapas, Mexico, 11 mi/18 km N of Tuxtla Gutiérrez; 16°57′N 93°05′W. The fertile soil around the Mezcalapa R. produces corn, beans, plantains, cacao, and wood prods. The road connects with the Pan-Amer. Highway 185 in Chiapa de Corzo. A Zoque Indian community.

Chicoloapan de Juárez (chee-ko-lo-AH-pahn dai HWAH-res), town (1990 pop. 13,790), Mexico state, central Mexico, on E shore of L. Texcoco, in the Zona Metropolitana de la Ciudad de México, 14 mi/23 km E of Mexico city; 19°25′N 98°54′W. Maguey, cereals; livestock. Also known as San Vicente Chicoloapan.

Chicomuselo (chee-ko-moo-SAI-lo), town (1990 pop. 3,238), Chiapas, S Mexico, on affluent of the Grijalva R., and 38 mi/61 km S of Venustiano Carranza; 15°48′N 92°16′W. Cereals, fruit.

Chiconamel (chee-ko-NAH-mel), town (1990 pop. 1,711), Veracruz, E Mexico, in E foothills of Sierra Madre Oriental, 17 mi/27 km SW of Tantoyuca; 21°18′N 98°27′W. Cereals, tobacco, sugar, fruit.

Chiconcuac de Juárez (chee-kon-KWAHK dai HWAH-res), town (1990 pop. 13,790), ⊙ Chiconcuac municipio, Mexico state, central Mexico, 16 mi/26 km NE of Mexico city, and a part of the Zona Metropolitana de la Ciudad de México. Maguey, cereals; livestock. Weaving (serapes, blankets). Light industry.

Chiconcuautla (chee-koh-KWOUT-lah), town (1990 pop. 2,084), Puebla, central Mexico, in Sierra Madre Oriental, 8 mi/12.9 km SE of Huauchinango. Sugar, coffee.

Chiconquiaco (chee-kon-kee-AH-ko), town (1990 pop. 2,412), Veracruz, E Mexico, in Sierra Madre Oriental, 21 mi/34 km NE of Xalapa Enríquez. Corn, coffee, fruit.

Chicontepec, Mexico: see CHICONTEPEC DE TEJEDA.

Chicontepec de Tejeda (chee-KON-te-pek dai te-HAI-dah), town (1990 pop. 3,380), ⊙ Chicontepec municipio, Veracruz, E Mexico, in Sierra Madre Oriental foothills, 50 mi/80 km W of Túxpam de Rodríguez Cano; 21°00′N 98°10′W. Corn, coffee, sugar, tobacco, fruit.

Chicopee (CHI-kuh-pee), city (1990 pop. 56,632), Hampden co., SW Mass., at the confluence of the Chicopee and Connecticut rivers; 42°11′N 72°34′W. Settled c.1641, set off from Springfield 1848, inc. as a city 1890. Includes the villages of Willimansett, Fairview, Aldenville, Chicopee Center, and Chicopee Falls. Paper and sporting goods, plastics, textiles, metal works, beverages, and machinery are among the city's manufactures. Seat of the Col. of Our Lady of the Elms. The author Edward Bellamy was born and lived in Chicopee Falls. Westover Air Base is nearby.

Chicopee (CHI-kuh-pee), village, Hall co., N Ga., 3 mi/ 4.8 km SW of Gainesville; 34°15′N 83°50′W.

Chicopee River (CHI-kuh-pee), c.18 mi/29 km long, S Mass.; formed at Three Rivers by junction of Quaboag and Ware rivers; flows W to the Connecticut R. at Chicopee.

Chicora (CHI-kor-ah), borough (1990 pop. 1,058), Butler co., W Pa., 10 mi/16 km NE of Butler, on Buffalo Creek; 40°56′N 79°44′W. Agr. (corn, hay; livestock; dairying); bituminous coal. Inc. 1855.

Chicot (CHEEK-o), county (□ 690 sq mi/1,787 sq km; 1990 pop. 15,713), extreme SE Ark.; ⊙ Lake Village; 33°16′N 91°17′W. Bounded S by La. state line and E by Mississippi R. (forms Miss. state line); drained by Boeuf R. and Bayou Macon. Mfg. at Lake Village and Endoras. As river changes its course, the state line remains straight, creating oxbow "pockets" of territory of opposing states on both sides of river. L. Chicot oxbow "pocket" was created before the state line was drawn. Includes L. Chicot State Park, in E by Mississippi R. (resort). Agr. includes rice, cotton, wheat, soybeans; cattle; lumber milling; catfish farming. Formed 1823.

Chicot, Lake (CHEEK-o), Chicot co., extreme SE Ark., 8 mi/12.9 km WSW of Greenville (Miss.). Largest natural lake in Ark. Crescent-shaped or oxbow lake, formed by cut off of Mississippi R. (to E); c.15 mi/ 24 km long, 1 mi/1.6 km wide. L. Chicot State Park is at N end. Resort (fishing, boating, bathing, hunting). Lake Village is on W shore.

Chicoutimi (shi-KOO-ti-mee), city (1991 pop. 62,670), S Que., E Canada, at the confluence of the Chicoutimi and Saguenay rivers; 48°26′N 71°04′W. The cultural and economic center of the Saguenay area. Aluminum plants, pulp, paper, and textile mills; wrought iron and leather goods. A Jesuit mission est. here in 1676. In the city is a branch of the Université de Québec.

Chicoutimi (shi-KOO-ti-mee), river, c.100 mi/161 km long, Que., E Canada; rises in the Laurentian Mts.; flows N into L. Kenogami, then E into the Saguenay R. at Chicoutimi. A hydroelectric facility on the falls (50 ft/15 m high) just above Chicoutimi supplies power to the region's aluminum and wood-processing industries.

Chicxulub, Mexico: see CHICXULUB PUEBLO.

Chicxulub Pueblo (cheeks-OO-loob PWAI-blo), town (1990 pop. 2,942), Yucatán, SE Mexico, 13 mi/21 km NE of Mérida. Henequen. Formerly Chicxulub.

Chidester (CHID-es-tuhr), village (1990 pop. 489), Ouachita co., S Ark., 13 mi/21 km NW of Camden; 33°42′N 93°01′W. Lumber. Poison Spring Wildlife Management Area and White Oak Lodge State Park to W; Poison Spring Battleground State Historic Monument to S.

Chidley, Cape, headland on the N coast of Lab., NE Canada, at the entrance to Hudson Strait. Named by the explorer John Davis in 1587.

Chiefland (CHEEF-luhnd), town (□ 3 sq mi/7.8 sq km; 1990 pop. 1,917), Levy co., N central Fla., 34 mi/55 km WSW of Gainesville; 29°28′N 82°51′W. Mfg. includes RR crossties, telephone poles.

Chietla (chee-AIT-lah), town (1990 pop. 6,367), Puebla, central Mexico, on RR, and 9 mi/14.5 km SW of Izúcar de Matamoros; 18°31′N 98°32′W. Agr. center (corn, rice, sugar, fruit; livestock.

Chiftak (CHIF-tak), village, SW Alaska, in Kuskokwim delta area.

Chigmecatitlán (cheeg-mai-kah-teet-LAHN), town (1990 pop. 1,165), Puebla, central Mexico, on Atoyac R., and 28 mi/45 km SSE of Puebla. Corn, sugar; livestock. Also known as Santa María Chigmecatitlán.

Chignahuapan (cheeg-nah-WAH-pahn), town (1990 pop. 10,242), Puebla, central Mexico, 55 mi/89 km N of Puebla; 19°51′N 98°02′W. Corn, wheat, barley, beans, maguey.

Chignautla (cheeg-NOUT-lah), town (1990 pop. 5,613), Puebla, central Mexico, 2 mi/3.2 km W of Teziutlán. Agr. center (corn, coffee, sugar, tobacco, fruit).

Chignecto (shig-NEK-to), isthmus connecting N.S. and E Canada, with the Can. mainland, bet. Chignecto Bay and Northumberland Strait; c.17 mi/27 km across at its narrowest point near Amherst, its chief city.

Chignecto Bay, inlet of the Bay of Fundy, bet. SE N.B. and N.S., E Canada; 50 mi/80 km long, 10 mi/16 km wide. NE sects. are Shepody Bay and Cumberland Basin. Noted for its high tides, sometimes rising 50 ft/ 15 m.

Chignecto, Cape (shig-NEK-to), on the Bay of Fundy, NW N.S., E Canada, bet. Chignecto Bay (N) and Minas Channel (S), 30 mi/48 km NW of Kentville; 45°20′N 64°57′W.

Chignecto Game Sanctuary (□ 85 sq mi/220 sq km), Cumberland co., N N.S., E Canada, at center of Chignecto Peninsula, 15 mi/24 km WSW of Springhill; 16 mi/26 km long, 8 mi/13 km wide.

Chignik (CHIG-nik), village (1990 pop. 188), SW Alaska, on Chignik Bay, on S Alaska Peninsula; 56°18′N 158°23′W. Salmon fishing and canning. Has Rus. Orthodox church.

Chignik Bay (CHIG-nik), SW Alaska, on E side of Alaska Peninsula, SW of Kodiak Isl.; 20 mi/32 km long, 18 mi/29 km wide at mouth; 56°23′N 158°10′W. Salmon canneries. Chignik village, S.

Chihuahua (chee-WAH-wah), state (□ 94,831 sq mi/ 245,612 sq km; 1990 pop. 2,441,873), N Mexico, on the U.S. (Texas) border; ⊙ Chihuahua; 26°36′N 103°11′W. Largest of the Mex. states, Chihuahua is divided into 2 regions—the mts. of the Sierra Madre Occidental to the W, and the vast, cactus-and-greasewood desert basins, broken by scattered barren ranges, to the N and E. In extreme E Chihuahua and W Coahuila is a desert basin, the Bolsón de Mapimí. Chihuahua is a leading natl. mineral producer; gold, zinc, lead, and other minerals constitute the state's most valuable industry. Cattle raising has been revived. The state has seen damming of some rivers for irrigation. Chihuahua is one of Mexico's chief agr. states. Foreign (particularly U.S.) corporations have taken advantage of the large and rapidly expanding pop. and built mfg. plants (*maquiladoras*). Among the prods. are electronics and motor vehicles. First known to the Spanish through the explorations of Cabeza de Vaca, and after the settlement of Durango in 1562 by Francisco de Ibarra, Chihuahua and Durango were called Nueva Vizcaya. Became a state after the Mex. revolution against Spain. During the 19th cent. Chihuahua was a center of Apache and Yaqui activity; today the Tarahumara and Tepehuan Indians inhabit some of the remote regions of Chihuahua. Of considerable importance to Chihuahua's economic and political development was the W expansion of the U.S.; during the 19th and early 20th cent. foreign investment was considerable, with the border city of Juárez as the commercial link. Occupied by Amer. forces in the Mex. War and played a prominent part in the turbulent years following the revolution in 1910. In

1961, in an attempt to open some of the most valuable timber and mining lands in the nation, Mexico inaugurated the 560-mi/901-km Chihuahua-Pacific RR, which borders the gigantic Barranca del Cobre (Copper Canyon). At Nuevo Casas Grandes, in NW Chihuahua, is Paquimé (Casas Grandes), a vast and important archaeological site.

Chihuahua (chee-WAH-wah), city (1990 pop. 516,153) and township, ⊙ Chihuahua state, N Mexico; 28°40′N 106°06′W. Commercial and processing center of a vast area. Agr., livestock, and mining are the economic mainstays of the surrounding region. The revolutionist Hidalgo y Costilla was executed here in 1811. Occupied briefly by U.S. forces in 1846 and served as the hq. of Benito Juárez until Fr. troops took it in 1865. Has many U.S. residents. There are several prime examples of 18th-cent. colonial architecture, including the aqueduct. Airport.

Chikaskia River (chi-KAS-kee-uh), 145 mi/233 km long, in Kansas and Okla.; rises in SW Kingman co. in S Kansas; flows E and SE into Okla., past Blackwell, to Salt Fork of Arkansas R. 5 mi/8 km SE of Tonkawa.

Chikindzonot (chee-KEEND-zo-not), town (1990 pop. 1,522), SE Yucatán, Mexico, 3.1 mi/5 km W of the Quintana Roo state border; 20°19′N 88°29′W. Tropical climate with pronounced dry season, tropical dry forest vegetation. Agr. (corn, beans, tropical fruit; livestock).

Chila (CHEE-lah), town (1990 pop. 2,079), ⊙ Chila municipio, Puebla, central Mexico, 20 mi/32 km SE of Acatlán. Sugar, corn, fruit; livestock. Also known as Chila de las Flores.

Chila de la Sal (CHEE-lah dai lah sahl), town (1990 pop. 1,295), Puebla, central Mexico, on central plateau, 37 mi/60 km S of Izúcar Matamoros; 17°59′N 97°51′W. Corn, fruit; livestock. Pyramids and stone idols are nearby.

Chila Honey, Mexico: see HONEY.

Chilac, Mexico: see SAN GABRIEL CHILAC.

Chilapa de Álvarez (chee-LAH-pah dai AHL-vah-res), city (1990 pop. 16,332) and township, Guerrero, SW Mexico, in Sierra Madre del Sur, 15 mi/24 km E of Chilpancingo de los Bravo, on Mexico Highway 93; 17°38′N 99°11′W. Agr. center (cereals, tobacco, coffee, fruit; livestock). Tanneries; mfg. of shoes, cotton shawls.

Chilapa River, small stream in Tabasco, SE Mexico; flows, with small Chilapilla R., into the lower Grijalva E of Villahermosa; 18°14′N 92°40′W.

Chilapilla River, Mexico: see CHILAPA RIVER.

Chilcautla (cheel-KAWT-lah), town (1990 pop. 947), Hidalgo, central Mexico, on Tula R., and 35 mi/56 km NW of Pachuca de Soto; 19°35′N 00°72′W. Corn, beans, fruit; livestock.

Chilchota (cheel-CHO-tah), town (1990 pop. 10,494), Michoacán state, central Mexico, 15 mi/24 km SE of Zamora de Hidalgo. Cereals, sugar, fruit; livestock.

Chilchotla, Mexico: see RAFAEL J. GARCÍA.

Chilcotin River (chil-KO-tin), 150 mi/241 km long, SW B.C., W Canada; rises in Coast Mts. W of Quesnel; flows SE to Fraser R. 30 mi/48 km W of Williams L.

Childersburg (CHIL-duhrz-buhrg), town (1990 pop. 4,579), Talladega co., E central Ala., on Coosa R., and 18 mi/29 km SW of Talladega. It developed with building of huge powder plant at nearby Coosa Pines. Plant was sold to private interests after World War II. Large rayon and newsprint mills have been built.

Childress, county (□ 713 sq mi/1,847 sq km; 1990 pop. 5,953), extreme N Texas, in SE Panhandle; ⊙ Childress; 34°32′N 100°12′W. In rolling prairies; drained by Prairie Dog Town Fork of Red R. (continues as Red R. and as Texas-Okla. state line to E). Agr. (cotton, wheat, grain sorghum, melons, peanuts; goats, ostriches). L. Childress and Baylor L. in W. Formed 1876. Acquired part of Harmon co. (Okla.) in relocation of 100th meridian (1930).

Childress, city (1990 pop. 5,055), ⊙ Childress co., extreme N Texas, in SE Panhandle, c.100 mi/161 km ESE of Amarillo, near Prairie Dog Town Fork of Red R.; 34°25′N 100°15′W. Elev. 1,877 ft/572 m. RR spur junction; trade and processing center for cattle, ostriches;

cotton, wheat region; meatpacking. L. Childress and Baylor L. to W. Inc. 1888.

Childs, village, Cecil co., NE Md., 19 mi/31 km WSW of Wilmington (Del.). Was Childs Station on the Baltimore and Ohio RR, named for George W. Childs, editor of the *Philadelphia Public Ledger*, who also owned the Marley paper mills here.

Chilhowee (chil-HOU-wee), town (1990 pop. 335), Johnson co., W central Mo., on RR, and 13 mi/21 km SSW of Warrensburg; 38°35′N 93°51′W. Corn, soybeans, hay; cattle.

Chilhowee Mountain (CHIL-HOU-ee), E Tenn., ridge (1,500 ft/457 m–3,000 ft/914 m) in Great Appalachian Valley, bordering Great Smoky Mts.; from point c.5 mi/8 km SW of Sevierville extends c.30 mi/48 km SW to Little Tennessee R. Sometimes considered a range of Unaka Mts. Summit at 35°45′N 83°45′W.

Chilhowie (CHIL-hou-wee), town (1990 pop. 1,971), Smyth co., SW Va., 10 mi/16 km WSW of Marion, near South Fork Holston R.; 36°47′N 81°40′W. Mfg. (carbide-mining tools, clothing, furniture, asphalt, fertilizer; textile cutting). Agr. (dairying; livestock; vegetables, fruit, corn, tobacco).

Chilkat Inlet (CHIL-kat), SE Alaska, NW arm of Lynn Canal, NNW of Juneau; 15 mi/24 km long; 59°07′N 135°23′W. Extends from point 12 mi/19 km SSE of Haines to mouth of Chilkat R. During 1890s it was the route to Chilkat Pass and Dalton Trail leading to the Klondike region. Chilkat Range extends on the inlet.

Chilkat Pass (CHIL-kat), in Coast Range, NW B.C., W Canada, near U.S. (Alaska) and Yukon borders, 50 mi/80 km WNW of Skagway. Discovered 1880; became important route from Haines (Alaska), to Yukon during Klondike gold rush in 1890s. Now crossed by Haines Cut-off, branch of Alaska Highway.

Chilkat River (CHIL-kat), c.50 mi/80 km long, SE Alaska; rises in Coast Range NW of Skagway; flows generally SE, past Klukwan, to Chilkoot Inlet, arm of Lynn Canal, 4 mi/6.4 km NW of Haines.

Chilko Lake (□ 75 sq mi/194 sq km), SW B.C., W Canada, in Coast Mts., 130 mi/209 km NNW of Vancouver, at foot of mts. Goodhope and Queen Bess; drained N into Chilcotin R. by Chilko R.; 40 mi/64 km long, 1 mi/2 km–4 mi/6 km wide; 51°15′N 124°05′W.

Chilkoot or **Port Chilkoot** (both: CHIL-koot), village (1990 pop. 221), SE Alaska, at head of Chilkoot Inlet, 13 mi/21 km SW of Skagway; 59°13′N 135°25′W.

Chilkoot Inlet (CHIL-koot), SE Alaska, NNW arm of Lynn Canal, NNW of Juneau; 20 mi/32 km long; 59°15′N 135°20′W. Extends from 12 mi/19 km SSE of Haines to Chilkoot. N of Haines, Taiya Inlet extends 12 mi/19 km NNE to Skagway. Route to Chilkoot Pass and Yukon during Klondike gold rush in 1890s.

Chilkoot Pass, c.3,500 ft/1,070 m, in the Coast Mts., on the U.S. (Alaska)–Canada (B.C.) border, 20 mi/32 km N of Skagway (Alaska); 59°43′N 135°08′W. Long used by the Chilkoot Native Americans as a link bet. the Pacific coast and the Yukon R. valley; the 1st non-Native traversed the pass in 1878. After the Klondike gold strike (1896), the pass became a much-used route to the interior (Chilkoot Trail). Subject of Jack London novels.

Chillicothe 1 (chi-li-KA-thee), city (1990 pop. 5,959), Peoria co., central Ill., on Illinois R., at N end of L. Peoria, and 15 mi/24 km NNE of Peoria; 40°55′N 89°30′W. In agr. and bituminous-coal area; sand, gravel pits; mfg. (clothing, concrete prods.). Inc. 1861. **2** (chi-luh-KO-thee), city (1990 pop. 8,804), ⊙ Livingston co., N central Mo., near Grand R., 70 mi/113 km NE of Kansas City; 39°47′N 93°32′W. Regional service center. Agr. includes grain, soybeans; cattle; dairy prods. Mfg. (wood, steel, machinery, meat prods., apparel, feeds; metal fabrication). Seat of business col.; has state correctional center (for women). Former RR junction. Founded 1837. **3** (CHI-li-KAH-thee), city (1990 pop. 21,923), ⊙ Ross co., S central Ohio, on the Scioto R.; 39°20′N 82°59′W. Trade and distribution center of a farm area that specializes in raising cattle and hogs and growing corn. Long noted for its large paper mills; transportation equip. Founded in 1796 by settlers from

Va., Chillicothe derives its name from the Shawnee word meaning "principal town." In 1800 it became the capital of NORTHWEST TERRITORY; capital of Ohio 1803–1810 and 1812–1816. Grew in the 19th cent. as an inland port on the Ohio and Erie Canal and a pork-packing center. During World War I, Camp Sherman, a large army training base, was built here. Notable are Adena State Memorial and Ross Co. Historical Society Mus. Just outside the city is Mound City Group Natl. Monument, containing prehistoric Native Amer. burial mounds. Has a state prison and a branch of Ohio Univ. Inc. 1802.

Chillicothe 1 town (1990 pop. 119), Wapello co., SE Iowa, on Des Moines R., and 8 mi/12.9 km NW of Ottumwa; 41°05′N 92°31′W. Feed milling. **2** (CHI-luh-ko-thee), town (1990 pop. 816), Hardeman co., N Texas, near Red R., 13 mi/21 km E of Quanah; 34°15′N 99°30′W. RR junction, in wheat, cotton area; grain elevators, cottonseed oil and flour mills. Has agr. experimental station. Nearby are L. Pauline to W (fishing, hunting) and Medicine Mound (Native Amer. relics) to SW. Settled 1886, inc. 1907.

Chilliwack (CHIL-i-wak), town (1991 pop. 49,531), SW B.C., W Canada, on the Fraser R., 65 mi/105 km W of Vancouver; elev. 10 m/33 ft; 49°10′N 121°57′W. Agr., dairying, and logging center. Fruit growing, hops. Main industry is food processing.

Chilmark (CHIL-mahrk), town (1990 pop. 650), Dukes co., SE Mass., on SW Martha's Vineyard, 12 mi/19 km WSW of Edgartown; 41°22′N 70°45′W. Fishing, agr.; resort. Includes village of Menemsha (resort and fishing harbor).

Chilocco (CHIL-AHK-o), village, Kay co., N Okla., near Kansas state line, 4 mi/6.4 km S of Arkansas City (Kansas).

Chilón (chee-LON), town (1990 pop. 3,661), Chiapas, S Mexico, in spur of Sierra Madre, 40 mi/64 km NE of San Cristóbal de las Casas. Corn, fruit; lumbering. In Tzeltal-Maya area.

Chiloquin (CHIL-uh-kwin), village (1990 pop. 673), Klamath co., S Oregon, 25 mi/40 km N of Klamath Falls, on Williamson R. at mouth of Sprague R.; 42°34′N 121°52′W. Elev. 4,189 ft/1,277 m. Timber; dairy prods.; potatoes; sheep, cattle. Upper Klamath and Agency lakes to SW. Crater L. Natl. Park to NW; Collier Memorial State Park to NW; parts of Winema Natl. Forest to E and W. Also nearby are Upper Klamath (SW) and Klamath Forest (NE) natl. wildlife refuges.

Chilpancingo de los Bravo (cheel-pahn-SEEN-go dai los BRAH-vo), city (1990 pop. 97,165) and township, ⊙ Guerrero state, S Mexico; 17°33′N 99°30′W. Serves as the regional center of agr. industry, producing primarily corn and bananas. Named in honor of its heroes in the war against Spain—3 brothers, of whom Nicolás Bravo was most prominent. During the war, the Congress of Chilpancingo, convened in 1813 by Morelos y Pavón, briefly established a constitutional republic based on the reforms of Hidalgo y Costilla.

Chilton (CHIL-tuhn), county (□ 700 sq mi/1,813 sq km; 1990 pop. 32,458), central Ala., ⊙ Clanton. Agr. area bounded on E by Coosa R., drained (SW) by Mulberry R. Cotton, hay; livestock; lumber milling. Part of Talladega Natl. Forest in SW. Formed 1868.

Chilton, town (1990 pop. 3,240), ⊙ Calumet co., E Wis., on branch of Manitowoc R., and 23 mi/37 km NE of Fond du Lac; 44°01′N 88°09′W. Trade center for dairying and farming area; mfg. (malt prods., cheese, pet food, machinery); dairy plants. Settled 1847, inc. 1877.

Chilton, uninc. village (1990 pop. 310), Falls co., E central Texas, 19 mi/31 km S of Waco. In agr. area; mfg. (cellulose insulation).

Chimacum (CHIM-uh-kuhm), uninc. town (1990 pop. 750), Jefferson co., NW Wash., 8 mi/12.9 km S of Port Townsend, in Chimcaum Valley, Quimper Peninsula, extension of Olympic Peninsula. Port Townsend bay, arm of Puget Sound, to NE. Bridge to Indian Isl. Naval Reservation to E. Nearby are Anderson L. (W) and Old Fort Townsend (N) state parks.

Chimalhuacán (chee-mahl-wah-KAHN), town (1990 pop. 235,587), Mexico state, central Mexico, on E shore of L. Texcoco, 13 mi/21 km E of Mexico city. A part of the Área Metropolitana de la Ciudad de México. Formerly a Dominican mission. Chimal Falls are nearby.

Chimaltitán (chee-mahl-teet-LAHN), town (1990 pop. 659), Jalisco, W Mexico, on N affluent of Santiago R., and 70 mi/113 km NW of Guadalajara. Grain, vegetables; livestock.

Chimayo (chi-mah-YO), uninc. town (1990 pop. 2,789), Santa Fe and Rio Arriba cos., N central N.Mex., in W foothills of Sangre de Cristo Mts., 21 mi/34 km N of Santa Fe; elev. 6,220 ft/1,896 m. Trading point in irrigated fruit region; also chiles, grain, vegetables, corn, alfalfa; mfg. (tortillas and tamales, wool blankets). Served as Span. frontier post 1598–1695. Nearby is El Santuário de Chimayó, adobe church built 1816. Santa Cruz Reservoir to S; part of Santa Fe Natl. Forest to E; Nambe and Pojoaque pueblos to S.

Chimney Point, Vt.: see ADDISON.

Chimney Rock, uninc. village, Rutherford co., SW N.C., 20 mi/32 km SE of Asheville, on Broad R. (forms L. Lure reservoir to E). Summer resort with Folk Art Center (rugs, pottery; wood carving). To S are Chimney Rock, a giant granite monolith ascended by trail and elevator, and Hickory Nut falls, c.404 ft/123 m high. Chimney Rock Park to S, overlooks Hickory Nut Gorge and Falls.

Chimney Rock National Historic Site, W Morrill co., W Nebr., 500-ft/150-m landmark on Oregon Trail. Authorized 1956.

Chimney Rock, Ky.: see CAMP NELSON.

China (CHEE-nah), town (1990 pop. 9,075), Nuevo León, N Mexico, in low country, 65 mi/105 km E of Monterrey, on Mexico Highway 40; 25°42′N 99°15′W. Cereals, cotton, sugarcane, cactus fibers.

China 1 resort town (1990 pop. 3,713), Kennebec co., S Maine, at N end of China L., 17 mi/27 km NE of Augusta; 44°24′N 69°32′W. South China village at S end of China L. Settled 1774; known as Harlem, 1796–1818. **2** town (1990 pop. 1,144), Jefferson co., SE Texas, 13 mi/21 km W of Beaumont; 30°03′N 94°20′W. Oil and natural gas. Agr. (rice, soybeans; cattle). Mfg. (plastic processing).

China Grove 1 town (1990 pop. 2,732), Rowan co., central N.C., suburb 7 mi/11.3 km NNE of Kannapolis; 35°34′N 80°34′W. Grain, tobacco, soybeans, sorghum; livestock, poultry; dairying. Mfg. (cotton yarn, ceramic magnets). **2** town (1990 pop. 872), Bexar co., S central Texas, suburb 8 mi/12.9 km ESE of downtown San Antonio, on Calaveras Creek; 29°23′N 98°20′W. Mfg. (bakery prods.). Calaveras L. reservoir to SE.

China Lake 1 NW San Bernardino co., S central Calif., playa in Mojave Desert, 8 mi/12.9 km NNE of Ridgecrest; c.11 mi/18 km long. Lake is in S part of 1 of 2 units of large China L. Naval Weapons Test Center; the other unit is c.25 mi/40 km E of Ridgecrest. **2** in Kennebec co., S Maine, in resort area near China, 15 mi/24 km NE of Augusta; 8 mi/12.9 km long.

Chinameca (chee-nah-ME-kah), town (1990 pop. 6,824), Veracruz, SE Mexico, on Isthmus of Tehuantepec, 9 mi/14.5 km WNW of Minatitlán. Fruit; livestock.

Chinampa de Gorostiza (chee-NAHM-pah dai go-ro-STEE-sah), town (1990 pop. 4,989), Veracruz, E Mexico, in Gulf lowland, 34 mi/55 km NW of Túxpam de Rodríguez Cano. Cereals, sugarcane, coffee, tobacco, fruit. Some Huastec-speaking pop.

Chinantla (chee-NAHN-tlah), town (1990 pop. 1,180), Puebla, central Mexico, 30 mi/48 km SE of Izúcar de Matamoros; 18°00′N 96°00′W. Cereals, sugarcane, fruit; livestock.

Chinati Mountains, Presidio co., extreme W Texas, generally parallel to the Rio Grande, c.35 mi/56 km SW of Marfa. Chinati Peak (7,730 ft/2,356 m) is highest point. Silver mining.

Chinatown, SE sect. of Lower Manhattan, SE N.Y. city, S of Little Italy; 40°43′N 73°59′W. Once an 8-block area S of Canal St., it now stretches to include over 65 blocks, spreading to sects. of Little Italy, Soho, and the Lower East Side. Over 100 years old, the neighborhood has the largest Asian community in N. Amer.; includes

Thais, Japanese, and Filipinos as well as Chinese. It has become more white-collar over time, as the financial resources and offices of banks, travel agencies, and accounting firms have been transferred here from Hong Kong. The streets are narrow, crowded, chaotic, noisy, and dirty, especially Mott St. (the main thoroughfare) and in Chatham Square. The influx of legal Chinese immigrants is c.30,000 per year; in addition, there are large numbers of illegals. Cantonese is the lingua franca, but since 1965 Mandarin and other dialects have grown more popular, partly because of the many recent immigrants from Taiwan and mainland China. Two other Chinatowns have sprung up in Flushing (Queens) and Sunset Park (Brooklyn).

Chinchilla (chin-CHI-lah), uninc. town (1990 pop. 1,300), Lackawanna co., NE Pa., suburb 5 mi/8 km N of Scranton, on Leggetts Creek; 41°28′N 75°40′W. Light mfg.

Chinchorro Bank, barrier reef in Caribbean Sea off E coast of Yucatán Peninsula, SE Mexico, 20 mi/32 km off Quintana Roo coast, 100 mi/161 km S of Cozumel Isl. Extends 28 mi/45 km N-S, 4 mi/6.4 km–10 mi/16 km wide. Lighthouses (Cayo Lobos and Cabeza de Coral) are on islets at 18°46′N 87°18′W.

Chincoteague (CHINK-uh-teeg), town (1990 pop. 3,572), Accomack co., E Va., 23 mi/37 km NE of Accomac, 29 mi/47 km SSW of Ocean City (Md.), on narrow Chincoteague Isl. (c.9 mi/14.5 km long, in Chincoteague Bay; 37°57′N 75°21′W. Surrounded by Chincoteague Natl. Wildlife Refuge, the isl. is sheltered from the Atlantic Ocean by Assateague Isl. (E) and connected by causeway to Delmarva Peninsula (W). Mfg. (seafood packaging and processing); oysters, clams, fish; tourism (hunting, fishing). Center for tourism, bird watching. Here annually (July) is held a "pony-penning," a roundup and auction of wild ponies from Chincoteague and Assateague isls. Assateague Isl. Natl. Seashore to E. NASA Wallops Flight Center to W. Town inc. 1908.

Chincoteague Bay (CHINK-uh-teeg) [Algonquin = large stream or inlet], Worcester co., E Md. and E Va., borders Atlantic shore, E of Snow Hill (Md.); 23 mi/37 km long; sheltered E by Assateague Isl. Chincoteague Inlet (channel to ocean) and Chincoteague Isl. are at S end. Fishing, shellfishing.

Chinese Camp, uninc. village, Tuolumne co., central Calif., 7 mi/11.3 km SSW of Sonora. In area are New Don Pedro (S), Tulloch (W), and New Melones (N) reservoirs. Cattle; hay, apples; timber. Sawmill.

Chiniak Bay (CHI-nee-yak), S Alaska, inlet of Gulf of Alaska, NE Kodiak Isl.; 10 mi/16 km long, 11 mi/18 km wide at mouth; 57°43′N 152°22′W. Kodiak village on N; Womens Bay (W arm) is site of Coast Guard base.

Chiniak, Cape (CHI-nee-yak), S Alaska, E extremity of Kodiak Isl., on Gulf of Alaska, 15 mi/24 km SSW of Kodiak; 57°37′N 152°10′W. Wild horses.

Chinicuila, Mexico: see VILLA VICTORIA.

Chínipas de Almada (CHEE-ni-pas de ahl-MAH-dah), town (1990 pop. 799), Chínipas municipio, Chihuahua, N Mexico, in Sierra Madre Occidental, 175 mi/282 km SW of Chihuahua; 27°22′N 108°32′W. Elev. 1,660 ft/506 m. Agr. (corn, wheat, beans; livestock); gold-placer mining; lumbering. Access by unimproved road.

Chinle (chin-lee), uninc. town, Apache co., NE Ariz., 90 mi/145 km NNE of Holbrook, on Chinle Creek, at mouth of Nazlini Creek, in Navajo Indian Reservation; elev. 5,058 ft/1,542 m. Cattle, sheep; crafts. Gateway to Canyon de Chelly Natl. Monument (E).

Chino (CHEE-no), city (1990 pop. 59,682), San Bernardino co., S Calif., suburb 32 mi/51 km E of downtown Los Angeles, and 4 mi/6.4 km SW of Ontario; 34°01′N 117°42′W. Business and processing center of a diversified farming (notably dairying) area. Mfg. (food processing, plastic prods., food and beverage machinery, household items, bldg. materials). City pop. nearly tripled 1970–1990. Chino Airport to SE. Boys Republic to W (boys town); Calif. Inst. for Men ("Prison Without Walls") in SE, Calif. Inst. for Women 6 mi/9.7 km to SE. Chino Hills

State Park to S. Prado Flood Control Basin (Santa Ana R.) to SE. Founded 1887, inc. 1910.

Chino Hills, city (1990 pop. 27,608), San Bernardino co., S Calif., residential suburb 30 mi/48 km E of Los Angeles, and 6 mi/9.7 km SW of Ontario, SE of Chino; 33°58′N 117°45′W. Chino Hills State Park to S; Prado Flood Control Basin to SE; Calif. Inst. for Men (prison) to E.

Chino Valley (CHEE-no), town (1990 pop. 4,837), Yavapai co., W central Ariz., 13 mi/21 km N of Prescott; 34°45′N 112°27′W. Cattle; wheat, corn, alfalfa, hay. Parts of Prescott Natl. Forest to E and W.

Chinobampo (chee-no-BAHM-po), town, Sinaloa, NW Mexico, in Río Fuerte basin (irrigation area), 18 mi/29 km ESE of El Fuerte. Sugarcane, corn, cotton, tomatoes, fruit.

Chinook (chuh-NUK), town (1990 pop. 1,512), ⊙ Blaine co., N Mont., on Milk R., near mouth of Lodge Creek, and 20 mi/32 km E of Havre; 48°35′N 109°14′W. Gas wells; livestock; dairying and poultry, grain, potatoes, sugar beets. Oil fields to S and SW. Inc. 1901, first called Belknap. Bear's Paw Battlefield Natl. Monument, Chief Joseph's surrender site of 1877, 14 mi/23 km to S, near Bear's Paw Mts., Blaine Co. Mus.

Chinook (shi-NOOK), village, SE Alta., W Canada, 45 mi/72 km ESE of Hanna. Grain elevators; lumbering; farming.

Chinook, uninc. village (1990 pop. 710), Pacific co., SW Wash., 7 mi/11.3 km NNW of Astoria (Oregon), on estuary of Columbia R., near Pacific Ocean. Astoria Bridge, 4 mi/6.4 km long (U.S. Hwy. 101), 4 mi/6.4 km to SE. Mfg. (fresh and frozen seafood).

Chinook, Lake, Oregon: see BILLY CHINOOK, LAKE.

Chinook Pass (shuh-NOOK), elev. 5,440 ft/1,658 m, Pierce/Yakima co. line, W central Wash., through crest of Cascade Range, just E of Mt. Rainier, on E boundary of Mt. Rainier Natl. Park. State Highway 410 here.

Chipley, town (□ 3 sq mi/7.8 sq km; 1990 pop. 3,866), ⊙ Washington co., NW Fla., c.45 mi/72 km NNE of Panama City; 30°46′N 85°32′W. Shipping center for farm and timber area; lumber milling, brick mfg. Nearby is egg-laying experiment station. Falling Water, 4 mi/6.4 km S, is one of the state's few waterfalls.

Chipman, village (1991 pop. 208), central Alta., W Canada, on Beaver Creek, and 35 mi/56 km ENE of Edmonton. Mixed farming; dairying.

Chipola River (CHIP-uh-luh), c.125 mi/201 km long, in Ala. and Fla.; rises in several branches near Dothan (SE Ala.); flows S, across NW Fla., past Marianna, through Dead L., to Apalachicola R. 10 mi/16 km SE of Wewahitchka.

Chippawa (CHIP-uh-wo), village, S Ont., central Canada, just above Niagara Falls; 43°05′N 79°03′W. Settled in 1794. Scene of an Amer. victory (1814) in the War of 1812.

Chippawa River, Ont.: see WELLAND RIVER.

Chippewa 1 (CHI-pe-wuh), county (□ 2,698 sq mi/6,988 sq km; 1990 pop. 34,604), E Upper Peninsula, Mich.; ⊙ SAULT SAINTE MARIE. Bounded E by St. Mary's R., N by Whitefish Bay, and S by L. Huron; 46°19′N 84°31′W. Includes Sugar, Neebish, and Drummond isls., vehicle ferry service to all 3. Drained by Tahquamenon and Munuscong rivers. Port of entry, and mfg. and shipping at Sault Ste. Marie. Agr. (potatoes, forage crops, oats; cattle, sheep, poultry); dairying; lumbering. Resorts. Bay Mills Indian Reservation, W unit on L. Superior, NW of Brimley, E unit on Sugar Isl., in NE. Parts of Tahquamenon Falls State Park in NW, Brimley State Park in N center; part of Hiawatha Natl. Forest in W; Fort Brady, and a waterfowl refuge; several small lakes in W and NW. Formed 1826. **2** (CHIP-wah), county (□ 587 sq mi/1,520 sq km; 1990 pop. 13,228) SW Minn.; ⊙ Montevideo; 45°01′N 95°33′W. Bounded W by Minnesota R. (flows NW to SE). Drained by Chippewa R. Agr. area (wheat, corn, oats, soybeans, sugar beets, alfalfa; hogs, sheep). Part of Lac qui Parle Wildlife Area in NW; Shakopee L., on Shakopee Creek, in N. Formed 1862. **3** county (□ 1,041 sq mi/2,696 sq km; 1990 pop. 52,360), W central Wis.; ⊙ Chippewa Falls; 45°04′N 91°16′W. Drained by

Chippewa R. Dairying; barley, oats, soybeans, brans, alfalfa, hay; cattle, sheep, poultry. Mfg. at Chippewa Falls (site of hydroelectric plant). Several small lakes, largest being L. Wissota. Brunet Isl. State Park in NE; L. Wissot State Park in S center. Formed 1845.

Chippewa Bay, resort village (1990 pop. 350), St. Lawrence co., N N.Y., 33 mi/53 km N of Watertown, on St. Lawrence R., in Thousand Isls. resort region; 44°27′N 75°46′W. Cedar Isl. State Park nearby.

Chippewa Falls, city (1990 pop. 12,727), ⊙ Chippewa co., W central Wis., on the Chippewa R., a satellite community 9 mi/14.5 km NNE of Eau Claire; 44°55′N 91°23′W. Originally a lumbering town, Chippewa Falls once had the world's largest sawmill. It remains a trade and transportation center in a region of beef- and dairy-cattle farms. Mfg. (foam prods., wood and coal furnaces, supercomputers, fire apparatus, paper prods., shoes, electronic prods., furniture; printing). Settled 1837, inc. as a city 1869. L. Wissota State Park to NE, on L. Wissota.

Chippewa Lake or **Chippewa-on-the-Lake,** village (1990 pop. 271), Medina co., N Ohio, 5 mi/8 km SSW of Medina, on small Chippewa L. Resort.

Chippewa, Lake, Sawyer co., NW Wis., on Chippewa R., 22 mi/35 km SE of Hayward; 12 mi/19 km long, max. 5 mi/8 km wide, with many sprawling arms; 45°53′N 91°04′W. Contains several islets. Partially in Lac Court Oreilles Indian Reservation; Chequamegon Natl. Forest on NE.

Chippewa River 1 (CHI-pe-wuh), c.200 mi/322 km long, Wis.; rising in several forks in the lake region of SW Ashland co., N Wis.; flows SW to the Mississippi R., which it enters at the foot of L. Pepin (responsible for lake's natural impoundment). Eau Claire and Chippewa Falls are on its banks. Chippewa L., L. Wissota, and Holcombe Flowage are major reservoirs. The river was once important in the lumbering industry. **2** c.80 mi/129 km long, central Mich.; rises in NE Mecosta co.; flows generally ESE, past Barryton and Mt. Pleasant, to Tittabawassee R. at Midland; 43°44′N 85°08′W. **3** (CHIP-wah), c.120 mi/193 km long, in W and SW Minn.; rises in lake region 7 mi/11.3 km NW of Alexandria in Chippewa L.; 44°56′N 95°43′W; flows 1st W through Devils, Little Chippewa, Stowe, Long and Erwin lakes, turns S in Albert L., flows through Peterson, Hjermenrud and Ellingson lakes, past Hoffman and Benson, to Minnesota R. at Montevideo. East Branch Chippewa R. rises in SE Douglas co., W Minn., 7 mi/11.3 km SE of Alexandria, flows S through Leven, Villard, Amelia, Marlu, and Gilchrist lakes, turns W before joining Chippewa R. at Benson; c.90 mi/145 km long. Little Chippewa R. rises in L. Reno, 5 mi/8 km N of Glenwood in N Pope co., W Minn., flows NE into Maple L. before turning W and SW; joins Chippewa R. 10 mi/16 km E of Morris; c.45 mi/72 km long.

Chiputneticook Lakes (chip-uht-NE-ti-kuk), E Maine and SW N.B., 28-mi/45-km chain extending NW from Vanceboro (Maine) along U.S.–Canada (N.B.) border; include North, Grand (17 mi/27 km long), Spednik, and Palfrey lakes. Source of St. Croix R. Formerly called Schoodic Lakes.

Chiquihuitlán de Benito Juárez, Mexico: see SAN JUAN CHIQUIHUITLÁN.

Chiquihuitlán, Santa Ana, Mexico: see SANTA ANA CUAUHTÉMOC.

Chiquilistlán (chee-kee-lees-TLAHN), town (1990 pop. 2,820), Jalisco, W Mexico, on central plateau, 32 mi/51 km SSE of Ameca. Grain, sugarcane, fruit; livestock.

Chiquita, Mount, Colo.: see MUMMY RANGE.

Chireno (1990 pop. 415), Nacogdoches co., E Texas, 19 mi/31 km ESE of Nacogdoches, near Attoyac Bayou; 31°30′N 94°20′W. Farm trade point (poultry; dairying); timber. Angelina Natl. Forest and Sam Rayburn reservoir to S.

Chiricahua Mountains, E Cochise co., SE Ariz., c.40 mi/64 km long, running N-S, c.46 mi/74 km NE of Douglas, just W of N.Mex state line; rises to 9,795 ft/2,986 m at Chiracahua Peak in S center of range. Most of range is in sect. of Coronado Natl. Forest. Chiracahua Natl.

Monument is in N center, area of unusual rock formations, and Fort Bowie Natl. Historic Site is in N. Apache Pass, in N, separates range from Dos Cabezas Mts. which angle westward, a continuation of the Chiracahuas.

Chiricahua National Monument (□ 18 sq mi/ 47 sq km), Cochise co., SE Ariz., in Chiracahua Mts., 33 mi/53 km SE of Willcox. Unusually shaped rock formations created by volcanic activity millions of years ago. Bounded N, E, and S by Coronado Natl. Forest. Authorized 1924.

Chirikof Island (CHIR-ri-kof), S Alaska, in N Pacific, S of Alaska Peninsula, 180 mi/290 km SW of Kodiak; 11 mi/18 km long, 3 mi/4.8 km–7 mi/11.3 km wide; 55°48′N 155°37′W.

Chisago (shuh-SAH-go), county (□ 442 sq mi/ 1,145 sq km; 1990 pop. 30,521), E Minn.; ⊙ Center City; 45°30′N 92°53′W. Agr. area bounded E by St. Croix R. (Wis. state line). Drained by Sunrise R., watered in S by several small lakes, including Rush L. in NW. Cattle, poultry; hay, corn, oats, rye, alfalfa; dairying. Carlos Avery Wildlife Area in center and SW; part of Lower St. Croix Natl. Scenic Riverway is in center. St. Croix Natl. Scenic Riverway along St. Croix R. in NE. On St. Croix R. are St. Croix Wild River (NE) and Interstate (E) state parks. Swed. settlement. Formed 1851.

Chisago City (shuh-SAH-go), town (1990 pop. 2,009), Chisago co., E Minn., 31 mi/50 km NNE of St. Paul; 45°22′N 92°53′W. Grain; cattle, poultry; dairying; mfg. (tree-transplanting machines, boat lifts). Resort area. Early Swed. settlement. Carlos Avery Wildlife Area to W; L. Chisago to SE, Green L. to SW.

Chisana (chee-SAH-nuh), village, E Alaska, 100 mi/ 161 km SSE of Tanacross, at foot of Wrangell Mts.

Chisasibi or **Fort-George,** village (1991 pop. 2,306), NW Que., E Canada, on E shore of James Bay, at mouth of La Grande R. James Bay Hydro Project is to E. Town was relocated from isl. at mouth of river to N side, due to increased flow from project. Road connection from S. Pop. is mainly Cree and Inuit.

Chisholm, town (1990 pop. 5,290), St. Louis co., NE Minn., in Mesabi Iron Range, 5 mi/8 km NNE, near source of East Swan R.; 47°29′N 92°52′W. Trading and mining point. Mfg. (pulpwood, apparel, drill bits, foods); timber; dairying; alfalfa. Iron mines in area. Minn. Mus. of Mines here. George Washington State Forest to NW; McCarthy Beach State Park to NW; Superior Natl. Forest to N. Inc. as town 1901, as city 1934.

Chisholm or **Chisholm Mills** (CHI-zhum), village, central Alta., W Canada, on Athabaska R., and 40 mi/64 km WNW of Athabaska; 54°55′N 114°10′W. Wheat; livestock.

Chisholm, Maine: see JAY.

Chisholm Trail, route over which vast herds of cattle were driven from N Texas to the railheads in Kansas after the Civil War. Named for Jesse Chisholm, a part-Cherokee trader who, in the spring of 1866, drove his wagon, heavily loaded with buffalo hides, from N Texas through what is now Okla., to Wichita, Kansas; the S terminus was Abilene, Texas. For the 2 decades that followed, hundreds of thousands of Texas longhorns were driven over the trail annually. The development of RRs and wire fencing ended the trail's use, and it became the subject of Western folklore.

Chisos Mountains (CHEE-sos), N-S range (□ c.40 sq mi/104 sq km) in S Brewster co., extreme W Texas, lying within the Big Bend of the Rio Grande; 3d-highest range in state. Center of Big Bend Natl. Park; noted for unusual geological formations. Highest point is Emory Peak (7,825 ft/2,385 m); just NE is Lost Mine Peak (7,535 ft/2,297 m).

Chistochina (CHIS-tuh-CHEE-nuh), village (1990 pop. 60), E Alaska, on upper Copper R., and at mouth of Chistochina R. (50 mi/80 km long), 110 mi/177 km NE of Valdez; 62°33′N 144°41′W. Formerly spelled Chestochina.

Chitina (CHI-ti-nuh), village (1990 pop. 49), S Alaska, on Copper R., at mouth of Chitina R., and 65 mi/105 km ENE of Valdez; 61°31′N 144°29′W. SE terminus of Edgerton Highway, branch of Richardson Highway.

Tourism; salmon fishing. Established division point on line of former Copper R. and Northwestern RR (abandoned). Unimproved road to Kennecott.

Chitina River (CHI-ti-nuh), 120 mi/193 km long, S Alaska; rises in St. Elias Mts. near 61°00′N 141°40′W, at foot of Logan Glacier; flows WNW to Copper R. at Chitina. Lower course is paralleled by Copper R. and Northwestern RR (abandoned). Flows through Wrangell–St. Elias Natl. Park. Formerly a major mining region.

Chittenango (chi-tuh-NAING-go), village (□ 2 sq mi/ 5.2 sq km; 1990 pop. 4,734), Madison co., central N.Y., 15 mi/24 km E of Syracuse; 43°02′N 75°52′W. Agr. and dairying area. Summer resort. Chittenango Falls village, and a state park (□ 122 acres/49 ha) with scenic Chittenango Falls on small Chittenango Creek, are just S.

Chittenango Falls, N.Y.: see CHITTENANGO.

Chittenden (CHIT-in-din), county (□ 619 sq mi/ 1,603 sq km; 1990 pop. 131,761), NW Vt., bounded W by L. Champlain, with Green Mts. in E; ⊙ Burlington; 44°28′N 73°04′W. Mfg. (textiles, wood and metal prods., electronics, bldg. materials, clothing), dairy and maple prods., fruit; granite. Lake and mt. resorts. Drained by Winooski and Lamoille rivers. Organized 1782.

Chittenden (CHIT-in-din), town (1990 pop. 1,102), Rutland co., W central Vt., 6 mi/9.7 km N of Rutland, partly in Green Mt. Natl. Forest; 43°43′N 72°54′W.

Chivirico (chee-vee-REE-ko), small port, Santiago de Cuba prov., SE Cuba, on Caribbean Sea; 19°58′N 76°24′W. Surrounded by coffee groves, beaches.

Chloride, village, Mohave co., W Ariz., 17 mi/27 km NNW of Kingman, on W side of Ceebat Mts.; elev. c.4,000 ft/1,219 m. Turquoise mines.

Chóapam, Mexico: see SANTIAGO CHÓAPAM.

Choc (SHUHK), village (1991 pop. 28), NW St. Lucia, 2 mi/3.2 km NNE of Castries, on Choc Bay. Limes, coconuts.

Chocamán (cho-kah-MAHN), town (1990 pop. 7,753), ⊙ Chocamán municipio, Veracruz, E Mexico, at E foot of Pico de Orizaba, on RR, and 10 mi/16 km NW of Córdoba; elev. 4,442 ft/1,354 m. Corn, coffee, sugarcane, fruit.

Chocholá (cho-cho-LAH), town (1990 pop. 3,567), Yucatán, SE Mexico, 20 mi/32 km SW of Mérida; 20°45′N 90°27′W. Henequen; tropical fruit; cattle.

Chocolate Mountains 1 in La Paz and Yuma cos., SW Ariz., W of Castle Dome Mts., E of Colorado R., and NE of Yuma; rise to 2,820 ft/860 m. Continuation of Chocolate Mts. (Calif.), W of Colorado R. **2** in Imperial co., SE Calif., NW of Yuma (Ariz.), desert range extending c.70 mi/113 km NW-SE along E side of Salton Sea and the Imperial Valley; mts. rise to c.2,000 ft/ 610 m. Gold mines. Barren Mts. are a spur at SE end, near Colorado R. Another range of the same name, c.30 mi/48 km to E of this one, is Ariz.

Chocorua (chi-KOO-ruh), village, Carroll co., E N.H., 26 mi/42 km NE of Laconia, and 2 mi/3.2 km ENE of Tamworth village, in town of Tamworth, on Chocorua R. (forms Chocorua L. to N). Timber. Dairying; livestock. Mfg. (pumps; commercial printing). White Mt. Natl. Forest to N.

Chocowinity (chahk-o-WI-nuh-tee), village (1990 pop. 624), Beaufort co., E N.C., 4 mi/6.4 km SSW of Washington, near Pamlico R.; 35°30′N 77°05′W. RR junction. Tobacco, cotton, peanuts, sweet potatoes, grain; livestock. Mfg. (furniture).

Choctaw 1 (CHAWK-taw), county (□ 920 sq mi/ 2,383 sq km; 1990 pop. 16,018), SW Ala.; ⊙ Butler. In Black Belt, bordering on Miss., bounded E by Tombigbee R. Cotton, corn; livestock. Textiles; paper, lumber milling; crude oil production. Formed 1847. **2** county (□ 419 sq mi/1,085 sq km; 1990 pop. 9,071), central Miss.; ⊙ Ackerman; 33°21′N 89°15′W. N boundary formed in part by Big Black R.; drained by Noxubee and Yockanookany rivers (source of both). Agr. (cotton, corn, lespedeza, sweet potatoes; cattle; timber). Natchez Trace Natl. Parkway crosses co.; part of Tombigbee Natl. Forest in SE. Formed 1833. **3** county (□ 800 sq mi/2,072 sq km; 1990 pop. 15,302), SE Okla.; ⊙

Hugo; 34°01′N 95°32′W. Bounded S by Red R., here forming Texas state line; drained by Muddy Boggy and Clear Boggy creeks and by Kiamichi R. Agr. (soybeans, vegetables, corn). Mfg. and vegetable processing at Hugo. Timber. Has Boswell (in W) and Raymond Gary (in E) state parks. Hugo L. (recreation). Formed 1907.

Choctaw (CHAWK-taw), city (1990 pop. 8,545), Oklahoma co., central Okla., residential suburb 14 mi/ 23 km E of downtown Oklahoma City, on North Canadian R.; 35°28′N 97°16′W. In agr. area; mfg. (magnets). John Miskelly State Park is here.

Choctawhatchee Bay (chawk-taw-HA-chee), NW Fla., arm (c.30 mi/48 km long, 3 mi/4.8 km–5 mi/8 km wide) of the Gulf of Mexico, 35 mi/56 km E of Pensacola, connected with Pensacola Bay via Santa Rosa Sound; E end of Santa Rosa Isl. extends almost across its mouth. Receives Choctawhatchee R. (E). Forms part of Gulf Intracoastal Waterway.

Choctawhatchee River (chawk-taw-HA-chee), 174 mi/ 280 km. long, SE Ala. and NW Fla.; rises in central Barbour co., Ala.; flows SSW to Geneva (here joined by Pea R.), thence S into Fla. and W to E end of Choctawhatchee Bay.

Choiceland, town (1991 pop. 434), central Sask., W Canada, 22 mi/35 km WNW of Nipawin. Dairying; wheat.

Choiseul (SHWAH-zhuhl), village (1991 pop. 381), SW St. Lucia, 16 mi/26 km SSW of Castries; 13°47′N 61°02′W. Coconuts, fruit; fishing. Local craft center.

Choix (cho-EESH), city (1990 pop. 5,333) and township, Sinaloa, NW Mexico, in W outliers of Sierra Madre Occidental, 28 mi/45 km NE of El Fuerte; 26°45′N 108°23′W. Corn, cotton. The municipality has had mining activity.

Choke Canyon Lake, reservoir, McMullen and Live Oak cos., S Texas, on Frio R., 65 mi/105 km ESE of San Antonio; 28°32′N 98°25′W. Max. capacity 1,096,261 acre-ft. Formed by Choke Canyon Dam (141 ft/43 m high), built (1982) by the Bureau of Reclamation for water supply; also used for recreation. Choke Canyon State Park near dam.

Chokio (shuh-KEI-yo), village (1990 pop. 521), Stevens co., W Minn., 13 mi/21 km W of Morris; 45°34′N 96°10′W. Wheat, corn, oats, soybeans, sunflowers; hogs, cattle; light mfg.

Cholla Bay, Mexico: see PUERTO PEÑASCO.

Cholula de Rivadabia (cho-LOO-lah dai ree-vah-DAH-bee-yah), city (1990 pop. 53,673) and historic site, ⊙ San Pedro Cholula municipio, Puebla state, E central Mexico; 19°05′N 98°20′W. The site of the famous *Teocali de Cholula*, a pre-Columbian pyramid of great antiquity, the city was an old Toltec center and an Aztec sacred city devoted to the worship of Quetzalcoatl. Today, a suburb of Puebla, its pyramid, the most massive in the Americas, is now crowned by a church. Site of dozens of R.C. churches, many in disrepair. The picturesque site remains a place of pilgrimage and attracts many tourists.

Chontla (CHON-tlah), town (1990 pop. 2,183), Veracruz, E Mexico, in Sierra Madre Oriental foothills, 40 mi/ 64 km NW of Túxpam de Rodríguez Cano. Cereals, sugarcane, fruit. Some Huastec-speaking pop.

Chopawamsic Recreational Area, Va.: see DUMFRIES.

Choptank River, c.70 mi/113 km long, in W Del. and E Md.; rises in Del. W of Dover, in W Kent co.; flows generally SSW, into Md., past Greensboro (head of navigation), Denton, and Cambridge (Senator Malkus, Jr. Bridge here), to Chesapeake Bay S of Tilghman Isl. Tidal estuary to Denton, more than 4 mi/6.4 km wide at mouth; Tred Avon R., Broad Creek, and Harris Creek are N branch estuaries near its mouth. Fishing, oystering.

Choteau (chuh-TO), town (1990 pop. 1,741), ⊙ Teton co., NW central Mont. on Teton R., near mouth of Deep Creek, and 50 mi/80 km NW of Great Falls; 47°49′N 112°11′W. In ranching region. Dairying; cattle, sheep, hogs; wheat, barley, oats. Teton Spring Creek Bird Preserve to NW; Pishkun Reservoir to SW; Freezeout L. to SE; Pine Butte Swamp, Preserve to W. Inc. 1913.

Choteau, Okla.: see CHOUTEAU.

Choudrant (SHOO-draw), village (1994 pop. 731), Lincoln parish, N La., 8 mi/13 km E of Ruston; 32°32′N 92°31′W. In agr. area.

Chouteau (chou-TO), county (□ 3,997 sq mi/ 10,352 sq km; 1990 pop. 5,452), N central Mont.; ⊙ Fort Benton; 47°53′N 110°26′W. Agr. area drained by Missouri, Teton, and Marias rivers. Arrow Creek forms SE border. Wheat, barley, oats, hay; cattle, hogs. Several lakes in S center of co. Part of Rocky Boy's Indian Reservation in NE; part of Lewis and Clark Natl. Forest in S; small part of Benton L. Natl. Wildlife Refuge in SW; Upper Missouri Natl. Wild and Scenic R. begins at Fort Benton, in center of co.; it follows Missouri R. E into Blaine and Fergus cos. Formed 1865.

Chouteau (CHO-to), town (1990 pop. 1,771), Mayes co., NE Okla., 37 mi/60 km E of Tulsa. Market center for farm area which includes concentration of Amish, esp. in village of Mazie 4 mi/6 km to S which hosts annual Amish festival. Mfg. (machinery, wooden prods.; meatpacking). Fort Gibson L. reservoir (Neosho R.) to E. Formerly spelled Choteau.

Chowan (chuh-WAHN), county (□ 233 sq mi/ 603 sq km; 1990 pop. 13,506), NE N.C.; ⊙ Edenton; 36°7′N 76°35′W. In coastal plain area; bounded W by Chowan R., S by Albemarle Sound. Agr. (peanuts, cotton, tobacco, corn, hay, sorghum, wheat, oats, soybeans, sweet potatoes; chickens, cattle, hogs); timber (pine, gum). Fishing; mfg. at Edenton. Drummand Point in SE corner. Formed 1672.

Chowan River (chuh-WAHN), 52 mi/84 km long, NE N.C.; formed 11 mi/18 km N of Winton, at Va. state line, on Gates/Hartford co. (N.C.) border, by confluence of Nottaway and Blackwater rivers; flows generally SSE past Winton, to W end of Albemarle Sound 4 mi/ 6.4 km W of Edenton (bridged); mouth of Roanoke R. enters sound 5 mi/8 km to S.

Chowchilla, city (1990 pop. 5,930), Madera co., central Calif., in San Joaquin Valley, 35 mi/56 km NW of Fresno; 37°07′N 120°16′W. Cottonseed oil, evaporated milk; dairying; potatoes, vegetables, apples, grapes, figs; cotton; grain, nuts; cattle, poultry; publishing and printing. Inc. 1923.

Chowchilla River, c.65 mi/105 km long, central Calif.; formed by short East and West forks (each flow S, c.15 mi/24 km), rising in S Mariposa co., join in NW Madera co., c.30 mi/48 km NW of Madera; flows SW and then W to join San Joaquin R. 18 mi/29 km SSW of Merced. Site of Buchanan Dam of Central Valley project. Forms part of border bet. Mariposa and Madera cos. for most of its course.

Chown, Mount (10,930 ft/3,331 m), W Alta., W Canada, near B.C. border, in Rocky Mts., in Jasper Natl. Park, 70 mi/113 km WNW of Jasper; 53°24′N 119°25′W.

Chrisman, city (1990 pop. 1,136), Edgar co., E Ill., 11 mi/ 18 km N of Paris; 39°47′N 87°40′W. Trade and shipping center in agr. area (corn, soybeans, sorghum; cattle, hogs). Plotted 1872, inc. 1873.

Chrisney, town (1990 pop. 511), Spencer co., SW Ind., 8 mi/12.9 km N of Rockport; 38°01′N 87°02′W. In agr. and bituminous-coal area.

Christian 1 county (□ 715 sq mi/1,852 sq km; 1990 pop. 34,418), central Ill.; ⊙ Taylorville; 39°32′N 89°16′W. Bounded N by Sangamon R.; drained by South Fork of Sangamon R. Agr. (corn, wheat, soybeans, sorghum). Bituminous-coal mining; oil. Mfg. (paper); commercial rose growing. Formed 1839 as Dane; became Christian in 1840. Sangchris L. State Park in NW, L. Taylorville SE of co. **2** county (□ 724 sq mi/ 1,875 sq km; 1990 pop. 68,941), SW Ky., on Tenn. (S) state line; ⊙ HOPKINSVILLE; 36°53′N 87°29′W. Bounded NE by Pond R.; drained by Tradewater, Little, South, and North forks Little West Fork Pond and West Fork of Red R. Gently rolling agr. area (dark and burley tobacco, corn, wheat, soybeans, hay, alfalfa; cattle, poultry; dairying); coal mines, gas wells; hardwood timber; mfg. at Hopkinsville. Part of Fort Campbell Military Reservation in S and NW (extends into Tenn.). Pennyrile Forest State Resort Park in NW. Formed 1796. **3** county (□ 567 sq mi/1,469 sq km; 1990 pop. 32,644), SW Mo., in the Ozark Mts.; ⊙ Ozark; 36°58′N 93°11′W.

Drained by tributaries of White R. Agr. (corn, wheat, hay, berries, apples, peaches); dairying; cattle, horses; timber. Mfg. at Ozark and Nixa, part of Mark Twain Natl. Forest in SE quarter. Urban growth from Springfield to N. Formed 1860.

Christian, village, in Chandalar dist., NE Alaska, 60 mi/ 97 km N of Fort Yukon; 67°30′N 145°20′W. Trapping and gold prospecting, at edge of Venetie Indian Reservation.

Christian, Cape, E Baffin Isl., SE Franklin dist., N.W.T., N Canada, on Davis Strait; 70°32′N 68°17′W. Clyde River trading post 9 mi/14 km SW. Site of former U.S. Naval Station, closed 1975.

Christian Island, S central Ont., central Canada, in Georgian Bay of L. Huron, on E side of entrance of Nottawasaga Bay, 40 mi/64 km ENE of Owen Sound; 10 mi/16 km long, 5 mi/8 km wide; 44°50′N 80°12′W.

Christiana, town (1991 pop. 7,235), Manchester parish, W central Jamaica, resort in uplands, 14 mi/14.5 km N of Mandeville; 18°21′N 74°29′W. Elev. c.2,500 ft/762 m. Ginger-growing center; also produces bananas, coffee, pimento, annatto, honey. Settled by Germans 1836–1842.

Christiana (KRIS-tee-A-nah), borough (1990 pop. 1,045), Lancaster co., SE Pa., 9 mi/14.5 km WSW of Coatesville, on East Branch Octoraro Creek; 39°57′N 76°00′W. Mfg. (gears, machinery). Agr. (grain, soybeans; poultry; livestock; dairying). Settled 1691, laid out 1833, inc. 1894.

Christiana River, Del.; see CHRISTINA RIVER.

Christiansburg, uninc. city (1990 pop. 15,004), ⊙ Montgomery co., SW Va., 27 mi/43 km WSW of Roanoke, 7 mi/11.3 km S of Blacksburg, near W base of the Blue Ridge, drained by Crab Creek; 37°08′N 80°24′W. Mfg. (stone processing, yarn twisting, machining, printing and publishing; bldg. materials, machinery, electric and electronic equip., clothing, furniture, canned goods, lumber); in agr. area (corn, apples, alfalfa; livestock; dairying). Founded 1792, inc. 1916.

Christiansburg, village (1990 pop. 599), Champaign co., W central Ohio, 9 mi/14 km E of Troy; 40°03′N 84°01′W. In agr. area.

Christiansted (KRIS-chuhn-sted), town (1990 pop. 2,555), chief city of St. Croix, U.S.V.I. Shipping port for sugar and rum; tourism is the leading industry. Founded in 1733, Christiansted served briefly as capital of the Dan. West Indies.

Christiansted Historic Site, on St. Croix, U.S.V.I. Commemorates the isls.' colonial development, especially under Dan. rule (18th–19th cent.). Authorized 1952.

Christina Lake, Douglas and Grant cos., W Minn., 23 mi/37 km NW of Alexandria; 5 mi/8 km long, 2 mi/ 3.2 km wide; 46°05′N 95°43′W. Dam at SW end raises lake level. Drains through short stream to Pelican L., which drains into Pelican Creek. Also called L. Christina.

Christina River, c.35 mi/56 km long, in Pa., Md., and Del.; rises in Chester co. (Pa.), flows SE and NE across tip of Md., through N Del. to Delaware R. at Wilmington, whose harbor it forms. Receives Brandywine Creek near mouth. Formerly Christiana R.

Christine, village (1990 pop. 368), Atascosa co., SW Texas, 41 mi/66 km S of San Antonio; 28°47′N 98°30′W. Farm trade point.

Christmas, town, Orange co., E central Fla., 20 mi/ 32 km E of Orlando; 28°34′N 81°03′W. Light mfg. St. Johns Natl. Wildlife Refuge and numerous lakes nearby.

Christmas Cove, Maine: see SOUTH BRISTOL.

Christopher, city (1990 pop. 2,774), Franklin co., S Ill., 5 mi/8 km WSW of Benton; 37°58′N 89°02′W. RR junction. In bituminous-coal-mining, oil, and agr. section. Agr. (grain and livestock); mfg. (boat trailers, mining equip.). Inc. 1903.

Christopher, uninc. village, Perry co., SE Ky., in Cumberland foothills, on North Fork Kentucky R. 1 mi/ 1.6 km SE of Hazard. Bituminous-coal-mining area.

Christoval, uninc. village (1990 pop. 216), Tom Green co., W Texas, 26 mi/42 km S of San Angelo, and on

South Concho R. In ranch, farm area. Tourist trade; mineral wells. Twin Buttes Reservoir to N.

Chubb Crater, Que.: see CRATER LAKE.

Chubbuck, town (1990 pop. 7,791), Bannock co., SE Idaho, residential suburb 3 mi/4.8 km N of downtown Pocatello, near Partneuf R.; 42°55′N 112°28′W. Bounded on N by Fort Hall Indian Reservation. American Falls Reservoir (Snake R.) to NW.

Chucándiro (choo-KAHN-dee-ro), town (1990 pop. 2,091), Michoacán, central Mexico, on W bank of L. Cuitzeo, 18 mi/29 km NW of Morelia. Cereals; fruit; livestock.

Chuckwalla Mountains, Riverside co., SE Calif., small desert range just N of the Chocolate Mts., 30 mi/48 km N of Calipatria, and S of Desert Center; max. elev. 4,490 ft/1,369 m. The lower Little Chuckwalla Mts. are to SE (Imperial co.).

Chugach Islands (CHOO-gach), group of 3 small mountainous islands, S Alaska, off S Kenai Peninsula, in Gulf of Alaska; 59°08′N 151°40′W. Consists of Chugach, Pearl, and Elizabeth isls.

Chugach Mountains (CHOO-gach), one of the Pacific coastal ranges, S Alaska, extending from the St. Elias Mts., on the U.S. (Alaska)–Canada (Yukon) border, NW to the Manuska R. Mt. Marcus Baker, 13,176 ft/4,016 m, is the highest peak. Rugged, with forested lower slopes (the S slope is a natl. forest) and glacier-covered summits, the Chugach are a barrier for movement inland from the coast. The Richardson and Parks highways and the Copper R. are corridors through the range.

Chugach National Forest (CHOO-gach) (□ 7,500 sq mi/19,425 sq km), S Alaska, on S slope of Chugach Mts., on N shore of Prince William Sound, bet. Cape Suckling (E) and SE tip of Kenai Peninsula (W). Includes offshore isls. Virgin forest, mainly western hemlock and Sitka spruce. Est. 1907.

Chuginadak Island (choo-GI-nuh-dak), largest of Isls. of Four Mts., Aleutian Isls., SW Alaska, 25 mi/40 km W of Umnak Isl.; 14 mi/23 km long, 3 mi/4.8 km–8 mi/12.9 km wide; 52°50′N 169°44′W. Rises to 5,675 ft/1,730 m on Mt. Cleveland (W), active volcano which erupted violently on June 10, 1944.

Chugwater, village (1990 pop. 192), Platte co., SE Wyo., on Chugwater Creek, and 43 mi/69 km N of Cheyenne; 41°45′N 104°49′W. Elev. 5,288 ft/1,612 m. In ranching area; agr. (wheat; cattle); mfg. (foods). Holds an annual chili cook-off.

Chugwater Creek, 81 mi/130 km long, SE Wyo.; rises in E Albany co.; flows generally N, past Chugwater, to Laramie R. 7 mi/11.3 km NE of Wheatland.

Chula (CHOO-luh), town (1990 pop. 183), Livingston co., N central Mo., 10 mi/16 km NNE of Chillicothe; 39°55′N 93°28′W.

Chula Vista (CHOO-lah VIS-tah), city (1990 pop. 135,163), San Diego co., S Calif., suburb 8 mi/12.9 km SSE of downtown San Diego, 8 mi/12.9 km to N of Tijuana (Mexico), on San Diego Bay (W); 32°38′N 117°02′W. A port of entry, the city lies in an area of citrus fruit– and vegetable-growing, and it has grown considerably with the aircraft industry in neighboring San Diego. Mfg. (apparel, bldg. materials, electrical items, machinery, transportation equip.). Chula Vista was marked by a pop. increase of 61% 1980–1990. It has a large percentage of Mex.-Amer. residents due to the proximity of the Mex. border to the S. Seat of Southwestern Col. (2-year). Silver Strand State Beach to W; Sweetwater R. to N, Otay R. to S. Inc. 1911.

Chulitna River (choo-LIT-nuh), 80 mi/129 km long, S central Alaska; rises in McKinley glacier system, Alaska Range, near 62°54′N 150°00′W; flows S to Susitna R. at Talkeetna.

Chuluota (choo-loo-O-duh), town (□ 2 sq mi/5.2 sq km; 1990 pop. 1,441), Seminole co., E central Fla., 15 mi/24 km NE of Orlando; 28°38′N 81°07′W. Econlockhatchee State Forest nearby.

Chumatlán (choo-mah-TLAHN), town (1990 pop. 1,376), Veracruz, E Mexico, in E foothills of Sierra Madre Oriental, 23 mi/37 km SW of Papantla de Ogarte. Corn, coffee, sugar.

Chumayel (choo-MAH-yel), town (1990 pop. 2,384), Yucatán, SE Mexico, 18 mi/29 km E of Ticul. Henequen, sugarcane, fruit.

Chunky, village (1990 pop. 292), Newton co., E central Miss., 13 mi/21 km W of Meridian, on Chunky Creek; 32°19′N 88°55′W. Agr. (cotton, corn; poultry, cattle).

Chunky Creek, c.50 mi/80 km long, E central Miss.; rises in SE Neshoba co.; flows S and SE, past Chunky, to Okatibbee Creek at Enterprise, where they form Chickasawhay R.

Chupadera Mesa (choo-puh-DER-uh MAI-suh), high tableland (6,000 ft/1,829 m–9,000 ft/2,743 m) largely in E Socorro co., central N.Mex. Extends N from Sierra Oscura. Game is abundant.

Chupara Point (chu-PAH-rah), cape, N Trinidad, Trinidad and Tobago, 14 mi/23 km NE of Port of Spain; 10°48′N 61°22′W.

Church Butte (BYOOT) (6,351 ft/1,936 m), eroded sandstone cliffs in Sweetwater co., SW Wyo., c.45 mi/72 km W of Rock Springs. They rise 75 ft/23 m above surrounding plain, in form of cathedral.

Church Creek, town (1990 pop. 113), Dorchester co., E Md., on Eastern Shore of Chesapeake Bay, 6 mi/9.7 km SW of Cambridge, on inlet of Little Choptank R.; 38°31′N 76°09′W. Blackwater Natl. Wildlife Refuge is S. Shipbuilding was a major industry until 1875 when the area's white oak was depleted.

Church Hill 1 town (1990 pop. 481), Queen Annes co., E Md., 25 mi/40 km W of Dover, (Del.); 39°08′N 75°59′W. In agr. area at the head of Southeast Creek. **2** town (1990 pop. 4,834), Hawkins co., NE Tenn., on Holston R., 9 mi/14 km WSW of Kingsport; 36°31′N 82°42′W. Inc. 1958.

Church Point, town (1990 pop. 4,677), Acadia parish, S La., 16 mi/26 km NNE of Crowley; 30°24′N 92°13′W. In agr. area (rice, soybeans, corn); mfg. (gasoline, apparel). Oil and gas field nearby.

Churchbridge, town (1991 pop. 919), SE Sask., W Canada, near Man. border, 33 mi/53 km SE of Yorkton. Mixed farming.

Churchill, county (□ 5,023 sq mi/13,010 sq km; 1990 pop. 17,938), W central Nev., in Great Basin; ⊙ Fallon; 39°36′N 118°20′W. Irrigated agr. area watered in W by Carson R. and diversions from Truckee R.; forms Lahontan Reservoir on W border. Alfalfa, cantaloupes, hay, vegetables; diatomite, salt, sand and gravel, lime gypsum, silica sand. Carson Sink is in N. Clan Alpine Mts. are in E. Stillwater Range is N center; part of W Humboldt, including Humboldt Sink, on N border; part of Walker Indian Reservation in SW; part of Lahontan State Recreation Area in W; Fallon Naval Air Station SE of Fallon and 4 separate sects. in W. Formed 1861.

Churchill, village (1991 pop. 1,143), N Man., central Canada, on Hudson Bay, at mouth of Churchill R., and c.600 mi/966 km NNE of Winnipeg; 58°47′N 94°12′W. RR terminal; major grain-shipping port, serving N Man. Shipping season mid-Aug.–mid-Oct. Thoroughfare for annual polar bear migrations along Hudson Bay coast. Mouth of Churchill R. was discovered 1619 by Jens Munck; Hudson's Bay Co. established trading post here, 1688; burned and abandoned soon after. Wooden Fort Churchill est. 1718, replaced (1733) by nearby Fort Prince of Wales, heavily fortified stone structure. Long-time Br. stronghold in N Canada, though captured for short period by the French under La Pérouse in 1782. Remains of fort are now historic memorial. Construction of Hudson Bay RR was begun 1911: original terminal of Port Nelson was abandoned (1927) in favor of Churchill. Line was completed 1929, and grain shipments begun 1931.

Churchill, uninc. village (1990 pop. 2,691), Trumbull co., NE Ohio, 11 mi/18 km SE of Warren, and 4 mi/6 km N of Youngstown, on Interstate 80; 41°10′N 80°40′W.

Churchill, borough (1990 pop. 3,883), Allegheny co., SW Pa., E suburb of Pittsburgh; 40°26′N 79°50′W. Inc. 1933.

Churchill 1 river, c.600 mi/966 km long, Lab., NE Canada; issues as the Ashuanipi R. from Ashuanipi L., SW Lab.; flows in an arc N, then SE through a series of lakes to Churchill Falls and McLean Canyon, then NE past Goose Bay and through Melville L. and Hamilton Inlet to the Atlantic Ocean near Rigolet. The river has probably the greatest hydroelectric power potential of any river in N. Amer., and Churchill Falls is the site of one of the world's largest hydroelectric power plants. Formerly known as the Hamilton R., it was renamed (1965) in honor of Sir Winston Churchill. **2** river, c.1,000 mi/1,609 km long, Sask. and Man., central Canada; issues from Methy L., NW Sask.; flows SE, E, and NE across the lowlands of N Sask. and N Man. to Hudson Bay at Churchill. It meets the Beaver R., its chief tributary, at Lac Île-à-la-Crosse (Sask.). Once a famous fur-trade route, it was 1st explored (1619) by Jens Munck, a Scandinavian sent by Christian IV, king of Denmark and Norway, to search for the Northwest Passage. In 1717 the Hudson's Bay Co. established a trading post, later called Fort Prince of Wales, which eventually became a Br. stronghold in the region. Captured (1782) by the French under Jean La Pérouse, the fort was regained by the British and renamed Fort Churchill; its ruins are preserved in Fort Prince of Wales Natl. Historic Park. Exploration of the upper reaches of the river was carried on by the Frobishers, Peter Pond, and Alexander Henry, all of the North West Co. A hydroelectric power station on the upper river supplies power for mining operations in Man. Modern port of Churchill is at the mouth.

Churchill, Cape, N Man., central Canada, on Hudson Bay, 33 mi/53 km E of Churchill; 58°47′N 93°15′W.

Churchill Downs, Ky.: see LOUISVILLE.

Churchill Falls, spectacular waterfalls of the upper Churchill R., 245 ft/75 m high, SW Lab., NE Canada; known as Grand Falls until renamed (1965) in honor of Sir Winston Churchill. Four mi/6 km above the falls, the Churchill R. narrows to 200 ft/61 m and negotiates a series of rapids before dropping into McLean Canyon, from which sheer cliffs rise several hundred feet on either side. The river flows 12 mi/19 km through the canyon over a series of rapids. The total drop from the rapids above the main falls to the end of McLean Canyon is 1,038 ft/316 m. Because of their isolated location and harsh surroundings, the falls never became a tourist attraction. Churchill Falls has one of the largest hydroelectricity-generating capacities (5,225,000 kw) in the world. It was completed in 1974 and most of the power is sent to the Montreal area. First explored (1839) by John McLean, a trader of the Hudson Bay Co.

Churchill Lake (□ 213 sq mi/552 sq km), NW Sask., W Canada, on Churchill R., 210 mi/338 km N of North Battleford; 25 mi/40 km long, 14 mi/23 km wide.

Churchill Lake, Piscataquis co., N central Maine, 64 mi/103 km SW of Presque Isle, in wilderness recreational area; triangular, with 3-mi/4.8-km sides. Joined by Allagash R. to Eagle and Umsaskis lakes. Part of Allagash Wilderness Waterway.

Churchill Peak (10,500 ft/3,200 m), N B.C., W Canada, in Rocky Mts.; 58°19′N 125°08′W.

Churchs Ferry, village (1990 pop. 118), Ramsey co., NE central N.Dak., 19 mi/31 km NW of Devils L.; 48°16′N 99°11′W. L. Irvine to NE. RR junction. L. Alice Natl. Wildlife Refuge to NE.

Churchton, village, Anne Arundel co., central Md., near Chesapeake Bay, 13 mi/21 km S of Annapolis. Post office est. 1885.

Churchville, uninc. town (1990 pop. 4,255), Bucks co., SE Pa., residential suburb 17 mi/27 km NNE of Philadelphia; 40°12′N 75°00′W. Science and technology research center. U.S. Naval Air Development Center to NW.

Churchville, residential village (□ 1 sq mi/2.6 sq km; 1990 pop. 1,731), Monroe co., W N.Y., 16 mi/26 km SW of Rochester; 43°06′N 77°52′W. Agr. area; mfg. of vacuum pump fluids. Frances E. Willard b. here.

Churdan, town (1990 pop. 423), Greene co., central Iowa, 10 mi/16 km NNW of Jefferson; 42°08′N 34°94′W.

Churintzio (choo-REEN-tsee-o), town (1990 pop. 3,080), Michoacán, central Mexico, 12 mi/19 km S of La Piedad de Cabadas. Cereals, fruit; livestock.

Churubusco (choo-roo-BOOS-ko), SE section of Mexico city, central Mexico. Residential suburb of lovely gardens and fine colonial architecture. Has old Franciscan monastery (1678), natl. invasion mus. A Mex. War battle took place here, Aug. 20, 1847. Center of Mex. film and television industry. Was anc. Aztec religious center dedicated to war-god Hutzilopochtli. Hydroelectric plant nearby.

Churubusko, town (1990 pop. 1,781), Whitley co., NE Ind., 11 mi/18 km NE of Columbia City; 41°14′N 85°19′W. In agr. area; ships vegetables. Mfg. (fabricated metal equip., machinery, transportation equip.).

Churumuco de Morelos (choo-roo-MOO-ko dai mo-RAI-los), town (1990 pop. 3,800), ⊙ Churumuco municipio, Michoacán, central Mexico, near Río Balsas, 38 mi/61 km SW of Tacámbaro; 18°36′N 101°40′W. Cereals, sugarcane, fruit.

Chuska Mountains, in Navajo Indian Reservation, Apache co., NE Ariz. and San Juan co., NW N.Mex. Chief peaks are Matthews Peak (9,512 ft/2,899 m) and Roof Butte (9,784 ft/2,982 m), both in Ariz.

Chute aux Outardes (SHYOOT o-zoo-TAHRD), village (1991 pop. 2,162), E Que., E Canada, on Outardes R., near its mouth on the St. Lawrence R., and 12 mi/19 km SW of Baie Comeau; 49°07′N 68°23′W. Hydroelectric station.

Chute Shipshaw (shyoot SHIP-sho) or **Racine** (ruh-SEEN), town (1991 pop. 556), central Que., E Canada, on Aulnets R., and 5 mi/8 km NW of Jonquière; 48°28′N 71°14′W. Hydroelectric-power center.

Chuviscar River (choo-VEES-kar), c.100 mi/161 km long, Chihuahua, N Mexico; rises in E outliers of Sierra Madre Occidental NW of Chihuahua; flows E, past Aldama, to Conchos R. 8 mi/12.9 km N of Julimes. Irrigation.

Ciales (see-AH-les), town (1990 pop. 18,084), N central P.R., on the Manatí R. Valley, and 24 mi/39 km WSW of San Juan. Coffee-growing center in the hills, considered best coffee in P.R. Agr. (plantains, bananas); light mfg. P.R. natl. poet Juan Antonio Corretjer b. here.

Cibao (see-BOU), lowland, N Dominican Republic, a broad valley bet. the Cordillera Setentrional (N) and Cordillera Central (S), along Yaque del Norte and Yuna rivers; extends 145 mi/233 km ESE from Monte Cristi to Sánchez on Samaná Bay. The most fertile and densely populated region of the country. Agr. (cacao, coffee, tobacco, corn, sugarcane, rice, tropical fruit). Its E sect. is sometimes called La Vega Real valley, a name given by Columbus.

Cibao Mountains, Dominican Republic: see CENTRAL, CORDILLERA.

Cibecue, uninc. town (1990 pop. 1,254), Navaho co., E central Ariz., 60 mi/97 km SSW of Holbrook, in Fort Apache Indian Reservation, on Cibicue Creek. Sheep, cattle.

Cibola (SEE-bo-luh), county (□ 4,542 sq mi/11,764 sq km; 1990 pop. 23,794), W N.Mex.; ⊙ Grants; 34°55′N 107°59′W. Created 1981 from Valencia co. Cattle, sheep; hay, alfalfa, triticale, some wheat, oats, barley, rye. Uranium, gypsum. Bounded on W by Ariz. Drained by Rio San Jose. Part of San Mateo Mts. in NE, part of Zuni Mts. in NW. Parts of Cibola Natl. Forest in NW and NE. Acoma and parts of Laguna and Canoncito Indian Reservations in W. El Morro Natl. Monument (Inscription Rock) in W; El Malpais Natl. Monument and lava field, La Ventura Natural Arch and Bandera Volcano and Ice Caves at center. Bluewater L. State Park on N border. Continental Divide runs N-S through W center of co.

Cibola, mythical grouping of seven "cities of gold" sought by 16th-cent. Span. explorers. Stories of possibly wealthy Native Amer. cities in the American Southwest brought to Mexico by survivors of Cabeza de Vaca's transcontinental trek (1528–1536) resulted in 1539 expedition to N.Mex. by Father Marcos de Nina. De Nina withdrew when his party met hostile reception, but his reports inflated the legend of "cities" he had only seen from a distance. Myth shattered by 1540 expedition under Francisco Coronado which established the "cities" as subsistence-economy Pueblo communities. Spaniards later applied the term *cibola* to the entire Pueblo

country, as far as and including the Great Plains (buffalo were *vacas de Cibola*, "the cows of Cibola"). In the 19th cent. anthropologists established the Pueblo community at Zuni (N.Mex.) is called "Shivola" in Zuni. Other terms related to the legend were found to be corruptions of Zuni meanings.

Cibolo (SIB-o-lo), town (1990 pop. 1,757), Guadalupe co., S central Texas, suburb 18 mi/29 km NE of San Antonio, on Cibolo Creek; 29°34′N 98°13′W. Agr. area. Mfg. (wood prods., paper prods., consumer goods, electronic equip., bldg. materials, machinery).

Cibolo Creek 1 (SIB-o-lo), c.125 mi/201 km long, in S central Texas; rises on Edwards Plateau in Bexar co., W of Boerne; flows generally E, then SE, passing city of San Antonio to the N and NE, then to San Antonio R., 5 mi/8 km NNE of Karnes City. **2** c.40 mi/64 km long, in extreme W Texas; rises S of Marfa; flows S to the Rio Grande at Presidio.

Ciboux Island (see-BOO), islet, NE N.S., E Canada, off NE Cape Breton Isl., 4 mi/6 km NE of Cape Dauphin; 46°23′N 60°22′W.

Cicero 1 town (1990 pop. 67,436), Cook co., NE Ill., an industrial and residential suburb 11 mi/18 km W of downtown Chicago; 41°50′N 87°45′W. Industry has been steadily declining since the 1970s. Mfg. (foods, furniture, paper goods, dampers and shutters, fabricated metal prods., signs; printing). Seat of Morton Col. Sportsmans Race Track here. Site of civil-rights march through blue-collar neighborhoods led by Dr. Martin Luther King, Jr. (1967). Once site of huge Western Electric factory, touted as a city within a city, closed 1970s and since demolished. Al Capone lived here. Inc. 1867. **2** town (1990 pop. 3,268), Hamilton co.; central Ind., on Cicero Creek, near Morse Reservoir, and 7 mi/11.3 km N of Noblesville; 40°07′N 86°01′W. In agr. area.

Cicero (SI-suh-ro), residential village (1990 pop. 1,100), Onondaga co., central N.Y., near Oneida L., 9 mi/14.5 km N of Syracuse; 43°09′N 76°03′W. Limited agr. (vegetables, grain). Cicero Swamp and State Wildlife Management Area 2 mi/3.2 km SE.

Cicero Creek, c.40 mi/64 km long, central Ind.; rises in W Tipton co.; flows NE to Tipton, then S to West Fork of White R. near Noblesville.

Cidra (SEE-druh), town, Matanzas prov., W Cuba, on RR, and 9 mi/14.5 km SSE of Matanzas; 22°54′N 81°31′W. Sugarcane, fruit; cattle.

Cidra (SEE-drah), town (1990 pop. 35,601), E central P.R., on N slopes of the Sierra de Cayey, 9 mi/14.5 km WSW of Caguas. Summer resort in fine mt. setting. Growing industrial area, mfg. (clothing, beverages, medicines, plastic prods.). Some agr. (plantains, ornamental plants). Horse raising. Mental-health hosp. and L. Cidra nearby.

Ciego de Ávila (see-AI-go dai AH-vee-luh), province (□ 4,030 sq mi/6,485 sq km), central Cuba; ⊙ Ciego de Ávila. Bordered by Old Bahama Channel, S by the Gulf of Ana María (arm of the Caribbean Sea), E by Camagüey prov., and W by Sancti Spíritus prov. Comprised mainly of rich-soiled flatlands; produces c.10% of Cuba's sugar and 7% of the country's citrus crops. Minerals include large gypsum deposits and oil fields. Important cities include Ciego de Ávila, Morón. Includes Cayo Coco, in Camagüey Archipelago (N) and Cayos de Ana María (S). Formed in 1976 through joining W Camagüey prov. with part of old prov. of Las Villas.

Ciego de Ávila (see-AI-go dai AH-vee-luh), city, (1995 est. pop. 91,000), ⊙ Ciego de Ávila prov., central Cuba; 21°50′N 78°45′W. An important processing center in a sugarcane region, it is also one of Cuba's leading producers of pineapples and oranges. Cattle raising is another major industry. Has good road and RR communications, though the natl. highway has not yet reached it. Founded in 1840.

Ciénaga de Flores (see-YAI-nah-gah dai FLOR-ais), town (1990 pop. 5,658), Nuevo León, N Mexico, on Inter-Amer. Highway 85, on Pesquería R., and 22 mi/35 km NNE of Monterrey; 26°00′N 100°10′W. Grain, cotton, sugarcane.

Ciénaga, La, Mexico: see CIÉNEGA DE ZIMATLÁN.

Ciénega de Zimatlán (see-AI-nai-gah dai zee-maht-LAHN), town (1990 pop. 3,504), in central Oaxaca, Mexico, 12 mi/20 km SSW of Oaxaca de Juárez; elev. 4,692 ft/1,430 m. Agr. (corn, beans, coffee, fruits); wood prods. Road and RR connections with Oaxaca. Formerly La Cíenaga.

Cienfuegos (see-ain-FWAI-goz), province, central Cuba; ⊙ Cienfuegos. Bordered NE by Villa Clara prov., S by Caribbean Sea, SE by Sancti Spíritus prov., and W and NW by Matanzas prov. (across Hanábana R., in part). Drained by Damují R. Next to Havana City, Cuba's most significant industrial region. Has 50 sq mi/130 sq km of arable land, of which pasture and sugarcane account for 36% and 30%, respectively; one of the slowest pop. growth rates in Cuba (grew from 211,000 in 1953 to 360,000 in 1993); good potential for economic growth, esp. in capital.

Cienfuegos (see-ain-FWAI-goz), city (1995 est. pop. 125,000), ⊙ Cienfuegos prov., central Cuba, a port on the Caribbean Sea; 22°08′N 80°27′W. Handles 30% of sugar exports; modern port facilities for bulk grain and liquid (mostly molasses) cargo. Marketing and processing center of a region producing sugarcane, tobacco, coffee, and rice; it also has rum distilleries and fish canneries. Also a major fishing port. Only deepwater access port (up to 3 km/9,842 ft) on Cuba's S coast. Major industrial facilities include the Soviet-built Jaraguá nuclear power unit, Carlos Manuel de Céspedes thermoelectric plant, a submarine base, the Carlos Marx cement plant, and the Cienfuegos oil refinery. Founded in 1819 by Fr. emigrants from La. and named for 1 of the original founders, Cienfuegos was destroyed by a tropical storm in 1825 and later rebuilt.

Cifuentes (see-FWEN-taiz), town, Villa Clara prov., central Cuba, RR junction 15 mi/24 km N of Santa Clara; 22°40′N 80°03′W. In agr. region (sugarcane; cattle). Has 5 sugar mills within a 15-mi/24-km radius. Iron and manganese deposits and mineral springs nearby.

Cihuatlán (see-wah-TLAHN), town (1990 pop. 13,333), in SW Jalisco, Mexico, 26 mi/42 km NW of Manzanillo, Colima; 19°14′N 104°33′W. Located 6 mi/10 km from where the Cihuatlán R. meets the Pacific Ocean. Agr. (tropical plants, coconuts, plantains); livestock (pork) and forestry. Beautiful beaches and tourist area.

Cimarron (SI-muh-rahn), county (□ 1,841 sq mi/4,768 sq km; 1990 pop. 3,301), W Okla. Panhandle; ⊙ Boise City; 36°44′N 102°31′W. Only co. in the U.S. to be bounded by 4 states. Bounded N by Colo. and Kansas (NE corner touches Kansas), W by N.Mex., S by Texas. Comprised of high plains (elev. c.4,000 ft/1,219 m); includes the Black Mesa (elev. 4,973 ft/1,516 m), highest point in Okla. in NW corner. Drained by Cimarron and North Canadian (Beaver) rivers. Livestock raising; agr. (wheat, sorghum). Westernmost of 3 Panhandle cos.; includes part of Rita Blanca Natl. Grassland in NW. Old Santa Fe Trail runs NE-SW across NW part of co.; Central/Mountain time zone boundary follows N and W borders. Black Mesa State Park and small L. Etling reservoir in NW. Formed 1907.

Cimarron 1 (SI-muh-rahn), town (1990 pop. 1,626), ⊙ Gray co., SW Kansas, on Arkansas R., and 18 mi/29 km W of Dodge City; 37°48′N 100°20′W. Elev. 2,600 ft/792 m. Grain; livestock. Inc. 1885. **2** town (1990 pop. 774), Colfax co., NE N.Mex., 38 mi/61 km SW of Raton, on Cimarron R. (smaller of 2 Cimarron rivers in region), in E foothills of Sangre de Cristo Mts., on Santa Fe Historical Trail; 36°30′N 104°54′W. Elev. 6,228 ft/1,898 m. Cattle, sheep; alfalfa, grain; mfg. (lumber). Ruins of Maxwell House, famous frontier hotel, are here. Cimarron Canyon State Park to W; Eagle Nest Reservation and Angel Fire Ski Area to W; Vietnam Veterans Chapel at Palo Flechado Pass to W; Philmont Scout Ranch to SW.

Cimarron (SI-muh-rahn), river, N.Mex., Colo., and Okla., 698 mi/1,123 km long; rises in NW part of Union co., NE N.Mex., 3 mi/4.8 km S of Colo. state line; flows generally E, into Okla., through N part of Cimarron co., in W end of Okla. panhandle, angles NE through SE corner of Colo. (Baca co.), into Kansas, through

Cimarron Natl. Grasslands, past Satanta, then SE, into E part of Okla. panhandle, NE of Brause, reenters Kansas S of Ashland, then enters Okla. a 3d time, passing SW of Enid and N of Oklahoma City, past Guthrie, and Cushing, joins Arkansas R. 15 mi/24 km W of Tulsa, where it forms W arm of Keystone L. reservoir. North Fork Cimarron R. rises in Baca co., SE Colo., 3 mi/4.8 km NNW of Campo, in Comanche Natl. Grassland, flows ENE into Kansas, past Ulysses, then SE, joining Cimarron R., 5 mi/8 km W of Satanta. The Santa Fe Trail, pioneer route, follows river for many miles in Kansas. Crooked Creek and North Fork are among the Cimarron's tributaries. Sects. of its bed are dry during most of the year.

Cimarron River (SI-muh-rahn), 60 mi/97 km long, NE N.Mex.; rises at Palo Flechado Pass, 16 mi/26 km E of Taos, in W Colfax co.; flows N to Eagle Nest L., then E, through Cimarron Canyon (State Park), past Cimarron and Springer, to Canadian R. 6 mi/9.7 km ESE of Springer. Eagle Nest Dam (140 ft/43 m high; built 1918), 2 mi/3.2 km SE of Eagle Nest village, is private project used for power and irrigation; forms Eagle Nest L. (capacity c.100,000 acre-ft.). Source of the larger Cimarron R. is c.50 mi/80 km NE of Springer.

Cimarron, Territory of (SI-muh-rahn), now the Panhandle of Okla. Settled in the early 19th cent. by cattle ranchers, many of them squatters. To protect their claims they attempted, in 1887, to create a separate territorial govt. at Beaver, Okla. After subsequent efforts toward this end failed in the U.S. Congress, Cimarron became part of the Okla. Territory in 1890.

Cinantécatl, Mexico: see TOLUCA, NEVADO DE.

Cincinnati, city (1990 pop. 364,040), ⊙ Hamilton co., extreme SW Ohio, on the Ohio R. opposite Newport and Covington (Ky.); 39°08′N 84°30′W. Near the midpoint of the Ohio R. and on the Mason-Dixon line. The 3d-largest city in the state, Cincinnati is the industrial, commercial, and cultural center for an extensive area including numerous suburbs in Ohio, Ky., and Ind. Port of entry with a large river front and good transportation facilities. Mfg. includes machinery, consumer goods, transportation equip., electronic and electronic equip., musical instruments, fabricated metal goods; meat packaging. Other important private sectors include insurance, food, telecommunications, utilities, banks, linen services, retailing, communication. Mfg. research center (machine and process design to mitigate pollution) located here. Founded in 1788 as Losantiville; in 1790 Arthur St. Clair, the 1st governor of the Northwest Territory, renamed it Cincinnati for the Society of Cincinnati, a group of Revolutionary War officers. It was the 1st seat of the legislature of the Northwest Territory. After the opening of the Ohio and Erie Canal (c.1832), the city developed as a shipping point for farm prods. and meat. In the mid–19th cent. it was the world's largest pork-packing center and was nicknamed "Porkopolis." A crime wave, the result of corrupt politics and lax law enforcement, provoked the Cincinnati riot in March 1884, and G. B. Cox, a political boss, gained firm control of the city. A reform movement culminated in the establishment (1924) of the city-manager type of govt. (notable managers were Clarence A. Dykstra and Clarence O. Sherrill). The Univ. of Cincinnati, Edgecliff Col., Xavier Univ., and several other educational institutions are here. William Howard Taft and his son Robert A. Taft b. here. Landmarks are the Taft Mus.; Eden Park, with the Cincinnati Art Mus.; a mus. of natural history; and zoological gardens. The Cincinnati zoo is one of the better zoos in the nation. The city also has a symphony orchestra, a music conservatory, an art acad., and a large public lib. Cincinnati suffered disastrous floods in 1884 and 1937; Federal and state flood-control projects were built to prevent further danger. Home to the Cincinnati Reds, the nation's oldest professional baseball team, and the Bengals football team. Inc. as a city 1819.

Cincinnati, town (1990 pop. 363), Appanoose co., S Iowa, near Mo. state line, 7 mi/11.3 km SSW of Centerville; 40°37′N 92°55′W.

Cincinnatus (sin-sin-NA-tuhs), village (1990 pop. 400), Cortland co., central N.Y., on Otselic R., 15 mi/24 km ESE of Cortland; 42°31′N 75°55′W.

Cinco Bayou (SEEN-ko BEI-yoo), village (1990 pop. 322), Okaloosa co., NW Fla., 36 mi/58 km E of Pensacola; 30°25′N 86°36′W.

Cinco de Mayo (SEEN-ko dai MAH-yo), town, ⊙ Xochiapulco municipio, N Puebla, Mexico, 8 mi/12 km SW of Tlatlauquitepec. Mountainous terrain which is well irrigated. Temperate to hot humid climate. Agr. (corn, beans, wheat, coffee, sugarcane, fruits); fine wood, construction lumber, straw textiles. Undeveloped roads. Indigenous zone of Huasteca-Totonaca.

Cinco Leguas, Cayos de las (SEEN-ko LAI-gwahz, KAI-yoz dai lahs), keys, c.12 mi/19 km long E-W, off N Matanzas prov., NW Cuba, forming N bar of Santa Clara Bay, 20 mi/32 km ENE of Cárdenas; 23°08′N 80°55′W.

Cinnaminson, township (1990 pop. 14,583), Burlington co., S N.J., 7 mi/11.3 km SW of Willingboro; 40°00′N 74°59′W. Light industry, residential and commercial. Inc. 1860.

Cinnamon Mountain (13,328 ft/4,062 m), San Juan co., SW Colo., in San Juan Mts., 10 mi/16 km NE of Silverton. Cinnamon Pass is nearby.

Cinnamon Pass (c.12,600 ft/3,840 m), in San Juan Mts., on border bet. San Juan and Hindsdale cos., SW Colo., near Cinnamon Mt., 11 mi/18 km NE of Silverton. Crossed by road.

Cintalapa de Figueroa (seen-tah-LAH-pah dai fee-gai-RO-ah), city (1990 pop. 29,303), ⊙ Cintalapa municipio, Chiapas, S Mexico, on N slopes of Sierra Madre, 40 mi/64 km W of Tuxtla Gutiérrez; 16°41′N 93°43′W. Agr. center (corn, beans, sugarcane, fruit; livestock); forest prods.; alcohol and liquor distilling.

Circle, town (1990 pop. 805), ⊙ McCone co., E Mont., on Redwater R., and 45 mi/72 km NW of Glendive; 47°25′N 105°35′W. In ranching region. Shipping point for wheat, barley, oats, alfalfa; sheep, cattle, hogs, poultry; dairying. Dry Arm of Fort Peck Reservoir (Missouri R.) and Charles M. Russell Natl. Wildlife Refuge which surrounds lake, to NW; Big Sheep Mts. to SE.

Circle, village (1990 pop. 73), NE Alaska, on Yukon R., and 130 mi/209 km ENE of Fairbanks, on the Yukon R.; 65°49′N 144°04′W. NE terminus of Steese Highway from Fairbanks. Supply center for trapping, mining, hunting, fishing, tourism. School; airfield. Est. in 1890s following gold discovery on nearby Birch Creek.

Circle Hot Springs, village, NE Alaska, near Yukon R., 100 mi/161 km ENE of Fairbanks, on branch of Steese Highway. Tourism; mining. Resort; hot mineral springs nearby. Airfield.

Circle Pines, town (1990 pop. 4,704), Anoka co., E Minn., suburb 12 mi/19 km NE of downtown Minneapolis; 45°08′N 93°09′W. Drained by Rice Creek, which forms Golden and Baldwin lakes in E. Mfg. (printing and publishing, industrial engraving; electronic equip.).

Circleville, city (1990 pop. 11,666), ⊙ Pickaway co., S central Ohio, on the Scioto R.; 39°36′N 82°56′W. Corn, hogs, and poultry are processed here. Laid out in 1810 within the remains of a circular fort allegedly erected by mound builders. Its growth was spurred by the building of the Ohio and Erie Canal 6 mi/9.7 km from Chief Logan monument. Inc. 1853.

Circleville 1 village (1990 pop. 153), Jackson co., NE Kansas, 7 mi/11.3 km NW of Holton; 39°30′N 95°51′W. Livestock; grain. **2** village (1990 pop. 417), Piute co., S Utah, on Sevier R., and 5 mi/8 km SSW of Junction; 38°09′N 112°15′W. Elev. 6,063 ft/1,848 m. Alfalfa; dairying; cattle, sheep; mfg. (apparel). Circleville Mt. (11,440 ft/3,487 m) is 7 mi/11.3 km WNW, in Tushar Mts. Dixie Natl. Forest to SE; Fishlake Natl. Forest to NW. Boyhood home of Butch Cassidy.

Cirque Mountain (SIRK) (5,500 ft/1,676 m), NE Lab., NE Canada, highest peak of Torngat Mts.; 58°55′N 63°33′W. Area of proposed Torngat Natl. Park.

Cirrus, Mount, Colo.: see NEVER SUMMER MOUNTAINS.

Cisco, town (1990 pop. 3,813), Eastland co., N central Texas, c.45 mi/72 km E of Abilene; elev. 1,608 ft/490 m; 32°23′N 98°58′W. Shipping, processing center for agr. area (peanuts, melons, vegetables); mfg. (machinery, bldg. materials, apparel); oil, natural gas wells nearby. Seat of Cisco Jr. Col.; L. Cisco (swimming, fishing; state fish hatchery) is 5 mi/8 km N. Mobley Astell (1916), Conrad Hilton's 1st hotel, purchased in 1919. Had oil boom, 1918. Settled 1851, inc. 1919.

Cisco 1 village, Placer co., E Calif., in the Sierra Nevada, 40 mi/64 km NE of Auburn, in Tahoe Natl. Forest. Burrau Ridge Ski Area is here. **2** village (1990 pop. 282), Piatt co., central Ill., near Robert Allerton Park, 16 mi/26 km NE of Decatur; 40°00′N 88°43′W. In rich agr. area.

Cisco, Lake, reservoir, Eastland co., N central Texas, on Sandy Creek, 5 mi/8 km NNW of Cisco; c.2 mi/3.2 km long; 33°26′N 98°59′W. Max. capacity 45,000 acre-ft. Drains N to Hubbard Creek Reservoir. Impounded by dam. Recreation; fishing.

Cisne, village (1990 pop. 645), Wayne co., SE Ill., 11 mi/18 km NNW of Fairfield; 38°30′N 88°26′W. In agr. area; oil wells.

Cissna Park (SIS-nah), village (1990 pop. 805), Iroquois co., E Ill., 18 mi/29 km SSW of Watseka; 40°34′N 87°53′W. In agr. area; grain; livestock.

Citlaltépec, Mexico: see CITLALTÉPETL.

Citlaltépec, San Nicolás, Mexico: see CITLALTÉPETL.

Citlaltépetl (seet-lahl-TAI-petl), town (1990 pop. 4,737), ⊙ Citlaltepec municipio, Veracruz, E Mexico, in Sierra Madre Oriental foothills, 38 mi/61 km NW of Túxpam de Rodríguez Cano; elev. 886 ft/270 m. Cereals, sugarcane, tobacco, fruit; livestock. Meat producers. Oil deposits. Also known as Citlaltépec or San Nicolás Citlaltépec.

Citlaltépetl, or *Pico de Orizaba*, peak (18,405 ft/5,610 m), in the Cordillera de Anáhuac, E Mexico, on the border bet. Veracruz and Puebla states; 19°01′N 97°11′W. It is the highest peak in Mexico and the 3d-highest in N. Amer. This snow-capped volcano is inactive; the last eruption occurred in 1687. The peak was 1st climbed in 1848.

Citronelle (sit-ruh-NEL), town (1990 pop. 3,671), Mobile co., SW Ala., 30 mi/48 km NNW of Mobile. In timber, livestock, and agr. area (cotton, vegetables, corn); resort with mineral springs; lumber, turpentine, tung oil (tung trees introduced 1906).

Citrus, county (□ 773 sq mi/2,002 sq km; 1990 pop. 93,515), W central Fla., on Gulf of Mexico, and bounded N and E by Withlacoochee R.; ⊙ Inverness; 28°51′N 82°31′W. Its swampy coast is dotted by Homosassa Isls.; contains Tsala Apopka L. in E. Agr. (corn, peanuts, citrus fruit; cattle, hogs); fishing; lumbering; quarrying (phosphate, limestone, clay). Formed 1887.

Citrus, uninc. town (1990 pop. 9841), Sacramento co., central Calif., residential suburb 13 mi/21 km ENE of downtown Sacramento, on American R. Mather Air Force Base to S; 34°07′N 117°54′W. Large area of dredge tailings to E and SE.

Citrus Heights, uninc. city (1990 pop. 107,439), Sacramento co., central Calif., residential suburb 14 mi/23 km NE of downtown Sacramento; 38°42′N 121°17′W. Folsom L. reservoir and State Recreation Area to E. Citrus; dairying; poultry; grain. Mfg. (printing).

Citrus Springs, town (□ 4 sq mi/10.4 sq km; 1990 pop. 2,213), Citrus co., N central Fla., 15 mi/24 km NW of Inverness; 29°00′N 82°28′W. Numerous lakes nearby.

City Island, SE N.Y., in L.I. Sound off E shore and part of Bronx borough of N.Y. city; 40°51′N 73°48′W. Connected with mainland by causeway. Mfg. (boatbuilding). Boating center; known for its seafood restaurants.

City of Industry, Calif.: see INDUSTRY, CITY OF.

City of Rocks National Historic Landmark (□ c.22 sq mi/57 sq km), Cassia co., S Idaho. Granite spires, columns, rock formations (c.600 ft/183 m). Authorized 1988.

City of the Dalles, Oregon: see THE DALLES.

City Point, Va.: see HOPEWELL.

City View, town (1990 pop. 1,490), Greenville co., NW S.C., 2 mi/3.2 km WNW of downtown Greenville; 34°51′N 82°25′W

Ciudad Acuña, Mexico: see ACUÑA.

Ciudad Adolfo López Mateos (syoo-DAHD ah-DOL-fo LO-paiz mah-TAI-os), city (1990 pop. 315,5059) and township, ⊙ Atizapán de Zaragoza municipio, Mexico state, central Mexico, on RR, and 12 mi/19 km NW of Mexico City; 19°28′N 00°14′W. Cereals; livestock. An important mfg. center of Mexico state. Municipio is part of the Zona Metropolitana de la Ciudad de México.

Ciudad Altamirano (syoo-DAHD ahl-tah-mee-RAH-no), city (1990 pop. 16,697) and township, ⊙ Pungarabato township, Guerrero, SW Mexico, on Cutzamala R. (Michoacán border), near its confluence with the Río Balsas, and 70 mi/113 km W of Iguala de la Independencia, on Mexico Highways 51 and 130. Agr. center (cereals, tobacco, coffee, sugarcane, tropical fruit, resin, vanilla). Pungarabato until 1936. Also called Altamirano.

Ciudad Benito Juárez (syoo-DAHD HWAHR-res), city (1990 pop. 9,151), Juárez municipio, Nuevo León, N Mexico, 13 mi/21 km E of Monterrey. Chickpeas, grain; livestock.

Ciudad Camargo, city (1990 pop. 7,370) and township, ⊙ Camargo municipio, Tamaulipas, NE Mexico, on San Juan R., in the Rio Grande basin, on RR, and 7 mi/11.3 km S of Rio Grande City (Texas), on Mexico Highway 2; 26°12′N 98°45′W. Agr. center (cotton, sugar, corn; cattle).

Ciudad Cerralvo (syoo-DAHD sai-RAHL-vo), town (1990 pop. 6,473), Nuevo León, NE Mexico, in NE foothills of Sierra Madre Oriental, 50 mi/80 km NE of Monterrey, on Mexico Highway 54; 26°10′N 99°40′W. Corn, cotton, sugar.

Ciudad Chetumal, Mexico: see CHETUMAL.

Ciudad Constitución (syoo-DAHD kon-stee-too-SYON), city (1990 pop. 34,692) and township, ⊙ Comondú municipio, Baja California Sur, NW Mexico, 160 mi/257 km NW of La Paz, on Mexico Highway 1; 26°02′N 111°49′W. Copper mining; livestock raising.

Ciudad Cuauhtémoc (syoo-DAHD kwou-TAI-mok), city (1990 pop. 8,612) and township, ⊙ Pueblo Viejo municipio, Veracruz, E Mexico, on Tampico Lagoon, near the Gulf of Mexico, 3 mi/4.8 km SE of Tampico, on Mexico Highway 180. Petroleum drilling and refining. Bellavista petroleum-refining plant nearby.

Ciudad Cuauhtémoc, Mexico: see SAN PEDRO PIEDRA GORDA.

Ciudad de La Habana (syoo-DAHD dai lah ah-BAH-nah), province, W Cuba, centered around the city of Havana, on the Straits of Florida; ⊙ Havana. Surrounded on 3 sides by La Habana prov. Created as part of the jurisdictional reorganization of the isl. in 1976, this is the most densely settled part of Cuba. Its roughly 650,000 non-metropolitan residents are distributed among a well-integrated network of small towns outside the metro. limits of Havana City. The prov. straddles both the Florida Straits on its N shore and the Caribbean Sea on its S side, with an average width of just 31 mi/50 km. Rolling topography, with hills 300 ft/91 m–900 ft/274 m high, transects the prov. along an E-W pattern. The S side opens to marshlands while the N end has good beaches. Agr. and light industry characterize its economy, the latter noted for 2 major textile centers in Alquizar and Ariguanabo. A key resource is the 53 billion cu ft/1.5 billion cu m of underground water, plus another 13.3 million cu ft/375 million cu m in reserves. Demand for fresh water for growing urban areas threatens to draw salt water into the wells of Cuenca Sur, El Gato, and Ariguanabo.

Ciudad de las Casas, Mexico: see SAN CRISTÓBAL DE LAS CASAS.

Ciudad de México, Mexico: see MEXICO, city.

Ciudad de Río Grande, Mexico: see RÍO GRANDE.

Ciudad del Carmen (syoo-DAHD del KAHR-men), city (1990 pop. 83,806), ⊙ Carmen municipio, Campeche, SE Mexico, port on W tip of Carmen Isl., at channel linking Gulf of Campeche with Laguna de Términos, 120 mi/193 km SW of Campeche, on Mexico Highway 180; 18°38′N 91°50′W. Mexico's most important shrimp port. Agr. (corn, beans, plantains, fruit); trading in and shipping of chicle and timber. Mfg. (fertilizers), sawmilling; works in hides, lizard and shark skins.

Ciudad del Maíz (syoo-DAHD del mah-EES), city (1990 pop. 6,907) and township, San Luis Potosí, N central Mexico, in E outliers of Sierra Madre Oriental, 40 mi/64 km NE of Río Verde; 22°26′N 99°36′W. Corn, wheat, beans, cotton, maguey. Sometimes Maíz.

Ciudad Dolores Hidalgo Cuna de la Independencia National, Mexico: see DOLORES HIDALGO.

Ciudad Fernández (syoo-DAHD fer-NAHN-des), city (1990 pop. 20,882) and township, San Luis Potosí, N central Mexico, on the Río Verde, and just NW of Río Verde. Corn, wheat, cotton, beans, fruit; livestock.

Ciudad González, Mexico: see SAN FELIPE.

Ciudad Guadalupe Victoria (syoo-DAHD gwah-dah-LOO-pai veek-TO-ree-ah), city (1990 pop. 12,831) and township, ⊙ Guadalupe Victoria municipio, Durango, N Mexico, on interior plateau, and 45 mi/72 km NE of Victoria de Durango on Mexico Highway 40; 24°30′N 104°08′W. Agr. center (corn, wheat, cotton, fruit; livestock).

Ciudad Guzmán (syoo-DAHD gooz-MAHN), city (1990 pop. 72,619), Jalisco state, SW Mexico, 37 mi/60 km NNE of Colima, on Mexico Highway 54; elev. 4,944 ft/1,507 m; 19°42′N 113°28′W. Marketing and processing center, esp. for hogs, with some minor industries. Starting point for ascents of the Nevado de Colima (14,206 ft/4,330 m) and the smoking volcano, Colima (12,992 ft/3,960 m). Beans, corn, wheat. Formerly called Zapotlán el Grande, Ciudad Guzmán was a center of the pre-Columbian kingdom of Zapotlán, which was conquered by the Spanish in 1526.

Ciudad Hidalgo 1 (syoo-DAHD ee-DAHL-go), city (1990 pop. 48,476) and township, ⊙ Hidalgo municipio, Michoacán, central Mexico, on central plateau surrounded by peaks, 35 mi/56 km E of Morelia, on Mexico Highway 15; 19°40′N 100°34′W. Agr. center (grain, sugarcane, beans, fruit; livestock). Tanning; lumbering; flour milling; soapmaking; forest prods. (resins, turpentine). It is the old Tarascan town Taximaroa. Sometimes Hidalgo. **2** city (1990 pop. 9,893), ⊙ Suchiate municipio, Chiapas, S Mexico, in Pacific lowland, opposite Ayutla (Guatemala), 16 mi/25 km SSE of Tapachula, on Mexico Highway 19; 14°40′N 92°11′W. RR terminus. Customhouse. Also known as Suchiate.

Ciudad Huitzuco (syoo-DAHD weet-ZOO-ko), city (1990 pop. 6,733), ⊙ Huitzuco de los Figueroa municipio, Guerrero, SW Mexico, 13 mi/21 km E of Iguala de la Independencia; elev. 6,791 ft/2,070 m. Mercury mining. Cereals, sugarcane, fruit; timber.

Ciudad Ixtepec (syoo-DAHD eesh-TE-pek), city (1990 pop. 20,818) and township, Oaxaca, S Mexico, in Pacific lowland of Isthmus of Tehuantepec, 18 mi/29 km NE of Santo Domingo Tehuantepec, on RR; 16°32′N 95°10′W. Elev. 397 ft/121 m. Lumbering, processing, and agr. center (rice, sugarcane, coffee, tobacco, fruit, vegetables); sawmilling, coffee processing, sugar refining. Formerly San Jerónimo Ixtepec.

Ciudad Juárez, Mexico: see JUÁREZ.

Ciudad Lázaro Cárdenas (syoo-DAHD LAH-zah-ro KAHR-dai-nahs), city (1990 pop. 53,581), in extreme S central Michoacán, Mexico, on the Pacific Ocean, 30 mi/48 km S of Arteaga, on Mexico Highway 200. A heavy industrial center specializing in iron, steel, and petrochemicals; also an important port.

Ciudad Lerdo (syoo-DAHD LER-do), city (1990 pop. 46,593) and township, Durango, N Mexico, in fertile irrigated area, on Nazas R., 4 mi/6.4 km W of Torreón, on Mexico Highways 40 and 49, on RR; 25°34′N 103°30′W. Processing and agr. center (cotton, grain, wine, fruit, vegetables, sugarcane, tobacco); cotton ginning, flour milling, fruit canning, wine and liquor making; foundries. Also Lerdo.

Ciudad López Mateos, Mexico: see CIUDAD ADOLFO LÓPEZ MATEOS.

Ciudad Madero (syoo-DAHD mah-DAI-ro), city (1990 pop. 160,331) and township, Tamaulipas, NE Mexico, just N of Tampico, on Mexico Highway 180; 22°19′N 97°50′W. Petroleum-producing and -refining center. Formerly Villa de Cecilia.

Ciudad Mante (syoo-DAHD MAHN-tai), city (1990 pop. 76,799) and township, ⊙ El Mante municipio, Tamaulipas, NE Mexico, on Inter-Amer. Highway 85 and Mexico Highway 80, 80 mi/129 km NW of Tampico; 22°44′N 98°59′W. Agr. center (cereals, sugarcane, fruit; livestock); tanning, sugar refining, alcohol distilling. Formerly Villa Juárez.

Ciudad Manuel Doblado (syoo-DAHD MAHN-wel do-BLAH-do), city (1990 pop. 10,381) and township, ⊙ Manuel Doblado municipio, Guanajuato, central Mexico, on central plateau, 33 mi/53 km SW of León. Wheat-growing center; flour milling.

Ciudad Melchor Múzquiz, Mexico: see MÚZQUIZ.

Ciudad Mendoza (syoo-DAHD mehn-DO-sah), city (1990 pop. 32,012) and township, ⊙ Camerino Z. Mendoza municipio, Veracruz, E Mexico, in valley of Sierra Madre Oriental, at S foot of Pico de Orizaba, on RR, and 8 mi/12.9 km WSW of Orizaba, on Mexico Highway 150; 18°49′N 97°14′W. Textile-milling and agr. center (coffee, sugarcane, tobacco, fruit). Formerly Santa Rosa. Sometimes Mendoza.

Ciudad Miguel Alemán (syoo-DAHD mee-GEL ah-le-MAHN), city (1990 pop. 17,030), N Tamaulipas, 7 mi/12 km W of Gustavo Díaz Ordaz, on Mexico Highway 2, and on the Nuevo León state and U.S. (Texas) border. Marte R. Gómez Dam here has improved agr. and cattle. Active business influenced by the border bridge between here and the U.S. city of Roma (Texas).

Ciudad Morelos, Mexico: see CUAUTLA.

Ciudad Nezahualcóyotl (syoo-DAHD ne-sah-wahl-KO-yotl), city (1990 pop. 1,255,456), ⊙ Nezahualcóyotl municipio, Mexico state, S central Mexico. One of Mexico city's largest and poorest suburban municipalities. Constructed on the drained bed of former L Texcoco. A part of the Área Metropolitana de la Ciudad de México. Also Netzahualcóyotl.

Ciudad Obregón (syoo-DAHD o-brai-GON), city (1990 pop. 219,980), ⊙ Cajeme municipio, Sonora, NW Mexico, in irrigated lowland of Gulf of California (Yaqui R. delta), on RR, and 65 mi/105 km SE of Guaymas, on Mexico Highway 15; 27°28′N 109°59′W. Agr. center (rice, fruit, winter vegetables, cotton; cattle); rice and flour milling, fruit canning. Copper mines nearby. Sometimes called Cajeme.

Ciudad Porfirio Díaz, Mexico: see PIEDRAS NEGRAS.

Ciudad Santos, Mexico: see TANCANHUITZ DE SANTOS.

Ciudad Serdán (syoo-DAHD ser-DAHN), city (1990 pop. 17,273) and township, ⊙ Chalchicomula de Sesma municipio, Puebla, central Mexico, near W foot of Pico de Orizaba, 50 mi/80 km E of Puebla, on Mexico Highway 144; 18°59′N 97°26′W. Elev. 8,333 ft/2,540 m. RR junction. Wheat- and corn-growing center; livestock raising; textile milling; salt quarrying. Sometimes Serdán.

Ciudad Trujillo, Dominican Republic: see SANTO DOMINGO.

Ciudad Valles (syoo-DAHD VAH-yes), city (1990 pop. 91,402) and township, ⊙ Ciudad Valles municipio, San Luis Potosí, E Mexico, in fertile Gulf dist., on RR, on Inter-Amer. Highway 85, and 75 mi/121 km WSW of Tampico; 21°59′N 99°58′E. Elev. 312 ft/95 m. Agr. center (coffee, tobacco, sugarcane, cereals, fruit; cattle). Taninul sulphur spas are 7 mi/11.3 km E. Sometimes Valles.

Ciudad Venustiano Carranza (syoo-DAHD vai-noos-tee-AH-no kah-RAHN-sah), city (1990 pop. 4,122), Jalisco, W Mexico, 13 mi/21 km SE of Sayula. Agr. center (grain, beans, sugarcane, fruit; livestock). Formerly San Gabriel.

Ciudad Victoria (syoo-DAHD veek-TO-ree-ah), city (1990 pop. 194,996) and township, ⊙ Victoria municipio and Tamaulipas state, NE Mexico, on the San Marcos R., on the Inter-Amer. Highway 85, on a major RR line,and at the foot of the Sierra Madre Oriental; 23°43′N 99°10′W. Agr. prods. are processed here, in addition to lumber. Founded in 1750.

Ciudamar (syoo-dah-MAHR), SE residential suburb of Santiago de Cuba, Santiago de Cuba prov., E Cuba, 19°58′N 75°51′W. Famous El Morro Castle is 1 mi/1.6 km away. Runway of Antonio Maceo Intl. Airport ends just .9 mi/1.5 km to the E.

Clackamas (KLAK-uh-muhs), county (□ 1,879 sq mi/ 4,867 sq km; 1990 pop. 278,850), NW Oregon; ⊙ Oregon City; 45°11′N 122°12′W. Cascade Range to E, drained by Willamette, Molalla, Sandy, and Clackamas rivers. Bounded in SW by Butte Creek. Highly urbanized in NW corner, from city of Portland to N. Agr. (apples, cherries, pears, plums, peaches, grapes, berries, wheat, oats, barley, corn, potatoes; sheep, hogs, cattle); nurseries. Part of Mt. Hood Natl. Forest in E, including Mt. Hood (11,239 ft/3,426 m), the highest mt. in Oregon, on border bet. Clackamas and Hood cos. Table Rock Wilderness Area in S; Milo McIver State Park in N center. Molalla R., Mary S. Young, and part of Tryon Creek state parks in NW. Founded in 1843.

Clackamas (KLAK-uh-muhs), uninc. town (1990 pop. 2,578), Clackamas co., NW Oregon, industrial suburb 8 mi/12.9 km SE of downtown Portland, near Clackamas R.; 45°24′N 122°32′W. Mfg. (meat processing, consumer goods, foods, labels, paper goods, transportation equip., wood stoves, bldg. materials). Camp Withycombe (Natl. Guard) to E.

Clackamas River (KLAK-uh-muhs), c.85 mi/137 km long, NW Oregon; rises in E. Marion co., 55 mi/89 km ESE of Salem, 10 mi/16 km N of Mt. Jefferson, in Cascade Range; flows NW, through North Fork Reservoir, where it receives North Fork from E (c.15 mi/24 km long), past Estacada, to Willamette R. near Oregon City. Used for hydroelectric power.

Cladonia, Mount (kluh-DO-nee-uh) (5,100 ft/1,554 m), NE Lab., NE Canada, on S shore of Nachvak Fiord; 58°58′N 63°34′W.

Claflin (KLAF-lin), town (1990 pop. 678), Barton co., central Kansas, 15 mi/24 km NE of Great Bend; 38°31′N 98°32′W. In grain and poultry region. Oil wells nearby. Cheyenne Bottoms L. and State Park to SW.

Claiborne (KLAI-buhrn), parish (□ 766 sq mi/ 1,984 sq km; 1990 pop. 17,405), N La., on Ark. (N) state line; ⊙ Homer; 32°48′N, 93°04′W. Drained by Bayou D'Arbonne (forms L. Claiborne reservoir in center of parish), its Middle Fork, and Corney Bayou (forms Corney L. in NE corner). Oil wells, natural gas. Logging. Agr. (hay, watermelons, nursery crops, grains; cattle, poultry, hogs; dairying). L. Claiborne State Park at SE end, 2 small units of Kisatchie Natl. Forest in NE and N center, part of 3d unit on SW border. Named after the 1st gov. of La. Formed 1828.

Claiborne 1 (KLAI-buhrn), county (□ 501 sq mi/ 1,298 sq km; 1990 pop. 11,370), SW Miss; ⊙ Port Gibson; 31°58′N 90°54′W. Bounded W by Mississippi R. (La. state line), N by Big Black R.; drained by Bayou Pierre. State line extends W of Mississippi R. to Yocatan L., oxbow lake and former river channel. Agr. (cotton, corn, soybeans; cattle; timber). Grand Gulf Military Park in W, on Mississippi R. Grand Gulf 1 nuclear power plant is 25 mi/40 km S of Vicksburg, uses cooling water from the Mississippi R., and has a max. dependable capacity of 1143 mw. Formed 1802. **2** county (□ 445 sq mi/1,153 sq km; 1990 pop. 26,137), NE Tenn.; ⊙ Tazewell; 36°29′N 83°40′W. Bounded N by Ky. and Va., S by Clinch R.; drained by Powell R. Includes part of Norris Reservoir. Traversed by Cumberland Mt. in NW; rest of co. has ridges and valleys of the Appalachians. Oil wells; coal mining; lumbering, woodworking; farming (livestock; corn, hay, apples, tobacco). Formed 1801.

Claiborne (KLAI-buhrn), uninc. town (1990 pop. 8,300), Ouachita parish, 5 mi/8 km W of Monroe; 32°30′N 92°11′W. Suburb of Monroe; pine forests and oil field in the area.

Claiborne, resort village, Talbot co., E Md., 22 mi/35 km NNW of Cambridge, on Eastern Bay. Terminus of ferry to Kent Isl. Founded by William Claiborne as a trading post in 1631.

Claiborne, Lake 1 reservoir (□ 9 sq mi/23.3 sq km), on border bet. Monroe and Clark cos., SW Ala., on Alabama R., 15 mi/24 km WNW of Monroeville; 31°37′N 87°33′W. Max. capacity 96,360 acre-ft. Extends N to Miller co. Formed by Claiborne Lock and Dam (100 ft/ 30 m), built (1969) by Army Corps of Engineers for navigation. **2** reservoir (□ 10 sq mi/26 sq km), Claiborne co., NW La., on Bayou d'Arbonne, 50 mi/80 km ENE of Shreveport; 32°44′N 92°54′W. Max. capacity 200,000 acre-ft. Formed by L. Claiborne Dam, built (1966) for water supply.

Clair Engle Lake, reservoir (□ 28 sq mi/73 sq km), Trinity co., N Calif., on Trinity R., bet. Salmon (W) and Trinity (E) mts., in Whiskeytown Shasta–Trinity Natl. Recreation Area, in Trinity Natl. Forest, 24 mi/39 km NW of Redding; c.15 mi/24 km long; 40°48′N 122°44′W. Max. capacity 2,761,000 acre-ft. Formed by Trinity Dam (458 ft/140 m high), built (1962) by the Bureau of Reclamation for irrigation, flood control, and power generation.

Claire City, village (1990 pop. 85), Roberts co., NE S.Dak., 13 mi/21 km N of Sisseton. Sica Hollow State Park to SW; in L. Traverse (Sisseton Wahpeton) Indian Reservation.

Claire, Lake (□ 545 sq mi/1,412 sq km), NE Alta., W Canada, W of L. Athabaska, in Wood Buffalo Natl. Park; 40 mi/64 km long, 28 mi/45 km wide; 58°30′N 112°00′W. Drains E into L. Athabaska through Mamawi L. Formerly a deep lake, it is now much silted up.

Clairemont, uninc. village (1990 pop. 15), Kent co., NW Texas, 30 mi/48 km NNE of Snyder, and bet. Salt Fork (N) and Double Mt. Fork (S) of Brazos R. In cattle; cotton, wheat and oil, gas region.

Clairemont, suburban section of San Diego city, San Diego co., S Calif., 6 mi/9.7 km N of downtown San Diego, residential area E of Mission Bay. Miramar Naval Air Station to NE; Montgomery Field airport to E. Tecolote Canyon Natural Park to E.

Clairton (KLER-tuhn), city (1990 pop. 9,656), Allegheny co., SW Pa., suburb 12 mi/19 km SSE of downtown Pittsburgh, on the Monongahela R.; 40°17′N 79°53′W. Mfg. (bldg. materials, plastic prods., machinery, coke prods.). Coal mines are in the area. Allegheny Co. Airport to NW. Seat of Community Col. of Allegheny Co.–South Campus to NW. Settled 1770, inc. 1903.

Clallam (KLA-luhm), county (□ 2,676 sq mi/ 6,931 sq km; 1990 pop. 56,464), NW Wash.; ⊙ Port Angeles; 48°07′N 123°56′W. In the Olympic region. Bounded W by Pacific Ocean and N by Strait of Juan de Fuca, forms U.S.–Canada (B.C.) border. Drained by Elwha, Dungeness, Bogachiel, Calawah, and Sol Duc (Soleduck) rivers. Fish; timber; dairying; paper, pulp mills; resorts. Dungeness Natl. Wildlife Refuge in E; Dungeness and Sequim Bay state parks in E; Bogachiel State Park in W. Cape Flattery in NW tip of co. L. Crescent (Olympic Natl. Park) in N. Olympic Mts. rise in S. Includes part of Olympic Natl. Park in S, part of coastal sect. of Olympia Natl. Park in W, including L. Ozette. Makah, Ozette, and Quilleute (Quillayute) Indian reservations; Lower Elwha Indian reservation in N. Formed 1854.

Clallam Bay (KLA-luhm), uninc. town (1990 pop. 850), Clallam co., NW Wash., on Olympic Peninsula, 38 mi/ 61 km WNW of Port Angeles, on Clallam Bay, arm of Strait of Juan de Fuca. Halibut, herring, crabs, oysters. Olympic Mts. and Olympic Natl. Forest to S; L. Ozette, in coastal sect. of Olympic Natl. Park, and Ozette Indian Reservation to SW; Cape Flattery and Makah Indian Reservation to NW. Slip Point Lighthouse to NE.

Clam River, c.40 mi/64 km long, NW and central Mich., drains L. Cadillac in Wexford co; flows SE, through forest and farm region, to Muskegon R. in NW Clare co.; 44°15′N 85°14′W.

Clan Alpine Mountains, W central Nev., in Churchill co., E of Humboldt Sink. Highest peak is Mt. Augusta (9,966 ft/3,038 m), 45 mi/72 km E of Fallon.

Clancy, village (1990 pop. 100), Jefferson co., SW central Mont., on Prickly Pear Creek, at mouth of Clancy Creek, and 9 mi/14.5 km S of Helena. In silver-mining dist. Parts of Helena Natl. Forest to E and W. First called Prickly Pear, then Alahambra (a name now given to a nearby hot-spring resort).

Clandonald, village, E Alta., W Canada, 16 mi/26 km NNE of Vermilion; 53°35′N 110°43′W. Grain; livestock.

Clanton, town (1990 pop. 7,669), ⊙ Chilton co., central Ala., 38 mi/61 km NNW of Montgomery. In cotton and fruit area; apparel mfg, consumer goods, transportation equip., furniture. Small power dams are on nearby Coosa R. Inc. 1873.

Clapperton Island, S central Ont., central Canada, one of the Manitoulin Isls., in the North Channel of L. Huron, just N of Manitoulin Isl., 14 mi/23 km W of Little Current; 6 mi/10 km long, 3 mi/5 km wide; 46°02′N 82°13′W.

Clara Barton Historic Site, Glen Echo, Montgomery co., SW Md. Home (built 1890) of Clara Barton, founder of the Amer. Red Cross; natl. hq. of the organization 1897–1904. Also known as Barton House. Designated Jan. 12, 1965.

Clara City, town (1990 pop. 1,307), Chippewa co., SW Minn., 19 mi/31 km SW of Willmar, on Hawk Creek; 44°57′N 95°22′W. Grain, soybeans, sugar beets; hogs, sheep; mfg. (fertilizer, tool and die, cereal prods., machinery).

Clare (KLER), county (□ 575 sq mi/1,489 sq km; 1990 pop. 24,952), central Mich.; ⊙ Harrison; 43°59′N 84°50′W. Drained by Muskegon, Tobacco, and Cedar rivers. Cattle, hogs, sheep; forage crops; dairy prods.; wheat, oats, soybeans, potatoes, corn, beans. Some mfg. at Clare. Many lakes, especially in SW; resorts. Wilson State Park and Snowsnake Ski Area in center, and Mott Mt. Ski Area in S. Organized 1871.

Clare 1 (KLER), town (1990 pop. 161), Webster co., central Iowa, 10 mi/16 km NW of Fort Dodge; 42°35′N 94°20′W. Livestock; grain. **2** town (1990 pop. 3,021), Clare co., central Mich., on Tobacco R., and 15 mi/ 24 km N of Mt. Pleasant; 43°49′N 84°46′W. In agr. area. (dairy prods.; grain; livestock). Mfg. (steel, transportation equip., theatrical equip., machinery). Mott Mt. Ski Area to W. Inc. as village 1879, as city 1891.

Claremont 1 city (1990 pop. 32,503), Los Angeles co., S Calif., at the foot of the San Gabriel Mts.; 34°07′N 117°43′W. In a citrus farm area diminished by urban development; mainly residential. Mfg. (dairy prods., fabricated metal, glass and opthalmic goods, flavoring extract, electrical equip.). Education center, it is the seat of Claremont branches of Pomona Col., Claremont cols. (school extensions), Scripps, Harvey Mudd, Pitzer, and the Southern Calif. School of Theology. A large botanical garden is also here. Marshall Canyon Regional Park to N; Angeles Natl. Forest to N; Cucamonga Wilderness Area to NE. Inc. 1907. **2** city (1990 pop. 13,902), Sullivan co., SW N.H., 40 mi/64 km WNW of Concord; 43°22′N 72°20′W. Drained by Sugar R., bounded W by Connecticut R. (Vt. state line). Mfg.(footwear, apparel, brushes, consumer goods, bldg. materials, textiles, bldg. materials, machinery, paper, fabricated metal prods.); agr. (nursery crops, hay, corn, apples; cattle, poultry; timber). The oldest R.C. church in the state (begun 1823) is here, and in nearby West Claremont is Union Church, the state's oldest Episcopal church (begun 1773). A replica of a pre-Revolutionary fort complex is nearby in Charlestown. Two covered bridges in E. Seat of Claremont Technical Col. Green Mt. (2,005 ft/611 m) in NE. Inc. 1764.

Claremont, town (1991 pop. 2,154), St. Ann parish, N Jamaica, 8 mi/12.9 km S of St. Ann's Bay; 18°23′N 77°10′W. In agr. region (citrus fruit, corn, pimento, coffee; cattle). Former bauxite-mining town.

Claremont 1 town (1990 pop. 980), Catawba co., W central N.C., 11 mi/18 km E of Hickory; 35°42′N 81°09′W. Agr. area (grain, soybeans; poultry, livestock; dairying). Mfg. (electronic equip. and cables, foam rubber, wooden prods., furniture, paper prods., foods). **2** town (1990 pop. 135), Brown co., NE S.Dak., 27 mi/43 km NE of Aberdeen. **3** town (1990 pop. 358), Surry co., SE Va., on James R., 25 mi/40 km E of Petersburg; 37°13′N 76°58′W. Mfg. (lumber); agr. (peanuts, grain, melons; livestock). Claremont manor house, here, dates from mid–17th cent.

Claremont, village, S Ont., central Canada, in city of Pickering, suburb 24 mi/39 km NE of Toronto; 43°58′N 79°07′W. Dairying; fruit (apples) growing; cattle.

Claremont 1 village (1990 pop. 256), Richland co., SE Ill., 6 mi/9.7 km E of Olney; 38°43′N 87°58′W. In agr. area (grain and livestock); mfg. agr. machines. **2** village

(1990 pop. 530), Dodge co., SE Minn., 11 mi/18 km E of Owatonna, near Dodge Center Creek; 44°22'N 93°00'W. Corn, soybeans, peas; livestock, poultry; dairying; light mfg. Rice L. State Park to NW; South Branch Middle Fork Zumbo R. to N.

Claremore, city (1990 pop. 13,280), ⊙ Rogers co., NE Okla., 25 mi/40 km ENE of Tulsa; 36°18'N 95°37'W. RR junction. In cattle and agr. area; dairying; mfg. (machinery, tubing, fabricated metal prods., wood prods., dry docks/boat lifts, sinker bars, transportation equip., cheese; printing). Health resort, with mineral springs. Oil, gas wells; sandstone quarries, strip coal mines. Will Rogers b. nearby; lived 10 mi/16 km NNW; a memorial to him was dedicated in 1938. J. M. Davis Gun Mus. and Rogers State Col. (2-year) here. Settled in late 19th cent. on site of a Native Amer. town. Inc. as town 1896, as city 1908.

Clarence, city (1990 pop. 1,026), Shelby co., NE Mo., near North Fork of Salt R., 25 mi/40 km NNE of Moberly; 39°44'N 92°15'W. Corn, wheat, soybeans; cattle, hogs; mfg. (machinery). Founded 1857.

Clarence, town (1990 pop. 936), Cedar co., E Iowa, 9 mi/14.5 km NNE of Tipton; 41°53'N 91°03'W.

Clarence 1 (KLER-ens), village (1990 pop. 577), Natchitoches parish, NW central La., 5 mi/8 km NE of Natchitoches, on Red R. Clear L.; 31°49'N 93°02'W. State Wildlife Area to NE. Kisatchie Natl. Forest to E. Agr. (cotton, rice, sorghum, soybeans; cattle, poultry); catfish, crawfish. **2** village (1990 pop. 2,100), Erie co., W N.Y., 15 mi/24 km ENE of Buffalo; 43°01'N 38°78'W. Mfg. (machinery, medical equip., precision small parts).

Clarence, Cape, NE extremity of Somerset Isl., E Franklin dist., N.W.T., N Canada, on Lancaster Sound, at N end of Prince Regent Inlet; 73°52'N 90°08'W.

Clarence Center, village (□ 2 sq mi/5.2 sq km; 1990 pop. 1,376), Erie Co., W N.Y., 12 mi/19 km NE of Buffalo; 43°00'N 78°37'W. Mfg. (machinery).

Clarence Head, cape, SE Ellesmere Isl., NE Franklin dist., N.W.T., N Canada, on Baffin Bay; 76°50'N 77°45'W.

Clarence King, Mount, Calif.: see KING, MOUNT CLARENCE.

Clarence, Port, bay of Bering Strait, W Alaska, in W Seward Peninsula; 15 mi/24 km long, 12 mi/19 km wide; 65°15'N 166°49'W. Teller village on E shore. SW side of bay protected by narrow spit of land. Ice-free June–Oct.

Clarence Strait, SE Alaska, in Alexander Archipelago, E of Prince of Wales Isl., extends 125 mi/201 km NW from Dixon Entrance to Summer Strait.

Clarence Town, town, S central Bahama Isls., on S Long Isl., 210 mi/338 km SE of Nassau; 23°07'N 74°59'W. Livestock (goats, pigs, sheep); sisal.

Clarenceville, village, S Que., E Canada, near Richelieu R., 14 mi/23 km WSW of Bedford. Dairying; pig raising.

Clarenceville, village, Oakland co., SE Mich., a NW suburb of Detroit, 3 mi/4.8 km ESE of Farmington, on the R. Rouge; 42°26'N 83°20'W. Now part of city of Farmington Hills.

Clarendon, parish (1991 pop. 211,447), Middlesex co., Jamaica; ⊙ May Pen; 17°44'N 77°09'W–18°12'N 77°29'W. Bounded on N by St. Ann, W by Manchester, E by St. Catherine parishes, S by the Caribbean Sea. RR through May Pen to Chapelton facilitates connection with Frankfield area. Rio Minho Valley area is famous for production of cedar, mahoe, mahogany and giant cotton trees. Mocho Mts. rise 2,000 ft/610 m, while farther N Bull Head Mt. rises 3,600 ft/1,097 m. The Clarendon Works and Alcoa Minerals, Inc. est. 1963 at Woodside because of the extensive bauxite and copper deposits. Famous Milk River Spa noted for its high therapeutic value is at Round Hill near Vere. Airstrip at Vernamfield was 1st Jamaican car-racing track. Sugar works at Kellits. Denbigh is famous for annual Natl. Agr. Show. Historic ruins at the Rock R. Dam site. Portland Point Lighthouse, a landmark on the summit of Portland Ridge at 17°44'N 77°10'W. Agr. (cotton, indigo, sugar, bananas, coffee, cocoa, tobacco); dairy farming; fish farming. Significant bauxite exports.

Clarendon (KLA-ruhn-duhn), county (□ 695 sq mi/1,800 sq km; 1990 pop. 28,450), E central S.C.; ⊙ Manning; 33°39'N 80°13'W. Bounded S by L. Marion; drained by Black and Pocotaligo rivers. Mfg. of sand, clay, gravel. Agr. area for chickens, eggs, cattle, corn, wheat, rye, tobacco, soybeans, hay, cotton, timber.

Clarendon 1 town (1990 pop. 2,072), ⊙ Monroe co., E central Ark., c.55 mi/89 km E of Little Rock, at junction of Cache and White rivers; 34°42'N 91°18'W. In rich agr. (cotton, soy beans, rice) area; timber; mfg. (transport containers for dairy and bakery industry, shoes, lumber). Dagmar Wildlife Management Area to N. Settled c.1819. **2** town (1990 pop. 2,067), ⊙ Donley co., extreme N Texas, in the Panhandle, 40 mi/64 km S of Pampa; 34°56'N 100°53'W. Elev. 2,727 ft/831 m. Commercial, processing, and shipping center for cattle; peanuts, sorghum, wheat, and cotton region. Greenbelt Reservoir (Salt Fork of the Red R.) to N, also to N, in Gray co., is McClellan Creek Natl. Grassland. Founded 1878, moved to present site on RR 1887. Inc. 1901. **3** town (1990 pop. 2,835), Rutland co., W central Vt., on Otter Creek, just S of Rutland; 43°31'N 72°58'W. Mineral springs are here.

Clarendon, borough (1990 pop. 650), Warren co., NW Pa., 5 mi/8 km SE of Warren; 41°46'N 79°05'W. Oil and natural gas. Mfg. (plastic prods., steel drums, light bulbs, boilers). Agr. includes livestock. Surrounded by Allegheny Natl. Forest. Chapman State Park to SW.

Clarendon Hills, village (1990 pop. 6,994), Du Page co., NE Ill., suburb 17 mi/27 km WSW of downtown Chicago, and 17 mi/27 km E of Aurora; 41°47'N 87°57'W. Some remnant agr., mainly corn. Inc. 1924.

Clarendon River, c.15 mi/24 km long, W Vt.; rises near Tinmouth; flows N to Castleton R. W of Rutland.

Clarenville, town (1986 pop. 2,967), in long picturesque arm on W side Trinity Bay, N.F., E Canada; 48°09'N 53°58'W. Amalgamation of several smaller communities settled in 19th cent. RR and transportation center of Bonarista region. Shipbuilding, asphalt and creosote mfg.; agr.; tourism.

Claresholm (KLERZ-hom), town (1991 pop. 3,297), S Alta., W Canada, 75 mi/121 km SSE of Calgary; 50°02'N 113°35'W. Dairying; barley, wheat, oats; cattle; cereal-foods mfg. Some logging to W.

Claridge (KLER-rij), uninc. town (1990 pop. 1,200), Penn township, Westmoreland co., SW Pa., 3 mi/4.8 km N of Jeanette, on Bushy Run; 40°21'N 79°37'W. Corn, hay; livestock; dairying. Bushy Run Battlefield Historic Site to S.

Clarinda, city (1990 pop. 5,104), ⊙ Page co., SW Iowa, on Nodaway R., and 17 mi/27 km E of Shenandoah; 40°44'N 95°02'W. Mfg. (printing; fabricated metal prods., bldg. materials, transportation equip.). Bituminous coal mines nearby. Seat of Iowa Western Community Col. and Clarinda Treatment Center (for mentally handicapped). Extensive flooding in area in 1993. Inc. 1866.

Clarington, village (1990 pop. 406), Monroe co., E Ohio, on the Ohio R., and 18 mi/29 km SSW of Woodsfield; 39°46'N 80°52'W. In agr. area.

Clarion (KLER-ee-uhn), county (□ 608 sq mi/1,575 sq km), W central Pa.; ⊙ Clarion; 41°11'N 79°25'W. Coal-mining plateau area, drained by Clarion R.; bounded SW by Allegheny R., S by Red Bank Creek. Settled after 1800 by Scotch-Irish. Growth due to iron, lumber, and oil industries in 19th cent. Bituminous coal; some mfg. at Clarion; clay, gas, oil; timber. Agr. (corn, wheat, oats, barley, hay, alfalfa, potatoes, apples; sheep, hogs, cattle; dairying). Part of Cook Forest State Park in NE. Formed 1839.

Clarion, city (1990 pop. 2,703), ⊙ Wright co., N central Iowa, 28 mi/45 km NE of Fort Dodge; 42°43'N 93°43'W. RR junction; livestock-shipping point. Mfg. (machinery, consumer goods). Hog farming. Has 4-H Historical Mus. and L. Cornelia State Park and Elm L. to NE. Inc. 1881.

Clarion (KLER-ee-uhn), borough (1990 pop. 6,457), ⊙ Clarion co., W central Pa., 60 mi/97 km NE of Pittsburgh, on Clarion R.; 41°12'N 79°22'W. RR terminus. In natural gas, bituminous coal, clay area. Mfg. (printing and publishing; lumber, bldg. materials, glass prods., metal prods.); surface bituminous coal mining; agr. (potatoes, corn, hay; livestock; dairying). Seat of Clarion Univ. of Pa. Clarion Co. Airport to W. Cook Forest State Park to NE. Laid out 1840, inc. 1841.

Clarion Island, Mexico: see REVILLAGIGEDO ISLANDS.

Clarion River (KLER-ee-uhn), c.110 mi/177 km long, W central Pa.; formed at Johnsonburg by confluence of East and West branches; flows generally SW, past Ridgway and Clarion, to Allegheny R. 5 mi/8 km S of Emlenton; 41°29'N 78°40'W. East Branch rises in S McKean co., 8 mi/12.9 km ESE of Mount Jewett, flows c.20 mi/32 km SW through East Branch L. reservoir (Elk State Forest) and Bradingo State Park. West Branch rises in S McKean co. at Mount Jewett, flows c.20 mi/32 km S past Wilcox.

Clarissa (KLA-ris-suh), village (1990 pop. 637), Todd co., central Minn., 12 mi/19 km NNW of Long Prairie, on Eagle Creek; 46°07'N 94°57'W. Grain, beans, potatoes; livestock, poultry; dairying. Light mfg. (consumer goods).

Clark 1 county (□ 882 sq mi/2,284 sq km; 1990 pop. 21,437), S central Ark.; ⊙ Arkadelphia; 34°02'N 93°10'W. Little Missouri R. forms S border, Antoine R. forms most of W border. Drained by Ouachita (forms parts of E border), Caddo R., and Terre Noire Creek. Agr. (soybeans; cattle, hogs); timber. Mfg. at Arkadelphia. Large DeGray L. (Caddo R.) and DeGray L. State Park in N. Formed 1823. **2** county (□ 1,765 sq mi/4,571 sq km; 1990 pop. 762), E Idaho, on Mont. (N) border; ⊙ Dubois; 44°17'N 112°23'W. Mt. area on Continental Divide. Drained by Camas, Medicino Lodge and Birch creeks, all flow into Snake R. Plain Aquifer S of co. Livestock (sheep, horses, cattle), agr. (potatoes, wheat, alfalfa, hay); lumber. Deposits of gold, iron, and silver mines. U.S. Sheep Experimental Station in E center. Part of Targhee Natl. Forest in W and N center, small part of Salmon Natl. Forest in SW corner; Lidy Hot Springs in S center; Sheridan Reservoir in NE. Formed 1919. **3** county (□ 504 sq mi/1,305 sq km; 1990 pop. 15,921), E Ill.; ⊙ Marshall; 39°19'N 87°47'W. Bounded SE by Wabash R.; drained by North Fork Embarras R. and Mill Creek. Agr. (corn, wheat, soybeans; cattle, hogs). Mfg. of paper prods., machinery, electronic equip. Formed 1819. Lincoln Trail State Park here. On historic Natl. Road. **4** county (□ 376 sq mi/974 sq km; 1990 pop. 87,777), SE Ind.; ⊙ Jeffersonville; part of Louisville metropolitan area (also referred to as Falls City Area); 38°29'N 85°43'W. Bounded SE by Ohio R. (here forming Ky. state line); drained by Silver Creek and other small tributaries of the Ohio. Agr. (soybeans, corn, tobacco; hogs, cattle). Mfg. at Charlestown and at Jeffersonville (river port). Part of Clark State Forest in NW. Formed 1801. **5** county (□ 977 sq mi/2,530 sq km; 1990 pop. 2,418), SW Kansas; ⊙ Ashland; 37°14'N 99°49'W. Located in Red Hills region, bordered S by Okla.; drained (S) by Cimarron R. and Bluff Creek. Grain, wheat, sorghum, alfalfa; cattle. Clark State Fishing L. in N; St Jacobs Well and Big Basin in W. Formed 1885. **6** county (□ 255 sq mi/660 sq km; 1990 pop. 29,496), central Ky.; ⊙ Winchester; 37°58'N 84°09'W. Bounded S by Kentucky R.; drained by Stoner Creek. Gently rolling agr. area, in Bluegrass region (burley tobacco, hay, alfalfa, soybeans, wheat, corn; hogs, cattle; dairying); limestone quaries. Mfg. at Winchester. Fort Boonesborough and Boone's Station state parks in SW. Formed 1792. **7** county (□ 509 sq mi/1318 sq km; 1990 pop. 7,547), extreme NE Mo.; ⊙ Kahoka; 40°24'N 91°44'W. Bounded E by Mississippi and Des Moines rivers; drained by Fox and Wyaconda rivers. Soybeans, corn; sheep, cattle, hogs. Flooding in 1993 heavily damaged E parts. Battle of Athens state park in N. Formed 1836. **8** county (□ 8,091 sq mi/20,956 sq km; 1990 pop. 741,459), SE Nev.; ⊙ Las Vegas; 36°12'N 115°01'W. Mining and livestock-grazing area bordering on Ariz. (E) and Calif. (SW). Colorado R. forms Ariz. state line except in NE. Drained by Virgin R. in NE. Magnesium deposits; sand and gravel, lime, gypsum, silicon sand; some dairying; cattle; vegetables. Gambling and entertainment at center of co.'s economy. For 30 years among fastest growing cos. in U.S. Sheep Range in N. Highland Range central bighorn habitat area in S; Moapa R. Indian Reservation and Valley of Fire State Park in NE; part of Toiyabe Natl. Forest, including Spring Mts. and Mt. Charleston, in W; part of Desert Natl. Wildlife Range in NW, overlaps large tract of Nellis Air Force Bombing and Gunnery Range; Indian Springs Air Force Base in NW; Nellis Air Force Base in E, at North Las Vegas. L. Mead, created by Hoover Dam, is in E; L. Mead Natl. Recreation Area surrounds lakes Mead and Mohavy (Davis Dam) as Ariz state line. Ariz. state line is also Pacific/Mountain time zone boundary. Lowest point in Nev. (469 ft/143 m) on Colorado R. at S tip of co. Formed 1909. **9** county (□ 402 sq mi/1,041 sq km; 1990 pop. 147,548), W central Ohio; ⊙ SPRINGFIELD; 39°55′N 83°46′W. Intersected by Mad and Little Miami rivers and by small Buck, Beaver, and Honey creeks. Includes George Rogers Clark Memorial Park. In the Till Plains physiographic region. Agr. (corn, soybeans; dairy prods.; livestock); mfg. at Springfield (textiles, plastics, metal prods., transportation equip.; commercial printing). Limestone quarrying; sand and gravel pits. Formed 1818. **10** county (□ 967 sq mi/2,505 sq km; 1990 pop. 4,403), E central S.Dak.; ⊙ Clark. Agr. area in the Côteau des Prairies ("Hill of the Prairies"), an area of high ground bet. Minn. (NE) and James (W) rivers, sources of numerous small creeks. Dairy prods.; poultry, cattle, hogs; corn, wheat, rye, soybeans, oats, hay, potatoes. Formed 1873. **11** county (□ 656 sq mi/1,699 sq km; 1990 pop. 238,053), SW Wash.; ⊙ Vancouver; 45°46′N 122°30′W. Rolling hills sloping S to valley of Columbia R. Bordered on S and W by Columbia R., on N by Lewis R., forms L. Merwin reservoir in N and Yale L. in NE. Blueberries, raspberries, lettuce, potatoes, alfalfa, hay, barley, oats; dairying; poultry. Ridgefield Natl. Wildlife Refuge in W, on Columbia R. Small part of Gifford Pinchot Natl. Forest on E border. Nearby are Reed Isl. (SE), Battle Ground L. (center), and Paradise (NW) state parks. Formed 1844. **12** county (□ 1,219 sq mi/3,157 sq km; 1990 pop. 31,647), central Wis.; ⊙ Neillsville; 44°43′N 90°36′W. Drained by Black and S Fork Eau Claire rivers. Principally a dairying area. Dairying; cattle, hogs, sheep, poultry; barley, oats, corn, alfalfa, hay, cranberries; cheese is chief product. Also lumbering; vegetable canning. Bruce Mound Ski Area in SW. Formed 1853.

Clark, city (1990 pop. 257), Randolph co., N central Mo., 10 mi/16 km SSE of Moberly; 39°16′N 92°20′W. Lumber. Amish area to E.

Clark, town (1990 pop. 1,292), ⊙ Clark co., E central S.Dak., 30 mi/48 km W of Watertown. Trade center for grain and cattle area; dairy prods.; potatoes and potato processing; poultry. Founded 1882.

Clark, borough (1990 pop. 610), Mercer co., Pa., 5 mi/8 km NE of Sharon, on Shenango R. L. reservoir (bridged); 41°17′N 80°24′W. Corn, hay, potatoes; livestock; dairying.

Clark, township (1990 pop. 14,629), Union co., NE N.J., 3 mi/4.8 km W of Linden; 40°37′N 74°18′W. Mfg. (machinery, metal prods., consumer prods., bldg. materials, chemical prods., gypsum board). Inc. 1864.

Clark Canyon Reservoir, Beaverhead co., extreme SW Mont., where Red Rock R. and Medicine Lodge Creek meet to form Beaverhead R., 19 mi/31 km SSW of Dillon; 5 mi/8 km long; 45°00′N 112°25′W. Max. capacity 329,000 acre-ft. Formed by Clark Canyon Dam (125 ft/38 m high), built (1964) by the Bureau of Reclamation for irrigation and flood control. Cattail Marsh Nature Trail; campgrounds. Lewis and Clark Memorial at N end.

Clark Fork, village (1990 pop. 448), Bonner co., N Idaho, 35 mi/56 km S of Bonners Ferry, 1 mi/1.6 km upstream (E) of Pend Oreille, and on Clark Fork R; 48°09′N 116°11′W. Elev. 2,100 ft/640 m. Center of agr.; lumber area. Cabinet Mts. Wilderness Area (Mont.) to E; Kaniksu Natl. Forest to NE; Coeur d'Alene Natl. Forest to SE; Cabinet Gorge Dam to SE.

Clark Fork, river, c.360 mi/579 km long, in Mont. and Idaho, part of Columbia R. system; rises in SW Mont. as Silver Bow Creek with joining of Basin and Blacktail creeks near downtown Butte, Silver Bow co.; flows W then N; changes name in Deer Lodge co., 7 mi/11.3 km E of downtown Araconda; continues N past Deer Lodge, then NW past Missoula and Thompson Falls, through Noxon and Cabinet Gorge reservoirs, and enters panhandle region of N Idaho, where it flows 12 mi/19 km to E side of L. Pend Oreille at village of Clark Fork. Segments of the Clark Fork were known by different names in the past, prominently including the Missoula R. Principal tributaries are the Blackfoot (enters from E, 5 mi/8 km to E of Missoula), Bitterroot, and Flathead rivers. Sometimes defined to include Pend Oreille R., which flows out of NW corner of Pend Oreille L. to Columbia R. Total length of Pend Oreille R. and the Clark Fork is 479 mi/771 km; their drainage basins total □ 25,820 sq mi/66,874 sq km.

Clark, Fort, Texas: see BRACKETTVILLE.

Clark Island (□ c.¼sq mi/c.7/10sq km), Knox co., S Maine, just E of St. George, and 8 mi/12.9 km S of Thomaston. Bridge to mainland.

Clark, Lake, S Alaska, 140 mi/225 km WSW of Anchorage, on W slope of Aleutian Range; 50 mi/80 km long, 1 mi/1.6 km–4 mi/6.4 km wide; 60°18′N 154°10′W. Nondalton village (S) and Tanalian Point (E) are game-fishing resorts.

Clark Mills, residential village (1990 pop. 1,303), Oneida co., central N.Y., on Oriskany Creek, 7 mi/11.3 km W of Utica; 43°04′N 75°22′W. Mfg. (apparel).

Clark, Mount (4,733 ft/1,443 m), W Mackenzie dist., N.W.T., N Canada, near Mackenzie R., 50 mi/80 km SE of Fort Norman; 64°25′N 124°11′W; highest peak of Franklin Mts.

Clarkdale, town (1990 pop. 2,144), Yavapai co., central Ariz., 28 mi/45 km NE of Prescott, and on Verde R; 34°45′N 112°03′W. Elev. 3,550 ft/1,082 m. Sheep, cattle; timber; mfg. (navigation systems). Tuzigoot Natl. Monument is to NE. Jerome State Historic Park to SW; Dead Horse Ranch State Park to SE; area surrounded by Prescott Natl. Forest.

Clarkdale, mill village, Cobb co., NW central Ga., 15 mi/24 km WNW of Atlanta; 33°49′N 84°38′W. Thread mfg.

Clarke 1 county (□ 1,252 sq mi/3,243 sq km; 1990 pop. 27,240), SW Ala.; ⊙ Grove Hill. Heavily forested area in Black Belt; bounded W by Tombigbee R., SE by Alabama R. Hay, corn; livestock; textile and lumber milling; crude oil and natural gas prods. Formed 1812. **2** county (□ 125 sq mi/324 sq km; 1990 pop. 87,594), NE central Ga.; ⊙ Athens; 33°57′N 83°22′W. Piedmont agr. (vegetables) area; cattle, hogs, poultry; dairying; textile mfg. Drained by Oconee R. Formed 1801. **3** county (□ 431 sq mi/1,116 sq km; 1990 pop. 8,287), S Iowa; ⊙ Osceola; 41°01′N 93°46′W. Rolling prairie agr. area (hogs, cattle, poultry; corn) with bituminous-coal deposits. Drained by Chariton and South rivers and Whitebreast Creek. Unit of Stephen State Forrest in SE. Formed 1846. **4** county (□ 693 sq mi/1,795 sq km; 1990 pop. 17,313), E Miss., on Ala.(E) state line; ⊙ Quitman; 32°02′N 88°41′W. Drained by Chickasawhay R. (formed in NW by joining of Chunky and Okatibbee creeks), also drained by Bucatunna Creek. Agr. (cotton, corn; cattle; timber). Clarke Co. State Park in N center; Bucatunna Wildlife Management Area in NE and E. Formed 1833. **5** county (□ 178 sq mi/461 sq km; 1990 pop. 12,101), N Va., in N Shenandoah Valley, on W.Va. (NE) state line; ⊙ Berryville; 39°07′N 78°00′W. Blue Ridge in SE; drained by Shenandoah R. and short Opequon Creek. Rich agr. area (apples, peaches, corn, wheat, barley, soybeans, hay, alfalfa); horse breeding is important. Appalachian Trail follows SE border; part of Sky Meadows State Park in S. State Arboretum of Va. in S. Formed 1836.

Clarkes Harbour, town (1991 pop. 1,076), SW N.S., E Canada, on W coast of Cape Sable Isl., 30 mi/48 km SW of Shelburne; 43°27′N 65°38′W. Fishing port. Also spelled Clark's Harbour.

Clarkesville, resort city (1990 pop. 1,151), ⊙ Habersham co., NE Ga., 11 mi/18 km WNW of Toccoa; 34°37′N 83°31′W. Mfg. includes clothing and textiles, transportation equip., toys; apple packing and shipping; sawmilling and printing. Also spelled Clarksville.

Clarkfield, town (1990 pop. 924), Yellow Medicine co., SW Minn., 13 mi/21 km W of Granite Falls; 44°47′N 95°48′W. Grain, soybeans, sugar beets; livestock; mfg. (apparel).

Clarks 1 village (1990 pop. 650), Caldwell parish, N La., 35 mi/56 km S of Monroe; 32°02′N 92°08′W. Timber. **2** village (1990 pop. 379), Merrick co., E central Nebr., 12 mi/19 km NE of Central City, and on Platte R; 41°13′N 97°50′W. Dairy and poultry prods.; livestock; grain; wood shavings. Mfg. (machinery, cedar and cottonwood). Mormon Trail State Wayside Area to S.

Clarks Fork (of Yellowstone R.), river, c.150 mi/241 km long, Mont. and Wyo.; rises in Beartooth Range, 4 mi/6 km NE of Cooke City and SW of Granite Peak, S Mont., in Gallatin Natl. Forest; flows SE into Shoshone Natl. Forest (Wyo.), thence NE back into Mont., past Bridger and Fromberg, to Yellowstone R. near Laurel.

Clarks Green, borough (1990 pop. 1,603), Lackawanna co., NE Pa., 6 mi/9.7 km NNW of Scranton; 41°30′N 75°42′W. Residential suburb.

Clarks Grove, village (1990 pop. 675), Freeborn co., S Minn., 9 mi/14.5 km N of Albert Lea; 43°45′N 93°19′W. Agr. area (poultry, cattle, hogs, sheep; corn, oats, alfalfa, soybeans; dairying); mfg. (concrete).

Clark's Harbour, N.S., Canada: see CLARKES HARBOUR.

Clarks Hill, town (1990 pop. 716), Tippecanoe co., W central Ind., 15 mi/24 km SE of Lafayette; 40°15′N 86°43′W. Agr. area.

Clarks Hill Dam, Ga. and S.C.: see J. STROM THURMOND LAKE.

Clarks Point, fishing village (1990 pop. 60), SW Alaska, on Nushagak Bay, inlet of Bristol Bay, 16 mi/26 km S of Dillingham; 58°51′N 158°31′W.

Clarks River, 8 mi/12.9 km long, W Ky.; formed in E McCracken co. by junction of East and West forks; flows N to Tennessee R. 4 mi/6.4 km SE of Paducah, 1 mi/1.6 km SE of Tennessee R. confluence with Ohio R. East Fork rises in NW Henry co., NW Tenn., flows c.60 mi/97 km N into Ky., past Murray and Benton, then NW to West Fork; West Fork rises in central Calloway co., SW Ky., flows 32 mi/51 km N.

Clarks Summit, borough (1990 pop. 5,433), Lackawanna co., NE Pa., 7 mi/11.3 km NNW of Scranton; 41°29′N 75°42′W. Mfg. (salt, furniture, machinery, rubber prods., concrete prods., fabricated metal prods., paper coatings; electroplating, printing and publishing). Agr. (vegetables; cattle; dairying). Lackawanna State Park to N; several small lakes and ponds in area, including Griffin Reservoir to E. Settled 1799, inc. 1911.

Clark's Town, town (1991 pop. 3,139), Trelawny parish, N Jamaica, 8 mi/12.9 km SE of Falmouth; 18°25′N 77°34′W. Sugarcane, ginger, pimento, fruit. Long Pond sugar estates and factory.

Clarksburg 1 city (1990 pop. 358), Moniteau co., central Mo., 6 mi/9.7 km W of California; 38°39′N 92°40′W. Soybeans, corn; cattle, poultry. **2** city (1990 pop. 18,059), ⊙ Harrison co., N W.Va., on the West Fork of the Monongahela R., at mouth of Elk Creek. Industrial and shipping center for an area of coal mines and oil and natural gas fields. Agr. (corn, nursery crops); cattle, poultry; dairying. Mfg. (glass prods., fabricated metal prods., graphite specialty items, welding equip., machinery, transportation equip., bldg. materials; printing and publishing). Salem-Teikyo Univ. is S. Watters Smith Memorial State Park to S; E terminus of N. Bend State Trail to W. Was an important Union supply base in the Civil War, and remains of Federal earthworks are preserved in Lowndes Hill park. Stonewall Jackson b. here; a plaque designates the site. FBI Fingerprint Identification Center to N. Inc. 1795.

Clarksburg, town (1990 pop. 1,745), Berkshire co., NW Mass., 22 mi/35 km NNE of Pittsfield, near Vt. state line; 42°43′N 73°07′W. Briggsville village is pop. center.

Clarksburg, village, S Ont., central Canada, near Georgian Bay, 23 mi/37 km E of Owen Sound; 44°43′N 80°27′W. Dairying; mixed farming.

Clarksburg 1 uninc. village, Yolo co., central Calif., on

Sacramento R., and 10 mi/16 km S of Sacramento. Sugar beets, corn, rice, beans; mfg. (beet sugar refining). Sacramento Deep Water Channel passes to W. **2** village (1990 pop. 523), Ross co., S Ohio, 15 mi/24 km NW of Chillicothe; 39°30′N 83°09′W. In agr. area.

Clarksdale, city (1990 pop. 19,717), ⊙ Coahoma co., NW Miss., 68 mi/109 km SSW of Memphis (Tenn.), on the Sunflower R.; 34°12′N 90°34′W. Processing and distributing center for agr. (cotton, corn, rice, soybeans; cattle), its main resource; mfg. (soybean prods., wire, prefabricated homes, paper prods., machinery, chemicals, wood prods., apparel, foods; printing and publishing). Major center for rhythm-and-blues music; the stackhouse repository for blues recordings on Delta and Rooster Blues labels. Archaeological Mus., Delta Blues Mus. Inc. 1882.

Clarksdale, town (1990 pop. 287), De Kalb co., NW Mo., 18 mi/29 km SSW of Maysville; 39°48′N 94°32′W. Feed supplements.

Clarkson 1 village (1990 pop. 611), Grayson Co., W central Ky., 25 mi/40 km WSW of Elizabethtown, and 4 mi/6.4 km ENE of Leitchfield; 37°29′N 86°13′W. Agr. area (burley, tobacco, grain; honey; livestock; dairying); mfg. (fertilizers, beekeeping supplies, fabricated metal prods.). **2** village (1990 pop. 699), Colfax co., E Nebr., 20 mi/32 km NNW of Schuyler, and on branch of Elkhorn R; 41°43′N 97°07′W. Feed, grain.

Clarkson Valley, city (1990 pop. 2,508), St. Louis co., E Mo., residential suburb 22 mi/35 km W of downtown St. Louis; 38°37′N 90°35′W. Babler State Park to NW; Rockwoods Reservation (nature reserve) to SW. Office complex in S part.

Clarkston 1 town (1990 pop. 5,385), DeKalb co., NW central Ga., 9 mi/14.5 km ENE of Atlanta; 33°49′N 84°14′W. Mfg. includes packaged foods, wood prods., vending machines; rubber processing. **2** town (1990 pop. 6,753), Asotin co., SE Wash., 22 mi/35 km S of Pullman, and on Snake R., opposite (2 mi/3.2 km W of) Lewiston (Idaho), and opposite mouth of Clearwater R. (from Idaho); 46°25′N 117°03′W. Wheat, barley, alfalfa; mfg. (lumber, furniture, fabricated structural metal). Chief Timothy State Park in W; Lower Granite L. reservoir (Snake R.) to NW. Inc. 1902.

Clarkston 1 village (1990 pop. 1,005), Oakland co., SE Mich., suburb 9 mi/14.5 km NW of Pontiac; 42°44′N 83°25′W. In farm and lake resort area. Mfg. (storage tanks, plastic molding). Pine Knob Ski Area to N. **2** village (1990 pop. 645), Cache co., N Utah, on Clarkston Creek, 17 mi/27 km NW of Logan, near Idaho state line; 41°55′N 112°02′W. Elev. 4,450 ft/1,356 m. Trading point for dairying and irrigated agr. area (wheat, alfalfa; cattle). Small part of Caribou Natl. Forest to NW.

Clarkston Creek, 20 mi/32 km long, rises in NW Cache co., N Utah, near Idaho state line; flows SE, past Clarkston, to Bear R. near Newton. Newton Dam and Reservoir (101 ft/31 m high, 3,360 ft/1,024 m long, including dike; completed 1946), on creek 3 mi/4.8 km N of Newton, is main unit in Newton irrigation project. Dam was built to replace structure constructed (1871) by Mormon pioneers.

Clarksville 1 city (1990 pop. 19,833), Clark co., S Ind., suburb 2 mi/3.2 km N of downtown Louisville (Ky.), and 2 mi/3.2 km W of Jeffersonville, on Ohio R. at mouth of Silver Creek; 38°19′N 85°46′W. Mfg. (asphalt, machine tools, printing cylinders). Founded 1783. **2** city (1990 pop. 480), Pike co., E Mo., on Mississippi R. and 16 mi/26 km E of Bowling Green; 39°22′N 90°54′W. Corn, soybeans; hogs; mfg. (hydraulic cement). Lock and Dam No. 24 on river. **3** city (1990 pop. 75,494), ⊙ Montgomery co., NW Tenn., on the Cumberland and Red rivers, 40 mi/64 km NW of Nashville; 36°21′N 87°21′W. In a farm, livestock, and tobacco region. Market and processing center for dark and burley tobacco. Cattle is also raised, meat is packed, zinc is processed. Other mfg. includes snuff, footwear, clothing, brake systems, and cooling and heating equip. Austin Peay State Univ. is here. Part of U.S. Fort Campbell is within the city limits. Dunbar Cave is to the NE. Platted 1784, inc. as a city 1855.

Clarksville 1 town (1990 pop. 5,833), ⊙ Johnson co., NW Ark., 23 mi/37 km NW of Russellville, near Arkansas R. (L. Dardanelle); 35°27′N 93°28′W. In agr. area (cotton, fruit; livestock, poultry); lumber milling, coal mines. Mfg. (machinery, shoes, fabricated metal prods., hosiery, frozen foods, bricks, lumber; poultry processing). Major grocery distribution center. Ozark Natl. Forest in N. Seat of Univ. of the Ozarks. **2** town (1990 pop. 1,382), Butler co., N central Iowa, on Shell Rock R., 20 mi/32 km NW of Cedar Falls; 42°46′N 92°40′W. RR junction; feed; metal. Limestone quarries, sand and gravel pits nearby. Henry Woods State Park just S. Inc. 1874. **3** town (1990 pop. 232), Coos co., N N.H., 38 mi/61 km NNW of Berlin; 45°01′N 71°18′W. Bounded W and N by Connecticut R., which forms Vt. state line in SW corner and L. Francis (dam) in N. Logging; timber; hay; poultry, cattle; dairying. Clarksville Pond in center. Recreational area. **4** town (1990 pop. 4,311), ⊙ Red R. co., NE Texas, 30 mi/48 km E of Paris; 33°36′N 95°03′W. Elev. 442 ft/135 m. Agr. area (cotton, soybeans, wheat; cattle, hogs, poultry); lumber area; mfg. (aluminum doors, windows and skylights, boat trailers, clothing). Settled 1828, inc. 1837. **5** town (1990 pop. 1,243), Mecklenburg co., S Va., 20 mi/32 km ESE of South Boston, on Roanoke R. (Buggs Isl. L. reservoir; bridged); 36°37′N 78°34′W. Mfg. (textile finishing, machining, packaging; textiles, chocolate candies, wooden prods., lumber); agr. (tobacco, grain; livestock, poultry; dairying); tobacco market; timber. Occoneechee State Park to E.

Clarksville 1 village, Kootenai co., N Idaho, suburb 4 mi/6.4 km NW of Coeur d'Alene. **2** village (1990 pop. 360), Ionia co., S central Mich., 13 mi/21 km SW of Ionia; 42°50′N 85°14′W. In farm area; sawmill. RR junction to W. **3** village (1990 pop. 485), Clinton Co., SW Ohio, 7 mi/11 km SW of Wilmington; 39°24′N 83°59′W.

Clarksville, borough (1990 pop. 211), Greene co., SW Pa., 9 mi/14.5 km WSW of Brownsville, on Tenmile Creek, at mouth of South Fork Tenmile Creek; 39°58′N 80°02′W. Livestock, dairying.

Clarksville, Ga.: see CLARKESVILLE.

Clarkton, city (1990 pop. 1,113), Dunklin co., in the bootheel of extreme SE Mo., in Mississippi alluvial plain and 16 mi/26 km NNE of Kennett; 36°27′N 89°58′W. Cotton, rice, soybeans.

Clarkton, town (1990 pop. 739), Bladen co., S N.C., 23 mi/37 km SE of Lumberton; 34°29′N 78°39′W. Cotton, peanuts, tobacco, grain, poultry, livestock. Settled c.1760. Mfg. (yarn).

Clason Point, residential sect. of S Bronx borough of N.Y. city, SE N.Y., at mouth of Bronx R. on East R.; 40°58′N 73°52′W. Sometimes called Clason's Point.

Clatonia (kluh-TO-nee-uh), village (1990 pop. 296), Gage co., SE Nebr., 16 mi/26 km NNW of Beatrice, near Big Blue R; 40°27′N 96°50′W.

Clatskanie (klat-SKAI-nee), town (1990 pop. 1,629), Columbia co., NW Oregon, 30 mi/48 km E of Astoria and on Clatskanie R., 3 mi/4.8 km S of its confluence with the Columbia R.; 46°06′N 123°12′W. Clatsop State Forest to W.

Clatsop (KLAT-suhp), county (□ 1,084 sq mi/2,808 sq km; 1990 pop. 33,301), NW Oregon; ⊙ Astoria; 46°00′N 123°42′W. NW extremity of state, bounded N by Columbia R. (forms Wash. state boundary) and W by Pacific Ocean; drained by Nehalem R. Bridge from Astoria to Wash. state (4 mi/6.4 km long). Fur farms. Poultry, sheep, cattle. Fishing. Wineries. Coast Range to E. Ecola and Hug Point State Parks and Tolovona Beach State Wayside in SW. Fort Clatsop Natl. Memorial, Fort Stevens State Park and Del Rey Beach State Wayside in NW. Bradley State Wayside in NE. Saddle Mt. State Park at center. Lewis and Clark Natl. Wildlife Refuge on marshy isls. in Columbia R. in NE. Camp Rilea Military Reservation in NW. Parts of Clatsop State Forest in E and NE; parts of Tillamook State Forest in S and SE. Formed 1844.

Clatsop Spit (KLAT-suhp), Clatsop co., NW Oregon, narrow arm of land at mouth of Columbia R., at extreme NW corner of Oregon, in Fort Stevens State Park. Extends 2.5 mi/4 km N, separates estuary (E) from Pacific Ocean (W).

Claude, town (1990 pop. 1,199), ⊙ Armstrong co., extreme N Texas, in the Panhandle, 25 mi/40 km ESE of Amarillo; 35°06′N 101°21′W. Elev. 3,397 ft/1,035 m. Trade, shipping center for (cattle; wheat, cotton, hay) area. Has semi-annual stock shows. Co. mus.

Claverack, village (1990 pop. 1,000), Columbia co., SE N.Y., 3 mi/4.8 km SE of Hudson; 42°13′N 73°40′W. Fine old bldgs. include Van Rensselaer manor house; former co. courthouse (built 1786).

Clawson, city (1990 pop. 13,874), Oakland co., SE Mich., a residential suburb 15 mi/24 km NNW of downtown Detroit and 8 mi/12.9 km SE of Pontiac; 42°32′N 83°09′W. Mfg. (automated mfg. systems, industrial controls). Oakland Troy Airport to W. Settled c.1833, inc. 1920.

Clawson, village (1990 pop. 151), Emery co., central Utah, 7 mi/11.3 km SSW of Castle Dale; 39°07′N 111°05′W. Cattle, alfalfa; coal mining in area. Manti-La Sal Natl. Forest to W.

Claxton (KLAKS-tuhn), town (1990 pop. 2,464), Evans co., E central Ga., 20 mi/32 km SSW of Statesboro, near Canoochee R.; 32°10′N 81°55′W. Specialized food mfg.; concrete production, galvanized steel; lumber. Located in agr. cotton and tobacco area.

Claxton Bay, village, W Trinidad, Trinidad and Tobago, on the Gulf of Paria, 23 mi/37 km S of Port of Spain; 10°21′N 61°28′W. Petroleum refining.

Clay 1 county (□ 606 sq mi/1,570 sq km; 1990 pop. 13,252), E Ala.; ⊙ Ashland, 33°16′N 85°51′W. Mt. Cheaha (2,407 ft/734 m) in Talladega Mts. (W) is highest point in state. Part of Talladega Natl. Forest is in W and N. Hay, hogs, poultry, corn; textiles, lumber milling. Formed 1866. **2** county (□ 641 sq mi/1,660 sq km; 1990 pop. 18,107), extreme NE Ark.; ⊙ Piggott and Corning; 36°22′N 90°23′W. Bordered N and E (St. Francis R.) by Mo. line, by Current R. on part of W boundary; drained by Cache, Black, and Little Black rivers. Agr. (cotton, rice, wheat, soybeans, corn, sorghum, cattle, hogs). Mfg. at Piggott, Corning. Fish hatchery at Corning. Hardwood timber. Part of Dave Donaldson-Black R. Wildlife Management Area in SW. Crowley's Ridge intersects the co. Formed 1873. **3** county (□ 643 sq mi/1,665 sq km; 1990 pop. 105,986), NE Fla.; ⊙ Green Cove Springs, 29°58′N 81°51′W. Bounded E by St. Johns R.; contains many small lakes in SW. Stock raising, dairying, farming (corn, vegetables, peanuts), lumbering; clay pits. Formed 1858. **4** county (□ 224 sq mi/580 sq km; 1990 pop. 3,364), SW Ga.; ⊙ Fort Gaines, 31°37′N 84°59′W. Bounded W by Ala. line, formed here by Chattahoochee R. Coastal plain agr. known for cotton, corn, truck, peanuts, cattle, hogs. Formed 1854. **5** county (□ 469 sq mi/1,215 sq km; 1990 pop. 14,460), S central Ill.; ⊙ Louisville; 38°50′N 88°29′W. Agr. (wheat, soybeans, sorghum; cattle). Oil, natural-gas wells. Mfg. (apparel, lighting equip., auto parts, paints, plastic bottles). Drained by Little Wabash R. Formed 1824. **6** county (□ 364 sq mi/943 sq km; 1990 pop. 24,705), W Ind.; ⊙ Brazil; 39°24′N 87°07′W. Agr. area (livestock, grain), with bituminous-coal mining, clay pits; mfg. at Brazil. Drained by Eel R. and small Birch Creek. Formed 1825. **7** county (□ 572 sq mi/1,481 sq km; 1990 pop. 17,585), NW Iowa; ⊙ Spencer; 43°05′N 95°09′W. Rolling prairie agr. area (hogs, cattle, sheep, poultry; corn, oats, soybeans) drained by Little Sioux and Ocheyedan rivers. Mfg. at Spencer. NE part of Clay in Iowa lakes district (glacial origins) which includes Elk L., Round L., Trumbull L., Lost Island L. (on boundary of Palo Alto co.), Dan Greene Slough (lake). Flooding in area in 1993. Formed 1851. **8** county (□ 655 sq mi/1,696 sq km; 1990 pop. 9,158), N Kansas; ⊙ Clay Center; 39°21′N 97°10′W. Rolling to hilly agr. region, drained by Republican R. Wheat, sorghum, cattle, hogs, sheep, poultry, corn, soybeans. Formed 1866. **9** county (□ 471 sq mi/1,220 sq km; 1990 pop. 21,746), SE Ky.; ⊙ Manchester; 37°09′N 83°42′W. In Cumberland foothills; drained by South Fork Kentucky R. and its headstreams, including Goose, Collins Fork, Red Bird, and Sexton creeks. Mt. agr. area (burley tobacco, corn, hay;

hogs, cattle). Bituminous coal mines; hardwood timber. Beech Creek Wildlife Management Area in E center; all but W end of co. is in Daniel Boone Natl. Forest. Formed 1806. **10** county (□ 1,052 sq mi/2,725 sq km; 1990 pop. 50,422), W Minn.; ⊙ Moorhead; 46°53′N 96°29′W. Bounded W by Red R. of the North (N.Dak. state boundary); drained by Buffalo R. and South Branch Wild Rice R. Agr. area (alfalfa, hay, oats, barley, soybeans, beans, sunflowers, wild rice, sugar beets; hogs, cattle, poultry; dairying). Buffalo R. State Park in center; Barnesville Wildlife Area in SE. Formed 1862. **11** county (□ 416 sq mi/1,077 sq km; 1990 pop. 21,120), E Miss.; ⊙ West Point; 33°38′N 88°46′W. Tombigbee R. forms E boundary (Tennessee-Tombigbee Waterway; Columbus L. reservoir in SE corner); drained by Line Creek (forms part of S boundary) and Chookatonchee Creek. Agr. (cotton, soybeans, corn, hay; cattle; dairying; timber). Formed 1871. **12** county (□ 413 sq mi/1070 sq km; 1990 pop. 153,411), W Mo., bounded S by Missouri R.; ⊙ Liberty; 39°19′N 94°24′W. Corn, soybeans, pumpkins and produce farming; cattle; mfg.; coal deposits, limestone. Immense underground mined-out space used for wholesaling and frozen-food storage. Part of Kansas City occupies SW quadrant; other major cities: Liberty, North Kansas City, Excelsior Springs (mfg. in all). Kansas City municipal airport in SW; Smithville Lake (reservoir) in NW; Watkins Mill in NE. Major theme park in S. Highly urbanized in S, rural in N. Formed 1822. **13** county (□ 573 sq mi/1,484 sq km; 1990 pop. 7,123), S Nebr.; ⊙ Clay Center; 40°32′N 98°03′W. Agr. area drained in SW by Little Blue R. Cattle, hogs, corn, wheat, sorghum, alfalfa, dairy prods. U.S. Meat Animal Research Center W of Clay center. Oregon Trail crosses SW corner. Formed 1871. **14** county (□ 220 sq mi/570 sq km; 1990 pop. 7,155), W N.C.; ⊙ Hayesville; 35°03′N 83°45′W. Mt. region; bounded S by Ga. state line and Chattahoochee Natl. Forest (Ga.), NE in part by Nantahala R.; drained by Hiwassee R. Most of co. in Nantahala Natl. Forest in E, N, and SW. Farming (corn, hay, apples, tobacco, cattle, chickens, some diarying), lumbering; resorts. Appalachian Trail crosses SE corner. Formed 1861. **15** county (□ 4,163 sq mi/10,782 sq km; 1990 pop. 13,186), SE S.Dak., on Nebr. state line; ⊙ Vermillion, 42°44′N 96°58′W. Agr. area drained by Vermillion R. and bounded S by Missouri R. (Nebr. state line). Corn, soybeans, hay; cattle, hogs; dairy prods.. Univ. of S.D. Clay co. State Rec. Area in S, on Missouri R. Formed 1862. **16** county (□ 264; 1990 pop. 7,238), N Tenn.; ⊙ Celina; 36°33′N 85°33′W. Bounded N by Ky.; drained by Obey and Cumberland rivers. Includes part of Dale Hollow Reservoir. Coal mining, lumbering, tobacco, grains, livestock raising. Formed 1870. **17** county (□ 1,116 sq mi/2,890 sq km; 1990 pop. 10,024), N Texas; ⊙ Henrietta; 33°47′N 98°12′W. Bounded N by Red R. (Okla. line); drained by Wichita and Little Wichita rivers. Livestock, agr., and oil and gas producing area: cattle; dairying; wheat, cotton, pecans, peaches; mesquite. Mfg. at Henrietta. L. Arrowhead (Little Witchita R.) reservoir and State Park on W boundary. Formed 1857. **18** county (□ 344 sq mi/891 sq km; 1990 pop. 9,983), central W.Va.; ⊙ Clay; 38°27′N 81°04′W. On Allegheny Plateau; drained by Elk R. Agr. (alfalfa, hay); cattle; timber; coal mines. Parts of B.J. Taylor and Wallback Wildlife Management Areas in N. Formed 1858.

Clay, town (1990 pop. 1,173), Webster co., W Ky., 21 mi/34 km WNW of Madisonville, near Slover Creek. Agr. (burley and dark tobacco, grain; hogs, cattle); mfg. (mine machine parts, coal processing, lumber); coal; timber.

Clay, village (1990 pop. 592), ⊙ Clay co., central W. Va., on Elk R., 32 mi/51 km ENE of Charleston. Agr. (alfalfa); cattle. Mfg. (lumber, metal fabricating). B.J. Taylor and Wallback Wildlife Management Areas to NW.

Clay Center, city (1990 pop. 4,613), ⊙ Clay co., N Kansas, on Republican R. and 30 mi/48 km NW of Manhattan; 39°22′N 97°07′W. Shipping center for agr. and dairying area; flour milling, meat packing, bottling. Mfg. (farm machinery, grain-handling equip., business forms, wood buildings). Laid out 1862, inc. 1875.

Clay Center, town (1990 pop. 825), ⊙ Clay co., S Nebr., 18 mi/29 km ESE of Hastings; 40°31′N 98°02′W. RR terminus. Small trade center; dairy prods., grain. U.S. Meat Animal Research Center to W.

Clay Center, village (1990 pop. 289), Ottawa co., N Ohio, 11 mi/18 km ESE of Toledo; 41°34′N 83°22′W.

Clay City 1 town (1990 pop. 929), Clay co., W Ind., near Eel R., 16 mi/26 km S of Brazil; 39°17′N 87°07′W. In agr. area; mfg. (hardwood, preserves, pottery); clay pits, bituminous coal mines. Settled 1873, inc. 1888. **2** town (1990 pop. 1,173), Powell co., E central Ky., on Red R. and 35 mi/56 km ESE of Lexington; 37°28′N 87°49′W. Agr. area (tobacco, corn; cattle); mfg. (typewriter and printer ribbons, cash registers, hardwood lumber, uniform shorts, archery supplies); oil wells, coal mines, oak timber. Ironworks formerly here. Red River Historical Mus. Pilot Knub State Nature Preserve to W.

Clay City, village (1990 pop. 929), Clay co., S central Ill., near Little Wabash R., 10 mi/16 km SE of Louisville; 38°41′N 88°20′W. Trade and shipping center; fruit, livestock, corn, wheat; oil, natural-gas wells. Settled in early 1830s; inc. 1869. Had oil boom in 1937.

Clay, Mount, N.H.: see PRESIDENTIAL RANGE.

Clayburn, rural village, SW B.C., Canada, in Fraser valley, immediately N of Abbotsford, and 4 mi/6 km SSE of Mission. Brick and tile making, clay quarrying, fruit-growing.

Claycomo (klai-KO-mo), town (1990 pop. 1,668), Clay co., W Mo., suburb 6 mi/9.7 km N of downtown Kansas City, near Mo. R.; 39°12′N 94°28′W. Mfg. (ornamental iron prods.). Town's name derived from the combination of Clay co., Mo.

Claymont, uninc. city (1990 pop. 9,800), New Castle co., NE Del., 6 mi/9.7 km NE of Wilmington on Delaware R., at mouth of Naaman Creek; 39°47′N 75°27′W. Mfg. (chemical preparations, steel foundry).

Clayoquot Sound, SW B.C., Canada, inlet of the Pacific extending c.60 sq mi/155 sq km along W central coast of Vancouver Isl., 50 mi/80 km W of Port Alberni; 49°10′N 126°09′W. Logging, fishing, tourism. Contains the isls. of Flores, Meares, and Vargas. Several arms extend inland: Sydney Inlet, Shelter Inlet, and Herbert Inlet (N), Calmus Passage and Bedwell Sound (E), and Fortune Channel and Tofino Inlet (S). Hot springs at Hot Springs Cave. Site of highly publicized encounters bet. loggers and environmentalists. Confrontation began in 1984 at Meares Isl., has involved sabotage of cutting operations and smashed car windows in Tofino.

Claypool 1 uninc. town (1990 pop. 1,942), Gila co., E central Ariz., 70 mi/113 km E of Phoenix and 3 mi/4.8 km WNW of Globe. Copper mining district; cattle, hay. RR terminus. Pinal Mts. to S; Tonto Natl. Forest to N, W, and S; San Carlos Indian Reservation to E. **2** town (1990 pop. 411), Kosciusko co., N Ind., 8 mi/12.9 km S of Warsaw; 41°08′N 85°53′W. In agr. area.

Claypool Hill, uninc. town, Tazewell co., SW Va., 15 mi/24 km WSW of Tazewell, near Clinch R.; 37°04′N 81°45′W. Agr. (livestock, dairying; tobacco, alfalfa); bituminous coal; timber. Part of Jefferson Natl. Forest to SE.

Claysburg, uninc. town (1990 pop. 1,399), Greenfield township, Blair co., central Pa., 15 mi/24 km S of Altoona, on Frankstown Branch Juniata Creek; 40°17′N 78°27′W. Mfg. (plastic prods., mobile homes, commercial printing, food). Agr. (corn, hay; livestock, dairying); Blue Knob State park to SW.

Claysville, borough (1990 pop. 962), Washington co., SW Pa., 9 mi/14.5 km WSW of Washington, on Dutch Fork Buffalo Creek; 40°07′N 80°24′W. Mfg. (food, conveyors and feeders, monument engraving). Agr. (apples, corn, hay; livestock, dairying). Dutch Fork L. reservoir to W.

Clayton 1 (KLAI-tuhn), county (□ 144 sq mi/373 sq km; 1990 pop. 182,052), NW central Ga.; ⊙ Jonesboro; 33°32′N 84°22′W. Drained by Flint R. Rapidly growing Atlanta suburban co. Location of Atlanta Hartsfield Internatl. airport largest employer in county. Formed 1858. **2** county (□ 792 sq mi/2,051 sq km; 1990 pop. 19,054), NE Iowa, bounded E by Mississippi R. (here forming Wis. line); ⊙ Elkader; 42°51′N 91°20′W. Dairying and agr. area (cattle, hogs, poultry; corn, hay), with rugged, wooded "Little Switzerland" dist. in N; drained by Turkey and Volga rivers. Limestone quarries, sand and gravel pits, lead and zinc deposits. Miss. R. Lock and Dam No. 10 at Guttenberg. Turkey R. Mounds State Preserve in SE; Pikes Peak and McGregor Heights State Parks in NE; Conservation Center on Volga R. near Osborne; Upper Miss. Natl. Wildlife Refuge. Formed 1837.

Clayton 1 city (1990 pop. 7317), Contra Costa co., W Calif., suburb 18 mi/29 km ENE of downtown Oakland and 4 mi/6.4 km SE of Concord. Mt. Diablo State Park to S; 37°57′N 121°56′W. Apples, walnuts, nursery stock. Mfg. (sand and gravel processing, crushed limestone). **2** city (1990 pop. 13,874), ⊙ St. Louis co., E Mo., 7 mi/11.3 km W of downtown; a suburb of St. Louis; 38°38′N 90°19′W. Considered a "downtown" of St. Louis area; high-rise office bldgs., hotels, shopping centers, result of building boom begun in 1960s to rival downtown St. Louis city. Several major firms are headquartered here; mfg. (printing, food prods., shoes). Washington Univ., Fontbonne Col., Concordia Seminary. Inc. 1919.

Clayton 1 town (1990 pop. 1,564), ⊙ Barbour co., SE Ala., 18 mi/29 km of Eufaula. Lumber, fiberboard, clothing mfg. Founded 1833. **2** town (1990 pop. 1,163), Kent co., central Del., 11 mi/18 km NNW of Dover, near Smyrna R.; 39°17′N 75°37′W. Agr. area. RR junction. Blackiston Wildlife Area to SW. **3** town (1990 pop. 1,613), ⊙ Rabun co., extreme NE Ga., 21 mi/34 km N of Toccoa, in Blue Ridge Mts. and Chattahoochee Natl. Forest; 34°53′N 83°24′W. Mfg. includes clothing and textiles. Resort. Inc. 1821. Machine shops. **4** town (1990 pop. 610), Hendricks co., central Ind., 6 mi/9.7 km S of Danville; 39°41′N 86°31′W. Fruit, grain. **5** town (1990 pop. 41), Clayton co., NE Iowa, on the Mississippi and 14 mi/23 km E of Elkader; 42°53′N 91°09′W. In hog and dairy area. **6** town (1990 pop. 917), Concordia parish, E central La., on Tensas R., 11 mi/18 km NNW of Vidalia; 31°43′N 91°33′W. In agr. area (rice, soybeans, sweet potatoes; cattle); catfish. **7** town (1990 pop. 2,484), ⊙ Union co., NE N.Mex., near Texas (SE) and Okla. (NE) state lines, 83 mi/134 km SE of Raton; 36°27′N 103°10′W. Elev. 5,050 ft/1,539 m. Trade and shipping center in grain, cattle, sheep, alfalfa, and sorghum region; Mfg. (agr. equip.). Laid out 1887, inc.1908. Clayton L. State Park to NW; Kiowa Natl. Grassland to E (becomes Rita Blanca Natl. Grassland in Texas/Okla). Rabbit Ear Mt. (6,062 ft/1,848 m) to N **8** town (1990 pop. 4,756), Johnston co., central N.C., 13 mi/21 km SE of Raleigh; timber; 35°38′N 78°27′W. Mfg. (electrical switches, machinery, folding cartons, sportswear, plastic insulation and tubing, intravenous nutrition prods.). Agr. area (tobacco, cotton, peanuts, grain, poultry, cattle, hogs). Atkinson's Mill, est. 1757, to E. Clemmons Educational State Forest to NW.

Clayton 1 village (1990 pop. 726), Adams co., W Ill., 25 mi/40 km ENE of Quincy; 40°01′N 90°57′W. Corn, wheat, soybeans, livestock. **2** village (1990 pop. 91), on Decatur-Norton co. line, NW Kansas, on Prairie Dog Creek and 15 mi/24 km SW of Norton; 39°44′N 100°10′W. Agr., cattle, grain. **3** village (1990 pop. 384), Lenawee co., SE Mich., 10 mi/16 km WSW of Adrian; 41°51′N 84°14′W. Lake Hudson State Recreation Area to S. **4** resort and recreational village (□ 2 sq mi/5.2 sq km; 1990 pop. 2,160), Jefferson co., N N.Y., on St. Lawrence R., in Thousand Isls. region, 20 mi/32 km NNW of Watertown; 44°14′N 76°05′W. Mfg. (snowplows, graphic-meter charts; boat repairing). N. Amer. freshwater craft at Antique Boat Mus., similar to one at Mystic, Conn.; Thousand Isls. Mus.; Clayton Historic Dist. Inc. 1872. **5** village (1990 pop. 713), Montgomery co., W Ohio, 11 mi/18 km NW of Dayton; 39°52′N 84°21′W. **6** village (1990 pop. 636), Pushmataha co., SE Okla., 34 mi/55 km SE of McAlester, and on Kiamichi R.; 34°35′N 95°21′W. In agr. and lumbering area; lumber milling; charcoal. Clayton L. State Park to SE (fishing); large Sardis L. to N; Kiamichi Mts. to E; Jack Fork Mts. to NW. **7** village (1990 pop. 450), Polk co., NW Wis., 23 mi/37 km SW of Rice L.; 45°19′N 92°10′W. In lake-resort and dairying area. Dairy prods.

Clayton, borough (1990 pop. 6,155), Gloucester co., SW N.J., 4 mi/6.4 km S of Glassboro; 39°39′N 75°04′W. Mfg. (bottles, water conditioning equip.; food containers); truck farming. Settled c.1775, inc. 1924.

Claytor Lake, Va.: see NEW RIVER.

Claytor Lake (□ 7 sq mi/18.1 sq km), Pulaski co., SW Va., on New R., 36 mi/58 km WSW of Roanoke; 37°05′N 80°35′W. Max. capacity 232,000 acre-ft. Formed by Claytor Dam (99 ft/30 m high), built (1939) for power generation.

Clayville 1 village (1990 pop. 463), Oneida co., central N.Y., 9 mi/14.5 km S of Utica; 42°59′N 75°15′W. Mfg. (metal powders, refrigeration and cold storage doors; inert-gas processing). **2** village, Scituate town, R.I.; 41°46′N 71°41′W.

Cle Elum (klee EL-uhm), city (1990 pop. 1,778), Kittitas co., central Wash., 22 mi/35 km NW of Ellensburg and on Yakima R.; mouth of Cle Elum R. 3 mi/4.8 km W; 47°11′N 120°56′W. Junction of RR spur to Roslyn and Ronald. Potatoes, fruit; sheep, cattle; dairying; timber; mfg. (lumber, ornamental metal work, transportation equip.). Cle Elum L. reservoir to NW; Wenatchee Natl. Forest to N and S; Easton and Iron Horse state parks to W. Founded 1885, inc. 1904.

Cle Elum Lake, reservoir (□ 8 sq mi/20.7 sq km), Kittitas co., central Wash., on Cle Elum, on E flank of Cascade Mts., 30 mi/48 km NW of Ellensburg; 47°25′N 121°07′W. Max. capacity 710,000 acre-ft. Formed by Cle Elum Dam (165 ft/60 m high), built (1933) by the Bureau of Reclamation for irrigation. Wenatchee Natl. Forest nearby.

Cle Elum River (klee EL-uhm), c.28 mi/45 km long, Chelan co., central Wash.; rises in Cascade Range, NW Chelan co.; flows generally S to Cle Elum L. (8 mi/12.9 km long; Cle Elum Dam, 160 ft/49 m high, at S end), thence SE, to Yakima R., 3 mi/4.8 km W of Cle Elum.

Clear, village (1990 pop. 504), central Alaska, 14 mi/23 km SW of Nenana, near Nenana R., on spur road from George Parks Highway (Rt. 3). Clear Air Force Station ballistic missile early warning station. Services at Anderson, 6 mi/9.7 km NW.

Clear Boggy Creek, c.125 mi/201 km long, SE Okla.; rises near Ada in Pontotoc co.; flows SE, receiving Muddy Boggy Creek in Choctaw co., to Red R. 8 mi/12.9 km SW of Hugo.

Clear Brook, uninc. village, Frederick co., N Va., 7 mi/11.3 km NNE of Winchester, near W.Va. state line; 39°15′N 78°05′W. Mfg. (limestone prods., wooden bldgs., flotation devices, abrasive coatings, steam boilers and irons); agr. (apples, grain; livestock, dairying).

Clear Creek, county (□ 396 sq mi/1,026 sq km; 1990 pop. 7,619), N central Colo.; ⊙ Georgetown; 39°41′N 105°38′W. Mining and sheep-grazing area; drained by Clear Creek. Gold, silver, lead, copper, zinc mines. Includes parts of Pike Natl. Forest in N, S, and W and Arapaho Natl. Forest in SW and Front Range. Mt. Evans State Wildlife Area in SE, bounded on W by Continental Divide. Popular winter and summer tourist area. Formed 1861.

Clear Creek 1 68 mi/109 km long, N central Colo.; rises in NW Clear Creek co., near Grays Peak, Front Range; flows E, past Idaho Springs and Golden, to South Platte R. N of Denver. **2** c.80 mi/129 km long, in N Wyo.; formed by its headstreams near Cloud Peak in Bighorn Mts., Johnson co.; flows NE, past Buffalo and Clearmont, to Powder R. Sheridan co., Wyo., near Mont. line, 22 mi/35 km NE of Clearmont.

Clear Creek Reservoir, Chaffee co., central Colo., on Clear Creek, in San Isabel Natl. Forest, 36 mi/58 km NNW of Salida; 2 mi/3.2 km long; 39°01′N 106°21′W. Max. capacity of 13,560 acre-ft. Formed by Clear Creek Dam (80 ft/24 m high), built (1970) by the City of Pueblo for irrigation.

Clear Fork of Brazos River, Texas: see BRAZOS RIVER.

Clear Lake, city (1990 pop. 8,183), Cerro Gordo co., N Iowa, 9 mi/14.5 km W of Mason City; 43°08′N 93°22′W.

On Clear L. (c. 5 mi/8 km long; state park, fish hatchery); popular summer resort; bakery and concrete prods. Sand and gravel pits (E). Inc. 1871.

Clear Lake 1 town (1990 pop. 272), Steuben co., extreme NE Ind., near Mich. and Ohio lines, on small Clear L.; 41°44′N 84°50′W. Resort area. **2** town (1990 pop. 1,247), ⊙ Deuel co., E S.Dak., 23 mi/37 km ESE of Watertown and on Hidewood Creek. Grain; dairy prods.; livestock; mfg. (medical equip.; signs). Cochrane State Rec. Area to SE. Annual co. fair. **3** uninc. town (1990 pop. 1,100), Skagit co., NW Wash., 5 mi/8 km NE of Mt. Vernon, on Clear L., near Skagit R. Dairying, cattle, berries, vegetables. Mfg. (metal plate work).

Clear Lake 1 village (1990 pop. 315), Sherburne co., central Minn., 12 mi/19 km SE of St. Cloud, near Mississippi R.; 45°27′N 94°00′W. Agr. area (grains; livestock; mfg. (meat processing, tool and die, industrial valves). **2** village (1990 pop. 932), Polk co., NW Wis., 31 mi/50 km NE of Hudson; 45°15′N 92°16′W. In dairying and stock-raising area; mfg. (vegetables, harvesting machines, cheeses, coatings).

Clear Lake (7 mi/11 km long, 3 mi/5 km wide), SW Man., Canada, at SE edge of Riding Mt. Natl. Park, 30 mi/48 km S of Dauphin. Drains W into Minnedosa R.

Clear Lake 1 (□ 65 sq mi/168 sq km), W Calif., in Lake co., Calif., 90 mi/145 km NW of San Francisco. Drained from SE by Cache R. It is the largest freshwater lake entirely within Calif. and is a fishing resort. Mt. Konocti rises nearly 3,000 ft/914 m on the W shore. Clear L. State Park on S shore. Towns of Lakesport on W side, Lucerne on E side. Residential communities of Clearlake Park, Clearlake Highlands and Clearwater Oaks at SE end. **2** natural lake in extreme NE Ind., Steuben co., near the Mich. and Ohio state lines. Glacially formed. Average depth is 107 ft/33 m.

Clear Lake, reservoir, Natchitoches parish, NW La., on Black Bayou, mostly in NW La. State Game and Fish Preserve, 8 mi/12.9 km NW of Natchitoches; c.14 mi/23 km long; 31°51′N 92°57′W. Joins Clear L. (SE) with Black L. (NW). Receives Black L. Bayou in NW; drains SE through outlet to Saline Bayou.

Clear Lake, Ont., Canada: see STONY LAKE.

Clear Lake City, locality, Harris and Galveston cos., SE Texas. Name used for general area of suburban Houston, c.25 mi/40 km SE of downtown Houston. Comprised of municipalities of Clear L. Shores, Kemah, Seabrook, El Lago, Taylor L. Village, Nassau Bay, Webster and extensions of cities of Houston, Pasedena, and League City. Bounded on E by Galveston Bay; traversed in center by Clear Creek, which forms Clear L. near its mouth. NASA Johnson Space Ctr. and Univ. of Houston–Clear L. City Campus are here.

Clear Lake Reservoir, Modoc co., NE Calif., formed by dam on Lost R., 35 mi/56 km SE of Klamath Falls, Oregon; c.10 mi/16 km long. Surrounded by Modoc Natl. Forest. Lake and shore areas protected by Clear L. Natl. Wildlife Refuge.

Clear Lake Shores, town (1990 pop. 1,096), Galveston co., SE Texas, residential suburb 12 mi/19 km NW of Texas City and 21 mi/34 km SE of Houston, on S shore of Clear L., near Galveston Bay. Located in area known as Clear Lake City.

Clear Spring, town (1990 pop. 415), Washington co., W Md., at E base of Bear Pond Mts., 12 mi/19 km W of Hagerstown; 39°40′N 77°56′W. In agr. area. Founded by Martin Meyers in 1821. Nearby are Fort Frederick State Park, Big Spring, Indian Spring, and Green Spring furnace.

Clearbrook, village (1990 pop. 650), Clearwater co., NW Minn., 12 mi/19 km N of Bagley; 47°41′N 95°25′W. Agr. (dairying, poultry, cattle, sheep, sunflowers, grain, alfalfa). Pine L. to W; Red Lake Indian Reservation to N.

Clearfield, county (□ 1,153 sq mi/2,986 sq km; 1990 pop. 78,097), central Pa.; ⊙ Clearfield; 41°00′N 78°28′W. Hilly upland, drained by West Branch of Susquehanna R. (forms Curwenville L. reservoir in center). Bituminous coal; mfg. at Clearfield and Du Bois; agr. (corn, some wheat, oats, barley, hay, alfalfa;

sheep, cattle, dairying); natural gas, sandstone; recreation. Parker Dam State Park in N; S.B. Elliott State Park in N center; parts of Moshannon State Forest in N. Formed 1804.

Clearfield, city (1990 pop. 21,435), Davis co., N Utah, suburb 10 mi/16 km SSW of Ogden, 21 mi/34 km NNW of Salt Lake City near Great Salt L.; 41°06′N 112°01′W. Hill Air Force Base to NE, Utah's largest employer with 17,000 employees. Diversified Mfg. At center of city is Freeport Center, Utah's largest industrial park, 89 businesses and 7,000 employees. Causeway to Antelope Island State Park to W. First settled in 1877, called Sandridgel; inc. 1922.

Clearfield 1 town (1990 pop. 417), on Taylor-Ringgold co. line, SW Iowa, 16 mi/26 km NE of Bedford; 40°47′N 94°28′W. Feed. **2** town (1990 pop. 1,250), Rowen co., NE Ky., residential suburb 2 mi/3.2 km S of Morehead. Area surrounded by Daniel Boone Natl. Forest.

Clearfield, borough (1990 pop. 6,633), ⊙ Clearfield co., central Pa., 35 mi/56 km N of Altoona, on West Branch of Susquehanna R., 2 mi/3.2 km W of mouth of Clearfield Creek; 41°01′N 78°26′W. Bituminous coal in area; clay. Mfg. (wood prods., electronic card connectors, concrete, iron castings, powdered metals, commercial printing, signs, sportswear). Clearfield-Lawrence Airport to NE. Laid out 1805, inc. 1840.

Clearlake, city (1990 pop. 11,804), Lake co., NW Calif., 35 mi/56 km N of Santa Rosa, at E end of Clear L. (Cache Creek), N of dam; 38°58′N 122°38′W. Residential area comprising communities of Clearlake Park and Clearlake Highlands. Mendocino Natl. Forest to N. Walnuts, grapes, pears, oats, cattle.

Clearlake Oaks, uninc. town (1990 pop. 2,419), Lake co., NW Calif., 39 mi/63 km N of Santa Rosa, 4 mi/6.4 km NW of Clearlake, on NE shore of Clear L. (Cache Creek); 39°01′N 122°40′W. Mendocino Natl. Forest to N. Residential community.

Clearmont, town (1990 pop. 175), Nodaway co., NW Mo., on Nodaway R. and 14 mi/23 km NW of Maryville; 40°30′N 95°01′W. Soybeans, grain; livestock.

Clearmont, village (1990 pop. 119), Sheridan co., N Wyo., on Clear Creek and 30 mi/48 km ESE of Sheridan; 44°38′N 106°22′W. Elev. 3,921 ft/1,195 m. In irrigated agr. region.

Clearview, village (1990 pop. 622), Ohio co., N W.Va., 6 mi/9.7 km N of Wheeling, on Ohio R.; 40°8′N 80°41′W. Livestock; dairying; grain. Wheeling Airport to E.

Clearwater 1 county (□ 2,488 sq mi/6,444 sq km; 1990 pop. 8,505), N Idaho; ⊙ Orofino; 46°40′N 115°40′W. Mt. area bounded on E by Bitterroot Range and state of Mont. Crossed by North Fork of Clearwater R; drained in SW corner by Clearwater R.; Lola Creek forms SW part of S boundary. Timber; stock raising (cattle); alfalfa; barley, wheat; silver, lead. Mont. state boundary forms boundary bet. Pacific (W) and Mountain (E) time zones. Clearwater Natl. and Clearwater Mts. extend over ½ of co. Dwurshak Dam, Reservoir, Fish Hatchery and State Park in W; Bald Mt. Ski Area and First Idaho Gold Discovery site at Pierce, in center of co.; part of Nez Perce Indian Reservation in SW. Formed 1911. **2** county (□ 1,029 sq mi/2,665 sq km; 1990 pop. 8,309), NW Minn.; ⊙ Bagley; 47°34′N 95°22′W. Bounded in NE corner by Lower Red L. reservoir; drained by Clearwater R. (center), Red Lake R. (N), Wild Rice R. and Mississippi R. (S). Agr. area (oats, wheat, barley, hay, alfalfa, potatoes, sunflowers; sheep, cattle, poultry; dairying); timber. Includes part of Red L. Indian Reservation in N, part of White Earth Indian Reservation in SW. Itasca State Park in SE corner includes L. Itasca, source of the Mississippi R.; parts of White Earth and Mississippi Headwaters state forests in S. Formed 1902.

Clearwater, residential and resort city (□ 37 sq mi/96 sq km; 1990 pop. 98,784), seat of Pinellas co., W central Fla., on the Pinellas peninsula, on Clearwater Bay and the Gulf of Mexico; 27°58′N 82°46′W. The city's pop. has expanded, particularly that of retired citizens. Its thriving tourist industry dates from 1896. A landscaped causeway connects the city proper with a 4-mi/6.4 km-long isl. of white sand beaches fronting on the Gulf. Clearwater was settled after the establishment of Fort Harrison in 1841. It is linked with Tampa by a causeway across Old Tampa Bay to the E. It is the seat of Clearwater Christian Col. and a junior col., and has an art center, a theater, and many recreational facilities. Inc. 1891.

Clearwater 1 town (1990 pop. 1,875), Sedgwick co., S Kansas, near Ninnescah R., 15 mi/24 km SW of Wichita; 37°30'N 97°30'W. In dairy and grain area. Oil wells in vicinity. Satellite Community of Wichita. **2** uninc. town (1990 pop. 4,731), Aiken co., SW S.C., residential suburb 5 mi/8 km ENE of Augusta, Ga., and 9 mi/14.5 km WSW of Aiken; 33°30'N 81°54'W. Mfg. of kaolin clay; agr. includes cotton, peanuts, grain, soybeans, livestock, poultry.

Clearwater 1 village (1990 pop. 597), Wright co., S central Minn., on Mississippi R. at mouth of Clearwater R., and 12 mi/19 km SSE of St. Cloud; 45°24'N 94°02'W. Grain; livestock, poultry; dairying; mfg. (plastic vacuum molding, feeds). Clearwater L. to SW, numerous small natural lakes to S. **2** village (1990 pop. 401), Antelope co., NE Nebr., 10 mi/16 km WNW of Neligh and on Elkhorn R; 42°10'N 98°11'W. Livestock, poultry, grain; edible beans, popcorn.

Clearwater, river, c.75 mi/121 km long, Idaho; formed by joining of South and Middle Forks at Kooskia, N Idaho co.; flows NW past Kaniah and Orofino, receives North Fork from NE, then flows W past Spalding to Snake R. at Lewinston. All but lower 5 mi/8 km within Nez Perce Indian Reservation. South Fork (c.65 mi/105 km long) rises in central Idaho co., N Idaho, flows W then N, joining Middle Forks at Kooskia to form Clearwater R. Middle Fork (c.25 mi/40 km long), formed at Lowell, N Idaho co., N Idaho, by joining of Selway and Lochsa rivers, flows W to join South Fork. North Fork rises in extreme SE Shoshone co., N Idaho, near Mont. border, flows SW into Clearwater co., then NW and again SW, passing through Dworshak Reservoir (54 mi/87 km long), impounded by Dworshak Dam only 5 mi/8 km NE of its confluence with Clearwater R. near Orofino. Dworshak Natl. Fish Hatchery near mouth. The gold-mining era in Idaho began in 1860, when gold was discovered and mining camps were set up on the river's South Fork.

Clearwater Lake, E B.C., Canada, in Cariboo Mts., in Wells Gray Provincial Park, 100 mi/161 km N of Kamloops; 16 mi/26 km long, 1 mi/2 km–2 mi/3 km wide; 52°15'N 120°13'W. Drains S into North Thompson R.

Clearwater Lake 1 central Minn., forms part of Wright-Stearns co. line, c.45 mi/72 km NW of Minneapolis; 5 mi/8 km long, 2.5 mi/4 km wide; 45°18'N 94°07'W. Fed and drained by small Clearwater R. Fishing resorts. **2** reservoir, mostly in Reynolds co. and on Wayne co. border, SE Mo., on Black R., 30 mi/48 km NW of Poplar Bluff; 8 mi/12.9 km long; 37°07'N 90°46'W. Max. capacity 413, 000 acre-ft. Logan Creek forms 3-mi/4.8-km NW arm. Formed by Clearwater Dam (154 ft/47 m high); built (1948) for flood control and recreation.

Clearwater Mountains, largely in Idaho co., N central Idaho, generally E of Grangeville. Bounded S and W by Salmon R., E by the Crags Mts. and Moose Ridge. Includes parts of Nez Perce and Clearwater natl. forests. Chief elevations (7,000 ft/2,134 m–8,000 ft/2,438 m) are in S near Salmon R; Pilot Knob (7,136 ft/2,175 m), Gospel Peak (8,135 ft/2,480 m). Gold, silver, lead, and copper are mined. Source of South Fork Clearwater R.

Clearwater River 1 230 mi/370 km long, NW Sask. and NE Alta., Canada; rises S of L. Athabaska in lat. 58°N; flows S, then W, crossing into Alta., to Athabaska R. at Fort McMurray. On its course are numerous rapids. Formerly an important link in the Churchill-Athabaska canoe route. **2** 130 mi/209 km long, W Alta., Canada; rises in Rocky Mts. S of Mt. Willingdon in Banff Natl. Park; flows in a winding course generally NE to North Saskatchewan R. at Rocky Mountain House.

Clearwater River 1 205 mi/330 km long, NW Minn.; rises W of Bagley, in Clearwater co.; flows E, past Bagley, NE through Clearwater L., and W past Plummer. Receives Poplar R. from SE, to Red Lake R. at town of Red Lake Falls. **2** 20 mi/32 km long, S central Minn.; rises in Clear L., in N Meeker co.; flows NNE, through Clearwater L., to Mississippi R. at Clearwater.

Cleaton (KLEET-uhn), uninc. village (1990 pop. 400), Muhlenberg co., W Ky., 3 mi/4.8 km SSE of Central City. Bituminous coal; agr. area (tobacco, grain; livestock).

Clebit (KLEB-it), village, McCurtain co., SE Okla., 32 mi/51 km NNW of Idabel, W of Battliest, in Ouachita Mts.

Cleburne 1 (KLEE-buhrn), county (□ 561 sq mi/1,453 sq km; 1990 pop. 12,730), E Ala.; ⊙ Heflin. Piedmont region crossed by Tallapoosa R., bordering on Ga. Part of Talladega Natl. Forest in W and N. Soybeans, corn, livestock (especially poultry); lumber milling. Formed 1866. **2** county (□ 591 sq mi/1,531 sq km; 1990 pop. 19,411), N central Ark.; ⊙ Heber Springs; 35°32'N 92°01'W. Drained by Little Red R. and its tributaries; situated in Ozark region. Cattle, chickens, lumber milling; limestone. Mfg. at Heber Springs. Part of large Greer Ferry L. in W part of co., Greers Ferry Dam and fish hatchery (on Little Rock R.) at center of co. Formed 1883.

Cleburne, city (1990 pop. 22,205), ⊙ Johnson co., 27 mi/43 km SSW of Fort Worth, N Texas; 32°21'N 97°24'W. Elev. 764 ft/233 m. It is a RR, processing, and medical center in a farming area (wheat, dairying; livestock). The city has large RR shops, cotton mills, limestone-processing plants, and mfg. (apparel). Hosts 2 annual rodeos. L. Pat Cleburne and Cleburne State Park to SW. Inc. 1907.

Cleghorn, town (1990 pop. 275), Cherokee co., NW Iowa, 9 mi/14.5 km WNW of Cherokee; 42°48'N 95°42'W.

Cleland Heights, uninc. town (1990 pop. 1,120), New Castle co., NE Del., residential suburb 3 mi/4.8 km SW of downtown Wilmington, near Christina R.; 39°44'N 75°34'W. New Castle County Airport to S.

Clementon, borough (1990 pop. 5,601), Camden co., SW N.J., 11 mi/18 km SE of Camden; 39°47'N 74°59'W. Makes concrete, plastic prods. Inc. 1925.

Clements, village (1990 pop. 191), Redwood co., SW Minn., 30 mi/48 km WNW of New Ulm; 44°22'N 95°02'W. Corn, oats, soybeans; livestock; mfg. (fertilizers, plastic molds).

Clementsport, village, NW N.S., Canada, on Annapolis Basin, 7 mi/11 km SW of Annapolis Royal. Fishing port; apple growing. First settled 1784 by United Empire Loyalists.

Clementsvale, village, NW N.S., Canada, 10 mi/16 km SSW of Annapolis Royal. Dairying, mixed farming; apples.

Clemmons, town (1990 pop. 6,020), Forsyth co., N central N.C., residential suburb 10 mi/16 km SW of downtown Winston-Salem, near Yadkin R; 36°01'N 80°23'W. Agr. area (tobacco, grain, cattle, dairying). Mfg. (cookies, furniture assembly, light mfg.). Tanglewood Park to SW.

Clemons, town (1990 pop. 173), Marshall co., central Iowa, 13 mi/21 km WNW of Marshalltown; 42°06'N 93°09'W. In agr. area.

Clemson, city (1990 pop. 11,096), Oconee and Pickens cos., NW S.C., 28 mi/45 km WSW of Greenville on Seneca R; 34°40'N 82°48'W. Mfg. includes drill chucks, sheets, twist drills, concrete in agr. area for dairying, poultry, hogs, corn. Location of Clemson Univ. After 1940, absorbed adjacent town of Calhoun.

Clendenin (klen-DEN-uhn), town (1990 pop. 1,203), Kanawha co., W central W. Va., on Elk R., 19 mi/31 km NE of Charleston; 38°29'N 81°20'W. Coal mines, oil and natural-gas wells. Agr. (corn, tobacco); cattle; poultry. Mfg. (lumber). Wallback Wildlife Management Area to NE. Inc. 1904.

Clendening Lake (klen-DE-ning), reservoir, Harrison co., E Ohio, on branch of Stillwater R., 9 mi/14.5 km SSE of Uhrichsville; c.9 mi/14.5 km long; 40°15'N 81°16'W. Max. capacity 54,000 acre-ft. Formed by Clendening Dam, built for flood control.

Cleo Springs, or **Cleo**, village (1990 pop. 359), Major co., NW Okla., 32 mi/51 km W of Enid, on Eagle Chief Creek near its confluence with Cimarron R.; 36°24'N 98°26'W. In grain and livestock area. Homesteaders Sod House Mus. to N.

Cleona (KLEE-o-nah), borough (1990 pop. 2,322), Lebanon co., SE central Pa., 3 mi/4.8 km W of Lebanon, on Quittapahilla Creek; 40°20'N 76°28'W. Light mfg. Agr. (grain; poultry, livestock, dairying).

Clèricy (klai-ree-SEE), village, W Que., E Canada, 12 mi/19 km NE of Rouyn-Noranda; 48°22'N 78°52'W. Gold mining.

Clermont (KLER-mahnt), county (□ 458 sq mi/1,186 sq km; 1990 pop. 150,187), SW Ohio; ⊙ Batavia, 39°03'N 84°09'W. Bounded SW by Ohio R. (here forming Ky. state line), NW by Little Miami R.; intersected by East Fork of Little Miami R. In the Till Plains physiographic region. Agr. (livestock, corn, soybeans, tobacco, fruit; dairy prods.); some diversified mfg. at Batavia, Bethel, Milford, New Richmond; nurseries. Formed 1800.

Clermont, city (□ 5 sq mi/13 sq km; 1990 pop. 6,910), Lake co., central Fla., 24 mi/39 km W of Orlando; 28°33'N 81°45'W. Citrus-fruit shipping point with cannery. Diatomite found nearby.

Clermont 1 (KLER-mahnt), town (1990 pop. 402), Hall co., NE central Ga., 12 mi/19 km NNE of Gainesville; 34°28'N 83°46'W. Mfg. of playground equip.; sawmilling. **2** town (1990 pop. 1,678), Marion co., central Ind.; 39°49'N 86°19'W. Laid out 1849. **3** town (1990 pop. 523), Fayette co., NE Iowa, on Turkey R., and 9 mi/14.5 km ENE of West Union; 43°00'N 91°39'W. Concrete; feeds; sand and gravel pits. Montauk Historic Governor's Home.

Clermont, village (1991 pop. 3,385), E Que., Canada, on Malbaie R. and 4 mi/6 km NW of La Malbaie; 47°41'N 70°14'W. Copper mining.

Clermont, uninc. village (1990 pop. 200), Bullitt co., NW Ky., 5 mi/8 km SSE of Shepherdsville. Mfg. (alcoholic beverages). Bernheim Arboretum and Research Forest to SE.

Clermont Harbor, village, Hancock co., SE Miss., 5 mi/8 km SW of Bay St. Louis, near Mississippi Sound. Beach resort area. Buccaneer State Park to NE.

Clevedale, village, Spartanburg co., NW S.C., 4 mi/6.4 km W of Spartanburg.

Cleveland 1 county (□ 598 sq mi/1,549 sq km; 1990 pop. 7,781), S central Ark.; ⊙ Rison; 33°53'N 92°11'W. Bounded W by Moro Bayou; intersected by Saline R. Agr. (cattle, hogs, chickens). Formed 1873. Mark Mills Battleground State Historic Monument in SW. **2** county (□ 468 sq mi/1,212 sq km; 1990 pop. 84,714), SW N.C.; ⊙ Shelby; 35°20'N 81°33'W. Bounded S by S.C.; drained by Broad and Fr. Broad rivers and its affluents. In Piedmont region; agr. area (cotton, corn, wheat, soybeans, hay, sorghum, chickens, turkeys, cattle, hogs, some dairying) region; timber. Mfg. at Shelby, Kings Mountain and Grover. Formed 1841. **3** county (□ 558 sq mi/1,445 sq km; 1990 pop. 174,253), central Okla.; ⊙ Norman; 35°12'N 97°19'W. Bounded SW by Canadian R.; drained by Little R. (forms L. Thunderbird reservoir). Part of Okla. City Metro Area, Okla. City has annexed N margin of co. Diversified agr. (alfalfa, fruit, melons, wheat; horses, cattle, dairying). Mfg. at Norman and Moore. Oil and natural-gas fields. Little River State Park on L. Thunderbird, in N at Norman. L. Stanley Draper reservoir in N (in Oklahoma City). Norman is seat of Univ. of Okla. Formed 1890.

Cleveland 1 city (1990 pop. 15,384), ⊙ Bolivar co. (seat shared with Rosedale), W Miss., 30 mi/48 km NE of Greenville; 33°44'N 90°43'W. Agr. (cotton, corn, rice, wheat, soybeans; cattle); mfg. (medical equip., ceramic tile, metal parts and prods., food and beverage processing, printing and publishing). Delta State Univ., including Wiley Planetarium and Mus. of Natural History. Inc. as city since 1930. **2** city (1990 pop. 505,616), ⊙ Cuyahoga co., NE Ohio, a port of entry on L. Erie at the mouth of the Cuyahoga R.; 41°28'N 81°40'W. Ohio's 2d largest city and the center of the state's largest metropolitan area, it is an ore port and a Great Lakes shipping point. In spite of a dramatic decline in mfg., Cleveland remains to some extent dependent on heavy

Cross references are shown in SMALL CAPITALS. The pronunciation key is on page xv. The dates of population figures are on page xii.

industry, including steel milling, machinery, engineered steel, automotive stampings, furnishings, engines, parts and accessories; guided missiles and space vehicles. There are numerous research firms; the Natl. Aeronautics and Space Administration has a large research center here, and the research laboratory hq. of the General Electric Co. is in nearby Nela Park. Cleveland Advanced Mfg. Program has extensive outreach to transfer technology to regional manufacturers. Biotechnology and biomedical start-up center. Cleveland also houses some of the nation's largest law firms. The health-care industry is the fastest growing segment of Cleveland's economy, largely due to the presence of the Cleveland Clinic, a world-famous medical research and treatment facility and the city's largest employer. Important private employment sectors: utilities, banks, automotive, chemicals, metals, aircraft parts, paint, plastics, greeting cards, wholesaling. Cleveland grew rapidly after the opening of the first sect. of the Ohio and Erie Canal in 1827 and the arrival of the RR in 1851. Cleveland and its factories attracted large numbers of immigrants throughout the 19th cent., including Irish, Germans, Italians, Poles, Czechs, Hungarians, and many others. Its central location midway bet. the coal and oil fields of Pennsylvania and (via the Great Lakes) the Minnesota iron mines spurred its industrialization; it was there that John D. Rockefeller began his oil dynasty. Large numbers of Afr. Americans migrated to Cleveland from the South after World War I. Cleveland is the seat of Case Western Reserve Univ., Cleveland State Univ., John Carroll Univ., Notre Dame Col., St. John Col. of Cleveland, Ursuline Col., Ohio Col. of Podiatric Medicine, St. Mary Seminary, the Cleveland Inst. of Art, the Cleveland Inst. of Music, and Cuyahoga Community col. The many points of interest include the Mall (civic center); the Terminal Tower; the Western Reserve Historical Society Mus.; the mus. of natural history, with a planetarium; Wade Park, with the Cleveland Mus. of Art and the Fine Arts Garden; Rockefeller Park, enclosing the Shakespeare and Cultural Gardens; Severance Hall, where concerts of the internationally famous Cleveland Symphony Orchestra are performed; Gordon Park, with an aquarium; a mus. of historical medicine; Cleveland Zoo; Rock and Roll Hall of Fame and Mus. The city also has a notable public library. The Cleveland *Plain Dealer* is a nationally known newspaper. In L. View Cemetery are the graves of James A. Garfield, Mark Hanna (who made his fortune in Cleveland), John Hay, and John D. Rockefeller. The city was plagued during the 1960s by racial disorders, especially in the Hough and Glenville sections; riots in the summer of 1968 resulted in 11 deaths and much property damage. In 1967, Cleveland became the first major U.S. city to elect an Afr.-Amer. mayor, Carl B. Stokes. As mfg. rapidly declined in the 1960s, 1970s, and 1980s, Cleveland went through a period of massive decay; numerous factories shut down and the city suffered from the outmigration of people and businesses to the suburbs. Cleveland's pop. declined 44% bet. 1950 and 1990. In 1979, Cleveland defaulted on $15.5 million in municipal loans. In the 1980s, the city was able to attract investment downtown and revitalize some sections. In 1991 construction began on a downtown sports complex to house Cleveland's professional baseball (1994 first season at Jacob Field) and basketball teams (Gund Arena). Laid out (1796) by Moses Cleaveland, chartered as a city 1836. **3** city (1990 pop. 30,354), ⊙ Bradley co., SE Tenn., c.26 mi/42 km ENE of Chattanooga; 35°10'N 84°51'W. Agr. (fruits, vegetables, wheat, tobacco) is the economic mainstay. Mfg. includes furniture, hosiery, batteries, chemicals, and textiles. Lee Col. is here. Cleveland is hq. of Cherokee Natl. Forest. To the S are Red Clay state historic area, home of the Cherokee people in the 1830s, and a portion of the Trail of Tears, the Cherokee's route W during their forced removal by order of President Andrew Jackson. Inc. 1838. **4** city (1990 pop. 7,124), Liberty co., SE Texas, on San Jacinto R., c.45 mi/72 km NNE of Houston; 30°20'N 95°04'W. RR junction, timber; oil wells; oil refineries, lumber mills; mfg. of wood prods.; rice soybeans; cattle. Sam Houston Natl. Forest to NW. Inc. 1929.

Cleveland 1 town (□ 5 sq mi/13 sq km; 1990 pop. 2,896), Charlotte co., SW Fla., 3 mi/4.8 km ENE of Punta Gorda; 26°56'N 81°59'W. **2** town (1990 pop. 1,653), ⊙ White co., NE Ga., 20 mi/32 km N of Gainesville, in Blue Ridge foothills; 34°36'N 83°46'W. Mfg. includes fiberglass fabric, clothing and textiles, candles, dolls, zippers; hardwood lumber. **3** town (1990 pop. 3,156), Pawnee co., N Okla., 29 mi/47 km WNW of Tulsa, near Arkansas R., headwaters of Keystone L. reservoir; 36°17'N 96°27'W. In oil- and natural-gas-producing and agr. area (grain, cattle); mfg. (gas-well-drilling materials, concrete). Feyodi Creek State Park to SE. Settled 1893. **4** town (1990 pop. 214), Russell co., SW Va., on Clinch R., 6 mi/9.7 km WNW of Lebanon; 36°56'N 82°09'W. Mfg. (lumber); agr. (tobacco, corn; cattle, sheep); timber. **5** town (1990 pop. 1,398), Manitowoc co., E Wis., 13 mi/21 km N of Sheboygan, near L. Michigan; 43°55'N 87°45'W. Dairying; grain, vegetables, fruit. Mfg. (fiberglass reinforced plastic prod.).

Cleveland 1 village, Conway co., central Ark., 26 mi/42 km ENE of Russellville. Ozark Natl. Forest to NW; Gulf Mt. Wildlife Management Area to N. **2** village (1990 pop. 283), Henry co., NW Ill., on Rock R. and 12 mi/19 km E of Rock Isl.; 41°30'N 90°19'W. Agr. (corn, soybeans, cattle, hogs; dairying). **3** village (1990 pop. 699), LeSueur co., S Minn., near Minnesota R., 14 mi/23 km NE of Mankato, on Cherry Creek; 44°19'N 93°50'W. Corn, oats, soybeans, peas; poultry; dairying; mfg. (meteorological satellite stations). Small lakes in area; Scotch L. to E. **4** village (1990 pop. 506), Cass co., W Mo., 12 mi/19 km WNW of Harrisonville and 28 mi/45 km S of downtown Kansas City, on Kansas border. Agr. area; mfg. (pipe organs). **5** village (□ 1 sq mi/2.6 sq km; 1990 pop. 784), Oswego co., N central N.Y., on N shore of Oneida L., 22 mi/35 km W of Rome; 43°14'N 75°53'W. Agr. area (dairy prods.; fruit). **6** village (1990 pop. 696), Rowan co., W central N.C., 11 mi/18 km WNW of Salisbury; 35°43'N 80°40'W. RR junction to E. In agr. area (tobacco, poultry, grain, livestock, dairying). Mfg. (motor-vehicle bodies, lumber, feeds). **7** village (1990 pop. 121), Stutsman co., central N.Dak., 20 mi/32 km W of Jamestown; 46°53'N 99°07'W. **8** uninc. village, Greenville co., NW S.C., in the Blue Ridge, 17 mi/27 km NNW of Greenville. Several state parks to W. **9** village (1990 pop. 498), Emery co., central Utah, 6 mi/9.7 km E of Huntington; 39°21'N 110°51'W. Elev. 5,735 ft/1,748 m. Alfalfa; cattle. Desert L. to NE; Huntington L. and State Park to W. Cleveland Lloyd Dinosaur Quarry to E.

Cleveland Heights, city (1990 pop. 54,052), Cuyahoga co., NE Ohio, a residential suburb of Cleveland; 41°30'N 81°34'W. Inc. 1903. It is known for its beautiful homes and interesting shops. Forest Hills Park, once part of an estate owned by John D. Rockefeller, offers recreational facilities.

Cleveland, Mount 1 Alaska: see CHUGINADAK ISLAND. **2** Mont.: see LEWIS RANGE.

Cleveland Park, residential sect., NW Washington, D.C., along Connecticut Ave. N of Rock Creek. Development of this exclusive neighborhood began in the 1880s, and was named for President Grover Cleveland, who owned a home and land here. Diplomats from nearby Embassy Row and numerous govt. officials have resided in the community.

Cleveland Peninsula, SE Alaska, extends c.35 mi/56 km SW into the Alexander Archipelago N of Ketchikan. On its Clarence Strait shore is fishing village Myers Chuck.

Clever (KLE-vuhr), town (1990 pop. 580), Christian co., SW Mo., in the Ozarks, near James R., 16 mi/26 km W of Ozark; 37°01'N 93°28'W. Limestone quarry.

Cleves, village (1990 pop. 2,208), Hamilton co., extreme SW Ohio, on Great Miami R. and 13 mi/21 km W of Cincinnati; 39°10'N 84°45'W. Petroleum refining. Plotted 1818. William Henry Harrison Memorial Park nearby.

Clewiston (KLOO-is-tuhn), town (□ 4 sq mi/10.4 sq km; 1990 pop. 6,085), Hendry co., S central Fla., c.55 mi/89 km W of W. Palm Beach, on SW shore of L. Okeechobee (diked here); 26°45'N 80°56'W. Sugar-refining and molasses center in a large cane-growing region. Founded 1921.

Cliff, village (1990 pop. 300), Grant co., SW N.Mex., on Gila R., E of Ariz. state line, 28 mi/45 km NW of Silver City. Cattle, alfalfa, grain; agr. Parts of Gila Natl. Forest to S and NE; Mogollon Mts. are N; Bill Evans Lake Reservoir to SE.

Cliff Haven, summer-resort village (1990 pop. 475), Clinton co., extreme NE N.Y., on W shore of L. Champlain, 4 mi/6.4 km S of Plattsburg; 44°40'N 73°26'W.

Cliff Island, SW Maine, fishing and resort isl. in Casco Bay, NE of Portland; c.2 mi/3.2 km long. Sometimes called Crotch Isl.

Clifford, town (1990 pop. 308), Bartholomew co., S central Ind., 5 mi/8 km NNE of Columbus; 39°17'N 85°52'W. Agr. area. Near Bakalar airport.

Clifford, village (1991 pop. 784), S Ont., Canada, 16 mi/26 km SE of Walkerton. Dairying, milling.

Clifford 1 village (1990 pop. 354), Lapeer co., E Mich., 19 mi/31 km NNE of Lapeer; 43°18'N 83°10'W. In agr. area; mfg. (shafts and gears). **2** village (1990 pop. 51), Traill co., E N.Dak.,11 mi/18 km SSW of Maysville; 47°21'N 97°24'W. RR terminus. KTHI-TV tower (2,063ft/629m high), N. Amer.'s tallest structure standing 6 mi/9.7 km ESE.

Cliffside, uninc. village, Rutherford co., SW N.C., near Broad R., 13 mi/21 km WSW of Shelby. Mfg. (denim fabric). RR spur terminus. Grain, soybeans, sorghum; poultry, livestock.

Cliffside Park, borough (1990 pop. 20,393), Bergen co., NE N.J., 12 mi/19 km NNE of Jersey City, on the palisades above the Hudson R., opposite New York City; 40°49'N 73°59'W. A residential suburb, it has some light industry. Inc. 1895.

Clifftop, uninc. village (1990 pop. 100), Fayette co., S central W.Va., 20 mi/32 km S of Summersville. Babcock State Park to SW.

Cliffwood or **Cliffwood Beach**, residential village, Monmouth co., E N.J., near Raritan Bay near Keyport.

Clifton 1 industrial city (1990 pop. 71,742), Passaic co., NE N.J., on the Passaic R.; set off from Passaic; 40°51'N 74°09'W. It has steel, textile equip., chemical, plastics, clothing, and electronic industries. Settled 1685 and inc. 1917 **2** city (1990 pop. 620), Wayne co., S Tenn., on Tennessee R. and 14 mi/23 km NW of Waynesboro; 35°22'N 87°59'W. Lumbering; mfg. machinery, children's clothing.

Clifton 1 town (1990 pop. 2,840), ⊙ Greenlee co., SE Ariz., on San Francisco R., 5 mi/8 km NE of its confluence with Gila R. near N.Mex. state line, 4 mi/6.4 km SE of Morenci; 33°01'N 109°17'W. Elev. 3,464 ft/1,056 m. Copper mining; cattle; grain, alfafa. Hot springs here. Town settled 1872. Apache-Sitgreaves Natl. Forest to N; Gila Box Riparian Natl. Conservation Area to SW; San Carlos Indian Reservation to NW. **2** town (1990 pop. 607), Penobscot co., S Maine, 11 mi/18 km E of Bangor; 44°49'N 68°31'W. Wood prods. **3** town (1990 pop. 3,195), Bosque co., central Texas, on Bosque R. and 30 mi/48 km NW of Waco; 31°46'N 97°34'W. Elev. 670 ft/204 m. In cotton, grain, pecans, peaches; cattle area; limestone processing. Texas Safari Wildlife Park here. Small Nor. village of Norse, 5 mi/8 km W; L. Whitney reservoir to NE; Meridian State Park to NW. Settled 1880, inc. 1902. **4** town (1990 pop. 176), Fairfax co., N Va., suburb 20 mi/32 km WSW of Washington, D.C., c.6 mi/9.7 km SW of Fairfax; 38°46'N 77°23'W. Light mfg. Bull Run Regional Park to SW, on Bull Run creek.

Clifton 1 village (1990 pop. 12,671), Mesa co., W Colo., near Colorado R. and 6 mi/9.7 km E of Grand Junction; 39°04'N 108°27'W. Elev. c.4,710 ft/1,436 m. Fruit-shipping point. Light mfg. Colorado River State Park to S. **2** village (1990 pop. 228), Franklin co., SE Idaho, 10 mi/16 km NW of Preston; 42°11'N 112°01'W. Elev. 4,893 ft/1,491 m. Dairying; cattle, sheep; sugar beets; wheat, barley. Caribou Natl. Forest to W. **3** village (1990 pop. 1,347), Iroquois co., E Ill., 12 mi/19 km SSW of

Kankakee; 40°56′N 87°55′W. In agr. area (corn, soybeans, sorghum; cattle, hogs). **4** village (1990 pop. 561), on Clay-Washington co. line, N Kansas, on Republican R. and 19 mi/31 km E of Concordia; 39°34′N 97°16′W. RR junction. Grain, livestock. **5** village (1990 pop. 165), on Greene-Clark co. line, SW central Ohio, 9 mi/14 km S of Springfield and on Little Miami R.; 39°48′N 83°49′W. **6** village, Spartanburg co., NW S.C., on Pacolet R. and 7 mi/11.3 km ENE of Spartanburg. In agr. area; textile mills.

Clifton, sect. of Staten Isl. borough of N.Y. city, SE N.Y., in port dist. of NE Staten Isl.; 40°37′N 74°04′W.

Clifton, former city, Campbell co., N Ky., annexed in 1935 by Newport. One of 4 places so named in Ky.

Clifton, Mass.: see MARBLEHEAD.

Clifton Forge, independent city (□ 3 sq mi/7.8 sq km; 1990 pop. 4,679), NW Va., separate from surrounding Alleghany co., in the Allegheny Mts., 37 mi/60 km N of Roanoke, on Jackson R. 5 mi/8 km N of Confluence with Cow Pasture R. where James is formed; 37°49′N 79°49′W. RR junction (shops). Mfg. (lumber, printing); coal-mining dist. Dabney S. Lancaster Community Col. Douthat State Park to N. Settled 1880, inc. 1884.

Clifton Heights, borough (1990 pop. 7,111), Delaware co., SE Pa., suburb 7 mi/11.3 km WSW of downtown Philadelphia, on Darby Creek; 39°55′N 75°17′W. Mfg. (fabricated metal prods., commercial printing, diverse light mfg.). Settled c.1850, inc. 1885.

Clifton Hill, town (1990 pop. 108), Randolph co., N central Mo., 12 mi/19 km W of Moberly; 39°26′N 92°40′W. Grain; lumber; pecans. Bison ranch to S.

Clifton Springs, village (□ 1 sq mi/2.6 sq km; 1990 pop. 2,175), Ontario co., W central N.Y., 28 mi/45 km SE of Rochester; 42°57′N 77°07′W. Mfg. of solenoids and flame arresters. Though no longer in operation, Clifton Springs Sanitarium here is on Natl. Register of Historic Places. Inc. 1859.

Cliftondale, Mass.: see SAUGUS.

Climax, town (1990 pop. 226), Decatur co., SW Ga., 8 mi/12.9 km ESE of Bainbridge; 30°53′N 84°26′W. Mfg. of horse trailers.

Climax, village (1991 pop. 226), SW Sask., Canada, 30 mi/48 km S of Shaunavon, near Mont. border; 49°12′N 108°23′W. Elev. 3,064 ft/934 m. Wheat.

Climax 1 village, Lake co., central Colo., at Continental Divide (to N) in Rocky Mts., in San Isabel Natl. Forest, 10 mi/16 km NNE of Leadville. Elev. c.11,320 ft/3,450 m. Mine here is one of the world's leading producers of molybdenum, one of 2 mines in Colorado that extract equal tonnages. High-elev. observatory here. Highway and RR run through Fremont Pass (11,318 ft/3,450 m) here. Quandary Peak and Mt. Lincoln nearby. Tourism. Copper Mt. Ski Resort to N. White River Natl. Forest to N, beyond Divide. **2** village (1990 pop. 57), Greenwood co., SE Kansas, near Fall R., 7 mi/11.3 km SSE of Eureka; 37°43′N 96°13′W. Fall River L. reservoir to E. **3** village (1990 pop. 677), Kalamazoo co., SW Mich., 13 mi/21 km ESE of Kalamazoo; 42°14′N 85°20′W. In agr. area (fruit, grain; livestock). **4** village (1990 pop. 264), Polk co., NW Minn., 14 mi/23 km SW of Crookston, on Sand Hill R., E of confluence with Red R.; 47°36′N 96°48′W. Grain; livestock; dairying; mfg. (fertilizer blending).

Climax Springs, town (1990 pop. 91), Camden co., central Mo., 18 mi/29 km WNW of Camdenton; near Lake of the Ozarks; 38°06′N 93°02′W. Mfg. (bearings).

Clinch, county (□ 796 sq mi/2,062 sq km; 1990 pop. 6,160), S Ga., on Fla. state line; ⊙ Homerville; 30°55′N 82°42′W. Flatwoods area drained by Suwannee R.; E part included in Okefenokee Swamp. Industry includes timber; cattle and hogs; tobacco and sweet potatoes. Formed 1850.

Clinch, river, c.300 mi/483 km long, SW Va. and NE Tenn.; rises in NE Tazewell co., Va.; flows SW past Tazewell and St. Paul, Va., enters Tenn., then flows through Norris L. reservoir where it receives Powell R. and Yellow R., then flows past Clinton and SE to Oak Ridge, through Melton Hill L. reservoir to Tennessee R. (Watts Bar L. Reservoir), 2 mi/3.2 km W of Kingston.

Clinch Mountain, ridge, SW Va. and NE Tenn., in Appalachian Mts., bet. Clinch R. (NW) and Holston R. (SE); extends c. 145 mi/233 km SW from Burkes Garden, Va. to near Knoxville. Elev. 2,000 ft/610 m in SW, 3,000 ft/914 m–4,700 ft/1,433 m in NE.

Clinchco, town (1990 pop. 534), Dickenson co., SW Va., 23 mi/37 km NE of Norton. Agr. (tobacco, cattle); in bituminous-coal region. John W. Flanagan Reservoir (Pound R.) to NW.

Clinchfield 1 village, Houston co., central Ga., 7 mi/11.3 km SE of Perry; 32°24′N 83°38′W. Mfg. of cement. **2** uninc. village, McDowell co., W N.C., 2 mi/3.2 km NE of Marion.

Clinchport, town (1990 pop. 67), Scott co., SW Va., 18 mi/29 km SSW of Norton, on Clinch R.; 36°40′N 82°44′W. RR junction. Agr. (dairying; livestock; tobacco, corn). Natural Tunnel State Park to N.

Cline, uninc. village, Uvalde co., SW Texas, 19 mi/31 km W of Uvalde, Cline Mt. (1,250 ft/381 m) to S.

Cline, Mount (11,027 ft/3,361 m), SW Alta., Canada, in Rocky Mts., near edge of Banff Natl. Park, 80 mi/129 km SE of Jasper; 52°05′N 116°42′W.

Clingmans Dome, Tenn., see GREAT SMOKY MOUNTAINS.

Clint, town (1990 pop. 1,035), El Paso co., extreme W Texas, near the Rio Grande, 20 mi/32 km SE of El Paso; 31°35′N 106°13′W. Irrigated agr. area (pecans, cotton; dairying, cattle); mfg. (turpentine and pine oil, meat processing).

Clinton 1 county (□ 503 sq mi/1,303 sq km; 1990 pop. 33,944), S Ill., bounded S by Kaskaskia R.; ⊙ Carlyle; 38°36′N 89°25′W. Agr. area (corn, wheat, sorghum). Mfg. (metal, wood, plastics, and food prods.). Bituminous coal mines. Formed 1824. L. Carlyle, important weekend and day recreational area in NE; South Shore and Eldon Hazlet State Parks on lake. Centralia Correctional Center and Kaskaskia Col. in SE. **2** county (□ 405 sq mi/1,049 sq km; 1990 pop. 30,974), central Ind.; ⊙ Frankfort; 40°18′N 86°29′W. Agr. area (soybeans, apples, corn, wheat, oats; cattle, hogs, sheep), with diversified mfg. at Frankfort, including farm-prods. processing; oil refining at Frankfort. Drained by Sugar Creek and forks of Wildcat Creek. Formed 1830. **3** county (□ 710 sq mi/1,839 sq km; 1990 pop. 51,040), E Iowa; ⊙ Clinton; 41°53′N 90°31′W. Bounded E by Mississippi R. (forms Ill. state line here) and SW and S by Wapsipinicon R. Prairie agr. area (hogs, cattle; corn, oats); limestone quarries. Mfg. at Clinton. Lock and Dam No. 13 above Clinton. Flooding along Miss. R. and tributaries in 1993. Formed 1840. **4** county (□ 205 sq mi/531 sq km; 1990 pop. 9,135), S Ky.; ⊙ Albany; 36°43′N 85°07′W. Bounded S by Tenn., NW corner by Cumberland R. (arm of L. Cumberland in N); drained by several creeks. Includes arm of Dale Hollow L. reservoir in SW. Hilly agr. region, in Cumberland foothills (burley tobacco, hay, alfalfa, soybeans, corn; hogs, cattle, poultry; dairying); coal mines; stone quarrying; timber. Formed 1836. **5** county (□ 574 sq mi/1,487 sq km; 1990 pop. 57,883), S central Mich.; ⊙ St. Johns. Part of city of Lansing surrounds it in S; 42°56′N 84°36′W. Drained by Maple, Looking Glass, and Grand rivers, and by small Stony Creek. Agr. (soybeans, corn, wheat, oats, vegetables, sugar beets, peppermint, beans, apples; cattle, hogs, sheep, poultry; dairying). Mfg. at St. Johns and Ovid. Sleepy Hollow State Park in E. Formed 1839. **6** county (□ 420 sq mi/1,088 sq km; 1990 pop. 16,595), NW Mo.; ⊙ Plattsburg; 39°36′N 94°24′W. Drained by Little Platte R. Corn, wheat, soybeans; cattle, sheep, hogs; natural gas. Smithville Lake (reservoir) in SW; Wallace State Park in NE. Formed 1833. **7** county (□ 1,059 sq mi/2,743 sq km; 1990 pop. 85,969), extreme NE N.Y.; ⊙ Plattsburgh; 44°44′N 73°40′W. Bounded N by Que. border, E by L. Champlain (here forming Vt. border). Includes N Adirondacks; situated partly in Adirondack State Park and forest preserve. Has many mt. and lake resorts and Ausable Chasm on Ausable R.; drained also by Saranac and Great Chazy rivers. Popular summer and winter recreational area. Lumbering and paper milling have historically been the important foundations of the economy, much as they are today, along with tourism. Other mfg., located primarily in Plattsburgh and Rouses Point, is limited. Dairy farming occupies the St. Lawrence and Champlain lowland portions of the co. Iron mining and granite quarrying, once important industries, no longer exist. Named for George Clinton, 1st governor of N.Y. state. Samuel de Champlain was the 1st European to pass through the region and explored the lake that bears his name. Area was part of New France. Treaty of Paris ceded land to England. Lakes Champlain and George and their combined valley figured prominently in the Fr. and Indian Wars, Amer. Revolution, and the War of 1812, as a strategic corridor of movement. Completion of Champlain Canal in 1823 bet. L. George and Champlain spurred development of the co. and region, as did coming of the RR. Formed 1788. **8** county (□ 412 sq mi/1,067 sq km; 1990 pop. 35,415), SW Ohio; ⊙ Wilmington, 39°24′N 83°49′W. Drained by forks of Little Miami R. and small Caesar Creek. In the Till Plains physiographic region. Stock raising (cattle, hogs), farming (corn, soybeans), dairying; mfg. at Wilmington and Sabina (paper prods., hand and edge tools, semiconductors, surgical appliances and supplies). U.S. air force base at Wilmington. Includes Fort Anc. State Memorial Park. Formed 1810. **9** county (□ 898 sq mi/2,326 sq km; 1990 pop. 37,182), N central Pa.; ⊙ Lock Haven; 41°14′N 77°38′W. Forested mt. area, drained by West Branch of Susquehanna R. (forms part of SW boundary in W) and Bald Eagle and Sinnemahoning creeks; Bald Eagle Mt. crosses SE part. Beech Creek forms part of SW boundary. Clay, bituminous coal, limestone; timber; mfg. at Lock Haven; agr. (corn, wheat, oats, barley, hay, alfalfa, some apples; hogs, cattle, dairying). Sproul State Forest in N half; part of Bald Eagle State Forest in S; part of Tiadaghton State Forest in SE; part of Bucktail State Park follows Susquehanna R. from Lock Haven NW and Sinnemahoning Creek to Emporium; Ravensburg State Park in SE; Hyner Run and Hyner View state parks in NE center; Kettle Creek State Park in NW. Formed 1839.

Clinton 1 city (1990 pop. 7,437), ⊙ De Witt co., central Ill., 19 mi/31 km N of Decatur; 40°08′N 88°57′W. RR junction. Trade center in agr. area (corn, soybeans; livestock); mfg. (hoses, lamps, freight cars). Settled 1836, inc. 1855. Lincoln practiced law here. Nuclear-power station nearby. Weldon Springs State Park to SE; Clinton L. reservoir and recreation area 6 mi/9.7 km E. **2** city (1990 pop. 5,040), Vermillion co., W Ind., on Wabash R. and 14 mi/23 km N of Terre Haute; 39°40′N 87°24′W. Italian immigrants. Mfg. (pharmaceuticals, agr. prods.). Settled 1818, laid out 1824. **3** city (1990 pop. 29,201), ⊙ Clinton co., E central Iowa, on the Mississippi; 41°50′N 90°13′W. In a corn and livestock area. Town of Camanche adjoins to SW. An industrial and RR center and junction, it has food-processing (especially corn and corn prods.) and diverse mfg. industries (milk cartons, metal shelving, plastic film, plastic fittings, pet foods, wood furniture, cotton prods.). Clinton grew as a lumbering town and in the 1880s became a great sawmill center in the Midwest. Due to the depletion of wood, the above agr. and mfg. have come to dominate the city's economy. Lock and Dam No. 13 is upstream. Mt. St. Clare Col. and Clinton Community Col. and the Showboat Mus. are here. Inc. 1859. **4** city (1990 pop. 21,847), Hinds co., W Miss., suburb 9 mi/14.5 km WNW of Jackson; 32°20′N 90°19′W. Mfg. (wooden, plastic, and metal prods., food and beverages). Seat of Mississippi Col. Natural Springs, including Rubinson Spring. On Natchez Trace (Natl.) Parkway (13 mi/21 km incomplete sect. from here ENE to Ridgeland). Settled c.1823 on site of an early Indian agency. **5** city (1990 pop. 8,703), ⊙ Henry co., W central Mo., near South Grand R., 37 mi/60 km SW of Sedalia; 38°22′N 93°46′W. Corn, wheat, soybeans; cattle; mfg. (crushed limestone, cheese prods., boat seats). N of S Grand Arm of Truman Lake. Plotted 1837. **6** city (1990 pop. 8,204), ⊙ Sampson co., SE central N.C., 32 mi/51 km ESE of Fayetteville, bet. Great Coharrit (W) and Six Run (E) creeks; sawmilling; 35°00′N 78°19′W. Timber; cotton, tobacco, peanuts, potatoes, sweet potatoes, grain, poultry, livestock. Mfg. (meat processing, metal prods., yarn, clothing). Sampson Community Col. Laid out 1818.

Clinton, town (1991 pop. 3,187), S Ont., Canada, on Bayfield R. and 13 mi/21 km SE of Goderich; light mfg. Salt wells nearby.

Clinton 1 town (1990 pop. 2,213), ⊙ Van Buren co., N central Ark., c.60 mi/97 km N of Little Rock, at confluences of Archeys Fork and S Fork of Little Red R.; Greens Ferry Reservoir to SE; 35°34′N 92°27′W. In diversified agr. area. Mfg. (concrete, poultry processing, cards and card sets, plastic molding, boat trailers). Gulf Mt. Wildlife Management Area and Ozark Natl. Forest to W. Inc. as city 1938. **2** town (1990 pop. 12,767), Middlesex co., S Conn., on L.I. Sound; 41°17′N 72°31′W. Summer tourism; agr.; a winery; fishing; mfg. includes consumer goods, plastics, wire, and small-boat building. Settled 1663, set off from Killingworth and inc. 1838. **3** town (1990 pop. 1,547), ⊙ Hickman co., W Ky., 23 mi/37 km WSW of Mayfield; 36°40′N 88°59′W. Mfg. (feeds, women's and children's clothing, ham and bacon, appliance motors, wooden prods.). Columbus Belmont Battlefield State Park is to NW, on Mississippi R. Plotted 1826, inc. 1831. **4** town (1994 pop. 2,134), ⊙ East Feliciana parish, SE central La., on Comite R., 31 mi/50 km NNE of Baton Rouge; 30°52′N 91°01′W. In agr. area (peaches; cattle, horses, hogs; dairying); timber; mfg. of lumber. Winery, Clinton Confederate Cemetery here. Located 1825, inc. 1830, inc. as town 1852. **5** town (1990 pop. 3,332), Kennebec co., S Maine, 27 mi/43 km NNE of Augusta and on Sebasticook R.; 44°39′N 69°31′W. Wood prods. Settled c.1775, inc. 1795. **6** town (1990 pop. 13,222), Worcester co., central Mass., on S branch of Nashua R., and 12 mi/19 km NNE of Worcester; 42°25′N 71°42′W. Metal prods., chemicals, medical prods., and furniture. Settled 1654, inc. 1850. Formerly had one of largest cotton mills in U.S. Wachusett Reservoir is just S. **7** town (1990 pop. 2,475), Lenawee and Washtenaw cos., SE Mich., on Raisin R., and 12 mi/19 km NNE of Adrian; 42°04′N 83°58′W. In fertile farm area; mfg. (bean and grain processing, sawmilling, glass encapsulating). Wamplers L. (resort) and Walter J. Hayes State Park to W. Inc. 1838. **8** town (1990 pop. 9,298), Custer co., W Okla., c.80 mi/129 km W of Okla. City, and on Washita R.; 35°30′N 98°58′W. RR junction. Mfg. and shipping center for stock-raising, dairying, and agr. area (wheat, cotton); mfg. (food prods., textiles, printing, fracturing fluids, metal windows and door frames). Historic growth of town related to Route 66. Western Trails Mus. and Oklahoma Route 66 Mus. (commemorating John Steinbeck's *Highway of the O'Kier*) here. Foss L. reservoir to W. Founded 1903, inc. 1909. **9** town (1990 pop. 7,989), Laurens co., NW S.C., 33 mi/53 km S of Spartanburg; 34°28′N 81°52′W. Mfg. includes epsom salts, papermaking felts, parquet flooring, apparel, blinds, church furniture, printing and publishing, roller bearings. Center of agr. area (grain, soybeans, vegetables; dairying; poultry). Seat of Presbyterian Col. and state school for mentally retarded. **10** town (1990 pop. 8,972), ⊙ Anderson co., E Tenn., near Clinch R., 15 mi/24 km NW of Knoxville; 36°06′N 84°08′W. Trade and shipping point for timber, orchard, farm area; makes hosiery, resins, metal parts. Oak Ridge, Norris Dam, and State fish hatchery are nearby. **11** town (1990 pop. 7945), Davis co., N Utah, suburb 8 mi/12.9 km SW of Ogden, near Great Salt Lake, and 24 mi/39 km NW of Salt Lake City; 41°08′N 112°03′W. Elev. 4,450 ft/1,356 m. Hill Air Force Base to E; Howard Slough Waterfowl Management Area to W. Settled 1880. **12** uninc. town (1990 pop. 1,564), Island co., NW Wash., 6 mi/9.7 km W of Everett, at SE end of Whidbey Isl., on Possession Sound, N extension of Puget Sound; 47°59′N 122°22′W. Terminus of ferry from Mukilteo, on mainland, landing 3 mi/4.8 km to SE. **13** town (1990 pop. 1,849), Rock co., S Wis., 9 mi/14.5 km NE of Beloit, near Ill. state line; 42°33′N 88°52′W. In dairying and farming area. RR junction. Mfg. (steel forgings, meat processing).

Clinton, village (1991 pop. 662), S B.C., Canada, 32 mi/51 km NNE of Lillooet; 51°05′N 121°35′W. In logging, gold- and silver-mining region. Gold-rush settlement on Cariboo Wagon Road.

Clinton 1 village, Jones co., central Ga., 13 mi/21 km NNE of Macon; 32°59′N 83°33′W. **2** village (1990 pop. 574), Big Stone co., W Minn., 10 mi/16 km N of Ortonville; 45°27′N 96°26′W. Agr. area (grain, alfalfa, soybeans; hogs); mfg. (fertilizers). **3** village (1990 pop. 200), Missoula co., W Mont., 14 mi/23 km SE of Missoula, on Clark Fork river. Logging. Cattle, alfalfa. Welcome Creek Wilderness to S; Beavertail Hill State Park to SE; Garnet Range to the N; surrounded by Lolo Natl. Forest. **4** village (1990 pop. 33), Sheridan co., NW Nebr., 7 mi/11.3 km ENE of Rushville; 42°45′N 102°20′W. **5** village (1990 pop. 2,238), Oneida co., central N.Y., on Oriskany Creek, and 8 mi/12.9 km WSW of Utica; 43°02′N 75°22′W. Mfg. (clothing, food prods.). Seat of Hamilton Col. Elihu Root was b. here. Clinton Village Historic Dist. Inc. 1843. **6** village (1990 pop. 1,175), Summit co., NE Ohio, 12 mi/19 km SSW of Akron, and on Tuscarawas R.; 40°55′N 81°38′W.

Clinton or **Hell's Kitchen**, SE N.Y., an often-overlooked neighborhood along Hudson R., on W side of Manhattan borough, N.Y. city; bounded by 8th Ave. on E, W. 34th St. on S, Hudson R. on W, and W 57th St. on N; 40°46′N 73°59′W. Named for DeWitt Clinton Park in its NW corner. From the Civil War to World War II, the neighborhood (then called Hell's Kitchen) was one of the city's most notorious precincts, as evidenced by some of the street names: Battle Row, Cockroach Row, Mulligan Alley, Poverty Lane, and Death Ave. (the colloquial name for 10th Ave.). Its domination by gangster rule, slaughterhouses, docks, freight yards, and factories established its character, which has changed little even to the present day—and residents take a perverse pride in the roughness of their neighborhood. The wharves that lined the Hudson shoreline here have all disappeared, except for 3 finger piers, bet. W. 48th St. and W. 52nd St., serving cruise ships. Also called the Middle West Side and the Theater Dist.

Clinton, township (1990 pop. 10,816), Hunterdon co., W N.J., on South Branch of Raritan R., and 9 mi/14.5 km NNW of Flemington; 40°38′N 74°50′W. State reformatory nearby. Settled in mid–18th cent., inc. 1865. Spruce Run Reservoir to NW. Several state parks in area.

Clinton 1 Nuclear Power Plant, Illinois: see DE WITT, co.

Clinton Corners, resort village (1990 pop. 450), Dutchess co., SE N.Y., 13 mi/21 km NE of Poughkeepsie; 41°50′N 73°46′W. Small lakes nearby.

Clinton Lake 1 reservoir (□ 8 sq mi/20.7 sq km), Dewitt co., central Ill., on Salt Creek, 32 mi/51 km W of Champaign-Urbana; 40°08′N 88°52′W. Max. capacity 250,000 acre-ft. Has 2 branches. Formed by Clinton Lake Dam (also known as Clinton Station; 65 ft/20 m high), built (1977) for water supply; also used for recreation. Clinton Lake State Recreation area on N shore. **2** reservoir (□ 11 sq mi/28 sq km), Douglas co., NE Kansas, on Wakarusa R., 5 mi/8 km W of Lawrence; 38°55′N 95°20′W. Max. capacity 368,700 acre-ft. Formed by Clinton Dam (116 ft/35 m high), built (1977) by Army Corps of Engineers for flood control; also used for recreation and water supply. Clinton State Park on N shore.

Clinton River, SE Mich., rises in small lakes near Pontiac in Oakland co., flows c.30 mi/48 km E, past Pontiac, Rochester, and Sterling Heights to Anchor Bay of L. St. Clair 5 mi/8 km E of Mt. Clemens; 42°47′N 83°24′W.

Clinton Township, suburb, Macomb co., SE Mich., 18 mi/29 km NE of downtown Detroit, near L. St. Clair. Drained by Clinton and North Br. Clinton rivers. Berz-Macomb Airport to NW. Heavy Mfg.

Clinton-Colden Lake, E Mackenzie Dist., N.W.T., Canada, NE of Great Slave L.; 20 mi/32 km long, 5 mi/8 km–20 mi/32 km wide; 64°N 107°30′W. Drains S through Artillery L. into Great Slave L.

Clintondale, village (□ 5 sq mi/13 sq km; 1990 pop. 1,394), Ulster co., SE N.Y., 6 mi/9.7 km W of Poughkeepsie; 41°41′N 74°02′W. In fruit-growing region.

Clintonville, town (1990 pop. 4,351), Waupaca co., E central Wis., on Pigeon L., tributary of the Embarrass R. and 30 mi/48 km NNW of Appleton; 44°37′N 88°45′W. In farm area; mfg. (motor vehicle prods. and parts, food prods., machinery). Settled c.1855, inc. 1887. Birthplace of North Central Airlines.

Clintonville (KLIN-tuhn-vil), borough (1990 pop. 520), Venango co., NW Pa., 13 mi/21 km S of Franklin, on Scrubgrass Creek; 41°12′N 79°52′W. Agr. (corn, hay; livestock, dairying). Part of Clear Creek State Forest to W.

Clintwood, town (1990 pop. 1,542), ⊙ Dickenson co., SW Va., near Ky. state line, 17 mi/27 km NNE of Norton; 37°08′N 82°27′W. Mfg. (clothing, printing, meat processing); agr. (tobacco, potatoes; cattle); timber; bituminous coal. John W. Flanagan Reservoir (Pound R.) to NE. Inc. 1894.

Clio 1 (KLEE-O), town (1990 pop. 1,365), Barbour co., SE Ala., 16 mi/26 km SW of Clayton. Hospital gowns mfg. here. **2** town (1990 pop. 103), Wayne co., S Iowa, near Mo. state line, 11 mi/18 km SW of Corydon; 40°37′N 93°27′W. In agr. area. **3** town (1990 pop. 2,692), Genesee co., SE central Mich., 11 mi/18 km NNW of Flint; 43°10′N 83°44′W. In agr. area; light mfg. Inc. as village 1873, as city 1928. **4** town (1990 pop. 882), Marlboro co., NE S.C., 8 mi/12.9 km ESE of Bennettsville; 34°34′N 79°32′W. Mfg. of fiberboard; agr. includes cotton, grain, vegetables; hogs.

Clipperton Island, isolated, uninhabited island (□ c.2 sq mi/5.2 sq km), in the Pacific Ocean, c.800 mi/1,300 km SW of Mexico and 1,802 mi/2,900 km W of Panama Canal; 10°18′N 109°13′W. An "almost atoll" with single spire of volcanic rock. May be developed as fishing base. It was used as a base by John Clipperton, an Eng. pirate. The French claimed it in 1858, the Americans held it for a time in the Span.-Amer. War, and Mex. troops occupied it in 1897. The conflict bet. France and Mexico was referred to the king of Italy for arbitration in 1908. The award was made (1931) in favor of France, and Mexico surrendered the isl. in 1932. Dependency of France.

Clitherall (KLI-thruhl), village (1990 pop. 109), Otter Tail co., W Minn., 21 mi/34 km E of Fergus Falls, at N end of Clitherall L.; 46°16′N 95°37′W. Grain; livestock; dairying. Battle L. to N.

Clitherall, Lake, Otter Tail co., W Minn., 18 mi/29 km E of Fergus Falls; 3.5 mi/5.6 km long, 1 mi/1.6 km wide; 46°15′N 95°39′W. Drains N into Battle L. through short stream. Fishing; resort area. Village of Clitherall at NE end of lake.

Clive, village (1991 pop. 414), S central Alta., Canada, 21 mi/34 km NE of Red Deer; 52°29′N 113°27′W. Lumbering; dairying; farming.

Clontarf (KLAWN-tahrf), village (1990 pop. 172), Swift co., W Minn., near Chippewa R., and 6 mi/9.7 km NW of Benson; 45°22′N 95°40′W. Grain; poultry; dairying; mfg. (fertilizers).

Cloquet (klo-KAI), city (1990 pop. 10,885), Carlton co., NE Minn., on St. Louis R., 18 mi/29 km WSW of Duluth; 46°43′N 92°29′W. RR junction. Dairying; poultry; oats, alfalfa; mfg. (matches, giftware, concrete, calcium carbonate, ceiling tile, knitwear, printing and publishing). Fond du Lac Indian Reservation to W. Almost entirely destroyed (1918) by forest fire, rebuilt with state aid. Inc. as village 1880, as city 1904.

Cloquet River (klo-KAI), 100 mi/161 km long, NE Minn.; rises in Cloquet Lake in Lake co., 55 mi/89 km NNE of Duluth (46°51′N 92°34′W); flows SW, through part of Superior Natl. Forest, and Cloquet Valley State Forest, through Island L. reservoir (9 mi/14.5 km long, 4.5 mi/7.2 km wide) to St. Louis R. 10 mi/16 km NNW of Cloquet.

Closplint (KLOZ-plint), village (1990 pop. 324), Harlan co., SE Ky., on Clover Fork of Cumberland R., and 14 mi/23 km ENE of Harlan. Bituminous coal.

Closter, residential borough (1990 pop. 8,094), Bergen co., NE N.J., near Hudson R., 10 mi/16 km NE of Paterson; 40°58′N 73°57′W. Mfg. (curtains, concrete prods.). Inc. 1903.

Cloud, county (□ 718 sq mi/1,860 sq km; 1990 pop.

11,023), N Kansas; ☉ Concordia; 39°28′N 97°39′W. Plains region, drained by Republican R. (N) and Solomon R. (SW). Wheat growing; cattle, hogs, sheep; sorghum, soybeans, alfalfa, hay, corn. Part of Republican Waterfowl Management Unit in NW corner. Formed 1867.

Cloud, Mount (6,113 ft/1,863 m), SE Alaska, in Coast Range, 50 mi/80 km ESE of Wrangell; 56°17′N 131°09′W.

Cloud Peak (13,167 ft/4,013 m), on border of Big Horn and Johnson cos., N Wyo., 30 mi/48 km SSW of Sheridan. Highest point in Bighorn Mts.; is partly glaciated at summit. Located in Cloud Peak Wilderness Area of Bighorn Natl. Forest.

Cloudcroft, village (1990 pop. 636), Otero co., S N.Mex., 21 mi/34 km ENE of Alamogordo, in Lincoln Natl. Forest (in Sacramento Mts.); 32°57′N 105°44′W. Elev. 8,663 ft/2,640 m. Cloudcraft Ski Area; Sunspot Observatory to S; Mescalero Apache Indian Reservation to N.

Clouds Rest, Calif.: see YOSEMITE NATIONAL PARK.

Clover 1 town (1990 pop. 3,442), York co., N S.C., 8 mi/12.9 km N of York; 35°6′N 81°13′W. Mfg. of apparel, textiles and textile machinery, rubber and metal prods.; agr. includes cotton, grain, soybeans, peaches; dairying; poultry, livestock. Kings Mt. Natl. Military Park and state part to W. **2** town (1990 pop. 198), Halifax co., S Va., 14 mi/23 km NE of South Boston, near Roanoke R.; 36°49′N 78°43′W. Mfg. (synthetic yarns); in agr. area (grain, soybeans, tobacco; cattle)

Clover Fork, river, c.35 mi/56 km long, SE Ky.; rises in the Cumberlands in E Harlan co.; flows WSW past Highsplint, Evarts, and Harlan; receives Martin's Fork before joining Poor Fork just N of Harlan to form Cumberland R.

Cloverdale, city (1990 pop. 4,924), Sonoma co., W Calif., 30 mi/48 km NNW of Santa Rosa, on Russian R.; 38°48′N 123°01′W. Grapes, apples, grain, dairying; poultry. Mfg. (winery, truck bodies, fabricated rubber goods).

Cloverdale 1 town (1990 pop. 1,681), Putnam co., W central Ind., 9 mi/14.5 km SSE of Greencastle. Hogs, cattle grain. Mfg. (plastics). Limestone quarries, crushed stone. Cagles Mill Reservoir, Lieber State Recreational Area and Cataract Falls to SW. **2** uninc. town, Botetourt co., W central Va., suburb, 7 mi/11.3 km N of downtown Roanoke; 37°21′N 79°54′W. Mfg. (wood veneers, steel fabricating, cement, refractory shapes); agr. (grain, soybeans, apples; livestock, dairying); timber. Limestone. Appalachian Trail passes to N; parts of Jefferson Natl. Forest to NW and NE.

Cloverdale, village, SW B.C., Canada, 18 mi/29 km SE of Vancouver; 49°06′N 122°44′W. Mixed farming; poultry; fruit; hops.

Cloverdale, village (1990 pop. 270), Putnam co., NW Ohio, 18 mi/29 km S of Defiance, near Auglaize R., in agr. region; 41°01′N 84°18′W.

Cloverport town (1990 pop. 1,207), Breckinridge co., NW Ky., 27 mi/43 km E of Owensboro, on Ohio R. (Cannelton Locks and Dam town); 37°49′N 86°37′W. Agr. area (corn, burley tobacco, hay; livestock); mfg. (furniture). Founded 1808.

Clovis 1 (KLO-vis), city (1990 pop. 50,323), Fresno co., central Calif., suburb 7 mi/11.3 km NE of downtown Fresno, near Dry Creek; 36°49′N 119°42′W. Calif. State Univ. (Fresno) to W; Fresno Airport to S. Dairying, cattle, fruit, tomatoes, grain, almonds. Diversified Mfg. **2** city (1990 pop. 30,954), Curry co., E N.Mex., 104 mi/167 km SW of Amarillo, Texas, and c.105 mi/169 km NE of Roswell, N.Mex.; 34°24′N 103°12′W. RR junction. Cattle, dairying, sheep; peanuts, potatoes, corn, wheat, pumpkins, alfalfa, vegetables. Mfg. (prefabricated metal prods., food and beverages, printing and publishing, household items). Cannon Air Force Base to SW. Blackwater Draw Natl. Archaeological Site and Oasis State Park to SW.

Club Med Columbus Isle, resort, San Salvador Isl., Bahamas. All inclusive resort. Major expansion of facility undertaken in 1995.

Cluny (KLOO-nee), village (1991 pop. 103), S Alta., Canada, near Bow R., 55 mi/89 km ESE of Calgary. Wheat, stock.

Clute, town (1990 pop. 8,910), Brazoria co., S Texas, near Brazos R., suburb 5 mi/8 km N of Freeport and 2 mi/3.2 km ESE of Lake Jackson City on Oyster Creek; 29°01′N 95°24′W. Elev. 10 ft/3 m. In Brazosport industrial area (circuit board assembly, printing).

Clutier (kloo-TEER), town (1990 pop. 219), Tama co., central Iowa, 11 mi/18 km NE of Toledo; 42°04′N 92°24′W. Mfg. of farm equip.

Clyde, city (1990 pop. 5,776), Sandusky co., N Ohio, 17 mi/27 km W of Sandusky; 41°18′N 82°58′W. Trade center for agr. area (grain, fruit, truck); canned foods. Major appliance mfg. Settled c.1820.

Clyde 1 town (1990 pop. 793), Cloud co., N Kansas, on Republican R., and 12 mi/19 km E of Concordia; 39°35′N 97°24′W. In wheat region. RR junction to SE. Inc. 1869. **2** town (1990 pop. 71), Nodaway co., NW Mo., near Platte R., 13 mi/21 km SE of Maryville; 40°16′N 94°40′W. **3** town (1990 pop. 1,041), Haywood co., W N.C., on Pigeon R., and 20 mi/32 km W of Asheville; 35°31′N 82°54′W. Agr. area (corn, tobacco, cattle, hogs, dairying). Parts of Pisgah Nat. Forest to NW and SE. **4** town (1990 pop. 3,002), Callahan co., central Texas, 16 mi/26 km E of Abilene; 32°23′N 99°30′W. Sorghum, peanuts; mfg. (steel tanks); oil and gas. Clyde L. to SE.

Clyde, village (1991 pop. 441), central Alta., Canada, 40 mi/64 km N of Edmonton. Wheat, barley, livestock.

Clyde, village (☐ a sq mi/5.2 sq km; 1990 pop. 2,409), Wayne co., W central N.Y., on the Barge Canal and Clyde R., 18 mi/29 km NW of Auburn; 43°04′N 76°52′W. In dairying and fruit-growing area; mfg. (pallets, boxes, and cathode ray tubes). Inc. 1835.

Clyde Hill, town (1990 pop. 2,972), King co., W Wash., residential suburb 5 mi/8 km ENE of downtown Seattle, 1 mi/1.6 km NW of Bellevue, on peninsula on E shore of L. Washington; 47°38′N 122°13′W. Evergreen Point Bridge to Seattle to W.

Clyde Park, village (1990 pop. 282), Park co., S Mont., on Shields R. and Cottonwood Creek, 15 mi/24 km N of Livingston; 45°53′N 110°37′W. Barley, oats, vegetables, horses, cattle. Bridger Bowl Ski Area to W; Gallatin Natl. Forest To W and NE. Formerly called Sunnyside.

Clyde River or **Kangirtugaapik**, trading post (1991 pop. 565), E Baffin Isl., SE Franklin Dist., N.W.T., Canada, on R. Clyde, inlet (70 mi/113 km long, 7 mi/11 km wide at mouth) of Davis Strait; 70°28′N 68°34′W. Radio station. Hudson's Bay Co. post was est. 1924. Hunting, trapping; carvings. Scheduled air service. At Cape Christian, 9 mi/14 km NE, is U.S. Naval Station (closed 1975) and govt. meteorological station (built 1924).

Clyde River 1 c.37 mi/60 km long, W central N.Y.; continuation of outlet of Canandaigua L.; flows generally E from Lyons, past Clyde, to Seneca R., 7 mi/11.3 km NE of Seneca Falls. Partly utilized by N.Y. State Barge Canal. **2** c.25 mi/40 km long, in NE Vt.; rises in Island Pond in Essex co.; flows NW, past Charleston, to L. Memphremagog opposite Newport.

Clyman, village (1990 pop. 370), Dodge co., S central Wis., 12 mi/19 km SSE of Beaver Dam; 43°18′N 88°43′W. In dairying region. RR junction. Mfg. (vegetable processing, California olives, cherries).

Clymer, village (1990 pop. 600), Chautauqua co., extreme W N.Y., 21 mi/34 km WSW of Jamestown, near Pa. line; 42°02′N 79°35′W.

Clymer (KLEI-muhr), borough (1990 pop. 1,499), Indiana co., W central Pa., 8 mi/12.9 km ENE of Indiana on Two Lick Creek; 40°40′N 79°00′W. Subsurface bituminous coal, clay; mfg. (meat processing). Agr. area (corn, hay; poultry, livestock; dairying). Inc. 1905.

Coacalco de Berriozábal (ko-ah-KAL-ko dai be-ree-o-SAH-bahl), city (1990 pop. 151,255) and township, ☉ Coacalco municipio, Mexico state, central Mexico, 14 mi/23 km N of Mexico City; 19°38′N 99°06′W. A part of the Área Metropolitana de la Ciudad de México.

Coachella, city (1990 pop. 16,896), Riverside co., S Calif., in Coachella Valley, suburb 3 mi/4.8 km SE of Indio, and 70 mi/113 km ESE of Riverside; 33°41′N 116°10′W.

Irrigated agr. area (dates, citrus, peppers; nursery stock); mfg. (iron and steel forgings, date processing). Coachella canal and Colorado R. Aqueduct are to NE. Torrez Martinez Indian Reservation to S. Salton Sea, inland saltwater lake (below sea level), 12 mi/19 km ESE; Salton Sea State Recreation Area on NE shore; Joshua Tree Natl. Monument to NE; San Bernardino Natl. Forest to SW. Inc. 1946.

Coachella Valley, irrigated arid region, central Riverside co., SE Calif., NW of the Salton Sea. Water is brought into the region by artesian wells; the Coachella Canal (123 mi/198 km long), a branch of the All-American Canal built bet. 1938 and 1948; the Colorado R. Aqueduct, which carries water from Parker Dam on the Colorado R. to Los Angeles and San Diego, and runs through the NE side of the valley; and intermittent Whitewater R. flowing through the valley. More than 100,000 acres/40,470 ha have been irrigated. Vegetables, especially peppers, avocados, dates (the majority of U.S. production), citrus fruits, grain, and cotton are grown in the region; also nursery stock and poultry. The prods. are shipped from the city of Coachella, which serves as a distribution point for the valley. Includes rapidly growing resort communities of Palm Springs, Palm Desert, and others. Coachella and Indio are in S part.

Coacoatzintla (kwa-kwat-SEEN-tlah), town (1990 pop. 3,092), Veracruz, E Mexico, in Sierra Madre Oriental, 9 mi/14.5 km N of Xalapa Enríque. Coffee.

Coahoma (ko-HO-muh), county (☐ 583 sq mi/1,510 sq km; 1990 pop. 31,665), NW Miss.; ☉ Clarksdale; 34°13′N 90°35′W. Bounded NW and W by Mississippi R. (Ark. state line); drained by Sunflower R. Rich agr. area (soybeans, corn, rice, sorghum, wheat; cattle; timber). Moon L. in NW, an oxbow lake, near Mississippi R. and source of Sunflower R., a prehistoric channel of the Mississippi R.; De Soto L., in SW, also an oxbow, forms part of Ark.-Miss. state line. Formed 1836.

Coahoma (KO-uh-ho-muh), town (1990 pop. 1,133), Howard co., W Texas, 10 mi/16 km ENE of Big Spring; 32°17′N 101°18′W. In cattle-ranching, agr. (vegetables), and oil and gas region; natural-gas processing.

Coahoma (ko-HO-muh), village (1990 pop. 254), Coahoma co., NW Miss., 11 mi/18 km NNE of Clarksdale, near Sunflower R.; 34°22′N 90°31′W. Cotton, corn, rice; cattle. Moon L. to N.

Coahuayana de Hidalgo (ko-ah-wah-YAH-nah de ee-DAHL-go), town (1990 pop. 5,828), ☉ Coahuayana municipio, Michoacán, W Mexico, on Tuxpan (or Coahuayana) R., 35 mi/56 km SSE of Colima. Rice, sugarcane, and fruit are grown. Formerly called Coahuayana.

Coahuayana River, W Mexico: see TUXPAN RIVER.

Coahuayutla de Guerrero (ko-ah-wah-YOU-tla de ge-RE-ro), town (1990 pop. 1,281), ☉ Coahuayutla de José María Izazaga municipio, Guerrero, SW Mexico, in NW outliers of Sierra Madre del Sur, 39 mi/63 km ENE of Lázaro Cárdenas; 18°19′N 101°42′W. Elev. 1,175 ft/358 m. Fruit; silver deposits.

Coahuayutla de José María Izazaga, Mexico: see COAHUAYUTLA DE GUERRERO.

Coahuila (ko-ah-WEE-lah), officially Coahuila de Zaragoza, state (☐58,067 sq mi/150,394 sq km; 1990 pop. 1,972,340), N Mexico, on the N bulge of the Rio Grande, S of Texas; ☉ SALTILLO; 26°51′N 100°57′W. Bounded on N by U.S., on E by Nuevo León state, on S by Zacatecas and Durango states, and on W by Durango and Chihuahua states. Arid to semi-arid climate. Across W Coahuila and E Chihuahua lie vast, arid plains (some of them recently irrigated), which are broken by barren hills; most notable of these plains is the Bolsón de Mapimí, extending into Chihuahua. South of the Bolsón is a fertile lake region, center of a large basin of interior drainage with no outlet to the sea. A considerable portion of the LAGUNA DISTRICT lies in this area. TORREÓN is the chief metropolis. In the E part of the state, where peaks of the Sierra Madre Oriental rise, are quantities of silver, copper, lead, iron, and zinc. Coahuila is an important coal-producing state and a leading natl. producer of iron and steel.

Lumbering is important, and NE of the mts., in the drainage area of the Rio Grande, there is considerable cattle raising. Coahuila produces cotton, corn, and grapes; the state is noted for its wines. Exploration of the territory began in the 16th cent. but was hampered by Native Amer. hostility. After playing some part in the war against Spain, Coahuila was combined (1830) with Texas, an action that caused dissatisfaction among the U.S. minority and contributed to the Texas Revolution (1835–1836). During the Mexican War, Saltillo was of strategic importance, and the battle of Buena Vista was fought nearby. Joined with Nuevo León by the constitution of 1857, Coahuila regained its separate status in 1868. The revolutionary leaders Francisco I. Madero and Venustiano Carranza were born in the state.

Coahuitlán, Mexico: see PROGRESO DE ZARAGOZA.

Coajomulco, Mexico: see CUAXOMULCO.

Coakley Town, Bahama Isls.: see FRESH CREEK.

Coal, county (□ 521 sq mi/1,349 sq km; 1990 pop. 5,780), S central Okla.; ⊙ Coalgate; 34°36′N 96°17′W. Drained by Clear Boggy and Muddy Boggy creeks. Agr. (corn, sorghum; cattle, hogs, poultry). Some mfg. (apparel) at Coalgate, former coal-mining town (last mine closed 1958). Formed 1907.

Coal Center, borough (1990 pop. 184), Washington co., SW Pa., suburb, 1 mi/1.6 km W of California, on Monongahela R., at mouth of Pike Run; 40°04′N 79°54′W. Bituminous coal.

Coal City, uninc. town (1990 pop. 1,876), Raleigh co., S W.Va., 7 mi/11.3 km S of Beckley; 37°40′N 81°12′W. Agr. (corn; nursery crops; cattle); bituminous coal.

Coal City 1 village (1990 pop. 3,907), Grundy co., NE Ill., 21 mi/34 km SW of Joliet; 41°17′N 88°16′W. In agr. area; mfg. (apparel, metal prods.). Founded 1875, inc. 1881. Recreational use and strip mines in area. **2** village, Owen co., SW central Ind., 8 mi/12.9 km NNW of Worthington. Bituminous-coal area. Old surface coal mines nearby. Laid out 1875.

Coal Creek, village, SE B.C., Canada, in Rocky Mts., 5 mi/8 km E of Fernie; 49°28′N 114°56′W. Coal mining; cattle.

Coal Creek, village (1990 pop. 157), Fremont co., S central Colo., near Ark. R., just NE of Wet Mts., 30 mi/48 km WNW of Pueblo; 38°21′N 105°09′W. Elev. 5,600 ft/1,707 m. Part of San Isabel Natl. Forest to SW. Sometimes spelled Coalcreek.

Coal Creek, Tenn.: see LAKE CITY.

Coal Fork, uninc. town (1990 pop. 2,100), Kanawha co., W central W.Va., a suburb 6 mi/9.7 km SE of Charleston; 38°19′N 81°31′W.

Coal Grove, village (1990 pop. 2,251), Lawrence co., S Ohio, just N of Ashland, Ky., across Ohio R.; 38°29′N 82°38′W.

Coal Hill, town (1990 pop. 912), Johnson co., NW Ark., 10 mi/16 km W of Clarksville near Ark. R. (upper reach of L. Dardanelle); 35°26′N 93°40′W. In agr. area.

Coal River, W.Va.: see BIG COAL RIVER.

Coal Run Village, village (1990 pop. 262), Pike co., E Ky., residential suburb, 1 mi/1.6 km N of Pikesville, on Russell Fork R.;37°30′N 82°33′W. RR junction. Coal-mining region.

Coal Valley, village, W Alta., Canada, in Rocky Mts., near Jasper Natl. Park, 40 mi/64 km SW of Edson. Coal; cattle.

Coal Valley, village (1990 pop. 2,683), Rock Island co., NW Ill., 7 mi/11.3 km SE of Rock Isl.; 41°27′N 90°27′W. In agr. area.

Coalcomán de Matamaros, Mexico: see COALCOMÁN DE VÁZQUEZ PALLARES.

Coalcomán de Vázquez Pallares (ko-ahl-ko-MAHN de VAHS-kez pa-YAR-es), town (1990 pop. 7,520), Michoacán, W Mexico, in NW foothills of Sierra Madre del Sur, 50 mi/80 km SE of Colima; 18°46′N 103°08′W. Cereals, fruit, coffee, sugarcane. Formerly called Coalcomán de Matamaros.

Coaldale, town (1991 pop. 5,310), S Alta., Canada, 10 mi/16 km E of Lethbridge; 49°44′N 112°37′W. Coal mining; wheat, sugar beets, flax.

Coaldale, village, Fremont co., S central Colo., on Ark.

R., just E of Sangre de Cristo Mts., and 30 mi/48 km WSW of Cañon City; elev. 6,480 ft/1,975 m. Coal mines. Part of San Isabel Natl. Forest to SW.

Coaldale 1 (KOL-dail), borough (1990 pop. 143), Bedford co., S Pa., 17 mi/27 km NE of Bedford, on Six Mile Run; 40°10′N 78°13′W. Livestock, dairying; coal. **2** borough (1990 pop. 2,531), Schuylkill co., E central Pa., 11 mi/18 km NE of Pottsville; 40°49′N 75°55′W. Steel fabrication; anthracite coal; agr. (grain); poultry, livestock; dairying). Settled 1868, inc. 1871.

Coalgate, town (1990 pop. 1,895), ⊙ Coal co., S central Okla., 31 mi/50 km ESE of Ada, near Muddy Boggy Creek; 34°31′N 96°13′W. Elev. 623 ft/190 m. Supply center for farm area (corn, sorghum; livestock); mfg. (apparel); meat packing. Formerly a coal-mining center; Mining Mus. here.

Coalgood, uninc. village, Harlan co., SE Ky., in the Cumberland Mts., 6 mi/9.7 km SE of Harlan, near Martin's Fork Cumberland R. Bituminous coal in area; coal processing.

Coalhurst, village (1991 pop. 1,322), S Alta., Canada, 5 mi/8 km NW of Lethbridge. Coal mining; oil and gas; wheat, sugar beets, flax.

Coalinga, city (1990 pop. 8,212), Fresno co., central Calif., in NE foothills of Coast Ranges, 50 mi/80 km SW of Fresno; 36°08′N 120°21′W. RR terminus. Cholame Hills to SW, Kettleman Hills to SE, Black Mts. to N. Calinga Oil Fields to W and N. Oil field center; oil refining; mfg. of oil well supplies; petroleum refinery. Also dairying, cattle, grain. Seat of Coalinga Community Col. R.C. Baker Memorial Mus. Inc. 1906.

Coalmont, city (1990 pop. 813), Grundy co., SE central Tenn., 31 mi/50 km NW of Chattanooga; 35°20′N 85°42′W.

Coalmont, village, SW B.C., Canada, in Cascade Mts., on Tulameen R., 5 mi/8 km NW of Princeton, and 5 mi/8 km W of Penticton; 49°31′N 120°41′W. Now a ghost town.

Coalmont, village, Jackson co., N Colo., on N. Platte R. and Little Grizzly Creek, 14 mi/23 km SW of Walden; elev. 8,209 ft/2,502 m. Rail terminus. Strip mining of coal; sheep, hay, timber. Routt Natl. Forest to W and SE.

Coalmont (KOL-mahnt), borough (1990 pop. 109), Huntingdon co., S Pa., 21 mi/34 km SSW of Huntingdon, on Shoup Run; 40°12′N 78°02′W. Bituminous coal.

Coalport (KOL-port), borough (1990 pop. 578), Clearfield co., central Pa., 17 mi/27 km NNW of Altoona, on Clearfield Creek; 40°45′N 78°31′W. Bituminous coal; light mfg. Prince Gallitzin State Park, including Glendale L. reservoir, to S. Inc. 1883.

Coalspur, village, W Alta., Canada, in Rocky Mts., near Jasper Natl. Park, 35 mi/56 km SW of Edson; 53°11′N 117°01′W. RR junction; coal mining; cattle.

Coalton 1 village (1990 pop. 359), Montgomery co., S central Ill., 13 mi/21 km NE of Hillsboro; 39°16′N 89°17′W. In agr. and bituminous-coal area. **2** village (1990 pop. 553), Jackson co., S Ohio, 25 mi/40 km SE of Chillicothe; 39°07′N 82°37′W. In agr. and coal mining area. **3** village (1990 pop. 277), Randolph co., E central W.Va., 7 mi/11.3 km WSW of Elkins; 38°53′N 79°57′W. Mfg. (coal processing); agr. (grain; livestock, poultry); bituminous coal. Official name of village is Womelsdorf.

Coalville, town (1990 pop. 1065), ⊙ Summit co., N Utah, on Weber R., at S end of Echo Reservoir, and 37 mi/ 60 km SE of Ogden, at center of vast area generally surrounded by Wasatch Natl. Forest; 40°55′N 111°23′W. Elev. 5,586 ft/1,703 m. Livestock (cattle, sheep) and poultry area; alfalfa; oil and natural gas; dairying; mfg. (dairy prods.; natural gas liquids). Coal mine nearby. Natl. forests in vicinity. Rockport Reservoir and State Park to S.

Coalwood, uninc. town (1990 pop. 900), McDowell co., S W. Va., 6 mi/9.7 km SW of Welch on Clear Creek, in coal region.

Coamo (ko-AH-mo), town (1990 pop. 33,837), S central P.R., on the Coamo R. Poultry center; livestock, horses; textile mfg. Just SSW is Baños de Coamo or Coamo Springs, natural hot baths. The town was founded in

the 16th cent. Has 18th-cent. church; historical mus. Internatl. San Blas marathon held here every year.

Coamo River (ko-AH-mo), c.20 mi/32 km long, S central P.R.; rises in the Cordillera Central; flows S, past Coamo, to the Caribbean W of Santa Isabel.

Coapilla (ko-wah-PEE-yah), town (1990 pop. 2,177), Chiapas, S Mexico, in N spur of Sierra Madre, 25 mi/ 40 km N of Tuxtla Gutiérrez. Corn, fruit. A Zoque Indian town.

Coast Fork, river, c.55 mi/89 km long, W Oregon; rises in N Douglas co., on W slope of Cascade Range; flows N, through Cottage Grove Reservoir, past Cottage Grove and Creswell, joining Middle Fork 4 mi/6.4 km SE of Eugene to form Willamette R. Cottage Grove Dam, 6 mi/9.7 km S of Cottage Grove, consists of rolled-earth embankment (1,750 ft/533 m long, 95 ft/ 29 m high) and concrete sect. (360 ft/110 m long, 100 ft/ 30 m high); total length 2,110 ft/643 m. Completed 1942 as unit in flood-control and navigation project in Willamette R. basin. Forms small reservoir. On a tributary (Row R.) is Dorena Dam (145 ft/44 m high, 3,388 ft/ 1,033 m long), begun in 1947.

Coast Mountains, moutain range, W B.C., Canada, and SE Alaska, extending c.1,000 mi/1,610 km parallel to the Pacific coast, from the mts. of Alaska near the Yukon border to the Cascade Range near the Fraser R. Mt. Waddington (13,260 ft/4,042 m) is the highest peak. The geologically complex range, composed mainly of metamorphic rocks, slopes steeply to the Pacific Ocean, where the shoreline is deeply indented by fjords. The Coast Mts. have been heavily eroded by mt. glaciers; numerous rivers, including the Fraser, the Skeena, and the Stikine, have cut deep gorges across the range. The average annual precipitation of c.90 in/ 230 cm makes the region one of the wettest parts of Canada. Its slopes are heavily forested, and lumbering is important. In the Coast Mts. is Kemano, one of Canada's largest hydroelectric plants. The Coast Mts. are sometimes confused with the geologically distinct COAST RANGES.

Coast Ranges, series of mountain ranges along the Pacific coast of N. Amer. extending from SE Alaska to Baja California; from 2,000 ft/610 m–20,000 ft/6,100 m high. The ranges include the St. Elias Mts. in SE Alaska and SW Yukon, which have the highest elevations; a partially submerged portion that forms the isls. off the coast of SE Alaska and B.C.; the Olympic Mts. in Wash.; the Coast Ranges in Oregon; the Klamath Mts., Coast Ranges, and Los Angeles Ranges in Calif.; and the Peninsular Range in Baja Calif. The Coast Ranges are rugged, geologically young mts. formed by faulting and folding and are composed mainly of granitic rock; the N third is glaciated. N of San Francisco the ranges are humid and thickly forested; the S parts are dry and covered with brush and grass. Lumbering, mining, and tourism are important.

Coatecas Altas (ko-ah-TE-kahs AHL-tahs), town (1990 pop. 1,984), in S Oaxaca, Mexico, 6 mi/10 km E of Ejutla de Crespo; 16°15′N 96°40′W. Elev. 4,872 ft/ 1,485 m. Mountainous terrain. Primarily subsistence agr. Zapotec Indian pop.

Coatepec (ko-AH-te-pek), city (1990 pop. 36,692) and township, ⊙ Coatepec municipio, Veracruz, E Mexico, at E foot of Cofre de Perote, in Sierra Madre Oriental, 5 mi/8 km SSW of Xalapa Enríquez; 19°27′N 96°57′W. Elev. 4,108 ft/1,252 m. RR junction. Center for agr. (corn, sugarcane, coffee, oranges) and processing (sugar refining, coffee roasting, alcohol distilling, wine making; textile milling). Picturesque Indian town in densely forested area; famed for orchids.

Coatepec (ko-AH-te-pek), town (1990 pop. 895), Puebla, central Mexico, in SE foothills of Sierra Madre Oriental, 22 mi/35 km ESE of Huauchinango. Sugarcane, fruit, cereals; wood. Humid climate.

Coatepec Harinas (ko-AH-te-pek ah-REE-nas), town (1990 pop. 5,264), Mexico state, central Mexico, 21 mi/ 34 km S of Toluca de Lerdo; 18°56′N 99°41′W. Agr. center (sugarcane, fruit, cereals, livestock). Sometimes Coatepec de las Bateas or San Nicolás Coatepec.

Coates, village (1990 pop. 186), Dakota co., SE Minn.,

suburb, 16 mi/26 km S of downtown St. Paul; 44°43′N 93°02′W. Agr. area (grains, livestock; dairying). Mississippi R. to NE.

Coatesville (KOTS-vil), city (1990 pop. 11,038), Chester co., SE Pa., on West Branch Brandywine Creek (near source); 39°58′N 75°49′W. Mfg., esp. steel- (has steel plant) and paper-related. Agr. area (grain, soybeans, apples, vegetables; poultry, livestock; dairying). Marsh Creek Reservoir and State Park to NE; Embreeville State Hospital to SE; Chester Co. Carlson Airport to W. Settled c.1717; inc. as a city 1916.

Coatesville, town (1990 pop. 469), Hendricks co., central Ind., 9 mi/14.5 km WSW of Danville; 39°41′N 40°86′W. In dairy, grain, and livestock area; timber. Mfg. (lawn mowers).

Coaticook (ko-A-ti-kook), town (1991 pop. 6,637), ⊙ Stanstead co., S Que., Canada, on Coaticook R., and 19 mi/31 km SSE of Sherbrooke, near Vt. border; 45°08′N 71°48′W. Milling, lumbering; mfg. of textile prods., consumer goods, furniture.

Coatlán del Río (ko-aht-LAHN del REE-o), town (1990 pop. 2,146), Morelos, central Mexico, 18 mi/29 km SW of Cuernavaca. Rice, sugarcane, fruit.

Coats, town (1990 pop. 1,493), Harnett co., central N.C., 8 mi/12.9 km NNW of Dunn, near South R.; 35°24′N 78°40′W. Tobacco, cotton, sweet potatoes, grain; poultry, livestock. Light mfg.

Coats, village (1990 pop. 127), Pratt co., S Kansas, 10 mi/16 km SSW of Pratt; 37°30′N 98°49′W. Wheat, livestock.

Coats Island (□ 1,544 sq mi/3,999 sq km), E Keewatin dist., N.W.T., Canada, in N part of Hudson Bay, S of Southampton Isl., across Fisher and Evans straits; 80 mi/129 km long, 13 mi/21 km–30 mi/48 km wide; 62°35′N 83°00′W. Became reindeer reserve, 1920.

Coatsburg, village (1990 pop. 201), Adams co., W Ill., 15 mi/24 km ENE of Quincy; 40°01′N 91°09′W. In agr. area; ships grain, livestock.

Coatzacoalcos (ko-aht-sah-ko-AHL-kos), city (1990 pop. 198,817), Veracruz state, E central Mexico, at the mouth of the Coatzacoalcos R.; 18°10′N 94°25′W. A port on the Gulf of Campeche, as well as the N terminus of RR traffic across the Isthmus of Tehuantepec. Good highway communications. With Minatitlán the center of Mexico's petroleum and petrochemical industry. Oil, petrochemical prods., sulfur, and timber are produced and exported. Formerly called Puerto México.

Coatzacoalcos River (ko-aht-sah-ko-AHL-kos), c.175 mi/282 km long, in Oaxaca and Veracruz, SE Mexico, the most important river of the Isthmus of Tehuantepec; rises in headstreams in Sierra Madre del Sur N of Ciudad Ixtepec; flows NNE in meandering course, past Minatitlán, to Gulf of Campeche at Coatzacoalcos. Navigable 125 mi/201 km. Its lower course was early explored by Cortés.

Coatzingo (ko-aht-SEEN-go), town (1990 pop. 2,824), Puebla, central Mexico, near Atoyac R., 18 mi/29 km E of Izúcar de Matamoros. Agr. center (corn, sugarcane, rice; livestock).

Coatzintla (ko-aht-SEEN-tlah), town (1990 pop. 20,493), Veracruz, E Mexico, near Cazones R., 10 mi/16 km WNW of Papantla de Olarte; 20°30′N 97°28′W. Petroleum. In Totonac Indian area.

Cobá (ko-BAH), historic site (□ 80 sq mi/207 sq km), in N Quintana Roo, Mexico, 27 mi/44 km NW of Tulum. Cobá is on the Maya Route. The Cobá ruins surround L. Cobá and 4 small lakes outside of the village of Cobá. This ceremonial center dates A.D. 600–900 and is believed to have had 50,000 residents at its peak. Nochul Mul, a 138-ft/42-m-high pyramid is the tallest in N Yucatán.

Cobalt (KO-bolt), town (1991 pop. 1,470), E Ont., Canada, NE of Sudbury, near L. Timiskaming; 47°23′N 79°41′W. Once a center for cobalt and silver mining. Mining mus. and an annual Miner's Festival.

Cobb, county (□ 345 sq mi/894 sq km; 1990 pop. 447,745), NW central Ga.; ⊙ Marietta; 33°56′N 84°35′W. Bounded SE by Chattahoochee R.; includes part of Allatoona Reservoir in NW. Major suburban

county in Atlanta region. Significant white-collar employment. Home of Lockheed-Ga. aircraft mfg. facility. Contains Kennesaw Mt. Natl. Battlefield Park and Marietta Natl. Military Cemetery. Formed 1832.

Cobb, uninc. town (1990 pop. 1,471), Lake co., NW Calif., 16 mi/26 km NE of Healdsburg, on Kelsey Creek; 38°51′N 122°43′W. Cobb Mt. to SW; Boggs Mt. State Forest to NE; Clear L. to N. Timber.

Cobb, village (1990 pop. 440), Iowa co., SW Wis., near source of Pecatonica R., 10 mi/16 km W of Dodgeville; 42°58′N 90°19′W. Black Hawk L. reservoir to NE.

Cobb Island, Northampton co., E Va., barrier isl. off Atlantic Ocean shore, 13 mi/21 km ENE of Cape Charles city; 5 mi/8 km long. Coast Guard station, lighthouse. Cobb Isl. Bay to W. Great Machipongo Inlet and Hog Isl. to N, Sand Shoal Inlet and Wreck Isl. to S.

Cobble Hill, village, SW B.C., Canada, on SE Vancouver Isl., 22 mi/35 km NW of Victoria; 48°41′N 123°36′W. Lumbering, mixed farming, fruit growing.

Cobble Hill, W. central sect. of borough of Brooklyn, N.Y. city, SE N.Y., S of Atlantic Ave., N of Carroll Gardens, and just below Brooklyn Heights. Brownstone dist. whose roots date to 17th-cent. Du. farm country; filled with comfortable row houses built in mid–19th cent. and occupied largely by Germans and Italians, followed by an influx of Syrians and Lebanese after World War I. Atlantic Ave., known as "Swedish Broadway" at turn of cent., is now famous for its many Middle Eastern businesses; it is known as N.Y. city's Middle East. Fort Cobbleskill figured prominently in the American Revolution's Battle of Long Isl. The dist. was in the forefront of N.Y. city's preservationist "Brownstone Revolution"; here, 22 blocks of preserved bldgs. constitute the Cobble Hill Historic Dist. There are also many Victorian houses, esp. along Clinton St.

Cobble Mountain Reservoir, SW Mass., c.5 mi/8 km long; impounded by Cobble Mt. Dam (263 ft/80 m high, 730 ft/223 m long; completed 1932) in short Little R., 15 mi/24 km W of Springfield, to which it supplies water and power.

Cobbosseecontee, Lake (kuh-bahs-ee-KAHN-tee), Kennebec co., S Maine, summer and winter resort center, 8 mi/12.9 km WSW of Augusta; 9 mi/14.5 km length, 1 mi/1.6 km average width, with many isls. Drains SE through Cobbosseecontee Stream into Pleasant Pond.

Cobbtown, village (1990 pop. 338), Tattnall co., E central Ga., 25 mi/40 km WSW of Statesboro; 32°17′N 82°08′W. Light mfg.

Cobden, village (1991 pop. 1,026), SE Ont., Canada, at SE end of Muskrat L., 18 mi/29 km SE of Pembroke; 45°37′N 76°53′W. Dairying, lumbering.

Cobden 1 (KAHB-din), village (1990 pop. 1,090), Union co., S Ill., 36 mi/58 km N of Cairo; 37°31′N 89°15′W. In fruit-growing area; ships fruit, vegetables, wheat, corn; mfg. of food prods. Inc. 1875. Near Shawnee Nat'l Forest. **2** village (1990 pop. 62), Brown co., SW Minn., 19 mi/31 km W of New Ulm, on Sleepy Eye Creek; 44°16′N 94°50′W. Grain; livestock; dairying.

Cobequid Bay (KAH-buh-kwid), E arm (30 mi/48 km long, 6 mi/10 km wide) of the Minas Basin, central N.S., Canada, extending E to Truro. Receives Shubenacadie R.

Cobequid Mountains, range in N N.S., Canada, extending 120 mi/193 km E-W along Northumberland Strait, bet. Minas Basin and Antigonish; rises to 1,100 ft/335 m, 12 mi/19 km W of Westville.

Cobleskill (KO-buhl-skil), village (□ 3 sq mi/7.8 sq km; 1990 pop. 5,268) in Cobleskill town (1990 pop. 7,270), Schoharie co., E central N.Y., 36 mi/58 km W of Albany; 42°40′N 74°29′W. Dairying; mfg. (construction materials, textiles, molded plastics, metalwork). Seat of State Univ. of N.Y. Col. of Agr. and Technology at Cobleskill. Cobleskill Historic Dist. Howe Caverns at Howes Cave (6 mi/9.7 km E). Settled 1752, inc. 1868.

Coboconk (KO-bo-kahngk), village, S Ont., Canada, near Balsam L., 20 mi/32 km NNW of Lindsay; 44°40′N 78°48′W. Dairying, mixed farming.

Cobourg (KO-buhrg), town (1991 pop. 15,079), ⊙ Northumberland. co., S Ont., Canada, on L. Ontario, 65 mi/105 km ENE of Toronto; 43°58′N 78°10′W. Commuter suburb of Toronto. Port, with mfg. (plastics, fabricated metal prods., machinery, lighting fixtures, chemicals, paper prods.); mixed farming (esp. apples), dairying; popular resort and agr. market.

Cobourg Island or **Coburg Island** (both: KO-buhrg) (22 mi/35 km long, 4 mi/6 km–14 mi/23 km wide), E Franklin Dist., N.W.T., Canada, in Baffin Bay, at entrance of Jones Sound, bet. Ellesmere and Devon isls.; 75°58′N 79°30′W. Mountainous. Large numbers of murres breed here.

Cobre, El (KO-brai, AIL), town, Santiago de Cuba prov., SE Cuba, in a high valley of the Sierra Maestra; 20°03′N 75°57′W. Once famous for rich copper mines (hence the name El Cobre), it is chiefly noted for a shrine to Our Lady of Charity (*La Virgen de la Caridad del Cobre*), Cuba's patron saint. Near headwaters of R. bearing same name.

Cobre River, St. Catherine parish, central and S Jamaica; rises 8 mi/12.9 km S of Port Maria, flows c.35 mi/56 km S and E, past Linstead, Bog Walk, Spanish Town, and Gregory Park, to Kingston Harbour, 4 mi/6.4 km W of Kingston; 17°59′N 76°52′W. Used for irrigation. Also called Rio Cobre.

Cobre, Sierra del (KO-brai, see-ER-uh dail), Santiago de Cuba prov., E Cuba, the E sect. of the SIERRA MAESTRA, just W of Santiago de Cuba, with town of Cobre (copper deposits) on its slopes; 20°01′N 76°02′W. San Pedro peak (3,599 ft/1,097 m) is the highest point. A Can. mining company holds exploration rights to the area. Cojímar R. has carved out a striking gorge at W end of this range and flows a short distance to the Caribbean Sea.

Cobscook Bay (KAHBS-kuk), Washington co., E Maine, inlet of Passamaquoddy Bay lying W of Eastport; c.7 mi/11.3 km long. Average tidal range, 18 ft/5 m. Dams of Passamaquoddy Bay tidal power project were built here.

Cobscook River, Maine: see DENNYS BAY.

Coburg 1 town (1990 pop. 58), Montgomery co., SW Iowa, near East Nishnabotna R., 7 mi/11.3 km S of Red Oak; 40°55′N 95°16′W. In agr. region. **2** (KO-buhrg), town (1990 pop. 763), Lane co., W Oregon, 5 mi/8 km N of Eugene, near McKenzie R.; 44°08′N 123°03′W. Nurseries; dairy prods.; berries, fruit, grain; poultry, livestock.

Coburg Island, Canada: see COBOURG ISLAND.

Coburn Gore (KO-buhrn GOR), town, on Que. (Canada) border, Franklin co., W Maine, 32 mi/51 km WSW of Jackman. Includes lumbering village of Moosehorn. Customs post.

Coburn Mountain (KO-buhrn) (3,718 ft/1,133 m), Somerset co., W Maine, 14 mi/23 km SE of Jackman. In hunting, fishing area. Inactive lookout station.

Cocheco River (kuh-CHEE-ko), E N.H., rises in N Strafford co., flows 30 mi/48 km SE, past Rochester and Dover (water power), to junction with Salmon Falls R., forming the Piscataqua.

Cochetopa Pass (10,067 ft/3,068 m), on Continental Divide, Saguache co., SW central Colo. Crossed by country road. Rio Grande Natl. Forest (SE), Gunnison Natl. Forest (NW).

Cochinos Bay (ko-CHEE-noz), Eng. Bay of Pigs, Caribbean inlet (15 mi/24 km long N-S, up to 5 mi/8 km wide), Matanzas prov., S Cuba, cutting off Zapata Peninsula (W), 45 mi/72 km W of Cienfuegos; 22°05′N 81°10′W. Site of ill-fated anti-Castro invasion (1961). Land surrounding bay may be future nature preserve.

Cochise (co-CHEES), county (□ 6,219 sq mi/16,107 sq km; 1990 pop. 97,624), SE Ariz.; ⊙ Bisbee; 31°53′N 109°44′W. Bounded by N.Mex., on E, and Mex. (Sonora state) on S. Copper mined near Warren and Bisbee, in SW. Silver, gold, gypsum. Irrigated farming along San Pedro R. and San Simon Creek (cotton, alfalfa, hay, wheat, corn, sorghum, lettuce; cattle, hogs); mfg. at Sierra Vista and Douglas. Chief ranges are Chiricahua, Dos Cabezas, Dragoon, and Mule mts. Includes

Chiricahua Natl. Monument and Fort Bowie Natl. Historic Site in E and several parts of Coronado Natl. Forest scattered throughout co. Coronado Natl. Monument and San Pedro Riparian Natl. Conservation Area in SW; historic town of Tombstone and Tombstone Courthouse State Historical Park in W center. Fort Huachuca, important in economy, very close to Sierra Vista urban area in SW. Formed 1881.

Cochise Head, Ariz.: see CHIRICAHUA MOUNTAINS.

Cochiti (KO- chi-tee), pueblo (□ 35 sq mi/91 sq km; 1990 pop. 434), Sandoval co., N central N.Mex; on W bank of the Rio Grande and 23 mi/37 km WSW of Santa Fe in Santo Domingo Indian Reservation; 35°36′N 106°20′W. Elev. 5,236 ft/1,596 m. Pueblo Indians here make pottery and raise livestock and corn. Festival of San Buenaventura, patron saint, takes place in July in connection with rain dance. San Buenaventura de Cochití Mission dates from 17th cent. Village named by Juan de Oñate in 1598 after hearing kotyete, which means stone kiva.

Cochiti Lake (KO- chi-tee), uninc. village, Sandoval co., N central N.Mex., 25 mi/40 km W of Santa Fe, on Rio Grande, near S end of Cochiti L. reservoir, in Santo Domingo Indian Reservation. Recreation. Bandelier Natl. Monument to N.

Cochituate, Mass.: see WAYLAND.

Cochituate, Lake (ko-CHIT-choo-wuht), reservoir, at Natick, Middlesex co., E Mass., on Sudbury R., 16 mi/26 km WSW of Boston; c.3 mi/4.8 km long; 42°18′N 71°22′W. Originally part of water-supply system for Boston area. Cochituate village to NE. Lake Cochituate State Park on E shore.

Cochran, county (□ 775 sq mi/2,007 sq km; 1990 pop. 4,377), NW Texas; ⊙ Morton; 33°36′N 102°49′W. On Llano Estacado, and bounded W by N.Mex. border; elev. 3,500 ft/1,067 m–3,800 ft/1,158 m. Cattle ranching, agr. (cotton, grain sorghum, wheat). Oil and gas wells. Formed 1876.

Cochran (KAHK-ruhn), town (1990 pop. 4,390), ⊙ Bleckley co., central Ga., 34 mi/55 km SSE of Macon; 32°23′N 83°21′W. Mfg. of wooden prods., textiles, fixtures; cotton processing. Middle Ga. Col., a unit of the Univ. System of Ga., located here. Inc. 1870.

Cochrane (KAH-kruhn), district (□ 52,237 sq mi/135,294 sq km; 1991 pop. 93,917), NE Ont., Canada, on Que. border, and on James Bay of the Hudson Bay; ⊙ Cochrane; 50°30′N 83°00′W.

Cochrane 1 (KAH-kruhn), town (1991 pop. 5,265), S Alta., Canada, on Bow R., and 20 mi/32 km NW of Calgary. Mixed farming, wheat, barley; cattle; hydroelectricity. Dormitory town for Calgary. **2** town (1991 pop. 4,585), ⊙ Cochrane dist., NE Ont., Canada, 45 mi/72 km NNE of Timmins; 49°04′N 81°01′W. Commercial center of NE Ont. and W Que. mining region, with machinery mfg., pulp and paper milling, lumbering, woodworking; dairy. Passenger train service, "The Polar Bear Express," to Moosonee, on Hudson Bay. Starting point of prospecting and hunting parties. Founded 1908.

Cochrane (KUH-kruhn), village (1990 pop. 475), Buffalo co., W Wis., near the Mississippi, 13 mi/21 km NW of Winona, Minn.; 44°13′N 91°50′W. In dairy and livestock area; timber. Merrick State Park to SE. Lock and Dam No. 5 to S. Mfg. (oat processing, cheese).

Cochrane Dam (KAHK-ruhn), Cascade co., W central Mont., on the Missouri R., 7 mi/11.3 km NE of Great Falls; 102 ft/31 m high; 47°33′N 111°10′W. Built (1957) by the Mont. Power Co. for power generation. Forms minor reservoir with max. capacity 9,900 acre-ft. Power plant on N side.

Cochranton (KAHK-rahn-tuhn), borough (1990 pop. 1,174), Crawford co., NW Pa., 10 mi/16 km SE of Meadville, on French Creek; 41°31′N 80°02′W. Mfg. (machinery, lumber, plastic prods., concrete prods., tool and die); agr. (grain, potatoes; livestock, dairying).

Cockburn Harbour, town (1990 pop. 1,198), Turks and Caicos Islands, South Caicos Isl.; 21°29′N 71°32′W. Only town on South Caicos Isl. Harbor and fishing center.

Cockburn Island, Canada: see MANITOULIN ISLANDS.

Cockburn Town (1990 pop. 350), Turks and Caicos Islands, Grand Turk Isl.; 21°28′N 71°08′E. Site of govt. offices for the colony.

Cocke (KAHK), county (□ 434 sq mi/1,124 sq km; 1990 pop. 29,141), E Tenn.; ⊙ Newport; 35°56′N 83°07′W. Borders SE on N.C.; Great Smoky and Bald mtn. ranges are along state border. Includes sections of Great Smoky Mts. Natl. Park, Cherokee Natl. Forest, and Douglas Reservoir. Drained by French Broad, Pigeon, and Nolichucky rivers. Forest and farm region, with active barite mines and idle iron-ore and granite quarries; corn, tobacco, tomatoes, apples; dairy prods.; livestock. Formed 1797.

Cockeysville (KOK-eez-vill), village (1990 pop. 18,668), Baltimore co., N Md., near Loch Raven Reservoir, 13 mi/21 km N of downtown Baltimore; 39°29′N 76°38′W. In dairying area; mfg. wood prods., prepared foods. The marble quarries here provided stones used in the Washington Monument and St. Patrick's Cathedral (N.Y. city). Gunpowder Meeting House (Quaker, built 1773) is nearby, as is Sherwood Episcopal Church (c.1830). Now a densely populated residential suburb of Baltimore. Greater Baltimore Industrial Park includes McCormick Spice Co. world hq.

Cockpit Country, hilly region (□ c.200 sq mi/518 sq km), Trelawny parish, on plateau, W central Jamaica; 18°18′N 77°43′W. Composed of limestone rock, the region has many sink holes, caverns, and subterranean streams.

Cockrell Hill, town (1990 pop. 3,746), Dallas co., N Texas, residential suburb, 5 mi/8 km WSW of downtown Dallas; 32°44′N 96°53′W. Community surrounded by city of Dallas.

Cockspur Island, Chatham co., SE Ga., in mouth of Savannah R., bet. Tybee Isl. and Savannah; 32°01′N 80°53′W. At E end is FORT PULASKI.

Coco Bay, cruise-ship port, Bahamas, located on a private island N of Freeport and SW of Nassau belonging to the Royal Caribbean Cruise Line. Features snorkeling and swimming.

Coco, Cayo (KO-ko, KAI-yo), coral island (25 mi/40 km long E-W, up to 8 mi/12.9 km wide) off E Cuba, in Old Bahama Channel, 25 mi/40 km N of Morón; separated by narrow strait from Cayo Romano (E); belongs to Camagüey Archipelago; 22°30′N 18°30′W. Low and swampy. Fishing. Tourist hotels built in 1990s; linked to small airstrip and causeway connecting isl. to Ciego de Ávila and Camagüey provs.

Cocoa (KO-ko), city (□ 9 sq mi/23.3 sq km; 1990 pop. 17,722), Brevard co., E central Fla., on the Indian R. (a lagoon), a segment of the Intracoastal Waterway; 28°22′N 80°45′W. It is a tourist center in a region where citrus fruits are grown. An 8-mi/12.9-km causeway leads from the city over Indian R. to Merritt Island, Cocoa Beach, and the Cape Canaveral space-launch complex. Brevard Community Col. is in the city. Patrick Air Force Base is nearby. Inc. 1895.

Cocoa Beach (KO-ko), resort town (□ 15 sq mi/39 sq km; 1990 pop. 12,123), Brevard co., E central Fla., on barrier beach bet. Banana R. and the Atlantic, 8 mi/12.9 km ESE of Cocoa, and 4 mi/6.4 km S of Cape Canaveral; 28°20′N 80°37′W.

Coconino (ko-ko-NEE-no), county (□ 18,662 sq mi/48,335 sq km; 1990 pop. 96,591), N Ariz.; ⊙ Flagstaff; 35°50′N 111°46′W. Bounded by Utah on N, Mogollon Rim escarpment (runs E-W) on SE; Colorado R. forms part of NW boundary, and along with the Little Colorado R., also drains the area; Kaibab Creek forms part of NW boundary. Plateau and mesa area; highest elev. in Ariz. reached in San Francisco Peaks, at Humphrey Peak (12,643 ft/3,854 m), S center, N of Flagstaff. Includes part of Grand Canyon Natl. Park in N and NW; part of Painted Desert extends NE of Little Colorado R.; Wupatki, Sunset Crater, and Walnut Canyon natl. monuments are in S corner of the co., as are parts of Navajo and Hopi Indian reservations in NE. Lumber; sheep, cattle; hay. Formed 1891. Second largest co. in U.S in land area. Part of Glen Canyon Natl. Recreation Area, including Glen Canyon Dam, on Colorado R., in N; Havasupai Indian Reservation and part of Hualapai

Indian Reservation in W; part of Kaibab Indian Reservation in NW corner; parts of Kaibab Natl. Forest in N, center, and S; Coconino Natl. Forest in S; parts of Prescott Natl. Forest on S boundary and Apache-Sitgreaves Natl. Forest in SE; Meteor Crater (Diablo Crater) in SE; parts of Paria Canyon-Vermillion Cliffs Wilderness Area in N.

Coconino Plateau, high tableland (c.6,000 ft/1,829 m) in Coconino co., N Ariz., S of Colorado R. and Grand Canyon. Extends throughout much of Coconino co. and includes parts of Kaibab Natl. Forest in E and SE.

Coconut Creek, city (□ 11 sq mi/28 sq km; 1990 pop. 27,485), Broward co., SE Fla., located 10 mi/16 km NNW of Fort Lauderdale; 26°16′N 80°10′W. Site of major suburban development since 1980.

Coconut Island, in Kaneohe Bay, NE Oahu isl., Honolulu co., Hawaii. Site of Hawaii Inst. of Marine Biology of the Univ. of Hawaii. Setting for television series Gilligan's Island. Also see HILO BAY. Formerly Moku O Loe.

Cocopás, Sierra de los (ko-ko-PAHS), precipitous range in N Lower California, NW Mexico, 10 mi/16 km SW of Mexicali; extends c.40 mi/64 km SE from U.S. border, E of Laguna Salada and Hardy R., S of Imperial Valley; rises to 3,475 ft/1,059 m. Sulphur deposits. Sometimes spelled Cucopas or Cucapahs.

Cocorite (ko-ko-REET), W suburb of Port of Spain, NW Trinidad, Trinidad and Tobago. Was seaplane base on the Gulf of Paria.

Cocos Bay (ko-KOS), E coast of Trinidad, Trinidad and Tobago; 10°27′N 61°00′W. Sandy bay bet. Manzanilla to the N and Pt. Radix to the S. Bordered by Nariva Swamp.

Cocotitlán (ko-ko-tee-TLAHN), town (1990 pop. 6,959), ⊙ Cocotitlán municipio, Mexico state, central Mexico, 23 mi/37 km SE of Mexico city, and within the Zona Metropolitana de la Ciudad de México. Corn, alfalfa, cereals, vegetables; livestock.

Cocula (ko-KOO-lah), city (1990 pop. 11,835) and township, Jalisco, W Mexico, on central plateau, and 35 mi/56 km SW of Guadalajara on Mexico Hwy. 80; 20°23′N 103°49′W. Elev. 4,698 ft/1,432 m. Orange growing center; wheat, sugarcane, beans, alfalfa; livestock. The mariachis of Cocula are famous.

Cocula (ko-KOO-lah), town (1990 pop. 4,342), ⊙ Cocula municipio, Guerrero, SW Mexico, on affluent of the Río Balsas, and 11 mi/18 km SW of Iguala de la Independencia, on railroad. Cereals, sugarcane, tobacco, tropical fruit.

Cod, Cape, Mass.: see CAPE COD.

Cod Island or **Ogualik Island** (o-GWAH-lik), NE Lab., Canada; 57°45′N 61°45′W. The isl. is 11 mi/18 km long and 10 mi/16 km wide. Kaumajet Mts., rising to 4,000 ft/1,219 m, cover entire surface of isl.

Coderre, village (1991 pop. 68), S Sask., Canada, 40 mi/64 km WSW of Moose Jaw; 50°08′N 106°23′W. Wheat.

Codington, county (□ 717 sq mi/1,857 sq km; 1990 pop. 22,698), E S.Dak.; ⊙ Watertown; 44°58′N 97°10′W. Agr. area drained by Big Sioux R.; has numerous lakes; includes S extremity of triangular L. Traverse (Sisseton Wahpeton) Indian Reservation in N. Mfg. at Watertown. On Coteau des Prairies plateau. Dairy prods.; corn, flax, wheat, soybeans; turkeys, cattle, hogs, sheep. Pelican State Rec. Area in S; Sandy Shore State Rec. Area at center. Formed 1877.

Codrington, village (1991 pop. 814), central Barbuda, Antigua and Barbuda Republic, West Indies, 37 mi/60 km N of St. John's, Antigua; 17°38′N 61°50′W.

Cody, town (1990 pop. 7,897), ⊙ Park co., NW Wyo., c.105 mi/169 km WSW of Sheridan, on the Shoshone R; 44°31′N 109°02′W. In a sheep, cattle, and irrigated farm area; rail terminus. It is a tourist resort c.45 mi/72 km E of the eastern entrance to Yellowstone Natl. Park, with dude ranches and a colorful old frontier town flavor. Mfg. concrete, furniture, gypsum prods., lumber, prepared foods, printing and publishing. Cody is hq. for the Shoshone Natl. Forest (to W); includes North Absaroka Wilderness Area. Of interest are the Buffalo Bill Historical Center, the Whitney Gall. of Western Art, and an annual rodeo. Buffalo Bill Reservoir (Shoshone R.) and State Park to W. Shoshone

Canyon and the Shoshone project are nearby. Founded and inc. 1901 by William F. Cody (Buffalo Bill).

Cody, village (1990 pop. 177), Cherry co., N Nebr., 35 mi/ 56 km W of Valentine, near S.Dak. border; 42°56′N 101°15′W. Trading center for Rosebud Indian Reservation, S.Dak.; grain, cattle. Recreation area nearby.

Coeburn, town (1990 pop. 2,165), Wise co., SW Va., 5 mi. E of Norton, on Guest R., at N edge of Jefferson Natl. Forest; 36°57′N 82°28′W. Agr. (cattle; tobacco, hay); timber; coal.

Coeneo de la Libertad (ko-NAI-o dai lah lee-bahr-TAHD), town (1990 pop. 4,498), ⊙ Coeneo municipio, Michoacán, central Mexico, 30 mi/48 km WNW of Morelia; elev. 6,234 ft/1,900 m. Cereals, fruit; livestock; cheese.

Coétzala (ko-AIT-sah-lah), town (1990 pop. 835), Veracruz, E Mexico, 7 mi/11.3 km S of Córdoba. Coffee, fruit.

Coeur d'Alene (KOOR da-LAIN), city (1990 pop. 24,563), ⊙ Kootenai co., N Idaho, 30 mi/48 km E of Spokane Wash.; 47°42′N 116°47′W. Elev. 2,187 ft/667 m. A tourist and lumbering center situated on the N end of Coeur d'Alene L., at the outlet of Spokane R., W of the Coeur d'Alene Mts.; gateway to a beautiful summer and winter resort area. Lumber; meat processing; printing and publishing; concrete mfg. Fort Coeur d'Alene (later Fort Sherman) est. 1876. The city grew around the fort after the discovery (1883) of rich silver, lead, and zinc lodes and after the mining boom of 1884. Hq. of Coeur d'Alene Natl. Forest and seat of North Idaho Jr. Col. Inc. 1907.

Coeur d'Alene Lake, Kootenai co., N Idaho, 30 mi/ 48 km E of Spokane, Wash.; 24 mi/39 km long, 1 mi/ 1.6 km–3 mi/4.8 km wide. Fed by Coeur d'Alene and St. Joe rivers, drained by Spokane R. City of Coeur d'Alene is at N end of lake. S end extends into Coeur d'Alene Indian Reservation and Benewah co.

Coeur d'Alene Mountains, N Idaho, extending S along Mont. state line from Pend Oreille L. to St. Joe R., largely in Shoshone co. Coeur d'Alene Natl. Forest extends throughout most of range. Chief elevations (6 ft/ 1.8 m–7,000 ft/2,134 m) are in E. Coeur d'Alene mining district, including several mines in vicinity of Kellogg (smelting, refining center), is leading producer of lead, silver, and zinc.

Coeur d'Alene River, N Shoshone co., N Idaho, rises near Mont. state line, flows SE, then WSW, to Coeur d'Alene L. at Harrison; c.110 mi/177 km long.

Coeymans (KWEE-muhnz), village (1990 pop. 1,000), Albany co., E N.Y., on W bank of Hudson R., 12 mi/ 19 km S of Albany; 42°30′N 73°52′W.

Coffee 1 (KAH-fee), county (□ 680 sq mi/1,761 sq km; 1990 pop. 40,240), SE Ala., ⊙ Elba and Enterprise, 31°25′N 86°00′W. Coastal plain region drained by Pea R. Corn, peanuts; poultry, hogs; timber; textiles mfg. Formed 1841. **2** county (□ 613 sq mi/1,588 sq km; 1990 pop. 29,592), S central Ga., ⊙ Douglas; 31°33′N 82°51′W. Bounded N by Ocmulgee R. Coastal plain farming (tobacco, cotton, corn, peanuts); cattle, hogs, poultry; dairying; marble; timber. Drained by Satilla R. Formed 1854. **3** county (□ 435 sq mi/1,127 sq km; 1990 pop. 40,339), central Tenn.; ⊙ Manchester; 35°30′N 86°04′W. Partly in the Cumberlands; bounded SE by Elk R., drained by Duck R. Timber tracts, coal deposits. Agr. (corn, cotton, hay, soybeans, tobacco, potatoes), livestock, dairying. Mfg. at Manchester and Tullahoma. Arnold Air Force Base and Engineering Development Center is here. Formed 1836.

Coffee City, village (1990 pop. 216), Henderson co., E Texas, 17 mi/27 km SSW of Tyler, on W shore of L. Palestine reservoir (Neches R.); 32°07′N 95°28′W. Agr. area. Recreation.

Coffee Springs, town (1990 pop. 294), Geneva co., SE Ala., 10 mi/16 km NNW of Geneva; 31°10′N 85°54′W.

Coffeen, city (1990 pop. 736), Montgomery co., S central Ill., 7 mi/11.3 km SE of Hillsboro; 39°05′N 89°23′W. In agr. and bituminous-coal area.

Coffeeville 1 (KAH-fee-vil), town (1990 pop. 431), Clarke co., SW Ala., near Tombigbee R., 20 mi/32 km W of Grove Hill; 31°45′N 88°05′W. **2** town (1990 pop. 825), ⊙ Yalobusha co. (seat shared with Water Valley), N central Miss., 20 mi/32 km NNE of Grenada; 33°58′N 89°40′W. Grenada L. reservoir and Hugh White State Park to S; sect. of Holly Springs Natl. Forest to W. Agr. (cotton, corn, soybeans, watermelons; cattle); mfg. (cultured marble, apparel).

Coffeeville Lock and Dam (KAH-fee-vil), Choctaw co., NW Ala.; 52 ft/16 m gravity construction, built in 1962 by the Army Corps of Engineers for navigational purposes; forms reservoir used for recreational purposes with a max. capacity of 190,800 acre-ft.

Coffey (KAW-fee), county (□ 654 sq mi/1,694 sq km; 1990 pop. 8,404), E Kansas; ⊙ Burlington; 38°14′N 95°43′W. Rolling plains area, drained by Neosho R. Cattle, poultry; corn, wheat, sorghum, soybeans, hay, grain. Wolf Creek nuclear power plant (initial criticality May 22, 1985) is 3.5 mi/5.6 km NE of Burlington, uses cooling water from the Wolf Creek Cooling L., and has a max. dependable capacity of 1,135 MWe. Large John Redmond Reservoir, surrounded by Flint Hills Natl. Wildlife Refuge, in NW ¼ of co. Formed 1859.

Coffey, town (1990 pop. 131), Daviess co., NW Mo., near Grand R., 14 mi/23 km N of Gallatin; 40°06′N 94°00′W.

Coffeyville (KAW-fee-vil), city (1990 pop. 12,917), Montgomery co., SE Kansas, on the Verdigris R., near the Okla. state line, 15 mi/24 km SE of Independence; 37°02′N 95°37′W. In a farm and oil area, Coffeyville is a trading and distributing center, with dairying, flour milling, mfg. (mostly machinery), and petrol refining. With the coming of the RR (1870), Coffeyville grew as a cattle-shipping point. Oil and natural gas were discovered in the area in 1902. The city was the scene (1892) of a famous shoot-out with the notorious Dalton gang during an attempted bank robbery. Of interest are the Dalton graves and the Dalton Museum. Coffeyville Community Col. here. Inc. 1872.

Coffin Island, in the Gulf of St. Lawrence, E Que., Canada, one of the Magdalen Isls., 80 mi/129 km NNE of Prince Edward Isl.; 47°33′N 61°31′W. The isl. is 4 mi/ 6 km long and 1 mi/2 km wide.

Cofield (KO-feeld), village (1990 pop. 407), Hertford co., NE N.C., 43 mi/69 km ESE of Roanoke Rapids, near Chowan R; 36°21′N 76°54′W. Peanuts, tobacco, cotton, grain; chickens, hogs. Mfg. (concrete).

Cofre de Perote National Park (KO-frai dai pe-RO-tai) (□ 29,000 acres/11,736 ha), central Veracruz, Mexico, 15 mi/24 km W of Xalapa Enríquez. The park is centered around a peak, Cofre de Perote, elev. 13,943 ft/ 4,250 m, a volcano in the Sierra Madre Oriental to the N of Pico de Orizaba. Its slopes are covered with pine forests. A paved road on Mexican Route 140 gives access to the E, N, and W of the park. The peak is also known as Nauhcampatépetl.

Coggon, town (1990 pop. 645), Linn co., E Iowa, on Buffalo Creek, and 22 mi/35 km NNE of Cedar Rapids; 42°16′N 91°31′W. Dairy prods.

Cogswell, village (1990 pop. 184), Sargent co., SE N.Dak., 15 mi/24 km E of Oakes; 46°06′N 97°46′W. Grain, livestock, dairy prods.

Cohansey Creek (ko-HAN-zee), SW N.J., rises in SE Salem co., flows c.35 mi/56 km S, past Bridgeton, and W to Delaware Bay. Navigable to Bridgeton.

Cohasset (ko-HA-sit), town (1990 pop. 7,075), including Cohasset village, in exclave of Norfolk co. in Plymouth co., E Mass., on Massachusetts Bay, and 16 mi/ 26 km SE of Boston; 42°17′N 70°47′W. Includes village of North Cohasset. Summer resort with summer theater; boat building. Estates along shore. Minots Ledge lighthouse maintained offshore since 1850; part of Wompatuck State Park. Settled c.1647, inc. 1770.

Cohasset (ko-HA-set), village (1990 pop. 762), Itasca co., N central Minn., 6 mi/9.7 km WNW of Grand Rapids, on Mississippi R. W of Mesabi Iron Range, in lake resort region; 47°15′N 93°37′W. Blackwater L. to SW, Bass L. to N. Light mfg.

Cohetzala, Mexico: see SANTA MARÍA COHETZALA.

Cohocton (ko-HAHK-tuhn), village (□ 1 sq mi/ 2.6 sq km; 1990 pop. 859), Steuben co., W central N.Y.,

on Cohocton R., 15 mi/24 km NNE of Hornell; 42°30′N 77°30′W. In agr. area; dairy prods.; sand and gravel.

Cohocton River (ko-HAHK-tuhn), W central and S N.Y., rises in Livingston co., flows c.55 mi/89 km generally SE, past Bath, joining Tioga R. to form Chemung R. at Painted Post.

Cohoes (kuh-HOZ), city (□ 4 sq mi/10.4 sq km; 1990 pop. 16,825), Albany co., E N.Y., near Albany, at confluence of Mohawk and Hudson rivers; 42°46′N 73°42′W. Retailing and outlet center. Its mfg. includes textiles (made there since 1840), cabinetry, meat packing, plastic prods., paper prods., machinery, consumer goods. The world's 1st power-operated knitting mill was opened here in 1832. Van Schaick Mansion (1735), now a mus., was used as hq. by Gen. Horatio Gates during the Amer. Revolution. Settled by Dutch 1665, inc. 1869.

Cohuecán (ko-wai-KAHN), town (1990 pop. 1,505), SE Puebla, Mexico, on the Morelos state border; elev. 5,577 ft/1,700 m. Mild climate. Agr. (sugarcane, rice, cereals, fruits, vegetables, citrus); various woods. Road access from Morelos.

Cohutta (kuh-HUHT-uh), town (1990 pop. 529), Whitfield co., Ga., 14 mi/23 km N of Dalton; 34°57′N 84°57′W. Mfg. of yarns and industrial chemicals.

Coicoyán de las Flores (koi-ko-YAHN de lahs FLO-res), town (1990 pop. 1,357), in W Oaxaca, Mexico, 19 mi/31 km W of Santiago Juxtlahuaca, and on the Guerrero border; 17°15′N 98°18′W. Elev. 8,530 ft/ 2,600 m. Cold climate. In Mixteca Alta region, Mixtec Indians. Grande R. (also known as the Puzmetocan) starts here.

Coin, town (1990 pop. 278), Page co., SW Iowa, near Tarkio R., 12 mi/19 km SW of Clarinda; 40°39′N 95°14′W.

Coinjock (KOIN-jahk), uninc. village, Currituck co., extreme NE N.C., 14 mi/23 km E of Elizabeth City, on Albemarle and Chesapeake Canal, Intercoastal Waterway. Resort (hunting, fishing). Soybeans, grain, cotton, peanuts; hogs.

Coixtlahuaca, Mexico: see SAN JUAN BAUTISTA COIXTLAHUACA.

Cojímar (ko-HEE-mahr), town, Ciudad de La Habana prov., W Cuba, at mouth of small Cojímar R., 4 mi/ 6.4 km ENE of Havana; 23°12′N 82°17′W. Large public housing complexes built here in early 1960s. Fishing. Its small fort (built 1646) was taken by Eng. forces in 1762.

Cojumatlán de Régules (ko-hoo-maht-LAHN de RE-goo-lais), town (1990 pop. 6,736), Michoacán, central Mexico, on SE shore of L. Chapala, and 17 mi/27 km SSW of Ocotlán on Mexico Hwy. 15. Cereals, fruit; livestock; lumbering.

Cokato (kuh-KAI-do), town (1990 pop. 2,180), Wright co., S central Minn., 16 mi/26 km WSW of Buffalo; 45°04′N 94°11′W. Trading and shipping point in agr. area (dairying; poultry; vegetables, soybeans, grain, garlic); mfg. (prepared foods, animal feeds, fabricated metal prods., electronic equipment). Inc. 1878.

Coke, county (□ 928 sq mi/2,404 sq km; 1990 pop. 3,424), W Texas; ⊙ Robert Lee; 31°52′N 100°31′W. Colorado R. crosses NW-SE, N Concho R. passes through SW corner; elev. c.2,000 ft/610 m. Ranching area (sheep, goats, beef cattle); agr. (cotton, grain, sorghum, hay, cotton). Some oil, natural gas, sand and gravel. Oak Creek Reservoir in NE corner; EV Spence Reservoir (Colorado R.) dominates NW ¼ of co. Formed 1889.

Cokeburg (KOK-buhrg), borough (1990 pop. 724), Washington co., SW Pa., 10 mi/16 km ESE of Washington, on South Branch Pigeon Creek; 40°06′N 80°04′W. Mfg. (machinery parts); coal; agr. (soybeans, grain; livestock, dairying). Inc. 1906.

Cokedale, village (1990 pop. 116), Las Animas co., S Colo., on Purgatoire R., near N.Mex. line, and 7 mi/ 11.3 km WSW of Trinidad; 37°08′N 104°37′W. Elev. c.6,200 ft/1,890 m. In coal-mining region; coke. Trinidad Reservoir and Trinidad State Park to E.

Cokeville, village (1990 pop. 493), Lincoln co., SW Wyo., on Bear R., near Idaho state line, and 29 mi/47 km NW of Kemmerer; 42°04′N 110°57′W. Elev. c.6,191 ft/ 1,887 m. Ranching (cattle and sheep), dairying; wool mfg. Pine Creek Ski Area to NE; Bridger-Teton Natl. Forest to NE.

Colbert (KAHL-buhrt), county (□ 623 sq mi/ 1,614 sq km; 1990 pop. 51,666), NW Ala.; ⊙ Tuscumbia. Bounded W by Miss.; in N are Pickwick Landing Reservoir and L. Wilson, both on Tennessee R. TVA developments have stimulated industry in region. Sheffield is mfg. center. Agr. includes cotton, corn, soybeans; poultry and hogs. There are deposits of asphalt, bauxite, and limestone. Fall line crosses co. N-S. Formed 1867.

Colbert, town (1990 pop. 1,043), Bryan co., S Okla., 12 mi/19 km SW of Durant, near Red R., which forms L. Texoma; 33°51′N 96°30′W. Rail junctions to S; mfg. (metal fabrication). Denison Dam is 4 mi/6.4 km W (upstream).

Colbert, village (1990 pop. 443), Madison co., NE Ga., 12 mi/19 km ENE of Athens; 34°02′N 83°13′W. Mfg. includes motor vehicles, fabricated metal prods., and wood prods.

Colborne (KOL-buhrn), village (1991 pop. 2,043), S Ont., Canada, on L. Ontario, 25 mi/40 km WSW of Belleville; 44°01′N 77°53′W. Food canning, dairying.

Colborne, Cape, SE Victoria Isl., SW Franklin dist., N.W.T., Canada, on narrow passage bet. Dease Strait and Queen Maud Gulf, 12 mi/19 km SSW of Cambridge Bay; 68°58′N 104°59′W.

Colby 1 town (1990 pop. 5,396), ⊙ Thomas co., NW Kansas, 35 mi/56 km E of Goodland; 39°23′N 101°02′W. RR junction. Trading and shipping center for wheat and cattle region. Sheep. Colby Community Col. Nearby are Kansas State Agr. Experimental Center and Thomas County Mus. Inc. 1886. **2** town (1990 pop. 1,532), on Clark-Marathon co. line, central Wis., 34 mi/ 55 km WSW of Wausau; 44°54′N 90°19′W. In dairying region; cheese, butter, canned foods. Also metal fabrication, paper prods.

Colchester (KOL-chis-tuhr), county (□ 1,451 sq mi/ 3,758 sq km; 1991 pop. 47,683), N N.S., Canada, bet Northumberland Strait and the Bay of Fundy; ⊙ Truro; 41°59′N 82°56′W.

Colchester (KOL-ches-tuhr), city (1990 pop. 1,645), McDonough co., W Ill., 6 mi/9.7 km WSW of Macomb; 40°25′N 90°47′W. Clay pits; agr. (corn, wheat, hay; livestock); mfg. (agricultural implements). Inc. 1867. Near Argyle Lake State Park.

Colchester 1 (KOL-ches-tuhr), town (1990 pop. 10,980), including Colchester borough, New London co., SE central Conn., on Salmon R., and 14 mi/23 km WNW of Norwich; 41°33′N 72°20′W. Agr.; mfg. (clothing, leather prods., fabricated metal prods., construction materials). Includes villages of North Westchester and Westchester. Settled and inc. 1699, borough inc. 1824. **2** town (1990 pop. 14,731), Chittenden co., NW Vt., on L. Champlain, just N of Burlington and Winooski; 44°33′N 73°12′W. Small boats; agr.; dairy prods. Ira Allen built mills and iron forge in area after 1783. Included Winooski until 1922. Malletts Bay recreation area on L. Champlain.

Colcord (KAHL-kord), village (1990 pop. 628), Delaware co., NE Okla., 11 mi/18 km NW of Siloam Springs, Ark.; 36°16′N 94°41′W. Agr. and timber area. Upper Spavinaw State Park to NW. Recreation.

Cold Bay, village (1990 pop. 148), SW Alaska, near SW end of Alaska Peninsula, on Cold Bay, extension of Pacific Ocean. Bristol Bay of Bering Sea 5 mi/8 km NW across isthmus. Formerly Fort Randall. Frosty Peak (5,784ft/1,763m) to SW. Fishing.

Cold Bay, inlet (20 mi/32 km long, 4 mi/6.4 km–8 mi/ 12.9 km wide) of N Pacific in SW Alaska Peninsula, SW Alaska; 55°11′N 162°33′W. Air base, built here early in World War II, played important part in repulse of initial Japanese attack on Aleutian Isls.

Cold Brook, village (1990 pop. 310), Herkimer co., central N.Y., 14 mi/23 km NE of Utica; 43°14′N 75°02′W.

Cold Harbor, uninc. village, Hanover co., E central Va., c.10 mi/16 km NE of Richmond. Civil War battlesites

(Gaines's Mill — one of the Seven Days Battles — and New Cold Harbor) to W, SW.

Cold Lake, town (1986 pop. 3,195), on Cold L., 180 mi/ 290 km NE of Edmonton, Alta., Canada; 52°18′N 112°41′W. Can. Forces base and testing range, satellite tracking unit for NORAD. Oil production since 1985; also tar and sand extraction. Fishing and tourist resort.

Cold Lake (□ 136 sq mi/352 sq km), on Alta.-Sask. border, Canada; 54°35′N 110°00W. The lake is 16 mi/26 km long and 11 mi/18 km wide.

Cold Mountain, Mont.: see ABSAROKA RANGE.

Cold River, small stream, SW N.H., rises in S Sullivan co., flows SW c.20 mi/32 km to the Connecticut R. above Walpole.

Cold Spring 1 or **Cold Springs**, town (1990 pop. 2,880), Campbell co., N Ky., a suburb 7 mi/11.3 km SSE of Cincinnati, Ohio, and 6 mi/9.7 km SE of Covington, Ky.; 39°01′N 84°26′W. Mfg. (fabricted metal prods., paper prods., printing). **2** town (1990 pop. 2,459), Stearns co., central Minn., 15 mi/24 km SW of St. Cloud, on Sank R., at its exit from Cedar Isl. L.; 45°27′N 94°25′W. Grain; livestock; dairying; mink. Mfg. (food and beverages; furniture). Granite quarries nearby. Several small natural lakes in area.

Cold Spring, village (1990 pop. 1,998), Putnam co., SE N.Y., on E bank of Hudson R., 6 mi/9.7 km S of Beacon; 41°25′N 73°57′W. Mfg. (metal prods.); in dairying area. Settled before the Amer. Revolution; inc. 1846.

Cold Spring Harbor, village (□ 3 sq mi/7.8 sq km; 1990 pop. 4,789) in Huntington town, Suffolk co., SE N.Y., on N shore of W L.I., on Cold Spring Harbor (SE arm of Oyster Bay), just W of Huntington village, in affluent summer-residence area; 40°51′N 73°27′W. Site of Cold Spring Harbor Laboratory (neurobiology genome, plant genetics, and cancer research), DNA Learning Center, world's 1st biotech mus., and Cold Spring Harbor Fish Hatchery and Aquarium. Was 19th-cent. whaling port.

Cold Spring Lake (□ 17 sq mi/44 sq km), S N.F., Canada, 50 mi/80 km SSE of Buchans; 7 mi/11 km long, 4 mi/6 km wide. Drains E into Round Pound.

Cold Springs, Ky.: see COLD SPRING.

Cold Stream Pond, reservoir, at Enfield, Penobscot co., central Maine, on Cold Stream, 35 mi/56 km NNE of Bangor; c.4 mi/6.4 km long; 45°16′N 68°33′W. Has NE arm. Three small Upper Cold Stream Ponds (connected by Cold Stream) to NE.

Colden, Mount (4,713 ft/1,437 m), Essex co., NE N.Y., in the High Peaks sect. of the Adirondacks Mts., just W of Mt. Marcy, 11 mi/18 km S of L. Placid village; 44°08′N 73°58′W.

Coldspring, village (1990 pop. 538), ⊙ San Jacinto co., E Texas, near San Jacinto R., c.60 mi/97 km NNE of Houston, surrounded by, except NE, Sam Houston Natl. Forest; 30°35′N 95°07′W. Agr., cattle, timber area. L. Livingston reservoir (Trinity R.) to NE.

Coldstream, district municipality (1986 pop. 6,872), 1.2 mi/1.9 km SE of Vernon, B.C., Canada. Glass mfg.; lumber mills. Formerly Coldstream ranch and in 1891 purchased by Earl of Aberdeen for fruit cultivation.

Coldwater 1 town (1990 pop. 939), ⊙ Comanche co., S Kansas, c.50 mi/80 km SE of Dodge City; 37°15′N 99°20′W. Trade center for wheat and livestock area. Inc. 1884. **2** town (1990 pop. 9,607), ⊙ Branch co., S Mich., on Coldwater R., and 28 mi/45 km SSE of Battle Creek; 41°56′N 85°00′W. Trade center in grain-growing, livestock, and dairying area. Mfg. (chemicals, consumer prods., furniture, machinery, prepared foods, publishing). Aiport. Many lakes nearby; Coldwater L., the largest, is at head of Coldwater R., 10 mi/16 km S. Settled 1830; inc. as village in 1837, as city in 1861. **3** town (1990 pop. 1,502), Tate co., NW Miss., 26 mi/42 km S of Memphis, Tenn., near E end of Arkabutla Reservoir (Coldwater R.); 34°41′N 89°58′W. Agr. (cotton, grain, soybeans; cattle; dairying); mfg. (machinery, cultured marble).

Coldwater, village (1991 pop. 1,254), S Ont., Canada, on Coldwater R., and 14 mi/23 km NW of Orillia; 44°43′N 79°49′W. Dairying, mixed agr.; resort.

Coldwater, village (1990 pop. 4,335), Mercer co., W

Ohio, 5 mi/8 km SW of Celina; 40°29′N 84°38′W. In agr. area; mfg. (agr. machinery, apparel, food prods.).

Coldwater River 1 c.25 mi/40 km long; S Mich.; rises in Coldwater L. (c.3 mi/4.8 km long, 1 mi/1.6 km wide; resort) in Branch co. near Ind. border, flows NE, through Long, Mud, Middle, and Marble lakes then NW, past Coldwater, through South, Randall, and Morrison lakes, to St. Joseph R. at Union City; 41°50′N 84°59′W. **2** 220 mi/354 km long; NW Miss., rises in NE Marshall co., flows W past Coldwater and through Arkabutla Reservoir, then generally S to Tallahatchie R. 6 mi/9.7 km SE of Marks.

Cole, county (□ 385 sq mi/997 sq km; 1990 pop. 63,579), central Mo.; ⊙ Jefferson City (also the state capital); 38°30′N 92°16′W. Bounded by Missouri R. (N) and Osage R. (E). Urban growth from Jefferson City. N part of co. is urbanized; parts of downtown Jefferson City damaged in 1993 flood. Wheat, hay, corn; dairying; poultry, livestock; mfg. centered at Jefferson City; limestone quarries. Formed 1820.

Cole, village (1990 pop. 355), McClain Co., central Okla., 10 mi/16 km SW of Norman; 35°06′N 97°34′W. Agr. area (dairying; cattle; cotton, soybeans).

Cole Camp, city (1990 pop. 1,054), Benton co., central Mo., 17 mi/27 km S of Sedalia, at N edge of Ozark region; 38°27′N 93°12′W. Corn, wheat; hogs, cattle. Settled by German immigrants 1830s.

Colebrook 1 resort town (1990 pop. 1,365), Litchfield co., NW Conn., in Litchfield Hills, on Mass. line, and 13 mi/ 21 km N of Torrington; 42°00′N 73°04′W. In Colebrook village. 18th-cent. houses include home of younger Jonathan Edwards, pastor here 1795–1799. Includes small villages of North Colebrook, Mill Brook, and Robertsville. State forest. **2** (KOL-bruk), town (1990 pop. 2,444), Coos co., NW N.H., 32 mi/51 km NW of Berlin; 44°53′N 71°24′W. Bounded W by Connecticut R. (Vt. state line); drained by Mohawk R., which flows into Connecticut R. Agr. (dairying; poultry, cattle; vegetables, nursery crops); mfg. (medical prods.). Beaver Brook Falls in NW. Shrine of Our Lady of Grace is here. Granted 1770, inc. 1795.

Coleen River (KO-leen), c.160 mi/257 km long, NE Alaska; rises in Davidson Mts., flows S to Porcupine R. at 67°04′N 142°29′W.

Coleharbor, village (1990 pop. 88), McLean co., central N.Dak., 20 mi/32 km NNW of Washburn, on S end of U.S. 83 causeway that divides L. Sakakawea (on W) from Audubon L. (E); 47°32′N 101°13′W. Audubon Natl. Wildlife Refuge to NE. Garrison Dam to SW.

Coleman, county (□ 1,281 sq mi/3,318 sq km; 1990 pop. 9,710), central Texas; bounded S by Colorado R. (forms L. O.H. Ivie in SW) and drained by Jim Ned and Hords creeks and Pecan bayou; ⊙ Coleman; 31°46′N 99°27′W. Agr. (especially oats); also wheat, grain sorghums, cotton; mesquite); livestock (cattle, sheep, goats, hogs). Oil, natural gas wells; silica (glass mfg.), limestone, clay mining; coal deposits. L. Coleman reservoir is in N; Hords Creek L. reservoir is in W. Formed 1858.

Coleman, city (1990 pop. 137), Randolph co., SW Ga., 9 mi/14.5 km SW of Cuthbert; 31°40′N 84°53′W.

Coleman, town, SW Alta., Canada, near B.C. border, in Rocky Mts., on Crowsnest R., and 100 mi/161 km SSW of Calgary; elev. 4,312 ft/1,314 m. Coal mining, logging, ranching, dairying; tourism.

Coleman 1 town (1990 pop. 1,237), Midland co., E central Mich., 19 mi/31 km NW of Midland; 43°45′N 84°35′W. In dairy and agr. area; mfg. (machinery, plastic prods.). Inc. 1905. **2** town (1990 pop. 5,410), ⊙ Coleman co., central Texas, 26 mi/42 km W of Brownwood; 31°49′N 99°25′W. Elev. 1,710 ft/521 m. Commercial, processing, shipping center for agr. (cotton, wheat, oats, mesquite), livestock (cattle, sheep, goats, hogs), oil and gas producing region; mfg. (construction materials, machinery, office and school supplies). Hords Creek L. to W, Coleman L. to N. Founded 1876, inc. 1877. **3** town (1990 pop. 839), Marinette co., NE Wis., 20 mi/32 km W of Marinette; 45°04′N 88°01′W. Dairying center; mfg. canned vegetables. Mt. Labett Ski Area to W.

Coleman, Mount (10,262 ft/3,128 m), SW Alta., Canada,

in Rocky Mts., near NE edge of Banff Natl. Park, 70 mi/113 km SE of Jasper; 52°07′N 116°56′W.

Colerain (KOL-rain), village (1990 pop. 139), Bertie co., NE N.C., near Chowan R., and 13 mi/21 km ESE of Ahoskie; 36°12′N 76°46′W. Cotton, peanuts; livestock; mfg. (fish processing, light mfg.).

Coleraine (KOL-rain), town (1990 pop. 1,041), Itasca co., N central Minn., 6 mi/9.7 km NE of Grand Rapids, in W end of Mesabi Iron Range, at N end of Trout L.; 47°18′N 93°25′W. Trading point and company town; iron mining, ore concentration. Chippewa Natl. Forest to NW.

Coleraine, village, S Que., Canada, 10 mi/16 km SE of Thetford Mines. Chromite mining.

Coleridge (KOL-rij), village (1990 pop. 596), Cedar co., NE Nebr., 10 mi/16 km SSE of Hartington; 42°30′N 97°12′W. Dairy and poultry prods.; livestock; grain; alfalfa pellets.

Coles (KOLS), county (□ 510 sq mi/1,321 sq km; 1990 pop. 51,644), E central Ill.; ⊙ Charleston; 39°30′N 88°13′W. Drained by Kaskaskia, Embarrass, and Little Wabash rivers; includes L. Charleston, Paradise L. port of Mattoon. Agr. (corn, wheat, soybeans; livestock). Diversified mfg. Formed 1830. Lakeland Community Col. near Mattoon. Eastern Illinois Univ. at Charleston.

Colesburg, town (1990 pop. 439), Delaware co., E Iowa, 17 mi/27 km NE of Manchester; 42°38′N 91°12′W. Dairy prods.

Coleta (ko-LEE-tah), village (1990 pop. 154), Whiteside co., NW Ill., 9 mi/14.5 km NW of Sterling, 12 mi/19 km NE of Morrison; 41°54′N 89°47′W. In agr. area (corn; cattle, hogs); mfg. sporting goods.

Coleville, uninc. village, Mono co., E Calif., 17 mi/27 km SE of Markleeville; Nevada state line 3 mi/4.8 km to NE. Toiyabe Natl. Forest to W, S, and E. Cattle.

Coleyville (KO-lee-vil), town (1991 pop. 3,320), Manchester parish, central Jamaica, 10 mi/16 km N of Mandeville; 18°13′N 77°30′W. Agr. town in strawberry-growing area. Forest reserve just NW of town.

Colfax 1 county (□ 418 sq mi/1,083 sq km; 1990 pop. 9,139), E Nebr.; ⊙ Schuyler; 41°34′N 97°05′W. Agr. area bounded S by Platte R. Cattle, hogs, poultry; corn, soybeans, alfalfa; dairying. Formed 1869. **2** (KOL-FAKS), county (□ 3,768 sq mi/9,759 sq km; 1990 pop. 12,925), NE N.Mex., bordering on Colo.; ⊙ Raton; 36°36′N 104°38′W. Livestock, coal-mining area; cattle, sheep; hay, alfalfa, wheat, oats, barley, millet. Drained by Canadian, Cimarron, and Vermejo rivers. Includes part of Raton Mts. in N, Sangre de Cristo Mts. in W (crest forms W boundary). Maxwell Natl. Wildlife Refuge in center; small part of Kiowa Natl. Grassland on S boundary in SE; Sugarite Ski Area and Sugarite State Park in N; Eagle Nest Lake Reservoir and Cimarron Canyon State Park in W; small parts of Cibola Natl. Forest in NW and SW; Angel Fire Ski Area in SW; Philmont Scout Ranch in W. Formed 1869.

Colfax 1 city (1990 pop. 1,306), Placer co., E central Calif., near Bear R., c.45 mi/72 km NE of Sacramento; 39°06′N 120°57′W. Fruit, nuts; cattle, sheep; mfg. (concrete). Tahoe Natl. Forest to E. **2** city (1990 pop. 2,462), Jasper co., central Iowa, on Skunk R., and 10 mi/16 km E of Newton; 41°40′N 93°14′W. Mfg. (packed poultry and eggs; feed; beverages). Developed with the exploitation of mineral wells. Inc. 1875.

Colfax 1 town (1990 pop. 727), Clinton co., central Ind., 10 mi/16 km SW of Frankfort; 40°11′N 86°40′W. In agr. area; meat processing. **2** (KOL-faks), town (1990 pop. 1,696), ⊙ Grant parish, central La., on Red R., and 22 mi/35 km NW of Alexandria; 31°31′N 92°43′W. In agr. area (cattle, horses; vegetables, sweet potatoes, corn, cotton, pecans, watermelon). Mfg. (apparel, birdhouses); logging. Colfax riot (1873) was a bloody incident of the Reconstruction period. Lake Iatt reservoir is NE. Named for vice president under Grant. Founded c.1870, inc. 1878. **3** town (1990 pop. 2,713), ⊙ Whitman co., SE Wash., 50 mi/80 km S of Spokane and on Palouse R., at mouth of South Fork Palouse R.; in the Palouse region; 46°53′N 117°22′W. RR junction. Wheat, peas, barley, oats, lentils; mfg. (farm machinery). Steptoe Butte (3,613 ft/1,101 m) State Park to NE; Kamiak Butte (3,641 ft/1,110 m) to E. **4** town (1990 pop. 1,110), Dunn co., W Wis., on Red Cedar R., and 17 mi/27 km NW of Eau Claire; 45°00′N 91°43′W. Dairying. Mfg. (malted milk prods., wood prods.). Deepwood Ski Area to W; Hoffman Hills State Recreational Area to S; Tainter L. reservoir to W.

Colfax 1 village (1990 pop. 854), McLean co., central Ill., on Mackinaw R., and 20 mi/32 km ENE of Bloomington; 40°34′N 88°37′W. In rich agr. area (corn, soybeans; cattle). Site of defunct coal mine. **2** uninc. village, Guilford co., N central N.C., suburb 13 mi/21 km W of Greensboro, and 12 mi/19 km E of Winston-Salem. Mfg. (doors, fabricated metal prods.). Piedmont Triad International Airport to E.

Colihaut (KUH-lee-ho), village (1991 pop. 887), NW Dominica, B.W.I., 14 mi/23 km NNW of Roseau; 15°29′N 61°29′W. Limes, cacao.

Colima (ko-LEE-mah), state (□ 2,010 sq mi/5,206 sq km; 1990 pop. 428,510), SW Mexico, on the Pacific Ocean; ⊙ COLIMA; 19°27′N 103°30′W. The 2d smallest in pop. and one of the smallest in area of the Mexican states, Colima is wedged bet. Jalisco, which nearly surrounds it, and Michoacán. It includes the isls. of Revillagigedo off the coast. The port is MANZANILLO. Most of the state lies within the cool highlands of the Sierra Madre Occidental. The smoking volcano, Colima (12,533 ft/3,820 m), and the neighboring peak, Nevado de Colima (13,911 ft/4,240 m), are just across the border in Jalisco. Sugarcane, bananas, tropical fruits, as well as some of Mexico's finest coffee, are Colima's primary agr. prods. Colima is also one of Mexico's largest iron-producing states, with the ore processed at Lázaro Cárdenas. Economic development has been hindered by inadequate communications, although tourism is being developed along the coast. Once part of the anc. Aztec kingdom of Colima, the region was conquered by the Spanish in the 16th cent. Wars bet. conservative and liberal forces during the 19th cent. brought much fighting to the state.

Colima (ko-LEE-mah), city (1990 pop. 106,967) and township, ⊙ Colima state, SW Mexico; 19°14′N 103°41′W. On Mexico highways 54 and 110, and on RR. It is a marketing and processing center for the surrounding agr. region. The city was founded in 1523 by the Span. explorer Gonzalo de Sandoval.

Colima, Nevado de (ko-LEE-mah), inactive volcano (13,911 ft/4,240 m), Jalisco, W Mexico, near Colima border, 13 mi/21 km SW of Ciudad de Guzmán. Just S is the Volcán de Colima, an active volcanic peak (12,533 ft/3,820 m), which erupted violently in 1941, with many lives lost.

Colinton (KAH-lin-tuhn), village, central Alta., Canada, on Tawatinaw R., and 7 mi/11 km S of Athabaska; mixed farming (including wheat; livestock).

Colipa (ko-LEE-pah), town (1990 pop. 2,571), Veracruz, E Mexico, in Sierra Madre Oriental foothills, 31 mi/50 km NNE of Xalapa Enríquez. Elev. 1,083 ft/330 m. Corn, beans, sugarcane, coffee. Oil and coal deposits.

Coliseo (ko-lee-SAI-o), town, Matanzas prov., W Cuba, 10 mi/16 km SW of Cárdenas; 22°55′N 81°17′W. Located at RR junction and on central highway in sugarcane and cattle region. Victoria de Yaguajay and Granma sugar mills to NW.

Collbran, village (1990 pop. 228), Mesa co., W Colo., on branch of Colorado R., and 35 mi/56 km ENE of Grand Junction; 39°14′N 107°57′W. Elev. 5,987 ft/1,825 m. Cattle, sheep; wheat, hay, beans; mfg. (electronic equipment). Pueblo Indian ruins nearby. Parts of Grand Mesa Natl. Forest to N and S, Vega Reservoir and State Park to E.

College, locality (1990 pop. 4,403), central Alaska, 4 mi/6.4 km W of downtown Fairbanks, on Deadman Slough of Chena R. Site of Univ. of Alaska-Fairbanks; mus., agr. experiment station, Mt. McKinley viewpoint on campus. Creamers Field (formerly Fairbanks) Wildlife Refuge to NE. Tanana Valley Fairgrounds to E. Fairbanks Internatl. Airport and Parks Highway to S. Service center for surrounding suburbs.

College Corner, village (1990 pop. 379), on Preble-Butler co. line, SW Ohio, at Ind. border, adjacent to West Col. Corner (Ind.) and 23 mi/37 km W of Middletown; 39°34′N 84°49′W.

College Heights, village, Darlington co., NE S.C., residential suburb 2 mi/3.2 km NE of Hartsville.

College Mound, uninc. community, Macon co., N central Mo., near Thomas Hill L., 10 mi/16 km SSW of Macon. Center of a former coal-mining area.

College Park 1 city (1990 pop. 20,457), Clayton and Fulton cos., NW Ga., a residential suburb of S Atlanta, on RR line near internatl. airport; 33°38′N 84°28′W. Mfg. includes soft drinks, printing and publishing, metal fabrication, concrete, machinery parts, oils, aircraft engine parts. Georgia Military Acad. (1900). Inc. 1891. **2** city (1990 pop. 23,714), Prince Georges co., W central Md., a residential suburb of Wash., D.C.; 39°00′N 76°56′W. It is the seat of the Univ. of Md., founded in 1856 as Md. Agr. Col. by Charles B. Calvert, a descendant of the Lords Baltimore. All of the univ.'s 70 principal bldgs. are in Georgian-Colonial style. Also here is Md. Agr. Experimental Station, est. 1887 as the first in the nation under federal enabling law. The College Park Airport, which now services light planes, is both the first airport built in the U.S. and the first military air training field in the world. The Wright Brothers established operations here after their first successful flight at Kitty Hawk. The city's economy is centered around the university, research institutions, electronics plants, and newspaper printing plant. Settled 1745, inc. 1945.

College Place, town (1990 pop. 6,308), Walla Walla co., SE Wash., 2 mi/3.2 km SW of Walla Walla, on Mill Creek, 3 mi/4.8 km N of Oregon state line; 46°02′N 118°23′W. RR junction. Vegetables, potatoes, alfalfa; dairying; cattle, hogs; mfg. (medical equipment, printing). Fort Walla Walla Mus. to E; Whitman Mission Natl. Historical Site to W. State penitentiary to NE. Seat of Walla Walla Col. Settled 1870, inc. 1878.

College Point, residential and mfg. sect. of N Queens borough of N.Y. city, SE N.Y., on Flushing Bay; 40°47′N 73°51′W. Site of Chisholm Mansion (1848). Newspaper printing.

College Springs, town (1990 pop. 230), Page co., SW Iowa, near Mo. state line, 9 mi/14.5 km SSW of Clarinda; 40°37′N 95°07′W.

College Station, city (1990 pop. 52,456), Brazos co., 80 mi/129 km NW of Houston, E central Texas; 30°36′N 96°18′W. In a prosperous livestock and cotton region. College Station has been marked by steady growth, and the pop. more than doubled from 1970 to 1990. Texas A and M Univ. is here, on common boundary with (sister) city of Bryan (NW). Inc. 1938.

College Station, village, Pulaski co., Ark. on Fourche Creek; part of city of Little Rock, in E part of city. Little Rock Port Industrial Park to E; Adams Field Airport to N.

Collegedale, city (1990 pop. 5,048), Hamilton co., SE Tenn., 13 mi/21 km E of Chattanooga; 35°04′N 85°03′W. Mfg. prepared foods. Has Southern Missionary Col. Red Clay State historic area, site of last Cherokee council before forced removal W in 1838, in E.

Collegeville 1 village (1990 pop. 993), Jasper co., NW Ind., on Iroquois R., and just S of Rensselear; 40°55′N 87°10′W. Seat of St. Joseph's Col. **2** village, Stearns co., central Minn., on North Fork Watab R., 9 mi/14.5 km W of St. Cloud; 45°35′N 94°21′W. Agr. and dairying area. St. John's Univ. (R.C.) is here.

Collegeville, borough (1990 pop. 4,227), Montgomery co., SE Pa., 7 mi/11.3 km NW of Norristown, on Perkiomen Creek; 40°11′N 75°25′W. Mfg. (light manufacturing, consumer prods., printing and publishing, machinery, pharmaceuticals); agr. (grain, soybeans, apples, alfalfa; livestock; dairying). Pa. State Correctional Institute at Graterford to N; Ursinus Col. and Evansburg State Park to E.

Collegiate Range, Colo.: see SAWATCH MOUNTAINS.

Colleton (KUHL-uht-in), county (□ 1,133 sq mi/2,934 sq km; 1990 pop. 34,377), S S.C.; ⊙ Walterboro; 32°50′N 80°39′W. Bounded by Edisto R. to SE, Combahee and Salkehatchie rivers to W, and St. Helena Sound to S. South Edisto R. and St. Helena Sound part of Intracoastal Waterway. Mfg. of peat, sand, clay; rural agr. area, producing timber, chickens, eggs, corn, wheat, rye, tobacco, hay, watermelons; hogs. Area known for hunting, fishing, tourism. Formed 1798.

Colleyville, city (1990 pop. 12,724), Tarrant co., N Texas, residential suburb 14 mi/23 km NE of downtown Fort Worth; 32°53′N 97°09′W. Bounded N by Big Bear Creek.; drained S by Little Bear Creek. Dallas–Fort Worth Airport to E.

Collier (KOL-yer), county (□ 2,305 sq mi/5,970 sq km; pop. 152,099), SW Fla., on Gulf of Mexico; ⊙ East Naples; 26°04′N 81°24′W. Co. area mostly covered by Big Cypress Swamp and the Everglades; Ten Thousand Isls. along SW coast. Rapidly expanding metropolitan area at Naples. Major resort development from Naples N along Gulf, and on Marco Isl. 10 mi/16 km SE of Naples. Farming, fishing, lumbering. Oil wells at Sunniland. Formed 1923.

Collierville (KAWL-yur-vil), town (1990 pop. 14,427), Shelby co., SW Tenn., 20 mi/32 km ESE of Memphis; 35°03′N 89°40′W. In cotton, livestock, dairying region; furniture, fabricated metal prods.

Collin, county (□ 885 sq mi/2,292 sq km; 1990 pop. 264,036), N Texas; ⊙ McKinney. In rich blackland prairie agr. region; drained by East Fork of the Trinity. A leading Texas corn-growing co.; also cotton, wheat, hay; cattle, horses. Stone quarries. Mfg. in McKinney and Plano. City of Dallas has annexed into SW corner of co. from S. This corner is highly urbanized and entire SW ¼ of co. is in rapidly growing urban fringe. L. Lavon reservoir and headwaters of L. Ray Hubbard (East Fork Trinity R.) in SE. Formed 1846.

Collingdale, borough (1990 pop. 9,175), Delaware co., SE Pa., suburb, 7 mi/11.3 km SW of downtown Philadelphia, on Darby Creek; 39°54′N 75°16′W. Mfg. (wood prods., fabricated metal prods., food). Inc. 1891.

Collingswood, borough (1990 pop. 15,289), Camden co., SW N.J.; 39°55′N 75°04′W. Largely residential, the borough has some light industry. Settled 1682 by Quakers, inc. 1888;

Collingsworth, county (□ 919 sq mi/2,380 sq km; 1990 pop. 3,573), extreme N Texas, in the Panhandle, on Okla. state line; ⊙ Wellington; 34°58′N 100°16′W. Drained by Salt Fork and Elm Fork of Red R. Agr. (cotton, wheat, peanuts; beef cattle). Oil and gas. Formed 1876; acquired parts of Beckham and Harmon cos., Okla., in resurvey of 100th meridian (1930).

Collingwood, town (1991 pop. 13,505), S Ont., Canada, at the S end of Georgian Bay, an arm of L. Huron; 44°30′N 80°13′W. Shipbuilding center, with one of the largest dry docks on the Great Lakes. Famous for its Blue Mt. pottery, made from Georgian Bay clay. Winter ski resort.

Collingwood Channel (10 mi/16 km long, 1 mi/2 km–2 mi/3 km wide), SW B.C., Canada, central entrance of Howe Sound from Strait of Georgia, separating Bowen Isl. (E) and Keats Isl. (W).

Collins 1 town (1990 pop. 455), Story co., central Iowa, 11 mi/18 km SE of Nevada; 41°53′N 93°18′W. In agr. area. **2** town, Story co., central Iowa, 11 mi/18 km SE of Nevada. In agr. area. **3** town (1990 pop. 2,541), ⊙ Covington, S central Miss., on Okatoma Creek, and 28 mi/45 km NNW of Hattiesburg; 31°38′N 89°33′W. Agr. (soybeans; timber; dairying); mfg. (apparel, wood prods., transportation equip.). **4** town (1990 pop. 144), St. Clair co., W Mo., 12 mi/19 km SSE of Osceola; 37°53′N 93°37′W.

Collins 1 village, Drew co., SE Ark., 14 mi/23 km SE of Monticello. Seven Devils Swamp L. Reservoir to N; Cut-off Creek Wildlife Management Area to S. **2** village (1990 pop. 528), Tattnall co., E central Ga., 18 mi/29 km E of Vidalia; 32°11′N 82°07′W. Mfg. of clothing and playground equip. **3** village (1990 pop. 500), Erie co., W N.Y., on Cattaraugus Creek, 30 mi/48 km S of Buffalo, near Cattaraugus Indian Reservation; 42°29′N 78°51′W.

Collins Bay, town, SE Ont., Canada, suburb, 6 mi/10 km W of Kingston, on N end of Collins Bay, arm of North Channel, L. Ontario; 44°14′N 76°37′W. Mixed farming. Penitentiary.

Collins Landing, village, Jefferson co., N N.Y., 22 mi/35 km N of Watertown, on St. Lawrence R., here spanned by Thousand Isls. Internatl. Bridge to a point 9 mi/14.5 km E of Gananoque, Ont.; 44°18′N 75°59′W.

Collins Park, uninc. town (1990 pop. 2,100), New Castle co., N Del., residential suburb, 4 mi/6.4 km S of downtown Wilmington, and 1 mi/1.6 km N of New Castle, near Del. R.; 39°41′N 75°33′W. Del. Memorial Bridge 1 mi/1.6 km NE.

Collinston 1 (KAHL-in-stuhn), village (1990 pop. 375), Morehouse parish, NE La., 6 mi/10 km SSE of Bastrop; 32°42′N 91°52′W. RR junction; agr. and lumbering; mfg. of go-carts. Coulee State Game Refuge to SE. **2** village, Box Elder co., N Utah, near Bear R., 18 mi/29 km N of Brigham City. Elev. 4,460 ft/1,359 m. Shipping center for grain, and cattle-raising area; alfalfa, wheat, barley; sheep. Wasatch Natl. Forest, including Wellsville Mt. Wilderness Area to S. RR junction.

Collinsville, city (1990 pop. 22,446), Madison and St. Clair cos., SW Ill., 10 mi/16 km S of Edwardsville; 38°40′N 90°00′W. Once a coal-mining center, food prods. and apparel are now Collinsville's manufactures. Nearby are the Cahokia Mounds Historic Site, with its Native Amer. earthworks, and the Edwardsville campus of Southern Ill. Univ. Settled 1817, inc. 1855.

Collinsville 1 farming town (1990 pop. 1,429), De Kalb co., NE Ala., 15 mi/24 km SW of Fort Payne; 34°16′N 85°51′W. Poultry processing, apparel mfg. **2** uninc. town (1990 pop. 1,364), Lauderdale co., E Miss., 12 mi/19 km NW of Meridian; 32°29′N 88°50′W. Agr. area (cotton, corn; cattle, hogs). Okatibbee L. reservoir to E.

Collinsville, city (1990 pop. 3,612), Tulsa co., NE Okla., suburb, 17 mi/27 km NNE of downtown Tulsa, near Caney R.; 36°22′N 95°51′W. In agr. area (grain, soybeans; cattle, horses); mfg. (tallow, fiberglass boats, food prods.); oil, natural-gas wells.

Collinsville 1 town (1990 pop. 1,033), Grayson co., N Texas, 19 mi/31 km WSW of Sherman; 33°33′N 96°54′W. Oil wells; cattle. L. Kiowa to W; L. Ray Roberts to SW. **2** uninc. town, Henry co., S Va., suburb, 3 mi/4.8 km NNW of Martinsville; 36°43′N 79°54′W. Printing, furniture, other light mfg.

Collinsville, uninc. village, Sonoma co., W Calif., 5 mi/8 km NW of Antioch, on Sacramento R. estuary, E of its entrance to Suisun Bay. Van Sickle Isl. marsh area to W. Safflower, sunflowers, sugar beets, fruit, grain; cattle, lambs.

Collinsville, Conn.: see CANTON.

Collinwood, city (1990 pop. 1,014), Wayne co., S Tenn., 11 mi/18 km S of Waynesboro; 35°10′N 87°44′W. In hilly timber region.

Collyer (KAHL-yuhr), village (1990 pop. 144), Trego co., W central Kansas, 11 mi/18 km W of Wakeeney; 39°02′N 100°07′W.

Colma, city (1990 pop. 1,103), San Mateo co., W Calif., residential suburb 8 mi/12.9 km SSW of downtown San Francisco, on Colma Creek; 37°40′N 122°27′W. Large flower-growing industry, ornamentals, vegetables. Much of land in cemeteries (2.2 sq mi/5.7 sq km necropoli), known as "City of Souls"; Thornton State Beach to W; San Francisco Bay 4 mi/6.4 km to E, Pacific Ocean 2 mi/3.2 km to W; part of Golden Gate Natl. Recreation Area to S. Formerly Lawndale, it took (1941) name of former town of Colma, which had been absorbed (1936) by Daly City.

Colman, village (1990 pop. 482), Moody co., E S.Dak., 12 mi/19 km WSW of Flandreau. Grain market; dairy prods.; livestock, poultry; mfg. (electrical equip.).

Colmar (KOL-mahr), uninc. town (1990 pop. 800), Montgomery co., SE Pa., 22 mi/35 km NNW of Philadelphia; 40°16′N 75°15′W. Mfg. includes fabricated metal prods., printing. Agr. includes dairying, livestock, grain.

Colmar Manor, town (1990 pop. 1,249), Prince Georges co., central Md., NE suburb of Wash., D.C., on Anacostia R.; 38°56′N 76°57′W. Colmar Manor is the terminus of the old Route One in Md.

Colmesneil, village (1990 pop. 569), Tyler co., E Texas,

9 mi/14.5 km N of Woodward; 30°54′N 94°25′W. Lumbering, agr. area. Angelina Natl. Forest to N; B.A. Steinhagen L. to E.

Colo, town (1990 pop. 771), Story co., central Iowa, 17 mi/27 km E of Nevada; 42°01′N 93°19′W. Grain milling.

Cologne, village (1990 pop. 563), Carver co., S central Minn., 29 mi/47 km SW of Minneapolis; 44°46′N 93°47′W. Agr. area (grain, soybeans; livestock, poultry; dairying); light mfg.

Coloma (ko-LO-mah) or **La Coloma**, town, Pinar del Río prov., on S coast of W Cuba, on Ensenada de la Coloma, and part of Gulf of Batabanó, 14 mi/23 km SE of Pinar del Río; 22°14′N 88°34′W. Fishing; lobster canning, food processing.

Coloma (kuh-LO-muh), town (1990 pop. 1,679), Berrien co., extreme SW Mich., on Paw Paw R., and 9 mi/14.5 km NE of Benton Harbor; 42°11′N 86°18′W. In fruit-growing region; mfg. (prepared foods, fabricated metal prods., paper prods., steel). Nearby is Paw Paw L., 2 mi/3.2 km inland from L. Michigan (resort; c.3 mi/4.8 km long). City laid out 1855; inc. as village 1893, as city 1942.

Coloma 1 uninc. village, El Dorado co., E Calif., on South Fork Amer. R., and 45 mi/72 km NE of Sacramento. At Sutter's Mill here, James W. Marshall discovered gold on Jan. 24, 1848. Marshall Gold Discovery State Historic Monument commemorates the event. Eldorado Natl. Forest to E, Folsom L. State Recreation Area to W. **2** (kuhl-O-muh), village (1990 pop. 383), Waushara co., central Wis., 28 mi/45 km W of Wisconsin Rapids; 44°01′N 89°31′W. In dairy area; non-cash grain, field crops; fisheries; mfg. (geodesic domes, meat processing).

Colombia, village (1990 pop. 281), Nuevo León, N Mexico, on the Rio Grande opposite Darwin (Texas), on RR, and 20 mi/32 km NW of Nuevo Laredo; 27°42′N 99°45′W. Elev. 673 ft/205 m. A bridge crosses the Rio Grande here, and the town is a Minoe border crossing point.

Colome (KUH-lom), village (1990 pop. 309), Tripp co., S S.Dak., 10 mi/16 km SE of Winner; 43°15′N 99°43′W. Grain; livestock, poultry. Dog Ear L. to SSW.

Colón (ko-LON), city (1994 est. pop. 44,000), Matanzas prov., W central Cuba; 22°43′N 80°54′W. RR hub and commercial center for the surrounding agr. region. Food processing and bottling industries. Sugar industry has declined since the mid–19th cent., although it remains an important part of the economy. Founded in 1836.

Colón (ko-LON), city (1990 pop. 5,331) and township, Querétaro, central Mexico, 27 mi/43 km NE of Querétaro. Agr. center (wheat, corn, sugarcane, cotton, beans, chicle, tobacco, fruit; livestock).

Colon (KO-luhn), town (1990 pop. 1,224), St. Joseph co., SW Mich., on St. Joseph R., and 11 mi/18 km ENE of Centreville, bet. Sturgeon L. (N) and Palmer L. (S); 41°57′N 85°19′W. In mint-growing area; mfg. (apparel, transportation equip.). Lake resort.

Colon 1 (KO-luhn), village (1990 pop. 128), Saunders co., E Nebr., 5 mi/8 km N of Wahoo, S of Platte R.; 41°17′N 96°36′W. **2** uninc. village, Lee co., central N.C., 3 mi/4.8 km N of Sanford. RR junction. Tobacco, grain; livestock, poultry.

Colona, village (1990 pop. 2,237), Henry co., NW Ill., suburb, 9 mi/14.5 km E of Moline, on Green R. and Hennepin Canal State Trail; 41°28′N 90°20′W. In agr. area (cattle, hogs; corn, soybeans).

Colonarie River, rivulet, E St. Vincent, West Indies, c.5 mi/8 km NE of Kingstown; 13°14′N 61°07′W. Site of hydroelectric plant.

Colonel Hill, town, S Bahama Isls., on central Crooked Isl., 250 mi/402 km SE of Nassau; 22°45′N 74°15′W. Produces cascarilla bark.

Colonia Calles, Mexico: see SAN JOSÉ DE GRACIA, Aguascalientes.

Colonia Manuel González (ko-LO-nee-ah mahn-WEL gon-ZAH-lez), town (1990 pop. 203), ⊙ Zentla municipio, E central Veracruz, Mexico, 7 mi/12 km SE of the city of Huatusco, and a short distance from the ruins of El Castillo; 19°06′N 96°50′W. Elev. 2,575 ft/

785 m. While president of Mexico in 1882, General Manuel González founded this town for Italian immigrants. Coffee, sugarcane, plantains, oranges, corn. Temperate climate.

Colonial Beach, town (1990 pop. 3,132), Westmoreland co., E Va., 28 mi/45 km E of Fredericksburg, on Potomac R. estuary; 38°15′N 76°58′W. Monroe bay to S. Mfg. (oyster processing, concrete); agr. (grain, soybeans; cattle); resort area. "Wakefield," George Washington Birthplace Natl. Monument, is 5 mi/8 km SSE. Ingleside Plantation Winery to S, near Oak Grove. Inc. 1892.

Colonial Heights, independent city (□ 8 sq mi/20.7 sq km; 1990 pop. 16,064), SE Va., separate from adjacent Chesterfield, Prince George cos., 21 mi/34 km S of Richmond, 2 mi/3.2 km N of Petersburg, on Appomattox R.; 37°15′N 77°24′W. Mfg. (printing and publishing, chemicals, consumer prods., fabricated metal prods., whiskey); agr. area (peanuts, grain, soybeans, tobacco; cattle). Violet Bank Lib. and Mus., with its famous giant cucumber tree, site of Confederate Army hq. during siege of Petersburg (1864), across Appomattox R. Va. State Univ. to SW; John Tyler Community Col. (Chester campus) to N. Inc. 1948.

Colonial Heights, town (1990 pop. 6,716), Sullivan co., NE Tenn., on Holston R., 5 mi/8 km SW of Kingsport, 36°29′N 82°30′W. Warriors Path State Park is nearby.

Colonial National Historical Park, (□ 14.6 sq mi/37.8 sq km), SE Va., in York, James City, Surrey cos., and independent cities of Williamsburg, Virginia Beach; 1 sect. on the peninsula bet. York and James rivers and 1 sect. at S side of mouth of Chesapeake Bay, at Ft. Story Military Reservation. Created 1930 as Colonial Natl. Monument, renamed 1936. Includes 23-mi/37-km Colonial Parkway connecting historic towns of Yorktown (12 mi/19 km ESE of Williamsburg) and Jamestown, 1st permanent Eng. settlement (1607) in U.S. (5 mi/8 km SW of Williamsburg). Park includes Jamestown Isl. and shoreline opposite, turning N from Kingsmill Neck to downtown Williamsburg, turning due E to York R., following shoreline to Yorktown. Yorktown Natl. Cemetery adjoins park. Separate unit at Cape Henry, Virginia Beach, 18 mi/29 km ENE of Norfolk, added 1939; Cape Henry Memorial marks 1st landing of Jamestown colonists (1607).

Colonial Park, uninc. city (1990 pop. 13,777), Dauphin co., S Pa., residential suburb, 4 mi/6.4 km NE of Harrisburg; 40°17′N 76°48′W.

Colonial Terrace, town (1990 pop. 1,050), Jefferson co., N Ky., residential suburb, 9 mi/14.5 km E of downtown Louisville.

Colonie (ka-la-NEE), village (□ 3 sq mi/7.8 sq km; 1990 pop. 8,019), Albany co., E N.Y., 6 mi/9.7 km NW of downtown Albany; 42°43′N 73°49′W. The growth and configuration of major highways, the flat, well-drained topography, and favorable economic-political climate make Colonie more than just a suburb of Albany, but rather a significant community in its own right. The area N and W of Albany in general is experiencing both retail and residential growth. Inc. 1921.

Colony 1 village (1990 pop. 447), Anderson co., E Kansas, 11 mi/18 km N of Iola; 38°04′N 95°21′W. In grain, livestock, and dairy region. **2** village (1990 pop. 163), Washita co., W central Okla., 19 mi/31 km SE of Clinton; 35°21′N 98°40′W. Agr. area. Crowder L. State Park to NW.

Colora (ko-LO-ruh), village, Cecil co., NE Md., 8 mi/12.9 km N of Havre de Grace. The name comes from that of a home built by Lloyd Balderston who settled here in 1842–1843. Large numbers of Federal troops camped here during the Civil War.

Colorada, La, Mexico: see LA COLORADA.

Colorado, state (□ 104,100 sq mi/269,616 sq km; 1995 est. pop. 3,746,585), W central U.S., one of the Rocky Mt. states; ⊙ DENVER. Admitted as the 38th state of the Union in 1876 (and therefore known as the "Centennial State"). Denver is the largest city and the center of state and regional activity. Other major cities are COLORADO SPRINGS, AURORA, LAKEWOOD, BOULDER, and PUEBLO. Colo. is bounded on the N by Wyo. and Nebr., on the E by Nebr. and Kansas, on the S by Okla. and N.Mex., and on the W by Utah. The plains of Colo.'s E sect. (roughly ½ of state) are part of the High Plains sect. of the Great Plains. On their W edge the plains give way to the Rocky Mts., which run N-S through central Colo. The mts. are divided into several ranges that make up 2 generally parallel belts, with the Front Range and a portion of the Sangre de Cristo Mts. on the E and the Park Range and Sawatch and San Juan mts. on the W. Mt. Elbert (14,433 ft/4,399 m) c.85 mi/137 km SW of Denver, is the highest peak in the U.S. Rocky Mts. The mt. ranges are separated by high valleys and basins sometimes called parks, because of the grassy vegetation. These include North Park, Middle Park, South Park, Estes Park, and San Luis Park. The Continental Divide runs N-S through the Rocky Mts. in Colo. One of the most scenic states in the country, Colo.'s recreational parks include Rocky Mt. Natl. Park (N), Black Canyon of the Gunnison Natl. Monument (W) with its narrow gorge cut by the Gunnison R., Dinosaur Natl. Monument in NW Colo. (extends into Utah), and Great Sand Dunes Natl. Monument in S central Colo. Mesa Verde Natl. Park, once the home of Native Amer. cliff dwellers, is located in the SW corner of the state, a beautiful but formidable area of mesas and canyons. Arapahoe Natl. Recreational Area is SW of Rocky Mt. Natl. Park, and Curecanti Natl. Recreational Area is along the Gunnison R. in W. Most of W Colo. is dominated by the Colo. Plateau, where many canyons have been formed by the action of the Colorado, Gunnison, and other rivers. Colo. has a mean elev. of c.6,800 ft/2,073 m and has 52 of the 80 peaks in N. America of 14,000 ft/4,267 m or higher, thus laying claim to the name "top of the world." Melting snows from the mts. form important river systems that deliver water to the Great Plains and the Southwest. A broad timber belt, largely coniferous and mostly protected as natl. forest reserves, covers large sections of the mts. Among Colorado's natl. forests are Roosevelt and Routt (N), White River, Arapaho, Grand Mesa, Pike, and Gunnison (center), Uncompahgre, San Juan, San Isabel, and Rio Grande (S). Colo. has 2 natl. grasslands, Pawnee in NE and Comanche in SE. The mighty Colorado R. originates in Rocky Mt. Natl. Park, and the headwaters of the N Platte, S Platte, Arkansas, and Rio Grande also gather in Colo.'s mts. The average annual rainfall in Colo. is only 16.6 in/43 cm, but by means of irrigation the state has been able to develop otherwise unusable land and ranks high among the states in irrigated acres. The Colorado–Big Thompson project and the Fryingpan-Arkansas project are 2 major water-diversion systems that carry water by tunnel across the Continental Divide to farms on the plains of E Colo. Agr., especially the raising of cattle and sheep, is economically important in the state. Crops include wheat, hay, corn, and sugar beets. Since the 1950s mfg. has been the major source of income in the state. Food processing is a major industry; other important industries include the manufacture of computer equip., aerospace prods., transportation equip., and electrical equip.; printing and publishing; and the production of fabricated metals, chemicals, and lumber. Denver, Colorado Springs, and other mt. communities have attracted research organizations and institutes (or think tanks). Tourism also plays a vital role in the economy. Colo.'s climate, colorful scenery, and extensive recreational facilities bring millions of visitors to the state annually. Numerous resorts in towns such as VAIL and ASPEN attract visitors year-round in addition to the annual winter flood of skiers. Besides fine hunting, fishing, and skiing there are many special events held in the state, including rodeos and fairs. Gold, the lure to exploration and settlement of Colo., was the first of many useful minerals to be discovered there. Leading minerals are petroleum, coal, silver, molybdenum, sand and gravel, oil shale, and uranium. Gold is no longer mined extensively. Large coal and oil deposits, as well as hydroelectric power, provide considerable resources for the generation of electricity. Colo.'s earliest inhabitants were the Basket Makers, Native Americans who settled in the mesa country before the beginning of the Christian era. Later people known as cliff dwellers inhabited the area, building their pueblos in canyon walls. The first European to enter the region was probably the Span. conquistador Francisco Vásquez de Coronado in the 16th cent. Spain subsequently claimed (1706) the territory, although no Span. settlements were established there. Part of the area was also claimed for France as part of the Louisiana Territory. At the end of the French and Indian Wars (1763), France secretly ceded the Louisiana Territory, including much of Colo., to Spain. The French regained the whole area in 1800 by the secret Treaty of San Ildefonso concluded with Spain. The U.S. bought the area N of the Arkansas R. and E of the Rocky Mts. in the Louisiana Purchase of 1803. The Federal govt. sent expeditions to Colo. which generated some public interest in the new territory, and they explored routes opened earlier by the famous mountain men, trappers, and fur traders who included William H. Ashley, James Bridger, Jedediah S. Smith, Kit Carson, and the Bent brothers. Bent's Fort, in Colo., was one of the best-known Western trading posts. Settlement in the area did not begin, however, until the U.S. acquired the remainder of present-day Colo. from Mexico by the Treaty of Guadalupe Hidalgo in 1848. In the early 1800s a small farming settlement had been est. in the San Luis valley, but most settlers pushing W across the Great Plains continued on to the more fertile lands of Oregon, Wash., and Calif. It was the discovery of gold that first brought large numbers of settlers to Colo. Prospectors led by Green Russell discovered gold in 1858 at Cherry Creek, where the city of Denver stands, and after another strike the following year, the mining boom began. At the time of the gold rush the area in which the gold fields were located was part of the U.S. Kansas Territory. A group of miners organized the gold fields as Arapahoe co. of Kansas Territory. The region was divided into districts, and miners' and people's courts were set up to provide quick justice. The miners sought separate territorial status in 1859 and formed the illegal Territory of Jefferson, which operated until the bill for territorial status was passed by Congress in 1861. William Gilpin, the first territorial governor, chose the name Colorado [Span. = red colored]. Measures proposing statehood for Colo. were introduced in the U.S. Congress in 1864, and again in 1866 and 1867 when they were vetoed by Andrew Johnson. A bill granting Colorado's statehood was finally passed by Congress in 1876. When the first settlers came to Colo., the Ute lived in the mt. areas, while the Comanche, Cheyenne, Arapaho, and Kiowa inhabited the Great Plains. (Ute Mt. and Southern Ute Indian Reservations are in SW along N.Mex. border, both large in area.) Warfare bet. plains and mt. ethnic groups was continuous. The tribes of the plains combined their forces in 1840 to halt the invasion of their homelands and hunting grounds by settlers, and violence ensued. The warfare finally culminated in the Native Americans' defeat after the Indian Wars (1861–1869) and the Buffalo War (1873–1874). (Colo.'s Native Americans now live mainly on the Southern Ute reservation and in the Denver area.) While Colo. was seeking to establish a govt. and engaged in conflict with Native Americans, the state's mining boom was in sharp decline. The surface gold had been extracted in the middle 1860s, and mining areas became, and in many cases remain, studded with ghost towns—the machinery abandoned and shacks deserted. Other towns, such as Central City with its famous opera house dating from the city's days of opulence, managed to stay alive. The completion (1870) of a RR link from Denver to the Union Pacific in Cheyenne, Wyo., and later RR construction helped to stimulate the extension of farming and the growth of huge cattle ranches as well as to encourage an influx of settlers. Bet. 1870 and 1880 pop. increased almost 5-fold. Denver briefly became the largest receiving market for sheep, and a smelting industry was est. In the 1870s the discovery of silver-bearing lead carbonite ore at Leadville started a new mining boom. Prosperity was short-lived, however, for in the 1890s, despite a rich silver strike at Creede and the discovery of the state's richest gold field at Cripple Creek, Colo. suffered a depression. In 1893 the U.S. govt. stopped buying silver in order to restore confidence in the nation's currency, which had been placed on the gold standard in 1873. The silver market subsequently collapsed, dealing a severe blow to Colo.'s economy. Labor conflicts, disputes over RR franchises, and warfare bet. sheep and cattle interests also plagued the state at the turn of the cent. Many of labor's battles in this period were fought in the mines of Colo., and the lawlessness and ruthlessness that prevailed among both employers and miners were reminiscent of the early days of the mining camps. When the silver market broke, Colo. turned politically to fusion Populist-Democratic leaders advocating a return to bimetallism. The free-silver movement, however, was unsuccessful, and by 1910, with the improvement of natl. economic conditions, Colo. settled down to a predominantly agr. economy. The establishment of large natl. parks in the early 1900s provided an additional source of revenue in tourism. During World War I the price of silver soared again and the economy prospered. The stock-market crash of 1929 and the droughts of 1935 and 1937 brought hardship to many. The economy recovered again during World War II, when the state produced food and valuable minerals and metal prods. for the war effort. In the mid-1960s Colo. experienced a large influx of new residents and rapid urban growth and development, especially along a strip (c.150 mi/240 km long) centered on Denver and stretching from Fort Collins and Greeley in the N to Pueblo in the S. This growth combined with the area's high elev. have caused enormous pollution problems, most notably smog. The discovery and exploitation of oil shales created a boom in the state's economy in the 1970s. However, when oil prices collapsed in the early 1980s, so did much of Colo.'s affluence. Oil shale fields are found in W and NW, including U.S. Naval Oil Shale Reserve NW of Rifle. Major military installations include Fort Carson Military Reservation and U.S. Air Force Acad., both near Colorado Springs. U.S. Army Depot and Dept. of Transportation High Speed Ground Test Facility NE of Pueblo. Colo.'s state govt. is based on the constitution drawn up in 1876 and since amended. The governor of the state is popularly elected and serves for a term of 4 years. The legislature is made up of a senate with 35 members elected for 4-year terms and a house of representatives with 65 members elected for 2-year terms. Colo. is represented in the U.S. Congress by 2 senators and 6 representatives and has 8 votes in the electoral col. Among Colo.'s institutions of higher learning are the Univ. of Colo., at Boulder; the Univ. of Denver, at Denver; Colo. State Univ., at Fort Collins; and the U.S. Air Force Academy, at Colo. Springs. Colo. has 63 cos.: ADAMS, ALAMOSA, ARAPAHOE, ARCHULETA, BACA, BENT, BOULDER, CHAFFEE, CHEYENNE, CLEAR CREEK, CONEJOS, COSTILLA, CROWLEY, CUSTER, DELTA, DENVER, DOLORES, DOUGLAS, EAGLE, ELBERT, EL PASO, FREMONT, GARFIELD, GILPIN, GRAND, GUNNISON, HINSDALE, HUERFANO, JACKSON, JEFFERSON, KIOWA, KIT CARSON, LAKE, LA PLATA, LARIMER, LAS ANIMAS, LINCOLN, LOGAN, MESA, MINERAL, MOFFAT, MONTEZUMA, MONTROSE, MORGAN, OTERO, OURAY, PARK, PHILLIPS, PITKIN, PROWERS, PUEBLO, RIO BLANCO, RIO GRANDE, ROUTT, SAGUACHE, SAN JUAN, SAN MIGUEL, SEDGWICK, SUMMIT, TELLER, WASHINGTON, WELD, YUMA.

Colorado, county (☐ 973 sq mi/2,520 sq km; 1990 pop. 18,383), S Texas; ⊙ Columbus; 29°37′N 96°31′W. Bounded on E in part by San Bernard R., bounded in extreme W by Navidad R.; drained by Colorado R. A leading Texas rice producing co.; cotton, wheat, corn, grain sorghum, peanuts, soybeans; livestock raising, dairying. Large gravel and sand-mining industry; natural gas and oil production, uranium; pine and cedar timber. Eagle L.; waterfowl refuges; Attwater Prairie Chicken Natl. Wildlife Refuge in E. Formed 1836.

Colorado, Arroyo, stream, extreme S Texas, flows c.50 mi/80 km NE from vicinity of Mercedes, Hidalgo co., through Cameron co., to Laguna Madre area of Gulf of Mexico, 25 mi/40 km NNW of Port Isabel. Canalized for c.20 mi/32 km of lower course to allow barge access from Harlingen to Gulf Intracoastal Waterway.

Colorado City 1 town (1990 pop. 2,426), Mohave co., NW Ariz., 33 mi/53 km ESE of St. George, Utah, at Utah state line; 36°58′N 112°58′W. Elev. 4,980 ft/1,518 m. Mfg. (apparel). Mormon community here noted for polygamy. Kaibab Indian Reservation to E; Pipe Spring Natl. Monument to SE; Zion Natl. Park (Utah) to N. Community has grown with influx of retired citizens, especially to SW of Utah. **2** uninc. town (1990 pop. 1,149), Pueblo co., S central Colo., 21 mi/34 km N of Walsenburg, on Greenhorn Creek; 37°56′N 104°50′W. Wet Mts. and San Isabel Natl. Forest to W. Residential community. **3** town (1990 pop. 4,749), ⊙ Mitchell co., W Texas, 65 mi/105 km W of Abilene and on Colorado R.; 32°23′N 100°51′W. Agr. (grain, alfalfa, cotton; beef cattle, sheep), oil and gas producing region; mfg. (agr. tools). L. Colorado City State Park to W. Champion Creek Reservoir to SW. Inc. 1907.

Colorado Creek, district, W Alaska, N of Kuskokwim R., 45 mi/72 km NNW of McGrath; 63°33′N 156°00′W. Placer gold mining.

Colorado Desert, in SE Calif., and N Baja Calif., Mexico; depressed arid region (☐ c.2,000 sq mi/5,180 sq km–3,000 mi/4,828 km), part of Great Basin, W of Colorado R., NW of Gulf of Calif., S extension of larger Mojave Desert; traversed by scattered mtn. ranges. Includes Imperial Valley, Coachella Valley (irrigated agr.), and Salton Sea.

Colorado National Monument (☐ 20,454 acres/8,278 ha), W Colo., 5 mi/8 km W of Grand Junction. Eroded sandstone formations, many of them vividly colored, include huge monoliths, stratified ramparts, and steep-walled canyons. Notable features are Independence Rock (500 ft/152 m sandstone shaft), Window Rock, and Cold Shivers Point, 1,000 ft/305-m deep canyons in SE. Dinosaur fossils and prehistoric Indian remains have been discovered in monument area. Est. 1911.

Colorado Plateau, vast arid upland (☐ c.150,000 sq mi/388,500 sq km), SW U.S., drained by the Colorado R. system, and including much of Ariz. and Utah and smaller parts of Colo. and N.Mex. Elev. 5,000 ft/1,524 m–11,000 ft/3,353 m. It is bounded E by the S Rocky Mts. and the valley of the Rio Grande, W by the Great Basin, N by the Wasatch and Uinta mts, and is one of the least populated and most inaccessible regions of the U.S. The deep canyons and high plateaus that contribute to its scenic beauty have made RR construction impossible over most of the plateau, and roads are few. Composed mainly of generally horizontal Paleozoic sediments (sand-stones, shales, conglomerates, and limestones), the plateau is underlain by very anc. (pre-Cambrian) metamorphic rocks (exposed in Grand Canyon) and is overlaid in places by later formations (Mesozoic, Tertiary) and volcanic materials. Faulting has raised portions above the general plateau surface, and the Colorado and its tributaries (Grand, Green, Gunnison, Little Colorado, San Juan rivers) have carved magnificent canyons, chief among them the stupendous Grand Canyon of the Colorado in NW Ariz. Brilliantly colored strata carved by erosion into fantastic shapes are also exhibited in Bryce Canyon Natl. Park, Zion Natl. Park, and Cedar Breaks Natl. Monument in Utah; in Ariz. are the Painted Desert, Meteor Crater, and the Petrified Forest; Rainbow Bridge Natl. Monument (Utah) contains the largest known natural bridge; Mesa Verde Natl. Park (Colo.), Canyon de Chelly Natl. Monument (Ariz.) preserves anc. cliff dwellings. In NE Ariz., S Utah, and NW N.Mex. are the vast, arid, colorful lands of the "Navajo country," containing the Navajo and Hopi Indian reservations, where sheep herds, a little agr., and handicrafts support an increasing Indian pop. Indian reservations occupy about ⅓ of the mostly semiarid and sparsely vegetated area; about ½ of the public land is used for grazing. Regional resources have been little developed for the most part, although some minerals are produced in Utah and Colo. portions. Good stands of pine grow at high elevs. of Ariz. and N.Mex., and there is some lumbering.

Colorado River 1 1,450 mi/2,333 km long; SW U.S., rising in the Rocky Mts. of N Colo., in NW Rocky Mt. Natl. Park, NE Grand co., 25 mi/40 km NNE of Granby, 65 mi/105 km NW of Denver, and flowing generally SW through Colo., Utah, Ariz., bet. Nev. and Ariz., and Ariz. and Calif., and then into Mexico, emptying into the Gulf of California; drains c.244,000 sq mi/631,960 sq km. Source is surrounded on 3 sides by Continental Divide; flows S through Grand L. (Shadow Mt. Reservoir) and L. Granby reservoirs, then generally SW past Glenwood Springs, Rifle, and Grand Junction, Colo., where it receives the Gunnison R. from SE, into Utah, where it forms the S boundary of Arches Natl. Park at Moab, then through Canyonlands Natl. Park, where it receives the Green R., its longest tributary from the N. The Colorado then enters Glen Canyon Natl. Recreational Area and L. Powell, formed by the Glen Canyon Dam at Page, in extreme NE Ariz., and at 26,997,000,000 cu ft/764,015,100 cu m, the 2d largest reservoir in U.S. Receives the San Juan R. from E. Below Glen Canyon Dam, the river enters Marble Canyon and Grand Canyon natl. parks. (The river and part of L. Powell form NW boundary of Navajo Indian Reservation.) Due to major park expansion in 1975, the river flows c.140 mi/225 km through the park, through Marble Canyon and the spectacular Grand Canyon; then for another 100 mi/161 km it forms the S boundary of the W extension of the park and N boundary of Hualapai Indian Reservation. It then enters L. Mead Natl. Recreational Area (at 28,253,000,000 cu ft/799,559,900 cu m, L. Mead, formed by Hoover Dam, is the largest reservoir in the U.S). The lake and L. Mohave below it, formed by Davis Dam, form the Ariz.-Nev. state line. The large N arm of L. Mead receives the Virgin R. from the NE. Below Hoover, the river flows almost due S. Below Davis Dam, it flows through Fort Mohave Indian Reservation and becomes Calif.-Ariz. state line. It forms boundary of Havasu Natl. Wildlife Refuge (E) and Chemehueva Indian Reservation (W), flowing past L. Havasu City and through L. Havasu, formed by Parker Dam. Below Parker Dam, the river flows past Parker; through Colorado Indian Reservation; through Cibola and Imperial natl. wildlife refuges; forms E and S boundary of Ft. Yuma Indian Reservation; and past Yuma, Ariz. Around Yuma, the Colorado passes through Imperial, Laguna, and Morelos dams, each with minor reservoirs, the volume of the river having been reduced by diversion to major cities and irrigation projects in Calif., Nev., and Ariz. Just E of Yuma, the Colorado receives the Gila R. from E. For c.20 mi/32 km below Yuma, the river forms part of the U.S.-Mexico border (Ariz. to E, Baja California Norte to W). Its final 95 mi/153 km, reduced to a braided trickle, flows through Mexico, forming border bet. Baja California Norte and Sonora states, entering the N end of the Gulf of California. In its small delta is Isla Montague. Many natl. parks, monuments, and recreational areas are located along the river banks. The Colorado's waters are used for power and irrigation, especially by means of the Colorado R. storage project, the Colorado–Big Thompson project, Hoover Dam, Davis Dam, Imperial Dam, the All-American Canal, Parker Dam, and Glen Canyon Dam. Controversies over water rights on the Colorado have long raged bet. the U.S. and Mexico and among the bordering states; treaties and compacts regulate the river's use. **2** 894 mi/1,439 km long; SW U.S., rising in Border co., in the Llano Estacado, NW Texas, from a combination of intermittent streams from the NW, and flowing SE to Matagorda Bay, an inlet of the Gulf of Mexico; drains c.41,500 sq mi/107,485 sq km. The source of numerous and frequent destructive floods brought about by heavy

Texas thunderstorms. As a result a series of flood control dams have been built, which also provide energy for power plants and water for irrigation. From its source, the Colorado flows through Lake J.B. Thomas (Borden/Scurry cos.), E.V. Spence Reservoir (Coke co.), Lake O.H. Ivie (Coleman, Runnels, Concho cos.), L. Buchanan, Inks L., L. Marble Falls (Llano/Burnet cos.), and L. Travis and L. Austin, as well as the city of Austin (Travis co). Major tributaries include the Concho, Llano, and Pedernales rivers.

Colorado River Aqueduct, great water supply system for Los Angeles basin, S Calif.; has its head at Parker Dam on the lower Colorado. Main aqueduct (242 mi/389 km long), with pumping stations raising water 1,600 ft/488 m, leads W, across Colorado Desert and through San Jacinto Mts., to L. Mathews S of Riverside; San Diego Aqueduct branches S from it, c.25 mi/40 km ESE of Riverside; gravity then carries flow through 150 mi/241 km of distribution lines to cities of Los Angeles area. Constructed by Metropolitan Water Dist. of S Calif. A major engineering achievement, it was begun in 1932, and the aqueduct completed in 1939; 1st water delivered to users in 1941.

Colorado River Storage Project, a multipurpose plan, undertaken by the U.S. Bureau of Reclamation in 1956, to control the flow of the upper Colorado and its tributaries and to aid in the development of the rugged, remote upper Colorado R. basin; includes parts of Wyo., Utah, Colo., Ariz., and N.Mex. The Colorado R. Compact of 1922 est. the division bet. the upper and lower basins and stipulated that the upper basin's water consumption be contingent on the delivery of a set amount of water to the lower basin. Since the flow of the Colorado is erratic, a storage project was needed to maintain an even flow of water to the lower basin in dry years. A series of dams regulates stream flow, provides storage reservoirs, creates hydroelectric power, and irrigates both new and previously developed acreage. The 4 major units of the project are Glen Canyon Dam (forms L. Powell), on the Colorado R. in Ariz.; Flaming Gorge Dam, on the Green R. in Utah; Navajo Dam, on the San Juan R. in N.Mex.; and the Curecanti dams on the Gunnison R. in Colo. The 3 reservoirs (Blue Mesa, Morrow Point, and Crystal) of the Curecanti unit are included in the Curecanti Natl. Recreation Area.

Colorado Springs, city (1990 pop. 281,140), ⊙ El Paso co., central Colo., 60 mi/97 km SSE of Denver, on Monument and Fountain creeks, at the foot of Pikes Peak; 38°51′N 104°45′W. Elev. 6,008 ft/1,831 m. RR junction. Colorado Springs is a residential and year-round vacation and health resort, with thriving industries that produce a wide variety of prods. Mfg. (aerospace development and equip., computer equip., fabricated metal prods., machinery, medical equip., prepared food prods., printing and publishing). The town of El Dorado (later Colorado City) was founded on Fountain Creek by gold miners in 1859. In 1871, Gen. William Palmer and the Denver and Rio Grande RR est. the modern city of Fountain Colony nearby; the name was changed to Colorado Springs because of the many mineral springs in the area. The city grew as a resort, absorbing the earlier community of Colorado City in 1917. It has undergone extensive economic growth as well as a boom in pop. since the 1970s. It is the seat of Colo. Col., the Univ. of Colo. at Colorado Springs, and Pikes Peak Community Col. The city is also the hq. of Pike Natl. Forest. U.S. Air Force Academy to N; U.S. Fort Carson (est. 1942) to S. Cheyenne Mt. Zoo, Will Rogers Shrine, Pro Rodeo Hall of Fame, Fine Arts Center, Pioneer Mus., World Figure Skating Hall of Fame are here. Colorado Springs Airport to SE. Garden of the Gods, rock formations, and Cave of the Winds to NW. Natl. Carvers Mus. to N. Pike Natl. Forest and Pikes Peak to W. Inc. 1886.

Colorado–Big Thompson Project, constructed by the U.S. Bureau of Reclamation to divert water from the headstreams of the Colorado R. to irrigate c.720,000 acres/291,400 ha of land in NE Colo. and to supply power; built 1938–1956. Water is diverted by several dams, notably Granby Dam on the Colorado and Green Mt. Dam on the Blue R. Water is stored in Granby Reservoir, Shadow Mt. L., and Grand L. before it is pumped through the Alva B. Adams Tunnel (13 mi/21 km long), to flow down the E slope of the Continental Divide into the Big Thompson R., a tributary of the South Platte. Dams E of Divide, near Fort Collins and Estes Park, collect the water for local use. Flatiron, Estes, Pole Hill, and Green Mt. dams generate hydroelectric power.

Colorados, Los, archipelago off NW Cuba, Pinar de Río prov., a chain of low coral reefs and keys stretching for c.140 mi/225 km from Cape San Antonio (W) along the coast, endangering navigation and prohibiting good ports; 22°45′N 84°03′W. On several islets are lighthouses. The group is also called Guaniguanico or Santa Isabel.

Coloso (ko-LO-so) or **Central Coloso**, locality, NW P.R., 1.5 mi/2.4 km E of Aguada. Sugar mill.

Colotlán (ko-lo-TLAHN), city (1990 pop. 10,041) and township, Jalisco, N central Mexico, on affluent of the Santiago, near Zacatecas border, and 60 mi/97 km SW of Zacatecas; 22°08′N 103°15′W. Agr. center (cereals, alfalfa, vegetables, fruit; livestock).

Colp, village (1990 pop. 235), Williamson co., S Ill., 3 mi/4.8 km W of Herrin; 37°48′N 89°01′W. In bituminous-coal-mining and agr. area.

Colquitt (KAHL-kwit), county (☐ 563 sq mi/1,458 sq km; 1990 pop. 36,645), S Ga.; ⊙ Moultrie; 31°11′N 83°46′W. Bounded E by Little R.; drained by Ochlockonee R. and its affluents. Coastal plain agr. (cotton, tobacco, corn, soybeans, wheat, melons, peanuts; cattle, hogs, poultry; timber). Formed 1856.

Colquitt (KAHL-kwit), town (1990 pop. 1,991), ⊙ Miller co., SW Ga., 21 mi/34 km NNW of Bainbridge and on Spring Creek; 31°10′N 84°44′W. Mfg. of apparel; meat and peanut processing. Agr. includes peanuts, cotton; cattle. Founded 1856, inc. 1860.

Colrain (KOL-rain), town (1990 pop. 1,757), Franklin co., NW Mass., in hills, 4.3 mi/6.9 km NW of Greenfield; 42°41′N 72°43′W. Includes villages of Griswoldville (cotton prods.) and Shattuckville. Settled 1735, inc. 1761.

Colstrip, town (1990 pop. 3,036), Rosebud co., SE Mont., 52 mi/84 km SW of Miles City; 45°54′N 106°38′W. Terminus of RR spur from nearby Forsyth. Agr. in area (cattle, sheep; wheat, alfalfa). Large quantities of lignite coal taken from strip mine, SE of town. Northern Cheyenne Indian Reservation to S. "Energy Capital of Montana." Visitor center.

Colt, village (1990 pop. 334), St. Francis co., E Ark., 8 mi/12.9 km N of Forrest City; 35°07′N 90°48′W.

Colton, city (1990 pop. 40,213), San Bernardino co., S Calif., a suburb 54 mi/87 km E of downtown Los Angeles, and 5 mi/8 km SSW of San Bernardino; 34°04′N 117°19′W. Drained by Santa Ana Wash. RR junction and center in a rich fruit- and vegetable-growing region; being replaced by urban development. Mfg. (frozen fruits and vegetables, construction materials, paints, RR equipment). A city marked by growth, Colton's pop. doubled from 1970 to 1990. Colton Airport in W, Tri-City Airport to E. Loma Linda Univ. to E. Inc. 1887.

Colton, town (1990 pop. 657), Minnehaha co., E S.Dak., 20 mi/32 km NNW of Sioux Falls; 43°47′N 96°55′W. Grain; livestock; dairy prods., feed.

Colton, village (1990 pop. 325), Whitman Co., SE Wash., 12 mi/19 km S of Pullman, on Union Flat Creek; 46°34′N 117°08′W. In agr. region; grain, livestock.

Coltons Point, summer-resort village, St. Marys co., S Md., on the Potomac and 8 mi/12.9 km SW of Leonardtown. Nearby is St. Clements State Park on St. Clements Isl., site of the first Pilgrim landing in Md. 1634. The blessing of the oyster fleet is held here each Sept. as the new oyster season begins.

Colts Neck, township (1990 pop. 8,559), Monmouth co., NE N.J., 5 mi/8 km W of Eatontown; 40°17′N 74°10′W. Inc. 1847.

Columbia 1 county (☐ 766 sq mi/1,984 sq km; 1990 pop. 25,691), SW Ark.; ⊙ Magnolia; 33°13′N 93°13′W. Bounded S by La. state line; drained by Bayou Dorcheat (forms part of W boundary). Agr. (cattle, hogs, chickens); timber; oil wells, oil and gas bromine. Cotton ginning, oil refining; some mfg. L. Columbia Reservoir in NW; Logoly State Park in N. Formed 1852. **2** county (☐ 801 sq mi/2,075 sq km; 1990 pop. 42,613), N central Fla., on Ga. state line, bet. Suwannee (NW) and Santa Fe (S) rivers; ⊙ Lake City; 30°13′N 82°37′W. Flatwoods area partly containing Okefenokee Swamp (N) and Osceola Natl. Forest (E). Agr. (corn, peanuts, cotton, tobacco; livestock) and forestry (lumber, naval stores); phosphate deposits in S. Formed 1832. **3** county (☐ 306 sq mi/793 sq km; 1990 pop. 66,031), E Ga.; ⊙ Appling; 33°33′N 82°16′W. Bounded E by Savannah R. (forms S.C. state line here) and N by Little R. Cotton, corn, potatoes; cattle; timber; farming area intersected by the fall line. Clark Hill Dam to NE in the Savannah R. Formed 1790. **4** county (☐ 648 sq mi/1,678 sq km; 1990 pop. 62,982), SE N.Y.; ⊙ Hudson; 42°15′N 73°37′W. Bordered E by Mass., W by Hudson R.; drained by Kinderhook Creek. Dairy and beef cattle raising; fruit. Other crops include sweet corn, potatoes, and hay. Sand and gravel, peat and limestone. Named in honor of Christopher Columbus. Involved in the bitter and violent land claim disputes bet. N.Y. state and Mass. after the Amer. Revolution. Has summer and winter resorts; includes part of Taconic State Park and several small lakes. Formed 1786. **5** county (☐ 688 sq mi/1,782 sq km; 1990 pop. 37,557), NW Oregon; ⊙ St. Helens; 45°57′N 123°04′W. Located in Coast Range region. Columbia R. forms N and E boundary (Wash. state). Mfg. at St. Helens. Agr. (fruit, berries, corn, wheat, oats; poultry, sheep, cattle); dairy prods.; timber; salmon. Trojan Nuclear Power Plant in NE at Prescott on Columbia R. has been shut down. Small parts of Clatsop State Forest in NW, SW, and center. Formed 1854. **6** county (☐ 484 sq mi/1,254 sq km), E central Pa.; ⊙ Bloomsburg; 41°02′N 76°24′W. Hilly region extending from Pocono plateau (N), Little Mt. and Big Mt. ridges in S. Anthracite coal field in S; bounded SW by South Branch Roaring Creek; drained by Susquehanna R. and Roaring and Fishing creeks. Mfg. at Berwick and Bloomsburg. Agr. (corn, wheat, oats, barley, hay, alfalfa, soybeans, potatoes, apples; poultry, sheep, hogs, cattle; dairying). More than 20 covered bridges in co. Formed 1813. **7** county (☐ 873 sq mi/2,261 sq km; 1990 pop. 4,024), SE Wash., on Oregon line; ⊙ Dayton; 46°18′N 117°55′W. Plateau area, with Blue Mts. in S; drained by Tucannon and Touchet rivers and bounded N by the Snake R. (Little Goose dam forms L. Bryan). Wheat, barley, oats, peas, alfalfa, hay, apples; hogs, cattle; timber. Part of Umatilla Natl. Forest in S, including part of Wenaha-Tucannon Wilderness Area. Camp William D. Wooten State Park in E; Ski Bluewood Alpine Ski Area in S. Formed 1875. **8** county (☐ 795 sq mi/2,059 sq km; 1990 pop. 45,088), S central Wis.; ⊙ Portage; 43°28′N 89°19′W. Drained by Wisconsin, Fox, Crawfish, and Baraboo rivers; contains resort lakes, notably L. Wisconsin (Wisconsin R.), and part of Baraboo Range in W. Barley, oats, wheat, soybeans, peas, beans, tobacco; hogs, sheep, poultry, cattle; dairying. Vegetable canning, other mfg. Wisconsin Dells, canyon feature of Wisconsin R. and popular tourist area, in NW. Formed 1846.

Columbia 1 city (1990 pop. 5,524), Monroe co., SW Ill., 12 mi/19 km S of East St. Louis, suburb of St. Louis; 38°27′N 90°13′W. In agr. area (wheat, sorghum, soybeans; apples; dairying); limestone quarries. Urban growth has occurred since 1980s. Inc. as village in 1859, as city in 1903. Well-known for its Ger. heritage, restaurants, taverns. Municipal airport. Near Jefferson Barrocks cemetary and park (in Mo.) **2** city (1990 pop. 75,883), Howard co., central Md., located bet. Washington, D.C., and Baltimore; 39°12′N 76°52′W. Columbia arose out of farmland as a complete "New Town" in 1966–1967, a planned community developed by the Rouse Co. It incorporates 9 villages around a main downtown along with schools, churches, a mall with more than 200 stores, recreational park, and business and cultural facilities. Numerous, diverse mfg. firms provide local employment. The Post-Merriweather

Outdoor Pavilion attracts well-known entertainment. **3** city (1990 pop. 69,101), ⊙ Boone co., central Mo., near Mo. R.; 38°57′N 92°19′W. The major trade center of central Mo., it is the seat of the main campus of the Univ. of Mo., Stephens Col. and Columbia Col. Mfg. (meat processing, transportation equip., electrical equip., beverages, consumer goods, plastic prods., publishing). Offices of several insurance companies. The city is a medical center, with the univ. hosp., the State Cancer Hosp., a state regional mental health center, a federal veteran's administration hosp., a county hosp., and a private regional hosp. Airport is to SE. Transportation and travel center on I-70, midpoint between St. Louis and Kansas City. Rock Bridge State Park to S; Finger Lakes State Park to N (reclaimed strip mine). Plotted 1821, inc. 1826. **4** city (1990 pop. 98,052), ⊙ S.C. and Richland co., central S.C., at the head of navigation on the Congaree R.; 34°02′N 80°53′W. Largest city in the state and an important trade and commercial point in the heart of a fertile farm region. Airport at Pineridge to W. Its industries include electric equip., paper prods., fabricated metal prods., construction materials, printing and publishing, stainless steel, apparel, boatbuilding. A trading post flourished nearby in the early 18th cent. In 1786 the site was chosen for the new state capital because of its central location; the legislature 1st met in its new quarters in 1790. During the Civil War, Gen. Sherman's army entered Columbia on Feb. 17, 1865. That night most of the city was burned by drunken Union soldiers and was almost totally destroyed. An educational city, Columbia is the seat of the Univ. of S.C., Benedict Col., Columbia Col., Allen Univ., Columbia Bible Col. and Lutheran Theological Southern Seminary. Also in the city is the state hosp. and Riverbanks Zoological Gardens. Notable bldgs. include the statehouse (begun 1855, damaged in 1865, completed 1901), the Horseshoe in the Univ. of S.C. campus, President Woodrow Wilson's boyhood home (1870), and several antebellum houses. Also of interest are the S.C. State Mus.; the Columbia Mus. of Art and Science; and the Midlands Exposition Park, with historical exhibits. E of the city is Fort Jackson Military Reservation, a major infantry training center. L. Murray reservoir is nearby. Inc. 1805. **5** city (1990 pop. 133), Brown co., NE S.Dak., 14 mi/23 km NE of Aberdeen, and on James R.; 45°36′N 98°18′W. Columbia Road Dam & Reservoir and Sand L. Natl. Wildlife Refuge to N; trading point for agr. area. **6** city (1990 pop. 28,583), ⊙ Maury co., central Tenn., on the Duck R., c.45 mi SSW of Nashville; 35°37′N 87°02′W. Once a noted racing-horse center, it still has an annual mule auction. It is the trade and processing hub of a fertile area producing burley tobacco, and a shipping point for the region's limestone and phosphate deposits. Mfg. includes computer systems, metal and plastic prods. Location of the Columbia State Community Col. Many fine antebellum homes, such as the James K. Polk House (1816). Inc. 1817.
Columbia 1 town (1990 pop. 922), Houston co., SE Ala., on Chattahoochee R. (here forming Ga. state line) and 17 mi/27 km ENE of Dothan; 31°18′N 85°06′W. Apparel, fishing equip. mfg. **2** town (1990 pop. 1,799), Tuolumne co., central Calif., 4 mi/6.4 km N of Sonora; 38°02′N 120°24′W. Cattle; hay; apples; timber. In 1849 Calif. Gold Rush region country; famous old gold-mining town which lost the race for state capital in 1854; its old bldgs. are well preserved. Columbia Airport to W, Columbia Col. (2-year). Stanislaus Natl. Forest to NE; New Melones L. reservoir to W. **3** town (1990 pop. 4,510), Tolland co., E central Conn., on Hop R., just W of Willimantic; 41°41′N 72°18′W. Agr. Includes small Columbia L. (resort), Hop R., and Chestnut Hill villages. Eleazer Wheelock est. a school here for Native Americans, which became Dartmouth Col. Settled c.1695, organized 1804. **4** town (1990 pop. 3,845), ⊙ Adair co., S Ky., 36 mi/58 km ENE of Glasgow, on Russell R.; 37°06′N 85°18′W. Agr. (burley tobacco, grain; hogs; cattle; poultry; dairying; timber); mfg. (lumber, apparel, feeds, asphalt, machinery, poultry processing; printing and publishing). Colonel Adair

County Airport to W. Seat of Lindsey Wilson Col. Pleasant View Baptist Church, oldest log church in Ky.; Trabue Russell House and Mus. Green River L. reservoir and State Park to N. Settled c.1793; est. 1801. **5** town (1994 pop. 516), ⊙ Caldwell parish, NE central La., 28 mi/45 km S of Monroe and on Ouachita R.; 32°06′N 92°05′W. In agr. area (cotton, soybeans; cattle); logging; mfg. (apparel, lumber). Columbia lock and dam nearby. Boeuf State Wildlife Area to E. **6** town (1990 pop. 437), Wash. co., E Maine, 16 mi/26 km WSW of Machias; 44°40′N 67°48′W. In blueberry-growing area. Great Heath, largest heath (raised bog) in Maine; birdwatching. **7** town (1990 pop. 6,815), ⊙ Marion co., S Miss., 32 mi/51 km W of Hattiesburg, and on Pearl R.; 31°15′N 89°49′W. In agr. area (cotton, corn; cattle; dairying; timber); mfg. (concrete, asphalt, paper prods., lumber, apparel, furniture). Was capital Miss. for part of 1821. **8** town (1990 pop. 661), Coos co., NW N.H., 31 mi/50 km NW of Berlin; 44°51′N 71°28′W. Bounded on W by Connecticut R. (Vt. state line). Timber; livestock, poultry; dairying. Covered bridge; part of Nash Stream State Forest in E; Blue Mt. (3,723 ft/ 1,135 m) in S. **9** town (1990 pop. 836), ⊙ Tyrrell co., E N.C., 28 mi/45 km E of Plymouth, on Scuppernong R., inlet of Albemarle Sound; 35°55′N 76°15′W. Fish, crabs, oysters. Agr. area (grain, soybeans, peanuts, potatoes, cotton; hogs). Mfg. (crab meat processing). Pettigrew State park and Somerset Place State Historical Site to SW. A trading post before 1700; named Columbia in 1810. **10** town (1990 pop. 58), Fluvanna co., central Va., 25 mi/40 km SE of Charlottesville on James R., at mouth of Rivanna R.; 37°45′N 78°10′W. Mfg. (lumber, building materials); agr. (grain, tobacco; livestock); timber.
Columbia, village, Warren co., NW N.J., on Delaware R., at mouth of Paulins Kill (hydroelectric dam here), opposite Portland, Pa., 12 mi/19 km NNW of Belvidere. Delaware Water Gap is 4 mi/6.4 km NNW.
Columbia, borough (1990 pop. 10,701), Lancaster co., SE Pa., 10 mi/16 km W of Lancaster, on Susquehanna R. (bridged), which forms L. Clarke reservoir, Soft Harbor Dam 8 mi/12.9 km S (downstream); 40°01′N 76°30′W. Mfg. (paper prods., wood prods., fabricated metal prods., apparel, machinery). Wrights Ferry Mansion (1738). Two covered bridges to NE on Chickies Creek. Settled 1730, laid out 1788, inc. 1814.
Columbia, river, c.1,210 mi/1,947 km long, rising in Columbia L., SE B.C., Canada. It flows first NW in the Rocky Mt. Trench, then hooks sharply about the Selkirk Mts. to flow S through Upper Arrow L. and Lower Arrow L. and receive the Kootenai R. (spelled Kootenay in Canada) before entering the U.S. after a course of 465 mi/748 km. It continues S through Wash. and just below the mouth of the Spokane R. is forced by lava beds to make a great bend W before veering S again, running the while entrenched in a narrow valley through the Columbia Plateau. Its chief tributary, the Snake R., joins it just before it turns W again. The Columbia then forms part of the Wash.-Oregon border before entering the Pacific Ocean through a wide estuary W of Portland, Oregon. The Columbia R. has created regal gorges by cutting through the Cascades and the Coast Ranges; it is fed by the Cowlitz and Willamette rivers, which drain the Puget trough bet. those ranges. Grand Coulee, now a reservoir in the COLUMBIA BASIN PROJECT, was a former stream channel of the Columbia R. It was created during the Ice Age when the Columbia's course was blocked by ice, forcing it to cut a new channel through the Columbia Plateau. When the ice receded the river resumed its former channel. The Columbia R., commanding one of the great drainage basins of N. America (c.259,000 sq mi/ 670,800 sq km), was visited by Robert Gray, an Amer. explorer, in 1792 and is named for his vessel, the *Columbia*. It was first actually entered by a British naval officer, William R. Broughton, later the same year. Long before this time Native Americans were fishing salmon from the river; today fish are still caught here, but heavy settlement along the river and its tributaries, the construction of dams, and human use have reduced the

salmon runs. The first whites to arrive overland were the members of the Lewis and Clark expedition and the fur traders (notably David Thompson of the North West Co. and the founders of Astoria). The river was the focus of the Amer. settlement that created Oregon, and the river was itself sometimes called the Oregon R. or the R. of the West. Irrigation was begun early, and some tributaries were used to water cropland and orchards, as in, e.g., the valleys of the Wenatchee and Yakima rivers. After 1932 plans gradually developed to use the Columbia R. to its ultimate possibility and the Columbia basin project was est. Its purpose was to establish flood control, which would alleviate the destruction seen in the Columbia's greatest flood, that of 1894, and somewhat lesser but damaging floods, such as that of 1948; to improve navigation; to extend irrigation in order to make optimum use of the water of the Columbia and its tributaries; and to produce hydroelectric power to supply the Pacific Northwest. There are 6 Federal and 5 non-Federal dams on the Columbia R. Grand Coulee Dam (the key unit of the Columbia basin project) and Chief Joseph Dam, on the river's upper course, provide power, flood control, and irrigation. Priest Rapids, Wanapum, Rock Island, Rocky Reaches, and Wells dams are on the middle course; all are among the largest non-Federal hydroelectric facilities in the U.S. Bonneville, The Dalles, John Day, and McNary dams, on the lower course, were designed as power, flood control, and navigation projects; these dams provide a 328-mi/528-km slack-water navigation channel up the Columbia R. from the Pacific Ocean to the Snake R. With these Federal projects and non-Federal dams on the Columbia, hydroelectric plants on the river have a potential generating capacity of about 21 million kw. The development of hydroelectric power has had a significant effect on the economic pattern of the Pacific Northwest.
Columbia Basin Project, waterway, central Wash.; a multi-purpose development of the U.S. Bureau of Reclamation providing irrigation, hydroelectric power, and flood control. Its key unit, the Grand Coulee Dam (forms Franklin D. Roosevelt Reservoir), provides the project with power and pumps the waters of the Columbia R. into an irrigation system comprising a series of lakes, reservoirs, and numerous canals. Irrigation was begun in 1948. In 1969 the project had an installed hydroelectric power generation capacity of 2,333,000 kw. O'Sullivan Dam (200 ft/61 m high; 19,000 ft/ 5,791 m long; completed 1949) on Crab Creek, the project's southernmost dam, is one of the largest earthfill dams in the U.S. and impounds Potholes Reservoir. Water is diverted to SW from behind Grand Coulee Dam into Grand Coulee, a previously dry valley, creating large Banks L. reservoir and braided canal system below it. Recreation; Coulee Dam Natl. Recreation Area extends length of reservoir, almost to Can. border.
Columbia Bay (5 mi/8 km long, 3 mi/4.8 km wide), S Alaska, on Prince William Sound, 30 mi/48 km WSW of Valdez; 60°58′N 147°05′W. Receives scenic Columbia Glacier.
Columbia, Cape, N Ellesmere Isl., NE Franklin Dist., N.W.T., Canada, on the Arctic Ocean; 83°07′N 70°28′W; northernmost point of Canada. Only N tip of Greenland is farther N.
Columbia City (1990 pop. 5,706), ⊙ Whitley co., NE Ind., 20 mi/32 km WNW of Fort Wayne; 41°10′N 85°29′W. In agr. area (grain, soybeans; livestock, poultry; dairy prods.); mfg. (transportation equip., machinery, plastics, primary metals).
Columbia City or **Columbia**, town (1990 pop. 1,003), Columbia co., NW Oregon, on Columbia R. 2 mi/ 3.2 km N of St. Helens; 45°53′N 122°48′W. Fruit, berries, nuts; poultry, sheep, cattle; dairy prods. Trojan Nuclear Power Plant (shut down) to N.
Columbia, District of: see WASHINGTON, D.C.
Columbia Falls 1 town (1990 pop. 552), Wash. co., E Maine, on Pleasant R. and 14 mi/23 km WSW of Machias; 44°40′N 67°42′W. Agr.; blueberry canning. **2** town (1990 pop. 2,942), Flathead co., NW Mont., on Flathead R., and 15 mi/24 km NNE of Kalispell;

48°22′N 114°11′W. Barley, alfalfa; hogs; mfg. (primary metals, logging, lumber, furniture, printing and publishing); tourism. Swan Range and parts of Flathead Natl. Forest to NE and W; Stillwater Game Preserve to S; Big Sky Water Park. Glacier National Park to NE. Formerly called Monaco.

Columbia Heights, city (1990 pop. 18,910), Anoka co., SE Minn., residential suburb, 4 mi/6.4 km N of downtown Minneapolis; adjoins Minneapolis E of the Miss. R.; 45°02′N 93°15′W. Mfg. Inc. 1921.

Columbia Icefield, mass of ice (☐ 116 sq mi/300 sq km), covering plateau bet. Mt. Columbia (12,293 ft/3,747 m) and Mt. Athabasca (11,453 ft/3,491 m) on boundary of Banff and Jasper natl. parks, B.C./Alta., Canada. Astride Great Divide, hydrographic apex of N. Amer., nourishes N. Sask., Columbia, Athabasca, and Fraser river systems. Largest icefield in Rocky Mts. 328 ft/100 m–1,198 ft/365 m deep.

Columbia, Mount (12,294 ft/3,747 m), on Alta.–B.C. border, Canada,, in Rocky Mts., at S edge of Jasper Natl. Park, 60 mi/97 km SSE of Jasper, in Columbia Icefield; 52°09′N 117°26′W. Athabaska R. rises here.

Columbia, Mount (14,073 ft/4,289 m), in Collegiate Range of Rocky Mts., Chaffee co., W central Colo. In San Isabel Natl. Forest, E of Continental Divide, also including Yale, Harvard, Princeton, and Oxford peaks.

Columbia Mountains, Canada: see ROCKY MOUNTAINS.

Columbia Plateau, physiographic region of N. Amer. (☐ c.100,000 sq mi/259,000 sq km), NW U.S., bet. the Rocky Mts. and the Cascade Range in Wash., Oregon, and Idaho. Most of the plateau is underlaid by deposits, more than 10,000 ft/3,048 m thick in places, of lava (mainly basalt) interbedded with sedimentary rock; older rocks outcrop in the Blue and Wallowa mts. Young lavas, scattered cinder cones, volcanic ash, and barren landscapes (including Craters of the Moon Natl. Monument) are features of the Snake R. plain in S. Older, decayed lavas, much modified by accumulations of loess, occur in N in the Columbia basin sect.; coulees (dry river canyons) and scablands (extensively eroded basalt surfaces), both carved by glacial meltwaters, are features of the region. The Columbia Plateau is an important agr. and grazing area and is a major source of hydroelectric power.

Columbia Road Reservoir (☐ 10 sq mi/26 sq km), Brown co, NE S.D., on James R., 15 mi/ 24 km NNE of Aberdeen; 45°40′N 98°19′W. Extends N-S toward Mud L. Reservoir and N.Dak. border. Formed by Columbia Road Dam (10 ft/3 m high), built (1939) as Fish and Wildlife Pond; owned and operated by Fish and Wildlife Service of the Dept. of the Interior.

Columbiana (kuh-LUM-bee-AN-uh), county (☐ 535 sq mi/1,386 sq km; 1990 pop. 108,276), E Ohio; ⊙ Lisbon; 40°45′N 80°45′W. Bounded E by Pa. state line, SE by Ohio R.; also drained by Little Beaver R. and by small Sandy and Yellow creeks. Primarily in the Glaciated Plain physiographic region; the S portion of the county is in the Unglaciated Plain region. Agr. area (livestock; dairy prods.; fruit, corn, vegetables); mfg. at East Liverpool, Salem, East Palestine, Wellsville (meat packing, plastic prods., glass, fabricated metal prods., optical instruments and lenses); coal mines, clay pits, oil and gas extraction. Formed 1803.

Columbiana, town (1990 pop. 2,968), ⊙ Shelby co., central Ala., 25 mi/40 km SSE of Birmingham; 33°10′N 86°35′W. In corn and cotton area; textiles, wire mfg. Founded c.1825.

Columbiana, village (1990 pop. 4,961), Columbiana co., E Ohio, 15 mi/24 km S of Youngstown; 40°53′N 80°41′W. Settled 1802.

Columbiaville, village (1990 pop. 934), Lapeer co., E Mich., on Flint R., and 9 mi/14.5 km NW of Lapeer; 43°09′N 83°24′W. In agr. area.

Columbine Valley, town (1990 pop. 1,071), Arapahoe co., N central Colo., residential suburb, 9 mi/14.5 km SSW of downtown Denver, on South Platte R.; 39°36′N 105°01′W. Elev. 5,280 ft/1,609 m. Chatfield L. and State Park to SW.

Columbus, county (☐ 953 sq mi/2,468 sq km; 1990 pop. 49,587), SE N.C.; ⊙ Whiteville; 34°15′N 78°40′W. Bounded SW by S.C. state line, NW by Lumber R., extreme NE by Cape Fear R.; forested and partly swampy tidewater area; drained by Waccamaw R. (forms L. Waccamaw in NE center). Farming (tobacco, wheat, cotton, peanuts, soybeans, sorghum, hay, corn, sweet potatoes; cattle, hogs); timber. L. Waccamaw State Park in NE center; Lumber R. State Park on NW boundary. Formed 1808.

Columbus 1 city (1990 pop. 179,278), ⊙ Muscogee co., W Ga., at the head of navigation on the Chattahoochee R.; 32°31′N 84°52′W. The 2d largest city in the state, it is a port of entry situated at the foot of a series of falls that extend more than 30 mi/48 km and provide extensive water power. An important industrial and shipping center; large textile industry since 1938; iron works, food-processing plants; mfg. (lumber, chemicals, furniture, hosp. equip., concrete, wood and rubber prods., printing and publishing, paper prods., fabricated metal prods., machinery). Was a busy river port until the arrival of the RRs in the 1850s; its river traffic has been revitalized with the completion of a series of locks and dams that provide access to the Gulf of Mexico. During the Civil War, Columbus was captured by Union troops one week after Lee's surrender at Appomattox. Its industry grew with the development of 20th-cent. hydroelectric power plants. Many antebellum homes and Columbus Col. are in the city. Fort Benning is to the S. Settled on the site of a Creek village; inc. 1828. **2** city (1990 pop. 31,802), ⊙ Bartholomew co., S central Ind., on the East Fork of the White R.; 39°13′N 85°55′W. Mfg. (transportation equip., pharmaceutical and medical devices, food and beverages, plastic prods., electronic prods., machinery, aluminum smelting, asphalt, paper prods.). In the Civil War, Columbus served as a depot for Union armies. The city is known for its outstanding architecture, including bldgs. designed by world-renowned architects from the late 1930s onward. Branch of Ind. Vocational Technical Col. (Ivy Tech); Camp Atterbury 8 mi/12.9 km NW. Inc. 1821. **3** city (1990 pop. 23,799), ⊙ Lowndes co., NE Miss., 125 mi/201 km NE of Jackson, on the Tombigbee R. (Tennessee-Tombigbee Waterway); 88°31′N 56°34′W. RR junction and yards. It is the trade, processing, and shipping center of a cotton, cattle, dairy, and timber area. Mfg. (wood and stone prods., paper prods., furniture, transportation equip., prefabricated bldgs., chemicals, medical equipment, agr. tools, printing and publishing); marble and granite processing. Franklin Acad., the first free school in the state, was opened in 1821. Seat of Miss. Univ. for Women; Columbus Air Force Base to N; Golden Triangle Airport to W. Tourists are attracted to the city's many beautiful antebellum homes. Columbus L. reservoir, on Tombigbee, to NW; Columbus Lock and Dam; Riverboat Julie (excursions). L. Lowlands State Park to SE. Tennessee Williams b. here. Inc. 1821. **4** city (1990 pop. 19,480), ⊙ Platte co., E Nebr., 70 mi/113 km W of Omaha, on N side of confluence of Loup and Platte rivers; 41°25′N 97°21′W. Elev. 1,449 ft/442 m. RR junction, mfg. and trade center. Mfg. (printing, medical instruments, fabricated metal prods., electronic equip., agr. equipment, chemicals, food prods., printing, transportation equip., construction materials); agr. (grain; livestock; dairy and poultry prods.). Hq. for publicly owned power project on Loup R. Municipal airport. Platte Creek Agr. Society Park E of town. L. North and L. Bulcock N of town. City founded 1856. **5** city (1990 pop. 632,910), ⊙ Ohio and Franklin co., central Ohio, on the Scioto R.; 39°59′N 82°59′W. Columbus has surpassed Cleveland in pop., thus making it Ohio's largest city. Port of entry, accessed by RR, highway, and an internatl. airport, major industrial and trade center in a fertile agr. region. Mfg. includes consumer goods, aircraft, engines, transportation equip., glass, food, textiles, primary metals, fabricated metal prods., machinery. Govt. agencies and many research and education centers add to the economy. Major private employment sectors: utilities, banks, leisure, food, metals, retailing, insurance. Immense industrial growth characterized the city from the 1940s. Columbus was laid out as state ⊙ in 1812, but did not take over the govt. from Chillicothe until 1816. Growth was stimulated by the development of transportation facilities—a feeder canal to the Ohio and Erie Canal, opened in 1831; the Natl. Road, which reached the city in 1833; and the RR, which arrived in 1850. The city is the seat of Ohio State Univ., Capital Univ., Ohio Dominican Col., Franklin Univ., a business univ., state schools for the deaf and blind, and Battelle Memorial Inst. (for industrial research in metallurgy, the graphic arts, ceramics, and other fields). Edison Welding Inst. is a research center for joining technologies. Landmarks include the state capitol bldg.; the state office bldg. and its lib.; the Columbus Gallery of Fine Arts; a large science and industry mus.; the lib. and mus. of the state archaeological and historical society; the hq. of the Amer. Rose Society, with one of the world's largest rose gardens; Camp Chase Confederate cemetery, with the graves of soldiers who died in the Civil War prison camp there; and the vast state fair grounds. Also in the city are U.S. Fort Hayes (est. 1863) and a state penitentiary. The Griggs, O'Shaughnessy, and Hoover reservoirs are the center for park and recreational activities. The city also has racetracks and a variety of annual cultural events. Inc. as a city 1834. James Thurber b. here 1895.

Columbus 1 town (1990 pop. 3,268), ⊙ Cherokee co., extreme SE Kansas, 18 mi/29 km SSW of Pittsburg; 37°10′N 94°50′W. Elev. 910 ft/277 m. RR junction. Trade center for diversified agr. region; dairying; mfg. (transportation equip., paper prods.); construction. Coal mines and deposits of zinc and lead in vicinity. Inc. 1871. **2** town (1990 pop. 1,573), ⊙ Stillwater co., S Mont., on Yellowstone R., opposite mouth of Stillwater R., at mouth of Keyser Creek, and 38 mi/61 km WSW of Billings; 45°38′N 109°15′W. Trade and shipping point; quarries and platinum group smelter; wheat, barley, sugar beets, beans; cattle, sheep, hogs; mfg. (silver jewelry). Cooney Reservoir State Park to S; Hailstone Natl. Wildlife Refuge and Halfbreed Natl. Wildlife Refuge to N; Big L. to N. Formerly called Eagle's Nest, Sheep Dip, and Stillwater. **3** town (1990 pop. 812), ⊙ Polk co., W N.C., 15 mi/24 km SE of Hendersonville, near S.C. state line; 35°15′N 82°12′W. Agr. area (peaches, grain, sweet potatoes; poultry, cattle); mfg. (knit prods., yarns). **4** town (1990 pop. 3,367), ⊙ Colorado co., S Texas, c.70 mi/113 km W of Houston and on Colorado R; 29°41′N 96°32′W. Elev. 207 ft/63 m. Agr. area (rice, corn, grain, sorghum, peanuts); timber; gas, oil; mfg. (concrete prods., prefabricated metal buildings, machinery). Attwater Prairie Chicken Natl. Wildlife Refuge to E. Founded 1823, inc. 1928. **5** town (1990 pop. 4,093), Columbia co., S central Wis., on Crawfish R., and 27 mi/43 km NE of Madison; 43°20′N 89°01′W. In diversified farming area; dairy prods. Mfg. (printing, machinery, food prods., fabricated metal prods., rubber prods.). Louis H. Sullivan designed a local bank bldg. (1919). Lazy L. to NW. Settled c.1840, inc. 1874.

Columbus 1 village (1990 pop. 88), Adams co., W Ill., 13 mi/21 km E of Quincy; 39°59′N 91°09′W. Agr. (corn, wheat; livestock; dairying). Vigorously competed with Quincy for seat of Adams co. in 19th century. **2** village (1990 pop. 252), Hickman co., W Ky., on the Miss. R., and 28 mi/45 km W of Mayfield, Ky., near Mo. R.; 36°45′N 89°05′W. Agr. area; mfg. (wire rope). Columbus Belmont Battlefield State Park is to S; former site of Columbus was a Confederate fortification early in Civil War, later occupied by Union forces. **3** village, Burlington co., W N.J.,7 mi/11.3 km E of Burlington; farm and flea market center. **4** village (1990 pop. 641), Luna co., SW N.Mex., 30 mi/48 km S of Deming, 70 mi/113 km W of El Paso,Texas; 31°49′N 107°38′W. Port of entry 3 mi/4.8 km N of Mex. (Chihuahua) border, and Las Palomas, Mexico. Mining in Cedar Mts. to W; cattle. Florida Mts. to N; Pancho Villa State Park to S on border; Flying W Mt. (6,217 ft/1,895 m) to W. **5** village (1990 pop. 223), Burke co., NW N.Dak., 26 mi/42 km WNW of Bowbells; 48°53′N 102°46′W. Livestock; wheat, grain, oats, potatoes. **6** uninc. village (1990 pop. 700), Warren co., NW Pa., 3 mi/4.8 km ENE of Corry on Brolenstraw Creek; 41°56′N 79°34′W. Mfg.

includes feeds, sheet metal fabricating; agr. includes dairying, livestock; potatoes, grain.

Columbus Bank, shoal, Bahama Isls., E and S of Great Ragged Isl.; c.50 mi/80 km NE-SW, up to 20 mi/32 km wide. Continues Great Bahama Bank towards SE.

Columbus Belmont Battlefield State Park, Ky.: see COLUMBUS, city.

Columbus City, town (1990 pop. 328), Louisa co., SE Iowa, near Iowa R., 10 mi/16 km NW of Wapello; 41°15′N 91°22′W.

Columbus Grove, village (1990 pop. 2,231), Putnam co., NW Ohio, 13 mi/21 km N of Lima; 40°55′N 84°03′W. In agr. area.

Columbus Junction, town (1990 pop. 1,616), Louisa co., SE Iowa, on Iowa R., and 10 mi/16 km NW of Wapello.

Colusa, county (□ 1,151 sq mi/2,981 sq km; 1990 pop. 16,275), N central Calif.; ⊙ Colusa; 39°11′N 122°14′W. Rises from lowlands of Sacramento and Colusa rivers (E boundary formed by Sacramento and Butte rivers) to Coast Ranges in W. Farming (rice, beans, wheat, oats, barley, corn, sugar beets, almonds, walnuts, tomatoes); cattle raising. Sand and gravel quarrying. Hunting (waterfowl, pheasant, deer). Tehama Colusa Canal (irrigation) passes N-S through center of co.; East Park Reservoir (Stony R.) in NW; Colus-Sacramento River State Recreation Area in NE, N of Colusa. Includes part of Mendocino Natl. Forest (NW); Sacramento Natl. Wildlife Refuge (N); Delevan Natl. Wildlife Refuge in NE, Colusa Natl. Wildlife Refuge in E center. Formed 1850.

Colusa, city (1990 pop. 4,934), ⊙ Colusa co., N central Calif., on Sacramento R., and 52 mi/84 km NW of Sacramento; 39°13′N 122°01′W. Irrigated agr. (rice, fruit, wheat, barley, oats, almonds, walnuts, sugar beets); mfg. (rice milling, wiring prods.). Sutter Buttes to E; Colusa-Sacramento R. State Recreation Area to N; Colusa Natl. Wildlife Refuge to SW; Delevan Natl. Wildlife Refuge to NW. Inc. 1870.

Colver (KOL-vuhr), uninc. town (1990 pop. 1,024), Cambria co., W central Pa., 5 mi/8 km NW of Ebensburg; 40°32′N 78°47′W. Agr. area (grain, potatoes; livestock; dairying).

Colville, town (1990 pop. 4,360), ⊙ Stevens co., NE Wash., 65 mi/105 km NW of Spokane and on Colville R.; 48°32′N 117°54′W. Wheat, barley, oats; dairying; mfg. (machinery, lumber, boatbuilding, sawmill, printing and publishing, various light mfg.); silver; timber. Fish hatchery. Parts of Colville Natl. Forest to NE and SE; Little Pond Oreille Natl. Wildlife Refuge to SE; Crystal Falls State Park to E; Fort Colville Monument to NE of town. Founded 1826 as a Hudson's Bay Co. post, U.S. Fort Colville built 1859, inc. 1890.

Colville (KOL-vil), river, c.375 mi/600 km long, rising in the De Long Mts. of the Brooks Range, NW Alaska, and flowing across the tundra, E then N, to the Arctic Ocean. All of its major tributaries rise on the N slope of the Brooks Range. The river, frozen for most of the year, floods each spring as ice on its upper course melts. Umiat is the airport along its banks. Coal, oil, and natural gas are found in the valley. In N separates Natl. Petroleum Reserve–Alaska to W and Arctic Natl. Wildlife Refuge to E.

Colville Indian Agency, uninc. village (1990 pop. 160), Okanogan co., N central Wash., 11 mi/18 km N of Coulee Dam, on Nespelem R., near its entrance to Columbia R. (2 mi/3.2 km W), in S part of Colville Indian Reservation. Reservation hq.

Colville, Lake, NW Mackenzie Dist., N.W.T., Canada, NW of Great Bear L.; 67°10′N 126°00W. Extends 25 mi/40 km in length, 15 mi/24 km in width. Outlet: Anderson R.

Colville Lake, Wash.: see SPRAGUE.

Colville River, c.60 mi/97 km long; NE Wash.; rises in S Stevens co., at junction of Sheep and Deer creeks, flows NW, past Chewelah and Colville, to Columbia R. (Franklin D. Roosevelt L. reservoir), 4 mi/6.4 km SW of Kettle Falls.

Colvin, Mount (4,074 ft/1,242 m), Essex co., NE N.Y., in the High Peaks sect. of the Adirondack Mts., c.4 mi/-

6.4 km ESE of Mt. Marcy, c.15 mi/24 km SE of L. Placid village; 44°06′N 73°51′W.

Colwell, town (1990 pop. 94), Floyd co., N Iowa, 8 mi NE of Charles City; 43°09′N 92°35′W. Creamery.

Colwich, village (1990 pop. 1,091), Sedgwick co., S Kansas, 13 mi/21 km WNW of Wichita; 37°46′N 97°32′W. In wheat region.

Colwyn (KOL-win), borough (1990 pop. 2,613), Delaware co., SE Pa., residential suburb, 5 mi/8 km SW of downtown Philadelphia; 39°54′N 75°15′W. Located on Darby Creek at confluence of Cobbs Creek. Mfg. (machinery, scale models).

Comal, county (□ 574 sq mi/1,487 sq km; 1990 pop. 51,832), S central Texas; ⊙ New Braunfels; 29°48′N 98°16′W. Elev. 600 ft/183 m–1,500 ft/457 m. Crossed SW-NE by Balcones Escarpment, separating broken hilly region from agr. prairies of S and SE. Bounded on SW by Cibolo Creek; drained by Guadalupe R., here receiving spring-fed Comal R. Ranching (sheep, goats, hogs, cattle, exotic animals); agr. (corn, sorghum, wheat). Timber (esp. cedar); limestone. Mfg. (stone, sand and gravel) at New Braunfels. Urbanization from San Antonio area has developed in S corner of co. Formed 1846.

Comal River, only 2.5 mi/4 km long, in Comal co., S central Texas. In New Braunfels; spring-fed, flows to Guadalupe R. Called shortest river in U.S.

Comala (ko-MA-lah), town (1990 pop. 7,570), Colima, W Mexico, in foothills, 7 mi/11.3 km NW of Colima. Corn, rice, beans, sugarcane, coffee, tobacco, fruit; livestock.

Comalapa, Mexico: see FRONTERA COMALAPA.

Comalcalco (ko-mahl-KAHL-ko), city (1990 pop. 31,878) and township, Tabasco, SE Mexico, on the Río Seco (arm of Grijalva R.), and 28 mi/45 km NW of Villahermosa; 18°16′N 93°10′W. Agr. center (rice, coffee, beans, fruit; livestock).

Comanche 1 (kuh-MAN-chee), county (□ 789 sq mi/2,044 sq km; 1990 pop. 2,313), S Kansas; ⊙ Coldwater; 37°11′N 99°16′W. In Red Hills region. Level to rolling prairie region, bordered S by Okla.; drained by Salt Fork of Ark. R., Cinnamon R., and Bluff Creek. Cattle raising; wheat, barley, alfalfa. Formed 1885. **2** county (□ 1,083 sq mi/2,805 sq km; 1990 pop. 111,486), SW Okla.; ⊙ Lawton; 34°39′N 98°27′W. Drained by Cache, West Cache, and Beaver creeks. Includes most of the Wichita Mts. (on W part of N boundary). Fort Sill U.S. Military Reservation is at center, N of Lawton; L. Lawtonka reservoir with Medicine Park resort is in N center; L. Ellsworth reservoir is on N boundary; Wichita Mts. Natl. Wildlife Refuge to NW. Some agr. (peanuts, wheat, hay, oats, sorghum; cattle; dairying). Mfg. at Lawton. Limestone quarries; sand and gravel pits. Named for nomadic Native American tribe, the Comanche. Formed 1907. **3** county (□ 947 sq mi/2,453 sq km; 1990 pop. 13,381), central Texas; ⊙ Comanche; 31°56′N 98°33′W. Drained by Leon R; mts. (c.1,800 ft/549 m) in SW. Livestock raising (beef and dairy cattle, sheep, goats); peanuts, pecans, grain, vegetables, hay, fruit; wool, mohair marketed. Oil, natural gas wells; clay. Formed 1856.

Comanche 1 town (1990 pop. 1,695), Stephens co., S Okla., 9 mi/14.5 km S of Duncan; 34°22′N 97°58′W. In oil, farm, and ranch area; mfg. (fabricated metal prods., printing). Small Comanche L. is 4 mi/6.4 km E; Waurika L. reservoir to SW. Founded 1892 on site of Indian village. **2** town (1990 pop. 4,087), ⊙ Comanche co., central Texas, 26 mi/42 km ENE of Brownwood; 31°53′N 98°35′W. Elev. 1,358 ft/414 m. Diversified agr. area (grains, peanuts, pecans; livestock; dairying); oil and gas. Proctor L. reservoir (Leon R.) to NE. Founded 1858, inc. 1873.

Comanche Peak 1 Nuclear Power Plant, Texas: see SOMERVELL, CO.

Comapa (ko-MAH-pah), town (1990 pop. 1,139), Veracruz, E Mexico, in Sierra Madre Oriental, 5 mi/8 km E of Huatusco. Fruit.

Combahee River (KUHM-bee), 40 mi/64 km long, S S.C.; formed 15 mi/24 km SW of Walterboro by junction of Salkehatchie and Little Salkehatchie rivers; flows

SE to Coosaw R. near its mouth on St. Helena Sound at the Atlantic Ocean. Navigable. Prosperous antebellum rice plantations in its lower reaches. Salkehatchie R. (60 mi/97 km long) rises NNW of Barnwell in Barnwell co.; Little Salkehatchie R. (55 mi/89 km long) rises NNE of Barnwell.

Comber (KAHM-buhr), village, S Ont., Canada, 24 mi/39 km E of Windsor; 42°14′N 82°33′W. Agr.

Combermere, Cape (KUHM-buhr-meer), SE Ellesmere Isl., NE Franklin Dist., N.W.T., Canada, on Baffin Bay; 76°59′N 78°15′W.

Combes, town (1990 pop. 2,042), Cameron co., extreme S Texas, residential suburb, 5 mi/8 km NNW of Harlingen; 26°14′N 97°43′W. In irrigated agr. area. Rio Grande Valley Internatl. Airport to E.

Combine, town (1990 pop. 1,329), Dallas and Kaufman cos., N Texas, residential suburb, 19 mi/31 km SE of downtown Dallas; 32°35′N 96°30′W. Agr. area on urban fringe (cotton, vegetables, peanuts; cattle).

Combined Locks, town (1990 pop. 2,190), Outagamie co., E Wis., on Fox R., suburb, 6 mi/9.7 km E of Appleton; 44°16′N 88°18′W. Paper mill. Mfg. (oils and coolants).

Combs (KOOMZ), uninc. town (1990 pop. 900), Perry co., SE Ky., 2 mi/3.2 km NW of Hazard, in Cumberland foothills, on North Fork Kentucky R. Bituminous coal; mfg. (explosives). One of 2 places so named in Ky.

Come By Chance, town (1991 pop. 296), SE N.F., Canada, 65 mi/105 km WNW of St. John's, on W side of isthmus of Avalon Peninsula, at mouth of Come By Chance R. on Placentia Bay; 47°51′N 53°59′W. Failed oil refinery turned this former fishing village into ghost town in late 1980s.

Comendador, town (1993 pop. 7,714), ⊙ Elías Piña prov., W Dominican Republic, near Haiti border, on Santo Domingo–Port-au-Prince highway, and 120 mi/193 km WNW of Santo Domingo; 18°57′N 71°43′W. In agr. region of San Juan valley (cotton, sugarcane, coffee, fruit). Also called Elías Piña.

Comer (KO-muhr), town (1990 pop. 939), Madison co., NE Ga., 16 mi/26 km ENE of Athens; 34°04′N 83°08′W. Mfg. of clothing and machinery.

Comerford Dam, N.H.: see FIFTEEN MILE FALLS RESERVOIR.

Comerío (ko-me-REE-o), town (1990 pop. 20,265), E central P.R., in the Cordillera Central, on La Plata R., and 13 mi/21 km W of Caguas. Plantains, vegetables; mfg. (tobacco prods., shoes, electronics).

Comet Falls, W central Wash., waterfall more than 200 ft/61 m high in small headstream of Nisqually R., on S slope of Mt. Rainier, in Mt. Rainier Natl. Park.

Cometa, Punta (ko-ME-tah), cape in Oaxaca, S Mexico, 4 mi/6.4 km W of Puerto Angel; 15°58′N 96°35′W.

Comfort, town (1990 pop. 1,477), Kendall co., S central Texas, on Edwards Plateau, c.45 mi/72 km NW of San Antonio and on Guadalupe R; 29°58′N 98°54′W. Elev. 1,437 ft/438 m. In ranching (sheep, angora goat) area; tourism; mfg. (printing, machinery). Fishing, hunting nearby. Memorial to Civil War Union soldiers.

Comfort, Cape, NE Southampton Isl., E Keewatin Dist., N.W.T., Canada, on Foxe Channel; 65°08′N 83°20′W.

Comfort, Point, Monmouth co., E N.J., peninsula marking E limit of Raritan Bay, 8 mi/12.9 km ESE of South Amboy; site of Keansburg borough.

Comfrey, village (1990 pop. 433), Brown co., SW Minn., 26 mi/42 km SW of New Ulm; 44°06′N 94°54′W. Agr. area (grain, soybeans, peas; dairying; poultry, livestock); mfg. (machinery). Wood L. to E.

Comitán de Domínguez (ko-mee-TAHN de do-MEEN-ges), city (1990 pop. 48,299) and township, Chiapas, S Mexico, in Sierra Madre, near Guatemala border, 45 mi/72 km SE of San Cristóbal de las Casas on Inter-American Highway 190; 16°18′N 92°09′W. A substantial Tojolabal Maya pop. lives in the rural areas. Trading, processing, and agr. center (lemons, corn, cotton sugarcane; livestock); alcohol and liquor distilling; textile milling. Has colonial churches. Frequently Comitán.

Comite (KO-meet), river, c. 65 mi/105 km long; SW Mo. and SE La., formed by the joining of Comite Creek and Little Comite Creek, S. of Centervillle, Mo; flows S past

Clinton, La., joins Amite R. E of Baton Rouge. With a 296 mi/476 km perimeter, its basin has an area of 722 sq mi/1,869 sq km, 95% forested. Along with the Amite R., it is subject to frequent flooding.

Commack, uninc. town (☐ 12 sq mi/31 sq km; 1990 pop. including E. Huntington 36,124), in towns of Huntington and Hempstead, Suffolk co., SE N.Y., on central L.I.; 40°50′N 73°16′W. Chiefly residential.

Commerce, city (1990 pop. 12,135), Los Angeles co., S Calif., a suburb 5 mi/8 km ESE of downtown Los Angeles; 34°00′N 118°09′W. An important transportation hub for S California, Commerce is the home of several large corporations. Mfg. (food processing, apparel, and plastic, wood, textile, and fabricated wire prods.). Los Angeles R. to SW. Inc. 1960.

Commerce 1 town (1990 pop. 4,108), Jackson co., NE central Ga., 17 mi/27 km NNW of Athens; 34°13′N 83°28′W. Late 19th-cent. RR market town and gateway to NE Ga. mts. Now a booming outlet mall center on I-85 corridor NE of Atlanta. Mfg. includes textiles, clothing, furniture, machinery. Inc. 1883. **2** town (1990 pop. 173), Scott co., SE Mo., on Mississippi R., and 8 mi/12.9 km NNE of Benton; 37°09′N 89°27′W. Heavily damaged in floods of 1993 and 1995. **3** town (1990 pop. 2,426), Ottawa co., extreme NE Okla., 5 mi/8 km N of Miami; 36°55′N 94°52′W. In lead- and zinc-mining region; agr. (grain, fruit; poultry, livestock; dairying); mfg. (arrows). **4** town (1990 pop. 6,825), Hunt co., NE Texas, 15 mi/24 km NE of Greenville; 33°14′N 95°54′W. Trade, shipping point in cotton area. Mfg. (fabricated metal prods., wood prods., medical supplies). Seat of EastTexas State Univ. (main campus). Settled 1874.

Commerce, village, Oakland co., SE Mich., 12 mi/19 km W of Pontiac; 42°35′N 83°29′W.

Commerce City (1990 pop. 16,466), Adams co., N central Colo., suburb, 7 mi/11.3 km NE of downtown Denver, on South Platte R.; 39°52′N 104°52′W. Elev. 5,150 ft/1,570 m. Mfg. (construction materials, flour, gasoline and petroleum refining, consumer goods, steel). Rocky Mt. Arsenal to E; state fish hatchery to N.

Commerce Township, suburb, Oakland Co., SE Mich., 30 mi/48 km NW of downtown Detroit, and 10 mi/16 km WSW of Pontiac. Numerous small natural lakes, esp. in E and to N. Proud L. State Recreation Area (2 units) in SW and NE; Highland State Recreation Area to NW; Alpine Valley Ski Area to N. Light mfg.

Commercial, township (1990 pop. 5,026), Cumberland co., S N.J., 8 mi/12.9 km S of Millville; 39°16′N 75°02′W. Rural area with oyster packing and light industry. Inc. 1874.

Commercial Point, village (1990 pop. 405), Pickaway co., S central Ohio, 13 mi/21 km S of Columbus; 39°46′N 83°03′W.

Commissioners Lake, S central Que., Canada, 18 mi/29 km S of Roberval; drains N into L. St. John by Quiatchouanish R. Its length is 20 mi/32 km, and its width, 2 mi/3 km.

Committee Bay, N.W.T., Canada, inlet (130 mi/209 km long, 80 mi/129 km wide at mouth) of the Gulf of Boothia, in W side of Melville Peninsula; 67°10′–69°18′N 85°30′–88°20′W.

Commonwealth, uninc. town, Albermarle co., N central Va., residential suburb, 4 mi/6.4 km N of Charlottesville, near Rivanna R.; 38°04′N 78°29′W.

Como (KO-mo), town (1990 pop. 1,387), Panola co., NW Miss., 42 mi/68 km S of Memphis, Tenn.; 34°30′N 89°56′W. In agr. (cattle; cotton, corn, soybeans; timber) area; mfg. (fabricated metal prods., furniture). John W. Kyle State Park., on Sardis L. reservoir to SE.

Como (KO-mo), village, SW Que., Canada, on L. of the Two Mountains, 7 mi/11 km NW of Vaudreuil; 45°27′N 74°07′W. Dairying, potato growing.

Como 1 (KO-mo), village, Park co., central Colo., on headstream of Tarryall Creek, in Rocky Mts., and 55 mi/89 km SW of Denver. Elev. c.9,790 ft/2,984 m. Small-scale placer mining for gold. Pike Natl. Forest to NW. **2** village (1990 pop. 71), Hertford co., NE N.C., 36 mi/58 km E of Roanoke Rapids, near N.C. state line; 36°30′N 77°00′W. Tobacco, cotton, peanuts; poultry, livestock. **3** village (1990 pop. 563), Hopkins co., NE Texas, 9 mi/14.5 km SE of Sulphur Springs; 33°03′N 95°28′W. Agr. area; mfg. (livestock feed, wood prods., petroleum prods.).

Como Lake, resort lake in Walworth co., SE Wis., just N of L. Geneva; 3 mi/4.8 km long, ½ mi/⁸⁄₁₀ km wide.

Comondú, Mexico: see CIUDAD CONSTITUCIÓN.

Comonfort, city (1990 pop. 18,327) and township, Guanajuato, central Mexico, on Laja R., and 37 mi/60 km SE of Guanajuato on Mexico Highway 51; 20°48′N 100°46′W. On RR. Agr. center (wheat, corn, alfalfa, beans, sugarcane, fruit; livestock). Formerly Chamacuero de Comonfort.

Comox (KO-mahks), town (1991 pop. 8,253), SW B.C., Canada, on E central Vancouver Isl. with a harbor on Strait of Georgia at mouth of Courtenay R., 110 mi/177 km NW of Victoria; 49°41′N 124°56′W. Lumbering, farming, dairying.

Compañía, La, Mexico: see LA COMPAÑÍA.

Compostela (kom-po-STAI-lah), city (1990 pop. 15,175) and township, ⊙ Compostela municipio, Nayarit, W Mexico, in a valley at W end of Transverse Volcanic Axis, 20 mi/31km from the Pacific coast, on RR, and 20 mi/32 km S of Tepic on Mexico Highway 200; 21°14′N 104°52′W. Elev. 1,837 ft/560 m. Mining (silver, gold, copper) and agr. center (corn, tobacco, beans, sugarcane, coffee, rice; pork); tobacco factories. Founded 1535. Has San Jago church, built 1539 of red volcanic stone. Compostela was 1st capital of of Nueva Galicia, early Span. colony.

Comptche, uninc. village, Mendocino co., NW Calif., 20 mi/32 km NW of Ukiah, in Coast Ranges. Fruit, grapes, beans, nursery stock; cattle; dairying. Mfg. (medical equip.).

Compton, county (☐ 933 sq mi/2,416 sq km), S Que., Canada, on N.H. border; ⊙ Cookshire; 45°20′N 71°30′W.

Compton, city (1990 pop. 90,454), Los Angeles co., S Calif., a residential and industrial suburb, predominantly Afr. Amer., 10 mi/16 km S of downtown Los Angeles, and 8 mi/12.9 km NNW of Long Beach; 33°54′N 118°14′W. It has aircraft, electronic, and steel industries, mfg. household items and other consumer goods; food processing, building materials, and textiles. Compton Airport, Compton Community Col. are there. Los Angeles R. to E. Inc. 1888.

Compton, village (1991 pop. 899), S Que., Canada, on Coaticook R., and 12 mi/19 km SSE of Sherbrooke. Livestock; dairying.

Compton, village (1990 pop. 343), Lee co., N Ill., 23 mi/37 km ESE of Dixon; 41°41′N 89°05′W. In rich agr. area (corn, soybeans; cattle).

Comstock 1 village, Kalamazoo co., SW Mich., on Kalamazoo R., and suburb 4 mi/6.4 km E of Kalamazoo; 42°17′N 85°30′W. Automotive assembly plant. Settled 1831. **2** village (1990 pop. 123), Clay co., W Minn., near Red R., 15 mi/24 km S of Fargo, N.Dak.; 46°39′N 96°45′W. Grain; dairying; mfg. (fertilizers). **3** (KAWM-stawk), village (1990 pop. 135), Custer co., central Nebr., 23 mi/37 km NE of Broken Bow and on Middle Loup R.; 41°33′N 99°14′W. Dairy prods.; livestock; grain. **4** village, Washington co., E N.Y., 12 mi/19 km NE of Glens Falls; 43°28′N 73°26′W. **5** uninc. village (1990 pop. 375), Val Verde co., SW Texas, near the Rio Grande, 27 mi/43 km NW of Del Rio. Goat-, cattle-, sheep-raising area. Seminole Canyon State Park to W; Amistad Reservoir (Rio Grande) and Amistad Natl. Recreation Area to E, S, and SW.

Comstock Lode, richest known U.S. silver deposit, Storey co., W Nevada, at Mt. Davidson in the Virginia Range. It is said to have been discovered in 1857 by Ethan Allen Grosh and Hosea Ballou Grosh, sons of a Pa. minister and veterans of the Calif. gold fields who died under tragic circumstances before their claims were recorded. Henry T. P. Comstock, known as Old Pancake, was a sheepherder and prospector who took possession of the brothers' cabin and tried to find their old sites. He and others searching for gold laid claim to sections of the Comstock (1859) but soon sold them for insignificant sums. The lode did not become really profitable until its bluish sand was assayed as silver. Yielded gold 1859–1865; 2d rush 1873–1882; declined after much lower levels were flooded. Peak years were 1876–1878, $36,000,000 annually. Ultimately yielded one billion dollars' worth of silver and gold. News of the discovery spread rapidly, attracting promoters and traders as well as miners, and the lode was the scene of feverish activity. Among early arrivals was William Morris Stewart, who later became one of Nev.'s first senators. Camps and trading posts in the area became important supply centers, and Virginia City, a mining camp on the mt., was for several decades the "capital" of the lode and a center of fabulous luxury. Great fortunes were made by the "silver kings," John W. Mackay, James Graham Fair, James C. Flood, and William S. O'Brien, and by Adolph Sutro, George Hearst, and Eilley Orrum Bowers. Silver determined the economy and development of Nev. until exhaustion of the mines by wasteful methods of mining and the demonetization of silver started a decline in the 1870s. By 1898 the Comstock was virtually abandoned.

Comstock Park, town (1990 pop. 6,530), Kent co., SW Mich., suburb, 4 mi/6.4 km N of downtown Grand Rapids, on Grand R.; 43°02′N 85°40′W. Mfg. (machinery, wood prods., asphalt, plastic prods., construction materials).

Con Mine, Canada: see YELLOWKNIFE.

Conanicut Island, suburb and resort island, Newport co., S R.I., coextensive with JAMESTOWN, c. 9 mi/14.5 km long, 1 mi/1.6 km–2 mi/3.2 km wide, in Narragansett Bay W of Newport. Bridge connects with mainland and Newport (Aquidneck Isl.).

Conasauga River (kahn-uh-SAW-guh), c.90 mi/145 km long, in Ga. and Tenn.; rises in the Blue Ridge, Fannin co., N Ga., flows NW across Tenn. state line, then SSW into Ga., past Tilton to confluence with Coosawattee R. 3 mi/4.8 km NE of Calhoun, forming Oostanaula R.; 34°51′N 84°35′W.

Concepción Bay, inlet of Gulf of Calif., on E coast of Lower Calif., NW Mexico, 95 mi/153 km SE of Guaymas; 22 mi/35 km long, 2 mi/3.2 km–5 mi/8 km wide.

Concepción Buenavista (kon-sep-see-ON bwe-nah-VEES-tah), town (1990 pop. 405), in the state of Oaxaca, Mexico, 27 mi/43 km ENE of Huajuapam de León, bordering the state of Puebla; 17°51′N 97°24′W. Elev. 6,644 ft/2,025 m. Mountainous with many streams flowing to the Papaloapan R. Corn, beans, wheat, fruits; woods; livestock. Connected by road to Inter-American Highway 190.

Concepción de Buenos Aires (kon-sep-see-ON de BWE-nos AI-rees), town (1990 pop. 4,147), Jalisco, central Mexico, in Sierra Madre Occidental, 20 mi/32 km ENE of Sayula. Grain, beans, fruit; livestock.

Concepción de la Vega, Dominican Republic: see LA VEGA, city.

Concepción del Oro (kon-sep-see-ON del O-ro), city (1990 pop. 7,784) and township, Zacatecas, N central Mexico, on interior plateau, near Coahuila border, 60 mi/97 km SW of Saltillo, and a short distance W of Mexico Highway 54; 24°36′N 101°25′W. Elev. 6,791 ft/2,070 m. RR terminus and mining center (silver, copper, gold, lead, mercury, iron), with copper smelters.

Concepción Pápalo (kon-sep-see-ON PAH-pah-lo), town (1990 pop. 1,100), in the state of Oaxaca, Mexico, 6 mi/10 km NE of San Juan Bautista Cuicatlán in a rugged upland in the Río Santo Domingo drainage; 17°51′N 96°42′W. Elev. 2,625 ft/800 m. Corn, beans, wheat, fruits; woods. Important asbestos deposits at Pegaso. Road to San Juan Bautista Cuicatlán.

Concepción River, Mexico: see MAGDALENA RIVER.

Conception, uninc. town, Nodaway co., NW Mo., on Platte R., 11 mi/18 km SE of Maryville. Mfg. (greeting cards). Benedictine abbey and seminary.

Conception Bay, inlet (50 mi/80 km long, 20 mi/32 km wide at entrance), SE N.F., Canada, in N part of Avalon Peninsula, 10 mi/16 km W of St. John's; 47°45′N 53°00′W. Near SW shore is Bell Isl., with once important iron mines. Chief towns on bay are Harbour Grace and Carbonear. There are numerous fishing settlements.

Cross references are shown in SMALL CAPITALS. The pronunciation key is on page xv. The dates of population figures are on page xii.

Conception Bay South, town (1986. pop. 15,531), SE shore Conception Bay, N.F., Canada, on Avalon Peninsula. Comprises smaller former settlements which ring shoreline. Once a string of fishing villages and summer homes for St. John's residents, the town is now a commuter center for St. John's.

Conception Island, islet, central Bahama Isls., 15 mi/24 km NW of Rum Cay, 160 mi/257 km SE of Nassau; 23°50′N 75°08′W. Lighthouse. Santa María de la Concepción was the name Columbus gave to Rum Cay.

Conception Junction, town (1990 pop. 236), Nodaway co., NW Mo., on Platte R., and 10 mi/16 km ESE of Maryville; 40°16′N 94°41′W. Corn, soybeans; cattle.

Conception, Point, Santa Barbara co., SW Calif., promontory at entrance to Santa Barbara Channel, 12 mi/19 km long. Lighthouse.

Conchas Lake (KAWN-chuhs), reservoir (□ c.25 sq mi/65 sq km), San Miguel co., NE N.Mex., on Canadian R. at confluence of Conchas R. (W arm), 28 mi/45 km WNW of Tucumcari; 35°24′N 104°11′W. The reservoir is c.13 mi/21 km long, with a max. capacity of 600,000 acre-ft. Formed by Conchas Dam (concrete; 235 ft/72 m high, 1,250 ft/381 m long), built (1940) by U.S. Army Corps of Engineers for flood control and irrigation. Conchas L. State Park is here.

Concho, county (□ 993 sq mi/2,572 sq km; 1990 pop. 3,044), W central Texas, on N Edwards Plateau; ⊙ Paint Rock; 31°19′N 99°51′W. Elev. c.1,600 ft/488 m–2,100 ft/640 m. Bounded NE by Colorado R. (forms L. O.H. Ivie); drained by Concho R. and Brady and Kickapoo creeks. Livestock raising (sheep, goats, cattle); wool, mohair marketed; some irrigated agr. (wheat, grain sorghum, cotton). Oil and gas, stone. Formed 1858.

Concho, village, Canadian co., central Okla., near North Canadian R., 6 mi/9.7 km N of El Reno. Now part of city of El Reno.

Concho River, W Texas, formed at San Angelo by North Concho and Middle Concho rivers, flows c.55 mi/89 km generally E to the Colorado R. (forms L. O.H. Ivie), 18 mi/29 km SE of Ballinger. L. Nasworthy (capacity 10,500 acre-ft.; municipal water supply) is impounded by dam at confluence of the Middle and South Concho just SW of San Angelo. Twin Buttes Reservoir is actually 2 reservoirs, upstream from L. Nasworthy, on both South and Middle branches, joined by narrow channels.

Conchos, Mexico: see VALLE DE ZARAGOZA.

Conchos River 1 (KON-chos), c.350 mi/563 km long, Chihuahua, N Mexico; rises in Sierra Madre Occidental near Sonora border NE of Bocoyna, flows first E, through L. Toronto, then N and NE, past Camargo, to join Rio Grande at Ojinaga opposite Presidio (Texas). Largely used for irrigation of arid but fertile plateaus. Along its middle course, near L. Toronto, are several dams and hydroelectric stations, including Boquilla. Receives Chuviscar and Florido rivers. **2** c.175 mi/282 km long, Tamaulipas, NE Mexico; rises on E slopes of Sierra Madre Oriental SW of Linares (Nuevo León), flows E, past Méndez and San Fernando, to Laguna Madre, lagoon on Gulf of Mexico. Forms cascades in upper course. Navigable on small scale at mouth. Sometimes called San Fernando R.

Conconully (kahn-KAHN-uh-lee), village (1990 pop. 153), Okanogan co., N Wash., 18 mi/29 km NW of Okanogan, on N shore of Conconully L.; 48°33′N 119°45′W. Resort community.

Concord 1 city (1990 pop. 111,348), Contra Costa co., W central Calif., suburb, 14 mi/23 km NE of downtown Oakland, 5 mi/8 km S of Suisun Bay; 37°58′N 122°00′W. In an oil refining and farm region (nursery stock; apples), displaced by urban development. Mokelumne Aqueduct passes through the city. Petroleum refining and hundreds of other companies with 25 or less employees. The city is the E terminus for rapid transit to the San Francisco Bay area. A junior col. is there, and a U.S. naval station and ammunition depot is nearby, which contains Port Chicago Natl. Memorial. Mount Diablo State Park to SE. Settled c.1852, inc. 1906. **2** city (1990 pop. 36,006), ⊙ state and Merrimack co., S central N.H., 15 mi/24 km N of Manchester, on both sides of the Merrimack R., bounded SE by Soucook R.; 43°13′N 71°33′W. Drained by Contoocook R. Famous for its granite quarrying. Mfg. (electronic equip., millwork, metal prods., dairy prods., porcelain pottery, printing and publishing, consumer goods); insurance. Agr. in N and W (nursery prods., vegetables, apples; poultry; dairying). It became the state capital in 1808, and its growth was further aided by the building of locks and dams on the Merrimac R. connecting it with the Middlesex Canal in 1815. State Lib. Capitol bldg. (State House). St. Paul's school (preparatory), the house and grave of President Franklin Pierce (a mus.), and the Christa McAuliffe Planetarium are in Concord. Mary Baker Eddy was born a few mi/km away, at Bow. N.H. Technical Inst. N.H. State Hosp. N.H. Historical Society. N.H. Natl. Guard and Municipal Airport in E. Peacock L. in W. Settled 1725–1727, inc. as Rumford, Mass., in 1733 (Count Rumford later took his title from this name) and as Concord, N.H., in 1765. **3** city (1990 pop. 27,347), ⊙ Cabarrus co., central N.C., 20 mi/32 km NE of Charlotte R; 35°24′N 80°35′W. Twin city to Kannapolis 6 mi/9.7 km NNW, near the edge of the Piedmont region. Mfg. (concrete forms, plastics, textiles, apparel, bldg. materials, consumer prods., paper prods., food and beverage processing). Read Gold Mine State Historical Site to SE, first U.S. gold strike (1799); Concord Motor Speedway is here with seating capacity of over 160,000. Concord is the seat of Barber-Scotia Col. Rowan-Cabarrus Community Col. to NW. Settled 1796, inc. 1837.

Concord 1 town (1990 pop. 17,076), Middlesex co., E Mass., a high-income suburb, 14 mi/23 km NW of Boston, on the Concord R.; 42°28′N 71°22′W. Electronic instruments, computer software, apparel, metal and wood prods. are made here. The site of the Revolutionary battle of Concord on April 19, 1775, is marked by Daniel Chester French's bronze *Minuteman.* Concord has many old houses, some opened as memorials to noted occupants—Emerson, the Alcotts, Hawthorne, and Thoreau. Seat of Concord Academy and Middlesex School. An antiquarian mus. and the Old Manse, built in 1769 by Emerson's grandfather and made famous by Thoreau, and the place where Ephraim Bull developed the Concord grape are here. Walden pond is in Concord with Walden Pond State Park. State Prison. Concord Bridge is administered by the Natl. Park Service. Inc. 1635. **2** town (1990 pop. 1,093), including Concord village, Essex co., NE Vt., 6 mi/9.7 km E of St. Johnsbury, and on Moose R.; 44°26′N 71°50′W. Includes villages of East Concord, North Concord and Miles Pond. Chartered 1781, settled 1788.

Concord 1 (KAHN-kord), village (1990 pop. 211), Pike co., W central Ga., 15 mi/24 km SW of Griffin; 33°05′N 84°26′W. **2** village (1990 pop. 172), Morgan co., W central Ill., 10 mi/16 km NW of Jacksonville; 39°49′N 90°22′W. In agr. area (corn, wheat, sorghum; cattle, hogs). **3** village (1990 pop. 65), Lewis co., NE Ky., 14 mi/23 km ENE of Maysville, on Ohio R.; 38°41′N 83°29′W. Tobacco, grain; dairying. One of 5 places so named in Ky. **4** (kuhn-kord), village (1990 pop. 944), Jackson co., S Mich., on Kalamazoo R., and 13 mi/21 km SW of Jackson; 42°10′N 84°38′W. In livestock, poultry, and grain area; grain milling; mfg. **5** (KAHN-kord), village (1990 pop. 156), Dixon co., NE Nebr., 10 mi/16 km N of Wayne; 42°22′N 96°59′W. **6** uninc. village, Campbell and Appomattox cos., SW central Va., 11 mi/18 km ESE of Lynchburg. Mfg. (wood prods., crushed stone, wine); agr. (dairying, livestock; grain, soybeans); limestone.

Concord, River, c.15 mi/24 km long, NE Mass., a short tributary of the Merrimack, which it joins at Lowell. On April 19, 1775, colonial militia fired some of the 1st shots of the Amer. Revolution at the British over a bridge across the river at Concord, Mass. Henry David Thoreau's first book, *A Week on the Concord and Merrimack Rivers* (1849), records a boat trip with his brother. Concord Bridge is administered by the Natl. Park Service.

Concordia (kuhn-KOR-dee-uh), parish (□ 709 sq mi/1,836 sq km; 1990 pop. 20,828), E central La.; ⊙ Vidalia; 31°34′N 91°27′W. Bounded E by the Mississippi, W by Black (Ouachita) and Tensas rivers, S by Red R. (outflow channel to Mississippi R. passes through S part). Drained by Bayou Cocodrie. Oil and natural gas fields; lumber; sand and gravel pits. Logging; mfg. of chemicals. Agr. (cotton, corn, sorghum, hay, pecans, rice, soybeans, sweet potatoes, vegetables, wheat; cattle, horses, exotic fowl). Fishing (catfish). Cocodrie Lake in W center, Concordia and St. John lakes in NE (oxbow lakes of Black and Mississippi rivers). Red R. and Three Rivers State Wildlife Area in S, Bayou Cocodrie Natl. Wildlife Refuge in center. La Salle called the area New Paradise. Formed 1805.

Concordia, city (1990 pop. 6,660) and township, Sinaloa, NW Mexico, in coastal lowland, 23 mi/37 km ENE of Mazatlán on Mexico Highway 40; 23°18′N 106°02′W. Agr. center (cotton, corn, tobacco, chickpeas, tomatoes, fruit); silver, gold, copper mining. Also known as Villa de San Sebastían.

Concordia, city (1990 pop. 2,160), Lafayette co., W central Mo., 25 mi/40 km NW of Sedalia; 38°59′N 93°34′W. Corn, wheat, soybeans, sorghum; cattle, hogs; mfg. (prepared foods, apparel). Settled by Ger. immigrants in 1850s. Has Lutheran acad. and junior col. (St. Paul's Col.). Plotted 1868.

Concordia (kahn-KOR-dee-uh), town (1990 pop. 6,167), ⊙ Cloud co., N Kansas, on Republican R., and 45 mi/72 km N of Salina; 39°34′N 97°39′W. Elev. 1,380 ft/421 m. RR junction. Trade center for wheat, livestock, and poultry region; dairying; mfg. (metal prods., industrial machinery; brick and tile). Cloud Co. Community Col., Brown Grand Opera House (1906) here. Inc. 1872.

Concordia, La, Mexico: see LA CONCORDIA.

Concordville (KON-kurd-vil), uninc. village, Delaware co., SE Pa., suburb, 18 mi/29 km WSW of Philadelphia, on West Branch Chester Creek; 39°53′N 75°31′W. Mfg. includes commercial printing, food, machinery, fabricated metal prod., aggregates. Agr. area on urban fringe. Brandywine Battlefield State Historical Site to W.

Concourse Village, section of borough of Bronx, N.Y. city, SE N.Y. Formerly populated mostly by Jews, the area suffered from severe dislocation problems caused by Robert Moses's Manhattan slum clearance policies, which drove low-income people (chiefly Afr. Americans and Puerto Ricans) into the South Bronx; the building of the Cross Bronx Expressway further increased tensions. Mitchell-Lama, a middle-income housing development between 156th and 158th Sts. just E of Grand Concourse in the South Bronx, opened in 1968 with 6 bldgs. featuring 25 stories and 1,855 apartments; the project successfully integrated minorities and whites in public housing.

Concow, uninc. town (1990 pop. 1,392), Butte co., N central Calif., residential community, 5 mi/8 km ENE of Paradise, on Concow Reservoir (Concow Creek); 39°45′N 121°30′W. Timber.

Concrete, village (1990 pop. 735), Skagit co., NW Wash., 35 mi/56 km ESE of Bellingham, at confluence of Baker and Skagit rivers; 48°32′N 121°45′W. Situated below Lower Baker Dam (forms L. Shannon); Upper Baker Dam (forms Baker L.) 7 mi/11.3 km N. Logging; sawmill. North Cascades Natl. Park to NE; parts of Mt. Baker Natl. Forest to N, E, and S. Mt. Baker (10,775 ft/3,284 m) and Mt. Baker Natl. Recreation Area to N; Rockport State Park to SE.

Conda, village (1990 pop. 200), Caribou co., SE Idaho, 8 mi/12.9 km NE of Soda Springs. Elev. 6,100 ft/1,859 m. RR spur terminus to E. Phosphate mines; cattle, sheep; alfalfa, grain. Caribou Natl. Forest to E; Blackfoot Reservoir to N.

Condado (kon-DAH-do), beach and S residential sect. of San Juan, NE P.R. Tourism. Famous for its hotel facilities, casinos, convention centers, and beaches.

Conde (kon-DEE), village (1990 pop. 203), Spink co., NE central S.Dak., 30 mi/48 km NE of Redfield and on Timber Creek; 45°09′N 98°05′W. Grain; dairy prods.; poultry, cattle in area.

Condon (KAHN-duhn), village (1990 pop. 635), ⊙ Gilliam co., N Oregon, 35 mi/56 km S of Columbia R. at Arlington; 45°14′N 120°10′W. Elev. 2,844 ft/867 m. Shipping point for wheat, barley, oats, cattle. Printing, publishing. Dyer Wayside State Park to S; J.S. Burres State Park to NW.

Conecuh (KAH-nuh-kuh), county (□ 850 sq mi/ 2,202 sq km; 1990 pop. 14,054), S Ala.; ⊙ Evergreen; 31°25′N 86°59′W. Coastal plain region drained by Sepulga R. Corn, peanuts; lumber milling, crude oil and natural gas production. Formed 1818.

Conecuh River (KAH-nuh-kuh), 231 mi/372 km long, SE Ala. and NW Fla.; rises near Union Springs, Ala., flows SW into Fla. near Century, then S to Escambia Bay, an arm of Pensacola Bay. In Fla. it is known as Escambia R. Dredged in lower course.

Conehatta (ko-nuh-HAT-uh), uninc. town (1990 pop. 925), Newton co., E central Miss., 10 mi/16 km NW of Newton; 32°27′N 89°16′W. Cotton, corn; poultry, cattle; dairying. Mfg. (wire harnesses).

Conejos, county (□ 1,290 sq mi/3,341 sq km; 1990 pop. 7,453), S. Colo.; ⊙ Conejos; 37°12′N 106°11′W. Irrigated agr. area on N.Mex. state line; bounded E by Rio Grande; drained by Conejos R. (forms Platoro Reservoir in NW), Rio De Lapinos, and La Jura Creek (forms La Jura Reservoir in W center). Sheep, cattle; wheat, hay, oats, barley, potatoes, vegetables. San Luis Valley extends N-S. Includes part of San Juan Mts. and parts of Rio Grande. Small part of San Isabel Natl. Forest to W. Formed 1861.

Conejos, village, S Colo., ⊙ Conejos co., in SE foothills of San Juan Mts., on Conejos R., and 27 mi/43 km SSW of Alamosa, and 1 mi/1.6 km NW of Antonito, in San Luis Valley. Elev. 7,901 ft/2,408 m. Church of Our Lady of Guadalupe (1856) here. Founded 1854, town is one of the oldest in Colo.

Conejos Peak (13,172 ft/4,015 m), in San Juan Mts., Conejos co., S Colo., in Rio Grande Natl. Forest.

Conejos River, c.75 mi/121 km long, S Colo.; rises at Continental Divide, in S San Juan Mts. in NW Conejos co., in Rio Grande Natl. Forest; flows first NE through Platoro Reservoir, then SE and NE again, past Conejos and Manassa, to Rio Grande, 10 mi/16 km E of Sanford.

Conemaugh (KON-maw), river, c.70 mi/113 km long, formed by joining of Little Conemaugh and Stony Creek rivers at Johnstown; 40°19′N 78°55′W. Flows WNW past Morrellville and Blairsville, joins Loyalhanna R., from S, at Saltsberg where it forms Kiskiminetas R., which continues NW to Allegheny R., SW Pa. Federal flood-control works on the river and its tributaries include Conemaugh R. Dam.

Conestee (KAHN-uhs-tee), uninc. village (1990 pop. 550), Greenville co., NW S.C., on Reedy R., suburb 6 mi/9.7 km S of Greenville. Mfg. includes textile machinery, metal finishing.

Conestoga (KAH-nuh-STO-gah), uninc. village, Conestoga township, Lancaster co., SE Pa., 7 mi/11.3 km SSW of Lancaster; 39°56′N 76°20′W. Mfg. (dairy prods.); agr. (grain; livestock). Once site of Native American village. Gave its name to Conestoga wagon, developed in this region before the Amer. Revolution.

Conestoga River (KAH-nuh-STO-gah), c.50 mi/80 km long, SE Pa.; rises in S Berks co. near Morgantown; flows SW, past Lancaster, to Susquehanna R. at Safe Harbor; 40°9′N 75°53′W.

Conesus Lake (kuh-NEE-suhs), in W central N.Y., westernmost of Finger Lakes, 30 mi/48 km S of Rochester; 42°47′N 77°43′W. The lake is 8 mi/ 12.9 km long. It drains NW through outlet to Genesee R.

Conesville, town (1990 pop. 334), Muscatine co., SE Iowa, near Cedar R., 15 mi/24 km W of Muscatine; 41°22′N 91°20′W.

Conesville, village (1990 pop. 420), Coshocton co., central Ohio, on Muskingum R., and 7 mi/11 km SSW of Coshocton; 40°11′N 81°54′W.

Coneto de Comonfort (ko-NAI-to de ko-mon-FORT), town (1990 pop. 1,097), Durango, N Mexico, 65 mi/ 105 km N of Victoria de Durango. Mining (silver, especially tin).

Conetoe (KAHN-uh-to), village (1990 pop. 292), Edgecombe co., E central N.C., 7 mi/11.3 km SE of Tarboro; 35°49′N 77°27′W. Tobacco, peanuts, cotton, grain; poultry, livestock; mfg. (textile cutting).

Conewago Heights (KAH-nuh-WAI-go), uninc. town (1990 pop. 950), York co., S Pa., 9 mi/14.5 km N of York on Conewago Creek, and 1 mi/1.6 km SW of its mouth on Susquehanna R.; 40°05′N 76°43′W. Agr. area for dairying, livestock; grain, soybeans. Three Mile Isl. Nuclear Power Plant 4 mi/6.4 km N.

Conewango (kuh-uh-WAIN-go), village (1990 pop. 150), Cattaraugus co., W N.Y., on Conewango Creek, 15 mi/24 km NE of Jamestown; 42°12′N 79°00′W.

Conewango Creek (kuh-uh-WAIN-go), c.65 mi/ 105 km long, in N.Y. and Pa., rises in W Cattaraugus co., W N.Y., flows NW, then generally S, past Kennedy and Frewsburg (N.Y.), to Allegheny R. at Warren, Pa.

Coney Island, swimming beach, amusement center, and neighborhood of S Brooklyn borough of N.Y. city, SE N.Y., on the Atlantic Ocean; 40°35′N 74°00′W. The tidal creek that once separated the isl. from the mainland has been filled in, making the area a peninsula. A seaside resort from the mid–19th cent., RR service made it an extremely popular resort. Although it no longer has hotels, its beach still attracts hundreds of thousands of visitors on hot summer days. The beach stretches from Norton Point on Lower N.Y. Bay E almost 4.5 mi/7.2 km to the residential communities of Brighton Beach and Manhattan Beach S of Sheepshead Bay. The 2-mi/3.2-km boardwalk, the N.Y. Aquarium, and the many notable eating places are other attractions. Most of its pop. is Afr.-Amer. and Hispanic; many residents are poor and elderly. High-rise apartments (many fallen into decay) have replaced much of amusement area since 1950s. Although it remains popular, Coney Isl. has declined considerably since its heyday in the 1920s and 1930s.

Confluence, borough (1990 pop. 873), Somerset co., SW Pa., 20 mi/32 km SW of Somerset, on Youghiogheny R. (forms Youghiogheny River L. reservoir to S), at mouth of Casselman R.; 39°48′N 79°20′W. Mfg. apparel, printing). Agr. (corn, oats, hay; livestock, dairying). Ohiopyle State Park to W. Borough of Ursina adjoins to E. Inc. 1873.

Congaree River (KAHNG-uh-ree), 52 mi/84 km long, central S.C.; formed at confluence of Broad and Saluda rivers at Columbia, flows SE, past Congaree Natl. Monument, joins Wateree R. 10 mi/16 km NE of St. Mathews to form Santee River. Navigable.

Congaree Swamp National Monument (KAHNG-uh-ree), Richland co., central S.C., 20 mi/32 km SE of Columbia on Congaree R. Contains last significant tract of S bottomland hardwood forest designated a Biosphere Reserve in 1983. Authorized 1976, 22,200 acres/ 8,984 ha.

Conger (KAWNG-guhr), village (1990 pop. 143), Freeborn co., S Minn., near Iowa state line, 9 mi/14.5 km WSW of Albert Lea; 43°37′N 93°31′W. Grain; poultry; dairying; mfg. Lower and Upper Twin lakes to SE.

Congers (KAHN-guhrz), village (□ 3 sq mi/7.8 sq km; 1990 pop. 8,003), Rockland co., SE N.Y., 3 mi/4.8 km S of Haverstraw, 41°08′N 73°57′W. State park on W bank of Hudson R. nearby.

Congerville (KAHN-ger-vil), village (1990 pop. 397), Woodford co., central Ill., 14 mi/23 km NW of Bloomington, near Mackinaw R.; 40°37′N 89°12′W. Corn, soybeans; cattle; metal fabricating. Mackinaw R. State Fish and Wildlife Area to SW.

Congress 1 uninc. village, Yavapai co., W central Ariz., 30 mi/48 km SW of Prescott. Cattle. Date Creek Mts. to NW. **2** village (1990 pop. 162), Wayne co., N central Ohio, 10 mi/16 km NNW of Wooster, in agr. area; 40°55′N 82°03′W.

Conimicut, neighborhood of E Warwick, Kent co., R.I.

Coniston (KAH-nis-tuhn), town, SE central Ont., Canada, on Wanapitei R., and 7 mi/11 km E of Sudbury; 46°29′N 80°51′W. Copper, nickel mining and smelting; hydroelectric station.

Conkal (kon-KAL), town (1990 pop. 5,083), Yucatán, SE Mexico, 10 mi/16 km NE of Mérida; 21°06′N 89°42′W. Henequen, corn, beans, tropical fruit.

Conklingville, village, Saratoga co., E N.Y., in foothills of Adirondacks, 14 mi/23 km W of Glens Falls; 43°19′N 73°56′W. On Sacandaga R. here, Conklingville Dam (1,100 ft/335 m long, 115 ft/35 m high; completed 1930 for river control, power) impounds Sacandaga Reservoir.

Conley, suburb (1990 pop. 5,528) S of Atlanta, Clayton co., Ga., c.2 mi/3.2 km NE of Forest Park. Mfg. of machinery, transportation equip., construction materials, chemicals, animal feeds, food prods., apparel, fabricated metal prods.; millwork.

Connaught Tunnel (26,517 ft/8,082 m long), SE B.C., Canada, in Selkirk Mts., under Mt. Macdonald, in Glacier Natl. Park, on Can. Pacific RR, just NE of Glacier. Completed 1916.

Conneaut (KAHN-ee-AHT), city (1990 pop. 13,241), Ashtabula co., extreme NE Ohio, on L. Erie, near the Pa. border; 41°55′N 80°34′W. It is a port of entry—an important ore-receiving port and a limestone- and coal-loading center—and a vacation resort. Conneaut has a RR mus., with antiques of the steam era. Settled 1799, inc. 1834.

Conneaut Creek (KAH-nee-aht), c.50 mi/80 km long, in Pa. and Ohio; rises in W central Crawford co., NW Pa. (41°40′N 80°23′W), flows N past Conneautville, turns W 2 mi/3.2 km NW of Albion, flows into NE Ohio, turns NE at Kingsville, flows past Conneaut, to Conneaut harbor, 2 mi/3.2 km NE of downtown Conneaut, and 1.5 mi/2.4 km W of Ohio-Pa. state line.

Conneaut Lake (KAH-nee-aht), borough (1990 pop. 699), Crawford co., NW Pa., 8 mi/12.9 km WSW of Meadville at S end of Conneaut L., largest natural lake (929 acres/376 ha) in Pa.; 41°36′N 80°18′W. Rail spur terminus. Mfg. (winery, tool and die); agr. area (corn, hay; livestock; dairying). Conneaut Lake Airport to SW; Conneaut L. Park (theme park) to N.

Conneaut Lakeshore (KAH-nee-aht), uninc. town (1990 pop. 1,852), Crawford co., NW Pa., residential development on E shore of Conneaut L.; 41°37′N 80°18′W. Conneaut L. Park (theme park) to NW.

Conneautville (KAH-nee-aht-vil), borough (1990 pop. 822), Crawford co., NW Pa., 13 mi/21 km NW of Meadville, on Conneaut Creek; 41°45′N 80°22′W. Mfg. (printing and publishing, furniture, transportation equip.); agr. (corn, hay, potatoes, soybeans; livestock, dairying). Conneaut L. (natural) to SE; Pymatuning Reservoir and State Park to SW.

Connecticut, state (□ 5,543 sq mi/14,358 sq km; 1995 est. pop. 3,274,662), NE U.S., southernmost of the New England states, one of the 13 colonies; ⊙ HARTFORD; 41°48′N 72°43′W. BRIDGEPORT is the largest city, with Hartford and NEW HAVEN next in size. Generally rectangular in outline, the state extends c.90 mi/145 km from E to W and c.55 mi/90 km from N to S; it is bounded on the N by Mass., on the E by R.I., on the S by Long Isl. Sound, and on the W by N.Y. Conn. is divided into 3 roughly equal sects., usually called the eastern highland, the western highland, and the Conn. valley lowland. The Connecticut R., which flows through only the N ½ of the valley, veers off to the SE at Middletown in central Conn. Along the L.I. Sound there is a low, rolling coastal plain. The W highland, with the Taconic Mts. and the Litchfield Hills, is more rugged than the E highland. A few isolated peaks in the W are more than 2,000 ft/610 m high. The Thames and the rivers emptying into it drain the E highland, and the Housatonic, with its chief tributary, the Naugatuck, drains the W highland. Though famed for its rural loveliness, Conn. is well industrialized. In spite of significant recent decline, the state still depends on industries for much of its economic health. The state's principal industries produce jet engines and parts, electronics and electrical machinery, computer equipment, and helicopters. There is also varied and abundant light mfg. Much of Conn.'s mfg. is still produced for the military, although cutbacks in federal defense spending beginning in the late 1980s has forced some restructuring and downsizing. Firearms and ammunition, 1st

---

produced in Conn. at the time of the Amer. Revolution, are still manufactured in the state. Groton is an important center for submarine building. Agr. accounts for only a small share of income in the state; dairy prods., eggs, vegetables, tobacco, and apples are the leading farm items. High-grade broadleaf tobacco, used in making cigar wrappers, has been a speciality of Conn. agr. since the 1830s. Largely shade-grown in the fertile Conn. valley, it remains a specialty crop although production has been adversely affected by new methods of cigar production. Many varieties of fish, as well as oysters, lobsters, and other shellfish, are caught in L.I. Sound, but the fishing industry is small and has been further hampered by pollution of the waters. The only commercial fishing fleet in the state is based in STONINGTON. Few minerals are produced; stone, sand, and gravel account for most income derived from mining. Insurance, historically, is an important industry in Conn., and the Hartford metropolitan area has been known as one of the world's largest insurance centers, with the home offices of many insurance companies. However, mergers and downsizings of the 1990s have trimmed the insurance company payrolls and caused some operations to be relocated to other states. Financial, real estate, and service industries are also of major importance. The most recent growth business in Conn. has been gambling, since the 1991 opening of Foxwoods Resort and Casino on the Mashantucket reservation next to LEDYARD in SE Conn. Foxwoods held the unofficial title of world's largest casino in 1996. Another casino was under construction nearby on the newly authorized Mohegan reservation at MONTVILLE. A proposal to build a non-reservation casino in Bridgeport, however, failed to gain the approval of the state's legislature in 1995, in spite of the governor's support of the casino as a way to rebuild the economically depressed city's financial health. The Conn. shore is a popular summer resort area, and the protected waters of L.I. Sound lure boating enthusiasts to the state. Another prominent summer attraction is the Stratford Shakespeare Festival, which has been operating since 1965. Institutions of higher learning in Conn. include Yale Univ., at New Haven; Trinity Col., at Hartford; Wesleyan Univ., at Middletown; the Univ. of Conn., at Storrs; and the U.S. Coast Guard Acad. and Conn. Col., at New London. In 1614, Adriaen Block, a Dutchman, sailed through L.I. Sound and explored the Connecticut R. The Dutch built a small fort in 1633 on the site of present-day Hartford, but they abandoned it in 1654 as Eng. settlers moved into the area in increasing numbers. Edward Winslow of Plymouth Colony was apparently the first Englishman to visit (1632) Conn., and in 1633 members of the Plymouth Colony established a trading post on the site of WINDSOR. This small Pilgrim enterprise was soon absorbed by Puritan settlers from the Massachusetts Bay Colony. These settlers had been attracted to the area by the excellent reports brought back by one of their members, John Oldham, in 1633. Oldham returned to the Conn. area in 1634 and established still another trading post, which became WETHERSFIELD. The following year Puritans flocked in great numbers to the Conn. valley. In 1636, Thomas Hooker and his congregation left Newtown and settled near the Du. trading post that had been established on the site of Hartford. The Pequot resisted white settlement, but they were defeated by the English in the short Pequot War of 1637. Relations remained relatively peaceful until King Philip's War in 1675–1676. In 1638–1639 representatives of the 3 Connecticut R. towns—Hartford, Windsor, and Wethersfield—met at Hartford and formed the colony of Conn. They also adopted the Fundamental Orders, which established a govt. for the colony. A second colony, SAYBROOK, had been established at the mouth of the Connecticut R. in 1635 by a group of Englishmen. The colony's founders (who included Viscount Saye and Sile and Baron Brooke, for whom the colony was named) sold the Saybrook settlement to Conn. colony in 1644. Conn.'s pop. expanded gradually, and by 1662 the colony included over a dozen towns, including Saybrook, NEW LONDON, FAIRFIELD, and NORWALK as well as East Hampton and Southampton on L.I. Another Puritan settlement, NEW HAVEN, was est. in 1638. It was not connected with the Conn. colony. In 1643, New Haven and Conn. colonies joined with Mass. Bay colony and Plymouth colony to form the New England Confederation, a loose union for mutual defense. In 1662, Conn. sent its governor, John Winthrop (1606–1676), to London to secure a royal charter for the colony. He obtained the charter, by which Conn. not only won its legal right to exist as a corporate colony but also acquired New Haven. The years from 1750 to 1776 saw much bitter disagreement bet. radicals and conservatives in the colony. In 1776, the patriot governor, Jonathan Trumbull, was reelected almost unanimously (Conn. and R.I. were the only colonies privileged to elect their chief executives), and he was the only governor of any colony to be retained in office after the outbreak of the Amer. Revolution. There was little fighting in Conn. during the Revolution—skirmishes at Stonington (1775), DANBURY (1777), New Haven (1779), and New London (1781)—but the state was the principal supply area for the Continental Army. After the war the state relinquished (1786) to the U.S. its claims to W land, except the WESTERN RESERVE (an area in Ohio). The claim was retained until part of the land was given to Conn. citizens in 1792 and the remainder sold in 1795. In 1799, Conn.'s long dispute with Pa. over the WYOMING VALLEY was finally settled. Conn. was one of the first states to approve the Federal Constitution. The Embargo Act of 1807, passed during the administration of Thomas Jefferson, was vehemently denounced throughout New England; the ports on L.I. Sound and on the Connecticut R. had developed a lively carrying trade with which the embargo interfered. The War of 1812 was also so unpopular that New England Federalists, meeting at the Hartford Convention in late 1814, considered secession. In 1818 the Jeffersonians came into power in the state, and a new constitution, replacing the old charter of 1662, was adopted. It disestablished the Congregational Church and greatly extended the franchise, although universal manhood suffrage was not proclaimed until 1845. Meanwhile, after Conn.'s shipping industry had been ruined by the embargo and the war, the state turned to mfg. Artisans and craftsmen had become increasingly numerous in late colonial days, and from native iron ore Conn. forges had produced guns for the patriot soldiers. Modern mass production had its beginning in the state when Eli Whitney, probably the best known of Conn.'s inventors, estab. (1798) at New Haven a firearms factory that began making guns with standardized, interchangeable parts. Earlier, in 1793, he had invented and manufactured the cotton gin at New Haven. The manufacture of notions (buttons, pins, needles, metal goods, and clocks) gave rise to the enterprising "Yankee peddler," who, with horse and team, covered the nation hawking his wares. Conn.'s insurance industry also developed during this period, and in 1810 the Hartford Fire Insurance Co. was established. Conn., which had placed limitations on slavery in 1784 and abolished it in 1848, supported the Union during the Civil War with nearly 60,000 troops and a secretary of the navy, Gideon Welles. During and after the war, industry expanded greatly. Immigration provided a cheap labor supply as English, Scottish, and many Irish immigrants, who had arrived in large numbers even before the war, were followed by Fr. Canadians and, in the late 19th and early 20th cent., by Italians, Poles, and others. During World Wars I and II Conn. prospered, providing munitions and other supplies for the war effort. However, bet. the 2 wars the Great Depression left many unemployed in the state. In the 1930s and 1940s the construction of many highways began to carry much of the commuter traffic to N.Y. city, causing a decline in the use of trains. Conn.'s industries have continued to grow and develop since the end of World War II, and in 1954 the world's first nuclear-powered submarine was launched at Groton. In the 1970s, as mfg. began to decline, Conn.'s major cities fell into a state of decay. A boom in defense spending and the growth of financial, insurance, real estate, and service industries helped make Conn. one of the wealthiest states in the nation throughout the 1980s. This wealth, however, has been enjoyed primarily by the state's affluent suburban communities while the central cities have further crumbled, as evidenced by Bridgeport's bankruptcy filing in 1991. Prior to 1965, Conn.'s constitution provided for a bicameral legislature with a house of representatives elected on the basis of geographical distribution. No town or city had less than 1 or more than 2 representatives, thus the larger cities wereunderrepresented. The 1965 constitution remedied this situation by providing for the election of both houses of the general assembly, as the legislature is called, on the basis of election districts apportioned according to pop. Conn.'s state senate has 36 members and its house of representatives has 151; members of both houses are elected for 2-year terms. The state executive branch is headed by a governor elected for a term of 4 years; Ella T. Grasso, a Democrat, elected governor in 1974, was the 1st woman governor elected in her own right. Conn. is represented in the U.S. Congress by 6 Representatives and 2 Senators and has 8 electoral votes. Conn. has 8 cos., although most governmental authority is vested in the individual towns. The counties, which mostly administer the court system, are: FAIRFIELD, HARTFORD, LITCHFIELD, MIDDLESEX, NEW HAVEN, NEW LONDON, TOLLAND, and WINDHAM.

Connecticut Lakes, reservoirs, Coos co., N N.H., 3 lakes at source of Connecticut R. and linked by it. Includes FIRST CONNECTICUT LAKE, Second Connecticut L. (3 mi/4.8 km long; 45°07'N 71°11'W), and Third Connecticut L. (1 mi/1.6 km long; 45°14'N 71°12'W), source of the Connecticut R., near Can. (Que.) border. Connecticut Lakes State Forest lies bet. Second and Third lakes. Hunting, fishing, and logging area. Also known, respectively, as First, Second, and Third lakes.

Connell, town (1990 pop. 2,005), Franklin co., SE Wash., 30 mi/48 km NNE of Pasco; 46°40'N 118°52'W. RR junction. In Columbia basin agr. region (wheat, corn, alfalfa, asparagus, potatoes, beans; sheep, hogs); mfg. (corn milling, frozen fruits and vegetables); sand, gravel. Juniper Dunes Wilderness Area to S; Scootenay Reservoir to W.

Connellsville (kah-NELS-vil), city (1990 pop. 9,229), Fayette co., SW Pa., 10 mi/16 km NE of Uniontown, on the Youghiogheny R. in the Allegheny Mts; 40°01'N 79°35'W. A significant producer of coal and coke, the city also has RR shops. Mfg. (machinery, chemicals, printing and publishing, paper prods.); agr. (corn, hay; livestock, dairying). The attack on Henry C. Frick by the anarchist Alexander Berkman occurred (1892) in Connellsville during the Homestead Strike. A branch of Pa. State Univ. is S of the city. Connellsville Airport to SW; Ohiopyle State Park to SE. Settled c.1770, inc. as a borough 1806, as a city 1911.

Connelly Springs, town (1990 pop. 1,349), Burke co., W central N.C., 11 mi/18 km E of Morganton, and 10 mi/16 km W of Hickory; 35°45'N 81°30'W. Grain, soybeans; chickens, hogs. Mfg. (apparel, fabricated metal prods.). L. Rhodhiss reservoir (Catawba R.) to N.

Connelsville, uninc. community, Adair co., N Mo., on Chariton R., and 8 mi/12.9 km NW of Kirksville.

Connersville, city (1990 pop. 15,550), ⊙ Fayette co., E central Ind., on West Fork of Whitewater R.; 39°40'N 85°08'W. Agr. (corn, hogs); mfg. (machinery, feeds and fertilizers, chemicals, fabricated metal prods., transportation equip.). Nearby are a state park and two historic covered bridges. Founded 1813; inc. as a city 1870.

Connoquenessing (KAH-no-kwe-NES-sing), borough (1990 pop. 507), Butler co., W Pa., 7 mi/11.3 km WSW of Butler; 40°49'N 80°00'W. Mfg. (fabricated metal prods.). Agr. (apples, soybeans, grain; livestock, dairying). Also spelled Conoquenessing.

Connoquenessing Creek (KAH-no-kwe-NES-sing), c.50 mi/80 km long, W Pa.; rises in E Butler co., 40°59'N 79°52'W, flows SW, through L. Oneida reservoir, past Butler and Zelienople, and NW, past Ellwood

City, where it receives Slippery Rock Creek from NE before entering Beaver R. just W of Ellwood City.

Connors Pass, Nev.: see SCHELL CREEK RANGE.

Conococheague Creek (KAH-no-KAH-cheek), c.80 mi/129 km long; rises at Franklin-Adams co. border, S Pa., flows W past Fayetteville and Chambersburg and S, through Cumberland Valley to W of Greencastle, Pa., and Hagerstown, Md., to the Potomac R. at Williamsport, Md; 39°58′N 77°24′W. West Branch rises in N Franklin co., Pa., flows c.45 mi/72 km generally S past Mercersburg, enters main stream 3 mi/4.8 km N of the Md. state line.

Conodoguinet Creek (KAH-no-DAH-gah-net), c.75 mi/121 km long, S Pa.; rises in mts. in N Franklin co., flows first SE, then generally ENE, passes N of Newville and past Carlisle and Camp Hill, to Susquehanna R. at West Fairview; 39°56′N 77°52′W. Lower course is extremely serpentine.

Conoquenessing, Pa.: see CONNOQUENESSING.

Conover, city (1990 pop. 5,465), Catawba co., W central N.C., suburb, 7 mi/11.3 km ESE of Hickory, and 2 mi/3.2 km N of Newton; 35°42′N 81°13′W. Agr. area (grain, soybeans, sorghum; poultry, livestock, dairying). Mfg. (electrical equip.; wood, plastic, and fabricated metal prods.; textiles; medical equip.; furniture; apparel). Hickory Motor Speedway to SW.

Conover (KUH-no-vuhr), village, Vilas co., N Wis., 30 mi/48 km NE of Rhinelander. In wooded lake region; trade center for resort area. Gateway Ski Area to N; Nicolet Natl. Forest to E; Northern Highland State Forest to W.

Conowingo (kaw no-WING-o), village, Cecil co., NE Md., 9 mi/14.5 km NNW of Havre de Grace. In the Susquehanna is Conowingo Dam, a hydroelectric dam which carries U.S. Route 1 across the river. The name comes from the Indian word meaning "at the rapids," rapids which blocked John Smith's further explorations of the Susquehanna R. in 1606.

Conowingo Dam, 4,648 ft/1,417 m long, 102 ft/31 m high, on the Susquehanna R., Cecil Co., NE Md. Completed in 1928, the dam created the 14-mi/23-km long Conowingo L., and covered the old crossing at Bald Friar Lafayette, used by Lafayette, the Comte de Rochambeau, and their troops on their way to Yorktown in 1781. It is one of the largest non-Federal hydroelectric power plants in the U.S. A platform extending the entire length of the powerhouse accomodates shad fishermen. The dam forms a reservoir with a max. capacity of 310,000 acre-feet. Electric power here flows to the Pa. Power Company's station near Philadelphia. The name comes from the Indian word meaning "at the rapids."

Conquest, village (1991 pop. 224), S central Sask., Canada, 32 mi/51 km E of Rosetown; 51°32′N 107°15′W. RR junction. Wheat.

Conrad 1 (KAHN-rad), town (1990 pop. 2,891), ⊙ Pondera co., N Mont., 55 mi/89 km NNW of Great Falls; 48°10′N 111°57′W. Shipping point for grain and sugar beets; hogs, sheep, poultry; oil wells; mfg. (transportation equip.). L. Elwell reservoir to NE. Inc. 1910. Formerly called Pondera. **2** town (1990 pop. 964), Grundy co., central Iowa, on Wolf Creek, and 10 mi/16 km SSW of Grundy Center; 42°13′N 92°52′W. In agr. area. Limestone quarry nearby.

Conrath, village (1990 pop. 92), Rusk co., N Wis., 35 mi/56 km NE of Chippewa Falls; 45°22′N 91°02′W. Dairying; cheese.

Conroe, city (1990 pop. 27,610), ⊙ Montgomery co., SE Texas, 40 mi/64 km N of Houston, near North Fork of San Jacinto R; 30°19′N 95°28′W. Elev. 213 ft/65 m. RR junction. Long a pine-lumbering town, it prospered after oil was discovered in 1932. The Conroe oil field is one of the significant producers in the state. Other natural resources in the area are timber, clays, and oil and gas. Farm prods. include beef and dairy cattle; nursery and greenhouse prods.; resorts and mfg. (machinery, rubber prods., chemicals). L. Conroe reservoir to NW; Co. Heritage Mus.; Sam Houston Natl. Forest to NE. Inc. 1885.

Conroe, Lake, reservoir, Montgomery and Walker cos., E Texas, on West Fork of San Jacinto R., 7 mi/11.3 km WNW of Conroe; 20 mi/32 km long; 30°21′N 96°33′W. Max. capacity 780,000 acre-ft. Formed by Conroe Dam (71 ft/22 m high), built (1973) by the San Jacinto R. Authority for water supply and irrigation.

Consecon (kahn-SEE-kuhn), village, SE Ont., Canada, on Wellar Bay of L. Ontario and on Consecon L. (5 mi/8 km long), 14 mi/23 km SW of Belleville; 44°00′N 77°31′W. Fishing, fruit growing.

Conshohocken (KAHN-shuh-HAH-ken), borough (1990 pop. 8,064), Montgomery co., SE Pa., suburb 11 mi/18 km NW of downtown Philadelphia, on the Schuylkill R.; 40°04′N 75°17′W. Mfg. (food, fabricated metals, electronic prods., commercial printing). Inc. 1850.

Consolación del Sur (kon-so-lah-see-ON dail soor), town, Pinar del Río prov., W Cuba, on Central Highway, and 12 mi/19 km NE of Pinar del Río; 22°30′N 83°31′W. Commercial center in Vuelta Abajo tobacco-growing region; produces also bananas, pineapples, vegetables. Mfg. of cigars. Has airfield. Sulphurous springs and clay quarries nearby.

Consort, village (1991 pop. 714), SE Alta., Canada, near Sask. border, 60 mi/97 km S of Wainwright; 52°01′N 110°48′W. Grain elevators, lumber and stockyards.

Constableville, village (□ 1 sq mi/2.6 sq km; 1990 pop. 307), Lewis co., N central N.Y., 30 mi/48 km N of Rome; 43°33′N 75°25′W. In timber and dairying area.

Constancia del Rosario (kon-STAHN-see-ah del ro-SAH-ree-o), town (1990 pop. 617), in the state of Oaxaca Mexico; 1 mi/2 km NW of Putla de Guerrero. Elev. 3,937 ft/1,200 m; steep terrain. Agr. (coffee, corn, beans); fine woods, lumber; unmined minerals and mezcal. Bordering the state of Guerrero in S Mixteca Alta. High percentage of pop. are Mixtec Indians. Poor roads.

Constant Spring, town (1991 pop. 12,369), St. Andrew parish, SE Jamaica, extends N of Halfway Tree to various residential areas in the Stoney Hills suburbs, 5 mi/8 km N of Kingston; 18°03′N 76°47′W. Dairying.

Constantia (kuhn-STAN-shah), village (□ 2 sq mi/5.2 sq km; 1990 pop. 1,140) in Constantia town (1990 pop. 4,868), Oswego co., N central N.Y., on N shore of Oneida L., 28 mi/45 km W of Rome; 43°15′N 76°00′W. State fish hatchery for warm-water fish and walleyes.

Constantine, town (1990 pop. 2,032), St. Joseph co., SW Mich., on St. Joseph R., and 31 mi/50 km SSW of Kalamazoo; 41°50′N 85°40′W. In agr. area (grain, vegetables; livestock, poultry; dairy prods.). Mfg. (paper and plastic prods.). Settled 1828; inc. 1837.

Constantine, Mount (10,290 ft /3,136 m), SW Yukon, Canada, near Alaska border, in St. Elias Mts., 200 mi/322 km WNW of Whitehorse; 61°25′N 140°36′W.

Constanza (kon-STAHN-zah), town (1993 pop. 17,073), La Vega prov., central Dominican Republic, in the Cordillera Central, on affluent of the Yaque del Sur, and 27 mi/43 km SW of La Vega; 18°52′N 70°42′W. Mt. resort in wheat-growing region. Airport nearby.

Constitution Gardens, park, Wash., D.C., located on the Mall, S of Constitution Ave. bet. 17th St. and Bacon Drive, NW, near the Rainbow Pool. Until their demolition in 1966, temporary wartime office bldgs. stood on the site. In 1976 Constitution Gardens, a memorial to the signers of the Declaration of Independence, was completed. Contains monuments, the Vietnam Veterans Memorial among them.

Constitution Island, in Hudson R. opposite West Point, SE N.Y.; 41°24′N 73°57′W. Part of U.S. Military Acad. The ruins of Fort Constitution, built 1775, are here. During the Amer. Revolution, a chain was stretched across Hudson R. here to prevent the ascent of Br. ships.

Consuelo (kon-SWAI-lo), locality (1993 pop. 18,277), San Pedro de Macorís prov., SE Dominican Republic, 8 mi/12.9 km N of San Pedro de Macorís city. Sugar mill.

Contepec (KON-te-pek), town (1990 pop. 3,963), Michoacán, central Mexico, 13 mi/21 km NNW of El Oro de Hidalgo. Cereals; livestock.

Continental, village (1990 pop. 1,214), Putnam co., NW Ohio, 14 mi/23 km SSE of Defiance; 41°05′N 84°16′W. In diversified agr. area; food prods., tile.

Continental Divide, uninc. village, McKinley co., NW N.Mex., 26 mi/42 km ESE of Gallup, at Continental Divide. Cattle, sheep. Mfg. (apparel). Sources of Rio San Jose to E and Rio Puerco to W. Part of Cibola Natl. Forest to S.

Continental Divide, the "backbone" of the continent, in N. Amer., from N Alaska to N.Mex., it moves along the crest of the Rocky Mts., which separates westward-flowing streams from eastward-flowing waters. In SW N.Mex. the divide crosses an area of low relief; it becomes more distinct in N Mexico, where it follows the Sierra Madre Occidental. In the U.S. it has been called the Great Divide, a name also occasionally used to designate the whole Rocky Mt. system, especially the S sect. where the high, rugged ranges presented an almost impenetrable barrier to westbound explorers and settlers. Glacier, Yellowstone, and Rocky Mt. natl. parks lie on the Continental Divide.

Contla (KON-tlah), town (1990 pop. 17,340), ⊙ Contla de Juan Cuamatzi municipio, Tlaxcala, central Mexico, 5 mi/8 km E of Tlaxcala; 19°20′N 98°10′W. Elev. 7,549 ft/2,300 m. Agr. center (corn, wheat, alfalfa, maguey; livestock). Also called San Bernardino Contla.

Contla de Juan Cuamatzi, Mexico: see CONTLA.

Contoocook, village, N.H.: see HOPKINTON.

Contoocook River (kuhn-TUH-kuk), c.60 mi/97 km long, S N.H.; rises in SE Cheshire co., flows generally NE to Merrimack R. at Penacook. Furnishes water power at Hillsboro, Peterboro, and other mfg. towns.

Contoy Island (□ 1.6 sq mi/4.1 sq km), in Yucatán Channel, off NE coast of Yucatán Peninsula, SE Mexico, 17 mi/27 km ESE of Cape Catoche; 21°32′N 86°49′W. The isl. is 4 mi/6.4 km long and c.$\frac{1}{2}$ mi/$\frac{8}{10}$ km wide.

Contra Costa, county (□ 720 sq mi/1,865 sq km; 1990 pop. 803,732), W Calif.; ⊙ Martinez; 37°56′N 121°57′W. Bounded on W by San Francisco Bay and San Pablo Strait, NW by San Pablo Bay, N by Carquinez Strait, Suisun Bay, San Joaquin/Sacramento estuary, and San Joaquin R., E by Old San Joaquin R. (old channel). Important ports (notably Richmond) and industrial cities (Pittsburg, with large steelworks; Antioch, Port Chicago, Martinez, Crockett, Hercules); and large oil refineries, shipyards, food processing, and other diversified mfg. plants. Highly urbanized and growing in W, center, and N. Berkeley Hills are along SW boundary; Mt. Diablo State Park is in S center. In NE is part of fertile delta of San Joaquin R. Asparagus, tomatoes, apples, walnuts; wheat, oats, barley, corn; nursery stock. Quarrying of stone, clay, sand, gravel, pumice; natural gas wells. County crossed E-W by Mokelumne Aqueduct. Formed 1850.

Contra Costa Canal, 48 mi/77 km long, Contra Costa co., W Calif., a unit (completed 1947) of Central Valley project, fed by pumped San Joaquin–Sacramento R. water from the delta near Oakley; flows W to Mallard Reservoir at Martinez. Used for irrigation and for industrial and urban supply in East Bay region. Closely paralleled by Mokelumne Aqueduct to S.

Contra Estaca (KON-trah es-TAH-kah), mining settlement (1990 pop. 14), Sinaloa, NW Mexico, in W outliers of Sierra Madre Occidental, 55 mi/89 km NNE of Mazatlán.

Contramaestre (kon-truh-mei-AIS-trai), town, (1994 pop. 30,000), Santiago de Cuba prov., SE Cuba, on Central Highway and RR, 3 mi/4.8 km N of Carlos Manuel de Céspedes L.; 20°18′N 76°14′W. América Libre sugar mill is 1 mi/1.6 km SE.

Contrecoeur (kon-truh-KUHR), village (1991 pop. 5,501), S Que., Canada, on the St. Lawrence, and 30 mi/48 km NNE of Montreal; 45°51′N 73°14′W. Dairying, cattle raising; fruit, potatoes. Opposite, in the St. Lawrence, are the Contrecoeur Isls., group of 6 islets.

Controller Bay, S Alaska, in Gulf of Alaska, SE of Katalla. Width is 18 mi/29 km.

Contwoyto Lake, central Mackenzie Dist., N.W.T., Canada; near 66°00′N 110°00′W. It is c.80 mi/129 km long and 2 mi/3 km–10 mi/16 km wide; drained N into Bathurst Inlet by Burnside R. (c.150 mi/241 km long).

Convent, uninc. village (1990 pop. 2,045), ⊙ St. James

parish, SE central La., on E bank (levee) of the Mississippi, and 45 mi/72 km W of New Orleans; 30°01′N 90°49′W. Mfg. (gas and liquid oxygen, chemicals, gasoline). Named after the Convent du Sacre Coeur, founded in 1825.

Convent Station, village, Morris co., N N.J., 2 mi/3.2 km SE of Morristown. Col. of St. Elizabeth (Catholic; 1899) here. Residential area.

Converse, county (□ 4,265 sq mi/11,046 sq km; 1990 pop. 11,128), E Wyo.; ⊙ Douglas; 42°58′N 105°30′W. Grain and livestock area (alfalfa, hay; sheep, cattle), drained by N Platte R. Coal and oil here. Part of Laramie Mts. and Medicine Bow Natl. Forest in S; Ayers Park and Natural Bridge in S center; part of Thunder Basin Natl. Grassland in NE corner. Formed 1888.

Converse, city (1990 pop. 8,887), Bexar co., S central Texas, suburb, 12 mi/19 km NE of downtown San Antonio; 29°30′N 98°18′W. Shipping point in agr. area; mfg. (aluminum and steel fabrication, concrete blocks, metal components). Randolph Field Air Force Base, one of world's largest military air fields, is just NE.

Converse, town (1990 pop. 1,144), Miami co., N central Ind., 14 mi/23 km SE of Peru; 40°35′N 85°53′W. In livestock and grain area; canned goods.

Converse 1 village (1990 pop. 436), Sabine parish, W La., 50 mi/80 km S of Shreveport; 31°47′N 93°42′W. Timber; dairying; oil wells. Toledo Bend reservoir on Sabine R. (Texas state line) to SW. **2** uninc. village, Spartanburg co., NW S.C., on Pacolet R., and 5 mi/8 km ENE of Spartanburg. Agr. area.

Convoy, village (1990 pop. 1,200), Van Wert co., W Ohio, 7 mi/11 km WNW of Van Wert, near Ind. state line; 40°55′N 84°42′W.

Conway, county (□ 566 sq mi/1,466 sq km; 1990 pop. 19,151), central Ark.; ⊙ Morrilton; 35°15′N 92°42′W. Bounded S in part by Arkansas R., E in part by Cadron Creek. Agr. (chickens, cattle, hogs; wheat, soybeans); timber. Some mfg. at Morrilton. Petit Jean State Park in SW corner; Arthur V. Ormond Lock and Dam (on Arkansas R.) in S; small part of Ozark Natl. Forest in NW corner. Formed 1825.

Conway 1 city (1990 pop. 26,481), ⊙ Faulkner co., central Ark., 27 mi/43 km NNW of Little Rock, near Arkansas R.; 35°05′N 92°27′W. Toad Suck Lock and Dam to E; in a farm and cotton area. It is a trade and industrial center. Mfg. (machinery, paper prods., wood prods., transportation equip., chemicals, consumer goods, printing, apparel, furniture). Seat of Hendrix Col., the Univ. of Central Ark., and Central Baptist Col. of Ark. Conway Reservoir to SE, offers excellent hunting and fishing. Settled (c.1865) near the site of a French trading post (c.1770). Inc. 1873. **2** city (1990 pop. 9,819), ⊙ Horry co., E S.C., on Waccamaw R. (head of navigation), and 90 mi/145 km NNE of Charleston; 33°50′N 79°03′W. Mfg. includes electronic equip., furniture, fabricated metal prods., lumber, textiles, consumer goods; agr. area for tobacco, watermelons, vegetables; tourism area, hunting, fishing. Coastal Carolina Univ.

Conway 1 town (□ 3 sq mi/7.8 sq km; 1990 pop. 13,159), Orange co., central Fla., located 6 mi/9.7 km SE of Orlando; 28°30′N 81°19′W. **2** town (1990 pop. 57), Taylor co., SW Iowa, 7 mi/11.3 km NE of Bedford; 40°45′N 94°37′W. In agr. region. **3** agr. town (1990 pop. 1,529), Franklin co., W Mass., 7 mi/11.3 km SW of Greenfield; 42°31′N 72°43′W. **4** town (1990 pop. 629), Laclede co., S central Mo., in the Ozarks, 15 mi/24 km SW of Lebanon. Wheat, corn, hay; cattle. **5** town (1990 pop. 7,940), Carroll co., E N.H., 34 mi/55 km NE of Laconia; 44°00′N 71°04′W. Bounded E by Maine state line; drained by Saco and Swift rivers. Agr. (livestock, poultry; dairying; nursery crops); mfg. (concrete, apparel, machinery, printing and publishing, furniture); winter sports and summer resort. Part of White Mt. Natl. Forest in W and N; Mt. Cranmore Ski Area in N; Echo L. State Park and Cathedral Ledge rock formation in W; 2 covered bridges at Conway village in S. Includes villages of North Conway and Center Conway. Settled 1764, inc. 1765. **6** town (1990 pop. 759), Northampton co., NE N.C., 11 mi/18 km NNE of Jackson, 25 mi/40 km E of Roanoke Rapids; 36°26′N 77°13′W. Timber; tobacco, peanuts, cotton, grain; poultry, livestock. Mfg. (wood prods.).

Conway 1 village, Emmet co., NW Mich., on W end of Crooked L., and 6 mi/9.7 km NE of Petoskey; 45°25′N 84°52′W. Resort Area. Nubs Nob Ski Area to N. **2** village (1990 pop. 24), Walsh co., NE N.Dak.,18 mi/29 km SW of Grafton; 48°13′N 97°40′W. RR junction.

Conway (KAHN-wai), borough (1990 pop. 2,424), Beaver co., W Pa., 20 mi/32 km NW of Pittsburgh and 3 mi/4.8 km NNE of Aliquippa, on Ohio R.; 40°39′N 80°14′W. Agr. (grain; dairying); mfg. (millwork).

Conway Springs, town (1990 pop. 1,384), Sumner co., S Kansas, 16 mi/26 km WNW of Wellington; 37°23′N 97°38′W. RR junction. In wheat region; dairying.

Conyers (KAHN-yuhrz), city (1990 pop. 7,380), ⊙ Rockdale co., N central Ga., 22 mi/35 km ESE of Atlanta; 33°40′N 84°01′W. Original RR-oriented community now restored as Olde Town Conyers. Modern-day Conyers is a booming residential and commercial suburb of Atlanta astride I-20. Site of Ga. Internatl. House Park, built for equestrian venues from the 1996 Summer Olympic Games. Mfg. includes gases, chemicals, electronic equip., machinery, paper prods., construction materials, consumer goods. Inc. 1854.

Conyngham (KAH-ning-ham), borough (1990 pop. 2,060), Luzerne co., E central Pa., 4 mi/6.4 km NW of Hazleton, on Little Nescopeck Creek; 40°59′N 76°03′W. Agr. (grain, potatoes; dairying). Hazleton Municipal Airport to E.

Cooch's Bridge, historic site, New Castle co., N Del. Site of only Revolutionary battle on Del. soil (Sept. 1777). 2 mi/3.2 km S of Newark.

Cook 1 county (□ 226 sq mi/585 sq km; 1990 pop. 13,456), S Ga.; ⊙ Adel; 31°09′N 83°26′W. Drained by Little and Withlacoochee rivers. Coastal plain. Tobacco, watermelons, cotton, corn, peanuts, fruit; cattle, hogs. Mfg. at Adel. Pine timber. Formed 1918. **2** county (□ 945 sq mi/2,447 sq km; 1990 pop. 5,105,067), NE Ill.; ⊙ Chicago, 3d-largest city of U.S. and center of vast metropolitan area extending far beyond co. boundaries; 41°53′N 87°39′W. Bounded E by L. Michigan and Ind. state line; traversed by Chicago and Des Plaines rivers and other links in Chicago Sanitary and Ship Canal system. Numerous suburban cities include Evanston, Arlington Heights, Skokie, Cicero, Oak Park, Des Plaines, Schaumburg, Mt. Prospect, Chicago Heights, and Oak Lawn. Industries of Chicago and suburbs earn co. rank among top mfg. cos. of U.S.; also contains many residential communities, recreational areas. Remnant agr. (corn, soybeans) in extreme NW and SW corners. O'Hare Internatl. Airport in NW on DuPage co. line. Midway Airport in SW part of Chicago. Several prominent univs., including Loyola, Northwestern, Univ. of Chicago, and De Paul, are here. Formed 1831. **3** county (□ 3,339 sq mi/8,648 sq km; 1990 pop. 3,868), extreme NE Minn.; ⊙ Grand Marais; 47°43′N 90°26′W. Bounded SE by L. Superior and on N by chain of lakes along Ont. border; watered by many lakes, including Brule and Saganaga. Agr.; resort area; fisheries; timber. Lies largely within Superior Natl. Forest (except for SW and E corners), includes part of Boundary Waters Canoe Area in N and NW, and is part of famous recreational area known as "Arrowhead Country" for its triangular shape, wedged bet. Canada (N) and L. Superior (SE); also called "North Shore." Grand Portage Indian Reservation and Grand Portage Natl. Monument are in extreme E. Taconite Harbor in SSW, RR to lake transfer point of iron ore from Mesabi Iron Range (St. Louis co.). Seven state parks and state waysides (NE to SW on lakeshore): Grand Portage and Judge C.R. Magney state parks and Kodonce R. State Wayside in E, Cascade R. State Park in S, Ray Berglund State Wayside, Temperance R. State Park and Cross R. State Wayside, are in SW; part of Finland State Forest in SW corner, Grand Portage State Forest in E. Eagle Mt. (2,301 ft/701 m), highest point in Minn., at center, L. Superior (602 ft/183 m) is Minn. lowest point (shared with Lake and St. Louis cos.); highest and lowest point separated by 13 mi/21 km (1,699 ft/518 m variation). County formed 1874.

Cook 1 village (1990 pop. 680), Saint Louis co., NE Minn., on North Branch of Little Fork R., 25 mi/40 km NNW of Virginia; 47°51′N 92°41′W. Timber; hay; cattle; mfg. (wood prods., feeds). Granite quarries nearby. Part of Superior Natl. Forest to S; W extension of Vermilion L. to NE; Kabetogama State Forest to N and E; Sturgeon R. State Forest to W. **2** village (1990 pop. 333), Johnson co., SE Nebr., 10 mi/16 km N of Tecumseh; 40°30′N 96°09′W. Grain, fruit; livestock. Beef and pork slaughter; poultry prods.

Cook 1 and 2 Nuclear Power Plants, Michigan: see BERRIEN, CO.

Cook, Cape, SW B.C., Canada, at W extremity of Brooks Peninsula, NW Vancouver Isl., 55 mi/89 km SW of Alert Bay; 50°07′N 127°55′W.

Cook Inlet, S Alaska, inlet of Gulf of Alaska, on W side of Kenai Peninsula; 59°10′– 61°10′N 150°–154°W. Length is 150 mi/241 km, width 9 mi/14.5 km–80 mi/129 km. From head at Anchorage, Turnagain Arm extends ESE, Knik Arm extends NE. Receives Susitna R. Sea lane to W Kenai Peninsula and Anchorage. Salmon, herring fisheries. Explored (1778) by Capt. James Cook.

Cook, Mount (13,760 ft/4,194 m), Canada, on Yukon-Alaska border, in St. Elias Mts., 170 mi/274 km WSW of Whitehorse, on SE edge of Seward Glacier; 60°11′N 139°58′W.

Cooke, county (□ 898 sq mi/2,326 sq km; 1990 pop. 30,777), N Texas; ⊙ Gainesville; 33°38′N 97°12′W. Bounded N by Red R. (here the Okla. state line), headwaters of L. Texoma (recreation) in NE. Drained by Elm Fork of Trinity R and Clear Creek. Agr. (peanuts, hay, and, especially, small sorghum, wheat, corn); dairying, livestock (cattle, hogs, horses, sheep); oil, natural gas wells; sand and gravel; some timber. Mfg., processing at Gainesville. Moss L. in N near Red R.; L. Kiowa in E; part of L. Ray Roberts in SE. Formed 1848.

Cooke City or **Cooke**, village, Park co., S Mont., near Wyo. state line and Yellowstone Natl. Park to SW, in Absaroka Range, 55 mi/89 km SE of Livingston. Elev. 7,651 ft/2,332 m. Formerly a center for gold mining, trade and shipping. Now dependent upon tourism. Absaroka-Beartooth Wilderness Area to N and E; Grasshopper Glacier to N. Southern terminus of Beartooth Scenic Highway.

Cooke Dam Pond, reservoir, Alcona co., N Mich., on Au Sable R., 38 mi/61 km S of Alpena; 44°28′N 85°34′W. Formed by Cooke Dam (50 ft/15 m high), built (1912) for power generation; also used for recreation.

Cookes Range, N Luna co., SW N.Mex., S extension of Mimbres Mts. Highest at Cooke's Peak (8,408 ft/2,563 m), 17 mi/27 km N of Deming. Lead and zinc mined.

Cookeville, city (1990 pop. 21,744), ⊙ Putnam co., N central Tenn., 70 mi/113 km E of Nashville; 36°10′N 85°30′W. A farm trade center; also mfg. of transportation equip., construction materials, clothing, and fabricated metal prods. Tenn. Technological Univ. is here. Inc. 1854.

Cooks Falls, village (1990 pop. 200), Delaware co., S N.Y., in Catskill Mts., on Beaver Kill, c.50 mi/80 km ESE of Binghamton; 41°57′N 73°59′W. Mfg. (chemicals, charcoal); lime.

Cooksburg, uninc. village, Forest co., W central Pa., on Clarion R., 14 mi/23 km NNW of Brookville, at entrance to Cook Forest State Park (to N); 41°20′N 79°12′W. Hq. for recreational area.

Cookshire, town (1991 pop. 1,552), ⊙ Compton co., S Que., Canada, on Eaton R., a tributary of St. Francis R., and 14 mi/23 km E of Sherbrooke; 45°25′N 71°37′W. Metalworking, lumbering. Agr. region (dairying; cattle, pigs).

Cookstown, village, S Ont., Canada, 15 mi/24 km S of Barrie; 44°11′N 79°42′W. Dairying, mixed farming.

Cooksville, village, S Ont., Canada, 12 mi/19 km WSW of Toronto; 43°34′N 79°37′W. Residential and commercial suburb of Toronto.

Cooksville, village (1990 pop. 211), McLean co., central Ill.,14 mi/23 km ENE of Bloomington; 40°32′N 88°43′W. In rich agr. area.

Cool Valley, city (1990 pop. 1,407), St. Louis co., E Mo., residential suburb, 8 mi/12.9 km NW of downtown St. Louis; 38°43′N 90°17′W. City of Ferguson to N, Univ. of Mo., St. Louis campus to S.

Cooleemee (KOOL-uh-mee), town (1990 pop. 971), Davie co., W central N.C., 12 mi/19 km NNW of Salisbury on South Fork of Yadkin R; 35°48′N 80°33′W. In agr. area (tobacco, grain, soybeans; chickens, livestock; dairying).

Cooley, village, Itasca co., N Minn., 19 mi/31 km ENE of Grand Rapids, 2 mi/3.2 km SW of Nashwauk; 47°21′N 93°11′W. Iron ore refining; iron mines nearby. In Mesabi Iron Range; Swan L. to S.

Coolidge (KOOL-ij), city (1990 pop. 610), Thomas co., S Ga., 14 mi/23 km NE of Thomasville; 31°01′N 83°52′W.

Coolidge 1 town (1990 pop. 6,927), Pinal co., S central Ariz., near Gila R., 21 mi/34 km NE of Casa Grande; 32°58′N 111°31′W. In irrigated cotton and alfalfa area served by Coolidge Dam; cotton ginning; mfg. (machinery, printing, chemicals, petroleum refining). Casa Grande Natl. Monument to N, and "Valley Farms" (U.S. resettlement project) nearby. Central Ariz. col. (2-year); Gila R. Indian Reservation to NW; Picacho Reservoir to S. Inc. since 1940. **2** town (1990 pop. 748), Limestone co., E central Texas, 32 mi/51 km NE of Waco; 31°45′N 96°39′W. Farm area (cotton, corn; cattle). Mfg. (machinery, furniture). L. Mexia to S. Settled 1903, inc. 1905.

Coolidge, village (1990 pop. 90), Hamilton co., SW Kansas, on Arkansas R., and 15 mi/24 km WNW of Syracuse, near Colo. border; 38°02′N 102°00′W.

Coolidge Dam, Ariz., see SAN CARLOS, LAKE.

Coolin, uninc. village (1990 pop. 100), Bonner., N Idaho, 19 mi/31 km NW of Sandpoint, at S end of Priest L. Timber; cattle. Chase L. to SE; Priest L. State Park and Upper Priest L. Scenic Area to N; Kaniksu Natl. Forest to E and W.

Coolville, village (1990 pop. 663), Athens co., SE Ohio, on Hocking R., and 17 mi/27 km ESE of Athens; 39°13′N 81°48′W.

Coon Rapids, city (1990 pop. 52,978), Anoka co., SE Minn., suburb 13 mi/21 km N of downtown Minneapolis–St. Paul, on the Mississippi R.; 45°10′N 93°18′W. Drained by Coon Creek. RR junction. Mfg. (transportation equip., fabricated metal prods., medical equip., consumer goods, printing and publishing, machinery). Anoka Ramsey Community Col. is here. Part of Bunker Hills Park Reserve in NE; Coon Rapids Dam State Park to S. Inc. 1952.

Coon Rapids, town (1990 pop. 1,266), Carrol co., W central Iowa, on Middle Raccoon R., and 17 mi/27 km SSE of Carroll; 41°52′N 94°40′W. Hybrid seed corn, feed, concrete prods.. Inc. 1882.

Coon Valley, village (1990 pop. 817), Vernon co., SW Wis., on small Coon Creek (tributary of the Mississippi R.), and 14 mi/23 km SE of La Crosse; 43°42′N 91°00′W. In tobacco-growing and dairying area. Mfg. (fabricated metal prods.). Hq. of Coon Creek soil conservation project.

Co-op City, NE section of borough of Bronx, N.Y. city, SE N.Y., near Westchester co. border, bet. Bruckner Expressway (I-95) and Pelham Bay Park; 40°53′N 73°50′W. A gargantuan Mitchell-Lama project built 1968–1970 on 300 acres/121 ha of filled marshland owned by the Port Authority of New York; the nation's largest cooperative apartment complex includes over 15,000 apartments in 35 bldgs., 236 clustered 2-family houses, 5 schools, a power plant, 3 shopping centers, 8 parking garages, and a fire station; there are c.55,000 middle-income inhabitants. Construction of the project coincided with both the decay of Brooklyn's older neighborhoods and the destruction of neighborhoods in the South Bronx and parts of the central Bronx caused by Robert Moses's drive to complete the Cross-Bronx Expressway. Co-op City functioned as a cheap, safe escape from neighborhoods that were coming apart, socially and physically; although originally built to house whites fleeing the decay of the South Bronx, today the complex is racially mixed.

Cooper (KU-puhr), county (□ 563 sq mi/1,458 sq km;

1990 pop. 14,835), central Mo.; ⊙ Boonville; 38°51′N 92°48′W. Bounded N by Missouri R.; drained by Lamine and Blackwater rivers. Wheat, corn, soybeans, peaches; dairying; cattle, turkeys; limestone; mfg. at Boonville. Formed 1818.

Cooper 1 town (1990 pop. 124), Wash. co., E Maine, 21 mi/34 km N of Machias; 45°00′N 67°25′W. In outdoor recreation area. **2** town (1990 pop. 2,153), ⊙ Delta co., NE Texas, 21 mi/34 km SSW of Paris; 33°22′N 95°41′W. Elev. 495 ft/151 m. Cotton area; "vetch capital of the world"; mfg. (transportation equip.). Cooper L. State Park (Cooper L. reservoir) to S. Settled in 1870s.

Cooper City, town (□ 6 sq mi/15.5 sq km; 1990 pop. 20,791), Broward co., SE Fla., located 10 mi/16 km WSW of Fort Lauderdale; 26°02′N 80°17′W. Site of major suburban development since 1990. Mfg.

Cooper Island, islet, Br. Virgin Isls., 4 mi/6.4 km SE of Tortola isl., bet. Salt Isl. (W) and Ginger Isl. (E); 18°23′N 64°30′W.

Cooper Lake 1 Kenai Peninsula Borough, S Alaska, in Chugach Natl. Forest, on Cooper Creek, 20 mi NNW of Seward; 60°24′N 149°46′W. Max. capacity 82,000 acre-ft. Formed by Cooper Lake Dam (60 ft/18 m high), built (1962) by the Chugach Electric Company for the generation of hydroelectricity. **2** reservoir (□ 30 sq mi/78 sq km), Hopkins and Delta cos., NE Texas, on Sulphur R., 20 mi/32 km S of Paris; 33°20′N 96°26′W. Max. capacity 797,300 acre-ft. Formed by Cooper Dam (79 ft/24 m high), built (1991) by Army Corps of Engineers for water supply; also used for flood control and recreation. Cooper Lake State Park near dam.

Cooper Landing, village, S Alaska, 30 mi/48 km NNW of Seward, on Kenai R. Road to Soldatna. Sports fishing, hiking, tourism.

Cooper Mountain (10,100 ft/3,078 m), SE B.C., Canada, in Selkirk Mts., 50 mi/80 km N of Nelson; 50°11′N 117°11′W.

Cooper River, SE S.C.; rises in Berkeley co. and joins Ashley R. to form Charleston Harbor. Many prosperous plantations situated along this waterway during the colonial antebellum periods.

Cooper Station Nuclear Power Plant, Nebr.: see NEMAHA, CO.

Co-Operative, village (1990 pop. 190), McCreary co., S Ky., 8 mi/12.9 km W of Whitley City, in Daniel Boone Natl. Forest. Timber; coal. Big South Fork Natl. R. and Recreational Area to E.

Cooper's Creek, c.20 mi/32 km long, Camden co., SW N.J.; rises near Lindenwold, flows generally NW, through Camden, to Delaware R. Navigable 8 mi/12.9 km above mouth.

Coopersburg (KOO-puhrs-buhrg), borough (1990 pop. 2,599), Lehigh co., E Pa., 8 mi/12.9 km SE of Allentown; 40°30′N 75°23′W. Agr. area (potatoes, apples, soybeans; livestock, poultry; dairying); mfg. (printing, apparel, electronic prods.). Allentown Col. of St. Francis de Sales to N at Center Valley. Settled 1780 as Fryburg, renamed 1832, inc. 1879.

Cooperstown, town (1990 pop. 1,247), ⊙ Griggs co., E central N.Dak., 37 mi/60 km NNW of Valley City, near Sheyenne R.; 47°26′N 98°07′W. Livestock; dairy prods.; wheat, barley. Mfg. (machinery, fabricated metal prods.). Settled 1882, inc. 1906.

Cooperstown, residential village (□ 1 sq mi/2.6 sq km; 1990 pop. 2,180), ⊙ Otsego co., E central N.Y., on Susquehanna R., and at S end of Otsego L.; 42°42′N 74°55′W. Founded by William Cooper, who brought his family here in 1787. His son, James Fenimore Cooper, made his home here after returning from abroad in 1833, and the region is described in his Leatherstocking Tales. Popular tourist destination. Fenimore House is the hq. of N.Y. State Historical Assn. Other attractions include Farmers' Mus. and the famous Natl. Baseball Hall of Fame and Mus., which commemorates the founding (1839) of baseball here by Abner Doubleday. Glimmerglass State Park and Glimmerglass Opera (in the architecturally distinctive 920-seat Alice Busch Opera Theater) at the N end of Otsego L. Inc. 1807.

Cooperstown (KOO-puhrs-toun), borough (1990 pop.

506), Venango co., NW Pa., 10 mi/16 km NW of Oil City, on Sugar Creek; 41°30′N 79°52′W. Mfg. (sand and gravel prods.). Agr. (corn, hay; dairying).

Coopersville, town (1990 pop. 3,421), Ottawa co., SW Mich., 15 mi/24 km N of Grand Rapids, and 18 mi/29 km SE of Muskegon; 43°04′N 85°55′W. In orchard and farm area (apples, peaches, grain; poultry; dairy prods.); food processing; mfg. (paper, wood, and fabricated metal prods., including bird houses and feeders). Settled 1845; inc. 1871.

Cooperton, village (1990 pop. 15), Kiowa co., SW Okla., 16 mi/26 km SE of Hobart, W of Wichita Mts; 34°51′N 98°52′W. In agr. area. Tom Steed L. reservoir and Great Plains State Park to SW; Wichita Mts. Natl. Wildlife Refuge to SE.

Coos 1 (KO-waws), county (□ 1,831 sq mi/4,742 sq km; 1990 pop. 34,828), N N.H., bounded W by Connecticut R. (forms Vt. state line), bounded NW and N by Can. (Que.), bounded E by Maine state line; ⊙ Lancaster; 44°41′N 71°17′W. Recreational and forestry region, including Presidential Range of White Mts. and parts of White Mt. Natl. Forest in S and S center, with many resorts; hunting, fishing in Connecticut Lakes region in N. Mfg. (pulp and paper, wood prods.) in Berlin and Groveton; timber, agr. (potatoes, nursery crops, vegetables, hay, apples; cattle, poultry; dairying). Drained by Androscoggin (water power), Connecticut, and Upper Ammonoosuc rivers. Coleman and L. Francis state parks in N. Nash Stream State Forest and Cape Horn State Forest in W center; Forest L. State Park and Weeks State Park in SW; Connecticut Lakes State Forest in N; Umbagog L. on E boundary (with Maine); Milan Hill and Nansen Wayside state parks in N center; Dixville Notch State Park in N center. Formed 1803. **2** (KOOZ), county (□ 1,806 sq mi/4,678 sq km; 1990 pop. 60,273), SW Oregon; ⊙ Coquille; 43°10′N 124°05′W. Bounded W by the Pacific Ocean. Indented in W by Coos Bay, bow-shaped estuary of Coos R., drained by Coquille R. and its N, S, E, and middle forks. Dairy prods. Food processing. Timber, millwork. Poultry, sheep, cattle. Fisheries. Cranberries. Coast Range in E. Part of Elliott State Forest in NE; part of Siskiyou Natl. Forest in S; S part of Oregon Dunes Natl. Recreational Area in NW. Numerous state parks, including William M. Tugman in NW, Cape Arago and Bandon in W, Coquille Myrtle Grove in S. Formed 1853.

Coos Bay (KOOZ), city (1990 pop. 15,076), Coos co., SW Oregon, a port of entry on Coos Bay, 70 mi/113 km SW of Eugene; 43°22′N 124°13′W. City extends across peninsula on S side of Coos Bay, formed by curve in estuary. Town of North Bend adjoins Coos Bay in N. Pacific Ocean and mouth of Coos Bay 5 mi/8 km to W. Mfg. (frozen shrimp and crab, seafood processing; wood prods., printing and publishing, plastic prods., fabricated metal prods., shipbuilding). Shipping, tourism, fishing, and canning are important industries. It is a worldwide lumber-shipping port that ships many of its prods. to Japan. Due to environmental concerns, however, Coos Bay industry has experienced a depressed market and sluggish growth since the 1980s. Southwestern Oregon Community Col. is here. Golden and Silver Falls State Park and Elliott State Forest to NE; Oregon Dunes Natl. Recreation Area to N. Seven Devils Wayside, Cape Arago, Sunset Bay, and Shore Acres state parks to SW. Founded 1854 as Marshfield, inc. 1874, renamed 1944.

Coos Bay (KOOZ), SW Oregon, an indentation in Pacific coast, 13 mi/21 km long, c.1 mi/1.6 km wide. Coos River rises in Coast Range, flows 60 mi/97 km W, entering the bay opposite Coos Bay city. North Bend and Coos Bay are trade and shipping points.

Coos River, Oregon: see COOS BAY, bay.

Coosa (KOO-suh), county (□ 666 sq mi/1,725 sq km; 1990 pop. 11,063), E central Ala.; ⊙ Rockford. Bounded W by Coosa R. Hay, corn; livestock; marble, granite; lumber; textiles. Formed 1832.

Coosa (KOO-suh), river, 286 mi/460 km long, rising in NW Ga. and flowing SW through E Ala., joining the Tallapoosa near Montgomery, Ala., to form the Alabama R.; 34°15′N 85°10′W. Locks and dams make the river navigable for barges to Rome, Ga. Jordan, Lay, and Mitchell dams on the river generate electricity.

Coosa Pines, Ala.: see CHILDERSBURG.

Coosaw River (KOO-suh), Beaufort co., S S.C., tidal channel bet. head of Broad R. channel (W) and St. Helena Sound (E), N of Port Royal and Lady's Isl.; E part of river is part of Intracoastal Waterway. Also called Coosa River.

Coosawattee River (koo-suh-WAH-tee), c.50 mi/ 80 km long, N Ga.; formed at Ellijay by union of small Ellijay and Cartecay rivers, flows WSW to confluence with Conasauga R., 3 mi/4.8 km NE of Calhoun, forming Oostanaula R.; 34°41′N 84°29′W.

Coosawhatchie River (kooz-uh-WAH-chee), c.50 mi/ 80 km long, S S.C.; rises W of Allendale in Allendale co., flows SE to Broad R., tidal channel N of Port Royal Sound.

Cooter (KOO-tuhr), town (1990 pop. 451), Pemiscot co., in the bootheel of extreme SE Mo., near Mississippi R., 13 mi/21 km SW of Caruthersville; 36°02′N 89°48′W. Cotton, rice, corn, soybeans.

Copainalá (ko-pah-ee-nah-LAH), city (1990 pop. 4,792) and township, Chiapas, S Mexico, in Chiapas Valley, 23 mi/37 km NNW of Tuxtla Gutiérrez; 17°08′N 93°11′W. Corn, sugarcane, tobacco, fruit; livestock. A Zoque Indian town.

Copake (KO-paik), village (1990 pop. 1,200), Columbia co., SE N.Y., 15 mi/24 km SE of Hudson; 42°07′N 73°32′W. In summer recreational area. Copake Falls village is just NE. Taconic State Park is 1 mi/1.6 km E. Copake L. (c.1.5 mi/2.4 km long) is c.2 mi/3.2 km NW.

Copala (ko-PA-lah), town (1990 pop. 5,772), Guerrero, SW Mexico, in Pacific lowland, 55 mi/89 km E of Acapulco de Juárez; 16°38′N 99°04′W. Sugarcane, cotton, coffee, fruit; livestock.

Copalillo (ko-pa-LEE-yo), town (1990 pop. 4,896), Guerrero, SW Mexico, on affluent of Mezcala R. (Río Balsas system), 40 mi/64 km NE of Chilpancingo de los Bravo; 18°01′N 99°09′W. Cereals, sugarcane, fruit, forest prods. (vanilla, resins).

Copalis Beach (kuh-PAL-les), uninc. town (1990 pop. 900), Grays Harbor co., W Wash., 15 mi/24 km NW of Hoquiam, on Pacific Ocean, at mouth of Copalis R. Timber. Beach resort area. Griffith-Priday and Pacific Beach state parks to N.

Copan (ko-PAN), town (1990 pop. 809), Wash. co., NE Okla., 10 mi/16 km N of Bartlesville; 36°53′N 95°55′W. In farm area. Copan L. reservoir to W; L. Hulah reservoir and Wah-Sha-She State Park farther to W in Osage co.

Copanatoyac (ko-pa-na-TO-yahk), town (1990 pop. 1,720), Guerrero, SW Mexico, in Sierra Madre del Sur, 38 mi/61 km SE of Chilapa de Alvarez. Cereals, fruit; livestock.

Copándaro de Galeana (ko-PAHN-dah-ro de ga-lai-AHN-ah), town (1990 pop. 3,836), ⊙ Copándaro municipio, in E central Michóacan, Mexico, near Cuitzco lake, 14 mi/22 km N of morelia. Corn, wheat, chiles; horticulture.

Copano Bay, Texas: see ARANSAS BAY.

Cope, village (1990 pop. 124), Orangeburg co., S central S.C., 11 mi/18 km SW of Orangeburg near Edisto R; 33°22′N 81°00′W. Agr. includes cotton, peanuts, grain; poultry, livestock.

Copeland, village (1990 pop. 290), Gray co., SW Kansas, 23 mi/37 km SW of Cimarron; 37°32′N 100°37′W. In grain area.

Copemish (KOP-mish), village (1990 pop. 222), Manistee co., NW Mich., on small Bear Creek, and 26 mi/ 42 km NE of Manistee; 44°28′N 85°55′W. In agr. area; mfg. (construction materials, plastic prods.). Crystal Mts. Ski Area to NW.

Copenhagen (KO-pen-HAI-guhn), village (☐ 1 sq mi/ 2.6 sq km; 1990 pop. 876), Lewis co., N central N.Y., 12 mi/19 km ESE of Watertown; 43°53′N 75°40′W. In dairying, cheese-making, and timber area.

Copiague, uninc. residential town (☐ 3 sq mi/7.8 sq km; 1990 pop. 20,769), Suffolk co., SE N.Y., on S shore of L.I.; 40°40′N 73°23′W.

Copiah (kuh-PEI-uh), county (☐ 779 sq mi/2,018 sq km;

1990 pop. 27,592), SW Miss.; ⊙ Hazlehurst; 31°51′N 90°26′W. Bounded E by Pearl R.; also drained by Homochitto R. and Bayou Pierre. Agr. (cotton, corn, soybeans; cattle, poultry; dairying; timber); sand and gravel. Part of Homochitto Natl. Forest in SW corner. Formed 1823.

Coplay (KO-plai), borough (1990 pop. 3,267), Lehigh co., E Pa., residential suburb, 6 mi/9.7 km NNW of downtown Allentown, on Lehigh R.; 40°40′N 75°30′W. RR junction. Light mfg. Agr. area (apples, corn; poultry, livestock; dairying). Cement Industry Mus. at former cement industrial site.

Copleston (KAH-puhlz-tuhn), village, S Ont., Canada, 3 mi/5 km NNW of Petrolia; 42°55′N 82°10′W. Former oil boom area, late 1800s and early 1900s.

Coplin, plantation (1990 pop. 120), Franklin co., W central Maine, on branch of Carrabassett R., and 35 mi/ 56 km NNW of Farmington; 45°04′N 70°28′W. In hunting area.

Coppel, city (1990 pop. 16,881), Dallas and Denton cos., N Texas, suburb, 16 mi/26 km NW of downtown Dallas; 32°57′N 96°59′W. Mfg. (transportation equip., fabricated metal prods., paper prods.). Bounded by Denton Creek (N), Elm Fork Trinity R. (E); drained by Grapevine Creek (S). Dallas–Fort Worth Internatl. Airport to SW. North L. reservoir to S.

Copper, river, c.300 mi/480 km long, rising in the Wrangell Mts., SE Alaska, and flowing S through the Chugach Mts. to the Gulf of Alaska. The indigenous pop. obtained copper from the deposits near the upper river; these deposits attracted the attention of the Russians and later the Americans, but exploration was difficult because of the river's currents and the glaciers near its mouth. The great Kennecott mine (discovered 1898) was developed and made reachable by the building (1908–1911) of the Copper R. and Northwestern RR from Cordova, through Chiting to Kennecott and McCarthy on the Chitina R., which followed the river along part of its lower valley. The mine was abandoned in 1938.

Copper Canyon, valley, Chihuahua, Mexico. One part of the Sierra Tarahumara system of canyons in the Sierra Madre Occidental that forms the largest canyon complex in N. Amer. and rivals the Grand Canyon in depth. Copper Canyon is the section of the Sierra Tarahumara canyon system that is traversed by the Chihuahua-Pacific RR, which makes it a prime tourist attraction. The canyon is named for the copper hue of the canyon walls.

Copper Center, village (1990 pop. 449), S Alaska, on Copper R., at mouth of Klutina R., and 70 mi/113 km NNE of Valdez, on Richardson Highway; 61°58′N 145°20′W. Tourism. Settled 1896, it became important when copper was discovered (1898) in region.

Copper City, village (1990 pop. 198), Houghton co., NW Upper Peninsula, Mich., 14 mi/23 km NE of Houghton, on Keweenaw Peninsula; 47°16′N 88°23′W.

Copper Cliff, town, SE central Ont., Canada, 4 mi/6 km WSW of Sudbury; 46°28′N 81°04′W. Part of city of Sudbury. World's largest known concentration of nickel. Nickel mining and smelting. Copper refinery, one of largest in Commonwealth. Mfg. (concrete, fabricated metal). Site of 30 ft/9 m high Big Nickel, replica of 1951 Can. 5-cent piece, located on N side of Trans-Can. Highway.

Copper Falls State Park (☐ 3.9 sq mi/10.1 sq km), Ashland co., N Wis., 4 mi/6.4 km N of Mellen, in wooded area. Central features are 4 spectacular falls, including Copper Falls (40 ft/12 m high) on Bad R.

Copper Harbor, village, Keweenaw co., Upper Peninsula, Mich., on L. Superior and 19 mi/31 km ENE of Eagle R.; 47°28′N 87°53′W. Terminus of U.S. Highway 41 (and road system) 3 mi/4.8 km E. Passenger ferry to Rock Harbor Lodge, Isle Royale Natl. Park. Old Fort Wilkins (1844–1863) is to E, Fort Wilkins State Park. Popular Copper Harbor Lodge 3 mi/4.8 km SW of town.

Copper Mountain, village, S B.C., Canada, in Cascade Mts., on Similkameen R., and 45 mi/72 km WSW of Penticton; 49°19′N 120°32′W. Copper mining.

Copper Range, in Wis. and Mich., trap-rock ridge traceable for c.300 mi/483 km from Minn.-Wis. state line NE of Minneapolis, across NW Wis. and NW Upper Peninsula of Mich. near its Superior shore, and along the backbone of Keweenaw Peninsula (where it is most prominent) to its tip. On Keweenaw Peninsula (where it is sometimes called Keweenaw Range or Trap Range), its elev. is generally c.1,300 ft/396 m; rises to 1,534 ft/ 468 m (Mt. Horace Greeley) S of Eagle Harbor. Here range is heart of the Mich. "copper country," where huge quantities of copper, a large part of U.S. supply, were produced in late 19th and early 20th cent.; peak production was in 1916–1917. Timms Hill (1,951 ft/ 595 m), Price co., Wis.

Copper River, village, W B.C., Canada, on Skeena R., and 5 mi/8 km ENE of Terrace; 54°33′N 128°29′W. Logging; cattle. Also called Zymoetz River (ZI-mets).

Copper River Highway, 48 mi/77 km long, S Alaska, from Cordova, on Orca Street, in W to Miles L., 33 mi/ 53 km ENE. Designated as part of Alaska Route 10; N section of Route 10 (Edgerton Highway) terminates at Chitina, 62 mi/100 km N of Miles L. Copper R. Highway is linked to remainder of Alaska highway system by ferry from Cordova. The highway runs parallel to Gulf of Alaska, Pacific Ocean, about 5 mi/8 km inland, at base of Chugach Mts. In its short course, it crosses the braided deltas of Scott and Sheridan glaciers as it heads E, then makes a 10 mi/16 km crossing of the Copper R. delta via Long Isl., before terminating at the Million Dollar Bridge, which crosses Copper R. at its exit from Miles L. Construction on the highway began in 1945, following the bed of the abandoned Copper R. and Northwestern RR. The Good Friday Earthquake in 1964 damaged the road and knocked out the N span of the bridge. Although repairs were made on the road, the bridge was only temporarily repaired and construction never resumed. Only W part is paved.

Copperas Cove, town (1990 pop. 24,079), Coryell co., central Texas, suburb, 12 mi/19 km W of Killern; 31°07′N 97°54′W. Elev. 1,086 ft/331 m. A growing farm and ranch center, agr. area to W (livestock); light mfg. Adjoins large Fort Hood Military Reservation on its W side, to which it owes much of its existence since est. in 1942.

Coppercrown Mountain (10,218 ft/3,114 m), SE B.C., Canada, in Selkirk Mts., 70 mi/113 km NE of Nelson; 50°18′N 116°22′W.

Copperhill, city (1990 pop. 362), Polk co., SE Tenn., near Ga.-N.C.-Tenn. border, on Ocoee R. (here dammed), and 50 mi/80 km E of Chattanooga, in copper-mining region; 34°59′N 84°22′W. Major whitewater recreation area and site of the 1996 Summer Olympics kayaking events.

Coppermine, town (1991 pop. 1,059), N Mackenzie dist., N.W.T., Canada, on Coronation Gulf of the Beaufort Sea, at mouth of Coppermine R.; 67°40′N 115°05′W. Fishing, hunting, trapping. Trading post; govt. radio and meteorological station, Royal Can. Mounted Police post; site of Anglican and R.C. missions. Extensive copper deposits in region. Hudson's Bay Company store opened 1927; Anglican mission built 1928. Scheduled air service.

Coppermine River, 525 mi/845 km long, rising in Lac de Gras, Fort Smith Region, N.W.T., Canada, and winding NW to enter the Arctic Ocean at Coronation Gulf. Coppermine, a trading post, is at its mouth.

Coppock, town (1990 pop. 50), on Henry-Jefferson-Wash. co. line, SE Iowa, on Skunk R., and 9 mi/14.5 km S of Wash.; 41°09′N 91°42′W. Limestone quarry.

Coquihalla Highway (KO-kee-AH-lah), 190 mi/306 km long, SW B.C., Canada; runs from Hope in S to 4 mi/ 6 km W of Kamloops in N. Completed in 1987, the 4-lane divided toll highway provides alternative to Fraser Canyon route. Engineering feat includes wildlife underpasses, deep mt. road cuts.

Coquille (ko-KEEL), town (1990 pop. 4,121), ⊙ Coos co., SW Oregon, on Coquille R., and 12 mi/19 km S of Coos Bay, 10 mi/16 km W of Pacific Ocean; 43°10′N 124°10′W. Elev. 45 ft/14 m. Dairy prods; timber, veneer.

Fish hatcheries to E. Maria C. Jackson State Park to E. Inc. 1901.

Coquille River (ko-KEEL), 35 mi/56 km long, SW Oregon; formed by confluence of North Fork with South Fork near Myrtle Point; flows NW past Coquille and W through Klamath Mts. (Coast Range) to Pacific Ocean at Brandon. The North Fork (42 mi/68 km) rises in NE Coos co. and flows generally SW, receiving East Fork (c.30 mi/48 km long); the South Fork (64 mi/103 km long) rises in Siskiyou Natl. Forest, S Coos co., and flows N, receiving Middle Fork (c.40 mi/64 km long).

Coquimatlán (ko-kee-mah-TLAHN), town (1990 pop. 9,702), ⊙ Coquimatlán municipio, Colima, W Mexico, on affluent of Armería R., and 9 mi/14.5 km SW of Colima. Elev. 899 ft/274 m. On RR. Rice, corn, beans, sugarcane, coffee, fruit; livestock.

Coquitlam, city (1991 pop. 84,021), SW B.C., Canada, residential suburb, 12 mi/19 km E of downtown Vancouver. Located bet. E end of Burrard Inlet on N and Fraser R. on S. Rapid growth in 1970s and 1980s. Wineries; mfg. (prepared foods, electrical machinery); petroleum refinery.

Corail (ko-REI), town (1982 pop. 1,991), Grande-Anse dept., SW Haiti, on NW coast of Jacmel Peninsula, 16 mi/26 km ESE of Jérémie; 18°34'N 73°53'W. Agr. (manioc, coffee, sugarcane, cacao); bauxite deposits nearby. Fishing port.

Coral Gables, city (□ 17 sq mi/44 sq km; 1990 pop. 40,091), Dade co., SE Fla., 5 mi/8 km SW of Miami; 25°41'N 80°15'W. Founded at the height of the Fla. land boom, Coral Gables is a splendid example of a planned city. Originally exclusively residential, a major business area has grown and contains many inter-Amer. (in particular Latin Amer.) offices of large corporations. Its proximity to Miami Internatl. Airport aids the city's development and promotes regional tourism. The Univ. of Miami is in Coral Gables. Inc. 1925.

Coral Harbour, trading post (1991 pop. 578), S Southampton Isl., E Keewatin Dist., N.W.T., Canada, on Hudson Bay; 64°07'N 83°14'W. Furs (polar bear, fox, seal); walrus and seal hunting. Royal Can. Mounted Police post. Site of Anglican and R.C. missions. Hudson's Bay Company store est. 1924. Coral Harbour U.S. Air Force Base is 5 mi/8 km NW, at Munn Bay; 64°09'N 83°17'W. Est. during World War II as base. Scheduled air service.

Coral Springs, city (□ 23 sq mi/60 sq km; 1990 pop. 79,443), Broward co., SE Fla.; 26°16'N 80°15'W. Largely residential, it is a city that has grown rapidly along with the S Fla. and Fort Lauderdale area. The pop. of Coral Springs nearly doubled bet. 1980 and 1990. Inc. 1963.

Coralville, town (1990 pop. 10,347), Johnson co., E Iowa, a suburb of Iowa City, adjoins it 2 mi/3.2 km to NW of downtown on Iowa R.; 41°41'N 91°35'W. Mfg. (electronic equip.). Univ. of Iowa Oakdale campus and Iowa Security Medical Facililty are here. Coralville L. (Iowa R.) to NE; Amana Colonies 20 mi/32 km to NW.

Coralville Reservoir, reservoir, Johnson Co., E Iowa, on Iowa R., 4 mi/6.4 km N of Iowa City/Coralville; 41°42'N 91°31'W. Max. capacity 585,000 acre-ft.; c.15 mi/24 km long. Formed by Coralville Dam (78 ft/24 m high), built (1958) by the Army Corps of Engineers for flood control. L. McBride State Park to NE.

Coram (KOR-uhm), village (1990 pop. 330), Flathead co., NW Mont., on Flathead R., and 22 mi/35 km NNE of Kalispell. Teakettle Mt. to W, Flathead Range to E. Surrounded by Flathead Natl. Forest. Part of Flathead Natl. Wild and Scenic R. to NE; Glacier Natl. Park to NE.

Coraopolis (ko-rai-AH-po-lis), borough (1990 pop. 6,747), Allegheny co., W Pa., industrial suburb, 10 mi/16 km NW of downtown Pittsburgh, on Ohio R. (bridged to Neville Isl.); 40°30'N 80°09'W. Mfg. (cement prods., printing, apparel; fabricated metal prods., structural steel, aluminum and clay refractories). Pittsburgh Internatl. Airport to W; Robert Morris Col. to W. Settled c.1760, inc. 1886.

Corazal Point (ko-RAH-zahl), Trinidad, Trinidad and Tobago, 12 mi/19 km NE of Port-of-Spain. Westernmost point along the N range.

Corbin, town (1990 pop. 7,419), Knox and Whitley cos., SE Ky., in Cumberland foothills, near Laurel R., 33 mi/53 km NW of Middlesboro; 36°56'N 84°06'W. RR junction; trade center; shipping point for bituminous-coal mining; agr. (corn, tobacco; livestock), and timber area; mfg. (paper prods., transportation equip., fabricated metal prods., consumer goods, construction materials, crude oil and natural gas processing, printing and publishing). London-Corbin Airport 8 mi/12.9 km N, near London. The original Kentucky Fried Chicken restaurant still open here. Cumberland Falls Resort State Park to SW, Levi Jackson Wilderness Road State Park to NE; Laural River L. reservoir and Daniel Boone Natl. Forest to W. Situated on old Wilderness Road, Corbin developed with RR's arrival (1883); inc. 1894.

Corbin, village, SE B.C., Canada, near Alta. border, in Rocky Mts., 18 mi/29 km E of Fernie; 49°30'N 114°44'W. Coal mining.

Corbin City (KOR-bin) (1990 pop. 412), Atlantic co., SE N.J., on Tuckahoe R., and 18 mi/29 km WSW of Atlantic City, in cranberry region; 39°17'N 74°42'W.

Corcoran, city (1990 pop. 13,364), Kings co., S central Calif., in San Joaquin Valley, 15 mi/24 km S of Hanford, near Cross Creek; 36°05'N 119°34'W. RR junction. Agr. (grapes, plums, peaches, nectarines; pistachios, almonds; grain; cotton); winery. Tulare L. irrigation reservoir is just W. Kern Natl. Wildlife Refuge to S, Pixley Natl. Wildlife refuge to SE; Colonel Allensworth State Historical Park to SE. Inc. 1914.

Corcoran (KOR-kuh-ruhn), town (1990 pop. 5,199), Hennepin co., E Minn., residential suburb, 17 mi/27 km NW of downtown Minneapolis, SE of Crow R.; 45°07'N 93°35'W. Mfg. (fabricated metal prods.); agr. (dairying; poultry; grain, nursery prods.). Crow Hassan Recreation Park to NW.

Corcoran, Mount, Calif.: see LANGLEY, MOUNT.

Cordaville, Mass.: see SOUTHBORO.

Cordele (kor-DEEL), city (1990 pop. 10,321), ⊙ Crisp co., S central Ga.; 31°58'N 83°46'W. It is a shipping, commercial, and processing center. Mfg. include machinery, apparel, peanut production and processing, pecan processing, asphalt, fiberglass prods.; agr. prods. include watermelons, cantaloupes, and corn; timber area. Annual Watermelon Days festival. Known as the Watermelon Capital of the World. Founded and inc. 1888.

Cordell, town, ⊙ Washita co., W Okla., 16 mi/26 km S of Clinton. Elev. 1,560 ft/475 m. In agr. area (cotton, wheat; livestock). Cotton ginning; mfg. (textiles, machinery).

Cordell Hull Lake, reservoir, Smith, Jackson, and Clay cos., N Tenn., on Cumberland R., 20 mi/32 km ENE of Lebanon; 36°16'N 85°55'W. Max. capacity 310,900 acre-ft; c.65 mi/105 km long. E arm formed by Obey R. Formed by Cordell Hull Dam (83 ft/25 m high), built (1973) by the Army Corps of Engineers for navigation, flood control, and power generation.

Corder, city (1990 pop. 485), Lafayette co., W central Mo., near Missouri R., 14 mi/23 km SE of Lexington; 39°06'N 93°38'W. Corn, wheat; cattle.

Córdoba (KOR-do-bah), city (1990 pop. 130,695) and township, Veracruz state, E central Mexico, on RR, on Mexico Hwy. 150; 18°55'N 96°55'W. It is the commercial and processing center of a fertile coffee, sugarcane, and tropical fruit region. Sugar milling is the chief industry. The city is also a popular tourist spot. Córdoba was founded in 1617. The Spanish viceroy O'Donojú and the Mexican revolutionary Agustín de Iturbide signed a treaty here in 1821 that established Mexico's independence. The city suffered extensive damage in 1973 from an earthquake.

Cordova 1 (kor-DO-vuh), town (1990 pop. 2,623), Walker co., NW central Ala., on Mulberry Fork, 8 mi/12.9 km SE of Jasper; 33°45'N 87°11'W. In coal area; steel fabrication. Inc. 1902. **2** town (1990 pop. 2,110), S Alaska, on Prince William Sound, 150 mi/241 km ESE of Anchorage; 60°33'N 145°46'W. Fishing; fish cannery, cold-storage plant. Has hosp. Founded 1908 as terminus of 197-mi/317-km Copper R. and Northwestern RR (ceased operations 1938), serving copper-mining region, notably Kennicott area. Harbor was explored and named by Spaniards (1792).

Cordova 1 (kor-DO-vuh), village (1990 pop. 638), Rock Isl. co., NW Ill., on the Mississippi, and 18 mi/29 km NE of Rock Isl.; 41°40'N 90°19'W. In agr. area. **2** village (1990 pop. 147), Seward co., SE Nebr., 19 mi/31 km SW of Seward, near West Fork of Big Blue R; 40°43'N 97°20'W. **3** uninc. village, Richmond co., S N.C., 3 mi/4.8 km SW of Rockingham, near Pee Dee (Great Pee Dee) R. Timber; tobacco, cotton, grain; livestock; mfg. (textiles, paper prods.). **4** village (1990 pop. 135), Orangeburg co., central S.C., 5 mi/8 km SW of Orangeburg; 33°26'N 80°55'W. Agr. includes cotton, corn, peanuts; poultry.

Cordova (1990 pop. 36,743), suburb, Shelby Co., SW Tenn., E of Memphis. Part inc. by Memphis in 1990.

Cordova Mines (KOR-do-vuh), village, SE Ont., Canada, 32 mi/51 km NW of Belleville; 44°33'N 80°27'W. Diatomite mining.

Core Banks, E N.C., long narrow sand barrier isl. c. 30 mi/48 km long, 1 mi/1.6 km wide, periodically broken by hurricanes and other storms. Part of the Outer Banks lying bet. Core Sound (NW) and the Atlantic Ocean and extends from Drum Inlet SW to Cape Lookout (lighthouse); S end of bank has a NW hook-shape. Core Sound extends c.30 mi/48 km from Pamlico Sound NE to Beaufort harbor (SW). Part of Cape Lookout Natl. Seashore.

Corell (kor-REL), village (1990 pop. 60), Big Stone co., SW Minn., 15 mi/24 km ESE of Ortonville. Grain; hogs. Marsh L. (Minnesota R.) to S, in Lac qui Parle Wildlife Area; Artichoke L. to N.

Corfu (KOR-fyoo), village (1990 pop. 755), Genesee co., W N.Y., 12 mi/19 km WSW of Batavia; 42°57'N 78°24'W.

Corinna (kor-IN-nuh), town (1990 pop. 2,196), Penobscot co., S central Maine, 25 mi/40 km WNW of Bangor; 44°57'N 69°15'W. Wood prods. Inc. 1816.

Corinne (kor-IN), village (1990 pop. 639), Box Elder co., N Utah, 5 mi/8 km NW of Brigham City near Bear R., N of its entrance to Bear R. Bay, Great Salt L.; 41°32'N 112°07'W. Elev. 4,238 ft/1,292 m. Wheat, barley, alfalfa; fruit, vegetables, sugar beets; dairying; cattle, sheep. Public Shooting Grounds Waterfowl Management Area to W; Bear R. Bay Migratory Bird Refuge to SW. Est. 1869 with construction of RR, same year as Golden Spike event (completion of 1st transcontinental RR, 25 mi/40 km to WNW).

Corinth (KO-rinth), city (1990 pop. 11,820), ⊙ Alcorn co., extreme NE Miss., 85 mi/137 km ESE of Memphis, Tenn., near the Tenn. state line; 34°56'N 88°31'W. RR junction. In an agr. area (cotton, corn, soybeans; cattle, hogs); mfg. (construction materials; machinery; furniture; apparel; transportation equip.; prepared foods;, wood, vinyl, and paper prods.; meat processing; consumer prods.). During the Civil War, Corinth was a strategic RR center, abandoned to Gen. H. W. Halleck's Union Army in May 1862, after the battle of Shiloh. General Rosecrans repulsed the Confederates under generals Earl Van Doren and Sterling Price in heavy fighting here, Oct. 3–4, 1862. Corinth Natl. Cemetery (est. 1866) has 6,000 graves. NE Miss. Mus.; Bastery Rubinette Civil War battle site. Founded c.1855.

Corinth 1 town (1990 pop. 136), Heard co., W Ga., 13 mi/21 km NNE of La Grange; 33°14'N 84°56'W. **2** town (1990 pop. 1,244), Orange co., E central Vt., 11 mi/18 km ENE of Chelsea; 44°01'N 72°17'W.

Corinth 1 village (1990 pop. 137), Grant co., N Ky., 10 mi/16 km S of Williamstown, in Bluegrass agr. region; 38°30'N 84°33'W. **2** village (□ 1 sq mi/2.6 sq km; 1990 pop. 2,760), Saratoga co., E N.Y., in the Adirondack foothills, on the Hudson R., and 11 mi/18 km SW of Glens Falls; 43°15'N 73°49'W. Mfg. of metal lockers, gym bleachers; paper milling. Inc. 1886.

Corinth, township (1990 pop. 2,177), Penobscot co., S central Maine, 18 mi/29 km NW of Bangor; 44°58'N 69°00'W. In agr., recreational area. Includes village of East Corinth, hamlets of West Corinth and South Corinth.

Cormack's Lake, SW N.F., Canada, 50 mi/80 km S of Corner Brook; 6 mi/10 km long, 2 mi/3 km wide.

Cormorant Island, Canada: see ALERT BAY.

Cormorant Lake (□ 141 sq mi/365 sq km), NW Man., Canada, 30 mi/48 km NE of the Pas; 18 mi/29 km long, 14 mi/23 km wide.

Cormorant Lake (KOR-muh-ruhnt), Becker co., W Minn., 9 mi/14.5 km WSW of Detroit Lakes city; 4.5 mi/7.2 km long, 2.5 mi/4 km wide; 46°46′N 96°03′W. Just W is Upper Cormorant L. (2.5 mi/4 km long, 1 mi/1.6 km wide). This and adjacent lakes have no definable outflow, common with W Minn. lakes. Little Cormorant L. to NE. Also known as Big Cormorant L.

Corn, village (1990 pop. 548), Washita co., W central Okla., 10 mi/16 km SE of Clinton, near Washita R.; 35°22′N 98°46′W. Agr. area. Crowder L. State Park to E.

Corn Belt, major agr. region of the U.S. Midwest where corn acreage once exceeded that of any other crop. It is now commonly called the Feed Grains and Livestock Belt. Located in the north central plains, it is centered in Iowa and Illinois and extends into S Minn., SE S.Dak., E Nebr., NE Kansas, N Mo., Ind., and W Ohio. Large-scale commercial and mechanized farming prevails in this region of deep, fertile, well-drained soils and long, hot, humid summers. The belt produces much of the U.S. corn crop, but agr. has diversified; soybeans are an important yield. Winter wheat and alfalfa are also significant crops in the area.

Cornelia (kor-NEEL-yuh), town (1990 pop. 3,219), Habersham co., NE Ga., 12 mi/19 km WSW of Toccoa; 34°31′N 83°32′W. Trade center for apple-growing dist.; mfg. of textiles and apparel; concrete prods., poultry processing, fabricated metal prods., go-carts, wooden materials for furniture building. Inc. 1887.

Cornelius 1 (kor-NEEL-yuhs), town (1990 pop. 2,581), Meckenburg co., S N.C., 17 mi/27 km N of Charlotte; 35°28′N 80°52′W. Tobacco, grain, soybeans; livestock; mfg. (plastic prods., wood prods., machinery, clocks). L. Norman reservoir (Catamba R.) to W. Settled 1880; inc. 1905. **2** town (1990 pop. 6,148), Wash. co., NW Oregon, suburb, 18 mi/29 km W of Portland, and 4 mi/6.4 km W of Hillsboro, near Tualatin R.; 45°31′N 123°02′W. Fruit, nuts, berries; poultry; dairy prods.

Cornell, town (1990 pop. 1,541), Chippewa co., W central Wis., on Chippewa R., and 19 mi/31 km NE of Chippewa Falls; 45°09′N 91°09′W. RR spur terminus. In dairying region; mfg. (paper, wood prods., construction materials). Brunet Isl. State Park nearby. Inc. 1913.

Cornell, village (1990 pop. 556), Livingston co., central Ill., near Vermilion R., 9 mi/14.5 km NNW of Pontiac; 40°59′N 88°43′W. In agr. area.

Corner Brook, city (1991 pop. 22,410), W central N.F., Canada, on the Humber R.; 48°57′N 57°56′W. It is N.F.'s 2d-largest city and has a large pulp and paper mill. Other industries include lumbering, salmon fishing, and quarrying. Nearby is Gros Morne Natl. Park.

Cornersville, town (1990 pop. 683), Marshall co., central Tenn., 8 mi/13 km SW of Lewisburg; 35°22′N 86°50′W. In farm area.

Cornettsville (KORN-ets-vil), uninc. village, Perry co., SE Ky., 10 mi/16 km S of Hazard, on North Fork of Kentucky R. Tobacco. Bituminous coal. Mfg. (pontoon boats).

Corney Bayou (KOR-nee), c.70 mi/113 km long, in SW Ark. and N La.; rises in E of Magnolia, Columbia co., Ark.; flows SE, into Claiborne and Union parishes, La., emptying into Bayou d'Arbonne L. just W of Farmerville. Dam impounds Corney L. (c.5 mi/8 km long) 7 mi/11.3 km NW of Bernice, La., in unit of Kisatchie Natl. Forest; 32°52′N 92°45′W.

Corney Lake, La.: see CORNEY BAYOU.

Cornfield Point, peninsula in Old Saybrook town, S Conn., at W side of Connecticut R. mouth, on Long Isl. Sound; 2.5 mi/4 km long. Summer resort, beaches; a residential section of Old Saybrook.

Cornillon (kor-nee-YONG) or **Grand-Bois**, town (1982 pop. 3,804), Ouest dept., S Haiti, 25 mi/40 km ENE of Port-au-Prince; 18°40′N 71°57′W. Fruit, coffee, lumber region.

Corning 1 city (1990 pop. 5,870), Tehama co., N Calif., near Sacramento R., 17 mi/27 km S of Red Bluff; 39°56′N 122°11′W. Extensive olive-growing area; walnuts, prunes, grain; cattle; mfg. (canned fruits and vegetables). Woodson Bridge State Recreation Area to E. Tehama Colusa Canal passes to E and W of Sacramento R. Inc. 1907. **2** city, ⊙ Adams co., SW Iowa, on East Nodaway R., and 20 mi/32 km WSW of Creston; 40°59′N 94°44′W. Grain-shipping center; mfg. (feed, concrete, fabricated metal prods., machinery, paper prods.). Bituminous-coal mines, limestone quarries nearby. An Icarian communist settlement, founded 1858 by Etienne Cabet, was situated near here until 1898. L. Icaria reservoir 4 mi N. Plotted 1855, inc. 1871. **3** city (□ 3 sq mi/7.8 sq km; 1990 pop. 11,938), Steuben co., S N.Y., on Chemung R.; 42°08′N 77°03′W. In a dairy and vineyard region. The glass industry, for which the city is famous, began in 1868. Corning, Inc. (formerly Corning Glass) has hq. here. Corning glass prods. are used in advanced technology industries, such as fiber optics. The Corning glass mus. is a major tourist attraction. Corning Community Col. and the Rockwell Mus., the largest collection of Western art in the E U.S. and the world's largest collection of Steuben glass, are located in the city, and a number of state parks are in the area. In 1972 the city was heavily damaged by flooding in the wake of Hurricane Agnes. Settled 1788; inc. as a city 1890.

Corning 1 town (1990 pop. 3,323), ⊙ Clay co., extreme NE Ark., 24 mi/39 km NNW of Paragould, near Black R., at Mo. state line; 36°24′N 90°35′W. In diversified farming area. Mfg. (electrical equip., wood prods., fabricated metal prods.). Fish hatchery. Dave Donaldson–Black R. Wildlife Management Area to SW. **2** town (1990 pop. 88), Holt co., NW Mo., on Missouri R., and 15 mi/24 km NW of Mound City; 40°15′N 95°27′W. Flooded 1993.

Corning 1 village (1990 pop. 142), Nemaha co., NE Kansas, 12 mi/19 km S of Seneca; 39°39′N 96°01′W. Livestock; grain. **2** village (1990 pop. 703), Perry co., central Ohio, 23 mi/37 km S of Zanesville, and on small Sunday Creek; 39°36′N 82°05′W.

Cornish 1 town (1990 pop. 1,178), York co., SW Maine, on Ossipee R., and 23 mi/37 km N of Alfred; 43°46′N 70°49′W. Settled 1776, inc. 1794. **2** town (1990 pop. 1,659), Sullivan co., W N.H., 8 mi/12.9 km N of Claremont; 43°28′N 72°19′W. Bounded W by Connecticut R. (Vt. state line); drained by Mill Brook. Resort, art and literary colony. Mfg. (construction materials, fire trucks). American sculptor Augustus St. Gaudens's estate "Aspet" in Saint-Gaudens Natl. Historic Site, in NW. Salmon P. Chase b. here. Three covered bridges. Croydon Peak (2,781 ft/848 m) on E boundary. Inc. 1763.

Cornish 1 village, Weld co., N Colo., 16 mi/26 km ENE of Greeley on Crow Creek. Elev. 4,712 ft/1,436 m. **2** village (1990 pop. 164), Jefferson co., S Okla., 26 mi/42 km W of Ardmore; 34°09′N 97°35′W. In farm area. **3** village (1990 pop. 205), Cache co., N Utah, near Idaho state line, 20 mi/32 km NNW of Logan and on Bear R.; 41°58′N 111°57′W. Grain; dairying; cattle.

Cornlea (KORN-lee), village (1990 pop. 39), Platte co., E central Nebr., 20 mi/32 km NNW of Columbus, and on branch of Elkhorn R; 41°40′N 97°34′W.

Cornucopia, village, Bayfield co., extreme N Wis., on L. Superior, and 45 mi/72 km NE of Superior. Fishing, resort area. Siskiwit Falls. Mainland shore unit of Apostle Isls. Natl. Lakeshore to NE; Red Cliff Indian Reservation to NE; Chequamegon Natl. Forest.

Cornucopia (kor-nuh-KO-pee-uh), locality, Baker co., NE Oregon, 35 mi/56 km ENE of Baker City on Pine Creek in Wallowa-Whitman Natl. Forest. Elev. 4,800 ft/1,463 m. Important historical mining town.

Cornville 1 uninc. town (1990 pop. 2089), Yavapai co., central Ariz., 30 mi/48 km ENE of Prescott, bet. Verde R. and Oak Creek, in Prescott Natl. Forest. Timber; cattle. Page Springs Fish Hatchery to NE. **2** town (1990 pop. 1,008), Somerset co., central Maine, just N of Skowhegan; 44°51′N 69°40′W. Agr.

Cornwall, county (□ 1,565 sq mi/4,053 sq km; 1991 pop. 555,417), W Jamaica, 18°15′N 77°54′W. Occupies W 3d of the isl. and consists of St. Elizabeth, Trelawny, St. James, Hanover, and Westmoreland parishes. Set up 1758 for assize purposes, it is now a regional unit without administrative status.

Cornwall, mfg. city (1991 pop. 47,137), SE Ont., Canada, on the St. Lawrence R.; 45°01′N 74°44′W. Mfg. includes cotton and rayon textiles, paper, chemicals, furniture, and electronic equipment. The hq. of the Can. St. Lawrence Seaway Authority here. The historical Native Amer. village of St. Regis is across the river on the Que.-N.Y. boundary.

Cornwall 1 town (1990 pop. 1,414), Litchfield co., NW Conn., in Litchfield Hills, on Housatonic R., and 10 mi/16 km W of Torrington; 41°51′N 73°19′W. Agr.; residential community, resorts; fishing; winter sports center at Mohawk Mt. State Park, on Appalachian Trail. Includes villages of Cornwall, Cornwall Center, Cornwall Bridge, Cornwall Hollow, North Cornwall, and West Cornwall. State forests in town include Cathedral Pines, one of finest U.S. stands of white pine. **2** town (1990 pop. 1,101), Addison co., W Vt., near Otter Creek, 5 mi/8 km SW of Middlebury; 43°57′N 73°12′W. Agr.

Cornwall, village (1990 pop. 3,093), Orange co., SE N.Y., near W bank of the Hudson R., 5 mi/8 km S of Newburgh; 41°25′N 74°03′W. Mfg. of apparel. Seat of N.Y. Military Acad., and private schools. Bet. Cornwall and the Hudson R. is village of Cornwall on the Hudson (1990 pop. 3,093) or Cornwall-on-Hudson. Inc. 1884.

Cornwall, borough (1990 pop. 3,231), Lebanon co., SE central Pa., 4 mi/6.4 km SSE of Lebanon; 40°16′N 76°24′W. Rich deposits of magnetite (mining stopped in 1972); mfg. (transportation equip., machinery); winery. Agr. area (grain, soybeans, apples; livestock; dairying). Mt. Hope Estate and Winery to S (Lancaster co.); Cornwall Iron Furnace historical site, operated 1742–1883; Keller Brothers Airport to E. Inc. 1926.

Cornwall Island 1 (□ 720 sq mi/1,865 sq km), N Franklin Dist., N.W.T., Canada, in the Arctic Ocean; separated from Amund Ringnes Isl. (NW) by Hendriksen Strait and from Devon Isl. (S) by Belcher Channel; 77°28′–77°49′N 93°50′–97°15′W. Isl. is 50 mi/80 km long, 8 mi/13 km–24 mi/39 km wide; rises to over 1,000 ft/305 m. **2** SE Ont., Canada, in the St. Lawrence, just S of Cornwall, at W end of L. St. Francis, opposite N.Y.-Que. border; 5 mi/8 km long, 1 mi/2 km wide.

Cornwallis Island (□ 2,592 sq mi/6,713 sq km), Parry Isls., central Franklin Dist., N.W.T., Canada, in the Arctic Ocean, separated from Bathurst Isl. (W) by McDougall Sound and Crozier Strait, from Devon Isl. (E) by Wellington Channel, and from Somerset Isl. (S) by Barrow Strait; 74°37′–75°38′N 93°40′–97°30′W. It is 70 mi/113 km long, 30 mi/48 km–60 mi/97 km wide. On SE coast is U.S.–Can. weather station at Resolute (74°42′N 94°34′W), which is transshipment point to outer isls., making it communications center of Arctic Archipelago.

Cornwallis River, 30 mi/48 km long, W central N.S., Canada; rises in North Mts., flows E, past Kentville, to Minas Basin at Wolfville.

Cornwall-on-Hudson, N.Y.: see CORNWALL.

Cornwells Heights, uninc. town (1990 pop. 2,600), Bucks co., SE Pa., residential suburb, 13 mi/21 km NE of Philadelphia on Poquessing Creek; 40°04′N 74°56′W. Mfg. includes chemicals, machining. Philadelphia Park Race Track (horse racing) to N. Eddington to SE.

Corona, city (1990 pop. 76,095), Riverside co., S Calif., suburb 14 mi WSW of Riverside, and 40 mi ESE of downtown Los Angeles; 33°52′N 117°34′W. The city developed as a primary citrus-fruit producer and shipping center. There is also light mfg. (canned foods, plastic prods., wooden prods., pharmaceuticals). The name Corona ("circle") was derived from the 3-mi/4.8-km circular drive around the city that was once used for car racing. Corona Municipal Airport in N. Calif. Inst. for Men and Women to NE (prisons). L. Mathews Reservoir to E; Prado Flood Control Basin to NW. Cleveland Natl. Forest is on Corona's SW boundary, and Glen Ivy Hot Springs to S; Chino Hills State Park to W. Inc. 1896.

Corona 1 (kuh-RO-nuh), village (1990 pop. 215), Lincoln

co., central N.Mex., 45 mi/72 km NNE of Carrizozo; 34°15′N 105°35′W. Elev. 6,685 ft/2,038 m. Trade and shipping point in agr. area. Sheep, cattle; alfalfa, hay, grain; copper, lead, zinc mining. Gallinas Peak, in Cibola Natl. Forest, 10 mi/16 km W. **2** village (1990 pop. 118), Roberts co., NE S.Dak., 26 mi/42 km SE of Sisseton; 45°19′N 96°46′W. Near N Fork Whetstone Creek.

Corona, section of N Queens borough of N.Y. city, SE N.Y.; 40°45′N 73°52′W. Residential; mfg. Large Hispanic pop.

Corona del Mar, section of Newport Beach city, in SE corner of city, Orange co., S Calif., on Pacific Ocean, E side of entrance to Newport Bay. Extends NE into San Joaquin Hills. Residential area; light mfg. Corona del Mar State Beach is here.

Corona, Villa, Mexico: see VILLA CORONA.

Coronaca (kor-uh-NAHK-uh), village, Greenwood co., NW S.C., 6 mi/9.7 km NE of Greenwood. Produces poultry, livestock, hay. L. Greenwood reservoir and L. Greenwood state park nearby.

Coronado, city (1990 pop. 26,540), San Diego co., S Calif., residential suburb, 2 mi/3.2 km SW of downtown San Diego, on Silver Strand (Coronado) peninsula, which separates San Diego Bay from Pacific Ocean, on the W side of San Diego Bay; 32°38′N 117°10′W. It is a well-known beach resort; mfg. (printing and publishing). The city is linked to San Diego by the Coronado Bay Bridge at the N end of the Silver Strand Peninsula. Bay entrance to W, Coronado (North Island) U.S. Naval Air Station, also to W, and Coronado Naval Amphibious Base to S. Of note is the Hotel del Coronado, a state historical monument. Cabrillo Point and Cabrillo Natl. Monument, on opposite side of bay entrance, to W; Silver Styrand State Beach to S. Inc. 1890.

Coronado (ko-ro-NAH-do), town (1990 pop. 1,142), Chihuahua, N Mexico, on Florido R., and 35 mi/56 km ESE of Hidalgo del Parral; 26°45′N 105°10′W. Cereals, cotton, fruit.

Coronado Islands or **Los Coronados** (ko-ro-NAH-do), small archipelago (□ 3 sq mi/7.8 sq km), off Pacific coast of Lower California, NW Mexico, 20 mi/32 km SSW of San Diego, Calif.; 2 mi/3.2 km long and ½ mi/⅘ km wide; 23°32′N 18°08′W. Four barren rocks, rising to 672 ft/205 m. Guano deposits. Known for deep-sea fishing.

Coronado National Memorial (7 sq mi /18.1 sq km), Cochise co., 15 mi/24 km S of Sierra Vista, on Mex. (Sonora) border, SE Ariz. Bounded N and W by Coronado Natl. Forest. Authorized 1952. Area near Francisco Vásquez de Coronado's point of entry (1540–1542) into what is now the U.S., first Eur. exploration of SW U.S. Includes desert flora and fauna.

Coronados, Los, isls. of Mexico: see CORONADO ISLANDS.

Coronango, Mexico: see SANTA MARÍA CORONANGO.

Coronation, town (1991 pop. 1,184), SE Alta., Canada, 100 mi/161 km E of Red Deer; 52°05′N 111°27′W. Grain elevators, dairying. In coal- and oil-bearing region.

Coronation Gulf, SW Franklin dist., N.W.T., Canada, arm of the Arctic Ocean, separating Victoria Isl. (N) from Mackenzie dist.; 130 mi/209 km long, 50 mi/80 km-70 mi/113 km wide; 67°42′–68°35′N 108°50′–113°30′W. Leads from Dolphin and Union Strait (W) to Queen Maud Gulf (E). Bathurst Inlet extends 120 mi/193 km S. Gulf receives Coppermine R. at Coppermine village. It forms part of Northwest Passage through the Arctic Archipelago; passage was 1st completed by Roald Amundsen, 1903–1906.

Coroneo (ko-ro-NAI-o), city (1990 pop. 2,437) and township, ⊙ Coroneo municipio, Guanajuato, central Mexico, 30 mi/48 km SSE of Querétaro. Elev. 4,777 ft/1,456 m. Grain, corn, wheat, beans, fruit, vegetables, sugarcane; livestock; wood.

Corozal (ko-ro-ZAHL), town (1990 pop. 33,095), N central P.R., 15 mi/24 km SW of San Juan. Industrial and commercial area; light mfg. Agr. (sugarcane, tobacco, coffee, plantains, bananas). Oil and copper deposits in vicinity.

Corporation of Ranson, W.Va.: see RANSON.

Corpus Christi, city (1990 pop. 257,453), ⊙ Nueces co., S Texas, 165 mi/266 km SE of San Antonio; 27°42′N 97°17′W.Elev. 35 ft/11 m. A busy port of entry on Corpus Christi Bay at the entrance to Nueces Bay (an inlet at the mouth of the Nueces R.); the main cargoes handled are cotton, oil, grain, and chemicals. The city is a RR junction and a petroleum and natural gas center, with much heavy industry. It has oil refineries, smelting plants, chemical works, and food-processing establishments. Excellent sports-fishing facilities, beaches, and a mild climate make Corpus Christi a well-known tourist center. It is the gateway to Padre Isl. Natl. Seashore; causeway crosses Laguna Madre to Padre Isl. to SE (Padre and Mustang isls. are long sand barrier isls., connected by land, just N of causeway.) Tradition holds that the bay was named by the Span. explorer Alonzo Alvarez de Pineda, who founded it on Corpus Christi Day in 1519, but there is evidence that it was named instead by the 1st settlers, who arrived from the lower Rio Grande valley in the 1760s. In 1839, Col. H. L. Kinney founded a trading post there, and traders, adventurers, and ne'er-do-wells collected in a raffish colony on land claimed by both Texas and Mexico. The small port and terminus for overland wagon-train traffic boomed during the Mexican War. It was briefly captured by the U.S. navy in the Civil War and later served as a supply and shipping point for sheep and cattle. It developed industrially after the discovery of oil in the area and the completion (1926) of a deepwater channel (Intracoastal Waterway) past Mustang Isl. Its remarkable growth is evidenced by a spectacular bridge (235 ft/72 m high; completed 1959) over the entrance to Nueces Bay, that links Portland to N, and by a large dam on the Nueces R. (L. Corpus Christi, 35 mi/56 km NW) that has increased local water supply. The city has many historical points of interest and is the seat of Del Mar Col. (2 year; E and W campuses) and Texas A and M Univ.—Corpus Christi. Corpus Christi Naval Air Station is on the S shore of Corpus Christi. Mustang Isl. State Park is 14 mi/23 km ESE of downtown, but within city limits; Texas State Aquarium, Greyhound Racetrack, Exposition Hall and Coliseum, Convention Center. There are also 2 Naval Air landing fields in the city, Nueces co. Airport is to W in nearby Robstown, Corpus Christi Internatl. Airport is W of downtown. The city has suffered from occasional hurricanes; it is partially protected from flooding by a sea wall 12,300 ft/3,749 m long, built bet. 1939 and 1941 to a ht. 14 ft/4 m beyond the high-water mark of a devastating 1919 hurricane. Inc. 1852.

Corpus Christi Bay, S Texas, an arm of Gulf of Mexico, forming harbor of Corpus Christi; c.25 mi/40 km long E-W, 3 mi/4.8 km–10 mi/16 km wide. Mustang Isl. lies bet. bay and the Gulf. Traversed by deepwater Corpus Christi ship channel and by Intracoastal Waterway, which links it to Redfish Bay (N) (leads to Aransas Bay), Laguna Madre (S). Supplies oyster shell to chemical plants. Nueces Bay is W arm, crossed at entrance by bridge bet. Corpus Christi and Portland; receives Nueces R.

Corral Nuevo (kor-RAHL NWAI-vo), village, Matanzas prov., W Cuba, on RR, and 5 mi/8 km W of Matanzas; 23°08′N 81°41′W. Sugarcane; cattle.

Corrales (kuh-RA-luhs), town (1990 pop. 5,453), Sandoval co., N central N.Mex., suburb 10 mi/16 km N of downtown Albuquerque, on Rio Grande, in Sandia Pueblo land grant; 35°13′N 106°37′W. Chiles; cattle, sheep; dairying. Diversified light mfg.

Corralillo (kor-rahl-EE-yo), town, Villa Clara prov., central Cuba, near N coast, on RR, and 35 mi/56 km WNW of Sagua la Grande, adjacent to Matanzas prov.; 22°59′N 80°35′W. In agr. (sugarcane, fruit; cattle; pasture) region.

Corralitos, uninc. town (1990 pop. 2,513), Santa Cruz co., W Calif., 10 mi/16 km E of Santa Cruz, in SW foothills of Santa Cruz Mts.; 37°00′N 121°48′W. Forest of Nisene Marks State Park to NW. Berries, apples, flowers, nursery stock, vegetables.

Correctionville, town (1990 pop. 897), Woodbury co., W Iowa, on Little Sioux R. and 32 mi/51 km E of Sioux City; 42°28′N 95°46′W. In livestock and grain area; mfg. (concrete prods., feed). Sand and gravel pits nearby.

Corregidora, Mexico: see EL PUEBLITO.

Corrick's Ford, W.Va.: see PARSONS.

Corrientes, Cape (kor-ree-AIN-tais), headland of S Guanahacabibes Peninsula, Pinar del Río prov., W Cuba, 30 mi/48 km E of Cape San Antonio across Corrientes Bay; 21°46′N 84°31′W. Lighthouse.

Corrientes, Cape, Pacific headland, Jalisco, Mexico, at S entrance to Banderas Bay; 20°25′N 105°43′W.

Corrigan, town (1990 pop. 1,764), Polk co., E Texas, 24 mi/39 km S of Lufkin; 31°00′N 94°49′W. Lumbering center; cattle. Inc. 1938.

Corriganville, village, Allegany co., W Md., on Wills Creek, and 3 mi/4.8 km NW of Cumberland. Limestone quarry here produces crushed stone for roads and other construction projects. Formerly known as Kriegbaum, the name was changed when Matthew Corrigan became the postmaster in 1869.

Corry (KOR-ee), city (1990 pop. 7,216), Erie co., NW Pa., 25 mi/40 km SE of Erie, near South Branch of French Creek; 41°55′N 79°38′W. Mfg. (fabricated metal prods., printing and publishing, machinery, plastic prods., rubber prods.); agr. (hay, corn; livestock, poultry; dairying). Lawrence Airport to S; state fish hatchery to W. Settled 1795, inc. as borough 1863, as city 1866.

Corsica, town (1990 pop. 619), Douglas co., SE S.Dak., 8 mi/12.9 km NNW of Armour. In agr. area (dairy prods.; livestock, poultry; grain); mfg.

Corsica, borough (1990 pop. 337), Jefferson co., W central Pa., 7 mi/11.3 km WNW of Brookville; 41°10′N 79°12′W. Mfg. (sand and gravel processing). Agr. (hay, corn; dairying).

Corsicana, city (1990 pop. 22,911), ⊙ Navarro co., E central Texas, 48 mi/77 km SSE of Dallas; 32°04′N 96°27′W. Elev. 411 ft/125 m. The city is an oil center; other mfg. (glass and rubber prods., clothing, electronics, paper prods., livestock equipment). Cotton, small grains, and cattle and emus grown/raised in the surrounding rich blackland farm area. The discovery of oil when a city water well was being dug (1894) led to the drilling (1895) of the first commercial oil well W of the Mississippi. This site has been preserved as Petroleum Park. Mobil Oil originated in Corsicana as Magnolia Oil with the construction of the first oil refinery in Texas built 1897. The refinery was the first of its kind in the West. Corsicana is home to Navarro Col. (2 year) and to Pioneer Village, a complex of 7 restored log structures. Inc. 1848.

Corson, county (□ 2,529 sq mi/6,550 sq km; 1990 pop. 4,195), N S.Dak., borders N.Dak. on N; ⊙ McIntosh; 45°43′N 101°10′W. Borders Missouri R. on E; also Mountain-Central time zone boundary. Entire county is within Standing Rock Indian Reservation, which also includes all of Sioux co., N.Dak., to N. Cheyenne R. Indian Reservation to S (Dewey and Ziebach cos). Agr. and cattle-raising area, with Standing Rock Indian Reservation in NE; drained by Grand R. and Oak, Rock, and other creeks. Lignite mines; wheat, flax, soybeans, hay. Formed 1909.

Corsons Inlet, SE N.J., passage from the Atlantic to Ludlam Bay (SW) and Intracoastal Waterway channel, 4 mi/6.4 km N of Sea Isle City; crossed by highway bridge. State park here.

Cortazar (kor-ta-SAHR), city (1990 pop. 45,579) and township, Guanajuato, central Mexico, in the Bajío, on Apaseo R., and 11 mi/18 km WSW of Celaya; 20°28′N 101°20′W. Sugarcane center.

Corte Madera (kor-TAY mah-dare-ah), city (1990 pop. 8,272), Marin co., W Calif., N residential suburb, 12 mi/19 km NNW of downtown San Francisco, and 3 mi/4.8 km S of San Rafael; 37°55′N 122°31′W. Mfg. (plastic prods., printing). N end of San Francisco Bay 2 mi/3.2 km to E; Mt. Tamalpais State Park to W; Muir Woods Natl. Monument to SW. Inc. 1916.

Cortés, Ensenada de (kor-TAIZ, ain-suh-nah-dah dai) or **Bahía de Cortés**, shallow inlet off Pinar del Río prov., SW Cuba, 20 mi/32 km SW of Pinar del Río; 22°08′N 83°50′W. The Laguna de Cortés is on its SW shore. Forms W part of Gulf of Batabanó.

Cortés, Sea of, Mexico: see CALIFORNIA, GULF OF.

Cortez 1 (kor-TEZ), town (1990 pop. 7,284), ⊙ Montezuma co., SW Colo., 40 mi/64 km W of Durango; 37°21′N 108°34′W. Elev. 6,201 ft/1,890 m. Trade center in peaches, grain, sheep, cattle region; timber. Mfg. (concrete, meat processing, flour, Indian pottery). Hoverweep Natl. Monument to W; McPher Reservoir to N; Mesa Verde Natl. Park and Yucca House Natl. Monument to SE; Ute Mountain Indian Reservation to S. County airport to SW. Founded 1887, inc. 1902. **2** town (□ 5 sq mi/13 sq km; 1990 pop. 4,509), Manatee co., W central Fla., 6 mi/9.7 km W of Bradenton; 27°28′N 82°40′W. Mfg. includes marine ladders.

Cortez Mountains, N central Nev., in Eureka co., extends SW into Lander Co., S of Humboldt R. Mt. Tenabo (9,162 ft/2,793 m), highest point, is 38 mi/61 km SSE of Battle Mountain (town).

Cortland, county (□ 501 sq mi/1,298 sq km; 1990 pop. 48,963), central N.Y.; ⊙ Cortland; 42°36′N 76°04′W. Dairying and farming area (cabbage and sweet corn); sheep and lambs, hogs, pigs, and poultry; maple sugar. Diversified mfg., esp. at Cortland, despite recent loss of several major employers. Drained by Tioughnioga R. Several major ski centers are in the area. Formed 1808.

Cortland 1 city (□ 3 sq mi/7.8 sq km; 1990 pop. 19,801), ⊙ Cortland co., central N.Y.; 42°36′N 76°10′W. In fertile farm area. Mfg. (paper, metal prods., sports equip.) supplements the city's agr. income. The State Univ. Col. at Cortland is a major employer. Former site of Mohegan colony, a summer resort founded by anarchists in 1923 and designed by Lewis Mumford. There are also several ski resorts in the surrounding area. Settled 1791, inc. as a city 1900. **2** city (1990 pop. 5,666), Trumbull co., NE Ohio, 15 mi/24 km N of Youngstown, on Mosquito Creek Reservoir; 41°20′N 80°43′W.

Cortland, town (1990 pop. 963), De Kalb co., N Ill., 4 mi/6.4 km S of Sycamore; 41°55′N 88°41′W. In rich agr. area.

Cortland, village (1990 pop. 393), Gage co., SE Nebr., 17 mi/27 km N of Beatrice; 40°30′N 96°42′W. Dairy and poultry prods.; livestock; grain.

Corunna, town, SW Ont., Canada, suburb of Sarnia, 7 mi/11 km S of downtown Sarnia, on E bank of St. Clair R. Oil refinery. Mixed farming, dairying.

Corunna 1 (kuh-ROO-nuh), town (1990 pop. 241), DeKalb co., NE Ind., 7 mi/11.3 km NW of Auburn; 41°26′N 85°08′W. In agr. area. Mfg. (copper wire). **2** town (1990 pop. 3,091), ⊙ Shiawassee co., S central Mich., on Shiawassee R., 21 mi/34 km W of Flint, and 3 mi/4.8 km E of Owosso; 42°58′N 84°07′W. In agr. area (beans, soybeans, corn, wheat). Mfg. (transportation equip., paper prods., construction materials). Inc. as village 1858, as city 1869.

Corvallis (kor-VAL-is), city (1990 pop. 44,757), ⊙ Benton co., NW Oregon, on the Willamette R., 27 mi/43 km SSW of Salem; 44°34′N 123°16′W. Elev. 224 ft/68 m. RR junction. Engineering firms contribute to the city's economy. Mfg. (food and beverages, lumber, millwork, chemicals, wood prods., furniture, printing and publishing, construction, computers). Agr. (apples, pears, plums, peaches, cherries). Corvallis is the seat of Oregon State Univ. and the hq. for Siuslaw Natl. Forest to SW. William L. Finley Natl. Wildlife Refuge to S; McDonald State Forest to NW. Inc. 1857.

Corwin, village (1990 pop. 225), Warren co., SW Ohio, 18 mi/29 km SSE of Dayton and on Little Miami R.; 39°31′N 84°04′W.

Corwith, town (1990 pop. 354), Hancock co., N Iowa, on Boone R., and 20 mi/32 km WSW of Garner; 42°59′N 93°57′W. In livestock and grain area.

Corydon 1 (KAWR-uh-duhn), town (1990 pop. 2,661), ⊙ Harrison co., S Ind., on Indian Creek, and 17 mi/27 km WSW of New Albany; 38°13′N 86°08′W. Center of fruit, grain, dairy, and poultry area; lumber milling; mfg. of furniture; glass; electrical prods., fabricated metal prods., automotive parts, poultry prods.; limestone quarries; timber. Wyandotte Cave is nearby. Laid out 1808; was territorial capital during 1813–1816, and capital of Ind. until 1825. Ind.'s first state capital. Scene of Ind.'s only battle of Civil War (July 8, 1863), when Confederate troops attacked. **2** town (1990 pop. 1,675), ⊙ Wayne co., S Iowa, 18 mi/29 km S of Chariton; 40°45′N 93°19′W. Mfg. (electrical equip., automotive parts, machinery). Coal mines to E. Bob White L. and state park to SW. Inc. 1862. **3** (KOR-uh-duhn), town (1990 pop. 790), Henderson co., W Ky., 9 mi/14.5 km SW of Henderson; 37°44′N 87°42′W. Agr. (tobacco, soybeans, grain; livestock); mfg. (chemicals, fabricated metal prods., plastic prods.); bituminous coal.

Coryell, county (□ 1,056 sq mi/2,735 sq km; 1990 pop. 64,213), central Texas; ⊙ Gatesville; 31°23′N 97°47′W. Drained by Leon R. Agr. (hay, sorghum, pecans, peaches, grapes); livestock (cattle, sheep, goats, horses), turkey raising; sand and gravel. Hunting, fishing. Includes Mother Neff State Park and part of L. Bolton reservoir in SE corner; part of large Fort Hood Military Reservation dominates S part of co. Formed 1854.

Corzo, Villa, Mexico: see VILLA CORZO.

Cos Cob, Conn.: see GREENWICH.

Cosalá (ko-sah-LAH), city (1990 pop. 5,285), ⊙ Cosalá municipio, Sinaloa, NW Mexico, in W outliers of Sierra Madre Occidental, 55 mi/89 km ESE of Culiacán Rosales; 20°23′N 106°41′W. Elev. 656 ft/200 m. Agr. (corn, sugarcane, chickpeas; livestock); thermal waters. Silver and lead deposits.

Cosamaloapan, Mexico: see COSAMALOAPAN DE CARPIO.

Cosamaloapan de Carpio (ko-sa-ma-lo-AH-pahn de KAHR-pee-o), city (1990 pop. 26,751) and township, ⊙ Cosamaloapan municipio, Veracruz, SE Mexico, on Papaloapan R., in Gulf lowland, and 40 mi/64 km W of San Andrés Tuxtla; 18°21′N 95°48′W. Elev. 315 ft/96 m. RR terminus. Agr. center (sugarcane, bananas; livestock).

Cosautlán de Carvajal (ko-sah-oo-TLAHN de kar-va-HAHL), town (1990 pop. 4,150), ⊙ Cosautlán de Carvajal municipio, Veracruz, E Mexico, in Sierra Madre Oriental, 14 mi/23 km S of Xalapa Enríquez. Elev. 4,295 ft/1,309 m. Coffee, fruit, sugarcane; fine woods and construction lumber.

Cosby, town (1990 pop. 121), Andrew co., NW Mo., on Platte R., and 8 mi/12.9 km SE of Savannah; 39°51′N 94°40′W. Meat processing.

Coscomatepec, Mexico: see COSCOMATEPEC DE BRAVO.

Coscomatepec de Bravo (kos-ko-MAH-te-pek de BRAH-vo), city (1990 pop. 1,588) and township, ⊙ Coscomatepec municipio, Veracruz, E Mexico, in Sierra Madre Oriental, at E foot of Pico de Orizaba, 14 mi/23 km NNW of Córdoba, on Mexico Highway 125; 19°04′N 97°02′W. Elev. 5,210 ft/1,588 m. Agr. center (corn, coffee, sugarcane, cereals, fruit, tobacco; woods).

Coshocton (kuh-SHAHK-tuhn), county (□ 562 sq mi/1,456 sq km; 1990 pop. 35,427), central Ohio; ⊙ Coshocton; 40°18′N 81°55′W. Drained by Muskingum, Tuscarawas, and Walhonding rivers. Agr. (livestock; dairy prods.; grain); mfg. at Coshocton (city); coal deposits, sand and gravel pits, oil pools. Formed 1811.

Coshocton (kuh-SHAHK-tuhn), city (1990 pop. 12,193), ⊙ Coshocton co., central Ohio, where the Tuscarawas and Walhonding rivers meet to form the Muskingum; 40°16′N 81°51′W. Its diverse manufactures include prods. made from paper, rubber, plastic, and enamel. The site was laid out in 1802 and called Tuscarawas; in 1811 it was renamed Coshocton and made the county seat. Of interest is Roscoe Village, a restored canal town on the Ohio-Erie Canal. Inc. 1833.

Cosío (ko-SEE-o), city (1990 pop. 3,197), ⊙ Cosio municipio, Aguascalientes, on Mexico Highway 45, N central Mexico, 33 mi/53 km N of Aguascalientes. Elev. 6,890 ft/2,100 m. Corn, fruit, vegetables. Gold, copper, zinc deposits.

Cosmopolis, town (1990 pop. 1,372), Grays Harbor co., W Wash., on Chehalis R., 2 mi/3.2 km SE of Aberdeen; 46°58′N 123°46′W. Sawmills; other millwork.

Cosmos, village (1990 pop. 610), Meeker co., S central Minn., 15 mi/24 km SW of Litchfield, on South Fork of Crow R.; 44°56′N 94°42′W. Agr. area (poultry; grain, soybeans, beans, peas; dairying); mfg. (metalworking machining).

Cosolapa (ko-so-LAH-pah), town (1990 pop. 6,181), ⊙ Cosolapa municipio, Oaxaca, S Mexico, in N foothills of Sierra Madre del Sur, near Veracruz border, 32 mi/51 km SE of Córdoba. Agr. center (cereals, fruit, sugarcane, tobacco; livestock); tanning, alcohol distilling. Some Malatec-speaking pop.

Cosoleacaque (ko-so-le-ah-KAH-kai), town (1990 pop. 21,501), ⊙ Cosoleacaque municipio, Veracruz, SE Mexico, 6 mi/9.7 km W of Minatitlán, on Mexico Highway 180. Agr. center (rice, coffee, fruit, corn, beans; livestock).

Cosoltepec (ko-SOL-te-pek), town (1990 pop. 420), in the state of Oaxaca, Mexico, 25 mi/40 km N of Huajuapam de León. Bordering the state of Puebla. Mountainous area of Mixteca Alta region; elev. 5,900 ft/1,800 m. Agr. (corn, beans, sugarcane, rice); woven straw textiles, livestock and poultry breeding and raising. Limited access by road.

Cossayuna, resort village (1990 pop. 350), Wash. co., E N.Y., on Cossayuna L. (c.3 mi/4.8 km long), 14 mi/23 km SE of Glens Falls; 43°11′N 73°25′W.

Costa Alegre (KOS-tah ah-LE-grai), region, Jalisco, Colima, Mexico; name for the Pacific Coast between Puerto Vallarta on W and Manzanillo on E; developed during the 1970s as one of the country's premier tourist centers, the coast is dotted with upscale beach resorts. Mexico Highway 200 serves the area and there is commercial air service between Manzanillo and Puerto Vallarta.

Costa Mesa, city (1990 pop. 96,357), Orange co., S Calif., a suburb 30 mi/48 km SE of downtown Los Angeles, and 10 mi/16 km S of Anaheim, on Pacific Ocean; 33°40′N 117°55′W. At mouth of and drained by Santa Ana R. A transportation hub, the city is marked by residential growth and mfg. (apparel, canned foods, electronics, pharmaceuticals, audio prods.). In addition to the research laboratories here, huge corporate complexes and shopping areas were constructed in the 1980s, contributing to a economic boon in the county. Orange Coast Col. (2-year) is in Costa Mesa, as is a mus. featuring innovative cars. John Wayne (Orange co.) Airport to E. Huntington State Beach in W Newport Bay to S. Site of South Coast Plaza/Crystal Court, one of the largest shopping centers in the U.S. The city was named for its coastal location. Inc. 1953.

Costilla, county (□ 1,230 sq mi/3,186 sq km; 1990 pop. 3,190), S Colo.; ⊙ San Luis; 37°16′N 105°25′W. Irrigated agr. area borders N.Mex. on S; bounded W by Rio Grande. Drained by Trindera and Culebra Creeks (forms Mountain, Home, and Smith reservoirs in N). Cattle, sheep; wheat, hay, oats, barley, potatoes, vegetables. Part of San Luis Valley in W and of Sangre de Cristo Mts. in E. Formed 1861.

Costilla (kos-TEE-uh), uninc. village (1990 pop. 400), Taos co., N N.Mex., on Costilla Creek, in W foothills of Sangre de Cristo Mts., at S tip of San Luis Valley, and 40 mi/64 km N of Taos, on Colo. state line. Elev. 7,815 ft/2,382 m. Cattle, sheep; wheat, alfalfa, hay. Ute Peak is 8 mi/12.9 km WSW. Ski Rio Ski Area to SE.

Costilla Creek (kos-TEE-uh), c.50 mi/80 km long, Taos co., N N.Mex. and NE Costilla co, S Colo.; rises in Sangre de Cristo Mts., N.Mex., 35 mi/56 km NNE of Taos; flows SW through Costilla L., then NW, past Costilla, N.Mex., and into Colo., then W and SW, crossing back into N.Mex. just before joining Rio Grande NW of Ute Peak. Also known as Rio Costilla and Costilla R.

Cosumnes River, c.50 mi/80 km long, central Calif.; formed in W foothills of Sierra Nevada on El Dorado–Amador co. line by joining of its North and South Forks, 35 mi/56 km E of Sacramento; flows SW to Mokelumne R. 5 mi/8 km W of Galt. North Fork c.45 mi/72 km long, South Fork c.25 mi/40 km long; both rise in central El Dorado co., and flow W. Middle Fork c.40 mi/64 km long rises in S central El Dorado co., flows W, joins South Fork 1 mi/1.6 km E of confluence with North Fork.

Cotati (ko-TA-ti), city (1990 pop. 5,714), Sonoma co., W Calif., suburb, 7 mi/11.3 km S of Santa Rosa; 38°20′N 122°43′W. Fruit, grapes, apples, grain, nursery prods.;

chickens, turkeys; dairying; mfg. (lighting fixtures, motor vehicles, electrical equip.).

Cotaxtla (ko-TAHSH-tlah), town (1990 pop. 949), Veracruz, E Mexico, in Gulf lowland, 30 mi/48 km SW of Veracruz. Fruit.

Cote Blanche Island (kot BLAHNSH), one of the 5 isls., in St. Mary parish, S La., a salt dome rising from sea marshes on N shore of West Cote Blanche Bay, 19 mi/31 km SSE of New Iberia; 29°45′N 91°42′W. Village of Louisa on isl.

Coteau des Prairies (kuh-to de PRER-EES), plateau, NE S.Dak. and SW Minn.; begins as continuation of Drift Prairie, N.Dak.; extends S, past L. Traverse and Big Stone L., area of high ground bet. James and Minnesota rivers, to Blue Earth R., N Iowa. Elev. 2,000 ft/610 m. Occupies grain and livestock region. Pipestone Natl. Monument (Minn.) in S part, quarry source for Indian peace pipes. Numerous small lakes, most natural and glacial in origin, lie sparsely scattered through region. Drained by Big Sioux R.

Coteau du Missouri (KO-to doo), plateau, central N.Dak. and N central S.Dak.; E of Missouri R. and W of James R.; 46°00′N 99°00′W. Elev. 2,000 ft/610 m. Grain and livestock region. Deposits of lignite, sodium sulphate, and bentonite here. Small midsized kettle lakes scattered sparsely throughout plateau.

Coteau-du-Lac (ko-TO duh LAHK), suburban town (1991 pop. 4,193), SW Que., Canada, on the St. Lawrence, opposite Valleyfield; 45°17′N 74°10′W. Agr. (dairying; pigs, potatoes); steel mill; resort.

Coteau-Landing (ko-TO), village (1991 pop. 1,552), ⊙ Soulanges co., SW Que., Canada, on L. St. Francis, opposite Valleyfield; 45°16′N 74°14′W. RR workshops; agr. (dairying; pigs, potatoes). SW terminus of Soulanges Canal.

Côteaux (ko-TO), agr. town (1982 pop. 1,504), Sud dept., SW Haiti, on SW coast of Jacmel Peninsula, 19 mi/31 km W of Les Cayes; 18°12′N 74°02′W. Coffee, limes. Fishing port. Sometimes Les Côteaux.

Côtes-de-Fer (kot–duh–FER), town (1982 pop. 1,877), Sud-Est dept., SW Haiti, a minor port on Caribbean, 32 mi/51 km W of Jacmel; 18°11′N 73°00′W. Agr. (coffee, bananas, tobacco, cotton); manganese deposits nearby. Fishing port.

Cotesfield, village (1990 pop. 60), Howard co., E central Nebr., 15 mi/24 km NW of St. Paul, and on Calamus R; 41°21′N 98°37′W.

Cotija de la Paz (ko-TEE-hah de lah PAHS), city (1990 pop. 12,553), ⊙ Cotija municipio, Michoacán, central Mexico, on central plateau, 35 mi/56 km SW of Zamora de Hidalgo; 19°48′N 102°52′W. Agr. center (corn, sugarcane, fruit, tobacco; stock).

Cotilla Caves (ko-TEE-yuh), caverns, c.15 mi/24 km SE of Havana, La Habana prov., W Cuba, part of large Karstic plain and one of the most accessible to the capital.

Coto de Caza (ko-to dai kah-zah), uninc. town (1990 pop. 2,853), Orange co., S Calif., residential suburb, 50 mi/80 km SE of Los Angeles, 5 mi/8 km E of Mission Viejo; 33°36′N 117°36′W. Part of Cleveland Natl. Forest to NE. Citrus, avocados, nursery prods.

Cotorro (ko-TOR-o), town, La Habana prov., W Cuba, 7.5 mi/12.1 km SE of Havana; 23°05′N 82°18′W. Dairying, sugar growing. Has mineral springs.

Cottage, Cape, SW Maine, promontory on Casco Bay, just S of South Portland. Site of U.S. Fort Williams and Portland Head, with oldest lighthouse on Maine coast (1791).

Cottage City, town (1990 pop. 1,236), Prince Georges co., central Md., suburb, just NE of Washington, D.C., on Anacostia R.; 38°57′N 76°57′W. Development began here around 1920 by a builder who put up 1-story cottages.

Cottage Grove, city (1990 pop. 22,935), Washington co., SE Minn., residential suburb, 11 mi/18 km SE of downtown St. Paul, on Mississippi R., mouth of the St. Croix R., 6 mi/9.7 km to SE; 44°49′N 92°55′W. Cattle, sheep; corn, soybeans; mfg. (chemicals, machinery, printing and publishing). Cottage Grove Ravine Regional Park is here. Lock and Dam No. 2 to SE; forms Spring L.; Afton State Park to NE. Inc. 1965.

Cottage Grove 1 town (1990 pop. 7,402), Lane co., W Oregon, 17 mi/27 km S of Eugene, on Coast Fork of Willamette R.; 43°47′N 123°03′W. RR junction. Bakery prods. Timber. Cottage Grove Dam and Reservoir, on Coast Fork, to S (100 ft/30 m high, 2,110 ft/643 m long; completed 1942). Basin project for flood control and navigation is 6 mi/9.7 km S. Dorena Dam and Reservoir on Row R. to E. **2** town (1990 pop. 85), Henry co., NW Tenn., 9 mi/14 km NW of Paris; 36°22′N 88°28′W. **3** town (1990 pop. 1,131), Dane co., S Wis., near small Koskonong Creek, 9 mi/14.5 km E of Madison; 43°05′N 89°12′W. In dairy region. Mfg. (chemicals, motor vehicle parts). W terminus of Glacial Drumlin State Trail.

Cottage Hills, uninc. village (1990 pop. 1,261), Madison co., SW Ill., residential suburb of St. Louis, 5 mi/8 km ENE of downtown Alton; 38°54′N 90°04′W,

Cottageville, village (1990 pop. 572), Colleton co., S S.C., 10 mi/16 km ENE of Walterboro; 32°56′N 80°28′W. Mfg. includes sand processing and lumber; agr. includes timber; livestock; grain, watermelons.

Cottel Island, Canada: see COTTLE ISLAND.

Cotter 1 town (1990 pop. 867), Baxter co., N Ark., 10 mi/16 km WSW of Mountain Home, on White R., in the Ozarks; 36°16′N 92°31′W. Mfg. (apparel, consumer goods). **2** town (1990 pop. 53), Louisa co., SE Iowa, 12 mi/19 km E of Washington; 41°17′N 91°28′W. Limestone quarries nearby.

Cottle, county (□ 901 sq mi/2,334 sq km; 1990 pop. 2,247), NW Texas; ⊙ Paducah; 34°04′N 100°16′W. Rolling country, drained by North, Middle, and South Pease and North Wichita rivers. Agr. (cotton, grains, alfalfa); beef cattle, horses. Formed 1876.

Cottle Island or **Cottel Island** (both: KAH-tuhl) (□ 7 sq mi/18 sq km), E N.F., Canada, in Bonavista Bay, 30 mi/48 km NW of Cape Bonavista; 48°50′N 53°44′W; 6 mi/10 km long, 2 mi/3 km wide. Fishing.

Cottle Knob, mountain (3,048 ft/929 m), Nicholas co., central W.Va., a summit of the Allegheny Mts., 12 mi/19 km NE of Summersville.

Cottleville, village (1990 pop. 2,936), St. Charles co., E Mo., residential suburb 7 mi/11.3 km W of St. Charles; 38°45′N 90°39′W. Located in urban growth area, this once rural village was inc. c.1979 to avert annexation by St. Peters.

Cotton, county (□ 641 sq mi/1,660 sq km; 1990 pop. 6,651), S Okla.; ⊙ Walters; 34°16′N 98°22′W. Bounded S by Red R., here forming Texas line; drained by the Deep Red Run and by Beaver and Cache creeks. Agr. (cotton, wheat, oats; cattle, sheep). Light mfg. at Walters and Temple. Oil wells. Formed 1912.

Cotton, town, Mitchell co., SW Ga., 10 mi/16 km SE of Camilla; 31°09′N 84°04′W. Mfg. of trampolines.

Cotton Belt, former agr. region of the SE U.S., where cotton was the main cash crop throughout the 19th and much of the 20th cent. Located on the Atlantic and Gulf coastal plains and on the Piedmont upland, it extended through N.C., S.C., Ga., Ala., Miss., W Tenn., E Ark., La., E Texas, and S Okla., and also into small areas of SE Miss., SW Ky., N Fla., and SE Va. Cotton is still grown in certain parts of the region, but it has ceased to be the dominant crop. The intensive production of corn, wheat, soybeans, peanuts, beans, and livestock has largely replaced it. Commercial timber production is also widespread on many former cotton plantations. Until the invention of the cotton gin in 1793, the Cotton Belt was confined to the coastal areas of S.C. and Ga.; by the mid-1800s, it extended from S Va. to E Texas. The belt's climatic conditions allowed cotton to thrive, but post–Civil War reforms, soil depletion, and the boll weevil (a type of beetle that eats cotton) combined to push cotton W, leading, in the 20th cent., to the more aptly named "Broken Cotton Belt." Today the majority of cotton is irrigated and grown in the Southwest—W Texas, S N.Mex., S Ariz., and S Calif. (see BLACK BELT; IMPERIAL VALLEY). The dryness of those areas makes it easier to control insect pests. Texas, Miss., and Ark. are the leading producers of the old cotton belt; Calif. ranks after Texas nationally.

Cotton Plant, town (1990 pop. 1,150), Woodruff co., E central Ark., 26 mi/42 km W of Forrest City; 35°00′N 91°15′W. In agr. area (cotton, rice, soybeans). Civil War battle took place here in 1862. Laid out 1840.

Cotton Valley, town (1990 pop. 1,130), Webster parish, NW La., 29 mi/47 km NE of Shreveport, near Bayou Dorcheat; 32°49′N 93°25′W. In oil and natural gas area; petroleum refineries. Bodcan State Wildlife Area to W.

Cottondale, village (□ 1 sq mi/2.6 sq km; 1990 pop. 900), Jackson co., NW Fla., 9 mi/14.5 km W of Marianna; 30°48′N 85°22′W. Fertilizer mfg.

Cottonport, town (1994 pop. 1,998), Avoyelles parish, E central La., 32 mi/51 km SE of Alexandria; 31°00′N 92°03′W. In cotton and sugarcane area; also vegetables, corn, sorghum, soybeans.

Cottonwood, county (□ 648 sq mi/1,678 sq km; 1990 pop. 12,694), SW Minn.; ⊙ Windom; 44°00′N 95°10′W. Watered by Des Moines R. Agr. area (soybeans, alfalfa; hogs, cattle, sheep). Talcot L. Wildlife Area in SW; numerous small lakes in area, especially in W and SE. Co. formed 1857.

Cottonwood 1 town (1990 pop. 1,385), Houston co., SE Ala., near Fla. line, 13 mi/21 km SSE of Dothan. Shirts. **2** town (1990 pop. 5,918), Yavapai co., central Ariz., on Verde R., 29 mi/47 km NE of Prescott; 34°43′N 112°01′W. Mfg. (electrical equip., machinery parts, metal prods., printing and publishing). Fish hatchery to E at Page Springs; Tuzigoot Natl. Monument to NE; Dead Horse Ranch State Park to SE; area surrounded by Prescott Natl. Forest. **3** uninc. town (1990 pop. 1,747), Shasta co., N Calif., 12 mi/19 km SSE of Redding, on Cottonwood R., 4 mi/6.4 km W of its confluence with Sacramento R.; 40°23′N 122°17′W. Walnuts, plums, olives, stawberries, grain; cattle. **4** town (1990 pop. 822), Idaho co., W Idaho, 12 mi/19 km WNW of Grangeville; 46°03′N 116°21′W. In grain (wheat, barley; alfalfa), livestock (cattle, sheep), lumbering (timber, logs) area; feeds. Nez Perce Indian Reservation to N. **5** town (1990 pop. 982), Lyon co., SW Minn., 13 mi/21 km NNE of Marshall, on S shore of Cottonwood L.; 44°36′N 95°40′W. Agr. area (dairying; livestock; grain, soybeans, alfalfa); light mfg. (cabinets).

Cottonwood, village (1990 pop. 12), Jackson co., SW central S.Dak., 22 mi/35 km WNW of Kadoka. Near Cottonwood Creek; on N edge of Buffalo Gap Natl. Grassland. Has substation of State Col. of Agr.

Cottonwood Creek 1 c.50 mi /80 km long, in S Calif., and N Baja California, Mexico. Rises in Laguna Mts. of San Diego co., Calif.; flows generally SW to Tijuana R. E of Agua Caliente, Mexico. In U.S. sect. are 2 water supply reservoirs for San Diego city: Barrett Reservoir is impounded by Barrett Dam (192 ft/59 m high, 750 ft/229 m long; completed 1922); Morena Reservoir is formed by Morena Dam (279 ft/85 m high, 550 ft/168 m long; completed 1930). **2** creek, Inyo co., Calif.; rises in SE Sierra Nevada; flows E into Owens R. and L. Original home of Calif. golden trout.

Cottonwood Falls, town (1990 pop. 889), ⊙ Chase co., E central Kansas, on Cottonwood R., 20 mi/32 km W of Emporia; 38°22′N 96°32′W. RR junction. Trade and shipping center for livestock, poultry, and grain area. Chase State Fishing L. to W. Founded 1858 by Free State settlers, inc. 1872.

Cottonwood River 1 c.140 mi /225 km long, in E central Kansas; rises in Marion co.; flows SE through Marion Reservoir, past Marion and Florence, then ENE and E, past town of Cottonwood Falls, to Neosho R. 7 mi/11.3 km E of Emporia. **2** 120 mi/193 km long, SW and S central Minn.; rises in S Lyon co., c.15 mi/24 km SW of Marshall; 44°17′N 94°24′W; flows E, past Lamberton and Springfield to Minnesota R. S of New Ulm. **3** N Calif.; formed by joining of North and South Forks 12 mi/19 km S of Redding, on Shasta/Tehama co. line; flows 9 mi/14.5 km E past Cottonwood to Sacremento R., 14 mi/23 km SSE of Redding. North Fork rises 15 mi/24 km W of Redding in W Shasta co., in Trinity Mts.; flows c.30 mi/48 km SE. South Fork rises 40 mi/64 km W of Red Bluff, W Tehama co.; flows c.50 mi/

80 km NE; Middle Fork rises 35 mi/56 km WSW of Redding, SW corner Shasta co.; flows E 40 mi/64 km, joining North Fork 15 mi/24 km SSW of Red co., forms part of Shasta-Tehama co. line for most of its course.

Cotuí (ko-TWEE), town (1993 pop. 41,682), ⊙ Sánchez Ramírez prov., E central Dominican Republic, in fertile La Vega Real valley, 27 mi/43 km ESE of La Vega; 19°00′N 70°10′W. In rice- and cacao-growing region. Founded 1505. Silver, gold, and copper were mined nearby in early colonial period. There are also iron pyrites, amber, and graphite deposits in vicinity.

Cotuit, Mass.: see BARNSTABLE, town.

Cotulla, town (1990 pop. 3,694), ⊙ La Salle co., SW Texas, on Nueces R., c.65 mi/105 km NNE of Laredo; 28°26′N 99°14′W. Cattle area; peanuts, watermelons, corn, sorghum; gas, oil fields nearby. Tourism. Chaparrel Wildlife Management Area. Inc. 1910.

Couchiching Lake (KOO-chi-ching) (10 mi/16 km long, 3 mi/5 km wide), S Ont., Canada, in Muskoka L. region, 60 mi/97 km N of Toronto, and just N of L. Simcoe, with which it is joined. Drained N into Georgian Bay by Severn R. Resort; scene of annual conference for discussion of public questions.

Couderay (kood-uh-RAI), village (1990 pop. 92), Sawyer co., N Wis., 29 mi/47 km E of Spooner; 45°47′N 91°17′W. Mfg. (consumer goods). Lac Court Oreilles to NW and Lac Court Oreilles Indian Reservation to N. Fishing. Al Capone's North Woods Hideout was here. Near Tuscolin State Trail.

Coudersport (KOU-duhrs-port), borough (1990 pop. 2,854), ⊙ Potter co., N Pa., 35 mi/56 km ESE of Bradford, on Allegheny R.; 41°46′N 78°00′W. Mfg. (consumer goods, printing and publishing, fabricated metal prods.); agr. (potatoes, corn, hay; livestock; dairying); timber. Hunting, fishing nearby. Coudersport Ice Mine to E (ice forms in 40 ft/12 m shaft into summer); Susquehanna State Forest to SW; Prouty Place and Patterson State Parks to SE; Denton Hill State Park and Pa. Lumber Mus. 10 mi/16 km to E; Denton Hill Ski Area to E; Potato City Airport to E. Laid out 1807, inc. 1848.

Coudres, Île aux (KOO-druh, eel o) or **Coudres Island** (7 mi/11 km long, 3 mi/5 km wide), in the St. Lawrence, SE central Que., Canada, opposite Baie St. Paul, 55 mi/89 km NE of Quebec; 47°24′N 70°23′W. Farming, fruit growing. At S end of isl. is village. Cartier landed here 1535.

Cougar Reservoir, Lane co., W central Oregon, on McKenzie R., 40 mi/64 km E of Eugene; 6 mi/9.7 km long; 44°07′N 122°13′W. Max. capacity 219,000 acre-ft. Formed by Cougar Dam (467 ft/142 m high), built (1964) by the Army Corps of Engineers for power generation, flood control, and irrigation.

Coulee City (KOO-lee), village (1990 pop. 568), Grant co., E central Wash., 47 mi/76 km ENE of Wenatchie, in the Grand Coulee, 28 mi/45 km SW of Grand Coulee Dam; 47°37′N 119°17′W. Wheat, apples; timber. Sun Lakes State Park, to SW, including Dry Falls, prehistoric falls site on former channel of Columbia R., Steamboat Rock State Park, on peninsula in Banks L. reservoir, to NNE. Banks L. formed by water diverted from Grand Coulee Dam, 28 mi/45 km NE.

Coulee Dam (KOO-lee), town (1990 pop. 1,087), Okanogan co., central Wash., on Columbia R., adjacent to Grand Coulee Dam (river flows W, turns N at dam); 47°58′N 118°58′W. Hq. for Coulee Dam Natl. Recreational Area (□ 153.9 sq mi/398.6 sq km; est. 1946). Town located within recreation area. Colville Indian Reservation borders recreation area to N and E.

Coulee Dam National Recreation Area (KOO-lee) (□ 157 sq mi/407 sq km), NE Wash., in Ferry, Grant, Lincoln, Okanogan, and Stevens cos. Franklin D. Roosevelt L., formed by the Grand Coulee Dam in the Columbia R. Basalt rock formations. Includes both shores of 130-mi/209-km reservoir. Authorized 1946.

Coulonge River (koo-LAHNJ), 120 mi/193 km long, SW Que., Canada; rises in a series of small lakes in the Laurentians; flows SSE past Fort Coulonge, to Ottawa R. at Fort Coulonge.

Coulter, town (1990 pop. 252), Franklin co., N central

Iowa, 7 mi/11.3 km W of Hampton; 42°43′N 93°22′W. Livestock; feeds.

Coulterville 1 uninc. village, Mariposa co., central Calif., 30 mi/48 km NNE of Merced. Old mining camp of gold rush days. Cattle, sheep. Stanislaus Natl. Forest to NE; L. McClare reservoir to SW. **2** village (1990 pop. 984), Randolph co., SW Ill., 14 mi/23 km NW of Pinckneyville; 38°10′N 89°35′W. RR junction. Corn, wheat; cattle; dairy prods.; bituminous-coal mines. Inc. 1874.

Council, town (1990 pop. 831), ⊙ Adams co., W Idaho, 40 mi/64 km NE of Weiser, and on Weiser R.; 44°44′N 116°26′W. Lumber; cattle; alfalfa, oats, barley, apples, plums; sawmill prods. Parts of Payette Natl. Forest to E and W.

Council 1 village (1990 pop. 8), W Alaska, on S Seward Peninsula, 60 mi/97 km NE of Nome; 64°54′N 163°39′W. Placer gold mining. Airstrip, road from Council to Teller through Nome. **2** village, Bladen co., SE N.C., 34 mi/55 km ESE of Lumberton on Waccamaw R., near its source. Cotton, tobacco; livestock.

Council Bluffs, city (1990 pop. 54,315), ⊙ Pottawattamie co., SW Iowa, on and below bluffs overlooking the Missouri R., opposite Omaha (Nebr.), in Omaha metropolitan area; 41°14′N 95°51′W. It was 1st settled by whites when the Mormons came in 1846 and dubbed the site Kanesville; when they left in 1852, the settlement was renamed Council Bluffs. An important supply point during the gold rush (1849–1850), Council Bluffs was made the E terminus of the Union Pacific RR in 1863. The city has become an important trade and industrial center for a large agr. area. It has grain elevators, and mfg. includes processed foods, fabricated metal prods., farm equip., chemicals, walnut and oak wood prods., consumer goods, and furniture. Among the points of interest in the city are Dodge House (Natl. Historic Landmark), the former home of Gen. G. M. Dodge, founder of the Union Pacific RR; the Lewis and Clark Monument to N; and the Lincoln Monument, built in honor of Abraham Lincoln's visit to Council Bluffs. Iowa Western Community Col. and Bluff Run Greyhound Race Track are there. L. Manawa State Park lies within the city limits on S, and Crescent Hills Ski Area is 10 mi/16 km N. Widespread flooding occurred along Missouri R. and its Iowa tributaries. Inc. 1853.

Council Grove, town (1990 pop. 2,228), ⊙ Morris co., E central Kansas, on Neosho R., 24 mi/39 km NW of Emporia; 38°39′N 96°29′W. Trade center for grain and livestock area; mfg. (machinery, prints). Treaty with Osage Indians was concluded (1825) on site of city, which later became important camping station on Santa Fe Trail. Methodist Indian mission (1849) is still standing. Council Grove L. Reservoir to NW, Kaw Mission Mus., Madonna of the Trail Monument. Settled as trading post in 1847, inc. 1858.

Council Grove Reservoir (□ 5 sq mi/13 sq km), Morris co., E central Kansas, on Neosho R., 25 mi/40 km NW of Emporia; 38°41′N 97°00′W. Max. capacity 229,120 acre-ft. Formed by Council Grove Dam (96 ft/29 m high), built (1964) by Army Corps of Engineers for flood control; also used for water supply and recreation. Kaw Mission Mus. nearby.

Council Hill, village (1990 pop. 139), Muskogee co., E Okla., 21 mi/34 km SW of Muskogee; 35°33′N 95°39′W. In agr. area. N arm of Eufala L. reservoir to S.

Country Club, uninc. town (1990 pop. 9,325), San Joaquin co., central Calif., residential suburb 4 mi/6.4 km N of Stockton, near Bear Creek; 37°58′N 121°20′W.

Country Club, village (1990 pop. 1,755), Andrew co., NW Mo., residential suburb, 4 mi/6.4 km N of St. Joseph. Near Missouri R.

Country Club Acres, town (1990 pop. 3,408), Palm Beach co., SE Fla., 3 mi/4.8 km SW of Delray Beach; 26°24′N 80°08′W.

Country Club Hills, city (1990 pop. 15,431), residential suburb, 22 mi/35 km SSW of Chicago, 4 mi/6.4 km E of Tinley Park; 41°33′N 87°43′W. Light mfg.

Country Club Hills, village (1990 pop. 1,348), St. Louis co., E Mo.; residential suburb, 7 mi/11.3 km NNW of St. Louis; 38°43′N 90°16′W. Surrounded by Jennings.

Country Homes, uninc. town (1990 pop. 5,126), Spokane co., E Wash., residential suburb, 5 mi/8 km N of Spokane, near Deadman Creek; 47°45′N 117°25′W. Seat of Whitworth Col. Spokane Fish Hatchery to NW.

Country Life Acres, village (1990 pop. 101), St. Louis co., E Mo.; residential suburb, 17 mi/27 km W of St. Louis, surrounded by city of Town and Country; 38°37′N 90°27′W.

Countryside 1 city (1990 pop. 5,716), Cook co., NE Ill., suburb, 14 mi/23 km WSW of Chicago, near Des Plaines R.; 41°46′N 87°52′W. Mfg. (chemicals, machinery, food). **2** city (1990 pop. 312), Johnson co., E Kansas, suburb 5 mi/8 km SSW of Kansas City, Kansas; 39°01′N 94°39′W.

Countryside, uninc. town, Loudoun co., NE Va., residential suburb, 7 mi/11.3 km ESE of Leesburg, 25 mi/40 km WNW of Washington, D.C., on Potomac R.; 39°02′N 77°25′W. George Washington Univ. (Va. Campus) to W.

Coupeville (KOOP-vil), town (1990 pop. 1,377), ⊙ Island co., NW Wash., on Whidbey Isl., 25 mi/40 km NW of Everett; 48°13′N 122°41′W. Grain; dairying; poultry. Resort. S side of Penn Cove, Saratoga Passage. Ebey's Landing Natl. Historical Reserve encompasses all of town (no official acreage). County Historical Mus. Fort Ebey State Park to W; Fort Casey State Park to S.

Courtdale, borough (1990 pop. 784), Luzerne co., NE central Pa., suburb 3 mi/4.8 km N of Wilkes-Barre, on Huntsville Creek; 41°17′N 75°55′W. Mfg. (metal fabrication). Frances Slocum State Park to N. Inc. 1897.

Courtenay (KORT-nee), city (1991 pop. 11,652), SW B.C., Canada, on E central Vancouver Isl., on Comox Harbour or Strait of Georgia, at mouth of Courtenay R., 110 mi/177 km NW of Victoria; 49°41′N 125°00′W. RR terminus, center of coal-mining, logging, mixed-farming, and dairying area; sawmilling; lumber-shipping port.

Courtenay (KORT-nee), village (1990 pop. 70), Stutsman co., central N.Dak., 23 mi/37 km NNE of Jamestown; 47°13′N 98°34′W. Arrowwood Natl. Wildlife Refuge to W.

Courtland 1 town (1990 pop. 803), Lawrence co., NW Ala., near Tennessee R., 20 mi/32 km WNW of Decatur, 14 mi/23 km N of Moulton. Pulp and paper mill; cotton ginning. **2** town (1990 pop. 1091), ⊙ Southampton co., SE Va., on Nottoway R., 8 mi/12.9 km WNW of Franklin; 36°42′N 77°3′W. Mfg. (food processing, chemicals, machinery); agr. area (livestock; grain, cotton, peanuts, melons).

Courtland 1 uninc. village, Sacramento co., central Calif., on Sacramento R., 15 mi/24 km S of Sacramento. Fruit, vegetables, corn, rice, beans, sugar beets; cattle; poultry; dairying. **2** village (1990 pop. 343), Republic co., N Kansas, 15 mi/24 km WSW of Belleville, near Republican R.; 39°46′N 97°54′W. RR junction. In grain area. State park nearby. Waterfowl Management Unit to S; Pawnee Indian village to N. **3** village (1990 pop. 412), Nicollet co., S Minn., 6 mi/9.7 km ESE of New Ulm; 44°16′N 94°20′W. Mfg. (concrete prods., lumber). Swan L. to NE. **4** village (1990 pop. 329), Panola co., NW Miss., 32 mi/51 km N of Grenada; 34°14′N 89°56′W. In agr. (cotton, corn; poultry, cattle, hogs; timber) area.

Courtney (KORT-nee), uninc. village, Union township, Washington co., SW Pa., on Monongahela R., 15 mi/24 km S of Pittsburgh, 2 mi/3.2 km NW of Monongahela; 40°13′N 79°58′W. Bituminous-coal area; mfg. (machining).

Courtright, village, S Ont., Canada, on St. Clair R., 12 mi/19 km SSW of Sarnia; 42°49′N 82°28′W. Sugar beets, corn; dairying.

Coushatta (koo-SHA-tuh), town (1990 pop. 1,845), ⊙ Red R. parish, NW La., 40 mi/64 km SE of Shreveport, and on Red R.; 32°01′N 93°20′W. In agr. area (cotton, vegetables, peaches, watermelons, cattle); cotton shipping point; mfg. (lumber, electric irons, seafood pies). Black L. and NW La. State Fish and Game Preserve to SE. Settled c. 1870.

Cousins Island, resort island, SW Maine, in Casco Bay off Yarmouth, just NE of Portland; 2 mi/3.2 km long.

Bridge connects with Littlejohn Isl., also bridged to mainland.

Coutts (koots), village (1991 pop. 355), S Alta., Canada, on Mont. border, near Milk R., 65 mi/105 km SE of Lethbridge; 49°00'N 111°57'W. Wheat, sugar beets; cattle.

Couva (KOO-vah), village, W Trinidad, Trinidad and Tobago, on RR, 17 mi/27 km S of Port of Spain; 10°25'N 61°27'W. Sugar mill. Now dormitory community.

Cove 1 village (1990 pop. 346), Polk co., W Ark., 14 mi/23 km SW of Mena, near Okla. line; 34°26'N 94°24'W. Mfg. (lumber, posts and poles). Ouachita Natl. Forest to E and NW. **2** village (1990 pop. 507), Union co., NE Oregon, 13 mi/21 km E of La Grande, on Mill Creek, near its confluence with Grande Ronde R.; 45°17'N 117°48'W. Agr. (cherries, apples, grain, potatoes, livestock). Cove Hot Springs are here. Part of Wallowa-Whitman Natl. Forest, including Eagle Cap Wilderness Area, to E. **3** village (1990 pop. 402), Chambers co., SE Texas, suburb 30 mi/48 km E of Houston, on Old River L., slough of Trinity R., 4 mi/6.4 km inland from Trinity Bay, Gulf of Mexico; 29°48'N 94°49'W. Urban growth area. Agr. (rice, soybeans; cattle).

Cove City, village (1990 pop. 497), Craven co., SE N.C., 16 mi/26 km WNW of New Bern; 35°11'N 77°19'W. In agr. area (cotton, tobacco, grain, potatoes; livestock).

Cove Island (4 mi/6 km long, 2 mi/3 km wide), S central Ont., Canada, in Lucas Channel, bet. L. Huron and Georgian Bay, 3 mi/5 km N of extremity of Saugeen Peninsula, 60 mi/97 km NW of Owen Sound; 45°18'N 81°44'W.

Cove Mountain, ridge (c.1,500 ft/457 m–2,000 ft/610 m) in the Appalachian Mts., S Pa. and NW Md.; 39°48'N 77°58'W–40°01'N 77°55'W. Joins Bear Pond Mt. on Pa.-Md. state boundary, extends c.15 mi/24 km from Bear Pond Mt., on Pa.-Md. state boundary in S, N to W part of Franklin co., Pa., where it merges with Tuscarora Mt. from SSW.

Cove Neck, village (□ 1 sq mi/2.6 sq km; 1990 pop. 332), in Oyster Bay town, Nassau co., SE N.Y., on N shore of L.I., on Cove Neck peninsula (c. 1.5 mi/2.4 km long), extending N into Oyster Bay; 40°52'N 73°30'W. "Sagamore Hill," home of Theodore Roosevelt, is here.

Cove Point, Calvert co., S Md., on W shore of Chesapeake Bay at N side of Patuxent R. mouth, 15 mi/24 km SE of Prince Frederick. Cove Point lighthouse, built here in 1828, is often photographed and is one of the few remaining tower lighthouses, still working, in the country. Calvert Cliffs State Park is just NW.

Covelo, uninc. town (1990 pop. 1,057), Mendocino co., NW Calif., 43 mi/69 km N of Ukiah; 39°48'N 123°15'W. Cattle and sheep raising; farming; timber; hunting, fishing. Round Valley Indian Reservation is to N. Mendocino Natl. Forest to E.

Covena (ko-VEE-nuh), agr. town, Emanuel co., E central Ga., 9 mi/14.5 km SW of Swainsboro; 32°29'N 82°26'W.

Coventry 1 town (1990 pop. 10,063), Tolland co., E central Conn., on Willimantic R., 22 mi/35 km ENE of Hartford; 41°46'N 72°20'W. Agr.; mfg. (textiles, medical equip., silk goods, and small industries). Monument to Nathan Hale, b. here, state park. Near South Coventry village (1990 pop. 1,257) is site of flood-control dam in the Willimantic, called Wangumbaug L. Settled c.1700, inc. 1711. **2** uninc. town (1990 pop. 1,165), New Castle co., N Del., residential suburb 7 mi/11.3 km SW of Wilmington, 4 mi/6.4 km W of New Castle; 39°40'N 75°38'W. New Castle County Airport to E. **3** town (1990 pop. 31,083), Kent co., W R.I.; 41°42'N 71°40'W. Formerly a noted lace center, now primarily residential and comprising several connected villages, including Anthony and Washington. It still has textile industries, but mfg. such as glass, chemicals, and pharmaceuticals has become important. Coventry's many historic structures include the Paine House (1668), a 19th-cent. tavern, and Nathanael Greene's homestead (1774). Settled 1643, set off from Warwick and inc. 1741.

Coventry Center, village, Coventry town, R.I.; 41°42'N 71°38'W. Seat of town govt.

Covina, city (1990 pop. 43,207), Los Angeles co., S Calif., suburb 20 mi/32 km ENE of Los Angeles; 34°05'N 117°53'W. Citrus fruits are processed, but a newer economic base includes the mfg. of varied prods., including medical supplies and fabricated metals. The area was settled in 1842, citrus crops were introduced in 1886, and the citrus industry reached its peak in the 1930s, when Covina was one of the world's largest producers. Citrus prods. are still produced. Inc. 1901.

Covington 1 (KUH-ving-tuhn), county (□ 1,043 sq mi/2,701 sq km; 1990 pop. 36,478), S Ala., ⊙ Andalusia. Coastal plain area bordering on Fla., drained by Conecuh R. and Patsaliga Creek. Cotton, corn, peanuts, soybeans; poultry, cattle, hogs. Mfg. at Andalusia. Trucking, textiles, and lumber; crude oil production. Part of Conecuh Natl. Forest in S. Formed 1822. **2** county (□ 414 sq mi/1,072 sq km; 1990 pop. 16,527), S central Miss., ⊙ Collins; 31°37'N 89°32'W. Drained by Leaf R. and by Oakohay, Okatoma, and Bowie creeks; Bowie Creek forms E part of SW boundary. Agr. (cotton, corn; cattle, poultry; timber). L. Mike Conner State L.in SW. Formed 1819.

Covington 1 (KUHV-ing-tuhn), city (1990 pop. 10,026), ⊙ Newton co., N central Ga., 32 mi/51 km ESE of Atlanta; 33°36'N 83°51'W. Emerging suburb of Atlanta on I-20. Mfg. includes machinery, plastics, medical supplies, food, consumer goods, printing, and packaging prods. and supplies. Known for its magnificent plantation homes. Annual Tour of Plantation Homes here. Inc. as town 1822, as city 1854. Oxford Col. of Emory Univ. nearby. **2** city (1990 pop. 2,747), ⊙ Fountain co., W Ind., on the Wabash, and 25 mi/40 km NW of Crawfordsville; 40°08'N 87°23'W. In agr. and bituminous coal area; ships farm produce, fruit. Mfg. (consumer goods). Sand and gravel pits. Laid out 1828. **3** city (1990 pop. 43,264), ⊙ Kenton co., N central Ky., suburb 2 mi/3.2 km S of Cincinnati (Ohio), on the Ohio R. (opposite Cincinnati; bridged), at mouth of Licking R.; 39°02'N 84°30'W. The 4th-largest city in Ky. Mfg. (consumer goods, metal prods., automotive parts, sheet metal fabrication, lumber, paper and plastic prods., food processing, printing and publishing, machinery). Among its points of interest are the Roebling Suspension Bridge to Cincinnati (designed by J. A. Roebling, it was the prototype of his design of the Brooklyn Bridge in N.Y. city); Devou Park, with Behringer-Crawford Mus. (focusing on natural and cultural history); Cathedral Basilica of the Assumption; the tiny Monte Casino chapel; the Garden of Hope; the Carnegie Art Center; and the Carneal House (1815). Main Strasse village theme park in W; Covington landing entertainment area, with Star of Cincinnati cruise boat. Frank Duveneck was born in Covington, and the city has a mus. devoted to his paintings. The artist and naturalist Daniel Carter Beard was also born (and lived) in Covington. Thomas More Col. (formerly Villa Madonna Col.) is to SW in Crestview Hills. Cincinnati–Northern Ky. Internatl. Airport (Greater Cincinnati Airport) is 8 mi/12.9 km to W, in Boone co. Area settled 1793, a ferry and a tavern were est. here c.1801, and the city was est. 1812; inc. 1815. **4** city (1994 pop. 8,317), ⊙ St. Tammany parish, SE La., 37 mi/60 km N of New Orleans, on the Bogue Falaya, near L. Pontchartrain; 30°29'N 90°07'W. RR terminus of line from Slidell. In agr. area (blueberries, cotton, oranges); mfg. (machinery, consumer goods, concrete); printing and publishing; catfish; resort. Historic dist. with 19th-cent. bldg. St. Joseph's Seminary and Abbey here. Fairview-Riverside State Park to SW. Settled 1769, inc. 1813. **5** city (1990 pop. 7,487), ⊙ Tipton co., W Tenn., 35 mi/56 km NE of Memphis; 35°34'N 89°39'W. In cotton-growing and timber area; bldg. materials, beverages. **6** independent city (□ 5 sq mi/13 sq km; 1990 pop. 6,991), NW Va., ⊙ Alleghany co. but separate from co., 35 mi/56 km N of Roanoke, on Jackson R., in the Allegheny Mts.; 37°46'N 79°59'W. Mfg. (packaging materials, bldg. materials, printing and publishing, metal fabrication, pulp and paper prods.; textile plants; flour milling); limestone quarrying; iron and coal fields nearby. Surrounded by George Washington Natl. Forest. Laid out 1819; inc. 1902.

Covington 1 village (1990 pop. 2,603), Miami co., W Ohio, 6 mi/10 km WSW of Piqua, at junction of Stillwater R. and Greenville Creek; 40°07'N 84°21'W. Settled 1807, inc. 1835. **2** village (1990 pop. 590), Garfield co., N Okla., 17 mi/27 km ESE of Enid; 36°18'N 97°35'W. Wheat; livestock; dairying. Oil and natural gas wells. **3** uninc. village, Tioga co., N Pa., 4 mi/6.4 km S of Mansfield, on Tioga R.; 41°44'N 77°04'W. Formerly a borough. Mfg. of modular bldgs., metal prods, commercial printing. Agr. includes dairying; livestock; corn, hay. Tioga State Forest to S. **4** village (1990 pop. 238), Hill co., N central Texas, 13 mi/21 km NNW of Hillsboro; 32°10'N 97°15'W. Agr. area (cotton; cattle; dairying). Oil and natural gas.

Covington Mills (KUHV-ing-tuhn), town, Newton co., N central Ga., 2 mi/3.2 km E of Covington.

Cow Creek, 77 mi/124 km long, S central Kansas, rises in Barton co., flows SE through Hutchinson to Arkansas R., 7 mi/11.3 km SE of Hutchinson.

Cowan (KOU-uhn), city (1990 pop. 1,738), Franklin co., S Tenn., at edge of Cumberland Plateau, 7 mi/11 km E of Winchester; 35°10'N 86°01'W. In agr. area (soybeans, wheat, corn); fabrics, lime, cement, pallets. Settled 1826; inc. 1921.

Cowan Lake (KOU-uhn), central Sask., Canada, W of Prince Albert Natl. Park, 70 mi/113 km NW of Prince Albert, 32 mi/51 km long, 1 mi/2 km wide. Drains NW through Beaver R. into Churchill R.

Cowans Ford Dam, N.C.: see NORMAN, LAKE.

Cowansville, town (1991 pop. 11,982), S Que., Canada, on the Yamaska R., SE of Montreal; 45°12'N 72°45'W. Mfg. (textiles, furniture, pottery, and plastics).

Coward, village (1990 pop. 532), Florence co., NE central S.C., 15 mi/24 km S of Florence, near Lynches R; 33°58'N 79°45'W. Mfg. of apparel; agr. includes cotton, tobacco, vegetables, grain; hogs, poultry. Lynches R. State Park to N.

Cowboy Trail, multiuse recreational trail, Nebr.; projected by Nebr. Game and Parks Commission to use former right of way of Chicago and Northwest RR from Norfolk to Merriman. There will be sects. for hikers, horseback riders, and mountain bikers; planned to connect with established parks and other recreational facilities and to be the longest such trail in the country.

Cowden, village (1990 pop. 599), Shelby co., central Ill., covered bridge to E near Kaskaskia R., 12 mi/19 km SSW of Shelbyville; 39°15'N 88°51'W. Agr. (corn, wheat, soybeans, sorghum; cattle; dairying).

Cowee Bald, N.C.: see COWEE MOUNTAINS.

Cowee Mountains (KO-ee), transverse ridge of the Appalachians, W N.C., along Macon-Jackson co. boundary; from Tuckasegee R. near Bryson City, they extend SSE to a point near Highlands; included in Nantahala Natl. Forest. Rise to 5,127 ft/1,563 m in Yellow Mt., 5 mi/8 km N of Highlands, to 4,944 ft/1,507 m in Cowee Bald, 7 mi/11.3 km WSW of Dillsboro.

Cowen (KO-wen), village (1990 pop. 549), Webster co., central W.Va., 18 mi/29 km NE of Summersville; 38°24'N 80°33'W. RR junction. Agr. (potatoes); cattle. Mfg. (coal processing, lumber). Coal mining. Monongahela Natl. Forest to SE; Big Ditch Wildlife Management Area to W.

Cowesett (ko-WEE-set), neighborhood, Kent co., E R.I., in town of Warwick, on Greenwich Bay. Reputedly located where a Pequot Indian path crossed the Maskerchugg R.

Coweta (kuh-WEE-tuh), county (□ 443 sq mi/1,147 sq km; 1990 pop. 53,853), W Ga.; ⊙ Newnan; 33°21'N 84°46'W. Bounded NW by Chattahoochee R. Mfg. of textiles; stone quarries; sawmills. Agr. includes melons, pecans, peaches; cattle, hogs, and poultry. Formed 1826.

Coweta (kuh-WEE-tuh), town (1990 pop. 6,159), Wagoner co., E Okla., 24 mi/39 km SE of Tulsa, on Arkansas R.; 35°57'N 95°39'W. In agr. area (grain, corn; cattle); mfg. (concrete, consumer goods, marble prods., machining). Settled by Indians; inc. 1900.

Cowgill (KOU-gil), town (1990 pop. 257), Caldwell co., NW Mo., 9 mi/14.5 km SE of Kingston; 39°33'N 93°55'W.

Cowichan Lake (KOU-i-chuhn) (□ 24 sq mi/62 sq km), SW B.C., Canada, on S Vancouver Isl., 15 mi/24 km WNW of Duncan, in lumbering area; 20 mi/32 km long, 1 mi/2 km–2 mi/3 km wide; 48°54′N 124°20′W. Drained E into Strait of Georgia by Cowichan R. (28 mi/45 km long). L. Cowichan village at E end, is trade center and fishing resort.

Cowles, village (1990 pop. 42), Webster co., S Nebr., 8 mi/12.9 km NNE of Red Cloud; 40°10′N 98°27′W. RR junction to S.

Cowley, county (□ 1,132 sq mi/2,932 sq km; 1990 pop. 36,915), S Kansas; ⊙ Winfield; 37°13′N 96°50′W. Located in Flint Hills region, gently rolling to hilly area, bordering S on Okla.; drained in W by Arkansas and Walnut rivers. Cattle, hogs, sheep; wheat, sorghum, alfalfa, apples, hay. Mfg. (plastic prods.). Extensive oil and natural gas fields. Formed 1870.

Cowley, village (1990 pop. 477), near Shoshone R. and Mont. line, 5 mi/8 km NW of Lovell; 44°53′N 108°28′W. Elev. 3,976 ft/1,212 m. In irrigated agr. region; sugar beets, beans, hay.

Cowlington, town (1990 pop. 756), Le Flore co., SE Okla., 19 mi/31 km NNW of Poteau; 35°16′N 94°43′W. In agr. area. Robert S. Kerr L. nearby; Lock and Dam to N, on Ark. R.

Cowlitz, county (□ 1,166 sq mi/3,020 sq km; 1990 pop. 82,119), SW Wash.; ⊙ Kelso; 46°11′N 122°41′W. Bounded on SW by Columbia R. (forms Oregon state line); bounded on S by Lewis R. (forms L. Merwin and Yale L. reservoirs in SE). Rolling hill area rising to foothills of Cascade Range in E; watered by Cowlitz, Toutle, Kalama, and Coweeman rivers. Peas, carrots, hay; dairying; poultry; limestone; timber; salmon. Part of Mt. Saint Helens Natl. Volcanic Monument in E (Mt. Saint Helens to E of co. line); part of Gifford Pinchot Natl. Forest in E; Seaquest State Park, on shore of Silver L. reservoir, in NW. Formed 1854.

Cowlitz River, c.130 mi/209 km long, SW Wash.; rises in Cascade Range SE of Mt. Rainier; flows W through Riffe L. reservoir (Mossyrock Dam) and Mayfield L. reservoir (Mayfield Dam), and S, past Castle Rock and Kelso, to Columbia R. near Longview.

Cowpasture River, c.75 mi/121 km long, NW Va.; rises in the Allegheny Mts., in NE Highland co., near W.Va. state line, in George Washington Natl. Forest; flows SW, joins Jackson R. 2 mi/3.2 km SE of Iron Gate to form James R. Bullpasture R. parallels upper course to W and joins Cowpasture from NW at Williamsville.

Cowpens (KOU-penz), town (1990 pop. 2,176), Spartanburg co., NW S.C., 9 mi/14.5 km ENE of Spartanburg; 35°01′N 81°47′W. Mfg. includes chemicals, textiles, metal prods.; bldg. materials; agr. includes dairying; livestock; grain, soybeans, peaches, apples. Located 6 mi/9.7 km N is Cowpens Natl. Battlefield Site (1 acre/0.4 ha; est. 1929) marking battle here (Jan. 17, 1781) in Carolina Campaign of Revolutionary War, in which British under Tarleton were defeated by Morgan.

Cowpens National Battlefield, NW S.C., Cherokee co., 6 mi/9.7 km N of town of Cowpens near N.C. state line. Authorized 1929, 842 acres/341 ha. Site of an Amer. militia victory over Br. infantry and cavalry forces in the Revolutionary War battle of Cowpens (Jan. 17, 1781).

Coxcatlán 1 (kosh-kat-LAHN), town (1990 pop. 4,863), Puebla, central Mexico, 21 mi/34 km SE of Tehuacán, on Mexico Highway 131; 18°15′N 97°08′W. Corn, sugarcane, fruit; livestock. **2** town (1990 pop. 1,867), San Luis Potosí, E Mexico, in fertile Gulf lowland, 32 mi/51 km SSE of Ciudad Valles; 21°32′N 98°55′W. Coffee, sugarcane, tobacco, fruit; livestock.

Coxquihui (kosh-KEE-wee), town (1990 pop. 4,023), Veracruz, E Mexico, in Sierra Madre Oriental foothills, on Puebla border, 26 mi/42 km SW of Papantla de Olarte; 20°12′N 97°38′W. Agr. center (corn, sugarcane, coffee, tobacco, fruit; livestock).

Coxsackie (kuhk-SA-kee), village (□ 2 sq mi/5.2 sq km; 1990 pop. 2,789), Greene co., SE N.Y., near W bank of Hudson R., 21 mi/34 km S of Albany; 42°21′N 73°48′W.

In diversified-farming area. Mfg. of sheet metal goods. Franklin air-cooled automobile engine invented here. Settled by the Dutch before 1700; inc. 1867.

Coxton (KAHKS-tuhn), uninc. village (1990 pop. 400), Harlan co., SE Ky., 2 mi/3.2 km E of Harlan, in the Cumberland Mts., on Clover Fork of Cumberland R. Bituminous-coal area.

Coyame (ko-YAH-mai), town (1990 pop. 733), Chihuahua, N Mexico, on affluent of Conchos R., 80 mi/129 km NE of Chihuahua, on Mexico Highway 16; 29°29′N 105°07′W. Corn, fruit; livestock.

Coycoyan, Sierra de (koi-KO-yahn), range along Oaxaca-Guerrero border, S Mexico, 30 mi/48 km W of Tlaxiaco; c.45 mi/72 km long; rises to 9,317 ft/2,840 m. Also spelled Coicoyan.

Coyle (KOIL), village (1990 pop. 289), Logan co., central Okla., 12 mi/19 km NE of Guthrie, on Cimarron R.; 35°57′N 97°14′W. In agr. area.

Coyoacán (ko-yo-ah-KAHN), one of 16 delegaciones (dists.) within the Distrito Federal (1990 pop. 640,066). An ancient Mex. city, today a middle-class suburb of Mexico city. The homes of Frida Kahlo and León Trotsky have been turned into mus. This area has become one of the most active cultural centers of Mexico city and a very popular destination for weekend excursions.

Coyomeapan, Mexico: see SANTA MARÍA COYOMEAPAN.

Coyote Creek, c.60 mi/97 km long, W Calif.; rises in E Santa Clara co.; flows S, then turns W and NW at joining of East and Middle Forks, then c.15 mi/24 km long; rise in Diablo Mts., through Coyote and Anderson reservoirs, into Santa Clara Valley c.25 mi/40 km SE of San Jose, and through San Jose, to San Francisco Bay. Also called Coyote R.

Coyote River, Calif.: see COYOTE CREEK.

Coyotepec (ko-YO-te-pek), town (1990 pop. 22,769), Mexico state, central Mexico, 25 mi/40 km N of Mexico city, and part of the Zona Metropolitana de la Ciudad de México; 19°42′N 99°12′W. Elev. 7,644 ft/2,330 m. Agr. center (grain, maguey, fruit; livestock).

Coyotepec 1 Mexico: see SAN BARTOLO COYOTEPEC. **2** Mexico: see SAN VICENTE COYOTEPEC.

Coytesville (KOITS-vil), residential village, Bergen co., NE N.J., near Hudson R., just N of Fort Lee, on S end of The Palisades.

Coyuca de Benítez (ko-YOO-ka de be-NEE-tes), city (1990 pop. 9,788), ⊙ Coyuca de Benitez municipio, Guerrero, SW Mexico, in Pacific lowland, 26 mi/42 km NW of Acapulco de Juárez, on Mexico Highway 200; 17°00′N 100°05′W. Rice, sugarcane, fruit; livestock.

Coyuca de Catalán (ko-YOO-kah de kah-tah-LAHN), city (1990 pop. 6,128), ⊙ Cayuca de Catalán municipio, Guerrero, SW Mexico, on Río Balsas, and 2 mi/3.2 km SW of Ciudad Altamirano; 18°20′N 100°41′W. Elev. 689 ft/210 m. Cereals, cotton, sugarcane, fruit; wood. Minerals are principal resource: gold, silver, copper. Ruins nearby.

Coyuca Lagoon, on Pacific coast of Guerrero, SW Mexico, just NW of Acapulco de Juárez, 20 mi/32 km long.

Coyutla (ko-YOO-tlah), town (1990 pop. 7,252), Veracruz, E Mexico, in Sierra Madre Oriental foothills, 25 mi/40 km SW of Papantla de Olarte; 20°18′N 97°41′W. Agr. center (corn, beans, sugarcane, tobacco, coffee; stock). In Totonac Indian area.

Coyville (KOI-vil), village (1990 pop. 78), Wilson co., SE Kansas, on Verdigris R., and 10 mi/16 km NNW of Fredonia; 37°41′N 95°54′W. Livestock; grain. Toronto L. and State Park to N.

Cozad, town (1990 pop. 3,823), Dawson co., S central Nebr., 13 mi/21 km WNW of Lexington, on Platte R; 40°51′N 99°59′W. Trading; dairy and poultry prods.; livestock. Mfg. (animal feed, machinery, food, fabricated metal prods.). Gallagher Canyon State Recreation Area to S. Old Oregon Trail across river. Founded 1874.

Cozumel (ko-zu-MEL), city (1990 pop. 44,903) and township, Quintana Roo, SE Mexico, on Cozumel Isl., 11 mi/18 km E of Yucatán Peninsula coast, in Caribbean Sea, 175 mi/282 km ESE of Mérida; 20°30′N 86°57′W. Corn, beans, fruit. Trades in chicle, fine woods, stock. Tourist center. Sometimes called San Miguel Cozumel.

Cozumel (ko-zu-MEL), island (□ c.190 sq mi/492 sq km; 1990 pop. 33,884), off the E coast of the Yucatán Peninsula, Caribbean Sea; 20°35′N 86°44′W. Ebony, fruits, palms, henequen, corn, manioc. A resort isl., it is known for its beautiful beaches and coral reefs. The isl. was inhabited by the Maya before the arrival of the Spanish. Discovered 1517 by Fernández de Córdoba, it has many Maya remains. Juan de Grijalva landed here in 1518. It was visited by the conquistador Hernán Cortes in 1519. Cozumel's long coral reef has long been a favored destination for sports diving, although the isl. was not extensively developed for tourism until the 1960s. It is an internationally known resort and major cruise-ship port. Internatl. airport on SE end.

Crab Orchard 1 town (1990 pop. 825), Lincoln co., central Ky., 20 mi/32 km SE of Danville, near Dix R., in Cumberland foothills; 37°27′N 84°30′W. Health resort, with mineral springs; agr. (tobacco, grain; livestock; dairying); mfg. (metal fabrication). On old Wilderness Road. William Whitley House (c.1785), state historic site, to NW. **2** uninc. town (1990 pop. 2,919), Raleigh co., SW W.Va., suburb, 3 mi/4.8 km S of Beckley; 37°44′N 81°13′W. Coal region. Mfg. (metal fabricating; mining equip.).

Crab Orchard, village (1990 pop. 47), Johnson co., SE Nebr., 12 mi/19 km W of Tecumseh; 40°19′N 96°25′W.

Crab Orchard Lake, reservoir, Williamson co., S Ill., on Crab Orchard Creek, in Crab Orchard Natl. Wildlife Refuge, 4 mi/6.4 km E of Carbondale; 9 mi/14.5 km long; 37°43′N 89°08′W. Formed by Crab Orchard Dam, built (1939) for recreation. Little Grassy Fish Hatchery to S.

Crab Orchard Mountains, ridge (2,000 ft/610 m–3,100 ft/945 m) of the Cumberlands, E Tenn., W of Harriman, 35°57′N 84°47′W. Range lies bet. Pine Mt. (NE), Walden Ridge (SW), Cumberland Plateau (N), and Great Appalachian Valley (S); highest point is 11 mi/18 km W of Rockwood. Source of Sequatchie R. Crab Orchard stone, an extensively mined, high-calcium limestone that is used in cement, glass, and agr. lime.

Crabtree (KRAB-tree), uninc. town (1990 est. pop. 1,000), Westmoreland co., SW Pa., 6 mi/9.7 km NE of Greensburg, on Crabtree Creek; 40°21′N 79°28′W. Bituminous coal in area. Grain; livestock; dairying.

Crabtree Bald, peak (5,280 ft/1,609 m) of Great Smoky Mts., Haywood co., W N.C., 20 mi/32 km WNW of Asheville.

Cracroft Island (□ 90 sq mi/233 sq km), SW B.C., Canada, on N side of Johnstone Strait, at E end of Queen Charlotte Strait, opposite Vancouver Isl., 15 mi/24 km E of Alert Bay; 20 mi/32 km long, 1 mi/2 km–5 mi/8 km wide. On Port Harvey, bay on SE coast, is Cracroft fishing village.

Crafton (KRAF-tuhn), borough (1990 pop. 7,188), Allegheny co., SW Pa., residential suburb, 3 mi/4.8 km W of Pittsburgh, near Ohio R.; 40°25′N 80°04′W. Inc. 1894.

Craftsbury (KRAFS-buhr-ee), town (1990 pop. 994), Orleans co., N Vt., on Black R., 22 mi/35 km SSW of Newport; 44°38′N 72°24′W. Dairy prods.; winter sports. Craftsbury Acad. (1829) is here.

Cragsmoor, resort village (1990 pop. 500), Ulster co., SE N.Y. in the Shawangunk range, 3 mi/4.8 km S of Ellenville; 41°40′N 74°23′W.

Craig 1 county (□ 764 sq mi/1,979 sq km; 1990 pop. 14,104), NE Okla.; ⊙ Vinita; 36°45′N 95°13′W. Bounded N by Kansas line; Neosho R. forms boundary in extreme NE, drained by small Cabin Creek. Agr. (soybeans, hay, corn; cattle; dairy prods.). Mfg. at Vinita. Coal mines. Formed 1907. **2** county (□ 330 sq mi/855 sq km; 1990 pop. 4,372), SW Va.; ⊙ New Castle; 37°29′N 80°13′W. In the Allegheny Mts., most of co. in Jefferson Natl. Forest; bounded W by W.Va. state line; drained by Craig Creek. Agr. (grain, hay; cattle, sheep; timber; iron-ore deposits, sand, gravel. Mt. resorts; mineral springs; hunting, fishing. Appalachian Trail passes through S edge. Formed 1851.

Craig, city (1990 pop. 346), Holt co., NW Mo., near Missouri R., 40 mi/64 km NW of St. Joseph; 40°11′N

95°22′W. Corn, wheat; hogs, cattle. Major flooding in area in 1993.

Craig 1 town (1990 pop. 1,260), SE Alaska, on W coast of Prince of Wales Isl., 60 mi/97 km W of Ketchikan; 55°29′N 133°09′W. Fishing. **2** town (1990 pop. 8,091), ⊙ Moffat co., NW Colo., on Yampa R., at mouth of Fortification Creek, 145 mi/233 km WNW of Denver; 40°31′N 107°32′W. Elev. 6,186 ft/1,885 m. RR terminus. Sawmill, logging; cattle, wheat, barley, oats; gas and oil wells. Elkhead Reservoir to NE; Routt Natl. Forest to NE; White R. Natl. Forest to S. Inc. 1908. **3** town (1990 pop. 116), Plymouth co., NW Iowa, 10 mi/16 km NW of Le Mars; 42°53′N 96°18′W. Livestock; grain.

Craig, village (1990 pop. 228), Burt co., E Nebr., 7 mi/11.3 km W of Tekamah, on branch of Elkhorn R; 41°46′N 96°21′W. Livestock; grain.

Craig Beach, village (1990 pop. 1,402), Mahoning co., E Ohio, 17 mi/27 km W of Youngstown, near Milton Reservoir; 41°07′N 80°59′W.

Craig Creek, c.75 mi/121 km long, SW Va.; rises in N Montgomery co.; flows generally NE past New Castle, to James R. at Eagle Rock.

Craig Harbour, trading post, SE Ellesmere Isl., NE Franklin dist., N.W.T., Canada, on Jones Sound of the Arctic Ocean; 76°12′N 81°02′W. Former Royal Can. Mounted Police post.

Craig, Mount (13,250 ft/4,039 m), SW Yukon, Canada, near Alaska border, in St. Elias Mts., 200 mi/322 km WNW of Whitehorse; 61°15′N 140°51′W.

Craig Springs, locality, Craig co., SW Va., in the Allegheny Mts., 22 mi/35 km NW of Roanoke, in Jefferson Natl. Forest, near W.Va. state line. Mineral springs.

Craighead, county (□ 713 sq mi/1,847 sq km; 1990 pop. 68,956), NE Ark.; ⊙ Jonesboro and Lake City; 35°49′N 90°37′W. Bounded by Mo. in NW corner. Intersected by Crowley's Ridge, drained by St. Francis (E) and Cache (W) rivers. Agr. (cotton, soybeans, sorghum, rice, fruit; cattle, hogs). Mfg. at Jonesboro. Gravel pits. Parts of St. Francis Sunken Lands Wildlife Management Area in E on St. Francis R. Formed 1859.

Craigmont, village (1990 pop. 542), Lewis co., W Idaho, 28 mi/45 km ESE of Lewiston; 46°14′N 116°28′W. Lumber; grain, potatoes; cattle; mfg. (wood prods.). In Nez Perce Indian Reservation.

Craigmyle (KRAIG-meil), village, S central Alta., Canada, 24 mi/39 km NE of Drumheller; 51°40′N 112°14′W. Coal; wheat, flax.

Craignish Hills (KRAI-nish), range in SW Cape Breton Isl., E N.S., Canada; 20 mi/32 km long, rises to 1,030 ft/314 m on McIntyre Mt., 12 mi/19 km N of Port Hawkesbury.

Craigsville 1 town (1990 pop. 812), Augusta co., NW Va., on Little Calfpasture R., 17 mi/27 km WSW of Staunton; 38°4′N 79°22′W. Agr. (apples, grain, soybeans; livestock; dairying). Augusta Correctional Center; Jefferson Natl. Forest to NW. **2** uninc. town (1990 pop. 1,955), Nicholas co., central W.Va., 11 mi/18 km ENE of Summersville, near Gauley R.; 38°19′N 80°39′W. Agr. (corn, apples; livestock); mfg. (machining); timber. Monongahela Natl. Forest to E.

Craigville, locality, Cape Cod, SE Mass. Site of Craigville Beach State Park.

Craik, town (1991 pop. 481), S Sask., Canada, near Arm R., 50 mi/80 km NNW of Moose Jaw. Grain elevators; lumbering.

Crainville, village (1990 pop. 1,019), Williamson co., S Ill., 5 mi/8 km SSW of Herrin; 37°45′N 89°03′W. In bituminous coal–mining and agr. area. Crab Orchard L. is S.

Cramerton, town (1990 pop. 2,371), Gaston co., S N.C., 6 mi/9.7 km ESE of Gastonia, 13 mi/21 km W of Charlotte on South Fork Catawba R., which forms arm of L. Wylie reservoir (Catawba R.); 35°13′N 81°04′W. Mfg. (textiles).

Cranberry (KRAN-ber-ee), township (1990 pop. 14,186), Butler co., W Pa., 18 mi/29 km NNW of Pittsburgh; 40°41′N 80°06′W. Drained by Brush Creek. Includes community of Fernway in SW and is considered a residential suburb of Pittsburgh.

Cranberry Glades, W.Va.: see RICHWOOD.

Cranberry Island, Knox co., S Maine, in Muscongus Bay, SSW of Friendship, 15 mi/24 km ESE of Wiscasset; c.1 mi/1.6 km long.

Cranberry Isles, resort town (1990 pop. 189), Hancock co., S Maine, on Great Cranberry, Little Cranberry, Baker (with lighthouse), and Sutton isls., just S of Mt. Desert Isl., 21 mi/34 km SSE of Ellsworth; 44°13′N 68°12′W. Islesford village, here, has Sawtelle Mus.

Cranberry Lake, village (1990 pop. 500), St. Lawrence co., N N.Y., at N end of Cranberry L. reservoir, 49 mi/79 km S of Massena; 44°13′N 73°51′W. Summer and winter resort.

Cranberry Lake, reservoir and resort lake, St. Lawrence co., N N.Y., on Oswegatchie R., in Adirondack Mts. and Adirondack Park, 33 mi/53 km SSE of Potsdam; c.8 mi/12.9 km long; 44°13′N 74°50′W. River enters from SW, drains from NW. Formed by dam at N end, near village of Cranberry Lake.

Cranbrook, city (1991 pop. 16,447), SE B.C., Canada, 49°31′N 115°46′W. Lumbering, tourism, and lead- and zinc-mining center.

Cranbury, township (1990 pop. 2,500), Middlesex co., central N.J., 15 mi/24 km NE of Trenton, in agr. region (fruit, vegetables); 40°18′N 74°31′W. Mfg of pharmaceutical supplies, cosmetics, fertilizer. Cranbury Inn (built 18th cent.) and 1st Presbyterian Church (1734) here. David Brainerd, Indian missionary, lived nearby.

Crandall 1 town, Murray co., NW Ga., 14 mi/23 km ENE of Dalton; 34°52′N 84°44′W. Mfg. includes metal fabrication and textiles. **2** town (1990 pop. 147), Harrison co., S Ind., on Indian Creek, 7 mi/11.3 km NE of Corydon; 38°17′N 86°04′W. In agr. area. **3** town (1990 pop. 1,652), Kaufman co., NE Texas, 22 mi/35 km ESE of Dallas, near E Fork of Trinity R.; 32°37′N 96°27′W. Cotton, corn, nurseries; cattle area. Mfg. (motor vehicle parts, aluminum castings).

Crandon, town (1990 pop. 1,958), ⊙ Forest co., NE Wis., 25 mi/40 km ESE of Rhinelander; 45°34′N 88°54′W. Resort in wooded-lake, lumbering, dairying, and potato-growing region; mfg. (wood prods., cutlery, pulp); sawmilling, woodworking. At N end of L. Metonga; Nicolet Natl. Forest to N and E; Mole L. Indian Reservation to SW. Reservation is proposed site for large zinc and copper mine. Inc. 1898.

Crane, county (□ 785 sq mi/2,033 sq km; 1990 pop. 4,652), W Texas; ⊙ Crane. Elev. c.2,000 ft/610 m. On W part of Edwards Plateau, and bounded S by Pecos R. Oil- and natural gas–producing and ranching (cattle, goats, sheep) region. Includes Castle Mt., historic Castle Gap, and Horsehead Crossing of the Pecos. Formed 1887.

Crane, city (1990 pop. 1,218), Stone co., SW Mo., in the Ozarks, on branch of James R., 27 mi/43 km SW of Springfield; 36°53′N 93°34′W. Cattle, poultry; dairying; fruit. Mfg. (food processing, plastic prods.).

Crane 1 town (1990 pop. 216), Martin co., SW Ind., 10 mi/16 km SSE of Bloomfield; 38°54′N 86°54′W. Heavily forested. Situated on the NW corner of the Crane Naval Weapons Support Center, which manufactures ordnance and microwave systems. **2** town (1990 pop. 3,533), ⊙ Crane co., W Texas, on the Edwards Plateau, 45 mi/72 km SSW of Midland; 31°23′N 102°20′W. Elev. 2,555 ft/779 m. Trade, shipping point of oil-producing region with ranches (sheep, cattle), mfg. (natural-gas processing). Founded 1926, inc. 1933.

Crane or **the Crane,** village, SE Barbados, B.W.I., 11 mi/18 km E of Bridgetown; 13°06′N 59°26′W. Popular bathing resort (Crane Beach). Once a shipping place. Historic Sam Lord's Castle, now a hotel, is just NE.

Crane, uninc. village, Harney co., E central Oregon, 25 mi/40 km SE of Burns. Elev. 4,132 ft/1,259 m. Wheat; sheep, cattle, horses. Malheur L. to W.

Crane Island, Canada: see GRUES, ÎLE AUX.

Crane Lake, St. Louis co., NE Minn., 40 mi/64 km NW of Ely, near Can. (Ont.) border; 5 mi/8 km long, 3 mi/4.8 km wide; 48°17′N 92°28′W. Has small isls. and fishing and hunting resorts. Receives Vermilion R. from SW, drains N through King Williams Narrows to Little

Cross references are shown in SMALL CAPITALS. **The pronunciation key is on page xv. The dates of population figures are on page xii.**

Vermilion L. N shore of lake is in Voyagers Natl. Park, remainder is in Superior Natl. Forest (coincides with Kabetogama State Forest); road and seaplane access on S end.

Crane Neck, N.Y.: see SMITHTOWN BAY.

Crane Prairie Reservoir (□ 8 sq mi/20.7 sq km), Deschutes co., central Oregon, on Deschutes R., in Deschutes Natl. Forest, on SE edge of Three Sisters Wilderness Area, 30 mi/48 km SW of Bend; 43°28′N 121°46′W. Max. capacity 68,800 acre-ft. Formed by Crane Prairie Dam (36 ft/11 m high), built (1940) by the Bureau of Reclamation and U.S. Dept. of Agr. Forest Service for irrigation; also used for recreation. Wickiup Reservoir downstream.

Cranesville (KRAINS-vil), borough (1990 pop. 598), Erie co., NW Pa., 20 mi/32 km SW of Erie, 1 mi/1.6 km NE of Albion, on East Branch of Conneaut Creek; 41°53′N 80°20′W. Mfg. (metal fabrication); agr. (apples, corn, hay; livestock; dairying). RR yards.

Craney Island (□ c.4 sq mi/10.4 sq km), SE Va.; isl. (partly artificial) joined to mainland; in Hampton Roads harbor, on W side of mouth of Elizabeth R., 17 mi/27 km NNW of downtown Portsmouth. Craney Isl. Corps of Engineers (Army) Disposal Area, fuel depot, Craney Isl. Naval Station.

Cranfill's Gap, village (1990 pop. 269), Bosque co., central Texas, 42 mi/68 km WNW of Waco; 31°46′N 97°49′W. Agr. area (cattle, dairying; grain).

Cranford, residential township (1990 pop. 22,633), Union co., NE N.J., 10 mi/16 km W of Elizabeth; 40°39′N 74°17′W. Printing, mfg. (metal prods., fire extinguishers). Union County col. here. Inc. 1871.

Cranston, industrial city (1990 pop. 76,060), Providence co., central R.I., residential suburb of Providence; 41°46′N 71°29′W. Its mfg. includes machinery, plastics, rubber prods., and chemicals. The city was named for Samuel Cranston, a colonial governor of R.I. In the 19th cent., Cranston was an important textile center. The Friends Meeting House (1729) and several pre-Revolutionary bldgs. still stand. The R.I. Adult Correctional Institute (state prison) is here. Inc. as a town 1754, as a city 1910.

Crapaud (KRA-po), village (1991 pop. 323), S P.E.I., Canada, 18 mi/29 km W of Charlottetown; 46°11′N 63°27′W. Mixed farming; dairying; potatoes.

Crary (KRER-ee), village (1990 pop. 145), Ramsey co., NE central N.Dak., 10 mi/16 km E of Devils L.; 48°04′N 98°38′W. Devils L. Sioux Indian Reservation to S.

Crater Lake, N Que., Canada, in Ungava, near Hudson Strait, 850 ft/259 m deep; 61°16′N 73°40′W. Occupies bottom of Chubb Crater, of meteoric origin and 1,350 ft/411 m in depth. Discovered 1949, the crater surpasses Meteor Crater, Ariz., in size.

Crater Lake, Oregon: see CRATER LAKE NATIONAL PARK.

Crater Lake National Park (□ 183,224 sq mi/4/4,550 sq km), SW Oregon, mainly in W Klamath co., extends into Douglas (N) and Jackson (W) cos., in the Cascade Range. Crater L. (20 mi/32 km) lies in a volcanic caldera that was created when the top of Mt. Mazama emptied violently c.4,800 B.C. The deepest lake (1,932 ft/589 m) in the U.S., Crater L. is 6 mi/9.7 km wide, lies 6,177 ft/1,883 m above sea level, and is surrounded by cliffs that are from 500 ft/152 m to 2,000 ft/610 m high. Having no inlet or outlet, the lake was formed by rain and snowfall, and its level remains fairly constant. The lake was found in 1853 by prospectors, who called it Deep Blue L. because of the intense blue of the water; it was renamed Crater L. in 1869. A scenic highway follows the rim of the crater. Wizard Isl., a cinder cone (763 ft/233 m high, with a 328 ft/100 m crater) near the lake's W shore, was formed by later eruptions. Noted for pure, clear water. Bounded by Winema Natl. Forest on S, E, and NE and by Rogers R. Natl. Forest on W and NW. Pacific Crest Trail winds through W part of park. Est. 1902.

Craters of the Moon National Monument (□ 84 sq mi/218 sq km), S central Idaho, mainly in Butte co., extends 5 mi/8 km into Blaine co., 60 mi/97 km NW of Pocatello, 18 mi/29 km SW of Arco. This region, composed of several closely grouped volcanoes, is suggestive of a telescopic view of the moon. Volcanic activity dating back c.2,100 years, along 60 mi/97 km fissure system, has left behind cinder cones, tree molds, craters, ice-lined lave tubes, and caves. Est. 1924.

Craven (KRAI-vuhn), county (□ 761 sq mi/1,971 sq km; 1990 pop. 81,613), E N.C., near Atlantic coast; ⊙ New Bern; 35°07′N 77°04′W. Tidewater area drained by Neuse and Trent rivers; Nuese R. estuary forms SE boundary. Part of Croatan Natl. Forest in S. Agr. area (tobacco, wheat, oats, barley, soybeans, hay, potatoes, cotton, peanuts, corn; poultry, cattle, hogs); timber (pine). Cherry Point Marine Corps Air Station in SE. Includes several small natural lakes in swampy area; Catfish, Long, Great, Little, and Ellis Simon lakes. Intracoastal Waterway canal crosses extreme SE corner, forms small part of boundary. Formed 1712.

Crawfish River, c.50 mi/80 km long, central Wis.; rises in Columbia co.; flows SE past Columbus, to Rock R. at Jefferson.

Crawford 1 county (□ 604 sq mi/1,564 sq km; 1990 pop. 42,493), NW Ark.; ⊙ Van Buren; 35°34′N 94°15′W. Bounded W by Okla. line, S by Arkansas R., E in part by Mulberry R. Cattle, hogs, poultry; wheat, soybeans. Mfg. at Van Buren. Hardwood timber. Mt. resorts. James W. Trimble Lock and Dam (Arkansas R.) in S, L. Fort Smith State Park in NE, Ozarks in N. Separate units of Ozark Natl. Forest are in NE and NW corners. Formed 1820. **2** county (□ 313 sq mi/811 sq km; 1990 pop. 8,991), central Ga.; ⊙ Knoxville; 32°43′N 83°59′W. Bounded SW by Flint R., NE by small Echeconnee Creek. Intersected by the fall line. Agr. includes cotton, corn, vegetables, peaches, pecans, wheat; cattle and poultry. Formed 1812. **3** county (□ 445 sq mi/1,153 sq km; 1990 pop. 19,464), SE Ill.; ⊙ Robinson; 39°00′N 87°45′W. Bounded E by Wabash R.; drained by Embarras R. Agr. (livestock; wheat, soybeans, hay). Oil drilling, refining; mfg. of pottery, food prods., rubber prods., metal prods. Wabash R. ports were important trade centers in 19th cent. Formed 1816. Crawford County Conservation Area. Robinson Correctional Center. Lincoln Trail Community Col. **4** county (□ 308 sq mi/798 sq km; 1990 pop. 9,914), S Ind.; ⊙ English; 38°17′N 86°28′W. Bounded S by Ohio R. (here forming Ky. line); drained by Blue R. and small Little Blue R. Agr. area (dairy prods.; cattle, poultry; tobacco). Mfg. (lime, wood prods.). Timber; limestone quarries. Hoosier Natl. Forest occupies W ¾ of co.; Harrison-Crawford State Forest in SE (including Wyandotte Caves). Marengo Cave in N. Newton-Stewart State Rec. Area and Patoka L. reservoir (Patoka R.) in NW. Formed 1818. **5** county (□ 715 sq mi/1,852 sq km; 1990 pop. 16,775), W Iowa; ⊙ Denison; 42°02′N 95°22′W. Prairie agr. area (hogs, cattle, poultry, sheep; corn, oats, barley) drained by Boyer R.; bituminous-coal deposits. Formed 1851. **6** county (□ 595 sq mi/1,541 sq km; 1990 pop. 35,568), SE Kansas; ⊙ Girard; 37°30′N 94°50′W. Agr. area located in the Osage Questas region, bordering E on Mo. Stock; wheat, cattle, sorghum, soybeans, corn, hay. Motor vehicles and equip. Extensive coal deposits. Formed 1867. **7** county (□ 563 sq mi/1,458 sq km; 1990 pop. 12,260), N central Mich.; ⊙ Grayling; 44°40′N 84°36′W. Drained by North, Middle, and South branches of Au Sable R., and by Manistee R. Agr. (potatoes, oats); lumber mills, industrial machinery. Includes part of Huron Natl. Forest in SE ¼, 2 state forests, part of Camp Grayling Mich. Natl. Guard Military Reservation in W, including L. Margrethe and Hanson Ski Area; Artillery Range in N; Skyline Ski Area in S; Hartwick Pines State Park in NW. Organized 1879. **8** county (□ 760 sq mi/1,968 sq km; 1990 pop. 19,173), E central Mo.; ⊙ Steelville; 37°58′N 91°17′W. In the Ozarks; drained by Meramec R. Wheat, corn, hay, grapes; cattle; oak timber; fire clay. Mfg. at Cuba, Steelville, and Sullivan. Wineries. Tourism, canoeing, fishing. Mark Twain Natl. Forest in SE; Onondaga Cave State Park and Huzzah State Forest in E. Pop. center of U.S. 1990 is 9.7 mi/15.6 km SE of Steelville. Formed 1829. **9** county (□ 404 sq mi/1,046 sq km; 1990 pop. 47,870), N central Ohio; ⊙ Bucyrus, 40°51′N 82°55′W. Drained by Sandusky and Olentangy rivers and small Sycamore Creek. In the Till Plains physiographic region. Agr. area (livestock, dairy prods., corn, soybeans); mfg. at Bucyrus, Galion, and Crestline (lamps, machinery, boatbuilding, construction machinery); hardwood timber; limestone quarries. Formed 1815. **10** (KRAW-fuhrd), county (□ 1,037 sq mi/2,686 sq km; 1990 pop. 86,169), NW Pa.; ⊙ Meadville; 40°40′N 80°06′W. Bounded W by Ohio state line. Mfg. and agr. area, drained by Shenango R. and French Creek. Pymatuning Reservoir (Shenango R.) is in W and SW part, on Ohio border, includes residential developments and Pymatuning State Park. Mfg. at Meadville and Saegertown; oil, gas, sand and gravel. Agr. (corn, wheat, oats, barley, hay, alfalfa, soybeans, potatoes; sheep, hogs, cattle; dairying). Conneaut L. (natural) in W center. Allegheny Col. Formed 1800. **11** county (□ 599 sq mi/1,551 sq km; 1990 pop. 15,940), SW Wis.; ⊙ Prairie du Chien; 43°13′N 90°55′W. Bounded W by Mississippi R. (here forming Iowa line), S by Wisconsin R., which enters the Mississippi at SE corner of co.; drained by Kickapoo R. Dairying; corn, alfalfa, hay, tobacco; cattle, hogs, sheep; cheese making, processing of farm prods., other mfg. Lock and Dam No. 9 N of Prairie du Chien; Snow Bowl Ski Area in E; Kickapoo Indian Cave in S. Formed 1818.

Crawford 1 town (1990 pop. 694), Oglethorpe co., NE Ga., 14 mi/23 km SE of Athens; 33°53′N 83°10′W. Mfg. includes electrical equip., wood prods., printing and publishing. **2** town (1990 pop. 89), Washington co., E Maine, on Crawford L. (5 mi/8 km long), 23 mi/37 km NNW of Machias; 45°01′N 34°67′W. **3** town (1990 pop. 668), Lowndes co., E Miss., 18 mi/29 km SW of Columbus; 33°17′N 88°37′W. Agr. (cotton, grain, soybeans; cattle). Noxubee Natl. Wildlife Refuge to W. **4** town (1990 pop. 1,115), Dawes co., NW Nebr., 22 mi/35 km SW of Chadron, and on White R; 42°41′N 103°24′W. RR junction. In irrigated grazing region; livestock; grain. Toadstool Park, badlands with toadstool-shaped rock formations, in Oglalla Natl. Grasslands to NW. Ft. Robinson State Park, historic military outpost, to W; Nebr. Natl. Forest and Cochran State Wayside Area to S. Relics of prehistoric man found in vicinity. Inc. 1885.

Crawford 1 village (1990 pop. 221), Delta co., W Colo., on Smith Fork of Gunnison R., in W foothills of West Elk Mts., 25 mi/40 km E of Delta; 38°42′N 107°36′W. Elev. 6,520 ft/1,987 m. Potatoes, vegetables, timber. Black Canyon of the Gunnison Natl. Monument to SW (N entrance); Crawford Reservoir and State Park to SW; Gunnison Natl. Forest to E. **2** village (1990 pop. 631), McLennan co., E central Texas, 18 mi/29 km W of Waco, of Middle Bosque R.; 31°31′N 97°26′W. Cotton, corn, grain area; limestone quarries.

Crawford Notch, scenic pass (1,773 ft/540 m) in the White Mts., N central N.H., in extreme NW Carroll co., through which the Saco R. flows, W of Presidential Range and 17 mi/27 km NW of Conway; c.5 mi/8 km long. It is named for Abel Crawford, an early settler. Discovered 1771; 1st highway built during Amer. Revolution. In Crawford Notch State Park (est. 1911). Area surrounded by White Mt. Natl. Forest. U.S. Highway 302 passes through. Appalachian Trail crosses valley E-W. Winter sports.

Crawford Purchase, land purchase, Coos co., N central N.H., 19 mi/31 km SW of Berlin, in White Mt. Natl. Forest. Drained by Ammonoosuc R. Timber; tourism. Bretton Woods Ski Area in NW.

Crawfordsville, city (1990 pop. 13,584), ⊙ Montgomery co., W central Ind.; 40°02′N 86°54′W. It is the trading center of an agr. and dairy region. Printing and binding is a major industry. Steel, wire, plastic, and metal prods. are made. Other mfg. (paper prods. metal prods., offset printing, plastic prods., automobile parts, steel sheet metal, food). Wabash Col. and the Lew Wallace Study are in the city. Shades State Park 10 mi/16 km SW. Laid out 1823, near Sugar Creek. Inc. 1866.

Crawfordsville, town (1990 pop. 265), Washington co., SE Iowa, 10 mi/16 km SE of Washington; 41°12′N 91°32′W. Feeds.

Crawfordsville, village (1990 pop. 617), Crittenden co., E Ark., 19 mi/31 km WNW of Memphis (Tenn.); 35°13′N 90°19′W. Mfg. (rice milling).

Crawfordville, village (1990 pop. 577), ⊙ Taliaferro co., NE Ga., 38 mi/61 km SE of Athens; 33°33′N 82°54′W. Sawmilling; apparel. Mfg. of treated lumber. Alexander H. Stephens Memorial State Park (with Liberty Hall, his home) is here. Inc. 1826.

Crazy Mountains, range of Rocky Mts., S central Mont., mainly in Sweet Grass Park and Meagher cos.; rise just S of Musselshell R., extend c. 30 mi/48 km S toward Yellowstone R. Lie within part of Gallatin and Lewis and Clark Natl. forests, c.40 mi/64 km NE of Bozeman. Highest point, Crazy Peak (11,214 ft/3,418 m.).

Creal Springs, city (1990 pop. 791), Williamson co., S Ill., 10 mi/16 km SE of Marion; 37°37′N 88°50′W. Some agr. In Shawnee Natl. Forest.

Crean Lake (kreen), central Sask., Canada, in Prince Albert Natl. Park, 60 mi/97 km NNW of Prince Albert. Lake is 12 mi/19 km long, 2 mi/3 km–9 mi/14 km wide. Drains NE through Montreal L. and Montreal R. into Churchill R.

Credit River, 60 mi/97 km long, S Ont.; Canada, rises near Orangeville; flows SE past Orangeville and Georgetown, to L. Ontario at Port Credit.

Crediton (KREH-di-tuhn), village, S Ont., Canada, on Ausable R., 26 mi/42 km NW of London; 43°18′N 81°33′W. Dairying, fruit growing.

Cree Lake (□ 555 sq mi/1,437 sq km), N Sask., Canada; 57°30′N 107°W; 50 mi/80 km long, up to 35 mi/56 km wide. Drains N into Dubawnt R. through Cree R.

Creede, village (1990 pop. 362), ⊙ Mineral co., SW Colo., on upper reach of Rio Grande, in area surrounded N, W, and S by Continental Divide, in San Juan Mts., 65 mi/105 km NW of Alamosa; 37°51′N 106°55′W. Elev. 8,957 ft/2,730 m. Surrounded by Rio Grande Natl. Forest. RR terminus (from Almosa). Timber, tourism, recreation. Town founded 1890, when silver was discovered; had pop. of 8,000 in 1893. Mines closed down after 1893 with decline in price of silver; some have been worked since late 1920s. Nearby is former (1908–1950) Wheeler Natl. Monument, an area of fantastic rock formations and deep gorges created by volcanic action and erosion. Recreational area here is now administered by U.S. Forest Service.

Creedmoor, town (1990 pop. 1,504), Granville co., N N.C., 15 mi/24 km NE of Durham; 36°07′N 78°41′W. Tobacco, grain, soybeans; livestock; dairying. Mfg. (textiles, lumber, medical prods.). Camp Butner Natl. Guard Base to W; Falls L. reservoir to S.

Creek, county (□ 969 sq mi/2,510 sq km; 1990 pop. 60,915), central Okla.; ⊙ Sapulpa; 35°53′N 96°22′W. Drained by Cimarron and Arkansas rivers and by the Deep Fork. Diversified agr. (grain, peanuts, sorghum); poultry, cattle; dairying. Extensive oil and natural gas fields; pipelines. Mfg. at Sapulpa, Drumright, and Bristow. Heyburn L. and State Park near center; part of Keystone L. reservoir (Arkansas and Cimarron rivers) on N boundary, including Keystone State Park. Heyburn L. here. Formed 1907.

Creekside, borough (1990 pop. 337), Indiana co., W central Pa., 5 mi/8 km NNW of Indiana, on Crooked Creek; 40°40′N 79°11′W. Mfg. (bldg. equip.). Agr. (corn; livestock; dairying).

Creel (kreel), settlement (1990 pop. 3,000), Chihuahua, N Mexico, 112 mi/180 km SW of Chihuahua in the Sierra Madre Occidental; on paved highway, on Chihuahua-Pacific RR; 27°44′N 107°38′W. Elev. 7,671 ft/2,338 m. A RR stop, popular tourist center for visitors to the Tarahumara Indian country and Copper Canyon. Named for Enrique Creel, 19th-cent. RR entrepreneur.

Creemore (KREE-mor), village (1991 pop. 1,327), S Ont., Canada, 40 mi/64 km SE of Owen Sound; 44°19′N 80°06′W. Dairying; lumbering; fruit packing.

Creighton 1 (KRAI-tuhn), town (1990 pop. 289), Cass co., W Mo., near South Grand R.,18 mi/29 km SE of Harrisonville; 38°30′N 94°04′W. **2** town (1990 pop. 1,223), Knox co., NE Nebr., 40 mi/64 km NNW of Norfolk and on Bazile Creek; 42°28′N 97°54′W. Dairy and poultry prods.; grain; livestock. Mfg. Laid out 1885.

3 uninc. town (1990 pop. 1,558), East Deer Township, Allegheny co., W central Pa., suburb, 15 mi/24 km NE of Pittsburgh, on Allegheny R.; 40°35'N 79°46'W. Mfg. (chemicals, bldg. materials, motor vehicle parts, textiles). Agr. to N (corn, hay; livestock; dairying).

Creighton Mine (KREI-tuhn), village, SE central Ont., Canada, 10 mi/16 km ESE of Sudbury. Nickel mining.

Crenshaw (KREN-shaw), county (□ 610 sq mi/ 1,580 sq km; 1990 pop. 13,365), S central Ala.; ⊙ Luverne. Level farm region drained by Conecuh R. and Patsaliga Creek. Peanuts, corn; livestock (esp. poultry); lumber milling. Formed 1866.

Crenshaw, town (1990 pop. 978), Panola co., NW Miss., 45 mi/72 km S of Memphis, Tenn.; 34°30'N 90°11'W. In agr. area (cotton, grain, soybeans; cattle); mfg. (clay and rubber processing).

Creola (kree-O-luh), city (1990 pop. 1,896), Mobile co., SW Ala., 15 mi/24 km N of Mobile; 30°54'N 88°00'W.

Cresaptown (KRES-ip-toon), village (1990 pop. 4,586), Allegany co., W Md., on North Branch of the Potomac, and 6 mi/9.7 km SW of Cumberland; 39°35'N 78°52'W. Named after Col. Thomas Cresap, who settled here in 1741 in a fort and home known as Skiptown (now Oldtown) near Cumberland.

Cresbard, village (1990 pop. 185), Faulk co., NE central S.Dak., 13 mi/21 km NE of Faulkton. In agr. area (wheat, barley, oats).

Crescent, city (1990 pop. 1,236), Logan co., central Okla., 11 mi/18 km WNW of Guthrie; 35°57'N 97°35'W. In oil-producing and agr. area (wheat, fruit; livestock). Mfg. (feed, concrete). Settled 1891, inc. 1893.

Crescent (KRES-uhnt), town (1990 pop. 500), McIntosh co., Ga., 12 mi/19 km NNE of Darien; 81°22'N 31°30'W. Seafood processing.

Crescent, village (1990 pop. 113), Pottawattamie co., SW Iowa, 7 mi/11.3 km N of Council Bluffs; 41°22'N 95°51'W. In agr. area. Crescent Hills Ski Area to N. Highway service center (interchange of I-29 and I-680) to W.

Crescent Beach, village, Horry co., E S.C., 13 mi/21 km NE of Myrtle Beach on Atlantic Ocean, in Grand Strand Beach resort area.

Crescent City, city (1990 pop. 4,380), ⊙ Del Norte co., NW Calif., on Pacific coast, 18 mi/29 km S of Oregon line, c.65 mi/105 km N of Eureka; 41°45'N 124°12'W. Fish, urchins; timber (redwood); cattle; grapes, apples, asparagus, tomatoes, walnuts; nursery stock. Dairying; logging; hunting, game fishing in region. Battery Point Lighthouse Mus., Jack McNamara Airport to N. 6 Rivers Natl. Forest to E; Earl L., inlet of Pacific Ocean, to N; L. Earl State Park to NW, Jedediah Smith Redwoods State Park to NE, Del Norte Coast Redwoods State Park to SE; N part of Redwood Natl. Park to E. Laid out 1852, inc. 1854.

Crescent City, town (□ 2 sq mi/5.2 sq km; 1990 pop. 1,859), Putnam co., NE Fla., 20 mi/32 km SE of Palatka, on Crescent L.; 29°26'N 81°31'W. Orange-growing center and resort.

Crescent City, village (1990 pop. 541), Iroquois co., E Ill., 7 mi/11.3 km W of Watseka; 40°46'N 87°51'W. In rich agr. area.

Crescent City North, uninc. town (1990 pop. 3,853), Del Norte co., NW Calif., residential suburb, 1 mi/1.6 km NW of Crescent City, near Pacific Ocean; 41°46'N 124°13'W. Point St. George to NW.

Crescent Heights, uninc. village, West Pike Run township, Washington co., SW Pa., 5 mi/8 km S of Charleroi; 40°03'N 79°56'W.

Crescent, Lake 1 Clallam co., NW Wash., in Olympic Natl. Park, 15 mi/24 km W of Port Angeles, 6 mi/9.7 km S of Strait of Juan de Fuca; c.9 mi/14.5 km long. Drained from NW end by Lyre R. U.S. Highway 101 follows S shore. **2** on Flagler-Putnam co. line, NE Fla., 6 mi/9.7 km NE of L. George; c.14 mi/23 km long, 1 mi/ 1.6 km–3 mi/4.8 km wide; drains into St. Johns R. through short outlet in N. Crescent City on W shore.

Crescent Park, village (1990 pop. 364), Kenton co., N Ky., residential suburb 6 mi/9.7 km SW of Cincinnati (Ohio), and 4 mi/6.4 km SW of Covington; 39°02'N 84°34'W.

Crescent Springs, town (1990 pop. 2,179), Kenton co., suburb 6 mi/9.7 km SW of Cincinnati (Ohio), and 4 mi/6.4 km WSW of Covington; 39°02'N 84°34'W. Mfg. (food). Cincinnati–Northern Ky. Internatl. Airport to W.

Cresco, city (1990 pop. 3,669), ⊙ Howard co., NE Iowa, near Turkey R., 17 mi/27 km WNW of Decorah; 43°22'N 92°07'W. Agr. trade and mfg. center; farm equip. (livestock and horse trailers); dairy and wood prods., feed, lime. Inc. 1868.

Cresco (KRES-ko), uninc. village, Barrett township, Monroe co., NE Pa., 12 mi/19 km NNW of Stroudsburg; 41°9'N 75°16'W. Mt. resort (elev. 1,203 ft/367 m). Mfg. (pottery, commercial printing).

Cresskill, suburban borough (1990 pop. 7,558), Bergen co., NE N.J., near the Hudson, 5 mi/8 km NE of Bergenfield; 40°56'N 73°57'W. Inc. 1894.

Cresson (KRE-suhn), borough (1990 pop. 1,784), Cambria co., W central Pa., 10 mi/16 km WSW of Altoona; 40°27'N 78°35'W. Surface bituminous coal; light mfg; resort. Mt. Aloysius Jr. Col. to West Lawrence Flick State Hosp. to SE. Allegheny Portage RR Natl. Historical Site to E. Birthplace of Robert E. Peary. Inc. 1906.

Cresson, uninc. village (1990 pop. 208), Hood co., N central Texas, 23 mi/37 km SW of Fort Worth. Elev. 1,047 ft/319 m. RR junction, in agr. area; mfg. (fertilizers, stucco).

Cressona (kre-SO-nah), borough (1990 pop. 1,694), Schuylkill co., E central Pa., suburb 1 mi/1.6 km W of Schuylkill Haven, on Schuylkill R.; 40°37'N 76°11'W. Mfg. (metal fabrication; apparel). Agr. (corn, hay, apples; livestock; dairying). Laid out 1847, inc. 1857.

Crest Hill, city (1990 pop. 10,643), Will co., NE Ill., suburb 2 mi/3.2 km N of Joliet, on Des Plaines R.; 41°34'N 88°06'W. Mfg. (motor vehicle parts, machinery, fiberglass boats, consumer goods). Stateville Correction Center to N.

Crested Butte, town (1990 pop. 878), Gunnison co., W central Colo., on Slate R., in Rocky Mts., 22 mi/35 km N of Gunnison; 38°52'N 106°58'W. Elev. 8,885 ft/ 2,708 m. Ski and summer resort and coal-mining point; sheep; mfg. (food). Historical sect. includes a 2-story outhouse. Rocky Mt. Biological Laboratory nearby. Growth stimulated by discovery of gold nearby in 1880s. Mt. Crested Butte Ski Area and Crested Butte Natl. Landmark. Surrounded by Gunnison Natl. Forest.

Crested Butte, peak (12,162 ft/3,707 m) in Rocky Mts., Gunnison co., W central Colo., just NE of Crested Butte town.

Crestline, uninc. town (1990 pop. 8,594), San Bernardino co., S Calif., in San Bernardino Mts., suburb, 9 mi/ 14.5 km N of San Bernardino; 34°15'N 117°18'W. At upper end of Waterman Canyon, in San Bernardino Mts., in San Bernardino Natl. Forest. Resort area. L. Gregory reservoir to E.

Crestline, village (1990 pop. 4,934), Crawford co., N central Ohio, 11 mi/18 km W of Mansfield; 40°51'N 82°44'W. RR junction; oil. Laid out 1851.

Creston, city (□ 5 sq mi/13 sq km; 1990 pop. 7,911), ⊙ Union co., S Iowa, c.55 mi/89 km SW of Des Moines, near sources of Little Platte and Grand rivers, in a bluegrass region; 41°03'N 94°21'W. RR junction. Commercial center and RR divisional hq. (since 1869) with repair shops; dairy prods., food processing, animal feeds, candy, lubricators, concrete blocks. Southwestern Community Col. is there. Summit L. reservoir and Green Valley State Park are to the NW. Inc. 1871.

Creston, town (1991 pop. 4,205), SE B.C., Canada, near Wash. border, at foot of Selkirk Mts., near Kootenay R. and S end of Kootenay L., 45 mi/72 km SE of Nelson; 49°06'N 116°31'W. Agr. center (strawberries, vegetables), with canneries, seed nurseries; woodworking.

Creston 1 village (1990 pop. 535), Ogle co., N Ill., 24 mi/ 39 km SSE of Rockford; 41°55'N 88°53'W. In rich agr. area. **2** village (1990 pop. 220), Platte co., E Nebr., 20 mi/32 km N of Columbus, on branch of Elkhorn R; 41°42'N 97°21'W. **3** village (1990 pop. 1,848), Wayne co., N central Ohio, 13 mi/21 km N of Wooster; 40°58'N

81°54'W. Basket making. **4** village (1990 pop. 230), Lincoln co., E Wash., 50 mi/80 km WNW of Spokane; 47°46'N 118°31'W. In Columbia basin agr. region. Franklin D. Roosevelt L. (Grand Coulee Dam, Columbia R.) to N.

Crestone, village (1990 pop. 39), Saguache co., S central Colo., 25 mi/40 km ESE of Saguache; 37°59'N 105°42'W. Elev. c.7,863 ft/2,397 m. Just E in Sangre de Cristo Mts. are Crestone Peak (14,294 ft/4,357 m) and Crestone Needle (14,197 ft/4,327 m). Great Sand Dunes Natl. Monument to SE; Rio Grande Natl. Forest to NE; San Isabel Natl. Forest to NE, beyond mt. ridge.

Crestview, town (□ 10 sq mi/26 sq km; 1990 pop. 9,886), ⊙ Okaloosa co., NW Fla., c.45 mi/72 km ENE of Pensacola; 30°45'N 86°34'W. RR junction; clothing factory, fruit cannery. Choctawhatchee Natl. Forest is nearby. Eglin Air Force Base is 20 mi/32 km S.

Crestview, village (1990 pop. 356), Campbell co., N Ky., residential suburb, 7 mi/11.3 km SE of Cincinnati (Ohio); 39°01'N 84°25'W. Agr. area (tobacco, corn, soybeans; cattle).

Crestview Hills, town (1990 pop. 2,546), Kenton co., N Ky., residential suburb, 8 mi/12.9 km SW of Cincinnati (Ohio), and 6 mi/9.7 km SW of Covington; 39°01'N 84°34'W. Seat of Thomas More Col.

Crestwood, city (1990 pop. 11,234), St. Louis co., E central Mo., suburb 13 mi/21 km SW of St. Louis; 38°33'N 90°22'W. Mostly residential with some light industry. Mfg. (printing, machining). The Thomas Sappington House (1808; restored 1965) is a worthy example of Federal architecture. Inc. as a city 1949.

Crestwood, town (1990 pop. 1,435), Oldham co., N Ky., suburb, 15 mi/24 km ENE of Lousville; 38°20'N 85°28'W. Agr. area (tobacco, grain; livestock; dairying). Mfg. (heating equip., diversified light mfg.).

Crestwood, village (1990 pop. 10,823), Cook co., NE Ill., suburb, 15 mi/24 km SSW of Chicago, on Calumet Sag Channel; 41°38'N 87°44'W. Remnant agr.; mfg. (machinery, metal prods.).

Creswell 1 town (1990 pop. 361), Washington co., NE N.C., 20 mi/32 km E of Plymouth, on Scuppernong R., in Albermarle Sound, Bull Bay, to N; 35°52'N 76°23'W. Mfg. (wood prods., fertilizers). Pettigrew State Park and Somerset Place State Historical Site to S, on Phelps L. **2** town (1990 pop. 2,431), Lane co., W Oregon, 10 mi/ 16 km SSE of Eugene, near Coast Fork Willamette R.; 43°55'N 123°01'W. Mfg. (food processing). Nurseries. Dairy prods. Agr. (fruit, nuts, berries, grains; poultry, sheep, hogs, cattle). Elijah Bristow State Park to E.

Creswell Bay, SE Somerset Isl., E Franklin dist., N.W.T., Canada, arm (45 mi/72 km long, 50 mi/80 km wide at mouth) of Prince Regent Inlet; 72°30'N 93°00'W.

Crete, town (1990 pop. 4,841), Saline co., SE Nebr., 20 mi/32 km SW of Lincoln, on Big Blue R; 40°37'N 96°57'W. RR junction. Livestock; grain. Mfg. (pet food, cereals, and feeds; food processing, hides). Doane Col. Satellite community of Lincoln. City inc. 1871.

Crete, village (1990 pop. 6,773), Will co., NE Ill., near Ind. line, suburb, 30 mi/48 km S of Chicago, on S boundary of urban growth; 41°27'N 87°37'W. In agr. area (corn, soybeans; livestock; dairying); mfg. locks. Platted 1849, inc. 1880. Balmoral Park racetrack is to SE.

Creve Coeur (KREEV-kuhr), city (1990 pop. 12,289), St. Louis co., E Mo., near the Missouri R.; mostly residential suburb, 17 mi/27 km NW of St. Louis. Mfg. (consumer goods). Mo. Baptist Col.; major hosp. center; Monsanto Corp. World Hq. (chemicals).

Creve Coeur, village (1990 pop. 5,938), Tazewell co., central Ill., on Illinois R., suburb, 4 mi/6.4 km S of Peoria; 40°38'N 89°35'W. In agr. area; mfg. locomotives. Inc. 1921. Nearby is site of old Fort Crève Coeur, built 1680 by La Salle.

Crewe (KROO), town (1990 pop. 2,276), Nottoway co., central Va., 16 mi/26 km W of Farmville; 37°10'N 78°07'W. Mfg. (milling equip., apparel; printing and publishing; agr. area (grain, soybeans, tobacco; livestock; dairying); timber. Inc. 1888.

Cricket, town (1990 pop. 2,015), Wilkes co., NW N.C.,

residential community 2 mi/3.2 km NW of Wilkesboro, on Yadkin R.; 36°10′N 81°11′W.

Cridersville (KREI-duhrz-vil), village (1990 pop. 1,885), Auglaize co., W Ohio, 7 mi/11 km SSW of Lima; 40°39′N 84°08′W.

Criehaven, Maine: see MATINICUS ISLE.

Crillon, Mount (12,726 ft/3,879 m), SE Alaska, in Fairweather Range, 100 mi/161 km WNW of Juneau, in Glacier Bay Natl. Monument; 58°39′N 137°10′W.

Crimora, uninc. town, Augusta co., NW Va., 6 mi/9.7 km N of Waynesboro, on South R.; 38°09′N 78°50′W. Mfg. (wood prods.); agr. (apples, grain, soybeans; livestock; dairying). Shenandoah Natl. Park to E, Grand Cavern Regional Park to N.

Cripple Creek, village, ⊙ Teller co., central Colo.; 38°45′N 105°10′W. Elev. 9,494 ft/2,894 m. Primarily a summer resort, it was once a great gold-mining town. N terminus of narrow-gauge RR to Victor. The discovery of gold (1891) on a cattle ranch created one of the richest camps of a major gold-producing area. In 1901 the dist. had an est. pop. of 50,000. Gold production declined after that year; yet the opening of a drainage tunnel in 1941 reactivated formerly flooded mines and led to the discovery of new veins. Violence marked miners' strikes in 1893 and 1904. The old mines are tourist attractions. Casino gambling. Pikes Peak and Pike Natl. Forest to E; Mueller State Park to N; Florissant Fossil Beds Natl. Monument to N. Inc. 1892.

Crisenberry Dam, Ill.: see KINKAID LAKE.

Crisfield (KRIS-field), city (1990 pop. 2,880), Somerset co., SE Md., on the Eastern Shore, 31 mi/50 km SSW of Salisbury, and on inlet of Tangier Sound; 37°59′N 75°52′W. RR terminus; port of entry; ferries to Smith Isl. and Tangier Isl. (Va.). A center of seafood industry (fish, crabs, oysters) of Md. and Va. Since the RR arrived in the 1860s, Crisfield has been the self-styled "Seafood Capital of the Country." Crisfield has the largest Chesapeake Bay fishing fleet, extensive processing, canning, and shipping facilities, although the number of packing houses has declined from more than 150 to fewer than 20. Sport fishing, duck hunting. Mfg. of fishing equip., boats, clothing. Hinterland is rich farming, dairying, poultry-raising area. Orginally surveyed by John Roach and Benjamin Summers (Somers) in 1663, it was called Somers Cove until 1868, when the Eastern Shore RR and John W. Crisfield, its principal financier, arrived. Hard crab races, with the crabs named for contenders in presidential election years, are held over the Labor Day holiday.

Crisp, county (□ 281 sq mi/728 sq km; 1990 pop. 20,011), S central Ga.; ⊙ Cordele; 31°56′N 83°46′W. Bounded W by Flint R. (forms L. Blackshear here). Coastal plain agr. that includes cotton, corn, peanuts, pecans, soybeans, wheat; cattle, hogs, poultry. Formed 1905.

Cristal, Sierra del (kree-STAHL, see-ER-uh dail), low range, Holguín prov., E Cuba, extending 20 mi/32 km WSW from Sagua de Tánamo; 20°30′N 75°12′W. Pico de Cristal rises to c.4,039 ft/1,231 m (rain forest at E foothills). Yields lumber. Numerous quarries; Nicaro nickel mines at N foot.

Cristo (KREE-sto), town, Santiago de Cuba prov., E Cuba, on RR, 8 mi/12.9 km NNE of Santiago de Cuba; 20°07′N 75°45′W. Manganese mining, with large concentration plant. Also called El Cristo.

Crittenden 1 (KRIT-uhn-duhn), county (□ 636 sq mi/1,647 sq km; 1990 pop. 49,939), E Ark.; ⊙ Marion; 35°12′N 90°18′W. Situated in delta region bet. the Mississippi (E and SE boundary) and the St. Francis. Agr. (cotton, rice, soybeans, hay). Mfg. at West Memphis. Hardwood timber. Wapanocca Natl. Wildlife Refuge in NE. Porter L. and large Horseshoe L., backwater lakes (oxbows) of Mississippi R., in far S; traversed by small Tyronza R. Formed 1825. **2** county (□ 370 sq mi/958 sq km; 1990 pop. 9,196), W Ky.; ⊙ Marion; 37°21′N 88°05′W. Bounded NW by Ohio R. (Ill. state line), NE by Tradewater R., SW corner by Cumberland R.; drained by Crooked Creek. Rolling agr. area (hogs, cattle, poultry; burley tobacco, hay, alfalfa, soybeans, wheat, corn); limestone quarries. Formed 1824.

Crittenden (KRIT-uhn-duhn), village (1990 pop. 731), Grant co., N Ky., 16 mi/26 km E of Warsaw; 38°46′N 84°36′W. Agr. (burley tobacco; livestock; dairying); mfg. (metal fabrication). Lloyd Wildlife Management Area to SE; Bullock Pen L. reservoir to NW.

Crivitz (KRI-vitz), town (1990 pop. 996), Marinette co., NE Wis., on Peshtigo R., 21 mi/34 km NW of Marinette; 45°13′N 88°00′W. RR junction. Mfg. (concrete, sport equip.); tourist center; fishing. Thunder R. State Fish Hatchery to W; Winterset Ski Area to W.

Croatan Sound (kro-uh-TAN), passage, Dare co., N E N.C., connects Albemarle (N) and Pamlico (S) sounds; Roanoke Isl. to E, mainland to W; bridged at N entrance; c.15 mi/24 km long, 4 mi/6.4 km wide. Roanoke Sound on E side of Roanoke Isl.

Croche River (krosh), 110 mi/177 km long, S central Que., Canada; rises W of L. St. John; flows S to St. Maurice R. 5 mi/8 km N of La Tuque.

Crocheron (KRO-she-ron), fishing village, Dorchester co., E Md., on Fishing Bay and Tedious Creek, 23 mi/37 km S of Cambridge. Packs oysters, crabs. Named after Nathan Crocheron, who settled here in the mid–19th cent. Many of its residents previously lived on Holland and Bloodsworth Isls. in the Bay. They settled here when subsiding land on the isls. endangered (and sometimes destroyed) their houses.

Crocker, agr. city (1990 pop. 1,077), Pulaski co., central Mo., in the Ozarks, near Gasconade R., 28 mi/45 km ENE of Lebanon; 37°57′N 92°16′W. Cattle; timber; mfg. (bldg. materials).

Crocker Mountain (4,168 ft/1,270 m), Franklin co., W Maine, 30 mi/48 km NNW of Farmington.

Crockett 1 (KRAH-kit), county (□ 269; 1990 pop. 13,378), W Tenn.; ⊙ Alamo; 35°49′N 89°08′W. Bounded NE by Middle Fork, SW by South Fork of Forked Deer R. Cotton, corn, soybeans, sorghum; livestock. Formed 1871. **2** county (□ 2,807 sq mi/7,270 sq km; 1990 pop. 4,078), W Texas; ⊙ Ozona; 30°43′N 101°24′W. Rough prairies and woodlands of Edwards Plateau, bounded W by Pecos R. Elev. c.1,500 ft/457 m–4,000 ft/1,219 m. Drained by Live Oak and Howards creeks, Johnson's Run, and Buckhorn Draw. Oil, natural gas, livestock region (sheep, Angora goats, cattle). Fort Richardson, state historic site, in W, on Pecos R. Founded 1875.

Crockett 1 uninc. town (1990 pop. 3,228), Contra Costa co., W Calif., residential suburb 14 mi/23 km N of Oakland, on Carquinez Strait (here bridged, to Vallejo), 9 mi/14.5 km NE of Richmond; 38°03′N 122°13′W. Large sugar refinery; port facilities. San Pablo Bay to W, Suisun Bay to E. **2** town (1990 pop. 7,024), ⊙ Houston co., E Texas, 33 mi/53 km SSE of Palestine. Horses, cattle; cotton, timber, watermelon, peanuts. Mfg. (apparel, bldg. materials; food processing). Davy Crockett Natl. Forest to E; Mission Tejas State Historical Park to NE; Houston County L. reservoir to NW. City founded in 1830s.

Crocus Hill, village, W Anguilla, B.W.I., 18°13′N 63°05′W.

Crofton 1 village (1990 pop. 699), Christian co., SW Ky., 13 mi/21 km N of Hopkinsville; 37°02′N 87°28′W. Agr. (tobacco, grain; livestock; dairying; timber); mfg. (wood prods.). Pennyrile Forest State Resort Park to W. **2** village (1990 pop. 820), Knox co., NE Nebr., 12 mi/19 km SSW of Yankton, S.Dak., near Gavins Point Dam (N) on Missouri R; 42°43′N 97°30′W. Santee Indian Reservation to W. Lewis and Clark L. (Missouri R.) State Recreation Area to N.

Croft's Hill, town (1991 pop. 2,994), Clarendon parish, central Jamaica, 11 mi/18 km NNE of May Pen; 18°08′N 77°13′W. Road junction town.

Croghan, village (1990 pop. 664), Lewis co., N central N.Y., on Beaver R., 8 mi/12.9 km NE of Lowville; 43°53′N 75°23′W. Timber harvesting. Amer. Maple Mus.

Croil Island, St. Lawrence co., N N.Y., in the St. Lawrence R., at Ont. line, c.4 mi/6.4 km NW of Massena; 44°58′N 74°59′W. Isl. is c.3.5 mi/5.6 km long, 0.75 mi/1.21 km–1.75 mi/2.82 km wide.

Croix-des-Bouquets (krwah–dai–boo-KE), town (1982 pop. 4,365), Ouest dept., S Haiti, 8 mi/12.9 km ENE of Port-au-Prince; 18°35′N 72°14′W. Agr. (coffee, limes, sisals, cotton, sugar); essential oils distillery.

Cromona (kruh-MO-nuh) or **Haymond**, uninc. town (1990 pop. 800), Letcher co., SE Ky., 3 mi/4.8 km W of Jenkins. Mfg. (printing and publishing); bituminous coal. Pop. figure includes nearby Potters Fork

Crompton, industrial village in West Warwick town, Kent co., central R.I., 11 mi/18 km SSW of Providence. Mfg.

Cromwell 1 town (1990 pop. 12,286), including Cromwell village, Middlesex co., central Conn., on Mattabesset and Connecticut rivers, just N of Middletown; 41°36′N 72°39′W. Hothouse flowers, consumer goods, hardware, tools. A retail center. Settled c.1650, set off from Middletown 1851. **2** town (1990 pop. 520), Noble co., NE Ind., near L. Wawasee, 10 mi/16 km W of Albion; 41°24′N 85°37′W. In agr. area. Mfg. (wire prods.). **3** town (1990 pop. 120), Union co., S Iowa, 5 mi/8 km W of Creston; 41°02′N 94°27′W. Livestock; grain.

Cromwell 1 uninc. village (1990 pop. 250), Ohio co., W Ky., 7 mi/11.3 km SE of Beaver Dam, on Green R. Tobacco, grain; livestock; timber. Bituminous coal. Mfg. (apparel, concrete, coal processing). **2** village (1990 pop. 221), Carlton co., E Minn., 37 mi/60 km W of Duluth; 46°40′N 92°52′W. Dairying; poultry; oats, alfalfa; mfg. (furniture). Fon du Lac State Forest to E; Fond du Lac Indian Reservation to E; Island L. to SE, Prairie L. to N. **3** village (1990 pop. 268), Seminole co., central Okla., 11 mi/18 km NNE of Wewoka; 35°20′N 96°27′W. In agr. area.

Cronin Mountain (KRO-nin) (7,827 ft/2,386 m), central B.C., Canada, 16 mi/26 km NE of Smiters; 54°56′N 126°51′W. Highest peak of Babine Mts.

Cronstadt Island (KRON-stahdt), islet off NW Trinidad, Trinidad and Tobago, in the Gulf of Paria, just W of Carrera Isl., with which it forms the San Diego Isls., 7 mi/11.3 km W of Port of Spain; 10°39′N 61°38′W. Bathing resort.

Crook 1 county (□ 2,987 sq mi/7,736 sq km; 1990 pop. 14,111), central Oregon; ⊙ Prineville; 44°07′N 120°21′W. Drained by Crooked R. Poultry, sheep, cattle; potatoes, wheat, oats, barley. Timber. Mercury. Parts of Ochoco Natl. Forest are in N, center, and SE corner, including Mill Creek Wilderness Area in NW. Ochoco L. and Prineville Reservoir State Parks and Ochoco State Wayside in W. Formed 1882. **2** county (□ 2,870 sq mi/7,433 sq km; 1990 pop. 5,294), NE Wyo.; ⊙ Sundance; 44°35′N 104°33′W. Borders S.Dak. (E) and Mont. (N); watered by Belle Fourche and Little Missouri rivers. Lowest point in Wyo., 3,125 ft/953 m in NE, where Belle Fourche R. enters S.Dak. Grain, livestock region (wheat, hay, alfalfa, oats; sheep, cattle); timber, coal. Devils Tower Natl. Monument in W center; Missouri Buttes also in W center; Belle Fourche R. forms Keyhole Reservoir in SW; Keyhole State Park on E shore. Bear Lodge Mts. at center, part of Black Hills in SE; parts of Black Hills Natl. Forest at center and in SE. Formed 1875.

Crook, village (1990 pop. 148), Logan co., NE Colo., on South Platte R., 26 mi/42 km NE of Sterling, near Nebr. line; 40°51′N 102°47′W. Elev. c.3,711 ft/1,131 m. Livestock; corn, sugar beets, beans, sunflowers. Julesburg Reservoir to NE.

Crook, Lake, Texas: see PINE CREEK.

Crooked Creek 1 village (1990 pop. 106), W Alaska, on Kuskokwim R., 60 mi/97 km ESE of Holy Cross; 61°52′N 158°04′W. **2** uninc. village, Middlebury township, Huntingdon co., S central Pa., 8 mi/12.9 km NNE of Wellsboro, on Crooked Creek; 40°29′N 78°04′W.

Crooked Creek 1 c.50 mi/80 km long, in S Ill.; rises in Marion co.; flows S and SW, past Central City, to Kaskaskia R. 8 mi/12.9 km SSW of Carlyle; 38°32′N 88°45′W. **2** c.50 mi/80 km long, W central Pa.; rises in central Indiana co., 4 mi/6.4 km NE of Indiana; 40°41′N 79°04′W; flows first N, then generally W, through Crooked Creek L. reservoir to Allegheny R. 2 mi/3.2 km SSW of Ford City.

Crooked Creek, Kansas and Okla.: see CIMARRON, river.

Crooked Island, island (□ 93 sq mi/241 sq km; 1990 pop. 412), 250 mi/400 km SE of New Providence Isl., SE Bahamas; 22°45′N 74°10′W. A sparsely populated isl.

producing aloe vera and cascarilla bark. Pop. figure includes neighboring Long Cay. Tourist development is very limited, and emigration has reduced the pop. by 75% since 1901. Visited by Columbus on Oct. 21, 1492. Amer. loyalists settled here and grew cotton in the 1780s, but later abandoned their plantations because of insect infestation.

Crooked Island Passage, deep channel, S central Bahama Isls., bounded by Samana Isl. (NE), Crooked Isl. (E), and Long Isl. (SW). Channel is c.60 mi/97 km long NE-SW. Used by ships on way to Panama Canal.

Crooked Lake (□ 22 sq mi/57 sq km), S central N.F., Canada, 40 mi/64 km SE of Buchans; 48°22′N 56°15′W. S part of lake is called Great Burnt L. Connects N with Isl. Pond (4 mi/6 km long, 2 mi/3 km wide).

Crooked Lake 1 in Polk co., central Fla., 5 mi/8 km S of L. Wales; c.7 mi/11.3 km long, 2 mi/3.2 km wide. Formerly also called L. Caloosa. **2** in Emmet co., NW Mich., 6 mi/9.7 km NE of Petoskey, in wooded resort area; c.4 mi/6.4 km long, 1.5 mi/2.4 km wide; 45°24′N 84°49′W. Joined by streams to Pickerel (SE) and Burt (E) lakes. **3** in St. Louis and Lake cos., Minn. and W Ont. (Canada), 20 mi/32 km N of Ely in chain of lakes on Can. border; 25 mi/40 km long, 4.5 mi/7.2 km wide; 48°14′N 91°54′W. Includes numerous isls. and inlets and has extremely irregular shoreline. Bounded on S by Superior Natl. Forest (includes Boundary Waters Canoe Area) and N by Quetico Provincial Park. Connected by short river to Iron L. (W), by Basswood R. to Basswood L. (SE). **4** natural, glacially formed lake in Steuben co., NE Ind., 4 mi/6.4 km NW of Angola. This is the 5th-largest natural lake in Indiana. Resort area.

Crooked River 1 c.40 mi/64 km long, in SW Maine; rises in Songo Pond, W Oxford co.; flows generally S to Sebago L. **2** c.60 mi/97 km long, in W central Mo.; rises in Clinton co.; flows SE to the Missouri 4 mi/6.4 km E of Lexington. **3** c.105 mi/169 km long, central Oregon; formed by joining of North and South Forks c.40 mi/64 km ESE of Prineville, in E Crook co.; flows W through Prineville Reservoir, then N past Prineville, and W through Crooked R. Natl. Grassland to Deschutes R. in L. Chinook Reservoir, 6 mi/9.7 km SW of Madras. North Fork rises in N Crook co.; then flows S c.25 mi/40 km South Fork rises in S Crook co.; then flows N c.40 mi/64 km.

Crooks, village (1990 pop. 671), Minnehaha co., SE S.Dak., 8 mi/12.9 km NNW of Sioux Falls; 43°39′N 96°48′W. Agr. area. Mfg. (food).

Crooks Tower, mountain peak (7,140 ft/2,176 m), Lawrence co., W S.Dak., in Black Hills, 16 mi/26 km SW of Lead.

Crookston, town (1990 pop. 8,119), ☉ Polk co., NW Minn., 24 mi/39 km SE of Grand Forks, N.Dak., on Red L. R.; 47°46′N 96°36′W. Elev. 867 ft/264 m. RR junction, trade center and shipping point in agr. area (grain, sugar beets, potatoes, sunflowers; livestock; dairying); mfg. (food processing, concrete pipe, machinery, printing and publishing). Univ. of Minn.–Crookston Campus. Stock and produce show takes place annually. Settled 1872, inc. 1879.

Crookston, village (1990 pop. 99), Cherry co., N Nebr., 10 mi/16 km WNW of Valentine, on branch of Niobrara R., near S.Dak. line; 42°55′N 100°45′W.

Crooksville, village (1990 pop. 2,601), Perry co., central Ohio, 12 mi/19 km SSW of Zanesville; 39°46′N 82°05′W.

Crosby, county (□ 901 sq mi/2,334 sq km; 1990 pop. 7,304), NW Texas; ☉ Crosbyton; 33°36′N 101°17′W. On edge of Llano Estacado, with E-facing Caprock escarpment curving from SW to N. Elev. 2,100 ft/640 m–3,400 ft/1,036 m. Drained by White R. (forms White R. L. reservoir in SE) and North Fork Double Mt. Fork of Brazos R. Cattle ranching. Heavily irrigated region, agr. (cotton, grain, sorghum, wheat, hay); hogs, sheep. Formed 1876.

Crosby 1 town (1990 pop. 2,073), Crow Wing co., central Minn., 15 mi/24 km NE of Brainerd, in Cuyuna Iron Range, on NW shore of Serpent L., near Mississippi R.;

46°29′N 93°57′W. Iron-mining; recreation; mfg. (machinery). Town's growth dates from 1st shipment (1911) of iron ore. Craft Mine Historical Park. Numerous small lakes in area; parts of Crow Wing State Forest to N and E; Mille Lacs L. to SE. **2** town (1990 pop. 1,312), ☉ Divide co., NW N.Dak., 55 mi/89 km NNE of Williston, near Can. border; 48°54′N 103°17′W. Trade center; port of entry in farming area; concrete. Inc. 1911. **3** town (1990 pop. 1,811), Harris co., SE Texas, industrial suburb, 24 mi/39 km ENE of Houston, near San Jacinto R. (forms L. Houston to NW); 29°54′N 95°03′W. Oil and natural gas. Mfg. (furniture, chemicals, industrial chemical processing, steel fabricating).

Crosby, village (1990 pop. 465), Amite and Wilkinson cos., SW Miss., 26 mi/42 km SE of Natchez, in Homochitto Natl. Forest; 31°16′N 91°03′W. Trade center for agr. (cattle) and timber area. Until 1934 called Stephenson.

Crosby, Mount, Wyo.: see ABSAROKA RANGE.

Crosbyton, town (1990 pop. 2,026), ☉ Crosby co., NW Texas, on the Llano Estacado, 35 mi/56 km E of Lubbock; 33°38′N 101°14′W. Elev. 3,108 ft/947 m. In cotton, wheat, sorghum; sheep, cattle, hogs; agribusiness; mfg. (meat processing). White R. L. Reservoir State Park to SE. Founded 1908.

Crosland, town, Colquitt co., S Ga., 12 mi/19 km NE of Moultrie; 31°18′N 83°38′W.

Cross, county (□ 622 sq mi/1,611 sq km; 1990 pop. 19,225), E Ark.; ☉ Wynne; 35°17′N 90°46′W. Intersected by Crowley's Ridge; drained by St. Francis and L'Anguille rivers. Agr. (hogs, cattle; rice, wheat, soybeans); hardwood timber. Mfg. at Wynne. Village Creek State Park in S; Darkin Arch State Park in E. Formed 1862.

Cross City, town (□ 1 sq mi/2.6 sq km; 1990 pop. 2,041), ☉ Dixie co., N Fla., c.50 mi/80 km WNW of Gainesville; 30°45′N 86°34′W. Trade center for lumbering, farming, and fishing area. Inc. 1924.

Cross Hill, town (1990 pop. 469), Laurens co., NW central S.C., 14 mi/23 km S of Laurens, 14 mi/23 km NNE of Greenwood; 34°17′N 81°58′W. Mfg. of timber, pontoon boats. L. Greenwood reservoir to SW.

Cross Island, Arctic islet, NE Alaska, in Beaufort Sea, 30 mi/48 km E of Beechey Point; 70°29′N 147°50′W.

Cross Lake, town (1990 pop. 1,132), Crow Wing co., central Minn., 22 mi/35 km N of Brainerd, on W shore of Cross L.; 46°39′N 94°06′W. Reservoir. Mfg. (logging equip.); agr. (dairying; cattle; alfalfa, timber). Whitefish L. to NW. Crow Wing State Forest to E and S.

Cross Lake, central Man., Canada, 60 mi/97 km N of L. Winnipeg. Lake is 68 mi/109 km long, 6 mi/10 km wide. Drained N by Nelson R.

Cross Lake 1 reservoir, Crow Wing co., central Minn., 22 mi/35 km N of Brainerd; 4.5 mi/7.2 km long, 1 mi/1.6 km wide. Drained SE by Pine R. to Mississippi R. Resort area. Town of Crosslake is E shore. Crow Wing State Forest to E. **2** reservoir, Caddo parish, NW La., on Cross Bayou, 3 mi/4.8 km W of Shreveport; c.8 mi/13 km long; 32°30′N 93°48′W. Formed by dam built for water supply and recreation. **3** reservoir, Onondaga and Seneca cos., central N.Y., on Seneca R., 17 mi/27 km WNW of Syracuse; 4.5 mi/7.2 km long N-S, max. 1 mi/1.6 km wide; 43°06′N 76°27′W. Part of Erie Barge Canal on this part of the river. River enters from SW, drains from SE.

Cross Lake, Maine: see FISH RIVER LAKES.

Cross Lanes, uninc. town (1990 pop. 10,878), Kanawha co., W central W.Va., residential suburb 12 mi/19 km NW of Charlestown, 2 mi/3.2 km E of Nitro, near Kanawha R.; 38°26′N 81°46′W. Light mfg. Tri-State Greyhound Park racetrack is nearby.

Cross Mountain (3,630 ft/1,106 m), in the Cumberlands, E central Tenn., 22 mi/35 km NW of Knoxville.

Cross Plains 1 town (1990 pop. 1,063), Callahan co., central Texas, 40 mi/64 km SE of Abilene; 32°07′N 99°10′W. In oil-producing and agr. area (cattle; wheat, peanuts, sorghum). Settled c.1876, inc. 1911. **2** town (1990 pop. 2,098), Dane co., S Wis., 15 mi/24 km W of Madison; 43°06′N 89°39′W. In dairy farm area. Mfg. (butter).

Cross Roads, borough (1990 pop. 322), York co., S Pa., 13 mi/21 km SE of York; 39°49′N 76°34′W. Agr. (grain, apples; livestock; dairying).

Cross Roads, village (1990 pop. 361), Henderson co., E Texas, 44 mi/71 km WSW of Tyler; 33°13′N 96°59′W. Agr. area (nursery crops, vegetables, melons; cattle, horses, hogs).

Cross Roads, N suburb of Kingston, St. Andrew parish, SE Jamaica; 17°59′N 76°47′W. Mfg. of borax. Reservoirs, cols., and movie theaters.

Cross Sound, SE Alaska, bet. Chichagof Isl. (S) and the mainland, extends 30 mi/48 km NE from the Gulf of Alaska to Icy Strait.

Cross Timbers, town (1990 pop. 168), Hickory co., W central Mo., 10 mi/16 km NE of Hermitage; 38°01′N 93°13′W.

Cross Village, village, Emmet co., NW Mich., on bluffs above L. Michigan, 19 mi/31 km NNW of Petoskey; 45°38′N 85°02′W. Resort area. Native Amer. inhabitants hold annual festival and dances. Wilderness State Park to NE.

Crossett (KRAWS-et), town (1990 pop. 6,282), Ashley co., SE Ark., 40 mi/64 km ESE of El Dorado; 33°07′N 91°58′W. Resenthal Natl. Wildlife Refuge to W, includes Resenthal Lock and Dam (Ouachita R.), impounds L. Jack Lee. Lower Ouachita Wildlife Management Area to SW. A lumbering "company town," also producing chemicals, paper prods., fabricated steel, meat packing, adhesives.

Crossfield, town (1991 pop. 1,739), S central Alta., Canada, 25 mi/40 km N of Calgary; 51°26′N 114°02′W. Grain elevators; wheat, barley, flax.

Crossnore, village (1990 pop. 271), Avery co., NW N.C., 23 mi/37 km NW of Morganton, near Linville R.; 36°01′N 81°55′W. Tobacco, corn, potatoes, cattle. Linville Falls and Caverns to S. Pisgah Natl. Forest to W, N, and E.

Crossville, city (1990 pop. 6,930), ☉ Cumberland co., E central Tenn., 25 mi/40 km E of Sparta, in the Cumberlands; 35°57′N 85°02′W. In region of stone quarries, coal mines, timber, and small farms; makes wood and stone prods., food, clothing, ceramics. Scenic state park and Cumberland Homesteads (est. 1934 by Roosevelt administration) nearby. Founded c.1856; inc. 1901.

Crossville (KRAHS-vil), town (1990 pop. 1,350), De Kalb co., NE Ala., 20 mi/32 km SW of Fort Payne. Ala. Polytechnic Inst. has an agr. experiment station here.

Crossville, village (1990 pop. 805), White co., SE Ill., 8 mi/12.9 km NE of Carmi; 38°09′N 88°03′W. Agr. (corn, wheat; livestock).

Crosswicks, village, Burlington co., W N.J., on Crosswicks Creek, 7 mi/11.3 km SE of Trenton. Has 18th-cent. Quaker meetinghouse. Settled before 1700. Hessians quartered here during the Amer. Revolution. Area becoming suburban.

Crosswicks Creek, c.25 mi/40 km long, W N.J.; rises S of New Egypt, flows N and WNW to Delaware R. near Bordentown.

Croswell (KRAHZ-wel), town (1990 pop. 2,174), Sanilac co., E Mich., on Black R., 13 mi/21 km SE of Sandusky, 5 mi/8 km W of L. Huron; 43°16′N 82°37′W. In agr. area (sugar beets, grain; dairy prods.); beet sugar refining; mfg. (filters, food, automotive parts). Inc. as village 1881, as city 1905.

Crotch Island, Maine: see CLIFF ISLAND.

Crothersville, town (1990 pop. 1,687), Jackson co., S Ind., 12 mi/19 km SE of Brownstown; 38°48′N 85°50′W. Mfg. (shoes).

Croton, village (1990 pop. 418), Licking co., central Ohio, 19 mi/31 km NW of Newark, in agr. area. Also called Hartford.

Croton Dam Pond, reservoir (□ 2 sq mi/5.2 sq km), Newaygo co., central Mich., on Muskegon R., in Manistee Natl. Forest, 19 mi/31 km SSW of Big Rapids; 43°25′N 85°48′W. Max. capacity 2,600 acre-ft. Formed by Croton Dam (50 ft/15 m high), built (1907) for power generation; also used for recreation.

Croton Falls, village (1990 pop. 970), Westchester co., SE N.Y., 12 mi/19 km WSW of Danbury (Conn.); 41°21′N 73°40′W. At S end of Croton Falls Reservoir (water supply for N.Y. city), impounded in a branch of Croton R. by Croton Falls Dam (1,100 ft/335 m long, 167 ft/51 m high; completed 1911).

Croton Point, Westchester co., SE N.Y., peninsula (c.1.5 mi/2.4 km. long) extending into Hudson R. from its E bank, just above mouth of Croton R., S of Croton-on-Hudson; 41°11′N 73°54′W. Recreational park here.

Croton River, SE N.Y.; rises in S Dutchess co. in West, Middle, and East branches, which flow S through Putnam co. to join near Westchester co. line; combined stream continues SW to Hudson R. at Croton Point. New Croton Dam (2,168 ft/661 m long, c.297 ft/91 m high; completed 1905 to replace earlier structure), 3 mi/4.8 km above mouth, impounds Croton L. (c.20 mi/32 km long). Lake's waters, with those of West Branch, Middle Branch, East Branch, Croton Falls, Titicus, Cross R., Amawalk, and Bog Brook reservoirs (and others in river's watershed), are carried to N.Y. city by Croton Aqueduct.

Croton-on-Hudson, residential village (□ 10 sq mi/26 sq km; 1990 pop. 7,018), Westchester co., SE N.Y., on E bank of Hudson R., 3 mi/4.8 km N of Ossining; 41°12′N 73°53′W. Mfg. (machinery, industrial diamonds; metal fabrication). Seat of Hessian Hills School. Includes Amtrak and Metro-North RR yards. During 1920s, fashionable haven for intellectuals, e.g., Edna St. Vincent Millay, Doris Stevens, Stuart Chase, and John Reed. Van Cortlandt Manor, a restored 18th-cent. Du.-Eng. manor house on 20 acres/8 ha of what was once 86,000-acres/34,804-ha estate is located here. Settled 1609, inc. 1898.

Crouch, village (1990 pop. 75), Boise co., SW Idaho, 30 mi/48 km NE of Emmett, on Middle Fork Payette R.; 44°07′N 115°58′W. Agr., cattle raising, lumbering. Surrounded by units of Boise Natl. Forest. Inc. 1951.

Crouse (KROUS), uninc. village (1990 pop. 700), Lincoln co., SW N.C., 4 mi/6.4 km SSW of Lincolnton. Cotton, grain; dairying; chickens, cattle, hogs.

Crow Agency, town (1990 pop. 1,446), Big Horn co., SE Mont., on Little Bighorn R., 11 mi/18 km SSE of Hardin; 45°36′N 107°28′W. In irrigated agr. region; grain, sugar beets; cattle. Trading center and hq. of Crow Indian Reservation located in NE part of reservation. Little Bighorn (formerly Custer) Battlefield Natl. Monument to SE; Big Horn Canyon Natl. Recreation Area to SW.

Crow Creek, 140 mi/225 km long, SE Wyo. and NE Colo.; rises in Laramie Mts., SW Laramie co., Wyo.; flows E past Cheyenne, then S into Colo., passes between units of Pawnee Natl. Grassland, joins South Platte R. in Weld co., 13 mi/21 km E of Greeley, Colo.

Crow River, S central Minn.; formed by confluence of North Fork and South Fork near Rockford, SE central Minn., 24 mi/39 km WNW of Minneapolis; 45°04′N 93°45′W; flows 30 mi/48 km NE to Mississippi R. 7 mi/11.3 km NW of Anoka. South Fork rises in Wagonga L. in central Kandiyohi co.; flows 100 mi/161 km generally E, through Big Kandiyohi L. past Hutchinson, Lester Prairie, and Watertown to join North Fork, which rises in lake region of W Stearns co.; flows 120 mi/193 km ESE past Paynesville, through Rice L. and L. Koronis, passes Buffalo to S, to join South Fork. Middle Fork, rises in Crow L. near Belgrade, SW Stearns co.; flows c.50 mi/80 km first S through Mud and Nest lakes, then E, through Green L., to North Fork in Meeker co., c.10 mi/16 km NNW of Litchfield.

Crow Wing (kro WING), county (□ 1,156 sq ft/107 sq m; 1990 pop. 44,249), central Minn.; ⊙ Brainerd; 46°29′N 94°04′W. Drained by Mississippi R. and watered by numerous lakes. Resort and agr. area (dairying; cattle, poultry; hay, alfalfa, oats, wild rice). Iron mining in E, near Crosby. Crow Wing State Forest in N centre, Emily and part of Land O'Lakes state forests in NE; Crow Wing State Park in SW; Mille Lacs L. on E boundary, in SE; part of Cuyuna Iron Range in E, near Crosby. Formed 1857.

Crow Wing River, 100 mi/161 km long, NW central Minn.; rises in 12th Crow Wing L., in Hubbard co., 7 mi/11.3 km SW of Walker; 47°00′N 94°44′W; flows SW through chain of 12 lakes (Twelfth Crow Wing through First Crow Wing lakes), then S and SE, past Motley (receives Leaf R. from W above Motley, Long Prairie R. from S at Motley) and Pillager, receives Gull R. from N before entering Mississippi R. 9 mi/14.5 km SW of Brainerd R.

Crowder (KROU-duhr), town (1990 pop. 758), Panola and Quitman cos., NW Miss., 25 mi/40 km E of Clarksdale, on Yocona R.; 34°10′N 90°08′W. In rich agr. area (cattle, cotton, rice, sorghum, soybeans; timber); mfg. (furniture).

Crowder, village (1990 pop. 339), Pittsburg co., SE Okla., 14 mi/23 km NNE of McAlester, on L. Arrowhead reservoir; 35°07′N 95°40′W. In agr. area.

Crowell, town (1990 pop. 1,230), ⊙ Foard co., N Texas, c.65 mi/105 km W of Wichita Falls; 33°58′N 99°43′W. Elev. 1,463 ft/446 m. RR, processing center in cattle ranching and agr. area (wheat, cotton, alfalfa; oil, natural gas wells; mfg. (apparel). L. Copper Breaks and Copper Breaks State Park to N. Settled 1887, inc. 1908; rebuilt after destructive tornado in 1942.

Crowley, county (□ 800 sq mi/2,072 sq km; 1990 pop. 3,946), SE central Colo.; ⊙ Ordway; 38°19′N 103°47′W. Irrigated agr. region (cattle; wheat, sorghum, vegetables, melons). Arkansas R. (forms part of S boundary in W) drained by Horse and Bob Creeks. Formed 1911.

Crowley, town (1990 pop. 6,974), Tarrant co., N Texas, suburb 12 mi/19 km S of Fort Worth; 32°34′N 97°21′W. Agr. to W and S (dairying; cattle; corn); urban-growth area on Benbrook L. reservoir (to NW). Mfg. (marble, plastic prods.; oil well equip.).

Crowley, village (1990 pop. 225), Crowley co., SE central Colo., near Arkansas R., 5 mi/8 km WSW of Ordway; 38°11′N 103°51′W. Elev. c.4,347 ft/1,325 m. In irrigated agr. region; feed, vegetables.

Crowley, Lake, Calif.: see OWENS RIVER.

Crowley's Ridge (KRO-leez), SE Mo. and NE Ark., long narrow ridge (c.180 mi/290 km long, 2 mi/3.2 km–12 mi/19 km wide) extending S from Scott co., Mo., to Phillips co., Ark., just W of Helena. Highest point c.250 ft/76 m above surrounding alluvial plain. Rich fruit-growing region; loess-capped; contains many fossil beds. Crowley's Ridge State Park (est. 1934) is on W slope near Walcott, Ark. Outlyer of Ozark Plateau.

Crown City, village (1990 pop. 445), Gallia co., S Ohio, 16 mi/26 km SSW of Gallipolis, and on the Ohio; 38°35′N 82°17′W.

Crown Heights, E section (□ 2 sq mi/5.2 sq km; pop. 3,200) of borough of Brooklyn, N.Y. city, SE N.Y.; borders Prospect Park and the Brooklyn Botanic Gardens to NE; bet. Atlantic Ave. (to N) and Empire Boulevard and East New York (to S); 41°38′N 73°56′W. Until 1916, it was known as Crow Hill, a derisive reference to the Afr.-Amer. colony along Hunterfly (Weeksville) Road. Ethnically the community is mixed. The large majority of the pop. is comprised of Afr. Americans (many of whom are of West Indian origin), but a significant Hasidic Jewish community is also firmly rooted here, centered around the Eastern Parkway. The area is the site of the world hq. of the Lubavitcher Hasidic sect. Beginning in July 1991, the neighborhood suffered from a series of racial riots following the death of a West Indian boy injured by a car driven by a Hasidic man.

Crown Point, city (1990 pop. 17,728), ⊙ Lake co., extreme NW Ind., 12 mi/19 km S of Gary, residential suburb of Chicago and Gary; 41°25′N 87°22′W. Some mfg. (metal fabrication, paper prods., machinery). Settled 1834, inc. 1868.

Crown Point, town (□ 80 sq mi/207 sq km; 1990 pop. 1,963), Essex co., NE N.Y., on L. Champlain; 43°57′N 73°31′W. Summer resort on historic site. The French began building Fort St. Frederic in 1731. In the Fr. and Indian Wars the fort successfully resisted (1755–1756) early Eng. attacks but was demolished (1759) before the advance of Jeffrey Amherst. The British began building a new fort, Fort Amherst (renamed Crown Point), in 1759. Early in the Amer. Revolution, Crown Point was captured (May 12, 1775) by Seth Warner and a detachment of Green Mt. Boys. It was finally abandoned (June 21, 1777) to Gen. John Burgoyne in the Saratoga campaign. Crown Point Reservation, with bathing and fishing facilities, a mus. and ruins of colonial forts, is nearby.

Crown Point, headland at SW tip of Tobago, Trinidad and Tobago, 8 mi/12.9 km WSW of Scarborough; 11°08′N 60°50′W. Adjoining is the Crown Point civil airfield. Nearby with fine beach are the ruins of Milford Fort and the so-called Robinson Crusoe's Cave. Cape is also called Brown's Point.

Crown Prince Frederick Island, SE Franklin dist., N.W.T., Canada, in the Gulf of Boothia, at W entrance of Fury and Hecla Strait, off NW Baffin Isl., 22 mi/35 km long, 6 mi/10 km wide; 70°08′N 86°40′W.

Crownpoint, uninc. town (1990 pop. 2,108), McKinley co., MW N.Mex., 32 mi/51 km ENE of Gallup; 35°41′N 108°09′W. Cattle, sheep; alfalfa; Navajo rugs. Navajo Indian Reservation to NW; Chaco Culture Natl. Historical Park to N. Continental Divide to S and SE; Hoska Butte (8,620 ft/2,627 m), on the Continental Divide, to S.

Crownsville, village (1990 pop. 1,514), Anne Arundel co., central Md., near Severn R., 7 mi/11.3 km WNW of Annapolis; 39°01′N 76°36′W. Crownsville State Hosp. here.

Crows Nest, residential suburb (1990 pop. 114) of Indianapolis, Marion co., central Ind., 5 mi/8 km N of downtown, on White R.; 39°51′N 86°10′W. Joined Indianapolis in 1970.

Crowsnest Mountain (9,138 ft/2,785 m), SW Alta., Canada, near B.C. border, in Rocky Mts., 6 mi/10 km NW of Coleman.

Crowsnest Pass (4,450 ft/1,356 m), in Rocky Mts. bet. Alta. and B.C., Canada, 20 mi/32 km NE of Fernie; 49°38′N 114°42′W. At E end of pass is village of Crows Nest or Crowsnest, B.C. Pass was discovered 1858 by the Palliser expedition; later used extensively by Northwest Mounted Police.

Crowsnest River, 100 mi/161 km long, SE B.C. and SW Alta., Canada; rises in Rocky Mts.; flows S to Crowsnest Pass, where it turns E and crosses into Alta., flowing past Coleman and Blairmore to Oldman R. near Macleod.

Croydon 1 (KROI-duhn), town (1990 pop. 627), Sullivan co., W N.H., 7 mi/11.3 km N of Newport; 43°26′N 72°12′W. Drained by Croydon and Beaver brooks. Nursery crops, hay, corn, apples; cattle, poultry. Croydon Peak (2,781 ft/848 m) on W boundary. **2** uninc. town (1990 pop. 9,967), Bristol township, Bucks co., SE Pa., suburb 15 mi/24 km NE of Philadelphia and 11 mi/18 km SW of Trenton (N.J.), on Neshaminy Creek at its entrance to Delaware R.; 40°05′N 74°54′W. Mfg. (consumer goods, electronic equip., paper prods., plastics, machining, concrete pipes, printing; metal fabrication).

Crozet, uninc. town, Albermarle co., N central Va., 12 mi/19 km WNW of Charlottesville; 38°04′N 78°42′W. Mfg. (furniture, lumber, food processing); agr. (dairying; livestock; grain, apples, peaches); timber. Shenandoah Natl. Park to NW, George Washington Natl. Forest to SW, Appalachian Trail and Blue Ridge Parkway pass to W.

Crozier Channel, Canada: see FITZWILLIAM STRAIT.

Cruce de los Baños (KROO-sai dai loz BAHN-yoz), agr. town, Santiago de Cuba prov., SE Cuba, at confluence of small rivers in mountainous Sierra Maestra; 20°09′N 76°15′W.

Cruces (KROO-sais), town, Cienfuegos prov., central Cuba, on RR, 13 mi/21 km SW of Santa Clara; 22°20′N 80°16′W. Agr. trading center (sugarcane, tobacco; livestock). There are 5 sugar mills within 8-mi-/12.9-km radius. Mineral springs nearby (SE).

Crucible (KROO-si-buhl), uninc. town (1990 pop. 900), Cumberland township, Greene co., SW Pa., on the Monongahela R., 12 mi/19 km ENE of Waynesburg; 39°56′N 79°57′W. Agr. includes hay, corn; sheep, livestock; dairying. Bituminous coal in area.

Cruger (KROO-guhr), village (1990 pop. 548), Holmes co., central Miss., 14 mi/23 km S of Greenwood, near Yazoo R.; 33°19′N 90°13′W. Agr. (soybeans, cotton, corn; cattle). Mathews Brake Natl. Wildlife Refuge to N, Morgan Brake Natl. Wildlife Refuge to S.

Crugers, village (1990 pop. 1,500), Westchester co., SE N.Y., near the Hudson R., 4 mi/6.4 km S of Peekskill; 41°14′N 73°55′W. FDR Veterans Administration Hosp.

Cruillas (krou-EE-yas), town (1990 pop. 483), Tamaulipas, NE Mexico, 65 mi/105 km ESE of Linares (Nuevo León); 24°45′N 98°31′W. Corn, sugar; livestock.

Crum Lynne (KRUHM-lin), uninc. village, Delaware co., SE Pa., residential suburb 11 mi/18 km SW of Philadelphia, and 2 mi/3.2 km NE of Chester; 39°52′N 75°19′W. Mfg. (concrete blocks, wooden fencing).

Crummies (KRUHM-eez), uninc. village (1990 pop. 300), Harlan co., SE Ky., in the Cumberland Mts., 31 mi/50 km ENE of Middlesboro. Bituminous coal.

Crumpler (KRUHMP-luhr), uninc. village (1990 pop. 500), McDowell co., S W.Va., 14 mi/23 km E of Welch, in coal region.

Crumpton, village, Queen Annes co., E Md., on Chester R., 22 mi/35 km WNW of Dover (Del.). The village was laid out as a 19th-cent. development planned by James C. Shepperd and Maurice Walsh of Salem, N.J., around McAllister's Ferry before the existing bridge was built. An 1877 map shows white-frame houses on tree-lined streets and 600 or more unoccupied lots. Thought to be named after William Crump.

Cruz Bay (KROOZ), main town on St. John Isl., U.S.V.I., resort on fine bay at W extremity of the isl., on Pillsbury Sound, 18 mi/29 km E of Charlotte Amalie (St. Thomas); 18°20′N 64°47′W. Ferry to St. Thomas.

Cruz, Cabo (KRUZ, KAH-bo), S coast of Cuba, Granma prov., at S entrance of the Gulf of Guacanayabo, 50 mi/80 km SW of Manzanillo; 19°50′N 77°44′W. Lighthouse. Adjoining airfield.

Cruz del Padre, Cayo (KRUZ dail PAH-drai, KEI-yo), key off Matanzas prov., NW Cuba, just outside Cárdenas Bay, 23 mi/37 km NE of Cárdenas; 23°16′N 80°55′W. Northernmost lighthouse in Cuba.

Cruz Grande, town (1990 pop. 8,547), ⊙ Florencio Villarreal municipio, Guerrero, SW Mexico, in Pacific lowland, 50 mi/80 km E of Acapulco de Juárez; 16°42′N 99°09′W. Sugarcane, fruit; livestock.

Cruz, La, Mexico: see LA CRUZ.

Crysler, village, SE Ont., Canada, on South Nation R., 30 mi/48 km NW of Cornwall. Dairying, mixed farming.

Crystal, town (1990 pop. 303), Aroostook co., E central Maine, 27 mi/43 km WSW of Houlton; 46°00′N 68°22′W.

Crystal, village (1990 pop. 199), Pembina co., NE N.Dak., 14 mi/23 km S of Cavalier, on Cart Creek; 48°36′N 97°40′W.

Crystal, residential suburb (1990 pop. 23,788) of Minneapolis, 5 mi/8 km NW of downtown, Hennepin co., E Minn.; 45°02′N 93°21′W. RR junction. Mfg. (textiles, light mfg.). Crystal Airport in N; Twin L. in NE.

Crystal Bay (KRI-stuhl), uninc. town (1990 pop. 2,600), Washoe co., W Nev., 13 mi/21 km WNW of Carson City, at Calif. state line, on N end of L. Tahoe, on W side of Crystal Bay. One of several gambling resort towns scattered along Nev. border. Tourism. Toiyabe Natl. Forest to NE; Tahoe Natl. Forest (Calif.) to W.

Crystal Beach, uninc. village (1990 pop. 787), Galveston co., SE Texas, 18 mi/29 km NE of Galveston, on Bolivar Peninsula, bet. Gulf of Mexico (S) and Intracostal Waterway and East Bay, arm of Galveston Bay (both N). Resort area.

Crystal Beach, village, S Ont., Canada, on L. Erie, 8 mi/12.9 km WSW of Fort Erie; 45°03′N 79°24′W. Resort.

Crystal Caverns, Va.: see STRASBURG.

Crystal City, city (1990 pop. 4,088), Jefferson co., E Mo., on Mississippi R., 30 mi/48 km S of St. Louis; part of Festus/Crystal City twin cities satellite; 38°13′N 90°22′W. Mfg. (machinery, fertilizer). Silica (industrial) sandstone mines. Commercial area suffered damage in 1993 from a flood along Joachim Creek. Inc. 1911.

Crystal City, town (1990 pop. 8,263), ⊙ Zavala co., SW Texas, 95 mi/153 km SW of San Antonio, near Nueces R; 28°41′N 99°49′W. Shipping center and RR spur junction in irrigated area; tomatoes, peppers, onions; pecans; cotton; cattle, sheep, goats, exotic fowl (emus,

ostriches); vegetable canneries. Known as the "spinach capital of the world," town has a statue of the cartoon character Popeye. State experimental farm nearby.

Crystal City, village (1991 pop. 437), S Man., Canada, in Pembina Mts., 65 mi/105 km SSW of Portage la Prairie, near N.Dak. border; 49°08′N 98°57′W. Wheat; lumbering.

Crystal Falls, town (1990 pop. 1,922), ⊙ Iron co., SW Upper Peninsula, Mich., 15 mi/24 km E of Iron R. city, near falls on Paint R.; 46°06′N 88°19′W. Lumbering; dairy farming; mfg. (wood prods.). Its many lakes attract tourists. Crystella Ski Area to SW; Bewabic State Park to W. Inc. as village 1889, as city 1899.

Crystal I, air base, N Que., Canada, on Caniapiscau (Koksoak) R., near its mouth on Ungava Bay, 6 mi/10 km SW of Kuujjuaa (Fort Chimo); 58°07′N 68°26′W. North Warning System here.

Crystal II, Canada: see IQALUIT.

Crystal III, Canada: see BROUGHTON ISLAND.

Crystal Lake, city (1990 pop. 24,512), McHenry co., NE Ill., satellite community of Chicago; 42°13′N 88°19′W. RR junction. In agr. area (corn, soybeans). Electrical components and tools are manufactured, also plastic molds, machinery, and medical equip. McHenry County Community Col. is here. Inc. 1914.

Crystal Lake 1 town (□ 2 sq mi/5.2 sq km; 1990 pop. 5,300), Washington co., NW Fla., 19 mi/31 km N of Panama City; 28°02′N 81°54′W. Numerous lakes in the immediate area. **2** town (1990 pop. 266), Hancock co., N Iowa, 13 mi/21 km NW of Garner, on Crystal L. (1 mi/1.6 km long; main source of Iowa R.) and in Crystal L. State Park; 43°13′N 93°47′W. Summer resort; has creamery.

Crystal Lake 1 in Benzie co., NW Mich., 25 mi/40 km SW of Traverse City, 2 mi/3.2 km NE of Frankfort, near L. Michigan; c.8 mi/12.9 km long, 2 mi/3.2 km wide; 44°39′N 89°09′W. It and its neighboring lakes have been formed by blockage of rivers, flowing into L. Michigan by natural sand dune deposits along lakeshore. Tourism and recreation. **2** in town of Barton, Orleans co., N Vt., in Crystal L. State Park, 23 mi/37 km NNW of St. Johnsbury; c.3 mi/4.8 km long; 44°44′N 72°09′W. Source of Barton R. 3 mi/4.8 km SE. Resorts.

Crystal Lake, Conn.: see ELLINGTON.

Crystal Lake Park, village (1990 pop. 506), St. Louis co., E Mo., residential suburb 16 mi/26 km W of downtown St. Louis; 38°37′N 90°25′W.

Crystal Lakes, uninc. village (1990 pop. 1,613), Clark co., SE Ohio, 5 mi/8 km NE of Dayton; 39°53′N 84°01′W.

Crystal River, fishing town (□ 4 sq mi/10.4 sq km; 1990 pop. 4,044), Citrus co., N central Fla., on Crystal R. (c.7 mi/11.3 km long) near its mouth on the Gulf, 34 mi/55 km WSW of Ocala; 28°53′N 82°35′W.

Crystal River, c.40 mi/64 km long, W central Colo.; rises in Elk Mts., NW Gunnison co., near Marble; flows N to Roaring Fork R. at Carbondale.

Crystal Rock Caves, Ohio: see SANDUSKY.

Crystal Springs, town (1990 pop. 5,643), Copiah co., SW Miss., 24 mi/39 km SSW of Jackson. Agr. (cotton, corn, soybeans, tomatoes; poultry, cattle; dairying); mfg. (apparel, sand and gravel processing, furniture, concrete, meat processing).

Cuajimalpa de Morelos (kwah-hee-MAHL-pah de mor-E-los), delegación (1990 pop. 119,669), Federal Dist., central Mexico, 13 mi/21 km SW of Mexico city; 19°26′N 99°17′W. At the foot of the Cumbres de Ajusco, this is one of the least urbanized parts of the Federal Dist. On the main Mexico City–Toluca de Lerdo Highway.

Cuajinicuilapa (kwa-hee-nee-kwee-LAH-pah), town (1990 pop. 8,439), Guerrero, SW Mexico, in Pacific lowland, 14 mi/23 km S of Ometepec. Fruit, sugarcane; livestock. Also known as Santa María.

Cualác (kwah-LAK), town (1990 pop. 1,428), Guerrero, SW Mexico, in Sierra Madre del Sur, 40 mi/64 km ENE of Chilapa de Álvarez. Cereals, fruit.

Cuanalá (kwah-nah-LAH), town (1990 pop. 4,081), ⊙ Juan C. Bonilla municipio, S central Puebla, Mexico, 6 mi/10 km NW of the city of Puebla. Rugged steep

terrain with water from the Atoyac R. Temperate climate with colder temperatures at higher elevations. Agr. (cereals, fruits, vegetables); handmade pottery and woolen fabrics. Language spoken is Náhuatl. Nearby roads connect with Atlixco and Puebla.

Cuapiaxtla (kwah-pee-AHSH-tlah), town (1990 pop. 5,200), ⊙ Cuapiaxtla municipio, Tlaxcala, central Mexico, on Puebla border, 33 mi/53 km NE of Puebla. Elev. 8,146 ft/2,483 m. Cereals, alfalfa; stock; wood, medicinal plants; arts and crafts.

Cuapiaxtla de Madero (kwah-pee-AHSH-tlah de mah-DE-ro), town (1990 pop. 3,885), central Puebla, Mexico, 7 mi/11 km SW of Tepeaca. Elev. 6,321 ft/2,050 m. Temperate climate. Resources are irrigated agr. (cereals, fruits), marble mines, horticulture, woods, cattle raising. Famous for fruit wines.

Cuatrociénegas (kwah-TRO-see-E-ne-gahs) or **Cuatro Ciénegas de Carranza**, town (1990 pop. 8,454), ⊙ Cuatrociénegas municipio, Coahuila, N Mexico, on RR, 130 mi/209 km NE of Torreón; 26°58′N 102°4′W. Elev. 2,434 ft/742 m. Cattle raising. Mines extract silver, copper, and lead.

Cuauhtémoc (kwou-TE-mok), delegación (1990 pop. 595,960) of Federal Dist., Mexico, N of Paseo de la Reforma, on which stands the statue of Cuauhtémoc, last Aztec emperor. One of 4 original delegaciones of the city, it includes most of downtown Mexico city, including Plaza de la Constitución (Zócalo), Alameda Park, and tourist zones.

Cuauhtémoc (kwou-TE-mok), city (1990 pop. 69,895) and township, Chihuahua, N Mexico, in Sierra Madre Occidental, 50 mi/80 km WSW of Chihuahua; 28°26′N 106°50′W. Elev. 6,893 ft/2,101 m. RR junction, agr. center (corn, wheat, beans, fruit; livestock). Mennonite farm cos. nearby.

Cuauhtémoc (kwou-TE-mok), town (1990 pop. 6,938), Colima, W Mexico, in W outliers of Sierra Madre Occidental, 10 mi/16 km NE of Colima. Agr. center (corn, beans, rice, sugarcane, fruit; livestock).

Cuauhtémoc, Mexico: see SAN PEDRO PIEDRA GORDA.

Cuauhtémoc, Villa, Mexico: see VILLA CUAUHTÉMOC.

Cuautempan, Mexico: see SAN ESTEBAN CUAUTEMPAN.

Cuautepec (kwou-TE-pek), town (1990 pop. 2,701), Guerrero, SW Mexico, in Pacific lowland, 55 mi/89 km E of Acapulco de Juárez. Sugarcane, fruit; livestock.

Cuautepec (kwou-TE-pek), suburb, Federal Dist., central Mexico, 8 mi/12.9 km N of Mexico city. Part of Gustavo A. Madero delegación.

Cuautepec de Hinojosa (kwou-TE-pek de ee-no-HO-sah), town (1990 pop. 11,574), ⊙ Cuautepec municipio, Hidalgo, central Mexico, on RR, 28 mi/45 km ESE of Pachuca de Soto. Cereals, maguey; livestock.

Cuautinchán (kwou-teen-CHAHN), town (1990 pop.1,350), central Puebla, Mexico, 12 mi/18 km E of San Francisco Totimehuacan. Temperate climate. Agr. (beans, wheat, corn, fruits); cattle; marble.

Cuautitlán (kwou-tee-TLAHN), city (1990 pop. 313,238), ⊙ Cuautitlán municipio, Mexico state, central Mexico, 20 mi/32 km N of Mexico city; 19°40′N 99°10′W. Elev. 7,388 ft/2,252 m. Wool and cotton textiles; other mfg. A part of the Área Metropolitan de la Ciudad de México.

Cuautitlán (kwou-tee-TLAHN), town (1990 pop. 1,926), in S central Jalisco, Mexico; 19°26′N 104°26′W. Near La Huerta, Cihuatlán, and the state of Colima. S flank of Sierra Manantlan. Agr. (wood prods., corn, beans; livestock). Has unmined iron and manganese resources. Sometimes Pueblo Nuevo.

Cuautitlán Izcalli (kwou-tee-TLAHN ees-KAH-yee), city (1990 pop. 41,172), adjoins Cuautitlán on the W, Atizapan on the N; part of the Zona Metropolitana de la Ciudad de México; 19°38′N 99°13′W. Rapidly urbanizing.

Cuautitlán River, canalized stream, c.35 mi/56 km long, Mexico state, central Mexico; draining former L. Texcoco and L. Zumpango to Tula R. (Pánuco R. system) via Tequixquiac tunnel.

Cuautla (KWOU-tlah), city (1990 pop. 110,242) and township, Morelos state, S Mexico, in the Cuautla R. valley; 18°48′N 98°57′W. It is a highway junction and the heart of a sugarcane- and rice-growing dist. Cuautla's hot springs and lovely scenery make it a popular resort and tourist attraction. Historically, Cuautla is famous for the heroic defense made here in 1812 by patriot forces under José María Morelos y Pavón, who cut through Span. troops besieging the town. The city is sometimes called Ciudad Morelos.

Cuautla (KWOU-tlah), town (1990 pop. 1,513), Jalisco, W Mexico, 35 mi/56 km SW of Ameca. Spa with sulphur springs.

Cuautlancingo, Mexico: see SAN JUAN CUAUTLANCINGO.

Cuaxomulco (kwa-ho-MOOL-ko), town (1990 pop. 1,877), Tlaxcala, central Mexico, 7 mi/11.3 km NE of Tlaxcala. Corn, wheat, maguey; stock. Also known as San Antonio Cuaxomulco. Sometimes spelled Coajomulco.

Cuayuca de Andrade, Mexico: see SAN PEDRO CUAYUCA.

Cub Hill, village, Baltimore co., N Md., 10 mi/16 km NE of downtown Baltimore.

Cub Run, uninc. village (1990 pop. 500), Hart co., central Ky., 9 mi/14.5 km WNW of Munfordville. Tobacco, grain; livestock; dairying. Mfg. (animal feeds). Nolin R. L. reservoir to NW; Mammoth Cave Natl. Park to S.

Cuba, republic (☐ 42,804 sq mi/110,922 sq km; 1991 est. pop. 10,705,000, including Isla de Juventud), consisting of the isl. of Cuba and numerous adjacent isls.; ⊙ HAVANA (Span. *La Habana*). Cuba is the largest of the Greater Antilles and westernmost country in the West Indies and lies strategically at the entrance of the Gulf of Mexico, with the W sect. only 90 mi/145 km S of Key West, Fla. The S coast is washed by the Caribbean Sea, the N coast by the Atlantic Ocean, the Fla. Straits, and the Gulf of Mexico, and in the E the Windward Passage separates Cuba from Haiti. The shores are often marshy and are fringed by coral reefs and keys. There are many fine seaports—Havana (the chief import point), CIENFUEGOS, MATANZAS, CÁRDENAS, NUEVITAS, SANTIAGO DE CUBA, , and GUANTÁNAMO (a U.S. naval base since 1903). Cuba has 3 mt. regions: the Sierra Maestra in the E, rising to 6,560 ft/2,000 m in the Pico Turquino; a lower range, the scenic Sierra de los Órganos, in the W; and the Sierra de Trinidad, or Escambray, a picturesque mass of hills amid the plains and rolling country of central Cuba, a region of vast sugar plantations. The rest of the isl. is level or rolling terrain. The topography, the semitropical and generally uniform climate, and the soil are suitable for various crops, but sugarcane has been dominant since the early 19th cent.; it is grown on about ⅔ of all cropland. Some attempts at diversification have been made, but the program of agr. reform established by the Castro govt. did not lessen the continued dominance of sugar. Sugar and its derivatives account for bet. 65% and 75% of the value of all exports. Other important exports include nickel, fish, citrus fruits, and cigars. High-quality tobacco is grown, especially in the VUELTA ABAJO region of Pinar del Río prov., and coffee, rice, corn, citrus fruits, and sweet potatoes are important. However, the emphasis on export crops (sugar and, to a lesser degree, tobacco) necessitates the importation of much food. Petroleum was also a major import when the USSR was supporting the Cuban economy and, in the mid-1990s, Cuba continued to trade sugar for Rus. oil. Large-scale fishing operations have been encouraged in recent decades, and that industry is now one of the largest in Lat. Amer. Livestock raising has also been highly developed. Mfg. is centered chiefly in the processing of agr. prods.; sugar milling has long been the largest industry. Some consumer goods (e.g., textiles, fertilizer, cement) are also manufactured, as well as chemicals and steel. Mining has never been of major importance, although Cuba's nickel deposits are among the largest in the world and are gaining in importance. Extraction is difficult because of the presence of other metals in the nickel ore, but production has nevertheless increased considerably and nickel is the country's 2d most valuable export item (after sugar). Large amounts of copper, chromite, and cobalt are also mined, as well as lesser quantities of salt, lead, zinc, gold, silver, and petroleum. There is also oil drilling near Veradero Beach. Limestone, clay, gypsum, and sulfur production easily meet the country's needs. There are immense iron reserves, but problems of extraction and purification are even greater than with nickel, and iron production is still slight. The country's main trading partners are Mexico and Canada (the latter's investments in Cuba's hotels and nickel mines is in defiance of the U.S. embargo). Cuba's attempts to promote tourism have met with limited success ever since the loss of U.S. business in the 1960s and because of the low quality of hotels and other services. From a low of less than 30,000 in the mid-1970s, the number of tourists surpassed 1,000,000 in 1997 for the first time since the 1959 revolution. Tourists from the Soviet bloc have been replaced recently by Europeans (esp. Italians and Spaniards), while Eur. investment has refurbished hotels. The isl. was inhabited by several different Native Amer. groups when it was visited in 1492 by Christopher Columbus. The Span. conquest began in 1511 under the leadership of Diego de Velázquez, who founded BARACOA and other major settlements. Cuba served as the staging area for Span. explorations of the Americas. As an assembly point for treasure fleets, it offered a target for Fr. and Br. buccaneers, who attacked the isl.'s cities incessantly. The indigenous pop. were quickly destroyed under Span. rule, soon replaced as laborers by black Afr. slaves, who contributed much to the cultural evolution of the isl. and sustained the sugar economy. Despite pirate attacks and the trade restrictions of Span. mercantilist policies, Cuba, "the Pearl of the Antilles," prospered. In the imperial wars of the 18th cent. other nations coveted the Span. possession, and in 1762 a Br. force captured Havana; England returned Cuba to Spain (1763) in exchange for Florida. Cuba remained a Span. colony even as most of Spain's possessions became (early 19th cent.) independent republics. The slave trade expanded rapidly, reaching its peak in 1817. Sporadic uprisings were brutally suppressed by the Spaniards. Cuban discontent with Span. rule grew and finally erupted (1868) in the unsuccessful Ten Years War. Failing to achieve substantive change, revolutionary leaders, many in exile in the U.S., planned a 2d war of independence, launched in 1895 with the writer José Martí as its leader. There was strong Amer. sentiment in favor of the rebels, which, after the suspicious sinking of the U.S. battleship *Maine* in Havana harbor, led the U.S. to declare war on Spain. The Span. forces capitulated, and a treaty, signed in 1898, set the stage for Cuba to become an independent republic. U.S. military occupation of the isl. continued until 1902, and economic and political influence prevailed until 1958. Cuba became an independent republic in 1902 with Estrada Palma as its 1st president, but the isl. remained under U.S. protection, and the U.S. also had the right to intervene in Cuban affairs. U.S. investment in Cuban enterprises increased, and plantations, refineries, RRs, and factories passed to U.S. ownership. This economic dependence led to charges of "Yankee imperialism," strengthened when a revolt headed by José Miguel Gómez led to a further U.S. military occupation (1906–1909) and again in 1912 to assist putting down Afro-Cuban protests against discrimination. Sugar production increased, and in World War I the near destruction of Europe's beet-sugar industry raised sugar prices and created explosive economic growth in Cuba in the early 1920s. The boom (called *vacas gordas*) was followed by collapse, however, and wild fluctuations in prices brought repeated hardship. Politically, the country suffered from fraudulent elections and increasingly corrupt administrations. The reforms of President Gerardo Machado (1925–1933) were followed by the era of Fulgencio Batista, a former army sergeant who dominated the political scene until 1959, either directly as president or indirectly as army chief of staff. In the 1930s, the U.S. changed tariff rulings to favor Cuba. However, economic problems continued, complicated by the difficulties of U.S. ownership of many of the sugar mills and the continuing need for diversification. Batista seized power through a military coup in 1952. An attack on July 26, 1953, by Fidel Castro and a few dozen guerrilla fighters against the Moncada jail (in Santiago de Cuba) was abortive. In 1956, however, Castro came by boat to E Cuba from Mexico and took to the Sierra Maestra. There, aided by Ernesto "Che" Guevara and others, he reformed his ranks and waged a much publicized guerrilla war. The U.S. withdrew military aid to Batista in 1958, and he finally fled on Jan. 1, 1959. Castro was soon in control of the nation. Despite its popular support, the revolutionary govt. proceeded with a severe program of political purges and suppressed all remaining public opposition. The new govt. concentrated on the provision of adequate medical care and education to the majority of the pop., with great success. Less successful, however, have been its attempts to diversify agr. production and achieve a self-sufficient economy. The expropriation of U.S. landholdings, banks, and industrial concerns led to the breaking (Jan. 1961) of diplomatic relations by the U.S. govt. That same year Castro declared his allegiance with the Eastern bloc. Opposition to Cuba's Communist alignment was strong in the U.S., which responded with a trade embargo and sponsorship of the Bay of Pigs incident (April 1961), when CIA-trained forces landed on Girón Beach in an attempt to invade Cuba. The invasion was quickly crushed—a debacle esp. humiliating to the U.S. because of its direct involvement. Cuba's significance in the Cold War was further dramatized the following year when the USSR began to buttress Cuba's military power and to build missile bases on the isls. In a dramatic confrontation, U.S. President John F. Kennedy demanded (Oct. 1962) the dismantling of the missiles and ordered naval vessels to blockade the isl. After a period of great world tension, Soviet Premier Khrushchev agreed to withdraw the missiles. Cuba's relations with other Lat. Amer. countries deteriorated quickly during this period because of its explicit intention of spreading the revolution to those countries by guerrilla warfare. In Feb. 1962, the OAS formally excluded Cuba from its council, and by Sept. 1964, all Lat. Amer. nations except Mexico had broken diplomatic and economic ties with Cuba. Cuban attempts to encourage revolution in other countries later abated, and by the early 1970s several nations resumed diplomatic relations. In the late 1960s and 1970s Cuba's govt. policies went through a significant reformulation, including an increased leadership role among less-developed nations, an active program of military support for revolutionary movements around the world, and a reorganization of its domestic political and economic systems. In the 1970s and early 1980s, Cuban troops fought with revolutionary groups in Angola and Mozambique, resulting in the loss of thousands of Cuban soldiers. From 1961 to the late 1980s Cuba was heavily dependent on economic and military aid from the Soviet Union. In the late 1980s Cuban-Soviet relations became more distant as the Soviets moved toward a more liberal position, and with the dissolution of the Soviet Union, Cuba faced extreme economic difficulties as it lost its primary source of aid. Castro has remained in firm control; most of those who had initially opposed him have fled, and, despite economic disappointments, he has long enjoyed a large measure of popularity. However, the decision to allow emigration in 1980 resulted in an exodus of more than 125,000 people from Mariel, Cuba, to Fla. before it was halted, awakening the govt. itself as much as the outside world to the discontent of much of the Cuban pop. The Castro govt. has succeeded in providing free universal health care and education, as well as subsidized housing, but the economic difficulties caused by the collapse of Soviet aid and a continuing U.S. embargo have made it difficult for the govt. to overcome the dissatisfaction of segments of the pop. The collapse of the Soviet Union forced Cuba into the so-called Special Period in a Time of Peace, consisting of food and power shortages, factory closings, and an overall deterioration of social services (especially health care and education) and transportation. In 1993, local use of the U.S. dollar was legalized, as were more than 100 types of private-sector jobs. Though natl. leaders pledge allegiance to a socialist system, a free-market (and illegal black-market) economy flourishes. Foreign joint-venture projects have transformed the look of Havana and tourist resorts in the 1990s. Economic liberalization, however, did not stop thousands of rafters from leaving Cuba in 1994. In Aug. of that same year, a civil disturbance broke out on the Malecón, the seaside promenade of Havana, over food scarcities, power outages, and related difficulties. By 1997, the Cuban govt. had sought and formalized more than 200 joint-venture firms which seek to generate hard currency. The U.S. reversed its policy of granting automatic political exile status to all Cubans in 1994 and instead placed thousands in refugee camps in Guantánamo, Panama, and elsewhere. Principal institutions of higher learning are the Univ. of Havana (founded 1728, reorganized 1943 and 1960) and José Antonio Echeverría Polytechnic Inst. in Havana; Universidad de Oriente, in Santiago de Cuba; and Central Universidad de las Villas, in Santa Clara.

Cuba 1 city (1990 pop. 1,440), Fulton co., W. central Ill., 8 mi/12.9 km NNW of Lewiston; 40°29′N 90°11′W. In agr. and bituminous coal–mining area. Inc. 1853. **2** city (1990 pop. 2,537), Crawford co., E central Mo., in the Ozarks, near Meramec R., 70 mi/113 km SW of St. Louis; 38°03′N 91°24′W. Elev. 1,035 ft/315 m. Resort, agr. center. Corn, wheat, grapes; cattle; wine; mfg. (wood prods., fabricated metal prods.). Inc. 1877.

Cuba 1 (KYOO-buh), town (1990 pop. 390), Sumter co., W Ala., near Miss. line, 16 mi/26 km SW of Livingston. **2** town (1990 pop. 760), Sandoval co., NW N.Mex., on the Rio Puerco, 40 mi/64 km NW of Los Alamos; 36°01′N 106°57′W. Elev. 6,908 ft/2,106 m. Cattle, sheep; alfalfa, chiles, timber; mfg. (sawmill). Santa Fe Natl. Forest to E; small sects. to W; Nacimiento Peak 7 mi/ 11.3 km ENE. Jemez Indian Reservation to S; Jicarilla Apache Indian Reservation to NW. Continental Divide to NW.

Cuba 1 (KYOO-buh), village (1990 pop. 242), Republic co., N Kans., 9 mi/14.5 km ESE of Belleville; 39°47′N 97°27′W. RR junction. In corn and wheat region. **2** village (□ 1 sq mi/2.6 sq km; 1990 pop. 1,690), Allegany co., W N.Y., near Cuba L. (c.2 mi/3.2 km long), 12 mi/19 km NE of Olean; 42°13′N 78°16′W. Mfg. (cheese, machinery, feed). Seneca Oil Spring, where oil was 1st noted by Jesuit missionaries in early 17th cent., is nearby; the spring was the precursor of the "Pennsylvania field," the 1st oil field in the U.S. Inc. 1850.

Cuba City, town (1990 pop. 2,024), Grant co., extreme SW Wis., 19 mi/31 km NE of Dubuque (Iowa); 42°36′N 90°25′W. In agr. area (livestock; corn, alfalfa); processes dairy and farm prods. Inc. 1925.

Cuba Lake, N.Y.: see CUBA.

Cube, Mount (KYOOB) (2,911 ft/887 m), Grafton co., W N.H., 6 mi/9.7 km ESE of Orford. Formerly called Mt. Cuba.

Cubero (koo-BER-o), village (1990 pop. 300), Cibola co., W central N.Mex., near San Jose R., just S of San Mateo Mts., bet. Laguna and Acomita, in Laguna Indian Reservation, 25 mi/40 km E of Grants. Elev. 6,191 ft/ 1,887 m. Cibola Natl. Forest just N.

Cubitas (koo-BEE-tahz), small town, Camagüey prov., E central Cuba, on RR line, N of Camagüey city; 21°44′N 77°45′W. Sugarcane at foot of hills of same name.

Cubitas, Sierra de (ku-BEE-tahz, see-ER-uh dai), low range, Camagüey prov., E Cuba, 17 mi/27 km N of Camagüey, on RR line/32 km long WNW-ESE; 21°39′N 77°47′W. Of calcareous formations with caverns. Chromite deposits and tropical hardwoods here. Average elev. is 750 ft/229 m; Cerro Tuabaquey (1,083 ft/330 m) is the max. elev. of the range and the highest point in Camagüey prov.

Cucamonga, uninc. village, San Bernardino co., S Calif., residential suburb 38 mi/61 km E of Los Angeles, and 17 mi/27 km W of San Bernardino, NE of Ontario, in foothills of the San Gabriel Mts. Wineries; citrus fruit–growing area; greatly urbanized 1970s–1990s. Site of Calif.'s oldest winery. Ontario Internatl. Airport to S, Ontario Motor Speedway to S. San Gabriel Mts. and Angeles Natl. Forest to N.

Cucharas River, c.70 mi/113 km long, S Colo.; rises in Sangre de Cristo Mts., SW Huertano co., near Cucharas Pass (9,941 ft/3,030 m) SSW of La Veta; flows NE past Walsenburg, through Cucharas Reservoir, to Huerfano R. 25 mi/40 km S of Pueblo.

Cucurpe (koo-KOR-pe), town (1990 pop. 423), Sonora, NW Mexico, on San Miguel R., 90 mi/145 km N of Hermosillo; 30°18′N 110°41′W. Agr. center (wheat, corn, fruit; livestock). Agr. center (wheat, corn, fruit; livestock).

Cudahy 1 (KUD-uh-hee), city (1990 pop. 22,817), Los Angeles co., S Calif., suburb, 6 mi/9.7 km SE of Los Angeles, bounded on E by Los Angeles R.; 33°58′N 118°11′W. Mfg. (fabricated metal prods., paper prods., electrical equip.). **2** city (1990 pop. 18,659), Milwaukee co., SE Wis., an industrial suburb, 6 mi/9.7 km SSE of Milwaukee, on L. Michigan; 42°57′N 87°51′W. It was founded in 1892 by John and Patrick Cudahy as a site for their meat-packing enterprise, which remains a significant industry. Mfg. (metal fabrication, bldg. equip., meat prods., hides, machinery). Gen. Mitchell Internatl. Airport to W in Milwaukee. Inc. 1906.

Cuddy (KUH-dee), uninc. town (1990 pop. 1,050), South Fayette township, Allegheny co., W Pa., residential suburb, 11 mi/18 km SW of Pittsburgh, on Millers Run; 40°20′N 80°09′W. Mfg. (paper prods.; metal fabricating).

Cudjoe Key (KUD-djo), island (1990 pop. 1,714), Monroe co., lower Fla. Keys, 22 mi/35 km NE of Key West; 24°40′N 81°30′W.

Cudworth, town (1991 pop. 727), S central Sask., Canada, 50 mi/80 km NE of Saskatoon; 52°29′N 105°43′W. Mixed farming; dairying.

Cuencamé, Mexico: see CUENCAMÉ DE CENICEROS.

Cuencamé de Ceniceros (kwen-kah-ME de se-nee-SE-ros), town (1990 pop. 6,945), in the E central part of Durango state, Mexico, 48 mi/78 km SSW of Torreón, on Mexico Highway 49; 24°53′N103°41′W. The important Velardeña mining dist. is in the municipio (mainly silver, lead, and zinc, with some gold). Sometimes Cuencamé.

Cuerámaro (kwe-RAH-mah-ro), city (1990 pop. 11,741), in SW Guanajuato, Mexico, 39 mi/63 km W of Irapuato, on Mexico Highway 90–110. Elev. 3,822 ft/ 1,165 m. Agr. (beans, wheat, peaches, garbanzos). Dry warm climate.

Cuernavaca (kwer-nah-VAH-kah), city (1990 pop. 279,187) and township, ⊙ Morelos state, S Mexico, in the Cuernavaca Valley; 18°57′N 99°15′E. The city has flour mills and beverage, textile, and cement industries. Cuernavaca is also a popular tourist and health resort. Many Span.-language programs for foreigners here. In the city are beautiful churches, monasteries, a 16th-cent. Franciscan convent, a palace built by Hernán Cortés and decorated with murals by Diego Rivera, and a formal garden that was frequented by Emperor Maximilian and Empress Carlotta. Nearby is the Toltec ruin, Xochicalco, built over limestone caves.

Cuero (KWER-oo), town (1990 pop. 6,700), ⊙ De Witt co., S Texas, 28 mi/45 km NW of Victoria, near Guadalupe R.; 29°05′N 97°17′W. Oil and natural gas in area. Agr. (dairying, hogs, poultry, wheat, sorghum, peaches, pecans). Mfg. (animal feed, cotton and polyester fabrics, light mfg.).

Cueto (KWAI-to), agr. town, Holguín prov., E Cuba, at highway crossroads; 20°39′N 76°03′W. In sugarcane region.

Cuetzala del Progreso (kwet-ZAH-lah del pro-GRE-so), town (1990 pop. 2,746), N central Guerrero, Mexico, located on the left bank of the Cuetzala R., 42 mi/ 67 km SW of Iguala de la Independencia. Agr. produces corn, beans, avocados, plantains, mango, sugarcane, peanuts, and papaya. Cattle raising.

Cuetzalan del Progreso (kwet-ZAH-lahn del pro-GRE-so), town (1990 pop. 4,345), N Puebla, Mexico, 20 mi/30 km N of Tlatlauquitepec, NE of the Sierra de Zacapoaxtla (part of the Sierra Madre Oriental), headwaters of the Apulco R., which enters the Tecolutla R. Elev. 3,353 ft/1,022 m. Hot humid climate. Agr. (corn, coffee, plantains), and cattle.

Cuevas de Bellamar (KWAI-vuhz dai bai-yah-MAHR),

large subterranean caverns, Matanzas prov., W Cuba, 1.5 mi/2.4 km SE of Matanzas, with an entrance at Matanzas Bay; 23°03′N 81°15′W. Their extent is still unknown. Famed for their beautiful limestone stalactites and stalagmites. Best-known cavern is the Gothic Temple, 250 ft/76 m long, 80 ft/24 m wide.

Cuevas de Camuy (KWAI-vahs dai kah-MOO-ee) or **Camuy Caves**, cave system in NW P.R., in karst region W of Arecibo. One of the largest cave systems in the Western Hemisphere, comprised of a series of limestone sinkholes (including Sumidero de Tres Pueblos), connected by the Camuy R. World's highest peak discharge of an underground river. Very large sinkholes occur along its underground path towards the Atlantic. Important tourist attraction, with visitors center at Parque de las Cavernas.

Cuicatlán, Mexico: see SAN JUAN BAUTISTA CUICATLÁN.

Cuichapa (koo-ee-CHAH-pah), town (1990 pop. 2,427), ⊙ Cuichapa municipio, Veracruz, E Mexico, in Sierra Madre Oriental, on RR, 9 mi/14.5 km SSE of Córdoba. Elev. 2,106 ft/642 m. Corn, beans, fruit, coffee, sugarcane; livestock; wood.

Cuicuilco, Mexico: see TLALPAN.

Cuilapam de Guerrero (koo-ee-LAH-pahm de ge-RE-ro), town (1990 pop. 8,561), Oaxaca, S Mexico, in Sierra Madre del Sur, 6 mi/9.7 km SW of Oaxaca de Juárez. Fruit- and vegetable-growing dist. Has fine colonial church and ruins of Dominican monastery (begun 1555, destroyed 1604 by earthquake). Vicente Guerrero, revolutionary hero, was executed here Feb. 14, 1831. Formerly Cuilapan de Guerrero.

Cuilipan de Guerrero, Mexico: see CUILAPAM DE GUERRERO.

Cuitláhuac (kweet-LAH-wak), city (1990 pop. 10,510), Veracruz, E Mexico, 15 mi/24 km ESE of Córdoba; 18°50′N 96°41′E. Coffee, sugarcane, fruit. Formerly San Juan de la Punta.

Cuitzeo de Abasolo, Mexico: see ABASOLO, Guanajuato state.

Cuitzeo de Hidalgo, Mexico: see ABASOLO, Guanajuato state.

Cuitzeo del Porvenir (KWEET-sai-o del por-VE-nir), town (1990 pop. 7,879), ⊙ Cuitzeo municipio, Michoacán, central Mexico, on W peninsula of L. Cuitzeo, 19 mi/31 km N of Morelia; 19°59′N 101°10′W. Resort and agr. trade center; cereals, fruit; livestock; timber.

Cuitzeo, Lake (□ 160 sq mi/414 sq km), Michoacán, central Mexico, on central plateau, 15 mi/24 km N of Morelia; of irregular shape, 30 mi/48 km long (W-E), 2 mi/3.2 km–7 mi/11.3 km wide (depending on time of year). Elev. 6,010 ft/1,832 m. Resort and agr. region.

Cuivre River (KWI-vuhr), c.55 mi/89 km long, E Mo.; formed in Lincoln co. by junction of West Fork and North Fork; flows SE to Mississippi R. NW of St. Louis. Cuivre R. State Park (□ 6,271 acres/2,538 ha) is near Troy.

Culberson, county (□ 3,812 sq mi/9,873 sq km; 1990 pop. 3,407), extreme W Texas; ⊙ Van Horn; 31°26′N 104°31′W. The 4th-largest co. in state; scenic mt. and plateau region, bounded N by N.Mex. line. Cattle-ranching region, with tourist trade; also sheep, goat raising; vegetables, melons, pecans; cotton (salt flats W of Guadalupe Mts. figured in Salt War of 1877); talc, sulphur, marble. In N are Guadalupe Mts. (Guadalupe Peak, 8,749 ft/2,667 m, is highest point in Texas); Delaware and Apache mts. run NW-SE; part of Sierra Diablo is in W; Van Horn Mts. in SW; part of Guadalupe Mts. Natl. Park in NW. NW corner of co. is in Mountain time zone, remainder in Central. 2 cos. to W (Hudspeth and El Paso) also in Mountain. Formed 1911.

Culberson (KUHL-buhr-suhn), uninc. village, Cherokee co., W N.C., 12 mi/19 km SW of Murphy, at Ga. state line, at edge of Nantahala Natl. Forest to NE.

Culbertson, town (1990 pop. 796), Roosevelt co., NE Mont., near Missouri R., 33 mi/53 km NNW of Sidney, 41 mi/66 km W of Willston (N.D.); 48°09′N 104°31′W. Wheat, barley, oats, corn, safflower; cattle, sheep. Culbertson Bridge (1,169 ft/356 m long), spanning Missouri R., to SE. Fort Peck Indian Reservation to NW. Culbertson Mus.

Culbertson, village (1990 pop. 795), Hitchcock co., SW Nebr., 11 mi/18 km W of McCook, on Republican R., at mouth of Frenchman Creek; 40°13′N 100°50′W. RR junction. Dairy prods., grain; livestock.

Culdesac (kul-de-sak), village (1990 pop. 280), Nez Percé co., NW Idaho, 18 mi/29 km E of Lewiston; 46°22′N 116°40′W. Shipping point for agr. area (cattle; potatoes, vegetables, alfalfa, wheat, barley). In Nez Percé Indian Reservation.

Cul-de-Sac (kyoo–duh–SAK), plain, S Haiti, extending from Port-au-Prince to the depression of Étang Saumâtre and L. Enriquillo. Well irrigated, it is most fertile region of Haiti, with greatest pop. density. Grows mostly sugarcane, cotton, fruit, tobacco, and subsistence crops; sisal in NW.

Cul-de-Sac (kuhl-duh-SAHK), valley, W St. Lucia, 2 mi/3.2 km S of Castries. Site of 1,600-acres/648-ha banana plantation that was owned by Geest but now run as St. Lucian cooperative.

Culebra, P.R.: see DEWEY.

Culebra Island (koo-LAI-brah) (□ 11 sq mi/28 sq km; 1990 pop. 1,542), belonging to P.R., 20 mi/32 km E of the main isl., 50 mi/80 km ESE of San Juan; c.7 mi/11.3 km long, 2 mi/3.2 km wide. Rises to 650 ft/198 m. An almost barren volcanic isl., lacking in water; some coconut groves. Has good harbor. Tourism. Main town is Dewey, formerly called Culebra. Lighthouse on E end. Reached by plane from San Juan and Fajardo and by ferry from Fajardo. Culebra Natl. Wildlife Reserve (□ c.1,480 acres/599 ha), comprised of 23 offshore isls. and 4 tracts of Culebra land. Has large seabird colony. U.S.Naval Reservation on isl.

Culebra Peak (14,047 ft/4,282 m), S Colo., in Culebra Range of Sangre de Cristo Mts., 35 mi/56 km W of Trindad.

Culebra Range, Colo.: see SANGRE DE CRISTO MOUNTAINS.

Culebrinas River (koo-le-BREE-nahs), c.25 mi/40 km long, W P.R.; rises SW of Lares; flows WNW to Mona Passage SSW of Aguadilla.

Culebrita Island (koo-lai-BREE-tah), islet of E P.R., just off E shore of Culebra Isl. Lighthouse (18°18′N 65°14′W).

Culiacán, Cerro (koo-lee-ah-KAHN, SE-ro), peak (9,160 ft/2,792 m), Guanajuato, central Mexico, in Sierra Madre, 15 mi/24 km SW of Celaya; 20°20′N 100°58′W.

Culiacán River (koo-lee-ah-KAHN), 50 mi/80 km long, Sinaloa, NW Mexico; formed near Culiacán, Rosales, dammed by Adolfo López Matteos Dam; flows SW through coastal lowlands, past Navolato, to Gulf of Calif. Its waters used for irrigation by many coastal, lowland communities.

Culiacán Rosales (koo-lee-ah-KAHN ro-SAH-les), city (1990 pop. 415,046) and township, ⊙ Culiacán municipio, ⊙ Sinaloa state, NW Mexico, in semitropical lowland, 30 mi/48 km from the coast, on Culiacán R., on Mexico Highway; 15; 24°48′N 107°23′W. RR junction; commercial and agr. center (corn, cotton, tobacco, sugarcane, chickpeas, tomatoes, fruit); leather and textile industry; lumbering (dyewood, rubber). Mining nearby (gold, silver, copper, lead, cobalt, iron). Altata, 35 mi/56 km WSW, serves as its port. Culiacán was a stronghold of Colhua Indians in preconquest times. Founded 1533 by Nuño Beltrán de Guzmán, it played an important part in early Span. colonial era, serving as base for the Coronado expedition (1540) up the Gulf of Calif. A well-built city with spacious plazas, cathedral, and luxuriant Rosales Park.

Cullen (KUH-len), town (1990 pop. 1,642), Webster parish, NW La., near Ark. line, 45 mi/72 km NE of Shreveport; 32°58′N 93°27′W. Cotton; cattle; dairying; logging; mfg. (mulch). Bodcan Bureau Wildlife Area to W.

Cullendale, village, Ouachita co., S Ark., 3 mi/4.8 km S of Camden, near Ouachita R.; annexed by Camden. Mfg. of paper and paper prods.

Cullison, village (1990 pop. 120), Pratt co., S Kansas, 7 mi/11.3 km W of Pratt; 37°37′N 98°54′W. Wheat, grain.

Cullman, county (□ 754 sq mi/1,953 sq km; 1990 pop. 67,613), N Ala.; ⊙ Cullman. Hilly agr. area bounded on E by Mulberry Fork. Cotton, corn, peanuts; poultry and cattle; lumber milling. Coal deposits. Formed 1877.

Cullman, city (1990 pop. 13,367), ⊙ Cullman co., N Ala. Apparel, electronic prods.; motor vehicle parts, wood prods., paper; poultry processing. Ave Maria Grotto, at the St. Bernard Abbey, contains more than 125 models of famous churches, bldgs., and shrines. Inc. 1875.

Culloden (kuhl-O-duhn), city (1990 pop. 242), Monroe co., central Ga., 26 mi/42 km W of Macon; 32°52′N 84°05′W.

Culloden (kuhl-O-duhn), uninc. town (1990 pop. 2,907), Cabell co., W.Va., 23 mi/37 km WNW of Charleston; 38°25′N 82°4′W. Agr. (corn, tobacco, potatoes); poultry, cattle. Mfg. (concrete, printing and publishing, electrical equip., glass prods.). Mill Creek Wildlife Management Area to NW.

Cullom, village (1990 pop. 568), Livingston co., E central Ill., 18 mi/29 km E of Pontiac; 40°52′N 88°16′W. In agr. area.

Cullowhee (KUHL-uh-wee), uninc. village (1990 pop. 4,029), Jackson co., W N.C., on Tuckasegee R., 5 mi/8 km SSE of Sylva, in Nantahala Natl. Forest; 35°18′N 83°10′W. Cattle, corn, tobacco; timber. Seat of Western Carolina Univ. Thorpe L. reservoir to S. Mountain Heritage Center.

Culmore, uninc. town, Fairfax co., NE Va., residential suburb, 6 mi/9.7 km WSW of Washington, D.C.; 38°51′N 77°08′W. L. Barcroft reservoir to SW.

Culpeper, county (□ 382 sq mi/989 sq km; 1990 pop. 27,791), N Va.; ⊙ Culpeper; 38°29′N 77°57′W. In the Piedmont region; bounded S by Rapidan R., E and NE by Rappahannock R.; the 2 rivers meet in SE corner of co. Drained by Hazel R. Rich agr. area (apples, peaches, barley, wheat, corn, soybeans, hay, alfalfa; cattle, sheep, poultry; dairying). Formed 1748; Madison co. separated 1792, Rappahannock co. separated 1833.

Culpeper, town (1990 pop. 8,581), ⊙ Culpeper co., N Va., 30 mi/48 km WNW of Fredericksburg; 38°28′N 78°00′W. RR and highway shipping center. Mfg. (fabricated metal prods., lumber, flour, concrete, feeds and fertilizers, automotive parts, furniture, wine, printing and publishing, wood prods., textiles, clothing). Agr. area (livestock; dairying; fruit, grain). Natl. cemetery nearby. Culpeper minutemen organized (1775). Several Civil War engagements fought nearby, notably at Brandy Station to NE. Founded 1759; inc. 1898.

Cultus Lake (KUHL-tuhs), SW B.C., Canada, 6 mi/10 km SSE of Chilliwack; 49°03′N 121°58′W. Lake is 3 mi/5 km long, 1 mi/2 km wide. Drained into Fraser R. by Chilliwack R. Summer resort area.

Culver, town (1990 pop. 1,404), Marshall co., N Ind., on L. Maxinkuckee, 10 mi/16 km SSW of Plymouth; 41°13′N 86°25′W. Agr. (livestock; dairy prods.; apples); mfg. (transportation equip., pharmaceuticals); summer resort. Site of Culver Military Acad.

Culver 1 village (1990 pop. 162), Ottawa co., N central Kansas, on Saline R., 10 mi/16 km S of Minneapolis; 38°58′N 97°45′W. Livestock; grain. **2** village (1990 pop. 570), Jefferson co., central Oregon, 10 mi/16 km SSW of Madras, E of Cascade Range; 44°31′N 121°12′W. Elev. 2,633 ft/803 m. Poultry, sheep, cattle; potatoes, grain. Crooked R. Natl. Grassland to S. Haystack Reservoir to SE. L. Chinook Reservoir to W. Cove Palisades State Park to NW.

Culver City, city (1990 pop. 38,793), Los Angeles co., S Calif., a suburb 9 mi/14.5 km W of downtown Los Angeles, surrounded by city of Los Angeles; 34°01′N 118°24′W. It is a center of the U.S. motion-picture industry, which began in the city c.1915. Mfg. (rubber prods., computers, printing, textiles). West Los Angeles Col. (2-year), 1 mi/1.6 km to E in Los Angeles and a private law school,. Directly S of the city is Los Angeles Internatl. Airport. Hollywood dist. (Los Angeles) to NE; Pacific Ocean 4 mi/6.4 km to W, including Venice City Beach (state park) and Marina del Rey boat harbor. Inc. 1917.

Culvers Lake (KUHL-vuhrz), reservoir, Sussex co., NW N.J., 8 mi/12.9 km N of Newton; 1.5 mi/2.4 km long; 41°10′N 74°46′W. Town of Culvers Lake on SW shore.

Cumana (koo-MAH-nah) or **Redhead**, village, Trinidad, Trinidad and Tobago, NE corner of isl.; 5 mi/8 km S of Galera Pt.

Cumana Bay (koo-MAH-nah) or **Matura Bay**, Trinidad, Trinidad and Tobago, NE corner of island; 10°40′N 61°34′W.

Cumanayagua (koo-mahn-ah-YAHG-wah), town, Cienfuegos prov., central Cuba, 15 mi/24 km E of Cienfuegos; 22°07′N 80°12′W. Tobacco, sugarcane. Copper, zinc, gold, and molybdenum deposits nearby.

Cumberland, county (□ 1,683 sq mi/4,359 sq km; 1991 pop. 34,284), N N.S., Canada, on N.B. border, bet. Northumberland Strait and the Bay of Fundy; ⊙ Amherst.

Cumberland 1 county (□ 347 sq mi/899 sq km; 1990 pop. 10,670), SE central Ill.; ⊙ Toledo; 39°16′N 88°15′W. Agr. (livestock, hay, soybeans, corn, dairying, wheat). Light mfg. Drained by Embarras R. Formed 1843. On historic Natl. Road. **2** county (□ 310 sq mi/803 sq km; 1990 pop. 6,784), S Ky.; ⊙ Burkesville, 36°48′N 85°24′W. Bounded S by Tenn.; drained by Cumberland R. and Marrowbone Creek. Hilly agr. area, in Cumberland foothills (hay, alfalfa, soybeans, corn; cattle, poultry; dairying). Part of Dale Hollow L. reservoir and State Park in SE corner. Formed 1798. **3** county (□ 1,217 sq mi/3,152 sq km; 1990 pop. 243,135), SW Maine, most densely populated in state; ⊙ PORTLAND; 43°51′N 70°20′W. Mfg. (paper and wood prods., apparel, furniture, textiles); dairying. CASCO BAY and Sebago L.– Long L. area are resort centers. Rivers: Fore (harbor of Portland), Presumpscot (water power), Nonesuch, Royal, Stroudwater. Formed 1760. **4** county (□ 676 sq mi/1,751 sq km; 1990 pop. 138,053), S N.J., bounded SW by Delaware Bay; ⊙ Bridgeton, 39°19′N 75°07′W. Mfg. (fabricated metal prods., construction materials, glass, paper, rubber, plastic prods., transportation equip., machinery, textiles, food, chemicals); agr. (poultry, fruit, berries, beans, corn, dairying); seafood. Drained by Maurice R. and Cohansey Creek. Formed 1748. **5** county (□ 658 sq mi/1,704 sq km; 1990 pop. 274,566), S central N.C.; ⊙ Fayetteville; 35°02′N 78°49′W. Sand-hill region; bounded E by South R., drained by Cape Fear R. and Little R. (forms part of N boundary). Agr. (cotton, wheat, oats, barley, soybeans, sorghum, hay, potatoes, peanuts, chickens, turkeys, cattle, hogs, tobacco, corn); timber (pine, gum). Textile mfg., sawmilling. Part of Fort Bragg Military Reservation in NW. Pope Air Force Base in NW. Formed 1754. **6** county (□ 551 sq mi/1,427 sq km; 1990 pop. 195,257), S Pa.; ⊙ CARLISLE, 40°10′N 77°16′W. Agr. and mfg. area, bounded NE by Susquehanna R. and SE by Yellow Breeches Creek; drained by Conodoguinet Creek. Blue Mt. ridge runs along N boundary; bet. them lies Cumberland Valley (part of Great Appalachian Valley), famous 18th-cent. route to W territories. Mfg. at Camp Hill, Mechanicsburg and Shippensburg; clay, limestone. Agr. (corn, wheat, hay, alfalfa, soybeans, apples; poultry, hogs, cattle, dairying, eggs). NE part of co. urbanized, part of Harrisburg metropolitan area. Pine Grove Furnace State park in S; Colonel Denning State Park in N; part of Michaux State Forest in SW; Appalachian Trail crosses co. N-S in E center and follows S boundary. Formed 1750. **7** county (□ 679; 1990 pop. 34,736), E central Tenn.; ⊙ Crossville; 35°57′N 85°00′W. On Cumberland Plateau; drained by Sequatchie R. and short Obed R. Stone quarries, coal deposits, timber tracts (lumbering); agr. (corn, hay, potatoes, tobacco, apples, livestock). Formed 1855. **8** county (□ 299 sq mi/774 sq km; 1990 pop. 7,825), central Va.; ⊙ Cumberland, 37°30′N 78°14′W. Bounded S and SE by Appomattox R., NE by James R.; drained by small Willis R. Some mfg. in S, at Farmville; agr. (mainly tobacco; also wheat, corn, hay, alfalfa; dairying; cattle); timber. Bear Creek Lake State Park, Cumberland State Forest in W center. Formed 1749.

Cumberland, city (1991 pop. 2,220), SW B.C., Canada, on E Vancouver Isl., 4 mi/6 km SSW of Courtenay; 49°37′N 125°01′W. Coal-mining center, with mines W end of city; logging, farming, vegetables, dairying. Coal, discovered 1891 in the area, has declined in importance.

Cumberland, city (1990 pop. 23,706), ⊙ Allegany co., NW Md., on the North Branch of the Potomac; 39°39′N 78°46′W. It is an important RR and shipping center for a coal-mining area. Its manufactures include textiles, rubber, glass, paper prods., and plastics. Cumberland grew around the site of a trading post, est. (1750) by the Ohio Co. at a natural gateway, through the Appalachians to the Ohio valley. Fort Cumberland (built 1754) was the base of operations for the ill-fated Braddock expedition (1755) against the Fr. and Native Amer. forces and the site of George Washington's first military hq. (1757). The city became the E terminus of the Cumberland Road, or NATIONAL ROAD; a division point for the Baltimore and Ohio RR (completed 1842); and the W terminus of the Chesapeake and Ohio Canal (completed 1850), which runs through Green Ridge State Forest. Construction of both the RR and the canal was spurred by the Erie Canal, which threatened Baltimore's competive edge over New York. Completion of the RR first—and at considerably cheaper cost—meant the iron horse rather than the canal barge would open the W to settlement and commerce. The town was occupied by Union troops as a strategic transportation point during the Civil War under the command of Gen. Lew Wallace, later the author of *Ben Hur*. One of the first great labor strikes in which federal troops were brought in occurred in Cumberland in 1876. Local attractions include the Site of Fort Cumberland; the Washington Historic District; Gephardt House (c.1840); Allegany County Public Lib. (c.1850); the Monastary of the German Redemptorist Fathers (c.1848); the old toll gate house (c.1833); and the Narrows, a magificent gorge through the Appalachians to the Ohio valley. Frostburg State Univ. is W. Settled 1750, inc. 1815.

Cumberland 1 town (1990 pop. 4,557), Marion co., central Ind., suburb, 9 mi/14.5 km E of downtown Indianapolis, on Hancock co. boundary; 39°47′N 85°57′W. Now part of City of Indianapolis. **2** town (1990 pop. 295), Cass co., SW Iowa, 12 mi/19 km SE of Atlantic; 41°16′N 94°52′W. In agr. area. **3** town (1990 pop. 3,112), Harlan co., SE Ky., 20 mi/32 km SE of Hazard, in the Cumberland Mts., near Pine Mt., on Poor Fork of Cumberland R.; 36°58′N 82°59′W. RR junction. Bituminous coal mining, some agr. (corn, tobacco, potatoes); light mfg. Airport. Southeast Community Col. (Univ. of Ky.) Kingdom Come State Park to N; Jefferson Natl. Forest to E; Black Mt. (4,139 ft/1,262 m) to SE, highest point in Ky. Settled as Poor Fork; renamed Cumberland 1926. **4** town (1990 pop. 5,836), Cumberland co., SW Maine, c.10 mi/16 km N of Portland; 43°45′N 70°11′W. Includes waterfront community of Cumberland Foreside. Inc. 1821. **5** town (1990 pop. 29,038), Providence co., NE R.I., on the Blackstone R. and the Mass. line. Included in Mass. until 1746, inc. as a R.I. town 1747; 41°58′N 71°25′W. Mfg. includes textiles and metal and fiberglass prods.. The Ballou Meetinghouse dates from c.1740. Previously known as Attleboro Gore, the name was changed to honor Prince William, Duke of Cumberland. **6** town (1990 pop. 2,163), Barron co., NW Wis., on Beaverdam L., 13 mi/21 km W of Rice L.; 45°32′N 92°01′W. In dairying and farming area; light mfg. Numerous small lakes in area. Settled 1874, inc. 1885.

Cumberland 1 village, Webster co., central Miss., 25 mi/40 km W of West Point. Natchez Trace Parkway passes to W. **2** village (1990 pop. 318), Guernsey co., E Ohio, 13 mi/21 km SW of Cambridge; 39°51′N 81°39′W. **3** uninc. village, ⊙ Cumberland co., central Va., 15 mi/24 km NNE of Farmville; 37°30′N 78°15′W. Mfg. (lumber); agr. area (tobacco, grain; livestock; dairying). Bear Creek Lake State Park, Cumberland State Forest to N. Also called Cumberland Court House.

Cumberland Basin, SE arm (15 mi/24 km long, 3 mi/5 km wide) of Chignecto Bay, bet. SE N.B. and N.S. Near its head are Sackville and Amherst.

Cumberland Bay, NE N.Y., inlet in W shore of L. Champlain, just NE of Plattsburgh; c.2.5 mi/4 km wide at entrance, 3 mi/4.8 km long; 44°42′N 73°25′W. Here, on Sept. 11, 1814, was fought the naval engagement of battle of Plattsburgh, in which Macdonough's Amer. ships routed the Br. Cumberland Beach is a bathing resort.

Cumberland Court House, Va.: see CUMBERLAND, village.

Cumberland Falls State Resort Park (c.1,675 acres/678 ha), Whitley and McCreary cos., SE Ky., in Daniel Boone Natl. Forest, on Cumberland R., 24 mi/39 km SW of London. Cumberland Falls (67 ft/20 m high, c.150 ft/46 m wide), in river here, are noted for "moonbows" on full moon nights; also Little Eagle Falls (40 ft/12 m), on small tributary. Park Lodge; nature preserve. Estab. 1930.

Cumberland Gap, town (1990 pop. 210), Claiborne co., NE Tenn., in the Cumberlands, at Va. line, 45 mi/72 km NNE of Knoxville; 36°36′N 83°41′W. Near Cumberland Gap, natural passage (NW).

Cumberland Gap, natural passage through the Cumberland Mts., near the point where Virginia, Kentucky, and Tennessee meet. The gap was formed by the erosive action of a stream that once flowed here. It was explored and named in 1750 by Dr. Thomas Walker, leader of a land company exploration party. Daniel Boone's WILDERNESS ROAD ran through the gap. A strategic point in the Civil War, the gap was held alternately by Confederate and Union forces. Cumberland Gap Natl. Historic Park estab. 1955.

Cumberland Gap Historic Park, national historical park (20,274 acres/8,205 ha), Bell and Harlan cos., Ky., Claiborne co., Tenn., and Lee co., Va.; elev. 1,631 ft/497 m. Mt. pass, 800 ft/244 m deep, (Ky.-Va. state line) of the Wilderness Road used by pioneers, which followed the Warriors Path primarily used by American Indians. Includes Hemsley settlement, restored 1904 farmstead. Cumberland Gap Tunnel Project (completed 1996); U.S. Highway 25E and RR pass through. Authorized 1940.

Cumberland House, village (1991 pop. 738), E central Sask., Canada, 95 mi/153 km ENE of Nipawin, 60 mi/97 km SSW of Flin Flon, Man.; 53°57′N 102°16′W. Terminus of road from Carrot R. Located on isl. where Saskatchewan R. flows E out of Cumberland L. Cumberland House Prov. Historical Park, site of first inland Hudson's Bay Co. post, 1774, and first permanent settlement in Sask., 1796. Wheat, timber; sport fishing.

Cumberland Island, largest (c.23 mi/37 km long, bet. 1 mi/1.6 km and 5 mi/8 km wide) of the Sea Isls., in Camden co., extreme SE Ga., just off the coast, bet. mouths of Satilla and St. Marys rivers; 30°51′N 81°26′W. Jekyll Isl. is to its N, the Fla.-Ga. state line to its S. Mostly undeveloped; undisturbed maritime forest and beach. Only access of ferry. Once owned by Carnegie family from Pittsburgh. Now managed by the Natl. Park Service as the Cumberland Isl. Natl. Seashore. Visitors center and access by ferry from St. Marys, Ga.

Cumberland Island National Seashore (☐ 56 sq mi/145 sq km), extreme SE Ga., largest island off Georgia located bet. Jekyll Isl. to the N and the Ga.-Fla. state line to the S; 30°52′N 81°30′W. Once privately owned, this natl. seashore is a preserve for wild horses, birds, deer, and alligators. Protected breeding area for loggerhead turtles. Accessible only by boat, the isl. is a pristine example of beaches, sand dunes, marshes, and lakes as they were before the discovery of the New World. Authorized 1972. Access from St. Mary's, Ga.

Cumberland, Lake, reservoir (c.80 mi/129 km long), mostly in Russell co., S Ky., on Cumberland R., 16 mi/26 km/ WNW of Monticello; 36°53′N 85°08′W. Formed by Wolf Creek Dam, built (1950) for flood control and power generation. Lake Cumberland State Resort Park on NW shore.

Cumberland Mills, region, Cumberland co., SW Maine, just W of Portland. Part of Westbrook.

Cumberland Narrows, Md.: see WILLS MOUNTAIN.

Cumberland Peninsula, SE Baffin Isl., SE Franklin Dist., N.W.T., Canada, extends c.200 mi/322 km E into Davis Strait, opposite Greenland, forming N shore of Cumberland Sound; 64°56′-67°57′N 61°56′-68° W. Up to 150 mi/241 km wide. Surface is mountainous, rising higher than 8,500 ft/2,591 m. Pangnirtung trading post on S coast.

Cumberland Plateau, Cumberland Mountains, southwestern division of the Appalachian Mtn. system, extending NE to SW through parts of West Virginia, Virginia, Kentucky, and Tennessee into N Alabama. Black Mt., Ky., is the highest point (4,145 ft/1,263 m). On the east the plateau rises sharply from the Great Valley of E Tennessee; on the west the slope is rough and broken. The plateau is the source of the Cumberland R. and several tributaries of the Tennessee R.. The surrounding region, which is sparsely populated, yields various minerals, such as coal, limestone, and sandstones. The region is also laden with trees, and the forests make for an important resource. There are some agr. subsistence settlements in the area. Cumberland Gap provides a natural passage through the Cumberland Mts., a ridge of the plateau.

Cumberland River, 720 mi/1,159 km long, rising in E Ky., in SE letcher co. Flows generally WSW past Harlan and Williamsburg, receives Laurel R. from E (Laurel River L. reservoir immediately upstream); flows through L. Cumberland reservoir (Wolf Creek Dam), and past Burkesville, enters Tenn., and turns W as it flows through Condell Hull L. reservoir., continues through Old Hickory L. reservoir and city of Nashville, then turns NW and flows through Cheatham L. reservoir, past Clarksville and Dover, reenters Ky. as it flows through L. Barkley reservoir (past Eddyville, Ky.), passes through Barkley Dam 26 mi/42 km above its confluence with Ohio R. at Smithland, 12 mi/19 km upstream (ENE) of mouth of Tennessee R. Neck of land bet. L. Barkley and Kentucky L. (Kenlake), on Tennessee R., to W, known as Land Between the Lakes (40 mi/64 km long; 7 mi/11.3 km wide), a recreation area managed by the TVA, short channel connects 2 lakes just above Barkley and Kentucky dams. The river is navigable for small craft for much of its length. The TVA markets hydroelectric power produced by the dams on the Cumberland and Tennessee rivers and their tributaries. The Cumberland valley was the scene of several important Civil War battles in 1860s.

Cumberland Sound, SE Baffin Isl., SE Franklin Dist., N.W.T., Canada, inlet (170 mi/274 km long, 100 mi/161 km wide at mouth) of Davis Strait; 63°58′-66°30′N 64°37′-68°W. On N shore is Pangnirtung trading post.

Cumberland Valley, 75 mi/121 km long and from 15 mi/24 km to 20 mi/32 km wide, part of the great Appalachian valley, bet. the Potomac and Susquehanna rivers, N Md. and S Pa. It is a fertile farming area that is becoming urbanized. Chambersburg and Carlisle, Pa., and Hagerstown, Md., are in the valley. Locally still called the Hayerstown Valley in Md.

Cumberland-Galleria, suburban downtown, Cobb co., NW of Atlanta, Ga., near the intersection of I-75 and the I-285 beltway. Cumberland Mall, opened in the 1970s, a major retail shopping center. Offices, hotels, and additional retail activity have given the area a distinctive skyline and prominence as a work center.

Cumbres de Ajusco National Park (KOOM-bres de ah-HOOS-ko), a national park, in Tlalpan, Distrito Federal, Mexico; elev. 12,890 ft/3,929 m. The highest in a chain of volcanoes which form the S Sierra de Ajusco. Only a central core remains of this volcano. The slopes are covered with pine forests. A popular site for weekend excursions from Mexico City.

Cumbres de Majalca (KOOM-bres dai mah-HAHL-kah), a national park (11,932 acres/4,829 ha), in central Chihuahua, Mexico, 19 mi/30 km NW of the city of Chihuahua on Mexican highway 45, then 19 mi/30 km NW on an improved gravel road. This park features Salsipuedes Canyon, with fantastically eroded geological formations within oak and evergreen forests.

Cumbres de Monterrey (KOOM-bres dai mon-te-RAI), a national park (616,250 acres/249,396 ha), in central Nuevo León, Mexico, SW of Monterrey, on the Saltillo Highway. Mexico's largest natl. park. The park extends from the W edge of Monterrey to the peaks of the Sierra Madre Oriental, ranging in elev. from 2,300 ft/701 m to 11,500 ft/3,505 m. The park contains many different habitats and a high degree of biodiversity.

Cross references are shown in SMALL CAPITALS. The pronunciation key is on page xv. The dates of population figures are on page xii.

Cumby, village (1990 pop. 571), Hopkins co., NE Texas, 15 mi/24 km E of Greenville; 33°07′N 95°50′W. In agr. area.

Cuming, county (□ 574 sq mi/1,487 sq km; 1990 pop. 10,117), NE Nebr.; ⊙ West Point; 41°55′N 96°47′W. Agr. area drained by Elkhorn R. Cattle, dairying, hogs, corn, alfalfa. Part of Omaha Indian Reservation in NE corner. Formed 1855.

Cumming 1 town (1990 pop. 2,828), ⊙ Forsyth co., N Ga., 33 mi/53 km NNE of Atlanta; 34°13′N 84°08′W. Mfg. includes fabricated metal prods., printing and publishing, food, apparel. Near L. Lanier recreation area. Access to Atlanta by way of Ga. 400 highway. **2** town (1990 pop. 132), Warren co., S central Iowa, 11 mi/18 km SW of Des Moines, just beyond urban fringe; 41°28′N 93°45′W. In agr. area. Badger Creek State Park to W.

Cummington, agr. town (1990 pop. 785), Hampshire co., W Mass., in hills, on Westfield R., and 16 mi/26 km NW of Northampton; 42°28′N 72°55′W. William Cullen Bryant b. here; his home is a memorial. Deer Hill State Reservation.

Cumpas (KOOM-pas), town (1990 pop. 3,102), Sonora, NW Mexico, on affluent of Yaqui R., and 95 mi/153 km NE of Hermosillo; 30°00′N 109°48′W. Agr. center (wheat, corn, livestock).

Cumulus, Mount, Colo.: see NEVER SUMMER MOUNTAINS.

Cumuto (koo-MOO-to), village, N central Trinidad, Trinidad and Tobago, 21 mi/34 km ESE of Port of Spain. In cacao-growing region.

Cuncunul (koon-KOO-nool), town (1990 pop. 934), Yucatán, SE Mexico, 7 mi/11.3 km SW of Valladolid. Sugarcane, henequen.

Cunduacán (koon-doo-ah-KAHN), city (1990 pop. 12,645) and township, Tabasco, SE Mexico, on arm of Grijalva R., and 18 mi/29 km WNW of Villahermosa. Cacao-growing center.

Cundys Harbor, Maine: see HARPSWELL.

Cunningham 1 village (1990 pop. 535), Kingman co., S Kansas, on South Fork Ninnescah R., and 12 mi/19 km W of Kingman; 37°38′N 98°25′W. Wheat. Kingman State Fishing L. to E. **2** uninc. village (1990 pop. 600), Carlisle co., W Ky., 20 mi/32 km SW of Paducah, near Mayfield Creek. Tobacco, grain, livestock, poultry, dairying.

Cunningham Mountain (3,316 ft/1,011 m), highest peak in Dome Rock Mts., La Paz co., SW Ariz., near Colorado R. (Calif. line), 60 mi/97 km NNE of Yuma.

Cupar (KOO-puhr), town (1991 pop. 636), S Sask., Canada, 40 mi/64 km NE of Regina; 50°57′N 104°12′W. Grain elevators, flour mills.

Cupertino, city (1990 pop. 40,263), Santa Clara co., W Calif., in Santa Clara Valley, a suburb, 8 mi/12.9 km W of downtown San Jose; 37°19′N 122°03′W. In Silicon Valley, known for its computer-based economy. Mfg. (computer equip., electronic equip.). Purtola and Castle Rock State Park to SW; Stevens Creek Reservoir and Park and Santa Cruz Mts. to SW.

Cupids, town (1986 pop. 789), SW Conception Bay, on Avalon Peninsula, N.F., Canada. Cod fishery and annual sea hunt. Historic site. Originally Cupers Cove (1612), site of Sea Forest Plantation established by John Guy in 1610.

Cuquío (koo-KEE-o), town (1990 pop. 3,615), Jalisco, central Mexico, 28 mi/45 km NE of Guadalajara. Bean-growing center; grain, fruit, livestock.

Curaçao (kyoo-ruh-SOU), island (1989 est. pop. 146,100), 178 sq mi/461 sq km, largest and most populous of the Neth. Antilles, West Indies; 12°10′N 69°00′W. Willemstad is ⊙ of the Neth. Antilles. Curaçao is semiarid; most of the plant life is of desert character. Oil refining is the principal industry, and the isl. has one of the world's largest refineries, receiving oil from the enormous reserves at nearby L. Maracaibo, Venezuela. Other major industries include tourism (Curaçao is a free port) and ship repairing. Curaçao's ship repair dry dock is one of the largest in the Americas. Visited by Alonso de Ojeda and Amerigo Vespucci in 1499, Curaçao was not settled by the Spanish until

1527. The Dutch captured it in 1634 and remained in possession except for a brief period of British rule during the Napoleonic Wars. In the 18th cent. Curaçao was a base for a flourishing Dutch entrepôt trade. Willemstad has the oldest synagogue in continuous use in W Hemisphere, also a Jewish historical and cultural mus. Economic prosperity declined after the abolition of slavery in 1863 but revived with the introduction of the petroleum industry in the early 20th cent.; also produces aloes and Curaçao liqueur. Curaçao was the scene of severe racial strife and rioting in 1969. Today there are resort-casino complexes in the Willemstad area. It is a duty free port and cruise ship dock. Foreign investment services and off-shore banking are offered.

Curecanti National Recreation Area, Gunnison and Montrose cos., E Colo., Blue Mesa, Morrow Point, and Crystal reservoirs, along 40 mi/64 km of Gunnison R., in the upper Black Canyon (above Black Canyon of the Gunnison Natl. Monument). Administered by cooperative agreement between Dept. of Interior and Bureau of Land Management. Hiking, fishing, boating. Authorized 1965.

Curepe (kyu-REE-pee), residential suburb, NW Trinidad, Trinidad and Tobago, 6 mi/9.7 km E of Port of Spain.

Curlew, town (1990 pop. 56), Palo Alto co., NW Iowa, 10 mi/16 km S of Emmetsburg; 42°58′N 94°44′W.

Curling, town, W N.F., Canada, on Humber R. estuary and 3 mi/5 km W of Corner Brook; 48°58′N 58°00′W. Fishing port; lumbering.

Curllsville (KUHRS-vil), uninc. village, Monroe township, Clarion co., W central Pa., 8 mi/12.9 km SSW of Clarion; 41°05′N 79°26′W.

Currant (KUHR-uhnt), uninc. village, Nye co., central Nev., 45 mi/72 km SW of Ely. Cattle, sheep. Duckwater Indian Reservation to NW; parts of Humbolt Natl. Forest to N and S; RR Valley Wildlife Management Area to SW.

Current River, flows c.225 mi/362 km generally SE, in SE Mo. and N Ark.; rises in the Ozarks in Dent co., Mo., to Black R. just E of Pocahontas, Ark. Many large springs empty into it. The Ozark Natl. Scenic Riverways lie along much of its course through Missouri. A major recreational river for canoeing, floating, fishing. Forms larger part of Ozark National Scenic Riverways.

Currie 1 village (1990 pop. 303), Murray co., SW Minn., 7 mi/11.3 km NE of Slayton, on Des Moines R.; 44°04′N 95°40′W. Grain, soybeans; livestock, poultry; dairying. L. Shetek State Park to NW; mouth of Beaver Creek to NW. **2** uninc. village, Pender co., SE N.C., 18 mi/29 km NNW of Wilmington. Mfg. (machinery, printing and publishig, apparel). Moores Creek Natl. Battlefield to W, commorating battle (Feb. 1776) of Moores Creek Bridge, in which N.C. Loyalists were defeated by Patriots.

Currituck (KUHR-uh-tuhk), county (□ 525 sq mi/1,360 sq km; 1990 pop. 13,736), extreme NE N.C.; ⊙ Currituck; 36°21′N 75°56′W. Bounded N by Va. state line, E by the Atlantic Ocean, SE by Carrituck Sound, S by Albemarle Sound, SW by North R. estuary. Agr. (corn, wheat, peanuts, hogs, sorghum, potatoes, soybeans, cotton); timber (pine, gum); fishing; resorts along coast (duck hunting). Co. consists of a mainland section in NW (part of Dismal Swamp), 25 mi/40 km peninsula extending SE bet. North R. estuary and Currituck Sound and a section of Outer Banks sand barrier in E, includes Currituck Beach (lighthouse) bet. Currituck Sound and Atlantic Ocean. 4 mi/6.4 km section of Albermarle and Chesapeake canal crosses base of peninsula, Intracoastal Waterway passes through canal and NW part of Currituck Sound, part of Mackay Isl. Natl. Wildlife Reserve in N. Formed 1672.

Currituck (KUHR-uh-tuhk), uninc. village, ⊙ Currituck co., extreme NE N.C., on Currituck Sound, 15 mi/24 km NE of Elizabeth City. Fishing and hunting resort. Cotton, grain, peanuts, hogs. Free ferry crosses Currituck Sound (Intracoastal Waterway) to Knotts Isl. village.

Currituck Sound (KUHR-uh-tuhk), NE N.C. and SE

Va., (c.30 mi/48 km long, 5 mi/8 km wide) N of Albermarle Sound, arm of the Atlantic Ocean, behind (W of) N part of Outer Banks sand barrier; Intracoastal Waterway in NW; opens (NE) into Back Bay (N), both extned into city of Virginia Beach, Va. Intracoastal Waterway passes through North Landing R. estuary bet. sections of Albermanle and Chesepeake Canal.

Curry 1 (KUHR-ee), county (□ 1,407 sq mi/3,644 sq km; 1990 pop. 42,207), E N.Mex.; ⊙ Clovis; 34°34′N 103°20′W. Drained by Blanco Creek. Cattle, dairying, sheep, peanuts, potatoes, cotton, corn, sorghum, hay, alfalfa, wheat, pumpkins, peas, spinach, cabbage, green beans, blue corn, triticale, caliche. Formed 1909. Bordering on Texas (E), Central/Mountain time zone boundary; N.Mex. is in Mountain time zone. Blackwater Draw Natl. Archaeological Site in S; Cannon Air Force Base in S. **2** county (□ 1,988 sq mi/5,149 sq km; 1990 pop. 19,327), SW Oregon; ⊙ Gold Beach; 42°28′N 124°13′W. SW extremity of state, bounded W by Chatco R. and by Pacific Ocean, S by Calif. Drained by Rogue R. and Illinois R. (State Scenic Waterways). Seafood processing (salmon, tuna, halibut, urchins, crabs, shrimp). Timber. Nurseries. Poultry, sheep, cattle. Co. has 11 state parks; 10 are coastal, including Cape Blanco and Hamburg Mt. State Parks in NW, Samuel H. Boardman and Capt. Sebastian State Parks in W, Loeb State Park in SW on Chatco R. Siskiyou Natl. Forest dominates co. except for coastal margin in W and extreme N and NE, including Wild Rogue Wilderness Area in NE, part of Kalmiopsis Wilderness Area in E, and Grassy Knob Wilderness Area in NW. Formed 1855.

Curry 1 village, S Alaska, on Susitna R., and 100 mi/161 km N of Anchorage. Center of fishing and hunting region. **2** resort village, Sullivan co., SE N.Y., near Neversink R., in the Catskills, 9 mi/14.5 km NE of Liberty; 41°52′N 74°35′W.

Curryville, town (1990 pop. 261), Pike co., E Mo., 8 mi/12.9 km W of Bowling Green; 39°21′N 91°20′W. Amish community nearby.

Curtis, village (1990 pop. 791), Frontier co., S Nebr., 30 mi/48 km SSE of North Platte, and on Medicine Creek; 40°37′N 100°30′W. Dairy prods., grain. Nebr. Col. of Technical Agr. (2 years).

Curtiss, village (1990 pop. 173), Clark co., central Wis., 40 mi/64 km W of Wausau, in dairying region; 44°57′N 90°26′W.

Curtisville (KUHR-tis-vil), uninc. town (1990 pop. 1,285), West Deer township, Allegheny co., W Pa., residential suburb, 14 mi/23 km NE of downtown Pittsburgh, on Little Deer Creek; 40°38′N 79°50′W. Light mfg. Agr. (corn, hay; poultry, livestock, dairying). Deer Lake Regional Airport to E.

Curwensville (KUHR-wins-vil), borough (1990 pop. 2,924), Clearfield co., W central Pa., 5 mi/8 km SW of Clearfield, on West Branch of Susquehanna R., at mouth of Anderson Creek; 40°58′N 78°31′W. Mfg. (apparel); sandstone, surface bituminous coal mining; agr. (corn, hay; livestock, dairying). Curwensville L. reservoir to S. Settled c.1800, inc. c.1832.

Cushing, city (1990 pop. 7,218), Payne co., N central Okla., 18 mi/29 km ESE of Stillwater, near Cimarron R.; 35°58′N 96°45′W. Trade and industrial center for petroleum-producing, diversified agr., and stock-raising area; dairying. Oil and gas wells. Diversified mfg. Settled 1892; inc. as town 1894, as city 1913.

Cushing 1 town (1990 pop. 220), Woodbury co., W Iowa, 38 mi/61 km E of Sioux City; 42°28′N 95°40′W. Livestock; grain. **2** resort town (1990 pop. 988), Knox co., S Maine, on peninsula, and 9 mi/14.5 km SW of Rockland; 44°00′N 69°15′W. Includes Pleasant Point village.

Cushing 1 village (1990 pop. 25), Howard co., E central Nebr., 7 mi/11.3 km NNE of St. Paul, near the junction of Middle Loup and North Loup rivers, which here form Loup R; 41°17′N 98°22′W. **2** village (1990 pop. 587), Nacogdoches co., E Texas, near Angelina R., 18 mi/29 km NW of Nacogdoches; 31°48′N 94°50′W. Poultry; dairying; timber.

Cushing Island, resort and residential island (c.1 mi/

1.6 km long), in Casco Bay, SW Maine, off Cape Elizabeth. Settled c.1682.

Cushman, village (1990 pop. 428), Independence co., NE central Ark., 9 mi/14.5 km NW of Batesville; 35°51′N 91°46′W. Marble.

Cushman Dam, Wash.: see SKOKOMISH RIVER.

Cushman, Lake, reservoir, Mason co., W Wash., on N. Fork of Skokomish R., in Olympic Natl. Forest, 26 mi/42 km NNE of Shelton; 47°26′N 123°14′W. Max. capacity 473,400 acre-ft. Formed by Cushman #1 Dam (235 ft/72 m high), built (1926) for power generation; also used for flood control and recreation. Mt. Skokomish Wilderness Area and Olympic Natl. Park, just N. System includes Cushman #2 Dam, to NW.

Cusick (KYOO-sik), village (1990 pop. 195), Pend Oreille co., NE Wash., 16 mi/26 km NW of Newport, and on Pend Oreille R.; 48°20′N 117°17′W. Alfalfa; cattle; timber. Calispell L. to S. Kalispell Indian Reservation to E and N. Parts of Kaniksa Natl. Forest to E and W.

Cusihuiríachic, Mexico: see CUSIHUIRÍACHI.

Cusihuiriáchici (koo-see-wee-ree-AH-chee-see), town (1990 pop. 183), ⊙ Cusihuiriáchic municipio, Chihuahua, N Mexico, at E foot of Sierra Madre Occidental, 55 mi/89 km SW of Chihuahua; 28°14′N 106°50′W. Elev. 6,512 ft/1,985 m. Produces corn, wheat, beans, potatoes, fruit; livestock; gold, silver, copper mining. Formerly Cusihuiriáchic.

Cusseta (kuh-SET-uh), town (1990 pop. 1,107), ⊙ Chattahoochee co., W Ga., 17 mi/27 km SE of Columbus, near Ala. line; 32°18′N 84°47′W.

Custar (KUH-stuhr), village (1990 pop. 209), Wood co., NW Ohio, 11 mi/18 km SW of Bowling Green, in agr. area; 41°17′N 83°51′W.

Custer 1 county (□ 739 sq mi/1,914 sq km; 1990 pop. 1,926), S central Colo.; ⊙ Westcliffe; 38°05′N 105°21′W. Sheep, cattle-grazing area, drained Grape Creek (forms Dewees Reservoir in N). Source of St. Charles R. in SE (forms L. San Isabel). Parts of Sangre de Cristo Mts. in W; part of Wet Mts. and of San Isabel Natl. Forest in E and W. Mt. Cliffe Ski Area in W. Formed 1877. **2** county (□ 4,936 sq mi/12,784 sq km; 1990 pop. 4,133), central Idaho; ⊙ Challis; 44°14′N 114°17′W. Mt. area crossed by Salmon R; Big Creek forms part of NE boundary, Middle Fork Salmon R. forms part of NW boundary; drained by Big Lost R. Livestock raising (cattle); alfalfa, hay; barley, oats; mining (gold, molybdenum, silver, lead, copper). Summer recreation area. In Sawtooth Natl. Forest. Lost R. Range is in E, site of Borah Peak (12,662 ft/3,859 m) highest point in Idaho; Salmon R. Mts. and Natl. Forest are on NE boundary, in Challis Natl. Forest; Sawtooth, including White Cloud Peaks, and Pioneer Mts. are in S, part of Sawtooth Wilderness Area in SW corner; most of Sawtooth Natl. Recreation Area in SW; small part of Salmon Natl. Forest on NE boundary; part of Frank Church R. of No Return Wilderness Area in NW. Formed 1881. **3** county (□ 3,793 sq mi/9,824 sq km; 1990 pop. 11,697), SE Mont.; ⊙ Miles City; 46°16′N 105°35′W. Agr. region drained by Yellowstone, Tongue, and Powder rivers and Pumpkin and Mizpah creeks. Wheat, oats, hay, corn, sugar beets, horses, cattle sheep. Fort Keogh Agr. Experiment Station in W. Pirogue Isl. State Park in W, on Yellowstone R. Formed 1877, present boundaries est. 1919. **4** county (□ 2,576 sq mi/6,672 sq km; 1990 pop. 12,270), central Nebr.; ⊙ Broken Bow, in Loess Hills and Sand Hills regions; 41°23′N 99°43′W. Agr. region drained by Middle Loup and South Loup rivers and Mud Creek. Cattle, dairying, hogs, corn, wheat, sorghum, alfalfa. Arnold Lake State Recreation Area in W. Formed 1877. **5** county (□ 1,002 sq mi/2,595 sq km; 1990 pop. 26,897), W Okla.; ⊙ Arapaho; 35°38′N 99°00′W. Drained by Washita and Canadian rivers and Deer Creek. Agr. area (wheat, cotton, sorghum, barley, peanuts, oats; cattle). Mfg. at Clinton and Weatherford; oil and gas (Anadarko Basin). Washita Natl. Wildlife Refuge to W; Foss L. reservoir and Foss State Park in W. Formed 1907. **6** county (□ 1,552 sq mi/4,020 sq km; 1990 pop. 6,179), SW S.Dak., borders Wyo. line on W; ⊙ Custer. Agr. and mining area; includes S part of Black Hills and part of Black Hills Natl. Forest; watered by Cheyenne R. (part of E boundary); also French, Battle, and Bed Canyon creeks. Mines at Custer; dairy prods., livestock, poultry, grain, timber. Places of interest are Wind Cave Natl. Park and Custer State Park in center; Jewel Cave Natl. Monument to W; part of Buffalo Gap Natl. Grassland in E. Work continues in 1995 on mountain sculpture of Crazy Horse mounted on his horse, designed and started in 1947 by Polish-American Korczak Ziolkowski (1908–1982); to be focal point of a large cultural center and univ. at its base. Co. formed in 1875.

Custer, town (1990 pop. 1,741), ⊙ Custer co., SW S.Dak., 30 mi/48 km SW of Rapid City, in Black Hills, within Black Hills Natl. Forest. Elev. 5,301 ft/1,616 m. Resort; dairy prods., livestock, poultry, grain; timber, feldspar, gold, rose quartz, mica, gypsum; lumber; mineral sands. Annual historical pageant celebrates discovery of gold (1874) in French Creek. Custer State Hospital 5 mi/8 km S. Nearby are Custer State Park, Harney Peak, Mt. Rushmore Natl. Memorial to NE, Wind Cave Natl. Park to SE, Jewel Cave and Natl. Monument to W. Crazy Horse Monument to N. Est. 1875.

Custer 1 village (1990 pop. 312), Mason co., W Mich., 12 mi/19 km E of Ludington, near Pere Marquette R.; 43°57′N 86°13′W. In farm and resort area; meat processing. RR junction to E at Walhalla. Manistee Natl. Forest to E. **2** uninc. village (1990 pop. 500), Whatcom co., NW Wash., 12 mi/19 km NW of Bellingham, 5 mi/8 km S of Canada (B.C.) border. Dairying, berries, vegetables, flowers. Mfg. (plastic prods.). Petroleum tank farm. Birch Bay State Park to W.

Custer City, town (1990 pop. 443), Custer co., W Okla., 11 mi/18 km NNE of Clinton; 35°39′N 98°53′W. Wheat, cotton.

Custer State Park (114 sq mi/295 sq km), Custer co., SW S. Dak., in Black Hills, 20 mi/32 km SSW of Rapid City; 43°42′N 103°26′W. Wind Cave Natl. Park adjoins to S, Black Hills Natl. Forest adjoins to W and N. Third-largest state park in U.S. after Baxter, Maine (314 sq mi/813 sq km), and Chugach, Alaska (774 sq mi/2,004 sq km). Drained by French Creek. The 14-mi/23-km-long Needles Highway (St. Highway 87) is noted for its tunnels and pigtail curves in which the road bridges itself. State Game Lodge, summer home of President Calvin Coolidge, has accommodations and services; also at Sylvan L., Legion L., and Blue Bell Lodge. Black Hills Playhouse and hist. Gordon Stockade are within park. Large bison herd, pronghorn antelope, wild burros, prairie dogs, elk, deer.

Cut and Shoot, town (1990 pop. 903), Montgomery co., SE Texas, 8 mi/12.9 km E of Conroe, at SW of Sam Houston Natl. Forest; 30°20′N 95°20′W. Timber; oil and natural gas; cattle.

Cut Bank, town (1990 pop. 3,329), ⊙ Glacier co., N Mont., on Cut Bank Creek (joins to Medicine R. 11 mi/18 km SE to form Marias R.), and 92 mi/148 km NNW of Great Falls; 48°38′N 112°20′W. Cattle, wheat, barley, oats, alfalfa. Located amid oil and gas fields, supply gas for use in homes in Great Falls, Helena, Anaconda, and Butte, and has replaced coal in metal reduction plants. At E entrance (U.S. Highway 2) to large Blackfeet Indian Reservation. Inc. 1911.

Cut Knife, town (1991 pop. 588), W Sask., Canada, 32 mi/51 km W of North Battleford; 52°45′N 109°01′W. Elev. 2,096 ft/639 m. Grain elevators. Cutknife Hill, 6 mi. NE, was scene of engagement (1885) bet. NW Mounted Police and Cree Indians in the Riel Rebellion.

Cut Off, uninc. town (1990 pop. 5,325), Lafourche parish, La., 34 mi/55 km SE of Thibodeaux; 29°32′N 90°20′W. Elev. 8,038 ft/2,450 m. A line village along Bayou Lafourche (continuous with Larose); has oil and gas field nearby; shrimping. Holds Cajun Heritage Festival. Named for a short-cut canal to New Orleans.

Cutchogue, village (□ 8 sq mi/20.7 sq km; 1990 pop. including New Suffolk 2,627), Suffolk co., SE N.Y., on NE L.I., 11 mi/18 km NE of Riverhead; 41°00′N 72°29′W. Farm, summer resort, and recreation area. Center of a thriving and growing region of vineyards and wineries.

Cuthbert (KUHTH-buhrt), town (1990 pop. 3,730), ⊙ Randolph co., SW Ga., c.50 mi/80 km SSE of Columbus; 31°46′N 84°47′W. Light mfg. Agr. trade center, with lumber and veneer mills. Location of private community col., Andrews Col. Inc. 1834.

Cutler 1 uninc. town (1990 pop. 4,450), Tulare co., S central Calif., in San Joaquin Valley, 14 mi/23 km N of Visalia; 36°32′N 119°17′W. RR junction. Vegetables, citrus, olives, nuts, grain; cotton; cattle, poultry; dairying. **2** fishing town (1990 pop. 779), Washington co., E Maine, 14 mi/23 km ESE of Machias; 44°38′N 67°13′W. Military installation.

Cutler, village (1990 pop. 523), Perry co., SW Ill., 12 mi/19 km WSW of Pickneyville; 38°01′N 89°34′W. In agr. and bituminous coal-mining area.

Cutler Reservoir, reservoir, Box Elder and Cache cos., NW Utah, on Bear R., 14 mi/23 km NW of Logan; 12 mi/19 km long; 41°50′N 112°02′W. Max. capacity 223,000 acre-ft. Bear R. enters from SE. Formed by Arthur V. Watkins Dam (28 ft/9 m high), built (1964) by Bureau of Reclamation for irrigation, flood control, and water supply.

Cutler Ridge, uninc. city (□ 4 sq mi/10.4 sq km; 1990 pop. 21,268), Dade co., SE Fla., a residential suburb, 12 mi/19 km SW of Miami; 25°34′N 80°20′W. The town has grown and developed since the 1970s, and a large shopping center was constructed here. Sustained major devastation in 1992 when eye of Hurricane Andrew struck; rebuilding effort completed by mid-1990s.

Cutten, uninc. town (1990 pop. 1,516), Humboldt co., NW Calif., residential suburb, 2 mi/3.2 km SSE of Eureka; 40°46′N 124°08′W. Redwood Acres Fairground to NE.

Cuttingsville, Vt.: see SHREWSBURY.

Cutts Grant, land grant, Coos co., N central N.H., 20 mi/32 km SW of Berlin, in White Mt. Natl. Forest. Bounded E by Dry R.

Cuttyhunk Island, Mass.: see ELIZABETH ISLANDS.

Cutzamala de Pinzón (koot-sah-MAH-lah de peen-SON), town (1990 pop. 5,195), Guerrero, SW Mexico, on Cutzamala R., in Río Balsas basin, and 7 mi/11.3 km NE of Ciudad Altamirano. Cereals, tobacco, coffee, sugarcane, fruit.

Cuxabexis Lake (kuhks-uh-BEKS-is), Piscataquis co., N central Maine, 47 mi/76 km NNW of Greenville, in wilderness recreational area; 2 mi/3.2 km long, 1 mi/1.6 km wide. Stream connects with Chesuncook L. to SW.

Cuyaguateje River (koo-yah-gwah-TAI-hai), flows c.35 mi/56 km S, Pinar del Río prov., W Cuba; rises in the Sierra de los Órganos; flows past Guane, to the Ensenada de Cortés; 22°15′N 84°05′W. Upper course is partly subterranean.

Cuyahoga (kei-HO-guh), county (□ 456 sq mi/1,181 sq km; 1990 pop. 1,412,140), N Ohio; ⊙ CLEVELAND; 41°26′N 81°40′W. Bounded N by L. Erie; drained by Cuyahoga and Rocky rivers. In the Till Plains physiographic region. Agr. area (vegetables, poultry; dairying); mfg., especially at Cleveland (food, apparel, wood prods., machinery, fabricated metal prods., electronic equip.). Sand and gravel pits; salt wells. Formed 1810.

Cuyahoga (KEI-uh-HO-guh), river, c.80 mi/129 km long, flowing SW through Cuyahoga Falls, then N to L. Erie, NE Ohio, forming part of Cleveland harbor; 41°30′N 81°42′W. Heavy industry located along the river near the mouth. By the late 1960s, the Cuyahoga was one of the most polluted rivers in the United States; in 1969 the river actually caught on fire. This was a major cause of L. Erie's deterioration. By the late 1970s, however, antipollution measures took effect, and the status of the Cuyahoga was much improved. Cuyahoga Valley Natl. Recreation Area was established in 1974 in the lower river valley bet. Akron and Cleveland. Upper valley has much less industrial pollution with river flowing through agricultural communities.

Cuyahoga Falls, city (1990 pop. 48,950), Summit co., NE Ohio, on the Cuyahoga R.; 41°10′N 81°31′W. On its course through the city, the river drops 220 ft/67 m through a series of falls and rapids. A suburb of Akron, Cuyahoga Falls is both residential and industrial, with factories that manufacture metals, rubber, chemicals, pharmaceuticals, and machinery. The city greatly expanded its area by annexing Northampton township in the 1980s. Blossom Music Center, the summer home of the Cleveland orchestra. A natl. park is to the north. Inc. 1836.

Cuyahoga Heights, industrial village (1990 pop. 682), Cuyahoga co., N Ohio, a S suburb of Cleveland; 41°26′N 81°39′W.

Cuyahoga Valley Recreation Area, NE Ohio, authorized 1974, 50 sq mi/130 sq km. Preserves rural character of Cuyahoga River Valley. Trails, folk music, ski slopes, steam RR. Hale Farm, mid-19th-cent. restored village. Western Reserve, interpretive bldgs. and early industry demonstrations are nearby.

Cuyama River, SW Calif., flows c.85 mi/137 km NW and SW; rises in N Ventura co., bet. the Coast Ranges, to Santa Maria R. just E of Santa Maria; flow is intermittent. Oil field in its valley was developed in 1948–1949.

Cuyamaca Peak, mountain (6,512 ft/1,985 m), in San Diego co., S Calif., 35 mi/56 km ENE of San Diego, in Cuyanaca Rancho State Park (c.24,709 acres/10,000 ha).

Cuyamecalco Villa de Zaragoza (koo-yah-me-KAHL-ko VEE-yah de sah-rah-GO-sah), town (1990 pop. 1,604), in the state of Oaxaca, Mexico, 16 mi/25 km NE of San Juan Bautista Cuicatlán. Mountainous region irrigated by Grande River. Temperate climate. Agr. (corn, beans, wheat, fruits); wood prods.

Cuyoaco (koo-yo-AH-ko), town (1990 pop. 1,372), Puebla, central Mexico, 24 mi/39 km SW of Teziutlán. Corn, maguey.

Cuyuna (kei-YOO-nuh), village (1990 pop. 172), Crow Wing co., central Minn., near Mississippi R., 18 mi/29 km NE of Brainerd, in region of woods and lakes; 46°30′N 93°55′W. Located at center of Cuyuna Iron Range, iron mining dist. Area surrounded by Crow Wing State Forest.

Cuyuna Iron Range (kei-YOO-nuh), Crow Wing and Aitkin cos., N central Minn. Runs c.30 mi/48 km E–W parallel with Mississippi R., N of Aitkin; 46°22′N 94°10′W. Includes iron mines at Cuyuna and Trommald; production has declined.

Cuzamá (koo-sah-MAH), town (1990 pop. 2,653), Yucatán, SE Mexico, 25 mi/40 km SE of Mérida. Henequen.

C. W. McConaughy, Lake, reservoir (□ 50 sq mi/130 sq km), Keith co., W central Nebr., on North Platte R., c.50 mi/80 km W of North Platte; 27 mi/43 km long, average width 2 mi/3.2 km; 41°13′N 101°40′W. Max. capacity 2,000,000 acre-ft. Formed by Kingsley Dam (earthfill; 162 ft/49 m high, c.1 mi/1.6 km thick at base), built (1941) for power generation and irrigation. Water is diverted through conduit and canal to Sutherland Reservoir and power plant on South Platte R. (30 mi/48 km SE). L. C.W. McConaughy and L. Ogallala state recreation areas here.

Cygnet, village (1990 pop. 560), Wood co., NW Ohio, 9 mi/14 km S of Bowling Green, in agr. area; 41°14′N 83°38′W.

Cylinder, town (1990 pop. 112), Palo Alto co., NW Iowa, 7 mi/11.3 km E of Emmetsburg; 43°05′N 94°32′W. Livestock, grain.

Cynthiana 1 (sin-thee-AN-uh), town (1990 pop. 669), Posey co., SW Ind., 20 mi/32 km NNE of Mount Vernon; 38°11′N 87°43′W. In agr. area. **2** town (1990 pop. 6,497), ⊙ Harrison co., N Ky., on South Fork of Licking R., and 27 mi/43 km NNE of Lexington, in Bluegrass area; 38°23′N 84°17′W. Agr. (grain, burley tobacco; livestock; poultry; dairy prods.); mfg. (construction materials, fabricated metal prods.). Cynthiana–Harrison Co. Airport to S. Raided (1862, 1864) by Gen. John Hunt Morgan in Civil War. Points of interest: log house (1790) where Henry Clay appeared as a lawyer; covered bridge (c.1837); burying ground (estab. 1793); Cynthiana–Harrison Co. Mus. Quiet Trails State Nature Preserve to N, at sunrise. Founded 1793; inc. 1806.

Cypress, city (1990 pop. 42,655), Orange co., S Calif., suburb, 17 mi/27 km SE of downtown Los Angeles and 9 mi/14.5 km ENE of Long Beach; 33°49′N 118°02′W. Forest Lawn–Cypress, a branch of the famous cemetery in Glendale, Calif., is a major employer. Mfg. (printing and publishing, fabricated metal prods., computer equip., machinery). The city's pop. has grown with the development of the area. Cypress Jr. Col. (2-year) and Los Alamitos Racetrack and the Los Alamitos Naval Air Station are S. San Gabriel R. to W. Inc. 1956.

Cypress, town (□ 2 sq mi/5.2 sq km; 1990 pop. 1,343), Jackson co., NW Fla., 10 mi/16 km ESE of Marianna, in agr. area; 27°15′N 80°48′W.

Cypress 1 village (1990 pop. 275), Johnson co., S Ill.,

8 mi/12.9 km SW of Vienna; 37°22′N 89°01′W. In rich agr. area. Cache R. State Natural Area nearby. **2** uninc. village (1990 pop. 260), Harris co., SE Texas, suburb, 22 mi/35 km NW of downtown Houston. Oil and natural gas. Agr. area; light mfg.

Cypress Gardens, town (□ 5 sq mi/13 sq km; 1990 pop. 9,188), Polk co., central Fla., just SE of Winter Haven; 28°00′N 81°41′W.

Cypress Hills, range, SW Sask. and SE Alta., Canada, extends 100 mi/161 km E–W along Mont. border, SE of Medicine Hat; rises to 4,810 ft/1,466 m 30 mi/48 km SE of Medicine Hat. In E part of range is the Shaunavon coal-mining area.

Cypress, Point, Calif.: see MONTEREY PENINSULA.

Cypress River, village, SW Man., Canada, on Cypress R., and 45 mi/72 km ESE of Brandon; 49°33′N 99°05′W. Grain, livestock, poultry; lumbering.

Cypress Springs, Lake, reservoir, Franklin co., NE Texas, impounded W arm (Big Cypress Creek Arm) of L. Bob Sandlin reservoir, 13 mi/21 km WSW of Mt. Pleasant; 8 mi/12.9 km long; 33°03′N 95°09′W. Max. capacity 125,051 acre-ft. Formed by Cypress Springs Dam (67 ft/20 m high), built (1971) for recreation and is adjacent to L. Bob Sandin.

Cypress Swamp or **Great Pocomoke Swamp**, in S Del. and SE Md., freshwater swamp covering □ c.50 sq mi/130 sq km, mainly in S Sussex co., Del.; source of Pocomoke R., flows S, and Pepper Creek flows NE; 38°29′N 75°18′W. Once yielded much cypress timber. Timber harvesting and disastrous peat fire (1930) destroyed much vegetation. Also called Big Cypress Swamp.

Cyr (SIR), plantation (1990 pop. 142), Aroostook co., NE Maine, S of Van Buren, 27 mi/43 km N of Presque Isle; 47°05′N 67°59′W.

Cyril (SIR-uhl), town (1990 pop. 1,072), Caddo co., SW central Okla., 13 mi/21 km S of Anadarko; 34°53′N 98°12′W. In cotton, wheat, and cattle producing area; light mfg.

Cyrus, village (1990 pop. 328), Pope co., W Minn., 17 mi/27 km WSW of Glenwood, on Chippewa R.; 45°37′N 95°44′W. Grain, soybeans, beans; dairying; poultry; mfg. (feeds).

Czar (zahr), village (1991 pop. 182), E Alta., Canada, 26 mi/42 km S of Wainwright; 52°27′N 110°50′W. Grain, mixed farming.

D

Dacoma (duh-KOM-uh), village (1990 pop. 182), Woods co., NW Okla., 11 mi/18 km SE of Alva, on Eagle Chief Creek; 36°39′N 98°33′W. In agr. area (wheat; cattle).

Dacono, town (1990 pop. 2,228), Weld co., N central Colo., 24 mi/39 km N of Denver; elev. c.5,017 ft/ 1,529 m; 40°04′N 104°56′W. In agr. area (cattle, corn, beans, fruit, vegetables). Mfg. (construction materials). RR junction to S.

Dacula (duh-KYOO-luh), town (1990 pop. 2,217), Gwinnett co., N central Ga., 32 mi/51 km NE of Atlanta, near Apalachee R; 33°59′N 83°53′W. Mfg. includes machinery and light mfg.

Dade 1 county (□ 2,429 sq mi/6,291 sq km; 1990 pop. 1,937,094), SE Fla.,⊙ Miami; 25°36′N 80°30′W. Lowland area bordered by Fla. Keys enclosing Biscayne Bay (E) and part of Fla. Bay (S). Coastal fringe is the heavily urbanized Miami metropolitan area. Interior lies in the Everglades and includes part of Everglades Natl. Park. Mfg. includes food and wood prods., construction materials, textiles. S anchor of the urban area that lines the coast of SE Fla.; has received infusion of immigrants since 1970s, mainly from Central and S. Amer. Natl. Hurricane Center of the National Weather Service is located here in the uninc. suburb of Sweetwater, c.7 mi/11.3 km W of central Miami. Formed 1836. In late 1997 its name was changed to Miami-Dade co. **2** county (□ 165; 1990 pop. 13,147), extreme NW Ga.; ⊙ Trenton; 34°51′N 85°30′W. Bounded N by Tenn., W by Ala.; drained by Lookout Creek; crossed by Lookout Mtn. (coal mining) and Sand Mtn. Agr. (fruit, vegetables, corn, grain, cotton, cattle, poultry) and timber area. Formed 1837. **3** county (□ 504 sq mi/1,305 sq km; 1990 pop. 7,449), SW Mo.; ⊙ Greenfield; 37°25′N 93°50′W. In Ozark region, drained by Sac R. Wheat, hay, corn, sorghum, fruit, soybeans; dairying; livestock; coal, limestone. Mfg. at Greenfield and Lockwood. Stockton Lake Reservoir NE part of co., with recreation. Formed 1841.

Dade City, town (□ 3 sq mi/7.8 sq km; 1990 pop. 5,633), ⊙ Pasco co., W central Fla., 32 mi/51 km NE of Tampa; 28°21′N 82°12′W. Shipping center (citrus fruit, vegetables); has packing houses and large citrus cannery. Dade Memorial Park is 20 mi/32 km N, near Bushnell.

Dadeville 1 (DAID-vil), town (1990 pop. 3,276), ⊙ Tallapoosa co., E Ala., 13 mi/21 km SE of Alexander City, near L. Martin, in timber and agr. area. Inc. 1837. Textiles, plastics. State monument, 10 mi/16 km, at Horseshoe Bend (in Tallapoosa R.), marks site of battle in which Andrew Jackson defeated Creek Indians (March, 1814). **2** town (1990 pop. 220), Dade co., SW Mo., 28 mi/45 km NW of Springfield; 37°28′N 93°40′W. On large peninsula formed by Stockton L. Soybeans, hay, wheat; dairying; cattle.

Daggett, county (□ 723 sq mi/1,873 sq km; 1990 pop. 690), NE Utah; ⊙ Manila; 40°53′N 109°30′W. Mt. area bordering on Wyo. (N) and Colo. (E), crossed by Green R. (enters co. from Wyo. to N, exits into Colo. to E). Uinta Mts. and Ashley Natl. Forest extend throughout most of co. Sheep; tourism. Utah's least-populated co. Flaming Gorge Dam, 17 mi/27 km ESE of Manila, forms large Flaming Gorge Reservoir; reservoir and Flaming Gorge Natl. Rec. Area extend deep into Wyo. Browns Park Waterfowl Management Area in E, near Colo. boundary. Formed 1918.

Daggett 1 village, San Bernardino co., S Calif., in Mojave Desert, 8 mi/12.9 km E of Barstow, on Mojave R. Silver mines near by. RR junction. Calico Ghost Town to N. Solar I (?is)& II solar power plant to the SW. **2** village (1990 pop. 260), Menominee co., SW Upper Peninsula, Mich., on Little Cedar R., and 25 mi/40 km N of Menominee; 45°27′N 87°35′W.

Dagsboro, village (1990 pop. 398), Sussex co., SE Del., 13 mi/21 km SSE of Georgetown near Pepper Creek;

38°32′N 75°15′W. Distributing point in poultry region. Cypress Swamp to SW.

Dagus Mines (DA-guhs), uninc. village, Fox township, Elk co., N central Pa., 8 mi/12.9 km SE of Ridgway; 41°21′N 78°36′W.

Dahlgren 1 village (1990 pop. 512), Hamilton co., SE Ill., 11 mi/18 km NW of McLeansboro; 38°12′N 88°40′W. In agr. area. **2** uninc. village, King George co., E Va., 21 mi/ 34 km E of Fredericksburg, 25 mi/40 km S of Washington, D.C., on Potomac R. Agr. (grain, soybeans; cattle; dairying). Governor Nice Memorial bridge to Newburg, Md., 2 mi/3.2 km to NE. Caledon Natural Area to W. Dahlgren Naval Surface Weapon Center to E.

Dahlonega (duh-LAHN-uh-guh), town (1990 pop. 3,086), seat of Lumpkin co., N Ga., 17 mi/27 km NNW of Gainesville; 34°32′N 83°59′W. Mfg. includes transportation equipment, textiles, wines; trade center; gold mining, sawmilling. North Georgia Col. here. Settled with opening of gold and copper mines in 1829; had U.S. mint 1836–1861. Former courthouse houses Gold Mus. operated by Georgia Dept. of Natural Resources. Tourism important to local economy. N Ga. Col. and State Univ., a unit of the Univ. System of Ga. Inc. 1833.

Daingerfield, town (1990 pop. 2,572), ⊙ Morris co., NE Texas, c.40 mi/64 km NNW of Marshall; 33°01′N 94°43′W. Elev. 402 ft/123 m. In agr. (cattle, poultry; peanuts, watermelons; hay), timber area; mfg. (fabricated metal prods., construction materials). About 10 mi/16 km S are iron-ore deposits. Ellison Creek Reservoir and L. O'the Pines to S; Daingerfield State Park to SE.

Dainzú (dain-ZOO), historic site, in central Oaxaca, Mexico, 16 mi/25 km SE of Oaxaca, on a dirt road, off Mexican Highway 190, bet. Oaxaca and Mitla. These ruins date from 600 A.D. and are currently being excavated. The site was occupied until A.D. 900. There is a huge pyramid structure and a ballcourt with art work portraying the ball players. There are also 50 carved stones, made around 300 B.C., at the base of the pyramid. The site has not been restored.

Daiquirí (dei-kee-REE), village, Santiago de Cuba prov., E Cuba, on the Caribbean Sea, 14 mi/23 km ESE of Santiago de Cuba; 19°52′N 75°38′W. Copper and iron deposits nearby. In Spanish-American War, U.S. troops landed at nearby Siboney. Allegedly, the name of the famous rum drink derives from here.

Dairyland, resort village (1990 pop. 65), Ulster co., SE N.Y., in the Catskills, 13 mi/21 km WNW of Ellenville; 41°45′N 74°33′W.

Dais Mountain (dais), (10,612 ft/3,235 m), SW Alta., near B.C. border, in Rocky Mts., in Jasper Natl. Park, 45 mi/ 72 km SSE of Jasper; 52°16′N 117°39′W.

Daisetta (1990 pop. 969), Liberty co., SE Texas, 32 mi/51 km W of Beaumont; 30°06′N 94°38′W. In farm, timber, oil area. Big Thicket Natl. Preserve to N and NE. Inc. since 1940.

Daisy 1 village (1990 pop. 122), Pike co., SW Ark., c.43 mi/69 km SW of Hot Springs, on the shore of Lake Greeson Reservoir (Little Missouri R.); 34°13′N 93°44′W. Daisy State Park nearby. **2** village (1990 pop. 138), Evans co., E central Ga., 20 mi/32 km S of Statesboro; 32°09′N 81°50′W.

Daisytown, borough (1990 pop. 367), Cambria co., W central Pa., suburb, 1 mi/1.6 km ESE of Johnstown, near Stonycreek R.; 40°19′N 78°54′W. Mfg. (food, fiberglass prods.).

Daisytown, village, Washington co., SW Pa., 6 mi/9.7 km S of Charleroi; 40°03′N 79°55′W.

Dajabón (dah-hah-BON), province (□ 344 sq mi/ 890 sq km; 1993 pop. 63,995), NW Dominican Republic, on Haiti border; ⊙ DAJABÓN; 19°30′N 71°35′W. Drained by Massacre R., and on N flank of Cordillera Central. Main prods.: rice, coffee, corn, fruit; stock; hides; beeswax, honey; timber. Highway to Haiti. The area was heavily disputed during struggles against Spain and Haiti. Formerly part of Monte Cristi prov.; set up 1938 as a separate prov. Formerly called Libertador prov.

Dajabón (dah-hah-BON), city (1993 pop. 12,436), ⊙ Dajabón prov., NW Dominican Republic, on Haiti border, opposite Ouanaminthe, on Massacre R., and 20 mi/ 32 km S of Monte Cristi; 19°32′N 71°42′W. Trades in timber, hides; bananas, honey, coffee. Center of resistance in struggle against Spain and Haiti. Since 1938, ⊙ prov.

Dajabón River, Dominican Republic and Haiti: see MASSACRE RIVER.

Dakota 1 county (□ 586 sq mi/1,518 sq km; 1990 pop. 275,227), SE Minn.; ⊙ Hastings; 44°40′N 93°03′W. Bounded NE and N (in part) by Mississippi R., and NW by Minnesota R.; drained by Vermilion and Cannon (forms part of S boundary) rivers. Agr. area (hay, alfalfa, oats, corn, soybeans, peas; sheep, cattle, hogs, poultry; dairying); sand and gravel. Food processing and mfg. at Hastings, Burnsville, Eagan, other municipalities. N part of co. is adjacent to St. Paul (N) and Minneapolis (NW) and is highly urbanized. Part of Richard J. Dorer Memorial Hardwood State Forest in SE; part of Gores Pool No. 3 Wildlife Area in SE; part of Fort Snelling State Park in NW; numerous small lakes in NW part of co. Formed 1859. **2** county (□ 267 sq mi/692 sq km; 1990 pop. 16,742), NE Nebr.; ⊙ Dakota City; 42°23′N 96°33′W. Agr. region bounded E and NE by Missouri R., form Iowa and S.Dak. line. Mfg. at S Sioux City and Dakota City. Food, leather prods., fabricated metal prods., machinery; corn, cattle, hogs. Formed 1855.

Dakota, town (1990 pop. 549), Stephenson co., N Ill., 8 mi/12.9 km NE of Freeport; 42°23′N 89°31′W. In agr. area (dairying).

Dakota, village (1990 pop. 360), Winona co., SE Minn., 17 mi/27 km SE of Winona, on Mississippi R.; 43°54′N 91°21′W. Dairying; poultry; grain; light mfg. Richard J. Dorer Memorial Hardwood State Forest to W; Upper Mississippi Wildlife Refuge on river margins and isls.; O.L. Kipp State Park to NW. Lock and Dam No. 7 to SE.

Dakota City 1 town (1990 pop. 1,024), ⊙ Humboldt co., N central Iowa, on East Des Moines R., just E of Humboldt; 42°43′N 94°12′W. Agr. (livestock; grain); mfg. (furniture). Humboldt co. Historical Museum in town; Winter World Ski Area to E. **2** town (1990 pop. 1,470), ⊙ Dakota co., NE Nebr., suburb 5 mi/8 km S of Sioux City, Iowa, on Missouri R; 42°25′N 96°25′W. RR junction. Grain; mfg. (machinery, transportation equip., food, electronic equip.). First Lutheran church in Nebr. (1860) is here.

Dakota Dunes, village, Union co., New community featuring upscale living, recreation (golf, boating, fishing), commerce and finances, on Missouri R. 1 mi/1.6 km NW of Sioux City, Iowa.

Dalark (dal-AHRK), village, Dallas co., S central Ark., 12 mi/19 km SE of Arkadelphia.

Dale, county (□ 562 sq mi/1,456 sq km; 1990 pop. 49,633), SE Ala.; ⊙ Ozark. Coastal plain drained by Choctawhatchee R. Peanuts, corn, poultry, hogs; lumber. Formed 1824.

Dale, town (1990 pop. 1,553), Spencer co., SW Ind., 18 mi/ 29 km N of Rockport; 38°10′N 86°59′W. Hardwoods, plastic prods. Near Lincoln Boyhood Natl. Memorial and Lincoln State Park.

Dale 1 borough (1990 pop. 1,642), Cambria co., SW central Pa., on Stony Creek, surrounded by city of Johnstown; 40°18′N 78°54′W. Coal mines. Inc. 1891. **2** borough (1990 pop. 1,642), Cambria co., W central Pa., residential suburb, 1 mi/1.6 km SE of Johnstown, near Stonycreek R.; 40°18′N 78°54′W.

Dale City, uninc. city, Prince William co., NE Va., residential suburb, 23 mi/37 km SW of Washington, D.C., 12 mi/19 km SW of Manassas; 38°38′N 77°20′W. Light mfg. Northern Va. Community Col. (Woodbridge Campus) to SE; Quantico Marine Corps Base to SW.

Dale Hollow, town, Clay co., N Tenn.

Dale Hollow Lake, reservoir (□ 48 sq mi/124 sq km), N Tenn. and S Ky., on Obey R., 7 mi/11 km above its mouth, in foothills of Cumberland Mts., 4 mi/6.4 km E of Celina; c.50 mi/80 km long; 36°32′N 85°27′W. Max. capacity 1,706,000 acre-ft. Has 2 arms, E (East Fork) and SE (Wolf Creek). Formed by Dale Hollow Dam (concrete, straight gravity construction; 200 ft/61 m high), built (1943) by Army Corps of Engineers for flood control and power generation.

Dale Lake, dry lake, San Bernardino co., S Calif., in Mojave Desert, 18 mi/29 km E of Twentynine Palms; 34°11′N 115°50′W. Its saline deposits yield chemicals.

Daleville, city (1990 pop. 5,117), Dale co., SE Ala., 8 mi/12.9 km E of Enterprise; 31°18′N 85°43′W. Fort Rucker lies just N.

Daleville 1 town (1990 pop. 1,681), Delaware co., E Ind., 10 mi/16 km SW of Muncie; 40°07′N 85°34′W. Agr. area. Light mfg. **2** uninc. town, Botetourt co., W central Va., 10 mi/16 km N of Roanoke; 37°25′N 79°55′W. Mfg. (concrete); agr. (dairying, livestock; grain, apples); limestone. Appalachian Trail crosses valley to S, parts of Jefferson Natl. Forest to E and NW.

Dalhart, town (1990 pop. 6,246), ⊙ Dallam co., and partly in Hartley co., extreme N Texas, on high plains of the Panhandle, 70 mi/113 km NW of Amarillo; 36°03′N 102°30′W. Elev. 3,985 ft/1,215 m. In irrigated farm area; RR junction; diversified light mfg. Founded 1901, inc. 1903. Nearby, a dam in Rita Blanca Creek forms Rita Blanca L. (to S), used for irrigation, recreation.

Dalhousie (dal-HOU-zee), town (1991 pop. 4,775), ⊙ Restigouche co., N N.B., at head of Chaleur Bay, at mouth of Restigouche R., 160 mi/257 km NW of Moncton; 48°04′N 66°23′W. Ferry to Pte. Miguasha, Que. Fishing port (lobster, cod, salmon, smelt); lumbering and newsprint milling, pulp export; mixed farming. Seed potatoes are grown in region. Resort. Inc. 1905.

Dall Island (DAWL) (43 mi/69 km long, 2 mi/3.2 km–8 mi/12.9 km wide), SE Alaska, in Alexander Archipelago, W of Prince of Wales Isl.; 54°58′N 133°02′W. Rises to 2,443 ft/745 m. View Cove village in E. Fishing, limestone quarrying.

Dall, Mount (DAWL) (8,756 ft/2,669 m), S central Alaska, in Alaska Range, 130 mi/209 km NW of Anchorage; 62°37′N 152°19′W.

Dall, Point (DAWL), cape, W Alaska, on Bering Sea, 150 mi/241 km WNW of Bethel; 61°37′N 166°8′W.

Dallam, county (□ 1,505 sq mi/3,898 sq km; 1990 pop. 5,461), extreme N Texas; ⊙ Dalhart; 36°17′N 102°35′W. Elev. 3,800 ft/1,158 m–4,700 ft/1,433 m. In high, treeless, wheat and cattle plains of the Panhandle, on Okla. (N) and N.Mex. (W) lines. Drained by Carrizo, Rita Blanca, and Coldwater creeks. Highly irrigated area, cattle; sorghum, wheat, pinto beans. Part of Rita Bleanca Natl. Grassland in N ½ of co. Formed 1876.

Dallas, plantation (1990 pop. 161), Franklin co., W central Maine, near Rangeley L., 31 mi/50 km NW of Farmington; 45°00′N 70°34′W.

Dallas 1 county (□ 993 sq mi/2,572 sq km; 1990 pop. 48,130), S central Ala.; ⊙ Selma. Drained by Alabama and Cahaba rivers; in Black Belt. Cotton, soybeans, dairy prods., livestock, lumber. Formed 1818. **2** county (□ 668 sq mi/1,730 sq km; 1990 pop. 9,614), S central Ark.; ⊙ Fordyce; 33°58′N 92°39′W. Drained by Ouachita and Saline rivers, and by Moro Bayou (forms part of E boundary). Agr. (cattle, poultry; timber); sawmilling, mfg. of wood prods. Hunting, fishing. Formed 1845. **3** county (□ 591 sq mi/1,531 sq km; 1990 pop. 29,755), central Iowa; ⊙ Adel; 41°41′N 94°02′W. Prairie agr. area (cattle, poultry; corn, oats, soybeans) drained by Raccoon R. system and by Beaver Creek; coal mines. Forrest Park and Museum in N; Deer Run Ski Area in SW corner. Flooding occurred in 1993, esp. Raccoon R. Formed 1846. **4** county (□ 542 sq mi/1,404 sq km; 1990 pop. 12,646), SW central Mo.; ⊙ Buffalo; 37°40′N 93°01′W. In the Ozarks; drained by Niangua and Little Niangua rivers. Agr. area; cattle, poultry; oak timber; mfg. at Buffalo. Bennett Spring State Park in E, trout hatchery. Formed 1842. **5** county (□ 908 sq mi/2,352 sq km; 1990 pop. 1,852,810), N Texas; ⊙ DALLAS, 2d largest Texas city, (after Houston); 32°46′N 96°46′W. A financial, commercial, industrial center. Other important suburban cities include Irving, Grand Prairie (part), Garland, Mesquite, and Carrollton (part). Rich blackland prairie, wooded in W; drained by Trinity R., here formed by Elm and West forks; East Fork Trinity drains E part (forms L. Ray Hubbard in NE). Most remaining agr. is in the SE and S margin of co., horticultural crops, grains, hay, cotton, much fruit, vegetables, pecans; dairying; horses. Clay. City of Dallas dominates center of co. Nearly all of co. is highly urbanized, rapid growth having occured in W, N, and E during 1970s–1990s. Diversified industries in Dallas metropolitan area. Dallas Naval Air Station in W; Dallas–Fort Worth Internatl. Airport in NW on Tarrant-Dallas co. boundary. Mountain Creek L. in W; part of L. Joe Pool (with Cedar Hill State Park) in SW; White Rock L. in NE center, in Dallas; North L. in NW corner. Formed 1846.

Dallas, city (1990 pop. 1,006,877), ⊙ Dallas co., N Texas, city limits also extend N into Collin and Denton cos., a detached extension E into Kaufman and Rockwall cos., on the Trinity R., near the junction of its E and W forks; elev. 512 ft/156 m. The city is also drained by White Rock, Five Mile, and Mountain creeks. The 2d-largest city in Texas (after Houston) and the 8th-largest in the nation, Dallas is an important commercial, industrial, and financial center with a diverse economy. Its mfg. includes aerospace equipment, electronic equipment, bldg. materials, cosmetics, food and beverage processing, textiles, chemicals, leather goods, as well as aircraft, automobiles, and other transportation equipment. The Dallas–Fort Worth metropolitan area (known as the Metroplex with Dallas being the dominant of the two cities, Fort Worth being 30 mi/48 km E in Tarrant co., their city limits come within 5 mi/8 km of each other) has been a leader in high-technology industries, esp. computers, and receives a substantial number of defense contracts. Oil is refined, and there are meat-packing plants. With its many large banks and insurance company hq., Dallas serves as the Southwest's center for those industries. Publishing and printing are also important to the city's economy. The Dallas–Fort Worth Internatl. Airport is one of the busiest in the nation and is located to the NW on Tarrant/Dallas co. boundary. Dallas Love Field, located NW of downtown, is still used for private and commuter flights. Founded c.1841, Dallas was early populated by French artisans and gentlemen who abandoned the nearby Fourierist community, La Réunion. The city was named in 1846 after George Mifflin Dallas, who was Vice President under President James K. Polk. Dallas developed as a cotton market in the 1870s. Dallas became known as a center for retail stores, including Neiman-Marcus Co., which was founded in 1907 and is home to the Galleria, Northpark Center, and Valley View Center, 3 of the largest shopping centers in the U.S. Southern Methodist Univ., (in University Park suburb), Texas A and M Research Center and Univ. of Texas at Dallas, both at suburban Richardson, also Dallas Baptist Col., Mountain View Col. (2 year), Paul Quinn Col., Cedar Valley Col., Eastfield Col. (Mesquite), Brookhaven Col. (at Farmers Brand), North Luke Col. and Univ. of Dallas (both at Irving), Richland Col. (2 year), and El Centro Col. (2 year). A noted fashion center, the city is also known for its museums, its musical activities, and its interest in literature and drama (the Dallas Theatre Center boasts the only public theater ever designed by Frank Lloyd Wright). In the 1980s, Dallas helped revitalize its downtown through the creation of an arts district, which includes the impressive Dallas Mus. of Art (1984) and the Morton H. Meyerson Symphony Center (1989), designed by I. M. Pei. Dallas was one of the fastest growing U.S. metropolitan areas in the 1980s, as evidenced by the construction of many large, postmodern office buildings which dramatically changed the city's skyline. North Dallas, a sprawling, affluent sector of suburban growth, continues to expand. The annual Texas State Fair is held in Dallas, E of downtown, as well as the annual Cotton Bowl football game, stadium located on State Fairgrounds, Dallas Cowboys football team play in Texas Stadium at Irving to NW, Texas Rangers baseball team play at the Ballpark in Arlington (W) (near Fort Worth). Dallas Naval Air Station is in W part of city on Mt. Creek L. Major reservoirs include L. Ray Hubbard to E, Mountain Creek L. in W, L. Joe Pool (with Cedar Hill State Park on its SE shore) in SW; L. Lewisville State Park is to NW, L. Lavon is to NE, White Rock L. is in NE part of city and has a large city park. President John F. Kennedy was assassinated in Dallas on Nov. 22, 1963. Inc. 1871.

Dallas 1 town (1990 pop. 2,810), ⊙ Paulding co., NW Ga., 29 mi/47 km WNW of Atlanta; 33°55′N 84°50′W. Located on urban fringe of Atlanta. Mfg. includes carpet production, construction materials, food, light mfg. Several Civil War battles fought in the area, including New Hope Church, Pickett's Mill, and Dallas. Pickett's Mill is well preserved and site of battle reenactments each May. Inc. 1854. **2** town (1990 pop. 3,012), Gaston co., S N.C., residential suburb, 3 mi/4.8 km N of Gastonia, near South Fork Catawba R; 35°18′N 81°10′W. Seat of Gaston Col. (2yr). Geston Co. Mus. of Art and History. Inc. 1848. **3** town (1990 pop. 9,422), ⊙ Polk co., NW Oregon, 13 mi/21 km W of Salem on Rickreall Creek; 44°55′N 123°18′W. Elev. 325 ft/99 m. Mail terminal. In fruit and grain area of Willamette Valley. Mfg. (printing, fixtures, lumber); tourism. Wineries; grapes, corn, brans; poultry, sheep, hogs, cattle; dairy prods. Baskett Slough Natl. Wildlife Refuge to NE; small part of Siaslaw Natl. Forest to W. Founded 1852; inc. 1874.

Dallas 1 village (1990 pop. 142), Gregory co., S S.Dak., 4 mi/6.4 km W of Gregory. **2** village (1990 pop. 452), Barron co., NW Wis., 34 mi/55 km NNW of Eau Claire; 45°15′N 91°48′W. In dairying area.

Dallas 1 borough (1990 pop. 2.567), Luzerne co., NE central Pa., 7 mi/11.3 km NW of Wilkes-Barre; 41°19′N 75°58′W. Mfg. of textiles; some agr. Seat of Col. Misericordia. Inc. 1879. **2** borough (1990 pop. 2,567), Luzerne co., NE central Pa., suburb, 7 mi/11.3 km NW of Wilkes-Barre on Toby Creek; 41°20′N 75°57′W. Mfg. includes printing and publishing, fabricated metal prods., ordnance; agr. includes dairying, livestock; corn, apples. Co. Misericordia. Huntsville Reservoir to SW and Frances Slocum State Park to E. Inc. 1879.

Dallas Center, town (1990 pop. 1,454), Dallas co., central Iowa, 5 mi/8 km NNE of Adel; 41°40′N 93°58′W. Feed mfg., livestock vaccines.

Dallas City, city (1990 pop. 1,037), in Hancock and Henderson cos., W Ill., on the Mississippi, and 16 mi/26 km N of Carthage; 40°37′N 91°09′W. In agr. and bituminous-coal-mining area; corn, wheat, soybeans, livestock, dairy prods. Sand pits. Inc. 1859.

Dallas, Lake, Texas: see TRINITY RIVER.

Dallastown, borough (1990 pop. 3,974), York co., S Pa., suburb, 6 mi/9.7 km SE of York; 39°53′N 76°38′W. Mfg. (fabricated metal prods., electronic equip., wood prods., paper prods., concrete, machinery). Agr. area (wheat, corn, alfalfa, poultry, apples, livestock, dairying). Inc. 1867.

Dalles of the St. Croix, Wis. and Minn.: see INTERSTATE STATE PARK.

Dalles of the Wisconsin, Wis.: see DELLS OF THE WISCONSIN.

Dalles, the oregon: see THE DALLES.

Dallesport (DALZ-port), uninc. village (1990 pop. 590), Klickitat co., S Wash., residential suburb, 1 mi/1.6 km N of the Dalles, Oregon, on the Columbia R. (Bonneville reservoir). The Dalles Dam and Bridge 2 mi/3.2 km upstream (E). The Dalles Airport to E, in Wash.

Dalmatia (dal-MAI-shuh), uninc. village, Lower Mahaney township, Northumberland co., E central Pa., 16 mi/26 km SSW of Sunbury, on Susquehanna R., at mouth of Dalmatia Creek; 40°39′N 76°54′W. Mfg. (electronic equip.). Agr. (corn, hay; livestock, dairying).

Dalmeny (DAL-muh-nee), town (1991 pop. 1,436), S central Sask., 16 mi/26 km NNW of Saskatoon; 52°20′N 106°47′W. Wheat.

Dalquier (dahl-KYAI), village, W Que., 8 mi/13 km N of Amos; 48°42′N 78°07′W. Gold, copper mining.

Dalton, city (1990 pop. 21,761), ⊙ Whitfield co., extreme NW Ga., in the Appalachian valley; 34°46′N 84°59′W. It is a highly industrialized city specializing in tuft carpet mfg. (often refered to as the carpet capital of the world). Its large tufted-textile industry was begun in the late 1800s and still remains important. Mfg. also includes printing and publishing, food, and concrete. In the Civil War, Dalton (Confederate hq. after the Chattanooga campaign) fell to Gen. Sherman in the Atlanta campaign (1864). Dalton Col., a 2-year institution of the Univ. System of Ga. located here. The Chickamauga and Chattanooga Natl. Military Park is nearby, as is a state park. Inc. 1847.

Dalton 1 town (1990 pop. 7,155), including Dalton village, Berkshire co., W Mass., in the Berkshires, 5 mi/8 km ENE of Pittsfield; 42°29′N 73°09′W. Resort; mfg. (paper). Settled 1755, inc. 1784. **2** town (1990 pop. 38), Chariton co., N central Mo., near Missouri R., 8 mi/12.9 km E of Brunswick; 39°23′N 92°59′W. **3** town (1990 pop. 827), Coos co., NW N.H., 9 mi/14.5 km NE of Littleton; 44°22′N 71°40′W. Bounded NW by Connecticut R.; drained by Johns R. Agr. (nursery crops, vegetables, apples; livestock, poultry; dairying; timber). Includes Dalton Mt. (2,142 ft/653 m) in center. Forest Lake State Park in S. Includes village of Cushman in W.

Dalton 1 village (1990 pop. 234), Otter Tail co., W Minn., 11 mi/18 km SE of Fergus Falls; 46°10′N 95°55′W. Dairying; poultry; grain, alfalfa, sunflowers; light mfg. Numerous small lakes in area. **2** village (1990 pop. 282), Cheyenne co., W Nebr., 20 mi/32 km N of Sidney, S of North Platte R; 41°24′N 102°58′W. Grain, livestock. On Oregon Trail. **3** village (1990 pop. 1,377), Wayne co., N central Ohio, 13 mi/21 km E of Wooster, in agr. area; 40°48′N 81°42′W.

Dalton (DAHL-tuhn), borough (1990 pop. 1,356), Lackawanna co., NE Pa., 10 mi/16 km NNW of Scranton; 41°32′N 75°44′W. Mfg. (food). Agr. (vegetables, corn, hay, dairying); Lackawanna State Park to NE; several small lakes to N; Keystone Jr. Col. to NW at LaPlume. Inc. c.1890.

Dalton City, village (1990 pop. 573), Moultrie co., central Ill., 10 mi/16 km SE of Decatur; 39°42′N 88°48′W. In agr. area.

Dalton Gardens, town (1990 pop. 1,951), Kootenai co., N Idaho, residential suburb, 3 mi/4.8 km N of Coeur d'Alene, at SW end of Hayden L.; 47°44′N 116°46′W. Coeur d'Alene Natl. Forest to E.

Dalton Highway, road, N central to N Alaska, project road for the Trans-Alaska Pipeline. The gravel road begins in S on Elliot Highway, W of Livengood, 60 mi/97 km N of Fairbanks. The 414–mi/666–km road was constructed in only 5 months in 1974 by the Alyeska Pipeline Company. From Livengood to its S terminus at Valdez, the pipeline follows the preexisting Elliot, Steese, and Richardson highways. Going N, the road crosses the Yukon R., the Arctic Circle, and the Brooks Range before terminating at Prudhoe Bay/Deadhorse, on the Arctic Ocean. Center for oil and gas development activities. The first 211 mi/340 km N to Disaster Creek, in the Brooks Range, gives access to Gates of the Arctic Natl. Park and Preserve. This is the only highway in the Alaska system that extends N of Yukon R. and the only U.S. highway to reach the Arctic Circle.

Dalvey, town (1991 pop. 2,742), St. Thomas parish, SE Jamaica, 35 mi/56 km E of Kingston; 17°54′N 76°15′W.

Dalworthington Gardens, town (1990 pop. 1,758), Tarrant co., N Texas, residential suburb, 10 mi/16 km ESE of downtown Fort Worth; 32°41′N 97°09′W. It and neighboring Pantego (N) completely surrounded by city of Arlington.

Daly City, city (1990 pop. 92,311), San Mateo co., W Calif., a residential suburb, 6 mi/9.7 km SW of downtown San Francisco; 37°42′N 122°28′W. San Francisco Bay 4 mi/6.4 km to E, Pacific Ocean 2 mi/3.2 km to W. Settled in 1906 by refugees from the San Francisco earthquake, Daly City is still primarily residential and marked by a steady growth in population since the 1970s. Mfg. (printing, chemicals, plastic prods.). The Livestock Exhibition Bldg., the "Cow Palace," (near San Francisco city limits) scene of the 1964 Republican Natl. Convention, is there. Daly City is the southern terminus of the Bay Area Rapid Transit System. Part of Golden Gate Natl. Recreation Area to S, Thornton

State Beach to W; San Bruno Mts. to SE. San Andreas Fault runs SE-NW to W of city. Inc. 1911.

Daly, Mount, peak (c.13,193 ft/4,021 m) in Rocky Mts., Pitkin co., W central Colo., NE of Capital Peak, and 13 mi/21 km W of Aspen.

Dalzell, village, Sumter co., central S.C., 9 mi/14.5 km NW of Sumter. Agr. includes cotton, soybeans, quail, quail eggs, squab. Mfg. includes apparel, fabricated metal prods.

Damar (duh-MAHR), village (1990 pop. 112), Rooks co., N central Kansas, 17 mi/27 km SW of Stockton; 39°19′N 99°34′W. Wheat, livestock.

Damariscotta (da-muhr-SKAHT-uh), resort town (1990 pop. 1,811), Lincoln co., S Maine, 7 mi/11.3 km E of Wiscasset, and on E bank of Damariscotta R.; 44°01′N 69°30′W. Clamming. Damariscotta Mills village is site of St. Patrick's church, said to be oldest R.C. church in New England (1803). Site of early trading posts; settled permanently c.1640.

Damariscotta Lake (da-muhr-SKAHT-uh), S Maine, narrow lake (10 mi/16 km long); center of resort area in central Lincoln co.

Damariscotta River (da-muhr-SKAHT-uh), Lincoln co., S Maine, inlet extending c.20 mi/32 km inland from point bet. Boothbay Harbor and South Bristol.

Damariscove Island (dam-AHR-is-kov), Lincoln co., S Maine, narrow isl. (2 mi/3.2 km long), 5 mi/8 km SSE of Boothbay Harbor.

Damascus, town (1990 pop. 918), Washington co., SW Va., near Tenn. state line, 20 mi/32 km SW of Marion, near South Fork Holston R.; 36°37′N 81°47′W. Mfg. (apparel, printing and publishing, wood prods.); agr. area (corn, alfalfa; livestock, poultry; dairying); timber. White Top Mtn. and Mt. Rogers are E. Appalachian Trail passes through; Mt. Rogers Natl. Recreation Area to E; Cherokee Natl. Forest (Tenn.) to S. Settled 1892; inc. 1904.

Damascus (duh-MASK-uhs), village (1990 pop. 290), Early co., SW Ga., 14 mi. ESE of Blakely; 31°18′N 84°43′W. Mfg. includes feeds, fertilizers, peanut production.

Dame-Marie (dahm–mah-REE), town (1982 pop. 4,320), Grande-Anse dept., SW Haiti, on W coast of Jacmel Peninsula, 20 mi/32 km WSW of Jérémie; 18°34′N 74°25′W. Coffee, cacao; bauxite deposits nearby. Fishing port.

Dame-Marie, Cape, on W tip of Jacmel Peninsula, SW Haiti, 20 mi/32 km W of Jérémie; 18°38′N 74°26′W.

Dames Quarter, village, Somerset co., SE Md., on the Eastern Shore, 21 mi/34 km SW of Salisbury, on Monie Bay (N arm of Tangier Sound). Fishing, farming. The area was formerly known as Damned Quarter, perhaps because of its proximity to Devil Isl., later known as Deal Isl. Wildlife Management Area here.

Damien (dah-MYANG), suburb, Ouest dept., S Haiti, 2 mi/3.2 km NE of Port-au-Prince; 18°36′N 72°18′W. Tobacco, fruit; meat processing.

Damují River (dah-moo-HEE), central Cuba; rises in Villa Clara prov., W of Santa Clara; flows c.35 mi/56 km SW and S, past Rodas and Abreus, to Cienfuegos Bay 6 mi/9.7 km NW of Cienfuegos; 22°20′N 80°32′W. Lower course is sometimes called Rodas.

Dan River, in Va. and N.C.; rises in the Piedmont region in NW Patrick co., S Va., in Meadows of Dan; flows SE into N.C., NE past Eden, N.C. into Va. past Danville, again briefly SE into N.C., then NE and E past South Boston, Va., to Roanoke R. (also called Staunton R.) 14 mi/23 km E of South Boston; lower 8 mi/12.9 km is arm of Kerr Reservoir (Buggs Isl. L.); c.180 mi/290 km long.

Dana 1 town (1990 pop. 612), Vermillion co., W Ind., 7 mi/11.3 km W of Newport, near Ill. line; 39°49′N 87°29′W. Ernie Pyle State Memorial. **2** town (1990 pop. 71), Greene co., central Iowa, 9 mi/14.5 km NE of Jefferson; 42°06′N 94°14′W. In agr. area. **3** former town, Worcester co., central Mass.; site inundated 1937 by Quabbin Reservoir. Main water source for Boston.

Dana (DAY-nah), village (1990 pop. 165), La Salle co., central Ill., 28 mi/45 km S of Ottawa; 40°57′N 88°57′W. In agr. area.

Dana, Mount, peak (13,053 ft/3,979 m) of the Sierra Nevada, on Mono-Tuolomne co. line, E Calif., 8 mi/12.9 km SSW of Mono L., on E boundary of Yosemite Natl. Park. Inyo Natl. Forest to E.

Dana Point, city (1990 pop. 31,896), Orange co., S Calif., suburb, 47 mi/76 km SE of downtown Los Angeles, and 7 mi/11.3 km SE of Laguna Beach, on Pacific Ocean, near Dana Pt. Doheny State Beach to E, San Juan Capistrano Mission to NE; 33°28′N 117°42′W. Recreation area. Mfg. (transportation equip.).

Dana Point, high coastal promontory, Orange co., S Calif., just SW of San Juan Capistrano, and W of Dana Point city.

Danboro (DAN-buh-ro), uninc. town (1990 pop. 950), Bucks co., SE Pa., suburb, 3 mi/4.8 km N of Doylestown; 40°21′N 75°07′W. Mfg. includes machinery; agr. includes dairying; livestock, poultry; alfalfa, hay, corn, wheat, apples.

Danburg, town, Wilkes co., NE Ga., 11 mi/18 km NE of Washington; 33°52′N 82°39′W.

Danbury, city (1990 pop. 65,585), Fairfield co., SW Conn.; 41°23′N 73°28′W. Settled 1685, inc. as a city 1889. Mfg. in this growing residential city includes electronic equipment, plastics, fabricated metal prods., machinery, electronic equip., printing and publishing, pharmaceuticals, chemicals, furniture. Once the country's leading hat center dating from 1780, the industry is now gone. Danbury is a commuting area of New York City. An early military depot, Danbury was the object of Gen. William Tryon's 1777 raid, repulsed but resulting in destruction of the settlement and the death of David Wooster; Wooster is buried in Wooster Cemetery. The famous Danbury Hatters' Case (1902) resulted in a U.S. Supreme Court ruling (1908) prohibiting boycotts by labor unions. In the city are Western Connecticut State Univ. and a Federal prison. Of note are the David Taylor House (1750) and the Dodd House (1770), both included in the Scott-Fanton Mus. The city was known for its annual state fairs that were held since the 1800s; however, these ended in 1981.

Danbury 1 town (1990 pop. 430), Woodbury co., W Iowa, c.40 mi/64 km ESE of Sioux City; 42°14′N 95°43′W. Concrete mfg. **2** town (1990 pop. 881), Merrimack co., S central N.H., 28 mi/45 km NW of Concord; 43°31′N 71°52′W. Drained by Smith R. Agr. (nursery crops; poultry; dairying; timber). Ragged Mt. Ski Area on S boundary. Tinkham Hill (2,280 ft/695 m) in N. **3** town (1990 pop. 1,447), Brazoria co., SE Texas, suburb, 8 mi/12.9 km NE of Angleton, in Brazosport Area, near Flores Bayou; 29°13′N 95°20′W. Agr. area (rice, cotton, pecans, soybeans).

Danbury 1 village (1990 pop. 109), Red Willow co., S Nebr., 15 mi/24 km SE of McCook, and on Beaver Creek, near Kansas line; 40°02′N 100°24′W. **2** village (1990 pop. 119), ⊙ Stokes co., N N.C., on Dan R., and 21 mi/34 km N of Winston-Salem; 36°24′N 80°12′W. Tobacco, grain, poultry, livestock. Hanging Rock State Park to W. **3** village, Burnett co., NW Wis., on St. Croix R., and 25 mi/40 km NW of Spooner. Governor Knowles State Forest to SW; St. Croix Natl. Scenic Riverway on St. Croix R.

Danby, town (1990 pop. 1,193), Rutland co., S central Vt., in valley bet. Green Mts. (E) and the Taconics, on Otter Creek, and 18 mi/29 km S of Rutland; 43°21′N 73°03′W. Wood prods., dairying, marble quarrying. Chartered 1761, settled 1765.

Danby Lake, San Bernardino co., SE Calif., intermittently dry lake, in Mojave Desert, 50 mi/80 km SW of Needles; c.15 mi/24 km long. Colorado R. Aqueduct passes to S. Turtle Mts. to E, Old Woman Mts. to N.

Dandridge, town (1990 pop. 1,540), ⊙ Jefferson co., E Tenn., on Douglas Reservoir, 28 mi/45 km E of Knoxville; 36°01′N 83°25′W. Canned vegetables, hosiery, luggage; zinc deposits.

Dane, county (□ 1,238 sq mi/3,206 sq km; 1990 pop. 367,085), S Wis.; ⊙ Madison; 43°04′N 89°25′W. Bounded NW by Wisconsin R; drained by Yahara and Sugar rivers and by Waterloo and Koshkonong creeks. Urbanized at center around city of Madison (state capital). Dairy-farming region; barley, oats, wheat, corn, soybeans, peas, beans, alfalfa, hay; cattle, hogs, sheep, poultry); mfg. in Madison, Sun Prairie, and Stoughton. Includes several large lakes, notably the FOUR LAKES (Mendota, Monona, Waubesa, Kegonsa). Blue Mound State Park on W boundary; W part of Glacial Drumlin State Trail in E; eastern half of Military Ridge State Trail in SW; L. Kegonsa State Park in SE; Governor Nelson State Park on N shore of L. Mendota. Formed 1836.

Dane, village (1990 pop. 621), Dane co., S Wis., 13 mi/21 km NNW of Madison, in dairy region; 43°15′N 89°30′W. Mfg. (plastic prods.).

Danforth, town (1990 pop. 710), Washington co., E Maine, c.70 mi/113 km NNW of Machias, near Chiputneticook Lakes; 45°37′N 67°50′W. Lumber milling. Settled 1829, inc. 1860.

Danforth, village (1990 pop. 457), Iroquois co., E Ill., 13 mi/21 km WNW of Watseka; 40°49′N 87°58′W. In agr. area (corn, soybeans, cattle, hogs).

Dania (DAIN-yuh), town (□ 5 sq mi/13 sq km; 1990 pop. 13,024), Broward co., SE Fla., on Atlantic coast, just S of Fort Lauderdale, 20 mi/32 km N of Miami; 26°03′N 80°09′W. Canning, packing, and shipping center (vegetables, citrus fruit); mfg. of machinery. Settled 1896 by Danes. Site of Ft. Lauderdale Intl. Airport and jai alai fronton.

Daniels, county (□ 1,426 sq mi/3,693 sq km; 1990 pop. 2,266), NE Mont.; ⊙ Scobey; 48°48′N 105°33′W. Agr. area bordering on Canada (Sask.), the southern ⅕ of the county incorporates part of the Fort Peck Indian Reservation. Drained by the E and W forks of the Poplar R. Wheat, barley, oats, hay, cattle. Formed 1920.

Daniels, uninc. town (1990 pop. 1,714), Raleigh co., S W.Va., 6 mi/9.7 km SE of Beckley; 37°43′N 81°07′W. Cattle; grain. Mfg. (lumber). Little Beaver State Park to NE.

Daniels 1 village, Howard co., central Md., on Patapsco R., and 11 mi/18 km W of downtown Baltimore. Renamed 1940 from Alberton. There was an important textile mill here as far back as 1829, run by the Albert Co. The whole town was bought by the Daniels Co. in 1940. Hurricane Agnes in 1972 demolished the mill factory. In 1977 a fire destroyed the remains. Little remains of the town today. **2** uninc. village, Lincoln co., W central N.C., 5 mi/8 km NW of Lincolnton.

Danielson, industrial borough (1990 pop. 4,441) in Killingly town, Windham co., NE Conn., on Quinebaug R., and 18 mi/29 km NE of Willimantic; 41°48′N 71°53′W. Textiles, machinery, rubber prods. Inc. 1854. A postal section of Killingly.

Danielsville, uninc. town (1990 pop. 750), Lehigh township, Northampton co., E Pa., 5 mi/8 km NE of Slatington; 40°47′N 75°31′W. Mfg. (apparel, fabricated metal prods.). Appalachian Trail passes to N in Blue Mt. ridge.

Danielsville, village (1990 pop. 318), ⊙ Madison co., NE Ga., 14 mi/23 km NE of Athens; 34°07′N 83°13′W, Mfg. includes transportation equip., furniture.

Danish West Indies: see VIRGIN ISLANDS of the U.S.

Dannebrog, village (1990 pop. 324), Howard co., E central Nebr., 7 mi/11.3 km SW of St. Paul, and on Middle Loup R; 41°07′N 98°32′W. In grain and cattle region. Named by Danish settlers, adopted home of Roger Welsch, folklorist and TV and radio performer.

Dannemora (dan-ah-MAWR-ah), village (□ 1 sq mi/2.6 sq km; 1990 pop. 4,005), Clinton co., extreme NE N.Y., in the Adirondacks, 13 mi/21 km W of Plattsburgh; 44°43′N 73°43′W. Site of Clinton Correctional Facility. Inc. 1881.

Dans Mountain, in NW Md. and S Pa. (2,898 ft/883 m), part of the E escarpment of the Allegheníes, at Dans Rock c.5 mi/8 km SW of Cumberland, Md. Runs NE c.30 mi/48 km from North Branch of the Potomac just E of Westernport, Md., to Hyndman, Pa. Named after Daniel Cresap, identified by different sources as the father and son of Col. Thomas Cresap who settled nearby after the Revolutionary War. Daniel may been killed there in a gunfight or in a struggle with a mother bear and her 2 cubs.

Dansville 1 village (1990 pop. 437), Ingham co., S central Mich., 8 mi/12.9 km ESE of Mason; 42°33′N 84°17′W. In agr. area. **2** village (□ 2 sq mi/5.2 sq km; 1990 pop. 5,002), Livingston co., W central N.Y., on Canaseraga Creek, 40 mi/64 km S of Rochester; 42°33′N 77°42′W. Mfg. (apparel, electronic equipment, fabricated metal prods.); agr. (beans, potatoes). Clara Barton founded (1881) 1st local chapter of the Amer. Red Cross here. Letchworth State Park nearby. Settled 1795, inc. 1845.

Dante 1 (DAHN-tee), village (1990 pop. 98), Charles Mix co., SE S.Dak., 20 mi/32 km SE of L. Andes, and on Choteau Creek, in Yankton Indian Reservation. **2** (DANT), uninc. village, Russell co., SW Va., in the Allegheny Mts., 19 mi/31 km E of Norton. Agr. area (tobacco, corn, soybeans; cattle, sheep); bituminous coal.

Danube, village (1990 pop. 562), Renville co., SW Minn., 6 mi/9.7 km W of Olivia; 44°47′N 95°05′W. Dairying; poultry, livestock; grain, soybeans; sand and gravel.

Danvers (DAN-vuhrz), town (1990 pop. 24,174), Essex co., NE Mass.; 42°34′N 70°57′W. Settled in the 1630s, set off from Salem 1752, inc. as a town 1757. Danvers has light mfg. (electronic equip., food, chemicals, machinery, apparel). The Salem witchcraft incidents began there in 1692; more than ½ of the victims were from Danvers. The Danvers Archival Center has the largest collection of writings about witchcraft. John Greenleaf Whittier spent his later years in the town, and the Amer. Revolutionary Gen. Israel Putnam was born in Danvers. Numerous bldgs. of historical and architectural interest are preserved, several dating from the 1600s.

Danvers 1 village (1990 pop. 981), McLean co., central Ill., 9 mi/14.5 km WNW of Bloomington; 40°31′N 89°10′W. In rich agr. area (corn, wheat, soybeans; cattle; dairying). **2** village (1990 pop. 98), Swift co., W central Minn., 8 mi/12.9 km WSW of Benson; 45°16′N 95°45′W. Grain; dairying.

Danville 1 city (1990 pop. 31,306), Contra Costa co., W Calif., a residential suburb 15 mi/24 km E of downtown Oakland; 37°49′N 121°58′W. In agr. region (apples, walnuts; nursery stock); mfg. (machinery, food). Eugene O'Neill Natl. Historic Site; Diablo State Park to NE; Las Trampas Regional Park to W. **2** city (1990 pop. 33,828), ⊙ Vermilion co., E Ill., on the Vermilion R., at the Ind. line; 40°08′N 87°37′W. It is a commercial and industrial center in a dairy, farm, and coal area. Coal was once a central industry. Agr. and industry have become predominant. Agr. (corn, soybeans, cattle; dairying); mfg. (chemicals, food, concrete, printing and publishing). Abraham Lincoln maintained a law office in Danville for 5 years. Lake View Nursing Col., Danville Area Community Col., Danville Natl. Cemetary are here. Danville Correctional Center to E (on state boundary). Kickapoo State Park to W. Vermilion Co. Airport. Inc. 1839. **3** city (1990 pop. 12,420), ⊙ Boyle co., central Ky.; 37°38′N 84°46′W. RR junction. Agr. (burley tobacco, grain; livestock, poultry; dairying); mfg. (apparel, electronic equip., construction materials, concrete, machinery, feeds, printing and publishing). One of the oldest settlements in Kentucky. Of note is the Dr. Ephraim McDowell House, pioneer surgeon. Centre Col., and the Kentucky School for the Deaf (opened 1823) are also here. Danville Natl. Cemetery and Constitution Square State Historic Site are here; Herrington L. (Dix Dam) to NE. Settled 1775, inc. 1836. **4** independent city (□ 44 sq mi/114 sq km; 1990 pop. 53,056), S central Va., on N.C. state line, 53 mi/85 km NE of Greensboro, N. C., on Dan R.; separate from adjoining Pittsylvania co; 36°34′N 79°24′W. RR junction. Mfg. (asphalt, transportation equip., textiles, tobacco processing, lumber, printing and publishing, fabricated metal prods., concrete, foods); agr. area (tobacco, especially bright leaf variety; grain, soybeans, alfalfa; cattle; dairying). During the Civil War, site of Confederate military facilities. Also, historical landmark Sutherlin Mansion, the "Last Capitol of the Confederacy," housed Jefferson Davis and his cabinet fleeing Richmond (April, 1865). Home of Lady Nancy Witcher (Langhorne) Astor, born in Danville. Averett Col., Danville Community Col., National Business Col., Danville campus. Natl. Tobacco and Textile Mus.; Danville Mus. of Fine Arts. Danville Regional Airport in E. Founded 1793, inc. 1870.

Danville 1 town (1990 pop. 1,585), shares ⊙ functions with Dardanelle Yell co., W central Ark., 22 mi/35 km SW of Russellville, and on Petit Jean R.; 35°02′N 93°23′W. Cotton, lumber; mfg. (food, fabricated metal prods.). Ozark Natl. Forest to N; Ouachita Natl. Forest to S; Petit Jean Wildlife Management Area to E. Founded 1841. **2** town (1990 pop. 480), Twiggs and Wilkinson cos., central Ga., 8 mi/12.9 km SE of Jeffersonville; 32°37′N 83°15′W. **3** town (1990 pop. 4,345), ⊙ Hendricks co., central Ind., on a fork of Whitelick Creek, and 20 mi/32 km W of Indianapolis; 39°46′N 86°31′W. In agr. area. Residential community of Indianapolis. Settled 1824, inc. 1835. **4** town (1990 pop. 926), Des Moines co., SE Iowa, 10 mi/16 km WNW of Burlington; 40°51′N 91°18′W. In agr. area. Geode State Park nearby. **5** uninc. town, Montgomery co., E central Mo., 5 mi/8 km S of Montgomery City. An important point on the Boonslick Trail until burned 1864 during the Civil War. **6** town (1990 pop. 2,534), Rockingham co., SE N.H., 10 mi/16 km SW of Exeter; 42°55′N 71°07′W. Light mfg; agr. (vegetables, nursery crops; cattle, poultry; dairying). **7** town (1990 pop. 1,917), Caledonia co., NE Vt., just W of St. Johnsbury; 44°25′N 72°07′W. Lumber, wood prods. Thaddeus Stevens b. here. West Danville village is resort on Joe's Pond. Settled 1784.

Danville, village (1991 pop. 1,782), S Que., 5 mi/8 km W of Asbestos, 25 mi/40 km N of Sherbrooke; 45°47′N 72°01′W. Asbestos mining, woodworking.

Danville 1 village (1990 pop. 56), Harper co., S Kansas, 12 mi/19 km NE of Anthony; 37°17′N 97°53′W. In wheat region. **2** village (1990 pop. 1,001), Knox co., central Ohio, 13 mi/21 km ENE of Mt. Vernon, in agr. area; 40°26′N 82°16′W. **3** village (1990 pop. 170), Ferry co., NE Wash., port of entry on Canada (B.C.) border, 25 mi/40 km NNE of Republic, and 3 mi/4.8 km SW of Grand Forks, B.C., opposite Cascade, B.C. Parts of Colville Natl. Forest to E and W. **4** village (1990 pop. 595), Boone co., W central W.Va., 1 mi/1.6 km N of Madison; 38°04′N 81°49′W. Bituminous coal. Mfg. (printing and publishing).

Danville, borough (1990 pop. 5,165), ⊙ Montour co., E central Pa., 29 mi/47 km SE of Williamsport, on Susquehanna R. (bridged to Riverside, to SW); 40°57′N 76°36′W. Mfg. (furniture, transportation equip., apparel, printing and publishing, textiles, fabricated metal prods.). Agr. area (corn, hay; poultry, livestock; dairying). E end of Montour Ridge to W; Danville State Hosp. to SE; Geisinger Medical Center; Danville Airport to SW (Northumberland co.). Laid out 1790, inc. 1849.

Daphne (DAF-nee), farming city (1990 pop. 11,290), Baldwin co., SW Ala., on E shore of Mobile Bay, a suburb, 10 mi/16 km SE of Mobile.

D'Arbonne, Bayou (dahr-BON, BEI-yoo), river, c.90 mi/145 km long, in N La.; rises in Claiborne parish; flows SE to Ouachita R. just N of Monroe; navigable; 32°34′N 92°08′W. Receives Middle Fork (c.50 mi/80 km long) from NW in N Lincoln parish and Corney Bayou from NW in L. D'Arbonne reservoir in Union parish. Forms L. Claiborne reservoir SE of Homer in Claiborne parish. Also called Slow Bayou.

Darby, village (1990 pop. 625), Ravalli co., W Mont., 16 mi/26 km S of Hamilton, near Idaho line and Bitterroot Range to W; 46°01′N 114°11′W. In rich agr. valley of Bitterroot R. Oats, alfalfa; cattle, sheep, llamas; gold mining, forest industries, tourism. Alta Ranger Station, one of the first forest-ranger stations in U.S. (built in 1899), at Painted Rocks State Park to SW. L. Como to NW. Parts of Bitterroot Natl. Forest to E and W; Selway-Bitterroot Wilderness Area to W. Pioneer Memorial Mus., Darby Historical Ranger Station.

Darby, borough (1990 pop. 11,140), Del. co., SE Pa., residential suburb, 6 mi/9.7 km SW of Philadelphia, on Darby Creek; 39°55′N 75°15′W. Mfg. includes paper prods., chemicals, food.

Darby Creek, W central Ohio; rises in Logan co.; flows c.70 mi/113 km generally SE to Scioto R. just above Circleville. Sometimes called Big Darby Creek.

Area in square miles is shown by the symbol □ capital city or county seat by ⊙

Darbyville, village (1990 pop. 272), Pickaway co., S central Ohio, 11 mi/18 km WNW of Circleville, and on Darby Creek, in agr. area; 39°42′N 83°07′W.

Dardanelle (dahrd-uh-NEL), town (1990 pop. 3,722), shares ⊙ functions with Danville, Yell co., W central Ark., 4 mi/6.4 km SSW of Russellville, and on Arkansas R., opposite Russellville; 35°13′N 93°10′W. In farm area; mfg. (construction materials, food). Mt. Nebo State Park to W; Holla Bend Natl. Wildlife Refuge to SE; Mt. Nebo State Park (recreation area) is nearby.

Dardanelle, Lake (dahrd-uh-NEL), Yell and Pope cos., NW central Ark., on the Arkansas R., 3 mi/4.8 km SW of Russellville, at city limit; c.40 mi/64 km long; 35°15′N 93°10′W. Max. capacity of 486,200 acre-ft. Big Piney Creek forms N arm. Formed by Dardanelle Lock and Dam, built (1969) by the Army Corps of Engineers for navigation and hydroelectric generation.

Dardanelles Cone, peak (9,524 ft/2,903 m), SW Alpine co., E Calif., in the Sierra Nevada, 18 mi/29 km SSW of Markleeville.

Dare, county (□ 1,561 sq mi/4,043 sq km; 1990 pop. 22,746), NE N.C.; ⊙ Manteo, on Roanoke Isl; 35°41′N 75°43′W. Bounded S and E by the Altantic Ocean, N by Albemarle Sound, W by Alligator R. estuary; SW by Pamlico Sound. Jockey's Ridge State Park and Wright Brothers Natl. Memorial in E, on Outer Banks, large part of Cape Hatteras Natl. Seashore in E and SE, on Outer Banks, inc. Cape Hatteras lightouse. Forested (pine, cypress) and swampy tidewater area; farming (grapes, oats, soybeans), fishing. Fort Raleigh Natl. Historic Site is in E, on Roanoke Isl. Pea Isl. Natl. Wildlife Refuge in E, on Outer Banks. Co. consists of 2 main sections, a marshy peninsula of mainland and a large section of the Outer Banks, bridge by way of Roanoke Isl. Intracoastal Waterway passes through Alligator R. estuary, crosses entrance to Albermarle Sound, and continues N to North R. estuary. Formed 1870.

Darfur (DAHR-fuhr), village (1990 pop. 128), Watonwan co., S Minn., 11 mi/18 km WNW of St. James, bet. Watonwan (S) and North Fork Watonwan (N) rivers; 44°02′N 94°50′W. Mfg. (chemicals).

Darien (DE-ree-EN), city (1990 pop. 18,341), Du Page co., NE Ill., suburb, 19 mi/31 km WSW of downtown Chicago; 41°45′N 87°58′W. Mfg. (electronic equip., machinery). Argonne Natl. Laboratory to S.

Darien 1 (DE-ree-EN), residential town (1990 pop. 18,196), Fairfield co., SW Conn., on Long Island Sound, settled c.1641, inc. 1820; 41°02′N 73°28′W. Darien has been marked by a growing economic base as it has become a principal commuter suburb for those who work in New York City. Many 18th-cent. houses remain. Home to many country, yacht, hunting, tennis, curling, and swim clubs. **2** (DAI-ree-uhn), town (1990 pop. 1,783), ⊙ McIntosh co., SE Ga., c.17 mi/27 km. NNE of Brunswick, 6 mi/9.7 km W of the mouth of Altamaha R., on the Atlantic; 31°22′N 81°26′W. Fishing port; seafood canning, sawmilling. Annual Blessing of the Fleet ceremony held each year. State park and site of Fort King George (1721–1727), the 1st English settlement in Ga., are nearby. Founded 1736 by Scotch Highlanders recruited by James Oglethorpe to supersede Spanish influence in the area. Important export center for cotton, rice, and timber before and after the Civil War. Fort Darien site and Waterfront Tabby has ruins of early 19th-cent. cotton factories and warehouses. **3** (DE-ree-EN), town (1990 pop. 1,158), Walworth co., SE Wis., 17 mi/27 km ESE of Janesville; 42°36′N 88°42′W. In dairying and hog-raising region. Mfg. (wood prods., plastic prods.).

Dark Harbor, Maine: see ISLESBORO.

Darke, county (□ 605 sq mi/1,567 sq km; 1990 pop. 53,619), W Ohio; ⊙ Greenville; 40°08′N 84°37′W. Drained by Greenville Creek, Stillwater and Mississinewa rivers. In the Till Plains physiographic region. Rich agr. area (poultry, corn, soybeans, tobacco, tomatoes, fruit); mfg. at Greenville (textiles, electronic equipment, transportation equip., machinery); clay and gravel pits. Formed 1816.

Darley Woods, uninc. town (1990 pop. 1,220), New Castle co., NE Del., residential suburb, 6 mi/9.7 km NE of

downtown Wilmington, and 2 mi/3.2 km NW of Claymont, at Pa. state line; 39°49′N 75°28′W.

Darling, Lake, reservoir (□ 18 sq mi/47 sq km), mainly in Renville co., N central N.Dak., on Souris R., 18 mi/29 km NNW of Minot; 48°28′N 101°35′W. Max. capacity 227,400 acre-ft. Formed by Dam #83 (39 ft/12 m high), built (1936) by Fish and Wildlife Service, Dept. of the Interior for fish and wildlife, within Upper Souris Natl. Wildlife Refuge.

Darlingford, village, S Man., Canada, 50 mi/80 km S of Portage la Prairie, in Pembina Mts.; grain, stock.

Darlington, county (□ 567 sq mi/1,469 sq km; 1990 pop. 61,851), NE S.C.; ⊙ Darlington; 34°19′N 79°57′W. Bounded E by Pee Dee R. Sand and clay. Agr. includes cattle; dairying; wheat, rye, oats, soybeans, hay, corn; hogs, timber. Formed 1785.

Darlington 1 town (1990 pop. 740), Montgomery co., W central Ind., on Sugar Creek, and 7 mi/11.3 km NE of Crawfordsville; 40°07′N 86°47′W. **2** town, (1990 pop. 104), Gentry co., NW Mo., on Grand R., and 4 mi/6.4 km SW of Albany. **3** town (1990 pop. 7,311), ⊙ Darlington co., NE S.C., 9 mi/14.5 km NW of Florence; 34°17′N 79°52′W. Mfg.of asphalt, lumber, concrete, fabricated metal prods., food, textiles, paper prods.; agr. (poultry, livestock; dairying; grain, soybeans). Florence-Darlington Technical Col. is here. Settled 1798, inc. 1835. **4** town (1990 pop. 2,235), ⊙ Lafayette co., S Wis., on Pecatonica R., and 24 mi/39 km WNW of Monroe; 42°40′N 90°07′W. Dairying; feed, cheese; mfg. (concrete). Inc. 1877.

Darlington 1 village, Harford co., NE Md., near the Susquehanna, 33 mi/53 km NE of Baltimore. The Deer Creek Friends Meeting House was built in 1737, rebuilt in 1784, and restored in 1888. Octagon House, with its false windows and "widow's walk" — a balcony for wives to look for their husbands' ships — was built by William Hensel, a ship's carpenter in the early 18th cent., presumably from old ship timber. Susquehanna State Park is just SE. **2** village, Passaic co., NE N.J., on Ramapo R., just NW of Ramsey. Seat of Immaculate Conception Seminary.

Darlington, borough (1990 pop. 311), Beaver co., W Pa., 6 mi/9.7 km WNW of Beaver Falls, on North Fork Little Beaver Creek; 40°48′N 80°25′W. Mfg. (wood prods., plastic prods., glass prods.). Agr. (corn, hay; livestock, dairying); timber. Darlington L. reservoir to NE.

Darlington, locality, S central Ontario, Canada, located within city of Newcastle, 14 mi/23 km E of Oshawa. Site of Darlington Nuclear Power Generating Plant.

Darliston, town (1991 pop. 1,435), Westmoreland parish, W Jamaica, 10 mi/16 km ENE of Savanna-la-Mar; 18°14′N 77°58′W. Sugarcane, rice, breadfruit; livestock.

Darmstadt, town (1990 pop. 1,346), Vanderburgh co., SW Ind., 8 mi/12.9 km N of Evansville; 38°05′N 87°35′W. Wheat, corn. Estab. 1860.

Darnley Bay, NW Mackenzie dist., N.W.T., Canada, inlet (28 mi/45 km long, 20 mi/32 km wide at mouth) of Amundsen Gulf, on E side of Parry Peninsula; 69°40′N 123°45′W.

Darr, uninc. village, Dawson co., S central Nebr., 7 mi/11.3 km WNW of Lexington, on Platte R. Feeds.

Darrell's Island (2.5 mi/4 km long, ⅛ mi/ km wide), W Bermuda, in Great Sound, 2.5 mi/4 km WSW of Hamilton.

Darrington, town (1990 pop. 1,042), Snohomish co., NW Wash., on Sauk R., 24 mi/39 km E of Arlington; 48°15′N 121°36′W. RR terminus. Logging. Parts of Mt. Baker–Snoqualmie Natl. Forest to NW, SW, and E, including Boulder R. Wilderness Area to SW and Glacier Peak Wilderness Area to E.

Darrouzett, village (1990 pop. 343), Lipscomb co., N Texas, 28 mi/45 km E of Perryton, on Kiowa Creek; 36°27′N 100°19′W. Oil and gas; cotton, wheat; cattle.

Dartmouth, city (1991 pop. 67,798), S N.S., Canada, on Halifax harbor, an inlet of the Atlantic Ocean; 44°40′N 63°34′W. Large sugar and oil refineries; mfg. includes shipbuilding, transportation equip.

Dartmouth, residential and resort town (1990 pop. 27,244), Bristol co., SE Mass., on Buzzards Bay, in a

dairy region, and 8 mi/12.9 km SSE of Fall River; 41°37′N 71°00′W. Settled c.1650, inc. 1664. Farming, fishing, boat building, and tourism are its economic mainstays. Other industry includes electronic equip. The town was practically annihilated in King Philip's War but was rebuilt and later became a shipbuilding center. Southeastern Massachusetts Univ. is in North Dartmouth, and a state park faces Buzzards Bay. Includes villages of Nonquitt, North Dartmouth, and South Dartmouth.

Dartmouth, Mount, peak (3,721 ft/1,134 m), Coos co., N N.H., White Mts., 15 mi/24 km SW of Berlin, c.5 mi/8 km WNW of Mt. Washington, in White Mt. Natl. Forest.

Darwin, village (1990 pop. 252), Meeker co., S central Minn., 6 mi/9.7 km ESE of Litchfield; Washington L. to SE; 45°06′N 94°24′W. Dairying; poultry, livestock; grain, soybeans, beans, peas; mfg. (concrete).

Darwin Peak, Wyo.: see GROS VENTRE RANGE.

Dashwood, village, S Ont., Canada, 30 mi/48 km NW of London; dairying, mixed farming.

Dassel (DA-suhl), town (1990 pop. 1,082), Meeker co., S central Minn., 10 mi/16 km ESE of Litchfield; 45°04′N 94°18′W. Grain, soybeans, peas, beans; livestock, poultry; dairying; light mfg. Lake resort. Washington L. to W.

Dasserat, Lake (dah-suh-RAH) (7 mi/11 km long, 3 mi/5 km wide), W Que., Canada, 17 mi/27 km W of Rouyn, near Ont. border; 48°15′N 79°24′W. On shore are gold mines.

Datil (DAI-tuhl)), uninc. village (1990 pop. 150), Catron co., W N.Mex., near Gallinas Mts., 62 mi/100 km WNW of Socorro; in plains of San Agustin. Elev. c.7,900 ft/2,408 m. Trade and supply point in ranching region. Part of Cibola Natl. Forest nearby. Datil Mts. to N; Cibola Natl. Forest to N and W; Datil Well Natl. Recreation Site to W.

Datto (DAT-o), village (1990 pop. 120), Clay co., extreme NE Ark., 16 mi/26 km NE of Pocahontas, bet. Black and Current rivers; 36°23′N 90°43′W. Dave Donaldson-Black R. Wildlife Management Area to SE.

Daufuskie Island (duh-FUHS-kee), Beaufort co., S S.C., one of Sea Isls., at mouth of New R., 12 mi/19 km E of Savannah, Ga.; c.5 mi/8 km long. Daufuskie Isl. Resort Center with village on S shore. Intracoastal Waterway runs between isl. and mainland.

Dauphin (DAW-fin), county (□ 557 sq mi/1,443 sq km; 1990 pop. 237,813), S central Pa.; ⊙ Harrisburg; 40°24′N 76°47′W. Bounded W by Susquehanna R., S by Conewago Creek, N by Mahantango Creek; drained by Swatara Creek. Gently rolling farmland in S, urbanized in SW, E-W running mt. ridges in N, including (N to S) Mahantango, Berry, Peters, Stony, Second, and Blue Mt. ridges. Long stone-arch bridge crosses Susquehanna R. at Rockville. Mfg. at Harrisburg, Steelton, Hershey, and Middletown. Agr. (corn, wheat, hay, alfalfa, vegetables, soybeans, apples; poultry, sheep, hogs, cattle, dairying). Limestone. Three Mile Isl. nuclear power plant (initial criticality June 5, 1974) is 10 mi/16 km SE of Harrisburg. Appalachian Trail passes E-W in N center, on Peters Mt. ridge. Formed 1785.

Dauphin (DO-fin), town (1991 pop. 8,453), SW Man., Canada, on the Vermilion R.; 51°09′N 100°03′W. It is the retail and distribution center for an agr., lumbering, and fishing area.

Dauphin (DAW-fin), borough (1990 pop. 845), Dauphin co., S central Pa., 8 mi/12.9 km NNW of Harrisburg, on Susquehanna R., at mouth of Stony Creek; 40°22′N 76°55′W. Agr. (soybeans, apples, corn, hay, wheat; poultry, livestock, dairying). Rockville Bridge (RR; Susquehanna R.) 2 mi/3.2 km to S. Appalachian Trail passes to N on Peters Mt. ridge. Fort Hunter Mansion (1814) to S.

Dauphin, Cape (DO-fin), NE N.S., Canada, on NE coast of Cape Breton Isl., bet. St. Ann's Bay (W) and Great Bras d'Or (E), 12 mi/19 km NW of Sydney Mines; 46°21′N 60°25′W.

Dauphin Island (DAW-fin), town (1990 pop. 824), Mobile co., SW Ala., on DAUPHIN ISLAND, in the Gulf of Mexico; 30°14′N 88°10′W.

Cross references are shown in SMALL CAPITALS. The pronunciation key is on page xv. The dates of population figures are on page xii.

Dauphin Island (DAW-fin), barrier beach (c.15 mi/24 km long, average width $\frac{1}{2}$ mi/$\frac{8}{10}$ km) in Gulf of Mexico at entrance to Mobile Bay, SW Ala. Est. as Fr. base (1699) for colonization of La.; seized (1813) by Gen. Wilkinson for U.S. Now part of Mobile co. Fort Gaines, at E end of isl., was captured (1864) by Admiral Farragut during battle of Mobile Bay. E end of isl. has a bird sanctuary and Univ. of S Alabama Marine Research Station. Deep-sea fishing pier (850 ft/259 m).

Dauphin Lake (□ 200 sq mi/518 sq km), W Man., Canada, 11 mi/18 km E of Dauphin; 26 mi/42 km long, 12 mi/19 km wide. Drains N into L. Winnipegosis.

Daveluyville (dah-vuhl-WEE-vil), village (1991 pop. 1,114), S Que., Canada, on Bécancour R., and 23 mi/37 km E of Nicolet; dairying, cattle; wheat, potatoes.

Davenport 1 city (1990 pop. 1,529), Polk co., central Fla., 4 mi/6.4 km NNE of Haines City; 28°09'N 81°35'W. Food prods. **2** city (1990 pop. 95,333), seat of Scott co., E central Iowa, on the Mississippi R.; 41°33'N 90°35'W. Bridges connect it with the Illinois cities of Rock Island and Moline. Davenport is the largest of the Quad Cities, which also includes Rock Isl., Moline (Ill.), and Bettendorf (Iowa). Davenport is a RR, commercial, and industrial center. Mfg. (food, fabricated metal prods., concrete, fixtures, apparel; printing and publishing). An early trading post was on the site, and the treaty ending the Black Hawk War was signed there in 1832. Davenport prospered with the arrival (1856) of the first RR to bridge the Mississippi and had heavy river traffic in the late 19th cent. It is the seat of St. Ambrose Col., Marycrest Col., Scott Community Col. in surburban Riverdale 4 mi/64 km. E, and the Palmer Col. of Chiropractic (developed by the son of D. D. Palmer). Also in the city are a municipal art gallery (Putnam Mus.); a public mus.; the Mississippi Valley Fair Grounds; a zoo; and several parks, including Credit Isl., a battle site in the War of 1812. A large roller-gate dam, Lock and Dam No. 15, and several locks, built there by the Federal govt., raise the water level of the river. Lock and Dam No. 14 is 8 mi/12.9 km. upstream. Downtown Davenport, denied the benefit of a floodwall for aesthetic reasons, was severely damaged in the flood of 1993. Inc. 1836.

Davenport 1 town (1990 pop. 979), Lincoln co., central Okla., 7 mi/11.3 km E of Chandler; 35°42'N 96°46'W. Agr. and oil-producing area. **2** town (1990 pop. 1,502), ⊙ Lincoln co., E Wash., 35 mi/56 km W of Spokane, on Hawk Creek; 47°39'N 118°09'W. In agr. region; wheat, barley, oats, rye, alfalfa; mfg. (printing and publishing). Spokane Indian Reservation N of river; Little Falls and Long L. dams (both Spokane R.) to NW. Spokane R. arm of Franklin D. Roosevelt L. reservoir (Coulee Dam Natl. Recreation Area) to N. Fort Spokane, at confluence of Spokane and Columbia rivers, 20 mi/32 km NNW.

Davenport 1 uninc. village, Santa Cruz co., W Calif., on the Pacific Ocean, 9 mi/14.5 km WNW of Santa Cruz. Fowers, nursery prods.; apples, vegetables; mfg. (hydraulic cement). Big Basin Redwoods State Park to N. **2** village (1990 pop. 383), Thayer co., S Nebr., 15 mi/24 km NW of Hebron; 40°18'N 97°48'W. **3** village (1990 pop. 218), Cass co., SE N.Dak., 17 mi/27 km SW of Fargo; 46°42'N 97°04'W. RR junction.

Davenport Center, village (1990 pop. 220), Delaware co., S N.Y., in the Catskills, on Charlotte R., 7 mi/11.3 km E of Oneonta; 42°27'N 74°54'W.

Davey, village (1990 pop. 160), Lancaster co., E Nebr., 11 mi/18 km N of Lincoln; 40°58'N 96°40'W.

David Berger Affiliated Area, natl. monument, NE Ohio, authorized 1980, Site honors Israeli athletes killed at the 1972 Olympic Games in Munich.

David City, town (1990 pop. 2,522), ⊙ Butler co., E Nebr., 24 mi/39 km N of Seward, in prairie region S of the Platte; 41°15'N 97°07'W. RR junction. Farm trade center. Livestock, grain. Mfg. (food, transportation equip.). Inc. 1878.

David D. Terry Lock and Dam, Pulaski co., central Ark. Dam is 39 ft/12 m high and is on the Arkansas R. It was built by the Army Corps of Engineers for navigational purposes. The reservoir it creates has a max. capacity of 59,600 acre-ft. It is near Pine Bluff.

David's Island, N.Y.: see NEW ROCHELLE.

Davidson 1 county (□ 566 sq mi/1,466 sq km; 1990 pop. 126,677), central N.C.; ⊙ Lexington; 35°47'N 80°12'W. In Piedmont region; bounded W and SW by Yadkin R., forms High Rock L. and Tuckertown L. reservoirs in SW. Agr. (tobacco, corn, wheat, hay, soybeans, sorghum, chickens, dairying, cattle, hogs), timber (pine, oak). Mfg. at Lexington and Thomasville (especially furniture); sawmilling. Small part of Uwharrie Natl. Forest in SE corner; Boone's Cave State Park in W. Formed 1822. **2** county (□ 532 sq mi/1,378 sq km; 1990 pop. 510,784) N central Tenn.; ⊙ NASHVILLE; 36°10'N 86°47'W. Intersected by Cumberland R. Limestone processing; livestock, small grains, dairy prods., tobacco, tomatoes, fruit; diversified mfg. at Nashville, Goodlettsville, Madison, and Old Hickory. Formed 1783, merged with city of Nashville 1963.

Davidson, town (1991 pop. 1,115), S central Sask., Canada, 65 mi/105 km NNW of Moose Jaw; 51°16'N 105°58'W. Grain elevators.

Davidson, town (1990 pop. 4,046), Mecklenburg co., S N.C., 18 mi/29 km N of Charlotte; 35°30'N 80°50'W. Mfg. (electronic equip., fabricated metal prods., machinery). Tobacco, grain, soybeans, livestock. Seat of Davidson Col. (1837). L. Norman reservoir (Catawba R.) to W.

Davidson, village (1990 pop. 473), Tillman co., SW Okla., 11 mi/18 km SSW of Frederick, near Red R.; 34°14'N 99°04'W. In agr. area (peanuts, vegetables, cotton).

Davidson Glacier, SE Alaska, arm of Muir Glacier, at W side of mouth of Chilkat Inlet; 59°05'N 135°27'W.

Davidson, Mount (7,864 ft/2,397 m), Storey co., W Nev., in Virginia Range, just W of Virginia City. Site of famed COMSTOCK LODE and location of Virginia City. named after either Calif. State Geologist Donald Davidson or Professor George Davidson, head of Coast and Geodetic Survey and founder of Univ. of Calif. Geography dept.

Davidson Mountains (8,000 ft/2,438 m.), NE Alaska, NE part of Brooks Range, S of Arctic Ocean; 68°30'–69°N 141°30'–144°W.

Davidsville, uninc. town (1990 pop. 1,167), Somerset co., SW Pa., 7 mi/11.3 km S of Johnstown; 40°13'N 78°56'W. Mfg includes fabricated metal prods.; coal mining. Agr. includes dairying, livestock; grain, potatoes. Bituminous coal in area. Quemahoning Reservoir to S.

Davie, county (□ 266 sq mi/689 sq km; 1990 pop. 27,859), central N.C.; ⊙ Mocksville; 35°55'N 80°32'W. In Piedmont region; bounded E by the Yadkin R., S by South Fork Yadkin R. Agr. (tobacco, wheat, corn, soybeans; chickens; dairying, cattle, hogs; hay); timber. Formed 1836.

Davie (DAI-vee), suburb (□ 33 sq mi/85 sq km; 1990 pop. 47,217) of Fort Lauderdale, Broward co., S Fla., 8 mi/12.9 km SW of city center; 26°04'N 80°17'W.

Daviess 1 (DAY-vuhs), county (□ 436 sq mi/1,129 sq km; 1990 pop. 27,533), SW Ind., bounded S by East Fork of White R., W by West Fork of White R.; ⊙ Washington; 38°42'N 87°05'W. Agr. and bituminous-coal area. Corn, soybeans, watermelon, fruit; cattle, turkeys; with mfg. at Washington; natural-gas and oil wells; nurseries. Glendale State Fish and Wildlife Area (including East Fork State Fish Hatchery) in SE; W. Boggs Creek reservoir in E. Formed 1817. **2** (DAI-veez), county (□ 476 sq mi/1,233 sq km; 1990 pop. 87,189), NW Ky; ⊙ OWENSBORO; 37°43'N 87°05'W. Bounded N by Ohio R. (Ind. state line), W by Green R.; drained by Panther Creek and its N and S forks. Rolling agr. area (burley and dark tobacco, a leading co. in Ky. tobacco production; corn, wheat, sorghum, hay, alfalfa, soybeans; cattle, hogs, poultry; dairying). Oil and gas wells, coal mines. Industries at Owensboro. Lock and Dam No. 45, Ohio R., at Owensboro in N; Ben Hawes State Park in N, to W of Owensboro. Formed 1815. **3** county (□ 563 sq mi/1,458 sq km; 1990 pop. 7,865), NW Mo.; ⊙ Gallatin; 39°57'N 93°59'W. Drained by Grand R. Corn, wheat, hay, soybeans; cattle, sheep, hogs; dairy prods. Amish community near Jamesport. Formed 1836.

Davis 1 county (□ 504 sq mi/1,305 sq km; 1990 pop. 8,312), SE Iowa, on Mo. state line (S); ⊙ Bloomfield; 40°45'N 92°24'W. Stock-raising (sheep, hogs, cattle, poultry) and agr. (corn, soybeans, hay) area, drained by Des Moines, Fox, North Fabius, and Wyaconda rivers; bituminous-coal deposits mined in NE. Includes L. Wapello State Park in NW and 3 small units of Stephens State Forrest also in NW. Formed 1843. **2** county (□ 633 sq mi/1,639 sq km; 1990 pop. 187,941), N Utah; ⊙ Farmington; 41°00'N 112°07'W. Irrigated agr. area; includes part of SE corner of Great Salt L. (with Antelope Isl.) and Antelope Isl. State Park in W and part of Wasatch Range and Wasatch Natl. Forest in E. Apples; alfalfa, wheat, barley, hay; sugar beets, cherries, peaches, berries, apricots, vegetables; cattle, sheep; food processing; gravel, coal, salt. Hill Air Force Base in N. Howard Slough and Farmington Bay Wildlife Management areas on Great Salt L. shore. Causeway extended from Syracuse to Antelope Isl. built early 1990s. Highly urbanized area bet. Salt Lake City (S) and Ogden (N); numerous communities have grown rapidly in 1970s through 1990s; agr. remains important. Smallest co. in Utah, 3rd largest in pop. Formed 1850.

Davis, city (1990 pop. 46,209), Yolo co., central Calif., 12 mi WSW of Sacramento, on Putah Creek; 38°33'N 121°45'W. RR junction. It is an education center with light industry, mfg. (printing and publishing, machinery, food, computer equip.). The extensive Univ. of California at Davis, which has a major agr. research center as well as schools of veterinary medicine, law, medicine, and engineering, is here. The Natl. Primate Center is near Davis, State Nursery to E. Settled in the 1850s, inc. 1917.

Davis 1 town (1990 pop. 2,543), Murray co., S Okla., at N base of the Arbuckle Mts., 8 mi/12.9 km W of Sulphur, and on Washita R.; 34°28'N 97°07'W. In dairying area; mfg. (transportation equip., concrete). Chickasaw Natl. Recreation Area and Arbuckle Reservoir to SE; Price Falls Park to S; Turner Falls Park nearby. Settled 1889. **2** town (1990 pop. 799), Tucker co., NE W.Va., 12 mi/19 km ENE of Parsons, near Md. state line; 39°07'N 79°28'W. Highest community in state (elev. 3,101 ft/945 m). Light mfg. Blackwater Outdoor Center is here. Blackwater Falls State Park to SW; Fairfax Stone State Monument to N; Canaan Valley State Park to S; Monongahela Natl. Forest to SW; Canaan Valley and Timberline Ski areas to S. Inc. 1889.

Davis 1 village (1990 pop. 541), Stephenson co., N Ill., 14 mi/23 km NE of Freeport; 42°25'N 89°25'W. In agr. area (corn; cattle, hogs; dairying); cheese factories. **2** village (1990 pop. 87), Turner co., SE S.Dak., 12 mi/19 km SSE of Parker. In grain-growing area.

Davis Bridge Dam, Davis Bridge Reservoir, Vt.: see HARRIMAN RESERVOIR.

Davis City, town (1990 pop. 257), Decatur co., S Iowa, near Mo. state line, on Thompson R., and 8 mi/12.9 km SSW of Leon; 40°38'N 93°48'W. In livestock and grain area. Nine Eagles State Park to SE.

Davis Dam, NW Ariz. and SE Nev., 200 ft/61 m high, 1,600 ft/488 m long, on Colorado R. (here forming the state border), 55 mi/89 km S of Hoover Dam and 30 mi/48 km W of Kingman, Ariz., in S end of Lake Mead Natl. Recreation Area; 35°09'N 114°34'W. Recreation Area. Rockfill and earthfill; built (1949) for hydroelectric power and for regulation of water from L. Mead for Parker and Imperial dams, downstream. Forms L. Mohave reservoir (max. 4 mi/6.4 km wide), which extends c.55 mi/89 km N to Hoover Dam.

Davis Inlet, bay (20 mi/32 km long, 1 mi/2 km wide) of the Atlantic, E Lab., Canada; 55°55'N 60°50'W. In entrance of bay is UKASIKSALIK ISLAND, with fishing village of Davis Inlet.

Davis Junction, village (1990 pop. 246), Ogle co., N central Ill., 12 mi/19 km S of Rockford; 42°06'N 89°05'W. RR junction. Grain; livestock, dairying; mfg. (leather).

Davis, Mount, peak, 3,213 ft/979 m high, Somerset co., SW Pa., in the Allegheny Mts., 38 mi/61 km SSW of Johnstown; 39°47'N 79°10'W. Highest point in Pa., in Forbes State Forest.

Davis Mountains, mainly in Jeff Davis co., W Tex., Mt. Livermore (8,378 ft/2,554 m) is the highest peak, c.150 mi/241 km SE of El Paso. Forested slopes, great springs, and deep canyons attract tourists; Davis Mts. State Park is in SE part. On the summit of Mt. Locke, 6,791 ft/2,070 m high, is the Univ. of Texas McDonald Observatory, with the world's 3d-largest (107 in./272 cm) reflector telescope. Fort Davis, estab. 1854 as a border outpost, is a natl. historic site in SE.

Davis-Besse Nuclear Power Plant, Ohio: see OTTAWA, co.

Davisboro, city (1990 pop. 407), Washington co., E central Ga., 12 mi/19 km E of Sandersville; 32°59′N 82°37′W.

Davis-Monthan Air Force Base, Ariz.: see TUCSON.

Davison, county (□ 436 sq mi/1,129 sq km; 1990 pop. 17,503), SE central S.Dak.; ⊙ Mitchell. Agr. area watered by James R. and Firesteel Creek. Mfg. at Mitchell. Corn, wheat, hay; cattle, hogs; dairy prods. Formed 1873.

Davison, town (1990 pop. 5,693), Genesee co., SE central Mich., suburb 9 mi/14.5 km E of Flint; 43°01′N 83°31′W. In agr. area; mfg. (machinery, printing and publishing). Has Rosemoor Park, with race track. Settled 1836; inc. as village 1889, as city 1939.

Daviston, town (1990 pop. 261), Tallapoosa co., E Ala., near Tallapoosa R., 17 mi/27 km NNE of Dadeville; lumber.

Davisville 1 Mass.: see FALMOUTH. **2** R.I.: see NORTH KINGSTOWN.

Davy, village (1990 pop. 403), McDowell co., S W. Va., 5 mi/8 km NW of Welch, on Tug Fork R.; 37°28′N 81°39′W. Semi-bituminous coal. Mfg. (fabricated metal prods.).

Davy Crockett Lake, Tenn.: see NOLICHUCKY.

Dawes, county (□ 1,400 sq mi/3,626 sq km; 1990 pop. 9,021), NW Nebr.; ⊙ Chadron; 42°42′N 103°08′W. Grazing and recreational area with a little irrigation, drained by White and Niobrara rivers; bounded N by S.Dak. Cattle, wheat, alfalfa, hogs, dairy and poultry, beans, potatoes. Fort Robinson State Park on W boundary; part of Oglalla Natl. Grasslands in NW corner; Pine Ridge unit of Nebr. Natl. Forest crosses co. from E center to SW; Chadron State Park in E, S of Chadron; Chadron State Col.; Cochran State Wayside Area in W, S of Crawford; Box Butte Reservoir State Recreation Area in S, E of Marsland. Formed 1885.

Dawson 1 county (□ 213 sq mi/552 sq km; 1990 pop. 9,429), N Ga.; ⊙ Dawsonville; 34°26′N 84°10′W. Blue Ridge (N) and piedmont (S) area drained by Etowah and Chestatee rivers. Mfg. of apparel and textiles. Agr. (corn, hay, sweet potatoes; cattle, hogs, poultry); timber. Chattahoochee Natl. Forest (N). Formed 1857. **2** county (□ 2,383 sq mi/6,172 sq km; 1990 pop. 9,505), E Mont.; ⊙ Glendive; 47°16′N 104°54′W. Agr. region drained by Yellowstone R. Wheat, barley, oats, hay, corn, beans, sugar beets, potatoes; cattle, sheep, hogs; poultry (chickens, geese, ducks, turkeys). Oil field (NW) discovered 1951. Makoshika State Park in SE center; rare paddle fish are found in the Yellowstone R.; dinosaur fossils incl. triceratops. Formed 1869, present boundaries est. 1919. **3** county (□ 1,019 sq mi/2,639 sq km; 1990 pop. 19,940), S central Nebr.; ⊙ Lexington; 40°52′N 99°48′W. Agr. area in Platte River Valley drained by Platte and Wood rivers. Corn, alfalfa, wheat, soybeans; hogs; dairy and poultry prods. Gallagher Canyon State Recreation Area in SW; Johnson L. State Recreation Area on S boundary. Formed 1871. **4** county (□ 902 sq mi/2,336 sq km; 1990 pop. 14,349), NW Texas, ⊙ Lamesa, on high plains, with E-facing Caprock escarpment in E; co.; 32°44′N 101°57′W. Elev. c.2,600 ft/792 m–3,200 ft/975 m. Drained by intermittent Sulphur Springs Draw and Tobacco Creek (leads into Colorado R. to E). Irrigated agr. (wheat, sorghum, cotton); livestock (cattle, hogs). Oil and natural gas wells. Hunting. Formed 1876.

Dawson or **Dawson City**, city (1991 pop. 972), W Yukon Territory, Canada, at the confluence of the Yukon and Klondike rivers; 64°04′N 139°25′W. Trade center of the Klondike mining region and a tourist center. During the gold rush of 1898 Dawson was a boom town, reported to have a pop. of about 20,000. Named for George M. Dawson, a Can. geologist. The territorial capital was moved from Dawson to Whitehorse in 1952.

Dawson 1 town (1990 pop. 5,295), ⊙ Terrell co., SW Ga., 22 mi/35 km NW of Albany; 31°46′N 84°26′W. Mfg. of apparel, food, transportation equip., fertilizers, concrete. Agr. includes corn and wheat. Center for soul music. Settled 1856, inc. 1872. **2** town (1990 pop. 174), Dallas co., central Iowa, on Raccoon R., and 10 mi/16 km NW of Adel; 41°50′N 94°13′W. In agr. area. **3** town (1990 pop. 1,626), Lac qui Parle co., SW Minn., 9 mi/14.5 km SE of Madison on West Fork Lac qui Parle R., near its confluence to E with Lac qui Parle R.; 44°55′N 96°02′W. Trade center and shipping point for agr. area (grain, soybeans; livestock, poultry; dairying). Lac qui Parle Wildlife Area and State Park to NE, on Minnesota R. Inc. as village 1885, as city 1911. **4** town, Tulsa co., NE Okla., just E of Tulsa. Part of Tulsa; SW of Tulsa Airport. Inc. 1923. **5** town (1990 pop. 766), Navarro co., E central Texas, 19 mi/31 km SW of Corsicana; 31°53′N 96°42′W. In farm area (cotton, corn; cattle; dairying). Navarro Mills L. to NW. Settled c.1882, inc. 1908.

Dawson 1 village (1990 pop. 536), Sangamon co., central Ill., 10 mi/16 km ENE of Springfield; 39°51′N 89°27′W. In agr. area (corn, sorghum, cattle, hogs; dairying); oil and natural gas. **2** village (1990 pop. 157), Richardson co., SE Nebr., 10 mi/16 km WNW of Falls City, and on North Fork of Big Nemaha R; 40°07′N 95°49′W. Grain, livestock. **3** village (1990 pop. 78), Kidder co., central N.Dak., 8 mi/12.9 km E of Steele; 46°52′N 99°45′W. Slade Natl. Wildlife Refuge to SE.

Dawson, borough (1990 pop. 535), Fayette co., SW Pa., 5 mi/8 km WNW of Connellsvile, on Youghiogheny R.; 40°02′N 79°39′W. Some agr.

Dawson Creek, city (1991 pop. 10,981), E B.C., Canada, near the Alta. border, on Dawson Creek and NE of Prince George; 55°46′N 120°14′W. Important grain-shipping center; S terminus of Alaska Highway.

Dawson, Mount (11,123 ft/3,390 m), SE B.C., Canada, in Selkirk Mts., in Glacier Natl. Park, 35 mi/56 km ENE of Revelstoke: 51°09′N 117°25′W.

Dawson Springs, town (1990 pop. 3,129), Hopkins co., W Ky., on Tradewater R., and 25 mi/40 km NNW of Hopkinsville; 37°10′N 87°41′W. RR junction. Health resort with mineral springs, in coal-mining and agr. area; light mfg. Airport to NE. Dawson Springs Mus. and Art Center. L. Beshear reservoir and Pennyrile Forest State Resort Park to S; Tradewater Wildlife Management Area 1 mi/1.6 km to S, Jones-Keeney Wildlife Management Area to W.

Dawsonville, village (1990 pop. 467), ⊙ Dawson co., N Ga., 19 mi/14.5 km WNW of Gainesville; 34°25′N 84°07′W. Mfg. includes apparel, rubber and paper prods.

Day, county (□ 1,091 sq mi/2,826 sq km; 1990 pop. 6,978), NE S.Dak.; ⊙ Webster. Agr. region watered by numerous lakes, nearly all of them in E half; largest is Waubay L. Located on E slope of Coteau des Prairies; part of L. Traverse (Sisseton Wahpeton) Indian Reservation in E. Resorts. Corn, flax, soybeans, wheat; dairying; cattle, hogs. Waubay Natl. Wildlife Refuge and Pickerel L. State Rec. Area in E. Amsden Dam State Lakeside Use Area in W. Formed 1875.

Day Valley, uninc. town (1990 pop. 2,824), residential suburb, Santa Clara co., Calif., c.20 mi/32 km S of San Jose and 6 mi/9.7 km S of Morgan Hill, in Santa Clara Valley; 37°02′N 121°52′W. Santa Cruz Mts. to W. Wineries in area. Grapes, fruit, vegetables, grain, dairying, poultry.

Daykin, village (1990 pop. 188), Jefferson co., SE Nebr., 13 mi/21 km NNW of Fairbury; 40°19′N 97°17′W. RR terminus. Grain, livestock. Alexandria Lakes State Recreation Area to S.

Daysland, town (1991 pop. 674), central Alta., Canada, 27 mi/43 km ESE of Camrose; 52°52′N 112°15′W. Grain elevators, food mfg.

Dayton 1 city (1990 pop. 182,044), ⊙ Montgomery co., SW Ohio, on the Great Miami R., where it is joined by the Stillwater R.; 39°46′N 84°11′W. Port of entry; the industrial, trade, and distributing point for a fertile farm area; and an aviation center. Its chief prods. are computers, machinery, fabricated metal prods., paper and rubber prods., transportation equip., printing and publishing. Dayton grew with the extension of canals (1830s and 40s) and RR (1850s), and with the industrial demands of the Civil War. First large city to adopt (1913) the city-manager form of govt. Home of the Wright brothers, and after their flight near Kitty Hawk, N.C., the brothers established a research aircraft plant in Dayton. The city's educational institutions include Wright State Univ., the Univ. of Dayton, Sinclair Community Col., a theological seminary, and a business col. Among the points of interest are the home of the poet Paul Laurence Dunbar, and Carillon Park, which contains a restored Wright brothers' airplane and a Carillon tower with 32 bells. Dayton has an art institute, a symphony orchestra, a natural history mus., and the Dayton Mall (one of the largest shopping centers in the U.S.). Wright-Patterson Air Force Base is nearby. Air Force Mus. has most diverse collection of aircraft in the world. Materials research center and avionics laboratory at Wright-Patterson Air Force Base. Edison Materials Technology Center and Wright Technology Network transfer technology to civilian mfg. firms. Inc. 1805. **2** city (1990 pop. 5,671), ⊙ Rhea co., E Tenn., near Tenn. R., 35 mi/56 km NNE of Chattanooga; 35°30′N 85°01′W. In fruit, coal, timber region; mfg. of apparel, consumer goods. William Jennings Bryan Univ. here. In 1925, scene of the Scopes trial. Founded c. 1884.

Dayton 1 town (1990 pop. 77), Marengo co., W Ala., 10 mi/16 km NE of Linden. **2** town (1990 pop. 996), Tippecanoe co., W central Ind., 6 mi/9.7 km SE of Lafayette; 40°23′N 86°47′W. Corn, wheat, cattle. **3** town (1990 pop. 818), Webster co., central Iowa, 17 mi/27 km SSE of Fort Dodge; 42°15′N 94°04′W. **4** town (1990 pop. 6,576), Campbell co., N Ky., suburb, 2 mi/3.2 km ENE of downtown Cincinnati, Ohio, on the Ohio R.; 39°06′N 84°27′W. Mfg. (printing and publishing, machinery). Settled 1848; inc. 1867. **5** town (1990 pop. 4,443), Hennepin co., E Minn., residential suburb, 17 mi/27 km NW of downtown Minneapolis on Mississippi R.; 45°11′N 93°28′W. E of mouth of Crow R. Mfg. (transportation equip., food). Part of Elm Creek Regional Park in SE. **6** uninc. town (1990 pop. 2,217), Lyon co., W Nev., on Carson R., and 10 mi/16 km ENE of Carson City; 39°15′N 119°34′W. Elev. 4,400 ft/1,341 m. Cattle, sheep, poultry; dairying; vegetables, potatoes, hay; mfg. (electronic equip.); silver mining. Includes Dayton State Park. Settled c. 1850 as a mining town; capital of Lyon co. until 1911. **7** town (1990 pop. 1,526), Yamhill co., NW Oregon, 6 mi/9.7 km E of McMinnville, and on Yamhill R. near its mouth in Willamette R.; 45°13′N 123°04′W. Fruit, vegetables; poultry; dairy prods. Willamette Mission and Maud Williamson State Parks to S. **8** town (1990 pop. 5,151), Liberty co., E Texas, near Trinity R., 33 mi/53 km ENE of Houston; 30°03′N 94°54′W. Trade, processing point in oil producing and agr. area (rice, soybeans; cattle); mfg. (chemicals, construction materials, fabricated metal prods.). Inc. 1925. **9** town (1990 pop. 921), Rockingham co., NW Va., in Shenandoah Valley, suburb, 4 mi/6.4 km SW of Harrisonburg; 38°25′N 78°56′W. Mfg. (electronic equip., lumber, food); agr. (grain, apples, peaches, soybeans; poultry, livestock; dairying). **10** town (1990 pop. 2,468), ⊙ Columbia co., SE Wash., 25 mi/40 km NE of Walla Walla, and on Touchet R., at mouth of Patit Creek; 46°19′N 117°59′W. Wheat, peas; timber; mfg. (food). Lewis and Clark Trail State Park. Historical Train Depot. Camp William T. Wooten State Park to E; Umatilla Natl. Forest to SE, including Wenaha-Tucannon Wilderness Area. Inc. 1871.

Dayton 1 village (1990 pop. 357), Franklin co., SE Idaho, 5 mi/8 km WNW of Preston; 42°07′N 111°59′W. Elev. 4,818 ft/1,469 m. Sugar beets; barley, wheat; cattle, sheep; dairying. Caribou Natl. Forest to W; Western Canyon to SW. **2** village (1990 pop. 100), Lake co., NW Mont., 13 mi/21 km NNW of Polson, in Flathead Indian Reservation, on W shore of Flathead L., at mouth of Dayton Creek. Winery. Tourism. Wild Horse Isl. Unit of Flathead L. State Park to E; Black L. to W.

3 village (1990 pop. 4,321), Middlesex co., central N.J., 9 mi/14.5 km SSW of New Brunswick; 40°22′N 74°30′W. In rapidly suburbanizing area. **4** village (1990 pop. 565), Sheridan co., N Wyo., on Tongue R., just E of Bighorn Mts. and Bighorn Natl. Forest, near Mont. line, and 15 mi/24 km WNW of Sheridan. Elev. 3,926 ft/1,197 m. To W are Tongue R. Canyon, a gorge 2,000 ft/610 m deep, and The Fallen City, picturesque jumble of rocks left on hillside by glacier. Crow Indian Reservation to N (Mont.). Livestock.

Dayton, borough (1990 pop. 572), Armstrong co., W central Pa., 15 mi/24 km ENE of Kittanning; 40°52′N 79°14′W. Mfg. (wood prods.); agr. (corn, hay; livestock, dairying). Mahoning Creek L. reservoir to N and NE.

Daytona Beach (dai-TO-nuh), city (□ 36 sq mi/93 sq km; 1990 pop. 61,921), Volusia co., E central Fla., on the Atlantic coast and Halifax R. (a lagoon); 29°11′N 81°02′W. The center of a major urban area comprising 8 cities, Daytona Beach is a popular year-round resort. Its economy, long oriented to tourism, has become more diversified with the growth of space-related industries. The city was founded in 1870 in an area settled by Span. Franciscans in the late 16th and 17th cents. Noted for its hard, white beach, the city has been the scene of automobile racing since 1902; a famous event is the Daytona-500. Its institutions of higher education include an aeronautical univ. Inc. 1876.

Daytona Beach Shores (dai-TO-nuh), town (1990 pop. 2,335), Volusia co., E central Fla., 3 mi/4.8 km S of Daytona Beach; 29°10′N 80°58′W.

Dayville, village (1990 pop. 144), Grant co., NE central Oregon, 28 mi/45 km W of John Day, and on John Day R. at mouth of its South Fork; 44°28′N 119°31′W. Timber. Grain; livestock. Parts of Malheur Natl. Forest to NE and SE; part of Ochoco Natl. Forest to SW; John Day Fossil Beds Natl. Monument (Sheep Rock Unit) to NW.

Dazey (DAIZ-ee), village (1990 pop. 129), Barnes co., E central N.Dak., 21 mi/34 km NNW of Valley City; 47°11′N 98°12′W.

De Baca (DE BAH-kuh), county (□ 2,334 sq mi/6,045 sq km; 1990 pop. 2,252), E N.Mex.; ⊙ Fort Sumner; 34°20′N 104°25′W. Cattle, sheep, sorghum, hay, alfalfa, wheat, oats, barley, millet. Watered by Pecos R. Conejos Mesa (5,000 ft/1,524 m) in center. Formed 1917. Fort Sumner State Monument and Grave of Billy the Kid in NE; Sumner L. Reservoir and State Park, on Pecos R., on N boundary.

De Bary (duh-BA-ree), town (□ 7 sq mi/18.1 sq km; 1990 pop. 7,176), Volusia co., E central Fla., 8 mi/12.9 km NW of Sanford; 28°52′N 81°18′W.

De Beque (da-BECK), village (1990 pop. 257), Mesa co., W Colo., on Colorado R. at mouth of Roan Creek, and 26 mi/42 km NE of Grand Junction; 39°19′N 108°12′W. Elev. 4,935 ft/1,504 m. Trade center in livestock region. Prehistoric fossils found nearby. Oilshale fields in vicinity. Grand Valley Dam, unit in Grand Valley irrigation project, is 14 mi/23 km SSW. Cattle, sheep, wheat, oats, hay, honey. Grand Mesa Natl. Forest to E; Isl. Acres State Park to SW.

De Borgia (duh BOR-juh), village (1990 pop. 75), Mineral co., W Mont., on St. Regis de Borgia R. (St. Regis R.), and 75 mi/121 km NW of Missoula near Idaho line. In the Bitterroot Range surrounded by the Lolo Natl. Forest. Nearby is Savenac Forest Nursery, with annual capacity of 6,000,000 trees.

De Cade, Lake (duh KAID), Terrebonne parish, SE La., 14 mi/23 km SW of Houma, in marshy coastal region; c.5 mi/8 km long, 1 mi/2 km–2 mi/3 km wide; 29°23′N 90°51′W. Connected by waterways with Intracoastal Waterway (N) and Gulf of Mexico (S).

De Chartres, Fort, Ill.: see PRAIRIE DU ROCHER.

De Chien, Bayou (de-SHEN, BEI-yoo), or **Bayou du Chien**, stream W Ky., flows c.35 mi/56 km generally W to the Mississippi R., 2 mi/3.2 km NE of Hickman. Rises in S Graves co., at Tenn. state line

De Cordova Bend Dam, Texas: see GRANBURY, LAKE.

De Forest, town (1990 pop. 4,882), Dane co., S Wis., on Yahara R., and 12 mi/19 km N of Madison; 43°15′N 89°20′W. In tobacco growing and dairying region; mfg. (plastic prods.). Agr. research station to N.

De Funiak Springs (duh-FOONEE-ak), town (□ 10 sq mi/26 sq km; 1990 pop. 5,120), ⊙ Walton co., NW Fla., c.45 mi/72 km NW of Panama City, in farm and timber area; 30°43′N 86°07′W.

De Graff 1 village (1990 pop. 149), Swift co., SW Minn., 8 mi/12.9 km SE of Benson; 45°15′N 95°28′W. Grain; livestock, poultry; dairying; light mfg. **2** village (1990 pop. 1,331), Logan co., W central Ohio, 9 mi/14 km WSW of Bellefontaine, and on Great Miami R., in agr. area; 40°19′N 83°55′W. Sometimes spelled Degraff.

De Haven Point, SE extremity of Victoria Isl., S Franklin dist., N.W.T., Canada, on Queen Maud Gulf, at S end of Victoria Strait; 69°39′N 101°34′W.

De Kalb 1 (duh KAHLB), county (□ 778 sq mi/2,015 sq km; 1990 pop. 54,651), NE Ala.; ⊙ Fort Payne, 34°27′N 85°47′W. Hilly region bordering on Ga. Corn, soybeans, hay, livestock (poultry, cattle, hogs); deposits of coal, iron, limestone, fuller's earth. Sand Mtn. extends throughout most of co. Formed 1836. **2** county (□ 635 sq mi/1,645 sq km; 1990 pop. 77,932), N Ill.; ⊙ Sycamore; 41°54′N 88°46′W. Agr. (sheep, hogs, corn, soybeans, poultry). Mfg. (food, asphalt, electronic equip., plastic prods.). Drained by branches of Kishwaukee R. Formed 1837. Northern Illinois Univ. is at De Kalb. Kishwaukee Community Col. is near Malta. **3** (dee KAB), county (□ 423 sq mi/1096 sq km; 1990 pop. 9,967), NW Mo., ⊙ Maysville; 39°53′N 94°25′W. Drained by branches of Grand and Platte rivers. Agr. (corn, wheat, soybeans; cattle). Pony Express L. in S. Formed 1845. **4** (de KAB), county (□ 317; 1990 pop. 14,360), central Tenn.; ⊙ Smithville; 35°58′N 85°51′W. Drained by Caney Fork of Cumberland R. and includes part of Center Hill Reservoir. Lumber; livestock; corn, small grains, soybeans, fruit, tobacco; dairying. Formed 1837.

De Kalb, city (1990 pop. 34,925), De Kalb co., N Ill., 6 mi/9.7 km SSW of Sycamore; 41°55′N 88°45′W. In a farm area; inc. 1861. Mfg. includes food, machinery, electronic equip., plastics. The growth of the city was stimulated in the 1870s by the development and manufacture of workable barbed wire by a resident, Joseph F. Glidden. Seat of Northern Illinois Univ.

De Kalb 1 (dee KALB), town (1990 pop. 1,073), ⊙ Kemper co., E Miss., 28 mi/45 km N of Meridian, near Sucarnoochie Creek; 32°46′N 88°39′W. Agr. (cotton, corn; cattle); mfg. (construction materials, transportation equip., food, apparel). Sciples Mill (1790); Kemper County L. (state lake) to NW; Sam Dale Memorial State Historic Site to S. **2** (dee KAB), town (1990 pop. 222), Buchanan co., NW Mo., near Missouri R., 12 mi/19 km SSW of St. Joseph; 39°35′N 94°55′W. Tobacco, corn, cattle. **3** town (1990 pop. 1,976), Bowie co., NE Texas, near Red R., 34 mi/55 km W of Texarkana; 33°30′N 94°37′W. In cotton, vegetable area; timber.

De Land (dee LAND), resort city (□ 9 sq mi/23.3 sq km; 1990 pop. 16,491), ⊙ Volusia co., E central Fla., 20 mi/32 km SW of Daytona Beach; 29°02′N 81°17′W. It has dairies, citrus packing plants, and lumber mills. Other prods. are electronic equip., apparel, and medical supplies. De Land is the seat of Stetson Univ. Inc. 1882.

De Land, village (1990 pop. 458), Piatt co., central Ill., 7 mi/11.3 km NNW of Monticello; 40°07′N 88°38′W. In corn, soybeans, and livestock area.

De Leon, town (1990 pop. 2,190), Comanche co., central Texas, near Leon R., near headwaters of Proctor L. reservoir (S), 35 mi/56 km NE of Brownwood; 32°06′N 98°32′W. Shipping; processing center of peanuts and pecans; dairying; cattle, hogs. Founded 1887, inc. as city 1919.

De Leon Springs (duh LEE-on), town (1990 pop. 1,481), Volusia co., E central Fla., 22 mi/35 km W of Daytona Beach; 29°07′N 81°20′W. Site of Ponce de Leon Springs.

De Long Mountains (duh-LAWNG) (5,000 ft/1,524 m), NW Alaska, W part of Brooks Range, N of Kotzebue Sound; extend c.150 mi/241 km E from Chukchi Sea, to 68°30′N. Noatak R. separates De Long from Baird Mts.

De Pere (di PIR), city (1990 pop. 16,569), Brown co., E central Wis., a suburb, 5 mi/8 km SSW of Green Bay on the Fox R.; 44°26′N 88°04′W. A channel 20 ft/6 m wide allows port traffic from Green Bay as far as De Pere, the last upstream dock. Agr. and industrial center; mfg. (transportation equip., pharmaceuticals, feeds, fabricated metal prods., fixtures, printing and publishing, electronic equip., machinery, food). A mission, founded here (1671) by Father Allouez, was burned, rebuilt (1685), and used until 1717. De Pere grew in the 19th cent. as a lumber town, port, and commercial center. St. Norbert Col. is here. Heritage Hill State Park to NE; Oneida Indian Reservation to W. De Pere and West De Pere consolidated 1890. Inc. 1857

De Queen, town (1990 pop. 4,633), ⊙ Sevier co., SW Ark., c.45 mi/72 km NNW of Texarkana, near Okla. line; 34°02′N 94°20′W. RR junction; mfg. (printing and publishing; concrete, plastic prods.; food; lumber). Inc. 1897. DeQueen L. reservoir to NW.

De Queen Lake, reservoir (□ 3 sq mi/7.8 sq km), Sevier co., W central Ark., on Rolling Fork R., near Okla. border, 50 mi/80 km NNW of Texarkana; 34°06′N 94°21′W. Max. capacity 370,600 acre-ft. Formed by De Queen Dam (160 ft/49 m high), built (1977) by Army Corps of Engineers for water supply, recreation, and as a fish and wildlife pond.

De Quincy (duh KWIN-see), city (1990 pop. 3,474), Calcasieu parish, SW La., 20 mi/32 km NW of Lake Charles city; 30°27′N 93°27′W. In oil-producing and agr. area (soybeans, sorghum, hay; cattle, horses); RR junction; mfg. includes paper prods., lumber. Settled 1898, inc. 1902.

De Ridder (duh RID-er), city (1990 pop. 9,868), ⊙ Beauregard parish, W La., c.45 mi/72 km N of Lake Charles city; 30°51′N 93°17′W. RR junction; wool market, and trade and processing center for lumbering, timber, and diversified farming area (soybeans, grain, blueberries, watermelons, squash, cattle; dairying); printing and publishing. Oil field nearby. Bundick's Fish and Game Preserve to SE, Boise-Vernon State Wildlife Area to NW, Kisatchie Natl. Forest and Fort Polk Military Reserve to NE. Inc. 1907.

De Russy, Fort, military reservation, S Oahu, Honolulu Co., Hawaii, at Waikiki; 2.5 mi/4 km SE of downtown Honolulu; SE of intersection of Kalakaua Ave. and Ala Moana Boulevard; on coast. Former hq. of Hawaiian Coast Artillery Command; estab. 1908. U.S. Army Mus.

De Ruyter (duh ROI-tuhr), village (1990 pop. 568), Madison co., central N.Y., 25 mi/40 km SSE of Syracuse; 42°46′N 75°53′W.

De Smet, town (1990 pop. 1,172), ⊙ Kingsbury co., E central S.Dak., 42 mi/68 km SW of Watertown. Center of dairying area; livestock, grain; light mfg. Site of Laura Ingalls Wilder Homestead. Lakes dist. to E. Inc. 1880.

De Smet, Lake, reservoir, 4 mi/6.4 km long, 1 mi/1.6 km wide, Johnson co., N Wyo., on Piney Creek, 8 mi/12.9 km N of Buffalo; 44°29′N 106°44′W. Bighorn Mts. to W.

De Soto (duh SO-to), county (□ 648 sq mi/1,678 sq km; pop. 23,865), central Fla.; ⊙ Arcadia. Rolling terrain, partly swampy, with many small lakes; drained by Peace R. Agr. (citrus fruit, vegetables, corn); cattle and poultry raising. Formed 1887.

De Soto (duh SO-to), parish (□ 899 sq mi/2,328 sq km; 1990 pop 25,346), NW La.; ⊙ Mansfield; 32°02′N 93°42′W. Bounded W by Texas line, SW by Sabine R. (here forming Toledo Bend Reservoir and Texas boundary), N by Bayou Pierre. Agr. (cotton, blueberries, hay; poultry, cattle; dairying); oil and natural gas; logging; wood prods., paper prods.; other mfg. at Mansfield. Named after Hernando de Soto, the Span. explorer who discovered the Mississippi R. Formed 1843. Clear L. and Smithport L. in NE, Wallace L. on N boundary. Includes Mansfield State Commemorative Area near center of parish.

De Soto (duh SO-to), county (□ 478 sq mi/1,238 sq km; 1990 pop. 67,910), extreme NW Miss.; ⊙ Hernando; 34°53′N 89°59′W. Bounded W in part by Mississippi R., (Ark. state line); and N by Tenn. state line. Drained by Coldwater R., forms part of S boundary, and Arkabutla

L. reservoir, on S boundary. Agr. (cotton, corn, sorghum, wheat, soybeans; cattle; dairying). Mfg. at Olive Branch and Hernando. N edge of co. is urbanized, adjacent to Memphis, Tenn. to N. Formed 1836.

De Soto 1 (duh-SO-to), city (1990 pop. 5,993), Jefferson co., E Mo., bet. Mississippi and Big rivers; satellite community, 35 mi/56 km SSW of St. Louis; 38°08′N 90°33′W. RR shops; mfg. (fabricated metal prods., transportation equip.); stone quarries. Washington State Park to SW. Founded 1857. **2** city (1990 pop. 30,544), Dallas co., N Texas, suburb, 12 mi/19 km S of downtown Dallas; 32°36′N 96°51′W. Mfg. (construction materials, apparel, chemicals). Drained by Tenmile Creek. L. Joe Pool and Cedar Hill State Park to W.

De Soto 1 town (1990 pop. 1,033), Dallas co., central Iowa, 7 mi/11.3 km S of Adel; 41°31′N 94°00′W. In agr. area. **2** town (1990 pop. 2,291), Johnson co., E Kansas, on Kansas R., 20 mi/32 km SW of Kansas City, Kansas, and 13 mi/21 km E of Lawrence; 38°58′N 94°57′W. Dairying, general agr. Mfg. (electronic equip., chemicals). Satellite community of Kansas City.

De Soto 1 village (1990 pop. 1,500), Jackson co., SW Ill., 7 mi/11.3 km NE of Murphysboro; 37°49′N 89°13′W. RR junction. In bituminous-coal mining and agr. area (livestock, wheat, sorghum; dairying). **2** village (1990 pop. 326), on Crawford-Vernon co. line, SW Wis., on the Mississippi R., and 28 mi/45 km S of La Crosse; 43°25′N 91°12′W. Black Hawk bridge to Lansing (Iowa) nearby. Upper Mississippi R. Wildlife and Fish Area on river; (Army Corps of Engineers) Blackhawk Recreational Area to N.

De Soto National Memorial (duh SOH-toh), natl. monument, W central Fla., just NW of Bradenton, authorized 1948, commemorates the landing (1539) of Hernando De Soto in Fla. and his exploration of S U.S.

De Tour Village, village (1990 pop. 407), Chippewa co., E Upper Peninsula, Mich., c.40 mi/64 km SE of Sault Ste. Marie, and on Detour Passage, L. Huron (S end of St. Marys R.) opposite Drummond Isl. (car ferry; E); 45°59′N 83°54′W. Lighthouse here. Fueling point for commercial shipping; resort. Caribou L. to W.

De Valls Bluff (duh VAHLZ), town (1990 pop. 702), ⊙ (with Des Arc), Prairie co., E central Ark., 20 mi/32 km NNE of Stuttgart, and on White R.; 34°47′N 91°27′W. In agr. area (rice, hay). Wattensaw Wildlife Management Area to NW.

De Witt 1 county (□ 405 sq mi/1,049 sq km; 1990 pop. 16,516), central Ill.; ⊙ Clinton; 40°10′N 88°54′W. Grain-growing area, produces corn, soybeans; livestock. Mfg. (fabricated metal prods., printing and publishing). Clinton 1 nuclear power plant, initial criticality Feb. 27, 1987, is 6 mi/10 km E of Clinton; uses cooling water from Salt Creek and has a max. dependable capacity of 930 MWe. Co. created 1839. **2** county (□ 910 sq mi/2,357 sq km; 1990 pop. 18,840), S Texas; ⊙ Cuero; 29°04′N 97°21′W. Drained by Guadalupe R. Agr. (peaches, pecans; corn, grain, sorghum, hay, oats, wheat); a leading poultry and egg producing co. of state; also beef cattle, hogs; dairying. Oil, natural gas, sand, gravel. Formed 1846.

De Witt 1 city (1990 pop. 3,553), ⊙ (with Stuttgart) Arkansas co., E central Ark., 39 mi/63 km E of Pine Bluff, near Little Bayou; 34°17′N 91°20′W. In agr. area (rice, soybeans); rice milling, sawmilling, mfg. (food, machinery, apparel). Federal bird refuge nearby. Inc. as city in 1933. **2** city (1990 pop. 4,514), Clinton co., E Iowa, 17 mi/27 km W of Clinton; 41°49′N 90°32′W. Livestock shipping; mfg. (printing and publishing, concrete, limestone). Settled 1837, platted 1841, inc. 1858. **3** city (1990 pop. 125), Carroll co., NW central Mo., on Missouri R., and 15 mi/24 km E of Carrollton; 39°22′N 93°13′W. Soybeans, wheat; hogs.

De Witt, town (1990 pop. 3,964), Clinton co., S central Mich., 7 mi/11.3 km N of Lansing and on Looking Glass R.; 42°50′N 84°34′W. In agr. area. Capital City Airport to SW.

De Witt 1 village (1990 pop. 122), De Witt co., central Ill., 10 mi/16 km ENE of Clinton; 40°10′N 88°47′W. In agr. area. Near Clinton L. **2** village (1990 pop. 598), Saline co., SE Nebr., 12 mi/19 km NW of Beatrice, and on Big Blue R; 40°23′N 96°55′W. RR junction. Flour, grain; dairying; poultry, livestock. Light mfg.

De Witt, residential suburb (1990 pop. 8,244) of Syracuse, Onondaga co., central N.Y., 4 mi/6.4 km ESE of city center; 43°02′N 76°04′W.

Dead Diamond River, N.H.: see SWIFT DIAMOND RIVER.

Dead Indian Peak, Wyo.: see ABSAROKA RANGE.

Dead Lake, Otter Tail co., W Minn., lake (□ 12 sq mi/31 sq km), 16 mi/26 km NE of Fergus Falls; 8.5 mi/13.7 km long, 4 mi/6.4 km wide, including 3 mi/4.8 km long N arm; 46°28′N 95°45′W. Fed from NW by short stream from Star L.; drains S through 2 outlets, both with small dams, of Dead R., Walker and Otter Tail lakes.

Dead Lake, reservoir, Gulf and Calhoun cos., NW Fla., on Chipola R., at Wewahitchka, 25 mi/40 km E of Panama City; c.10 mi/16 km long, 1 mi/1.6 km wide; 30°08′N 85°10′W. Linked by channel with Apalachicola R. (1 mi/1.6 km E). Dead Lakes State Recreation Area on W shore.

Dead River, township, Somerset co., W central Maine, 30 mi/48 km NW of Skowhegan.

Dead River 1 45 mi/72 km long; rising on the Can. border, NW Maine; and flowing NE through a hunting and fishing region to the Kennebec R. Flagstaff Dam creates Flagstaff Lake (15 mi/24 km long). **2** 6 mi/9.7 km long, in Androscoggin co., SW Maine. Small stream through which Androscoggin L. drains into Androscoggin R. **3** c.40 mi/64 km, in NW Upper Peninsula, Mich.; rises in NW Marquette co.; flows out of Silver L. Basin, SE through 10 mi/16 km Long Dead R. Storage Basin (both reservoirs built to serve mining dist.), to L. Superior 2 mi/3.2 km N of Marquette; 46°39′N 87°59′W. Power dams.

Dead River Storage Basin, reservoir (□ 3 sq mi/7.8 sq km), La Salle co., N Mich., on Upper Peninsula, on the Dead R., 7 mi/11 km WNW of Marquette; 46°39′N 87°50′W. Max. capacity 160,000 acre-ft. Formed by Silver Lake Dam (35 ft/11m high), built (1912) for power generation.

Deadman's Cay, islet and town, S central Bahama Isls., off W Long Isl., 17 mi/27 km NW of Clarence Town; 23°14′N 75°15′W. Stock raising, salt panning.

Deadwood, town (1990 pop. 1,830), ⊙ Lawrence co., W S.Dak., in the Black Hills, 30 mi/48 km NW of Rapid City, surrounded by Black Hills Natl. Forest; settled 1876 after discovery of gold. It is a tourist center that features legalized gambling and a trading hub; lumbering, stock-raising, and mining operations. The graves of Wild Bill Hickok (shot in the back in a saloon here during a card game) and Calamity Jane are in Deadwood. Town retains characteristics of Wild West.

Deadwood Reservoir, Valley co., W central Idaho, on Deadwood R., in Boise Natl. Forest., 55 mi/89 km NE of Boise, 4 mi/6.4 km long, 2 mi/3.2 km wide; 44°16′N 115°36′W. Max. capacity c.164,000 acre-ft. Formed by concrete-arch Deadwood Dam (165 ft/50 m high, 749 ft/228 m long; completed 1930), unit in Payette div. of Boise irrigation project.

Deaf Smith (DEEF smith), county (□ 1,498 sq mi/3,880 sq km; 1990 pop. 19,153), extreme N Texas; ⊙ Hereford; 34°58′N 102°35′W. Elev. 3,700 ft/1,128 m–4,400 ft/1,341 m. In high plains of the Panhandle, on N.Mex. line; Drained by Palo Duro and Tierra Blanca creeks. A leading Texas cattle and wheat co.; irrigated lands produce sorghum, wheat, oats, barley, corn; cotton, vegetables (especially onions), sunflowers. Includes Buffalo L. (recreation). County named for Erastus (Deaf) Smith, French scout at Battle of San Jacinto. Formed 1876.

Deal, resort borough (1990 pop. 1,179), Monmouth co., E N.J., on coast, 15 mi/24 km E of Freehold; 40°15′N 74°00′W. Deal L. (c.2 mi/3.2 km long) is just SW.

Deal Island, small isl., Somersett co., SE Md., off the W shore of Delmarva peninsula. Fishing, oystering. Marshes make the isl. uninhabitable except for 2 small clusters of late 19th and early 20th cent. houses in the villages of Deal and Winoma.

Deal Lake, N.J.: see DEAL.

Deandale, village, Jefferson co., E Ohio, on the Ohio R., 5 mi/8 km S of Steubenville.

Dearborn, county (□ 307 sq mi/795 sq km; 1990 pop. 38,835), SE Ind.; ⊙ Lawrenceburg; 39°09′N 84°59′W. Bounded E by Ohio line and SE by Ky. line (here formed by Ohio R.); some urban growth around Lawrenceburg from nearby Cincinnati 15 mi/24 km E. Drained by Whitewater R. and Laughery Creek. Agr. (cattle, tobacco), with some mfg. (food, wood prods., liquor). Formed 1803.

Dearborn 1 city (1990 pop. 89,286), Wayne co., SE Mich., suburb, 6 mi/9.7 km W of downtown Detroit, borders city of Detroit on E and N; 42°18′N 83°12′W. Drained by R. Rouge and Lower R. Rouge; parkways on both rivers. The city's economy is principally tied to the automobile industry. Mfg. (plastic prods., fabricated-metal prods., apparel, chemicals, electronic equip., printing and publishing, food). Automotive research and development are also important. Largely residential despite its industry, Dearborn is famous for the Edison Institute of Technology, which includes Greenfield Village, the birthplace of Henry Ford. Ford's large estate, Fair Lane, is a natl. historic landmark and has become part of the Univ. of Michigan's Dearborn campus. Site of Fairlane Town Center, one of the largest shopping centers in the U.S. Two museums and Henry Ford Community Col. and Detroit Col. of Business are in the city. Settled 1795, consolidated with the city of Fordson in 1928, inc. as a city 1929. **2** city (1990 pop. 480), Platte co., W Mo., 17 mi/27 km S of St. Joseph; 39°31′N 94°46′W. Corn, tobacco, soybeans; cattle; shale and refractory materials.

Dearborn, Fort, Ill.: see FORT DEARBORN.

Dearborn Heights, city (1990 pop. 60,838), Wayne co., SE Mich., residential suburb, 10 mi/16 km W of downtown Detroit; 42°19′N 83°16′W. Gerrymandered corporate limits surround W end of city of Dearborn; N and S sections of city connected by narrow strip. Drained by Middlw R. Rouge in N. Light mfg.

Dearing 1 village (1990 pop. 547), McDuffie co., E Ga., 22 mi. W of Augusta; 33°25′N 82°23′W. Lumber. **2** village (1990 pop. 428), Montgomery co., SE Kansas, 5 mi/8 km WNW of Coffeyville, near Okla. line; 37°03′N 95°42′W. In stock-raising and general agr. region. Oil and gas fields nearby.

Deary, village (1990 pop. 529), Latah co., N Idaho, 21 mi/34 km ENE of Moscow; 46°48′N 116°34′W. Shipping point for lumber, agr. (sheep, cattle; alfalfa, barley, oats), mining area. St. Joe Natl. Forest to N.

Dease Lake (deez), (25 mi/40 km long, 1 mi/2 km wide), NW B.C., Canada, 160 mi/257 km E of Juneau, Alaska; drained N into Liard R. by Dease R. At S end of lake is trading post of Dease L.; 58°27′N 130°02′W.

Death Valley Junction, uninc. village, Inyo co., E Calif., in Amargosa Desert, near Nev. state line, across Amargosa Range from Death Valley (W), E entrance to Death Valley Natl. Monument. Borax works. Ash Meadows Wildlife Management Area (Nev.) to NE. Also called Amargosa.

Death Valley National Monument, 3,231 sq mi/8,368 sq km; (Calif. 3,057 sq mi/7,918 sq km, Nev. 173 sq mi/448 sq km), Inyo and San Bernardino cos., SE Calif., Nye and Esmeralda cos., SW Nev., c.170 mi/274 km NNE of Los Angeles and c.100 mi/161 km W of Las Vegas. A deep, arid basin, 140 mi/225 km long, bordered on the W by the Panamint Range, NW by the Cottonwood Mts., and on the E by the Amargosa Range (latter 2 within monument boundary). Small separate unit at Devils Hole, 10 mi/16 km NE of Death Valley Junction, in Nev. In summer the valley has radiated some of the highest air and ground temperatures in the world. Hottest temperature recorded in U.S. was at Greenland Ranch near monument, 134°F/56.6° C on, July 10, 1913. Less than 2 in/5.1 cm of rain falls annually; the small Amargosa R. and Furnace Creek disappear into the sands. Salt and alkali flats, unique rock formations, and briny pools are found here. Badwater, in the south central part of Death Valley, is 282 ft/86 m below sea level at Badwater Basin, the lowest point in the Western Hemisphere; Telescope Peak, in the Panamint Range, is 11,049 ft/3,368 m high. Death Valley was named by gold seekers who undertook to cross this desolate region in 1849 on their way to the California gold fields. The valley yielded gold and silver in the 1850s, and in the 1880s borax was discovered and taken out by mule-drawn wagons. In spite of the harsh environment, a large variety of small animals and exotic desert plants are found in Death Valley; they have attracted much scientific attention. Native Americans of Panamint descent, an offshoot of the Shoshone, are the only group ever to be self-subsisting in the region. The valley was much publicized by the Amer. adventurer Walter Scott ("Death Valley Scotty"), whose palatial home, Scotty's Castle, is a major attraction, in far NW of monument. Stovepipe Wells in N center; Funeral Peak (6,384 ft/1,946 m) in SE; Ubehebe Crater in NW. Estab. 1933.

Deaver, village (1990 pop. 199), Big Horn co., N Wyo., near Mont. line, 12 mi/19 km NE of Powell; 44°53′N 108°35′W. Elev. 4,105 ft/1,251 m. RR junction. Supply point in oil and ranching area; sugar beets, beans, grain.

Debden (DEHB-duhn), village (1991 pop. 416), S central Sask., 50 mi/80 km WNW of Prince Albert; 53°31′N 106°52′W. Mixed farming, dairying.

Debe (DAI-bai) or **Débé**, village, SW Trinidad, Trinidad and Tobago, 4 mi/6.4 km S of San Fernando. Marketing place in sugar-growing region. Petroleum deposits are nearby (E). Also spelled Dibe.

Debert (duh-BER), agr. village, N central N.S., Canada, on Debert R., and 10 mi/16 km ENE of Truro. Air base. Site of major archaeological discovery.

Debert River, flows 25 mi/40 km S, past Debert, to Cobequid Bay, 12 mi/19 km W of Truro, N central N.S., Canada; rises in Cobequid Mts.

Deblois (duh-BLOI), village (1990 pop. 73), Washington co., E Maine, on Narraguagus R., and 29 mi/47 km W of Machias; 44°43′N 67°59′W.

Deborah, Mount (DE-buh-rah) (12,339 ft/3,761 m), E Alaska, peak in Alaska Range, 90 mi/145 km S of Fairbanks; 63°38′N 147°14′W.

Debruce, resort village, Sullivan co., SE N.Y., on small Willowemoc Creek, 5 mi/8 km E of Livingston Manor; 41°55′N 74°44′W.

Decatur 1 (duh-KAI-tuhr), county (□ 467; 1990 pop. 25,511), SW Ga.; ☉ Bainbridge; 30°53′N 84°35′W. Bounded S by Fla. state line; intersected by Flint R. Coastal plain agr. (corn, cotton, tobacco, wheat, sugarcane, peanuts, pecans; cattle, hogs, poultry); timber. Formed 1823. **2** county (□ 373 sq mi/966 sq km; 1990 pop. 23,645), SE central Ind.; ☉ Greensburg; 39°18′N 85°30′W. Drained by Flatrock R. and small Salt, Clifty, and Sand creeks. Agr. (corn, soybeans; hogs, cattle); limestone quarries. Mfg. at Greensburg; RR junction. Formed 1821. **3** county (□ 533 sq mi/1,380 sq km; 1990 pop. 8,338), S Iowa, on Mo. line; ☉ Leon, 40°45′N 93°47′W. Rolling prairie agr. area (hogs, cattle, poultry; corn, alfalfa), with bituminous-coal deposits; drained by Thompson and Weldon rivers. Nine Eagles State Park in S. Local flooding occurred in 1993. Formed 1846. **4** county (□ 894 sq mi/2,315 sq km; 1990 pop. 4,021), NW Kansas; ☉ Oberlin; 39°48′N 100°28′W. Flat to rolling area, bordered N by Nebr.; watered by Sappa, Prairie Dog, and Beaver creeks and North Fork Solomon R. (extreme SE). Wheat, sorghum, corn, alfalfa; cattle, hogs. Formed 1879. **5** county (□ 346 sq mi/896 sq km; 1990 pop. 10,472), W Tenn., ☉ Decaturville; 35°37′N 88°07′W. Bounded E and S by Tennessee R.; drained by its tributaries. Includes part of Kentucky Reservoir. Livestock, dairying; cotton, corn, hay. Formed 1845.

Decatur 1 (duh-KAI-tuhr), city (1990 pop. 48,761), ☉ Morgan co., N Ala., on the Tennessee R. Commercial and mfg. center, with shipyards, port traffic, steel and diverse industries. The city thrived due to power supplied by the TVA. A settlement inc. in 1820 as Rhodes Ferry was here; it was chartered in 1826 and renamed in honor of Stephen Decatur, U.S. naval hero in the

War of 1812. During the Civil War, Decatur was continually raided by Federal forces; 2 houses and the imposing state bank (1832) survive. John C. Calhoun State Community Col. is in Decatur, and Brownsferry Nuclear Power Plant is nearby. Wheeler Natl. Wildlife Refuge lies NE of Decatur. The present city was formed (1927) by the union of Decatur and Albany (formerly New Decatur); inc. 1826. **2** city (1990 pop. 17,336), ☉ DeKalb co., NW Ga., a residential suburb of Atlanta.; 33°46′N 84°18′W. Important co. govt. center. Mfg. includes fabricated metal prods., plastics, chemicals, fixtures, food, toys, paper prods. Named for the U.S. war hero, Stephen Decatur. Agnes Scott Col., Columbia Theological Seminary; Emory Univ. nearby; Battle of Atlanta fought nearby during the Civil War. Carved on the side of nearby Stone Mountain, in a memorial park, are the figures of Robert E. Lee, Stonewall Jackson, and Jefferson Davis. Inc. 1823. **3** city (1990 pop. 83,885), ☉ Macon co., central Ill., on the Sangamon R. (dammed there to form L. Decatur), 75 mi/121 km SSE of Peoria; 39°51′N 88°55′W. Inc. 1839. A RR and industrial center in a fertile farm and livestock area, Decatur has RR repair shops and huge plants for processing corn and soybeans. Other mfg. includes transportation equip., machinery. Coal deposits underlie the area. Of interest are the Lincoln Log Cabin Courthouse, where Abraham Lincoln practiced law; Lincoln Square, where he received his 1st endorsement for the presidential nomination; and the city library, with its Lincoln collection. The site of Lincoln's 1st home in Illinois is in a state park nearby. The Grand Army of the Republic was organized in Decatur in April 1866. Millikin Univ. and Richland Community Col. are in the city. Spitler Wood State Natural Area nearby. **4** city (1990 pop. 8,644), ☉ Adams co., E Ind., on St. Marys R., and 21 mi/34 km SSE of Fort Wayne; 40°50′N 84°56′W. Agr. area; mfg. (cement, machinery, food, construction materials, fabricated metal prods., wood prods.); timber. Laid out 1836. City was a former home of Gene Stratton Porter.

Decatur 1 (duh-KAIT-uhr), town (1990 pop. 918), Benton co., extreme NW Ark., 18 mi/29 km W of Rogers, in the Ozarks; 36°20′N 94°27′W. Mfg. (machinery, food). **2** town (1990 pop. 1,760), Van Buren co., SW Mich., 8 mi/12.9 km SSW of Paw Paw; 42°06′N 85°58′W. In farm area (grains, vegetables, fruit; livestock); light mfg. Small (resort) lakes nearby, especially SE. Inc. 1861. **3** town (1990 pop. 1,248), ☉ Newton co., E central Miss., 24 mi/39 km WNW of Meridian; 32°26′N 89°06′W. Agr. (cotton, corn; cattle, poultry; dairying; timber); mfg. (electronic prods.). East Central Community Col. is here. **4** town (1990 pop. 1,361), ☉ Meigs co., SE Tenn., 45 mi/72 km NE of Chattanooga; 35°31′N 84°47′W. In farm area. **5** town (1990 pop. 4,252), ☉ Wise co., N Texas, 37 mi/60 km NNW of Fort Worth; 33°13′N 97°35′W. Elev. 1,097 ft/334 m. Trade, shipping center for dairying, livestock, agr. area (peanuts, pecans, grains, sorghum); mfg. (fabricated metal prods.). Was seat of Decatur Baptist Col. (1892), is now Wise co. Heritage Mus.

Decatur (duh-KAI-tuhr), village (1990 pop. 641), Burt co., NE Nebr., 15 mi/24 km N of Tekamah, and on Missouri R; 42°00′N 96°15′W. Livestock, grain. At S edge of Omaha Indian Reservation. Bridge to Onawa, Iowa. Blackbird State Wayside Area to N.

Decatur City, town (1990 pop. 177), Decatur co., S Iowa, 3 mi/4.8 km W of Leon; 40°44′N 93°49′W. In livestock area. Limestone quarries nearby.

Decaturville, town (1990 pop. 879), ☉ Decatur co., W Tenn., 38 mi/61 km E of Jackson, near Kentucky Reservoir; 35°35′N 88°07′W. Sawmills, limestone quarries; mfg. of apparel.

Deception Pass, Wash.: see WHIDBEY ISLAND.

Decew Falls (duh-KOO), village, S Ont., Canada, on Welland R., and 4 mi/6 km SE of St. Catharines; hydroelectric power center.

Decherd (DEH-kuhrd), town (1990 pop. 2,196), Franklin co., S Tenn., 13 mi/21 km SSE of Tullahoma; 35°13′N 86°05′W.

Decker, town (1990 pop. 281), Knox co., SW Ind., on

White R., and 11 mi/18 km S of Vincennes; 38°31′N 87°31′W. In agr. area.

Deckerville 1 village, Poinsett co., NE Ark., 9 mi/14.5 km SE of Marked Tree. **2** village (1990 pop. 1,015), Sanilac co., E Mich., 8 mi/12.9 km NE of Sandusky; 43°31′N 82°44′W. In farm area (livestock, poultry; grain; dairy prods.); mfg. (transportation equip., plastic, chrome, and rubber prods.). RR junction to N at Palms.

Declo, village (1990 pop. 279), Cassia co., S Idaho, 10 mi/16 km E of Burley, near Snake R.; 42°31′N 113°38′W. RR terminus. Wheat, sugar beets. Parts of Sawtooth Natl. Forest to S.

Decorah, city (1990 pop. 8,063), ☉ Winneshiek co., NE Iowa, on Upper Iowa R., and 60 mi/97 km NNE of Waterloo; 43°18′N 91°47′W. Mfg. (fabricated-metal prods., food, plastic prods.). Seat of Luther Col. (coeducational; 1861), with Norwegian Mus. devoted to early history of the city. Inc. 1857.

Dedham 1 (DED-uhm), town (1990 pop. 264), Carroll co., W central Iowa, 12 mi/19 km S of Carroll; 41°54′N 94°49′W. **2** town (1990 pop. 1,229), Hancock co., S Maine, 16 mi/26 km NW of Ellsworth, includes Lucerne-in-Maine, resort village near Phillips L.; 44°41′N 68°35′W. **3** town (1990 pop. 23,782), ☉ Norfolk co., E Mass., on the Charles R.; a primarily residential suburb of Boston.; 42°15′N 71°11′W. Film production support business. America's oldest frame house, the Fairbanks house (1636), is in Dedham, which is said to have had the 1st public school in America (1649). The county courthouse was the scene of the Sacco-Vanzetti trial (1921). Horace Mann practiced law in Dedham, and Fisher Ames was born here. Inc. 1636.

Deemston, borough (1990 pop. 770), Washington co., SW Pa., 15 mi/24 km SE of Washington, near Monongahela R.; 40°01′N 80°01′W. Bounded on SW by Tenmile Creek.

Deep Creek, former village, SE Va., now part of independent city of CHESAPEAKE, 6 mi/9.7 km S of Portsmouth, on short Deep Creek and Dismal Swamp Canal.

Deep Creek Lake, reservoir, Garrett co., NW Md., on Deep Creek, tributary of Youghiogheny R., in Allegheny Mts., 7 mi/11.3 km N of Oakland and 4 mi/6.4 km E of W.Va. border; 12 mi/19 km long; c.4,000 acres/1,619 ha; 39°30′N 79°23′W. Elev. 2,427 ft/740 m. Largest freshwater lake in Md. Formed by a hydroelectric dam (built 1923–1926). McHenry village and Wisp Ski Area at N end; Deep Creek State Park on NE side. Waters diverted by tunnel through Marsh Hill (3,100 ft/945 m), to NW.

Deep Creek Mountains, Tooele and Juab cos., W Utah and White Pine co., E Nev., SW of Great Salt L. Desert. Haystack Peak (12,100 ft/3,688 m) is highest point. Goshute Indian Reservation (Utah/Nev.) to W.

Deep Fork, river c.220 mi/354 km long, in central and E Okla.; rises in Oklahoma co.; flows NE, E, and SE, past Okmulgee, to North Canadian R. (Eufala L.), c.6 mi/9.7 km N of Eufaula. Full name, Deep Fork of the Canadian R.

Deep Gap, mountain pass (3 ft/⁹⁄₁₀ m), NW N.C., Blue Ridge Mts., 20 mi/32 km NW of Wilkesboro, U. S. Highway 421 passes through, crosses by Blue Ridge Parkway.

Deep Red Run, stream in SW Okla., c.55 mi/89 km long, generally SE. Rises in W Comanche co., through Tillman (through L. Frederick) and Cotton cos., flows generally SE to West Cache Creek, 10 mi/16 km SSW of Walters. Also called Deep Red Creek.

Deep River, town (1991 pop. 4,571), SE Ont., Canada, near Ottawa R., and 100 mi/161 km WNW of Ottawa; 46°06′N 77°30′W. Residential town for nearby Chalk R. atomic research center.

Deep River 1 town (1990 pop. 4,332), Middlesex co., S Conn., on the Connecticut R., and 16 mi/26 km SE of Middletown; 41°22′N 72°27′W. Includes Deep River village. Agr.; mfg. plastic prods., electronic prods., printing and publishing, and wood prods. State forest here. Settled 1635 as Saybrook colony on site of present OLD

SAYBROOK; colony was sold to Conn. in 1644, and present town was inc. as Saybrook in 1899. Name changed 1947 to Deep River. **2** town (1990 pop. 345), Poweshiek co., central Iowa, 9 mi/14.5 km E of Montezuma; 41°34′N 92°22′W. In agr. area.

Deep River, c.125 mi/201 km long, N central N.C., in W Guilford co.; rises E of Kernersville; flows SE past High Point and Randleman, passes NE of Asheboro, then E pass N of Sanford, joins Haw R. near Haywood to form Cape Fear R.

Deep Run, uninc. village, Lenoir co., E N.C., 12 mi/19 km SW of Kinston. In agr. area. Light mfg.

Deephaven (DEEP-ha-vuhn), town (1990 pop. 3,653), Hennepin co., E Minn., residential suburb, 13 mi/21 km W of downtown Minneapolis, on E shore of L. Minnetonka (Lower Lake), indented by Carson Bay; 44°55′N 93°31′W. Mfg. (printing and publishing). Minnetonka city to E.

Deepstep, town (1990 pop. 111), Washington co., E central Ga., 10 mi/16 km WNW of Sandersville, in agr. area; 33°01′N 82°58′W.

Deepwater, city (1990 pop. 441), Henry co., W central Mo., on S side of South Grand Arm of Truman Lake, 8 mi/12.9 km S of Clinton; 38°15′N 93°46′W.

Deepwater, village, Salem co., SW N.J., on Del. R., and 8 mi/12.9 km N of Salem. Terminus of Del. Memorial Bridge and of N.J. Turnpike.

Deer Creek, former town, St. Louis co., Mo.: see LADUE.

Deer Creek 1 village (1990 pop. 630), in Tazewell co., central Ill., 15 mi/24 km ESE of Peoria; 40°37′N 89°19′W. In agr. area. **2** village (1990 pop. 303), Otter Tail co., W Minn., 36 mi/58 km ENE of Fergus Falls, near Deer Creek; 46°23′N 95°19′W. Agr. area (dairying; poultry, livestock; grain, sunflowers, sugar beets). **3** village (1990 pop. 124), Grant co., N Okla., 13 mi/21 km W of Blackwell; 36°48′N 97°31′W. In grain and cattle-producing area.

Deer Creek 1 c.50 mi/80 km long, flows W in N central Ind.; rises in S Miami co., flows W. past Delphi, to the Wabash just SW of Delphi. **2** c.70 mi/113 km long, in S central Ohio; rises in Madison co., flows SE past Mt. Sterling and Williamsport, to Scioto R. in Ross co.; 39°27′N 83°00′W. **3** c.50 mi/80 km long, S Pa. and NE Md.; rises in S York co., SE Pa., E of Shrewsbury; flows ESE, across Harford co., Md., to the Susquehanna R., 6 mi/9.7 km NNW of Havre de Grace, in Susquehanna State Park; 39°46′N 76°40′W.

Deer Creek Dam, Utah: see PROVO RIVER.

Deer Flat Reservoir, Idaho: see LOWELL, LAKE.

Deer Grove, village (1990 pop. 44), Whiteside co., NW Ill., near Green R., 20 mi/32 km SE of Morrison; 41°36′N 89°40′W. In agr. area.

Deer Island 1 in Passamaquoddy Bay of the Bay of Fundy, SW N.B., Canada, just off Maine coast, 6 mi/10 km SSE of St. Andrews, N of Campobello Isl.; 44°52′N 66°57′W. Surrounded by rocky islets. Pollock, sardine, herring, lobster fishing. **2** (3 mi/5 km long, 1 mi/2 km wide), E N.F., Canada, in Bonavista Bay, 35 mi/56 km E of Gander; 48°55′N 53°45′W; fishing.

Deer Island, in E Mass., former isl., connected in 1936 to Winthrop to N by filling in Shirley Gut, bet. Boston Bay (W) and Mass. Bay (E); c.1 mi/1.6 km long. Site of Mass. Water Resource Authority (New) Sewage Treatment Plant and Park.

Deer Isle 1 resort isl., Hancock co., S Maine, in Penobscot Bay, 20 mi/32 km SE of Belfast; 10 mi/16 km long, 3 mi/4.8 km–5 mi/8 km wide. Reached by a bridge. Deer Isl. (N) and Stonington (S). Crockett Cove Woods is a spruce and tamarack preserve. Beyond Stonington, to the S, is Isle au Haut, part of Acadia Natl. Park. **2** Piscataquis co., W central Maine (□ c.2.25 sq mi/5.83 sq km) near S end of Moosehead L. and 35 mi/56 km NW of Dover-Foxcroft. Site of settlement of Capens. **3** Harrison co., SE Miss., marshy isl. in the Gulf of Mexico just SE of Biloxi; c.5 mi/8 km long.

Deer Lake, town (1991 pop. 4,327), W N.F., Canada, at N end of Deer L., 27 mi/43 km NE of Corner Brook, on Humber R., and at W end of Newfoundland Canal; lumbering, sawmilling center. Site of hydroelectric station, Buchans mines. Airport.

Deer Lake, borough (1990 pop. 550), Schuylkill co., E central Pa., 11 mi/18 km ESE of Pottsville, on Deer L. (Pine Creek); 40°37′N 76°03′W. Agr. (corn, hay; poultry, livestock, dairying). Schuylkill Airport to N; Hawk Mt. Sanctuary to E; Appalachian Trail passes to SE.

Deer Lake 1 (□ 28 sq mi/73 sq km; 15 mi/24 km long, 3 mi/5 km wide), W N.F., Canada, on Humber R., and 15 mi/24 km ENE of Corner Brook. W terminal of Newfoundland Canal, which links it with Grand L. **2** (35 mi/56 km long, 5 mi/8 km wide), NW Ont., Canada, in Patricia dist., near Man. border; 52°39′N 94°15′W. Elev. 1,014 ft. Drained by Severn R.

Deer Lake, Itasca co., N central Minn., 11 mi/18 km NNW of Grand Rapids; 5 mi/8 km long, 1.5 mi/2.4 km wide; 47°30′N 94°06′W. Elev. 1,309 ft/399 m. Drains W through Deer R., joined 1 mi/1.6 km W by outflow of Moose L. Fishing resorts. Small isls. in SE, including Picnic Isl. in S; Moose L. to N, Bass L. to S.

Deer Lodge, county (□ 741 sq mi/1,919 sq km; 1990 pop. 10,278), SW Mont.; ⊙ Anaconda; 46°04′N 113°05′W. Mining and agr. area drained by the Clark Fork R. and Dutchman Creek, Big Hole R. forms part of S boundary, Pintler Creek forms SW boundary. Continental Divide crosses co., E-W through middle and forms part of W boundary and parts of E boundary (SE and extreme E). Cattle, hay; mining. Lost Creek State Park in N center; Anaconda Stack State Park and Mt. Haggin Wildlife Management Area in SE; Georgetown L. on W boundary; part of Anaconda-Pintler Wilderness Area in SW, part (NW, SE and E) of Beaverhead Natl. Forest on S and SW; parts of Deerlodge Natl. Forest throughout. Flint Creek and Anaconda ranges in N and SW, respectively. Formed 1865, present boundaries est. 1903.

Deer Lodge, town (1990 pop. 3,378), ⊙ Powell co., W central Mont., 30 mi/48 km NNW of Butte, and on the Clark Fork, E of Flint Creek Range; 46°24′N 112°44′W. RR center. Lead and silver mines; lumber mill; livestock, dairying, hay, grain; mfg. (lumber, furniture, ordnance). Mont. State Prison. Grant-Kohrs Ranch Natl. Historic Site to N. Lost Creek State Park to SW; parts of Deerlodge Natl. Forest to W and SE; Helena Natl. Forest to NE. Powell Co. Historical Mus., Mont. Law Enforcement Mus., Old Mont. Prison, closed 1979, now a mus.; Towe Ford Mus., antique cars; Yesterday's Playthings Mus. Founded as Cottonwood, named La Barge City 1862, named Deer Lodge City 1863 (shortened to Deer Lodge in 1896). Inc. 1883.

Deer Park, city (1990 pop. 27,652), Harris co., SE Texas, an industrial and residential suburb, 14 mi/23 km ESE of downtown Houston. On Buffalo Bayou–Houston Ship Channel. Mfg. (chemicals, rubber prods.).

Deer Park 1 uninc. town (1990 pop. 1,825), Napa co., W Calif., residential community, 2 mi/3.2 km NW of St. Helena, in Napa Valley; 38°32′N 122°28′W. Bale Grist Mill State Historic Park to NW. Grapes, walnuts, poultry, dairying, cattle. Winery. **2** town (1990 pop. 419), Garrett co., W Md., in the Alleghenies S of Deep Creek L., 35 mi/56 km WSW of Cumberland; 39°25′N 79°20′W. Mt. resort (elev. c.2,500 ft/762 m). **3** uninc. town (□ 6 sq mi/15.5 sq km; 1990 pop. 28,840), Suffolk co., SE N.Y., on L.I.; 40°45′N 73°19′W. Substantial and very diverse mfg., much of it derived from supporting aircraft-aerospace industries. **4** town (1990 pop. 2,278), Spokane co., E Wash., 20 mi/32 km N of Spokane; 47°58′N 117°26′W. Wheat, barley, oats, rye, alfalfa; dairying; mfg. (wood prods.). Municipal Airport to E. Inc. 1908.

Deer Park 1 village (1990 pop. 2,887), Lake co., NE Ill., on Cook Co. boundary, residential suburb, 29 mi/47 km NW of downtown Chicago, S of Lake Zürich city; 42°10′N 88°05′W. **2** village (1990 pop. 6,181), Hamilton co., extreme SW Ohio, a NE suburb of Cincinnati; 39°12′N 84°23′W. **3** village (1990 pop. 237), St. Croix co., W Wis., 23 mi/37 km NE of Hudson; 45°11′N 92°23′W. Dairying.

Deer Pond (7 mi/11 km long, up to 4 mi/6 km wide), SE N.F., Canada, 30 mi/48 km SSW of Gander; 48°31′N 54°45′W. Drains into L. St. John.

Deer River, town (1990 pop. 838), Itasca co., N central Minn., 14 mi/23 km WNW of Grand Rapids, and 1 mi/1.6 km N of Zemple, near Mississippi R., N of White Oak L.; 47°20′N 93°47′W. In region of lakes and forests; resort area; supply point in timber area; mfg. (lumber, pulpwood prods.). Leech L. Indian Reservation to S and W. Chippewa Natl. Forest to S, W, and N; Deer L. to NE, Bass L. to E; Mud Goose Wildlife Area to SW.

Deer Trail, village (1990 pop. 476), Arapahoe co., E central Colo., 50 mi/80 km E of Denver, E of Bijou Creek; 39°37′N 104°02′W. Elev. c.5,183 ft/1,580 m. On RR and interstate highway. Wheat, beans, cattle.

Deerfield 1 town (1990 pop. 5,018), NW Mass., on the Deerfield R., 2 mi/3.2 km S of Greenfield. Old Deerfield St. is lined with 18th-cent. houses. Deerfield Acad., one of the country's foremost private secondary schools located here. Includes South Deerfield village (1990 pop. 1,906). The town's industries include printing and publishing, food, chemicals, other light mfg. Inc. 1677. **2** town (1990 pop. 3,124), Rockingham co., SE N.H., 16 mi/26 km SE of Concord; 43°08′N 71°15′W. Drained by Lamprey and North Branch rivers. Agr. (nursery crops, vegetables, apples; cattle, poultry; dairying); light mfg. Part of Bear Brook State Park in W; part of Pawtuckaway State Park in E. **3** town (1990 pop. 1,617), Dane co., S Wis., 15 mi/24 km E of Madison; 43°02′N 89°04′W. In agr. area; dairying. Light mfg. On Glacial Drumlin State Trail.

Deerfield 1 village (1990 pop. 17,327), Lake co., NE Ill., a residential suburb of Chicago; 42°10′N 87°50′W. Inc. 1903. The huge Sara Lee Bakery is its major industry; other light mfg. **2** village (1990 pop. 677), Kearny co., SW Kansas, on Ark. R., and 8 mi/12.9 km ENE of Lakin; 37°58′N 101°07′W. Grain, cattle. **3** village (1990 pop. 922), Lenawee co., SE Mich., 13 mi/21 km E of Adrian, near R. Raisin; 41°53′N 83°46′W. In farm area.

Deerfield, river, 70 mi/113 km long, rising in S Vt. and flowing S into NW Mass., then SE to the Connecticut R. at Greenfield, Mass. The river has hydroelectric facilities.

Deerfield Beach, city (□ 10 sq mi/26 sq km; 1990 pop. 46,325), extreme NE Broward co., SE Fla., on the Atlantic coast; 26°18′N 80°07′W. The development of high-technology industry and commerce has expanded the town and more than doubled its pop. from 1970 to 1990. Deerfield Beach has one of the largest retirement communities in the U.S. Inc. 1925

Deerfield Dam, S.Dak.: see CASTLE CREEK.

Deering 1 (DEE-reeng), town (1990 pop. 1,707), Hillsborough, co., S N.H., 17 mi/27 km WSW of Concord; 43°04′N 71°50′W. Drained by Contoocook R. Piscataquog R., flows out of Deering L. in center. Agr. (nursery crops, vegetables, apples; livestock, poultry; dairying). **2** uninc. town, Pemiscot co., extreme SE Mo., in Mississippi alluvial plain, 13 mi/21 km W of Caruthersville.

Deering 1 village (1990 pop. 157), NW Alaska, on S shore of Kotzebue Sound, N Seward Peninsula, 60 mi/97 km S of Kotzebue; 66°04′N 162°43′W. **2** village (1990 pop. 99), McHenry co., N central N.Dak., 16 mi/26 km NE of Minot, on Little Deep R; 48°23′N 101°02′W.

Deersville, village (1990 pop. 86), Harrison co., E Ohio, 10 mi/16 km WNW of Cadiz; 40°18′N 81°11′W. Livestock.

Deerwood, village (1990 pop. 524), Crow Wing co., central Minn., 17 mi/27 km NE of Brainerd, on E end of Serpent L.; 46°28′N 93°54′W. In Cuyuna Iron Range mining dist.; mfg. (machinery, lumber, food). Crow Wing State Forest to N and E.

Deeth, uninc. village (1990 pop. 125), Elko co., NE Nev., 27 mi/43 km NE of Elko, on Humboldt R., at mouth of Marys R. Cattle, sheep. Part of Humboldt Natl. Forest, including Hole in the Mt. Peak (11,306 ft/3,446 m), in Ruby Mts., to SE.

Deferiet (duh-FER-ee-et), village (1990 pop. 293), Jefferson co., N N.Y., on Black R. (water power), 12 mi/19 km NE of Watertown; 44°01′N 75°40′W.

Defiance, county (□ 410 sq mi/1,062 sq km; 1990 pop. 39,350), NW Ohio; ⊙ Defiance, 41°20′N 84°27′W. Bounded W by Ind. line; intersected by Maumee, Auglaize, and Tiffin rivers. Primarily in the Lake Plains physiographic region, the NW portion in the Till Plains region. Agr. (poultry, hogs, cattle; corn, soybeans); diversified mfg., especially at Defiance. Formed 1845.

Defiance, city (1990 pop. 16,768), ⊙ Defiance co., NW Ohio, at the confluence of the Auglaize and Maumee rivers, in a farm area; 41°19'N 84°22'W. Mfg. includes machinery, food, fabricated-metal prods., glass prods. Gen. Anthony Wayne built Fort Defiance in 1794. Defiance Col. is in the city. A Johnny Appleseed festival is held annually in Defiance. Settled 1790, inc. 1836.

Defiance, town (1990 pop. 312), Shelby co., W Iowa, 13 mi/21 km N of Harlan; 41°49'N 95°20'W. In agr. area.

Degollado (de-go-YAH-do), town (1990 pop. 9,299), ⊙ Degollado municipio, Jalisco, central Mexico, 10 mi/16 km NW of La Piedad de Cabadas, on Mexico Highway 90. Elev. 5,594 ft/1,705 m. Rich soil in agr. region; orange-growing center, wheat; livestock.

DeGray Lake (duh-GRAI), Clark and Hot Springs cos., SW central Ark., on the Caddo R., 9 mi/14.5 km NNW of Arkadelphia; 34°12'N 93°06'W. Max. capacity of 1,377,000 acre-ft. Formed by DeGray Dam (238 ft/73 m high), built (1969) by the Army Corps of Engineers for the generation of hydroelectric power, flood control and water supply. DeGray Lake State Park on shores.

DeKalb 1 (duh-KAB), county (□ 271 sq mi/702 sq km; 1990 pop. 545,837), NW central Ga., ⊙ Decatur; 33°46'N 84°14'W. Largest suburban co. in metropolitan Atlanta. Pioneered urban co. concept whereby co. provides most services to its residents; not an inc. municipality. Bisected by I-285 beltway and is site of largest suburban downtown. Perimeter center is the most important corporate location in metropolitan area as well as a leading retail center. Most ethnically diverse co. in Atlanta region with a large African-Amer., Hispanic, and Asian pop. Home of Emory Univ., the Amer. Cancer Society hq., and the Center for Disease Control and Prevention (CDCAP). Founded 1822. **2** county (□ 363 sq mi/940 sq km; 1990 pop. 35,324), NE Ind., bounded E by Ohio line; ⊙ Auburn; 41°24'N 85°00'W. Agr. area (cattle, sheep, poultry, soybeans; corn, wheat, oats; dairying). Mfg., especially at Auburn, Butler, and Garrett. Drained by small Cedar and Fish creeks and by St. Joseph R. Small natural lakes, Story Cedar, Lintz and Indian lakes in NW, part of NE Ind. Lake Region, glacial in origin. Formed 1837.

Dekoven (de-KO-ven), uninc. village, Union co., W Ky., 12 mi/19 km SSW of Morganfield, near Ohio R. Agr. (grain; livestock).

Del Aire, uninc. town (1990 pop. 8,040), Los Angeles co., S Calif., suburb, 10 mi/16 km SW of downtown Los Angeles, on San Diego Freeway, SW of Los Angeles Internatl. Airport, W of Hawthorne; 33°55'N 118°22'W. Pacific Ocean coast at El Segundo 3 mi/4.8 km to W.

Del Bonita (del buh-NEE-tuh), village, Glacier co., N Mont., port of entry at Canada (Alta.) border, 32 mi/51 km NW of Cut Bank near Milk R., on N edge of Blackfeet Indian Reservation.

Del City, city (1990 pop. 23,928), Oklahoma co., central Okla., a residential suburb, 6 mi/9.7 km E of downtown Oklahoma City; on Canadian R.; 35°27'N 97°26'W. Mfg. (transportation equip., electronic equip.); Tinker Air Force Base to SE; Rose State Univ. to E. Inc. 1948.

Del Mar, city (1990 pop. 4,860), San Diego co., S Calif., on Pacific Ocean, 18 mi/29 km N of downtown San Diego, at mouth of San Dieguito R.; 32°58'N 117°16'W. Race track; mfg. (electronic prods., beeswax). Torrey Pines State Beach and Reserve to S.

Del Monte Forest, town (1990 pop. 5,069), Monterey co., W Calif., residential suburb, 1 mi/1.6 km E of Seaside, on Monterey Peninsula, near Monterey Bay; 36°36'N 121°57'W. Fort Ord Military Reservation to E.

Del Norte, county (□ 1,008 sq mi/2,611 sq km; 1990 pop. 23,460), NW Calif.; ⊙ Crescent City; 41°45'N 123°58'W. Bounded N by Oregon state line, W by Pacific Ocean; mountainous (Siskiyou and Klamath mts.), except for narrow coastal strip. Drained by Smith R. (NW), Klamath R. (SW). Includes part of Six Rivers Natl. Forest in all but coastal strip in W. Site of Smith R., Crescent City, and Lower Klamath Indian reservations. Redwood trees are preserved in Jedidiah Smith Redwoods and Del Norte Coast redwoods state parks in W center. Lumbering and sawmilling (especially redwood); timber; dairying; cattle; grapes, apples, asparagus, tomatoes, walnuts; nursery stock; mining (silver, gold), quarrying (sand and gravel). Ocean fisheries (salmon, halibut, sole, crabs). Game fishing (salmon, steelhead, trout) and hunting attract vacationers. Processing industries (lumber, fish, dairy prods.). Pelican State Beach in NW corner; part of Redwood Natl. Park in W and SW, along coast. Formed 1857.

Del Norte, town (1990 pop. 1,647), ⊙ Rio Grande co., S Colo., on Rio Grande, just E of San Juan Mts., and 30 mi/48 km NW of Alamosa; 37°40'N 106°20'W. Elev. 7,874 ft/2,400 m at the airport. In irrigated agr. area. Dairying and vegetables, wheat, cattle. Light mfg. Gold and silver mines in vicinity. Rio Grande Natl. Forest nearby. Settled 1871–1872, inc. 1885.

Del Norte Peak (12,400 ft/3,780 m), in San Juan Mts., Almosa co., SW Colo., 13 mi/21 km WSW of Del Norte.

Del Park Manor, uninc. town (1990 pop. 1,550), New Castle co., N Del., residential suburb 5 mi/8 km WSW of downtown Wilmington, on White Clay Creek; 39°43'N 75°39'W. Del. Park Race Track to SW.

Del Rey, uninc. town (1990 pop. 1,150), Fresno co., central Calif., in San Joaquin Valley, 12 mi/19 km SE of Fresno; 36°40'N 119°36'W. Raisins and dried fruits; cattle; dairying, sugar beets, grapes, figs, almonds, grain; cotton.

Del Rey Oaks, city (1990 pop. 1,661), Monterey co., W Calif., residential suburb, 1 mi/1.6 km S of Seaside; 36°36'N 121°51'W. Fort Ord Mil. Reservation to E; Monterey Peninsula Airport to W.

Del Rio, city (1990 pop. 30,705), ⊙ Val Verde co., W Texas, 145 mi/233 km W of San Antonio, a port of entry on the Rio Grande opposite Ciudad Acuña, Mexico; 29°22'N 100°54'W. Elev. 948 ft/289 m. It is the marketing and distributing center for a region known for its sheep, Angora goats, wools, and mohair; cattle; grapes, winery. Light mfg. The internatl. bridge to Mex. has made Del Rio important in tourist traffic. Laughlin Air Force Base, a jet training command, is to the E. The Internatl. Amistad Reservoir and Amistad Natl. Recreation Area are to NW. Founded 1868; inc. 1911.

Del Rio (dehl REE-oh), village, Cocke co., E Tenn., on French Broad R., and 10 mi/16 km ESE of Newport, in Bald Mts.

Delafield, town (1990 pop. 5,347), Waukesha co., SE Wis., 10 mi/16 km. WNW of Waukesha, on small lake in truck farming region; 43°04'N 88°23'W. St. John's Military Acad. and a state fish hatchery are nearby.

Delagua, abandoned town site, Las Animas co., S Colo., just E of Culebra Range of Sangre de Cristo Mts., 14 mi/23 km NW of Trinidad. Elev. c.6,700 ft/2,042 m. Town site is midway up Canyon del Agua, 4 mi/6.4 km S of Aguilar.

Delake (duh-LAIK), uninc. town, Lincoln co., W Oregon, 2 mi/3.2 km S of Lincoln City on the Pacific Ocean, at the outlet of Devils L. Devils L. State Park to NE. Name is short for "Devils Lake."

Delanco (duh-LAN-ko), village (1990 pop. 3,316), Burlington co., SW N.J., on Del. R., N of mouth of Rancocas Creek, and 12 mi/19 km NE of Camden; 40°02'N 74°57'W. Largely residential.

Delano (de-LAY-no), city (1990 pop. 22,762), Kern co., S central Calif., 29 mi/47 km NNW of Bakersfield, in the fertile San Joaquin valley; 35°46'N 119°15'W. The city's economy is based on irrigated agr. (melons, grapes, tomatoes, beans, nuts, grain; cotton; cattle; dairying); mfg. (plastics prods., machinery). Colonel Allensworth State Historical Park to NW; Kern Natl. Wildlife Refuge to W. Friant-Kern Canal passes to E. Inc. 1915.

Delano (DE-luh-no), town (1990 pop. 2,709), Wright co., E Minn., on Crow R., and 27 mi/43 km W of Minneapolis; 45°02'N 93°47'W. Grain, soybeans; livestock, poultry; dairying; mfg. (wood prods., concrete, chemicals). Inc. 1885.

Delano (duh-LAH-no), uninc. village, Delano township, Schuylkill co., E central Pa., 4 mi/6.4 km NE of Mahanoy City; 40°50'N 76°04'W. RR junction. Mfg. (chemicals, plastic prods., electronic equip.). Anthracite coal region.

Delano Peak (duh-LAWN-o), highest point (12,173 ft/3,710 m.) in Tushar Mts., Beaver-Piute co. line, SW central Utah, 32 mi/51 km SSW of Richfield. In Fishlake Natl. Forest.

Delanson, village (1990 pop. 361), Schenectady co., E N.Y., 13 mi/21 km WSW of Schenectady; 42°45'N 74°10'W.

Delaplaine (del-uh-PLAIN), village (1990 pop. 146), Greene co., NE Ark., 18 mi/29 km NW of Paragould; 36°13'N 90°43'W. Dave Donaldson-Black R. Wildlife Management Area to NW.

Delarof Islands (DE-luh-rawf), SW Alaska, group of 7 small isls. of the Aleutians, in N Pacific, bet. Andreanof Isls. (E) and Amchitka Pass (W); 51°33'N 178°49'W. Main isls. are Gareloi, Ogliuga (emergency airfield), Ulak, and Amatignak. Amatignak Isl. is the southernmost point in Alaska.

Delaronde Lake (DEH-luh-rahnd) (29 mi/47 km long, 3 mi/5 km wide), central Sask., Canada, 65 mi/105 km NE of Prince Albert. Drains N into Beaver R.

Delavan (DELL-ah-vahn), city (1990 pop. 1,642), Tazewell co., central Ill., 23 mi/37 km S of Peoria; 40°22'N 89°32'W. In agr. area. Founded 1837, inc. 1888.

Delavan (DEL-uh-ven), town (1990 pop. 6,073), Walworth co., SE Wis., on Turtle Creek, and 20 mi/32 km E of Janesville; 42°37'N 88°37'W. In dairying and stock raising area; mfg. (food, transportation equip., printing and publishing, fabricated metal prods., electrical equip., cigars). Settled 1836, inc. 1897. Just E of the city is Delavan L. (3 1/2 mi. long), with the resort village Delavan L. on its shores; winter and summer sports. Wis. School for the Deaf.

Delavan (DE-luh-van), village (1990 pop. 245), Faribault co., S Minn., 10 mi/16 km NE of Blue Earth; 43°46'N 94°01'W. Grain, soybeans; livestock; mfg. (feed, fertilizers). Rice L. to NW.

Delaware, state (□ 2,489 sq mi/6,447 sq km; 1995 est. pop. 717,197), E U.S., one of the Middle Atlantic states and one of the 13 original U.S. states; ⊙ DOVER. The only sizeable city is WILMINGTON in N (Philadelphia, Pa., to NE). Together with E Md. and the E shore of Va., the state occupies the Delmarva peninsula bet. Chesapeake Bay and Delaware Bay. The Chesapeake and Delaware Canal connect the 2 bays (crosses base of peninsula) S of Wilmington (part of Intracoastal Waterway). Delaware is situated on the NE portion of the peninsula, facing the Delaware R., which broadens into Delaware Bay; the bay, in turn, joins the Atlantic Ocean at Cape Henlopen, opposite Cape May, N.J. Del. Bay and R. forms N.J.–Delaware state line. Elsewhere, Del. is bounded N by Pa. and W and S by Md., E by Atlantic Ocean (in SE). Its 38 mi/61 km beach-lined coastal strip includes Rehoboth, Dewey, and Bethany beaches; has 3 large back bays, Rehoboth, Indian R., and part of Assawoman bays. The second smallest inland area of all U.S. states after R.I., Del. is sometimes called the Diamond State, in reference to its small size but significant value to the nation. Many small rivers flow across the state, including Christina, Murderkill, St. Jones, and Broadkill (flow E) and Nanticoke, Choptank (flow SW). In the N the Christina and Brandywine rivers flow into the Delaware; in the S the Nanticoke R. flows SW to Chesapeake Bay. The land is low-lying, none of it far from saltwater, from the sand dunes in the S to the pleasant little hills on the border of Pa. in the N; the average elev. is c.60 ft/18 m, and the highest point (unnamed), at Centerville (NW of Wilmington and almost on the Pa. border) is only 442 ft/135 m high. Del. is chiefly an industrial state, although agr. is still important. Industry is heavily concentrated in the N, while farming is carried on throughout the state. Chief agr. prods. are broilers, soybeans, corn, and dairy prods. Potatoes and other vegetables are also grown. Much of the state's wealth comes from industries around Wilmington, especially the chemicals industry that was founded by the Du Pont family in the 19th cent. and that continues to be one of the largest chemical companies in the world. In addition to chemicals, mfg. includes food, rubber and plastic prods., and transportation equip. Because of Del.'s lenient laws

Area in square miles is shown by the symbol □ capital city or county seat by ⊙

governing business taxation, some of the nation's largest corporations, and other companies, have their home offices in the Wilmington area, while actual mfg. is done elsewhere. The banking and finance industries have especially profitted. Del. has a small fishing industry and the principal species caught are menhaden, oysters, clams, and lobsters. Regional tourism, especially from cities of Baltimore and Wash., also contributes to the economy. Long before Europeans explored the Del. area, it was inhabited by several Native Amer. groups, notably the Nanticoke in the S and the Minqua in the N. In 1609, Henry Hudson, in the service of the Du. East India Co., sailed into Delaware Bay. A year later the Br. captain Sir Samuel Argall, bound for the colony of Va., also sailed into the bay. Argall named one of the capes Cape La Warre after the governor of Va., Thomas West, Baron De la Warr. From the time of its discovery, the region was contested by the Du. and English. The first settlement was established by Du. patroons, or proprietors, in partnership with the Dutch navigator David Pietersen de Vries; it was called Swanendael and was est. (1631) on the site of the town of Lewes. However, within a year it was destroyed by a Native Amer. attack. This attack notwithstanding, the Native Americans were generally friendly and willing to trade with the newcomers. The Du. West India Co., organized in 1623, was more interested in trade on the South R., as the Delaware R. was called at that time, than in settlement (the North R. was the Hudson, in the Du. colony of New Netherland). Several Dutch men, interested in settling the area, put their services at the disposal of Sweden and colonized the area for that country. The best known of these was Peter Minuit, who had been governor of New Amsterdam. In 1637–1638 Minuit directed the colonizing expedition for the Swedes that organized NEW SWEDEN. Fort Christina was founded in 1638 on the site of Wilmington and was named in honor of the queen of Sweden. The colony grew with the arrival of Swed., Finn., and Du. settlers. Eng. colonists from Conn. tried to establish trading posts in the Delaware R. region and failed, but Dutch interests in the area were not disposed of as easily. Peter Stuyvesant, governor of New Netherland, sailed to the Del. region in 1651 and established Fort Casimir on the Del. shore at the site of present-day New Castle. The Swedes captured the fort by surprise in 1654, but their triumph was brief; Stuyvesant returned with an expedition in 1655 and conquered all New Sweden. The Du. West India Co. sold part of New Sweden to the Du. city of Amsterdam in 1656 and the rest in 1663. In 1664 the English seized the Dutch holdings on the Del. The Dutch recaptured the colony in 1673 and although they held Del. only briefly, they set up 3 district courts that marked the beginning of Del.'s division into 3 cos. The colony was returned to the English in 1674 and remained in their hands until the Amer. Revolution. The English Duke of York (later James II) annexed the region to N.Y., land granted him earlier by Charles II. In 1682 the Duke transferred the claim to William Penn, who wanted to secure a navigable water route from his new colony of Pa. to the ocean. The 3 cos. of Del. thus became the 3 Lower Counties (or Territories, as Penn called them) of Pa. The individual cos. were called New Castle, Kent (formerly St. Jones), and Sussex (formerly Hoornkill, also known as Whorekill, and Deale). The English proprietors of Md. contested Penn's claim to Del., and the boundary dispute was not fully settled until 1750. The inhabitants of the Del. cos. were at first unwilling to be joined to the "radical" Quaker colony of Pa. or to have their affairs settled in Philadelphia. They finally accepted the Penn charter of 1701 after provisions were added giving the 3 Lower Counties the right to a separate assembly, which first met in 1704. Del. maintained quasi-autonomy until the Amer. Revolution. The 2 colonies maintained strong ties, however, and 2 of Del.'s leading statesmen during the Revolution — Thomas McKean and John Dickinson — were also prominent in Pa. affairs. Although there were many Loyalists in Del. just prior to the Amer. Revolution, Del. supported independence, with 2 of its 3 delegates to the Continental Congress — Caesar Rodney and Thomas McKean — voting for independence. George Read, the 3d Del. delegate, voted against independence, fearing that Loyalist sentiment was too strong in the colonies. However, Read subsequently signed the Declaration of Independence. In 1776 the colony of Del. became a state, with a president as its chief executive. Regiments from the state rendered valiant service to the patriot cause, especially the Del. 1st Regiment, which was nicknamed the Blue Hen's Chickens — originally because they carried with them gamecocks bred by a famous hen of Kent and later because they themselves showed the fighting quality of gamecocks. Del. was a leader in the movement for revision of the form of govt. under the Articles of Confederation and in 1787 became the first state to ratify the new Constitution of the U.S. The late 18th cent. also marked the beginning of industry in Del. with the establishment of gristmills on the Brandywine and Christina rivers. Wilmington became a center for the manufacture of cloth, paper, and flour prods. that helped to build the industrial economy of N Del. that flourished in the 19th cent. Shortly thereafter, in 1802, Eleuthère Irénée Du Pont established a gunpowder mill on the Brandywine R. The state constitution of 1776 was superseded by a new constitution in 1792, which provided that the chief executive be a governor rather than a president. Prior to the Civil War, Del. was a slave state, but in the early 19th cent. the number of slaves in the state declined, while the number of free blacks increased. Many citizens of Del. favored manumission of slaves and belonged to the American Colonization Society, but there were few who sympathized with the growing abolitionist movement and there was strong sentiment for separation of whites and blacks. In the Civil War, Del. remained loyal to the Union, but pro-Southern feeling increased rather than diminished during the course of the war. Del. refused to accept an emancipation proposal made by Lincoln in 1861 and did not ratify the Thirteenth, Fourteenth, and Fifteenth amendments to the U.S. Constitution until 1901. Del. Democrats subsequently became divided, and the Republican Party emerged in 1905 to assume a leading political role for some years. A new state constitution in 1897 reflected the political strength as well as conservatism of Delaware's farmers through provisions that kept the political strength of Wilmington at a min. and that of rural areas at a max. Many European immigrants came to the state in the late 19th and early 20th cent., settling in the Wilmington area. The pop. of S Del. continued to be made up largely of blacks and persons of Eng. origin. Industries flourished during the 19th cent. as transportation facilities improved. Industry continued to expand in the 20th cent., especially during World Wars I and II. The chemical industry built by the Du Pont family was broken up by a Federal antitrust suit in 1912, but became large enough to buy control of General Motors corporation in the 1920s and hold it for many years. Racial tensions appeared in the state in the 1950s and 1960s as Del.'s schools became racially integrated, and after the assassination of Martin Luther King in 1968, rioting erupted in Wilmington. In the 1980s, Gov. Pierre S. Du Pont fought to liberalize the state's usury laws and won. As a result, many large N.Y. banks set up subsidiaries in Del. (especially the Wilmington area), and thousands of jobs were created. Under the provisions of the 1897 constitution, the governor is elected to a 4-year term. The state legislature, called the general assembly, is made up of a senate of 21 members elected to serve for 4 years and a house of representatives with 41 members elected for 2 years. In the 1960s the general assembly was reapportioned on the basis of pop., thus giving a greater influence to urban areas and reducing the rural influence. Del. is represented in the U.S. Congress by 2 Senators and 1 Representative and has 3 electoral votes. Pierre S. Du Pont, a Republican, was elected governor in 1976 and reelected in 1980. He was succeeded by Michael Castle, also a Republican, in 1984. Castle was reelected in 1988. Democrat Tom Carper was elected in 1992. The leading institutions of higher education are the Univ. of Del., at Newark, and Del. State Univ. Del. has several state parks and state forests, some of them coastal; also important are Bombay Hook and Prime Hook Natl. wildlife refuges, both on Del. Bay. Del. has 3 cos.: KENT, NEW CASTLE, SUSSEX.

Delaware 1 county (□ 395 sq mi/1,023 sq km; 1990 pop. 119,659), E Ind.; ⊙ Muncie; 40°14′N 85°24′W. Drained by Mississinewa R., West Fork of White R., and small Kill Buck, Bell, and Buck creeks. Agr. (corn, wheat, oats; hogs; soybeans, tomatoes; dairying). Diversified mfg. and shipping at Muncie; petroleum field. Prairie Creek Reservoir in SE. Formed 1827. **2** county (□ 579 sq mi/1,500 sq km; 1990 pop. 18,035), E Iowa; ⊙ Manchester; 42°28′N 91°22′W. Prairie agr. area (hogs, cattle, poultry; corn, oats) drained by Maquoketa R.; limestone quarries. Backbone State Park in NW corner. Flooding along rivers in 1993. Formed 1837. **3** county (□ 1,468 sq mi/3,802 sq km; 1990 pop. 47,225), S N.Y.; ⊙ Delhi. Named for the Del. R., situated in the W Catskills; bounded NW by Susquehanna R., SW by Delaware R. (here the Pa. border), which is formed in co. by junction of E and W branches; also drained by Beaver Kill and Charlotte R. Once a leading dairying co. of N.Y., it no longer ranks even among the top 20, having lost 48% of its dairy farms bet. 1985 and 1995 largely due to the Federal Dairy Termination Program. Also produces hay, cauliflower, potatoes, poultry; bluestone quarrying; some lumbering. Diversified mfg. at Sidney, Walton, Hancock. At one time co. was state's leading wool producer. As settlement of co. was based on leasing property, it was the center of the mid-19th-cent. anti-rent war, where armed bands disguised as Native Americans prevented the sheriff from collecting rents. Many former farms have been purchased by "Downstaters" as 2d homes and summer residences. With Otsego co., it represents the northernmost extension of Appalachia and the application of benefits that originated with President Lyndon Johnson's Great Society programs. Formed 1797. **4** county (□ 459 sq mi/1,189 sq km; 1990 pop. 66,929), central Ohio; ⊙ Delaware; 40°11′N 83°00′W. Intersected by Olentangy and Scioto rivers, and by small Big Walnut and Alum creeks. Agr. area (livestock, dairying, grain, fruit); mfg. at Delaware; limestone quarries. Formed 1808. **5** county (□ 792 sq mi/2,051 sq km; 1990 pop. 28,070), NE Okla.; ⊙ Jay; 36°24′N 94°47′W. Bounded E by Ark. and Mo. state lines. L. Spavinaw and L. Eucha reservoirs (water supply for Tulsa) in W part, and also part of L. of the Cherokees (Neosha R.) in N, here receiving Elk R. Some agr. (hay, cattle, chickens; dairying); mfg. (food, transportation equip.). Bernice and Honey Creek state parks in N; Upper Spavinaw State Park near center. Formed 1907. **6** county (□ 190 sq mi/492 sq km; 1990 pop. 547,651), SE Pa.; ⊙ Media; 39°55′N 75°24′W. Highly urbanized residential and industrial area bet. cities of Philadelphia (NE) and Wilmington, Delaware (SW). Bounded E by city of Philadelphia (boundary formed by Darby and Cobbs creeks), SE by Del. R. (N.J. state boundary), S by Del. state boundary, SW by Brandywine Creek. Drained by Darby, Crum, Ridley, and Chester creeks. First settlement in Pa. at ESSINGTON, 1643. Battle of Brandywine, 1777. Oil refining, shipbuilding; mfg. at Folcroft, Ridley Park, Chester, Marcus Hook, other communities. Some agr. in W (hay, alfalfa; cattle, dairying). Ridley Creek State Park and Springdon Reservoir in NW; Philadelphia Internatl. Airport (Tinicum Isl.) in SE corner; Valley Forge State Forest, on Little Tinicum Isl., on Del. R., in SE. Formed 1789.

Delaware, city (1990 pop. 20,030), ⊙ Delaware co., central Ohio, on the Olentangy R.; 40°17′N 83°05′W. A trade center in a fertile farm area, it also has some mfg. (transportation equip.). Ohio Wesleyan Univ. is here. Also the birthplace of President Rutherford B. Hayes. During the War of 1812, the city served as Gen. William Henry Harrison's hq. Inc. as a city 1903.

Delaware, town (1990 pop. 176), Delaware co., E Iowa, 5 mi/8 km E of Manchester; 42°28′N 91°20′W. In livestock area.

Delaware, village (1990 pop. 434), Nowata co., NE Okla.,

5 mi/8 km N of Nowata; 36°46′N 95°38′W. Ships wheat, cattle, corn.

Delaware and Hudson Canal, historic waterway, 107 mi/172 km long, bet. Honesdale, Pa., and Kingston, N.Y.; built 1825–1829 to link Pa. anthracite coal fields with Hudson R. valley and N.Y. City; 41°36′N 74°26′W–41°40′N 74°24′W. It operated profitably until the 1860s; increasing RR competition caused its abandonment in 1899. The 1st locomotive in the U.S. ran in 1829 on a RR line built to serve the canal. No longer in use.

Delaware and Lehigh Navigation Canal National Affiliated Area (LEE-hei), E Pa.; 19th-cent. canals used for transportation. Authorized 1988.

Delaware and Raritan Canal, abandoned canal, 45 mi/72 km long, bet. Bordentown, Trenton and New Brunswick, N.J., connecting the Delaware and the Raritan rivers; opened in 1834. Once an important inland waterway, it was superseded by RR in the latter half of the 19th cent.

Delaware Aqueduct, SE N.Y., 105 mi/169 km long, carrying water from Rondout Reservoir, Sullivan co., SE into the N.Y. city water system at the Hillview Reservoir, Westchester co.; built 1937–1962. The tunnel taps the Delaware R. basin and supplies more than ½ of N.Y. city's water. The aqueduct's deep, gravity-flow construction requires little maintenance. The Rondout Reservoir receives water from other Del. basin reservoirs through a tunnel system. In 1965 the aqueduct was extended.

Delaware Bay, entrance bet. Cape Henlopen, Del. (SW), and Cape May, N.J. (NE), is 12 mi/19 km wide; bay expands to 25 mi/40 km just inside entrance, tapers to c.7 mi/11.3 km to NW to become Delaware R. estuary. Intracoastal Waterway traverses length of bay, from Chesapeake and Delaware Canal, which enters Delaware R. from W, to canal crossing Cape May.

Delaware City, town (1990 pop. 1,682), New Castle co., N Del., 10 mi/16 km S of Wilmington, on Delaware R.; 39°34′N 75°35′W. Mfg. (chemicals, plastic prods.). Fort Delaware State Park is on Pea Patch Isl. in Del. R., to NE; Fort Dupont State Park to SE. Canal Natl. Wildlife Refuge follows length of canal; Augustine Wildlife Area to SE. E entrance to Chesapeake and Delaware Canal is 2 mi/3.2 km S. Laid out 1826, inc. 1851.

Delaware, Fort, Del.: see PEA PATCH ISLAND.

Delaware Memorial Bridge, New Castle co., N Del. and Salem co., SW N.J., crosses Del. R., 3 mi/4.8 km NNE of New Castle, Del., and Pennsville, N.J., and 3 mi/4.8 km SSE of Wilmington, Del.; 39°41′N 75°31′W. Overall length is 3.5 mi/5.6 km, with center span 2,150 ft/655 m long. Completed 1951; twin span completed 1968.

Delaware Mountains, Culberson co., extreme W Texas, barren range extending c.35 mi/56 km SSE from Guadalupe Pass at S end of Guadalupe Mts., rises to 5,870 ft/1,789 m near S end. Part of E boundary of Diablo Bolson; playas (salt flats) are just W.

Delaware National Scenic River, Pa. and N.J. (□ 3 sq mi/7.8 sq km). Swimming, boating, and fishing along 41 mi/66 km of Del. R. within the Delaware Water Gap Natl. Recreation Area; 40°07′N 74°56′W–41°04′N 74°59′W. Authorized 1978.

Delaware River 1 c.280 mi/451 km long; rising in the Catskills, SE N.Y., in E and W branches, which meet at Hancock. It flows SE along the N.Y.-Pa. border to Port Jervis, then bet. Pa. and N.J. generally S to Delaware Bay, an estuary (52 mi/84 km long) bet. N.J. and Del. A migratory bird protection zone has been established over the bay. Reservoirs and dams on the river's headstreams provide flood control and water supply; part of N.Y. city's water supply comes from the Delaware R. The diversion of large amounts of water from the upper Del. R. has increased the salinity of Delaware Bay. The Delaware R. Basin Compact was formed (1961) to regulate the use of water in the entire river basin. The Delaware R. cuts through Kittatinny Mt. near Stroudsburg, Pa., forming the Delaware Water Gap, a scenic resort and recreation area. The lower Delaware R., from Trenton, N.J. (the head of navigation), past Philadelphia (an ocean port), to Wilmington, Delaware, flows through a highly industrialized area; water pollution is a problem here. The Delaware R. has long been significant in commerce and carries a significant amount of tonnage. The Chesapeake and Delaware Canal links it with Chesapeake Bay. **2** 80 mi/129 km long, in NE Kansas, rises in NE Nemaha co., near Sabetha, flows past Valley Falls through the large Perry Lake Reservoir, to Kansas R. 15 mi/24 km E of Topeka.

Delaware Water Gap, borough (1990 pop. 733), Monroe co., E Pa., 3 mi/4.8 km E of Stroudsburg, on Delaware R. at mouth of Brodhead Creek; 40°58′N 75°08′W. Some mfg. Appalachian Trail passes through town and crosses river here. Recreation and tourism are important industries.

Delaware Water Gap, scenic gorge, 2 mi/3.2 km long, cut by the Delaware R. through Kittatinny Mt., on the N.J.-Pa. state line; located in a mt. resort area. The gap, part of the wooded Kittatinny Mt., several isls, and c.40 mi/64 km of river bank are included in Delaware Water Gap Natl. Recreation Area.

Delaware Water Gap National Recreation Area, N.J., and Pa., authorized 1965 (104 sq mi/269 sq km). Scenic DELAWARE WATER GAP.

Delbarton (del-BAHR-tuhn), village (1990 pop. 705), Mingo co., SW W.Va., 5 mi/8 km ENE of Williamson; 37°42′N 82°11′W. Bituminous-coal region. Coal processing.

Delburne, village (1991 pop. 564), S central Alta., Canada, on small lake, 25 mi/40 km E of Red Deer; 52°12′N 113°14′W. Coal mining; oil and gas; wheat, barley, oats; hogs, cattle.

Delcambre (del-KAHMB), town (1990 pop. 1,978), S La., 8 mi/13 km E of Abbeville, in the Acadian country, and 9 mi/14 km N of Vermilion Bay, Gulf of Mexico; 29°57′N 92°00′W. Elev. 6 ft/2 m on Vermilion-Iberia parish line. Rice, sugarcane, soybeans; cattle; frozen-shrimp processing. Scenic Gardens to NE. Settled by Spanish in 1790. Hosts the Delcambre Shrimp Festival. Inc. 1907.

Delco, uninc. village, Columbus co., SE N.C., 17 mi/27 km WNW of Wilmington. Light mfg. Tobacco, grain, peanuts, livestock.

Deleau (duh-LO), village, SW Man., Canada, 35 mi/56 km WSW of Brandon; grain, stock.

Delgada, Point, SW Humboldt co., NW Calif., 50 mi/80 km S of Eureka on Pacific Ocean.

Delhi (DEHL-hei), town (1991 pop. 15,852), S Ont., Canada, on Big Creek, and 34 mi/55 km E of St. Thomas; 42°51′N 80°30′W. Tobacco processing, natural-gas production, lumbering.

Delhi 1 (DEL-ee), uninc. town (1990 pop. 3,280), Merced co., central Calif., 4 mi/6.4 km SE of Turlock, near Merced R.; 37°26′N 120°47′W. Dairying, poultry, grain, alfalfa, sugar beets, sweet potatoes, tomatoes, almonds, melons, cotton. **2** (DELL-high), town (1990 pop. 485), Del. co., E Iowa, near Maquoketa R., 8 mi/12.9 km SE of Manchester; 42°25′N 91°19′W. **3** (DEL-ee), town (1990 pop. 3,169), Richland parish, NE La., 36 mi/58 km E of Monroe, and on Bayou Macon; 32°28′N 91°30′W. In agr. area (cotton, soybeans, corn, rice; cattle); mfg. (fabricated metal prods., apparel). Fishing nearby.Tensas R. Natl. Wildlife Refuge to SE. Settled before the Civil War. Originally called Deerfield.

Delhi 1 (DEL-hei), village (1990 pop. 69), Redwood co., SW Minn., near Minnesota R., 7 mi/11.3 km NW of Redwood Falls; 44°36′N 95°12′W. Grain. **2** village (□ 3 sq mi/7.8 sq km; 1990 pop. 3,064), ⊙ Del. co., S N.Y., in the Catskills, on W. Branch of the Delaware R., 14 mi/23 km SE of Oneonta; 42°16′N 74°54′W. In dairying and summer residence and recreation area. Seat of State Univ. of N.Y. Col. of Technology at Delhi. Delaware Co. Historical Assn. Mus. 2 mi/3.2 km NE. Settled c.1785, inc. 1821.

Delia (DEE-lyuh), village (1991 pop. 171), S central Alta., Canada, 18 mi/29 km NE of Drumheller; grain elevators, flour mills; cattle, wheat, barley.

Delia (DEEL-yuh), village (1990 pop. 172), Jackson co., NE Kansas, 19 mi/31 km SW of Holton; 39°14′N 95°57′W. Livestock, grain area. Potawatomic Indian Reservation to NE.

Delicias (de-LEE-see-ahs), city (1990 pop. 87,412), ⊙ Delicias municipio, Chihuahua, N Mexico, in irrigation area of Conchos R. valley, on RR, and 45 mi/72 km SE of Chihuahua; 28°10′N 105°30′W. Elev. 3,842 ft/1,171 m. Important agr. region, dams at La Boquilla on the Conchos R. and at Francisco I. Madero on San Pedro R. have enabled great irrigation development. Cotton-growing center, wheat, grapevines. Also known as Ciudad de Delicias.

Delicias (dai-LEE-see-uhz), town, Las Tunas prov., E Cuba, near Atlantic inlet, 28 mi/45 km NW of Holguín; 21°10′N 76°35′W. Sugar-milling center; Antonio Gutieras and Jesús Menéndez sugar mills to N; yeast factory.

Delight, village (1990 pop. 311), Pike co., SW Ark., 25 mi/40 km WSW of Arkadelphia; 34°01′N 93°30′W. Light mfg.

Delisle (duh-LEIL), town (1991 pop. 874), S central Sask., Canada, 24 mi/39 km SW of Saskatoon; 51°55′N 107°07′W. Grain elevators.

Délisle (dai-LEEL) or **Saint Coeur de Marie** (seh kuhr duh mah-REE), village (1991 pop. 4,281), central Que., Canada, on Saguenay R., and 7 mi/11 km NNW of St. Joseph d'Alma; dairying, pig raising.

Dell 1 village (1990 pop. 258), Mississippi co., NE Ark., 9 mi/14.5 km SW of Blytheville on Left Hand Chute (irrigation canal); 35°51′N 90°01′W. Big Lake Wildlife Management Area and Natl. Wildlife Refuge to NW. **2** village (1990 pop. 25), Beaverhead co., extreme SW Mont., on Red Rock R., at mouth of Big Sheep Creek, and 35 mi/56 km S of Dillon. Sheep, cattle, alfalfa, potatoes. Tendoy Mts. of the Bitterroot Range just W; Clark Canyon Reservoir (Red Rock R.) to N; Beaverhead Natl. Forest to W and S.

Dell City, village (1990 pop. 569), Hudspeth co., extreme W Texas, 70 mi/113 km ENE of El Paso, near N Mexico boundary (N); 31°56′N 105°12′W. Cattle-ranching area. Guadalupe Mts. Natl. Park to E.

Dell Creek, c.15 mi/24 km long, Sauk co., S central Wis.; rises c.20 mi/32 km NW of Baraboo, flows SE, then NE, to Wisconsin R. near L. Delton town. Near its mouth, the stream widens to form L. Delton (2 mi/3.2 km long, ½ mi/⅘ km wide) and Mirror L. (2.5 mi/4 km long, c.¼ mi/⅖ km wide), separated by a dam.

Dell Rapids, town (1990 pop. 2,484), Minnehaha co., E S.Dak., 20 mi/32 km N of Sioux Falls, and on Big Sioux R. Rock quarries, diversified farming; animal feed, grain. Nearby are the Dells of the Sioux, beautiful ravines cut by the river. Settled 1868, inc. 1879.

Dellroy, village (1990 pop 314), Carroll co., E Ohio, 17 mi/27 km SSE of Canton, on Atwood Reservoir; 40°33′N 81°11′W.

Dells of the Wisconsin, or **the Dells**, or **the Wisconsin Dells**, scenic part of the Wisconsin R., central Wis., NW of Portage. The river has cut a deep gorge through 8 mi/12.9 km of sandstone, which is carved into caves, pinnacles, and other interesting shapes, some of which are beautifully colored. Rocky Arbor and Mirror Lake State Parks lie N and S of the Dells. The Dells is a major recreation area of the Midwest. Town of Wisconsin Dells at center of area.

Dellview, town (1990 pop. 10), Gaston co., S N.C., 10 mi/16 km NE of Shelby; 35°23′N 81°24′W.

Dellwood, city (1990 pop. 5,245), St. Louis co., E Mo., residential suburb, 9 mi/14.5 km NNW of downtown St. Louis; 38°45′N 90°16′W. Bordered on all sides except E by city of Ferguson.

Dellwood, town (1990 pop. 887), Washington co., E Minn., residential suburb, 12 mi/19 km NE of downtown St. Paul; 45°06′N 92°58′W. Agr. area (cattle, sheep; corn, oats, alfalfa). On NE shore of White Bear L. Northport Airport to SE. Numerous small natural lakes in area.

Delmar 1 town (1990 pop. 962), Sussex co., SW Del., 12 mi/19 km S of Seaford at Md. state line, opposite Delmar, Md.; 38°27′N 75°34′W. Agr. area (poultry, livestock; dairying, fruit, vegetables). **2** town (1990 pop. 517), Clinton co., E Iowa 23 mi/37 km WNW of Clinton; 42°00′N 90°36′W. Light mfg. **3** town (1990 pop. 1,430), on Md.-Del. state line, Wicomico co., Md., 7 mi/

11.3 km N of Salisbury, Md.; 38°27′N 75°34′W. Mfg. of apparel. In 1859, when the town was founded and the Delaware RR reached here, the area was still a pine forest. The name is a compound of the first syllables of Md. and Del., and the town has 2 mayors, councils, and school systems in both states, although only 1 (federal) post office. The main street divides Md. and Del.

Delmar, suburban village (□ 4 sq mi/10.4 sq km; 1990 pop. 8,360), Albany co., E N.Y., 5 mi/8 km SW of downtown Albany; 42°37′N 73°49′W. Mfg. of construction materials.

Delmarva, peninsula, E Va., E Md., central and S Del., c.180 mi/290 km long, separating Chesapeake Bay on the W from Delaware Bay and the Atlantic Ocean on the E; 38°30′N 75°30′W. Name derived from abbreviations of 3 states that comprise it (Del., Md., and Va.). Referred to in Md. and Va. as the Eastern Shore (of Chesapeake Bay). The W coast of the peninsula is jagged and marshy, deeply indented by river estuaries, branches of Chesapeake Bay. The E shore has a relatively even coastline, with beaches and barrier isls. with backwater bays. The Chesapeake and Delaware Canal (part of Intracoastal Waterway) crosses the Delmarva's narrow neck (16 mi/26 km base); 12 mi/19 km SSW of Wilmington, Del. The Chesapeake Bay Bridge–Tunnel links Cape Charles, Va., at the S tip of the peninsula, with Norfolk, Va. Poultry raising, fruit and vegetable farming, fishing, and tourism are major industries. Dover, Del., and Salisbury, Md., are the main cities of the peninsula. On the Delmarva's E shore is Assateague Isl. Natl. Seashore (Md., Va.) and Chincoteague Natl. Wildlife Refuge, both famous for wild horses.

Delmont 1 village, Cumberland co., S N.J., in marshland near Delaware Bay, 13 mi/21 km SSE of Millville. **2** village (1990 pop. 235), Douglas co., SE S.Dak., 10 mi/16 km ESE of Armour, near Choteau Creek. Ships cattle, grain.

Delmont (DEL-mahnt), borough (1990 pop. 2,041), Westmoreland co., SW Pa., 8 mi/12.9 km N of Greensburg and 22 mi/35 km E of Pittsburgh; 40°24′N 79°34′W. Mfg. (fabricated metal prods., machinery, transportation equip., lumber, plastic prods., construction materials). Agr. (corn, hay; livestock, dairying). Beaver Run Reservoir, on Beaver Run, to N.

Deloit, town (1990 pop. 296), Crawford co., W Iowa, on Boyer R., and 6 mi/9.7 km N of Denison; 42°06′N 95°19′W.

Deloraine (deh-luh-RAIN), town (1991 pop. 1,045), SW Man., Canada, 50 mi/80 km SW of Brandon; 49°11′N 100°30′W. Wheat, barley, stock.

Deloro (duh-LO-ro), village (1991 pop. 208), SE Ont., Canada, 27 mi/43 km NNW of Belleville; 44°31′N 77°37′W. Cobalt and arsenic smelting; dairying.

Delphi, city (1990 pop. 2,531), ⊙ Carroll co., NW central Ind., on Deer Creek, near the Wabash, and 17 mi/27 km NE of Lafayette; 40°35′N 86°40′W. In agr. area; mfg. (fabricated metal prods., transportation equip., construction materials, food); poultry hatcheries; RR junction. Laid out 1828.

Delphos, city (1990 pop. 7,093), on Allen-Van Wert co. line, W Ohio, 14 mi/23 km WNW of Lima; 40°51′N 84°20′W. Transportation equip., food, furniture, fabricated metal prods., wood prods. Limestone quarries; also grain and dairy farming in region. Laid out 1845.

Delphos, town (1990 pop. 23), Ringgold co., S Iowa, near Grand R., 6 mi/9.7 km SW of Mount Ayr; 40°39′N 94°20′W.

Delphos (DEL-fos), village (1990 pop. 494), Ottawa co., N central Kansas, on Solomon R., and 12 mi/19 km N of Minneapolis; 39°16′N 97°46′W. In livestock and grain region.

Delran (del-RUHN), township (1990 pop. 13,178), Burlington co., S N.J., 1 mi/1.6 km SW of Willingboro; 40°00′N 74°57′W. Residential, light industry, and commercial areas. Inc. 1880.

Delray Beach (DEL-rai), city (□ 15 sq mi/39 sq km; 1990 pop. 47,181), Palm Beach co., SE Fla., 8 mi/13 km N of Boca Raton, on the Atlantic coast; 26°26′N 80°05′W. Mostly residential, Delray Beach is also the trade center for a citrus-fruit and vegetable-growing region. The

city's flower farms are noted for chrysanthemums and gladiolas. Delray Beach has undergone significant suburban economic development and has a large retirement community. The city's pop. more than doubled from 1970 to 1990. Settled 1895, inc. 1911.

Delson, town (1991 pop. 6,063), S Que., Canada, near the St. Lawrence, 8 mi/13 km SSE of Montreal; 45°22′N 73°33′W. Suburb.

Delta 1 county (□ 1,148 sq mi/2,973 sq km; 1990 pop. 20,980), W Colo.; ⊙ Delta; 38°51′N 107°51′W. Coal-mining and agr. area, drained by Gunnison R. Cattle, sheep, wheat, hay, beans, oats, corn, fruit, vegetables. Crawford State Park in S; Grand Mesa Natl. Forest in N; part of Gunnison Natl. Forest in SE; part of Grand Mesa Lakes in NW; numerous reservoirs (c.100 in number) to either side of Mesa/Delta co. line in the area. Formed 1883. **2** county (□ 1,991 sq mi/5,157 sq km; 1990 pop. 37,780), S Upper Peninsula, Mich.; ⊙ Escanaba. Bounded S by L. Michigan and arms (Big Bay De Noc, Little Bay De Noc) of Green Bay; 45°46′N 86°52′W. Drained by Ford, Escanaba, and Whitefish rivers and small Days R. Lumbering, dairying. Agr. (beans, barley, oats, potatoes; cattle, hogs, poultry). Mfg. at Escanaba and Gladstone. Ships grain. Resorts. Part of Hiawatha Natl. Forest in E ⅔; Gladstone Ski Area near Gladstone; Fayette State Park in SE on Garden Peninsula. W boundary W Dickinson co., marks Central and Eastern time zone boundary; Delta co. is in Eastern time zone. Organized 1861. **3** county (□ 277 sq mi/717 sq km; 1990 pop. 4,857), NE Texas; ⊙ Cooper; 33°23′N 95°40′W. Rich prairie agr. region, small, triangular co., bet. N and S forks of Sulphur R., which join to form Sulphur R. at E tip. Cotton, hay, wheat, soybeans; dairying; cattle. Some lumbering. Formed 1870.

Delta, city (1991 pop. 88,978), SW B.C., Canada, suburb 13 mi/21 km SE of downtown of Vancouver, on S bank of Fraser R.; 50°11′N 98°19′W. Boundary Bay to S. Bridge to Richmond and New Westminster/Burnaby. River port; logging collection point. Fruit; dairying; mfg. (lumber, chemicals, electronic equipment, furniture, plastic prods., shipbuilding).

Delta 1 town (1990 pop. 3,789), ⊙ Delta co., W Colo., on Gunnison R., at mouth of Uncompahgre R., and 35 mi/56 km SE of Grand Junction; 38°44′N 108°04′W. Elev. 4,961 ft/1,512 m. RR junction spur to Montrose. Trade and shipping center for diversified farming region. Mfg. (food, concrete). City is hq. for Uncompahgre Natl. Forest to SW. On Surface Creek, 8 mi/12.9 km NE, is Fruit Growers Dam (55 ft/17 m high, 1,520 ft/463 m long; for irrigation; completed 1938). Some of the largest dinosaur bones were found W of Delta. Black Canyon of the Gunnison Natl. Monument to SE; Switzer Lake State Park to SE; Grand Mesa Natl. Forest to NE. Originally Uncompahgre. Inc. 1882. **2** town (1990 pop. 409), Keokuk co., SE Iowa, 6 mi/9.7 km W of Sigourney; 41°19′N 92°19′W. Livestock, grain. **3** town (1990 pop. 450), Cape Girardeau co., SE Mo., in Miss. alluvial plain, 15 mi/24 km SSE of Jackson; 37°12′N 89°44′W. **4** town (1990 pop. 2,998), Millard co., W central Utah, in Sevier Desert, and c.80 mi/129 km SW of Provo in Sevier Desert; 39°21′N 112°34′W. Elev. 4,649 ft/1,417 m. Trade and shipping center in livestock and irrigated agr. area, once a swampy delta area of Sevier R. when it entered prehistoric Bonneville L. Alfalfa, barley, wheat, sugar beets; dairying; cattle. Mfg. (food, fabricated metal prods.); limestone, beryllium ore mining. Fort Deseret State Historical Park to SW; part of Fishlake Natl. Forest to E. Gunnison Massacre Monument to SW; Great Basin Natl. Park (Nev.) 90 mi/145 km WSW (including former Lehman Caves Natl. Monument). Topaz Marsh Waterfowl Management Area to NW. Intermountain Power Plant (coal) 18 mi/29 km N. Junction of RR spur to Fillmore. Settled 1906.

Delta, village, SE Ont., Canada, bet. small Upper and Lower Beverly lakes, 20 mi/32 km SSE of Smiths Falls; dairying, mixed farming.

Delta 1 village (1990 pop. 234), Madison parish, NE La., on the Mississippi, opposite Vicksburg (Miss.); 32°19′N

90°55′W. In agr. area (cotton, rice, soybeans, cattle, hogs); crawfish. **2** village (1990 pop. 2,849), Fulton co., NW Ohio, 24 mi/39 km WSW of Toledo; 41°34′N 84°00′W.

Delta, borough (1990 pop. 761), York co., S Pa., 28 mi/45 km SE of York, on Md. state line; 39°43′N 76°19′W. RR junction. Mfg. (apparel); slate and marble quarries. Agr. (corn, wheat, hay, apples; livestock, dairying).

Delta Junction, town (1990 pop. 652), E central Alaska, c.100 mi/161 km SE of Fairbanks, on Delta R., S of its influence with Tanana R.; 64°03′N 145°42′W. Elev. 1,180 ft/360 m. Located on Alaska Highway (Rt. 2) at N terminus of Richardson Highway (Rt. 4). State agr. project begun in 1978 has led to establishment of over 12,000 acres/4,856 ha of privately owned cultivated land. Barley is main crop; also grown are oats, potatoes, grass seed and hay; dairying; pigs, beef cattle; fishing. Tourism. Fort Greeley cold weather testing center.

Delta River, 50 mi/80 km, E Alaska; rises in glaciers on N slope of Alaska Range, at 63°31′N 145°52′W; flows to Tanana R. at Big Delta. Paralleled by Richardson Highway; before construction of highway, river when frozen was part of trail to interior gold fields.

Delta Township, suburb, Eaton co., S central Mich., 5 mi/8 km W of downtown Lansing; 42°43′N 84°39′W. Includes former suburbs of Millette and Delta Mills. State Secondary Govt. Complex to S.

Delta-Mendota Canal, runs 120 mi/193 km S, central Calif. An irrigation unit of CENTRAL VALLEY project; has its head NW of Stockton, where it receives water pumped at Tracy Pumping Plant from Delta Cross Channel. Flows through W part San Joaquin Valley, to San Joaquin R., 30 mi/48 km W of Fresno.

Delton, Lake, Wis.: see DELL CREEK.

Deltona (del-TO-nuh), town (□ 55 sq mi/142 sq km), Volusia co., E central Fla., located 28 mi/45 km N of Orlando; 28°54′N 81°12′W. Mfg. includes transportation equip., concrete.

Demarcation Point, small promontory, NE Alaska, just W of Yukon border, on Beaufort Sea of the Arctic Ocean; 69°42′N 141°18′W. Marks boundary with Canada; narrowest point on the Interior Plains of N. America.

Demarest, suburban borough (1990 pop. 4,800), Bergen co., NE N.J., near Hudson R., 4 mi/6.4 km N of Englewood. Inc. 1903.

Deming (DEM-eeng), city (1990 pop. 10,970), ⊙ Luna co., SW N.Mex., on Mimbres R., 85 mi/137 km NW of El Paso, Texas; 32°15′N 107°45′W. Elev. 4,337 ft/1,322 m. RR junction; trade center in grain and livestock region; cattle, cotton, chile and jalapeño peppers, vegetables, beans, grain, corn, sorghum, alfalfa, grapes, melons, fruit, nuts; mfg. (food and beverages). Mining dist. (copper, zinc) to NW in Grant co.; fluorspar deposits. Mimbres R., flowing underground here, is tapped for irrigation and drinking water. Continental Divide runs N-S c.20 mi/32 km to W; City of Rocks State Park to NW; Rock Hound State Park, in Fla. Mts., to SE; S end of Mimbre Mts., including Cooke's Peak, to NE. Settled 1880, inc. 1902.

Democrat, Mount, peak (14,148 ft/4,312 m) in Park Range, central Colo., 10 mi/16 km NW of Leadville, in Pike Natl. Forest.

Demopolis (dem-AH-puh-lis), city (1990 pop. 7,512), ⊙ Marengo co., W Ala., on Tombigbee R., at mouth of Black Warrior R., and 50 mi/80 km SSW of Tuscaloosa. Wood prods., apparel, fertilizers, food, paper prods., plastic prods. Navigation lock and dam begun 1950 on the Tombigbee here. Founded 1817 by Bonapartist exiles. Has fine Greek Revival homes built by cotton planters.

Demopolis, Lake, reservoir (□ 16 sq mi/41 sq km), on Marengo-Sumter co. border, W central Ala., on Tombigbee R., 3 mi/4.8 km W of Demopolis; 32°31′N 87°53′W. E arm extends N along Hale (E shore) and Greene (W shore) cos.; W arm extends NNW along Green (N shore) and Sumter (S shore) cos. Formed by Demopolis Lock and Dam (64 ft/20 m high), built (1955) by Army Corps of Engineers for navigation.

Demorest (DEM-uh-rest), town (1990 pop. 1,088), Habersham co., NE Ga., 13 mi/21 km W of Toccoa, in apple-growing area; 34°34′N 83°33′W. Piedmont Col. here. Mfg. of construction materials, machinery.

DeMotte, town (1990 pop. 2,482), Jasper co., NW Ind., 20 mi/32 km SSW of Valparaiso, near Kankakee R. Dairying, soybeans, grain. Mfg. (animal feed).

Dempster Highway, runs fom Dawson, Yukon Territory, to Fort McPherson, N.W.T., Canada, 447 mi/719 km through formidable and beautiful terrain. Begun in 1959, 1st of Can. "roads to resources." Open to public in spring 1979.

Denair, uninc. town (1990 pop. 3,693), Stainislaus co., central Calif., in San Joaquin Valley, 13 mi/21 km SE of Modesto; 37°32′N 120°48′W. Dairying, irrigated farming (vegetables, fruit, melons; grain; poultry, cattle); poultry processing.

Denali (de-NAH-lee), former townsite and mining camp, on Valdez Creek, E Alaska, on upper Susitna R., and 120 mi/193 km S of Fairbanks. Visible from Denali Highway. Supply point; airfield; gold actively mined until late 1980s. The Athabascan Indian name of Mt. MCKINLEY is Denali. Town is on a summer only road, Denali Highway, which connects George Parks Highway to Richardson Highway.

Denali National Park and Preserve (de-NAH-lee), park (7,370 sq mi/19,088 sq km), preserve (2,049 sq mi/5,037 sq km) in the Alaska Range, S central Alaska. Located in a region of spectacular mt. scenery, the park contains Mt. McKinley (Denali), the highest point in N. Amer. (20,320 ft/6,194 m). Many peaks exceed 10,000 ft/3,048 m. The park includes glaciers, tundra, and abundant wildlife (moose, Dall sheep, grizzly bears, and wolves). Major tourist destination; numerous hotels near entrance to park. Name changed and park expanded 1980. Also, 2,969 sq mi/7,689 sq km designated as wilderness; designated Biosphere Reserve 1976. Estab. 1917 as Mt. McKinley Natl. Park; Denali Natl. Monument est. 1978.

Denbigh, former village, formerly capital of Warwick co., SE Va., now part of independent city of NEWPORT NEWS, 12 mi/19 km NNW of downtown Newport News.

Dendron (DEN-drawn), town (1990 pop. 305), Surry co., SE Va., 30 mi/48 km SE of Petersburg, near Blackwater R.; 37°01′N 76°55′W. Agr. (peanuts, grain; livestock).

Denham, village (1990 pop. 36), Pine co., E Minn., on Split Rock R., and 47 mi/76 km SW of Duluth; 46°21′N 92°56′W.

Denham Springs (DEN-uhm), city (1994 pop. 9,066), Livingston parish, SE La., on Amite R., and 14 mi/23 km E of Baton Rouge; 30°29′N 90°56′W. In agr. area (cucumbers, peppers; cattle, poultry, exotic fowl; dairying); mfg. (plastics, chemicals, concrete, food, fixtures, construction materials, fabricated-metal prods.). Settled in early 19th cent. around mineral springs.

Denio (DEN-ee-o), uninc. village (1990 pop. 35), Humboldt. co., N Nev., 80 mi/129 km NW of Winnemucca and 85 mi/137 km ESE of Lakeview, Oregon, at Oregon state boundary. Cattle, sheep; mercury. Remote desert outpost. Sheldon Natl. Wildlife Refuge to W; Summit L. Indian Reservation to SW. Duffer Peak (9,397 ft/2,864 m), in Pine Forest Range, to S. Annual 4th of July craft fair and rock swap.

Denison 1 city (1990 pop. 6,604), ⊙ Crawford Co., W Iowa, on Boyer R., and c.60 mi/97 km NNE of Council Bluffs; 42°01′N 95°20′W. RR junction. Light mfg; agr. (pork). Inc. 1876. **2** city (1990 pop. 21,505), Grayson co., N Texas, 8 mi/12.9 km NNE of Sherman, near the Red R.; 33°45′N 96°33′W. Elev. 767 ft/234 m. It is a RR center with mfg. of machinery, apparel, fabricated metal prods; winery. The town was founded by the RR in 1872 on the site of an old stagecoach station. Wealth from industry has preserved the beauty of the city's well-shaded streets, and local funds have converted (1968) the downtown area into a modern shopping park. Eisenhower Birthplace State Historic Site is here. Grayson Community Col. is to SW. L. Texoma, NW of the city, is impounded on the Red R. by the huge Denison Dam.

Eisenhower State Park to NW and Hagerman Wildlife Refuge to W. Inc. 1873.

Denison, village (1990 pop. 225), Jackson co., NE Kansas, 8 mi/12.9 km SE of Holton; 39°23′N 95°37′W. In livestock and grain region.

Denison Dam, Okla.: see TEXOMA, LAKE.

Denman Island (□ 19 sq mi/49 sq km), SW B.C., Canada, in Strait of Georgia just off E coast of Vancouver Isl., 9 mi/14 km SE of Courtenay; 12 mi/19 km long; lumbering, fishing. Just E is Hornby Isl.

Denmark 1 town (1990 pop. 855), Oxford co., W Maine, on the Saco, and 23 mi/37 km SW of South Paris; 43°58′N 70°48′W. Farming, resort area. **2** town (1990 pop. 3,762), Bamberg co., S central S.C., 20 mi/32 km SW of Orangeburg; 33°19′N 81°08′W. Light mfg; agr. includes grain, watermelons, soybeans, dairying, livestock. Settled 1896, inc. 1903. **3** town, Madison co., W Tenn., 12 mi/19 km SW of Jackson, in farm area. **4** town (1990 pop. 1,612), Brown co., E Wis., at base of Door Peninsula, 15 mi/24 km SE of Green Bay City; 44°21′N 87°49′W. In dairy and farm area. Mfg. (food, printing and publishing).

Denmark, village, Lee co., SE Iowa, 7 mi/11.3 km N of Fort Madison. In agr. area.

Dennery, village (1991 pop. 2,481), E St. Lucia, landing 9 mi/14.5 km SE of Castries. Limes, bananas, tropical fruit; fishing.

Denning, village (1990 pop. 206), Franklin co., NW Ark., 15 mi/24 km W of Clarksville, near Arkansas R.; 35°25′N 93°45′W.

Dennis, resort town (1990 pop. 13,864), Barnstable co., SE Mass., extending across central Cape Cod, 6 mi/9.7 km ENE of Barnstable; 41°43′N 70°10′W. Cranberries. Has summer theater, Cape Playhouse (1927). Includes villages of Dennis Port (1990 pop. 2,775), East Dennis (1990 pop. 2,584), South Dennis (1990 pop. 3,559), and West Dennis (1990 pop. 2,307). West Dennis Beach. Settled 1639, set off from Yarmouth 1793.

Dennis, village, Tishomingo co., NE Miss., near Ala. state line, and 35 mi/56 km NE of Tupelo. Timber; mfg. (wood prods.). Tishomingo State Park to NE.

Dennis, township (1990 pop. 5,574), Cape May co., S N.J., 18 mi/29 km N of Cape May, on Del. Bay; 39°12′N 74°49′W. Inc. 1827.

Dennis Acres, village (1990 pop. 157), Newton co., SW Mo., residential suburb of Joplin, 37°02′N 94°30′W. Surrounded by city of Joplin.

Dennis Port, Mass.: see DENNIS.

Dennison 1 village (1990 pop. 152), Goodhue and Rice cos., SE Minn., 13 mi/21 km NE of Fairbault; 44°23′N 93°01′W. Poultry, cattle, sheep, hogs; grain; dairying; mfg. (food). **2** village (1990 pop. 3,282), Tuscarawas co., E Ohio, on Stillwater Creek, opposite Uhrichsville; 40°23′N 81°19′W. Founded 1864. About 5 mi/8 km SE, a flood-control dam impounds Tappan Reservoir in Little Stillwater Creek.

Dennistown, plantation (1990 pop. 32), Somerset co., W Maine, on Que. (Canada) line just NW of Jackman, in wilderness area; 45°41′N 70°20′W. Hunting, fishing.

Dennisville, village, Cape May co., SE N.J., 19 mi/31 km SE of Millville. Adjoins Great Cedar Swamp, which has giant prehistoric white cedars preserved in the wetlands.

Denny Island (□ 51 sq mi/132 sq km), 11 mi/18 km long, 6 mi/10 km wide, SW B.C., Canada, in NE part of Queen Charlotte Sound; 52°07′N 128°00′W. On NE coast is Bella Bella village.

Denny Terrace, uninc. town (1990 pop. 1,750), Richland co., central S.C., residential suburb 4 mi/6.4 km N of downtown Columbia, near Broad R. Columbia. Internatl. Univ. to NW.

Dennys Bay (DEN-neez), Washington co., E Maine, inlet of Cobscook Bay; extends c.10 mi/16 km N-S bet. Dennysville and Whiting. Formerly called Cobscook R.

Dennys River, c.17 mi/27 km long, Washington co., E Maine; rises in Meddybemps L.; flows S and E to Dennys Bay below Dennysville. Noted for salmon fishing.

Dennysville, town (1990 pop. 355), Washington co., E Maine, on Dennys R. and Dennys Bay, and 17 mi/27 km

NE of Machias; 44°57′N 67°15′W. Noted for salmon fishing.

Dent, county (□ 756 sq mi/1,958 sq km; 1990 pop. 13,702), SE central Mo.; ⊙ Salem; 37°36′N 91°30′W. In the Ozarks; drained by Meramec R. to N and Current R. to S; corn, wheat, hay; cattle; oak, pine timber; lead deposits in E. Mfg. in Salem. Tourism, canoeing. Indian Trail State Forest in NE; Montauk State Park in SW; Part of Mark Twain Natl. Forest in E part. Formed 1851.

Dent, village (1990 pop. 177), Otter Tail co., W Minn., 25 mi/40 km NE of Fergus Falls, in small lakes region; 46°32′N 95°43′W. Dairying; light mfg. Maplewood State Park to W.

Denton, county (□ 957 sq mi/2,479 sq km; 1990 pop. 273,525), N Texas, ⊙ Denton; 33°12′N 97°07′W. Drained by Elm Fork of Trinity R. Rich agr. area (cotton, wheat, hay, sorghum, peanuts); beef cattle, horses. Natural gas; clay, sand, and gravel deposits. Site of L. Lewisville State Park in SE, a 2 million acre-ft. reservoir for flood control, water supply to Lewisville and recreation; part of L. Ray Roberts reservoir (Elm Fork Trinity R.) in N; part of Grapevine L. reservoir in S. Formed 1846.

Denton, city (1990 pop. 66,270), ⊙ Denton co., 40 mi/64 km NW of Dallas, 35 mi/56 km NNE of Fort Worth N Texas. Elev. 620 ft/189 m. The city lies in an agr. and industrial region; mfg. (construction materials, wood and plastic prods.), but the economy is based on education and research. North Texas State Univ., Texas Woman's Univ. (largest women's univ. in U.S.), and the Denton State School for the mentally retarded are here. Denton is also known as the city of roses. The North Texas State Fair is held here annually. The city is also the site of the first federally-sponsored regional emergency and disaster center, where preparedness operations are undertaken. L. Lewisville State Park to E, Ray Roberts L. State Park to NE. Inc. 1866.

Denton 1 town (1990 pop. 2,977), ⊙ Caroline co. (since 1791), E Md., 26 mi/42 km NE of Cambridge, and on Choptank R.; 38°53′N 75°49′W. Originally named Eden-Town after Sir Robert Eden, the last royal governor of Md. Settled c.1765. Denton has long been a crossing point on the Choptank R. **2** town (1990 pop. 1,292), Davidson co., central N.C., 15 mi/24 km SSE of Lexington; 35°38′N 80°06′W. Tobacco, soybeans, grain, sweet potatoes, poultry, livestock, dairying. Mfg. (apparel, furniture). High Rock L. reservoir (Yadkin R.) to W. Uwharris Natl. Forest to SE.

Denton 1 village (1990 pop. 335), Jeff Davis co., SE central Ga., 11 mi/18 km SSW of Hazelhurst; 31°43′N 82°42′W. **2** village (1990 pop. 166), Doniphan co., extreme NE Kansas, 9 mi/14.5 km WSW of Troy; 39°43′N 95°16′W. Apples. **3** village (1990 pop. 350), Fergus co., central Mont., on Wolf Creek, near mouth of Coyote Creek and 31 mi/50 km NW of Lewistown; 47°19′N 109°57′W. Wheat, barley, oats, alfalfa; cattle, sheep, hogs. **4** village (1990 pop. 161), Lancaster co., SE Nebr., 9 mi/14.5 km WSW of Lincoln; 40°44′N 96°50′W. Conestoga L. State Recreation Area to NW.

Denton Creek, c.75 mi/121 km long, N Texas, a W tributary of Elm Fork of Trinity R.; rises in Montague co. flows SE. Creek forms Grapevine Reservoir, 20 mi/32 km NE of Fort Worth, a unit of Trinity R. flood-control, conservation development.

Dentsville, uninc. city (1990 pop. 11,839), Richland co., central S.C., residential suburb 5 mi/8 km NE of downtown Columbia, on Gills Creek, from Garys L. reservoir to S; 34°04′N 80°57′W. Fort Jackson Military Reservation to SE. Sesquicentennial State Park to NE.

Denver, county (□ 154 sq mi/399 sq km; 1990 pop. 467,610), N central Colo., ⊙ Denver; 39°46′N 104°52′W. Bounded on N by Adams co., S by Arapahoe co., W by Jefferson co. The co. boundary is contiguous with the Denver city limits except for new annexations by city into the neighboring cos.; Denver co. boundary is adjusted every decennial year to coincide with city boundary. 1960 land area was 66 sq mi/171 sq km. It is currently the smallest co. in land area in Colo.

Denver, city (1990 pop. 467,610), N central Colo.; ⊙ of state and of Denver co., 39°46′N 104°52′W. Elev. 5,280 ft/1,609 m. City limits coextensive with Denver co. boundary except for new annexation into Adams, Arapaho, and Jefferson cos., which remain in those cos. until decennial years, when Denver co. is adjusted to conform with city units, reducing land areas of neighboring cos. (recent extension by city to Denver Internatl. Airport to NE, opened in 1995, to be bounded by year 2000). On the South Platte R. at the mouth of Cherry Creek. It is the largest city in the state, a port of entry, and a processing, shipping, and distributing point for an extensive agr. area. It is also the financial, administrative, and transportation center of the Rocky Mt. region, and the location of numerous Federal agencies. Denver area has many electronics plants and is a major livestock market; foremost among its mfg. aeronautics and other high-technology prods. Mfg. (transportation equip., electronic equip., computers, food, printing and publishing, chemicals). With the famous ski resorts of Aspen and Vail within easy driving distance, Denver is an important tourist center. The city was made territorial capital in 1867. The rich gold and silver strikes of the late 1870s and the 1880s brought prosperity to the city, and it became the metropolis for bonanza kings such as H.A.W. Tabor, who built the Tabor Grand Opera House. In the late 1890s, Denver's development as an important metropolis began. After World War II, Denver experienced rapid growth; a 23% increase in pop. in the 1950s and 1960s. This sudden growth combined with the city's high elev. created environmental problems, and by the late 1970s Denver had one of the worst smog problems in the nation. Denver boomed again during the oil shocks of the late 1970s and early 1980s when the city became the center of oil shales exploration and the city quickly built many new office bldgs. in anticipation of further growth in this field. But when oil prices fell dramatically in the early 1980s, Denver was hard hit economically and experienced outmigration. The metropolitan area (especially the suburbs) has continued to grow however, the city center underwent a renaissance in 1990s with construction of new office bldgs., and the opening of a new baseball stadium, mus. and public library. In 1995, a huge new airport NE of the city was completed. The previous airport, Stapleton, has been redeveloped for warehouses, food production, and a video/film studio. Among the city's educational institutions are the Univ. of Denver, Loretto Heights Col., Regis Col., Colo. Women's Col., Metropolitan State Col., and the Univ. of Colo. Medical Center. Points of interest include a park system with many mt. areas; the Denver Art Mus., new public library (1994); the Colo. State Historical Mus.; Denver Mus., of Natural History and Denver Zoo are at City Park E of downtown, Denver Botanical Garden SE of downtown; a performing arts center; the state capitol; Lower downtown (LoDo), the skidrow area, now gentrified, is site of Coors Field (1995), home field of major league Colorado Rockies baseball team. W of downtown is Mile High Stadium, home of the Broncos, Denver's Natl. Football League team; and the zoological gardens. The U.S. Denver mint is downtown, the Rocky Mt. Arsenal is to NE, and the U.S. Army Fitzsimmons General Hosp. (scheduled to close) are there. In E part of city is Lowry Air Force Base. Referred to as the Mile High City and Gateway to the Rockies located just E of the front Range, Denver is both a major tourist attraction and gateway to Rocky Mt. Natl. Park, several natl. forests and ski resorts located in the nearby mts. Denver Federal Center is to W in Lakewood. Cherry Creek State Park to SE, Barr Lake State Park to NE, Chatfield State Park to SW. Black American West Mus., Childrens Mus., Colo. Convention Center all near downtown. Denver Coliseum and Natl. Western Stock Show Complex both N of downtown. Inc. 1861.

Denver 1 town (1990 pop. 504), Miami co., N central Ind., on Eel R., and 8 mi/12.9 km N of Peru; 40°52′N 86°05′W. Poultry, fruit, dairy prods., grain. **2** town (1990 pop. 1,600), Bremer co., NE Iowa, 8 mi/12.9 km ESE of Waverly; 42°40′N 92°19′W. Creamery, feed mill, machine shop. **3** town (1990 pop. 53), Worth co., NW Mo., on East Fork of Grand R., and 6 mi/9.7 km SSE of Grant City; 40°23′N 94°19′W.

Denver, uninc. village, Lincoln co., S N.C., 13 mi/21 km NE of Lincolnton. Cotton, grain, poultry, livestock. Mfg. (construction equip., machinery, rubber prods.). L. Norman reservoir (Catawba R.) to E.

Denver, borough (1990 pop. 2,861), Lancaster co., SE Pa., 14 mi/23 km SW of Reading, on Cocalico Creek; 40°13′N 76°08′W. Mfg. (wooden prods., apparel, concrete, chemicals); agr. (soybeans, grain; poultry, livestock, dairying). Middle Creek L. (reservoir) Waterfowl Management Area to NW. Settled 1863, inc. 1990.

Denver City, town (1990 pop. 5,145), Yoakum co., NW Texas, on the Llano Estacado, 68 mi/109 km SW of Lubbock; 32°58′N 102°49′W. Trade, supply point for oil and gas region. Cattle; cotton, sorghum, wheat, peanuts; salt. Inc. after 1940.

Denville, resort village and township (1990 pop. 13,812), Morris co., N central N.J., on small Indian L. (c.5 mi/.8 km long), 6 mi/9.7 km N of Morristown; 40°53′N 74°29′W. Largely residential.

Denzil (DEHN-zil), village (1991 pop. 207), W Sask., Canada, 70 mi/113 km SW of North Battleford; 52°14′N 109°39′W. Wheat.

Depew (duh-PYOO), village (1990 pop. 502), Creek co., central Okla., 26 mi/42 km SW of Sapulpa; 35°47′N 96°30′W. In agr. area; oil and natural gas extraction.

Depew, suburb (□ 5 sq mi/13 sq km; 1990 pop. 17,673) of Buffalo, Erie co., W central N.Y., 8 mi/12.9 km ENE of city center; 42°54′N 78°42′W. Diverse mfg. that includes plastics, food, machinery, apparel, furniture, transportation equip. Founded in 1892 as a village, it was named for Chauncey M. Depew, a RR executive and later a U.S. senator. Inc. 1894.

Depoe Bay (DEE po), town (1990 pop. 870), Lincoln co., W Oregon, 13 mi/21 km N of Newport, on Depoe Bay, arm of Pacific Ocean; 44°48′N 124°03′W. Resort area. Fish (salmon). Depoe Bay State Park is here; part of Siuslaw Natl. Forest to NE.

Deport, town (1990 pop. 746), Lamar and Red R. cos., NE Texas, 17 mi/27 km SE of Paris; 33°31′N 95°19′W. Trade point in agr. area (cotton, cattle, soybeans, peanuts).

Deposit, resort village (□ 1 sq mi/2.6 sq km; 1990 pop. 1,936), on Broome-Del. co. line, S N.Y., on W. Branch of the Del. R., 25 mi/40 km ESE of Binghamton, near Pa. line; 42°03′N 75°25′W. Bluestone and sandstone quarrying. Cannonsville Reservoir (10 mi/16 km long), part of N.Y. city's water supply, created by damming W. Branch of the Del. R., 2 mi/3.2 km E of village. Settled 1785, inc. 1811.

Depot Harbour (DEE-po), village, S central Ont., Canada, on Parry Sound, inlet of Georgian Bay, 4 mi/6 km WSW of Parry Sound town; 45°19′N 80°05′W. Port; resort.

Deptford (DET-fuhrd), township (1990 pop. 24,137), Gloucester co. SW N.J., 10 mi/16 km SE of Camden; 39°49′N 75°07′W. Suburban area with retail businesses and light industry. Site of Gloucester Co. Col.

Depue (de-PUH), village, Bureau co., N Ill., on Illinois, R. and 8 mi/12.9 km ESE of Princeton; 41°19′N 89°18′W. In agr. area; zinc plant. L. Depue (c.3 mi/4.8 km long), a bayou of Illinois R., is S. Inc. 1867.

Dequen (duh-KAH), village, central Que., Canada, 11 mi/18 km SSE of Roberval; silica mining.

Derby 1 city (1990 pop. 12,199), New Haven co., SW Conn., at the confluence of the Naugatuck and Housatonic rivers, opposite Shelton; 41°19′N 73°04′W. Founded 1642 as a trading post, inc. as a city 1893. Its copper industry and pin manufactures date from the 1830s. Mfg. includes electronic equip., machinery. **2** city (1990 pop. 14,699), Sedgwick co., S Kansas, on Arkansas R., a suburb 11 mi/18 km SSE of downtown Wichita; 37°32′N 97°15′W. Wheat. Called El Paso until 1930.

Derby 1 town (1990 pop. 135), Lucas co., S Iowa, near Chariton R., 10 mi/16 km SW of Chariton; 40°55′N 93°27′W. **2** town (1990 pop. 4,479), Orleans co., N Vt., at Que. line, just NE of Newport; 44°57′N 72°07′W. Includes villages of Derby Center, Beebe Plain, and Derby Line. Derby Line, on high (1,029 ft/314 m) plateau, is customs post and port of entry; has Can.-Amer. World War memorial.

Derby 1 village (1990 pop. 6,043), Adams co., N central Colo., a NE suburb of Denver now part of Commerce City, W of Rocky Mt. Arsenal; 39°50′N 104°55′W. **2** village (1990 pop. 1,200), Erie co., W N.Y., near L. Erie, 15 mi/24 km SSW of Buffalo; 42°41′N 78°58′W. In grape-growing region. Light mfg.

Derby (DUHR-bee), settlement (1991 pop. 1,221), E N.B., Canada, on Southwest Miramichi R., and 9 mi/14 km SW of Newcastle; 46°54′N 65°39′W. Logging, sport fishing; salmon.

Derby Line, Vt.: see DERBY, town.

Dering Harbor, village (1990 pop. 28), Suffolk co., SE N.Y., on N Shelter Isl.; 41°05′N 72°20′W. In summer-resort area.

Derma, town (1990 pop. 959), Calhoun co., N central Miss., 30 mi/48 km E of Grenada, near Yalobusha R.; 33°51′N 89°17′W. Agr. (cotton, corn, sorghum, soybeans; cattle).

Dermott (DUHR-muht), town (1990 pop. 4,715), Chicot co., extreme SE Ark., 22 mi/35 km WNW of Greenville, Miss., near the Bayou Bartholomew; 33°31′N 91°26′W. RR junction. In agr. area. Mfg. (food). Delta Regional Correctional Unit SE of town. Cut-off Creek Wildlife Management Area to SW. Settled 1832.

Derry, town (1990 pop. 29,603), Rockingham co., SE N.H., 9 mi/14.5 km SE of Manchester, and 10 mi/16 km NE of Nashua; 42°53′N 71°16′W. Rapid pop. growth has changed it from a small town to a suburb. Drained by Beaver Brook. Mfg. (chemicals, electronic equip., construction materials, printing and publishing, apparel); agr. (vegetables, apples; cattle, poultry; dairying; timber). Robert Frost farmed and taught school in Derry (farm in SE). Set off from Londonderry 1827. Section along West Running Brook settled as Londonderry by Scots-Irish in 1719.

Derry, borough (1990 pop. 2,950), Westmoreland co., SW central Pa., 13 mi/21 km E of Greensburg; 40°19′N 79°17′W. Mfg. (fabricated metal prods., chemicals, plastic prods.); sandstone. Agr. (corn, hay; livestock, dairying). Keystone State Park to NW; Chestnut Ridge to SE. Inc. 1881.

Derwent, village (1991 pop. 109), E Alta., Canada, 22 mi/35 km NNW of Vermilion; wheat, oats, dairying, lumbering.

Des Allemands (DAIZ AL-uh-maw), uninc. town (1990 pop. 2, 095), St. Charles parish, La., 11 mi/18 km SW of Hahnville; 29°55′N 90°34′W. Site of the La. Catfish Festival, calls itself the Catfish Capital of the Universe.

Des Allemands, Bayou, La.: see DES ALLEMANDS, LAC.

Des Allemands, Lac (DAIZ AL-uh-maw), lake, c.7 mi/11 km long, 6 mi/10 km wide, SE La., 26 mi/42 km W of New Orleans, near the Mississippi R.; 29°55′N 90°34′W. Mostly in St. John the Baptist parish, on boundary of St. Charles and Lafourche parishes. Joined by Bayou Des Allemands (c.20 mi/32 km long) to L. Salvador (SE).

Des Arc 1 (dez-AHRK), town (1990 pop. 2,001), shares ⊙ (with De Valls Bluff), Prairie co., E central Ark., 23 mi/37 km SE of Searcy, and on White R.; 34°58′N 91°30′W. In diversified farm area. Mfg. (apparel, lumber). Bayou Des Arc Wildlife Management Area to N; Wattensaw Wildlife Management Area to S. Prairie Co. Mus. State Historical Site here. Settled in 1820s, inc. 1854. **2** (DEZ-AHRK), town (1990 pop. 173), Iron co., SE Mo., in the St. Francois Mts. 22 mi/35 km S of Ironton; 37°16′N 90°37′W.

Des Arc, Bayou (dez-AHRK), river, c.60 mi/97 km long, in central Ark.; rises in White Co. W of Searcy flows SE, to White R. just N of Des Arc. Bayou Des Arc Wildlife Management Area near its mouth.

Des Cannes, Bayou (DAI KAIN, BEI-yoo), stream, c.50 mi/80 km long, in S La.; rises in Evangeline parish flows S, joining Bayou Nezpique to form Mermentau R. just above Mermentau; 30°12′N 92°34′W. Navigable for lower 8 mi/13 km. Receives Bayou Plaquemine Brule (navigable) near mouth. Shallow-draft port at mouth.

Des Joachims (dai zho-ah-SHEH), locality, SW Que., Canada, on Ottawa R. (rapids), and 40 mi/64 km NW of Pembroke: hydroelectric-power center.

Des Lacs (duh LAKS), village (1990 pop. 216), Ward co., NW central N.Dak., 13 mi/21 km WNW of Minot; 48°15′N 101°33′W.

Des Lacs Lake, in SE Sask., Canada, and N N.Dak., extends NE and NW from Kenmare; largest of the Des Lacs lakes, sources of Des Lacs R.; 30 mi/48 km long, ½mi. wide. Migratory waterfowl project is here.

Des Lacs River (duh LAKS), 42 mi/68 km long, N N.Dak.; flows SE rises in Des Lacs lakes near Kenmare, flows S to Souris R. 6 mi/9.7 km WNW of Minot; 48°35′N 100°59′W. Also known as Rivière des Lacs. Part of the river N of Coulee, including Lower and Upper Des Lacs Lakes, is in Des Lacs Natl. Wildlife Refuge.

Des Moines, county (□ 429 sq mi/1,111 sq km; 1990 pop. 42,614), SE Iowa; ⊙ Burlington; 40°55′N 91°10′W. Bounded E by the Mississippi R. (forms Ill. state line here) and S by Skunk R. Prairie agr. area (hogs, cattle; corn, soybeans); gypsum and limestone quarries. Mfg. at Burlington and W. Burlington. Lock and Dam No. 18, upstream from Burlington. Extensive flooding occurred in 1993, along Mississippi and tributaries. Formed 1834.

Des Moines 1 city (1990 pop. 193,187), ⊙ Iowa and Polk co., S central Iowa, at the junction of the Des Moines and the Raccoon rivers; 41°34′N 93°37′W. Iowa's largest city, it is an industrial, transportation, and govt. center in the heart of the Feed Grains and Livestock Belt. Among its many industries include mfg. (printing and publishing, transportation equip., machinery, fabricated metal prods., construction materials, textiles, plastic prods., apparel, food). The city is also the home office of numerous insurance companies. Settled by homesteaders, Des Moines became the capital of Iowa in 1857. It is the seat of Drake Univ., the Col. of Osteopathic Medicine and Surgery, Amer. Institute of Business and Grand View Col., among other educational institutions. Places of interest include the capitol (1871–1884); the Des Moines Art Center; the Center of Science and Industry; the State Historical Mus.; the Des Moines Art Center; the Equitable Bldg.; the Iowa Mus. of Agr.; the Living History Farm, 8 mi/12.9 km W at Urbandale; the state fairgrounds; and acres of park land. The Des Moines Internatl. Airport is in SW. The city suffered several floodings in the 1950s; dams and reservoirs were later constructed on the Des Moines R. to provide flood control. Extensive flooding occurred in 1993 to the city, and surrounding communities and farmlands. More flooding occurred in early 1994. This was one of the hardest hit areas of Midwest floods. Inc. as Fort Des Moines in 1851, chartered as Des Moines in 1857. **2** (di MOIN), city (1990 pop. 17,283), King co., W Wash., residential suburb 13 mi/21 km S of downtown Seattle and 13 mi/21 km NW of downtown Tacoma, bet. Puget Sound (W) and Green R. (E); 47°24′N 122°19′W. Seat of Highline Community Col. Salt Water State Park to S. Seattle Tacoma (SeaTac) Internatl. Airport to N.

Des Moines (de MOIN), village (1990 pop. 168), Union co., NE N.Mex., 35 mi/56 km ESE of Raton; 36°45′N 103°49′W. Elev. 6,645 ft/2,025 m. In agr., ranching region. Source of Cimarron R. (larger of 2 Cimarron rivers in area) c.15 mi/24 km to NW. Capulin Volcano Natl. Monument to W.

Des Moines River (duh MOIN), 535 mi/861 km long, Minn. and Iowa; rises in Curant L., NW Murray co., SW Minn. at 44°05′N 95°41′W; flows NE before turning SE across Iowa to the Mississippi R. at Keokuk, SE Iowa. Flows through fertile farmland. Flows through Long Shetek and Talcot lakes, then turns NE, then SE again, past Windom and Jackson, Minn., enters N central Iowa, flows past Estherville and Emmetsburg, receives East Fork Des Moines from N, S of Humboldt, past Fort Dodge and Boone, through Saylorville Reservoir and city of Des Moines, continues SE through Red Rock Reservoir and city of Ottumwa, enters Mississippi R. at Keokuk, Iowa; lower c.25 mi/40 km forms Mo./Iowa boundary. Receives Boone R. from N., 18 mi/29 km N of Boone, receives Raccoon R. from W at Des

Moines. Des Moines R. and its tributaries were central to the Great Floods of 1993. Heavy rainfalls of up to 5 in/12.7 cm–8 in/20.3 cm fell repeatedly in spring and summer in S Minn., all of Iowa, and N Mo. Des Moines was heavily damaged; its water purification plant was flooded for 11 days.

Des Peres (duh-PER), town (1990 pop. 8,395), St. Louis co., E Mo., W suburb of St. Louis; 15 mi/24 km W of downtown St. Louis; 38°36′N 90°27′W. Mfg. (chemicals, printing and publishing). Inc. 1934.

Des Plaines (dez-PLAINS), city (1990 pop. 53,223), Cook co., NE Ill., a suburb of Chicago on the Des Plaines R.; 42°01′N 87°54′W. Inc. 1869. Mfg. (chemicals, electronic equip). It was founded in the 1830s as the town of Rand; the name was changed in 1869, and Riverview was annexed in 1925. Oakton Community Col. is here. O'Hare Internatl. Airport is to the S.

Des Plaines (des PLAINZ), river, 110 mi/177 km long, rising in SE Wis., and flowing S and SW through NE Ill. past cities of Des Plaines, Maywood, and Brookfield, joining the Kankakee R. S of Joliet, Ill., to form the Illinois R. The lower Des Plaines is part of the Illinois Waterway.

Désarmes (dai-ZAHRM), village (1982 pop. 10,132), Artibonite dept., central Haiti, 21 mi/34 km ESE of Saint-Marc; 19°00′N 72°23′W. Limes.

Desbiens (dai-BYEH) or **Saint Emilien** (seht-ai-mee-LYEH), town (1991 pop. 1,265), central Que., Canada, on S shore of L. St. John, at mouth of Metabetchouan R., 16 mi/26 km SW of St. Joseph d'Alma; 48°25′N 71°57′W. Hydroelectric station; dairying, pig raising.

Descanto, uninc. village (1990 pop. 680), San Diego co., S Calif., 35 mi/56 km E of San Diego. Cuyamaca Rancho State Park to N; Anza-Borrego Desert State Park to NE; Capitan Grande and Viejas Indian reservations to W. Cleveland Natl. Forest surrounds area. Cattle. Mfg. (leather prods.).

Deschaillons-sur-Saint-Laurent (dai-shah-YOH), village (1991 pop. 1,072), S Que., Canada, on the St. Lawrence, and 26 mi/42 km NE of Trois Rivières; 46°33′N 72°07′W. Dairying, pig raising. Adjoining is Deschaillons sur St. Lauren.

Deschambault (dai-shahm-BO), village (1991 pop. 1,213), S central Que., Canada, on the St. Lawrence, and 45 mi/72 km WSW of Quebec; 46°38′N 71°55′W. Dairying; cattle, pigs, poultry.

Deschambault Lake (42 mi/68 km long. 1 mi/2 km–12 mi/19 km wide), E Sask., Canada, near Man. border, 50 mi/80 km W of Flin Flon. Drains N into Churchill R.

Deschênes, Lake (dai-SHAIN), expansion (6 mi/10 km long, up to 3 mi/5 km wide) of Ottawa R., Que. and Ont., Canada, 6 mi/10 km WSW of Ottawa.

Deschutes (di-SHOOTS), county (□ 3,054 sq mi/7,910 sq km; 1990 pop. 74,958), central Oregon; ⊙ Bend; 43°54′N 121°13′W. Drained by Deschutes R. Agr. (potatoes, alfalfa, wheat, oats, barley; poultry, sheep, cattle); dairy prods.; wineries. Recreation. Diatomite quarrying; manganese, lead, zinc deposits. Deschutes Natl. Forest covers large part of co. in W and S, including parts of Three Sisters and Mt. Jefferson Wilderness Areas. Pilot Butte and Tumalo State Parks in center; Clint Falls and Smith Rock State Parks and Ogden Scenic State Wayside in N; LaPine State Recreation Area in SW; Newberry Natl. Volcanic Monument, including Newberry Crater, in S. Includes part of Cascade Range (W). Formed 1916.

Deschutes River 1 (di-SHOOTS), river, c. 240 mi/386 km long, rising in several lakes in the Cascade Range, SW Deschutes co., W central Oregon. Flows S through Crane Prairie and Wickiup reservoirs, then flows NE through part of Bend, through lakes Chinook and Simtustus to the Columbia R. L. Chinook is formed by Round Butte Dam, where it receives Crooked R. and L. Simtustusis formed by (Pelton Dam) and part of Maupin R. Forms E boundary of Warm Springs Indian Reservation, below round Butte Dam. Deschutes River State Scenic Waterway runs from Pelton Dam to its mouth. The U.S. Bureau of Reclamation has developed the upper river and its main tributary,

the Crooked R., for hydroelectric power and irrigation (c.100,000 acres/40,470 ha). **2** in W Wash., rises in Snoqualmie Natl. Forest 25 mi/40 km E of Chehalis, in N central Lewis co., flows c.50 mi/80 km NW to Budd Inlet, arm of Puget Sound at Olympia.

Descubierta, La, Dominican Republic: see LA DESCUBIERTA.

Desdemona, uninc. village (1990 pop. 180), Eastland co., N central Texas, c.45 mi/72 km NNE of Brownwood, near Leon R. Cotton; vegetables, peanuts; cattle; oil and gas.

Desecheo Island (de-se-CHAI-o), small islet (□ c.1 sq mi/2.6 sq km) belonging to P.R., in Mona Passage, 17 mi/27 km W of main isl.; 18°23′N 67°28′W. Bird sanctuary.

Deseret (dez-UHR-et), a proposed state of the U.S., organized 1849 by a convention of Mormons; it would have included present-day Utah and much of the Southwest below the 42d parallel; proposed capital was Salt L. City. It was refused recognition by Congress, which instead set up Utah Territory (1850).

Deseret Peak (dez-UHR-et) (11,031 ft/3,362 m), in Stansbury Mts., E Tooele co., NW Utah, 19 mi/31 km WSW of Tooele. In unit of Wasatch Natl. Forest, including Deseret Peak Wilderness Area, W of summit.

Deseronto (dehz-uh-RAHN-to), town (1991 pop. 1,862), SE Ont., Canada, near Bay of Quinte of L. Ontario, 25 mi/40 km W of Kingston; 44°12′N 77°02′W. Food canning, dairying, plastics mfg. Former lumbering center. Indian reservation nearby.

Desert Center, uninc. village, Riverside co., S Calif., highway service center on Interstate highway 10, about halfway between Indio (W) and Blythe (E) c.45 mi/72 km each way. Chuckwilla Mts. to S; Palen Mts. and Palen L. (dry) to NE. Joshua Tree Natl. Monument to NW. Colorado R. Aqueduct passes to NW.

Desert Hot Springs, city (1990 pop. 11,668), Riverside co., 10 mi/16 km N of Palm Springs and 50 mi/80 km E of Riverside, S Calif., in N Coachella Valley; 33°58′N 116°30′W. Resort Area, with growing pop. and development. Colorado R. Aqueduct passes to N. Hot thermal springs; Joshua Tree Natl. Monument to E; Morongo Indian Reservation to W; San Bernardino Mts. to NW.

Desert of Maine, Maine: see FREEPORT.

Desert Peak, Utah: see NEWFOUNDLAND MOUNTAINS.

Desert View Highlands, uninc. town (1990 pop. 2,154), Los Angeles co., S Calif., residential suburb 36 mi/58 km N of downtown Los Angeles, at S edge of Antelope Valley; 34°36′N 118°09′W. Irrigated agr. area. California Aqueduct passes to S. Fruit, grain, alfalfa; dairying, cattle, poultry.

Desha (duh-SHAI), county (□ 819 sq mi/2,121 sq km; 1990 pop. 16,798), SE Ark.; ⊙ Arkansas City; 33°49′N 91°15′W. Bounded E by Mississippi R.; drained by Arkansas and White rivers, both form part of N boundary. Agr. (cotton, rice, wheat, soybeans; cattle). Rice and lumber milling. Part of White R. Natl. Wildlife Refuge in far N. Formed 1838.

Deshaies (dai-ZAI), town, NW Basse-Terre isl., Guadeloupe, 22 mi/35 km NNW of Basse-Terre. In agr. region (coffee, cacao, vanilla); exports bananas. Sometimes spelled Deshayes.

Deshayes, Guadeloupe: see DESHAIES.

Deshler 1 village (1990 pop. 892), Thayer co., S Nebr., 7 mi/11.3 km W of Hebron, and on branch of Little Blue R., near Kansas line; 40°08′N 97°43′W. Dairy and poultry prods., grain, livestock. Light mfg. **2** village (1990 pop. 1,876), Henry co., NW Ohio, 17 mi/27 km SW of Bowling Green; 41°12′N 83°54′W.

Desierto Central de Baja California, a proposed biological reserve in S Central Baja California, Mexico. Traversed by Mexico Highway 1 between Guayaquil and Rosarito. The reserve would protect a wild and varied desert landscape. This area is one of most picturesque on the peninsula. Not officially recognized as of 1993.

Desierto de los Leones (de-see-ER-to de los lai-ON-es), natl. park in Federal dist., central Mexico, 18 mi/29 km SW of Mexico city. Pine-forested mt. scenery;

has ruins of old Carmelite monastery (built 1606). A popular destination for weekend trips.

Desierto del Carmen National Park (de-see-ER-to del KAR-men), a natl. park, in S México, Mexico, 4 mi/6 km SW of Tenancingo de Degollado and 4.5 mi/7 km SW of Malinalco on paved road. This is a 1790 Classical-style Carmelite monastery. It is in a wooded mt. setting and there is a spectacular view of the Malinalco Valley (Valle de Malinalco).

Désirade (dai-zee-RAHD), coral island (□ 10.5 sq mi/28 sq km), dependency of Guadeloupe dept., Fr. West Indies, 5 mi/8 km ENE of Grande-Terre; 7 mi/11.3 km long, c.1 mi/1.6 km wide. Rises to c.930 ft/283 m. Of little economic importance, it produces some sugarcane, cotton, sisal, and livestock. Coastal fishing. Its principal settlement, Grande-Anse, is W. Sometimes called La Désirade.

Desloge (duh-LOZH), town (1990 pop. 4,150), St. Francois co., E Mo., just SE of Bonne Terre; 37°52′N 90°31′W. Former lead-mining area. Light mfg. Inc. 1940.

Desmeloizes (dai-mehl-WAHZ), village, W Que., Canada, 33 mi/53 km NNW of Duparquet, near Ont. border; 48°57′N 79°29′W. Gold, copper, zinc mining.

Desolation Valley (□ c.65 sq mi/168 sq km), El Dorado and Placer cos., E. Calif., in the Sierra Nevada, just SW of L. Tahoe. Elev. c.7,000 ft/2,134 m. Lake-dotted, forested glacial valley, of the Rubicon R. which flows NW to Hell Hole Reservoir, accessible only by trails; preserved as a Desolation Wilderness Area in El Dorado Natl. Forest.

DeSoto (duh-SO-to), village (1990 pop. 258), Sumter co., SW central Ga., 13 mi/21 km SE of Americus; 31°57′N 84°04′W. Mfg. (chemicals, food).

DeSoto Park (duh-SO-to), village, Floyd co., NW Ga.

Despard (des-PAHRD), town (1990 pop. 1,018), Harrison co., N W.Va., suburb 2 mi/3.2 km E of Clarksburg; 39°17′N 80°19′W.

d'Espoir, Bay (dehs-PER, Fr. dehs-PWAHR), inlet (30 mi/48 km long, 4 mi/6 km wide at entrance), S N.F., Canada, N arm of Hermitage Bay; fishing, logging. In it is Bois Isl. On shore are fishing settlements; town of St. Albans on W shore.

d'Espoir, Cape, at E end of Gaspé Peninsula, E Que., Canada, on N side of entrance of Chaleur Bay, 30 mi/48 km SSE of Gaspé; 48°24′N 64°19′W.

Dessalines (dai-sah-LEEN), town (1982 pop. 7,984), Artibonite dept., central Haiti, on Artibonite Plain, 18 mi/29 km SE of Gonaïves; 19°17′N 72°30′W. Agr. (coffee, cotton, limes, rice); cattle; timber.

Destin (DES-stin), town (□ 8 sq mi/20.7 sq km; 1990 pop. 8,080), Okaloosa co., NW Fla., 10 mi/16 km E of Fort Walton Beach; 30°23′N 86°28′W. Mfg. includes machinery, printing and publishing, transportation equip., fabricated metal prods. Apalachicola Natl. Forest is nearby.

Destor (dehs-TOR), village (1991 pop. 421), W Que., Canada, 13 mi/21 km NNE of Rouyn; gold, copper mining.

Destrehan (DES-truh-han), unincorp. village (1990 pop. 8,031), St. Charles parish, SE La., on E bank (levee) of the Mississippi R., and 16 mi/26 km W of New Orleans; 29°58′N 90°22′W. RR junction; mfg. (food); oil refining in area. Internatl. highway bridge to Luling.

Detour, Point, Mich.: see GARDEN PENINSULA.

Detroit, city (1990 pop. 1,027,974), ⊙ Wayne co., SE Mich., on the Detroit R., and bet. lakes St. Clair (E) and Erie (S); 42°22′N 83°05′W. Inc. as a city 1815. City borders Macomb and Oakland cos., on N. Metro area includes Wayne, Macomb, Oakland, St. Clair, and Monroe cos. Drained by R. Rouge in W and S. Michigan's largest city and the 7th largest in the nation, Detroit is a port of entry and a major Great Lakes shipping and RR center. Its early carriage industry helped Henry Ford and others to make Detroit the "automobile capital of the world." Mfg. of motor vehicles and motor vehicle parts, steel prods., food and beverages, fabricated metal prods., chemicals, paper prods., and printing and publishing. Detroit is a very diverse city ethnically, and has the nation's largest community of Arab Americans. Extensive salt mines lie under the SW sect. of the city. A Fr. fort and fur-trading settlement founded there in 1701 by Antoine de la Mothe Cadillac and called *Ville d'étroit* [city of the strait] were captured by the British in 1760. Three years later the British withstood a long siege there in Pontiac's rebellion. Amer. control, resulting from Jay's Treaty, was established in 1796. Detroit was 1st the territorial and then the state capital from 1805 to 1847. Fire in 1805 nearly destroyed all of the several hundred buildings in the town, but the settlement was rebuilt from a design by Pierre C. l'Enfant. Detroit was surrendered in 1812 to Br. forces, but was recovered by Gen. (later President) William Henry Harrison in 1813. With the development of land and water transportation, the city grew rapidly during the 1830s. It assumed great importance after the mid–19th cent. as a shipping, shipbuilding, and mfg. center. Detroit's factories attracted immigrants from around the world, including Poles, Italians, Germans, Serbs, Croats, and others. Large numbers of people from the South, especially African Americans, also migrated to Detroit as the factory production increased rapidly. Detroit was a leading producer for the military during World Wars I and II. In 1943, the Natl. Guard was called in as race riots broke out in the city. Race riots erupted again in 1967, killing 43 and causing property damage estimated at $150 million. Detroit's dependence on the declining automobile industry combined with high crime and dramatic suburban growth resulted in massive outmigration in the 1970s and 1980s. Detroit's pop. declined 32% from 1970 to 1990 and scores of businesses left or closed. In 1979 the struggling Chrysler Corporation, based in nearby Highland Park, received $1.5 billion in federal loan guarantees to save it from bankruptcy. Large revitalization projects during this period were largely failures, especially the Renaissance Center (1977), built on bank of Detroit R., with a 73-story circular hotel at its core, and 4 39-story office bldgs. surrounding it, it dominates the skyline. Other projects, including high-rise apartments and the revitalization of the city's theater district, have had more success. Detroit's notable mayors include James Couzens (1919–1922) and Frank Murphy (1930–1933). Wayne State Univ., Wayne County Community Col., Marygrove Col., Sacred Heart Seminary, and the Univ. of Detroit Mercy are located there. Michigan State Fairgrounds is on N part of city. Detroit has a symphony orchestra, organized in 1914. Points of interest include the Detroit Inst. of Arts, one of the nation's finest; a historical mus.; the Fox Theater, a huge renovated movie palace; a civic center, with Cobo Hall, one of the world's largest exhibition halls; Joe Louis Arena, where the Natl. Hockey League's Red Wings play; and Fort Wayne (1849). Tiger Stadium, home of the city's professional baseball team, is currently in nearby "Corktown," but a new stadium is being planned for the downtown area. A new stadium is also being built for the Detroit Lions Natl. Football League team. Belle Isle in the Detroit R., near its exit from L. St. Clair, is a park with flower gardens, a conservatory, a children's zoo, an aquarium, and the Detroit-Windsor Tunnel. It is also the site of the annual Detroit Grand Prix auto race and summer ethnic festivals. The Ambassador Internatl. Bridge (the world's longest internatl. suspension bridge) and a vehicular tunnel link Detroit with Windsor, Ont. (Canada).

Detroit, town (1990 pop. 751), Somerset co., central Maine, 20 mi/32 km E of Skowhegan; 44°46′N 69°17′W.

Detroit 1 village (1990 pop. 126), Pike co., W Ill., 7 mi/11.3 km E of Pittsfield; 39°37′N 90°40′W. In agr. area (corn, wheat, soybeans, sorghum, cattle, hogs). **2** village (1990 pop. 331), Marion co., NW Oregon, 43 mi/69 km ESE of Salem, on Detroit L. reservoir, North Santiam R.; 44°43′N 122°09′W. Timber. Tourism. Area surrounded by Willamette Natl. Forest. Bull of the Woods Wilderness Area to N; Detroit L. State Park to W. **3** village (1990 pop. 706), Red R. co., NE Texas, 16 mi/26 km E of Paris; 33°39′N 95°16′W. Cotton, corn, soybeans; cattle; timber; lumber mills.

Detroit, river, 32 mi/51 km long, flowing from L. St. Clair S into L. Erie bet. Detroit, Mich., and Windsor, Ont. (Canada); it forms part of the U.S.-Canada boundary; 42°21′N 82°55′W. It is one of the most heavily industrialized waterways in the U.S. Steel and chemical plants run along its coast.

Detroit Beach, village (1990 pop. 2,113), Monroe co., SE Mich., 5 mi/8 km ENE of Monroe; 41°55′N 83°19′W. Sterling State Park to S.

Detroit Dam oregon: see DETROIT LAKE.

Detroit Harbor, NE Door Co., NE Wis., arm of L. Mich. Village of Washington Island on shore.

Detroit Lake 1 Becker co., W Minn.; 3 mi/4.8 km long, 2.5 mi/4 km wide. Town of Detroit Lakes on N shore; 46°47′N 95°49′W. Resort area. Lake has no outflow; fed by small stream from lakes Melissa and Sallie, to SW. **2** reservoir (□ 5 sq mi/13 sq km), Linn and Marion cos., NW Oregon, on N. Santiam R., on western edge of Mt. Hood and Willamette natl. forests, 42 mi/68 km ESE of Salem; 44°46′N 122°15′W. Max. capacity 455,000 acre-ft. Formed by Detroit Dam (463 ft/141m high), built (1955) by Army Corps of Engineers and U.S. Department of Agr. Forest Service for power generation; also used for flood control, irrigation, and recreation. S. Shore Detroit Lake State Park located on S shore.

Detroit Lakes, town (1990 pop. 6,635), ⊙ Becker co., W Minn., 41 mi/66 km E of Moorhead, at N end of Detroit L., at inflow of Pelican R.; 46°48′N 95°50′W. Elev. 1,300 ft/396 m. RR junction and trade center for farm and lake-resort area; livestock, poultry; dairying; grain, wild rice, sunflowers, sugar beets, beans; light mfg. There are 2 hospitals. Municipal Airport to W. Tamarac Natl. Wildlife Refuge and Hubbel Pond Wildlife Area to NE; White Earth Indian Reservation to N; numerous small natural lakes in area. Settled c.1858, inc. as village 1880, as city 1900.

Deuel 1 (DOO-el), county (□ 440 sq mi/1,140 sq km; 1990 pop. 2,237), W Nebr.; Platte River valley, bounded S by Colo.; drained by Lodgepole Creek and South Platte R; 41°06′N 102°19′W. Cattle, hogs; wheat, sorghum, sunflower seed. Old Oregon Trail passes through co. Formed 1888. **2** (DOO-IL), county (□ 636 sq mi/1,647 sq km; 1990 pop. 4,522), E S.Dak., on Minn. line; ⊙ Clear Lake; 44°45′N 96°40′W. Agr. area watered by Hidewood Creek and W Fork Lac qui Parle R. Has numerous lakes, especially in NW and SE. Corn, wheat, flax, soybeans, potatoes; dairying; cattle, hogs. Formed 1862.

Deux Montagnes (duh moh-TAH-nyuh), county (□ 279 sq mi/723 sq km), S Que., Canada, on the St. Lawrence; ⊙ Ste Scholastique; 45°40′N 74°00′W.

Deux Rivières, village, E central Ont., Canada, on Ottawa R. and 20 mi/32 km E of Mattawa. Lumbering.

Deux Rivières, Que., Canada: see SAINT STANISLAS DE CHAMPLAIN.

Devens, Fort, Mass.: see AYER.

Devers, village (1990 pop. 318), Liberty co., SE Texas, 30 mi/48 km W of Beaumont; 30°01′N 94°35′W. In oil-producing area; cattle; rice, soybeans.

Deville (duh-VIL), uninc. town (1990 pop. 1,113), Rapides parish, 17 mi/27 km NE of Alexandria; 31°21′N 92°09′W. In agr. and timber area.

Devil's Den State Park, Washington Co., NW Ark. Recreational area (2.6 sq mi/6.9 sq km) in Boston Mts. in Ozark Natl. Forest , 7 mi/11.3 km W of Winslow, 22 mi/35 km S of Fayetteville. Caves, unusual rock formations.

Devils Elbow, W Alaska, bend on lower Yukon R. and 50 mi/80 km N of Bethel; 61°33′N 162°W.

Devils Head, mountain (9,174 ft/2,796 m), SW Alta., Canada, near B.C. border, in Rocky Mts. near E edge of Banff Natl. Park, 18 mi/29 km NE of Banff; 51°21′N 115°16′W.

Devils Lake, town (1990 pop. 7,782), ⊙ Ramsey co., NE central N.Dak., 90 mi/ 145 km W of Grand Forks, on N shore of Devils L.; 48°06′N 98°52′W. RR junction and resort (hunting and fishing). Mfg. (machinery, food). Grain; livestock, dairy prods., poultry. State school for deaf; branch campus of Univ. of N.Dak. Devils Lake Sioux Indian Reservation (formerly Fort

Totten Indian Reservation) to the S. Camp Grapton on lake. Fort Totten Historic Site and Skyline Slyway to W. Sully Hill Natl. Game Preserve to SE. Univ. of N.Dak.-Lakes Region Campus. Settled 1882, inc. 1887.

Devils Lake, village, Lenawee co., SE Mich., on N end of Devils L. and 19 mi/31 km SSE of Jackson.

Devils Lake 1 in Lenawee co., SE Mich., 15 mi/24 km NW of Adrian; c.3 mi/4.8 km long. Summer resort. Devils L. village is at N end. Town of Manitou Beach on W side. **2** in NE central N.Dak., largest (□ 30 sq mi/78 sq km) of group of lakes which includes East Devils L. and Stump L; 48°01′N 98°55′W. Forms Benson/Ramsey co. line. Occupies irregular basin 30 mi/48 km long; max. depth, 7 ft/2.1m. No longer used for commercial shipping, lake size has been fluctuating since turn of cent. Water is salty. Devils L. Sioux Indian Reservation and Sully Hill Natl. Game Preserve are on S shore. Town of Devils Lake is on N shore. Popular for fishing. **3** in Devils L. State Park (13 sq mi/34 sq km, 1 mi/1.6 km long), central Wis., 3 mi/4.8 km S of Baraboo. The clear, oval-shaped lake is ringed by bluffs, 400 ft/122 m–500 ft/152 m high. Native Amer. mounds rest on its shores. The lake is a year-round resort.

Devils Paw, mountain (8,584 ft/2,616 m) on Alaska-B.C. (Canada) border, in Coast Range, 35 mi/56 km NE of Juneau; 58°44′N 133°50′W.

Devil's Postpile National Monument (1.2 sq mi/3.2 sq km; elev. 7,600 ft/2,316 m), NE Madera co., E Calif., 70 mi/113 km NE of Fresno, in Sierra Nevada, on Middle Fork of San Joaquin R., near its source. Bounded all sides by Sierra Natl. Forest. Cluster of basalt columns 40 ft/12 m–60 ft/18 m high on face of basaltic cliff. Rainbow Fall (140 ft/43 m drop) is 2 mi/3.2 km downstream. Resembles pipe organ. Yosemite Natl. Park is NW. Pacific Rim Natl. Scenic Trail passes through monument (John Muir Trail). Est. 1911.

Devil's River, flows c.100 mi/161 km generally S, SW Texas; rises in Sutton co., out of Buckborn Draw (intermittent stream), to the Rio Grande NW of Del Rio. L. Walk has been inc. into Devil's River Arm of L. Amistad.

Devils Thumb, mountain (9,077 ft/2,767 m), on Alaska-B.C. (Canada) border, in Coast Range, 30 mi/48 km NE of Petersburg; 57°05′N 132°22′W.

Devils Tower National Monument (1,347 acres/545 ha), Crook co., NE Wyo., 20 mi/32 km NW of Sundance, to W of Bear Lodge Mts. U.S. first natl. monument (est. 1906). The monument's central feature, Devils Tower, is 865 ft/264 m high and varies in width from 1,000 ft/305 m at its base to 250 ft/76 m at its summit. The tower may be a volcanic plug, the hardened core of an extinct volcano, composed of dense columnar basalt, and stripped of the surrounding volcanic material that once formed the volcano itself. Devils Tower has played a significant role in shaping Native Amer. legends and folklore. The tower is a popular challenge for experienced rock climbers. Prairie dog villages and a variety of bird life are found on the grounds of the monument. Missouri Buttes to W; Belle Fourche R. passes to E through mounument.

Devil's Woodyard, volcanic region, S central Trinidad, Trinidad and Tobago, 10 mi/16 km E of San Fernando. Known for its tiny mud volcanoes, which erupt regularly.

Devine, town (1990 pop. 3,928), Medina co., SW Texas, 32 mi/51 km SW of San Antonio; 29°08′N 98°54′W. Elev. 670 ft/204 m. In irrigated agr. area (livestock; cotton; vegetables, peanuts); oil and gas; light mfg. Inc. 1904.

Devol (duh-VAHL), village (1990 pop. 165), Cotton co., S Okla., near Red R., 19 mi/31 km SW of Walters, near Red R; 34°11′N 98°35′W. In agr. area.

Devola, uninc. village (1990 pop. 2,736), Washington co., SE Ohio, just N of Marietta, and on Muskingham R.; 39°28′N 81°28′W. Also spelled De Vola.

Devon 1 (DEH-vuhn), town (1990 pop. 3,691), 19 mi/31 km SW of Edmonton, Alta., Canada. A 1947 grainfield, then discovery of Leduuc No. 1 oilfield brought Imperial Oil to establish town site to service oil fields. Planned town with orderly development; still oil and gas center. Also commuter suburb for Edmonton. **2** residential town, S N.B., Canada, on St. John R. opposite Fredericton; 45°59′N 65°37′W. Inc. 1917.

Devon, town, Manchester parish, W central Jamaica, in uplands, 9 mi/14.5 km N of Mandeville; 18°11′N 77°31′W. Tropical fruit, spices.

Devon (DE-vuhn), uninc. town, Chester co., SE Pa., residential suburb 14 mi/23 km WNW of Philadelphia; 40°02′N 75°25′W. Mfg. includes printing and publishing, electronic equip., concrete. Jenkins Arboretum in N. Berwyn is 1 mi/1.6 km to W.

Devon Island (□ c.20,900 sq mi/54,100 sq km), E Baffin region, N.W.T., Canada, bet. Baffin and Ellesmere isls.; 75°00′N 86°00′W.

Devonshire, parish (1991 pop. 7,371), central Bermuda; 32°18′N 64°45′W.

Devonshire, uninc. town (1990 pop. 2,120), New Castle co., N Del., residential suburb 5 mi/8 km N of downtown Wilmington, near Pa. state line; 39°49′N 75°32′W. Highest point in Del. (442 ft/135 m) 1 mi/1.6 km to NE, on Ebright Road.

DEW Line, generic term for 3 sets of radar sites est. by the U.S. and Can. govts. in the 1950s to warn against possible Soviet air attack on N. Amer. The Distant Early Warning Line (originally 78 sites, later fewer) was aligned across Alaska, Canada, and Greenland on 70°N. The acronym DEW gave name to entire complex. Operational 1957 as an initial alert system, and modernized as Northern Warning System (13 sites) in late 1970s, it remains active. In 1950s the Mid-Canada Line (98 sites) was built along 55°N as a confirmation system, but was shut down in 1965 as redundant under new technologies. The Pine Tree Line (39 sites), operational from 1954 along 50°N as intercept tracking system, was phased out as technologically outmoded in 1980s. Although most sites were on Can. soil, the N and S lines were primarily Amer. built and operated. The central line was entirely Can. The N Distant Early Warning Line was the largest Arctic construction and manning project ever attempted.

Dewar (DOO-uhr), town (1990 pop. 921), Okmulgee co., E central Okla., 3 mi/4.8 km NE of Henryetta and 12 mi/19 km S of Okmulgee; 35°27′N 95°57′W. In agr. area.

Dewdney, village, SW B.C., Canada, in lower Fraser R. valley, 5 mi/8 km ENE of Mission; 49°10′N 122°12′W. Logging, dairying; vegetables, fruit, hops.

Dewees Island (duh-WEES), Charleston co., SE S.C., swampy isl. (c.2 mi/3.2 km long), 13 mi/21 km ENE of Charleston, bet. Intracoastal Waterway channel (NW) and the Atlantic Ocean (SE).

Deweese (duh-WEEZ), village (1990 pop. 74), Clay co., S Nebr., 13 mi/21 km SW of Clay Center, and on Little Blue R; 40°21′N 98°08′W. Oregon Trail passes through here.

Dewey 1 county (□ 1,008 sq mi/2,611 sq km; 1990 pop. 5,551), W Okla.; ⊙ Taloga; 35°59′N 99°00′W. Intersected by South Canadian and North Canadian rivers. Agr. (wheat, sorghum); cattle. Oil and natural-gas extraction. Formed 1891. **2** county (□ 2,310 sq mi/5,983 sq km; 1990 pop. 5,523), N central S.Dak.; ⊙ Timber L.; 45°09′N 100°52′W. Agr. and cattle-raising area drained by Moreau R. Bounded on E by Missouri R. Little Moreau State Rec. Area at N center. Lignite mines. Flax, wheat; dairy produce; cattle, hogs. In Mountain time zone; Mountain/Central time zone boundary coincides W Missouri R. and E county boundary. All of Dewey co. and neighboring Ziebach co. to W comprise the large Cheyenne River Indian Reservation (4,279 sq mi/11,083 sq km). Formed 1883.

Dewey 1 town (1990 pop. 3,326), Washington co., NE Okla., suburb 4 mi/6.4 km NE of Bartlesville; 36°47′N 95°55′W. In farm, oil, and natural-gas area; mfg. (printing and publishing, fabricated metal prods.). Has annual fair and rodeo. Tom Mix Mus. here. Named for Admiral George Dewey. Founded 1899. **2** town, of P.R., on S Culebra Isl., 55 mi/89 km E of San Juan; 18°17′N 65°18′W. U.S. naval base. Called Culebra until c.1940.

Dewey, uninc. village, Yavapai co., W central Ariz., 13 mi/21 km E of Prescott, on headstream of Aqua Fria R. Cattle, sheep, hay, alfalfa; mfg. (food). Prescott Natl. Forest to E and W.

Dewey Beach, village (1990 pop. 204), Sussex co., SE Del., 17 mi/27 km E of Georgetown, on Atlantic Ocean; 38°41′N 75°04′W. Beach resort area. Tourism; light mfg. Rehoboth Bay To SW; Del. Seashore State Park to S.

Dewey Lake, reservoir, Floyd co., E Ky., on Johns Creek, E tributary of Levisa Fork R., 7 mi/11.3 km SE of Paintsville; 8 mi/12.9 km long; 37°44′N 82°43′W. Max. capacity 88,000 acre-ft. Formed by Dewey Dam (118 ft/36 m high, 920 ft/280 m long), built (1946) for flood control. Jenny Wiley State Resort Park on S shore.

Deweyville, town (1990 pop. 1,218), Newton co., SE Texas, on Sabine R., opposite Starks, La., and 26 mi/42 km NE of Beaumont.; 30°18′N 93°45′W. Timber; peaches, vegetables.

Deweyville, village (1990 pop. 318), Box Elder co., N Utah, near Bear R., 14 mi/23 km N of Brigham City; 41°41′N 112°05′W. Elev. 4,323 ft/1,318 m. Wheat, barley, sugar beets; dairying; cattle, sheep. Wasatch Natl. Forest including Wellsville Mt. Wilderness Area to E.

Dexter, city (1990 pop. 7,559), Stoddard co., SE Mo., on Crowley's Ridge and 25 mi/40 km E of Poplar Bluff; 36°47′N 89°57′W. Cotton, rice, soybeans; sand and gravel; light mfg. Founded 1873.

Dexter 1 town (1990 pop. 475), Laurens co., central Ga., 11 mi/18 km SW of Dublin; 32°26′N 83°04′W. Light mfg. **2** town (1990 pop. 628), Dallas co., central Iowa, 14 mi/23 km SW of Adel; 41°31′N 94°13′W. In agr. area. Light mfg. **3** industrial town (1990 pop. 4,419), including Dexter village, Penobscot co., central Maine, c.30 mi/48 km NW of Bangor, on Wassookeag L.; 45°02′N 69°16′W. Settled 1800, inc. 1816. **4** town (1990 pop. 1,497), Washtenaw co., SE Mich., 8 mi/12.9 km NW of Ann Arbor, and on Huron R.; 42°19′N 83°52′W. In agr. area (fruit; poultry, livestock; dairying); lumbering; mfg. (machinery, printing and publishing, fabricated metal prods.). Pickney State Recreation Area to N. Settled 1823; inc. 1855. **5** town (1990 pop. 898), Chaves co., SE N. Mex., near Pecos R., 16 mi/26 km SSE of Roswell; 33°11′N 104°22′W. In alfalfa area. Dexter Natl. Fish Hatchery at La Van to NE; Bottomless Lakes State Park to N.

Dexter 1 village (1990 pop. 320), Cowley co., SE Kansas, 15 mi/24 km ESE of Winfield; 37°10′N 96°43′W. First helium deposit in U.S. discovered here. **2** uninc. village, Calloway co., W Ky., near East Fork Clarks R., 9 mi/14.5 km N of Murray. **3** village (1990 pop. 303), Mower co., SE Minn., 14 mi/23 km ENE of Austin; 43°43′N 92°42′W. Dairying; corn, soybeans; cattle, sheep, hogs, poultry. **4** village (1990 pop. 1,030), Jefferson co., N N.Y., at mouth of Black R., on Black R. Bay of L. Ontario, 7 mi/11.3 km W of Watertown; 44°00′N 76°02′W. Inc. 1855.

Dexter City, village (1990 pop. 161), Noble co., E Ohio, 17 mi/27 km N of Marietta, and on small Duck Creek; 39°39′N 81°28′W.

D'Hanis (DUH-hai-nis), uninc. village (1990 pop. 548), Medina co., SW Texas, c.50 mi/80 km W of San Antonio. In ranch and farm area.

Diablo (dee-AHB-lo), hamlet, Whatcom co., NW Wash., at site of Diablo Dam, on Skagit R., and 65 mi/105 km E of Bellingham, in Cascade Range. In Ross L. Natl. Recreation Area. Parts of North Cascade Natl. Park to SE and NW.

Diablo Bolson, Culberson co., extreme W Texas, basin with interior drainage into playas (salt flats) at W base of Guadalupe Mts.; elev. 3,500 ft/1,067 m–5,000 ft/1,524 m. Bounded E by Guadalupe and Delaware Mts., E and S by Sierra Diablo, SW and W by Finlay Mts., W by Hueco Mts. Salt lakes here, worked for centuries, were disputed in Salt War, 1877. Also called Diablo Plateau.

Diablo Canyon 1 and 2 Nuclear Power Plants, California: see SAN LUIS OBISPO CO.

Diablo Crater, Ariz.: see METEOR CRATER.

Diablo Lake (dee-AHB-lo), reservoir, Whatcom co., NW Wash., on Skagit R. in Ross Lake Natl. Recreation Area, 65 mi/105 km E of Bellingham; 4 mi/6.4 km long; 48°41′N 121°06′W. Ross Dam at E end. Thunder Creek forms 3-mi/4.8-km S arm. Formed by Diablo Dam (386 ft/118 m high), built (1930) for power generation; owned by City of Seattle.

Diablo, Mount, peak (2,750 ft/838 m), central Jamaica, forms parish boundary bet. St. Catherine and St. Ann on the N boundary of the Rio Cobre Gorge, 27 mi/43 km NW of Kingston; 18°12′N 77°06′W. At its N foot is the resort Moneague.

Diablo, Mount, isolated peak (3,849 ft/1,173 m), Contra Costa co., W Calif. at N end of Diablo Range, c.20 mi/32 km E of Oakland, in Mt. Diablo State Park (16,577 acres/6,709 ha; recreational facilities). Road to summit.

Diablo Plateau, Texas: see DIABLO BOLSON.

Diablo Range, 3,000 ft/915 m–4,000 ft/1,220 m; rises to 5,239 ft/1,597 m in San Benito Mt., W central Calif. One of the Coast Ranges, forms W wall of Central Valley for c.180 mi/290 km from solitary Mt. Diablo E of Oakland to N end of Temblor Range in NW Kern co. In N, range widens; its W arm (Mount Hamilton Range), which includes Mt. HAMILTON, E of San Jose and Santa Clara Valley, and is disected on N-S axis by several intermittent streams, or arroyos. Hetch Hetchy Aqueduct, from Sierra Nevada to San Francisco, crosses range NE of San Jose.

Diablotin, Morne (dee-A-blo-TER, MAWN), peak (4,747 ft/1,447 m), of Dominica, center, 15 mi/24 km N of Roseau; 15°30′N 61°25′W.

Diagonal, town (1990 pop. 298), Ringgold co., S Iowa, 18 mi/29 km NW of Mount Ayr; 40°48′N 94°20′W. Livestock, grain; burial vaults.

Diamant (dee-ah-MAWNG), town, S Martinique, on bay overlooking Rocher du Diamant (Diamond Rock), 9 mi/14.5 km SSE of Fort-de-France. Fishing; rum distilling. Sometimes called Le Diamant.

Diamant, Rocher du (dee-ah-MAWNG, raw-SHAI dyoo), or **Diamond Rock**, SW promontory of Martinique 10 mi/16 km S of Fort-de-France, French West Indies. During war bet. Britain and France (1804), held successfully by Br. seamen.

Diamond (DEL-muhnd), town (1990 pop. 775), Newton co., SW Mo., 12 mi/19 km SE of Joplin; 37°00′N 94°19′W. George Washington Carver Natl. Monument to W.

Diamond 1 village (1990 pop. 1,077), Grundy co., NE Ill., 9 mi/14.5 km SE of Morris; 41°17′N 88°15′W. In agr. area (corn, soybeans). **2** uninc. village (1990 pop. 100), Kanawha co., W W. Va., on Kanawha R., 12 mi/19 km SE of Charleston.

Diamond Bar, city (1990 pop. 52,672), Los Angeles co., S Calif., residential suburb 22 mi/35 km E of downtown Los Angeles, at E end of Puente Hills; 34°00′N 117°49′W. Mfg. (paper prods., chemicals, construction materials).

Diamond, Cape, on the St. Lawrence R., S Que., Canada, at mouth of Charles R.; site of QUEBEC city.

Diamond Caverns, Ky.: see PARK CITY.

Diamond Head, peak, (762 ft/232 m), along the rim of an extinct volcano, SE Oahu island, Honolulu Co., Hawaii; 6 mi/9.7 km SE of downtown Honolulu. Diamond Head, as seen from Waikiki Beach to NW, is Hawaii's signature landmark. A prominent point in the Honolulu skyline, Diamond Head State Monument protects W and S slopes from the commercial development along world-famous Waikiki Beach. Fort Ruger Park is at the northern end of the crater's floor. The crater was the site of an anc. Hawaiian burial ground.

Diamond Island (□ c.5 sq mi/13 sq km), Henderson co., NW Ky., in Ohio R., 10 mi/16 km WNW of Henderson. Agr. Bandit refuge in early 19th cent.

Diamond Mountains, central Nev., NE of Eureka, former White Pine/Eureka co. line. Diamond Peak (10,614 ft/3,235 m), highest point, is 9 mi/14.5 km NE of Eureka.

Diamond Peak, mountain (8,750 ft/2,667 m), Lane and Klamath cos., W Oregon, in Cascade Range, 40 mi/64 km N of Crater L., in Diamond Peak Wilderness Area.

Diamond Rock, Martinique: see DIAMANT, ROCHER DU.

Diamond Springs, uninc. town (1990 pop. 2,872), El Dorado co., E central Calif., 3 mi/4.8 km S of Placerville, near Weber Creek; 38°42′N 120°49′W. In timber area; light mfg; cattle, sheep, lambs, poultry; apples, walnuts. El Dorado Natl. Forest to E.

Diamondhead, uninc. town (1990 pop. 2,661), Hancock co., SE Miss., 5 mi/8 km NNW of Bay St. Louis, near N shore of St. Louis Bay, Gulf of Mexico, near mouth of Jordan R.; 30°22′N 89°22′W. Cotton, corn; timber. Mfg. (wood prods., machinery).

Diamondville, town (1990 pop. 864), suburb 1 mi/1.6 km S of Kemmerer, Lincoln co., SW Wyo., on Hams Fork; 41°46′N 110°32′W. Elev. c.6,880 ft/2,097 m. Coal mines nearby.

Diana, uninc. village (1990 pop. 200), Upshur co., NE Texas, 14 mi/23 km N of Longview. Oil and natural gas; timber; agr. Light mfg.

Díaz Ordaz, Mexico: see VILLA DÍAZ ORDAZ.

Dibble, village (1990 pop. 181), McClain co., central Okla., 15 mi/24 km SW of Norman; 35°01′N 97°37′W. In agr. area. Inc. 1937.

D'Iberville (dee-EI-buhr-vil), town (1990 pop. 6,566), Harrison co., SE Miss., residential suburb 2 mi/3.2 km N of Biloxi, on Back Bay of Biloxi (bridge to Biloxi); 30°26′N 88°54′W. Bounded by Tchoutacabouffa R. on N. Formerly called North Biloxi.

Diboll, town (1990 pop. 4,341), Angelina co., E Texas, near the Neches, and 11 mi/18 km SSW of Lufkin. RR junction in lumbering area; mfg. (chemicals). Davy Crockett Natl. Forest to W, Angelina Natl. Forest to E.

Dickens, county (□ 905 sq mi/2,344 sq km; 1990 pop. 2,571), NW Texas; ⊙ Dickens; 33°37′N 100°46′W. Elev. 1,900 ft/579 m–3,000 ft/914 m. Rolling plains, just below Caprock escarpment of Llano Estacado. Drained by N and S Wichita rivers, by Croton and Duck creeks, all intermittent. Cattle and goat ranching and agr. area, including parts of huge Matador, Spur, and Pitchfork ranches. Cotton, peanuts. Gypsum, caliche, gravel deposits. Formed 1876.

Dickens 1 town (1990 pop. 214), Clay co., NW Iowa, 6 mi/9.7 km E of Spencer; 43°07′N 95°01′W. In livestock and grain area. **2** town (1990 pop. 322), ⊙ Dickens co., NW Texas, on plain below Caprock escarpment, c.60 mi/97 km E of Lubbock; 33°37′N 100°50′W. Elev. 2,468 ft/752 m. Agr. (cotton, peanuts, goats, cattle).

Dickens, village (1990 pop. 16), Lincoln co., SW central Nebr., 25 mi/40 km SSW of North Platte; 40°49′N 100°59′W.

Dickenson, county (□ 334 sq mi/865 sq km; 1990 pop. 17,620), SW Va.; ⊙ Clintwood; 37°07′N 82°20′W. Bounded NW, N by Ky. state line; Cumberland Mts. in NW; drained by Russell Fork and Pound rivers (John W. Flannagan Reservoir, on Pound R. in NW). Agr. (hay, potatoes, tobacco; cattle); timber; bituminous-coal mining. Part of Jefferson Natl. Forest in NW; Breaks Interstate Park in far N. Formed 1880.

Dickey, county (□ 1,143 sq mi/2,960 sq km; 1990 pop. 6,107), SE N.Dak.; ⊙ Ellendale; 46°06′N 98°29′W. Agr. area drained by James and Maple rivers. Wheat, barley, rye and dairy prods.; poultry, cattle, hogs. Trinity Bible Col. Formed 1881. Whitestone Battlefield Historic Site in NW.

Dickey, town, Calhoun co., SW Ga., 27 mi. W of Albany; 31°33′N 84°39′W.

Dickey, village (1990 pop. 53), La Moure co., SE central N.Dak., 15 mi/24 km NNW of La Moure, on James R.; 46°32′N 98°28′W.

Dickey Peak, Idaho: see LOST RIVER RANGE.

Dickeyville, town (1990 pop. 862), Grant co., extreme SW Wis., 8 mi/12.9 km NNE of Dubuque, Iowa; 42°37′N 90°35′W. In agr. area. Mfg. (concrete). An elaborately constructed shrine of Christ and His Mother is here. Lock and Dam No. 11 (Mississippi R.) to SW.

Dickinson 1 county (□ 403 sq mi/1,044 sq km; 1990 pop. 14,909), NW Iowa, on Minn. line; ⊙ Spirit L.; 43°22′N 95°09′W. Prairie agr. area (cattle, hogs, poultry; corn, oats, hay) drained by Little Sioux R. Chief lake region, which is glacial in origin (Big Spirit in N, East and West Okoboji lakes at center, Swan L. in E, Silver L. in

W) of Iowa, with many state parks and preserves (Mini-Waken and Marble Beach State Parks (Big Spirit L.); Isthmus Access State Park and Gardner Sharp State Preserve (East Okoboji L.); Pikes Point, Gull Point, Pillsbury Point and Emerson Bay State Parks (West Okoboji L.); Trappers Bay State Park (Silver L.); Cayler Prairie State Preserve (SW of Montgomery). Tourism; some lumbering; sand and gravel pits. Formed 1851. **2** county (□ 852 sq mi/2,207 sq km; 1990 pop. 18,958), central Kansas; ⊙ Abilene, located in the Flint Hills region; 38°51′N 97°09′W. Gently rolling area, drained by Smoky Hill R. Soybeans, alfalfa, sorghum, rye, wheat; cattle, sheep, poultry; machinery. Arm of Milford L. Reservoir in NE corner. Formed 1857. **3** county (□ 777 sq mi/2,012 sq km; 1990 pop. 26,831), SW Upper Peninsula, Mich.; ⊙ Iron Mountain. Bounded SW by Wis. line; 46°00′N 87°52′W. Drained by Menominee, Ford, and Escanaba rivers. Dairying and agr. area (cattle; potatoes; hay). Mfg. at Iron Mountain. Some lumbering. Resorts (hunting, fishing, winter sports). One of 4 Mich. cos. in central time zone; N boundary and N part of E boundary coincide with Central/Eastern time zone boundary. Pine Mt. Ski Area in SW; Iron Mt. Iron Mine in S at Norway (tourist attraction). Organized 1891.

Dickinson 1 city (1990 pop. 16,097), ⊙ Stark co., SW N.Dak., on the Heart R., 100 mi/161 km W of Bismarck; 46°53′N 102°46′W. Elev. 2,420 ft/738 m. It is a processing and shipping center for a livestock, dairy, and wheat region. Service center for Williston Basin oil industry. Dickinson State Univ. and state experimental livestock and agr. stations are in the city. Mfg. (furniture, food, printing and publishing, transportation equip.). Airport. Patterson L. Reservoir to SW. Inc. 1919. **2** city (1990 pop. 9,497), Galveston co., S Texas, suburb 9 mi/14.5 km NW of Texas City and 23 mi/37 km SE of downtown Houston, on Dickinson Bayou; 29°26′N 95°04′W. Cattle; rice; light mfg.; oil wells.

Dickson, county (□ 486 sq mi/1,259 sq km; 1990 pop. 35,061), N central Tenn.; ⊙ Charlotte; 36°09′N 87°22′W. Bounded NE by Cumberland R.; drained by Harpeth R. Livestock, dairying, field crops, tobacco; timber; iron-ore deposits. Mfg. of fabricated-metal prods., wood prods., and textiles. Formed 1803.

Dickson, city (1990 pop. 8,791), Dickson co., N central Tenn., 33 mi/53 km W of Nashville; 36°05′N 87°23′W. In timber, iron, oil, and farm area; mfg. of apparel, wood prods., fabricated metal prods. Montgomery Bell recreation area nearby. Inc. 1899.

Dickson, town (1990 pop. 942), Carter co., S Okla., 8 mi/12.9 km E of Ardmore, near Washita R.; 34°11′N 96°59′W. Agr. and oil-production area.

Dickson City, borough (1990 pop. 6,276), Lackawanna co., NE Pa., residential suburb 5 mi/8 km NNE of downtown Scranton, on Lackawanna R.; 41°28′N 75°37′W. Former anthracite coal-mining center. Mfg. (wood prods., fixtures). Founded 1859, inc. 1875.

Dickson Mounds Museum, central Ill., 3 mi/4.8 km SE of Lewistown. Here once were extensive excavations of prehistoric burials, with skeletons and artifacts left in original positions. Since reburied. Mus. features Native American ways of life.

Didsbury, town (1991 pop. 3,355), S central Alta., 40 mi/64 km N of Calgary; 51°40′N 114°08′W. Stock and dairy prods. shipping center; food mfg.

Diefenbaker, Lake, T-shaped reservoir created from 2 separate rivers in SW Sask., Canada. Gardiner Dam, 55 mi/89 km SSW of Saskatoon, blocks the South Saskatchewan R. as it flows N; the Qu'Apelle Dam, 85 mi/137 km S of Saskatoon, blocks the headwaters of the Qu'Apelle R. as it flows SE. The backed up waters of the 2 rivers meet about midway bet. the dams at village of Elbow. From here, the main part of the reservoir extends WSW on the South Saskatchewan R. to Saskatchewan Landing Prov. Park, 30 mi/48 km NNW of Swift Current. Total length from lake head to Gardiner Dam, 85 mi/137 km; length of Qu'Apelle arm, 10 mi/16 km Power generating station and Danielson Prov. Park at Gardiner Dam; Douglas Prov. Park at Qu'Apelle Dam. Named for Can. Prime Minister John Diefenbaker, 1957–1963.

Cross references are shown in SMALL CAPITALS. The pronunciation key is on page xv. The dates of population figures are on page xii.

Diego Martin (DAI-go), residential suburb, NW Trinidad, Trinidad and Tobago, 5 mi/8 km NNW of Port of Spain; 10°42'N 61°35'W. In cacao-growing region. To the W was former site of U.S. naval base (Chaguaramas Bay). Blue Basin waterfalls are 2 mi/3.2 km ENE.

Diehlstadt (DEEL-stat), town (1990 pop. 145), Scott co., SE Mo., near Mississippi R., 5 mi/8 km NW of Charleston; 36°57'N 89°25'W.

Dieppe, town (1991 pop. 10,463), SE N.B., Canada, E residential suburb of Moncton renamed in honor of World War II landing site of Can. troops in France; 46°06'N 64°45'W. Situated on NE bank of Petitcodiac R. Moncton Airport; Champlain Center, largest single-story shopping center E of Quebec City (being expanded to 800,000 sq ft/74,320 sq m); Crystal Palace Entertainment Centre; Champlain Raceway; Dieppe Industrial Park. Mfg. (food, paper prods., construction equip., fixtures); distribution facilities; agr. and fish processing in area. Formerly Leger Corner.

Dieppe Bay, village, N St. Kitts, West Indies, 10 mi/16 km NW of Basseterre. Fishing. Sometimes called Dieppe Bay Town.

Dierks (DUHRKS), town (1990 pop. 1,263), Howard co., SW Ark., 16 mi/26 km NW of Nashville; 34°07'N 94°01'W. In timber and agr. area. Mfg. (lumber); logging. Inc. 1907.

Dieterich (DEE-trick), village (1990 pop. 568), Effingham co., SE central Ill., 10 mi/16 km ESE of Effingham; 39°03'N 88°22'W. Redtop seed-cleaning plant; agr. (corn, wheat; dairying; livestock; lumber.

Dietrich, village (1990 pop. 127), Lincoln co., S Idaho, 7 mi/11.3 km E of Shoshone, near Little Wood R; 42°55'N 114°16'W. Cattle; grain; alfalfa.

Digby, county (□ 970 sq mi/2,512 sq km; 1991 pop. 21,250), W N.S., Canada, on the Bay of Fundy; ⊙ Digby; 44°36'N 65°45'W.

Digby, town (1991 pop. 2,311), ⊙ Digby co., W N.S., Canada, on Annapolis Basin of the Bay of Fundy, 60 mi/97 km NNE of Yarmouth; fishing center (herring, scallops); seaside resort; terminal of car ferry from St. John, N.B. Lumbering, woodworking. Extending SW from Digby is Digby Neck peninsula. Founded 1785 by United Empire Loyalists; inc. 1890.

Digby Neck, peninsula (2 mi/3 km wide) on the Bay of Fundy, W N.S., Canada; extends 30 mi/48 km SW from Digby, forming St. Mary Bay. Opposite SW extremity is Long Isl.

Diggins, town (1990 pop. 258), Webster co., S central Mo., in the Ozarks, 12 mi/19 km S of Marshfield; 37°10'N 92°50'W.

Dighton 1 (DEI-tuhn), town (1990 pop. 1,361), ⊙ Lane co., W central Kansas, 40 mi/64 km NNE of Garden City; 38°28'N 100°28'W. Grain, cattle. Inc. 1887. **2** town (1990 pop. 5,631), Bristol co., SE Mass., at mouth of Taunton R., 6 mi/9.7 km S of Taunton; 41°51'N 71°09'W. Chemicals, textiles. Formerly shipbuilding. Inscriptions, probably Native American, on Dighton Rock, a state park, across the river have caused much speculation. Includes village of North Dighton. Settled 1678, inc. 1712.

Dike, town (1990 pop. 875), Grundy co., central Iowa, 10 mi/16 km NE of Grundy Center; 42°27'N 92°37'W. In agr. area.

Dildo (DIL-do), village, SE N.F., Canada, at head of Trinity Bay, 40 mi/64 km W of St. John's; fishing port; 47°33'N 53°03'W. Sawmills nearby.

Dill, Okla.: see DILL CITY.

Dill City or **Dill**, village (1990 pop. 622), Washita co., W Okla., 8 mi/12.9 km W of Cordell; 35°16'N 99°07'W. In cotton and grain area.

Dillard (DIL-uhrd), village (1990 pop. 199), Rabun co., extreme NE Ga., on Little Tennessee R., 15 mi W of the S.C. state line, 1 mi/1.6 km S of the N.C. state line, and 7 mi/11.3 km N of Clayton, in the Blue Ridge and Chattahoochee Natl. Forest; 34°58'N 83°23'W.

Dillard, uninc. community, Crawford co., E central Mo., in the Ozarks, 18 mi/29 km SSE of Steelville. Timber; tourism. Surrounded by Mark Twain Natl. Forest; historic Dillard Mill to S.

Diller, village (1990 pop. 298), Jefferson co., SE Nebr.,

12 mi/19 km E of Fairbury or 15 mi/24 km SW of Beatrice; 40°06'N 96°56'W. Dairy and poultry prods., livestock, grain.

Dilley, town (1990 pop. 2,632), Frio co., SW Texas, c.65 mi/105 km SW of San Antonio; 28°40'N 99°10'W. Cattle and winter vegetable farming (peas, melons, tomatoes, peanuts, corn). Mfg. (machinery). Settled 1880, inc. 1920.

Dillingham, village (1990 pop. 2,017), SW Alaska, on N shore of Nushagak Bay, inlet of Bristol Bay; 59°01'N 158°31'W. Tourism; fishing; cannery; supply center for Nushagak R. trapping region. Main settlement and airport for Bristol Bay.

Dillon, county (□ 406 sq mi/1,052 sq km; 1990 pop. 29,114), NE S.C.; ⊙ Dillon; 34°23'N 79°22'W. Bounded NE by N.C.; drained by Little Pee Dee R. Agr. includes hogs, cattle, corn, rye, soybeans, hay, cotton. Formed 1910.

Dillon 1 town (1990 pop. 3,991), ⊙ Beaverhead co., SW Mont., on Beaverhead R., at mouth of Blacktail Deer Creek, and 55 mi/89 km S of Butte; 45°13'N 112°38'W. Wool-shipping point; gold, silver, lead, copper mines; sheep, cattle, potatoes, barley, alfalfa; tourism. Maverick Mt. Ski Area to NW; part of Beaverhead Natl. Forest to NW; Bannack State Park to W; Clark Canyon Reservoir and Lewis and Clark Memorial to SW; Beaverhead Rock State Park to NE. Seat of Western Mont. Col. of the Univ. of Mont.; Beaverhead County Mus., Western Mont. Col. Gallery and Mus. City founded 1880, inc. 1885. **2** town (1990 pop. 6,829), ⊙ Dillon co., NE S.C., 27 mi/43 km NE of Florence; 34°25'N 79°22'W. Mfg. includes transportation equip., printing and publishing, food; shipping center for agr. area (cotton, corn, timber, grain, paprika). Founded c. 1886.

Dillon, village (1990 pop. 553), Summit co., N central Colo., on Blue R. and Dillon Reservoir, in Gore Range, and 9 mi/14.5 km N of Breckenridge; 39°37'N 106°02'W. Elev. c.8,700 ft/2,652 m. Summer and ski resort. Gold, silver mines nearby. Continental Divide and Eisenhower Memorial Tunnel to E. Surrounded by Arapaho Natl. Forest. Keystone, Silver Plume, Loveland, and Arapaho Basin ski resorts to E.

Dillon Lake, reservoir (□ 2 sq mi/5.2 sq km), Muskingum co., E central Ohio, on Licking R., 5 mi/8 km NW of Zanesville; 40°00'N 82°05'W. Max. capacity 274,000 acre-ft. Formed by Dillon Dam (118 ft/36 m high), built (1960) by Army Corps of Engineers for flood control; also used for recreation and as a fish and wildlife pond. Dillon State Park on NE shore

Dillon Reservoir, Summit co., N central Colo., on Blue R., in Arapaho Natl. Forest, 55 mi/89 km W of Denver; 4 mi/6.4 km long, with 2-mi/3.2-km long SW arm; 39°37'N 106°02'W. Max. capacity of 252,678 acre-ft. Formed by Dillon Dam (240 ft/73 m high), built (1959) by the Denver Water Board for water supply. Harold D. Roberts Tunnel (23 mi/37 km long) delivers water across Continental Divide to North Fork of South Platte R. Resort communities of Dixon and Silverthorne on N shore, near dam, Frisco at SW end.

Dillonvale, village (1990 pop. 857), Jefferson co., E Ohio, 12 mi/19 km SSW of Steubenville, near Ohio R.; 40°11'N 80°46'W.

Dillsboro, town (1990 pop. 1,200), Dearborn co., SE Ind., 12 mi/19 km SSW of Lawrenceburg; 39°01'N 85°04'W. In agr. area; timber.

Dillsboro, village (1990 pop. 95), Jackson co., W N.C., on Tuckasegee R., and 2 mi/3.2 km W of Sylva, in Nantahala Natl. Forest; 35°22'N 83°15'W. Cattle, tobacco, corn; light mfg. Great Smoky Mts. Scenic RR is here.

Dillsburg (DILS-buhrg), borough (1990 pop. 1,925), York co., S Pa., 14 mi/23 km SW of Harrisburg; 40°06'N 77°01'W. Light mfg; agr. (grain, soybeans, apples; livestock, poultry, dairying). Appalachian Trail passes to W. Laid out 1880, inc. 1833.

Dillwyn (DIL-win), town (1990 pop. 458), Buckingham co., central Va., 32 mi/51 km N of Farmville; 37°32'N 78°27'W. RR spur terminus. Light mfg; agr. (grain, tobacco, apples; cattle); timber. Bear Creek L. State Park to E.

Dilworth, town (1990 pop. 2,562), Clay co., W Minn., in

Red R. valley, suburb 5 mi/8 km E of Fargo, N. Dak., and 4 mi/6.4 km E of Moorhead Minn.; 46°52'N 96°42'W. Corn, wheat, barley, potatoes, sugar beets, beans, sunflowers; cattle, sheep, hogs, poultry; dairying; mfg. (fertilizers).

Dime Box, uninc. village (1990 pop. 313), Lee co., S central Texas, near E. Yegua Creek, c.55 mi/89 km E of Austin. Cattle, hogs; cotton, corn, peanuts, soybeans. Mfg. (food). Old Dime Box is 3 mi/4.8 km NW. Somerville L. reservoir to E.

Dimmit, county (□ 1,334 sq mi/3,455 sq km; 1990 pop. 10,433), SW Texas, on plains of the Rio Grande; ⊙ Carrizo Springs; 28°25'N 99°45'W. Drained by Nueces R. In vegetable growing area, irrigated by artesian wells; ships onions, carrots, spinach, other vegetables, some citrus; hay; pecans; also cattle. SW corner of co. is within 4 mi/6.4 km of Rio Grande (Mex. border). Formed 1858.

Dimmitt, town (1990 pop. 4,408), ⊙ Castro co., NW Texas, on Llano Estacado, 55 mi/89 km SSW of Amarillo; 34°32'N 102°19'W. Elev. 3,854 ft/1,175 m. RR terminus; wheat, corn; cotton; cattle, sheep, hogs; light mfg. Estab. 1891.

Dimondale, uninc. town (1990 pop. 1,247), Eaton co., S central Mich., suburb 7 mi/11.3 km SW of Lansing and on Grand R.; 42°38'N 84°39'W. In farm area; light mfg.

Dimsdale, village, W Alta., Canada, 8 mi/13 km W of Grande Prairie; coal mining; oats, wheat.

Dinant (DI-nuhnt), village, central Alta., Canada, 8 mi/13 km N of Camrose; coal mining; wheat, oats, rye.

Dingmans Ferry (DEENG-muhns), uninc. town (1990 pop. 1,200), Delaware township, Pike co., NE Pa., on Delaware R. (bridged), 24 mi/39 km NE of Stroudsburg in Delaware Water Gap Natl. Recreation Area (Pa.-N.J.); 41°13'N 74°52'W. Dingmans Falls, Silverthread Falls, and Fulmer Falls, on Dingman Creek, to W.

Dinosaur, village (1990 pop. 324), Mofatt co., NW Colo., near Utah line, 75 mi/121 km WSW of Craig, Colo., and 30 mi/48 km ESE of Vernal, Utah; 40°14'N 109°00'W. Elev. c.5,900 ft/1,798 m. S gateway to Dinosaur Natl. Monument 15 mi/24 km N. Artesian springs in area. Formerly Artesia, name change c.1965.

Dinosaur National Monument, Uinta co., NE Utah, Moffat co., NW Colo. Authorized 1915, 329 sq mi/852 sq km. Rich quarries of well-preserved fossils of dinosaurs, other animals; Visitor Center at W entrance. Area bisected by canyons of Green and Yampa rivers. Entrances: E, 50 mi/80 km W of Craig, Colo.; Middle, 15 mi/24 km N of Dinosaur, Colo.; W, 10 mi/16 km E of Vernal. Total: Utah, 210,844 acres/85,329 ha; Colo., 156,398 acres/63,294 ha.

Dinsmore, village (1991 pop. 374), S central Sask., Canada, 65 mi/105 km SW of Saskatoon; wheat, livestock.

Dinuba, city (1990 pop. 12,743), Tulare co., S central Calif., in San Joaquin Valley, 25 mi/40 km SE of Fresno; 36°33'N 119°23'W. Packing houses (raisins, figs, grapes, peaches, citrus; pistachios, walnuts, almonds; nursery prods.); mfg. (printing and publishing, food, furniture). Inc. 1906.

Dinwiddie, county (□ 507 sq mi/1,313 sq km; 1990 pop. 22,319), SE central Va.; ⊙ Dinwiddie, 37°04'N 77°37'W. Petersburg is inside but independent of co. Bounded N by Appomattox R., SW by Nottoway R. Agr. (tobacco, barley, wheat, corn, soybeans, peanuts, cotton, hay; hogs; cattle; dairying); lumber milling, granite quarrying. Battlefields at Five Forks and in Petersburg vicinity to NE were among the last struggles (April 1865) of Civil War. Part of Fort Pickett Military Reservation in W, Poplar Grove Natl. Cemetery in NE. Formed 1752.

Dinwiddie (DIN-wid-ee), uninc. village, ⊙ Dinwiddie co., SE central Va., 14 mi/23 km SW of Petersburg. Light mfg; agr. (grain, peanuts, tobacco; livestock). Site of Civil War Battle of Dinwiddie Court House (March 31, 1865), followed (April 1) by Battle of Five Forks to NW. Dinwiddie Correctional Unit.

Diomede, village, Alaska: see LITTLE DIOMEDE ISLAND.

Diomede Islands (DEI-yo-meed), pair of rocky isls. in Bering Strait bet. Alaska and Siberia. The larger isl., Big Diomede (Ratmanov), is Russian, while the smaller is

---

part of Alaska. At 2 mi/3.2 km apart, the Diomedes represent the closest approach of U.S. and Russian land masses. Inuit settlement on Little Diomede; Big Diomede is not inhabited.

Dirty Devil River, 80 mi/129 km long, SE central Utah, formed by confluence of Muddy Creek and Fremont R., 2 mi/3.2 km W of Hanksville. Flows SE and S through Wayne and Garfield cos. to Colorado R. 17 mi/27 km E of Mt. Hillers, through Wayne and Garfield cos. Sometimes called part of Fremont R. Lower 20 mi/32 km in Glen Canyon Natl. Recreation Area.

Disappointment, Cape, projecting into the Pacific Ocean, Pacific co., SW Wash., on N side of the entrance to estuary of the Columbia R. It was named in 1788 by English Capt. John Meares, who rounded it when searching for the fabled R. of the West and was "disappointed" because he could not enter the river (see NORTHWEST PASSAGE). Fort Canby Historical State Park and Lewis and Clark Interpretive Center are on the cape. Fort Columbia State Park to E. Town of Ilwaco at base of cape, on river.

Discovery, village, NW B.C., Canada, 6 mi/10 km E of Atlin; 59°36′N 133°25′W. Originally called Pine Creek. Now a ghost town and tourist destination.

Discovery Bay, town (1991 pop. 2,230), St. Ann parish, N Jamaica, 20 mi/32 km W of Ocho Rios; 18°28′N 77°24′W. Resort town. Site of Christopher Columbus landing. Bauxite shipping port. Marine research lab.

Discovery Bay, uninc. town (1990 pop. 5,351), Contra Costa co., W Calif., planned residential community 13 mi/21 km SE of Antioch, 5 mi/8 km ESE of Brentwood; 37°55′N 121°36′W. Subdivision built entirely on man-made necks of land in man-made Discovery Bay, on Indian Slough, giving all residences water access.

Discovery Harbour, small bay on N side of Lady Franklin Bay, near its entrance on Robeson Channel, NE Ellesmere Isl., Franklin Dist., N.W.T., Canada; 81°44′N 64°45′W. First entered by Nares, whose expedition vessel *Discovery* wintered here, 1875–1876. Greely established his expedition hq. and meteorological station, FORT CONGER, at head of inlet, 1881; it was also one of principal bases of Peary's expedition, 1898–1902. Visited 1934–1935 by Oxford Univ. Ellesmere Land Expedition. Entrance is protected by small Bellot Isl.

Discovery Island, islet, SW B.C., Canada, in S part of Haro Strait, just off SE Vancouver Isl., 4 mi/6 km E of Victoria; 48°25′N 123°15′W. Lighthouse.

Discovery Passage, 26 mi/42 km long, channel on E coast of Vancouver Isl., SW B.C., Canada, joining Johnstone Strait with main body of Strait of Georgia at Campbell R. village. Narrowest part of the channel, Seymour Narrows (700 yd/640 m wide), is just NE of Bloedel. Strong tidal currents.

Disenchantment Bay (20 mi/32 km long), SE Alaska, at head of Yakutat Bay, 20 mi/32 km NE of Yakutat; 60°N 139°32′W. Russell Fiord extends 35 mi/56 km SSE from head of bay. Named by Ital. navigator and explorer Alessandro Malaspina, in the service of Spain, 1791, when it proved not to be the Northwest Passage he was seeking.

Dishman, uninc. town (1990 pop. 9,671), Spokane co., E Wash., residential suburb 6 mi/9.7 km E of downtown Spokane; 47°40′N 117°17′W. RR junction. Spokane Interstate Raceway to W. Dishman Hills Natural Area to S.

Dismal River, 75 mi/121 km long, central Nebr., rises in Grant co., flows E to Middle Loup R. near Dunning, through Sand Hills Region. Nebraska Natl. Forest near mouth. Exceptional even flow for rivers of Sand Hills.

Dismal Swamp (□ 600 sq mi/1,554 sq km), SE Va. and NE N.C., in Chesapeake and Suffolk independent cities, Va., and Gates, Pasquotank, Camden, and Currituck cos., N.C. With dense forests and tangled undergrowth, a favorite site for sportsmen and naturalists. Once covering nearly 2,200 sq mi/5,698 sq km, reduced by drainage to less than 600 sq mi/1,554 sq km. Surveyed in 1763 by George Washington. Dismal Swamp Canal, 22 mi/35 km long, now part of the Intracoastal Waterway, was completed in 1828; it connects Chesapeake Bay with Albemarle Sound. L. Drummond, Va., c.3 mi/4.8 km in diameter, is in the center of the swamp and is its highest elev. Great Dismal Swamp Natl. Wildlife Refuge (Va./N.C.) covers W part.

Dismal Swamp Canal, c.22 mi/35 km long, SE Va. and NE N.C., Chesapeake city, Va. and Camden co., N.C., W branch of Intracoastal Waterway; connects Hampton Roads harbor and Chesapeake Bay in N (via Elizabeth R. estuary and its S branch and Deep Creek) with Albemarle Sound (via Pasquotank R. estuary); completed 1828 through then–densely wooded Dismal Swamp, or Great Dismal Swamp.

Disney, village (1990 pop. 257), Mayes co., NE Okla., 13 mi/21 km SSE of Vinita, near W end of Pensacola Dam (Neosho R.), which forms L. of the Cherokees; 36°28′N 95°01′W. Recreation area. Little Blue–Disney State Park to S; Cherokee State Park at dam.

Disputanta, uninc. village, Prince George co., SE Va., 11 mi/18 km SE of Petersburg, near Blackwater R.; 37°07′N 77°13′W. Mfg. (lumber, chemicals); agr. (peanuts, grain, melons; livestock, poultry).

Disraeli (diz-RAI-lee), town (1991 pop. 2,749), S Que., Canada, on St. Francis R., at N end of L. Aylmer, 30 mi/48 km NW of Megantic; 45°54′N 71°21′W. Woodworking; dairying, cattle, potato-growing region; resort.

District Heights, town, Prince Georges co., central Md., SE suburb of Washington, D.C. Suburban development began here in 1925. Inc. 1936.

District of Columbia, Federal district (□ c.68 sq mi/177 sq km; 1995 est. pop. 554,256), on the E bank of the Potomac R., coextensive with the city of WASHINGTON, D.C. (capital of the U.S.); 38°54′N 77°01′W. The District was established by congressional acts of 1790 and 1791 on a site selected by George Washington. It was originally a 10 mi/16 km square (100 sq mi/259 sq km), with Md. and Va. granting land on each side of the river, including the town of Georgetown and the co. of Alexandria respectively. The "Federal City" was laid out at its center. Alexandria co., at the request of its inhabitants, was returned to Va. in 1846. The city continued to grow on the E bank of the river and in 1878, when Georgetown became a part of Washington (although it continued to operate as a separate city until 1895), the city of Washington and the District of Columbia became one and the same. Although "Washington" is the name known throughout the world, the city is more commonly called "the District" by its own residents. The District has no legal subdivisions, but has been geographically divided into quadrants centered on the U.S. CAPITOL. Northeast (NE) comprises the area E of North Capitol St. and N of East Capitol St. The area is largely residential, but also includes a large part of Washington's small industrial sector — printing and publishing firms, bakeries, machine shops, and warehouse facilities. The Natl. Arboretum is here. Northwest (NW) is the largest quadrant, and includes all areas W of North Capitol St. and N of the NATIONAL MALL. This area contains the WHITE HOUSE, GEORGETOWN, many govt. offices, Embassy Row, most of downtown Washington's office blocks, and extensive residential areas. Large apartment complexes line the main arteries, and exclusive neighborhoods are found in "upper" NW. Southeast (SE) comprises the area E of South Capitol St. and S of East Capitol St. Primarily a residential area stretching from the upscale town houses on CAPITOL HILL to ANACOSTIA, where many of the city's poorer housing projects are located. The Washington Navy Yard and Fort Dupont Park are also here. Southwest (SW) is the smallest quadrant, and includes the area W of South Capitol St. and S of the NATIONAL MALL. Bolling Air Force Base is here, and parts of the waterfront have been redeveloped to include condominiums, restaurants, and marina facilities. For more information, see WASHINGTON, D.C.

Divernon (die-VER-on), village (1990 pop. 1,178), Sangamon co., central Ill., 15 mi/24 km S of Springfield; 39°34′N 89°39′W. In agr. area. Oil wells. Inc. 1900.

Divide, county (□ 1,294 sq mi/3,351 sq km; 1990 pop. 2,899), extreme NW N.Dak., borders Sask., Canada, on N and Mont. on W; ⊙ Crosby; 48°48′N 103°29′W. Hilly area watered by small creeks and lakes, drained by Long Creek in N. Lignite mines; farming, cattle, wheat, barley. Includes Writing Rock State Historic Site in SW. Mountain/Central time zone boundary on W. Formed 1910.

Divide 1 village, Teller co., central Colo., in Front Range, on Rule Creek, and 20 mi/32 km WNW of Colorado Springs; elev. 9,160 ft/2,792 m. Pikes Peak 10 mi/16 km SE. Pike Natl. Forest to SE and N; Mueller State Park to S; Florissant Fossil Beds Natl. Monument to W. **2** village, Silver Bow co., SW Mont., 20 mi/32 km SSW of Butte, and on Big Hole R., just NE of Pioneer Mts. Cattle, forest industries, mining. Humbug Spires Primitive Area to E. Parts of Beaverhead Natl. Forest to W and NW. Deerlodge Natl. Forest to E.

Dividing Creek, village, Cumberland co., S N.J., on small stream, and 13 mi/21 km SE of Bridgeton, in farm area.

Divisaderos (dee-vee-sah-DE-ros), town (1990 pop. 884), Sonora, NW Mexico, 20 mi/30 km SE of Moctezuma; 29°38′N 109°34′E. Ranching, grazing, and farming area. Access by unpaved road to Moctezuma and Sahuaripa.

Dix 1 village (1990 pop 456), Jefferson co., S central Ill., 9 mi/14.5 km NNW of Mt. Vernon; 38°26′N 88°56′W. Wheat, sorghum; cattle; lumber; oil- and coal-producing region. **2** village (1990 pop. 229), Kimball co., W Nebr., 8 mi/12.9 km E of Kimball and on Lodgepole Creek; 41°13′N 103°29′W.

Dix, Fort, N.J.: see FORT DIX.

Dix Island, Knox co., S Maine, in Penobscot Bay, 3 mi/4.8 km SE of South Thomaston; ½ mi/⅘ km long.

Dix Mountain (4,842 ft/1,476 m), Essex co., NE N.Y., in the High Peaks sect. of the Adirondacks, 8 mi/12.9 km ESE of Mt. Marcy, and 18 mi/29 km SE of L. Placid village; 44°05′N 73°48′W.

Dix River (DIKS), 77 mi/124 km long, central Ky.; rises in Rockcastle co., W of Mount Vernon bet. Staford and Lancaster, flows generally NW, through Herrington L. reservoir, formed by Harrodsburg Dam, enters Kentucky R. 8 mi/12.9 km ENE of Harrodsburg, at High Bridge.

Dixfield, town (1990 pop. 2,574), including Dixfield village, Oxford co., W Maine, on the Androscoggin, 22 mi/35 km N of South Paris; 44°32′N 70°22′W. In farming, recreational area; wood prods. Settled 1787–1789, inc. 1803.

Dixiana (dik-see-A-nuh), village, Jefferson co., N central Ala., 16 mi/26 km NNE of Birmingham.

Dixie, county (□ 863 sq mi/2,235 sq km; 1990 pop. 10,585), N Fla., on Gulf of Mexico (S, W) and bounded E by Suwannee R.; ⊙ Cross City; 29°35′N 83°11′W. Flatwoods area, with swamps in central part and small lakes in NE. Cattle, lumbering, farming (corn, peanuts), and fishing. Formed 1921.

Dixie, town, Brooks co., S Ga., 20 mi. ESE of Thomasville, near Fla. state line; 30°47′N 83°39′W.

Dixie Caverns, Va.: see SALEM.

Dixmont (DIX-mawnt), town (1990 pop. 1,007), Penobscot co., S Maine, 18 mi/29 km WSW of Bangor; 44°41′N 69°07′W. In agr. region.

Dixmoor, village (1990 pop. 3,647), Cook co., NE Ill., suburb 16 mi/26 km SSW of downtown Chicago; 41°37′N 87°40′W. Mfg. (transportation equip.). Inc. 1922.

Dixon, county (□ 482 sq mi/1,248 sq km; 1990 pop. 6,143), NE Nebr.; ⊙ Ponca; 42°30′N 96°52′W. Agr. region bounded N by Missouri R. and S.Dak.; watered by Logan Creek. Cattle, hogs, corn, soybeans, alfalfa, oats, poultry; food processing, dairy prods. Ponca State Park in NE; small part of Winnebago Indian Reservation in extreme SE corner. Formed 1888.

Dixon 1 city (1990 pop. 10,401), Solano co., central Calif., in Sacramento Valley, 20 mi/32 km WSW of Sacramento; 38°26′N 121°49′W. Cattle, sheep; grain, tomatoes, sugar beets, beans, grains, safflowers, sunflowers; light mfg. Monticello Dam on Putah Creek to NW, forms L. Berryessa reservoir. Inc. 1878. **2** city (1990 pop. 15,144), ⊙ Lee co., N Ill., on the Rock R.; 41°51′N 89°28′W. Founded 1830, inc. 1853. Agr. (corn, soybeans, cattle; dairying); light mfg. On the site of the Dixon

Blockhouse is a statue of Abraham Lincoln as a youthful captain in the Black Hawk War. Pres. Ronald Reagan's boyhood home. The Dixon Developmental Center, a hosp. for the mentally retarded and the blind and (the co-educational) Dixon Correctional Center are here. Sauk Valley Col. 6 mi/9.7 km WSW. **3** city (1990 pop. 1,585), Pulaski co., central Mo., in the Ozarks, near Gasconade R., 18 mi/29 km W of Rolla; 38°00′N 92°05′W. Ships livestock; dairying; cattle, poultry; light mfg.

Dixon, town (1990 pop. 202), Scott co., E Iowa, 17 mi. NW of Davenport; 41°44′N 90°46′W. Light mfg. Limestone quarries nearby.

Dixon 1 village (1990 pop. 552), ⊙ Webster co., W Ky., 24 mi/39 km SSW of Henderson, near source of Slover Creek; 37°31′N 87°41′W. Agr. (tobacco, grain; cattle, hogs); light mfg; coal mining. **2** village (1990 pop. 145), Sanders co., W Mont., on Flathead R. at mouth of Jocko R., and 35 mi/56 km NNW of Missoula. Agr. (vegetables); RR junction; mfg. (lumber). Located in the Flathead Indian Reservation. Lolo Natl. Forest to SW. Natl. Bison Range to E. Formerly called Jocko City. **3** village (1990 pop. 87), Dixon co., NE Nebr., 12 mi/19 km N of Wayne, and on Logan Creek; 42°25′N 96°59′W. **4** uninc. village (1990 pop. 800), Rio Arriba co., N N.Mex., 33 mi/53 km N of Santa Fe, near Rio Grande. Chiles, grapes, alfalfa, cattle, sheep. Light mfg. Parts of Carson Natl. Forest to N. San Lorenzo Pueblo to E. **5** village (1990 pop. 70), Carbon co., S Wyo., on Little Snake R., near Colo. line, and 55 mi/89 km S of Rawlins; 41°01′N 107°31′W. Elev. 6,324 ft/1,928 m. Hay. Medicine Bow Natl. Forest to E.

Dixon Entrance, strait (c.50 mi/80 km long, c.50 mi/80 km wide) in N Pacific at Alaska-Canada boundary, bet. Alexander Archipelago (N) and Queen Charlotte Isls. (S); leads from the ocean to Hecate Strait and the Inside Passage; 54°30′N. Forms main approach to Prince Rupert.

Dixon Lane–Meadow Creek, uninc. town (1990 pop. 2,531), Inyo co., E Calif., residential community 2 mi/3.2 km NW of Bishop; 37°23′N 118°25′W. Bishop Indian Reservation to S. Cattle.

Dixonville (DIK-suhn-vil), uninc. town (1990 pop. 1,000), Indiana co., W central Pa., 10 mi/16 km NE of Indiana on Dixon Run Creek; 40°42′N 79°00′W. Agr. includes dairying, livestock; corn, hay.

Dix's Grant, land grant, Coos co., N N.H., 32 mi/51 km N of Berlin. Bounded W by Dixville town. Wilderness area drained by Swift Diamond R.

Dixville, town, Coos co., N N.H., 27 mi/43 km NNW of Berlin. Drained by Mohawk R. and Clear Stream. Dairying; cattle, poultry. Dixville Notch pass (1,871 ft/570 m), in Dixville Notch State Park, in S center. Balsams-Wilderness Ski Area in S. Every presidential election year, the town has the tradition of being the first to cast its vote, just after midnight, in the N.H. primary in March. Also known as Dixville Notch.

Dixville, village (1991 pop. 440), S Que., Canada, on Coaticook R., and 5 mi/8 km SSE of Coaticook, near Vt. border; dairying.

Dixville Notch, Coos co., N N.H., scenic pass in outlying range of White Mts., c.25 mi/40 km NNE of Lancaster; c.2 mi/3.2 km long. State forest area; resorts at Dixville Notch village.

D'Lo (DEE-lo), village (1990 pop. 421), Simpson co., S central Miss., 27 mi/43 km SE of Jackson, near Strong R.; 31°59′N 89°54′W. Agr. (cotton, corn; poultry, cattle).

Dobbins Heights, town (1990 pop. 1,144), Richmond co., S N.C., residential suburb 6 mi/9.7 km ESE of Rockingham; 34°54′N 79°41′W.

Dobbs Ferry, suburb (□ 3 sq mi/7.8 sq km; 1990 pop. 9,940) of N.Y. city, Westchester co., SE N.Y., 16 mi/26 km N of the city, on the Hudson R.; 41°00′N 73°52′W. It is mostly residential but has a chemical research laboratory. Dobbs Ferry is the site of Livingston Manor, where George Washington and Marshal Rochambeau of France are said to have planned the Yorktown Campaign. Seat of Mercy Col. and Masters School for Girls; Children's Village, a rehabilitation school for boys, is also there. Inc. 1873.

Dobson, town (1990 pop. 1,195), ⊙ Surry co., N N.C., 12 mi/19 km SSW of Mt. Airy; 36°23′N 80°43′W. Agr. (tobacco, grain, soybeans, chickens, cattle, hogs, dairying); mfg. (hosiery, poultry processing, apparel).

Doce Leguas, Cayos de las (DO-sai LEG-wahz, KEI-yoz dai lahz), coral reefs and keys off Caribbean coast of E Cuba, 70 mi/113 km SW of Camagüey; 20°58′N 79°00′W. The keys form 2 groups: Cayos de las Doce Leguas (NW) and Laberinto de las Doce Leguas (SE), divided by the Canal de Caballones, and forming in their entirety the Jardines de la Reina (c.85 mi/137 km long NW-SE).

Docena (duh-SEE-nuh), Jefferson co., N central Ala., a NW suburb of Birmingham.

Dochet Island, Maine: see SAINT CROIX ISLAND.

Doctor Arroyo (ah-RO-yo), city (1990 pop. 6,025) and township, S Nuevo León, N Mexico, on the Mesa Central, 30 mi/48 km E of Matehuala (San Luis Potosí); 23°40′N 100°10′W. Elev. 5,794 ft/1,766 m. Ranching, grazing, farming area. Small industry in city.

Doctor Belisario Domínguez (be-lee-SAH-ree-o do-MEEN-ges), town (1990 pop. 695), Chihuahua, N Mexico, 40 mi/64 km SW of Chihuahua; 28°03′N 106°30′W. Small farming, livestock. Copper deposits. Formerly San Lorenzo.

Doctor Coss, town (1990 pop. 1,100), Nuevo León, N Mexico, on San Juan R., and 60 mi/90 km W of Reynosa (Tamaulipas); 25°55′N 99°10′W. Cotton, sugarcane, corn, cactus fibers.

Doctor González (gon-SAH-les), town (1990 pop. 1,957), Nuevo León, N Mexico, 26 mi/42 km NE of Monterrey on Mexico Highway 54. Cereals, cactus fibers, livestock.

Doctor Mora (MO-rah), city (1990 pop. 3,222), Guanajuato, central Mexico, 20 mi/32 km SE of San Luis de la Paz. Grain, sugar, fruit, livestock. Also called Charcas.

Doctor Phillips, suburb of Orlando (□ 5 sq mi/13 sq km; 1990 pop. 7,963), Orange co., central Fla., located just E of Walt Disney World; 28°26′N 81°29′W.

Doctor's Cave, resort of Montego Bay, St. James parish, N Jamaica; 18°30′N 77°54′W. Famous as a bathing beach with curative powers, helped to make Montego Bay a prime tourist area.

Dodd City, village (1990 pop. 350), Fannin co., NE Texas, 6 mi/9.7 km E of Bonham; 33°34′N 96°04′W. In agr. area. Bonham State Park to SW.

Doddridge (DAHD-rij), county (□ 321 sq mi/831 sq km; 1990 pop. 6,994), W W.Va.; ⊙ West Union; 39°15′N 80°42′W. On Allegheny Plateau; drained by Middle Island creek, McElroy creek, and South Fork of Hughes R. Agr. (potatoes, alfalfa, hay, apples); cattle; poultry. Some bituminous coal; timber. North Bend State Trail passes E-W through center of co. Formed 1845.

Dodds, locality, central Alta., Canada, 19 mi/31 km NE of Camrose; coal mining; wheat, oats, rye.

Doddsville, village (1990 pop. 149), Sunflower co., W Miss., 22 mi/35 km WNW of Greenwood, near Sunflower R.; 33°39′N 90°31′W. In cotton area.

Dodge 1 county (□ 503 sq mi/1,303 sq km; 1990 pop. 17,607), S central Ga.; ⊙ Eastman; 32°10′N 83°10′W. Bounded SW by Ocmulgee R.; drained by Little Ocmulgee R. Cotton, corn, peanuts, pecans, soybeans, tobacco, wheat; cattle, hogs; lumber; textile mfg. at Eastman. Formed 1870. **2** county (□ 439 sq mi/1,137 sq km; 1990 pop. 15,731), SE Minn.; ⊙ Mantorville; 44°01′N 92°51′W. Drained by South Fork Zumbro, Middle Fork Zumbro, and South Branch Middle Fork Zumbro rivers. Agr. area (soybeans, corn, oats, peas; sheep, hogs, cattle, poultry); dairying. Mfg. at Dodge Center and Kasson. Part of Rice Lake State Park on W boundary. Formed 1855. **3** county (□ 543 sq mi/1,406 sq km; 1990 pop. 34,500), E Nebr.; ⊙ Fremont; 41°34′N 96°39′W. Agr. region bounded S by Platte R.; drained by Elkhorn R. and Logan Creek. Cattle, hogs, corn, soybeans, sorghum, alfalfa, dairy, and poultry prods. Mfg. in Fremont. Dead Timber State Recreation Area in N; Fremont Lakes State Recreation Area in SE, W of Fremont. Formed 1854. **4** county (□ 907 sq mi/2,349 sq km; 1990 pop. 76,559), S central Wis.; ⊙ Juneau; 43°25′N 88°42′W. Drained by Rock R. and its tributaries, including Crawfish R.; contains Beaver Dam, Fox, and Sinissippi lakes. Horicon Natl. Wildlife Refuge and Horicon Marsh State Wildlife Area in N. Agr. (barley, oats, soybeans, peas, beans, alfalfa, hay, cherries; cattle, hogs, sheep, poultry); dairying. Processing of farm prods., light mfg., iron mining. Formed 1836.

Dodge, Mass.: see CHARLTON.

Dodge 1 village (1990 pop. 693), Dodge co., E Nebr., 27 mi/43 km NW of Fremont; 41°43′N 96°52′W. Grain, livestock; cheese. **2** village (1990 pop. 135), Dunn co., W central N.Dak., 20 mi/32 km WNW of Beulah and on Spring Creek; 47°18′N 102°12′W. **3** uninc. village (1990 pop. 150), Walker co., E Texas, 10 mi/16 km E of Huntsville, in N edge of Sam Houston Natl. Forest. In cotton growing, lumbering area. L. Somerville reservoir to N and NE.

Dodge, Camp, Iowa: see JOHNSTON.

Dodge Center, town (1990 pop. 1,954), Dodge co., SE Minn., 20 mi/32 km W of Rochester, near Dodge Center Creek; 44°01′N 92°50′W. Shipping point for agr. area (livestock, poultry; dairying; grain, soybeans, peas); mfg. (concrete mixers, printing and publishing). Settled 1853, inc. 1872.

Dodge City, city (1990 pop. 21,129), ⊙ Ford co., SW Kansas, on the Arkansas R.; elev. 2,484 ft/757 m; 37°45′N 100°01′W. RR junction. Distributing center for an extensive wheat and livestock area. Mfg. (truck, farm machinery, gears, printing and publishing, meat packing, feeds, fertilizers, agr. equip.). Laid out in 1872 near Fort Dodge (1864) on the old Santa Fe Trail, it flourished as the Santa Fe RR head and became a wild cow town; Wyatt Earp and Bat Masterson were among those who helped to curb lawlessness. Fort Dodge has become a soldiers' home. The city hall, formerly located on Boot Hill, an early cowboy burial ground, has been removed to permit enlargement of that tourist attraction. Front Street, with its famous Long Branch Saloon, has been restored. Dodge City Community Col. holds an annual rodeo. Inc. 1875.

Dodgeville, town (1990 pop. 3,882), ⊙ Iowa co., S Wis., 38 mi/61 km WSW of Madison; 42°57′N 90°07′W. Trade center for farm area (livestock, poultry), dairying. Mfg. (solar cells, wood prods.). Hq. of Land's End catalog sales. Architect Frank Lloyd Wright's houses, Taliesin and House on the Rock, to N. Black Hawk L. reservoir to NW; W terminus of Military Ridge State Trail; Governor Dodge State Park to N. Was center of early lead-mining industry. Settled 1827; inc. as village in 1858, as city in 1889.

Dodgeville, village, Houghton co., NW Upper Peninsula, Mich., 3 mi/4.8 km S of Houghton; 47°05′N 88°34′W. In former copper-mining area.

Dodsland, village (1991 pop. 269), SW Sask., Canada, 27 mi/43 km NE of Kindersley; 51°48′N 108°50′W. RR junction; wheat, livestock.

Dodson 1 (DAHD-suhn), village (1990 pop. 350), Winn parish, N central La., 12 mi/19 km N of Winnfield; 32°05′N 92°40′W. In agr., lumber, and gas field area. **2** village (1990 pop. 137), Phillips co., N Mont., on Milk R., and 17 mi/27 km W of Malta; 48°24′N 108°15′W. Cattle, wheat; mining. Fort Belknap Indian Reservation to SW. Weigand Reservoir to SW. Dodson Creek joins Milk R. 5 mi/8 km E. **3** village (1990 pop. 113), Collingsworth co., extreme N Texas, near Okla. line, 25 mi/40 km NNE of Childress and near Salt Fork of Red R.; 34°45′N 100°01′W. In wheat and cattle area.

Doe Hill, uninc. village, Highland co., NW Va., 28 mi/45 km NW of Staunton, near W. Va. state line; 38°25′N 79°26′W. Mfg. (organic maple syrup, fruit processing); agr. (sugar maples, fruit, alfalfa). George Washington Natl. Forest to SE.

Doe River, c.30 mi/48 km long, rises on Roan Mtn. in Carter co., NE Tenn., flows NNW around S end of Iron Mts. to Watauga L. at Elizabethton; 36°21′N 82°12′W.

Doerun (DO-ruhn), town (1990 pop. 899), Colquitt co., S Ga.,12 mi/19 km NW of Moultrie; 31°19′N 83°55′W.

Dog Island, islet of Leeward group, B.W.I., on Anegada Passage, 12 mi/19 km W of Anguilla; 18°17′N 63°16′W.

Dog Island (c.7 mi/11.3 km long), Franklin co., NW Fla., in the Gulf of Mexico; partly shelters St. George Sound.

Dog Lake (16 mi/26 km long, 5 mi/8 km wide), W Ont.,

Canada, 22 mi/35 km NW of Port Arthur; drained S by Kaministikwia R. into L. Superior.

Dog River, in Ala. and Miss.: see ESCATAWPA RIVER.

Dog River, c.25 mi/40 km long, rises in SW Washington co., central Vt., and flows NNE to the Winooski R. at Montpelier.

Dolan Springs, uninc. town (1990 pop. 1,090), Mohave co., NW Ariz., 29 mi/47 km NNW of Kingman, at N end of Cerbat Mts. Cattle; copper, molybdenum. Hoover Dam (forms L. Mead on Colorado R.) to NW.

Doland, village (1990 pop. 306), Spink co., NE central S.Dak., 20 mi/32 km E of Redfield; 44°53′N 98°05′W. Trade and wool-shipping point in productive agr. region. Grain; dairy produce; livestock, poultry.

Dolbeau (dahl-BO), town (1991 pop. 8,181), S central Que., Canada, on Mistassini R., near L. St. John, 60 mi/97 km NW of Jonquière; 48°52′N 72°14′W. Pulp and paper milling; dairying market. Inc. 1927.

Dolgeville, village (□ 1 sq mi/2.6 sq km; 1990 pop. 2,452), on Fulton-Herkimer co. line, central N.Y., on E. Canada Creek, 23 mi/37 km E of Utica; 43°06′N 74°46′W. Mfg. (textiles, wood prods., sporting goods, apparel, piano parts). Inc. 1891.

Dollar Bay, village, Houghton co., NW Upper Peninsula, Mich., 4 mi/6.4 km E of Houghton, on Portage L.; 44°07′N 88°30′W. Mfg. (wood flooring).

Dollar Point, uninc. town (1990 pop. 1,449), Placer co., E Calif., 3 mi/4.8 km NE of Tahoe City, on NW shore of L. Tahoe, at Dollar Point. Tahoe Nordic Ski Center is here; 39°11′N 120°07′W.

Dollard (DAH-luhrd), village (1991 pop. 33), SW Sask., Canada, in the Cypress Hills, 8 mi/13 km W of Shaunavon; elev. 3,029 ft/923 m; coal mining.

Dolliver, town (1990 pop. 103), Emmet co., NW Iowa, near Minn. state line, 12 mi/19 km ENE of Estherville; 43°27′N 94°36′W. State park on nearby Tuttle L.

Dollywood, family entertainment park, in Pigeon Forge, Sevier co., E Tenn., on the Little Pigeon R., and 7 mi/11 km S of Sevierville. Built by country singer Dolly Parton. Showcases Appalachian crafts, music, and traditions.

Dolomite (DAH-luh-meit), village, Jefferson co., N central Ala., a suburb just SW of Birmingham.

Dolores, county (□ 1,068 sq mi/2,766 sq km; 1990 pop. 1,504), SW Colo.; ⊙ Dove Creek, bounded by Utah on W; 37°45′N 108°31′W. Drained by Dolores R. (source in E part of co.). Zinc mining; cattle, wheat, hay, beans, sheep. San Miguel Range in NE. Includes parts of San Juan Natl. Forest in center and E. Formed 1881.

Dolores, town (1990 pop. 866), Montezuma co., SW Colo., on Dolores R. (forms McPhee Reservoir to NW), at mouth of Lost Canyon Creek, and 37 mi/60 km WNW of Durango; 37°28′N 108°30′W. Elev. 6,936 ft/2,114 m. In livestock region; aspen-wood paneling, lumber. Anasazi Heritage Center and Dominguez and Escalante Ruins to W on shore of McPhee Reservoir; Mesa Verde Natl. Park to S.

Dolores Hidalgo (do-LO-res ee-DAHL-go), city (1990 pop. 40,001) and township, Guanajuato, central Mexico, on central plateau, on RR, and 23 mi/37 km NE of Guanajuato on Mexico Highways 51 and 110; 21°10′N 100°56′W. Agr. center (wheat, corn, sugarcane, vegetables, fruit, livestock); flour milling; tanning; chinaware. Miguel Hidalgo y Costilla here initiated struggle for independence on Sept. 16, 1810. Formerly Ciudad Dolores Hidalgo Cuna de la Independencia Nacional.

Dolores, Mission, Calif.: see SAN FRANCISCO, city.

Dolores Peak, Colo.: see SAN MIGUEL MOUNTAINS.

Dolores River, c.250 mi/402 km long; in Colo. and Utah; rises near Dolores Peak and Mt. Wilson in San Miguel Mts., E Dolores co., San Juan Natl. Forest, SW Colo.; flows SW then NNW through McPhea Reservoir past Gateway, Colo., to Colorado R., 20 mi/32 km NE of Moab, Utah. Receives San Miguel R. 22 mi/35 km SSE of Gateway.

Dolphin and Union Strait (DAHL-fin), SW Franklin dist., N.W.T., Canada, arm of the Arctic Ocean, bet. Amundsen Gulf (W) and Coronation Gulf (E), separating Victoria Isl. (N) from Mackenzie dist. mainland; 100 mi/161 km long, 20 mi/32 km–40 mi/64 km wide; 69°N 113°30′–116°30′W. Strait forms part of Northwest Passage through the Arctic Isls.

Dolton 1 village (1990 pop. 23,930), Cook co., NE Ill., on the Little Calumet R., S of Chicago; 41°37′N 87°35′W. Mfg. (steel, aluminum prods., glass, chemicals). Settled 1832, inc. 1892. **2** village (1990 pop. 43), Turner co., SE S.Dak., 14 mi/23 km WNW of Parker; 43°29′N 97°22′W.

Dome Mines, Canada: see PORCUPINE.

Dome Peak (9,000 ft/2,743 m), SW Mackenzie dist., N.W.T., Canada, in Mackenzie Mts.; 61°32′N 126°56′W.

Dome Rock Mountains, N extension of Trigo Mts., in La Paz co., SW Ariz., E of Colorado R. (Calif. state line), SE of Colorado River Indian Reservation. Rises to 3,316 ft/1,011 m at Cunningham Mt.

Domingo Arenas, town, ⊙ Domingo Arenas municipio, Puebla, Mexico, 17 mi/27 km WNW of Puebla on E slopes of Iztaccihuatl volcano; 19°09′N 98°26′W. Elev. 8,038 ft/2,450 m. Poor road access. Agr., small farming (mainly for subsistence).

Domingues Hills, uninc. residential suburb of Los Angeles, Los Angeles co., S Calif, 8 mi/12.9 km S of city center, part of Carson city. Calif. State Univ. at Domingues Hill; educational software industry.

Dominica (do-MI-ni-kuh), island republic (1991 pop. 71,183) (□ 305 sq mi/790 sq km), ⊙ Roseau, in the Windward Isls., West Indies; 15°30′N 61°20′W. Roseau is the chief port. The isl., of volcanic origin, is mountainous and forested, with fertile soil, and is noted for its numerous (365) rivers. Bananas are the chief commercial crop and export, although citrus fruits and coconut oil are also exported, and farmers have begun growing marijuana as well. Economic progress was set back severely by 2 major hurricanes in 1979 and 1980, and although tourism is a growing industry, Dominica remains one of the poorest Caribbean nations. The isl. was sighted by Columbus in 1493. English and French attempts at settlement were thwarted by the Caribs, who had taken it earlier from the Arawaks. An Anglo-French treaty of 1748 left Dominica in Carib hands, but both powers continued to covet it. The island definitively passed to the British in 1815. Hostilities bet. the British and the Caribs led to the virtual extinction of the Caribs, who number about 500 and occupy a reservation on the eastern side of the island. Dominica gained independence in 1978. In 1981 there were 2 attempted political coups, both of which failed.

Dominica Passage, channel (c.20 mi/32 km wide) in Lesser Antilles, West Indies, bounded by Guadeloupe and Marie-Galante (N) and Dominica (S).

Dominican Republic, republic (1993 pop. 7,089,041), 18,700 sq mi/48,433 sq km, West Indies, ⊙ Santo Domingo; on the eastern ⅔ of the island of Hispaniola; 19°00′N 70°40′W. With a moderate subtropical climate, ample rainfall, and fertile soil, the country is predominantly agr. Sugarcane is the chief crop, and sugar is the chief product and export. Other major crops are coffee, cocoa, bananas, tobacco, and rice. There are deposits of rock salt, bauxite, copper, gold, silver, and nickel; mining; light industries. Tourism has become increasingly important: international resort areas include Puerto Plata on the N coast, and Boca Chica and La Romana on the S coast. The U.S. and Great Britain are the main trading partners. The majority of the pop. is of mixed African and European descent. Spanish is the official language and Roman Catholicism the state religion. Pop. growth is a problem, and emigration to the U.S., particularly to New York City, has been high. The 2 major parties are the Reformist party and the Dominican Revolutionary party. The history of the country has been turbulent and closely linked with that of the neighboring republic of Haiti. After Spain ceded the colony of Santo Domingo to France (1795), the area now known as the Dominican Republic was conquered by Haitians under Toussaint L'Ouverture. France, Haiti, and Spain fought for control until 1844, when the Haitians were defeated, a constitution was promulgated, and a republic was established under Pedro Santana. Frequent revolts as well as continued Haitian attacks led Santana to make his country a province of Spain in 1861, but opposition was so severe that Spain withdrew in 1865. When the U.S. Senate failed to ratify a treaty of annexation, all semblance of order vanished. A long (1882–1899), ruthless dictatorship under Ulíses Heureaux ended with his assassination and was followed by more revolutions. The republic was bankrupt by 1905 and faced intervention by European powers. U.S. President Theodore Roosevelt arranged a U.S. customs receivership. Disorder continued, however, and the country was occupied by U.S. marines in 1916. They were withdrawn in 1924 and the customs receivership terminated in 1941. In 1930, Rafael Trujillo Molina became dictator. In 1937, Dominican troops massacred thousands of immigrant Haitians and war was narrowly averted. Material improvements in roads, agr., sanitation, and education contributed to the prolongation of the regime. Feuds with other Caribbean nations developed. In 1961, Trujillo was assassinated. Joaquín Balaguer, who had been named president by Trujillo in 1960, initiated democratization measures, withstood attempts by the Trujillo family to regain power, and promulgated (1962) a new constitution. In Dec. 1962, in their first free election since 1924, the Dominicans elected Juan Bosch president by a substantial majority. Right-wing opposition led to his overthrow in 1963. In 1965 military supporters of Bosch toppled the govt. In 1966, with Bosch and Balaguer the leading candidates, an election was held. Balaguer, the Social Christian Reform party (PRSC) candidate, won and took office on July 1. The authoritarianism of the Trujillo period continued under Balaguer, who enjoyed the support of the right, the military, and the church. Balaguer was reelected in 1970 and 1974. The political climate, however, remained uneasy, with the economy stagnant and many workers emigrating to the U.S. and Puerto Rico. From 1978 to 1986 the Dominican Revolutionary party (PRD) won the presidency. However, rising prices resulting from a program of economic austerity cost the PRD, as Balaguer was elected in 1986 and again in 1990. In 1996 Leonel Fernández was elected to succeed him.

Dominion, town (1991 pop. 2,517), NE N.S., Canada, on NE coast of Cape Breton Isl., near E side of Glace Bay, 15 mi/24 km E of Sydney; 46°13′N 60°01′W. Coal-mining center. Inc. 1906.

Dominion, Md.: see KENT ISLAND.

Dominion City, village, S Man., Canada, on Roseau R., and 50 mi/80 km S of Winnipeg; 49°08′N 97°09′W. Grain elevators, lumbering.

Domino Harbour, settlement on Isl. of Ponds (10 mi/16 km long, 9 mi/14 km wide), off SE Lab., Canada; 53°27′N 55°45′W; fishing port and seaplane anchorage. Lighthouse.

Domremy, village (1991 pop. 150), central Sask., Canada, near small Pelican L., 28 mi/45 km S of Prince Albert; 52°47′N 105°44′W. Mixed farming, dairying.

Don Martín Dam, Mexico: see PRESA VENUSTIANO CARRANZA.

Don Pedro Lake, c.30 mi/48 km long; Tuolumne co., E Calif., on Tuolumne R., 33 mi/53 km WNW of Modesto, at W edge of Sierra Nevada mts.; elev. 801 ft/244 m; 37°41′N 120°24′W. Extends N (crossed here by Hetch Hetchy Aqueduct); max. capacity 2,030,000 acre-ft. Formed by Don Pedro Dam (513 ft/156 m high), built (1971) for hydroelectricity and irrigation.

Doña Ana (DON-yuh A-nuh), county (□ 3,804 sq mi/9,852 sq km), S N.Mex.; ⊙ Las Cruces. Irrigated agr. and livestock area; watered by Rio Grande; bounded S by Texas and Mexico (Chihuahua state). Cattle, sheep; dairying; chiles, jalapenos, onions, lettuce, pecans, cotton, corn, hay, alfalfa, sorghum wheat, spinach, triticale, melons, cabbage, fruit, nuts. Stone. Organ Mts. in E, part of White Sands Natl. Monument in NE. Formed 1852. Acquirre Springs Natl. Recreation Area in E; Leasburg Dam State Park and Fort Selden State Monument in N center; part of large White Sands Missile Range, including White Sands Space Harbor (landing site of space shuttle), in NE corner.

Dona Ana (DON-uh A-nuh), uninc. town (1990 pop. 1,202), Dona Ana co., S N.Mex., suburb 4 mi/6.4 km

NNW of Las Cruces, near Rio Grande; 32°23′N 106°49′W. Irrigated area with varied agr. Mfg. (cement slabs).

Doña Juana (DO-nah HWAH-nah), cascades, rivulet, reservoir, mt. (over 3,500 ft/1,067 m), and recreational area, central P.R., 32 mi/51 km SW of San Juan. Nearby (W) is one of the Toro Negro hydroelectric plants.

Donahue, town (1990 pop. 316), Scott co., E Iowa, 12 mi/19 km NNW of Davenport. In agr. area.

Donald, village (1990 pop. 316), Marion co., NW Oregon, 20 mi/32 km NNW of Salem, and 25 mi/40 km SSW of Portland; 45°13′N 122°50′W. Fruit, vegetables; dairy prods. Champoeg State Park to W.

Donalda (duh-NAL-duh), village (1991 pop. 221), S central Alta., Canada, near Buffalo L., 30 mi/48 km SSE of Camrose; 52°35′N 112°34′W. Coal mining; oil and gas; wheat, oats, barley, cattle.

Donalds, village (1990 pop. 326), Abbeville co., NW S.C., 18 mi/29 km ESE of Anderson; 34°22′N 82°20′W. Mfg. includes machining, hardwood lumber.

Donaldson 1 village (1990 pop. 57), Kittson co., NW Minn., 14 mi/23 km S of Hallock, in Red R. valley; 48°34′N 96°54′W. Grain, sugar beets, mustard; mfg. (mustard processing, mustard seeds). Red R. 11 mi/18 km to W. **2** uninc. village, Frailey township, Schuylkill co., E central Pa., 12 mi/19 km WSW of Pottsville, and 1 mi/1.6 km NW of Tremont, on Good Spring Creek; 40°38′N 76°24′W.

Donaldsonville (DAH-nuhld-suhn-vil), city (1990 pop. 7,949), ⊙ Ascension parish, SE La., on W bank (levee) of the Mississippi R., at the exit of Bayou Lafourche, and 27 mi/43 km SSE of Baton Rouge; 30°06′N 91°00′W. RR junction to W. In agr. area (sugarcane, vegetables; cattle, ostriches, crawfish, alligators; sugar milling; mfg. (ammonia, carbon dioxide, pipes, fittings, agr. equipment, snack foods); printing; oil and natural gas wells nearby. Architect H. H. Richardson b. nearby. Area known for antebellum plantations. The Catholic church possesses records from 1772, the oldest in the state. Founded 1806 as trading post; inc. 1822; temporary state capitol, 1830.

Donalsonville (DAHN-uhl-suhn-vil), town (1990 pop. 2,761), ⊙ Seminole co., extreme SW Ga., 21 mi/34 km WNW of Bainbridge; 31°02′N 84°53′W. Mfg. includes peanut and almond processing equip., cotton and peanut processing, fertilizer, clothing. Inc. 1897.

Donato Guerra (do-NAH-to GE-rah), town (1990 pop. 804), Mexico state, central Mexico, 30 mi/48 km W of Toluca de Lerdo; 24°38′N 104°40′W. Grain, fruit, livestock. Formerly Asunción Donato Guerra.

Dondon (DONG-DONG), agr. town (1982 pop. 3,419), Nord dept., N Haiti, in the Massif du Nord, 18 mi/29 km S of Cap-Haïtien; 19°32′N 72°14′W. Oranges, limes, cacao, coffee growing and processing.

Donegal (DAH-nuh-guhl), borough (1990 pop. 212), Westmoreland co., SW Pa., 13 mi/21 km ESE of Mount Pleasant; 40°06′N 79°22′W. Some agr. (livestock, dairying). Forbes State Forest to SE; Donegal L. reservoir to NE; Chestnut Ridge to NW; Laurel Hill ridge to SE.

Donelson (DAH-nuhl-suhn), village, Davidson co., N central Tenn., a residential suburb 6 mi/10 km E of Nashville; 36°10′N 86°40′W.

Doneraile (DAHN-uh-rail), village, Darlington co., NE S.C., suburb 2 mi/3.2 km NW of Darlington.

Dongan Hills, sect. of State Isl. borough of N.Y. city, SE N.Y., on E Staten Isl., 4 mi/6.4 km SSW of St. George; 40°35′N 74°08′W. Todt Hill (elev. c.409 ft/125 m), highest point of isl., is here.

Dongola (don-GO-lah), village (1990 pop. 728), Union co., S Ill., 8 mi/12.9 km SE of Jonesboro; 37°21′N 89°09′W. Fruit, sweet potatoes, vegetables.

Doniphan (DAH-ni-fuhn), county (□ 397 sq mi/1,028 sq km; 1990 pop. 8,134), extreme NE Kansas; ⊙ Troy; 39°47′N 95°09′W. Fertile agr. area in the Loess Hills region (hilly in E), bounded E and N by Missouri R. and Mo. Poultry, cattle, hogs, corn, wheat, strawberries, hay, apples; dairying. Iowa Sac and Fox Indian Mission E of Highland. NE co. touches Nebr. border. Formed 1855.

Doniphan (DAH-ni-fuhn), city (1990 pop. 1,713), ⊙ Ripley co., S Mo., in Ozark region, on Current R., and 27 mi/43 km WSW of Poplar Bluff; 36°37′N 90°49′W. Resort, recreation. Agr. center. Apples; lumber prods.; gravel quarries; mfg. (steel forging, vinyl prods.); tourism. Mark Twain Nat'l Forest to NE. Settled c.1847.

Doniphan (DAW-ni-fen), village (1990 pop. 736), Hall co., S central Nebr., 10 mi/16 km S of Grand Island, and near Platte R; 40°46′N 9°22′W. Mfg. (small arms ammunition, sports equipment). Mormon Isl. State Wayside to N.

Donjek River (DAHN-jek), SW Yukon, Canada, 150 mi/241 km long, rises in St. Elias Mts. near 61°15′N 139°35′W, flows generally N to White R., 20 mi/32 km NE of Snag.

Donkin (DAHNG-kin), village, NE N.S., Canada, on Glace Bay, 2 mi/3 km SE of Glace Bay town; 46°11′N 59°52′W. Coal mining.

Donley, county (□ 933 sq mi/2,416 sq km; 1990 pop. 3,696), N Texas, in the Panhandle; ⊙ Clarendon. Lies just below the high plains; elev. 2,500 ft/3,200 ft–762 m/975 m; 34°57′N 100°48′W. Traversed by Salt Fork of Red R. (forming Greenbelt Reservoir in W center). Wheat, hay, cotton, peanuts, sorghum; cattle, horses, and hogs. Formed 1876.

Donna, city (1990 pop. 12,652), Hidalgo co., extreme S Texas, 12 mi/19 km E of McAllen, in lower Rio Grande valley; elev. 88 ft/27 m; 26°10′N 98°02′W. A shipping, processing center in rich irrigated farmland (citrus, vegetables); cotton; mfg. (signs, canned tomatoes, and chili). Santa Ana Nat'l Wildlife Refuge to SW. Founded c.1902.

Donnacona (dah-nuh-KO-nuh), town (1991 pop. 5,659), S Que., Canada, on St. Lawrence R., at mouth of Jacques Cartier R., and 26 mi/42 km WSW of Quebec; 46°40′N 71°47′W. Pulp milling, dairying center.

Donnan, town (1990 pop. 7), Fayette co., NE Iowa, 5 mi/8 km SW of West Union. RR junction.

Donnellson, town (1990 pop. 940), Lee co., SE Iowa, 12 mi/19 km W of Fort Madison; 40°38′N 91°33′W. In livestock and grain area.

Donnellson, village (1990 pop. 167), in Montgomery co., S central Ill., 20 mi/32 km WNW of Vandalia; 39°01′N 89°28′W. In agr. area (corn, wheat; dairy prods.; livestock). Near Coffeen L.

Donnelly (DAHN-nuh-lee), village (1991 pop. 421), W Alta., Canada, 35 mi/56 km S of Peace R.; 55°44′N 117°07′W. Highway junction. Logging; mixed farming, oats, wheat.

Donnelly 1 village (1990 pop. 135), Valley co., W Idaho, 52 mi/84 km NE of Weiser, on E side of Cascade Reservoir (North Fork Payette R.), bridged here; 44°44′N 116°05′W. Timber; cattle; tourism. Parts of Payette Nat'l. Forest to E and W; parts of Boise Natl. Forest to SE and SW. **2** village (1990 pop. 221), Stevens co., W Minn., 8 mi/12.9 km NW of Morris; 45°41′N 96°00′W. Grain, sunflowers; livestock; mfg. (fertilizer, draperies).

Donnelsville, village (1990 pop. 276), Clark co., W central Ohio, 6 mi/10 km W of Springfield; 39°55′N 83°57′W.

Donner Lake, glacial lake (c.3 mi/4.8 km long; elev. 5,939 ft/1,810 m), Nevada co., E Calif. In summer and winter resort in the Sierra Nevada, 12 mi/19 km NNW of Tahoe City, 3 mi/4.8 km W of Truckee. Site of Donner Memorial State Park (Nev.-Placer cos.) in honor of ill-fated Donner Party, a group of pioneer emigrants who perished at Donner Pass to W (1846); 352 acres/142 ha N of Donner L. was site of the first encampment, on historic Emigrant Trail. Tahoe Donner Ski Area to N.

Donner Pass (elev. 7,239 ft/2,206 m), mountain pass in the Sierra Nevada, Nevada co., E Calif., c.35 mi/56 km WSW of Reno, Nev. Between Truckee R. system (E) and Yuba R. system (W). Interstate Highway 80 (formerly U.S. Highway 40) passes through. U.S. Weather Bureau observatory here. Norden Tunnel carries RR under summit of pass. Donner L. is just E. Site of attempted crossing of Donner Party wagon train, winter of 1846–1847; many members starved or froze to death. Emigrant Trail Mus.

Donner und Blitzen River, c.60 mi/97 km long, Harney co., SE Oregon; rises on W side of Steens Mt.; flows N to Malheur L. (no outlet). Most of lower course is marshy, and within Malheur Natl. Wildlife Refuge.

Donnybrook, village (1990 pop. 106), Ward co., NW central N.Dak., 34 mi/55 km W of Minot, and on Des Lacs R.; 48°30′N 101°53′W. Des Lacs Natl. Wildlife Refuge to NW and Upper Souris Natl. Wildlife Refuge to NE.

Donora (duh-NOR-ah), borough (1990 pop. 5,928), Washington co., SW Pa., 19 mi/31 km SSE of Pittsburgh, on Monongahela R.; 40°10′N 79°51′W. Printing, ammonium nitrate, rebuilt mining equipment, refuse-hauling equipment, plastics, apparel; corn, hay; livestock, dairying. Inc. 1901.

Donovan, village (1990 pop. 361), Iroquois co., E Ill., 20 mi/32 km SE of Kankakee, near Ind. line; 40°53′N 87°36′W. Agr. (corn, soybeans).

Dooling, town (1990 pop. 28), Dooly co., Ga., 11 mi/18 km ENE of Andersonville; 32°14′N 83°56′W.

Doolittle, village, (1990 pop. 599), Phelps co., central Mo., 5 mi/8 km W of Rolla, near Little Piney Creek. On N edge of Mark Twain Natl. Forest. Timber. Recreation.

Dooly, county (□ 394; 1990 pop. 9,901), central Ga.; ⊙ Vienna; 32°10′N 83°48′W. Bounded W by Flint R. Coastal plain agr. Cotton, corn, soybeans, wheat, peanuts, pecans; cattle, hogs, poultry; timber. Formed 1821.

Dooms, uninc. town, Augusta co., NW Va., 3 mi/4.8 km N of Waynesboro, on South R.; 38°06′N 78°50′W. Dairying, livestock; apples, grain, soybeans.

Doon, town (1990 pop. 476), Lyon co., NW Iowa, 11 mi/18 km SSW of Rock Rapids, near confluence of Little Rock and Rock rivers, in livestock and grain area; 43°16′N 96°13′W.

Doon, village, S Ont., Canada, 6 mi/10 km SE of Kitchener. Dairying, mixed farming.

Door, county (□ 2,369 sq mi/6,136 sq km; 1990 pop. 25,690), NE Wis., on Door Peninsula, bounded E by L. Michigan, W by Green Bay; ⊙ Sturgeon Bay; 45°01′N 87°00′W. Includes Washington and Chambers isls. Fishing; dairying; barley, oats, wheat, peas, beans, cherries, cranberries, apples; quarrying at Sturgeon Bay city. A resort area, the co. contains Peninsula State Park in W center and Potawatomi State Park in SW. Newport and Rock Isl. state parks in NE; Whitefish Dunes State Park in E center; N end of Ahnapee State Trail in S. Formed 1851.

Door Peninsula, 80 mi/129 km long, 25 mi/40 km wide at base, NE Wis., bet. Green Bay (W) and L. Michigan (E); a canal at Sturgeon Bay bisects the peninsula about halfway. Includes all of Door co. and parts of Kewaunee and Browa cos.Tourism is the chief industry. Also cherries; dairying.The peninsula was visited as early as the 17th cent. by Fr. explorers and missionaries. Later settled by Icelandic people, especially at N end. Sturgeon Bay, Algoma, Ellison Bay, Fish Creek, and Egg Harbor are among the towns located on the peninsula (city of Green Bay is at W side of its base). Potawomi, Peninsula, Whitefish Dunes, and Newport state parks. Rock Isl. State Park is beyond end of peninsula.

d'Or, Cape (dor), on Bay of Fundy, NW N.S., Canada, on N side of entrance of Minas Channel, 20 mi/32 km NW of Kentville; 45°18′N 64°46′W.

Dora, town (1990 pop. 2,214), Walker co., NW central Ala., 14 mi/23 km ESE of Jasper. In industrial area.

Dora (DOR-uh), uninc. village (1990 pop. 167), Roosevelt co., E N.Mex., 17 mi/27 km S of Portales; 33°55′N 103°20′W. Livestock, grain, alfalfa, vegetables, cotton. Grulla Natl. Wilderness Refuge to NE.

Dora, Lake (DOR-ruh), c.6 mi/9.7 km long, 1 mi/1.6 km wide, Lake co., central Fla., near Tavares. Connected by waterways with Eustis L. (N) and Apopka L. (S), it is part of central Fla. lake system drained by Oklawaha R.

Dorado (do-RAH-do), town (1990 pop. 30,759), N P.R., at mouth of the La Plata, 10 mi/16 km W of San Juan. Tourist resort. Light mfg. Many residents travel to San Juan to work. Airport 1.5 mi/2.4 km W.

Doran (DOR-uhn), village (1990 pop. 78), Wilkin co., W Minn., 7 mi/11.3 km SE of Breckenridge, bet. Otter Tail and Bois de Sioux rivers, near Doran Slough; 46°11'N 96°29'W. Grain, sunflowers; livestock; mfg. (plant fertilizer).

Doraville (DOR-uh-vil), town (1990 pop. 7,626), De Kalb co., NW central Ga., suburb 11 mi/18 km NNE of Atlanta; 33°55'N 84°16'W. Rapidly diversifying demographic mix of Hispanic, Asian, and Afr.-Amer. pops. Mfg. includes motor vehicle assembly, printing, concrete, contact lenses, paper prods., plastics, air filtration systems. Major gasoline storage tank farm. Site of the northernmost station on the metropolitan Atlanta Rapid Transit Authority's NE RR line.

Dorcheat, Bayou (dor-CHEET), river, c.115 mi/185 km long, in Ark. and La.; rises in Nevada co., SW Ark.; flows generally S into La., through Webster parish, to N end of L. Bistineau.

Dorchester (DOR-chis-tuhr), county (☐ 842 sq mi/ 2,181 sq km), S Que., Canada, on Maine border; ☉ Ste. Hénédine; 46°25'N 70°35'W.

Dorchester 1 (DOR-che-stuhr), county (☐ 982 sq mi/ 2,543 sq km; 1990 pop. 30,236), E Md.; ☉ Cambridge; 38°25'N 76°05'W. Marsh-fringed peninsula on the Eastern Shore, bounded E by Del. state line. Isls. belonging to co. in Chesapeake Bay include Barren, Hooper, and Bloodsworth. Shores are indented by many inlets. The rolling land is well suited for growing fruit (especially cantaloupes) because of the loamy clay soil as well as the long, hot summers; also vegetables (especially tomatoes), barley, soybeans, corn, wheat. Dairy prods., poultry; large seafood industry (fish, crabs, oysters); vegetable and seafood canneries and packing houses; lumber and flour mills; boatyards. Marshes (W ½ of co.) are center of state's muskrat-trapping industry. Sport fishing, duck hunting, yachting attract visitors. Includes Blackwater Natl. Wildlife Refuge, which is a resting and feeding area for migrant and wintering waterfowl, notably huge flocks of Canada geese. Rare Delmarva fox squirrel may be seen. Twenty percent of the area of the co. is water, but its land area makes it the largest co. on the E shore. **2** county (☐ 577 sq mi/ 1,494 sq km; 1990 pop. 83,060), S S.C.; ☉ Saint George. In Outer Coastal Plain region, bounded S by Edisto R. Mfg. includes polypropylene fabric, fuel injectors, portland cement, office supplies, food casings. Corn, soybeans; hogs; cattle; timber. Named after town founded in 1697 on Ashley R. Tabby ruins of colonial fort, ruins of Saint George's Parish Church, and tombstones at Old Fort Dorchester State Park. Health resorts attracted tourists (early 18th–mid-20th cent.) Proximity to Charleston and Middleton Gardens on Ashley R. stimulates contemporary tourism.

Dorchester, town (1990 pop. 392), Grafton co., W central N.H., 12 mi/19 km W of Plymouth; 43°46'N 71°59'W. Drained by South Branch Baker and Mascoma rivers. Poultry, cattle; dairying; nursery crops; timber. Part of Province Road State Forest in SE.

Dorchester, village (1991 pop. 848), ☉ Westermorland co., SE N.B., Canada, on Memramcook R., just above its mouth on Shepody Bay, 18 mi/29 km SE of Moncton; 45°54'N 64°31'W. In wheat-growing region. Dominion penitentiary. Near by are sandstone quarries, salt and copper mines.

Dorchester 1 village (1990 pop. 145), Macoupin co., SW Ill., 20 mi/32 km NE of Alton; 39°05'N 89°53'W. In agr. and bituminous coal area. **2** (DOR-che-stuhr), village (1990 pop. 614), Saline co., SE Nebr., 17 mi/27 km S of Seward; 40°38'N 97°06'W. Flour, grain. **3** village (1990 pop. 697), Clark co., central Wis., 34 mi/55 km WNW of Wausau; 45°00'N 90°19'W. In dairying region: cheese, butter; dairy equipment; manufactured homes, forage boxes; poultry hatchery; stone quarries.

Dorchester, Mass.: see BOSTON.

Dorchester Bay, Mass.: see BOSTON BAY.

Dorchester, Cape (DOR-chis-tuhr), SW Baffin Isl., N.W.T., Canada, NW extremity of Foxe Peninsula, on Foxe Channel; 65°29'N 77°50'W.

Dorchester Station, village, S Ont., Canada, on Middle Thames R., and 10 mi/16 km E of London. Dairying, mixed farming, fruitgrowing.

Doré Lake (do-RAI) (☐ 248 sq mi/642 sq km), central

Sask., Canada, 120 mi/193 km NNW of Prince Albert; 24 mi/39 km long, 18 mi/29 km wide.

Dorena Dam oregon: see COAST FORK.

Dorgali, , village, Cumberland co., S N.J., on Maurice R., and 9 mi/14.5 km SSE of Millville. Shipbuilding; sand pits.

Dorion (DAH-ree-o), suburban town (1991 pop. 5,920), S Que., Canada, on Ottawa R., opposite Ile Perrot, 25 mi/40 km WSW of Montreal; 45°23'N 74°01'W. Vegetable gardening. Bridge to Ile Perrot and Montreal Isl.

Dorion Peak, Idaho: see LOST RIVER RANGE.

Dorion Station, village, W central Ont., Canada, on Black Bay of L. Superior, 40 mi/64 km NE of Thunder Bay. Mixed farming.

Dormont (DOR-mahnt), borough (1990 pop. 9,772), Allegheny co., SW Pa., residential suburb 4 mi/6.4 km SW of downtown Pittsburgh; 40°23'N 80°02'W. Bakery prods. Settled c.1790, inc. 1909.

Dorneyville (DOR-nee-vil), uninc. town (1990 pop. 1,460), Lehigh co., E Pa., residential suburb 4 mi/ 6.4 km SW of Allentown, near Little Lehigh Creek; 40°34'N 75°31'W. Dorney Park (theme park) to W; Bieber Farmhome historical site to S; Allentown Queen City airport to W.

Dorothy, uninc. village (1990 pop. 500), Raleigh co., S W.Va., 20 mi/32 km SSE of Charleston, in coal-mining region. Has Union cemetery.

Dorrance (DOR-uhns), village (1990 pop. 195), Russell co., central Kansas, 15 mi/24 km E of Russell, near Smoky Hill R.; 38°51'N 98°35'W. In livestock and grain region. Wilson L. Reservoir and Wilson State Park to N.

Dorris, city (1990 pop. 892), Siskiyou co., N Calif., 20 mi/ 32 km SSW of Klamath Falls, Oregon and 35 mi/56 km ENE of Yreka, 4 mi/6.4 km S of Oregon state boundary; 41°58'N 121°55'W. Agr. (cattle, sheep; grain). Klamath Natl. Forest to S and SE; Lower Klamath Natl. Wildlife Refuge to E, Tule L. Natl. Wildlife Refuge to E, beyond Lower Klamath; Lava Beds Natl. Monument 20 mi/32 km to SE.

Dorrisville, Ill.: see HARRISBURG.

Dorset, town (1990 pop. 1,918), Bennington co., SW Vt., just N of Manchester, in a valley of Taconic Mts.; resort, with Bromley Mt. ski area nearby; 43°16'N 73°02'W. Lumber, dairy prods., maple sugar. Dorset Peak (3,804 ft/1,159 m) is NE of Dorset village. First commercial marble quarry in U.S. opened here, 1785. Conventions which led to independent Vt. held in Dorset, 1775 and 1776.

Dortches (DORCH-uhs), town (1990 pop. 840), Nash co., NE central N.C., residential suburb 5 mi/8 km NW of Rocky Mount; 36°00'N 77°51'W. Nash Community Col. to SW.

Dorton, uninc. town (1990 pop. 800), Pike co., E Ky., 13 mi/21 km SSW of Pikeville. Bituminous coal. Coal processing.

Dorval (dor-VAHL), city (1991 pop. 17,249), S Que., Canada, on the S shore of Montreal Isl., and on the St. Lawrence R.; 45°27'N 73°45'W. Site of 1 of Montreal's intl. airports.

Dos Bocas (DOS BO-kahs), hydroelectric project, NW central P.R., at confluence of Arecibo and Caonillas rivers, 10 mi/16 km S of Arecibo. Consists of artificial lake, dam, and hydroelectric plant. Completed 1943. Caonillas dam, reservoir, and hydroelectric plant, just SE, dedicated 1949.

Dos Cabezas, uninc. village, Cochise co., SE Ariz., 14 mi/23 km SE of Willcox. Chiricahua Natl. Monument is SE; Fort Bowie Natl. Historic Site is E; Dos Cabezas Mts. to N.

Dos Cabezas Mountains, Cochise co., SE Ariz., c.15 mi/ 24 km E of Willcox. Separated from Chiricahua Mts. by Apache Pass. Highest point is Dos Cabezias, peak with 2 summits, 8,369 ft/2,551 m and 8,363 ft/2,549 m.

Dos Caminos (DOS kah-MEE-noz), town, Santiago de Cuba prov., E Cuba, on RR, and 12 mi/19 km N of Santiago de Cuba; 20°11'N 75°48'W. Sugarcane, coffee, fruit.

Dos Palos, city (1990 pop. 4,196), Merced co., central

Calif., in San Joaquin Valley, 20 mi/32 km SSW of Merced; 37°00'N 120°39'W. Dairying; alfalfa; melons, sweet potatoes, beans, tomatoes, grain; poultry. Merced and San Luis natl. wildlife refuges to N. Inc. 1935.

Dos Ríos (DOS REE-oz), sugar-mill town, Santiago de Cuba prov., E Cuba, 40 mi/64 km NW of Santiago de Cuba; 20°14'N 76°00'W. Site of 1895 battle in which Martí, hero of Cuban independence, was killed. Has monument to him.

Dos Ríos (dos REE-os), town (1990 pop. 137), central E Veracruz, Mexico, 9 mi/14 km SE of Xalapa Enríquez on Mexico Highway 140; ☉ Emiliano Zapata municipio. Elev. 2,904 ft/885 m. Hot humid climate. Agr. (corn, beans, coffee, chile, sugarcane, fruits), cattle, poultry raising, and woods.

Dosewallips River (do-see-WAH-lips), c.35 mi/56 km long, in NW Wash.; rises in S part of Olympic Natl. Park near Mt. Anderson (7,365 ft/2,245 m), flows E through Olympic Natl. Forest to Hood Canal.

Dosquet (dahs-KAI), village, S Que., Canada, 28 mi/ 45 km SW of Quebec; 46°28'N 71°31'W. Lumbering, dairying.

Doswell, uninc. village, Hanover co., E central Va., 7 mi/ 11.3 km N of Ashland, near North Anna R; 37°51'N 77°27'W. RR junction. Mfg. (feeds, mulch processing, lumber and paper, crushed stone, metal racks); agr. (grain, soybeans, tobacco; poultry, cattle, dairying); limestone. King's Dominion Amusement Park to S.

Dot Lake, village (1990 pop. 53), E central Alaska, c.50 mi/80 km SE of Delta Junction, near Tanana R.; 63°38'N 144°03'W. Services center on Alaska Highway almost midway bet. Delta Junction and Tok (to 3E). Headquarters of Dot Lake (Athabascan) Indian Corporation.

Dothan (DO-thuhn), city (1990 pop. 53,589), ☉ Houston co., SE Ala., near the Fla. state line, in a timber and peanut-growing area. Industrial and farm trade center. Diverse mfg. includes fertilizer, motor vehicle parts, food processing. Farley Nuclear Power Plant, George C. Wallace State Community Col., and Troy State Univ. at Dothan are here. Hot mineral springs. A natl. peanut festival is held here every Nov. Inc. 1885.

Dotsero, village, Eagle co., NW Colo., on Colorado R., at mouth of Eagle R., and 12 mi/19 km W of Eagle; elev. c.6,160 ft/1,878 m. Dotsero cutoff (completed 1934) is 38 mi/61 km stretch of RR track extending NE from Dotsero along Colorado R. It links 2 RRs and, with Moffat Tunnel, shortens route from Denver to Salt Lake City, Utah, by 173 mi/278 km. Glenwood Canyon to W. Rail junction to S. Parts of White River Natl. Forest to W and SE.

Double Mer (DOO-bluh MER), lake (35 mi/56 km long, 4 mi/6 km wide, SE Lab., Canada, N of L. Melville, and W of Hamilton Inlet, into which it drains at Rigolet, through 20 mi/32 km long channel; 54°5'N 59°W.

Double Springs, town (1990 pop. 1,138), ☉ Winston co., NW Ala., 32 mi/51 km W of Cullman. Lumber, mobile home mfg., fiberglass tubs, industrial trailers, windows.

Double Top Mountain (3,905 ft/1,190 m), Ulster co., SE N.Y., in the Catskills, 27 mi/43 km WNW of Kingston; 42°02'N 74°32'W.

Doubletop Peak (11,715 ft/3,571 m), on Teton-Sublette cos. boundary, W Wyo., 26 mi/42 km ESE of Jackson. Highest point in Gros Ventre Range.

Doucette, uninc. village (1990 pop. 131), Tyler co., E Texas, c.55 mi/89 km NNW of Beaumont, and 3 mi/ 4.8 km N of Livingston. In agr. and timber area.

Dougherty (DO-uhr-tee), county (☐ 335 sq mi/ 868 sq km; 1990 pop. 96,311), SW Ga.; ☉ Albany; 31°32'N 84°13'W. Intersected by Flint R. Coastal plain agr. (corn, soybeans, peanuts, pecans, cotton, wheat); cattle, dairying; limestone quarries; timber. Formed 1853.

Dougherty 1 village (1990 pop. 308), Cerro Gordo co., N central Iowa, 16 mi/26 km. SSE of Mason City; 42°55'N 93°02'W. Dairying; cattle, corn, hogs. **2** (DO-uhr-tee), village (1990 pop. 138), Murray co., S Okla., 9 mi/14.5 km SSW of Sulphur, on Washita R.; 34°23'N 97°02'W. Dairying. Recreation. Arbuckle Reservoir and Chicksaw Natl. Recreation Area to NE.

Douglas 1 county (□ 842 sq mi/2,181 sq km; 1990 pop. 60,391), central Colo.; ⊙ Castle Rock; 39°21′N 104°55′W. Located between Denver (N) and Colorado Springs (S). Bounded on W by South Platte R. (forms Chatfield and Cheesman reservoirs). W part extends into Front Range of the Rocky Mts., including part of Pike Natl. Forest; remainder of co. on W edge of Great Plains. Drained by Plum and Cherry creeks. Agr. (wheat, oats, fruit, vegetables; cattle); timber. NW corner has experienced some urbanization from Denver area to N. Castlewood Canyon State Park in E; Roxborough State Park in NW. **2** county (□ 200 sq mi/518 sq km; 1990 pop. 71,120), W Ga.; ⊙ Douglasville; 33°42′N 84°46′W. Suburban community W of Atlanta. Cattle, poultry. **3** county, (474 sq mi/1,228 sq km; 1990 pop. 81,798) E Kansas; ⊙ Lawrence; 38°52′N 95°17′W. Rolling prairie; hilly near rivers. Bounded on N, and drained by, Kansas (Kaw) R. and by Wakarusa R., which forms the large Clinton Lake, a recreational area for Univ. of Kansas and city of Lawrence. Clinton State Park on N shore. Douglas State Fishing L. in SE. Cattle, corn, sorghum, soybeans. Limestone quarries. Mfg. at Lawrence. **4** county (□ 719 sq mi/1,862 sq km; 1990 pop. 28,674), W Minn.; ⊙ Alexandria; 45°56′N 95°27′W. Watered by Long Prairie, Chippewa, and Little Chippewa rivers. Resort and agr. area (wheat, corn, oats, barley, alfalfa, hay; sheep, hogs, cattle, poultry; dairying). Lake Carlos State Park in E center; numerous natural lakes, including L. Miltona in NE, L. Christina in NW corner. **5** county (□ 809 sq mi/2,095 sq km; 1990 pop. 11,876), S Mo.; ⊙ Ava; 36°55′N 92°30′W. In the Ozarks; drained by North Fork of White R. Corn, hay, apples; dairy and beef cattle, poultry; oak timber; tourism. Mfg. at Ava. Parts of Mark Twain Natl. Forest in E and SW corners. Formed 1857. **6** county (□ 339 sq mi/878 sq km; 1990 pop. 416,444), E Nebr.; ⊙ Omaha; 41°17′N 96°09′W. Industrial region bounded W by Platte R., E by Missouri R. and Iowa; drained by Elkhorn R. Mfg. and food processing at Omaha; cattle, dairying, hogs, corn. Two Rivers State Recreation Area in SW; Glen Cunningham L. and Standing Bear L. both local recreation areas NW of Omaha (city limits extend out to them). Boys Town, municipality administered by homeless boys and girls, estab. 1919 by Father Flanagan, W of city. Highly urbanized in and around Omaha, primarily in SE. Some flooding occurred along rivers during flood of 1993. Formed 1854. **7** county (□ 737 sq mi/1,909 sq km; 1990 pop. 27,637), W Nev.; ⊙ Minden; 38°55′N 119°36′W. Irrigated region bordering on Calif. (W and SW), and watered by Carson R. (E and W forks) and W Walker R. Dairy; poultry, cattle, sheep; sand and gravel. Foothills of Sierra Nevada throughout, part of L. Tahoe, in NW, forms W boundary with Calif. Gambling, entertainment, and tourism at L. Tahoe. Formed 1851. **8** county (□ 5,134 sq mi/13,297 sq km; 1990 pop. 94,649), SW Oregon; ⊙ Roseburg; 43°17′N 123°10′W. Mt. area bounded NW by the Pacific Ocean; crossed by Umpqua R. Agr. (apples, cherries, pears, plums, peaches, grapes; poultry, sheep, cattle); dairy prods.; nurseries, wineries. Timber, wood prods. Fish (in W). Part of Siuslaw Natl. Forest is W, in Coast Range; part of Umpqua Natl. Forest is E, in Cascade Range; parts of Siuslaw Natl. Forest and Elliott State Forest in NW; Umpqua Wayside State Park in NW; Camas Mt. Wayside State Park in SW; Umpqua Lighthouse State Park and part of Oregon Dunes Natl. Recreation Area on coast, in NW. Formed 1852. **9** county (□ 435 sq mi/1,127 sq km; 1990 pop. 3,746), SE S.Dak.; ⊙ Armour; 43°23′N 98°21′W. Agr. and cattle-raising area. Drained by Choteau Creek. Corn, wheat, soybeans, oats; cattle, hogs, poultry; dairy produce. Formed 1883. **10** county (□ 1,848 sq mi/4,786 sq km; 1990 pop. 26,205), central Wash.; ⊙ Waterville; 47°45′N 119°42′W. Plateau area bounded N and W by Columbia R. Alfalfa, hay, wheat, barley, oats, rye; cattle, sheep. E boundary zigzags SW-NE along NW side of Grand Coulee (valley), touching Banks L. at several points. Lincoln Rock State Park in SW; Grand Coulee Dam 1 mi/1.6 km beyond NE corner of co.; part of Coulee Dam Natl. Recreation Area is here, including Crown Point observation point. Formed 1883. **11** county (□ 1,480 sq mi/3,833 sq km; 1990 pop. 41,758), extreme NW Wis.; ⊙ Superior; 46°27′N 91°54′W. Bounded W by Minn., N by St. Louis R. (on Minn. border) and L. Superior. Generally wooded lake area, drained by St. Croix, Eau Claire, Amnicon, Bois Brule, and Black rivers. Cattle, poultry, limited farming on cutover forest land. Heavy industry at Superior, a major port. Pattison State Park containing Big Manitou Falls in W; Mont Du Lac Ski Area in NW corner; Amnicon Falls State Park in N; Lucine Woods State Park in SE; Brule River State Forest in E and NE; St. Croix Natl. Scenic Riverway in S, from dam at St. Croix Flowage (reservoir) SW into Burnett co. Formed 1854.

Douglas 1 city (1990 pop. 12,822), Cochise co., SE Ariz., at the Mexican (Sonora state) border; elev. 3,990 ft/1,216 m; 31°20′N 109°31′W. The mining and smelting of copper have been important since 1900; the city grew around a copper smelter which has since been abandoned and largely dismantled. Douglas is also a ranching center and a border station, with mfg. (transformers, wiring devices, electronic components, apparel). Gypsum and tungsten mines and limestone quarries in the area. RR terminus transfer point to Mex. rail system. The city has Cochise col. (2-year) as well as an internatl. airport. Its sister city is Agua Prieta, Mexico. San Bernadino Natl. Wildlife Refuge to E; part of Coronado Natl. Forest to NE. Inc. 1905. **2** city (1990 pop. 10,464), ⊙ Coffee co., S central Ga.; 31°31′N 82°51′W. Mfg. includes yarns, asphalt, aluminum doors, printing and publishing, marble prods., dairy products, jet engine parts, apparel; lumber. S. Georgia Col., a unit of the Univ. System of Ga.; General Coffee State Park nearby. Inc. 1895.

Douglas 1 town (1990 pop. 5,438), Worcester co., S Mass., 14 mi/23 km SSE of Worcester, near R.I. line; 42°03′N 71°45′W. Woolens. Settled c.1721, inc. 1746. Includes village of East Douglas (1990 pop. 1,945). **2** town (1990 pop. 5,076), ⊙ Converse co., E central Wyo., on North Platte R., and 50 mi/80 km E of Casper; 42°45′N 105°23′W. Elev. 4,815 ft/1,468 m. Trade center in livestock and oil region; clover seed. Mfg. (canvas prods.; printing and publishing; drill bits). State fairgrounds. Nearby are Ayer's Park Natural Bridge to W and site of Fort Fetterman to NW, important supply depot (1867–1882) during Indian Wars. Town square has a Jackalope statue, legendary cross between antelope and jackrabbit. Town laid out 1886 with coming of RR.

Douglas 1 village, Lincoln co., SE Ark., on Arkansas R., and 29 mi/47 km ESE of Pine Bluff. **2** village (1990 pop. 1,040), Allegan co., SW Mich., 10 mi/16 km SW of Holland, and on Kalamazoo R. near its mouth on L. Michigan; 42°38′N 86°12′W. Resort area. Mfg. (fiberglass boats, hinges). **3** village (1990 pop. 199), Otoe co., SE Nebr., 20 mi/32 km SE of Lincoln, and on branch of Little Nemaha R.; 40°35′N 96°23′W. **4** village (1990 pop. 93), Ward co., central N.Dak., 28 mi/45 km SSW of Minot, on Douglas Creek; 47°51′N 101°30′W. **5** village (1990 pop. 55), Garfield co., N Okla., 15 mi/24 km SE of Enid; 36°15′N 97°40′W. In agr. area.

Douglas, Cape, S Alaska, at base of Alaska Peninsula, at N end of Shelikof Strait, 80 mi/129 km NNW of Kodiak; 58°51′N 153°16′W.

Douglas, Fort, Utah: see SALT LAKE CITY.

Douglas Island (18 mi/29 km long, 3 mi/4.8 km–7 mi/11.3 km wide), SE Alaska, bet. Admiralty Isl. (NE) and mainland (SW), W of Juneau, across Gastineau Channel (bridge); 58°16′N 134°30′W. Rises to 3,515 ft/1,071 m. Douglas town in E. Fishing, fish processing. Site of famous Treadwell mine.

Douglas Lake, Cheboygan co., N Mich., 10 mi/16 km SW of Cheboygan, in wooded resort area; c.4 mi/6.4 km long, 2 mi/3.2 km wide; 45°34′N 84°41′W. Fishing, boating.

Douglas Lake, reservoir (□ 49 sq mi/127 sq km), Sevier, Jefferson, Cocke, and Hambler cos., E Tenn., on French Broad R., 22 mi/35 km E of Knoxville; c.45 mi/72 km long; 35°57′N 83°32′W. Max. capacity 1,514,100 acre-ft. Nolichucky R. forms 15 mi/24 km long NE arm. Formed by Douglas Dam (202 ft/62 m high), built (1943) by TVA for flood control and power generation.

Douglas Station, village, SW Man., Canada, 12 mi/19 km ENE of Brandon; 49°53′N 99°42′W. Grain, livestock.

Douglass, town (1990 pop. 1,722), Butler co., SE Kansas, on Walnut R., and 22 mi/35 km SSW of El Dorado; 37°31′N 97°00′W. Livestock, grain. Oil wells nearby. Mus.

Douglass Hills, town (1990 pop. 5,549), Jefferson co., N Ky., residential suburb 9 mi/14.5 km E of downtown Louisville; 38°14′N 85°32′W.

Douglassville (DUHG-luhs-vil), uninc. town (1990 pop. 1,200), Berks co., SE central Pa., suburb 4 mi/6.4 km W of Pottstown, on Schuylkill R.; 40°15′N 75°43′W. Mfg. includes construction equipment, steel fabricating, investment castings, crushed stone. Agr. includes dairying, livestock, poultry; grain, apples, plums. French Creek State Park and Hopewell Furnace Natl. Historic Site to SE.

Douglassville, village (1990 pop. 192), Cass co., NE Texas, 26 mi/42 km SW of Texarkana; 33°11′N 94°20′W. Natural gas processing. Wright Patman L. reservoir (Sulphur R.) to N. Atlanta State Park to NE.

Douglaston, residential sect. of NE Queens, borough of N.Y. city, SE N.Y., on Little Neck Bay; 40°45′N 73°45′W. Includes Douglas Manor, a community on Long Isl. Sound.

Douglastown, village (1991 pop. 1,556), NE N.B., Canada, on Miramichi R., and 3 mi/5 km W of Chatham; 47°02′N 65°30′W. Timber shipping port; logging; salmon.

Douglasville, city (1990 pop. 11,635), ⊙ Douglas co., NW central Ga., 21 mi/34 km W of Atlanta; 33°45′N 84°45′W. Bedroom community for the greater Atlanta area. Mfg. of pipe, copper wire; printing and publishing; gardening tools; oil refining. Inc. 1875.

Doullut Canal, La.: see EMPIRE.

Dousman (DOUS-muhn), town (1990 pop. 1,277), Waukesha co., SE Wis., on Bark R., and 28 mi/45 km W of Milwaukee; 43°00′N 88°28′W. In farm and resort area. Furniture, veal feeds. On Glacial Drumlin State Trail; N end of S unit of Kettle Moraine State Forest.

Douthat (DO-thaht) or **Century**, uninc. village, Ottawa co., extreme NE Okla., 7 mi/11.3 km NNE of Miami, S of Pitcher. Lead and zinc deposits.

Dove Creek, village (1990 pop. 643), ⊙ Dolores co., SW Colo., bet. Dolores R. (E) and Utah line (W), 65 mi/105 km NW of Durango; elev. c.6,843 ft/2,086 m; 37°46′N 108°54′W. Diversified farming; beans, wheat, sheep, cattle. San Juan Natl. Forest to E.

Dover 1 city (1990 pop. 27,630), ⊙ Del. and Kent co., central Del., on the St. Jones R., which forms Silver Lake reservoir N of downtown; 39°09′N 75°31′W. In a fertile farming and fruit-growing region, it is a shipping and canning center. Lumber, fabricated metal, and glass prods.; printing and publishing; feeds, paints; paper mill. Dover Air Force Base to SE, including a base mus. Dover Base Housing (1990 pop. 4,376) for base personnel is just S of the city limits. The State House (now the Old Statehouse) was finished in 1792. A new Legislature Hall was built in 1933, but the Old Statehouse is used for some official functions. Numerous historic houses and sites remain. Historic preservation and landscaping have helped the downtown area retain an attractive small town, colonial appearance. The State Mus. is in the Old Presbyterian Church (1790). Seat of Del. State Univ. and Wesley Col. Del. Technical and Community Col. (Terry campus). Chandelle Estates Airport to NE; Little Creek Wildlife Area to E; Bombay Hook Wildlife Area to NE; N.G. Wilder Wildlife Area to SW; Dover Downs race track to N. Founded 1683 on orders of William Penn, laid out 1717, inc. as a city 1929, state capital since 1977. **2** city (1990 pop. 25,042), ⊙ Strafford co., SE N.H., 32 mi/51 km ENE of Manchester, and 8 mi/12.9 km SSE of Rochester; bounded E and drained by Cocheco R., bounded SE by Piscataqua R. (tidal; Maine state boundary), SW in part by Bellamy R; 43°11′N 70°52′W. The 30 ft/9 m falls of the Cocheco R. here have powered industry since the late 1700s. Mfg.

(electrical equip., plastic fabricating, shoes, business equip., printing and publishing, tool and die); insurance. Regarded by some as the first permanent settlement in N.H., Lord Saye and Sele and his group had large holdings here (1633–41). A massacre by Native Americans occurred in 1689. In 1812 the first cotton factory was established and the town thrived as a textile center. Attractions include the garrison house (late 1600s); the Hale house (1806), where Lafayette and James Monroe stayed; and a library organized in 1792. Seat of McIntosh Col. Woodman Inst. is here. Covered bridges in N. Settled 1623, inc. as a city 1855. **3** city (1990 pop. 11,329), Tuscarawas co., E Ohio, just NW of New Philadelphia, and on Tuscarawas R.; 40°31′N 81°28′W. In mining (coal, fire clay) area; mfg. of clay prods., chemicals, cheese, wood prods.; oil refining. Laid out 1807. Dover Reservoir (capacity 203,000 acre-ft.) is impounded by nearby flood control dam on the Tuscarawas R. **4** city (1990 pop. 1,341), ⊙ Stewart co., NW Tenn., on Cumberland R., and 27 mi/43 km W of Clarksville; 36°29′N 87°50′W. In agr. area (tobacco, corn, beans); mfg. children's clothing. Fort Donelson Natl. Military Park is nearby.

Dover 1 town (1990 pop. 1,055), Pope co., N central Ark., 8 mi/12.9 km N of Russellville, near Illinois Bayou; 35°23′N 93°06′W. Ozark Natl. Forest to N. **2** town (□ 2 sq mi/5.2 sq km; 1990 pop. 2,606), Hillsborough co., W central Fla., 15 mi/24 km E of Tampa; 27°59′N 82°13′W. **3** town (1990 pop. 4,915), Norfolk co., E Mass., on Charles R., and 14 mi/23 km SW of Boston; 42°14′N 71°17′W. Residential. Settled c.1635, set off from Dedham 1784. **4** town (1990 pop. 115), Lafayette co., W central Mo., near Missouri R., 10 mi/16 km E of Lexington; 39°11′N 93°41′W. Apples, corn, cattle, hogs. **5** town (1990 pop. 994), Windham co., SE Vt., 13 mi/21 km NW of Brattleboro, and 10 mi/16 km W of Newfane; 42°57′N 72°50′W. Partly in Green Mtn. Natl. Forest. West Dover has mtn., ski resort.

Dover 1 village (1990 pop. 294), Bonner co., N Idaho, 3 mi/4.8 km W of Sandpoint, on Pend Oreille R. at its outflow from L. Pend Oreille; 48°15′N 116°36′W. RR junction; cattle; oats, alfalfa. Kaniksu Natl. Forest to NW. **2** village (1990 pop. 163), Bureau co., N Ill., 6 mi/9.7 km NE of Princeton; 41°25′N 89°24′W. In agr. area. **3** village (1990 pop. 297), Mason co., NE Ky., on the Ohio, and 10 mi/16 km NW of Maysville; 38°45′N 83°52′W. Agr. (tobacco, grain; livestock; dairying); mfg. (airboat propellers). Dover Covered Bridge (1835) to SE. **4** village (1990 pop. 416), Olmsted co., SE Minn., 17 mi/27 km ESE of Rochester; 43°58′N 92°07′W. Dairying; poultry; livestock; grain, soybeans; mfg. (concrete). Whitewater State Park and Whitewater Wilderness Area to NE. **5** village (1990 pop. 451), Craven co., E N.C., 9 mi/14.5 km SE of Kinston; 35°13′N 77°25′W. Cotton, tobacco, peanuts, grain, poultry, livestock. Mfg. (apparel). **6** village (1990 pop. 376), Kingfisher co., central Okla., 9 mi/14.5 km N of Kingfisher, on Cimarron R.; 35°58′N 97°54′W. Oil fields. Livestock.

Dover, borough (1990 pop. 1,884), York co., S Pa., 6 mi/9.7 km WNW of York. Mfg. (food, metal prods., counter tops, business forms). Agr. (grain, soybeans, apples; livestock, poultry; dairying). Conewango Mts. to W; Gifford Pinchot State Park to NW.

Dover, industrial township (1990 pop. 76,371), Morris co., N central N.J., on the Rockaway R.; 39°59′N 74°10′W. In an iron ore area, the town grew as an iron mfg. center on the old Morris Canal. It still has iron- and steelworks as well as a wide variety of mfg. The U.S. Army Picatinny Arsenal is nearby. Morris Co. Col. Settled 1722, inc. as town 1869.

Dover, Maine: see DOVER-FOXCROFT.

Dover Base Housing, Del.: see DOVER.

Dover Plains, village (□ 1 sq mi/2.6 sq km; 1990 pop. 1,847), Dutchess co., SE N.Y., near Conn. border, 19 mi/31 km ENE of Poughkeepsie; 41°45′N 73°34′W. Dairy prods.; vegetables. Terminus of Harlem line of Metro-North commuter RR.

Dover-Foxcroft, town (1990 pop. 4,657) including Dover-Foxcroft village, ⊙ Piscataquis co., central Maine, c.35 mi/56 km NW of Bangor, astride Piscataquis R.;

45°10′N 69°12′W. Formed 1922 by union of Foxcroft (settled 1806, inc. 1812) and Dover (settled 1803, inc. 1822).

Dovray (DO-vrai), village (1990 pop. 60), Murray co., SW Minn., 12 mi/19 km ENE of Slayton; 44°02′N 95°32′W. Dairying; grain; mfg. (feeds).

Dow City, town (1990 pop. 439), Crawford co., W Iowa, on Boyer R., and 9 mi/14.5 km SW of Denison; 41°55′N 95°29′W. In agr. area.

Dowager Island (□ 53 sq mi/137 sq km), SW B.C., Canada, in SE arm of Hecate Strait, 20 mi/32 km NNW of Bella Bella; 52°25′N 128°22′W; 10 mi/16 km long and 5 mi/8 km wide; rises to 2,360 ft/719 m.

Dowagiac (de-WAH-zhak), town (1990 pop. 6,409), Cass co., SW Mich., 17 mi/27 km NE of Niles, near Dowagiac R.; 41°58′N 86°06′W. In farm area (wheat, corn, soybeans). Mfg. (metal prods., furniture, aluminum and zinc die); timber. Resort. Airport to W. Southwestern Mich. Col. (2-year). Settled 1848; inc. as village 1863, as city 1877.

Dowell, village (1990 pop. 465), Jackson co., SW Ill., 14 mi/23 km NNE of Murphysboro; 37°56′N 89°14′W. Mining. In bituminous coal and agr. area.

Dowelltown (DOUL-tuhn), town (1990 pop. 308), De Kalb co., central Tenn., 8 mi/13 km NW of Smithville; 36°00′N 85°56′W.

Dowling Lake (6 mi/10 km long, 5 mi/8 km wide), SE central Alta., Canada, 35 mi/56 km NE of Drumheller, and 8 mi/13 km S of Sullivan L. Drains S into Red Deer R.

Downers Grove, village (1990 pop. 46,858), Du Page co., NE Ill.; 41°47′N 88°01′W. Settled 1832, inc. 1873. Population growth and commercial development include the construction of new office complexes. Mfg (baked goods, plastic and metal prods., electrical components). The Avery Coonley School, a private, progressive elementary school, and Midwestern Univ. are here. Argonne Natl. Laboratory and Morton Arboretum are nearby.

Downey, city (1990 pop. 91,444), Los Angeles co., S Calif., residential and industrial suburb 9 mi SE of downtown Los Angeles; 33°57′N 118°08′W. Bounded E by San Gabriel R, Los Angeles R. to W. Metal prods., rubber goods, communications equipment; dairy prods. Aerospace mfg. in area. Inc. 1957.

Downey, village (1990 pop. 626), Bannock co., SE Idaho, 15 mi/24 km NE of Malad City; elev. 4,854 ft/1,479 m; 42°26′N 112°07′W. In agr. and grazing area. Part of Caribou Natl. Forest to SW; Devil Creek Reservoir to S.

Downieville, uninc. village (1990 pop. 500), ⊙ Sierra co., NE Calif., 80 mi/129 km NE of Sacramento, in the Sierra Nevada, on North Yuba R. In Tahoe Natl. Forest region. Winter sports area nearby. Tahoe Natl. Forest to S and W, Plumas Natl. Forest to N.

Downing, city (1990 pop. 359), Schuyler co., N Mo., near North Fabius R., 9 mi/14.5 km ESE of Lancaster; 40°29′N 92°22′W. Soybeans, corn; hogs, sheep.

Downing, village (1990 pop. 250), Dunn co., W Wis., 14 mi/23 km NW of Menomonie; 45°02′N 92°07′W. Dairying.

Downingtown, borough (1990 pop. 7,749), Chester co., SE Pa., 28 mi/45 km W of Philadelphia, on east branch of Brandywine Creek; 40°00′N 75°42′W. Mfg. (machining, steel fabricating, chemicals, crushed limestone, plastics, packaging materials, paper mill). Agr. area (grain, hay, apples; livestock; dairying). Marsh Creek Reservoir and State Park to N. Inc. 1859.

Downs, town (1990 pop. 1,119), Osborne co., N Kansas, on North Fork Solomon R. at its entrance to N arm of Wakonda Lake, and 9 mi/14.5 km ENE of Osborne; 39°30′N 98°32′W. RR junction. Produce packing center in grain and livestock area.

Downs, village (1990 pop. 620), McLean co., central Ill., 8 mi/12.9 km SE of Bloomington; 40°23′N 88°52′W. In rich agr. area (corn, wheat, soybeans, sorghum, cattle). Subdivisions encroaching from NW.

Downsville (DOUNZ-vil), town (1990 pop. 82), Union parish, N La., 10 mi/16 km S of Farmerville; 32°37′N 92°24′W. Agr. area; cattle and poultry. Settled in 1840s

by immigrants from Alabama and Georgia; an early cotton growing area.

Downsville 1 village (1990 pop. 1,100), Delaware co., S N.Y., c.45 mi/72 km E of Binghamton, in a resort area of the Catskills; 42°05′N 75°00′W. Downsville Dam impounds Pepacton Reservoir and Bear Spring Mt. nearby. **2** village, Dunn co., W Wis., on Red Cedar R., and 7 mi/11.3 km S of Menomonie; granite quarrying. Timber, wood prods. Lumbering Mus.

Dows, town (1990 pop. 660), on Franklin-Wright co. line, N central Iowa, on Iowa R., and 14 mi/23 km ESE of Clarion; 42°39′N 93°30′W. Animal feed.

Doylestown 1 village (1990 pop. 2,668), Wayne co., N central Ohio, 12 mi/19 km SW of Akron; 40°58′N 81°42′W. **2** village (1990 pop. 316), Columbia co., S central Wis., near Crawfish R., 17 mi/27 km SE of Portage; 43°25′N 89°09′W. In farm area. Hunting and state wildlife area.

Doylestown (DOI-uhls-toun), borough (1990 pop. 8,575), ⊙ Bucks co., SE Pa., 23 mi/37 km N of Philadelphia; 40°18′N 75°07′W. Mfg. (printing and publishing, machining, tool and die, furniture). Agr. area (grain, hay, soybeans, apples; livestock, poultry; dairying). Seat of Delaware Valley Col. of Science and Agr.; Warrington Airport to S; Doylestown Airport to N; Mercer Mus.; L. Galena reservoir to W. Settled 1735, laid out 1778, inc. 1838.

Doyline (DOI-lein), village (1994 pop. 1,004), Webster parish, NW La., 20 mi/32 km E of Shreveport; 32°31′N 93°25′W. In agr. area (cotton, vegetables, sweet potatoes; cattle; dairying). Lake Bistineau State Park to S.

Dozier (DO-zhuhr), town (1990 pop. 483), Crenshaw co., S Ala., on Conecuh R., and 16 mi/26 km SSW of Luverne. Saw mill, clothing.

Dracut (DRAI-kuht), town (1990 pop. 25,594), Middlesex co., NE Mass., near the N.H. state line, 2 mi/3.2 km N of Lowell; 42°41′N 71°18′W. A growing commercial center of a fertile farm region; mfg. (plastics, concrete). Settled 1664, inc. 1702.

Dragerton, village, Carbon co., central Utah, adjacent to East Carbon City, 22 mi/35 km E of Price. Coal-mining area. Combined with former village of Columbia to form East Carbon City in the 1970s.

Dragon Run, Va.: see PIANKATANK RIVER.

Dragoon Mountains, small range in Cochise co., 25 mi/40 km long, SE Ariz., SSW of Willcox, in section of Coronado Natl. Forest. Mt. Glen (7,512 ft/2,290 m) is highest point. Cochise stronghold memorial park near peak; historic town of Tombstone to SW. Little Dragoon Mts. to SE.

Drain, town (1990 pop. 1,011), Douglas co., SW Oregon, 30 mi/48 km SSW of Eugene, on Elk Creek; 43°39′N 123°18′W. Cottage Grove Reservoir to E. Wood prods.; timber; fruit; sheep, cattle.

Drake, village (1990 pop. 361), McHenry co., central N Dak., 48 mi/77 km WNW of Harvey; 47°55′N 100°22′W. Diversified farming, livestock, wheat. RR junction. Small lakes to NNE.

Drake's Bay, inlet of the Pacific Ocean, on S side of Point Reyes Peninsula, Marin co., W Calif., c.25 mi/40 km NW of San Francisco. San Andreas Fault passes to E of bay forming base of peninsula (Bolinas and Tomales bays are formed by fault). Point Reyes to W forms outer arm of peninsula. The bay reportedly was visited by Sir Francis Drake in 1579.

Drakes Branch, town (1990 pop. 565), Charlotte co., S Va., 40 mi/64 km SE of Lynchburg; 36°59′N 78°35′W. Mfg. (saw blades, wooden pallets, lumber, cloth); tobacco; timber.

Drakes Creek, c.26 mi/42 km long, in S Ky. and N. Tenn., formed in S Warren co., Ky., by junction of West Fork and Trammel Fork creeks; flows generally N to Barren R., 5 mi/8 km E of Bowling Green, Ky. Trammel Fork rises in NW Macon co., N Tenn., flows c.45 mi/72 km NNW into Ky. West Fork rises in NW Sumner co., N Tenn., flows c.50 mi/80 km N into Ky. past Franklin, then NE.

Drakesboro, village (1990 pop. 565), Muhlenberg co., W Ky., 8 mi/12.9 km SSE of Central City, on Pond Creek;

37°13'N 87°02'W. Tobacco, grain; livestock; timber; mfg. (industrial equipment). Bituminous coal.

Drakesville, town (1990 pop. 172), Davis co., SE Iowa, near Fox R., 4 mi/6.4 km NW of Bloomfield; 40°47'N 92°28'W. In sheep-raising area. L. Wapello State Park to W.

Draper, town (1990 pop. 7,257), Salt Lake and Utah cos., N central Utah, suburb 18 mi/29 km S of Salt Lake City, and 20 mi/32 km NW of Provo, on Jordan R.; 40°30'N 111°51'W. Elev. 4,200 ft/1,280 m. Sugar beets, vegetables, alfalfa; dairying; poultry, cattle; mfg. (computer peripherals, dairy prods., signs). Alpine Peak (11,253 ft/3,430 m) is 5 mi/8 km E in Wasatch Range. Wasatch and Uinta Natl. Forests in Wasatch range to E. Camp Williams Military Reservation to SW.

Draper 1 uninc. village, Rockingham co., N N.C., near Dan R. and Va. state line, 11 mi/18 km N of Reidsville. Inc. 1949. **2** village (1990 pop. 123), Jones co., S central S.Dak., 32 mi/51 km SSW of Pierre; 6 mi/9.7 km E of Mountain/Central Time Zone boundary; 43°55'N 100°32'W. Small trading point. Grain; dairy produce; livestock, poultry. Fort Pierre Natl. Grassland to NE. **3** uninc. village, Pulaski co., SW Va., 3 mi/4.8 km SSE of Pulaski, on New R. (Clayton L. reservoir). Agr. area (corn; livestock; dairying); timber. New River Trail State Park passes through town.

Draperville, uninc. village, Linn co., W Oregon, 4 mi/6.4 km E of Albany, on Truax Creek.

Dravosburg (DRAH-vos-buhrg), borough (1990 pop. 2,377), Allegheny co., SW Pa., residential suburb 8 mi/12.9 km SE of downtown Pittsburgh, and 2 mi/3.2 km W of McKeesport, on Monongahela R.; 40°21'N 79°53'W. Light mfg. Allegheny co. airport to W. Inc. 1903.

Drayton 1 town (1990 pop. 961), Pembina co., NE N.Dak.,14 mi/23 kmNE of Grafton, on Red R. of the North, on Minn. boundary; 48°33'N 97°10'W. Livestock, wheat, sugar beets, potatoes. Food processing. **2** uninc. town (1990 pop. 1,443), Spartanburg co., NW S.C., residential suburb, 2 mi/3.2 km ENE of Spartanburg.

Drayton (DRAI-tuhn), village (1991 pop. 1,181), S Ont., Canada, 23 mi/37 km NNW of Kitchener. Farming.

Drayton Plains, residential village, Oakland co., SE Mich., suburb 5 mi/8 km NW of Pontiac, and on Clinton R.; 42°41'N 83°22'W. In area of many lakes. Has state fish hatchery. Settled 1823. Part of the inc. city of Waterford Township.

Drayton Valley, town (1986 pop. 5,290), 75 mi/121 km SW of Edmonton, Alta., Canada; 53°13'N 114°59'W. Oil and gas; forestry. Developed as center for Pembina oil field in 1950s. Planned as model town but grew too quickly.

Dreher Shoals Dam, S.C.: see MURRAY, LAKE.

Dresden (DREZ-duhn), town (1991 pop. 2,646), S Ont., Canada, on Sydenham R., and 12 mi/19 km N of Chatham; 42°35'N 82°10'W. Food prcessing; dairying; natural-gas production. Hydroelectric power.

Dresden 1 (DREZ-duhn), town (1990 pop. 1,332), Lincoln co., S Maine, on the Kennebec R., and 7 mi/11.3 km NW of Wiscasset; 44°04'N 69°44'W. Boatbuilding; summer camps. **2** town (1990 pop. 2,488), ⊙ Weakley co., NW Tenn., 21 mi/34 km SE of Union City; 36°18'N 88°42'W. Trade center in timber, clay, agr. area (cotton, corn, sweet potatoes, tobacco); footwear; printing and publishing. Laid out 1825.

Dresden 1 (DREZ-den), village (1990 pop. 73), Decatur co., NW Kansas, 15 mi/24 km SW of Oberlin; 39°37'N 100°25'W. In agr. and livestock area. **2** village (1990 pop. 339), Yates co., W central N.Y., on W shore of Seneca L., 12 mi/19 km S of Geneva; 42°40'N 76°57'W. **3** village (1990 pop. 1,581), Muskingum co., central Ohio, 12 mi/19 km N of Zanesville, at head of navigation on the Muskingum R.; 40°07'N 82°01'W. Tourism. Basket mfg.

Dresden 2 and 3 Nuclear Power Plants, Illinois: see GRUNDY.

Dresser, village (1990 pop. 614), Polk co., NW Wis., 26 mi/42 km N of Hudson, near St. Croix R.; 45°21'N 92°37'W. In dairying area. Cheese; dies and fixtures; mechanical assembly. St. Croix Falls and Osceola Fish Hatcheries on river. Interstate State Park to N. Trollhaugen Ski Area nearby. Until 1940, called Dresser Junction.

Drew, plantation (1990 pop. 43), Penobscot co., central Maine, 60 mi/97 km NE of Bangor; 45°34'N 68°05'W. Lumbering. Mattawamkeag R. traverses plantation.

Drew, county (☐ 835 sq mi/2,163 sq km; 1990 pop. 17,369), SE Ark.; ⊙ Monticello; 33°35'N 91°43'W. Saline R. forms part of W boundary. Drained by the Bayou Bartholomew R. and Cut-Off Creek. Cotton, ricc, wheat, soybeans; cattle; timber. Cut-Off Creek Wildlife Management Area in SE; Seven Devils Swamp L. Reservoir in E. Formed 1846.

Drew, town (1990 pop. 2,349), Sunflower co., W Miss., 28 mi/45 km NW of Greenwood; 33°48'N 90°31'W. In rich agr. area (cotton, rice, soybeans; cattle); mfg. (apparel, furniture).

Drewsey (DROO-zee), uninc. village, Harney co., E Oregon, 37 mi/60 km NE of Burns on Malheur R., at mouth of Stinking Water Creek; elev. 3,516 ft/1,072 m.

Drexel (DREK-suhl), city (1990 pop. 936), Cass co., W Mo., 19 mi/31 km SW of Harrisonville, on Kansas border; 38°28'N 94°36'W. Wheat, soybeans; livestock; gas wells, oil field.

Drexel (DREK-suhl), town (1990 pop. 1,746), Burke co., W central N.C., 5 mi/8 km E of Morganton; 35°45'N 81°36'W. Agr. area (grain, soybeans; chickens, hogs); mfg. (apparel, furniture). L. Rhodhiss reservoir (Catawba R.).

Drexel, uninc. village (1990 pop. 5,143), Montgomery co., SW Ohio, 6 mi/10 km W of Dayton, on Highway 35; 39°45'N 84°17'W.

Drexel Hill (DREK-suhl), uninc. city (1990 pop. 29,744), Upper Darby township, Delaware co., SE Pa., suburb 7 mi/11.3 km W of downtown Philadelphia, on Darby Creek; 39°57'N 75°17'W. Mfg. (medical supplies, trophies, electrical equipment, food industry equipment).

Drift, uninc. village (1990 pop. 600), Floyd co., E Ky., 12 mi/19 km S of Prestonsburg, on Beaver Creek. Livestock; coal. Mfg. (industrial batteries).

Drift Prairie, in N N.Dak. and S Man., Canada; sandy, rolling plain, varies in width from 70 mi/113 km–100 mi/161 km; extends S to headwaters of James and Sheyenne rivers; in N is Devils L. basin, basis of an interior drainage system.

Driftless Area, c.13,000 sq mi/33,670 sq km, largely in SW Wis. but extending into SE Minn., NE Iowa, and NW Ill. The continental glacier which covered most surrounding regions did not touch this area, which abounds in caves and sinkholes and has residual, well-drained soil. Because it was an important lead-mining region, the Federal govt. prohibited farming in the Driftless Area until the 1840s. It was then settled by European immigrants. Its existence has led geologists (gromorphologists) to believe that the Ice Age was more complex than 1st thought, a series of separate ice sheets advancing at different times, rather than one single ice sheet or event. Baraboo Mts. extend across eastern part of area.

Drifton, uninc. town (1990 pop. 750), Luzerne co., E central Pa., 5 mi/8 km NE of Hazleton, in anthracite coal region; 41°00'N 75°54'W.

Driftwood, village, Alfalfa co., N Okla., 18 mi/29 km ENE of Alva. In grain and livestock area.

Driftwood, borough (1990 pop. 116), Cameron co., N central Pa., 12 mi/19 km SSE of Emporium, at confluence of Driftwood and Bennett branches of Sinnemahoning Creek, forming main stream, surrounded by Elk State Forest; 41°20'N 78°08'W. Lumber; cattle; timber. Bucktail State Park to SE, Sinnemahoning State Park to NE.

Driggs, town (1990 pop. 846), ⊙ Teton co., E Idaho, near Wyo. state line, c.50 mi/80 km ENE of Idaho Falls, in valley of Teton R.; 43°44'N 111°07'W. Trade center for farm area (cattle; potatoes, beans, alfalfa, barley), some dairying. Large coal bed nearby; tourism. Targhee Natl. Forest to E (Wyo.) and W; Grand Targhee Ski Area to NE (Wyo.).

Drinnan (DRI-nuhn), village, W Alta., Canada, in Rocky Mts., near E side of Jasper Natl. Park, on Athabaska R.,

adjacent to Hinton, and 45 mi/72 km NE of Jasper; 53°26'N 117°32'W. Coal mining, logging; cattle.

Dripping Springs, town (1990 pop. 1,033), Hays co., S central Texas, 22 mi/35 km WSW of Austin; 30°11'N 98°05'W. Livestock (cattle, sheep, goats) and agr. (cotton, wheat) area; light mfg.

Driscoll, village (1990 pop. 688), Nueces co., S Texas, 23 mi/37 km WSW of Corpus Christi; 27°40'N 97°45'W. Oil, cotton, cattle in area.

Driskill Mountain (DRI-skuhl), Bienville parish, NW La., 5 mi/8 km ESE of Bryceland; highest point (535 ft/163 m) in state; 32° 25'N 92° 53'W.

Droop Mountain Battlefield State Park, Pocahontas co., E W.Va., 3 mi/4.8 km SW of Hillsboro, at Droop village. Here on slope of Droop Mtn. (c.3,100 ft/945 m) is preserved 287 acres/116 ha of the battlefield where Union troops defeated (Nov. 6, 1863) a Confederate army.

Drowning Creek, N.C. and S.C.: see LUMBER RIVER.

Druif (DROIF), village, NW Aruba, Neth. Antilles, 2 mi/3.2 km NW of Oranjestad. Petroleum refinery.

Drum, Fort, N.Y.: see FORT DRUM.

Drum Inlet, Carteret co., E N.C., channel through the Outer Banks, connects Core Sound with the Atlantic Ocean 3 mi/4.8 km E of Atlantic town.

Drum, Mount (12,010 ft/3,661 m), E Alaska, in Wrangell Mts., 85 mi/137 km NE of Valdez; 62°8'N 144°38'W.

Drum Point, low headland, Calvert co., S Md., on N shore of Patuxent R. estuary and 18 mi/29 km SSE of Prince Frederick. Lighthouse.

Drumbo (DRUHM-bo), village, S Ont., Canada, 16 mi/26 km S of Kitchener; 43°14'N 80°33'W. Dairying; farming.

Drumheller, city (1991 pop. 6,277), SE Alta., Canada, on the Red Deer R.; 51°28'N 112°42'W. Once a coal mining town, now an agr. area. Site of the Tyrrell Mus. of Paleontology, which houses the largest display of complete dinosaur skeletons in the world. Badlands to SW along Rosebud R. and SE along Red Deer R. major geological attraction, source of fossils. In 1984 a dinosaur skull was found in carved trenches at Kneehill Creek, 5 mi/8 km away; many other fossils have been found here as well.

Drummond, county (☐ 532 sq mi/1,378 sq km; 1991 pop. 79,654), S Que., Canada, on St. Francis R.; ⊙ Drummondville; 45°50'N 72°30'W.

Drummond 1 village (1990 pop. 37), Fremont co., E Idaho, 15 mi/24 km E of St. Anthony; 44°00'N 111°20'W. Elev. 5,607 ft/1,709 m. Dry farming (wheat). Teton Dam Site, on Teton R. to SW, site of dam collapse (June 5, 1976) which killed 11 people. Targhee Natl. Forest to NE. **2** village, Chippewa co., Mich; on Drummond Island, on Potagannissing Bay, which indents isl.'s NW shore; 46°01'N 83°43'W. Resort (hunting, fishing, hiking, boating); lumbering; dolomite quarrying. Occupied by Br. troops in 1815, became Amer. in 1828. **3** village (1990 pop. 264), Granite co., W Mont., on the Clark Fork R., opposite mouth of Flint Creek, and 46 mi/74 km SE of Missoula; 46°40'N 113°09'W. Silver, sapphires, and garnets; cattle; alfalfa. Helena Natl. Forest to E; Deerlodge Natl. Forest to S; Lolo Natl. Forest to W; Garnet Range to N. Garnet Ghost Town 13 mi/21 km NW. **4** village (1990 pop. 408), Garfield co., N Okla., 11 mi/18 km SW of Enid, and near Turkey Creek; 36°17'N 98°02'W. In agr. area. **5** village (1990 pop. 417), Bayfield co., N Wis., 25 mi/40 km SW of Ashland, in Chequamegon Natl. Forest; 46°19'N 91°17'W. Lumbering. Univ. of Wis. Forest Station to W at Pigeon L.

Drummond Island, c.20 mi/32 km long, 11 mi/18 km wide, Chippewa co., SE Upper Peninsula, Mich., bet. North Channel and main body of L. Huron, just E of St. Marys R.; only major U.S. isl. of the Manitoulin Isl.; 46°00'N 83°40'W.

Drummond, Lake, Va.: see DISMAL SWAMP.

Drummondville, city (1991 pop. 35,462), S Que., Canada, on the St. Francis R., NE of Montreal; 45°53'N 72°29'W. Textiles, paper, wood prods., rubber goods.

Drumright, town (1990 pop. 2,799), Creek co., central Okla., 9 mi/14.5 km E of Cushing; 35°59'N 96°35'W. In oil region; mfg. (toys; concrete, fiberglass, metal prods.; oil-well pumps). Founded c.1913 as an oil boom town.

Dry Bay, inlet (10 mi/16 km long, 14 mi/23 km wide at mouth) of Gulf of Alaska, SE Alaska, 50 mi/80 km SE of Yakutat; 59°10′N 138°25′W. Moraine delta at mouth of Alsek R.

Dry Branch, village, Bibb co., central Ga., 7 mi/11.3 km E of Macon; 32°48′N 83°29′W. Mfg. (trampolines and clay processing).

Dry Falls State Park, Wash.: see COULEE CITY.

Dry Fork, river, c.35 mi/56 km long, in S W.Va.; rises in S McDowell, near Va. state line, 15 mi/24 km W of Bluefield; flows NW past War and Bradshaw to Tug Fork R. at Iaeger.

Dry Harbour, village, St. Ann parish, N Jamaica, 13 mi/21 km W of St. Ann's Bay, on fine bay, where Christopher Columbus on his 2d voyage made his 1st landing in Jamaica (May 4, 1494) and took possession of the isl. for Spain; 18°28′N 77°24′W. Columbus named the actual spot which he landed Horseshoe Bay, because of the peculiar shape of the land. This was changed to Dry Harbour and eventually, a final name change was made to Discovery Bay. There are caves with aboriginal remains nearby. The adjoining interior uplands are called Dry Harbour Mts.

Dry Mills, Maine: see GRAY.

Dry Prong, village (1990 pop. 380), Grant parish, central La., 20 mi/32 km NNW of Alexandria, in Kisatchie Natl. Forest; 31°35′N 92°32′W.

Dry Ridge, town (1990 pop. 1,601), Grant co., N Ky., 4 mi/6.4 km NNW of Williamstown; 38°40′N 84°35′W. Agr. (tobacco; livestock; dairying); mfg. (camping stoves, industrial pumps, concrete). Williamstown L. reservoir to SE, Boltz L. reservoir to NW, Lloyd Wildlife Management Area to NE, Mullins Wildlife Management Area to S.

Dry Run, uninc. village (1990 pop. 5,389), Scioto co., S Ohio, 5 mi/8 km NW of Portsmouth; 39°06′N 84°20′W.

Dry Tortugas (tor-TOO-guss), island group in the Gulf of Mexico, off lower Fla. Keys, 60 mi/97 km W of Key West. Named by the Span. explorer Ponce de León in 1513, the isls. later became a pirate base. They are famous for their bird and marine life. Loggerhead Key is the largest isl. On Garden Key are Fort Jefferson Natl. Monument and a U.S. bird refuge. Accessible by boat and seaplane from Key West.

Dryberry Lake (22 mi/35 km long, 6 mi/10 km wide), W Ont., Canada, 20 mi/32 km E of Lake of the Woods, 30 mi/48 km ESE of Kenora.

Dryden, town (1991 pop. 6,505), NW Ont., Canada, on Wabigoon L., 75 mi/121 km E of Kenora; 49°47′N 92°50′W. Paper, pulp, lumber milling; dairying. Site of govt. experimental farm. In gold-mining region.

Dryden 1 village, Craighead co., NE Ark., 11 mi/18 km W of Jonesboro. **2** village (1990 pop. 628), Lapeer co., E Mich., 12 mi/19 km SE of Lapeer; 42°57′N 83°07′W. Trade center for agr. and horse-breeding area. Mfg. (automotive accessories). **3** residential village (1990 pop. 1,908), Tompkins co., W central N.Y., in Finger Lakes region, 10 mi/16 km ENE of Ithaca; 42°29′N 76°17′W. Mfg. (copier equipment); agr. (fruit; poultry). Seat of Tompkins-Cortland Community Col. Residential and retail growth occurring along Dryden-Ithaca axis.

Du Bois (DOO BOIZ), city (1990 pop. 8,286), Clearfield co., central Pa., 55 mi/89 km NNE of Johnstown, on Sandy Lick Creek, in the region of the Allegheny plateau; 41°07′N 78°45′W. Varied mfg. A commercial and industrial center of a farming area where coal also is still mined. Pa. State Univ. Du Bois Campus (2-year). Du Bois Reservoir to E, Treasure L. reservoir and residential development to NE; part of Moshannon State Forest to NE; S.B. Elliot State Park to E. Inc. 1881.

Du Bois 1 (DOO BOIZ), village, Washington co., SW Ill., 13 mi/21 km SE of Nashville; 38°13′N 89°12′W. In agr. area (wheat, corn, soybeans, sorghum; hogs); coal, oil. **2** (DOO BOIZ), village (1990 pop. 119), Pawnee co., SE Nebr., 7 mi/11.3 km SE of Pawnee City and on S

Fork Big Nemaha R., near Kansas state line; 40°01′N 96°02′W.

Du Chien, Bayou, Ky.: see DE CHIEN, BAYOU.

Du Large, Bayou (doo LAHRZH, BEI-yoo), c.35 mi/56 km long, stream in Terrebonne parish, SE La.; rises S of Houma; flows SW past Theriot to an outlet to the Gulf of Mexico, SW of Caillou L.; partly navigable for shallow-draft vessels. In lower course, joined by channels to Mechant and Caillou lakes.

Du Page (due PAGE), county (□ 336 sq mi/870 sq km; 1990 pop. 781,666), NE Ill., in Chicago suburban area; ⊙ Wheaton, bounds Des Plaines R. on SE; 41°51′N 88°05′W. Agr. being replaced by rapid urban growth; remnant agr. (grain). Residential communities. Diversified mfg.; RR shops; limestone quarries; nurseries. Drained by Du Page R. Formed 1839. Argonne Natl. Lab. in S; Fermi Natl. Acceleration Lab. in W. Part of Chicago's "Collan counties."

Du Page River, NE Ill., rises in 2 branches W of Chicago, flows c.30 mi/48 km SW from their junction N of Joilet to Des Plaines R. just above its confluence with Kankakee R.; 41°42′N 88°08′W. West Branch (c.30 mi/48 km long) flows generally S, past Naperville. East Branch (c.20 mi/32 km long) flows S and SW to West Branch.

Du Pont (doo PAHNT), village (1990 pop. 592), Pierce co., W Wash., residential suburb 15 mi/24 km W of downtown Tacoma, near Puget Sound, bounded N, E, and S by Fort Lewis Military Reservation. Mfg. (semiconductors). Nisqually Indian Reservation to W.

Du Pont, Fort, Del.: see DELAWARE CITY.

Du Quoin (doo KOIN), city (1990 pop. 6,697), Perry co., SW Ill., 9 mi/14.5 km SE of Pinckneyville; 38°00′N 89°14′W. RR junction. Trade and mfg. center in bituminous-coal mining and agr. area; machinery, high voltage cable; sorghum, wheat, cattle; dairying. Site of Du Quoin State Fair, popular for its harness racing and rival to state fair in Springfield. Inc. 1861.

Du Ross Heights, uninc. village (1990 pop. 650), New Castle co., N Del., residential suburb 5 mi/8 km SW of Wilmington, on Christina R., on W side of New Castle County Airport; 39°40′N 75°37′W.

Duane Arnold Nuclear Power Plant, Iowa: see LINN.

Duarte (DWAHR-tai), province (□ 1,090 sq mi/2,823 sq km; 1993 pop. 272,277), central Dominican Republic; ⊙ San Francisco de Macorís. Camú R. here forms fertile E sect. of La Vega Real valley, bounded by Cordillera Setentrional (N) and Cordillera Central (S). Densely pop. agr. region: cacao, coffee, rice, tropical fruit. Iron deposits near Cotuí. Traversed by Sánchez-Santiago RR. The prov., formerly Pacificador dist., was set up 1936.

Duarte, city (1990 pop. 20,688), Los Angeles co., S Calif., suburb 17 mi/27 km NE of Los Angeles; 34°10′N 117°57′W. Drained by San Gabriel R. It is a growing residential city with light industry (motor vehicle parts, aircraft parts, telephone and broadcasting equip.) and warehousing. The City of Hope Natl. Medical Center. Morris and San Gabriel reservoirs to NE; Angeles Natl. Forest to N. Settled c.1841, inc. 1957.

Duarte, Pico (DWAHR-tai, PEE-ko), peak (10,115 ft/3,083 m), central Dominican Republic, in the Cordillera Central, 35 mi/56 km SW of Santiago; 19°3′N 70°58′W. Sometimes considered highest elev. in the West Indies, though Monte Tina, to SE, is said to be 10,301 ft/3,140 m.

Dubach (DOO-bahk), town (1990 pop. 843), Lincoln parish, N La., 11 mi/18 km N of Ruston, near Bayou D'Arbonne; 32°42′N 92°40′W. In agr. area (cattle, poultry; peaches); timber; logging, lumber milling, mfg. of wooden pallets. Home of state Chicken Festival.

Dubawnt (doo-BONT), river, 580 mi/933 km long, rising in Wholdaia L., Keewatin region, N.W.T., Canada, and flowing NE to Dubawnt L., then E to Baker L. at the head of Chesterfield Inlet of Hudson Bay.

Dubawnt Lake, one of the largest lakes of Canada (□ c.1,600 sq mi/4,140 sq km), W Keewatin region, N.W.T. The Dubawnt R. flows through it. Located N of the tree line, the lake is icebound most of the summer.

Dubberly (DUH-buhr-lee), town (1990 pop. 253), Webster parish, La., 6 mi/9.7 km SE of Minden; 32°32′N 93°14′W. In agr. area (cotton, vegetables); oil fields nearby. Est. 1883 as RR station.

Dublán (doob-LAHN), village, Chihuahua, N Mexico, on Casas Grandes R. (irrigation), and 2 mi/3 km N of Nuevo Casas Grandes, on RR; 30°28′N 107°53′W. Cotton-growing center; cereals; cattle. Site of Mormón colony (estab. 1888).

Dublin 1 city (1990 pop. 23,229), Alameda co., W Calif., a suburb 19 mi/31 km ESE of Oakland on South San Ramon Creek; 37°43′N 121°55′W. Mfg. (wire drawing, power transformers). **2** city (1990 pop. 16,312), ⊙ Laurens co., central Ga., on the Oconee R.; 32°32′N 82°55′W. Commercial and industrial center; largest city on I-16 bet. Macon and Savannah. Diversified mfg.; lumbering. Major center for cotton processing and distribution prior to decline of cotton economy in 1920s. Inc. 1812.

Dublin 1 town (1990 pop. 805), Wayne co., E Ind., 17 mi/27 km W of Richmond; 39°49′N 85°13′W. In agr. area. **2** resort town (1990 pop. 1,474), Cheshire co., SW N.H., 10 mi/16 km ESE of Keene; 42°53′N 72°04′W. Dublin Pond in W center. One of state's highest towns (elev. 1,485 ft/453 m). *Old Farmer's Almanac* published here. Nursery crops, vegetables; cattle, sheep, poultry; dairying. Seat of Dublin School, preparatory school. Monadnock Mt. is SW. **3** town (1990 pop. 3,190), Erath co., N central Texas, c.45 mi/72 km NE of Brownwood; 32°05′N 98°20′W. Elev. 1,493 ft/455 m. RR junction in agr., dairying, cattle ranching region; peanuts, grains. Peanut and sugar processing. First Dr. Pepper bottling plant (1891). Proctor L. reservoir to SW. Founded 1856, inc. 1889. **4** town (1990 pop. 2,012), Pulaski co., SW Va., 7 mi/11.3 km WSW of Radford; 37°06′N 80°41′W. Mfg. (heavy trucks, motor vehicle components, textiles, electroplating, furniture); agr. area (corn; livestock; dairying); timber. New River Valley Airport to N. Part of Radford Army Ammunition Plant to E. New River Community Col.

Dublin, village (1990 pop. 246), Bladen co., SE N.C., 16 mi/26 km E of Lumberton; 34°39′N 78°43′W. In agr. area (cotton, peanuts, tobacco, poultry, livestock); peanut processing. Cape Fear R. to NE.

Dublin, borough (1990 pop. 1,985), Bucks co., SE Pa., 6 mi/9.7 km NW of Doylestown; 40°22′N 75°12′W. Pet food, horseradish processing, marble prods. Grain, soybeans, apples, horseradish; livestock; poultry; dairying. Ralph Stover State Park to NE, Nockamixon State Park to NW; L. Galena reservoir and Peace Valley Winery to S.

Dubois (DOO-boiz), county (□ 435 sq mi/1,127 sq km; 1990 pop. 36,616), SW Ind.; ⊙ Jasper; 38°22′N 86°53′W. Bounded partly in N by East Fork of White R.; drained by Patoka R. (Patoka Dam and Lake in NE) and small Huntley Creek. Corn, soybeans; cattle, poultry, hogs. Bituminous coal, clay pits, timber, and stone quarries; diversified mfg. Lick Fork State Recreation Area around Patoka Dam; Hoosier Natl. Forest in NE corner; Ferdinand State Forest in SE. Formed 1817.

Dubois (DOO-boiz), town (1990 pop. 895), Fremont co., W Wyo., on Wind R., in Wind R. Range, and 65 mi/105 km NW of Lander; 43°32′N 109°38′W. Elev. 6,917 ft/2,108 m. Sheep, cattle; hay; lumber. Bighorn Natl. Sheep Center and largest sheep herd in U.S. Wind R. Indian Reservation to E; Shoshone Natl. Forest to N, W, and S.

Dubois 1 village (1990 pop. 420), ⊙ Clark co., E Idaho, 35 mi/56 km NW of Rexburg; 44°10′N 112°14′W. Elev. 5,145 ft/1,568 m. Sheep, cattle, horses; potatoes; wheat; alfalfa, hay. U.S. Sheep Experimental Station to N. Parts of Targhee Natl. Forest to W and N; Camas Natl. Wildlife Refuge to S; Lidy Hot Springs to W. **2** village, Dubois co., SW Ind., on Patoka R., and 8 mi/12.9 km NE of Jasper. Agr.; poultry feed, furniture, processed eggs.

Dubois, Ill.: see DU BOIS.

Duboistown (DOO-boiz-town), borough (1990 pop. 1,201), Lycoming co., N central Pa., residential suburb, 2 mi/3.2 km WSW of Williamsport, on West Branch of Susquehanna R. (bridged to Williamsport's W end);

41°13′N 77°02′W. Susquehanna State Park to NW; part of Tiadaghton State Forest to S. Settled 1773, inc. 1878.

Dubuisson (duh-bwee-SON), village (1991 pop. 1,480), W Que., Canada, on L. Dubuisson (6 mi/10 km long, 5 mi/8 km wide), 6 mi/10 km WSW of Val d'Or; 48°06′N 77°54′W. Gold mining.

Dubuque, county (□ 616 sq mi/1,595 sq km; 1990 pop. 86,403), E Iowa, bounded E by Mississippi R. (forms Wis. and Ill. lines here); ☉ Dubuque; 42°28′N 90°53′W. Prairie agr. area (hogs, cattle; corn, oats) drained by North Fork Maquoketa R.; lead and zinc deposits around Dubuque city; many limestone quarries. Lock and Dam No. 11 at Dubuque city. Flooding on Mississippi R. and tributaries occurred in 1993. Formed 1834.

Dubuque, city (1990 pop. 57,546), seat of Dubuque co., NE Iowa, on the Mississippi R.; 42°30′N 90°41′W. Trade, industrial, RR center, and a river port for an agr. and dairy area. Shipyards, food-processing plants, brewery, and mfg. (metal prods., water-purification equip., bldg. prods., chemicals, machinery, printing). One of the oldest cities in the state, it was named for Julien Dubuque, who had settled nearby c.1788. Native Amer. title to the territory ended with the Black Hawk Treaty of 1832, and white settlers began to pour in. Iowa's first newspaper, the Du Buque *Visitor*, was est. in 1836. The town was first a mining town, then a lumbering and milling center. It is the seat of the Univ. of Dubuque, Clarke Col., Wartburg Theological Seminary, Dubuque Community Col. Ctr. and Loras Col. Of interest are the library, with a collection of paintings; St. Raphael's Cathedral (1857); the Ham House Mus.; and Eagle Point Park. Nearby are Crystal L. Cave; Lock and Dam No. 11 on the Mississippi R.; the grave of Julien Dubuque (with a memorial tower built 1897); Dubuque Greyhound Park racetrack, on an island on the river; and a Trappist monastery, New Melleray Abbey, 3 mi/4.8 km SW of city. Some flooding occurred in area in 1993. Chartered 1841.

Duchesnay (duh-shai-NAI), village, S central Que., Canada, on L. St. Joseph (4 mi/6 km long), 20 mi/ 32 km WNW of Quebec; gold mining.

Duchesne (doo-SHAIN), county (□ 3,256 sq mi/ 8,433 sq km; 1990 pop. 12,645), NE Utah; ☉ Duchesne; 40°16′N 110°26′W. Agr. area bordering on Colo. and served by irrigation projects on Strawberry and Duchesne rivers and L. Fork. Wheat, barley, alfalfa, sugar beets, dairy prods.; cattle, sheep. Kings Peak (13,528 ft/ 4,123 m), highest point in Utah, in N edge of co., in Uinta Range. Widely scattered parts of Uintah and Ouray Indian Reservaton in N central and S central parts of co. Small part of Wasatch Natl. Forest in NW corner. Starvation Reservoir and State Park near center. Large part of Ashley Natl. Forest, including part of Uinta Range and part of High Uintas Wilderness Area, in N. Smaller part of Ashley Natl. Forest in S center. Formed 1914.

Duchesne (doo-SHAIN), town (1990 pop. 1308), ☉ Duchesne co., NE Utah, 45 mi/72 km NNE of Price, on Duchesne R., at mouth of Strawberry R.; 40°10′N 110°23′W. Elev. 5,517 ft/1,682 m. Ranch-outfitting center in irrigated agr. area; wheat, barley, alfalfa; dairying; cattle, sheep; oil and natural gas. Starvation Reservoir and State Park to NW; parts of Uintah and Ouray Indian Reservation to N, NE, and S. Settled 1904.

Duchesne River (doo-SHAIN), river, c.100 mi/161 km long, in NE Utah; rises in foothills of Uinta Mts., NW Duchesne co., 30 mi/48 km NW of Duchesne at junction of North and West Forks; flows generally E, past Duchesne and Myton, to Green R. 22 mi/35 km SE of Roosevelt. Strawberry R. joins Duchesne R. near Duchesne. Small irrigation dam and dike are 10 mi/16 km E of Duchesne on Strawberry R. River skirts through edge of fragmented Uintah and Ouray Indian Reservation.

Duchess, village (1991 pop. 477), S Alta., Canada, 70 mi/ 113 km NW of Medicine Hat; 50°44′N 111°54′W. Ranching.

Duck Hill, town (1990 pop. 586), Montgomery co., central Miss., 10 mi/16 km N of Winona; 33°37′N 89°42′W.

Cotton, corn, soybeans; cattle; mfg. (strand board). Camp McCain Natl. Guard base to NE.

Duck Island 1 (3 mi/5 km long, 2 mi/3 km wide), E N.F., Canada, in Notre Dame Bay, 35 mi/56 km SE of Cape St. John; 49°31′N 55°07′W. Chief fishing settlement is Exploits, on NE coast. **2** islet just off SW N.F., Canada, 3 mi/5 km SW of Burgeo; 47°35′N 57°42′W. Lighthouse.

Duck Island, Maine: see ISLES OF SHOALS.

Duck Islands, Ont., Canada: see GREAT DUCK ISLAND and WESTERN DUCK ISLAND.

Duck Lake, town (1991 pop. 661), central Sask., Canada, near Duck L. (6 mi/10 km long), 33 mi/53 km SW of Prince Albert; 52°48′N 106°13′W. Lumbering, woodworking, grain.

Duck Lake, small lake, central Sask., Canada, SW of Prince Albert. It was the scene of the 1st encounter in Riel's Rebellion, 1885. A large group of métis (persons of mixed Fr. and Native Amer. descent) under Gabriel Dumont defeated a detachment of Northwest Mounted Police.

Duck Lake, c.3 mi/4.8 km long, 1.5 mi/2.4 km wide, Grand Traverse co., NW Mich., just SE of Interlochen, in resort area; 44°37′N 85°44′W. Joined by stream to Green L. (W). Interlochen State Park and forest here; camping, fishing. Interlochen Center for the Arts (Natl. Music Camp).

Duck Mountain, range, W Man., Canada, extends 50 mi/80 km N-S along Sask. border. Highest point is Baldy Mt. (2,727 ft/831 m), 36 mi/58 km NW of Dauphin.

Duck River, c.50 mi/402 km long, in central Tenn.; rises c.15 mi/24 km NNW of Manchester; flows S and generally WNW, past Shelbyville, Columbia, and Centerville, to Kentucky Lake (Tennessee R.) 7 mi/11 km SW of Waverly. Receives Buffalo R.

Duckabush River, c.30 mi/48 km long, Jefferson co., NW Wash.; rises in Olympic Natl. Park at Mt. Duckabush (6,250 ft/1,905 m), N of L. Cushman; flows generally E through Olympic Natl. Forest to Hood Canal arm of Puget Sound.

Ducktown, city (1990 pop. 421), Polk co., SE Tenn., near Ga.-N.C.-Tenn. border, 50 mi/80 km E of Chattanooga; 35°02′N 84°23′W. Smelting center in coppermining region; large sulphuric acid plant. Smelter fumes, by destroying plant growth, have caused deep erosion of region.

Ducktown, town, Forsyth co., N Ga., 12 mi/19 km E of Canton; 34°14′N 84°14′W.

Ducos (dyoo-KO), town, S Martinique, 6 mi/9.7 km ESE of Fort-de-France. Bananas; rum distilling.

Dudley 1 town (1990 pop. 9,540), Worcester co., S Mass., 17 mi/27 km SSW of Worcester, near Conn. border; 42°04′N 71°57′W. Eyewear, furniture, woolens, paper. Has Nichols Col. Quinebaug R. skirts township. Settled 1714, inc. 1732. Includes Merino Village and Perryville. **2** town (1990 pop. 271), Stoddard co., SE Mo., in Mississippi alluvial plain, 7 mi/11.3 km W of Dexter; 36°47′N 90°05′W. Mfg. (wood cabinets and doors).

Dudley 1 village (1990 pop. 430), Laurens co., central Ga., 10 mi/16 km W of Dublin; 32°32′N 83°05′W. Mushroom cultivation; clothing; lumber. **2** uninc. village, Wayne co., E central N.C., 8 mi/12.9 km SSW of Goldsboro. Timber. Lumber, plywood.

Dudley (DUHD-lee), borough (1990 pop. 232), Huntingdon co., S central Pa., 22 mi/35 km S of Huntingdon, on Shoup Run; 40°12′N 78°10′W. Raystown Reservoir and Trough Creek State Park to N.

Dudleyville, uninc. town (1990 pop. 1,356), Pinal co., S central Ariz., 50 mi/80 km NNE of Tuscon, on San Pedro R. Cattle, sheep; copper, molybdenum, silver, gold. San Carlos Indian Reservation to NE; Aravaipa Canyon Wilderness Area to E; Tortilla Mts. to W.

Due West, town (1990 pop. 1,220), Abbeville co., NW S.C., 16 mi/26 km SE of Anderson; 34°19′N 82°23′W. Agr. area (poultry, livestock; dairying; grain, soybeans). Seat of Erskine Col.

Duenweg (DUHN-uh-weg), town (1990 pop. 940), Jasper co., SW Mo., suburb 6 mi/9.7 km E of downtown

Joplin; 37°04′N 94°24′W. Residential and commercial area. Light mfg.

Dufferin (DUH-fuh-rin), county (□ 557 sq mi/ 1,443 sq km; 1991 pop. 39,897), S Ont., Canada, on Grand R.; ☉ Orangeville; 44°05′N 80°10′W.

Duffield, town (1990 pop. 54), Scott co., SW Va., 17 mi/ 27 km SW of Norton, in Jefferson Natl. Forest; 36°43′N 82°47′W. Industrial minerals, coal mining equip., automotive components. Dairying; livestock; tobacco Bituminous coal. Natural Tunnel State Park to SE.

Dufresnoy (duh-fren-WAH), village, W Que., Canada, 10 mi/16 km NE of Rouyn; copper, zinc, pyrite mining.

Dufrost (DOO-frost), village, SE Man., Canada, 35 mi/ 56 km S of Winnipeg; 49°21′N 97°03′W. Dairying; grain.

Dufur (DUHF-uhr), village (1990 pop. 527), Wasco co., N Oregon, 10 mi/16 km S of the Dalles, on Fifteenmile Creek; 45°27′N 121°07′W. In agr. area (wheat, apples, cherries, grapes; hogs, cattle). Mt. Hood Natl. Forest to W.

Dugald (DOO-guhld), village, SE Man., Canada, 14 mi/ 23 km E of Winnipeg; dairying; grain.

Dugdemona River (duhj-duh-MO-nuh), c.85 mi/ 137 km long, N central La., rises in Lincoln parish, SW of Ruston, flows SE through Jackson-Bienville State Wildlife Area, joining Castor Creek to form Little R. just above Rochelle; 31°47′N 92°21′W. Forms boundary of Kisatchie Natl. Forest in S.

Dugger, town (1990 pop. 936), Sullivan co., SW Ind., 8 mi/12.9 km E of Sullivan; 39°04′N 87°16′W. In agr. area; crushed stone, bituminous coal.

Dugway, uninhabited town site, Tooele co., NW Utah, 32 mi/51 km SW of Tooele, at E edge of Great Salt Desert. Located within E boundry of Dugway Proving Grounds (860,000 acres/348,000 ha), used for testing of military vehicles and chemical warfare. Pop. in 1950 was c.1,500.

Duke, village, Jackson co., SW Okla., 13 mi/21 km WNW of Altus, near East Duke. Mfg. (gypsum wallboard, sprayers).

Duke Center, uninc. town (1990 pop. 850), Otto township, McKean co., N Pa., 8 mi/12.9 km E of Bradford; 41°57′N 78°28′W. In oil-producing area; timber.

Duke Island (12 mi/19 km long, 8 mi/12.9 km wide), in Gravina Isls., Alexander Archipelago, SE Alaska, 30 mi/ 48 km SSE of Ketchikan; 54°56′N 131°20′W. Rises to 1,778 ft/542 m; just N of border with Canada.

Dukes, county (□ 490 sq mi/1,269 sq km ; 1990 pop. 11,639), SE Mass.; ☉ Edgartown; 41°22′N 70°42′W. Comprises isl. of Martha's Vineyard and the Elizabeth Islands; former lying c.5 mi/8 km S of SW angle of Cape Cod. Summer resorts; some agr. Fishing. Formed 1695.

Dulac (DOO-lak), uninc. town (1990 pop. 3,273), Terrebonne parish, La., 15 mi/24 km S of Houma. On road through the marsh to Cocodrie; on S shore of Bayou Dulac. Shrimp, alligators. Swamp activities. Heliport.

Dulce (DOOL-sai), uninc. town (1990 pop.2,438), Rio Arriba co., NW N.Mex., on Navajo R., near Colo. state line, 62 mi/100 km ENE of Farmington; 36°55′N 107°00′W. Elev. 6,769 ft/2,063 m. Sheep, cattle; chiles, hay. Hq. of Jicarilla Indian Reservation in N. Continental Divide to E. Southern Ute Indian Reservation (Colo.) to N. Part of Carson Natl. Forest to W.

Dulles International Airport, airport, Fairfax and Loudoun cos., NE Va., about 24 mi. W of Washington, D.C., 3 mi/ 4.8 km SW of Herndon, Va.; 38°56′N 77°27′W. Opened on Nov. 19, 1962, it covers more than 16 sq mi/41 sq km and has three runways over 10,000 ft/3,048 m long. In 1995 it handled more than 10 million passengers with 245 daily flights; its 26 scheduled carriers serve 98 destinations. Major cargo hub.

Duluth (duh-LOOTH), city (1990 pop. 85,493), ☉ St. Louis co., NE Minn., on St. Louis Bay, at W end of L. Superior, 140 mi/225 km NNE of Minneapolis, opposite Superior, Wis.; 46°46′N 92°07′W. Westernmost port in Great Lakes–St. Lawrence Seaway Navigation system. A commercial, industrial, and cultural center of N Minn., as well as a major port on the Great Lakes, convention center, and the gateway to resort region to

N. Large amounts of grain, iron ore (especially taconite), oil, and bulk cargo are shipped on lake freighters and ocean vessels. Fish processing, grain elevator services, specialty fabricating; steel, concrete, piping, chemical lime, paper, hand tools, consumer goods. Tourism is important, and the military air-defense installation at Duluth International Airport is valuable to the economy. Native Americans were found here in the 1670s by the early explorers and fur traders, and included the Sieur Duluth (for whom the city was named). Permanent settlement began c.1852. Built largely on rocky bluffs overlooking the lake, the city was at first a trade and shipping center for timber. Discovery of iron (1865) in the Mesabi range made it the chief shipping point for ore for the nation's steel mills. With the opening of the St. Lawrence Seaway (1959), it became one of the leading ports on the Great Lakes for the export of grain. It is the seat of the Col. of St. Scholastica, the Duluth Institute of Technology, and a branch of the Univ. of Minnesota. It has a symphony orchestra, a community theater, various museums, including L. Superior Maritime Mus., and the St. Louis County Heritage and Arts Center. Wade Municipal Stadium in SW. Of interest are the large Aerial Lift Bridge, which dominates skyline (crosses harbor entrance), linking the city to 7 mi/11.3 km of sand beach on Park Point (Minnesota Ave.); the Skyline Parkway, winding along escarpment above the city for 15 mi/24 km; Scenic State Highway 61 follows lakeshore NE to Thunder Bay, Ontario, also called the North Shore drive; and Leif Erikson Park on lake shore. Jay Cooke State Park to SW; Cloquet Valley State Forest to N; Spirit Mt. Ski Area to SW; Fond du Lac Indian Reservation to W. Inc. 1870.

Duluth (duh-LOOTH), town (1990 pop. 9,029), Gwinnett co., N central Ga., suburb 21 mi/34 km NE of Atlanta; 34°00′N 84°09′W. Major retail center. Diverse mfg. SE RR mus. Gwinnett co. civic and cultural center.

Dumas, city (1990 pop. 12,871), ⊙ Moore co., N Texas, in high plains of the Panhandle, 45 mi/72 km N of Amarillo; 35°51′N 101°57′W. Elev. 3,668 ft/1,118 m. Oil, natural gas, and helium production; cattle; wheat, corn. L. Meredith Natl. Recreation Area to SE. Settled 1892, inc. 1930.

Dumas (DOO-muhs), town (1990 pop. 5,520), Desha co., SE Ark., 39 mi/63 km SE of Pine Bluff; 33°52′N 91°29′W. In agr. area. Light mfg. Founded c.1876.

Dumas (DOO-muhs), village (1990 pop. 407), Tippah co., N Miss., 9 mi/14.5 km SE of Ripley; 34°38′N 88°50′W. Timber; cotton, corn, soybeans; cattle; dairying. Mfg. (furniture, lumber).

Dumbarton, uninc. city, Henrico co., E central Va., residential suburb 5 mi/8 km NW of downtown Richmond; 37°36′N 77°30′W.

Dume, Point, Los Angeles co., S Calif., promontory on N shore of Santa Monica Bay, 5 mi/8 km W of Malibu and 18 mi/29 km W of Santa Monica. In Santa Monica Mt. Natl. Recreation Area.

Dumfries (DUHM-freez), town (1990 pop. 4,282), Prince William co., NE Va., near Potomac R., 15 mi/24 km SE of Manassas; 38°34′N 77°19′W. Mfg. (concrete, consumer prods.); agr. (grain, soybeans; livestock; dairying). Prince William Forest Park to W; Leesylvania State Park to NE. Quantico Marine Corps Base, Quantico Natl. Veterans Cemetery to SW; Chopawamsic Recreation Area to S.

Dummer, town (1990 pop. 327), Coos co., N N.H., 10 mi/16 km N of Berlin; 44°40′N 71°15′W. Drained by Androscoggin R. (forms Pontook Reservoir). In hunting, fishing, logging region. Livestock; timber.

Dummerston, town (1990 pop. 1,863), Windham co., SE Vt., on the Connecticut R., 6 mi/9.7 km SE of Newfane; 42°55′N 72°35′W. Wood prods.

Dumont, town (1990 pop. 705), Butler co., N central Iowa, 9 mi/14.5 km W of Allison; 42°45′N 92°58′W. Creamery.

Dumont (DOO-mawnt), village (1990 pop. 126), Traverse co., W Minn., 7 mi/11.3 km SE of Wheaton, on West Branch Mustinka R.; 45°43′N 96°25′W. Dairy prods.

Dumont (DOO-muhnt), borough (1990 pop. 17,187), Bergen co., NE N.J.; 40°57′N 73°59′W. Residential suburb of Hackensack. Settled 1677 by the Dutch; inc. 1894.

Dunbar, town (1990 pop. 8,697), Kanawha co., W central W.Va., on Kanawha R. (bridged), suburb 6 mi/9.7 km WNW of downtown Charleston; 38°22′N 81°44′W. Coal-mining region; oil wells. Steel fabricating, machining, printing, asphalt. Inc. 1921.

Dunbar, village (1990 pop. 171), Otoe co., SE Nebr., 8 mi/12.9 km W of Nebraska City, and on branch of Little Nemaha R; 40°40′N 96°01′W.

Dunbar, borough (1990 pop. 1,213), Fayette co., SW Pa., 3 mi/4.8 km SSW of Connellsville, and 8 mi/12.9 km NE of Uniontown on Dunbar Creek, near Youghiogheny R. Light mfg.; surface coal; agr. (corn, hay; livestock; dairying). Connellsville Airport to SW. Ohiopyle State Park to SE; Chestnut Ridge to SE.

Dunbarton 1 (DUHN-bahr-tuhn), town (1990 pop. 1,759), Merrimack co., S central N.H., 8 mi/12.9 km SW of Concord; 43°06′N 71°36′W. Maple syrup; pottery; vegetables, apples; poultry, livestock; dairying; maple trees, timber. Part of Hopkington Everett Flood Control reservoir on W boundary. Gorham L., on Gorham Brook, in SW. **2** former town, Barnwell co., W S.C., 25 mi/40 km SSE of Aiken. In area taken over (1951–1952) by U.S. Atomic Energy Commission for its Savannah River Plant (hydrogen-bomb materials).

Duncan, city (1991 pop. 4,301), SW B.C., Canada, SE Vancouver Isl., on Cowichan R., near its mouth on Saanich Inlet, and 30 mi/48 km NW of Victoria; 48°47′N 123°42′W. RR junction; trade center for dairying, ranching, and poultry-raising area; lumbering; woodworking.

Duncan, city (1990 pop. 21,732), ⊙ Stephens co., SW Okla., 23 mi/37 km ESE of Lawton; 34°31′N 97°58′W. Elev. 1,126 ft/343 m. In oil, farm, and cattle area; electronics, concrete, printing and publishing, apparel. Oil industry. During the late 19th cent., Duncan was a stopping-off place for cattlemen driving their herds from Texas to the railhead in Abilene, Kansas. Inc. 1892.

Duncan, town (1990 pop. 2,152), Spartanburg co., NW S.C., 12 mi/19 km W of Spartanburg; 34°56′N 82°08′W. Light mfg. Dairying; poultry, livestock; grain, soybeans, sorghum, peaches, apples.

Duncan 1 village (1990 pop. 662), Greenlee co., SE Ariz., on Gila R., near N.Mex. state line, and 31 mi/50 km SSE of Clifton; 32°44′N 109°05′W. Elev. 3,535 ft/1,077 m. Trade center, cattle-shipping point in irrigated agr. area (wheat, barley, alfalfa). Peloncillo Mts. to SW. **2** village (1990 pop. 416), Bolivar co., NW Miss., 15 mi/24 km SW of Clarksdale; 34°02′N 90°44′W. In agr. area (cotton, corn, rice, soybeans; cattle). **3** village (1990 pop. 387), Platte co., E central Nebr., 6 mi/9.7 km WSW of Columbus, and on Platte R; 41°23′N 97°29′W. Feeds.

Duncan Canal, inlet (30 mi/48 km long, 2 mi/3.2 km wide) in S coast of Kupreanof Isl., Alexander Archipelago, SE Alaska.

Duncan Falls, village, Muskingum co., central Ohio, on Muskingum R., and 7 mi/11 km SE of Zanesville. Oil wells.

Duncan Lake, reservoir, Stephens co., S Okla., on small branch of Wildhorse R., 5 mi/8 km E of Duncan; c.3.5 mi/5.6 km long; 34°31′N 97°49′W.

Duncan Town, settlement on Great Ragged Isl. or Ragged Isl., S Bahama Isls., c.225 mi/362 km SE of Nassau; 22°12′N 75°44′W. Salt panning.

Duncannon (duhn-KA-nuhn), borough (1990 pop. 1,450), Perry co., S central Pa., 13 mi/21 km NW of Harrisburg, on Susquehanna R., 1 mi/1.6 km SW of (below) mouth of Juniata R. (both rivers bridged at confluence). Mfg. (concrete, furniture); agr. (corn, hay; dairying; livestock, poultry). Appalachian Trail descends from Peters Mt. ridge (Susquehanna R. flows through gap in mt.) to cross both rivers, passes through to W. Inc. 1844.

Duncans, town (1991 pop. 1,849), Trelawny parish, N Jamaica, near the coast, 8 mi/12.9 km E of Falmouth; 18°28′N 77°32′W. Sugarcane, ginger, pimento, fruit. Adjoining NE is the now abandoned Braco airfield.

Duncansville (DUHN-kuhns-vil), borough (1990 pop. 1,309), Blair co., S central Pa., residential suburb 5 mi/

8 km SSW of Altoona, on Blair Gap Run creek. Light mfg. Blue Knob Valley Airport to S. Allegheny Portage RR Natl. Historic Site to W. Laid out 1831.

Duncanville, city (1990 pop. 35,748), Dallas co., N Texas, suburb 11 mi/18 km SW of downtown Dallas; 32°38′N 96°54′W. Drained by Tenmile Creek. It is mostly residential with some mfg. Lake Joe Pool and Cedar Hill State Park to SW. Estab. 1882, inc. 1947.

Duncombe, town (1990 pop. 488), Webster co., central Iowa, 10 mi/16 km ESE of Fort Dodge; 42°28′N 94°00′W.

Dundalk, city (1990 pop. 65,800), Baltimore co., NE Md., a suburb of Baltimore, on the Patapsco R.; 39°16′N 76°30′W. Has one of the world's largest steel plants (Sparrows Point Mill) and a 9-berth marine terminal, operated by the Md. Port Authority. Electronic parts, auto bodies, yachts. Named after Dundalk, Ireland. The first house built (c.1665) in the city was burned by the British after their march on Washington (1814) during the War of 1812. U.S. Fort Holabird is nearby. Inc. 1946.

Dundalk (duhn-DOK, -DOLK), village (1991 pop. 1,677), S Ont., Canada, 35 mi/56 km SE of Owen Sound; 44°10′N 80°23′W. Dairying; lumber.

Dundarrach (DUHN-duh-rach), uninc. village, Hoke co., S N.C., 18 mi/29 km SW of Fayetteville. Tobacco, cotton; livestock.

Dundas (DUHN-duhs), county (□ 384 sq mi/995 sq km), SE Ont., Canada, on St. Lawrence R. and on N.Y. state line; ⊙ Cornwall; 45°00′N 75°17′W. Part of United County of Stormont, Dundas, and Glengarry.

Dundas (DUHN-duhs), town (1991 pop. 21,868), S Ont., Canada, suburb of Hamilton; 43°16′N 79°56′W. At the head of the disused Desjardins Canal, which formerly gave it water connection with Hamilton and other ports.

Dundas (DUHN-duhs), village (1990 pop. 473), Rice co., S Minn., on Cannon R., and 10 mi/16 km NNE of Faribault; 44°25′N 93°12′W. Agr. area (corn, oats; livestock, poultry; dairying); mfg. (brass hardware, ventilation equip.).

Dundas, Cape, N Prince of Wales Isl., central Franklin dist., N.W.T., Canada, on Barrow Strait; 73°58′N 99°57′W.

Dundas Harbour (DUHN-duhs), trading post, SE Devon Isl., E Franklin Dist., N.W.T., Canada, on Lancaster Sound; 74°31′N 82°25′W.

Dundas Islands, W B.C., Canada, group of 4 isls. and numerous islets and rocks, in Dixon Entrance of the Pacific, NW of Prince Rupert. Largest is Dundas Isl. (□ 58 sq mi/150 sq km; 14 mi/23 km long, 8 mi/13 km wide; rising to 1,523 ft/464 m), is 25 mi/40 km NW of Prince Rupert and 12 mi/19 km S of Cape Fox, S extremity of Alaska mainland, separated from Can. mainland by Chatham Sound (15 mi/24 km wide); 69°18′N 94°20′W. Just SE are the small Baron, Dunira, and Melville isls.

Dundee 1 (duhn-DEE), town (□ 3 sq mi/7.8 sq km; 1990 pop. 2,335), Polk co., central Fla., 7 mi/11.3 km E of Winter Haven; 28°01′N 81°37′W. Citrus fruit packing. **2** town (1990 pop. 174), Delaware co., E Iowa, on Maquoketa R., and 7 mi/11.3 km NW of Manchester; 42°34′N 91°32′W. Backbone State Park with fish hatchery (N). **3** town (1990 pop. 2,664), Monroe co., extreme SE Mich., 14 mi/23 km WNW of Monroe, and on Raisin R.; 41°57′N 83°39′W. RR junction in agr. area (grain, vegetables; livestock, poultry; dairy prods.). Poultry hatcheries; auto parts, portland cement, tool and die. Settled 1827; inc. 1855. **4** town (1990 pop. 1,663), Yamhill co., NW Oregon, 10 mi/16 km NE of McMinnville; 45°16′N 123°00′W. Vegetables, grapes, berries, wheat, nuts; poultry; dairy prods.; wineries.

Dundee, Ill.: see EAST DUNDEE and WEST DUNDEE.

Dundee 1 (duhn-DEE), village (1990 pop. 107), Nobles co., SW Minn., Des Moines R. to NE, 17 mi/27 km NNE of Worthington; 43°50′N 95°28′W. Grain; livestock, poultry; dairying. Small natural lakes in area. **2** village (1990 pop. 1,588), Yates co., W central N.Y., 24 mi/39 km S of Geneva, in Finger Lakes region; 42°31′N 76°58′W. In grape-growing area; processing of apple and grape concentrates and juices, canned and bottled vegetables, and snack foods. Inc. 1847. **3** uninc. village (1990 pop. 40), Archer co., N Texas, 25 mi/40 km WSW of Wichita Falls. Oil and gas.

Dundurn (duhn-DUHRN), town (1991 pop. 496), S Sask., Canada, 23 mi/37 km SSE of Saskatoon; 51°48′N 106°30′W. Wheat.

Dundy, county (□ 920 sq mi/2,383 sq km; 1990 pop. 2,582), SW Nebr.; ☉ Benkelman; 40°10′N 101°41′W. Agr. area bordering on Kansas and Colo.; drained by Republican R. Cattle, hogs; corn, wheat, beans, sorghum. Central/Mountain time zone boundary follows E boundary. Fish hatchery N of Benkelman, another fish hatchery at Rock Creek State Recreation Area at center of co. Formed 1873.

Dune Acres, town (1990 pop. 263), Porter co., NW Ind., on L. Michigan, 14 mi/23 km NNE of Valparaiso; 41°38′N 87°06′W. Adjacent to Indiana Dunes State Park.

Dunean (duh-NEEN), uninc. town (1990 pop. 4,637), Greenville co., NW S.C., residential suburb 2 mi/3.2 km S of downtown Greenville; 34°49′N 82°25′W. Co. fairgrounds to W. Donaldson Center Airport to SE.

Dunedin (duh-NEED-in), resort city (1990 pop. 34,012), Pinellas co., W central Fla., on the Gulf Coast and St. Joseph Sound (part of the Intracoastal Waterway); 28°02′N 82°48′W. A growing commercial center; processing site for citrus fruit. City pop. doubled from 1970 to 1990. Connected to Dunedin Beach, an isl., by a causeway. Founded by Scots in 1870, inc. 1898.

Dunellen (duh-NE-luhn), borough (1990 pop. 6,528), Middlesex co., NE N.J., 18 mi/29 km SW of Newark, adjoining Plainfield; 40°35′N 74°28′W. Industrial machinery, adhesives, pumps; commercial printing. Residential. Inc. 1887.

Dunes City, town (1990 pop. 1,081), Lane co., W Oregon, 35 mi/56 km N of Coos Bay, 2 mi/3.2 km inland (E), between Siltcoos (S) and Woahink (N) lakes; 43°54′N 124°05′W. Resort area. Tourism. Oregon Dunes Natl. Recreation Area to W; Siuslaw Natl. Forest to E; Honeyman Memorial State Park to N.

Dunfermline (duhn-FUHRM-lin), village (1990 pop. 259), Fulton co., W central Ill., 28 mi/45 km SW of Peoria and 3 mi/4.8 km S of Canton; 40°29′N 90°01′W. Corn, wheat, soybeans; cattle. Bituminous coal.

Dungannon (duhn-GA-nuhn), town (1991 pop. 1,412), S Ont., Canada, 10 mi/16 km NE of Goderich. Dairying; mixed farming.

Dungannon, town (1990 pop. 250), Scott co., SW Va., 12 mi/19 km SE of Norton, on Clinch R.; 36°49′N 82°28′W. Light mfg.; dairying; livestock; tobacco, corn; timber.

Dungeness (DUHN-juh-nes), uninc. village, Clallam co., NW Wash., on Strait of Juan de Fuca, at mouth of Dungeness R. (c.35 mi/56 km long), and 15 mi/24 km ENE of Port Angeles. Fish, clams, oysters, crabs; dairying; alfalfa. New Dungeness Light, to N, and Dungeness Natl. Wildlife Refuge, to NW; the narrow peninsula forms Dungeness Bay. Dungeness State Park to W. Dungeness Spit has lighthouse.

Dunham (DUH-nuhm), town (1991 pop. 3,226), S Que., Canada, 9 mi/14 km ENE of Bedford. Dairying; pig raising.

Dunkerton, town (1990 pop. 746), Black Hawk co., E central Iowa, 10 mi/16 km ENE of Waterloo; 42°34′N 92°09′W. In agr. area.

Dunkirk 1 city (1990 pop. 2,739), on Jay-Blackford co. line, E Ind., 16 mi/26 km NNE of Muncie; 40°22′N 85°13′W. In agr. area (livestock; dairy; poultry farms; soybeans, grain); mfg. (brick, tile, glass). **2** city (□ 41 sq mi/106 sq km; 1990 pop. 13,989), Chautauqua co., SW N.Y., on L. Erie; 42°34′N 79°19′W. It is a port of entry and trades extensively with other Great Lakes ports. Located in the grape belt, the city produces wines and other grape prods.; mfg. (steel, food prods., apparel). In 1946, it developed a program to help Dunkerque, France (for which it was named), recover from World War II. Other U.S. cities followed, and established a program, called the One World Plan, to aid

war-damaged European cities. Founded c.1800, inc. as city 1880.

Dunkirk, village (1990 pop. 869), Hardin co., W central Ohio, 24 mi/39 km E of Lima; 40°47′N 83°38′W. In agr. area; transportation equip.

Dunklin, county (□ 543 sq mi/1,406 sq km; 1990 pop. 33,112), in boot heel of extreme SE Mo.; ☉ Kennett; 36°16′N 90°05′W. Bounded W by St. Francis R.; in Mississippi alluvial plain, with drainage channels. Land surface modified by New Madrid earthquakes of 1811–1812. Grows and processes cotton; rice, corn, wheat, melons, fruit, popcorn, soybeans; poultry. Mfg. at Kennett, Malden, Senath. Formed 1845.

Dunlap, city (1990 pop. 3,731), ☉ Sequatchie co., E Tenn., on Sequatchie R., and 23 mi/37 km N of Chattanooga; 35°23′N 85°23′W. In fertile agr., livestock, timber, coal-mining region; mfg. (wood prods., small engines, zippers, parachutes).

Dunlap, town (1990 pop. 1,251), Harrison co., W Iowa, 18 mi/29 km NE of Logan; 41°51′N 95°35′W. Feed mill. Inc. 1871.

Dunlap 1 village (1990 pop. 851), Peoria co., central Ill., 14 mi/23 km NNW of downtown Peoria, on Rock Island State Trail; 40°51′N 89°40′W. Corn, soybeans; light mfg. **2** village (1990 pop. 5,705), Elkhart co., N Ind., 6 mi/9.7 km NW of Goshen; 41°38′N 85°55′W. Suburb of Elkhart. **3** village (1990 pop. 65), Morris co., E central Kansas, near Neosho R., 8 mi/12.9 km SE of Council Grove; 38°34′N 96°22′W. In grazing and farming region.

Dunleith, uninc. town (1990 pop. 2,600), New Castle co., N Del., residential suburb 2 mi/3.2 km S of Wilmington, near Christina R.; 39°42′N 75°33′W. Delaware Memorial Bridge 2 mi/3.2 km SE.

Dunlevy (DUHN-lee-vee), borough (1990 pop. 417), Washington co., SW Pa., 3 mi/4.8 km SE of Charleroi, on Monongahela R.; 40°06′N 79°51′W. Some agr.

Dunlo (DUHN-lo), uninc. town (1990 pop. 850), Adams township, Cambria co., SW central Pa., 10 mi/16 km E of Johnstown, on Sulphur Creek; 40°17′N 78°43′W. Some agr.

Dunlow, uninc. village, Wayne co., W W.Va., 21 mi/34 km S of Huntington. Corn, tobacco; cattle. Bituminous coal. Coal processing. East Lynn L. reservoir and Wildlife Management Area to NE. Cabwaylingo State Forest to SE.

Dunmore (duhn-MOR), borough (1990 pop. 15,403), Lackawanna co., NE Pa., an industrial suburb 2 mi/3.2 km NE of downtown Scranton, near Lackawanna R.; 41°25′N 75°36′W. Declining coal-mining industry. Food processing; printing and publishing; apparel, automotive batteries, textile equip., fabricated metal. Pa. State Univ.–Worthington Scranton (2-year) campus near Scranton corporate limits. Moosic Mts. to SE; Scranton L. reservoir to S. Inc. 1783.

Dunmore, Lake, in Addison co., W Vt., lake (3.5 mi/5.6 km long) and resort village, 8 mi/12.9 km SSE of Middlebury, partly in Green Mt. Natl. Forest.

Dunmore Town, chief settlement of Harbour Isl., central Bahama Isls., 33 mi/53 km NE of Nassau; 25°30′N 76°38′W. Winter resort with fine harbor; tomatoes, fruit.

Dunn 1 county (□ 1,992 sq mi/5,159 sq km; 1990 pop. 4,005), W central N.Dak.; ☉ Manning; 47°21′N 102°37′W. Missouri R. (L. Sakakawea Reservoir) forms NE boundary; Little Missouri Bay of L. Sakakawea and Little Missouri R. cross N part and form Mountain/ Central time zone boundary (N part of co. is in Central time zone). Agr. area drained by Little Missouri and Knife rivers and Spring Creek. Cattle; dairy prods.; wheat, oats. Fort Berthold Indian Reservation in N. Little Missouri State Primitive Park and Killdeer Battlefield Historic Site in NW. Lake Ilo Natl. Wildlife Refuge at center. Formed 1883, organized 1908. **2** county (□ 863 sq mi/2,235 sq km; 1990 pop. 35,909), W Wis.; ☉ Menomonie; 44°57′N 54°91′W. Drained by Red Cedar and Chippewa rivers. Predominantly a dairying region, with some stock raising and lumbering; barley, oats, corn, soybeans, beans, alfalfa, hay; cattle, hogs, sheep, poultry; mfg. at Menomonie. Hoffman Hills

State Recreational Area in E; Red Cedar State Trail runs N-S in S center. Formed 1854.

Dunn, town (1990 pop. 8,336), Harnett co., central N.C., 23 mi/37 km NE of Fayetteville, 33 mi/53 km S of Raleigh, near South R.; 35°18′N 78°37′W. RR spur junction. Agr. area (cotton, tobacco, grain, sweet potatoes, peppers; poultry, livestock). Diverse mfg. Aversboro Battleground State Historical Site to S.

Dunn Center, village (1990 pop. 128), Dunn co., W central N.Dak., 34 mi/55 km NNE of Dickinson, on Spring Creek; 47°21′N 102°10′W. Killdeer Mts. to NW. Lake Ilo Natl. Wildlife Refuge to W.

Dunn Loring, uninc. town, Fairfax co., NE Va., residential suburb 10 mi/16 km W of Wash., D.C., 4 mi/6.4 km NE of Fairfax; 38°53′N 77°13′W. Stop on Orange line of Washington Metro.

Dunn Point, promontory, SE N.F., Canada, at S end of Merasheen Isl., in Placentia Bay; 47°25′N 54°22′W.

Dunnell (duh-NEL), village (1990 pop. 187), Martin co., S Minn., near Iowa state line, 18 mi/29 km WSW of Fairmont; 43°33′N 94°46′W. Grain, soybeans; livestock. East Fork Des Moines R. to N.

Dunnellon (duh-NEL-uhn), town (□ 4 sq mi/10.4 sq km; 1990 pop. 1,624), Marion co., N central Fla., on Withlacoochee R., and 22 mi/35 km WSW of Ocala; 29°03′N 82°27′W. Sawmilling, quarrying (phosphate, limestone); fertilizer mfg. Rainbow Springs nearby. Inc. 1909.

Dunning, village (1990 pop. 131), Blaine co., central Nebr., 15 mi/24 km SW of Brewster, and on Middle Loup R., at mouth of Dismal R; 41°49′N 100°05′W. Livestock; dairy and poultry prods. (turkeys); fruit. Nebr. Natl. Forest of mainly planted ponderosa pine and red cedar to W, campground (NE).

Dunning Mountain, ridge (1,900 ft/579 m–2,200 ft/ 671 m), runs N-S c.15 mi/24 km, S from Halter Creek, W of Roaring Spring, Blair co., S central Pa., to 8 mi/ 13 km N of Bedford, Bedford co., where it joins Evitts Mt., from SE. Quartzite; 40°14′N 78°26′W–40°18′N 78°26′W. Dunning Cove Valley NE of Bedford.

Dunn's River Falls, St. Ann parish, N central Jamaica, 2 mi/3 km W of Ocho Rios; 18°25′N 77°08′W. Cascading series of falls and pools which drop 600 ft/183 m down a hillside to the beach. The site is a popular tourist attraction.

Dunnstown, uninc. town (1990 pop. 1,486), Clinton co., N central Pa., residential suburb 2 mi/3.2 km ENE of Lock Haven, on West Branch Susquehanna R.; 41°08′N 77°25′W. Sproul State Forest to N.

Dunnville, town (1991 pop. 12,131), S Ont., Canada, on Grand R., near its mouth on L. Erie, and 27 mi/43 km SSE of Hamilton; 42°54′N 79°37′W. Port. Food processing; dairying; light mfg.

Dunnville, village (1990 pop. 165), Casey co., central Ky., on Green R. and 20 mi/32 km WNW of Somerset. Tobacco; livestock; dairying; light mfg.

Dunraven, Mount, Colo.: see MUMMY RANGE.

Dunraven Pass, Wyo.: see WASHBURN RANGE.

Dunrea (duhn-RAI), village, SW Man., Canada, 30 mi/ 48 km SSE of Brandon. Grain; livestock.

Dunreith, town (1990 pop. 205), Henry co., E Ind., 9 mi/ 14.5 km SSW of New Castle; 39°48′N 85°26′W. In agr. area. Laid out 1865.

Dunseith (duhn-SEETH), village (1990 pop. 723), Rolette co., N. Dak., port of entry, 21 mi/34 km WSW of Rolla and S of Turtle Mt.; 48°48′N 100°03′W. 14 mi/ 23 km N, on Can. border, is Internatl. Peace Garden. Turtle Mt. Indian Reservation to E. Lake Metigoshe State Park to NW.

Dunsmuir (DUHN-stuh-buhl), city (1990 pop. 2,129), Siskiyou co., N Calif., 42 mi/68 km N of Redding in canyon of Sacramento R., near W base of Cascade Range, 15 mi/24 km S of Mt. Shasta; 41°14′N 122°16′W. Hunting, fishing resort. Castle Crags State Park is SW. Parts of Shasta Natl. Forest to W, S and E, Klamath Natl. Forest to N. Inc. as town in 1909, as city in 1935.

Dunstable (DUHN-stuh-buhl), farming town (1990 pop. 2,236), Middlesex co., NE Mass., 8 mi/12.9 km WNW of Lowell; 42°41′N 71°30′W.

Dunstan, Maine: see SCARBOROUGH.

Dunwoody (DUHN-wud-ee), suburb (1990 pop. 26,302), De Kalb co., Ga., NE of Atlanta, 2 mi/3.2 km NE of Sandy Springs. Upper-middle-class residential area first developed in 1960s and 1970s. Borders Perimeter Center and suburban downtown. Commercial printing.

Duparquet (duh-pahr-KAI), town (1991 pop. 680), W Que., Canada, on L. Duparquet (6 mi/10 km long, 6 mi/10 km wide), 20 mi/32 km NNW of Rouyn. Gold-mining center.

Duplin (DUHP-lin), county (□ 819 sq mi/2,121 sq km; 1990 pop. 39,995), E N.C.; ⊙ Kenansville; 34°56′N 77°55′W. Forested (pine, gum), partly swampy coastal plain; drained by Northeast Cape Fear R. Tobacco; corn, cotton, wheat, oats, soybeans, sorghum, hay, cucumbers, peppers, sweet potatoes; poultry, cattle, hogs; timber. Formed 1749.

Dupo (DOO-po), village (1990 pop. 3,164), St. Clair co., SW Ill., near the Mississippi R., and 6 mi/9.7 km S of East St. Louis; suburb of St. Louis, within St. Louis metropolitan area; 38°31′N 90°12′W. Large RR yard; limestone quarries. Mfg. crushed stone; agr. (apple orchards, soybeans). Inc. 1907.

DuPont (doo-PAHNT), town (1990 pop. 177), Clinch co., S Ga., 27 mi/43 km ENE of Valdosta, and on small Suwanoochee Creek; 30°59′N 82°52′W.

Dupont, town, Jefferson co., SE Ind., 12 mi/19 km NW of Madison. Agr. area. Laid out 1849.

Dupont, village (1990 pop. 279), Putnam co., NW Ohio, 15 mi/24 km S of Defiance, and on Auglaize R.; 41°03′N 84°18′W.

Dupont (doo-PAHNT), borough (1990 pop. 2,984), Luzerne co., NE Pa., 6 mi/9.7 km SW of Scranton and 10 mi/16 km NE of Wilkes-Barre. Former anthracite coal mining area. Machining. Wilkes-Barre Scranton Internatl. Airport to NE. Inc. 1917.

Dupont Manor, uninc. town (1990 pop. 1,059), Kent co., central Del., residential suburb 2 mi/3.2 km NNW of Dover; 39°11′N 75°33′W. Campus of Del. State Univ. to S. Dover Downs Race Track to E. Agr. area (vegetables, fruit; dairying; poultry).

Duprat (duh-PRAH), village, W Que., Canada, 5 mi/8 km NW of Rouyn; gold, copper, zinc, pyrite mining.

Dupree, village (1990 pop. 484), ⊙ Ziebach co., N central S.Dak., 80 mi/129 km NW of Pierre, on Elm Creek; 45°02′N 101°35′W. Trading center; supply center for S part of large Cheyenne River Indian Reservation. Flax, wheat; dairy produce; livestock, poultry.

Dupuy (duh-PWEE), village, W Que., Canada, 45 mi/72 km NNW of Rouyn, near Ont. border; 48°50′N 79°22′W. Gold, copper, zinc mining.

Dupuyer (duh-POO-yuhr), village (1990 pop. 100), Pondera co., N Mont., on Dupuyer Creek, and 26 mi/42 km W of Conrad. Supply point in rich cattle, hogs, sheep region. Blackfeet Indian Reservation to NW; Lewis and Clark Natl. Forest to W; numerous small lakes to W.

Duquesne (doo-KAIN), city (1990 pop. 8,525), Allegheny co., SW Pa., residential suburb 10 mi/16 km SE of Pittsburgh, on the Monongahela R. (bridged), opposite (1 mi/1.6 km N of) McKeesport; 40°22′N 79°50′W. In a coal region; light mfg. Settled 1789, laid out by the Duquesne Steel Co. in 1885, inc. as a city 1917.

Duquesne (doo-KAIN), town (1990 pop. 1,229), Jasper co., SW Mo., residential suburb 4 mi/6.4 km E of downtown Joplin; 37°04′N 94°27′W.

Duquesne, Fort, Pa.: see FORT DUQUESNE.

Duran (duh-RAN), village, Torrance co., central N.Mex., 50 mi/80 km SW of Santa Rosa. Elev. 6,273 ft/1,912 m. Cattle; grain, alfalfa. Part of Cibola Natl. Forest to SW.

Durand (duh-RAND), city (1990 pop. 4,283), Shiawassee co., S central Mich., 15 mi/24 km SW of Flint; 42°54′N 83°59′W. RR junction in farm area (beans, corn, wheat, soybeans); light mfg. Inc. as village 1887, as city 1933.

Durand 1 (duh-RAND), town, Meriwether co., W Ga., 16 mi/26 km ESE of La Grange; 32°55′N 84°46′W. **2** town (1990 pop. 2,003), ⊙ Pepin co., W Wis., on Chippewa R., and 27 mi/43 km SW of Eau Claire; 44°37′N 91°57′W. In dairy and livestock area: dairy prods., vegetables, feed, beverages. Lumber. Settled c.1850, inc. 1887.

Durand, village (1990 pop. 1,100), Winnebago co., N Ill., 17 mi/27 km NW of Rockford; 42°26′N 89°19′W. In dairying and grain area.

Durango (doo-RAHN-go), state (□ 47,691 sq mi/123,520 sq km; 1990 pop. 1,349,378), N central Mexico; ⊙ Victoria de Durango (also Durango); 24°24′N 105°08′W. Fourth largest state, with 6% of total land surface of Mexico; 39 municipios. The W half of the state is dominated by the Sierra Madre Occidental. These mts. contain deposits of many different minerals; mining activities extend N into Chihuahua and S into Zacatecas. Highest mt. is Cerro Huehuento (10,335 ft/3,150 m). At N are basins and isolated mt. ranges. NE of Victoria de Durango, at Malpais de la Breña, is large zone covered with many small volcano cones. Elev. on plain 6,234 ft/1,900 m. Arid to semiarid climate with greatest rainfall on W slopes of Sierra Madre Occidental, decreasing to E and N to arid Bolsón de Mapimí, the driest part of state. State is a leading natl. producer of ferrous metals. The semiarid plains (E) afford good ranching and livestock raising. Lumbering is also economically important. On the border of Coahuila is the fertile Laguna district, where vast desert basin lands are irrigated by water from the Nazas R. Gómez Palacio is the chief settlement in this region. Cotton, wheat, sugarcane, tobacco, corn, and vegetables are grown here. Although known early to the Spanish, Durango was not opened up until 1562, when Francisco de Ibarra undertook its exploration and colonization. The early European settlers of Durango and Chihuahua (which were then called Nueva Viscaya) were strongly resisted by the native pop., but the mines and grazing lands continued to attract colonists. Durango became a separate state in 1823, shortly after the Mexican revolution against Spain.

Durango, city (1990 pop. 12,430), ⊙ La Plata co., SW Colo., on the Animas R., 120 mi/193 km SSE of Grand Junction and 35 mi/56 km NE of Farmington, N. Mex.; 37°17′N 107°52′W. Elev. 6,512 ft/1,985 m. S terminus of Durango and Silverton Narrow Gauge RR. Computer software, printing and publishing, diversified light mfg. Durango is the gateway to Mesa Verde Natl. Park (W) and is the hq. for the San Juan Natl. Forest (N). Fort Lewis Col. is here. Southern Ute Indian Reservation to S. Vallecits and Lemon reservoirs to NE. Chapman/Tophack Hill Ski Area to E. Inc. 1881.

Durango, town (1990 pop. 34), Dubuque co., E Iowa, 6 mi/9.7 km NW of Dubuque; 42°33′N 90°46′W.

Durant, city (1990 pop. 12,823), ⊙ Bryan co., central S Okla., 20 mi/32 km ESE of Ardmore; 33°58′N 96°23′W. Elev. 657 ft/200 m. RR junction. Commercial and processing center for an agr. region (peanuts, cotton, wheat; cattle), oil production; mfg. (plastics, wood prods., trailers, food processing, apparel). Red R. valley farm area to SW. Blue R. to NE. Durant is the seat of Southeastern Okla. State Univ. The ruins of Fort Washita to NW, on nearby L. Texoma, include 48 buildings. L. Texoma State Park and Lodge to W. Inc. 1873.

Durant 1 (doo-RANT), town (1990 pop. 1,549), Cedar co., E Iowa, 16 mi/26 km SE of Tipton; 41°36′N 90°54′W. Dairy prods., feed, iron castings. **2** town (1990 pop. 2,838), Holmes co., central Miss., 36 mi/58 km SSE of Greenwood, and on Big Black R.; 33°04′N 89°51′W. RR junction to S. Soybeans; timber; light mfg. Holmes County State Park to SW. Founded 1858.

Durbin, village (1990 pop. 278), Pocahontas co., E W.Va., 27 mi/43 km NNE of Marlinton, on Greenbriar R., in Monongahela Natl. Forest; 38°32′N 79°49′W. Lumber, crushed limestone.

Durfee Hill (804 ft/245 m), NW R.I., in Glocester town, 17 mi/27 km WNW of Providence.

Durham (DUH-ruhm), county (□ 629 sq mi/1,629 sq km), S Ont., Canada, on L. Ontario; ⊙ Port Hope; 44°00′N 78°40′W.

Durham (DUHR-uhm), county (□ 298 sq mi/772 sq km; 1990 pop. 181,835), N central N.C.; ⊙ Durham; 36°02′N 78°52′W. In Piedmont region; drained by Flat and Eno rivers, which join on E boundary to form Neuse R., forming Falls Lake reservoir on E boundary. Urbanized co. dominated by city of Durham in SW center. Tobacco, wheat, hay, soybeans, corn; cattle; pine forests; mfg. at Durham. Timber. Part of Camp Butner Natl. Guard Base in NE. Eno River State Park on W boundary; L. Michie reservoir (Flat R.) in N. Formed 1881.

Durham (DUHR-uhm), city (1990 pop. 136,611), ⊙ Durham co., N central N.C., in the Piedmont region, 22 mi/35 km NW of Raleigh; 35°58′N 78°54′W. Once a major tobacco and textile center, Durham is a research and education center. Medical, computer, electronic, and telecommunications equip.; sheet metal and bldg. materials; printing and publishing; plastic, paper, and lumber prods.; aircraft components; apparel. Gen. Joseph E. Johnston surrendered nearby to Gen. William T. Sherman during the Civil War. After the war the tobacco industry began with James B. Duke as the leading manufacturer. Major research and economic development at Research Triangle Park 5 mi/8 km to SSE. Durham is the seat of Duke Univ., N.C. Central Univ., and Durham Technical Community Col. Of interest are the Sarah P. Duke Memorial Gardens and the N.C. Mus. of Life and Science. Falls L. State Recreation Area on Falls L. reservoir, to E; Eno R. State Park to NW. Carolina Theater (1926). Bennett Place State Historical Site to W. Raleigh-Durham Internatl. Airport 13 mi/21 km to SE. Camp Butner Natl. Guard Base to NE. Stagville Preservation Center, Afr.-Amer. history, to NE. The area was settled c.1750; inc. 1867.

Durham, town (1991 pop. 2,558), S Ont., Canada, 28 mi/45 km SSE of Owen Sound; 44°11′N 80°49′W. Dairying; lumbering; light mfg.

Durham 1 (DUHR-uhm), uninc. town (1990 pop. 4,784), Butte co., N central Calif., in Sacramento Valley, 6 mi/9.7 km S of Chico, on Butte R.; 39°36′N 121°50′W. RR junction. Plums, prunes, peaches, kiwi fruit, walnuts, almonds, olives; rice. **2** town (1990 pop. 5,732), Middlesex co., S central Conn., 5 mi/8 km S of Middletown; 41°27′N 72°40′W. Metal cabinets, electrical supplies, tools; farming. State park here. Public library dates from 1733. Settled 1698, inc. 1708. **3** town (1990 pop. 2,842), Androscoggin co., SW Maine, on the Androscoggin R., and 10 mi/16 km SE of Auburn; 43°57′N 70°07′W. In agr. area. **4** town (1990 pop. 11,818), Strafford co., SE N.H., 5 mi/8 km SSW of Dover; 43°07′N 70°55′W. Drained by Oyster R. (in center) and Lamprey R. (in S); bounded SE by Great Bay, tidal estuary of Atlantic Ocean. Computer software; boats; vegetables, apples; poultry, cattle; dairying. Seat of Univ. of N.H.; has 18th-cent. home of Gen. John Sullivan. Settled 1635 as Oyster R. parish of Dover, inc. as town 1732. Settlement suffered greatly in Indian wars. **5** town (1990 pop. 748), Washington co., NW Oregon, residential suburb 9 mi/14.5 km SSW of Portland, bet. Tigard (N) and Tualatin (S), near Tualatin R.; 45°23′N 122°45′W. RR junction.

Durham (DUHR-uhm), village (1990 pop. 119), Marion co., central Kansas, on Cottonwood R., and 15 mi/24 km NW of Marion; 38°29′N 97°13′W. Grain, live stock.

Durham Sud, village (1991 pop. 1,051), S Que., Canada, 16 mi/26 km SSE of Drummondville. Dairying.

Durhamville, village (1990 pop. 500), Oneida co., central N.Y., on Oneida Creek, just NW of Oneida; 43°07′N 75°40′W.

d'Urville, Cape (DUHR-vil), E Ellesmere Isl., NE Franklin dist., N.W.T., Canada, on Kane Basin, at entrance of small Allman Bay; 79°28′N 74°10′W. Peary's expedition vessel the *Windward* wintered offshore, 1898–1899.

Duryea (duhr-REE-ah), borough (1990 pop. 4,869), Luzerne co., NE Pa., 6 mi/9.7 km WSW of Scranton, and 10 mi/16 km NE of Wilkes-Barre on Lackawanna R., 1 mi/1.6 km NE of its mouth on the Susquehanna R. Former anthracite coal center; light mfg. Wilkes-Barre Scranton Internatl. Airport to E. Inc. 1891.

Dushore (doo-SHOR), borough (1990 pop. 738), Sullivan co., NE Pa., 17 mi/27 km S of Towanda. Hay, corn; dairying; lumber; light mfg.; printing and publishing.

Duson (DOO-suhn), town (1990 pop. 1,465), Lafayette parish, S La., 10 mi/16 km W of Lafayette; 30°14′N

92°11'W. In agr. area (sugarcane, rice, sweet potatoes, vegetables, corn, sorghum); crawfish; mfg. (solar panels, chemical additives); oil and natural-gas field nearby.

Dustin, village (1990 pop. 429), Hughes co., central Okla., 11 mi/18 km SSW of Henryetta; 35°16'N 96°01'W. In agr. area.

Dutch Harbor–Unalaska (oo-nuh-LAS-kuh), port (1990 pop. 250), SW Alaska, on Unalaska Bay, N side of Unalaska Isl., on Aleutian Isl. chain, 3 mi/4.8 km W of town of Unalaska, with which it is now unified. Major internatl. fishing port for Bering Sea and North Pacific (is the biggest commercial fishing port in the U.S. in terms of tonnage); fishing center with 5 fish processing plants (1994). King crab became depleted in 1980s; groundfish is now a major catch. Vessels from Russia, China, Taiwan, Japan, South Korea, Seattle, and elsewhere unload fish and secure services. Makushin Volcano (4,420 ft/1,347 m) to NW.

Dutch Island, S R.I., small island (c.1 mi/1.6 km long) in Narragansett Bay, c.1 mi/1.6 km W of Conanicut Isl. Site of old Fort Greble (1863). Entire isl. is a State Park Management Area. Lighthouse on southernmost tip.

Dutchess, county (□ 825 sq mi/2,137 sq km; 1990 pop. 259,462), SE N.Y.; ⊙ Poughkeepsie; 41°45'N 73°45'W. Bounded W by the Hudson R., E by Conn. border; includes part of Taconic Mts. (state park here) and part of highlands of the Hudson R. Drained by Wappinger and Fishkill creeks. Dairying, poultry raising, diversified farming (fruit, grain, potatoes); hothouse flowers; sand and gravel, and shale (bluestone). Mfg. primarily at Poughkeepsie, Milton, Pleasant Valley, Beacon. Includes small lakes, resorts. Named in honor of Mary Beatrice D'Este, Duchess of York, wife of James II; it was one of the 10 original cos. of N.Y. state. Originally occupied by Wappingers; succeeded by large influx of Fr. Huguenots in 1720. At Hyde Park, the home and grave of Franklin D. Roosevelt and the Vanderbilt Mansion are natl. historic sites. Eleanor Roosevelt's home at Val-Kill is the only natl. historic site dedicated to a U.S. president's wife. Formed 1683.

Dutchman Peak oregon: see SISKIYOU MOUNTAINS.

Duthie, village, Shoshone co., N Idaho, 16 mi/26 km NE of Wallace and 5 mi/8 km NE of Murray, near Mont. line, in mt. region. Elev. 4,100 ft/1,250 m. Silver, lead, zinc.

Dutton, village (1991 pop. 1,201), S Ont., Canada, near L. Erie, 18 mi/29 km WSW of St. Thomas. Food processing; dairying; lumber.

Dutton, village (1990 pop. 392), Teton co., N central Mont., 30 mi/48 km NW of Great Falls; 47°51'N 111°43'W. Teton R. to N, Teton Ridge to S. Cattle, sheep, hogs; wheat, barley, oats, alfalfa. Founded in 1905; inc. 1935.

Dutton, Mount (11,041 ft/3,365 m), NW Garfield co., SW Utah, S of East Fork Sevier R., and 20 mi/32 km NNW of Panguitch, in Dixie Natl. Forest.

Duval 1 (doo-VAHL), county (□ 918 sq mi/2,378 sq km; 1990 pop. 672,971), NE Fla., on the Atlantic; coextensive (since 1968) with ⊙ Jacksonville; 30°19'N 81°39'W. Lowland area bordered by Talbot Isl. (E) and drained by St. Johns R.; coast partly swampy. Dairy and poultry prods.; corn, vegetables. Forestry (naval stores; lumber; furniture), and fishing. Mfg. at Jacksonville. Resorts along coast. Formed 1822. **2** county (□ 1,795 sq mi/4,649 sq km; 1990 pop. 12,918), S Texas; ⊙ San Diego; 27°40'N 98°31'W. Beef, dairy cattle. Oil, and a leading natural-gas producing co. of Texas. Cotton, hay, grain sorghum, vegetables. Salt, uranium. Hunting. Formed 1858.

Duvalierville, Haiti: see CABARET.

Duvall (doo-VAHL), town (1990 pop. 2,770), King co., W central Wash., 18 mi/29 km NE of Seattle, near Snoqualmie R; 47°44'N 121°58'W. Berries; dairying; poultry; mfg. (printing, farm machinery, aluminum foundry); timber. Snoqualmie Natl. Forest to E.

Duvergé (doo-ver-GAI), town (1993 pop. 8,175), Baho-ruco prov., SW Dominican Republic, near E shore of L. Enriquillo, 8 mi/12.9 km S of Neiba; 18°18'N 71°30'W. In fertile, irrigated agr. region (corn, coffee, rice, fruit); lumbering. Salt and gypsum mines nearby.

Duwamish River (duh-WAH-mish), c.12 mi/19 km long, a continuation of the Green R., in W Wash., changes name in S Seattle suburb of Tukwila, flows N to Elliott Bay at Seattle. Lower sect. (dredged channel) is part of Seattle harbor. Lower navigable portion known as Duwamish Waterway.

Duxbury 1 (DUHKS-be-ree), town (1990 pop. 13,895), Plymouth co., E Mass., on Duxbury Bay and 30 mi/48 km SE of Boston; 42°02'N 70°42'W. Summer resort; poultry, cranberries. Formerly shipbuilding. Plymouth colonists here included Miles Standish, William Brewster, John Alden. Alden's house is still standing. Settled c.1624, inc. 1637. Includes villages of Millbrook and South Duxbury (1990 pop. 3,017). **2** town (1990 pop. 976), Washington co., N central Vt., 11 mi/18 km NW of Montpelier, in Green Mts.; 44°17'N 72°49'W. Camels Hump peak (4,083 ft/1,244 m) is here; Camels Hump State Park is in village of North Duxbury.

Duxbury Bay, Mass.: see PLYMOUTH BAY.

Dwight 1 village (1990 pop. 4,230), Livingston co., NE central Ill., 19 mi/31 km NE of Pontiac; 41°06'N 88°25'W. In agr. area; granite prods. Seat of Keeley Inst. Nearby is the state prison for women. Inc. 1869. **2** village (1990 pop. 365), Morris co., E central Kansas, 18 mi/29 km SE of Junction City; 38°50'N 96°35'W. In grazing and agr. region. **3** village (1990 pop. 227), Butler co., E Nebr., 13 mi/21 km NNE of Seward; 41°04'N 97°01'W. **4** village (1990 pop. 83), Richland co., SE N.Dak., 7 mi/11.3 km WNW of Wahpeton, on Wild Rice R.; 46°17'N 96°44'W.

Dworshak Reservoir, Clearwater co., NW Idaho, on N. Fork Clearwater R., 3 mi/4.8 km NW of Orofino; c.40 mi/64 km long; 46°30'N 116°17'W. Max. capacity 3,468,000 acre-ft. Formed by Dworshak Dam (645 ft/ 197 m high), built (1972) by the Army Corps of Engineers for power generation and flood control. SW end (dam) in Nez Perce Indian Reservation and near Dworshak State Park, NE end in Clearwater Natl. Forest.

Dycusburg (DEI-kuhs-buhrg), village (1990 pop. 47), Crittenden co., W Ky., on Cumberland R., and 13 mi/ 21 km SSW of Marion; 37°09'N 88°10'W. Tobacco; livestock.

Dyer (DEI-uhr), county (□ 527 sq mi/1,365 sq km; 1990 pop. 34,854), NW Tenn.; ⊙ Dyersburg; 36°04'N 89°25'W. Bounded W by the Mississippi R., SW by Forked Deer R.; drained by Obion R. Fertile agr. area. Cotton, sorghum, corn, wheat; livestock raising; timber, sand and gravel, clay. Mfg. at Dyersburg. Formed 1823.

Dyer, city (1990 pop. 2,204), Gibson co., NW Tenn., 6 mi/ 10 km N of Trenton; 36°04'N 88°59'W. In farm area; mfg. (shoes, small engines).

Dyer, town (1990 pop. 10,923), Lake co., extreme NW Ind., near Ill. line, 9 mi/14.5 km NW of Crown Point; 41°30'N 87°31'W. Machinery parts.

Dyer, village (1990 pop. 502), Crawford co., NW Ark., 17 mi/27 km NE of Fort Smith, near Arkansas R.; 35°29'N 94°08'W.

Dyer Brook (DEI-uhr), town (1990 pop. 243), Aroostook co., E Maine, 18 mi/29 km WSW of Houlton; 46°04'N 68°13'W. Agr.

Dyer, Cape, E extremity of Baffin Isl., SE Franklin Dist., N.W.T., Canada, at tip of Cumberland Peninsula, on Davis Strait; 66°37'N 61°19'W.

Dyer Island (DEI-uhr), Knox co., S Maine, just W of and bridged to Vinalhaven Isl.; ½ mi/⅕ km long.

Dyersburg, city (1990 pop. 16,317), ⊙ Dyer co., NW Tenn., near the Mississippi R., 70 mi/113 km NNE of Memphis; 36°02'N 89°21'W. A processing and industrial center for a fertile cotton and farm area. Mfg. (wood, metal, and rubber prods.). Inc. 1850.

Dyersville, city (1990 pop. 3,703), on Delaware-Dubuque co. line, E Iowa, on North Fork Maquoketa R., and 22 mi/35 km W of Dubuque; 42°28'N 91°07'W. Livestock shipping; mfg. (shirts, concrete blocks, butter tubs). Limestone quarries nearby. Settled 1837; laid out 1851; inc. 1892.

Dyerville, village, Humboldt co., NW Calif., at junction of Eel R. and its South Fork, 33 mi/53 km SSE of Eureka. Humboldt State Redwood Park to W.

Dysart, town (1990 pop. 1,230), Tama co., central Iowa, 22 mi/35 km S of Waterloo; 42°10'N 92°18'W. Feed milling, corn processing.

Dysart (1991 pop. 243), S Sask., Canada, 40 mi/ 64 km NE of Regina. Wheat, mixed farming.

Dzam, Mexico: see DZAN.

Dzan (ZAHN), town (1990 pop. 3,648), Yucatán, SE Mexico, 4 mi/6.4 km E of Ticul. Henequen, sugarcane, corn. Sometimes Dzam.

Dzemul (ze-MOOL), town (1990 pop. 2,830), Yucatán, SE Mexico, 27 mi/43 km NE of Mérida. Henequen, corn, beans, tropical fruit.

Dzibilchaltún (zeeb-eel-chahl-TOON) [= written on flat stone], national park, in NW Yucatán, Mexico, 9 mi/15 km N of Mérida on Mexican Highway 261. Mexico's largest archaeological site with over 8,000 structures, which have been partly restored. The city was continuously inhabited for 2,500 years and most important during the 7th–10th cents. It is the Yucatán Peninsula's oldest inhabited ceremonial center. The terrain is dry with palms and cacti. Birds nest in the area of Xlacah Cenote (pool) which has a depth of 738 ft/ 225 m; many artifacts have been found in its depths.

Dzidzantún (zeed-san-TOON), town (1990 pop. 7,126), Yucatán, SE Mexico, 40 mi/64 km ENE of Mérida; 21°14'N 89°2'W. Henequen, sugarcane, corn.

Dzilám de Bravo (zee-LAHM de BRAH-vo), town (1990 pop. 1,941), ⊙ Dzilám de Bravo municipio, Yucatán, SE Mexico, on a bar off the coast, 30 mi/48 km N of Izamal; 21°24'N 88°52'W. Coastal road links to Puerto Progreso, other roads to Izamal and Merida-Valladolid Highway. Main product has been salt since pre-Hispanic times. Was important capital and port of Maya Ah Kin Chel. Picturesque fishing village and tourist resort with fine beaches; best fishing at "Bocas de Dzilám."

Dzilám González (zee-LAHM gon-SAH-les), town (1990 pop. 4,893), Yucatán, SE Mexico, 50 mi/80 km ENE of Mérida. Henequen, small farming.

Dzitás (zee-TAHS), town (1990 pop. 2,812), ⊙ Dzitás municipio, Yucatán, SE Mexico, 23 mi/37 km NW of Valladolid; 20°50'N 88°31'W. RR links with Valladolid and Mérida. Henequen, corn, sugarcane.

Dzitbalché (zeet-bal-CHAI), village (1990 pop. 7,628), Calkiní municipio, Campeche, SE Mexico, on NW Yucatán peninsula, 55 mi/89 km SW of Mérida; 20°19'N 90°02'W. Corn, sugarcane, henequen, tobacco, fruit; livestock. Road and RR links with cities of Campeche and Mérida.

Dzoncauich (zon-ka-WEECH), town (1990 pop. 2,189), ⊙ Dzoncahuich municipio, Yucatán, SE Mexico, 16 mi/ 26 km NNE of Izamal; 21°15'N 89°30'W. Henequen, corn, beans, tropical fruit.

Eads, town (1990 pop. 780), ⊙ Kiowa co., E Colo., 55 mi/ 89 km NE of La Junta; 38°28′N 102°46′W. Elev. 4,213 ft/ 1,284 m. Wheat, sunflowers, sorghum; cattle, poultry. Sand Creek Massacre site to NE. Cluster of reservoirs, to S; including Thurston, Kin, Net So Pah, Ner Grande, Ner Noshe, and Ner Shah (the Nee Reservoirs).

Eagan (E-guhn), city (1990 pop. 47,409), Dakota co., SE Minn., suburb 8 mi/12.9 km SSW of downtown St. Paul, and 11 mi/18 km SSE of downtown Minneapolis; 44°49′N 93°09′W. Bounded by Minnesota R. in NW; Mississippi R. to N and E. Mfg. (consumer goods, construction materials, printing and publishing, computers, fixtures); steel fabricating. Lebanon Hills Park on S boundary; Minnesota Zoo to S; part of Fort Snelling State Park in NW. Numerous small lakes in city.

Eagar (EE-guhr), town (1990 pop. 4,025), Apache co., E Ariz., on headstream of Little Colorado R., and 27 mi/ 43 km S of St. Johns; 34°06′N 109°17′W. Cattle; logging; sawmill. Apache-Sitgreaves Natl. Forest to S; Fort Apache Indian Reservation to SW.

Eagerville, village (1990 pop. 127), Macoupin co., SW Ill., 13 mi/21 km SSE of Carlinville; 39°06′N 89°46′W. In agr. and bituminous coal area.

Eagle, county (□ 1,691 sq mi/4,380 sq km; 1990 pop. 21,928), W central Colo.; ⊙ Eagle; 39°37′N 106°42′W. Continental Divide forms part of SE boundary. Sheep-grazing and mining area, drained by Colorado, Eagle, and Fryingpan rivers (forms Ruedi Reservoir on S boundary). Silver, gold, lead, copper, zinc. Gypsum mining. Timber. Includes parts of White R. Natl. Forest in E, S, and in NW corner. Ranges of Rocky Mts. are in E and S. Sylvan L. State Park in S. Ski-resort towns of Vail and Avon in E. Formed 1883.

Eagle 1 town (1990 pop. 1,580), ⊙ Eagle co., W central Colo., on Eagle R., at mouth of Brush Creek, and 40 mi/64 km NW of Leadville; 39°39′N 106°49′W. Elev. 6,602 ft/2,012 m. Mfg. (printing); grain, potatoes; sheep; silver, gold mines. White River Natl. Forest to S; Sylvan L. State Park to S. **2** town (1990 pop. 3,327), Ada co., SW Idaho, suburb 7 mi/11.3 km NW of downtown Boise, on Boise R.; 43°42′N 116°21′W. Light mfg. Bogus Basin Ski Area to NE; Eagle Isl. State Park is here. **3** town (1990 pop. 1,182), Waukesha co., SE Wis., 15 mi/ 24 km SW of Waukesha; 42°52′N 88°28′W. In agr. and lake-resort region. Light mfg. At E edge of Kettle Morain State Forest (S unit); Eagle L. is SE.

Eagle 1 village (1990 pop. 35), E Alaska, near Yukon (Canada) border, on Yukon R., and 90 mi/113 km NW of Dawson; 64°47′N 141°06′W. Tourism; fur-trading post and supply center for placer gold-mining operations on upper Yukon. Old Fort Egbert Natl. Preserve (army base abandoned 1911). Has school, airfield, mus. Historic riverboat landing; Yukon Queen continues summer tourist service to Dawson. Former gold rush town (1898 pop. 1,700); inc. as city 1901. **2** village (1990 pop. 120), Clinton co., S central Mich., 13 mi/21 km WNW of Lansing, near Grand R.; 42°48′N 84°47′W. **3** village (1990 pop. 1,047), Cass co., SE Nebr., 18 mi/ 29 km E of downtown Lincoln; 40°49′N 96°25′W. Auto racing.

Eagle Bay, resort village (1990 pop. 200), Herkimer co., N central N.Y., in the Adirondacks, on Fourth L. (part of Fulton Chain of Lakes), c.50 mi/80 km NNE of Utica; 43°46′N 74°50′W.

Eagle Bend, village (1990 pop. 524), Todd co., W central Minn., 16 mi/26 km NW of Long Prairie, on Eagle Creek; 46°10′N 95°01′W. Grain, beans, potatoes; livestock, poultry; dairying.

Eagle Butte, village (1990 pop. 489), Dewey co., N central S.Dak., 30 mi/48 km SSW of Timber L.; 44°59′N 101°13′W. Grain, livestock. Cheyenne R. Community Col.

Eagle Cap oregon: see WALLOWA, town.

Eagle Creek, 87 mi/140 km long, N Ky.; rises in central Scott co.; flows NNW to W of Williamstown, then SW, past Sparta and Worthville, to Kentucky R. just SW of Worthville. One of 6 streams so named in Ky.

Eagle Grove, city (1990 pop. 3,671), Wright co., N central Iowa, near Boone R., 18 mi/29 km NE of Fort Dodge; 42°40′N 93°54′W. RR junction; livestock shipping. Mfg. (prepared food, animal feed, agr. chemicals, wood and metal prods.); soybean processing; poultry packing. Sand and gravel pits nearby. Location of Iowa Central Community Col. Inc. 1882

Eagle Harbor, town (1990 pop. 38), Prince Georges co., central Md., on the Patuxent R., and 15 mi/24 km E of La Plata; 38°34′N 76°42′W. Inc. 1929.

Eagle Harbor, resort village, Keweenaw co., NW Upper Peninsula, Mich., on L. Superior, and 30 mi/48 km NE of Houghton; 44°27′N 88°09′W. Former copper-shipping point.

Eagle Island, small island in Casco Bay, Cumberland co., SW Maine, SW of Harpswell. Site of Admiral Peary's summer home, containing many trophies.

Eagle Lake 1 town (1990 pop. 1,758), Polk co., central Fla., 8 mi/12.9 km NE of Bartow, near several small lakes; 27°58′N 81°45′W. **2** town (1990 pop. 942), including Eagle L. village, Aroostook co., N Maine, on Eagle L., and 15 mi/24 km S of Fort Kent; 47°03′N 68°37′W. In hunting, fishing area. Seat of Northern Maine General Hosp. Settled 1840, inc. 1911. **3** town (1990 pop. 3,551), Colorado co., S Texas, 60 mi/97 km W of Houston, and on Eagle L. (c.2.5 mi/4 km long); 29°35′N 96°19′W. Elev. 170 ft/52 m. RR junction. Cotton; rice, soybeans, peanuts, sorghum; timber; mfg. (concrete prods.). Attwater Prairie Chicken Natl. Wildlife Refuge to N. Founded c.1840.

Eagle Lake, village (1990 pop. 1,703), Blue Earth co., S Minn., 6 mi/9.7 km E of Mankato, at S end of Eagle L.; 44°09′N 93°52′W. Agr. area (corn, oats, alfalfa, soybeans; livestock); mfg. (livestock equip.).

Eagle Lake (□ 130 sq mi/337 sq km), W Ont., Canada, 10 mi/16 km WSW of Dryden, in gold-mining region; 30 mi/48 km long, 10 mi/16 km wide. At N end is Vermilion Bay village.

Eagle Lake 1 central Lassen co., NE Calif., 12 mi/19 km NNW of Susanville; 15 mi/24 km long, 2 mi/3.2 km– 6 mi/9.7 km wide. Receives Pine R. from W. Eagle L. Resort at S end. Lassen Natl. Forest to W, refuge for osprey. **2** Piscataquis co., N central Maine, 80 mi/ 129 km N of Dover-Foxcroft, in wilderness recreational area; 9 mi/14.5 km long, 2 mi/3.2 km wide. Joined to Churchill and Chamberlain lakes. Part of Allagesh Wilderness Waterway.

Eagle Lake, Aroostook co., Maine: see FISH RIVER LAKES.

Eagle, Mount, highest peak (1,165 ft/355 m) of St. Croix Isl., U.S. Virgin Isls., 7 mi/11.3 km W of Christiansted; 17°45′N 64°49′W.

Eagle Mountain, uninc. town (1990 pop. 1,890), Riverside co., S Calif., c.40 mi/64 km ENE of Indio, and 10 mi/16 km NNW of Desert Center, on Colorado R. Aqueduct. Joshua Tree Natl. Monument to N and W. Desert resort area.

Eagle Mountain Lake, reservoir (□ 15 sq mi/39 sq km), Tarrant and Wise cos., N Texas, on W Fork Trinity R. above L. Worth, 12 mi/19 km NW of Fort Worth; 32°51′N 97°30′W. Lake is 13 mi/21 km long; max. capacity 716,000 acre-ft. Formed by Eagle Mt. Dam (earth fill; 127 ft/39 m high), built (1933) for flood control, irrigation, and water supply for Fort Worth. State fish hatchery. Fort Worth Nature Center and Refuge below dam.

Eagle Mountains, Texas: see EAGLE PEAK.

Eagle Nest, village (1990 pop. 189), Colfax co., N N.Mex., in Sangre de Cristo Mts., 20 mi/32 km ENE of Taos; 36°32′N 105°15′W. Elev. 8,203 ft/2,500 m. Cattle, sheep; coal. Eagle Nest L. (dam) on Cimarron R. just S; Wheeler Peak, part of Carson Natl. Forest, to W. Called Therma until 1935. Angel Fire Ski Area to S; Cimarron Canyon Ski Area to E; Pueblo de Taos Indian Reservation to SW.

Eagle Nest Dam, N.Mex.: see CIMARRON RIVER.

Eagle Park, uninc. village, Madison co., SW Ill., S of Madison, at W end of Horseshoe L. Residential area.

Eagle Pass, city (1990 pop. 20,651), ⊙ Maverick co., SW Texas, 52 mi/84 km SSE of Del Rio, a port of entry on the Rio Grande opposite Piedras Negras, Mexico; 28°42′N 100°29′W. Elev. 726 ft/221 m. Tourist center and shipping and processing point for the area's agr. (cattle; wheat, pecans, oats). The city has also prospered from mineral processing and internatl. trade. Oil and gas; sand and gravel, mfg. (small arms, apparel, concrete). Site of a U.S. Army camp during the Mexican War, it was on one of the main routes to Calif. during the gold rush. In 1855 trouble with the Mexicans led to the burning of Piedras Negras. Fort Duncan (1849), part of which still stands in restored stone bldgs., was a base for raids against Mexicans and Native Americans and it housed thousands of U.S. troops during the Villa revolution in Mex. just before World War I. Inc. 1888.

Eagle Pass, pass, through Gold Range in Monashee Mts., 7 mi/11.3 km SW of Revelstoke, B.C., Canada, bet. Shuswap L. and Columbia R.; elev. 1,804 ft/550 m. Canadian Pacific RR route and Trans-Canada Highway route.

Eagle Peak 1 mountain (11,845 ft/3,610 m) in Mono co., E Calif., in the Sierra Nevada, 18 mi/29 km NW of Mono L., Eldorado Natl. Forest. **2** mountain (9,802 ft/ 2,988 m) in Catron co., W N.Mex., in Tularosa Mts., 11 mi/18 km E of Reserve; W of Continental Divide, in Gila Natl. Forest. **3** mountain (7,510 ft/2,289 m) in S Hudspeth co., extreme W Texas, near the Rio Grande, 16 mi/26 km SW of Van Horn; highest peak of Eagle Mts., small range (c.15 mi/24 km long NW-SE) lying bet. Quitman Mts. (NW) and Van Horn Mts. (SE).

Eagle Peak 1 Calif.: see YOSEMITE NATIONAL PARK. **2** Calif.: see WARNER MOUNTAINS.

Eagle Point, town (1990 pop. 3,008), Jackson co., SW Oregon, 10 mi/16 km N of Medford, on Little Butte Creek; 42°28′N 122°47′W. Riverboat mfg. Part of Rogue R. Natl. Forest to E; TouVelle State Park to SW.

Eagle River, town (1990 pop. 1,374), ⊙ Vilas co., N Wis., on small Eagle R., and 20 mi/32 km NE of Rhinelander; 45°55′N 89°15′W. In dairying and lumbering area; year-round resort and sports center. Light mfg.; printing and publishing. Nearby is a chain of 27 lakes. Chanticleer Ski Area to E; Nicolet Natl. Forest to E; American Legion State Forest to W. Inc. as village in 1923, as city in 1937.

Eagle River, village, ⊙ Keweenaw co., NW Upper Peninsula, Mich., 24 mi/39 km NE of Houghton, on L. Superior on NW shore of Keweenaw Peninsula. Summer resort area.

Eagle River, c.70 mi/113 km long; W central Colo.; rises in SE Eagle co., at Continental Divide; flows NW past Minturn and W, past Eagle, to Colorado R. at Dotsero, West Eagle co.

Eagle River Peak, Colo.: see JACQUE PEAK.

Eagle Rock, uninc. village, Botetourt co., W.Va., 25 mi/ 40 km N of Roanoke, on James R., near mouth of Craig Creek, in Jefferson Natl. Forest. Mfg. (machinery, apparel); agr. (livestock); timber; limestone quarrying.

Eagle Rock, N residential sect. of Los Angeles city, Los Angeles co., S Calif., 5 mi/8 km N of downtown Los Angeles. Glendale to N, Pasadena to E. Seat of Occidental Col. Annexed 1923 by Los Angeles.

Eagles Mere, borough (1990 pop. 123), Sullivan co., NE Pa., 28 mi/45 km ENE of Williamsport, on Eagles Mere L.; 41°24′N 76°34′W. Elev. 2,000 ft/610 m. Eagle Mere Airport to SW. Wyoming State Forest to N; Worlds End State Park to N.

Eaglesham (EE-guhl-shuhm), village (1991 pop. 184), W Alta., Canada, near Peace R., 40 mi/64 km SW of Peace R. town; 55°47′N 117°54′W. Lumbering, mixed, farming, wheat.

Eagleton Village, village, Blount co., E Tenn., 2 mi/3 km E of Alcoa.

Eagleville, city (1990 pop. 462), Rutherford co., central Tenn., 16 mi/26 km SW of Murfreesboro; 35°45′N 86°39′W.

Eagleville 1 town (1990 pop. 275), Harrison co., NW Mo., 14 mi/23 km N of Bethany; 40°28′N 93°59′W.

2 uninc. town (1990 pop. 3,637), Montgomery co., SE Pa., residential suburb 18 mi/29 km NW of Philadelphia; 40°09′N 75°24′W. Agr. includes dairying, livestock; grain, nursery stock. Evansburg State Park to NW.

Eakly (EEK-lee), village (1990 pop. 277), Caddo co., W central Okla., 23 mi/37 km NW of Anadarko; 35°18′N 98°33′W. In agr. area; mfg. (peanut processing). Fort Cobb L. reservoir to SE. Inc. 1930.

Eardley (UHRD-lee), village, SW Que., Canada, on L. Deschênes, 18 mi/29 km WNW of Ottawa; molybdenum mining.

Earl, village (1990 pop. 230), Cleveland co., S N.C., 6 mi/9.7 km S of Shelby, near S.C. state boundary; 35°11′N 81°31′W. Cotton, grain, soybeans, poultry, livestock.

Earl Grey, village (1991 pop. 289), S Sask., Canada, 33 mi/53 km N of Regina; wheat, livestock.

Earl Park, town (1990 pop. 443), Benton co., W Ind., on small Sugar Creek, and 7 mi/11.3 km NW of Fowler; 40°41′N 87°25′W. In agr. area. Laid out 1872.

Earle, town (1990 pop. 3,393), Crittenden co., E Ark., 27 mi/43 km WNW of Memphis, Tenn.; 35°16′N 90°27′W. In cotton- and rice-growing area. Light mfg.; rice milling. Inc. 1905.

Earlham, town (1990 pop. 1,157), Madison co., S central Iowa, 13 mi/21 km NNW of Winterset; 41°29′N 94°07′W. In agr. area. Limestone quarries nearby.

Earlimart, uninc. town (1990 pop. 5,881), Tulare co., S central Calif., in San Joaquin Valley, 22 mi/35 km S of Tulare; 35°53′N 119°16′W. Cotton; citrus orchards, grapes, sugar beets, grains, nuts; cattle, hogs, poultry. Pixley Natl. Wildlife Refuge to NW; Colonel Allensworth State Historical Park to SW.

Earling, town (1990 pop. 466), Shelby co., W Iowa, 10 mi/16 kmi. NNW of Harlan; 41°46′N 95°25′W. Hybrid-seed corn.

Earlington, town (1990 pop. 1,833), Hopkins co., W Ky., 5 mi/8 km S of Madisonville; 37°16′N 87°31′W. In coal mining and agr. (dairy prods.; livestock) area. Fishing in nearby small lake.

Earlsboro, village (1990 pop. 535), Pottawatomie co., central Okla., 8 mi/12.9 km SE of Shawnee; 35°19′N 96°47′W. Corn, peanuts; oil wells.

Earlton, village (1990 pop. 69), Neosho co., SE Kansas, 7 mi/11.3 km S of Chanute; 37°35′N 95°28′W. Stock raising, agr.

Earlville, city (1990 pop. 1,435), La Salle co., N Ill., 16 mi/26 km NNW of Ottawa; 41°35′N 88°55′W. In agr. area; RR junction. Food processing; corn, soybeans, livestock. Founded c.1854, inc. 1869.

Earlville, town (1990 pop. 822), Delaware co., E Iowa, 10 mi/16 km E of Manchester; 42°28′N 91°16′W. Creamery, poultry hatchery.

Earlville, village (□ 1 sq mi/2.6 sq km; 1990 pop. 883), on Madison-Chenango co. line, central N.Y., at junction of Chenango and Sangerfield rivers, 28 mi/45 km SSW of Utica; 42°44′N 75°32′W. In dairying area. Earlville Opera House is a Natl. Historic Landmark and is part of Earlville Historic Dist.

Early, county (□ 526 sq mi/1,362 sq km; 1990 pop. 11,854), SW Ga.; ⊙ Blakely; 31°20′N 84°55′W. Bounded W by Ala. state line, formed here by Chattahoochee R. Coastal plain. Agr. includes cotton, corn, peanuts, pecans, soybeans, sorghum, wheat; cattle, hogs, lumber. Drained by Spring Creek. Formed 1818.

Early 1 town (1990 pop. 649), Sac co., W Iowa, near Boyer R., 8 mi/12.9 km WNW of Sac City; 42°27′N 95°09′W. Grain elevator. **2** town (1990 pop. 2,380), Brown co., central Texas, 3 mi/4.8 km E of Brownwood; 31°44′N 98°56′W. Agr. area near Pecan Bayou (cattle, sheep, goats; peanuts, pecans, wheat, vegetables). Light mfg.

Earlysville, uninc. village, Albermarle co., N central Va., 9 mi/14.5 km N of Charlottesville; 38°09′N 78°28′W. Mfg. (aircraft instrumentation, electrical equip.). Charlottesville-Albermarle Co. Airport is here.

Earth, town (1990 pop. 1,228), Lamb co., NW Texas, 23 mi/37 km NNW of Littlefield; 34°13′N 102°24′W. Cattle, sheep; cotton; oil and gas; light mfg.

Earth City, uninc. industrial area, St. Louis co., E Mo.,

17 mi/27 km NW of downtown St. Louis, on Missouri R. opposite city of St. Charles. Bordered on N and E by Bridgeton; on S by Maryland Hts. A major floodplain economic development protected by river levees. Has office complexes. Mfg. (RR freight cars, automation systems, conveyor belts, drilling rigs, printing, barcoded labels, industrial marking equip., sheet-metal fabricator, truss connectors, sportswear, envelopes, plastic sheets and tubes, dental instruments). No residential land use.

Earthquake Lake, Gallatin and Madison cos., SW Mont.: see QUAKE LAKE.

Easington, town (1991 pop. 2,378), St. Thomas parish, SE Jamaica, 14 mi/23 km E of Kingston; 17°55′N 76°36′W. In fruit-growing region (bananas, coconuts, sugarcane, coffee).

Easley, city (1990 pop. 15,195), Pickens co., NW S.C., 12 mi/19 km W of Greenville in the foothills of the Blue Ridge Mts.; 34°49′N 82°35′W. Mfg. includes textiles, industrial machinery, plastic prods., electronics, transportation equip., and printing. Agr. includes dairying, poultry, eggs, hogs, corn. Inc. 1874.

East Albany (AWL-buh-nee), village (1990 pop.), Dougherty co., SW Ga., near Albany; 31°34′N 84°6′W.

East Alliance, village, Mahoning co., E Ohio, adjacent to Alliance, on Mahoning R.

East Alton (AHL-tuhn), village (1990 pop. 7,063), Madison co., SW Ill., on the Mississippi, and 4 mi/6.4 km E of Alton, suburb of St. Louis; 38°52′N 90°06′W. Mfg. (transportation equip. construction materials, copper sheeting, ammunition). Inc. 1894.

East Andover, N.H.: see ANDOVER.

East Angus (ANG-guhs), town (1991 pop. 3,639), S Que., Canada, on St. Francis R., and 13 mi/21 km ENE of Sherbrooke; 45°29′N 71°40′W. Pulp and paper milling, brick making; dairying, pig-raising region.

East Ann Arbor, uninc. city, Washtenaw co., SE Mich., suburb 4 mi/6.4 km E of Ann Arbor.

East Arcadia, village (1990 pop. 468), Bladen co., SE N.C., 27 mi/43 km WNW of Wilmington; 34°22′N 78°19′W. Cape Fear R. (Lock No. 1) to NE. Cotton, peanuts, tobacco, corn, sweet potatoes; poultry, livestock.

East Ashtabula (ASH-tuh-BYOO-luh), village, Ashtabula co., NE Ohio.

East Aspetuck River (AS-pe-tuhk), c.18 mi/29 km long, W Conn.; rises in W Litchfield co. N of Warren; flows generally S, joining West Aspetuck R. just above junction with the Housatonic near New Milford. Aspetuck R. is S, in Fairfield co.

East Aurora, suburban village (□ 2 sq mi/5.2 sq km; 1990 pop. 6,647), Erie co., W N.Y., 15 mi/24 km SE of Buffalo; 42°46′N 78°37′W. Mfg. (industrial equip., electrical and electronic equip., consumer goods), metal fabrication. Seat of Christ the King Seminary. Site (1895–1939) of the Roycroft Shops, founded by Elbert Hubbard. Restored home of Millard and Abigail Fillmore as a Natl. Historic Landmark. Inc. 1874.

East Baldwin, hamlet of Baldwin township, Cumberland co., SW Maine, c.25 mi/40 km WNW of Portland; 43°48′N 70°40′W.

East Bangor (BANG-gor), borough (1990 pop. 1,006), Northampton co., E Pa., 13 mi/21 km N of Easton; 40°52′N 75°11′W. Agr. (grain, soybeans, potatoes; livestock, dairying).

East Bank, town (1990 pop. 892), Kanawha co., W central W.Va., on the Kanawha R., 14 mi/23 km SE of Charleston; 38°13′N 81°27′W. Coal-mining region.

East Barre (BER-ee), village of Barre town, Washington co., central Vt.; granite. Flood-control dam of Winooski R. system here.

East Baton Rouge (BA-tuhn ROOZH), parish (□ 462 sq mi/1,197 sq km; 1990 pop. 380,105), SE central La.; ⊙ Baton Rouge; 30°27′N 91°08′W. Shipping, industrial, and commercial center for large region. Bounded E by Amite R., S in part by Bayou Manchac, W by Mississippi R. Drained by Comite R. Diversified industry; oil and gas fields; sand and gravel; timber. In agr. area (home gardens, peas, sugarcane, vegetables;

cattle, horses, poultry, goats, exotic fowl; dairying); alligators. One of the Fla. parishes of SE La., former Br. colony of W Florida. Port Hudson State Commemorative Area in NW corner. Formed 1810.

East Battle Lake, Minn.: see BATTLE LAKE.

East Bay, Texas: see GALVESTON BAY.

East Bend, village (1990 pop. 619), Yadkin co., NW N.C., 16 mi/26 km NW of Winston-Salem; 36°13′N 80°30′W. Tobacco, grain, soybeans, poultry, livestock, dairying. Mfg. (wooden furniture).

East Berlin, village, Hartford co., Conn.: see BERLIN.

East Berlin (BUHR-lin), borough (1990 pop. 1,175), Adams co., S Pa., on Conewago R.,13 mi/21 km W of York, on Conewago Creek, at mouth of Beaver Creek; 39°56′N 76°58′W. Mfg. (telecommunications components, fertilizer, furniture, wood prods.); agr. (grain, soybeans, potatoes, apples; poultry, livestock, dairying) L. Meade reservoir (residential development) to NW.

East Bernard, town (1990 pop. 1,544), Wharton co., S Texas, 15 mi/24 km N of Wharton; 29°31′N 96°03′W. In agr. (rice, cotton), cattle and poultry ranching area; mfg. (machine-tool accessories, kites, cabinets).

East Bernstadt (BUHRN-stat), uninc. town (1990 pop. 950), Laurel co., SE Ky., in Cumberland foothills, 4 mi/6.4 km NNW of London, 5 mi/8 km ENE of Bernstadt. Agr. (tobacco; livestock; dairying); mfg. (bathroom fixtures, whiskey-barrel staves, wood prods.); coal region. Wood Creek L. reservoir and part of Daniel Boone Natl. Forest to W.

East Berwick (BUHR-wik), uninc. town (1990 pop. 2,128), Salem township, Luzerne co., E central Pa., residential suburb 1 mi/1.6 km E of Berwick, on Susquehanna R.; 41°03′N 76°13′W.

East Bethel (BE-thel), town (1990 pop. 8,050), Anoka co., E Minn., residential suburb 25 mi/40 km N of downtown Minneapolis; 45°20′N 93°12′W. Mfg. (trophies); agr. (alfalfa, rye, dairying, poultry). Andover L. and part of Coon L. in SE corner. Carlos Avery Wildlife Area to E.

East Bloomfield, village (1990 pop. 541), Ontario co., W central N.Y., 20 mi/32 km SSE of Rochester; 42°53′N 77°25′W. In fruit-growing region. Mfg. of hunting and sporting goods.

East Blythe, uninc. town (1990 pop. 1511), Riverside co., S Calif., 2 mi/3.2 km E of Blythe; Colorado R. 3 mi/4.8 km to E.; 33°37′N 114°35′W. Colorado R. Indian Reservation (Calif./Ariz.) to N. Hwy service center (I-10). Cotton, grain, alfalfa.

East Borough, village (1990 pop. 896), Sedgwick co., S Kansas, suburb 4 mi/6.4 km E of downtown Wichita; 37°40′N 97°15′W. Oil discovered here in 1930.

East Boston, Mass.: see BOSTON.

East Brady (BRAI-dee), borough (1990 pop. 1,047), Clarion co., W central Pa., 13 mi/21 km NE of Butler, on Allegheny R. (bridged) in sharp bend in river; 40°58′N 79°36′W. Mfg. includes machining; agr. (corn, hay, potatoes; livestock, dairying). bituminous coal, limestone; timber. Laid out 1866.

East Brainerd, town (1990 pop. 11,594), Hamilton co., SE Tenn., suburb 6 mi/10 km SE of Chattanooga, 34°59′N 85°09′W.

East Braintree, Mass.: see BRAINTREE.

East Branch Clarion River Lake, reservoir (□ 2 sq mi/5.2 sq km), Elk co., NW Pa., on Clarion R., in Elk State Forest, 26 mi/42 km ESE of Bradford; 41°34′N 78°36′W. Max. capacity 103,000 acre-ft. Formed by E. Branch Dam (184 ft/56 m high), built (1952) by Army Corps of Engineers for flood control; also used for recreation.

East Brewster, Mass.: see BREWSTER.

East Brewton, city (1990 pop. 2,579), Escambia co., S Ala., c.65 mi/105 km NE of Mobile, near Conecuh R.; 31°5′N 87°3′W. suburb of Brewton. Veneer prods.

East Bridgewater, town (1990 pop. 11,104), including East Bridgewater village, Plymouth co., E Mass., 23 mi/37 km S of Boston, just SE of Brockton; 42°02′N 70°57′W. Machinery mfg.; dairying, fruit farming. Settled 1649, set off from Bridgewater 1823.

East Brimfield Dam, Mass.: see QUINEBAUG RIVER.

East Brimfield Lake, reservoir, Worcester co., S central Mass., on Quinebaug R., 8 mi/13 km W of Southbridge;

42°07′N 72°08′W. Max. capacity 71,000 acre-ft. Formed by E. Brimfield Dam (48 ft/15 m high), built (1960) by Army Corps of Engineers for flood control; also used for recreation. Holland Pond Recreational Area on SE part of reservoir.

East Brookfield, town (1990 pop. 2,033), Worcester co., S central Mass., 12 mi/19 km WSW of Worcester; 42°12′N 72°03′W. Settled 1664, set off from Brookfield 1920.

East Brooklyn, village (1990 pop. 80), Grundy co., NE Ill., 25 mi/40 km SSW of Joliet, in agr. area (corn, soybeans; dairying); 41°10′N 88°16′W.

East Brooklyn, Conn.: see BROOKLYN, town.

East Broughton (BRO-tuhn), village (1991 pop. 1,278), S Que., Canada, 15 mi/24 km NE of Thetford Mines; 46°13′N 71°08′W. Asbestos mining, lumbering, maple-sugar making. 1 mi/2 km NW is village of East Broughton Station; mfg. (apparel).

East Brunswick, township (1990 pop. 43,548), Middlesex co., central N.J., 2 mi/3.2 km S of New Brunswick; 40°25′N 74°25′W. Residential and commercial. Inc. 1860.

East Burke, Vt.: see BURKE.

East Butler, borough (1990 pop. 725), Butler co., W Pa., suburb 3 mi/4.8 km ENE of Butler, on Bonnie Creek; 40°52′N 79°50′W. Agr. (corn, hay; dairying; livestock); some light mfg.

East Caicos, uninhabited isl., Turks and Caicos Isls., E of Middle Caicos, on Turk Isl. Passage; 21°40′N 71°30′W.

East Canaan, Conn.: see NORTH CANAAN.

East Canada Creek, c.35 mi/56 km long, E central N.Y., rises in the Adirondacks in S Hamilton co., flows generally SW, past Dolgeville, to Mohawk R. 4 mi/6.4 km W of St. Johnsville. Dams impound small lakes in lower course.

East Canton, village (1990 pop. 1,742), Stark co., E central Ohio, 5 mi/8 km E of Canton; 40°47′N 81°17′W. Tiles, bricks, and plastic-parts manufactures. Founded 1805.

East Cape Girardeau, village (1990 pop. 451), Alexander co., S Ill., on Mississippi R. (bridged here) opposite Cape Girardeau, Mo.; 37°17′N 89°28′W. Wheat. Shawnee Natl. Forest to E.

East Carbon City, town (1990 pop. 1,270), Carbon co., central Utah, 22 mi/35 km E of Price; 39°32′N 110°24′W. Service center for coal mining at Sunnydale, 3 mi/4.8 km NE. Est. in 1970s from combining Dragerton and Columbia.

East Caroga Lake, N.Y.: see CAROGA LAKE.

East Carondelet (ka-RON-do-LET), village (1990 pop. 630), St. Clair co., SW Ill., near the Mississippi R. 5 mi/8 km S of E. St. Louis, suburb of St. Louis; 38°32′N 90°14′W. Agr. (soybeans, hogs); mfg. paints. Damaged in floods of 1993.

East Carroll, parish (☐ 432 sq mi/1,119 sq km; 1990 pop. 9,709), extreme NE La.; ⊙ Lake Providence; 32°49′N 91°11′W. Bounded by the Mississippi R., W by Bayou Macon, N by Ark. line, in Delta region. Source of Tensas R. Agr. (cotton, corn, sorghum, home gardens, rice, soybeans, wheat, pecans; cattle); logging. Bayou Macon State Wildlife Area in NW. Named after James Carroll, signer of the Declaration of Independence. Formed 1877.

East Chain of Lakes, S Minn., N Iowa: See MIDDLE CHAIN OF LAKES.

East Chicago, city (1990 pop. 33,892), Lake co., extreme NW Ind., on L. Michigan; 41°39′N 87°27′W. In the industrialized Calumet region, adjoining Gary, Hammond, and Whiting; inc. 1889. It is a very large port, and its Indiana Harbor on L. Michigan is connected with the Grand Calumet R. by a ship and barge canal. The city's mfg. base is dominated by heavy industry such as steelworks, scrap-iron processing, RR-equip. shops, and chemical plants, but its pop. has decreased by nearly 12% since the 1970s.

East Chillicothe (CHI-li-KAH-thee), village, Ross co., S central Ohio.

East Chop, headland, Oak Bluffs, N Martha's Vineyard,

SE Mass., on E side of entrance to harbor of Vineyard Haven. Lighthouse.

East Cleveland, city (1990 pop. 33,096), Cuyahoga co., NE Ohio, a suburb of Cleveland; inc. 1911; 41°32′N 81°35′W. Mostly residential, it has some declining light industry. Site of a General Electric lamp factory and research laboratory.

East Cleveland, village, Bradley co., SE Tenn.

East Columbia, Texas: see WEST COLUMBIA.

East Compton, uninc. town (1990 pop. 7967), Los Angeles co., S Calif., residential suburb 10 mi/16 km SSE of downtown Los Angeles and 2 mi/3.2 km E of Compton, on Los Angeles R.; 33°54′N 118°11′W.

East Conemaugh (KON-maw), borough (1990 pop. 1,470), Cambria co., W central Pa., residential suburb 3 mi/4.8 km NE of Johnstown, on Little Conemaugh R.; 40°21′N 78°53′W. Coal mining. Inc. 1891.

East Cote Blanche Bay (kot BLAHNSH), arm of the Gulf of Mexico, in St. Mary parish, S La., c.30 mi/48 km SSE of New Iberia; 12 mi/19 km wide at entrance; 29°33′N 91°38′W. Passage connects it with W. Cote Blanche Bay to NW. Marsh Isl. is to W, mainland to N and E, gulf to S, Atchafalaya Delta to E. Oil and gas field nearby.

East Coulée (koo-LAI), town, S Alta., Canada, on Red Deer R., and 14 mi/23 km SE of Drumheller; 51°20′N 112°29′W. Coal mining; cattle, wheat. Near Badlands area.

East Dennis, Mass.: see DENNIS.

East Detroit, Mich.: see EASTPOINTE.

East Douglas, Mass.: see DOUGLAS.

East Dublin (DUHB-lin), town (1990 pop. 2,524), Laurens co., Ga., 1 mi/1.6 km E of Dublin; 32°33′N 82°52′W. Mfg. includes concrete block, meat by-products, carpet.

East Dubuque (duh-BYOOK), residential city (1990 pop. 1,914), Jo Daviess co., extreme NW Ill., near Wis. state line, on the Mississippi R., opposite Dubuque, Iowa (connected by bridge); 42°29′N 90°38′W. In agr. area (cattle, hogs, sheep; dairy prods.); mfg. (iron castings, ammonia solutions). Popular ski resort. A natl. wildlife refuge is nearby. Inc. 1857.

East Duke, village (1990 pop. 360), Jackson co., SW Okla., 8 mi/12.9 km WNW of Altus, near Duke; 34°39′N 99°34′W.

East Dundee (duhn-DEE), village (1990 pop. 2,721), Kane co., NE Ill., on Fox R., and satellite community c.35 mi/56 km WNW of Chicago; 42°06′N 88°15′W. In agr. area (dairy prods.; livestock); mfg. (asphalt, fences). Inc. 1887. With WEST DUNDEE, across river, area generally known as Dundee.

East Durham, village (1990 pop. 600), Greene co., SE N.Y., in the Catskills, 16 mi/26 km NW of Catskill; 42°23′N 74°06′W.

East Earl, uninc. village, Lancaster co., SE Pa., 15 mi/24 km ENE of Lancaster, in Pa. Du. region; 40°06′N 76°01′W. Mfg. includes lumber, wooden cabinets, concrete, pet food; agr. includes dairying, livestock; grain, apples; timber.

East Ellijay (EL-i-jai), town (1990 pop. 303), Gilmer co., N Ga., just SE of Ellijay; 34°41′N 84°28′W. Mfg. of concrete blocks.

East Ely (EE-lei), village, White Pine co., E Nev., just NE of Ely; part of Ely; elev. 6,386 ft/1,946 m. Part of Ely city.

East End, Cayman Isls., B.W.I.: see GRAND CAYMAN.

East Falmouth, Mass.: see FALMOUTH.

East Farnham (FAHR-nuhm), village (1991 pop. 528), S Que., Canada, near Yamaska R., 12 mi/19 km SSW of Granby; dairying.

East Feliciana (fuh-LEE-shee-an-uh), parish (☐ 454 sq mi/1,176 sq km; 1990 pop. 19,211), SE central La.; ⊙ Clinton; 30°52′N 91°01′W. Bounded E by Amite R., W by Thompson Creek, N by Miss. state line. Drained by Comite R. Agr. (blueberries, peaches, corn, hay, sweet potatoes; cattle, horses, hogs; dairying); 2 wineries in area; sod production; logging. One of Fla. parishes of SE La. Clinton Confederate Cemetery at Clinton, Centenary State Commemorative Area in W. Has

many antebellum homes, including Asphodel and Milbank. Formed 1824.

East Flat Rock, uninc. town (1990 pop. 3,218), Henderson co., SW N.C., 4 mi/6.4 km SSE of Hendersonville and 2 mi/3.2 km ENE of Flat Rock; 35°16′N 82°25′W. Agr. area (tobacco, corn, soybeans, fruit, potatoes, hogs, cattle); mfg. (cardboard cartons, hosiery, screen printing).

East Flatbush, N.Y.: see FLATBUSH.

East Foothills, uninc. city (1990 pop. 14,898), Santa Clara co., W Calif., residential suburb 7 mi/11.3 km NE of downtown San Jose, in W foothills of Diablo Range, on Penitencia Creek; 37°23′N 121°49′W. Youth Science Inst. is here. Orchard area.

East Fork, Minn. and Iowa: see DES MOINES RIVER.

East Fork Lake, reservoir, Richland co., SE Ill., on E. Fork Fox R., 2 mi/3.2 km NNE of Olney; 3 mi/4.8 km; 38°45′N 88°06′W. Max. capacity of 27,600 acre-ft. Formed by East Fork Dam (55 ft/17 m high), built (1971) for water supply purposes for Olney.

East Fork of Trinity River, Texas: see TRINITY RIVER.

East Fork of White River, Ind.: see WHITE RIVER.

East Fork Owyhee River, c.110 mi/177 km long, in Nev. and Idaho; rises in N part of Elko co., NE Nev.; flows NW, past Mountain City and Owyhee, into Owyhee co., SW Idaho, and joins South Fork Owyhee R. near Oregon state line. Artificial reservoir in upper course, 12 mi/19 km SE of Mountain City.

East Fork Sevier River (suh-VIR), 90 mi/145 km long, S Utah; rises in NW Kane co., Dixie Natl. Forest, in Paunsaugunt Plateau SW of Bryce Canyon Natl. Park; flows N, past Antimony, receives Otter Creek from NE, then W, through Sevier Plateau, to Sevier R. near Junction. Dam on lower course forms Otter Creek Reservoir.

East Fork Virgin River, 50 mi/80 km long, SW Utah; rises in NW Kane co., W of Alton; flows S, then W through SE end of Zion Natl. Park, joining North Fork just SW of Zion Natl. Park at Springdale to form Virgin R.

East Freetown, Mass.: see FREETOWN.

East Gaffney or **Limestone**, uninc. town (1990 pop. 3,278), Cherokee co., N S.C., 1 mi/1.6 km E of Gaffney; 35°04′N 81°37′W.

East Galesburg, village (1990 pop. 813), Knox co., NW central Ill., just E of Galesburg; 40°56′N 90°18′W. Formerly Randall.

East Germantown, town (1990 pop. 372), Wayne co., E Ind., 11 mi/19 km W of Richmond; 39°49′N 85°08′W. In agr. area.

East Gillespie (gil-ES-pee), village (1990 pop. 205), Macoupin co., SW central Ill., just N of Gillespie; 39°08′N 89°48′W. In agr. and bituminous-coal area.

East Glacier Park, village (1990 pop. 326), Glacier co., NW Mont., 43 mi/69 km WSW of Cut Bank; at W edge of Blackfeet Indian Reservation; 48°27′N 113°13′W. Resort. Lewis and Clark Natl. Forest to S; Glacier Natl. Park to W. U.S. Highway 2 passes through village and skirts around S end of Glacier Natl. Park. Two Medicine Road (dead end) leads NW to Two Medicine L. in corner of Glacier Natl. Park. Formerly Glacier Park.

East Glenville, village (1990 pop. including Alplaus 6,518), Schenectady co., E. N.Y., 6.5 mi/10.5 km N of Schenectady; 42°54′N 73°56′W.

East Granby, town (1990 pop. 4,302), Hartford co., N Conn., 13 mi/21 km N of Hartford; 41°57′N 72°44′W. Industries include mfg. and quarrying. Newgate Prison, copper mine used as prison 1773–1827, is here. Set off from Granby 1858.

East Grand Forks, town (1990 pop. 8,658), Polk co., NW Minn., 1 mi/1.6 km NE of Grand Forks, N. Dak., twin city to Grand Forks, on Red R. at mouth of Red Lake R.; 47°55′N 97°01′W. Wheat, potatoes, sugar beets, sunflowers; mfg. (dried beet pulp, potato processing, metering valves, grain milling, lumber). Settled 1870.

East Grand Rapids, city (1990 pop. 10,807), Kent co., SW Mich., residential suburb 3 mi/4.8 km SE of downtown Grand Rapids; 42°57′N 85°36′W. Reeds Lake in N part of city. Settled 1835; inc. as village 1891, as city 1926.

East Greenbush, suburban village (☐ 2 sq mi/5.2 sq km;

1990 pop. 3,784), Rensselaer co., E N.Y., 10 mi/16 km S of Troy; 42°35′N 73°42′W. Rapidly expanding residential area SE of Albany with easy commuter access to center of the capital.

East Greenville, borough (1990 pop. 3,117), Montgomery co., SE Pa., 14 mi/23 km S of Allentown, near Perkiomen Creek, which forms Green Lane Reservoir to S; 40°24′N 75°30′W. Agr. (grain, soybeans, apples; livestock, dairying); mfg. (plastic bottles, chocolate prods., commercial printing, pulverized minerals, chairs and desks, plumbing and heating prods., wooden pallets, knitting mill). Settled 1850, inc. 1875.

East Greenwich, town (1990 pop. 11,865), ⊙ Kent co., central R.I., on Greenwich Bay, and 11 mi/18 km S of Providence; 41°38′N 71°30′W. Industrial center (Quonset Point and Davisville Industrial Complex) in agr. area; textiles and shipbuilding; potatoes; clam and oyster fisheries. East Greenwich Acad. (1802) here; former site of Naval Air Station at nearby QUONSET POINT. Includes village of East Greenwich. Inc. 1677.

East Greenwich (GRE-nich), township (1990 pop. 5,258), Gloucester co., S N.J., 8 mi/12.9 km NW of Glassboro; 39°47′N 75°14′W. Inc. 1881.

East Griffin, village (1990 pop.), Spalding co., W central Ga., near Griffin; 33°14′N 84°13′W.

East Gull Lake, village (1990 pop. 687), Cass co., central Minn., 8 mi/12.9 km WNW of Brainerd, at S end of Gull L. and N end of L. Sylvan; 46°24′N 94°20′W. Timber; dairying; poultry, cattle, sheep; oats, alfalfa; resort area. Pillsbury State Forest to NW.

East Haddam, town (1990 pop. 6,676), Middlesex co., S Conn., on the Connecticut (here bridged), at mouth of Salmon R., and 12 mi/19 km SE of Middletown; 41°28′N 72°23′W. Mfg. (machinery, fish nets, printing, bicycles, plumbing and heating prods., boats, concrete); summer resorts surrounding various lakes and rivers, farming. Home of Goodspeed Opera House where many Broadway plays are perfected before opening in New York City. Includes MOODUS, Leesville, and Millington villages, Devil's Hopyard State Park. Settled c.1670, set off from Haddam 1734.

East Hampstead, village (1990 pop. 950) in town of Hampstead, Rockingham co., SE N.H., 8 mi/12.9 km NNE of Salem and 2 mi/3.2 km E of Hampstead village. Mfg. (microwave components, tortillas, automation systems, printing and publishing). Angle Pond to NW.

East Hampton, town (1990 pop. 10,428), Middlesex co., S central Conn., 8 mi/12.9 km ENE of Middletown; 41°34′N 72°30′W. Agr. (fruit, dairy prods.; poultry). Middle Haddam village, once a shipbuilding center, is 3 mi/4.8 km SSW. Pocotopaug L. (resort) formed by dam on the Pocotopaug R., state park here. Settled c.1710, inc. 1767 as Chatham, renamed 1915.

East Hampton, resort and residential village (□ 4 sq mi/ 10.4 sq km; 1990 pop. 1,402), Suffolk co., SE N.Y., near S shore of L.I., 6 mi/9.7 km SE of Sag Harbor; 40°57′N 72°12′W. Summer homes; diversified farming; mfg. of septic systems, jetties, stone revetments; sand and gravel. Fashionable, upper-income area. Birthplace of John Howard Payne, whose home is now a mus. The village has 3 historic bldgs. containing other significant bldgs. Settled 1648, inc. 1920.

East Hanover, township (1990 pop. 9,926), Morris co., N N.J., 7 mi/11.3 km W of Montclair; 40°49′N 74°22′W. Mfg. (food prods., electronic parts, lubricants, pharmaceuticals, office machines, and plastics). Inc. 1928.

East Hartford, urban town (1990 pop. 50,452), Hartford co., central Conn., on the Connecticut R. opposite Hartford; settled c.1640, inc. 1783; 41°45′N 72°37′W. East Hartford is a trucking and warehousing center. The town is heavily industrialized and also has technology-based facilities. Among the chief manufactures are fabricated steel, precision parts, aircraft engines, appliances, paper, television and radio parts, stamp and die plates, small tools, machinery, metal-working, bulk oil storage and distribution, storage warehouses, retail sales, auto dealerships, and banking and insurance.

East Hartland, Conn.: see HARTLAND.

East Harwich, Mass.: see HARWICH.

East Haven 1 town (1990 pop. 26,144), New Haven co.,

S Conn., on Long Island Sound, a residential suburb of New Haven; 41°17′N 72°51′W. In a farm area; inc. 1785. Light industry, wholesale distribution and warehousing, electronic components and equipment, architectural castings, high-tech welding equipment, printing, insurance, investments research and development form the town's economic basis. Of interest are an early-18th-cent. stone church and a trolley museum. **2** town (1990 pop. 269), Essex co., NE Vt., on Passumpsic R., and 20 mi/32 km WNW of Guildhall; 44°39′N 71°49′W.

East Hazel Crest, village, Cook co., NE Ill., S suburb of Chicago, just E of Hazel Crest; 41°34′N 87°38′W.

East Helena, town (1990 pop. 1,538), Lewis and Clark co., SW central Mont., on Prickly Pear Creek, suburb 5 mi/8 km E of Helena; 46°35′N 111°55′W. Silver, zinc, lead, and gold ores (much of it from S. America) are reduced, mfg. (cuprous oxide, cement). L. Helena and Huaser L. to N. Helena Regional Airport to NW. Parts of Helena Natl. Forest to S, W, and NE; Canyon Ferry Lake (Missouri R.) and State Park to E. Inc. 1927.

East Hemet, uninc. city (1990 pop. 17,611), S Calif., residential suburb 2 mi/3.2 km E of Hemet and 29 mi/ 47 km SE of Riverside; 33°45′N 116°57′W. Soboba Indian Reservation to NE. Citrus, avocados, grain, nursery stock, dairying, poultry.

East Highland Park, uninc. city, Henrico co., E central Va., residential suburb 5 mi/8 km NE of downtown Richmond, near Chickahominy R.; 37°34′N 77°22′W.

East Hills, suburban village (□ 2 sq mi/5.2 sq km; 1990 pop. 6,746), Nassau co., SE N.Y., on W L.I., 4 mi/ 6.4 km NNE of Mineola; 40°47′N 73°37′W. Inc. 1931.

East Hodge, town (1990 pop. 421), Jackson parish, 2 mi/ 3.2 km N of Jonesboro; 32°16′N 92°42′W.

East Hope, village (1990 pop. 215), Bonner co., N Idaho, 11 mi/18 km ESE of Sandpoint and 1 mi/1.6 km SE of Hope, on E shore of Pend Oreille L.; 48°14′N 116°17′W. Timber. Site of Thompson's Trading Post (1809); Kaniksu Natl. Forest to NE.

East Humboldt Range (HUHM-buhlt), NE Nev., in Elko co., E of Elko. Lies in part of Humboldt Natl. Forest. Ruby Range, N extension of Ruby Range. Hole in Mt.'s Peak (11,306 ft/3,446 m).

East Indian Island (□ 4 sq mi/10.4 sq km), E N.F., Canada, at mouth of Notre Dame Bay, 3 mi/5 km S of Fogo Isl.; 49°32′N 54°14′W; 2 mi/3 km long, 2 mi/3 km wide. On N coast is fishing settlement of Indian Island Harbour. Just W is West Indian Isl.

East Islip, village (□ 4 sq mi/10.4 sq km; 1990 pop. 14,325), Suffolk co. SE N.Y., near S shore of L.I., just E of Islip, in summer resort area; 40°43′N 73°11′W. Heckscher State Park on Great South Bay is immediately S.

East Jewett, resort village (1990 pop. 200), Greene co., SE N.Y., in the Catskills, 9 mi/14.5 km W of Catskill; 42°14′N 74°08′W.

East Jordan, town (1990 pop. 2,240), Charlevoix co., NW Mich., 13 mi/21 km SSE of Charlevoix, at mouth of Jordan R. at S end of South Arm of L. Charlevoix; 45°09′N 85°07′W. In fruit-growing and dairying area. Mfg. (castings, canned fruits and vegetables, automotive systems). Resort; fishing. Airport to S. Inc. as village 1889, as city 1911.

East Juliette, town (1990 pop.)), Jones co., central Ga., 20 mi/32 km NNW of Macon, on Ocmulgee R.; 33°6′N 83°47′W.

East Keansburg, village, Monmouth co., E N.J., just E of Keansburg, and 15 mi/24 km NNE of Freehold. On Sandy Hook Bay. Largely residential.

East Kennebago Mountain (ken-uh-BAI-go), (3,825 ft/ 1,166 m), Franklin co., W Maine, 37 mi/60 km NNW of Farmington.

East Kingsford, village, Dickinson co., SW Upper Peninsula, Mich., 1 mi/1.6 km E of Kingsford; 45°47′N 88°03′W.

East Kingston, town (1990 pop. 1,352), Rockingham co., SE N.H., 5 mi/8 km SW of Exeter; 42°55′N 71°00′W. Mfg. (sheet metal work); agr. (nursery crops; poultry, cattle; dairying; timber).

East Knox (NAHKS), hamlet, (1990 pop. 681), Knox

township, Waldo co., S Maine, 11 mi/18 km NW of Belfast. In agr., recreational area.

East La Mirada, uninc. town (1990 pop. 9,367), Orange co., S Calif., residential suburb 17 mi/27 km SE of downtown Los Angeles, 2 mi/3.2 km E of La Mirada (Los Angeles co.); 33°55′N 118°00′W. West Coyote Hills and oil field in N.

East Lake, village, Dare co., NE N.C., 33 mi/53 km S of Elizabeth City and on Alligator R. estuary (bridged), near its entrance to Albermarle Sound (N). Durant Isl. to N.

East Lansdowne (LANS-doun), borough (1990 pop. 2,691), Delaware co., SE Pa., residential suburb 6 mi/ 9.7 km WSW of downtown Philadelphia, near Cobbs Creek; 39°56′N 75°15′W. Mfg. (skin-care prods.).

East Lansing, city (1990 pop. 50,677), Ingham co., S central Mich., a suburb 3 mi/4.8 km E of Lansing, on the Red Cedar R.; 42°44′N 84°28′W. Rail junction; mfg. (resins and adhesives, light mfg.). The city was first known as College Park, but was renamed when it was incorporated. It is a residential city that adjoins the state capital of Lansing and is the seat of Michigan State Univ. Abrams Planetarium. Inc. 1907.

East Las Vegas, uninc. city (1990 pop. 11,087), Clark co., SE Nev., residential suburb 4 mi/6.4 km ESE of downtown Las Vegas; 36°06′N 115°02′W. Sunrise Mt. Natural Area to NE.

East Laurinburg (LAW-ruhn-buhrg), village (1990 pop. 302), Scotland co., S N.C., suburb 1 mi/1.6 km SE of Laurinburg, 34°46′N 79°27′W.

East Layton, town, Davis co., N Utah, E of Layton. Now part of city of Layton.

East Lee, Mass.: see LEE.

East Livermore, Maine: see LIVERMORE FALLS.

East Liverpool, industrial city (1990 pop. 13,654), Columbiana co., E central Ohio, on the Ohio R. near the Pa. and W.Va. borders; settled 1798 as St. Clair, called Fawcett's Town until its incorporation as East Liverpool in 1834; 40°38′N 80°34′W. Extensive clay deposits in the area are used in making pottery, brick, and tile. A ceramics center since about 1839; mus. housing historical pottery collection.

East Longmeadow, town (1990 pop. 13,367), Hampden co., SW Mass., a suburb of Springfield; 42°04′N 72°30′W. Settled c.1740, set off from Longmeadow and inc. 1894. It is chiefly residential. Industries include saws and blades, toys, electric machinery and components.

East Los Angeles, uninc. city (1990 pop. 126,379), Los Angeles co., S Calif., residential suburb 5 mi/8 km E of downtown Los Angeles; 34°02′N 118°10′W. In industrial area.

East Lyme, town (1990 pop. 15,340), New London co., SE Conn., on L.I. Sound, c. 7 mi/11.3 km WNW of New London; settled c.1660, inc. 1839; 41°21′N 72°13′W. The town has diversified light industry. Its many colonial bldgs. include the restored Thomas Lee House (c.1660). Rocky Neck State Park is here. Includes village of Niantic (1990 pop. 3,048).

East Lynn Lake, reservoir, Wayne co., SW W.Va., on Twelvepole R., 20 mi/40 km S of Huntington; 37°37′N 81°17′W. Max. capacity 3,700 acre-ft. Formed by E. Lynn Dam (110 ft/34 m high).

East Lynne, town (1990 pop. 289), Cass co., W Mo., 6 mi/9.7 km E of Harrisonville; 38°40′N 94°13′W.

East Machias (muh-CHEI-uhs), town (1990 pop. 1,218), Washington co., E Maine, on E. Machias R., and just E of Machias, 10 mi/16 km from the ocean; 44°46′N 67°25′W. Lumbering, canning. Inc. 1826.

East Machias River (muh-CHEI-uhs), c.35 mi/56 km long, E Maine; rises in lakes of central Washington co.; flows generally SE to Machias Bay at East Machias.

East Marion, uninc. village, McDowell co., W N.C., 1 mi/1.6 km E of Marion.

East Massapequa, uninc. town (□ 3 sq mi/7.8 sq km; 1990 pop. 19,550), Nassau co., SE N.Y., on S shore of L.I.; 40°40′N 73°26′W. It is chiefly residential. Pop. figure also includes Arlyn Oaks, Crown Village, and Nassau Shores.

East Mattapoisett, Mass.: see MATTAPOISETT.

East McKeesport (mah-KEES-port), borough (1990 pop. 2,678), Allegheny co., SW Pa., residential suburb 11 mi/18 km SE of downtown Pittsburgh and 3 mi/4.8 km NE of McKeesport; 40°22′N 79°48′W. Mfg. (machinery). Inc. 1895.

East Meadow, uninc. residential city (☐ 6 sq mi/15.5 sq km; 1990 pop. 36,909), Nassau co., SE N.Y., on W L.I.; 40°43′N 73°33′W.

East Middletown, village (☐ 3 sq mi/7.8 sq km; 1990 pop. 4,974), Orange co., SE N.Y.; 41°27′N 74°23′W.

East Millinocket (mil-uh-NAHK-et), town (1990 pop. 2,166), Penobscot co., central Maine, on the W branch of the Penobscot, and 55 mi/89 km N of Bangor; 45°38′N 68°34′W. Inc. 1907, when dam and paper mill were built.

East Millstone, town, Somerset co., central N.J., on Millstone R., and 5 mi/8 km SSE of Somerville. In rapidly suburbanizing area.

East Milton, Mass.: see MILTON.

East Moline, city (1990 pop. 20,147), Rock Island co., NW Ill., E of Moline, on the Mississippi R.; 41°30′N 90°25′W. Inc. 1907. East Moline, Moline, Rock Island (all in Ill.), and Davenport, Iowa, are known as the Quad Cities, due to their formation as an industrial complex. Near East Moline are significant RR-repair shops. The city has East Moline Correctional Center.

East Montpelier (mahnt-PEEL-yuhr), town (1990 pop. 2,239), Washington co., central Vt., on Winooski R., just E of Montpelier; 44°17′N 72°30′W. First settled c.1788, set off from Montpelier 1848.

East Moriches, village (☐ 5 sq mi/13 sq km; 1990 pop. 4,021), Suffolk co., SE N.Y., on SE L.I., on Moriches Bay, just E of Center Moriches; 40°48′N 72°45′W. In shore-resort area.

East Mountain, town (1990 pop. 762), Gregg co., E Texas, 8 mi/12.9 km NW of Longview; 32°35′N 94°51′W. Cattle, horses; oil and natural gas; timber.

East Mountain (1,840 ft/561 m), SW Mass., in East Mt. State Forest (1,553 acres/628 ha), just SE of Great Barrington, in the Berkshires. Recreation.

East Musquash Lake (MUHS-kwahsh), Washington co., E Maine, on East Branch Musquash Stream, 29 mi/47 km NW of Calais. 2.5 mi/4 km long; 45°23′N 67°47′W. Musquash Mt. (1,238 ft/377 m) to S. W. Musquash L. (3.5 mi/5.6 km long; 45°18′N 67°49′W) is 4 mi/6.4 km SW.

East Naples, city (☐ 14 sq mi/36 sq km; 1990 pop. 22,951), ⊙ Collier co., SW Fla.; 26°07′N 81°45′W.

East New Market, town (1990 pop. 153), Dorchester co., E Md., 9 mi/14.5 km ENE of Cambridge; 38°36′N 75°55′W. The entire community is a Historic Dist. listed in the Natl. Register of Historic Places. Originally settled in 1640 as a trading post on the Choptank Indian Trail. Some 75 homes represent architectural styles of 3 centuries, from the mid-18th to the 20th. Many of the brick walkways laid in 1884 are still in use. Among the notable homes are Friendship Hall (c.1740) and the House of the Hinges (c.1750). Inc. 1832.

East New York, residential section of N Brooklyn borough of N.Y. city, SE N.Y. Pop. mostly Afr.-Amer. and Hispanic. Economically depressed area.

East Newark (NOO-uhrk), borough (1990 pop. 2,157), Hudson co., NE N.J., across Passaic R. from Newark; 40°45′N 74°09′W. Mfg. (clothing, textiles, yarn, metal prods.). Inc. 1895.

East Newnan, village (1990 pop. 1,173), Coweta co., W Ga., near Newnan; 33°21′N 84°46′W.

East Ninnekah (NIN-uh-kuh), town (1990 pop. 1,016), Grady co., central Okla., 7 mi/11.3 km S of Chickasha. Agr. and mfg. (farm equipment).

East Nishnabotna River, Iowa: see NISHNABOTNA RIVER.

East Norriton (NOR-i-tuhn), township (1990 pop. 13,324), Montgomery co., SE Pa., residential suburb 15 mi/24 km NNW of Philadelphia, and 2 mi/3.2 km NE of Norristown; 40°08′N 75°20′W. Agr. includes dairying, livestock; corn, wheat.

East Northfield, Mass.: see NORTHFIELD.

East Northport, uninc. residential town (☐ 5 sq mi/13 sq km; 1990 pop. 20,411), Suffolk co., SE N.Y., on N shore of L.I.; 40°52′N 73°19′W.

East Okoboji Lake, Iowa: see OKOBOJI.

East Omaha, NE suburb of Omaha, Douglas co., E Nebr., on Missouri R. at E end of Carter L., 3 mi/4.8 km NE of downtown. Site of Eppley Airfield, Omaha's main airport. Part of Omaha.

East Orange, city (1990 pop. 73,552), Essex co., NE N.J.; settled 1678, separated from Orange and inc. 1863; 40°46′N 74°12′W. A residential city adjacent to Newark, its mfg. includes metals, paint, electrical equip., and bldg. materials. East Orange is the seat of Upsala Col., which is about to be closed.

East Orleans, Mass.: see ORLEANS.

East Otto, village (1990 pop. 300), Cattaraugus co., W N.Y., 36 mi/58 km S of Buffalo; 42°23′N 78°45′W.

East Palatka (puh-LAT-kuh), town (☐ 4 sq mi/10.4 sq km; 1990 pop. 1,989), Putnam co., NE Fla., on St. Johns R., opposite Palatka; 29°38′N 81°35′W. Shipping (citrus fruit, vegetables); lumber milling.

East Palestine (PA-luhs-tein), city (1990 pop. 5,168), Columbiana co., E Ohio, at Pa. line, 20 mi/32 km SSE of Youngstown; 40°50′N 80°32′W. Clay prods., fireproofing materials, metal prods., tires, models and patterns, furniture. Clay pits. Founded 1828; inc. as city in 1875.

East Palo Alto, city (1990 pop. 23,451), San Mateo co., W Calif., residential suburb 27 mi/43 km SE of downtown San Francisco and 2 mi/3.2 km NE of Palo Alto, on San Francisco Bay, drained by San Francisco Creek; 37°28′N 122°08′W. Palo Alto Airport to E. Dunbarton Bridge and Hetch Hetchy Aqueduct both cross bay to N.

East Park Dam, Calif.: see STONY CREEK.

East Parsonfield, Maine: see PARSONSFIELD.

East Pasadena, uninc. town (1990 pop. 5910), Los Angeles co., S Calif., residential suburb 3 mi/4.8 km ESE of Pasadena and 11 mi/18 km NE of downtown Los Angeles, along Rosemead Boulevard; 34°08′N 118°05′W.

East Patchogue, suburban residential village (☐ 8 sq mi/20.7 sq km; 1990 pop. including W. Bellport 20,195), Suffolk co., SE N.Y., on S L.I., on Great South Bay just E of Patchogue; 40°46′N 72°58′W. In shore-resort area. Mfg. (stamps, tapes, labels, and engraved plates).

East Paterson (PA-tuhr suhn), borough, Bergen co., NE N.J., industrial suburb of Paterson, across Passaic R. Mfg. (paper prods., leather goods, metal prods., cement pipes); dairying. Inc. 1916.

East Peoria, city (1990 pop. 21,378), Tazewell co., N central Ill., on the Illinois R. Suburb opposite Peoria; 40°40′N 89°32′W. Dam forms Peoria L. Inc. 1884. It is a RR and warehousing center for central Illinois. Agr. in area (corn, soybeans, cattle, hogs; dairying); mfg. (electrical fixtures, gauges, machinery, advertising specialties, book printing). Illinois Central Col. and a U.S. Coast Guard base are here. Festival of Lights during Christmas season, beginning Thanksgiving weekend.

East Pepperell, Mass.: see PEPPERELL.

East Peru, town (1990 pop. 132), Madison co., S central Iowa, 30 mi/48 km SSW of Des Moines; 41°13′N 93°55′W. In agr. area.

East Petersburg, borough (1990 pop. 4,197), Lancaster co., SE Pa., residential suburb 4 mi/6.4 km N of Lancaster, on Little Conestoga Creek; 40 6′N 76°20′W. Mfg. (concrete blocks, fertilizer, asphalt, control room equip.). Inc. 1946.

East Pittsburgh (PITS-buhrg), borough (1990 pop. 2,160), Allegheny co., SW Pa., SE residential suburb 9 mi/14.5 km ESE of downtown Pittsburgh, on Turtle Creek, 1 mi/1.6 km NE of its entrance to Monongahela R.; 40°23′N 79°50′W. Mfg. (rolled steel, chocolate candy, machining). Braddock defeated near here (1755) by French and Native Americans. Inc. 1895.

East Point, city (1990 pop. 34,402), Fulton co., NW Ga., blue-collar industrial suburb of Atlanta located on RR line; 33°40′N 84°28′W. Textiles, machinery, chemicals, and paper. Atlanta Christian Col. is here. Natl. Archives—SE region, Federal-records facility; Fort McPherson adjacent to the city. Inc. 1887.

East Point 1 cape at E extremity of P.E.I., Canada, on the Gulf of St. Lawrence, 15 mi/24 km NE of Souris; 46°27′N 61°58′W; lighthouse. **2** cape at E extremity of Anticosti Isl., E Que., Canada, on the Gulf of St. Lawrence; 49°8′N 61°41′W.

East Point, promontory, Nahant, E Mass., Essex co., 6 mi/9.7 km NE of Boston, Mass., at farthest end of tombolo bet. Lynn Harbor and Swampscott Harbor. Former site of coastal artillery during World War II. Marine Research Station and Education Facility for Northeastern Univ.; town park.

East Porterville, uninc. town (1990 pop. 5,790), Tulare co., S central Calif., residential suburb 2 mi/3.2 km E of Porterville, on Tule R.; 36°04′N 118°58′W. L. Success reservoir to E. Orchard area.

East Prairie, city (1990 pop. 3,416), Mississippi co., extreme SE Mo., in Mississippi alluvial plain, 10 mi/16 km S of Charleston; 36°46′N 89°22′W. Cotton, soybeans, corn, wheat, rice; mfg. (business forms, mufflers).

East Prospect, borough (1990 pop. 558), York co., S Pa., 12 mi/19 km E of York, near Cabin Creek; Susquehanna R. 1 mi/1.6 km to E. Samuel S. Lewis State Park to NW; 39°53′N 76°31′W.

East Providence, city (1990 pop. 50,380), Providence co., E R.I., on the Providence and Seekonk rivers; 41°48′N 71°22′W. Inc. as a city 1958. A wholesale and distribution center for petroleum prods. in the S New England area, East Providence also has factories that manufacture metal goods, jewelry, plastics, and machinery. A petrochemical-production facility has been constructed, adding impetus to the economy. Originally part of Seekonk, Mass., it was inc. as a town of R.I. in 1862.

East Quincy, uninc. town (1990 pop. 1,600), Plumas co., NE Calif., 5 mi/8 km E of Quincy. Area surrounded by Plumas Natl. Forest. Timber; cattle, alfalfa. Statistically reported as Quincy-East Quincy (1990 pop. 4271).

East Quogue, resort village (☐ 10 sq mi/26 sq km; 1990 pop. including W. Tiana 4,372), Suffolk co., SE N.Y., on SE L.I., on Shinnecock Bay, 6 mi/9.7 km SE of Riverhead; 40°51′N 72°34′W. Yachting. Region originally occupied by Native Amer. tribe of Shinnecocks because of rich hunting and fishing. Nearby Hampton Bays was called Good Ground until 1922. Settled in 1686, when known as Fourth Neck, then Atlanticville, until adoption of present name in 1891.

East Randolph, village (☐ 1 sq mi/2.6 sq km; 1990 pop. 629), Cattaraugus co., W N.Y., 15 mi/24 km ENE of Jamestown; 42°10′N 78°57′W. State trout hatchery 2 mi/3.2 km SE of village.

East Richmond Heights, uninc. town (1990 pop. 3,266), Contra Costa co., W Calif., residential suburb 9 mi/14.5 km N of downtown Oakland, 2 mi/3.2 km NE of Richmond, on Wildcat Creek; 37°57′N 122°19′W.

East Ridge, city (1990 pop. 21,101), Hamilton co., SE Tenn., a chiefly residential suburb just S of Chattanooga, near the Ga. border, 34°59′N 85°13′W. Inc. 1921.

East River, village, Conn.: see MADISON.

East River, tidal strait, 16 mi/26 km long and 600 ft/183 m–4,000 ft/1,219 m wide, connecting Upper N.Y. Bay and L.I. Sound, N.Y. city, and separating boroughs of Manhattan and the Bronx from Brooklyn and Queens. The East R. is linked with the Hudson R. at N end of Manhattan isl. by the Harlem R. Isls. of Roosevelt (formerly Welfare), Wards, Randalls, Rikers, N. Brother, and S. Brother, all located in the East R., have city institutions, parks, and recreation areas. Roosevelt Isl. was developed as a residential area in the early 1970s. Hell Gate, at the junction of the Harlem and East rivers, was named for its treacherous currents and rocky reefs (now removed). A total of 8 bridges, including the historic Brooklyn Bridge, span the river; subway, RR, and vehicular tunnels pass beneath it.

East River Mountain, Bland and Giles cos. in SW Va. and Mercer co. in SE W.Va., ridge (elev. c.3,000 ft/914 m–4,000 ft/1,219 m) from point SW of Bluefield extends c.35 mi/56 km NE along state line to gorge of New R. Its NE continuation is Peters Mt. Highest peak is Buckhorn Knob (elev. 4,069 ft/1,240 m) at center.

East Riverdale, village (1990 pop. 14,187), Prince Georges co., central Md., NE of Wash., D.C.; 38°58′N 76°55′W.

East Rochester, village (□ 1 sq mi/2.6 sq km; 1990 pop. 6,932), Monroe co., W N.Y., 7 mi/11.3 km SE of Rochester; 43°06′N 77°29′W. Mfg. (leather handles, builders hardware, industrial ceramics, precision tool and die mfg. machinery, filters, measuring devices, packing tools). Expanding suburban housing area. Inc. 1906.

East Rochester (RAH-ches-tuhr), borough (1990 pop. 672), Beaver co., W Pa., suburb 1 mi/1.6 km E of Rochester, on Ohio R. (bridged); 40°42′N 80°16′W.

East Rockaway, village (□ 1 sq mi/2.6 sq km; 1990 pop. 10,152), Nassau co., SE N.Y., on SW L.I.; 40°38′N 73°40′W. It is mostly residential with some light mfg. Settled c.1688, inc. 1900.

East Rupert, Vt.: see RUPERT.

East Rutherford (RUH-thuhr-fuhrd), industrial borough (1990 pop. 7,902), Bergen co., NE N.J., 8 mi/12.9 km NNE of Newark; 40°49′N 74°04′W. Clothing, chemicals, metal prods. Includes Carlton Hill, mfg. village. Site of the Meadowlands Sports Complex. Operated by the N.J. Sports and Exposition Authority, created 1971, the complex includes the Meadowlands Racetrack, Giants Stadium, and Continental Airlines Meadowlands Arena, on a 750-acre/304-ha tract. Inc. 1894.

East Ryegate, Vt.: see RYEGATE.

East Saint Louis, city (1990 pop. 40,944), St. Clair co., SW Ill., on the Mississippi R. opposite St. Louis, with which it is connected by 4 bridges (of which one is closed to traffic); 38°36′N 90°07′W. Inc. 1865. Once a major RR and transportation hub, with stockyards (in adjacent Natl. City), warehouses, and important industries, East St. Louis entered a period of serious economic decline beginning in the 1990s. The city was subsequently hit hard with growing unemployment and significant urban flight. Mfg. (fluorides, RR ties, lumber, feed). Riverboat gambling started in 1994 to boost economy, and the state began to take steps to help improve the city's schools and financial prospects. Pop. is now almost entirely Afr.-Amer. Metro Link light RR system (inaugurated 1993) connects East St. Louis with St. Louis. The 1st settlement was in 1765. Cahokia Creek was bridged in 1795, and a ferry across the Mississippi began operation shortly thereafter. East St. Louis was plagued by devastating floods until its 1st dike was completed in 1909. The Old Cathedral (1834) and Old Courthouse (1839) have been preserved. Branch of S. Ill. Univ. here. Frank Holten State Park and CAHOKIA MOUNDS State Historical Site (site of prehistoric Indian mounds) are nearby. Riverfront area has been acquired from RRs for extension of Jefferson Natl. Expansion Memorial. Community col.

East Salinas, uninc. village, Monterey co., W Calif., adjoining Salinas. Settled after 1933 by migratory agr. workers from the Midwest.

East San Gabriel, uninc. city (1990 pop. 12,736), Los Angeles co., S Calif., residential suburb 10 mi/16 km ENE of downtown Los Angeles and 2 mi/3.2 km ENE of San Gabriel, on Rosemead Boulevard; 34°08′N 118°05′W.

East Sandwich, Mass.: see SANDWICH.

East Saugus, Mass.: see SAUGUS.

East Setauket, village (1990 pop. 1,350), Suffolk co., SE N.Y., on N L.I., on Port Jefferson Harbor, bet. Port Jefferson (E) and Setauket; 40°56′N 73°08′W. In summer resort area.

East Side, borough (1990 pop. 330), Carbon co., E Pa., 14 mi/23 km SSE of Wilkes-Barre, on Lehigh R. opposite (E of) White Haven. Hickory Run State Park to SE; 41°3′N 75°45′W.

East Sonora, uninc. town (1990 pop. 1,675), Tuolumne co., E central Calif., 1 mi/1.6 km E of Sonora; 37°59′N 120°20′W. Timber, cattle, dairying.

East Spanish Peak, Colo.: see SPANISH PEAKS.

East Sparta, village (1990 pop. 771), Stark co., E central Ohio, 9 mi/14 km S of Canton, and on small Nimishellen Creek; 40°40′N 81°21′W.

East Spencer, town (1990 pop. 2,055), Rowan co., W

central N.C., suburb 2 mi/3.2 km E of Salisbury and 1 mi/1.6 km SE of Spencer; 35°40′N 80°25′W. Tobacco, grain, poultry, livestock, dairying. Mfg. (face brick). High Rock L. reservoir to E.

East Springfield, uninc. town (1990 pop. 800), Erie co., NW Pa., 20 mi/32 km WSW of Erie, L. Erie 3 mi/4.8 km to NW; 40°57′N 80°24′W. Agr. (potatoes; livestock, dairying); mfg. (plastic prods.).

East Springfield, resort village, Otsego co., central N.Y., 11 mi/18 km NNE of Cooperstown; 42°50′N 74°49′W. Otsego L. is 4 mi/6.4 km SW.

East Stanwood, village, Snohomish co., NW Wash., 12 mi/19 km NNW of Everett, 1 mi/1.6 km E of Stanwood. Peas, berries; dairying; poultry, cattle.

East Stroudsburg (STROUDS-buhrg), borough (1990 pop. 8,781), Monroe co., E Pa., 22 mi/35 km N of Easton, 1 mi/1.6 km E of Stroudsburg, on Brodhead Creek, 1 mi/1.6 km W of its mouth on Delaware R.; 41°0′N 75°10′W. Agr. (grain; livestock, dairying); mfg. (steel stairs and ladders, carbon and graphite prods., hardware, industrial-cleaning compounds, cosmetics, iron castings, printing and publishing, water heaters and drying equip., steel-pallet racks). Stroudsburg-Pocono Airpark to N. Site of East Stroudsburg Univ. of Pa. Shawnee Mt. and Fernwood Ski Areas to NE; Worthington State Forest (N.J.) to E; part of Delaware Gap Recreational Area to SE; Middle Delaware Natl. Scenic River to E; Appalachian Trail passes to S. Settled 1737, inc. 1870.

East Sumner, Maine: see SUMNER.

East Sumter, uninc. town (1990 pop. 1,590), Sumter co., central S.C., residential suburb 3 mi/4.8 km E of downtown Sumter; 33°55′N 80°17′W.

East Syracuse, suburban village (□ 1 sq mi/2.6 sq km; 1990 pop. 3,343), Onondaga co., central N.Y., just E of Syracuse; 43°03′N 76°04′W. Industrial mfg. heart of Syracuse region. Diverse light and heavy industries include aluminum castings and molds, industrial electroplating, gears and gear boxes, transmissions, doors and windows, meat packing, glass and wooden containers, tissue paper, gas analysis equip.; machining, screws, steel prods., pharmaceuticals. Inc. 1881.

East Tallassee, village, Tallapoosa co., E Ala., across Tallapoosa R. from Tallassee. Clothing mfg.

East Taunton, Mass.: see RAYNHAM.

East Tavaputs Plateau (TA-vah-poots), high tableland (7,000 ft/2,134 m–9,000 ft/2,743 m) in Grand and Uintah cos., E Utah. Descends into Grand Valley at Roan Cliffs and Book Cliffs, to S and SE, bounded S by Book Cliffs, W by Green R. and West Tavaputs Plateau. Forms W continuation of Roan Plateau to E (Colo./Utah).

East Tawas (TAH-WAHS), town, Iosco co., NE Mich., 2 mi/3.2 km NE of Tawas City, on Tawas Bay; 44°16′N 83°29′W. In agr. area (grain; livestock; potatoes); mfg. (concrete, automotive parts, metal stampings, cutting tools). Resort. Tawas Airport to NE. Huron Natl. Forest to N; Tawas State Park to N; Tawas L. to N. Settled 1864; inc. as village 1887, as city 1895.

East Templeton, village, SW Que., Canada, on Ottawa R., and 7 mi/11 km ENE of Hull; quartz mining.

East Templeton, Mass.: see TEMPLETON.

East Texas, uninc. village, Lehigh co., E Pa., 6 mi/9.7 km SW of Allentown on Lehigh Creek; 40°32′N 75°33′W. Mfg. includes business organizers; agr. includes dairying, livestock; corn, wheat. A winery is located N.

East Thermopolis, village (1990 pop. 221), Hot Springs co., N central Wyo., 2 mi/3.2 km E of Thermopolis, on Bighorn R; 43°38′N 108°12′W.

East Thomaston, village (1990 pop.), Upson co., W central Ga., just NE of Thomaston; 32°53′N 84°18′W.

East Timbalier Island, La.: see TIMBALIER ISLAND.

East Troy, town (1990 pop. 2,664), Walworth co., SE Wis., on Honey Creek (tributary of Fox R.) and 30 mi/48 km SW of Milwaukee; 42°47′N 88°24′W. In dairy and livestock area; steel prods., condensed milk, feed. Mfg. (canvas prods., meat prods., steel tubing, industrial ovens, castings). Resort lakes nearby. Alpine Valley Ski Area to SW.

East Tupelo (TOO-puh-lo), town, Lee co., NE Miss., just E of Tupelo. Part of city of Tupelo.

East Uniontown, uninc. town (1990 pop. 2,822), Fayette co., SW Pa., residential suburb 2 mi/3.2 km E of Uniontown; 39°53′N 79°42′W.

East Vandergrift (VAN-duhr-grift), borough (1990 pop. 787), Westmoreland co., W central Pa., 25 mi/40 km ENE of Pittsburgh, 1 mi/1.6 km E of Vandergrift, on Kiskiminetas R; 40°36′N 79°33′W. Agr. (corn, hay; dairying). Inc. 1901.

East Verde River, central Ariz.; rises at Mogollon Rim, S edge of Mogollon Mesa; flows c.50 mi/80 km SW and W to Verde R. 37 mi/60 km S of Cottonwood. Entirely in Tonto Natl. Forest.

East View, uninc. town (1990 pop. 950), Harrison co., N W.Va., a suburb 2 mi/3.2 km E of Clarksburg.

East Village, section of borough of Manhattan, N.Y. city, SE N.Y. Bounded on N by E. 14th St., on S by Houston St., by the Bowery (4th Ave.) on the W, and on the E by the East R., this is one of the older parts of N.Y. city and a neighborhood that is as familiar, at least in name, to non–New Yorkers as it is to residents. Characterized by the "bohemian" lifestyle, replete with often-struggling artists, writers, and students. A section that was formerly Pol. and Ukr. began losing its ethnic flavor in the 1960s and 1970s, becoming first a bastion of hippies, then punks; in more recent years, it has been altered and gentrified. The Cooper Union Foundation Bldg. is named after Peter Cooper, its founder and benefactor, who helped develop telegraph technology. Other significant historic figures connected with the East Village include Jacob Riis, Peter Stuyvesant, and John Jacob Astor.

East Village, Mass.: see WEBSTER.

East Walker River, c.75 mi/121 km long, in E Calif. and W Nev.; rises in Sierra Nevada near Mono L., E Calif.; at NE boundary of Yosemite Natl. Park; flows NE past Bridgeport, through Bridgeport Reservoir, and into Nevada, then N.

East Wallingford, Vt.: see WALLINGFORD.

East Walpole, Mass.: see WALPOLE.

East Wareham, Mass.: see WAREHAM.

East Washington, borough (1990 pop. 2,126), Washington co., SW Pa., residential suburb 1 mi/1.6 km E of Washington; 40°10′N 80°13′W. Brady Tunnel (RR; 1 mi/1.6 km long) to E. Inc. 1892.

East Weissport (WEIS-port), uninc. town (1990 pop. 1,843), Franklin township, Carbon co., E Pa., 1 mi/1.6 km E of Weissport, 2 mi/3.2 km E of Lehighton; 40°50′N 75°41′W. Beltzville State Park to E.

East Wellington, village, SW B.C., Canada, on SE Vancouver Isl., 4 mi/6 km WNW of Nanaimo; 45°11′N 124°06′W. Coal mining; mixed farming.

East Wenatchee (wen-ACH-ee), town (1990 pop. 2,701) Douglas co., central Wash., across Columbia R. (here bridged) from WENATCHEE, to W; 47°25′N 120°17′W. Apples, wheat, barley, oats, alfalfa. Lincoln Rock State Park, at Rocky Reach Dam, to N; Badger Mt. Ski Area to E. Pangborn Airport to E.

East Weymouth, Mass.: see WEYMOUTH.

East Williston, residential village (1990 pop. 2,515), Nassau co., SE N.Y., on W L.I., just N of Mineola; 40°45′N 73°37′W. Inc. 1926.

East Wilmington, uninc. village, New Hanover co., SE N.C., near Wilmington.

East Windham, resort village (1990 pop. 65), Greene co., SE N.Y., in the Catskills, 17 mi/27 km NW of Catskill; 42°20′N 74°10′W.

East Windsor (WIN-zuhr), town (1990 pop. 10,081), Hartford co., N Conn., on Connecticut (here bridged) and Scantic rivers, and 10 mi/16 km NNE of Hartford; 41°53′N 72°33′W. Residential; agr.; support-system facilities. Mfg. small tools, paper boxes, electronics, aluminum by-products, farm implements, and fertilizers. Set off from Windsor 1768. Includes village of Broad Brook (1990 pop. 3,585).

East Windsor (WIN-zuhr), township (1990 pop. 22,353), Mercer co., central N.J., 1 mi/1.6 km W of Hightstown; 40°15′N 74°31′W. Inc. 1798.

East Windsor (WIN-zuhr), E suburb of Windsor, S

Ont., Canada, on Detroit R. opposite Detroit; motor-vehicle-mfg. center. Formerly one of the Border Cities, it was named Ford in 1913, later became Ford City. Name was changed to East Windsor 1929; merged with Windsor 1935.

East York, uninc. town (1990 pop. 8,487), York co., S Pa., residential suburb 3 mi/4.8 km ENE of York; 39°58′N 76°40′W.

East York, borough (1991 pop. 102,696), borough of Metropolitan Toronto, S central Ont., Canada, 3 mi/5 km NE of downtown Toronto. Bisected N-S by Don R. and Don Valley Pkwy. Residential.

East Youngstown, Ohio: see CAMPBELL.

Eastanollee (eest-uh-NAHL-ee), town (1990 pop. 365), Stephens co., Ga., c.52 mi/84 km N of Athens; 34°31′N 83°15′W. Mfg. includes particle board, cabinet components, wooden furniture parts. Recreation area in NE Ga. mts. region near Toccoa.

Eastbrook, town (1990 pop. 289), Hancock co., S Maine, 13 mi/21 km NE of Ellsworth; 44°41′N 68°13′W. In recreational area.

Eastchester, residential town (□ 5 sq mi/13 sq km; 1990 pop. 18,537), Westchester co., SE N.Y., just E of Yonkers; includes Bronxville and Tuckahoe villages; 40°57′N 73°48′W. Growing Asian community in the area. Once a township (formed 1788) extending from the present Bronx N to Scarsdale; Mt. Vernon city was separated from it in 1892; the sect. S of Mt. Vernon was annexed by N.Y. city in 1895.

Eastchester, village, S Alaska, residential suburb just SE of Anchorage; absorbed by Anchorage metro area.

Eastchester Bay, an inlet of L.I. Sound in E shore of the Bronx borough of N.Y. city, SE N.Y.; sheltered on E by Rodman's Neck and City Isl.; 40°51′N 73°49′W. Receives Hutchinson R. Pelham Bay Park is on its shores.

Eastend, town (1991 pop. 622), SW Sask., Canada, in the Cypress Hills, on Frenchman R., and 20 mi/32 km WSW of Shaunavon; 49°31′N 108°49′W. Coal and clay mining; grain elevators.

Eastend, village, E St. John Isl., U.S. Virgin Isls., 17 mi/27 km E of Charlotte Amalie; 18°21′N 64°40′W. A Moravian settlement, with school.

Eastern Bay, Talbot co., E Md., irregular Chesapeake Bay inlet (c.5 mi. long, 7 mi. wide), indenting the Eastern Shore to S and E of Kent Isl.; connected with Chester R. (N) by narrow channel. Miles R., Wye R., other estuaries enter it. Bennett's Point, at the entrance to the Wye, was the home of Richard Bennett, son of Md.'s one Puritan governor and father of another Richard, the richest American of his time. Oystering, fishing.

Eastern Island (□ 6 sq mi/16 sq km), one of the St. Barbe or Horse Isls., NE N.F., Canada, at entrance of White Bay, 20 mi/32 km NW of Cape St. John; 50°13′N 55°47′W; 4 mi/6 km long, 2 mi/3 km wide, rises to 550 ft/168 m.

Eastern Neck Island, sparsely wooded isl. (c.3 mi/4.8 km long, c.2 mi/3.2 km wide), Kent co., E Md., in Chesapeake Bay c.15 mi/24 km ENE of Annapolis. Separated from mainland by narrow channel (bridged). Eastern Neck is Natl. Wildlife Refuge; hunting permitted.

Eastern Panhandle, NE W.Va., (□ c.3,500 sq mi/9,065 sq km), E arm of state, extends NE bet. Md. (N) and Va. (S and E); Potomac R. and its N Branch form N border. Includes Pendleton, Grant, Mineral, Hardy, Hampshire, Morgan, Berkeley, and Jefferson cos., also parts of Tucker and Randolph cos.; Martinsburg is largest city. Near its W base are highest summits of the Allegheny Mts. (including Spruce Knob); to E, beyond Allegheny Front and Allegheny Mt., are ridges of the Appalachian Mts.; in extreme E is part of Great Appalachian Valley. Drained by Shenandoah, Cacapon, Moorefield, and S Branch Potomac rivers. In W is part of Monongahela Natl. Forest, including scenic Smoke Hole Caverns, Seneca Caverns, Seneca Rocks, and Blackwater Falls State Park.

Eastern Point, Mass.: see GLOUCESTER.

Eastern River, S Maine; rises in NW Lincoln co.; flows 18 mi/29 km SW to Kennebec R. near Dresden.

Eastern Shore, Md. and Va., the tidewater region along E shore of CHESAPEAKE BAY; includes all of Md. and Va. E of the bay, and, with Del., comprises DELMARVA peninsula.

Eastern Townships, region, located in S central Que., Canada, bet. Montreal and Quebec City, S of St. Lawrence R. valley, Granby to L. Megantic. Mining, hydroelectricity, mfg. and tourism relpaced marginal agr.

Eastford, town (1990 pop. 1,314), Windham co., NE Conn., on Natchaug R. and 16 mi/26 km NNE of Willimantic; 41°53′N 72°05′W. Metal fabrication, dairy farms, and horticulture. State park, state forest here.

Eastgate, uninc. town (1990 pop. 4,434), King co., W Wash., residential suburb 9 mi/14.5 km ESE of downtown Seattle, bet. Sammamish L. (E) and L. Washington (W); 47°34′N 122°08′W.

Eastham (EES-tuhm), town (1990 pop. 4,462), Barnstable co., SE Mass., on N arm of Cape Cod, 19 mi/31 km ENE of Barnstable; 41°51′N 70°00′W. Summer resort; agr. Formerly shipping and fishing port. Has lighthouse and coast guard station. Settled 1644, inc. 1651. Includes North Eastham village (1990 pop. 1,570). Hq. and visitor center Cape Cod Natl. Seashore.

Easthampton (ees-TAM-tuhn), town (1990 pop. 15,537), Hampshire co., W Mass.; 42°16′N 72°40′W. It is primarily a mfg. town with diversified light industry including plastics, chemicals, furniture parts and cleaning items. Easthampton was settled as early as 1664. In the 1820s the town's textile industry was founded by Samuel Williston; a preparatory school there was later named for him. Includes village of Mt. Tom (site of state park and ski area). Inc. 1809.

Eastlake, city (1990 pop. 21,161), Lake co., NE Ohio, a suburb of Cleveland, on the Chagrin R. and L. Erie; inc. 1949; 41°39′N 81°26′W. Diversified light mfg. industries.

Eastlake or **East Lake**, village (1990 pop. 473), Manistee co., NW Mich., 1 mi/1.6 km E of Manistee, across Manistee L., at entrance of Manistee R.; 44°15′N 86°17′W. Resort Area. Orchard Beach State Park to NW; Manistee Natl. Forest to E.

Eastland, county (□ 931 sq mi/2,411 sq km; 1990 pop. 18,488), N central Texas; ⊙ Eastland; 32°19′N 98°49′W. Drained by Leon R. Agr. (esp. peanuts; also melons; hay; vegetables); cattle, poultry. Oil, natural-gas wells, stone, clay, sand and gravel; mfg., processing at Ranger, Cisco, Eastland. Includes L. Cisco in NW (recreation) and L. Leon in E center. Formed 1858.

Eastland, town (1990 pop. 3,690), ⊙ Eastland co., N central Texas, on Leon R. and c.50 mi/80 km E of Abilene; 32°23′N 98°49′W. Elev. 1,421 ft/433m.Trade, processing center in petroleum-producing and agr. area (peanuts, melons, vegetables); mfg. (cotton prods.); oil and gas. Kendrick Religious Mus.; L. Leon to SE. Laid out 1875, inc. 1897.

Eastlawn, uninc. village, Washtenaw co., SE Mich, suburb 3 mi/4.8 km ESE of Ypsilanti; 42°14′N 83°35′W. Willow Run Airport to E.

Eastlawn Gardens, uninc. town (1990 pop. 1,794), Northampton co., E Pa., residential suburb 1 mi/1.6 km E of Nazareth and 6 mi/9.7 km NW of Easton; 40°45′N 75°17′W.

Eastmain (EEST-main), river, c.510 mi/820 km long; rises in the Otish Mts., central Que., Canada; flows W into James Bay; 3 miles/5 km from its mouth is East Main (founded 1685), one of the oldest Hudson's Bay Co. posts.

Eastman, town (1990 pop. 5,153), ⊙ Dodge co., S central Ga., c.50 mi/80 km SSE of Macon; 32°12′N 83°11′W. Mfg. includes specialty apparel, paper prods., printing, candy; lumber. Home of the original Stuckey's roadside store. Founded 1871, inc. 1873.

Eastman, village (1991 pop. 710), S Que., Canada, on Missiquoi R., and 20 mi/32 km ESE of Granby; 45°18′N 72°19′W. Dairying.

Eastman, village (1990 pop. 369), Crawford co., SW Wis., 10 mi/16 km NE of Prairie du Chien; 43°09′N 91°01′W. In livestock and dairy area.

Easton, city (1990 pop. 26,276), ⊙ Northampton co., E Pa., 50 mi/80 km N of Philadelphia and 8 mi/12.9 km ENE of Bethlehem, on Delaware R., opposite (W of) Phillipsburg, N.J., at mouth of Lehigh R.; 40°41′N 75°13′W. Easton is a part of the industrial Lehigh Valley. Rail junction. The surrounding area has limestone. Mfg. (crushed stone, food prods., apparel, printing and publishing, wood prods., electrical equip., fabricated metal prods., textiles, writing implements, insulation). Native American peace conferences held here in 1756 and 1761, and Easton served as an outpost during the Amer. Revolution. Lafayette Col., the First United Church of Christ (1776), and the restored house (1757) of George Taylor, a signer of the Declaration of Independence, are in Easton. Easton Airport to N. Canal Mus. and restored sect. of Lehigh Canal mark the city's canal days, and a park lies along the banks of the old Lehigh Canal. Bushkill Park theme park to NW; Kressler Memorial Colonial Gardens; Jack Nicholas House (c.1807); Illick Historical Library; County Historical Society. Founded 1751 by Thomas Penn, inc. as a city 1886.

Easton 1 uninc. town (1990 pop. 1871), Fresno co., central Calif., 6 mi/9.7 km S of Fresno; 36°39′N 119°48′W. Dairying, cattle, grapes, nectarines, almonds, grain, sugar beets, beans, vegetables. Wineries in area. **2** town (1990 pop. 6,303), Fairfield co., SW Conn., residential community on Aspetuck R., and 8 mi/12.9 km NW of Bridgeport; 41°16′N 73°17′W. Settled c.1757. **3** agr. town (1990 pop. 1,291), Aroostook co., NE Maine, just E of Presque Isle; 46°38′N 67°51′W. Inc. 1864. **4** town (1990 pop. 9,372), ⊙ Talbot co., E Md., on the Eastern Shore at head of Tred Avon R., 15 mi/24 km N of Cambridge; 38°46′N 76°04′W. Trade center for agr. (wheat, corn, tomatoes); canneries; clothing mfg. and lumber plants. Airport nearby. Waterfront plantations in the area have been bought by wealthy vacationers from New York, Cleveland, Pittsburgh, and the town has become a center of fashionable summer and hunting-season activities. Easton arose around the still functioning Talbot County Court House (c.1794), and for many years was the most progressive on the Eastern Shore, with the first newspaper (1790), first bank (1805), and the first steamboat line to Baltimore (1807). The town is filled with historic bldgs., among them: Third Haven Quaker Meeting House, erected in 1682–1684 and enlarged in 1792; the Old Market House (c.1791); Bullitt or Chamberlain House, built in 1790 by an ancestor of William C. Bullitt, ambassador to the USSR (1933–1936) and France (1936–1941); Stevens House (c.1800); and Thomas Perrin Smith House (c.1803). Once served as the seat of govt. for the entire E shore of Md. Inc. 1790. **5** town (1990 pop. 19,807), Bristol co., SE Mass., 6 mi/9.7 km SW of Brockton; 42°02′N 71°07′W. Machinery; glass, beverages, and aerosol prods.; dairying. Includes village of North Easton. Borderland State Park nearby. Former site of Ames Shovel Factory. Settled 1694, inc. 1725. **6** town (1990 pop. 232), Buchanan co., NW Mo., near Platte R., 11 mi/18 km E of St. Joseph; 39°43′N 94°38′W. **7** town (1990 pop. 223), Grafton co., NW N.H., 16 mi/26 km SSW of Littleton; 44°07′N 71°47′W. Drained by Wild Ammonoosuc R. and Ham Branch Gale R. In recreational area. Cattle; dairying; timber.

Easton 1 village (1990 pop. 351), Mason co., central Ill., 12 mi/19 km ESE of Havana; 40°13′N 89°50′W. In agr. area (corn, wheat, soybeans); mfg. (feed, fertilizer). **2** village (1990 pop. 405), Leavenworth co., NE Kansas, on small affluent of Kansas R., and 11 mi/18 km WNW of Leavenworth, on Stranger Creek; 39°21′N 95°07′W. Grain, livestock. **3** village (1990 pop. 229), Faribault co., S Minn., 13 mi/21 km NE of Blue Earth; 43°46′N 93°54′W. Livestock; soybeans, grain. Minnesota L. to N. **4** village (1990 pop. 401), on Gregg-Rusk co. line, E Texas, 17 mi/27 km E of Kilgore; 32°22′N 94°35′W. Dairying; cattle; vegetables, watermelons; timber; oil and gas. L. Cherokee reservoir to S.

Eastover 1 uninc. town (1990 pop. 1,243), Cumberland co., S central N.C., residential suburb 8 mi/12.9 km NE of downtown Fayetteville, near Cape Fear R.; 35°06′N 78°46′W. **2** town (1990 pop. 1,044), Richland co., central S.C., 20 mi/32 km ESE of Columbia; 33°52′N 80°42′W. Mfg. (fine paper and steel joists).

Eastpoint, town (□ 7 sq mi/18.1 sq km; 1990 pop. 1,577), Franklin co., NW Fla., located 8 mi/13 km E of Apalachicola on Apalachicola Bay; 29°45′N 84°52′W. Mfg. includes seafood processing (esp. oysters). Apalachicola Natl. Forest to N, St. Vincent Natl. Wildlife Refuge to W, St. George Isl. to E.

Eastpointe, Macomb co., SE Mich., a suburb 9 mi NE of downtown Detroit. Borders Detroit on S; 42°28′N 82°57′W. Mfg. (specialty machinery, meat processing). Mostly residential, it has been marked by a decrease in pop. since the 1970s, as Detroit's industrial and economic growth has faltered. Its name was changed from East Detroit in 1992. Inc. 1925 as Halfway village, renamed and inc. as a city 1929.

Eastport, city (1990 pop. 1,965), Washington co., E Maine, on Moose Isl. in SE PASSAMAQUODDY BAY 24 mi/39 km SSE of Calais; 44°55′N 67°00′W. Fishing and textiles are important to the local economy; resort activities. Port of entry. A causeway connects to mainland. Tides c.25 ft/8 m keep the bay ice-free throughout the year. Has artists' colony. First sardine cannery in U.S. built here c.1875. Marine-trades center. Site of old Fort Sullivan (1808). With Lubec, the easternmost community in U.S. Customs Post. Settled c.1780, town inc. 1798, city 1893.

Eastport 1 village (1990 pop. 125), Boundary co., N Idaho, port of entry (at Can. border), 22 mi/35 km NNE of Bonners Ferry, and 18 mi/29 km ESE of Creston, B.C., Canada, opposite Kingsdale, B.C. In Kaniksu Natl. Forest; Kootenai Natl. Forest, including Northwest Peak Scenic area, to E (in Mont.). **2** village, Anne Arundel co., central Md., on Severn R. just SE of Annapolis. Boatyards. Long a working-class community of watermen, it is now home to upper-class commuters living in restored "Annapolis vernacular" homes as well as high-rise condominiums. It is named after the hometown—Eastport, Maine—of Charles Murphy, who retired from the Navy in 1893 and became a pioneer real-estate developer in the Annapolis area. **3** village (1990 pop. 1,600), Suffolk co., SE N.Y., on SE L.I., on Moriches Bay, 15 mi/24 km E of Patchogue; 40°49′N 72°43′W. In summer resort area.

Eastside, town, Coos co., SW Oregon, suburb 3 mi/4.8 km E of Coos Bay, across Isthmus Slough, at White Park in SE end of Coos Bay.

Eastside, village, Jackson co., SE Miss., near the coast just NE of Pascagoula. Now part of cities of Pascagoula and Moss Point.

Eastsound, uninc. town (1990 pop. 1,100), San Juan co., NW Wash., on Orcas Isl., 18 mi/29 km W of Bellingham, at E end of East Sound, on isthmus (1.5 mi/2.4 km long) that connects E and W sections of islands. Fish, crabs, oysters. Tourism. Moran State Park to SE. Orcas Isl. Historical Mus.

Eastvale, borough (1990 pop. 328), Beaver co., W Pa., on Beaver R., bridged to Beaver Falls, to W; 40°46′N 80°19′W. Agr. (corn, hay; dairying; livestock).

Eastville 1 town, Oconee co., NE central Ga., 9 mi/14.5 km SW of Athens; 33°52′N 83°30′W. **2** town (1990 pop. 185), ⊙ Northampton co., E Va., 7 mi/11.3 km NE of Cape Charles town; 37°21′N 75°56′W. Chesapeake Bay to W, Cobb Isl. Bay to E (both are arms of Atlantic Ocean). Mfg. (crab-meat processing); agr. (grain, vegetables; livestock, poultry); seafood. Co. records beginning 1632 are preserved here.

Eaton, county (□ 579 sq mi/1,500 sq km; 1990 pop. 92,879), S central Mich.; ⊙ Charlotte; 42°35′N 84°50′W. Drained by Grand and Thornapple rivers, and by Battle Creek. Part of Metropolitan Lansing, urbanized in NE corner. Agr. area (wheat, corn, beans, soybeans, vegetables, fruit; cattle, hogs, poultry); dairy prods.; stock-breeding. Mfg. at Charlotte, Eaton Rapids, and Grand Ledge. Mineral springs. Organized 1837.

Eaton, city (1990 pop. 7,396), ⊙ Preble co., W Ohio, 23 mi/37 km W of Dayton, and on small Seven Mile Creek; 39°45′N 84°38′W. Trading center for agr.; mfg. (food prods.). Fort St. Clair State Park is nearby. Founded 1806.

Eaton 1 town (1990 pop. 1,959), Weld co., N Colo., near Lone Tree Creek, 7 mi/11.3 km N of Greeley; 40°31′N

104°42′W. Elev. 4,839ft/1,475 m. In grain and cattle region. Beet sugar, sunflowers, wheat, potatoes, beans, livestock; mfg. (processed foods, food-mixing equipment, hoists). Artifacts of Yuma man and Folsom man discovered nearby. Pawner Natl. Grassland to NE. Founded 1881, inc. 1892. **2** town (1990 pop. 1,614), Delaware co., E Ind., on Mississinewa R., and 11 mi/18 km N of Muncie; 40°20′N 85°21′W. Livestock, grain; mfg. (paper prods., chipboard, canned goods). **3** town (1990 pop. 362), Carroll co., E N.H., 32 mi/51 km NE of Laconia; 43°54′N 71°02′W. Bounded E by Maine state line. Mfg. (hardwood furniture at village of Eaton Center); agr. (vegetables; livestock, poultry; dairying; timber). Conway L. on N boundary, Crystal L. in center.

Eaton Centre, shopping mall, downtown Toronto, Ont., Canada. Surrounded by office towers. Built in 1970s, designed by Zeidler partnership and Bregman and Hamann. Atrium, multistoried interior focus integrated with existing downtown.

Eaton, Lake, NE central Hamilton co., N central N.Y., in the Adirondacks, c.2 mi/3.2 km W of Long Lake village; c.1 mi/1.6 km in diameter; 43°58′N 74°27′W.

Eaton Rapids, town (1990 pop. 4,695), Eaton co., S central Mich., 17 mi/27 km SSW of Lansing, and on Grand R.; 42°30′N 84°39′W. In sheep-raising area. Mfg. (woolen goods, metal parts, food prods.); dairy, poultry; mfg. (plastic compounds and adhesives, small engine parts, corrugated packing). Mineral springs. Settled 1837; inc. as village 1871, as city 1881.

Eatonia (ee-TO-nee-uh), town (1991 pop. 505), SW Sask., Canada, 20 mi/32 km SW of Kindersley; wheat, stock.

Eatons Neck, irregular sandspit (¼ mi/ km–1.5 mi/2.4 km wide), SE N.Y., extending c.3.5 mi/5.6 km NW from N shore of W L.I., and sheltering Huntington and Northport bays (W); 40°56′N 73°23′W. At its tip is Eatons Neck Point (lighthouse). Site of Asharoken (resort).

Eatonton (EET-uhn-tuhn), town (1990 pop. 4,737), ⊙ Putnam co., central Ga., 37 mi/60 km NNE of Macon; 33°19′N 83°23′W. Prosperous agr. region, especially dairy cattle and field crops. Mfg. includes upholstered furniture, concrete, apparel, fiberglass prods.; lumber. Has monument to Joel Chandler Harris, who was b. here. Inc. 1809.

Eatontown, borough (1990 pop. 13,800), Monmouth co., E central N.J.; inc. 1926; 40°17′N 74°03′W. A residential borough, it is named for Thomas Eaton, who built a gristmill here c.1670. The mill's site is a landmark.

Eatonville 1 town (□ 1 sq mi/2.6 sq km; 1990 pop. 2,170), Orange co., central Fla., 7 mi/13 km N of Orlando; 28°37′N 81°23′W. Mfg. includes wooden cabinets. **2** town (1990 pop. 1,374), Pierce co., W central Wash., 28 mi/45 km SSE of Tacoma, in foothills of Cascade Range; 46°52′N 122°16′W. Agr.; dairying; poultry; timber. Parts of Mt. Baker-Snoqualmie Natl. Forest to E, including Glacier View Wilderness Area; part of Gifford Pinchot Natl. Forest to S; Mt. Rainier Natl. Park to E; Northwest Trek Wildlife Park to N. Pioneer Farm Mus. to W. La Grande and Alder dams, on Nisqually R., to S.

Eau Claire (o KLER), county (□ 645 sq mi/1,671 sq km; 1990 pop. 85,183), W central Wis.; ⊙ Eau Claire; 44°43′N 91°17′W. Drained by Chippewa and Eau Claire rivers. Dairying (most important industry), cattle, barley, corn, oats, soybeans, peas. Eau Claire city has diversified mfg. L. Eau Claire reservoir in E. Formed 1856.

Eau Claire (o KLER), city (1990 pop. 56,856), ⊙ Eau Claire co., 75 mi/121 km E of St. Paul, Minn., in Eau Claire and Chippewa cos., W central Wis., on the Chippewa at the mouth of the Eau Claire R., in a hilly lake region; inc. 1872; 44°49′N 91°29′W. Once a lumber-based economy, the city has turned to producing items such as rubber tires, processed foods, and dairy goods. Mfg. (automotive controls, concrete, window systems, frozen pizza, video display monitors, printing, paper prods., labels, mattresses, bed frames, horseradish prods., detergents, cleaners, coiled cords, household appliances, baby formula, aviation-towing tractors). A trading port was here in the late 18th cent. The city

grew from several sawmills established on the Eau Claire R. in the mid-19th cent. It is the seat of the Univ. of Wis. at Eau Claire and a technical inst. Eau Claire Airport in N part of city. Chippewa Valley Mus. Carson Park, on a nearby peninsula of Oxbow L., contains a memorial to logging days.

Eau Claire (o-KLER), town, Richland co., central S.C.; N residential suburb of Columbia. Seat of Columbia Col. and Lutheran Theological Southern Seminary. Inc. 1897.

Eau Claire (AW KLER), village (1990 pop. 494), Berrien co., extreme SW Mich., 11 mi/18 km SE of St. Joseph; 41°58′N 86°17′W. Mfg. (machining, fruit juices, zinc and lead castings).

Eau Claire (o-KLER), borough (1990 pop. 371), Butler co., W Pa., 19 mi/31 km NNE of Butler; 41°8′N 79°47′W. Agr. (grain, potatoes, dairying; livestock).

Eau Claire River 1 (o KLER), in central Wis.; rises in lake region in Langlade co.; flows c.55 mi/89 km generally SW to Wisconsin R. (L. Wausau reservoir) at Schofield, 2 mi/3.2 km S of Wausau. Little Eau Claire R. rises in SW Marathon co., central Wis.; flows 20 mi/32 km SW to Wisconsin R. (Du Bay reservoir) 20 mi/32 km S of Wausau. **2** in Wis., formed by 2 forks joining near Eau Claire–Clark co. line; flows c.40 mi/64 km W to Chippewa R. at Eau Claire. Both N Fork (c.25 mi/40 km) and S Fork (c.35 mi/56 km) rise at boundary of Taylor and Clark cos., central Wis.; and flows SW meeting in E Eau Claire co.; flows c.40 mi/64 km W through Eau Claire L. and L. Altoona to Chippewa R. at Eau Claire.

Eau Galle River (o GAWL), in W Wis.; rises in SE St. Croix co.; flows c.35 mi/56 km SE through George L. (Eau Galle Dam Recreation Area, Corps of Engineers) near its source, past Elmwood, to Chippewa R. SW of Durand.

Ebano (e-BAH-no), city (1990 pop. 24,340) and township, San Luis Potosí, E Mexico, in fertile gulf plain, on RR, and 35 mi/56 km W of Tampico, on Mexico Highway 70; 22°16′N 98°26′W. Sugarcane, tobacco, coffee, vegetables, fruit; cattle. Oil and forestry main industries.

Ebbegunbaeg, Lake (12 mi/19 km long, 1 mi/2 km wide), S central N.F., Canada, 50 mi/80 km SSE of Buchans; 48°12′N 56°28′W. Drains NW into Meelpaeg L.

Ebbetts Pass, E Calif., mt. pass (elev. 8,731 ft/2,661 m) across the Sierra Nevada, in Alpine co., c.40 mi/64 km S of Carson City, Nev. State Highway 4 passes through. Source of North Fork Makelumne R., flows W.

Ebenezer 1 (eb-uh-NEE-zuhr), village, Holmes co., central Miss., 20 mi/32 km ENE of Yazoo City. **2** village, Erie co., N.Y., 6 mi/9.7 km SE of Buffalo; 42°50′N 78°45′W. Former industrial-RR satellite town in Greater Buffalo area. It is now a residential area. **3** village, York co., N S.C.; NW residential suburb of Rock Hill.

Ebensburg (E-buhns-buhrg), borough (1990 pop.), ⊙ Cambria co., W central Pa., 15 mi/24 km NE of Johnstown; 40°29′N 78°43′W. Mfg. (wood prods., electronic equip., food, metal fabrication); agr. (corn, hay, potatoes; dairying; livestock); timber; summer resort; bituminous-coal mining. Cambria co. Historic Site Mus. William Run Reservoir to N. Settled 1796, laid out 1806, inc. 1825.

Ebey's Landing National Historical Reserve (EEB-eez), Whidbey Isl., Wash.; encompasses town of Coupeville. Natural and historic features of one of state's oldest towns. Authorized 1978.

Éboulements, Les (lai-zai-bool-MAH), village (1991 pop. 1,013), E Que., Canada, on the St. Lawrence R., and 7 mi/11 km ENE of Baie St. Paul; dairying, lumbering; hydroelectric station.

Ecatepec de Morelos (ai-KAH-tai-pek dai mo-RAI-los, city (1990 pop. 1,218,135) and township, ⊙ Ecatepec municipio, Mexico state, S central Mexico, part of the Área Metropolitana de la Ciudad de México. It is an industrial center. Ecatepec was the site of an Indian kingdom (est. 12th cent.). The Mexican revolutionary hero Morelos y Pavón was executed by the Spanish at Ecatepec in 1815; a monument to him stands in the city.

Ecatzingo de Hidalgo (ee-kaht-SEEN-go dai ee-DAHL-go), town (1990 pop. 4,215), ⊙ Ecatzingo municipio, Mexico state, central Mexico, 40 mi/64 km SE of Mexico City and in the Zona Metropolitana de la Ciudad de México. Sugarcane, cereals, stock. Also known as San Pedro Ecatzingo.

Eccles (EK-uhlz), uninc. town (1990 pop. 1,162), Raleigh co., S W.Va., 4 mi/6.4 km W of Beckley. Coal area. Stevens L. reservoir to W.

Echo 1 village (1990 pop. 304), Yellow Medicine co., SW Minn., 15 mi/24 km SSE of Granite Falls; 44°37'N 95°24'W. Livestock; grain, soybeans, alfalfa; mfg. (fertilizers). **2** village (1990 pop. 499), Umatilla co., N Oregon, 20 mi/32 km WNW of Pendleton, and on Umatilla R.; 45°44'N 11°119'W. Agr. (apples, plums, peaches, vegetables, wheat; sheep, hogs, cattle). Mfg. beeswax. **3** uninc. village (1990 pop. 70), Summit co., N Utah, NNW of Coalville, and on Weber R., at Echo Dam. Elev. 5,461 ft/1,665 m. Dairying; cattle, sheep. Echo Reservoir to S. Intersection of Highway I-80 and I-84; rail junction. Est. 1853 as stagecoach station.

Echo Dam, Utah: see WEBER RIVER, Echo.

Echo Lake, El Dorado co., E Calif., small lake in the Sierra Nevada, 7 mi/11.3 km S of L. Tahoe. In Eldorado Natl. Forest. Narrow point in lake divides it into upper (W) and Lower (E) Echo lakes. Echo L. village (resort) is near S shore. Fallen Leaf L. bet. Tahoe and Echo lakes. Echo Peak (8,895 ft/2,711 m) N of lake's W end, Echo Summit Pass (7,377 ft/2,249 m) to SE (U.S. Highway 50).

Echo Lake, N.H.: see FRANCONIA NOTCH.

Echols (EK-uhlz), co. (□ 425; 1990 pop. 2,334), S Ga., on Fla., line; ⊙ Statenville; 30°43'N 82°54'W. Coastal-plain agr. (corn, cotton, tobacco); cattle; lumber. Area drained by Alapaha and Suwannee rivers. Formed 1858.

Eckert, Colo.: see ORCHARD CITY.

Eckhart Mines, village, Allegany co., W Md., in the Alleghenies, 8 mi/12.9 km W of Cumberland. Named after the Eckhart family who acquired lots here after the Revolutionary War. Coal was mined here early when the "Big Vein" was opened in 1820. The coal was originally transported by flatboats knocked together on the headwaters of the Potomac, and abandoned after reaching the RR in Cumberland. Declined after horse-drawn tramlines were built to carry the coal to the RR directly from the mines.

Eckley 1 (EK-lee), village (1990 pop. 211), Yuma co., NE Colo., 14 mi/23 km W of Wray, in the Sand Hills; 40°06'N 102°29'W. Elev. 3,894 ft/1,187 m. **2** uninc. village, Luzerne co., E central Pa., 6 mi/9.7 km ENE of Hazleton; 40°59'N 75°51'W. In former anthracite-coal-mining region. Eckley Mining Village Historic site, 19th-cent. mining town.

Eckman 1 village, Bottineau co., N N.Dak., 31 mi/50 km WSW of Bottineau; 48°39'N 101°03'W. Cut Bank Creek to S. **2** uninc. village (1990 pop. 300), McDowell co., S W.Va., 7 mi/11.3 km ESE of Welch; semibituminous coal.

Eckville, agr. town (1991 pop. 899), S central Alta., Canada, on Medicine R., and 24 mi/39 km W of Red Deer; oil and gas; cattle, hogs, wheat, barley.

Eclectic, town (1990 pop. 1,087), Elmore co., E central Ala., near L. Martin, 13 mi/21 km NE of Wetumpka; 32°38'N 86°1'W. Cabinets.

Eclipse Sound, N Baffin Isl., SE Franklin Dist., N.W.T., Canada, arm (60 mi/97 km long, 40 mi/64 km wide) of Baffin Bay, S of Bylot Isl.; 72°30'N 80°W.

Economy, town (1990 pop. 151), Wayne co., E Ind., on a fork of Whitewater R., and 15 mi/24 km NW of Richmond; 39°59'N 85°05'W. In agr. area. Mfg. (concrete drain tile).

Economy, village, N central N.S., Canada, on Cobequid Bay, at mouth of Economy R., 30 mi/48 km W of Truro; 45°23'N 63°55'W. Dairying, mixed farming.

Economy, borough (1990 pop. 9,519), Beaver co., Pa., 5 mi/8 km E of Aliquippa, 16 mi/26 km NNW of Pittsburgh; 40°38'N 80°11'W. Borough covers 18 sq mi/47 sq km of mainly rural area, bounded S by Big Sewickley Creek.

Ecorse (EK-ors), city (1990 pop. 12,180), Wayne co., SE Mich., on the Detroit R., at mouth of Ecorse R., 7 mi/11.3 km SW of downtown Detroit. Borders Detroit on W; 42°15'N 83°08'W. Rolled and sheet metal, packaging, meat processing are the chief manufactures, but the city has suffered from the economic and pop. decline of the surrounding region. Settled c.1815, inc. as a city 1941.

Ecru (EK-roo), village (1990 pop. 696), Pontotoc co., N Miss., 8 mi/12.9 km N of Pontotoc; 34°21'N 89°01'W. In agr. area; mfg. (furniture, mattresses, pool tables).

Ector, county (□ 901 sq mi/2,334 sq km; 1990 pop. 118,934), W Texas; ⊙ Odessa; 31°52'N 102°32'W. Here S Llano Estacado meets Edwards Plateau. Elev. c.2,800 ft/853 m–3,300 ft/1,006 m. A leading petroleum-producing co. of Texas, with great fields in Odessa region. Oil refining, mfg. of oil-field supplies at Odessa; also natural gas, stone. Cattle ranching, horses; pecans; hay. Large potash deposits. S of Odessa is huge meteor crater; sand dunes in SW. Formed 1887.

Ector, village (1990 pop. 494), Fannin co., NE Texas, 5 mi/8 km W of Bonham; 33°34'N 96°16'W. In agr. area. Mfg. (surge protection hardware).

Ecuandureo (ai-kwahn-doo-RAI-o), town (1990 pop. 324), ⊙ Ecuandureo municipio, Michoacán, central Mexico, on central plateau, 14 mi/23 km SW of La Piedad de Cabadas. Elev. 5,151 ft/1,570 m. Located on N slope of inactive volcano. On paved highway between La Piedad de Cabadas and Zamora de Hidalgo. An agr. community in Tarascan Indian area.

Edam (EE-dam), village (1991 pop. 425), W Sask., Canada, on Turtlelake R., and 35 mi/56 km NW of N. Battleford; 53°11'N 108°46'W. Wheat, mixed farming.

Edberg, village (1991 pop. 135), S central Alta., Canada, 17 mi/27 km S of Camrose; coal mining; oil and gas; wheat, oats, barley.

Edcouch, town (1990 pop. 2,878), Hidalgo co., extreme S Texas, in the lower Rio Grande valley, 12 mi/19 km E of Edinburg; 26°17'N 97°57'W. In irrigated citrus, vegetables, cotton area; mfg. (Mex.-style dried beef). Inc. 1928.

Eddington 1 agr. town (1990 pop. 1,947), Penobscot co., S Maine, on the Penobscot, just N of Bangor; 44°49'N 68°37'W. **2** (E-ding-tuhn), uninc. town (1990 pop. 1,000), Bucks co., SE Pa., suburb 13 mi/21 km NE of Philadelphia on Delaware R. at mouth of Neshaminy Creek; 40°05'N 74°56'W. Mfg. includes machining, tool and die; candies. Neshaminy State Park is here.

Eddiville, village, Kootenai co., N Idaho, 4 mi/6.4 km SSE of Coeur d'Alene, on S shore of E arm of Coeur d'Alene L. Coeur d'Alene Natl. Forest 1 mi/1.6 km SE.

Eddy 1 county (□ 4,197 sq mi/10,870 sq km; 1990 pop. 48,605), SE N.Mex.; ⊙ Carlsbad; 32°28'N 104°17'W. Irrigated agr. and livestock region; watered by Pecos R.; borders on S Texas (Central/Mountain time zone boundaries, N.Mex. in Mountain Time Zone). Cattle, sheep; dairying; chiles, pecans, cotton, corn, sorghum hay, alfalfa, wheat, oats, barley, millet, rye; potash and salt mining dist. in E center, near Carlsbad. Carlsbad Caverns Natl. Park in SW part of Guadalupe Mts., in part of Lincoln Natl. Forest in SW. Formed 1889. Living Desert State Park in center near Carlsbad. Brantley L. State Park in center NW of Carlsbad. N part of Red Bluff Reservoir (Pecos R.) on S boundary, in SE, lowest point in N.Mex., 2,842 ft/866 m, (3rd highest state low point in U.S.). **2** county (□ 635 sq mi/1,645 sq km; 1990 pop. 2,951), central N.Dak.; ⊙ New Rockford. Agr. area drained by Sheyenne and James rivers; 47°43'N 98°54'W. Sunflowers, dairy prods., wheat, rye, flax, poultry, cattle. Formed 1885. Part of Devils L. Sioux Indian Reservation in N; N of Sheyenne R.; Coe L. and other small lakes in E.

Eddy, town (1990 pop. 1,075), McLennan co., E central Texas, 18 mi/29 km SSW of Waco. Cattle, dairying, grain, cotton.

Eddystone (E-dee-ston), borough (1990 pop. 2,446), Delaware co., SE Pa., suburb 11 mi/18 km SW of downtown Philadelphia, and 2 mi/3.2 km E of Chester, on Delaware R.; 39°51'N 75°19'W. RR shops. Mfg. (apparel, industrial gases, plastic prods., fabricated metal prods.). Inc. 1889.

Eddyville 1 (ED-ee-vil), town (1990 pop. 1,010), on Mahaska-Wapello co. line, S central Iowa, on Des Moines R. and 15 mi/24 km NW of Ottumwa; 41°09'N 92°37'W. Feed milling. Bituminous-coal mines, limestone quarries nearby. **2** town (1990 pop. 1,889), ⊙ Lyon co., W Ky., 27 mi/43 km E of Paducah, on Cumberland R. (L. Barkley reservoir); 37°04'N 88°04'W. In agr. area with limestone quarries; light mfg. Entire town was relocated (c.1960) 4 mi/6.4 km to NW with construction of Barkley Dam and reservoir (completed 1966). State penitentiary here. Rose Hill Mansion (1832). Barkley Dam 6 mi/9.7 km to W; Kentucky Dam (Tennessee R.) 9 mi/14.5 km to W; Mineral Mounds State Park to SE; Land Between the Lakes Recreation Area (TVA) to S, across L. Barkley.

Eddyville 1 village (1990 pop. 151), Pope co., extreme S Ill., 12 mi/19 km NNW of Golconda; 37°30'N 88°35'W. Agr. (cattle; timber). In Shawnee Natl. Forest. **2** village (1990 pop. 102), Dawson co., S central Nebr., 15 mi/24 km NNE of Lexington, and on Wood R; 41°00'N 99°37'W.

Eden (EED-uhn), city (1990 pop. 15,238), Rockingham co., N N.C., 32 mi/51 km N of Greensboro, on Dan R., at Va. state line; 36°30'N 79°44'W. Agr. area (tobacco, grain, soybeans, poultry, livestock, dairying). Mfg. (printing and publishing; yarns, bedding, apparel; lumber; beer).

Eden 1 town, St. Clair co., NE central Ala., 28 mi/45 km ENE of Birmingham. **2** town (1990 pop. 750), Effingham co., Ga., 20 mi/32 km WNW of Savannah; 32°10'N 81°23'W. Mfg. includes concrete blocks, pumps. **3** town (1990 pop. 1,567), Concho co., W central Texas, on Edwards Plateau, c.40 mi/64 km ESE of San Angelo; 31°13'N 99°50'W. Trade, shipping center in ranch, farm area (sheep, cattle, goats; cotton, wheat). **4** town (1990 pop. 840), Lamoille co., N Vt., in Green Mts., 24 mi/39 km SW of Newport. L. Eden (2 mi/3.2 km long) here; 44°42'N 72°32'W. Includes village of Eden Mills.

Eden 1 (EED-uhn), village (1990 pop. 314), Jerome co., S Idaho, 18 mi/29 km SE of Jerome, near Snake R.; 42°37'N 114°13'W. Potatoes, onions, beets, sugar beets; dairying; cattle, sheep; corn, wheat, barley. Wilson L. reservoir to NE; Shoshone Falls (212 ft/65 m) to W, on Snake R. **2** village (1990 pop. 88), Yazoo co., W central Miss., 11 mi/18 km NNE of Yazoo City, near Yazoo R.; 32°59'N 90°19'W. Hillside Natl. Wildlife Refuge to NE. **3** residential village (□ 5 sq mi/13 sq km; 1990 pop. 3,088), Erie co., W N.Y., 18 mi/29 km S of Buffalo; 42°38'N 78°54'W. Mfg. (various brass mfg., tools and dies, electronic measuring devices). The "Original Amer. Kazoo" is still made here, and though the factory itself may no longer be toured, there is still a visitors center that explains modern production methods as well as West Afr. origins of the instrument. Est. in 1916, this is now the world's only metal kazoo factory. **4** village (1990 pop. 97), Marshall co., NE S.Dak., 20 mi/32 km SE of Britton; 45°37'N 97°25'W. Fort Sisseton State Park to W, Roy L. State Park to N. **5** village (1990 pop. 610), Fond du Lac co., E Wis., 6 mi/9.7 km SE of Fond du Lac; 43°41'N 88°21'W. In farm area; canned vegetables. Kettle Moraine State Forest (N unit) to SE. **6** village, Sweetwater co., SW central Wyo., near Sandy Creek, 33 mi/53 km NNW of Rock Springs. Elev. 6,590 ft/2,009 m. On fertile, irrigated plateau extensively cultivated by state agr. experiment station; alfalfa, oats; cattle, sheep. Big Sandy Reservoir and Eden Valley Reservoir to N. Big Sandy State Recreation area to N.

Eden Park (EE-duhn), borough, Allegheny co., SW Pa., on Youghiogheny R., just SE of McKeesport. Inc. 1944; 40°19'N 79°50'W.

Eden Prairie, city (1990 pop. 39,311), Hennepin co., E Minn., suburb 12 mi/19 km SW of downtown Minneapolis, on Minnesota R., drained by Purgatory Creek, several small lakes in city; 44°51'N 93°27'W. Mfg. (computer accessories, metallic balloons, printing and publishing, software, hearing aids, medical equip., chemicals, electronic sensors, workstations, seed cleaning equip., envelopes, packaging machinery, laser printers, medical optical sensors, motion controls, heating equip., power supplies). S Suburban Hennepin Co. Technical Col. is here. Flying Cloud Airport in S.

Eden Valley, village (1990 pop. 732), Meeker and Stearns cos., S central Minn., 14 mi/23 km N of Litchfield; 45°19′N 94°32′W. In natural lake region. Dairying; poultry, cattle, sheep, hogs, mink; grain, soybeans; mfg. (toy animals, mink feeders, fertilizers). L. Koronis to W, Rice L. to NW.

Edenborn (EE-duhn-born), uninc. village, Fayette co., SW Pa., 9 mi/14.5 km WSW of Uniontown; 39°53′N 79°52′W. Some agr.; coal.

Edenburg, Pa.: see KNOX.

Edenton (EED-uhn-tuhn), town (1990 pop. 5,628), ⊙ Chowan co., NE N.C., on inlet of Albemarle Sound, 27 mi/43 km SW of Elizabeth City, near Chowan R. mouth (bridged) to Edenhouse to W. Rail terminus; 36°03′N 76°35′W. Trade center for agr. (peanuts, cotton) area; mfg. (boats, wood processing, lumber, packaged nuts, textile prods., cotton yarn, metal connector plates). Has St. Paul's Church (1736), old court house (1767), other historic bldgs. Bridge across Albermarle Sound 7 mi/11.3 km to SE. Iredell State Historical Site (1776). Was capital of N.C. 1722–1743. Settled c.1658, inc. 1722.

Edenville, Iowa; see RHODES.

Edgar, county (□ 624 sq mi/1,616 sq km; 1990 pop. 19,595), E Ill., on Ind. line (E); ⊙ Paris; 39°40′N 87°45′W. Agr. (corn, soybeans, sorghum; cattle, hogs). Food processing; mfg. (in Paris) of farm machinery. Drained by small tributaries of the Wabash. Formed 1823. Jenison Correctional Center N of Paris.

Edgar, town (1990 pop. 1,318), Marathon co., central Wis., 16 mi/26 km W of Wausau; 44°55′N 89°57′W. Cheese, processed meat, wood prods. Mfg. (juvenile bassinettes, cradles, etc.).

Edgar, village (1990 pop. 600), Clay co., S Nebr., 11 mi/18 km SSE of Clay Center; 40°22′N 97°58′W. Rail junction. Grain.

Edgar Allan Poe National Historic Site (½ acre/⅕ ha), Philadelphia co., in city of Philadelphia, SE Pa., 532 N. 7th St., downtown, 3 bldg.-complex. In 1843, Edgar Allan Poe lived here and wrote several of his most famous stories. Authorized 1978.

Edgard (ED-gahrd), uninc. village (1990 pop. 2,753), ⊙ St. John the Baptist parish, SE La., on the Mississippi R., and 28 mi/45 km WNW of New Orleans; 30°02′N 90°34′W. In sugarcane area, also vegetables; cattle; catfish, crawfish, alligators; mfg. of molasses. Toll ferry to Reserve deepwater port. Lac Des Allemands to S. Originally known as Edgar but as another town had the same name, a *d* was added.

Edgartown (ED-guhr-toun), town (1990 pop. 3,062), ⊙ Dukes co., SE Mass., on SE Martha's Vineyard, and 27 mi/43 km SE of New Bedford; 41°23′N 70°32′W. Main center of the isl.; summer resort, fishing community; good harbor and lighthouse. Boatbuilding, canning; state forest. Includes CHAPPAQUIDDICK ISLAND. Old homes, built when town was whaling port, survive. Site of famed Edgartown Regatta. Settled 1642, inc. 1671.

Edge Hill, Pa.: see CHELTENHAM.

Edgecliff, town (1990 pop. 2,715), Tarrant co., N Texas, residential suburb, 7 mi/11.3 km SE of downtown Fort Worth, bounded on all sides by Fort Worth, near Sycamore Creek; 32°39′N 97°20′W.

Edgecomb (EJ-kom), town (1990 pop. 993), Lincoln co., S Maine, just SE of Wiscasset; includes North Edgecomb village; 43°58′N 69°37′W. Fort Edgecomb, wooden block-house built 1808–1809, is nearby.

Edgecombe (EJ-kuhm), co. (□ 506 sq mi/1,311 sq km; 1990 pop. 56,558), E central N.C.; ⊙ Tarboro; 35°54′N 77°35′W. On coastal plain; drained by Tar R. and Fishing Creek (forms part of N boundary). Timber (pine, gum), partly swampy; agr. (tobacco, peanuts, cotton, corn, wheat, oats, barley, sorghum, hay, soybeans, sweet potatoes; chickens, cattle, hogs). Tobacco markets, industries at Rocky Mount and Tarboro. Formed 1735.

Edgecumbe, Cape (EJ-kuhm), SE Alaska, SW tip of Kruzof Isl., on Gulf of Alaska, at mouth of Sitka Sound, 20 mi/32 km W across Sitka Sound from Sitka; 57°N 135°51′W.

Edgecumbe, Mount (EJ-kuhm), extinct volcano (3,201 ft/976 m), SE Alaska, on S Kruzof Isl., 16 mi/26 km W of Sitka; 57°3′N 135°45′W.

Edgefield, county (□ 506 sq mi/1,311 sq km; 1990 pop. 18,375), W S.C.; ⊙ Edgefield; 33°46′N 81°58′W. Bounded SW by Savannah R.; includes part of Sumter Natl. Forest. Some mfg. of textiles. Sparsely settled agr. region known for cotton, peaches; chickens, eggs, hogs, cattle, dairying; corn, wheat, rye, oats, soybeans, sorghum, hay. Some mfg. textiles. Formed 1785.

Edgefield, town (1990 pop. 2,563), ⊙ Edgefield co., W S.C., 20 mi/32 km NNW of Aiken; 33°47′N 81°55′W. In agr. area; poultry, livestock, dairying, grain, peaches, soybeans. Settled in 18th cent.

Edgefield (EJ-feeld), village (1990 pop. 207), Red River parish, NW La., 38 mi/61 km SE of Shreveport; 32°03′N 93°20′W. In agr. area (cotton, soybeans, vegetables, peaches, watermelons; cattle).

Edgeley (EJ-lee), village (1990 pop. 680), La Moure co., SE central N.Dak., 20 mi/32 km W of La Moure; 46°21′N 98°42′W. Grain, dairy prods. Terminus for RR from La Moure.

Edgely, uninc. village, Bristo township, Bucks co., SE Pa., residential suburb, 20 mi/32 km NE of downtown Philadelphia, and 6 mi/9.7 km SE of Levittown, on Delaware R.; 40°07′N 74°50′W.

Edgemere, section of S Queens borough of N.Y. city, SE N.Y., near base of Rockaway Peninsula; 40°36′N 73°46′W.

Edgemere (EJ-mir), suburban industrial village (1990 pop. 9,226), Baltimore co., central Md., on Back R., adjacent to Sparrows Point, and 10 mi/16 km ESE of downtown Baltimore; 39°13′N 76°28′W. Makes wooden boxes, welding rods.

Edgemont 1 uninc. town (1990 pop. 950), Dauphin co., S Pa., residential suburb, 2 mi/3.2 km NE of Harrisburg; 40°17′N 76°50′W. **2** town (1990 pop. 906), Fall R. co., SW S.Dak., 20 mi/32 km SW of Hot Springs, just S of Black Hills, and on Cheyenne R., near Wyo. line; 43°17′N 103°49′W. At N edge of Buffalo Gap Natl. Grasslands; Black Hills Natl. Forest to N. Black Hills Army Depot 8 mi/12.9 km at Provo. Trading point for agr. area; sandstone quarries; RR junction.

Edgemont, village, Cleburne co., N central Ark., 33 mi/53 km WSW of Batesville, on N shore of Greers Ferry L. Recreation.

Edgemont, summer resort, Washington co., W Md., at foot of South Mt., 10 mi/16 km ENE of Hagerstown.

Edgemoor, uninc. town (1990 pop. 5,853), New Castle co., N Del., residential suburb, 2 mi/3.2 km NE of downtown Wilmington, on Delaware R.; 39°45′N 75°30′W. Mfg. (compressors); RR yards. Fox Point State Park to SE. Former site of Edgemoor Iron Co., which produced iron used for the Brooklyn Bridge.

Edgemoor, village, Chester co., N S.C., 8 mi/12.9 km S of Rock Hill. Mfg. includes filters, printing and publishing, fibers, lighting fixtures, yarns, transformers, lumber; agr. includes logging, timber; livestock, poultry; grain.

Edgerton, city (1990 pop. 565), Platte co., W Mo., on Platte R., and 28 mi/45 km N of Kansas City; 39°30′N 94°37′W. Corn, tobacco; cattle.

Edgerton 1 (ED-guhr-tuhn), town (1990 pop. 1,106), Pipestone co., SW Minn., 12 mi/19 km SE of Pipestone, on Rock R., at mouth of Chanarambie Creek; 43°52′N 96°07′W. Soybeans, grain; livestock, poultry; dairying; mfg. (printing, feeds, filters). **2** town (1990 pop. 4,254), Rock co., S Wis., 23 mi/37 km SE of Madison, near L. Koshkonong (resort to E); 42°50′N 89°04′W. In tobacco-growing area; mfg. (aerosols, salt-glazed stoneware, wood trusses); tobacco warehouses. Settled 1836, laid out 1854, inc. 1883.

Edgerton, village (1991 pop. 353), E Alta., Canada, near Sask. border, 18 mi/29 km ESE of Wainwright; 52°45′N 110°27′W. Mixed farming, grain, oats, rye.

Edgerton 1 (ED-guhr-tuhn), village (1990 pop. 1,244),

Johnson co., E Kansas, 14 mi/23 km SW of Olathe, and 29 mi/47 km SW of Kansas City, Kansas; 38°45′N 95°00′W. Dairying, farming. Douglas State Fishing L. to W. Near N end of Hillsdale L. Reservoir. **2** village (1990 pop. 1,896), Williams co., extreme NW Ohio, on St. Joseph R., and 10 mi/16 km W of Bryan, near Ind. line; 41°26′N 84°45′W. **3** village (1990 pop. 247), Natrona co., central Wyo., on Salt Creek, and 40 mi/64 km N of Casper; 43°24′N 106°15′W. In oil field. Teapot Dome to S.

Edgerton Highway (ED-guhr-tuhn), S Alaska, extends 39 mi/63 km NW from Chitina to Richardson Highway, 60 mi/97 km NE of Valdez. Serves fishing; tourism.

Edgewater, resort city (□ 7 sq mi/18.1 sq km; 1990 pop. 15,337), Volusia co., E central Fla., near the Atlantic, on Hillsborough R. (lagoon), and 17 mi/27 km SSE of Daytona Beach; 28°58′N 80°54′W.

Edgewater, town (1990 pop. 4,613), Jefferson co., N central Colo.; suburb, 4 mi/6.4 km WNW of downtown Denver; 39°45′N 105°03′W. Elev. 5,353 ft/1,632 m. Bounded by Denver on E, Wheat Ridge on N, Lakewood on W and S. Inc. 1904 as town.

Edgewater, village, Jefferson co., N central Ala., near Birmingham.

Edgewater, borough (1990 pop. 5,001), Bergen co., NE N.J., on Hudson R., just S of Fort Lee; 40°49′N 73°58′W. Mfg. (chemicals, food prods., boats, automobile parts, metal prods., linseed oil). Inc. 1899.

Edgewater Park, township (1990 pop. 8,388), Burlington co., S N.J., 2 mi/3.2 km W of Burlington, on Delaware R.; 40°02′N 74°54′W. Inc. 1924.

Edgewater Park, resort, Harrison co., SE Miss., on Mississippi Sound, c.5 mi/8 km W of Biloxi. Part of city of Biloxi (W part).

Edgewood, village, S B.C., Canada, on Lower Arrow L. (Columbia R.), 40 mi/64 km NW of Nelson; 49°47′N 118°08′W. Silver, lead, zinc mining.

Edgewood 1 town (1990 pop. 1,062), Orange co., central Fla., 4 mi/6.4 km S of Orlando; 28°29′N 81°22′W. **2** town (1990 pop. 2,057), Madison co., E central Ind., on W edge of Anderson; 40°06′N 85°44′W. **3** town (1990 pop. 776), on Clayton-Delaware co. line, NE Iowa, 15 mi/24 km S of Elkader; 42°38′N 91°24′W. Mfg. (dairy prods., packed poultry, feed). Limestone quarry nearby. Bixby State Park is N. **4** town (1990 pop. 8,143), Kenton co., N Ky., residential suburb, 8 mi/12.9 km SSW of Cincinnati, Ohio, and 6 mi/9.7 km SSW of Covington, Ky.; 39°00′N 84°33′W. Mfg. (fire apparatus, light mfg.). Thomas More Col. to NW. **5** uninc. town (1990 pop. 3,324), Santa Fe co., N central N.Mex., 28 mi/45 km E of Albuquerque; 40°25′N 79°52′W. Cattle, sheep, grain, corn, alfalfa. Sandia Mts., in part of Cibola Natl. Forest, to W. **6** uninc. town (1990 pop. 2,719), Coal township, Northumberland co., E central Pa., residential suburb, 1 mi/1.6 km W of Shamokin; 40°47′N 76°34′W. **7** town (1990 pop. 1,284), Van Zandt co., NE Texas, 24 mi/39 km E of Terrell; 32°41′N 95°52′W. Elev. 460 ft/140 m. In agr. area (grains, vegetables, sweet potatoes; cotton, nurseries; dairying; cattle, hogs); mfg. (trailers). L. Tawakoni State Park to NW. **8** uninc. town (1990 pop. 2,657), Pierce co., W Wash., residential suburb, 7 mi/11.3 km E of downtown Tacoma.

Edgewood 1 village (1990 pop. 502), Effingham co., SE central Ill., 15 mi/24 km SSW of Effingham; 38°55′N 88°39′W. In agr. area (corn, soybeans, wheat). Rail junction nearby. **2** village (1990 pop. 23,903), Harford co., NE Md., near Bush R., 19 mi/31 km ENE of Baltimore; 39°25′N 76°18′W. Nearby Army Chemical Center (adjacent to Aberdeen Proving Ground) on Chesapeake Bay is part of Edgewood Arsenal, est. in 1917. Gunpowder State Park is just S. **3** uninc. village (1990 pop. 5,189), Ashtabula co., NE Ohio, near Ashtabula; 41°52′N 80°45′W.

Edgewood, borough (1990 pop. 3,581), Allegheny co., SW Pa., residential suburb, 6 mi/9.7 km E of downtown Pittsburgh; 40°25′N 79°52′W. Inc. 1888.

Edgeworth, borough (1990 pop. 1,670), Allegheny co.,

W Pa., residential suburb, 13 mi/21 km NW of Pittsburgh, on Ohio R., at mouth of Little Sewickley Creek; 40°32′N 80°11′W. First municipality in Pa. to adopt borough-manager govt. Site of Dashields Lock and Dam, on Ohio R. Inc. 1904.

Edina 1 (ee-DI-nuh), city (1990 pop. 46,070), Hennepin co., E Minn., a residential suburb, 7 mi/11.3 km SW of downtown Minneapolis; 44°53′N 93°21′W. Mfg. (electronic insulators, leather gift items, signs, microwave foods, lighting controls, folding tables, feed supplements, printing and publishing). Site of the Southdale Shopping Center, the 1st covered and one of the largest shopping centers in the U.S., designed by Victor Gruen in the 1950s. Several small lakes in area; Cornelia and Edina lakes in SE. **2** city (1990 pop. 1,283), ⊙ Knox co., NE Mo., on South Fabius R., and 20 mi/32 km E of Kirksville; 40°10′N 92°10′W. Corn, soybeans; cattle, hogs; lumber; mfg. (crushed stone, leather prods.). Inc. 1857.

Edinboro (E-din-buhr-o), borough (1990 pop. 7,736), Erie co., NW Pa., 17 mi/27 km S of Erie, on Conneauttee Creek, forms Edinboro L. Reservoir on N; 41°52′N 80°7′W. Agr. (grain, soybeans, potatoes; livestock, dairying); mfg. (fabricated metal prods., furniture, heating elements, electrical equip.). Seat of Edinboro Univ. of Pa. Mt. Pleasant Ski Area to SE.

Edinburg, city (1990 pop. 29,885), ⊙ Hidalgo co., extreme S Texas, suburb, 7 mi/11.3 km NE of McAllen; 26°18′N 98°09′W. Elev. 91 ft/28 m. It is a processing center in the irrigated portion of the lower Rio Grande valley. Agr. prods. include, citrus fruits, vegetables, and cotton. Oil and gas are produced from surrounding fields; mfg. (food processing, fertilizers, corrugated boxes, rebuilt engines, concrete). Univ. of Texas–Pan Amer. is in Edinburg. International Racetrack Association drag racing. Inc. 1919.

Edinburg, town (1990 pop. 860), Shenandoah co., NW Va., near North Fork of Shenandoah R., 5 mi/8 km SW of Woodstock; 38°49′N 78°33′W. Mfg. (clothing, microwave filters, pocket folders, poultry processing, poultry houses, wine, roofing insulation); agr. (grain, soybeans, apples, peaches, grapes; poultry, livestock; dairying).

Edinburg 1 village (1990 pop. 982), Christian co., central Ill., 15 mi/24 km SE of Springfield; 39°39′N 89°23′W. Agr. (wheat, corn, soybeans). Sangchris L. and State Park to W on Sangamon-Christian co. line. **2** village (1990 pop. 284), Walsh co., NE N.Dak., 22 mi/35 km WNW of Grafton; 48°30′N 97°51′W.

Edinburgh, town (1990 pop. 4,536), on Johnson-Bartholomew co. line, S central Ind., 9 mi/14.5 km SSE of Franklin and on East Fork of White R.; 39°21′N 85°58′W. In grain, livestock, and dairying area. Mfg. of wood prods., plastic parts, flexible package materials. U.S. Camp Atterbury. Atterbury Fish and Wildlife Area and Driftwood State Fishing Area are just W. Settled 1821.

Edison, city (1990 pop. 88,680), Middlesex co., NE N.J., 4 mi/6.4 km NE of New Brunswick; 40°31′N 74°22′W. Residential; mfg. of chemicals, metal prods., electrical and electronic equip., machinery, and instruments. Newspaper printing. Site of Middlesex Community Col.

Edison 1 uninc. town (1990 pop.), Kern co., S central Calif., residential suburb, 6 mi/9.7 km E of downtown Bakersfield. Greenhorn Mts. (Sierra Nevada), and Sequoia Natl. Forest to NE. Diverse irrigated agr. area. Mfg. (machined parts). **2** town (1990 pop. 1,182), Calhoun co., SW Ga., 32 mi/51 km W of Albany; 31°34′N 84°44′W. Mfg. of uniforms.

Edison 1 village (1990 pop. 148), Furnas co., S Nebr., 7 mi/11.3 km ESE of Arapahoe, and on Republican R; 40°16′N 99°46′W. Dairying; livestock, grain. **2** village (1990 pop. 488), Morrow co., central Ohio, 13 mi/21 km E of Marion, in agr. area; 40°33′N 82°52′W.

Edisto (ED-is-to), uninc. town (1990 pop. 2,815), also known as Edisto Isl., Charleston co., S S.C., 25 mi/40 km SW of Charleston, in E center of Edisto Isl; 33°28′N 80°54′W. Mfg. includes oyster and clam processing. Atlantic Ocean to SE, Edisto Beach State Park to S.

Edisto Beach (ED-is-to), village (1990 pop. 340), Colleton co., S S.C., 30 mi/48 km SW of Charleston on Atlantic Ocean near entrance to St. Helena Sound; 32°29′N 80°19′W.

Edisto Island (ED-is-to), Charleston and Colleton cos., S S.C., one of Sea Isls., 22 mi/35 km SW of Charleston; c.10 mi/16 km long, 10 mi/16 km wide. Highway connects with Little Edisto Isl. (just N) and mainland. Edisto Isl. village, Edisto Beach (resort), and Edisto Beach State Park (c.1,250 acres/506 ha) are here. Antebellum plantation area; vegetable farming, fishing.

Edisto River (ED-is-to), S S.C., formed 15 mi/24 km S of Orangeburg by junction of its North and South forks; flows 90 mi/145 km SE and S dividing into 2 channels as it enters the Atlantic Ocean, called North Edisto R. (15 mi/24 km long) and South Edisto R. (12 mi/19 km long) which form Edisto Isl. South Fork (c.65 mi/105 km long) rises SE of Johnston and flows ESE; North Fork rises W of Batesburg. Navigable. Drains □ 6,150 sq mi/15,929 sq km.

Edith Cavell, Mount (KA-vuhl), (11,033 ft/3,363 m), W Alta., Canada, near B.C. border, in Rocky Mts., in Jasper Natl. Park, 15 mi/24 km S of Jasper; 52°40′N 118°3′W.

Ediz Hook, Wash.: see PORT ANGELES.

Edmeston (ED-muh-stuhn), village (1990 pop. 600), Otsego co., central N.Y., 28 mi/45 km S of Utica; 42°42′N 75°15′W. In farming and dairying area; makes artists' paints.

Edmond, city (1990 pop. 52,315), Oklahoma co., central Okla.; suburb, 15 mi/24 km N of downtown Okla. City, near North Canadian R.; 35°40′N 97°24′W. Trading center with a huge oil field and many small industries; mfg. (concrete, furniture, asphalt, pet foods, wood prods., petroleum prods.). The city's pop. nearly tripled from 1970 to 1990. Univ. of Central Okla.; Okla. Christian Univ. of Science and Arts to S. Part of Arcadia L. reservoir in SE part. South of the city in Memorial Park is the grave of Wiley Post, who died along with Will Rogers in a plane crash near Point Barrow, Alaska, in 1935. Settled 1889.

Edmond, village (1990 pop. 37), Norton co., NW Kansas, on North Fork Solomon R., and 14 mi/23 km SSE of Norton; 39°37′N 99°49′W. Wheat, barley, rye; cattle.

Edmonds, city (1990 pop. 30,744), Snohomish co., NW Wash., a suburb, 14 mi/23 km N of downtown Seattle, and 15 mi/24 km SW of Everett, on Puget Sound; 47°50′N 122°22′W. Edmonds is primarily a residential city that has grown with the development of Seattle. Mfg. (lighting equip., machinery, laboratory apparatus, boatbuilding). Inc. 1890.

Edmondson, village (1990 pop. 286), Crittenden co., E Ark., 15 mi/24 km W of Memphis (Tenn.); 35°06′N 90°18′W.

Edmonson (ED-muhn-suhn), county (□ 308 sq mi/798 sq km; 1990 pop. 10,357), central Ky.; ⊙ Brownsville; 37°12′N 86°15′W. Drained by Green and Nolin rivers and Bear Creek. Agr. (burley tobacco; hay, alfalfa, soybeans, wheat, corn; hogs, cattle, poultry; dairying). Resorts include most of MAMMOTH CAVE NATIONAL PARK in E. Numerous limestone caves in area; part of Nolin River L. reservoir in NE. Formed 1825.

Edmonston (ED-muhns-tuhn), town (1990 pop. 851), Prince Georges co., central Md., NE of Wash., D.C.; 38°57′N 76°56′W.

Edmonton (ED-muhn-tuhn), city (1991 pop. 616,741), provincial ⊙, central Alta., Canada, on the North Saskatchewan R.; 53°33′N 113°30′W. The largest metropolitan area in Alberta, Edmonton, known as the "Gateway to the North," is located in the center of the prov. bet. the fertile valleys of the S and the rich resources of the N. It is a major market center for farm and petrochemical prods., and has an economy based on the production of oil, coal, and natural gas. Other industries include lumbering, meat packing, flour milling, and dairying. The dominant center for the W fur trade during the 19th cent., Edmonton grew slowly in the 20th cent., relying on its agr.-based economy. Before World War II it was only the 9th-largest city in Canada, but the discovery (1947) of petroleum at Leduc, Redwater, and Pembina transformed Edmonton into one of the fastest-growing cities in Canada. Its pop. increased more than sixfold from 1941 to 1987. The city is on the site of Edmonton House, an important 19th-cent. trading post, and is also the site of the West Edmonton Mall (1981), the world's largest. The Univ. of Alta. (1906) and Athabasca Univ. (1972) are here. Edmonton's professional hockey team, the Edmonton Oilers, was the dominant team of the Natl. Hockey League in the 1980s, winning five championships (1984–1985, 1987–1988, 1990).

Edmonton (ED-muhn-tuhn), town (1990 pop. 1,477), ⊙ Metcalfe co., S Ky., 17 mi/27 km E of Glasgow; 36°58′N 85°37′W. In agr. area (corn, burley tobacco, wheat; cattle, hogs, poultry; dairying; timber). Mfg. (hunting jackets, industrial uniforms, lumber, magnet wire, electric wire harnesses). Sulphur Wells (artesian) to E. Est. 1800.

Edmore, town (1990 pop. 1,126), Montcalm co., central Mich., 18 mi/29 km SW of Mt. Pleasant; 43°24′N 85°02′W. In dairy and grain area; light mfg.

Edmore, village (1990 pop. 329), Ramsey co., NE N.Dak., 28 mi/45 km NE of Devils L; 48°24′N 98°27′W. Livestock; poultry; dairy prods., grain.

Edmunds, county (□ 1,151 sq mi/2,981 sq km; 1990 pop. 4,356), N central S.Dak.; ⊙ Ipswich; 45°24′N 99°12′W. Agr. area drained by Snake Creek and other creeks. Wheat, flax, barley, other grains; dairy produce; cattle, hogs, poultry. Mina State Rec. Area in E. L. Parmley reservoir on E boundary (Snake Creek). Formed 1873.

Edmunds, village, Washington co., E Maine, on Dennys Bay, and 18 mi/29 km NE of Machias. Township includes part of Moosehorn Natl. Wildlife Refuge.

Edmundson, town (1990 pop. 1,111), St. Louis co., E Mo., mainly residential suburb, 11 mi/18 km NW of downtown St. Louis; 38°43′N 90°22′W. Major hotels adjacent to airport terminal.

Edmundston (ED-muhn-stuhn), city (1991 pop. 10,835), NW N.B., Canada, at the confluence of the St. John and Madawaska rivers, at the U.S. border; 47°22′N 68°20′W. Large pulp mill; RR center; hunting and fishing base. Col. of St. Louis is here. Settled c.1785 by Acadians; known as Petit Sault to the French and Little Falls to the English before being named in 1850 for Sir Edmund Head, later gov. gen. of Canada.

Edna, town (1990 pop. 5,343), ⊙ Jackson co., S Texas, 35 mi/56 km NE of Victoria; 28°58′N 96°39′W. Elev. 90 ft/27 m. In oil, cattle, rice, and cotton area; light mfg. L. Texana reservoir and State Park to E. Inc. 1926.

Edna, village (1990 pop. 438), Labette co., SE Kansas, 15 mi/24 km SW of Oswego; 37°03′N 95°21′W. Dairying, general agr.

Edna Bay, village, SE Alaska, on SE shore of Prince of Wales Isl., 38 mi/61 km NNW of Craig.

Edon (EE-duhn), village (1990 pop. 880), Williams co., extreme NW Ohio, 13 mi/21 km WNW of Bryan; 41°33′N 84°46′W. Machine tools, poultry equip., food prods.

Edson (ED-suhn), town (1991 pop. 7,323), W Alta., Canada, near McLeod R., 120 mi/193 km W of Edmonton; 53°35′N 116°25′W. In coal-mining region; oil and natural gas; also logging, lumber milling; wheat, cattle.

Eduardo Neri, Mexico: see ZUMPANGO DEL RÍO.

Edward, uninc. village, Beaufort co., E N.C., 18 mi/29 km SE of Washington.

Edwards 1 county (□ 222 sq mi/575 sq km; 1990 pop. 7,440), SE Ill.; ⊙ Albion; 38°25′N 88°03′W. Agr. (cattle; wheat, sorghum); oil. Mfg. auto parts. Fisheries. Drained by Little Wabash R. and Bonpas Creek (E boundary); SE corner touches Wabash R. Formed 1814. One of 17 Ill. cos. to retain southern-style commission form of govt. **2** county (□ 622 sq mi/1,611 sq km; 1990 pop. 3,787), S central Kansas; ⊙ Kinsley; 37°52′N 99°17′W. Prairie area, drained by Arkansas R. Wheat, cattle, hogs; corn, soybeans, alfalfa. Formed 1874. **3** county (□ 2,120 sq mi/5,491 sq km; 1990 pop. 2,266), SW Texas; ⊙ Rocksprings; 29°58′N 100°17′W. On Edwards Plateau. Elev. c.2,000 ft/610 m–2,500 ft/762 m. Nueces R. forms part of E boundary, drained by S

Llano (N) and W Nueces (S) rivers. A leading Texas co. in Angora goat raising; also sheep, cattle, horses. Some oil, gas; deposits of silver, iron, sulphur, coal, kaolin. Hunting, fishing. Formed 1858.

Edwards, town (1990 pop. 1,279), Hinds co., W Miss., 16 mi/26 km E of Vicksburg, near Big Black R.; 32°19′N 90°35′W. In agr. (cattle, poultry; cotton, corn, soybeans; timber) area; mfg. (egg processing, wooden pallets). Southern Christian Inst. is here. The Civil War battle of Champion's Hill (May 1863) in Grant's Vicksburg campaign was fought nearby.

Edwards, village (1990 pop. 487), St. Lawrence co., N N.Y., on Oswegatchie R., 28 mi/45 km. SSE of Ogdensburg; 44°19′N 75°15′W. In dairying area.

Edwards Air Force Base, U.S. military installation, (1990 pop. 7,423), 301,000 acres/121,815 ha, Kern, Los Angeles, and San Bernardino cos., S Calif., c.20 mi/ 32 km NE of Lancaster; c.35 mi/56 km long E-W, c.15 mi/24 km wide; 34°55′N 117°56′W. In Mojave Desert. It is one of the largest air force bases in the U.S. The base houses the Air Force Flight Test Center, which researches and develops aerospace weapons and rocket-propulsion systems, and NASA's Flight Research Center. The base is also the proving ground for military aircraft. It has been the landing point for several space shuttle missions; on Sept. 5, 1983, the Challenger made the first nighttime landing of a spacecraft there. Rogers L. (dry) in center, Rosamond L. (dry) in SW. Est. 1933.

Edwards Plateau, SW Texas, SE extension of the Great Plains, lying to S and SE of the South Plains (S Llano Estacado), and bounded on S by the Rio Grande valley, SE by the Balcones Escarpment, overlooking the coastal plain; drained by Colorado, Concho, San Saba, Llano, Nueces, Guadalupe rivers. Max. elev. c.2,500 ft/762 m (in Edwards co.). W extension, across canyon of Pecos R., is the Stockton Plateau country (elev. c.2,000 ft/ 610 m–4,000 ft/1,219 m) of W Texas bounded S by the Rio Grande and W by Davis Mts. Much of it semiarid, plateau is largely devoted to stock raising (cattle, sheep, goats) and is chief mohair producing area of state. In region just above escarpment on SE, streams have carved the scenic terrain of the hill country, known for its many springs and its wild game hunting.

Edwards River, NW Ill., rises in SE Henry co., flows c.75 mi/121 km WNW and generally W, through Mercer co., to the Mississippi, just S of New Boston; 41°09′N 89°59′W. Bishop Hill Historic Site on S branch.

Edwardsburg, village (1990 pop. 1,142), Cass co., SW Mich., 10 mi/16 km ESE of Niles, near Ind. line; 41°47′N 86°04′W. In farm and lake area; mfg. (tool and die, van conversions, wood cabinets, R.V. bathtubs).

Edwardsport, town (1990 pop. 380), Knox co., SW Ind., on West Fork of White R., and 17 mi/27 km ENE of Vincennes; 38°49′N 87°15′W. In agr. area (wheat, corn); oil, natural gas, and bituminous-coal area.

Edwardsville 1 city (1990 pop. 14,579), ⊙ Madison co., SW Ill.; 38°47′N 89°57′W. Inc. 1819. It is mainly residential, with many citizens commuting to St. Louis. A campus of Southern Illinois Univ. is here. **2** city (1990 pop. 3,979), Wyandotte co., NE Kansas, on Kansas R., a suburb, 10 mi/16 km WSW of Kansas City, Kansas; 39°04′N 94°49′W. General agr.

Edwardsville, town, S Ont., Canada, on St. Lawrence R. Canadian terminus of Ogdensburg Prescott Internatl. Bridge from Ogdensburg, New York. Town fully owned by the N. Y. State Thruway Authority, which owns the approaches on the Canadian side of the border. The town disputes rent payments to the Authority.

Edwardsville, town (1990 pop. 118), Cleburne co., E Ala., 6 mi/9.7 km NE of Heflin; 33°42′N 85°30′W. Talladega Natl. Forest nearby.

Edwardsville, village (1990 pop. 700), Floyd co., S Ind., 5 mi/8 km WSW of New Albany. Cattle, poultry.

Edwardsville (ED-wuhrds-vil), borough (1990 pop. 5,399), Luzerne co., NE central Pa., suburb, 2 mi/3.2 km NW of downtown Wilkes-Barre on Huntsville Creek, at its entrance to Susquehanna R. Mfg. (scrap metal processing, machinery). Inc. 1884.

Edwight, uninc. village (1990 pop. 30), Raleigh co., S

W.Va., 20 mi/32 km WNW of Beckley, on Marsh Fork R. Coal area.

Edzná (ed-SNAH), an historic site, in N Campeche, Mexico, 6 mi/10 km SE of Campeche. This is a classical Maya site although the area was inhabited as early as 600 B.C. Most of the dates found on monuments range from 550–810 A.D. This site is representative of the Puuc architectural style. The entire zone covers 1.2 sq mi/3 sq km and has been partly reconstructed.

Eek (EEK), Eskimo village (1990 pop. 254), W Alaska, at head of Kuskokwim Bay, 45 mi/72 km SSW of Bethel; 60°13′N 162°01′W.

Eel River 1 in NW Calif.; rises in NE Mendocino co., N of Hall Mt., in Medocino co.; flows SE and W, through L. Pillsbury reservoir, then NW, past Round Valley Indian Reservation, Rio Dell, and Fortuna, to the Pacific 13 mi/21 km SSW of Eureka; c.200 mi/322 km long. Upper course formerly called South Eel R. Receives South Fork (c.90 mi/145 km long), c.14 mi/23 km SE of Rio Dell flows past Redway and through part of Humboldt Redwoods State Park. **2** in W central and SW Ind.; rises in Boone co., as a fork of Big Walnut Creek; flows generally SW, passing near Greencastle, to SW Putnam co. where Mill Creek joins it to form the Eel River. It continues into central Clay co., then SE to West Fork of White R. at Worthington; 110 mi/177 km long. **3** in N central Ind.; rises in NW Allen co.; flows c.100 mi/161 km SW to the Wabash at Logansport.

Effie, village (1990 pop. 130), Itasca co., N Minn., 42 mi/ 68 km N of Grand Rapids, near Big Fork R.; 47°50′N 93°38′W. Timber; cattle; alfalfa. Big Fork State Forest to W; Koachiching State Forest to N.

Effigy Mounds National Monument, park (2 sq mi/ 5.2 sq km), NE Iowa, atop bluffs overlooking Mississippi R, just N of McGregor. Prehistoric Indian mounds 2 ft/0.6 m–4 ft/1.2 m high, up to 200 ft/61 m in diameter; many of them are in shapes of birds and bears, and are believed to be burial mounds. Artifacts (including bone, copper, and stone tools) have been found. Est. 1949.

Effingham 1 (E-fing-ham), county (□ 480 sq mi/ 1,243 sq km; 1990 pop. 25,687), E Ga.; ⊙ Springfield; 32°22′N 81°20′W. Bounded E by Savannah R. (forms S.C. line here) and W by Ogeechee R. Coastal plain agr. including corn, soybeans, peanuts, fruit, tobacco, wheat, cotton; cattle, hogs; timber. Formed 1777. **2** county (□ 479 sq mi/1,241 sq km; 1990 pop. 31,704), SE central Ill.; ⊙ Effingham; 39°03′N 88°35′W. Agr. area (corn, wheat, sorghum, soybeans, hogs, cattle; dairying). Mfg. (dairy and other food prods., lumber and wood prods., leather gloves and mittens, telephone directory printing, tables, air conditioners, fertilizers, housing components). Oil field. Drained by Little Wabash R. Formed 1831.

Effingham, city (1990 pop. 11,851), ⊙ Effingham co., SE central Ill., 26 mi/42 km SSW of Mattoon, and 100 mi/ 161 km ENE of St. Louis; 39°07′N 88°32′W. Trade, railroad, and mfg. center (food prods., lumber, specialty knives, industrial machinery, gloves, telephone directory printing, tables, air conditioners, fertilizers, housing components). Situated in agr. area (dairy prods.; corn, wheat, sorghum, hogs, cattle). L. Sara reservoir 4 mi/6.4 km NW; Little Wabash R. to W. Inc. 1861. Major highway junction.

Effingham (E-fing-ham), town (1990 pop. 941), Carroll co., E N.H., 30 mi/48 km NE of Laconia; 43°44′N 71°02′W. Bounded E by Maine state line, N by Ossipee R. In resort area. Agr. (nursery prods., vegetables; livestock, poultry; dairying). Green Mt. (1,907 ft/581 m) in N. Pine River State Forest in S. Effingham Falls village, in the N part of town, on Ossipee R., at its outlet from Broad Bay of Ossipee L.

Effingham 1 (E-fing-ham), village (1990 pop. 540), Atchison co., extreme NE Kansas, 15 mi/24 km W of Atchison; 39°31′N 95°24′W. In corn belt; corn, livestock. **2** uninc. village, Florence co., NE central S.C., 8 mi/ 12.9 km S of Florence, on Lynches R. Lynches River State Park to S. Mfg. includes burial vaults, pine lumber, canned vegetables; agr. includes cotton, tobacco, vegetables, grain, hogs, chickens, timber.

Egan, village (1990 pop. 208), Moody co., E S.Dak., 5 mi/ 8 km SSW of Flandreau, and on Big Sioux R.; 44°00′N 96°39′W.

Egan Range, (6,000 ft/1,829 m–10,000 ft/ 3,048 m), E Nev., in White Pine co. Highest point, Ward Mts. (10,936 ft/3,333 m), 9 mi/14.5 km SW of Ely in small sect. of Humboldt Natl. Forest. Copper mines near Ely.

Eganville (EE-guhn-vil), village (1991 pop. 1,292), SE Ont., Canada, on Bonnechére R., and 20 mi/32 km S of Pembroke; 45°32′N 77°06′W. Pulp and lumber milling, dairying, lime production.

Egavik (EE-guh-vik), Inuit village, W Alaska, on E shore of Norton Sound, 13 mi/21 km N of Unalakleet.

Egegik (EE-ge-gik), village (1990 pop. 122), SW Alaska on W shore of Alaska Peninsula, at mouth of King Salmon R., 40 mi/64 km SSW of Naknek; 58°13′N 157°23′W. Salmon fishing and canning.

Egeland (EG-land), village (1990 pop. 103), Towner co., N N.Dak.,11 mi/18 km NNE of Cando; 48°37′N 99°05′W. RR junction.

Egg Harbor, village (1990 pop. 183), Door co., NE Wis., on Door Peninsula, on Green Bay, 16 mi/26 km NNE of Sturgeon Bay city; 45°02′N 87°17′W. Chief Oshkosh Indian Mus.

Egg Harbor City, inland city (1990 pop. 4,583), Atlantic co., SE N.J., 15 mi/24 km NW of Atlantic City; 39°33′N 74°35′W. Wine-making center, yacht construction; fruit, poultry, vegetables. Annual agr. fair. Great Egg Harbor Bay lies S, near Ocean City, and Little Egg Harbor NE, near Tuckerton. Settled 1854 by Germans, inc. 1856.

Egg Island, islet in central Bahama Isls., off N tip of Eleuthera Isl., just W of Royal Isl., 40 mi/64 km NE of Nassau; 25°30′N 76°53′W. Belongs to Spanish Wells dist.

Egg Island Point, S N.J., low headland with lighthouse, on N shore of Delaware Bay, 7 mi/11.3 km SW of Port Norris.

Eggemoggin Reach (EG-uh-mahg-uhn), Hancock co., S Maine, passage bet. Deer Isl. and Brooklin and Sargentville towns; connects Penobscot and Jericho bays; c.12 mi/19 km long.

Eggertsville, village, Erie co., W N.Y., just N of Buffalo; 42°58′N 78°48′W.

Eglinton Island (□ 504 sq mi/1,305 sq km), Parry Isls., W Franklin Dist., N.W.T., Canada, in the Arctic Ocean; 75°28′–76°10′N 117°35′–119°30′W; separated from Melville Isl. (E) by Kellett Strait and from Prince Patrick Isl. (W) by Crozier Channel; 50 mi/80 km long, 10 mi/ 16 km–20 mi/32 km wide.

Egmont Bay, inlet (12 mi/19 km long, 19 mi/31 km wide at entrance) of Northumberland Strait, W P.E.I., Canada, 17 mi/27 km W of Summerside, bet. West Point and Cape Egmont.

Egmont, Cape (EG-mahnt), W extremity of P.E.I., Canada, on Northumberland Strait, on S side of Egmont Bay, 17 mi/27 km W of Summerside; 46°24′N 64°8′W. Lighthouse (built 1833).

Egmont Key, c.2 mi/3.2 km long, W central Fla., 2 mi/ 3.2 km N of Anna Maria Isl., at entrance to Tampa Bay; 27°36′N 82°45′E. Lighthouse.

Egmont (E-gruh-mawnt), resort town (1990 pop. 1,229), Berkshire co., SW Mass., in the Berkshires, 21 mi/34 km SSW of Pittsfield, near N.Y. line; 42°10′N 73°26′W. Its villages are North Egremont and South Egremont. State Reservation.

Egypt, uninc. town (1990 pop. 1,350), Whitehall township, Lehigh co., E Pa., suburb, 6 mi/9.7 km NNW of Allentown, near Lehigh R; 40°40′N 75°31′W. Agr. area (grain, apples; livestock, poultry, dairying).

Egypt, village, Plymouth co., Mass.: see SCITUATE.

Ehrenberg, uninc. town (1990 pop. 1,226), La Paz co., W Ariz., 60 mi/97 km N of Yuma, on Colorado R. (bridged). Elev. 277 ft/84 m. Cattle; mfg. (truck bodies). Blythe, Calif., 5 mi/8 km to W; Colorado R. Indian Reservation to N; N end of large Yuma Proving Grounds to SE; Dome Rock Mts. to E.

Ehrenfeld (AI-ruhn-feld), borough (1990 pop. 307),

Cambria co., central Pa., 7 mi/11.3 km ENE of Johnstown, on Little Conemaugh R; 40°22′N 78°46′W. Agr. (corn, hay, dairying).

Ehrhardt (ER-hahrt), village (1990 pop. 442), Bamberg co., S central S.C., 29 mi/47 km SSW of Orangeburg; 33°06′N 81°00′W. Mfg. of fertilizer, timber.

Eielson Air Force Base (EI-yel-suhn), central Alaska, 23 mi/37 km SE of Fairbanks, on Richardson Highway; 64°39′N 147°06′W. Constructed in 1943; expanded in 1950s and 1980s. Major air force fighter training center for the Pacific. Air natl. guard refueling squadron. Named for bush pilot Carl Ben Eielson.

Eight-Mile Rock, town, Grand Bahama Isl., NW Bahama Isls., on SW shore of the isl., at picturesque Hawksbill Creek, 27 mi/43 km SE of West End. Fishing, lumbering.

Eighty Eight, uninc. village (1990 pop. 150), Barren co., S Ky., 8 mi/12.9 km SE of Glasgow. Burley tobacco, grain, livestock, dairying.

Eighty Four, uninc. village (1990 pop. 700), Washington co., SW Pa., 20 mi/32 km SSW of Pittsburgh, and 6 mi/9.7 km E of Washington on Little Chartiers Creek; 40°10′N 80°08′W. Mfg. of composite and powder metals, chemicals, wood prods., corrugated boxes, machinery, plastic prods., fabricated metal prods. Agr. includes dairying. Area rich in bituminous coal. Site of the original Eighty Four lumber store chain.

Eisenhower Memorial Tunnel, tunnel, N central Colo.; 8,941 ft/2,725 m. 2nd longest land vehicular tunnel in U.S. Opened in 1973.

Eisenhower, Mount, (9,390 ft/2,862 m), SW Alta., Canada, near B.C. border, in Rocky Mts., in Banff Natl. Park, 18 mi/29 km WNW of Banff; 51°18′N 115° 56′W. Renamed 1946 from Castle Mt.

Eisenhower National Historic Site (690 acres/279 ha), 3 mi/4.8 km SW of Gettysburg, near Marsh Creek, S Pa. Home and farm of President Dwight D. Eisenhower, only home ever owned by the former president and wife Mamie, used as retreat during presidency and as retirement residence. Authorized 1969.

Eitzen (EIT-suhn), village (1990 pop. 221), Houston co., extreme SE Minn., 9 mi/14.5 km SSE of Caledonia, on Iowa state line; 43°30′N 91°27′W. Mfg. (feeds). In S part of Richard J. Dorer Memorial Hardwood State Forest.

Ejutla (e-HOOT-lah), town (1990 pop. 1,253), Jalisco, W Mexico, on central plateau, 18 mi/29 km NE of Autlán de Navarro. Small farming; livestock.

Ejutla de Crespo (e-HOOT-lah dai KRAIS-po), city (1990 pop. 7,633) and township, ⊙ Ejutla de Crespo municipio, Oaxaca, S Mexico, in Atoyac valley, 40 mi/60 km S of Oaxaca on Mexico Highway 175; 16°33′N 96°13′W. Elev. 4,593 ft/1,400 m. Regional administrative center. Agr. center (cereals, coffee, sugarcane, vegetables, fruit; livestock); makes vegetable oils. Silver, gold, and copper deposits. Once called Ejutla Santa Maria.

Ekalaka (e-kuh-LA-kuh), village (1990 pop. 439), ⊙ Carter co., SE Mont., 70 mi/113 km SE of Miles City; 45°54′N 104°33′W. S terminus of State Highway 7. Timber, livestock, grain. Carter Co. Mus. houses a world-renowned collection of dinosaur remains, including the only Pachycephalosaurus ever discovered. Parts of Custer Natl. Forest to S and E; Medicine Rocks State Park to NE. Named for Ijkalaka, niece of Sitting Bull, who lived here until her death (1901).

Eklutna (e-KLOOT-nuh), village (1990 pop. 381), S Alaska on Knik Arm, 25 mi/40 km NE of Anchorage, on Glenn Highway; 61°28′N 149°20′W. Tourism. Orthodox church, cemetery, mus.

Eklutna Lake (e-KLOOT-nuh), Greater Anchorage Borough, S Alaska, on Eklutna R., 30 mi/48 km NE of Anchorage, in N part of Chugach State Park; 61°26′N 148°38′E. Max. capacity of 280,00 acre-ft. Fed by Eklutna Glacier (SE). Formed by Eklutna Dam (39 ft/12 m high), built (1965) by the Bureau of Reclamation for the generation of hydroelectricity.

Ekron (EK-ruhn), village (1990 pop. 110), Meade co., NW Ky., 24 mi/39 km NW of Elizabethtown; 37°55′N 86°10′W. Agr. (tobacco; livestock); mfg. (rebuilt rail cars).

Ekwan River (E-kwahn), N Ont., Canada; rises in Patricia dist.; flows 300 mi/483 km NE and E to James Bay opposite Akimiski Isl.

Ekwok (EK-wawk), village (1990 pop. 77), SW Alaska on Nushagak R., and 40 mi/64 km NE of Dillingham; 59°21′N 157°28′W.

El Aguacero National Park (el ah-gwah-SER-o), a natl. park, in W Chiapas, Mexico, 12 mi/20 km W of Ocozocuautla. Partly developed around a waterfall (98 ft/30 m in ht. and 164 ft/50 m wide), which falls down the side of the Río La Venta Canyon over the Las Flores River.

El Arenal (ah-re-NAHL), town (1990 pop. 2,721), Hidalgo, central Mexico, 13 mi/21 km NW of Pachuca de Soto, and on the Inter-Amer. Highway 85. Corn, beans, maguey; livestock.

El Arenal (ah-re-NAHL), village (1990 pop. 7,504), Jalisco, W Mexico, on RR, and 24 mi/39 km WNW of Guadalajara on Mexico Highway 15. Elev. 4,600 ft/1,402 m. Small farming; livestock.

El Barrio de la Soledad (el BAH-ree-o dai lah so-le-DAHD), town (1990 pop. 11,535), Oaxaca, SE Mexico, 7 mi/11 km SW of Matías Romero; road connections to Mexico Highway 185 (Transisthmian Highway); 16°48′N 95°05′W. Elev. 617 ft/200 m. Lowland tropical climate, agr. (small farming, tropical fruit, manioc, corn, livestock).

El Bosque (BO-skai), town (1990 pop. 3,522), Chiapas, S Mexico, in spur of Sierra Madre, 33 mi/53 km NE of Tuxtla Gutiérrez. Cereals, fruit. In Tzotzil Maya-speaking area.

El Cajon, city (1990 pop. 88,693), San Diego co., S Calif., suburb, 12 mi/19 km NE of downtown San Diego; 32°48′N 116°58′W. Electronic equip., aircraft parts, irrigation equip., furniture, men's suits, orthopedic supplies, and metal prods. are among its various manufactures. El Cajon is a rapidly growing city; its population increased by nearly 70% bet. 1970 and 1990. Grossmont Col. (2-year) and Cuyamaca Col. (2-year) are here. Gillespie Field Airport to N. Inc. 1912.

El Camino Real, generically, "The Royal Road," there was a Camino Real in most Span. possessions, including at least three in the American SW. Trail most associated with the name was the 700 mi/1,100 km New Mexico Trail, from Santa Barbara in N.Mex. to Santa Fe, pioneered by Juan de Onate in 1598, becoming lifeline for N. Mex. colony. Trail later originated in Chihuahua and was extended S to Mexico City. Part of trail on upper Rio Grande through 90 mi/145 km of waterless waste became known as Jornada del Muerte ("Journey of Death"). Other branches of Camino Real extended from Saltillo and Monterrey into Texas at San Antonio, and from Santiago de Mexico to Tucson and San Diego.

El Campo, city (1990 pop. 10,511), Wharton co., S Texas, c.65 mi/105 km SW of Houston, 29°11′N 96°16′W. Elev. 110 ft/34 m. Trade, processing, market center; mfg. (fertilizers, styrofoam cups, sleepwear, machinery, aluminum extrusions); oil-producing, cattle ranching, dairying, agr. area (rice, cotton, sorghum); poultry. Mus. of Art, Science and History. Founded 1884, inc. 1905.

El Caney, Cuba: see CANEY.

El Cano, Cuba: see CANO.

El Capitan, peak (8,085 ft/2,464 m) in W Texas, in Guadalupe Mts.

El Capitan, Calif.: see YOSEMITE NATIONAL PARK.

El Capitan Dam, Calif.: see SAN DIEGO RIVER.

El Carmen Tequexquitla, Mexico: see TEQUEXQUITLA.

El Carro, Mexico: see VILLA GONZÁLEZ ORTEGA.

El Centro, city (1990 pop. 31,384), ⊙ Imperial co., SE Calif., 10 mi N of the Mex. border; 32°48′N 115°34′W. It is a RR junction and a processing and shipping center for a heavily irrigated agr. region (vegetables, tomatoes, sugar beets, dates, corn, wheat, alfalfa; cotton; cattle, sheep); mfg. (electronic components, printing and publishing, signs, concrete). Imperial Valley Col. (2-year) at Imperial, to N, and El Centro Naval Air Station to W. Natl. Parachute Test Range to NW. Inc. 1908.

El Cercado (el ser-KAH-do), officially San Pedro del Cercado, town (1993 pop. 4,791), San Juan prov., W Dominican Republic, on N slopes of the Sierra de Neiba, 19 mi/31 km WSW of San Juan; 18°42′N 71°28′W. In agr. region (coffee, bananas, potatoes, vegetables); sawmilling.

El Cerrito, city (1990 pop. 22,869), Contra Costa co., W Calif., on San Francisco Bay; 37°55′N 122°18′W. It is primarily residential. Mfg. (lumber, nuts and bolts). Golden Gate Fields Racetrack to SW, on bay shore; Charles Les Tilden and Wildcat Canyon regional parks to E. Inc. 1917.

El Cerrito, uninc. town (1990 pop. 4,490), Riverside co., S Calif., residential suburb, 9 mi/14.5 km WSW of Riverside, 4 mi/6.4 km SE of Corona, in Temescal Valley; 33°51′N 117°31′W. L. Mathews reservoir to E. Santa Ana Mts., in Cleveland Natl. Forest, to SW. Glen Ivy Hot Springs to S.

El Chamizal (el chah-mee-ZAHL), N Chihuahua, Mexico, across the Bridge of the Americas, on the Avenida de las Américas, at the city of Juárez, Mexico. It is a strip of land on the edge of the Río Bravo del Norte (Río Grande) on the border bet. the U.S. and Mexico. The river changed its course over the years and 600 acres/243 ha of land which belonged to Mexico became U.S. territory. In July 1963, President John F. Kennedy visited Mexico City and agreed to transfer this land back to Mexico. It is now El Chamizal Internatl. Park with a mus. and botanical park. The river is now canalized.

El Chichonal (el chee-cho-NAHL), active volcano, Chiapas, Mexico, 40 mi/59 km SSW of Villahermosa; 17°21′N 93°14′W. Elev. 3,478 ft/1,060 m. Erupted violently in 1982, causing loss of life and damage to local roads, crops, and bldgs.

El Chico (el CHEE-ko), a natl. park, in SW Hidalgo, Mexico, 7 mi/11 km N of Pachuca de Soto. This park was est. as a forest reserve in 1898. It is claimed to be Mexico's oldest natl. park. The park contains the old mining center of El Chico, along with a variety of natural vegetation and geologic formations.

El Chico, Mexico: see MINERAL DEL CHICO.

El Cimatario (el see-mah-TAH-ree-o), a national park, in W Querétaro, Mexico, 5 mi/8 km SW of Querétaro City. It is in a mountainous region that is part of the Sierra de Amealco. A road reaches the summit of Cerro Cimatorio, one of three forested peaks in the park.

El Cobre, Cuba: see COBRE, EL.

El Dara, village (1990 pop. 94), Pike co., W Ill., 29 mi/47 km SE of Quincy; 39°37′N 90°59′W. In agr. area.

El Diente Peak (14,159 ft/4,316 m), in Rocky Mts., Dolores co., SW Colo.

El Dorado, county (□ 1,712 sq mi/4,434 sq km; 1990 pop. 125,995), E central Calif.; ⊙ Placerville, 38°47′N 120°32′W. Rises from the Sierra Nevada foothills (W) to crest of range; includes Pyramid Peak (10,020 ft/3,054 m), Freel Peak (10,900 ft/3,322 m). Many lakes and reservoirs, among them L. Tahoe (bounds Nev. on NE) and small Fallen Leaf and Echo lakes. Part of W boundary formed by American R. and its reservoir, Folsom L., part of N boundary formed by North Fork American and Rubicon rivers, part of S boundary formed by Cosumnes R. and its South Fork. Drained by American, Rubicon, and Cosumnes rivers. Popular resort area at South Lake Tahoe. Winter sports, hunting, fishing, camping, hiking. Lumbering; limestone quarrying; gold mining. Grapes, apples, walnuts; cattle, lambs, poultry; timber; tourism. Coloma, site of gold discovery (1848) which began the gold rush, and other old mining towns of the Mother Lode survive. Parts of Eldorado Natl. Forest in E, including part of Desolation Valley Wilderness Area; part of Folsom L. State Recreation Area on W boundary; Marshall Gold Discovery State Historical Park at Coloma, near center; Emerald Bay State Park in NE, on SW shore of L. Tahoe. Formed 1850.

El Dorado 1 city (1990 pop. 23,146), ⊙ Union co., S central Ark.; 33°13′N 92°39′W. Inc. 1845. The discovery of oil in 1921 made it the oil center of the state. The city has oil refineries, chemical plants, and poultry-packing houses. Mfg. (electrical cable for mining industry, gym seats, wooden containers, poultry packing,

---

automotive rubber goods, printing, paper bags, lumber, fiberboard, sodium bromide and bromine, bromide compounds, electrical motor sockets, asphalt, petroleum prods., fiberglass pipes, filing accessories, structural steel, lighting fixtures, plastic bathtubs). South Ark. Community Col. **2** (el duhr-AID-uh), city (1990 pop. 11,504), ⊙ Butler co., SE Kansas, on Walnut R., El Dorado Dam and Lakes to NE, and 26 mi/42 km ENE of Wichita; 37°49′N 96°51′W. RR junction. Trade and oil-refining center. Mfg. (oil and gas field machinery, plastics production, asphalt, metal doors, gas distribution, concrete, fabricated rubber prods., petrol refining). Oil and natural-gas fields nearby. Grew as refining and shipping point for petroleum after discovery (1915) of oil in vicinity. Butler Co. Community Col. Inc. 1870.

El Dorado (el do-RAH-do), village, NW Trinidad, Trinidad and Tobago, 8 mi/12.9 km E of Port of Spain.

El Dorado Hills, uninc. town (1990 pop. 6395), El Dorado co., E central Calif., 23 mi/37 km ENE of Sacramento and 5 mi/8 km E of Folsom; 38°42′N 121°05′W. Folsom L. reservoir and State Recreation Area to N. Apples, walnuts, cattle, poultry. Mfg. (printing and publishing, special machinery, light mfg.).

El Dorado Lake, reservoir (□ 13 sq mi/34 sq km), Butler co., S central Kansas, on Walnut R., 30 mi/48 km SW of Emporia; 37°51′N 96°49′W. Max. capacity 236,200 acre-ft. Formed by El Dorado Lake Dam (99 ft/30 m high), built (1981) by Army Corps of Engineers for flood control; also used for water supply and recreation. El Dorado State Park near dam.

El Espinal (el es-pee-NAHL), town (1990 pop. 7,079), in SE Oaxaca, Mexico; 16°29′N 95°08′W. Previously known as Espinal Santa Cruz. 3.5 mi/5.7 km N of Juchitán de Zaragoza; 16°29′N 95°02′W. Hot climate. Agr. (corn, beans, sesame) and livestock. A Zapotec Indian community.

El Fuerte (FWER-tai), city (1990 pop. 10,279) and township, Sinaloa, NW Mexico, on the Río Fuerte (irrigation area), and 43 mi/70 km NNE of Los Mochis; 26°28′N 108°35′W. Sugarcane center; corn, chickpeas, tomatoes, fruit.

El Gabriel, Cuba: see GABRIEL.

El Gogorrón (el go-go-RON), a natl. park (62,500 acres/25,294 ha), in S San Luis Potosí, Mexico, 30 mi/48 km S of the city of San Luis Potosí, and near Santa María del Río. Hot springs are here, intended to be therapeutic for various ailments. The climate is semiarid, with mesquite, cacti, and nopal plants. Mexican Route 57 S of San Luis Potosí leads to the park.

El Granada, uninc. town (1990 pop. 4,426), San Mateo co., W Calif., residential suburb c.20 mi/32 km SSW of downtown San Francisco, on Half Moon Bay of Pacific Ocean; 37°31′N 122°28′W. Half Moon Bay Airport is NW. Santa Cruz Mts. and San Francisco State Fish and Game Refuge to NE; Half Moon Bay State Beach to SE.

El Grullo (GROO-yo), city (1990 pop. 17,881) and township, Jalisco, W Mexico, in W outliers of Sierra Madre Occidental, 9 mi/14.5 km SE of Autlán de Navarro. Agr. center (grain, sugarcane, cotton, fruit, livestock).

El Guaje, Mexico: see VILLAGRÁN, Guanajuato.

El Higo (el EE-go), village (1990 pop. 8,386), NW Veracruz, Mexico, 15 mi/24 km SW of Tampico, in the Huasteca region where the Río Tempoal enters the Moctezuma R. 7 mi/12 km from Mexico Highway 180. Hot climate. Important because of sugar refinery, "El Higo," which produces sugar and alcohol prods. Irrigated sugarcane production.

El Jovero, Dominican Republic: see MICHES.

El Lago, town (1990 pop. 3,269), Harris co., SE Texas, residential suburb 23 mi/37 km SE of downtown Houston in area referred to as Clear Lake City, at confluence of Taylor L. (Taylor Bayou) and Clear L. (Clear Creek); 29°34′N 95°02′W. NASA Johnson Space Center to W.

El Limón (lee-MON), town (1990 pop. 3,140), Jalisco, W Mexico, in W outliers of Sierra Madre Occidental, 12 mi/19 km NE of Autlán de Navarro; 22°50′N 99°00′E. Grain, sugarcane, fruit, tobacco.

El Malpais (el MAL-pei), natl. monument, Cibola co., W N.Mex., 6 mi/9.7 km S of Grants. Authorized 1987; □ 178 sq mi/461 sq km. In volcanic area; also rich in Pueblo history. Lava flow area. [Span. = the badlands].

El Mamey, Mexico: see MINATITLÁN, Colima.

El Mante, Mexico: see CIUDAD MANTE.

El Marqués, Mexico: see LA CAÑADA.

El Mirage, town (1990 pop. 5,001), Maricopa co., central Ariz., residential suburb 18 mi/29 km NW of downtown Phoenix; 33°35′N 112°19′W. Luke Air Force Base to SW.

El Modena, urbanized sect. of Orange city, Orange co., S Calif., 2 mi/3.2 km E of downtown Orange, in area annexed by Orange 1960s and 1970s. Citrus fruit groves.

El Molino, Mexico: see VISTA HERMOSA DE NEGRETE.

El Monte, city (1990 pop. 106,209), Los Angeles co., S Calif. A suburb 12 mi/19 km, E of downtown Los Angeles; 34°04′N 118°02′W. Residential, industrial, and commercial city in the San Gabriel Valley. Bounded by San Gabriel R. on SE. El Monte manufactures such diverse items as furniture, electronic equip., semiconductors, chemicals, and plastic and metal prods. Urbanization has replaced the walnut groves it was once known for. The pop. here has increased by more than 40% 1970–1990. Continued growth limited by other municipalities that now surround it. El Monte was founded in 1852 by westward-bound pioneers on the Santa Fe Trail. Angeles Natl. Forest to N. Inc. 1912.

El Morro (el MO-ro), natl. monument (□ 1 sq mi/2.6 sq km), Cibola co., W N.Mex.; 42 mi/68 km W of Grants, in Ramah Navajo Indian Reservation. Anasazi villages were once situated on this mesa. Sandstone "Inscription Rock" with inscriptions of Spanish explorers and American pioneers and cent.-old Indian petroglyphs. Also pre-Columbian petroglyphs and pueblo ruins. Proclaimed 1906.

El Nayar, Mexico: see JESÚS MARÍA NAYARIT.

El Ocote Ecological Reserve (el o-KO-tai), a biological reserve, in NW Chiapas, Mexico, S of Lago Netzahualcóyotl.

El Oro, Mexico: see EL ORO DE HIDALGO.

El Oro, Mexico: see SANTA MARÍA DEL ORO DURANGO.

El Oro de Hidalgo (el O-ro de ee-DAHL-go), city (1990 pop. 2,347) and township, ⊙ El Oro municipio, Mexico state, central Mexico, on central plateau near Michoacán border, on RR, and 70 mi/113 km NW of Mexico city; 19°48′N 100°8′W. Elev. 8,957 ft/2,730 m. Corn, wheat, pears; livestock. Silver, gold, and copper mining; shoe mfg., tanning. Sometimes Real del Oro.

El Paso 1 county (□ 2,129 sq mi/5,514 sq km; 1990 pop. 397,014), E central Colo.; ⊙ Colorado Springs; 38°50′N 104°31′W. Wheat and livestock area, drained by Fountain Creek and Big Sandy creeks. Cattle, wheat, oats, sorghum. Coal mining; mfg. and tourist trade at Colorado Springs. Includes part of Pike Natl. Forest in W. Pikes Peak in W is a prominent landmark. Garden of the Gods rock formations in W. U.S Air Force Acad. in NW; part of Fort Carson Military Reserve in SW. Ramah State Wildlife Area in NE. Urbanized in W center (Colorado Springs area). Formed 1861. **2** county (□ 1,014 sq mi/2,626 sq km; 1990 pop. 591,610), westernmost co. of Texas; ⊙ El Paso; 31°46′N 106°14′W. Commercial, transportation, industrial, tourist center of border region. Bounded N by N.Mex. line, W (in W, old channel forms N.Mex. line) and S by the Rio Grande (Mex. border). Co. is urbanized in W, agr. and mts. in E and SE. Irrigated agr. (water from Elephant Butte Reservoir, N.Mex.) in Rio Grande valley. A leading cotton-producing co.; also alfalfa; poultry, dairying; cattle ranching, hogs. Some minerals (limestone, sand and gravel). High plateau (elev. 3,500 ft/1,067 m–7,200 ft/2,195 m), with Hueco Mts. and Hueco Tanks State Park (natural rain-collecting rock basins) in NE, Franklin Mts. and Franklin Mts. State Park in NW. Large Fort Bliss Military Reservation extends across N part of co. and into N.Mex. Includes Ysleta (now part of El Paso city), Socorro, and San Elizario, oldest communities in Texas. One of only 2 Texas cos. entirely within Mountain time zone. Formed 1850.

El Paso 1 city (1990 pop. 2,499), Woodford co., central Ill., 13 mi/21 km N of Bloomington; 40°44′N 89°00′W. In agr. area; ships grain, hybrid seed corn. Poultry hatchery; mfg. (canned foods). Inc. 1861. Originally a RR junction. **2** city (1990 pop. 515,342), ⊙ El Paso co., extreme W Texas, on the Rio Grande opposite Ciudad Juárez, Mexico; 31°51′N 106°26′W. Elev. 3,762 ft/1,147 m. A large city area extends to N.Mex. state boundary to N. Located in a region of cattle ranches and cotton and vegetable farms (irrigated from the Elephant Butte Reservoir), the city is a port of entry and a commercial, industrial, financial, and mining center. Among the city's diverse manufactures are refined petroleum, processed copper, metals, plastics, tool and die, foodstuffs, clothing ("jeans capital of the world"), vacuum cleaners, and machinery. The dry warmth of the area also attracts a significant tourist industry along with a number of seasonal winter residents. One of the largest of the border cities, El Paso is a blend of the U.S. and Mex., and its history is linked to that of its twin Mex. city, Ciudad Juárez. The 2 cities are in the region once known as El Paso del Norté, so called because of the route through the mts. to the N. In the 16th and 17th cents. missionaries, soldiers, and traders came to the region. Although missions were founded at Ysleta and elsewhere N of the river, the major settlement was on the S (Juárez) bank. Not until 1827 was the first house built on the site of El Paso. After the U.S.-Mex. border was set, settlement increased, and the coming of the RR in 1881 prefaced the arrival of cowboys, exiles, border traders, and adventurers to the city. As a result of the settlement in 1963 of the Chamizal border dispute, a small area of El Paso was transferred to Mexico. The city is the seat of the Univ. of Texas (Sun Bowl football stadium) at El Paso and El Paso Community Col.; large Fort Bliss and air defense center extends from city center NE into N.Mex.; a large hosp.; and the White Sands Missile Range are in El Paso's vicinity. El Paso Internatl. Airport NE of downtown. Old missions include Nuestra Señora del Carmen and Nuestra Señora de la Concepción del Socorro, both to SE. Chamizal Natl. Monument E of downtown; Tigua Indian Reservation in SE part of city; Biggs Army Airfield also NE of downtown; Franklin Mts. State Park in N part of city. Inc. 1873.

El Paso del Norte, Mexico: see JUÁREZ CHIHUAHUA.

El Plan Grande, Mexico: see PROGRESO DE ZARAGOZA.

El Plateado, Mexico: see GENERAL JOAQUÍN AMARO.

El Portal (el por-TAHL), town (1990 pop. 2,457), Dade co., SE Fla., 5 mi/8 km N of Miami; 25°51′N 80°12′W.

El Porvenir de Velazco Suárez (el por-vai-NIR dai ve-LAS-ko soo-AH-res), town (1990 pop. 836), ⊙ El Porvenir municipio, Chiapas, S Mexico, in Sierra Madre, 8 mi/12.9 km N of Motozintla de Mendoza; 15°46′N 93°22′W. Elev. 9,186 ft/2,800 m. Beans, wheat, fruit; livestock; fine woods and construction lumber. Cool climate with summer rains. Unpaved roads.

El Potosí (el po-to-SEE), natl. park, San Luis Potosí, Mexico, 44 mi/70 km E of San Luis Potosí. Community of Santa Catarina is within the park, which incorporates portions of the Cañada Grande (a portion of the Río Verde watershed), along with the Valle de las Fantásmas (Valley of the Ghosts), a forested valley with a wide range of forest types. There are practically no public facilities and road access is largely limited to dirt tracks.

El Potrero (el po-TRAI-ro), village (1990 pop. 160), Acultzingo municipio, Veracruz, E Mexico, in foothills of Sierra Madre Oriental, 20 mi/32 km N of Tantoyuca; 23°42′N 101°52′W. Elev. 5,512 ft/1,680 m. Has sugar plantations and huge refinery.

El Prado (el PRAH-do), uninc. town (1990 pop. 200), Taos co., N N.Mex., suburb 2 mi/3.2 km N of Taos, in Pueblo de Taos Indian Reservation. Mfg. (cement, sand and gravel processing). Taos Pueblo to E. Rio Grande Gorge Bridge to W.

El Progreso Industrial or **Progreso**, town (1990 pop. 6,541), Nicolás Romero municipio, Mexico state, central Mexico, 3 mi/5 km NW of Nicolás Romero on Mexico Highway 13. Paper-milling and pulp-mfg. center.

El Pueblito 1 (el pwaib-LEE-to), town (1990 pop. 23,022), ⊙ Corregidora municipio, Querétaro, central

Mexico, on central plateau, 4 mi/6.4 km SW of Querétaro; 20°32′N 100°27′W. Elev. 6,014 ft/1,833 m. Agr. center (wheat, corn, alfalfa, sugarcane, beans, fruit, livestock). Anc. Indian ruins. Shrine of Our Lady of Pueblito here. Called Villa Corregidora bet. 1946–1989. **2** town (1990 pop. 23,033), ⊙ Cor egidora municipio, Querétaro, N central Mexico, 4 mi/7 km SW of Querétaro on Mexico Highway 45. Elev. 6,070 ft/1,850 m. Formerly an agr. community, now becoming a suburb of Querétaro. Formerly Villa Corregidora.

El Reno, city (1990 pop. 15,414), ⊙ Canadian co., central Okla., satellite community 23 mi/37 km W of downtown Oklahoma City, on North Canadian R. Elev. 1,359 ft/414 m. RR junction. Agr. area (wheat, cattle, dairying). Mfg. (aircraft services and prods., mobile home parts; oil-field services, chemicals, publishing and printing). Redlands Community Col. and co. historical mus. are located here. Historic Ft. Reno in W part of city.

El Rio, uninc. town (1990 pop. 6,419), Ventura co., S Calif., suburb 4 mi/6.4 km N of Oxnard and 4 mi/6.4 km ESE of Ventura, 5 mi/8 km NE of Pacific Ocean; 34°14′N 119°10′W. Near Santa Cruz R. Citrus, avocados; flowers, nursery prods.; apiary prods.

El Rito (el REE-to), village, Rio Arriba co., N.Mex., in S foothills of San Juan Mts., 45 mi/72 km SE of Tierra Amarilla. Elev. c.7,000 ft/2,134 m. Trading point in livestock and agr. region; grain, beans. Part of Carson Natl. Forest nearby.

El Rosario (el ro-SAH-ree-o), city (1990 pop. 12,764) and township, Sinaloa, NW Mexico, in coastal lowland, on Baluarte R., and 38 mi/61 km SE of Mazatlán on Mexico Highway 15, on RR; 23°00′N 105°51′W. Silver-mining center; agr. (cotton, sugarcane, fruit, vegetables).

El Rosario (el ro-SAH-ree-o), village, Baja Calif., NW Mexico, near Pacific coast, 140 mi/225 km SSE of Ensenada on Mexico Highway 1; 30°02′N 115°46′W. Some agr. (maguey, livestock). Founded 1774 as Dominican mission. First mission in Baja Calif. Also later (1802) mission ruins.

El Sabinal, natl. park, Nuevo León, Mexico. SE of Cerralvo off Mexico Highway 54, this small (20 acres/8 ha) park preserves stands of sabinos (Monterrey cypresses) and provides habitat for local wildlife.

El Sacromonte National Park (el sah-kro-MON-tai), a natl. park, in SE Mexico, Mexico, located on the outskirts of the town of Amecameca. The Shrine of the Sacred Mt. has an excellent view of the 2 volcanoes, Ixtaccíhuatl and Popocatépetl. This small park contains a church built around a cave where a conquistador, Fráy Martín de Valencia, once lived. It is one of Mexico's most venerated religious sites.

El Salado (el sah-LAH-do), village (1990 pop. 26), Ebano municipio, San Luis Potosí, N Mexico, on central plateau, on RR, and 80 mi/129 km S of Saltillo. Elev. 6,033 ft/1,839 m. Main prod. is salt. Troops of General Pancho Villa once defended this area (1914). RR station from San Luis Potosí to Tampico 56 mi/90 km from port.

El Salto 1 (el SAHL-to), town (1990 pop. 15,116), ⊙ Pueblo Nuevo municipio, Durango, N Mexico, in Sierra Madre Occidental, 55 mi/89 km WSW of Victoria de Durango on Mexico Highway 40; 23°46′N 105°21′W. Elev. 8,563 ft/2,610 m. On RR; agr. center (corn, cotton, sugarcane, tobacco, vegetables, fruit; livestock). Important sawmill here. **2** town (1990 pop. 11,546), ⊙ E Salto municipio, in E central Jalisco, Mexico; 23°47′N 105°22′W. Elev. 4,921 ft/1,500 m. On the left bank of the Santiago R.; 22 mi/36 km SE of Guadalajara. Agr. (corn, beans); poultry breeding and livestock.

El Salvador, sugar-mill town, Guantánamo prov., SE Cuba, on RR line, and 5 mi/8 km N of Guantánamo city, at the foot of Guaso Meseta; 20°13′N 75°14′W.

El Salvador (el sahl-VAH-dor), congregación (1990 pop. 1,334), ⊙ El Salvador municipio, Zacatecas, N central Mexico, on RR, and 65 mi/105 km S of Saltillo near borders of Zacatecas with San Luis Potosí and Coahuila; 24°32′N 100°53′W. Maguey, corn, stock. Sometimes San Salvador.

El Santo, Cuba: see SANTO, EL.

El Seco, Mexico: see SAN SALVADOR EL SECO.

El Segundo, city (1990 pop. 15,223), Los Angeles co., S Calif., industrial suburb 12 mi/19 km SW of downtown Los Angeles, on Santa Monica Bay, Pacific Ocean; 33°55′N 118°25′W. Its prods. include navigation systems, computer systems, semiconductors, aircraft parts and toys, office machines, telephone apparatus, and refined oil prods.; also aerospace research. It was founded (1911) as an oil refinery town. Hq. Hughes Electronics. A U.S. air force missile station is there. Los Angeles Internatl. Airport is adjacent to the city to N. Dockweiler State Beach to N, Manhattan State Beach to S. Inc. 1917.

El Seibo, Dominican Republic: see SEIBO, EL.

El Sobrante (so-brahn-tai), uninc. city (1990 pop. 9,852), Contra Costa co., W Calif., residential suburb 11 mi/18 km N of downtown Oakland and 4 mi/6.4 km NE of Richmond, 3 mi/4.8 km SE of San Pablo Bay, drained by San Pablo Creek; 37°59′N 122°17′W. San Pablo Ridge to S, Sobrante Ridge to E. Mfg. (printing and publishing).

El Socorro (el so-KO-ro), village, NW Trinidad, Trinidad and Tobago, 3 mi/4.8 km E of Port of Spain. In agr. region (coconuts).

El Tajín, ruins, Papantla de Olarte, Veracruz state, E central Mexico; 20°28′N 97°28′W. This site is the remains of pre-Columbian Totonac civilization (fl. 9th–13th cents). The site is partly restored. The most impressive relic is Pyramid of the Niches or El Tajín, a spectacular pyramid in 7 rectangular tiers, one for each day of the year, lined with niches that contained small idols.

El Tepeyac (el te-pe-YAHK), a natl. park, in N Distrito Federal, Mexico, in the NE suburb of Mexico city known as Villa de Guadalupe. The park includes the Basilica of Our Lady of Guadalupe, Mexico's most important religious shrine. On Dec. 12th, there is a nationwide celebration in honor of the Virgin de Guadalupe.

El Tepozteco National Park (el te poz-TE-ko), a natl. park (60,000 acres/24,282 ha), in SW Morelos, Mexico, 20 mi/32 km NE of Mexico city. The terrain is volcanic basalt ridges covered in places by pine and oak trees. This area was favored by the Tlahuica Indians who built the Tepozeco Pyramid which can be seen here. It is accessible from México Route 115-D, near the village of Tepoztlán.

El Toro, uninc. city (1990 pop. 62,685), Orange co., S Calif., residential suburb 14 mi/23 km SE of Santa Ana and 40 mi/64 km SE of downtown Los Angeles, near Aliso Creek; 33°39′N 117°41′W. Rapidly growing area adjacent to Los Angeles. Irrigated agr. U.S. Marine Corps Air Station to NW scheduled to close and be converted to internatl. airport. Santa Ana Mts. and Cleveland Natl. Forest to NE.

El Triunfo or **Triunfo**, (tree-OON-fo), village (1990 pop. 339), La Paz municipio, Baja Calif. Sur, NW Mexico, 28 mi/45 km SSE of La Paz; 24°09′N 110°18′W. Elev. 33 ft/10 m. Corn, beans; livestock.

El Triunfo Ecological Reserve (el tree-OON-fo), a nature reserve, in S central Chiapas, Mexico, on the S slope of the Sierra Madre de Chiapas, E of Escuintla in S Chiapas state.

El Tuito (el too-EE-to), town, in W Jalisco, Mexico, ⊙ Cabo Corrientes municipio, 31 mi/50 km SW of Puerto Vallarta, and off Mexico Highway 200; 20°20′N 105°25′W. On Tuito R.

El Tule (el TOO-lai), town, (1990 pop. 1,085), Chihuahua, N Mexico, in wide valley on E slopes of Sierra Madre Occidental, 34 mi/55 km W of Hidalgo del Parral. Corn, cotton, sugarcane, beans, cattle. Formerly San Antonio del Tule.

El Vado (el VAH-do), uninc. village, Rio Arriba co., N N.Mex., 12 mi/19 km SW of Tierra Amarilla, on Rio Chama, S of (below) El Vado Dam and Reservoir. Sheep, cattle.

El Vado Dam, N.Mex.: see RIO CHAMA.

El Valle 1 Mexico: see VALLE DE JUÁREZ. **2** Mexico: see BUENAVENTURA.

El Verano, uninc. town (1990 pop. 3,498), Sonoma co., W Calif., 17 mi/27 km SE of Santa Rosa and 1 mi/1.6 km W of Sonoma, on Sonoma Creek; 38°18′N 122°30′W. Dairying; poultry, sheep; nursery prods.; grapes, apples, vegetables, grain. Sonoma Mission State Historical Park to E.

El Vizcaíno Biosphere Reserve (el veez-kah-EE-no), a biological reserve in Baja Calif. Sur, Mexico, just S of the Baja Calif. state line. There are 6.1 million acres/2.5 million ha of the Vizcaíno Desert protected here, supposedly the largest reserve in Lat. Amer., decreed in 1988, includes the Parque Nacional Ballena Gris (a reserve for gray whales in Ojo de Liebre estuary on Sebastián Vizcaíno Bay, NW of Baja Calif. Sur).

El Yunque (el YOON-kai), peak, P.R.: see YUNQUE, EL.

El Zapotal, Mexico: see SAN LUCAS.

El Zócalo, Mexico: see PLAZA DE LA CONSTITUCIÓN.

Elaine (ee-LAIN), town (1990 pop. 846), Phillips co., E Ark., 21 mi/34 km SW of Helena, near the Mississippi R.; 34°18′N 90°50′W. White River Natl. Wildlife Refuge to W.

Eland (ee-LAND), village (1990 pop. 247), Shawano co., E central Wis., 22 mi/35 km ESE of Wausau; 44°52′N 89°12′W. In lumbering and agr. area.

Elba, city (1990 pop. 4,011), ⊙ Coffee co., SE Ala., on Pea R. and 15 mi/24 km NW of Enterprise. Trading point in cotton, peanut, and livestock area; agr. equip., lumber; clothing mfg., trailer truck mfg., forklifts, meat prods. Became co. seat 1852.

Elba 1 village (1990 pop. 220), Winona co., SE Minn., 22 mi/35 km ENE of Rochester, on Whitewater R.; 44°05′N 92°01′W. Dairying; poultry; grain. Whitewater State Park to SW; Whitewater Wildlife Area to N and E. **2** village (1990 pop. 196), Howard co., E central Nebr., 7 mi/11.3 km NW of St. Paul, and on North Loup R; 41°16′N 98°34′W. **3** village (□ 1 sq mi/2.6 sq km; 1990 pop. 703), Genesee co., W N.Y., on Oak Orchard Creek, 5 mi/8 km N of Batavia; 43°04′N 78°11′W. In agr. area.

Elberfeld, town (1990 pop. 635), Warrick co., SW Ind., 9 mi/14.5 km NW of Boonville; 38°10′N 87°27′W. In agr. and bituminous-coal area. Surface mines.

Elberon, town (1990 pop. 203), Tama co., central Iowa, 8 mi/12.9 km N of Belle Plaine; 42°00′N 92°19′W. In agr. area.

Elbert 1 county (□ 1,851 sq mi/4,794 sq km; 1990 pop. 9,646), E central Colo.; ⊙ Kiowa, 39°16′N 104°07′W. Drained by Big Sandy, Beaver, Baxrider, Kiowa, E and W Bijon creeks. Cattle; wheat, hay, oats, sunflowers. Formed 1874. **2** county (□ 362 sq mi/937 sq km; 1990 pop. 18,949), NE Ga.; ⊙ Elberton; 34°07′N 82°49′W. Bounded E by S.C. line formed here by Savannah R. and W by Broad R. Agr includes cotton, fruit, soybeans, wheat; cattle, poultry; granite-quarrying (ELBERTON) area. Formed 1790.

Elbert, Mount (14,433 ft/4,399 m), Lake co., central Colo., 12 mi/19 km SW of Leadville in San Isabel Natl. Forest. Highest point in Colo. and tallest peak in the U.S. Rocky Mts.

Elberta (el-BER-tah), village (1990 pop. 478), Benzie co., NW Mich., opposite Frankfort (1 mi/1.6 km SE) on Betsie R. at its mouth on L. Michigan; 44°37′N 86°13′W.

Elberton, town (1990 pop. 5,682), ⊙ Elbert co., NE Ga., 31 mi/50 km ENE of Athens, near S.C. line; 34°07′N 82°52′W. A major granite-quarrying and processing center of the U.S.; the so-called Granite Capital of the World. Mfg. of monuments, clothing, yarns, tapestry, machinery. Elberton Granite Mus. Settled 1780s.

Elberton, uninc. village (1990 pop. 35), Whitman co., SE Wash., 8 mi/12.9 km NE of Colfax and on Palouse R., at mouth of Silver Creek.

Elbing, village (1990 pop. 184), Butler co., SE central Kansas, 12 mi/19 km E of Newton; 38°02′N 97°07′W. Grain, livestock.

Elbow, village (1991 pop. 327) S Sask., Canada, on South Saskatchewan R., and 70 mi/113 km NW of Moose Jaw; 51°07′N 106°36′W. Grain.

Elbow Lake, town (1990 pop. 1,186), ⊙ Grant co., W Minn., 43 mi/69 km NE of Fergus Falls; 45°59′N 95°58′W. Elev. 1,212 ft/369 m. Farm trading point (poultry, livestock; grain, sugar beets, beans, alfalfa; dairying); mfg.

(automotive grease, fertilizer machining). Pomme de Terre L. to NE, Elbow L. to NW.

Elbow Lake, Becker co., W Minn., 25 mi/40 km NE of Detroit Lakes city; 5 mi/8 km long, ½ mi/⅘ km wide. In White Earth Indian Reservation and White Earth State Forest.

Elbridge, village (□ 1 sq mi/2.6 sq km; 1990 pop. 1,219), Onondaga co., central N.Y., 16 mi/26 km W of Syracuse; 43°01′N 76°26′W. In agr. area. State rearing station for brown, brook, and rainbow trout.

Elburn, village (1990 pop. 1,275), Kane co., NE Ill., 8 mi/12.9 km W of Geneva; 41°53′N 88°28′W. In agr. area; meat-packing plant. Subdivision encroaching from E.

Elcho (EL-ko), village, Langlade co., NE Wis., 20 mi/32 km N of Antigo, in wooded lake region. Resort.

Elco (EL-ko), borough (1990 pop. 373), Washington co., SW Pa., 4 mi/6.4 km S of Charleroi, on Monongahela R.; 40°5′N 79°52′W. Agr. (dairying).

Elden, Mount, peak (9,280 ft/2,829 m), in Coconino Natl. Forest, Coconino co., N central Ariz., just NE of Flagstaff. Pueblo ruins at base of mt.

Elderon (EL-duhr-ahn), village (1990 pop. 175), Marathon co., central Wis., 23 mi/37 km SE of Wausau; 44°46′N 89°15′W. In dairying region.

Elderton (EL-duhr-tuhn), borough (1990 pop. 371), Armstrong co., W central Pa., 12 mi/19 km SE of Kittanning, near Plum Creek. Agr. (grain; livestock; dairying); bituminous-coal mining. Keystone L. reservoir to NE, on Plum Creek. 1896.

Eldon (EL-duhn), town (1990 pop. 1,070), Wapello co., SE Iowa, on Des Moines R., and 12 mi/19 km SE of Ottumwa; 40°55′N 92°13′W. Fertilizers. Bituminous-coal mines nearby. Inc. 1877.

Eldon, city (1990 pop. 4,419), Miller co., central Mo., near Osage R., 28 mi/45 km SW of Jefferson City, at N edge of Ozarks; 38°21′N 92°34′W. Corn, soybeans; cattle, poultry; mfg. (coin-operated rides, motors, wood beds, optical lenses). Founded c.1880.

Eldora, city (1990 pop. 3,038), ⊙ Hardin co., central Iowa, on Iowa R., and 24 mi/39 km NNW of Marshalltown; 42°21′N 93°05′W. Mfg. (screw machine prods., funnel tanks and garden sprayers, feeds, athletic clothing, furniture). Has state training school for boys. Pine L. State Park (with fish hatchery) and Steamboat Rock State Park, both to NE. Limestone quarries, sand pits in area. Settled 1851, inc. 1896.

Eldora, village, Boulder co., N central Colo., in Front Range, 35 mi/56 km NW of Denver. Elev. 8,641 ft/2,634 m. Picturesque gold mining town from 19th cent. Eldora Ski Area is here. Area surrounded by Roosevelt Natl. Forest. L. Eldora to E.

Eldorado (EL-duh-RAI-do), city (1990 pop. 4,536), Saline co., SE Ill., 7 mi. NE of Harrisburg; 37°48′N 88°26′W. Trade center of bituminous-coal-mining and agr. area; corn, wheat, oats; poultry. Inc. 1873.

Eldorado 1 town (1990 pop. 49), Dorchester co., E Md., 16 mi/26 km E of Cambridge and on Marshyhope Creek; 38°35′N 75°48′W. The name comes from a farm which presumably had gold under it. An old factory here that once produced tapestries and tweeds now houses several small businesses. A modern factory also produces RR cars. **2** town (1990 pop. 2,019), ⊙ Schleicher co., W Texas, on the Edwards Plateau, 40 mi/64 km S of San Angelo; 30°51′N 100°35′W. Shipping point for cattle, sheep; goat-ranching region; cotton, grain, milo, hay; oil and gas; mfg. (natural-gas processing). Founded nearby as Verand; moved here and changed name, 1895.

Eldorado 1 (EL-duh-RAI-duh), village (1990 pop. 549), Preble co., W Ohio, 14 mi/23 km SSW of Greenville; 39°54′N 84°40′W. **2** village (1990 pop. 573), Jackson co., SW Okla., 21 mi/34 km SW of Altus, near Red R. (Texas state line); 34°28′N 99°39′W. In agr. area (grain, cotton); livestock.

Eldorado, N.W.T., Canada, : see PORT RADIUM.

Eldorado Mountains (el-do-RAH-do) (3,000 ft/914 m—4,000 ft/1,219 m), Clark co., SE Nev., W of Colorado R., S of Boulder City, c.30 mi/48 km long. Gold, silver, copper, and lead have been mined. Sometimes written El Dorado.

Eldorado Springs, city (1990 pop. 3,830), Cedar co., W Mo., 19 mi/31 km E of Nevada. Former health resort. Corn, soybeans, hay, sorghum; cattle; mfg. (jackets, metal fabrication, cheese and dehydrated food, printing). Founded 1881.

Eldred (EL-drid), village (1990 pop. 254), Greene co., W Ill., near Illinois R., 8 mi/12.9 km W of Carrollton; 39°17′N 90°32′W. In agr. area (corn, wheat, soybeans, sorghum, cattle, hogs; dairying).

Eldred (EL-dred), borough (1990 pop. 869), McKean co., N Pa., 8 mi/13 km SSE of Olean, N.Y., on Allegheny R.; 41°57′N 78°22′W. Agr. (corn, hay, dairying); light mfg.; oil; natural gas. Inc. 1880.

Eldred Passage, S Alaska, arm (10 mi/16 km long) of Kachemak Bay, S Kenai Peninsula, 10 mi/16 km ENE of Seldovia. Salmon fishing.

Eldridge 1 uninc. town (1990 pop. 1,144), Sonoma co., NW Calif., 5 mi/8 km NW of Sonoma Creek (Valley of the Moon); 38°20′N 122°31′W. Sonoma State Hosp. is here; to NW; Jack London State Historical Park to NW. Wineries in area. **2** town (1990 pop. 3,378), Scott co., E Iowa, 8 mi/12.9 km N of Davenport; 41°38′N 90°34′W. In agr. area.

Eleanor, town (1990 pop. 1,256), Putnam co., W central W.Va., 21 mi/34 km NW of Charlestown, on Kanawha R. (bridged; 2 mi/3.2 km NW, across from Winfield); 38°32′N 81°55′W. Agr. (corn, tobacco); livestock; poultry. Mfg. (coal-mining equip., prefabricated metal bldgs.).

Eleanor, Lake, reservoir, Tuolumne co., E Calif., on Eleanor Creek, 22 mi/35 km NW of Yosemite Village, in NW part of Yosemite Natl. Park; 3 mi/4.8 km long; 37°57′N 119°53′W. Elev. 4,656 ft/1,419 m. Formed by Lake Eleanor Dam. Supplies water to San Francisco. Cherry Lake reservoir 1 mi/1.6 km to W.

Eleanor Roosevelt, historic site, Val-Kill, Hyde Park, Dutchess co., on E side of Hudson R., S N.Y.; 41°46′N 73°54′W. Authorized as Natl. Historic Site 1977. Her personal retreat, including 2 restored bldgs., tennis court, rose garden, and playhouse on 180 acres/73 ha, lies 2 mi/3.2 km E of Roosevelt Home. After the death of FDR in 1945, she lived here until her death in 1962. This is the only natl. historic site dedicated to a president's wife. Cottage was built for her by her husband in 1925.

Electra, town (1990 pop. 3,113), Wichita co., N Texas, 26 mi/42 km WNW of Wichita Falls; 34°01′N 98°55′W. In oil, agr. region; mfg. (natural-gas processing, gas-processing equip.). Founded 1890, inc. 1910; oil boom, 1911.

Electra Lake, La Plata co., SW Colo., on Elbert Creek (sidestream of Animas R.), 17 mi/27 km NNE of Durango; 37°31′N 107°47′W. Max. storage capacity of 29,934 acre-ft. Formed by Electra Dam (53 ft/16 m high), built (1972) by the Western Colo. Power Company for flood control.

Electric City, town (1990 pop. 910), Grant co., E central Wash., near the Columbia, 5 mi/8 km SW of Grand Coulee Dam, 2 mi/3.2 km W of town of Grand Coulee, at NE end of Banks L. reservoir formed by water diverted from Columbia R.; 47°56′N 119°02′W. Wheat, barley, oats, alfalfa; cattle. Steamboat Rock State Park, to SW, on peninsula in Banks L.

Electric Mills, village, Kemper co., E Miss., 32 mi/51 km NNE of Meridian, near Ala. state line. In agr. and timber area.

Electric Peak (10,992 ft/3,350 m), highest point in Gallatin Range, Park co., SW Mont., in NW part of Yellowstone Natl. Park near Wyo. boundary, c.45 mi/72 km S of Bozeman, Mont.

Eleele (AI-lai-AI-lai), town (1990 pop. 1,489), S Kauai, Kauai Co., Hawaii, 14 mi/23 km WSW of Lihue, on Hanapepe R., on Kaumualii highway; 21°54′N 159°34′W. Opposite Hanapepe sugarcane plantation; sugarcane plantations to E; mfg. (cane sugar processing); agr.

Elephant Butte (BYOOT), uninc. village (1990 pop. 500), Sierra co., SW N.Mex., 5 mi/8 km ENE of Truth or Consequences, on Rio Grande, at S end of Elephant Butte Dam. Grapes, grain, livestock. Winery . Elephant

Butte L. reservoir and State Park to N; Sierra Caballo to S; Elephant Butte (4718ft/1438m) to E.

Elephant Butte Dam (BYOOT), at Elephant Butte village, Sierra and Socorro cos., SW N.Mex., on Rio Grande, 5 mi/8 km ENE of Truth or Consequences; c.30 mi/48 km long; 33°09′N 107°10′W. Max. capacity 2,195,000 acre-ft. Formed by Elephant Butte Dam (186 ft/57 m), built (1916) by U.S. Govt. for irrigation, power generation, and flood control.

Elephant Point, village, W Alaska, on S shore of Eschscholtz Bay, 55 mi/89 km SE of Kotzebue.

Eleuthera (ee-LOO-thuh-ruh) [Gr. = place of freedom], isl. (□ 187 sq mi/484 sq km; 1990 pop. 7,993), 50 mi/80 km ENE of New Providence Isl., central Bahamas; 24°56′N 76°10′W. A narrow, crescent-shaped isl. c.1 mi/1.6 km wide, but 110 mi/177 km long. Known for its beautiful beaches. The first Eur. settlement in the Bahamas was built here in 1649 by the British. Many of the original settlers emigrated to Boston in 1680 after being driven out by the Spanish. Today, three airfields give tourists access to numerous resorts. Hurricane Andrew damaged many areas of the isl. in 1992. Main settlements include Governor's Harbour, Rock Sound, and Tarpum Bay. Agr. prods.

Eleva (el-EE-vah), village (1990 pop. 491), Trempealeau co., W Wis., on Buffalo R., and 16 mi/26 km S of Eau Claire; 44°34′N 91°28′W. In dairy, poultry, and grain area. Mfg. (meat processing, cheese). On Buffalo R. State Trail.

Eleven Point River, S Mo. and N Ark.; rises in Howell co.; Mo., flows c.115 mi/185 km E and S through the Ozarks to Spring R. above Black Rock, Ark. Large springs feed into the river; canoeing; fishing; recreation.

Elevenmile Reservoir, Park co., central Colo., on South Platte R., in Eleven-Mile State Recreation Area, 60 mi/97 km SSW of Denver; 6 mi/9.7 km long, 1 mi/1.6 km wide; 38°54′N 105°26′W. Elev. c.8,564 ft/2,610 m. Formed by Elevenmile Dam (112 ft/34 m high), built for Denver water supply. SE end in Pike Natl. Forest; Elevenmile Canyon downstream from dam, to E.

Elfers, town (□ 3 sq mi/7.8 sq km; 1990 pop. 12,356), Pasco co., W central Fla., 29 mi/47 km NNW of Tampa; 28°12′N 82°43′W.

Elfin Cove, village, SE Alaska, on NW tip of Chicagof Isl., on Cross Sound, 70 mi/113 km W of Juneau. Fishing, fish processing.

Elfros (EL-frahs), village (1991 pop. 181), SE central Sask., Canada, near the Quill Lakes, 15 mi/24 km E of Wynyard; mixed farming, dairying.

Elgin (EL-gin), co. (□ 720 sq mi/1,865 sq km; 1991 pop. 75,423), S Ont., Canada, on L. Erie, and on Thames R.; ⊙ St. Thomas; 42°45′N 81°10′W.

Elgin, city (1990 pop. 77,010), Kane and Cook cos., NE Ill., on the Fox R.; 42°02′N 88°17′W. Inc. 1854. Elgin is a RR, trade, and industrial city marked by a steady pop. growth. The city was home of the Elgin Watch Co. (est. 1864). Remnant agr. (corn, soybeans); mfg. (gauging instruments, precious metal platings, ball bearings, auto and truck parts, switches, pharmaceuticals, printing, zinc and aluminum castings, vacuums and sweepers, guitar accessories, screws, kitchen equip., metal cans, doors, margarine, therapy tables). Casino here. Judson Col. and Elgin Community Col. are here.

Elgin 1 (EL-jin), town (1990 pop. 637), Fayette co., NE Iowa, on Turkey R., and 9 mi/14.5 km E of West Union; 42°57′N 91°37′W. Feed mill. **2** town (1990 pop. 118), Chautauqua co., SE Kansas, on Caney R., at Okla. line, and 6 mi/9.7 km W of Chautauqua; 37°00′N 96°16′W. Livestock, grain. **3** town (1990 pop. 765), Grant co., S N.Dak., 60 mi/97 km SW of Bismarck; 46°23′N 101°50′W. Livestock; dairy farms, grain, wheat. L. Tschida to N. **4** town (1990 pop. 975), Comanche co., SW Okla., suburb 14 mi/23 km NNE of Lawton; 34°46′N 98°17′W. In agr. area. Fort Sill Military Reservation to SW; L. Ellsworth reservoir to NW. **5** town (1990 pop. 1,586), Union co., NE Oregon, 20 mi/32 km NNE of La Grande, and on Grande Ronde R.; 45°33′N 117°55′W. Elev. 2,670 ft/814 m. Shipping point for apples, cherries, timber. Minam State Recreation Area to

NE; Wallowa-Whitman Natl. Forest and Wallowa Mts. to SE; Umatilla Natl. Forest and Blue Mts. to NW. **6** uninc. town (1990 pop. 2,196), Lancaster co., N S.C., 4 mi/6.4 km SE of Lancaster, in agr. area. Mfg. includes fiberglass industrial parts, industrial belts, agr. chemicals, pine chips; agr. includes poultry, cattle, grain, soybeans. **7** (EL-gin), town (1990 pop. 4,846), Bastrop co., S central Texas, 23 mi/37 km ENE of Austin; 30°21'N 97°22'W. RR junction and processing center for agr. area (cattle; wheat, corn, grain sorghum); clay prods.; lignite mines; mfg. (bricks and tiles). Settled 1867, inc. 1890.

Elgin 1 village, SW Man., Canada, on Elgin Creek and 30 mi/48 km SSW of Brandon; grain, stock. **2** village, SE Ont., Canada, 30 mi/48 km NE of Kingston; dairying, mixed farming.

Elgin 1 (EL-jin), village (1990 pop. 733), Wabasha co., SE Minn., 13 mi/21 km NE of Rochester; 44°07'N 92°15'W. Dairying; mfg. (lumber, cabinet, feeds). Carley State Park and Whitewater Wildlife Area to E. **2** village (1990 pop. 731), Antelope co., NE central Nebr., 10 mi/16 km S of Neligh, and on branch of Elkhorn R; 41°58'N 098°04'W. Dairy prods.; livestock; grain. **3** village (1990 pop. 71), Van Wert co., W Ohio, 10 mi/16 km SSE of Van Wert; 40°45'N 84°28'W. **4** (EL-gin), village (1990 pop. 622), Kershaw co., N central S.C., 19 mi/31 km NE of Columbia, Fort Jackson Military Reservation to S; 34°10'N 80°47'W. Agr. interests include poultry, cattle, corn, rye, cotton, timber.

Elgin (EL-jin), borough (1990 pop. 229), Erie co., NW Pa., 5 mi/8 km WSW of Corry, near South Branch French Creek.; 41°54'N 79°44'W. Agr. (corn, hay, potatoes; livestock, dairying).

Elías Piña (e-LEE-ahs PEE-nah), prov. (□ 788 sq mi/ 2,041 sq km; 1993 pop. 59,321), W Dominican Republic, on Haiti border; ⊙ Comendador; 19°00'N 71°35'W. Bounded by the Cordillera Central (N) and Sierra de Neiba (S); watered by Artibonito R. Agr. region (corn, rice, cotton, coffee, sugarcane, fruit); also goats, hides, timber. Prov. was set up 1942. Sometimes called San Rafael or La Estrelleta.

Elida 1 (e-LEE-duh), village (1990 pop. 201), Roosevelt co., E N.Mex., 25 mi/40 km SW of Portales; 33°56'N 103°39'W. Cattle, sheep, in ranching region; wheat, oats, millet, alfalfa, barley, rye, cotton. **2** (EE-lei-duh), village (1990 pop. 1,486), Allen co., W Ohio, 6 mi/10 km WNW of Lima, and on Ottawa R.; 40°47'N 84°11'W.

Elim (EE-lim), uninc. town (1990 pop. 3,861), Cambria co., W central Pa., residential suburb 2 mi/3.2 km S of downtown Johnstown on Stonycreek R.; 40°17'N 78°56'W.

Elim (EE-lim), village (1990 pop. 264), W Alaska, on SE Seward Peninsula, at mouth of Norton Bay, 95 mi/ 153 km E of Nome; 64°37'N 162°15'W. In Elim Indian Reserve.

Eliot, town (1990 pop. 5,329), York co., extreme SW Maine, on Piscataqua R. and 23 mi/37 km S of Alfred; 43°08'N 70°47'W. Includes South Eliot village (1990 pop. 3,112). Set off from Kittery 1810.

Eliot, village, Middlesex co., Mass.: see NEWTON.

Eliot, Mount (4,554 ft/1,388 m), E Lab., Canada, 10 mi/ 16 km N of Nachvak Fiord; 59°10'N 63°49'W.

Elizabeth, city (1990 pop. 110,002), Union co., NE N.J., 8 mi/12.9 km SW of Newark; 40°40'N 74°11'W. Large industrial city and port; mfg. (furnaces, plastics, chemicals, copper and other metal prods.; tea, food prods., paperboard boxes, pharmaceuticals). Inc. 1855.

Elizabeth 1 town (1990 pop. 818), Elbert co., central Colo., on Boulder Creek, 35 mi/56 km SE of Denver; 39°21'N 104°35'W. Elev. 6,448 ft/1,965 m. Cattle. **2** town (1990 pop. 153), Harrison co., S Ind., 11 mi/18 km SE of Corydon; 38°08'N 85°58'W. In agr. area. **3** town (1990 pop. 414), Allen parish, SW central La., 34 mi/ 55 km SW of Alexandria; 30°52'N 92°48'W. Mfg. (pilings and poles); logging; paper milling. West Bay State Wildlife Area to S. **4** town (1990 pop. 900), ⊙ Wirt co., NW W.Va., on Little Kanawha R., 17 mi/27 km SE of Parkersburg; 39°3'N 81°24'W. Agr. (corn, tobacco) cattle; poultry. Timber. Mfg. (life preservers, aluminum extrusion). Beauchamp-Newman Mus. in old courthouse (1840). Hughes R. Wildlife Management Area to NE; Palestine State Fish Hatchery (158 acres/64 ha) to S.

Elizabeth 1 village (1990 pop.), Cobb co., NW central Ga., just N of Marietta; 33°58'N 84°32'W. **2** village (1990 pop. 641), Jo Daviess co., NW Ill., 13 mi/21 km SE of Galena, above Apple R.; 42°19'N 90°13'W. Grain, livestock; dairying; mfg. (smoked sausage, DC power supplies, transformers). Long Hollow Scenic Overlook Tower to NW. **3** village, Jo Daviess co, Ill., 14 mi/23 km SE of Galena, Ill. Dairy prods.; lead mines; timber. **4** village (1990 pop. 152), Otter Trail co., W Minn., on Pelican R., 7 mi/11.3 km N of Fergus Falls; 46°22'N 96°07'W. Dairying; grain. Numerous small lakes to E.

Elizabeth, borough (1990 pop. 1,610), Allegheny co., SW Pa., suburb 13 mi/21 km SSE of Pittsburgh, on Monongahela R. (bridged). Light mfg.; limestone, bituminous coal; agr. Pioneer boat construction center after 1778. Settled 1769, inc. 1834.

Elizabeth City 1 former co., SE Va.; is now part of independent city of HAMPTON. **2** city (1990 pop. 14,292), ⊙ Pasquotank co., NE N.C., 40 mi/64 km SSE of Portsmouth, Va., and c.100 mi/161 km ENE of Rocky Mount at head of Pasquotank R. estuary; 36°17'N 76°13'W. Intracoastal Waterway passes through estuary N to Dismal Swamp Canal to Portsmouth, Va. It is the largest city in the Albemarle Sound area. Shipyards. The city is also a trade and shipping center for the region's diversified farm prods. Mfg. (printing and publishing, lumber, industrial equip., wooden cabinets, flow meters, crab meat processing, paper boxes, cotton yarn, horticultural growing media, aerostats). The area was first visited (1584) and mapped by a scouting expedition from Roanoke Isl. The first Gen. Assembly of Carolina met there in 1665. In the Civil War, Elizabeth City was occupied (1862) by Federal troops and burned. It is the seat of Elizabeth City State Univ. and the Col. of the Albemarle (2-year). Mus. of Albermarle here. A large U.S. Coast Guard air station is NE. Dismal Swamp Natl. Wildlife Refuge to NW. Elizabeth City Municipal Airport to SE. Settled mid-1600s, inc. 1793.

Elizabeth Islands, chain of small isls. off Cape Cod that form the S boundary of Buzzards Bay; SE Mass. Naushon is the largest isl. Cuttyhunk Isl. (with famous fishing and resort village of same name) was settled in 1641. Most of the isls. are privately owned. Includes Pasque Isl. and Penikese Isl.

Elizabeth River, SE Va., short tidal river, S arm of Hampton Roads (harbor in James R. estuary), bet. cities of Norfolk (E) and Portsmouth (W), port facilities on both sides (bridged and tunnel); c.25 mi/40 km long. West Branch (c.20 mi/32 km long), East Branch (c.25 mi/40 km long), South Branch (c.40 mi/64 km long); South Branch receives Albemarle-Chesapeake Canal (Intracoastal Waterway) from SE. Lafayette R. estuary (c.20 mi/32 km long) enters from E.

Elizabethton (e-LIZ-uh-BETH-tuhn), city (1990 pop. 11,931), ⊙ Carter co., NE Tenn., on the Watauga R., 8 mi/13 km E of Johnson City; 36C°20'N 82°15'W. An industrial center where rayon and other synthetics, clothing, boxes, crushed stone, and hand tools are produced. Agr. includes tobacco, fruit, and Christmas trees. The region was one of the earliest settled in Tennessee. In 1772 the Watauga Assn. was organized there; Sycamore Shoals Monument commemorates this event, the treaty Richard Henderson made with the Cherokee in 1775, and the formation of a Revolutionary force that later took part in the battle of Kings Mountain. Nearby lakes have Tennessee Valley Authority dams, and the area was developed for recreational use. Inc. 1799.

Elizabethtown, city (1990 pop. 18,167), ⊙ Hardin co., central Ky., 38 mi/61 km S of Louisville; 37°42'N 85°52'W. Elev. 731 ft/223 m. Originally developed as a trade center for agr., whiskey, and tobacco, the city now manufactures a variety of prods. (automotive parts, glass packaging equip., organic pigment, flooring insulation materials, magnets, fuses, adhesives, men's slacks, motor controls, rubber belts, metal tanks, wooden kitchen cabinets, freight car bearings, steel guard rails, crushed limestone, telephone cables). Addington Field airport to W. Points of interest include an old church (1789); the Lincoln Heritage House, built by Thomas Lincoln, Abraham Lincoln's father c.1800; a restored stagecoach inn that was built c.1825, now a historical library; Black History Gall.; Coca-Cola Memorabilia Mus.; Pine Valley Golf Mus.; Model "A" Ford Mus. Elizabethtown Community Col. (Univ. of Ky.). Fort Knox Military Reservation and Gold Bullion Depository to N. Vernon-Douglas State Nature Preserve to E; Freeman L. reservoir to N. Inc. 1797.

Elizabethtown 1 town (1990 pop. 495), Bartholomew co., S central Ind., 8 mi/12.9 km SE of Columbus; 39°08'N 85°49'W. In agr. area. **2** town (1990 pop. 3,704), ⊙ Bladen co., SE N.C., on Cape Fear R. (head of navigation), and 33 mi/53 km SSE of Fayetteville; 34°37'N 78°36'W. In agr. area (cotton, peanuts, tobacco, grain, soybeans, turkeys, cattle, hogs), timber area; mfg. (textile dyeing and finishing, blueberry processing, commercial lumber and wooden-furniture components, printing and publishing, dehumidifying equip., farming equip.). Bladen Lakes State Forest to NE; Jones Lake State Park to N; Turnbull Creek Educational State Forest to SE. Lock No. 2 downstream (SE). Several lakes in area, including White L to E. Settled c.1738.

Elizabethtown 1 village (1990 pop. 427), ⊙ Hardin co., extreme SE Ill., on Ohio R., and 23 mi/37 km SSE of Harrisburg; 37°27'N 88°17'W. Farming (wheat, corn; livestock). Cave in Rock State Park is E. Shawnee Nat'l Forest nearby. **2** resort village (1990 pop. 950), ⊙ Essex co., NE N.Y., in the Adirondacks, on Bouquet R., 34 mi/ 55 km SSW of Plattsburgh; 44°10'N 73°37'W.

Elizabethtown, borough (1990 pop. 9,952), Lancaster co., SE central Pa., 16 mi/26 km SE of Harrisburg. Agr. (grain, soybeans, potatoes; dairying; livestock, poultry); mfg. (air filters, commercial printing, mobile homes, meat processing, electroplating, cough drops and hard candy, wood prods., feeds). Elizabethtown-Marietta Airport to S. Masonic Homes Arboretum to SW. Olmstead Air Force Base to W; Three Mile Isl. nuclear plant to W. Laid out 1751, inc. 1827.

Elizabethville, borough (1990 pop. 1,467), Dauphin co., S central Pa., 20 mi/32 km NNE of Harrisburg, near Wicanisco creek.; 40°32'N 76°49'W. Agr. (grain; dairying, livestock, poultry); mfg. (crushed stone, wood prods., fabricated metal prods., apparel, truck frames); limestone. Part of Weiser State Forest to SE; Berry Mt. ridge to S. Settled 1817.

Elk 1 county (□ 650 sq mi/1,684 sq km; 1990 pop. 3,327), SE Kansas; ⊙ Howard; 37°27'N 96°14'W. Gently rolling agr. area, partly located in the Flint Hills region, watered by Elk, Caney, and Fall rivers. Cattle, oat, wheat, hay, corn. Oil and natural-gas fields. Formed 1875. **2** county (□ 832 sq mi/2,155 sq km; 1990 pop. 34,878), N central Pa.; ⊙ Ridgway. Forested upland. Drained by Clarion R. and Bennett Branch Sinnemahoning Creek. Agr. (corn, oats, barley, hay, alfalfa; dairying); bituminous coal, clay, sandstone, limestone. Mfg. at St. Marys and Ridgeway. Part of Allegheny Natl. Forest in W; parts of Moshannon State Forest in S, parts of Elk State Forest in SE and NE; Bendigo State Park in NE center, Elk State Park in NE; East Branch L. reservoir in NE. Formed 1843.

Elk Basin, village, Park co., NW Wyo., near Mont. line, 12 mi/19 km NNW of Powell, in E foothills of Beartooth Range of Absaroka Range Mts. Landing strip. Elk Basin oil field nearby.

Elk City, city (1990 pop. 10,428), Beckham co., W Okla., 27 mi/43 km WSW of Clinton, and on Elk Creek; 35°23'N 99°24'W. Processing and distribution center for agr. area (peanuts, cotton); horses. Mfg. (disk substrates, publishing and printing, personal computers, boats). An important quarter-horse raising region. Once an important oil area; oil and natural gas declining. Annual Rodeo. Old Town Mus. and Oil Mus. here. Inc. 1907.

Elk City 1 uninc. village (1990 pop. 450), Idaho co., N Idaho, 33 mi/53 km ESE of Grangeville, on South Fork Clearwater R., near its source in Clearwater Mts.

Timber. Area surrounded by Nez Perce Natl. Forest. Sleway-Bitterroot Wilderness Area to NE; Frank Church–River of No Return Wilderness Area to S; Gospel Hump Wilderness Area to SW. **2** village (1990 pop. 334), Montgomery co., SE Kansas, on Elk R., and 12 mi/19 km WNW of Independence; 37°17′N 95°54′W. Livestock, grain. Oil and gas fields in vicinity. Elk City Lake to SE.

Elk City Lake, reservoir (□ 7 sq mi/18.1 sq km), Montgomery co., SE Kansas, on Elk City R., 11 mi/16 km W of Independence; 37°17′N 96°47′W. Max. capacity 284,300 acre-ft. Formed by Elk City Dam (107 ft/33 m high), built (1966) by Army Corps of Engineers for flood control; also used for water supply. Elk City State Park near dam.

Elk Creek, village (1990 pop. 116), Johnson co., SE Nebr., 5 mi/8 km SSE of Tecumseh, and on North Fork of Big Nemaha R; 40°17′N 96°07′W.

Elk Creek, river in SW Okla.; rises in E Beckham co.; flows c.65 mi/105 km SE and S, past Elk City, to North Fork of Red R. 15 mi/24 km S of Hobart.

Elk Falls, village (1990 pop. 122), Elk co., SE Kansas, on Elk R. and 8 mi/12.9 km SSE of Howard; 37°22′N 96°11′W. Livestock, grain.

Elk Garden, village (1990 pop. 261), Mineral co., NE W. Va., 9 mi/14.5 km WSW of Keyser; 39°23′N 79°9′W. Jennings Randolph L. reservoir on N. Branch Potomac R. (W.Va.-Md. line) to N.

Elk Grove, uninc. city (1990 pop. 17,483), Sacramento co., central Calif., a suburb 12 mi/19 km SE of downtown Sacramento, near Cosumnes R.; 38°24′N 121°22′W. Citrus, pears, vegetables; cattle, poultry; dairying; mfg. (fertilizers, wood cabinets, concrete, prefabricated wood bldgs.). Rancho Seco nuclear power plant here recently closed.

Elk Grove Village, city (1990 pop. 33,429), Cook and Du Page cos., NE Ill., a suburb of Chicago; inc. 1956; 42°00′N 87°59′W. With a pop. of c.100 at the time of its establishment on open farmland, the village has grown dramatically and steadily, largely because of its industrial park. Its many manufactures include electronics. Adjacent to O'Hare Internatl. Airport.

Elk Hills Reserve, huge oil reserve near Bakersfield, Calif. that played a major role in the Teapot Dome scandal during the Harding Administration. The U.S. govt. acquired 78% of the reserve in the 1960s as the "Elk Hills Naval Petroleum Reserve," and large-scale oil production was accomplished by the introduction of new techniques after the energy crisis of 1973–1974. The govt. interest was sold to a private company in 1997. Natural gas also produced.

Elk Horn, town (1990 pop. 672), Shelby co., W Iowa, 15 mi/24 km E of Harlan; 41°35′N 95°03′W. In agr. area (grain, meal). Elk Horn and neighboring Kimballton (Audubon co.) are known as Danish Villages.

Elk Island National Park, 75 sq mi/194 sq km, central Alta., Canada, near Edmonton, est. 1913. It occupies a wooded rolling region in the midst of level farmland. Canada's major fenced preserve for buffalo and other prairie animals. Numerous small lakes offer summertime recreation.

Elk Lake, NW Mich., 12 mi/19 km NE of Traverse City, in resort area; c.9 mi/14.5 km long, 2 mi/3.2 km wide; 44°52′N 85°23′W. Drains W into E Arm of Grand Traverse Bay through Elk R. (c.2 mi/3.2 km long). Joined by passage to L. Skegemog (SE; 3.5 mi/5.6 km in diameter), then to Torch L. (E). S part marks boundary Bet. Antrim (E) and Grand Traverse (W) cos. As with Torch L. (to E) and the E and W arms of Grand Traverse Bay, to W, Elk L. was formed by S-bound glacial lobe.

Elk Mills, village, Cecil co., NE Md., on Elk R. near Del. line and 17 mi/27 km WSW of Wilmington, Del., which was originally the site of Elk Forge (c.1760), which manufactured bar iron from pig iron produced in Lancaster co., Pa. The forge later turned out guns for the Continental Army. Daniel Lord built the Elk Mills cotton factory here (c.1846) as well as stone housing for factory workers.

Elk Mound, village (1990 pop. 765), Dunn co., W Wis.,

10 mi/16 km WNW of Eau Claire, on sandy plain; 44°52′N 91°41′W. Mfg. (trailers). Hoffman Hills State Recreational Area to NW.

Elk Mountain, village (1990 pop. 174), Carbon co., S Wyo., on Medicine Bow R., and 45 mi/72 km ESE of Rawlins; 41°41′N 106°24′W. Elev. c.7,000 ft/2,134 m. Elk Mt. 7 mi/11.3 km to SW; Medicine Bow Natl. Forest to S.

Elk Mountain 1 mountain peak (6,423 ft/1,958 m) in Custer co., 11 mi/18 km SE of New Castle, Wyo.; 43°33′N 103°29′W. W S.Dak., near Wyo. line, in Black Hills. Lookout. **2** outlying peak (11,156 ft/3,400 m) in NNW tip of Medicine Bow Mts., S Wyo., 7 mi/11.3 km SW of Elk Mountain town. Peak has long served as a prominent landmark for travelers, formerly along the Cherokee Trail, now on Interstate Highway 80.

Elk Mountains, range of Rocky Mts. in Pitkin and Gunnison cos., W central Colo., just W of Sawatch Mts. and W of Continental Divide. Chief peaks include Sopris Peak (12,660 ft/3,859 m), Pyramid Peak (14,018 ft/4,273 m), Snowmass Peak (14,092 ft/4,295 m), Capitol Peak (14,130 ft/4,307 m), and Maroon Peak (14,156 ft/4,315 m); Mt. Carbon (14,265 ft/4,348 m; also called Castle Peak) is highest point in range. SW extension, called West Elk Mts., rises to 12,714 ft/3,875 m in Mt. Gunnison.

Elk Neck, Cecil co., NE Md., peninsula c.12 mi/19 km long, at head of Chesapeake Bay bet. Northeast R. and Elk R., just SW of Elkton; terminates at Turkey Point. The lighthouse here (c.1833) is an important mark for ships coming up the Bay to the Chesapeake and Del. Canal. It once had the only female lighthouse keeper in the country. It is also a state forest and park.

Elk Park, village (1990 pop. 486), Avery co., NW N.C., 17 mi/27 km WSW of Boone, near Tenn. state line in Pisgah Natl. Forest. Mt. resort; 36°09′N 81°58′W. Corn, potatoes, tobacco; livestock. Appalachian Trail passes to W on state line.

Elk Point, town (1991 pop. 1,341), E Alta., Canada, near North Saskatchewan R., 40 mi/64 km N of Vermilion; 53°54′N 110°54′W. Wheat, dairying, lumbering.

Elk Point, town (1990 pop. 1,423), ⊙ Union co., SE S. Dak., 17 mi/27 km SE of Vermillion, 20 mi/32 km NW of Sioux City, Iowa, near Missouri R. (Nebr. line) in SW, and Big Sioux R. (Iowa line) to NE; 42°40′N 96°40′W. Grain; livestock, poultry; mfg. (low-bed trailers and cleaning systems). Founded 1861.

Elk Rapids, village (1990 pop. 1,626), Antrim co., NW Mich., 13 mi/21 km NE of Traverse City, bet. Elk L. and East Arm of Grand Traverse Bay; 44°53′N 85°24′W. Agr. (potatoes, beans, cherries); mfg. (fruit prods., cutting tools); resort.

Elk Ridge, town (1990 pop. 771), Utah co., N central Utah, 14 mi/23 km S of Provo and 2 mi/3.2 km SE of Payson; 40°00′N 111°40′W. Elev. c.5,500 ft/1,676 m. Dairying, cattle, sheep, fruit. Uinta Natl. Forest to S. Settled late 1800s, inc. 1976.

Elk Ridge (c.1,500 ft/457 m), NW Md., N continuation of the Blue Ridge of Va.; begins at the Potomac R. in Washington co. (near Harpers Ferry), just S of Keedysville, Md., and runs NW for c.10 mi/16 km.

Elk River, city (1990 pop. 11,143), ⊙ Sherburne co., E Minn., 28 mi/45 km NW of Minneapolis, on Mississippi R., at mouth of Elk R.; 45°19′N 93°34′W. Elev. 891 ft/272 m. Grain, soybeans, alfalfa, potatoes; hogs; mfg. (ordnance, tool and die, sand and gravel, motors, machining, grinders, aerospace parts, printing and publishing). Site of Elk River Nuclear Power Plant. Sand Dunes State Forest and Sherburne Natl. Wildlife Refuge to NW. Platted 1865, inc. 1881.

Elk River, village (1990 pop. 149), Clearwater co., N Idaho, 21 mi/34 km N of Orofino, on Elk Creek; 46°47′N 116°11′W. Grazing (cattle); alfalfa; lumber. Dworshak Reservoir (N Fork Clearwater R.) to S and E.

Elk River 1 in SE Kansas, formed by confluence of several headstreams in Elk co. near Howard, flows c.80 mi/129 km ESE, past Howard and Elk City through Elk City Lake Reservoir, to Verdigris R. just N of Independence. **2** in central Minn.; rises in marshy area of N

Benton co.; flows 70 mi/113 km first S bet. Foley and St. Cloud, to its joining the Mississippi R. at Elk River city, then SE through Elk L.; roughly paralleling Mississippi R. to Elk River city; 45°49′N 93°55′W. **3** in SW Mo. and NE Okla.; rises in McDonald co., Mo.; flows 80 mi/129 km W to Grand L. of the Cherokees in Delaware co., Okla. **4** estuary, Cecil co., NE Md., NE arm of Chesapeake Bay; 41°33′N 78°22′W. One of northernmost extensions of bay, c.15 mi/24 km long, 2 mi/3.2 km wide, separated from bay by Elk Neck peninsula; Chesapeake and Delaware Canal, part of Intracoastal Waterway, enters estuary from E (connects Chesapeake and Delaware bays across base of Delmarva Peninsula.); estuary fed from N by Big Elk Creek (c.25 mi/40 km long) and Little Elk Creek (c.20 mi/32 km long), both rise in SW Chester co., Pa., and both share common mouth at Elkton, at head of estuary. **5** in S Tenn. and N Ala.; rises on W slope of Cumberland Mts. in Grundy co., Tenn.; meanders c.200 mi/322 km generally WSW past Fayetteville, into Ala., to Wheeler Reservoir (Tennessee R.) 6 mi/10 km E of Wheeler Dam; 34°45′N 87°15′W. Impounded in Franklin and Moore cos. to form Tims Ford L.; lower course also forms part of reservoir. **6** 172 mi/277 km long, central W.Va. Rises in central Pocahontas co., in the Allegheny Mts., N of Marlinton; flows N then W, past Webster Springs, generally NW through Sutton L. reservoir (Elk R. Wildlife Management Area), past Sutton, then SW past Clay and Clendenin, to Kanawha R. at Charleston.

Elk Run Heights, town (1990 pop. 1088), Blackhawk co., E central Iowa, suburb 5 mi/8 km ESE of Waterloo, near Cedar R.; 42°28′N 92°15′W. Residential area.

Elkader, town (1990 pop. 1,510), ⊙ Clayton co., NE Iowa, on Turkey R. (bridged here), and 29 mi/47 km ENE of Oelwein; 42°51′N 91°24′W. Livestock shipping; mfg. (wine specialties, farm bldgs., luggage); limestone quarries. Nearby are ruins of Communia, a cooperative town settled c.1850. Flooding occurred here in 1993. Inc. 1868.

Elkford, town (1991 pop. 2,846), SE B.C., Canada, located in Rocky Mts. on Elk R. at confluence of Fording R., 20 mi/32 km N of Sparwood; 49°55′N 114°51′W. Town grew from a cluster of mobile homes in 1971 with opening of subsurface coal mine. Cattle; tourism. Highway terminus.

Elkhart, county (□ 467 sq mi/1,210 sq km; 1990 pop. 156,198), N Ind., bounded N by Mich. line; ⊙ Goshen; 41°36′N 85°52′W. Agr. area (dairy prods.; hogs, cattle; soybeans, corn, wheat, oats, potatoes, hay, mint, onions); diversified mfg. (at Elkhart, Nappanee, and Goshen); timber. Drained by Elkhart and St. Joseph rivers. One of the leading mfg. cos. in Ind. Formed 1830.

Elkhart, city (1990 pop. 43,627), Elkhart co., N Ind., at the confluence of the Elkhart and St. Joseph rivers. One of the leading mfg. cities in Ind. The city's status as a chief producer of band instruments began in 1875 by Charles Conn, who manufactured brass parts. Other major prods. include pharmaceuticals (the industry dates from 1884), machinery, electrical equip., metal fabricating, auto parts, packaging, office furniture, recreational vehicle parts, saxophones, mobile homes, cargo trailers, van conversions, steel tubing, motor homes, and fire protection equip. Agr. and livestock are also prevalent. Laid out 1832, inc. 1877.

Elkhart 1 town (1990 pop. 388), Polk co., central Iowa, 15 mi/24 km NNE of Des Moines; 41°47′N 93°30′W. In agr. area. **2** town (1990 pop. 2,318), ⊙ Morton co., extreme SW Kansas, at Okla. line, 50 mi/80 km W of Liberal; 37°00′N 101°53′W. In grain region. Cimarron Natl. Grassland to NE. Inc. 1913. **3** town (1990 pop. 1,076), Anderson co., E Texas, near the Trinity, 10 mi/16 km S of Palestine; 31°37′N 95°34′W. Light mfg.

Elkhart, village, (1990 pop. 475), Logan co., central Ill., 17 mi/27 km NNE of Springfield; 40°01′N 89°28′W. In agr. area. Richard J. Oglesby b. and buried here. Bituminous-coal area.

Elkhart Lake, town (1990 pop. 1,119), Sheboygan co., E

Wis., on Elkhart L. (resort), 16 mi/26 km NW of Sheboygan; 43°49′N 88°00′W. In dairy and grain area. Mfg. (aluminum castings, sausage, metal fabrication, plastic and metal windows, labels); cannery. Large co. park nearby. Summer resort.

Elkhart River, N Ind.; rises in E Noble co.; flows c.100 mi/161 km generally W and NW, past Goshen, to St. Joseph R. at Elkhart.

Elkhead Reservoir, Moffat and Routt cos., NW Colo., on Elkhead Creek, in Elkhead State Wildlife Area, 9 mi/14.5 km ENE of Craig; 3 mi/4.8 km long; 40°33′N 107°24′W. Max. storage capacity of 18,900 acre-ft. Formed by Elkhead Creek Dam (41 ft/12 m high), built (1972) by the Colo. Div. of Wildlife for recreation.

Elkhorn 1 uninc. town (1990 pop. 1,458), Monterey co., W Calif., 6 mi/9.7 km S of Watsonville, on Elkhorn Slough, 4 mi/6.4 km E of Pacific Ocean; 36°49′N 121°43′W. Elkhorn Slough Natl. Estuaries Research Inst. is here. Artichokes, vegetables, grain, dairying. **2** town (1990 pop. 1,398), Douglas co., E Nebr., 15 mi/24 km W of Omaha and on Elkhorn R., near Platte R; 41°16′N 96°14′W. Mfg. (cabinets, apparel, animal health prods.). **3** town (1990 pop. 5,337), ⊙ Walworth co., SE Wis., near L. Geneva, 40 mi/64 km SW of Milwaukee; 42°40′N 88°32′W. In dairy, grain, and poultry area; mfg. (band instruments and equip., rubber prods., concrete, drafting tables, electric motors, undercarriage components, leather packings, industrial packaging); canneries; fish hatchery. Resort lakes near by. Settled 1837, inc. as village in 1852, as city in 1897.

Elkhorn, village (1991 pop. 505), SW Man., Canada, 60 mi/97 km W of Brandon; 49°58′N 101°15′W. Grain elevators; dairying, livestock raising.

Elkhorn, uninc. village (1990 pop. 350), McDowell co., S W.Va., 10 mi/16 km. SE of Welch. Coal area.

Elkhorn City, town (1990 pop. 813), Pike co., E Ky., 15 mi/24 km SSE of Pikesville, near Va. state line, on Russell Fork river; 37°17′N 82°20′W. Bituminous-coal-mining region; coal processing. Pine Mt. Canyon, in Breaks Interstate Park, and Jefferson Natl. Forest to SE. Est. 1825.

Elkhorn Creek 1 in NW Ill.; rises in W Ogle co.; flows c.55 mi/89 km generally SW and S to Rock R. c.5 mi/8 km SW of Sterling; 47°07′N 89°39′W. **2** in N Ky.; rises in Fayette co. S of Lexington; flows 85 mi/137 km NW to Kentucky R. 9 mi/14.5 km N of Frankfort; receives N Fork Elkhorn Creek, NE of Frankfort.

Elkhorn, Mount (7,200 ft/2,195 m), SW B.C., Canada, on central Vancouver Isl., in Strathcona Provincial Park, 40 mi/64 km WNW of Courtenay; 49°47′N 125°51′W.

Elkhorn Ridge, NE Oregon, range of Blue Mts. in Baker co., W of Baker City. Chief peaks: Angell Peak (8,646 ft/2,635 m), Twin Mt. (8,897 ft/2,712 m), and ROCK CREEK BUTTE (9,106 ft/2,776 m). Lies in Wallowa-Whitman Natl. Forest.

Elkhorn River, NE Nebr.; rises in Rock co.; flows 333 mi/536 km ESE and S, past O'Neill, Norfolk, and West Point, to Platte R. near Omaha. Logan Creek enters from N at Winslow. Numerous cattle feedlots on terraces along river. S Fork Elkhorn enters from W at Ewins, Holt co.

Elkhorn Tavern, Ark.: see PEA RIDGE.

Elkin, town (1990 pop. 3,790), Surry co., N N.C., on Yadkin R. and 35 mi/56 km WNW of Winston-Salem; 36°15′N 80°50′W. In agr. area (dairying; cattle, hogs, chickens; grain, soybeans, tobacco); mfg. (textiles and apparel, candles, wooden furniture, crushed stone, strand board).

Elkins, town (1990 pop. 7,420), ⊙ Randolph co., E central W.Va., on Tygart R., 36 mi/58 km SE of Clarksburg; 38°55′N 79°50′W. RR junction (shops); airport; trade and distributing center for coal-mining and timber area. Mfg. (lumber, hardwood furniture, wooden flooring, clothing, printing and publishing, asphalt, concrete, crushed limestone); agr. (grain, soybeans); livestock; poultry; dairying. Halliehurst Mus. is here. Has Davis and Elkins Col., state home for children. A gateway to Monongahela Natl. Forest to E. Inc. 1890.

Elkins Park, uninc. village, in CHELTENHAM township, Montgomery co., SE Pa., 8 mi/12.9 km N of downtown Philadelphia, on Tacony Creek; 40°04′N 75°07′W. Light mfg. (book publishing, wood prods.). Has Quaker meetinghouse built 1682.

Elkland, borough (1990 pop. 1,849), Tioga co., N Pa., 17 mi/27 km NW of Mansfield, on N.Y. state boundary, on Cowanesque R.; 41°59′N 77°18′W. Agr. (corn, hay; dairying, livestock); mfg. (apparel, plastic prods.). Cowananesque L. reservoir to E. Inc. 1850.

Elkmont, town (1990 pop. 389), Limestone co., N Ala., 9 mi/14.5 km N of Athens, near Elk R. and Tenn. line.; 34°55′N 86°58′W. Mfg. (Automotive wire, baseball caps); poultry.

Elko, county (□ 17,204 sq mi/44,558 sq km; 1990 pop. 33,530), NE Nev.; ⊙ Elko; 41°07′N 115°20′W. Mt. and plateau area crossed by Humboldt R., bordering on Idaho (N) and Utah (E). Both boundaries near Pacific/Mt. Time Zone boundary; Nev. is in Pacific on Idaho line. Gold, silver, sand and gravel; cattle, sheep; Part of Duck Valley Indian Reservation is in N; South Fork Indian Reservation, 1 unit in S, other in SW. Part of Duck Valley Indian Reservation in N, on Idaho boundary. Sections of Humboldt Natl. Forest are in S (in Ruby Mts.) and N. Livestock grazing. Formed 1869. Fourth largest co. in U.S. in land area. Natl. Basque Fortress; large Basque-Amer. pop. Wild Horse Reservation in N. Part of Ruby L. Natl. Wildlife on S boundary.

Elko, city (1990 pop. 14,736), ⊙ Elko co., NE Nev., on Humboldt R., and c.200 mi/322 km W of Salt L. City, and c.215 mi/346 km ENE of Reno; 40°50′N 115°45′W. Elev. 5,067 ft/1,544 m.Trade center and shipping point for cattle, sheep, and wool. RR center. Gold, silver mines in vicinity. Founded 1868, when RR arrived; inc. 1917. Univ. of Nevada (now at Reno) was here 1873–1885. Great Basin Col. South Fork Indian Reservation to S. Parts of Humboldt Natl Forest to N and SE. Wild Horse Reservation to N.

Elko, town (1990 pop.), Houston co., central Ga., 8 mi/12.9 km S of Perry; 32°19′N 83°42′W.

Elko, village, SE B.C., on Elk R., and 14 mi/23 km SSW of Fernie; 49°18′N 115°07′W. Iron, coal, copper deposits.

Elko 1 village (1990 pop. 223), Scott co., SE Minn., 28 mi/45 km S of Minneapolis; 44°34′N 93°19′W. Poultry; grain; dairying; light mfg. Race track here. Small lakes in area. **2** village (1990 pop. 214), Barnwell co., W S.C., 10 mi/16 km N of Barnwell; 33°22′N 81°22′W. Agr. includes livestock, poultry, grain, cotton, peanuts.

Elkport, town (1990 pop. 82), Clayton co., NE Iowa, near confluence of Turkey and Volga rivers, 9 mi/14.5 km WSW of Guttenberg; 42°44′N 91°16′W. Limestone quarries nearby.

Elkridge 1 village (1990 pop. 12,953), Howard co., central Md., on Patapsco R. and 8 mi/12.9 km SW of downtown Baltimore; 39°12′N 76°45′W. Residential. The name comes from a spiny, thickly wooded ridge that turns E to the valley of the Patapsco. A forge here produced guns during the Revolution and the Marquis de Lafayette camped here with his troops on the way to Yorktown. **2** uninc. village (1990 pop. 100), McDowell co., W.Va.: adjoining village of Algoma.

Elkton, city (1990 pop. 1,789), ⊙ Todd co., S Ky., 17 mi/27 km ESE of Hopkinsville; 36°48′N 87°09′W. Agr. area (burley tobacco, grain, fruit; cattle); mfg. (oak furniture, refrigerator doors, aluminum die castings, blue jeans, crushed limestone, beef processing, camp chairs); stone quarries; timber. Robert Penn Warren Birthplace; Milliken Memorial Community House (1929); Jefferson Davis State Historic Site is W, at Fairview. Est. 1820.

Elkton 1 town (1990 pop. 9,073), ⊙ Cecil co. (since 1786), NE Md., at head of navigation on Elk R., and 19 mi/31 km WSW of Wilmington, Del.; 39°36′N 75°49′W. In wheat-growing area, with large sand and gravel pits. Mfg. (rubber toys, paper, clothing, fireworks, spark plugs, radios). Until 1938, when Md. passed a revised marriage law, Elkton was the "Let's get married right away" capital of the East Coast for couples who did not want to wait 48 hours for a wedding license. Eloping couples were met at the train by taxi drivers who hurried them first to the court for a license and then to one of the "marrying parsons" on Main Street. Originally called Head of Elk, because it is near the source of the Elk R., the town was overrun during the Revolution by both rebel and royal troops. Original maps of British fortifications are in the Cecil co. Public Library. Two 18th-cent. homes are in the town, Partridge Hill (c. pre–1776) and Gilpin Manor (c.1760), as well as the site of Fort Hollingsworth, a small redoubt constructed by citizens during the War of 1812. Nearby are Md. terminus of Chesapeake and Del. Canal and Elk Neck, site of a state forest, state park, and Turkey Point Lighthouse (erected 1834). Founded 1681. **2** town (1990 pop. 958), Huron co., E Mich., 14 mi/23 km W of Bad Axe, near Saginaw Bay; 43°49′N 83°10′W. In agr. area; dairy prods.; mfg. metal stampings. **3** town (1990 pop. 602), Brookings co., E S.Dak., 16 mi/26 km ESE of Brookings, near Minn. line; 44°13′N 96°28′W. Dairy produce, poultry, livestock, grain. **4** town (1990 pop. 448), Giles co., S Tenn., near Ala. line, 13 mi/21 km SE of Pulaski; 35°03′N 86°54′W. **5** town (1990 pop. 1,935), Rockingham co., NW Va., in Shenandoah Valley, on South Fork of Shenandoah R., 14 mi/23 km E of Harrisonburg; 38°24′N 78°37′W. Mfg. (hospital sheets and uniforms, beer, clothing, pharmaceuticals, lumber); agr. (grain, soybeans, apples, peaches; dairying; livestock, poultry). Massanutten Resort to W; Massanutten Mt., in George Washington Natl. Forest to NW; Shenandoah Natl. Park to SE. Inc. 1908.

Elkton 1 village (1990 pop. 142), Mower co., SE Minn., 13 mi/21 km E of Austin; 43°39′N 92°42′W. Corn, oats, soybeans; dairying. **2** village (1990 pop. 172), Douglas co., W Oregon, on Umpqua R. at mouth of Elk Creek, and 32 mi/51 km NNW of Roseburg; 43°38′N 123°34′W Trading point in agr. area. Timber. Fruit; sheep, cattle. Siaslaw Natl. Forest to NW; Elliott State Forest to SW.

Elkview, uninc. town (1990 pop. 1,047), Kanawha co., W central W.Va., 11 mi/18 km NE of Charlestown, on Elk R.; 38°25′N 81°28′W. Agr. (corn, tobacco); cattle; poultry. Bituminous coal. Mfg. (hand-blown glass, mining machinery).

Elkville, village (1990 pop. 958), Jackson co., SW Ill., 12 mi/19 km NNE of Murphysboro; 37°54′N 89°14′W. Bituminous-coal mining; agr. (grain, fruit, vegetables).

Ellamar (E-luh-mahr), village, S Alaska, on Prince William Sound, 20 mi/32 km SW of Valdez. Fishing, canning.

Ellaville (EL-uh-vil), town (1990 pop. 1,724), ⊙ Schley co., W central Ga., 12 mi/19 km NNW of Americus; 32°14′N 84°19′W. Mfg. of modular buildings, trusses, leather goods, wire shelving.

Ellef Ringnes Island (□ 4,266 sq mi/11,049 sq km), Sverdrup Isls., N Franklin dist., N.W.T., Canada, in the Arctic Ocean; bet. 77°44′N–79°25′N and 99°00′W–106°30′W; separated from Axel Heiberg Isl. (NE) by Peary Channel, from Amund Ringnes Isl. (SE) by Hassel Sound, from Bathurst Isl. (S) by Maclean Strait, and from Borden Isl. (W) by the Gustav Adolph Sea. Isl. is 150 mi/241 km long, 20 mi/32 km–70 mi/113 km wide; surface rises to c.2,000 ft/610 m on central plateau. Isachsen Peninsula (□ 1,008 sq mi/2,611 sq km; 55 mi/89 km long, 40 mi/64 km wide), extending NW, was formerly believed to be separate isl. Cape Isachsen is nearby.

Ellen, Mount, peak (11,522 ft/3,512 m) highest point in Henry Mts., Garfield co. near Wayne co. line, S Utah, 20 mi/32 km SSW of Hanksville.

Ellen, Mount, summit in Vt.: see LINCOLN MOUNTAIN.

Ellenboro 1 village (1990 pop. 514), Rutherford co., SW N.C., 12 mi/19 km W of Shelby; 35°19′N 81°45′W. RR spur junction. Grain, soybeans, poultry, livestock; mfg. (modular bldgs., business forms, plastic molding). **2** village (1990 pop. 453), Ritchie co., NW W.Va., 5 mi/8 km N of Harrisville; 39°16′N 81°2′W.

Ellendale, town (1990 pop. 1,798), ⊙ Dickey co., SE N.Dak., 64 mi/103 km S of Jamestown, near S.Dak. state line; 46°00′N 98°31′W. Dairy prods., livestock. Trinity Bible Col. here. Inc. as a village 1883; inc. as a city in 1889. Whitestone Battlefield Historic Site to NW.

Ellendale 1 village (1990 pop. 313), Sussex co., S central Del., 7 mi/11.3 km S of Milford at source of Gravelly Creek; 38°48′N 75°25′W. Ellendale Swamp, in Ellendale State Forest, to SE; Redden State Forest to S. Formerly an important lumber center. **2** village (1990 pop. 549), Steele co., SE Minn., 15 mi/24 km SSW of Owatonna; 43°52′N 93°17′W. Agr. area (poultry; grain, soybeans; dairying); mfg. (electric fence insulations).

Ellensburg, city (1990 pop. 12,361), ⊙ Kittitas co., central Wash., 28 mi/45 km N of Yakima, on the Yakima R.; 47°00′N 120°33′W. RR junction. It is the trade and processing center for a region in which cattle raising and diverse, irrigated farming are predominant. Potatoes, wheat, alfalfa, peas; dairying; mfg. (printing and publishing, wood pallets, meat packing, frozen fruits and vegetables). Roza Dam, Yakima R., 19 mi/31 km S; Wanapum Dam, on Columbia R., 30 mi/48 km ESE. Bowers Airport to N. U.S. Military Reserve, Yakima Training Center to SE. Spurgeon Art Mus.; Anthropology Mus. here. Central Wash. Univ. here, and an annual rodeo is held in the city. Ginkgo Petrified Forest and Wanapum state parks to E. Parts of Wenatchee Natl. Forest to N and W; Olmstead Place State Park to SE. Inc. 1886.

Ellenton, town (□ 4 sq mi/10.4 sq km; 1990 pop. 2,573), Manatee co., W central Fla., 13 mi/21 km N of Sarasota; 27°31′N 82°31′W. Mfg. includes concrete and mattresses.

Ellenton, village (1990 pop. 227), Colquitt co., S Ga., 11 mi/18 km E of Moultrie; 31°11′N 83°35′W. Mfg. of farm equip.

Ellenton, locality, Aiken co., SW S.C., near Savannah R., 23 mi/37 km S of Aiken. In former town taken over (1951–1952) by U.S. Atomic Energy Commission for huge Savannah R. Nuclear Plant (hydrogen-bomb materials).

Ellenville, village (□ 9 sq mi/23.3 sq km; 1990 pop. 4,243), Ulster co., SE N.Y., in the Shawangunk range, 25 mi/40 km SW of Kingston; 41°42′N 74°21′W. Changing lifestyles forced the closing of the large hotels of this resort village. Today it is a popular gathering place for mountaineers and rock climbers tackling the Shawangunk Mts. Area remains a popular recreational destination in summer. Inc. 1856.

Ellenwood, town (1990 pop. 400), Clayton co., Ga., suburb of Atlanta, c.2 mi/3.2 km SE of Forest Park. Mfg. includes bone meal, food prods., wooden cabinets.

Ellerbe (EL-uhr-bee), town (1990 pop. 1,132), Richmond co., S N.C., 9 mi/14.5 km N of Rockingham; 35°04′N 79°45′W. Tobacco, cotton, grain, sweet potatoes; poultry, livestock. Mfg. (lingerie, nylon socks, synthetic yarn).

Ellerslie (E-luhrz-lee), village, W P.E.I., Canada, near Malpeque Bay, 16 mi/26 km NW of Summerside; lobster fishing.

Ellerslie, village, Allegany co., W Md., on Wills Creek at Pa. line, 5 mi/8 km NNW of Cumberland. Limestone quarries nearby. Post office est. in 1868. Named after Ellerslie, Scotland, the birthplace of Sir William Wallace, a Scots hero.

Ellesmere Island National Park Reserve, NE N.W.T., Canada, on N end of Ellesmere Isl., (15,251 sq mi/39,500 sq km), 1,553 mi/2,500 km NE of Yellowknife. Includes territory N of line from SW end of Lady Franklin Bay W to NE extremity of Tanquary Fjord, and E of 77°30′W; excludes large area around Cape Union, on NE. Tundra, glaciers, ice caps of Br. Empire and U.S. Ranges; L. Hazen, 60 mi/97 km long, largest lake N of Arctic circle. Thermal oasis surrounds lake, maintaining plant, animal community typical of areas further S. Fragile ecosystem throughout park. Musk ox, caribou, polar bears, Arctic fox, wolves. Outfitting.

Ellettsville, town (1990 pop. 3,275), Monroe co., S central Ind., 7 mi/11.3 km NW of Bloomington; 39°14′N 86°37′W. In agr. area; limestone, timber. Mfg. (medical prods., concrete blocks).

Ellice Island (E-lis) (24 mi/39 km long, 4 mi/6 km–11 mi/18 km wide), NW Mackenzie Dist., N.W.T., Canada, in Beaufort Sea of the Arctic Ocean, off mouth of Mackenzie R.; 65°5′N 135°40′W.

Ellicott City (E-li-kut), village (1990 pop. 41,396), ⊙ Howard co., in Baltimore and Howard cos., central Md., on Patapsco R., and 11 mi/18 km WSW of downtown Baltimore; 39°16′N 76°50′W. Trade center in agr. area (wheat, corn, hay); mfg. (doughnut machines, prepared flour mixes, feed, shirts). The community grew up around Ellicotts' Mills, one of whose founders, Joseph Ellicott, was the father of the surveyor, Andrew Ellicott, who redrew L'Enfant's plans of Washington for Thomas Jefferson. Ellicott was helped by Benjamin Banneker, his protegé and an early black scientist. Ellicott also surveyed the boundaries of several states, among them Florida's. Another brother, Joseph, founded Buffalo, N.Y. The exterior of the stone Baltimore and Ohio station has changed little since the first horse-cars were hauled here from Baltimore on May 24, 1830. The private Doughoregan Manor (c.1735–1745), the home of Charles Carroll of Carrollton, the only Catholic to sign the Declaration of Independence, contains a richly furnished Catholic chapel from the days when public celebration of Mass was forbidden. Other notable sights include the Log Cabin (c.1780) and Angelo Cottage (c.1831) and the gutted walls of Patapsco Female Inst. (c.1829). Patapsco State Park nearby. Flour mill built here (1774) was nucleus of settlement of Ellicott Mills; inc. and renamed 1867; reverted (1935) to uninc. status.

Ellicottville, village (1990 pop. 513), Cattaraugus co., W N.Y., 9 mi/14.5 km NNE of Salamanca; 42°16′N 78°40′W. In dairying and poultry area; some mfg. (lumber, furniture, sporting goods, automotive and industrial hand tools, cutlery). Inc. 1881.

Ellijay (EL-i-jai), town (1990 pop. 1,178), ⊙ Gilmer co., N Ga., on Coosawattee R., and c.50 mi/80 km NE of Rome; 34°41′N 84°29′W. Center of apple-production region; recreation area. Mfg. of carpeting and textiles, clothing, yarns, wire assemblies, poultry processing, trophies; lumber and wood prods. such as log homes, hardwood flooring. Inc. 1834.

Ellinger, village (1990 pop. 200), Fayette co., S central Texas, 28 mi/45 km SW of Brenham, near Colorado R. In agr. area. L. Fayette reservoir to N.

Ellington 1 town (1990 pop. 11,197), Tolland co., N Conn., 15 mi/24 km NNE of Hartford; 41°54′N 72°27′W. Agr. Settled c.1720, inc. 1786. Includes village of Crystal Lake (1990 pop. 1,175). **2** town (1990 pop. 994), Reynolds co., SE Mo., in the Ozarks, 14 mi/23 km S of Centerville; 37°14′N 90°58′W. Cattle. Recreation area. Nearly surrounded by state forests.

Ellington, village (1990 pop. 500), Chautauqua co., extreme W N.Y., 11 mi/18 km NE of Jamestown; 42°12′N 79°07′W. In dairying and fruit-growing area.

Ellinwood, town (1990 pop. 2,329), Barton co., central Kansas, on Arkansas R., and 10 mi/16 km E of Great Bend; 38°21′N 98°34′W. RR junction. Founded 1871, inc. 1878. Boomed in 1930s with development of oil fields.

Elliott, county (□ 235 sq mi/609 sq km; 1990 pop. 6,455), NE Ky.; ⊙ Sandy Hook; 38°07′N 83°05′W. Drained by Little Sandy R. (source in SW; upper reach of Grayson L. reservoir in NE) and several creeks. Hilly agr. area (burley tobacco, hay, alfalfa; cattle); coal mines. Daniel Boone Natl. Forest immediately W of co. Formed 1869.

Elliott 1 town (1990 pop. 399), Montgomery co., SW Iowa, on East Nishnabotna R., and 10 mi/16 km NNE of Red Oak; 41°08′N 95°09′W. In agr. region. **2** uninc. town (1990 pop. 900), Grenada co., N central Miss., 6 mi/9.7 km SSE of Grenada. Timber; cotton, corn; dairying. Mfg. (hardware, lumber, wood preserving, scrap metal). Camp McCain Natl. Guard base to E.

Elliott 1 village (1990 pop. 309), Ford co., E central Ill., 9 mi/14.5 km W of Paxton; 40°27′N 88°16′W. In rich agr. area. **2** village (1990 pop. 32), Ransom co., SE N.Dak., 7 mi/11.3 km WSW of Lisbon; 46°23′N 97°48′W. Fort Ransom State Park and Historic Site to NW. **3** uninc. village, Lee co., central S.C., c.10 mi/16 km NE of Sumter. Agr. includes cotton, corn, livestock, peanuts.

Elliott Bay, King co., W Wash., inlet of Puget Sound forming harbor of Seattle; 6 mi/9.7 km wide at entrance, 4 mi/6.4 km long. Receives Duwamish R. from S. Ferry terminal. Downtown Seattle fronts bay.

Elliott Highway (72 mi/116 km long), central Alaska, road connecting Fairbanks, Livengood, and Manley Hot Springs.

Elliott Key, island in S Biscayne Bay, SE Fla., c.20 mi/32 km S of Miami; c.8 mi/12.9 km long.

Elliott Lake, city (1991 pop. 14,089), S central Ont., Canada, W of Sudbury; 46°23′N 82°39′W. Center of a large uranium-mining area. Formerly known as the "uranium capital of the world," its last active mine closed in 1996. The pop. peaked at 25,000 in the late 1950s. Now it is a retirement community and summer recreation area.

Elliottsville, township, Piscataquis co., central Maine, 17 mi/27 km NW of Dover-Foxcroft, in wilderness area. Hunting, fishing. Includes Onawa village on L. Onawa (3 mi/4.8 km long).

Ellis 1 county (□ 900 sq mi/2,331 sq km; 1990 pop. 26,004), W central Kansas; ⊙ Hays; 38°55′N 99°18′W. Smoky Hills region, drained in N by Saline R., in S by Smoky Hill R., and Big Creek at center. Wheat, cattle, hogs, oil, natural gas. Mfg. of granite prods. Oil fields in NE. Formed 1867. **2** county (□ 1,231 sq mi/3,188 sq km; 1990 pop. 4,497), NW Okla.; ⊙ Arnett; 36°12′N 99°45′W. Bounded W by Texas state line, S by Canadian R.; boundary reaches North Canadian R. in far N; drained (SE) by South Canadian R. and Wolf Creek. Agr. area (barley, sorghum, oats; cattle, dairying); oil and gas. Formed 1907. **3** county (□ 951 sq mi/2,463 sq km; 1990 pop. 85,167), N Texas; ⊙ Waxahachie; 32°21′N 96°47′W. In rich blackland agr. region; bounded E by Trinity R., drained by Chambers and Waxahachie (forms Bardwell L.) (SE) creeks. Cotton, corn, wheat, hay; dairying, livestock (cattle, sheep, horses); honey. Limestone quarrying; oil and gas. Mfg. Waxahachie, Ennis, Ferris. Formed 1849.

Ellis, town (1990 pop. 1,814), Ellis co., W central Kansas, on the Big Creek, and 14 mi/23 km WNW of Hays; 38°56′N 99°33′W. In wheat and livestock region. Oil wells nearby. Founded 1867, inc. 1888.

Ellis Grove, village (1990 pop. 353), Randolph co., SW Ill., near the Mississippi, 7 mi/11.3 km NNW of Chester; 38°00′N 89°54′W. In agr. area. Fort Kaskaskia State Historical Site nearby.

Ellis Island (□ 27.5 acres/11.1 ha), SE N.Y., in Upper N.Y. Bay, c.1 mi/1.6 km SW of the Battery of Manhattan; 40°42′N 74°02′W. Ferry connections. Govt. property since 1808, it was 1st site of an arsenal and fort, later (1892–1943) the chief immigration station of U.S.; located just N of the Statue of Liberty. Between 1892 and 1954, 12 million immigrants were processed here. Today, over 40% of Americans can trace their roots to ancestors who came through here. Under the Statue of Liberty–Ellis Isl. Foundation, Inc., founded in 1982, major projects have been completed; others are still under way. These include restoration of the Main Bldg. on Ellis Isl. (the largest restoration project in U.S. history); creation of the Ellis Isl. Immigration Mus. featuring such things as taped interviews and interactive artifacts and photos; creation of the Amer. Family Immigration History Center with data on 20 million immigrants, such as ship names, dates of arrival, cities and countries of origin, and relatives in U.S.; and bldg. of Amer. Immigrant Wall of Honor inscribed with over 500,000 names of immigrants who entered through Ellis Isl. or other gateways. This will be the largest wall of names in the world and will include George Washington's great-grandfather; Miles Standish; Priscilla Alden; the great-grandparents of John F. Kennedy, and relatives of Gregory Peck, Cicely Tyson, Jay Leno, and Barbra Streisand. While the isl. is owned by the Federal govt., N.J. claims state jurisdiction over 24.5 acres/9.9 ha of its total area. The original 3 acres/1.2 ha were owned by N.Y. state in accordance with an 1834 pact bet. the 2 states setting the median line of the Hudson R. as the boundary. The Federal govt. expanded the isl. in 1890 (using fill from underwater land bought from N.J.) to build the immigration center. The fact that N.J. "land" was used is the basis for the state's claim and for its desire to get any future tax revenues from 30 unrestored bldgs. occupying the land. The dispute is before the

Supreme Court; an arbitrator appointed by the court is currently attempting to determine a "clean and workable" boundary line that the justices can approve.

Ellis River, 14 mi/23 km long, E N.H.; rises in S Coos co., on Mt. Washington, in White Mts.; flows S to Saco R. 6 mi/9.7 km E of Bartlett. Glen Ellis Falls (70 ft/21 m), scenic feature on side stream.

Ellisburg, village (□ 1 sq mi/2.6 sq km; 1990 pop. 246), Jefferson co., N N.Y., 20 mi/32 km SSW of Watertown, near L. Ontario; 43°44'N 76°07'W.

Ellison Bay, village, Door co., NE Wis., on Door Peninsula, on Green Bay, 33 mi/53 km NE of Sturgeon Bay city. Door Co. Maritime Mus. Newport State Park to E.

Elliston, uninc. town, Montgomery co., SW Va., 16 mi/26 km W of Roanoke, on South Fork Roanoke R.; 37°12'N 80°13'W. Mfg. (feeds, cable assembly, log homes); agr. (grain, apples; livestock, dairying); timber. Dixie Caverns to NE.

Elliston, village (1990 pop. 180), Powell co., W central Mont., on Little Blackfoot R. at its confluence with Elliston Creek, 20 mi/32 km W of Helena, Continental Divide to E. Cattle, hay; trade center, formerly for a gold-mining dist., later the site of a lime quarry and mill. Parts of Helena Natl. Forest to N and S.

Ellisville, city (1990 pop. 7,545), St. Louis co., E Mo., residential suburb 21 mi/34 km W of St. Louis; 38°35'N 90°35'W. Mfg. (electrical fuses, metal tanks). Rockwoods Reservation (nature reserve) to SW; Babler Memorial State Park to NW.

Ellisville, town (1990 pop. 3,634), ⊙ Jones co. (a seat shared with Laurel), SE Miss., 7 mi/11.3 km SSW of Laurel, near Tallahala Creek; 31°36'N 89°12'W. Agr. (cotton, corn, poultry, dairying, timber); mfg. (trusses, lumber, oil-rig drive shafts); oil and natural gas. Seat of a Jones County Jr. Col. Part of De Soto Natl. Forest to E.

Ellisville, village (1990 pop. 116), Fulton co., W central Ill., on Spoon R. (bridged here), and 18 mi/29 km NNW of Lewiston; 40°37'N 90°18'W. In agr. and bituminous-coal area.

Elloree (E-nuh-ree), town (1990 pop. 939), Orangeburg co., central S.C., 17 mi/27 km E of Orangeburg Santee State Park on L. Marion Reservoir; 33°31'N 80°34'W. Mfg. of veneer and distribution center for grocery chain store; agr. includes timber, livestock, poultry, grain, cotton, tobacco, peanuts, peaches.

Ellport, borough (1990 pop. 1,243), Lawrence co., W Pa., suburb 1 mi/1.6 km E of Ellwood City, on Connoquenessing Creek.; 40°51'N 80°15'W. Agr. (grain, corn, hay, dairying); light mfg.

Ellsinore, town (1990 pop. 405), Carter co., S Mo., in Ozark region, 17 mi/27 km SE of Van Buren; 36°55'N 90°45'W. Mfg. (self-lighting charcoal), lumber. Surrounded by Mark Twain Nat'l Forest.

Ellston, town (1990 pop. 44), Ringgold co., S Iowa, 11 mi/18 km NE of Mt. Ayr; 40°50'N 94°06'W. Livestock, grain.

Ellsworth, county (□ 723 sq mi/1,873 sq km; 1990 pop. 6,586), central Kansas; ⊙ Ellsworth; 38°42'N 98°12'W. Smoky Hills region, drained by Smoky Hill R. Cattle, sheep, hogs, wheat, sorghum, hay; industrial valves. Oil and gas fields. Kanopolis L. Reservoir and Kanopolis State Park in SE. Formed 1867.

Ellsworth, city (1990 pop. 5,975), ⊙ Hancock co., S Maine, bet. Bangor and Mt. Desert Isl., on Union R. (falls here); 44°35'N 68°30'W. Resort and retail center. Green L. Natl. Fish Hatchery (Atlantic salmon) is here. Black Mansion (1802) is colonial mus. Settled 1763; inc. as a town, 1800; as a city, 1869.

Ellsworth 1 town (1990 pop. 451), Hamilton co., central Iowa, on Skunk R., and 17 mi/27 km SE of Webster City; 42°18'N 93°34'W. **2** town (1990 pop. 2,294), ⊙ Ellsworth co., central Kansas, on Smoky Hill R., and 35 mi/56 km WSW of Salina; 38°44'N 98°13'W. Elev. 1,540 ft/469 m. RR junction. Marketing center for cattle and winter-wheat region. Mfg. (industrial valves, feeds). Oil and gas fields in vicinity. Inc. 1868. **3** town (1990 pop. 74), Grafton co., central N.H., 7 mi/11.3 km NNW of Plymouth, in White Mt. Natl. Forest; 43°54'N 71°46'W. Mt. Kineo (3,320 ft/1,012 m) in W. Ellsworth Pond in center. **4** town (1990 pop. 2,706), ⊙ Pierce co., W Wis., 13 mi/21 km N of Red Wing, Minn.; 44°44'N 92°28'W. Dairying; livestock raising. Mfg. (contract mfg., concrete lawn ornaments). Inc. 1887.

Ellsworth 1 village (1990 pop. 224), McLean co., central Ill., 14 mi/23 km E of Bloomington; 40°27'N 88°43'W. In rich agr. area. **2** village (1990 pop. 418), Antrim co., NW Mich., 10 mi/16 km S of Charlevoix; 45°10'N 85°14'W. In resort and farm area. Mfg. (wooden pallets). **3** village (1990 pop. 580), Nobles co., SW Minn., on Iowa state line, 23 mi/37 km WSW of Worthington, near Kanasanzi Creek; 43°31'N 96°01'W. Grain, corn, soybeans; sheep, cattle, hogs; dairying; mfg. (feeds, sausages).

Ellsworth, borough (1990 pop. 1,048), Washington co., SW Pa., 12 mi/19 km ESE of Washington, adjoins Bentleyville to NE. Agr. (grain; dairying); mfg. (glass-making machinery). Inc. 1900.

Ellwood City, borough (1990 pop. 8,894), Beaver and Lawrence cos., W central Pa., on Connoquenessing Creek (enters Beaver R. 3 mi/4.8 km to W); Slippery Rock Creek enters Connoquenessing from NE. Mfg. (electrical prods., chemicals, printing and publishing, sheet-metal fabrication, plastic prods.). Agr. area (corn, hay, apples; dairying). Coal mines are in the area. McConnells Mill State Park to NE. Inc. 1892.

Elm City, town (1990 pop. 1,624), Wilson co., E central N.C., 6 mi/9.7 km NNE of Wilson, and 10 mi/16 km SSW of Rocky Mount; 35°48'N 77°51'W. Tobacco, cotton, peanuts, grain, sweet potatoes, poultry, livestock. Mfg. (wire cable).

Elm Creek, village (1990 pop. 852), Buffalo co., S central Nebr., 15 mi/24 km W of Kearney, and on Platte R; 40°43'N 99°22'W. Dairy and poultry, produce, grain, livestock. Mfg. (alfalfa pellets).

Elm Creek, 60 mi/97 km long, rises N of Jackson, NE Jackson co., SW Minn.; flows E through area of small lakes of glacial origin, through Green L., to Blue Earth R. at Winnebago; 43°47'N 95°02'W.

Elm Fork, Texas and Okla.: see NORTH FORK OF RED RIVER.

Elm Grove, city (1990 pop. 6,261), Waukesha co., SE Wis., a suburb 7 mi/11.3 km W of downtown Milwaukee; 43°02'N 88°05'W. Mfg. (trade bindery).

Elm Grove, uninc. town, Ohio co., N W.Va., residential suburb 4 mi/6.4 km SE of downtown Wheeling.

Elm Springs, town (1990 pop. 893), Washington co., NW Ark., 10 mi/16 km NNW of Fayetteville; 36°12'N 94°13'W. Mfg. (oil-field valves).

Elma 1 town (1990 pop. 653), Howard co., NE Iowa, 18 mi/29 km SW of Cresco; 43°15'N 92°26'W. Concrete blocks. Limestone quarry and gravel pits nearby. **2** town (1990 pop. 3,011), Grays Harbor co., W Wash., 25 mi/40 km W of Olympia, near Chehalis R.; 47°01'N 123°24'W. RR junction. Lumber; mfg. (plywood, chemicals). Harbor Speedway to E. Settled c.1886.

Elmdale 1 village (1990 pop. 83), Chase co., E central Kansas, on Cottonwood R., and 6 mi/9.7 km W of Cottonwood Falls; 38°22'N 96°39'W. RR junction. Livestock, grain. Chase State Fishing L. to E. **2** village (1990 pop. 130), Morrison co., central Minn., 11 mi/18 km SW of Little Falls, on North Branch Two Rivers (S) and Little Two Rivers (N), separate streams; 45°50'N 94°29'W.

Elmendorf, village (1990 pop. 568), Bexar co., S central Texas, 15 mi/24 km SE of San Antonio, near Medina R.; 29°15'N 98°19'W. In agr. area (cattle; wheat, corn, peanuts, nursery crops). Bravnig L. reservoir to W, Calaveras L. reservoir to NE.

Elmendorf Field (EL-men-dorf), air force base, S Alaska, near Knik Inlet, 4 mi/6.4 km NE of center of Anchorage; 61°15'N 149°51'W.

Elmer, town (1990 pop. 91), Macon co., N central Mo., on Chariton R., and 18 mi/29 km NW of Macon; 39°57'N 92°39'W.

Elmer, village (1990 pop. 132), Jackson co., SW Okla., 10 mi/16 km S Altus, at Salt Fork Red R., at its entrance into Red R.; 34°28'N 99°20'W. In cotton and grain area.

Elmer, borough (1990 pop. 1,571), Salem co., SW N.J., 15 mi/24 km E of Salem; 39°35'N 75°10'W. Agr. shipping center (vegetables). Inc. 1893.

Elmer City, village (1990 pop. 290), Okanogan co., N Wash., on the Columbia 2 mi/3.2 km below (N) Grand Coulee Dam, in S part of Colville Indian Reservation, on Rufus Woods L. reservoir; 48°00'N 118°57'W. Mfg. (concrete).

Elmhurst, city (1990 pop. 42,029), Du Page co., NE Ill., a suburb of Chicago; 41°53'N 87°56'W. Settled 1843, inc. 1882. A residential city, it also has 3 industrial parks. Elmhurst Col. is here, as is a mus. of lapidary art that displays numerous minerals and gemstones.

Elmhurst, township (1990 pop. 834), Lackawanna co., NE Pa., 6 mi/9.7 km ESE of Scranton, on Roaring Brook, forms Elmhurst Reservoir to SE; 41°22'N 75°32'W. Mfg. (concrete, wood prods.). Moosic Mts. to NW. Former borough reverted to township status, 1941.

Elmhurst, section of N Queens borough of N.Y. city, SE N.Y.; 40°39'N 73°53'W. Mainly residential, with a growing pop. of Asians and Latinos; some mfg.

Elmira (el-MEI-ra), city (□ 7 sq mi/18.1 sq km; 1990 pop. 33,724), ⊙ Chemung co., extreme S central N.Y., on the Chemung R.; 42°05'N 76°48'W. It is a distributing and mfg. center with plants that make electronic and fire-fighting equip., automotive parts, and iron and steel prods. Formerly Newtown, renamed for Elmira Teall, an innkeeper's daughter. The Treaty of Painted Post, ending warfare bet. settlers and the Iroquois confederation, was signed here in 1791. The city was the site of a Confederate prison camp in 1864–1865; 3,000 Confederate prisoners are buried here. The well-known Elmira Correctional Facility (est. 1876) led the way in prison reform. Mark Twain spent many summers in Elmira and is buried here. Places of interest include his study, built in the shape of a riverboat pilot's house; the Arnot Art Mus.; and a Native Amer. historical mus. Seat of Elmira Col. and a business inst. Nearby are Harris Hill, site of an annual natl. glider contest; and Newtown Battlefield State Park, with a John Sullivan Monument. Settled 1788, inc. 1864.

Elmira (el-MEI-ruh), town, S Ont., Canada, 11 mi/18 km N of Kitchener; mfg. center; dairying, wood working.

Elmira (el-MEI-ruh), town (1990 pop. 70), Ray co., NW Mo., on Crooked R., and 18 mi/29 km NNW of Richmond; 39°30'N 94°09'W.

Elmira Heights, village (□ 1 sq mi/2.6 sq km; 1990 pop. 4,359), Chemung co., S N.Y., just N of Elmira; 42°07'N 76°49'W. Settled 1779, inc. 1896.

Elmo, town (1990 pop. 179), Nodaway co., NW Mo., near Nodaway R., 18 mi. NW of Maryville; 40°31'N 95°07'W. Grain, livestock.

Elmo 1 village (1990 pop. 267), Emery co., central Utah, 16 mi/26 km NE of Castle Dale; 39°23'N 110°49'W. Cattle. Desert L. to SE. **2** village, Carbon co., S Wyo., 15 mi/24 km N of Medicine Bow Mts., 38 mi/61 km ENE of Rawlins and 2 mi/3.2 km E of Hanna. Elev. c.6,780 ft/2,067 m.

Elmont, uninc. city (□ 3 sq mi/7.8sq km; 1990 pop. 28,612), Nassau co., SE N.Y., on L.I.; 40°42'N 73°42'W. Although chiefly residential, Elmont has some light industry. Belmont Park racetrack is nearby.

Elmore 1 co. (□ 657 sq mi/1,702 sq km; 1990 pop. 49,210), E central Ala.; ⊙ Wetumpka; 32°36'N 86°08'W. Coastal plain bounded on E and S by Tallapoosa R., drained by Coosa R. Part of L. Martin is in NE; fall line crosses co. E-W. Cotton, corn, livestock; textiles. Formed 1866. **2** co. (□ 3,100 sq mi/8,029 sq km; 1990 pop. 21,205), SW Idaho; ⊙ Mountain Home; 43°20'N 115°28'W. Bounded N by Boise (including Arrow Rock Reservoir and part of Lucky Peak Reservoir) and Middle and North Forks Boise rivers, S by Snake R. (C.J. Strike Dam and Reservoir in SW), which drains SE corner. Livestock-grazing region (sheep, cattle); contains deposits of gold. Irrigated agr. regions (potatoes, vegetables, sugar beets; alfalfa, hay; wheat) are in NW, around ARROW ROCK RESERVOIR, and in SE (King Hill project). Mountain Home Air Force Base in SW. Three Isl. Crossing State Park in SE; parts of Sawtooth and Boise natl. forests in N, including part of Sawtooth Wilderness Area in NE corner; Long Tom, Little

Camas, and Anderson Ranch (on South Fork Boise) dams at center of co. Formed 1889.

Elmore, town (1990 pop. 573), Lamoille co., N central Vt., 19 mi/31 km N of Montpelier; 44°30′N 72°30′W. Includes L. Elmore, resort on small L. Elmore; Putnam State Forest nearby.

Elmore 1 village (1990 pop. 709), Faribault co., S Minn., 9 mi/14.5 km S of Blue Earth on West Branch of Blue Earth R., on Iowa state line; 43°30′N 94°05′W. Grain, soybeans; livestock; mfg. (grain processing). **2** village (1990 pop. 1,334), Ottawa co., N Ohio, 18 mi/29 km SE of Toledo, and on Portage R.; 41°28′N 83°17′W.

Elmore City or **Elmore**, village (1990 pop. 493), Garvin co., S central Okla., 13 mi/21 km SW of Pauls Valley; 34°37′N 97°24′W. In agr. area (soybeans, peanuts; sheep).

Elmsford, residential suburban village (□ 1 sq mi/ 2.6 sq km; 1990 pop. 3,938), Westchester co., SE N.Y., 3 mi/4.8 km NW of White Plains; 41°02′N 73°48′W. Mfg. (abrasives, foods, knitting machines, electron tubes, gas detectors, fire-protection equip., copying and collating machines, umbrellas, batteries, publishing, jewel bearings, wallpapers and fabric, precision-rubber molded prods.). Inc. 1910.

Elmvale, village (1991 pop. 1,678), S Ont., Canada, 23 mi/ 37 km W of Orillia; 44°35′N 79°52′W. Dairying.

Elmwood, village, S Ont., Canada, 23 mi/37 km S of Owen Sound; dairying, mixed farming.

Elmwood, city (1990 pop. 1,841), Peoria co., central Ill., 19 mi/31 km WNW of Peoria; 40°46′N 89°58′W. In agr., bituminous-coal mining, and timber area. Inc. 1867. Lorado Taft b. here; his statue *Pioneers of the Prairies* (1928) is in city park.

Elmwood, town (1990 pop. 775), Pierce co., W Wis., on Eau Galle R., and 13 mi/21 km SW of Menomonie; 44°46′N 92°09′W. In lumbering, dairying, and poultry-raising area; mfg. (syringes, serum bottles); hydroelectric plant.

Elmwood 1 village (1990 pop. 584), Cass co., SE Nebr., 25 mi/40 km WSW of Plattsmouth, and on Weeping Water Creek; 40°50′N 96°17′W. Livestock, grain. Mfg. (pickup flatbeds). **2** village, Atlantic co., SE N.J., 9 mi/ 14.5 km N of Mays Landing. Formerly named E. Paterson; name changed to Elmwood in 1972.

Elmwood Park 1 village (1990 pop. 23,206), Cook co., NE Ill., a suburb of Chicago; inc. 1914; 41°55′N 87°49′W. It is chiefly residential. On Des Plaines R. **2** village (1990 pop. 534), Racine Co., SE Wis., residential suburb 4 mi/ 6.4 km SE of Racine; 42°41′N 87°49′W. In urban growth area.

Elmwood Park, borough (1990 pop. 17,623), Bergen co., NE N.J., 2 mi/3.2 km E of Paterson; 40°53′N 74°07′W. Inc. 1916.

Elmwood Place, village (1990 pop. 2,937), Hamilton co., extreme SW Ohio, near Kentucky border, within but administratively independent of Cincinnati, Ohio; 39°11′N 84°29′W. Machinery, foundry prods. Settled 1875, inc. 1890.

Elnora, town (1990 pop. 679), Daviess co., SW Ind., near West Fork of White R., 15 mi/24 km NNE of Washington; 38°53′N 87°05′W. In farming and dairying area; cheese, cargo trailers.

Elnora (el-NO-ruh), village (1991 pop. 265), S central Alta., Canada, 32 mi/51 km SE of Red Deer; wheat, mixed farming.

Eloise (el-o-EEZ), village, Wayne co., SE Mich., 2 mi/ 3.2 km E of Wayne, and on a branch of the R. Rouge; 42°17′N 83°20′W. Area has been absorbed by cities of Wayne, Westland, and Inkster, all Detroit suburbs.

Elon College (EE-lahn), town (1990 pop. 4,394), Alamance co., N central N.C., suburb 4 mi/6.4 km W of Burlington; 36°05′N 79°30′W. Tobacco, grain, potatoes, chickens, hogs, dairying. Mfg. (industrial valves, textile machinery, textile chemicals, ham processing, hosiery). Seat of Elon Col.

Elora (e-LO-ruh), village (1991 pop. 3,261), S Ont., Canada, on Grand R., and 14 mi/23 km NW of Guelph; 43°41′N 80°26′W. Cattle center; mfg. of farm implements, furniture; resort.

Elota, Mexico: see LA CRUZ.

Elota River, c.100 mi/161 km long, W Mexico; rises in Sierra Madre Occidental in Durango near Sinaloa border; flows SW through fertile coastal lowlands of Sinaloa, past El Roble and La Cruz, to the Pacific 4 mi/ 6.4 km SW of La Cruz.

Eloxochitlán 1 (e-lo-ho-chee-TLAN), town (1990 pop. 821), Hidalgo, central Mexico, in Sierra Madre Oriental, 20 mi/32 km NNW of Metztitlán. Cereals, beans, fruit, livestock. Also known as San Agustín. **2** town (1990 pop. 1,331), Puebla, central Mexico, on E slope of Sierra Madre, on Veracruz border, 30 mi/48 km E of Tehuacán. Corn, sugarcane, livestock.

Eloxochitlán de Flores Magón (e-lo-ho-chee-TLAN de FLO-res mah-GON), town (1990 pop. 1,443), in the N of the state of Oaxaca, Mexico, 14 mi/22 km ENE of Teotitlán de Flores Magón. Rugged terrain in Río Papaloapan drainage; 18°11′N 96°52′W. Elev. 8,497 ft/ 2,590 m. Agr. (corn, beans, wheat, chiles, potatoes, fruits, woods), livestock and poultry breeding and raising. No direct road access. Formerly San Antonio Eloxochitlán.

Eloy, town (1990 pop. 7,211), Pinal co., S Ariz., on Santa Cruz R., 48 mi/77 km NW of Tucson, and 12 mi/19 km SE of Casa Grande; 32°45′N 111°36′W. Elev. 1,565 ft/ 477 m. Agr. area (wheat, alfalfa, cotton, cantaloupe, lettuce); cattle, sheep, poultry, hogs; vegetable packing; cotton mill; sawmill. Inc. 1940. Tohono O'odham (Papago) Indian Reservation to W; Picacho Reservoir to NE; Picacho Mts. to E; Picacho Peak State Park to SE.

Elrosa (el-RO-zuh), village (1990 pop. 205), Stearns co., central Minn., 37 mi/60 km W of St. Cloud; 45°33′N 94°57′W. Grain, poultry, livestock; dairying.

Elrose, town (1991 pop. 577), SW Sask., Canada, 50 mi/ 80 km ESE of Kindersley; 51°12′N 108°02′W. Wheat, mixed farming.

Elroy 1 uninc. town (1990 pop. 4,028), Wayne co., E central N.C., residential suburb 6 mi/9.7 km ESE of downtown Goldsboro; 35°19′N 77°55′W. Seymour-Johnson Air Force Base to W. **2** town (1990 pop. 1,533), Juneau co., S central Wis., on Baraboo R., and 45 mi/ 72 km ESE of La Crosse; 43°44′N 90°16′W. In timber and farm area (dairy prods.; poultry, livestock). Light mfg. E terminus of La Crosse State Trail. Settled 1854, inc. 1885.

Elsa, town (1990 pop. 5,242), Hidalgo co., extreme S Texas, in lower Rio Grande valley, 10 mi/16 km E of Edinburg; 26°18′N 97°59′W. Trade, shipping center in irrigated citrus, vegetables, cotton area; mfg. (vertical and mini blinds). Settled 1927, inc. 1933.

Elsa, uninc. locality (1986 pop. 294), 67 mi/108 km NE of Klondike Highway, and 281 mi/452 km N of Whitehorse, Yukon Territory, Canada. Silver- and lead-mining service center.

Elsah (EL-zuh), village (1990 pop. 851), Jersey co., W Ill., on the Mississippi R., and 10 mi/16 km WNW of Alton; 38°57′N 90°20′W. In agr. area. Seat of Principia Col.

Elsberry, city (1990 pop. 1,898), Lincoln co., E Mo., near Mississippi R., 17 mi/27 km NW of Troy; 39°10′N 90°47′W. Corn, soybeans, apples; hogs, cattle; light mfg.; limestone prods. Has a U.S. nursery (plant materials center). Est. 1871.

Elsie 1 (el-SEE), village (1990 pop. 957), Clinton co., S central Mich., 11 mi/18 km NE of St. Johns, on Maple R.; 43°05′N 84°23′W. In farm area (dairy prods.; grain, sugar beets). Mfg. seat tracks. **2** village (1990 pop. 153), Perkins co., SW central Nebr., 18 mi/29 km E of Grant; 40°51′N 101°23′W. Feeds and fertilizer; custom handguns and rifles.

Elsinore, village (1990 pop. 608), Sevier co., central Utah, on Sevier R., 8 mi/12.9 km SSW of Richfield; 38°40′N 112°09′W. Elev. 5,335 ft/1,626 m. Sugar beets. Pavant Mts. WNW. Historic White Rock School (1898); part of Fishlake Natl. Forest to SE and NW. Settled 1874.

Elsinore, Lake, Calif.: see LAKE ELSINORE.

Elsmere 1 (ELZ-mir), town (1990 pop. 5,935), New Castle co., N Del., residential suburb 2 mi/3.2 km W of downtown Wilmington; 39°44′N 75°35′W. **2** town (1990 pop. 6,847), Kenton co., N Ky., a residential suburb 9 mi/14.5 km SW of Cincinnati, Ohio, and 7 mi/11.3 km SW of Covington, Ky.; 38°59′N 84°35′W. Cincinnati–Northern Ky. Internatl. Airport to NW. Turfway Park racetrack to NW.

Elsmere, suburban village (1990 pop. 4,200), Albany co., E N.Y., 4 mi/6.4 km SW of downtown Albany; 42°37′N 73°49′W.

Elsmore, village (1990 pop. 91), Allen co., SE Kansas, 16 mi/26 km SE of Iola; 37°47′N 95°09′W. In livestock, grain, and dairy region.

Eltingville, sect. of Richmond borough of N.Y. city, SE N.Y., on SE Staten Isl., 8 mi/12.9 km SW of St. George; 40°33′N 74°10′E. Great Kills Park is just E.

Elton (EL-tuhn), town (1990 pop. 1,277), Jefferson Davis parish, SW La., 35 mi/56 km NE of Lake Charles city; 30°29′N 92°42′W. In agr. area (rice, sweet potatoes, soybeans; livestock); catfish, crawfish; mfg. of milled rice; natural gas field nearby.

Elvaston, village (1990 pop. 198), Hancock co., W Ill., 6 mi/9.7 km WSW of Carthage; 40°23′N 91°15′W. In agr. area.

Elverson, borough (1990 pop. 470), Chester co., SE Pa., 13 mi/21 km SSE of Reading. Agr. (grain, apples; dairying; livestock, poultry); mfg. (textiles, furniture, machinery, wooden gazebos). French Creek State Park to NE.

Elvins, city (1990 pop. 1,391), St. Francois co., E Mo. Merged with Flat River, Rivermines, and Esther to become PARK HILLS, 1993; 37°50′N 90°31′W.

Elvira, Cape (el-VEI-ruh), NE extremity of Victoria Isl., central Franklin Dist., N.W.T., Canada, on Viscount Melville Sound; 73°16′N 107°5′W.

Elwell, Lake, Liberty and Toole cos., N Mont., on Marias R., 35 mi/56 km ESE of Shelby; c.30 mi/48 km long; 48°18′N 111°04′W. Max. capacity 1,425,000 acre-ft. Willow Creek forms 10-mi/16-km N arm. Formed by Tiber Dam (190 ft/58 m), built (1956) by the Bureau of Reclamation for flood control, water supply, and recreation. Formerly Tiber Reservoir.

Elwell, Mount (7,812 ft/2,381 m), peak of the Sierra Nevada, Sierra co., NE Calif., 13 mi/21 km SW of Portola. In recreational region; trail to summit.

Elwha River (EL-wah), c.30 mi/48 km long, NW Wash.; rises at Mt. Olympus; flows generally N through L. Mills (Glines Canyon Dam) and L. Aldwell (Elisha Dam) before entering Strait of Juan de Fuca 5 mi/8 km W of Port Angeles; near source, Glines Canyon Dam (completed 1927; 210 ft/64 m high, 508 ft/155 m long) forms reservoir, furnishes power. Lower Elwha Indian Reservation E of mouth.

Elwood, city (1990 pop. 9,494), Madison co., central Ind., 15 mi/24 km NW of Anderson; 40°17′N 85°50′W. It has large canneries and plants that make a variety of metal, electrical, and machine goods, including jewelry, automotive fuel tanks, paint, safety equip., wire prods., and metal platings. Birthplace of Wendell L. Willkie. Est. 1853. Inc. 1872.

Elwood, town (1990 pop. 1,079), Doniphan co., extreme NE Kansas, on right bank of Missouri R.; 39°45′N 94°52′W. Residential suburb of St. Joseph, Mo. 1 mi/ 1.6 km W (across river). Mfg. (asphalt, animal health prods., concrete prods.). Sawmill. Flooding occurred here in 1993. Founded 1856, inc. 1873.

Elwood 1 village, (1990 pop. 951), Will co., NE Ill., 9 mi/ 14.5 km S of Joliet; 41°24′N 88°06′W. In agr. area. U.S. Army arsenal, now abandoned, nearby. Much of arsenal to become tall-grass prairie. **2** village (1990 pop. 679), ⊙ Gosper co., S Nebr., located in the Platte River valley, 14 mi/23 km SW of Lexington; 40°35′N 99°51′W. Grain, livestock. Elmwood Reservoir immediately N, Johnson Reservoir and Johnson L. State Recreation Area further N at co. boundary, on Tri-County Supply Canal. Johnson Canyon Power Plant, part of tri-co. irrigation and power project. **3** village (1990 pop. 575), Box Elder co., N Utah, 14 mi/23 km NNW of Brigham City on Bear R.; 41°40′N 112°08′W. Elev. 4,285 ft/ 1,306 m. Sugar beets, barley, wheat; dairying; cattle, sheep. Wasatch Natl. Forest, including Wellsville Mt. Wilderness Area, to E. Settled 1868, named 1900.

Elwyn (EL-win), uninc. town, Del. co., SE Pa., residential suburb 13 mi/21 km WSW of Philadelphia; 39°54′N 75°24′W. Light mfg. Franklin Mint and Mus. to W.

Area in square miles is shown by the symbol □ capital city or county seat by ⊙

Ely (EE-lee), city (1990 pop. 4,756), ⊙ White Pine co., E Nev., in E foothills of Egan Range; 39°15′N 114°52′W. Elev. 6,427 ft/1,959 m. Trade center for mining, dairying, cattle, sheep area. Extremely productive, large copper pit mine at Ruth, 5 mi/8 km to W, and gold, silver, lead mines nearby; mfg. (petroleum, refining). Great Basin Natl. Park, including Wheeler Peak is SE, in Snake Range. Settled 1868, inc. 1907. Ward Charcoal Ovens State Historical Site to S; Schell Creek Range to E; parts of Humboldt Natl. Forest to E and SW. Hq. and S terminus of Northern Nevada RR, junction of spurs to Ruth (W), and McGill (NNE); Northern Nevada RR is both a working short line and mus.

Ely 1 (EE-lee), town (1990 pop. 517), Linn co., E Iowa, 8 mi/12.9 km SSE of Cedar Rapids; 41°52′N 91°35′W. Feed milling. **2** town (1990 pop. 3,968), St. Louis co., NE Minn., 75 mi/121 km of Duluth, 16 mi/26 km SW of S shore of Shagawa L., at E end of Vermilion Iron Range; 47°54′N 91°50′W. In Superior Natl. Forest. Iron-mining center, with mines within city limits; dairying; poultry; oats, hay; mfg. (printing, parkas, varied light mfg.); resort activities; outfitting center for canoe expeditions. Hq. of Superior Natl. Forest. Bear Lake State Park and Kabetogama State Forest to SW; Bear Isl. State Forest to S; Burntside State Forest to NW; Indian Valley Ski Area to E; parts of Boundary Waters Canoe Area to NW, N, and E. Inc. as village 1888, as city 1891.

Elyria (ee-LIR-ee-uh), city (1990 pop. 56,746), ⊙ Lorain co., N Ohio, on the Black R.; inc. 1833; 41°22′N 82°06′W. It is an industrial center in a farm region. Its manufactures include plastics, automotive parts, motors, tools, and machine and foundry prods. Cascade Park, with waterfalls, caves, nature trails, and a zoo, is in the heart of the city. Also in Elyria are a junior col. and Elyria Memorial Hosp.

Elyria (el-IR-ee-uh), village (1990 pop. 61), Valley co., central Nebr., 7 mi/11.3 km NNW of Ord, and on North Loup R; 41°40′N 99°00′W. Ft. Hartsuff State Historical Park to N.

Ely's Harbour, inlet, W Bermuda, bet. Somerset Isl. and NW end of Bermuda Isl.

Elysburg (EE-lais-buhrg), uninc. town (1990 pop. 1,890), Northumberland co., E central Pa., 5 mi/8 km N of Shamokin; 40°52′N 76°32′W. Mfg. includes apparel, carbide cutting tools. Agr. includes dairying, livestock, poultry; corn, hay.

Elysian (e-LEE-zhuhn), village (1990 pop. 445), Le Sueur co., S Minn., 16 mi/26 km E of Mankato, on ½ mi/⅘ km wide neck of land bet. L. Elysian reservoir (S) and E end of L. Frances (N); 44°12′N 93°40′W. Grain, soybeans, peas; livestock, poultry; dairying; mfg. (plastic molding, light mfg.). Numerous small lakes in area.

Emanuel (em-AN-yoo-uhl), county (1990 pop. 20,546), E central Ga., ⊙ Swainsboro; 32°35′N 82°18′W. Bounded NE by Ogeechee R.; drained by Ohoopee and Canoochee rivers. Coastal agr. plain specializing in cotton, corn, tobacco, wheat, soybeans, peanuts; hogs, cattle; timber. Formed 1812.

Emaus, Pa.: see EMMAUS.

Embarcadero de Banes (em-bahr-kah-DER-o dai BAH-naiz), port for Banes Holguín prov., E Cuba, on sheltered Banes Bay, 38 mi/61 km E of Holguín; 20°52′N 75°42′W. Agr. (sugar, tropical fruit); bulk grain and liquid cargo transfer.

Embarras River (AM-brah), 185 mi/298 km long, in E Ill.; rises near Urbana; flows generally S and SE, past Newton and Lawrenceville, to the Wabash 6 mi/9.7 km SW of Vincennes, Ind.; 40°05′N 88°15′W. Receives North Fork (55 mi/89 km long) SE of Newton.

Embarrass, village (1990 pop. 461), Waupaca co., central Wis., on Embarrass R., and 8 mi/12.9 km SSW of Shawano; 44°40′N 88°42′W. Lumbering. Mfg. (furniture). Navarino Hills ski area to E.

Embarrass River, c.45 mi/72 km long., in E central Wis.; formed by North (20 mi/32 km), Middle (40 mi/64 km), and South (26 mi/42 km) branches, all rising in Shawano co. and converging NE of Marion; flows E and S to Wolf R. at New London.

Embden, town (1990 pop. 659), Somerset co., central

Maine, on the Kennebec R., and 12 mi/19 km NNW of Skowhegan; 44°55′N 69°55′W. Resort area.

Embreville or **Embreeville**, village, Washington co., NE Tenn., on Nolichucky R., and 11 mi/18 km SSW of Johnson City; iron, lead, zinc, manganese deposits.

Embro, village, S Ont., Canada, on Middle Thames R., and 8 mi/13 km WNW of Woodstock. Agr. (dairying; grain).

Embrun (EM-bruhn), village, SE Ont., Canada, 23 mi/37 km ESE of Ottawa. Agr. (dairying).

Embudo (em-BOO-do), uninc. village (1990 pop. 400), Rio Arriba co., N N.Mex., 34 mi/55 km N of Santa Fe, on Rio Grande. Agr. (cattle, sheep; alfalfa, chilies). Mfg. (pottery). Parts of Carson Natl. Forest to N and S.

Emden, village (1990 pop. 459), Logan co., central Ill., 12 mi/19 km NNW of Lincoln; 40°17′N 89°29′W. In agr. area.

Emerado, village (1990 pop. 483), Grand Forks co., E N.Dak., 16 mi/26 km W of Grand Forks; 47°55′N 97°21′W. Service center for Grand Forks Air Force Base, to NW.

Emerald Bay 1 uninc. village, El Dorado co., E Calif., in the Sierra Nevada, on Emerald Bay (at SW end of L. Tahoe). Emerald Bay State Park to Rubicon Point (N). **2** uninc. village, Orange co., S Calif., residential suburb 38 mi/61 km SE of downtown Los Angeles, and 2 mi/3.2 km NW of Laguna Beach, on Emerald Bay, Pacific Ocean; bounded NW and SE by Laguna Beach corporate limits.

Emerald Coast, local name for the Gulf of Mexico coast of NW Fla. bet. Pensacola on the W and Panama City on the E, centered on Fort Walton Beach and Destin. Named for the emerald green color often seen in the Gulf's nearshore waters.

Emerald Island, W Franklin dist., N.W.T., Canada, in Ballantyne Strait of the Arctic Ocean, at mouth of Fitzwilliam Strait, bet. Prince Patrick Isl. and Melville Isl.; 76°46′N 114°30′W. Isl. is c.20 mi/32 km long and 5 mi/8 km–10 mi/16 km wide.

Emerald Isle, town (1990 pop. 2,434), Carteret co., E N.C., 15 mi/24 km WSW of Morehead City, on Atlantic Ocean; 34°40′N 77°01′W. Beach resort area. Bogue Sound to N (Intercoastal Waterway). N.C. Aquarium and Theodore Roosevelt State Natural Area to E. Bridge to mainland 7 mi/11.3 km to W.

Emerald Lake, resort village, SE B.C., Canada, near Alta. prov. border, in Rocky Mts., in Yoho Natl. Park, on small Emerald L., 4 mi/6 km NW of Field; 63°33′N 131°13′W.

Emerald Lake Hills, uninc. town (1990 pop. 3,328), San Mateo co., W Calif., residential suburb 22 mi/35 km S of downtown San Francisco, and 2 mi/3.2 km WSW of Redwood City, in E foothills of Santa Cruz Mts.; 37°28′N 122°16′W. Hetch Hetchy Aqueduct passes to N. San Francisco State Fish and Game Refuge to W, including Upper and Lower Crystal Springs reservoirs, which lie on San Andreas Fault.

Emerson, town (1991 pop. 721), SE Man., Canada, on Red R., and 65 mi/105 km S of Winnipeg, at Minn.-N.Dak. state line; 49°00′N 97°12′W. Dairying; mixed farming; livestock.

Emerson 1 town (1990 pop. 1,201), Bartow co., NW Ga., 4 mi/6.4 km SE of Cartersville; 34°08′N 84°44′W. Mfg. (pesticides). **2** town (1990 pop. 476), Mills co., SW Iowa, 19 mi/31 km E of Glenwood; 41°01′N 95°24′W. Agr. region (corn; livestock).

Emerson 1 village (1990 pop. 317), Columbia co., SW Ark., 13 mi/21 km S of Magnolia; 33°06′N 93°12′W. Mfg. (lumber, bark, and sawdust). **2** village (1990 pop. 791), Dakota, Dixon, Thurston cos., NE Nebr., 23 mi/37 km SW of Sioux City, Iowa, near Logan Creek; 42°16′N 96°43′W. Livestock; grain.

Emerson, borough (1990 pop. 6,930), Bergen co., NE N.J., 6 mi/9.7 km N of Hackensack; 40°58′N 74°01′W. Settled 1875, inc. 1909. Largely residential.

Emery, county (□ 4,461 sq mi/11,554 sq km; 1990 pop. 10,332), central Utah; ⊙ Castle Dale; 38°59′N 110°41′W. Drained by Price, San Rafael, and Muddy rivers, bounded on E by Green R. Elev. 6,247 ft/1,904 m. Alfalfa, peaches, melons (at Green R. in E); cattle; coal.

Part of Wasatch Plateau and Manti–La Sal Natl. Forest in NW; small part of Capitol Reef Natl. Park in SW corner. Huntington and Millsite state parks, Goblin Valley State Park in S. Green R. State Park on E boundary. Formed 1880.

Emery 1 village (1990 pop. 417), Hanson co., SE central S.Dak., 22 mi/35 km ESE of Mitchell; 43°36′N 97°37′W. In agr. area. **2** village (1990 pop. 300), Emery co., central Utah, 25 mi/40 km SSW of Castle Dale. Manti–La Sal Natl. Forest to NW; Fishlake Natl. Forest to W; 38°55′N 111°15′W. Settled 1881.

Emeryville, city (1990 pop. 5,740), Alameda co., W Calif., on San Francisco Bay, 2 mi/3.2 km N of downtown Oakland, at E end of San Francisco–Oakland Bay Bridge; 37°51′N 122°18′W. Mfg. (beet-sugar refining; dairy prods.; plastics; pharmaceuticals; furniture; compressors; structural metalwork); software development and printing and publishing. Petroleum research laboratory. Golden Gate Fields Race Track to N. Inc. 1896.

Emhouse, village (1990 pop. 195), Navarro co., E central Texas, 8 mi/12.9 km NW of Corsicana, near Chambers Creek; 32°09′N 96°34′W. In agr. area.

Emigrant Gap, uninc. village, Placer co., E Calif., at pass (Emigrant Gap) near crest of the Sierra Nevada, 35 mi/56 km NE of Auburn, near Bear Creek; elev. 5,250 ft/1,600 m. Timber; hunting, fishing. An emigrant (Donner Party) trail passed here. Tahoe Natl. Forest to N and S.

Emigrant Lake, Tuolumne co., E Calif., in the Sierra Nevada, on West Fork Cherry Creek, 38 mi/61 km ENE of Sonora; c.2 mi/3.2 km long. S of Granite Dome and N of Yosemite Natl. Park.

Emigrant Pass, N Eureka co., N central Nev., 27 mi/43 km WSW of Elko, in S. Elev. 6,114 ft/1,864 m. Part of Tuscarora Mts., in Humboldt R. Interstate Highway 80 (formerly U.S. 40) passes through. Important point on Humboldt Trail; used by pioneer settlers headed for Calif. in 1840s and 1850s.

Emigsville, uninc. town (1990 pop. 2,580), Manchester township, York co., S Pa., suburb 4 mi/6.4 km N of York. Agr. (grain, dairying, livestock); mfg. (electronic components, pharmaceuticals, metal plating, concrete blocks, fabricated metal prods.). John Rudy Co. Park to NE.

Emiliano Zapata (e-mee-lee-AH-no zah-PAH-tah), city (1990 pop. 14,833) and township, Tabasco, SE Mexico, on Usumacinta R., and 80 mi/129 km ESE of Villahermosa; 17°42′N 91°46′W. Rubber, rice, tobacco, fruit, timber.

Emiliano Zapata 1 (e-mee-lee-AH-no zah-PAH-tah), town (1990 pop. 19,354), ⊙ Emiliano Zapata municipio, Morelos, central Mexico, 7 mi/12 km SSE of Cuernavaca. Sugarcane, cereals, fruit, livestock. **2** town (1990 pop. 7,996), in extreme SE of Hidalgo, Mexico, 28 mi/45 km SE of Pachuca de Soto near Apan; 19°40′N 98°32′W; elev. 6,755 ft/2,059 m. On Mexico Highway 115, indirect access to Mexico City by highway, rail service.

Emiliano Zapata, Mexico: see DOS RÍOS.

Emily, village (1990 pop. 613), Crow Wing co., central Minn., 27 mi/43 km NNE of Brainerd, on W shore of Emily L.; 46°43′N 93°57′W. Light mfg; agr. (dairying; poultry; oats, alfalfa). Emily State Forest to E; Land O' Lakes State Forest to N. Numerous small lakes in area.

Emily, Lake, Pope co., W Minn., 27 mi/43 km SSW of Alexandria; 5 mi/8 km long, 1 mi/1.6 km wide; 45°30′N 95°38′W. Elev. 1,078 ft/329 m. Drains W into Chippewa R.

Eminence 1 town (1990 pop. 2,055), Henry co., N Ky., 21 mi/34 km NW of Frankfort, in Bluegrass region, near source of Little Kentucky R.; 38°22′N 85°10′W. Agr. (tobacco, grain; horses, cattle, hogs, poultry; dairying); mfg. (golf bags, electronic equipment, copper and brass bars, steel processing). **2** town (1990 pop. 582), ⊙ Shannon co., S Mo., in the Ozarks, on Jacks Fork of Current R., and 35 mi/56 km S of Salem; 37°08′N 91°21′W. Resort; former copper mines; lumber prods. Tourism. Outfitting center for canoeing and fishing. Large springs and caves nearby. At center of Ozark Natl. Scenic Riverways.

Cross references are shown in SMALL CAPITALS. The pronunciation key is on page xv. The dates of population figures are on page xii.

Eminence, village, Morgan co., central Ind., 13 mi/21 km NW of Martinsville. Agr. area (corn, soybeans; hogs). Settled 1855.

Emington, village (1990 pop. 135), Livingston co., E central Ill., 15 mi/24 km ENE of Pontiac; 40°58′N 88°21′W. In agr. area.

Emlenton (EM-len-tuhn), borough (1990 pop. 834), Venango co., W central Pa., 15 mi/24 km SSE of Franklin, on Allegheny R. Agr. (dairying); light mfg. (lumber); bituminous coal. Kahle L. reservoir to NE.

Emma, Mount (7,698 ft/2,346 m), Mohave co., NW Ariz., near Colorado R., c.80 mi/129 km SW of Kanab, Utah, in W extension of Grand Canyon Natl. Park.

Emmastad (E-mahs-taht), town, E central Curaçao, Neth. Antilles, on Schottegat harbor, just N of Willemstad; 12°08′N 68°55′W. Site of one of the world's largest oil refineries.

Emmaus (E-mous), borough (1990 pop. 11,157), Lehigh co., E Pa., a suburb 5 mi/8 km SSW of downtown Allentown, on Little Lehigh Creek; 40°32′N 75°30′W. It is chiefly residential, with some light mfg. (textiles, pumps, heating equip., apparel, printing and publishing). Allentown Queen City Municipal Airport to N. Bieber Farmhouse (1734) to NW. Founded in 1740 by Moravians. Inc. 1859.

Emmet 1 county (□ 402 sq mi/1,041 sq km; 1990 pop. 11,569), NW Iowa, on Minn. boundary; ⊙ Estherville; 43°22′N 94°40′W. Rolling prairie region, in Iowa Lakes Region (glacial origin), with Swan, Ingram, and High lakes in S, Twelve Mile L. in SW, L. Okamandpeedan (also called Turtle L.) in NE of Minn. Boundary and drained by East and West Des Moines rivers. Includes Fort Defiance State Park in W; Okamanpeedan State Park in NE. Agr. (cattle, hogs, poultry; corn, oats, soybeans); sand and gravel pits. Formed 1851. **2** county (□ 882 sq mi/2,284 sq km; 1990 pop. 25,040), NW Mich.; ⊙ Petoskey. Bounded W by Little Traverse Bay and L. Michigan, N by the Straits of Mackinac; 45°34′N 84°58′W; drained by small Maple R. Agr. (dairy prods.; potatoes; cattle, poultry). Mfg. at Petoskey. Sawmills, fisheries. Year-round resorts (hiking, fishing, camping, winter sports). Includes Wycamp, Pickerel, Crooked, and Paradise lakes; Walloon L. in SW, forms part of boundary bet. W Charlevoix co.; Wilderness State Park in N, Fort Michilimackinac State Park in NE corner, Petoskey State Park at Bay View. Organized 1853.

Emmet 1 village (1990 pop. 446), Nevada co., SW Ark., 8 mi/12.9 km NE of Hope near Terre Rouge Creek; 33°43′N 93°28′W. **2** village (1990 pop. 70), Holt co., N Nebr., 7 mi/11.3 km W of O'Neill, and on Elkhorn R; 42°28′N 98°48′W.

Emmetsburg, city (1990 pop. 3,940), ⊙ Palo Alto co., NW Iowa, resort on Five Island L., 23 mi/37 km E of Spencer, near West Des Moines R.; 43°06′N 94°40′W. RR junction; mfg. (animal feeds; dairy prods.; mattresses, electrical transformers, crushed limestone; printing). Has a branch of Iowa Lakes Community Col. Founded 1856.

Emmett, town (1990 pop. 4,601), ⊙ Gem co., W Idaho, on Payette R. (Black Canyon Dam to NE), and 25 mi/40 km NW of Boise; 43°52′N 116°29′W. RR junction; in agr. area (grain; fruit [esp. apples, plums]; dairying); mfg. (sawmills, plywood, concrete). Settled as trading post 1864, inc. as village 1900, as city 1909. Surrounding region lies within Boise irrigation project.

Emmett 1 village (1990 pop. 165), Pottawatomie co., NE Kansas, 20 mi/32 km ESE of Westmoreland; 39°18′N 96°03′W. **2** village (1990 pop. 297), St. Clair co., E Mich., 17 mi/27 km W of Port Huron; 42°59′N 82°46′W. In agr. area.

Emmitsburg, town (1990 pop. 1,688), Frederick co., N Md., near Pa. state line, on Toms Creek, 21 mi/34 km NNE of Frederick; 39°42′N 77°20′W. In agr. area (grain; dairy prods.). Seat of Mt. St. Mary's Col., founded in 1808, and the alma mater of Monseigneur John McCloskey, the first American cardinal, and Edward Douglass White, who became (1910) the first southerner named chief justice of the Supreme Court since the Civil War. The Stone House, in which Mother Elizabeth Seton founded the Sisters of Charity in 1808, has been preserved and is open to the public. The academy she founded here was the first in the Catholic parochial school system of the U.S. Mother Seton became the first American to be canonized a saint of the Catholic Church in 1975. The Grotto of Lourdes, an almost exact replica of the famous shrine in Lourdes, France, also is here. Area settled c.1734 as Poplar Fields. Town was laid out in 1785.

Emmonak (EE-mo-nak), village (1990 pop. 642), W Alaska, c.160 mi/257 km NNW of Bethel, near S channel of Yukon Delta; 62°46′N 164°32′W. Village of Alakanuk to S. Bering Sea coast 5 mi/8 km W. Air service. Fishing, hunting, trapping.

Emmons, county (□ 1,503 sq mi/3,893 sq km; 1990 pop. 4,830), S N.Dak., borders S.Dak. on S; ⊙ Linton; 46°16′N 100°14′W. Agr. area drained by Beaver, Little Beaver, and Long Lake Creeks. Wheat, barley; cattle; dairying. Formed 1879; organized 1883. L. Oahe of the Missouri R. forms W border and also Mountain/Central time zone boundary.

Emmons, village (1990 pop. 439), Freeborn co., S Minn., on Iowa state line, 11 mi/18 km SW of Albert Lea, in lake region; 43°30′N 93°28′W. Agr. (grain, soybeans, alfalfa; livestock, poultry; dairying); mfg. (agr. equipment). State Line L. to E.

Emmons Glacier, Wash.: see MOUNT RAINIER NATIONAL PARK.

Emmons, Mount, Duchesne co., NE Utah (13,440 ft/4,097 m): see UINTA RIVER. In High Uintas Wilderness Area, Ashley Natl. Forest, 35 mi/56 km NNW of Roosevelt.

Emo (EE-mo), town (1991 pop. 1,275), W Ont., Canada, on Rainy R., and 20 mi/32 km W of Fort Frances; 48°37′N 93°50′W. Dairying; mixed farming; lumber.

Emory 1 town (1990 pop. 963), ⊙ Rains co., NE Texas, 45 mi/72 km NW of Tyler; 32°52′N 95°46′W. Elev. 464 ft/141 m. In agr. area (cattle; vegetables; cotton); light mfg. L. Tawakoni reservoir to W; L. Fork reservoir to E. **2** uninc. town, Washington co., SW Va., 9 mi/14.5 km NE of Abingdon, 2 mi/3.2 km NE of Meadowview; 36°46′N 81°50′W. Agr. (dairying; livestock, poultry; corn, alfalfa). Seat of Emory and Henry Col.

Emory, Lake, N.C.: see FRANKLIN, town.

Emory Peak, Texas: see CHISOS MOUNTAINS.

Empalme (em-PAHL-mai), city (1990 pop. 35,954) and township, ⊙ Empalme municipio, Sonora, NW Mexico, on Empalme Bay, Gulf of California, 7 mi/12 km ENE of Guaymas; 27°58′N 110°50′W. Elev. 6.6 ft/2 m. On Mexico Highway. 15. Agr. (cotton, fruit). Rapid development because of increasing shrimp fishing.

Empire 1 town, Dodge co., S central Ga., 12 mi/19 km NW of Eastman; 32°20′N 83°17′W. **2** former town, Coos co., SW Oregon, W side of city of Coos Bay (merged with Coos Bay in 1960s, giving city 2 downtown areas), on Coos Bay, 3 mi/4.8 km NW of downtown Coos Bay. Paper mill.

Empire 1 uninc. village, Stanislaus co., central Calif., 5 mi/8 km E of Modesto, on Tuolumne R. Irrigated agr. area. Modesto Main Canal to N. **2** village (1990 pop. 401), Clear Creek co., N central Colo., near source of Clear Creek, in Front Range, and 35 mi/56 km W of Denver; elev. 8,601 ft/2,622 m; 39°45′N 105°40′W. Mining point surrounded by Arapaho Natl. Forest. Berthoud Pass to NW; Continental Divide to W. **3** village (1990 pop. 2,654), Plaquemines parish, extreme SE La., on W bank (levee) of the Mississippi R., and 50 mi/80 km SE of New Orleans, in the delta; 29°25′N 89°37′W. Elev. 4 ft/1 m. Hunting, fishing (fish, shrimp, crabs, oysters); mfg. (fish meal, machinery). Doullut Canal, with lock through the Mississippi levee here, connects river with waterways leading S into Gulf of Mexico. Oil field in vicinity. Named after the Empire Canal built in 1885. **4** village (1990 pop. 355), Leelanau co., NW Mich., 22 mi/35 km WNW of Traverse City, on L. Michigan; 44°48′N 86°03′W. In cherry-and grape- growing region; winery; apple juice and fruit processing. Resort area. Sleeping Bear Dunes Natl. Lakeshore to N and S; Timber L. ski area to E. **5** uninc. village (1990 pop. 300), Washoe co., NW Nev., 72 mi/116 km NNE of Reno, and 6 mi/9.7 km S of Gerlach. Gypsum mining. Pyramid L. Indian Reservation to SW. Mud L. to SE. **6** village (1990 pop. 364), Jefferson co., E Ohio, 10 mi/16 km N of Steubenville, and on Ohio R.; 40°31′N 80°37′W.

Empire City, village (1990 pop. 219), Stephens co., S central Okla., 6 mi/9.7 km SW of Duncan; 34°27′N 98°02′W. Oil production and cattle-raising region.

Empire State Building, bldg. in central Manhattan, N.Y. city, on Fifth Ave. bet. 33d and 34th sts. Designed by the firm of Shreve, Lamb, and Harmon and built 1930–1931. For many years it was the tallest bldg. in the world, having 102 stories. In 1951 a television mast was added, raising its height from 1,250 ft/381 m to 1,472 ft/449 m. An office bldg., it accommodates some 25,000 tenants. On a very clear day the view from its highest observation tower embraces an area with a circumference of nearly 200 mi/322 km.

Emporia 1 (em-POR-ee-uh), city (1990 pop. 25,512), ⊙ Lyon co., E central Kansas, in the Flint Hills bet. the Neosho and Cottonwood rivers, 50 mi/80 km SW of Topeka on Kansas Turnpike; 38°24′N 96°11′W. Elev. 1,150 ft/351 m. Commercial and shipping (RR and highway) center for a large cattle and grain area. Mfg. (soybean oil, engines, printing machinery, baked goods, meat prods., vehicular lighting equipment, pet foods, fabricated metal prod., ceramic insulation, valves, hose fittings). Emporia State Univ. in the city. William Allen White (locally renowed editor) made the small-town *Emporia Gazette* a nationally known newspaper. William Allen White home and sculpture park here. Lyon State Fishing L. to NE. Inc. 1857. **2** independent city (□ 7 sq mi/18.1 sq km; 1990 pop. 5,306), ⊙ Greensville co., S Va. (separate from surrounding Greensville co.), on Meherrin R., 38 mi/61 km SSW of Petersburg, near N.C. state line; 36°41′N 77°32′W. RR junction; mfg. (wooden wall panels, plywood, printing and publishing, iron castings, poultry processing, textile dyeing and finishing, clothing); shipping; processing center for agr. (cotton, peanuts, tobacco, grain, melons, soybeans; poultry, livestock); timber area. Co. courthouse dates from 1787. Emporia Municipal Airport to E. Inc. 1887. Est. as independent city in 1967.

Emporium (em-POR-ee-uhm), borough (1990 pop. 2,513), ⊙ Cameron co., N central Pa., 65 mi/105 km WNW of Williamsport, on Driftwood Branch, at mouth of Sinnemahoning Portage Creek; at NW end of Buctnil State Park, which extends from Lock Haven in Clinton co.; 41°30′N 14°78′W. Mfg. (powdered metal prods., tool and die, lumber, machinery, custom forgings); timber. Surrounded by sects. of Elk State Forest. Settled 1810, laid out 1861, inc. 1864.

Empress, village (1991 pop. 189), SE Alta., Canada, on Sask. border, on Red Deer R., and 70 mi/113 km NNE of Medicine Hat; 50°58′N 110°01′W. Wheat; ranching.

Emsworth (EMS-wuhrth), borough (1990 pop. 2,892), Allegheny co., SW Pa., residential suburb 7 mi/11.3 km NW of downtown Pittsburgh, on Ohio R. Emsworth Dam, on Ohio R., is here. Settled 1803; inc. 1897.

Encampment, village (1990 pop. 490), Carbon co., S Wyo., on Encampment R., on NE edge of Sierra Madre, and 47 mi/76 km SSE of Rawlins. Elev. 7,323 ft/2,232 m. Lumber. Once trade center of busy copper-mining area. Grand Encampment Mus. is here. Battle Pass on Continental Divide (9,955 ft/3,034 m) to W; parts of Medicine Bow Natl. Forest to SW and E.

Encampment River, 42 mi/68 km long, rises at Continental Divide, Routt Natl. Forest, in Park Range, N Colo.; flows N into S Wyo. and Medicine Bow Natl. Forest, past Encampment town, to North Platte R. 10 mi/16 km SSE of Saratoga.

Encantada, Cerro La, Mexico: see SAN PEDRO MÁRTIR, SIERRA.

Encanto, suburban section of San Diego city, San Diego co., S Calif., residential area 6 mi/9.7 km E of downtown San Diego. Sweetwater Reservoir to E.

Encarnación de Díaz (en-kahr-nah-see-ON dai DEE-ahz), city (1990 pop. 18,629) and township, ⊙ Encarnación de Díaz municipio, Jalisco, central Mexico, on RR, and 27 mi/43 km S of Aguascalientes on Mexico Highway. 45; 21°31′N 102°14′W. Elev. 6,115 ft/1,864 m.

Hot, dry climate. Important agr. center (corn, wheat, grapes, beans, chilis; livestock); mfg. (clay earthenware, wool serapes).

Enchanted Mesa, Span. *Mesa Encantada*, sandstone butte, 430 ft/131 m high, Cibola co., central N.Mex., near the pueblo of Acoma; also called *Katzimo* by Native Americans. According to one Pueblo legend, the mesa was the home of their people until an earthquake destroyed the only approach; investigation does not support the legend.

Encinal, village (1990 pop. 620), La Salle co., SW Texas, 38 mi/61 km N of Laredo; 28°02'N 99°20'W. Watermelons, peanuts, corn; cattle.

Encinitas, city (1990 pop. 55,386), San Diego co., S Calif., on coast, a suburb 23 mi/37 km N of downtown San Diego; 33°03'N 117°16'W. Agr. (avocados, fruits, vegetables); mfg. (lighting equipment, light mfg.); flower growing; beach resort area.

Encino 1 (en-SEE-no), village (1990 pop. 131), Torrance co., central N.Mex., 48 mi/77 km ESE of Estancia; 34°38'N 105°27'W. Elev. 6,200 ft/1,890 m. Trade center in agr. and livestock region. Pedernal Peak (7,576 ft/2,309 m) to NW. **2** uninc. village (1990 pop. 110), Brooks co., S Texas, 50 mi/80 km N of McAllen. Cattle; natural-gas processing.

Encino, suburban sect. of LOS ANGELES city, Los Angeles co., S Calif., in San Fernando Valley, 17 mi/27 km NW of downtown Los Angeles. Residential. Van Nuys Airport to N. Sepulveda Dam Flood Control Area (Los Angeles R.) to N. Site of Los Encinos State Historical Park; Encino Reservoir to SW, in Santa Monica Mts. Recreation area.

Encrucijada (en-kroo-see-HAH-dah), town, Villa Clara prov., central Cuba, on RR, and 15 mi/24 km NNE of Santa Clara. Sugar-growing center; also tobacco, fruit; livestock. Four sugar centrals nearby.

Endeavor, village (1990 pop. 316), Marquette co., S central Wis., 11 mi/18 km N of Portage, on Buffalo L.; 43°42'N 89°28'W. Mfg. (plastic molding).

Endeavour, Mount (9,300 ft/2,835 m), NW B.C., Canada, near Alaska border, in Coast Mts., 75 mi/121 km NNE of Wrangell; 57°25'N 131°30'W.

Enderby (EN-duhr-bee), city (1991 pop. 2,128), S B.C., Canada, on Shuswap R., and 21 mi/34 km NNE of Vernon; 50°33'N 119°08'W. Dairying; lumbering; brick making.

Enderlin, town (1990 pop. 997), Ransom and Cass cos., SE N.Dak., 13 mi/21 km NNE of Lisbon, and on Maple R.; 46°37'N 97°35'W. RR junction to SE; dairy prods.; sunflowers; livestock. Inc. 1897.

Endicott 1 (EN-di-kawt), village (1990 pop. 163), Jefferson co., SE Nebr., 5 mi/8 km SE of Fairbury, and on Little Blue R; 40°04'N 97°05'W. RR junction. Mattresses and box springs. **2** village (□ 3 sq mi/7.8 sq km; 1990 pop. 13,531), Broome co., S central N.Y., on the Susquehanna R.; 42°06'N 76°03'W. Mfg. (shoes, leather). Settled c.1795; inc. 1906. **3** village (1990 pop. 320), Whitman co., SE Wash., 18 mi/29 km W of Colfax; 46°56'N 117°41'W. Agr. (wheat, oats, barley; sheep, cattle).

Endicott Mountains, N central Alaska, central part of Brooks Range, extends c.150 mi/241 km E-W in lat. 68°N; rise to 8,800 ft/2,682 m.

Endicott River, 20 mi/32 km long, SE Alaska, rises in Muir Glacier, near 58°50'N 135°44'W; flows SE to W side of Lynn Canal at 58°47'N 135°15'W.

Endless Caverns, Va.: see NEW MARKET.

Endwell, residential village (□ 3 sq mi/7.8 sq km; 1990 pop. 12,602), Broome co., S N.Y., on the Susquehanna R., bet. Endicott and Johnson City; 42°07'N 76°01'W. Mfg. of electronic parts and components. Also called Hooper.

Energy, village (1990 pop. 1,106), Williamson co., S Ill., 8 mi/12.9 km NW of Marion; 37°46'N 89°01'W. In coal-mining and agr. area.

Enfield 1 town (1990 pop. 45,532), Hartford co., N Conn., on the Connecticut R., near the Mass. state line; 41°58'N 72°33'W. Industry includes mfg. of water-filtration systems, specialized machinery, aluminum and magnesium castings, wooden reels for wire and cables, silk screening, games, greeting cards, tools and gauges, envelopes, laser-beam welding, warehouse distribution of toys, clothing, pharmaceuticals, manufacture and assembly of computer parts, food and dairy processing, insurance; tobacco and vegetable farming. Settled c.1680, originally part of Massachusetts, Enfield was annexed to Connecticut in 1749. The town hall was built in 1775. A community col. was opened in 1972. Includes villages of Thompsonville (1990 pop. 8,458) and Hazardville (1990 pop. 5,179). **2** town (1990 pop. 1,476), Penobscot co., central Maine, near the Penobscot R., 33 mi/53 km N of Bangor; 45°16'N 68°35'W. In hunting, fishing, lumbering area. Inc. 1835. **3** former town, Hampshire co., W central Mass.; inundated in 1937 by Quabbin Reservoir. **4** town (1990 pop. 3,979), Grafton co., W N.H., 5 mi/8 km E of Lebanon; 43°36'N 72°07'W. Drained by Mascoma R. Agr. (nursery crops, vegetables, apples, corn; cattle, poultry; dairying; timber). Mascoma L. in W; Crystal L. in E. Former Shaker Village and Shrine of Our Lady of La Salette on SW shore of Mascoma L. Settled 1761. **5** town (1990 pop. 3,082), Halifax co., NE N.C., 18 mi/29 km NNE of Rocky Mount near Fishing Creek; 36°10'N 77°40'W. Agr. area (peanuts, soybeans, tobacco, cotton, grain, potatoes; chickens, hogs); mfg. (lumber, auto windshields, infant clothing). Medoc Mountain State Park to NW. Settled before 1750.

Enfield, village (1990 pop. 683), White co., SE Ill., 10 mi/16 km WNW of Carmi; 38°06'N 88°20'W. In agr. area.

Engadine (en-ga-DEIN), village, Mackinac co., SE Upper Peninsula, Mich., 44 mi/71 km NW of St. Ignace; 46°07'N 85°34'W. Supply point for timber area; wood prods.

Engaño, Cape (en-GAH-no), E-most tip of Hispaniola isl. and the Dominican Republic, on Mona Passage, 50 mi/80 km ESE of Seibo; 18°36'N 68°19'W.

Engelhard (ENG-uhl-hahrd), uninc. village, Hyde co., E N.C., 35 mi/56 km E of Belhaven, on Pamlico Sound. L. Mattamuskeet Natl. Wildlife Refuge to W.

Engineer Mountain, peak (13,218 ft/4,029 m) in San Juan Mts., Ainsdale and Duray cos., SW Colo., just N of San Juan co. line, 12 mi/19 km NNE of Silverton.

England, town (1990 pop. 3,351), Lonoke co., central Ark., 22 mi/35 km SE of Little Rock; 34°32'N 91°58'W. In agr. area; mfg. (lumber and building materials, shoes). Wabbuska Bayou to W; Clear L. (oxbow lake) to W.

Englebright Reservoir (□ 7 sq mi/18.1 sq km), Yuba co., N Calif., on N. Yuba R., 19 mi/30 km ENE of Marysville; 39°21'N 121°14'W. Max. capacity 960,000 acre-ft. Formed by New Bullards Bar Dam (635 ft/194 m high), built (1969) for water supply, power generation, recreation, and as a fish and wildlife pond.

Englefield, Cape, NW extremity of Melville Peninsula, SE Franklin dist., N.W.T., Canada, on Gulf of Boothia, at W end of Fury and Hecla Strait; 69°51'N 85°39'W.

Englehart, town (1991 pop. 1,726), E Ont., Canada, on Englehart R., and 29 mi/47 km NNW of Haileybury; 47°49'N 79°52'W. Silver and cobalt mining; dairying.

Engleside, uninc. city, Fairfax co., NE Va., residential suburb 6 mi/9.7 km S of Alexandria, 12 mi/19 km S of Washington, D.C., drained by Little Hunting Creek; 38°43'N 77°07'W. Fort Belvoir Military Reservation to W; Mt. Vernon historical site to S.

Englewood 1 city (1990 pop. 29,387), Arapahoe co., N central Colo., on the South Platte R., a residential and industrial suburb 7 mi/11.3 km S of downtown Denver; 39°38'N 104°59'W. Elev. 5,306 ft/1,617 m. Englewood Speedway to W in Sheridan. Inc. 1903. **2** city (1990 pop. 24,850), Bergen co., NE N.J.; 40°53'N 73°58'W. Residential area with light industry in a variety of metals and chemical prods. The area was founded in the 17th cent. Inc. as a city 1899. **3** city (1990 pop. 11,432), Montgomery co., W Ohio, 10 mi/16 km NW of Dayton and on Stillwater R.; 39°52'N 84°18'W. Englewood Dam (4,700 ft/1,433 m wide, 125 ft/38 m high) was completed in 1922 for flood control on the Stillwater.

Englewood, town (1990 pop. 1,611), McMinn co., SE Tenn., 6 mi/10 km ESE of Athens; 35°26'N 84°29'W. In timber and farm area. Settled 1819; inc. 1919.

Englewood, village, SW B.C., Canada, on N Vancouver Isl., on Johnstone Strait, 3 mi/5 km SE of Alert Bay; 50°33'N 126°53'W. Lumber-shipping port; sawmilling.

Englewood 1 village, Lawrence co., S Ind., near Bedford. **2** village (1990 pop. 96), Clark co., SW Kansas, near Okla. line, 17 mi/27 km SW of Ashland; 37°02'N 99°59'W. Wheat; cattle.

Englewood Cliffs, residential borough (1990 pop. 5,634), Bergen co., NE N.J., on Hudson R. just ESE of Englewood and 4 mi/6.4 km E of Hackensack, on the Palisades; 40°52'N 73°57'W. Mfg of tea and pharmaceuticals.

Englewood Dam, Montgomery co., SW Ohio, on the Stillwater R.; 132 ft/40 m high; 39°52'N 84°16'W. Built (1922) for flood control. Reservoir is dry except during floods; extends N into Miami co.; potential max. capacity 413,000 acre-ft.

English, town (1990 pop. 614), ⊙ Crawford co., S Ind., 36 mi/58 km W of New Albany; 38°20'N 86°28'W. In agr. and timber area; some mfg.

English Bay or **Alexandrovsk**, Kenai Indian village (1990 pop. 158), S Alaska, W Kenai Peninsula, on Cook Inlet, 10 mi/16 km SW of Seldovia; 59°21'N 151°54'W. Fishing. Has Orthodox church.

English Harbour, village and bay (1991 pop. 614), S Antigua, Antigua and Barbuda Republic, West Indies, 8 mi/12.9 km SSE of St. John's; 17°00'N 61°46'W. Tourist resort and marina. Has historic dockyard, where Br. admiral Horatio Nelson served 1784–1787.

English River, 330 mi/531 km long, W Ont., Canada, issues from Lac Seul, flows SW and W to Winnipeg R. just E of Man. border.

English River, c.35 mi/56 km long, SE Iowa, formed by forks rising in Poweshiek co. and joining W of Kalona; flows generally E to Iowa R. 12 mi/19 km S of Iowa City; 85 mi/137 km long, including longest headstream.

English Turn, historic site, 10 mi/16 km SE of New Orleans, La.; 29°52'N 55°89'W. Here Bienville stopped the English in 1699 as they progressed up the Mississippi R. intent on establishing a colony (Carolana). The French later built a fort at the bend. One of the last naval battles of the Civil War occurred here.

Englishman Bay, Washington co., E Maine, inlet of the Atlantic lying bet. Roque Isl. and Roque Bluffs; 4 mi/6.4 km long, 2 mi/3.2 km wide.

Englishtown, fishing village, NE N.S., Canada, N Cape Breton Isl., on St. Ann's Bay, 20 mi/32 km WNW of Sydney. First permanent white settlement on Cape Breton Isl., a French post was established here 1629, named St. Ann, for Anne of Austria. In 1713 Fort Dauphin and naval base were built. Fort was destroyed (1745) by Warren's fleet.

Englishtown, borough (1990 pop. 1,268), Monmouth co., E N.J., 5 mi/8 km NW of Freehold; 40°17'N 74°21'W. Amer. troops camped here just before the battle of Monmouth (1778). Site of thoroughbred race track.

Enhaut (EN-hout), uninc. town (1990 est. pop. 1,600), Swatara township, Dauphin co., S central Pa., residential suburb 4 mi/6.4 km SE of downtown Harrisburg and 1 mi/1.6 km NE of Bressler, near Susquehanna R.; 40°13'N 76°49'W. Light mfg.

Enid (EE-nid), city (1990 pop. 45,309), ⊙ Garfield co., N central Okla., 58 mi/93 km NNW of Okla. City; 36°24'N 97°52'W. Elev. 1,246 ft/380 m. Major RR junction and center. It is an important trade and processing center for an area rich in wheat, dairy cattle, poultry, and oil; mfg. (flour milling, Mexican foods, meat processing, machining, publishing and printing, steel fittings, transfer trailers, drilling rigs, pre-processing of industrial steel, agr. equipment). Oil fields are nearby, and there are foundries and machine shops and other oil-related industries in the city. Phillips Univ., a state hosp., and Mus. of the Cherokee Strip, are in Enid. Vance Air Force Base is nearby. Inc. 1893.

Enid (EE-nid), uninc. village, Tallahatchie co., NW central Miss., 11 mi/18 km NE of Charleston. Agr. (cotton, grain; cattle). Enid L. reservoir on Yocona R., and George Payne Cossar State Park to NE.

Enid Lake (EE-nid), reservoir (□ 10 sq mi/26 sq km),

Yalobusha co., N central Miss., on Yocona R., 35 mi/ 56 km S of Batesville; 34°10′N 89°49′W. Max. capacity 1,213,500 acre-ft. Formed by Enid Dam (110 ft/34 m high), built (1952) by Army Corps of Engineers for flood control; also used for recreation. George P. Cosse State Park near dam.

Enigma (e-NIG-muh), town (1990 pop. 611), Berrien co., S Ga., 12 mi/19 km E of Tifton; 31°25′N 83°20′W.

Enilda (e-NIL-duh), village, W central Alta., Canada, 70 mi/113 km SE of Peace R., 10 mi/16 km W of Lesser Slave L.; 55°25′N 117°19′W. Lumbering, mixed farming.

Enka (ENK-uh), uninc. village, Buncombe co., W N.C., 7 mi/11.3 km SW of Asheville. Mfg. (industrial fibers, plastic moldings, crushed stone). Pisgah Natl. Forest to S.

Enloe, uninc. town (1990 pop. 113), Delta co., NE Texas, 16 mi/26 km SSW of Paris, near North Fork of Sulphur R.

Ennadai Lake (52 mi/84 km long, 3 mi/5 km–14 mi/ 23 km wide), SW Keewatin dist., N.W.T., Canada, near Mackenzie and Man. borders; 60°55′N 101°15′W. Drained N by Kazan R.

Ennery (en-REE), town (1982 pop. 982), Artibonite dept., N central Haiti, 14 mi/23 km E of Gonaïves; 19°29′N 72°29′W. In agr. region (sugarcane, cotton).

Ennis, city (1990 pop. 13,883), Ellis co., N Texas, 31 mi/ 50 km SSE of Dallas; 32°20′N 96°37′W. Elev. 548 ft/ 167 m. Trading, financial, rail, and processing center in a fertile blackland area that produces cattle; dairying; cotton, grain. Mfg. (chemicals, building materials, auto parts, printing). The city, which was settled by Czechs, sponsors a natl. polka festival each May. Nearby L. Bardwell (on Waxahachie Creek) to SW, offers recreational activities. Inc. 1872.

Ennis, town (1990 pop. 773), Madison co., SW Mont., on Madison R., and 41 mi/66 km SW of Bozeman; 45°21′N 111°44′W. Cattle, sheep, hogs; potatoes, vegetables, sugar beets, alfalfa; tourism, mining. Ennis Natl. Fish Hatchery 12 mi/19 km to SW. Ennis L. reservoir to N. Gravelly and Tobacco Root ranges to the W; Madison Range to the E. Parts of Beaverhead Natl. Forest to SW, NW, and SE; parts of Gallatin Natl. Forest to NE; parts of Lee Metcalf Wilderness Area to NE and E. Wildlife Mus. of the West.

Ennis Lake, reservoir, Madison co, SW Mont., on Madison R., 32 mi/51 km SW of Bozeman; 45°29′N 111°56′W. Max. capacity 42,053 acre-ft. Formed by Madison Dam (39 ft/12 m high), built (1907) for power generation; also used for flood control, water supply, and recreation.

Enoch, town (1990 pop. 1,947), Iron co., SW Utah, 7 mi/ 11.3 km NNE of Cedar City; 37°45′N 113°02′W. Elev. c.5,400 ft/1,646 m. Dairying; cattle, sheep; barley, alfalfa. Iron Mission State Historic Park to S; Dixie Natl. Forest to SE. Settled in 1851 as Johnson's Springs; temporarily abandoned until 1854 due to conflicts with Native Americans.

Enochville (EE-nahk-vil), uninc. town (1990 pop. 2,901), Rowan co., W central N.C., residential suburb 5 mi/ 8 km NW of Kannapolis, near Rocky R; 35°31′N 80°40′W. Agr. area.

Enola (EE-no-lah), uninc. town (1990 pop. 5,961), East Pennsboro township, Cumberland co., S central Pa.; 40°17′N 76°56′W. Suburb 3 mi/4.8 km NW of downtown Harrisburg, across Susquehanna R. Mfg. (machinery, electronic prods., sheet-metal fabrication). Ridge of the Blue Mts. to N.

Enon (EE-nahn), village (1990 pop. 2,605), Clark co., W central Ohio, 7 mi/11 km WSW of Springfield; 39°52′N 83°56′W.

Enon Valley (EE-nuhn), borough (1990 pop. 355), Lawrence co., W Pa., 12 mi/19 km SSW of New Castle, on Honey Creek; 40°51′N 80°27′W. Agr. (apples; dairying); mfg. (machinery, dairy prods.).

Enoree (E-nuh-ree), uninc. village (1990 pop. 1,107), Spartanburg co., NW S.C., on Enoree R., and 20 mi/ 32 km S of Spartanburg. Agr. (dairying; poultry, hogs; grain, soybeans, peaches, apples); mfg. (vermiculite prods., cotton fabric, cotton yarns, chemicals).

Enoree River (E-nuh-ree), 85 mi/137 km long, NW S.C.;

rises in the Blue Ridge foothills N of Greenville in Greenville co.; flows SE, past Enoree and Whitmire through part of Sumter Natl. Forest, to Broad R. 15 mi/ 24 km NE of Newberry.

Enosburg (EE-nuhs-buhrg), town (1990 pop. 2,535), Franklin co., NW Vt., 15 mi. NE of St. Albans, and on Missisquoi R.; 44°52′N 72°45′W. Includes village of Enosburg Falls. Dairying; sheep farming; dairy prods. Annual dairy festival. Chartered 1780.

Enriquillo (en-ree-KEE-yo), town (1993 pop. 5,068), Barahona prov., SW Dominican Republic, on the Caribbean, 24 mi/39 km SSW of Barahona; 17°55′N 71°15′W. Coffee; hardwoods.

Enriquillo, Lago (en-ree-KEE-yo), salt lake, SW Dominican Republic, the largest lake of HISPANIOLA, c.110 ft/ 34 m below sea level. Lago Enriquillo has a large and varied wildlife pop., including flamingos and iguanas. Near Haitian border.

Ensenada (en-sai-NAH-dah), city (1990 pop. 259,979) and township, Baja California state, NW Mexico on Mexico Highway 1; 31°53′N 116°35′W. Developed in the 19th cent., Ensenada is the oldest deep-sea port in Baja California and is one of the most important ports in Mexico. It is a primary processing and shipping point for the region's agr. produce, which includes grains, cotton, and fish. Ensenada also possesses a broad-based mfg. industry created largely through foreign investment. The city is also a popular tourist destination.

Ensenada (en-sai-NAH-dah), village, SW P.R., West of Guánica Bay, part of Guánica, 21 mi/34 km W of Ponce. Former sugar milling center.

Ensenada de la Broa (en-sai-NAH-dah dai lah BRO-ah), off SE La Habana and W Matanzas provs., W Cuba, NE inlet (c.30 mi/48 km long E–W, 15 mi/24 km wide) of the Gulf of Batabanó, bounded SE by Zapata Peninsula; 22°30′N 82°00′W. Drains the western coastal plain of SW Cuba (La Habana prov.), as well as the Zapata Swamp (Matanzas prov.).

Ensenada Honda (en-sai-NAH-dah ON-dah), small, deep bay in E P.R., opposite Vieques Isl., 2 mi/3.2 km S of Ceiba. Surrounded by Roosevelt Roads, U.S. naval station. Fort Bundy is on N shore.

Ensign (EN-sin), village (1990 pop. 192), Gray co., SW Kansas, 12 mi/19 km SSE of Cimarron; 37°38′N 100°13′W. In grain region.

Ensley (ENZ-lee), city (□ 11 sq mi/28 sq km; 1990 pop. 16,362), Escambia co., NW Fla., 10 mi/16 km NNW of Pensacola; 30°31′N 87°16′W.

Enterprise, city (1990 pop. 20,123), Coffee co., SE Ala.; 31°19′N 85°50′W. Peanut-shipping center with many peanut-processing plants; lumber; textile mills; concrete. The region's diversified farming began after the boll weevil destroyed the cotton (1910–1915); in gratitude for the resulting prosperity, the city erected a monument to the boll weevil in 1919. Enterprise State Junior Col. located here. Inc. 1896.

Enterprise 1 uninc. town, Shasta co., N Calif., suburb 2 mi/3.2 km SE of Redding, on Sacramento R.; 39°33′N 121°20′W. **2** town (1990 pop. 865), Dickinson co., central Kansas, on Smoky Hill R., and 5 mi/8 km ESE of Abilene; 38°53′N 97°07′W. RR junction. Flour milling; mfg. (machinery, plastic prods.). **3** town (1990 pop. 1,905), ⊙ Wallowa co., NE Oregon, on Wallowa R., 7 mi/11.3 km NNW of Wallowa L., and 40 mi/64 km ENE of La Grande; 45°25′N 117°16′W. Elev. 3,757 ft/ 1,145 m. Trade center for nearby ranches. Agr. (potatoes, wheat, barley, oats; sheep, hogs, cattle). Timber. State fish hatchery is here. Hq. for Wallowa-Whitman Natl. Forest, parts to S and N. Inc. 1889. **4** town (1990 pop. 936), Washington co., SW Utah, 33 mi/53 km NNW of St. George, 37°34′N 113°42′W. Elev. 5,380 ft/ 1,640 m. Alfalfa, potatoes; cattle. Enterprise Reservoir and Lower Reservoir to SW; Dixie Natl. Forest to S and W. Settled 1891. **5** uninc. town (1990 pop. 1,058), Harrison co., N W.Va., 11 mi/18 km NNE of Clarksburg, on West Fork R.; 39°25′N 80°16′W. Agr. (corn; dairying; cattle, poultry.), mfg. (mining equipment). Bituminous coal.

Enterprise, village (1990 pop. 477), Clarke co., E Miss., 15 mi/24 km SSW of Meridian, and on Chickasawhay

R., formed here by joining of Chunky and Okatibbee creeks; 32°10′N 88°48′W. Agr. (cotton, corn; cattle; timber); mfg. (lumber).

Entiat (en-tee-AHT), village (1990 pop. 449), Chelan co., central Wash., on the Columbia R. (L. Entiat, formed by Rocky Reach Dam, 10 mi/16 km SSW) at mouth of the Entiat, and 19 mi/31 km N of Wenatchee; 47°41′N 120°13′W. Mfg. (sporting goods, aluminum foundry). Daroga State Park to N; Lincoln Rock State Park, at Rocky Reach Dam, to S; Wenatchie Natl. Forest to SW, W, and NW.

Entiat, Lake, reservoir, Chelan co., central Wash., on Columbia R., 7 mi/11.3 km N of Wenatchee; 40 mi/ 64 km long; 47°31′N 120°17′W. Elev. 708 ft/216 m. Max. capacity 412,000 acre-ft. Formed by Rocky Reach Dam (120 ft/37 m high), built (1962) for power generation. Rocky Reach Fish Hatchery at dam. Daroga and Lincoln state parks here; Wenatchee Natl. Forest on W shore.

Entiat River (en-tee-AHT), c.50 mi/80 km long, central Wash.; rises in the Cascades W of L. Chelan, in NW Chelan co., Wenatchee Natl. Forest; flows SE, bet. Chelan (E) and Entiat (W) ranges, to the Columbia R. at Entiat. Apples are grown in the narrow irrigated river valley.

Entwistle (EN-twi-suhl), village (1991 pop. 460), S central Alta., Canada, near Pembina R., 60 mi/97 km W of Edmonton; 53°31′N 114°58′W. Mixed farming; lumber.

Enumclaw (EE-nuhm-klaw), town (1990 pop. 7,227), King co., W central Wash., near White R., suburb 22 mi/35 km E of Tacoma, and 30 mi/48 km SSE of Seattle, in foothills of Cascade Range; 47°12′N 122°00′W. Agr. (timber, dairying); mfg. (printing and publishing, power cylinders, furniture, salad dressings). Mt. Rainier Natl. Park to SE; Mud Mountain Dam, on White R., to SE; Federation Forest State Park to E; Kanaskat-Palmer and Nolte state parks to N. Founded 1885.

Eola (ee-O-luh), uninc. village, Avoyelles parish, E central La., on small Bayou Boeuf, 4 mi/6 km SW of Bunkis, and 30 mi/48 km SE of Alexandria; 30°54′N 92°12′W; in agr. area. Oil field nearby. Formerly a RR town.

Eolia (ee-OL-ee-uh), uninc. village (1990 pop. 600), Letcher co., SE Ky., 5 mi/8 km S of Whitesburg, near Poor Fork river, in Jefferson Natl. Forest, near Va. state line. Bituminous coal; lumber.

Eolus, Mount (14,083 ft/4,292 m), La Plata co., SW Colo., in San Juan Mts., 12 mi/19 km SSE of Silverton, in San Juan Natl. Forest.

Epatlán, Mexico: see SAN JUAN EPATLÁN.

Epazoyucan (e-pah-so-YOO-kan), town (1990 pop. 2,158), Hidalgo, central Mexico, 10 mi/16 km SE of Pachuca de Soto. On paved road, 3 mi/5 km off Mexico Hwy. 130. Corn, maguey; livestock.

Epes (eps), town (1990 pop. 267), Sumter co., W Ala., on Tombigbee R. and 8 mi/12.9 km NNE of Livingston; 32°41′N 88°07′W. Hardwood veneer.

Ephesus (EF-uh-suhs), town (1990 pop. 324), Heard co., Ga., 12 mi/19 km NE of Franklin; 33°25′N 85°16′W.

Ephraim (EE-fruhm), city (1990 pop. 3,363), Sanpete co., central Utah near San Pitch R., in irrigated Sanpete Valley, just W of Wasatch Plateau, 60 mi/97 km S of Provo; 39°21′N 111°34′W. Elev. 5,543 ft/1,690 m. Agr. (alfalfa, barley, wheat; dairying; hogs, cattle, sheep); mfg. (turkey processing, lumber). Snow Col. and museum of Native American relics are here. Manti–La Sal Natl. Forest just E; part of Uinta Natl. Forest to NW. Settled 1854; inc. 1868.

Ephraim (EE-fruhm), village (1990 pop. 261), Door co., NE Wis., on Door Peninsula, on Green Bay, 24 mi/ 39 km NE of Sturgeon Bay City; 45°09′N 87°10′W. Annual regatta is held here. Founded 1853 as Moravian colony. Peninsula State Park is to W. Orchards.

Ephrata (ee-FRAI-tuh), town (1990 pop. 5,349), ⊙ Grant co., central Wash., 35 mi/56 km E of Wenatchee, at S end of the Grand Coulee Dam; 47°19′N 119°32′W. Irrigated agr. area (wheat, alfalfa, vegetables, sugar beets, mint, potatoes, beans); mfg. (animal feeds, printing and publishing). County Historical Mus. Airforce training base in World War II. Inc. 1909.

Ephrata (ee-FRAI-tah), borough (1990 pop. 12,133), Lancaster co., SE Pa., 11 mi/18 km NE of Lancaster on Cocalico Creek; 40°10′N 76°10′W. In a prosperous farm area. Mfg. (textiles, stone prods., foods, machinery, printing and publishing, metal fabrication, apparel, mobile homes). A noted religious community was founded (c.1732) here by Seventh-day Baptists under the leadership of Johann Conrad Beissel. This austere colony, the Ephrata Cloisters, is a state historic site.

Epitacio Huerta (e-pee-TAH-see-o WER-tah), town (1990 pop. 783), in extreme NE Michóacan, Mexico, 29 mi/47 km E of Acámbaro, 32 mi/52 km S of Querétaro. Temperate climate with average annual temperature 72°F/22°C. A rural community of small farms.

Epping, town (1990 pop. 5,162), Rockingham co., SE N.H., 15 mi/24 km W of Portsmouth; 43°02′N 71°04′W. Drained by Lamprey R. and Piscassic R. Agr. (nursery crops, vegetables; cattle, poultry; dairying); mfg. (aluminum awnings, signs, boats, aircraft components, boat trailers). Separated from Exeter in 1741.

Epping, village (1990 pop. 64), Williams co., NW N.Dak., 16 mi/26 km NE of Williston, near Epping-Spring Brook dam, large earthfill dam; 48°16′N 102°21′W. Lewis and Clark State Park on L. Sakakawea Reservoir, to SE.

Epps, village (1990 pop. 541), West Carroll parish, NE La., 37 mi/60 km ENE of Monroe; 32°37′N 91°29′W. In agr. area. Gas field nearby. Poverty Point State Commemorative Area to NE, 3,000-year-old Native American cultural site.

Epsom (EP-suhm), town (1990 pop. 3,591), Merrimack co., S central N.H., 10 mi/16 km E of Concord; 43°13′N 71°20′W. Drained by Suncook and Little Suncook rivers. Agr. (vegetables, nursery crops, apples; poultry, livestock; dairying); mfg. (machining, concrete structures, metal coatings). Includes Gossville village near center.

Epworth, town (1990 pop. 1,297), Dubuque co., E Iowa, 13 mi/21 km WSW of Dubuque; 42°27′N 90°55′W. In agr. area. Mfg. (toys). Divine Word Col. is located here.

Equality, village (1990 pop. 748), Gallatin co., SE Ill., on Saline R. and 8 mi/12.9 km W of Shawneetown; 37°44′N 88°20′W. In agr. area. Formerly county seat and site of salt works.

Equinox, Mount (EEK-hwin-awks) (3,816 ft/1,163 m), SW Vt., highest peak of Taconic Mts., W of Manchester, in resort area. Road to summit.

Erasmus, Mount (10,700 ft/3,261 m), SW Alta., Canada near B.C. border, in Rocky Mts., in Banff Natl. Park, 80 mi/129 km NW of Banff; 51°57′N 116°55′W.

Erath, county (□ 1,089 sq mi/2,821 sq km; 1990 pop. 27,991), N central Texas; ⊙ Stephenville; 32°13′N 98°13′W. Drained by Bosque R. Rich diversified agr. area (peanuts, grain, sorghum), horticultural crops; a leading dairying co.; beef cattle, horses. Oil, natural gas; coal deposits formerly worked. Formed 1856.

Erath (er-ath), town (1990 pop. 2,428), Vermilion parish, S La., 6 mi/10 km E of Abbeville, in Cajun country; 29°58′N 92°02′W. Boatbuilding. Inc. 1889.

Erebus Bay, SW Devon Isl., E central Franklin dist., N.W.T., Canada, small inlet of Barrow Strait, at S end of Wellington Channel; 74°42′N 91°50′W. Contains Beechey Isl.

Erebus, Mount (E-ri-buhs) (10,234 ft/3,119 m), W Alta., Canada, near B.C. border, in Rocky Mts., in Jasper Natl. Park, 19 mi/31 km SW of Jasper; 52°37′N 118°16′W.

Erhard (ER-hahrd), village (1990 pop. 181), Otter Tail co., W Minn., 14 mi/23 km N of Fergus Falls, on Pelican R.; 46°28′N 96°05′W. Grain; dairying. Maplewood State Park to NE.

Eric Cove, Canada: see WOLSTENHOLME.

Erick, town (1990 pop. 1,083), Beckham co., W Okla., 14 mi/23 km WSW of Sayre, near the N Fork of Red R.; 35°12′N 99°52′W. Agr. (cotton, wheat, peanuts; cattle, horses); mfg. (candles, honey). Natural gas field nearby. Inc. 1903.

Ericson, village (1990 pop. 111), Wheeler co., NE central Nebr., 10 mi/16 km SW of Bartlett and on Cedar R; 41°46′N 98°40′W.

Erie 1 county (□ 1,226 sq mi/3,175 sq km; 1990 pop. 968,532), W N.Y., ⊙ Buffalo; 42°45′N 78°46′W. Drained by Cattaraugus and Tonawanda creeks and small Buffalo and Cayuga creeks. Includes parts of Cattaraugus and Tonawanda reservations. Agr. (dairy prods.; poultry, livestock; field corn and hay; sweet corn, beans, potatoes, tomatoes, strawberries, grapes); extensive mfg. (including stone and gypsum quarrying). Named for Erie tribe. In 1821 Samuel Wilkinson completed a breakwater to form an artificial harbor, and in 1825, the Erie Canal connected the city to N.Y. harbor. Wells Fargo Express was formed in Buffalo in 1851. The first air conditioner and transfer elevator were made here. Laurence D. Bell founded Bell Aircraft here in 1935. Numerous vocational/technical schools reflect the industrial nature of the region, which, with Niagara co., is referred to as the Niagara Frontier. Formed 1821. **2** county (□ 264 sq mi/684 sq km; 1990 pop. 76,779), N Ohio, ⊙ SANDUSKY; 41°21′N 82°36′W. Bounded N by L. Erie; drained by Huron and Vermilion rivers and small Pipe Creek. Includes Kelleys Isl. In the Lake Plains physiographic region. Agr. area (corn, soybeans, fruits; livestock); mfg. at Sandusky, Huron, Vermilion (sausages and other prepared meats, paints, rubber prods., steel foundries, food prods., machinery, vehicular lighting equip.). Limestone quarries; fisheries. Summer resorts. Formed 1838. **3** county (□ 1,558 sq mi/4,035 sq km; 1990 pop. 275,572), NW Pa., ⊙ Erie. Bounded N by L. Erie, NE by N.Y., W by Ohio; drained S by Elk and French creeks. Agr. (grapes, cherries, apples, corn, wheat, oats, barley, potatoes, hay, alfalfa; hogs, cattle; dairying; timber); mfg. (limestone, sand and gravel). Mfg. at Erie, Corey, and Fairview. Pa.'s only co. on Great Lakes. Site of Millcreek Mall, one of the largest shopping centers in the U.S. Fr. forts built 1753 at Presque Isle and Le Boeuf (at Waterford) occupied 1760 by British. Pesque Isle State Park in N, on L. Erie. Claims to Erie Triangle ceded 1781–1785 to U.S. govt. by N.Y. and Mass.; sold 1788 to Pa. Formed 1800.

Erie, city (1990 pop. 108,718), ⊙ Erie co., NW Pa., on L. Erie, 120 mi/193 km N of Pittsburgh and 80 mi/129 km WSW of Buffalo, N.Y.; 42°07′N 80°05′W. Pa.'s only port on the Great Lakes; has natural harbor in Presque Isle Bay, which opens on lake to NE; U.S. Coast Guard Station at harbor entrance. Erie is a busy shipping point for coal, iron ore, grain, petroleum, machinery, and lumber. Mfg. (hosp. equip., locomotives, paper prods., bearings, food prods., plastic products, fish processing, wood products, chrome plating, industrial heaters). Fort Presque Isle was built in 1753 by the French, occupied and rebuilt in 1760 by the English, and destroyed during Pontiac's Rebellion in 1763. A peace conference bet. the British and Native Americans was held in 1764, but the town was not laid out until 1795. Oliver Hazard Perry's fleet was launched at Crystal Point before his victory over the British during the battle of L. Erie in 1813. Gannon Univ., Mercyhurst Col., Villa Maria Col., and Pa. State Univ. – Behrend Campus to E. Erie International Airport to W. Millcreek Mall (□ 1,500,058 sq ft/139,355 sq m), the 45th-largest shopping center in U.S. Many historic buildings remain in Erie. Erie Historical Mus. and Planetarium, Erie Art Mus., Erie Playhouse, Erie Philharmonic, Perry Memorial House, Historic Cashiers House (Erie History Center). Flagship *Niagara* (U.S. brig). Presque Isle State Park, on Presque Isle peninsula to N, across Presque Isle Bay. Inc. as a city 1851.

Erie 1 town (1990 pop. 1,258), Weld co., N Colo., near Boulder Creek, 20 mi/32 km N of Denver and 18 mi/29 km E of Boulder; elev. c.5,038 ft/1,536 m; 40°01′N 105°02′W. Diversified farming, sugar beets, fruits, vegetables, beans, wheat, sunflowers; cattle. Mfg. (corrugated boxes, plastics prods.). **2** town (1990 pop. 1,276), ⊙ Neosho co., SE Kansas, on Neosho R. and 14 mi/23 km SE of Chanute; 37°34′N 95°14′W. RR junction. Shipping and trading point in oil producing and general farming region. Mfg. (farm machinery). Oil and gas wells in vicinity. Neosho State Fishing L. to S; Neosho Waterfowl Refuge to SE. Inc. 1870.

Erie, village, SE B.C., Canada, on Beaver Creek, at mouth of Erie Creek, 19 mi/31 km ENE of Trail; 49°10′N 117°23′W. Mining (gold, silver, lead, zinc).

Erie, village (1990 pop. 1,572), Whiteside co., NW Ill., near Rock R. (bridged here), 13 mi/21 km SSE of Morrison; 41°39′N 90°04′W. In agr. area. Inc. 1872.

Erie Canal, artificial waterway, c.360 mi/579 km long, from Tonawanda on L. Erie to Cohoes on Hudson R. in N.Y. Locks were built to overcome the 571 ft/174 m difference bet. the level of the river and that of L. Erie. The N.Y. State Barge Canal follows part of the Erie Canal's course. After the Amer. Revolution, the need for an all-Amer. water route bet. the Great Lakes and the Atlantic coast was evident. Political unity, easy and inexpensive transportation, and increased trade (free from Can. competition) were the anticipated benefits of such a route. Several land surveys for a canal followed, and by 1810, the issue was paramount in the N.Y. state legislature, where De Witt Clinton lent his political support. A canal commission, including Clinton, Gouverneur Morris, Stephen Van Rensselaer, and Thomas Eddy, among others, formed by the legislature, recommended (1811) an Erie rather than an Ontario canal. The canal bill, drawn up by Clinton in 1815, was debated in the legislature (1816–1817), with N.Y. city and the L. Ontario interests opposing it vigorously. Although a presidential veto of a natl. waterway project forced the proposed canal's financial burden onto N.Y. state, the canal bill passed the state legislature in April 1817. Work on the canal was done by gangs of workers, many of whom were European immigrants. The canal's course was entirely enclosed; streams and lakes were not incorporated into the waterway. The Erie Canal's middle sect. (Utica to Salina) completed 1820; its E sect. through the Mohawk R. Valley was finished in 1823. Elaborate celebrations marked the 1825 opening of the canal, heralded as the "8th Wonder of the World"; Clinton and other notables sailed from Buffalo to N.Y. city, where Clinton emptied a barrel of L. Erie water into the Atlantic Ocean. The canal was enlarged beginning in 1835; its most important branches, the Champlain (opened 1819), the Oswego (1828), and the Cayuga and Seneca (1829), were also enlarged. RR competition, beginning in the 1850s eventually destroyed the canal's long-haul advantages; however, for many years the Erie Canal was a profitable route, amassing income from tolls. The tolls were abolished in 1882 because of the canal's state of disrepair and in order to lure more traffic. Although some improvements in the canal were made (1884–1894), its inadequate navigability, the competition of Can. routes, and the disclosure of fraudulent canal administration (the "Canal Ring") brought about plans for its complete renovation and subsequent conversion (1904–1918) into a large, modern barge canal. By the 1970s a large amount of tonnage was still being shipped across the waterway. The Erie Canal contributed to N.Y. city's financial development, opened E markets to Midwest farm prods. and encouraged immigration to that region, and helped to create numerous large cities (including Buffalo, Rochester, Utica, and Syracuse), making N.Y. a U.S. commercial center in mid–19th cent. Its initial success started a wave of canal bldg. in the U.S. The present commercial usage of the canal is 500,000 tons/453,500 metric tons per year, and all of that is bet. Three Rivers (named for the confluence of the canalized Oneida, Seneca, and Oswego rivers, 12 mi/19 km NNW of Syracuse) and Albany. There are many problems with the canal, including high maintenance costs, antiquated systems, and the shortness of the season. To address these problems, the N.Y. State Thruway Authority's Canal Recreation Commission was created in 1992 to control the management of the canal. A possible option is to turn it into a recreational waterway, and some sects. may be closed.

Erie, Lake (□ 9,940 sq mi/25,745 sq km), 241 mi/388 km long and 30 mi/48 km–57 mi/92 km wide, bordered on the N by S Ont., Canada, on the E by W N.Y., on the S by NW Pa. and N Ohio, and on the W by SE Mich. and NW Ohio; 4th-largest of the GREAT LAKES. It is 572 ft/174 m above sea level and has a max. depth of 210 ft/64 m, making it the shallowest of the Great Lakes and the only one with a floor above sea level. It is part of the Great Lakes–St. Lawrence Seaway system and is linked to L. Huron by the Detroit R., L. St. Clair, and St. Clair R., and with L. Ontario by the Niagara R. (L. Erie's only natural outlet) and the Welland Canal. The New York State Barge Canal links the lake with the Hudson R. Several small rivers, including the Maumee, Sandusky, and Cuyahoga, flow into the lake from the south; the Grand R. enters from Ontario. L. Erie is partially icebound in winter and is usually closed to navigation from mid-December to the end of March. Rich agr. lands border the Can. shore, where the chief towns are Port Colbourne and Port Stanley. The principal U.S. cities on the lake are Buffalo, N.Y.; Erie, Pa.; and Cleveland and Toledo, Ohio, all of which are ports with heavy industry. Untreated industrial and municipal wastes from lakeshore cities—and from Detroit, whose wastes enter the western end of the lake—polluted the waters and created a foul smell in the surrounding areas. A U.S.-Can. pact (1972) ended the discharge of contaminating materials into the water, and the environmental damage has since abated. Numerous recreation facilities are provided at natl. (Point Pelee and Fort Malden in Canada), state, and provincial parks located on the lake's islands and shores. The first European to see the lake was French explorer Louis Jolliet in 1669. The British and the French, and later the British and the Americans, fought for its control. The battle of L. Erie (Sept. 10, 1813), a naval engagement in the War of 1812, led successfully by the U.S. leader Oliver H. Perry against the British, was fought at Put-in Bay.

Erie Railroad, RR transportation line designed to connect the mouth of the Hudson R. with the Great Lakes region. The N.Y. and Erie RR Co. was enfranchised and inc. in 1832 and construction began in 1835 near Deposit, N.Y. In 1851, 446 mi/718 km of trunkline across N.Y. state was completed to Dunkirk, N.Y., on L. Erie, at a huge cost. The RR was extended to Jersey City, N.J., and to Buffalo, N.Y., but in 1861 the company failed and was reorganized as the Erie Railway Co. The company gained sound financial footing during the Civil War before it became the subject of a tremendous financial battle. An alliance was formed among Daniel Drew, Jay Gould, and James Fisk, and from 1866 to 1868, with the aid of unauthorized stock issues, political chicanery, and incessant litigation, they outmaneuvered Cornelius Vanderbilt to keep control of the Erie Railway Co. Drew lost his control to Gould, who during his presidency (1868–1872) further weakened the Erie Railway Co. After further financial trickery, the Erie Railway Co. went bankrupt and was reorganized (1878) as the N.Y., L. Erie, and Western Railway Co. By 1880 branch lines were built to Chicago. The N.Y., L. Erie, and Western went into receivership after the Panic of 1893 and was reorganized (1895) as the Erie RR Co. Under the presidency of Frederick D. Underwood (1901–1927), the Erie continued to suffer losses. After a major reorganization in 1941, the RR yielded a dividend in 1942 for the 1st time in 69 years. On Oct. 15, 1960, the Erie merged with the Delaware, Lackawanna, and Western RR to form the Erie-Lackawanna. In 1976 this organization and 5 other lines that had gone bankrupt were merged to form the Conrail system.

Erieau (EER-ee-o), village (1991 pop. 474), S Ont., Canada, on L. Erie, 17 mi/27 km SE of Chatham; 42°15′N 81°55′W. Dairying.

Erieville, resort village (1990 pop. 400), Madison co., central N.Y., 25 mi/40 km SE of Syracuse; 42°51′N 75°45′W. Lakes, reservoirs nearby.

Erin, city (1990 pop. 1,586), ⊙ Houston co., NW Tenn., 23 mi/37 km SW of Clarksville; 36°19′N 87°42′W. Mfg. (men's shirts; lumbering).

Erin, village (1991 pop. 2,489), S Ont., Canada, 10 mi/16 km S of Orangeville; 43°46′N 80°04′W. Dairying; potatoes.

Erin, village, SW Trinidad, Trinidad and Tobago, on the Serpent's Mouth, and 19 mi/31 km SW of San Fernando; 10°05′N 61°38′W. Coconuts. Sometimes called San Francique. Erin Point is just SE.

Erlanger (UHR-lang-uhr), city (1990 pop. 15,979), Kenton co., N central Ky., suburb 8 mi/12.9 km SW of Cincinnati, Ohio, and 6 mi/9.7 km SW of Covington, Ky.; 39°00′N 84°35′W. Mfg. (chemicals, sheet metal fabrication, medical supplies, lumber processing, sports equip., jewelry, aerospace equip., construction materials, paper, food prods.). Cincinnati–Northern Ky. International Airport to NW. Turfway Park racetrack to NW.

Erling, Lake, Lafayette co., SW Ark., on Bodcau Creek (Bodcau Bayou), 23 mi/37 km SW of Magnolia and 3 mi/4.8 km N of La. border; 15 mi/24 km long; 33°03′N 93°31′W. Extends NNW; max. capacity 140,000 acre-ft. Formed by Percy Cobb Dam (12 ft/4 m high), built (1965) by the Internatl. Paper Co. for industrial water supply. Lafayette Wildlife Management Area on W shore.

Ernest, borough (1990 pop. 492), Indiana co., W central Pa., 4 mi/6.4 km N of Indiana, on McKee Run. Agr. (corn, hay, potatoes; dairying; livestock).

Ernest Sound, SE Alaska, bet. Cleveland Peninsula (SE) and Etolin Isl. (NW), N of Myers Chuck; opens S into Clarence Strait at 55°51′N 132°22′W.

Erongarícuaro (e-ron-gah-REE-kwah-ro), town (1990 pop. 2,456), Michoacán state, central Mexico, on W shore of L. Pátzcuaro, near RR and 36 mi/58 km WSW of Morelia. Cereals, fruits; livestock; timber.

Eros (er-OS), town (1990 pop. 177), Jackson parish, N central La., 20 mi/32 km WSW of Monroe; 32°23′N 92°25′W. In agr. area.

Errol (E-ruhl), town (1990 pop. 292), Coos co., N N.H., 30 mi/48 km N of Lancaster; 44°46′N 71°07′W. Bounded E by Maine state line, Magallaway R. flows into Umbagog L., which drains into Androscoggin R. Agr. (vegetables; cattle, poultry; dairying; timber). Errol Hill (2,313 ft/705 m) in center; Androscoggin State Wayside Park in SW.

Erskine (UHRS-kin), village (1990 pop. 422), Polk co., NW Minn., 29 mi/47 km ESE of Crookston; 47°39′N 96°00′W. RR junction. Agr. (wheat, potatoes, sunflowers; dairying); mfg. (drill hitches, pallets). Small lakes in area.

Erving (UHR-veeng), town (1990 pop. 1,372), Franklin co., NW Mass., on Millers R., and 10 mi/16 km E of Greenfield; 42°37′N 72°25′W. Paper prods. Includes part of Millers Falls village. Erving is known for the Mohawk Trail, Route 2, and the French King Bridge spanning the Conn. R. gorge, 787 ft/240 m long, 140 ft/43 m high. Settled 1801; inc. 1838.

Ervings Location, locality, Coos co., N N.H., 9 mi/14.5 km SE of Colebrook. Wilderness area in N part of White Mts.; drained by Phillips Brook. Muise Mt. (3,610 ft/1,100 m) here.

Erwin, city (1990 pop. 5,015), ⊙ Unicoi co., NE Tenn., on Nolichucky R. and 12 mi/19 km S of Johnson City, near Bald Mts. and N.C. state line; 36°09′N 82°25′W. Fruit and timber area; RR shops; mfg.: pottery, clothing, electric motors. U.S. fish hatchery and mtn. recreation areas nearby. Settled c.1775; inc. 1903.

Erwin (UHR-win), town (1990 pop. 4,061), Harnett co., central N.C., 4 mi/6.4 km WNW of Dunn, on Cape Fear R.; South R. to E; 35°19′N 78°40′W. RR spur terminus. Agr. (tobacco, cotton, grain; poultry, livestock); mfg. (textiles, sand and gravel processing, utility trailers). Averasboro Battleground State Historical Site to S.

Erwin, village (1990 pop. 42), Kingsbury co., E central S.Dak., 9 mi/14.5 km NE of De Smet; 44°29′N 97°26′W.

Esbon (ES-buhn), village (1990 pop. 167), Jewell co., N Kansas, 12 mi/19 km WNW of Mankato; 39°49′N 98°25′W. In grain and livestock region.

Escalante (es-kuh-LAN-tee), town (1990 pop. 818), Garfield co., S Utah, on Kaiparowits Plateau, on Escalante R., and c.45 mi/72 km E of Panguitch; 37°45′N 111°35′W. Elev. 5,268 ft/1,606 m. Trading point in cattle-grazing area. Dixie Natl. Forest to N and W; Box-Death Hollow Wilderness Area to N. Escalante State Park (petrified forest) to N; Escalante Canyons to E. Settled 1875 by Mormons.

Escalante River (es-kuh-LAN-tee), c.80 mi/129 km long, S Utah; rises in Escalante Mts. of W central Garfield co. c.20 mi/32 km W of Escalante; flows SE past Escalante, through the Escalante Canyons, through a large section of Glen Canyon Natl. Recreation Area to Colorado R., 8 mi/12.9 km N of mouth of San Juan R.; 40 mi/64 km NE of Page, Ariz. Lower 10 mi/16 km section of river is arm L. Powell (L. Powell formed by Glen Canyon Dam, Ariz.).

Escalante, Villa, Mexico: see SANTA CLARA DEL COBRE.

Escalon, city (1990 pop. 4,437), San Joaquin co., central Calif., 19 mi/31 km SE of Stockton, near Stanislaus R.; 37°48′N 121°00′W. Agr. (wine growing; fruits, vegetables, nuts, grain, hay; cattle; dairying); mfg. (food processing). Woodward Reservoir to NE.

Escambia 1 (es-KAM-bee-uh), county (☐ 953 sq mi/2,468 sq km; 1990 pop. 35,518), S Ala.; ⊙ Brewton. Coastal plain bordering on Fla., drained by Conecuh (or Escambia) R. Cotton, peanuts, corn; livestock. Part of Conecuh Natl. Forest in E. Formed 1868. **2** county (☐ 893 sq mi/2,313 sq km; 1990 pop. 262,798), extreme NW Fla.; ⊙ Pensacola; 30°36′N 87°19′W. Bounded by Ala. line on W (here formed by Perdido R.) and N, Gulf of Mexico on S, Escambia R. on E. Rolling terrain in N, lowlands in S around Pensacola and Perido bays, and white sandy beaches along Gulf shore. Agr. (corn, peanuts, cotton, vegetables; dairying); mfg. (forestry [lumber, naval stores]); fishing. Shipyards and other industry at Pensacola. Formed 1821.

Escambia Bay (es-KAM-bee-uh), N arm of Pensacola Bay, extreme NW Fla.; 9 mi/14.5 km long, 3 mi/4.8 km–6 mi/9.7 km wide; crossed by RR and I-10 bridge. Receives Escambia (Conecuh) R.

Escanaba (es-KAN-ah-bah), city (1990 pop. 13,659), ⊙ Delta co., W Upper Peninsula, N Mich., on Little Bay de Noc, 48 mi/77 km NE of Menominee; 45°45′N 87°04′W. It is a RR and mfg. center (soft drinks, automotive parts, concrete prods.); stores and exports coal and petrochemicals from its harbor. Lumber and its by-products, however, are the chief economic mainstay. Municipal airport to SW. The Upper Peninsula State Fair is held annually in Escanaba, Bay de Noc Community Col. Hiawatha Natl. Forest to E, across bay. Settled 1852; inc. 1883.

Escanaba River (es-KAN-ah-bah), c.40 mi/64 km long, central Upper Peninsula, Mich., formed by junction of branches in SE Marquette co.; flows SE to Little Bay de Noc of Green Bay, 2 mi/3.2 km N of Escanaba. Middle Branch rises NE of L. Michigamme; flows c.50 mi/80 km SE. West Branch rises SE of Republic; flows c.30 mi/48 km SE. East Branch rises SW of Ishpeming; flows c.35 mi/56 km E and S to Middle Branch at Gwinn; 46°16′N 87°26′W.

Escatawpa (es-kuh-TAW-puh), uninc. town (1990 pop. 3,902), Jackson co., SE Miss., residential suburb 8 mi/12.9 km N of Pascagoula, on E channel of Pascagoula R.; 30°29′N 88°32′W. Mfg. (steel boats). Pascagoula Airport here.

Escatawpa River (es-kuh-TAW-puh), c.90 mi/145 km long, in SW Ala. and SE Miss.; rises in Washington co., Ala.; flows S to Pascagoula Bay, Miss. Sometimes known as Dog R. Forms part of harbor of Pascagoula city at mouth.

Escholtz Bay, Alaska: see ESCHSCHOLTZ BAY.

Eschscholtz Bay (E-sholts) (30 mi/48 km long, 7 mi/11.3 km–16 mi/26 km wide), NW Alaska, SE arm of Kotzebue Sound, NE Seward Peninsula, 50 mi/80 km SE of Kotzebue; 66°20′N 161°25′W. Trapping and fishing; Elephant Point village on S shore. Contains Chamisso Isl. (2 mi/3.2 km long), bird sanctuary. Sometimes spelled Escholtz.

Escobedo (es-ko-BAI-do), town (1990 pop. 669), Coahuila state, N Mexico, in E outliers of Sierra Madre Oriental, 22 mi/35 km N of Monclova. Cattle, sheep; cereals. Also known as Villa Escobedo.

Escobosa (es-ko-BO-suh), uninc. village, Bernalillo co., N central N.Mex., 18 mi/29 km SE of Albuquerque.

Chiles, corn, grain; cattle; dairying. Isleta Indian Reservation to W; Manzano Mts. to W; parts of Cibola Natl. Forest to NW and SW.

Escocesa Bay (es-ko-SAI-sah), small inlet on N coast of Dominican Republic, bounded by Samaná Peninsula (SE); 19°25′N 69°45′W. At its head is Matanzas.

Escoheag, R.I.: see WEST GREENWICH.

Escondido, city (1990 pop. 108,635), San Diego co., S Calif., suburb 30 mi/48 km NNE of downtown San Diego; 33°08′N 117°04′W. RR terminus. Located in a grain, citrus fruit, and grape growing valley, Escondido produces cereal prods. and has fruit-packing houses and one of the world's largest avocado processing plants. The city's light industries manufacture goods such as pens, musical instruments, electronics, communications equip., and machine tools. Escondido is one of the fastest-growing U.S. cities, marked by a population increase of nearly 70% bet. 1980 and 1990. Site of North County Fair, one of the largest shopping centers in U.S. A huge wild animal park was constructed just S of the city and draws numerous tourists to the area. To the E is San Pasqual Battlefield State Monument, commemorating the battle fought in Dec. 1846 bet. U.S. forces under Gen. Stephen W. Kearny and Californians under Andrés Pico. San Pasqual and Rincon Indian Reservations to NE. Cleveland Natl. Forest to E. Inc. 1888.

Escoumins, Les (laiz-es-kuh-ME), village (1991 pop. 2,212), E Que., Canada, on the St. Lawrence, at mouth of Escoumins R., and 40 mi/64 km NNE of Riviére du Loup. Lumbering.

Escuinapa or **Escuinapa de Hidalgo** (es-kwee-NAH-pah), city (1990 pop. 25,086) and township, Sinaloa state, NW Mexico, in coastal lowland, on RR to Mexico City and 45 mi/72 km SE of Mazatlán on Mexico Hwy. 15; 22°50′N 105°46′W. Commercial and agr. center (corn, sugarcane, chickpeas, cotton, fruits, vegetables).

Escuintla (es-KWEEN-tlah), city (1990 pop. 7,392) and township, ⊙ Escuintla municipio, Chiapas state, S Mexico, in Pacific lowland, on RR, and 38 mi/61 km NW of Tapachula on Mexico Highway 200; 15°18′N 92°39′W; elev. 361 ft/110 m. Sugarcane; corn, coffee, fruits.

Escuminac Bay (es-KOO-min-ak), tidal estuary (24 mi/39 km long) of Restigouche R., N N.B., Canada; enters Chaleur Bay at Dalhousie. Campbellton is on S shore.

Escuminac Point, promontory on the Gulf of St. Lawrence, E N.B., Canada, at N entrance to Northumberland Strait, 30 mi/48 km. ENE of Chatham; 47°05′N 64°49′W.

Eska (ES-kah), village, S Alaska, in Matanuska Valley, on RR spur and 16 mi/26 km NE of Matanuska village. Coal deposits.

Eskdale, uninc. village (1990 pop. 350), Kanawha co., W central W.Va., 21 mi/34 km SE of Charleston. Coal and agr. area.

Esker, settlement, W Lab., Canada, 65 mi/105 km NNE of Labrador City, on E side of Menihek Locks. Situated on Que. N shore and Labrador RR; development road from Goose Bay and Churchill Falls. Service center for mining and hydroelectric projects.

Eskridge, village (1990 pop. 518), Wabaunsee co., E central Kansas, 26 mi/42 km SW of Topeka; 38°51′N 96°05′W. Trade center for grain region. Mfg. (counter tops).

Esmeralda (ez-muh-RAHL-duh), county (□ 3,589 sq mi/9,296 sq km; 1990 pop. 1,344), S Nev.; ⊙ Goldfield; 37°47′N 117°37′W. Mining and livestock-grazing area bordering on Calif. (SW). Lithium, gold, silver, diatomite, clay. Silver Peak Mts. in W. Formed 1861. Columbia Salt Marsh is in NW. Small parts of Inyo Natl. Forest in W, including Boundary Peak (13,140 ft/4,005 m) on Calif. boundary. Small parts of Death Valley Natl. Monument in far S.

Esmeralda (es-mah-RAHL-dah), town, Camagüey prov., E Cuba, on RR and 37 mi/60 km NNW of Camagüey; 21°52′N 78°08′W. In agr. region (sugarcane, coconuts, fruits, tobacco). Sugar central of Brasil, one of largest in Cuba, is 13 mi/21 km E.

Esmeralda or **La Esmeralda** (es-me-RAHL-dah), village (1990 pop. 146), Acuña municipio, Coahuila state, N Mexico, on RR spur, and 125 mi/201 km N of Torreón. Road junction. Zinc and lead mines.

Esmond 1 (EZ-muhnd), village (1990 pop. 196), Benson co., N central N.Dak., 25 mi/40 km W of Minnewaukan; 48°01′N 99°45′W. Buffalo L. Natl. Wildlife Refuge to W. RR terminus. **2** (EZ-mond), village in Smithfield town, Providence co., NE R.I., on Woonasquatucket R. (bridged here) and 6 mi/9.7 km NW of Providence. **3** village, Kingsbury co., E central S.Dak., 13 mi/21 km SW of De Smet; 44°15′N 97°46′W.

Esopus (uh-SO-puhs), village (1990 pop. 650), Ulster co., SE N.Y., on W bank of the Hudson R., 7 mi/11.3 km SSE of Kingston; 41°51′N 73°59′W. In grape-growing and resort area. Seat of Mt. St. Alphonsus Theological Seminary. John Burroughs lived near here. Town was formed in 1811, and was partly annexed by Kingston in 1818.

Esopus Creek, c.65 mi/105 km long, SE N.Y.; rises in the Catskills in central Ulster co.; flows N, then SE, to Ashokan Reservoir; the creek emerges on the S side of the reservoir and continues SE, then NE, to the Hudson R. at Saugerties.

Espaillat (es-pei-YAT), province (□ 433 sq mi/1,121 sq km; 1993 pop. 197,617), N Dominican Republic, on the coast; ⊙ Moca; 19°30′N 70°27′W. Crossed by Cordillera Septentrional and including central sect. of Cibao region (La Vega Real). One of the most fertile and densely populated parts of the country. Agr. (coffee, cacao, tobacco, rice, corn). Highway passes through Moca from Santo Domingo. Other centers are Salcedo, Tenares, Veragua. Originally a part of La Vega prov.; created 1885.

España (es-PAHN-yuh) or **España Repúblicana**, sugar-mill village, Matanzas prov., W Cuba, on RR, and 40 mi/64 km ESE of Matanzas; 22°48′N 81°01′W.

Españita (es-pahn-YEE-tah), town (1990 pop. 1,708), ⊙ Españita municipio, Tlaxcala state, central Mexico, 16 mi/26 km NW of Tlaxcala; elev. 7,247 ft/2,209 m. Maguey.

Española (es-pahn-YO-luh), city (□ 7 sq mi/18.1 sq km; 1990 pop. 8,389), Rio Arriba and Santa Fe cos., N central N.Mex., 22 mi/35 km NNW of Santa Fe, on the Rio Grande, in the heart of pueblo country; 36°00′N 106°04′W. A shipping point for sheep and cattle. Mfg. (pumice, lumber, concrete, printing and publishing). An annual 3-day fiesta in July commemorates the establishment nearby of a settlement by Juan de Oñate on July 11, 1598. Many scenic, historic, archaeological, and Native American attractions abound in the area. San Juan Indian Reservation to N; Santa Clara Indian Reservation to W; Puye cliff dwellings to W; Nambe and Pojoaque pueblos to SE; San Juan Pueblo to N; Santa Clara and San Idefonso pueblos to S; part of Santa Fe Natl. Forest to E and W. Founded 1880; inc. 1964.

Espanola (es-puh-NO-luh), town (1991 pop. 5,527), S central Ont., Canada, on Spanish R., and 40 mi/64 km WSW of Sudbury; 46°15′N 81°46′W. Nickel, copper, gold mining; lumbering.

Esparto, uninc. town (1990 pop. 1487), Yolo co., central Calif., 30 mi/48 km WNW of Sacramento, near Cache Creek; 38°42′N 122°01′W. Berryessa Peak (3,057 ft/932 m) to W. Fruits, nuts, grapes, vegetables, wheat, sugar beets, beans. Winery.

Espenberg, Cape (ES-puhn-buhrg), NW Alaska, N Seward Peninsula, on S side of entrance to Kotzebue Sound, 40 mi/64 km SW of Kotzebue, on Arctic Circle; 66°32′N 163°47′W.

Esperance, village (1990 pop. 324) in Esperance town (1990 pop. 2,101), Schoharie co., E central N.Y., 16 mi/26 km W of Schenectady; 42°45′N 74°15′W.

Esperanza (es-pai-RAHN-sah), town, Villa Clara prov., central Cuba, on RR and 10 mi/16 km W of Santa Clara; 22°25′N 80°07′W. Trading and agr. center (sugarcane, tobacco, fruits; livestock); mfg. (cigars; canned foods). Seven sugar mills to SW.

Esperanza (es-pai-RAHN-sah), town (1993 pop. 33,071), Santiago prov., N Dominican Republic, in fertile Cibao valley, 26 mi/42 km WNW of Santiago; 19°38′N 71°03′W. Agr. (cacao, coffee, tobacco, divi-divi; beeswax; hides).

Esperanza (es-pai-RAHN-sah), town (1990 pop. 6,347), ⊙ Esperanza municipio, Puebla state, central Mexico, near S foot of Pico de Orizaba, 20 mi/32 km W of Orizaba; 27°32′N 109°55′W. Elev. 8,268 ft/2,520 m. RR junction and on Mexico Hwy. 150. Corn, wheat, beans; livestock; wool.

Esperanza Inlet (es-puh-RAN-zuh) (22 mi/35 km long), on W coast of Vancouver Isl., B.C., Canada, separates Nootka Isl. from Vancouver Isl.; 49°48′N 127°10′W. At head of its Zeballos Arm (N) is Zeballos, a gold-mining center. Logging. Hecate Channel (E) connects inlet with Tahsis Inlet of Nootka Sound.

Esperanza, La, Cuba: see PUERTO ESPERANZA.

Esperanzas, Las, Mexico: see LAS ESPERANZAS.

Espinal (es-pee-NAHL), town (1990 pop. 2,684), Veracruz state, E Mexico, on Tecoutla R., and 15 mi/24 km SSW of Papantla de Olarte. Corn, coffee, sugarcane. Also El Espinal.

Espíritu Santo Bay (es-PEE-ree-too SAHN-to), inlet of Caribbean Sea on E coast of Yucatán Peninsula, Quintana Roo state, SE Mexico, 10 mi/16 km S of Ascensión Bay, 30 mi/48 km SE of Felipe Carrillo Puerto.

Espíritu Santo Bay, S Texas, inlet sheltered from Gulf of Mexico by Matagorda Isl.; c.17 mi/27 km long, 2 mi/3.2 km–4 mi/6.4 km wide. Joined by Gulf Intracoastal Waterway to Matagorda Bay (NE) and San Antonio Bay (SW).

Espíritu Santo Island (es-PEE-ree-too SAHN-to), (□ 43 sq mi/111 sq km), in Gulf of California, off E coast of Baja California, NW Mexico, 16 mi/26 km N of La Paz; 7.5 mi/12.1 km long, 2 mi/3.2 km–5 mi/8 km wide; rises to 1,886 ft/575 m. Uninhabited. Of volcanic origin; desert climate. Surrounding sea has oysters and pearls.

Espíritu Santo Tamazulapan, Mexico: see TAMAZULA-PAM DEL ESPÍRITU SANTO.

Espita (es-PEE-tah), town (1990 pop. 8,279), ⊙ Espita municipio, Yucatán state, SE Mexico, 23 mi/37 km NNW of Valladolid; 21°0′N 88°18′W. Elev. 72 ft/22 m. Agr. center (henequen, chicle, sugarcane, corn, fruits; livestock); mfg. (lumber).

Espy (ES-pee), uninc. town (1990 pop. 1,430), Scott township, Columbia co., E central Pa., residential suburb 2 mi/3.2 km ENE of Bloomsburg on Susquehanna R.; 41°00′N 76°25′W.

Esquimalt (SKWEI-molt), regional district (1991 pop. 16,129), on Vancouver Island, SW B.C., Canada, just SW of Victoria. W Canada's chief naval station and naval dockyard are located here. Station est. by the Brit. govt. in 1855 and taken over by Canada in 1906.

Essex, county (□ 707 sq mi; 1991 pop. 327,365), S Ont., Canada, on L. Erie, L. St. Clair, and Mich. border; ⊙ Windsor; 42°10′N 82°49′W.

Essex, town (1991 pop. 6,759), S Ont., Canada, 14 mi/23 km SE of Windsor, in fruit-growing region. Mfg. (food processing, lumbering, light mfg.).

Essex 1 county (□ 828 sq mi/2,145 sq km; 1990 pop. 670,080), NE Mass.; ⊙ Salem, Newburyport, and Lawrence; 42°38′N 70°52′W. On the coast, bounded N by N.H.; intersected by Merrimack and Ipswich rivers. Agr. (nursery prods., fruits; livestock; mfg. (shoes, textiles, metal prods., electronics). Industrial centers are Lynn, Lawrence, Haverhill, Newburyport, Salem, Beverly. Resorts on coast include Gloucester and Cape Ann area, Swampscott, Marblehead. Formed 1643. **2** county (□ 129 sq mi/334 sq km; 1990 pop. 778,206), NE N.J., bounded W, N, and E by Passaic R., SE by Newark Bay, ⊙ Newark, state's largest city and industrial, commercial, transportation center; 40°47′N 74°15′W. Varied mfg. (chiefly food prods., apparel, furniture, paper prods., esp. chemicals, printing, rubber and plastic products, metal prods., industrial machinery, measuring devices, surgical instruments, jewelry, electronic equip.). Formed 1675. **3** county (□ 1,916 sq mi/4,962 sq km; 1990 pop. 37,152), NE N.Y., ⊙ Elizabethtown; 44°06′N 73°46′W. Situated in the High Peaks sect. of the Adirondack range; Mt. Marcy, highest peak (5,344 ft/1,629 m) in state, is in co. Bounded E by L.

Champlain; drained by Hudson R. (rising here), Ausable R., and other streams. Includes L. Placid, Saranac L., and other noted recreational areas. Agr. (potatoes, hay; livestock); mfg. (dairy prods; lumbering); wollastonite, titanium, and garnet deposits. Named for Essex co., England. Region figured strongly in Fr. and Indian Wars, Amer. Revolution, and War of 1812. Strategic forts at Crown Point and Ticonderoga. L. Champlain–L. George–Hudson R. was a strategic route to be won and protected. Iron mfg. utilizing Adirondack ore began in 1801 with the production of anchors at Willsborough Falls. The Elba Iron Works were constructed in 1809, and by the mid-1800s the forges, rolling mills, and nail factories were among the most extensive in the nation. Thick forests resulted in paper and lumber mills, and the clear mt. air attracted those seeking a cure for tuberculosis, including Robert Louis Stevenson. With the exception of paper mills and lumber mills ringing the Adirondacks, the granite quarries, iron ore, and graphite and talc mines are largely gone. Formed 1799. **4** county (□ 673 sq mi/1,743 sq km; 1990 pop. 6,405), NE Vt., on Que. border, bounded E by Connecticut R.; ☉ Guildhall; 44°43′N 71°43′W. Mfg. (paper and wood prods.); Agr. (dairying; lumbering; hunting and fishing). Drained by Moose, Nulhegan, and Clyde rivers. Formed 1792. Encompasses most of Vermont's "Northeast Kingdom." **5** county (□ 285 sq mi/738 sq km; 1990 pop. 8,689), E Va., ☉ Tappahannock. In Tidewater region; bounded NE, E by Rappahannock R.; 37°56′N 76°57′W. Agr. (barley, wheat, soybeans, corn, hay; cattle). Formed 1692.

Essex 1 uninc. city (1990 pop. 40,872), Baltimore co., NE Md., a suburb of Baltimore, 8 mi/12.9 km NE of downtown; 39°18′N 76°27′W. When the Glen Martin Plant opened in 1914 the area began to develop and grew considerably during World War II when the plant manufactured airplanes for the army. The community is dominated by moderate-income houses and apartments. **2** city (1990 pop. 531), Stoddard co., SE Mo., in Mississippi alluvial plain, 6 mi/9.7 km E of Dexter; 36°48′N 89°51′W. Cotton, rice, soybeans.

Essex 1 town (1990 pop. 5,904), including Essex village, Middlesex co., S Conn., on the Connecticut R., and 20 mi/32 km SE of Middletown; 41°21′N 72°25′W. Mfg. (tools, electrical equip., boats and boat repair, turbine blades, machine parts, naval equip., wire prods., publishing). Summer resort (yachting). Steamtrain carries tourists along banks of Connecticut R. Named "Best Small Town in America," 1995. Includes Centerbrook and Ivoryton villages. Est. 1852. **2** town (1990 pop. 916), Page co., SW Iowa, near East Nishnabotna R., 5 mi/8 km NE of Shenandoah; 40°49′N 95°17′W. Fertilizer. **3** town (1990 pop. 3,260), Essex co., NE Mass., on tidewater inlet, and 10 mi/16 km NE of Salem; 42°38′N 70°47′W. Resort; boatbuilding; fishing. Settled 1634; inc. 1819. Includes village of South Essex. **4** town (1990 pop. 16,498), Chittenden co., NW Vt., just E of Burlington, and on the Winooski; 44°30′N 73°03′W. Includes Essex Junction village. Chartered 1763; settled 1783.

Essex 1 village (1990 pop. 482), Kankakee co., NE Ill., 16 mi/26 km WNW of Kankakee; 41°10′N 88°11′W. In agr. area (grain). **2** resort village (1990 pop. 400), Essex co., NE N.Y., 28 mi/45 km S of Plattsburgh, on W shore of L. Champlain; 44°16′N 73°24′W. Ferry to Charlotte, Vt.

Essex Fells, borough (1990 pop. 2,139), Essex co., NE N.J., 9 mi/14.5 km NW of Newark; 40°49′N 74°16′W. Residential. Inc. 1902.

Essex Junction, village (1990 pop. 8,396) of Essex town, Chittenden co., NW Vt., just E of Burlington, and on Winooski R.; 44°29′N 73°06′W. Bldg. materials, electronics, and food, maple, and wood prods. Annual Champlain Valley Exposition here.

Essexville, town (1990 pop. 4,088), Bay co., E Mich., suburb 2 mi/3.2 km ENE of Bay City and near mouth of Saginaw R., on Saginaw Bay; 43°36′N 83°50′W. Cement and asphalt mfg. Area was part of an Indian reservation, 1819–1837. Inc. as village 1883; as city 1934.

Essington (E-seeng-tuhn), uninc. village, Tinicum

township, Delaware co., SE Pa., suburb, 9 mi/14.5 km SW of downtown Philadelphia, on Delaware R., at mouth of Darby Creek, on Tinicum Isl.; 39°51′N 75°17′W. Mfg. (plastic prods., helicopter research and development). Philadelphia International Airport to E. First white settlement in Pa. made 1643 by Swedes on Tinicum Isl. just offshore. Valley Forge State Forest to S, on Little Tinicum Isl.

Essondale, village, SW B.C., Canada, near lower Fraser R., 5 mi/8 km ENE of New Westminster. Lumbering; dairying; fruit growing.

Estacada (es-tuh-KAI-duh), town (1990 pop. 2,016), Clackamas co., NW Oregon, 12 mi/19 km ESE of Oregon City, on Clackamas R.; 45°17′N 122°19′W. Berries; lumber; sheep, cattle. North Fork Reservoir to SE. Milo McIver State Park to W; Mt. Hood Natl. Forest to E and SE.

Estancia (es-TAHN-see-uh), town (1990 pop. 792), ☉ Torrance co., central N.Mex., 40 mi/64 km SE of Albuquerque; 34°45′N 106°03′W. Elev. 6,107 ft/1,861 m. In agr. and cattle region. Mfg. (handcrafted tile, wax castings, printing and publishing). Cibola Natl. Forest and Manzano Mts. are W; Laguna del Perro just SE.

Estanzuela, Mexico: see GARCÍA DE LA CADENA.

Este, Pico del (AI-ste, PEE-ko dai), peak (3,448 ft/1,051 m), NE P.R., in the Sierra de Luquillo, 27 mi/43 km ESE of San Juan.

Estell Manor, city (1990 pop. 1,404), Atlantic co., S N.J., bet. Tuckahoe and Great Egg Harbor rivers, 18 mi/29 km WSW of Atlantic City, in large rural area; 39°21′N 74°46′W. Includes Estelville (or Estellville) village and a game preserve.

Estelle, uninc. city (1990 pop. 14,091), Jefferson parish, La., 5 mi/8 km SW of Gretna; 29°50′N 90°06′W. On road to Lafitte; Estelle Canal.

Estelline, town (1990 pop. 658), Hamlin co., E S.Dak., 18 mi/29 km NNW of Brookings, near Big Sioux R.; 44°34′N 96°54′W. Grain; dairy produce; livestock, poultry. Lake Poinsett State Rec. area 7 mi/11.3 km to W.

Estelline, village (1990 pop. 194), Hall co., NW Texas, 15 mi/24 km NW of Childress, near Prairie Dog Town Fork of Red R.; 34°32′N 100°26′W. In cotton, peanuts and cattle region. Baylor L. and L. Childress to SE.

Ester, suburb, Tanana valley, central Alaska, 8 mi/12.9 km W of Fairbanks. Gold mining; tourism.

Esterhazy (E-stuhr-hai-zee), town (1991 pop. 2,896), SE Sask., Canada, 40 mi/64 km SSE of Yorkton; 50°39′N 102°05′W. Wheat, livestock; potash mining.

Estero (e-STER-ro), town (□ 6 sq mi/15.5 sq km; 1990 pop. 3,177), Lee co., SW Fla., 15 mi/24 km S of Fort Myers, near Estero Bay (a lagoon of the Gulf of Mexico partly enclosed by narrow Estero Isl.); 26°26′N 81°48′W. Grows citrus fruit, vegetables, and bamboo. Bathing beach on Estero Isl. Founded 1894.

Estero Bay, San Luis Obispo, SW Calif., broad open bay of the Pacific Ocean, 12 mi/19 km WNW of San Luis Obispo. Vessels load oil from pipelines here. Morro Bay, E arm of Estero Bay, separated from ocean by 4 mi/6.4 km sand spit, town of Morro Bay is here.

Estes Park, town (1990 pop. 3,184), Larimer co., N Colo., in Front Range of Rocky Mts., on Big Thompson R., at mouth of Fall R., and 24 mi/39 km W of Loveland, and 50 mi/80 km NNW of Denver; 40°22′N 105°31′W. Elev. 7,522 ft/2,293 m. Mfg. (pewter jewelry; printing and publishing). Noted resort; hq., and E entrance for Rocky Mt. Natl. Park (just W). Local mus. contains geological and botanical specimens from park. Nearby are Horseshoe Falls and state fish hatchery. Roosevelt Natl. Forest to N, E, and S. L. Ester to E. Settled 1859, inc. 1917.

Estevan (ES-tuh-van), city (1991 pop. 10,240), S Sask., Canada, on the Souris R., near N.Dak. border; 49°09′N 103°00′W. Lignite mining; mfg. of clay and plastic prods. Oil, discovered in the 1950s, important to the economy.

Estevan Islands, W B.C., Canada, group of 7 isls. (□ 51 sq mi/132 sq km), and several islets in Hecate Strait just S of Banks Isl.

Esther, Mo.: see PARK HILLS.

Estherton (ES-tuhr-tuhn), uninc. town (1990 pop. 1,240), Dauphin co., Pa. residential suburb, 3 mi/4.8 km N of Harrisburg, on Susquehanna R. RR yards here. Wildwood L. reservoir to W; Fort Hunter Mansion (1814) to N.

Estherville, city (1990 pop. 6,720), ☉ Emmet co., NW Iowa, near Minn. state line, on West Des Moines R., and 23 mi/37 km NE of Spencer; 43°23′N 94°49′W. RR junction. Mfg., trade, and shipping center; industries (meat packing, rendering plants, feed mills, bottling works, RR shops); mfg. (wood and plastic prods., bldg. materials, neon signs, fishing lines, egg processing, golf carts). Sand and gravel pits (S). Iowa Lakes Community Col. (main campus) is here. Just W is site of Fort Defiance (1862), preserved in a state park. Meteorite fell nearby in 1879; large fragments are in mus. in London, Vienna, and at Univ. of Minn. Settled 1857; inc. 1881 as town, 1894 as city.

Estherwood (E-stuhr-wud), village (1990 pop. 745), Acadia parish, S La., 6 mi/10 km WSW of Crowley; 30°11′N 92°28′W. Ships rice and other agr. prods.

Estill (EST-il), county (□ 255 sq mi/660 sq km; 1990 pop. 14,614), E central Ky.; ☉ Irvine; 37°41′N 83°57′W. Drained by Kentucky R. (forms NW boundary; Red R. forms part of N boundary) and Station Camp and Red Lick creeks. Hilly agr. area (burley tobacco, hay, alfalfa, soybeans, corn; hogs, cattle). Daniel Boone Natl. Forest in E and S. Formed 1808.

Estill (EST-il), town (1990 pop. 2,387), Hampton co., SW S.C., 19 mi/31 km S of Allendale; 32°45′N 81°14′W. Mfg. (apparel, lumber, trailers, vegetable oil processing); agr. (cotton, soybeans, watermelons, grains; livestock).

Estill Springs, town (1990 pop. 1,408), Franklin co., S Tenn., on Elk R. arm of Tims Ford L., 7 mi/11 km SE of Tullahoma; 35°16′N 86°08′W. Medicinal springs.

Eston, town (1991 pop. 1,210), SW Sask., Canada, 75 mi/121 km NW of Swift Current; 51°09′N 108°45′W. Grain; livestock.

Estral Beach (ES-tral), village (1990 pop. 430), Monroe co., extreme SE Mich., 9 mi/14.5 km NE of Monroe, on L. Erie; 41°59′N 83°14′W.

Étang du Nord (ai-TAH duh NOR) or **L'Étang du Nord** village (1991 pop. 3,044), E Que., Canada, on W Grindstone Isl., one of the Magdalen Isls.; 47°23′N 61°57′W. Fishing port.

Étang Saumâtre, Haiti: see SAUMÂTRE, ÉTANG.

Etawney Lake or **Etawnei Lake** (ee-TO-nee) (□ 546 sq mi/1,414 sq km), N Man., Canada, 30 mi/48 km N of Northern Indian L.

Etchemin River (E-chuh-min), 50 mi/80 km long, SE Que., Canada; issues from L. Etchemin (3 mi/5 km long), 45 mi/72 km SE of Quebec; flows NW to the St. Lawrence opposite Quebec.

Etchojoa (e-cho-HO-ah), town (1990 pop. 7,253), Sonora, NW Mexico, in lowland near Gulf of California, on lower Mayo R. (irrigation), and 100 mi/161 km SE of Guaymas; 26°56′N 109°40′W. Agr. center (chickpeas, corn, rice, fruit; livestock).

Eternity Cape, Fr. *Cap Eternité*, SE central Que., Canada, on Saguenay R., 30 mi/48 km above its mouth, 36 mi/58 km ESE of Chicoutimi; 1,700 ft/518 m high; 48°20′N 70°16′W. Just WNW is Trinity Cape.

Ethan, village (1990 pop. 312), Davison co., SE central S.Dak., 10 mi/16 km S of Mitchell; 43°32′N 97°58′W.

Ethel, town (1990 pop. 71), Macon co., N central Mo., near Chariton R., 18 mi/29 km NW of Macon; 39°53′N 92°44′W.

Ethel 1 village (1990 pop. 454), Attala co., central Miss., on Yockanookany R., and 9 mi/14.5 km ENE of Kosciusko; 33°07′N 89°27′W. Agr. (cotton, corn, soybeans; cattle); mfg. (lumber). Natchez Trace Parkway passes to W. **2** uninc. village (1990 pop. 700), Logan co., SW W.Va., 4 mi/6.4 km ENE of Logan; in coal-mining region.

Ethete (EE-thuh-tee), village (1990 pop. 1,059), Fremont co., W central Wyo., on Sage Creek, branch of Popo Agie R., near Wind R. Range, and 14 mi/23 km N of Lander, in S part of Wind R. Indian Reservation; 43°01′N 108°45′W. Elev. c.5,500 ft/1,676 m.

Etiwanda, uninc. village, San Bernardino co., S Calif.,

suburb, 43 mi/69 km E of downtown Los Angeles, and 12 mi/19 km W of San Bernardino, in the S foothills of San Gabriel Mts. (San Bernardino Natl. Forest). Mfg. (industrial glass, concrete and wood prods., metal plate work). Glen Helen Regional Park to NE.

Etla, Mexico: see VILLA DE ETLA.

Etna, city (1990 pop. 835), Siskiyou co., N Calif., near Scott R., 22 mi/35 km SW of Yreka, in a valley of Klamath Mts.; 41°28′N 122°58′W. Cattle, lambs; grain, onions, sugar beets; hunting, fishing. Klamath Natl. Forest to N, W, and S, including Marble Mt. Wilderness Area to SW.

Etna, town (1990 pop. 977), Penobscot co., S central Maine, 16 mi/26 km W of Bangor; 44°47′N 69°07′W. In agr., recreational area.

Etna, village, Lincoln co., W Wyo., on Salt R., near Idaho line, and 22 mi/35 km N of Afton, in Star Valley. Elev. c.5,600 ft/1,707 m. Sheep, cattle; barley. Salt R. Range to E; Bridger-Teton Natl. Forest to E.

Etna (ET-nah), borough (1990 pop. 4,200), Allegheny co., SW Pa., residential suburb, 5 mi/8 km NE of downtown Pittsburg, on Allegheny R. (bridged), at mouth of Pine Creek. Light mfg. Ironmaking began here 1832. Lock and Dam No. 2 here. Inc. 1868.

Etna Green, town (1990 pop. 578), Kosciusko co., N Ind., 10 mi/16 km WNW of Warsaw; 41°17′N 86°03′W. In agr. area. Mfg. (modular wooden houses and mobile homes).

Etobicoke, city (1991 pop. 309,993), borough of Metropolitan Toronto, S central Ont., Canada, 5 mi/8 km W of downtown Toronto; 43°42′N 79°34′W. Borders L. Ontario on S, Humber R. on E. Toronto Internatl. Airport (Malton) to W. Woodbine Racetrack. Highly industrialized, diversified economy. Mfg. (motor vehicles and transportation equip., machinery, rubber prods., medical equip., food processing, apparel, ordances, chemicals, electrical wiring, telephone equip.). Book publishing; greenhouse agr.

Etolin Island (E-duh-lin), SE Alaska, in Alexander Archipelago, bet. Prince of Wales Isl. (W) and mainland (E), SW of Wrangell Isl.; 30 mi/48 km long, 10 mi/16 km–22 mi/35 km wide; 56°5′N 132°20′W. Rises to 4,000 ft/1,219 m; fishing, hunting.

Etolin Strait (E-duh-lin), W Alaska, bet. Nunivak Isl. (W) and Nelson Isl. and mainland (E), extends SE-NW bet. Kuskokwim Bay and Bering Sea; 60 mi/97 km long, 30 mi/48 km–50 mi/80 km wide.

Eton (EET-uhn), village (1990 pop. 315), Murray co., NW Ga., 13 mi/21 km ENE of Dalton; 34°49′N 84°46′W. Mfg. includes carpets and textiles.

Etowah, county (□ 548 sq mi/1,419 sq km; 1990 pop. 99,840), NE Ala.; ⊙ Gadsden. Hilly region crossed by Coosa R. Mfg. (iron and steel prods.) at Gadsden and Attalla. Corn, soybeans, cotton; poultry. Deposits of coal, iron, limestone, fuller's earth, manganese, barites. Formed 1866.

Etowah, city (1990 pop. 3,815), McMinn co., SE Tenn., 10 mi/16 km SSE of Athens; 35°20′N 84°32′W. Mfg. of textiles. Cherokee Natl. Forest nearby.

Etowah (ET-uh-wah), uninc. town (1990 pop. 1,997), Henderson co., SW N.C., 8 mi/12.9 km W of Hendersonville, on French Broad R.; 35°19′N 82°35′W. Tobacco, corn, potatoes, soybeans; hogs, cattle; dairying. Mfg. (plastic molding; machining). Pisgah Natl. Forest to NW; Holmes Educational State Forest to S. Blue Ridge Mts. to SE.

Etowah, village (1990 pop. 33), Cleveland co., central Okla., residential suburb, 14 mi/23 km ESE of Norman; 35°07′N 97°10′W.

Etowah (ET-uh-wah), river, 141 mi/227 km long; rising in the Blue Ridge Mts., N Ga.; flowing SW to Rome, Ga., where it joins the Oostanaula R. to form the Coosa; 34°39′N 84°07′W. Allatoona Dam, built for flood control and hydroelectric power, is important in the development and growth of mfg. in N Ga. and N Ala. Etowah Mounds, a natl. historic landmark, is a group of prehistoric Native Amer. earthworks 60 ft/18 m high, located on the river near Cartersville, Ga.

Etter, uninc. village (1990 pop. 160), Moore co., extreme N Texas, 60 mi/97 km N of Amarillo. RR junction. Gas

and oil; cattle; wheat, sorghum. Former site of U.S. Ordnance plant.

Ettrick, uninc. town (1990 pop. 5,290), Chesterfield co., E central Va., suburb 2 mi/3.2 km NW of Petersburg, across Appomattox R.; 37°14′N 77°25′W Seat of Va. State Univ.

Ettrick, village (1990 pop. 461), Trempealeau co., W Wis., on tributary of Black R., and 24 mi/39 km N of La Crosse; 44°10′N 91°16′W. In dairy and livestock area; flour mills.

Etzatlán (et-saht-LAHN), city (1990 pop. 11,339) and township, Jalisco, W Mexico, on interior plateau, near L. Magdalena, RR terminus, 50 mi/80 km W of Guadalajara; 20°48′N 104°05′E. Mining center (silver, gold, lead, zinc).

Eubank (YOO-bank), village (1990 pop. 354), Pulaski co., S Ky., 14 mi/23 km NNW of Somerset; 37°16′N 84°39′W. Agr. (tobacco, grain; livestock; hardwood timber); mfg. (lumber, wooden pallets).

Eucha, Lake, Okla.: see SPAVINAW LAKE.

Euclid, city (1990 pop. 54,875), Cuyahoga co., NE Ohio, a suburb adjoining Cleveland, on L. Erie; 41°35′N 81°31′W. Named for the famous Gr. mathematician, the industrial city manufactures metal goods, electrical supplies and equip., airplane and automobile parts, and machinery. The Natl. Amer. Shrine of Our Lady of Lourdes is here. Settled 1798, inc. 1848.

Euclid Heights (YOO-klid), residential suburb, Garland co., central Ark., adjacent to Hot Springs, part of city (SE side).

Eudora 1 (yoo-DOR-uh), town (1990 pop. 3,155), Chicot co., extreme SE Ark., 24 mi/39 km SSW of Greenville (Miss.), on Bayou Macon, near the Mississippi R.; 33°07′N 91°15′W. Mfg. of hardwood prods., apparel, and processed catfish. Inc. 1904. **2** town (1990 pop. 3,006), Douglas co., E Kansas, on Kansas R., at mouth of Wakarusa R., and 8 mi/12.9 km E of Lawrence; 38°56′N 95°05′W. Grain; mfg. (surgical supplies, meat packing), printing.

Eufaula (yoo-FAW-luh), city (1990 pop. 13,220), ⊙ Barbour co., SE Ala., on Chattahoochee R. (here forming Ga. line), and c.50 mi/80 km NNE of Dothan. Trade and shipping center, with boat connections, for cotton, peanut, pecan, and livestock area. Mfg. includes textiles, lumber prods., food processing, oil extraction, fertilizer, consumer goods. Sparks State Technical Col. Settled in 1830s. Has many fine plantation homes.

Eufaula (yoo-FAW-luh), town (1990 pop. 2,652), ⊙ McIntosh co., E Okla., 34 mi/55 km SSW of Muskogee, on W side of Eufaula L. (confluence of Canadian and North Canadian rivers); 35°17′N 95°35′W. Elev. 617 ft/188 m. Mfg. (boat docks,apparel). Site of Eufaula Reservoir in the Canadian R. (a unit of Arkansas R. basin development plan) is E. Fountainhead State Park to N; Arrowhead State Park to S. Founded c.1872 near site of a Creek settlement.

Eufaula Lake (yoo-FAW-luh), on McIntosh-Haskill co. border, and in Pittsburg and Hughes cos., E Okla., on Canadian R., 30 mi/48 km S of Muskogee; c.40 mi/64 km long; 35°18′N 95°20′W. Max. capacity 3,848,000 acre-ft. Three arms formed by North Canadian R. (N), Deep Fork Canadian R. (N), Gaines Creek (S). Formed by Eufaula Dam (99 ft/30 m high), built by the Army Corps of Engineers for flood control, navigation, and power generation. Fountainhead (NE shore of N arm) and Arrowhead (W shore of S arm) state parks here.

Eufaula, Lake, Ala. and Ga., see WALTER F. GEORGE RESERVOIR.

Eugene (YOO-jeen), city (1990 pop. 112,669), ⊙ Lane co., W Oregon, 65 mi/105 km S of Salem, on the Willamette R.; elev.422 ft/129 m; 44°02′N 123°06′W. RR junction. Twin city of Springfield adjoins Eugene on E. A processing and shipping center located in a farming area, it has huge lumbering facilities. Mfg. (food and beverage processing, wood and plastic prods., furniture, chemicals, construction materials, transportation equip. consumer goods, primary metals, machinery, computer chips); mill work. Agr. (nuts, grains, fruit,

oats; poultry, sheep, cattle; dairy prods.); nurseries. Eugene has a tourist industry based on its attractive environment and river recreational areas. The city has been marked by steady pop. growth. Eugene is the seat of the Univ. of Oregon, with its noted mus. of art and natural history, NW Christian Col., Lane Community Col., Willamette Science and Technology Center (WISTEC), and the Oregon Aviation and Space Center. Fern Ridge Reservoir to W. Willamette Natl. Forest to E; Siuslaw Natl. Forest to W; Armitage State Park to N; Elijah Bristow State Park to SE; Hendricks Bridge State Park to E. Inc. 1862.

Eugene, town (1990 pop. 141), Cole co., central Mo., near Osage R., 20 mi/32 km SW of Jefferson City; 38°21′N 92°24′W.

Eugene O'Neill National Historic Site, Contra Costa co., N Calif., near Danville. Covers 13 acres/5 ha. Restored home (Tao House) of the playwright, lived here 1937–1944; limited guided tours. Authorized 1976.

Eugenia Point (ee-ou-HAI-nee-ah), cape on Pacific coast of Lower California, NW Mexico, at W entrance of Sebastián Vizcaíno Bay; 27°50′N 115°05′W.

Euharlee (yoo-HAHR-lee), town (1990 pop. 850), Bartow co., Ga., 10 mi/16 km WSW of Cartersville; 34°08′N 84°56′W.

Euless, city (1990 pop. 38,149), Tarrant co., N Texas, a suburb, 15 mi/24 km ENE of downtown of Fort Worth; 32°51′N 97°04′W. Drained in N by Little Bear Creek. Euless has grown in 1970s and 1980s along with the surrounding Dallas–Fort Worth area. Mfg. (electronics, aircraft parts, plastic prods., consumer goods). Dallas–Fort Worth Internatl. Airport adjoins it to E.

Eunice 1 (YOO-nis), city (1990 pop. 11,162), St. Landry parish, S central La., 28 mi/45 km NW of Lafayette, near Bayou des Cannes; 30°30′N 92°25′W. RR junction. In an oil and agr. area (sugarcane, rice, cotton; dairying). Mfg. includes concrete prods., primary metals, machinery, apparel; printing and publishing. La. State Univ. is here (at Eunice). Inc. 1895. **2** city (1990 pop. 2,676), Lea co., SE N.Mex., on Llano Estacado, near Texas line, 18 mi/29 km S of Hobbs; 32°26′N 103°11′W. In ranching region; cattle, sheep; dairying; grain; alfalfa, cotton; mfg. (meat packing); carbon black. Oil wells and pipe lines nearby. Settled 1909, plotted 1927, inc. 1935.

Eunola (yoo-NO-luh), town (1990 pop. 199), Geneva co., SE Ala.; suburb of Geneva.

Eupora (yoo-POR-uh), town (1990 pop. 2,145), Webster co., central Miss., 25 mi/40 km WNW of Starkville, near Big Black R.; 33°32′N 89°16′W. In agr. (cotton, corn, soybeans; cattle; timber) area; mfg. (transportation equip., apparel, furniture, plastic prods., lumber). Natchez Trace (Natl.) Parkway passes to SE. Settled 1887, inc. 1889.

Eureka, (yoo-REE-kuh), county (□ 4,180 sq mi/10,826 sq km; 1990 pop. 1,547), N central Nev.; ⊙ Eureka; 39°58′N 116°16′W. Mt. region crossed in N by Humboldt R. Gold, silver; cattle. Chief ranges are Diamond Mts., form E central boundary, and Cortez Mts. (S of Humboldt R.). Part of Antelope Valley is in S. Formed 1873. Part of Toiyabe Natl Forest is SW, in Monitor Range. Former central mining dist. to Eureka. Geyser basin in N, on S side of Humboldt, c. 20 mi/32 km E of Battle Mt. Parts of Tuscarora Mts. and Emigrant Pass on far N.

Eureka 1 (yoo-REE-kuh), city (1990 pop. 27,025), ⊙ Humboldt co., NW Calif., 1,856 acres/751 ha W of Redding, 2 mi/3.2 km W of Pacific Ocean coast, on Humboldt Bay; 40°48′N 124°10′W. It is a port of entry. Lumbering and fishing are chief industries; tourism and some dairy farming, also cattle, sheep, lambs; timber; mfg. (machinery, paper and pulp, consumer goods, printing and publishing). A 40-acre/16-ha redwood park lies within the city limits. Eureka Municipal Airport to S, Clarke Memorial Mus. In Eureka is the Col. of the Redwoods (2-year); Humboldt State Univ. 5 mi/8 km NE, near Arcata. Humboldt Redwoods State park to S; Humboldt Natl. Wildlife Refuge to SW; Redwoods Natl. Park to N; Six Rivers Natl. Forest to E. Inc. 1856. **2** city (1990 pop. 4,435), ⊙ Woodford co., central

Ill., 17 mi/27 km E of Peoria; 40°43′N 89°16′W. Farm trade center; agr. (corn, wheat, soybeans, vegetables; livestock; dairy prods.); food processing. Seat of Eureka Col. Founded in 1830s, inc. 1859. Ronald Reagan graduated from Eureka Col.

Eureka 1 (yoo-REE-kuh), town (1990 pop. 2,974), ⊙ Greenwood co., SE Kansas, on Fall R., and c.55 mi/89 km E of Wichita; 37°49′N 96°17′W. Elev. 1,000 ft/305 m. Shipping and trade center for cattle, grain, and oil- and natural-gas-producing region. Eureka Downs, quarterhorse racetrack here. Fall River L. Reservoir and State Park to SE. Laid out 1867, inc. 1870. **2** town (1990 pop. 4,683), St. Louis co., E Mo., on Meramec R., suburb, 24 mi/39 km WSW of downtown St. Louis. Agr. (cattle; corn); limestone quarries; mfg. (crushed limestone, concrete, rotary cutting dies, printing roller). Annexed area includes community of Allenton in W. Six Flags Over Mid-America theme park in W; Hidden Valley Ski Area to NW; Rockwoods reservation (nature preserve) to N and W; Babler State Park to N; Castlewood State Park to NE. Former town of Times Beach adjoins town on NE, dioxin contaminated area; town has been removed. **3** town (1990 pop. 1,043), Lincoln co., NW Mont., on Tobacco R., near Canada (B.C.) border; 48°53′N 115°03′W. Berries, alfalfa, some livestock; logging; mfg. (lumber). Roosville, B.C., is 10 mi/16 km to N. L. Koocanusa reservoir (Kootenai R.) to W, formed by Libby Dam; lake is bridged 10 mi/16 km WSW. Kootenai Natl. Forest to W, S, and E, and 59 mi/95 km NW of Kalispell. **4** town (1990 pop. 1,197), McPherson co., N S.Dak., 60 mi/97 km WNW of Aberdeen; 45°46′N 99°37′W. Shipping center for grain and livestock; agr. (wheat, barley, oats; dairy produce); mfg. (feeds, swimming pool accessories, sports equip.); cement blocks. Agr. experiment station is here. Founded 1886.

Eureka 1 (yoo-REE-kuh), uninc. village (1990 pop. 550), ⊙ Eureka co., central Nev., 58 mi/93 km WNW of Ely; elev. 6,481 ft/1,975 m. Gold, silver, lead; cattle ranching. Diamond Peak (10,614 ft/3,235 m) is 9 mi/14.5 km NE. Town grew as a lead mining center; had pop. of 9,000 in 1870s. Eureka Sentinel Mus. here. **2** village (1990 pop. 282), Wayne co., E central N.C., 12 mi/19 km NNE of Goldsboro; 35°32′N 77°52′W. Tobacco, cotton, grain, poultry; livestock. **3** village, Chester co., S.C., 2 mi/3.2 km NNE of Chester. Agr. **4** village (1990 pop. 562), Juab co., central Utah, SW of Utah L., 30 mi/48 km SW of Provo, in mt. region; 39°57′N 112°07′W. Elev. 6,442 ft/1,964 m. Trade center for rich mining area (gold, silver, lead, zinc, copper). Utah L. 13 mi/21 km NE; unit of Wasatch Natl. Forest to W. Located in the Tintic Mining Dist.; Tintic Mining Mus. Settled 1870.

Eureka, SE Ohio: see CHAMBERSBURG.

Eureka Mill (yoo-REE-kuh), uninc. town (1990 pop. 1,738), Chester co., N S.C., residential suburb, 2 mi/3.2 km NE of Chester; 34°43′N 81°11′W.

Eureka Sound, N Franklin Dist., N.W.T., Canada, arm of the Arctic Ocean, bet. Axel Heiberg Isl. and Ellesmere Isl.; 180 mi/290 km long, 8 mi/13 km–30 mi/48 km wide; 79°N 87°W. Extends N from Norwegian Bay. Several arms radiate from it.

Eureka Springs (yoo-REE-kuh), town (1990 pop. 1,900), shares ⊙ functions with Berryville, Carroll co., NW Ark., 33 mi/53 km NE of Fayetteville, near Mo. line, in Ozark region; 36°23′N 93°44′W. Tourism; health resort with mineral springs. Diverse light mfg. Beaver L. Dam (White R.) to W. Settled 1879.

Eustace, village (1990 pop. 662), Henderson co., E Texas, 42 mi/68 km W of Tyler; 32°18′N 96°00′W. Agr. area. Oil and natural gas. Mfg. (apparel); natural gas processing. Cedar Creek Reservoir to SW; Purtis Creek State Park to N.

Eustatius Island, Neth. Antilles: see SAINT EUSTATIUS.

Eustis 1 (YOO-stis), town (□ 8 sq mi/20.7 sq km; 1990 pop. 12,967), Lake co., central Fla., 27 mi/43 km NW of Orlando, on L. Eustis; 28°51′N 81°41′W. Resort; shipping center for citrus fruit; packing houses, citrus-fruit canneries, creamery. Inc. 1925. **2** town (1990 pop. 616),

Franklin co., W central Maine, on Dead R., in recreational, lumbering area, and 40 mi/64 km NW of Farmington; 45°10′N 70°29′W. Mfg. (tools, wood prods.) at Stratton village.

Eustis (YOOS-tis), village (1990 pop. 452), Frontier co., S Nebr., 17 mi/27 km SW of Lexington, and on branch of Platte R; 40°39′N 100°01′W. Dairy prods., livestock, grain.

Eustis, Fort, Va., U.S. Army base along James R., in Newport News, at mouth of Warwock R. Base of approximately 10 sq mi/26 sq km occupies Mulberry Isl. and is used for army transportation services and training.

Eustis, Lake (YOO-stis), Lake co., central Fla.; c.5 mi/8 km long, 3 mi/4.8 km wide. Eustis city is on E shore. Part of connected lake system (Lakes Griffin, Harris, Dora, Apopka) drained by Oklawaha R.

Eutaw (YOO-taw), town (1990 pop. 2,281), ⊙ Greene co., W Ala., near Black Warrior R., c.30 mi/48 km SW of Tuscaloosa. In corn area; mfg. (paper prods., apparel). Greyhound racing track here. Settled 1818.

Eutaw Springs, S.C.: see EUTAWVILLE.

Eutawville (YOO-taw-vil), village (1990 pop. 350), Orangeburg co., SE central S.C., 30 mi/48 km ESE of Orangeburg, near L. Marion reservoir; 33°23′N 80°20′W. Santee-Cooper hydroelectric and navigation development is E. Mfg. includes wood treatments; agr. (timber; cotton, peanuts, tobacco, grain; livestock, poultry). Nearby was fought the Revolutionary battle of Eutaw Springs (Sept. 8, 1781).

Eutsuk Lake (OOT-suhk), (□ 96 sq mi/249 sq km), W central B.C., Canada, in Coast Mts., in Tweedsmuir Park, 150 mi/241 km WSW of Prince George; 48 mi/77 km long, 1 mi/2 km–8 mi/13 km wide. Elev. 2,817 ft/859 m. Contains John Buchan and Lady Susan isls. Connected with Whitesail L. (NW). Drains E into Nechako R. through Tetachuck L.

E.V. Spence Reservoir, Coke co., W central Texas, on Colorado R., 32 mi/51 km NNW of San Angelo, and 3 mi/4.8 km W of Robert Lee; 16 mi/26 km long; 31°53′N 100°31′W. Max. capacity 950,000 acre-ft. Formed by E.V. Spence Dam (123 ft/37 m high), built (1969) by the Colorado R. Municipal Water Dist. for water supply.

Evadale, town (1990 pop. 1,422), Jasper co., SE Texas, 20 mi/32 km NNE of Beaumont, on Neches R.; 30°20′N 94°03′W. Timber. Cattle. Mfg. (pulp and paperboard). Big Thicket Natl. Preserve follows course of river. Village Creek State Park to SW.

Evan, village (1990 pop. 83), Brown co., SW Minn., 19 mi/31 km W of New Ulm; 44°21′N 94°50′W. Dairying; livestock; grain.

Evandale, village (1990 pop. 3,175), Hamilton co., extreme SW Ohio, an E suburb of Cincinnati; 39°15′N 84°25′W.

Evangeline (uh-VAN-juh-leen), parish (□ 672 sq mi/1,740 sq km; 1990 pop. 33,274), S central La.; ⊙ Ville Platte; 30°42′N 92°17′W. Cocodrie L. on N boundary, part of W boundary formed by Bayou Nezpique, and part of S boundary formed by Bayou des Cannes. Agr. area, esp. rice (cotton, corn, hay, sugarcane, sweet potatoes; home gardens; cattle; dairying); fishing (crawfish, alligators); logging; mfg. (apparel, oil and gas field machinery, carbon black); sand and gravel. Formed 1910. Named for the heroine of Longfellow's poem. Includes Chicot State Park in NE, La. State Arboretum NW of park, Crooked Creek State Recreation Area in N center.

Evans, county (□ 186; 1990 pop. 8,724), E central Ga.; ⊙ Claxton; 32°10′N 81°53′W. Coastal plain agr. (cotton, corn, soybeans, wheat, tobacco, peanuts; cattle, hogs, poultry; timber). Drained by Canoochee R. Formed 1914.

Evans 1 town (1990 pop. 5,877), Weld co., N Colo., on South Platte R., suburb, 3 mi/4.8 km S of Greeley; 40°22′N 104°42′W. Elev. 4,651 ft/1,418 m. In irrigated agr. region. Lower Latham Reservoir to SE. **2** town (1990 pop. 13,713), Columbia co., Ga., 12 mi/19 km NW

of Augusta; 33°32′N 82°02′W. Mfg. includes consumer goods, bldg. materials, lumber; commercial printing.

Evans City or **Evansburg**, borough (1990 pop. 2,054), Butler co., W Pa., 10 mi/16 km SW of Butler. RR junction to W. Agr. area (grain, soybeans; dairying; livestock;); mfg. (boron compounds, food, fabricated metal prods.). Settled 1796, laid out 1836, inc. 1882.

Evans Mills, village (1990 pop. 661), Jefferson co., N N.Y., 10 mi/16 km NE of Watertown; 44°05′N 75°48′W.

Evans, Mount (10,460 ft/3,188 m), W Alta., Canada, near B.C. border, in Rocky Mts., in Jasper Natl. Park, 30 mi/48 km S of Jasper; 52°27′N 118°8′W. Just S is Hooker Icefield.

Evans, Mount (14,264 ft /4,346 m), in Clear Creek co., N central Colo., in the Front Range of the Rocky Mts., 35 mi/56 km WSW of Denver. At its summit was the Inter-Univ. High Altitude Laboratory. In Pike Natl. Forest. Road to summit (from Idaho Springs) is highest in U.S.

Evansburg, uninc. town (1990 pop. 1,047), Montgomery co., SE Pa., 5 mi/8 km NNE of Phoenixville, on Perkomen Creek; 40°10′N 75°25′W. Agr. (dairying; livestock; grain, apples, vegetables). Evansburg State Park to E.

Evansburg, Pa.: see EVANS CITY.

Evansdale, town (1990 pop. 4,638), Black Hawk co., E central Iowa, on Cedar R., suburb, 3 mi/4.8 km SE of downtown Waterloo; 42°27′N 92°16′W. Meat processing. Inc. after 1940.

Evanston 1 residential city (1990 pop. 73,233), Cook co., NE Ill., on L. Michigan; 42°02′N 87°41′W. A largely residential suburb N of Chicago, Evanston has businesses and manufactures goods such as books and published documents, paper, paint, chemicals, and medical supplies. Settled 1826, inc. 1857. It is also the natl. hq. of many companies and organizations, including the Woman's Christian Temperance Union, the Natl. Merit Scholarship Corporation, Rotary Internatl., and various agencies of the United Methodist Church. Evanston is an education center: Northwestern Univ., the Natl. Col. of Education, Kendall Col., 2 theological seminaries, and a junior col. Frances E. Willard lived in the city, and her home is a natl. landmark. The house of Vice President Charles G. Dawes seats the Evanston Historical Society. **2** city (1990 pop. 10,903), ⊙ Uinta co., extreme SW Wyo., on Bear R., and 50 mi/80 km E of Ogden, Utah, and 90 mi/145 km WSW of Rock Springs, Wyo.; 41°15′N 110°57′W. Elev. 6,748 ft/2,057 m. Trade center, RR division point in farm and oil-producing region. Mfg. (lumber; printing; petroleum prods.; concrete; wire harnesses). Historic Depot Square and historic dist. Bear River State Park to E; Bear River Divide (mt. range) to N. Settled 1869, inc. 1888, founded as Bear River City. Developed with arrival of RR.

Evansville, city (1990 pop. 126,272), ⊙ Vanderburgh co., extreme SW Ind., a port on the Ohio R.; 37°59′N 87°32′W. Inc. 1819. It is a RR and river shipping and commercial center for a coal, oil, and farm region. Machinery, plastics, primary metals, pharmaceuticals, food prods., consumer goods, and fabricated-metal items are among its many manufactures. The Univ. of Evansville, the Univ. of South Ind., several technical cols., and a state mental hosp. are there. The city has a mus. of arts and sciences, a large shopping plaza, a zoo, a philharmonic orchestra, and an aviary. A nearby Native Amer. mound site is a state memorial (Angel Mounds State Memorial).

Evansville 1 town (1990 pop. 3,174), Rock co., S Wis., 20 mi/32 km S of Madison; 42°46′N 89°17′W. In agr. area (tobacco; livestock, poultry; dairy prods.); mfg. (iron castings, exercise equip. (barbells), metal bldgs.). Settled 1839; inc. as village in 1866, as city in 1896. **2** town (1990 pop. 1,403), Natrona co., central Wyo., on North Platte R., and suburb, 1 mi/1.6 km E of Casper; 42°52′N 106°15′W. Elev. c.5,200 ft/1,585 m. Chemicals, petroleum prods. Hogaden Ski Area to S.

Evansville 1 village (1990 pop. 844), Randolph co., SW Ill., on Kaskaskia R. (bridged), and 14 mi/23 km NNW of Chester; 38°05′N 89°55′W. In agr. and bituminous coal area. **2** village (1990 pop. 566), Douglas co., W Minn., 18 mi/29 km NW of Alexandria; 46°00′N 95°40′W. Dairying; poultry; grain, soybeans, alfalfa. L. Christian and Pelican L. to NW, numerous small natural lakes in region.

Evant, village (1990 pop. 444), Coryell co., central Texas, 35 mi/56 km NW of Killeen; 31°28′N 98°09′W. Cattle, sheep; grains, pecans.

Evart, town (1990 pop. 1,744), Osceola co., central Mich., 26 mi/42 km SSW of Cadillac, and on Muskegon R.; 43°53′N 85°16′W. In agr. area (dairy prods.; livestock; corn); mfg. (automotive parts). Indian mounds nearby. Inc. as village 1872, as city 1938.

Evarts (EV-uhrts), town (1990 pop. 1,063), Harlan co., SE Ky., 7 mi/11.3 km E of Harlan, on Clover Fork of Cumberland R., near Pine Mt. in the Cumberland Mts.; 36°51′N 83°12′W. Bituminous coal; timber; mfg. (lumber processing). Settled c.1800; inc. 1915.

Eveleth, town (1990 pop. 4,064), St. Louis co., NE Minn., 4 mi/6.4 km S of Virginia, in Mesabi Iron Range; 47°27′N 92°32′W. RR junction to SW. Cattle; oats, alfalfa; dairying; mfg. (snowmobile parts, vinyl windows, hardwood panels); shipping point for iron ore. Iron mines nearby. Growth dates from beginning of mining operations (c.1900). Virginia Eveleth Airport to SE; annual winter carnival; U.S. Hockey Hall of Fame. Superior Natl. Forest to N. Settled 1892, inc. 1893.

Evening Shade, village (1990 pop. 328), former capital shared with town of Hardy, consolidated and moved to Ash Flat, Sharp co., N Ark., 20 mi/32 km N of Batesville near Strawberry R.; 36°04′N 91°37′W. In agr. area.

Everest, village (1990 pop. 310), Brown co., extreme NE Kansas, 13 mi/21 km SSE of Hiawatha, 39°40′N 95°25′W. Agr. (grain; poultry, livestock; dairying).

Everett 1 city (1990 pop. 35,701), Middlesex co., E Mass., an industrial suburb of Boston, on the Mystic R.; 42°25′N 71°03′W. A deepwater port, Everett has petroleum storage facilities and foundries and plants that manufacture rubber prods., metals, transportation equip., chemicals, and paper. Other industries include bookbinding and printing, and lasers; electric power generation. Nearby education centers, such as Harvard Univ. and the Mass. Inst. of Technology, have spurred research development in Everett. Settled c.1643, set off from Malden 1870, inc. as a city 1892. **2** city (1990 pop. 69,961), ⊙ Snohomish co., NW Wash., suburb 28 mi/45 km N of Seattle, on Possession Sound, arm of Puget Sound, near mouth of the Snohomish R.; 47°58′N 122°12′W. RR junction. A port of entry with a natural harbor, it is an important lumber-shipping center. Other industries include commercial fishing (fish, oysters, crabs) and aircraft mfg.; sand and gravel. Navy homeport. Mfg. (medical and dental equip., food and beverage processing, plastics, machinery, metal fabrication, electronics, lumber, furniture, transportation equip., consumer goods, paper prods.); bookbinding, iron foundry. Inc. 1893. Tourism is also significant; the city is a gateway to both the Cascade Mts. and the offshore isls.; Boeing Tour Center. Everett Community Col. Tulalip Indian Reservation to N; Snoqualmie Natl. Forest to E.

Everett (E-vuh-ret), borough (1990 pop. 1,777), Bedford co., S Pa., 7 mi/11.3 km E of Bedford, on Raystown Branch of Juniata R. Agr. (corn, oats, hay, apples; livestock; dairying); mfg. (lumber, wood prods., metal fabrication, fertilizers, limestone); printing and publishing. Tussy Mt. ridge to W. Laid out 1795, inc. 1873.

Everett, Mount (EV-ret), mountain (2,602 ft/793 m), extreme SW Mass., in the Berkshires, near N.Y. and Conn. lines, 7 mi/11.3 km SSW of Great Barrington. Observation tower on summit. Surrounding peak is Mt. Everett State Reservation; covers 1,000 acres/400 ha and is crossed by Appalachian Trail; hiking and ski trails.

Everetts, village (1990 pop. 143), Martin co., NE N.C., 6 mi/9.7 km W of Williamston; 35°49′N 77°10′W. Tobacco, cotton, peanuts, grain; poultry, livestock.

Everglades, marshy, low-lying tropical savanna area (□

c.4,000 sq mi/10,360 sq km), interior S and SW Fla., extending from L. Okeechobee S to Fla. Bay. Characterized by water, sawgrass, hammocks (islandlike masses of vegetation), palms, pine and mangrove forests, and solidly packed black muck (resulting from millions of years of vegetation decay in near-stagnant water), the Everglades receives an annual average rainfall of more than 60 in/152 cm, mainly in the summer. Big Cypress Swamp, to the NW, and L. Okeechobee are the chief sources of water for the Everglades. Limestone rims the area, acting as a natural retaining wall against the sea. Large tracts of land were drained in the late 19th and early 20th cents., when the Everglades was considered a potentially rich agr. region, but only the area immediately bordering L. Okeechobee was farmed. Winter vegetables and sugarcane are now the main crops; some cattle are raised. A ring dike was constructed around the entire shore of L. Okeechobee in the 1920s to prevent hurricanes from blowing water out of the lake. This, in addition to land development in Big Cypress Swamp, has disrupted the natural flow of water into the Everglades, creating water shortages that have damaged much of its plant and animal life. In the 1980s, Fla. began a massive conservation project in the Everglades; it called for reflooding drained swampland and restoring areas to their natural state that had been cleared for agr. and development. At the S end of Fla. is Everglades Natl. Park (□ 2,354 sq mi/6,097 sq km), the 3d-largest natl. park; est. 1947. Big Cypress Natl. Preserve (est. 1974) is to the N. Fla. Bay, with its many islets and the Ten Thousand Isls., is part of the park. A great variety of flora and fauna are found in the park, which is also a haven for such endangered species as the alligator, egret, and bald eagle. The Tamiami Trail (completed 1928), a highway N of the park, links Miami with the W coast of Fla. Farther N, I-75 links the W coast with Fort Lauderdale.

Everglades City, village (□ 1 sq mi/2.6 sq km; 1990 pop. 321), ⊙ Collier co., SW Fla., c.30 mi/51 km SE of Naples, on Gulf coast, opposite Ten Thousand Isls.; 25°51′N 81°23′W. RR terminus; resort and fishing port. Seafood canning.

Evergreen, city (1990 pop. 3,911), ⊙ Conecuh co., S Ala., 25 mi/40 km N of Brewton. Mfg. includes fabricated metal prods., apparel, textiles, meat processing, motor vehicles). Settled c.1820.

Evergreen 1 town (1990 pop. 283), Avoyelles parish, E central La., 32 mi/51 km SE of Alexandria; 30°57′N 92°07′W. In cotton-growing area. **2** town (1990 pop. 4,109), Flathead co., NW Mont., residential suburb, 2 mi/3.2 km E of Kalispell, on Flathead R., at mouth of Whitefish R.; 48°14′N 114°16′W. Stillwater Game Preserve to NE.

Evergreen 1 uninc. village (1990 pop. 7,582), Jefferson co., N central Colo., on Bear Creek, in Front Range suburb, 20 mi/32 km WSW of downtown Denver; 39°37′N 105°20′W. Elev. 7,040 ft/2,146 m. Resort center. Diverse light mfg. Pike Natl. Forest to W. **2** uninc. village, Columbus co., SE N.C., 16 mi/26 km SSE of Lumberton. Tobacco, peanuts, grain; livestock. Lumber River State Park to W.

Evergreen Park, village (1990 pop. 20,874), Cook co., NE Ill., a residential suburb 10 mi/16 km SW of downtown Chicago; 41°43′N 87°42′W. Mfg. advertising novelties. Inc. 1893. St. Xavier Col. nearby.

Everly, town (1990 pop. 706), Clay co., NW Iowa, near Ocheyedan R., 9 mi/14.5 km W of Spencer; 43°09′N 95°19′W. Feed milling; fertilizer.

Everman, town (1990 pop. 5,672), Tarrant co., N Texas, residential suburb, 9 mi/14.5 km SSE of downtown Fort Worth, near Village Creek; 32°37′N 97°16′W. Surrounded by city of Fort Worth. Light mfg.

Everson, town (1990 pop. 1,490), Whatcom co., NW Wash., 12 mi/19 km NE of Bellingham, and on Nooksack R., 5 mi/8 km S of Canada (B.C.) border; 48°55′N 122°21′W. In agr. region (vegetables, berries, alfalfa; poultry, cattle; dairying; mfg. (lumber, log homes, nylon twine).

Everson (E-vuhr-suhn), borough (1990 pop. 939), Fayette co., SW Pa., 5 mi/8 km N of Connellsville, and 1 mi/1.6 km S of Scottdale on Jacobs Creek. Agr. (corn, hay; livestock; dairying); light mfg. Mt. Pleasant–Scottdale Airport to NE. Laid out 1874.

Everton (E-vuhr-tuhn), city (1990 pop. 325), Dade co., SW Mo., 25 mi/40 km WNW of Springfield; 37°20′N 93°42′W. Wheat, hay; cattle; dairying.

Everton 1 village (1990 pop. 150), Boone co., N Ark., 12 mi/19 km ESE of Harrison; 36°09′N 92°54′W. Glasssand deposits nearby. **2** uninc. village (1990 pop. 500), Fayette co., E Ind., 6 mi/9.7 km SSE of Connorsville. Corn, wheat; hogs.

Evesham (EEV-shuhm), township (1990 pop. 35,309), Burlington co., S N.J., 12 mi/19 km E of Camden; 39°51′N 74°53′W. Rapidly expanding residential area. Inc. 1798.

Evitts Creek, c.30 mi/48 km long, in S Pa. and NW Md.; rises in central Bedford co., Pa.; flows SW bet. Evitts Mt. ridge (E) and Wills Mt. ridge (W), through Koon and Gordon reservoirs, into Md., to North Branch of the Potomac R. 2 mi/3.2 km SE of Cumberland, Md.; 39°55′N 78°36′W.

Evitts Mountain, S Pa., NE-SW ridge of the Appalachian system, runs c.23 mi/37 km NE from Md. state line through center of Bedford co., joins Dunning Mt. ridge in N part of Bedford co.; 39°55′N 78°43′W–40°08′N 78°27′W. Elev. 2,000 ft/610 m–2,400 ft/730 m.

Ewa (EI-vah), town, S Oahu, Honolulu Co., Hawaii, 12 mi/19 km WNW of Honolulu, 3 mi/4.8 km inland from S coast. Barbers Point Naval Air Station to SW. Pearl Harbor Naval Reservation to E.

Ewa Beach (EI-vah), city (1990 pop. 14,315), S Oahu isl., Honolulu co., Hawaii, on S coast, 8 mi/12.9 km W of Honolulu, 3 mi/4.8 km SSE of Ewa, 3 mi/4.8 km W of entrance to Pearl Harbor; 21°19′N 158°00′W. Residential and service center for military operations in area. Mfg. (meat packing); agr. (dairying; poultry). Barbers Point Naval Air Station to W, Pearl Harbor Naval Reservation to E. Pacific Tsunami Warning Center located here.

Ewansville (YOO-uhnz-vil), village, Burlington co., W N.J., on Rancocas Creek, and 3 mi/4.8 km ESE of Mt. Holly, in agr. area that is rapidly suburbanizing.

Ewarton (1991 pop. 8,742), St. Catherine parish, central Jamaica, at S foot of Mt. Diablo, 17 mi/27 km NW of Spanish Town; 18°11′N 77°05′W. RR terminus in agr. region. Processes and exports citrus fruit. Famous St. Clair's Cave to S.

Ewauna, Lake (uh-WAHN-uh), Klamath co., S Oregon, at city of Klamath Falls, S of Upper Klamath L. (linked by 2-mi/3.2-km Link R.); c.2 mi/3.2 km long; 42°14′N 121°47′W. Drained by Klamath R.

Ewell, Md.: see SMITH ISLAND.

Ewen (YOO-en), village, Ontonagon co., NW Upper Peninsula, Mich., 24 mi/39 km S of Ontonagon; 46°32′N 89°16′W. In dairy area. Area surrounded by, but not included in, Ottawa Natl. Forest.

Ewing (YOO-ing), town (1990 pop. 463), Lewis co., NE Mo., near Middle Fabius R., 6 mi/9.7 km S of Monticello; 40°00′N 91°42′W.

Ewing 1 village (1990 pop. 264), Franklin co., S Ill., 7 mi/11.3 km NNE of Benton; 38°05′N 88°50′W. In bituminous-coal-mining, oil, and agr. area. Rend L. to W. **2** village (1990 pop. 449), Holt co., N Nebr., 20 mi/32 km SE of O'Neill, and on Elkborn R.; 42°15′N 98°20′W. Dairying; livestock, grain; concrete. **3** uninc. village, Lee co., SW Va., 49 mi/79 km SW of Norton, on Indian Creek, bet. Ky. (N) and Tenn. (S) state lines; one of the westernmost communities in Va.; 36°37′N 83°25′W. Mfg. (apparel, limestone processing); agr. (tobacco, corn; cattle); coal, limestone. Cumberland Gap Natl. Historic Park to W; Cumberland Gap pass (1,700 ft/518 m), 13 mi/21 km WSW of Ewing.

Ewing, township (1990 pop. 34,185), Mercer co., central N.J., 6 mi/8 km N of Trenton. Printing establishments. Inc. 1834. Col. of N.J., formerly Trenton State Col.

Ewingsville (YOO-ings-vil), uninc. village, Collier township, Allegheny co., W Pa., residential suburb, 7 mi/

11.3 km SW of downtown Pittsburgh, on Robinson Run; 40°23′N 80°06′W.

Excel (ek-SEL), town (1990 pop. 571), Monroe co., SW Ala., 8 mi/12.9 km S of Monroeville.

Excelsior, town (1990 pop. 2,367), Hennepin co., E Minn., residential suburb, 16 mi/26 km WSW of downtown Minneapolis; 44°53′N 93°34′W. On Gideon Bay, S shore of L. Minnetonka. Mfg. (farm equip., trusses, millwork, baked goods, diverse light mfg.). Experimental fruit farm nearby.

Excelsior Mountain, peak (12,446 ft/3,794 m) of the Sierra Nevada, on Mono-Tuolumne co. line, E Calif., 8 mi/12.9 km W of Mono L. On E boundary of Yosemite Natl. Park.

Excelsior Mountains (ek-SEL-syor), in Mineral co., W Nev. extends slightly into Mono co., E Calif., S of Hawthorne, Nev., Toiyabe Natl. Forest; an E spur of Sierra Nevada. Highest point, Moho Mts. (8,805 ft/2,684 m). Toiyabe Natl Forest is in W part.

Excelsior Springs, city (1990 pop. 10,354), on Ray-Clay co. line, W Mo., 25 mi/40 km NE of Kansas City; 39°20′N 94°14′W. Health resort, mineral springs; former coal mines. Corn, wheat, wheat milling; mfg. (transportation equip., machinery, sealants and adhesives). Satellite community of Kansas City. Founded 1880, inc. 1903. Jesse James b. nearby.

Exchequer Dam; Exchequer Reservoir, Calif.: see MERCED RIVER.

Excursion Inlet, village, SE Alaska, 30 mi/48 km N of Hoonah; 58°25′N 135°27′W. Fishing; cannery.

Exeland (EKS-land), village (1990 pop. 180), Sawyer co., N Wis., 34 mi/55 km ESE of Spooner; 45°40′N 91°14′W. In cutover forest area; farming.

Exeter (EK-suh-tuhr), town (1991 pop. 4,338), S Ont., Canada, 30 mi/48 km NNW of London; 43°21′N 81°29′W. Food canning; dairying.

Exeter, city (1990 pop. 7,276), Tulare co., S central Calif., 8 mi/12.9 km E of Visalia, near Keawah R., in Sierra Nevada foothills, at edge of San Joaquin Valley; 36°17′N 119°08′W. RR junction. Shipping center for citrus and deciduous fruit dist.; also olives, alfalfa, cotton; cattle, hogs; mfg. (machinery and coated paper). Sequoia Natl. Park is c.20 mi/32 km NE; Sequoia Natl. Forest to E. Inc. 1911.

Exeter 1 town (1990 pop. 597), Barry co., SW Mo., in the Ozarks, 4 mi/6.4 km W of Cassville; 36°40′N 93°56′W. **2** town (1990 pop. 12,481), ⊙ Rockingham co., SE N.H., 11 mi/18 km SW of Portsmouth; 42°59′N 70°57′W. Town center on Exeter R. at head of navigation and falls (site of early mills), continues N as tidal Squamscott R. Mfg. (computers, leather goods, leather tanning chemicals, medical and electrical equip., bldg.

materials; printing and publishing); agr. (apples, nursery crops, vegetables; poultry; dairying). Seat of N.H. govt. from 1774 to 1784. Seat of Phillips Exeter Acad. (opened 1783). Founded 1638 by John Wheelwright; noted in the Revolution for its patriot activities. **3** town (1990 pop. 5,461), Washington co., SW central R.I., on Queen R., and 18 mi/29 km SSW of Providence; 41°34′N 71°38′W. Poultry, dairy prods. Fisherville and Hallville historic and archaeological dists. are of interest. R.I. Veterans Cemetery here. Set off from North Kingston; inc. 1743.

Exeter 1 village (1990 pop. 59), Scott co., W central Ill., 13 mi/21 km W of Jacksonville; 39°43′N 90°30′W. In agr. area. **2** village (1990 pop. 661), Fillmore co., SE Nebr., 11 mi/18 km NE of Geneva; 40°38′N 97°27′W. Dairy prods.; livestock; grain.

Exeter (EK-suh-tuhr), borough (1990 pop. 5,691), Luzerne co., NE central Pa., 6 mi/9.7 km NNE of Wilkes-Barre, on Susquehanna R. Mfg. (wire and wire rope, furniture); some anthracite. Frances Slokum State Park to NW. Settled 1790, inc. 1884.

Exeter (EK-suh-tuhr), township (1990 pop. 937), Penobscot co., S central Maine, 22 mi/35 km NW of Bangor; 44°58′N 69°08′W. In agr. region. Includes villages of Exeter Center and Exeter Corners.

Exeter River, 30 mi/48 km long, Rockingham co., SE N.H.; rises at Chester, 12 mi/19 km SE of Manchester; flows E and NE, through Exeter, to Swampscott R., tidal river leading N to Great Bay. Falls at Exeter.

Exira, town (1990 pop. 955), Audubon co., W central Iowa, on East Nishnabotna R., and 10 mi/16 km S of Audubon; 41°35′N 94°52′W. Settled 1852; laid out 1857; inc. 1880.

Exline, town (1990 pop. 187), Appanoose co., S Iowa, near Mo. line, 6 mi/9.7 km S of Centerville; 40°38′N 92°50′W.

Exmore, town (1990 pop. 1,115), Northampton co., E Va., 20 mi/32 km NE of Cape Charles town, in Eastern Shore area, bet. Atlantic Ocean (E) and Chesapeake Bay (W); 37°31′N 75°49′W. Mfg. (consumer goods, fiberglass boats and tanks, asphalt); agr. area (vegetables, grain; poultry, livestock).

Experiment, town (1990 pop. 3,762), Spalding co., W central Ga., 2 mi/3.2 mi NW of Griffin; 33°15′N 84°16′W.

Exploits, river, c.150 mi/240 km long, SW N.F., Canada; rising in the Long Range, SW; flowing NE to Exploits Bay, an arm of Notre Dame Bay. On the river are Grand Falls and Bishop's Falls, sites of large hydroelectric power plants.

Exploits, Bay of, inlet of Notre Dame Bay, E N.F., Canada; 30 mi/48 km long, 2 mi/3 km–6 mi/10 km wide.

Receives Exploits R. estuary 5 mi/8 km S of Botwood, near head of bay. At entrance of bay is Thwart Isl.

Exploits River, 200 mi/322 km long, N.F., Canada; rises as Lloyds R. in SW part of isl.; flows ENE through King George IV L., Lloyds L., and Red Indian L., past Grand Falls (hydroelectric power) and Bishop's Falls, to Bay of Exploits (5 mi/8 km S of Botwood). Receives Victoria R. in Red Indian L.

Export, borough (1990 pop. 981), Westmoreland co., SW central Pa., 19 mi/31 km E of Pittsburgh, on Turtle Creek. Agr. (corn, hay; livestock; dairying); mfg. (electrical equip., energy management systems, machinery, plastic and fabricated metal prods.); coal. Beaver Run Reservoir to NE. Inc. 1911.

Extension, village, SW B.C., Canada, on SE Vancouver Isl., 4 mi/6 km S of Naniamo; 49°06′N 123°57′W. Coal mining; mixed farming.

Exton (EKS-tuhn), uninc. town (1990 pop. 2,550), Chester co., SE Pa., suburb, 25 mi/40 km WNW of Philadelphia, on Valley Creek; 40°01′N 75°37′W. Mfg. (bldg. materials, consumer goods, paper prods., chemicals, machinery, plastic prods., furniture); printing, metal fabrication.

Exuma and Cays: see BAHAMAS.

Exuma Sound, deep Atlantic channel, in central Bahama Isls., c.100 mi/160 km long NW-SE, c.40 mi/64 km wide. Bordered by Eleuthera Isl. (NE), Cat Isl. (E), Great Exuma Isl. (SW).

Eyak (EE-yok), village (1990 pop. 172), S Alaska, 4 mi/6.4 km E of Cordova, on small L. Eyak; 60°31′N 145°35′W. Resort and residential dist. for Cordova.

Eynon (EL-nuhn), uninc village, Lackawanna co., NE Pa., suburb, 7 mi/11.3 km NE of Scranton, and part of Archbald borough, 2 mi/3.2 km W of Archbald center; 41°29′N 75°34′W. Mfg. includes bridal gowns, metal caskets, military tanks. Archbald Pothole State Park to N.

Eyota (ei-YO-duh), town (1990 pop. 1,448), Olmsted co., SE Minn., 12 mi/19 km E of Rochester; 43°59′N 92°13′W. RR junction to W. Poultry, livestock; grain, soybeans; dairying; mfg. (feeds). Part of Richard J. Dorer Memorial Hardwood State Forest to S.

Ezel (EEZ-el), uninc. village (1990 pop. 400), Morgan co., E Ky., 31 mi/50 km ESE of Mt. Sterling city. In coal and agr. (tobacco, corn; cattle) area. Upper reach of Cave Run L. reservoir to NE.

Ezequiel Montes (ee-ZEE-kee-el mon-TEZ), town (1990 pop. 7,705), E Querétaro, Mexico, 19 mi/30 km E of the city of Querétaro; elev. 6,677 ft/2,035 m. In the central plateau; limited surface water. Temperate to hot climate. Resources are agr., cattle, and minerals. Connected by road to Querétaro and Cadereyta de Montes.

F

Fabens, town (1990 pop. 5,599), El Paso co., extreme W Texas, port of entry near the Rio Grande, 27 mi/43 km SE of El Paso; 31°30′N 106°09′W. Shipping, processing center in irrigated farm area (cotton, pecans; dairying, cattle). Mfg. (jeans).

Fabius, village (1990 pop. 310), Onondaga co., central N.Y., 16 mi/26 km SE of Syracuse; 42°50′N 75°59′W. In dairying area. Ski centers nearby.

Fabius River (FAI-bee-uhs), 1 mi/1.6 km long, NE Mo.; formed by 3 branches, North, Middle, and South Fabius rivers; main river formed by junction of the North and the South Fabius just below Quincy, Ill., empties into the Mississippi R. North Fabius R. (c.130 mi/209 km) rises near Moulton, Iowa, flows SE. Middle Fabius R. (c.90 mi/145 km) rises in Scotland co., flows SE to the North Fabius. South Fabius R. (c.100 mi/161 km) rises in Knox co., flows SE, N, and E. Portions of all 3 branches have been straightened by channelization.

Fabre (FAH-bruh), village, W Que., Canada, near L. Timiskaming, 22 mi/35 km SE of Haileybury; 47°12′N 79°22′W. Copper mining.

Fabyan House, N.H.: see CARROLL, town.

Factoryville, borough (1990 pop. 1,310), Wyoming co., NE Pa., 12 mi/19 km NNE of Scranton, on South Branch Tunkhannock Creek; 41°33′N 75°46′W. Agr. (grain; dairying; livestock; timber). Mfg. (wood prods., stainless steel fabrication). Lackawanna State Park to E; L. Winola reservoir to S. Settled 1798.

Fair Bluff, town (1990 pop. 1,068), Columbus co., SE N.C., on Lumber R., and 21 mi/34 km S of Lumberton, near S.C. state line; 34°18′N 79°01′W. Grain, tobacco, peanuts, livestock. Mfg. (construction materials, apparel). Lumber River State Park to NE.

Fair Grove, town (1990 pop. 919), Greene co., SW Mo., 13 mi/21 km NE of Springfield; 37°22′N 93°09′W. Satellite community of Springfield near West Branch of Pomme de Terre R. Agr. area. Light mfg.

Fair Harbor, N.Y.: see FIRE ISLAND.

Fair Haven, town (1990 pop. 2,887), including Fair Haven village, Rutland co., W Vt., 15 mi/24 km W of Rutland, and on Castleton R.; 43°37′N 73°16′W. Slate quarries (1st in Vt.; opened 1839); dairy prods. Settled c.1780.

Fair Haven 1 village (1990 pop. 1,505), St. Clair co., E Mich., 13 mi/21 km NE of Mount Clemens, on Anchor Bay of L. St. Clair; 42°40′N 82°39′W. Mfg. (plastics, machinery, boats). **2** resort village (□ 2 sq mi/5.2 sq km; 1990 pop. 895), Cayuga co., W central N.Y., on Little Sodus Bay of L. Ontario, 14 mi/23 km SW of Oswego; 43°19′N 76°42′W. Nearby is Fair Haven Beach State Park.

Fair Haven, borough (1990 pop. 5,270), Monmouth co., E N.J., on Navesink R., and 2 mi/3.2 km NE of Red Bank; 40°21′N 74°02′W. Largely residential. Inc. 1912.

Fair Hill, hamlet, Cecil co., NE Md., near Pa. state line, 17 mi/27 km E of Wilmington, Del. Early names of the town included Fairhill Crossroads and Fayette.

Fair Island (□ 1 sq mi/3 sq km), E N.F., Canada, in Bonavista Bay, 40 mi/64 km W of Gander; 48°58′N 53°45′W. Fishing.

Fair Lawn, borough (1990 pop. 30,548), Bergen co., NE N.J., across the Passaic R. from Paterson; 40°56′N 74°07′W. It is residential with light industries. Includes the Radburn "new town," a suburban housing development that separates pedestrian and vehicle traffic. It was constructed in the 1920s. Inc. 1924.

Fair Oaks, town (1990 pop. 1,133), Wagner and Rogers cos., NE Okla., residential suburb 15 mi/24 km E of downtown Tulsa, on Verdigris R.; 36°08′N 95°42′W. Agr. to E and S.

Fair Oaks 1 village (1990 pop. 6,996), Cobb co., NW central Ga., just SE of Marietta; 33°54′N 84°32′W. Also

called Machinery City. **2** uninc. village, Henrico co., E central Va., near Chickahominy R., 7 mi/11.3 km E of Richmond. Scene of indecisive Civil War battle, sometimes called Battle of Seven Pines (May 31–June 1, 1862). Seven Pines Natl. Cemetery to SE. Richmond Internatl. Airport to S.

Fair Oaks, residential suburb (1990 pop. 26,867) of Sacramento, Sacramento co., N central Calif., 13 mi/21 km NE of downtown Sacramento, on the American R.; 38°39′N 121°15′W. In a citrus fruit and farm (vegetables; dairying; poultry) area. Folsom L. reservoir and State Recreation Area to NE.

Fair Plain, city (1990 pop. 8,051), Berrien co., SW Mich., residential suburb of St. Joseph/Benton Harbor, 2 mi/3.2 km SE of St. Joseph, S of Benton Harbor; 42°04′N 86°27′W.

Fair Play, city (1990 pop. 442), Polk co., SW central Mo., 9 mi/14.5 km W of Bolivar; 37°37′N 93°34′W. Dairy and poultry market; wheat, soybeans; cattle.

Fair Port, uninc. village, Northumberland co., E Va., 75 mi/121 km SE of Fredericksburg, on Chesapeake Bay, at entrance to Great Wicomico R. estuary. Fish, crabs, oysters. Ferry from Tangier Isl. terminates at Reedville, 2 mi/3.2 km to NE.

Fairacres, uninc. town (1990 pop. 700), Dona Ana co., S N.Mex., residential suburb 3 mi/4.8 km W of downtown Las Cruces, on Rio Grande. In irrigated agr. area; winery.

Fairbank, town (1990 pop. 1,018), on Buchanan-Fayette co. line, E Iowa, on Little Wapsipinicon R., and 17 mi/27 km NE of Waterloo; 42°38′N 92°02′W. Feed, meat processing. Amish-Mennonite settlement.

Fairbank 1 village, Talbot co., Md. The community was originally "bounty land" given Edward Ned Fairbanks for fighting in the War of 1812. See TILGHMAN ISLAND. **2** uninc. village, Luzerne township, Fayette co., SW Pa., 7 mi/11.3 km NW of Uniontown, on Dunlap Creek; 39°56′N 79°50′W. Agr. (corn, hay; dairying). Mfg. (wire material handling prods.).

Fairbanks, city (1990 pop. 30,843), E central Alaska, on the Chena R. near its confluence with the Tanana; 64°50′N 147°39′W. Lying SW of the trans-Alaskan oil pipeline from the Prudhoe Bay fields to Valdez, Fairbanks's economic mainstay is govt., mining, tourism, oil business; some farming; light mfg.; lumbering. The 1974–1977 construction of oil pipeline and Dalton Highway to Prudhoe Bay brought boom to area. Gold was discovered in 1902, and Fairbanks grew rapidly as a mining camp. The building of the Alaskan RR allowed significant access to the city from Seward and Anchorage. Fort Wainwright and Eielson Air Force Base are central to the area's development. NW terminus of Richardson and Alaska highways from Dawson Creek, B.C. S terminus of Dalton Highway to Prudhoe Bay. Univ. of Alaska-Fairbanks is at College. Dog-sled races are a popular annual event, including the Yukon Quest. Of notable interest is "Alaskaland," a 40 acres/16 ha local site that includes a Gold Rush town, mining, a mus., art galleries, and a theater. Creamers Field Wildlife Refuge. Fairbanks North Star borough has 80,000 people. Inc. 1903.

Fairbanks North Star, borough (□ 7,362 sq mi/19,068 sq km; 1990 pop. 77,720), central Alaska, drained by Chena and Nanana R.'s, city of Fairbanks in W center. Upper Chatanika State Recreation Area in N; Fort Wainwright Military Reserve in E; Eielson Air Force Base in center. Alaska Pipeline runs N-S through center. Mfg. at Fairbanks.

Fairborn, city (1990 pop. 31,300), Greene co., SW Ohio, 5 mi/8 km NE of Dayton; 39°48′N 84°01′W. Major employers are Wright State Univ. in nearby Dayton and the huge Wright-Patterson Air Force Base. Cement production. Air Force Mus. nearby. Settled 1799, inc. 1950 with the merging of Osborn and Fairborn.

Fairburn, city (1990 pop. 4,013), Fulton co., NW central Ga., 18 mi/29 km SW of Atlanta; 33°34′N 84°35′W. Suburb of S Atlanta. Mfg. (concrete, electrical equip., machinery, canvas and vinyl prods., furniture, construction materials, plastics, sheet metal fabrication). Inc. as town 1854, as city 1925.

Fairburn, village (1990 pop. 62), Custer co., SW S.Dak., 20 mi/32 km ESE of Custer, and on French Creek; 43°41′N 103°12′W.

Fairbury, city (1990 pop. 3,643), Livingston co., E central Ill., 12 mi/19 km SSE of Pontiac; 40°45′N 88°30′W. In agr. area; corn, wheat, soybeans, livestock, poultry; dairy prods. Mfg. (clothing). Gravel pits. Inc. 1890.

Fairbury (FER-buhr-ee), town (1990 pop. 4,335), ⊙ Jefferson co., SE Nebr., 50 mi/80 km SSW of Lincoln, and on Little Blue R., near Kansas state line; 40°08′N 97°10′W. Elev. 1,319 ft/402 m. RR junction. Trade center for agr. area. Concrete and clay prods.; meat, poultry, and dairy prods.; livestock, grain. Mfg. (chemicals, food prods., quarry tile, printing, agr. equip., apparel). Old Oregon Trail passes to NE, Rock Creek Station historical site to SE on trail. Alexandria Lakes State Recreation Area to NW. Founded 1869.

Fairchance, borough (1990 pop. 1,918), Fayette co., SW Pa., 6 mi/9.7 km SSW of Uniontown; 39°49′N 79°45′W. Agr. (corn, hay; dairying, livestock). Light mfg. Forbes State Forest to SE.

Fairchild, village (1990 pop. 504), Eau Claire co., W central Wis., 31 mi/50 km SE of Eau Claire; 44°36′N 90°57′W. In hilly stock-raising region. E terminus of Buffalo R. State Trail.

Fairchild, Mount, Colo.: see MUMMY RANGE.

Fairdale 1 town (1990 pop. 6,563), Jefferson co., N Ky., residential suburb, 11 mi/18 km S of downtown Louisville; 38°06′N 85°45′W. Agr. area (tobacco, grain, livestock). Mfg. (construction materials, concrete prods., metal fabricating). **2** uninc. town (1990 pop. 2,049), Greene co., SW Pa., residential community 1 mi/1.6 km W of Carmichaels; 39°53′N 79°58′W. **3** uninc. town, Raleigh co., S central W.Va., 8 mi/12.9 km W of Beckley. Bituminous coal. Mfg. (coal processing). Stephens L. reservoir to NE.

Fairdale, village (1990 pop. 76), Walsh co., NE N.Dak., 39 mi/63 km W of Grafton; 48°29′N 98°13′W.

Fairfax, county (□ 406 sq mi/1,052 sq km; 1990 pop. 818,584), N Va.; ⊙ Fairfax (independent city, not part of co.); 38°49′N 77°16′W. Bounded SW by the Bull Run creek and Occoquan R., SE, E (in part), and NE by Potomac R. (Md. state line). Fairfax co. excludes Arlington co. (uninc. city) and independent cities of Alexandria, Falls Church to NE (W of Wash., D.C.), and Fairfax at center. Chiefly residential; some agr. in W (cattle, poultry, hay, nursery stock). Co. has become almost totally urbanized since 1960s, part of Washington, D.C., urban area; growth mainly residential, commercial, and offices. Mount Vernon and Gunston Hall (1755) historical sites in SE. Civil War engagements (notably battles of Bull Run) were fought in W. Dulles Internatl. Airport on NW boundary. Wolf Trap Farm Park for the Performing Arts (natl. park unit) in N center. Mason Neck, George Washington's Grist Mill Historical State Parks, and Mason Neck Natl. Wildlife Refuge in SE. Ft. Belvoir Military Reservation in SE. Formed 1742.

Fairfax 1 city (1990 pop. 6,931), Marin co., W Calif., residential suburb 18 mi/29 km NW of downtown San Francisco, adjacent to San Anselmo, and 3 mi/4.8 km W of San Rafael; 38°00′N 122°36′W. Alpine L. reservoir to SW; Point Reyes Natl. Seashore to W. Inc. 1931. **2** city (1990 pop. 699), Atchison co., NW Mo., on Tarkio R., and 7 mi/11.3 km S of Tarkio; 40°20′N 95°23′W. Soybeans, corn, wheat; hogs, cattle. **3** independent city (□ 6 sq mi/15.5 sq km; 1990 pop. 19,622), ⊙ Fairfax co. (but separate from surrounding co.), NE Va., a residential suburb 14 mi/23 km W of Wash., D.C.; 38°51′N 77°17′W. Mfg. (printing and publishing, diverse light mfg.). Old courthouse (built 1799; restored 1967) houses the wills of George and Martha Washington. George Mason Univ. is located S of Fairfax, including Center for the Arts. Inc. 1892, as a city (separate from co.) 1961.

Fairfax 1 uninc. town (1990 pop. 2,075), New Castle co., N Del., residential suburb 3 mi/4.8 km N of downtown Wilmington; 39°47′N 75°32′W. **2** town (1990 pop. 780), Linn co., E Iowa, 8 mi/12.9 km SW of Cedar Rapids; 41°55′N 91°46′W. Sausage. **3** town (1990 pop. 1,276),

Renville co., S Minn., 19 mi/31 km E of Redwood Falls near Fort Ridgely Creek; 44°31′N 94°43′W. Agr. (grain; livestock, poultry). Mfg. (beach cleaning machines, toys). Fort Ridgely State Park to S on Minnesota R. **4** town (1990 pop. 1,749), Osage co., N Okla., on Salt Creek, near Arkansas R., 22 mi/35 km WSW of Pawhuska; 36°34′N 96°42′W. In oil area, also producing grain and cattle, hogs. Mfg. (petroleum prods., food prods.). Founded c.1905, inc. 1909. **5** town (1990 pop. 2,317), Allendale co., SW S.C., 5 mi/8 km SE of Allendale; 32°57′N 81°14′W. Mfg. (apparel, hardwood lumber, veneer, commercial ice-making equipment, feeds). Agr. (hogs, grain, watermelons, cotton, peanuts). Settled 1876, inc. 1898. **6** rural town (1990 pop. 2,486), Franklin co., NW Vt., 10 mi/16 km SSE of St. Albans, and on Lamoille R.; 44°41′N 73°00′W. Dairy prods. Granted 1763, settled 1783.

Fairfax, village (1990 pop. 144), Gregory co., S S.Dak., 23 mi/37 km ESE of Burke; 43°01′N 98°53′W.

Fairfield 1 county (□ 837 sq mi/2,168 sq km; 1990 pop. 827,645), SW Conn., on L.I. Sound and N.Y. state line, bounded E by Housatonic R.; ⊙ Bridgeport and Danbury; 41°13′N 73°22′W. Many residential communities lie within N.Y. city commuting radius. Mfg. centers include Bridgeport (state's leading industrial city), Danbury, Fairfield, Stamford, and Stratford. Mfg. (electrical equip., firearms, hats, machinery, metal prods., apparel, textiles, chemicals, rubber, paper, wood and glass prods.). Home to many major corporate hq. Agr. (fruit, truck, dairy prods.). Resorts on shore and L. Candlewood. Drained by Housatonic, Norwalk, Aspetuck, and Poquonock rivers. Constituted 1666. **2** county (□ 505 sq mi/1,308 sq km; 1990 pop. 103,461), central Ohio; ⊙ Lancaster; 39°45′N 82°36′W. Drained by Hocking R. and small Rush and Little Walnut creeks; includes part of Buckeye L. (recreation). Primarily in the Till Plains physiographic region, the SE portion in the Unglaciated Plain region. Agr. (sheep, hogs, poultry; corn, soybeans, fruit). Mfg. at Lancaster and Bremen (plastic and leather prods., gray and ductile iron foundries, industrial machinery); oil wells, sand and gravel pits; timber. Substantial retailing hq. Formed 1800. **3** county (□ 709 sq mi/1,836 sq km; 1990 pop. 22,295), N central S.C.; ⊙ Winnsboro; 34°23′N 81°07′W. Bounded by Broad R. (W), Wateree Pond (E). Includes part of Sumter Natl. Forest. Gold, silver, sand, clay, granite. Agr. (cattle, corn, hay, cotton); timber. Formed 1785.

Fairfield 1 city (1990 pop. 12,200), Jefferson co., N central Ala., W of Birmingham; 33°28′N 86°55′W. Founded (1910) by the U.S. Steel Corp., its steel industry has greatly declined, and the economy has faltered. Still some steel working; lumber, asphalt shingles, toy mfg. Inc. 1919. **2** city (1990 pop. 77,211), ⊙ Solano co., W Calif., 38 mi/61 km SW of Sacramento; 38°15′N 122°02′W. Elev. 19 ft/6 m. In extremely productive and varied agr. area (irrigated); cattle, lambs; fruits, sugar beets, almond, sunflowers, safflower, grain; nursery prods. Mfg. (metal prods., explosives, candy, plastic prods. medical equip.); brewery. Travis (formerly Fairfield-Suisun) Air Force Base to NE. Founded 1859, inc. 1903. **3** city (1990 pop. 5,439), ⊙ Wayne co., SE Ill., 30 mi/48 km E of Mt. Vernon; 38°22′N 88°22′W. In agr. area (cattle, soybeans, sorghum, wheat; poultry; dairy prods.). Mfg. (auto parts, pumps, picture frames); oil wells. Frontier Community Col. nearby. **4** city (1990 pop. 9,786), ⊙ Jefferson co., SE Iowa, 23 mi/37 km E of Ottumwa; 41°00′N 91°58′W. Residential, trade, and mfg. center (consumer goods, machinery, farm equip., apparel, feed, dairy prods). Bituminous-coal mines nearby. First annual Iowa State Fair held here in 1854. Has Maharish, an internatl. univ. (Hindu), on former Parsons Col. campus; and Old Settlers' Park (with log cabin built in 1836). Inc. 1847.

Fairfield 1 town (1990 pop. 53,418), Fairfield co., SW Conn., on L.I. Sound; 41°10′N 73°16′W. Chiefly residential, but with diverse light mfg. The town was settled on the site of the last battle (1637) in the Pequot War. During the Revolution much of it was burned (1777) by the British. Fairfield has three colonial historical dists., as well as resort beaches and a large marina. Site of Sacred Heart Univ. and Fairfield Univ. Settled 1639, chartered 1947. **2** mfg. town (1990 pop. 6,718), including Fairfield village, Somerset co., S Maine, on the Kennebec just NE of Waterville; 44°38′N 69°40′W. Wood and paper prods. Kennebec Valley Technical Col. is here. Includes Fairfield Center and Hinckley. Settled 1774, inc. 1788. **3** town (1990 pop. 660), Teton co., NW central Mont., 35 mi/56 km WNW of Great Falls, near Greenfield Main Irrigation Canal, just SE of Freezeout L. and the Freezeout L. Wildlife Management Area; 47°37′N 111°59′W. Trading center for the farmers of Greenfield Bench. Cattle, sheep; wheat, hay. **4** uninc. town (1990 pop. 1,100), Erie co., NW Pa., residential suburb 5 mi/8 km ENE of Erie on Lake Erie; 42°10′N 80°00′W. Agr. (dairying, livestock; corn, apples). **5** town (1990 pop. 3,234), ⊙ Freestone co., E central Texas, 32 mi/51 km SE of Corsicana; 31°43′N 96°10′W. Elev. 461 ft/141 m. Highway junction in cattle, timber area. Agr. (peaches, vegetables, melons, pecans). Mfg. (meat processing). Fairfield Lake State Park to NE. Inc. 1933. **6** town (1990 pop. 1,680), Franklin co., NW Vt., 7 mi/11.3 km E of St. Albans; 44°48′N 72°56′W. Maple sugar, dairy prods. Chester A. Arthur b. here. Granted 1763, settled 1787.

Fairfield, township (1990 pop. 7,615), Essex co., NE N.J., 6 mi/9.7 km SW of Patterson; 40°52′N 74°18′W. Mfg. (fishing tackle, textiles, sheet metal prods., packaging, apparel). Inc. 1798.

Fairfield 1 village (1990 pop. 371), ⊙ Camas co., S Idaho, 25 mi/40 km SW of Hailey; 43°21′N 114°48′W. Elev. 5,065 ft/1,544 m. In livestock (cattle) and grain (alfalfa, hay, barley) area. Gold and silver mines nearby. Sawtooth Natl. Forest is N; Soldier Mt. Ski Area to N; Mormon Reservoir to S. **2** village (1990 pop. 142), Nelson co., central Ky., 9 mi/14.5 km NNE of Bardstown; 37°55′N 85°22′W. Agr. (tobacco, grain; livestock). **3** village (1990 pop. 458), Clay co., S Nebr., 7 mi/11.3 km SSW of Clay Center; 40°25′N 98°05′W. Livestock, grain. **4** village (1990 pop. 446), Spokane co., E Wash., 20 mi/32 km SE of Spokane; 47°23′N 117°10′W. Wheat, peas, alfalfa. Coeur d'Alene Indian Reservation to E, in Idaho.

Fairfield, borough (1990 pop. 524), Adams co., S Pa., 8 mi/12.9 km SW of Gettysburg; 39°47′N 77°22′W. Agr. (grain, apples; poultry, livestock, dairying). Mfg. (book printing, lumber, crushed limestone). Mt. Alto State Forest to W; Ski Liberty ski resort to SW; Adams Co. Winery to N.

Fairfield City, city (1990 pop. 39,707), Butler co., Ohio, suburb of Hamilton. Diverse mfg.

Fairfield-Suisun Air Force Base, Calif.: see FAIRFIELD.

Fairforest, uninc. village (1990 pop. 600), Spartanburg co., NW S.C., suburb 4 mi/6.4 km W of Spartanburg. Mfg. (textiles and textile by-products, knitted fabrics, specialty boxes, prestressed concrete, industrial chemicals).

Fairgrove, village (1990 pop. 592), Tuscola co., E Mich., 8 mi/12.9 km WNW of Caro; 43°31′N 83°32′W. In agr. area.

Fairhaven (fer-HAI-vuhn), residential town (1990 pop. 16,132), Bristol co., SE Mass., at the mouth of the Acushnet R., on Buzzards Bay, opposite New Bedford; 41°38′N 70°52′W. A former whaling center, from which Herman Melville sailed in 1841, Fairhaven has commercial fishing industries, boatyards, and plants making machinery, tires, mattresses, and nails. It is also a summer resort. Fort Phoenix, a pre-Revolutionary War fort, is here. Settled 1670, set off from New Bedford and inc. 1812.

Fairhope, city (1990 pop. 8,485), Baldwin co., SW Ala., on E shore of Mobile Bay, 13 mi/21 km SE of Mobile; 30°30′N 87°52′W. Summer and winter resort (boating, fishing, hunting). Mfg. (lumber, bricks, furniture). Founded 1894–1895 by followers of Henry George; inc. 1908.

Fairhope, uninc. town (1990 est. pop. 2,000), Washington township, Fayette co., SW Pa., 24 mi/39 km S of Pittsburgh, and 3 mi/4.8 km SE of Monesson, near Monogahela R.; 40°06′N 79°50′W. Agr. (corn, hay, alfalfa; livestock, dairying).

Fairland, town (1990 pop. 916), Ottawa co., extreme NE Okla., 8 mi/12.9 km S of Miami; 36°45′N 94°50′W. In agr. area (livestock; hay, grain). L. of the Cherokees (Neosho R.) is just E. Bernice State Park to S.

Fairland, village, Shelby co., central Ind., 7 mi/11.3 km NW of Shelbyville. Agr. area. Mfg. (wooden cabinets, fiberglass insulation, diesel piston parts).

Fairlawn, city (1990 pop. 5,779), Summit co., NE Ohio, 4 mi/6 km NW of Akron; 41°07′N 81°37′W.

Fairlawn, uninc. town (1990 pop. 2,399), Pulaski co., SW Va., residential suburb 2 mi/3.2 km N of Radford, on New R. (bridged), opposite Radford; 37°08′N 80°33′W.

Fairlea (FER-lee), uninc. town (1990 pop. 1,743), Greenbrier co., SE W.Va., 1 mi/1.6 km S of Lewisburg, near Greenbrier R.; 37°46′N 80°27′W. Agr. (grain, tobacco); livestock; poultry. Bituminous coal. Mfg. (electronic mining monitors). Site of W.Va. State Fairgrounds.

Fairlee, town (1990 pop. 883), Orange co., E Vt., on the Connecticut R., and 25 mi/40 km SE of Barre; 43°56′N 72°10′W. Dairying. Nearby lakes Fairlee and Morey have resorts. Samuel Morey said to have built steamboat here, 1793.

Fairlee (FAIR-lee), village, Kent co., E Md., 24 mi/39 km E of Baltimore. Originally Bel Air, the name was changed to avoid confusion with Bel Air in Harford co. The Kent volunteers skirmished with a small force of Br. troops under the command of Sir Peter Parker here in 1814. Nearby is St. Paul's Church (est. 1713).

Fairlee, Lake orange co., E Vt., 17 mi/27 km NNE of White River Junction, and 2 mi/3.2 km W of Connecticut R. (N.H. border), where towns of Thetford, Fairlee, and W. Fairlee meet; c.2 mi/3.2 km long; 43°53′N 72°13′W.

Fairless Hills, uninc. town (1990 pop. 9,026), Bucks co., SE Pa., suburb 22 mi/35 km NE of Philadelphia, and 6 mi/9.7 km WSW of Trenton, N.J.; 40°10′N 74°50′W. Drained by Queen Creek. Former large steel-rolling mill now engaged only in steel fabricating. Mfg. (polyurethane foam, machinery, chemicals, plastic molds, transportation equip., dollies). Sesame Place theme park to NW. Historic Fallsington with restored bldgs. to E.

Fairmont 1 city (1990 pop. 11,265), ⊙ Martin co., S Minn., 40 mi/64 km SW of Mankato, near Iowa state line, at center of Middle Chain of Lakes, on E side of (N-S) L. George, Sisseton L., Budd L., and Hell L.; 43°38′N 94°27′W. Elev. 1,187 ft/362 m. RR junction and shipping point for agr. area (grain, soybeans; livestock). Mfg. (lumber, electrical equip., stained glass windows, prepared foods, machinery, asphalt, printing and publishing); resorts. Fairmont Municipal Airport to E. Courthouse has pioneer relics. Plotted 1857, inc. as village 1878, as city 1902. **2** city (1990 pop. 20,210), ⊙ Marion co., N W.Va., 115 mi/185 km NE of Charleston, at confluence of the West Fork and Tygart rivers, which form Monongahela R; 39°28′N 80°09′W. Mining, industrial, and commercial center in bituminous-coal field, where large shaft mines are in decline. RR junction. Mfg. (transportation equip., construction materials, electrical equip., metal fabricating, printing and publishing, machinery, glass, nylon fiber). Agr. (corn, apples); livestock; poultry. FBI Fingerprint Identification Center to S. Fairmont State Col.; state hosp. Fairmont Municipal Airport to SW. Scenic Valley Falls State Park, in gorge of Tygart R. to SE; Prickett's Fort State Park to NE; Buffalo Creek Covered Bridge to NW. A Union supply depot in the Civil War, Fairmont was raided by Confederate cavalry in 1863. In 1907 a tragic mine explosion nearby resulted in almost 400 deaths. Founded 1843 as union of earlier communities.

Fairmont, town (1990 pop. 2,489), Robeson co., SE N.C., 10 mi/16 km SSW of Lumberton; 34°30′N 79°07′W. Agr. area (grain, tobacco, soybeans, sunflowers; cattle, hogs); Mfg. (apparel, wooden furniture components, fiberglass boats). Lumber R. State Park to SE.

Fairmont 1 village (1990 pop. 708), Fillmore co., SE Nebr., 7 mi/11.3 km N of Geneva; 40°38′N 97°34′W. Dairy prods., grain. Crosstrail State Wayside Area to S.

2 village (1990 pop. 129), Garfield co., N Okla., 10 mi/16 km ESE of Enid; 36°21′N 97°42′W. RR junction. In agr. area. **3** uninc. village, Spartanburg co., NW S.C., on Tyger R., and 8 mi/12.9 km WSW of Spartanburg.

Fairmont City, village (1990 pop. 2,140), St. Clair co., SW Ill., NE suburb of East St. Louis, suburb of St. Louis, within St. Louis metropolitan area; 38°38′N 90°05′W. Some agr. (corn, cattle). Cahokia Mounds State Historical Site (formerly state park) to E; Gateway Natl. Raceway to NW. Founded 1910, inc. 1914.

Fairmount 1 town (1990 pop. 657), Gordon co., NW Ga., 28 mi/45 km ENE of Rome; 34°26′N 84°42′W. Mfg. (waterproof liners, flame retardants, carpets, printing). **2** town (1990 pop. 3,130), Grant co., E central Ind., 10 mi/16 km S of Marion; 40°25′N 85°39′W. In agr. area. Mfg. (wire prods., fire fighting equip.); gas wells.

Fairmount 1 village (1990 pop. 678), Vermilion co., E Ill., 12 mi/19 km WSW of Danville; 40°02′N 87°49′W. In agr. (corn, soybeans, cattle) and bituminous-coal area. **2** village, Somerset co., SE Md., on the Eastern Shore, near Big Annemessex R., 23 mi/37 km SSW of Salisbury. Fishing. The church was originally on Holland Isl., but taken apart and rebuilt here when the isl. was abandoned in 1922 following severe storms. Nearby is Fairmount Wildlife Management Area. **3** suburban village (☐ 3 sq mi/7.8 sq km; 1990 pop. 12,266), Onondaga co., central N.Y., just W of Syracuse; 43°02′N 76°15′W. There is considerable retail activity in this otherwise residential area. Pop. figure also includes Sherwood Knolls, Stanley Manor, and West Genessee Terrace. **4** village, (1990 pop. 427), Richland co., SE N.Dak., 15 mi/24 km S of Wahpeton; 46°03′N 96°36′W. RR junction to W.

Fairmount Heights, town (1990 pop. 1,238), Prince Georges co., central Md., E of Wash., D.C.; 38°54′N 76°55′W. One of the city's older suburbs.

Fairplains, uninc. town (1990 pop. 2,339), Wilkes co., NW N.C., 3 mi/4.8 km N of Wilkesboro; 36°12′N 81°09′W. Agr. area (tobacco, grain; poultry, hogs, dairying).

Fairplay, village (1990 pop. 387), ⊙ Park co., central Colo., on South Platte R. (source is 10 mi/16 km NW), in Rocky Mts., and 15 mi/24 km E of Leadville; 39°13′N 106°00′W. Elev. c.9,953 ft/3,034 m. Marketing center for area. Gold mines; cattle, sheep. Twenty log homes survive from the 1800s. Mt. Lincoln (14,286 ft/4,354 m) is 10 mi/16 km NW. Pike Natl. Forest to W and N.

Fairport 1 village, Muscatine co., SE Iowa, on Mississippi R., and 7 mi/11.3 km E of Muscatine. U.S. fish hatchery here; Wildcat Den State Park is nearby. **2** suburban village (☐ 1 sq mi/2.6 sq km; 1990 pop. 5,943), Monroe co., W N.Y., on the Barge Canal, 10 mi/16 km SE of Rochester; 43°06′N 77°26′W. Mfg. (electronic prods., chemicals, plastics, transportation equip., machinery). Nurseries; agr. (apples, peaches, potatoes; honey). Inc. 1867.

FairPort, Ohio: see FAIRPORT HARBOR.

Fairport Harbor, village (1990 pop. 2,978), Lake co., NE Ohio, on L. Erie at mouth of Grand R., 29 mi/47 km NE of Cleveland; 41°44′N 81°16′W. Shipping. Resort, beaches. Laid out 1810. Also known as FairPort.

Fairton, village (1990 pop. 1,359), Cumberland co., SW N.J., on Cohansey Creek, and 4 mi/6.4 km S of Bridgeton; 39°22′N 75°12′W. Canned vegetables.

Fairview, city (1990 pop. 4,210), Williamson co., central Tenn., 23 mi/37 km SW of Nashville; 35°58′N 87°07′W. In hilly farm area. Mfg. (transformers, ballasts). Inc. 1959.

Fairview, town (1991 pop. 3,023), W Alta., Canada, 45 mi/72 km WSW of Peace R.; 56°04′N 118°24′W. Lumbering, mixed farming.

Fairview 1 uninc. town (1990 pop. 9,045), Contra Costa co., W Calif., residential suburb 11 mi/18 km SE of downtown Oakland, and 3 mi/4.8 km NE of Hayward; 37°41′N 122°02′W. Walpert Ridge to SE. **2** town (1990 pop. 298), Newton co., SW Mo., in the Ozarks, 16 mi/26 km E of Neosho; 36°49′N 94°04′W. **3** town (1990 pop. 869), Richland co., NE Mont., on N.Dak. state line, and 10 mi/16 km NNE of Sidney, on the Lower Yellowstone Project Main Canal, near Yellowstone R., its junction with Missouri R. 11 mi/18 km NNE in N. Dak.; 47°51′N 104°03′W. State boundary forms Central/Mountain time zone boundary, Mont. is in mountain time zone. Agr. and mining (lignite). Fort Union Trading Post Natl. Historic Site 10 mi/16 km N; Little Missouri Natl. Grassland to SE (N.Dak.). **4** uninc. town (1990 pop. 1,830), Union co., S N.C., 18 mi/29 km ESE of Charlotte; 35°31′N 82°24′W. Agr. area (cotton, sorghum, soybeans, grain; poultry, livestock). Mfg. (electrical compounds). **5** town (1990 pop. 2,936), ⊙ Major co., NW Okla., 35 mi/56 km WSW of Enid; 36°16′N 98°28′W. In grain and livestock area. Mfg. (flatbed platforms, street sweepers). Settled 1893; inc. as town 1901, as city 1909. **6** town (1990 pop. 2,391), Multnomah co., NW Oregon, 11 mi/18 km E of Portland, on Fairview Creek, near Columbia R.; 45°32′N 122°25′W. Multnomah Kennel Club Race Track to SE. **7** uninc. town (1990 pop. 1,500), Northumberland co., E central Pa., residential suburb 1 mi/1.6 km W of Shamokin; 40°47′N 76°34′W. **8** town (1990 pop. 1,554), Collin co., N Texas, residential suburb 25 mi/40 km NNE of downtown Dallas, and 3 mi/4.8 km S of McKinney, near Wilson Creek; 33°08′N 96°37′W. L. Lavon reservoir to SE. **9** town (1990 pop. 960), Sanpete co., central Utah, on San Pitch R., and 45 mi/72 km SSE of Provo, in irrigated Sanpete Valley; 39°37′N 111°26′W. Elev. 6,023 ft/1,836 m. Agr. (barley, wheat, alfalfa; dairying; cattle, sheep, poultry); sand, gravel. Wasatch Range to E in Manti–La Sal Natl. Forest. White Sand Dunes and Little Sahara Recreation Area to SW. Uinta Natl. Forest to W. Electric L. reservoir to E. Fairview Mus. of History and Arts; Natl. Shrine to Love and Devotion. Settled 1859 by Mormons, inc. 1872.

Fairview 1 village (1990 pop. 510), Fulton co., W central Ill., 17 mi/27 km N of Lewiston; 40°38′N 90°09′W. In agr. (corn, wheat, sorghum, soybeans; cattle) and bituminous coal-mining area. Ships grain. **2** village (1990 pop. 306), Brown co., NE Kansas, 11 mi/18 km W of Hiawatha; 39°50′N 95°43′W. Trading point in agr. region. **3** village (1993 pop. 119), Christian and Todd cos., SW Ky., 10 mi/16 km E of Hopkinsville; 39°00′N 84°28′W. Agr. (tobacco, grain; livestock). Birthplace of Jefferson Davis (1808), confederate President 1861–1865, commemorated by Jefferson Davis State Historic Site. One of 9 places so named in Ky. **4** uninc. village, Rio Arriba co., N N.Mex., 24 mi/39 km N of Santa Fe, on Rio Grande, opposite mouth of Rio Chama, in San Juan Pueblo Indian Reservation. Cattle, sheep. Mfg. (solid waste handling equip.). San Juan Pueblo to N. **5** village (☐ 3 sq mi/7.8 sq km; 1990 pop. 4,811), Dutchess co., SE N.Y., just NE of Poughkeepsie; 41°43′N 73°54′W. **6** village (1990 pop. 79), on Guernsey-Belmont co. line, E Ohio, 19 mi/31 km E of Cambridge; 40°03′N 81°14′W. In agr. and coal-mining area. **7** village (1990 pop. 73), Lincoln co., SE S. Dak., 8 mi/12.9 km SSE of Canton, and on Big Sioux R.; 43°13′N 96°29′W. Newton Hills State Rec. Area to W **8** village (1990 pop. 513), Marion co., N W.Va., 10 mi/16 km NW of Fairmont; 39°35′N 80°15′W. Bituminous-coal area. Mfg. (coal processing, mining equip.). **9** village, Lincoln co., W Wyo., on branch of Salt R., near Idaho line, and 3 mi/4.8 km SW of Afton, in Star Valley. Elev. c.6,000 ft/1,829 m. Sheep, cattle; barley, oats. Bridger-Teton Natl. Forest to E and S.

Fairview 1 borough (1990 pop. 10,733), Bergen co., NE N.J.; 40°49′N 74°00′W. Apparel and embroideries. Settled 1860, inc. 1894. **2** borough (1990 pop. 224), Butler co., W Pa., 17 mi/27 km NE of Butler; 41°01′N 79°44′W. Agr. (grain; dairying, livestock); oil. **3** borough (1990 pop. 1,988), Erie co., NW Pa., 10 mi/16 km WSW of Erie; 42°01′N 80°15′W. Agr. (grain, soybeans; dairying, livestock). Mfg. (electronic equip., wood prods., fabricated metal prods., plastic prods., machinery). L. Erie 2 mi/3.2 km to NW; state fish hatchery on Trout Run to SW.

Fairview Heights, city (1990 pop. 14,351), St. Clair co., SW Ill., suburb 12 mi/19 km E of downtown St. Louis, Mo., 5 mi/8 km N of Belleville; 40°38′N 90°11′W. Commercial and office center of E metro area. Mfg. (electric prods.). Also known as Fairview. Formerly called Lincoln Heights.

Fairview Park, city (1990 pop. 18,028), Cuyahoga co., NE Ohio; 41°26′N 81°51′W. A residential suburb of Cleveland. Inc. 1950.

Fairview Park, town (1990 pop. 1,446), Vermillion co., W Ind., near Wabash R., 13 mi/21 km S of Newport; 39°40′N 87°24′W. In agr. and bituminous-coal area. Laid out 1902.

Fairville, SW suburb of St. John, SW N.B., Canada, on W bank of mouth of St. John R.

Fairwater, village (1990 pop. 302), Fond du Lac co., E central Wis., on Grand R., and 20 mi/32 km W of Fond du Lac; 43°44′N 88°52′W. In farm area. Mfg. (frozen vegetables).

Fairway, city (1990 pop. 4,173), Johnson co., E Kansas, residential suburb 4 mi/6.4 km S of downtown Kansas City, Kansas; 39°01′N 94°37′W. Inc. after 1950.

Fairway Rock, bare islet (1 mi/1.6 km long), NW Alaska, in Bering Strait, near Russian boundary, 12 mi/19 km SSE of Little Diomede Isl., 20 mi/32 km W of Cape Prince of Wales; 65°37′N 168°44′W.

Fairweather, Cape, SE Alaska, on Gulf of Alaska, 85 mi/137 km SE of Yakutat; 58°50′N 137°57′W.

Fairweather, Mount (15,300 ft/4,663 m), on border bet. SE Alaska and B.C. (Canada), in Fairweather Range of St. Elias Mts., 17 mi/27 km NE of Cape Fairweather, 90 mi/145 km SE of Yakutat, at SW end of Glacier Bay Natl. Monument; 58°54′N 137°32′W.

Fairweather Range, SE Alaska, S mountain group of St. Elias Mts., paralleling Gulf of Alaska for c.35 mi/56 km from 59°N 137°30′W to 58°35′N 137°W. Highest peak, Mt. Fairweather (15,300 ft/4,663 m).

Fairy Stone State Park, Patrick and Henry cos., S Va., recreational area (c.4,570 acres/1,849 ha), 14 mi/23 km NW of Martinsville, on slope of Fairy Stone Mtn. Camping, bathing, boating, fishing. Here are found cross-shaped twinned crystals of staurolite ("fairy stones"). Philpott Reservoir to NE.

Faison (FAI-suhn), village (1990 pop. 701), Duplin co., E central N.C., 20 mi/32 km SSW of Goldsboro; 35°07′N 78°08′W. Cucumber market; ships local produce; peppers, tobacco, grain; poultry, livestock. Mfg. (pickles, duffel bags, turkey processing).

Faith 1 village (1990 pop. 553), Rowan co., central N.C., 5 mi/8 km S of Salisbury; 35°35′N 80°27′W. Tobacco, grain; poultry, livestock, dairying. Mfg. (bird baths). **2** village (1990 pop. 548), Meade co., W central S.Dak., 85 mi/137 km NE of Sturgis; 45°01′N 102°02′W. Livestock-shipping point and trade center; animal fodder. At W entrance to Cheyenne R. Indian Reservation.

Fajardo (fah-HAHR-do), town (1990 pop. 36,882), NE P.R. Tourism, commercial, yachting center. Has several marinas. Ferry to Vieques and Culebra isls. Airport. Las Cabezas de San Juan Nature Reserve (also known as El Faro, for an 1882 lighthouse restored as scientific research center) on peninsula nearby (NNE). Historic supply depot for pirates.

Falco (FAHL-ko), town, Covington co., S Ala., 20 mi/32 km SW of Andalusia, near Fla. state line.

Falcon 1 village (1990 pop. 167), Quitman co., NW Miss., 22 mi/35 km NE of Clarksdale; 34°23′N 90°15′W. Cotton, corn, rice; cattle. Pecan L. to NE. **2** village (1990 pop. 216), Cumberland co., S central N.C., 15 mi/24 km NE of Fayetteville, on South R.; 35°11′N 78°39′W Tobacco, cotton, grain; poultry, livestock.

Falcon Heights, town (1990 pop. 5,380), Ramsey co., E Minn., residential suburb 4 mi/6.4 km NW of downtown St. Paul and 4 mi/6.4 km E of downtown Minneapolis; 44°59′N 93°10′W. Mississippi R. to SW. Univ. of Minn. Agr. Col. and Minn. State Fairgrounds are here.

Falcon Island, W Ont., Canada, in L. of the Woods, just W of Aulneau Peninsula, 4 mi/6 km SSW of Kenora; 8 mi/13 km long, 4 mi/6 km wide.

Falconbridge, village, SE central Ont., Canada, 10 mi/16 km NE of Sudbury; 46°34′N 80°49′W. Nickel and copper mining.

Falconer (FAWLK-nur), village (☐ 1 sq mi/2.6 sq km; 1990 pop. 2,653), Chautauqua co., extreme W N.Y., just

NE of Jamestown; 42°07′N 79°12′W. Mfg. (furniture, machinery, transportation equip., wood prods.). Settled 1807, inc. 1891.

Falfurrias (fal-FYOOR-ee-uhs), town (1990 pop. 5,788), ⊙ Brooks co., S Texas, 28 mi/45 km SW of Kingsville; 27°13′N 98°09′W. Elev. 109 ft/33 m. RR terminus, shipping, trade center for rich vegetable farming, dairying area, with oil and natural gas wells. Mfg. (apparel). Holds large annual rodeo. Inc. after 1940.

Falher, town (1991 pop. 1,183), W Alta., Canada, 35 mi/56 km S of Peace R. Lumbering, mixed farming, wheat.

Falkland (FAWK-luhnd), town (1990 pop. 108), Pitt co., E N.C., 10 mi/16 km NW of Greenville, near Tar R.; 35°42′N 77°30′W. Tobacco; chickens, livestock. Mfg. (surgical garments).

Falkner (FAWK-ner), village (1990 pop. 232), Tippah co., N Miss., 7 mi/11.3 km N of Ripley; 34°51′N 88°55′W. Timber; cotton, corn, soybeans; cattle. Mfg. (upholstered furniture). Holly Springs Natl. Forest to W.

Falkner Island, S Conn., islet in L.I. Sound, off Guilford, New Haven co. Lighthouse.

Falkville, town (1990 pop. 1,337), Morgan co., N Ala., 17 mi/27 km SSE of Decatur; 34°22′N 86°54′W.

Fall City, uninc. town (1990 pop. 1,582), King co., W Wash., 18 mi/29 km E of Seattle, on Snoqualmie R., in W foothills of Cascade Range; 47°34′N 121°54′W. Dairying, poultry; berries, vegetables.

Fall Creek, town (1990 pop. 1,034), Eau Claire co., W central Wis., 12 mi/19 km ESE of Eau Claire; 44°45′N 91°16′W. Dairying, stock raising. Near Eau Claire R.

Fall Creek Falls, waterfall at NW end of Fall Creek L., in Fall Creek Falls State Park, Van Buren co., S central Tenn., 23 mi/37 km E of McMinnville; 35°39′N 85°21′W. At 256 ft/78 m, it is tallest waterfall E of the Rocky Mts.

Fall Creek Reservoir, Lane co., W central Oregon, on Fall Creek, 18 mi/29 km SE of Eugene; 5 mi/8 km long; 44°06′N 122°45′W. Max. capacity 125,000 acre-ft. Winberry Creek forms 3-mi/4.8-km SE arm. Formed by Fall Creek Dam (181 ft/55 m high), built (1965) by the Army Corps of Engineers for flood control, power generation, and irrigation.

Fall Lake, NE Minn., Lake co. (Squaw Bay at W end extends into St. Louis co.), 4 mi/6.4 km NE of Ely; 6 mi/9.7 km long, 1 mi/1.6 km wide, in Superior Natl. Forest; 47°56′N 91°45′W. Fed and drained (S to N) by Kawishiwi R.; also fed from SW by Shagawa R. from Shagawa L. Fishing resorts. Village of Winton is at SW end of lake. Far NE end in Boundary Waters Canoe Area.

Fall Line, in E U.S., zone at outer border of the PIEDMONT region, where streams, passing from the more resistant rocks to softer coastal plain deposits, flow over rapids and waterfalls. As it marks head of navigation on rivers and good sites for industries needing water power, many cities (Trenton, N.J.; Baltimore; Philadelphia; Wash., D.C.; Richmond; Raleigh, N.C.; Columbia, S.C.; and Augusta, Macon, and Columbus, Ga.) have grown up along the Fall Line.

Fall River, county (□ 1,749 sq mi/4,530 sq km; 1990 pop. 7,353), SW S.Dak., on Wyo. and Nebr. state lines; ⊙ Hot Springs; 43°15′N 103°31′W. Agr. area drained by Cheyenne R. and numerous creeks. Buffalo Gap Natl. Grassland in W, S, and E; S part of Black Hills Natl. Forest in N. Wheat, hay; cattle; sandstone quarries. Black Hills Army Depot in SW. Angosturn Reservoir State Recreational Area at center. Formed 1883.

Fall River (fawl-RI-vuhr), industrial city (1990 pop. 92,703), Bristol co., SE Mass., a port of entry on Mt. Hope Bay, at the mouth of the Taunton R.; 41°43′N 71°07′W. It was once the foremost cotton textile center in the U.S.; the 1st cotton mill was built in 1811. Textiles and clothing are the leading manufactures. The city's industries have diversified, however, and a variety of prods. are made, including metals and chemicals. The Bradford Durfee Col. of Technology and a junior col. are in Fall River. The U.S.S. *Massachusetts*, the state's official World War II memorial, is berthed in the harbor, at the site of Fall River. The city was the scene (1892) of the famous trial of Lizzie Borden, accused of murdering her parents in the family's home here. Heritage State Park. Settled 1656, set off from Freetown 1803, inc. as a city 1854.

Fall River, town (1990 pop. 842), Columbia co., S central Wis., on Crawfish R., and 23 mi/37 km SE of Portage; 43°23′N 89°02′W. Agr. Mfg. (machining, foundry, printing). Lazy L. to NE.

Fall River, village (1990 pop. 113), Greenwood co., SE Kansas, on Fall R., and 20 mi/32 km SE of Eureka; 37°36′N 96°01′W. Cattle, grain; dairying. Fall River L. Reservoir and State Park to N.

Fall River 1 c.25 mi/40 km long, NE Calif.; rises in SW Plumas co.; flows SW to Middle Fork Feather R., on arm of L. Oroville reservoir, 29 mi/47 km NW of Nevada City. Feather Falls, on Fall R., is c.3 mi/4.8 km from confluence of the rivers (village of Feather Falls is here). Another Fall River, affluent of the Pit, is in Shasta co.; its waters are diverted through a tunnel to a hydroelectric plant on Pit R. near Fall River Mills village. **2** c.90 mi/145 km long, SE Kansas; rises in N Greenwood co.; flows SE, past Eureka, through Fall River L. Reservoir, and past Fredonia, to Verdigris R. just SE of Neodesha.

Fall River Lake, Greenwood co., SE Kansas, on Fall R., 18 mi/29 km SE of Eureka; 6 mi/9.7 km long; 37°38′N 96°03′W. Max. storage capacity 11,500 acre-ft. Formed by Fall River Dam (83 ft/25 m high) built by the city of Eureka for flood control and water supply. Fall River State Park at dam.

Fall River Mills, uninc. village, Shasta co., N Calif., on Pit R. at mouth of Fall R., forms Big L. reservoir to N, and 53 mi/85 km NE of Redding. Logging; dairying; grain; cattle. Mfg. (wild-rice processing). Lassen Natl. Forest to S, part of Shasta Natl. Forest to N and W; Ahjumawi Lava Springs State Park to NE.

Fallbrook, city (1990 pop. 22,095), San Diego co., S Calif., near Santa Margarita R., 15 mi/24 km NE of Oceanside; 33°22′N 117°14′W. Thermal belt here produces avocados, citrus fruit, ornamental plants; dairying; poultry. Mfg. (machinery, light mfg.). Camp Pendelton Marine Corps Base to W.

Fallen Leaf Lake, El Dorado co., E Calif., in the Sierra Nevada, 2 mi/3.2 km S of L. Tahoe, and 5 mi/8 km WSW of S Lake Tahoe; c.3 mi/4.8 km long. In Eldorado Natl. Forest; Desolation Wilderness Area to W.

Fallen Timbers State Park, Lucas co., NW Ohio, on Maumee R., near Maumee. Marks site of battle of Fallen Timbers (1794), in which Anthony Wayne defeated the Indians and opened S and E Ohio for settlement.

Falling Spring, W. Va.: see RENICK.

Fallingwater, historic site near Mill Run, Fayette co., SW Pa., 13 mi/21 km E of Uniontown, in Bear Run Nature Reserve. House designed by Frank Lloyd Wright. Fallingwater (1936–1939) is an architectural tour de force of Wright's organic philosophy, whereby a bldg. should be completely integrated with its environment. Seen from below, the house is boldly cantilevered over a waterfall, with its powerful balconies and terraces seemingly suspended in midair.

Fallingwaters or **Falling Waters**, uninc. village, Berkeley co., NE W.Va., 8 mi/12.9 km NNE of Morgantown, on Potomac R. Agr. (grain, apples); livestock; dairying. Mfg. (resin grouts).

Fallis (FAL-is), village, Lincoln co., central Okla., 28 mi/45 km NE of Oklahoma City, on Deep Fork Canadian R; 35°45′N 97°07′W. In agr. area.

Fallon, county (□ 1,623 sq mi/4,204 sq km; 1990 pop. 3,103), E Mont.; ⊙ Baker; 46°21′N 104°25′W. Agr. region bordering on N.Dak. and S.Dak.; drained by O'Fallon, Sandstone, Pennel, and Little Beaver creeks. Oil and gas. Agr. (wheat, barley, oats, corn, hay, beans, sugar beets; hogs, cattle, sheep). Formed 1913. Present boundaries est. 1919.

Fallon (FA-luhn), town (1990 pop. 6,438), ⊙ Churchill co., W Nev., on Carson R., and c.55 mi/89 km E of Reno, N of Carson L. and SW of Carson Sink; 39°28′N 118°46′W. Elev. 3,963 ft/1,208 m. Trade and processing center for dairying, livestock, and irrigated agr. area (cantaloupes). Mfg. (printing and publishing). RR terminus. State fairgrounds and Stillwater Natl. Wildlife Refuge to E; Fallon Natl. Wildlife Refuge to NE; Stillwater Wildlife Management Area to NE. Grew with development (1903–1908) of Newlands irrigation project, supplied by Truckee River and Carson River. Sheckler Reservoir to W; sects. of Fallon Naval Air Station to SE and SW; Lahontan Reservoir and State Recreation Area to W; Walker R. Indian Reservation to S. Inc. 1908.

Fallon, village (1990 pop. 235), Prairie co., E Mont., on Yellowstone R., at mouth of O'Fallon Creek, and 27 mi/43 km SW of Glendive. RR junction to SW. Diversified farming (wheat, barley, corn, oilseed, alfalfa, sugar beets; cattle, sheep); gravel.

Falls, county (□ 773 sq mi/2,002 sq km; 1990 pop. 17,712), E central Texas; ⊙ Marlin; 31°15′N 96°55′W. Mainly blackland prairies; drained by Brazos R. (Falls on the Brazos Park). Agr. (cotton, corn, grain sorghum); cattle, hogs, sheep, goats. Natural gas, some oil, stone. Once a health resort, with hot artesian wells. Formed 1850.

Falls Church, independent city (□ 2 sq mi/5.2 sq km; 1990 pop. 9,578), NE Va., a residential suburb 7 mi/11.3 km W of Washington, D.C., separate from adjoining Fairfax and Arlington cos.; 38°53′N 77°10′W. Mfg. (telecommunications equip., printing, diverse light mfg.). George Washington and George Mason (author of the Va. Bill of Rights) were members of Falls Church (built 1767–1769). Inc. as a town 1875, as a city 1948.

Falls City 1 town (1990 pop. 4,769), ⊙ Richardson co., extreme SE Nebr., 42 mi/68 km SSE of Nebraska City, and on Nemaha R., near Missouri R. and Kansas state line; 40°04′N 95°35′W. RR division point, trade center for agr. area; cattle feed; dairy, meat, and poultry prods.; grain; livestock. Mfg. (metal, prods., food, machinery). Falls of Big Nemaha R. nearby. Sac and Fox Indian Reservation and Iowa Indian Reservation to SE. Founded 1857, inc. 1858. **2** town (1990 pop. 818), Polk co., NW Oregon, 6 mi/9.7 km SW of Dallas, on Little Luckiamute R.; 44°52′N 123°26′W. Agr. (dairy prods.; poultry). Valsetz L. Reservoir to W. Small unit of Siuslaw Natl. Forest to NW.

Falls City, village (1990 pop. 478), Karnes co., S Texas, 42 mi/68 km SE of San Antonio, on San Antonio R; 28°58′N 98°01′W. Agr. (cattle, dairying; wheat, corn). Mfg. (feeds, fertilizer).

Falls Creek, borough (1990 pop. 1,087), Jefferson and Clearfield cos., W central Pa., 3 mi/4.8 km NW of Du Bois, near Sandy Lick Creek. Mfg. (powdered-metal compactors). Kyle L. Reservoir to NW. Inc. 1900.

Falls Lake Reservoir (□ 18 sq mi/47 sq km), Wake and Durham cos., central N.C., on Neuse R., 15 mi/24 km ESE of Durham; 35°56′N 78°35′W. Max. capacity 1,020,980 acre-ft. Formed by Falls L. Dam (88 ft/27 m high), built (1981) by Army Corps of Engineers for water supply; also used for recreation and as a fish and wildlife pond. Falls L. State Recreational Area at S end of reservoir, by dam.

Falls of Baleine, waterfall, St. Vincent, St. Vincent and the Grenadines, West Indies. Freshwater cascades 60 ft/18 m to natural pool, N end of isl., accessible only by boat.

Falls River, c.50 mi/80 km long, in NW Wyo. and E Idaho; rises in SW corner of Yellowstone Natl. Park (Teton co., Wyo.); flows W and WSW to Henrys Fork 7 mi/11.3 km SW of Ashton, Idaho. Cave Falls are at Bechler townsite, Yellowstone Park, near mouth of Bechler R. Falls R. Basin.

Falls View or **Fallsview**, uninc. village (1990 pop. 500), Fayette co., S central W.Va., on Kanawha R., 25 mi/40 km SE of Charleston.

Falls Village, Conn.: see CANAAN, town.

Fallsburg, resort village (1990 pop. 800), Sullivan co., SE N.Y., 7 mi/11.3 km NW of Monticello; 41°44′N 74°36′W.

Fallsington, uninc. village (1990 pop. 342), Bucks co., SE Pa., residential suburb 4 mi/6.4 km SW of Trenton, N.J., and 24 mi/39 km NE of Philadelphia; 40°11′N 74°49′W. Mfg. (textiles, plastic prods.). Historic section with restored bldgs. here.

Fallston 1 village (1990 pop. 5,730), Harford co., NE Md., near Little Gunpowder Falls (stream), 19 mi/31 km NNE of Baltimore; 39°31′N 76°26′W. Mfg. (vegetable canneries, apparel). Little Falls Quaker Meeting House (c.1843) was a station on the Underground RR before the Civil War. The Quaker community here was established as branch of Gunpowder Meeting in 1748, but formed own meeting in 1815. **2** village (1990 pop. 498), Cleveland co., S N.C., 11 mi/18 km N of Shelby.; 35°25′N 81°30′W. Cotton, grain, soybeans; poultry, livestock. Mfg. (fabric converting, furniture lighting fixtures, lingerie).

Fallston, borough (1990 pop. 392), Beaver co., W Pa., residential suburb 2 mi/3.2 km N of Beaver, and 3 mi/4.8 km S of Beaver Falls, on Beaver R., at mouth of Brady Run, opposite New Brighton; 40°43′N 80°18′W. Agr. (dairying).

Falmouth, village (1991 pop. 272), S Antigua, Antigua and Barbuda Republic, West Indies, 7 mi/11.3 km SE of St. John's, on fine bay; 17°01′N 61°46′W. Sometimes called Falmouth Harbour. Was once a prosperous town.

Falmouth, village, W central N.S., Canada, on Avon R., opposite Windsor. Apples.

Falmouth, town (1991 pop. 7,955), ⊙ Trelawny parish, N Jamaica, seaport on N coast at mouth of the Martha Brae R., 17 mi/27 km E of Montego Bay, 65 mi/105 km NW of Kingston; 18°30′N 77°39′W. Trades in sugar, rum, coffee, ginger, pimento, bananas, honey, dyewood. Resort. In colonial times an important shipping point serving surrounding sugar estates.

Falmouth 1 (FAL-muhth), town (1990 pop. 2,378), ⊙ Pendleton co., N Ky., 30 mi/48 km SSE of Covington, on Licking R., at mouth of its South Fork, in Bluegrass region; 38°40′N 84°19′W. Agr. area (dairying, poultry, sheep; hay, corn, tobacco; honey). Mfg. (fitness equip., machinery, concrete, transportation equip.). Gene Snyder Airport to NW. Ky. Wool Festival (Oct.). Kincaid L. State Park to NE. Settled 1776; town founded 1799. **2** town (1990 pop. 7,610), Cumberland co., SW Maine, on Presumpscot R. and Casco Bay, and just NE of Portland; 43°44′N 70°16′W. Includes villages of Falmouth Foreside and West Falmouth. Old town of Falmouth, site of one of Maine's earliest settlements (c.1632), included Portland until 1786. Inc. 1718. **3** (FAWL-muhth), town (1990 pop. 27,960), Barnstable co., SE Mass., on Cape Cod; 41°36′N 70°36′W. Once a whaling and boatbuilding center, the town has become a popular tourist summer resort. Falmouth was attacked by the British in the Revolutionary War and again in the War of 1812. Historic structures include the Ship's Bottom Roof House (1678); the Congregational church on the town green (1756; restored), with a bell cast by Paul Revere; and the Julia Wood House (1790). The town includes the community of Woods Hole, seat of the Oceanographic Inst. and Marine Biological Laboratories. Includes villages of Davisville, East Falmouth (1990 pop. 5,577), Falmouth Heights (site of Nopsha Lighthouse), Hatchville, Mara Vista, North Falmouth (1990 pop. 2,625), Silver Beach, Teaticket (1990 pop. 1,856), Waquoit. Settled c.1660, inc. 1686. **4** (FAL-muhth), uninc. town (1990 pop. 3,541), Stafford co., N Va., at falls of Rappahannock R. (bridged) 2 mi/3.2 km N of Fredericksburg; 38°20′N 77°28′W. Mfg. (plastic, concrete, printing, asphalt, foods). Agr. (grain, soybeans; cattle, poultry, dairying). A thriving mfg. and trade center for almost a cent. Chatham Manor, part of Fredericksburg and Spotsylvania Natl. Military Park, served as Federal hq. here in Civil War battle of Fredericksburg (1862). Founded 1727 as port.

Falmouth Heights, Mass.: see FALMOUTH, town.

False Pass, village (1990 pop. 68), on E shore of Unimak Isl., Aleutian Isls., SW Alaska, opposite SW tip of Alaska Peninsula; 54°52′N 163°24′W. Narrow False Pass connects Bering Sea (Bechevie Bay) to Pacific Ocean.

False Presque Isle (presk), peninsula in L. Huron, NE Mich., 14 mi/23 km NNE of Alpena, and 4 mi/6.4 km SE of Presque Island village; c.2 mi/3.2 km long, 1.5 mi/2.4 km wide; 45°15′N 83°23′W. Part of Presque Isle co.

False River, La.: see NEW ROADS.

Falso, Cabo (FAHL-so, KAH-bo) or **Point Agujas**, headland on Caribbean coast of SW Dominican Republic, 50 mi/80 km SW of Barahona; 17°47′N 71°43′W.

Fancy Farm, uninc. town (1990 pop. 900), Graves co., W Ky., 10 mi/16 km WNW of Mayfield, on West Fork Mayfield Creek. In agr. area (tobacco; livestock; timber). Mfg. (hams, wooden cabinets).

Fannin 1 (FAN-in), county (□ 396; 1990 pop. 15,992), N Ga., on Tenn. and N.C. state lines; ⊙ Blue Ridge; 34°52′N 84°19′W. In the Blue Ridge and partly (W) in Chattahoochee Natl. Forest. Mfg. (apparel, textiles, wood prods., dairy prods.). Agr. (cattle, poultry, hogs; fruit, corn, hay, potatoes). Resort area drained by Toccoa R. (forms L. Blue Ridge here). Copper mines of adjacent Polk co.,Tenn., are a major employer of Fannin co. pop. Formed 1854. **2** county (□ 899 sq mi/2,328 sq km; 1990 pop. 24,804), NE Texas; ⊙ Bonham; 33°35′N 96°06′W. Bounded N by Red R. (Okla. state line); drained by S Sulphur and N Sulphur rivers and Bois d'Arc Creek (forms L. Bonham at center). Rich prairie agr. area (cotton, corn, wheat, sorghum, peanuts; cattle). Caddo Natl. Grassland in NE; Bonham State Park at center of co. Formed 1837.

Fanny Bay, village, SW B.C., Canada, on E central Vancouver Isl., on Strait of Georgia, 14 mi/23 km SE of Courtenay; 49°30′N 124°50′W. Lumber-shipping port.

Fanshaw, Cape, SE Alaska mainland, on Frederick Sound N of Kupreanof Isl.; 57°11′N 133°34′W. Post office and cannery here.

Fanshawe (FAN-shaw), village (1990 pop. 331), Le Flore co., E Okla., 17 mi/27 km WSW of Poteau; 34°58′N 94°52′W. Agr. and timber area in Ouchita Mts. L. Wister reservoir to SE.

Fantino (fahn-TEEN-oh), town (1993 pop. 8,307), 13 mi/20km NE of Bonao, Sánchez Ramírez prov., central Dominican Republic; 19°07′N 70°18′W. Market town in rice-producing region.

Fanwood, residential borough (1990 pop. 7,115), Union co., NE N.J., 9 mi/14.5 km WSW of Elizabeth; 40°38′N 74°23′W. Mfg. (packaging, air hoses). Settled before 1780, inc. 1895.

Far Hills, borough (1990 pop. 657), Somerset co., N central N.J., on North Branch of Raritan R., and 8 mi/12.9 km N of Somerville; 40°41′N 74°37′W. In country-estate area that is rapidly suburbanizing

Far Rockaway, residential sect. of S Queens borough of N.Y. city, SE N.Y., at base of Rockaway Peninsula; 40°36′N 73°45′W. Once a popular beach resort, it now has a mainly elderly and immigrant pop., mostly from Lat. Amer.

Farallon Islands or **Farallones**, Calif., 2 groups of waterless rocky islets in the Pacific, 26 mi/42 km W of San Francisco, and 20 mi/32 km S of Point Reyes, part of San Francisco city and co. On Southeast Farallon, the only inhabited isl., are a lighthouse and a U.S. navy radio-beam compass and radar station. Farallon Natl. Wildlife Refuge has seabird rookeries and seal colonies. In early 19th cent., Rus. sealers est. a colony here.

Farber, town (1990 pop. 418), Audrain co., NE central Mo., near West Fork of Cuivre R.,18 mi/29 km ENE of Mexico; 39°16′N 91°34′W. Soybeans; cattle, hogs. Mfg. (fire bricks).

Farewell (FER-wel), former air base, S central Alaska, on N slope of Alaska Range, near Mt. McKinley Natl. Park, 160 mi/257 km NW of Anchorage, on South Fork Kuskokwina R., 90 mi/145 km SW of Mt. McKinley (outside preserve); 62°31′N 153°58′W.

Fargo, city (1990 pop. 74,111), seat of Cass co., E N.Dak., on the Red R., opposite Moorhead, Minn; 46°52′N 96°49′W. A RR hub, RR junction, regional airport, and regional finance center, and regional medical center, Fargo is also the trade and distribution center of a spring-wheat and livestock region. Mfg. (computer software, farm tools, agr. prods., transportation equip.). The city was founded (1871) with the coming of the Northern Pacific RR and named for William G. Fargo of the Wells-Fargo Express Company. In the city are N.Dak. State Univ. and historical mus. The nearby suburb of West Fargo has minor stockyards and meat-packing plants. Cass Co. Historical Mus. Hector Internatl. Airport in N. Inc. 1875.

Fargo 1 village, Clinch co., S Ga., 26 mi/42 km SSE of Homerville, and on Suwannee R., at edge of Okefenokee Swamp; 30°41′N 82°33′W. Mfg. (mulch packaging). **2** village (1990 pop. 299), Ellis co., NW Okla., 13 mi/21 km WSW of Woodward, near Wolf Creek; 36°22′N 99°37′W. In livestock and grain area.

Faribault (FER-uh-bo), county (□ 721 sq mi/1,867 sq km; 1990 pop. 16,937), S Minn.; ⊙ Blue Earth; 43°40′N 93°57′W. Bounded on S by Iowa; drained by Blue Earth R. and its East and West forks. Agr. area (corn, oats, soybeans, alfalfa, peas; hogs, cattle, sheep, poultry). Food processing at Faribault. Rice and Minnesota lakes in N, Walnut L. in E center. Formed 1855.

Faribault (FER-uh-bo), city (1990 pop. 17,085), ⊙ Rice co., SE Minn., 45 mi/72 km S of Minneapolis, on Cannon R., at mouth of Straight R.; 44°17′N 93°16′W. Elev. 1,000 ft/305 m. Mfg. (transportation equip., asphalt, apparel, machinery, printing and publishing). Agr. (large floral nurseries, esp. peony farms). The city was founded in 1826 by Alexander Faribault, a French fur trader. In the city are state schools for the blind, the deaf, and the mentally challenged. Seat of Faribault Tech. Col. Municipal Airport to NW. River Bend Nature Center to SE; Nerstrand Big Woods State Park to NE; Wells and Cannon lakes to SW, on Cannon R. Inc. 1872.

Farina (fa-REI-nah), village (1990 pop. 575), Fayette co., S central Ill., 20 mi/32 km ESE of Vandalia; 38°49′N 88°46′W. In agr. area.

Farisita, village, Huerfano co., S Colo., on Huerfano R., in foothills of Wet Mts., and 17 mi/27 km NW of Walsenburg. Elev. c.6,960 ft/2,121 m. Chapel of Penitentes nearby. Part of San Isabel Natl. Forest to N.

Farley 1 town (1990 pop. 1,354), Dubuque co., E Iowa, 17 mi/27 km WSW of Dubuque; 42°26′N 91°00′W. Mfg. (metal, leather, concrete, plastic prods., dairy prods.); limestone quarries, gravel pit. **2** town (1990 pop. 217), Platte co., W Mo., on Missouri R., and 20 mi/32 km NW of downtown Kansas City; 39°16′N 94°49′W. Tobacco, corn, wheat; cattle.

Farley 1 and 2 Nuclear Power Plants, Alabama: see HOUSTON, CO.

Farm Island, S Ont., Canada, in St. Clair R., 7 mi/11.3 km SW of Sarnia; 2 mi/3.2 km long.

Farmer, village (1990 pop. 23), Hanson co., SE S.Dak., 17 mi/27 km E of Mitchell; 43°43′N 97°41′W.

Farmer City, city (1990 pop. 2,114), De Witt co., central Ill., 18 mi/29 km ENE of Clinton; 40°14′N 88°38′W. In agr. area; corn, wheat, soybeans; livestock. Seed-processing plant. Inc. 1869.

Farmers, village (1990 pop. 180), Rowan co., NE Ky., 7 mi/11.3 km WSW of Morehead, on Licking R., and 2 mi/3.2 km below (N of) Cave Run Dam. Clay mining and agr. area. Morehead/Rowan Co. Airport here. Daniel Boone Natl. Forest to E and S.

Farmers Branch, city (1990 pop. 24,250), Dallas co., N Texas, suburb 11 mi/18 km NNW of downtown Dallas, adjacent to city of Dallas; 32°55′N 96°52′W. Elev. 633 ft/193 m. Mfg. (printing, tiles, plastic prods., bakery prods.). Dallas–Fort Worth Internatl. Airport to W; bounded by Elm Fork Trinity R. on W; seat of Brookhaven Col. (2 year); has local Historical Park. Settled 1841, inc. 1946

Farmersburg 1 town (1990 pop. 1,159), Sullivan co., SW Ind., 11 mi/18 km N of Sullivan; 39°15′N 87°23′W. Trading center in agr. (livestock, grain), oil, and gas area; lumber milling. Laid out 1853, inc. 1871. **2** town (1990 pop. 291), Clayton co., NE Iowa, 8 mi/12.9 km NNE of Elkader; 42°57′N 91°22′W. In hog and dairying region; makes cheese.

Farmersville, city (1990 pop. 6,235), Tulare co., S central Calif., in San Joaquin Valley, 5 mi/8 km ESE of Visalia; 36°18′N 119°13′W. Orchards, citrus groves, nuts, grapes; grain; cattle, hogs.

Farmersville, town (1990 pop. 2,640), Collin co., N Texas, 36 mi/58 km NE of Dallas; 33°09′N 96°21′W. RR junction. Cotton; cattle, horses. Mfg. (packaging material, light mfg.).

Farmersville 1 village (1990 pop. 698), Montgomery co., S central Ill., 23 mi/37 km S of Springfield; 39°26′N

89°39′W. In agr. and bituminous-coal area. **2** village (1990 pop. 932), Montgomery co., W Ohio, 13 mi/21 km WSW of Dayton; 39°40′N 84°25′W. In agr. area.

Farmerville, town (1990 pop. 3,334), ⊙ Union parish, N La., 25 mi/40 km NW of Monroe, and on Bayou D'Arbonne (navigable; here forming Bayou D'Arbonne L., incl. L. D'Arbonne State Park to W); 32°46′N 92°24′W. Trade center for agr. area (cotton, corn, vegetables; cattle; dairying); logging, lumber mfg. La. Watermelon Festival held here. Union State Wildlife Area to N.

Farmingdale, town (1990 pop. 2,918), Kennebec co., S Maine, on the Kennebec R. below Augusta; 44°15′N 69°49′W. Inc. 1852.

Farmingdale, village (□ 1 sq mi/2.6 sq km; 1990 pop. 8,022), Nassau co., SE N.Y., on W L.I., 10 mi/16 km E of Mineola; 40°43′N 73°27′W. Mfg. (machinery, printing equip., electrial equip., ammunition, electronics; metal fabrication). Seat of State Univ. of N.Y. at Farmingdale. Republic Airport is located just E of community. Bethpage State Park is just N. Settled 1695, inc. 1904.

Farmingdale, borough (1990 pop. 1,462), Monmouth co., E N.J., near Manasquan R., 7 mi/11.3 km SE of Freehold; 40°12′N 74°10′W. Mfg. (concrete prods.). Naval Ammunition Depot just N.

Farmington 1 city, Oconee co., NE central Ga., 13 mi/21 km S of Athens; 33°46′N 83°23′W. **2** city (1990 pop. 2,535), Fulton co., W central Ill., 21 mi/34 km W of Peoria; 40°42′N 90°00′W. RR junction. Bituminous-coal mines. Agr. (corn, soybeans, sorghum, soybeans; cattle). Mfg. (prepared food, machinery). Laid out 1834, inc. 1857. **3** city (1990 pop. 10,132), Oakland co., SE Mich., suburb 19 mi/31 km WNW of downtown Detroit, and 13 mi/21 km SSW of Pontiac, on the R. Rouge; 42°27′N 83°22′W. Residential. Mfg. (machinery, transportation equip.). Settled 1824; inc. as village 1867, as city 1926. **4** city (1990 pop. 11,598), ⊙ St. Francois co., E Mo., in the St. Francois Mts. near St. Francis R., 58 mi/93 km S of St. Louis; 37°46′N 90°25′W. Regional service center. Mixed farming. Mfg. (metal prods., outdoor furniture, bank vaults, shoes, crushed limestone); flour mills. Southeast Mo. Mental Health Center and a state correctional facility. St. Joe State Park to W. Settled 1799, laid out c. 1822. **5** city (1990 pop. 33,997), San Juan co., NW N.Mex., 182 mi/293 km NW of Albuquerque, at the mouths of the San Juan, Animas, and La Plata rivers; 36°45′N 108°11′W. Trade center of an oil, natural gas, and irrigated farm area (cattle, sheep, potatoes, grain, pumpkins, blue corn, alfalfa). Mfg. (machinery, fencing, asphalt, electronic equip., concrete, consumer goods, printing and publishing). San Juan Community Col. is in Farmington. San Juan Downs Racetrack here. Aztec Ruins Natl. Monument (NE) and Salmon Ruins (E) are nearby. Navajo Indian Reservation immediately to SW; Ute Mt. Indian Reservation to NW. Inc. 1901.

Farmington 1 town (1990 pop. 20,608), Hartford co., central Conn., on the Farmington R.; 41°43′N 72°50′W. Mainly residential with some light industries. Miss Porter's boarding school for girls, Tunxis Community Col., and the Univ. of Conn. Medical Hosp. (a teaching hosp.) are here. Of interest are the Congregational Church (1770) and 2 mus.—the Hillstead Mus. houses a small, but notable, collection of Fr. impressionist paintings. Inc. 1645. **2** town (1990 pop. 655), Van Buren co., SE Iowa, near Mo. state line, on Des Moines R., and 15 mi/24 km SE of Keosauqua; 40°38′N 91°44′W. Pickle processing. Coal mines, limestone quarries nearby. State parks in vicinity **3** town (1990 pop. 7,436), ⊙ Franklin co., W central Maine, on Sandy R., and 30 mi/48 km NW of Augusta resort and agr. trade center; 44°40′N 70°08′W. Light mfg. A Univ. of Maine campus is here. Birthplace (mus.) of Lillian Nordica here. Gateway to Rangeley Lakes and Dead R. areas. Settled 1781, inc. 1794. **4** town (1990 pop. 5,940), Dakota co., SE Minn., suburb 19 mi/31 km S of downtown St. Paul, on Vermillion R.; 44°39′N 93°10′W. Shipping point for agr. area on S fringe of Twin Cities region (dairying; grain, soybeans; poultry, livestock). Mfg. (electrical equip., plastic prods.). **5** town (1990 pop. 5,739), Strafford co., SE N.H., 7 mi/11.3 km NW of Rochester; 43°21′N 71°04′W. Drained by Cocheco R. and Mad R. Mfg. (machinery, asphalt, sand and gravel processing, septic tank, shoes [industry began 1835], metal prods.). Agr. (nursery crops, apples, vegetables; cattle; dairying). Part of Blue Hills Range in SW. Henry Wilson b. here. Set off from Rochester 1797. **6** uninc. town (1990 pop. 800), Lehigh co., E Pa., residential suburb 2 mi/3.2 km SE of Allentown near Lehigh R.; 40°35′N 75°25′W. **7** town (1990 pop. 9,028), ⊙ Davis co., N Utah, near Great Salt L., suburb 15 mi/24 km N of Salt Lake City, and 15 mi/24 km S of Ogden, just W of Wasatch Range; 40°59′N 111°53′W. Elev. 4,302 ft/1,311 m. Agr. (apples, berries, cherries, peaches, vegetables; dairying; cattle). Lagoon Resort and Amusement Park, Farmington Bay (Great Salt L.). Waterfowl Management Area to SW. Settled 1848 by Mormons; originally called North Cottonwood. Disastrous floods of 1923 and 1930 led to soil-conservation and reforestation project nearby.

Farmington 1 village (1990 pop. 122), Kent co., W central Del., 4 mi/6.4 km S of Harrington; 38°52′N 75°34′W. In agr. area. Mfg. (industrial machinery). Del. State Forest and Raceway to N. **2** uninc. village, Wharlon township, Fayette co., SW Pa., 10 mi/16 km SE of Uniontown; 39°48′N 79°33′W. Agr. (livestock, dairying). Light mfg. (printing and publishing); surface coal. Fort Necessity Natl. Battlefield Site 1 mi/1.6 km to W. **3** village (1990 pop. 126), Whitman co., SE Wash., 18 mi/29 km NE of Colfax, on Pine Creek, near Idaho state line; 47°05′N 117°03′W. Grain, peas, lentils. Coeur d'Alene Indian Reservation (Idaho) to NE; St. Joe Natl. Forest (Idaho) to E. **4** village (1990 pop. 414), Marion co., N W. Va., 17 mi/27 km WNW of Fairmont; 39°30′N 80°15′W. Agr. (corn, apples); livestock. Mfg. (mining equip.). Coal-mining and oil-producing region.

Farmington Hills, city (1990 pop. 74,652), Oakland co., SE Mich., suburb 20 mi/32 km NNW of downtown Detroit and 12 mi/19 km SSW of Pontiac; 42°29′N 83°22′W. Drained by Upper R. Rouge. Borders Wayne co. on S. Mfg. (machinery, transportation equip., electronics assembly, rubber and plastic prods., security control equip., metal prods.).

Farmington River, c.40 mi/64 km long, N Conn.; formed at New Hartford by junction of West Branch (c.30 mi/48 km long), rising in S Mass., and East Branch (c.14 mi/23 km long); flows SE to Farmington, thence N and SE to the Connecticut above Hartford. Water is supplied to Hartford and suburbs from Barkhamsted and East Branch reservoirs on East Branch and Nepaug Reservoir (c.3 mi/4.8 km long), S of New Hartford on a short W tributary. Recreational tubing at New Hartford. Some success with salmon restoration.

Farmland, town (1990 pop. 1,412), Randolph co., E Ind., 7 mi/11.3 km WNW of Winchester; 40°11′N 85°08′W. Agr. area. Mfg. (foil stamping).

Farmville 1 town (1990 pop. 4,392), Pitt co., E N.C., 12 mi/19 km W of Greenville, near Contentnea Creek; 35°35′N 77°35′W. Tobacco warehouses in declining tobacco-growing area; peanuts, grain, cotton, sweet potatoes; chickens, cattle, hogs. Mfg. (pharmaceuticals, transportation equip., apparel, paper prods., feeds, textiles). Settled 1860; inc. 1872. **2** town (1990 pop. 6,046), Prince Edward and Cumberland cos., central Va., ⊙ Prince Edward co., on Appomattox R., 40 mi/64 km E of Lynchburg; 37°17′N 78°24′W. Mfg. (apparel, lumber, wood prods., machinery, shoes, textiles). Tobacco market; processing center for agr. area (tobacco, grain; livestock; dairying). Medicinal springs nearby. Seat of Longwood Col.; Hampden-Sydney Col. is 5 mi/8 km SW, at Hampden Sydney. Sailor's Creek Battlefield State Historical Park to E; Twin Lakes State Park, Gallion State Forest to SE. Inc. 1912.

Farnam, village (1990 pop. 188), Dawson co., S central Nebr., 25 mi/40 km WSW of Lexington; 40°42′N 100°13′W. Grain.

Farnams, Mass.: see CHESHIRE.

Farnham (FAHR-nuhm), town (1991 pop. 6,146), S Que., Canada, on Yamaska R., and 14 mi/23 km E of St. Jean; 45°17′N 72°58′W. RR shops. Mfg.; refining; dairying.

Farnham, village (□ 1 sq mi/2.6 sq km; 1990 pop. 427), Erie co., W N.Y., near L. Erie, 15 mi/24 km NE of Dunkirk; 42°36′N 79°04′W. Mfg. (canned foods, textiles).

Farnham, Mount (11,342 ft/3,457 m), SE B.C., Canada, in Selkirk Mts., 65 mi/105 km SW of Banff; 50°29′N 116°30′W.

Farnhamville, town (1990 pop. 414), Calhoun co., central Iowa, 20 mi/32 km SW of Fort Dodge; 42°16′N 94°24′W. Feed; foods; fertilizers.

Farnumsville, Mass.: see GRAFTON.

Faro, town (1991 pop. 1,221), central Yukon Territory, Canada, 80 mi/129 km NE of Whitehorse, on N side of Pelly R. Spur road connects with Campbell Highway 5 mi/8 km S. Silver-lead and zinc mined 1969–1982; reopened 1986. One of the largest lead producers in world; part of Anvil dist., Anvil Range mts. Scheduled air service.

Farr West, town (1990 pop. 2,178), Weber co., N Utah, residential suburb 6 mi/9.7 km NW of Ogden, near Great Salt L.; 41°17′N 112°01′W. Elev. 4,269 ft/1,301 m. Agr. area (vegetables, fruit, alfalfa, barley, wheat; dairying, cattle). Ogden Defense Depot to SE. Town named for pioneers Lorin Farr and Chauncey West. Settled 1858.

Farragut, town (1990 pop. 498), Fremont co., SW Iowa, 7 mi/11.3 km SW of Shenandoah; 40°43′N 95°28′W. In agr. area (grain; livestock, poultry).

Farrar (fuh-RAHR), town, Jasper co., central Ga., 12 mi/19 km NNE of Monticello; 33°27′N 83°25′W.

Farrell, city (1990 pop. 6,841), Mercer co., W central Pa., 11 mi/18 km NE of Youngstown, Ohio, and 2 mi/3.2 km S of Sharon, its larger twin city, on the Shenango R., near the Ohio state line; 41°12′N 80°30′W. A RR center; steel and iron works industries have declined. Mfg. (metal fabrication, machinery, rolled steel, food). Sharon Airport to E, West Middlesex Airport to S. Shenango River L. reservoir to N. Inc. 1901.

Farwell, town (1990 pop. 1,373), ⊙ Parmer co., NW Texas, on Llano Estacado, on state line contiguous to Texico, N.Mex., and 10 mi/16 km E of Clovis, N.Mex.; 34°23′N 103°02′W. Elev. 4,375 ft/1,334 m. RR junction, in wheat and cattle region; light mfg.

Farwell 1 village (1990 pop. 851), Clare co., central Mich., 17 mi/27 km NNW of Mt. Pleasant, and on Tobacco R.; 43°50′N 84°52′W. In lake and farm area; fishing. Mfg. (plastic prods.). Mott Mt. Ski Area outside of town. **2** village (1990 pop. 74), Pope co., W Minn., 13 mi/21 km NW of Glenwood at E end of Pike L.; 45°45′N 95°37′W. Grain; dairying.

Fate, village (1990 pop. 475), Rockwall co., NE Texas, 25 mi/40 km NE of Dallas; 32°56′N 96°23′W. In agr. area.

Father Marquette National Memorial, Mackinac co., N Mich., (□ 52 acres/21 ha); 43°56′N 86°27′W. Located in Straits State Park near St. Ignace on the Straits of Mackinac. Commemorates Father Jacques Marquette who founded a Jesuit mission here (1671) and explored much of the area; buried here, 1678. Authorized 1975.

Faulk, county (□ 1,005 sq mi/2,603 sq km; 1990 pop. 2,744), N central S.Dak.; ⊙ Faulkton; 45°04′N 99°09′W. Agr. area watered by intermittent streams, branches at James R.; wheat, other grains; livestock. L. Faulkton Reservoir and State Lakeside Use Area to S. Formed 1873.

Faulkland Heights, uninc. town (1990 pop. 1,300), New Castle co., N Del., residential suburb 4 mi/6.4 km W of downtown Wilmington, on Red Clay Creek; 39°44′N 75°38′W.

Faulkner, county (□ 664 sq mi/1,720 sq km; 1990 pop. 60,006), central Ark.; ⊙ Conway; 35°08′N 92°20′W. Bounded SW by Arkansas R.; drained by Cadron Creek (forms part of W boundary). Agr. (cattle, hogs; wheat, soybeans); timber. Mfg. at Conway. Toad Suck Lock and Dam (Arkansas R.) in SW; Woolly Hollow State Park in N; L. Conway Reservoir, Bell Slough Wildlife Management Area, Camp Robinson Wildlife Management Area, and part of Camp Robinson Natl. Guard Training Area in S. Formed 1873.

Faulkton, city (1990 pop. 809), ⊙ Faulk co., N central S.Dak., 45 mi/72 km SW of Aberdeen, and on branch of James R.; 45°01′N 99°07′W. Livestock, grain. Nearby is L. Faulkton, artificial lake used for recreation.

Faunsdale (FAWNS-dail), town (1990 pop. 96), Marengo co., W Ala., 14 mi/23 km ESE of Demopolis; 32°27′N 87°35′W. Farming.

Fauquier (fawk-YIR), county (☐ 651 sq mi/1,686 sq km; 1990 pop. 48,741), N Va.; ⊙ Warrenton; 38°44′N 77°48′W. Mainly in the Piedmont region, with part of Blue Ridge in NW; bounded S and SW by Rappahannock R.; drained by Little R. in N. Rich agr. area (wheat, barley, corn, soybeans, hay, alfalfa, apples, peaches; cattle, hogs); noted for stock raising (esp. horses, in Warrenton sect.) and dairying; oak, hickory, and pine timber. Appalachian Trail follows NW boundary. Sky Meadows State Park in far N. Vint Hill Farm Military Reservation in E, part of Quantico Marine Corps Base in SE. Formed 1759.

Favourable Lake, village, NW Ont., Canada, in Patricia dist., near Favourable L. (16 mi/26 km long, 4 mi/6 km wide); 52°50′N 93°38′W. Gold mining.

Fawcett, Mount (6,213 ft/1,894 m), on Alaska-B.C. (Canada) border, in Coast Range, 35 mi/56 km E of Wrangell; 56°33′N 131°28′W.

Fawn Grove, borough (1990 pop. 489), York co., S Pa., 23 mi/37 km SE of York, at Md. state border; 43°39′N 76°27′W. Agr. (grain, apples; dairying, livestock).

Faxon, uninc. town (1990 pop. 1,635), Loyalsock township, Lycoming co., N central Pa., residential suburb 2 mi/3.2 km E of Williamsport, on West Branch Susquehanna R.; 41°15′N 76°58′W.

Faxon (FAK-suhn), village (1990 pop. 127), Comanche co., SW Okla., 14 mi/23 km SW of Lawton, on West Cache Creek; 34°27′N 98°34′W. In agr. area.

Fayette 1 (FAI-yet), county (☐ 629 sq mi/1,629 sq km; 1990 pop. 17,962), W Ala.; ⊙ Fayette; 33°44′N 87°43′W. Agr. region drained by Sipsey and North rivers, crossed (N-S) by fall line. Cotton, corn, livestock; lumber milling; crude oil and natural gas prods. Deposits of coal, sandstone, fuller's earth. Formed 1824. **2** county (☐ 199 sq mi/515 sq km; 1990 pop. 62,415), W central Ga.; ⊙ Fayetteville; 33°25′N 84°29′W. Bounded E by Flint R. Piedmont agr. includes pecans, peaches; dairy; cattle. Formed 1821. **3** county (☐ 725 sq mi/1,878 sq km; 1990 pop. 20,893), S central Ill.; ⊙ Vandalia; 39°01′N 89°02′W. Agr. area (corn, wheat, soybeans, sorghum; cattle; dairy prods.), with petroleum and natural gas wells. Mfg. (rubber and plastics prods.). Drained by Kaskaskia R. Formed 1821. Ramsey L. State Park in NW; Carlyle Wildlife Management Area and N end of L. Carlyle, in SW. Vandalia is site of Vandalia State House Historic Site and Vandalia Correctional Center. Historic Natl. Road ended at Vandalia, the 2d of 3 Ill. capitals. **4** county (☐ 215 sq mi/557 sq km; 1990 pop. 26,015), E Ind.; ⊙ Connersville; 39°38′N 85°11′W. Corn, soybeans, wheat; cattle, hogs. Mfg. at Connersville. Drained by West Fork Whitewater R. Formed 1819. **5** county (☐ 731 sq mi/1,893 sq km; 1990 pop. 21,843), NE Iowa; ⊙ West Union, 42°52′N 91°51′W. Prairie agr. area (hogs, cattle, poultry; corn, oats; dairying) drained by Volga, Maquoketa, and Turkey rivers, and by Buffalo Creek. Limestone quarries, sand and gravel pits. Mfg. at West Union and Oelwein. Echo Valley State Park is N central; Volga River State Park is center; Brush Creek Canyon State Preserve is SE. General flooding occurred in 1993. Formed 1837. **6** county (☐ 285 sq mi/738 sq km; 1990 pop. 225,366), central Ky.; ⊙ Lexington; 38°03′N 84°27′W. Bounded SE by Kentucky R.; drained by Elkhorn Creek and its North Branch. Gently rolling upland agr. area, in heart of Bluegrass region; has hundreds of thoroughbred and saddle horse farms. Agr. (tobacco, hay, alfalfa, soybeans, wheat, corn; hogs, cattle; bluegrass seed); limestone quarries. Mfg. at Lexington, an important commercial center. Co. is coterminus with the city limits of Lexington. Ky. Horse Park (State Park) in N. Formed 1780 from old Kentucky co., Va. **7** county (☐ 406 sq mi/1,052 sq km; 1990 pop. 27,466), S central Ohio; ⊙ Washington Court House, 39°33′N 83°27′W. Drained by Paint Creek and small Sugar and Rattlesnake creeks. In the Till Plains physiographic region. Agr. (sheep; dairy prods.; grain, soybeans, fruit). Mfg. at Washington Court House (plastic prods., fabricated metal prods., machinery, medical appliances and supplies). Formed 1810. **8** county (☐ 797 sq mi/2,064 sq km; 1990 pop. 145,351), SW Pa.; ⊙ Uniontown; 39°55′N 79°39′W. Bounded S by W.Va. and Md. state boundaries, W by Monongahela R., Laurel Hill forms part of E boundary; drained by Youghiogheny R. (forms Youghiogheny River L. reservoir on SE boundary). Agr. (corn, wheat, oats, barley, hay, alfalfa, apples; sheep, hogs, cattle, dairying); timber. Bituminous coal; natural gas; limestone. Mfg. at Uniontown and Connellsville. First settled 1752 by Virginians. Whiskey Rebellion put down here in 1794. Friendship Hill Natl. Historic Site in SW; Fort Necessity Natl. Battlefield in S center; historic Cumberland Road passed through co. Chestnut Ridge crosses center of co. NE-SW; part of Laurel Ridge State Park in NE; large Ohiopyle State Park in E; Forbes State Forest in several small sects. in S, including Que. Run Wilderness Area; part of Cheat L. reservoir, on Cheat R., in SW corner; L. Courage reservoir in SE. Formed 1783. **9** county (☐ 704 sq mi/1,823 sq km; 1990 pop. 25,559), SW Tenn.; ⊙ Somerville; 35°11′N 89°25′W. Bounded S by Miss.; drained by Loosahatchie and Wolf rivers. Agr. (cotton, livestock, corn, soybeans, sorghum, pecans, fruit). Formed 1824. **10** county (☐ 959 sq mi/2,484 sq km; 1990 pop. 20,095), S central Texas; ⊙ La Grange; 29°51′N 96°55′W. Drained by Colorado R. and headwaters of Navidad R. Cattle, poultry, dairying; agr. (corn, grain sorghum, peanuts, pecans). Some timber; oil wells. Monument Hill State Park in center; L. Fayette in E. Formed 1837. **11** county (☐ 668 sq mi/1,730 sq km; 1990 pop. 47,952), S central W.Va.; ⊙ Fayetteville, 38°03′N 81°06′W. On Allegheny Plateau; drained by Kanawha R. and Gauley R. (part of N border); Meadow R. forms NE border. Part of New R. Gorge Natl. R. in S and center; Babcock State Park in center; Hawks Nest State Park in NW center; part of Gauley R. Natl. Recreation Area in N; Plum Orchard Wildlife Management Area in SW. Bituminous-coal mining. Agr. (corn, oats, alfalfa, hay; cattle, sheep). Some timber. Mfg. at Oak Hill. Formed 1831.

Fayette 1 (FAI-yet), city (1990 pop. 4,909), ⊙ Fayette co., NW Ala., on Sipsey R., and c.60 mi/97 km WNW of Birmingham; 41°33′N 87°49′W. Mfg. (apparel, tile, yarn, machinery); lumber; gas and oil production. Bevill State Community Col. here. Inc. 1821. **2** (fai-YET), city (1990 pop. 2,888), ⊙ Howard co., central Mo., near Missouri R., 23 mi/37 km NW of Columbia; 39°08′N 92°41′W. Agr. center. Corn, wheat, soybeans; cattle. Mfg. (apparel). Central Methodist Col. Founded 1823.

Fayette 1 (FAI-yet), town (1990 pop. 1,317), Fayette co., NE Iowa, on Volga R., and 12 mi/19 km NNE of Oelwein; 42°50′N 91°47′W. Feed milling; steel fabrication. Limestone quarries nearby. Seat of Upper Iowa Univ. (coed., 1857). Volga River State Park to E. **2** town (1990 pop. 855), Kennebec co., SW Maine, 16 mi/26 km NW of Augusta; 44°26′N 70°03′W. In resort area; agr., lumbering. **3** town (1990 pop. 1,853), ⊙ Jefferson co., SW Miss., 45 mi/72 km SSW of Vicksburg; 31°42′N 91°03′W. Agr. (cotton, corn, soybeans; cattle; timber). Mfg. (wood furniture parts). Natchez Trace (Natl.) Parkway passes to W. Springfield Plantation (c.1788), site of Andrew Jackson's marriage to Rachel Robards (1791).

Fayette 1 (FAI-yet), village (1990 pop. 1,248), Fulton co., NW Ohio, c.40 mi/64 km W of Toledo, near Mich. state line; 41°40′N 84°19′W. **2** village (1990 pop. 183), Sanpete co., central Utah, on S end Sevier Bridge Reservoir, and 5 mi/8 km N of Gunnison; 39°13′N 111°50′W. Grain; livestock. Mfg. (medical supplies). Painted Rock and Yuba State Parks to NW.

Fayette City (FEI-yet), borough (1990 pop. 713), Fayette co., SW Pa., 25 mi/40 km S of Pittsburgh, and 4 mi/6.4 km SE of Monessen, on Monongahela R; 40°06′N 79°50′W. Agr. (grain, alfalfa; livestock, dairying); coal. Settled 1794.

Fayetteville 1 (FAI-uht-vuhl), city (1990 pop. 42,099), ⊙ Washington co., NW Ark., in the Ozarks, 45 mi/72 km NNE of Fort Smith; 36°04′N 94°09′W. It is a farm trade and agr. center with canneries and food processing. Mfg. (concrete, machinery, electronic equip., prepared food, transportation equip., dairy prods., apparel, lumber, printing, paper prods.). The Univ. of Ark. is here and maintains an agr. experimental farm here. Several battles occurred in the area during the Civil War, including at Pea Ridge and Prairie Grove. Tourism, recreation area. Beaver L. reservoir to NW; Ozark Natl. Forest to W and S; Devil's Den State Park to S; Prairie Grove Battlefield State Park to SW. Core of Fayetteville–Springdale–Rogers metropolitan areas, one of country's fastest growing areas. Inc. 1836. **2** (FAI-et-vuhl), city (1990 pop. 75,695), ⊙ Cumberland co., S central N.C., 55 mi/89 km SSW of Raleigh at the head of navigation on the Cape Fear R.; 35°04′N 78°54′W. An inland port (it is connected by a channel to the Intracoastal Waterway). Mfg. (printing and publishing; concrete, plastic, and lumber prods.; machinery, feeds, textiles, apparel; steel fabrication, food, industrial chemicals, automotive parts.) Settled as 2 towns (1739) by Highland Scots, it was a Tory center during the Amer. Revolution. The 2 towns were merged during the war, and in 1783 they were renamed for the Marquis de Lafayette. The city was state capital 1789–1793 and the scene (1789) of the state convention that ratified the U.S. Constitution. In 1831 fire destroyed nearly 600 bldgs. During the Civil War, Sherman occupied the town and razed its arsenal (1865). The city is the seat of Fayetteville State Univ., Methodist Col., and Fayetteville Tech. Community Col.; it also has a symphony orchestra. Fort Bragg Military Reserve and Pope Air Force Base to NW. Fayetteville Regional Airport to S. Mus. of the Cape Fear. Inc. 1783. **3** (FAI-et-vil), city (1990 pop. 6,921), ⊙ Lincoln co., S Tenn., on Elk R., and 36 mi/58 km SW of Manchester, near Ala. state line; 35°09′N 86°34′W. Shipping and trade center in timber, livestock, tobacco, dairying, apple-growing region. Mfg. (apparel, textiles, metal products; lumber milling. U.S. fish hatchery nearby.

Fayetteville 1 (FAI-et-vil), town (1990 pop. 5,816), ⊙ Fayette co., W central Ga., 22 mi/35 km SSW of Atlanta; 33°27′N 84°28′W. Suburb of S Atlanta. Mfg. (transportation equipment, printing and publishing, concrete, diversified light mfg.). **2** (FEI-yet-vil), uninc. town (1990 pop. 3,033), Franklin co., S Pa., 6 mi/9.7 km E of Chambersburg, near Conococheague Creek; 39°54′N 77°34′W. In agr. area (grain, potatoes, apples; livestock, poultry, dairying). Mfg. (sand and gravel processing, light mfg.). Appalachian Trail passes to E; parts of Michaux State Forest to NE and SE; Caledonia State Park to E; Mt. Alto State Park to S. **3** town (1990 pop. 2,182), ⊙ Fayette co., S central W.Va., near New R., 35 mi/56 km SE of Charleston; 38°02′N 81°06′W. Bituminous-coal mining. Agr. (grain, alfalfa); livestock. Timber. New R. Gorge Natl. R. to E (includes Canyon Rim visitor center). Babcock State Park to SE; Hawks Nest State Park to N. Settled 1818.

Fayetteville 1 (FAI-et-vil), village (1990 pop. 283), Fayette co., S central Texas, 23 mi/37 km SW of Brenham; 29°54′N 96°40′W. Elev. 411 ft/125 m. In agr. area. L. Fayette reservoir to W. **2** village (1990 pop. 371), St. Clair co., SW Ill., 15 mi/24 km SE of Belleville; 38°22′N 89°47′W. In bituminous-coal and agr. area. On Kaskaskin R. **3** suburban village (☐ 1 sq mi/2.6 sq km; 1990 pop. 4,248), Onondaga co., central N.Y., 7 mi/11.3 km E of Syracuse; 43°01′N 76°00′W. Mfg. (machinery, paper prods.). Agr. (dairy prods.). Green Lakes State Park NE of village. Inc. 1844. **4** village (1990 pop. 393), Brown co., SW Ohio, 30 mi/48 km E of Cincinnati, and on East Fork of Little Miami R.; 39°11′N 83°56′W.

Fayston, resort town (1990 pop. 846), Washington co., central Vt., in Green Mts., 10 mi/16 km SW of Montpelier; 44°13′N 72°52′W. Mad R. Glen, Sugarbush North, and Tucker Hill (touring) ski areas are here.

Fear, Cape, Brunswick co., SE N.C., S tip of Bald Head Isl. on the Atlantic Ocean, 27 mi/43 km S of Wilmington, E of mouth of Cape Fear R. Lighthouse 3 mi/

4.8 km NW of Cape; Frying-Pan Shoals extend c.20 mi/32 km S and SE from cape.

Fearrington (FEER-ing-tuhn), uninc. town (1990 pop. 1,101), Chatham co., central N.C., suburb, 17 mi/27 km SW of Durham, near Haw R.; 35°48′N 79°04′W. Agr. area (grain, tobacco; poultry, livestock). Jordan L. reservoir, on New Hope R., to E. Original townsite of Farrington, on W shore.

Feasterville-Trevose (FEE-stuhr-vil–TREE-vos), uninc. town (1990 pop. 6,696), Bucks co., SE Pa., suburb 16 mi/26 km NNE of Philadelphia. Mfg. (packaging, printing, machinery, sheet metal fabricating, plastic prods., food, telecommunications equip.).

Feather Falls, Butte co., N central Calif., waterfall (640 ft/195 m drop) branch of South Fork Feather R. (L. Oroville), 18 mi/29 km NE of Oroville. Plumas Natl. Forest to N and E.

Feather River, 80 mi/129 km long, N central Calif.; rises in 3 forks in the Sierra Nevada; all three uniting 5 mi/8 km NE of Oroville, in L. Oroville reservoir (Middle Fork joins South Fork 3 mi/4.8 km E of confluence of North and South forks) and flowing S past Oroville and Yaba City/Marysville to Sacramento R., NNW of Sacramento. The Feather R. basin was a rich source of gold in the mid-19th cent. The Feather R. project (1957–1968), which includes Oroville Dam, furnishes central and S California with water and provides flood control, recreation, and hydroelectricity in the river basin.

Federal, former lead-mining company town, St. Francois co., E Mo., just S of Flat R., 1 mi/1.6 km S of center of Park Hills. Merged with Flat River (now Park Hills) c.1970.

Federal Dam, village (1990 pop. 118), Cass co., N central Minn., 18 mi/29 km NE of Walker, on Leech Lake R., in Chippewa Natl. Forest; 47°14′N 94°13′W. Dairying; cattle, sheep; oats; timber. Leech L. and Leech L. Indian Reservation to N, W, and S. Dam just W on Leech R. Battleground State Forest to S and Bowstring State Forest to N.

Federal Hall, memorial, in lower Manhattan borough of N.Y. city, SE N.Y., authorized 1939. Site of the 1st seat of the federal govt. and George Washington's inauguration (1789).

Federal Heights, town (1990 pop. 9,342), residential suburb 9 mi/14.5 km N of downtown Denver, Adams co., N central Colo., bounded E by Thornton, W by Westminster; 39°52′N 105°01′W.

Federal Way, city (1990 pop. 67,554), King co., W Wash., suburb 20 mi/32 km S of Seattle, and 7 mi/11.3 km ENE of Tacoma, on Puget Sound; 47°19′N 122°20′W. Mfg. (printing and publishing, rubber prods., apparel, metal prods., food). Rhododendron Botanical Garden is here.

Federalsburg, town (1990 pop. 2,365), Caroline co., E Md., on Delmarva Peninsula 19 mi/31 km ENE of Cambridge, and on Marshyhope Creek; 38°42′N 75°46′W. In agr. area (vegetable canneries, poultry-dressing plants). Mfg. (buttons, cutlery, plastics). Settled 1789 as Northwest Fork Bridge. Idylwild Wildlife Management Area is just N.

Feeding Hills, Mass.: see AGAWAM.

Felchville, Vt.; see READING.

Felicity (fuh-LI-si-tee), village (1990 pop. 856), Clermont co., SW Ohio, 29 mi/47 km SE of Cincinnati, near Ohio R.; 38°50′N 84°05′W.

Felipe Carrillo Puerto (fe-LEE-pe kah-REE-yo PWER-to), town (1990 pop. 12,704), Quintana Roo, SE Mexico, on E Yucatán Peninsula, 80 mi/129 km NNE of Chetumal; 19°36′N 88°02′W. Exports henequen, chicle, tropical hardwood. Former capital of territory. Santa Cruz de Bravo until 1935.

Felix, Cape, N extremity of King William Isl., S Franklin dist., N.W.T., Canada, on James Ross and Victoria straits; 69°55′N 97°50′W.

Felix Harbour, SE Boothia Peninsula, SE Franklin dist., N.W.T., Canada, small bay of the Gulf of Boothia; 70°00′N 91°52′W. John Ross's *Victory* wintered here (1829–1830 and 1830–1831).

Fellsmere (FELZ-mir), town (□ 1 sq mi/2.6 sq km; 1990 pop. 2,179), Indian R. co., E central Fla., 16 mi/26 km NW of Vero Beach; 27°46′N 80°35′W. Sugar-milling center in large cane-growing area.

Felsenthal (FEL-sen-thahl), village (1990 pop. 95), Union co., S Ark., 31 mi/50 km ESE of El Dorado, at W end of Felsenthal Lock and Dam (Ouachita R.); impounds L. Jack Lee to N; 33°03′N 92°09′W. Felsenthal Natl. Wildlife Refuge to N; Lower Ouachita Wildlife Management Area to SE.

Felton, uninc. town (1990 pop. 5,350), Santa Cruz co., W Calif., in Santa Cruz Mts., 6 mi. NNW of Santa Cruz, 5 mi/8 km NE of Pacific Ocean coast; 37°02′N 122°04′W. Printing and publishing. Big Basin Redwoods State Park to NW, Forest of Nisene Marks State Park to E.

Felton (FAIL-ton), village, Holguín prov., E Cuba, on E inlet of Nipe Bay, and 45 mi/72 km E of Holguín; 20°44′N 75°38′W. Refining of chromium and iron mined in the Sierra de Nipe 15 mi/24 km SSW.

Felton 1 village (1990 pop. 683), Kent co., central Del., 10 mi/16 km SSW of Dover; 39°00′N 75°35′W. Shipping point in agr. region; dairying. N.G. Wilder Wildlife Area to NW: Killen's Pond State Park to SE. **2** village (1990 pop. 211), Clay co., W Minn., 20 mi/32 km NE of Fargo N.Dak., in Red R. valley; 47°04′N 96°30′W. Agr. (grain, sunflowers; dairying; poultry, livestock. Mfg. (fertilizers).

Felton (FEL-tuhn), borough (1990 pop. 438), York co., S Pa., 12 mi/19 km SE of York, on North Branch Muddy Creek. Agr. (grain, apples; livestock, poultry, dairying). Mfg. (plastic molding).

Fenelon Falls (FEH-nuh-lahn), village (1991 pop. 1,888), S Ont., Canada, on Fenelon R., bet. Cameron L. (N) and Sturgeon L. (S), 12 mi/19 km N of Lindsay, in Muskoka dist.; 44°32′N 78°45′W. Light mfg.; lumbering; resort.

Fennimore, town (1990 pop. 2,378), Grant co., extreme SW Wis., 26 mi/42 km ESE of Prairie du Chien; 42°58′N 90°39′W. In farm area (livestock, poultry; grain); dairy prods., feed. Mfg. (cheese). Has hq. of a U.S. soil conservation project. Eagle River Nature Preserve to NW. Inc. 1919.

Fennville, village (1990 pop. 1,023), Allegan co., SW Mich., 13 mi/21 km WNW of Allegan; 42°35′N 86°06′W. In fruit-growing and dairying area. Mfg. (food processing, automotive parts).

Fenton 1 town (1990 pop. 346), Kossuth co., N Iowa, 14 mi/23 km NW of Algona; 43°13′N 94°25′W. Animal feed. **2** town (1990 pop. 8,444), Genesee co., SE central Mich., 15 mi/24 km S of Flint, and on Shiawassee R.; 42°47′N 83°42′W. In agr. area (dairy prods.; livestock; apples, grain). Mfg. (plastic and rubber prods., motor vehicle parts, insulated glass). L. Fenton to N. Settled 1834, inc. 1863. **3** town (1990 pop. 3,346), St. Louis co., E Mo., an industrial and commercial suburb 16 mi/26 km on the Meramec R., and SW of downtown St. Louis; 38°32′N 90°27′W. Mfg. (metal prods., telecommunications equip., machinery, transportation equip., baked specialties, food prods., medical supplies, fireproofing materials, consumer goods,). Weiss Airport. Fenton area extends into Jefferson co.

Fenton (FEN-tuhn), village (1990 pop. 265), Jefferson Davis parish, SW La., 20 mi/32 km ENE of Lake Charles city; 30°22′N 92°55′W. In agr. area (rice, sweet potatoes, sorghum, soybeans); logging. Red beans and rice festival.

Fentress (FEN-tris), county (□ 499; 1990 pop. 14,669), N Tenn.; ⊙ Jamestown; 36°23′N 84°56′W. In the Cumberlands; drained by forks of Obey and Cumberland rivers. Includes part of Dale Hollow Reservoir. Lumbering (hardwoods), agr. (corn, tobacco, fruit, vegetables), dairying, livestock raising. Oil and gas; bituminous-coal mines, dimension sandstone. Formed 1823.

Fentress, uninc. village (1990 pop. 85), Caldwell co., S central Texas, 11 mi/18 km SW of Lockhart, and on San Marcos R.

Fenwick, Conn.: see OLD SAYBROOK.

Fenwick Island, resort town (1990 pop. 186), Sussex co., SE Del., on Atlantic Ocean, just N of Md. state line; 38°27′N 75°03′W. Beach resort. Fenwick Isl. State Park to N and S of town.

Fenwood, village (1990 pop. 214), Marathon co., central Wis., 20 mi/32 km WSW of Wausau; 44°52′N 90°00′W. Lumbering, dairying, livestock raising.

Ferdinand, town (1990 pop. 2,318), Dubois co., SW Ind., 11 mi/18 km S of Jasper; 38°14′N 86°52′W. In agr. area; timber; stone quarries. Mfg. (furniture, machinery, paper prods., construction materials). Seat of Convent of Immaculate Conception. Near Ferdinand State Forest. Laid out 1840.

Ferdinand, village (1990 pop. 135), Idaho co., W Idaho, 10 mi/16 km SW of Nezperce; 46°09′N 116°23′W. Livestock; timber. Mfg. (wooden cabinets). In S part of Nez Perce Indian Reservation, near Lawyer's Creek.

Fergus (FUHR-guhs), county (□ 4,350 sq mi/11,267 sq km; 1990 pop. 12,083), central Mont.; ⊙ Lewistown; 47°16′N 109°13′W. Irrigated agr. region, mountainous in S; drained by Judith R., bounded N by Missouri R., including part of Upper Missouri Natl. Wild and Scenic River; Arrow Creek forms W boundary. Agr. (grain, wheat, barley, oats, hay; cattle, sheep, hogs). Part of Charles M. Russell Natl. Wildlife Refuge in NE; sect. of Lewis and Clark Natl. Forest in S. Formed 1886. Present boundaries est. 1925.

Fergus, town (1991 pop. 7,940), S Ont., Canada, on Grand R., and 13 mi/21 km NNW of Guelph; 43°42′N 80°22′W. Mfg. (domestic appliances).

Fergus Falls, city (1990 pop. 12,362), ⊙ Otter Tail co., W central Minn., 105 mi/169 km NW of St. Cloud, on the Otter Tail R.; 46°16′N 96°04′W. Elev. 1,194 ft/364 m. RR junction. Agr. is central to the economy (poultry, livestock; grain, sunflowers, sugar beets); dairying. Mfg. (furniture, food and beverages, printing, consumer goods). Fergus Falls Community Col., a Lutheran seminary, and a state hosp. are in the city. Municipal airport (Elmer Mickelson Field) to W. Inc. 1872.

Ferguson, city (1990 pop. 22,286), St. Louis co., E Mo., a suburb 10 mi/16 km NW of downtown St. Louis; 38°45′N 90°17′W. Primarily residential. Light mfg. Florissant Valley Community Col. Inc. 1894.

Ferguson 1 town (1990 pop. 166), Marshall co., central Iowa, 8 mi/12.9 km SSE of Marshalltown; 41°56′N 92°51′W. In agr. area. **2** town (1990 pop. 934), Pulaski co., S Ky., 2 mi/3.2 km S of Somerset, in Cumberland foothills; 37°04′N 84°35′W. Agr. (tobacco, grain; livestock, poultry; dairying). Mfg. (transportation equip., ceramic bathroom fixtures). Before 1947, called Luretha.

Ferintosh (FEH-rin-tahsh), village (1991 pop. 115), central Alta., Canada, 19 mi/31 km SSW of Camrose; 52°46′N 112°58′W. Wheat, dairying.

Ferland (FUHR-luhnd), village, NW Ont., Canada, near N shore of L. Nipigon, 200 mi/322 km NNE of Thunder Bay; 50°19′N 88°25′W.

Ferme Neuve (ferm NUHV), village (1991 pop. 2,267), SW Que., Canada, in the Laurentians, on Lièvre R., and 11 mi/18 km N of Mont Laurier, at foot of Mt. Sir Wilfrid; 46°42′N 75°27′W. Dairying, lumbering.

Fermi 2, Michigan: see MONROE, county.

Fermin, Point, promontory, Los Angeles co., S Calif., San Pedro sect. of city of Los Angeles. Los Angeles Harbor breakwater extends E from Cabrillo Beach Park, E side of promontory. U.S. Fort MacArthur Military Reservation is here. San Pedro Bay to E.

Fermont, town (1991 pop. 3,735), E central Que., Canada, 20 mi/32 km SW of Labrador City, on Lab. border. Terminus of RR spur from Gagnon. Iron mining center.

Fern Creek, uninc. city (1990 pop. 16,406), Jefferson co., N Ky., residential suburb 10 mi/16 km SE of downtown Louisville, at fringe of urbanized area; 38°09′N 85°35′W. Agr. to S and E (grain, nursery prods.; livestock).

Fern Park, town (□ 2 sq mi/5.2 sq km; 1990 pop. 8,294), Seminole co., central Fla., 10 mi/16 km N of Orlando, and just SE of Altamonte Springs; 28°38′N 81°20′W. Mfg. (printing and publishing).

Fern Ridge Reservoir (□ 15 sq mi/39 sq km), Lane co., W central Oregon, on Long Tom R., 5 mi/8 km W of Eugene; 44°07′N 123°18′W. Max. capacity 121,000 acre-ft. Formed by Fern Ridge Dam, built (1941) by Army

Corps of Engineers for flood control; also used for recreation. Mahlon Sweet Airport just N.

Fernan Lake, village (1990 pop. 170), Kootenai co., N Idaho, residential suburb 4 mi/6.4 km E of Coeur d'Alene L. to S; 47°40′N 116°45′W. Coeur d'Alene Natl. Forest to E.

Fernández, Ciudad, Mexico: see CIUDAD FERNÁNDEZ.

Fernandina Beach (fer-nuhn-DEEN-ah), town (1990 pop. 8,765), ⊙ Nassau co., extreme NE Fla., on Amelia Isl., near mouth of St. Marys R., 25 mi/40 km NE of Jacksonville; 30°39′N 81°27′W. Major resort area; port of entry; fishing (oysters, shrimp, menhaden) and pulp-milling center. Mfg. (fish meal, oil; seafood canning). Exports phosphate, lumber, naval stores, cottonseed. Nearby is Fort Clinch, built 1847–1861, now a state park. Isl. was also site of a Span. fort built in 1680s. N terminus of Fla. Highway A1A, which runs along state's Atlantic shore.

Ferndale 1 city (1990 pop. 1,331), Humboldt co., NW Calif., 16 mi/26 km SSW of Eureka, 3 mi/4.8 km SE of Pacific Ocean, and on delta of Eel R.; 40°35′N 124°16′W. Dairying; cattle, sheep; timber. Humboldt Bay Natl. Wildlife Refuge to N. An April 1992 earthquake (7.0 magnitude), centered near here, destroyed many 19th-cent. Victorian houses. Town again badly damaged, by floods, in 1995, which killed much livestock. **2** city (1990 pop. 25,084), Oakland co., SE Mich., a suburb 9 mi/14.5 km NW of downtown Detroit; borders Detroit city and Wayne co. on S; 42°27′N 83°07′W. Mfg. (automobile parts, machinery, pharmaceuticals). Mich. State Fairgrounds to S. Inc. as a city 1927.

Ferndale 1 uninc. town (1990 est. pop. 1,400), Northumberland co., E central Pa., residential suburb 1 mi/1.6 km W of Shamokin; 40°46′N 76°34′W. **2** town (1990 pop. 5,398), Whatcom co., NW Wash., 9 mi/14.5 km NW of Bellingham, and on Nooksack R. 10 mi/16 km S of Canada (B.C.) border; 48°51′N 122°35′W. Agr. (vegetables, berries, grain; dairying; poultry). Mfg. (apparel, meat packing, aluminum products, kayaks, industrial gases, wood prods.). Petroleum tank farms to W. Lummi Indian Reservation and Lummi Isl. to SSW.

Ferndale 1 resort village (1990 pop. 850), Sullivan co., SE N.Y., 2 mi/3.2 km S of Liberty; 41°46′N 74°44′W. **2** suburban village (1990 pop. 16,355), Anne Arundel co., central Md., 8 mi/12.9 km S of downtown Baltimore; 39°11′N 76°38′W. Washington-Baltimore Internatl. (B.W.I.) Airport nearby.

Ferndale, borough (1990 pop. 2,020), Cambria co., SW central Pa., residential suburb 2 mi/3.2 km SSW of Johnstown, near Stonycreek R; 40°17′N 78°55′W. State rehabilitation center is here. Inc. 1896.

Fernie (FUHR-nee), city (1991 pop. 5,012), SE B.C., Canada, in Rocky Mts., on Elk R., and 120 mi/193 km SSW of Calgary, at foot of Mt. Fernie (7,850 ft/2,393 m); 49°30′N 115°03′W. Elev. 3,313 ft/1,010 m. Coal mining, coke making, logging. Tourist center. Snow Valley Ski Hill.

Fernley (FUHRN-lee), uninc. village (1990 pop. 5,164), Lyon co., W Nev., near Truckee R., 31 mi/50 km E of Reno in irrigated agr. area; 39°34′N 119°12′W. Elev. 4,153 ft/1,266 m. Trading point and feeding base for livestock; mining center; cattle, sheep; hay. Mfg. (construction materials, paper prods., cement, plastics prods., diatomite mining and processing, modified bitumen. Pyramid L. Indian Reservation to NW.

Fernway, uninc. town (1990 pop. 9,072), Butler co., W Pa., suburb 17 mi/27 km NNW of Pittsburgh; 40°41′N 80°07′W. Mfg. (electrical equip., polyurethane processing equip. and materials, machinery, plastic prods., metal fabricating). Agr. (dairying, livestock; grain, apples).

Fernwood 1 village (1990 pop. 315), Benewah co., N Idaho, 14 mi/23 km SSE of St. Maries, on St. Maries R. Garnet sand mining. St. Joe Natl. Forest to SW; Hobo Cedar Grove Botanical Area to SE; North-South Bowl Ski Area to W. **2** village (1990 pop. 600), Pike co., SW Miss., 3 mi/4.8 km S of McComb. Agr. (cotton, corn; cattle; dairying; timber. Mfg. (lumber, wirebound boxes, apparel, portable steel bldgs.). **3** uninc. village, Upper Darby township, Delaware co., SE Pa., 4 mi/-

6.4 km WSW of downtown Philadelphia, on Cobbs Creek; 39°56′N 75°15′W. Mfg. (machinery, diazo-coated paper).

Ferolle Point (FEH-rol), promontory, NW N.F., Canada, at N edge of St. John Bay; 51°01′N 57°06′W.

Ferrelview, village (1990 pop. 338), Platte co., W Mo., suburb 16 mi/26 km NNW of downtown Kansas City; 39°18′N 94°40′W. Surrounded by Kansas City; 1 mi/1.6 km E of Kansas City Internatl. Airport.

Ferriday (FER-e-dai), town (1990 pop. 4,111), Concordia parish, E central La., 10 mi/16 km NW of Natchez (Miss.), near Mississippi R.; 31°38′N 91°34′W. In agr. area (cotton, pecans, corn; dairy prods.; cattle, horses). RR shops. Mfg. (apparel, culverts, lumber, publishing and printing). Oil and gas fields nearby. L. Concordia, oxbow lake, to NE. Bayou Cocodrie Natl. Wildlife Refuge to SW. Location selected by the RR. Founded 1903; inc. as village in 1905, as town in 1927.

Ferrier (fe-ree-AI), town (1982 pop. 2,586), Nord dept., NE Haiti, 5 mi/8 km SE of Fort Liberté, near Dominican Republic border; 19°37′N 71°47′W. Oranges, limes, tobacco; timber.

Ferris, town (1990 pop. 2,212), Ellis co., N Texas, suburb 18 mi/29 km SSE of downtown Dallas, on S fringe of Dallas–Fort Worth metropolitan area; 32°32′N 96°39′W. In rich blackland agr. area (cattle; dairying; cotton, grain, honey). Mfg. (transportation equip., consumer goods). Settled 1870, inc. 1874.

Ferris, village (1990 pop. 177), Hancock co., W Ill., 4 mi/6.4 km NNW of Carthage; 40°28′N 91°10′W. In agr. area.

Ferrisburg, town (1990 pop. 2,317), Addison co., W Vt., 15 mi/24 km N of Middlebury, and on L. Champlain, at mouth of Otter Creek; 44°12′N 73°16′W. Lumber. Includes Basin Harbor (resort). Granted 1762, settled 1785.

Ferron, town (1990 pop. 1,606), Emery co., central Utah, 11 mi/18 km SW of Castle Dale, on Ferron Creek; 39°05′N 111°07′W. Elev. 5,996 ft/1,828 m. Alfalfa, peaches; cattle. Millsite Reservoir and State Park to W. Manti–La Sal Natl. Forest to W. Settled 1877.

Ferrum, uninc. town, Franklin co., S Va., 9 mi/14.5 km SW of Rocky Mount; 36°55′N 80°01′W. Mfg. (apparel, furniture, lumber, components). Agr. (tobacco, grain, apples, peaches; cattle); timber. Ferrum Col., Blue Ridge Inst. Philpott Reservoir, Fairy Stone State Park to S. Blue Ridge Parkway passes to W.

Ferry, county (☐ 2,257 sq mi/5,846 sq km; 1990 pop. 6,295), NE Wash., on Canada (B.C.) border; ⊙ Republic; 48°28′N 118°31′W. Forested mt. area watered by Sanpoil and Kettle rivers. Bounded on S and E by Columbia R. (Franklin D. Roosevelt L. reservoir); Kettle R. forms part of E boundary, in N. Coulee Dam Natl. Recreation Area surrounds reservoir. Timber; gold, silver. Agr. (hay, alfalfa, barley, oats; dairying; cattle). Part of large Colville Indian Reservation covers S ½ of co., and parts of Colville Natl. Forest throughout N ½ of co. Curlew L. reservoir and State Park, in NW center. Formed 1899.

Ferry, village, Ferry co., NE Wash., port of entry on Canada (B.C.) border, 25 mi/40 km N of Republic, 2 mi/3.2 km SE of Midway, B.C., on Kettle R. Alfalfa, barley; timber. Parts of Colville Natl. Forest to W, S, and E.

Ferry Pass, city (☐ 14 sq mi/36 sq km; 1990 pop. 26,301), Escambia co., NW Fla., 8 mi/13 km N of Pensacola; 30°31′N 87°12′W.

Ferryland, village (1991 pop. 717), SE N.F., Canada, on SE coast of Avalon Peninsula, 40 mi/64 km SSW of St. John's; fishing port; 47°01′N 52°55′W. Lord Baltimore est. settlement here 1624. In 1638 Sir David Kirke, count palatine of isl., est. his capital here. Settlement was raided 1673 by the Dutch.

Ferrysburg, town (1990 pop. 2,919), Ottawa co., SW Mich., suburb 1 mi/1.6 km N of Grand Haven, also 11 mi/18 km S of downtown Muskegon, opposite Grand Haven on Spring L., near its outlet to L. Michigan (across bridge from Grand Haven); 43°05′N 86°13′W. Mfg. (boilers).

Ferryville, village (1990 pop. 154), Crawford co., SW Wis., on the Mississippi R., and 32 mi/51 km S of La

Crosse; 43°20′N 91°04′W. In livestock and dairy area; cheese. Near Rush Creek Natural Area and bridge to Lansing, Iowa, 6 mi/9.7 km NW.

Fertile 1 town (1990 pop. 382), Worth co., N Iowa, on Lime Creek, and 15 mi/24 km SW of Northwood; 43°15′N 93°25′W. In onion-growing region. **2** town (1990 pop. 853), Polk co., NW Minn., 22 mi/35 km SE of Crookston, on Sand Hill R.; 47°31′N 96°17′W. RR terminus. Diversified farming area (grain, sunflowers, potatoes; dairying; poultry, livestock). Small lakes to NE.

Fessenden, village (1990 pop. 655), ⊙ Wells co., central N.Dak., 28 mi/45 km NW of Carrington, near James R; 47°38′N 99°37′W. Wheat, barley, rye; dairying. Seat of annual agr. exposition. Plotted 1893.

Festina, village, Winneshiek co., NE Iowa, 14 mi/23 km SSW of Decorah. Animal feed.

Festus (FES-tuhs), city (1990 pop. 8,105), Jefferson co., E Mo., on Mississippi R., and 30 mi/48 km S of St. Louis; 38°13′N 90°24′W. Satellite city of St. Louis. Part of Festus/Crystal City twin cities; urban growth area. Mfg. (electronic equip., cement). Agr. (vegetable farming). Part of commercial area suffered flood damage 1993 along Joachim Creek. Plotted 1878.

Fever River, Wis. and Ill.: see GALENA RIVER.

Fidalgo Island (fi-DAHL-go), Skagit co., NW Wash., irregular isl., separated from mainland by Swinomish Channel; c.8 mi/12.9 km long. City of Anacortes on N end of isl. Deception Pass connects S shore with Whidbey Isl. Two highway bridges. Ferry terminal for San Juan Isls., Wash., and Vancouver Isl., B.C., at NW tip. Bounded S by Skagit Bay (arm of Puget Sound) and Deception Pass, W by Rosario Strait, N by Padilla Bay and Guemes Channel. Swinomish Indian Reservation in SE.

Fidalgo, Port (fee-DAL-go), S Alaska, bay on E shore of Prince William Sound, 30 mi/48 km NW of Cordova; 25 mi/40 km long, 2 mi/3.2 km wide; 60°47′N 146°30′W.

Fidelity 1 village (1990 pop. 66), Jersey co., W Ill., 18 mi/29 km N of Alton; 39°08′N 90°09′W. Apples. **2** village (1990 pop. 235), Jasper co., SW Mo., 10 mi/16 km E of Joplin; 37°04′N 94°18′W. Wheat, hay; cattle.

Field, village, SE B.C., Canada, near Alta. border, in Rocky Mts., in Yoho Natl. Park, on Kicking Horse R. and 40 mi/64 km WNW of Banff; 51°24′N 116°29′W. Elev. 4,075 ft/1,242 m. Resort. Bet. this point and Hector the Can. Pacific RR passes through the Spiral Tunnels.

Fieldale (FEEL-dail), uninc. town (1990 pop. 1,018), Henry co., S Va., 3 mi/4.8 km W of Martinsville, in foothills of the Blue Ridge, on Smith R.; 36°42′N 79°56′W. Mfg. (polyester films, textiles); agr. (tobacco; poultry, cattle).

Fielden Peninsula, NE Ellesmere Isl., NE Franklin dist., N.W.T., Canada, extends 10 mi/16 km NE into Lincoln Sea of the Arctic Ocean; 3 mi/5 km–6 mi/10 km wide; 82°50′N 64°00′W. At NE extremity is Cape Joseph Henry.

Fielding, village (1990 pop. 422), Box Elder co., N Utah, 22 mi/35 km NNW of Brigham City, near Bear R., at mouth of Malad R.; 41°48′N 112°07′W. Elev. 4,367 ft/1,331 m. Sugar beets; dairying; cattle, sheep.

Fieldon, village (1990 pop. 277), Jersey co., W Ill., 9 mi/14.5 km W of Jerseyville; 39°06′N 90°30′W. In apple-growing area.

Fields Landing, uninc. village, Humboldt co., NW Calif., on Humboldt Bay, suburb 4 mi/6.4 km S of Eureka. Humboldt Bay Natl. Wildlife Refuge is to W.

Fieldsboro, borough (1990 pop. 579), Burlington co., W N.J., on Delaware R., and 6 mi/9.7 km S of Trenton; 40°08′N 74°43′W. Light mfg. Mainly residential.

Fierro (fee-ER-o), village, Grant co., SW N.Mex., in Pinos Altos Mts., 16 mi/26 km ENE of Silver City. Elev. 6,658 ft/2,029 m. Iron-ore deposits nearby. Terminus of mining RR spur from Hurley. Gila Natl. Forest to W, N, and E. Black Peak, or Continental Divide, to NW.

Fife, town (1990 pop. 3,864), Pierce co., W Wash., suburb 5 mi/8 km E of downtown Tacoma, near Puyallup R.;

47°14′N 122°22′W. Dairying; poultry; berries. Mfg. (vehicles, cranes).

Fife Lake, village (1990 pop. 394), Grand Traverse co., NW Mich., on small Fife L., and 18 mi/29 km SE of Traverse City; 44°34′N 85°20′W. Resort; mfg.

Fifield (FEI-feeld), village, Price co., N Wis., 4 mi/6.4 km SSE of Park Falls, near Chequamegon Natl. Forest. Ships Christmas trees. Unit of Chequamegon Natl. Forest to E; Flambeau R. State Forest to W and N.

Fifteen Mile Falls Reservoir, reservoir, NW N.H. and NE Vt., on Connecticut R., 7 mi/11.3 km S of St. Johnsbury, Vt.; 8 mi/12.9 km long; 44°19′N 72°00′W. Max. capacity 223,582 acre-ft. Moore Dam at E end. Formed by Comerford (KUH-muhr-fuhrd) Dam (169 ft/52 m high), built (1957) by the New England Power Company for power generation.

Fifth Avenue, famous N-S street of thc borough of Manhattan, N.Y. city, SE N.Y. It begins at Washington Sq. and ends at the Harlem R. The sect. bet. 34th St. and 59th St. is lined with fashionable dept. stores and specialty shops. Fronting the avenue are the Empire State Bldg., the N.Y. Public Lib., Rockefeller Center, St. Patrick's Cathedral, and the Guggenheim Mus. From 59th to 110th streets Fifth Ave. borders Central Park; on its E side are tall apartment houses (interspersed with formerly private homes), built on the site of elegant 1940s-era mansions. On the W side of the avenue bet. 80th and 84th streets is the Metropolitan Mus. of Art. The strip of avenue N of the park runs through Marcus Garvey Park and Harlem.

Fifty Lakes, village (1990 pop. 299), Crow Wing co., central Minn., 26 mi/42 km NNE of Brainerd; 46°45′N 94°05′W. Resort area; dairying; cattle, poultry; alfalfa. Whitefish L. to SW; Crow Wing State Forest to S; numerous small lakes.

Fig Garden, suburban section of Fresno, Fresno co., central Calif., residential suburb 6 mi/9.7 km NNW of downtown Fresno, on Kings R. Residential area.

Fighting Island, islet, S Ont., Canada, in Detroit R., 7 mi/11 km SW of Windsor.

Figuery (fi-guh-REE), village, W Que., Canada, near Okikeska L., 7 mi/11 km SSE of Amos; 48°28′N 78°04′W. Gold mining.

Filbert, uninc. village, Redstone township, Fayette co., SW Pa., 7 mi/11.3 km NW of Uniontown, on Dunlap Creek; 39°56′N 79°51′W. Dairying.

Filbert, locality, McDowell co., S W.Va., 8 mi/12.9 km S of Welch; part of Gary, W.Va. Coal area.

Filer, town (1990 pop. 1,511), Twin Falls co., S Idaho, 9 mi/14.5 km W of Twin Falls; 42°34′N 114°37′W. In irrigated agr. area noted for Idaho white beans; tree fruit (apples, cherries, peaches); wheat, barley, corn; potatoes; sheep, cattle; dairying; mfg. (fabricated metal prods., animal feeds); seed plants. Commercial fish hatcheries. Inc. 1909.

Filer City, village, Manistee co., NW Mich., 3 mi/4.8 km SE of Manistee, and on Little Manistee R.; 44°12′N 86°17′W. Mfg. (paper prods., chemicals). Manistee Natl. Forest to E.

Filley (FIL-ee), village (1990 pop. 157), Gage co., SE Nebr., 10 mi/16 km E of Beatrice; 40°17′N 96°31′W.

Fillmore 1 county (□ 862 sq mi/2,233 sq km; 1990 pop. 20,777), SE Minn.; ⊙ Preston; 43°40′N 92°05′W. Watered by Root R. and by its South, Middle, and North branches; bounded on S by Iowa. Agr. area (poultry, cattle, sheep, hogs; corn, soybeans, oats, alfalfa, hay; dairying; limestone. Parts of Richard J. Dorer Memorial Hardwood State Forest in N, center, and E. Formed 1853. **2** county (□ 576 sq mi/1,492 sq km; 1990 pop. 7,103), SE Nebr.; ⊙ Geneva; 40°31′N 97°35′W. Part of Loess Plain, marked by several poorly drained depressions in major Rainwater Basin, some wet areas preserved as wildlife refuges. Agr. region drained by branches of Big Blue R. Corn, soybeans, sorghum; cattle, hogs; dairy and poultry prods. Formed 1871.

Fillmore, city (1990 pop. 11,992), Ventura co., S Calif., 45 mi/72 km NW of Los Angeles and 21 mi/34 km NE of Oxnard, on Santa Clara R.; 34°24′N 118°55′W. Citrus, avocados; flowers, nursery prods., apiary prods.; mfg. (ornamental metal work, concrete, pencils); oil fields

nearby. Santa Susana Mts. to S; Los Padres Natl. Forest to N, including Condor Refuge. Inc. 1914.

Fillmore 1 town (1990 pop. 497), Putnam co., W central Ind., 5 mi/8 km ENE of Greencastle, near source of Deer Creek; 39°40′N 86°45′W. Hogs, cattle. Mfg. Laid out 1837. **2** town (1990 pop. 256), Andrew co., NW Mo., near Nodaway R., 6 mi/9.7 km NW of Savannah; 40°01′N 94°58′W. **3** town (1990 pop. 1,956), ⊙ Millard co., W central Utah, 60 mi/97 km SSW of Nephi; 38°58′N 112°20′W. Elev. 5,135 ft/1,565 m. Alfalfa, barley, wheat, potatoes; cattle, poultry. Capital of Utah Territory 1851–1856. Pavant Mts. just E, in Fishlake Natl. Forest; Clear L. Waterfowl Management Area to NW; Black Rock Desert to W; Kanosh Indian Reservation to S. Territorial Statehouse State Historical Park located here. Settled 1851.

Fillmore, village (1991 pop. 328), SE Sask., Canada, 24 mi/39 km NE of Weyburn; 49°53′N 103°26′W. Mixed farming, dairying.

Fillmore 1 village (1990 pop. 326), Montgomery co., S central Ill., 12 mi/19 km ESE of Hillsboro; 39°07′N 89°16′W. In agr. and bituminous-coal area. **2** village (1990 pop. 455), Allegany co., W N.Y., on Genesee R., 20 mi/32 km S of Warsaw; 42°28′N 78°06′W. In agr. and timber area; fish traps and netting.

Fillmore Glen State Park (c.850 acres/344 ha), Cayuga co., W central N.Y., in glen along small Fillmore Creek, near S end of Owasco L., c.18 mi/29 km N of Ithaca; 42°42′N 76°25′W. Waterfalls here. Camping, hiking, swimming, picnicking facilities. President Millard Fillmore b. in Locke, just S of here.

Filomeno Mata (fee-lo-ME-no MAH-tah), town (1990 pop. 7,274), Veracruz, E Mexico, in Sierra Madre Oriental, on Puebla border, 30 mi/48 km SW of Papantla de Olarte. Cereals, sugarcane, coffee, tobacco, fruit. Poor road access. In Totonac Indian area. Formerly Santo Domingo.

Fincastle 1 (FIN-kas-uhl), town (1990 pop. 838), Jefferson co., N Ky., residential suburb 12 mi/19 km ENE of downtown Louisville; 38°18′N 85°32′W. E.P. Tom Sawyer State Park to SW. **2** town (1990 pop. 236), ⊙ Botetourt co., W central Va., 15 mi/24 km N of Roanoke; 37°30′N 79°52′W. Mfg. (plastic prods., printing and publishing); agr. area (fruit; dairying); timber.

Fincastle, village, Putnam co., W central Ind., 12 mi/19 km N of Greencastle, on Ramp Creek. Agr. area.

Finch, village (1991 pop. 456), SE Ont., Canada, 20 mi/32 km NW of Cornwall; 45°08′N 75°05′W. Dairying, mixed farming.

Findlay (FIN-lee, FIND-lee), city (1990 pop. 35,703), ⊙ Hancock co., NW Ohio, on the Blanchard R.; 41°02′N 83°38′W. Petroleum prods., tires, washing machines, heavy machinery, and plastic goods are among its many manufactures; appliance mfg. and tire mfg. are major employers. Gas and oil discovered in the 1880s, but by 1900 the supply had greatly diminished. The city is the home of Findlay Col. Inc. 1887.

Findlay (FIN-lee), village (1990 pop. 787), Shelby co., central Ill., near Kaskaskia R. and L. Shelbyville, 8 mi/12.9 km SW of Sullivan; 39°31′N 88°45′W. In agr. area; ships grain.

Findlay Islands, group of 4 isls., NW Franklin dist. N.W.T., Canada, in the Arctic Ocean, N of Bathurst Isl.; largest is Lougheed Island.

Findlay, Mount (FIN-lee) (10,780 ft/3,286 m), SE B.C., Canada, in Selkirk Mts., 55 mi/89 km NE of Nelson; 50°04′N 116°28′W.

Findley Lake, resort village (1990 pop. 800), Chautauqua co., extreme W N.Y., on small Findley L., 26 mi/42 km W of Jamestown; 42°06′N 79°44′W. In dairying area.

Fingal (FING-uhl), village (1990 pop. 138), Barnes co., SE N.Dak., 15 mi/24 km SE of Valley City; 46°45′N 97°47′W. RR junction to SE at Lucca.

Finger Lake, Patricia dist., NW Ont., Canada; 20 mi/32 km long, 7 mi/11 km wide; 53°09′N 93°30′W. Drained by Severn R.

Finger Lakes, group of 11 long, narrow, glacial lakes in N-S valleys, W central N.Y. They range from Conesus L. in the W to Otisco, 72 mi/116 km to the E. Cayuga and Seneca, both more than 35 mi/56 km long, are the

largest and deepest lakes. Keuka L. is the center of the N.Y. state wine industry. Fertile soil, sunny hillside locations, broad interlake upland, and the moderating effect of the lakes themselves make the Finger Lakes an important viticulture and vegetable-farming region. Skaneateles and Hemlock lakes are the source of water for Syracuse and Rochester, respectively. The Finger Lakes region is a major recreational area with many historical attractions, summer residences, and state parks.

Fingerville, uninc. village, Spartanburg co., NW S.C., near N.C. state line, 13 mi/21 km N of Spartanburg.

Finland, village, Bamberg co., S central S.C., 4 mi/6.4 km NE of Denmark. Named by RR company. Agr. includes cotton and soybeans.

Finlay Mountains, Hudspeth co., extreme W Texas, NW-SE range c.25 mi/40 km long, generally parallel to the Rio Grande (c.15 mi/24 km away), and c.40 mi/64 km SE of El Paso; rises to c.5,700 ft/1,737 m. Partly bounds Diablo Bolson (E).

Finlay River (FIN-lee), 210 mi/338 km long, N B.C., Canada, chief tributary of Peace R.; rises in Stikine Mts. at about 57°30′N 126°30′W, flows SE to Finlay Forks (56°00N 123°45′W), where it joins Parsnip R. to form Peace R.

Finlayson (FIN-luh-suhn), village (1990 pop. 242), Pine co., E Minn., 26 mi/42 km N of Pine City; 46°12′N 92°55′W. Cattle, sheep, poultry; oats, alfalfa; dairying; mfg. (plastic prods.). Banning State Park to E; several small lakes to SW.

Finley, village (1990 pop. 543), ⊙ Steele co., E N.Dak., 48 mi/77 km SW of Grand Forks; 47°30′N 97°50′W. Grain; livestock; dairy prods.; mfg. (baking prods.). Willow L. to N.

Finleyson, town (1990 pop. 1,126), Pulaski co., S central Ga., 11 mi/18 km S of Hawkinsville; 32°07′N 83°30′W.

Finleyville (FIN-lee-vil), borough (1990 pop. 446), Wash. co., SW Pa., 13 mi/21 km S of Pittsburgh, on Peters Creek; 40°15′N 80°00′W. Agr. (grain; livestock; dairying); timber; mfg. (steel storage tanks, wood prods.); bituminous coal. Finleyville Airport to SW.

Finney, county (□ 1,302 sq mi/3,372 sq km; 1990 pop. 33,070), SW Kansas; ⊙ Garden City; 38°02′N 100°45′W. Rolling prairie region. Second largest co. in land area in Kansas; drained by Arkansas and Pawnee rivers. Wheat, sorghum, soybeans, alfalfa; sugar beets in irrigated area (S) along Arkansas R; cattle. State Buffalo Game Preserve in W center. Formed 1884.

Fircrest, town (1990 pop. 5,258), Pierce co., W central Wash., residential suburb 4 mi/6.4 km W of downtown Tacoma, near the Narrows, Puget Sound; 47°14′N 122°31′W.

Fire Island, narrow barrier island, 32 mi/51 km long, off S shore of L.I., SE N.Y., separating Great South Bay from the Atlantic Ocean; 40°45′N 72°50′W. Robert Moses State Park and several resort communities sit astride the barrier isl., ranging from Saltaire in the NE (34 mi/55 km SW of Riverhead) through Ocean Beach, Point of Woods, Cherry Grove, and Fair Harbor. Once accessible only by boat or ferry, Fire Isl. enjoyed a rare privacy until the construction of a bridge in 1959 linked the E end of the isl. with L.I. Another bridge was later built. Motor vehicles are banned from much of the isl. Fire Isl. is known for the large numbers of artists and gays and lesbians among its summer residents. Fire Isl. Natl. Seashore (est. 1964) covers 30 sq mi/78 sq km of the isl. and includes wooded areas, marshes, and Sunken Forest, an area of unusual plant and animal life.

Firebaugh, city (1990 pop. 4,429), Fresno co., central Calif., 38 mi/61 km WNW of Fresno, and on San Joaquin R.; 36°51′N 120°27′W. Melons, vegetables, sugar beets, figs, nectarines, beans, grain; cotton; cattle; dairying. Delta Mendota Canal passes to SW.

Fireco (FEIR-ko), uninc. village (1990 pop. 180), Raleigh co., S W.Va., 9 mi/14.5 km S of Beckley. Coal-mining region.

Firehole River, 28 mi/45 km long, NW Wyo.; rises in SW part of Yellowstone Natl. Park at Continental Divide, flows N, through geyser area, joining Gibbon R.

to form Madison R., at Madison Junction (to W of Old Faithful Geyser).

Firestone, town (1990 pop. 1,358), Weld co., N Colo., 27 mi/43 km N of Denver; 40°07'N 104°55'W. Elev. c.4,970 ft/1,515 m. In the Spindle Oil Field. Barbour Ponds State Park to NW.

First Connecticut Lake, reservoir (□ 4 sq mi/ 10.4 sq km), Coos co., extreme N N.H., on upper course of Connecticut R., 42 mi/68 km N of Berlin, near Can. (Que.) border; 4 mi/6.4 km long; 45°09'N 71°29'W. Max. capacity 114,000 acre-ft. Formed by First Connecticut L. Dam (46 ft/14 m high), built (1930) for water supply and recreation; owned by New England Power Company.

First Eel Lake (□ 3 sq mi/8 sq km), SW N.B., Canada, near Maine border, 20 mi/32 km SSW of Woodstock; 3 mi/5 km long, 2 mi/3 km wide. Just S is Second Eel L. (3 mi/5 km long). Both drain into St. John R. by the short Eel R.

First Roach Pond, Piscataquis co., central Maine, 18 mi/ 29 km NE of Greenville; 6 mi/9.7 km long, 1.5 mi/ 2.4 km wide. In hunting, fishing area. Formerly called Kokadjo L.

Firth 1 village (1990 pop. 429), Bingham co., SE Idaho, 10 mi/16 km NE of Blackfoot, and on Snake R.; 43°19'N 112°11'W. Elev. 4,566 ft/1,392 m. Sugar beets, grain, potatoes; cattle, sheep; dairying; mfg. (prepared foods). Fort Hall Indian Reservation to S. **2** village (1990 pop. 471), Lancaster co., SE Nebr., 20 mi/32 km SSE of Lincoln, and on North Fork of Big Nemaha R; 40°31'N 96°35'W.

Firthcliffe, industrial village (□ 3 sq mi/7.8 sq km; 1990 pop. 4,127), Orange co., SE N.Y., 5 mi/8 km SW of Newburgh; 41°26'N 74°01'W. Carpet mfg.

Fish Creek, village, Door co., NE Wis., on inlet of Green Bay, on Door Peninsula, 21 mi/34 km NNE of Sturgeon Bay city. Fishing and agr.; mfg. (moccasins). Peninsula State Park to NE.

Fish Creek, c.30 mi/48 km long, central Mich.; rises near Sheridan in Montcalm co.; flows E and S, past Carson City, to Maple R. just S of Hubbardston; 43°21'N 84°55'W.

Fish Hook River, W Minn., rises in series of small creeks, out of NE Becker co.; flows as Hay Creek from Two Inlets L., SE through Island, Eagle, and Potato lakes to Fish Hook L., continues S as Fish Hook R., through town of Park Rapids, receives Straight R. from W; joins Shell R., SW of Long L. Small dam at Park Rapids.

Fish Lake, reservoir, Sevier co., S central Utah, on Fremont R., in Fishlake Natl. Forest, 11 mi/18 km NE of Koosharem; 6 mi/9.7 km long, 1 mi/1.6 km wide; 38°35'N 111°40'W. Elev. c.8,845 ft/2,696 m. Fish Lake Hightop Plateau to NW. Fishing resorts.

Fish Lake Plateau, S central Utah, high tableland in Fishlake Natl. Forest, Sevier and Wayne cos. Watered by Fish L. and Fremont R. Reaches max. elev. in Mt. Marvine (11,610 ft/3,539 m). Other peaks are Mt. Hilgard (11,533 ft/3,515 m) and Mt. Terrill (11,547 ft/ 3,520 m). Also known as Fish L. Mts. Thousand L. Mt. (11,306 ft/3,446 m) is in S outlier. N part of Capitol Reef Natl. Park in SE margin of plateau.

Fish River, c.50 mi/80 km long, Aroostook co., N Maine; rises 35 mi/56 km NW of Presque Isle; flows SE, then N, connecting Fish R. Lakes to Saint John R. near Fort Kent.

Fish River Lakes, NE Maine, chain in NE Aroostook co., linked by Fish R.; includes Fish River L. (4 mi/ 6.4 km long), Portage L. (4.5 mi/7.2 km long), St. Froid L. (7 mi/11.3 km long), Eagle L. (14 mi/23 km long), Square L. (7 mi/11.3 km long), Cross L. (5.5 mi/8.9 km long), Long L. (11 mi/18 km long). Noted for excellent fishing, canoeing.

Fish Village, W Alaska, on Yukon R., near its mouth on Bering Sea, 23 mi/37 km SE of Kwiguk. Salmon fishing.

Fisher, county (□ 901 sq mi/2,334 sq km; 1990 pop. 4,842), NW central Texas; ⊙ Roby; 32°44'N 100°24'W. Rolling plains drained by Double Mt. and Clear forks of Brazos R. Agr. and livestock region, producing some oil and natural gas; cotton, wheat, hay, alfalfa; beef cattle, hogs, Angora goats. Gypsum quarried. Formed 1876.

Fisher, town (1990 pop. 277), Sabine parish, La., 6 mi/ 9.7 km S of Many; 31°27'N 93°27'W. In agr. (cattle) and oil and gas area. Originally owned by La. Long Leaf Lumber Company and named after its president O.W. Fisher.

Fisher 1 village (1990 pop. 245), Poinsett co., NE Ark., 29 mi/47 km SSW of Jonesboro, near Bayou DeView; 35°29'N 90°58'W. **2** village (1990 pop. 1,526), Champaign co., E Ill., near the Sangamon (bridged here) and 14 mi/23 km NNW of Champaign; 40°19'N 88°20'W. In agr. area. **3** village (1990 pop. 413), Polk co., NW Minn., 9 mi/14.5 km W of Crookston, on Red Lake R. at head of Grand Marais R. (side channel of Red Lake R.); 47°47'N 96°47'W. Grain, potatoes, sunflowers; livestock; dairying.

Fisher, Mount (9,245 ft/2,818 m), SE B.C., Canada, in Rocky Mts., 17 mi/27 km ENE of Cranbrook, overlooking the Kootenay valley; 49°36'N 115°56'W.

Fisher Peak (10,015 ft/3,053 m), SW Alta., Canada, in Rocky Mts., 35 mi/56 km SE of Banff; 50°50'N 115°02'W.

Fisherman Island, in Lincoln co., S Maine, narrow island 4 mi/6.4 km SE of Boothbay Harbor; 1 mi/1.6 km long.

Fishermans Island, Northampton co., E Va., low island just off S tip of Cape Charles, at entrance to Chesapeake Bay, separated from Cape Charles (mainland) by Fishermans Inlet; c.1.5 mi/2.4 km long. Site of Fishermans Isl. Natl. Wildlife Refuge. Chesapeake Bay Bridge-Tunnel crosses isl.

Fishers or Fishers Station, town (1990 pop. 7,508), Hamilton co., central Ind., 6 mi/9.7 km S of Noblesville; 39°57'N 86°01'W. Mfg. (concrete, machinery, prepared foods, wood prods.). Suburb of Indianapolis.

Fishers Island, Suffolk co., SE N.Y., in E L.I. Sound, 11 mi/18 km off NE tip of L.I., and 7 mi/11.3 km SE of New London, Conn.; c.8 mi/12.9 km long, average width c.1 mi/1.6 km; 41°15'N 71°58'W. Ferry connections. Separated from SE Conn. by Fishers Isl. Sound (2 mi/3.2 km–3 mi/4.8 km wide). Summer resort and residential area. Fishers Isl. village.

Fishers Lake, W N.S., Canada, 18 mi/29 km ESE of Digby; 8 mi/13 km long, 1 mi/2 km wide. Outlet: Mersey R.

Fishers Peak, Colo.: see RATON MOUNTAINS.

Fishers Station, Ind.: see FISHERS.

Fishersville, uninc. town, Augusta co., NW Va., 5 mi/ 8 km WNW of Waynesboro, 6 mi/9.7 km ESE of Staunton; 38°06'N 78°58'W. Mfg. (lumber, wood prods., machinery, fabricated metal prods., resin figurines); agr. area (grain, soybeans, apples; livestock, poultry; dairying); timber. De Jarnette Center for Human Development.

Fisherville, Mass.: see GRAFTON.

Fishhook Lake, Hubbard co., W Minn., 2 mi/3.2 km N of Park Rapids; 3 mi/4.8 km long, 1 mi/1.6 km wide; 46°57'N 95°03'W. Drains S through Fish Hook R. to Shell R. Fed from N by short stream from Potato L. Fishing resorts.

Fishing Bay, E Md., inlet of Tangier Sound, indenting the Eastern Shore in S Dorchester co.; c.14 mi/23 km long, 2 mi/3.2 km–4 mi/6.4 km wide. Receives Blackwater and Transquaking rivers.

Fishing Creek, c.75 mi/121 km long, N N.C., rises 4 mi/ 6.4 km NE of Henderson, in E Vance co., flows generally ESE past Warrenton to Tar R., 3 mi/4.8 km N of Tarboro.

Fishing Creek, Md.: see HOOPER ISLANDS.

Fishing Islands, group of c.20 islets, S Ont., Canada, in L. Huron, just off foot of Saugeen Peninsula, 8 mi/ 13 km W of Wiarton.

Fishing Lakes, group of 4 contiguous lakes in SE Sask., Canada, on Qu'Appelle R., 35 mi/56 km NE of Regina; total length 28 mi/45 km, average width 1 mi/ 2 km. Bet. the central lakes is Fort Qu'Appelle. Lakes are noted for whitefish.

Fishing River, c.40 mi/64 km long, W Mo., rises in Clay co., flows NE and SE to the Missouri R., 25 mi/40 km E of Kansas City, in Ray co.

Fishkill, village (1990 pop. 1,957), Dutchess co., SE N.Y.,

on Fishkill Creek, 5 mi/8 km ENE of Beacon; 41°31'N 73°53'W. Mfg. of concrete bldg. material, computer equip. Fishkill Correctional Facility. Nearby village of Fishkill Landing joined Matteawan (1913) to form Beacon city.

Fishkill Creek, c.35 mi/56 km long, SE N.Y., rises in Dutchess co. E of Poughkeepsie, flows SW to the Hudson R. just S of Beacon.

Fishkill Landing, N.Y.: see BEACON.

Fishtrap Lake, reservoir, Pike co., extreme E Ky., on Levisa Fork river, 7 mi/11.3 km SE of Pikeville; c.10 mi/ 16 km long; 37°24'N 82°24'W. Max. capacity 164,360 acre-ft. Formed by Fishtrap Dam (125 ft/38 m high), built (1972) by the Army Corps of Engineers for flood control.

Fisk, town (1990 pop. 422), Butler co., SE Mo., on St. Francis R., and 11 mi/18 km E of Poplar Bluff; 36°46'N 90°12'W. Cotton, rice, soybeans; mfg. (consumer goods).

Fiskdale, Mass.: see STURBRIDGE.

Fiskeville, village, Scituate town and Cranston city, R.I., on North Branch of Pawtuxet R.; 41°44'N 71°33'W.

Fitch Bay, village, S Que., Canada, on arm of L. Memphremagog, 10 mi/16 km SSW of Magog. Resort; dairying.

Fitchburg 1 industrial city (1990 pop. 41,194), ⊙ Worcester co., N Mass., on North Branch of Nashua R.; 42°35'N 71°49'W. Its important paper industry dates from approximately 1805. Other prods. include fabricated steel, machinery, textiles, clothing, shoes, and plastics. Fitchburg State Col. is here. Settled c.1730, inc. as a city 1872. **2** city (1990 pop. 15,648), Dane Co., S central Wis., suburb 5 mi/8 km S of Madison; 42°59'N 89°25'W. Mixture of residential and agr. (dairying; grain, vegetables). Nevin State Fish Hatchery in N part. Mfg. (tube and wire fabrication).

Fitchville, Conn.: see BOZRAH.

Fithian (FITH-ih-an), village (1990 pop. 512), Vermilion co., E Ill., 12 mi/19 km W of Danville; 40°06'N 87°52'W. In agr. and bituminous-coal area.

Fitzgerald, city (1990 pop. 8,912), ⊙ Ben Hill co., S central Ga., c.50 mi/80 km NE of Moultrie; 31°43'N 83°15'W. Tobacco market and processing center for diversified farm area. Mfg. of plastics, clothing, foods and beverages, printing and publishing, machinery. Nearby is Jefferson Davis State Park , where Davis was taken prisoner by Federal troops. Settled 1895 by Union veterans. Inc. 1896.

Fitzgerald, Canada: see FORT FITZGERALD.

Fitzwilliam (fits-WIL-yuhm), town (1990 pop. 2,011), Cheshire co., S N.H., 13 mi/21 km SE of Keene; 42°45'N 72°09'W. Bounded S by Mass. state line. Diversified mfg.; granite quarries; agr. (nursery crops, vegetables; cattle, poultry; dairying; timber). Little Monadnock Mt. (1,883 ft/574 m) and Rhododendron State Park in W. Bowkep Pond source of South Branch of Ashuelot R.

Fitzwilliam Island, S central Ont., Canada, one of the Manitoulin Isls., in L. Huron, just SE of Manitoulin Isl., separated from Saugeen Peninsula by 15 mi/24 km-wide channel; 8 mi/13 km long, 4 mi/6 km wide.

Fitzwilliam Strait, W Franklin Dist., N.W.T., Canada, arm of the Arctic Ocean, bet. Melville Isl. and Prince Patrick Isl.; 60 mi/97 km long, 15 mi/24 km–40 mi/ 64 km wide; 76°10'–76°40'N 114°30'–117°30'W. At NE end is Emerald Isl. At SW end of Fitzwilliam Strait is Eglinton Isl., where strait divides into Crozier Channel (65 mi/105 km long) and Kellett Strait (60 mi long).

Five Forks, uninc. village, Dinwiddie co., SE central Va., 12 mi/19 km SW of Petersburg. Site of last important Civil War battle (April 1, 1865), where the Union victory led to the fall of Petersburg, the capture of Richmond, and the surrender of Lee's army at Appomattox Court House.

Five Island Harbour, bay, W Antigua, Antigua and Barbuda Republic, West Indies, 2 mi/3.2 km WSW of St. John's; 17°06'N 61°54'W. Resort area.

Five Island Lake, Palo Alto co., NW Iowa; c.5 mi/8 km long. Emmetsburg is at S end.

Five Islands, village, N central N.S., Canada, on Minas

Basin, 30 mi/48 km SSE of Amherst; 45°25′N 64°02′W. Dairying, mixed farming; port. Just offshore are several islets.

Five Islands, archipelago (319 acres/129 ha) off NW Trinidad, Trinidad and Tobago, in Gulf of Paria, c.7 mi/11.3 km W of Port of Spain. Consists, actually, of 6 tiny islets: Caledonia, Nelson, Lenagan, Rock, Pelican, and Craig (joined to Caledonia by narrow reef). Bathing and fishing resort. Also known as Las Cotorras.

Five Islands, S La., name given to 5 salt domes, forming low rises or isls., scattered through coastal marshes of St. Mary and Iberia parishes. Isls. contain large rock-salt mines, oil and gas wells. Include Avery Island (with noted bird sanctuary and gardens), Belle Isle, Cote Blanche Island, Jefferson Island, Weeks Island. Cayenne peppers grown and processed on Avery Isl.

Five Islands, Maine: see GEORGETOWN.

Five Points 1 town (1990 pop. 200), Chambers co., E Ala., 9 mi/14.5 km NNE of Lafayette; 33°01′N 85°20′W. **2** uninc. town, Bernalillo co., N.Mex. residential suburb, 2 mi/3.2 km SW of downtown Alburquerque, near Rio Grande.

Five Towns of Long Island, cluster of 5 highly affluent communities within the town of Hempstead, Nassau co., SE N.Y., SE of JFK Internatl. Airport; 40°38′N 73°44′W. Includes Cedarhurst, Hewlett, Inwood, Lawrence, and Woodmere.

Fixed Link, Canada: see PRINCE EDWARD ISLAND BRIDGE.

Flagler (FLAG-luhr), county (□ 571 sq mi/1,479 sq km; 1990 pop. 28,701), NE Fla., on the Atlantic (E), and partly bounded W by Crescent L.; ⊙ Bunnell; 29°28′N 81°17′W. Lowland agr. (corn, vegetables, citrus fruit; livestock) and forestry (lumber, naval stores) area, with swamps and small lakes. Very rapid growth since 1980; has become center of the coastal strip known as Palm Coast, located bet. Daytona Beach and St. Augustine. Formed 1917.

Flagler, village (1990 pop. 564), Kit Carson co., E Colo., 43 mi/69 km W of Burlington; 39°17′N 103°04′W. Elev. 4,931 ft/1,503 m. Cattle, mfg. (pet food, printing). Small Flagler Reservoir and Flagler State Wildlife Area to E. Airport to SW.

Flagler Beach (FLAG-lurr), resort town (□ 4 sq mi/10.4 sq km; 1990 pop. 3,820), Flagler co., NE Fla., 30 mi/48 km S of St. Augustine, on the Atlantic; 29°28′N 81°17′W.

Flagler, Fort, Wash.: see PORT TOWNSEND.

Flagstaff, former plantation, Somerset co., W Maine, inundated 1949–1950 by reservoir (Flagstaff L.) impounded by Long Falls Dam in Dead R.

Flagstaff, city (1990 pop. 45,857), ⊙ Coconino co., N Ariz., 120 mi/193 km NNE of Phoenix, near the San Francisco Peaks; 35°11′N 111°37′W. Elev. 6,905 ft/2,105 m. City is bounded on all sides by Coconino Natl. Forest; part of Kaibab Natl. Forest to W. Lumbering, ranching, and a lively tourism thrive in the region; fish hatchery to SW. Flagstaff Symphony Orchestra. Flagstaff Municipal Airport (Pulliam Field) in SW. Flagstaff also has facilities for astronomy, such as the Lowell observatory at Mars Hill, in W part of city, Riordan State Historic Park. The Mus. of Northern Ariz., Pioneer History Mus., and Northern Ariz. Univ. are in the city. Flagstaff Aboretum to S. Walnut Canyon Natl. Monument is E of city; San Francisco Mts. to N, including Ariz. Snow Bowl ski area and Humphreys Peak (12,643 ft/3,854 m), the highest point in Ariz.; Mormon L. to SE; Sunset Crater and Wupatki Natl. Monuments to NE; Slide Rock State Park to S. Inc. 1894.

Flagstaff Lake, reservoir (□ 28 sq mi/73 sq km), Somerset and Franklin cos., W Maine, on Dead R., 37 mi/60 km NW of Madison; 45°13′N 70°12′W. Max. capacity 435,000 acre-ft. Formed by Flagstaff Dam (43 ft/13 m high), built (1948) for power generation.

Flagstaff Mountain (2,497 ft/761 m), Somerset co., W Maine, near Flagstaff L. (2.25 mi/3.7 km long), 25 mi/40 km NW of Bingham.

Flambeau Reservoir (□ 28 sq mi/73 sq km), Iron co., N Wis., on Flambeau R., 45 mi/72 km NW of Rhinelander; 46°04′N 90°13′W. Max. capacity 215,000 acre-ft. Formed by Flambeau Dam (also called Turtle Dam; 33 ft/10 m high), built (1920) for power generation. Recreation. Lac Du Flambeau Indian Reservation to E; Chequamegon Natl. Forest just S. Reservoir also known as Turtle-Flambeau Flowage.

Flambeau River (FLAM-bo), c.115 mi/185 km long, N Wis., rises in lake region near Mich. state line, flows NW, through large irregular Turtle-Flambeau Flowage reservoir (E of Butternut), then SW, past Park Falls and Ladysmith, to Chippewa R. (Holcombe Flowage reservoir) 27 mi/43 km NNE of Chippewa Falls. Longest branch is sometimes called North Fork in upper course. South Fork (c.55 mi/89 km long) rises in NE Price co., joins North Fork at Rusk-Sawyer co. line N of Hawkins. Has hydroelectric plants. Formerly important for logging. Whitewater canoeing. North Fork flows through Flambeau River State Forest.

Flaming Gorge Reservoir, NE Utah and SW Wyo., in Flaming Gorge Canyon of the Green R., in Flaming Gorge Natl. Recreation Area, 30 mi/48 km N of Vernal (Utah); c.80 mi/129 km long, max. 4 mi/6.4 km wide; 40°55′N 109°31′W. In Wyo., Blacks Fork R. forms 15-mi/24-km NW arm and Henrys Fork enters from W, forming 8-mi/12.9-km arm. Widest point 26 mi/42 km WNW of dam. Formed by Flaming Gorge Dam, built (1958–1963) by the U.S. Bureau of Reclamation as a major unit in the Colorado R. storage project for water storage and hydroelectricity. Canyon named in 1869 by the U.S. explorer John Wesley Powell because the brilliant red gorge, from a distance, looked as if it were on fire. Ashley Natl. Forest and foothills of Uinta Mts. on S.

Flamingo, southernmost settlement on Fla.'s mainland in Everglades Natl. Park, Monroe co., extreme S Fla., just E of Cape Sable. Site of ranger station and visitor's center at terminus of the Natl. Park's main road.

Flanagan, village (1990 pop. 987), Livingston co., N central Ill., 11 mi/18 km W of Pontiac; 40°52′N 88°51′W. In agr. area; grain, dairy prods., poultry.

Flanders Bay, N.Y.: see GREAT PECONIC BAY.

Flandreau, town (1990 pop. 2,311), ⊙ Moody co., E S.Dak., 35 mi/56 km N of Sioux Falls, and on Big Sioux R.; 44°02′N 96°35′W. Large cooperative creamery; grain; dairy prods.; livestock, poultry; mfg. Flandreau Indian School and Flandreau Indian Reservation are here. Permanently settled 1869.

Flasher, village (1990 pop. 317), Morton co., S N.Dak., 33 mi/53 km SW of Bismarck and on Louise Creek; 46°27′N 101°13′W.

Flat, village, W Alaska, near Iditarod R., and 60 mi/97 km ENE of Holy Cross; 62°27′N 158°01′W. Airfield.

Flat Brook, c.20 mi/32 km long, NW N.J.; rises in NW Sussex co., flows SW in the Appalachians, to the Delaware c.15 mi/24 km above Delaware Water Gap. Hunting, fishing in valley.

Flat Creek, village, Walker co., NW central Ala., 20 mi/32 km WNW of Birmingham.

Flat Island (□ 1 sq mi/3 sq km), in Placentia Bay, SE N.F., Canada, 20 mi/32 km NE of Burin; 3 mi/5 km long; 47°17′N 54°56′W. Fishing.

Flat Mountain (9,204 ft/2,805 m), peak in Continental Divide, in S part of Yellowstone Natl. Park, Teton co., Wyo., S of Flat Mt. arm of Yellowstone L.

Flat River 1 c.60 mi/97 km long, in central Mich.; rises in N Montcalm co., flows SSW, past Greenville and Belding, to Grand R. at Lowell; 43°26′N 85°08′W. **2** c.7 mi/11.3 km long, in W central R.I.; small stream in Coventry town, dammed to form Flat R. Reservoir (c.4 mi/6.4 km long) E of Coventry village. Reservoir drained from E by South Branch of Pawtuxet R.

Flat River, Mo.: see PARK HILLS.

Flat Rock, city (1990 pop. 7,290), Wayne co., SE Mich., suburb 19 mi/31 km SSW of downtown Detroit, and on Huron R.; 42°06′N 83°16′W. Mfg. of vehicles, sheet metal. Oakwood and Willow Metro parks to W. Settled 1824, inc. 1923.

Flat Rock, uninc. town (1990 pop. 1,812), Henderson co., SW N.C., in the Blue Ridge Mts., 4 mi/6.4 km S of Hendersonville; 36°30′N 80°34′W. Agr. area (tobacco, corn, potatoes, soybeans; hogs, cattle; dairying). Light mfg. Has church built in 1832. Nearby is Bonclarken, with church assembly grounds. Holmes Educational State Forest to W (235 acres/95 ha). Carl Sandburg Home Natl. Historical Site. Flat Rock Playhouse with the Vagabond Players. Blue Ridge Community Col.

Flat Rock, village (1990 pop. 421), Crawford co., SE Ill., 8 mi/12.9 km SSE of Robinson; 38°53′N 87°40′W. In agr. area (corn, wheat; livestock, poultry).

Flat Top, Va.: see OTTER, PEAKS OF.

Flatbush, a residential section of central Brooklyn borough of N.Y. city, SE N.Y.; 40°39′N 73°59′W. Name derived from *Vlackebos* [Du. = flat plain]. Was a Du. village in 17th cent.; annexed to Brooklyn 1694. Has several 18th-cent. bldgs., including Erasmus Hall Acad. (1786) and Reformed Protestant Du. Church. Seat of Brooklyn Col. Site of former Ebbets Field, which was replaced by housing development when Brooklyn Dodgers left for Los Angeles in 1957. Also here is Prospect Park South, an upscale suburban community planned and built c.1900; from the 1920s to the 1950s, it was the home of many prominent actors, musicians, and writers, including Mary Pickford. Barbra Streisand and Mary Tyler Moore grew up in this neighborhood. Kings Co. Hosp. and Downstate State Hosp. are in adjacent East Flatbush.

Flathead, county (□ 5,256 sq mi/13,613 sq km; 1990 pop. 59,218), NW Mont.; ⊙ Kalispell; 48°17′N 114°01′W. Agr. region bordering on far N on Canada (B.C), bounded E by Continental Divide (in N, it runs SE-NW through center of Glacier Natl. Park). Drained by Flathead R. and its North, Middle, and South forks, also by Stillwater, Whitefish, and Little Bitterroot rivers. Fruit (including cherries), wheat, barley, rape seeds, hay, potatoes, peas, lentils, mint, Christmas trees; cattle, horses, hogs, llamas; forest industries; mining; mfg. (furniture, pre-fabricated log houses); tourism. Flathead Natl. Wild and Scenic River (on Middle Fork of Flathead R.) in E, along perimeter of Glacier Park. Sections of Flathead Natl. Forest in SE, S, and N; part of Glacier Natl. Park in NE; ranges of Rocky Mts. throughout; parts of Lolo and Kootenai natl. forests in SW; Whitefish L. with Whitefish L. State Park at S end, in center; Lone Pine State Park in S center; N part of Flathead L. in S with Wayfarers Unit of Flathead L. State Park on NE shore; parts of Bob Marshall and Great Bear wilderness areas in SE; Hungry Horse Reservoir on South Fork of Flathead R. in E center; Coal Creek State Forest in N; part of Stillwater State Forest in NW; part of Flathead Indian Reservation in S. Formed 1893. Present boundaries est. 1923.

Flathead, river, c.240 mi/390 km long, rising as the North Fork, in SE B.C., Canada, and flowing generally SE through NW Mont., to Coram, where it is joined by the Middle Fork (c.85 mi/140 km long) and the South Fork (c.80 mi/130 km long). It continues S through Flathead L., then W and S to Clark Fork R. Hungry Horse Dam and Kerr Dam are the centers of hydroelectric, irrigation, and flood-control projects in the river's basin.

Flathead Lake (□ 197 sq mi/510 sq km), Lake and Flathead cos., NW Mont.; 28 mi/45 km long. Largest natural lake in Mont. Formed by glacial scouring and moraine damming of the Flathead R., which flows through it from N to S. Flathead L. has an irregular shoreline and many small isls. S ½ of lake in Flathead Indian Reservation, town of Polson at S end, city of Kalispell 9 mi/14.5 km NW of N end, 6 units of Flathead L. State Park scattered about lake shore, Swan R. at NE end. RR termini at both ends of lake, transfer of goods across lake. Surrounded by mts., the lake is a noted recreation area. Kerr Dam, 4 mi/6.4 km downstream from S end, provides hydroelectric power and water for irrigation.

Flathead Lake State Park (total land □ 2,466 acres/998 ha), Lake and Flathead cos., NW Mont., 6 separate units scattered along shore of Flathead L., SE of Kalispell. Big Arm Unit (55 acres/22 ha), Lake co., Flathead Indian Reservation, 10 mi/16 km NW of Polson, boat access to Wild Horse Isl. Finley Point Unit (24 acres/10 ha), Lake co., Flathead Indian Reservation, 6 mi/9.7 km NE of Polson, conifer forest on peninsula on

SE shore. Wayfarers Unit (68 acres/28 ha), Flathead co., at Bigfork, 16 mi/26 km SE of Kalispell, at mouth of Swan R.; resort area. West Shore Unit (146 acres/59 ha), Lake co., on Table Bay, 18 mi/29 km SSE of Kalispell; rock formations. Wild Horse Isl. Unit (2,163 acres/ 875 ha), Lake co., Flathead Indian Reservation, at entrance to Big Arm, 10 mi/16 km N of Polson; bighorn sheep, deer, coyote, wild horses, bald eagles, ospreys. Yellow Bay Unit (10 acres/4 ha), Lake co., Flathead Indian Reservation, 14 mi/23 km NE of Polson; camping and cherry orchards.

Flathead Pass (elev. 6,981 ft/2,128 m), in Bridger Range, Gallatin co., S Mont., 20 mi/32 km N of Bozeman. Gallatin Natl. Forest.

Flathead Range, in Rocky Mts. of NW Mont., mainly Flathead co., extends from N Powell co. in S, NNW to West Glacier (Flathead co.) in N. Bet. South Fork of Flathead R., and Hungry Horse Reservoir (to SW), and Middle Fork of Flathead R. (NE) and Continental Divide (SE). Glacier Natl. Park to NE. Highest point: Silvertip Mt. (8,890 ft/2,710 m), 46 mi/74 km E of Polson. Most of range is in Great Bear Wilderness Area of Flathead Natl. Forest.

Flatlands, residential section of S Brooklyn borough of N.Y. city, SE N.Y., near W shore of Jamaica Bay; 40°37′N 73°55′W. Much of the area developed 1910–1960s along the suburban model.

Flatonia, town (1990 pop. 1,295), Fayette co., S central Texas, 28 mi/45 km N of Yoakum; 29°41′N 97°06′W. Elev. 458 ft/140 m. RR junction, in agr. area (poultry, cattle; dairying; pecans, peanuts); mfg. (food processing, machining). Founded 1874, inc. 1875.

Flatrock River, c.90 mi/145 km long, E and central Ind., rises in NE Henry co., flows SW and S to East Fork of White R. at Columbus.

Flattery, Cape, Clallam co., NW Wash., at the rocky entrance to Strait of Juan de Fuca; discovered in 1778 by Capt. James Cook. Cape Flattery Lighthouse, on Tatoosh Isl., 1 mi/1.6 km off cape town of Neah Bay on N side of peninsula. Makah Indian Reservation occupies cape, where cliffs rise 120 ft/37 m above the Pacific Ocean.

Flatwoods, town (1990 pop. 7,799), Greenup co., NE Ky., a suburb 6 mi/9.7 km NW of Ashland and 4 mi SW of Ohio R.; 38°31′N 82°43′W. Agr. (tobacco, grain; cattle); light mfg. Greenbo Lake State Resort Park to W.

Flatwoods, village (1990 pop. 324), Braxton co., central W.Va., 6 mi/9.7 km NNE of Sutton; 38°43′N 80°39′W. Agr. (grain, apples); livestock. Sutton L. reservoir, in Elk R. Wildlife Management Area, to S.

Flaxton, village (1990 pop. 121), Burke co., NW N.Dak., 10 mi/16 km NW of Bowbells; 48°53′N 102°23′W. RR junction.

Flcoton, uninc. village, Northumberland co., E Va.; 37°48′N 76°16′W. Ferry from Tangier Isl. terminates at Reedville 2 mi N.

Fleetwood, borough (1990 pop. 3,478), Berks co., SE central Pa., 9 mi/14.5 km NE of Reading. Agr. (apples, plums, mushrooms, grain; livestock, poultry, dairying); mfg. (food prods., machinery). L. Ontelaunee reservoir to W. Founded 1800, inc. 1873.

Fleetwood Hill, Va.: see BRANDY STATION.

Fleischmanns (FLEISH-muhnz), resort village (1990 pop. 351), Delaware co., S N.Y., in the Catskills, 31 mi/ 50 km WNW of Kingston; 42°09′N 74°31′W.

Fleming, county (□ 351 sq mi/909 sq km; 1990 pop. 12,292), NE Ky.; ⊙ Flemingsburg; 38°22′N 83°41′W. Bounded W by Licking R., NE by North Fork of Licking R; drained by Fleming Creek. Gently rolling upland agr. area, in N part of Bluegrass region (burley tobacco, corn, hay, alfalfa, soybeans, wheat; hogs, cattle, poultry; dairying). Fleming Wildlife Management Area in E; Goddard Hillsboro and Ringo's Mills covered bridges in SE. Formed 1798.

Fleming, town (1991 pop. 118), SE Sask., Canada, on Man. border, 9 mi/14 km SE of Moosomin; 50°04′N 101°31′W. Mixed farming.

Fleming, village (1990 pop. 344), Logan co., NE Colo., near South Platte R., 20 mi/32 km E of Sterling;

40°40′N 102°50′W. Elev. 4,240 ft/1,292 m. Corn, beans, sunflowers; cattle. Sand Hills nearby to N.

Fleming-Neon, town (1990 pop. 759), Letcher co., SE Ky., 22 mi/35 km SW of Pikesville, in the Cumberland Mts., on North Fork of Kentucky R. Some agr.

Flemingsburg, town (1990 pop. 3,071), ⊙ Fleming co., NE Ky., 16 mi/26 km S of Maysville, in N part Bluegrass region; 38°25′N 83°44′W. Mfg. (crushed limestone, shoes, concrete, mobile homes). Fleming Wildlife Management Area to E; Goddard "White" Covered Bridge to SE, Hillsboro Covered Bridge to S, Ringo's Mills Covered Bridge to SE; Fox Valley L. to SE. Settled 1796.

Flemington, city (1990 pop. 279), Liberty co., SE Ga., just SE of Hinesville; 31°51′N 81°34′W.

Flemington, town (1990 pop. 141), Polk co., SW Mo., 3 mi/4.8 km E of Humansville; 37°47′N 93°30′W. Hay; cattle.

Flemington, village (1990 pop. 352), Taylor co., N W.Va., 7 mi/11.3 km SW of Grafton; 39°16′N 80°07′W. Alfalfa; cattle. Tygart L. reservoir and State Park to E.

Flemington 1 borough (1990 pop. 4,047), ⊙ Hunterdon co., W N.J., 20 mi/32 km NNW of Trenton; 40°30′N 74°51′W. Farm-market center (poultry, vegetables); mfg. (metal prods., fur coats, consumer goods, concrete prods., plastics, dairy prods., rubber goods, chemicals). Large-scale discount shopping center. Agr. fairs held here since 1930. Scene (1935) of Hauptmann's trial for kidnapping and murder of Charles A. Lindbergh, Jr. Settled c.1730, inc. 1910. **2** borough (1990 pop. 1,321), Clinton co., N central Pa., residential suburb 2 mi/ 3.2 km SW of Lock Haven, on Bald Eagle Creek; 41°07′N 77°28′W. Inc. 1864.

Flensburg, village (1990 pop. 213), Morrison co., central Minn., 8 mi/12.9 km W of Little Falls; 45°57′N 94°31′W. Grain, sunflowers, beans; livestock, poultry; dairying.

Flesherton, village (1991 pop. 543), S Ont., Canada, 23 mi/37 km SW of Collingwood; 44°15′N 80°33′W. Milling, lumbering.

Fletcher 1 town (1990 pop. 2,787), Henderson co., SW N.C., 12 mi/19 km SSE of Asheville, near French Broad R., in the Blue Ridge Mts; 35°25′N 82°30′W. Agr. area (dairying; cattle, hogs; potatoes, corn, soybeans, tobacco). Mfg. (printing, construction materials, transportation equip., lumber, limestone processing, wooden furniture, consumer goods). **2** town (1990 pop. 1,002), Commanche co., SW Okla., 18 mi/29 km NNE of Lawton; 34°49′N 98°14′W. Mfg. (concrete). L. Ellsworth reservoir to W. **3** town (1990 pop. 941), Franklin co., NW Vt., 12 mi/19 km SE of St. Albans, near Lamoille R.; 44°42′N 72°54′W.

Fletcher, village (1990 pop. 545), Miami co., W Ohio, 6 mi/10 km E of Piqua, in agr. area; 40°08′N 84°07′W.

Fletcher Pond (□ 11 sq mi/28 sq km), Alpena co., N Mich., on Upper South Branch of Thunder Bay R., 21 mi/34 km W of Alpena; 45°01′N 83°47′W. Max. capacity 40,100 acre-ft. Formed by Upper South Dam (20 ft/6 m high), built (1930) for power generation.

Flin Flon (flin flahn), city (1991 pop. in Man., 7,119; in Sask., 330), on the Man.-Sask. border, Canada; 54°46′N 101°53′W. A mining and smelting center in a region producing copper, zinc, silver, gold, and cadmium; also serves a lumbering and fishing area.

Flinders, Cape, NE Mackenzie Dist., N.W.T., Canada, on Coronation Gulf, at entrance of Bathurst Inlet, at W extremity of Kent Peninsula; 68°13′N 108°46′W.

Flint 1 city (1990 pop. 1,033), Morgan co., N Ala., on inlet of Wheeler Reservoir (on Tennessee R.), and 6 mi/ 9.7 km S of Decatur; 34°31′N 86°58′W. Lurleen Wallace Developmental Hosp. here. **2** city (1990 pop. 140,761), ⊙ Genessee co., SE Mich., on the Flint R.; 43°01′N 83°41′W. Elev. 750 ft/229 m. RR junction. Mfg. (transportation equip., fabricated metal prods., chemicals, publishing, meat processing, consumer goods). Since 1902 it has been one of the chief automobile-mfg. centers of the world, paralleling the success of the nearby Detroit auto industry. The huge General Motors Corp. had its beginnings (1908) in Flint, and many other major automobile makers (Chrysler, Chevrolet, Nash,

Champion, Buick) also started here. The early fur-trading post (1819) was succeeded by a settlement with lumbering and then cart and carriage making as Flint's major industry. In 1937, sitdown strikes by the United Auto Workers (UAW) in the factories of General Motors led to widespread labor organization. The auto industry has faltered in the latter 20th cent., in part due to foreign competition, and during the 1980s massive layoffs at General Motors devastated Flint's single-industry economy. Attempts at economic diversification and revitalization have had limited success. Bishop Internat. Airport in SW city. In the city are a branch of the Univ. of Mich., Charles Stewart Mott Community Col., Art Institute, Mich. School for the Deaf, Alfred P. Sloan Mus., a planetarium, I.M.A. Sports Arena, Guy Houston Stadium, and a nature preserve. Inc. 1855.

Flint Creek, 45 mi/72 km long, SW Mont.; rises in Georgetown L., on Deer Lodge–Granite co. line, flows N, past Philipsburg, bet. Flint Creek Range and John Long Mts., to the Clark Fork R. at Drummond. Almost entirely in Granite co.

Flint Creek Range, in Rocky Mts. of W Mont., extends from E Granite co. just S of the Clark Fork, c.25 mi/ 40 km S to near Anaconda. Elevs. of 8,000 ft/2,438 m–10,400 ft/3,170 m. In Deerlodge Natl. Forest. Manganese, silver, and coal mined.

Flint Hills, in N Okla. and E Kansas, a low, hilly strip extending c.200 mi/322 km bet. Arkansas R. (S) and Kansas R. (N), and rising 300/91 m–500 ft/152 m above plain. Essentially an E-facing, limestone escarpment, capped by thin layer of flint gravel. Important grazing area.

Flint River 1 150 mi/241 km long, Ga.; rises in upper Piedmont in W central Ga., just S of Atlanta; flows S to the SE corner of the state; 33°39′N 84°25′W. Major flood in Albany, Ga., in 1994 when the river crested at 43 ft/13 m and 23,000 residents were evacuated. Historically, the head of navigation was Bainbridge. At the confluence of the Chattahoochee and Flint rivers, at the Fla.-Ala. border, the Jim Woodruff Lock and Dam creates L. Seminole. To the S the river is called the Apalachicola. **2** c.71 mi/114 km long, in E central Mich.; formed in Lapeer co. near Columbiaville by union of North (c.20 mi/32 km long) and South (c.25 mi/40 km long) branches, flows SW through Moll L. reservoir, to Flint, then NW, past Flushing, to Shiawassee R. just S of Saginaw; 43°10′N 83°22′W. **3** c.60 mi/97 km long, in S Tenn. and N Ala.; rises in SE Lincoln co., Tenn., flows S to Wheeler Reservoir, on Tennessee R., 16 mi/26 km S of Huntsville, Ala.; 34°30′N 86°31′W.

Flintridge, Calif.: see LA CAÑADA FLINTRIDGE.

Flintstone, town (1990 pop. 350), Walker co., Ga., c.100 mi/161 km NW of Atlanta; 34°56′N 85°20′W. Fabrics processing and light mfg.

Flintstone, village, Allegany co., W Md., in the Appalachians near Pa. border, and 11 mi/18 km ENE of Cumberland. Gateway to small-game refuges and Green Ridge State Forest (c.17,000 acres/6,880 ha; E). Hunting, fishing. Name presumably came from huge stone on the nearby Warriors' Path from which Indians chipped flints. The Marquis de Lafayette, Henry Clay, and Theodore Roosevelt were among the many travelers on the Cumberland Road who stayed at the Flintstone Hotel (c.1807), now an apartment house.

Flippin (FLIP-in), town (1990 pop. 1,006), Marion co., N Ark., 13 mi/21 km WSW of Mt. Home, in the Ozarks, near White R.; 36°16′N 92°35′W. Mfg. (electrical equip., plastic prods., boats). Bull Shoals Dam and L. and State Park to N.

Flomaton (FLO-muh-tuhn), town (1990 pop. 1,811), Escambia co., S Ala., on Fla. border, near Escambia R., 14 mi/23 km SW of Brewton; 31°01′N 87°15′W. Meat curing, lumber milling; clothing.

Flood, village, S B.C., Canada, on Fraser R., and 25 mi/ 40 km NE of Chilliwack; 49°21′N 121°27′W. Logging; tourism.

Floodwood, village (1990 pop. 574), St. Louis co., NE central Minn., 38 mi/61 km WNW of Duluth, on St. Louis R., at mouths of Floodwood and East Savanna rivers; 46°55′N 92°55′W. Dairying; poultry; oats, alfalfa;

mfg. Prairie L. to S; Savanna State Forest to W and SW; Fond du Lac Indian Reservation to SE.

Flora, city (1990 pop. 5,054), Clay co., S central Ill., 7 mi/11.3 km S of Louisville; 38°40′N 88°28′W. Industrial and farmers' cooperative center, in agr., oil- and natural-gas area; mfg. (apparel); fruit, redtop seed, soybeans; livestock. Inc. 1867.

Flora 1 town (1990 pop. 2,179), Carroll co., W central Ind., 8 mi/12.9 km ESE of Delphi; 40°32′N 86°31′W. In livestock and grain area; plumbing prods., cement prods.; timber. Laid out 1872, inc. 1898. **2** town (1990 pop. 1,482), Madison co., central Miss., 19 mi/31 km NNW of Jackson and 17 mi/27 km WSW of Canton; 32°32′N 90°18′W. Agr. (cotton, corn, soybeans; cattle, poultry; dairying); mfg. (machinery, lumber, paper prods.). Site of Miss. Petrified Forest, 36-million-year-old petrified trees.

Flora Vista, uninc. town (1990 pop. 1,021), San Juan co., NW N.Mex., residential suburb 8 mi/12.9 km NE of Farmington and 6 mi/9.7 km WSW of Aztec, on San Juan R.; 36°47′N 108°04′W. Irrigated agr. area.

Floral City, town (□ 7 sq mi/18 sq km; 1990 pop. 2,609), Citrus co., W central Fla., 13 mi/21 km S of Inverness, near Tsala Apopka L.; 28°44′N 82°17′W. Citrus-fruit packing; phosphate quarrying.

Floral Park, residential suburb (□ 1 sq mi/2.6 sq km; 1990 pop. 15,947) of N.Y. city, Nassau co., SE N.Y., on L.I.; 40°43′N 73°42′W. Inc. 1908.

Floral Park, locality, Silver Bow co., SW Mont., a S suburb of Butte, now part of city of Butte.

Florala (flo-RAH-luh), city (1990 pop. 2,075), Covington co., S Ala., 23 mi/37 km SSE of Andalusia, at Fla. border, near Conecuh Natl Forest; 31°01′N 86°18′W. Forest. Lumber milling, mfg. (wood prods., apparel, construction materials); peanut, soybean, and tung oil; cotton.

Flordell Hills, town (1990 pop. 950), St. Louis co., E Mo., residential suburb 7 mi/11.3 km NW of downtown St. Louis; 38°43′N 90°16′W. Surrounded by Jennings.

Florence 1 county (□ 803 sq mi/2,080 sq km; 1990 pop. 114,344), E central S.C.; ⊙ Florence; 34°01′N 79°42′W. Bounded E by Pee Dee R.; drained by Lynches R. Mfg. includes sand and clay at Florence and Lake City. Agr. area (chickens, hogs; corn, wheat, rye, oats, tobacco, sorghum, hay, cotton, vegetables; timber). Formed 1888. **2** county (□ 497 sq mi/1,287 sq km; 1990 pop. 4,590), extreme NE Wis.; ⊙ Florence; 45°51′N 88°24′W. Bounded N by Brule R. and E by Menominee R. (both on Mich. boundary). Contains sect. of Nicolet Natl. Forest in W, and several lakes. Lumbering, dairying, potato growing. Keyes Park Ski Area in N center. Formed 1882.

Florence 1 city (1990 pop. 36,426), ⊙ Lauderdale co., NW Ala., on Tennessee R. Near Muscle Shoals and adjacent to Wilson Dam (a natl. historic landmark). It is a cotton and mineral area. Mfg. center served by power from Wilson Dam (2.5 mi/4 km E), in region yielding coal, iron, bauxite, and asphalt. Makes cotton fabrics, machinery, furniture, clothing, meat packing, dairying, bottling. The dam and the state dock installations have stimulated the growth of diverse industries. Large Listerhill aluminum plant (built 1941) nearby. Univ. of N Ala. is in the city. Oscar DePriest, 1st Afr.-Amer. man to serve in Congress, b. here. Of interest are Pope's Tavern (1811), once a stagecoach stop and later a Civil War hosp. and a Native American mound with mus. Laid out 1818, inc. 1826. **2** uninc. city (1990 pop. 57,147), Los Angeles co., S Calif., residential suburb 6 mi/9.7 km S of downtown Los Angeles; 33°58′N 118°14′W. In industrial dist. Designated Florence-Graham by Census Bureau. **3** city (1990 pop. 18,624), Boone co., N Ky., suburb 10 mi/16 km SW of Cincinnati, Ohio, and 8 mi/12.9 km SW of Covington, Ky., in N part of Bluegrass region; 38°59′N 84°38′W. Mfg. (chemicals, construction materials, machinery, plastic prods., furniture, transportation equip., consumer prods., food, paper prods., printing and publishing). Cincinnati–Northern Ky. Internatl. Airport to NW. Turfway Park thoroughbred racetrack is here; Anderson ferry crosses Ohio, to N at Constance. Big Bone Lick State Park to SW. **4** city (1990 pop. 29,813), ⊙ of Florence co., NE S.C., 75 mi/121 km ENE of Columbia, in a farm and timber area. Important RR junction (with extensive repair shops and yards); developed as an industrial and trade distribution center. Airport. Mfg. includes wide variety of goods, and tobacco and cotton are grown. During the Civil War it was a transportation and supply point and served as the site of a prison camp. It is the seat of Francis Marion Univ., a technical institute, and a branch of the Univ. of S.C. An experimental station affiliated with Clemson Univ. and a U.S. agr. laboratory are also here. Florence has museums, and nearby is a Natl. Civil War Cemetery. Inc. 1871.

Florence 1 town (1990 pop. 7,510), ⊙ Pinal co., S central Ariz., on Gila R., and 50 mi/80 km SE of Phoenix; 33°02′N 111°22′W. Elev. 1,490 ft/454 m. Agr. area irrigated from San Carlos Reservoir of Coolidge Dam 50 mi/80 km ENE. RR junction to NW. Cotton, wheat, alfalfa, cantaloupes; cattle, poultry, sheep, hogs; mfg. McFarland State Historic Park is here. Casa Grande Natl. Monument to W, near Coolidge. Founded 1866, inc. 1906. **2** town (1990 pop. 2,990), Fremont co., S central Colo., on Arkansas R., just NE of Wet Mts., and 30 mi/48 km WNW of Pueblo; 38°23′N 105°07′W. Elev. 5,187 ft/1,581 m. Livestock; fruit, vegetables; mfg. (fabricated-metal prods., cement). Coal mines nearby. Start of the Gold Belt Scenic Tour. Part of San Isabel Natl. Forest to SW; Indian Petroglyphs State Historical Site to NE. Fort Carson Military Reserve to NE. Federal maximum security prison is here. Inc. 1887. **3** town (1990 pop. 1,831), Rankin co., central Miss., 10 mi/16 km SSE of Jackson; 32°08′N 90°07′W. Agr. area (vegetables, cotton, corn; poultry, cattle); mfg. (transportation equip., fabrics, diversified light mfg.). **4** town (1990 pop. 5,162), Lane co., W Oregon, 50 mi/80 km W of Eugene and 40 mi/64 km N of Coos Bay, on Siuslaw R., 1 mi/1.6 km inland (E) from Pacific Ocean; 43°59′N 124°05′W. Timber; printing and publishing, dairy prods. Tourism. Heceta Head Cape and lighthouse to N. Oregon Dunes Natl. Recreation Area to SW; Siuslaw Natl. Forest to N and E; Honeyman Memorial State Park to S; Darlington State Wayside to N. **5** town (1990 pop. 829), Williamson co., central Texas, 19 mi/31 km SSW of Killeen; 30°50′N 97°47′W. Agr. area (cattle; cotton, corn, wheat); limestone; mfg. (candy, wooden cabinets). **6** town, ⊙ Florence co., extreme NE Wis., 11 mi/18 km NW of Iron Mt. (Mich.). In wooded area. Dairying; livestock raising; cabinetmaking; light mfg. Keyes Park Ski Area to SW; Nicolet Natl. Forest to W.

Florence 1 village (1990 pop. 45), Pike co., W Ill., on Illinois R. (bridged here), and 10 mi/16 km ENE of Pittsfield; 39°37′N 90°36′W. In agr. area (corn, wheat, soybeans; cattle, hogs). **2** village (1990 pop. 636), Marion co., E central Kansas, on Cottonwood R., and 8 mi/12.9 km SE of Marion; 38°14′N 96°55′W. In grain and livestock region. Plotted 1870, inc. 1872. **3** village on Mill R., in Northampton town, Hampshire co., W central Mass. Station on Underground RR until 1861. **4** village (1990 pop. 53), Lyon co., SW Minn., 20 mi/32 km SW of Marshall; 44°14′N 96°02′W. RR junction. Grain, soybeans; livestock; dairying. **5** village (1990 pop. 250), Ravalli co., W Mont. in Bitterroot Valley, 17 mi/27 km S of Missoula, and on Bitterroot R. Bitterroot Range and Idaho border to W. Sapphire Mts. to E. Parts of Bitterroot Natl. Forest to E and W; Selway-Bitterroot Wilderness Area to SW. Agr. and forest industries. **6** village (1990 pop. 192), Codington co., NE S.Dak., 15 mi/24 km NW of Watertown; 45°03′N 97°19′W.

Florence, industrial township (1990 pop. 10,266), Burlington co., W N.J., on the Delaware R., and 8 mi/12.9 km S of Trenton; 40°06′N 74°47′W. Pipe foundry; mfg. of dairy prods. Residential.

Florence, Lake (4 mi/6.4 km long), SE Alaska, on Admiralty Isl.; 57°48′N 134°38′W. Fishing, hunting.

Florence Lake, reservoir, Fresno co., E central Calif., on South Fork of San Joaquin R., in the Sierra Nevada Mts., NW of Kings Canyon Natl. Park, 60 mi/97 km NE of Fresno; 3 mi/4.8 km long; 37°16′N 118°57′W. Elev. 7,329 ft/2,234 m. Formed by Florence L. Dam (154 ft/47 m high, 3,106 ft/947 m long), built (1926) by Southern Calif. Edison Company for power generation. Ward Tunnel delivers water to Huntington L. (12 mi/19 km W).

Florenceville, village (1991 pop. 694), W N.B., Canada, on St. John R., and 20 mi/32 km NNW of Woodstock; 46°23′N 67°36′W. Lumbering; mixed farming (notably Irish potatoes). Home of McCain Corp., one of Canada's largest food processors. Settled 1832. Named for Florence Nightingale.

Florencia de Bénito Juárez, Mexico: see BENITO JUÁREZ.

Florencio Villarreal, Mexico: see CRUZ GRANDE.

Flores Island (FLO-riz) (□ 60 sq mi/155 sq km), SW B.C., Canada, in Clayoquot Sound, just off W central Vancouver Isl., 10 mi/16 km NW of Tofino; 10 mi/16 km long, 6 mi/10 km wide; 49°20′N 126°10′W. Copper, gold, silver mining. On SE coast is village of Ahousat.

Flores, Villa, Mexico: see VILLAFLORES.

Floresville, town (1990 pop. 5,247), ⊙ Wilson co., S Texas, 29 mi/47 km SE of San Antonio, and on San Antonio R.; 29°08′N 98°09′W. Trade, shipping, processing center for agr. area (vegetables, peanuts, watermelons); dairying; light mfg. Canary Islanders Cemetery, est. 1732, by Atlantic islander immigrants.

Florham Park (FLOR-uhm), borough (1990 pop. 8,521), Morris co., N.J., 5 mi/8 km E of Morristown; 40°46′N 74°24′W. Chiefly residential. Light industry, petroleum research. Campus of Farleigh Dickinson Univ. and Col. of St. Elizabeth. Site of Little Red Schoolhouse (1897) now on Natl. Registry. Inc. 1899.

Florida, state (□ 65,758 sq mi/170,313 sq km; 1995 est. pop. 14,165,570), extreme SE U.S., admitted 1845 as the 27th state of the Union; ⊙ TALLAHASSEE. JACKSONVILLE, MIAMI, TAMPA, SAINT PETERSBURG, ORLANDO, and HIALEAH are the largest cities. A long, low peninsula, with an equally long N panhandle, Fla. is bounded on the E by the Atlantic Ocean, on the W by the Gulf of Mexico and Ala., and on the N by Ga. and Ala. (where the SAINT MARYS river in the NE and the PERDIDO RIVER in the NW form part of the boundary). Fla. is separated from Cuba to the S by the Straits of Fla. Much of the E coast is shielded from the Atlantic by narrow barrier isls. that protect shallow lagoons, rivers, and bays. Immediately inland, pine and palmetto flatlands stretch from the Ga. border almost to the S tip of the state, but rapid coastal urbanization has pushed all vegetation inland. The N tier of Fla. is a gently rolling area known as the Panhandle, cut into by deep swamps along the coast. Central Fla. abounds in lakes, with LAKE OKEECHOBEE being the largest. The EVERGLADES, which includes BIG CYPRESS SWAMP, is a unique wilderness region of subtropical plant growth and animal life and extends over the center of the S part of the peninsula S and SW of L. Okeechobee. Fla.'s lower Gulf coast is dotted with tiny isls., and the FLORIDA KEYS, arching SW from the SE tip of the Fla. peninsula, are linked to each other and the mainland by a series of bridges. Warmed by the surrounding subtropical and tropical waters and cooled by the trade winds, Fla. is famous for its hot climate, abundant sunshine, and scenery. Tourism plays a primary role in the state's economy; in the mid-1990s visitors to Fla. spent over $30 billion. Walt Disney World, a massive theme park near Orlando, is one of the world's most popular tourist attractions. Beautiful beaches, such as those at MIAMI BEACH, DAYTONA BEACH, PENSACOLA, PANAMA CITY, and FORT LAUDERDALE, attract millions of vacationers annually, and abundant recreational facilities have made tourism a year-round enterprise. Other attractions include Everglades Natl. Park, with its unusual plant and animal life; PALM BEACH, with its palatial estates; and SANIBEL ISLAND, with shelling and picturesque resorts. Famous also for its citrus fruits, Fla. leads the nation in production of oranges, grapefruits, and tangerines. Other important crops are tomatoes and sugarcane. Fla. also supplies much of the country with many varieties of winter vegetables, and cattle and dairy prods. are important. Fla.'s leading mfg. includes food prods., printing and publishing, electrical and electronic equip., and transportation equip. Lumber and wood prods. are also important. Most of the state's timber is yellow pine. Fla.'s mineral resources include phosphate rock, sand, and gravel. Commercial fishing is important; species caught include crabs, lobsters, and shrimp. Fla.'s institutions of higher education include the Univ. of Fla., at GAINESVILLE; the Univ. of Miami, at CORAL GABLES; Fla. State Univ. and Fla. Agr. and Mechanical Univ., at Tallahassee; Univ. of Central Fla., at Orlando; Rollins Col., at WINTER PARK; the Univ. of Tampa and the Univ. of S. Fla., at Tampa; Fla. Southern Col., at LAKELAND; Stetson Univ., at DE LAND; Barry Univ., at MIAMI SHORES; and Bethune-Cookman Col., at Daytona Beach. Juan Ponce de León, landing near the site of St. Augustine in 1513, is credited as the 1st European to visit the peninsula. He claimed the land, which he thought was an isl., for Spain and named it Florida, probably because it was then the Easter season (*Pascua Florida*). Later Span. explorers established that Fla. was not an isl., and the whole region comprising most of the SE U.S. was claimed for Spain and given the same name. Fr. encroachment on the Fla. peninsula during the 1560s led to the Spanish actually settling here. Pedro Menéndez de Aviles, sent to Fla. to drive the French out of the area, est. St. Augustine in 1565. Spain was compelled to hold Fla., regardless of the land's apparent infertility and lack of precious metals, because of its strategic location along the Straits of Fla. through which rich treasure ships from points S and W sailed for Spain. Spain lost Fla. to the British in 1763 as a result of its last-minute entry into the Seven Years War, but gained it back in 1783. Spain's hold over Fla., however, was extremely tenuous, and boundary disputes developed with the U.S. In the War of 1812, Pensacola served as a Br. base until captured (1814) by Andrew Jackson. In 1819, Spain reluctantly signed the Adams-Onis treaty, ceding Fla. to the U.S. in return for U.S. assumption of $5 million in damage claims by Amer. citizens against Spain. Official U.S. occupation took place in 1821, and Fla., with its present boundaries, was organized as a territory in 1822. Settlers from neighboring states quickly established a flourishing plantation economy in the area surrounding Tallahassee, the new capital. As settlement expanded S, wars with the indigenous Seminoles resulted in their forced relocation to the West. A small band, however, fled to the interior Everglades, and their descendants live on scattered reservations there today. Fla. was admitted to the Union in 1845 as a slaveholding state. It seceded from the Union in 1861; during the Civil War the state furnished vital supplies (particularly salt and cattle) to the Confederacy. The most important Civil War engagement fought in Fla. was the battle of Olustee (Feb. 20, 1864), a Confederate victory. After the war, Fla. was placed under military rule by Congress and readmitted to the Union in 1868. In 1881 the state sold 6,250 sq mi/ 16,188 sq km of land to real-estate promoters, and Northern developers built RRs and hotels. During the latter half of the 19th cent., Cubans rebelling against Spain received sanctuary and aid in Fla., and its ties to Cuba became even stronger in the 20th cent. Miami has been profoundly influenced by the massive influx of Cubans and other Caribbean peoples, both culturally and commercially. The city functions as the trade center of Lat. Amer. The drainage of the Everglades, begun in 1906, precipitated one of the state's periodic land booms, but environmental degradation due to farming has prompted restoration through reflooding. The most famous of these land booms started after World War I and reached its peak in 1925, when land values achieved fantastic heights only to collapse the following year when a hurricane nearly destroyed Miami. Fla. weathered the Depression of the 1930s with the help of the Federal govt., and prospered during World War II from army, navy, and air force installations. After the war the state enjoyed phenomenal growth. Mfg., particularly industries related to aerospace, developed at an extraordinary rate. CAPE CANAVERAL became famous as the site of the John F. Kennedy Space Center, a missile-testing and space-research center, and many defense- and scientific-research companies were drawn to the area. Virtually unlimited water resources, as well as the mild climate, were important factors in attracting new industries. In terms of pop., Fla. has been one of the fastest- growing U.S. states for many decades. During the 1980s it surpassed Ohio, Ill., and Pa. to become the 4th-largest state. Thousands of retired persons have settled here, particularly S of Tampa along the W coast (the "Sun Coast") and on the E coast from WEST PALM BEACH to the vicinity of Miami, nicknamed the "Gold Coast." The central interior of the state is growing fastest, particularly the corridor along Interstate Highway 4 that stretches from the Tampa Bay–St. Petersburg area through Orlando to Daytona Beach. Fla. has 67 cos.: ALACHUA, BAKER, BAY, BRADFORD, BREVARD, BROWARD, CALHOUN, CHARLOTTE, CITRUS, CLAY, COLLIER, COLUMBIA, DADE, DE SOTO, DIXIE, DUVAL, ESCAMBIA, FLAGLER, FRANKLIN, GADSDEN, GILCHRIST, GLADES, GULF, HAMILTON, HARDEE, HENDRY, HERNANDO, HIGHLANDS, HILLSBOROUGH, HOLMES, INDIAN RIVER, JACKSON, JEFFERSON, LAFAYETTE, LAKE, LEE, LEON, LEVY, LIBERTY, MADISON, MANATEE, MARION, MARTIN, MONROE, NASSAU, OKALOOSA, OKEECHOBEE, ORANGE, OSCEOLA, PALM BEACH, PASCO, PINELLAS, POLK, PUTNAM, SAINT JOHNS, SAINT LUCIE, SANTA ROSA, SARASOTA, SEMINOLE, SUMTER, SUWANNEE, TAYLOR, UNION, VOLUSIA, WAKULLA, WALTON, and WASHINGTON.

Florida, town (1995 pop. 45,000), Camagüey prov., E Cuba, on Central Highway, and 23 mi/37 km WNW of Camagüey; 21°33′N 78°14′W. RR junction, trading and agr. center (sugarcane, oranges; cattle). Three sugar mills within 6 mi/9.7 km: the large Central Argentina is just N; the Central Agramonte is S.

Florida, town (1990 pop. 742), Berkshire co., NW Mass., 21 mi/34 km NNE of Pittsfield, and on Deerfield R.; 42°41′N 73°01′W. Resort area. Includes village of Hoosac Tunnel, at E end of RR tunnel through Hoosac Range.

Florida (flo-REE-dah), village (1990 pop. 8,689), N P.R., 13 mi/21 km SE of Arecibo. Mfg. plastic prods., juices. Many residents commute to nearby towns. Agr. (pineapples, coffee; livestock). Located in the Karst region.

Florida 1 village (☐ 1 sq mi/2.6 sq km; 1990 pop. 2,497), Orange co., SE N.Y., 5 mi/8 km SSW of Goshen; 41°19′N 74°20′W. In onion-growing area. William H. Seward was b. here. **2** village (1990 pop. 304), Henry co., NW Ohio, on Maumee R., 6 mi/10 km SW of Napoleon; 41°19′N 84°12′W.

Florida, uninc. community, Monroe co., NE central Mo., on Salt R., 28 mi/45 km SW of Hannibal; 39°29′N 91°47′W. Mark Twain (Samuel L. Clemens) b. here; Mark Twain State Park includes Mark Twain's cabin. Surrounded on 3 sides by Mark Twain L. Historic area, tourism, recreation.

Florida Bay, shallow body of water ringing the S end of the Fla. peninsula, and partly sheltered S and E from the Atlantic by the Fla. Keys; opens into Biscayne Bay (NE) and the Gulf of Mexico (W). Bay has dredged navigation channels. Most of bay and its many small isls. are included in Everglades Natl. Park.

Florida City, town (☐ 2 sq mi/5.2 sq km; 1990 pop. 5,806), Dade co., SE Fla., 29 mi/47 km SW of Miami; 25°26′N 80°28′W. Vegetable-produce shipping. S terminus of Fla.'s Turnpike Extension, and gateway to the Fla. Keys via U.S. 1. Town destroyed by Hurricane Andrew in 1992 and subsequently rebuilt. Inc. 1913.

Florida Current, warm ocean current of North Atlantic Ocean, constituting initial sect. of Gulf Stream system. Formed by union of Antilles Current and of the major current component issuing from Gulf of Mexico through Straits of Fla., the Fla. Current flows N along SE coast of U.S. to area of Cape Hatteras, where it becomes the Gulf Stream proper. It issues from the Gulf as dark indigo–blue water of c.80°F moving at a surface velocity of 4–6 mi per hour. The initial transport of 26,000,000 cu mm per second rapidly increases and reaches its max. in the Gulf Stream proper.

Florida Keys, chain of small coral and limestone islands and reefs, c.100 mi/161 km long, extending from Key Largo at the SE corner of the Fla. peninsula to Key West, and forming the S extremity of Fla. Bet. the keys and the mainland lies Fla. Bay; they are separated from Cuba by the Straits of Fla. Many of the isls., which are generally covered by dense growths of low trees and shrubs, have become resort developments. The best known isls. are Key Largo and Key West, on which is the city of Key West. The Fla. Keys are noted for their commercial fisheries, resort areas, tropical vegetation, and extensive varieties of small wildlife. The 1st U.S. underseas park is along the coast of Key Largo and has noted coral formations. Most of the isls. are joined to each other and to the mainland by U.S. 1 or the Overseas Highway (completed in 1938), which has 42 bridges.

Florida Mountains, Luna co., SW N.Mex., extend N-S, SE of Deming. Chief peak, Florida Peak (7,448 ft/ 2,270 m). Manganese deposits.

Florida Panhandle, the continental portion of the state of Fla. that does not lie on the Fla. peninsula. Stretches W for c.375 mi/603 km from metropolitan Jacksonville on the Atlantic coast to metropolitan Pensacola in Fla.'s NW corner. Bounded on the N by Ga. and Ala. (which also forms the W border of the Panhandle). Bounded on the SW by the Gulf of Mexico and on SE by the Fla. Peninsula, which begins S of the line connecting Perry and St. Augustine.

Florida Peak, peak (7,448 ft/2,270 m) in Florida Mts., Luna co., SW N.Mex., 13 mi/21 km SE of Deming.

Florida Peninsula, the portion of Fla., SE of the Fla. Panhandle, that juts outward into the Atlantic coast and Gulf of Mexico for more than 350 mi/563 km, generally aligned NNW-SSE and averaging c.100 mi/ 161 km in width. S terminus is Cape Sable in Monroe co.

Florida, Straits of, passage, c.90 mi/145 km wide, bet. the Fla. Keys in the N and Cuba in the S. It connects the Gulf of Mexico with the Atlantic Ocean, and is the source area for the Gulf Stream ocean current.

Florida's Turnpike, one of the 3 major N-S expressways in Fla. This toll road begins at Interstate Highway 75 in Wildwood, 50 mi/80 km NW of Orlando and then passes through the city as it crosses the center of the peninsula, reaching the Atlantic coast at Fort Pierce. It then runs parallel to the Eastern Seaboard for about 100 mi/161 km S of Golden Glades at the N edge of Maimi. An extension of the turnpike branches off just N of Golden Gates, swings W of Miami, and terminates 30 mi/48 km S of Miami at Fla. City, from where U.S. 1 leads to the Fla. Keys that begin 20 mi/ 32 km farther S.

Florido River (flo-REE-do), c.140 mi/225 km long, N Mexico; rises in Sierra Madre Occidental SW of Hidalgo del Parral, on Durango-Chihuahua border, flows in arc N, past Villa Coronado, Villa López, and Jiménez, to Conchos R. at Camargo.

Florien (FLOIR-ee-uhn), town (1990 pop. 626), Sabine parish, La., 9 mi/14.5 km S of Many; 31°26′N 93°27′W.

Florin, uninc. city (1990 pop. 24,330), Sacramento co., central Calif., residential suburb 8 mi/12.9 km SE of downtown Sacramento; 38°30′N 121°24′W. Sacramento Army Depot to N. Agr. region (nursery prods., grain; poultry; dairying).

Floris, town (1990 pop. 172), Davis co., SE Iowa, 9 mi/ 14.5 km NNE of Bloomfield; 40°51′N 92°19′W. In sheep-raising area.

Florissant (FLOR-i-sint), city (1990 pop. 51,206), St. Louis co., E Mo., a residential and commercial suburb 17 mi/27 km NW of downtown St. Louis, near the Missouri R.; 38°47′N 90°19′W. Light mfg.; limestone quarries in area. It was settled by Fr. farmers and fur trappers c.1769, but the 1st civil govt. there was established in 1786 by the Spanish. The Spanish called the city San Ferdinand; its traditional Fr. name, *fleurissant* [flowering or flourishing], was officially adopted in 1939. Of interest are Old St. Ferdinand's Shrine and Convent (founded 1789; rebuilt 1820), and the historic Fr. homes, some dating from 1790. St. Louis Christian Col. and St. Stanislaus Seminary are in the city. Inc. 1829.

Florissant, village, Teller co., central Colo., in Rocky Mts., 25 mi/40 km WNW of Colorado Springs. Elev. c.8,170 ft/2,490 m. Tourist point. Dude ranches and petrified forest nearby. Lumber. Pikes Peak 15 mi/24 km to SE. Eleven Mile Canyon Reservoir and Eleven Mile State Park to W; Pike Natl. Forest to W and N; Florissant Fossil Beds Natl. Monument to S.

Florissant Fossil Beds National Monument (□ 5,998 acres/2,427 ha), Teller co., central Colo., S of Florissant, 25 mi/40 km WNW of Colorado Springs. Well-preserved insect, seed, and leaf fossils of the Oligocene period; petrified sequoia tree stumps. Authorized 1969.

Flossmoor (FLAAS-more), village (1990 pop. 8,651), Cook co., NE Ill., suburb 23 mi/37 km SSW of downtown Chicago; 41°32′N 87°40′W. Mfg. Inc. 1924.

Flourtown (FLOU-wuhr-toun), uninc. town (1990 pop. 4,754), Montgomery co., SE Pa., residential suburb 11 mi/18 km N of downtown Philadelphia, on Wissahikon Creek; 40°06′N 75°12′W. Mfg. (printing). Morris Arboretum to SW. Fort Wash. State Park to NW.

Flovilla (flo-VIL-uh), town (1990 pop. 602), Butts co., central Ga., 5 mi/8 km ESE of Jackson; 33°15′N 83°54′W.

Flower Hill, village (□ 1 sq mi/2.6 sq km; 1990 pop. 4,490), Nassau co., SE N.Y., near N shore of W L.I., 5 mi/8 km NNW of Mineola; 40°48′N 73°40′W. In shore-resort area. Inc. 1931.

Flower Lake, N.Y.: see SARANAC LAKE.

Flower Mound, city (1990 pop. 15,527), Denton co., N Texas, suburb 20 mi/32 km NW of downtown Dallas and 23 mi/37 km NE of downtown Fort Worth, in urban growth fringe of Dallas–Fort Worth Metroplex, on NE shore of Grapevine L. reservoir (Denton Creek); 33°01′N 97°05′W. Mfg. (fabricated metal prods.). Dallas–Fort Worth Internatl. Airport to S.

Flowery Branch, town (1990 pop. 1,251), Hall co., NE Ga., 9 mi/14.5 km SW of Gainesville; 34°11′N 83°55′W. Near L. Lanier and Interstate Highway 985. Mfg. includes paper prods., machinery, furniture, glass; chewing-gum plant.

Flowood, town (1990 pop. 2,860), Rankin co., central Miss., suburb 3 mi/4.8 km NE of downtown Jackson, on Pearl R. (forms Ross Barnett Reservoir to NE); 32°19′N 90°06′W. Mfg. (fabricated metal prods.). Allen C. Thompson Airport to E; LeFleur's Bluff State Park to W, in Jackson.

Floyd 1 county (□ 514 sq ft/48 sq m; 1990 pop. 81,251), NW Ga., on Ala. state line; ⊙ Rome; 34°16′N 85°13′W. Valley and ridge area, including part of Chattahoochee Natl. Forest (N); drained by Coosa, Etowah, and Oostanaula rivers. Cotton, corn, wheat, soybeans; cattle, hogs, poultry; stone quarrying. Formed 1832. **2** county (□ 148 sq mi/383 sq km; 1990 pop. 64,404), S Ind.; ⊙ New Albany; 38°19′N 85°54′W. Hilly region, bounded S by Ohio R. (here forming Ky. state line), and drained by small tributaries. Farming (corn, tobacco); cattle, poultry; dairying; timber; sand, gravel. Extensive mfg. at New Albany. Part of Louisville metropolitan area (also called Falls City Area). Formed 1819. **3** county (□ 501 sq mi/1,298 sq km; 1990 pop. 17,058), N Iowa; ⊙ Charles City; 43°03′N 92°47′W. Prairie agr. area (hogs, cattle, poultry; corn, soybeans, oats) drained by Shell Rock, Cedar, and Little Cedar rivers. Limestone quarries, some clay and gravel pits. Widespread flooding in 1993. Formed 1851. **4** county (□ 395 sq mi/1,023 sq km; 1990 pop. 43,586), E Ky.; ⊙ Prestonsburg; 37°33′N 82°45′W. In the Cumberland Mts.; drained by Levisa Fork and Beaver Creek. Bituminous-coal mining; oil and gas wells; some agr. (hay, corn; livestock). Dewey L. reservoir, on John's Creek, in N; Jenny Wiley State Resort Park on Dewey L. Formed 1799. **5** county (□ 992 sq mi/2,569 sq km; 1990 pop. 8,497), NW Texas, on Llano Estacado, with E-facing Caprock escarpment; ⊙ Floydada; 34°04′N 101°17′W. Elev. 2,800 ft/853 m–3,500 ft/1,067 m. Drained by White R. Agr. and livestock region; grain sorghum, corn, soybeans, sunflowers, pumpkins, cotton; cattle. Formed 1876. **6** county (□ 381 sq mi/987 sq km; 1990 pop. 12,005), SW Va.; ⊙ Floyd; 36°56′N 80°21′W. In the Blue Ridge; Blue Ridge Parkway follows E, SE boundary; drained by Little R., which forms part of NW boundary. Mfg. at Floyd; agr. (hay, alfalfa, corn, apples, peaches; cattle, sheep; dairying); arsenopyrite deposits. Formed 1831.

Floyd 1 town (1990 pop. 359), Floyd co., N Iowa, on Cedar R., and 5 mi/8 km NNW of Charles City; 43°07′N 92°44′W. Limestone quarries nearby. **2** town (1990 pop. 396), ⊙ Floyd co., SW Va., 33 mi/53 km SW of Roanoke, in Blue Ridge; 36°54′N 80°19′W. Mfg. (wine, textiles, apparel, lumber, meat processing); agr. (corn, apples; livestock; dairying); timber. Blue Ridge Parkway to SE.

Floyd, uninc. village (1990 pop. 117), Roosevelt co., E N.Mex., 14 mi/23 km WNW of Portales; 34°12′N 103°32′W. Livestock; grain, alfalfa, cotton, vegetables.

Floyd Bennett Field, park, SE N.Y., in SE Brooklyn borough of N.Y. city, on heavily polluted Jamaica Bay; 40°35′N 73°59′W. U.S. Coast Guard air station and U.S. Naval Reserve center. Formerly N.Y. city's 1st municipal airport. Named after flyer who 1st piloted Admiral Richard Byrd across North Pole in 1926. Part of the Gateway Natl. Recreation Area, 1,430 acres/579 ha of the park has been run by Natl. Park Service since 1972.

Floyd River, 92 mi/148 km long, NW Iowa; rises near Sanborn in O'Brien co., flows generally SW, past Sheldon and Le Mars, to the Missouri at Sioux City. West Branch of Floyd R. rises near Boyden, flows c.40 mi/64 km SW to Floyd R. near Merrill.

Floydada, town (1990 pop. 3,896), ⊙ Floyd co., NW Texas, on Llano Estacado, 40 mi/64 km NE of Lubbock, near White R.; 33°58′N 101°20′W. Elev. 3,179 ft/969 m. In agr. area (grain sorghum, corn, soybeans, sunflowers, pumpkins; cattle); light mfg. Settled c.1889, inc. 1909.

Floyds Fork, river, c.65 mi/105 km long, N Ky., rises in SW Henry co., flows SW to SE of Louisville, past Shepherdsville, in Fort Knox Military Reservation.

Floyds Knobs, village (1990 pop. 600), Floyd co., S Ind., suburb 3 mi/4.8 km NW of New Albany, in Louisville metropolitan area. Fruit; cattle, poultry. Mfg. (plastic prods.).

Flume, the, N.H.: see FRANCONIA NOTCH.

Flushing, city (1990 pop. 8,542), Genesee co., SE central Mich., 9 mi/14.5 km WNW of Flint and on Flint R.; 43°03′N 83°50′W. In agr. area (dairy prods.; grain, beans, apples); flour milling; light mfg. Indian mounds nearby. Settled 1833, inc. 1877.

Flushing 1 former village, now in N Queens borough of N.Y. city, SE N.Y.; 40°46′N 73°49′W. Although chiefly residential, Flushing gained importance as a trading and mfg. center. It was chartered (as Vlissingen) by the chartered Du. West India Company to Eng. settlers, who anglicized the name. It is the seat of Queens Col. of the City Univ. of N.Y. and the Queens Botanical Gardens. The Bowne House (1661) and the Quaker meetinghouse (c.1696) are landmarks of the colonial period. Flushing Meadow (now a park) was the site of 2 N.Y. World's Fairs (1939–1940, 1964–1965) and temporary hq. of the UN (1946–1949). Shea Stadium, home of the N.Y. Mets (baseball), is here; it is also the site of the U.S. Open (tennis) championships. N.Y. Hall of Science is here. It is now a major retailing center with a large Asian (Chinese, Korean, Indian) and Latino pop. Chartered 1645, inc. into Greater N.Y. city with Queens in 1898. **2** village (1990 pop. 1,042), Belmont co., E Ohio, 20 mi/32 km W of Wheeling, W.Va., and on small Wheeling Creek, in coal-mining area; 40°08′N 81°04′W.

Flushing Bay, shallow inlet of East R., SE N.Y., in NW shore of L.I., in Queens borough of N.Y. city, bet. Corona (W) and Flushing and Col. Point (E); c.1 mi/1.6 km wide at entrance, 2 mi/3.2 km long; 40°47′N 73°52′W. On W shore is N.Y. city municipal airport (La Guardia Field); on S shore is Flushing Meadow Park, scene of 1939–1940 and 1964–1965 World's Fairs, and later the temporary home of the UN.

Fluvanna (floo-VAN-uh), county (□ 290 sq mi/751 sq km; 1990 pop. 12,429), central Va.; ⊙ Palmyra; 37°50′N 78°16′W. Bounded S by James R.; drained by Rivanna R. and Hardware R. Agr. (especially tobacco, with hay, alfalfa, wheat, corn; cattle); some timber; slate quarrying. L. Monticello reservoir in NW. Formed 1777.

Fluvanna, uninc. village (1990 pop. 180), Scurry co., NW central Texas, 15 mi/24 km NW of Snyder. In agr., cattle-ranching area; dairying; wheat, pecans.

Flying Hills, uninc. town (1990 pop. 1,526), Berks co., SE central Pa., residential suburb 3 mi/4.8 km SSE of Reading, near Schuylkill R.; 40°16′N 75°54′W.

Flying Point Neck, peninsula in Casco Bay, SW Maine, near Freeport. Resort area.

Foam Lake, town (1991 pop. 1,359), SE central Sask., Canada, near Foam L. (3 mi/5 km long, 3 mi/5 km wide), 55 mi/89 km NW of Yorkton; 51°39′N 103°32′W. RR junction. Woodworking, furniture mfg., flour milling, dairying.

Foard, county (□ 707 sq mi/1,831 sq km; 1990 pop. 1,794), N Texas; ⊙ Crowell; 33°58′N 99°46′W. Bounded N in part by Pease R., S in part by Wichita R. Broken in W and SW (cattle ranches); agr. in E (wheat, cotton, alfalfa, hay). Oil, natural-gas wells; copper deposits. Formed 1891.

Fogelsville (FO-guhls-vil), uninc. town (1990 pop. 900), Lehigh co., E Pa., 9 mi/14.5 km E of Allentown; 40°34′N 75°37′W. Light mfg.; agr. includes dairying; livestock, poultry; apples, grain. Clover Hill Winery to S.

Foggy Bottom, area W of the White House in NW Wash., D.C., along the Potomac R. and Rock Creek; 38°54′N 77°03′W. Built on what was originally low, swampy land and so named because of the haze from industries along the Potomac. George Washington Univ., the Kennedy Center, and the Watergate Bldg. are located here, as well as office bldgs. for the U.S. Dept. of State, the Dept. of the Interior, and the Federal Reserve. The source of State Dept. policy-making is often referred to as "Foggy Bottom."

Fogo Island (FO-go) (□ c.100 sq mi/260 sq km), at the entrance to Notre Dame Bay, E N.F., Canada. It rises to 382 ft/116 m. The town of Fogo (1991 pop. 1,030) is a fishing port and tourist attraction.

Folcroft, borough (1990 pop. 7,506), Delaware co., SE Pa., suburb 8 mi/12.9 km SW of downtown Philadelphia, on Darby Creek; 39°53′N 75°16′W. Mfg. (chemicals, costume jewelry, food, machinery, textile prods.). Philadelphia Internatl. Airport to SE. John Heinz Natl. Wildlife Refuge to SE. Inc. 1927.

Foley 1 town (1990 pop. 4,937), Baldwin co., SW Ala., 35 mi/56 km S of Bay Minette; 30°24′N 87°40′W. Diversified mfg. Large factory-outlet center here. **2** town (1990 pop. 1,854), ⊙ Benton co., central Minn., 14 mi/23 km NE of St. Cloud, on Stony Brook; 45°39′N 93°54′W. Elev. 1,136 ft/346 m. Grain, soybeans; livestock; dairying; mfg. (plastic prods., cabinets, other light mfg.). **3** town (1990 pop. 209), Lincoln co., E Mo., near Mississippi R., 12 mi/19 km NE of Troy; 39°02′N 90°44′W.

Folkestone (FOLK-stuhn), Natl. Marine Park, protected reef just N of Holetown, Barbados. Popular among divers and snorkelers.

Folkston (FOKS-tuhn), town (1990 pop. 2,285), ⊙ Charlton co., SE Ga., 33 mi/53 km SE of Waycross, near St. Marys R. (forms Fla. state line here); 30°50′N 82°01′W. Gateway to Okefenokee Swamp. Suwanee Canal Recreation Area and Okefenokee Natl. Wildlife refuge. Diversified mfg.

Follansbee (FAH-luhnz-bee), town (1990 pop. 3,339), Brooke co., N W.Va., in N Panhandle, 6 mi/9.7 km S of Weirton; 40°20′N 80°35′W. On Ohio R. (bridged to Steubenville, Ohio, 2 mi/3.2 km N). Agr. (grain, apples); cattle; dairying. Coal mines, oil and gas wells. Mfg. (coated steel prods., coal tar). Inc. 1906.

Follett, village (1990 pop. 441), Lipscomb co., extreme N Texas, in the Panhandle, 45 mi/72 km W of Woodward, Okla.; 36°25′N 100°08′W. In wheat, cattle region.

Folly Beach, town (1990 pop. 1,398), Charleston co., SE S.C., 9 mi/14.5 km S of downtown Charleston on Atlantic Ocean; 32°40′N 79°55′W. Beach resort area.

Folly Island, Charleston co., SE S.C., one of Sea Isls., 8 mi/12.9 km S of Charleston, on the Atlantic; separated by Folly R. channel (W); c.6.5 mi/10.5 km long. Highway bridged to James Isl. and mainland (N). On SE shore is Folly Beach (resort); naval reservation is on NE end.

Area in square miles is shown by the symbol □ capital city or county seat by ⊙

Folly Lake, N N.S., Canada, 18 mi/29 km NW of Truro; 1½ mi/2 km long, ½ mi/1 km wide. Village of Folly L. is on W side. Popular year-round recreation area. Downhill and cross-country ski facilities to N.

Folsom, city (1990 pop. 29,802), Sacramento co., central Calif., a suburb 20 mi/32 km ENE of downtown Sacramento, and on American R.; 38°41′N 121°10′W. In general agr. and citrus-fruit area; nursery stock, grain; poultry; dairying. Mfg. (computer equip., electronic equip.). Seat of a state prison. Folsom Dam is to NE, forms Folsom L. reservoir State Recreation Area. First steam RR in Calif. was built from here to Sacramento in 1856. Founded 1855 on road to the goldfields; inc. 1946.

Folsom (FOL-suhm), uninc. town (1990 pop. 8,173), Delaware co., SE Pa., residential suburb 10 mi/16 km SW of Philadelphia; 39°53′N 75°19′W. Mfg. includes machinery, security systems, light mfg.

Folsom 1 (FUL-suhm), village (1990 pop. 469), St. Tammany parish, SE La., 10 mi/16 km N of Covington L.; 30°38′N 90°12′W. Ramsey State Wildlife Area to W. **2** village (1990 pop. 71), Union co., NE N.Mex., source of Cimarron R. (larger of 2 Cimarron rivers in region) to NW, near Colo. state line, 48 mi/77 km NNW of Clayton; 36°51′N 103°55′W. Elev. 6,400 ft/1,951 m. Shipping point for cattle and sheep. Capulin Volcano Mt. Natl. Monument is 6 mi/9.7 km SSW. Artifacts of Folsom culture have been found in vicinity.

Folsom (FOL-suhm), borough (1990 pop. 2,181), Atlantic co., S N.J., near Great Egg Harbor R., and 13 mi/21 km NNW of Mays Landing; 39°35′N 74°50′W.

Folsom Lake, Sacramento co., central Calif., at junction of North Fork and South Fork American rivers, at Folsom, 20 mi/32 km NE of Sacramento; 38°41′N 121°09′W. Extends NE; has 2 arms: North Fork (c.15 mi/24 km long) and South Fork. Max. capacity 1,000,000 acre-ft. Formed by Folsom Dam (268 ft/82 m), built by U.S. Army Corps of Engineers for irrigation, power production, and flood control. Surrounded by Folsom L. State Recreation Area.

Fomento (fo-MAIN-to), town, Sancti Spíritus prov., central Cuba, on RR, and 27 mi/43 km SE of Santa Clara; 22°03′N 79°43′W. Agr. center (sugarcane, tobacco, coffee, fruit; livestock). Ramón Ponciano sugar mill just S.

Fond du Lac, county (□ 765 sq mi/1,981 sq km; 1990 pop. 90,083), E Wis.; ☉ Fond du Lac; 43°45′N 88°29′W. Dairying and agr. area (barley, oats, wheat, soybeans, peas, alfalfa, hay; cattle, hogs, sheep). Diversified mfg. at Fond du Lac, Ripon, Waupun; also vegetable canning, processing of dairy prods. S part of L. Winnebago (resorts) is in NE co. Drained by Milwaukee, Rock, Sheboygan, and Fond du Lac rivers. N tip of Horicon Natl. Wildlife Refuge in SW; part of Kettle Morain State Forest (N unit) in SE. Formed 1836.

Fond du Lac (fawn doo LAK), city (1990 pop. 37,757), ☉ Fond du Lac co., E central Wis., in a resort region at the S end of L. Winnebago; 43°46′N 88°27′W. RR junction. Highly diversified mfg. The city's economy is based on dairy farming and the manufacture of machine tools, leather goods, engines, and auto parts. A Fr. fur-trading post in the late 18th cent., it later grew into a lumbering town. After the arrival of the RR, it became an industrial city. Marian Col.; Moraine Park Technical Col.; and the Univ. of Wis., Fond du Lac campus, are here. Inc. 1852.

Fond du Lac (FAHN duh lak), village, N Sask., Canada, near N.W.T. border, at E end of L. Athabaska; 59°19′N 107°10′W; Hudson's Bay Company trading post. In summer Hudson's Bay Company steamers connect it with Fort Chipewyan; here begins canoe route to Churchill R. via Wollaston and Reindeer lakes. Formerly important fur-trading center.

Fonda, town (1990 pop. 731), Pocahontas co., N central Iowa, on Cedar Creek, and 14 mi/23 km SW of Pocahontas; 42°34′N 94°50′W.

Fonda, village (1990 pop. 1,007), ☉ Montgomery co., E central N.Y., on Mohawk R., and the Barge Canal, and 10 mi/16 km W of Amsterdam; 42°57′N 74°22′W. Formally a freight transfer point on the N.Y. Central RR.

Mfg. of aluminum prods., apparel, and textiles. Inc. 1850.

Fond-des-Blancs (fong–dai–BLAWNG), town (1982 pop. 1,932), Sud dept., SW Haiti, on Jacmel Peninsula, 23 mi/37 km SW of Petit-Goâve; 18°17′N 73°08′W. Sisal growing.

Fond-des-Nègres (fong–dai–NE-gruh), village, Sud dept., SW Haiti, on Jacmel Peninsula, 23 mi/37 km SW of Petit-Goâve; 18°21′N 73°14′W. Coffee growing and processing; essential-oils distillery.

Fonde (FAHN-dee), village, Bell co., SE Ky., in the Cumberland Mts. at Tenn. state line, 10 mi/16 km W of Middlesboro. Bituminous coal.

Fond-Parisien (fong–pah-ree-ZYANG), village (1982 pop. 9,171), Ouest dept., S Haiti, on S shore of the Étang Saumâtre, 22 mi/35 km E of Port-au-Prince; 18°31′N 71°59′W. Sugarcane, fruit.

Fonds-Saint-Denis (fong-sang–duh-NEE), town, NW Martinique, 9 mi/14.5 km NNW of Fort-de-France. Rum distilling.

Fond-Verrettes (fong–ve-RET), village (1982 pop. 1,401), Ouest dept., SE Haiti, near Dominican border, 30 mi/48 km ESE of Port-au-Prince; 18°24′N 71°51′W. Coffee growing; bauxite deposits nearby.

Fontana, city (1990 pop. 87,535), San Bernardino co., S Calif., suburb 45 mi/72 km E of downtown Los Angeles and 10 mi/16 km W of San Bernardino, at the S foot of the San Bernardino Mts.; 34°06′N 117°28′W. Mfg. (fabricated metal prods., construction materials, transportation equip.); small steel mill. Mormons farmed on the site in the 1850s; in the early 20th cent. extensive citrus orchards were planted. During World War II the Kaiser (steel) mill was built (closed 1982 and main section shipped to China, 1994) and Fontana began its transformation from an agr. to an industrial community. The city has grown extensively along with the development of S Calif., and the pop. has increased fourfold since the 1970s. Speedway Rialo Municipal Airport to NE. San Bernardino Natl. Forest, including San Gabriel Mts., to N.; Glen Helen Regional State Park to NE. Inc. 1952.

Fontana (fawn-TA-nuh), town (1990 pop. 1,635), Walworth co., SE Wis., at W end of L. Geneva, 23 mi/37 km ESE of Janesville; 42°32′N 88°34′W. Mfg. (canvas prods.). Resort area. Full name: Fontana on Geneva L.

Fontana (fahn-TAN-uh), village (1990 pop. 131), Miami co., E Kansas, 10 mi/16 km S of Paola, near Marais des Cygnes R.; 38°25′N 94°50′W. In livestock-raising and general agr. region.

Fontanelle, town (1990 pop. 712), Adair co., SW Iowa, 6 mi/9.7 km W of Greenfield; 41°17′N 94°33′W. Grain; livestock; feed milling.

Fontenelle Reservoir (fahnt-uh-NEL), Lincoln and Sublette cos., SW Wyo., on Green R., 30 mi/48 km NE of Kemmerer; c.25 mi/40 km long; 42°01′N 110°03′W. Max. capacity of 405,000 acre-ft. Formed by Fontenelle Dam (121 ft/37 m high), built (1964) by the Bureau of Reclamation for water supply, flood control, and power generation.

Fonthill, village, S Ont., Canada, 5 mi/8 km NNW of Welland; 43°02′N 79°17′W. Dairying, fruit growing.

Foothill Farms, uninc. city (1990 pop. 17,135), Sacramento co., central Calif., residential suburb 10 mi/16 km NE of downtown Sacramento, on Arcake Creek; 38°41′N 121°21′W. McClellan Air Force Base to W. Agr. to N (fruit, nuts, grain; cattle).

Foothills, village, W Alta., Canada, in Rocky Mts., near Jasper Natl. Park, 40 mi/64 km SSW of Edson; 53°04′N 116°47′W. Coal mining; cattle.

Footville, village (1990 pop. 764), Rock co., S Wis., 9 mi/14.5 km W of Janesville; 42°40′N 89°12′W. Farm trade center. Mfg.

Forada (for-RAI-duh), village (1990 pop. 171), Douglas co., W Minn., 7 mi/11.3 km S of Alexandria, in lake region, on N end of Maple L.; 45°47′N 95°21′W. Grain; poultry; dairying.

Foraker (FOR-uh-kuhr), village (1990 pop. 25), Osage co., N Okla., 19 mi/31 km NW of Pawhuska; 36°52′N 96°34′W.

Foraker, Mount (FOR-uh-kuhr) (17,400 ft/5,304 m), S

central Alaska, in Alaska Range, in Mt. McKinley Natl. Park, 130 mi/209 km NNW of Anchorage; 62°57′N 151°27′W.

Forbes, village (1990 pop. 56), Dickey co., S N.Dak., 13 mi/21 km WSW of Ellendale, at S.Dak. state line; 45°56′N 98°00′W.

Forbes, Mount (11,902 ft/3,628 m), SW Alta., Canada, near B.C. border, in Rocky Mts., in Banff Natl. Park, 75 mi/121 km NW of Banff; 51°52′N 116°56′W.

Ford 1 county (□ 486 sq mi/1,259 sq km; 1990 pop. 14,275), E central Ill.; ☉ Paxton; 40°35′N 88°13′W. Agr. (corn, soybeans, wheat; livestock); mfg. (machinery, brooms and brushes). Drained by Mackinaw R., North Fork of the Vermilion, and a headstream of the Sangamon. Formed 1859 from territory left over when surrounding counties formed. Last of Illinois's 102 counties to organize. **2** county (□ 1,099 sq mi/2,846 sq km; 1990 pop. 27,463), SW Kansas; ☉ Dodge City; 37°41′N 99°52′W. Gently sloping prairie region, drained by Arkansas R. Wheat, sorghum, corn, soybeans, alfalfa, sugar beets; cattle; food processing. Formed 1873.

Ford, village (1990 pop. 247), Ford co., SW Kansas, on Arkansas R., and 16 mi/26 km ESE of Dodge City; 37°38′N 99°45′W. Grain; cattle.

Ford City, uninc. town (1990 pop. 3,781), Kern co., S central Calif., suburb 2 mi/3.2 km N of Taft and 28 mi/45 km SW of Bakersfield; 35°10′N 119°28′W. In oil fields; also, cattle; grain, cotton, fruit, nuts, sugar beets. Midway Sunset Oil Field to S; Naval Petroleum Reserve 1 and 2 to N. Buena Vista L. irrigation reservoir to E.

Ford City, borough (1990 pop. 3,413), Armstrong co., W central Pa., 4 mi/6.4 km S of Kittanning, on Allegheny R.; 40°46′N 79°31′W. Agr. area (corn, hay; livestock; dairying). Mfg. (machinery, wood prods.). Crooked Creek L. reservoir and park to SE. Laid out 1871, inc. 1889.

Ford City, uninc. community, Gentry co., NW Mo., 8 mi/12.9 km SSE of Stanberry; 40°06′N 94°27′W.

Ford Cliff, borough (1990 pop. 450), Armstrong co., W central Pa., suburb 1 mi/1.6 km S of Ford City and 5 mi/8 km S of Kittanning, near Allegheny R.; 40°45′N 79°32′W.

Ford Heights, village (1990 pop. 4,259), Cook co., NE Ill., residential suburb 25 mi/40 km S of downtown Chicago, 3 mi/4.8 km E of Chicago Hts.; 41°30′N 87°35′W.

Ford Island, S Oahu, Hawaii, in Pearl Harbor. Site of U.S. Luke Field (est. 1919); bombed by Japanese (Dec. 7, 1941).

Ford River, c.100 mi/161 km long, SW Upper Peninsula, Mich.; rises SE of Channing in Dickinson co., flows generally SE to Green Bay 6 mi/9.7 km SW of Escanaba at village of Ford River; 46°08′N 88°07′W.

Fordham, a W business dist. of the Bronx borough of N.Y. city, SE N.Y.; 40°51′N 73°54′W. Fordham Univ. is here.

Fordland, city (1990 pop. 523), Webster co., S central Mo., in the Ozarks, 20 mi/32 km E of Springfield; 37°09′N 92°56′W. Fruit; dairying; cattle; timber; state correctional center.

Fordoche (fo-DOSH), town (1990 pop. 869), Pointe Coupee parish, SE central La., 25 mi/40 km WNW of Baton Rouge; 30°36′N 91°37′W. In agr. area (cotton, rice, soybeans, sugarcane, vegetables; cattle); timber; oil and gas. Atchafalaya Natl. Wildlife Refuge and Sherburne State Wildlife Area to SW.

Fords, industrial village in Woodbridge township, Middlesex co., NE N.J., near Raritan R., 3 mi/4.8 km WNW of Perth Amboy; 40°32′N 74°18′W. Chemicals, plastics, metal prods., clothing.

Fords Prairie, uninc. town (1990 pop. 2,480), Lewis co., W Wash., suburb 2 mi/3.2 km NW of Centralia, on Chehalis R., at mouth of Skookunchuck R.; 46°45′N 123°00′W. RR junction. Dairying; poultry; vegetables.

Ford's Theatre Historic Site, Wash., D.C., authorized 1970. Site of President Abraham Lincoln's assassination. Includes the Lincoln Mus.

Fordson, Mich.: see DEARBORN.

Fordsville, village (1990 pop. 522), Ohio co., W Ky., 24 mi/39 km ESE of Owensboro; 37°38′N 86°43′W. Agr.

(tobacco, grain; cattle, hogs; timber); mfg. (lumber, apparel, furniture); coal area. Depot Mus.

Fordville, village (1990 pop. 299), Walsh co., NE N.Dak., 23 mi/37 km SW of Grafton and on Forest R.; 48°13′N 97°47′W. Vegetables, grain; poultry; dairy prods. RR junction to W.

Fordwick, locality, Augusta co., NW Va., on Little Calfpasture R., 17 mi/27 km WSW of Staunton, just E of Craigsville.

Fordyce (FOR-deis), town (1990 pop. 4,729), ⊙ Dallas co., S central Ark., 37 mi/60 km SW of Pine Bluff; 33°49′N 92°24′W. In agr. area (cattle, poultry; timber); mfg. of wood and paper prods., furniture.

Fordyce (FOR-dis), village (1990 pop. 190), Cedar co., NE Nebr., 7 mi/11.3 km NW of Hartington; 42°42′N 97°21′W.

Fore River, c.5 mi/8 km long, SW Maine, inlet of Casco Bay (with dredged channel) forming inner harbor and S boundary of Portland. Receives Stroudwater R.

Foreman, town (1990 pop. 1,267), Little River co., extreme SW Ark., 27 mi/43 km NW of Texarkana, near Okla. boundary; 33°43′N 94°24′W. In agr. area. Sawmilling; limestone quarry; mfg. (portland cement, wood prods.).

Forest 1 county (□ 431 sq mi/1,116 sq km; 1990 pop. 4,802), NW Pa.; ⊙ Tionesta; 41°31′N 79°14′W. Forested region. Much of co. (N and E) is in Allegheny Natl. Forest. Drained by Allegheny R. (NW), Clarion R. along part of S boundary, and Tionesta Creek in N and W (forming Tionesta L. reservoir in W center). Settled by Moravian missionaries. Corn, oats, hay, alfalfa; cattle; dairying; timber; sand and gravel. Parts of Cook Forest State Park and Clear Creek State Forest in S. Formed 1848. **2** county (□ 1,046 sq mi/2,709 sq km; 1990 pop. 8,776), NE Wis., bounded partly N by Brule R. (on Mich. state line); ⊙ Crandon; 45°40′N 88°46′W. Most of co. is in Nicolet Natl. Forest (N ½ and SE ¼), and contains Sugarbush Hill, highest point (1,951 ft/595 m) in state, and many resort lakes. Lumber; limited dairying; potatoes. Mule L. Indian Reservation in SW; Potawatomi Indian Reservation in SE. Sheltered Valley Ski Area in NW. Formed 1885.

Forest, town (1991 pop. 2,787), S Ont., Canada, 22 mi/35 km ENE of Sarnia; 43°06′N 82°00′W. Dairying; food processing; fruit, flax. Resort.

Forest 1 town (1990 pop. 5,060), central Miss., 45 mi/72 km W of Meridian; ⊙ Scott co.; 32°21′N 89°28′W. Near source of Leaf R., in Bienville Natl. Forest, with hq. here. Lumber; electronics, feeds, bakery goods; poultry processing. Bienville Pines Scenic Area to SE. **2** uninc. town, Bedford co., SW central Va., suburb 5 mi/8 km WSW of Lynchburg; 37°22′N 79°16′W. Diverse light mfg. Dairying; livestock; grain, tobacco.

Forest 1 village (1990 pop. 263), West Carroll parish, NE La., 12 mi/19 km W of L. Providence town; 32°48′N 91°25′W. Agr. and timber area. Bayou Macon State Wildlife Area to NE. **2** village (1990 pop. 1,594), Hardin co., W central Ohio, 12 mi/19 km NNE of Kenton; 40°48′N 83°31′W. In agr. area.

Forest Acres, town (1990 pop. 7,197), Richland co., central S.C., residential suburb 3 mi/4.8 km E of downtown Columbia; 34°01′N 80°58′W.

Forest City 1 city (1990 pop. 4,430), ⊙ Winnebago co., N Iowa, on Lime Creek, and 23 mi/37 km WNW of Mason City; 43°15′N 93°38′W. Transportation equip., fabricated metal prods.; food processing. Waldorf Col. here. Pilot Knob State Park to E. Plotted 1856, inc. 1879. **2** city (1990 pop. 380), Holt co., NW Mo., on Missouri R., and 23 mi/37 km NW of St. Joseph; 39°58′N 95°11′W. Corn, wheat, soybeans; hogs. Flooding occurred here in 1993.

Forest City 1 town (1990 pop. 10,638), Seminole co., central Fla., 10 mi/16 km NNW of Orlando. **2** town (1990 pop. 7,475), Rutherford co., SW N.C., 18 mi/29 km W of Shelby; 35°20′N 81°52′W. Cotton, grain, soybeans, sorghum; poultry, livestock. Light mfg. (plastics, textiles).

Forest City 1 village (1990 pop. 321), Mason co., central Ill., 25 mi/40 km SSW of Peoria; 40°22′N 89°49′W. In

agr. area (corn, wheat, soybeans). Sand Ridge State Forest to NW. **2** village, Wash. co., E Maine, on Grand L., and c.65 mi/105 km NNW of Machias. Township has hunting, fishing camps.

Forest City, borough (1990 pop. 1,846), Susquehanna co., NE Pa., 6 mi/9.7 km NNE of Carbondale, on West Branch of Lackawanna R. Agr. (hay, corn; dairying); light mfg. (apparel); anthracite coal. Carbondale-Clifford Airport 5 mi/8 km to W. Elk Mt. Ski Area to NW; Merli Sarnoski Park to SW; Moosic Mts. to E; Stillwater L. reservoir to N. Laid out 1871.

Forest Glen, residential village, Montgomery co., central Md., N suburb of Wash., D.C., on Rock Creek near D.C. border. Now best known as the site of Walter Reed Army Hosp., the community began as a summer resort on the Baltimore and Ohio RR in the late 19th cent.

Forest Grove, city (1990 pop. 13,559), Wash. co., NW Oregon, 22 mi/35 km W of Portland, on Gales Creek, near its confluence with Tualatin R.; 45°31′N 123°05′W. RR junction. Food processing, millwork, wood prods.; printing and publishing. Berries, nuts, grapes; poultry, sheep, hogs, cattle; dairying; wineries. Seat of Pacific Univ. Tillamook State Forest to W. Founded 1849.

Forest Heights, town (1990 pop. 2,859), Prince Georges co., central Md., S suburb of Wash., D.C., near the Potomac R.; 38°49′N 77°00′W. Part of an original grant to John Addison in 1667, the town was named by a real estate firm in 1941.

Forest Hill, city (1990 pop. 11,482), Tarrant co., N Texas, residential suburb 6 mi/9.7 km SE of downtown Fort Worth, near Village Creek; 32°39′N 97°16′W. L. Arlington reservoir to NE. Inc. after 1940.

Forest Hill, village (1990 pop. 408), Rapides parish, central La., 19 mi/31 km SW of Alexandria; 31°03′N 92°31′W. Timber; cotton, corn, rice, sugarcane; cattle; dairying. Cocodrie L. to SE. Kisatchie Natl. Forest to W, Alexander State Forest to N.

Forest Hills, city (1990 pop. 4,231), Davidson co., central Tenn., residential suburb 7 mi/11 km S of Nashville; 36°03′N 86°50′W. Radnor Lake State Natural Area is nearby. Inc. 1957.

Forest Hills, uninc. village (1990 pop. 454), Pike co., E Ky., residential suburb 3 mi/4.8 km SW of Williamson, W.Va., in Cumberland Mts.; 38°13′N 85°34′W. Bituminous coal.

Forest Hills, borough (1990 pop. 7,335), Allegheny co., SW Pa., residential suburb 7 mi/11.3 km E of Pittsburgh. Inc. 1920.

Forest Hills, a middle-income residential section of central Queens borough of N.Y. city, SE N.Y.; 40°46′N 73°51′W. Some light mfg. Within Forest Hills lies Forest Hills Gardens (□ 142 acres/57 ha), planned by Olmsted as an Eng. village, with a green, and developed 1910–1923. It contains the West Side Tennis Club (built in 1923), the scene of natl. and internatl. matches (including the U.S. Open tennis tournament, which was held here for many years until 1978, when it was moved to the National Tennis Center at Flushing Meadow, Queens).

Forest Hills, uninc. suburb (1990 pop. 16,690) of Grand Rapids (5 mi/8 km ESE), Kent co., SW Mich., near Grand R.; 42°57′N 85°29′W. Residential.

Forest Homes, uninc. village (1990 pop. 1,701), Madison co., SW Ill., residential suburb 20 mi/32 km NNE of St. Louis, 4 mi/6.4 km ENE of Alton, on Wood R.; 38°54′N 90°05′W.

Forest Junction, village, Calumet co., E Wis., 13 mi/21 km ESE of Appleton. Barley; cheese.

Forest Lake, town (1990 pop. 5,833), Washington co., E Minn., residential suburb 24 mi/39 km NNE of St. Paul, at W end of Forest L.; 45°16′N 92°59′W. Agr. area; light mfg. Forest Lake Airport to S. Carlos Avery Wildlife Area to NW.

Forest Lake, uninc. village (1990 pop. 1,371), Lake co., NE Ill., residential suburb 32 mi/51 km NW of Chicago, NE of Lake Zürich, on Forest L.; 42°12′N 88°02′W.

Forest Lake, Washington co., E Minn., 24 mi/39 km NNE of St. Paul; 4 mi/6.4 km long, max. 1 mi/1.6 km wide; 45°16′N 92°56′W. Recreational facilities. Town of Forest Lake at W end of lake.

Forest Oaks, uninc. town (1990 pop. 3,054), Guilford co., N central N.C., residential suburb 8 mi/12.9 km SSE of Greensboro; 35°59′N 79°42′W.

Forest Park, city (1990 pop. 16,925), Clayton co., NW Ga., a suburb of Atlanta; 33°37′N 84°22′W. Major warehouse and distribution center adjacent to Atlanta Hartsfield Internatl. Airport. Sheet metal fabrication, asphalt, concrete, aluminum containers, paper prods., hats, handbags, foods. An army depot and a large state farmers' market are here. Inc. 1908.

Forest Park 1 town (1990 pop. 780), Dawson co., E Mont., suburb 3 mi/4.8 km WSW of Glendive (across Yellowstone R.). RR junction. Grain, alfalfa, sugar beets, beans; livestock. Makoshika State Park to SE. **2** town (1990 pop. 1,249), Oklahoma co., central Okla., residential suburb 6 mi/9.7 km NE of Oklahoma City, near North Canadian R.; 35°30′N 97°27′W.

Forest Park, village (1990 pop. 14,918), Cook co., NE Ill., residential suburb 10 mi/16 km W of Chicago, on Des Plaines R.; 41°52′N 87°48′W. Mfg. (bronze prods., burial vaults, cranes, hoists, power presses).

Forest River, village (1990 pop. 148), Walsh co., NE N.Dak., 15 mi/24 km S of Grafton, and on Forest R.; 48°13′N 97°28′W. RR junction.

Forest River, 90 mi/145 km long, in NE N.Dak., rises in Walsh co., flows SE and E, past Minto, to Red R. of the North; 48°12′N 97°48′. L. Ardoch, below Minto, formed on S slough of river.

Forest View, village (1990 pop. 743), Cook co., NE Ill., W suburb of Chicago; 41°48′N 87°46′W.

Forestbrook, uninc. town (1990 pop. 2,502), Horry co., E S.C., residential community 6 mi/9.7 km NW of Myrtle Beach, and 7 mi/11.3 km SE of Conway, near Intracoastal Waterway; 33°43′N 78°58′W.

Forestburg, village (1991 pop. 920), S central Alta., Canada, 45 mi/72 km SE of Camrose; 52°35′N 112°04′W. Agr.

Forestdale, suburb (1990 pop. 10,395), Jefferson co., N central Ala., just NW of Birmingham.

Forestdale 1 Mass.: see SANDWICH. **2** R.I.: see NORTH SMITHFIELD.

Forester, village, Scott co., W Ark., c.45 mi/72 km ESE of Waldron, in Ouachita Natl. Forest. Sawmilling.

Foresthill, uninc. town (1990 pop. 1,409), Placer co., E central Calif., 13 mi/21 km ENE of Auburn, near Middle Fork American R.; 39°00′N 120°50′W. Tahoe Natl. Forest to NE; El Dorado Natl. Forest to S. Timber; cattle.

Foreston 1 village (1990 pop. 354), Mille Lacs co., central Minn., 3 mi/4.8 km WSW of Milaca, on West Branch of Rum R.; 45°43′N 93°42′W. Poultry; grain; dairying; mfg. (cabinet components). **2** uninc. village, Clarendon co., E central S.C., 26 mi/42 km SE of Sumter.

Forestville, uninc. town (1990 pop. 2,443), Sonoma co., W Calif., 10 mi/16 km WNW of Santa Rosa, near Russian R.; 38°29′N 122°54′W. Apples, grapes, grain; dairying; poultry, sheep. RR terminus. Food processing.

Forestville 1 village, Hartford co., Conn. A postal branch of Bristol. **2** village (1990 pop. 153), Sanilac co., E Mich., 21 mi/34 km SE of Bad Axe, on L. Huron; 43°39′N 82°36′W. Resort, tourism. **3** village (1990 pop. 738), Chautauqua co., extreme W N.Y., 8 mi/12.9 km E of Dunkirk; 42°28′N 79°10′W. **4** uninc. village (1990 pop. 9,185), Hamilton co., extreme SW Ohio, suburb 8 mi/13 km E of Cincinnati, and c.2 mi/3 km W of U.S. Interstate 275; 39°04′N 84°20′W. **5** uninc. village, Cass township, Schuylkill co., E central Pa., 6 mi/9.7 km W of Pottsville; 40°41′N 76°18′W. **6** village, Door co., NE Wis., on Door Peninsula and on Ahnapee R., 11 mi/18 km SSW of Sturgeon Bay; 44°41′N 87°28′W. In dairying and fruit-growing area. Mfg. (dehydrated cherries, cranberries). On Ahnapee State Trail.

Forgan (FOR-guhn), village (1990 pop. 489), Beaver co., E Okla. Panhandle, 6 mi/9.7 km N of Beaver; 36°54′N 100°32′W. In grain and livestock area. Beaver State Park to S.

Forge Village, Mass.: see WESTFORD.

Forillon National Park (□ 92 sq mi/238 sq km), at the tip of Forillon Peninsula, SE Que., Canada, near Gaspé. Scenic coastal landscape on the Gulf of St. Lawrence. Est. 1970.

Foristell (FAHR-is-tuhl), village (1990 pop. 144), St. Charles co., E Mo., 12 mi/19 km W of O'Fallon; 38°49'N 90°58'W. Commercial highway services. Agr. area; mfg. (corrugated cartons, machining).

Fork Shoals, village, Greenville co., NW S.C., on Reedy R., and 16 mi/26 km S of Greenville. Poultry, livestock; grain, peaches.

Fork Union, uninc. village, Fluvanna co., central Va., 22 mi/35 km SE of Charlottesville. Mfg. (furniture); agr. (tobacco, grain; cattle). Military academy.

Forked Deer River (FOOR-ked DIR), W Tenn., formed 4 mi/6 km SW of Dyersburg by junction of North and South forks; flows c.10 mi/16 km SW to Obion R. near its mouth on the Mississippi. South Fork rises in McNairy co., flows c.100 mi/161 km NW past Jackson, to join North Fork, which rises in Carroll co. and flows c.50 mi/80 km W past Trenton and Dyersburg; receives Middle Fork (c.60 mi/97 km long).

Forked Lake (□ c.2 sq mi/5.2 sq km), Hamilton co., NE central N.Y., on Raquette R., 35 mi/56 km SW of Saranac Lake, in the Adirondack Mts., in Adirondack Park; 44°23'N 74°35'W. Near Raquette (SW), Long (NE), and Little Fork (N) lakes.

Forked River, resort village (1990 pop. 4,243), Ocean co., E N.J., near Barnegat Bay, 8 mi/12.9 km S of Toms River village, and on small Forked R. (navigable to village); 39°48'N 74°09'W. Fishing. State marina.

Forks, town (1990 pop. 2,862), Clallam co., NW Wash., near Sol Duc (Soleduck) R., Calawah R., and Pacific coast, c.45 mi/72 km WSW of Port Angeles; 47°57'N 124°23'W. Printing; cedar prods.; logging. Forks Timber Mus. Bogachiel State Park to S; part of Olympic Natl. Forest to E; Olympic Natl. Park to SE, coastal section of park to W. Inc. after 1940.

Forksville, borough (1990 pop. 160), Sullivan co., NE Pa., 30 mi/48 km NE of Williamsport, on Loyalsock Creek. Lumber; wood prods. Worlds End State Park to SE; parts of Wyoming State Forest to S and W.

Forman, village (1990 pop. 586), ⊙ Sargent co., SE N.Dak., 24 mi/39 km W of Lidgerwood; 46°06'N 97°38'W. Wahneton (Sisseton) Indian Reservation nearby.

Formoso (for-MO-suh), village (1990 pop. 128), Jewell co., N Kansas, 14 mi/23 km E of Mankato; 39°46'N 97°59'W. In grain and livestock area.

Forney, town (1990 pop. 4,070), Kaufman co., NE Texas, 17 mi/27 km E of Dallas, near E Fork Trinity R., just below (S) of L. Ray Hubbard dam; 32°45'N 96°28'W. In agr. area (cotton, peaches, corn, nurseries; cattle). Mfg. (corrugated paper, furniture, fishing tackle). Settled 1872, inc. 1910.

Forney Dam, Texas: see RAY HUBBARD, LAKE.

Forrest, county (□ 470 sq mi/1,217 sq km; 1990 pop. 68,314), SE Miss.; ⊙ Hattiesburg; 31°11'N 89°15'W. Drained by Leaf and Bowie rivers, Black and Tallahala creeks. Agr. (cotton, corn, poultry; timber); sand and gravel; oil and natural gas. Diverse mfg. at Hattiesburg. Most of S ½ of co. is in De Soto Natl. Forest; Paul B. Johnson State Park and Camp Shelby Natl. Guard base in center. Formed 1908.

Forrest, village (1990 pop. 1,124), Livingston co., E central Ill., 14 mi/23 km SE of Pontiac; 40°45'N 88°24'W. In agr. area.

Forrest City, city (1990 pop. 13,364), ⊙ St. Francis co., E central Ark., at the E edge of Crowley's Ridge; 35°00'N 90°47'W. It is a RR and trade center in an agr. (cotton, rice, vegetables, peaches) area. Diversified mfg. (machinery, agr. equip., televisions, metal fabrications, hunting accessories). East Ark. Community Col. Village Creek State Park to N. Inc. 1871.

Forrester Island (5 mi/8 km long, 1 mi/1.6 km wide), SE Alaska, in Alexander Archipelago, off SW Prince of Wales Isl., 50 mi/80 km SSW of Craig; 54°48'N 133°32'W.

Forreston, village (1990 pop. 1,361), Ogle co., N Ill., 15 mi/24 km WNW of Oregon; 42°07'N 89°34'W. In rich agr. area.

Forrestville, town (1991 pop. 3,946), E Que., Canada, on the St. Lawrence, at mouth of Sault au Cochon R., and 32 mi/51 km NW of Rimouski; 48°44'N 69°04'W. Lumbering, pulp milling, dairying.

Forsyth 1 (for-SEITH), county (□ 243 sq mi/629 sq km; 1990 pop. 44,083), N Ga., ⊙ Cumming; 34°13'N 84°08'W. Bounded E by Chattahoochee R. Agr. in the Piedmont region in decline. **2** (FOR-seith), county (□ 412 sq mi/1,067 sq km; 1990 pop. 265,878), N central N.C.; ⊙ Winston-Salem; 36°07'N 80°15'W. In the Piedmont; bounded W by Yadkin R. Agr. area (tobacco, corn, hay, wheat, oats; cattle); timber (pine, oak). Mfg. at Winston-Salem and Kernersville. Tanglewood Park in SW corner. County urbanized in center around Winston-Salem and in E. Formed 1849.

Forsyth 1 (for-SEITH), town (1990 pop. 4,268), ⊙ Monroe co., central Ga., 22 mi/35 km NW of Macon; 33°02'N 83°56'W. Textiles, yarn, computer hardware; wood chips, lumber. Bessie Tift Col. here. Piedmont Natl. wildlife refuge nearby. Inc. 1822. **2** (FOR-seith), town (1990 pop. 1,175), ⊙ Taney co., S Mo., in the Ozarks, 8 mi/12.9 km NE of Branson; 36°41'N 93°06'W. Resort area; fishing, boating. Mfg. (apparel, food supplements); tourism; retirement communities. Ozark Beach Dam on White R. impounds L. Taneycomo. **3** town (1990 pop. 2,178), ⊙ Rosebud co., SE central Mont., on Yellowstone R., and 43 mi/69 km WSW of Miles City; 46°16'N 106°41'W. Junction of RR spur to Colstrip to W. Cattle, sheep, hogs; wheat, barley, oats, alfalfa, sugar beets, beans. North Cheyenne Indian Reservation to S. Colstrip coal mine to S. Inc. 1904.

Forsyth, village (1990 pop. 1,275), Macon co., central Ill., suburb 4 mi/6.4 km N of Decatur; 39°55'N 88°57'W. Corn, soybeans; mfg. (farm chemicals).

Fort Abercrombie (AB-uhr-krahm-bee), U.S. Army post on the west bank of the Red R., 14 mi/23 km NNW of Wahpeton, at Abercrombie, N.Dak. Built to protect settlers in the Red R. Valley from attacks by the Dakotas (Sioux), the fort played an important role in opening the Dakota Territory to settlement. It was twice attacked unsuccessfully by the Sioux in 1862. With the signing of a treaty with the Ojibwa and the Sioux here in 1870, the fear of Indians declined and the fort was abandoned in 1877. Part of the former installation is now a state historical site. Est. 1857.

Fort Adams, village, Wilkinson co., SW Miss., near the Mississippi R., at mouth of Buffalo R., 33 mi/53 km SSW of Natchez. Here were Fr. mission (1698) and old Fort Adams (built 1798; traces remain). Large Creek Nature Area to SE.

Fort Albany, fur-trading post, N Ont., Canada, at the mouth of the Albany R. on James Bay. It was founded (before 1682) by the Hudson's Bay Company as one of its earliest forts. In the Anglo-Fr. struggle for the Hudson Bay trade, Fort Albany was taken by the French in 1686. It was recaptured by the British in 1693 and from 1697 to 1713 was the only post of the region in the Brit. company's possession. It has continued as an important fur-trading post.

Fort Ann, village (1990 pop. 419), Washington co., E N.Y., on Champlain division of the N.Y. State Barge Canal and 11 mi/18 km NE of Glens Falls; 43°24'N 73°29'W.

Fort Anne National Historic Park, Canada: see ANNAPOLIS ROYAL.

Fort Apache, uninc. town, Navajo co., E central Ariz., 50 mi/80 km NE of Globe, in Fort Apache Indian Reservation, on White R. Cattle, sheep, hogs; corn, alfalfa. Trading post, school. Est. 1870 as military post. Kinishba Ruins to W.

Fort Ashby, uninc. town (1990 pop. 1,288), Mineral co., NE W.Va., 9 mi/14.5 km S of Cumberland, Md., on Patterson Creek, in Allegheny Mts.; 39°30'N 78°46'W. Grain, tobacco; livestock, poultry. Springfield Wildlife Management Area to SE.

Fort Atkinson, city (1990 pop. 10,227), Jefferson co., S Wis., on both banks of Rock R., near confluence of Bark R., and 30 mi/48 km ESE of Madison; 42°55'N 88°50'W. Trade and shipping center for surrounding dairying area; food processing; light mfg. L. Koshkonong is SW. William D. Hoard began the *Hoard's Dairyman* publication here (1885). Indian mounds here. Settled c.1836, inc. 1878.

Fort Atkinson, town (1990 pop. 367), Winneshiek co., NE Iowa, on Turkey R., and 13 mi/21 km SW of Decorah; 43°08'N 91°55'W. Fort Atkinson State Preserve to W, built 1840 and partly restored.

Fort Beauséjour (bo-sai-ZHOOR), N.B., Canada, near Amherst (N.S.); 45°53'N 64°10'W. Built by the French bet. 1751 and 1755 to command Chignecto isthmus bet. N.S. and N.B., it was captured (1755) by Brit. and Amer. troops and renamed Fort Cumberland. Since 1926 the site of Fort Beauséjour Natl. Historic Park.

Fort Belknap Agency or **Fort Belknap**, village (1990 pop. 422), Blaine co., N Mont., in N part of Fort Belknap Indian Reservation (1990 pop. 2,508), 41 mi/66 km E of Havre and 3 mi/4.8 km SSE of Harlem, on Milk R.; 48°29'N 108°46'W. Sheep, cattle, grain, alfalfa, beans. Hqs. of reservation of Gros Ventre and Assiniboine nations. St. Paul's Mission is here.

Fort Bend, county (□ 886 sq mi/2,295 sq km; 1990 pop. 225,421), SE Texas; ⊙ Richmond; 29°31'N 95°46'W. SE extensions of city of Houston on NE boundary, fringe of urbanized area. Drained by Brazos (forms SE and NW boundaries) and San Bernard (forms SW boundary) rivers. Large oil, natural-gas, sulphur production; agr. (cotton, rice, corn, vegetables, soybeans, sorghum, nurseries); livestock (cattle, poultry). Formed 1837.

Fort Benning Military Reservation, U.S. Army post (□ 295 sq mi/764 sq km), W Ga., S of Columbus. One of the largest army posts in the U.S., it is the nation's largest infantry training center and the home of the Army Infantry School. Natl. Infantry Mus.; remains of old Federal Road crossing of the Chattahooche R., major route bet. New Orleans and Charleston. Est. 1918.

Fort Benton, town (1990 pop. 1,660), ⊙ Chouteau co., N central Mont., on Missouri R., and 35 mi/56 km NE of Great Falls; at upstream (W) end of Upper Missouri Natl. Wild and Scenic River (Missouri R. Breaks); 47°50'N 110°40'W. Trade center in grain and livestock region; tourism. First reached by steamboat in 1860. Important disembarkation point, and head of the Mullan Road. It was supply point for gold prospectors and cattlemen; served during Indian wars (after 1870) as military outpost. Old Fort Benton (1850–1887). Parts of trading post and blockhouse survive. Mus. of the Northern Great Plains, Mus. of the Upper Missouri, and the Wild and Scenic Upper Missouri Visitor's Center here. Founded as fur-trading post 1846, laid out 1865, inc. 1883.

Fort Bidwell, uninc. village, Modoc co., NE Calif., in Surprise Valley, 32 mi/51 km NE of Alturas. Nev. state line 6 mi/9.7 km E, Oregon state line 10 mi/16 km N. Fort Bidwell Indian Reservation, Warner Mts., and Modoc Natl. Forest to W; Upper Alkali L. (dry) to S.

Fort Bliss Military Reservation, U.S. Army post (□ 1,754 sq mi/4,543 sq km), extreme W Texas and S N.Mex., from just NE of downtown El Paso, Texas, extends NE c.70 mi/113 km into El Paso co., Texas, and Otero co., N.Mex.; in N.Mex. it extends almost to Rio Grande; 31°48'N 106°25'W. It includes Organ Mts. in N.Mex. and part of Hueco Mts. in Texas and N.Mex. Named for Col. William Bliss, Gen. Zachary Taylor's adjutant in the Mexican War. Originally strategically located near the only ice-free pass through the Rocky Mts., it guarded the U.S.-Mex. border and protected westbound gold seekers from hostile Indians; task forces against Cochise and Geronimo were based here. The fort's location has changed several times as a result of flooding; its present site, on a mesa, was est. 1890. In 1916, post commander Gen. John J. Pershing led an unsuccessful expedition into Mexico to catch the bandit Francisco (Pancho) Villa. Fort Bliss is now the Army Air Defense Center, training missile, artillery, and air-defense units. Hueco Tanks State Park, Texas, is located in SE part. Biggs Army Airfield is in SW part; has several museums. Est. 1849.

Fort Bowie National Historic Site (□ 1 sq mi/2.6 sq km), Cochise co., SE Ariz., in Chiricahua Mts., NW of Chiricahua Natl. Monument, 24 mi/39 km ESE of Willcox. Ruins of a fort (est. 1862) that was the base of military operations against Geronimo and his Apache followers. Authorized 1964.

Fort Bragg, city (1990 pop. 6,078), Mendocino co., NW Calif., on coast, c.140 mi/225 km NNW of San Francisco; 39°27′N 123°48′W. Fruit; cattle; logging. Named for army post (est. 1857) formerly here. Jackson State Forest to SE; Site of Mackerricher State Park.

Fort Bragg Military Reservation, U.S. Army base (□ 17.4 sq mi/45.1 sq km; 1990 pop. 34,744), Hoke and Cumberland cos., S central N.C., N of Fayetteville; 35°08′N 79°00′W. Bounded N by Little R. Originally an artillery post, it is now the principal U.S. army airborne-training center and the site of the Special Warfare School. Pope Air Force Base is in NE part of base; 82d Airborne Div. War Memorial Mus., history of first Airborne division. Est. 1918.

Fort Branch, town (1990 pop. 2,447), Gibson co., SW Ind., 6 mi/9.7 km S of Princeton; 38°15′N 87°34′W. RR junction. In agr. area; mfg. (concrete blocks, beef and pork processing).

Fort Branch, village (1990 pop. 100), Logan co., SW W.Va., 3 mi/4.8 km E of Logan, in coal-mining area.

Fort Bridger, village, Uinta co., SW Wyo., on Blacks Fork R., and 30 mi/48 km E of Evanston; elev. 6,657 ft/2,029 m. Fort Bridger State Historic Site (35 acres/14 ha) here. An important supply post on the Oregon Trail, fort was est. (1843) by Jim Bridger, famous guide and trader; held by Mormons 1853–1857. Later leased by Bridger to U.S. and used as fort until 1890. Some of the original bldgs. still survive.

Fort Bridger State Historic Site, Wyo.: see FORT BRIDGER.

Fort Calhoun, village (1990 pop. 648), Washington co., E Nebr., 9 mi/14.5 km SE of Blair, on Missouri R.; 41°27′N 96°01′W. Trade center for grain, livestock region. Mfg. (industrial precision prods., formed foil containers, plastic packaging). Stone monument in village park commemorates council held by Lewis and Clark with Native Americans. DeSoto Bend Natl. Wildlife Refuge to N (across Missouri R.) includes Oxbow Lake and former river bend (on Iowa side) belonging to Nebr. Fort Atkinson to E. Flooding occurred in area in 1993.

Fort Calhoun Nuclear Power Plant, Nebr.: see WASHINGTON county.

Fort Campbell Military Reservatioin, Ky. and Tenn.: see HOPKINSVILLE.

Fort Caswell, N.C.: see CASWELL BEACH.

Fort Chimo (shee-MO), village, N Que., Canada, on Koksoak R., near its mouth on Ungava Bay; 58°09′N 68°18′W. A Hudson's Bay Company post est. 1830. In region are rich iron deposits.

Fort Chipewyan (chip-uh-WEI-uhn), trading post, NE Alta., Canada, at the west end of L. Athabasca. The old Fort Chipewyan, on the south shore, was built for the North West Company at the urging of Alexander Mackenzie in 1788. It formed the base from which he set out on his expedition (1789) down the Mackenzie R. to the Arctic Ocean and in 1792 across the mountains to the Pacific Ocean. The present post, built in 1804 on the north shore, was taken over by the Hudson's Bay Company in 1821.

Fort Clark Springs, uninc. town (1990 pop. 1,070), Kinney co., SW Texas, 27 mi/43 km E of Del Rio. Resort and retirement community. Site of Fort Clark (1852–1944).

Fort Clatsop Historic Site (KLAT-suhp) (□ 125 sq mi/324 sq km), Clatsop co., NW Oregon, 4 mi/6.4 km SW of Astoria. Site of the winter encampment of the Lewis and Clark Expedition, 1805–1806. Authorized 1958.

Fort Cobb, village (1990 pop. 663), Caddo co., W central Okla., 11 mi/18 km W of Anadarko, and on Washita R.; 35°06′N 98°26′W. In farming area; mfg. (crushed limestone, fishing lights, canned fruits and vegetables, bottled drinks). Fort Cobb L. reservoir and Fort Cobb State Park to N.

Fort Cobb Lake, reservoir, Caddo co., W central Okla., on Pond Creek, 12 mi/19 km NW of Anadarko; 8 mi/12.9 km long; 35°09′N 98°25′W. Max. capacity 292,500 acre-ft. Formed by Fort Cobb Dam (95 ft/29 m high), built by the U.S. govt. for irrigation, flood control, and water supply. Fort Cobb State Park on E shore.

Fort Collins, city (1990 pop. 87,758), ⊙ Larimer co., N Colo., 60 mi/97 km NNW of Denver and 37 mi/60 km SSW of Cheyenne, Wyo., on the Cache la Poudre R., at the foot of the Rocky Mts.; 40°33′N 105°04′W. Elev. 4,984 ft/1,519 m. RR junction. It is a trading, shipping, and processing center of a rich agr. area (grain, sugar beets; lamb, sheep, cattle). Diversified mfg.; tourism. Colorado State Univ. Fort Collins Mus. Lory State Park and Horsetooth Reservoir to W; Picnic Rock State Park to NW; Boyd Lake State Park to SE; Roosevelt Natl. Forest and Rocky Mt. Natl. Park to W. Several dams nearby. Downtown Airpark to NE. The area was settled in 1864 around a fortification built to protect a strategic trading post; the city itself was named for the military commander there. Inc. as a city 1883.

Fort Collinson, trading post, W Victoria Isl., SW Franklin dist., N.W.T., Canada, on Walker Bay, inlet of Prince of Wales Strait; 71°35′N 117°49′W. At present unoccupied.

Fort Conger, locality, NE Ellesmere Isl., NE Franklin dist., N.W.T., Canada, on Robeson Channel, opposite Greenland coast, at mouth of Lady Franklin Bay; 81°43′N 64°43′W. Site of meteorological station est. 1881–1883 by A. W. Greely.

Fort Coulonge (koo-LOHZH), village (1991 pop. 1,647), SW Que., Canada, on Ottawa R. at mouth of Coulonge R., and 18 mi. E of Pembroke; 45°51′N 76°45′W. Dairying; cattle raising. Founded 1680 as fur-trading post.

Fort Covington, village (1990 pop. 1,200), Franklin co., N N.Y., on Salmon R., at Que. border, and 14 mi/23 km NW of Malone; 44°57′N 74°29′W. Port of entry.

Fort Davis, uninc. town (1990 pop. 1,212), ⊙ Jeff Davis co., extreme W Texas, in Davis Mts., 20 mi/32 km SSW of Marfa. Elev. 5,050 ft/1,539 m. Tourist center in cattle-ranching area. Goats, hogs; dairying; cotton, melons, corn, wheat; mfg. (rubber stamps). Nearby are ruins of old Fort Davis (frontier post 1854–1891), Davis Mts. State Park (recreation area) to W, and McDonald Observatory on Mt. Locke (10 mi/16 km NW). Fort Davis Natl. Historic Site is here.

Fort Davis National Historic Site, at town of Fort Davis, Jeff Davis co., W Texas. Key post in the defensive system of W Texas, guarding (1854–1891) the San Antonio–El Paso road through the Davis Mts., only ice-free passage through Rocky Mts. in U.S. Authorized 1961, est. 1963.

Fort de Chartres State Historic Site, Ill.: see PRAIRIE DU ROCHER.

Fort Dearborn, former U.S. Army post on the Chicago R., NE Ill. Est. 1803 and named for Secretary of War Henry Dearborn; 41°59′N 87°51′W. Threatened at the start of the War of 1812, the frontier post was ordered by Gen. William Hull to evacuate. On Aug. 15, 1812, as Capt. Nathan Heald led the small contingent of troops, militia, women, and children from the fort, a large Native Amer. force attacked. More than ½ of the people were killed and most of those remaining were taken prisoner; the fort was destroyed. Fort Dearborn was rebuilt in 1816–1817, and later abandoned.

Fort Defiance, uninc. town, Apache co., E Ariz., on Black Creek, in Navajo Indian Reservation, near N.Mex. line, 25 mi/40 km NW of Gallup, N.Mex. Former military post. Cattle, sheep; crafts. Natural bridge to W; Red L., on state boundary, to N.

Fort Defiance, uninc. village, Augusta co., NW Va., 7 mi/11.3 km NNE of Staunton. Military acad.

Fort Deposit, town (1990 pop. 1,240), Lowndes co., S central Ala., 14 mi/23 km S of Hayneville, in the Black Belt. Clothing, aircraft electrical components; pecan processing; lumber. Grew around fort built here c.1813 by Andrew Jackson.

Fort Dix, formerly U.S. Army training center (□ 142 sq mi/368 sq km), central N.J., 20 mi/32 km SE of Trenton, spanning from Lakehurst in the E to Juliustown in the W in the Pine Barrens of N.J.; est. 1917 as Camp Dix and named for U.S. statesman John A. Dix. In 1939, it was made a permanent garrison and renamed Fort Dix. During World War II, Fort Dix was the largest army-training center in the country. Converted in 1992 into minor military training center. Now houses federal and state prisoners. McGuire Air Force Base, adjacent to the fort, is a main East Coast terminal for domestic and European military flights.

Fort Dodge, city (1990 pop. 25,894), seat of Webster co., central Iowa, on the Des Moines R.; 42°30′N 94°10′W. Fort Clarke was built on the site in 1850 and renamed Fort Dodge the following year. In a gypsum-mining and agr. area. Fort Dodge is a RR junction and distributing center. Meat packing; farm equip., fertilizers, feeds, gypsum prods., construction equip., veterinary pharmaceuticals. Gypsum mills in city, and extensive gypsum beds in region. Iowa Central Community Col.; Blandon Art Gall.; Fort Dodge Historical Mus. Dolliver Memorial and Brush Creek State Parks to SE. Widespread field and river flooding occurred in this region in 1993. Settled c.1846; inc. 1869.

Fort Donelson, historic site, on the Cumberland R., at Dover, Tenn., Confederate fortification in the Civil War, commanding the river approach to Nashville. After capturing Fort Henry on the Tennessee R. (Feb. 6, 1862), Gen. Ulysses S. Grant, on Feb. 12, marched his men 12 mi/19 km to Fort Donelson, which he proceeded to invade. Although assisted by gunboats, his army was repulsed by the Confederates. The Confederates were thrown back by the Union forces on the next day, after attempting to retreat. The fort fell on Feb. 16, opening the way for the advance on Nashville. Fort Donelson Natl. Military Park and Natl. Cemetery are here.

Fort Dorchester, historic site on Ashley R., S S.C., in Dorchester co., 26 mi/42 km from Charleston. Tabby ruins mark the site of Dorchester town, est. 1697, and named after Dorchester, Mass. Town lasted for nearly 50 years and all materials from the town, except the fort, were removed.

Fort Drum, military installation (□ 168 sq mi/435 sq km; 1990 pop. 11,578), Jefferson co., N N.Y., 7 mi/11 km NE of Watertown; 44°02′N 75°46′W. The largest in N.Y. state, it was opened in 1908 as Pine Camp, a training ground (16 sq mi/41 sq km) along Black R., near the villages of Felts Mills, Great Bend, and Black River. Its 1st commander was Brig. Gen. Frederick D. Grant, son of Gen. Ulysses S. Grant; the base came to natl. attention in 1935, when the largest peacetime maneuvers (involving 36,500 soldiers), took place here. It grew considerably with the construction of 800 bldgs. during World War II. Gen. George Patton's Fourth Armored Division trained here; the base was also a prisoner-of-war camp. In 1951 it was renamed Camp Drum, after Lt. Gen. Hugh A. Drum, who commanded the First Army in World War II; in 1974, it was again renamed (as Fort Drum). The base was expanded to accommodate the reactivated Tenth Mt. (Light Infantry) Division; 130 new bldgs. were put up bet. 1986 and 1992.

Fort Duchesne (doo-SHAYN), uninc. village (1990 pop. 655), Uintah co., NE Utah, 20 mi/32 km SW of Vernal on Whitewater R.; 40°16′N 109°52′W. Sheep, cattle; oil, natural gas. Hq. for Uinta and Ouray reservations, in S extension of Unitah and Ouray Indian Reservation. Bottle Hollow Reservoir to W; Whiterocks State Fish Hatchery to N.

Fort Duquesne (DOO-kain), historic site, in Point State Park, downtown Pittsburgh, Allegheny co., W Pa., at the confluence of the Monongahela and Allegheny rivers, which form Ohio R.; 40°26′N 80°00′W. Because of its strategic location, it was a major objective in the last of the Fr. and Indian Wars. The fort was begun by a group of Virginians in 1754 at the insistence of Gov. Robert Dinwiddie. The French drove the Virginians away on April 17, 1754, and completed the fort; they named it after the Marquis de Duquesne, governor general of New France. George Washington's Va. militia had failed to reach the fort before the arrival of the French. Fort Duquesne was also the goal of an unsuccessful expedition under Eng. Gen. Edward Braddock in 1755. On Nov. 24, 1758, the French abandoned their position without a fight to advancing Br. troops led by Gen. John Forbes, and retreated N after burning Fort Duquesne. The English rebuilt it and renamed it Fort Pitt, around which Pittsburgh grew.

Fort Duvernette, islet, Young Isl., St. Vincent and the Grenadines, West Indies, off S pt. of Young Isl; 13°08′N 61°13′W. High rocky Br. fortress and historic monument. Uninhabited.

Fort Edward, village (□ 1 sq mi/2.6 sq km; 1990 pop. 3,561), Washington co., E N.Y., on the Hudson R. at its junction with Champlain division of the Barge Canal, and 2 mi/3.2 km S of Hudson Falls; 43°16′N 73°34′W. Paper milling; light mfg. Fort built here in 1755 to protect portage bet. the Hudson R. and L. Champlain; it was occupied by Burgoyne in 1777. Inc. 1849.

Fort Erie, town (1990 est. pop. 23,253), S Ont., Canada, on the Niagara R., opposite Buffalo, N.Y.; 42°54′N 78°56′W. A number of branch factories of U.S. firms are here. Connected to the U.S. by Peace and RR bridges. Lumber; steel; auto parts. Fort Erie was built in 1764 and was taken from the British in the War of 1812. In Aug. 1814, the Americans withstood a siege by a superior Br. force but afterward blew up and abandoned the stronghold. The modern town developed in 1932.

Fort Fairfield, town (1990 pop. 3,998), including Fort Fairfield village, Aroostook co., NE Maine, on Aroostook R., and 10 mi/16 km NE of Presque Isle; 46°46′N 67°50′W. Port of entry at N.B., Canada border. Potato-growing center. Settled 1816, inc. 1858.

Fort Fisher, state historic site, New Hanover co., SE N.C., c.20 mi/32 km S of Wilmington, near S tip of Pleasure Isl. Cape Fear R. estuary to W, Atlantic Ocean to E, Corncake Inlet to S. Confederate earthwork fortification, built by Gen. William Whiting in 1862 to guard the port of Wilmington, N.C.; scene of one of the last large battles of the Civil War. Because Wilmington was one of the few ports open to blockade-runners, a joint land-sea expedition under Gen. Benjamin Butler and Admiral David Porter was sent against Fort Fisher in Dec. 1864; the Union forces, however, failed to take it. A 2d attempt, with Gen. Alfred Terry replacing Butler, captured the fort on Jan. 15, 1865. The port was closed and Wilmington fell soon afterward. Fort Fisher State Recreation Area on Atlantic Coast (287 acres/116 ha) has 4 mi/6.4 km of beach. N.C. Aquarium nearby. Mus. and visitor center.

Fort Fitzgerald or **Fitzgerald**, village, NE Alta., Canada, near N.W.T. border, on Slave R., N of L. Athabaska, and 20 mi/32 km SE of Fort Smith; 59°52′N 111°37′W. Hudson's Bay Company trading post; transhipment point for Great Slave L., linked with Fort Smith by 2 portage roads, bypassing Slave R. rapids.

Fort Frances, town (1991 pop. 8,891), W Ont., Canada, 70 mi/113 km SE of Kenora, on N side of Rainy R., opposite International Falls, Minn.; 48°37′N 93°25′W. Important border-crossing and customs center. Admin. center for Rainy River District. Large paper mill. Staging area for sport fishing and hunting, canoeing. Agr. area to W (rye, oats, wheat; cattle). Rainy L. to E.

Fort Frances, Yukon, Canada: see FRANCES LAKE.

Fort Franklin, trading post (1991 pop. 551), W Mackenzie dist., N.W.T., Canada, on W shore of Great Bear L., at outlet of Great Bear R., 60 mi/97 km ENE of Fort Norman; 65°11′N 123°28′W. Est. 1932 on site of fort built 1799 by the North West Company. Winter hq. of Franklin expedition, 1825–1827.

Fort Fraser, village, central B.C., Canada, on Nechako R., near E end of Fraser L., 75 mi/121 km W of Prince George; 54°03′N 124°32′W. Lumbering. Trading post, est. here 1806 by Simon Fraser for the North West Company, was burned in 1817 and later rebuilt. Taken over by the Hudson's Bay Company, it was closed down c.1900.

Fort Fred Steele State Historic Site (□ 145 acres/59 ha), Carbon co., S Wyo., on North Platte R., and 15 mi/24 km E of Rawlins; elev. 6,515 ft/1,986 m. Includes original bldgs. of fort built 1868 to protect travelers on overland stage route. Also known as Fort Steele.

Fort Frederica (fred-uh-REEK-uh), natl. monument, SE Ga., on St. Simons Isl.; 31°13′N 81°23′W. It is the ruins of a fort built by James Oglethorpe in 1736 to guard the Eng. colony's S frontier from the Span.-held Florida. The fort's layout has been restored and the tabby walls are partially preserved. (Tabby is a cement-like mixture of lime, sand, and oyster shells used in coastal S.C. and Ga.) Soldiers from Fort Frederica successfully defended the English-held lands at the Battle of Bloody Marsh. Authorized 1936.

Fort Frontenac, Canada: see KINGSTON.

Fort Gaines, city (1990 pop. 1,248), ⊙ Clay co., SW Ga., WSW of Cuthbert, on Chattahoochee R. (bridged; forms Ala. state line here); 31°38′N 85°03′W. Agr. trade center; peanuts grown and shelled; sawmilling. Fort on bluffs overlooking Chattahoochee R. est. 1814. One of the oldest settlements in SE Ga. Inc. 1830.

Fort Garland, village, Costilla co., S Colo., on Ute Creek, near Trinchera Creek, in San Luis Valley, just W of Sangre de Cristo Mts., and 24 mi/39 km E of Alamosa. Elev. c.7,936 ft/2,419 m. Fort Garland Mus. here. San Isabel Natl. Forest to N, W, and E; Rio Grande Natl. Forest to NW; Smith Reservoir to SW; Mountain Home Reservoir to SE. Est. 1858 as military post and commanded (1866–1867) by Kit Carson. Part of original adobe fort still standing. State's oldest surviving military fort.

Fort Garry, 2 trading posts of the Hudson's Bay Company, built on the present-day site of Winnipeg, Man., Canada, at the confluence of the Red and Assiniboine rivers. The 1st, Upper Fort Garry, was built in 1822 on the site of Fort Gibralter, a post of the North West Company from 1809 to 1816. It was named for Nicholas Garry, the deputy governor of the Hudson's Bay Company. Damaged by flood, it was replaced by Lower Fort Garry (1831–1833) farther down on the Red R. Upper Fort Garry was rebuilt in 1835 and became the center of the Red R. fur trade. Fort Garry Natl. Historic Park contains a restoration of Lower Fort Garry.

Fort Gates, town (1990 pop. 818), Coryell co., central Texas, near Leon R., suburb of Gatesville, 36 mi/58 km W of Waco; 31°23′N 97°42′W. Agr. area (livestock; pecans, peaches). Located immediately N of large Fort Hood Military Reservation. Site of Fort Gates (1849).

Fort Gay, town (1990 pop. 852), Wayne co., W W.Va., on Big Sandy R. (bridged) opposite (E of) Louisa, Ky., and 11 mi/18 km SW of Wayne; 38°07′N 82°35′W. Corn, tobacco; livestock; lumber. Bituminous-coal region.

Fort George, river, c.480 mi/770 km long, rising in L. Nichicun, E Que., Canada. It flows W into James Bay at Fort George, a Hudson's Bay Company trading post.

Fort George, Canada: see PRINCE GEORGE.

Fort George G. Meade, U.S. Army post (□ c.21sq mi/54 sq km), Anne Arundel co., central Md., bet. Baltimore and Wash., D.C. Est. 1917 as a World War I induction center and rebuilt later for World War II. Named for the commanding general of Union forces during the Battle of Gettysburg, it is now hq. for First Army Command and the location of the Natl. Security Agency.

Fort Gibson, town (1990 pop. 3,359), Muskogee co., E Okla., E of confluence of Arkansas, Neosho, and Verdigris rivers (here forming Fort Gibson L.), suburb 9 mi/14.5 km E of Muskogee; 35°47′N 95°15′W. Agr. area. One of oldest settlements in state, founded 1824 as army post in preparation for coming of the Five Civilized Tribes; served as chief military center for Indian Territory until 1857. Old bldgs. of the Fort Gibson Stockade (abandoned 1890) have been restored. Fort Gibson Natl. Cemetery (est. 1868) is here. Fort Gruber Natl. Guard Training Facility to S; Fort Gibson Dam and reservoir to N.

Fort Gibson Lake, reservoir (□ 80 sq mi/207 sq km), on Cherokee-Wagoner co. border and in Mayes co., E Okla., on Neosho (Grand) R., 11 mi/18 km NE of Muskogee; c.35 mi/56 km long; 35°52′N 95°13′W. Max. capacity 922,000 acre-ft. Hudson (Markham Ferry) Dam at N tip. Formed by Fort Gibson Dam (110 ft/34 m high), built (1946) by Army Corps of Engineers for flood control and power generation. Sequoyah (E shore) and Sequoyah Bay (W shore) state parks are here, near dam.

Fort Good Hope, village (1991 pop. 602), W Mackenzie dist., N.W.T., Canada, on Mackenzie R. at mouth of Hare Indian R., and 90 mi/145 km NW of Norman Wells; 66°15′N 128°38′W. River port; terminus of winter road from Wrigley, future extension of Mackenzie Highway; govt. radio and meteorological station, Royal Can. Mounted Police Post; site of R.C. mission est. 1821. North West Company post est. 1805. Low temp. of −79°F was recorded here Dec. 1910. Scheduled air service.

Fort Gordon Military Reservation, fort, Augusta, Ga.; 33°25′N 82°09′W. Founded as Camp Gordon in World War II. Site of U.S. Army Signal Mus.

Fort Greene, a residential sect. of NW Brooklyn borough of N.Y. city, SE N.Y., near Wallabout Bay; 40°42′N 73°57′W. Monument commemorates Prison Ship Martyrs, who died in Br. hulks here during the Revolution. Brooklyn Acad. of Music and Pratt Inst. are here. Brooklyn Navy Yard is NW; it closed in the 1960s and now is an industrial development zone.

Fort Griffin, uninc. village (1990 pop. 96), Shackelford co., N central Texas, 14 mi/23 km N of Albany, and on Clear Fork of Brazos R. Elev. 1,275 ft/389 m. Fort Griffin State Park includes restored Fort Griffin (1867–1881), once an important frontier post. Agr. area; oil and gas.

Fort Hall, village (1990 pop. 600), Bingham co., SE Idaho, near Snake R., 9 mi/14.5 km N of Pocatello, at center of Fort Hall Indian Reservation. Est. 1834 by trader Nathaniel Wyeth. It was made a military post in 1849. Fort Hall was the main stopping point on the Oregon Trail W of Fort Bridger. It was destroyed by floods in 1862 and 1864.

Fort Hamilton, a residential sect. of Brooklyn borough of N.Y. city, SE N.Y.; 40°37′N 74°01′W. Here is U.S. Fort Hamilton (formerly Fort Lewis, opened 1831), on The Narrows opposite Fort Wadsworth, Staten Isl.

Fort Hancock, village (1990 est. pop. 400), Hudspeth co., extreme W Texas, 45 mi/72 km SE of El Paso, near the Rio Grande (Mex. border). In irrigated farm region (vegetables, cotton, hay, alfalfa; catle, hogs). Toll bridge. Ruins of old Fort Hancock are nearby.

Fort Henry, historic site, Confederate fortification on the Tennessee R., S of the Ky.-Tenn. state line; site of the first major Union victory of the Civil War (Feb. 6, 1862). The fort was attacked and reduced by Union gunboats commanded by Commodore Andrew Foote. Confederate commander Gen. Lloyd Tilghman, foreseeing capture, sent the bulk of his force to Fort Donelson before surrendering.

Fort Henry, Canada: see KINGSTON.

Fort Hill, Ohio: see SINKING SPRING.

Fort Hood, U.S. army post (□ 342 sq mi/886 sq km), Bill and Coryell cos., central Texas, adjacent (on N) to Killeen; 31°07′N 97°46′W. Drained by Cowhouse Creek and tributaries; bounded E by Belton L. reservoir (Leon R.). Est. 1942 on the site of old Fort Gates and named for Confederate Gen. John Hood. It is one of the army's largest installations and a major employer in the area. City of Temple to E. Has 2 museums.

Fort Huachuca, uninc. village, Cochise co., SE Ariz., near Mex. border, suburb 3 mi/4.8 km W of Sierra Vista, at NE boundary of Huachuca Mts. Elev. 4,763 ft/1,452 m. U.S. military post nearby. Historic mus.; Coronado Natl. Forest to SW.

Fort Île-aux-Noix, Canada: see ÎLE-AUX-NOIX.

Fort Jay, N.Y.: see GOVERNORS ISLAND.

Fort Jefferson, national monument (□ 101 sq mi/262 sq km), Garden Key, lowermost Fla. Keys, in the Dry Tortugas, 60 mi/97 km W of Key West, Fla. Authorized 1935. The largest all-masonry fort in the Western Hemisphere, built 1846.

Fort Jennings, village (1990 pop. 436), Putnam co., NW Ohio, 15 mi/24 km NW of Lima and on Auglaize R.; 40°54′N 84°17′W.

Fort Johnson, village (1990 pop. 615), Montgomery co., E central N.Y., on Mohawk R. and the Barge Canal, just W of Amsterdam; 42°57′N 74°14′W. Fort Johnson (1749), once home of Sir William Johnson, is now a mus.

Fort Jones, city (1990 pop. 639), Siskiyou co., N Calif., 13 mi/21 km SW of Yreka, on Scott R.; 41°37′N 122°51′W. Cattle, sheep, lambs; potatoes, sugar beets, onions, grain. Klamath Mts. to W; Klamath Natl. Forest to N, W, and S.

Fort Juliana, locality, E Ellesmere Isl., NE Franklin dist., N.W.T., Canada, on Hayes Fjord, W arm (25 mi/40 km long) of Hill Bay, an inlet of Buchanan Bay; 79°00′N 77°00′W. Site of hq. of Otto Sverdrup expedition, 1898–1899.

Fort Kent, town (1990 pop. 4,268), including Fort Kent village, Aroostook co., N Maine, on St. John R., at influx of Fish R., and 50 mi/80 km NNW of Presque Isle; 47°14′N 68°33′W. Port of entry; trade center at N.B. line; potato-processing center; lumbering. Seat of Univ. of Maine at Fort Kent. Terminus of U.S. Highway No. 1. Settled 1829 by Acadians, inc. 1869.

Fort Knox, U.S. military reservation (□ 172 sq mi/445 sq km), Hardin, Meade, and Bullitt cos., N Ky., 25 mi/40 km SSW of Louisville, near Ohio R. Drained by Salt and Rolling Fork rivers. City of Radcliffe to S, town of West Point to N. Est. 1917 as a training camp in World War I. It became a permanent post in 1932. Godman Army Airfield was opened in 1918. It currently serves as airport and heliport for training purposes. In the steel and concrete vaults of the U.S. Bullion Depository (W part), the bulk of the nation's gold bullion is stored. Of interest is the Patton Mus. of Cavalry and Armor. Tioga Falls Natl. Recreation Trail and Bridges to the Past, 3 stone bridges on old Louisville and Nashville Turnpike, in N part of reservation.

Fort Langley, village, SW B.C., Canada, on lower Fraser R., and 24 mi/39 km ESE of Vancouver. Lumbering, dairying, fruitgrowing. First Hudson's Bay Company post in S B.C. was est. here (1827) and played important part in securing British influence in the region; it was closed down c.1885. Fort was reconstructed as tourist center.

Fort Laramie (LA-ruhm-ee), village (1990 pop. 243), Goshen co., SE Wyo., on North Platte R., at mouth of Laramie R., and 20 mi/32 km NW of Torrington; 42°12′N 104°31′W. Elev. 4,230 ft/1,289 m. Cattle; sugar beets. Fort Laramie Natl. Historic Site is to W, across river. Prehistoric stone quarry region to N.

Fort Laramie National Historic Site (LA-rahm-ee) (□ 1.3 sq mi/3.4 sq km), Goshen co., at village of Fort Laramie, 22 mi/35 km NW of Torrington, SE Wyo., on North Platte R. Surviving bldgs. of a military past (1849–1890) on the Oregon and Overland Trails. Authorized 1938 as natl. monument; changed to natl. historic site 1960.

Fort Larned National Historic Site (LAHR-ned) (□ 1.1 sq mi/2.9 sq km), 3 mi/4.8 km W of Larned, Pawnee co., central Kansas. Protected travelers on the Santa Fe Trail; served as a military base during the Indian War (1868–1869) and later as an Indian Bureau administrative center. Fort est. 1859, deactivated 1878, sold at public auction 1884. Historic site authorized 1964; est. 1966.

Fort Lauderdale, residential and resort city (□ 35 sq mi/91 sq km; 1990 pop. 149,377), ⊙ Broward co., SE Fla., on the Atlantic coast; 26°08′N 80°08′W. Settled around a fort built (c.1837) in the Seminole War. A port of entry (Port Everglades), the city is located on New R. and a navigable canal to L. Okeechobee, and is interwoven with more than 270 mi/435 km of natural and artificial waterways. It has one of the largest marinas in the world and one of the most popular beaches in the country. The city's variety of mfg. includes boat and yacht production. Tourism and recreation are economic mainstays, and the city has experienced extensive development in these areas. Nova-Southeastern Univ., a branch campus of Fla. Atlantic Univ., and a community col. are here. Nearby are Port Everglades, a noted artificial port with heavy passenger (cruise ships) and freight traffic, and a state park. Fort Lauderdale Internatl. Airport in neighboring Dania has expanded and is now one of the state's main airports. Inc. 1911.

Fort Lawn, town (1990 pop. 718), Chester co., N S.C., near Catawba R., 18 mi/29 km E of Chester; 34°42′N 80°54′W. Mfg. (textile finishing machinery, cotton cloth, bedding).

Fort Leavenworth (LEV-en-wuhrth), U.S. military post (□ 9 sq mi/23.3 sq km), on the Missouri R., NE Kansas, 2 mi/3.2 km N of Leavenworth. Est. 1827 by Col. Henry Leavenworth to protect travelers on the Santa Fe Trail. The oldest U.S. military prison (est. 1874) and the U.S. Army Command and General Staff Col. are here.

Fort Lee, residential borough (1990 pop. 31,997), Bergen co., NE N.J., 4 mi/6.4 km SE of Hackensack, on the Palisades overlooking the Hudson R.; 40°51′N 73°58′W. The fort built here by the Americans as Fort Constitution to command the Hudson during the Revolution was abandoned on Nov. 20, 1776, by Gen. Greene after Fort Washington, on the opposite shore (in New York City), fell to the British. It was renamed Fort Lee and is now an historical park and mus. Fort Lee was an early center of the motion-picture industry. It is the W terminus of the George Washington Bridge and the N terminus of the New Jersey Turnpike. Nearly half the pop. now of Asian origin. Settled c.1700, inc. 1904.

Fort Lennox, Canada: see ÎLE-AUX-NOIX.

Fort Leonard Wood, U.S. Army post (□ 111 sq mi/287 sq km), Pulaski co., S central Mo., main entrance 20 mi/32 km SW of Rolla; 37°42′N 92°09′W. Est. 1940, it is one of the largest basic-training centers in the U.S. and also provides training for army engineers. Surrounded, except on N, by Mark Twain Natl. Forest; service center at Waynesville and St. Robert to N. Airport.

Fort Liard (LEE-ahrd), village (1991 pop. 485), SW Mackenzie dist., N.W.T., Canada, near B.C. and Yukon borders, on Liard R., at mouth of Petitot R.; 60°14′N 123°28′W. Liard Highway, connecting Alaska Highway in B.C. to Mackenzie Highway in N.W.T., opened 1983. Trading post; radio and TV stations; Royal Can. Mounted Police post. Hunting, trapping, fishing, mfg. (birch-bark and porcupine quill baskets). Outfitting for Nahanni Natl. Park. Est. c.1800. Trading post est. 1807; Hudson Bay Company took over in 1821. Scheduled air service.

Fort Liberté, town (1982 pop. 5,012), ⊙ Nord-Est dept., NE Haiti, port on small inlet of the Atlantic, 23 mi/37 km E of Cap–Haïten; 19°40′N 71°50′W. Agr. (sugarcane, oranges, limes); sisal processing; ships logwood. Fishing port.

Fort Lincoln New Town, residential sect. in NE Wash., D.C., S of Bladensburg Rd. at the Md. state line; 38°56′N 76°57′W. Originally planned (late 1960s) as a govt.-financed "new town," the site is instead being developed by private interests. It is a mix of town houses, high-rise apartments, and condominiums on hills overlooking much of Wash., D.C. Since 1975, some 1,600 housing units have been completed.

Fort Loramie (LO-ruh-mee), village (1990 pop. 1,042), Shelby co., W Ohio, 12 mi/19 km WNW of Sidney, on L. Loramie; 40°20′N 84°22′W. Fort Loramie built here (1794) by Anthony Wayne.

Fort Loudoun Lake (LOU-duhn), reservoir (□ 22.7 sq mi/58.8 sq km), Loudon, Knox, and Blount cos., E Tenn., on Tennessee R., where it is formed (4 mi/6.4 km E of Knoxville) by French Broad and Holston rivers, 20 mi/32 km SW of Knoxville and 1 mi/1.6 km E of Lenoir City; c.55 mi/89 km long; 35°46′N 84°14′W. Max. capacity 386,500 acre-ft. Formed by Fort Loudoun Lock and Dam (122 ft/37 m high), built (1943) by TVA for flood control and power generation.

Fort Lupton, town (1990 pop. 5,159), Weld co., N Colo., on South Platte R., and 25 mi/40 km NNE of Denver; 40°05′N 104°48′W. Elev. c.4,914 ft/1,498 m. Trade center for grain and dairy region; cattle, sugar beets, fruit, beans, sunflowers, wheat. Mfg. (aluminum casting). Site of Fort Lupton (1836–1844), fur-trading post, is nearby. Founded c.1872, inc. 1890.

Fort Lyon, village, SE Colo., 4 mi/6.4 km E of Las Almas on Arkansas R., near headwaters of John Martin Reservoir; elev. 3,870 ft/1,180 m. Cattle; wheat, barley, corn, sorghum, hay. Lake Harty State Park to E. RR junction to S across river, opposite mouth of Purgatoine R.

Fort Macleod (muh-KLOUD), town (1991 pop. 3,112), SW Alta., Canada, on Oldman R., and 25 mi/40 km W of Lethbridge; 49°44′N 113°24′W. Coal mining; oil and gas; dairying, ranching, mixed farming; wheat, flax, sugar beets; cattle. Fort Mus. Nearby was Fort Macleod (1874), first outpost of North West Mounted Police (later Royal Can. Mounted Police). Peigan Indian Reserve 20 mi/32 km SW.

Fort Macon State Park, N.C.: see BOGUE ISLAND.

Fort Madison, city (1990 pop. 11,618), ⊙ Lee co., SE Iowa, on the Mississippi R.; 40°37′N 91°20′W. The city is a river port for barge traffic as well as a RR, commercial, and industrial center with a wide variety of light mfg. (truck trailers, pens and mechanized pencils, concrete, furniture). Iowa State Penitentiary (1839) and Lee County Courthouse (1841) are here. Record flooding occurred along Mississippi R. in 1993. Fort Madison, a U.S. trading post, was est. in 1808 as the first fort west of the Mississippi and named for James Madison, then President. Inc. 1838.

Fort Massac State Park, Ill.: see METROPOLIS.

Fort Matanzas National Monument, Fla.: see SAINT AUGUSTINE.

Fort McClellan, military base (1990 pop. 4,128), Calhoun co., NE Ala., just N of Anniston. Hq. of the Army Military Police and Chemical Regiments; research and development center for chemical and biological weapons. Three military museums are located on Fort McClellan: the Military Police Corps Regimental Mus., the Army Chemical Corps Mus., and the Women's Army Corp Mus. Fort McClellan was recommended for closure by the Base Realignment and Closure committee in 1995.

Fort McHenry, former U.S. military post in Baltimore harbor, Md., located at the entry of the harbor at Whetstone Point. Built 1794–1805. In the War of 1812 it was bombarded (Sept. 13–14, 1814) by a Br. fleet under Sir George Cockburn, but the fort, commanded by Maj. George Armistead, resisted the attack. Its defense inspired Francis Scott Key to write "The Star-Spangled Banner." During the Civil War the fort was a Union prison camp. Restored in 1933, it was designated a Natl. Monument and Historic Site in 1939. Named after James McHenry, a Md. native who was secretary to George Washington during the Revolution and secretary of war (1796–1800).

Fort McKavett, uninc. village (1990 pop. 45), Menard co., W central Texas, 20 mi/32 km WSW of Menard, and on San Saba R. Elev. 2,155 ft/657 m. In cattle ranching area. Ruins of old Fort McKavett (1852) are here; Fort McKavett State Historic Site is to W (in Schleicher co.).

Fort McKenzie, village, N Que., Canada, near Kaniapiskau R.; 56°53′N 68°59′W. Hudson's Bay Company post.

Fort McKinley, uninc. village (1990 pop. 9,740), Montgomery co., SW Ohio, c.7 mi/11 km NW of Dayton; 39°48′N 84°15′W.

Fort McLeod, Canada: see MCLEOD, FORT.

Fort McMurray, town (1991 pop. 34,706), NE Alta., Canada, on the Athabasca and Clearwater rivers; 56°44′N 111°23′W. Oil refining; since the beginning of the Oil Sands Project in 1964, the pop. grew from 1,200 to almost 35,000 in 1986. It is an important river port and transshipment point for the N.W.T. Major center for tar, sand, and oil extraction as well.

Fort McPherson, village (1991 pop. 759), NW Mackenzie dist., N.W.T., Canada, near Yukon border, on Peel R., near its mouth on Mackenzie R., and 50 mi. S of Aklavik; 67°27′N 134°53′W. On Dempster Highway, completed 1978. Oil exploration activities along Dempster. Arts and crafts; hide garments, furs; fishing; canvas factory (tents, nylon bags). Hudson's Bay Company furtrading post (est. 1840); radio station, Royal Can. Mounted Police summer post; site of Anglican and R.C. missions. Scheduled air service.

Fort McPherson, U.S. military base, Ga., near Atlanta. Hq. of the U.S. Third Army.

Fort Meade, town (□ 3 sq mi/7.8 sq km; 1990 pop. 4,976), Polk co., central Fla., near Peace R., 10 mi/16 km S of Bartow; 27°45′N 81°47′W. Trade center for citrus-growing and phosphate-mining area.

Fort Meigs (megz), Amer. fortification on the Maumee R., near Perrysburg, N central Ohio, 10 mi/16 km S of

Toledo. Est. Feb. 1813 by Gen. William Henry Harrison across the river from Br. Fort Miami (Maumee, Ohio). Through the spring and summer of 1813, the Americans there held off Br. attacks. The fort was instrumental in safeguarding the W frontier in the War of 1812.

Fort Michie, N.Y.: see GULL ISLANDS.

Fort Mill, town (1990 pop. 4,930), York co., N S.C., 7 mi/ 11.3 km NE of Rock Hill, and 15 mi/24 km SSW of Charlotte, N.C., near the Catawba R; 35°00′N 80°56′W. Mfg. (plastics, chemicals, industrial machinery, textiles, computer software, inks).

Fort Mimms, temporary stockade near the confluence of the Tombigbee and Alabama rivers, Ala.; the scene of a massacre (Aug. 30, 1813) in which William Weatherford led a Native American force in the killing of c.500 whites.

Fort Mitchell, town (1990 pop. 7,438), Kenton co., N Ky., residential suburb 5 mi/8 km SW of Cincinnati, Ohio, and 3 mi/4.8 km SW of Covington, Ky.; 39°02′N 84°33′W. Mfg. (ice cream, beer, light assembly). Vent Haven Ventriloquist Mus.

Fort Monroe, historic fort, Hampton (independent city), SE Va., commanding the entrance to Hampton Roads harbor from Chesapeake Bay; named for President James Monroe. Fortress (□ 80 acres/32 ha) built (1819–1834) by U.S. govt. on site of English fortifications erected 1609 and 1727.

Fort Montgomery, village (□ 1 sq mi/2.6 sq km; 1990 pop. 1,450), Orange co., SE N.Y., on W bank of the Hudson R. (crossed here by Bear Mountain Bridge), and 12 mi/19 km S of Newburgh; 41°20′N 73°59′W. Just S is Bear Mtn. sect. of Palisades Interstate Park.

Fort Morgan, town (1990 pop. 9,068), ⊙ Morgan co., NE Colo., on South Platte R., and 70 mi/113 km NE of Denver; 40°16′N 103°47′W. Elev. c.4,330 ft/1,320 m. Trade center for sugar beet, grain, dairy, and cattle region; oil services; mfg. (printing and publishing). RR center located between Union Pacific (N) and Burlington Northern RR lines. Morgan Community Col. and Fort Morgan Mus. here. Bijou Reservoir to W. Established as military post on Overland Trail, named Fort Morgan in 1866, inc. 1887.

Fort Motte, village, Calhoun co., central S.C., 10 mi/ 16 km NE of Saint Matthews. Named after Revolutionary War battle. Cotton, soybeans, wheat.

Fort Moultrie (MOL-tree), at W end of Sullivans Isl., Charleston co., at the entrance to Charleston Harbor, 4 mi/6.4 km E of Charleston, S.C. Originally called Fort Sullivan. Constructed originally of sand and palmetto logs by Col. William Moultrie, the fort was renamed for him after he repulsed a heavy Br. naval attack in June 1776, in one of the most decisive battles of the Amer. Revolution. During the Seminole War, Osceola, a chief, and 200 Seminoles were imprisoned in the fort; Osceola's tomb is here. During the Civil War, Confederates held the fort until the evacuation of Charleston in 1865. It was Charleston's chief harbor defense until 1947, when it was abandoned. Fort Moultrie is part of Fort Sumter; together they form a Natl. Monument.

Fort Myers, city (□ 30 sq mi/78 sq km; 1990 pop. 45,206), ⊙ Lee co., SW Fla., on the Caloosahatchee R., near the Gulf of Mexico; 26°37′N 81°50′W. Tourism; light mfg.; shipping point for citrus fruits, winter vegetables, flowers (especially gladioli), and fish. The city grew up around Fort Harvie, built (c.1841) in the Seminole War, and lies in a region of tropical vegetation noted for its royal palms. Attractions include boat trips to the Everglades, local wildlife preserves, and extensive beach resorts. There is a community of retired people, and the city has been marked by rapid urban and economic growth since 1970. A new, major airport lies just SE of the city. Thomas Edison's estate is a mus., and an annual light show commemorates him. A campus of the Univ. of Fla. and a community col. are also here. Founded 1850, inc. 1905.

Fort Myers Beach, town (□ 7 sq mi/18.1 sq km; 1990 pop. 9,284), Lee co., SW Fla., 15 mi/24 km SW of Fort Myers; 26°26′N 81°55′W. Shrimp processing; light mfg. Resort on Gulf of Mexico.

Fort Nassau 1 (NA-saw), built (1623) by the Dutch on the E bank of the Delaware R. near present-day Gloucester City, N.J. The Dutch soon abandoned the fort, but after Swedish colonization in the area, the Dutch reoccupied it. Fear of Swed. competition in the fur trade caused Du. Gov. Peter Stuyvesant to take over (1655) the Swed. forts on the Delaware basin. After the Swedes evacuated Fort Elfsborg, the Dutch destroyed Fort Nassau. **2** on Castle Isl., in the Hudson R., S of Albany, N.Y. Built 1614, the fort served as a trading post for the Dutch until 1617, when it was destroyed by flood and replaced (1624) by Fort Orange, built on the site of Albany.

Fort Necessity (□ 1.4 sq mi/3.6 sq km), national battlefield, Fayette co., SW Pa., 9 mi/14.5 km SE of Uniontown, on SE side of Chestnut Ridge; 39°49′N 79°36′W. Entrenched camp of Col. George Washington and his Va. militia at Great Meadows defeated here July 3, 1754, in opening battle of Fr. and Indian War. Mt. Washington Tavern; Major Gen. Edward Braddock's grave and memorial. Est. 1931.

Fort Nelson, town (1991 pop. 3,804), NE B.C., Canada, at confluence of Muskwa R. and Sikanni Chief R., here forming Fort Nelson R., on branch of Alaska Highway; 58°49′N 122°32′W. Hudson's Bay Company post; lumbering. Est. c.1800, post was destroyed by Indians 1825, rebuilt 1865.

Fort Nelson River, NE B.C., Canada, 100 mi/161 km long, formed at Fort Nelson by confluence of Muskwa and Sikanni Chief rivers, flows generally NW to Liard R. at Nelson Forks.

Fort Niagara, post on the S shore of L. Ontario, at the mouth of the Niagara R., NW N.Y.; 43°16′N 79°08′W. It was strategically located on the water route to the fur lands. Fr. explorer Robert LaSalle erected a blockhouse on the river in 1679; in 1726 a stone fort overlooking the river was completed. A Br. force, led by Sir William Johnson, captured Fort Niagara in 1759 during the Fr. and Indian War. The British held the fort until 1796, when it was turned over to the U.S. by Jay's Treaty. During the War of 1812, the British captured Fort Niagara but returned it in 1815. The fort remained a U.S. military post until 1946. It is now a N.Y. state park.

Fort Norman, village (1991 pop. 375), W Mackenzie dist., N.W.T., Canada, on Mackenzie R., at mouth of Great Bear R., at foot of Franklin Mts.; 64°54′N 125°35′W. On winter road from Wrigley, future extension of Mackenzie Highway. River port; fur-trading post (est. 1810); govt. radio and meteorological station, hosp., Royal Can. Mounted Police Post. Hunting, fishing, trapping. Site of R.C. mission. Transshipment point for waterborne traffic for Great Bear L. region. Fort was est. 1810 by North West Company, taken over by Hudson's Bay Company 1821. Historic village and church. Scheduled air service. Oil center of Norman Wells is 45 mi/72 km NW.

Fort Oglethorpe (O-guhl-thorp), town (1990 pop. 5,880), Catoosa and Walker cos., extreme NW Ga., 7 mi/11.3 km SE of Chattanooga, Tenn., and near U.S. Fort Oglethorpe; 34°55′N 85°15′W. Mfg. (carpeting, furniture, yarns, sheet metal fabrication; printing).

Fort Ontario, N.Y.: see OSWEGO, city.

Fort Payne, city (1990 pop. 11,838), ⊙ De Kalb co., NE Ala., on branch of Coosa R., and 34 mi/55 km NE of Gadsden. Trade center for cotton, poultry, and fruit area; mfg. (clothing, lumber, sporting goods, paper prods.). Deposits of clay, coal, iron, and fuller's earth in vicinity. Alabama June Jam held here annually. Site of Cherokee settlement nearby. Fort Payne Opera House (1889) is oldest active theater in Ala. Founded 1889.

Fort Peck, village (1990 pop. 325), Valley co., NE Mont., below Fort Peck Dam (at W end), on Missouri R., and 15 mi/24 km SE of Glasgow; 48°01′N 106°27′W. On Fort Peck Reservoir, surrounded by Charles M. Russell Natl. Wildlife Refuge to S. Fort Peck Indian Reservation to NE. Built as permanent town for construction workers on Fort Peck Dam. Dinosaur and other fossils collected here.

Fort Peck Lake, reservoir, NE Mont., on Missouri R., 18 mi/29 km SE of Glasgow, forming Valley-McCone, Garfield-Valley, Phillips-Garfield, and Petroleum-Phillips co. borders; c.134 mi/216 km long; 48°00′N 106°25′W. Big Dry Creek forms c.35 mi/56 km long Dry Arm (S). Formed by Fort Peck Dam, one of the world's largest earth-filled dams (21,430 ft/6,532 m long, 250 ft/ 76 m high), built (1940) as part of the Missouri River Basin Project for irrigation, flood control, and power generation. Almost entirely surrounded by Charles M. Russell Natl. Wildlife Refuge, with U L Bend Natl. Wildlife Refuge on inside of sharp U L Bend, opposite mouth of Musselshell R. Hell Creek State Park at center of S shore.

Fort Phantom Hill, Lake, Jones co., W central Texas, reservoir impounded by dam in Cedar Creek, a small S tributary of Clear Fork of the Brazos, c.7 mi/11.3 km N of Abilene; c.74,000 acre-ft capacity. Fishing. City of Abilene has extended its corporate limits to include lake and its residential and recreational developments. Nearby are ruins of Fort Phantom Hill U.S. military post, est. 1851.

Fort Pickens, Civil War–era fortification, on the W end of Santa Rosa Isl., Escambia co., extreme NW Fla., at the entrance to Pensacola Bay.

Fort Pierce, city (□ 18 sq mi/47 sq km; 1990 pop. 36,830), ⊙ St. Lucie co., E central Fla., on Indian R. (a lagoon, part of the Intracoastal Waterway); 27°26′N 80°19′W. Located at an important junction of Fla.'s turnpike and I-95. With harbor and RR facilities, it is a distribution center for a cattle and farm area yielding citrus fruits and vegetables. Commercial fishing. Tourism. There are 2 bridges connecting the city with its ocean beach resorts. Fort Pierce has a junior col. and 2 mus. Settled in the 1860s around a fort. Inc. 1901.

Fort Pierre, town (1990 pop. 1,854), ⊙ Stanley co., central S.Dak., opposite Pierre, on the Missouri R. at mouth of Bad R.; 44°21′N 100°22′W. Grain and livestock. Mountain/Central time zone boundary follows Missouri R. S to Fort Pierre, then passes over land to W of it. Farm Island State Recreation Area to E; Fort Pierre Natl. Grassland to S. Nearby on bluff is the Vérendrye Monument, erected to recognize 1743 claim of surrounding territory by France. Founded 1817 as furtrading post; site of Fort Pierre (1832).

Fort Pillow, historic site, fortification on the Mississippi R., N of Memphis, Tenn.; built by Confederate Gen. Gideon Pillow in 1862. Evacuated by the Confederates after the fall of Island No. 10 to the N, the fort was occupied by Union troops on June 6, 1862. Confederate Gen. Nathan Forrest stormed and captured Fort Pillow on April 12, 1864, killing many Afr.-Amer. defenders. Often called the Fort Pillow Massacre, it became one of the greatest atrocity stories of the Civil War.

Fort Plain, village (□ 1 sq mi/2.6 sq km; 1990 pop. 2,416), Montgomery co., E central N.Y., on Mohawk R. and the Barge Canal, and 23 mi/37 km W of Amsterdam; 42°55′N 74°37′W. In dairying and poultry area. Settled 1723, inc. 1832.

Fort Point, national historic site, San Francisco, W Calif. (□ 29 acres/12 ha). Large brick and granite mid-19th-cent. coastal fortification on Golden Gate Strait E of S end of Golden Gate Bridge. Adjoins Golden Gate Natl. Recreation Area to W and N. Authorized 1970.

Fort Polk Military Reserve, U.S. Army post (□ 313 sq mi/811 sq km), Vernon parish, W La., E of Leesville. Major army warm-weather training center, est. 1941 and named for the Rev. Leonidas Polk. Polk Field airport in SW. Overlaps Kisatchie Natl. Forest to S.

Fort Providence, village (1991 pop. 645), S Mackenzie dist., N.W.T., Canada, on Mackenzie R., near W end of Great Slave L.; 61°21′N 117°39′W. At ferry crossing of Yellowknife Highway. Tourism. Trapping, fishing, some agr. (vegetables; cattle); moose-hair embroidery, porcupine-quill crafts. Trading post; airfield; govt. radio, TV, and meteorological stations; Royal Can. Mounted Police post; site of R.C. mission and boarding school. Est. 1861. Scheduled air service.

Fort Pulaski (puhl-AS-kee), historic site, brick fortification on Cockspur Isl., SE Ga., at the mouth of the Savannah R.; 32°01′N 80°56′W. Built 1829–1847 by the U.S. govt. and named for Casimir Pulaski. The fort was seized by Georgia troops during the Civil War in Jan. 1861, but fell to a Union force under Q. A. Gillmore on April 11, 1862, after a 2-day bombardment in which the Federals used rifled cannon for the first time in the war; the battle proved the superiority of rifled cannon over masonry forts. Fort Pulaski Natl. Monument was est. 1924.

Fort Qu'Appelle (for kah-PEHL), town (1991 pop. 1,953), SE Sask., Canada, on Fishing Lakes, 40 mi/64 km ENE of Regina; 50°46'N 103°47'W. Mixed farming. Former fur-trading post, est. c.1800, discontinued 1880.

Fort Rae, Canada: see RAE-EDZO.

Fort Raleigh National Historic Site (□ 157 acres/ 64 ha), Roanoke isl., Dare co., NE N.C., 3 mi/4.8 km NW of Manteo, on Albermarle Sound. Site of the first attempted settlement by the English in North Amer. (1585–1587), Sir Walter Raleigh's "Lost Colony," whose fate remains a mystery. Authorized 1941.

Fort Randall Dam, S.Dak.: see FRANCIS CASE, LAKE.

Fort Recovery, village (1990 pop. 1,313), Mercer co., W Ohio, 14 mi/23 km SW of Celina, and on Wabash R.; 40°25'N 84°46'W. Oil wells. Fort Recovery was est. here in 1791 by Anthony Wayne.

Fort Resolution, village (1991 pop. 515), S Mackenzie dist., N.W.T., Canada, on S shore of Great Slave L., near mouth of Slave R.; 61°11'N 113°41'W. E terminus of Fort Resolution Highway. Trapping, logging; sawmill. Fur-trading center; airfield, govt. radio, TV, and meteorological stations, Royal Can. Mounted Police post; site of R.C. mission (1852), hosp., and boarding school. Wood Buffalo Natl. Park extends S. At mouth of Slave R., 9 mi/14 km NNE of fort, is Res-delta, a river-lake transshipment point for Yellowknife mining region. Scheduled air service. Est. 1786 by the Hudson's Bay Company.

Fort Richardson, Alaska: see ANCHORAGE city.

Fort Riley, U.S. military post (□ 9 sq mi/23.3 sq km), Riley co., NE Kansas, on the Kansas R., 10 mi/16 km W of Manhattan. Milford L. Reservoir to W. Est. 1852 to protect travelers on the Santa Fe Trail from Indian attacks. Was first called Camp Center, but in 1853 it was renamed for Gen. Bennett Riley. It was a cavalry post and school until 1917, when it became a reserve-officer training center. Fort Riley is now a U.S. army staging and training area for transportation, supply, and service units. Custer house, officers quarters until 1974 (including Gen. Custer). Cavalry mus.

Fort Ripley, village (1990 pop. 92), Crow Wing co., central Minn., on Mississippi R., 15 mi/24 km SW of Brainerd; 46°10'N 94°21'W. Grain, potatoes; mfg. (exercise equipment). Camp Ripley Military Reservation, used by Minn. Natl. Guard, to W. Ruins of Old Fort Ripley (1850–1878) here. Crow Wing State Park to N.

Fort Ross, abandoned trading post, SE Somerset Isl., central Franklin Dist., N.W.T., Canada, on Prince Regent Inlet; 72°00'N 94°07'W.

Fort Ross, historic site, Sonoma co., W Calif., on Pacific coast, 28 mi/45 km W of Santa Rosa. In Fort Ross State Historic Park (□ 5 sq mi/13 sq km) are restored bldgs., including Rus. Orthodox chapel, of Rus. Fort Ross, a fur-trapping and trading post (1812–1841) which was southernmost Rus. outpost in Pacific Northwest. Sold to John Sutter by Russians.

Fort Rucker, military base (1990 pop. 7,593), Dale co., SE Ala., just N of Daleville. Home of Army Aviation, with training and operational units. Army Aviation Mus.

Fort Saint James, village, central B.C., Canada, on E shore of Stuart L., 70 mi/113 km NW of Prince George; 54°26'N 124°15'W. Trading post; lumbering; stock raising. Est. 1806 by North West Company, it was taken over (1821) by Hudson's Bay Company.

Fort Saint John, town (1991 pop. 14,156), NE B.C., Canada, on the Peace R., and the Alaska Highway; 56°15'N 120°50'W. The town is a supply point for nearby gas and oil fields. Trading post est. 1805.

Fort Sam Houston, U.S. Army base (□ 5 sq mi/ 13.3 sq km), in San Antonio, Bexar co., S Texas. Hq. of the Fourth Army. The city, long a military center, donated land in 1870 for the site of a permanent military post that was constructed from 1876 to 1890 and named for Gen. Sam Houston. The famous Brooke Army Medical Center, the major training center for army medics and the home of the Army Medical Service School, is located on the post. Site of Army Medical Mus. and Fort Sam Houston Mus.; Natl. Cemetery in N part of base. Est. 1876.

Fort San Cristóbal (chris-TO-bahl), historic site, NE P.R., N Old San Juan, 1 mi/1.6 km ESE of El Morro Castle, facing the Atlantic Ocean. Fort built (1630–1771) to protect the city of San Juan from land attacks by the enemies of Spain. The first shot of the Spanish-American War was fired from this fort. Local hq. of the U.S. Department of the Interior and of the State Civil Defense located here.

Fort Saskatchewan (sas-KA-chuh-wahn), city (1991 pop. 12,078), central Alta., Canada, on North Saskatchewan R., satellite community 15 mi/24 km NE of Edmonton; 53°43'N 113°13'W. Coal mining, oil and gas, iron ore, and nonferrous smelting and refining; mfg. (fertilizer); grain elevators, mixed farming, cattle, barley. First fort of the North West Mounted Police N of Calgary was established here. Elk Island Natl. Park is 10 mi/16 km ESE.

Fort Schuyler 1 (SKEI-luh), fort built on the site of Utica, N.Y., in 1758. **2** fort in Throgs Neck, N.Y., at E end of Pennyfield Ave.; 40°48'N 73°48'W. Built (c.1856) as part of the defenses of N.Y. Harbor, it was converted to the Maritime College in 1934–1938. Fort is now State Univ. of N.Y. Maritime Col.

Fort Schuyler, Rome, N.Y.: see FORT STANWIX.

Fort Scott, city (1990 pop. 8,362), ⊙ Bourbon co., SE Kansas, on Marmaton R., and 28 mi/45 km N of Pittsburg, near Mo. state line; 37°49'N 94°42'W. RR junction. Trade and shipping center for agr. region; mfg. (apparel, cement, metal prods.); wood planing. Quarries (cement rock, flagstone). Fort Scott Community Col. City grew up around military post that was est. 1842, abandoned in 1855, and rebuilt during Civil War. Inc. 1860.

Fort Scott Historic Site, SE Kansas; commemorates historic events in Kansas prior to and during the Civil War. Authorized 1965.

Fort Selkirk or **Selkirk**, trading post, SW Yukon, Canada, at confluence of Lewes and Pelly rivers, here forming Yukon R., 110 mi/177 km SE of Dawson; 62°46'N 137°23'W. Royal Can. Mounted Police post. Fort was est. 1848, destroyed by Indians 1852. Hudson's Bay Company re-established the post in 1938.

Fort Severn (SEH-vuhrn), village, NW Ont., Canada, on Hudson Bay, at mouth of Severn R.; 55°59'N 87°36'W. Trading post. Built by the British (1685), it was burned (1689) to prevent capture by the French. Fr. fort (1691) changed hands repeatedly, until handed over to Hudson's Bay Company under Treaty of Utrecht (1713).

Fort Shawnee, village (1990 pop. 4,128), Allen co., NW Ohio, 4 mi/6 km S of Lima; 40°41'N 84°08'W.

Fort Sill, U.S. military reservation (□ 148 sq mi/ 383 sq km), Comanche co., SW Okla., 4 mi/6.4 km N of Lawton; 25 mi/48 km long (E-W), c.5 mi/8 km wide. It is home of the U.S. Army Artillery and Missile Center. Est. 1869 by Gen. Philip Sheridan, the fort was named in memory of Joshua W. Sill, a Civil War general. The Wichita, Kiowa, Comanche, and other Native Amer. groups were ordered to live on the reservation and trained in agr.; Geronimo (buried in the Apache cemetery here) was imprisoned at the fort. Almost abandoned in 1904, it was revitalized by the establishment (1911) of a school that was to become the U.S. army's main field-artillery training base. There are 48 designated historic sites in the Fort Sill area. W entrance at Cache. Henry Post Army Airfield in S part; Wichita Mts. to NW. Fort Sill Mus.

Fort Simpson, village (1991 pop. 1,142), SW Mackenzie dist., N.W.T., Canada, on small isl. in Mackenzie R., at mouth of Liard R.; 61°52'N 121°21'W. River port; on Mackenzie Highway. Trapping, fishing. Trading post; site of agr. experiment station, Anglican and R.C. missions and schools; airfield; govt. radio, TV, and meteorological stations; hosp.; Royal Can. Mounted Police post. Oats, potatoes, barley, beets, vegetables are grown in vicinity. Founded 1804 by North West Company and named Fort of the Forks, it was renamed 1821, after being taken over by Hudson's Bay Company. Scheduled air service. Outfitting for Nahanni Natl. Park.

Fort Smith, SW region (□ 235,636 sq mi/610,455 sq km; 1991 pop. 27,553), N.W.T., Canada, ⊙ Fort Smith. The region extends E from the Yukon to the upper Thelon R. and N from Alta. to encompass most of Great Bear L. Encompassing the S Mackenzie Mts. and the S portion of the Mackenzie R., it is a transitional zone bet. the forests of the S and the arctic tundra of the N. The most prosperous and populous of the N regions, its main industries are mining, tourism, lumbering, fur trapping, and fishing. The Fort Smith region, formerly part of Mackenzie dist., was created by the territorial govt. in the early 1970s.

Fort Smith, city (1990 pop. 72,798), ⊙ (with Greenwood) Sebastian co., c.125 mi/201 km WNW of Little Rock, NW Ark., at the Okla. line where the Arkansas and the Poteau rivers join; 35°22'N 94°22'W. "Twin City" of Van Buren, Ark., to NE. It is the RR and trade center of a farm and livestock area and a most industrial city in Ark. Highly diversified mfg. (construction materials, food and beverages, textiles, furniture, hardware). Large Fort Chaffee Military Reservation to SE. Of interest are Fort Smith Natl. Historic Site, which includes the Old Fort Mus. and the "Hanging Judge" Isaac Parker's court; a natl. Civil War cemetery; and an annual rodeo. Westark Community Col. and a U.S. forest reserve are to the S. In 1969 the city was linked by the Arkansas R. project with the inland waterway to the Gulf of Mexico and the Great Lakes; James W. Trimble Lock and Dam (Arkansas R.) to E of city. Reservoir on nearby Lees Creek filled in 1996 to serve as water source for city. Founded as a military post in 1817, inc. 1842; an important supply point during the 1848 gold rush.

Fort Smith Historic Site, Sebastian co., NW Ark., S of Rogers Ave. Bridge in downtown Fort Smith, near Arkansas R. where it enters Okla. One of the first U.S. military posts in the Louisiana Purchase; maintained law and order in the Oklahoma Territory. Remains of 2 frontier forts and a federal courthouse. Authorized 1961.

Fort Snelling, historic site, on a W bluff above the junction of the Mississippi and Minnesota rivers, Hennipen co., SE Minn., 7 mi/11.3 km SSE of Minneapolis, and 7 mi/11.3 km SW of St. Paul, in Fort Snelling Park, at E edge of Minneapolis–St. Paul Internatl. Airport; 45°53'N 93°10'W. It served as a regional protective barrier and as a nucleus for settlement. Minneapolis and St. Paul grew N and E of the fort, beginning in the mid-1800s; now partially restored. Fort Snelling Natl. Cemetery to S. Est. 1820.

Fort Stanwix, colonial outpost on the site of Rome, N.Y., controlling a principal route from the Hudson R. to L. Ontario; 43°13'N 75°28'W. Originally a Fr. trading center, it was rebuilt by the English Gen. John Stanwix in 1758. The Br. colonial leader Sir William Johnson signed an important treaty with the Iroquois here in 1768. The fort fell into disrepair until early in the Amer. Revolution, when it was rebuilt by the patriots and called Fort Schuyler. In 1777 the fort was held against Br. and Tory forces until reinforcements under Benedict Arnold helped lift the siege. Fort Stanwix is a natl. monument.

Fort Steele, village, SE B.C., Canada, on Kootenay R., at mouth of St. Mary R., and 10 mi/16 km NE of Cranbrook; 49°37'N 115°38'W. Ranching, fruitgrowing. In mining (gold, silver, copper, iron, lead) region.

Fort Stewart Military Reservation (□ 463 sq mi/ 1,199 sq km), SE Ga., just W of Savannah and just N of Hinesville; home of the Third Infantry; has 2,000 bldgs. and over 15,000 active duty personnel with 24,099 dependents; employs 3,356 civilian workers. Est. 1940 by President Franklin D. Roosevelt for anti-aircraft training. It is the largest army base E of the Mississippi R. and played an important role during the Persian Gulf War.

Fort Stockton, town (1990 pop. 8,524), ⊙ Pecos co., extreme W Texas, c.150 mi/241 km WSW of San Angelo; 30°53′N 102°53′W. Elev. 2,954 ft/900 m. Trade and shipping center for cattle, sheep, and goats; oil area; light mfg. Old Fort Stockton (founded 1859; now in ruins) and Comanche Springs (Indian watering place; now used for irrigation) are nearby. Paisano Pete, large scale roadrunner statute.

Fort Sumner, town (1990 pop. 1,269), ⊙ De Baca co., E N.Mex., on Pecos R., and 60 mi/97 km W of Clovis; 34°28′N 104°14′W. Trade and shipping point in livestock and irrigated agr. region (cattle, sheep; grain, sorghum). Mfg. (feeds, windmills). Sumner L. Reservoir, on Pecos Bay, and Sumner Lake State Park, to NW. Ruins of Fort Sumner State Monument (built 1862). Cemetery containing remains of Billy the Kid (William H. Bonney) to SE.

Fort Sumter, fortification and historic site, on a shoal at the entrance to the harbor of Charleston, S.C., built 1829–1860, and named for Gen. Thomas Sumter. Scene of the opening engagement of the Civil War. Upon passing the Ordinance of Secession (Dec. 1860), S.C. demanded all Federal property within the state, particularly the forts of Charleston harbor — Fort Sumter, Fort Moultrie, and Castle Pinckney. On Dec. 26, 1860, Major Robert Anderson removed his U.S. army command of about 100 men from Fort Moultrie to Fort Sumter, a stronger defensive site. Gov. F. W. Pickens of S.C. had the other 2 forts, along with the Charleston arsenal, seized, and upon the refusal of President James Buchanan to order Anderson's evacuation, had guns trained on Fort Sumter. In Feb. 1861, the newly organized Confederate govt. assumed the state's part in the controversy, sending Gen. P. G. T. Beauregard to command Charleston. On April 8, 1861, Pickens received President Lincoln's notice that a naval expedition would be sent to provision the beleaguered garrison. After a 34-hour Confederate bombardment, begun at 4:30 A.M. on April 12, Anderson accepted terms, and on April 14 the garrison departed with the honors of war. Although no one was killed, the action made manifest the belligerent spirit in both the North and the South. In 1863, Union naval attacks on the fort were thoroughly repulsed. After Sherman forced the evacuation of Charleston, the U.S. flag was again raised over the fort by Anderson on April 14, 1865. Fort Sumter became a natl. monument in 1948; Fort Moultrie is part of the monument.

Fort Supply, village (1990 pop. 369), Woodward co., NW Okla., near mouth of Wolf Creek on North Canadian R., and 13 mi/21 km NW of Woodward; 36°34′N 99°34′W. Mfg. (overhead feed bins). Founded as U.S. Fort Supply in 1867. Fort Supply Dam and lake just S. Sometimes called just Supply.

Fort Supply Lake, reservoir, 4 mi/6.4 km long, Woodward co., NW Okla., on Wolf Creek 5 mi/8 km SW of its mouth on North Canadian (Beaver) R., 10 mi/16 km NW of Woodward and just S of Fort Supply; 36°32′N 99°33′W. Formed by Fort Supply Dam (82 ft/25 m high, 11,325 ft/3,452 m long), built (1942) for flood control and water supply.

Fort Thomas, city (1990 pop. 16,032), Campbell co., N Ky., a residential suburb 4 mi/6.4 km SE of Cincinnati (Ohio), on the Ohio R.; 39°04′N 84°27′W. Light mfg. Thomas More Col. to S. Named after an army post (est. 1890) that later became a veterans' hosp. Inc. 1867.

Fort Thompson, village (1990 pop. 1,088), Buffalo co., central S.Dak., 16 mi/26 km NNW of Chamberlain, and on Missouri R. at Big Bad Dam; in Crow Creek Indian Reservation hq.; 44°02′N 99°24′W. Lower Brule Indian Reservation and site of Fort Hale across river.

Fort Ticonderoga, N.Y.: see TICONDEROGA.

Fort Totten, village (1990 pop. 867), Benson co., NE central N.Dak., on Devils L., and 10 mi/16 km SSW of Devils L. city; 47°58′N 98°59′W. Hq. of Devils L. Sioux Indian Reservation. Original fort still stands and is a historical site. Tribal community col.

Fort Towson (TOU-suhn), village (1990 pop. 568), Choctaw co., SE Okla., 14 mi/23 km E of Hugo; 34°01′N 95°17′W. Trading point for farm area. Fort Towson Historical Site, with ruins of old Fort Towson (1824), is nearby. Raymond Gary State Park to S; Hugo L. reservoir (Kiamichi R.) to W.

Fort Union National Monument, Mora co., NW N.Mex., 25 mi/40 km NNE of Las Vegas, covers 721 acres/292 ha. Ruins of last of 3 U.S. Army forts built on this site on the Santa Fe Trail and occupied 1851–1891. It once was the largest military post in the SW U.S. Authorized 1954.

Fort Union Trading Post National Historic Site, Williams co., W N.Dak., and Roosevelt co., NE Mont. Reconstructed trading post of the American Fur Company, erected in 1828 (originally called Fort Floyd), on Missouri R. just NW of and opposite confluence of Yellowstone R. (□ 378 acres/153 ha in N.Dak., 64 acres/26 ha in Mont.). Controlled converging routes of travel from the Rocky Mts., for c.40 years it was the most important post in the U.S. fur trade and was under the control of Amer. fur trader Kenneth Mackenzie. When the U.S. army assumed control in 1868, Fort Union was torn down and Fort Buford, a military post, was erected nearby. Authorized 1966.

Fort Valley, town (1990 pop. 8,198), ⊙ Peach co., central Ga., 25 mi/40 km SW of Macon; 32°33′N 83°53′W. Market, shipping, and canning center for peach-growing area. Mfg. (motor vehicle bodies, textiles, chemicals, wire harnesses). Fort Valley State Univ., a unit of the Univ. System of Ga. here. Settled c.1836, inc. 1856.

Fort Vancouver National Historic Site (□ 209 acres/85 ha), Vancouver, Clark co., SW Wash., near Columbia R. Site of western hq. of Hudson's Bay Company (1825–1849) and later of a U.S. Army fort. Became the center of commercial, political, and cultural activities for Pacific Northwest. Authorized 1948 as natl. monument; changed to historic site 1961.

Fort Vermilion (vuhr-MIL-yuhn), village, N Alta., Canada, on Peace R., and 170 mi/274 km W of L. Athabaska; 58°24′N 116°00′W. Northernmost wheat producing area. Fort Vermilion wheat took 1st prize at Chicago World's Fair 1893. Trading post. Established on nearby site in 1798, it was taken over (1821) by Hudson's Bay Company; later removed to present site. Vermilion Falls (25 ft/8 m high) on Peace R. are 40 mi/64 km E.

Fort Wainwright, army base, Fairbanks, Alaska; 2d largest in Alaska. Light infantry units specially trained in cold weather warfare; 8,000 Lend Lease aircraft transferred here to Russians during World War II. Formerly Ladd Field.

Fort Walton Beach, city (□ 8 sq mi/20.7 sq km; 1990 pop. 21,471), Okaloosa co., NW Fla., on the Gulf of Mexico; 30°25′N 86°37′W. It is a year-round resort, with beaches and freshwater and deep-sea fishing. Mfg. includes electronic equip. and small boats. Eglin Air Force Base, on the city's outskirts, contributes significantly to the economy. The city grew around a fort constructed during the Seminole War (1835–1842). Its main growth came after 1941, when it developed as a resort center and the air force base was expanded. A natl. historic landmark here includes a mus. of Native Amer. culture. Inc. 1941.

Fort Washakie (WAHSH-uh-kee), village (1990 pop. 1,334), Fremont co., W central Wyo., on S. Fork Sage Creek, on branch of Popo Agie R., and 14 mi/23 km NNW of Lander, near Wind River Range; 43°00′N 108°55′W. Elev. 5,570 ft/1,698 m.

Fort Washington, uninc. town (1990 pop. 3,699), Montgomery co., SE Pa., in Upper Dublin township, suburb 13 mi/21 km N of Philadelphia, on Wissahickon Creek. Mfg. (food and dairy prods., display terminals, navigation equip., pharmaceuticals; printing and publishing). Fort Washington State Park to SW, with remains of Revolutionary fortifications. Childventure Mus.; Hope Lodge, 18th-cent. Georgian mansion; Highlands Mansion and Gardens.

Fort Washington, military post during the Amer. Revolution, situated on the highest point of Manhattan isl., N.Y. city, N.Y., overlooking the Hudson R. opposite Fort Lee, N.J. It was a hastily built earthwork with no water supply within its walls and no fortifications able to withstand a strong attack. It was, however, strategically located, and its maintenance was a mark of Amer. prestige. When Gen. George Washington was retreating before the Br. general William Howe, in 1776, he left a garrison under Gen. Nathanael Greene at Fort Washington. In spite of Washington's advice to abandon the fort, Greene chose to remain. Howe attacked and captured the fort on Nov. 16, 1776.

Fort Washington Park, Md., 9 mi/14.5 km SSE of Washington, D.C.; 38°43′N 77°02′W. The first fortification built for the defense of the capital was constructed here in 1809. Destroyed in the War of 1812, it was rebuilt in 1824. National park authorized 1930.

Fort Wayne, city (1990 pop. 173,072), ⊙ Allen co., NE Ind., where the St. Joseph and the St. Mary's rivers join to form the Maumee R.; 41°04′N 85°08′W. The city straddles land divide bet. Wabash (Mississippi) and Maumee (St. Lawrence) river systems; Wabash-Erie Canal, completed here in 1843, provided water link to W. It is the 2d largest city in the state, a major RR and shipping point, a wholesale and distribution hub, and a diverse mfg. center, with large high-technology electronics and automotive industries. The Kekionga people had their chief town at this strategic water intersection before the French founded (c.1680) a trading post there. In 1697 a Fr. fort was built; it remained under Fr. control until 1760, when it was surrendered to the British. The fort was held briefly by Native Americans in Pontiac's Rebellion. Later, they were subdued by Anthony Wayne, who built (1794) the fort named for him. The fur-trading center began to grow after the War of 1812. The city is the seat of several cols., the Indiana Inst. of Technology, and a branch of Ind. Univ.-Purdue Univ. The city has a philharmonic orchestra and numerous museums, including one devoted exclusively to Lincoln memorabilia. Also of interest are the Landing, the restored main street of the original frontier settlement; the sunken gardens at Lakeside Park; and the burial place of Johnny Appleseed (John Chapman). Baer Field Airport in SW part of city. Laid out 1824, inc. 1840.

Fort Wilkins State Park, Mich.: see COPPER HARBOR.

Fort William, Ont.: see THUNDER BAY.

Fort William Henry, historic site, at the S end of L. George, NE N.Y.; 43°25′N 75°43′W. Built by the English in 1755. In 1757, during the last conflict of the Fr. and Indian Wars, it was captured and destroyed. Although Fr. Gen. Louis Montcalm had promised safe-conduct from the fort, he was unable to control his Native Amer. allies, who attacked and killed many of those retreating from the garrison. Fort William Henry was rebuilt in 1953 and is now a mus.

Fort Wingate, uninc. village (1990 pop. 800), McKinley co., NW N.Mex., in NW foothills of Zuni Mts., 12 mi/19 km ESE of Gallup. Elev. 6,991 ft/2,131 m. Cattle, sheep; alfalfa, hay. Zuñi Indian Reservation to S; Navajo Indian Reservation to N; part of Cibola Natl. Forest to S.

Fort Worth, city (1990 pop. 447,619), ⊙ Tarrant co., N Texas; 32°45′N 97°20′W. Downtown Fort Worth is 30 mi/48 km W of downtown Dallas; a NNE extension of the city's corporate limits to S entrance of Dallas–Fort Worth Internatl. Airport (and to co. line) puts the city boundary within 5 mi/8 km of Dallas city limits. Most of the urban expansion of the Dallas–Fort Worth area has radiated out from Dallas; most of Fort Worth's growth has been to E and NE, toward Dallas. Drained by W Fork and Clear Fork of Trinity R., and several branch creeks. An army post was est. in 1847, and after the Civil War the settlement became a cow town. The first RR (completed 1876) helped establish it as a meat-packing and cattle-shipping point. Later in the 19th cent., the city became a prime center for milling and shipping grain. In 1919 oil was discovered W of here, and large refineries and other oil and gas installations were built. The city was financially revitalized by the construction of major industrial parks in the 1980s just N of the city. Oil, cattle, and grain remain important, but newer industries, such as aerospace and electronic equip mfg., wholesaling, transportation, communications, bldg. materials, and food processing, have led to great industrial and economic development. The aircraft industry is the largest in the Dallas–Fort Worth area. The Dallas–Fort Worth Internatl. Airport was the largest in the world when it was opened in early 1974. Specialized foreign air freight facility. Fort Worth is the seat of Texas Christian Univ. (Amon Carter Stadium), Texas Wesleyan Univ., Tarrant Co. Junior Col. (3 campuses around city) (S and NW campuses in city, NE campus in Hurst), and a Baptist seminary. Points of interest include Tarrant County Convention Center, Tarrant County Courthouse (1895), the Mus. of Science and History, the Health Mus., art museums and centers, Fort Worth Nature Center and Refuge to NW, Stockyards Historic Area; Eagle Mt. Natl. Guard Base to NW; a botanic garden, a zoo, an aquarium, a planetarium, National Cowgirl Hall of Fame, and Heritage Hall. Area reservoirs include Eagle Mt. L. and L. Worth to NW, Benbrook L. to SW, Grapevine L. to NE, L. Arlington on E boundary. Settled 1843, inc. 1873.

Fort Wright (fort REIT), uninc. town (1990 pop. 6,570, including Lookout Heights, to NW), Kenton co., N Ky., 4 mi/6.4 km SW of downtown Cincinnati (Ohio) and 2 mi/3.2 km SW of Covington. Mfg. (resins).

Fort Wrigley, Canada: see WRIGLEY.

Fort Yates, village (1990 pop. 183), ⊙ Sioux co., S N.Dak., on Missouri R. (L. Oahe Reservoir), and 50 mi/80 km SSE of Bismarck; 46°05′N 100°37′W. Livestock, grain. Agency hq. for Standing Rock Indian Reservation (N. and S.Dak.). Sitting Bull burial site nearby. Tribal casino, tribal community col. Mountain/Central time zone boundary, which follows Missouri R. to N and S, skirts around the village to W, putting it in Central zone, while remainder of Indian reservation is in Mountain zone.

Fort Yukon, village (1990 pop. 580), NE Alaska, on Yukon R. at mouth of Porcupine R., and 140 mi/225 km NE of Fairbanks, on the Yukon Flats, just N of Arctic Circle; 66°34′N 145°18′W. Fur-trading center and supply base for trappers. Has hosp., schools, airfield. A post est. here 1847 by Hudson's Bay Company, in agreement with Russians, was moved to Old Rampart House and later to British territory, after U.S. purchase of Alaska.

Fort-de-France (fawr–duh–FRAWNGS), city (1988 pop. 99,844), ⊙ the French overseas dept. of Martinique, West Indies; 14°36′N 61°05′W. Located on a large natural harbor, at the mouth (N) of Baie de Fort-de-France, with cruise ship pier, across the bay. It is a popular tourist resort and a free port, exporting mainly bananas, sugar, and rum. It was settled in 1762 by the French, who built Fort-Royal by the strategically situated harbor. Yellow fever hampered its prosperity, however, and Fort-de-France did not gain importance until after 1902, when the city of Saint-Pierre was destroyed by an eruption of Mont Pelée. Drainage of the swamps to control disease further stimulated Fort-de-France's growth. Empress Josephine, wife of Napoleon I, was born across the bay from the city.

Forteau Bay (for-TO), inlet (6 mi/10 km long, 4 mi/6 km wide at entrance) on Strait of Belle Isle, SE Lab., Canada; 51°27′N 56°55′W. On NE side of entrance is Amour Point. On W shore of bay is fishing settlement of Forteau.

Fortescue (FOR-tes-kioo), town (1990 pop. 46), Holt co., NW Mo., on Missouri R., and 12 mi/19 km NW of Oregon; 40°02′N 95°19′W. Mfg. (lead alloys and smelting). Squaw Creek wildlife refuge to E. Big Lake State Park to N. Area flooded 1993.

Fortierville (FOR-tyai-vil), village (1991 pop. 381), S Que., Canada, near the St. Lawrence, 26 mi/42 km ENE of Trois Rivières; 46°29′N 72°02′W. Lumbering. In agr. area.

Fortín de las Flores (for-TEEN de las FLO-res), city (1990 pop. 17,786), ⊙ Fortín municipio, Veracruz, E Mexico, in Sierra Madre Oriental, on RR, and 5 mi/8 km W of Córdoba on Mexico Highway 150; 18°54′N 97°00′W. Coffee-growing center. Famous for gardenias, orchids, camellias.

Fortine (FOR-teen), village (1990 pop. 130), Lincoln co., NW Mont., 48 mi/77 km NW of Kalispell, on Fortine and Deep creeks. RR tunnel through Salish Mts. to S. Timber; lumber. Area surrounded by parts of Kootenai Natl. Forest; Stillwater State Forest to SE. Murphy and Dickey lakes to SE.

Fortress Mountain, Wyo.: see ABSAROKA RANGE.

Fort-Royal, Martinique: see FORT-DE-FRANCE.

Fortson, town, Muscogee co., Ga., 12 mi/19 km NE of Columbus; 32°36′N 84°56′W. Asphalt, crushed stone; steel fabricating.

Fortuna, city (1990 pop. 8,788), Humboldt co., NW Cal., 13 mi/21 km S of Eureka, on Eel R., 8 mi/12.9 km E of its mouth on Pacific Ocean; 40°36′N 124°08′W. Timber; some dairying, stock raising (sheep, cattle); sawmill. Humboldt Bay Natl. Wildlife Refuge to NW. Inc. 1906.

Fortuna, village (1990 pop. 53), Divide co., NW N.Dak., port of entry 6 mi/9.7 km N of village on Can. border; 48°54′N 103°00′W. Writing Rock Historic Site to S.

Fortuna Ledge, Alaska: see MARSHALL.

Fortune, town (1991 pop. 2,177), S N.F., Canada, on SE shore of Fortune Bay, near its entrance, 4 mi. WSW of Grand Bank; 47°04′N 55°52′W. Fishing port.

Fortune Bay, arm of the Atlantic Ocean, c.80 mi/130 km long, S N.F., Canada. Its shores are lined with many fishing villages. The French islands of Miquelon and St. Pierre are at its mouth, and its NE arm is Belle Bay.

Fortune Island, Bahama Isls.: see LONG CAY.

Fortville, town (1990 pop. 2,690), Hancock co., central Ind., 11 mi/18 km NNW of Greenfield, satellite community of Indianapolis; 39°56′N 85°51′W. Mfg. (abrasives, feeders, brake shoes). Laid out 1849.

Forty Fort, borough (1990 pop. 5,049), Luzerne co., NE central Pa., residential suburb 2 mi/3.2 km NNE of Wilkes-Barre, on Susquehanna R. (bridged). Light mfg. Settled 1772 on site of Colonial fort in the Wyoming Valley. Settlers made last stand here in Wyoming Valley massacre, 1778.

Forty Mile or **Fortymile**, village, W Yukon, Canada, near Alaska border, on Yukon R. at mouth of Fortymile R., and 40 mi/64 km NW of Dawson; 64°27′N 140°33′W. Gold mining.

Foss, village (1990 pop. 148), Washita co., W Okla., 15 mi/24 km NW of Cordell; 35°27′N 99°10′W. In cotton and grain area. Foss L. reservoir and Foss State Park to N (Custer Creek).

Foss Lake, reservoir, 10 mi/16 km long, Custer co., W Okla., on Washita R., 13 mi/21 km WNW of Clinton; 35°33′N 99°08′W. Max. capacity 817,000 acre-ft. Formed by Foss Dam (128 ft/39 m high), built (1961) by the U.S. govt. for flood control and water supply. Foss State park at dam (SE); NW sect. in Washita Natl. Wildlife Refuge.

Fossil, village (1990 pop. 399), ⊙ Wheeler co., N central Oregon, 58 mi/93 km SE of the Dalles; 45°00′N 120°12′W. Alfalfa; sheep, cattle. John Day Fossil Beds Natl. Monument, Clarno Unit, and Clarno State Park to W. Dyer State Wayside to N; Shelton State Park to SE; Umatilla Natl. Forest to E.

Fossil Butte National Monument (BYOOT) (□ 13 sq mi/34 sq km), Lincoln co., W Wyo., 12 mi/19 km W of Kemmerer. Area containing Paleocene-Eocene fossil fish; most noteworthy freshwater-fish fossil site in U.S. Also contains fossilized turtles, bats, birds, insects, and plants. Authorized 1972.

Fosston (FAWS-tuhn), town (1990 pop. 1,529), Polk co., NW Minn., 40 mi/64 km WNW of Bemidji, on Poplar R.; 47°34′N 95°45′W. Grain, potatoes, carrots, sunflowers; livestock, poultry; dairying; mfg. (food processing; steel and aluminum fabrication). White Earth Indian Reservation to S; small lakes in area. Settled 1884.

Foster, village, S Que., Canada, on Centre Yamaska R., at N end of Brome L., 14 mi/23 km SE of Granby. Dairying; resort.

Foster, county (□ 646 sq mi/1,673 sq km; 1990 pop. 3,983), central N.Dak.; ⊙ Carrington; 47°27′N 98°52′W. Drift prairie drained by James R. and Pipestem Creek. Sunflowers, wheat, barley, flax; cattle; dairy prods.

Juanita L. in NE, small lakes in S. Formed 1873, organized 1883.

Foster 1 town (1990 pop. 161), Bates co., W Mo., near Marais des Cygnes R., 12 mi/19 km SW of Butler; 38°10′N 94°30′W. Former coal-mining area. **2** town (1990 pop. 4,316), Providence co., W R.I., on Conn. line, on Ponaganset and Moosup rivers, and 16 mi/26 km W of Providence, in rural hilly area; 41°48′N 71°45′W. Jerimoth Hill (812 ft/247 m) is state's highest point. Timber, gravel pits, granite quarries. Set off from Scituate and inc. 1781. Named for Theodore Foster, a US. Senator who owned property in the town.

Foster 1 village (1990 pop. 65), Bracken co., N Ky., on the Ohio R., 12 mi/19 km W of Augusta; 38°47′N 84°12′W. Mfg. (aluminum castings). Meldahl Lock and Dam on Ohio R. to E. **2** village (1990 pop. 57), Pierce co., NE Nebr., 8 mi/12.9 km NW of Pierce, and on branch of Elkhorn R; 42°16′N 97°40′W.

Foster City, city (1990 pop. 28,176), San Mateo co., W Calif., suburb 17 mi/27 km SSE of San Francisco Bay, at W end of San Mateo Bridge; 37°34′N 122°14′W. Mfg. (analytical instruments, printing and publishing, biological prods., computers, computer peripherals, photographic equipment, industrial instruments). Bay Meadows Racetrack to W.

Foster Peak (10,511 ft/3,204 m), SE B.C., Canada, in Rocky Mts., on W edge of Kootenay Natl. Park, 27 mi/43 km WSW of Banff; 51°04′N 116°10′W.

Fosterdale, resort village (1990 pop. 150), Sullivan co., SE N.Y., near Pa. line, 16 mi/26 km WNW of Monticello; 41°42′N 74°58′W.

Fostoria (fahs-TOR-ee-uh), city (1990 pop. 14,983), Hancock, Seneca, and Wood cos., NW Ohio; 41°09′N 83°25′W. A trade and shipping center for a livestock and farm area, Fostoria processes grain, flour, and soybeans. Mfg. (carbon prods., iron castings, automotive and electrical equip.). Inc. 1854.

Fostoria, town, Clay co., NW Iowa, 7 mi/11.3 km N of Spencer; 43°14′N 95°09′W. In livestock and grain area.

Fostoria, uninc. village (1990 pop. 482), Montgomery co., E Texas, c.40 mi/64 km NNE of Houston, near Peach Creek. In timber area. Sam Houston Natl. Forest to N.

Fouke (FOK), village (1990 pop. 634), Miller co., extreme SW Ark., 16 mi/26 km SE of Texarkana; 33°15′N 93°53′W.

Fountain, county (□ 397 sq mi/1,028 sq km; 1990 pop. 17,808), W Ind., ⊙ Covington; 40°07′N 87°14′W. Bounded W and N by Wabash R.; drained by small Coal Creek. Mfg. at Attica, Covington, and Veedersburg. Bituminous-coal mining, dairying, farming (wheat, corn, rye, soybeans, fruit, vegetables; cattle, hogs, sheep, poultry). Sand, gravel, clay pits. Portland Arch natural bridge in NW; part of Shades State Park in SE corner. Formed 1825.

Fountain, city (1990 pop. 9,984), El Paso co., central Colo., on Fountain Creek, and suburb 12 mi/19 km SSE of Colorado Springs; 38°40′N 104°41′W. Elev. 5,546 ft/1,690 m. Shipping point in irrigated alfalfa region; cattle; mfg. (computers, software assembly). Fort Carson Military Reserve to W.

Fountain 1 village (1990 pop. 165), Mason co., W Mich., 15 mi/24 km NE of Ludington, and on small Lincoln R.; 44°02′N 86°10′W. In farm and resort area; lumber; cheese; pallets and boxes. Manistee Natl. Forest to N and E. **2** village (1990 pop. 327), Fillmore co., SE Minn., near Root R., 25 mi/40 km SE of Rochester; 43°44′N 92°07′W. Poultry, livestock; grain, soybeans; dairying; timber. Richard J. Dorer Memorial Hardwood State Forest to W, S, and E. **3** village (1990 pop. 445), Pitt co., E N.C., 15 mi/24 km WNW of Greenville and 15 mi/24 km ESE of Wilson; 35°40′N 77°38′W. Tobacco, cotton, peanuts, grain, sweet potatoes; chickens, cattle, hogs. Mfg. (crushed stone, apparel).

Fountain City 1 town (1990 pop. 766), Wayne co., E Ind., on a fork of Whitewater R., 10 mi/16 km N of Richmond; 39°58′N 84°55′W. In livestock and grain area. Highest point in Ind. (1,257 ft/383 m) 3 mi/4.8 km to NE (unnamed). **2** town (1990 pop. 938), Buffalo co., N Wis., on Mississippi R., 7 mi/11.3 km NNW of Winona,

Minn., surrounded by bluffs; 44°07′N 91°42′W. Livestock; beer, dairy prods. Merrick State Park is to W; Lock and Dam No. 5 to NW, Lock and Dam No. 5A to SE.

Fountain City, village, Knox co., E Tenn., N suburb of Knoxville.

Fountain Creek, c.60 mi/97 km long, in central Colo., rises N of Pikes Peak in Front Range, flows in W El Paso co., at confluence of Catamount and Crystola creeks, SE of Manitou Springs and Colorado Springs, where it is joined by Monument Creek from N, continues SSE past Security-Widefield and Fountain, and S to Arkansas R. at Pueblo.

Fountain Green, village (1990 pop. 578), Sanpete co., central Utah, 12 mi/19 km SE of Nephi; 39°37′N 111°38′W. Sheep, cattle; wool. Elev. 5,994 ft/1,827 m. Uinta Natl. Forest to W; Fountain Green State Fish Hatchery to N. Settled 1859.

Fountain Hill, village (1990 pop. 195), Ashley co., SE Ark., 19 mi/31 km S of Monticello; 33°21′N 91°50′W.

Fountain Hill, borough (1990 pop. 4,637), Lehigh co., E Pa., suburb 4 mi/6.4 km E of Allentown, on Lehigh R.

Fountain Hills, town (1990 pop. 10,030), Maricopa co., central Ariz., residential suburb 21 mi/34 km ENE of Phoenix, in McDowell Mts.; 33°36′N 111°44′W. Mfg. (printing and publishing). Famed for a fountain that shoots water 560 ft/171 m high. City of Scottsdale to W; Salt R. Indian Reservation to S; Fort McDowell Indian Reservation to E, with Tonto Natl. Forest beyond it; McDowell Mt. Park to N.

Fountain Inn, town (1990 pop. 4,388), Greenville co., NW S.C., 16 mi/26 km SE of Greenville; 34°41′N 82°12′W. Textile-mfg. equip., apparel, resins, pumps, metal fabricating, commercial printing, RR equipment; baked goods. Agr. (poultry, livestock; grain, tomatoes, soybeans, peaches).

Fountain Run, village (1990 pop. 259), Monroe co., S Ky., near Tenn. state line, 20 mi/32 km S of Glasgow; 36°43′N 85°57′W. Agr. (tobacco, grain; livestock; dairying); mfg. (jeans; lumber). Barren River L. reservoir to NW.

Fountain Valley, city (1990 pop. 53,691), Orange co., S Calif., suburb 27 mi/43 km SE of Los Angeles, 13 mi/21 km ESE of Long Beach, and near Pacific coast; 33°43′N 117°57′W. Chiefly residential, it also produces consumer goods, apparel, computer equip., semiconductors, and medical equip. Coastline Community Col. U.S. Navy Helicopter Field. Bolsa Chica and Huntington state beaches. Inc. 1957.

Four Corners, uninc. city (1990 pop.12,156), Marion co., NW Oregon, residential suburb 3 mi/4.8 km ESE of Salem; 44°55′N 122°58′W.

Four Corners, uninc. village, San Bernardino co., S Calif., 30 mi/48 km W of Barstow. Highway junction (Calif. 58 and US 395) in Mojave Desert, at NE corner of Edwards Air Force Base. Cattle. Solar power plant just to NW.

Four Lakes, chain of lakes in Dane co., S Wis. All 4 connected by Rock R., in order, NW-SE going downstream, Mendota, Monona, Waubesa, and Kegonsa. City of Madison, the state capital, straddles low ridge bet. Mendota and Monona lakes. Largest of the four is Mendota, c.8 mi/12.9 km long, on which the Univ. of Wisconsin campus is located.

Four League Bay, La.: see ATCHAFALAYA BAY.

Four Mountains, Islands of, group of 5 small uninhabited volcanic isls. of the Aleutians, SW Alaska, in N Pacific, W of Umnak Isl.; 52°50′N 170°W. Consists of Chuginadak Isl., Carlisle Isl. (7,500 ft/2,286 m), Herbert Isl. (4,235 ft/1,291 m), Kagamil Isl., and Uliaga Isl. Group is noted for fog and strong sea currents. Aleuts on Uliaga Isl. were wiped out (1764) by Russians.

Four Oaks, town (1990 pop. 1,308), Johnston co., central N.C., 8 mi/12.9 km SW of Smithfield; 35°27′N 78°25′W. Agr. area (tobacco, cotton, grain, peanuts, potatoes, sweet potatoes; poultry, livestock). Mfg. (cabinets, sportswear, military uniforms; lumber). Holts L. reservoir to NE.

Four Paths, town, Clarendon parish, S Jamaica, in Vere Plain, on RR, and 3 mi/4.8 km E of May Pen; 17°57′N 77°21′W. Trades in citrus fruit.

Four Peaks, group of rocky points (highest 7,645 ft/2,330 m), Maricopa-Gila co. line, central Ariz., in S part of Mazatzal Mts., c.45 mi/72 km ENE of Phoenix, in Tonto Natl. Forest.

Four Roads, village, central Trinidad, Trinidad and Tobago, 5 mi/8 km SE of Port of Spain. In cacao-growing region.

Fourche (FOOSH), village (1990 pop. 55), Perry co., central Ark., 12 mi/19 km SW of Conway, near Arkansas R. at mouth of Fourche La Fave R.; 34°59′N 92°37′W.

Fourche La Fave River (foosh luh FAIV), 140 mi/225 km long, in W Ark., rises in S Scott co. in the Ouachita Mts., flows ENE past Perryville to Arkansas R. 23 mi/37 km NW of Little Rock. Harris Brake Dam (Harris Brake Wildlife Management Area) is 15 mi/24 km above mouth and Nimrod Reservoir (c.22 mi/35 km long), impounded by Nimrod Dam (995 ft/303 m long, 97 ft/30 m high; for flood control), is c.60 mi/97 km above river's mouth.

Fourmile Creek, c.50 mi/80 km long, in central Colo., rises in E Teller co., NW of Pikes Peak, 8 mi/12.9 km SSW of Woodland Park, flows generally SW through Wrights Reservoir, then S, joining Arkansas R. 3 mi/4.8 km E of Canon City.

Fourth Lake, resort village (1990 pop. 300), Herkimer co., N central N.Y., in the Adirondacks, on Fourth L. (□ c.3 sq mi/7.8 sq km); part of Fulton Chain of Lakes, c.50 mi/80 km NNE of Utica; 43°22′N 73°50′W.

Foux, Cap à (FOO, kah-pah), westernmost headland of N peninsula of Haiti, on Windward Passage, 10 mi/16 km SW of Môle-Saint-Nicolas; 19°42′N 73°27′W.

Fowler, city (1990 pop. 3,208), Fresno co., central Calif., in San Joaquin valley, 9 mi/14.5 km SE of Fresno; 36°37′N 119°40′W. Packs and ships raisins, grapes, nectarines, almonds; grain; dairying; cattle; mfg. (food containers, rubber goods); winery. Inc. 1908.

Fowler 1 town (1990 pop. 1,154), Otero co., SE central Colo., on Arkansas R., 33 mi/53 km ESE of Pueblo; 38°07′N 104°01′W. Elev. 4,341 ft/1,323 m. RR junction to NW. Shipping point in cattle, sugar beet region; light mfg., food processing. Pueblo Ordnance Depot and U.S. Dept. of Transportation High Speed Ground Test Center to NW. **2** town (1990 pop. 2,333), ⊙ Benton co., W Ind., 27 mi/43 km NW of Lafayette; 40°37′N 87°19′W. Corn, oats, soybeans; hogs, poultry; mfg. (paper bags, steel fabrication, concrete patio stone). Laid out 1872.

Fowler 1 village (1990 pop. 571), Meade co., SW Kansas, on Crooked Creek, 11 mi/18 km NE of Meade; 37°22′N 100°12′W. Shipping point in cattle and grain region. **2** village (1990 pop. 912), Clinton co., S central Mich., 9 mi/14.5 km W of St. Johns; 43°00′N 84°44′W. Farm area.

Fowlerton, town (1990 pop. 306), Grant co., E central Ind., 10 mi/16 km SSE of Marion; 40°25′N 85°34′W. In agr. area.

Fowlerville, town (1990 pop. 2,648), Livingston co., SE Mich., 25 mi/40 km ESE of Lansing, and on Red Cedar R.; 42°39′N 84°04′W. In agr. area (grain, corn; livestock; dairy prods.); nursery; mfg. (automotive parts). Settled c.1836, inc. 1871.

Fox, village, Tuscaloosa co., W central Ala., 7 mi/11.3 km ENE of Tuscaloosa.

Fox, river, 176 mi/283 km long, rising in S central Wis., flows SW to within 2 mi/3.2 km of Wisconsin R. near Portage (hence the town's name), then NE through Buffalo and Montello lakes, past Montello, through Packwaukee L., past Berlin, through L. Butte des Morts, through city of Oshkosh and L. Winnebago at its W side. It continues NE from N end of lake, past Appleton and Kaukauna to Green Bay, an arm of L. Michigan, at Green Bay, Wis.; receives Wolf R. from NW in L. Butte des Morts. The cities of Appleton and Oshkosh are on the Fox. Rapids at points along the river furnish water power. The river was a well-known route used by early explorers, missionaries, and fur traders to reach the NW and the Mississippi R. system from the Great Lakes. A barge canal links the Fox and Wisconsin rivers at Portage, forming a continuous waterway from L. Michigan to the Mississippi R.

Fox, Cape, SE Alaska, 10 mi/16 km W of entrance to Pearse Canal; 54°46′N 130°51′W. Southernmost cape of Alaska mainland.

Fox Chapel, borough (1990 pop. 5,319), Allegheny co., SW Pa., residential suburb 8 mi/12.9 km NW of Pittsburgh, near Allegheny R. Hartwood Acres Park to N. Inc. 1934.

Fox Island, Jefferson co., N N.Y., in E part of L. Ontario, 6 mi/9.7 km S of Cape Vincent; 44°03′N 76°25′W. Isl. is 1.5 mi/2.4 km long; max. width c.½ mi/⁸⁄₁₀ km.

Fox Islands, Mich., in L. Michigan, 10 mi/16 km SW of Beaver Isl. and c.40 mi/64 km W of Petoskey; part of Beaver Islands archipelago. Includes North Fox Isl. (2 mi/3.2 km long, 1 mi/1.6 km wide), 45°28′N 85°46′W; and South Fox Isl. (c.5 mi/8 km long, 1.5 mi/2.4 km wide), 45°25′N 85°51′W. A lighthouse on South Fox Isl. is located at 45°22′N 85°50′W.

Fox Islands, Alaska: see ALEUTIAN ISLANDS.

Fox Lake, city (1990 pop. 1,269), Dodge co., S central Wis., S end of Fox L., bet. Fox and Beaver Dam lakes, 8 mi/12.9 km NNW of Beaver Dam; 43°33′N 88°54′W. In dairying region. Mfg. (printed circuit boards, gun cases). Settled 1838, inc. as village in 1893, as city in 1930.

Fox Lake, village (1990 pop. 7,478), Lake and McHenry cos., NE Ill., on Fox and Pistakee lakes of Chain O' Lakes, 17 mi/27 km W of Waukegan; 42°25′N 88°10′W. Trade center in dairying, agr., and lake resort area; dairy prods. Rapidly suburbanizing area. State park and state natural area nearby. Inc. 1906.

Fox Lake Hills, village (1990 pop. 2,681), Lake co., NE Ill., residential suburb 45 mi/72 km NW of downtown Chicago, 8 mi/12.9 km SW of Antioch, on E shore of Fox L.; 42°24′N 88°07′W. Recreation.

Fox Point, village (1990 pop. 7,238), Milwaukee co., SE Wis., on L. Michigan, a suburb 7 mi/11.3 km NNE of Milwaukee; 43°09′N 87°54′W. Settled by Dutch c. 1846, inc. 1926. Cardinal Stritch Col.

Fox River 1 river, c.85 mi/137 km long, in SE Iowa and NE Mo., rises near Udell in Appanoose co., Iowa, flows E and SE, into Mo., to the Mississippi R. 10 mi/16 km SW of Keokuk. **2** 185 mi/298 km long, in SE Wis. and N Ill., rises in Waukesha co., Wis., flows generally S, past Waukesha and Burlington, enters Ill., continuing SSW, past Elgin and Aurora, to Illinois R. at Ottawa. Connects and drains Grant, Fox, Pistakee, and other lakes in Ill.

Fox River Grove, village (1990 pop. 3,551), McHenry co., NE Ill., on Fox R. (bridged here), and 11 mi/18 km NNE of Elgin; 42°12′N 88°13′W. In agr. and resort area; mfg. (dairy prods., cement blocks). In suburbanizing area.

Fox River Valley Gardens, village (1990 pop. 665), McHenry co., NE Ill., on Lake co. border, on Fox R.; 42°14′N 88°12′W. Residential suburb 6 mi/9.7 km E of Crystal Lake.

Fox Run, uninc. town (1990 pop. 2,384), Butler co., W Pa., residential suburb 18 mi/29 km NNW of Pittsburgh and 4 mi/6.4 km W of Mars; 40°42′N 80°04′W.

Fox Valley, village (1991 pop. 360), SW Sask., Canada, 40 mi/64 km N of Maple Creek; 50°28′N 109°29′W. Elev. 2,358 ft/719 m. Wheat; livestock.

Foxboro (FAWKS-buh-ro), city (1990 pop. 14,637), Norfolk co., SE Mass.; 42°04′N 71°15′W. Mfg. (precision instruments). Foxboro Stadium is home of the New England Patriots football team. Foxboro Horse-Raceway State Forest. During the Revolutionary War cannons and cannonballs were manufactured here. Settled 1704, inc. 1778.

Foxburg, borough (1990 pop. 262), Clarion co., W central Pa., 16 mi/26 km WSW of Clarion, on Allegheny R. Corn, hay, potatoes; livestock; dairying. Clarion R. ½mi/⅘ km to E, its mouth on Allegheny R. 2 mi/3.2 km to S. First golf course in the United States.

Foxcroft, Maine: see DOVER-FOXCROFT.

Foxe Basin, a widening of the waterway bet. Baffin isl. and the Melville peninsula, c.340 mi/550 km long and c.225 mi/360 km wide, Baffin region, N.W.T., Canada. The basin is shallow and is ice-clogged most of the year. Foxe Channel (c.200 mi/320 km long and c.90 mi/

140 km wide) connects it with Hudson Bay and Hudson Strait.

Foxe Channel, SE Franklin dist. and E Keewatin dist., N.W.T., Canada, arm (200 mi/322 km long, 90 mi/145 km–200 mi/322 km wide) of Hudson Bay, bet. Melville Peninsula and Southampton Isl. (W) and Foxe Peninsula of Baffin Isl. (E); bet. 63°30′N–66°00′N and 78°00′W–84°00′W. Connects Hudson Strait and Hudson Bay (S) with Foxe Basin (N).

Foxe Peninsula, SW Baffin Isl., SE Franklin dist., N.W.T., Canada, extends 150 mi/241 km W into Foxe Channel, bet. Foxe Basin and Hudson Strait; 50 mi/80 km–100 mi/161 km wide. W extremity is Cape Queen; 64°43′N 78°30′W. On SW coast is Cape Dorset trading post.

Foxfire Village, village (1990 pop. 334), Moore co., central N.C., 10 mi/16 km WSW of Southern Pines, on Drowning Creek; 35°10′N 79°34′W. Tobacco, grain; poultry, livestock.

Foxhome (FAUKS-hom), village (1990 pop. 160), Wilkin co., W Minn., 11 mi/18 km W of Fergus Falls; 46°16′N 96°18′W. RR spur terminus from Fergus Falls. Grain, sunflowers, sugar beets; livestock; mfg. (fertilizers). Orwell Wildlife Area to SE.

Foxpark, village, Albany co., SE Wyo., in Medicine Bow Mts., 33 mi/53 km SW of Laramie. Elev. c.9,100 ft/2,774 m. Supply point in timber region.

Foxton, village, Jefferson co., central Colo., 25 mi/40 km SSW of Denver, on Craig Creek, in foothills of Front Range. Elev. 6,460 ft/1,969 m. Mfg. of audio/visual programs. Pike Natl. Forest to S.

Foxwarren, village, SW Man., Canada, 65 mi/105 km SW of Dauphin. Wheat, mixed farming.

Foxworth, village, Marion co., S Miss., 2 mi/3.2 km WSW of Columbia, on opposite side of Pearl R. Timber; mfg. (wooden trusses, granite monuments).

Foyil (FOI-uhl), village (1990 pop. 86), Rogers co., NE Okla., 10 mi/16 km NE of Claremore; 36°25′N 95°31′W. In livestock-raising and agr. area. Oologah L. reservoir to NW.

Frackville (FRAK-vil), borough (1990 pop. 4,700), Schuylkill co., E central Pa., 7 mi/11.3 km NNW of Pottsville, near Mahanoy Creek. Agr. (corn, hay; livestock, poultry; dairying); mfg. (textiles, apparel, plastics, titanium wire and spooling, tool and die); anthracite coal. Locust Lake State Park to E. Settled 1852, laid out 1861, inc. 1876.

Fragoso, Cayo (frah-GO-so, KEI-yo), long narrow key (25 mi/40 km long, up to 3 mi/4.8 km wide), off Villa Clara prov., N central Cuba, 10 mi/16 km N of Caibarién, just E of the Sabana Archipelago and part of larger Camagüey Archipelago; 22°42′N 79°30′W. Broken into 3 parts. Lighthouse.

Fram Haven, small bay of Smith Sound, Ellesmere Isl., NE Franklin Dist., N.W.T., Canada, just S of Cape Rutherford, at S entrance of Buchanan Bay; 78°47′N 75°00′W. Winter quarters of Otto Sverdrup's expedition (1898–1899).

Framingham (FRAI-meeng-ham), town (1990 pop. 64,994), Middlesex co., E Mass., on the Sudbury R. bet. Worcester and Boston; 42°19′N 71°26′W. Framingham has a very diverse mfg. base (footwear, hats, loudspeakers, chemicals, rubber, paper, ice cream, printing and publishing, computer components, and software). Framingham State Col. was 1st state normal school in U.S. (1839). Min. security women's state prison. Many large retail malls. Callahan State Park; Garden in the Woods. Settled 1650, inc. 1700.

Francés, Cabo (frah-SAIS, KAH-bo), a cape in Pinar del Río prov., SW Cuba, 40 mi/64 km SW of Pinar del Río; 21°55′N 84°03′W. Lighthouse.

Francés, Cayo (frah-SAIS, KEI-yo), key (3 mi/4.8 km long, up to 1.5 mi/2.4 km wide), off Villa Clara prov., N central Cuba, E of Cayo Fragoso, 13 mi/21 km ENE of Caibarién; 22°42′N 79°12′W. Lighthouse on W tip.

Frances Lake, trading post, SE Yukon, Canada, on Frances L. (27 mi/43 km long, 1 mi/2 km–3 km wide), 200 mi/322 km E of Whitehorse; 61°16′N 129°18′W. Sometimes called Fort Frances. Frances R. (90 mi/145 km long) drains the lake S to Liard R.

Frances, Lake, reservoir, Pondera co., NW central Mont., 25 mi/40 km SW of Shelby; 5 mi/8 km long, 3 mi/4.8 km wide; 48°15′N 112°11′W. Dammed at E end; levee at NW end; joined by irrigation canals, near branch of Dry Fork Marias R. Village of Valier on N shore.

Francés Viejo, Cape (frahn-SAIS vee-AI-ho), headland, N Dominican Republic, 33 mi/53 km NE of San Francisco de Macorís, 2 mi/3.2 km NW of Cabrera; 19°42′N 69°55′W. Lighthouse.

Francestown, town (1990 pop. 1,217), Hillsborough co., S N.H., 17 mi/27 km W of Manchester. Drained by South Branch Piscataquog R. and Rand Brook. Apples, vegetables; poultry, livestock; dairying; timber. Mfg. (log homes, signs). Crotched Mt. (2,055 ft/626 m) in W.

Francesville, town (1990 pop. 969), Pulaski co., NW Ind., near Big Monon Creek, 14 mi/23 km ENE of Rensselaer; 40°59′N 86°53′W. Mfg. (truck wheels and rims, plastic tubing, feed, crushed stone prods.).

Francis, town (1991 pop. 205), SE Sask., Canada, 40 mi/64 km SE of Regina; 50°06′N 103°52′W. Grain elevators.

Francis 1 village (1990 pop. 346), Pontotoc co., S central Okla., 11 mi/12.9 km NNW of Ada, near Canadian R.; 34°52′N 96°35′W. In agr. area. **2** village (1990 pop. 381), Summit co., N Utah, on Provo R., in Wasatch Mts., 12 mi/19 km ESE of Park City; 40°36′N 111°16′W. Elev. c.6,500 ft/1,981 m. Jordanville Reservoir and State Park to W; part of Wasatch Natl. Forest (Uinta Mts.) to E. Settled Nov. 11, 1899.

Francis Case, Lake, reservoir (□ 185 sq mi/479 sq km), S central S.Dak., on Missouri R., 50 mi/80 km SSE of Mitchell; 43°04′N 98°34′W. Max. capacity 6,300,000 acre-ft. Formed by Fort Randall Dam (170 ft/52 m high), built (1957) by Army Corps of Engineers for flood control; also used for power generation, irrigation, navigation, and recreation. Yankton Indian Reservation and Fort Randall Historic Site near dam; Snake Creek and Platt Creek state recreational areas on NE shore.

Francis Creek, village (1990 pop. 562), Manitowoc co., E Wis., 8 mi/12.9 km N of Manitowoc; 44°12′N 87°43′W. Dairying; grain, vegetables, fruit. Hidden Valley Ski Area to N.

Francis E. Walter Lake, reservoir (□ 13 sq mi/34 sq km), Luzerne and Carbon cos., NE Pa., on Lehigh R., 11 mi/18 km SSE of Wilkes-Barre; 41°07′N 75°43′W. Max. capacity of 16,290 acre-ft. Formed by Francis E. Walter Dam (239 ft/73 m high), built (1961) by Army Corps of Engineers for flood control.

Francis, Lake, reservoir, at Pittsburg, Coos co., N N.H., on Connecticut R., below First Connecticut L.; 5 mi/8 km long; 45°02′N 71°23′W. Formed by dam.

Francisco, town (1990 pop. 560), Gibson co., SW Ind., 7 mi/11.3 km E of Princeton; 38°20′N 87°27′W. In agr., gas and oil, and bituminous-coal area.

Francisco Castro Ceruto (frahn-SEE-sko CAHS-tro sai-ROO-to), sugar-mill village, Granma prov., E Cuba, just NE of Campechuela, 10 mi/16 km SW of Manzanillo; 20°14′N 75°17′W.

Francisco I. Madero 1 (fran-SEES-ko ee mah-DE-ro), town (1990 pop. 26,227), Coahuila, N Mexico, near Nazas R., in irrigated Laguna dist., on RR, and 20 mi/32 km NE of Torreón; 25°48′N 103°18′W. Wine; cotton, vegetables, fruit, alfalfa, wheat. Formerly Chávez. **2** town (1990 pop. 4,655), ⊙ Pánuco de Coronado municipio, Durango, N Mexico, on RR and 33 mi/53 km NE of Victoria de Durango on Mexico Highway 40; 24°28′N 104°20′W. Agr. center (corn, wheat, cotton, vegetables, fruit).

Francisco I. Madero, municipio, Mexico: see TEPATEPEC.

Francisco León (frahn-SEES-ko le-ON), town (1990 pop. 3,903), in NW Chiapas, Mexico, 43 mi/69 km NW of San Cristóbal de las Casas. No road access.

Francisco Portillo, Mexico: see AQUILES SERDÁN.

Francisco R. Murguía 1 Mexico: see NIEVES. **2** Mexico: see NIEVES.

Francisco Z. Mena, Mexico: see METLATOYUCA.

Francks Peak, Wyo.: see ABSAROKA RANGE.

Francoeur (frah-KUHR), village, S Que., Canada, 45 mi/72 km SW of Quebec. Dairying; pigs, cattle.

Francois Lake (□ 91 sq mi/236 sq km), central B.C., Canada, 90 mi/145 km W of Prince George; 68 mi/109 km long, 2 mi/3 km wide. Drains E into Fraser R. through Nechako R.

Franconia, uninc. city, Fairfax co., NE Va., residential suburb, 6 mi/9.7 km WSW of Alexandria, 10 mi/16 km SW of Wash., D.C.; 38°45′N 77°09′W. Fort Belvoir Military Reservation to S.

Franconia (frain-KO-nee-yuh), resort town (1990 pop. 811), Grafton co., NW N.H., 7 mi/11.3 km SSE of Littleton; 44°09′N 71°39′W. Drained by Gale R., Ham Branch Gale R., and Lafayette Brook. Mfg. (apparel); agr. (nursery crops, sugar maples; cattle, poultry; dairying). Tourism. Robert Frost Home in NW. Franconia Notch State Park and Parkway in S; Franconia Inn's cross-country ski area in W; Franconia Notch Ski Area in S; part of White Mt. Natl. Forest in E and S; Appalachian Trail crosses S part.

Franconia (fran-KO-nee-ah), uninc. village, Montgomery co., SE Pa., 24 mi/39 km NNW of Philadelphia and 2 mi/3.2 km W of Souderton; 40°18′N 75°21′W. Ornamental iron, poultry processing; dairying; livestock, poultry; grain.

Franconia Mountains (frain-KO-nee-yuh), range in the White Mts., N N.H., rising to 5,249 ft/1,600 m at Mt. Lafayette, also Mt. Lincoln (5,106 ft/1,556 m), in White Mts. Natl. Forest. Franconia Notch, a scenic, narrow pass (6 mi/10 km long), is W of the range. Appalachian Trail crosses range N-S.

Franconia Notch (frain-KO-nee-yuh), Grafton co., NW N.H., pass (1,896 ft/578 m) in White Mts., 23 mi/37 km N of Plymouth, W of Franconia Mountains; c.6 mi/9.7 km long. Pemigewasset R. drains S; Lafayette Brook drains N. Tourism. Echo and Profile (source of Pemigewasset R.) lakes, and the Flume, a gorge with granite walls 70 ft/21 m high along Mt. Liberty (4,460 ft/1,359 m), are in the notch. Overlooking the pass is the Old Man of the Mountain, or Profile, jutting cliffs that form the "Great Stone Face" that inspired Nathaniel Hawthorne's story. E and W of pass are parts of White Mt. Natl. Forest. Pass is in Franconia Notch State Park. U.S. Highway 3 and Interstate Highway 93 are part of Franconia Notch Parkway. Cannon Mt. Ski area; New England Ski Mus.; Cannon Mt. Aerial Tramway; Franconia Inn to NW. Franconia, N.H., NW of the notch, is a ski resort.

Frank, village, SW Alta., Canada, near B.C. border, in Rocky Mts., on Crowsnest R., and 5 mi/8 km SE of Coleman. Elev. 4,212 ft/1,284 m. Coal mining, logging; cattle. Village was partly destroyed by landslide from Turtle Mt., April 29, 1903.

Frankclay, uninc. village, St. Francois co., SE Mo., 5 mi/8 km W of Park Hills, SW of Leadwood. Former lead-mining location.

Frankel City, uninc. city (1990 pop. 1,344), Andrews co., W Texas, 40 mi/64 km NW of Odessa, near N.Mex. border. In agr. area (cattle, cotton, sorghum, corn). Oil and natural gas.

Frankenmuth (FRAIN-ken-mooth), town (1990 pop. 4,408), Saginaw co., E central Mich., 12 mi/19 km SE of Saginaw, and on Cass R.; 43°19′N 83°44′W. In farm area; wineries; brewery; mfg. (printing, food processing, machine tools); tourism. Historical Mus., Military and Space Mus., antique-arts village, flour mill (1847), Holz-Brke covered bridge on Cass R., famous German Glockenspiel, 35-bell carillon. Settled 1845 by German Bavarians; inc. 1904.

Frankfield, town (1990 pop. 3,373), Clarendon parish, central Jamaica, on Minho R., and 17 mi/27 km NW of May Pen (linked by RR); 18°09′N 77°21′W. In agr. region (bananas, sugarcane, coffee; livestock).

Frankford, village (1991 pop. 2,114), SE Ont., Canada, on Trent R., and 11 mi/18 km WNW of Belleville; 44°12′N 77°36′W. Paper milling; food processing; hydroelectric station.

Frankford, city (1990 pop. 396), Pike co., E Mo., 7 mi/11.3 km SSE of New London; 39°29′N 91°19′W. Corn, wheat, soybeans; hogs. Wood prods.; limestone quarry.

Frankford, village (1990 pop. 591), Sussex co., SE Del., 15 mi/24 km SSE of Georgetown, near Pepper Creek; 38°31'N 75°13'W. Marketing center in agr. region (strawberries, fruit, vegetables); mfg. (feeds). Cypress Swamp to W.

Frankford, industrial sect. in NE Philadelphia co., SE Pa., on Frankford Creek; 40°28'N 80°26'W. Printing and publishing. Annexed by Philadelphia, 1845.

Frankford, township (1990 pop. 5,114), Sussex co., NW N.J., 2 mi/3.2 km N of Newton; 41°09'N 74°44'W. Inc. 1798.

Frankfort 1 (FRANK-fuhrt), city (1990 pop. 14,754), ⊙ Clinton co., central Ind., 40 mi/64 km NNW of Indianapolis; 40°17'N 86°31'W. Trading and distribution center in apple-growing and farming region (grain, livestock). Diversified light mfg. Major RR junction. Laid out 1830. **2** city (1990 pop. 25,968), ⊙ of state and of Franklin co., N central Ky., 45 mi/72 km E of Louisville, and 22 mi/35 km WNW of Lexington on both sides of the Kentucky R., in the heart of the Bluegrass region; 38°11'N 84°52'W. It is the trade and shipping center for an area yielding tobacco, livestock, and limestone. Mfg. (wire prods., air brake components, wooden prods., plastic molded parts, apparel, concrete, distilled beverages, asphalt, automotive equip., thermostats, printing and publishing). Thoroughbred horses are also raised here. Daniel Boone reached the site in 1770. The city was organized (1786) by the Va. legislature and was selected as the state capital in 1792. Many old homes and bldgs. have been preserved. Capital City Airport to W. Of interest are the Capitol Bldg. (1910), with a giant floral clock in its plaza; the old state house (1827–1830), which houses the state historical society; Liberty Hall (1796). Kentucky State Univ. is here. Switzer Covered Bridge to NE; State Penitentiary to N; Capitol View Park has Ky. Vietnam Veteran Memorial and State Lib.; Daniel and Rebecca Boone graves in Frankfort Cemetery. Ky. Fish and Wildlife Game Farm to W (includes Salato Wildlife Education Center); Ky. Natl. Fish Hatchery to N, on Elkhorn Creek; Frank Lloyd's Wright Zeigler House (1910); Ky. Military History Mus. Inc. 1796. **3** city (1990 pop. 1,546), Benzie co., NW Mich., 32 mi/51 km WSW of Traverse City, on L. Michigan at mouth of Betsie R.; 44°38'N 86°13'W. Resort, sport fishing. Ships fruit; processes fruits and juices; coils. Indian relics found nearby. Sleeping Bear Dunes Natl. Lakeshore to NE, across Crystal L. Settled 1870; inc. as village 1885, as city 1935.

Frankfort 1 (FRANK-fuhrt), town (1990 pop. 927), Marshall co., NE Kansas, on Black Vermillion R., and 15 mi/24 km SE of Marysville; 39°42'N 96°25'W. Trading center in grain area; feeds, meat prods. Founded 1867, inc. 1875. **2** town (1990 pop. 1,020), Waldo co., S Maine, on the Penobscot R., and 14 mi/23 km NNE of Belfast; 44°35'N 68°55'W. Granite quarried at nearby Mt. Waldo.

Frankfort 1 (FRANK-fort), village (1990 pop. 7,180), Will co., NE Ill., 11 mi/18 km E of Joliet, on Hickory Creek; 41°30'N 87°50'W. In rapidly suburbanizing area. **2** village (□ 1 sq mi/2.6 sq km; 1990 pop. 2,693), Herkimer co., central N.Y., on Mohawk R., and 9 mi. ESE of Utica; 43°02'N 75°04'W. Office and library equipment, threaded fittings, agr. and industrial hand tools. Settled 1723, inc. 1863. **3** village (1990 pop. 1,065), Ross co., S Ohio, 11 mi/18 km WNW of Chillicothe, and on small Paint Creek; 39°24'N 83°11'W. In livestock and grain area. **4** village (1990 pop. 192), Spink co., NE central S.Dak., 10 mi/16 km E of Redfield, and on James R.; 44°52'N 98°18'W. Terminus for RR span from Redfield. Fisher Grove State Park.

Frankfort Heights, Ill.: see WEST FRANKFORT.

Frankfort Springs, borough (1990 pop. 134), Beaver co., W Pa., 24 mi/39 km W of Pittsburgh. Corn, hay; dairying; livestock. Raccoon Creek State Park to N; Frankfort Mineral Springs to NE.

Franklin, former state (1784–1788), formed by inhabitants of Washington, Sullivan, and Greene cos., E Tenn., after N.C. ceded its W lands to the U.S. N.C. repealed the act ceding the lands, and the state of Franklin ceased to exist after its elected government's first term expired.

Franklin, district, provisional administrative division (land area □ 541,793 sq mi/1,403,244 sq km, total □ 549,253 sq mi/1,422,565 sq km) of the N.W.T., Canada, almost coextensive with the Arctic Archipelago, the northernmost region of N. Amer., bounded by Mackenzie and Keewatin dists. (S), the Arctic Ocean (W and N), and Greenland (E); 72°00'N 96°00'W. Comprises isls. of Ellesmere, Baffin, Devon, Axel Heiberg, Ellef Ringnes, Amund Ringnes, Borden, Prince Patrick, Melville, Victoria, Bathurst, Cornwallis, Cornwall, Byam Martin, Bylot, Banks, Prince of Wales, Somerset, and King William, and numerous smaller isls.; also Melville and Boothia peninsulas of the mainland. Entire area constitutes a vast game preserve (est. 1926); fur trapping and craft cooperatives are chief occupations of Inuit population. There are trading posts at Cambridge Bay, Repulse Bay, Cape Dorset, L. Harbour, Iqaluit (Frobisher Bay), Pangnirtung, Pond Inlet, Arctic Bay, Igloolik, Holman Isl., and Craig Harbour. Major employers are govt. services and education sectors. There are air bases on Frobisher Bay and Padloping Isl., and U.S.-Canadian weather stations at Cambridge Bay, Cornwallis Isl., Ellesmere Isl., Alert and Eureka, Prince Patrick Isl., Clyde R., Victoria Isl. (Byron Bay, Lady Franklin Point), and Melville Peninsula. Dist. was created 1895, named after Sir John Franklin; boundaries defined 1897. All but westernmost part, including Banks Isl. and NW Victoria Isl., to be included in territory of Nunavut (1999).

Franklin, village (1991 pop. 1,651), SW Man., Canada, 8 mi/13 km E of Minnedosa. Grain, mixed farming.

Franklin 1 county (□ 646 sq mi/1,673 sq km; 1990 pop. 27,814), NW Ala.; ⊙ Russellville; 34°27'N 87°51'W. Agr. and iron-mining region bordering on Miss., crossed (N-S) by fall line. Soybeans, corn, poultry. Deposits of coal, iron, limestone, bauxite; natural gas production. Part of William B. Bankhead Natl. Forest in SE. Formed 1818. **2** county (□ 619 sq mi/1,603 sq km; 1990 pop. 14,897), Ozark region, NW Ark.; ⊙ Charleston and Ozark; 35°33'N 93°52'W. Drained by Mulberry R. Intersected by Arkansas R. Ozark Zeta Taylor Lock and Dam SE of Ozark form the narrow Ozark L. Agr. area (cattle, hogs, poultry). Coal mining; timber. Part of Fort Chaffee Military Reservation in far SW corner; part of Ozark Natl. Forest in N; part of Ozark Natl. Forest and a game refuge are in co. Formed 1837. **3** county (□ 1,026 sq mi/2,657 sq km; 1990 pop. 8,967), NW Fla., on the Gulf of Mexico (S), bet. Apalachicola (W) and Ochlockonee (E) rivers; ⊙ Apalachicola; 29°48'N 84°49'W. Lowland area, partly swampy. Contains St. Vincent, St. George, and Dog isls., enclosing St. Vincent Sound, Apalachicola Bay, and St. George Sound. Fishing; forestry (lumber, naval stores); cattle. Formed 1832. **4** county (□ 269 sq mi/697 sq km; 1990 pop. 16,650), NE Ga., on S.C. state line; ⊙ Carnesville; 34°22'N 83°14'W. Piedmont agr. area (cotton, corn, hay, soybeans, wheat; cattle, hogs, poultry) drained by Broad R. Textiles; lumber. Formed 1784. **5** county (□ 668 sq mi/1,730 sq km; 1990 pop. 9,232), SE Idaho; ⊙ Preston; 42°11'N 111°49'W. Bounded by Utah on S. Agr. area (SW) along Bear R. (sugar beets, sweet corn, wheat, alfalfa, barley; cattle, sheep, horses, poultry; dairying). Weston Canyon in SW; Caribou Natl. Forest in W, Cache Natl. Forest in E. Formed 1913. **6** county (□ 431 sq mi/1,116 sq km; 1990 pop. 40,319), S Ill.; ⊙ Benton; 38°00'N 88°56'W. Bounded NW by Little Muddy R.; also drained by Big Muddy R. Bituminous coal fields. Agr. (livestock, poultry; corn, wheat, fruit). Mfg. (textiles, boats). Rend L. in N. Formed 1818. **7** county (□ 391 sq mi/1,013 sq km; 1990 pop. 19,580), SE Ind., bounded E by Ohio line; ⊙ Brookville; 39°25'N 85°04'W. Corn, wheat; dairying; cattle, hogs. Some mfg. at Brookville. Drained by Whitewater R. and its two forks. Brookville Reservoir and Mounds State Recreation Area in N; Whitewater Canal State Historic Site at Metamora. Formed 1811. **8** county (□ 583 sq mi/1,510 sq km; 1990 pop. 11,364), N central Iowa; ⊙ Hampton; 42°44'N 93°16'W. Drained by Iowa Branch and West Fork Cedar rivers. Rolling-prairie agr. area (cattle, hogs, poultry; corn, oats, soybeans); limestone quarries. Berds Lake State Park at center. This area was affected by widespread flooding in 1993. Formed 1855. **9** county (□ 576 sq mi/1,492 sq km; 1990 pop. 21,994), E Kansas; ⊙ Ottawa; 38°35'N 95°17'W. Rolling prairie region, drained by Marais des Cygnes R. Diversified agr. (cattle, hogs; sorghum, soybeans, wheat, hay, apples, corn); machinery, navigation equipment. Oil and gas fields. Formed 1855. **10** county (□ 212 sq mi/549 sq km; 1990 pop. 43,781), N central Ky.; ⊙ Frankfort; 38°14'N 84°52'W. Drained by Kentucky R. and by Elkhorn Creek and its North Branch. Gently rolling upland agr. area in the Bluegrass (burley tobacco, hay, alfalfa, corn; cattle, horses). Stone quarries, lead and zinc deposits. Mfg. at Frankfort. Ky. Natl. Fish Hatchery in N, on Elkhorn Creek. Buckley Hills Wildlife Management Area in SW. Formed 1794. **11** county (□ 1,744 sq mi/4,517 sq km; 1990 pop. 29,008), W Maine, bordering on Que. (Canada); ⊙ Farmington; 44°54'N 70°27'W. Agr., recreational, lumbering region. Paper and pulp mills, wood prods.; dairying; hunting, fishing; resorts and camps center on Rangeley L. The Androscoggin, near S boundary, is chief river. Formed 1838. **12** county (□ 724 sq mi/1,875 sq km; 1990 pop. 70,092), NW Mass.; ⊙ Greenfield; 42°35'N 72°35'W. Predominantly rural; hilly in N. Bisected by Connecticut R.; drained by Deerfield and Millers rivers. Food processing, wood prods., paper products, plastics, handtools and hardware, industrial machinery, silverware. Fruits, nursery products; cattle; dairying. Yankee-Rowe nuclear power plant, initial criticality August 19, 1960, 21 mi/34 km NE of Pittsfield, was the oldest nuclear power plant in the U.S., now decommisioned. Formed 1811. **13** county (□ 566 sq mi/1,466 sq km; 1990 pop. 8,377), SW Miss.; ⊙ Meadville; 31°28'N 90°54'W. Drained by Homochitto R., forms part of S boundary in SW. Cotton, corn; pine and hardwood timber; oil field. Large part of co. in Homochitto Natl. Forest, in W, S, and E center. Formed 1809. **14** county (□ 932 sq mi/2,414 sq km; 1990 pop. 80,603), E central Mo.; ⊙ Union; 38°26'N 91°04'W. Missouri R. on N; drained by the Meramec R. Wheat, corn, soybeans, hay, vegetables; dairying; cattle, hogs, horses, mules; lumber prods.; fire clay, limestone. Part of St. Louis metropolitan area in E half of county; scattered residential lake developments. Mfg. at Union, Washington, New Haven, Berger, Gerald, St. Clair, Sullivan, and Pacific. Meramec Caverns at Stanton; Meramec State Park and State Forest in S. Robertsville State Park in E. Major Ger. settlement 1830s–1860s. Formed 1818. **15** county (□ 576 sq mi/1,492 sq km; 1990 pop. 3,938), S Nebr.; ⊙ Franklin; 40°10'N 98°57'W. Bounded S by Kansas; drained by Republican R. Corn, wheat, soybeans, sorghum; livestock; dairy prods. Formed 1871. **16** county (□ 1,697 sq mi/4,395 sq km; 1990 pop. 46,540), NE N.Y.; ⊙ Malone; 44°36'N 74°18'W. Bounded N by Que. (Canada) border; S part is in the Adirondacks. Named for Benjamin Franklin. Drained by Saranac, St. Regis, Salmon, Little Salmon, Chateaugay, and Raquette rivers. Includes many lakes and resorts (notably Saranac L., Tupper L.), and part of St. Regis Indian Reservation. Dairying and farming in the N part, lying in the St. Lawrence lowland. Field corn, potatoes, hay; timber; cheddar cheese; hunting, fishing. N extension of the Adirondacks High Peaks sect. in S part of co. Canoe routes, hiking and ski trails. Formed 1808. **17** county (□ 494 sq mi/1,279 sq km; 1990 pop. 36,414), N central N.C.; ⊙ Louisburg; 36°04'N 78°16'W. Coastal plain area; bounded N by Fishing Creek; drained by Tar R. Agr. area (tobacco, corn, wheat, oats, barley, soybeans, sorghum, hay, sweet potatoes; chickens, cattle, hogs); timber, pine forests. Mfg. (asphalt, crushed stone, oil seals, wire harnesses, electronic components, mica processing, concrete, hardwood flooring). Mfg. at Louisburg and Youngsville. Laurel Mill (1769) in NE. Perry's Pond in S. Formed 1779. **18** county (□ 538 sq mi/1,393 sq km; 1990 pop. 961,437), central Ohio; ⊙ Columbus; 39°58'N 83°01'W. Intersected by Scioto and

Olentangy rivers, and small Alum, Darby, and Big Walnut creeks. In the Till Plains physiographic region. Livestock; dairy prods.; grain, fruit, vegetables. Mfg. at Columbus (food processing, machinery and equip., pharmaceuticals, electronic prods.); sand and gravel pits, limestone quarries. Formed 1803. **19** county (□ 772 sq mi/1,999 sq km; 1990 pop. 121,082), S Pa.; ⊙ Chambersburg; 39°55′N 77°43′W. Bounded S by Md. state line; Tuscarora Mt. ridge forms W boundary. Part of Cove Mt. lies in SW, part of South Mt. in SE, part of Blue Mt. in N; drained by Conococheague Creek. Corn, wheat, oats, barley, hay, alfalfa, soybeans; potatoes, apples; poultry and eggs; sheep, hogs, cattle; dairying; sand and gravel; recreation. Mfg. at Chambersburg, Mercersburg, Green Castle, and Waynesboro. Scene of many Indian massacres until end of Revolution; birthplace (1791) of James Buchanan (Buchanan Birthplace Historic State Park). Mont Alto State Park in E center; Caledonia State Park in E; part of Michaux State Forest in E; Appalachian Trail passes N-S in E part of co. Formed 1784. **20** county (□ 561 sq mi/1,453 sq km; 1990 pop. 34,725), S Tenn.; ⊙ Winchester; 35°09′N 86°06′W. Drained by Elk R. Bounded S by Ala.; Cumberlands in E area, here rising to 1,800 ft/549 m. Livestock; dairying; corn, cotton, hay, potatoes. Timber tracts, coal mines, crushed stone. Formed 1807. **21** county (□ 294 sq mi/761 sq km; 1990 pop. 7,802), NE Texas; ⊙ Mount Vernon; 33°10′N 95°13′W. Bounded N by Sulphur R.; drained by White Oak and Cypress creeks. Dairying; poultry; vegetables, watermelons, pumpkins, strawberries, peaches, hay. Oil, natural-gas wells; lignite. Formed 1875. **22** county (□ 692 sq mi/1,792 sq km; 1990 pop. 39,980), NW Vt., on Que. (Canada) border and L. Champlain, rising to Green Mts. in E; ⊙ St. Albans; 44°51′N 72°55′W. Farm machinery, textile equipment, paper and wood prods., medicines; dairy prods., maple sugar; resorts. Drained by Missisquoi and Lamoille rivers. Formed 1792. **23** county (□ 711 sq mi/1,841 sq km; 1990 pop. 39,549), S Va.; ⊙ Rocky Mount; 36°59′N 79°52′W. Partly in the Piedmont region; rises to the Blue Ridge in NW; Blue Ridge Parkway follows W boundary. Bounded NE by Roanoke R. and Smith Mountain Lake; drained by Blackwater and Pigg rivers. Mfg. at Rocky Mount. Agr. (tobacco, hay, alfalfa, barley, wheat, corn; apples, peaches; cattle); timber; mica mining. Franklin Airport to NE. Booker T. Washington Natl. Monument in NE. Philpott Reservoir on S boundary. Formed 1786. **24** county (□ 1,265 sq mi/3,276 sq km; 1990 pop. 37,473), SE Wash., in irrigated Columbia basin agr. region; ⊙ Pasco; 46°32′N 118°54′W. Bounded by Columbia R. (L. Wallala reservoir), SE by Snake R. (L. Sacajawea reservoir), on extreme NE by Palouse R. Wheat, alfalfa, hay, barley, oats, corn; onions, carrots, asparagus, potatoes, beans; sheep, hogs. Part of U.S. Dept. of Energy Hanford Site in NW. Juniper Wilderness Area in SE; Lyons Ferry State Park and part of Palouse Falls State Park in NE, on Palouse R.; Sacajawea State Park in S. Formed 1883.

Franklin, parish (□ 648 sq mi/1,678 sq km; 1990 pop. 22,387), NE La.; ⊙ Winnsboro; 32°10′N 91°43′W. Bounded E by Tensas R. and Bayou Macon, W by Boeuf R. and Big Creek, S in part by Deer Creek. Agr. (cotton, corn, sorghum, hay, rice, soybeans, wheat, sweet potatoes; cattle, hogs); catfish; logging; mfg. of food prods., apparel; boatbuilding. Part of oil and natural-gas field in N. Includes Turkey Creek L. reservoir in S, part of Big Lake State Wildlife Area in E. Named after Benjamin Franklin. Formed 1843.

Franklin 1 city (1990 pop. 876), ⊙ Heard co., W Ga., 17 mi/27 km NNW of La Grange, on Chattahoochee R.; 33°17′N 85°06′W. Mfg. (tire cords, gravel processing, aluminum prods., clothing). **2** city (1990 pop. 12,907), ⊙ Johnson co., central Ind.; 39°29′N 86°04′W. It is a farm trade center. Mfg. includes auto parts, plastic prods., air compressors, aluminum doors and windows, foundry products, and copper panels. Franklin Col. of Ind. is here. Laid out 1823. **3** city (1990 pop. 9,004), ⊙ St. Mary parish, S La., 20 mi/32 km NW of Morgan City, and on navigable Bayou Teche; 29°48′N 91°31′W. Commercial and processing center of rich sugarcane area; sugar milling; mfg. of fabricated metal; printing and publishing. Historic old houses. Allakanas Island State Wildlife Area to NE. Founded 1800. **4** city (1990 pop. 8,304), Merrimack co., S central N.H., 17 mi/27 km N of Concord, at junction of Winnipesaukee and Pemigewasset rivers (forming the Merrimack R.); 43°27′N 71°40′W. Equip. mfg., printing and publishing; agr. (nursery crops, vegetables, apples; livestock, poultry; dairying). Daniel Webster b. here, in sect. then in Salisbury. Franklin Falls Dam, on Pemigewasset R., forms Franklin Falls Reservoir. Webster L. (2 mi/3.2 km long) in N. Includes village of West Franklin. Settled 1764; town inc. 1828, city 1895. **5** city (1990 pop. 11,026), Warren co., SW Ohio, 5 mi/8 km N of Middletown, on the Great Miami R.; 39°33′N 84°18′W. In an agr. area; paper prods. It was a flourishing river port in the mid–19th cent. Inc. 1813. **6** city (1990 pop. 7,329), ⊙ Venango co., NW central Pa., 7 mi/11.3 km WSW of Oil City, on Allegheny R., at mouth of French Creek (both bridged). Machinery and equip. mfg.; oil wells, natural gas, bituminous coal. Site of Indian village and of early Fr., Br., and Amer. forts. Chess-Lamberton Airport to SW. Oil discovered 1860. Laid out 1795, inc. as borough 1828, as city 1868. **7** city (1990 pop. 20,098), ⊙ Williamson co., central Tenn., on Harpeth R., and 16 mi/26 km SSW of Nashville; 35°55′N 86°52′W. In farm, timber, phosphate-mining area; lumber milling; tobacco warehouses. Light mfg. Civil War fighting here in 1864. Has Confederate cemetery, antebellum homes. Area settled before 1800. **8** independent city (□ 8 sq mi/20.7 sq km; 1990 pop. 7,864), SE Va., separate from adjacent Southampton and Isle of Wight cos., on Blackwater R., 20 mi/32 km W of Suffolk; 36°40′N 76°56′W. RR junction. Peanut market. Mfg. (food containers and processing, printing and publishing, logging equip.). In agr. area (peanuts, fruit, grain, cotton; livestock); timber. Paul D. Camp Community Col. (Franklin campus). Inc. 1876. **9** city (1990 pop. 21,855), Milwaukee co., W central Wis., a residential suburb, 8 mi/12.9 km SSW of Milwaukee; 42°53′N 88°00′W. Machinery and equip. mfg. Rainbow Airport. Inc. 1956.

Franklin 1 town (1990 pop. 1,810), New London co., E Conn., on Yantic R., and 7 mi/11.3 km NW of Norwich; 41°37′N 72°08′W. Dairy prods., poultry, egg-processing plant, grain feed mills, truck terminals. Mushroom-growing facility. Farm Home Administration for New London and Middlesex counties here. Summer 4H camp nearby. **2** town (1990 pop. 152), Lee co., SE Iowa, 10 mi/16 km WNW of Fort Madison; 40°40′N 91°30′W. **3** town (1990 pop. 7,607), ⊙ Simpson co., S Ky., 21 mi/34 km SSW of Bowling Green, near West Fork Drakes R.; 36°43′N 86°34′W. Trade center and shipping point for timber and agr. area (tobacco, strawberries, grain; livestock; dairying). Mfg. (lumber, automotive components, office furniture and equip., feeds, color separations, leather dying, printing and publishing). Duncan Inn (c.1819) to S, former stagecoach stop. Dueling Grounds Racetrack to S. Founded 1820. **4** town (1990 pop. 1,141), Hancock co., S Maine, 10 mi/16 km ENE of Ellsworth, in recreational area; 44°36′N 68°13′W. Granite quarries. **5** residential town (1990 pop. 22,095), including Franklin village, Norfolk co., S Mass., 19 mi/31 km N of Providence, R.I.; 42°05′N 71°25′W. Suburb of Boston, connected by commuter RR. Textiles, foundry prods.; poultry; dairying. Dean Col. is here. Settled 1660, inc. 1778. **6** town (1990 pop. 2,626), Oakland co., SE Mich., residential suburb, 17 mi/27 km NW of Detroit, and 9 mi/14.5 km S of Pontiac; 42°31′N 83°17′W. **7** town (1990 pop. 181), Howard co., central Mo., just N of Boonville across the Missouri R. Former RR junction. It was the original E terminus of the Santa Fe Trail. It has the same name as the town est. in 1816, 2 miles away on the Missouri R., which was destroyed by floods in the 1820s. **8** town (1990 pop. 1,112), ⊙ Franklin co., S Nebr., 45 mi/72 km SW of Hastings, and 40 mi/64 km S of Kearny, on Republican R., near Kansas state line; 40°06′N 98°57′W. Feed; dairying; grain; poultry; livestock. Light mfg. Inc. 1879. **9** town (1990 pop. 2,873), ⊙ Macon co., W N.C., on Little Tennessee R., 55 mi/89 km WSW of Asheville, in Nantahala Natl. Forest (hq. here); 35°10′N 83°22′W. Mt. resort area; timber, mining (mica, corundum, kaolin), agr. area (tobacco, corn; cattle; dairying). Small L. Emory, formed by dam in river. Scaly Mt. Ski Area to S. Once active Cowee Valley Mines (gems), rockhounding. Appalachian Trail passes 12 mi/19 km to W. Franklin Gem and Mineral Mus. in restored Macon co. jail (1841) building. Bridal Veil Falls (120 ft/37 m), Dry Falls (75 ft/23 m), and Cullasaja Falls (250 ft/76 m) to SE. Inc. 1852. **10** town (1990 pop. 1,336), ⊙ Robertson co., E central Texas, c.55 mi/89 km SE of Waco; 31°01′N 96°29′W. In agr. area (cotton, grain, watermelon). Gas and oil; mfg. (fertilizer). Twin Oak Reservoir to N. Settled 1880, inc. 1912. **11** town (1990 pop. 1,068), Franklin co., NW Vt., 15 mi/24 km NE of St. Albans, at Que. (Canada) border; 44°58′N 72°54′W. Includes L. Carmi, resort. Granted 1789 as Huntsburg, renamed 1817. **12** town (1990 pop. 914), ⊙ Pendleton co., E W.Va., in Eastern Panhandle, on South Branch of the Potomac R., 33 mi/53 km SE of Elkins; 38°38′N 79°19′W. Corn, potatoes; livestock; poultry. Mfg. (textiles, leather).

Franklin 1 village (1990 pop. 205), Izard co., N Ark., 28 mi/45 km NNW of Batesville, on Strawberry R.; 36°10′N 91°46′W. Mfg. (wood furnaces). **2** village (1990 pop. 478), Franklin co., SE Idaho, near Utah state line, just S of Preston; 42°01′N 111°48′W. In dairying and vegetable growing area; canned vegetables, egg and chicken production. Cache Natl. Forest to E, Wasatch Natl. Forest (Utah) to SE. First permanent settlement and oldest town in Idaho; founded 1860 by Mormons, who introduced irrigation here. **3** village, Morgan co., central Ill., 12 mi/19 km SE of Jacksonville; 39°37′N 90°02′W. Agr. (corn, soybeans). **4** village, Crawford co., SE Kansas, near Mo. line, 8 mi/12.9 km N of Pittsburg. In coal-mining area. **5** village (1990 pop. 441), Renville co., SW Minn., near Minnesota R., 12 mi/19 km E of Redwood Falls; 44°31′N 94°53′W. Grain, sugar beets; livestock, poultry; dairying. **6** village, NE suburb of Virginia, St. Louis co., NE Minn., in Mesabi iron range. **7** village (1990 pop. 409), Delaware co., S N.Y., in the Catskills, 9 mi/14.5 km SW of Oneonta; 42°20′N 75°10′W. Farming; dairying.

Franklin 1 borough (1990 pop. 4,977), Sussex co., NW N.J., on Wallkill R., and 10 mi/16 km NE of Newton, in hill and lake region; 41°06′N 74°35′W. Textiles, clothing. Former zinc mines. A mus. here commemorates the area's mining past. Inc. 1913. **2** borough (1990 pop. 565), Cambria co., W central Pa., residential suburb, ENE of Johnstown, on Little Conemaugh R.

Franklin, township (1990 pop. 42,780), Somerset co., N N.J., 2 mi/3.2 km SE of New Brunswick; 40°28′N 74°32′W. Formerly farm area (corn, barley, wheat), now suburban development and service industries. Inc. 1798.

Franklin Bay, NW Mackenzie dist., N.W.T., Canada, inlet (30 mi/48 km long, 25 mi/40 km wide at mouth) of Amundsen Gulf, on W side of Parry Peninsula; 69°40′N 125°30′W. S part is called Langton Bay. Receives Horton R.

Franklin Center, uninc. village, Delaware co., SE Pa., on Chester Creek, residential suburb, 15 mi/24 km WSW of Philadelphia; 41°56′N 80°13′W. Light mfg. Franklin Mint and Mus. are here.

Franklin D. Roosevelt, historic site, SE N.Y., authorized 1944. Here is the N.Y. home (nicknamed the "Summer White House") and burial place of Franklin D. and Eleanor Roosevelt. See also HYDE PARK.

Franklin D. Roosevelt Lake, Wash.: see GRAND COULEE DAM.

Franklin D. Roosevelt State Park, at Warm Springs, Ga. Once a part of the 2,700-acre/1,093-ha Franklin Roosevelt farm, this 10,000-acre/4,047-ha park was created by the Civilian Conservation Corps, a New Deal relief initiative. The 23 mi/37 km long Pine Mt. Trail traverses the length of the park. New Callaway Gardens, the premier tourist destination in the area. Most of the park now covered by pine trees.

Area in square miles is shown by the symbol □ capital city or county seat by ⊙

Franklin Falls, reservoir (☐ 1 sq mi/2.6 sq km), Merrimack co., central N.H., on Pemigewasset R., just N of Franklin; 43°27′N 71°40′W. Max. capacity 222,000 acre-ft. Formed by Franklin Falls Dam (112 ft/34 m long), built (1943) by Army Corps of Engineers for flood control.

Franklin Falls Dam, N.H.: see PEMIGEWASSET RIVER.

Franklin Grove, village (1990 pop. 968), Lee co., N Ill., 9 mi/14.5 km E of Dixon; 41°50′N 89°17′W. In rich agr. area.

Franklin Island, S Maine, lighthouse isl. in Muscongus Bay, 6 mi/9.7 km SSW of Friendship.

Franklin, Lake (30 mi/48 km long, 2 mi/3 km–10 mi/16 km wide), N Keewatin dist., N.W.T., Canada, just S of head of Chantrey Inlet, into which it is drained by Back R.; 67°N 96°15′W.

Franklin Lake, NE Nev., shallow marsh in S Elko co., just E of Ruby Mts. Ruby L. is 10 mi/16 km S.

Franklin Lakes, borough (1990 pop. 9,873), Bergen co., NE N.J., in lake region, 6 mi/9.7 km NW of Paterson; 41°00′N 74°12′W. Mfg. village (Venetian blinds). Inc. 1922. Largely residential. Campgaw Mt. ski area nearby.

Franklin, Mount 1 in N.H.: see PRESIDENTIAL RANGE. **2** in Texas: see FRANKLIN MOUNTAINS.

Franklin Mountains, W Mackenzie dist., N.W.T., Canada, extend c.300 mi/483 km NW–SE along E bank of Mackenzie R., bet. Hare Indian R. (NW) and mouth of Liard R. (SE); highest peak, Mt. Clark (4,733 ft/1,443 m), 50 mi/80 km SE of Fort Norman.

Franklin Mountains, extreme W Texas, range extending N into Dona Ana co., N.Mex., from point just N of El Paso; highest point, Mt. Franklin (7,192 ft/2,192 m). Franklin Mts. State Park in city of El Paso, Texas.

Franklin Park, village (1990 pop. 18,485), Cook co., NE Ill., a suburb of Chicago; inc. 1892; 41°56′N 87°52′W. It is chiefly residential. On Des Plaines R.

Franklin Park, borough (1990 pop. 10,109), Allegheny co., W Pa., residential suburb, 11 mi/18 km NW of Pittsburgh; 40°35′N 80°05′W. Agr. in NW includes dairying.

Franklin Roosevelt, Mount, Colo.: see WILSON, MOUNT.

Franklin Springs, village (1990 pop. 475), Franklin co., NE Ga., 3 mi/4.8 km W of Royston; 34°17′N 83°09′W. Mfg.of paints, van conversions.

Franklin Square, uninc. city (☐ 2 sq mi/5.2 sq km; 1990 pop. 28,205) in town of Hempstead, Nassau co., SE N.Y., on L.I.; 40°42′N 73°40′W. Although chiefly residential, there is significant mfg., including fire extinguishers, partitions and laminates, wire prods., adhesives, hair prods., die castings, asphalt-block flooring and brick pavers, electrical machinery and equip., furniture, lighting fixtures, foundation garments, and hydraulic systems.

Franklin Strait, S Franklin dist., N.W.T., Canada, arm (110 mi/177 km long, 20 mi/32 km–60 mi/97 km wide) of the Arctic Ocean, bet. Boothia Peninsula and Prince of Wales Isl.; 72°N 97°W.

Franklinton 1 town (1994 pop. 4,359), ⊙ Washington parish, SE La., 17 mi/27 km W of Bogalusa and on the Bogue Chitto R.; 30°51′N 90°08′W. Trade and shipping center for timber, dairying, and agr. area (vegetables, watermelons, pumpkins, hay; cattle, exotic fowl); pulpwood, lumber milling; mfg. (dog food, vinyl windows, dairy prods., pants). Watermelon Festival. Laid out 1821, chartered 1861. **2** town (1990 pop. 1,615), Franklin co., N central N.C., 24 mi/39 km NNE of Raleigh; 36°06′N 78°27′W. Grain, soybeans, poultry, livestock; mfg. (women's hosiery, wooden crates, veneers, detergent).

Franklintown, borough (1990 pop. 373), York co., S Pa., 15 mi/24 km SW of Harrisburg; 40°4′N 77°1′W. Agr. (grain, livestock, dairying).

Franklinville 1 village, Gloucester co., SW N.J., on branch of Maurice R., and 16 mi/26 km SSE of Woodbury; vegetable farming. Founded 1800. **2** village (☐ 1 sq mi/2.6 sq km; 1990 pop. 1,739), Cattaraugus co., W N.Y., on Ischua Creek, and 17 mi/27 km N of Olean; 42°20′N 78°27′W. Mfg. of dairy prods., cutlery; lumber milling; agr. includes field corn, hay, and dairy farming. Settled 1806, inc. 1874. **3** village (1990 pop. 666), Randolph co., central N.C., 9 mi/14.5 km ENE of Asheboro on Deep R; 35°44′N 79°41′W. Agr. area (tobacco, grain, soybeans, poultry, livestock, dairying). Mfg. (wooden furniture frames, cushions, socks, meat processing, tool and die).

Franks Peak, Wyo.: see ABSAROKA RANGE.

Frankston, town (1990 pop. 1,127), Anderson co., E Texas, 21 mi/34 km NNE of Palestine, near Neches R. (dam forming L. Palestine to NE); 32°03′N 95°30′W. Timber; mfg. (paper boxes); melons, peaches, vegetables; dairying; cattle.

Franksville, uninc. town, Racine co., SE Wis., suburb, 7 mi/11.3 km WNW of Racine. Urban-growth area. Dairying and general farming to W. Mfg. (electronic-circuit boards, fractional motors, meat processing, packaging equip., ducklings).

Frankton, town (1990 pop. 1,736), Madison co., E central Ind., on small Pipe Creek, and 10 mi/16 km NNW of Anderson; 40°13′N 85°46′W. In agr. area.

Frankville, village, Winneshiek co., NE Iowa, 12 mi/19 km SE of Decorah.

Frannie, village (1990 pop. 148), Park and Big Horn cos., NW Wyo., on branch of Shoshone R., near Mont. state line, and 18 mi/29 km NE of Powell; 44°58′N 108°37′W. Elev. 4,219 ft/1,286 m. Lime processing.

Franz (frans), village, central Ont., Canada, on Hobon L. (4 mi/6 km long), 130 mi/209 km N of Sault Ste. Marie; 48°28′N 84°25′W. RR junction; gold mining.

Fraser, city (1990 pop. 13,899), Macomb co., SE Mich., a suburb, 15 mi/24 km NE of downtown Detroit; 42°32′N 82°57′W. Tools, dies, and jigs, plastic and plaster prods., heating equip., and steel prods. are manufactured here. Inc. as a village 1894, as a city 1957.

Fraser, town (1990 pop. 120), Boone co., central Iowa, on Des Moines R., and 6 mi/9.7 km NW of Boone; 42°07′N 93°58′W. In agr. area. State Forests nearby.

Fraser, village (1990 pop. 575), Grand co., N Colo., 28 mi/45 km W of Boulder, on Fraser R.; 39°56′N 105°47′W. Elev. 8,550 ft/2,606 m. Timber; tourism. Arapaho Natl. Forest to E and SW.

Fraser, chief river of B.C., Canada, c.850 mi/1,370 km long; rises in the Rocky Mts., at Yellowhead Pass, near the B.C.-Alta. line; flows NW through the Rocky Mt. Trench to Prince George, thence S and W to the Strait of Georgia at Vancouver. Its chief tributaries are the Nechako, Quesnel, Chilcotin, and Thompson rivers. It is navigable to Yale, c.80 mi/130 km upstream. The Fraser R. canyon, which begins at Yale, is noted for its scenery; its mountain walls rise more than 3,000 ft/914 m. The river contains the chief spawning grounds in N. America for the Pacific salmon. Logging is important along the upper course. The Fraser delta is the most fertile agr. region of B.C.; dairying and truck farming are important. The delta has the largest concentration of people in W Canada. Sections of the river are followed by oil and gas pipelines as well as transcontinental rail and highway routes. The Fraser R. was visited by Sir Alexander Mackenzie, the Can. explorer, who followed its upper course on his expedition (1793) to the Pacific Ocean and takes its name from Simon Fraser, the Can. explorer and fur trader, who followed (1808) the river to its mouth, establishing fur-trading posts along the way. The river valley was the domain of the fur traders until the gold rush of 1858. After the discovery of gold (1859) in the Cariboo dist., on the river's upper reaches, the govt. built a road to serve the valley, and settlement of the region followed.

Fraser Canyon, S central B.C., Canada, Fraser R., from its confluence with Thompson R. at Lytton, S 55 mi/89 km to Yale. Is 3,281 ft/1000 m deep at Hell's Gate. Can. Pacific RR laid tracks through canyon, 1880s; Can. Natl. RR laid tracks in 1910s; Trans-Canada Highway built in 1960s. All 3 transportation routes use tunnels, ledges, snow sheds (to catch avalanches). Precipitation rarely reaches canyon floor, resulting in variety of vegetation regimes; dry below, forested snow-capped mts. above.

Fraser Lake (12 mi/19 km long, 3 mi/5 km wide), central B.C., Canada, 75 mi/121 km W of Prince George.

Fraser Mills, village, SW B.C., Canada, on lower Fraser R., and 2 mi/3 km NE of New Westminster; pulp and paper milling, lumbering.

Fraser River, N central Colo.; rises at Berthond Pass, at Continental Divide, SE Grand co., in Arapaho Natl. Forest; flows c.40 mi/64 km NNW past Tabernash to Colorado R. just W of Granby.

Frayser's Farm, Va.: see GLENDALE.

Frazee (frai-ZEE), town (1990 pop. 1,176), Becker co., W Minn., on Otter Tail R., 9 mi/14.5 km SE of Detroit Lakes; 46°43′N 95°42′W. Dairying; poultry; wild rice, grain, sugar beets, sunflowers; timber. Mfg. (lumber, wild rice processing, turkey feed). Numerous small natural lakes in area.

Frazer (FRAI-zhuhr), uninc. town (1990 pop. 2,100), Chester co., SE Pa., 21 mi/34 km WNW of Philadelphia; 40°01′N 75°33′W. Mfg. (food, soaps, medical tables, fabricated metal prods., gantry cranes, chemicals, rolled steel, pharmaceuticals). Seat of Immaculata Col.

Frazer (FRAI-zhuhr), village (1990 pop. 403), Valley co., NE Mont., on Little Porcupine Creek, near its confluence with the Missouri R., and 32 mi/51 km ESE of Glasgow, in SW of Fort Peck Indian Reservation; 48°03′N 106°03′W. In irrigated grain region; wheat, barley, oats, alfalfa, cattle, sheep, hogs. Frazer L. reservoir to SE.

Frazer Point, S extremity of Bathurst Isl., central Franklin dist., N.W.T., Canada, on Barrow Strait; 75°N 98°50′W.

Frazeysburg, village (1990 pop. 1,165), Muskingum co., central Ohio, 13 mi/21 km NNW of Zanesville; 40°07′N 82°07′W.

Frazier Park, uninc. town (1990 pop. 2,201), Kern co., S central Calif., planned residential community, 35 mi/56 km S of Bakersfield in Cuddy Canyon, Los Padres Natl. Forest.; 34°49′N 118°57′W. San Emigdio Mts. to N.

Frederic, town (1990 pop. 1,124), Polk co., NW Wis., 37 mi/60 km WNW of Rice L.; 45°39′N 92°27′W. Dairy prods., canned vegetables; mfg. (plastic prods., printing and publishing). On Coon L.

Frederica (fred-uh-REE-kuh), town (1990 pop. 761), Kent co., E Del., 10 mi/16 km SSE of Dover, and on Murderkill R., at head of navigation; 39°00′N 75°27′W. In agr. area. Nearby is Barratt's Chapel (c.1780). Killen's Pond State Park to SW; Milford Neck Wildlife Area to SE. The town was a ship-construction center in the 1880s.

Frederica, Fort, Ga.: see FORT FREDERICA.

Frederick 1 county (☐ 667 sq mi/1,728 sq km; 1990 pop. 150,208), N Md.; ⊙ Frederick; 39°28′N 77°24′W. Bounded N by Pa. line, SW by the Potomac (Va. state line), NE by Monocacy R.; also drained by Catoctin Creek. The largest co. in Md., it was named either for Prince Frederick, son of George I or Frederick Calvert, the 6th Lord Baltimore, and settled primarily by Irish and Germans. Rolling piedmont area, with extreme W in the Blue Ridge (locally called South and Catoctin mts.) and Middletown Valley. Rich agr. area (wheat, corn, hay, dairy prods., fruit; poultry, livestock). Diversified industries, especially at Frederick. Mt. resorts; black-bass and trout fishing. Includes Sugar Loaf Mt., part of the abandoned Chesapeake and Ohio Canal, Gambrill State Park (W). and parts of Catoctin Recreational Demonstration Area, and Gathland and Washington Monument state parks. Formed 1748. **2** county (☐ 415 sq mi/1,075 sq km; 1990 pop. 45,723), N Va.; seat is Winchester (independent city separate from surrounding co.); 39°12′N 78°15′W. Bounded W and NE by W.Va. state line; mainly in Shenandoah Valley, with mt. ridges in W. Mfg. at Winchester; leading apple-growing co. of Va.; also wheat, corn, hay, alfalfa; cattle, sheep, hogs; dairying; limestone, sand and gravel. Formed 1738.

Frederick, city (1990 pop. 40,148), ⊙ Frederick co., NW Md.; near Monocacy R., 23 mi/37 km SE of Hagerstown. The processing center of a fertile farm area, it has canneries, milk-receiving stations, and plants that manufacture household items, aluminum, optical and glass prods., solar panels, leather goods, clothing, and electronic equip. Frederick was a supply and rendevous point for Br. troops under the command of Gen. Edward Braddock in 1755. During the Civil War, Frederick was in the path of both armies, and was occupied briefly in 1862 by Gen. Jubal Early of the Confederacy after his victory at the Battle of Monocacy. Mfg. became important only after World War II, but the most important influence on the community's economy was the Biological Warfare Laboratory at Fort Detrick. Biological warfare research stopped in 1973 and a branch of the Natl. Institutes of Health, specializing in cancer research, moved in. Other points of interest include the Frederick Co. Court House (c.1756), The Evangelical Lutheran Church (c.1753), Trinity Chapel (c.1764), All Saints Parish House (c.1812), and the Frederick Acad. of the Visitation (c.1845–1851). Hood Col. for Women and the Md. School for the Deaf are in the community along with Frederick Community Col. and several state parks. Monocacy Natl. Battlefield is nearby. Laid out 1745.

Frederick 1 town (1990 pop. 988), Weld co., N Colo., 25 mi/40 km N of Denver; 40°06′N 104°56′W. Elev. 4,962 ft/1,512 m. In cattle, grain, and sugar-beet region. Coal mines. **2** town (1990 pop. 5,221), ⊙ Tillman co., SW Okla., 38 mi/61 km WSW of Lawton; 34°23′N 99°00′W. Elev. 1,304 ft/397 m. RR junction; trade center for rich agr. area (wheat, cotton, alfalfa, peanuts); mfg. (lingerie, automotive sealings). Sand and gravel pits. Small Burts L. (fishing, swimming) is nearby; L. Frederick reservoir to NE.

Frederick 1 (FRED-rik), village (1990 pop. 18), Rice co., central Kansas, 11 mi/18 km N of Lyons; 38°30′N 98°16′W. RR junction. In wheat area. **2** village (1990 pop. 241), Brown co., N S.Dak., 25 mi/40 km N of Aberdeen and on Maple R.; 45°49′N 98°30′W.

Frederick Douglass Historic Site, Washington, D.C., authorized 1962. Home of the abolitionist and writer; contains original furnishings, photographs, lithographs, and his library.

Frederick Law Olmstead Historic Site (OLM-sted), E Mass., authorized 1979, Site of Olmstead's home and business, containing lithographs and original furnishings. Located in Brookline, Mass.

Frederick Sound, SE Alaska, bet. Kupreanof Isl. (S) and mainland, extends 50 mi/80 km E to W. Part of Inside Passage bet. Petersburg and Juneau.

Fredericksburg, independent city (□ 10 sq mi/26 sq km; 1990 pop. 19,027), N Va., 55 mi/89 m N of Richmond, on the Rappahannock R., separate from adjacent Stafford and Spotsylvania cos.; 38°17′N 77°29′W. Mfg. (mattresses, highway signs, steel doors and wire, millwork, roof and floor trusses, zinc die-castings, package printing, silicon crystals); agr. area (tobacco, grain, soybeans; cattle); tourism. Known for its historic dists.; historic bldgs. include the home of George Washington's mother, Mary Washington (1772–1789); "Kenmore," his sister's home; the Rising Sun Tavern (c.1760); the law office of James Monroe; and the home of John Paul Jones. Also, Fredericksburg Mus.; Fredericksburg and Spotsylvania Natl. Cemetery. Mary Washington Col. Shannon Airport to SE. Ft. A.P. Hill Military Reservation to SE. Nearby are WAKEFIELD (Washington's birthplace) and Fredericksburg and Spotsylvania Memorial Natl. Military Park, commemorating Civil War battles of Fredericksburg, Chancellorsville, and Spotsylvania Courthouse. Settled 1671, laid out 1727, inc. as a town 1781, as a city 1879.

Fredericksburg 1 (FRED-riks-buhrg), town (1990 pop. 155), Washington co., S Ind., on Blue R., and 13 mi/21 km SSW of Salem; 38°26′N 86°11′W. In agr. area. **2** town (1990 pop. 1,011), Chickasaw co., NE Iowa, on branch of Wapsipinicon R., and 10 mi/16 km SSE of New Hampton; 42°57′N 92°12′W. **3** uninc. town (1990 pop. 1,269), Crawford co., NW Pa., residential suburb, 2 mi/3.2 km W of Meadville, near Cussewago Creek; 41°38′N 80°10′W. **4** uninc. town (1990 pop. 2,338), Lebanon co., SE central Pa., 7 mi/11.3 km N of Lebanon; 40°27′N 76°25′W. Agr. (grain, soybeans, apples; poultry, livestock, dairying); mfg. (food prods.). Farmer's Pride Airport to W. Appalachian Trail passes to N, on Blue Mt. ridge. **5** town (1990 pop. 6,934), Gillespie co., S central Texas; c.65 mi/105 km W of Austin, in valley of Pedernales R. in hilly country of Edwards Plateau; 30°16′N 98°52′W. Elev. 1,743 ft/531 m. Cattle, turkeys; grains; 1st Texas co. in peach production. Mfg. (animal feeds, processed foods, millwork); granite (quarrying nearby); gypsum, sand, and gravel. Hunting, fishing attract visitors. Retains architecture, customs, language of Ger. settlers (1846). Bauer Toy Mus.; Admiral Nimitz State Historic Site is here; site of Fort Martin Scott (1848); Enchanted Rock State Natural Area to N; Lyndon B. Johnson Natl. Historical Park (LBJ Ranch Unit) is 13 mi/21 km ESE at Stonewall. Inc. 1928.

Fredericksburg, village (1990 pop. 502), Wayne co., N central Ohio, 9 mi/14 km SSE of Wooster; 40°40′N 81°52′W.

Fredericksburg Spotsylvania Memorial National Military Park (□ 12 sq mi/31 sq km), NE Va., authorized 1927; 38°17′N 77°44′W. Portions of 4 major Civil War battlefields W, SW, and E of Fredericksburg; also historical sites in Fredericksburg. Fredericksburg and Spotsylvania Natl. Cemetery (12 acres/5 ha) in Fredericksburg is separate. See FREDERICKSBURG, Va.

Fredericktown, city (1990 pop. 3,950), ⊙ Madison co., SE Mo., in the St. Francois Mts., on branch of St. Francis R., and 75 mi/121 km S of St. Louis; 37°33′N 90°17′W. Mixed farming, cattle; mining and processing of copper, nickel, and cobalt; mfg. (caps, fiberglass, wood prods., apparel). Continent's 1st lead mine in "Old Lead Belt," played out in 1972. Mark Twain Natl. Forest nearby. Founded 1819 adjacent to a French settlement called St. Michel (1800).

Fredericktown (FRED-rik-toun), uninc. town (1990 est. pop. 1,000), East Bethlehem township, Washington co., SW Pa., on the Monongahela, 17 mi. SE of Washington; 40°00′N 79°59′W. Mfg. (coal processing); subsurface coal.

Fredericktown 1 village, Cecil co., E Md., 17 mi/27 km SE of Havre de Grace, and on Sassafras R. Yachting; boatyards. Laid out in 1736, the same time as the town named Georgetown. The two towns were likely named after the English King and his son. The town became a new home for Acadian families of French descent whose exile from Nova Scotia in 1755 was immortalized in Henry W. Longfellow's narrative poem, *Evangeline.* It was nearly destroyed by the Br. in 1814. A monument near the bridge spanning the Sassafras R. commemorates John Smith's explorations along its shores. It remains today a popular boating center. **2** village (1990 pop. 2,443), Knox co., central Ohio, 7 mi/11 km NNW of Mount Vernon, and on Kokosing R., near Knox L. and Knox L. Wildlife Area; 40°28′N 82°32′W.

Fredericton, city (1991 pop. 46,466), ⊙ N.B., Canada, S central N.B., on the St. John R.; 45°57′N 66°38′W. It is a commercial and distribution center where wood prods., shoes, and bricks are manufactured. The city was founded by United Empire Loyalists in 1783 and was made the prov. capital in 1785. Of interest are the govt. buildings, the Beaverbrook Art Gallery, and the Playhouse Theatre. The Univ. of N.B. (1785), Canada's 1st univ., and St. Thomas Univ. (1910) are here. Nearby is a Forest Research Center for Atlantic Canada and a federal experimental farm.

Frederika, town (1990 pop. 188), Bremer co., NE Iowa, on Wapsipinicon R., 14 mi/23 km NE of Waverly; 42°52′N 92°18′W. Dairy prods., feed. Limestone quarries nearby.

Fredonia 1 (free-DOH-nia), town (1990 pop. 1,207), Coconino co., N Ariz., 135 mi/217 km NNW of Flagstaff, near Utah state border, and 5 mi/8 km S of Kanab, Utah, on Kanab Creek; 36°57′N 112°31′W. Elev. 3,502 ft/1,067 m. Cattle, sheep; logging. Kaibab Indian Reservation and Pipe Spring Natl. Monument to W; Kaibab Natl. Forest and Grand Canyon Natl. Park to S. **2** town (1990 pop. 201), Louisa co., SE Iowa, at confluence of Iowa and Cedar rivers, 10 mi/16 km N of Wapello; 41°16′N 91°20′W. In livestock area. **3** (fri-DON-ee-uh), town (1990 pop. 2,599), ⊙ Wilson co., SE Kansas, on Fall R., and 22 mi/35 km NNW of Independence; 37°31′N 95°49′W. Elev. 900 ft/274 m. RR junction. Trading center in agr. and oil-producing area; dairying; mfg. (industrial machinery, soybean oil and meal, wood furniture, printing, cement). Inc. 1871. **4** (fre-DO-nee-ah), town (1990 pop. 1,558), Ozaukee co., E Wis., on Milwaukee R., and 7 mi/11.3 km NW of Port Washington; 43°28′N 87°57′W. In farm area. Mfg. (screen printing, plastic dinnerware, machinery).

Fredonia 1 (fruh-DON-yuh), village (1990 pop. 490), Caldwell co., W Ky., 31 mi/50 km ENE of Paducah; 37°12′N 88°03′W. Agr. (tobacco, grain; livestock); mfg. (crushed limestone, wooden pallets); limestone quarries. **2** village (□ 5 sq mi/13 sq km; 1990 pop. 10,436), Chautauqua co., SW N.Y., near L. Erie; 42°26′N 79°19′W. Inc. 1829. Grape juice, wine, and canned foods are produced. Fredonia was the site of the 1st gas well in the U.S. The 1st local unit of the Natl. Grange (Patrons of Husbandry) Movement was also founded here. State Univ. of N.Y. at Fredonia here. **3** village (1990 pop. 66), Logan co., S N.Dak., 35 mi/56 km ESE of Napoleon; 46°19′N 99°05′W.

Fredonia (free-DO-nee-ah), borough (1990 pop. 683), Mercer co., W Pa., 7 mi/11.3 km N of Mercer, near Otter Creek. Agr. (corn, hay, potatoes; dairying); mfg. (concrete, cheese, gas detection equip.).

Freeborn, county (□ 722 sq mi/1,870 sq km; 1990 pop. 33,060), S Minn.; ⊙ Albert Lea; 43°40′N 93°20′W. Bounded by Iowa on S. Agr. area (cattle, sheep, hogs, poultry; dairying; hay, alfalfa, oats, corn, soybeans, peas, potatoes). Several natural lakes run N-S through center of co., Albert Lea L. in center; Freeborn L. in NW; Myre Big Island State Park near center, on Albert Lea L. Formed 1855.

Freeborn, village (1990 pop. 301), Freeborn co., S Minn.,12 mi/19 km NE of Alber Lea, at N end of Freeborn L.; Big Cobb R. exits lake to W; 43°45′N 93°33′W. Mfg. of feeds and fertilizers; agr. (dairying, poultry, livestock, grain, soybeans, alfalfa).

Freeborn Lake, natural lake, Freeborn co., S Minn., 11 mi/18 km NW of Albert Lea, of glacial origin; 3 mi/4.8 km long, 1.5 mi/2.4 km wide. Village of Freeborn at N end. Source of Big Cobb R., which exits lake from NW end.

Freeburg, town (1990 pop. 446), Osage co., central Mo., near Gasconade R., 12 mi/19 km S of Linn; 38°19′N 91°55′W. Hay, cattle. Mfg. (windows and doors). RR passes beneath Freeburg through a tunnel.

Freeburg, village (1990 pop. 3,115), St. Clair co., SW Ill., 8 mi/12.9 km SSE of Belleville; 38°25′N 89°54′W. Bituminous coal mines; corn, wheat, dairy prods., livestock, vegetables. Inc. 1859.

Freeburg, borough (1990 pop. 640), Snyder co., central Pa., 11 mi/18 km SW of Sunbury, on Susquehecka Creek; 40°45′N 76°56′W. Agr. (corn, hay, apples; dairying, poultry); mfg. (fine wooden furniture, food).

Freeburn, uninc. village (1990 pop. 525), Pike co., E Ky., in the Cumberland Mts., near Tug Fork R., 11 mi/18 km SE of Williamson. Bituminous coal.

Freedom 1 uninc. town (1990 pop. 8,361), Santa Cruz co., W Calif., a suburb, 5 mi/8 km N of Watsonville; 36°57′N 121°48′W. Apples, berries, artichokes, vegetables; flowers, nursery prods. Monterey Bay, Pacific Ocean 3 mi/4.8 km to W. **2** town (1990 pop. 593), Waldo co., S Maine, 15 mi/24 km NW of Belfast; 44°30′N 69°20′W. In agr., recreational area. **3** town (1990 pop. 935), Carroll co., E N.H., 33 mi/53 km N of Rochester; 43°49′N 71°04′W. Bounded E by Maine state line, S by Ossipee R. and Broad Bay, SW by Ossipee L. Agr. (vegetables; cattle, poultry; dairying). Resort, camps on Ossipee L.

Freedom 1 village (1990 pop. 264), Woods co., NW Okla., 25 mi/40 km W of Alva, and on Cimarron R.; 36°46′N 99°06′W. In grain and livestock area; mfg. (salt for water softening, concrete). Alabaster Caverns State Park to S. Annual rodeo. **2** village, Lincoln co., W Wyo., on Idaho line, on Salt R., and 18 mi/29 km NNW of Afton, in Star Valley. Elev. 5,556 ft/1,693 m. Agr. (barley, alfalfa; sheep, cattle); mfg. (lumber; hand guns). Salt R. Range just E; Bridger-Teton Natl. Forest to E.

Freedom, borough (1990 pop. 1,897), Beaver co., W Pa., 7 mi/11.3 km SSE of Beaver Falls, on Ohio R., opposite

Monaca. RR yards; 40 °40′N 80°15′W. Agr. (grain, soybeans; dairying, livestock); mfg. (machining). Settled 1832, inc. 1838.

Freehold, borough (1990 pop. 10,742), ⊙ Monmouth co., E central N.J.; 40°15′N 74°16′W. Settled c.1650, called Monmouth Courthouse (1715–1801), inc. as a town 1869, as a borough 1919. Freehold is a farm trade center, with some diversified industry, including telecommunications equip. Site of Freehold Raceway, thoroughbred horse racetrack. Of interest are the Monmouth Co. Historical Assn. Mus. and St. Peter's Episcopal Church (c.1683). The Revolutionary War battle of Monmouth took place in this area in 1778, notable in part because of Mary Ludwig (1754–1832), alias Molly Pitcher. The battle was fought at Monmouth Courthouse, which was part of the area that would become Freehold. As was the custom, women would carry water to the soldiers during battle. Such women were given the name "Molly Pitcher." While Mary Ludwig was performing this task, her husband, overcome by the heat, was unable to complete his fighting duties. Mary took his place for the remainder of the battle. In 1822 she was rewarded for her heroism with a soldier's pension.

Freel Peak (10,881 ft/3,317 m), E Calif., in the Sierra Nevada, just SE of L. Tahoe, on El Dorado–Alpine co. line. In Eldorado Natl. Forest.

Freeland, uninc. town (1990 pop. 1,278), Island co., NW Wash., on Whidbey Isl., on Holmes Harbor bay, 15 mi/24 km W of Everett; 48°01′N 122°32′W. Dairying, poultry, alfalfa. Mfg. (coated paper, store fixtures, ship construction).

Freeland (FREE-luhnd), borough (1990 pop. 3,909), Luzerne co., E central Pa., 16 mi/26 km S of Wilkes-Barre; 41°01′N 75°54′W. Agr. (corn, hay, potatoes; dairying); mfg. (food prods., commercial cooking equip.). Eckley Miners' Village, 19th-cent. coal-mining town, to S. Eagle Rock Ski Area to S. Laid out 1868, inc. 1876.

Freelandville, village, Knox co., SW Ind., 17 mi/27 km NE of Vincennes. In agr. area.

Freels, Cape, on E coast of N.F., Canada, at N end of Bonavista Bay, 40 mi/64 km NNW of Cape Bonavista; 49°14′N 53°29′W.

Freeman 1 town (1990 pop. 480), Cass co., W Mo., on South Grand R., and 9 mi/14.5 km W of Harrisonville; 38°37′N 94°30′W. **2** town (1990 pop. 1,239), Hutchinson co., SE S.Dak., 35 mi/56 km N of Yankton;40 mi/64 km SE of Mitchell; 43°21′N 97°25′W. Grain; dairy prods.; livestock, sausages, poultry; mfg. (milk powder, dust filters, feeds, printing, snowblowers).

Freeman, Lake, reservoir, Carroll co., NW central Ind., on Tippecanoe R., 14 mi/23 km NNE of Lafayette; 40°35′N 86°45′W. Extends N, c.10 mi/16 km, along White-Carroll co. border. Formed by Freeman Dam on Tippecanoe R. W of Yeoman. Power dam.

Freeman Peak, Colo.: see TARRYALL MOUNTAINS.

Freemansburg (FREE-muhns-buhrg), borough (1990 pop. 1,946), Northampton co., E Pa., residential suburb, 2 mi/3.2 km E of downtown Bethlehem, on Lehigh R.; 40°37′N 75°20′W. Settled c.1760, inc. 1856.

Freeport, city (1990 pop. 25,115), Grand Bahama Isl., Bahamas; 26°40′N 78°45′W. A popular resort area, it developed out of a 1955 agreement bet. the Bahamian colonial govt. and a private development company to create a free port and business area. The venture was a rapid success, resulting in the additional development of resort facilities, including casinos and duty-free shops. Princess casino is one of the world's largest. A petroleum-transshipment facility has also been built, and an internatl. airport is located here.

Freeport 1 city (1990 pop. 25,840), ⊙ Stephenson co., NW Ill., on the Pecatonica R.; 42°17′N 89°37′W. Inc. 1855. It is a trade and mfg. center in a fertile farm and dairy region. Agr. (corn, oats; cattle, hogs); mfg. (brass and aluminum forging, tires, switches, feeds, metal processing, window treatments, barbecue grills, snack foods). Freeport was the scene of the second Lincoln-Douglas debate (1858), in which Douglas expounded his famous "Freeport doctrine." Highland Community Col. is here. Albertus Airport to SE. **2** city (1990 pop. 11,389), Brazoria co., SE Texas, 9 mi/14.5 km SE of its twin city of Lake Jackson, on the Gulf of Mexico near the mouth of the Brazos R., on the Intracoastal Waterway; 28°56′N 95°21′W. Elev. 15 ft/5 m. The center of a thriving industrial area in a ranching, oil, and natural-gas region known as Brazosport, Freeport has large chemical and shrimping industries. One plant extracts magnesium from seawater. New port facilities were opened in 1955, and historic Velasco was annexed in 1957. The city's beaches and deep-sea fishing facilities attract tourists. San Bernard Natl. Wildlife Refuge to SW; Brazia Natl. Wildlife Refuge to NE; Bryan Beach State Park to S at mouth of the Brazos R. (formerly Velasco State Park). Inc. 1949.

Freeport 1 town (1990 pop. 6,905), including Freeport village, Cumberland co., SW Maine, on Casco Bay, 8 mi/12.9 km SW of Brunswick; 43°50′N 70°05′W. Factory-outlet shopping center and hq. of L. L. Bean mail-order company. In 1820 papers were signed here preliminary to admission of Maine into the Union as a state. Desert of Maine, spreading dune area, near here. Settled c.1700, inc. 1789. **2** town (☐ 4 sq mi/10.4 sq km; 1990 pop. 39,894), Nassau co., SE N.Y., on the S shore of L.I., a residential suburb of N.Y. city; 40°38′N 73°34′W. Settled as a village c.1650, inc. 1892. It is a resort and a deep-sea fishing and oystering center, with access to the Atlantic Ocean through Jones Inlet. Jones Beach State Park is nearby.

Freeport 1 village (1990 pop. 8), Harper co., S Kansas, 10 mi/16 km ENE of Anthony; 37°12′N 97°50′W. In wheat area. **2** village (1990 pop. 458), Barry co., SW Mich., 23 mi/37 km SE of Grand Rapids; 42°45′N 85°18′W. In agr. area; mfg. (lumber, trimming dies). **3** village (1990 pop. 556), Stearns co., central Minn., 25 mi/40 km WNW of St. Cloud; 45°39′N 94°41′W. Grain; poultry; dairying; mfg. (coal-mining filters, garage doors, machining, aviation fueling equip., agr. separating equip., industrial fans, pipe and duct work, showcase components, special machinery, printing and publishing). Birch L. State Forest to NW; Kings L. to N.

Freeport, borough (1990 pop. 1,983), Armstrong co., W central Pa., 22 mi/35 km NE of Pittsburgh, on Allegheny R. (bridged), at mouth of Buffalo Creek; mouth of Kiskiminetas R. 1 mi/1.6 km E; Lock and Dam No. 5, 1.5 mi/2.4 km NE; 40°40′N 79°40′W. Agr. (corn, hay; livestock, dairying); mfg. (tool and die, pewter dinnerware, printing and publishing, bricks, showcase glass); bituminous coal. Canal town in mid-19th cent. Settled c.1792, laid out c.1800.

Freeport, Wood co., N Ohio: see WAYNE.

Freer, town (1990 pop. 3,271), Duval co., S Texas c.70 mi/113 km W of Corpus Christi; 27°52′N 98°37′W. In oil, natural-gas fields; natural-gas processing; cattle ranching in area. Inc. 1938.

Freesoil, village, Mason co., W Mich., 16 mi/26 km NE of Ludington, near Big Sable R.; 44°10′N 86°21′W. Nearly surrounded by Manistee Natl. Forest. In farm and resort area.

Freestone, county (☐ 892 sq mi/2,310 sq km; 1990 pop. 15,818), E central Texas; ⊙ Fairfield. Bounded NE and E by Trinity R.; 31°41′N 96°09′W. Agr. (corn, pecans, peaches, melons, vegetables; hay), livestock (cattle, hogs, horses). Timber. Some gas and oil, iron ore. Fairfield L. State Park in NE; dam end of Richland Chambers Reservoir in N. Formed 1850.

Freetown, town (1990 pop. 8,522), Bristol co., SE Mass., 8 mi/12.9 km NE of Fall R.; 41°46′N 71°01′W. Settled 1675, inc. 1683. Includes villages of Assonet and East Freetown. Part of Long Pond is in NE. State forest nearby.

Freetown, village, central P.E.I., Canada, 9 mi/14 km E of Summerside; mixed farming, dairying, potatoes.

Freetown, village (1990 pop. 600), Jackson co., S central Ind., 12 mi/19 km W of Seymour. On E edge of Hoosier Natl. Forest. Vegetables, livestock. Timber. Near the Knobstone Escarpment.

Freeville, village (☐ 1 sq mi/2.6 sq km; 1990 pop. 437), Tompkins co., W central N.Y., 10 mi/16 km NE of Ithaca; 42°30′N 76°20′W. Seat of the George Junior Republic.

Freezeout Lake, reservoir, Teton co., NW central Mont., in Freezeout Lake Wildlife Management Area, 2 mi/3.2 km NW of Fairfield, and 35 mi/56 km WNW of Great Falls; 5 mi/8 km long, 1 mi/1.6 km wide; 47°40′N 112°02′W. Fed by branches of Sun R.

Freistatt (FREI-stat), town (1990 pop. 166), Lawrence co., SW Mo., in the Ozarks, 12 mi/19 km SSW of Mt. Vernon; 37°01′N 93°54′W. Settled by Germans.

Frelighsburg (FREH-ligz-buhrg), village (1991 pop. 1,066), S Que., Canada, 10 mi/16 km ESE of Bedford, near Vt.; dairying, pig raising.

Fremont 1 (FREE-mahnt), county (☐ 1,534 sq mi/3,973 sq km; 1990 pop. 32,273), S central Colo.; ⊙ Cañon City; 38°28′N 105°26′W. Sheep-grazing and mining area, drained by Arkansas R. Royal Gorge in center of co. Coal. Sheep, cattle, vegetables. Part of Fort Carson Military Reserve on E boundary. Includes parts of San Isabel Natl. Forest in S and SW; part of Pike Natl. Forest in NW; part of Sangre de Cristo Mts. in SW, of Wet Mts. in SE. Formed 1861. **2** county (☐ 1,895 sq mi/4,908 sq km; 1990 pop. 10,937), E Idaho; ⊙ St. Anthony; 44°13′N 111°29′W. Mt. area bordering on Mont. (N), Continental Divide and Wyo. (E); drained by Henrys Fork and Teton R.; part of S boundary formed by Teton R. Irrigation and dry farming in valleys. Wheat, barley; hay; sugar beets, potatoes; cattle, sheep; lumber. Teton Dam Site on Teton R., collapsed June 5, 1976, killing 11 people downstream. Grand Teton region in the E. Part of Targhee Natl. Forest in N and NE, small part of Yellowstone Natl. Park in NE corner; Island Park Reservoir with Harriman State Park in N center; Henrys L. Reservoir and State Park in N. Formed 1893. **3** county (☐ 516 sq mi/1,336 sq km; 1990 pop. 8,226), extreme SW Iowa, bounded by Mo. (S) and Nebr. (W; state line here formed by Missouri R.); ☐ Sidney; 40°44′N 95°35′W. Prairie agr. area (cattle, hogs, poultry; corn) with bituminous-coal deposits; drained by Nishnabotna R. Mfg. at Shenandoah. Includes Waubonsie State Park in SW; Forney L. State Preserve in NW. Formed 1847; annexed part of Otoe co., Nebr., in 1943. **4** county (☐ 9,266 sq mi/23,999 sq km; 1990 pop. 33,662), W central Wyo.; ⊙ Lander; 43°01′N 108°37′W. Grain, sugar beets, livestock (hay, barley, alfalfa, corn, beans; cattle, sheep) region; watered by Sweetwater, Popo Agie, Wind, and Bighorn rivers. Mfg. (timber). Coal, oil, uranium, natural gas, and iron ore found here. Wind River Mts. in W; Green Mts. in S. Bighorn R. forms Boysen Reservoir in N part; Boysen State Park on E shore. Castle Gardens, sandstone rock formations, and Gas Hills Uranium Mining Dist., in E. Continental Divide passes through SW and NW corners and forms most of W boundary. Parts of Shoshone Natl. Forest in SW and NW; part of Bridger-Teton Natl. Forest in NW corner. Sinks Canyon State Park in SW. Most of large Wind River Indian Reservation located in N center of co. Formed 1884.

Fremont 1 city (1990 pop. 173,339), Alameda co., W Calif., suburb, 22 mi/35 km SE of downtown Oakland and 17 mi/27 km NNW of downtown San Jose, on Alameda Creek, E of San Francisco Bay; 37°32′N 122°00′W. Long an agr. center, with champagne vineyards founded (1870) by Leland Stanford. Mfg. includes computer equip., semiconductors, electronics and electronic equip., computer-storage devices; a shipping point for fruits and vegetables. Its economy was transformed in 1963, however, when General Motors opened a huge automobile-assembly plant here; auto-parts mfg. at Irvingston, to E. With this industrial addition, Fremont has become one of the fastest-growing cities in the U.S. Mission San Jose de Guadalupe (1797) to SE, at Irvington, has been restored as a mus. The city has the Calif. School for the Deaf, Ohione Col. (2-year), Coyote Hills Regional Park to W on San Francisco Bay, and a 3,000-acre/1,214-ha aquatic park. Hetch Hetchy Aqueduct runs E-W in S. Inc. 1956. **2** city (1990 pop. 23,680), ⊙ Dodge co., E central Nebr., on the Platte R; 41°26′N 96°29′W. RR junction. It is a trade, shipping, and processing center for a grain, dairying, and livestock area. Mfg. (processed food, machinery, apparel; printing, agr. chemicals, animal feed, fertilizer, metal prods.)

Cross references are shown in SMALL CAPITALS. The pronunciation key is on page xv. The dates of population figures are on page xii.

Midland Lutheran Col. is here. Fremont Lakes State Recreation Area to W. Inc. 1858. **3** city (1990 pop. 17,648), ⊙ Sandusky co., N Ohio, on the Sandusky R.; 41°21′N 83°07′W. Inc. 1849. Trade and industrial center in an agr. region specializing in sugar-beet processing and canning. Battle of Fort Stephenson fought here (1813) during the War of 1812. Shipbuilding was an early industry. House and tomb of President Rutherford B. Hayes (a state memorial) are in Spiegel Grove State Park.

Fremont 1 town (1990 pop. 1,407), Steuben co., extreme NE Ind., 7 mi/11.3 km NNE of Angola, near Mich. state line; 41°44′N 84°56′W. Agr.; lumber milling; mfg. (aluminum auto wheels, camper axles, pressure tanks, steel wire, plastic containers, baked goods, machine forgings, gaskets). **2** town (1990 pop. 701), Mahaska co., S central Iowa, 13 mi/21 km SE of Oskaloosa; 41°12′N 92°25′W. In agr. area (seed, corn processing). **3** town (1990 pop. 3,875), Newaygo co., W central Mich., 23 mi/37 km NE of Muskegeon, on NE side of Fremont L.; 43°27′N 85°57′W. RR terminus and airport here. In dairying and fruit-growing area; food processing; baby-food processing. Native Amer. village sites and mounds, and several small lakes are nearby. Manistee Natl. Forest to W, N, and E. Settled 1855; inc. as village 1875, as city 1911. **4** (FREE-mahnt), uninc. town, Carter co., S Mo., in Ozark region, near Current R., 8 mi/12.9 km SW of Van Buren. In Mark Twain Natl. Forest. Peck Ranch Conservation Area to N. **5** town (1990 pop. 2,576), Rockingham co., SE N.H., 9 mi/14.5 km W of Exeter; 42°59′N 71°07′W. Drained by Exeter R. Agr. (cattle, poultry; vegetables; dairying; nursery crops); mfg. (patterns and molds, wooden barrels, machining, tool and die). **6** town (1990 pop. 1,710), Wayne co., E central N.C., 11 mi/18 km N of Goldsboro; 35°32′N 77°58′W. Tobacco, grain, cotton, peanuts, sweet potatoes, poultry, livestock. Mfg. (hosp. supplies, sportswear, shirts). Charles B. Acock Birthplace State Historical Site to S, former govt. bldg. built 1859.

Fremont, village (1990 pop. 632), Waupaca co., E central Wis., on Wolf R. and Partridge L., 22 mi/35 km NW of Oshkosh; 44°15′N 88°52′W. Lumbering, fishing; mfg. (buttons, golf T-shirts). In wildlife and resort area.

Fremont Island, **Disappointment Island**, or **Miller Island** (7 mi/11.3 km long, 2 mi/3.2 km wide), in Great Salt L., Weber co., NW Utah, 4 mi/6.4 km SE of Promontory Point (Box Elder co.), c.35 mi/56 km NW of Salt Lake City. Castle Rock, on isl. Elev. 4,493 ft/1,369 m. Location of Kit Carson's cross.

Fremont Pass (11,318 ft/3,450 m), central Colo., on Continental Divide, Lake/Summit co. line, in Park Range, 10 mi/16 km NE of Leadville. Crossed by State Highway 91. Village of Climax is here. Quandary Peak to NE and Mt. Lincoln to SE.

Fremont Peak (FREE-mahnt), peak (13,745 ft/4,189 m) in Wind R. Range, Fremont/Sublette cos., W central Wyo., c.45 mi/72 km NW of Lander.

Frémont Peak State Park, Calif.: see GABILAN RANGE.

Fremont River, rises just SW of Fish L. reservoir, Sevier co., S central Utah; flows 60 mi/97 km NE through Fish L. and Johnson Reservoir, then S past Loa, then E through Capitol Reef Natl. Park, joining Muddy Creek in Wayne co., N of Henry Mts., to form Dirty Devil R., which in turn flows SSE to the Colorado.

French Broad River, 210 mi/338 km long; rises in the Blue Ridge Mts., W Transylvania co., SW N.C.; flows NE past Brevard, then N through Asheville and through main range of Appalachian Mts. in Tenn., turns W; flows through Douglas reservoir, joins Holston R. 4 mi/6.4 km E of downtown Knoxville to form Tennessee R.

French Camp, uninc. town (1990 pop. 3,018), San Joaquin co., W Calif., suburb, 4 mi/6.4 km SSE of Stockton, on Lone Tree Creek, SE of its confluence with San Joaquin R.; 37°53′N 121°17′W. Fruit, nuts, pumpkins, grapes, grain, vegetables, dairying, cattle. Mfg. (concrete prods., plastic prods.).

French Camp, village (1990 pop. 320), Choctaw co., central Miss., 13 mi/21 km W of Ackerman, on Natchez Trace Natl. Parkway; 33°17′N 89°24′W. Agr. (cotton, corn; cattle); mfg. (wooden boxes). Rainwater Observatory to N, has 13 telescopes.

French Creek 1 village (1990 pop. 80), Chautauqua co., extreme W N.Y., 25 mi/40 km WSW of Jamestown; 42°02′N 79°42′W. **2** uninc. village (1990 pop. 100), Upshur co., central W.Va., 8 mi/12.9 km SSW of Buckhannon. Mfg. (wooden fence posts). W.Va. State Wildlife Center to S.

French Creek 1 80 mi/129 km long, in SW N.Y. and NW Pa.; rises in SW Chautauqua co., N.Y.; flows and S, past Meadville, Pa., and SE to Allegheny R. at Franklin, Pa. Pioneer route from Great Lakes to the Midwest. **2** 62 mi/100 km long, creek, in S.Dak., intermittent stream; rises near Custer in Black Hills; flows E through Custer State Park to Cheyenne R.; 43°46′N 103°43′W. Gold, discovered here 1874, is still extracted.

French Frigate Shoals, Honolulu Co., Hawaii, crescent atoll comprising 13 sand islets and 1 rock islet (La Perouse Pinnacle, elev. 122 ft/37 m), N Pacific, 520 mi/837 km WNW of Honolulu, Hawaii; 20 mi/32 km N of Tropic of Cancer; 23°45′N 166°10′W. Annexed 1895 by Republic of Hawaii. Includes World War II landing strip on Tern Isl. and Disappearing Isl. Part of Hawaiian Isls. Natl. Wildlife Refuge.

French Lake (7 mi/11 km long, 5 mi/8 km wide), S central N.B., Canada, 14 mi/23 km E of Fredericton; drains into St. John R. through Maquapit and Grand lakes.

French Lick, town (1990 pop. 2,087), Orange co., S Ind., 22 mi/35 km SSW of Bedford; 38°33′N 86°37′W. Agr. area (fruit, livestock, poultry); has noted mineral springs. Mfg. (wood furniture, pianos, plastic bottles). Stone quarries. Resort area.

French River, S central Ont., Canada, issues from L. Nipissing, flows 50 mi/80 km WSW to Georgian Bay 60 mi/97 km NW of Parry Sound.

French Settlement, town (1990 pop. 829), Livingston parish, SE La., 24 mi/39 km ESE of Baton Rouge, on Amite R.; 30°19′N 90°48′W. Elev. 14 ft/5 m. In agr. area; catfish, crawfish, alligators.

French Shore, part of N.F., Canada, coastline in which, under various treaties from 1713 to 1904, France was ceded fishing rights by Great Britain. It first extended from Cape Bonavista N to Cape Norman, thence S to Point Riche; later it was extended S to Cape Ray.

French West Indies: see WEST INDIES.

Frenchboro, Maine: see LONG ISLAND, plantation.

Frenchburg, village (1990 pop. 625), ⊙ Menifee co., E central Ky., 31 mi/50 km E of Winchester, in Daniel Boone Natl. Forest; 37°57′N 83°37′W. Agr. (cattle; timber); mfg. (lumber, valves); fishing nearby. Red R. Gorge in Red R. Natl. Geological Area to S; Cave Run L. reservoir to NE.

Frenchman Bay, Hancock co., S Maine, inlet of the Atlantic; extends inland c.20 mi/32 km bet. Mt. Desert Isl. and Schoodic Peninsula.

Frenchman Creek, in SE Logan co., NE Colo. and Nebr.; rises in NE Colo.; flows 151 mi/243 km ESE, past Holyoke, Colo., into S Nebr., through Enders Reservoir, past Wauneta and Palisade, Nebr., through Culbertson Dam (at Palisade), to Republican R. near Culbertson, 12 mi/19 km W of McCook. Enders Dam.

Frenchman Flat, Nev.: see INDIAN SPRINGS.

Frenchman River, SW Sask., Canada, and NE Mont.; rises in Cypress Hills; flows c.250 mi/402 km SE, past Eastend and Val Marie, crossing into Mont., to Milk R., 30 mi/48 km ENE of Malta.

Frenchmans Cay, islet, just off SW Tortola isl., Br. Virgin Isls., 5 mi/8 km SW of Road Town; 18°23′N 64°42′W. Agr. (livestock, fruit, vegetables). Sometimes called Frenchman Isl.

Frenchtown, village (1990 pop.140), Missoula co., W Mont., at mouth of Mill Creek, near the Clark Fork R., and 15 mi/24 km NW of Missoula. In irrigated agr. and mining region; cattle, alfalfa, forest industries. Parts of Lolo Natl. Forest to N and S; Frenchtown Pond State Park to W. June 24, St. John's Day, is celebrated in honor of the original Fr. Can. settlers.

Frenchtown, borough (1990 pop. 1,528), Hunterdon co., W N.J., on Del. R., and 10 mi/16 km W of Flemington; 40°31′N 75°03′W. Mfg. (electronics, office); hatcheries; poultry, fruit, grain; dairy and nursery prods. Inc. 1867.

Frenchville, agr. town (1990 pop. 1,338), Aroostook co., N Maine, on St. John R., 8 mi/12.9 km E of Fort Kent; 47°16′N 68°23′W. Potatoes shipped. Settled by Acadians, inc. 1869.

Fresh Creek, town, W Bahama Isls., on E shore of Andros Isl., 40 mi/64 km SW of Nassau; 24°42′N 77°45′W. Sponge fishing. Also known as Coakley Town.

Fresh Kills Landfill, landfill (□ 5 sq mi/13 sq km), on W central side of Staten Isl. borough, N.Y. city, SE N.Y., bet. Victory Boulevard (N) and Arthur Kill Road (S); 40°34′N 74°10′W. In marsh area drained by Fresh Kills Creeks into the Arthur Kill. The area is N.Y. city's sole remaining active garbage-disposal area. The world's largest man-made waste-disposal structure, the area is 6 times the size of La Guardia Airport, 4 times the size of Disneyland. Operating round-the-clock, 6 days per week, it handles N.Y. city's 16,000 tons/14,512 metric tons of daily garbage and incinerator ash brought by barge and truck at cost of $100 million per year. Produces, as waste gas, 5.7% of U.S. methane and 1.8% of world's; about 25% of gas is tapped and sold to Brooklyn Union Gas Co. utility. In mid-1980s engineers proposed permitting an accumulation that would produce a 505-ft/154-m-high mt., which would have been the highest point on Atlantic coast bet. Boston and Miami; present plans would allow height to reach 435 ft/133 m, 135 ft/41 m (higher than the Statue of Liberty). Known colloquially as Mt. Trash. A 12-member task force is under City Council mandate to complete plans for the closing of the landfill, scheduled for Dec. 31, 2001.

Freshfield, Mount (10,945 ft/3,336 m), on Alta.-B.C., Canada, border, in Rocky Mts., on W edge of Banff Natl. Park, 70 mi/113 km NW of Banff; 51°43′N 116°58′W.

Freshwater, Colo.: see GUFFEY.

Fresnillo (frez-NEE-yo), city (1990 pop. 75,118) and township, Zacatecas state, N central Mexico; 23°10′N 102°54′W. The city, on Mexico Highway 45-49, is the center of a rich mining area known especially for silver. It has a mining school. Agr. (cereals, beans) and cattle raising are other important economic activities. Fresnillo was founded in 1554 by Francisco de Ibarra. Also known as Fresnillo de González Echeverría.

Fresnillo de González Echeverría, Mexico: see FRESNILLO.

Fresnillo de Trujano (frez-NEE-yo de troo-HAH-no), town (1990 pop. 421), in far NW Oaxaca, Mexico, 37 mi/60 km WNW of Huajuapan de León. Elev. 3,346 ft/1,020 m. Near the Mixteco River. Mild climate. Agr. (corn, sugarcane, beans, chile, fruits); woods; straw textiles made from palms; livestock and poultry breeding and raising. In the Mixteca Baja.

Fresno, county (□ 5,963 sq mi/15,444 sq km; 1990 pop. 667,490), central Calif.; ⊙ Fresno; 36°45′N 111°37′W. Stretches across San Joaquin Valley from Diablo Range (W) to crest of the Sierra Nevada (E), where there are peaks over 14,000 ft/4,267 m. San Joaquin R. forms most of N boundary. Drained by Kings and Fresno rivers. FRIANT DAM is in co. Oil and natural-gas fields in SW (Coalinga dist.). Rich irrigated valley sect. produces raisins (large part of U.S. crop), table grapes; cotton, figs, nectarines, oranges, almonds, lettuce, garlic, tomatoes, sugar beets, rice, corn, beans; barley, oats, wheat; also has dairying and cattle. Diversified mfg. at Fresno. Sand and gravel, stone quarrying; oil and gas. Timber (pine, fir, cedar). Huntington, Shaver, Florence lakes (resorts); winter sports areas; and hunting and fishing attract vacationers. Delta Mendota Canal (irrigation) terminates in NW co., Calif. Aqueduct crosses co., in SW center; Pine Flat L. reservoir in E center, Millerton L. reservoir and State Recreation Area are on co. line, San Joaquin R. Large part of KINGS CANYON NATIONAL PARK and parts of Sierra and Sequoia natl. forests in E. Formed 1856.

Fresno, city (1990 pop. 354,202), ⊙ Fresno co., S central Calif., 120 mi/193 km ESE of San Jose, in San Joaquin Valley; 36°47′N 119°48′W. Settled in 1872 as a station on the Central Pacific RR, Fresno profited from irrigated farming in the 1880s. Due to the extensive and sophisticated agribusiness in the valley, the city dramatically expanded, becoming one of the fastest-growing cities in the U.S. Its pop. increased by more than 62% bet. 1980 and 1990. Substantial proportion of total pop. of Muong who live in U.S. are residents of Fresno, which is regarded by Muong as their internatl. capital. Fresno is the financial center of the San Joaquin valley, where food processing and shipping, service industries, and commercial activities have flourished. The city is laced with several irrigation canals. The variety of fruits, nuts, and vegetables in the valley include grapes, tomatoes, figs, olives, peaches, nectarines, sugar beets, grain, and corn. The area is also rich in cotton harvesting and production. Cattle are abundant, and dairy farming is important. Among the city's manufactures are beer, farm machinery, plastic prods., vending machines, and orthopedic appliances. Nearby oil and natural-gas fields further stimulate Fresno's economy. Fresno Airport in E, Chandler Municipal Airport in SW. The city is the seat of California State Univ., Fresno; Pacific Col.; and Fresno City Col. (the oldest junior col. in Calif.; est. 1910). Of interest are Forestiere Underground Gardens; Roeding Park, with a large zoo and amusements; wineries; co. fairgrounds; and an annual rodeo. Fresno Mus. of Natural History, Fresno Arts Center, Fresno Metropolitan Mus., and a philharmonic orchestra. City and its Armenian community subject of William Saroyan's writings. Sierra and Sequoia natl. forests to NE; a gateway to Kings Canyon and Sequoia natl. parks, both c.55 mi to E; Millerton L. reservoir and State Recreation Area to N. Inc. 1885.

Fresno, uninc. town (1990 pop. 3,182), Fort Bend co., SE Texas, suburb, 16 mi/26 km SSW of downtown Houston; 29°32′N 95°27′W. Urban fringe in agr. area. Oil and natural gas. Mfg. (oil field chemicals, steel fabricating, blasting equip.).

Fresno Reservoir, reservoir, Hill co., N central Mont., on Milk R., 12 mi/19 km WNW of Havre; c.25 mi/40 km long; 48°35′N 109°56′W. Max. capacity 262,000 acre-ft. Formed by Fresno Dam (earth construction; 75 ft/23 m high), built (1939) by the Bureau of Reclamation for irrigation, flood control, and water supply.

Fresno River, central Calif.; rises in NE Madera co., c.45 mi/72 km ENE of Merced; flows c.75 mi/121 km generally SW and W, past Madera. Much of its flow is directed into irrigation channels flowing S into San Joaquin Valley, c.20 mi/32 km WNW of Madera.

Frewsburg, village (☐ 1 sq mi/2.6 sq km; 1990 pop. 1,817), Chautauqua co., extreme W N.Y., on Conewango Creek and 5 mi/8 km SE of Jamestown; 42°03′N 79°09′W. Injection plastic molders; wood prods.; dairying.

Friant, uninc. village, Fresno co., central Calif., 17 mi/27 km NNE of Fresno, on San Joaquin R., below (S of) Friant Dam. Mfg. (concrete). Millerton L. State Recreation Area to N.

Friant, Calif., see MILLERTON LAKE.

Friant Dam, Calif., see MILLERTON LAKE.

Friant-Kern Canal, S central Calif., a unit of CENTRAL VALLEY project, conducts water by gravity for 153 mi/246 km from Friant Dam, along E side of San Joaquin Valley, to Kern R. near Bakersfield. Irrigates large agr. acreages in Fresno, Tulare, Kern cos.

Friars Point, town (1990 pop. 1,334), Coahoma co., NW Miss., 12 mi/19 km NNW of Clarksdale, and on Mississippi R., Sunflower R. to E; 34°22′N 90°38′W. In rich agr. (cotton, corn, rice, soybeans; cattle) and timber area; mfg. (concrete). Sometimes Friar Point.

Friday Harbor, town (1990 pop. 1,492), ⊙ San Juan co., NW Wash., on San Juan Isl., and 28 mi/45 km SW of Bellingham; on Friday Harbor, arm of San Juan Channel; 48°32′N 123°02′W. Port of entry; oceanographic laboratories. Hay; fish, crabs, oysters; dairying; cattle; mfg. (computer peripherals; printing and publishing); tourism. Ferries from Seattle and Anacortes, also to Orcas and Lopez isls. San Juan Isl. Natl. Historical Park, separate units at Friday Harbor, Wascott Bay (NW),

and Cattle Point (S). The Whale Mus.; St. Francis Xavier Mission. Lime Kiln Point State Park to W; Turn Isl. State Park to E.

Fridley, city (1990 pop. 28,335), Anoka co., SE Minn., a suburb, 7 mi/11.3 km N of downtown Minneapolis, on the Mississippi R. (bridged); 45°04′N 93°15′W. Drained by Rice Creek. A distribution center with RR yards and warehouses. Mfg. (rubber and plastics prods., electrical prods., electroplating, machinery, aircraft, cosmetics, computers, X-ray equip., ordnance and weapons systems). Settled 1847, inc. as a city 1957.

Fridtjof Nansen Sound, N.W.T., Canada: see NANSEN SOUND.

Friedens (FREE-dahns), uninc. town (1990 pop. 1,576), Somerset co., SW Pa., 6 mi/9.7 km NE of Somerset on Wells Creek; 40°02′N 79°00′W. Mfg. (popcorn); agr. (dairying, livestock; potatoes, apples; corn, oats, hay). Location of surface and subsurface bituminous coal. County airport to SW.

Friend, town (1990 pop. 1,111), Saline co., SE Nebr., 20 mi/32 km SW of Seward; 40°38′N 97°16′W. Grain, livestock. Mfg. (agr. chemical applicators, trailer parts, printing). Founded c.1873.

Friendly, village (1990 pop. 146), Tyler co., NW W.Va., 14 mi/23 km SW of New Martinsville, on the Ohio R., 8 mi/12.9 km WNW of Middlebourne; 39°30′N 81°3′W. Mfg. (aluminum recycling).

Friends Lake, reservoir and resort lake, Warren co., E N.Y., in the Adirondack Mts., in Adirondack Park, 23 mi/37 km NNW of Glens Falls; c.2 mi/3.2 km long; 43°38′N 73°50′W.

Friendship, city (1990 pop. 467), Crockett co., W Tenn., 11 mi/18 km SE of Dyersburg; 35°55′N 89°14′W. In farm, clay area.

Friendship 1 resort and fishing town (1990 pop. 1,099), Knox co., S Maine, on Muscongus Bay and SW of Rockland; 43°58′N 69°20′W. **2** town, ⊙ Adams co., central Wis., on Little Roche a Cri Creek (tributary of the Wisconsin R.), and 29 mi/47 km S of Wisconsin Rapids, in timber region. Mfg. (wood pallets). Roche a Cri State Park to N; Castle Rock L. Reservoir to W.

Friendship 1 village (1990 pop. 160), Hot Spring co., central Ark., 8 mi/12.9 km NNE of Arkadelphia; 34°13′N 93°00′W. Mfg. (pontoon boats, fishing boats, roof and floor trusses). **2** village (1990 pop. 1,423), Allegany co., W N.Y., 18 mi/29 km NE of Olean; 42°13′N 78°07′W. Agr.; mfg. (hosiery, textiles, auto bodies, metal and wood prods.); timber. Inc. 1898.

Friendship Hill National Historic Site, (675 acres/273 ha), Fayette co., SW Pa., 12 mi/19 km SW of Uniontown on Monongahela R., at mouth of Georges Creek. Home of Albert Gallatin, scholar and financier, U.S. Secretary of the Treasury (1801–1813) under Presidents Jefferson and Madison. Authorized 1978.

Friendship Island (☐ c.0.75 sq mi/1.9 sq km), Knox co., S Maine, in Muscongus Bay, just S of Friendship.

Friendsville, town (1990 pop. 577), Garrett co., extreme NW Md., in the Alleghenies on Youghiogheny R., and 35 mi/56 km W of Cumberland; 39°40′N 79°25′W. Records show John Friend (1732–1831), the first Eur. settler, bought land from peaceful Shawnee Indians in 1765. A recent architectural dig at the construction of the U.S. 48 interchange in Friendsville produced evidence of an Indian village.

Friendsville, borough (1990 pop. 102), Susquehanna co., NE Pa., 11 mi/18 km WNW of Montrose. Agr. (corn, hay; dairying; livestock; mfg. (meat packing, machining).

Friendswood, city (1990 pop. 22,814), Galveston and Harris cos., SE Texas, suburb, 16 mi/26 km NW of Texas City, and 17 mi/27 km SSW of downtown Houston; 29°30′N 95°12′W. Bounded by Clear Creek on NE. Diversified light mfg.

Fries (FREEZ), village (1990 pop. 690), Grayson co., SW Va., 4 mi/6.4 km NNW of Galax, in the Blue Ridge, at dam on New R.; 36°43′N 80°58′W. Mfg. (wooden pallets, clothing, lumber); in agr. area (dairying; livestock; tobacco, corn). Spur of New River Trail State Park passes to E. Inc. 1901–1902.

Friesland (FREES-land), village (1990 pop. 271), Columbia co., S central Wis., 20 mi/32 km ENE of Portage; 43°35′N 89°04′W. Farming, dairying.

Frigid, Cape, E extremity of Keewatin dist. mainland, N.W.T., Canada, on Roes Welcome Sound, at S entrance of Repulse Bay; 66°4′N 85°5′W.

Frio, county (☐ 1,134 sq mi/2,937 sq km; 1990 pop. 13,472), SW Texas; ⊙ Pearsall; 28°51′N 99°06′W. Drained by Frio and Leona rivers. Partly in irrigated Winter Garden vegetable-farming and fruit-growing area; peanuts, corn, grain sorghum. Cattle ranching. Oil and natural gas wells; stone. Formed 1858.

Frio Canyon, Texas: see FRIO RIVER.

Frio River, Texas; rises on Edwards Plateau in Real co.; flows S and SE c.220 mi/354 km; flows through Choke Canyon L. reservoir, and receives Atascosa R. just before joining the Nueces R. below Three Rivers. Recreational areas at Frio Canyon N of Uvalde (Garner State Park here).

Friona, town (1990 pop. 3,688), Parmer co., NW Texas, on the Llano Estacado, 22 mi/35 km SW of Hereford 34°38′N 102°43W. Shipping point for wheat and cattle area. Mfg. (beef processing, livestock feed).

Frisco 1 town (1990 pop. 1,601), Summit co., central Colo., on Tenmile Creek, entrance to Dillon Reservoir (formed by Blue R.), 25 mi/40 km NNE of Leadville, in Gore Range; 39°34′N 106°05′W. Elev. 9,097 ft/2,773 m. Small-scale gold and silver mining. Skiing, river rafting. Site was a Ute Indian Camp for 7,000 years. Surrounded by Arapaho Natl. Forest, Copper Mt. Ski Resort to S; Keystone Ski Resort to E. **2** uninc. town (1990 est. pop. 1,000), Franklin township, Beaver co., W Pa., suburb, 1 mi/1.6 km SE of Ellwood City, on Connoquenessing Creek; 40°50′N 80°16′W. **3** town (1990 pop. 6,141), Collin and Denton cos., N Texas, suburb, 26 mi/42 km N of downtown Dallas; 33°08′N 96°48′W. In agr. area (cotton, corn; cattle) in urban fringe; mfg. (lead smelting, polyethylene fusion tools, structural steel fabrication).

Frisco City, town (1990 pop. 1,581), Monroe co., SW Ala., 7 mi/11.3 km SW of Monroeville; 31°25′N 87°24′W. Woodworking, work pants, hospital garments.

Frissell, Mount (FRES-sel), peak, 2,380 ft/725 m high, extreme NW Conn., in the Taconic Mts., near the Mass.–N.Y. line. Highest point in Conn.

Fritch, town (1990 pop. 2,335), Hutchinson co., extreme N Texas, 32 mi/51 km NNE of Amarillo; 35°38′N 101°35′W. Elev. 3,200 ft/975 m. Oil and natural gas. Cattle; wheat, corn. Mfg. (natural gas processing). Recreation. Large L. Meredith reservoir (Canadian R.) to NW. Lake, surrounded by L. Meredith Natl. Recreation Area. Alibates Flint Quarries Natl. Monument to SW.

Frobisher Bay, town, E N.W.T., Canada, Franklin dist., S Baffin Isl. See also IQALUIT.

Frobisher Bay, arm of the Atlantic Ocean, 150 mi/240 km long and from 20 mi/32 km–40 mi/64 km wide, Baffin Region, N.W.T., Canada. Cutting deeply into SE Baffin Isl., it has steep, deeply indented shores and numerous islets. On its SW side the Grinnell and Southeast icecaps rise to c.3,000 ft/910 m, extending tongues into the bay. At its head are Frobisher Bay trading post (est. 1914) and an air base. The bay was explored (1576) by Sir Martin Frobisher; until 1860 it was believed to be a strait separating Baffin Isl. from another isl.

Frobisher Lake (24 mi/39 km long, 17 mi/27 km wide), NW Sask., Canada, just N of Churchill L., into which it drains; 56°20′N 108°20′W. Elev. 1,382 ft/421 m. Just N are Turnor and Wasekamio lakes.

Frohna (FRO-nuh), village, (1990 pop. 246), Perry co., SE Mo., 12 mi/19 km SSE of Perryville. Hilly area settled by Germans in 1830s. Laid out as a German *Strassendorf* (street village). Dairying; cattle; timber. Mfg. (hardwood and softwood lumber).

Froid, village (1990 pop. 195), Roosevelt co., NE Mont., on Sheep Creek, near Medicine L. and Big Muddy Creek, 58 mi/93 km ENE of Wolf Point, 42 mi/68 km WNW of Williston, N.D.; 48°20′N 104°29′W. Wheat, corn, hay, vegetables; cattle. Medicine Lake Natl. Wildlife Refuge to N includes Homestead L., to NW. Fort Peck Indian Reservation to W.

Fromberg (FRAHM-buhrg), village (1990 pop. 370), Carbon co., S Mont., on Clarks Fork Yellowstone R., near mouth of Bluewater Creek, and 34 mi/55 km SW of Billings; 45°23′N 108°55′W. Coal; oats, barley, corn (maize), sorghum; cattle, sheep. Formerly called Gebo.

Frome, town (1991 pop. 900), Westmoreland parish, W Jamaica, 7 mi/11.3 km NNW of Savanna-la-Mar; 18°18′N 78°09′W. Sugarcane, breadfruit; livestock. Has the West Indies Sugar Co., one of isl.'s largest sugar mills; exports unrefined sugar. Yeast factory nearby.

Front Range, an eastern range of the U.S. Rocky Mts., bordering the Great Plains, and extending c.300 mi/483 km S from SE Wyo. to the Arkansas R., S central Colo. It has several peaks, including Gray's Peak and Pikes Peak, that are more than 14,000 ft/4,267 m high. Also included are several lesser ranges, especially Rampart Range, NW of Colorado Springs, Green Ridge, W of Ft. Collins, and Medicine Bow Mts., W of Laramie. The Colorado, Arkansas, South Platte, and North Platte rivers are the largest streams rising in the range. Except for the lower Arkansas, the regions that these rivers flow through are either arid or semiarid, receiving little retainable rainfall, making the snowcapped Front Range one of the most significant water sources in N. Amer. Most of Colorado's pop. is located along the range's E foothills. The Front Range was scouted by U.S. explorers Zebulon Pike, in 1806–1807, and Stephen Long, in 1819–1820. In 1858 gold was discovered at Cripple Creek, Colo., and goldseekers rushed into the S Front Range. Most of the range is in natl. forests; Rocky Mt. Natl. Park is located in the north.

Front Royal, city (1990 pop. 11,880), ⊙ Warren co., N Va., 19 mi/31 km S of Winchester, near junction of South Fork and North Fork of Shenandoah R. (which form the river), at N end of Skyline Drive (Shenandoah Natl. Park extension of Blue Ridge Parkway); 38°55′N 78°10′W. RR junction. Mfg. (wooden doors, windows and cabinets, automotive paints, furniture, lumber, modular homes, concrete, fiberglass pipe and fittings, printing and publishing, chemicals, foods and beverages, canning); limestone quarrying. Skyline Caverns to S attract tourists. Part of George Washington Natl. Forest (Massanutten Mt.) is W. Site of Confederate victory during Shenandoah Valley campaign of Civil War. Christendon Col. to NE. Front Royal Warren Co. Airport to W. Inc. 1788.

Frontenac 1 (FRAHN-tuh-nak), county (□ 1,599 sq mi/4,141 sq km; 1991 pop. 129,089), SE Ont., Canada, on L. Ontario, and on the St. Lawrence R.; ⊙ Kingston. **2** county (□ 1,370 sq mi/3,548 sq km), S Que., Canada, on Maine border, on Chaudière R.; ⊙ Megantic.

Frontenac (FRAHN-tuh-nak), city (1990 pop. 3,374), St. Louis co., E Mo., residential and commercial suburb 12 mi/19 km W of downtown St. Louis; 38°37′N 90°25′W. Exclusive shopping dist.

Frontenac (FRAHN-tuh-nak), town (1990 pop. 2,588), Crawford co., SE Kansas, near Mo. line, suburb, 3 mi/4.8 km N of Pittsburg; 37°27′N 94°42′W. RR junction. In general agr. and coal-mining region. Mfg. (prepared meats). Crawford State Fishing L. to N. Laid out 1887, inc. 1895.

Frontenac, Fort, Canada,: see KINGSTON, Ont.

Frontera 1 (fron-TER-ah), city (1990 pop. 16,269) and township, ⊙ Centla township, Tabasco, SE Mexico, port at mouth of Grijalva R., 6 mi/9.7 km inland from the Gulf of Campeche, 40 mi/64 km NNE of Villahermosa, on Mexico Highway 180; 18°32′N 92°39′W. A cargo and fishing port. Trading, processing, and agr. center (sugar, tobacco, corn, coconut, rice, beans, cacao, bananas; livestock; timber). Tanning, sawmilling, vegetable oil pressing; mfg. of soap, footwear. Exports fruit, wood. Formerly Álvaro Obregón. **2** city (1990 pop. 56,216) and township, ⊙ municipio, Coahuila, N Mexico, in E outliers of Sierra Madre Oriental, adjoining Monclova, 115 mi/185 km NW of Monterrey; 26°59′N 101°30′W. Elev. 1,926 ft/587 m. City built around RR station. Agr. center (cereals, fruit; cattle; flour milling, wax mfg. Formerly Villa Frontera.

Frontera (fron-TER-ah), town, N Tabasco, Mexico, 5.6 mi/9 km NE of Benito Juárez, in the municipality of Centla, on Mexico Highway 180; 18°31′N 92°38′W. It is a maritime customs port, located on the E bank of the Grijalva River. The city is surrounded by extensive marshes. Hot climate. It is the most important port in the state with extensive cargo traffic. There are no public navigation services and not much cargo equip. for loading or unloading. Much of the traffic is private. Agr. (cereals, legumes). The principal resource is coconut. Other activities are the production of copra, cattle raising, woods, and fishing.

Frontera Comalapa or **Comalapa,** (fron-TER-ah ko-ma-LAH-pah), town (1990 pop. 8,310), Chiapas, S Mexico, in Sierra Madre, 40 mi/64 km S of Comitán de Domínguez, on the Inter-Amer. Highway 190. Coffee, citrus, tropical fruit.

Frontera Hidalgo (fron-TER-ah ee-DAHL-go), town (1990 pop. 2,377), Chiapas, S Mexico, on Guatemala border, 8 mi/12.9 km N of Ciudad Hidalgo, 11 mi/18 km SE of Tapachula on Mexico Highway 19. Coffee.

Frontera Point (fron-TER-ah), cape in Tabasco, SE Mexico, on Gulf of Campeche, at mouth of Grijalva and Usumacinta rivers, 7 mi/11.3 km NNW of Frontera; 18°37′N 92°38′W.

Fronteras (fron-TER-ahs), town (1990 pop. 962), Sonora, NW Mexico, on RR, and 32 mi/51 km S of Douglas, Ariz.; 30°51′N 109°33′W. Wheat, corn, alfalfa; cattle.

Frontier, county (□ 980 sq mi/2,538 sq km; 1990 pop. 3,101), S Nebr.; ⊙ Stockville; 40°31′N 100°23′W. Agr. region drained by Medicine Creek and other branches of Republican R. Corn, wheat, sorghum; livestock. Red Willow Recreation Area in SW (Hugh Butler L.); Medicine Creek Reservoir State Recreation Area in SE (Harry D. Struck L.). Formed 1872.

Frontier 1 village (1990 pop. 218), Cass co., E N.Dak., suburb, 5 mi/8 km S of Fargo, on Red R. of the N, at mouth of Wild Rice R.; 46°47′N 96°49′W. Residential. **2** village, Lincoln co., SW Wyo., on Hams Fork, 2 mi/3.2 km N of Kemmerer. Elev. 6,954 ft/2,120 m. Rail spur; coal mines.

Frood Mine, town, SE central Ont., Canada, 3 mi/5 km NW of Sudbury; nickel and copper mining.

Frost 1 village (1990 pop. 236), Faribault co., S Minn., 9 mi/14.5 km ESE of Blue Earth, near East Fork Blue Earth R., and near Iowa state line; 43°34′N 93°55′W. Livestock; grain, soybeans. **2** village (1990 pop. 579), Navarro co., E central Texas, 20 mi/32 km W of Corsicana; 32°04′N 96°48′W. In agr. area (cotton, corn). Navarro Mills L. to S.

Frostburg, resort and trading town (1990 pop. 8,075), Allegany co., W Md., in the Alleghenies, 9 mi/14.5 km W of Cumberland. Bituminous coal and clay mining; makes firebrick, clothing. Named for Meshach Frost who settled here in 1812 and around whose tavern on the Natl. Road the community grew. The Frost mansion, built in 1846 with a 3d story added in 1890, is now a funeral home. William Cullen Bryant described Frostburg in 1860 as a little town "flying high among the mountain ridges." Seat of Frostburg State Univ. and the Miners' Hosp. *Ripley's Believe It or Not* once claimed Frostburg had more bars — and churches — per capita than any other town in the U.S. Big Savage Mt. and Savage R. State Forest lie just W.

Frostproof, town (□ 2 sq mi/5.2 sq km; 1990 pop. 2,808), Polk co., central Fla., 13 mi/21 km S of Lake Wales, near several lakes; 27°45′N 81°31′W. Cans and packs citrus fruit.

Frozen Strait, E Keewatin dist., N.W.T., Canada, arm (50 mi/80 km long, 12 mi/19 km–20 mi/32 km wide) of Foxe Channel, bet. Melville Peninsula and Southampton Isl.; 65°50′N 84°30′W. Connects Foxe Channel (SE) with Repulse Bay and Roes Welcome Sound.

Fruit Cove, town (□ 17 sq mi/44 sq km; 1990 pop. 5,904), St. Johns co., NE Fla., 21 mi/34 km S of Jacksonville; 30°06′N 81°37′W. Chiefly residential.

Fruit Growers Dam, Colo.: see DELTA, city.

Fruit Heights, town (1990 pop. 3900), Davis co., N Utah, suburb near Great Salt L., 13 mi/21 km S of Ogden and 17 mi/27 km N of Salt Lake City; 41°01′N 111°54′W. Drained by Bear Creek. Fruit-growing area; dairying. Cherry Hill Camp and Amusement Park; Wasatch

Range and Natl. Forest to E. Francis Peak (9,265 ft/2,824 m) 4 mi/6.4 km E. Settled in 1850.

Fruit Hill, uninc. village (1990 pop. 4,101), Hamilton co., extreme SW Ohio, an E suburb of Cincinnati, near Ohio R.; 39°04′N 84°22′W.

Fruita, town (1990 pop. 4,045), Mesa co., W Colo., on Colorado R., near Utah line, and 10 mi/16 km NW of Grand Junction; 39°09′N 108°43′W. Elev. 4,498 ft/1,371 m. Trade center for irrigated sugar-beet and grain region; beans, fruit. Mfg. (fireproofing, light mfg.). Oil and gas wells, coal and gold mines in vicinity. Highline State Park to NW. Colo. Natl. Monument nearby. Inc. 1894.

Fruitdale 1 village, Washington co., SW Ala., on Escatawpa R., near Miss. line, and 50 mi/80 km NNW of Mobile. **2** village (1990 pop. 43), Butte co., W S.Dak., 8 mi/12.9 km E of Belle Fourche, just N of Black Hills, and on Belle Fourche R.; 44°40′N 103°42′W.

Fruithurst, town (1990 pop. 177), Cleburne co., E Ala., 10 mi/16 km NE of Heflin, near Ga. line; 33°43′N 85°25′W. Lumbering.

Fruitland 1 town (1990 pop. 2,400), Payette co., W Idaho, 6 mi/9.7 km SE of Payette, on Snake R., at mouth of Payette R., opposite Ontario, Oregon; 44°01′N 116°55′W. Dairying; sheep, cattle; sugar beets, potatoes; fruit (apples, plums, peaches), vegetables; mfg. (pine prods. and millwork, apple cider). **2** town (1990 pop. 3,511), Wicomico co., SE Md., 4 mi/6.4 km SSW of Salisbury; 38°19′N 75°38′W. Fruit and vegetable canneries, clothing factories, lumber mills. Fruitland won out over Phoenix as the town's name in a 1873 poll of residents. Auctions of holly and greenery from all Lower Shore communities held here before Christmas.

Fruitland, village (1990 pop. 800), San Juan co., NW N.Mex., on San Juan R., Colo. state line to N, and 10 mi/16 km W of Farmington. Elev. 5,118 ft/1,560 m. In irrigated region; grain, potatoes, pumpkins; cattle, sheep. Mfg. (power boats). Navajo Indian Reservation to S and W; Ute Mt. Indian Reservation (N.Mex./Colo.) to N.

Fruitland Park, town (□ 2 sq mi/5.2 sq km; 1990 pop. 2,754), Lake co., central Fla., 4 mi/6.4 km N of Leesburg, near L. Griffin, in citrus-fruit-growing area; 28°51′N 81°54′W.

Fruitlands, Mass.: see HARVARD.

Fruitport, town (1990 pop. 1,090), Muskegon and Ottawa cos., SW Mich., 9 mi/14.5 km SE of Muskegon, on N arm of Spring L.; 43°07′N 86°09′W. Mfg. (wood and metal patterns, castings, store fixtures and displays, electronic assemblies).

Fruitvale, town (1990 pop. 349), Van Zandt co., NE Texas, 9 mi/14.5 km NNE of Canton, near Sabine R.; 32°40′N 95°47′W. Agr. area (vegetables, cotton, grains; dairying; cattle). Timber.

Fruitvale, village (1991 pop. 2,062), S B.C., Canada, near Wash. border, on Beaver Creek, and 8 mi/13 km E of Trail; 49°07′N 117°33′W. Fruit, vegetables.

Fruitville, suburb (□ 7 sq mi/18.1 sq km; 1990 pop. 9,808) of Sarasota, Sarasota co., W cental Fla., 4 mi/6.4 km E of city center; 27°19′N 82°27′W.

Fryatt, Mount (FREI-uht) (11,026 ft/3,361 m), W Alta., Canada, near B.C. border, in Rocky Mts., in Jasper Natl. Park, 24 mi/39 km SSE of Jasper; 52°34′N 117°56′W.

Fryeburg (FREI-buhrg), town (1990 pop. 2,968), including Fryeburg village, Oxford co., W Maine, on the Saco R., and 27 mi/43 km SW of South Paris, near N.H. line; 44°02′N 70°56′W. Year-round resort center, mfg. (wood prods., canned foods). Fryeburg Acad. here. Settled 1762, inc. 1777.

Frying-Pan Shoals, N.C.: see FEAR, CAPE.

Fuerte, El, Mexico: see EL FUERTE.

Fuerte, Río (FWER-tai, REE-o), NW Mexico; formed in Chihuahua by Río Verde and Urique R.; flows W into Sinaloa, then SW, past El Fuerte and San Blas, to Gulf of Calif. 27 mi/43 km W of Los Mochis, at Lechuguilla Isl.; c.175 mi/282 km long; c.350 mi/563 km long with Río Verde.

Fulda (FUL-duh), town (1990 pop. 1,212), Murray co., SW Minn., 11 mi/18 km SE of Slayton, near Lime Creek;

43°52′N 95°35′W. Grain, soybeans; livestock, poultry; dairying; light mfg. Talcot Lake Wildlife Area to E.

Fulford Harbour, village, SW B.C., Canada, on SE Saltspring Isl., 11 mi/18 km E of Duncan; 48°46′N 123°27′W. Fishing port; mixed farming. Tourist, summer, and retirement residence center. Ferry to Swartz Bay and Vancouver Isl.

Fullarton (FUL-ahr-ton), village, SW Trinidad, Trinidad and Tobago, on the Gulf of Paria, 20 mi/32 km SW of San Fernando. In coconut-growing region.

Fullerton 1 city (1990 pop. 114,144), Orange co., S Calif., suburb, 21 mi/34 km SE of downtown Los Angeles, and 3 mi/4.8 km N of Anaheim, SE of Los Angeles; 33°53′N 117°56′W. The city is named for George H. Fullerton, head of a land company, who arranged to route the San Diego–Los Angeles–Santa Fe RR through the settlement in 1888. Oil was discovered near Fullerton in 1892, but the city's main growth came with the construction of the Santa Ana Freeway in the 1950s. Among Fullerton's manufactures are aerospace equip., canned food prods., electrical and electronic components, navigation systems, and laboratory instruments. Oil wells in city. Fullerton Municipal Airport to W. Fullerton Col. (2-year) and Calif. State Univ., Fullerton are in the city. Muckenthaler Center houses 2 symphony orchestras, a theater group, and art galleries. Coyote Hills to NW; Brea Reservoir in N, Fullerton Reservoir in NE. Founded 1887, inc. 1904. **2** uninc. city (1990 pop. 13,127), Whitehall township, Lehigh co., E Pa., residential suburb, 2 mi/3.2 km N of Allentown, on Lehigh R.; 40°37′N 75°29′W. Lehigh Valley Internatl. Airport to NE.

Fullerton, town (1990 pop. 1,452), ⊙ Nance co., E central Nebr., 32 mi/51 km W of Columbus, and on Loup R., in prairie region; 41°21′N 97°58′W. Dairying; grain. Platted 1878.

Fullerton 1 village (1990 pop. 950), Greenup co., NE Ky., on Ohio R. 1 mi/1.6 km SE of Portsmouth, Ohio (opposite side of river). In fruit-growing area. On site of part of Lower Shawneetown, one of last Indian settlements in Ky., built c.1729, deserted c.1753. **2** village (1990 pop. 94), Dickey co., SE N.Dak., 16 mi/26 km W of Oakes; 46°09′N 98°25′W.

Fullerton, Cape, E Keewatin dist., N.W.T., Canada, on Hudson Bay, at S end of Roes Welcome Sound; 63°58′N 88°47′W.

Fulshear, village (1990 pop. 557), Fort Bend co., SE Texas, 32 mi/51 km W of Houston, near Brazos R.; 29°41′N 95°52′W. Agr. area (rice, cotton, soybeans, vegetables). Oil and natural gas. Mfg. (piping systems assembly, injection molding).

Fulton 1 county (□ 620 sq mi/1,606 sq km; 1990 pop. 10,037), N Ark.; ⊙ Salem; 36°22′N 91°49′W. Bounded N by Mo. line; drained by Spring and Strawberry rivers. Agr. (cattle, hogs), hardwood timber. Arm of Norfork L. reservoir in SW part; Mammoth Spring State Park in NE. Formed 1842. **2** county (□ 523; 1990 pop. 648,951), NW central Ga.; ⊙ Atlanta; 33°47′N 84°28′W. Bounded NW by Chattahoochee R. Includes major part of Atlanta metropolitan area. City of Atlanta lies in its center. N and S portion largely uninc. but rapidly urbanizing. N Fulton is now home of the largest concentration of executive housing in the Atlanta urban area. While the city portion of the co. is largely Afr. Amer., the suburban portions of Atlanta house a white majority. The co. and city share many services and jointly fund many projects, such as the co. and city lib. system. Each maintain its own police force. Milton and Campbell cos. were annexed during the depression. Formed in 1853. **3** county (□ 882 sq mi/2,284 sq km; 1990 pop. 38,080), W central Ill.; ⊙ Lewistown; 40°28′N 90°12′W. Bounded SE by Illinois R.; drained by Spoon R.; includes group of bayou lakes (resorts) along Illinois R. Agr. (cattle; corn, wheat, soybeans, sorghum; dairy prods.). Bituminous-coal mining. Mfg. (textiles, furniture; metals). Clay deposits. Formed 1823. Many square miles disturbed by strip- mine efforts in search of coal. **4** county (□ 371 sq mi/961 sq km; 1990 pop. 18,840), N Ind.; ⊙ Rochester; 41°02′N 86°16′W. Agr. (vegetables, corn, soybeans; cattle, poultry, hogs; dairy prods.); some mfg. at Rochester and Akron; timber. L. resorts. Drained by Tippecanoe R. L. Manitou SE of Rochester. Nyona and South Mud (natural) lakes in S. Menominee State Fishing Area N of Rochester. Famous for its round barns. Formed 1835. **5** county (□ 230 sq mi/596 sq km; 1990 pop. 8,271), extreme W Ky.; ⊙ Hickman; 36°32′N 89°11′W. Bounded W by the Mississippi R. (Mo. state boundary), S by Tenn. state boundary; drained by Obion Creek and Bayou de Chien. Agr. area (cotton, corn, hay, alfalfa, soybeans, wheat, walnuts, dark tobacco; hogs; timber). Madrid Bend (westernmost part of state) totally separated from remainder of state, bounded by Mississippi R. (W, N, and E; Mo. state boundary) and by Tenn. (S), connected by road through Tenn. Part of Reelfoot Natl. Wildlife Refuge in SW, (Reelfoot L., large backwater lake formed by earthquake of 1811–1812, is in Tenn.). Formed 1845. **6** county (□ 532 sq mi/1,378 sq km; 1990 pop. 54,191), E central N.Y.; ⊙ Johnstown; 43°06′N 74°25′W. Situated in the Adirondacks; drained by E. Canada Creek and Sacandaga R. Includes Sacandaga Reservoir and several lakes (resorts). Dairying; poultry raising; farming; mfg. (leather and leather goods, knitting mill prods., furniture; baseball and softball bats). Co. was formerly the site of the major glove-making industry in the U.S. (mainly at Gloversville and Johnstown), but it has now largely disappeared. Formed 1838. Fulton-Montgomery Community Col. is in Johnstown. **7** county (□ 407 sq mi/1,054 sq km; 1990 pop. 38,498), NW Ohio; ⊙ Wauseon; 41°36′N 84°08′W. Bounded N by Mich. line; drained by Tiffin R. In the L. Plains physiographic region. Livestock, farming (soybeans, corn, tomatoes); diversified mfg. (furniture, plastics, steel pipe and tubes, sporting goods, motor vehicle parts and accessories). Formed 1850. **8** county (□ 438 sq mi/1,134 sq km; 1990 pop. 13,837), S Pa.; ⊙ McConnellsburg. Mountainous region, bounded S by Md. state line, with Tuscarora Mt. ridge on E boundary, Town Hill and Rays Hill ridges on W boundary; 39°55′N 78°06′W. Agr. (corn, wheat, oats, hay, alfalfa; hogs, cattle; dairying); bituminous coal, limestone. Mfg. at McConnellsburg. Sideling Hill ridge in W part, Meadow Grounds Mt. in E center; part of Cowans Gap State Park in NE; sects. of Buchanan State Forest in NE and NW. Settled in 1740s by Scotch-Irish; formed 1850.

Fulton 1 city (1990 pop. 3,698), Whiteside co., NW Ill., on the Mississippi (bridged here), 12 mi/19 km WNW of Morrison, 2 mi/3.2 km NE of Clinton, Iowa; 41°52′N 90°09′W. Trade and shipping center in agr. area (corn, wheat; cattle, hogs; dairy prods.); mfg. (chemicals, machinery). Limestone quarries. Inc. 1859. Lock and Dam No. 13 immediately upstream (N). **2** city (1990 pop. 10,033), ⊙ Callaway co., central Mo.; 38°51′N 91°57′W. In an agr. area; inc. 1859. Corn, wheat, soybeans; cattle, horses; mfg. (potato chips, publishing, textiles, switch gear, ball joints and drills, firebricks from nearby clay beds, refractories). On March 5, 1946, former Br. prime minister Winston Churchill delivered his famous "iron curtain" speech at Westminster Col. In 1992, past president of the former Soviet Union Mikhail Gorbachev spoke at the same col. on the lifting of the "iron curtain." In 1996, former Br. prime minister Lady Margaret Thatcher spoke at the same col. to commemorate the 50th anniversary of Churchill's "iron curtain" speech. Westminster Col. houses the Winston Churchill Memorial and Lib., including a reconstruction of a Christopher Wren church destroyed in the bombing of London. William Woods Col., state school for the deaf, and state mental hosp. are also here. Platted 1825; inc. 1859. **3** city (□ 4 sq mi/10.4 sq km; 1990 pop. 12,929), Oswego co., N central N.Y., on Oswego R. (water power) and the Barge Canal, and 10 mi/16 km SSE of Oswego; 43°19′N 76°25′W. Mfg. (confectionery, textiles, paper prods., firearms, machinery, cutlery, canned foods); sand and gravel. Ships dairy prods., fruit, vegetables, poultry. Battle Isl. State Park is 2.5 mi/4 km N. Inc. as village in 1835, as city in 1902.

Fulton 1 town (1990 pop. 384), Clarke co., SW Ala., 6 mi/9.7 km N of Grove Hill; 31°47′N 87°44′W. Lumber. **2** town (1990 pop. 371), Fulton co., N Ind., 14 mi/23 km NNE of Logansport; 40°57′N 86°16′W. Agr. area; light mfg. **3** town (1990 pop. 3,078), Fulton co., W Ky., 24 mi/39 km SW of Mayfield, Ky., at Tenn. state line, contiguous to South Fulton, Tenn. RR junction; 36°30′N 88°52′W. In agr. area (corn, dark tobacco, cotton; oak timber); mfg. (seeds, apparel, lumber, motor vehicle parts, dairy prods.). Fulton Airport to NW. Settled 1860; inc. 1874. **4** town (1990 pop. 3,387), ⊙ Itawamba co.; 34°15′N 88°24′W, NE Miss., 18 mi/29 km E of Tupelo, near (East Fork) Tombigbee R. and Tennessee-Tombigbee Waterway, both to W. In agr. area (soybeans, cotton, corn; cattle, poultry; timber); mfg. (furniture, wood prods., lumber, leather boots, printing and publishing, beef and pork processing, copper tubing). Itawamba Community Col. Whitten Historical Center. Lock C at Fulton, Lock D to N; Canal Section of John Bell Williams Wildlife Management Area to N. Settled 1848, inc. 1850. **5** town, Hanson co., SE central S.Dak., 10 mi/16 km E of Mitchell. **6** uninc. town (1990 pop. 763), Aransas co., S Texas, 28 mi/45 km NE of Corpus Christi, on Aransas Bay, which separates mainland from St. Joseph (San Jose) barrier isl.; 28°04′N 97°02′W. Mfg. (boats). Intracoastal Waterway traverses bay near mainland shore. Copano Bay to W. Fulton Mansion State Historic Park is here; Goose Isl. State Park and Aransas Natl. Wildlife Refuge are to NE. Copano Bay State Fishing Pier (on old causeway) to N. Aransas Co. Airport is to N.

Fulton 1 village (1990 pop. 269), Hempstead co., SW Ark., 18 mi/29 km NE of Texarkana, and on Red R. near mouth of Little R.; 33°36′N 93°48′W. Bois D'Arc Wildlife Management Area to E. **2** village (1990 pop. 191), Bourbon co., SE Kansas, near Mo. line, 10 mi/16 km N of Fort Scott; 38°00′N 94°43′W. In livestock-raising, dairying, and gen. agr. region. **3** village, Keweenaw co., Mich., ½ mi/⁸⁄₁₀ km S of Mohawk, 16 mi/26 km NE of Houghton; 44°17′N 88°21′W. **4** village (1990 pop. 325), Morrow co., central Ohio, 18 mi/29 km ESE of Marion; 40°28′N 82°49′W.

Fulton Chain of Lakes, group of 8 small lakes in the Adirondacks, N central N.Y., extending SW from vicinity of Raquette L.; 43°45′N 74°57′W. Lakes are connected by streams, and drained by Middle Branch of Moose R. Fourth L. (□ c.3 sq mi/7.8 sq km) is largest of group. Noted canoe route through hunting, fishing, and resort region. Old Forge, Inlet, and other resorts are here.

Fultondale, city (1990 pop. 6,400), Jefferson co., N central Ala., a N suburb of Birmingham; 33°37′N 86°47′W. Inc. since 1940.

Fultonville, village (1990 pop. 748), Montgomery co., E central N.Y., on Mohawk R. (bridged), opposite Fonda, and 10 mi/16 km W of Amsterdam; 42°57′N 74°22′W. Mfg. (apparel, textiles).

Fults (fullts), village (1990 pop. 45), Monroe co., SW Ill., 13 mi/21 km S of Waterloo; 38°09′N 90°12′W. In agr. area (wheat, corn, soybeans, sorghum). Heavily damaged in floods of 1993.

Fundición de Ávalos, Mexico: see ÁVALOS.

Fundy, Bay of, large inlet of the Atlantic Ocean, c.170 mi/270 km long and 30 mi/48 km/–50 mi/80 km wide, bet. N.B. and SW N.S., Canada. It is famous for its tide and tidal bore; in its upper arms, Chignecto Bay and the Mínas Basin, tides reach 40 ft/12 m–50 ft/15 m in ht. and create the reversing falls of the St. John R. At low tide, wide flats are laid bare, and the long estuaries of the rivers are drained. Many of the surrounding flats have been reclaimed and transformed into fertile farmland since Acadian settlers began to build dikes in the early 17th cent. Annapolis Royal, on the N.S. side of the bay, is the oldest settlement in Canada. St. John, N.B., is the chief port on the bay.

Fundy National Park, 80 sq mi/207 sq km, S N.B., Canada, on the Bay of Fundy, near St. John. It has a rugged terrain with a wooded interior and an irregular shoreline that is constantly being eroded by the bay's great tidal range. Est. 1947.

Funeral Mountains, Calif.: see AMARGOSA RANGE.

Funk, village (1990 pop. 198), Phelps co., S Nebr., 7 mi/11.3 km ENE of Holdrege; 40°27′N 99°15′W.

Funk Island, islet in the Atlantic, off E N.F., Canada, 37 mi/60 km E of Fogo Isl.; 49°45′N 53°14′W. Together with Two Islets, just W, it was one of the last breeding grounds of the now extinct great auk.

Funkley, village (1990 pop. 15), Beltrami co., N Minn., 30 mi/48 km NE of Bemidji; 47°47′N 94°25′W. Grain; livestock. Chippewa Natl. Forest to E and S.

Funkstown, town (1990 pop. 1,136), Washington co., W Md., on Antietam Creek just SSE of Hagerstown; 39°37′N 77°43′W. Originally called Jerusalem, it missed its opportunity to grow when Jonathan Hager rode to Annapolis in 1776 to have Hager-Town, later Hagerstown, made the co. seat. Named after Henry Funk, who was granted land by Frederick Calvert in 1754. According to local legend Funk also est. Funkstown or Hamburg on the present site of Washington, D.C. John Brown stayed at the site of Smith's Hotel in June 1859 while transporting pikes to arm slaves in the insurrection he was planning. Confederates held the hts. here (July 10–14, 1863) while waiting for the floodwaters of the Potomac R. to recede long enough for them to retreat back into Virginia after Gettysburg.

Funston, village (1990 pop. 248), Colquitt co., S Ga., 5 mi/8 km W of Moultrie; 31°12′N 83°52′W. Mfg. of cotton-fiber processing.

Funter (FUHN-tuhr), fishing village, SE Alaska, on N Admiralty Isl., on Icy Strait, 20 mi/32 km W of Juneau.

Fuquay-Varina (fyoo-kwai–vuh-REE-nuh), town (1990 pop. 4,562), Wake co., central N.C., 16 mi/26 km SSW of Raleigh; 35°35′N 78°47′W. Cotton, tobacco, grain; poultry, livestock. Harris L. reservoir to W. Mfg. (yarns, telephone cable accessories, children's apparel).

Furcy (fyoor-SEE), village, Ouest dept., S Haiti, mt. resort, 10 mi/16 km SSE of Port-au-Prince; 18°25′N 72°18′W.

Furman, village (1990 pop. 260), Hampton co., SW S.C., 45 mi/72 km N of Savannah (Ga.); 32°40′N 81°11′W. Mfg. (fertilizer). Tobacco, vegetables, watermelons, cotton; livestock.

Furnace Creek, Calif.: see DEATH VALLEY NATIONAL MONUMENT.

Furnas (FUHR-nes), county (□ 720 sq mi/1,865 sq km; 1990 pop. 5,553), S Nebr.; ☉ Beaver City; 40°10′N 99°54′W. Agr. region drained by Republican R. and Beaver and Sappa creeks; bounded S by Kansas. Cattle, hogs; dairying; corn, wheat, sorghum, alfalfa. Formed 1873.

Fury and Hecla Strait (HEK-luh), narrow channel, c.100 mi/160 km long and 10 mi/16 km–15 mi/24 km wide, N Canada, bet. Baffin Isl. and Melville Peninsula. It connects Foxe Basin with the Gulf of Boothia. It was explored (1822) by Sir William E. Parry and named for his ships. The strait is nearly always ice blocked.

Fury Point, cape, SE Somerset Isl., E Franklin dist., N.W.T., Canada, on Prince Regent Inlet, on NE side of Creswell Bay; 72°45′N 91°52′W.

Fussels Corner, town (□ 6 sq mi/15.5 sq km; 1990 pop. 3,840), Polk co., central Fla., 12 mi/19 km NE of Lakeland; 28°03′N 81°51′W.

Fyzabad (FEI-zah-bad), village, SW Trinidad, Trinidad and Tobago, 8 mi/12.9 km SSW of San Fernando. Oil wells.

G

Gaastra (GAH-struh), city (1990 pop. 376), Iron co., SW Upper Peninsula, Mich., 3 mi/4.8 km SSE of Iron R.; 46°03′N 88°36′W. Wood prods.

Gabarus Bay (ga-buh-ROOS), inlet, E N.S., Canada, on SE coast of Cape Breton Isl., SW of Louisburg; 45°50′N 60°06′W. Is 8 mi/13 km long, 5 mi/8 km wide at entrance.

Gabbro Lake, Minn.: see BALD EAGLE LAKE.

Gabbs, uninc. village (1990 pop. 667), Nye co., central Nev., 41 mi/66 km ENE of Hawthorne; 38°52′N 117°55′W. Cattle, sheep. Service center for gold mining dists. to E. Part of Toiyabe Natl. Forest to E. Sherman Peak (8,657 ft/2,639 m) to NE. Berlin-Ichthyosaur State Park, in Shoshone Mts., to E, marine reptile fossils.

Gabby Heights, uninc. town (1990 pop. 1,230), Washington co., SW Pa., residential suburb 1 mi/1.6 km SW of Washington; 40°09′N 80°15′W. Airport to SW.

Gabilan Range, one of the Coast Ranges, Monterey and San Benito cos., W Calif.; extends 50 mi/80 km SE from Pajaro R. at S end of Santa Cruz Mts. to near Lewis Creek and juncture with Diablo Range NE of King City. Rises to 3,455 ft/1,053 m at Mt. Johnson in center, Gabilan Peak (3,169 ft/966 m) is included in Frémont Peak State Park (□ 244 acres/99 ha) NE of Salinas. Salinas Valley to SW, upper San Benito R. Valley to NE, Santa Clara Valley to N; Pinnacles Natl. Monument in S center.

Gaboury (gah-boo-REE), village, W Que., Canada, 16 mi/26 km ESE of Haileybury. Gold mining.

Gabriel (gah-bree-EL), town, La Habana prov., W Cuba, 24 mi/39 km SSW of Havana; 22°49′N 82°28′W. Tobacco, fruit, vegetables. Commandante Manuel Fajardo sugar mill 2 mi/3.2 km NE. Also called El Gabriel.

Gabriel Zamora, Mexico: see LOMBARDÍA.

Gabriels, resort village (1990 pop. 250), Franklin co., NE N.Y., in the Adirondacks, 10 mi/16 km N of Saranac Lake village; 44°26′N 74°11′W. Several lakes are nearby.

Gabriola Island (ga-bree-O-luh) (□ 20 sq mi/52 sq km), Gulf Isls., SW B.C., Canada, in Strait of Georgia just off Vancouver Isl., 3 mi/5 km E of Nanaimo; 9 mi/14 km long, 2 mi/3 km wide; 49°10′N 123°47′W. Mixed farming. Village of Gabriola is at W tip.

Gabro Lake, Minn.: see BALD EAGLE LAKE.

Gackle (GAK-uhl), village (1990 pop. 450), Logan co., S N.Dak., 29 mi/47 km SW of Jamestown; 46°37′N 99°08′W.

Gadsby, village (1991 pop. 26), S central Alta., Canada, 15 mi/24 km E of Stettler; 52°18′N 112°21′W. Dairying; wheat growing.

Gadsden (GADZ-den), county (□ 528 sq mi/1,368 sq km; 1990 pop. 41,105), NW Fla., bounded N by Ga., E and S by Ochlockonee R. and L. Talquin, W by Apalachicola R.; ⊙ Quincy; 30°34′N 84°36′W. Rolling agr. area produces corn, peanuts, tobacco, vegetables; dairy prods.; poultry, hogs. Mfg. includes food prods., lumber, cigars, bldg. materials. Large deposits of fuller's earth mined near Quincy; also clay, sand, and gravel pits. Formed 1823.

Gadsden, city (1990 pop. 42,523), ⊙ Etowah co., NE Ala., on the Coosa R. Iron, coal, limestone, sand, clay, and timber are found in the area. Gadsden has metal and textile industries and a large tire and rubber plant; clothing, plumbing fixtures, motor vehicle parts, farm machinery. The city is home to Gadsden State Community Col. Settled in 1846, inc. 1871.

Gadsden, town (1990 pop. 561), Crockett co., W Tenn., 15 mi/24 km NW of Jackson, 35°47′N 88°59′W. In agr. area (cotton, beans, corn, strawberries); sand deposits.

Gaff Topsail, mountain (1,477 ft/450 m), W central N.F., Canada, on mi/32 km E of NE end of Grand L.; 49°09′N 56°38′W.

Gaffney (GAF-nee), city (1990 pop. 13,145), ⊙ Cherokee co., NW S.C., 18 mi/29 km ENE of Spartenburg near the N.C. state line; 35°04′N 81°39′W. In a cotton, grain, and peach region. Textiles and clothing, including yarns and fabrics, are its major prods. Other mfg. includes plastics, printing and engraving, rugs, machinery, and food. The city also has a large peach-packing plant and a variety of light mfg. Agr. includes livestock; dairying; wheat, soybeans, and peaches. Gaffney is the seat of Limestone Col. Cowpens Natl. Battlefield and Kings Mt. Natl. Military Park are nearby. Settled in the early 1800s, inc. 1873.

Gage, county (□ 859 sq mi/2,225 sq km; 1990 pop. 22,794), SE Nebr.; ⊙ Beatrice; 40°16′N 96°41′W. Agr. region drained by Big Blue R. and North Fork of Big Nemaha R.; bounded S by Kansas in Loess-Drift Hills region. Cattle, hogs; corn, wheat, soybeans, sorghum, alfalfa; dairy and poultry prods. Homestead Natl. Monument in W; Rockford L. State Recreation Area in E. Formed 1857.

Gage, village (1990 pop. 473), Ellis co., NW Okla., 22 mi/35 km SW of Woodward, on Wolf Creek; 36°19′N 99°45′W. In grain, livestock area.

Gages Lake, uninc. village (1990 pop. 8,349), Lake co., NE Ill., residential suburb 37 mi/60 km NW of Chicago, 7 mi/11.3 km W of Waukegan, on Gages L.; 42°21′N 87°58′W. Mfg.

Gagetown, village (1991 pop. 607), ⊙ Queens co., S N.B., Canada, on St. John R., 25 mi/40 km ESE of Fredericton; 45°46′N 66°09′W. In apple-growing and farming region.

Gagetown, village (1990 pop. 337), Tuscola co., E Mich., 13 mi/21 km NNE of Caro; 43°39′N 83°15′W.

Gagnon, town, E Que., Canada, 125 mi/201 km NW of Sept-Iles, SE end of L. Barbel; 51°48′N 68°10′W. Iron-mining center; RR terminus. Air service.

Gahanna (guh-HAN-uh), city (1990 pop. 27,791), Franklin co., central Ohio, growing residential suburb of Columbus; 40°01′N 82°52′W. Inc. 1881.

Gail, uninc. village (1990 pop. 202), ⊙ Borden co., NW Texas, just below Caprock escarpment of Llano Estacado, 30 mi/48 km W of Snyder, near Colorado R. In cattle-ranching area; cotton; wheat, milo, soybeans, pecans. L. J.B. Thomas reservoir to SE.

Gaillard, Lake (GAI-luhrd), reservoir, in North Branford town, S Conn. Dam at S end; drained by Branford R. Reservoir is 2.5 mi/4 km long.

Gaines, county (□ 1,502 sq mi/3,890 sq km; 1990 pop. 14,123), NW Texas; ⊙ Seminole; 32°44′N 102°38′W. Bounded W by N.Mex.; on the Llano Estacado. Elev. c.3,000 ft/914 m. Drained by Seminole Draw and McKenzie Draw. Cattle ranching; oil and some natural gas; sodium sulphate; agr. (major cotton and peanut producer, also sorghum, vegetables, grains); hogs, sheep. Cedar L. is in E. Formed 1876.

Gaines, village (1990 pop. 427), Genesee co., SE central Mich., 14 mi/23 km SW of Flint; 42°52′N 83°54′W.

Gaines, Fort, Ala.: see DAUPHIN ISLAND.

Gainesboro, town (1990 pop. 1,002), ⊙ Jackson co., N central Tenn., on Cumberland R., 17 mi/27 km NW of Cookeville; 36°21′N 85°39′W. Trade point in hilly region producing oil, timber, zinc, limestone, sand, farm prods. (corn, feed grain, tobacco). Center Hill and Dale Hollow dams nearby. Cordell Hull practiced law here.

Gainesville 1 city (□ 35 sq mi/91 sq km; 1990 pop. 84,770), ⊙ Alachua co., N central Fla.; 29°40′N 82°20′W. The Univ. of Fla., located here, is a major source of employment in the city. The mfg. of electronic equip. in addition to agr. add to the economy. A state mus. and a state school for the mentally handicapped are here as well. Inc 1869. **2** (GAINZ-vil), city (1990 pop. 17,885), ⊙ Hall co., NE central Ga., near Chattahoochee R., c.50 mi/80 km NE of Atlanta on L. Lanier in the foothills of the Blue Ridge Mts.; 34°17′N 83°49′W. Poultry-processing center; clothing and textiles, lumber, furniture, pharmaceuticals, food, feeds, printing and publishing, plastics. Brenau Col. and hq. of Chattahoochee Natl. Forest here; Riverside Military Acad. nearby. L. Lanier nearby. Becoming a commuter exurb of Atlanta. Located on I-985. Inc. 1821. **3** city (1990 pop. 14,256), ⊙ Cooke co., N Texas, 60 mi/97 km NNW of Dallas, on the Elm Fork of the Trinity R., Red R. to N; 33°38′N 97°09′W. Elev. 738 ft/225 m. It is the commercial and industrial hub of a farm and oil area. Mfg. (electrical equip., metal works, plastic and fiberglass prods., tools). Gainesville was founded (1850) on the California Trail; later it became a stopping point on the Chisholm Trail. Historical markers are on various houses, churches, and sites of early Native American raids. Cook County Col. Inc. 1873.

Gainesville 1 town (1990 pop. 449), Sumter co., W Ala., on Tombigbee R., 17 mi/27 km N of Livingston. Wood prods. **2** town (1990 pop. 659), ⊙ Ozark co., S Mo., in the Ozarks, 33 mi/53 km WSW of West Plains; 36°36′N 92°25′W. Lumber prods.; mfg. (wood prods.). Tourism center for recreation on nearby lakes.

Gainesville 1 village (1990 pop. 340), Wyoming co., W N.Y., 9 mi/14.5 km S of Warsaw; 42°38′N 78°08′W. In potato-growing area. Belva Ann Lockwood, suffragette leader and 1st woman presidential candidate, was b. nearby. **2** uninc. village, Prince William co., NE Va., 8 mi/12.9 km WNW of Manassas. Mfg. (bldg. materials, tools; metal fabrication); agr. (grain, soybeans; livestock; dairying). Manassas Natl. Battlefield Park to E.

Gainsborough, village (1991 pop. 301), SE Sask., Canada, near Man. and N.Dak. borders, 70 mi/113 km E of Estevan; 49°10′N 101°27′W. Mixed farming.

Gaithersburg (GAI-therz-buhrg), city (1990 pop. 39,542), Montgomery co., central Md., 20 mi/32 km NNW of Washington, D.C.; 39°08′N 77°13′W. In dairying area; vegetable cannery, feed mill, and biopharmaceuticals. Named for Benjamin Gaither, who settled here in 1802, it became a milling and trade center in 1873 when the Baltimore and Ohio RR came through. The U.S. Coast and Geodetic Survey observatory here in 1889 was one of 5 in the world located at 39°08′ latitude, all of which recorded the wobble of the Earth on its axis (which changes the latitudes of the planet with respect to fixed stars). The other observatories were in Calif., Japan, Turkistan, and Italy. Now part of the Washington, D.C., metropolitan area, the city is the site of the Inst. of Technology and Standards, the nation's arbiter of physical measurements. Seneca State Park, with its famed collection of peonies, is nearby.

Gakona (gah-KO-nuh), village (1990 pop. 25), S Alaska, on Copper R., 90 mi/145 km NNE of Valdez, on Tok Cut-off; 62°17′N 145°18′W.

Gakona River (gah-KO-nuh), 70 mi/113 km long, S central Alaska; rises in SE foothills of Alaska Range near 63°09′N 145°12′W, flows S to Copper R. at Gakona.

Galahad, village (1991 pop. 158), SE Alta., Canada, 50 mi/80 km WSW of Wainwright; 52°31′N 111°55′W. Grain; farming; dairying.

Galante (gah-LAWNGT), town, SE coast of Marie-Galante isl., Guadeloupe, Fr. West Indies.

Galata (guh-LAH-tuh), village (1990 pop. 25), Toole co., N Mont., 22 mi/35 km E of Shelby, on Willow Creek. Wheat, barley, oats, cattle. L. Elwell (Tiber Reservoir) to S.

Galatia 1 village (1990 pop. 983), Saline co., SE Ill., 8 mi/12.9 km NNW of Harrisburg; 37°50′N 88°36′W. In bituminous coal-mining and agr. region. **2** (guh-LAI-shuh), village (1990 pop. 47), Barton co., central Kansas, 22 mi/35 km NNW of Great Bend; 38°38′N 98°57′W. Wheat.

Galax (GAL-laks), independent city (□ 8 sq mi/20.7 sq km; 1990 pop. 6,670), SW Va., separate from adjacent Grayson and Carroll cos., in Blue Ridge Mts., 65 mi/105 km SW of Roanoke, near N.C. state line, on Chestnut Creek; 36°39′N 80°55′W. Mfg. (glass prods., furniture, lumber, yarn, clothing, printing and publishing); agr. area (dairying; cattle; corn, apples, peaches). Site of Old Fiddlers' Convention (est. 1935); Bluegrass Music Festival. S terminus of New R. Trail State Park. Founded 1903; inc. 1906.

Galeana (gah-le-AH-nah), city and township, Nuevo León, N Mexico, in Sierra Madre Oriental, 60 mi/97 km SSE of Monterrey; 24°51′N 100°08′W. Wheat-growing area.

Galeana (gah-le-AH-nah), town (1990 pop. 1,189), Chihuahua, N Mexico, in Sierra Madre Occidental, on Santa María R., 28 mi/45 km SSW of Nuevo Casas

Grandes; 30°08′N 107°38′W. Cereals, fruit, vegetables; cattle. Noted for white marble deposits said to be the equal of Carrara.

Galena, city (1990 pop. 3,647), ⊙ Jo Daviess co., extreme NW Ill., on Galena R. (bridged here), near the Mississippi, 12 mi/19 km ESE of Dubuque (Iowa); 42°25′N 90°25′W. Trade and shipping point in dairying region containing relict lead and zinc deposits. Agr. (cattle, hogs, sheep); mfg. (iron prods., electrical equip.). Lead mined here beginning early 18th cent. Settled c.1820 after the U.S. placed mines under govt. protection (1807); laid out and named (after Lat. word for lead ore) in 1826; inc. 1835. Until 1860s, Galena was active center of the lead-mining areas of NW Ill. and SW Wis. and one of the busiest steamboat ports on the upper Mississippi. Ulysses S. Grant lived here before and after Civil War; his home is a state historic site. Old Market House State Historic Site here. City is a major tourist destination year-round.

Galena 1 (guh-LEE-nuh), town (1990 pop. 3,308), Cherokee co., extreme SE Kansas, near Okla. line, 7 mi/11.3 km W of Joplin, 12 mi/19 km SE of Columbus; 37°04′N 94°38′W. In mining and agr. area; mfg. (chemicals, electrical equip.). RR junction to W. Founded in 1870s, when lead was discovered nearby; inc. 1877. **2** town (1990 pop. 324), Kent co., E Md., near Sassafras R., 23 mi/37 km NW of Dover, Del.; 39°20′N 75°53′W. Galena is a sulphide of lead, and a small deposit here was mined in the early 19th cent. to make spoons, coasters, and buckles. George Washington stopped at the site of Downs Cross Roads Tavern in 1774 on his way both to and from the 1st Continental Congress. **3** town (1990 pop. 401), SW Mo., ⊙ Stone co., in the Ozarks, on James R., 30 mi/48 km SSW of Springfield; 36°47′N 93°28′W. Corn, wheat, hay, fruit, vegetables, cattle; tourism; mfg. (medical equip.).

Galena 1 (gah-LEE-nuh), village (1990 pop. 833), W Alaska, on Yukon R., 140 mi/225 km W of Tanana; 64°45′N 156°56′W. Air force station. Founded c.1919 as supply point for Galena prospectors. **2** village (1990 pop. 1,231), Floyd co., S Ind., suburb 7 mi/11.3 km NW of New Albany, in Louisville metropolitan area; 38°21′N 85°56′W. Tobacco; cattle, poultry. **3** village (1990 pop. 361), Delaware co., central Ohio, 18 mi/29 km NNE of Columbus, on Hoover Reservoir; 40°13′N 82°53′W.

Galena Mountain, peak (13,278 ft/4,047 m) in San Juan Mts., E San Juan co., SW Colo., 5 mi/8 km E of Silverton.

Galena Park, city (1990 pop. 10,033), Harris co., SE Texas, suburb 6 mi/9.7 km E of Houston; 29°44′N 95°13′W. Near Buffalo Bayou/Houston Ship Channel. Mfg. (metal works, fertilizers, bldg. materials, chemicals; metal fabrication). Absorbed 1948 by Houston.

Galena River (guh-LEE-nah), c.35 mi/56 km long, in Wis. and Ill.; rises in W Lafayette co., SW Wis. Flows generally SW, past Galena (Ill.), to the Mississippi 3 mi/4.8 km S of Galena. Formerly Fever R.

Galeota Point (gah-lee-O-tah), headland on SE coast of Trinidad, Trinidad and Tobago, 50 mi/80 km SE of Port of Spain; 10°08′N 60°59′W. It was the 1st point of the isl. sighted by Columbus (July 31, 1498).

Galera Point (GAH-lir-ah), cape on NE coast of Trinidad, Trinidad and Tobago, 45 mi/72 km ENE of Port of Spain; 10°50′N 60°54′W. Lighthouse.

Galesburg, city (1990 pop. 33,530), ⊙ Knox co., W Ill.; 40°57′N 90°22′W. In agr. (corn, soybeans, sorghum; cattle, hogs, poultry; dairying) and coal area. A trade, RR, and industrial center, it has RR shops and plants that make paints, rubber hoses, apparel, and plastic prods. Galesburg was founded by Presbyterians from the Mohawk valley, N.Y., under the leadership of George Washington Gale. They established Knox Col., and in 1858 a debate bet. Abraham Lincoln and Stephen Douglas took place in Knox Old Main, the oldest bldg. on the campus. The birthplace of the poet Carl Sandburg (b. 1878) has been preserved as a state historical site in Galesburg, which also has Carl Sandburg Col., and Hill Correctional Center here or nearby. Chartered 1841.

Galesburg, town (1990 pop. 1,863), Kalamazoo co., SW Mich., 8 mi/12.9 km E of Kalamazoo, 12 mi/19 km WSW of Battle Creek, on Kalamazoo R.; 42°17′N 85°25′W. In agr. area (grain, fruit; livestock); mfg. (motor vehicle parts, plastic molding, machinery, dairy prods.). Settled 1829; inc. as village 1869, as city 1931.

Galesburg 1 village (1990 pop. 160), Neosho co., SE Kansas, 15 mi/24 km SSE of Chanute; 37°28′N 95°21′W. Livestock; grain; dairying. **2** village (1990 pop. 161), Traill co., E N.Dak., 16 mi/26 km S of Mayville, on Elm R.; 47°16′N 97°24′W.

Galesville, town (1990 pop. 1,278), Trempealeau co., W Wis., on tributary of Black R., 19 mi/31 km NNW of La Crosse. Dairy prods., timber, apples, feed; limestone quarries; mfg. (metal fabrication; furniture, canned food). Nearby L. Marinuka is to N. Settled 1854. Inc. as village in 1887, as city in 1942.

Galeton (GAIL-tuhn), borough (1990 pop. 1,370), Potter co., N Pa., in the Alleghenies, on Pine Creek, 19 mi/31 km E of Coudersport. Agr. (hay, potatoes; livestock; dairying; timber); mfg. (aircraft parts, lumber, leather prods.). Resort center for hunting, fishing region. Lyman Run State Park to W; Cherry Springs State Park to SW; Ole Bull State Park to S; parts of Susquehanna State Forest to NW and SW. Inc. 1896.

Galetta (guh-LE-tuh), village, SE Ont., Canada, on Mississippi R., near its mouth on L. des Chats, 27 mi/43 km W of Ottawa. Lead and zinc mining; hydroelectric power.

Galiano Island (ga-li-AH-no) (□ 22 sq mi/57 sq km), SW B.C., Canada, Gulf Isls., in Strait of Georgia off SE Vancouver Isl., bet. Valdes Isl. and Mayne Isl., 25 mi/40 km SW of Vancouver; 16 mi/26 km long, 1 mi/2 km–3 mi/5 km wide; 48°56′N 123°29′W. Mixed farming. Galiano village on S coast. Tourism, summer resort. Ferries to mainland (Tsawwassan).

Galien (GAI-len), village (1990 pop. 596), Berrien co., extreme SW Mich., 18 mi/29 km S of St. Joseph; 41°47′N 86°30′W. In agr. area (grain, fruit, peppermint, honey; dairy prods.; poultry); mfg. wood prods.

Galilee, village (1990 pop. 450) in Narragansett town, Washington co., SE R.I., west of Point Judith on Block Isl. Sound. An important but declining fishing fleet has its homeport here. Nearby are the Galilee Bird Santuary and Sand Hill Cove beach.

Galina Point, cape on N coast of Jamaica, St. Mary parish, 3 mi/4.8 km N of Port Maria; 18°24′N 76°53′W. Housing development. Garment industry outlet. Lighthouse at point.

Galion (GAL-yuhn), city (1990 pop. 11,859), Crawford co., N central Ohio; 40°44′N 82°48′W. Construction equip. is the chief mfg.; other prods. include electric conversion equip., motor vehicle parts, and pollution-control facilities. Inc. as a borough 1840, as a city 1878.

Galisteo (ga-lis-TAI-o), uninc. village, Santa Fe co., N central N.Mex., 15 mi/24 km S of Santa Fe. Cattle, sheep, grain, alfalfa. Mfg. (beverages).

Galiuro Mountains (ga-li-YOU-ro), Graham co., SE Ariz., NE of Tucson; extend c.55 mi/89 km SE-NW along right bank of San Pedro R. in sect. of Coronado Natl. Forest. Chief peaks are Kennedy Peak (7,549 ft/2,301 m.) and Bassett Peak (7,663 ft/2,336 m).

Gallatin 1 (GA-luh-tin), county (□ 328 sq mi/850 sq km; 1990 pop. 6,909), SE Ill., ⊙ Shawneetown; 37°45′N 88°13′W. Bounded NE by Wabash R. and SE by the Ohio (bridged here); drained by Saline R. Corn, soybeans. Bituminous-coal mining, oil, natural gas. S part is in Shawnee Natl. Forest. Formed 1812. Shawneetown State Historic Site here, marking the site of Old Shawneetown, once a major river port. Floods finally forced removal of much of sites to higher ground in 1937. **2** (GA-luh-tin), county (□ 104 sq mi/269 sq km; 1990 pop. 5,393), N Ky.; ⊙ Warsaw; 38°45′N 84°51′W. Bounded N by Ohio R. (Ind. state line), S by Eagle Creek. Gently rolling upland agr. area (burley tobacco, corn, hay, alfalfa, soybeans; cattle, poultry, horses; dairying), in N part of Bluegrass region. Some mfg. at Warsaw. Markland Locks and Dam, on Ohio R., in NW. Formed 1798. **3** (GA-luh-tin), county (□ 2,517 sq mi; 1990 pop. 50,463), SW Mont.; ⊙ Bozeman. Agr. area bordering on Idaho (S) and Wyo (SE); drained in S by Gallatin R. in NW by Madison R., in N by Sixteenmile Creek.; 45°34′N 111°10′W. Jefferson and Missouri rivers form NW boundary. Cattle, sheep, hogs, llamas; potatoes; hay, wheat, barley, oats. Forest industries; gold, talc, phosphate; mfg., commerce, tourism. Missouri R. formed in NW, near Three Forks, by junction of Gallatin R. with Jefferson and Madison rivers. Parts of Gallatin Natl. Forest in all of S ½ and in NE. Part of Gallatin Range in E; includes Mt. Blackmore (10,154 ft/3,095 m). Lee Metcalf Wilderness and Gallatin-Porcupine Wildlife Management Area in S central. Hebgen L. reservoir and Quake L. (formed by 1959 earthquake) in S. Part of Yellowstone Natl. Park in SE, town of West Yellowstone is W gateway to park, tourist center. Madison Buffalo Jump State Park in NW; Missouri Headwaters State Park and Monument on NW boundary; Bridger Ski Area in N. Formed 1865.

Gallatin 1 city (1990 pop. 1,864), ⊙ Daviess co., NW Mo., on Grand R. and 23 mi/37 km WNW of Chillicothe; 39°54′N 93°57′W. Corn, wheat, hay, soybeans; cattle, hogs; mfg. (metal fabrication; apparel). Adam-ondi-Ahman, a Mormon shrine and park, is to N. Laid out 1837. **2** (GA-luh-tin), city (1990 pop. 18,794), ⊙ Sumner co., N central Tenn., 23 mi/37 km NW of Nashville; 36°22′N 86°28′W. A livestock and agr. center that produces tobacco, Gallatin's mfg. includes motor vehicle parts, tobacco goods, furniture, boats, and bldg. equip. Nearby is Old Hickory L. (Cumberland R.), a fishing and recreation area. The city is named for Albert Gallatin, secretary of the treasury under Presidents Jefferson and Madison. Inc. 1815.

Gallatin, village (1990 pop. 368), Cherokee co., E Texas, 33 mi/53 km SSE of Tyler, on Angelina R.; 31°53′N 95°09′W. Agr. area (vegetables, peaches; cattle).

Gallatin (GA-luh-tin), river, c.120 mi/193 km long, rising in the Gallatin Range in the NW corner of Yellowstone Natl. Park, Park co., NW Wyo., and flowing generally NW through Gallatin Natl. Forest to join the Madison and Jefferson rivers at Three Forks, 30 mi/48 km NW of Bozeman.

Gallatin Gateway (GA-luh-tin), village (1990 pop. 260), Gallatin co., SW Mont., on Gallatin R., 11 mi/18 km SW of Bozeman. Tourist trade; mfg. (timber, homes, cheese); wheat, barley, oats, hay, potatoes; horses, cattle, sheep, hogs, poultry. Just S are Gallatin Canyon and Gallatin Natl. Forest, includes Lee Metcalf Wilderness Area (part) and Big Sky Ski Area both to SW. Yellowstone Natl. Park is 35 mi/56 km S. Originally called Salesville.

Gallatin Range (GA-luh-tin), in Rocky Mts., of NW Wyo. and SW Mont., rises S of Bozeman, Mont.; extends c.45 mi/72 km S, bet. Gallatin and Yellowstone rivers, into NW corner of Yellowstone Natl. Park, Wyo. Prominent peaks include Emigrant Peak, Mont. (10,960 ft/3,341 m); Electric Peak, Wyo. (10,992 ft/3,350 m); and Mt. Holmes, Wyo. (10,336 ft/3,150 m), the latter 2 in Yellowstone Natl. Park.

Gallia (GA-lee-uh), county (□ 471 sq mi/1,220 sq km; 1990 pop. 30,954), S Ohio; ⊙ Gallipolis, 38°49′N 82°20′W. Bounded E by Ohio R., here forming W.Va. state line; intersected by Raccoon Creek and small Symmes and Campaign creeks. In the Unglaciated Plain physiographic region. Agr. (cattle; corn, tobacco, fruit); mfg. at Gallipolis (motors and generators, motor vehicle parts, stone, clay, and glass prods.); coal mines; limestone, sand, gravel. Formed 1803.

Galliano (GA-lee-ahn-o), uninc. town (1990 pop. 4,291), Lafourche parish, 27 mi/43 km SE of Raceland; 29°26′N 90°17′W. On Bayou Lafourche, in fishing (shrimp, crabs) area. In agr. (sugarcane) area; oil fields nearby. Named after Salvador Galiano, a Spaniard who was the 1st settler in the area.

Gallina Peak (gai-EEN-uh) (8,977 ft/2,736 m), Rio Arriba co., central N.Mex., 66 mi/106 km NW of Santa Fe, near Rio Chama, rises from high tableland in Santa Fe Natl. Forest.

Gallinas Mountains (gei-EEN-ahs), W N.Mex., extends c.30 mi/48 km E-W in NW Socorro co., extends an additional 20 mi/32 km W into NE Catron co., as Datil Mts.; rises to 9,560 ft/2,914 m at Madre Mt. Peak in

Datil Mts.; in sects. of Cibola Natl. Forest. Continental Divide runs N-S to W of both ranges.

Gallinas River (gei-EEN-ahs), c.70 mi/113 km long, N central N.Mex.; rises in S Sangre de Cristo Mts. in NW San Miguel co., Santa Fe Natl. Forest, 20 mi/32 km ENE of Santa Fe, flows SE past Las Vegas to Pecos R. 21 mi/34 km NW of Santa Rosa. Also known as Gallinas Creek above Las Vegas.

Gallipolis (GA-luh-puh-LEES), city (1990 pop. 4,831), ⊙ Gallia co., S Ohio, on the Ohio, c.40 mi/64 km E of Portsmouth; 38°49′N 82°11′W. In agr. area; mfg. Settled 1790; inc. 1865 as city.

Gallipolis Ferry (GA-luh-puh-LEES), uninc. village, Mason co., NW W.Va., 5 mi/8 km SSW of Point Pleasant, on Ohio R., opposite (SE of) Gallipolis (Ohio). Agr. (grain, tobacco); livestock; dairying. Mfg. (chemicals).

Gallitzin (guh-LIT-sin), borough (1990 pop. 2,003), Cambria co., W central Pa., 7 mi/11.3 km W of Altoona. Agr. (timber); mfg. (bldg. materials); bituminous coal. Allegheny Portage RR Natl. Historic Site to S. Settled c.1796.

Gallman (GAHL-muhn), village, Copiah co., SW Miss., 28 mi/45 km SSW of Jackson. Mfg. (wire, bldg. equip.).

Galloo Island (guh-LOO), Jefferson co., N N.Y., in E part of L. Ontario, 12 mi/19 km W of Sackets Harbor village; 43°54′N 76°25′W. Isl. is 4 mi/6.4 km long, 0.5 mi/0.8 km–1.25 mi/2.01 km. wide. Lighthouse here.

Gallop's Island, in Quincy Bay sect. of Boston Harbor, E Mass., 6 mi/9.7 km SE of Boston; c.1 mi/1.6 km long. Abandoned communications training facility after World War II. Now reclaimed for recreation; part of Boston Harbor Isls. State Park.

Galloway (GA-lo-wai), township (□ c.90 sq mi/233 sq km; 1990 pop. 23,330), Atlantic co., S N.J., 7 mi/11.3 km N of Atlantic City; 39°29′N 74°28′W. Rural resort area, with rapid pop. growth in recent decades. Inc. 1798.

Gallup, city (1990 pop. 19,154), ⊙ McKinley co., NW N.Mex., 138 mi/222 km WNW of Albuquerque, on the Rio Puerco near the Ariz. state line; 35°31′N 108°44′W. Elev. 6,510 ft/1,984 m. It is a RR and trade center in a large mining, timber, and ranching area. Cattle, sheep; alfalfa, timber. Mfg. (Native Amer. jewelry and crafts, printing and publishing, concrete, bakery prods.). Located in a region populated by the Navajo, Zuñi, Hopi, and Pueblo, its economy is based on local trade. The city's principal employer is the U.S. Bureau of Indian Affairs. Uranium, oil, natural gas, and coal are among the minerals found and processed. Tourism is important. Founded as stagecoach stop, formerly coal mining center and site for early Westerns. Nearby natural and archaeological wonders draw many visitors, as does the intertribal ceremonial held every August. A U.S. public health service hosp. is in Gallup. Univ. of N.Mex., Gallup branch; Navajo Indian Capitol at Window Rock, Ariz., to NW; Navajo Indian Reservation to N (N.Mex.) and W (Ariz.); Zuñi Indian Reservation to S; Cibola Natl. Forest to SE; Red Rock State Park to E. Inc. 1891.

Galop Island, St. Lawrence co., N N.Y., in the St. Lawrence amid the Galops Rapids, at Ont. (Canada) border, c.1 mi/1.6 km SW of Cardinal (Ont.); c.1.5 mi/2.4 km long; 44°46′N 75°23′W.

Galops Rapids, N.Y. and Canada: see GALOP ISLAND.

Galt 1 city (1990 pop. 8,889), Sacramento co., central Calif., 25 mi/40 km SSE of Sacramento, on Dry Creek; 38°16′N 121°18′W. RR junction. Poultry; dairying; citrus, pears, tomatoes, corn, rice; nursery stock; mfg. (concrete, printing and publishing, food). Inc. 1946. **2** city (1990 pop. 296), Grundy co., N Mo., 13 mi/21 km ENE of Trenton; 40°07′N 93°23′W. Corn, wheat; cattle.

Galt, town (1990 pop. 43), Wright co., N central Iowa, 7 mi/11.3 km ESE of Clarion; 42°41′N 93°35′W. Livestock; grain.

Galt, Canada: see CAMBRIDGE.

Galva (GAL-vah), city (1990 pop. 2,742), Henry co., NW Ill., 13 mi/21 km SE of Cambridge; 41°10′N 90°02′W. Trade and industrial center in agr. area (cattle, hogs; corn, soybeans); mfg. (furniture, automotive prods.). Small L. Calhoun (resort) is S. Nearby is Bishop Hill

State Historic Site. Black Hawk Col. E campus 6 mi/9.7 km E. Founded 1854, inc. 1867.

Galva, town (1990 pop. 398), Ida co., W Iowa, near Maple R., 10 mi/16 km N of Ida Grove; 42°30′N 95°25′W. Rendering plant.

Galva, village (1990 pop. 651), McPherson co., central Kansas, 7 mi/11.3 km E of McPherson; 38°22′N 97°32′W. In wheat region. Oil field here.

Galveston, county (□ 876 sq mi/2,269 sq km; 1990 pop. 217,399), S Texas; ⊙ Galveston; 29°22′N 94°51′W. Port, industrial center, coast resort. Also important is Texas City, Galveston's mainland twin. Bounded N by Clear Creek and Clear L.; boundary crosses Galveston Bay from San Leon to Smith Point and follows N shore of East Bay; boundary crosses West Bay in SW at angle to pass S end of Galveston Isl.; bounded SE by Gulf of Mexico; includes Bolivar Peninsula and Galveston Isl. (site of Galveston), both sand barriers paralleling Gulf Coast. Sulphur, chemical, oil-refining industries; processing and shipping of cotton, wheat, metals, agr. prods. Irrigated agr. (rice, soybeans, sorghum, cotton, pecans); cattle, horses. Oil, natural gas fields; clay and gravel. Aquaculture; fisheries; shrimping; oysters; sport fishing. Urban growth in co.'s NW is due in part to the new presence of Houston. Intracoastal Waterway runs length of co. Galveston Isl. State Park in SW, in city of Galveston. Formed 1838.

Galveston, city (1990 pop. 59,070), ⊙ Galveston co., on Galveston Isl., SE Texas, 42 mi/68 km SE of Houston; 29°13′N 94°53′W. Twin city of Texas City, 8 mi/12.9 km NW The isl. lies across the entrance to Galveston Bay, an inlet of the Gulf of Mexico. City occupies all of 30 mi/48 km long barrier isl. except for small village of Pelican Beach, at mid-isl.; city also includes Pelican Isl. on bayside of N end, adjacent to downtown. Long causeways connect the city with the mainland, Houston, and Texas City; Intracoastal Waterway passes through Galveston and West bays, bet. isl. and mainland; free ferry NE to Port Bolivar Peninsula, opposite side of entrance to Galveston Bay; toll bridge connects SW end of isl. to Follets Isl. and mainland. Trains and trucks bring cotton, sulfur, rice, flour, and other prods. to Galveston to be stored, processed, and shipped all over the world. Despite the ship channel to the larger port at Houston, Galveston remains a key port of entry. Oil refining and shipbuilding are major industries, and the city has mfg. (metal fabrication, printing, concrete prods., steel containers, seafood processing). It is also a beach and fishing resort, with its attractions enhanced by pink and white oleanders, bougainvillea, and other subtropical blooms. The Spanish knew the bay and the isl. early; it was probably there that Cabeza de Vaca was shipwrecked in 1528. Settlement began in the 1830s. The natural port came gradually into its own despite scourges of yellow fever, hurricanes, and the occupation for a few months in 1862 by a small Union force. A 1900 hurricane resulted in thousands of deaths and left the city in ruins. An enormous 10-mi/16 km-long protective seawall was built to protect against future storms; however, in 1961 and later in the 1980s, hurricanes still caused much damage. Economic growth has largely bypassed Galveston because of its exposure to this kind of storm damage, favoring Texas City and other communities directly inland, only a few miles away. Of interest are the Texas Heroes monument and several old homes. A Coast Guard base and the Texas Maritime Acad. are in Galveston, as are Galveston Col. and the Univ. of Texas medical school, and Texas A and M Univ. at Galveston (Pelican Isl.) with a large group of hosps. Pelican Spit Military Reservation on Pelican Isl.; Scholes Field airport W of downtown; Galveston Isl. State Park near center of isl. Inc. 1839.

Galveston (gal-VES-tuhn), town (1990 pop. 1,609), Cass co., N central Ind., 15 mi/24 km SE of Logansport; 40°35′N 86°11′W. In agr. area.

Galveston Bay, S Texas, inlet of Gulf of Mexico c.20 mi/32 km SE of Houston, with its entrance bet. tip of Bolivar Peninsula and NE end of Galveston Isl.; c.35 mi/56 km long NE-SW; max. width c.19 mi/31 km. With deepwater channels from the gulf to harbors of

Galveston, Texas City, Houston, and other cities, and crossed by Gulf Intracoastal Waterway, near its entrance and along inland side of Bolivar Peninsula, bay is center of one of most important U.S. port and industrial regions. Bay supplies oyster shell for cement. Receives San Jacinto R. (Houston Ship Channel) in NW; Trinity Bay, NNE corner; receives Trinity R.; East Bay, NE arm, receives Intracoastal Waterway from Port Arthur. In E, it is divided by reefs from East Bay (c.22 mi/35 km long, 2 mi/3.2 km–5 mi/8 km wide), is separated from the gulf by Bolivar Peninsula; in SW, car passage (bridged) connects to West Bay (c.20 mi/32 km long, 3 mi/4.8 km–6 mi/9.7 km wide), separated from the gulf by Galveston and Follets isls. Anahuac Natl. Wildlife Refuge on N shore of East Bay.

Galveston Island, Texas: see GALVESTON.

Galway, village (1990 pop. 151), Saratoga co., E N.Y., 10 mi/16 km NE of Amsterdam; 43°01′N 74°01′W. In dairying area.

Gamaliel (guh-MAIL-yuhl), village (1990 pop. 462), Monroe co., S Ky., 7 mi/11.3 km SW of Tompkinsville, near East Fork of Barren R., joins West Fork 1 mi/1.6 km to W to form main stream, on Tenn. state line; 36°38′N 85°47′W. Agr. area (burley tobacco, grain; livestock; dairying). Timber. Mfg. (furniture, apparel). Old Mulkey Meeting House State Historical Site to NE.

Gambell (GAM-buhl), village (1990 pop. 525), on NW St. Lawrence Isl., W Alaska, c.200 mi/322 km W of Nome and c.15 mi/24 km from Internatl. Date Line; 63°46′N 171°41′W. Whaling. Cooperative store. School. Landing strip for aircraft.

Gambier (GAM-bir), village (1990 pop. 2,073), Knox co., central Ohio, 5 mi/8 km E of Mt. Vernon, on Kokosing R.; 40°22′N 82°23′W. Seat of Kenyon Col.

Gambier Island (GAM-bir) (□ 27 sq mi/70 sq km), SW B.C., Canada, in Howe Sound, 17 mi/27 km NW of Vancouver; 6 mi/10 km long, 5 mi/8 km wide. S part is deeply indented. Lumbering. Ferry from Langdale to Gambier Harbour on SW coast.

Gambo, town (1990 pop. 2,723), end of Freshwater Bay, Bonavista Bay, N.F., Canada; 48°47′N 54°13′W. Amalgamation of the 3 towns of Dark Cove, Middle Brook, and Gambo. Regional service center. Inc. 1980.

Gambo Lake (□ 8 sq mi/21 sq km), E N.F., Canada, 20 mi/32 km SE of Gander; 20 mi/32 km long; drains into Bonavista Bay.

Gamerco (guh-MER-ko), uninc. village (1990 pop. 800), McKinley co., NW N.Mex., 3 mi/4.8 km N of Gallup, near Ariz. state line. Elev. 6,724 ft/2,049 m. Coal mining; mfg. (concrete). Pueblo ruins nearby. Navajo Indian Reservation to N.

Gamewell, town (1990 pop. 3,357), Caldwell co., W central N.C., 5 mi/8 km SW of Lenoir; 35°52′N 81°35′W. Agr. area (tobacco, grain, potatoes; chickens, livestock). Tuttle Educational State Forest to SW.

Gammon Point (GAM-uhn), promontory, West Yarmouth, Mass., SW corner of Great Isl., separates Lewis Bay from Nantucket Sound. Abandoned lighthouse.

Ganado, town (1990 pop. 1,701), Jackson co., S Texas, 34 mi/55 km NE of Victoria; 29°02′N 96°30′W. In agr. area (rice, cotton; cattle); mfg. (furniture). L. Texana reservoir (Navidad R.) to S, State Park to SW. Founded 1883.

Ganado (gah-NAH-do), uninc. village, Apache co., NE Ariz., in Navajo Indian Reservation, 47 mi/76 km WNW of Gallup (N.Mex.), 64 mi/103 km NE of Holbrook. Elev. 6,439 ft/1,963 m. Trading post. Canyon de Chelly Natl. Monument to N; Hubbell Trading Post Natl. Historic Site is here; Gando Mission to N; Ganado L. to NE.

Gananoque (gan-uh-NAHK-wee), town (1991 pop. 5,209), SE Ont., Canada, on the St. Lawrence R.; 44°20′N 76°10′W. Steel- and copperworks. Summer resort, serving as a starting point for excursions to the Thousand Isls. and the Rideau Lakes.

Gananoque River, 15 mi/24 km long, SE Ont., Canada; issues from Gananoque L. (6 mi/10 km long), 8 mi/13 km NNE of Gananoque, flows SSW to the St. Lawrence at Gananoque.

Gander, town (1991 pop. 10,339), NE N.F., Canada;

48°57′N 54°33′W. Gander's airport, an important base in World War II and a hub for internatl. flights, later attracted many refugees hoping to defect to Canada. It was the site of a Dec. 1985 plane crash that killed 256 passengers, 248 of them U.S. soldiers coming back from the Middle East.

Gander Lake (□ 47 sq mi/122 sq km), E N.F., Canada, 35 mi/56 km E of Grand Falls, at confluence of NW Gander R. and Southwest Gander R., which form Gander R. here. Lake is 30 mi/48 km long, up to 3 mi/5 km wide.

Gander River, 110 mi/177 km long, E N.F., Canada; rises as NW Gander R. on Partridgeberry Hill, S of Grand Falls, flows NE to Gander L., where it receives Southwest Gander R., then flows NE to Gander Bay of the Atlantic, 25 mi/40 km N of Gander.

Gandy, village (1990 pop. 51), Logan co., central Nebr., 3 mi/4.8 km E of Stapleton, near South Loup R.; 41°28′N 100°27′W.

Ganges (GAN-jeez), village, SW B.C., Canada, on E Saltspring Isl., 11 mi/18 km ENE of Duncan; 48°51′N 123°30′W. Fishing port; mixed farming. Summer and retirement residents.

Gann Valley, village, ⊙ Buffalo co., central S.Dak., 20 mi/32 km NE of Chamberlain, near Crow Creek; Crow Creek Indian Reservation to W. Farm trading point; wheat.

Gannett, Mount (GA-nit) (9,500 ft/2,896 m), S Alaska, in Chugach Mts., 60 mi/97 km E of Anchorage; 61°13′N 148°11′W.

Gannett Peak (GA-nit) (13,804 ft/4,207 m), in Wind River Range, Fremont/Sublette cos., W central Wyo., 50 mi/80 km NW of Lander. Highest point in state.

Gans (GANZ), village (1990 pop. 218), Sequyah co., E Okla., 7 mi/11.3 km SSE of Sallisaw, near Arkansas R.; 35°23′N 94°41′W. Agr. area. Robert S. Kerr Dam 7 mi/ 11.3 km W on Arkansas R.

Ganthier (gawng-TYAI), agr. town, Ouest dept., S Haiti, on the Cul-de-Sac plain, 18 mi/29 km E of Port-au-Prince; 18°32′N 72°04′W. Limes, cotton are grown.

Gantt (GANT), uninc. city (1990 pop. 13,891), Greenville co., NW S.C., residential suburb 4 mi/6.4 km S of Greenville; 34°47′N 82°24′W. Fairgrounds to NW; Donaldson Center Airport to SE.

Gantts Quarry, town (1990 pop. 7), Talladega co., central Ala., 22 mi/35 km SSW of Talladega. Marble and limestone quarrying.

Gap, uninc. town (1990 pop. 1,226), Salisbury township, Lancaster co., SE Pa., 16 mi/26 km ESE of Lancaster. Agr. (grain, soybeans; livestock; dairying); mfg. (concrete, farm equip.). Nickel deposits (formerly mined) are SW.

Garber 1 town (1990 pop. 118), Clayton co., NE Iowa, at confluence of Turkey and Volga rivers, 10 mi/16 km SE of Elkader; 42°44′N 91°15′W. Creamery. **2** or **Garber City,** town (1990 pop. 959), Garfield co., N Okla., 16 mi/ 26 km ENE of Enid; 36°26′N 97°34′W. In wheat, livestock, and dairying area; oil and natural gas. Inc. as town 1901, as city 1920.

Garberville, uninc. town, Humboldt co., NW Calif., 54 mi/87 km SSE of Eureka, on South Fork of the Eel R. Town of Redway is 2 mi/3.2 km to NW. Benbow L. State Recreation Area to S. Cattle, sheep; timber.

García de la Cadena (gahr-SEE-ah dai lah kah-DE-nah), town (1990 pop. 2,266), ⊙ Trinidad García de la Cadena municipio, Zacatecas, N central Mexico, 40 mi/64 km SSW of Tlaltenango de Sánchez Román. Elev. 3,970 ft/1,210 m. Agr. (fruit, vegetables; livestock). Formerly called Estanzuela.

Garden, county (□ 1,731 sq mi/4,483 sq km; 1990 pop. 2,460), W Nebr.; ⊙ Oshkosh; 41°37′N 102°20′W. Agr. area drained by North Platte R. Cattle, hogs; corn, wheat, alfalfa, sugar beets. Oregon Trail follows S side of North Platte R. Ash Hollow State Historical Park (has Oregon Trail wagon ruts, gravesites) in SE corner; Crescent L. Natl. Wildlife Refuge in N central part, in Sandhill Lakes area, including and surrounded by numerous small natural lakes; abundant birds, beavers, reptiles. Formed 1910.

Garden, village (1990 pop. 268), Delta co., S Upper Peninsula, Mich., 25 mi/40 km E of Escanaba, on W side of Garden Peninsula, on E shore of Big Bay De Noc, L. Michigan; 45°46′N 86°32′W. Fresh and frozen fish. Fayette State Park to SW, with historic iron smelting village; Hiawatha Natl. Forest to N.

Garden Acres, uninc. town (1990 pop. 8,547), San Joaquin co., central Calif., residential suburb 4 mi/6.4 km SE of Stockton, near Mormon Slough; 37°58′N 121°14′W. Stockton Metropolitan Airport to S; Northern Calif. Youth Center to SE.

Garden City 1 city (1990 pop. 24,097), ⊙ Finney co., SW Kansas, on the Arkansas R.; 37°58′N 100°51′W. Elev. 2,839 ft/865 m. RR junction. A trade center in an irrigated farm and dairy region producing wheat, sugar beets, and alfalfa, it has a gas and an oil field, cattle feedlots, and hide-processing and meat-packing plants. Mfg. (farm machinery, concrete, cultured marble, fertilizers, corrugated boxes, animal fats and oils, natural gas distribution). The city has an agr. experiment station, a recreational park and zoo. Garden City Community Col. here. State Buffalo Game Preserve to SW. Inc. 1887. **2** city (1990 pop. 31,846), Wayne co., SE Mich., suburb 14 mi/23 km W of Detroit; 42°19′N 83°20′W. Chiefly residential but with a noted pop. decline, the city produces gauge systems and aluminum extrusions. Middle R. Rouge to immediate N. Inc. as a city 1934. **3** city (1990 pop. 1,225), Cass co., W Mo., 10 mi/16 km SE of Harrisonville; 38°33′N 94°11′W. Corn, soybeans, sorghum, wheat; cattle. Limestone quarry.

Garden City 1 town (1990 pop. 578), Cullman co., N central Ala., on Mulberry Fork, 12 mi/19 km SSE of Cullman. **2** town (1990 pop. 7,410), Chatham co., SE Ga., 5 mi/8 km NW of Savannah; 32°07′N 81°10′W. Residential town and site of port for Savannah. **3** town (1990 pop. 6,369), Ada co., SW Idaho, residential suburb 2 mi/3.2 km NW of Boise, on Boise R.; 43°39′N 116°16′W. Veterans Memorial State Park to W, across river; Western Idaho Fairgrounds to NW. **4** uninc. town (1990 pop. 6,305), Horry co., E S.C., 9 mi/14.5 km SW of Myrtle Beach, on Atlantic Ocean, in Grand Strand Beach resort area; 33°35′N 79°00′W. Tourism and furniture mfg.

Garden City 1 village (1990 pop. 199), residential suburb 2 mi/3.2 km SSE of Greeley, Weld co., N Colo.; 40°23′N 104°41′W. Elev c.4,670 ft/1,423 m. **2** village (□ 5 sq mi/ 13 sq km; 1990 pop. 21,686), Nassau co., SE N.Y., on L.I.; 40°43′N 73°38′W. It is a high-income residential community, with printing, publishing, and retailing as the major industries. Garden City was founded in 1869 and planned by the merchant Alexander Stewart. In 1927, Charles Lindbergh began his historic transatlantic flight from nearby Roosevelt Field. Adelphi Univ., Nassau community col., and a theology school are in the city. Site of Roosevelt Field Mall, one of the largest malls in the U.S. Inc. 1919. **3** uninc. village, Tulsa co., NE Okla., suburb 2 mi/3.2 km S of Tulsa, and on Arkansas R., across river from downtown. Inc. 1925. **4** village (1990 pop. 93), Clark co., E central S.Dak., 10 mi/16 km NE of Clark; 44°57′N 97°34′W. **5** uninc. village (1990 pop. 293), ⊙ Glasscock co., W Texas, 25 mi/40 km S of Big Spring. Elev. 2,630 ft/802 m. In livestock-ranching area; hydrocarbon processing. **6** village (1990 pop. 193), Rich co., N Utah, on W shore of Bear L., 26 mi/42 km NW of Logan, near Idaho state line; 41°55′N 111°24′W. Elev. 5,890 ft/1,795 m. Raspberry center of Utah; also alfalfa, wheat, barley; cattle, sheep; tourism. Bear L. State Park to N; Wasatch Natl. Forest, including Beaver Mt. Ski Area, to W.

Garden Grove, city (1990 pop. 143,050), Orange co., S Calif., suburb 25 mi/40 km SE of Los Angeles and 3 mi/ 4.8 km SW of Anaheim, the Santa Ana R. on E; 33°47′N 117°58′W. Many of its residents work in nearby aerospace and defense installations. Mfg. (hardware, botanical prods., medical instruments, loose-leaf binders, packaging machinery, paperboard cartons). Site of The Crystal Cathedral constructed of over 10,000 panes of glass. Los Alamitos Naval Air Station to W, Seal Beach

Navy Weapons Station to SW, U.S. Navy Helicopter Field to S. Founded 1877, inc. 1956.

Garden Grove, town (1990 pop. 229), Decatur co., S Iowa, near Weldon R., 10 mi/16 km NE of Leon; 40°49′N 93°36′W. In livestock and grain area. Settled 1846 by Mormons.

Garden Island, Mich.: see BEAVER ISLANDS.

Garden Island Bay, a bay at tip of Mississippi R. delta, extreme SE La.; 29°02′N 89°07′W. Along its marshy shores a rich sulphur deposit was found in 1951. Oil and gas fields nearby. Waters, shores, and isls. are within Pass a Loutre State Wildlife Area. North Pass to N, South Pass to W. Delta Natl. Wildlife Refuge to N.

Garden of the Gods, rock formations and park, central Colo., 4 mi/6.4 km WNW of Colorado Springs, 2 mi/ 3.2 km NE of Manitou Springs, within city limits of Colorado Springs. With 770 acres/312 ha, park is noted for its unusual, multihued red sandstone formations. Narrow-crested sandstone rocks and ridges have been eroded into fascinating groups with such fanciful names as Kissing Camels. Gray Rock serves as a natural amphitheater.

Garden Peninsula, irregular neck of land, Schoolcraft and Delta cos., Mich., extending c.20 mi/32 km S from the Upper Peninsula into L. Michigan SW of Manistique; 45°42′N 86°38′W. Shelters Big Bay De Noc on E. Max. width, c.9 mi/14.5 km. Point Detour is at its tip. Ski areas to E.

Garden Plain, town (1990 pop. 731), Sedgwick co., S Kansas, 18 mi/29 km W of Wichita; 37°39′N 97°40′W. In wheat region. Satellite community of Wichita.

Garden Ridge, town (1990 pop. 1,450), Comal co., S central Texas, suburb 17 mi/27 km NE of San Antonio, near Cibolo Creek; 29°37′N 98°17′W. Agr. area (cattle, sheep; wheat).

Garden View, uninc. town (1990 pop. 2,687), Old Lycoming township, Lycoming co., N central Pa., residential suburb 2 mi/3.2 km WNW of Williamsport, on Lycoming Creek.

Gardena, city (1990 pop. 49,847), Los Angeles co., SW Calif., residential and industrial suburb 10 mi/16 km SSW of Los Angeles; 33°54′N 118°18′W. Torrance to SW. Gardena is often called Freeway City because of its proximity to several major roads; San Diego Freeway to S and W, Harbor Freeway to E. Its diverse mfg. includes aircraft components, electronic equip., machinery, tools, communications equipment, metal items, clothing, and food prods. Gardena is also noted for its plant nurseries. The city has a sizeable Jap.-Amer. community, and an annual Jap. cultural exhibit is held here. El Camino Col. and Harbor Junior Col. are in Gardena. Inc. 1930.

Gardena (gahr-DEEN-uh), village (1990 pop. 41), Bottineau co., N N.Dak., 9 mi/14.5 km SSE of Bottineau; 48°42′N 100°30′W.

Gardendale, city (1990 pop. 9,251), Jefferson co., N central Ala., suburb 10 mi/16 km N of Birmingham; 33°40′N 86°48′W. Mfg. (medical supplies).

Gardendale, town (1990 pop. 1,103), Ector co., W Texas, 10 mi/16 km N of Odessa; 32°01′N 102°21′W. RR junction. Oil and natural gas. Agr. area (cattle, horses; pecans, hay).

Gardenville, suburban village, Erie co., W N.Y., 3 mi/ 4.8 km SE of Buffalo; 42°52′N 78°45′W.

Gardiner (GAHRD-nuhr), city (1990 pop. 6,746), Kennebec co., S Maine, on the Kennebec just S of Augusta; 44°11′N 69°47′W. Mfg. (shoes, paper, wood prods.) here and at South Gardiner. The poet Edward Arlington Robinson lived here as a boy; there is a memorial to him on the town green. Founded 1760; inc. as town 1803, city 1850.

Gardiner 1 (GAHRD-nuhr), village (1990 pop. 670), Park co., S Mont., on Yellowstone R., at N boundary of Yellowstone Natl. Park, 44 mi/71 km S of Livingston. Gallatin Natl. Forest and Absaroka-Beartooth Wilderness to N. Black Canyon of the Yellowstone to SE; Roosevelt Arch, drive-through portal at park entrance (1903), is just S. **2** resort village (1990 pop. 700), Ulster co., SE N.Y., on Small Wallkill R. and 12 mi/19 km W of Poughkeepsie; 41°42′N 74°11′W. A 17th-cent. gristmill is here.

Gardiner, Mount (12,907 ft/3,934 m), Fresno co., E Calif., in the Sierra Nevada, 15 mi/24 km W of Independence, in Kings Canyon Natl. Park.

Gardiner River, 20 mi/32 km long, in NW Wyo. and S Mont.; rises in Gallatin Range, entire river lies within NW part of Yellowstone Natl. Park; flows SE and N, past Mammoth Hot Springs, to Yellowstone R. at Gardiner, Mont.

Gardiners Bay, inlet of Block Isl. Sound, SE N.Y., bet. N and S peninsulas of L.I., and bet. Gardiners Isl. (E) and Shelter Isl. (W); 41°05′N 72°15′W. Inlet is c.10 mi/16 km long E-W, 8 mi/12.9 km wide. Connected by channels to Little Peconic and Great Peconic bays (W). Oyster beds; fishing; yachting.

Gardiners Island (□ c.5 sq mi/13 sq km), in Gardiners Bay bet. the 2 flukelike peninsulas of E L.I., SE N.Y.; 41°05′N 72°06′W. It was settled by colonist Lion Gardiner in 1639 as the 1st permanent Eng. settlement in N.Y. state and has been owned for 300 years by his descendants. The isl. is a private game preserve. Captain Kidd is said to have buried treasure here.

Gardner, city (1990 pop. 20,125), Worcester co., N central Mass.; 42°35′N 72°00′W. Its furniture and lumber industries date from c.1805. Diversified metal and electronics mfg. has also developed there and adds to the city's economic base. Includes village of Otter River. Community col. State Prison. Settled 1764, inc. as a city 1921.

Gardner, town (1990 pop. 3,191), Johnson co., E Kansas, 27 mi/43 km SW of Kansas City, 8 mi/12.9 km SW of Olathe; 38°48′N 94°55′W. Satellite community of Kansas City. Trading point in grain and livestock area. Mfg. (sporting goods, plastics prods., printing). Santa Fe and Oregon trails branched off here from their shared route from Independence.

Gardner 1 village, Huerfano co., S Colo., at point where Williams, Muddy, and Huertano creeks converge to form Huerfano R., 24 mi/39 km WNW of Walsenburg. Elev. 6,966 ft/2,123 m. Outfitting point for excursions, hunting, hiking, and rafting in nearby Sangre de Cristo Mts. Part of San Isabel Natl. Forest to N. **2** village (1990 pop. 1,237), Grundy co., NE Ill., 15 mi/24 km SSE of Morris; 41°11′N 88°18′W. In agr. area. Bituminous coal in area. **3** village (1990 pop. 85), Cass co., E N.Dak., 21 mi/34 km NNW of Fargo; 47°08′N 96°58′W.

Gardner Lake 1 (GAHRD-nuhr), in Washington co., E Maine, 6 mi/9.7 km NE of Machias; 7 mi/11.3 km long. **2** reservoir and resort lake, Bozrah, Salem, and Montville towns, New London co., SE Conn., on Gardner R., 8 mi/12.9 km W of Norwich; 1.2 mi/1.9 km long; 41°30′N 72°13′W. Minnie Sate Park on E shore.

Gardner Pinnacles, island in Hawaiian Isls., N Pacific, Honolulu co., Hawaii, 100 mi/161 km N of Tropic of Cancer, c.640 mi/1,030 km WNW of Honolulu; 25°N 167°55′W. Elev. 190 ft/58 m. Discovered 1820 by Amer. traders. Part of Hawaiian Isls. Natl. Wildlife refuge.

Gardnerville, uninc. town (1990 pop. 2,177), Douglas co., W Nev., 1 mi/1.6 km SE of Minden, 16 mi/26 km S of Carson City, on East Carson R.; 38°56′N 119°44′W. Mfg. (cabinets, printing and publishing, lumber); cattle, sheep; hay. Part of Toiyabe Natl. Forest to S.

Gardnerville Ranchos, uninc. town (1990 pop. 7,455), Douglas co., W Nev., residential suburb W of Gardnerville, in foothills of Sierra Nevada range; 38°53′N 119°44′W. Retirement community developed in 1980s.

Gareloi Island (GAW-re-loi), largest of Delarof Isls., Aleutian Isls., SW Alaska; 51°47′N 178°52′W. Isl. is 6 mi/9.7 km long, 5 mi/8 km wide. In center rises active volcano of Mt. Gareloi (5,160 ft/1,573 m).

Garfield 1 county (□ 2,956 sq mi/7,656 sq km; 1990 pop. 29,974), W Colo.; ⊙ Glenwood Springs; 39°36′N 107°54′W. A plateau area, bordering on Utah; drained by Colorado R. Cattle, sheep; hay, oats, timber. U.S. oil-shale reserve is near Grand Valley town. Glenwood Canyon in E; part of Grand Mesa Natl. Forest in S; parts of White R. Natl. Forest in NE and SE; part of Routt Natl. Forest in NE corner; Rifle Gap and Harvey Gap State Parks in center; Rifle Falls State Park in N center. Formed 1883. **2** county (□ 4,847 sq mi/12,554 sq km; 1990 pop. 1,589), E central Mont.; ⊙ Jordan; 47°17′N 107°00′W. Agr. area, bounded N by Missouri R., W by Musselshell R., drained by Big Dry Creek and Little Dry Creek. Wheat, barley, oats, hay; sheep, cattle, hogs. Fort Peck Reservoir to N, large part of Dry Arm of reservoir in NE. Reservoir surrounded by Charles M. Russell Natl. Wildlife Refuge. Hell Creek State Park, on Hell Creek Bay of Fort Peck Reservoir, and Hell Creek Fossil Area in N. Formed 1919. **3** county (□ 571 sq mi/1,479 sq km; 1990 pop. 2,141), central Nebr.; ⊙ Burwell; 41°53′N 98°58′W. Ranching area, some irrigation. Agr. area drained by Cedar, North Loup, Calamus, and Cedar rivers. Corn, wild hay; cattle, hogs. **4** county (□ 1,060 sq mi/2,745 sq km; 1990 pop. 56,735), N Okla.; ⊙ Enid; 36°22′N 97°46′W. Drained by tributaries of Cimarron and Turkey rivers and by the Salt Fork of Arkansas R. and Turkey co. Agr. area (wheat; cattle, sheep; dairying). Diversified mfg. at Enid. Oil and gas wells. Formed 1893. **5** county (□ 5,208 sq mi/13,489 sq km; 1990 pop. 3,980), S Utah; ⊙ Panguitch; 37°52′N 111°26′W. Mt. area bounded E by Colorado R. (L. Powell reservoir) and drained by Sevier, East Fork of Sevier, and Escalante rivers. Alfalfa, barley; cattle; timber; tourism. Antimony mining. Henry Mts. in NE; Paunsaugunt Plateau in W, including part of Bryce Canyon Natl. Park. Parts of 3 large units of Dixie Natl. Forest in W ½ of co. Long S extension (c.40 mi/64 km long) of Capitol Reef Natl. Park in E center. Escalante State Park (petrified forest) and Anusazi Indian Village State Historical Park at center of co. Small part of Fishlake Natl. Forest in NW corner. Main part of Bryce Canyon Natl. Park in SW; part of Canyonlands Natl. Park in extreme NE corner. Large sect. of Glen Canyon Natl. Recreation Area in SE and nearly length of E boundary along L. Powell (Colorado R.). Formed 1882. **6** county (□ 718 sq mi/1,860 sq km; 1990 pop. 2,248), SE Wash.; ⊙ Pomeroy; 46°26′N 117°32′W. In Palouse region. Rolling plateaus bounded by Oregon on S, on N by Snake R. (forms L. Bryan reservoir in NW and Lower Granite L. reservoir in NE) and rising to Blue Mts. in S. RR junction. Apples, wheat, hay, alfalfa, barley, oats; hogs. Part of Umatilla Natl. Forest in S, including part of Wenaha-Tucannon Wilderness Area. Smallest co. in pop. in Wash. Formed 1881.

Garfield, industrial city (1990 pop. 26,727), Bergen co., NE N.J., on the Passaic at its confluence with the Saddle R.; 40°52′N 74°06′W. Mfg. includes paper prods., rubber, and printing machinery. Settled 1679 by the Dutch; inc. 1898.

Garfield 1 village (1990 pop. 308), Benton co., extreme NW Ark., 10 mi/16 km NE of Rogers, in the Ozarks; 36°27′N 93°58′W. Pea Ridge Natl. Military Park to W; large Beaver L. Reservoir to SE. **2** village (1990 pop. 255), Emanuel co., E central Ga., 14 mi/23 km ENE of Swainsboro; 32°39′N 82°06′W. Mfg. (candy). **3** village (1990 pop. 236), Pawnee co., SW central Kansas, on Arkansas R., 11 mi/18 km SW of Larned; 38°04′N 99°14′W. Grain; livestock. **4** village (1990 pop. 203), Douglas co., W Minn., 7 mi/11.3 km WNW of Alexandria, in lake region; 45°56′N 95°29′W. Grain; poultry; dairying; mfg. (fertilizer, plastic sheets, wood trusses). L. Ida to NE. **5** village, Salt Lake co., N Utah, near Great Salt L., 15 mi/24 km W of Salt Lake City, at N tip of Oquirrh Mts. Elev. 4,234 ft/1,291 m. Copper mining and smelting; cobalt refining. In vicinity (S) of large Kennecott Corp. Tailings Pond. **6** village (1990 pop. 544), Whitman co., SE Wash., 13 mi/21 km NE of Colfax, near Idaho state line; 47°01′N 117°08′W. Barley, wheat, peas, oats; mfg. (farm machinery). Steptoe Butte State Park to W; St. Joe Natl. Forest (Idaho) to E.

Garfield Heights, village (1990 pop. 31,739), Cuyahoga co., NE Ohio, residential and industrial suburb adjacent to Cleveland; 41°25′N 81°36′W. Oil refineries and steel industry. Founded 1904, inc. 1932.

Gargathy Inlet, Va.: see ASSAWOMAN ISLAND.

Garibaldi (ga-ruh-BAHL-dee), town (1990 pop. 877), Tillamook co., NW Oregon, at N end of Tillamook Bay, E of its entrance to the Pacific Ocean, near mouth of Miami R., 7 mi/11.3 km NNW of Tillamook; 45°33′N 123°54′W. Shrimp and crab processing. Dairy prods.; cattle. Tourism. Inc. 1946.

Garibaldi, Mount (8,787 ft/2,678 m), SW B.C., Canada, in Coast Mts., in Garibaldi Park, 40 mi/64 km N of Vancouver.

Garibaldi Park, provincial park (□ 973 sq mi/2,520 sq km), SW B.C., Canada, in Coast Mts., 40 mi/64 km N of Vancouver. Mt. region; includes Mt. Weart (9,300 ft/2,835 m), Wedge Mt. (9,484 ft/2,891 m), Mt. Garibaldi (8,787 ft/2,678 m). Popular skiing region near Vancouver.

Garland, county (□ 734 sq mi/1,901 sq km; 1990 pop. 73,397), central Ark.; ⊙ Hot Springs; 34°34′N 93°09′W. Intersected by Ouachita R. Agr. (cattle, hogs). Health and recreation and retirement resorts. Hot Springs Natl. Park at Hot Springs, at center of co.; part of Ouachita Natl. Forest in W; L. Ouachita State Park in N center, at E end of L. Ouachita reservoir (Ouachita R.); L. Hamilton and part of L. Catherine in S, both reservoirs on Ouachita R. Formed 1873.

Garland, city (1990 pop. 180,650), Dallas co., extending NE into Rockwall and Collin cos., N Texas, suburb 12 mi/19 km NE of Dallas; 32°54′N 96°37′W. Elev. 551 ft/168 m. Bounds L. Ray Hubbard on SE and extreme NE; drained by Rowlett, Pittman and Duck creeks. Since World War II, Garland has grown from an agr. community into an important center for electronics research and for the production of electronic equip. Other mfg. include oil-field equip., chemicals, apparel, sheet-metal fabrication, and processed foods. An Air Force station is here. Garland remains one of the fastest growing cities in the U.S. Inc. 1891.

Garland 1 town (1990 pop. 1,064), Penobscot co., central Maine, 22 mi/35 km NW of Bangor; 45°02′N 69°09′W. In agr. region. **2** town (1990 pop. 746), Sampson co., SE central N.C., 15 mi/24 km SSW of Clinton, near South R; 34°47′N 78°23′W. Tobacco, cotton, peanuts, grain, berries, sweet potatoes; poultry, livestock. Mfg. (apparel). Bladen Lakes State Forest to SW. **3** town (1990 pop. 194), Tipton co., W Tenn., 5 mi/8 km WNW of Covington; 35°35′N 89°45′W. **4** town (1990 pop. 1637), Box Elder co., N Utah, 18 mi/29 km NNW of Brigham City; 41°44′N 112°09′W. Elev. 4,344 ft/1,324 m. Trade center for agr. area; wheat, barley, alfalfa, sugar beets; dairying. Sugar beet factory closed 1978. Settled 1905. Home of Bear R. High School.

Garland 1 village (1990 pop. 415), Miller co., extreme SW Ark., 18 mi/29 km ESE of Texarkana, on Red R.; 33°21′N 93°42′W. Livestock; oil and gas. **2** village (1990 pop. 247), Seward co., SE Nebr., 7 mi/11.3 km ENE of Seward; 40°56′N 96°59′W.

Garnacha, Ensenada de (gahr-NAHCH-uh, en-sai-NAH-dah dai), sheltered inlet, Pinar del Río prov., W Cuba, on the Gulf of Guanahacabibes, 45 mi/72 km WSW of Pinar del Río; 22°07′N 84°22′W. Mouth of Salado R.

Garnavillo, town (1990 pop. 727), Clayton co., NE Iowa, near the Mississippi, 10 mi/16 km E of Elkader; 42°52′N 91°14′W. In corn, hog, and dairy region.

Garner, city (1990 pop. 14,967), Wake co., central N.C., suburb 5 mi/8 km SSE of Raleigh; 35°41′N 78°37′W. N.C. State Univ. Farms to W. L. Benson reservoir to S, L. Wheeler reservoir to SW. Mfg. (food processing, sheet metal).

Garner, town (1990 pop. 2,916), ⊙ Hancock co., N Iowa, on East Branch of Iowa R., 20 mi/32 km W of Mason City; 43°06′N 93°35′W. RR junction. Mfg. (bldg. equip., metal prods., wood, feed). Clear L. and McIntosh Woods State Parks to E; Eagle L. to W. Inc. 1881.

Garnerville, village, Rockland co., SE N.Y., 2 mi/3.2 km NW of Haverstraw; 41°12′N 73°59′W. Part of West Haverstraw, but has its own post office.

Garnet Lake, resort village, Warren co., E N.Y., on small Garnet L. in the Adirondacks, 25 mi/40 km NW of Glens Falls; 43°32′N 74°01′W.

Garnett (GAHR-net), town (1990 pop. 3,210), ⊙ Anderson co., E Kansas, 23 mi/37 km S of Ottawa; 38°16′N 95°14′W. Elev. 1,050 ft/320 m. RR junction. Trade center for livestock, grain, and dairy region. Mfg. (furniture,

Cross references are shown in SMALL CAPITALS. The pronunciation key is on page xv. The dates of population figures are on page xii.

clothing, fabricated metal), food processing. Oil wells in vicinity. Edgar Lee Masters b. here. Founded 1856; inc. as town 1861, as city 1870.

Garrard (GAHR-uhrd), county (□ 233 sq mi/603 sq km; 1990 pop. 11,579), central Ky.; ⊙ Lancaster; 37°38′N 84°32′W. Bounded N by Kentucky R., W by Dix R. (forms Herrington L. reservoir in NW), NE by Paint Lick Creek (source in SE). Gently rolling upland in Bluegrass region. Agr. area (burley tobacco, corn, hay, alfalfa; hogs, cattle, poultry; dairying). Formed 1796.

Garretson, town (1990 pop. 924), Minnehaha co., E S.Dak., 16 mi/26 km NE of Sioux Falls and on Pipestone Creek, near Minn. state line; 43°43′N 96°30′W. Grain; dairy prods.; poultry. Palisades State Park to S.

Garrett, county (□ 656 sq mi/1,699 sq km; 1990 pop. 28,138), extreme W Md.; ⊙ Oakland; 39°32′N 79°16′W. Bounded SE by North Branch of the Potomac (forms W.Va. state line here), W by W.Va. state line, N by Pa. state line; drained by Youghiogheny, Casselman, Savage, and Stoney rivers. Backbone Mt. (3,360 ft/1,024 m), the highest point in Md., is in this Allegheny mt. co., as is Muddy Creek Falls (64 ft/20 m), the state's highest waterfall. Garrett co. was called "the Switzerland of America" by John W. Garrett, the president of the Baltimore and Ohio RR, who was the most powerful force in the development of its resort interests. The co. was named for him. Although only 200 mi/322 km away from the Eastern Shore, it has 9 times the average annual snowfall. Known for excellent hunting and fishing, the co. also includes Savage R., Swallow Falls, Potomac State Forest, and Deep Creek L., which is both a summer and winter resort. Mining (bituminous coal, fireclay) as well as some lumbering; agr. (dairy prods.; grain; livestock); maple sugar and syrup. The co.'s pop. density is low by comparison with the rest of the state. Formed in 1872.

Garrett, city (1990 pop. 5,349), DeKalb co., NE Ind., 4 mi/6.4 km W of Auburn; 41°21′N 85°08′W. Trading center in agr. area (grain, soybeans; livestock); mfg. of wood prods., silicone rubber, small motors, mobile homes, rubber prods.

Garrett 1 village (1990 pop. 169), Douglas co., E central Ill., 23 mi/37 km E of Decatur; 39°47′N 88°25′W. In agr. area. **2** uninc. village (1990 pop. 500), Floyd co., E Ky., in Cumberland foothills, 17 mi/27 km W of Pikeville. Bituminous coal; timber; oil and gas.

Garrett (GER-ret), borough (1990 pop. 520), Somerset co., SW Pa., 10 mi/16 km S of Somerset, on Casselman R., at mouth of Buffalo Creek. Agr. (livestock; corn, oats, hay, potatoes; dairying); bituminous coal. Negro Mt. ridge to NW.

Garrett Hill (GER-ret), uninc. village, Radnor township, Delaware co., SE Pa., residential suburb 10 mi/16 km NW of Philadelphia; 40°01′N 75°20′W. Villanova Univ. to N; Bryn Mawr Col. to E.

Garrett Park, town (1990 pop. 884), Montgomery co., central Md., NW suburb of Washington, D.C., on Rock Creek; 39°02′N 77°05′W. Named for John W. Garrett, president of the Baltimore and Ohio RR, it was laid out in 1887 along irregular lot lines and winding paths reminiscent of an Eng. village. Georgetown Preparatory School (founded 1789 by Jesuits) is nearby. Inc. 1891.

Garrettsville, village (1990 pop. 2,014), Portage co., NE Ohio, 25 mi/40 km NE of Akron and on small Eagle Creek; 41°17′N 81°05′W.

Garrison 1 town (1990 pop. 320), Benton co., E central Iowa, 6 mi/9.7 km E of Vinton; 42°08′N 92°08′W. Professional theater in old creamery; limestone quarries nearby. **2** town (1990 pop. 1,530), McLean co., N central N.Dak., 32 mi/51 km NNW of Washburn; 47°38′N 101°25′W. Lignite mines; grain, dairy prods. Garrison Dam in Missouri R. is near. Inc. 1920. Fort Stevenson State Park to S on L. Sakakawea Reservoir. Fort Berthold Indian Reservation to W. **3** town (1990 pop. 883), Nacogdoches co., E Texas, near Attoyac Bayou, 17 mi/27 km NNE of Nacogdoches; 31°49′N 94°29′W. In timber; cattle, poultry; dairying; clay area; mfg. (bldg. materials, furniture).

Garrison 1 uninc. village (1990 pop. 700), Lewis co., NE Ky., 7 mi/11.3 km E of Vanceburg, on Grassy Fork R., 1 mi/1.6 km S of its confluence with Ohio R. Timber. Tobacco, grain; livestock. Mfg. (lumber). **2** village (1990 pop. 5,045), Baltimore co., N Md., 11 mi/18 km NW of Baltimore; 39°24′N 76°45′W. In the vicinity are The Caves, home of Charles Carroll (c.1730), St. Thomas's Episcopal Church (c.1742), and The Stone Chapel (c.1786), a Methodist church. **3** village (1990 pop. 138), Crow Wing co., central Minn., on W shore of Mille Lacs L., 19 mi/31 km ESE of Brainerd; 46°17′N 93°49′W. Resort area; light mfg. Borden L. to W; Wealthwood State Forest to NE; Mille Lacs Indian Reservation (including Mille Lacs Indian Mus.) and Mille Lacs Kathio State Park to SE. Numerous small lakes in area. **4** (GER-i-suhn), village (1990 pop. 50), Powell co., W central Mont., on the Clark Fork R., at mouth of Little Blackfoot R., 10 mi/16 km NNW of Deer Lodge. RR junction. Helena Natl. Forest to the N and E; parts of Deerlodge Natl. Forest to SW and SE. **5** village (1990 pop. 71), Butler co., E Nebr., 6 mi/9.7 km SSW of David City, on branch of Big Blue R.; 41°10′N 97°09′W. **6** village (1990 pop. 800), Putnam co., SE N.Y., on E bank of the Hudson, 8 mi/12.9 km S of Beacon; 41°23′N 73°56′W.

Garrison Dam, N.Dak.: see SAKAKAWEA, LAKE.

Garry, Cape, SE Somerset Isl., E Franklin dist., N.W.T., Canada, on Prince Regent Inlet, on SE side of Creswell Bay; 72°16′N 93°23′W. Sometimes called Cape Clara.

Garry, Fort, Canada: see FORT GARRY.

Garry Island, NW Mackenzie dist., N.W.T., Canada, in Beaufort Sea of Arctic Ocean, off mouth of Mackenzie R. delta; 69°19′N 135°40′W. Isl. is 5 mi/8 km long, 4 mi/6 km wide.

Garry, Lake (□ 980 sq mi/2,538 sq km), NW Keewatin dist., N.W.T., Canada, near Mackenzie dist. boundary, just E of L. Pelly; 66°00′N 100°00′W; 60 mi/97 km long, 2 mi/3 km–38 mi/61 km wide. Drained E by Back R.

Garson, village, SE central Ont., Canada, 5 mi/8 km N of Sadbury. Nickel and copper mining.

Garson Quarry, village, SE Man., Canada, 23 mi/37 km NE of Winnipeg. Grain; dairying.

Garthby, village (1991 pop. 389), S Que., Canada, on L. Aylmer, 30 mi/48 km NW of Megantic. Asbestos, chrome mining; dairying; cattle raising; potato growing.

Garvin, county (□ 813 sq mi/2,106 sq km; 1990 pop. 26,605), S central Okla.; ⊙ Pauls Valley; 34°42′N 97°18′W. Intersected by Washita R. (forms part of S boundary), and by small Rush and Wildhorse creeks. Agr. (oats, fruit, corn, hay, peanuts, soybeans; sheep). Farm prods. processing, mfg. at Pauls Valley, Wynnewood, and Lindsay. Oil and natural gas; oil refining. Formed 1907.

Garvin 1 village (1990 pop. 149), Lyon co., SW Minn., 16 mi/26 km S of Marshall; 44°12′N 95°45′W. L. Shetek to SE. **2** village (1990 pop. 128), McCurtain co., extreme SE Okla., 9 mi/14.5 km WNW of Idabel, on Little R.; 33°57′N 94°56′W. In farm area.

Garwin, town (1990 pop. 533), Tama co., central Iowa, 9 mi/14.5 km NNE of Toledo; 42°05′N 92°40′W. Feed, wood prods.

Garwood, uninc. town (1990 pop. 965), Colorado co., S Texas, 21 mi/34 km SSE of Columbus, on Colorado R. Agr. area (rice, cotton, peanuts). Oil and natural gas.

Garwood, industrial borough (1990 pop. 4,227), Union co., NE N.J., 6 mi/9.7 km W of Elizabeth; 40°38′N 74°19′W. Mfg. (metal prods., vitamins, paper, and plastics). Inc. 1903.

Gary, city (1990 pop. 116,646), Lake co., NW Ind., a port of entry on L. Michigan; 41°36′N 87°20′W. Drained by Grand Calumet R., which flows W out of Grand Calumet R. Lagoon to join Calumet R. Mfg. (tin and steel prods., beverages, medical prods., iron and steel processing, consumer goods, dairy prods., paper prods., apparel, cement, lime, publishing). Gary was founded in 1906 by the U.S. Steel Corp., which purchased the land in 1905 and landscaped it for a city. In 1908 the 1st blast furnace was lit to begin the vast lakefront complex that was to dominate U.S. steel production and become one of the world's greatest steel centers. Gary steelworkers were esp. active in the nationwide steel strike of 1919, when federal troops occupied the city for several months. During the 1960s and 1970s, Gary underwent a series of economic, social, and political changes. The city's steel industry began a rapid decline soon afterward that continued throughout the 1980s, leading to large-scale plant closings and high unemployment. In the early 1990s city leaders and citizen groups proposed plans to replace the vacant mills and to revitalize the economy. The NW campus of Indiana Univ. is in Gary, as is a branch of the Ind. Vocational and Technical Col. (Ivy Tech). The city has an airport and a civic center, and the Ind. Dunes Natl. Lakeshore Park and State Park to E.

Gary, town (1990 pop. 1,355), McDowell co., S W.Va., 5 mi/8 km S of Welch; 37°21′N 81°32′W. Coal.

Gary 1 village (1990 pop. 200), Norman co., NW Minn., 13 mi/21 km ENE of Ada; 47°22′N 96°16′W. Agr. area (grain, sunflowers, potatoes, alfalfa); mfg. (feeds, fertilizers). White Earth India Reservation to E. **2** village (1990 pop. 274), Deuel co., E S.Dak., 12 mi/19 km ENE of Clear L., on Minn. state line; 44°47′N 96°27′W. Trading point for agr. area; dairy prods.; livestock; grain. **3** village (1990 pop. 271), Panola co., E Texas, 8 mi/12.9 km S of Carthage, near Murvaul Bayou; 32°01′N 94°22′W. Natural gas and oil. Poultry, cattle, hogs. Timber. Murvaul L. to W.

Garysburg, town (1990 pop. 1,057), Northampton co., NE N.C., 6 mi/9.7 km E of Roanoke Rapids, near Roanoke R.; 36°27′N 77°33′W. RR junction. Tobacco, grain, peanuts, cotton; livestock.

Garyton, village, Porter co., NW Ind., 5 mi/8 km ESE of Gary.

Garyville, uninc. town (1990 pop. 3,181), St. John the Baptist parish, SE La., 32 mi/51 km WNW of New Orleans, on E bank (levee) of the Mississippi R.; 30°05′N 90°37′W. In agr. area (sugarcane, vegetables, soybeans); crawfish, catfish, alligators; mfg. (gasoline, chemicals).

Garza, county (□ 896 sq mi/2,321 sq km; 1990 pop. 5,143), NW Texas; ⊙ Post; 33°10′N 101°17′W. Rolling plains at foot of Caprock escarpment (in W). Elev. 2,100 ft/640 m–3,000 ft/914 m. Drained by Salt and Double Mt. Forks of Brazos R., also North Fork of the Double Mt. Fork. Cattle ranching (in lower plains); some irrigation agr. (cotton, grains, hay; also poultry) on high plains above Caprock. Oil, natural gas wells. Formed 1876.

Garza Garciá (GAHR-sah gahr-see-AH), city (1990 pop. 113,017), Nuevo León, N Mexico, in foothills of Sierra Madre Oriental, 6 mi/9.7 km W of Monterrey; 25°40′N 100°25′W. Part of the Monterrey metropolitan area; has become an upper-middle-class to upper-class residential area with little industry.

Gas, village (1990 pop. 505), Allen co., SE Kansas, 3 mi/4.8 km E of Iola; 37°55′N 95°20′W. In cattle, hogs, grain, and dairy region. Gas fields here.

Gas City, city (1990 pop. 6,296), Grant co., E central Ind., 5 mi/8 km SSE of Marion; 40°29′N 85°37′W. In agr. area (livestock; grain, dairy); light mfg. Grew after a natural gas boom in 1887. Laid out 1867.

Gas Hills, mining district, E Fremont co., central Wyo., 35 mi/56 km ESE of Riverton, in the N foothills of Rattlesnake Range. Major open-pit uranium-mining area.

Gasconade, county (□ 520 sq mi/1347 sq km; 1990 pop. 14,006), E central Mo.; ⊙ Hermann; 38°26′N 91°30′W. In Ozark region, bounded N by Missouri R.; drained by Gasconade and Bourbeuse rivers. Corn, wheat, grapes; dairying; cattle, poultry; timber; fireclay, mines; tourism. Mfg. (grain prods., lumber prods., shoes). Ger.-settled region. Mfg. at Hermann, Owensville, and Bland. Canaan State Forest in SW. Wineries at Hermann. Historical Ger. community; annual Oktoberfest and Maifest attracts thousands of tourists. Formed 1820.

Gasconade (gas-kuh-NAID), town (1990 pop. 253), Gasconade co., E central Mo., at confluence of Missouri and Gasconade rivers, 8 mi/12.9 km W of Hermann; 38°40′N 91°33′W.

Gasconade River, c.265 mi/426 km long, central Mo.; rises in the Ozarks in Wright co., meanders in a deep valley NE to Missouri R. at Gasconade. Many large springs and caves along its upper ½.

Gascoyne (GA-skoin), village (1990 pop. 22), Bowman co., SW N.Dak., 16 mi/26 km E of Bowman; 46°07′N 103°04′W.

Gaspar (gahs-PAHR), town, Ciego de Ávila prov., central Cuba, on central RR line and just S of Central Highway, 16 mi/26 km S of Ciego de Ávila; 21°44′N 78°34′W. In sugar-producing region.

Gaspar Grande (GA-spuhr), islet off NW Trinidad, Trinidad and Tobago, outside Chaguaramas Bay, 9 mi/ 14.5 km W of Port of Spain; 10°40′N 61°39′W. Islet covers an area of 319 acres/129 ha. Bathing and fishing resort. Gasparillo (also called Little Gasparee) Isl. is off N coast.

Gaspar Hernández (gahs-PAHR er-NAHN-dez), town (1993 pop. 4,550), Espaillat prov., N Dominican Republic, near coast, 30 mi/48 km ENE of Santiago; 19°35′N 70°10′W. Agr. (cacao, rice, coffee, corn).

Gasparilla Island (gas-puh-RIL-uh), narrow barrier island in the Gulf of Mexico, SW Fla., at entrance to Charlotte Harbor (W), S of Gasparilla Pass (inlet connecting small Gasparilla Sound and the Gulf); c.6 mi/ 9.7 km long; 26°43′N 83°15′W. Contains a lighthouse, and villages of Gasparilla (ferry to mainland) in N, and Boca Grande (resort, port of entry, and fishing station) and South Boca Grande in S.

Gasparillo (GAS-pah-ril-lo), village, W Trinidad, Trinidad and Tobago, 22 mi/35 km SSE of Port of Spain; 10°40′N 61°39′W. Sugarcane, coconuts. Small, uninhabited Gasparillo (also called Little Gasparee) Isl. is just N of Gaspar Grande isl., 7 mi/11.3 km W of Port of Spain.

Gaspé (gas-PAI), city (1991 pop. 16,402), E Que., Canada, on Gaspé Bay near the E extremity of the Gaspé Peninsula; 48°50′N 64°29′W. Resort. Cartier landed here in 1534.

Gaspé Bay (gas-PAI), deep inlet of the Gulf of St. Lawrence, E Que., Canada, at the E end of the Gaspé Peninsula; 22 mi/35 km long and 6 mi/10 km wide. The village of Gaspé is near its head.

Gaspé, Cape (gas-PAI), E extremity of Gaspé Peninsula, E Que., Canada, on the Gulf of St. Lawrence, bet. mouth of the St. Lawrence R. (N) and Gaspé Bay (S), 16 mi/26 km ESE of Gaspé; 48°45′N 64°10′W. Lighthouse.

Gaspé East (gas-PAI), county (☐ 2,348 sq mi/ 6,081 sq km), E Que., Canada, at E end of Gaspé Peninsula, bet. the St. Lawrence (N) and Chaleur Bay (S); ☉ Percé; 48°40′N 64°45′W.

Gaspé Peninsula (gas-PAI) or **Gaspésie** (gahs-pai-ZEE), tongue of land, E Que., Canada, bet. the estuary of the St. Lawrence R. on the N and Chaleur Bay on the S, and extending E into the Gulf of St. Lawrence; 48°30′N 65°00′W. It is c.150 mi/240 km long and 60 mi/97 km—90 mi/145 km wide. Its backbone is an extension of the Appalachian mt. system and is known in its highest part as the Monts Chic-Chocs (Shickshock Mts.). Mt. Jacques-Cartier, or Tabletop Mt. (4,160 ft/1,268 m), is the highest elev. in SE Canada. The interior of the peninsula is a mt. wilderness, completely forested, and with numerous streams and lakes, offering excellent hunting and fishing. Copper mining near Murdochville, only sizable interior town, is nearly mined out. Settlement is almost wholly confined to the coastal rim, where there is a succession of picturesque villages. Declining agr., depleted mineral and forest resources, collapse of cod fisheries, and small tourist trade have all contributed to a high unemployment rate. Shrimp, herring, scallops, lobster, and crabs have spared economy from total collapse. Lumbering, pulp mills. The inhabitants on the N and NE are chiefly Fr. Can. (90%), Acadian, Scottish, Irish, and Eng. The coast, with its combination of mt. and sea and its many bold headlands, is famed for its beauty. The chief towns are Gaspé, Matane, Percé, Chandler, New Richmond, Grand Rivière, Cap-Chat, Ste. Anne-des-Monts. Gaspesian Provincial Park is in the Monts Chic-Chocs, and

there are bird sanctuaries off the E coast. Jacques Cartier landed on the peninsula in 1534. RR along S shore, Matapedia to Gaspé. Forillon Natl. Park on peninsula opposite town of Gaspé.

Gaspé West (gas-PAI), county (☐ 2,198 sq mi/ 5,693 sq km), E Que., Canada, on N side of Gaspé Peninsula, on the St. Lawrence; ☉ Ste. Anne des Monts; 48°53′N 65°45′W.

Gaspee Point, promontory in Warwick town, Kent co., E R.I., on Providence R. c.5 mi/8 km S of Providence. Br. sloop *Gaspee* burned here by patriots in 1772.

Gaspereau, Lake (GA-spuh-ro), W central N.S., Canada, 20 mi/32 km W of Windsor; drains into Minas Basin; 8 mi/13 km long, 4 mi/6 km wide.

Gasport, village (☐ 2 sq mi/5.2 sq km; 1990 pop. 1,336), Niagara co., W N.Y., on the Barge Canal, 25 mi/40 km NNE of Buffalo; 43°12′N 78°34′W. Mfg. reflects the region's longtime ties to the free fruit–processed vegetable farming and includes vegetable- and fruit-grading and -handling equip., computerized control systems, orchard-spray equip., pallets, and boxes. Limestone quarry.

Gassaway (GAS-uh-wai), town (1990 pop. 946), Braxton co., central W.Va., on Elk R., 50 mi/80 km NE of Charleston; 38°40′N 80°46′W. Agr. (grain, apples); livestock. Mfg. (lumber, concrete). Elk R. Wildlife Management Area to E (includes Sutton L. reservoir). Founded 1904.

Gassville, town (1990 pop. 1,167), Baxter co., N Ark., 7 mi/11.3 km WSW of Mountain Home, near White R., in the Ozarks; 36°16′N 92°29′W. Mfg. (shirts). Bull Shoals Dam, Reservoir, and State Park to NW (on White R.).

Gastineau Channel (GAS-ti-no), 20 mi/32 km long, SE Alaska, bet. Douglas Isl. and mainland; navigable at high tide. On it are Thane, Douglas, and Juneau. It has a 16-ft/5-m tide.

Gaston (GA-stuhn), county (☐ 363 sq mi/940 sq km; 1990 pop. 175,093), S N.C., ☉ Gastonia; 35°17′N 81°10′W. In Piedmont region; bounded S by S.C. state line, E by Catawba R. forms Mountain Isl. L. Wyle reservoirs; drained by South Fork of Catawba R. Largely agr. (cotton, wheat, hay, corn, soybeans, sweet potatoes, tobacco; poultry, chickens, hogs, cattle; dairying); timber (pine, oak). Stone quarrying. Produces much of combed cotton yarn made in U.S., with textile center at Gastonia; sawmilling. Mfg. at Gastonia, Stanley, Mt. Holly, other towns. Crowders Mt. State Park in SW. Formed 1846.

Gaston 1 town (1990 pop. 979), Delaware co., E central Ind., 12 mi/19 km NNW of Muncie; 40°19′N 85°30′W. Livestock; grain. Mfg. (furniture). **2** (GA-stuhn), town (1990 pop. 1,003), Northampton co., NE N.C., near Va. state line, 4 mi/6.4 km N of Roanoke Rapids, near Roanoke R; 36°30′N 77°38′W. Mfg. (wood, sheet metal). Tobacco, peanuts, cotton; chickens, cattle, hogs Roanoke Rapids Dam (Roanoke R.) 3 mi/4.8 km to W. Inc. 1950. **3** town (1990 pop. 984), Lexington co., central S.C., 13 mi/21 km S of Columbia; 33°49′N 81°05′W. Mfg. includes scrap metal processing, feeds, steel prods.; agr. includes poultry, hogs; dairying; grain, soybeans, peaches.

Gaston (GA-stuhn), village (1990 pop. 563), Washington co., NW Oregon, 25 mi/40 km WSW of Portland, on Tualatin R.; 45°26′N 123°08′W. Agr. (grapes, berries, cherries, apples, vegetables, potatoes; sheep, cattle); wineries. Timber. Oak furniture.

Gaston, Lake (GA-stuhn), reservoir, NE N.C. and SE Va., on Roanoke R., 10 mi/16 km WNW of Roanoke Rapids; c.35 mi/56 km long; 36°30′N 77°48′W. Max. capacity 813,120 acre-ft. John H. Kerr Dam (Va.) at WNW end. Formed by Gaston Dam (77 ft/23 m high), built (1962) by Va. Electric Power Co. for power generation. Roanoke Rapids L. reservoir below dam.

Gastonia (gas-TON-yuh), city (1990 pop. 54,732), ☉ Gaston co., SW N.C., 22 mi/35 km W of Charlotte; 35°15′N 81°10′W. An important textile mill center, Gastonia is a major producer of fine-combed cotton yarn. RR junction. Mfg. (textiles, chemicals, machinery,

poultry processing, beverages, electronic and automotive parts; paper, plastic, and steel prods.; fabric dyeing and finishing, consumer goods). Gaston Col. is in Dallas to N, as is Kings Mt. State Park to SW (in S.C.). Crowders Mt. State Park to SW. Municipal Airport to S. Amer. Military Mus., Schiele Nature Mus. Inc. 1877.

Gastonville, uninc. town (1990 pop. 3,090), Washington co., SW Pa., 12 mi/19 km S of Pittsburgh on Peters Creek; 40°15′N 80°00′W. Agr. includes dairying; livestock; hay, corn.

Gate, village (1990 pop. 159), Beaver co., Okla., in E Panhandle, 27 mi/43 km ENE of Beaver; 36°51′N 100°03′W. In grain-growing area.

Gate City, town (1990 pop. 2,214), ☉ Scott co., SW Va., 6 mi/9.7 km N of Kingsport (Tenn.), near North Fork of Holston R., near Tenn. state line; 36°38′N 82°34′W. Mfg. (printing and publishing, light mfg.); trade center; agr. (livestock region; tobacco, corn); timber, limestone. Natural Tunnel State Park to NW. Settled in late 18th cent.; inc. 1892.

Gates, county (☐ 345 sq mi/894 sq km; 1990 pop. 9,305), NE N.C.; ☉ Gatesville; 36°26′N 76°42′W. Coastal plain; bounded N by Va. state line, SW and W by Chowan R.; part of Dismal Swamp in E. Drained by Bennetts Creek. Agr. (wheat, barley, sorghum, hay, tobacco, peanuts, cotton, corn, soybeans; chickens, cattle, hogs); timber (gum, cedar pine, cypress). Merchants Millpond State Park at center; part of Dismal Swamp Natl. Wildlife Refuge in NE. Formed 1778.

Gates, town (1990 pop. 608), Lauderdale co., W Tenn., 13 mi/21 km S of Dyersburg; 35°50′N 89°24′W. In timber and farm region.

Gates, village (1990 pop. 499), Marion co., NW Oregon, 32 mi/51 km ESE of Salem, on North Santiam R.; 44°45′N 122°25′W. RR terminus. Timber; cattle, sheep, poultry; dairying. Detroit L. Reservoir and State Park 10 mi/16 km ESE; Willamette Natl. Forest to E; North Santiam State Park to W.

Gates Center, suburban village, Monroe co., W N.Y., just W of Rochester; 43°09′N 77°42′W. Nurseries and horticultural crops.

Gates Mills, village (1990 pop. 2,508), Cuyahoga co., N Ohio, 15 mi/24 km E of Cleveland and on Chagrin R.; 41°32′N 81°25′W.

Gates–North Gates, town (1990 pop. 14,995), Monroe co., W N.Y., 14 mi/23 km SW of Rochester; 43°10′N 77°42′W. Pop. figure includes Gates Center.

Gatesville, city (1990 pop. 11,492), ☉ Coryell co., central Texas, on Leon R., 37 mi/60 km W of Waco; 31°26′N 97°43′W. Elev. 795 ft/242 m. Trade, processing center for agr. (sorghum, pecans, peaches, grapes), livestock area; cedar timber; mfg. (laboratory equip., fiberglass prods., apparel, trailers). Fort Hood Military Reservation is to S. Ruins of Fort Gates (est. 1849) to S.

Gatesville, village (1990 pop. 308), ☉ Gates co., NE N.C., 30 mi/48 km WNW of Elizabeth City, on Bennetts Creek; 36°24′N 76°45′W. In agr. (peanuts, cotton, tobacco, grain; livestock) and timber area; hunting, fishing. Mfg. (lumber, sleepwear, cedar and cypress siding). Merchants Millpond State Park to E.

Gateway 1 village (1990 pop. 65), Benton co., extreme NW Ark., on Mo. boundary, 16 mi/26 km NE of Rogers; 36°29′N 93°56′W. Pea Ridge Natl. Military Park to SW; Beaver L. Reservoir to SE; Mark Twain Natl. Forest to NE (in Mo.). **2** village (1990 pop. 7,510), Mesa co., W Colo., near Utah state line, 35 mi/ 56 km SW of Grand Junction; 39°32′N 104°54′W. Elev. 4,595 ft/1,401 m. Uncompahgre Natl. Forest to E; Manti La Sal Natl. Forest to SW.

Gateway National Recreation Area (☐ 41 sq mi/ 106 sq km), N.Y. and N.J.; 40°36′N 73°52′W. Authorized 1972 as 1 of only 2 urban recreation areas in nation. Beaches, marshes, isls., and waters in and around N.Y. city. Comprised of Sandy Hook, N.J. (which includes sandy beach, historic lighthouse, and Fort Hancock); and 3 N.Y. city units: Breezy Point unit on Rockaway Peninsula (including Jacob Riis Park, Fort Tilden and westernmost point of peninsula); the Jamaica Bay unit (including Jamica Bay Wildlife Refuge in Queens and

Canarsie Pier, Plumb Beach, and Floyd Bennett Field in Brooklyn); and the Staten Isl. unit (consisting of Great Kills Park and Miller Field and beaches on the Atlantic Ocean).

Gathright Dam, Va.: see JACKSON RIVER.

Gatineau (GAT-i-no), city (1991 pop. 92,284), SW Que., Canada, at the junction of the Gatineau and Ottawa rivers, adjoining Hull (suburb of Ottawa); 45°29′N 75°39′W. The 5th-largest city in Que., it was created through the merger of 7 municipalities. Its diversified industrial base has led to rapid growth and extensive development since the mid-1970s. Mfg. (plastics, edible fats and oils, metal doors, structured lumber); pulp mill.

Gatineau (GAT-i-no), river, c.240 mi/390 km long, Canada; rising in the Laurentians, SW Que., and flowing S to the Ottawa R. at Hull, Ont. Several rapids with hydroelectric power plants.

Gatineau National Capital Commission Park (□ 56 sq mi/145 sq km), SW Que., Canada, SE tip of park on edge of Hull, extends NW 30 mi/48 km to beyond Lac La Peche. Park is 8 mi/13 km wide at center. Located in Canadian Shield, W of Gatineau R. valley. Est. 1934 to prevent environmental damage from firewood collectors during the Depression. Greatly expanded after 1950 when it was incorporated into the Natl. Capital Region master plan by urban planner Jacques Greber. Administered by N.C.C., it serves both as a recreational area for the Ottawa region and symbolizes the "green image" of the capital city and the country. Hardwood and conifer forests; large stands of oak, maple. Fishing, hiking, camping, bicycling, swimming, picnicking, skiing.

Gatliff, village, Whitley co., SE Ky., 8 mi/12.9 km ESE of Williamsburg, near Pine Mt. in the Cumberland Mts. Bituminous coal mining.

Gatlinburg, city (1990 pop. 3,417), Sevier co., E Tenn., 30 mi/48 km SE of Knoxville, in Great Smoky Mts. Natl. Park (hq. nearby); 35°43′N 83°31′W. Handicraft workshops (pottery, wood). Has several mus., an art school, and a settlement school. Mt. Le Conte is just SE. Inc. 1945.

Gattman (GAT-muhn), village (1990 pop. 120), Monroe co., E Miss., near Ala. state line and Buttahatchie R., 19 mi/31 km ENE of Aberdeen; 33°53′N 88°14′W. Agr. area (cotton, corn; cattle); mfg. (apparel).

Gauley Bridge, village (1990 pop. 691), Fayette co., S central W.Va., on Gauley R. (joins New R. 2 mi/3.2 km S to form Kanawha R.), 25 mi/40 km ESE of Charleston; 38°10′N 81°12′W. Includes locality of Charlton Heights. Hawks Nest State Park and 3-mi/4.8-km-long Hawks Nest Tunnel to SE, which diverts New R. waters (impounded here by Hawks Nest Dam) to a hydroelectric plant. In Civil War, Gen. Rosecrans defeated a Confederate force here in 1861.

Gauley Mountain, W.Va.: see BIG SPRUCE KNOB.

Gauley River 1 (GAW-lee), Natl. Recreation Area (□ 16 sq mi/41 sq km), Fayette and Nicholas cos., W.Va., 7 mi/11.3 km SW of Summersville. Passes through scenic valleys and gorges of Gauley and Meadow rivers. Authorized 1988. White-water rafting. **2** (GAW-lee), river, 104 mi/167 km long, SE W.Va.; rises in the Allegheny Mts. in W Pocahontas co., NW of Marlinton; flows generally WSW, past Summersville, and through Summersville L. reservoir (Wildlife Management Area) and Gauley R.; 38°24′N 80°14′W. Natl. Recreation Area, joins New R. 2 mi/3.2 km S of Gauley Bridge to form Kanawha R. Carnifex Ferry State Park (□ 275 acres/111 ha) is on its banks, 7 mi/11.3 km SW of Summerville; marks scene of Civil War engagement (1861) won by Union troops. White-water rafting.

Gaultois Island (GOL-tuhs) or **Long Island** (□ 34 sq mi/88 sq km), in Hermitage Bay, S N.F., Canada, 10 mi/16 km long, 2 mi/3 km–7 mi/11 km wide; 47°40′N 56′W. Rises to 725 ft/221 m (W). Gaultois, on E coast, is fishing settlement.

Gause, uninc. village (1990 pop. 400), Milam co., central Texas, 22 mi/35 km WNW of Bryan. In cotton, cattle, corn area.

Gautier (go-SHAI), city (1990 pop. 10,088), Jackson co.,

SE Miss., residential suburb 4 mi/6.4 km W of Pascagoula, on Mississippi Sound, Gulf of Mexico, at mouth of Pascagoula R. (bridged to Pascagoula); 30°23′N 88°38′W. Light mfg. Shepard State Park to SW; Mississippi Sandhill Crane Natl. Wildlife Refuge to NW. Seat of Mississippi Gulf Community Col., Jackson co. campus.

Gaviota, uninc. village, Santa Barbara co., SW Calif., on Santa Barbara Channel, 29 mi/47 km W of Santa Barbara. Fruit, vegetables, grains; flowers; cattle. Vessels load oil from offshore pipelines here, Gaviota State Park. Gaviota Pass crosses Santa Ynez Mts. to N. Part of Los Padres Natl. Forest to N; Refugio State Beach and El Capitan State Park to E.

Gay, town (1990 pop. 133), Meriwether co., W Ga., 26 mi/42 km ENE of La Grange; 33°05′N 84°34′W. Site of biannual festival, the Cotton Pickin' County Fair, held in May and Oct.

Gay, W.Va.: see MOUNT GAY.

Gay Head, town (1990 pop. 201), Dukes co., SE Mass., 15 mi/24 km WSW of Edgartown; 41°23′N 70°51′W. Resort area, fishing; pottery, brick. Lighthouse on colorful clay cliffs here since 1799. Most famous glacial clay cliffs on the East Coast. Wampanog Indian Territory in Gay Head. Famous site of brick industry. Settled 1669, inc. 1870.

Gayle, town (1991 pop. 3,205), St. Mary parish, N Jamaica, 8 mi/12.9 km SW of Port Maria; 18°20′N 77°00′W. Tropical fruit.

Gayle Mill, uninc. town (1990 pop. 1,037), Chester co., N S.C., residential suburb 2 mi/3.2 km SW of Chester; 34°42′N 81°14′W. Chester State Park to SW.

Gaylesville (GAILS-vil), farming town (1990 pop. 149), Cherokee co., NE Ala., on Chattooga R., near Ga. state line, 10 mi/16 km NE of Centre.

Gaylord 1 town (1990 pop. 3,256), ☉ Otsego co., N Mich., 27 mi/43 km SE of Petoskey; 45°01′N 84°40′W. Trade center for agr. (potatoes; livestock; dairying); lumbering; mfg. (wood prods., electronic equip., publishing); lake resort area. Airport to W. Otsego L. to S; Michawaye Slopes Ski Area to SE. Inc. as village 1881, as city 1922. **2** town (1990 pop. 1,935), ☉ Sibley co., S Minn., 55 mi/89 km SW of Minneapolis; 44°32′N 94°13′W. Elev. 996 ft/304 m. Trade point in agr. area (grain; livestock; dairying); mfg. (food, bldg. materials). Plotted 1881.

Gaylord, village (1990 pop. 173), Smith co., N Kansas, on North Fork of Solomon R., 9 mi/14.5 km SSW of Smith Center; 39°38′N 98°50′W. Cattle, hogs; wheat, rye, sorghum.

Gays, village (1990 pop. 237), Moultrie co., central Ill., 13 mi/21 km SSE of Sullivan; 39°27′N 88°30′W. In agr. area.

Gays Mills, village (1990 pop. 578), Crawford co., SW Wis., on Kickapoo R., 24 mi/39 km NE of Prairie du Chien; 43°19′N 90°50′W. In farm area. Apples; poultry; butter and other dairy prods.; flour, feed, concrete. Snow Bowl Ski Area to S.

Gayville, village (1990 pop. 401), Yankton co., SE S.Dak., 11 mi/18 km E of Yankton; 42°53′N 97°10′W. In agr. area.

Gearhart (GIR-hart), town (1990 pop. 1,027), Clatsop co., NW Oregon, 12 mi/19 km SSW of Astoria, on Pacific Ocean, at mouth of Neacoxie Creek, which parallels the Pacific Ocean E of coast; 46°01′N 123°55′W. Beach resort. Seafood. Saddle Mt. State Park to SE; Del Rey Beach State Wayside to N. Seaside State Airport to SE. Camp Rilea Military Reservation to N.

Geary (GIR-ee), county (□ 403 sq mi/1,044 sq km; 1990 pop. 30,453), E central Kansas; ☉ Junction City; 39°00′N 96°45′W. Region of low hills drained in W by Smoky Hill and Republican rivers, which join at Junction City to form Kansas R. Livestock; grain; electronic equip. Formed 1889.

Geary (GIR-ee), city (1990 pop. 1,347), on Blaine-Canadian co. line, central Okla., 22 mi/35 km WNW of El Reno, bet. Canadian and North Canadian rivers; 35°37′N 98°19′W. Trade and processing center for wheat, livestock, and dairy area. Founded 1898.

Geauga (jee-O-guh), county (□ 407 sq mi/1,054 sq km;

1990 pop. 81,129), NE Ohio; ☉ Chardon, 41°30′N 81°10′W. Drained by Cuyahoga, Chagrin, and Grand rivers; includes several small lakes. In the Glaciated Plain physiographic region. Agr. area (dairy prods., corn, fruit, poultry); mfg. at Chardon and Middlefield (chemical preparations, furniture, plastic prods., construction machinery). Formed 1805.

Gebhard State Park, Ill.: see MORRIS.

Gebo (JEE-bo), village, Hot Springs co., N central Wyo., near Bighorn R., 10 mi/16 km N of Thermopolis, 2 mi/3.2 km SW of Kirby. Elev. 4,570 ft/1,393 m. Coal mines. Gebo had a pop. of 200 in the 1960s, but is now virtually a ghost town.

Geddes, village (1990 pop. 280), Charles Mix co., S S.Dak., 10 mi/16 km NW of L. Andes; 43°15′N 98°42′W. Business center for agr. area; mfg. On W edge of Yankton Indian Reservation.

Geddes, Mount (GE-dis) (11,000 ft/3,353 m), SW B.C., Canada, in Coast Mts., 180 mi/290 km NW of Vancouver; 51°27′N 125°20′W.

Geiger (GEI-guhr), town (1990 pop. 270), Sumter co., W Ala., near Miss. state line, c.22 mi/35 km NNW of Livingston.

Geismar (GEIZ-muhr), uninc. village, Ascension parish, SE La., 16 mi/26 km SE of Baton Rouge, on E bank of Mississippi R.; 30°12′N 91°01′W. Agr. area known for its antebellum homes. Heavily industrialized area; mfg. includes chemicals.

Geist Reservoir, in Marion, Hamilton, and Hancock cos., central Ind., on Fall R., 12 mi/19 km NE of Indianapolis, 6 mi/9.7 km long; 39°52′N 85°59′W. Formed by Geist Dam, built by the Indianapolis Water Co. for water supply.

Geistown (GEIS-toun), borough (1990 pop. 2,749), Cambria co., W central Pa., residential suburb 3 mi/4.8 km SE of Johnstown. Johnstown-Cambria County Airport to NE; Univ. of Pittsburg–Johnstown Campus to SE. Part of Gallitzin State Forest to SE.

Gem, county (□ 565 sq mi/1,463 sq km; 1990 pop. 11,844), W Idaho; ☉ Emmett; 44°04′N 116°25′W. Irrigated agr. and timber area; drained by Payette R. and Squaw Creeks. Hay, alfalfa, oats, corn, barley, wheat, sugar beets, vegetables, potatoes, fruit (apples, pears, peaches, plums, cherries, nectarines); dairying. Located in Snake R. Plain. Part of Boise Natl. Forest in N end; Black Canyon Dam, on Payette, in S; mts. in N. Formed 1915.

Gem (JEM), village (1990 pop. 104), Thomas co., NW Kansas, near Prairie Dog Creek, 7 mi/11.3 km ENE of Colby; 39°25′N 100°54′W. Agr., livestock raising.

Gem Lake, village (1990 pop. 439), Ramsey co., E Minn., residential suburb 7 mi/11.3 km NNE of St. Paul; 45°03′N 93°01′W. White Bear L. to NE.

Genaro Codina (he-NAH-ro ko-DEE-nah), town (1990 pop. 1,552), ☉ Genaro Codina municipio, S Zacatecas, Mexico, 22 mi/35 km S of Zacatecas, 10 mi/16 km N of San Pedro Piedra Gorda on unpaved secondary road. Temperate climate. Agr. (corn, beans, chile, fruits), cattle and poultry breeding. Formerly known as San Jose de la Isla.

Gene Autry, village (1990 pop. 97), Carter co., S Okla., 8 mi/12.9 km NE of Ardmore, near Washita R. and mouth of Caddo R.; 34°16′N 97°02′W. In farm area; mfg. Formerly Berwyn; renamed for cowboy film star and Okla. native Gene Autry.

General Bravo (he-NE-rahl BRAH-vo), town (1990 pop. 4,980), ☉ General Bravo municipio, Nuevo León, N Mexico, on San Juan R. (irrigation), 70 mi/113 km ENE of Monterrey on Mexico Highway 40; 25°47′N 99°10′W. Elev. 492 ft/150 m. Cotton, sugarcane, cereals, cactus fibers.

General Canuto A. Neri, Mexico: see ACAPETLAHUAYA.

General Cepeda (he-NE-rahl se-PE-dah), town (1990 pop. 3,238), ☉ General Cepeda municipio, Coahuila, N Mexico, in Sierra Madre Oriental, on secondary road, on RR, 30 mi/48 km W of Saltillo; 25°24′N 101°30′W. Elev. 4,967 ft/1,514 m. Agr. center (corn, beans, alfalfa, istle fibers, candelilla wax; cattle).

General Enrique Estrada, town (1990 pop. 2,768), central Zacatecas, Mexico, 20 mi/29 km NW of Zacatecas on Mexico Highway 45-49; 23°00′N 102°43′W. Elev. 7,120 ft/2,170 m. Farming and livestock raising.

General Escobedo (he-NE-rahl es-ko-BE-do), town (1990 pop. 96,962), Nuevo León, N Mexico, on RR, 10 mi/16 km N of Monterrey; 25°50′N 100°21′W. Elev. c.1,640 ft/500 m. A working-class suburb of Monterrey; part of the Monterrey metropolitan area.

General Felipe Ángeles, Mexico: see SAN PABLO DE LAS TUNAS.

General Heliodoro Castillo, Mexico: see TLACOTEPEC.

General Joaquín Amaro (he-ne-RAHL wah-KEEN ah-MAHR-o), town (1990 pop. 606), Zacatecas, N central Mexico, 65 mi/105 km SW of Zacatecas. Elev. 6,253 ft/1,906 m. Grain, beans, fruits; livestock. Also known as El Plateado.

General Pánfilo Natera (he-NE-rahl PAHN-fee-lo nah-TE-rah), town (1990 pop. 3,591), Zacatecas, N central Mexico, 30 mi/48 km ESE of Zacatecas on Mexico Highway 49. Cereals, maguey; livestock; silver deposits. Also known as La Blanca.

General Pedro Antonio Santos, Mexico: see TANCANHUITZ DE SANTOS.

General Plutarco Elías Calles, Mexico: see SONOITA.

General Simón Bolívar (he-NE-rahl see-MON bo-LEE-vahr), congregación (1990 pop. 1,326) and township, Durango, N Mexico, on affluent of Aguanaval R., 60 mi/97 km SSE of Torreón on RR; 24°42′N 103°15′W. Antimony mining; silver, gold, lead deposits. Formerly called San Bartolo.

General Terán (he-NE-rahl te-RAHN), town (1990 pop. 6,139), Nuevo León, N Mexico, 45 mi/72 km SE of Monterrey on Río Pilón; 25°18′N 99°40′W. Agr. center (fruit, grain, cactus fibers; livestock).

General Treviño (he-NE-rahl tre-VEEN-yo), town (1990 pop. 1,612), Nuevo León, N Mexico, in lowland, 65 mi/105 km NE of Monterrey on Mexico Highway 54; 26°13′N 99°30′W. Corn, cotton, sugarcane, cactus fibers.

General Trías (he-NE-rahl TREE-ahs), town (1990 pop. 1,103), ⊙ General Trías municipio, Chihuahua, N Mexico, at W foot of Sierra Madre Occidental, 28 mi/45 km SW of Chihuahua; 28°20′N 106°20′W. Elev. 4,695 ft/1,431 m. Agr. (corn, fruit, beans; cattle). Formerly called Santa Isabel.

General Zaragoza, Mexico: see ZARAGOZA, Nuevo León.

General Zuazua (he-NE-rahl soo-ah-SOO-ah), town (1990 pop. 3,670), ⊙ General Zuazua municipio, Nuevo León, N Mexico, on Salinas R., 20 mi/32 km NE of Monterrey. Elev. 1,640 ft/500 m. Agr. (grain, cotton, sugarcane; livestock).

Genesee 1 (JE-nuh-SEE), county (□ 649 sq mi/1,681 sq km; 1990 pop. 430,459), SE central Mich.; ⊙ Flint; 43°01′N 83°42′W. Drained by Flint and Shiawassee rivers. Agr. (dairy prods.; cattle, poultry; apples, strawberries, corn, wheat, oats, soybeans, cucumbers, forage crops, beans). Mfg. at Flint. Summer resorts. Organized 1836. **2** county (□ 495 sq mi/1,282 sq km; 1990 pop. 60,060), W N.Y.; ⊙ Batavia; 43°00′N 78°11′W. Drained by Tonawanda and Oak Orchard creeks. Diversified mfg. at Batavia; agr. area (dairy prods.; poultry; fruit, wheat, beans, sweet corn, field corn, peas, hay); timber; sand and gravel; expanded perlite and natural gas; gypsum quarries. Name derived from Seneca word meaning "good valley," referring to the Genesee R. Valley. Co. originally included most of W N.Y. Ingram Univ., founded in 1837 but closed in 1902, was one of the 1st chartered univs. for women. Site of N.Y. State School for the Blind, which opened in 1865 in Batavia. In summer of 1826, Batavia resident William Morgan, a Mason, published secrets of Freemasonry. He was arrested, harassed, and finally kidnapped, and was never seen again. The resulting public outcry led to creation of Anti-Masonic Party. By 1832 other events eclipsed the issue. Includes part of Tonawanda Indian Reservation. Formed 1802.

Genesee, town (1990 pop. 725), Latah co., W Idaho, 12 mi/19 km SSE of Moscow; 46°33′N 116°56′W. RR terminus. Agr. (barley, oats). Nez Perce Indian Reservation to SE.

Genesee (JE-nuh-SEE), uninc. village, Genesee township, Potter co., N Pa., 16 mi/26 km NNE of Coudersport, on Genesee R., near N.Y. state line; 41°59′N 77°51′W. Agr. (grain; dairying; livestock); mfg. (furniture, hardware).

Genesee (JE-nuh-SEE), river, 158 mi/254 km long, Pa. and N.Y.; rises in the Allegheny Mts., in N central Potter co., Pa., at Ulysses; 41°53′N 77°43′W. Flows NNW into N.Y., past Wellsville, turns NNE at Houghton, through Mt. Morris reservoir, in Letchworth State Park, past Genesco and through city of Rochester, to L. Ontario 6 mi/9.7 km N of Rochester. The N.Y. State Barge Canal (Erie Canal) crosses river SW of Rochester.

Genesee Depot (JE-nuh-SEE), village, Waukesha co., SE Wis., 8 mi/12.9 km in agr. area. Mfg. (fireworks). Glacial Drumlin State Trail to N. Near Kettle Moraine State Forest (S unit) to SW.

Genesee Valley, W N.Y. A beautiful, broad valley with rich alluvial soils, it was already being used by the Seneca Nation prior to the Revolutionary War. Immediately after the war, postcolonial settlement occurred rapidly. With the completion of the Erie Canal, soon followed by RRs, the valley and region stretching to its W became the breadbasket not only of N.Y. state but for the whole country, with Rochester, the "flour city," as its center. Even today, grain growing remains an important industry; others include dairying, beef and horse raising, and growing and processing of vegetables. Valley has the cultural and historical legacy of the development of W N.Y. from the late 18th cent. onward.

Geneseo (je-nuh-SEE-o), city (1990 pop. 5,990), Henry co., NW Ill., near old Illinois and Mississippi Canal (now Hennepin Canal State Trail), 11 mi/18 km N of Cambridge; 41°27′N 90°09′W. Farm trade center in agr. (corn, oats, wheat; livestock) area. Mfg. (food prods.). Settled 1836, inc. 1855.

Geneseo 1 (je-nuh-SEE-o), village (1990 pop. 382), Rice co., central Kansas, 12 mi/19 km N of Lyons; 38°31′N 98°09′W. RR junction. In wheat area; oil refining. Oil and gas wells nearby. **2** village (□ 2 sq mi/5.2 sq km; 1990 pop. 7,187), ⊙ Livingston co., W central N.Y., on Genesee R., 28 mi/45 km SSW of Rochester; 42°47′N 77°48′W. Trade center in agr. area (peas, corn); mfg. (athletic clothing and sportswear); salt deposits. Major salt mine cave-in and diversion of surface drainage into subterranean channels occurred in 1995. Estates of the Wadsworth family, NE and S of village. Eng.-style Genesee Valley Hunt each fall. Summer residence and recreation at Conegus L. 7 mi/11.3 km E. Seat of State Univ. of N.Y. Col. at Geneseo. Settled c.1790, inc. 1832.

Geneva, county (□ 578 sq mi/1,497 sq km; 1990 pop. 23,647), SE Ala.; ⊙ Geneva. Coastal plain bordering on Fla., drained by Pea and Choctawhatchee rivers. Poultry; peanuts, corn, soybeans. Formed 1868.

Geneva 1 city (1990 pop. 12,617), ⊙ Kane co., NE Ill., on Fox R. (bridged here), satellite community 5 mi/56 km W of Chicago; 41°52′N 88°18′W. In agr. area (grain, livestock; dairy prods.); mfg. (RR accessories, printing). Illinois Youth Center to W. Founded c.1833, inc. 1867. **2** city (1990 pop. 14,143), Ontario co., W central N.Y., in the Finger Lakes region, at N end of Seneca L.; 42°52′N 76°59′W. Located in a farm area; mfg. (cans and canning machinery, paper containers, metal and optical prods., and water purification systems). It also has printing plants. Hobart Col. and William Smith Col. are in the city. N.Y. state est. an agr. experiment station here in 1882; in 1923, it became part of Cornell Univ. Settled 1788; inc. as village in 1812, as city in 1897. **3** city (1990 pop. 6,597), Ashtabula co., extreme NE Ohio, 8 mi/13 km WSW of Ashtabula; 41°48′N 80°57′W. Historic and operational wineries. Lake resort 5 mi/8 km N. Settled 1802; inc. 1867.

Geneva 1 town (1990 pop. 4,681), ⊙ Geneva co., SE Ala., at confluence of Choctawhatchee and Pea rivers, 32 mi/51 km SW of Dothan, near Fla. state line. Clothing, aluminum prods., lumber. Settled 1836, inc. 1872. **2** (juh-NEE-vuh), town (1990 pop. 182), Talbot co., W Ga., 27 mi/43 km ENE of Columbus; 32°35′N 84°33′W. **3** town (1990 pop 1,280), Adams co., E Ind., on the Wabash, 16 mi/26 km S of Decatur; 40°36′N 84°58′W. In agr. area. Mfg. (fabricated metal prods., refrigeration components). Gene Stratton Porter lived here (Limberlost State Memorial). **4** town (1990 pop. 169), Franklin co., N central Iowa, 6 mi/9.7 km SE of Hampton; 42°40′N 93°07′W. Livestock; grain. **5** town (1990 pop. 2,310), ⊙ Fillmore co., SE Nebr., 23 mi/37 km S of Fork, on branch of Big Blue R.; 40°31′N 97°35′W. Trade, cattle-shipping center; flour, feed; dairy and poultry prods., grain. Mfg. (vinyl and cloth medical supplies, steel tubing). Plotted 1858.

Geneva (juh-NEE-vuh), village (1990 pop. 444), Freeborn co., S Minn., 14 mi/23 km NNE of Albert Lea at N end of Geneva L. and S end of Titlow L.; 43°49′N 93°16′W. Dairying; poultry, cattle, hogs, sheep; corn, oats, soybeans; mfg. (crates). Rush R. State Park to E.

Geneva, Lake, resort lake, Walworth co., SE Wis., near Ill. state line; c.8 mi/12.9 km long, c.1 mi/1.6 km wide. Lake Geneva city, on NE shore, is largest resort; others are Fontana at W end and Williams Bay on N shore. Fishing, year-round lake sports. Drained by White R. Big Foot Beach State Park at E end.

Geneva-on-the-Lake (juh-NEE-vuh), resort village (1990 pop. 1,626), Astabula co., extreme NE Ohio, just N of Geneva, 8 mi/13 km W of Ashtabula, on L. Erie; 41°51′N 80°57′W. Site of Geneva State Park.

Genoa, city (1990 pop. 3,083), De Kalb co., N Ill., on South Branch of Kishwaukee R. (bridged here), 9 mi/14.5 km NNW of Sycamore; 42°06′N 88°41′W. RR junction. In rich agr. area (dairying; hogs, sheep; corn, soybeans); mfg. (tools, communication equip.). Inc. 1876.

Genoa 1 village (1990 pop. 167), Lincoln co., E central Colo., 10 mi/16 km E of Limon, near source of Hell Creek; 39°16′N 103°30′W. Elev. 5,602 ft/1,707 m. Wheat, sunflowers; cattle. **2** (juh-NO-uh), village (1990 pop. 1,082), Nance co., E central Nebr., 20 mi/32 km W of Columbus, near Loup R.; 41°27′N 97°43′W. RR junction. Dairy prods., grain. Pawnee Indian village excavated nearby. Diversion dam on Loup R. Settled 1857. **3** (juh-NO-uh), uninc. village, Douglas co., extreme W Nev., 12 mi/19 km SSW of Carson City, bet. Carson Range and Carson R., in foothills of Sierra Nevadas. Elev. 4,788 ft/1,459 m. Founded c.1849 as Mormon Station, renamed 1855. Was 1st permanent settlement in state. Was capital of Douglas co. 1861–1916. Old courthouse (1865) is now a mus. Toiyabe Natl. Forest to W; L. Tahoe 5 mi/8 km W; Mormon Station State Historical Park is here. Hot springs, pools est. 1862, remodeled 1929. **4** (juh-NO-uh), village (1990 pop. 500), Cayuga co., W central N.Y., in Finger Lakes region, 19 mi/31 km S of Auburn; 42°38′N 76°34′W. **5** village (1990 pop. 2,262), Ottawa co., N Ohio, 13 mi/21 km SE of Toledo; 41°31′N 83°22′W. Settled 1835 as Stony Ridge Station. **6** village, Harris co., S Texas, 12 mi/19 km SE of Houston. In vegetable farm area. Ellington Air Force Base, now closed, served as military air base in both World Wars. **7** (juh-NO-uh), village (1990 pop. 266), Vernon co., SW Wis., on the Mississippi, 17 mi/27 km S of La Crosse; 43°34′N 91°13′W. Fishing. Lock and Dam No. 8 on the Mississippi here. Upper Mississippi Wildlife and Fish Area along river.

Genoa City, town (1990 pop. 1,277), Kenosha and Walworth cos., SE Wis., on Ill. line, near small L. Elizabeth, 8 mi/12.9 km SE of Lake Geneva city; 42°30′N 88°19′W. In dairy-farm area. Mfg. (furnaces, food prods.).

Genola (je-NO-luh), town (1990 pop. 803), Utah co., N central Utah, just S of Utah L., 20 mi/32 km SW of Provo; 40°01′N 111°50′W. Fruit orchards. Uinta Natl. Forest to SE; Mona Reservoir to S. Settled early 1860s.

Genola (je-NO-luh), village (1990 pop. 85), Morrison co., central Minn., 13 mi/21 km E of Little Falls, near Skunk R.; 45°58′N 94°06′W. Agr. area (grain; dairying).

Gentilly (zhah-tee-YEE), village, S Que., Canada, on the St. Lawrence R., 14 mi/23 km ENE of Trois Rivières; 46°24′N 72°34′W. Dairying; pigs; lumbering.

Gentry, county (□ 488 sq mi/1264 sq km; 1990 pop. 6,848), NW Mo.; ⊙ Albany; 40°13′N 94°24′W. Drained by Grand R. Corn, soybeans; cattle, hogs, poultry. Light mfg. at Albany and Stanberry. Formed 1841.

Gentry 1 town (1990 pop. 1,726), Benton co., extreme

NW Ark., 6 mi/9.7 km NE of Siloam Springs, in the Ozarks; 36°16′N 94°28′W. Mfg. (plastic prods., food, furniture). Location of major electricity generation plant. Also called Gentry City. **2** town (1990 pop. 95), Gentry co., NW Mo., on Middle Fork of Grand R., 6 mi/9.7 km NW of Albany; 40°19′N 94°25′W.

Gentryville, town (1990 pop. 277), Spencer co., SW Ind., near Little Pigeon Creek, 15 mi/24 km N of Rockport; 38°07′N 87°02′W.

George, county (□ 483 sq mi/1,251 sq km; 1990 pop. 16,673), SE Miss.; ⊙ Lucedale; 30°52′N 88°38′W. Bordered E by Ala., W by De Soto Natl. Forest; drained by Pascagoula (formed by joining of Leaf and Chickasawhay rivers in NW) and Escatawpa rivers and Black and Red creeks. Agr. (vegetables, corn; timber). Part of Pascagoula R. Wildlife Management Area in S. Formed 1910.

George, town (1990 pop. 1,066), Lyon co., NW Iowa, near Little Rock R., 11 mi/18 km SE of Rock Rapids; 43°20′N 96°00′W. Inc. 1889.

George, village (1990 pop. 253), Grant co., E central Wash., 27 mi/43 km W of Moses Lake, on West Canal; Columbia R. to W; 47°05′N 119°52′W. Irrigated agr. area (vegetables, sugar beets, beans, potatoes, wheat). Winery. Major summer concert site.

George, river, c.345 mi/560 km long, Canada; rises in a lake on the Que.-Lab. boundary. It flows N through Indian L. (□ 125 sq mi/324 sq km) to Ungava Bay (an arm of Hudson Strait).

George Air Force Base, Calif.: see ADELANTO and VICTORVILLE.

George Bay, inlet of the Gulf of St. Lawrence, NE N.S., Canada, at E end of Northumberland Strait, forming SW shore of Cape Breton Isl. Bay is 20 mi/32 km long, 20 mi/32 km wide at entrance. Strait of Canso connects it with the Atlantic.

George, Cape, on Northumberland Strait, NE N.S., Canada, on W of entrance to George Bay, 18 mi/29 km NNE of Antigonish; 45°53′N 61°54′W.

George, Fort, Canada: see PRINCE GEORGE.

George Hill, summit (2,946 ft/898 m) of the Alleghenies, in Garrett co., extreme NW Md., SE of Accident.

George, Lake 1 (□ 3 sq mi/8 sq km), SW N.B., Canada, 20 mi/32 kim WSW of Fredericton, 3 mi/5 km long, 2 mi/3 km wide; drains into St. John R. **2** a widening of St. Marys R., in S central Ont., Canada, and E Upper Peninsula, Mich., 10 mi/16 km E of Sault Ste. Marie and E of Sugar Isl.; c.11 mi/18 km long, 2 mi/3 km–8 mi/13 km wide. Traversed by internatl. line.

George, Lake 1 a widening of St. Johns R., NE Fla., 19 mi/31 km S of Palatka; c.11 mi/18 km long, 5 mi/8 km–7 mi/11.3 km wide. **2** reservoir, Hobart city, Lake co., NW Ind., on Deep Creek; c.3 mi/4.8 km long; 41°31′N 87°14′W. Residential and recreational area. **3** glacial lake, in the foothills of the Adirondack Mts., NE N.Y., 33 mi/53 km long and 1 mi/1.6 km–3 mi/4.8 km wide; 43°33′N 73°38′W. It drains NE via rapids and waterfalls into L. Champlain. The lake was discovered in 1646 by Isaac Jogues, a Fr. Jesuit missionary, who named it Lac du St. Sacrement; the Eng. colonial leader Sir William Johnson renamed it for George III in 1755. During the Fr. and Indian War and the Amer. Revolution, the area around L. George was the scene of many battles. The ruins of Fort George (built 1759) and Fort William Henry are at the S end of the lake; historic Fort Ticonderoga, a natl. historic landmark, is at the N end. L. George, with numerous small isls., is noted for its scenery. The lake and the adjacent village of Lake George remain a center of a resort area that attracts tourists and vacationers year-round.

George Parks Highway or **Parks Highway**, running S to central Alaska. Formerly known as Anchorage-Fairbanks Highway; renamed and designated Alaska Route 3 in 1975, 4 years after its completion. Originates at Glenn Highway (Route 1), 25 mi/40 km NE of Anchorage, in delta of Matanuska Valley, Alaska's main agr. region. The paved highway 1st heads W to Wasilla and Houston, then gradually turns N. Beyond Willow, the highway follows the Susitna R., then it crosses the Chulitna R. by bridge. It passes through Denali State Park, affording views of Mt. McKinley (20,320 ft/6,193 m), highest point in N. Amer., and the Alaska Range. The Denali Highway. (Route 8), intersects it from E at Cantwell; then it passes the E end of Denali Natl. Park and Preserve. A restricted spur road goes W into the park to Wonder L. and Kantishna. The highway continues N, following in part the Nenana R., crossing the Tanana R. at village of Nenana. Turning to NE, it reaches Fairbanks, passing the Univ. of Alaska campus, ending at intersection of Alaska Highway, from SE, and Steese Highway, from N. The entire 358-mi/576-km length of the highway follows or closely parallels the Alaska RR.

George Richards, Cape, N extremity of Melville Isl., W central Franklin dist., N.W.T., Canada, on Hazen Strait; 76°50′N 109°10′W.

George Rogers Clark National Memorial and Historical Park, historic site, SW Ind., located near the site of old Fort Sackville, seized from British by Gen. G. R. Clark in 1779. Authorized 1966.

George Town, town (1989 pop. 12,921), ⊙ Cayman Isls., West Indies, on W end of Grand Cayman isl., 210 mi/338 km WNW of Montego Bay (Jamaica); 19°17′N 81°23′W. Major offshore banking and business center with some 500 banks. Many U.S. and internatl. companies have established subsidiaries here because of the tax advantages. Tourism, diving, and duty-free shopping are the town's other principal economic activities.

George Washington Birthplace, natl. monument, Westmoreland co., E Va., 32 mi/51 km E of Fredericksburg, on Potomac R.; 38°11′N 76°55′W. Covers an area of 538 acres/218 ha. Authorized 1930, includes Wakefield estate and reconstructed mansion; tombs of 3 previous generations of Washington's paternal ancestors.

George Washington Bridge, vehicular suspension bridge across the Hudson R., bet. Manhattan borough of N.Y. city and Fort Lee, N.J.; 40°51′N 73°57′W. Constructed 1927–1931. It is one of the longest suspension bridges in the world. Its main span is 3,500 ft/1,067 m long and 250 ft/76 m above the water. Cass Gilbert was the consulting architect, and O. H. Ammann was in general charge of the planning and construction. In 1962 a lower deck of 6 lanes was completed.

George Washington Carver Natl. Monument, at Diamond, Newton co., SW Mo. Birthplace and boyhood home of George Washington Carver, the monument is on 210 acres/85 ha of land. This Afr.-Amer. scientist developed hundreds of agr. prods. and taught scientific agr. Authorized 1943.

George Washington Memorial Parkway, passing through Fairfax and Arlington cos., N Va., and Montgomery co., SW Md.; 38°58′N 77°13′W. Parkway connecting landmarks associated with life of George Washington along both sides of Potomac R. from Great Falls to Mt. Vernon on Va. side and Great Falls to Chain Bridge on Md. side. Authorized 1930

George West, town (1990 pop. 2,586), ⊙ Live Oak co., S Texas, on Nueces R., 24 mi/39 km W of Beeville; 28°19′N 98°07′W. In cotton-, corn-, cattle-, and hog-raising area. Oil and gas; mfg. (feeds). L. Corpus Christi reservoir to SE. Inc. c.1940.

Georges Island, island, E Mass., Boston Harbor, SE of Boston, bet. Dorchester and Quincy bays. Site of Fort Warren (which saw action in the Civil War, World War I, and World War II). Hq. and visitor center of the Boston Harbor Isls. State Park. Summer ferry service from Boston.

Georges Islands, isl. group in Muscongus Bay, Knox co., S Maine, SW of Port Clyde; include Allen (1.5 mi/2.4 km long, ½ mi/⅘ km wide), Burnt (0.75 mi/1.2 km in diameter), and smaller Benner, Davis, and Thompson isls.

Georges Mills, resort village, Sullivan co., W N.H., in Sunapee town, at N end of L. Sunapee, 6 mi/9.7 km NE of Newport.

Georges Run, village, Jefferson co., E Ohio, on the Ohio, 4 mi/6 km S of Steubenville.

George-Town, town, central Bahama Isls., on E Great Exuma Isl., just above Tropic of Cancer, 140 mi/225 km SE of Nassau; 23°30′N 75°47′W. Livestock raising (sheep, goats, hogs). Has sheltered harbor. U.S. naval base was granted here 1940, but is now closed.

Georgetown 1 town, S Ont., Canada, 25 mi/40 km W of Toronto; 43°39′N 79°55′W. Now part of city of Halton Hills. Commuter suburb of Toronto. Paper milling; mfg. (confectionaries, refrigeration equip.); in dairying, sandstone-quarrying region. **2** town (1991 pop. 716), ⊙ Kings co., E P.E.I., Canada, on Cardigan Bay, on RR, 30 mi/48 km E of Charlottetown; 46°11′N 62°32′W. Fishing port; also ships agr. produce.

Georgetown, town (1989 est. pop. 7,521), E St. Vincent, West Indies, 10 mi/16 km NE of Kingstown; 13°16′N 61°07′W. In agr. region (sugarcane, cotton, arrowroot); sugar mill; also mfg. of rum and molasses.

Georgetown, county (□ 1,035 sq mi/2,681 sq km; 1990 pop. 46,302), E S.C.; ⊙ Georgetown; 33°24′N 79°17′W. Bounded by the Atlantic Ocean to the E; the Great Pee Dee R. to the NE, S by Santee R.; watered by Waccamaw, Sampit, and Black rivers; Winyah Bay in SE. Mfg. includes sand, clay, and limestone. Formerly a region of great plantations; economy is now based on timber, agr. includes cattle, corn, wheat, tobacco, hay, fishing, tourist trade. Formed 1798.

Georgetown 1 city (1990 pop. 3,678), Vermilion co., E Ill., near Little Vermilian R., 10 mi/16 km S of Danville; 39°58′N 87°37′W. Bituminous coal mines; agr. (corn, wheat, soybeans; livestock). Laid out 1827, inc. 1869. **2** city (1990 pop. 9,517), ⊙ Georgetown co., E S.C., 55 mi/89 km NE of Charleston at mouths of Sampit, Black, and Waccamaw rivers on Winyah Bay, c.15 mi/24 km from the ocean; 33°21′N 79°17′W. Historic port of entry and shipping center. Mfg. includes bailing wire, wire rods, lumber, textile printing, paper, auxiliaries, concrete, sportswear. Agr. includes livestock; grain, tobacco. Tourism is also a significant industry. The city was founded c.1734 as a shipping point for the plentiful rice and indigo prods. garnered from nearby plantations. Deepwater facilities were later added to the port. The Church of Prince George dates from the 1740s. Inc. 1805. **3** city (1990 pop. 14,842), ⊙ Williamson co., central Texas, at junction of North and South Forks to form San Gabriel R., 25 mi/40 km N of Austin; 30°38′N 97°41′W. Market for ranches (cattle) to W, farms to S and E (cotton, corn, wheat); mfg. limestone prods. Seat of Southwestern Univ. L. Georgetown to NW; Inner Space cavern on S side of city. Founded 1848, inc. 1871.

Georgetown 1 town (1990 pop. 891), ⊙ Clear Creek co., N central Colo., on headstream of Clear Creek, in Front Range, 40 mi/64 km W of Denver; 39°43′N 105°42′W. Elev. 8,519 ft/2,597 m. Georgetown Loop Narrow Gauge RR. Gold, silver, lead, copper mines. Tourism. Prior to 1878 one of most important silver camps in Colo. More than 200 original bldgs. still stand. Surrounded by Arapaho Natl. Forest. Eisenhower Tunnel (I-70) and Loveland Pass to W. **2** town (1990 pop. 3,732), ⊙ Sussex co., S Del., 33 mi/53 km S of Dover; 38°41′N 75°23′W. Junction of RR spur to Cape Henlopen. Market center for farm region; fruit, vegetables; livestock; poultry; dairying; mfg. (fruits and vegetables, communications equip., printing and publishing). Has historic bldgs., including Old Sussex County Courthouse. Del. Technical and Community Col. (Georgetown campus) is here. Sussex County Airport to E; Ellendale State Forest to NW; Redden State Forest to N. Inc. 1869. **3** town (1990 pop. 913), ⊙ Quitman co., SW Ga., on Chattahoochee R., 20 mi/32 km WNW of Cuthbert; 31°53′N 85°07′W. **4** town (1990 pop. 2,092), Floyd co., S Ind., 8 mi/12.9 km W of New Albany; 38°18′N 85°58′W. Agr. area; wood trusses. **5** town (1990 pop. 11,414), Scott co., N central Ky., 12 mi/19 km N of Lexington, in Bluegrass region, on North Elkhorn Creek; 38°12′N 84°32′W. In a rich agr., dairying, and livestock area; mfg. (crushed stone, motor vehicles, consumer goods, tools, mining equip., electrical equip., plastics). Georgetown–Scott County Regional Airport to E. Georgetown Col. here. Points of interest include City/County Mus., Royal Bridge on W Main St. (1796), Giddings Hall (c.1840). Was 1st "bourbon" whiskey made here by Reverend Elijah Craig, 1789, then part of Bourbon co., Va. Settled

1776, inc. 1790. **6** resort town (1990 pop. 914), Sagadahoc co., SW Maine, on several isls. at mouth of the Kennebec, 8 mi/12.9 km SSE of Bath; 43°48′N 69°45′W. Fishing. Includes Five Isls. and Robinhood villages. **7** town (1990 pop. 6,384), Essex co., NE Mass., 9 mi/14.5 km E of Lawrence; 42°43′N 71°00′W. Mfg. (shoes). State forest nearby. Includes Georgetown village. Settled 1639, inc. 1838. **8** town (1990 pop. 332), Copiah co., SW Miss., 30 mi/48 km S of Jackson, near Pearl R.; 31°52′N 90°09′W. In agr. (cotton, corn; cattle; dairying) and timber area; mfg. (hardwood lumber).

Georgetown 1 uninc. village, El Dorado co., E Calif., in the Sierra Nevada, 12 mi/19 km N of Placerville. Timber; gold; apples, walnuts; cattle, lamb, poultry. Was thriving gold camp in 1850s. Eldorado Natl. Forest to E. **2** village (1990 pop. 1,694), Fairfield co., SW Conn., on Norwalk R., 10 mi/16 km N of Norwalk; 41°15′N 73°25′W. Bicycle mfg. **3** village (1990 pop. 558), Bear Lake co., SE Idaho, 18 mi/29 km N of Paris, on Bear R.; 42°29′N 111°22′W. Elev. 6,006 ft/1,831 m. Center of agr. area (cattle, sheep; dairying; alfalfa, wheat, barley, oats). Meade Peak (10,541 ft/3,213 m) to E, Caribou Natl. Forest to E, Cache Natl. Forest to W. **4** village (1990 pop. 273), Grant parish, central La., 30 mi/48 km N of Alexandria, near Little R.; 31°46′N 92°23′W. Mfg. of jogging suits. Little R. State Wildlife Area to S, Catahoula Natl. Preserve and Kisatchie Natl. Forest to W. **5** village (1990 pop. 107), Clay co., W Minn., on Red R. at mouth of Buffalo R., 14 mi/23 km N of Fargo (N. Dak.); 47°04′N 96°47′W. Grain, potatoes, sugar beets, beans; livestock; dairying. **6** village (1990 pop. 3,627), ⊙ Brown co., SW Ohio, 36 mi/58 km SE of Cincinnati, on small White Oak Creek; 38°52′N 83°54′W. Laid out 1819. Boyhood home of Ulysses S. Grant is here; his birthplace (at Point Pleasant) is W. **7** uninc. village (1990 pop. 194), Luzerne co., NE central Pa., suburb 2 mi/3.2 km S of Wilkes-Barre; 41°12′N 75°52′W. In former anthracite coal–mining region; mfg. (plastics prods.), sand and gravel processing.

Georgetown, borough (1990 pop. 194), Beaver co., W Pa., on Ohio R., 4 mi/6.4 km ENE of East Liverpool (Ohio). Agr. (dairying; livestock; corn, hay). Raccoon Creek State Park to S.

Georgetown, residential section (since 1895) of Washington, D.C., on the Potomac R. near the confluence of Rock Creek; 38°54′N 77°04′W. Initially a river port, the town was part of the land granted by Md. in 1790 to the Federal govt. as the Federal Dist. of the natl. capital; in 1878 it became part of Washington, D.C. It is a bustling center for shopping, students, and tourists. Its picturesque old houses and colonial atmosphere (including the Dumbarton Oaks gardens, house, and mus.) lend it charm and attract Washington's elite. Wisconsin Ave., its main shopping street, attracts many tourists and has numerous restaurants and bars. Georgetown Univ., with its renowned foreign service school, is here. Settled c.1665, inc. as a town in 1789.

Georgetown, Trinidad and Tobago: see MOUNT SAINT GEORGE.

Georgetown Lake, reservoir, on border of Granite and Deer Lodge cos., SW Mont., in Deerlodge Natl. Forest, 15 mi/24 km WNW of Anaconda; 3 mi/4.8 km long, max. 3 mi/4.8 km wide; 46°11′N 113°16′W. Drained by Flint Creek. Fish hatchery.

Georgetown Township, suburb of Grand Rapids, Ottawa co., W Mich., 9 mi/14.5 km SW of city center; 42°50′N 85°49′W. Drained by Grand R. Grand Valley State Univ. to NW at Allendale.

Georgia, state (□ 59,441 sq mi/153,953 sq km; 1995 est. pop. 7,200,882), SE U.S., the last of the 13 colonies to be founded (1733); ⊙ ATLANTA (also largest city); 32°25′N 81°47′W. Other cities include COLUMBUS, SAVANNAH, MACON, BRUNSWICK, and ALBANY. Ga. is bounded on the N by Tenn. and N.C., on the E by S.C. and the Atlantic Ocean, on the S by Fla., and on the W by Ala. Several isls. that make up part of the Sea Isls. chain, including Jekyll, Sapelo, St. Simons, and Sea Isl., lie off Ga.'s coastline. Ga. is the largest state E of the Mississippi R. and has 3 main topographical areas in addition to the coastal isls. Extending inland from the coast is a low coastal plain that covers the S ½ of the state. In mountainous N Ga. are the Appalachian Plateau, the valley and ridge region, and the Blue Ridge region. Bridging these 2 sects. and embracing about ⅓ of the state is the Piedmont foothill region in central Ga. In the transition area bet. the Piedmont and Coastal Plain regions lies the Fall Zone, or Fall Line, which became home to 3 large mfg. cities that benefited from water power to drive industry; they are AUGUSTA, Macon, and Columbus. The Fall Zone is also a rich mineral area; kaolin and other clays were deposited in near-shore environments when the Coastal Plain was ocean; weathered and decomposed Appalachian Mt. rock material lies close to the surface. The state has a humid subtropical climate characterized by hot summers (average temperature 78°F/26°C) and mild winters (average temperature 44°F/7°C) with only a few inches of snowfall in the mts. and Piedmont region. The annual precipitation, highest (up to c.75 in/191 cm) in the extreme NE Blue Ridge, averages c.50 in/127 cm, with spring and fall relatively dry. There is a long growing season ranging (N-S) from 200 to 250 days except in the mts. (where it is c.180 days). Ga. is well drained by many rivers, including the SAVANNAH, which forms the boundary with S.C.; the OCMULGEE and the OCONEE, which merge in the SE to form the ALTAMAHA; the CHATTAHOOCHEE, which forms part of the Ala. boundary and joins with the FLINT in the extreme SW corner of the state to form the APALACHICOLA; and the SAINT MARYS, which rises in the large OKEFENOKEE SWAMP and forms part of the Ga.-Fla. state line. Although the trade and service industries supply the majority of jobs in Ga., mfg. and agr. remain important to the state's economy. Cotton, 1st planted in Ga. in 1733, reemerged as Ga.'s chief cash crop in 1994. Ga. is the 2d-largest producer of cotton nationally and is easily the nation's largest producer of peanuts. Tobacco is the main crop in the central and S sects. of the state, and peanuts rank 1st in the SW. Soybeans are also grown. Livestock raising accounts for the largest share of farm income; broilers, eggs, and cattle are the most important prods. The mfg. of textiles and textile prods. has long been Ga.'s leading industry, centering mainly around Columbus, Augusta, Macon, and ROME, but has declined in recent years. Other major mfg. includes transportation equip. (esp. aircraft), food prods., paper prods., and chemicals. Motor vehicle mfg. takes place in and around Atlanta. Much of Ga. is heavily forested with pine, and the state is a leading producer in the South of lumber and pulpwood. The state is rich in minerals, but mining is not as important as mfg. and agr. The most valuable minerals produced are various types of clays, including kaolin, stone, iron ore, sand, and gravel. Ga. is famous for its fine marble. Ga. ranks 5th nationally in nonfuel mineral production value, with kaolin accounting for 62%, and ranking 1st among all 50 states in kaolin and dimension stone; 2d in natl. bauxite production; 3d in mica and iron oxide pigments; 4th in feldspar; and 9th in masonry cement. With its moderate winter climate and its Southern charm and beauty, the state is a popular vacation area. The Sea Isls. are especially noted for their picturesque resorts. Warm Springs, established with the help of President Franklin D. Roosevelt for the treatment of poliomyelitis, is now a historical landmark. Ga.'s other attractions include OKEFENOKEE SWAMP, a large wilderness area; Chattahoochee and Oconee natl. forests, with facilities for hunting and fishing; Chickamauga and Chattanooga Natl. Military Park; Kennesaw Mt. Natl. Battlefield Park; and STONE MOUNTAIN MEMORIAL, near Atlanta, on which is carved the likenesses of Robert E. Lee, Stonewall Jackson, and Jefferson Davis. The Creek and Cherokee inhabited the Ga. area when Hernando De Soto and his expedition passed through the region c.1540. The Spanish later established missions and garrisons on the Sea Isls. In 1663, Charles II of England made a grant of land that included Ga. to the 8 proprietors of Carolina. However, Spain claimed the whole E ½ of the present U.S. and protested the grant. The English ignored the protest, and the Eng.-Span. contest for the territory bet. the Eng. Charleston (S.C.) hq. and the Span. St. Augustine (Fla.) fort continued intermittently for almost a cent. In June 1732, the Eng. philanthropist James E. Oglethorpe received a charter from George II (for whom the colony was named) to settle the colony of Ga. (as a refuge for Eng. debtors) and form a board of trustees to manage it. The 1st colonists, led by Oglethorpe, reached the mouth of the Savannah R. in Feb. 1733. On a bluff c.18 mi/29 km upstream, the colonists laid out the 1st town, Savannah. In 1739, war broke out bet. Spain and England. Fighting occurred in Ga., and in 1742, near Fort Frederica on St. Simons Isl., Oglethorpe defeated the Spanish in the Battle of Bloody Marsh, thereby effectively ending Spain's claim to the land N of the St. Marys R. Ga.'s early settlers included English, Welsh, Scots Highlanders, Germans, Italians, Piedmontese, and Swiss; Jews, Catholics, and settlers from other Amer. colonies were at 1st barred. At 1st slavery was prohibited, but this and other restrictions impeded the colony's growth, and by the time Ga. became a royal colony in 1754, most of the restrictions had been abolished. Ga. fitted well into the Br. mercantile system, exporting rice, indigo, deerskins, lumber, naval stores, beef, and pork to England and buying there the manufactured articles it needed. Ga.'s citizens were slower to resent those acts of the crown that exasperated the other colonies, but by June 1775, Georgian patriots had begun to organize, and the following month delegates were elected to the 2d Continental Congress. Ga.'s colonists were about equally divided into Loyalists and patriots during the Amer. Revolution, but the patriots, exposed to Loyalist Fla. on the S and the Indians on the W, fared badly. In Dec. 1778, the British captured Savannah, and by the end of 1779 held every important town in Ga. After Amer. independence had been won, Ga. was the 1st Southern state to ratify (1788) the Constitution. Ga. came into conflict with the Federal govt. over states' rights when the U.S. Supreme Court ruled, in *Chisholm* vs. *Georgia* (1793), that an individual could sue a state, a decision equally distasteful to other states as well as to Ga. (This decision was later nullified by the 11th Amendment to the U.S. Constitution.) Further difficulties with the Federal govt. stemmed from the related issues of the removal of Native Americans and land speculation. In 1827, the Cherokee in Ga. set themselves up as an independent nation. The U.S. Supreme Court held (1832) that the state had no jurisdiction over the Cherokee, but President Andrew Jackson declined to support the Chief Justice, and in 1838 the Cherokee were forced to migrate W to govt. land in present-day Okla. The path of their journey is known as the Trail of Tears. With the invention of the cotton gin (1793) by Eli Whitney, Ga. began to prosper as a cotton-growing state. Cotton was grown under the plantation system with labor supplied by slaves. By the 1840s a textile industry was established in the state. Although Ga. was committed to slavery before the Civil War, state leaders opposed secession. However, successive defeats on the natl. scene, culminating in the election of Lincoln as president, fostered separatist sentiment in the state. On Jan. 19, 1861, Ga. seceded from the Union and shortly afterward joined the Confederacy. The coast was soon blockaded by the Union navy, and in April 1862, Fort Pulaski (which had been seized by the state in Jan. 1861) was recaptured by Union forces. Ga. became a major Civil War battlefield when, in 1864, Union Gen. W. T. Sherman launched his successful Atlanta campaign. On Nov. 15, 1864, Sherman set fire to Atlanta, and his subsequent march through Ga. to the sea, culminating (Dec.) in the fall of Savannah, left in its path a scene of great destruction. During Reconstruction, Ga. initially refused to ratify the 14th Amendment and was consequently placed under military rule. During the period of military rule Rufus B. Bullock, a radical Republican, was elected governor. After the legislature approved the 15th Amendment (the 13th and 14th having been ratified earlier), Ga. was readmitted (1870) to the

Union, and Bullock resigned. The textile industry recovered from the effects of the war and was expanding by the 1880s. Atlanta, which had succeeded Milledgeville as capital in 1868, grew into a thriving industrial city, largely due to its importance as the center of an expanding regional RR network. Whereas Savannah had traditionally been the leading city in the state, that status shifted to Atlanta in the early 20th cent. as its pop. exceeded 100,000 for the 1st time. The Atlanta region reached 1,000,000 inhabitants in 1960, and approaches 4,000,000 in the late 1990s. The effect of the war on agr.—which formerly had depended on slave labor—was more serious. The breakup of large plantations resulted in the rise of tenant farming and sharecropping, systems often accompanied by poverty and abuse. A farm depression began in Ga. long before the Great Depression of the 1930s. The state weathered the Depression, but its subsequent history was marked by political and racial conflict. In 1941, Gov. Eugene Talmadge caused nationwide commotion by discharging 3 state univ. educators who were alleged to have advocated racial equality in the schools. Talmadge was defeated in the 1942 Democratic primary by Ellis G. Arnall. Under Arnall's administration, Ga. became the 1st state to grant the vote to 18-year-olds, and in 1946 (on the strength of a U.S. Supreme Court decision) Afr.-Americans voted for the 1st time in the Ga. Democratic primary. Among Arnall's other administrative acts was the adoption of a new constitution in Aug. 1945, which contained a provision for Ga.'s notorious co.-unit system. This system for nominating state officials in Democratic primaries led to the political control of urban areas by sparsely populated rural areas. The integration of public schools, following the 1954 Supreme Court decision, was strenuously opposed by many Georgians. However, in 1961 the legislature abandoned a "massive resistance" policy, and Ga. became the 1st state in the deep South to proceed with integration without a major curtailment of its public school system; however, racial tensions persisted. Ga.'s co.-unit system (held constitutional by the Supreme Court in April 1950) was finally abolished by Federal court order in 1962. In the 1972, Andrew Young became the 1st Afr.-Amer. elected to the U.S. Congress and later became mayor of Atlanta. Ga.'s urban centers, esp. Atlanta, have experienced rapid growth over the past 40 years. About ½ of the jobs and pop. in Ga. are located in the 20 cos. of the Atlanta metropolitan area. This urban growth has expanded the cultural and economic gap bet. Ga.'s rural and urban areas. Ga.'s constitution provides for an elected governor who serves for a term of 4 years. The legislature, called the general assembly, is made up of a Senate with 56 members and a House of Representatives with 180 members. Members of both houses are elected to terms of 2 years. Ga. sends 11 representatives and 2 senators to the U.S. Congress and has 13 electoral votes. The Democratic party in Ga. has dominated that state's politics since the end of Reconstruction. Jimmy Carter, a Democrat and the 39th president of the U.S., was governor of Ga. from 1970–1974. In 1990, Zell Bryan Miller, a Democrat, was elected governor. Leading educational institutions include the Univ. of Ga., at Athens; Ga. Inst. of Technology, Ga. State Univ., Emory Univ., Clark Col., Morehouse Col., Spelman Col., and Morris Brown Col., at Atlanta; Agnes Scott Col., at Decatur; Mercer Univ. and Wesleyan Col., at Macon; Savannah Col. of Art and Design; and several other state univs. Ga. has 159 cos.: APPLING, ATKINSON, BACON, BAKER, BALDWIN, BANKS, BARROW, BARTOW, BEN HILL, BERRIEN, BIBB, BLECKLEY, BRANTLEY, BROOKS, BRYAN, BULLOCH, BURKE, BUTTS, CALHOUN, CAMDEN, CANDLER, CARROLL, CATOOSA, CHARLTON, CHATHAM, CHATTAHOOCHEE, CHATTOOGA, CHEROKEE, CLARKE, CLAY, CLAYTON, CLINCH, COBB, COFFEE, COLQUITT, COLUMBIA, COOK, COWETA, CRAWFORD, CRISP, DADE, DAWSON, DECATUR, DEKALB, DODGE, DOOLY, DOUGHERTY, DOUGLAS, EARLY, ECHOLS, EFFINGHAM, ELBERT, EMANUEL, EVANS, FANNIN, FAYETTE, FLOYD, FORSYTH, FRANKLIN, FULTON, GILMER, GLASCOCK, GLYNN, GORDON, GRADY, GREENE,

GWINNETT, HABERSHAM, HALL, HANCOCK, HARALSON, HARRIS, HART, HEARD, HENRY, HOUSTON, IRWIN, JACKSON, JASPER, JEFF DAVIS, JEFFERSON, JENKINS, JOHNSON, JONES, LAMAR, LANIER, LAURENS, LEE, LIBERTY, LINCOLN, LONG, LOWNDES, LUMPKIN, MCDUFFIE, MCINTOSH, MACON, MADISON, MARION, MERIWETHER, MILLER, MITCHELL, MONROE, MONTGOMERY, MORGAN, MURRAY, MUSCOGEE, NEWTON, OCONEE, OGLETHORPE, PAULDING, PEACH, PICKENS, PIERCE, PIKE, POLK, PULASKI, PUTNAM, QUITMAN, RABUN, RANDOLPH, RICHMOND, ROCKDALE, SCHLEY, SCREVEN, SEMINOLE, SPALDING, STEPHENS, STEWART, SUMTER, TALBOT, TALIAFERRO, TATTNALL, TAYLOR, TELFAIR, TERRELL, THOMAS, TIFT, TOOMBS, TOWNS, TREUTLEN, TROUP, TURNER, TWIGGS, UNION, UPSON, WALKER, WALTON, WARE, WARREN, WASHINGTON, WAYNE, WEBSTER, WHEELER, WHITE, WHITFIELD, WILCOX, WILKES, WILKINSON, and WORTH.

Georgia, town (1990 pop. 3,753), Franklin co., NW Vt., just S of St. Albans, on L. Champlain; 44°43′N 73°07′W. Agr. Includes villages of East Georgia, Georgia Plains, and Oakland. Chartered 1763.

Georgia, Strait of, channel, c.150 mi/240 km long, Canada, bet. the mainland of B.C. and Vancouver Isl., bet. Puget Sound and Queen Charlotte Sound. It forms part of the inland steamship passage to Alaska.

Georgian Bay, large NE extension of L. Huron, S Ont., Canada, separated from L. Huron by Manitoulin Isl. and by the Bruce Peninsula; Lucas Channel is its chief connection with L. Huron; 45°15′N 80°50′W. Rivers draining the lake regions of S Ont. flow into it; they include the French R., which, with North Channel, the N connection of Georgian Bay with L. Huron, forms part of the old voyageur's trading route from Montreal to the NW. Georgian Bay is connected with L. Ontario by the Severn R. and Trent Canal. Christian Isl. is the largest in the bay. Many of the well-timbered, rockbound isls. of Georgian Bay are summer resorts. The Georgian Bay Isls. Natl. Park (5.4 sq mi/13.9 sq km), est. 1929, includes 40 of the isls. and part of the mainland, 5 mi/8 km N of Midland, in Georgian Bay of L. Huron. Includes Beausoleil Isl. (□ 2,711 acres/1,097 ha) and 76 smaller isls. in Severn Sound and off O'Donnell Point, 26 mi/42 km NNW of Midland. Flowerpot Isl. (□ 499 acres/202 ha), 4 mi/6 km E of Tobermory, Bruce Peninsula, became part of Bruce Peninsula Natl. Park (est. 1929) in 1986. Hiking, camping, fishing, boating, canoeing.

Georgiana, town (1990 pop. 1,933), Butler co., S central Ala., 15 mi/24 km SSW of Greenville. In poultry, peanut, and vegetable area; lumber milling, textiles. Settled 1824, inc. 1869.

Gerald, town (1990 pop. 888), Franklin co., E central Mo., in Ozark region, 17 mi/27 km W of Union; 38°23′N 91°19′W. Grain prods., livestock; mfg. (fabricated metal prods., paint, apparel).

Geraldine, town (1990 pop. 801), DeKalb co., NE Ala., 16 mi/26 km E of Guntersville; 34°22′N 86°00′W. Apparel mfg.

Geraldine (jer-uhl-DEEN), village (1990 pop. 299), Chouteau co., N central Mont., 50 mi/80 km E of Great Falls; 47°36′N 110°16′W. Wheat. Square Butte Special Recreation Management Area to S (5,684 ft/1,732 m). Part of Lewis and Clark Natl. Forest to SW.

Geraldton, town (1991 pop. 2,633), W central Ont., Canada, 140 mi/225 km NE of Thunder Bay; 49°43′N 86°58′W. Lumbering. Inc. 1937.

Gerber, uninc. village (1990 pop. 1,143), Tehama co., N Calif., 10 mi/16 km SSE of Red Bluff, bet. Sacramento R. (E) and Tehama Colusa Canal (W); 40°04′N 122°09′W. In livestock-raising area. Statistically reported as Gerber-Las-Flores.

Gerdine, Mount (guhr-DEEN) (12,580 ft/3,834 m), S Alaska, in Alaska Range, 90 mi/145 km WNW of Anchorage; 61°35′N 152°29′W.

Gering, town (1990 pop. 7,946), ⊙ Scotts Bluff co., W Nebr., 1 mi/1.6 km S of Scottsbluff across North Platte R.; 41°49′N 103°40′W. Twin city to Scottsbluff. RR division point, trade center for irrigated agr. area. Alfalfa,

grain, sugar beets; mfg. (printing, motor vehicles, irrigation equip., food processing, sheet metal). Oregon Trail Days, pageant celebrating movement W of pioneers, held here annually. Oregon Trail passes through city on S side of river. Scotts Bluff Natl. Monument to W; Wildcat Hills State Recreation Area to S. Founded 1887, inc. 1890.

Gerlach, uninc. village, Washoe co., NW Nev., in SW tip of Black Rock Desert, 78 mi/126 km NNE of Reno. Junctions of RR spur S to Empire. Gypsum prods.; art community. Gerlach-Empire Regional Park to N.

German Valley, village (1990 pop. 480), Stephenson co., N Ill., 9 mi/14.5 km SE of Freeport; 42°13′N 89°28′W. In agr. area; nursery.

Germanton, uninc. village, Stokes co., N N.C., 10 mi/16 km N of Winston-Salem. Hanging Rock State Park to N.

Germantown 1 city (1990 pop. 4,916), Montgomery co., W Ohio, 12 mi/19 km SW of Dayton, on small Twin Creek; 39°38′N 84°22′W. Laid out 1814. **2** city (1990 pop. 32,893), Shelby co., SW Tenn., suburb 12 mi/19 km E of Memphis; 35°05′N 89°47′W.

Germantown 1 village (1990 pop. 1,195), Clinton co., SW Ill., on Shoal Creek, 14 mi/23 km WSW of Carlyle; 40°46′N 89°28′W. In agr. area. **2** village (1990 pop. 213), Bracken and Mason cos., N Ky., 11 mi/18 km W of Maysville, in N part of Bluegrass region; 38°38′N 83°58′W. Agr. (tobacco, corn; dairying); mfg. (feeds). Annual (Aug.) fair and horse show dates from 1854. **3** village, Montgomery co., central Md., 9 mi/14.5 km NE of Rockville. Settled by Germans in the 1870s, it is now becoming a planned community marked by rapid development. Nearby are the Nuclear Regulatory Commission and Sherman Fairchild Technology Center, the largest corporation based in Md., although not the largest employer. **4** village, Washington co., SE Wis., on Menomonee R., suburb 16 mi/26 km NNW of Milwaukee; 43°14′N 88°07′W. Dairy prods.; mfg. (welders, metal prods., consumer goods, machinery, laminating equip., dairy prods., paper prods., metal processing, food processing; motor vehicle parts).

Germantown, residential section of NW Philadelphia, Philadelphia co., Pa., Wissahickon Creek to SW; 40°02′N 75°10′W. Settled by Dutch and Germans in 1683, Germantown became one of the earliest printing and publishing centers in the country. When the British occupied Philadelphia during the Amer. Revolution, the greater part of their army encamped at Germantown. George Washington's forces unsuccessfully attacked the camp on Oct. 4, 1777, in the last important engagement conducted by Washington before he took the army to Valley Forge for the winter. In 1854, Germantown was annexed to Philadelphia. The Howe House and other colonial houses, inns, and churches still stand. Awbury Arboretum, LaSalle Col., and Germantown Historical Society are here.

Germantown, suburb (1990 pop. 41,145) of Annapolis, Anne Arundel co., central Md.; 39°11′N 77°16′W. There is also a village called Germantown in Montgomery co.

Germantown Dam, Montgomery co., SW Ohio, on Twin Creek, 14 mi/23 km SW of Dayton; 39°38′N 84°24′W. Built in 1922 for flood control. Pool is dry except during flood periods; extends into Preble co.; max. potential capacity 865,000 acre-ft.

Germantown Hills, village (1990 pop. 1,518), town, Woodford co., central Ill., residential suburb 7 mi/11.3 km NE of Peoria; 40°45′N 89°28′W. Agr. area.

Germfask (JUHRM-fask), village, Schoolcraft co., S Upper Peninsula, Mich., on Manistique R. and 25 mi/40 km NE of Manistique, near Manistique L.; 46°14′N 85°55′W. Sawmill. Seney Natl. Wildlife Refuge immediately W; Manistique L. to E.

Geronimo (juhr-UH-ni-mo), town (1990 pop. 990), Comanche co., SW Okla., 8 mi/12.9 km S of Lawton; 34°28′N 98°22′W. In agr. area.

Gerry (GER-ee), resort village (1990 pop. 800), Chautauqua co., extreme W N.Y. 6 mi/9.7 km N of Jamestown and c.6 mi/9.7 km from Chautauqua L. (SW); 42°12′N 79°13′W.

Gerster (GUHR-stuhr), town (1990 pop. 40), St. Clair

co., W Mo., 12 mi/19 km SSE of Osceola; 37°57'N 93°34'W.

Gerty, village (1990 pop. 95), Hughes co., central Okla., 19 mi/31 km SSE of Holdenville; 34°50'N 96°17'W.

Gervais (JUHR-vuhs), town (1990 pop. 992), Marion co., NW Oregon, 12 mi/19 km NNE of Salem in Willamette Valley, bet. Willamette (W) and Pudding (E) rivers; 45°06'N 122°53'W. Agr. (berries, fruit, nuts, vegetables, grain; poultry); dairy prods. Concrete mfg.

Gethsemane (geth-SEM-uh-nee), village, Nelson co., central Ky., 17 mi/27 km ESE of Elizabethtown, near Rolling Fork R. At nearby Trappist is a Trappist monastery, Abbey of Our Lady of Gethsemani (or Gethsemani Farms), where cheese is made.

Gettysburg, town (1990 pop. 1,510), ⊙ Potter co., N central S.Dak., 50 mi/80 km NNE of Pierre; 45°00'N 99°57'W. Trade center for agr. region; flour mill, oil-compounding plant; wheat, corn, potatoes; dairy prods.; livestock, poultry; mfg. (feeds, printing and publishing); RR terminus. Founded 1881.

Gettysburg (GE-teez-buhrg), village (1990 pop. 539), Darke co., W Ohio, 7 mi/11 km E of Greenville and on Greenville Creek.

Gettysburg, borough (1990 pop. 7,025), ⊙ Adams co., S Pa., 35 mi/56 km SW of Harrisburg, near Rock Creek; 39°49'N 77°13'W. Mfg. (furniture, printing and publishing, fabricated metal prods., food, construction materials, machinery). Agr. (apples, cherries, grain, soybeans, potatoes; poultry, eggs; livestock; dairying). Gettysburg was settled c.1780 and is named for Gen. James Getty, to whom its site was granted (17th cent.) by William Penn. The Gettysburg Campaign (1863) was a turning point in the Civil War; Abraham Lincoln made his famous Gettysburg Address here. Separate sects. of Gettysburg Natl. Military Park in N and S, Gettysburg Natl. Cemetery in S, and Eisenhower Natl. Historic Site to SW are natl. historic shrines and popular tourist attractions. Seat of Gettysburg Lutheran Theological Seminary and Gettysburg Col. Adams Co. Winery to NW. L. Hermitage reservoir (residential development) to SE. S terminus of Gettysburg RR, scenic RR, to Biglerville (N). Inc. 1806.

Gettysburg National Military Park (6.2 sq mi/16 sq km), Adams co., S Pa.; 39°49'N 77°13'W. Comprising 2 main sects., N and S of Gettysburg; S part is largest sect.; drained by Rock Creek and Plum Run. Battle of Gettysburg here July 1–3, 1863; President Lincoln's Gettysburg Address given here Nov. 19, 1863; Gettysburg Natl. Cemetery (21 acres/8 ha), adjunct to S sect. and town. Eternal Lights Peace Memorial in N. Authorized 1895.

Geuda Springs (GOO-duh), village (1990 pop. 219), on Cowley-Sumner co. line, S Kansas, on Arkansas R. and 7 mi/11.3 km WNW of Arkansas City; 37°06'N 97°09'W. Grain, livestock.

Geyserville, uninc. town (1990 pop. 950), Sonoma co., W Calif., 20 mi/32 km NNW of Santa Rosa, on Russian R. Grapes, apples, dairying, poultry, grain. Wineries (6).

Ghent 1 (GENT), village (1990 pop. 365), Carroll co., N Ky., 8 mi/12.9 km NE of Carrollton, on Ohio R. opposite Vevay, Ohio; 38°44'N 85°03'W. Agr. (tobacco; horses, cattle, hogs); mfg. (fabricated metal prods.). **2** village (1990 pop. 316), Lyon co., SW Minn., on Three Mile Creek, 7 mi/11.3 km NW of Marshall; 44°30'N 95°53'W. Grain; livestock; dairying; mfg. (feeds). Early Belgian settlement.

Gholson, village (1990 pop. 692), McLennan co., E central Texas, 14 mi/23 km NNW of Waco, bet. Brazos R. and Aquilla Creek; 31°42'N 97°14'W. Agr. area (cattle, dairying, hogs, cotton, grains).

Ghost Mountain (10,512 ft/3,204 m), SE B.C., Canada, near Alta. border, in Rocky Mts., in Hamber Provincial Park, 40 mi/64 km SSE of Jasper, on edge of the Chaba Icefield; 52°18'N 117°53'W.

Giant City State Park, Ill.: see CARBONDALE.

Giant Mountain (4,622 ft/1,049 m), Essex co., NE N.Y., in the High Peaks sect. of the Adirondacks, E of Keene Valley and 10 mi/16 km ENE of Mt. Marcy; 44°10'N 73°44'W.

Gibara (hee-BAHR-ah), town, Holguín prov., E Cuba, port on N coast (Gibara Bay), 18 mi/29 km NNE of Holguín (linked by RR); 21°06'N 76°08'W. Seaside resort and trading center in agr. region (sugarcane, tobacco, corn, bananas, cattle); mfg. of cigars, lumbering. Gold, copper, and lead deposits in vicinity. Here the Span. troops embarked after Span.-Amer. War. The town was disputed during 1933 revolution. Nearby, at Gibara Bay, Columbus made his 1st landing on the isl. (1492).

Gibara River (hee-BAHR-ah), flows 20 mi/32 km N, Holguín prov., E Cuba, to Gibara Bay (Atlantic Ocean) SE of Gibara; 21°04'N 76°07'W. Lower course navigable for small vessels.

Gibbon, town (1990 pop. 1,525), Buffalo co., S Nebr., 13 mi/21 km ENE of Kearney and on Wood R.; 40°45'N 98°50'W. RR junction. Mfg. (feed, food). Windmill State Wayside Area to S.

Gibbon, village (1990 pop. 712), Sibley co., S Minn., 15 mi/24 km W of Gaylord; 44°32'N 94°31'W. Agr. area (poultry, livestock; grain, soybeans, alfalfa; dairying); mfg. (feeds, fabricated metal prods.). Clear L. to S.

Gibbon River, NW Wyo., rises in Washburn Range, Yellowstone Natl. Park, Park co., flows 37 mi/60 km SW, through geyser region, joining Firehole R. at Madison Junction to form Madison R. in W part of park. Gibbon Falls (84 ft/26 m) is in lower course.

Gibbons Creek Lake, reservoir (□ 32 sq mi/83 sq km), Grimes co., E Texas, on Gibbons Creek, 18 mi/29 km E of Bryan; 30°37'N 96°04'W. Max. capacity 320,084 acre-ft. Formed by Gibbons Creek Dam (50 ft/15 m high), built (1981) for power generation; also used for recreation.

Gibbs, town (1990 pop. 89), Adair co., N Mo., near North Fork of Salt R., 10 mi/16 km SE of Kirksville; 40°06'N 92°25'W.

Gibb's Hill, highest point (240 ft/73 m) of Bermuda, in Southampton parish, 4 mi/6.4 km WSW of Hamilton; 32°15'N 64°50'W. Gibb's Hill Lighthouse is the oldest cast-iron lighthouse in the world.

Gibbsboro (GIBZ-buh-ro), borough (1990 pop. 2,383), Camden co., SW N.J., 11 mi/18 km SE of Camden; 39°49'N 74°58'W.

Gibbstown (GIBZ-toun), village (1990 pop. 3,902), Gloucester co., SW N.J., near the Delaware, 7 mi/11.3 km W of Woodbury; 39°49'N 75°16'W.

Gibraltar, city (1990 pop. 4,297), Wayne co., SE Mich., suburb 18 mi/29 km SSW of downtown Detroit, immediately S of Trenton, on Detroit R.; 42°05'N 83°12'W. Boblo Isl. Amusement park in river; boat access only. Steel mill.

Gibraltar (ji-BRAHL-tuhr), uninc. village, Robeson township, Berks co., SE central Pa., on Schuylkill R., 5 mi/8 km SE of Reading; 40°17'N 75°52'W. Mfg. (chemicals).

Gibraltar Dam, Calif.: see SANTA YNEZ RIVER.

Gibsland (GIBZ-luhnd), town (1990 pop. 1,224), Bienville parish, NW La., 7 mi/11 km W of Arcadia; 32°33'N 93°03'W. RR junction; shipping center for farming (peaches, watermelons; cattle; dairying); timber; logging, lumber milling. Former plantation; site selected by RR. Founded c.1885.

Gibson 1 county (□ 499 sq mi/1,292 sq km; 1990 pop. 31,913), SW Ind.; ⊙ Princeton; 38°19'N 87°35'W. Bounded W by Wabash R. (here forming Ill. state line) and N by White R.; also drained by Patoka R., a small Black R. and Pigeon Creek. Agr. area (corn, wheat, barley, hogs, poultry, truck, melons); mfg. (concrete prods., food prods.). Natural-gas and oil wells; timber. Some flooding of Wabash, 1993. Formed 1813. **2** county (□ 607 sq mi/1,572 sq km; 1990 pop. 46,315), NW Tenn.; ⊙ Trenton; 36°00'N 88°56'W. Bounded NE by South Fork of Obion R., SW by Middle Fork of Forked Deer R. Fertile agr. area (cotton, corn, apples, peaches, soybeans, sorghum, vegetables, livestock). Mfg. at Humboldt and Milan. Timber tracts, clay pits. Formed 1823.

Gibson 1 town (1990 pop. 679), ⊙ Glascock co., E Ga., 37 mi/60 km WSW of Augusta; 33°14'N 82°36'W. **2** town (1990 pop. 281), Gibson co., NW Tenn., 18 mi/29 km N of Jackson; 35°52'N 88°50'W.

Gibson, village (1990 pop. 532), Scotland co., S N.C., 9 mi/14.5 km WSW of Laurinburg, at S.C. state line; 34°45'N 76°36'W. Tobacco, cotton, grain, chickens, hogs). Light mfg.

Gibson City, city (1990 pop. 3,396), Ford co., E central Ill., 16 mi/26 km W of Paxton; 40°28'N 88°22'W. Trade and processing center in rich agr. area (corn, wheat, soybeans, livestock, poultry). RR junction. Inc. 1894.

Gibson Dam, Mont.: see SUN RIVER.

Gibson Island, resort village, Anne Arundel co., central Md., on narrow neck bet. Chesapeake Bay and Magothy R., 14 mi/23 km NNE of Annapolis. Known for yachting. Named for Colonel Joseph Gibson, a local landowner, taken prisoner by the British in 1813. A monument on the isl. commemorates Stuart Symington (1884–1926), who established a settlement here in 1921. Nearby is Fort Smallwood, fortifications erected by the federal govt. in 1896, and subsequently turned over to the city of Baltimore as a 100–acre/40–ha public park with a view of the harbor. Also nearby is Fort Carroll where then Colonel Robert E. Lee supervised construction of fortifications from 1849 to 1852.

Gibsonburg, village (1990 pop. 2,579), Sandusky co., N Ohio, 11 mi/18 km W of Fremont; 41°23'N 83°19'W. Founded 1871.

Gibsonia 1 (gib-SO-nee-yuh), town (□ 3 sq mi/7.8 sq km; 1990 pop. 5,168), Polk co., central Fla., 5 mi/8 km N of Lakeland; 28°07'N 81°58'W. **2** (gib-SON-ee-ah), uninc town (1990 pop. 3,500), Allegheny co., W Pa., suburb 12 mi/19 km N of Pittsburgh on urban fringe area; 40°37'N 79°58'W. Light mfg.

Gibsons Landing, village, SW B.C., Canada, on Thornbrough Channel of Howe Sound, 20 mi/32 km WNW of Vancouver. Resort. Opposite Keats Isl.

Gibsonton (GIB-suhn tuhn), town (□ 8 sq mi/20.7 sq km; 1990 pop. 7,706), Hillsborough co., W central Fla., 12 mi/19 km SE of Tampa. Light mfg.

Gibsonville, town (1990 pop. 3,441), Guilord and Alamance cos., N central N.C., 13 mi/21 km E of Greensboro; 36°06'N 79°32'W. In agr. area (tobacco, grain, potatoes, sweet potatoes, chickens, hogs, dairying). Mfg. (apparel, plastic prods., textiles, chemicals, machinery).

Giddings, city (1990 pop. 4,093), ⊙ Lee co., S central Texas, c.45 mi/72 km E of Austin; 30°10'N 96°55'W. Elev. 520 ft/158 m. In agr. area (corn, peanuts, wheat, oats; cattle, hogs); mfg. (furniture, feed). Founded 1872 by Wends (Slavic branch).

Gideon, city (1990 pop. 1,104), New Madrid co., in the bootheel of extreme SE Mo., in Mississippi alluvial plain, 8 mi/12.9 km SSE of Malden; 36°27'N 89°54'W. Rice, soybeans; cattle. Inc. 1909.

Gifford 1 village (1990 pop. 845), Champaign co., E central Ill., 7 mi/11.3 km E of Rantoul; 40°18'N 88°01'W. Corn, soybeans. **2** village (1990 pop. 313) Hampton co., SW S.C., 12 mi/19 km SSE of Allendale; 32°51'N 81°14'W. Agr. includes vegetables, watermelons, cotton, peanuts, grain, livestock; timber.

Gifford Shores, town (□ / sq mi/18.1 sq km; 1990 pop. 6,278), Indian R. co., E central Fla., 3 mi/4.8 km N of Vero Beach; 27°40'N 80°24'W.

Gig Harbor, town (1990 pop. 3,236), Pierce co., W Wash., across the Narrows of Puget Sound (bridged from Tacoma) NW of Tacoma, on Kitsap Peninsula; 47°20'N 122°35'W. Fishing base; berries; poultry, eggs; timber, logging; mfg. (apparel, computer equip., printing and publishing). Penrose Point State Park to SW.

Giganta, La (hee-GAHN-tah), peak (9,631 ft/2,936 m), Guanajuato, central Mexico, in Sierra Madre Occidental, 9 mi/14.5 km NNW of Guanajuato.

Giganta, Sierra de la (hee-GAHN-tah), range in S Lower California, rises to 5,794 ft/1,766 m in Cerro de la Giganta, NW of Loreto, NW Mexico. Extends c.180 mi/290 km SE along E coast of Gulf of California, from Concepción Bay to La Paz Bay.

Gil Island (□ 89 sq mi/231 sq km; 16 mi/26 km long, 4 mi/6 km–8 mi/13 km wide), W B.C., Canada, in Hecate Strait bet. Pitt and Princess Royal isls.

Gila (HEE-la), county (□ 4,796 sq mi/12,422 sq km; 1990 pop. 40,216), E central Ariz.; ⊙ Globe; 33°47'N 110°49'W. Bounded by San Carlos and Gila rivers in S,

---

and Verde R. in extreme NW, Mogollon Rim escarpment forms part of N boundary. Chief ranges are Sierra Ancha and Mazatzal (W) and Pinal (S) Mts., drained by San Carlos, Black, White, and East Verde rivers, Theodore Roosevelt Dam and Reservoir on Salt R. in W, and Coolidge Dam and San Carlos Reservoir on Gila R. in S provide water for irrigation. Co. includes large part of Tonto Natl. Forest in NW and W and San Carlos and Fort Apache Indian reservations in NE (San Carlos and Black rivers form boundary bet. them). Only 2 small areas in S around Globe/Miami and in S tip, are outside natl. forest and Indian reservation. Copper gold, silver, vanadium are mined; cattle; hay. Tonto Natural Bridge State Park to NW. Formed 1881.

Gila (HEE-luh), village (1990 pop. 359), Grant co., SW N.Mex., on Gila R., just S of Mogollon Mts., and 28 mi/45 km NW of Silver City. Elev. 4,550 ft/1,387 m. Cattle, grain, alfalfa. Supply point for camping trips. Gila Cliff Dwellings Natl. Monument is 25 mi/40 km NE.

Gila (HEE-luh), river, 630 mi/1,014 km long, rises in the mts. of W N.Mex. in NW Sierra co., at Continental Divide, flows SW through Wall L. and Gila Natl. Forest, NW of Silver City, enters Ariz. where it turns generally W, flows past Duncan, receives San Fancisco R. near Clifton, continues past Safford, through San Carlos Indian Reservation and San Carlos L. reservoir, where it receives San Carlos R. from N. It continues past Winkelman and Florence, and flows through Gila R. Indian Reservation S of Phoenix, where it receives Santa Cruz R. from S and Salt R. from S, its main tributary, then WSW past Gila Bend and through Gila Bend Indian Reservation, past Wellton, joining Colorado R. 5 mi/8 km E of Yuma. The Gila valley was occupied by the ancestors of the Pima and Papago ethnic groups, who farmed the region by irrigation. The ruins of their dwellings are preserved in Casa Grande Ruins and Gila Cliff Dwellings natl. monuments. In the river's headwater region are Gila Natl. Forest and the government-preserved "unimproved" Gila Wilderness Area. The Gila and its tributaries have many dams to provide flood control, hydroelectricity, and water for irrigation in the arid SW (see SALT RIVER VALLEY). Coolidge and Painted Rock dams are the largest dams on the Gila R. Hayden-Rhodes Aqueduct carries water from Parker Dam, on Colorado R. over 200 mi/322 km E to Salt/Gila river system to increase its water volume for irrigation and other purposes. Gila monsters (poisonous reptiles) are numerous in the Gila valley.

Gila Bend, town (1990 pop. 1,747), Maricopa co., SW Ariz., near large bend in Gila R., 50 mi/80 km SW of Phoenix; 32°57′N 112°40′W. Cotton; citrus; cattle, sheep; mfg. (transportation equip.). Gila Indian Reservation is to NW across river. Painted Rocks Dam (Gila R.) to NW; large Barry M. Goldwater (formerly Luke) Air Force Range to S.

Gila Bend Mountains, rise to c.3,000 ft/914 m, Maricopa co., SW Ariz., near Gila R., SW of Phoenix. Woolsey Peak N of town of Gila Bend.

Gila Cliff Dwellings (HEE-luh), National Monument, Catron co., SW N.Mex., 44 mi/71 km N of Silver City, on West Fork Gila R., 533 acres/216 ha. Proclaimed 1907. Well-preserved cliff dwellings (occupied c.1280–1320) built by Indians of the Mogollon culture into a 150 ft/46 m cliff.

Gila Mountains 1 Graham co., SE Ariz., N of Safford; extend SE-NW, NE of Gila R.; rise to Gila Peak (6,340 ft/1,932 m). Forms part of S boundary of San Carlos Indian Reservation. **2** Yuma co., SW Ariz., NE of Yuma Desert, E of Yuma; extend N from Tinajas Altas Mts. to Gila R. and rise to Sheep Mt. (3,156 ft/962 m.).

Gilbert, city (1990 pop. 29,188), Maricopa co., S central Ariz., suburb, 18 mi/29 km SE of downtown Phoenix; 33°19′N 111°45′W. Irrigated agr. area on urban fringes (alfalfa, wheat, cotton, fruits, vegetables); mfg. (concrete, rubber and plastic prods., apparel, machinery). City crossed by several irrigation canals. Chandler municipal airport to S; Williams Air Force Base to SE; Ariz.-Boys Ranch to SE.

Gilbert 1 town (1990 pop. 796), Story co., central Iowa, 6 mi/9.7 km N of Ames; 42°06′N 93°39′W. Livestock; grain. **2** town (1990 pop. 1,934), St. Louis co., NE Minn., 47 mi/76 km NNW of Duluth, in Mesabi Iron Range, 4 mi/6.4 km SE of Virginia; 47°29′N 92°27′W. In iron mining area; poultry; oats, alfalfa; dairying; light mfg. Virginia-Eveleth Airport to SW. Superior Natl. Forest to N. Inc. 1909.

Gilbert 1 village (1990 pop. 43), Searcy co., N Ark., 27 mi/43 km SE of Harrison and on Buffalo R. (Buffalo Natl. River Natl. Park); 35°59′N 92°43′W. **2** village (1990 pop. 704), Franklin parish, NE La., 41 mi/66 km SE of Monroe, near Deer Creek; 32°03′N 91°40′W. In agr. area (cotton). Turkey Creek L. reservoir to SW. **3** village (1990 pop. 324), Lexington co., central S.C., 20 mi/32 km W of Columbia; 33°55′N 81°23′W. Light mfg.; agr. includes peaches, grain, vegetables, dairying, poultry. **4** village (1990 pop. 456), Mingo co., SW W. Va., 23 mi/37 km E of Williamson, on Guyandotte R.; 37°36′N 81°52′W. Forms R. D. Bailey L. reservoir (Wildlife Management Area) to E. Bituminous coal.

Gilbert Creek, uninc. town, Mingo co., SW W.Va., residential community, 22 mi/35 km ESE of Williamson, and 2 mi/3.2 km SW of Gilbert, on Gilbert Creek. Bituminous coal.

Gilbert Lake, c.½ mi/8/10 km long, Otsego co., central N.Y., 12 mi/19 km NNW of Oneonta; 42°35′N 75°08′W. State park here; camping, hiking.

Gilbert, Mount (10,200 ft/3,109 m), SW B.C., Canada, in Coast Mts., 120 mi/193 km NNW of Vancouver; 50°50′N 124°17′W.

Gilbert Plains, village (1991 pop. 741), W Man., Canada, on Valley R. and 19 mi/31 km W of Dauphin; 51°08′N 100°29′W. Dairying; lumber; grain, livestock; brick making, clay and marl quarrying; grain elevators.

Gilberton (GIL-buhr-tuhn), borough (1990 pop. 953), Schuylkill co., E central Pa., 8 mi/12.9 km NNW of Pottsville, on Mahanoy Creek. Agr. (corn, hay, poultry, dairying); light mfg.; anthracite coal. Inc. 1873.

Gilbertown (GIL-buhr-tuhn), town (1990 pop. 235), Choctaw co., SW Ala., 16 mi/26 km SSW of Butler.

Gilbertsville 1 uninc. town (1990 pop. 900), Marion co., W Ky., 16 mi/26 km ESE of Paducah, on Tennessee R. Kentucky Dam (forms Kentucky L. reservoir) and Kentucky Dam Village State Park to SE. Tourism, recreation; agr. (tobacco, grain, livestock); light mfg. **2** (GIL-buhrts-vil), uninc. town (1990 pop. 3,994), Montgomery co., SE Pa., 5 mi/8 km N of Pottstown; 40°19′N 75°36′W. Light mfg; agr. (dairying, livestock; apples, grain, soybeans).

Gilbertsville, village (□ 1 sq mi/2.6 sq km; 1990 pop. 388), Otsego co., central N.Y., 11 mi/18 km W of Oneonta; 42°28′N 75°19′W. In dairying and grain-growing area.

Gilbertville, town (1990 pop. 748), Black Hawk co., E central Iowa, on Cedar R. and 8 mi/12.9 km SE of Waterloo; 42°25′N 92°12′W. Light mfg.

Gilbertville, village, Worcester co., Mass.: see HARDWICK.

Gilboa 1 village (1990 pop. 200), Schoharie co., E central N.Y., in the Catskills, 40 mi/64 km SW of Albany; 42°25′N 74°27′W. Gilboa Dam here impounds Schoharie Reservoir in Schoharie Creek. **2** village (1990 pop. 208), Putnam co., NW Ohio, 15 mi/24 km W of Findlay and on Blanchard R.; 41°01′N 83°55′W.

Gilboa Upper Dam, N.Y.: see SCHOHARIE RESERVOIR.

Gilchrist (GIL-krist), county (□ 355 sq mi/919 sq km; 1990 pop. 9,667), N central Fla., bounded by Santa Fe (N) and Suwannee (W) rivers; ⊙ Trenton; 29°43′N 82°47′W. Flatwoods area with many small lakes. Farming (corn, vegetables, peanuts), cattle raising, lumbering. Formed 1925.

Gilchrist, uninc. town (1990 pop. 750), Galveston co., S Texas, on Gulf of Mexico shore of Bolivar Peninsula, 28 mi/45 km NE of Galveston, East Bay to NW (Intracoastal Waterway). Resort Area. Anahuac Natl. Wildlife Refuge to N.

Gilcrest, town (1990 pop. 1,084), Weld co., N Colo., near South Platte R., 10 mi/16 km SSW of Greeley; 40°16′N 104°46′W. Elev. 4,754 ft/1,449 m. In irrigated sugar beet, fruit, vegetables, beans, sunflowers region. Milton Reservoir to SE.

Gildersleeve, Conn.: see PORTLAND.

Gildford, village (1990 pop. 250), Hill co., N Mont., 29 mi/47 km W of Havre on Sage Creek. Grain, livestock.

Gilead (GIL-ee-uhd), town (1990 pop. 204), Oxford co., W Maine, on the Androscoggin and 25 mi/40 km NW of South Paris, partly in White Mt. Natl. Forest; 44°23′N 70°57′W.

Gilead (GIL-ee-ad), village (1990 pop. 37), Thayer co., SE Nebr., 10 mi/16 km E of Hebron, near Little Blue R.; 40°08′N 97°24′W.

Gilead, village, Tolland co., Conn.: see HEBRON.

Giles 1 (jeilz), county (□ 619 sq mi/1,603 sq km; 1990 pop. 25,741), S Tenn.; ⊙ Pulaski; 35°12′N 87°02′W. Bounded S by Ala.; drained by Elk R. and small Richland Creek. In fertile bluegrass region; produces dairy prods., livestock, hay, cotton, tobacco; phosphate mining. Mfg. at Pulaski. Formed 1809. **2** county (□ 360 sq mi/932 sq km; 1990 pop. 16,366), SW Va.; ⊙ Pearisburg; 37°19′N 80°42′W. In the Allegheny Mts.; bounded NW by W.Va. state line; parts of Jefferson Natl. Forest in W, N, and along SE boundary. Drained by New R. and Sinking Creek. Mfg. at Ripplemead; agr. (hay, alfalfa, apples; cattle, poultry); timber; some coal mining. Mt. L. Resort, White Rocks, and Cascade Falls Recreation Areas in E. Appalachian Trail crosses N part of co., follows W.Va. border, crosses through W part of co. Formed 1806.

Gilford, town (1990 pop. 5,867), Belknap co., central N.H., 4 mi/6.4 km NE of Laconia; 43°32′N 71°22′W. Bounded on N by L. Winnipesaukee, which dominates N part of town. Laconia Airport in N. Agr. (cattle, poultry; dairying; nursery crops); light mfg.; recreation, tourism. Ellacoya State Beach in NE; Belknap Mt. (2,384 ft/727 m); Belknap State Reservation in S; Gunstock Ski and Recreation Area in S.

Gilford Island (□ 159 sq mi/412 sq km), SW B.C., Canada, at E end of Queen Charlotte Strait, 15 mi/24 km ENE of Alert Bay; 21 mi/34 km long, 4 mi/6 km–12 mi/19 km wide. NE part of isl. rises to 4,820 ft/1,469 m on Mt. Read.

Gilham Lake, reservoir (□ 3 sq mi/7.8 sq km), Howard co., W central Ark., on Cossatot R., 60 mi/96 km SE of Hot Springs; 34°13′N 94°14′W. Max. capacity 221,800 acre-ft. Formed by Gilham Lake Dam (160 ft/49 m high), built (1975) by Army Corps of Engineers for water supply, recreation, and as a fish and wildlife pond.

Gill, agr. town (1990 pop. 1,583), Franklin co., NW Mass., on Connecticut R. and 7 mi/11.3 km NE of Greenfield; 42°38′N 72°31′W. Includes village of Riverside. Inc. 1793.

Gillespie, county (□ 1,061 sq mi/2,748 sq km; 1990 pop. 17,204), S central Texas; ⊙ Fredericksburg. In scenic hill country of Edwards Plateau; 30°18′N 98°57′W. Elev. c.1,400 ft/427 m–2,300 ft/701 m. Drained by Pedernales R. and several creeks. Ranching (cattle, goats, sheep); wool, mohair marketed; also some poultry. Agr. (wheat, oats, hay, grain sorghum), leading peach-producing co. in Texas. Hunting, fishing attracts visitors. Granite quarrying, gypsum, sand and gravel. Enchanted Rock State Natural Area in N; Lyndon B. Johnson Natl. Historical Park (LBJ Ranch Unit) and State Historic Site are in E. Formed 1848.

Gillespie (gil-ES-pee), city (1990 pop. 3,645), Macoupin co., SW Ill., 12 mi/19 km SSE of Carlinville; 39°07′N 89°49′W. Bituminous coal mining; agr. (dairy prods.; livestock, grain). Inc. 1859.

Gillespie Dam, Maricopa co., S central Ariz., on Gila R., 42 mi/68 km WSW of Phoenix; 21 ft/6 m high; 33°14′N 112°46′W. Built by the Painted Rock Development Co. for irrigation purposes in 1921; multi-arch construction. Formed reservoir (now completely silted in) that had a max. capacity of 260,000 acre-ft.

Gillett 1 (jil-ET), town (1990 pop. 883), Arkansas co., E central Ark., 26 mi/42 km SSE of Stuttgart; 34°07′N 91°22′W. RR terminus. Rice milling, light mfg. Arkansas Post Natl. Memorial to SE. **2** (gi-LET), town (1990 pop. 1,303), Oconto co., NE Wis., 30 mi/48 km NW of Green Bay city; 44°53′N 88°18′W. Mfg. (food, construction materials). Inc. as village in 1900, as city in 1944.

Gillette (ji-LET), city (1990 pop. 17,635), ⊙ Campbell co., NE Wyo., 80 mi/129 km ESE of Sheridan; 44°16′N 105°31′W. Elev. 4,544 ft/1,385 m. RR junction 10 mi/ 16 km to E. Trade center in grain (wheat, oats), livestock (sheep, cattle), and coal mining region; mfg. (feeds; printing and publishing; concrete; flour; dairy prods.). "Energy Capital" of U.S.; fairgrounds and airport located here. Small unit of Thunder Basin Natl. Grassland to NE.

Gillham (GIL-uhm), village (1990 pop. 210), Sevier co., SW Ark., 9 mi/14.5 km N of De Queen; 34°10′N 94°18′W. Gillham L. reservoir to NE (Howard co.); Dr. Quinn L. reservoir to W.

Gilliam (GIL-ee-uhm), county (☐ 1,222 sq mi/ 3,165 sq km; 1990 pop. 1,717), N Oregon; ⊙ Condon; 45°22′N 120°12′W. Bounded N by Columbia R. and L. Umatilla Reservoir (forms Wash. state boundary), and W by John Day R. State Scenic Riverway. Agr. (wheat, oats, barley; cattle). Formed 1885.

Gilliam, town (1990 pop. 212), Saline co., central Mo., near Missouri R., 13 mi/21 km NE of Marshall; 39°13′N 93°00′W. Limestone quarry. Corn, soybeans, cattle.

Gilliam (GIL-yuhm), village (1990 pop. 202), Caddo parish, NW La., 22 mi/35 km N of Shreveport, near Red R., between Red R. (E) and Black Bayou (W); 32°50′N 93°51′W. Cotton area; oil and natural gas field nearby.

Gills Rock, village, Door co., NE Wis., on tip of Door Peninsula on Green Bay, 36 mi/58 km NE of Sturgeon Bay city. Fishing; tourism. Passenger ferry service to Washington Isl.; car ferry from Northport 3 mi/4.8 km E. Newport State Park to S.

Gillsville, village (1990 pop. 113), Hall and Banks cos., NE Ga., 9 mi/14.5 km E of Gainesville; 34°19′N 83°38′W. Mfg. includes concrete, lumber, apparel.

Gilman (GILL-mahn), city (1990 pop. 1,816), Iroquois co., E Ill., 13 mi/21 km W of Watseka; 40°46′N 88°00′W. RR junction. In agr. area (corn, wheat, soybeans, livestock; dairy prods.). Inc. 1867.

Gilman, town (1990 pop. 586), Marshall co., central Iowa, 14 mi/23 km SSE of Marshalltown; 41°52′N 92°47′W.

Gilman 1 village, Eagle co., W central Colo., on Eagle R., in Gore Range, and 20 mi/32 km N of Leadville. Elev. 8,970 ft/2,734 m. Gold, silver, lead, zinc, and copper mining. Mt. of the Holy Cross is 7 mi/11.3 km SW. Vail ski resort to N. Area surrounded by White River Natl. Forest. **2** village (1990 pop. 192), Benton co., central Minn., 16 mi/26 km NE of St. Cloud, near Elk R.; 45°44′N 93°56′W. Mfg. of feeds; agr. (grains, soybeans, alfalfa, livestock, dairying). **3** village (1990 pop. 412), Taylor co., N central Wis., on Yellow R. and 40 mi/ 64 km NE of Eau Claire; 45°10′N 90°48′W. Chequamegon Natl. Forest to E. Dairying; lumber.

Gilman 1 village, New London co., Conn.: see BOZRAH. Postal branch of Bozrah. **2** village, Essex co., Vt.: see LUNENBURG.

Gilman City, city (1990 pop. 393), Harrison co., NW Mo., 12 mi/19 km SE of Bethany; 40°08′N 93°52′W. Corn, wheat; sheep, cattle.

Gilman Hot Springs, Calif.: see SAN JACINTO.

Gilmanton (GIL-muhn-tuhn), town (1990 pop. 2,609), Belknap co., central N.H., 7 mi/11.3 km SSE of Laconia; 43°25′N 71°22′W. Agr. (cattle, poultry; vegetables; dairying; nursery crops; sugar maples); mfg. (food). Iron formerly mined at Gilmanton Iron Works village. Home of the late author Grace Metallious who wrote the novel *Peyton Place*. Crystal L. in E; Shellcamp Pond in W.

Gilmer 1 county (☐ 439 sq mi/1,137 sq km; 1990 pop. 13,368), N Ga.; ⊙ Ellijay; 34°41′N 84°28′W. In the Blue Ridge and partly (N) in Chattahoochee Natl. Forest; drained by Coosawattee R. Corn; timber, cattle, hogs; and resort area; textile mfg. at Ellijay. Formed 1832. **2** (GIL-muhr), county (☐ 340 sq mi/881 sq km; 1990 pop. 7,669), central W.Va.; ⊙ Glenville; 38°55′N 80°50′W. On Allegheny Plateau; drained by Little Kanawha R. and tributaries. Oil and gas wells, coal mines. Agr. (corn, alfalfa, hay; cattle; poultry; sheep). Timber. Cedar Creek State Park in S. Formed 1845.

Gilmer, town (1990 pop. 4,822), NE Texas, near Little Cypress Bayou, 36 mi/58 km WNW of Marshall; ⊙

Upshur co. Elev. 370 ft/113 m. Trade center for agr. (dairying; poultry; vegetables, sweet potatoes); timber; oil area; oil refining; mfg. (lumber, machinery). Annual East Texas Yamboree, Oct. Settled 1858, inc. 1902.

Gilmore City, town (1990 pop. 560), on Humboldt-Pocahontas co. line, N central Iowa, 12 mi/19 km E of Pocahontas; 42°43′N 94°26′W. Livestock, grain.

Gilpin, county (☐ 150 sq mi/389 sq km; 1990 pop. 3,070), N central Colo.; ⊙ Central City; 39°51′N 105°31′W. Mining and livestock-grazing region; gold, silver, lead, copper, zinc. Tourism. Noted for old frontier towns of Central City and Black Hawk. Part of Golden Gate Canyon State Park in E; part Roosevelt Natl. Forest and Front Range in W.

Gilroy, city (1990 pop. 31,487), Santa Clara co., W Calif., between Uvas and Llagas creeks; 37°01′N 121°35′W. Located in the fertile Santa Clara valley, Gilroy supports diversified agr., including vineyards (6 wineries), orchards, dairy farms, plant nurseries, and mushrooms. Its chief prods. are food, fabricated metal prods., and paper prods. Annual Garlic Festival. Gilroy has also benefitted from the high-technology microelectronics industry in the area. Gavilan Col. is in the city. Mt. Madonna County Park, with its redwood stands, is to W; Mt. Madonna (1,897 ft/578 m) in Santa Cruz Mts. Gilroy Hot Springs and H.W. Coe State Park to NE; Coyote Reservoir, on Coyote Creek, to N. Inc. 1870.

Gilsum (GIL-suhm), town (1990 pop. 745), Cheshire co., SW N.H., 8 mi/12.9 km N of Keene; 43°02′N 72°15′W. Drained by Ashuelot R. Agr. (dairying; cattle, poultry; vegetables; nursery crops); light mfg.

Giltner (JILT-nurh), village (1990 pop. 367), Hamilton co., SE central Nebr., 15 mi/24 km SE of Grand Isl.; 40°46′N 98°09′W. Dairying; grain, livestock; light mfg.

Gimco City, town, Madison co., E central Ind., S suburb of Alexandria. Absorbed by Alexandria in 1973.

Gimie, Morne (zhee-mee, MAWRN), highest peak (3,145 ft/959 m) of St. Lucia, 10 mi/16 km S of Castries; 13°51′N 61°00′W.

Gimli (GIM-lee), town (1991 pop. 1,579), SE Man., Canada, on lower W shore of L. Winnipeg, 50 mi/80 km NNE of Winnipeg; 50°38′N 97°00′W. Settled by Icelanders, 1875. Administrative center for republic of New Iceland, 1878–1881; absorbed by prov. Large Viking statue towers above landscape. Fishing (pickerel), dairying, mixed farming; distillery. Royal Can. Air Force base W of town, 1948–1971.

Ginger Island, islet, Br. Virgin Isls., 3 mi/4.8 km SSW of Virgin Gorda isl., W of Cooper Isl; 18°24′N 64°28′W.

Gingerbread Ground, reef, NW Bahama Isls., on N Great Bahama Bank, halfway bet. Grand Bahama Isl. (N) and the Biminis (S), at 26°N.

Ginkgo Petrified Forest State Park, Wash.: see ELLENSBURG.

Ginna Station Nuclear Power Facility, power plant, Wayne co., central N.Y., 15 mi/24 km NE of Rochester; 43°17′N 77°19′W. It is 1 of 3 nuclear power-generating sites in the state; its 2 nuclear-heated steam generators began commercial operation in June 1970 and are capable of producing 470 MW of electricity. Located on S shore of L. Ontario, the plant uses lakewater to cool the nuclear reactor.

Girard 1 city (1990 pop. 2,164), Macoupin co., SW central Ill., 13 mi/21 km NNE of Carlinville; 39°27′N 89°46′W. In agr. and bituminous coal area; ships grain. RR junction. Inc. 1855. **2** (ji-RAHRD), city (1990 pop. 11,304), Trumbull co., NE Ohio, adjacent to Youngstown, on the Mahoning R.; 41°09′N 80°42′W. Its ironworks date from 1866. Mfg includes plastic prods., fabricated metal prods., and chemicals. Settled c.1800, inc. 1891.

Girard 1 (juh-RAHRD), town (1990 pop. 195), Burke co., E Ga., 19 mi/31 km E of Waynesboro; 33°02′N 81°43′W. **2** (juh-RAHRD), town (1990 pop. 2,794), ⊙ Crawford co., extreme SE Kansas, 11 mi/18 km NW of Pittsburg; 37°30′N 94°50′W. Elev 980 ft/299 m. Trade center for grain; fabricated metal prods. Light mfg. Crawford State Park to N; Crawford State Fishing L. to E. Inc. as town 1869, as city 1871.

Girard (JIR-rahrd), borough (1990 pop. 2,879), Erie co., NW Pa., 15 mi/24 km WSW of Erie, near Elk Creek.

Agr. (corn, hay; livestock; dairying); mfg. (concrete, machinery, fabricated metal prods., plastic prods.). Settled c.1800, inc. 1846.

Girard, Calif.: see WOODLAND HILLS.

Girardville (JIR-rahrd-vil), borough (1990 pop. 1,889), Schuylkill co., E central Pa., 9 mi/14.5 km NNW of Pottsville, on Mahanoy Creek. Agr. (corn, hay, poultry, dairying); anthracite coal. Settled c.1832, inc. 1872.

Girdletree (GUR-del-tree), village, Worcester co., SE Md., near Chincoteague Bay, 22 mi/35 km SSE of Salisbury. The name comes from girdling, a method of removing trees by cutting the bark. The village has a small seafood industry and canning plant.

Girdwood, village, S Alaska, on Turnagain Arm of Cook Inlet, 30 mi/48 km SE of Anchorage. Near Portage Glacier and ski resort.

Girouard, Mount (juh-RAHRD) (9,825 ft/2,995 m), SW Alta., Canada, near B.C. border, in Rocky Mts., in Banff Natl. Park, 8 mi/13 km ENE of Banff, overlooking L. Minnewanka; 51°14′N 115°24′W.

Gisburn Lake (☐ 9 sq mi/23 sq km), S N.F., Canada, N of Fortune Bay; 8 mi/13 km long, up to 3 mi/5 km wide; 47°48′N 54°51′W.

Gjoa Haven, N.W.T., Canada: see PETERSON BAY.

Glace Bay (glais), town (1991 pop. 19,501), E Cape Breton Island, N.S., Canada; 46°12′N 59°57′W. Exploitation of its coal mines began toward the end of the 19th cent., but declined in the 1960s. Its mines extended for several miles under the sea and were among the best equipped in the world. Glace Bay has a good harbor and relies heavily on its large deep-sea fishing fleet. The Marconi wireless tower at Table Head nearby was the transmitter in 1902 of the 1st transatlantic wireless message.

Glacier (GLAI-shur), county (☐ 3,037 sq mi/ 7,866 sq km; 1990 pop. 12,121), N Mont.; ⊙ Cut Bank; 48°42′N 113°01′W. Agr. area bordering on Alta.; drained by St. Mary, Milk, and Two Medicine rivers and Cut Bank Creek (latter 2 join in SE corner of co. to form Marias R.). Livestock, grain, wheat, barley, oats, hay, hogs; petroleum, natural gas. Blackfeet Indian Reservation covers all but E and W margins of co., extends S into Pondera co. Part of Glacier Natl. Park in W, Continental Divide forms W co. boundary and runs SE-NW through center of park. Part of Lewis and Clark Natl. Forest in SW corner. Formed 1919.

Glacier, resort village, SE B.C., Canada, in Rocky Mts., 35 mi/56 km NE of Revelstoke, in Glacier Natl. Park, at foot of Mt. Bonney (10,194 ft/3,107 m); 51°16′N 117°31′W. Elev. 3,817 ft/1,163 m. Just NE, on Can. Pacific RR transcontinental main line, is the Connaught Tunnel.

Glacier Bay National Park and Preserve, park (5,040 sq mi/13,052 sq km), preserve (90 sq mi/234 sq km), SE Alaska, NW of Juneau. Proclaimed as Glacier Bay Natl. Monument 1925; estab. as park and preserve 1980, designated Biosphere Reserve 1986. Glaciers descending from the towering snow-covered mts. into the bay create one of the world's most spectacular displays of ice (origin of icebergs). Among the bay's most famous glaciers is Muir Glacier, c.2 mi/3.2 km wide and rising c.265 ft/80 m above the water. Entire Glacier Bay was glacier-bound as recently as 1750. Wildlife includes bears, deer, mt. goats, whales, and water-fowl. Park lodge, camping 10 mi/16 km NW of Gustavas. Wilderness area 2,770,000 acres/1,121,019 ha.

Glacier Highway, scenic road (Highway 7), SE Alaska, extends 40.5 mi/65.2 km from Juneau NW along shore of Gastineau Channel and Lynn Canal; passes near Mendenhall Glacier and Auke Bay Ferry Terminal. Ends at Echo Cove. S extension (Thane Road) ends 5 mi/8 km SE of Juneau. No connection to outside road systems.

Glacier Island (9 mi/14.5 km long, 2 mi/3.2 km–5 mi/ 8 km wide), S Alaska, in Prince William Sound, 35 mi/ 56 km WSW of Valdez; 60°53′N 147°12′W.

Glacier Mountain (12,443 ft/3,793 m), Summit co., central Colo., 10 mi/16 km NE of Breckenridge, near Continental Divide.

Glacier National Park, 521 sq mi/1,349 sq km, SE B.C.,

Canada, in the Selkirk Mts.; estab. 1886. It contains extensive glaciated areas, including Illecilliwaet Glacier. Snow-capped peaks, with densely forested lower slopes include Mt. Bonney, with the resort village of Glacier at its base. The rugged terrain of the park is crossed by the main line of the Can. Pacific RR.

Glacier National Park (GLAI-shur) (1,584 sq mi/4,013 sq km), NW Mont., bounded by Canada (B.C. and Alta.) on N. North Fork Flathead R. forms boundary in W, Middle Fork Flathead R. forms SW boundary, U.S. Highway 2 skirts S perimeter of park. Many lakes, include McDonald, Harrison, Logging, Quartz, Bowman, and Kintla W of Continental Divide; Two Medicine, St. Mary, Sherburne, Glenns, and Waterton E of the Divide. Large mountainous area with the Continental Divide running SE-NW through its center, the park contains some of the most beautiful primitive wilderness in the U.S. and the most glaciated part of the U.S. Rocky Mts. There are about 50 glaciers, more than 200 glacier-fed lakes (L. McDonald and St. Mary L. are the largest), high peaks, sheer cliffs, waterfalls, large forests, much wildlife, and a great variety of wildflowers. Together with the adjacent Waterton Lakes Natl. Park (Alta., Canada), it forms Waterton-Glacier Internatl. Peace Park (estab. 1932). A variety of campgrounds, historical lodges, high-mt. chalets, and other accommodations in or near the park; 52 mi/84 km serpentine road bet. St. Mary (E) and West Glacier (W); crosses Divide into Logan Pass. Estab. 1910.

Glacier Peak 1 (10,541 ft/3,213 m), E Snohomish co., NW Wash., in Cascade Range, c.50 mi/80 km ENE of Everett, in Glacier Peak Wilderness Area of mt. Baker-Snoqualmie Natl. Forest. Pacific Crest Trail passes near N and W base of mt. Snowcapped extinct volcano. **2** (c.12,625 ft/3,848 m), on boundary bet. Summit co and Park co., central Colo., on Continental Divide, 8 mi/12.9 km E of Breckenridge.

Gladbrook, town (1990 pop. 881), Tama co., central Iowa, on Wolf Creek and 14 mi/23 km NE of Marshalltown; 42°11′N 92°42′W. Feed. Union Grove State Park to S.

Glade, village (1990 pop. 101), Phillips co., N Kansas, on N fork of Solomon R., 4 mi/6.4 km S of Phillipsburg; 39°40′N 99°18′W.

Glade Park, village, Mesa co., W Colo., near Utah state line, 10 mi WSW of Grand Junction; elev. c.6,750 ft/2,057 m. Grain, potatoes, beans. Colorado Natl. Monument to NE; small unit of Uncompahgre Natl. Forest to S.

Glade Spring, town (1990 pop. 1,435), Washington co., SW Va., 12 mi/19 km NE of Abingdon; 36°47′N 81°46′W. Light mfg.; agr. (livestock, poultry; dairying; corn, alfalfa).

Glades, county (□ 986 sq mi/2,554 sq km; 1990 pop. 7,591), central Fla., bounded E by L. Okeechobee; ⊙ Moore Haven; 26°56′N 81°11′W. Everglades cattle-raising area, with some farming and fishing. Crossed by Caloosahatchee R. Includes Seminole Indian Reservation. Formed 1921.

Gladewater, town (1990 pop. 6,027), Gregg and Upshur cos., E Texas, near Sabine R., 12 mi/19 km W of Longview; 32°32′N 94°57′W. Elev. 333 ft/101 m. In E Texas oil field; cattle; racehorses; timber; light mfg. L. Gladewater reservoir to N. Boomed after oil discovery, 1930. Settled 1870, inc. 1931.

Gladstone 1 city (1990 pop. 26,243), Clay co., W Mo., a suburb surrounded by Kansas City, 7 mi/11.3 km N of downtown Kansas City; 39°12′N 94°33′W. The city has diverse light industries. Founded c.1878, inc. 1952. **2** city (1990 pop. 10,152), Clackamas co., NW Oregon, expanding residential suburb 9 mi/14.5 km SSE of downtown Portland, 1 mi/1.6 km N of Oregon City, on Clackamas R., at confluence with Willamette R.; 45°23′N 122°35′W. Inc. 1911.

Gladstone, town (1991 pop. 928), S Man., Canada, on Whitemud R. and 35 mi/56 km WNW of Portage la Prairie; 50°14′N 98°57′W. Grain elevators; dairying; stock, poultry.

Gladstone, town (1990 pop. 4,565), Delta co., S Upper Peninsula, Mich., 8 mi/12.9 km NNE of Escanaba, on Little Bay De Noc; 45°51′N 87°01′W. Shipping point for grain; cattle; mfg. (wood prods., fabricated metal prods., concrete); fisheries. Agr. (potatoes). Resort. Hiawatha Natl. Forest to N and E. Founded 1887, inc. 1889.

Gladstone 1 village (1990 pop. 270), Henderson co., W Ill., 3 mi/4.8 km S of Oquawka; 40°51′N 90°57′W. Ships grain; limestone quarries. On Henderson Creek (bridged here). **2** village (1990 pop. 224), Stark co., W N.Dak., 10 mi/16 km E of Dickinson and on Green R. near its entrance to Heart R.; 46°51′N 102°34′W. **3** uninc. village, Nelson co., central Va., 23 mi/37 km NE of Lynchburg, on James R.; 37°32′N 78°50′W. Mfg. (paper prods., fabricated metal prods.); agr. (grain, tobacco, cotton, peanuts; livestock).

Gladwin, county (□ 516 sq mi/1,336 sq km; 1990 pop. 21,896), E central Mich.; ⊙ Gladwin; 43°59′N 84°23′W. Drained by Tittabawassee and Tobacco rivers and small Cedar R. Agr. (cattle, hogs, sheep, poultry; grain, seed, sugar beets, corn, wheat, oats); dairy prods.; industrial machinery. Co. has about 10 small lakes and reservoirs (called "ponds" in Mich.), largest is L. Lancer in N; Gladwin State Park in W; state forest, game refuge. Organized 1875.

Gladwin, town (1990 pop. 2,682), ⊙ Gladwin co., E central Mich., 40 mi/64 km NW of Bay City, and on small Cedar R.; 43°58′N 84°29′W. In livestock and dairy area; apples; light mfg. A dist. office of Mich. Conservation Dept. and Gladwin State Park on small Cedar R. to S. Recreation. Municipal airport. Settled 1865; inc. as village 1885, as city 1893.

Gladwyne, Pa.: see LOWER MERION.

Glandorf, village (1990 pop. 829), Putnam co., NW Ohio, c.22 mi/35 km W of Findlay and on Blanchard R.; 41°02′N 84°04′W.

Glasco 1 village (1990 pop. 556), Cloud co., N central Kansas, on Solomon R. and 16 mi/26 km SW of Concordia; 39°21′N 97°50′W. **2** village (□ 2 sq mi/5.2 sq km; 1990 pop. 1,538), Ulster co., SE N.Y., on W bank of the Hudson and 8 mi/12.9 km above Kingston; 42°02′N 73°57′W. Mfg. (textiles, apparel, construction materials).

Glascock (GLAS-kahk), county (□ 142; 1990 pop. 2,357), E Ga.; ⊙ Gibson; 33°14′N 82°37′W. Bounded W by Ogeechee R. Coastal plain agr. cotton, corn, soybeans, wheat; cattle, hogs. Formed 1857.

Glasford, village (1990 pop. 1,115), Peoria co., central Ill., 13 mi/21 km SW of Peoria, near Illinois R.; 40°34′N 89°48′W. Agr. (corn, cattle; dairying); bituminous coal–mining; wood prods. Banner Fish and Wildlife Area to S.

Glasgo, Conn.: see GRISWOLD.

Glasgow 1 (GLAS-go), city (1990 pop. 12,351), ⊙ Barren co., S central Ky.; 37°00′N 85°55′W. It is an agr. trade center that relies on dairying, livestock, tobacco, grain, timber; mfg. (apparel, printing and publishing, transportation equip., wooden prods., pharmaceuticals, concrete). The area's oil and gas fields add to Glasgow's economy. A state fish hatchery is to N. Municipal airport to NW. Western Ky. Univ.-Glasgow campus. Mus. of the Barrens. Barren River L. reservoir and State Resort Park to SW. Inc. 1799. **2** (GLAZ-go), city (1990 pop. 1,295), Howard co., central Mo., on Missouri R. and 10 mi/16 km NW of Fayette; 39°13′N 92°50′W. Ships grain by water and RR, cattle; canning factory; light mfg. RR bridge and highway bridge across Mo. R. damaged in flood of 1993. First all-steel bridge in the world completed in 1879, 2,700 ft/823 m in length (replaced in 1899). Laid out 1836, inc. 1845. Lewis Lib., built 1866, oldest building and exclusively as lib. W of Mississippi.

Glasgow 1 (GLAS-go), town (1990 pop. 3,572), ⊙ Valley co., NE Mont., 145 mi/233 km ESE of Havre and on Milk R.; 48°12′N 106°38′W. In extensively irrigated region. Shipping point for grain, sugar beets, cattle, sheep, hogs; mfg. (electronic equip., concrete); aircraft testing, tourism, retirement center. Valley Industrial Park 14 mi/23 km NNE at St. Marie. Fort Peck Lake and Dam (surrounded by Charles M. Russell Natl. Wildlife Refuge) to S. Growth of city stimulated by construction of dam. Former Glasgow Air Force Base, Glasgow Internatl. Airport N of town. Pioneer Mus.

Founded 1887, plotted 1888. Formerly called Siding 45. **2** town (1990 pop. 1,140), Rockbridge co., NW Va., 10 mi/16 km S of Lexington, in the Blue Ridge, on North R. near its mouth on Murry R., in George Washington Natl. Forest; 37°37′N 79°27′W. Light mfg.; agr. area (dairying; livestock; corn, soybeans, apples, peaches); limestone quarrying. Natural Bridge is 5 mi/8 km W. **3** (GLAS-go), town (1990 pop. 906), Kanawha co., W central W.Va., on the Kanawha R. 14 mi/23 km SE of Charleston; 38°12′N 81°25′W. Coal-mining region. Agr. (corn, tobacco); cattle; poultry.

Glasgow, village (1990 pop. 163), Scott co., W central Ill., 6 mi/9.7 km S of Winchester; 39°32′N 90°28′W. In agr. area (cattle, hogs, corn, soybeans, sorghum).

Glasgow (GLAS-go), borough (1990 pop. 74), Beaver co., W Pa., 11 mi/18 km W of Beaver and 4 mi/6.4 km ENE of East Liverpool, at Ohio state line.

Glasgow Junction, Ky.: see PARK CITY.

Glass Mountains, rise to 6,860 ft/2,091 m at Cathedral Mt., extreme W Texas, in Brewster and Pecos cos.; range extends c.25 mi/40 km ENE from point c.13 mi/21 km E of Alpine.

Glassboro, borough (1990 pop. 15,614), Gloucester co., SW N.J.; 39°42′N 75°06′W. It is a trade and processing center for a fruit-growing (especially apples) region and has light mfg. The founding industry, glass, is still important. Glassboro State Col. (renamed Rowan State Col. in 1992) was the site of a summit meeting (1967) bet. President Lyndon Johnson and Soviet Premier Aleksei Kosygin. Settled 1775, inc. 1920.

Glasscock, county (□ 901 sq mi/2,334 sq km; 1990 pop. 1,447), W Texas; ⊙ Garden City; 31°52′N 101°31′W. Elev. 2,400 ft/732 m–2,800 ft/853 m. Rolling prairies and woodlands, drained by Mustang Draw and North Concho R. Cattle; agr. (grain sorghum, hay; wheat; pecans; cotton). Some oil, natural gas. Formed 1887.

Glassport, borough (1990 pop. 5,582), Allegheny co., SW Pa., suburb 10 mi/16 km SSE of downtown Pittsburgh and 3 mi/4.8 km SW of McKeesport, on Monongahela R. Mfg. (fabricated metal prods.). Inc. 1902.

Glastenbury (GLAH-stuhn-buhr-ee), town, Bennington co., SW Vt., in the Green Mts. 10 mi/16 km NE of Bennington. Green Mt. Natl. Forest.

Glastonbury, town (1990 pop. 27,901), Hartford co., central Conn., a suburb of Hartford on the Connecticut R.; 41°41′N 72°32′W. Located in a farming region, the town has industries that include dairy, fruit, and poultry research and breeding as well as various light mfg. Several 17th-cent. houses still stand in Glastonbury, which was the birthplace of American politician Gideon Welles. Inc. 1690.

Glazier Lake (GLAI-zhuhr), Maine and N.B., on internatl. border 19 mi/31 km W of Fort Kent; 5 mi/8 km long.

Gleason, town (1990 pop. 1,402), Weakley co., NW Tenn., 28 mi/45 km SE of Union City; 36°13′N 88°37′W. In corn, cotton, livestock, tobacco area.

Gleichen (GLEE-chuhn), town (1991 pop. 331), S Alta., Canada, near Bow R., 45 mi/72 km ESE of Calgary; 50°52′N 113°03′W. Coal mining; wheat elevators; oats; ranching, cattle.

Glen Allen, uninc. town, Henrico co., E central Va., suburb 10 mi/16 km NNW of downtown Richmond, near Chickahominy R.; 37°39′N 77°28′W. Light mfg. Meadow Farm Mus. is here.

Glen Alpine, village (1990 pop. 563), Burke co., W central N.C., residential suburb 5 mi/8 km W of Morganton near Catawba R; 35°43′N 81°46′W. Grain, soybeans, chickens, hogs.

Glen Avon Heights, uninc. city (1990 pop. 12,633), Riverside co., S Calif., residential suburb 7 mi/11.3 km NW of Riverside; 34°01′N 117°30′W.

Glen Burnie, residential suburb (1990 pop. 37,305), Anne Arundel co., central Md., 10 mi/16 km S of downtown Baltimore; 39°10′N 76°36′W. Named in 1887 after the suburban estate of Judge Elias Glenn who owned the Curtis Creek Mining, Furnace and Mfg. Co. here. The Md. Dept. of Motor Vehicles in located here. Also the location of Harundale Mall, opened in 1958 as one of the 1st malls with a landscaped interior. Baltimore-Wash. Internatl. Airport is also nearby.

Glen Campbell, borough (1990 pop. 313), Indiana co., W central Pa., 22 mi/35 km NE of Indiana, on Cush Creek. Agr. (corn, hay; dairying; livestock); bituminous coal.

Glen Canyon Dam, Ariz., see POWELL, LAKE.

Glen Carbon, village (1990 pop. 7,731), Madison co., SW Ill., 12 mi/19 km NE of East St. Louis, suburb of St. Louis; 38°45′N 89°58′W. In agr. area (corn, wheat, cattle). Inc. 1892.

Glen Cove, city (□ 19 sq mi/49 sq km; 1990 pop. 24,149), Nassau co., SE N.Y., on the N shore of L.I., at the entrance to Hempstead Harbor; on L.I. Sound; 40°53′N 73°38′W. Settled 1668, attracted affluent class after Civil War. In 1920s it became core of the "Gold Coast" as mansions were built, including waterfront community on East Isl. at N end (once known as Morgans Isl. when owned by J.P. Morgan). In 19th cent. it attracted industry, including 1 of the world's largest starch factories. Now a high-income suburb with a diverse pop. Although chiefly residential, it has varied high-technology equip. and chemical industries. The Webb Inst. of Naval Architecture is here. Inc. as a city 1918.

Glen Dale, town (1990 pop. 1,612), Marshall co., NW.Va., in N. Panhandle, near the Ohio R., 4 mi/6.4 km N of Moundsville; 39°57′N 80°45′W. Mfg. (machinery, fabricated metal prods.). Reynolds Memorial Hosp. here. Inc. 1924.

Glen Echo, residential suburb (1990 pop. 234), Montgomery co., central Md., NW suburb of Washington, D.C., on the Potomac; 38°58′N 77°08′W. In the 1890s, the community was a Chautauqua meeting ground and a summer resort; during most of the 20th cent., it was an amusement park. The Chautauqua center is now run by the Natl. Park Service, which has preserved a bell tower and many old buildings. The home of Clara Barton, founder of the Amer. Red Cross, is nearby.

Glen Echo Park, village (1990 pop. 304), St. Louis co., E Mo., residential suburb 7 mi/11.3 km NW of downtown St. Louis; 38°42′N 90°17′W.

Glen Elder, village (1990 pop. 448), Mitchell co., N Kansas, on Solomon R. at Wakonda L. dam, and 11 mi/18 km WNW of Beloit; 39°30′N 98°18′W. Grain, livestock, poultry; dairying. Glen Elder State Park at Wakonda dam, to S.

Glen Ellen, uninc. town (1990 pop. 1,191), Sonoma co., W Calif., 11 mi/18 km SE of Santa Rosa and 15 mi/24 km N of San Pablo Bay, on Sonoma Creek; 38°22′N 122°33′W. Jack London State Historical Park to NW. Apples, grapes, grain, vegetables, dairying, poultry.

Glen Ellis Falls, N.H.: see ELLIS RIVER.

Glen Ellyn, village (1990 pop. 24,944), Du Page co., NE Ill., a residential suburb of Chicago, 41°52′N 88°03′W. Points of interest include Stacy Tavern, a 19th-cent. stagecoach stop on the Chicago-Galena route; a wildlife sanctuary; and an arboretum. Col. of Du Page is here, the largest community col. on one campus in the U.S. Inc. 1892.

Glen Ferris, uninc. village (1990 pop. 250), Fayette co., S central W.Va., on the Kanawha R. (power dam), 25 mi/40 km SE of Charleston.

Glen Flora 1 uninc. village (1990 pop. 210), Wharton co., S Texas, on Colorado R. 6 mi/9.7 km NW of Wharton. In oil, agr. area. **2** village (1990 pop. 108), Rusk co., N Wis., 11 mi/18 km ENE of Ladysmith; 45°30′N 90°53′W. Dairying; light mfg.

Glen Forks, uninc. village, Wyoming co., S W.Va., 18 mi/29 km WSW of Beckley. Bituminous-coal mining.

Glen Gardner, borough (1990 pop. 1,665), Hunterdon co., NW N.J., 12 mi/19 km E of Phillipsburg; 40°42′N 74°56′W. Voorhees State Park and Hagedorn Center for Geriatrics nearby.

Glen Haven, village, Leelanau co., NW Mich., 22 mi/35 km NW of Traverse City, bet. Glen L. (c.5 mi/8 km long) and L. Michigan; 44°54′N 86°01′W. Nearby is Sleeping Bear Point, with large sand dunes. A sand dune, c.480 ft/146 m above the level of the lake, is moving toward Glen L. Former fishing village. Townsite is

entirely within Sleeping Bear Dunes Natl. Lakeshore. Bldgs. are being preserved as historic site.

Glen Head, suburb (□ 1 sq mi/2.6 sq km; 1990 pop. 4,488), Nassau co., SE N.Y., on N shore of W L.I., just S of Glen Cove; 40°50′N 73°37′W.

Glen Hope, borough (1990 pop. 187), Clearfield co., central Pa., 20 mi/32 km NNW of Altoona and 4 mi/6.4 km NE of Coalport, on Clearfield Creek. Mfg. (lumber); bituminous coal. Also spelled Glenhope.

Glen Jean, uninc. village (1990 pop. 800), Fayette co., S central W. Va., 10 mi/16 km S of Fayetteville, in coal region.

Glen Lake, Mich.: see GLEN HAVEN.

Glen Lyn (GLEN-LIN), town (1990 pop. 170), Giles co., SW Va., 7 mi/11.3 km NW of Pearisburg, in Allegheny Mts. near New R., at W.Va. state line; 37°22′N 80°51′W. Light mfg.; coal. Large hydroelectric plant.

Glen Lyon, uninc. town (1990 pop. 2,082), Newport township, Luzerne co., E central Pa., near Susquehanna R., 5 mi/8 km WSW of Nanticoke. State correctional institute and hosp. to N.

Glen, Mount (7,512 ft/2,290 m), Cochise co., SE Ariz., highest peak in Dragoon Mts., 17 mi/27 km N of Tombstone in section of Coronado Natl. Forest. Cochise Stronghold Memorial Park is here.

Glen Park, village (1990 pop. 527), Jefferson co., N N.Y., on Black R., just NW of Watertown; 44°00′N 75°57′W.

Glen Raven, uninc. town (1990 pop. 2,616), Alamance co., N central N.C., suburb 3 mi/4.8 km NW of Burlington near Haw R.; 36°07′N 79°28′W. Light mfg.

Glen Ridge, residential borough (1990 pop 7,076), Essex co., NE N.J., 5 mi/8 km W of Newark; 40°47′N 74°12′W. Settled in early 19th cent., inc. 1895.

Glen Roberston, village, SE Ont., Canada, 25 mi/40 km NNE of Cornwall; 45°21′N 74°30′W. Dairying, mixed farming.

Glen Rock 1 borough (1990 pop. 10,883), Bergen co., NE N.J., a residential suburb of N.Y. city; 40°57′N 74°07′W. George Washington's army used the area for camping grounds during the Revolutionary War. Settled c.1710, inc. 1896. **2** borough (1990 pop. 1,688), York co., S Pa., 12 mi/19 km S of York. Agr. (grain, soybeans, apples; dairying, livestock, poultry); mfg. (electronic equip., machinery). Inc. 1860.

Glen Rogers, uninc. village (1990 pop. 500), Wyoming co., S W.Va., 11 mi. NNE of Pineville, in coal region; RR terminus.

Glen Rose, town (1990 pop. 1,949), ⊙ Somervell co., N central Texas, near junction of Paluxy Creek with Brazos R., 23 mi/37 km WSW of Cleburne; 32°14′N 97°45′W. Elev. 680 ft/207 m. Health and vacation resort, with mineral springs; bathing, fishing; dairying; peanuts; cattle; mfg. (construction materials). Squaw Creek L. to N; Dinosaur Valley State Park to NW, area known for its dinosaur fossils. Inc. 1926.

Glen, the, resort village, Warren co., E N.Y., in the Adirondacks, on the Hudson R. and 21 mi/34 km NNW of Glen Falls; 43°35′N 73°52′W.

Glen Ullin (UHL-lin), town (1990 pop. 927), Morton co., S central N.Dak. on Big Muddy Creek, 45 mi/72 km W of Mandan. Airport. Heart Butte Dam is 15 mi/24 km S on L. Tschida Reservoir on Heart R.; 46°48′N 101°49′W.

Glen White, uninc. village (1990 pop. 430), Raleigh co., S W. Va., 5 mi/8 km SW of Beckley. Agr., coal mining area.

Glenaire, village (1990 pop. 597), Clay co., W Mo., residential suburb 13 mi/21 km NE of downtown Kansas City, surrounded by city of Liberty; 39°13′N 94°27′W.

Glenallen, town (1990 pop. 96), Bollinger co., SE Mo., 3 mi/4.8 km NW of Marble Hill; 37°19′N 90°01′W.

Glenarden, town (1990 pop. 5,025), Prince Georges co., central Md., E of Wash., D.C.; 38°56′N 76°52′W. Originally a slum area, it was developed into a successful urban renewal area by black Washingtonians, recognized by the Dept. of Housing and Urban Development. Inc. in 1939.

Glenavon (gleh-NA-vuhn), village (1991 pop. 237), SE Sask., Canada, 33 mi/53 km SE of Indian Head; mixed farming.

Glenbeulah (glen-BYOO-lah), village (1990 pop. 386), Sheboygan co., E Wis., on small Mullet R. and 17 mi/27 km WNW of Sheboygan, at N end of Kettle Moraine State Forest; 43°47′N 88°02′W. In dairy and grain area. Light mfg. Sheboygan L. to N.; Old Wade House State Park to SW.

Glenboro, village (1991 pop. 674), SW Man., Canada, 35 mi/56 km SE of Brandon; 49°33′N 99°17′W. Grain elevators.

Glenbrook, uninc. town, Douglas co., W Nev., on E shore of L. Tahoe, 10 mi/16 km SW of Carson City. Resort area; tourism. L. Tahoe Nev. State Park to NE; Toiyabe Natl. Forest to E.

Glenburn, town (1990 pop. 3,198), Penobscot co., S Maine, just NW of Bangor; 44°55′N 68°51′W. In agr., recreational region.

Glenburn, village (1990 pop. 439), Renville co., N central N.Dak., 37 mi/60 km N of Minot; 48°30′N 101°13′W.

Glenburn, township (1990 pop. 1,242), Lackawanna co., NE Pa., 9 mi/14.5 km NNW of Scranton and 2 mi/3.2 km NW of Clarks Summit; 41°30′N 75°44′W. Agr. includes dairying, cattle; corn, hay, vegetables. Lackawanna State Park to N.

Glencliff, N.H.: see WARREN.

Glencoe (GLEHN-ko), village (1991 pop. 2,148), S Ont., Canada, 30 mi/48 km SW of London; 42°45′N 81°42′W. Mixed farming, dairying, woodworking; former oil production.

Glencoe 1 (GLEN-ko), town (1990 pop. 4,670), Etowah co., NE Ala., 5 mi/8 km SE of Gadsden. Light mfg.; concrete; limestone. Inc. 1939. **2** town (□ 8 sq mi/20.7 sq km; 1990 pop. 2,282), Volusia co., E central Fla., 3 mi/4.8 km W of New Smyrna Beach; 29°00′N 80°58′W. **3** town (1990 pop. 4,648), ⊙ McLeod co., S central Minn., 13 mi/21 km SE of Hutchinson, on Buffalo Creek; 44°46′N 94°09′W. Elev. 1,002 ft/305 m. Trading point in agr. area (grain, peas; poultry, livestock; dairying); mfg. (machinery, fabricated metal prods., food). Plotted 1855.

Glencoe 1 village (1990 pop. 8,499), Cook co., NE Ill., on L. Michigan, residential suburb 18 mi/29 km NW of downtown Chicago; 42°07′N 87°45′W. Glencoe is among the several scenic, upper income North Shore suburbs N of Chicago. It has light mfg. Inc. 1869. **2** village (1990 pop. 473), Payne co., N central Okla., 11 mi/18 km NE of Stillwater; 36°13′N 96°55′W. In agr. area (grazing and wheat).

Glendale 1 city (1990 pop. 148,134), Maricopa co., S central Ariz., suburb 7 mi/11.3 km NW of downtown Phoenix, adjacent to Phoenix; 33°34′N 112°12′W. Elev. 1,154 ft/352 m. It is located in a rich agr. region irrigated by the Salt R. project; immediate vicinity has been replaced by rapid urban growth. Glendale has become one of the fastest growing U.S. cities, marked by a pop. increase of more than 52% bet. 1980 and 1990. It has food-processing plants and is a shipping point for fruits and vegetables; mfg. (plastics, fabricated metal prods., wood prods., food). Luke Air Force Base, a large jet fighter training center, is in Glendale. Glendale Community Col., American Graduate School of Internatl. Management, and the Glendale Historical Society are also located here. Glendale Municipal Airport in SW. Inc. 1910 **2** city (1990 pop. 180,038), Los Angeles co., S Calif., a suburb 7 mi/11.3 km N of downtown Los Angeles, W of Pasadena; 34°11′N 118°15′W. Bounded S and NW by city of Los Angeles. Mfg. includes chemicals, apparel, electronic equip. Glendale is also within the area's film industry, dist.; Burbank to W, Hollywood (Los Angeles) to SW. The city was founded on part of a ranch that had been the 1st Spanish land grant in California (1784). Forest Lawn Memorial Park, a large cemetery, is there. Glendale Community Col. and a chiropractic col. Mt. Waterman Ski Area to N; Angeles Natl. Forest to N. Inc. 1906. **3** city (1990 pop. 5,945), St. Louis co., E Mo., suburb 10 mi/16 km WSW of downtown St. Louis; 38°35′N 90°22′W. **4** city (1990 pop. 14,088), Milwaukee co., SE Wis., a suburb 5 mi/8 km N of downtown Milwaukee, on the Milwaukee R.; 43°07′N 87°55′W. Light mfg. Inc. 1950.

Glendale 1 town (1990 pop. 2,453), Arapahoe co., N central Colo., residential suburb 4 mi/6.4 km SE of downtown Denver, on Cherry Creek, completely surrounded by Denver city and county; 39°42′N 104°55′W. Elev. 5,350 ft/1,631 m;. **2** uninc. town (1990 pop. 1,049), Spartanburg co., NW S.C., 4 mi/6.4 km E of Spartanburg. Agr. includes dairying, poultry, soybeans, sorghum, peaches.

Glendale 1 village, Daviess co., SW Ind., 7 mi/11.3 km SE of Washington. Agr. area. Glendale State Fish and Wildlife Area and the East Fork State Fish Hathchery are nearby to the E. **2** uninc. village (1990 pop. 23), Clark co., SE Nev., 45 mi/72 km NE of Las Vegas, on Muddy R. Farming community in Moapa Valley. Cattle, poultry, hay. **3** village (1990 pop. 2,445), Hamilton co., extreme SW Ohio, 11 mi/18 km N of downtown Cincinnati; 39°16′N 84°27′W. Inc. 1855. **4** village (1990 pop. 707), Douglas co., SW Oregon, 21 mi/34 km S of Roseburg, on Cow Creek; 42°44′N 123°25′W. Timber. Light mfg. **5** uninc. village, Scott township, Allegheny co., SW Pa., residential suburb 6 mi/9.7 km SW of downtown Pittsburgh, on Chartiers Creek; 40°23′N 80°05′W. **6** village (1990 pop. 282), Kane co., S Utah, 18 mi/29 km N of Kanab and on East Fork of Virgin R. Apples; cattle. Elev. 5,500 ft/1,676 m. Dixie Natl. Forest to N; Zion Natl. Park to W. **7** uninc. village, Henrico co., E central Va., 12 mi/19 km SE of Richmond. Site of inconclusive Civil War engagement (also called Battle of Frazier's Farm) of Seven Days Battles (June 30, 1862). Malvern Hill Battlefield, part of Richmond Natl. Battlefield Park; Glendale Natl. Cemetery.

Glendale, a sect. of W Queens borough of N.Y. city, SE N.Y., bounded on N by RR, on E by Woodhaven Blvd., on S by cemeteries, and on W by Fresh Pond Rd. Part of the old Newtown, which also encompassed present-day Jackson Heights, Corona, Elmhurst, Rego Park, Forest Hills, Maspeth, Middle Village, and Ridgewood. Known as a quiet residential area; its inhabitants are mainly of Ger. origin, though since 1980s many E Europeans have moved to the area.

Glendale, Mass.: see STOCKBRIDGE.

Glendale Heights, village (1990 pop. 27,973), Du Page co., NE Ill., suburb 23 mi/37 km WNW of downtown Chicago, 4 mi/6.4 km NNE of Wheaton; 41°55′N 88°04′W. Mfg. (plastic prods., machinery). De Vry Inst. of Technology to SE.

Glendive (GLEN-DEIV), town (1990 pop. 4,802), ⊙ Dawson co., E Mont., on Glendive Creek where it enters the Yellowstone R., and 70 mi/113 km NE of Miles City; 47°07′N 104°43′W. Trading and shipping point in irrigated grain and sugar beet region; cattle, sheep, hogs, wheat, barley, oats, corn sugar beets, beans, alfalfa. Lignite mines nearby; gas wells 20 mi/32 km S. Known for agates, fossils, and the primitive paddlefish in the Yellowstone. Frontier Gateway Mus., Merril Ave. Historic Dist., and Dawson Community Col. Lower Yellowstone Diversion Dam to NE. Makoshika State Park to S. Laid out 1880, inc. 1902.

Glendo, town (1990 pop. 195), Platte co., E Wyo., on W shore of Glendo Reservoir (N. Platte R.), 31 mi/50 km N of Wheatland; 42°30′N 105°01′W. Elev. 4,718 ft/1,438 m. Supply point in ranching region. Glendo State Park to SE.

Glendo Reservoir (□ 36 sq mi/93 sq km), Platte co., SE Wyo., on N. Platte R., c.80 mi/128 km ESE of Casper; 42°29′N 104°59′W. Max. capacity 1,118,653 acre-ft. Formed by Glendo Dam (190 ft/58 m high), built (1958) for flood control. Glendo State Park on E shore.

Glendon, village (1991 pop. 403), E Alta., Canada, 65 mi/105 km N of Vermilion; 54°15′N 111°10′W. Mixed farming, lumbering.

Glendon, borough (1990 pop. 391), Northampton co., E Pa., 2 mi/3.2 km SW of Easton, on Lehigh R.

Glendora, city (1990 pop. 47,828), Los Angeles co., S Calif., a residential suburb 22 mi/35 km ENE of downtown Los Angeles, at the S base of the San Gabriel Mts.; 34°09′N 117°51′W. Mfg of plastic prods., transportation equip., food. The region was declared open govt. land in 1869 and a rush of homesteaders began. By the early 1900s it was covered with magnificent groves of orange and lemon trees. Although some citrus fruit is still grown in the area, the housing boom following World War II converted the city into a bedroom community. Angeles Natl. Forest to N, including San Gabriel Wilderness Area; Morris and San Gabriel reservoirs. Inc. 1911.

Glendora (glen-DOR-uh), village (1990 pop. 165) Tallahatchie co., NW central Miss., near Tallahatchie R. and 23 mi/37 km NNW of Greenwood; 33°49′N 90°17′W. RR junction to N. Agr. (cotton, grain, soybeans; cattle).

Glenfield, borough (1990 pop. 201), Allegheny co., SW Pa., residential suburb 9 mi/14.5 km NW of downtown Pittsburgh, on Ohio R. (bridged), opposite Coraopolis.

Glenford, village (1990 pop. 208), Perry co., central Ohio, 16 mi/26 km W of Zanesville; 39°53′N 82°19′W.

Glengarry (glehn-GA-ree), county (□ 478 sq mi/1,238 sq km), SE Ont., Canada, on the St. Lawrence and on Que. border; ⊙ Cornwall; 45°15′N 74°35′W. Part of United County of Stormont, Dundas, and Glengarry.

Glenham, village, (1990 pop. 134) Walworth co., N S.Dak., 8 mi/12.9 km E of Mobridge, near Missouri R.; 45°31′N 100°16′W. L. Hiddenwood State Park to E; L. Oahe to SW.

Glenida, Lake, N.Y.: see CARMEL HAMLET.

Glenmont, village (1990 pop. 233), Holmes co., central Ohio, 28 mi/45 km SE of Mansfield; 40°31′N 82°05′W.

Glenmora (GLIN-mor-uh), town (1990 pop. 1,686), Rapides parish, central La., 24 mi/39 km SW of Alexandria; 30°58′N 92°35′W. In agr. area (vegetables, cotton, corn, sugarcane, sweet potatoes: poultry, cattle, exotic fowl). Oil and gas field nearby. Cocodrie L. to E. Kisatchie Natl. Forest to N. Settled 1898, inc. 1913.

Glenn, county (□ 1,315 sq mi/3,406 sq km; 1990 pop. 24,798), N central Calif.; ⊙ Willows; 39°36′N 122°23′W. E part is in Sacramento Valley; rises in W to Coast Ranges, where highest point in co. (Black Butte) is 7,450 ft/2,271 m. Part of E boundary formed by Butte Creek. Livestock (cattle, sheep); dairying; irrigated farming (sugar beets, rice, corn, beans, barley, olives, almonds, walnuts, pistachios, prunes, honey, citrus); timber. Waterfowl, pheasant, deer hunting. Includes part of Mendocino Natl. Forest (W). Watered by Sacramento R. (forms part of E boundary). Part of Sacramento Natl. Wildlife Refuge is in SE; Stone George Reservoir in W center, Black Butte Reservoir on N boundary, both on Stony Creek. Tehuma Colusa Canal crosses co. N-S in center. Formed 1891.

Glenn, village Allegan co., SW Mich., 19 mi/31 km W of Allegan, near L. Michigan; 42°31′N 86°13′W. Resort.

Glenn Heights, town (1990 pop. 4,564), Dallas and Ellis cos., N Texas, residential suburb 15 mi/24 km S of downtown Dallas; 32°32′N 96°50′W. Agr. area on fringe of rapidly growing Dallas–Fort Worth Metroplex. Dairying, cattle, cotton.

Glenn Highway, S Alaska, extends 189 mi/304 km ENE from Anchorage to Glennallen, where it joins Richardson Highway (to Fairbanks) 10 mi/16 km NNW of Copper Center. Follows course of Matanuska and Tazlina rivers along NW slope of Chugach Mts.; serves Eklutna, Palmer, Chickaloon, Sutton, and other localities in fertile Matanuska Valley.

Glenn Springs, uninc. village, Spartanburg co., NW S.C., 11 mi/18 km SSE of Spartanburg.

Glennallen, town (1990 pop. 928), S central Alaska, 75 mi/121 km NNE of Valdez, on Glenn Highway (Rt. 1), 2 mi/3.2 km W of S junction of Richardson Highway (Rt. 4). Situated near Tazlina R., branch of Copper R., to E. Elev. 1,460 ft/445 m. Trans-Alaska Pipeline passes N-S to E. Highway services center; several small farms in area. Radio station. Small Bible col.

Glenns, locality, Gloucester co., E Va., 11 mi/18 km NNW of Gloucester, near Piankatank R.; 37°33′N 76°36′W. Agr. (grain, soybeans; cattle). Rappahannock Community Col. (Glenns Campus).

Glenns Ferry, town (1990 pop. 1,304), Elmore co., SW Idaho, on Snake R. and 25 mi/40 km SE of Mountain Home; 42°57′N 115°18′W. Elev. 2,577 ft/785 m. RR center in irrigated agr. area (potatoes, onions, grain); food processing; mfg. (electronic equip.). Three Island Crossing State Park is 1 mi/1.6 km W. Laid out 1883, Snake R. crossing site of Oregon Trail, later became ferry station.

Glennville, town (1990 pop. 3,676), Tattnall co., E central Ga., 35 mi/56 km SSW of Statesboro; 31°56′N 81°56′W. Light mfg.

Glenolden, borough (1990 pop. 7,260), Delaware co., SE Pa., suburb 8 mi/12.9 km SW of downtown Philadelphia. Mfg. (fabricated metal prods., pharmaceuticals). Settled c.1654, inc. 1894.

Glenpool, town (1990 pop. 6,688), Tulsa co., NE Okla., suburb 14 mi/23 km S of downtown Tulsa; 35°57′N 96°00′W. In agr. area; mfg. (machinery, plastic prods., fabricated metal prods.). Founded as an oil boom town.

Glenrock, town (1990 pop. 2,153), Converse co., E central Wyo., on N Platte R. and 23 mi/37 km E of Casper; 42°51′N 105°51′W. Elev. 5,009 ft/1,527 m. In sheep and cattle region; alfalfa, hay. Oil wells, coal and vermiculite mines in vicinity. Nearby is site of Deer Creek Station, military post estab. 1861 on Oregon Trail. Ayers Park and Natural Bridge to SE; Laramie Mts. and Medicine Bow Natl. Forest to S.

Glens Falls, city (□ 3 sq mi/7.8 sq km; 1990 pop. 15,023), Warren co., E central N.Y., in the foothills of the Adirondack Mts. and on the Hudson R.; 43°18′N 73°39′W. Mfg. includes lumber, paper prods., electronic equip., portland cement, textiles, and apparel. Seat of Adirondack Community Col. Noteworthy is the Hyde collection of European and Amer. art. Charles Evans Hughes was b. here. Settled 1762, inc. as a city 1908.

Glenshaw, Pa.: see SHALER.

Glenshire-Devonshire, uninc. town (1990 pop. 2,133), Nevada co., E Calif., residential area 4 mi/6.4 km ENE of Truckee, on Truckee R.; 39°21′N 120°05′W. Area surrounded by parts of Tahoe Natl. Forest.

Glenside, uninc. town (1990 pop. 8,704), Montgomery co., SE Pa., part of Abington and Cheltenham townships, residential suburb 11 mi/18 km N of downtown Philadelphia on Tacony Creek. Light mfg. Seat of Beaver Col., and Reconstructionist and Rabbinical Col.; Curtis Arboretum.

Glenview, village (1990 pop. 37,093), Cook co., NE Ill., a suburb 16 mi/26 km NW of downtown Chicago; 42°04′N 87°49′W. Settled 1833, inc. 1899. The U.S. Coast Guard Air Facility is here, along with varied light industry. Mfg. (plastic prods., machinery, printing and publishing, electronic equip.). Peacock Prairie, a center for important botanical research, is nearby.

Glenville 1 town (1990 pop. 778), Freeborn co., S Minn., on Shell Rock R., near Iowa state line, and 6 mi/9.7 km SE of Albert Lea; 43°34′N 93°16′W. RR junction. Livestock, poultry; grain, soybeans, alfalfa; dairying. **2** town (1990 pop. 1,923), ⊙ Gilmer co., central W.Va., on the Little Kanawha, 21 mi/34 km WSW of Weston; 38°56′N 80°49′W. Agr. (corn; livestock; poultry). Mfg. (plastic prods., chemicals). Glenville State Col. here. Oil and gas fields. Cedar Creek State Park to S.

Glenville, Conn.: see GREENWICH.

Glenville, village (1990 pop. 304), Clay co., SE Nebr., on branch of Little Blue R. and 10 mi/16 km SE of Hastings. U.S. Meat Animal Research Center to NE.

Glenwillow, village (1990 pop. 455), Cuyahoga co., N Ohio, 15 mi/24 km SE of downtown Cleveland; 41°22′N 81°28′W.

Glenwood, city (1990 pop. 4,571), ⊙ Mills co., SW Iowa, on Keg Creek and 17 mi/27 km SSE of Council Bluffs, Mo. R. valley to W; 41°02′N 95°44′W. In grain and livestock area; RR junction to SW at Pacific Jct. Mfg. (plastic prods., food). Glenwood State Hosp. and School (1876). Flooding occurred here in 1993. Founded by Mormons as Rushville; renamed Coonsville in 1852 and Glenwood in 1853; inc. 1857.

Glenwood 1 town (1990 pop. 208), Crenshaw co., S Ala., near Conecuh R., 7 mi/11.3 km SE of Luverne. **2** town (1990 pop. 1,354), Pike co., SW Ark., on Caddo R., 31 mi/50 km WSW of Hot Springs; 34°19′N 93°32′W. Light mfg. Ouachita Natl. Forest to N. **3** town (1990 pop. 881), Wheeler co., SE central Ga., 15 mi/24 kmW of Vidalia; 32°11′N 82°40′W. **4** town, E Hawaii isl., Hawaii co., Hawaii, 15 mi/24 km SSW of Hilo, 15 mi/

24 km inland fro SE coast. Fruit, macadamia nuts. Residential area. Small unit of Hawaii Volcanoes Natl. Park to W; parts of Olaa Forest Reserve to NW and SW; Wao Kele O Puna Natural Area Reserve to SE. **5** town (1990 pop. 285), Rush and Fayette cos., E Ind., 8 mi/12.9 km W of Connersville; 39°19′N 85°18′W. Agr. area; fertilizers. **6** town (1990 pop. 2,573), ⊙ Pope co., W Minn., 17 mi/27 km S of Alexandria at NE end of L. Minnewaska; 45°38′N 95°22′W. Elev. 1,392 ft/424 m. RR junction. Resort in agr. area (poultry, livestock; grain, soybeans, beans; dairying); light mfg. Municipal airport to E. Plotted 1866, inc. as village 1881, inc. as city 1912. **7** town (1990 pop. 195), Schuyler co., N Mo., near Chariton R., 3 mi/4.8 km W of Lancaster; 40°31′N 92°34′W. **8** uninc. town (1990 pop. c. 3,200), Dauphin co., SE Pa. residential suburb 3 mi/4.8 km NE of Harrisburg; 40°17′N 76°50′W.

Glenwood 1 village (1990 pop. 9,289), Cook co., NE Ill., suburb 23 mi/37 km S of downtown Chicago, NE of Chicago Heights; 41°32′N 87°37′W. Light mfg. **2** uninc. village (1990 pop. 220), Catron co., SW N.Mex., 64 mi/103 km NW of Silver City on San Francisco R., 8 mi/12.9 km E of Ariz. state line, just W of Mogollon Mts. Elev. 4,712 ft/1,436 m. In hunting and fishing region. Prehistoric artifacts, thought to mark beginning of Mogollon culture, found nearby. Village is in Gila Natl. Forest. A fish hatchery is here. **3** uninc. village, McDowell co., W N.C., 5 mi/8 km SSE of Marion. Agr. area. Mfg. (leather prods.). **4** village (1990 pop. 437), Sevier co., central Utah, 5 mi/8 km E of Richfield; 38°45′N 111°59′W. Alfalfa, barley; dairying; cattle. Parts of Fishlake Natl. Forest to NW, S, and E. Utah State (Glenwood) Fish Hatchery to S. Historic bldgs. Settled 1863–1864, originally Glen Cove; abandoned 1867 during Blackhawk Indian War, resettled 1870.

Glenwood, plantation (1990 pop. 8), Aroostook co., E Maine, 26 mi/42 km SSW of Houlton; 45°48′N 68°05′W. In wilderness recreational area.

Glenwood City, town (1990 pop. 1,026), St. Croix co., W Wis., 17 mi/27 km NW of Menomonie; 45°03′N 92°10′W. Dairy prods., poultry, cement.

Glenwood Landing, village (1990 pop. 3,407), Nassau co., SE N.Y., on N shore of W L.I., overlooking Hempstead Harbor and just SW of Glen Cove; 40°49′N 73°38′W. In summer recreational and residential region, and agr. area; boat repairing. Large power station.

Glenwood Springs, town (1990 pop. 6,561), ⊙ Garfield co., W central Colo., on Colorado R., at mouth of Roaring Fork R., N of Elk Mts., and 75 mi/121 km NE of Grand Junction; 39°32′N 107°19′W. Elev. 5,746 ft/1,751 m. Light mfg. Resort, with hot mineral springs; hq. of White R. Natl. Forest (parts of forest to N and S). Potatoes, cattle, sheep, hay, oats. Oil-shale deposits in vicinity. Hydroelectric plant just NE receives water from dam and diversion tunnel on Colorado R.; supplies power to Denver. To E scenic Glenwood Canyon, 1,000 ft/305 m deep in places, extending 15 mi/24 km along Colorado R. Colorado Mountain Col. here. Sunrise Ski Resort to S. City laid out 1883, inc. 1885.

Glidden, town (1990 pop. 1,099), Carroll co., W central Iowa, near Middle Raccoon R., 7 mi/11.3 km E of Carroll; 42°03′N 94°43′W. Dairying.

Glidden 1 (GLID-uhn), village, Harlan co., SE Ky., in the Cumberlands 5 mi/8 km SE of Harlan. Bituminous coal. **2** village, Ashland co., N Wis., 34 mi/55 km SSE of Ashland, in submarginal farm area. Dairy prods., lumber, logging. Chequamegon National Forest to W.

Glines Canyon Dam, Wash.: see ELWHA RIVER.

Globe, town (1990 pop. 6,062), ⊙ Gila co., E central Ariz., 73 mi/117 km E of Phoenix; 33°22′N 110°45′W. Elev. 3,541 ft/1,079 m. Pinal Mts. to SW. Mining and ranching area. Settled 1876 as silver-mining center, developed as one of largest copper-producing centers in U.S. Copper, silver, gold mines in vicinity; cattle, hogs; mfg. (printing and publishing). San Carlos Indian Reservation is just E. Tonto Natl. Forest to N, W, and S.

Glocester (GLOS-ter), town (1990 pop. 9,227), Providence co., NW R.I., on Conn. state line, on Chepachet R. (bridged at Chepachet village) and 15 mi/24 km WNW of Providence; 41°54′N 71°42′W. Named for Glocester, England. Set off from Providence and inc. 1731.

Glomawr (GLAHM-uh-wah), village (1990 pop. 400), Perry co., SE Ky., in Cumberland foothills, on North Fork Kentucky R. and 3 mi/4.8 km SE of Hazard. Bituminous coal.

Glooscap Trail, scenic highway (200 mi/322 km long), N N.S., Canada. Starts at Windsor, runs ENE along S shore of Minas Basin to Truro, detouring the lower reaches of Shubenacadie R. From Truro it continues W along N shore of Minas Basin to Parrsboro, then N across base of Chignecto Peninsula through Springhill, ending at Amherst. 30 mi/48 km branch goes W from Parrsboro to Advocate Harbour, near Cape d'Or. High tides, waterfalls, mining mus., headlands, mud flats. Named for Micmac man-god Glooscap.

Gloria Dei National Affiliated Area, historic site (3.73 acres/1.51 ha), city of Philadelphia, Philadelphia co., SE Pa., at Delaware Ave. and Christian Street; 2d-oldest Swed. church in the U.S.; founded 1677, present bldg. erected c.1700. Authorized 1942.

Gloria Glens Park, resort village (1990 pop. 446), Medina co., N Ohio, on small Chippewa L., 7 mi/11 km SW of Medina; 41°03′N 84°54′W.

Glorieta, uninc. village (1990 pop. 300), Santa Fe co., N central N.Mex., 12 mi/19 km SE of Santa Fe, near Pecos R., in Sangre de Cristo Mts. Elev. 7,425 ft/2,263 m. Blankets. Trading point and RR loading station surrounded by Santa Fe Natl. Forest. A fish hatchery to E; Pecos Natl. Historical Park to E; Glorieta Mesa to S. Civil War battle fought here.

Gloster (GLAWS-tuhr), town (1990 pop. 1,323), Amite co., SW Miss., 34 mi/55 km SE of Natchez; 31°11′N 91°01′W. RR terminus. In timber and agr. (cattle, corn) region; light mfg. Homochitto Natl. Forest to N. Inc. 1884.

Gloucester (GLAH-stuhr), county (□ 1,854 sq mi/4,802 sq km; 1991 pop. 88,101), NE N.B., Canada, on Chaleur Bay and Gulf of St. Lawrence; ⊙ Bathurst. Includes Shippigan and Miscou isls.

Gloucester 1 (GLAH-stuhr), county (□ 336 sq mi/870 sq km; 1990 pop. 230,082), SW N.J., bounded W by Delaware R.; ⊙ Woodbury; 39°42′N 75°08′W. Mfg. (food, apparel, printing and publishing, chemicals, plastic prods., fabricated metal prods., machinery, electronic equip.); agr. (fruit). Drained by Maurice R. and Big Timber Creek. Formed 1686. NW part of co. in Camden metro area. **2** county (□ 288 sq mi/746 sq km; 1990 pop. 30,131), E Va.; ⊙ Gloucester; 37°23′N 76°31′W. In Tidewater region; bounded W and S by York R. estuary and E by Mobjack Bay, arms of Chesapeake Bay; many tidal inlets. Mfg. at Gloucester; agr. (barley, wheat, corn, hay, soybeans; some cattle); bulb growing; fisheries. Formed 1651.

Gloucester, city (1991 pop. 101,677), SE Ont., Canada, suburb of Ottawa, part of Ottawa-Carleton Regional Municipality (1991 pop. 678,147). Located 6 mi/10 km E and SE of downtown Ottawa. Borders Ottawa R. on NE, Rideau R. on SW. Ottawa Internatl. Airport in SW. Includes communities of Blackburn and ORLEANS. Mainly rural. Mfg. (transportation equip., electronic equip.); mixed farming, dairying.

Gloucester (GLAWS-tuhr), city (□ 41 sq mi/106 sq km; 1990 pop. 28,716), Essex co., NE Mass., on Cape Ann; settled 1623, inc. as a city 1873; 42°38′N 70°41′W. It is a port of entry at the head of Gloucester Harbor, which is protected by a breakwater built from Eastern Point (lighthouse here). The harbor has been used by fishing ships for over 3 cents., and Gloucester still bases much of its economy on the fishing, fishing research and development, and fish-processing industries; mfg. (machinery, electronic equip., apparel). Once an important shipbuilding center; the 1st schooner is said to have been built there in 1713. The picturesque old city is also a popular summer resort. Tourist attractions include the famous bronze *Fisherman,* a memorial to the thousands of Gloucestermen lost at sea; whale-watching excursions; Hammond Castle, which houses collections of medieval art; Cape Ann Historical Mus.; and numerous pre-Revolutionary houses and art galleries. The city has furnished material for authors (e.g., Rudyard Kipling in his *Captains Courageous*) as well as artists. Includes villages of Bass Rocks, Bay View, Lanesville, Magnolia, Riverdale, and W. Gloucester.

Gloucester, uninc. town (1990 pop. 2,118), ⊙ Gloucester co., E Va., 30 mi. N of Newport News, near Mobjack Bay, arm of Chesapeake Bay; 37°24′N 76°31′W. Mfg. (printing and publishing, construction materials, machinery); agr. (grain, soybeans; cattle); fish, oysters. Courthouse (1766) and old debtors' prison here. Also called Gloucester Courthouse. Founded 1769.

Gloucester (GLAH-stuhr), township (1990 pop. 53,797), Camden co., S N.J., 2 mi/3.2 km S of Camden; 39°47′N 75°02′W. Residential and commercial. Inc. 1798.

Gloucester City (GLAH-stuhr), city (1990 pop. 12,649), Camden co., SW N.J., on the Delaware R., a suburb adjoining Camden and opposite Philadelphia; 39°53′N 75°07′W. Site of Fort Nassau (built 1623 by the Dutch); settled c.1682 by Irish Quakers. The city has oil refining, light industry, and glass mfg. Inc. 1868.

Gloucester Point, uninc. town (1990 pop. 8,509), Gloucester co., E Va., residential suburb 17 mi/27 km N of Newport News, 10 mi/16 km W of mouth of York R. estuary, at narrows, on peninsula in Chesapeake Bay; 37°16′N 76°30′W. Bridge to Yorktown (S). Light mfg.

Glouster (GLOU-stuhr), village (1990 pop. 2,001), Athens co., SE Ohio, 12 mi/19 km N of Athens, and on small Sunday Creek; 39°30′N 82°05′W.

Glover, town (1990 pop. 820), including villages of Glover and West Glover, Orleans co., N Vt., on Barton R. and 16 mi/26 km S of Newport; 44°41′N 72°13′W. Agr.

Glover Island, N.F., Canada: see GRAND LAKE.

Gloversville, city (□ 5 sq mi/13 sq km; 1990 pop. 16,656), Fulton co., E central N.Y.; 43°02′N 74°20′W. Glove making, important since the late 19th cent., once accounted for 95% of all fine leather gloves made in the U.S.; now only 1 factory is left. Leather coats and other related goods are still made here; other mfg. includes tanning and textiles. Gloversville has a noteworthy colonial church bldg. The city is within easy access to Adirondack State Park. Inc. 1890.

Gloverville, uninc. town (1990 pop. 2,753), Aiken co., SW S.C., 6 mi/9.7 km WSW of Aiken; 33°31′N 81°48′W. RR junction. Mfg. of wood prods.; agr. includes cotton, peanuts, grain, soybeans, livestock, poultry. Kaolin clay mining.

Gluck, village, Anderson co., NW S.C., 4 mi/6.4 km S of Anderson. Agr. area.

Glyndon, town (1990 pop. 862), Clay co., W Minn., and 10 mi/16 km E of Fargo N.Dak., in Red R. valley near Buffalo R.; 46°52′N 96°34′W. RR junction. Grain. Buffalo R. State Park to E.

Glyndon (GLIN-duh), village, Baltimore co., N Md., 17 mi/27 km NW of Baltimore. In area of dairy farms and country estates. Sagamore Stables nearby, owned by the Alfred G. Vanderbilt family, is a horsebreeding and training farm where such famous racers as Native Dancer and Discovery were raised.

Glynn, county (□ 423; 1990 pop. 62,496), SE Ga.; ⊙ Brunswick; 31°13′N 81°29′W. Bounded E by the Atlantic, NE by Altamaha R., SW by Little Satilla R.; includes St. Simons, Little St. Simons, and Jekyll isls. Coastal plain fishing shrimp, conch, crabs; forestry; cattle, dairying. mfg. of seafood prods. at BRUNSWICK. Federal Law Enforcement Training Center located here. Area made famous by Sidney Lanier's poem "Marshes of Glynn." Home of the 1995 Golden Isles Bowl Classic Championship (football). Formed 1777.

Gnadenhutten (jin-AI-duhn-HUH-tuhn), village (1990 pop. 1,226), Tuscarawas co., E Ohio, 9 mi/14 km S of New Philadelphia, and on Tuscarawas R.; 40°21′N 81°26′W. State memorial park marks site of massacre (1782) of 96 Christian Indians by white men. The Moravian mission is the site of this park and mus. Founded as Christian Indian village in 1772.

Gnaw Bone, village, Brown co., S central Ind., 5 mi/8 km E of Nashville. Near Brown County State Park.

Goat Island 1 small lighthouse island, SW Maine, ½ mi/⅘ km off Kennebunkport. **2** small island in Newport harbor, SE R.I. Former site of U.S. naval torpedo station. Now site of resort hotel with good views of city and harbor. **3** W N.Y., in the Niagara R., dividing Niagara Falls into the Amer. and the Can. falls; 43°05′N 79°04′W.

Goat Island, Calif.: see YERBA BUENA ISLAND.

Goat Islands, Jamaica: see GREAT GOAT ISLANDS.

Goat Rock Dam, Ga.: see CHATTAHOOCHEE RIVER.

Goble (GO-buhl), village, Columbia co., NW Oregon, 13 mi/21 km NNW St. Helens, on Columbia R. Closed Trojan Nuclear Power Plant to N.

Gobler (GAH-bluhr), uninc. community, Dunklin and Pemiscot cos., extreme SE Mo., 12 mi/19 km SW of Kennett.

Gobles (GO-buls), village (1990 pop. 769), Van Buren co., SW Mich., 16 mi/26 km WNW of Kalamazoo; 42°21′N 85°52′W. In agr. area (fruit, potatoes, corn; livestock, poultry); wood milling. Small lakes in area; Timber Ridge Ski Area to NE.

Goddard (GAHD-uhrd), town (1990 pop. 1,804), Sedgwick co., S Kansas, 14 mi/23 km W of Wichita; 37°39′N 97°34′W. In wheat region. Mfg. (plastic containers, tool and die pigments; printing). Satellite community of Wichita. Afton Observatory to S.

Goddard (GAH-duhrd), village, SE Alaska, on W coast of Baranof Isl., 13 mi/21 km S of Sitka. Hot springs resort.

Goderich (GAHD-rich), town (1991 pop. 7,452), ⊙ Huron co., S Ont., Canada, on L. Huron, at mouth of Maitland R., and 60 mi/97 km NNW of London; 43°44′N 81°42′W. Major lake port, with grain elevators, saltworks; flour and lumber mills; mfg. of machinery, brass prods., chemicals. Also a resort and market in fruit-growing, farming, fishing region.

Godfrey 1 village, Morgan co., N central Ga., 10 mi/16 km SSW of Madison; 33°27′N 83°20′W. **2** village (1990 pop. 16,085), Madison co., SW Ill., suburb 22 mi/35 km N of downtown St. Louis, Mo., 3 mi/4.8 km NW of Alton; 38°57′N 90°11′W. Borders Jersey Co. (W, N), Mississippi R. (SW). Mfg. (plastic fabrication, glass containers, paper prods., machining). Site of Lewis and Clark Community Col.

Godley, village (1990 pop. 569), Johnson co., N central Texas, 10 mi/16 km NW of Cleburne; 32°27′N 97°31′W. In agr. area.

Godman Army Airfield, Ky.: see FORT KNOX.

Gods Lake (□ 432 sq mi/1,119 sq km), NE Man., Canada; 60 mi/97 km long, 18 mi/29 km wide; 54°30′N 94°W. Drained N by Gods R.

Gods River, 200 mi/322 km long, NE Man., Canada; issues from Gods L.; flows N and NW to Hayes R. 50 mi/80 km SSW of York Factory. Numerous rapids.

Godwin, village (1990 pop. 77), Cumberland co., SE central N.C., 15 mi/24 km NE of Fayetteville near Cape Fear R.; 35°13′N 78°40′W. Tobacco, grain; livestock. Mfg. (meat processing). Averasboro State Historical Site to N.

Goehner (GO-nuhr), village (1990 pop. 192), Seward co., SE Nebr., 8 mi/12.9 km SW of Seward; 40°49′N 97°13′W.

Goéland, Lac (go-eh-LAH, lahk), lake, W Que., Canada, 120 mi/193 km NNE of Val d'Or; 20 mi/32 km long, 12 mi/19 km wide.

Goessel (GES-uhl), village (1990 pop. 506), Marion co., E central Kansas, 12 mi/19 km N of Newton; 38°15′N 97°20′W. Agr. area (corn, wheat; cattle). Mfg. (home furnishings; printing). Mennonite Heritage Center.

Goethals Bridge (GAH-thuhlz), bridge over Arthur Kill bet. Staten Isl., N.Y., and Elizabeth, N.J.; 40°38′N 74°11′W. Cantilever structure 8,600 ft/2,621 m long, with a main span 672 ft/205 m long and 135 ft/41 m above water. Opened 1928.

Goff (GAHF), village (1990 pop. 156), Nemaha co., NE Kansas, 13 mi/21 km SSE of Seneca; 39°39′N 95°55′W. Livestock; grain.

Goffstown (GAWFS-toun), town (1990 pop. 14,621), Hillsborough co., S N.H., 7 mi/11.3 km WNW of Manchester and on Piscataquog R. W of Glen L. (formed by dam; hydroelectric power); 43°01′N 71°34′W. Mfg.

(metal fabrication, molded plastics); timber; agr. (nursery crops, vegetables, fruit; poultry, livestock; dairying). Site of Hillsborough County Farm. State Prison for Women near Grasmere village in E. First granted (1734) by Mass. as Narragansett No. 4, regranted 1748, inc. 1761.

Gogebic (go-GEE-bik), county (□ 1,476 sq mi/3,823 sq km; 1990 pop. 18,052), W Upper Peninsula, Mich.; ⊙ Bessemer. Bounded NW by L. Superior, S and SW by Wis.; 46°28′N 89°47′W. Drained by Montreal, Presque Isle, and Ontonagon rivers. Lumbering; agr. (cattle; dairying). Some mfg. at Ironwood. Resorts. Much of co. is in Ottawa Natl. Forest. L. Gogebic is on N boundary. Gogebic Range crosses N part of co. Many small lakes and waterfalls, especially in S and E. Indianhead Mt., Big Powderhorn Mt., and Mt. Zion ski areas in W; W part of Porcupine Mts. State Park in NW, Lake Gogebic State Park on W side of L. Gogebic; Ottawa Natl. Forest in all but W end of co. N boundary, W Ontonagon co., and L. Superior share Central/Eastern time zone boundary, 1 of only 4 cos. in Mich. (all on Upper Peninsula) within Central time zone. Organized 1887.

Gogebic (go-GEE-bik), E-W mountain range, 80 mi/129 km long and ½ mi/⁸⁄₁₀ km–1 mi/1.6 km wide, extending from the W Upper Peninsula, N Mich., into N Wis.; 46°17′N 90°46′W. It was known for its iron deposits (discovered in 1848), which are now depleted.

Gogebic Lake (go-GEE-bik), W Upper Peninsula, N Mich., 27 mi/43 km E of Ironwood, in Gogebic and Ontonagon cos., in Ottawa Natl. Forest; c.15 mi/24 km long, 2 mi/3.2 km wide; 46°30′N 89°34′W. Drained by West Branch of Ontonagon R. Lake Gogebic State Park on W side. Split roughly in ½ (E-W) by co. boundary and Eastern/Central time zone boundary.

Going-to-the-Sun Mountain, Mont.: see GLACIER NATL. PARK.

Golconda, city (1990 pop. 823), ⊙ Pope co., extreme SE Ill., on Ohio R. and 25 mi/40 km S of Harrisburg; 37°21′N 88°29′W. In rich agr. area (corn, wheat; livestock). Inc. 1845. Site of Ohio R. lock and dam.

Golconda (guhl-KAHN-duh), uninc. village, Humboldt co., N Nev., on Humboldt R. and 13 mi/21 km E of Winnemucca. RR junction to E. Cattle, sheep; tungsten deposits. Sonoma Peak (9,396 ft/2,864 m) to SW.

Gold Bar, town (1990 pop. 1,078), Snohomish co., NW Wash., 25 mi/40 km ESE of Everett, on Skykomish R.; 47°52′N 121°42′W. In agr., lumbering region; berries; dairying; poultry; salmon; logging. Part of Mt. Baker–Snoqualmie Natl. Forest to N, E, and SE; Wallace Falls State Park to NE; Spada L. reservoir to N.

Gold Beach, town (1990 pop. 1,546), ⊙ Curry co., SW Oregon, 55 mi/89 km W of Grants Pass, at mouth of Rogue R. on Pacific Ocean; 42°24′N 124°25′W. Elev. 71 ft/22 m. Fishing and beach resort. Mfg. (wooden boxes, aluminum prods.). Siskiyou Natl. Forest to E; Geisel Monument State Wayside to N; Cape Sebastian State Park to S. Inc. 1945.

Gold Bridge, village, SW B.C., Canada, in Coast Mts., on Bridge R. and 120 mi/193 km N of Vancouver; 50°51′N 122°50′W. Cattle. Gold and silver mining; logging; hydroelectricity.

Gold Coast, local name for the Atlantic coast of SE Fla. bet. the Upper Keys (Key Largo) on the S and Jupiter on the N. Includes numerous resort cities, among them Miami Beach, Fort Lauderdale, and Palm Beach. Source of name for the Pacific coastal strip of Australia's SE Queensland, which includes several towns named after seaside places in SE Fla.

Gold Hill, town (1990 pop. 964), Jackson co., SW Oregon, 11 mi/18 km NW of Medford, on Rogue R.; 42°25′N 123°02′W. RR terminus. Agr. (fruit, grain, hops; poultry, sheep, cattle). TouVelle State Park to E; Ben Hur Lampman State Wayside to S; Valley of the Rogue State Park to W.

Gold Hill 1 village, Boulder co., N central Colo., in E foothills of Front Range, near Left Hand Creek, 7 mi/11.3 km NW of Boulder; elev. c.8,296 ft/2,529 m. Summer resort and small-scale gold-mining point. Miners'

Hotel (1872) preserves old-time furnishings and decorations. **2** uninc. village, Storey co., W Nev., 10 mi/16 km NE of Carson City, 2 mi/3.2 km S of Virginia City. Once a rich gold town, near Comstock Lode. Historic bldgs. include bank, hotel, and mill. **3** uninc. village, Rowan co., central N.C., 13 mi/21 km SSE of Salisbury. Mfg. (aggregates, lumber, log homes).

Gold Lake, N Sierra co., NE Calif., in the Sierra Nevada, 11 mi/18 km NE of Downieville; c.1.5 mi/2.4 km long. Fishing and vacation resort in Tahoe Natl. Forest.

Gold Point, uninc. village, Martin co., E N.C., 10 mi/16 km W of Williamston. Grain, tobacco; poultry, livestock.

Goldcreek, village (1990 pop. 15), Powell co., W central Mont., on the Clark Fork R., at mouth of small Gold Creek, and 16 mi/26 km NW of Deer Lodge. Gold is still mined from Gold Creek area to SW, in Flint Creek Range, near alleged first gold discovery (c.1856) in Mont. Site of the spike driven in 1883 completing a RR line connecting the E and W coasts.

Golden, city (1990 pop. 13,116), ⊙ Jefferson co., N central Colo., on Clear Creek, just E of Front Range, a suburb 10 mi/16 km W of downtown Denver; 39°44′N 105°13′W. Elev. 5,674 ft/1,729 m. Resort and trading point in livestock and poultry region; mfg. (structural ceramics, medical equip., rock prods., radio and television software, beer, biological services). Coal and gold mines in vicinity. Colo. School of Mines here. Camp George West Military Reserve to NE. County fairgrounds to SE; Red Rocks Natural Amphitheater to S. Goden Gate State Park to NW. Grave of William F. Cody (Buffalo Bill) on Lookout Mt. to SW. City founded 1859 as mining town, served as territorial capital of 1862–1867, inc. 1886.

Golden, town (1991 pop. 3,721), SE B.C., Canada, on Columbia R., at mouth of Kicking Horse R., and 60 mi/97 km ENE of Revelstoke, on slope of Rocky Mts.; 51°18′N 116°58′W. Elev. 2,583 ft/787 m. Dairying, sheepraising center, in mining (silver, gold, lead, barites, zinc), fruit growing, and lumbering region. Hydroelectricity. Tourism; service center for Yoho and Glacier Natl. Parks.

Golden 1 village (1990 pop. 565), Adams co., W Ill., 24 mi/39 km ENE of Quincy; 40°06′N 91°01′W. In agr. area (corn, wheat, soybeans; livestock); makes seed sowers. **2** village (1990 pop. 202), Tishomingo co., extreme NE Miss., near Ala. state line and 33 mi/53 km ENE of Tupelo; 34°29′N 88°11′W. In agr. and timber area; mfg. (furniture, apparel, transportation equip.); sawmills.

Golden City, city (1990 pop. 794), Barton co., SW Mo., 20 mi/32 km NE of Carthage; 37°23′N 94°05′W. Corn, wheat, sorghum, hay, soybeans; cattle; mfg. (business forms). Several native bluestem praries in the area.

Golden Gate, suburb (□ 4 sq mi/10.4 sq km; 1990 pop. 14, 142) of Naples, Collier co., SW Fla., 7 mi/11.3 km NE of city center; 26°10′N 81°42′W.

Golden Gate, village, (1990 pop. 71), Wayne co., SE Ill., 8 mi/12.9 km E of Fairfield; 38°21′N 88°12′W. In agr. area.

Golden Gate, National Recreation Area, San Francisco, San Mateo, and Marin cos., W Calif. Covers 73,122 acres/29,592 ha; beaches, forests, and marshes along coastal margins of city of San Francisco and Marin Peninsula, W of Golden Gate Bridge and ALCATRAZ Isl. (historical prison, in San Francisco Bay). Includes mt. sect. beside (SW of) San Andreas Fault, SE of Pacifica, San Mateo co. Presidio of San Francisco added 1994. Includes former military bases of Fort Cronkhite, Fort Barry, and Fort Baker, also former James D. Phelan State Beach, San Francisco. One of the first 2 natl. urban recreation areas (also Gateway Natl. Recreation Area, New York City). Authorized 1972.

Golden Gate Bridge, San Franscisco/Marin cos., W Calif., crosses Golden Gate Strait from city of San Francisco (S) to Marin Peninsula (N). Built 1933–1937. Its overall length is 9,266 ft/2,824 m; its main span across the strait, 4,200 ft/1,280 m, is one of the longest bridges in the world. Joseph B. Strauss was the chief engineer.

Carries U.S. Highway 101. Golden Gate Natl. Recreation Area is generally W of bridge on both sides of strait.

Golden Glades, suburb (□ 4 sq mi/10.4 sq km; 1990 pop. 25,474), Dade co., SE Fla., 12 mi/19 km N of Miami; 25°54′N 80°12′W. Site of freeway convergence (I-95, Fla.'s Turnpike, and Palmetto Expressway) considered to be one of the most complex in the U.S.

Golden Grove, town (1991 pop. 2,761), St. Thomas parish, SE Jamaica, 35 mi/56 km E of Kingston; 17°56′N 76°16′W. In a sugar- and banana-producing area.

Golden Grove, uninc. town (1990 pop. 2,055), Greenville co., NW S.C., residential suburb 7 mi/11.3 km SSW of downtown Greenville, near Saluda R.; 34°43′N 82°26′W.

Golden Hills, uninc. town (1990 pop. 5,423), Kern co., S central Calif., planned residential community 3 mi/4.8 km WNW of Tehachapi; 35°08′N 118°30′W. Tehachapi Mts. to S; Tom Sawyer L. reservoir to N.

Golden Hinde, mountain (7,219 ft/2,200 m), SW B.C., Canada, on central Vancouver Isl.; highest peak in Strathcona Provincial Park, 30 mi/48 km W of Courtenay; 49°40′N 125°45′W.

Golden Meadow, town (1990 pop. 2,049), Lafourche parish, SE La., on Bayou Lafourche (navigable) and 40 mi/64 km SSW of New Orleans; 29°23′N 90°16′W. Shrimp processing; baking prods. Duck hunting, fur trapping nearby. Catfish L. to W. Pointe au Chien State Wildlife Area to NW.

Golden Prairie, village (1991 pop. 67), SW Sask., Canada, 22 mi/35 km NNW of Maple Creek; 50°13′N 109°37′W. Wheat.

Golden Shores, uninc. town, Mohave co., NW Ariz., 25 mi/40 km SW of Kingman and 7 mi/11.3 km SE of Needles, Calif., near Colorado R. (near arm of L. Havasu Resevoir). Planned community. Havasu Natl. Wildlife Refuge protects Ariz. shore of lake. Fort Mohave Indian Reservation to NW; Warm Springs Wilderness Area to E.

Golden Spike National Historic Site, (□ 4 sq mi/10.4 sq km), Box Elder co., N Utah, 40 mi/64 km NW of Ogden at Promontory, N of Great Salt L., at base of Pomontory Point peninsula. Covers 2,735 acres/1,107 ha; authorized 1957. Site where the Union Pacific RR and the Central Pacific RR joined to form the first transcontinental RR in N. Amer., May 10, 1869. The event is reenacted every year.

Golden Valley 1 county (□ 1,176 sq mi/3,046 sq km; 1990 pop. 912), central Mont.; ⊙ Ryegate; 46°23′N 109°10′W. Agr. area drained by Musselshell R. also Big Coulee and Swimming Woman creeks. Wheat, rye, hay; sheep, cattle, hogs, poultry. Part of Lewis and Clark Natl. Forest and the Snowy Mts. in NW. Formed 1920. **2** county (□ 1,014 sq mi/2,626 sq km 1990 pop. 2,108), W N.Dak., on Mont. state line, drained by Beaver Creek in N; ⊙ Beach; 46°56′N 103°50′W. Fertile agr. and grazing area (cattle; wheat); oil fields, lignite mines. Organized 1912. Little Missouri Natl. Grassland in E. Camel Hump Reservoir at center.

Golden Valley, city (1990 pop. 20,971), Hennepin co., SE Minn., a suburb 4 mi/6.4 km W of downtown Minneapolis; 44°59′N 93°21′W. RR junction. It is chiefly residential, with some industry (transportation equip., meat prods., machinery, marketing exhibits, cast metal prods., consumer goods; printing and publishing), research activity. Theodore Wirth Park in E. Inc. 1886.

Golden Valley, village (1990 pop. 239), Mercer co., central N.Dak.,14 mi/23 km W of Beulah and on Spring Creek; 47°17′N 102°03′W.

Goldendale, town (1990 pop. 3,319), ⊙ Klickitat co., S Wash., on Little Klickitat R. and 55 mi/89 km SSW of Yakima; 45°49′N 120°49′W. Timber; wheat, alfalfa; cattle. Aluminium mfg. County Historical Mus.; Goldendale Observatory State Park, public telescope. Fish hatchery to W. Maryhill State Park to S, on Columbia R.; John Day Dam to SSE; Yakima Indian Reservation to N; Brooks Memorial State Park to NE; Conboy L. Natl. Wildlife Refuge to NW. Settled c.1863.

Goldenrod, suburb (□ 2 sq mi/5.2 sq km; 1990 pop.

12,362) of Orlando, Seminole/Orange co., central Fla., 6 mi/9.7 km NE of city center; 28°36′N 81°17′W.

Goldens Bridge, suburb (1990 pop. 1,589), Westchester co., SE N.Y., on reservoir in Croton R., 7 mi/11.3 km NNE of Mount Kisco; 41°17′N 73°41′W. RR junction.

Goldenville, village, E N.S., Canada, on St. Mary R. and 30 mi/48 km SW of Guysborough; 45°07′N 62°01′W. Gold reserves in area.

Goldfield, town (1990 pop. 710), Wright co., N central Iowa, near Boone R., 10 mi/16 km W of Clarion; 42°44′N 93°55′W. Feed.

Goldfield 1 village, Teller co., central Colo., in Rocky Mts., 1 mi/1.6 km NE of Victor 20 mi/32 km WSW of Colorado Springs; elev. c.9,882 ft/3,012 m. Former shipping point in Cripple Creek gold dist., with pop. of 3,000 in 1890s. Much of the city stands empty; virtual ghost town. Pikes Peak 9 mi/14.5 km NNE. **2** uninc. village, ⊙ Esmeralda co., SW Nev., 24 mi/39 km; elev. 5,869 ft/1,789 m. A former gold-mining center. Gold was discovered there in 1902, and after an early period of disappointment, large yields of high-quality gold were extracted. A rush in 1903 built a remarkable city that had a theater, a large hotel (still standing), and fine residences. A strike by the miners caused Federal troops to be brought in Goldfield in 1907. Production reached its ht. in 1910. When the boom ended in 1918, Goldfield declined as fast as it had risen. Had 20,000 people in 1907. Nellis Air Force Bombing and Gunnery Range to E.

Goldfields, village, NW Sask., Canada, on N shore of L. Athabaska, near Alta. border; 59°27′N 108°29′W. Until 1943 gold was mined here; uranium ore mining was begun here later.

Goldonna (gol-DAH-nuh), village (1990 pop. 417), Natchitoches parish, NW central La., 20 mi/32 km NE of Natchitoches and on Saline R.; 32°01′N 92°55′W. Located in Kisatchie Natl. Forest. Saline Lake and NW La. State Wildlife Area to S.

Goldpines, village, NW Ont., Canada, on Chukuni R., at NW end of L. Seul, and 70 mi/113 km NW of Sioux Lookout; 50°38′N 93°10′W. Hydroelectric power center on the Ear Falls.

Goldroad, ghost town, in Black Mts., W Ariz., 20 mi/32 km SW of Kingman; elev., 5,225 ft/1,593 m. Former gold mining dist. S part in Mt. Naff Wilderness Area.

Goldsboro, city (1990 pop. 40,709), ⊙ Wayne co., E central N.C., 50 mi/80 km SE of Raleigh, on Little R., 3 mi/4.8 km N of its mouth on Neuse R.; 35°22′N 77°58′W. Goldsboro is a marketplace for bright-leaf tobacco and a shipping center for timber. Agr. area (tobacco, cotton, peanuts; grain; poultry, livestock; dairying); mfg. (textiles and apparel; transportation equip., machinery, roofing materials, lumber, dairy, rubber, baked prods., iron castings, feeds, greenhouses); sand processing. Wayne Community Col. here. Seymour-Johnson Air Force Base in SE. Goldsboro Wayne Municipal Airport to N. Waynesborough State Park 1 mi/1.6 km SW of downtown; Cliffs of the Nuese State Park to SE. Inc. 1847.

Goldsboro, town (1990 pop. 185), Caroline co., E Md., 16 mi/26 km WSW of Dover, Del.; 39°02′N 75°48′W. Once a crossroads called Oldtown, it became a canning center when the RR reached there in 1867. In 1870, it was renamed Goldsboro in honor of Dr. G. W. Goldsborough, a large landowner. Castle Hall, a 4-story brick house, was completed by Thomas Hardcastle, a co. justice, in 1781.

Goldsboro, borough (1990 pop. 458), York co., S Pa., 9 mi/14.5 km SE of Harrisburg, on Susquehanna R. Agr. (dairying). Olmstead Air Force Base to NE (Dauphin co.). Three Mile Isl. Nuclear Plant 1 mi/1.6 km to E in Susquehanna River Frederic L. reservoir, formed by York Haven Dam, 2 mi/3.2 km to SE.

Goldsby, town (1990 pop. 816), McClain co., central Okla., 5 mi/8 km SSW of Norman, near Canadian R.; 35°07′N 97°28′W. Agr. area; mfg. (wood roof trusses).

Goldsmith, village (1990 pop. 297), Ector co., W Texas, 15 mi/24 km NW of Odessa; 31°58′N 102°37′W. Oil and natural gas. Agr. (cattle, horses; pecans). Mfg. (oil and gas processing).

Goldston, village (1990 pop. 299), Chatham co., central N.C., 12 mi/19 km NW of Sanford; 35°35′N 79°19′W. Tobacco, grain, soybeans; poultry, livestock. Mfg. (lumber).

Goldthwaite, town (1990 pop. 1,658), ⊙ Mills co., central Texas, 30 mi/48 km SE of Brownwood; 31°26′N 98°34′W. Elev. 1,580 ft/482 m. Market, shipping center for diversified agr., ranching area (cattle, sheep, goats; dairying; grain; pecans); mfg. (leather prods., dried flowers).

Goleta, uninc. town, Santa Barbara co., SW Calif., on the coast, 8 mi/12.9 km W of Santa Barbara. Fruit, vegetables, avocados; flowers; cattle. Oil, natural gas fields nearby; mfg. (electronic equip.,telephone apparatus, aircraft parts, medical supplies). Los Padres Natl. Forest to N; Univ. of Calif. Santa Barbara to W.

Golf, village (1990 pop. 454), Cook co., NE Ill., N suburb of Chicago, 6 mi/9.7 km W of Evanston; 42°03′N 87°47′W.

Golf Manor, village (1990 pop. 4,154), Hamilton co., extreme SW Ohio, suburb c.6 mi/10 km N of downtown Cincinnati; 39°11′N 84°26′W. Inc. 1947.

Goliad, county (□ 859 sq mi/2,225 sq km; 1990 pop. 5,980), S Texas; ⊙ Goliad, one of state's oldest cities; 28°38′N 97°25′W. Bounded SW by Blanco R.; NE by Coleto Creek and Coleto Creek Reservoir; drained by San Antonio R. Cattle ranching, agr. (corn, grain, sorghum; hay). Oil, natural gas wells. Includes Goliad State Park in center of co.; Gen. Zaragoza State Historic Site; Fannin Battleground State Historic Site in E; Presidio la Bahia Church (est. 1749). Name is an anagram for (H)IDALGO; symbol of Anti-Mex. sentiment during Texas Revolution. Formed 1836.

Goliad, town (1990 pop. 1,946), ⊙ Goliad co., S Texas, 60 mi/97 km N of Corpus Christi, on the San Antonio R.; elev. 167 ft/51 m. It is a market for the surrounding farm region (cattle; corn, sorghum). Oil and gas; printing. A Spanish mission and presidio moved to Goliad in 1749. After the start of the Texas Revolution (1836), Goliad was seized by Texan forces under Col. J. W. Fannin. When Mex. troops advanced into Texas, Fannin evacuated Goliad with about 300 men but was overtaken. After a hopeless battle, he surrendered to the Mexicans on March 20, 1836; a week later most of the prisoners were shot. The Amer. settlement grew up across the river, and the restored mission and the ruins of the old presidio are in a state park. Coleto Creek Reservoir to NE; Fannin Battleground State Historic Site to E at Fannin; Goliad State Park and General Zaragoza State Historic Site S of town.

Golovin (GO-lo-vin), village (1990 pop. 127), NW Alaska, on S Seward Peninsula, on Golovnin Lagoon, N arm (25 mi/40 km long) of Norton Sound, 70 mi/113 km E of Nome; 64°34′N 162°59′W. Fishing, gold mining; supply center for mining region. Has school. Sometimes called Cheenik.

Goltry (GOL-tree), village (1990 pop. 297), Alfalfa co., N Okla., 18 mi/29 km WNW of Enid; 36°31′N 98°09′W. In grain-producing area.

Golva (GUHL-vuh), village (1990 pop. 101), Golden Valley co., W N.Dak., 13 mi/21 km S of Beach; 46°43′N 103°58′W.

Gómez Farías 1 (GO-mes fah-REE-ahs), town (1990 pop. 5,782), Jalisco, central Mexico, near RR, 6 mi/9.7 km N of Ciudad Guzmán on Mexico Highway 54. Alfalfa, cotton, sugarcane, grain, fruit; livestock. Formerly San Sebastián. **2** (GO-mes fah-REE-ahs), town (1990 pop. 889), Tamaulipas, NE Mexico, 45 mi/72 km S of Ciudad Victoria, 6 mi/10 km W of Mexico Highway 85. An isolated town in the Sierra Madre Oriental foothills. Elev. 1,148 ft/350 m. Agr. (cereals, henequen; livestock). **3** (GO-mes fah-REE-ahs), town (1990 pop. 4,884), W central Chihuahua, Mexico, 84 mi/135 km NW of Cuautemoc, on State Highway 28. Elev 4,921 ft/1,500 m. Mountainous region with water from the Papigochic R. Cold moderate climate. Agr. (corn, beans, wheat, potatoes, wood; fruit, cattle raising).

Gómez Palacio (GO-mes pah-LAH-see-yo), city (1990 pop. 164,092) and township, Durango, N Mexico, in fertile irrigated Laguna Dist., on Mexico Highway 45,

3 mi/4.8 km NW of Torreón across Nazas R.; 25°39′N 103°30′W. RR junction; processing and agr. center (cotton, corn, wheat, barley, wine, fruit, sugarcane, tobacco, vegetables). Wine and liquor distilling, vegetable-oil pressing, cotton ginning, flour and textile milling, tanning; iron and steel foundries; mfg. of agr. implements, explosives, chemicals, soap, clothing.

Gonaïves (go-nah-EEV), town (1982 pop. 34,209), ⊙ Artibonite dept., Haiti, 93 mi/150 km NNW of Port-au-Prince. Sugarcane growing; copper, bauxite, and manganese deposits nearby. Essential oils distillery, extraction of cottonseed oil, cotton manufacture. Port.

Gonaïves, Gulf of, on W coast of Haiti, E of Windward Passage, bet. N peninsula of Haiti and Jacmel Peninsula; c.75 mi/121 km wide; 19°00′N 73°30′W. On it are Gonaïves, Saint-Marc, and Port-au-Prince. Receives Artibonite R. In S is the Île de la Gonâve; Canal de la Gonâve (Gonâve Channel) or Canal du Sud (Southern Channel) separate the isl. from the mainland. Sometimes called Gulf of Gonâve.

Gonâve, Île de la (go-NAHV, EEL duh lah), long narrow island (□ 254 sq mi/658 sq km), belonging to Haiti, in the Gulf of Gonaïves, 32 mi/51 km WNW of Port-au-Prince; 35 mi/56 km long, c.8 mi/12.9 km wide; 18°51′N 73°03′W. Rises to 2,303 ft/702 m. Cotton, bananas, limes, sisal, subsistence crops; cattle. Largely covered by forests. Has bauxite deposits. Good fishing grounds. The channel S of it is called Canal de la Gonâve or Canal du Sud, channel due E is Canal de St. Marc.

Gonic (GAW-nik), village, Rockingham co., SE N.H., in city of Rochester, 2 mi/3.2 km S of city center, on Cocheco R. Mfg. (apparel, plastic prods., bricks, beverage processing).

Gonvick (GAWN-vik), village (1990 pop. 302), Clearwater co., NW Minn., 15 mi/24 km NNW of Bagley; 47°44′N 95°30′W. Grain, potatoes; poultry, cattle, sheep; dairying; mfg. (printing; food processing). Red Lake Indian Reservation to N; Lower Red L. to NE.

González, town (1990 pop. 10,249), Tamaulipas, NE Mexico, on Gulf plains, on RR and on Mexico Highway 81; 55 mi/89 km NW of Tampico; 22°50′N 98°25′W. Agr. (corn, henequen, fruit; livestock). Named after President Manuel González.

Gonzales, county (□ 1,069 sq mi/2,769 sq km; 1990 pop. 17,205), S central Texas; ⊙ Gonzales; 29°26′N 97°29′W. Drained by Guadalupe and San Marcos rivers. An important poultry-raising area (chickens, turkeys, eggs); also agr. (corn, grain sorghums, peanuts, pecans, wheat); cattle. Clay and kaolin mining, gravel; oil and gas; mineral springs (health resorts). Includes Palmetto State Park in NW, unique botanical community includes semitropical plants (site of 1st battle of Texas Revolution). Formed 1836.

Gonzales 1 city (1990 pop. 4,660), Monterey co., W Calif., in Salinas valley, 17 mi/27 km SE of Salinas, near Salinas R.; 36°31′N 121°27′W. Vegetables, grapes, strawberries, tomatoes; nurseries; dairying; cattle. Winery; vegetable packing and shipping. Pinnacles Natl. Monument to E. Inc. 1947. **2** (guhn-ZAH-luhs), city (1994 pop. 7,958), Ascension parish, SE La., 21 mi/34 km SE of Baton Rouge; 30°13′N 90°55′W. In agr. area (vegetables, sugarcane, strawberries; cattle); mfg. (fabricated metal prods., leather goods, apparel, machinery); oil wells.

Gonzales, town (1990 pop. 6,527), ⊙ Gonzales co., S central Texas, c.65 mi/105 km E of San Antonio, near mouth of San Marcos R. on the Guadalupe; 29°30′N 97°27′W. Elev. 292 ft/89 m. RR spur terminus; poultry-shipping and hatching center in livestock and agr. area (cattle; peanuts, pecans, wheat, sorghum, corn); mfg. (steel plate fabrication, food processing, feeds, thickening agents). Palmetto State Park is to NW, lakes impounded by dams in Guadalupe R. (used to generate power, and also for recreation). Gonzales Memorial Mus. and monument, site of 1st battle of Texas Revolution (1835), at Cost (6 mi/9.7 km SW). Founded 1825.

Gonzalez (guhn-ZAH-lez), town (□ 11 sq mi/28 sq km; 1990 pop. 7,669), Escambia co., extreme NW Fla.,

12 mi/19 km NNW of Pensacola; 30°34′N 87°17′W. Farm trade center.

González Cuidad, Mexico: see SAN FELIPE, city, Guanajuato.

González River, Mexico: see NUEVO, RÍO.

Goochland, county (□ 290 sq mi/751 sq km; 1990 pop. 14,163), central Va.; ⊙ Goochland; 37°43′N 77°55′W. Bounded S by James R. Agr. (tobacco, barley, wheat, corn, soybeans, hay; some dairying; cattle); timber. Historic estates. State penal farms. Formed 1727.

Goochland, uninc. village, ⊙ Goochland co., central Va., near James R., 25 mi/40 km WNW of Richmond. Mfg. (lumber, fertilizer); agr. (grain, tobacco, soybeans; cattle); timber. J. Sargent Reynolds Community Col. (Western campus). Virginia Correctional Center for Women to S, Powhatan Correctioinal Complex to SE (Powhatan co.).

Good Friday Gulf, N Franklin dist., N.W.T., Canada, arm (70 mi/113 km long, 35 mi/56 km–60 mi/97 km wide) of the Arctic Ocean, bet. Amund Ringnes Isl. and Axel Heiberg Isl.; 78°N 94°W.

Good Hope, town (1990 pop. 1,700), Cullman co., N Ala., 5 mi/8 km S of Cullman; 34°07′N 86°52′W.

Good Hope 1 village (1990 pop. 181), Walton co., N central Ga., 7 mi/11.3 km E of Monroe; 33°47′N 83°37′W. Textile mfg. **2** village (1990 pop. 416), McDonough co., W Ill., 6 mi/9.7 km N of Macomb; 40°33′N 90°40′W. In agr. area; ships grain. **3** uninc. village, St. Charles parish, SE La., 2 mi/3 km SE of Norco, 15 mi/24 km W of New Orleans, on Mississippi R.; 29°59′N 90°24′W.

Good Thunder, village (1990 pop. 561), Blue Earth co., S Minn., on Maple R. and 12 mi/19 km S of Mankato; 44°00′N 94°04′W. Grain, alfalfa, soybeans; hogs, cattle, sheep; mfg. (meat processing).

Goode, Mount (10,610 ft/3,234 m), S Alaska, in Chugach Mts., 65 mi/105 km E of Anchorage; 61°20′N 148°00′W.

Goodell, town (1990 pop. 201), Hancock co., N Iowa, 12 mi/19 km S of Garner; 42°55′N 93°36′W. Livestock; grain.

Goodeve, village (1991 pop. 77), SE Sask., Canada, in the Beaver Hills, 33 mi/53 km WSW of Yorkton. Mixed farming.

Goodfield, village (1990 pop. 454), Woodford co., central Ill., 10 mi/16 km E of Morton; 40°37′N 89°16′W. Grain, soybeans; cattle; dairying; mfg. (feeds, plows and other agr. equip.).

Goodhope, Mount (10,670 ft/3,252 m), SW B.C., Canada, in Coast Mts., 140 mi/225 km NNW of Vancouver, overlooking Chilko L.; 51°8′N 124°11′W.

Goodhue, county (□ 780 sq mi/2,020 sq km; 1990 pop. 40,690), SE Minn.; ⊙ Red Wing; 44°24′N 92°43′W. Drained by Cannon R. and bounded NE by Mississippi R. (forms Wis. boundary). Agr. area (hay, corn, oats, barley, alfalfa, soybeans, peas; sheep, hogs, cattle, poultry; dairying). Prairie Isl. Indian Reservation and part of Gore Pool No. 3 Wildlife Area in N; part of Richard J. Dorer Memorial Hardwood State Forest in N; Frontenac State Park in NE. Nuclear power plants: Prairie Isl. 1 (initial criticality Dec. 1, 1973; max. dependable capacity of 503 MWe) and Prairie Isl. 2 (initial criticality Dec. 17, 1974; max. dependable capacity of 500 MWe) are 28 mi/45 km SE of Minneapolis. Uses cooling water from the Mississippi R. County formed 1853.

Goodhue, village (1990 pop. 533), Goodhue co., SE Minn., 12 mi/19 km SSW of Red Wing; 44°23′N 92°37′W. Grain, alfalfa; poultry, livestock; dairying; mfg. (feeds, calf huts). Part of Richard J. Dorer Memorial Hardwood State Forest to N.

Gooding, county (□ 733 sq mi/1,898 sq km; 1990 pop. 11,633), S Idaho; ⊙ Gooding; 42°58′N 114°48′W. Located in Snake River Plain; agr. and livestock-raising area bounded S and SW by Snake R. Irrigated region around town of Gooding produces potatoes, dry beans, sugar beets; alfalfa; corn, wheat; watermelons, cranberries; sheep, cattle; dairying. Tableland in N slopes to Snake R. Plain in S; Bray L. reservoir in N center; Malad Gorge State Park in S; Thousand Springs in S near Snake R., waters from Big and Little Lost rivers,

c.100 mi/161 km NE, emerge from Snake R. Plain Aquifer in series of waterfalls in deep canyon. Formed 1913.

Gooding, town (1990 pop. 2,820), ⊙ Gooding co., S Idaho, on Big Wood R., at mouth of Little Wood R. and 30 mi/48 km NW of Twin Falls; 42°57′N 114°43′W. Elev. 3,576 ft/1,090 m. In irrigated agr. area (livestock; poultry; watermelons; grain; dairying). Malad Gorge State Park to SW. Founded 1883 as Toponis, renamed 1896.

Goodland 1 town, Collier co., SW Fla., c.15 mi/24 km SE of Naples, on Marco Isl. Connected by road with nearby mainland; fishing, clamming; resort. **2** town (1990 pop. 1,033), Newton co., NW Ind., 8 mi/12.9 km E of Kentland; 40°46′N 87°17′W. In agr. area (corn, soybeans; cattle; dairy prods.); mfg. (plastic molding, transformers); stone quarrying. **3** town (1990 pop. 4,983), ⊙ Sherman co., NW Kansas, 105 mi/169 km NNW of Garden City; 39°21′N 101°42′W. Elev. 3,683 ft/1,123 m. In agr. area (grain, hay; livestock); RR maintenance; soybean processing. Fossils have been found in vicinity. Sherman State Fishing L. to S. Inc. 1887.

Goodlettsville (GOOD-lets-vil), city (1990 pop. 11,219), Davidson and Sumner cos., N central Tenn., suburb 13 mi/21 km N of Nashville; 36°19′N 86°43′W.

Goodman 1 town (1990 pop. 1,256), Holmes co., central Miss., 24 mi/39 km NNE of Canton, near Big Black R.; 32°58′N 89°54′W. RR junction to N. Holmes Community Col. Holmes County State Park to N. **2** town (1990 pop. 1,094), McDonald co., extreme SW Mo., in the Ozarks, 10 mi/16 km S of Neosho; 36°44′N 94°24′W.

Goodman, village, Marinette co., NE Wis., 20 mi/32 km SW of Iron Mountain, Mich. Sawmilling, woodworking; hardwood forest prods. Nicolet Natl. Forest to W.

Goodnews Bay, village (1990 pop. 241), SW Alaska, on N side of Goodnews Bay, 110 mi/177 km S of Bethel; 59°06′N 161°34′W. Mining (platinum, gold, osmiridium); trapping.

Goodnews Bay, inlet (10 mi/16 km long, 1 mi/1.6 km–6 mi/9.7 km wide) of Kuskokwim Bay, SW Alaska, NW of Bristol Bay; 59°05′N 161°40′W. Village of Platinum at mouth. Region is rich in platinum and osmiridium placers.

Goodnight, uninc. village (1990 est. pop. 25), Armstrong co., extreme N Texas, on edge of high plains of the Panhandle, 20 mi/32 km WNW of Clarendon. Very small village in cattle and grain area.

Goodrich 1 village (1990 pop. 192), Sheridan co., central N.Dak., 23 mi/37 km SSW of Harvey; 47°28′N 100°07′W. **2** village (1990 pop. 239), Polk co., E Texas, 8 mi/12.9 km S of Livingston, near Trinity R. Timber; oil and natural gas. Recreation; L. Livingston reservoir and State Park to NW.

Goodridge, village (1990 pop. 115), Pennington co., NW Minn., 17 mi/27 km E of Thief River Falls; 48°08′N 95°47′W. Grain, sunflowers; sheep; mfg. (industrial controls).

Goodsir, Mount (11,686 ft/3,562 m), SE B.C., Canada, in Rocky Mts., on S edge of Yoho Natl. Park, 35 mi/56 km W of Banff; 51°12′N 116°23′W.

Goodsonville, uninc. village, Lincoln co., W central N.C., 3 mi/4.8 km ENE of Lincolnton.

Goodsprings, village, Walker co., NW central Ala., 12 mi/19 km SSE of Jasper.

Goodview, town (1990 pop. 2,878), Winona co., SW Minn., on Mississippi R. suburb 3 mi/4.8 km WNW of Winona, near Mississippi R. (Lock and Dam No. 5A to NE); 44°04′N 91°42′W. Max Conrad Field airport to N.

Goodwater, town (1990 pop. 1,840), Coosa co., E central Ala., 15 mi/24 km NE of Rockford. Mfg. (lumber, burial caskets); paper mill. Talladega Natl. Forest nearby. Inc. 1875.

Goodwell, town (1990 pop. 1,065), Texas co., central Okla. Panhandle, 11 mi/18 km SW of Guymon; 36°35′N 101°37′W. Grain; cattle. Seat of Okla. Panhandle State Univ. In Okla. Panhandle (formerly No Man's Land). No Man's Land Mus.

Goodwin, village (1990 pop. 126), Deuel co., E S.Dak., 13 mi/21 km E of Watertown; 44°52′N 96°50′W.

Goodwin's Mills, village, on Lyman/Dayton border, York co., SW Maine, 6 mi/9.7 km NW of Biddeford.

Goodyear, town (1990 pop. 6,258), Maricopa co., S central Ariz., suburb 20 mi/32 km W of downtown Phoenix, near Gila R.; 33°21′N 112°24′W. Cotton; mfg. (plastic prods., chemicals, electronic equip.). Inc. since 1940. Luke Air Force Base to N.

Goodyear Lake, reservoir, Otsego co., E central N.Y., on Susquehanna R., 5 mi/8 km NE of Oneonta; c.2 mi/3.2 km long; 42°31′N 74°59′W. Manmade lake created by Goodyear Dam at S end. Originally built in early 20th cent. for hydroelectric power generation, now entirely recreational. Bordered by mostly year-round residences (though some are seasonal).

Goose Bay, town, SE Lab., Canada, on Goose Bay, inlet of L. Melville, at mouth of Churchill (Hamilton) R.; 53°19′N 60°25′W. The large air base and radio station, built here in World War II (1941) as military and ferrying base, is now used by Can. commercial aircraft on transatlantic routes. Lumbering. Staging center for Churchill R. hydro plan. Consolidated with Happy Valley, 1975, now Happy Valley–Goose Bay.

Goose Creek, city (1990 pop. 24,692), Berkeley and Charleston cos., SE S.C., suburb 14 mi/23 km NNW of Charleston; 32°59′N 80°00′W. Mfg. in area includes paper, bldg. equip., chemicals, missile assembly; agr. in area includes poultry, livestock, grain, tobacco, cotton. Charleston Naval Base to E; Cypress Gardens to NE.

Goose Creek 1 in Nev. and Idaho; rises in NE Elko co., NE Nev., c.50 mi/80 km, NE of Wells; flows 70 mi/113 km NE, through extreme NW corner of Utah (Box Elder co.) and into Cassia co., S Idaho, through Lower Goose Creek Reservoir, formed by Oakley Dam, and past Oakley, entering Snake R. at Burley. **2** in N Wyo.; E and W forks rise in Bighorn Mts.; flows c.30 mi/48 km generally NE, past Sheridan (here receiving Little Goose Creek), to Tongue R. 8 mi/12.9 km N of Sheridan near Mont. state line.

Goose Egg, village, Natrona co., E central Wyo., 9 mi/14.5 km WSW of Casper, on North Platte R. Agr. area (sugar beets; cattle, sheep). Jackson's Canyon to SE.

Goose Island, Canada: see OIES, ÎLE AUX.

Goose Lake, town (1990 pop. 221), Clinton co., E Iowa, 13 mi/21 km NW of Clinton; 41°58′N 90°22′W. Concrete blocks; limestone quarry nearby.

Goose Lake, Lake co., S Oregon and Modoc co., N Calif., fluctuating body of water extending N-S across state line; 28 mi/45 km long, 9 mi/14.5 km wide. Elev. 4,701 ft/1,433 m; XL Ranch Indian Reservation at S end. Goose L. State Recreation Area on E side, Oregon. Modoc Natl. Forest, Calif., bounds SW shore. No outlet; North Fork Pit R., to S, former exit to Sacramento R. system.

Goose Lake, Ill.: see BANNER.

Goose River, 90 mi/145 km long, E N.Dak.; rises in Nelson co.; flows SE, past Northwood, Mayville and Hillsboro, to Red R. near Caledonia; 47°56′N 98°00′W.

Gooseberry Island, in Bonavista Bay, E N.F., Canada, 40 mi/64 km E of Gander; 2 mi/3 km long, 1 mi/2 km wide; 48°53′N 53°38′W.

Gorda, Sierra (GOR-dah), outlier range of Sierra Madre Oriental, in Guanajuato, central Mexico, 15 mi/24 km E of San Luis de la Paz; rises to 8,300 ft/2,530 m; 21°23′N 105°15′W. Has many Otomí and Nahuatl Indian communities.

Gordo, town (1990 pop. 1,918), Pickens co., W Ala., 12 mi/19 km NE of Carrollton. Sawmills.

Gordon, county (□ 358 sq mi/927 sq km; 1990 pop. 35,072), NW Ga.; ⊙ Calhoun; 34°30′N 84°52′W. Valley and ridge area drained by Oostanaula, Conasauga, and Coosawattee rivers. Agr. includes cotton, corn, soybeans, wheat; cattle, hogs, poultry. Part of Chattahoochee Natl. Forest and New Echota Marker Natl. Monument in W. Formed 1850.

Gordon 1 town (1990 pop. 493), Houston co., SE Ala., on Chattahoochee R. (here forming Georgia border) and 18 mi/29 km ESE of Dothan. **2** town (1990 pop.

2,468), Wilkinson co., central Ga., 18 mi/29 km ENE of Macon; 32°53′N 83°20′W. Mfg. includes apparel, bldg. materials, steel containers; Kaolin clay processing and mining center. **3** town (1990 pop. 1,803), Sheridan co., NW Nebr., 15 mi/24 km ENE of Rushville and on branch of Niobrara R. near S.Dak. border; 42°48′N 102°12′W. Trade and shipping point for grazing for agr. region; feeds; flour; dairy and poultry prods.; grain, livestock. Inc. 1921.

Gordon 1 village (1990 pop. 206), Darke co., W Ohio, 14 mi/23 km SSE of Greenville, in agr. area; 39°55′N 84°30′W. **2** village (1990 pop. 465), Palo Pinto co., N central Texas, c.60 mi/97 km WSW of Fort Worth; 32°32′N 98°22′W. In agr. area (cattle; peanuts, wheat); oil and gas; natural gas processing. L. Palo Pinto to NE. **3** village (1990 pop. 301), Douglas co., NW Wis., 31 mi/50 km SSE of Superior, on St. Croix R., on upstream (E) end of St. Croix Flowage Reservoir, in lake region; 46°12′N 90°45′W. Unit of Brule R. Sate Forest to E; St. Croix Natl. Scenic Riverway to W, below dam.

Gordon, borough (1990 pop. 768), Schuylkill co., E central Pa., 9 mi/14.5 km NW of Pottsville, on Little Mahony Creek. Agr. (corn, hay; poultry; dairying); mfg. (bottled water, wood prods.); anthracite coal. Settled 1856, inc. 1891.

Gordon Town, village (1991 pop. 1,049), St. Andrew parish, SE Jamaica, mt. resort, 7 mi/11.3 km NE of Kingston; 18°3′N76°42′W. Elev. c.2,000 ft/610 m.

Gordonhorne Peak (9,562 ft/2,914 m), SE B.C., Canada, 60 mi/97 km NNW of Revelstoke; 51°47′N 118°50′W.

Gordonsburg, town, Lewis co., central Tenn., 22 mi/35 km W of Columbia, just E of the Natchez Trace Parkway.

Gordonsville 1 town (1990 pop. 891), Smith co., N central Tenn., 20 mi/32 km E of Lebanon; 36°10′N 85°56′W. Cordell Hull and Center Hill Reservoirs are nearby. **2** town (1990 pop. 1,351), Orange co., N central Va., 18 mi/29 km NE of Charlottesville, on North Anna R.; 38°08′N 78°11′W. RR junction; mfg. (steel prods., lumber, plastic prods., wine, textiles; printing and publishing); trade point in country-estate and agr. area. (grain, soybeans, tobacco; livestock; dairying). Zachary Taylor's b. nearby.

Gordonville, city (1990 pop. 345), Cape Girardeau co., SE Mo., 8 mi/12.9 km W of Cape Girardeau; 37°18′N 89°40′W. Corn, soybeans; hogs; mfg. (advertising specialties).

Gore, village (1990 pop. 690), Sequoyah co., E Okla., 21 mi/34 km SE of Muskogee, and on Arkansas R.; 35°32′N 95°06′W. Mfg. (wooden shipping containers). Was once capital of the Cherokee Nation West. Greenleaf State Park to NW; Tenkiller L. State Park to NE. Cherokee Court House (SE of town); Fort Gruber Natl. Guard Training Facility to NW.

Gore Bay, town (1991 pop. 916), ⊙ Manitoulin dist., S central Ont., on Manitoulin Isl., in North Channel of L. Huron, 90 mi/145 km SW of Sudbury; 45°55′N 82°28′W. Fishing port, freezing plant, lumber mills; resort.

Gore Mountain, N.Y.: see NORTH CREEK.

Gore Pass (9,527 ft/2,904 m), N Colo., in Park Range at N end of Gore Range, 9 mi/14.5 km W of Kremmling. Crossed by State Highway 134. Arapaho Natl. Forest (NE); Routt Natl. Forest (SW).

Gore, Point, S Alaska, cape on Gulf of Alaska at S tip of Kenai Peninsula, 30 mi/48 km SE of Seldovia; 59°12′N 150°58′W.

Gore Range, part of Park Range in Routt, Grand, Summit, and Eagle cos., N central Colo.; extends SSE from Kremmling to Breckenridge, bet. Eagle and Blue rivers. Chief peaks are Red Peak (c.13,183 ft/4,018 m), Blue River Peak (c.13,000 ft/3,962 m), Mt. Powell (c.13,398 ft/4,084 m). Crossed in S by Shrine Pass (11,089 ft/3,380 m) and Vail Pass (10,666 ft/3,251 m). Occupies parts of Arapaho, Routt, and White River natl. forests.

Goree, village (1990 pop. 412), Knox co., N Texas, c.65 mi/105 km WSW of Wichita Falls; 33°28′N 99°31′W. In cotton, grain, cattle area. Millers Creek Reservoir to SE.

Goreville, village (1990 pop. 872), Johnson co., S Ill., 17 mi/27 km S of Herrin; 37°33′N 88°58′W. In fruit-growing region. Fern Clyffe State Park nearby. In Shawnee Natl. Forest.

Gorgas, village, Walker co., NW central Ala., on Mulberry Fork and 13 mi/21 km SSE of Jasper. There are 2 power plants nearby, on Black Warrior R.

Gorham 1 (GOR-uhm), town (1990 pop. 11,856), including Gorham village, Cumberland co., SW Maine, just W of Portland; 43°42′N 70°27′W. Seat of Univ. of Southern Maine. Includes part of South Windham village. Settled on land grant of 1728, inc. 1764. **2** (GOR-uhm), town (1990 pop. 3,173), Coos co., NE N.H., 5 mi/8 km S of Berlin; 44°23′N 71°12′W. Drained by Androscoggin and Peabody rivers. Agr. (cattle, poultry; dairying); mfg. (lumber, pulp, and paper). Parts of White Mt. Natl. Forest in S and NW; Moose Brook State Park in W. Settled c. 1805, inc. 1836.

Gorham 1 village (1990 pop. 290), Jackson co., SW Ill., 10 mi/16 km WSW of Murphysboro; 37°43′N 89°28′W. In agr. region. RR junction. Near Shawnee Nat'l Forest. **2** (GOR-uhm), village (1990 pop. 284), Russell co., central Kansas, 8 mi/12.9 km W of Russell; 38°52′N 99°01′W.

Gorin, Mo.: see SOUTH GORIN.

Gorman 1 town (1990 pop. 1,090), Durham co., N central N.C., residential suburb 8 mi/12.9 km NE of downtown Durham; 36°02′N 78°48′W. Camp Butner Natl. Guard Base to N, Falls Lake reservoir (Neuse R.) to NE. **2** town (1990 pop. 1,290), Eastland co., N central Texas, 38 mi/61 km NNE of Brownwood; 32°12′N 98°40′W. RR terminus; peanut producing and processing; feed mfg. Founded 1890, inc. 1902.

Gorman, uninc. village, Los Angeles co., S Calif., 60 mi/97 km NW of Los Angeles, on Gorman Creek, S of Tejoh Pass. Fort Tejon State Historical Park to N. Service center on Interstate 5.

Gorrie, village, S Ont., Canada, on Maitland R. and 30 mi/48 km ENE of Goderich. Dairying, mixed farming.

Goshen, county (□ 2,232 sq mi/5,781 sq km; 1990 pop. 12,373), SE Wyo.; ⊙ Torrington; 42°05′N 104°21′W. Agr. area bordering on Nebr.; watered by North Platte R. Agr. (beans, oats, corn, hay, sugar beets, alfalfa, wheat; cattle). Ft. Laramie Natl. Historic Site (W); Hawk Springs Reservoir and State Recreation Area (SE). Formed 1911.

Goshen, city (1990 pop. 23,797), ⊙ Elkhart co., N Ind., on the Elkhart R.; 41°35′N 85°50′W. Agr. and dairy region; poultry is also raised and processed. Mfg. (plastic agr. equip., livestock feeding and watering equip., transportation equip, electronic equip., paper, rubber, concrete, metal, and wood prods.). Amish and Mennonite colonies are in the area. Goshen Col. is here. Laid out 1831; inc. 1868.

Goshen 1 town (1990 pop. 302), Pike co., SE Ala., on Conecuh R., and 10 mi/16 km SW of Troy. **2** uninc. town (1990 pop. 1,809), Tulare co., S central Calif., 6 mi/9.7 km WNW of Visalia. Visalia Mun. Airport to SE. Fruit, vegetables, grain; dairying; cattle, poultry. RR junction. **3** town (1990 pop. 2,329), Litchfield co., NW Conn., in Litchfield Hills, 9 mi/11.3 km WNW of Torrington; 41°51′N 73°14′W. Dairying; produced cheese commercially after 1792. Children's camps. Mohawk State Forest, home to part of the Appalachian Trail. **4** town (1990 pop. 2,447), Oldham co., N Ky., 15 mi/24 km NW of Louisville, near Ohio R.; 38°24′N 85°35′W. Agr. (burley tobacco, soybeans, grain; livestock; dairying); mfg. (book printing). **5** agr. town (1990 pop. 830), Hampshire co., NW Mass., 13 mi/21 km NW of Northampton; 42°27′N 72°49′W. Maple sugar. State park nearby. D.A.R. State Forest. **6** town (1990 pop. 742), Sullivan co., SW N.H., 4 mi/6.4 km S of Newport; 43°17′N 72°06′W. Drained by South Branch Sugar R. Agr. (cattle, poultry; corn, nursery crops). **7** town (1990 pop. 226), Addison co., W central Vt., in Green Mts., 13 mi/21 km SSE of Middlebury; 43°52′N 73°00′W. **8** town (1990 pop. 366), Rockbridge co., NW Va., on Calfpasture R., 19 mi/31 km NNW of Buena Vista;

37°59'N 79°30'W. Mfg. (wood prods., textiles). Goshen Pass nearby (SE); a 4-mi/6.4-km river gap cut through a mt. ridge.

Goshen 1 (GO-shuhn), village, Cape May co., S N.J., near Delaware Bay, 4 mi/6.4 km N of Cape May Court House. Agr., fishing; wildlife management area nearby. **2** village (□ 3 sq mi/7.8 sq km; 1990 pop. 5,255) in Goshen town (1990 pop. 11,500), ⊙ Orange co., SE N.Y., 6 mi/9.7 km SE of Middletown; 41°23'N 74°19'W. In dairying and farming area; mfg. (veterinary pharmaceuticals, meatpacking). Resort, with lakes nearby. Good Time and Historic (or Harriman) harness-racing tracks are here; and the Hambletonian race is held here. Settled during 18th cent.; inc. 1809. **3** village (1990 pop. 578), Utah co., central Utah, 12 mi/19 km E of Eureka, near Currant Creek; 39°57'N 111°54'W. Fruit orchards; cattle, sheep. Elev. 4,530 ft/1,381 m. Utah Lake to N.; Mona Reservoir to S.

Goshen Hole, lowland region of Great Plains, Goshen co., E Wyo. and W Nebr., drained by North Platte R.; c.40 mi/64 km N-S, 120 mi/193 km E-W. Consists of mesas, buttes, and badland topography as well as irrigated agr. dists. (sugar beets, wheat, oats, potatoes; cattle). Scottsbluff, Torrington, and Mitchell are chief towns; crossed by Oregon Trail (mid–19th cent.).

Goshen Pass, Va.: see GOSHEN.

Gosier (gaw-ZYAI), town, SW Grande-Terre, Guadeloupe, on the Petit Cul de Sac, 3.5 mi/5.6 km SE of Pointe-á-Pitre. Tourist center, hotels, and casinos. Sometimes called Le Gosier.

Gosnold (GAWZ-nold), town (1990 pop. 98), Dukes co., SE Mass.; comprises Elizabeth Isls., extending 15 mi/24 km SW from Cape Cod, bet. Buzzards Bay and Vineyard Sound, SE of New Bedford; 41°26'N 70°51'W. Fishing community; resorts. Cuttyhunk, on westernmost isl., is only village. Named for explorer Bartholomew Gosnold, 1602. Settled 1641, inc. 1864.

Gosper, county (□ 462 sq mi/1,197 sq km; 1990 pop. 1,928), S Nebr.; ⊙ Elwood; 40°30'N 99°49'W. Borders (NE corner) Platte R. Agr. region (corn, wheat, sorghum; cattle, hogs). Elwood and Johnson reservoirs in N, latter is on Tri-County Supply Canal. Formed 1873.

Gosport, town (1990 pop. 764), Owen co., SW central Ind., on West Fork of White R., and 7 mi/11.3 km NE of Spencer, near Morgan and Monroe co. lines; 39°21'N 86°40'W. In agr. area (hogs, cattle; corn); mfg. (canvas prods. and tarpaulins).

Gossville, N.H.: see EPSOM.

Gotebo (GO-tee-bo), village (1990 pop. 370), Kiowa co., SW Okla., 13 mi/21 km ENE of Hobart; 35°04'N 98°52'W. In cotton and wheat area; sorghum; cattle, sheep.

Gotham, name for N.Y. city first used by Washington Irving and others in the *Salmagundi Papers,* with satirical reference to Gotham, England. The name was later immortalized by creators of cartoons such as *Batman,* whose "Gotham City" was a veiled representation of N.Y. city.

Gothenburg, town (1990 pop. 3,232), Dawson co., S central Nebr., 24 mi/39 km WNW of Lexington and on Platte R; 40°55'N 100°09'W. Agr. (dairying; livestock; grain); diversified mfg. Fur-trading post, built 1854, was moved here (1931) from nearby Oregon Trail. Pony Express Station at city park, bldg. moved from its original site. Settled 1882, inc. 1884.

Gothic Mountain 1 peak (12,625 ft/3,848 m) in Rocky Mts., Gunnison co., W central Colo., 6 mi/9.7 km NNW of Crested Butte, in Gunnison Natl. Forest. **2** peak (4,738 ft/1,444 m) in Essex co., NE N.Y., in the High Peaks sect. of the Adirondacks, c.3 mi/4.8 km ENE of Mt. Marcy, and c.9 mi/14.5 km SSE of Lake Placid village; 44°08'N 73°52'W.

Gott Peak (9,700 ft/2,957 m), S B.C., Canada, in Coast Mts., 80 mi/129 km NNE of Vancouver; 50°22'N 122°17'W.

Goudreau (goo-DRO), village, central Ont., Canada, 120 mi/193 km N of Sault Ste. Marie; 48°15'N 84°32'W. Gold, iron mining.

Gouin Reservoir (goo-EH), central Que., Canada, W of L. St. John; collective name of series of interconnected lakes with deeply indented shoreline, containing numerous isls.; 50 mi/80 km long, 30 mi/48 km wide. Drained by St. Maurice R.

Gould, town (1990 pop. 1,470), Lincoln co., SE Ark., 32 mi/51 km ESE of Pine Bluff; 33°59'N 91°33'W. In rice-growing area. Mfg. (wooden pallets, apparel). Cummins Correctional Unit to N at Varner.

Gould (GOOLD), village (1990 pop. 237), Harmon co., SW Okla., 7 mi/11.3 km W of Hollis, near Texas line; 34°40'N 99°46'W. In agr. area (cotton, grain, peanuts, vegetables).

Goulding (GHOUL-ding), town (□ 1 sq mi/2.6 sq km; 1990 pop. 4,159), Escambia co., extreme NW Fla., NW of Pensacola; 30°26'N 87°13'W.

Goulds (GHOULDZ), suburb (□ 2 sq mi/5.2 sq km; 1990 pop. 7,284) of Miami, Dade co., SE Fla., 18 mi/29 km SW of city center; 25°33'N 80°23'W. Agr. shipping.

Gouldsboro (GOOLDZ-buhr-o), resort town (1990 pop. 1,986), Hancock co., S Maine, on peninsula across Frenchman Bay from Bar Harbor, and 20 mi/32 km E of Ellsworth; 44°25'N 68°02'W. Inc. 1739. Sometimes Gouldsborough.

Gourbeyre (goor-BER), town, S Basse-Terre, Guadeloupe, 2 mi/3.2 km ESE of Basse-Terre. Coffee and cacao growing. Popular excursion point, with nearby thermal springs.

Gouverneur (guhv-uh-NOOR), village (□ 2 sq mi/5.2 sq km; 1990 pop. 4,604), St. Lawrence co., N N.Y., on Oswegatchie R., and 25 mi/40 km S of Ogdensburg; 44°20'N 75°28'W. Mfg. of textiles, clothing, paper, cheese, feed. The mineral sphalerite is extensively mined, yielding zinc, lead, and silver in sizable commerical amounts; talc, wollastonite, and limestone quarries; talc mills. Dairying. Named for Gouverneur Morris, whose mansion still stands. State prison. Laid out 1787, inc. 1850.

Gouyave (GWAHV), town, W Grenada, West Indies, 7 mi/11.3 km N of St. George's; 12°10'N 61°44'W. Cacao growing; fishing. Sometimes called Charlotte Town.

Govan (GO-vuhn), town (1991 pop. 318), S Sask., Canada, near Last Mountain L., 60 mi/97 km NNW of Regina; 51°19'N 105°00'W. Resort.

Govan (go-VAN), village (1990 pop. 84), Bamberg co., S central S.C., 9 mi/14.5 km SW of Bamberg; 33°13'N 81°10'W. Agr. area of grain and cotton; livestock.

Gove, county (□ 1,071 sq mi/2,774 sq km; 1990 pop. 3,231), W central Kansas; ⊙ Gove; 38°55'N 100°29'W. Located in Smoky Hills region, a level to sloping area, drained in S by Smoky Hill R., in N by Big Creek. Wheat, sorghum, cattle; farm machinery. Monument Rocks and Chalk Pyramids in SW; Castle Rock in SE, rock formations. Formed 1886.

Gove (GOV) or **Gove City,** village (1990 pop. 103), ⊙ Gove co., W Kansas, on affluent of Smoky Hill R., and 23 mi/37 km ESE of Oakley; 38°57'N 100°29'W. Grain and livestock area.

Governor's Harbour, town, central Bahama Isls., on small cay off central Eleuthera Isl., 70 mi/113 km E of Nassau; 25°10'N 76°13'W. Trading point; grows tomatoes, pineapples.

Governors Island, W N.F., Canada, on S side of the Bay of Isls., 20 mi/32 km WNW of Corner Brook; 2 mi/3 km long, 1 mi/2 km wide; 49°05'N 58°22'W.

Governors Island, in Upper N.Y. Bay, S of Manhattan Isl., SE N.Y.; covers 173 acres/70 ha; 40°41'N 74°01'W. Bought from the Native Americans by the Dutch in 1637, it was the site of an early New Neth. settlement. The isl. received its name in 1698 (officially 1784), when the British set it aside as the colonial governors' residence. Historic landmarks include Fort Jay (completed c.1800) and Castle William (1811), a Civil War military prison. Governors Isl. served as a U.S. military base and was the East Coast hq. and training center of the U.S. Coast Guard. Military base was closed in 1998, and isl. has already been converted for some civilian uses.

Gowanda, village (□ 1 sq mi/2.6 sq km; 1990 pop. 2,901), on Cattaraugus-Erie co. line, W N.Y., on Cattaraugus Creek and 20 mi/32 km E of Dunkirk; 42°27'N 78°56'W. In dairying area; mfg. (leather goods, maple syrup, agr. insecticides, power sprayers, electronics).

Natural-gas wells; sand and gravel. Nearby is Cattaraugus Indian Reservation. Gowanda Village Historic dist. Settled 1810, inc. 1848.

Gowanus, NW section of Brooklyn borough, N.Y. city, SE N.Y., bounded on E by 4th Ave., S by 14th St., W by Smith St., and N by Baltic Ave.; 40°41'N 73°59'W. Part of former S. Brooklyn; bisected N-S by Gowanus Canal. Originally settled by Dutch c.1640, grew rapidly as an industrial-warehousing dist. in 1840s with the construction of the canal. By late 19th cent., it was a tough, gritty, working-class neighborhood nicknamed the "Gashouse Dist." Unlike many of the surrounding neighborhoods such as Park Slope, Crown Heights, and Cobble Hill, Gowanus has not improved much over time, and its deterioration has been heightened by the decline in port activity in the area. The one bright spot has been the 10-acre/4-ha Brooklyn Piers, purchased by the Port Authority of N.Y. and N.J. in the 1950s and 1960s and now leased for stevedoring and warehousing of breakbulk cargoes. Smith St. is the principal thoroughfare. The Carroll St. Bridge crossing the canal is one of the few remaining examples of retractable bridges in the U.S.

Gowanus Canal, industrial canal, SE borough of Brooklyn, N.Y. city, SE N.Y.; 40°40'N 74°00'W. Heavily polluted, it runs from Hamilton Ave. at head of Gowanus Creek to Degraw St. in S. Brooklyn, where it empties into Gowanus Bay on E side of N.Y. Harbor's Upper Bay. Named after Gonwane, a Canarsie Indian. In the 17th cent., the Dutch found it to be a pristine tidal inlet bordered by rich saltmarsh from which foot-long oysters were supposedly taken; in 1774 the Colonial Assembly enacted a law to widen the creek, draining and filling adjacent marshes. By 1885 industrial use as a canal supported oil refineries, machine shops, chemical plants, wagon makers, cement and soap makers, and tanneries. In 1911 a system was opened to flush out the canal by bringing fresh water in via a tunnel from N.Y. Harbor, thereby getting the stagnant industrial waste and sewage moving; it worked for 50 years, but then broke down and was not repaired. The canal is sometimes referred to as "Lavender Lake" because of its floating chemicals and filth. Construction of the Gowanus Expressway through Brooklyn and subsequent increased use of trucks diminished the canal's importance, though some ships still use it today. Al Capone grew up nearby at Garfield Place and 4th Ave., robbing many banks in the area.

Gowen (GOU-en), village, Latimer co., SE Okla., 10 mi/16 km WSW of Wilburton. In agr. and timber area.

Gower (GOU-wuhr), town (1990 pop. 1,249), Clinton co., NW Mo., 9 mi/14.5 km WNW of Plattsburg; 39°36'N 94°35'W. Agr. (corn, hay; cattle; mfg. (concrete).

Gowganda (gou-GAN-duh), village, E Ont., Canada, on Gowganda L., 60 mi/97 km SSE of Timmins; 47°39'N 80°47'W. Silver and cobalt mining.

Gowganda Lake, E Ont., Canada, 80 mi/129 km N of Sudbury; drains N into Montreal R.; 6 mi/10 km long, 1 mi/2 km wide.

Gowrie, town (1990 pop. 1,028), Webster co., central Iowa, 16 mi/26 km SSW of Fort Dodge; 42°16'N 94°17'W. Inc. 1870.

Goyave (gwah-YAHV), town, E Basse-Terre isl., Guadeloupe, 12 mi/19 km NE of Basse-Terre. Agr. center (cacao, coffee); lumbering, liquor distilling.

Grabill, town (1990 pop. 751), Allen co., NE Ind., 13 mi/21 km NE of Fort Wayne; 41°13'N 84°58'W. In agr. area. Mfg. (furniture, reinforced fiberglass moldings, feed mixing, steering wheels).

Grace, town (1990 pop. 973), Caribou co., SE Idaho, 10 mi/16 km SW of Soda Springs and on Bear R.; 42°35'N 111°44'W. Elev. 5,226 ft/1,593 m. Dairying, cattle. Part of Cache Natl. Forest to SE.

Gracefield, village (1991 pop. 703), SW Que., Canada, on Gatineau R., and 50 mi/80 km NNW of Ottawa; 46°05'N 76°03'W. Dairying; cattle raising.

Gracemont, village (1990 pop. 339), Caddo co., W central Okla., 8 mi/12.9 km N of Anadarko, on Sugar

Creek; 35°11′N 98°15′W. In agr. area; L. Chickasha reservoir to E.

Graceville, town (□ 4 sq mi/10.4 sq km; 1990 pop. 2,675), Jackson co., NW Fla., near Ala. line and Holmes Creek, 21 mi/34 km NW of Marianna; 30°57′N 85°30′W. RR terminus; peanut shelling, lumber milling.

Graceville, village (1990 pop. 671), Big Stone co., W Minn., 18 mi/29 km N of Ortonville, at N end of Toqua L.; 45°34′N 96°26′W. Agr. area (grain, soybeans, alfalfa; hogs).

Gracey (GRAIS-ee), village (1990 pop. 250), Christian co., SW Ky., 11 mi/18 km W of Hopkinsville. In agr. area (tobacco, grain; livestock).

Grady 1 county (□ 460 sq mi/1,191 sq km; 1990 pop. 20,279), SW Ga.; ⊙ Newton; 30°53′N 84°14′W. Bounded S by Fla. state line. Coastal plain area drained by Ochlockonee R. Agr. tobacco, corn, peanuts, pecans, tung nuts, cotton, soybeans, wheat; cattle, hogs, poultry; forestry (lumber, naval stores). Mfg. at Cairo. Formed 1905. **2** county (□ 1,105 sq mi/2,862 sq km; 1990 pop. 41,747), central Okla.; ⊙ Chickasha; 35°01′N 97°53′W. Bounded N by Canadian R.; intersected by Washita R.; and drained also by small Rush Creek and Little Washita R. Diversified agr. (wheat, oats, winter hay, watermelons, alfalfa, peanuts, sorghum, corn, honey); cattle, sheep; dairying. Mfg. at Chickasha. Oil and natural gas. Formed 1907.

Grady 1 village (1990 pop. 586), Lincoln co., SE Ark., 20 mi/32 km ESE of Pine Bluff, near Arkansas R.; 34°04′N 91°42′W. Joe Hardin Lock and Dam to N. **2** village (1990 pop. 110), Curry co., E N.Mex., 35 mi/56 km NNW of Clovis; 34°49′N 103°19′W. Cattle, sheep.

Graettinger, town (1990 pop. 813), Palo Alto co., NW Iowa, near West Des Moines R., 10 mi/16 km NNW of Emmetsburg; 43°14′N 94°45′W. Mfg. (feed, concrete blocks). Sand and gravel pits nearby.

Graf, town (1990 pop. 78), Dubuque co., E Iowa, 10 mi/16 km W of Dubuque; 42°29′N 90°52′W.

Graford, village (1990 pop. 561), Palo Pinto co., N central Texas, c.55 mi/89 km WNW of Fort Worth, near the Brazos R.; 32°56′N 98°15′W. In cattle, agr. (peanuts, wheat); cedar timber area. Possum Kingdom L. reservoir to W.

Grafton, village, SE Ont., Canada, near L. Ontario, 8 mi/13 km ENE of Cobourg. Dairying, fruitgrowing.

Grafton, county (□ 1,750 sq mi/4,533 sq km; 1990 pop. 74,929), central and W N.H.; ⊙ Woodsville; 43°55′N 71°50′W. Bounded W and N by Connecticut R. Drained by Ammonoosuc, Pemigewasset, Gale, Mascoma, and Baker rivers. Summer and winter resort region, including large area of White Mts. and White Mt. Natl. Forest in center and NE. Second largest co. in N.H. in land area. Mfg. at Lebanon, West Lebanon, Plymouth, and Littleton; timber; agr. (nursery crops, hay, corn, vegetables, apples, sugar maples; poultry; dairying). Mica quarrying; sand and gravel, soapstone. Bedell Bridge State Park in W; Cardigan and Wellington (on Newfound L.) state parks in S; Franconia Notch State Park and Parkway in N center, including Old Man of the Mountain rock formation; Province Road State Forest in S; Black Mt. State Forest in W; Appalachian Trail crosses co. NE-SW. Formed 1769.

Grafton 1 city (1990 pop. 918), Jersey co., W Ill., at junction of Illinois and Mississippi rivers, 14 mi/23 km WNW of Alton; 38°58′N 90°25′W. In agr. area. Pere Marquette State Park (c.5,000 acres/2,024 ha) and Mark Twain Wildlife Refuge are W, along Illinois R. City suffered greatly during a devastating flood (1993). Inc. 1837. **2** city (1990 pop. 9,340), Ozaukee co., E Wis., on Milwaukee R., a surburb 19 mi/31 km N of downtown Milwaukee; 43°19′N 87°57′W. In farm area. Mfg. (transportation equip., tools, appliances, textiles, electronic equip., aluminum die castings, fabricated metal prods., chemicals; machining). Inc. 1896.

Grafton 1 town (1990 pop. 282), Worth co., N Iowa, 11 mi/18 km SE of Northwood; 43°19′N 93°04′W. Livestock, grain. **2** town (1990 pop. 13,035), Worcester co., S central Mass., 7 mi/11.3 km ESE of Worcester; 42°13′N 71°42′W. Leather prods. and abrasives are made there. Includes villages of Farnumsville, Fisherville, Saundersville. Built on the site of a Native Amer. village; est. c.1654 by Puritans, inc. 1731. **3** town (1990 pop. 923), Grafton co., W central N.H., 15 mi/24 km ESE of Lebanon; 43°34′N 71°58′W. Drained by Smith R. Agr. (dairying; cattle, poultry; vegetables; nursery crops). Halfmoon and Grafton ponds in W; Ruggles Mine in W center (tourist attraction). **4** town (1990 pop. 4,840), ⊙ Walsh co., NE N.Dak., 38 mi/61 km NNW of Grand Forks and on Park R.; 48°25′N 97°24′W. Center of rich agr. area and important shipping point; dairy prods.; livestock, poultry, grain, potatoes. Mfg. (printing and publishing, farm machinery and equip., batteries). RR junction. Inc. 1883. **5** town (1990 pop. 602), Windham co., SE Vt., 10 mi/16 km WNW of Bellows Falls, and on Saxtons R.; 43°11′N 72°37′W. Grafton State Forest and part of Dorand State Forest are here. Grafton Village resort community. **6** town (1990 pop. 5,524), ⊙ Taylor co., N W.Va., on Tygart R. and 12 mi/19 km SSE of Fairmont; 39°20′N 80°01′W. RR junction. Agr. (alfalfa; cattle); timber. Mfg. (concrete, chemicals, rubber prods., packaging, toys); printing and publishing, coal-mining. Grafton Natl. Cemetery is here. Tygart L. Reservoir and State Park to S; Valley Falls State Park to NW; historic Anna Jarvis Home (first Mother's Day celebration) to S. Settled 1852.

Grafton 1 village (1990 pop. 167), Fillmore co., SE Nebr., 9 mi/14.5 km NW of Geneva; 40°37′N 97°43′W. RR junction. Grafton Pond to SW, one of the lagoons of the Rainwater Basin, preserved in part as Morphy (federal) Wildlife Preserve. **2** resort village (1990 pop. 690), Rensselaer co., E N.Y., 13 mi/21 km ENE of Troy; 42°46′N 73°27′W. Small lakes nearby. **3** village (1990 pop. 3,344), Lorain co., N Ohio, 6 mi/10 km SSE of Elyria and on East Branch of Black R.; 41°17′N 82°02′W. **4** uninc. village, York co., SE Va., 9 mi/14.5 km NNW of downtown Hampton; 37°09′N 76°28′W. Mfg. (furniture, lighting equip., commercial printing). Williamsburg–Newport News Internatl. Airport to SW; Newport News Park to W; Chesapeake Bay to E.

Grafton, Mount, (10,990 ft/3,350 m), E Nev., on White Pine–Lincoln co. line, 40 mi/64 km SSE of Ely, in Egan Range, on Great Basin Divide, outlying sect. of Egan Schell Range.

Graham 1 county (□ 4,641 sq mi/12,020 sq km; 1990 pop. 26,554), SE Ariz.; ⊙ Safford; 32°56′N 109°53′W. Cotton, hay, wheat, corn, sorghum; cattle. Chief ranges are Gila (NE), Pinaleno (center), and Galiuro (SW) mts. Drained by Gila and San Carlos (forms NW boundary) rivers and San Carlos Reservoir at their confluence, on W boundary, which supply water for irrigation. Black R. forms part of N boundary. Part of San Carlos Indian Reservation is in N; parts of Coronado Natl. Forest are in SW; part of Gila Box Riparian Natl. Conservation Area in E; Roper L. State Park in center; part of Aravaipa Canyon Wilderness Area on W boundary, Safford Federal Prison in center. Formed 1909. **2** (GRAI-uhm), county (□ 898 sq mi/2,326 sq km; 1990 pop. 3,543), NW Kansas; ⊙ Hill City; 39°21′N 99°52′W. Rolling prairie region, drained by South Fork Solomon R. and Bow Creek. Wheat, sorghum, cattle. Formed 1880. **3** (GRAI-uhm), county (□ 301 sq mi/780 sq km, 1990 pop. 7,196), extreme W N.C.; ⊙ Robbinsville; 35°21′N 83°49′W. Bounded W by Tenn. state line, N by Little Tennessee R. (Cheoah and Fontana L. reservoirs) and by Great Smoky Mts. Natl. Park. Unicoi Mts. in W, Snowbird Mts. in S; entirely in Nantahala Natl. Forest except NW corner, including Joyce Kilmer Memorial Forest in NW; drained by Cheoah R. Agr. area (tobacco, hay; hogs, cattle), timber; resort area. Mfg. (paper, textiles and apparel, transportation equip., fabricated metal prods., consumer goods; machining, printing and publishing). Formed 1872.

Graham (GRAI-uhm), city (1990 pop. 10,426), ⊙ Alamance co., N central N.C., suburb 3 mi/4.8 km SE of Burlington, near Haw R; 36°03′N 79°23′W. Timber. Mfg. (paper, transportation equip., apparel, textiles, fabricated metal prods., electronic equip., machinery, consumer goods; printing and publishing). Alamance Community Col.; Alamance Battlegrouond State Historical Site to SW. Est. 1849.

Graham 1 (GRAI-uhm), town, Appling co., SE central Ga., 10 mi/16 km WNW of Baxley and 7 mi/11.3 km ESE of Hazelhurst; 31°49′N 82°30′W. **2** town (1990 pop. 204), Nodaway co., NW Mo., on Nodaway R., and 13 mi/21 km SW of Maryville; 40°12′N 95°02′W. Mfg. (concrete). **3** town (1990 pop. 8,986), ⊙ Young co., N Texas, c.55 mi/89 km S of Wichita Falls; 33°06′N 98°34′W. Elev. 1,045 ft/319 m. Commercial processing center for cattle; agr. and oil area; mfg. (computer and electronic equip., aluminum grandstands). Possum Kingdom L. 13 mi/21 km to SE, Possum Kingdom L. State Park is 17 mi/27 km to S; L. Graham reservoir to N. Founded 1872.

Graham 1 (GRAI-uhm), uninc. village (1990 pop. 500), Muhlenberg co., W Ky., 6 mi/9.7 km WNW of Greenville. Agr. (tobacco, grain; livestock); mfg. (detonating cords and fuses); bituminous coal. **2** uninc. village (1990 pop. 180), Pierce co., W Wash., 14 mi/23 km SSE of Tacoma. Agr. area (flower bulbs, berries; poultry; dairying); pottery prods. Fort Lewis Military Reservation to W. Pierce County Fairground is here.

Graham Island, island, NE Franklin dist., N.W.T., Canada, in Norwegian Bay of the Arctic Ocean, W of Ellesmere Isl.; c.15 mi/24 km long, 3 mi/5 km–7 mi/11 km wide; 77°15′N 90°50′W.

Graham Lake (GRAI-uhm), Hancock co., S Maine, just N of Ellsworth; 13 mi/21 km long. In hunting, fishing area.

Graham, Mount, highest peak (10,717 ft/3,267 m) in Pinaleno Mts., Graham co., SE Ariz., 13 mi/21 km SW of Safford, in Coronado Natl. Forest.

Grahn, uninc. village (1990 pop. 500), Carter co., NE Ky., 27 mi/43 km WSW of Ashland. Agr. (tobacco, corn; cattle); mfg. (safety bricks).

Grain Valley, town (1990 pop. 1,898), Jackson co., W Mo., satellite community of Kansas City 22 mi/35 km E of Kansas City; 39°00′N 94°12′W. Sorghum, wheat, corn; cattle; mfg. (RR communications equip.).

Grainfield, village (1990 pop. 357), Gove co., NW Kansas, 21 mi/34 km E of Oakley; 39°06′N 100°28′W.

Grainger (GRAIN-juhr), county (□ 310 sq mi/803 sq km 1990 pop. 17,095), E Tenn.; ⊙ Rutledge; 36°17′N 83°31′W. Traversed SW–NE by Clinch Mtn.; bounded N by Clinch R., E and S by Holston R. Includes part of Cherokee Reservoir. Farm and timber region; livestock, dairy prods., corn, tobacco. Lumbering, marble quarrying; mfg. mobile homes, furniture. Mineral springs (resorts). Formed 1796. "Marble" from here (actually a form of limestone) was used to build Natl. Gall. of Art and Supreme Court Bldg., in Washington, D.C.

Graingers, uninc. village, Lenoir co., E central N.C., 5 mi/8 km NE of Kinston, near Neuse R.

Grainola (grain-OL uh), village (1990 pop. 58), Osage co., N Okla., 26 mi/42 km NW of Pawhuska, on Salt Creek near Kansas line; 36°56′N 96°39′W. Grazing area.

Grainton (GRAIN-tuhn), village (1990 pop. 16), Perkins co., SW central Nebr., 23 mi/37 km E of Grant; 40°49′N 101°17′W.

Grambling (GRAM-bling), town (1994 pop. 6,267), Lincoln parish, N La., suburb 5 mi/8 km W of Ruston; 32°32′N 92°43′W. Timber and agr. area; mfg. of insulation, adhesives. Site of Grambling State Univ.

Gramercy (GRA-muhr-see), town (1990 pop. 2,412), St. James parish, SE central La., 36 mi/58 km WNW of New Orleans and on E bank (levee) of the Mississippi R.; 30°04′N 90°42′W. Mfg. (petroleum coke, processed food, fluorochemicals). Inc. 1940.

Gramercy Park, an affluent residential neighborhood of S central Manhattan borough of N.Y. city, SE N.Y., S of 23d St. and E of 4th Ave., and centering on small privately owned Gramercy Park.

Grampian (GRAM-pee-ahn), borough (1990 pop. 395), Clearfield co., W central Pa., 5 mi/8 km W of Curwensville. Agr. (corn, hay; dairying); surface coal mining.

Gran Banco de Buena Esperanza (grahn BAHNK-o dai BWAIN-ah es-pai-RAHN-zah), bank and reefs in center of Gulf of Guacanayabo, off Granma prov., E Cuba, c.20 mi/32 km W of Manzanillo; 20°25′N 77°30′W.

Gran Couva (KOO-vah), village, W central Trinidad, Trinidad and Tobago, at W foot of Montserrat Hills, 19 mi/31 km SE of Port of Spain. Cacao growing.

Gran Desierto de Pinacate (grahn de-see-ER-to dai PEE-nah-kah-tai), a desert biological reserve (□ 600 sq mi/1,554 sq km), W Sonora, Mexico, 30 mi/49 km W of Sonoita, Mexico, on the Ariz. state border. It comprises a huge area of lava flows and cinder cones. Much wildlife (puma, deer, antelope, wild boar, Gila monster, wild sheep, quail, and red-tailed eagle) inhabit the area. This area was used to train U.S. astronauts during the moon missions. Visitors are restricted to the Cerro Colorado and Elegante Crater areas.

Gran Morelos (grahn mo-RE-los), town (1990 pop. 950), Chihuahua, N Mexico, 37 mi/60 km SW of Chihuahua on an unpaved secondary road; 28°15′N 106°30′W. Corn; livestock. Formerly called San Nicolás de Carretas or San Nicolás.

Gran Piedra (grahn pee-AID-rah), mountain (3,710 ft/1,131 m), Santiago de Cuba prov., E Cuba, near S coast, 15 mi/24 km E of Santiago de Cuba; 21°00′N 75°42′W.

Granada 1 village (1990 pop. 513), Prowers co., SE Colo., near Arkansas R., near Kansas line, and 17 mi/27 km E of Lamar; 38°03′N 102°18′W. Elev. 3,484 ft/1,062 m. Trading point in cattle, grain and feed area. **2** (gruh-NAI-duh), village (1990 pop. 374), Martin co., S Minn., 6 mi/9.7 km ENE of Fairmont, on Center Creek; 43°41′N 94°20′W. Grain, soybeans; livestock; mfg. (fertilizer).

Granada Hills, suburban section of LOS ANGELES city, Los Angeles co., S Calif., residential area 21 mi/34 km NW of downtown Los Angeles, in San Fernando Valley. Bull Canyon in E; Van Norman Reservoir to NE. Mfg. (publishing and printing).

Granada Lake (gruh-NAID-uh), reservoir (□ 15 sq mi/39 sq km), Granada co., N Miss., on Yalobusha R., 5 mi/8 km NE of Granada; 33°49′N 89°46′W. Max. capacity 2,722,100 acre-ft. Formed by Grenada Dam (97 ft/30 m high), built (1954) by Army Corps of Engineers for flood control; also used for recreation. Hugh White State Park on S shore.

Granados (grah-NAH-dos), town (1990 pop. 1,259), Sonora, NW Mexico, on Bavispe R. in Sierra Madre Occidental, and 115 mi/185 km NE of Hermosillo. Irrigated agriculture and livestock raising.

Granbury, town (1990 pop. 4,045), ⊙ Hood co., N central Texas, 34 mi/55 km SW of Fort Worth and on Brazos R.; 32°26′N 97°47′W. Elev. 725 ft/221 m. In agr. area (cattle, horses; peanuts, pecans; hay); mfg. (rope, printing, steel machine parts). Acton State Historical Park, gravesite of Davy Crockett's 2d wife (E); L. Granbury reservoir to SE. Settled c.1860, inc. 1873.

Granbury, Lake, reservoir, Hood co., N central Texas, on Brazos R., 32 mi/51 km SW of Fort Worth; c.20 mi/32 km long; 32°22′N 97°42′W. Max. capacity 293,750 acre-ft. Formed by De Cordova Bend Dam (84 ft/26 m high), built (1969) by the Brazos River Authority for water supply. Acton State Park on NE shore.

Granby (GRAN-bee), city (1991 pop. 42,804), S Que., Canada, on the North Yamaska R., E of Montreal; 45°23′N 72°44′W. In farming area. Textile mills; mfg. includes furniture, tobacco and rubber prods., precision instruments, paper and printed materials, and food prods. Tourism.

Granby, city (1990 pop. 1,945), Newton co., SW Mo., in the Ozarks, 18 mi/29 km SE of Joplin; 36°55′N 94°15′W. Agr. center (fruit-growing, wheat; dairying; poultry); mfg. (sportswear); former zinc, lead mines. Settled 1850s. Pop. of 2,500 in 1874 at height of lead boom.

Granby 1 town (1990 pop. 966), Grand co., N Colo., on Fraser R., near its confluence with the Colorado R., and 55 mi/89 km NW of Denver; elev. 7,939 ft/2,420 m. Livestock and some vegetables, timber; wood prods., tourism. Just NE, on Colorado R., is Granby Dam (begun 1942; important unit in Colorado–Big Thompson project of Bureau of Reclamation). Dam is 300 ft/91 m high, 930 ft/283 m long; from Granby Reservoir (capacity 550,000 acre-ft.), water is pumped into Shadow Mountain L. and Grand L., then conducted through Alva B. Adams Tunnel to E slope of Continental Divide and used for irrigation and power in the South Platte Basin. L. Granby reservoir and Arapaho Natl. Recreation Area to NE; Rocky Mt. Natl. Park to NE; parts of Arapaho Natl. Forest to NW, E, and SW; W gateway to Rocky Mt. Natl. Park. Silver Creek Ski Area to SE. County airport here. **2** town (1990 pop. 9,369), Hartford co., N Conn., 15 mi/24 km NW of Hartford; 41°57′N 72°50′W. Agr. (tobacco). Residential community with retail service and office development necessary to support a residential community. Includes part of McLean Game Refuge. Settled c.1664, inc. 1786. **3** town (1990 pop. 5,565), Hampshire co., S central Mass., 7 mi/11.3 km SE of Northhampton; 42°16′N 72°30′W. Settled 1727, inc. 1768. **4** town (1990 pop. 85), Essex co., NE Vt., 10 mi/16 km W of Guildhall; 44°36′N 71°43′W. Hunting, fishing.

Granby, Lake, Grand co., N Colo., on Colorado R., in Arapaho Natl. Recreation Area, 6 mi/9.7 km NE of Granby; 8 mi/12.9 km long NW-SE; 40°08′N 105°52′W. Max. storage capacity of 540,000 acre-ft. River enters on NE, exits SW. Formed by Granby Dam, built (1950) by the Bureau of Reclamation for irrigation.

Grand 1 county (□ 1,869 sq mi/4,841 sq km; 1990 pop. 7,966), N Colo.; ⊙ Hot Sulphur Springs; 40°06′N 106°07′W. Bounded by Continental Divide on N, E, and SE. Sheep-grazing and farming area, bounded E by Front Range; drained by Colorado R. Part of Rocky Mt. Natl. Park in NE; Arapaho Natl. Recreation Area in NE, including Grand L., L. Granby Reservoir, and Shadow Mt. Reservoir; parts of Arapaho Natl. Forest in N, W, S, and E; part of Routt Natl. Forest in far W and NW. Silver Creek and Winter Park Ski Areas in E. **2** county (□ 3,694 sq mi/9,567 sq km; 1990 pop. 6,620), E Utah; ⊙ Moab, bounded W by Green R., drained by Colorado R.; 38°59′N 109°33′W. Some cattle and sheep-grazing area bordering on Colo. (E); oil and natural gas; salt, potassium. Mineral deposits (vanadium, uranium) near Moab, copper deposits in La Sal Mts. (SE). Includes much of East Tavaputs Plateau and Book Cliffs. Arches Natl. Monument is N of Moab. Dead Horse Point State Park on S boundary; very small section of Canyonlands Natl. Park in SW. Part of large Will Creek Extension unit of Uintah and Ouray Indian Reservation in NW; part of Manti-La Sal Natl. Forest in SE. Co. formed 1890.

Grand Bahama: see BAHAMAS.

Grand Bank, town (1991 pop. 3,528), S N.F., Canada, on SE shore of Fortune Bay, on Burin Peninsula, 150 mi/241 km WSW of St. John's; 47°05′N 55°46′W. Important base for Grand Banks fisheries. Site of govt. facilities. Fishing and lumbering nearby.

Grand Banks, submarine plateau rising from the continental shelf, c.36,000 sq mi/93,200 sq km, off SE N.F., Canada; c.300 mi/480 km long, c.400 mi/640 km wide; 47°00′N 52°00′W. Depths range from 20 to 100 fathoms. The cold Labrador Current flows over most of the banks; the warmer Gulf Stream sweeps along the E edge, sometimes crossing the S part. The Grand Banks are noted for the persistent dense fog (formed as warm air passes over cold water) that engulfs the area. The mingling of the 2 currents along with the shallowness of the water forms a favorable environment for plankton and other small sea life upon which cod, haddock, halibut, and other fish feed. Lobsters are also found here. Supplies have dwindled in recent years, however, leading to govt.-imposed limits on fishing. The Grand Banks were probably the world's most important internatl. fishing ground until 1977, when Canada extended its offshore jurisdiction to include most of the area. Until 1990s, the major concern was political. Canada declared a 200 mi/370 km exclusive zone that included most of the Grand Banks, in response to overfishing by foreign trawlers. It has extended a no-fishing moratorium beyond this limit and seized Eur. trawlers violating the moratorium. A large number of fishermen (50,000) and fish-processing workers lost their jobs as result of moratorium on fishing. A 14 mi/23 km territorial zone around the Fr. isls. of St. Pierre and Miquelon and a Fr. exclusive zone extending 186 mi/299 km SE from the isls., disputed by Canada, added to the problem. Reduced quotas failed to revive the fish stocks, lending to collapse of the cod industry in 1992–1993. Fog, icebergs, and the nearby transatlantic shipping lanes make fishing hazardous. Oil drilling began on the banks in the late 1970s but was slowed after the loss of the Ocean Ranger rig on Feb. 15, 1982. Continued exploration has brought a minor oil boom to Halifax and other parts (St. John's, N.F.); giant Hibernia oil and gas field on the banks. Earthquake and iceberg activity in the Banks pose potential ecological disaster.

Grand Bay, village (1986 pop. 3,319), 7 mi/11.3 km N of center of St. John, N.B., Canada; 45°18′N 66°12′W. Summer community after World War II, now suburb of St. John. Inc. 1972.

Grand Bay, village (1990 pop. 3,383), Mobile co., extreme SW Ala., 23 mi/37 km SW of Mobile; 30°28′N 88°20′W. Steel tank mfg.

Grand Beach, village (1990 pop. 146), Berrien co., extreme SW Mich., on L. Michigan, at Ind. line, 6 mi/9.7 km NE of Michigan City, Ind.; 41°46′N 86°47′W.

Grand Blanc, town (1990 pop. 7,760), Genesee co., SE central Mich., suburb 7 mi/11.3 km SSE of Flint; 42°55′N 83°37′W. In agr. area (livestock; soybeans, apples, grain, beans; dairy prods.). Mfg. (transportation equip., concrete blocks, environmental testing equip., chemicals). Settled 1823, inc. 1930.

Grand Cache, town (1986 pop. 3,646), 267 mi/430 km NW of Edmonton, Alta., Canada. Model planned resource town. Coking coal for Jap. market. Inc. 1966.

Grand Caicos, Turks and Caicos Isls.: see MIDDLE CAICOS.

Grand Caillou, Bayou (GRAWN kah-YOO, BEI-yoo), navigable waterway in SE La., extends from N Terrebonne parish c.35 mi/56 km generally S to Caillou Bay, an arm of the Gulf of Mexico. Partly canalized; linked by connecting waterways to Intracoastal Waterway, Caillou L., and other navigable bayous.

Grand Calumet River, Ill. and Ind.: see CALUMET RIVER.

Grand Cane, village (1990 pop. 233), De Soto parish, NW La., 29 mi/47 km S of Shreveport; 32°05′N 93°49′W. Agr. (cotton; cattle); timber; oil and gas. Founded in 1848.

Grand Canyon, uninc. town, in Grand Canyon Natl. Park, Coconino co., N Ariz., 65 mi/105 km NW of Flagstaff; elev. 6,866 ft/2,093 m. Hq. for park. Pop. made up of park service and concession personnel. Tourism; mfg. (printing and publishing); terminus of RR spur from Williams and part of Kaibab Natl. Forest (S); Havasupai Indian Reservation (W) at S rim of Grand Canyon.

Grand Canyon, N Ariz., Coconino co., extends W into Mohave co., c.65 mi/105 km NNW of Flagstaff, great gorge of the Colorado R., one of the great natural wonders of the world; c.1 mi/1.6 km deep, from 4 mi/6.4 km to 18 mi/29 km wide, and 277 mi/446 km long, N and central Ariz. The canyon shows in its rocks, exposed by more than 8 million years of chemical erosion, the repeated geological sequence of uplift, erosion (due to the constant wearing force of the Colorado R.), submergence, and deposition of materials. The multicolored rocks, the steep and embayed rims, and the isolated towers, mesas, "temples," and other eroded rock forms catch the contrast of sun and shadow and glow with constantly changing hues of great beauty. Plant life on the canyon walls varies from subtropical at the base to subarctic near the rims. Hundreds of anc. pueblos dot the lower canyon walls and the rim. The first European to see the canyon was the Span. explorer García López de Cárdenas in 1540. In 1869, U.S. explorer John W. Powell was the first man to lead a party through the canyon river bottom in a boat. The Grand Canyon, set aside by the U.S. govt. in 1908 as a natl. monument, was expanded in 1919 and designated

Grand Canyon National Park (1,904 sq mi/4,931 sq km), Coconino and Mohave cos., N Ariz. A separate Grand Canyon Natl. Monument was created 1940 to W of park; Marble Canyon Natl. Monument erected 1969 NE of park, both areas plus additional acreage absorbed into Grand Canyon Natl. Park in 1975. Along the forested N rim and the more accessible S rim are numerous lookouts, and trails wind to the canyon floor. Popular tourist activities include mule rides from rim to base of the canyon and raft and boat excursions along the canyon's river bottom. Lodge and other services at Grand Canyon village at S rim; lodge at N rim; connection bet. N and S rims by hiking trail only. More than 3 million tourists visit the park each year. One of the most popular natl. parks in U.S. and world.

Grand Canyon of the Arkansas, Colo.: see ROYAL GORGE.

Grand Canyon of the Snake River, Idaho: see SNAKE RIVER.

Grand Canyon of the Tuolumne, Calif.: see YOSEMITE NATIONAL PARK.

Grand Canyon of the Yellowstone, Wyo.: see YELLOWSTONE NATIONAL PARK.

Grand Cascapedia (ka-skuh-PEE-dee-uh), **Cascapedia**, or **Cascapédia** (kahs-kah-pai-dee-AH), village, E Que., Canada, S Gaspé Peninsula, on Cascapedia R., near its mouth on Chaleur Bay, and 26 mi/42 km NE of Dalhousie. Dairying; lumbering.

Grand Caverns, Va.: see GROTTOES.

Grand Cayman, largest of the Cayman islands (□ 71 sq mi/184 sq km, 1989 pop. 23,881), crown colony of Great Britain, West Indies, westernmost and largest of the Cayman group, 190 mi/306 km WNW of Jamaica; 17 mi/27 km long, 4 mi/6.4 km–7 mi/11.3 km wide, surrounded by coral reefs; 19°17′N 81°23′W. Chief settlements include George Town (capital of the Cayman Isls.), Bodden Town, West Bay, Prospect, and East End. Thriving offshore banking and hq. for thousands of corporate industry subsidiaries, attracted to Caymans as a tax haven. Excellent beaches, resorts, and scuba-diving facilities.

Grand Chenier (GRAWN SHEN-yai), town, in Cameron parish, La.; 29°46′N 92°59′W. Located on one of the cheniers (oak tree-covered ridges) that parallel the Gulf of Mexico coastline, this is a fishing, garden crop, and marsh hunting area.

Grand Codroy River, 30 mi/48 km long, SW N.F., Canada; rises in Anguille Mts.; flows SW to Cabot Strait 6 mi/10 km SE of Cape Anguille. Valley is one of most fertile regions of N.F.; sheep; potatoes, buckwheat, hay. Isolation has preserved unique folk culture.

Grand Coteau (kuh-TO), town (1990 pop. 1,118), St. Landry parish, S central La., 12 mi/19 km N of Lafayette; 30°25′N 92°02′W. In agr. area. Oil and gas nearby. Seat of Academy of the Sacred Heart (1821), 2d-oldest educational institution W of Mississippi R.

Grand Coulee (KOO-lee), town (1990 pop. 984), Grant co., NE central Wash., 75 mi/121 km WNW of Spokane and near Columbia R., on channel that diverts water from Grand Coulee Dam and Columbia R. into Grand Coulee, former channel of Columbia, forming Banks L. reservoir; 47°57′N 119°00′W. Wheat, barley, oats, alfalfa; cattle. Near W end of Grand Coulee Dam, opposite town of Coulee Dam. Steamboat Rock State Park to SW, on peninsula in Banks L. Coulee Dam Natl. Recreation Area adjoins town to N and E. Inc. 1935.

Grand Coulee Dam (KOO-lee), on Okanogan-Grant co. border, on Columbia R., N central Wash., 75 mi/121 km NW of Spokane; 550 ft/168 m high, 4,173 ft/1,272 m long; 47°57′N 118°59′W. One of the world's largest concrete dams. Built (1933–1942) as a key unit in the COLUMBIA BASIN PROJECT of the U.S. Bureau of Reclamation for flood control, irrigation, and power generation. Has the largest power-producing capacity (6,480 mw) in the U.S. Impounds Franklin D. Roosevelt L., 130-mi/209-km long and generally 1-mi/1.6-km wide, which extends E and N into Lincoln, Ferry, and Stevens cos. and to Can. (B.C.) border; it is 1 of the largest reservoirs in the U.S. Hydroelectricity is produced at the dam; and water is diverted into Grand Coulee, a walled gorge of formerly dry basaltic rock, c.30 mi/48 km long, the prehistoric main channel of the Columbia R., through the Columbia Plateau. Banks L., a large reservoir at N end of Grand Coulee gorge, controls water supply to more than 500,000 acres/202,350 ha to the valley and the plateau. Entire reservoir, including 35-mi/56-km long Spokane R. Arm (extends E to Little Falls Dam), is in Coulee Dam Natl. Recreation Area. Located on the Pacific flyway, a chief N-S migratory route, the area has a great variety of waterfowl and land birds. Grand Coulee (1990 pop. 1,150) and Coulee Dam (1990 pop. 1,087) were founded by the U.S. govt. in 1935–1936 as construction, operational, and housing bases for the dam.

Grand Cul de Sac (GRAHND kyoo duh SAHK), bay in N Guadeloupe, Fr. West Indies, bet. Basse-Terre and Grand-Terre, and linked by 4-mi/6.4-km-long Rivière Salée with Petit Cul de Sac; 16°20′N 61°35′W. Sometimes called Grand Cul de Sac Marin.

Grand Detour, village, Ogle co., N Ill., on Rock R., and 5 mi/8 km NNE of Dixon; 41°53′N 89°24′W. Founded 1835 by Leonard Andrus. In 1837, John Deere built 1st Grand Detour steel plow here; he established with Andrus Illinois' 1st plow industry, which remained in village until 1869 despite Deere's withdrawal and establishment in 1847 of factory at Moline. John Deere's home and workshop are now a mus.

Grand Etang (GRAN uh-TAING), lake (2.5 mi/4 km circumference; elev. 1,740 ft/530 m), central Grenada, West Indies, 5 mi/8 km NE of St. George's, in crater of an extinct volcano; 12°05′N 61°42′W. On it are a rest-house and sanatorium.

Grand Falls, city (1991 pop. 6,083), W N.B., Canada, on the St. John R. The nearby falls in the river and its 1-mi/2-km-long gorge attract many visitors. The falls power a large hydroelectric development.

Grand Falls, town (1991 pop. 14,693), central N.F., Canada, on the Exploits R. In the town are large pulp and paper mills that produce large amounts of newsprint.

Grand Falls, in central Ont., Canada, waterfalls (150 ft/46 m high) of the Mississagi R., 30 mi/48 km NW of Blind R.

Grand Falls, Canada: see CHURCHILL FALLS.

Grand Falls, plantation, Penobscot co., S central Maine, in wilderness area, 30 mi/48 km NW of Bangor.

Grand Forks, county (□ 1,439 sq mi/3,727 sq km; 1990 pop. 70,683), E N.Dak.; ⊙ Grand Forks, in Red R. Valley; 47°55′N 97°27′W. Bordered E by Red R. of the North (Minn. boundary), watered by Goose, Forest, and Turtle rivers. Agr. produce (wheat, barley, mustard, potatoes, sugar beets; cattle, hogs); mfg. at Grand Forks. Formed 1873. Grand Forks Air Force Base and Turtle River State Park near center.

Grand Forks, city (1991 pop. 3,610), S B.C., Canada, on Wash. border, on Granby R., and 35 mi/56 km W of Trail; 49°03′N 118°28′W. Fruit- and vegetable-growing center, with canneries and seed nurseries, in irrigated farming region; lumbering. Former mining center.

Grand Forks, city (1990 pop. 49,425), seat of Grand Forks co., E N.Dak., at the confluence of the Red R. of the North (N.Dak.-Minn. state line) and the Red Lake R. from East Grand Forks, Minn., on opposite side; 47°55′N 97°04′W. Agr. area (wheat, sugar beet, potato, and edible beans; livestock); grain elevators, state-operated flour mills, and plants that process and distribute meat, dairy prods., sugar beets, and potatoes. Mfg. (printing, fiberglass prods., beverage processing, farm equip., mustard processing). RR junction. The area was settled by Fr. fur traders who traveled the 2 rivers by canoe and camped at the junction. They called their campsite La Grandes Fourches [Fr. = the grand forks]. Euro-Americans arrived in 1868. Grand Forks became an important stop on the Great Northern RR after 1880. In 1928 the RR built huge switching and storage yards in the city. The Univ. of N.Dak. is here, as is a U.S. Dept. of Agr. human nutrition research laboratory and a regional Natl. Weather Service meteorological station. Grand Forks Air Force and Base to W. Sites of interest are Campbell House/Myra Mus. and N.Dak. Mus. of Art (official state art mus.). Fairgrounds. 1881. In April 1997 the Red R., swelled by melting snow, overflowed its banks, and the flood devastated Grand Forks and several other communities; most of the city's pop. was evacuated. Inc. 1881.

Grand Gorge, village (1990 pop. 1,000), Delaware co., S N.Y., in the Catskills, c.40 mi/64 km NW of Kingston, in resort and dairying area; 42°22′N 74°29′W.

Grand Gulf 1 Nuclear Power Plant, Miss.: see CLAIBORNE CO.

Grand Harbour, fishing village (1991 pop. 598), chief settlement of Grand Manan Isl., SW N.B., Canada, on E coast of isl., 30 mi/48 km SE of St. Andrews. Tourism.

Grand Haven, city (1990 pop. 11,951), ⊙ Ottawa co., SW Mich., 12 mi/19 km S of Muskegon, 32 mi/51 km WNW of Grand Rapids (in commuting distance of both cities), at the mouth of the Grand R.; 43°03′N 86°13′W. It is a port on L. Michigan that ships sand and gravel. Mfg. (fabricated metal prods., paper prods., consumer goods); popular resort area. Annual Coast Guard festival. Municipal Airport to SE; Tri-City Historical Mus., Grand Haven Ski Bowl, and Grand Haven State Park on L. Michigan in town; P.J. Hoffmaster State Park to NE (Muskegon co.). Inc. 1867.

Grand Island, city (1990 pop. 39,386), ⊙ Hall co., S Nebr., on the Wood R. near its junction with the Platte, 85 mi/137 km W of Lincoln; 40°55′N 98°22′W. RR junction. Agr. market (esp. livestock; grain, corn, dairy); also RR, and mfg. and shipping center. Mfg. (plastic prods., meat packing, agr. machinery, irrigation systems, transportation equip., bldg. materials, hides, trusses, food prods., printing and publishing). The Stuhr Mus. of the Prairie Pioneer, on an isl. in a nearby artificial lake, was designed by Edward Durrell Stone. Veteran's Home. Settled 1857 on the Platte by Germans, moved 1866 to its location on the Union Pacific RR, inc. c.1872.

Grand Island, town (□ 33 sq mi/85 sq km; 1990 pop. 17,561), Erie co., W N.Y., comprising Grand Isl. and adjacent small isls. in Niagara R. bet. N.Y. and Ont. (Canada), just NW of Buffalo; 7.5 mi/12.1 km long, 1 mi/1.6 km–6.5 mi/10.5 km wide; 43°01′N 78°57′W. Linked by bridges to N.Y. and Ont. Buckhorn Isl. State Park is on Grand Isl.'s N shore and small Buckhorn Isl.; Beaver Isl. State Park is on its S shore and adjacent Beaver Isl. Grand Isl. village is near S tip.

Grand Island 1 SE La., in Gulf of Mexico, in passage connecting L. Borgne (W) and Mississippi Sound (E); c.2 mi/3 km long. Grand Isl. Pass to N is principal deepwater navigation channel bet. sound and lake. **2** in Alger co., N Mich., in Trout Bay of L. Superior off the Upper Peninsula, 3 mi/4.8 km N of Munising; 46°31′N 86°40′W. One of largest Mich. isls. (c.13,000 acres/5,261 ha). Wooded area, with game refuge; resort.

Grand Isle, county (□ 194 sq mi/502 sq km; 1990 pop. 5,318), NW Vt., on a peninsula and several isls. in L. Champlain; ⊙ North Hero; 44°47′N 73°17′W. Dairying, apples, lumber; resorts. Includes North Hero Isl., Grand Isle, and Isle La Motte, site of state's 1st Eur. settlement (c.1665). Organized 1802.

Grand Isle 1 town (1990 pop. 1,455), in Jefferson parish, extreme SE La., c.50 mi/80 km S of New Orleans, on isl. of same name, bet. Gulf of Mexico (S) and Caminada Bay (NW) and Barataria Bay (NE); c.7 mi/11 km long, c.2 mi/3 km wide; W end bridged to mainland; 29°13′N 90°02′W. Mfg. of fabricated structural metal. Recreation. La. State Univ. marine laboratory is here. Isl. was hq. for Lafitte's pirates in early 19th cent. Grand Isle State Park on E end. **2** agr. town (1990 pop. 558), Aroostook co., NE Maine, on St. John R., and 20 mi/32 km E of Fort Kent; 47°15′N 68°07′W. Inc. 1869.

Grand Isle, island and town (1990 pop. 1,642), Grand Isle co., NW Vt., in L. Champlain, 12 mi/19 km SW of St. Albans; c.13 mi/21 km long; 44°43′N 73°17′W. Fruit, dairy prods., lumber; resort. Oldest Vt. log cabin here.

Isl. includes South Hero (S); bridged to North Hero Isl. and to mainland. Grand Isle State Park is here.

Grand Junction 1 city (1990 pop. 29,034), ⊙ Mesa co., W Colo., 195 mi/314 km WSW of Denver on Colorado R., at mouth of Gunnison R.; elev. 4,586 ft/1,398 m. RR junction. The shipping and processing center of a large ranch and irrigated farm region, it also serves the area's uranium, oil shale, gas, and coal-mining industries. Mfg. (electronic equip., candies, concrete, agr. machinery; printing); tourism. Grand Junction's airport permits access to many Colo. ski resorts. Walker Field airport to NE. The city is also a center during the regional hunting season and serves as hq. for Grand Mesa Natl. Forest to (E). Mesa Col. (2-year) is here. Uranium production was regulated in 1970 after a radiation hazard arose from radioactive wastes (tailings) used for construction fill in bldg. projects. Colorado Natl. Monument to W; Highline State Park to NW; Colorado R. State Park to E; Island Acres State Park to NE. Western Colo. Center for the Arts, Dinosaur Valley Mus., Mus. of Western Colo. here. Powderhorn Ski Area to E. Inc. 1891. **2** city (1990 pop. 365), Hardeman co., SW Tenn., near Miss. border, 45 mi/72 km E of Memphis; 35°02'N 89°11'W. Cotton, corn; livestock.

Grand Junction, town (1990 pop. 808), Greene co., central Iowa, 7 mi/11.3 km E of Jefferson; 42°01'N 94°14'W. Concrete prods. Sand pits nearby. Inc. 1873.

Grand Lake, village (1990 pop. 259), Grand co., N Colo., on Colorado R., in Front Range, and 33 mi/53 km WNW of Boulder; elev. 8,369 ft/2,551 m. Fishing and boating resort on Grand L., in Colorado–Big Thompson project. Largest glacial lake in Colo. Shadow Mtn. Reservoir and Granby Reservoir to S, downstream from Grand L. Town is at W entrance to Rocky Mt. Natl. Park. Cascade Falls Trail starts here. Rocky Mt. Natl. Park to N, E, and SE; Arapaho Natl. Forest to W; Arapaho Natl. Recreation Area to S.

Grand Lake, locality, central N.S., Canada, on Shubenacadie L., 17 mi/27 km N of Halifax; quartzite mining. Gold formerly mined.

Grand Lake 1 lake (□ 67 sq mi/174 sq km), S central N.B., Canada, 30 mi/48 km E of Fredericton; drains into St. John R. (S) by the short Jemseg stream; 20 mi/32 km long, 7 mi/11 km wide. Short streams drain into it from several smaller lakes nearby. Along N and W shore are important coal fields, whence coal was 1st shipped to New England in 1643. At N end of lake is hydroelectric power station. There are shad and alewife fisheries. In Fr. period, called Lac Freneuse. **2** lake (□ 129 sq mi/334 sq km; 60 mi/97 km long, 6 mi/10 km wide), W N.F., Canada, 15 mi/24 km SE of Corner Brook. Connected N with Sandy L. by narrow channel and with Deer L. by the Newfoundland Canal. In S part of lake is uninhabited Glover Isl. (□ 74 sq mi/192 sq km; 25 mi/40 km long, 3 mi/5 km wide).

Grand Lake 1 lake (12 mi/19 km long E-W, 7 mi/11 km wide), in Cameron parish, SW La., a widening of Mermentau R.; 29°53'N 92°44'W. Lacassine Natl. Wildlife Refuge to NW. **2** lake (c.30 mi/48 km long, 1 mi/2 km–2 mi/3 km wide); in Iberia, St. Martin, and St. Mary parishes, S La.; a widening of Atchafalaya River. **3** largest of CHIPUTNETICOOK LAKES, E Maine and N.B., Canada; 17 mi/27 km long. **4** in Presque Isle co., NE Mich., 13 mi/21 km N of Alpena. Separated from L. Huron (E) by narrow strip of land with Presque Isle village (resort) on it; c.8 mi/12.9 km long, 1.5 mi/2.4 km wide; 45°18'N 83°30'W.

Grand Lake Matagamon (mat-uh-GAM-uhn), lake in Piscataquis and Penobscot cos., N central Maine, 33 mi/53 km NNW of Millinocket; 8 mi/12.9 km long. Source of East Branch of Penobscot R.

Grand Lake of the Cherokees (□ 73 sq mi/189 sq km), Mayes, Del., and Ottawa cos., extreme NE Okla., on Neosho R., in Ozark Recreation Area, 55 mi/88 km NE of Tulsa; 36°28'N 95°02'W. Max. capacity 1,537,000 acre-ft. Formed by Pensacola Dam (150 ft/46 m high), built (1940) for power generation.

Grand Lake Saint Marys, reservoir, Mercer and Auglaize cos., W Ohio, on Beaver Creek, branch of Wabash R., 1 mi/1.6 km SE of Celina; 8 mi/12.9 km long, 3 mi/4.8 km wide. Formed by dams at E (40°31'N 84°25'W) and W (40°32'N 84°04'W) ends of lake; linked (E end) to St. Mary's R. by 2-mi/3.2-km channel. Grand Lake–St. Marys Park at E end; fish hatchery.

Grand Lake Seboeis (se-BOI-uhs), Penobscot co., N central Maine, 42 mi/68 km N of Millinocket; 7 mi/11.3 km long. Source of Seboeis R. Formerly spelled Seboois Lake (also the name of another lake in Piscataquis co.).

Grand Lake Stream, plantation (1990 pop. 174), Washington co., E Maine, near Grand L., 35 mi/56 km NNW of Machias; 45°13'N 67°43'W.

Grand Lake Victoria, SW Que., Canada, 120 mi/193 km NE of North Bay; 32 mi/51 km long, 3 mi/5 km wide. Elev. 1,051 ft/320 m; source of Ottawa R.

Grand Ledge, town (1990 pop. 7,579), Eaton co., S central Mich., suburb 10 mi/16 km WNW of Lansing and on Grand R.; 42°45'N 84°45'W. In agr. area (livestock; grain, beans, vegetables, hay; dairy prods.); mfg. (transportation equip., printing). Sandstone deposits. Settled c.1848; inc. as village 1871, as city 1893.

Grand Manan (muh-NAN), island c.16 mi/26 km long and c.7 mi/11 km wide, S N.B., Canada, in the Bay of Fundy. On the N and W sides are bold cliffs, rising from 200 ft/61 m to 400 ft/122 m high, visible from the Maine coast. The principal villages and harbors, North Head, Grand Harbor, and Seal Cove, are on the S and E sides. The chief occupation is fishing, and the isl. is a summer resort. It was settled after the Amer. Revolution by Loyalists; Brit. possession was disputed by the U.S. until 1817.

Grand Marais (muh-RAI), town (1990 pop. 1,171), ⊙ Cook co., NE Minn., 110 mi/177 km NE of Duluth, on Grand Marais Harbor, L. Superior, in Superior Natl. Forest; 47°45'N 90°20'W. Elev. 688 ft/210 m. Resort area, recreation; timber; mfg. (lumber [beech and cedar], wood chips). Cascade State Park to SW; Kodonce R. State Wayside to E; Grand Portage State Forest to NE. Eagle Mt. (2,301 ft/701 m) highest point in Minn., 13 mi/21 km NW. Devil Track L. to NW; Wild Flower Sanctuary to NE, on Devil Track R.

Grand Marais (ma-REI), resort village, Alger co., N Upper Peninsula, Mich., 37 mi/60 km NE of Munising, on harbor on L. Superior. Entrance (E) to Pictured Rocks Natl. Lakeshore; Au Sable Dunes 5 mi/8 km W; Muskallonge L. State Park 15 mi/24 km E (Luce co.); 45°40'N 85°59'W.

Grand Meadow, town (1990 pop. 967), Mower co., SE Minn., 20 mi/32 km E of Austin, on Deer Creek; 43°42'N 92°34'W. Grain, corn, oats, soybeans, peas; cattle, hogs, sheep, poultry; dairying; mfg. (utility trailers, fertilizers; printing). Limestone quarry nearby.

Grand Mesa (□ c.50 sq mi/130 sq km), one of the largest flat-topped mesas in the U.S., in Delta and Mesa cos., W Colo.; lies within part of Grand Mesa Natl. Forest. Elev. 10,000 ft/3,048 m. Deposits of coal and oil shale. Volcanic top layer protects the mesa from erosion. Over 200 lakes cover its top, which is 5,000 ft/1,524 m above the surrounding land.

Grand Monadnock, N.H.: see MONADNOCK MT..

Grand Mound, town (1990 pop. 619), Clinton co., E Iowa, 23 mi/37 km W of Clinton; 41°49'N 90°39'W. Metal prods.

Grand Mountain (10,842 ft/3,305 m), SE B.C., Canada, in Selkirk Mts., in Glacier Natl. Park, 35 mi/56 km SE of Revelstoke; 51°4'N 117°23'W.

Grand Narrows, resort village, NE N.S., Canada, central Cape Breton Isl., on Barra Strait (ferry), bet. Bras d'Or L. and Great Bras d'Or, 30 mi/48 km WSW of Sydney; 45°57'N 60°47'W.

Grand Pass, town (1990 pop. 53), Saline co., central Mo., near Missouri R., 14 mi/23 km NW of Marshall; 39°12'N 93°26'W. Corn, soybeans, wheat.

Grand Portage, village, Cook co., extreme NE Minn., 34 mi/55 km ENE of Grand Marais and 36 mi/58 km SSW of Thunder Bay, Ont., Canada; port of entry 5 mi/8 km ENE, on Grand Portage Bay, L. Superior, 3 mi/4.8 km S of Canada (Ont.) border, in Grand Portage (Chippewa) Indian Reservation. Elev. 1,348 ft/411 m. Fishing center. Was busy fur-trading point in 18th cent. and central depot for North West Company It was E terminus of the Grand Portage, 9 mi/14.5 km overland link bet. L. Superior and Pigeon R.; the route of the old trail, long used by Native Americans, explorers, and traders. Passenger ferry to Windigo, at S end of Isle Royale, Mich., Isle Royale Natl. Park, 25 mi/40 km E. Grand Portage Natl. Monument adjacent to village to S, on bay shore, also includes Grand Portage Trail to NW. Dedicated 1951 as a natl. historic site, now a natl. monument.

Grand Portage Monument, Cook co., NE Minn., 34 mi/55 km ENE of Grand Marais, on L. Superior, surrounded by Grand Portage Indian Reservation; 710 acres/287 ha. Portage on the route to the Northwest used by explorers, missionaries, and fur traders. Monument includes a reconstruction of North West Company trading post on L. Superior and 9 mi/14.5 km Grand Portage Trail to Pigeon R., 7 mi/11.3 km WNW of Grand Portage. Grand Portage State Park to SW. Authorized 1951.

Grand Prairie, city (1990 pop. 99,616), Dallas and Tarrant cos., N Texas, suburb 12 mi/19 km WSW of Dallas and 17 mi/27 km E of Fort Worth; 32°41'N 97°01'W. Elev. 528 ft/161 m. Drained by W Fork Trinity R. and Mountain and Bear creeks. Located in a highly urbanized and rapidly growing area, the city's boom caused its pop. to double from 1970 to 1990. Grand Prairie is a distribution center with a large aerospace industry. Other mfg. includes food packaging, tools, machinery, furniture, electronic equip., excavating equip.; printing and publishing. A nearby auto assembly plant adds to the city's economy. Dallas–Fort Worth Internatl. Airport to N; Grand Prairie Municipal Airport in W; Dallas Naval Air Station on Mountain Creek L., on E boundary; "Six Flags over Texas" amusement park is to W in Arlington. L. Joe Pool partially in city on S; Cedar Hill State Park on SE shore. Inc. 1909.

Grand Pré (gran prai) [Fr. = large field], village, W central N.S., Canada, on an arm of the Bay of Fundy. The area is famous for having been an early settlement of the Acadians, whose expulsion in 1755 is the subject of Longfellow's poem *Evangeline.* Grand Pré Natl. Historic Park contains several remains from the Acadian period. Sir Robert Borden, prime minister of Canada, 1911–1920, b. here.

Grand Rapids, city (1990 pop. 189,126), ⊙ Kent co., SW central Mich., 55 mi WNW of Lansing, on the Grand R.; 42°57'N 85°39'W. The 2d largest city in the state, it is a RR junction, distribution (consumer prods.), wholesale, and industrial center for an area that yields fruit, dairy prods., farm produce, gypsum, and gravel. Furniture mfg. (begun in 1859) remains an important industry. Among the city's other manufactures are appliances, electronic equip., automotive parts, aircraft and space navigation systems, and paper prod. Kent County Internatl. Airport to SE. It has an art gallery, the Gerald R. Ford Mus., a furniture mus., a planetarium, and a symphony orchestra. Also in Grand Rapids are Aquinas Col., Calvin Col. and Seminary, G.R. Baptist Col. and Seminary, a business col., and a school of design. Pando and Cannonsburg ski areas to NE; Graham Horticultural Research Center in W part of city; Blandford Nature Center; John Ball Park and Zoo. Minor league baseball and basketball. Inc. 1850.

Grand Rapids, town (1990 pop. 7,976), ⊙ Itasca co., N central Minn., c.75 mi/121 km NW of Duluth, on Mississippi R., forms Paper Mill Reservoir here; 47°13'N 93°31'W. Elev. 1,289 ft/393 m. Cattle; alfalfa; timber; mfg. (coated papers, corn cribbing, packaging, concrete, furniture, strand board, printing and publishing). Seat of Itasca Community Col. school of agr., experiment station of state univ., co. fairgrounds, and Forest History Center are here. Grand Rapids Itasca County Airport to SE. Schoolcraft State Park and Chippewa Natl. Forest to W; Leech L. Indian Reservation to NW; Golden Anniversary State Forest to SE; Pokegama L. to SW; Bass L. to NW. Settled 1877, inc. 1891.

Grand Rapids 1 village, La Moure co., SE central N.Dak., on James R., and 7 mi/11.3 km NNW of La Moure; 46°26'N 98°22'W. Capital until 1886. **2** village

(1990 pop. 955), Wood co., NW Ohio, 11 mi/18 km WNW of Bowling Green, and on Maumee R.; 41°25′N 83°52′W. Natural gas wells.

Grand Rapids, Wis.: see WISCONSIN RAPIDS.

Grand Reservoir, Ohio: see GRAND LAKE.

Grand Ridge 1 village (□ 1 sq mi/2.6 sq km; 1990 pop. 536), Jackson co., NW Fla., 50 mi/80 km W of Tallahassee; 30°43′N 85°01′W. Mfg. (animal feed). Numerous state parks located in area. **2** village (1990 pop. 560), La Salle co., N Ill., 7 mi/11.3 km S of Ottawa; 41°14′N 88°49′W. In agr. and bituminous coal area.

Grand River, town (1990 pop. 171), Decatur co., S Iowa, near Thompson R., 12 mi/19 km SSW of Leon; 40°49′N 93°57′W. In livestock and grain area. Limestone quarries nearby.

Grand River, village (1990 pop. 297), Lake co., NE Ohio, just W of Painesville, on L. Erie; 41°45′N 81°17′W. Formerly Richmond.

Grand River, c.165 mi/270 km long, Ont., Canada; rises in the highlands of the Ontario Peninsula, S Ont.; flows S past Kitchener and Brantford, then SE to L. Erie at Port Maitland. It is navigable for c.70 mi/110 km upstream. The river drains one of the most populated regions of Canada.

Grand River 1 in Colo. and Utah, a former name for the COLORADO RIVER above the mouth of Green R. **2** c. 215 mi/346 km long, S Iowa and NW Mo.; rises near Creston, Iowa; meanders SE to Missouri R. just below Brunswick, Mo. Receives Locust and Medicine creeks. **3** c. 50 mi/80 km long, S central La., fed by network of waterways in low swampy region bet. Atchafalaya R. and Mississippi R., SW of Baton Rouge; winds generally S to L. Palourde NW of Morgan City. Partly navigable; formerly part of Plaquemine–Morgan City Waterway, it is now part of the Port Allen–Morgan City Alternate Shipping Route. **4** c.75 mi/121 km long, NE Ohio; rises in SE Geauga co.; flows NE to West Farmington, through Trumbull co., then N and W, past Painesville, to L. Erie at Fairport Harbor; 41°45′N 81°16′W. **5** c.35 mi/56 km long, E central Wis.; rises in Fond du Lac co.; flows generally W, past Markesan, then NW to Fox R. near Montello. **6** 260 mi/418 km long, Mich.; rises in S Mich.; flows N to Lansing, then NW to L. Michigan at Grand Haven; 42°05′N 84°25′W. It is the longest river in the state and is navigable to the city of Grand Rapids, which grew there because of the availability of waterpower. **7** SW N.Dak. and NW S.Dak.; North Branch rises in S Bowman co.; flows c.80 mi/129 km ESE through Bowman Haley Reservoir, N.Dak.; 46°00′N 103°40′W. Grand R. flows another c.110 mi/177 km S to the Missouri R. opposite Mobridge. South Branch rises in W Harding co., NW S.Dak. and flows c.90 mi/145 km E, past Buffalo. Both branches meet at Shadehill Reservoir (1951), W of Shadehill, Perkins co., S.Dak. Lower 15 mi/24 km is Grand arm of L. Oahe Reservoir. L. Oahe and Shadehill were built for flood control and irrigation of Missouri R. basin project.

Grand River, Okla.: see NEOSHO RIVER.

Grand Rivers, village (1990 pop. 351), Livingston co., W Ky., 22 mi/35 km ESE of Paducah, bet. Tennessee R. (Kentucky L. reservoir) and Cumberland R. (L. Barkley reservoir); 37°00′N 88°14′W. Tourism; timber; limestone quarrying; mfg. (lumber, crushed stone, asphalt). Kentucky Dam Village State Resort Park to W, includes an airport. Thomas Lawson House, 1 of 2 houses remaining, out of 9 on "Millionaire's Row." Kentucky Dam to W, Barkley Dam to E, channel linking lakes to S; with Bridge to Land Between the Lakes Recreation Area (TVA).

Grand Saline, town (1990 pop. 2,630), Van Zandt co., NE Texas, near Sabine R., 32 mi/51 km NW of Tyler; 32°40′N 95°42′W. Elev. 407 ft/124 m. Salt mining, processing center, with one of largest U.S. salt mines. Oil and natural gas fields nearby. Cattle, dairying; sweet potatoes, vegetables; grain; cotton. Mfg. (mirrors and lenses, salt). L. Holbrook to W.

Grand Sentinel Dome, Calif.: see KINGS CANYON NATIONAL PARK.

Grand Staircase–Escalante National Monument (□

c.2,565 sq mi/4,137 sq km), Kane and Garfield cos., S Utah, c.60 mi/97 km E of Ceddar City, Utah, bounded on S by Arizona. Dixie Natl. Forest to N; Bryce Canyon Natl. Forest to W; Glen Canyon Natl. Recreation Area to E. Drained by Escalante R. Includes Escalante Canyons, Kaiparowits Plateau, and the Grand Staircase (a 7,000-ft/2,100-m incline of red sandstone); also 300 Native Amer. archaeological sites. Est. 1996.

Grand Terrace, city (1990 pop. 10,946), San Bernardino co., S Calif., residential suburb 55 mi/89 km E of downtown Los Angles and 6 mi/9.7 km S of San Bernardino; 34°02′N 117°19′W. Citrus-and vegetable-growing area in area of rapid urban growth (1980s and 1990s). Mfg. (pumps).

Grand Terre Island, Jefferson parish, extreme SE La., irregularly shaped island (c.6 mi/10 km long) 5 mi/ 8 km ENE of Grand Isle, c.45 mi/72 km SSE of New Orleans, bet. Barataria Bay (N) and Gulf of Mexico (S); 29°18′N 89°53′W. Barataria Bay lighthouse (29°16′N 89°57′W) is at SW end, near old Fort Livingston; 29°16′N 89°56′W (abandoned 1893).

Grand Teton National Park (TEE-tahn), Teton co., NW Wyo. The park (covers 310,443 acres/125,636 ha), which includes part of Jackson Hole Valley and Jackson L., embraces the E front of the glaciated, snow-covered Teton Range, one of the most scenic ranges of the Rocky Mts.; Grand Teton (13,772 ft/4,198 m) is the highest peak. Snake R. flows the length of the park, through Jackson L. (a natural lake dammed to enlarge its capacity) and the smaller Leigh and Jenny lakes. Hiking, floating down the Snake on rafts, camping, and mountain climbing are popular activities in the park. The Natl. Elk Refuge, adjacent to S end of park, protects the largest elk herd in U.S. Est. 1929.

Grand Tower, city (1990 pop. 775), Jackson co., SW Ill., on the Mississippi R. and 27 mi/43 km WSW of Herrin; 37°38′N 89°30′W. In agr. region. Named for rock (60 ft/ 18 m) in Mississippi R. here. Inc. 1872.

Grand Traverse, county (□ 601 sq mi/1,557 sq km; 1990 pop. 64,273), NW Mich.; ⊙ Traverse City. Grand Traverse Bay is in N; 44°43′N 85°32′W. Drained by Boardman and Betsie rivers. Fruit growing (esp. cherries, apples, plums, grapes). Agr. (potatoes; cattle, hogs, poultry). Mfg. at Traverse City. Fisheries. Resorts. Interlochen State Park and Center for the Arts in W; Traverse City State Park in N; Old Mission Peninsula in extreme N; Green, Duck, and Skegemog lakes. Organized 1851.

Grand Traverse Bay, arm of L. Michigan, W central Mich., 32 mi/51 km long and 10 mi/16 km wide; 45°05′N 85°28′W. The bay is known for its fishing and boating. The surrounding area is an important cherry-growing and resort region. Traverse City is located at the head of the bay. Old Mission Peninsula divides S part of bay into East and West Areas, Old Mission Lighthouse at N end.

Grand Turk, town and island (□ 9.4 sq mi/24.3 sq km; 1990 pop. 3,691), ⊙ Turks and Caicos Isls., crown colony of Great Britain, West Indies, 135 mi/217 km NNW of Cap-Haïtien (Haiti); 6.5 mi/10.5 km long, 2 mi/ 3.2 km wide; 21°30′N 71°10′W. Tourism, diving, fishing, and sailing center. Center for offshore financial offices. Seat of govt. of Turk and Caicos located at Cockburn Town on W side of isl.

Grand Valley, fertile fruit-growing region in Mesa co., W Colo., extending W c.50 mi/80 km along Colorado R., from Palisade almost to Utah state line. Grand Valley project, 14 mi/23 km SSW of De Beque, with dam on Colorado R. that diverts water into 55 mi/89 km canal, irrigates more than 40,000 acres/16,188 ha. Chief crop is peaches, grapes (wineries at Palisade). Grand Junction is marketing and shipping center.

Grand Valley, village (1991 pop. 1,517), S Ont., Canada, on Grand R., and 11 mi/18 km W of Orangeville; 43°54′N 80°19′W. Dairying; lumber milling.

Grand View, village (1990 pop. 330), Owyhee co., SW Idaho, 20 mi/37 km WSW of Mountain Home, on Snake R. (bridged here), downstream (W) of C.F. Strike Dam and Reservoir; 42°59′N 116°05′W. Irrigated agr. area. Mountain Home Air Force Base to NE. Bruneau

Dunes State Park to SE. Snake R. Birds of Prey Natural Area to NW.

Grand View-on-Hudson, village (□ 2 sq mi/5.2 sq km; 1990 pop. 271), Rockland co., SE N.Y., on W bank of the Hudson, and 2 mi/3.2 km S of Nyack; 41°03′N 73°54′W. Nearby is a sect. of Palisades Interstate Park.

Grand Wash Cliffs (1,000 ft/305 m–2,000 ft/610 m), in Mohave co., NW Ariz., extending N from the point near Music Mts. with Hualapai Indian Reservaton to E, to lat. 36°30′N. Bisected by Grand Canyon, N of Colo.; escarpment of Shivwits Plateau, near Nev. state line.

Grand-Bassin (grawng–bah-SANG), village, Nord-Est dept., Haiti, 19 mi/31 km SE of Cap-Haïtien; 19°35′N 71°56′W. Sugarcane and citrus fruit growing.

Grand-Bois, Haiti: see CORNILLON.

Grand-Bourg (grahnd–BOOR), town, SW Marie-Galante isl., Guadeloupe, 19 mi/31 km ESE of Basse-Terre. Minor port in sugar-growing region; sugar milling, alcohol distilling.

Grande Baie (grand BAI) or **Saint Alexis de la Grande Baie** (seht-ah-lehk-SEES duh lah grand BAI), village, S central Que., Canada, on Ha Ha Bay of the Saguenay, at mouth of Ha Ha R., and 13 mi/21 km SE of Chicoutimi. Dairying, lumbering center.

Grande Cayemite Island, Haiti: see CAYEMITES ISLANDS.

Grande de Añasco, Río, P.R.: see AÑASCO RIVER.

Grande de Arecibo, Río, P.R.: see ARECIBO RIVER.

Grande de Chiapa, Río, Mexico: see GRIJALVA RIVER.

Grande de Loíza, Río, P.R.: see LOÍZA RIVER.

Grande de Manatí, Río, P.R.: see MANATÍ RIVER.

Grande de Moa, Cayo (GRAHN-dai dai MO-ah, KEI-yo), small reef, off Holguín prov., NE Cuba, 35 mi/ 56 km NW of Baracoa; 2 mi/3.2 km long, ½ mi/⁹⁄₁₀ km wide; 20°41′N 74°52′W.

Grande de Santiago, Río, Mexico: see RAMOS RIVER.

Grande Ecaille, Lake, La.: see PORT SULPHUR.

Grande Prairie, city (1991 pop. 28,271), W Alta., Canada, NW of Edmonton; 55°10′N 118°48′W. Chief business center for the Peace R. valley farming area. The discovery of oil and natural gas in the region in the late 1970s led to a short boom, which dramatically increased the city's pop. Annual Northern Winter Carnival.

Grande, Río, river, c.25 mi/40 km, Portland parish, E Jamaica; rises in E Blue Mts.; flows NW, past Moore Town, to the N coast W of Port Antonio; 18°08′N 76°28′W.

Grande, Río, Mexico: see AGUANAVAL RIVER and RÍO GRANDE.

Grande, Rio, U.S. and Mexico: see RIO GRANDE.

Grande Rivière (grahd reev-YER), town (1991 pop. 3,979), E Que., Canada, on E Gaspé Peninsula, on Gulf of St. Lawrence, at mouth of Grand R., 30 mi/48 km S of Gaspé; 48°23′N 64°30′W. Fishing center; lumbering; dairying. Site of fishery research station of Laval Univ.

Grande Ronde River, c. 180 mi/290 km, NE Oregon–SE Wash.; rises in Blue Mts., SW Union co.; flows generally NE in separation course past La Grande, to the Snake R. in SE corner of Wash., 22 mi/35 km S of Lewiston, Idaho. Man-made channel NE of LaGrande cuts across torturous bend near cove.

Grande Soufrière, La, Basse-Terre, Guadeloupe: see SOUFRIÈRE.

Grande-Anse (grand ANS), village (1991 pop. 981), NE N.B., Canada, on Chaleur Bay, 30 mi/48 km NE of Bathurst; 47°48′N 65°11′W. Fishing port (herring, cod, mackerel, clams, oysters, smelt); fish packing (fresh, frozen). Popular beach resort.

Grande-Anse (grahnd–TAWNGS), village, SW Désirade isl., Guadeloupe dept., Fr. West Indies, 30 mi/48 km E of Pointe-à-Pitre. Sisal, cotton; fishing.

Grande-Anse (grawnd–AWNS), department (1982 pop. 489,957), SW Haiti, NW part of the Jacmel Peninsula; ⊙ Jérémie. Bounded on the N by the Gulf of Gonâives, E by Ouest dept., S by Sud dept., W by Caribbean Sea. Cocoa, coffee, sugarcane; beekeeping. Bauxite and manganese deposits.

Grande-Rivière-du-Nord   (grawnd–ree-VYER–dyoo–

NOR), town (1982 pop. 6,007), Nord dept., N Haiti, in foothills of the Massif du Nord, on the Grande Rivière du Nord (50 mi/80 km long), 13 mi/21 km S of Cap-Haïtien; 19°35′N 72°11′W. Cacao, coffee and fruit growing; cattle. Has colonial church. Birthplace of Jean Jacques Dessalines, Haiti's liberator. Copper, lead, zinc, silver deposits nearby.

Grandes Bergeronnes (grahd behr-zheh-RON), village (1991 pop. 623), E Que., Canada, on the St. Lawrence R. and 30 mi/48 km N of Rivière du Loup; 48°15′N 69°33′W. In mica-mining region; logging, dairying, blueberry canning.

Grande-Saline (grawnd–sah-LEEN), town (1982 pop. 1,161), Artibonite dept., W central Haiti, at mouth of Artibonite R. on Gulf of Gonaïves, 15 mi/24 km SSW of Gonaïves; 19°15′N 72°47′W. In salt marshes. Fishing port.

Grande-Terre (grahnd–TAHR), island (□ 218.63 sq mi/ 567 sq km), E ½ of Guadeloupe isl., Fr. West Indies, separated from Basse-Terre by narrow Rivière Salée channel; c.25 mi/40 km long; 16°20′N 61°25′W. It is of a low-lying limestone formation; water is scarce. Sugarcane is its principal prod. Resort hotels and large marinas along S shore. Pointe-à-Pitre, leading port and commercial center of Guadeloupe, is on SW coast.

Grandeza, La, Mexico: see LA GRANDEZA.

Grandfalls, village (1990 pop. 583), Ward co., extreme W Texas, in the Pecos R. valley, 38 mi/61 km E of Pecos; 31°20′N 102°50′W. In irrigated region (cotton, pecans, alfalfa; cattle, hogs, goats). Oil and natural gas; mfg. (silica sand processing). Imperial Reservoir to S on opposite side of river.

Grandfather, village (1990 pop. 34), Avery co., NW N.C., 12 mi/19 km SW of Boone, in Pisgah Natl. Forest; 36°06′N 81°50′W. Grandfather Mt. (2 mi/3.2 km to N); resort area.

Grandfather Mountain (5,964 ft/1,818 m), Caldwell, Avery, and Watawga co. lines converge on mt., NW N.C., in the Blue Ridge Mts., 16 mi/26 km SW of Boone.

Grandfield, town (1990 pop. 1,224), Tillman co., SW Okla., near Red R., 22 mi/35 km SE of Frederick; 34°13′N 98°41′W. In agr. area (cotton, vegetables, peanuts); mfg. (textiles). Inc. 1909.

Grand-Goâve (grawng–go-AHV), town (1982 pop. 2,357), Ouest dept., S Haiti, on NE coast of Jacmel Peninsula, 23 mi/37 km WSW of Port-au-Prince; 18°26′N 72°46′W. Coffee, cotton, sugarcane; fishing port.

Grand-Gosier (grawng–go-ZYAI), town, Ouest dept., SE Haiti, minor port on the Caribbean, 38 mi/61 km SE of Port-au-Prince; 18°11′N 71°55′W. Construction wood. Fishing port.

Grandin (GRAN-din), town (1990 pop. 233), Carter co., S Mo., in the Ozarks, near Current R., 16 mi/26 km SSE of Van Buren; 36°49′N 90°49′W. Lumber; historic lumber company town in early 1900s.

Grandin, agr. village (1990 pop. 213), Cass co., E N.Dak., 27 mi/43 km NNW of Fargo, near Elm R.; 47°14′N 97°00′W. Sunflowers, flax.

Grand-Mère (grahn-MEHR), city (1991 pop. 14,287), S Que., Canada, on the St. Maurice R., N of Trois Rivières; 46°38′N 72°41′W. The Grand-Mère Falls furnish power for paper and pulp mills. The city also has clothing and textile factories, and a growing service industry.

Grand'Rivière (GRAWNG–ree-VYER), town, N Martinique, at N foot of Mont Pelée, 20 mi/32 km NNW of Fort-de-France. Banana and cacao growing; rum distilling.

Grandview, town (1991 pop. 870), W Man., Canada, on Valley R., and 28 mi/45 km W of Dauphin. Grain elevators, stockyards. Mfg. (lumbering; dairying; mixed farming).

Grandview, city (1990 pop. 24,967), Jackson co., W Mo., suburb 13 mi/21 km S of downtown Kansas City; 38°52′N 94°31′W. Mfg. (hardware, chemicals, transportation equip., apparel, steel fabrication, food processing, consumer goods, machinery). Richards-Gebaur Airport (former A.F.B.) and Harry S. Truman farm are nearby. Inc. 1912.

Grandview 1 town (1990 pop. 761), Spencer co., SW Ind., on Ohio R., and 6 mi/9.7 km NE of Rockport; 37°56′N 86°59′W. In agr. area. Barge building and repair. **2** town (1990 pop. 514), Louisa co., SE Iowa, 6 mi/9.7 km N of Wapello; 41°16′N 91°11′W. In livestock area. **3** town (1990 pop. 1,245), Johnson co., N central Texas, 35 mi/ 56 km SSE of Fort Worth; 32°16′N 97°10′W. In cotton, grain, dairy area; mfg. (lumber, transportation equip.). **4** town (1990 pop. 7,169), Yakima co., S Wash., 35 mi/ 56 km SE of Yakima, on Sunnyside Canal; 46°14′N 119°55′W. RR junction. Vegetables, fruit; mfg. (feeds, thread mills, food and beverage processing); lumber. Horse Heaven Hills to S. Historic Château (Ste. Michele Winery); Yakima Indian Reservation to W. Founded 1905, inc. 1919.

Grandview, village (1990 pop. 1,647), Sangamon co., central Ill., residential suburb 1.5 mi/2.4 km NE of downtown Springfield; 39°49′N 89°37′W. In agr. area. Inc. 1939.

Grandview Heights, city (1990 pop. 7,010), Franklin co., central Ohio, a W suburb of Columbus; 39°58′N 83°02′W.

Grandview Park or **Grandview**, uninc. town (1990 pop. 2,170), Elk co., N central Pa., residential suburb 1 mi/ 1.6 km ESE of St. Marys; 41°25′N 78°32′W. St. Marys Municipal Airport to E.

Grandville, city (1990 pop. 15,624), Kent co., W Mich., suburb 6 mi/9.7 km SW of Grand Rapids, on the Grand R.; 42°53′N 85°45′W. In a farm area; mfg. (transportation equip., dies and molds, bldg. materials, paper, metal, and electrical prods., lumber, silver recovery equip.). Native Amer. mounds, some of which were opened in 1964, are preserved in the NE sect. of the city. Settled 1833, inc. as a city 1933.

Grange Hill, village (1991 pop. 6,530), Westmoreland parish, W Jamaica, 8 mi/12.9 km NNW of Savanna-la-Mar; 18°22′N 78°12′W. Sugarcane, fruit; livestock.

Granger, uninc. city (1990 pop. 20,241), St. Joseph co., N Ind., suburb 7 mi/11.3 km NE of South Bend, near Mich. boundary near Ind. East-West Toll Road (Interstate 80/90); 41°44′N 86°08′W. Mfg. (transportation equip., machinery, lumber, fabricated steel).

Granger 1 town (1990 pop. 624), Dallas co., central Iowa, 14 mi/23 km NE of Adel; 41°45′N 93°49′W. In agr. area. **2** town (1990 pop. 63), Scotland co., NE Mo., bet. North and South Wyaconda rivers, 10 mi/16 km E of Memphis; 40°28′N 91°58′W. Wood prods. **3** town (1990 pop. 1,190), Williamson co., central Texas, 37 mi/60 km NNE of Austin; 30°43′N 97°26′W. RR junction, in cotton, corn, sorghum, wheat area; mfg. clothing. Granger L. reservoir to E. **4** town (1990 pop. 2,053), Yakima co., S Wash., 22 mi/35 km SE of Yakima, on Yakima R., opposite mouth of Toppenish Creek; 46°20′N 120°11′W. Fruit, vegetables, potatoes, beans, wheat, barley, oats; dairying; cattle; mfg. (glass prods., sporting goods, winery). Toppenish Natl. Wildlife Refuge to W; Yakima Indian Reservation across river, to W.

Granger, village (1990 pop. 126), Sweetwater co., SW Wyo., on Blacks Fork, on Oregon Trail, at mouth of Hams Fork, and 26 mi/42 km W of Green R. town; 41°35′N 109°58′W. Elev. 6,240 ft/1,902 m. RR junction. Cattle, sheep. Seedskadee Natl. Wildlife Refuge to N.

Grangeville, town (1990 pop. 3,226), ⊙ Idaho co., central Idaho, 50 mi/80 km SE of Lewiston; 45°56′N 116°07′W. In fertile valley of Salmon R., trading point for wheat and livestock region. RR terminus. Lumber milling; mfg.; timber; sheep, cattle; wheat, barley, alfalfa. Hq. for Nez Perce Natl. Forest, to SE. Nez Perce Indian Reservation to N; Snowhaven Ski Area to S. Settled 1876, inc. 1897. Growth stimulated by discovery of gold (1898) nearby.

Granite (GRA-nit), county (□ 1,733 sq mi/4,488 sq km; 1990 pop. 2,548), W Mont.; ⊙ Philipsburg; 46°25′N 113°27′W. Georgetown L. on SE boundary, Garnet Range in NE, Continental Divide forms SE boundary (Anaconda Range), Sapphire Mts. form the W boundary. Mining and agr. region, drained N by the Clark Fork R. and by Flint and Rock creeks. Crater. Silver, sapphires; hay; cattle. Discovery Basin Ski Area in SE, Garnet Ghost Town in N; parts of Deerlodge Natl. Forest in center E, S, and SW; Flint Creek Range in E; part of Lolo Natl. Forest in NW. Formed 1893.

Granite, town (1990 pop. 1,844), Greer co., SW Okla., 9 mi/14.5 km NE of Mangum, near North Fork of Red R. (Altus L.), near W outliers of Wichita Mts.; 34°57′N 99°22′W. Mfg. (birdseed, granite monuments); gravel pits. State reformatory here; reservoir to SE. Settled and inc. 1900.

Granite 1 village, Chaffee co., central Colo., on Arkansas R., just E of Sawatch Mts., and 14 mi/23 km S of Leadville. Elev. 8,928 ft/2,721 m. Whitewater rafting. Scene of early gold discoveries. Gold is still dredged. San Isabel Natl. Forest to E and W. **2** village, Baltimore co., N Md., near Patapsco R., 14 mi/23 km WNW of downtown Baltimore. Granite quarries. Originally called Watersville, it was renamed Granite when Capt. Alexander Walters opened the quarries around 1820 before they were closed in 1925. Stones from the quarries went into the interior of the Washington Monument and the Treasury Bldg. Nearby is Patapsco Valley State Park and Liberty L. **3** village (1990 pop. 8), Grant co., NE Oregon, 27 mi/43 km W of Bend, on Granite Creek, on boundary of Umatilla (NW) and Wallowa-Whitman (SE) Natl. Forests; 44°48′N 118°25′W.

Granite City (1990 pop. 32,862), Madison co., SW Ill., an industrial suburb of St. Louis, on the Mississippi; 38°42′N 90°07′W. It has port and RR connections. Some metal prods. are manufactured; however, the suburb has been affected by the surrounding cities and area, which have become highly depressed economically due to declining industries. Lies next to Chain of Rocks Canal, a Mississippi R. bypass. Inc. 1896.

Granite Creek Desert, Nev.: see BLACK ROCK DESERT.

Granite Falls 1 town (1990 pop. 3,083), Chippewa and Yellow Medicine cos., SW Minn., at falls on Minnesota R., 13 mi/21 km SE of Montevideo; ⊙ Yellow Medicine co.; 44°48′N 95°32′W. Elev. 892 ft/272 m. RR junction; trade center in agr. area (grain, sugar beets, soybeans, alfalfa; livestock); mfg. (granite aggregates, machinery, transportation equip., printing and publishing). Hydroelectric plant here. Upper Sioux Indian Reservation and Upper Sioux Agency State Park and Monument to SE. Plotted 1872, inc. as village 1879, as city 1889. **2** town (1990 pop. 3,253), Caldwell co., W central N.C., 7 mi/ 11.3 km NW of Hickory, at dam of L. Rhodhiss reservoir (Catawba R.; lake to W); L. Hickory reservoir downstream (E); 35°47′N 81°25′W. Agr. area (tobacco, grain, potatoes; poultry, livestock); diversified mfg. **3** town (1990 pop. 1,060), Snohomish co., NW Wash., 15 mi/24 km NE of Everett, on South Fork of Stillaguamish R.; 48°05′N 121°58′W. Vegetables, berries; dairying; mfg. (construction machinery, wood prods.). L. Roesiger reservoir to S; Snoqualmie Natl. Forest to E, including Boulder River Wilderness Area.

Granite Hills, uninc. town (1990 pop. 3,157), San Diego co., S Calif., residential suburb 14 mi/23 km NE of downtown San Diego and 2 mi/3.2 km E of El Cajon; 32°48′N 116°54′W.

Granite Mountain (7,700 ft/2,347 m), Yavapai co., central Ariz., highest peak in the Sierra Prieta, 7 mi/11.3 km NW of Prescott. In Prescott Natl. Forest.

Granite Peak (GRA-nit) (12,799 ft/3,901 m), in S Mont., highest point in Mont., in Beartooth Mts. c.50 mi/ 80 km SE of Livingston, NE of Yellowstone Natl. Park. Grasshopper Glacier 4 mi/6.4 km to SW, in Absaroka-Beartooth Wilderness Area, on boundary of Gallatin and Custer Natl. forests.

Granite Peak, N.Mex.: see MOGOLLON MOUNTAINS.

Granite Quarry, town (1990 pop. 1,646), Rowan co., central N.C., 4 mi/6.4 km SSE of Salisbury; 35°36′N 80°27′W. Granite quarrying. Grain; poultry, livestock; dairying. Mfg. High Rock L. reservoir (Yadkin R.) to E.

Granite Range, (GRA-nuht), in NW Nev., in Washoe co., N of Smoke Creek Desert. Rises to 9,056 ft/2,760 m at Granite Peak, 11 mi/18 km NNW of Gerlach.

Granite Range, Mont.: see BEARTOOTH RANGE.

Granite Shoals, town (1990 pop. 1,378), Burnet co., central Texas, 45 mi/72 km WNW of Austin, on NE shore of L. Lyndon Baines Johnson reservoir (Colorado R.); 30°35′N 98°22′W. Residential and recreational community in agr. region.

Graniteville, uninc. town (1990 pop. 1,158), Aiken co., W S.C., 5 mi/8 km W of Aiken. Textile and dye plants mfg. apparel, yarns, fabrics, and textiles. Agr. prods. include cotton, peanuts, grain, peaches; livestock, poultry. Founded 1846 as one of 1st mill towns in the South.8

Graniteville, uninc. community, Iron co., SE central Mo., 5 mi/8 km N of Ironton in St. Francois Mts. Granite quarries. Elephant Rocks State Park.

Graniteville, a section of Staten Isl. borough of N.Y. city, SE N.Y., on N Staten Isl.; 40°38′N 74°09′W.

Graniteville 1 Mass.: see WESTFORD. **2** Vt.: see BARRE.

Granma (GRAHN-mah), province (1994 est. pop. 818,000), SE Cuba; ⊙ Bayamo. Bordered NE by Holguín prov., NW by Las Tunas prov., S by Caribbean Sea, E by Guantánamo prov., and W by the Gulf of Guacanayabo. One of five provs. created in 1976 from former Oriente prov. Drained in N by Cauto R. Important cities include Bayamo (pop. 132,000), Manzanillo (pop. 98,000). Sierra Maestra in SE. Cauto R. valley in Central prov. produces 40–50% of national rice production. Sugar mfg. at foot (N slope) of Sierra Maestra, with coffee production in the mts.

Grannis (GRAN-is), village (1990 pop. 507), Polk co., W Ark., 24 mi/39 km SSW of Mena, near Okla. state line; 34°14′N 94°19′W. Mfg. (poultry processing). Gillham L. reservoir (Cossatot R.) and Howard Co. Wildlife Management Area to E.

Grano (GRAIN o), village (1990 pop. 9), Renville co., N N.Dak., 30 mi/48 km NNW of Minot, near Souris R,; 48°37′N 101°35′W. L. Darling and Upper Souris Natl. Wildlife Refuge to W.

Grant 1 county (☐ 633 sq mi/1,639 sq km; 1990 pop. 13,948), central Ark.; ⊙ Sheridan; 34°17′N 92°25′W. Drained by Saline R. and Hurricane Creek (forms part of S boundary). Agr. (cattle, hogs, catfish). Jenkins Ferry Battleground State Historic Monument in SW. Formed 1869. **2** county (☐ 414 sq mi/1,072 sq km; 1990 pop. 74,169), E central Ind.; ⊙ Marion; 40°31′N 85°39′W. Agr. area (hogs, poultry; corn, vegetables, soybeans, oats, fruit, vegetables; dairy prods.). Diversified mfg. at Marion and Gas City. Natural-gas and oil wells. Drained by Mississinewa R. Miller Purdue Experimental Farm near E boundary. Formed 1831. **3** county (☐ 575 sq mi/1,489 sq km; 1990 pop. 7,159), SW Kansas; ⊙ Ulysses; 37°33′N 101°18′W. Gently rolling wheat area, drained by Cimarron R. (in S) and its North Fork. Corn, sorghum, alfalfa; cattle. Chemicals; feed. Small natural-gas fields. Formed 1888. **4** county (☐ 260 sq mi/ 673 sq km; 1990 pop. 15,737), N Ky.; ⊙ Williamstown; 38°38′N 84°36′W. Drained by Eagle, Fork Lick, and South Fork Grassy creeks. Gently rolling upland agr. area (burley tobacco, corn, hay, alfalfa; cattle, hogs, poultry; dairying), in Bluegrass region. Lloyd Wildlife Management Area in NE, Mullins Wildlife Management Area in E center; Williamstown L. reservoir in E. Formed 1820. **5** county (☐ 575 sq mi/1,489 sq km; 1990 pop. 6,246), W Minn.; ⊙ Elbow Lake; 45°55′N 96°00′W. Drained by Mustinka and Pomme de Terre rivers. Agr. area (alfalfa, wheat, corn, oats, barley, soybeans, sugar beets, beans, sunflowers; hogs, sheep, poultry; dairying). Numerous small lakes in co., notably Pomme de Terre and Pelican lakes in NE. Formed 1868. **6** county (☐ 783 sq mi/2,028 sq km; 1990 pop. 769), W central Nebr.; ⊙ Hyannis, in Sand Hills region; 41°55′N 101°44′W. Grazing region; cattle. Numerous small natural lakes throughout co., especially in N and SE. Formed 1887. **7** county (☐ 3,967 sq mi/10,275 sq km; 1990 pop. 27,676), SW N.Mex.; ⊙ Silver City; 32°43′N 108°22′W. Watered by Gila R.; borders on Ariz. on W in N part of co.; extreme SE corner within 4 mi/6.4 km of Mex. border. Livestock-grazing, copper- and silver-mining area. Cattle, some sheep; hay, alfalfa, oats, barley, millet. Continental Divide crosses co. twice, N-S in E part and E-W in S part. Includes Pinos Altos Mts. in NE; parts of Gila Natl. Forest in N and center; Black Range and Mimbres Mts. form E boundary in N part; City of Rocks State Park in E; Santa Rita Open Pit Copper Mine in E. Formed 1868. **8** county (☐ 1,666 sq mi/4,315 sq km; 1990 pop. 3,549), S N.Dak.; ⊙

Carson; 46°21′N 101°38′W. Agr. area watered by Heart and Cannonball rivers and Antelope Creek. Cattle, hogs; dairy prods.; barley, rye, wheat. Heart Butte Reservoir in NW. Bounded by Cedar Creek and Cannonball R. on S. Formed 1916. **9** county (☐ 1,003 sq mi/ 2,598 sq km; 1990 pop. 5,689), N Okla.; ⊙ Medford; 36°47′N 97°47′W. Bounded N by Kansas state line; intersected by Salt Fork of Arkansas R. Agr. area (wheat, cotton, sorghum; cattle). Some mfg. at Medford and Pond Creek. Oil and natural-gas wells. Formed 1893. **10** county (☐ 4,529 sq mi/11,730 sq km; 1990 pop. 7,853), E central Oregon; ⊙ Canyon City; 44°30′N 119°00′W. Mt. area drained by John Day R. and its N and S Forks, and by N Fork of Malheur R. Blue Mts. in E. Agr. (wheat, oats, barley; poultry, sheep, cattle). Timber. Mercury mining. Clyde Holliday State Park to center; John Day Fossil Beds Natl. Monument (Sharp Crick Unit) in W; parts of Malheur Natl. Forest in E, S, and center, including Strawberry Mt. Wilderness Area in SE center; part of Ochoco Natl. Forest in SW; part of Wallowa-Whitman Natl. Forest in NE; parts of Umatilla Natl. Forest in N and NW; parts of N Fork John Day Wilderness Area in NE. **11** county (☐ 687 sq mi/1,779 sq km; 1990 pop. 8,372), NE S.Dak., on Minn. state line; ⊙ Milbank; 45°10′N 96°46′W. Agr. area watered by North Fork of Whetstone R. and streams; part of L. Traverse (Sisseton Wahpeton) Indian Reservation in NW. Corn, wheat, sorghum, soybeans, flax; dairy prods.; cattle, hogs. Formed 1873. **12** county (☐ 2,791 sq mi/7,229 sq km; 1990 pop. 54,758), E central Wash., in Columbia basin agr. region; ⊙ Ephrata; 47°13′N 119°28′W. Grand Coulee Dam on Columbia R. is at NE corner; the Grand Coulee (including large Banks L. reservoir) is along NW border. Wheat, barley, oats, alfalfa, hay, potatoes, beans, corn, onions, peas, carrots, asparagus, peppermint, spearmint; cattle, sheep, hogs. Steamboat Rock State Park, on peninsula in Banks L. reservoir, in NE; Moses L. reservoir and State Park and Potholes Reservoir and State Park in SE. County bounded by Columbia R. on W and S; touches river in NE corner. Formed 1909. **13** county (☐ 480 sq mi/1,243 sq km; 1990 pop. 10,428), W.Va., in E Panhandle; ⊙ Petersburg; 39°06′N 79°12′W. Bounded NW by North Branch of Potomac R. (Md. state line); drained by South Branch of Potomac R. and Patterson Creek. Traversed by Allegheny Front (in W), by Knobly Mtn. ridge in center, and Patterson Creek Mtn. ridge on NE border. Includes part of Monongahela Natl. Forest in S. Agr. (corn, grains, hay, alfalfa, honey, nursery crops); livestock, poultry. Coal-mining. Some mfg. at Petersburg (wood prods., space industry). Smoke Hole Caverns in S; Mount Storm L. and Stony R. reservoirs in W; Fairfax Stone State Monument (land grant marker at junction of 3 cos.) on W corner. Formed 1866. **14** county (☐ 1,183 sq mi/3,064 sq km; 1990 pop. 49,264), extreme SW Wis.; ⊙ Lancaster; 42°51′N 90°42′W. Agr. (barley, oats, corn, soybeans, alfalfa, hay; cattle, hogs, sheep, poultry); mining (zinc, lead); some mfg. Bounded S by Ill. state line, N by Wisconsin R., W by the Mississippi R. (here forming Iowa state line); drained by Platte and Blue rivers, small Grant R. Contains Wyalusing State Park in NW. Lock and Dam No. 10 in W, Lock and Dam No. 11 in S, both on Mississippi R.; Nelson Dewey State Park and Stonefield State Historic Site in W; W end of Pecatonica State Trail in E, terminating at Platteville; Bull Run Ski Area and Eagle Valley Nature Preserve in N. Formed 1836.

Grant, parish (☐ 670 sq mi/1,735 sq km; 1990 pop. 17,526), central La.; ⊙ Colfax; 31°31′N 92°43′W. Bounded E by Little R., W and SW by Red R. Agr. (cotton, corn, soybeans, sweet potatoes, vegetables, watermelons, home gardens; cattle, horses); some mfg. at Colfax; logging, timber. Lakes Iatt and Nantachie in NW part. Part of Kisatchie Natl. Forest dominates E half of parish, part of Catahoula Natl. Preserve in N, Little River State Wildlife Area on E boundary. Part of Camp Livingston Military Reserve in SE. Named after President Ulysses S. Grant. Formed 1869.

Grant 1 town (1990 pop. 638), Marshall co., NE Ala.,

12 mi/19 km N of Guntersville, near Guntersville Reservoir; 34°31′N 86°15′W. Mfg. **2** town (1990 pop. 123), Montgomery co., SW Iowa, on West Nodaway R. and 15 mi/24 km NE of Red Oak; 41°08′N 94°59′W. **3** town (1990 pop. 1,239), ⊙ Perkins co., SW central Nebr., 19 mi/31 km S of Ogallala; 40°50′N 101°43′W. Dairying; livestock; grain, potatoes. Mfg. (fertilizers).

Grant 1 village (1990 pop. 764), Newaygo co., W central Mich., 5 mi/8 km S of Newaygo; 43°19′N 85°48′W. In dairy and fruit region. Mfg. Mainistee Natl. Forest to NE. **2** village, Choctaw co., SE Okla., 5 mi/8 km S of Hugo, near Red R. In farm area.

Grant City, town (1990 pop. 998), NW Mo., ⊙ Worth co., near Middle Fork of Grand R., 26 mi/42 km ENE of Maryville; 40°29′N 94°24′W. Wheat, soybeans; cattle; mfg. (apparel). Settled 1864.

Grant City, a section of Richmond borough of N.Y. city, SE N.Y., on E Staten Isl. bet. South and Midland Beach.

Grant Land, N part of Ellesmere Island, NE Franklin dist., N.W.T., Canada, bet. the Arctic Ocean (N), Nansen Sound (W), Greely Fjord (S), and Robeson Channel and Lady Franklin Bay (E). It is crossed by United States Range, rising to c.11,000 ft/3,353 m.

Grant, Mount, peak (11,245 ft/3,427 m), Mineral co., W Nev., 10 mi/16 km WNW of Hawthorne. In W part of Hawthorne Naval Ammunition Dump; highest in Wassuk Range.

Grant Park, village (1990 pop. 1,024), Kankakee co., NE Ill., 13 mi/21 km ENE of Kankakee; 41°14′N 87°38′W. In agr. area.

Grant Point, cape, NW Adelaide Peninsula, N Keewatin dist., N.W.T., Canada, on Queen Maud Gulf, at entrance of Simpson Strait; 68°20′N 98°54′W.

Grant Range, E Nev., in NE of Nye co., extends S into a corner of Lincoln co., SSW of Ely, S of White Pine Mts. Troy Peak (11,298 ft/3,444 m) and Timber Mt. (10,603 ft/3,232 m). Partly sect. of Humboldt Natl. Forest.

Grant Town, village (1990 pop. 694), Marion co., N W.Va., 4 mi/6.4 km N of Fairmont; 39°33′N 80°10′W. Coal-mining area. Agr. (corn, apples); livestock; poultry.

Grantfork, village (1990 pop. 273), Madison co., SW Ill., 16 mi/26 km E of Edwardsville; 38°49′N 89°40′W. In agr. area.

Grantham 1 (GRAN-thuhm), town (1990 pop. 1,247), Sullivan co., W N.H., 9 mi/14.5 km N of Newport; 43°31′N 72°09′W. Drained by Croydon Brook. Agr. (cattle, poultry; nursery crops; timber); mfg. (lumber, post and beams homes). Eastman Pond in NE; Snowhill at Eastman Ski Area in NE; Grantham Mt. (2,661 ft/811 m) in W. **2** (GRAN-thahm), uninc. town (1990 pop. c.2,000), Cumberland co., S Pa., residential suburb 9 mi/14.5 km SW of Harrisburg on Yellow Breeches Creek; 40°09′N 76°59′W. Agr. area (dairying; livestock, poultry; grain). Seat of Messiah Col. Williams Grove Amusement Park to W.

Grant-Kohrs Ranch, national historic site (2,3 sq mi/ 6.1 sq km), Powell co., W Mont., on Clark Fork R. Hq. of one of the largest ranches of the 19th cent., once actively grazed cattle in 4 states and Canada, includes elegant ranch house. Authorized 1972.

Grantley, uninc. town (1990 pop. 3,069), York co., S Pa., residential suburb 1 mi/1.6 km S of York; 39°56′N 76°43′W.

Grantley Adams International Airport, 8 mi/12.9 km ESE of Bridgetown, Barbados; 13°04′N 54°29′W. Major gateway to SE Caribbean with regular service from U.S., Can., and Eur. cities, including Concorde service from London during peak tourist season.

Granton, town (1990 pop. 379), Clark co., central Wis., 16 mi/26 km WSW of Marshfield; 44°35′N 90°27′W. Dairy prods.; lumber; mfg. (cheese, whey prods.).

Grants, town (1990 pop. 8,626), ⊙ Cibola co., W N.Mex., on Rio San Jose, near San Mateo Mts., 70 mi/113 km W of Albuquerque; 35°08′N 107°50′W. Elev. 6,460 ft/ 1,969 m. Trade and shipping point in ranching and agr. region (sheep, cattle; alfalfa, grain, triticale, vegetables, fruit); mfg. (printing and publishing, mattresses, pottery, gypsum prods.). Continental Divide to W; parts of Cibola Natl. Forest to W and E, including Mt. Taylor 15 mi/24 km ENE; El Malpais Natl. Monument to S; El Murro Natl. Monument to W; La Ventana Natural Arch to S; Bluewater L. State Park to NW.

Grants Pass, city (1990 pop. 17,488), ⊙ Josephine co., SW Oregon, 23 mi/37 km WNW of Medford, on the Rogue R., in a heavily forested area; 42°26′N 123°19′W. Elev. 948 ft/289 m. Tourism. Mfg. (meat processing, millwork, wood prods., furniture, printing and publishing, fiberglass prods., plastic prods., concrete, electronic equip.). Agr. (flower bulbs, fruits, nuts, vegetables); dairy prods. Rogue Community Col., Wiseman Art Gall. here. Valley of the Rogue State Park to E; parts of Siskiyou Natl. Forest to W and S; Oregon Caves Natl. Monument to S; Rogue R. State Scenic Waterway to NW. Hq. for Siskiyou Natl. Forest and gateway to nearby recreational area. Inc. 1887.

Grant's Pass, channel bet. Dauphin Isl. and Mobile co., SW Ala.; leads from Mississippi Sound of Gulf of Mexico to Mobile Bay; c.3 mi/4.8 km wide.

Grant's Tomb, memorial, on the Upper West Side of Manhattan in N.Y. city, SE N.Y., at Riverside Dr. and W. 122 St. Dedicated in 1897, authorized 1958. Tomb of President Ulysses S. Grant and his wife, Julia. The Neo-Classical structure (150 ft/46 m) is 2d-tallest mausoleum in W Hemisphere.

Grant's Town, S suburb of Nassau, New Providence Isl., Bahamas. Fruit and vegetable market.

Grantsburg, town (1990 pop. 1,144), ⊙ Burnett co., NW Wis., 26 mi/42 km N of St. Croix Falls; 45°46′N 92°40′W. Dairy prods.; poultry; mfg. (cheese, plastic prods., machinery, wood prods.). Governor Knowles State Forest. St. Croix Natl. Scenic Riverway to W and N.

Grantsdale, village (1990 pop. 150), Ravalli co., W Mont., 3 mi/4.8 km S of Hamilton, on Bitterroot R., at mouth of Skalkaho Creek. Grain, forage crops; horses, cattle, sheep, goats, llamas. Bitterroot Natl. Forest to E and W; fish hatchery to E; Sleeping Child Hot Springs to SE.

Grantsville 1 town (1990 pop. 505), Garrett co., W Md., in the Alleghenies near Casselman R. and Pa. state line; 22 mi/35 km W of Cumberland; 39°42′N 79°10′W. Named after Daniel Grant, a Baltimore native, it was settled by Ger.-speaking Mennonite and Amish families in the late 18th cent. Maple syrup and sugar are produced here in a climate comparable to New England's. The Casselman House, built as the Drovers' Inn in 1824, still offers food and shelter to travelers. The Fuller-Baker Log House (c.1814) is also another inn in the area near 2 abandoned stone arches of the Natl. Road. The Stanton Grist Mill (c.1798) is still operating, but with electrical power. Several Amish settlements are in the area. The Casselman R. Bridge State Park (1813) and Savage River State Forest are nearby. **2** town (1990 pop. 4,500), Tooele co., NW Utah, 6 mi/9.7 km S of Great Salt L., 10 mi/16 km NW of Tooele; 40°36′N 112°28′W. Grain, alfalfa, barley; cattle, turkeys; mfg. (salt; lime processing). Elev. 4,304 ft/1,312 m. Donner-Reed Memorial Mus., Donner Party artifacts. Unit of Wasatch Natl. Forest, including Deseret Peak Wilderness Area, to SW. Settled 1850 by Mormons, inc. 1867. **3** town (1990 pop. 671), ⊙ Calhoun co., central W.Va., on Little Kanawha R., 35 mi/56 km SE of Parkersburg; 38°55′N 81°05′W. Agr. (corn, potatoes); livestock, poultry. Mfg. (commercial printing). Natural-gas and oil wells. Timber. Laid out 1866.

Grantville, town (pop. 1,180), Coweta co., W Ga., 9 mi/14.5 km SW of Newnan, in farm area; 33°14′N 84°50′W. Mfg. of swimming pools and supplies; yarn.

Grantwood, village (1990 pop. 904), St. Louis co., E Mo., residential suburb 10 mi/16 km SW of downtown St. Louis; 38°32′N 90°20′W. Grant's Farm (owned by Anheuser-Busch) major tourist attraction; historic home of President Ulysses S. Grant.

Granum (GRA-nuhm), town (1991 pop. 343), S Alta., Canada, at foot of Porcupine Hills, 32 mi/51 km WNW of Lethbridge. Wheat, ranching.

Granville, village, W Yukon, Canada, 35 mi/56 km SE of Dawson. Gold mining.

Granville, county (□ 536 sq mi/1,388 sq km; 1990 pop. 38,345), N N.C., bounded by Va. state line; ⊙ Oxford; 36°17′N 78°39′W. In Piedmont region; drained by Tar R. Agr. area (especially tobacco; corn, wheat, oats, soybeans, sorghum; hogs, chickens, cattle; dairying); timber. Sawmilling. Arms of Fall L. reservoir extend into S part. Arms of large Buggs Island L. reservoir (Va.) extend into NW part. Part of Camp Butner Natl. Guard Base in SW. Formed 1746.

Granville, city (1990 pop. 236), McHenry co., central N.Dak., 21 mi/34 km E of Minot; 48°16′N 100°50′W. RR junction. Dairy prods.; livestock; grain. North L. and Buffalo Lodge L. to NE.

Granville 1 town (1990 pop. 298), Sioux co., NW Iowa, 10 mi/16 km E of Orange City; 42°58′N 95°52′W. Livestock; grain. **2** town (1990 pop. 1,403), Hampden co., SW Mass., 15 mi/24 km WSW of Springfield; 42°05′N 72°55′W. Includes state forest and village of Granville Center. **3** town (1990 pop. 309), Addison co., central Vt., on White R., and 17 mi/27 km E of Middlebury, in Green Mts.; 44°00′N 72°50′W. **4** town (1990 pop. 798), Monongalia co., N W.Va., on the Monongahela R., suburb 2 mi/3.2 km NW of Morgantown; 39°38′N 79°59′W. Mfg. (hunting rifles, countertops). Inc. after 1940.

Granville 1 village (1990 pop. 1,407), Putnam co., N central Ill., near the great bend of Illinois R., 5 mi/8 km E of Hennepin; 41°15′N 89°13′W. Corn, soybeans, wheat; poultry, livestock; dairy prods. Inc. 1861. **2** village (□ 1 sq mi/2.6 sq km; 1990 pop. 2,646), Wash. co., E N.Y., near Vt. border, 20 mi/32 km ENE of Glens Falls; 43°24′N 73°15′W. Slate quarrying; mfg. (slate prods., furniture, wood prods., chemicals). Settled 1870, inc. 1885. **3** village (1990 pop. 4,353), Licking co., central Ohio, 7 mi/11 km W of Newark, and on Raccoon Creek, in diversified farming area; 40°04′N 82°30′W. Seat of Denison Univ. Settled 1805, inc. 1832. **4** uninc. village, Grainsville township, Mifflin co., central Pa., 4 mi/6.4 km SW of Lewistown, on Juanita R.; 40°33′N 77°37′W. Mfg. (fiberglass prods.).

Granville Ferry, village, W N.S., Canada, on Annapolis Basin, opposite Annapolis; 44°45′N 65°31′W. Dairying; apples.

Grape Island, island, E Mass., part of Hingham, Mass., in Hingham Bay, SE of downtown Boston. Part of Boston Harbor Isls. State Park.

Grapeland, town (1990 pop. 1,450), Houston co., E Texas, 12 mi/19 km N of Crockett; 31°29′N 95°28′W. In oil, agr., timber area; mfg. Mission Tejas State Historical Park and Davy Crockett Natl. Forest are to the E; Houston Co. L. reservoir to SW. Inc. 1924.

Grapeville, uninc. village, Penn township, Westmoreland co., SW Pa., 1 mi/1.6 km E of Jeannette; 40°19′N 79°36′W.

Grapevine, city (1990 pop. 29,202), Tarrant and Dallas cos., N Texas, suburb 19 mi/31 km NE of downtown Fort Worth; 32°55′N 97°04′W. Elev. 650 ft/198 m. Drained by Denton Creek (N; forms Grapevine in N part of city) and by Big Bear Creek (S). Trade point in cotton, corn area; mfg. (paper prods., fabricated metal prods., construction materials). Dallas–Fort Worth Internatl. Airport adjoins city to E and S; NW runway extension splits city into 2 parts. Grapevine Recreation Area at Grapevine Dam. Settled 1854, inc. 1907.

Grapevine Mountains, Calif.: see AMARGOSA RANGE.

Grapevine Peak, Calif. and Nev.: see AMARGOSA RANGE.

Gras, Lac de (GRAH, lahk duh), lake (□ 345 sq mi/894 sq km), central Mackenzie dist., N.W.T., Canada; 40 mi/64 km long, 3 mi/5 km–18 mi/29 km wide; 64°30′N 110°30′W. Drains N through Contwoyto L. into Bathurst Inlet by Burnside R.

Grasmere, a section of Staten Isl. borough of N.Y. city, SE N.Y., on NE Staten Isl.; 40°36′N 74°05′W.

Grasmere, N.H.: see GOFFSTOWN.

Grasonville, village (1990 pop. 2,439), Queen Annes co., E Md., on the Eastern Shore, bet. inlets of Eastern Bay and Chester R.; 38°58′N 76°11′W. Named for William Grason (1786–1868), Md.'s 28th governor. Several seafood operators are the key to the town's survival.

Grass Lake, town (1990 pop. 903), Jackson co., S Mich.,

10 mi/16 km E of Jackson, on S end of small Grass L. (S and W); 42°15′N 84°12′W. In agr. and dairy area. Mfg. (transportation equip.). Waterloo State Recreation Area to N.

Grass Lake, uninc. village (1990 pop. 2,191), Lake co., NE Ill., suburb 48 mi/77 km NW of downtown Chicago, 4 mi/6.4 km SW of Antioch. Town located on isl. formed by "chain" of lakes: L. Marie (N), Grass L. (W), Fox L. (S), Petite and Bluff lakes (E). Chain O'Lakes State Park to NW.

Grass Lake, lake, Ill.: see CHAIN O' LAKES.

Grass River, c.60 mi/97 km long, NE N.Y., formed just S of Canton by small tributaries, flows generally NE, past Massena, to the St. Lawrence R. 12 mi/19 km NE of Massena.

Grass Valley, city (1990 pop. 9,048), Nevada co., E central Calif., 50 mi/80 km NE of Sacramento, on W slope of the Sierra Nevada; 39°13′N 121°04′W. Elev. c.2,400 ft/732 m. Center of gold-mining area (mines producing since 1850); mfg. (electronic, transportation, and scientific equip.). Timber; apples; nursery stock; cattle. Home of Lola Montez, who lived here (1852–1854), is preserved. Beale Air Force Base to SW; Eaglebright Reservoir to W; Tahoe Natl. Forest to E; Empire Mine State Historical Park to E. Inc. 1861.

Grass Valley, village (1990 pop. 160), Sherman co., N Oregon, 23 mi/37 km SE of The Dalles; 45°21′N 120°46′W. Grain. Deschutes R. State Recreation Area to W.

Grassflat, uninc. town (1990 pop. 850), Cooper township, Clearfield co., central Pa., 9 mi/14.5 km NE of Philipsburg; 41°00′N 78°06′W. Agr. (corn, hay; dairying). Also spelled Grass Flat.

Grasslands National Park (□ 350 sq mi/907 sq km), SW Sask., Canada, located on Montana border bet. Kildeer and Val Marie, in the Wood Mt. region. Traversed by Frenchman R. Under a 1981 agreement, oil and natural gas exploration would be allowed, with park acreage being purchased by govt. gradually until total area is acquired. Mixed-grass prairie. Kildeer Badlands, Seventy Mile Butte, prairie dog towns, antelope; remnant tepee rings from original inhabitants. Horseback riding, hiking. No facilities.

Grassrange, village (1990 pop. 159), Fergus co., central Mont., on South Fork of McDonald Creek. Cattle, sheep; hay. War Horse Natl. Wildlife Refuge to NE and 28 mi/45 km E of Lewistown. Also spelled Grass Range.

Grasston, village (1990 pop. 119), Kanabec co., E Minn., on Snake R., and 8 mi/12.9 km W of Pine City; 45°47′N 93°09′W. Dairying; mfg. (feeds).

Grassy Mountain, Ga.: see OGLETHORPE, MOUNT.

Grassy Narrows, Indian settlement (1986 pop. 740), Canada, afflicted with Minamata disease (mercury poisoning). Forestry; tourism.

Grassy Sound, S N.J., inlet of the Atlantic, bet. Cape May Peninsula and a barrier isl., W of North Wildwood; c.1 mi/1.6 km in diameter. Crossed by Intracoastal Waterway channel.

Gratiot (GRA-tee-o), county (□ 571 sq mi/1,479 sq km; 1990 pop. 38,982), central Mich.; ⊙ Ithaca; 43°17′N 84°35′W. Drained by Maple, Pine, and Bad rivers. Poultry, cattle, hogs; agr. (sugar beets, soybeans, grain, beans, corn; dairy prods.). Mfg. at Alma, Ithaca, and St. Louis. Petroleum refineries; mineral springs. State game area in SE. Organized 1855.

Gratiot 1 (GRA-shee-uht, GRAI-), village (1990 pop. 195), on Licking-Muskingum co. line, central Ohio, 11 mi/18 km W of Zanesville; 39°57′N 82°13′W. **2** (GRA-tee-aht), village (1990 pop. 207), Lafayette co., S Wis., on Pecatonica R., and 18 mi/29 km W of Monroe; 42°34′N 90°01′W. In livestock and dairy area.

Gratis (GRAT-is), town, Walton co., N central Ga., 17 mi/27 km WSW of Athens; 33°52′N 83°39′W.

Gratis, village (1990 pop. 998), Preble co., W Ohio, 21 mi/34 km WSW of Dayton and on small Twin Creek; 39°38′N 84°31′W.

Graton, uninc. town, (1990 pop. 1,409), Sonoma co., W Calif., 8 mi/12.9 km W of Santa Rosa; 38°27′N 122°52′W. Grapes, apples, grain; dairying; poultry, sheep.

Gratz, borough (1990 pop. 696), Dauphin co., S central Pa., 17 mi/27 km SSE of Sunbury; 40°36'N 76°43'W. Agr. (corn, hay; poultry; dairying); mfg. (construction materials). Mahantango Mt. ridge to N.

Gravelbourg (GRA-vuhl-buhrg), town (1991 pop. 1,226), S Sask., Canada, on Wood R., and 55 mi/89 km SW of Moose Jaw; 49°53'N 106°33'W. Grain elevators, flour and lumber mills.

Gravelly Range (GRAIV-lee), in Rocky Mts. of SW Mont., rises E of Ruby R., near Idaho state line; extends c.40 mi/64 km N to Virginia City. Largely within Beaverhead Natl. Forest. Highest peaks: Old Baldy (9,572 ft/2,918 m), Cascade Mt. (9,900 ft/3,018 m), Black Butte (10,545 ft/3,214 m). Major source of talc.

Gravenhurst (GRAI-vuhn-huhrst), town (1991 pop. 9,988), S Ont., Canada, N of Toronto; 44°55'N 79°22'W. Gateway to the Muskoka Lakes area. Light industry.

Graves, county (□ 556 sq mi/1,440 sq km; 1990 pop. 33,550), SW Ky.; ⊙ Mayfield; 36°43'N 88°39'W. Bounded S by Tenn. state line; drained by West Fork of Clarks R., Mayfield, West Fork Mayfield, and Obion creeks, and Bayou de Chien. Gentle rolling agr. area (dark and burley tobacco, sorghum, hay, alfalfa, soybeans, wheat, corn; hogs, cattle, poultry; dairying); clay; timber. Some mfg. at Mayfield. Formed 1821.

Graves, rock island, E Mass., E of Boston port. Site of lighthouse, Graves Light, 1 of 4 lighthouses marking entrance to Boston Harbor.

Gravesend, a residential section of SW Brooklyn borough of N.Y. city, SE N.Y., on Gravesend Bay (an arm of Lower N.Y. Bay), 40°36'N 73°57'W. Settled in 1643 by Lady Deborah Moody and her followers in search of religious freedom. Pop. is predominantly working- and lower-middle-class people, mainly Ital.-Amer.

Gravette (GRAV-et), town (1990 pop. 1,412), Benton co., extreme NW Ark., 30 mi/48 km NNW of Fayetteville, 19 mi/31 km WNW of Rogers, in the Ozarks; 36°25'N 94°27'W. Mfg. (machinery, chemicals, apparel, consumer goods).

Gravina Island (grah-VEE-nuh), SE Alaska, one of Gravina Isls., Alexander Archipelago, just W of Ketchikan; 20 mi/32 km long, 3 mi/4.8 km–9 mi/14.5 km wide; 55°15'N 131°45'W.

Gravina Islands (grah-VEE-nuh), part of Alexander Archipelago, SE Alaska, bet. Clarence Strait (W) and Revillagigedo Channel (E), S of Ketchikan. Largest isls. (N-S) are Gravina, Annette, and Duke. Largest settlement is Metlakatla on Annette Isl. Fishing, fish processing, lumbering.

Gravina, Port (grah-VEE-nuh), S Alaska, bay on E shore of Prince William Sound, 20 mi/32 km NW of Cordova; 15 mi/24 km long; 60°42'N 146°18'W.

Gravity, town (1990 pop. 218), Taylor co., SW Iowa, 6 mi/9.7 km N of Bedford; 40°45'N 94°44'W. Livestock; grain.

Grawn, village, Grand Traverse co., NW Mich., 7 mi/11.3 km SSW of Traverse City; 44°39'N 85°41'W. RR terminus. Pulpwood market; ships farm produce; fruit growing; mfg. (canned and frozen cherries, plums, apples; applesauce). Several lakes in area.

Gray 1 county (□ 869 sq mi/2,251 sq km; 1990 pop. 5,396), SW Kansas; ⊙ Cimarron; 37°44'N 100°25'W. Rolling plain region, drained by Arkansas R. Wheat, sorghum, corn, soybeans, alfalfa; cattle. Formed 1887. **2** county (□ 929 sq mi/2,406 sq km; 1990 pop. 23,967), extreme N Texas, in the Panhandle; ⊙ Pampa; 35°24'N 100°48'W. Elev. 2,500 ft/762 m–3,300 ft/1,006 m. Drained by North Fork of Red R. and McClellan Creek. One of state's most productive oil and natural gas cos. (oil well at Pampa), lying in huge Panhandle field; refineries, mfg. (oil well equipment and supplies, chemicals); cattle and wheat ranching; sorghum, corn, forage crops, hay. Hunting, fishing at L. McClellan (in McClellan Creek Natl. Grassland in S). Formed 1876.

Gray 1 town (1990 pop. 2,189), ⊙ Jones co., central Ga., 14 mi/23 km NNE of Macon; 33°01'N 83°32'W. Mfg. includes crushed stone, trusses, concrete, and peach-pitting equip. **2** town (1990 pop. 83), Audubon co., W central Iowa, 9 mi/14.5 km N of Audubon; 41°50'N 94°58'W. In agr. area; feed. **3** or **Grays**, town (1990 pop. 2,911), Knox co., SE Ky., in Cumberland foothills, 5 mi/8 km E of Corbin. In bituminous-coal region; agr. (tobacco; cattle). **4** town (1990 pop. 5,904), Cumberland co., SW Maine, 14 mi/23 km N of Portland; 43°52'N 70°21'W. Dry Mills village has large Fish and Wildlife Center and fish hatchery. Settled c.1750, inc. 1778.

Gray Court, town (1990 pop. 914), Laurens co., NW S.C., c.10 mi/16 km NW of Laurens; 34°36'N 82°06'W. Mfg. includes machining, crushed stone.

Grayland, uninc. town (1990 pop. 900), Grays Harbour co., W Wash., 16 mi/26 km WSW of Aberdeen, on Pacific Ocean, midway bet. Grays Harbor (N) and Willapa Bay (S). Beach resort. Grayland Beach State Park to S; Twin Harbors State Park to N.

Grayling, city (1990 pop. 1,944), ⊙ Crawford co., N central Mich., c.45 mi/72 km ESE of Traverse City and on Middle Branch of Au Sable R.; 44°39'N 84°42'W. Resort area (winter-sports and canoeing center); timber and farm area; lumber milling. A Natl. Guard training camp (camp Grayling) to W; state fish hatchery and Hartwick Pines State Park (c.9,672 acres/3,914 ha) to N. Sky (the ski area) to S; Huron Natl. Forest to SE. Inc. as village 1903, as city 1934.

Graymont, Ga.: see TWIN CITY.

Graymoor-Devondale (grai-mor–DEV-uhn-dail), uninc. town (1990 pop. 2,911), Jefferson co., N Ky., residential suburb 7 mi/11.3 km ENE of downtown Louisville; 38°16'N 85°37'W.

Grays, village, Woodruff co., E central Ark., 8 mi/12.9 km ESE of Augusta, on Cache R. Rex Hancock Black Swamp Wildlife Management Area to SW.

Grays, Ky.: see GRAY.

Grays Harbor, county (□ 2,224 sq mi/5,760 sq km; 1990 pop. 64,175), W Wash.; ⊙ Montesano; 47°09'N 123°50'W. Rolling hills, rising to Olympic Mts. in E; bounded W by Pacific Ocean. Drained by Chehalis R., also Hoquiam, Humptulips, Satsop, and North rivers. Peas, hay, cranberries; lumber, wood prods.; oysters, clams, salmon, other seafood. Grays Harbor, inlet of Pacific, in SW. Includes part of Chehalis Indian Reservation in SE and parts of Olympic Natl. Forest and Quinault Indian Reservation, NW; Ocean City, Griffiths-Friday, and Pacific Beach state parks, all on coast in W; Lake Sylvia State Park in S center; Westhaven and Westport Light state parks, on coast; Two Harbors State Park, on Grays Harbor, in SW; Copalis Natl. Wildlife Refuge offshore in NW part; small part of Olympic Natl. Park at L. Quinault in N. Formed as Chehalis co. 1854, renamed 1915.

Grays Harbor, W Wash., an inlet of Pacific Ocean; c.15 mi/24 km long, 13 mi/21 km wide, tapers toward E. Lumber shipping; fish, oysters, clams; logging. Hoquiam is on N shore, at mouth of Chehalis R. Entrance is 2 mi/3.2 km wide.

Grays Knob, uninc. village, Harlan co., SE Ky., 3 mi/4.8 km S of Harlan, in the Cumberland Mts. Mfg. (concrete, coal processing); bituminous coal.

Grays Peak (14,270 ft/4,349 m), Clear Creek and Summit cos., N central Colo., on Continental Divide, in Front Range, 45 mi/72 km W of Denver, and 17 mi/27 km ENE of Breckenridge. Loveland Pass to NW.

Grayslake, village (1990 pop. 7,388), Lake co., extreme NE Ill., 11 mi/18 km W of Waukegan; 42°21'N 88°02'W. In dairying, agr., and lake-resort area. Small Grays L. is here. Mfg. (cement and wood prods.). Col. of Lake County here. Inc. 1895.

Grayson, village (1991 pop. 256), SE Sask., Canada, 16 mi/26 km SSE of Melville. Mixed farming, livestock.

Grayson 1 county (□ 510 sq mi/1,321 sq km; 1990 pop. 21,050), W central Ky.; ⊙ Leitchfield; 37°27'N 86°20'W. Bounded N by Rough R. (forms Rough River L. reservoir; Rough R. Dam State Resort Park), SE by Nolin R. (forms Nolin River L. reservoir); drained by Bear and Caney creeks. Rolling agr. area (burley tobacco, hay, alfalfa, soybeans, wheat, corn; hogs, cattle, poultry, dairying; honey); asphalt; bituminous-coal mines, stone quarries. Formed 1810. **2** county (□ 979 sq mi/2,536 sq km; 1990 pop. 95,021), N Texas; ⊙ Sherman; 33°37'N 96°40'W. Bounded N by Red R. and L. Texoma (Okla. state line). Rich diversified agr., cattle, and dairying area (wheat, peanuts, some citrus); also hogs, poultry, horses. Some oil and gas; stone; timber. Mfg., farm-prods. processing at Sherman and Denison. Eisenhower Birthplace State Historic Site at Dennison; Eisenhower State Park in N near Dennison Dam; Hagerman Natl. Wildlife Refuge in N, on arm of L. Texoma; part of L. Ray Roberts reservoir in SW corner. Formed 1846. **3** county (□ 445 sq mi/1,153 sq km; 1990 pop. 16,278), SW Va.; ⊙ Independence; 36°38'N 81°13'W. Independent city of Galax on E boundary, separate from co. Bounded S by N.C. state line; Iron Mts., including White Top Mtn. and Mt. Rogers, highest peak in Va., are in N and W; part of Blue Ridge in SE corner. Drained by New R. Mfg. at Independence and Fries; agr. (tobacco, corn, hay, alfalfa; cattle, sheep, poultry; dairying); timber. Includes part of Jefferson Natl. Forest in W and N (mostly in Mt. Rogers Natl. Recreation Area), Appalachian Trail passes through W, small part of Blue Ridge Parkway passes through SE corner. Grayson Highlands State Park in W; spur of New River Trail State Park on E boundary. Formed 1778.

Grayson, town (1990 pop. 3,510), ⊙ Carter co., NE Ky., on Little Sandy R., and 20 mi/32 km WSW of Ashland; 38°19'N 82°56'W. Agr. (dairying; livestock, poultry; tobacco, corn, wheat) area; clay, coal, timber; mfg. (coal processing, lumber, meat processing, concrete). Seat of Ky. Christian Col. (1919). Camp Robert Webb Conservation Education Center to S. Carter Caves State Resort Park to W; Grayson L. reservoir and State Park to W; Greenbo L. State Resort Park to N. Est. 1844.

Grayson 1 village (1990 pop. 529), Gwinnett co., N central Ga., 25 mi/40 km ENE of Atlanta; 33°53'N 83°58'W. Mfg. includes medical diagnostic equip., crushed stone, asphalt. **2** village (1990 pop. 529), Caldwell parish, NE central La., 32 mi/51 km S of Monroe; 32°03'N 92°07'W. Mfg. of concrete; timber; soybeans, cotton; cattle.

Grayson, uninc. community, Clinton co., NW Mo., 6 mi/9.7 km SW of Plattsburg.

Grayson Lake, resevoir, Carter and Elliott cos., NE Ky., on Little Sandy R., 7 mi/11.3 km SSW of Grayson; c.7 mi/11.3 km long; 38°15'N 82°59'W. Max. capacity 118,990 acre-ft. Formed by Grayson Dam (60 ft/18 m high), built by the Army Corps of Engineers for flood control. Partially in Grayson L. State Park.

Graysville, city (1990 pop. 2,241), Jefferson co., N central Ala., 12 mi/19 km NW of Birmingham; 33°37'N 86°58'W. Coal mining.

Graysville 1 town (1990 pop. 120), Catoosa co., NW Ga., 17 mi/27 km NW of Dalton, on Tenn. state line, in agr. area; 34°58'N 85°08'W. Mfg. of rebuilt steel drums. **2** town (1990 pop. 1,301), Rhea co., E Tenn., 30 mi/48 km NNE of Chattanooga; 35°27'N 85°08'W. In coal, timber, fruit area.

Graysville, village (1990 pop. 89), Monroe co., E Ohio, 23 mi/37 km NE of Marietta, in agr. area; 39°40'N 81°10'W.

Grayville, city (1990 pop. 2,043), in White and Edwards cos., SE Ill., on Wabash R. at mouth of Bonpas Creek, and 16 mi/26 km SW of Mount Carmel; 38°15'N 88°00'W. Agr. (sorghum, wheat; cattle); mfg. auto accessories; coal, oil; fisheries. Inc. 1851. Since 1985 cut off from direct access to Wabash R. because of river shift (a natural event).

Great Abaco Island, constituting most of Abaco (or Abaco and Cays) dist. (including Little Abaco and Cays, □ 776 sq mi/2,010 sq km), N Bahama Isls., E of Grand Bahama Isl., 33 mi/53 km N of Nassau; forms roughly a right angle c.100 mi/161 km long, up to 14 mi/23 km wide. It is adjoined NW by Little Abaco Isl. and is surrounded by many small cays. Has several fine harbors. Largely wooded. Main prods. are timber, fish, boatbuilding, fruit. Many hotels and resorts throughout the area. Principal settlements: Hope Town (on E cay), Cherokee Sound and Marsh Harbour (E central), Green Turtle Cay (NE), Sandy Point (SW). The isl. was settled (1783) by loyalists from N.Y. city. At SE end, where NE and NW Providence channels join, is the "Hole in the Wall," a widely known perforated rock, now site of a lighthouse.

Great American Desert, in SW U.S. and NW Mexico, name formerly given to vast arid and semiarid region lying bet. W base of the Rockies and E base of the Sierra Nevada and the Cascades S of central Oregon; included parts of the Great Basin and Colo. Plateau regions, and the deserts (Colorado, Yuma, Mojave, and Sonoran) of SE Calif., SW Ariz., and N Sonora, Mexico.

Great Appalachian Valley, E N. Amer. longitudinal chain of lowlands of the Appalachian Mountains; extends from Canada on NE to Ala. on SW. Represented from NE to SW by the great St. Lawrence R. lowland, Richelieu R. valley, L. Champlain lowland, and the valley of the Hudson R. bet. the L. Champlain region and the point near Kingston, N.Y., where the Wallkill R. valley extends SW to meet the Kittatinny Valley of N N.J.; from Kittatinny Valley, it is continued by the Lebanon Valley (Pa.), Cumberland Valley (Pa. and Md.), Shenandoah Valley in Va., the Valley of E Tenn. (drained by Tennessee R.) in Tenn., and Coosa R. valley of Ala., where the lowland meets the Gulf coastal plain. It contains rich agr. land, notably in the Cumberland and Shenandoah valleys.

Great Averill Pond, in town of Averill, Essex co., NE Vt., 8 mi/12.9 km W of Canaan and 2 mi/3.2 km S of Can. (Que.) border; 2 mi/3.2 km long; 44°58′N 71°42′W. In hunting, fishing area. Little Averill Pond 2 mi/3.2 km SW.

Great Backbone Mountain, Md.: see BACKBONE MOUNTAIN.

Great Bahama Bank, large shoal in the Bahamas, SE of Fla., and S of Little Bahama Bank, from which it is separated by NW Providence Channel. Extends from just E of Miami (across Straits of Fla.) c.350 mi/563 km SE bet. Cuba and Andros Isl.

Great Barrington (BAR-reeng-tuhn), town (1990 pop. 7,725), including Great Barrington village, Berkshire co., SW Mass., on Housatonic R., and 18 mi/29 km SSW of Pittsfield, in the Berkshires; 42°13′N 73°20′W. Summer resort; ski center. Mfg.; dairying; poultry; timber. Has fine old houses. Settled 1726, set off from Sheffield 1761. Includes state forest, villages of Housatonic (1990 pop. 1,184) and Van Deusenville.

Great Basin, semiarid, N section of the Basin and Range prov., the intermontane plateau region of W U.S. and N Mexico. Lying mostly in Nev. and extending into Calif., Oregon, Idaho, and Utah, it is bordered by the Sierra Nevada on the W, the Columbia Plateau on the N, the Rocky Mts. on the NE, the Colo. Plateau on the E, and the Mojave Desert on the S. The region is a complex topographic basin, the surface of which is broken by numerous fault-block mountains, trending mostly N-S and rising sharply in places to more than 10,000 ft/3,048 m above dry, sediment-floored basins. Death Valley Natl. Monument, 282 ft/86 m below sea level, is the lowest basin; it is also the hottest (134°F/57°C in the shade is the highest temp. recorded) and one of the driest (less than 3 in/7.6 cm of rain annually) parts of N. Amer. Throughout the Great Basin rainfall is limited (2 in/5.1 cm–20 in/51 cm annually) and sporadic. The region was recognized as an area of interior drainage by J. C. Frémont, who explored (1843–1845) and named it. The rivers of the region have no outlet to the sea; they either dry up as they cross the parched terrain, like the Humboldt, or empty into large lakes or into playas that temporarily fill with water after heavy rain. Klamath and Utah lakes contain freshwater; most other lakes are brackish or salty. The lakes are remnants of a much larger system of anc. lakes that occupied the region during the Pleistocene epoch: Great Salt, Sevier, and Utah lakes are remnants of glacial L. Bonneville; North Carson, South Carson, Walker, Honey, Pyramid, and Winnemucca are remnants of glacial L. Lahontan; and glacial L. Manly is thought to have occupied Death Valley. Although Nev. and Utah experienced significant growth in the 1970s and 1980s, the Great Basin remains one of the least populated areas of the U.S. In recent decades, its traditional economic activities, mining and ranching, have been superseded by mfg. and tourism. In addition, several military installations, including a nuclear testing site in Nev., have been established since the 1950s, and a concentration of aerospace, defense, and electronics firms has sprung up around them. The mining industry in the Great Basin traces its roots to the 1850s, when gold and silver were discovered in Death Valley; the discovery of silver at the Comstock Lode near Virginia City, Nev., in 1859 attracted a new influx of settlers. The output of gold from mines in both Nev. and Utah remains high. Mercury and barite are also mined in Nev.; in Utah, beryllium, uranium, molybdenum, and silver are mined. Copper mines, formerly the mainstay of the regional economy, began to decline in the 1970s and have largely fallen into disuse. A variety of commercial salts are processed at chemical plants near the Great Salt L. Intensive forms of cattle production, based on irrigated feed crops, are concentrated along the Humboldt and Reese rivers and along streams draining into the margins of the Great Basin from the Wasatch Mts. and the Sierra Nevada.

Great Basin National Park (□ 120 sq mi/311 sq km), White Pine co., E Nev., authorized 1986, c.35 mi/56 km SE of Ely, 10 mi/16 km W of Utah border; covers 77,079 acres/31,194 ha. Features Lehman Caves (originally est. in 1922 as Lehman Caves Natl. Monument; was 640 acres/259 ha), an icefield on Wheeler Peak (13,063 ft/3,982 m, 2d-highest point in Nev.), an ancient bristlecone pine forest, and a limestone arch, known as Lexington Arch (75 ft/23 m high). Access from Baker, Nev., 5 mi/8 km to E.

Great Bay 1 inland tidal bay in SE N.H., Rockingham and Strafford cos., receives Swampscott, Lamprey, Oyster, and Bellamy rivers; exits N and E through Little Bay into tidal Piscataqua R., 6 mi/9.7 km NW of Portsmouth; 6 mi/9.7 km long, 4 mi/6.4 km wide. **2** inlet of the Atlantic in SE N.J., at mouth of navigable Mullica R., 9 mi/14.5 km NNE of Atlantic City; c.5 mi/8 km in diameter. Entered from Atlantic by Little Egg Inlet; traversed by Intracoastal Waterway channel.

Great Bear Lake, largest lake of Canada and 4th-largest of N. Amer. (□ c.12,275 sq mi/31,800 sq km), Fort Smith and Inuvik regions, N.W.T., on the edge of the Can. Shield; c.190 mi/310 km long and from 25 mi/40 km to 110 mi/177 km wide. It is drained to the W by the Great Bear R. (c.100 mi/160 km long), which flows into the Mackenzie R. Even though it is one of N. Amer.'s deepest (1,356 ft/413 m) lakes, its waters are open only about 4 months each year. The lake was explored (c.1800) by traders of the North West Company, and a trading post was later est. here. Fort Franklin, on the SW shore, was built by Sir John Franklin, a Br. explorer, in 1825. Discoveries of rich radium ores, which are now exhausted, on the E side of the lake in 1930 caused much mining activity in the years immediately following; the Eldorado Mines, at Port Radium, were located here.

Great Bend, city (1990 pop. 15,427), ⊙ Barton co., central Kansas, on a bend in the Arkansas R.; 38°21′N 98°48′W. Elev. 1,849 ft/564 m. RR junction. It is a trade and shipping center for a wheat and oil region. Mfg. (alfalfa pellets, farm machinery, concrete prods., consumer prods., plastic prods.). The city has Barton Co. Community Col. and a medical center. Great Bend was located on the old Santa Fe Trail. Fort Zarah to E. Settled and inc. 1872.

Great Bend 1 village (1990 pop. 650), Jefferson co., N N.Y., on Black R., and 10 mi/16 km ENE of Watertown; 44°02′N 75°43′W. Fort Drum (formerly Pine Camp, then Camp Drum) is nearby. **2** village (1990 pop. 108), Richland co., SE N.Dak., 12 mi/19 km SW of Wahpeton and on Wild Rice R.; 46°08′N 96°47′W.

Great Bend, borough (1990 pop. 704), Susquehanna co., NE Pa., 12 mi/19 km SE of Binghamton, N.Y., and 1 mi/1.6 km N of Hallstead, on Susquehanna R., opposite Hailstead, near N.Y. state line; 41°58′N 75°45′W. Agr. (corn, hay; livestock; dairying); mfg. (machinery). Salt Springs State Park to SW.

Great Boars Head, promontory, Rockingham co., SE N.H., on coast N of Hampton Beach, 2 mi/3.2 km SE of Hampton town center; ½ mi/⅘ km long. Little Boars Head is 3 mi/4.8 km N.

Great Bras d'Or, Canada: see BRAS D'OR LAKE.

Great Brewster Island, Mass.: see BREWSTER ISLANDS.

Great Burnt Lake, Canada: see CROOKED LAKE.

Great Cacapon (kuh-KAI-puhn), uninc. village (1990 pop. 500), Morgan co., NE W.Va., 21 mi/34 km NW of Martinsburg, in E Panhandle, on the Potomac R., at mouth of Cacapon R. Agr. (grain, apples); livestock, poultry. Glass-sand quarries.

Great Captain Island, SW Conn., in Long Isl. Sound, 3 mi/4.8 km offshore, S of Greenwich; mi/⁹⁄₁₀ km long. Lighthouse here since early 19th cent. Little Captain Isl. is E.

Great Cedar Swamp, N.J.: see DENNISVILLE.

Great Central Lake (□ 20 sq mi/52 sq km), SW B.C., Canada, in central Vancouver Isl., just S of Strathcona Park, in fishing, lumbering area 11 mi/18 km NW of Port Alberni. Great Central village, at E end, at head of RR spur, saws and ships lumber.

Great Chazy River (shai-ZEE), c.40 mi/64 km long, NE N.Y., issues from Chazy L., flows NE and E, past Champlain, to L. Champlain 4 mi/6.4 km S of Rouses Point.

Great Chebeague Island (she-BEEG) (□ c.3.1 sq mi/8.1 sq km), SW Maine, resort and residential isl. in Casco Bay. Chebeague Island village is on E shore.

Great Cloche Island (klosh), S central Ont., Canada, one of the Manitoulin Isls., in the North Channel of L. Huron, just off Little Current, Manitoulin Isl.; 10 mi/16 km long, 4 mi/6 km wide. Has RR connection with mainland and Little Current.

Great Colinet Island (ko-lee-NAI) (□ 5 sq mi/13 sq km), in St. Mary's Bay, SE N.F., Canada, 25 mi/40 km SE of Argentia; 5 mi/8 km long, 2 mi/3 km wide; 46°59′N 53°42′W. Fishing. Little Colinet Isl. (2 mi/3 km long) is 2 mi/3 km N.

Great Cranberry Island, Maine: see CRANBERRY ISLES.

Great Diamond Island (□ 0.6 sq mi/1.5 sq km), SW Maine, resort isl. in Casco Bay off Portland. Site of Fort McKinley. Sand spit connects with Little Diamond Isl.

Great Dismal Swamp, Va. and N.C.: see DISMAL SWAMP.

Great Divide Basin (□ c.2,500 sq mi/6,475 sq km), S central Wyo., primarily in NE Sweetwater co., extends into Fremont and Carbon cos.; 90 mi/145 km long E-W, 45 mi/72 km wide. Bounded on N by Antelope Hills and Green Mts. An area of sand dunes and alkali flats lying bet. branches of the Continental Divide; there is no river outlet from the basin to either the Atlantic or Pacific oceans. The only viable streams are Bear Creek, which flows SE into Bush L., and its North Fork and Sand Creek tributaries, all in NW corner of basin. Interstate Highway 80 and Union Pacific RR pass E-W through S; village of Wamsutter located in S.

Great Duck Island, S central Ont., Canada, one of the Manitoulin Isls., in L. Huron 8 mi/13 km S of Manitoulin Isl.; 5 mi/8 km long, 2 mi/3 km wide. Just SE is Outer Duck Isl. (2 mi/3 km long).

Great Duck Island, Maine: see LONG ISLAND, plantation.

Great East Lake, SW Maine and E N.H., 13 mi/21 km NW of Sanford, Maine, and just E of Wakefield, N.H.; c.4 mi/6.4 km long; 43°35′N 70°58′W. Source of Salmon Falls R.

Great Egg Harbor, SE N.J., inlet of the Atlantic, 8 mi/12.9 km SW of Atlantic City, entered from Atlantic by Great Egg Harbor Inlet (bridged) N of Ocean City, which is on Peck Beach bet. bay and ocean; c.5 mi/8 km long. Bay traversed by Intracoastal Waterway channel. Sometimes called Great Egg Harbor Bay. Receives from W Tuckahoe River, from NW Great Egg Harbor River, rising SE of Camden, flowing c.50 mi/80 km SE, past Mays Landing (head of navigation), to head of Great Egg Harbor Bay near Somers Point city. Sometimes called Great Egg R.

Great Exuma Island, main island of the Exuma isls. (1990 pop. 3,556, including Little Exuma), central Bahama Isls., adjoined SE by Little Exuma Isl., 120 mi/193 km SE of Nassau; c.40 mi/64 km long, 1 mi/1.6 km–2 mi/3.2 km wide; 23°32′N 75°50′W. Fringed by numerous cays and good harbors. Tourism is main industry; govt. approved $90 million residential and resort development in 1994; also livestock raising (sheep, goats, pigs). Among the settlements are George-Town (E), Moss Town (center), Rolleville (N). Originally settled by refugees from Europe, S.C., and E Fla., who planted cotton. A U.S. naval base (granted in 1940, now closed) is at George-Town.

Great Falls, city (1990 pop. 55,097), ⊙ Cascade co., N central Mont., 2d largest city in the state, at the confluence of the Missouri and Sun rivers and near the falls that give the city its name; 47°30′N 111°17′W. Ryan Dam site of Great Falls of the Missouri to NE on Missouri R. As the center of extensive hydroelectric power development, Great Falls is popularly called the "Electric City." There are a copper reduction plant and flour mills. The surrounding area has deposits of coal, natural gas, silver, and lead. Mfg. (printing and publishing, meat packing, feeds, fabricated metal prods., construction materials, consumer goods). The city is a market for an irrigated farm and livestock district and for the Sun R. project. Great Falls is also a wholesale and retail trade and service center. Great Falls Internatl. Airport W of city. Charles M. Russell Mus. Complex, includes paintings and log cabin studio, Paris Gibson Sq. Mus., Malmstrom Air Force Base Mus. Outside the city is Giant Springs, which discharges a large flow of water through Roe R., "shortest river in world" (201 ft/61 m long), into the Missouri R. The Univ. of Great Falls and the Mont. School for the Deaf and Blind are in the city, which also serves as the hq. for Lewis and Clark Natl. Forest; forest to SE and E. Tourists are drawn to the annual rodeo and state fair. Malmstrom Air Force Base (scheduled for closing in the late 1990s) is to E. Benton L. Natl. Wildlife Refuge to N; Ulm Pishkun State Park to W; Giant Springs Heritage State Park to NE. Inc. 1888.

Great Falls 1 town (1990 pop. 2,307), Chester co., N S.C., and 22 mi/35 km ESE of Chester on the Catawba R. in Great Falls and Dearborn Dam to S; 34°34′N 80°54′W. Textile mills. Power plants here generate electricity for towns and cities in wide area. Fishing Creek Dam N, Great Falls and Dearborn Dam S. Mfg. includes apparel, fabricated metal prods. Agr. area for poultry, livestock; dairying; grains, sorghum. **2** uninc. town, Fairfax co., N Va., residential suburb 14 mi/23 km NW of Wash., D.C., 5 mi/8 km NE of Reston, near Potomac R.; 39°00′N 77°17′W. Light mfg. Great Falls Regional Park to NE.

Great Falls, village, SE Man., Canada, on Winnipeg R. (waterfalls), and 60 mi/97 km NE of Winnipeg; 50°27′N 96°01′W. Hydroelectric-power center.

Great Falls, Canada: see CHURCHILL FALLS.

Great Falls of the Potomac, in Potomac R. (here forming state line bet. Md. and Va.), c.15 mi/24 km WNW of Wash., D.C. A 3 mi/4.8-km-long series of cascades (greatest drop 35 ft/11 m) and rapids in 200-ft/61-m gorge. Sometimes known as Great Falls. Power dam here. Great Falls Park (140 acres/57 ha) is recreational area on both banks of river; sect. in Md. side is crossed by old Chesapeake and Ohio Canal (now recreational waterway). A public mus. includes parts of an iron foundry and mill once owned by George Washington as well as the Great Falls Tavern. Nearby is the Central Intelligence Agency and the U.S. Naval Reserach and Development Center, where ship models are tested.

Great Falls Reservoir (□ 3.5 sq mi/9.1 sq km), on White-DeKalb co. border, central Tenn., on Caney Fork R., branch of Cumberland R., 11 mi/18 km NE of McMinnville; 4 mi/6.4 km long; 35°47′N 85°36′W. Max. capacity 54,500 acre-ft. Formed by Great Falls Dam (92 ft/28 m high), built (1916) for power generation, now owned by TVA. Forms small reservoir.

Great Goat Island, off S coast of Jamaica, St. Catherine parish, in Old Harbour and Galleon Bay, 18 mi/29 km WSW of Kingston; consisting of Great Goat Isl. (3 mi/4.8 km long) and adjacent to Little Goat Isl; 17°52′N 77°03′W. Leased to U.S. for 99 years in 1940.

Great Gott Island, Hancock co., S Maine, at entrance to Blue Hill Bay, just S of Mt. Desert Isl.; c.1 mi/1.6 km wide.

Great Guana Cay, long narrow islet (c.9 mi/14.5 km long), Bahama Isls., in center of Exuma isls., 90 mi/145 km SE of Nassau; 24°05′N 76°20′W.

Great Gull Island, N.Y.: see GULL ISLANDS.

Great Inagua Island or **Inagua Island**, island and district (including Little Inagua Isl., □ 560 sq mi/1,450 sq km), Bahama Isls., southernmost isl. of the Bahamas and one of the largest, 55 mi/89 km NE of Cape Maisí (E Cuba), 350 mi/563 km SE of Nassau; in lat. 21°N. Chief settlement is Matthew Town on its W tip. The isl. has a large, shallow lake in its center, which abounds in bird wildlife. Salt panning is the principal activity (25% of Inaguans work at Morton Salt Company) Half of the isl. is wildlife sanctuary with guest houses and camps. Little Inagua Isl. adjoins NE.

Great Isaac, cay, NW Bahama Isls., 20 mi/32 km NE of the Biminis, 65 mi/105 km ENE of Miami, Fla.; 26°02′N 79°06′W. Lighthouse. Sometimes called Great Isaacs.

Great Island, Yarmouth Mass., SW corner of Yarmouth in West Yarmouth, bet. Lewis Bay and Nantucket Sound. Private residential area, includes Gammon Point and abandoned lighthouse.

Great Island, Maine: see HARPSWELL.

Great Kills, a section of Staten Isl. borough of N.Y. city, SE N.Y., on SE Staten Isl.; 40°33′N 74°09′W.

Great Lakes, group of five freshwater lakes, central N. Amer., creating a natural border bet. the U.S. and Canada and forming the largest body of freshwater in the world, with a combined surface area of c.95,000 sq mi/246,050 sq km. From W to E they are Lakes SUPERIOR, MICHIGAN, HURON, ERIE, and ONTARIO, out of which flows the Saint Lawrence R. The distance from Duluth, Minn., at the W end of L. Superior, to the outlet of L. Ontario is 1,160 mi/1,867 km. The internatl. boundary passes approximately through the center of all the lakes except L. Michigan, which lies entirely within the U.S. The Great Lakes were formed approximately at the end of the Pleistocene period, when the glacier-carved lake basins were filled with meltwater from the retreating ice sheet. The lakes are connected to each other by straits, short rivers, and canals. The ht. above sea level of the lake surfaces varies from L. Superior's 602 ft/183 m to L. Ontario's 246 ft/75 m; the greatest sudden drop occurs at Niagara Falls (167 ft/51 m) bet. lakes Erie and Ontario. All the lake bottoms, except that of L. Erie, extend below sea level. Fr. traders were the first Europeans to see any of the Great Lakes; Étienne Brulé visited L. Huron c.1612. In 1614, Brulé and Fr. explorer Samuel de Champlain explored L. Huron and L. Ontario. In 1679, Fr. explorer Robert LaSalle sailed from L. Erie to L. Michigan. The Great Lakes region, rich in furs, was contested for many years by the French, English, and Americans. The close of the War of 1812 finally ended the struggle for possession of the Great Lakes, and settlement of the region rapidly followed. The opening of the Erie Canal in 1825 accelerated the development of commerce on the Great Lakes, which carry large quantities of iron ore and grain, coal, and petroleum, and manufactured articles from April until Dec., until ice closes most of the ports and winter storms hinder navigation. Large concentrations of pop. and industry along the lakes' shores have led to increasing pollution, especially of L. Erie. The large industrial lakefront cities include Toronto, Hamilton, Buffalo, Cleveland, Detroit, Gary, Milwaukee, and Chicago. The opening of the St. Lawrence Seaway in 1959 made the Great Lakes a truly internatl. water body. The Illinois Waterway connects the lakes with the Mississippi R. and the Gulf of Mexico; the N.Y. State Barge Canal joins the Great Lakes with the Hudson R. and the Atlantic Ocean. The Great Lakes region, with its natl. parks and lakeshores, state parks, and many natural and scenic features, has become an important year-round recreation area.

Great Lakes Naval Training Station, Lake co., NE Ill., at North Chicago, on L. Michigan. Training and processing center for new recruits of U.S. Navy. Veterans hosp.

Great Lakes–St. Lawrence Waterway, Canada: see SAINT LAWRENCE–GREAT LAKES WATERWAY.

Great Machipongo Inlet, Va.: see HOG ISLAND.

Great Meadows, Pa.: see FORT NECESSITY.

Great Miami River or **Miami** (mei-AM-uh, -ee), river, c.160 mi/257 km long, formed in W Ohio near Indian L. and flowing generally SW past Dayton to the Ohio R. at the Ind. state line; 39°06′N 84°48′W. The Miami R. system has large-scale flood-control projects. The Miami and Erie Canal (c.240 mi/386 km long; opened in the 1830s) linked the upper Miami R. with L. Erie and was the principal transportation route of W Ohio until the 1850s. The Little Miami R. (95 mi/153 km long) to the E and generally parallel, rises SE of Springfield and enters the Ohio R. at Cincinnati.

Great Misery Island (□ 98 acres/40 ha), NE Mass., in the Atlantic, c.5 mi/8 km ENE of Salem. With nearby Little Misery Isl., comprises state reservation.

Great Moose Lake, in Somerset co., Maine, 12 mi/19 km NE of Skowhegan; 5 mi/8 km long. Source of Sebasticook R.

Great Neck, village (□ 1 sq mi/2.6 sq km; 1990 pop. 8,745), a projection of land into L.I. Sound at the NW end of L.I.; bordered by Manhasset Bay on the E and Little Neck Bay on the W; 40°47′N 73°43′W. The area consists of a group of villages, all within North Hempstead township; collectively constitutes a high-income suburb of N.Y. city on the Nassau-Queens border. Includes the villages of Great Neck, Great Neck Estates, Great Neck Gardens, Great Neck Plaza, Harbor Hill, Kensington, Kings Point, Russell Gardens, Saddle Rocks, and Thomaston. There are diverse light and high-technology industries centered on village of Great Neck. The U.S. Merchant Marine Acad. is in nearby Kings Point. F. Scott Fitzgerald lived in Great Neck and placed *The Great Gatsby* in a setting based on this area.

Great Neck Estates, affluent residential village (1990 pop. 2,790), Nassau co., SE N.Y., on N shore of W L.I., just S of Great Neck; 40°46′N 73°44′W. Inc. 1911.

Great Neck Plaza, affluent suburban village (1990 pop. 5,897), Nassau co., SE N.Y., on N shore of W L.I., just S of Great Neck village; 40°47′N 73°43′W. Inc. 1930.

Great Northern Peninsula or **Petit Nord Peninsula**, comprising NW N.F. isl., Canada, extending 170 mi/274 km NE from Bonne Bay on the W to Cape Bauld at the tip; White Bay borders it on the E. The Long Range, along the W coast, rises to 2,651 ft/808 m in Gros Morne.

Great Onyx Cave, Ky.: see CAVE CITY.

Great Peconic Bay, SE N.Y., bet. N and S peninsulas of E L.I. and near their bases, just E of Riverhead; c.6 mi/9.7 km in diameter; 40°57′N 72°30′W. Receives Peconic R. in Flanders Bay, its W arm; Shinnecock Canal joins it to Shinnecock Bay (S). Connected by channels to Little Peconic Bay (E), thence to Gardiners Bay and Block Isl. Sound. Sometimes called Peconic Bay.

Great Pedro Bluff, headland, St. Elizabeth parish, S Jamaica, 60 mi/97 km WSW of Kingston; 17°51′N 77°44′W.

Great Pee Dee River, N.C. and S.C.: see PEE DEE RIVER.

Great Plains, extensive grassland region on the continental slope of central N. Amer. It extends from the Can. provinces of Alta., Sask., and Man. S through W central U.S. into W Texas. In the U.S. the Plains include parts of N.D., S.D., Mont., Wyo., Colo., Nebr., Kansas, Okla., N.Mex., and Texas. The Great Plains slope gently E from the foothills of the Rocky Mts. at an elev. of 6,000 ft/1,829 m to merge into the interior lowlands at an elev. of roughly 1,500 ft/457 m. The 1,500 ft/457 m contour line, the 100th meridian of longitude, and the 20 in/51 cm isohyet of precipitation are arbitrarily used to mark the region's transitional E border. In places, however, it is clearly marked by an escarpment. Much of the Great Plains was once covered by a vast inland sea, and sediments deposited by the sea make up the nearly horizontal rock strata that underlie the area. Intrusive igneous rocks account for sects. of higher elev. The Great Plains region has generally level or rolling terrain; its subdivisions include Edwards Plateau, the Llano Estacado, the High Plains, the Sand Hills, the Badlands, and the Northern Plains. The Black Hills and several outliers of the Rocky Mts. interrupt the region's undulating profile. The Saskatchewan, Missouri, Platte,

Cross references are shown in SMALL CAPITALS. The pronunciation key is on page xv. The dates of population figures are on page xii.

Republican, Arkansas, Cimarron, and Canadian rivers flow in wide beds, generally from W to E, and are important sources of water. Rainfall decreases from E to W. Except for its easternmost margin and the elevations, the Great Plains have a semiarid climate, averaging less than 20 in/51 cm of precipitation annually. There are wide seasonal temp. ranges and winds of high velocity. In the westernmost sects. the chinook, a warm winter wind, brings relief from bitterly cold and snowy winters. The dominant type of vegetation consists of shortgrass prairies; trees grow in moister areas and along water courses. Although overall the Great Plains sparsely populated, with much of the grassland devoted to farms and ranches, about half the people live in small to medium-sized urban areas; Edmonton, Alberta, and Denver, Colo., are the largest cities in the region. Soils throughout the region are fertile and very productive when water is available. The principal crop is wheat, concentrated in the Spring Wheat Belt (generally N of Nebr.), where the colder climate delays sowing until spring, and the Winter Wheat Belt (centered in Kansas and Okla.), where the milder climate allows for winter sowing. Other crops include sorghum, flax, and cotton. Cattle and sheep are raised throughout most of the Great Plains. Oil, natural gas, coal, and gold are among its mineral deposits. The Great Plains were long inhabited by Native Americans, who hunted the teeming herds of buffalo that roamed the grasslands and, due to wholesale slaughter by Eur. settlers, were nearly extinct by the end of the 19th cent. The region was explored by the Spanish in the 17th cent. Until well into the 19th cent., the central Great Plains were called the Great Amer. Desert. The first W-bound pioneers bypassed the Great Plains. The RRs were largely responsible for their development after the Civil War. An initial wave of settlement was followed by emigration in times of drought. By the mid-1930s, decades of overgrazing and poor soil management in many of the Plains states had resulted in dust storms and the devastation of crops.

Great Point, Mass.: see NANTUCKET, isl.

Great Pond, reservoir (□ 13 sq mi/34 sq km), Kennebec co., central Maine, on Belgrade Stream, c.7 mi/11 km W of Waterville; 44°32′N 69°53′W. Max. capacity 43,900 acre-ft. Formed by Great Pond Storage Dam (14 ft/4 m high), built (1886) for power generation.

Great Quittacas Pond (KWIT-uh-kuhs), reservoir, Plymouth co., SE Mass., on small stream draining N to Assawompsett Pond, 11 mi/18 km N of New Bedford; c.3.5 mi/5.6 km long; 41°48′N 70°53′W.

Great Ragged Island, islet, S Bahama Isls., in part of the archipelago usually called Ragged Isl. and Cays or Jumento Cays, adjoined S by Little Ragged Isl. and situated 70 mi/113 km N of Cuba and 225 mi/362 km SE of Nassau; c.4 mi/6.4 km long, up to 1.5 mi/2.4 km wide. Principal activity is salt panning; the surrounding sea abounds in fish. Chief settlement is Duncan Town (22°12′N 75°44′W).

Great Saint Lawrence, Canada: see SAINT LAWRENCE.

Great Salt Lake, shallow body of salt water, NW Utah, bet. the Wasatch Range on the E and the Great Salt L. Desert on the W; largest salt lake in N. Amer. Fed by the Weber (E), Jordan (S), and Bear (NE) rivers, the lake varies greatly in size and depth according to climate changes. Its average depth ranges from 13 ft/4 m to 24 ft/7 m with a mean elevation of 4,200 ft above sea level. From 1,000 sq mi/2,590 sq km in the period bet. 1955 and 1975, the lake expanded to its all-time max. of almost 2,500 sq mi/6,477 sq km by the mid-1980s. Storage of spring run-off in reservoirs to meet domestic and industrial demands for water have contributed to seasonal lake shrinkage. The salt content, nearly 10% at its greatest size, increases as the water level decreases. Magnesium chloride, potash, and common table salt have been commercially extracted from the lake. The heavy brine supports no life except brine shrimp and colonial algae. The Great Salt L. is a remnant of prehistoric L. Bonneville, which covered an extensive area of the Great Basin and was once c.1,000 ft/305 m deep. Its various levels are marked by former beachlines on

the mountains and by rich soil deposits on the terraces to the E, where irrigated farming is practiced. Antelope and Fremont isls. are the largest isls. in the lake; the smaller isls. are rookeries for sea gulls and other birds. Promontory Point, a mountainous peninsula 20 mi/32 km long, extends into the lake from the N; a RR cutoff on a causeway passes through the point as it crosses the lake E-W and the Great Salt L. Desert from Ogden to Lucin, Utah. Differing from all other sides of the lake, the E shore area, the base of Wasatch Mts., is wellwatered, agricultural, and well populated. Salt Lake City on SE shore, at mouth of Jordan R.; city of Ogden and other small cities near E shore. Channels drain excess water to Newfoundland Evaporation Channel c.25 mi/40 km to W in Great Salt L. Desert, once part of the prehistoric L. Bonneville. Actual shape and size of lake bears little resemblance to that shown on most maps. Several salt evaporation ponds, especially in S part of lake. Series of dikes in NE traps freshwater from inflowing rivers for human use and waterfowl management.

Great Salt Lake Desert, arid region in NW Utah, primarily in Tooele and Box Elder cos., just W of Great Salt L. in Great Basin, extending c.110 mi/177 km S from Grouse Creek Mts. and bordering on Nev. (W). Long an obstacle to W migration, now crossed by 1 highway (I-80) and 1 RR. Bonneville Salt Flats, extremely level stretch in W near Nev. state line, is known as Bonneville Speedway, site of automobile world speed records, set on the 10 mi/16 km circular track. Desert, along with Great Salt L. and Utah L., were once part of prehistoric L. Bonneville. Newfoundland Evaporation Basin in N captures flood overflow from Great Salt L.

Great Salt Plains Lake, reservoir, Alfalfa co., N Okla., on Salt Fork of the Arkansas R., in Great Salt Plains Natl. Wildlife Refuge, 23 mi/37 km NW of Enid; 10 mi/16 km wide, with 10-mi/16-km NW reach; 38°44′N 98°07′W. Formed by Great Salt Plains Dam, built (1936) by U.S. govt. for flood control. Great Salt Plains State Park on NE shore.

Great Saltpeter Caves, Ky.: see MOUNT VERNON.

Great Sand Dunes National Monument (□ 60 sq mi/156 sq km), Almosa and Saguache cos., S Colo. Entrance on S, 20 mi/32 km NE of Alamosa. Drained in S by Medano Creek, bounds Rio Grande Natl. Forest on E. Large, high sand dunes accumulated at the foot of the Sangre de Cristo Mts. over 15,000 years. Among highest dunes in U.S.; some dunes are over 700 ft/213 m high. Tours and a visitors center. Authorized 1932.

Great Sandy Desert, arid region, S Oregon, extending roughly NW-SE, from SE of Bend to Steens Mt.; 150 mi/241 km long, 30 mi/48 km–50 mi/80 km wide. S of Malheur L., occupies parts of L. and Harney cos. Area largely volcanic, on foundation of porous mantle rock into which surface waters disappear. Grazing in E near Harney and Malheur lakes. Desert punctuated with numerous buttes, peaks, alkali lakes, and dry lake beds.

Great Sitkin Island, Andreanof Isls., Aleutian Isls., SW Alaska, 20 mi/32 km NE of Adak Isl.; 12 mi/19 km long, 8 mi/12.9 km wide; 52°03′N 176°07′W. Active volcano in center.

Great Slave Lake, 2d-largest lake of Canada (□ c.10,980 sq mi/28,400 sq km), Fort Smith region, N.W.T., named for the Slave (Dogrib), a tribe of Native Americans; c.300 mi/480 km long, 12 mi/19 km–68 mi/109 km wide, 2,015 ft/614 m deep (it is the deepest lake of N. Amer.). The Hay and Slave rivers are its chief tributaries; it is drained by the Mackenzie R. The W shores are wooded, but the long E and N arms reach into tundralike country. Samuel Hearne, a British fur trader, explored the lake in 1771. Gold was discovered in the 1930s on the N shore, and the town of Yellowknife was established as a mining center. The area is still important for gold mining; lead and zinc are found near Pine Point on the S shore. The lake has commercial fisheries. Fort Providence, Hay R., and Fort Resolution are the chief towns on the lake.

Great Slave River, Canada: see SLAVE, river.

Great Smoky Mountains, part of the Appalachian system, on the N.C.-Tenn. border; highest range E of the Mississippi and one of the oldest uplands on earth; 35°35′N 83°30′W. The mountains are named for the smokelike haze that envelops them. More than 25 peaks rise over 6,000 ft/1,829 m. Mt. Chapman (6,417 ft/1,956 m), Clingmans Dome (6,642 ft/2,024 m), and Mt. Guyot (6,621 ft/2,018 m), the highest points in Tennessee, were named after geologists T.L. Clingman and Arnold Guyot, who explored the mountains in the late 1800s. The Great Smokies are noted for their many species of trees and a great variety of flowering plants. Nearly 40% of the forest is virgin growth. Black bears are among the most well known of the many animals and birds in the Great Smokies. Although the region's coves and valleys have been settled since pioneer times, they remained isolated and inaccessible until the 20th cent., when loggers began harvesting the virgin forest and significant tourism led to development of the area, such as the construction of scenic auto and hiking roads and routes. Increased industrialization in the surrounding states and acid rain have caused vegetation damage and resulted in environmental protection and awareness efforts. Great Smoky Mountains Natl. Park (520,269 acres/210,545 ha; est. 1930) straddles the crest of the Great Smokies for 71 mi/114 km. The park includes c.600 mi/965 km of trails (the Appalachian Trail follows the crest) and many streams and waterfalls. Former farmsteads with log cabins and barns and a grist mill have been preserved. Several museums.

Great Snow Mountain (9,500 ft/2,896 m), N central B.C., Canada, in Rocky Mts.; 57°27′N 124°01′W.

Great Sound, sheltered lagoon, W Bermuda; 6 mi/9.7 km long, 4 mi/6.4 km wide. Its brilliantly clear waters are dotted with small islets. Hamilton is on E shore.

Great Sound, S N.J., inlet of the Atlantic, just E of Cape May Court House; c.4 mi/6.4 km long. Sheltered from ocean by Seven Mile Beach isl., site of Avalon and Stone Harbor resort boroughs. Crossed by Intracoastal Waterway channel.

Great South Bay, arm of the Atlantic Ocean, c.45 mi/72 km long, bet. the S shore of L.I. and offshore barrier islands, SE N.Y.; 40°40′N 73°10′W. With the rapid pop. growth along its shores, the shallow bay has suffered accelerated deposition, pollution, and rampant growth of eel grass. Environmental efforts have sought to eliminate these problems. Major recreation areas on the bay include Jones Beach State Park and Fire Isl. Natl. Seashore.

Great South Beach, SE N.Y., extends along Atlantic (S) shore of Fire Isl.; 40°38′N 73°00′W. Extends from Robert Moses State Park 35 mi/56 km NE to dredged inlet to Moriches Bay. Part of Fire Isl. Natl. Seashore.

Great Stone Face, N.H.: see CANNON MOUNTAIN.

Great Thatch Island, uninhabited islet, Br. Virgin Isls., just W of Tortola and just N of St. John; 18°23′N 64°43′W.

Great Trading and War Path, major Native Amer. trading route, down the Shenandoah Valley to the New and Holston rivers in Tenn., then S on Coosa River to Ala., where it linked to the Creek Paths, regional trade routes of the tribes in the SE. Branches through the Cumberland Gap and Boone's Gap. Developed from old buffalo paths. From 1770s provided established routes for colonial emigrants moving SW from Pa. and Va.

Great Valley, village (1990 pop. 250), Cattaraugus co., W N.Y., 6 mi/9.7 km NE of Salamanca; 42°12′N 78°39′W. Wood prods., lumber.

Great Valley, Calif.: see CENTRAL VALLEY, valley.

Great Village, central N.S., Canada, near Cobequid Bay, 16 mi/26 km W of Truro; 45°25′N 63°36′W. Dairying, mixed farming.

Great Wass Island, Wash. co., E Maine, off Jonesport; 5 mi/8 km long, ½ mi/⁸⁄₁₀ km–1.5 mi/2.4 km wide.

Great Western Reservoir, Jefferson co., N central Colo., on Walnut Creek, 14 mi/23 km NNW of Denver; 1 mi/1.6 km long; 39°54′N 105°08′W. Formed by North Walnut Creek Dam (33 ft/10 m high), built (1974) by the U.S. Atomic Energy Commission for debris control. Rocky Flats Plant, U.S. Dept. of Energy, is 2 mi/3.2 km W.

Great Whale River, 365 mi/587 km long, N Que., Canada; rises E of L. Bienville, flows W, through L. Bienville, to Hudson Bay. At its mouth is Great Whale R. (55°17′N 77°47′W), Hudson's Bay Company trading post.

Great Works, Maine: see OLD TOWN.

Great Works River, c.27 mi/43 km long, SW Maine, rises in central York co., flows generally S to Salmon Falls R. 8 mi/12.9 km below Berwick.

Greater Antilles: see WEST INDIES.

Greeley 1 county (□ 783 sq mi/2,028 sq km; 1990 pop. 1,774), W Kansas; ⊙ Tribune; 38°28′N 101°47′W. Located in Smokey Hill R. valley, bordering W on Colo. Drained by White Women Creek. Agr. (cattle; wheat, corn, sorghum). One of 4 Kansas cos. in Mountain time zone; Mountain/Central time zone boundary on E. Formed 1887. **2** county (□ 570 sq mi/1,476 sq km; 1990 pop. 3,006), E central Nebr.; ⊙ Greeley; 41°33′N 98°31′W. Agr. area drained by Cedar and North Loup rivers. Cattle, hogs; dairying; soybeans, corn, alfalfa, dairy prods. Chalkmine State Wayside Area in SW corner. Formed 1872.

Greeley, city (1990 pop. 60,536), ⊙ Weld co., N Colo., 50 mi/80 km NNE of Denver, at the base of the Front Range of the Rocky Mts.; 40°25′N 104°44′W. Elev. 4,664 ft/1,422 m. Near confluence of South Platte and Cache La Powder rivers. Cattle, horses, fruit and vegetables, beans, sugar beets, sunflowers, wheat, corn. It is a growing RR, trade, and processing center for a rich irrigated farm area. Mfg. (bridges, food, apparel, printing and publishing, chemicals, software). Greeley was founded (1870) by Horace Greeley through his agent, Nathan C. Meeker, as an irrigated cooperative farm and temperance colony. Meeker was killed in the Ute uprising of 1879; his home is a mus. The city has Aims Community Col. and the Univ. of Northern Colo. It has a symphony orchestra, a theater, and an art gallery. Greeley also holds an annual rodeo. Pawnee Natl. Grassland to NE. Inc. 1885.

Greeley 1 village (1990 pop. 339), Anderson co., E Kansas, on Pottawatomie Creek, 10 mi/16 km NE of Garnett; 38°22′N 95°07′W. Livestock; grain; dairying. Mfg. (fabricated metal prods.). **2** village (1990 pop. 562), ⊙ Greeley co., E central Nebr., 45 mi/72 km NNW of Grand Isl; 41°32′N 98°31′W. Beef cattle, dairy prods.

Greeleyville, village (1990 pop. 464), Williamsburg co., E central S.C., 11 mi/18 km WSW of Kingstree; 33°34′N 79°59′W. Mfg. includes apparel; agr. includes livestock; grain, cotton, soybeans. Formerly spelled Greelyville.

Greelyville, S.C.: see GREELEYVILLE.

Green 1 county (□ 288 sq mi/746 sq km; 1990 pop. 10,371), central Ky.; ⊙ Greensburg; 37°15′N 85°32′W. Drained by Green and Little Barren rivers and Russell and Big Pitman creeks. Rolling agr. area (burley tobacco, hay, alfalfa, soybeans, wheat, corn; hogs, cattle, poultry; dairying); cedar timber. Mfg. at Greensburg. Formed 1792. **2** county (□ 584 mi/940 km; 1990 pop. 30,339), S Wis.; ⊙ Monroe; 42°40′N 89°35′W. Generally hilly area, bounded S by Ill. line. Dairying region, with mfg. (cheese, wood prods., feed, hardware); agr. (barley, oats, wheat, corn, soybeans, beans, alfalfa, hay; hogs, sheep, poultry). Drained by Sugar and Pecatonica rivers; includes New Glarus Woods State Park; Sugar R. State Trail crosses co. from E to N; Browntown-Cadiz State Recreation Area (forms Cadiz Springs State Park in SW). Formed 1836.

Green, village (1990 pop. 150), Clay co., N Kansas, 7 mi/11.3 km ENE of Clay Center; 39°25′N 97°00′W. In livestock and grain region.

Green, river, 730 mi/1,175 km long; rising in the Green R. Lakes near the Continental Divide, Sublette co., W Wyo., and flowing generally S through W Wyo., NW Colo., and E Utah to the Colorado R. in Canyonlands Natl. Park, SE Utah. It is the largest tributary of the Colorado. Most of its course flows through deep canyons, including Canyon of the Lodore in Dinosaur Natl. Monument. The White, Yampa, and San Rafael rivers are its main tributaries. The Colorado R. storage project of the U.S. Bureau of Reclamation has extensively developed the Green R. basin for irrigation, mining, and hydroelectric power; Flaming Gorge Reservoir (Utah/Wyo.) is the major unit in this project (surrounded by Flaming Gorge Natl. Recreation Area). Fontenelle Reservoir, formed in W Wyo., is the only other project unit on the Green.

Green Bay, city (1990 pop. 96,466), ⊙ Brown co., NE Wis., 90 mi/145 km N of Milwaukee, at the mouth of the Fox R. on Green Bay, L. Michigan; 44°31′N 87°59′W. A metropolitan area and important Great Lakes harbor, Green Bay is a port of entry, with heavy shipping and a large wholesale and jobbing trade. Mfg. (food, printing and paper prods., sheet metal processing, dairy processing, motor vehicle parts, fabricated metal prods., machinery, medical prods., lumber, furniture, paints). Jean Nicolet established a trading post on the site of Green Bay in 1634; many notable Fr. explorers and missionaries followed. The permanent settlement, the oldest in the state, dates from 1701. The key to the Fox-Wisconsin water route and thus an entry to the Midwest, Green Bay became a fur-trading center and was occupied successively by the French (1717), the British (1761), and the Americans (1816). With the settlement of the Old Northwest after the War of 1812 and the decline of the fur trade, Green Bay became the trade center of a lumber and farm area. Austin Straubel Airport to SW. Of interest are the Natl. RR Mus. and many historical bldgs., including the Tank Cottage (1776). A branch of the Univ. of Wis. and a technical col. are in the city, which is also the home of the Green Bay Packers (Lambeau Field stadium) professional football team. Inc. 1854.

Green Bay, W arm of L. Michigan, NE Wis. and NW Mich., c.100 mi/161 km long and from 10 mi/16 km–20 mi/32 km wide; separated from the lake by the Door and Garden peninsulas. The Fox R. flows into the head of the bay at the port city of Green Bay, Wis. A natl. and a state forest lie along a portion of the N shore.

Green Camp, village (1990 pop. 393), Marion co., central Ohio, 5 mi/8 km SW of Marion, on Scioto R.; 40°32′N 83°12′W.

Green Castle, city (1990 pop. 254), Sullivan co., N Mo., 16 mi/26 km WNW of Kirksville. Corn, soybeans; cattle, sheep. Platted 1857.

Green Cay, islet, S central Bahama Isls., E of Andros Isl., 75 mi/121 km S of Nassau; 24°01′N 77°20′W.

Green City, city (1990 pop. 671), Sullivan co., N Mo., 20 mi/32 km WNW of Kirksville; 40°16′N 92°57′W. Corn, soybeans; sheep, cattle. Platted 1880.

Green Cove Springs, town (□ 9 sq mi/23.3 sq km; 1990 pop. 4,497), ⊙ Clay co., NE Fla., on St. Johns R., 23 mi/37 km S of Jacksonville; 29°59′N 81°40′W. Trade center and resort with mineral springs, in stock-raising, farming, and lumbering area. Settled 1830.

Green Forest, town (1990 pop. 2,050), Carroll co., NW Ark., 20 mi/32 km WNW of Harrison, in the Ozarks; 36°20′N 93°25′W. Mfg. (fabricated metal prods., poultry processing).

Green Harbor, Mass.: see MARSHFIELD.

Green Hill, village, Maury co., central Tenn., 10 mi/16 km N of McMinnville.

Green Hills, borough (1990 pop. 21), Berks co., SE central Pa., 5 mi/8 km S of Reading, residential community on Green Hills L. reservoir; 40°07′N 80°18′W.

Green Island, town (1991 pop. 1,591), Hanover parish, W Jamaica, 24 mi/39 km WSW of Montego Bay; 18°23′N 78°17′W. Banana port. Tiny Green Isl. is just off coast.

Green Island, town (1990 pop. 54), Jackson co., E Iowa, 24 mi/39 km NNW of Clinton; 42°08′N 90°19′W. In agr. area.

Green Island, village and town (1990 pop. 2,490), Albany co., E N.Y., on Green Isl. (2 mi/3.2 km long) in the Hudson, bet. Troy and Watervliet (bridges to both cities); 42°45′N 41°73′W. Food prods., machinery. Inc. 1869.

Green Island, island in Knox co., S Maine, in entrance to Penobscot Bay and just SW of Vinalhaven Isl., 1.5 mi/2.4 km long.

Green Island, Canada: see VERTE, ÎLE.

Green Isle, village (1990 pop. 239), Sibley co., S Minn., 40 mi/64 km SW of Minneapolis; 44°40′N 94°00′W. Agr. area (grain, soybeans; livestock; dairying). Washington L. to E, Silver L. to S.

Green Lake, county (□ 380 sq mi/984 sq km; 1990 pop. 18,651), central Wis.; ⊙ Green Lake; 43°48′N 89°02′W. Predominantly farming area (vegetables, wheat, corn, soybeans, peas; hogs, poultry, sheep); mfg. in Berlin (canneries, creameries); fur farms. Drained by Fox and Grand rivers. Includes Green L. and L. Puckaway in center of co. (resorts). Formed 1858.

Green Lake, town (1990 pop. 1,064), ⊙ Green Lake co., central Wis., at E end of Green L., 26 mi/42 km W of Fond du Lac; 43°50′N 88°57′W. Boats, textiles; summer resort.

Green Lake 1 in Hancock co., S Maine, 6 mi/9.7 km NW of Ellsworth, 6 mi/9.7 km long. In hunting, fishing area. **2** in Grand Traverse co., NW Mich., just S of Interlochen, in resort area, c.3 mi/4.8 km long, 1 mi/1.6 km wide; 44°36′N 85°47′W. Joined by passage to Duck L. (E). Interlochen State Park and Center for the Arts on E shore. **3** Kandiyohi co., SW central Minn., 10 mi/16 km NE of Willmar; 4 mi/6.4 km wide. Elev. 1,155 ft/352 m. Drained E by Middle Fork of Crow R. Town of Spicer at SW end. **4** Calhoun co., SE Texas, 20 mi/32 km SSE of Victoria, in marshy coastal region just N of San Antonio Bay; c.3 mi/4.8 km long; 28°32′N 96°49′W. Drains SE into bay; Guadelupe R. immediately SW. **5** in Green Lake co., central Wis., 25 mi/40 km W of Fond du Lac; c.8 mi/12.9 km long, 2 mi/3.2 km wide. Summer homes on shores. Town of Green Lake on E end.

Green Lane, borough (1990 pop. 442), Montgomery co., SE Pa., 29 mi/47 km NW of Philadelphia, on Perkiomen Creek, which forms Green Lane Reservoir to NW. Agr. (grain; livestock; dairying); mfg. (wire prods., plastic molding).

Green Mountain Dam, Colo.: see BLUE RIVER.

Green Mountain Falls, village (1990 pop. 663), El Paso and Teller cos., central Colo., on Fountain Creek, 10 mi/16 km NW of Colorado Springs; 38°55′N 105°01′W. Elev. c.7,694 ft/2,345 m. Pikes Peak to S. Nearby cascades are of scenic interest. Surrounded by Pike Natl. Forest.

Green Mountains, range of the Appalachian Mts., extending 250 mi/402 km from N to S and extending from S Que. (Canada), to Vt. Mt. Mansfield (4,393 ft/1,339 m), in Vt., is the tallest peak. The range has low, rounded peaks, fertile valleys, and streams. Timber and maple syrup are the main prods. of the heavily forested mts., much of whose area is in natl. and state forests. The mts. also yield high-quality talc, asbestos, and granite, with world-famous quarries in Barre, Vt. The scenic Green Mts. are a year-round vacation area, well known for ski resorts. The Long Trail for hikers runs 261 mi/420 km from Mass. to Canada; the Appalachian Trail runs through the S part of the Green Mts.

Green Oaks, village (1990 pop. 2,101), Lake co., NE Ill., residential suburb 33 mi/53 km NNW of Chicago, 7 mi/11.3 km SW of Waukegan, near Des Plaines R.; 42°17′N 87°54′W.

Green Park, village, St. Louis co., E. Mo., residential suburb 9 mi/14.5 km SSW of St. Louis. Inc. 1995.

Green Peter Lake, reservoir, Linn co., W central Ore., on Middle Santiam R., 30 mi/48 km ESE of Corvallis; c.10 mi/16 km long; 44°24′N 122°42′W. Max. capacity 430,000 acre-ft. Quartzville Creek forms 3-mi/4.8-km N arm. Formed by Green Peter Dam (319 ft/97 m high), built by the Army Corps of Engineers (1967) for flood control, power generation, and irrigation.

Green Pond, village, Colleton co., S S.C., 12 mi/19 km S of Walterboro. Mfg. of chemicals; agr. includes livestock; grain.

Green Ridge 1 town (1990 pop. 452), Pettis co., central Mo., 11 mi/18 km SW of Sedalia; 38°37′N 93°24′W. Cattle; wheat, corn, hay, sorghum. **2** uninc. town (1990 pop. c. 4,000), Delaware co., SE Pa., residential suburb 13 mi/21 km SW of Philadelphia and 3 mi/4.8 km NW of Chester; 39°52′N 75°24′W. Tank farms in area.

Cross references are shown in SMALL CAPITALS. The pronunciation key is on page xv. The dates of population figures are on page xii.

Green Ridge State Forest, Md.: see FLINTSTONE.

Green River, city (1990 pop. 12,711), ⊙ Sweetwater co., SW Wyo., on Green R., near mouth of Bitter Creek and just above headwaters of Flaming Gorge Reservoir, 13 mi/21 km WSW of Rock Springs; 41°31′N 109°28′W. Elev. c.6,100 ft/1,859 m. RR center; shipping center for sheep and cattle in forest and agr. area. Mfg. (printing and publishing, consumer goods, bldg. materials). Trona mining, source of soda ash. Starting point of John Wesley Powell expedition (1869). Flaming Gorge Natl. Recreation Area to S (visitors' center in town). Developed with arrival of RR. Founded 1868 near Overland stage route; inc. 1891.

Green River, town (1990 pop. 866), Emery co., E Utah, 55 mi/89 km SE of Price, on Green R.; 38°58′N 110°05′W. Elev. 4,079 ft/1,243 m. Service center for trips on Green and Colorado rivers. Green R. State Park to S; part of Uintah and Ouray Indian Reservation to NE. Arches Natl. Park to SE; Goblin Valley State Park to SW. John Wesley Powell R. History Mus. here. Settled 1878.

Green River 1 c.110 mi/177 km long, in N and NW Ill.; rises NW of Shabbona, flows generally WSW past Amboy, to Rock R. E of Moline; 41°51′N 89°05′W. **2** c.30 mi/48 km long, in Vt. and Mass.; rises on E slope of Green Mts. in Windham co., SE Vt., flows SSE to Deerfield R. just S of Greenfield, Mass. **3** 60 mi/97 km long, W Wash.; rises in Cascade Range c.25 mi/40 km NE of Mt. Rainier, in SE King co., flows NW through Howard Hanson Reservoir to within 1 mi/1.6 km of White R., past Auburn, through Kent and Tukwila, in S suburbs of Seattle. Changes name to Duwamish R. N of Tukwila. **4** 370 mi/595 km long, in Ky. and Ind.; rises in central Lincoln co., Ky., flows SW past Liberty, then W through Green River L. reservoir, past Greensbury and Munfordville in central Ky., through Mammoth Cave Natl. Park, then NW past Morgantown and Calhoun to the Ohio R., 5 mi/8 km S of Evansville, Ind.

Green River Lake, reservoir, Taylor and Adair cos., central Ky., on Green R., 8 mi/12.9 km S of Campbellsville; c.10 mi/16 km long; 37°13′N 85°21′W. Max. capacity 723,200 acre-ft. NE arm (7 mi/11.3 km long) part of Robinson Creek. Formed by Green R. Dam (120 ft/37 m high), built (1969) by the Army Corps of Engineers for flood control.

Green Rock, city (1990 pop. 2,615), Henry co., NW Ill., suburb 7 mi/11.3 km ESE of Moline, on Rock R.; 41°28′N 90°21′W. Hennepin Canal crosses town.

Green Springs, village (1990 pop. 1,446), on Seneca-Sandusky co. line, N Ohio, 8 mi/13 km SSE of Fremont, on small Green Creek; 41°15′N 83°03′W. Health resort, with mineral springs.

Green Springs, natl. historic landmark district (☐ 8 sq mi/20.7 sq km), Louisa co., central Va., c.40 mi/64 km NW of Richmond; 38°05′N 78°06′W. Rural manor houses are a Natl. Historic Landmark. Affiliated area of natl. park system, authorized 1974.

Green Tree, borough (1990 pop. 4,905), Allegheny co., SW Pa., residential suburb 3 mi/4.8 km WSW of Pittsburgh, near Ohio R. Fort Pitt Tunnel (Interstate Highway 279) to NE. Inc. 1885.

Green Turtle Cay, islet and town, N Bahama Isls., just off NE Great Abaco Isl., 35 mi/56 km NW of Hope Town, 125 mi/201 km N of Nassau; 26°50′N 77°23′W. Fishing, some fruit growing (pineapples). Town is sometimes called New Plymouth.

Green Valley, uninc. city (1990 pop. 13, 231), Pima co., S Ariz., suburb 20 mi/32 km S of Tucson, on Santa Cruz R. Mostly a retirement community. Agr. (cattle; cotton); mfg. (metalworking machinery, printing and publishing). Part of Coronado Natl. Forest to SE, including Bog Springs and Smithsonian Astrophysical Observatory at Mt. Hopkins. Mt. Wrightson (9,453 ft/2,881 m) to E of observatory.

Green Valley, village (1990 pop. 745), Tazewell co., central Ill., 10 mi/16 km S of Pekin; 40°24′N 89°38′W. In agr. area.

Greenacres, city (☐ 4 sq mi/10.4 sq km; 1990 pop. 18,683), Palm Beach co., SE Fla., 8 mi/12.9 km SSW of West Palm Beach; 26°37′N 80°08′W.

Greenacres 1 uninc. town (1990 pop. 7,379), Kern co., S central Calif., residential suburb 4 mi/6.4 km W of Bakersfield, near Kern R.; 35°23′N 119°08′W. Irrigated agr. area (cotton, grain, fruit, nuts, vegetables, sugar beets, beans; dairying; cattle). **2** uninc. town (1990 pop. 4,625), Spokane co., E Wash., suburb 11 mi/18 km E of Spokane, on Spokane R., 5 mi/8 km W of Idaho state line. Mfg. (gypsum and lime prods., metal fabrication). Liberty L. to SE.

Greenawalds, uninc. town (1990 pop. 1,110), Lehigh co., E Pa., residential suburb 3 mi/4.8 km NW of Allentown, near Jordan Creek; 40°37′N 75°31′W.

Greenbank, uninc. town (1990 pop. 800), Island co., NW Wash., 13 mi/21 km S of Oak Harbor, on E side of Whidbey Isl., on Saratoga Passage, at entrance to Holmes Harbor bay; main channel of Puget Sound 1.5 mi/2.4 km to W. L. Hancock Military Firing Range to NW; South Whidbey State Park to SW.

Greenbelt, city (1990 pop. 21,096), Prince Georges co., W central Md., residential suburb of Washington, D.C.; 38°59′N 76°54′W. Greenbelt was planned and built by the federal govt. in the 1930s as an experimental model community for families whose annual income did not exceed $1,250. A total of 3,000 people were originally accommodated in "superblocks," which vehicles were prohibited from entering, and which were connected by pedestrian walks. During World War II, housing for another 4,000—without income restrictions—was built. The huge (☐ c.10,000 acres/4,047 ha) Natl. Agr. Center surounds the city on 2 sides, and NASA's Goddard Space Flight Center is nearby. Chartered 1937.

Greenbelt Park (☐ 1 sq mi/2.6 sq km), Prince George's co., central Md., SW of Greenbelt city. Authorized 1950.

Greenbrier, county (☐ 1,024 sq mi/2,652 sq km; 1990 pop. 34,693), SE W.Va.; ⊙ Lewisburg; 37°57′N 80°27′W. Bounded E by Va.; partly on Allegheny Plateau, with Allegheny Mts. along SE border, Grassy Knob and other summits are in NW; drained by Greenbrier and Meadow rivers. Mfg. at Ronceverte and Lewisburg. Coal mining, limestone quarrying. Agr. (honey, corn, oats, tobacco, potatoes, alfalfa, hay, apples, nursery crops); livestock; dairying. Resort region, with mineral springs (notably White Sulphur Springs resort in SE); parts of Monongahela Natl. Forest in N and E; includes Blue Bend Recreation Area in E; Lost World Caverns and Organ Caverns in S; Greenbrier State Forest in SE; Beartown State Park on NE border; Meadow R. Wildlife Management Area in W; S part of Greenbrier R. Trail in E center. Formed 1778.

Greenbrier 1 town (1990 pop. 2,130), Faulkner co., central Ark., 10 mi/16 km N of Conway; 35°13′N 92°22′W. Light mfg. Woolly Hollow State Park to NE. **2** (GREEN-brei-ur), town (1990 pop. 2,873), Robertson co., N Tenn., 18 mi/29 km N of Nashville; 36°25′N 86°47′W. In tobacco-growing region.

Greenbrier River, c.165 mi/266 km long, E W.Va., formed by junction of West Fork and East Fork (both c.15 mi/24 km long), just S of Durbin, in NE Pocahontas co.; flows generally SSW, past Marlinton, Ronceverte, and Alderson, to New R., just S of Hinton. Greenbrier R. Trail follows river's central course.

Greenbush 1 town (1990 pop. 1,309), Penobscot co., S central Maine, on the Penobscot, 20 mi/32 km N of Bangor; 45°04′N 68°35′W. Hunting, fishing area. Includes Olamon village. **2** town (1990 pop. 800), Roseau co., NW Minn., 22 mi/35 km SW of Roseau, on South Branch of Two Rivers, near its source; 48°42′N 96°10′W. Poultry, cattle, sheep; grain, sunflowers, alfalfa; dairying; timber; mfg. (feeds, wood furniture). Twin Lakes Wildlife Area to SW.

Greenbush, Mass.: see SCITUATE.

Greencastle, city (1990 pop. 8,984), ⊙ Putnam co., W central Ind., near Big Walnut Creek., c.40 mi/64 km WSW of Indianapolis; 39°38′N 86°50′W. RR, trade, and distribution center for livestock, grain, and dairy area; lumber, pulverized limestone; mfg. (motor vehicle parts, metal prods., dairy prods., cement, plastic prods.). Seat of DePauw Univ.; RR junction. Ger. V-1 rocket (buzz bomb) displayed on courthouse lawn. Laid out 1822.

Greencastle, borough (1990 pop. 3,600), Franklin co., S Pa., 10 mi/16 km SSW of Chambersburg, 10 mi/16 km N of Hagerstown (Md.), near Conocbooheague Creek. Agr. area (grain, potatoes, apples; livestock; dairying); mfg. (fabricated metal prods., glassware, paper prods., motor vehicle parts, food processing, machining; steel fabrication). Greencastle Military Reservation to SE. Laid out 1784, inc. 1805.

Greendale 1 city (1990 pop. 3,881), Dearborn co., SE Ind., suburb of Lawrenceburg, near Ohio R.; 39°07′N 84°52′W. Agr. area. **2** city (1990 pop. 15,128), Milwaukee co., SE Wis., suburb 7 mi/11.3 km SW of Milwaukee; 42°56′N 88°00′W. Mfg. (sheet metal, hardware, water softeners and filters). Greendale is one of 3 original Greenbelt low-cost, planned communities built by the federal govt. in the 1930s. Inc. 1938.

Greene 1 county (☐ 659 sq mi/1,707 sq km; 1990 pop. 10,153), W Ala.; ⊙ Eutaw, 32°51′N 87°59′W. Bounded N by the Sipsey R., W by Tombigbee R., and E by Black Warrior R.; in the Black Belt. Cattle; pecans, corn, soybeans, timber, potatoes. Formed 1819. **2** county (☐ 579 sq mi/1,500 sq km; 1990 pop. 31,804), NE Ark.; ⊙ Paragould; 36°07′N 90°33′W. Bounded E by St. Francis R.; drained by Cache R.; intersected by Crowley's Ridge. Agr. (cattle, hogs; sorghum, cotton, rice, wheat, soybeans), timber; gravel. Mfg. at Paragould. Includes Crowley's Ridge State Park (recreation) in S center; L. Frierson State Park on S boundary; small part of Dave Donaldson Black R. Wildlife Management Area in NW corner. Formed 1833. **3** county (☐ 404 sq mi/1,046 sq km; 1990 pop. 11,793), NE central Ga.; ⊙ Greensboro; 33°35′N 83°10′W. Piedmont area drained by Oconee, Ogeechee, and Apalachee rivers. Agr. (cotton, corn, grain, fruit; cattle, poultry); textile mfg.; timber. Formed 1786. **4** county (☐ 546 sq mi/1,414 sq km; 1990 pop. 15,317), SW central Ill.; ⊙ Carrollton; 39°21′N 90°24′W. Bounded W by Illinois R.; drained by Macoupin and Apple creeks. Agr. (cattle, hogs; corn, wheat, soybeans, sorghum, oats, fruit; dairy prods.). Potter's clay. Mfg. (paper prods.). Formed 1821. **5** county (☐ 545 sq mi/1,412 sq km; 1990 pop. 30,410), SW Ind.; ⊙ Bloomfield; 39°02′N 86°58′W. Drained by West Fork of White R. and Eel R. Agr. area (wheat, corn, soybeans; hogs, cattle), with bituminous coal mines, timber. Mfg. at Bloomfield, Jasonville, Linton. Part of Shakamak State Park in NW corner; Greene-Sullivan State Forest on W boundary. Formed 1821. **6** county (☐ 571 sq mi/1,479 sq km; 1990 pop. 10,045), central Iowa; ⊙ Jefferson, 42°02′N 94°24′W. Prairie agr. area (hogs, cattle, poultry; corn, soybeans) drained by Raccoon R., and with bituminous coal deposits; also has sand and gravel pits. Spring L. State Park in E. Flooding in area in 1993. Formed 1851. **7** county (☐ 718 sq mi/1,860 sq km; 1990 pop. 10,220), SE Miss.; ⊙ Leakesville; 31°13′N 88°38′W. Bordered E by Ala.; drained by Leaf and Chickasawhay rivers. Agr. (cotton, corn; cattle, poultry; timber). Parts of De Soto Natl. Forest in N and SW corner. Formed 1811. **8** county (☐ 677 sq mi/1753 sq km; 1990 pop. 207,949), SW Mo.; ⊙ Springfield; 37°16′N 93°21′W. In the Ozarks; drained by James, Sac, Little Sac, and Pomme de Terre rivers. Agr. (wheat, soybeans, vegetables, peaches, apples, strawberries, grapes, tomatoes); dairying; cattle, limestone. Mfg., tourist center for SW Ozarks; Southwestern Mo. State Univ. at Springfield. Springfield is the 3d-largest city in Mo. Fantastic Caverns N of Springfield; Wilson's Creek Natl. Battlefield in S. Formed 1833. **9** county (☐ 658 sq mi/1,704 sq km; 1990 pop. 44,739), SE N.Y.; ⊙ Catskill, 42°17′N 74°07′W. Mt.-resort area, with small lakes, situated mainly in the Catskills; bounded E by the Hudson, and drained by Schoharie and Catskill creeks. Named after Amer. Revolutionary general Nathaniel Greene. Farming (hay, field and sweet corn, tomatoes, apples), dairying; some timber. Includes part of Catskill State Park. *Catskill Packet*, begun Aug. 6, 1792, is today's *Greene County News*. Mfg. of brick, leather, and paper figured in the early growth of the co. Thomas Cole, who lived in Catskill from 1836 until his death in 1848, led America's 1st native art movement, "The Hudson River School," and is intimately connected with the painted landscapes of the Catskills. From 1894–1918, Otis Elevating RR was nation's 1st RR passenger lift, which took mt. vacationers from here to the Catskills. Formed 1800. **10** county (☐ 265 sq mi/686 sq km; 1990 pop. 15,384), E central N.C.; ⊙ Snow Hill; 35°29′N 77°40′W. On coastal plain; bounded NE by Nuese R., drained by Contentnea Creek, forms part of S boundary, in SE. Agr. area (esp. tobacco, corn, wheat, oats, soybeans, hay, sweet potatoes, peanuts, cotton; chicken, turkeys, cattle, hogs), timber prods. (pine, gum). Formed 1799. **11** county (☐ 416 sq mi/1,077 sq km; 1990 pop. 136,731), SW central Ohio; ⊙ Xenia, 39°41′N 83°54′W. Intersected by Little Miami and Mad rivers and small Caesar Creek. In the Till Plains physiographic region. Agr. area (corn, soybeans; hogs, poultry); mfg. at Xenia, Yellow Springs, Fairborn (commercial printing, aircraft engines). Sand and gravel pits, mineral springs. Formed 1803. **12** county (☐ 577 sq mi/1,494 sq km; 1990 pop. 39,550), SW Pa.; ⊙ Waynesburg; 39°51′N 80°13′W. Bounded S and W by W.Va. state line, E by Monongahela R., NW by Enlow Fork of Wheeling Creek, NE corner by Tenmile Creek. Agr. (corn, hay, alfalfa; sheep, hogs, cattle; dairying); bituminous coal, gas, oil; limestone, sandstone, clay, shale, sand. Area was in dispute bet. Pa. and Va. until 1784. Ryerson Station State Park in W. Formed 1796. **13** county (☐ 617 sq mi/1,598 sq km; 1990 pop. 55,853), NE Tenn.; ⊙ Greeneville; 36°10′N 82°51′W. Bounded SE by N.C., with Bald Mts. along border (rise to 4,889 ft/1,490 m in Big Butt); drained by Nolichucky R. Includes part of Cherokee Natl. Forest. State's leading tobacco grower; other agr. includes blueberries, strawberries, corn, hay; livestock raising, dairying; lumbering (oak, pine). Limestone, natural gas, oil, and silica deposits. Mfg. at Greeneville. Formed 1783. **14** county (☐ 156 sq mi/404 sq km; 1990 pop. 10,297), N central Va.; ⊙ Stanardsville, 38°17′N 78°28′W. Bounded NW by the Blue Ridge, NE by Rapidan R. and its Conway R. branch. Diversified agr. (corn, alfalfa, hay, tobacco, fruit; cattle, hogs, sheep, poultry; dairying); timber (oak, pine). Part of Shenandoah Natl. Park, includes sects. of Appalachian Trail and Skyline Drive (both follow NW co. line) Formed 1838.

Greene 1 town (1990 pop. 1,142), Butler co., N central Iowa, on Shell Rock R., 10 mi/16 km N of Allison; 42°53′N 92°47′W. Mfg. (feed, concrete blocks). Limestone quarries, sand pits nearby. Inc. 1879. **2** town (1990 pop. 3,661), Androscoggin co., SW Maine, on the Androscoggin, 10 mi/16 km NE of Auburn; 44°11′N 70°08′W.

Greene, village (☐ 1 sq mi/2.6 sq km; 1990 pop. 1,812), Chenango co., S central N.Y., on Chenango R., 17 mi/27 km NNE of Binghamton; 42°19′N 75°46′W. In dairying area; mfg. (fabricated metal prods., construction equip., electronic equip., wire). Settled 1792, inc. 1842.

Greenevers (GREEN-ev-uhrs), village (1990 pop. 512), Duplin co., E N.C., 7 mi/11.3 km NNE of Wallace; 34°49′N 77°55′W. Tobacco, cotton, grain, sweet potatoes; livestock.

Greeneville, town (1990 pop. 13,532), ⊙ Greene co., NE Tenn., 60 mi/97 km ENE of Knoxville; 36°10′N 82°50′W. Tobacco, dairy, and cattle area. It is a leading tobacco market with significant silica deposits. Diverse mfg. includes consumer prods., food, and fabricated and machined metals. In 1785, Greeneville succeeded Jonesboro as the capital of the State of Franklin. President Andrew Johnson's home, tailor shop, and grave are preserved at a natl. historic site. In the courthouse square are monuments to Civil War soldiers. Tusculum Col. is here. Founded 1783, inc. 1875.

Greenfield 1 city (1990 pop. 7,464), Monterey co., W Calif., in Salinas valley, 30 mi/48 km SE of Salinas; 36°19′N 121°14′W. Grapes, strawberries, vegetables; grain; winery. Sierra de Salinas to W; Los Padres Natl. Forest to W. Inc. 1947. **2** city (1990 pop. 1,162), Greene co., SW central Ill., 11 mi/18 km ENE of Carrollton; 39°20′N 90°12′W. In agr. area (corn, wheat, oats, soybeans; cattle, hogs). Inc. 1837. **3** city (1990 pop. 11,657), ⊙ Hancock co., central Ind., satellite community of Indianapolis, on small Brandywine Creek, 21 mi/34 km E of Indianapolis; 39°47′N 85°46′W. Agr. area (livestock; grain, vegetables); mfg. (clothing, paper prods., concrete, fiberglass insulation). James Whitcomb Riley birthplace. Laid out 1828, inc. 1850. **4** city (1990 pop. 1,416), ⊙ Dade co., SW Mo., near Sac R., 33 mi/53 km WNW of Springfield; 37°25′N 93°50′W. Wheat, hay, soybeans; dairying; cattle; mfg. (apparel, animal feed, grass seed). Stockton L. to N. Settled 1841. **5** city (1990 pop. 5,172), Highland co., SW Ohio, 22 mi/35 km W of Chillicothe, on Paint Creek; 39°21′N 83°23′W. In agr. area; mfg. of footwear, leather prods., consumer goods. Stone quarries. Platted 1798, inc. 1841. **6** city (1990 pop. 33,403), Milwaukee co., SE Wis., suburb 6 mi/9.7 km SW of Milwaukee; 42°57′N 88°00′W. City is 6 mi/9.7 km long E-W, 1 mi/1.6 km–2 mi/3.2 km wide. Residential; mfg. (metal fabrication).

Greenfield 1 town (1990 pop. 2,074), ⊙ Adair co., SW Iowa, near Middle Nodaway R., 42 mi/68 km WSW of Des Moines; 41°18′N 94°27′W. Trade and shipping center for cattle, corn, and poultry region. Mfg. (dairy prods., food, tools, farm machinery). Settled 1841, inc. 1876. **2** town (1990 pop. 267), Penobscot co., S central Maine, 22 mi/35 km NE of Bangor; 45°01′N 68°27′W. In hunting, fishing area. **3** town (1990 pop. 18,666), ⊙ Franklin co., NW Mass., at the confluence of the Deerfield and Green rivers, near their junction with the Connecticut; 42°37′N 72°36′W. The 1st cutlery factory in the U.S. was established here in the early 1800s. Other prods. include silverware, electronic components, fabricated metal prods., and lumber. Agr. and dairy farming are also important. The town, the E terminus of the Mohawk Trail, was the site of many Native Amer. attacks until 1735. Greenfield Community Col. and a historical mus. are in the town. Asher Benjamin was born there, and several bldgs. designed by him remain. Poet's Seat Tower provides a spectacular view of the town. Settled 1686, set off from Deerfield and inc. 1753. **4** town (1990 pop. 1,450), Hennepin co., E Minn., residential suburb 22 mi/35 km WNW of Minneapolis, on Crow R. On W fringe of Minneapolis–St. Paul (Twin Cities) urban area. Agr. (dairying; livestock; grain, nursery prods.). Small lakes in area. **5** town (1990 pop. 1,519), Hillsborough co., N.H., 21 mi/34 km WSW of Manchester; 42°56′N 71°52′W. Mfg. (fabricated metal prods., medical equip., software); agr. (vegetables, corn, nursery prods., fruit; cattle, hogs, poultry; dairying). Crotched Mt. Brain Injury Rehabilitation Center in N. Greenfield State Park in center. **6** town (1990 pop. 2,105), Weakley co., NW Tenn., 22 mi/35 km SSE of Union City; 36°09′N 88°48′W.

Greenfield, village (1990 pop. 200), Blaine co., W central Okla., 8 mi/12.9 km SSE of Watonga, near North Canadian R.; 35°43′N 98°22′W. In agr. area. Inc. 1930.

Greenfield Park, city (1991 pop. 17,652), S central Que., Canada, residential suburb 4 mi/6.4 mi ESE of Montreal, near SE shore of St. Lawrence R.; 45°30′N 73°29′W.

Greenfield Park, resort village (1990 pop. 500), Ulster co., SE N.Y., in the Catskills, 5 mi/8 km W of Ellenville; 41°44′N 74°29′W.

Greenfield Village, reproduction of an early Amer. village, Dearborn, Mich., created by Henry Ford as part of the Edison Inst.; 42°18′N 83°13′W. A white-spired church, a town hall, an inn, a school, a courthouse, a general store, and other bldgs. are grouped about a typical New England village green. Many of the structures were brought from their original location; others are reconstructions. Among them are Thomas Edison's Menlo Park workshop and his Fort Myers laboratory, a William McGuffey group including a school in which classes are regularly held, Noah Webster's birthplace, Stephen Foster's home, Luther Burbank's birthplace and office, and the Wright brothers' cycle shop and home. There are also mills and craft shops that illustrate early methods of production. The village has a blacksmith shop, a cobbler's shop, and a tintype studio. Nearby is the Henry Ford Mus., which has a large collection of Americana. Est. 1933.

Greenhills, village (1990 pop. 4,393), Hamilton co., extreme SW Ohio, N suburb of Cincinnati, near Winton L.; 39°16′N 84°31′W. Est. 1938 by Federal Resettlement Administration as experimental model community; inc. as village in 1939.

Greenhorn, uninc. village, Baker co., E Oregon, 35 mi/56 km W of Baker City, in Wallowa-Whitman Natl. Forest; 44°42′N 118°30′W.

Greenhorn Mountain, peak (12,347 ft/3,763 m) in Wet Mts., Pueblo and Huerfano cos., S Colo., 22 mi/35 km NW of Walsenburg, and in San Isabel Natl. Forest.

Greenland 1 town (1990 pop. 757), Washington co., NW Ark., 4 mi/6.4 km S of Fayetteville, in the Ozarks; 36°00′N 94°10′W. **2** (GREEN-luhnd), town (1990 pop. 2,768), Rockingham co., SE N.H., 5 mi/8 km SW of Portsmouth. Bounded NW by Great Bay; drained by Winnicut R. Dairying; cattle, poultry. Mfg. (textiles, paper prods., beverages).

Greenlawn, residential village (☐ 3 sq mi/7.8 sq km; 1990 pop. 13,208), Suffolk co., SE N.Y., on N shore of W L.I., 3 mi/4.8 km E of Huntington; 40°51′N 73°22′W.

Greenleaf 1 village (1990 pop. 648), Canyon co., SW Idaho, 7 mi/11.3 km W of Caldwell, bet. Boise R. (N) and Snake R. (SW); 43°40′N 116°49′W. Irrigated farming area. Fruit, potatoes, vegetables. **2** village (1990 pop. 353), Washington co., N Kansas, 8 mi/12.9 km SSE of Washington; 39°43′N 96°58′W. RR junction. Grain, livestock; dairying. Mfg. (food).

Greenlee, county (☐ 1,848 sq mi/4,786 sq km; 1990 pop. 8,008), SE Ariz.; ⊙ Clifton; 33°11′N 109°13′W. Mt. region drained by Blue, Gila, and San Francisco rivers. Crest of Peloncillo Mts. forms part of SW boundary; Black R. forms NW boundary. Some irrigation near Duncan. Morenci is mining center. Mining (copper, silver), cattle; alfalfa, hay, wheat, barley. Part of Apache-Sitgreaves Natl. Forest covers ⅔ of co. Formed 1909. Part of Gila Box Riparian Natl. Conservation Area in SW.

Greenly Island, islet, E Que., Canada, near Lab. border, in the Gulf of St. Lawrence, at SW end of Belle Isle Strait; 51°22′N 57°12′W. Fishing settlement. Lighthouse.

Greenmount, village, Carroll co., N Md., 27 mi/43 km NNW of Baltimore.

Greenock, uninc. town (1990 pop. 2,500), Allegheny co., SW Pa., on Youghiogheny R., 4 mi/6.4 km SE of McKeesport; 40°18′N 79°48′W. Agr. (corn, hay; dairying; poultry); mfg. (plastic prods.).

Greenpoint, residential and industrial section of N Brooklyn borough of N.Y. city, SE N.Y.; 40°44′N 73°56′W. Bounded on the N by Newtown Creek, to the S by the Brooklyn-Queens Expressway, and to the W by the East R. Once a major shipbuilding and chemical and oil storage center, now there are many abandoned industrial sites here that are polluted and require cleanup. The iron-clad ship *Monitor* was built here in 1862. Pipes for the Old Croton Aqueduct were constructed here as well.

Greenport, summer recreational village (☐ 1 sq mi/2.6 sq km; 1990 pop. 2,070) in Greenport town (1990 pop. 4,101), Suffolk co., SE N.Y., on N fluke of E L.I., 20 mi/32 km NE of Riverhead; 41°06′N 72°22′W. Mfg. of textiles; boat repair; fisheries (esp. oysters). By 1840 pursuit of offshore whaling, practiced by both Native Americans and Eur. residents, had turned into a way of industry with ships leaving Cold Springs Harbor, Sag Harbor, and Greenport on 3-year whaling voyages. A terminus of L.I. RR. Greenport Village Historic Dist. Inc. 1838.

Greens Fork, town, Wayne co., E Ind., on a fork of Whitewater R., 9 mi/14.5 km NW of Richmond. In agr. area. Laid out 1818.

Greens Grant, land grant, Coos co., N central N.H., 12 mi/19 km S of Berlin, in White Mt. Natl. Forest. Drained by Peabody R. Village of Glen House is here.

Greens Peak (10,133 ft/3,089 m), Apache co., E Ariz., in White Mts., 17 mi/27 km W of Eager, on boundary of Apache-Sitgreaves Natl. Forest (NE) and Fort Apache Indian Reservation (SW).

Greensboro, city (1990 pop. 183,521), ⊙ Guilford co., N central N.C., 25 mi/40 km E of Winston-Salem;

36°04′N 79°49′W. The city has an important textile industry and foundries and is a financial, insurance, and distribution center for the region. Mfg. (motor vehicle parts, electronic and telecommunications equip., food and beverages, printing and publishing, apparel and textiles, plastic, paper, and lumber prods., steel fabrication, pharmaceuticals, crushed granite, chemicals, machinery). Among its educational institutions are the Univ. of N.C. at Greensboro, Greensboro Col., Guilford Col. (to W), N.C. Agr. and Technical State Univ., and Bennett Col. N.C. Dolley Madison, O. Henry, and Edward R. Murrow were born in Greensboro. Greensboro Historic Mus., Natl. Science Center, Zane Planetarium. Colonial Heritage Center to NW. Greensboro was settled in 1749. Inc. 1829.

Greensboro 1 town (1990 pop. 3,047), ⊙ Hale co., W Ala., 18 mi/29 km NE of Demopolis, in Black Belt cotton area. Clothing, catfish processing, plastic bottles, food processing. Settled c.1816, inc. 1823. **2** town (1990 pop. 2,860), ⊙ Greene co., NE central Ga., 29 mi/47 km SSE of Athens; 33°34′N 83°11′W. Mfg. of textiles and apparel, canvas prods., fabricated metal prods., food processing, plastics; lumber. Laid out 1786, inc. 1803. **3** town (1990 pop. 204), Henry co., E central Ind., near Big Blue R., 6 mi/9.7 km SW of New Castle; 39°53′N 85°28′W. Agr. area. **4** town (1990 pop. 1,441), Caroline co., E Md., 20 mi/32 km SW of Dover (Del.), at head of navigation on Choptank R. A 1732 act called for laying out what was originally called Choptank Bridge, then Bridgetown. It tried unsuccessfully to become the co. seat but was defeated by Denton. When resurveyed in 1791, the name was changed to Greensboro. **5** town (1990 pop. 717), Orleans co., N Vt., 26 mi/42 km S of Newport; 44°36′N 72°17′W. Dairying; winter sports. Caspian L. is resort.

Greensboro, borough (1990 pop. 307), Greene co., SW Pa., 13 mi/21 km SW of Uniontown, on Monongahela R. Agr. (corn, hay; dairying; livestock).

Greensburg 1 city (1990 pop. 9,286), ⊙ Decatur co., SE central Ind., c.45 mi/72 km SSE of Indianapolis; 39°20′N 85°29′W. Trade center for agr.; mfg. (fabricated metal prods., motor vehicle parts, consumer goods, food, livestock feed, machinery); stone quarries. Laid out 1822, inc. 1859. **2** city (1990 pop. 16,318), ⊙ Westmoreland co., SW Pa., 24 mi/39 km SE of Pittsburgh; 40°18′N 79°32′W. Located in a coal area; mfg. (concrete, chemicals, printing and publishing, machinery, fabricated metal prods.). Col. Henry Bouquet defeated (1763) Native Americans near here, opening up W Pa. for settlement. Greensburg (originally New Town) was located midway bet. Fort Ligonier and Fort Pitt. It became co. seat in 1785. Seton Hill Col. and the Univ. of Pittsburgh at Greensburg are here. Westmoreland Mus. of Art; Old Hanna's Town Historic Site to N; Hillcrest Winery to SE. Chestnut Ridge to SE. Settled c.1770, inc. as a city 1928.

Greensburg 1 town (1990 pop. 1,792), ⊙ Kiowa co., S Kansas, 30 mi/48 km W of Pratt; 37°36′N 99°17′W. Elev. 2,240 ft/683 m. In grain and livestock region; feeds. Largest hand-dug well in the world, 109 ft/33 m deep (dug in 1885). Inc. 1886. **2** town (1990 pop. 1,990), ⊙ Green co., central Ky., 37 mi/60 km SE of Elizabethtown, on Green R.; 37°15′N 85°30′W. Agr. (burley tobacco, grain); cedar timber area; mfg. (furniture, apparel, beverages, lumber). Old courthouse (1803). Green R. L. reservoir and State Park to E. Settled c.1780 as Glovers Station.

Greensburg 1 village (1990 pop. 583), ⊙ St. Helena parish, SE La., near Tickfaw R., 40 mi/64 km NE of Baton Rouge; 30°50′N 90°40′W. In agr. area (vegetables; cattle, poultry; dairying); logging; mfg. (chemicals, steel fabricating). Hosts the Forest Festival. **2** uninc. village (1990 pop. 3,306), Summit co., NE Ohio, 10 mi/16 km NNW of Canton; 40°56′N 81°26′W.

Greenspond Island, E N.F., Canada, on N side of Bonavista Bay, 45 mi/72 km W of Gander, 2 mi/3 km long, 2 mi/3 km wide; 49°04′N 53°34′W. On S shore is fishing port of Greenspond.

Greensville, county (□ 296 sq mi/767 sq km; 1990 pop. 8,853), S Va.; ⊙ Emporia; 36°40′N 77°33′W. Independent city of Emporia is separate from co. Bounded S by N.C. state line, N by Nottoway R.; drained by Meherrin R. (forms part of E boundary) and Fontaine Creek branch. Mfg. (processing of farm prods.) at Emporia; agr. (esp. peanuts; also cotton, tobacco, hay, wheat, corn, soybeans, melons, eggs; cattle, hogs, poultry); timber. Formed 1781.

Greentop, town (1990 pop. 425), Schuyler and Adair cos., N Mo., 13 mi/21 km S of Lancaster; 40°21′N 92°34′W. Corn; cattle, sheep. Settled c.1849.

Greentown 1 town (1990 pop. 2,172), Howard co., central Ind., on Wildcat Creek, 9 mi/14.5 km E of Kokomo; 40°29′N 85°58′W. In agr. area (livestock; grain). Founded 1848. **2** uninc. town (1990 pop. 1,000), Pike co., NE Pa., 18 mi/29 km ESE of Scranton; 41°19′N 75°18′W. Mfg. includes electronics; agr. includes dairying; cattle. Also a resort area. Delaware State Forest to E.

Greenup, county (□ 354 sq mi/917 sq km; 1990 pop. 36,742), extreme NE Ky.; ⊙ Greenup; 38°32′N 82°55′W. Bounded N and E by Ohio R. (Ohio state line); drained by Little Sandy R. and Tygarts Creek. E part is urbanized and part of Huntington (W.Va.)–Ashland metropolitan area. Hilly agr. area (corn, burley tobacco, apples, hay, alfalfa, soybeans; cattle); iron deposits. Some mfg. at Russell. Greendo L. State Resort Park in center; Jesse Stuart State Nature Preserve in NE center, Bennett's Mill Covered Bridge in N, Old Town Covered Bridge in S. Formed 1803.

Greenup, town (1990 pop. 1,158), ⊙ Greenup co., NE Ky., on the Ohio R., at mouth of Little Sandy R., 14 mi/23 km SSE of Portsmouth (Ohio); 38°34′N 82°49′W. In agr. area (tobacco); light mfg. Co. courthouse, built 1811. Jesse Stuart State Nature Preserve to S; Greenbo L. State Resort Park to S; Greenup Lock and Dam (Ohio R.) 5 mi/8 km to N.

Greenup, village (1990 pop. 1,616), Cumberland co., SE central Ill., 5 mi/8 km ESE of Toledo; 39°15′N 88°09′W. In fruit-growing area. Founded 1836, inc. 1855. On the historic Natl. Road.

Greenvale, residential village (1990 pop. 1,450), Nassau co., SE N.Y., on W L.I., 5 mi/8 km N of Mineola; 40°49′N 73°37′W. C.W. Post campus of L.I. Univ.

Greenview, village (1990 pop. 848), Menard co., central Ill., 8 mi/12.9 km NE of Petersburg; 40°04′N 89°44′W. Grain; livestock.

Greenville, county (□ 797 sq mi/2,064 sq km; 1990 pop. 320,167), NW S.C.; ⊙ Greenville; 34°53′N 82°22′W. Bounded N by N.C. line, W by Saluda R.; drained by Enoree and Reedy rivers. Mfg. (esp. cotton textiles; also granite, sand, and gravel) in Greenville and its surrounding mill villages; agr. includes dairying; hogs, cattle; tomatoes, corn, wheat, soybeans, sorghum, hay, peaches. Summer resort area, with part of the Blue Ridge in N. Formed 1786.

Greenville 1 city (1990 pop. 7,492), ⊙ Butler co., S Ala., 42 mi/68 km SSW of Montgomery. Mfg. of clothing, wood prods., apparel; lumber milling, machinery, fertilizer. Agr. (pecans). Settled 1819. **2** city (1990 pop. 1,167), ⊙ Meriwether co., W Ga., 18 mi/29 km E of La Grange; 33°02′N 84°43′W. Mfg. includes clothing, lumber, cotton. **3** city (1990 pop. 4,806), ⊙ Bond co., SW central Ill., on East Fork of Shoal Creek, 40 mi/64 km E of Alton; 38°53′N 89°24′W. In agr. area (corn, wheat; dairy prods.; alfalfa); clothing. Seat of Greenville Col. Settled 1815, inc. 1855. **4** city (1990 pop. 45,226), ⊙ Washington co.; 33°23′N 91°02′W, W Miss., 88 mi/142 km NW of Jackson, on L. Ferguson, a backwater arm of the Mississippi R., used as river harbor (barge and towboat construction). It is the trade, processing, and shipping center of the Mississippi-Yazoo delta, a fertile region producing soybeans, oats, corn, timber, and esp. cotton. Cattle is raised. Mfg. (food processing, asphalt, wooden prods., fabricated steel, metal, rubber, and paper prods., textiles, chemicals, apparel). Greenville Municipal Airport to NE. Stoneville Natl. Wildlife Refuge to NE; Winterville Mounds State Park and Mus. to NW; Greenville Flood Mus., commemorates 1972 flood; casinos nearby. Inc. 1886. **5** city (1990 pop. 437), SE Mo., ⊙ Wayne co., in Ozark region, on St. Francis R., 24 mi/39 km N of Poplar Bluff; 37°07′N 90°27′W. Agr.; tourism, canoeing, fishing; mfg. (wood prods.); lumber. Original town site platted 1819, but was submerged by L. Wappapello. New, planned town platted 1942. Town is surrounded by Mark Twain Natl. Forest; located on upper reach of L. Wappapello (Reservoir); Sam A. Baker State Park and Coldwater State Forest to N. **6** city (1990 pop. 44,972), ⊙ Pitt co., E N.C., 77 mi/124 km ESE of Raleigh, on the Tar R.; 35°36′N 77°22′W. RR junction. Agr. area (sweet potatoes, tobacco, cotton, peanuts, grain; chickens, cattle, hogs). Mfg. (consumer goods, printing, apparel, food, pharmaceuticals, tobacco processing, bldg. materials, fishing boats, machining). East Carolina Univ. and Pitt Community Col. are here. Pitt Greenville Airport to N. Founded 1786. **7** city (1990 pop. 12,863), ⊙ Darke co., W Ohio; 40°06′N 84°37′W. In a farm area. Gen. Anthony Wayne built (1793) a fort here. In 1795 he negotiated the Treaty of Greenville with the major Ohio tribes, who relinquished a large part of their territory. NW part of Ohio remained Indian territory; remainder of Ohio was open for settlement. A memorial marks the site of the signing of the treaty, and a famous mural depicting the event hangs in the rotunda of the state capitol. Settled 1808, inc. as a city 1900. **8** city (1990 pop. 58,282), ⊙ Greenville co., NW S.C., on the Reedy R., in the Piedmont area, near the Blue Ridge Mts., 97 mi/156 km NW of Columbia; 34°50′N 82°22′W. Trade and processing center for agr. and livestock prods.; processing and packing of farm produce; mfg. of metals, textiles and apparel, paper, rubber prods., motor vehicles, chemicals, and electronic equip. Airport to NE at Lake Forest. Textile Hall is the scene of the biennial Southern Textile Exposition. Greenville is the seat of Furman Univ., Bob Jones Univ., a 2-year branch of Clemson Univ., a technical center, and a Shriners' hosp. for disabled children. It has an art mus., a symphony orchestra, Greenville zoo, and its popular Little Theater. Tourists are attracted to a historic park in the city, as well as to the 2 state parks and Blue Ridge Mts. area nearby. Laid out 1797, inc. as a city 1907. **9** city (1990 pop. 23,071), ⊙ Hunt co., E Texas, 45 mi/72 km NE of Dallas; 33°07′N 96°05′W. RR junction in a prosperous blackland cotton region; wheat, nursery crops; dairying; cattle. Among its mfg. are electronic systems, food processing, plastic prods., and oil field equip. E Texas State Univ. is at Commerce, 14 mi/23 km NE, L. Tawakoni is 20 mi/32 km SE, State Park on S shore. Inc. 1874

Greenville 1 town (1990 pop. 1,396), Plumas co., NE Calif., 14 mi/23 km N of Quincy, in the Sierra Nevada; 40°08′N 120°57′W. Timber; cattle; alfalfa, hay; gold mining; summer resort. L. Almanor reservoir is 7 mi/11.3 km NW. Surrounded by Lassen Natl. Forest. **2** town (1990 pop. 508), Floyd co., S Ind., 11 mi/18 km NW of New Albany; 38°22′N 85°59′W. In agr. area. **3** town (1990 pop. 84), Clay co., NW Iowa, 9 mi/14.5 km S of Spencer; 43°01′N 95°09′W. Farming center. **4** town (1990 pop. 4,689), ⊙ Muhlenberg co., W Ky., 37 mi/60 km S of Owensville, 8 mi/12.9 km SSW of Central City; 37°12′N 87°10′W. Trade and processing center for bituminous coal mining, agr. (corn, tobacco; livestock), limestone and timber area; mfg. (denim jackets, wooden prods., crushed limestone, mining equip.). Muhlenberg Co. Airport to N. L. Malone Reservoir State Park to SE. Est. 1799. **5** town (1990 pop. 1,884), Piscataquis co., central Maine, at S end of Moosehead L., 25 mi/40 km NW of Dover-Foxcroft; 45°27′N 69°32′W. Hq. for hunting, fishing, camping area. Municipal airport is W of Greenville center. Big Squaw Ski Resort is c.5 mi/8 km NW. Settled 1824, inc. 1836. **6** town (1990 pop. 8,101), Montcalm co., central Mich., 27 mi/43 km NE of Grand Rapids, on Flat R.; 43°10′N 85°15′W. Potato market, apples; mfg. (appliances, machinery, printing and publishing, plastics, steel fabrication). Resort. Airport to S. Inc. as village 1867, as city 1871. **7** town (1990 pop. 2,231), Hillsboro co., S N.H., 16 mi/26 km W of Nashua; 42°45′N

71°47′W. Drained by Souhegan R. Agr. (fruit, vegetables; livestock; dairying; nursery crops); mfg. (chemicals, fabricated metal prods., plastic prods., food). Set off from Mason 1872.

Greenville 1 village (□ 1 sq mi/2.6 sq km; 1990 pop. 950), Madison co., N central Fla., c.40 mi/64 km E of Tallahassee; 30°28′N 83°38′W. Plywood mfg. **2** resort village (1990 pop. 660), Greene co., SE N.Y., in foothills of the Catskills, 21 mi/34 km SW of Albany; 42°23′N 74°00′W. **3** village (1990 pop. 8,303), Smithfield town, Providence co., R.I.; 41°53′N 71°34′W. Providence reservoir nearby. **4** uninc. village, Augusta co., NW Va., 12 mi/19 km S of Staunton, on South R.; 38°00′N 79°09′W. Mfg. (metal fabrication; lumber); agr. (apples, grain; livestock; dairying). **5** uninc. village, Outagamie co., E Wis., suburb 6 mi/9.7 km WNW of Appleton. Dairying; poultry; general farming area. Mfg. (wood and metal prods.).

Greenville, borough (1990 pop. 6,734), Mercer co., NW Pa., 14 mi/23 km NNE of Sharon, on Shenango R. RR junction. Agr. (corn, hay, potatoes; livestock; dairying); mfg. (feeds, printing and publishing, machinery, fabricated metal prods., lumber). Seat of Thiel Col. Greenville Airport to N. Settled c.1796, laid out 1798, inc. 1837.

Greenville Creek, c.40 mi/64 km long, in Ind. and SW Ohio; rises in E Ind. near Ohio line, flows NE and E into Ohio, past Greenville and Gettysburg, to Stillwater R. at Covington; 40°07′N 84°21′W.

Greenville East, uninc. town (1990 pop. 1,419), Mercer co., NW Pa., residential suburb 1 mi/1.6 km ESE of Greenville; 41°23′N 80°21′W.

Greenwald, village (1990 pop. 209), Stearns co., central Minn., 34 mi/55 km W of St. Cloud; 45°36′N 94°51′W. Poultry, cattle, sheep, hogs; dairying; grain; mfg. (livestock feed).

Greenway, village (1990 pop. 212), Clay co., extreme NE Ark., 24 mi/39 km NE of Paragould; 36°20′N 90°13′W.

Greenwich (GREN-ich), residential town (1990 pop. 58,441), Fairfield co., SW Conn., on the Mianus and Byram rivers and L.I. Sound; 41°02′N 73°36′W. This attractive suburban community is noted as the home of many N.Y. city executives. The town is located near an active and growing business community and contains many corporate hq. Greenwich was long inhabited by farmers and oystermen. In the Amer. Revolution it was plundered (1779) by the British; a house (built 1731) from which Gen. Israel Putnam supposedly made a dramatic escape is still preserved. In the late 19th cent., Greenwich began to attract artists and summer residents. Comprised of numerous villages (including Greenwich, Riverside, Glenville, Quaker Ridge, Old Greenwich, and Cos Cob), it has over 32 mi/51 km of shoreline on L.I. Sound, with many harbors, beaches, and small isls. Of interest are the Bruce Mus. and the Audubon Center. Settled 1640, inc. 1955.

Greenwich 1 village and township (1990 pop. 911), Cumberland co., SW N.J., on Cohansey Creek, 7 mi/11.3 km WSW of Bridgeton; 39°23′N 75°22′W. Canneries. Seaport in 18th cent. Monument (1908) commemorates scene of tea-burning "party," 1774. **2** village (□ 1 sq mi/2.6 sq km; 1990 pop. 1,961), Washington co., E N.Y., on Batten Kill, 14 mi/23 km E of Saratoga Springs; 43°05′N 73°30′W. In farming and dairying area; mfg. (paper mill, paper prods.). Inc. 1809. **3** (GREEN-wich), village (1990 pop. 1,442), Huron co., N Ohio, 19 mi/31 km N of Mansfield; 41°02′N 82°31′W. Inc. 1879.

Greenwich Bay, arm of Narragansett Bay, E central R.I., just S of Warwick; 2 mi/3.2 km long, 3 mi/4.8 km wide. Center of suburbanized area, with several state and municipal parks, golf courses, beaches, and public fishing areas.

Greenwich Village, residential neighborhood of lower Manhattan, N.Y. city, extending S from 14th St. to Houston St. and W from Washington Sq. to the Hudson R.; 40°44′N 74°00′W. N of the main settlement of N.Y. city in colonial times, in the 1830s it became an exclusive residential sect., described in Henry James's novel *Washington Square* (1880). An influx of foreign immigrants settled there after 1880. Around 1910, the Village gained renown as the home and workshop of artists and of freethinkers. Barns, stables, and houses along the narrow, crooked streets were converted into studios, eating places, nightclubs, theaters, and shops, and the Village acquired a reputation for bohemianism. Interesting old bldgs., many dating from the early and mid-1800s, remain, although there is an increasing number of modern apartment houses. Washington Sq. Park, with its McKim, Mead, and White–designed arch (1892), is a popular meeting place. N.Y. Univ.'s campus surrounds the park. Outdoor art exhibits are held in the Village.

Greenwood 1 county (□ 1,152 sq mi/2,984 sq km; 1990 pop. 7,847), SE Kansas; ⊙ Eureka; 37°52′N 96°13′W. Rolling to hilly area, located in Osage Questas region, drained by Fall R. Cattle; hay, wheat, soybeans. Extensive oil and natural gas fields. Falls R. L. Reservoir and State Park in SE; part of Toronto L. Reservoir (with Toronto State Park) on E boundary. Formed 1862. **2** county (□ 462 sq mi/1,197 sq km; 1990 pop. 59,567), W S.C.; ⊙ Greenwood. Bounded NE by Saluda R., dammed in SE by Buzzard Roost Dam to form L. Greenwood; 34°09′N 82°07′W. Includes part of Sumter Natl. Forest. Has considerable mfg. (chiefly textiles) and some shale, sand, and granite production. Fertile agr. land (cotton, corn, fruit, lespedeza hay, grains); dairying. Formed 1897.

Greenwood, city (1991 pop. 725), S B.C., Canada, 6 mi/10 km N of Wash. border, on Border Creek, 45 mi/72 km W of Trail; 49°05′N 118°41′W. Elev. 2493 ft./748 m. Silver, lead, zinc mining. Mother Lode Mine. Tourism.

Greenwood 1 city (1990 pop. 26,265), Johnson co., central Ind., residential suburb of Indianapolis; 39°37′N 86°07′W. Greenwood is in a retail shopping area. Mfg. includes motor vehicle parts and metal prods. Settled 1823; laid out 1864; inc. as a city 1960. **2** city (1990 pop. 18,906), ⊙ Leflore co., W central Miss., 85 mi/137 km N of Jackson, on the Yazoo R. (formed by joining of Tallahatchie and Yalobusha rivers 2 mi/3.2 km to N), in the Mississippi Delta; 33°31′N 90°11′W. RR junction. It is a retail and trade center for a productive farm region, with a major cotton market. Mfg. (musical instruments, cable and concrete, apparel, motor vehicle parts, consumer goods, metal and wood prods., agr. equip., food processing, printing and publishing). The area's original inhabitants were the Choctaws; the city and co. derive their names from a Choctaw chief and cotton planter, Greenwood Leflore. After the area was ceded to the U.S. in 1830 by the Treaty of Dancing Rabbit Creek, settlers poured in, carving vast cotton plantations out of the delta swamplands. Campus of Miss. State Univ. 7 mi/11.3 km to W. Cottonlandia Mus., and several Native Amer. burial grounds are nearby. Florewood R. Plantation State Park to W; L. Henry to W; Malmaison Waterfowl Area and Wildlife Management Area to NE. Inc. 1844. **3** city (1990 pop. 20,807), ⊙ Greenwood co., W S.C., 65 mi/105 km WNW of Columbia; 34°11′N 82°09′W. RR center with mfg. (textiles, wood prods., commercial printing, consumer goods, meat packing). A trading post was est. here in 1751, and a Revolutionary War battle was fought at nearby Old Star Fort in 1775. The 1st RR came in 1852; by 1911, 5 lines were operating through the city. Lander Univ. and Piedmont Technical Col. are in the city. L. Greenwood State Park nearby. Settled 1824, inc. as a city 1927.

Greenwood 1 town (1990 pop. 3,984), shares ⊙ functions with Fort Smith, Sebastian co., W Ark., 14 mi/23 km SSE of Fort Smith; 35°12′N 94°14′W. Dairy; poultry; mfg. (paper prods., electrical equip., plastic moldings). Fort Chaffee Military Reservation to N. **2** town (1990 pop. 2,092), Caddo parish, NW La., 14 mi/23 km WSW of Shreveport, near Texas line; 32°27′N 93°58′W. In agr. and timber area; oil and natural gas; mfg. of oil-field equip. **3** town (1990 pop. 689), Oxford co., W Maine, 10 mi/16 km NW of South Paris; 44°19′N 70°40′W. In summer-resort area. Includes Locke Mills village. Settled 1802, inc. 1816. **4** town (1990 pop. 969), Clark co., central Wis., on Black R., 50 mi/80 km WSW of Wausau; 44°46′N 90°35′W. In dairying, lumbering, and farming area. Mfg. (animal feed; dairy prods., esp. cheese). Mead L. to W.

Greenwood 1 village (1990 pop. 578), Sussex co., SW Del., 25 mi/40 km SSW of Dover near Marshyhope Creek; 38°48′N 75°35′W. Shipping point for farm prods.; fruit, vegetables; livestock; dairying; mfg. (cotton processing, furniture, plastics prods.). **2** village (1990 pop. 531), Cass co., SE Nebr., 18 mi/29 km NE of Lincoln, on Salt Creek of Platte R; 40°57′N 96°26′W.

Greenwood, Mass.: see WAKEFIELD.

Greenwood Lake, village (1990 pop. 3,208), Orange co., SE N.Y., at N end of Greenwood L., 22 mi/35 km NW of Nyack; 41°13′N 74°17′W.

Greenwood Lake, resort lake (c.7 mi/11.3 km long), in SE N.Y. and N N.J., bisected by state line, c.20 mi/32 km NW of Paterson, N.J. In mt. resort area; fishing, winter sports. Greenwood Lake village at N end.

Greenwood, Lake, reservoir (c.20 mi/32 km long), in Newberry, Laurens, and Greenwood cos., W central S.C., on Saluda R. (Newberry/Greenwood co. border), 14 mi/23 km E of Greenwood; 34°12′N 81°55′W. Reedy R. forms N arm (6 mi/9.7 km long). Formed by Buzzard Roost Dam, built for hydroelectric power. Lake Greenwood State Park on SW shore.

Greenwood Village, town (1990 pop. 7,589), Arapahoe co., N central Colo., residential suburb 10 mi/16 km SSE of downtown Denver, adjoins Denver and Cherry Hills Village on N; 39°37′N 104°54′W. Elev. 5,422 ft/1,653 m. Agr. to S and SE. Mus. of Outdoor Art here. Cherry Creek L. and State Park to NE.

Greer, county (□ 643 sq mi/1,665 sq km; 1990 pop. 6,559), SW Okla.; ⊙ Mangum; 34°55′N 99°33′W. Bounded E by North Fork of Red R. (with Altus Dam in SE); drained also by the Elm and Salt forks of Red R. Quartz Mountain State Park in E, on Altus L. Peanuts; sheep; granite, clay. Mfg. at Mangum. Originally part of Texas. Formed 1907.

Greer, city (1990 pop. 10,322), Greenville and Spartanburg cos., NW S.C.; 34°56′N 82°13′W. In a farm region notable for peach production. It has textile mills, food-processing plants, and some light mfg.

Greer, uninc. village (1990 pop. 117), Apache co., E Ariz., in White Mts., on Little Colorado R., c.50 mi/80 km SSW of Saint Johns, in Apache-Sitgreaves Natl. Forest. Elev. 8,554 ft/2,607 m. Summer and winter resort village, and recreation area; tourism. Site of oldest continually operated lodge (Molly Butler Lodge) in Ariz. Three Greer lakes used for fishing and irrigation of Springerville and Eager. Sunrise Ski Resort 17 mi/27 km WSW. Mt. Baldy (11,403 ft/3,476 m) to SSW. Originally founded by Mormon pioneers for ice cutting, lumber, and cold crops.

Greers Ferry Lake, reservoir (□ 49 sq mi/127 sq km), Cleburne and Van Buren cos., N central Ark., on Little Red R., 50 mi/80 km N of Little Rock; 35°32′N 92°00′W. Max. capacity 2,844,000 acre-ft. Extends E-W. Fed by Middle Fork of the Little Red R. Formed by Greers Ferry Dam, built (1962) by Army Corps of Engineers for power generation, recreation, and as a fish and wildlife pond.

Greeson, Lake, reservoir (□ 11 sq mi/28 sq km), Pike co., SW Ark., on Little Missouri R., 40 mi/64 km SW of Hot Springs; 34°09′N 93°43′W. Max. capacity 600,600 acre-ft. Formed by Narrows Dam (196 ft/60m high), built (1950) by Army Corps of Engineers for flood control, power generation, and recreation. Daisy St. Park on NE shore.

Gregg, county (□ 276 sq mi/715 sq km; 1990 pop. 104,948), E Texas; ⊙ Longview; 32°28′N 94°48′W. Drained by Sabine R. (forms part of E boundary). In huge E Texas oil field (discovered 1930); a leading oil-producing co. of Texas. Also natural gas, sand and gravel, clay; timber; agr. (livestock); racehorses. Longview, Kilgore, Gladewater are industrial centers. L. Cherokee reservoir on S boundary. Formed 1873.

Gregory, county (□ 1,053 sq mi/2,727 sq km; 1990 pop. 5,359), S S.Dak., on Nebr. line; ⊙ Burke; 43°12′N 99°10′W. Agr. and livestock-raising region watered by

Ponca Creek and other streams and bounded NE by Missouri R. Corn, wheat, soybeans; dairy prods.; poultry, cattle, hogs. Fort Randall Dam in SE corner. Burke Lake State Rec. Area at center. Formed 1862.

Gregory 1 town (1990 pop. 1,384), Gregory co., S S.Dak., 42 mi/68 km SSW of Chamberlain, and 8 mi/12.9 km NW of Burke; 43°13′N 99°25′W. Trading point for livestock and agr. region. Grain; livestock. **2** town (1990 pop. 2,458), San Patricio co., S Texas suburb 14 mi/23 km N of Corpus Christi, across Corpus Christi Bay; 27°55′N 97°17′W. Agr. area (cattle, cotton). Oil and natural gas. Mfg. (fabricated metal prods., chemicals).

Gregory Park, village, St. Catherine parish, S Jamaica, on Cobre R., on RR and 5 mi/8 km WNW of Kingston; 18°00′N 76°53′W.

Gregory Town, town, central Bahama Isls., on N Eleuthera Isl., 25 mi/40 km NW of Governor's Harbour, 55 mi/89 km ENE of Nassau; 25°24′N 76°35′W. Pineapples, tomatoes.

Grenada (gre-NAI-duh), republic (1991 pop. 90,691), in the Windward Isls., West Indies; 12°07′N 61°40′W. The state includes the isl. of Grenada (□ 133 sq mi/344 sq km) and the S ⅓ of the archipelago known as the Grenadines (gren-nuh-DEENZ). The ⊙ is St. George's, also main port, and commercial center. Grenada is a volcanic, mountainous isl. with crater lakes. Its economy is primarily agr., and cocoa, bananas, nutmeg, mace, and fruit are exported. Tourism is a developing industry, although it suffered during the political unrest of the late 1970s and early 1980s. The Grenadines are a group of small isls. and islets N of Grenada in the Windward Isls. They are largely uninhabitable. From its sighting by Christopher Columbus in 1498 until Fr. settlement began in 1650, the Caribs prevented European colonization on Grenada. A point of dispute bet. England and France, the isl. became permanently Br. in 1783. The Br. imported Afr. slaves and established sugar plantations. In 1967, Grenada became an associated state of Britain with full internal self-government. When complete independence was achieved in Feb. 1974, Grenada became a full member of the Commonwealth of Nations. In 1979 a successful, bloodless coup established the People's Revolutionary Govt. (PRG) under Prime Minister Maurice Bishop. Its favorable stance toward Cuba and the Soviet Union strained relations with the U.S. and other nations in the region in the early 1980s. An internal coup in Oct. 1983 resulted in the execution of Bishop and the assumption of power by the army. That same month, the U.S. invaded and occupied Grenada under the rationale of protecting U.S. students studying at the St. George's Univ. School of Medicine. A general election held in Dec. 1984 reestablished democratic govt. Since then, financial aid from the U.S. and Europe has helped boost tourism; 2 world-class resorts, La Source and Rex Grenadian, opened in 1994.

Grenada, county (□ 449 sq mi/1,163 sq km; 1990 pop. 21,555), N central Miss.; ⊙ Grenada; 33°46′N 89°47′W. Drained by Yalobusha and Skuna rivers. Agr. (soybeans, cotton, corn; cattle; dairying; timber). Camp McCain Natl. Guard base in SE. Hugh White State Park; Mamaison Wildlife Management Area and Waterfowl Area in SW. Skuna enters Yalobusha in Grenada L. reservoir in NE center. Formed 1870.

Grenada (gruh-NAID-uh), city (1990 pop. 10,864), ⊙ Grenada co.; 33°46′N 89°48′W, N central Miss., on Yalobusha R., and 28 mi/45 km NE of Greenwood. RR junction to N. In agr. (cotton, corn, soybeans; cattle; dairying; timber); light mfg. Camp McCain Natl. Guard base in SE. Grenada Lake Mus. Hugh White State Park, on Grenada L. reservoir to NE. Settled in early 1830s, inc. 1836.

Grenada Reservoir or **Grenada Dam**, Miss.: see YALOBUSHA RIVER.

Grenadier Island (5 mi/8 km long, 1 mi/2 km wide), SE Ont., Canada, one of the Thousand Isls., in the St. Lawrence, 15 mi/24 km SW of Brockville.

Grenadier Island, Jefferson co., N N.Y., in E part of L. Ontario, Canada, 5 mi/8 km SSW of Cape Vincent;

44°03′N 76°02′W. Isl. is 2.25 mi./3.6 km long, 1.25 mi/2 km wide.

Grenadines, Grenada: see WINDWARD ISLANDS.

Grenell Island, Jefferson co., N N.Y., one of the Thousand Isls., c.7 mi/11.3 km SW of Alexandria Bay; 44°17′N 76°02′W. Isl. is c.½ mi/⁹⁄₁₀ km long. Grenell village is here.

Grenfell, town (1991 pop. 1,164), SE Sask., Canada, 34 mi/55 km E of Indian Head; 50°25′N 102°55′W. Grain elevators. Resort.

Grenloch (GREN-lawk), village, Camden co., SW N.J., on Big Timber Creek and 11 mi/18 km S of Camden; mfg. of fabricated metal prods, plastic prods. Residential.

Grenola (gruh-NO-luh), village (1990 pop. 256), Elk co., SE Kansas, on Caney R. and 30 mi/48 km ENE of Winfield; 37°21′N 96°27′W. Livestock, grain.

Grenora, village (1990 pop. 261), Williams co., NW N.Dak., 36 mi/58 km NNW of Williston, near Mont. line; 48°37′N 103°56′W.

Grenville, SE Ont., Canada: see LEEDS AND GRENVILLE UNITED COUNTIES.

Grenville, town, E Grenada, West Indies, 9 mi/14.5 km NE of St. George's, on Grenville Bay; 12°07′N 61°37′W. Cacao, coconuts. Also called La Baye.

Grenville, village (1991 pop. 1,362), S Que., Canada, on Ottawa R., opposite Hawkesbury; 45°38′N 74°36′W. Mining (magnesite, feldspar, graphite), limestone quarrying.

Grenville 1 village (1990 pop. 24), Union co., NE N.Mex., on Clearquilla Creek, and 26 mi/42 km WNW of Clayton; 36°35′N 103°36′W. Shipping point for ranch and farm prods. Grenville Caves nearby; Clayton L. to E. **2** village (1990 pop. 81), Day co., NE S. Dak., 11 mi/18 km NNE of Webster, near Waubay L.; 45°28′N 97°23′W. Trade center of agr. community.

Grenville Channel (55 mi/89 km long, 1 mi/2 km wide), W B.C., Canada, separating Pitt Isl. from mainland.

Grenville, Mount (10,200 ft/3,109 m), SW B.C., Canada, 120 mi/193 km NNW of Vancouver; 50°51′N 124°16′W.

Gresham (GRESH-uhm), city (1990 pop. 68,235), Multnomah co., NW Oregon, suburb 10 mi/16 km E of downtown Portland, near Columbia R.; 45°30′N 122°26′W. Drained by Fairview and Johnson creeks. Mfg. (construction materials, electronic equip.). Nuts, berries; poultry. Mt. Hood Community Col. Site of co. fair. Dabney State Park to E.

Gresham 1 (GRE-shuhm), village (1990 pop. 253), York co., SE central Nebr., 15 mi/24 km NE of York; 41°01′N 97°24′W. Dairying, livestock, grain. **2** village (1990 pop. 515), Shawano co., E central Wis., 10 mi/16 km NW of Shawano; 44°51′N 88°47′W. Lumbering; agr.; granite and marble prods. Strockbridge Indian Reservation to NW; Menominee Indian Reservation to N and NE.

Gressier (gre-SYAI), village (1982 pop. 1,780), Ouest dept., S Haiti, on Gonâve Channel, 10 mi/16 km W of Port-au-Prince; 18°33′N 72°31′W. Sugarcane, limes; sugar processing. Fishing port.

Gretna (GRET-nuh), city (1990 pop. 17,208), SE La., on the Mississippi R.; ⊙ Jefferson parish; 29°55′N 90°03′W. Elev. 5 ft/2 m. Suburb opposite and 1 mi/2 km SSE of downtown New Orleans. Ocean and river shipping port; RR junction. Ferry and bridge connection across river. Marble and granite production; mfg. of chemicals, food, printing and publishing. La. RR mus. Founded in 1836 as Mechanicsham, Gretna merged with McDonoghville in 1913.

Gretna 1 (GRET-nuh), town (□ 1 sq mi/2.6 sq km; 1990 pop. 1,981), Gadsden co., NW Fla., 6 mi/9.7 km WNW of Quincy; 30°36′N 84°39′W. **2** town (1990 pop. 2,249), Sarpy co., E Nebr., 17 mi/27 km WSW of Omaha; 41°08′N 96°14′W. Livestock, grain, dairy prods. Light mfg. Satellite community of Omaha. **3** town (1990 pop. 1,339), Pittsylvania co., S Va., 25 mi/40 km N of Danville; 36°57′N 79°21′W. Mfg. (transportation equip., furniture, apparel, lumber); trading point in tobacco-growing area; agr. (tobacco, grain; cattle; dairying). Leesville L. reservoir to NW.

Gretna, village (1991 pop. 620), SE Man., Canada, 65 mi/

105 km SSW of Winnipeg, on N.Dak. border; 49°00′N 97°33′W. Grain elevators, flour mills.

Grey, county (□ 1,708 mi/2,749 km; 1991 pop. 84,071), S Ont., Canada, on Georgian Bay of L. Huron; ⊙ Owen Sound; 44°20′N 80°45′W.

Grey Eagle, village (1990 pop. 353), Todd co., central Minn., 12 mi/19 km SE of Long Prairie; 45°49′N 94°45′W. Lake resort region; poultry; grain, potatoes; dairying. Big Birch L. to S.

Grey Forest, village (1990 pop. 425), Bexar co., S central Texas, residential suburb 17 mi/27 km NW of downtown San Antonio; 29°36′N 98°40′W. Agr. area. Oil and natural gas.

Grey Islands, group of 2 islands off NE N.F., Canada, in the Atlantic. Largest isl. is Bell Isl. or Grey Isl. South (□ 34 sq mi/88 sq km), 50 mi/80 km N of Cape St. John; 10 mi/16 km long, 7 mi/11 km wide; 50°44′N 55°35′W. Site of lighthouse (SW) and radio station. N of Bell Isl., 7 mi/11 km, is Groais Isl. or Grey Isl. North (□ 16 sq mi/41 sq km); 7 mi/11 km long, 4 mi/6 km wide. Both isls. are hilly, rising to over 500 ft/152 m. Village of Grey Islands Harbour at Rocky Bay, S end of Bell Isl.

Greybull, town (1990 pop 1,789), Big Horn co., N Wyo., on Bighorn R., at mouth of Greybull R., just W of Bighorn Mts., and 60 mi/97 km WSW of Sheridan; 44°29′N 108°03′W. Oil-refining point in livestock and irrigated agr. region; sugar beets; beans; flour; timber; concrete. Airport; dinosaur fossil beds to E, with exhibits at town mus. To NE, Antelope Butte Ski Area and Bighorn Mts. and Natl. Forest. Inc. 1912.

Greybull River, flows c.70 mi/113 km NE, NW Wyo.; rises in S in Absaroka Range, Park co. , past Meeteetse, to Bighorn R. at Greybull.

Greylock, Mount, Mass.: see BERKSHIRE HILLS.

Greys River, c.60 mi/97 km long, W Wyo.; rises in E Lincoln co. SE of Afton, flows generally N bet. Salt R. and Wyoming ranges, makes small turn to W before entering Snake R. just E of Idaho state line at Alpine.

Gribbell Island (□ 96 sq mi/249 sq km; 16 mi/26 km long, 2 mi/3 km–10 mi/16 km wide), W B.C., Canada, in Douglas Channel (N arm of Hecate Strait) just N of Princess Royal Isl.

Gridley, city (1990 pop. 4,631), Butte co., N central Calif., in Sacramento Valley, 17 mi/27 km N of Yuba City; 39°22′N 121°42′W. Prunes, peaches, kiwi fruit, olives, almonds, walnuts, wheat, rice, beans; livestock. Feather R. to E. Inc. 1905.

Gridley 1 village (1990 pop. 1,304), McLean co., central Ill., 18 mi/29 km NNE of Bloomington; 40°44′N 88°52′W. In agr. area. **2** village (1990 pop. 356), Coffey co., SE Kansas, 10 mi/16 km SW of Burlington; 38°06′N 95°52′W. In livestock and grain region. Oil fields nearby.

Griffin, city (1990 pop. 21,347), ⊙ Spalding co., W central Ga., in an agr. and cotton area experiencing transition into metropolitan Atlanta's economy; 33°14′N 84°16′W. The city has large textile and apparel industries, now experiencing decline. Other mfg. includes leather, plastics, transportation equip., printing and publishing. Nearby is a state agr. station. Inc. 1843.

Griffin, town (1990 pop. 171), Posey co., SW Ind., near the Wabash, 18 mi/29 km N of Mount Vernon; 38°12′N 87°55′W. In agr. and petroleum area. Near the Mumford Hills. Laid out 1881.

Griffin, Lake (c.9 mi/14.5 km long, 2 mi/3.2 km wide), Lake co., central Fla., linked by canal with nearby L. Eustis, it is part of lake system drained by Oklawaha R.

Griffiss Air Force Base, N.Y.: see ROME.

Griffith, town (1990 pop. 17,916), Lake co., extreme NW Ind.; 41°31′N 87°25′W. It is primarily a residential town in the Chicago metropolitan area. Mfg. includes fabricated metal prods., chemicals, electronic equip., construction materials. Settled c.1854. Inc. 1904.

Griffith Island (11 mi/18 km long, 7 mi/11 km wide), central Franklin dist., N.W.T., Canada, in Barrow Strait, off S Cornwallis Isl.; 74°35′N 95°25′W.

Griffith Mountain (11,568 ft/3,526 m), in Front Range, Clear Creek co., N central Colo. Summit 2 mi/3.2 km E of Georgetown. Mt. overlooks historic town.

Griffithville, village (1990 pop. 237), White co., central Ark., 11 mi/18 km SSE of Searcy; 35°07′N 91°39′W.

Grifton, town (1990 pop. 2,393), Pitt co., E N.C., 17 mi/27 km S of Greenville, on Contennea Creek; 35°22′N 77°25′W. Agr. area (tobacco, corn, peanuts, grain, cattle, hogs); mfg. (apparel, lumber).

Griggs, county (□ 709 sq mi/1,836 sq km; 1990 pop. 3,303), E central N.Dak.; ⊙ Cooperstown; 47°27′N 98°13′W. Wheat-growing area drained by Sheyenne R. and Bald Hill Creek. Cattle, dairy prods., wheat, rye. N part of L. Ashtabula Reservoir in SE corner. Red Willow L. and other small lakes in NW. Formed 1881.

Griggsville, city (1990 pop. 1,218), Pike co., W Ill., 8 mi/12.9 km NNE of Pittsfield; 39°42′N 90°43′W. In agr. area (corn, wheat, cattle, hogs, poultry; dairy prods.); light mfg. Inc. 1878.

Grimes, county (□ 801 sq mi/2,075 sq km; 1990 pop. 18,828), E central Texas; ⊙ Anderson; 30°33′N 95°58′W. Bounded W by Navasota and Brazos rivers. Diversified agr. (corn, fruit; hay; honey; cattle; dairying). Timber (mainly pine), hunting, fishing. Includes game preserve. Formed 1846.

Grimes, town (1990 pop. 2,653), Polk co., central Iowa, suburb, 12 mi/19 km NW of downtown Des Moines; 41°39′N 93°47′W. Mfg (food). Living History Farm to S.

Grimesland (GREIMZ-land), village (1990 pop. 469), Pitt co., E N.C., near Tar R., 11 mi/18 km ESE of Greenville; 35°33′N 77°11′W. Tobacco, cotton, peanuts, grain, chickens, cattle, hogs. Mfg. (apparel).

Grimsby (GRIMZ-bee), town (1991 pop. 18,520), S Ont., Canada, on L. Ontario, 15 mi/24 km ESE of Hamilton; 43°12′N 79°34′W. Part of city of Grimsby. Commuter suburb of Hamilton. Mfg. (machinery, transportation equip.), fruit processing, dairying; distillery and winery; nursery; in fruit-growing region. Resort.

Grimshaw, town (1991 pop. 2,812), W Alta., near Peace R., 13 mi/21 km W of Peace R.; 56°11′N 117°36′W. Lumbering, mixed farming, dairying, wheat, barley, cattle; gravel. Estab. as a town in 1953.

Grindstone, uninc. town (1990 pop. 1,500), Jefferson township, Fayette co., SW Pa., 10 mi/16 km NNW of Uniontown, on Redstone Creek; 40°00′N 79°49′W. Agr. (corn, hay, dairying); mfg. (machinery, lumber).

Grindstone, N.Y.: see GRINDSTONE ISLAND.

Grindstone Island, Jefferson co., N N.Y., one of largest of the Thousand Isls., in the St. Lawrence, at Ont. line, just N of Clayton, N.Y.; 44°17′N 76°07′W. Isl. is c.6 mi/9.7 km long, 1–2.5 mi/1.6–4 km wide. Grindstone village (resort) and Canoe Point and Picnic Point state parks are here.

Grinnell (gri-NELL), city (1990 pop. 8,902), Poweshiek co., central Iowa, 44 mi/71 km ENE of Des Moines; 41°44′N 92°43′W. RR junction. Mfg. (machinery, apparel, transportation equip., feeds, construction materials, wood prods.). Seat of Grinnell Col. (founded 1855, coed., nonsectarian). Founded 1854 by Josiah Bushnell Grinnell, and inc. 1865.

Grinnell (grin-EL), village (1990 pop. 348), Gove co., W central Kansas, 14 mi/23 km NW of Gove; 39°07′N 100°37′W. In grain and cattle area.

Grinnell, Cape (gri-NEHL), SW Devon Isl., E Franklin dist., N.W.T., Canada, on Wellington Channel; 75°10′N 92°15′W.

Grinnell Land, NE Franklin dist., N.W.T., Canada, NE part of ELLESMERE ISLAND, bet. Grant Land (N), Greely Fjord, (W), Ellesmere Land (S), and Kennedy Channel and Kane Basin (E).

Grissom Air Base, Miami co., N central Ind., 7 mi/11.3 km SW of Peru. Weather station.

Griswold 1 town (1990 pop. 10,384), including Jewett City borough (1990 pop. 3,349), New London co.; SE Conn., on Quinebaug R., and 7 mi/11.3 km NE of Norwich; 41°34′N 71°55′W. Agr. (poultry, fruit). Mfg. includes textiles, machinery, plastics, fabricated metal prods., and rubber prods. State forest here. Settled c.1690, inc. 1815; Jewett City inc. 1895. Includes village of Glasgo. **2** town (1990 pop. 1,049), Cass co., SW Iowa, 14 mi. SSW of Atlantic; 41°13′N 95°08′W. Shipping center for corn and livestock area; light mfg. Cold Springs State Park to NE. Inc. 1880.

Griswold (GRIZ-wold), village, SW Man., Canada, near Assiniboine R., 24 mi/39 km WSW of Brandon; 49°46′N 100°28′W. Grain, livestock.

Griswoldville, Mass.: see COLRAIN.

Grizzly Mountain, Colo.: see SAWATCH MOUNTAINS.

Grizzly Peak (13,738 ft/4,187 m), Dolores and San Juan cos., SW Colo., in San Juan Mts., 10 mi/16 km ENE of Rico.

Groais Island, N.F., Canada: see GREY ISLANDS.

Groesbeck, town (1990 pop. 3,185), ⊙ Limestone co., E central Texas, near Navasota R., 36 mi/58 km E of Waco; 31°31′N 96°31′W. Elev. 477 ft/145 m. RR junction; livestock (cattle, sheep, goats), agr. (hay, wheat, cotton, peaches, vegetables); some oil and natural gas; light mfg. Fort Parker State Park and Old Fort Parker State Historic Site to N; L. Mexia to NW; L. Limestone to SE.

Groesbeck, uninc. village (1990 pop. 6,684), Hamilton co., extreme SW Ohio, a W suburb of Cincinnati; 39°13′N 84°35′W.

Grondines or **Saint Charles des Grondines** (seh shahrl dai groh-DEEN), village (1991 pop. 654), S central Que., Canada, on the St. Lawrence R., and 16 mi/26 km WSW of Donnacona; dairying; livestock.

Groom, village (1990 pop. 613), Carson co., extreme N Texas, in the Panhandle, c.40 mi/64 km E of Amarillo; 35°12′N 101°06′W. In agr. (wheat, corn; hay); cattle; mfg. (food); oil and gas. McClellan L. and McClellan Creek Natl. Grassland to E.

Gros Islet (gros EE-let), fishing village (1991 pop. 1,351), NW St. Lucia, 6 mi/9.7 km NNE of Castries; 14°03′N 60°57′W. On fertile plain (limes, tropical fruit). Tourist mooring. Opens out to Rodney Bay.

Gros Morne (gro morn), mountain (2,644 ft/806 m), W N.F., Canada, in the Long Range N of Bonne Bay; 2d-highest point on N.F. Gros Morne Natl. Park is here.

Gros Morne National Park (□ 697 sq mi/1,805 sq km), W central N.F., Canada, 85 mi/137 km N of Corner Brook, on Gulf of St. Lawrence. Excludes margins surrounding numerous fishing villages. Landscape consists of flat-topped peaks, tablelands of Long Range Mts. (upthrust base earth mantle), contains Viking Trail (231 mi/372 km long) from Rocky Harbour to Anse aux Meadows, fjords, and deep valleys with glacial lakes (locally called ponds). Declared World Heritage Area, 1988. Estab. 1970.

Gros Pate, mountain (2,115 ft/645 m), in Long Range Mts., NW N.F., Canada, 35 mi/56 km S of Point Riche.

Gros Piton, St. Lucia: see PITONS, THE.

Gros Ventre Range (gro VAHNT), in Rocky Mts. of NW Wyo., just E of Snake R. and Jackson Hole. Prominent peaks are Sheep Mt. (11,190 ft/3,411 m), Pyramid Peak (11,087 ft/3,379 m), Doubletop Peak (11,715 ft/3,571 m, highest in range). Includes part of Bridger-Teton Natl. Forest.

Gros-Morne (GRO–MORN), town (1982 pop. 4,739), Artibonite dept., N Haiti, 16 mi/26 km N of Gonaïves; 19°40′N 72°41′W. Coffee, cotton, fruit; manganese, bauxite, copper deposits nearby.

Gross, village (1990 pop. 7), Boyd co., N Nebr., 14 mi/23 km E of Butte, near S.Dak. line and Missouri R; 42°57′N 98°34′W.

Grosse Ile (GROS eel), island, Wayne co., SE Mich., in Detroit R. E of Trenton, uninc. residential suburb 14 mi/23 km SSW of downtown Detroit; c.8 mi/12.9 km, 1.5 mi/2.4 km wide; 42°07′N 83°09′W. Light mfg. Free bridge from Trenton to middle of isl.; toll bridge from Riverview to N end of isl. Trenton Channel separates isl. from Mich. mainland to W; main channel Detroit R. and Canada (Ont.) boundary to E. Grosse Ile Municipal Airport at S end. Has 2 golf courses.

Grosse Ile, island, S central Que., Canada, at center of St. Lawrence R., 60 mi/97 km ENE of Que. city. Natl. Historic Site, 1988. Quarantine station for Irish immigrants fleeing famine, 1825–1937. Graves of thousands who died, esp. in epidemics of 1832 and 1847, at Cholera Bay. Military biological weapons research station, 1942–1957. Animal quarantine station, 1965 to present.

Grosse Îsle (gros) (3 mi/5 km long, 2 mi/3 km wide), in the Gulf of St. Lawrence, E Que., Canada, one of the Magdalen Isls., 80 mi/129 km NNE of P.E.I.; 47°37′N 61°31′W. Wolfe Isl., narrow spit of land, extends SW to Grindstone Isl.

Grosse Pointe (GROS), city (1990 pop. 5,681), Wayne co., SE Mich., suburb 9 mi/14.5 km ENE of downtown Detroit, on L. St. Clair; borders Detroit on NW; 42°22′N 82°54′W. Light mfg.

Grosse Pointe (GROS), name referring to 5 residential suburbs of Detroit, NE Wayne co., and SE of Macomb co., SE Mich.; 42°22′N 82°54′W. They include the city of Grosse Pointe, Grosse Pointe Farms, Grosse Pointe Park, Grosse Pointe Shores, and Grosse Pointe Woods. The area was originally settled, and called Grosse Pointe Park, by the Fr. along the lake shore c.1712. Farms clustered there became organized as Grosse Pointe township c.1846. As the nearby city of Detroit boomed with the auto industry, many wealthy industrialists established large estates in the outlying area. Henry Ford's family, including his son Edsel, built their homes there. Of interest in the Grosse Pointe area are the mansion of Russell A. Alger, now a war memorial center, and a branch of the Detroit Inst. of Arts.

Grosse Pointe Farms (GROS), city (1990 pop. 10,092), Wayne co., SE Mich., residential suburb 10 mi/16 km ENE of downtown Detroit, on L. St. Clair; 42°22′N 82°51′W. Mfg. (publishing and printing). Borders Detroit on W and N. Alger House, a branch of Detroit Inst. of Arts, is here. Inc. as village 1893, as city 1949.

Grosse Pointe Park (GROS), residential village (1990 pop. 12,857), Wayne co., SE Mich., suburb 8 mi/12.9 km NE of downtown Detroit, on L. St. Clair; 42°22′N 82°55′W. Inc. 1907.

Grosse Pointe Shores (GROS), village (1990 pop. 2,955), Wayne and Macomb cos., SE Mich., residential suburb 11 mi/18 km NE of Detroit, on L. St. Clair; 42°27′N 82°52′W. Borders Macomb co. on N. Inc. 1911.

Grosse Pointe Woods (GROS), residential village (1990 pop. 17,715), Wayne co., SE Mich., suburb 11 mi/18 km NE of downtown Detroit, near L. St. Clair; 42°26′N 82°54′W. Inc. 1926 as Lochmoor; name was changed 1939.

Grosse Tete (gros TEHT), village (1994 pop.704), Iberville parish, SE central La., 15 mi/24 km W of Baton Rouge; 30°25′N 91°27′W. In sugarcane, cattle, timber, and oil and gas area. On the Lafon Map of 1806.

Grossetete, Bayou (gros TEHT, BEI-yoo), c.36 mi/58 km long, SE central La.; rises in Pointe Coupee parish, flows SE past village of Grosse Tete, to Bayou Plaquemine, 8 mi/13 km below Plaquemine. Navigable. Intersected by Port Allen–Morgan City Alternate Shipping Route. Also Grose Tete Bayou.

Grosvenor Dale, Conn.: see THOMPSON.

Groswater Bay, E central Lab., Canada; arm of Labrador Sea, 140 mi/225 km NE of Goose Bay. Hamilton Inlet, outlet for L. Melville, and Double Mer enter at W end; Tom Luscombe Brook enters bay on NW. George Isl. is at bay entrance; Black Isl. is near N shore; Pompey Isl. is at W end.

Groton 1 town (1990 pop. 45,144), New London co., SE Conn., including the borough of Groton and the village of West Mystic (1990 pop. 3,595), on the Thames R. opposite New London; 41°21′N 72°01′W. Shipbuilding, mfg., and commercial fishing are among the town's industries; biomedical research facilities. The huge New London Naval Submarine Base is on the Thames. The *Nautilus*, the 1st nuclear submarine, was launched in Groton in 1954 and is commemorated with a mus. Groton is the site of Fort Griswold (1775), unsuccessfully defended against the British in 1781. Of interest are tours of the submarine base and a number of well-maintained colonial homes. A branch of the Univ. of Conn. is also in Groton. Silas Deane b. here. Settled c.1650; inc. 1705. **2** (GRAW-tuhn), town (1990 pop. 7,511), Middlesex co., N Mass., 14 mi/23 km WSW of Lowell; 42°37′N 71°34′W. Mfg. (paper, wood prods.). Agr. (lumber; apples; dairying, poultry). Seat of Groton preparatory school. Settled and inc. 1655; destroyed in King Philip's War and later rebuilt. **3** town (1990 pop. 318), Grafton co., W central N.H., 7 mi/11.3 km WSW of Plymouth; 43°44′N 71°51′W. Drained by Cockermouth R. Agr. (cattle, poultry; vegetables; dairying; timber). Sculptured Rocks Natural Area in S; part of Province Road State Forest in W. **4** town (1990 pop. 1,196), Brown co., NE S.Dak., 20 mi/32 km E of Aberdeen; 45°27′N 98°05′W. In rich agr. area. Settled 1881, inc. 1886. **5** (GRAH-tin), town (1990 pop. 862), Caledonia co., NE Vt., including Groton village, on Wells R., and 16 mi/26 km SW of St. Johnsbury; 44°15′N 72°15′W. Dairy prods. Winter sports. Groton Pond (2.5 mi/4 km long), in Groton State Forest, is resort.

Groton (GRAH-tin), village (□ 1 sq mi/2.6 sq km; 1990 pop. 2,398), Tompkins co., W central N.Y., in Finger Lakes region, 12 mi/19 km NE of Ithaca; 42°35′N 76°22′W. Agr. (dairy prods.; field and sweet corn, hay). Inc. 1860.

Grottoes, town (1990 pop. 1,445), Augusta and Rockingham cos., NW Va., in S Shenandoah Valley, 15 mi/24 km NE of Staunton; 38°16′N 78°49′W. Mfg. (machining, lumber, furniture, plastic prods.). Agr. area (dairying; livestock, poultry; grain, soybeans, apples). Grand Caverns and Grand Cavern Regional Park to SW; Shenandoah Natl. Park to E.

Grouse Creek Mountains (6,000 ft/1,829 m–8,000 ft/ 2,438 m), W Box Elder co., NW Utah, near Nev. line; extend 30 mi/48 km S from Raft R. Mts. Parallel to Grouse Creek, to W.

Grouse Mountain (3,701 ft/1128 m.), SW B.C., Canada, in Coast Range in W part of North Vancouver, 5 mi/ 8 km N of Vancouver. Winter ski facilities, aerial tramway, mountaintop chalet.

Grove, town (1990 pop. 4,020), Delaware co., NE Okla., 22 mi/35 km E of Vinita, near L. of the Cherokees (W) and Mo. state line (E); 36°36′N 94°47′W. Trade center and shipping point for agr. (grain, fruit) and recreation area. Mfg. (awnings, lead-acid batteries, printing and publishing). Honey Creek State Park to W.

Grove City, city (1990 pop. 19,661), Franklin co., central Ohio; 39°52′N 83°04′W. Some mfg. Horse racing.

Grove City, town (□ 2 sq mi/5.2 sq km; 1990 pop. 2,374), Charlotte co., SW Fla., 12 mi/19 km SSE of Venice; 26°54′N 82°19′W. Mfg. (commercial printing).

Grove City, village (1990 pop. 547), Meeker co., S central Minn., 8 mi/12.9 km W of Litchfield; 45°08′N 94°40′W. Agr. (poultry, livestock; grain, soybeans; dairying). Mfg. (aircraft drills, snowmobile attachments, fiberglass boats). Long L. to S.

Grove City, borough (1990 pop. 8,240), Mercer co., W Pa., 25 mi/40 km SSE of Greenville; 41°09′N 80°05′W. Agr. area (grain, potatoes; livestock, dairying). Mfg. (printing and publishing, machinery, food prods., wood prods., fabricated metal prods.); surface bituminous coal, limestone. Grove City Col. is here. Grove City Airport to W. Settled 1798, laid out 1844, inc. 1883.

Grove Hill, farming town (1990 pop. 1,551), ⊙ Clarke co., SW Ala., bet. Tombigbee and Alabama rivers, 65 mi/ 105 km SW of Selma; 31°41′N 87°46′W. Mfg. (woodworking, apparel).

Grove Place, agr. station, Manchester parish, central Jamaica, on Jamaica RR, and 50 mi/80 km WNW of Kingston; 18°07′N 77°32′W.

Groveland 1 town (□ 2 sq mi/5.2 sq km; 1990 pop. 2,300), Lake co., central Fla., 29 mi/47 km W of Orlando; 28°33′N 81°50′W. Citrus-fruit packing and canning. Inc. 1922. **2** residential town (1990 pop 5,214), including Groveland village, Essex co., NE Mass., on Merrimack R. opposite Haverhill (to SE); 42°46′N 71°01′W. Settled c.1639, inc. 1850.

Groveland, uninc. village, Tuolumne co., central Calif., in resort region of the Sierra Nevada, 58 mi/93 km ESE of Stockton. On Hetch Hetchy Aqueduct. Agr. (apples; hay; cattle); timber. Founded in gold rush, when it was known as First Garrote. Stanislaus Natl. Forest to E; Yosemite Natl. Park to E. Groveland–Big Oak Flat area had a combined 1990 pop. of 2,753.

Groveport, village (1990 pop. 2,948), Franklin co., central Ohio, 9 mi/14 km SE of Columbus; 39°52′N 82°54′W. In agr. area.

Grover 1 village (1990 pop. 135), Weld co., NE Colo., on Crow Creek, near Wyo. state line, and 40 mi/64 km

NE of Greeley; 40°52′N 104°13′W. Elev. 5,071 ft/1,546 m. Agr. (sugar beets, beans, wheat, sunflowers; cattle). Parts of Pawnee Natl. Grassland to SW, SE, and NE. **2** village (1990 pop. 516), Cleveland co., S N.C., 9 mi/ 14.5 km SSE of Shelby, at S.C. state line; 35°10′N 81°27′W. Agr. (cotton, grain, soybeans; poultry, livestock). Mfg. (consumer goods, transportation machinery, industrial battery grid machinery). Kings Mountain Natl. Military Park (S.C.) to SE. **3** village, Lincoln co., W Wyo., near Salt R. and Idaho state line, just W of Salt R. Range, 5 mi/8 km N of Afton. Elev. 6,167 ft/ 1,880 m. Agr. (barley, hay, alfalfa; sheep, cattle). Bridger-Teton Natl. Forest to E.

Grover, Ohio: see TILTONSVILLE.

Grover Beach, beach (1990 pop. 11,656), San Luis Obispo co., SW Calif., on the Pacific Ocean, 8 mi/12.9 km S of San Luis Obispo. Agr. (flowers, nursery stock; vegetables, apples, strawberries, avocados, grain; cattle). Mfg. (wire drawing, millwork, machinery).

Grover Hill, village (1990 pop. 518), Paulding co., NW Ohio, 18 mi/29 km SSW of Defiance; 41°01′N 84°28′W. In agr. area.

Groves, city (1990 pop. 16,513), Jefferson co., SE Texas; suburb 3 mi/4.8 km N of downtown Port Arthur, near Neches R. and Sabine L.; 29°56′N 93°55′W. Light mfg.

Grovespring, uninc. community, Wright co., S central Mo., in the Ozarks, 13 mi/21 km NNW of Hartville.

Groveton, uninc. city (1990 pop. 19,997), Fairfax co., N Va., residential suburb 3 mi/4.8 km SW of Alexandria, and 9 mi/14.5 km SSW of Washington, D.C. The city has grown rapidly since the 1970s. Huntley Meadows Park to SW.

Groveton, town (1990 pop. 1,071), ⊙ Trinity co., E Texas, c.30 mi/48 km SW of Lufkin; 31°03′N 95°07′W. Elev. 323 ft/98 m. Agr. (peaches, pecans, vegetables; poultry); timber; cattle. Mfg. (apparel). At S edge of Davy Crockett Natl. Forest; L. Livingston reservoir to SW.

Groveton, N.H.: see NORTHUMBERLAND.

Groveton Gardens, uninc. town, Fairfax co., N Va., residential suburb 4 mi/6.4 km SW of Alexandria, 10 mi/ 16 km SSW of Washington, D.C. Huntley Meadows Park to SW.

Grovetown, town (1990 pop. 3,596), Columbia co., Ga., 15 mi/24 km W of Augusta; 33°27′N 82°12′W. Mfg. includes pumps, trailers, sports equipment.

Groveville, village, Mercer co., W N.J., on Crosswicks Creek, and 5 mi/8 km SE of Trenton. Largely residential.

Growler Mountains, Pima co., extend N into Maricopa co., SW Ariz., W of Ajo; rise to 3,000 ft/914 m in N ½; extend S into Organ Pipe Cactus Natl. Monument. Middle part in Cabeza Prieta Natl. Wildlife Refuge.

Grubbs, village (1990 pop. 528), Jackson co., NE Ark., 12 mi/19 km ENE of Newport, and on Cache R.; 35°38′N 91°04′W.

Grubbs, Del.: see ARDEN.

Grues, Île aux (GRUH, eel o) or **Crane Island**, in the St. Lawrence, S Que., Canada, 35 mi/56 km ENE of Que. city; 5 mi/8 km long, 1 mi/2 km wide. Just NE is Île aux Oies.

Grullo, El, Mexico: see EL GRULLO.

Grundy 1 county (□ 430 sq mi/1,114 sq km; 1990 pop. 32,337), NE Ill.; ⊙ Morris; 41°17′N 88°25′W. Agr. (corn, soybeans; dairying). Clay, limestone. Mfg. (paper prods., aluminum prods., rubber and plastics products, chemicals and allied products). Drained by Illinois, Des Plaines, Kankakee, and Mazou rivers. Includes Gebhard Woods State Park on the Ill. and Mich. Canal Parkway. Formed 1841. Nuclear power plants: Dresden 2 (initial criticality Jan. 7, 1970; max. dependable capacity of 772 MWe) and Dresden 3 (initial criticality Jan. 31, 1971; max. dependable capacity of 773 MWe) are 9 mi/14.5 km E of Morris. Use cooling water from the Kankakee R. **2** county (□ 502 sq mi/1,300 sq km; 1990 pop. 12,029), central Iowa; ⊙ Grundy Center; 42°24′N 92°48′W. Rolling prairie agr. area (hogs, cattle; corn, soybeans, oats) drained by Blackhawk and Wolf creeks. Field and stream flooding in 1993. Formed 1851. **3** county (□ 435 sq mi/1,127 sq km; 1990 pop. 10,536), N Mo.; ⊙ Trenton; 40°07′N 93°34′W. Drained by

Thompson and Weldon rivers. Corn, wheat, cattle. Some mfg. at Trenton. North Central Mo. Col. at Trenton. Crowder State Park NW of Trenton. Formed 1841. **4** county (□ 358 sq mi/927 sq km; 1990 pop. 13,362), SE central Tenn.; ⊙ Altamont; 35°23′N 85°43′W. In the Cumberlands; drained by Elk R., and small Collins and Little Sequatchie rivers. Coal mining, lumbering; some agr. (apple growing). Includes Savage Gulf State Natural Area and the resort community known as Beersheba Springs. Formed 1844.

Grundy, town (1990 pop. 1,305), ⊙ Buchanan co., SW Va., 41 mi/66 km NE of Norton, on E bank of Levisa Fork R., in Appalachian Mts. near Ky. and W.Va. state lines; 37°16′N 82°05′W. Mfg. (apparel, printing and publishing). Agr. (cattle; potatoes, tobacco; hay). Breaks Interstate Park (Ky., Va.) to W. Former coalmining center. Subject to periodic floods (town center destroyed by floods 3 times in the last 6 decades). A plan exists to relocate the center from the riverbank to higher ground on the Appalachian slopes by the early 21st cent.

Grundy Center, town (1990 pop. 2,491), ⊙ Grundy co., central Iowa, 24 mi. WSW of Waterloo; 42°21′N 92°46′W. Agr. trade center with corn cannery. Mfg. (plastic prods.; printing; food prods.). Historic Herbert Quick School House is here. Inc. 1877.

Grupo de Maniabón (GROO-po dai mah-nee-uh-BON), mountain range, Holguín prov., E Cuba; 20°57′N 76°05′W. Collection of several small mountain ranges in E-W alignment. Small deposits of gold, feldspar, and limestone.

Grutas de Cacahuamilpa (GROO-tahs dai kah-kah-hwah-MEEL-pah), a national park, in SW Morelos, Mexico, at the intersection of Mexican highway 166 and Mexican highway 55. The caves include chambers that are 100 ft/30 m high and 200 ft/61 m long, which contain many interesting formations. Around 8 mi/ 12.9 km of the caves have been explored, but the end has never been found; ½ mi/⅓ km of the caves can be viewed from paved pathways.

Grutas de Juxtlahuaca (GROO-tahs dai hoosh-tlah-HWAH-kah), a national park, in central Guerrero, Mexico, 6 mi/10 km S of Chilpancingo de los Bravo. These caves have walls decorated with 3,000-year-old Olmec-style paintings. There are also unusual geological formations and underground ponds, which support myriad blind creatures. It takes 5 hours to complete the tour of these caves.

Gruver 1 town (1990 pop. 102), Emmet co., NW Iowa, 7 mi/11.3 km E of Estherville; 43°23′N 94°42′W. Livestock; grain. **2** town (1990 pop. 1,172), Hansford co., extreme N Texas, in high plains of the Panhandle, 80 mi/129 km NNE of Amarillo; 36°15′N 101°24′W. Ships wheat, corn, sorghum; cattle; gas and oil; helium. Palo Duro Reservoir to NE.

Grygla (GRI-gluh), village (1990 pop. 220), Marshall co., NW Minn., on Mud R., 29 mi/47 km NE of Thief R.; 48°17′N 95°37′W. Falls. Timber; cattle, sheep; grain. Mfg. (wood milling). Red Lake Indian Reservation to SE; Agassiz Natl. Wildlife Refuge to W; Thief L. Wildlife Area to N.

Guacanayabo, Gulf of (gwah-kahn-ah-YAH-bo), shallow inlet of Caribbean, S coast of Cuba, off Granma, Las Tunas, and Camagüey provs., N of Cape Cruz (Granma prov.); horseshoe-shaped, c.60 mi/97 km wide N-S, 60 mi/97 km long; 20°15′N 77°30′W. Dotted by coral reefs, with the Gran Banco de Buena Esperanza in its center. At its head is port of Manzanillo (Granma prov.). Receives Cauto R. Important fishing industries at Manzanillo, Santa Cruz del Sur, and Niguero, esp. commercial shrimp.

Guachinango (gwah-chee-NAN-go), town (1990 pop. 1,735), ⊙ Guachinango municipio, Jalisco state, W Mexico, 23 mi/37 km W of Ameca. Isolated community in S Sierra Madre Occidental. Not accessible by all-weather roads.

Guachochi (gwah-CHO-chee), town (1990 pop. 8,052), in S Chihuahua state, Mexico, 124 mi/200 km S of Cuauhtemoc, and 86 mi/138 km W of Hidalgo del Parral in Sierra Tarahumara; 26°51′N 107°51′W. Elev.

5,535 ft/1,687 m. Access by unpaved roads. In forested, mountainous area. Lumbering, small farming. Jesuit mission site to serve Tarahumara Indian pop.

Guadalajara (gwah-dah-lah-HAH-rah), city (1990 pop. 1,650,042) and township, ⊙ Jalisco state, SW Mexico, 2d largest city of Mexico; 20°40′N 103°20′W. Elev. 5,213 ft/1,589 m. Guadalajara is a beautiful, spacious city on a plain, surrounded by mts. It is a modern commercial metropolis with many picturesque survivals of the Span. colonial era. The mild, clear, dry climate has made it a popular health resort, and because of its charm it is often called "Perla del Occidente" [= Pearl of the West]. Guadalajara is also an important communications and industrial center. Industry is aided by direct RR and air service to the U.S., and by a hydroelectric plant utilizing the Juanacatlán falls on the Santiago R. Food processing; mfg. of xerographic and photographic equipment, plastics, chemicals, and electronic prods. are among the leading industries. The region around the city is important for agr. and livestock raising; some coal is also mined. Big tourist area. The most famous prods. of Guadalajara and its environs are intricately designed and finely worked glassware and pottery. Founded by Cristóbal de Oñate c.1530, Guadalajara was moved twice, before and during the Mixtón War, because of military pressure by the region's native inhabitants; it was permanently est. in 1542, the date chosen as its official founding. Guadalajara became the seat of the *audiencia* of Nueva Galicia. Easily captured in 1810 by Hidalgo y Costilla during the war against Spain, the city was the center of reform activities. Again in 1858, in the War of Reform, it was briefly occupied by the liberals under Benito Juárez. Miguel Hidalgo Internatl. airport to S. Its notable public bldgs. include the cathedral, finished in 1618 after more than 50 years of work, and the governor's palace, begun in 1643. The cathedral, which houses B. E. Murillo's *The Assumption of the Blessed Virgin*, has been partially destroyed several times by earthquakes and represents a conglomerate of architectural styles. The governor's palace, with murals by J. C. Orozco, is an excellent example of Span. colonial architecture. The Univ. of Guadalajara and the orphanage chapel also contain Orozco murals.

Guadalcázar (gwah-dahl-KAH-sahr), city (1990 pop. 1,146) and township, ⊙ Guadalcázar municipio, San Luis Potosí, N central Mexico, on interior plateau, 50 mi/80 km NE of San Luis Potosí, on paved road 9 mi/15 km E, off Mexico Highway 57/80; 22°50′N 100°45′W. Elev. 5,489 ft/1,673 m. Silver, lead, and phosphate deposits.

Guadalupe, town, Ciego de Ávila prov., E Cuba, in foothills of Sierra de Jatibonico, 20 mi/32 km W of Morón; 22°09′N 78°57′W. Cattle; tobacco. Has sulphurous springs; copper deposits nearby.

Guadalupe, city (1990 pop. 535,332) and township, Nuevo León state, NE Mexico, on the Santa Catalina R.; 25°43′N 100°15′W. A largely working-class suburb of Monterrey; part of Monterrey metropolitan area.

Guadalupe 1 town (1990 pop. 2,223), ⊙ Guadalupe municipio, Puebla state, central Mexico, 9 mi/14.5 km SW of Acatlán; 19°12′N 97°28′W. Elev. 3,980 ft/1,213 m. Sugarcane, corn, fruit; livestock. Formerly called Guadalupe Santa Ana. **2** town (1990 pop. 46,433), ⊙ Guadalupe municipio, Zacatecas, N central Mexico, on interior plateau, 3.7 mi/6 km, ESE of Zacatecas; 22°45′N 102°31′W. Elev. 7,431 ft/2,265 m; on RR. Agr. center (cereals, sugarcane, vegetables; livestock). Has old cathedral and Jesuit col. **3** (gwah-dah-LOO-pai), town (1990 pop. 3,803), Chihuahua state, N Mexico, on the Rio Grande, and 32 mi/51 km SE of Juárez; 31°25′N 106°00′W. Cotton, cereals; cattle. Sometimes called Guadalupe Bravo.

Guadalupe, village, Tijuana municipio, Baja California state, NW Mexico, 14 mi/23 km N of Ensenada; 32°4′N 116°35′W. Elev. 4,593 ft/1,400 m. Rus. agr. settlement in small irrigated valley (wheat, fruit; livestock).

Guadalupe 1 (gwah-dah-LOO-pe), county (□ 3,031 sq mi/7,850 sq km; 1990 pop. 4,156), E central N.Mex.; ⊙ Santa Rosa; 34°51′N 104°46′W. Barley, oats, cattle,

sheep, hay, alfalfa, some sorghum. Plateau area watered by Pecos R., which forms Sumner L. reservoir (formerly known as Alamogordo Reservoir) and by Pintada Arroyo. Formed 1891. **2** county (□ 714 sq mi/1,849 sq km; 1990 pop. 64,873), S central Texas; ⊙ Seguin; 29°34′N 97°57′W. Bounded by San Marcos R. (NE) and Cibolo Creek (SW); drained by Guadalupe R. Power dams form lakes (recreational areas), including L. McQueeney reservoir (Guadalupe R.) in NW. Agr. (cotton, corn, peanuts, grain sorghum, wheat, oats, pecans, vegetables, peaches, nursery crops, Christmas trees); livestock raising (cattle, horses, hogs, poultry, exotic animals); greyhound breeding. Oil, natural gas; clay mining; sand and gravel. Mfg. (farm prods. processing) Seguin. Hunting, fishing. Formed 1846.

Guadalupe (gwa-dah-loo-pay), city (1990 pop. 5,479), Santa Barbara co., SW Calif., 8 mi/12.9 km W of Santa Maria, 5 mi/8 km E of Pacific Ocean at mouth of Santa Maria R.; 34°58′N 120°34′W. RR junction. Dairying, farming (strawberries, avocados, vegetables, grain; cattle); mfg. (metal prods.). Inc. 1946.

Guadalupe, town (1990 pop. 5,458), Maricopa co., central Ariz., 8 mi/12.9 km SE of downtown Phoenix, on Highline canal; 33°22′N 111°57′W. Bounded by Phoenix (W), Tempe (N, E, S). Phoenix South Mt. Park to W.

Guadalupe Etla, town (1990 pop. 1,592), central Oaxaca state, Mexico, 7 mi/12 km NW of Oaxaca de Juárez; elev. 5,315 ft/1,620 m. In Etla arm of Oaxaca Valley on the Atoyac R. Temperate climate. Agr. (corn, wheat, beans, fruits; cattle and dairy farming; woods); palm textiles. Road and RR connections with Oaxaca de Juárez.

Guadalupe Hidalgo, Mexico: see BASILICA DE GUADALUPE.

Guadalupe Island (□ 102 sq mi/264 sq km), in the Pacific Ocean, c.150 mi/241 km off coast of Baja California, NW Mexico; 23 mi/37 km long, c.7 mi/11.3 km wide; rises to 4,593 ft/1,400 m; 30°43′N 118°24′W. Goat grazing.

Guadalupe Mountains, range of Sacramento Mts. in S N.Mex. and W Texas; c. 40 mi/64 km long and 10 mi/16 km wide (NNW–SSE). Highest peak, Guadalupe Peak (8,749 ft/2,667 m) in Guadalupe Mts. Natl. Park, is highest point in Texas; region also contains a limestone fossil reef. Guadalupe Mts. Natl. Park protects the Texas portion of the range (c.10 mi/16 km at S end); range continues SSE and becomes Delaware Mts. (Texas). Also includes Carlsbad Cavern Natl. Park (N.Mex.) and part of Lincoln Natl. Forest (N.Mex.); extends into Sacramento Mts. in N.Mex.

Guadalupe Mountains National Park, W Texas; covers 135 sq mi/350 sq km. Located in the S Guadalupe Mts., the park contains parts of the world's largest and most significant Permian limestone fossil reef. Peaks include McKittrick Canyon, Guadalupe Peak (8,749 ft/2,667 m and the highest point in Texas), and El Capitan (8,078 ft/2,462 m; which historically served as a landmark for W-traveling pioneers). Unique desert mt. flora and fauna. Authorized 1966, est. 1972.

Guadalupe Pass (5,426 ft/1,654 m), W Texas, highway pass bet. Guadalupe (N) and Delaware (S) mts., c.100 mi/161 km E of El Paso, just S of Guadalupe Mts. Natl. Park.

Guadalupe Peak (8,749 ft/2,667 m), W Texas, Guadalupe Mts., c.100 mi/161 km E of El Paso. Highest point in Guadalupe Mts. and in Texas. Salt lakes and flats are just W; Guadalupe Pass (S).

Guadalupe Ramírez (gwah-dah-LOO-pe rah-MEE-res), town (1990 pop. 1,615), in far NW Oaxaca state, Mexico, 28 mi/45 km W of Huajuapan de León; elev. 3,051 ft/930 m. In the Mixteca Baja, a Mixtec-speaking community. Straw textiles, aguardiente (liquor), and agr. (corn, beans, fruits). Poor roads.

Guadalupe River, c.356 mi/573 km long, Texas; rises in springs in W Kerr co. on Edwards Plateau; flows generally SE, past Kerrville, through Canyon L. reservoir (Comal R. c.30 mi/48 km N of San Antonio), past New Braunfels, through L. McQueeney, past Seguin, Gonzales, and Victoria, to head of San Antonio Bay. Receives Comal and San Marcos rivers in upper course,

San Antonio R. near its mouth. Hydroelectric plants; also used for irrigation and domestic water supply.

Guadalupe Santa Ana, Mexico: see GUADALUPE PUEBLA.

Guadalupe Victoria, Mexico: see CIUDAD GUADALUPE VICTORIA.

Guadalupe Victoria or **Nuevo Saltillo**, town (1990 pop. 7,166), Puebla state, central Mexico, 25 mi/40 km N of Ciudad Serdán. Cereals, fruit, maguey.

Guadalupe y Calvo (gwah-dah-LOO-pe ee KAHL-vo), town (1990 pop. 1,642), ⊙ Guadalupe y Calvo municipio, in far S Chihuahua, Mexico, 56 mi/90 km SE of Guachochi; 26°04′N 106°58′W. Elev. 7,598 ft/2,316 m. In a mountainous area of Sierra Tarahumara. Largely forested. Climate cold at high elevs. and temperate in the valleys. Agr. (cattle raising and wood prods.). On paved state highway. Jesuit mission site.

Guadeloupe Passage, channel in Leeward Isls., West Indies, bounded by Montserrat and Antigua (N) and Guadeloupe (S); c.35 mi/56 km wide.

Guadiana, Ensenada de (gwah-dee-AH-nuh, en-suh-NAH-dah dai), sheltered bay, off Pinar del Río prov., W Cuba, 35 mi/56 km ENE of Cape San Antonio, the E extension of the Gulf of Guanahacabibes; c.13 mi/21 km long, 10 mi/16 km wide; 22°04′N 88°24′W. Lobster fishing.

Guaico (GWEI-ko), village, N Trinidad, Trinidad and Tobago, on RR, and 25 mi/40 km ESE of Port of Spain. Cacao-growing region.

Guáimaro (GWAH-ee-mahr-o), town (1994 est. pop. 25,000), Camagüey prov., E Cuba, on Central Highway, and 40 mi/64 km ESE of Camagüey; 21°04′N 77°07′W. Lumbering and agr. center (fruit, sugarcane, cattle). Mfg. (dairy and meat prods.; sawmilling).

Guajaba, Cayo (gwah-HAH-bah, KEI-o), coral island, off Camagüey prov., E Cuba, in Old Bahama Channel, bet. Cayo Romano (NW) and Cayo Sabinal (SE), 22 mi/35 km NW of Nuevitas; 12 mi/19 km long, c.4 mi/6.4 km wide; 21°49′N 77°30′W. Charcoal burning, fishing. Part of Camagüey Archipelago.

Guajataca River (gwah-hah-TAH-kah), NW P.R.; rises just S of Lares; flows c.30 mi/48 km N, past Lares and through L. Guajataca, to the Atlantic 1.5 mi/2.4 km NW of Quebradillas. The artificial L. Guajataca (2.5 mi/4 km long), along its midcourse 5 mi/8 km S of Quebradillas, serves irrigation system of the NW. On a canal is Isabela hydroelectric project. Guajataca Forest Reserve just W of L. Guajataca.

Guajay, Cuba: see WAJAY.

Guaje, Llano del (GWAH-he, YA-no del), arid depression N outliers of Sierra Madre Oriental of Coahuila, N Mexico, NE of the Bolsón de Mapimí; elev. c.3,000 ft/914 m.

Guamaní River (gwah-mah-NEE), c.10 mi/16 km long, SE P.R.; flows S, past Guayama, to the Caribbean. Its source is linked through an artificial tunnel with L. Carite (on the La Plata), where water is diverted to feed the 3 Carite hydroelectric plants and irrigation channels.

Guamúchil (gwah-MOO-chil), city (1990 pop. 49,635), ⊙ Salvador Alvarado municipio, Sinaloa, NW Mexico, on Mocorito R., on RR, and 60 mi/97 km NW of Culiacán Rosales; 25°27′N 108°05′W. Elev. 148 ft/45 m. Irrigation from Eustaquio Balbuena Reservoir. In the Fuerte irrigation dist. Agr. center (chickpeas, sugarcane, tomatoes, fruit).

Guamutas (gwah-MOO-tahz), town, Matanzas prov., N Cuba, 23 mi/37 km SE of Cárdenas; 22°52′N 80°55′W. Sugarcane, fruit, sisal.

Guanabacoa (gwah-nah-bah-KO-uh), city, (1986 est. pop. 95,500), Ciudad de La Habana prov., W Cuba; 23°08′N 82°18′W. A residential and commercial suburb of Havana. Numerous mineral springs are located near Guanabacoa, whose Native Amer. name means "place of waters." Havana's Jewish cemetery is here, as is a folklore mus. The city was founded in 1555 on the site of a Native Amer. settlement.

Guanaceví (gwah-nah-se-VEE), mining settlement (1990 pop. 1,983) and township, Durango state, N Mexico, on E slopes of Sierra Madre Occidental, 70 mi/

113 km SSW of Hidalgo del Parral. Mining center (gold, silver, lead, copper).

Guanahacabibes, Gulf of (gwah-nuh-uh-kuh-BEE-bais), large, shallow body of water off W edge of Pinar del Río prov. in W Cuba; littered with coral reefs. Separates Cuba from deeper waters of Gulf of Mexico.

Guanahacabibes Peninsula (gwah-nah-hah-KEE-bais), Pinar del Río prov., W Cuba, westernmost part of the isl., facing Yucatán peninsula (Mexico); extends c.45 mi/72 km E from Cape San Antonio; 21°18′N 84°33′W. The region is sparsely populated. Important lobster and red snapper fishing grounds.

Guanahani, Bahamas: see SAN SALVADOR, island.

Guanajay (gwah-nah-HEI), city, La Habana prov., W Cuba, on Central Highway, on RR, and 25 mi/40 km SW of Havana; 22°55′N 82°41′W. In agr. region (sugarcane, tobacco, fruit); mfg. of cigars; heavy industry.

Guanajibo River (gwah-nah-HEE-bo), c.25 mi/40 km long, SW P.R., flows S and WNW, past San Germán, to Mona Passage 3 mi/4.8 km SW of Mayagüez.

Guanajuato (gwah-nah-HWAH-to), state (□ 11,805 sq mi/30,575 sq km; 1990 pop. 3,982,593), W central Mexico, on the central plateau; ⊙ GUANAJUATO. The state's high average elev. (6,000 ft/1,829 m) provides a moderately cool, healthful climate. Guanajuato is crossed in the N by transverse ranges of the Sierra Madre Occidental, some of which reach hts. of 11,000 ft/3,353 m. In the S are fertile plains supporting livestock raising and the cultivation of wheat, maize, other grain crops, and beans. The Lerma and its tributaries form the chief river system. Despite the steadily growing importance of agr., Guanajuato is noted primarily as Mexico's foremost mining state; much silver and some gold are extracted, and mercury, lead, tin, copper, fluorite, and opals are also produced. Industrial prods. from the cities—Guanajuato, Celaya, León, and Irapuato—include textiles, saddles and other leather goods, and foodstuffs. Oil refining is also a significant part of the economy. Joined with Querétaro, the state was a Span. intendancy until 1824. A leading silver producer of Span. Amer., Guanajuato declined in economic importance during the wars of the 19th cent.

Guanajuato (gwah-nah-HWAH-to), city (1990 pop. 73,108) and township, ⊙ Guanajuato state, W central Mexico, in the Cañada de Marfil [ivory ravine], a precipitous ravine encircled by barren hills, on Mexico Highway 110; 21°00′N 101°16′W. Elev. c.6,600 ft/2,012 m. Guanajuato has narrow, winding, steep cobblestone streets, sometimes pieced out by stone steps, and the ground underneath is honeycombed with silver-mine shafts. Its geographic position and economic importance as one of Span. Amer.'s chief silver-producing centers gave the city a key role in the wars and revolutions that wracked Mexico in the 19th and early 20th cent. Guanajuato has become a tourist center. There are several noteworthy colonial churches and bldgs., including the Alhóndiga de Granaditas, originally a granary that was besieged and captured (1810) by Hidalgo y Costilla at the outset of the war against Spain. Guanajuato is a natl. monument and a UNESCO World Heritage site.

Guane (GWAH-nai), town, Pinar del Río prov., W Cuba, on Cuyaguateje R. and 28 mi/45 km SW of Pinar del Río; 22°12′N 84°07′W. RR terminus and agr. center (sugar, tobacco, beeswax, honey); lumbering.

Guane River, Cuba: see CUYAGUATEJE RIVER.

Guánica (GWAH-nee-kah), town (1990 pop. 19,984), SW P.R., on well-protected Guánica Bay, 20 mi/32 km W of Ponce. Light industry; mfg. (electronics, fertilizer); aviculture. Port of entry. Site of 1st landing of U.S. troops (1898). Guánica Forest Reserve here; largest remaining tract of tropical dry coastal forest in the world and an Internatl. Biosphere Reserve. Originally settled 1510.

Guánica Lagoon (GWAH-nee-kah) (c.3 mi/4.8 km long), SW P.R., near the coast, 2 mi/3.2 km N of Ensenada, and linked with the Caribbean. Known for wild fowl.

Guaniguanico, Cuba: see COLORADOS, LOS.

Guaniguanico, Serranía de (gwah-nee-gwah-NEE-ko,

ser-rah-NEE-ah dai), low hilly range, Pinar del Río prov., W Cuba, extends c.40 mi/64 km NW from Mantua, forms outliers of the Sierra de los Órganos; 22°38′N 83°30′W. Rugged limestone formation. Sometimes, as Cordillera de Guaniguanico, it is considered to include the entire W range of the isl. with the Sierra de los Órganos and Sierra del Rosario.

Guantánamo (gwan-TAHN-ah-mo), easternmost province of W Cuba (□ 2,460 sq mi/6,370 sq km; pop. 535,000), ⊙ Guantánamo. Bordered NW by Holguín prov., NE by Atlantic Ocean, S by Caribbean Sea, and W by Santiago de Cuba prov. Drained by Guantánamo, Yumurí, and Toa rivers. Created as one of five provs. out of old Oriente prov. Important cities include Guantánamo (pop. 200,000), Baracoa. Windward Passage to E. U.S. naval base at Guantánamo Bay (SW). Mountainous area with up to 134 in/3,400 mm rainfall. Striking marine terraces at Maisí Cape, E point of isl. Mainly agr. economy but confined to lowlands of Guantánamo Basin and Caujerí Valley. About 161,429 acres/37,000 ha devoted to cacao and coffee in wet, mountainous areas. Just under ⅓ of prov. in capital city. Minimal RR and road networks due to topography.

Guantánamo (gwahn-TAHN-ah-mo), city (1994 est. pop. 200,000), ⊙ Guantánamo prov., SE Cuba, on the Guaso R.; 20°10′N 75°13′W. It is the processing center for a sugar- and coffee-producing region; has road and main RR connections with Santiago de Cuba. Publishing facility and furniture plant. Founded in the early 19th cent. by Frenchmen fleeing the slave rebellion in Haiti, Guantánamo retains many vestiges of Fr. architecture. The city is c.20 mi/32 km inland from its port, Caimanera, on landlocked Guantánamo Bay. U.S. naval base at mouth of bay will provide economic development potential when turned over to Cuba.

Guantánamo Bay (gwahn-TAHN-ah-mo), sheltered Caribbean Sea inlet, Guantánamo prov., SE Cuba, 8 mi/12.9 km S of Guantánamo, which is served by ports of Caimanera (W) and Boquerón (E), opposite each other on central narrows; 12 mi/19 km long, up to 5 mi/8 km wide; 21°56′N 75°10′W. The S basin with adjoining shoreline is site of the U.S. naval reserve and includes airfields (McCalla Field) and fortifications. Training center for ships of U.S. Atlantic fleet. Often called the "Pearl Harbor of the Atlantic," the base has naval installations covering c.45 sq mi/117 sq km. Its site was leased to the U.S. in 1903 by a treaty that was renewed in 1934; consent of both govts. is needed to revoke the agreement. Since 1960 the Cuban govt. has refused to accept the token annual rent ($5,000) from the U.S. and seeks the return of the land. Recently (1994–1996) used to house over 35,000 Haitian and Cuban refugees seeking entry to the U.S. Called Cumberland Harbor by the English when they landed (1741) here under Admiral Vernon and Gen. Wentworth. U.S. troops disembarked on the beach in Span.-Amer. War.

Guantánamo River (gwahn-TAHN-ah-mo), 118 mi/190 km long, draining 471 sq mi/1,221 sq km basin in Santiago de Cuba and Guantánamo provs., E Cuba; rises E of Santiago de Cuba; flows E and SSE to Guantánamo Bay near Caimanera (Guantánamo prov.); 20°00′N 75°12′W. Navigable for small vessels in lower course.

Guapo (GWAH-po), village, SW Trinidad, Trinidad and Tobago, on N shore of SW peninsula, 14 mi/23 km WSW of San Fernando. Petroleum wells nearby.

Guapo Bay (GWAH-po), Trinidad, Trinidad and Tobago, 16 mi/26 km WSW of San Fernando, bet. Point Fortin and La Brea; 10°12′N 61°40′W. Petroleum wells. Pitch L. nearby.

Guara (GWAH-rah), town, La Habana prov., W Cuba, on RR and expressway, 25 mi/40 km SSE of Havana; 22°48′N 82°12′W. In sugar- and vegetable-growing region.

Guarachita, Mexico: see VILLAMAR.

Guardalavaca (gwahr-dah-lah-VAH-kah), modern beach resort on N shore of Old Bahama Channel, Holguín prov., E Cuba; 21°08′N 75°50′W.

Guarico, Cape (gwah-REE-ko), headland, Holguín

prov., E Cuba, 24 mi/39 km NW of Baracoa; 20°37′N 74°44′W.

Guaro (GWAH-ro), town, Holguín prov., E Cuba, 9 mi/14.5 km W of Mayarí, near Nipe Bay; 20°40′N 75°47′W. Agr. settlement (sugarcane). Airstrip to NW.

Guasave (gwah-SAH-ve), city (1990 pop. 49,338) and township, Sinaloa state, W Mexico, on the Sinaloa R., within the Fuerte irrigation dist.; 25°34′N 108°27′W. The growing of irrigated cotton and maize and the raising of livestock are the chief occupations. The city was est. in 1595 as a Span. mission among the Guasave Indians. Also Guasabe.

Guasimal (gwah-see-MAHL), town, Sancti Spíritus prov., central Cuba, on RR, and 13 mi/21 km S of Sancti Spíritus; 21°45′N 79°27′W. Tobacco, sugarcane; livestock.

Guaso River (GWAH-so), 20 mi/32 km long, Guantánamo prov., E Cuba; rises 5 mi/8 km NNW of Jamaica, flows S, past Guantánamo, to Guantánamo Bay 4 mi/6.4 km N of Caimanera; 20°13′N 75°10′W. Navigable below Guantánamo for small boats.

Guasti (gwas-tee), village, San Bernardino co., S Calif., just E of Ontario. Wine production. Area annexed by Ontario.

Guatemala, town, Holguín prov., E Cuba, on E shore of Nipe Bay, 40 mi/64 km E of Holguín; 20°45′N 75°39′W. Sugar-milling center. Ships iron ore. Formerly called Preston.

Guavate (gwah-VAH-te) or **Carite Forest Reserve,** nature reserve (9.4 sq mi/24 sq km), SE P.R., c.10 mi/16 km N of Guayama. Has sierra palms, teak, mahogony. Includes Cerro La Santa, reserve's highest point (2,963 ft/903 m) with communications towers.

Guayabal (gwei-yuh-BAHL), minor port and small beach, SW Las Tunas prov., E Cuba, 38 mi/61 km SE of Camagüey, on Gulf of Guacanayabo; 20°41′N 77°37′W. Sugar bulk terminal capable of shipping 10,000 metric tons of sugar daily. Only Caribbean port in prov.

Guayabal, Lake (gwah-yah-BAHL), artificial reservoir, S P.R., in Cordillera Central, 2.5 mi/4 km N of Juana Díaz. A 2,800-ft/853-m tunnel diverts water into Toro Negro and Doña Juana rivers.

Guayaguayare (GWAI-yah-GWAI-yah-ree), village, SE Trinidad, Trinidad and Tobago, on beach, 3 mi/4.8 km W of Galeota Point, 45 mi/72 km SE of Port of Spain; 10°12′N 61°03′W. Coconuts, cacao. Oil fields nearby.

Guayama (gwah-YAH-mah), town (1990 pop. 41,588), SE P.R., founded 1736. Market and commercial center; petrochemicals. Guayama has been noted for its developments in irrigation, which increased agr. production, as well as in electrification. Two reservoirs here. Birth place of poet Louis Palés Matos.

Guayamouc River (gwah-yah-MOOK), c.70 mi/113 km long, central and E Haiti; rises in the Massif du Nord NW of Saint-Michel-de-l'Atalaye; flows S, through fertile plain, past Hinche, to the Artibonite at Dominican Republic border; 18°59′N 71°52′W. Not navigable.

Guayanilla (gwah-yah-NEE-yah), town (1990 pop. 21,581), S P.R., 10 mi/16 km W of Ponce. Petrochemicals; thermoelectric plants produce more than ½ electric power used on isl. Oil refinery. Playa de Guayanilla (port) is 1.5 mi/2.4 km SE. First settled 1511.

Guaymas, Mexico: see HEROICA GUAYMAS.

Guaynabo (gwei-NAH-bo), town (1990 pop. 92,886), N P.R., 6 mi/9.7 km SW of San Juan. Oil refinery; mfg. (pharmaceuticals, glass prods., cement, paper); construction industry. Ruins; historic mus.

Guayos (GWEI-yoz), town, Sancti Spíritus prov., central Cuba, on RR and 10 mi/16 km NNW of Sancti Spíritus; 22°04′N 79°28′W. Tobacco, sugarcane; cattle. Remberto Abad Alemán sugar mill just S. Natl. highway projected to pass through.

Guayubín (gwah-yoo-BEEN), town (1993 pop. 1,977), Monte Cristi prov., NW Dominican Republic, on the Yaque del Norte, and 20 mi/32 km SE of Monte Cristi; 19°37′N 71°20′W. In fertile agr. region (tobacco, coffee, cacao, divi-divi, cotton; fine hardwood, hides); mfg. of cheese and sweets.

Guazapares, Mexico: see TÉMORIS.

Guelatao de Juárez (we-LAH-tou de HWAH-rez), town (1990 pop. 590), in central Oaxaca state, Mexico, 39 mi/62 km NE of Oaxaca de Juárez, and 2 mi/3 km S of Ixtlán de Juárez near Mexico Highway 175; 17°18′N 96°29′W. Elev. 6,181 ft/1,884 m. Mountainous and cold. Birthplace of Benito Juárez, former president of a Zapotec Indian community. Agr. Road to Oaxaca de Juárez.

Guelph (gwehlf), city (1991 pop. 87,976), S Ont., Canada, on the Speed R.;43°33′N 80°15′W. Industrial and agr. center located in one of Canada's most densely populated regions. Mfg. includes electrical, construction, and farm equip.; textiles; clothing; fiberglass and tobacco prods. The Univ. of Guelph, comprising the Ont. Agr. Col. (1874) and other institutions, was founded in 1964. Founded in 1827 by the Scot. novelist John Galt.

Güémez (GWAI-mes), town (1990 pop. 1,790), Tamaulipas, NE Mexico, 16 mi/26 km NE of Ciudad Victoria. Silver, lead, copper mining.

Guerneville (gur-nee-vill), uninc. town (1990 pop. 1,966), Sonoma co., W Calif., 17 mi/27 km W of Santa Rosa and on Russian R.; 38°31′N 122°59′W. Apples, grapes, grain; poultry; sheep; dairying; quicksilver mining; timber, redwood lumbering in area; champagne production. Armstrong Redwoods State Park and Austin Creek State Recreation Area are to NW.

Guernewood Park (gur-nee-wood), uninc. town, Sonoma co., W Calif., on Russian R. and 17 mi/27 km W of Santa Rosa. Armstrong Redwoods State Reserve and Austin Creek State Recreation Area to N.

Guernsey, county (□ 529 sq mi/1,370 sq km; 1990 pop. 39,024), E Ohio; ⊙ Cambridge; 40°03′N 81°31′W. Drained by Wills Creek. In the Unglaciated Plain physiographic region. Agr. (cattle, poultry; corn, hay); mfg. (stone, clay, and glass prods.; computer equip., machinery); oil and gas extraction, clay mining, limestone quarrying. Formed 1810.

Guernsey, town (1990 pop. 70), Poweshiek co., central Iowa, 11 mi/18 km NE of Montezuma; 41°38′N 92°20′W. In agr. area.

Guernsey (GUHRN-zee), village (1990 pop. 1,155), Platte co., SE Wyo., on North Platte R.; 42°16′N 104°44′W. Elev. 4,354 ft/1,762 m. Junction of RR spur to Hartville (N); supply station; shipping point. Limestone quarries. Wyo. Natl. Guard summer training camp here. In town, Register Cliff has thousands of pioneers' names carved into it; also, Oregon Trail Natl. Historic Landmark, with its wagon trail ruts. Guernsey Reservoir (North Platte R.) and State Park are to NW.

Guernsey Island, W N.F., Canada, in the Bay of Islands, 25 mi/40 km NW of Corner Brook; 1 mi/2 km long, 1 mi/2 km wide; 49°12′N 58°23′W.

Guernsey Reservoir (GUHRN-zee), Platte co., SE Wyo., on North Platte R., 2 mi/3.2 km NW of Guernsey; c.25 mi/40 km long; 42°16′N 104°44′W. Max. capacity 46,000 acre-ft. Formed by Guernsey Dam (rock and earthfill; 105 ft/32 m high), built (1927) as unit in North Platte project for power generation and irrigation. Guernsey State Park on S shore.

Guerrero (ge-RE-ro), state (□ 24,887 sq mi/64,457 sq km; 1990 pop. 2,620,637), S Mexico, on the Pacific Ocean; ⊙ Chilpancingo de los Bravo; 16°17′N 98°04′E. Dominated by the Sierra Madre del Sur, which reaches 12,149 ft/3,703 m in the Pico de Teotepec, Guerrero is extremely mountainous except for a narrow coastal strip, which has a harbor at Acapulco de Juárez. The state's major river is the Río Balsas. The climate of the coast and the deep valleys is hot and seasonally rainy, but the highlands are temperate and drier. Tourism, centered at Acapulco de Juárez, is an economic mainstay. Agr. (the growing of coffee, tobacco, cotton, tropical fruits, and cereals), forest prods., and mining are the state's other chief economic activities. Mineral resources include gold, silver, lead, zinc, iron, coal, precious stones, and sulfur. The silverwork of Taxco de Alarcón is famous. Little industrialization has occurred in Guerrero, despite its abundant hydroelectric power. Historically, Guerrero was divided among the states of Michoacán, Mexico, Puebla, and Oaxaca; it did not

gain sovereignty until 1849. Some of the heaviest fighting of the Mex. war (1810–1821) against Spain took place in the area, which was later named for Vicente Guerrero, one of the revolutionary leaders. Has 75 municipios.

Guerrero (ge-RE-ro), city (1990 pop. 5,636) and township, Chihuahua state, N Mexico, in Sierra Madre Occidental, 85 mi/137 km W of Chihuahua. Elev. 6,560 ft/1,999 m. Silver, lead, copper mining. Also known as Ciudad Guerrero.

Guerrero (ge-RE-ro), town (1990 pop. 944), Coahuila state, N Mexico, near the Rio Grande (Texas border), 25 mi/40 km SSW of Piedras Negras. Grain and cattle center. Also known as Presidio de Río Grande.

Guerrero, Mexico: see NUEVA CIUDAD GUERRERO.

Guevea de Humboldt (we-VE-ah de UHM-bolt), town (1990 pop. 1,398), in E Oaxaca state, Mexico, 25 mi/73 km NNW of port of Salina Cruz. In the headwaters of the Los Perros R.; 16°47′N 95°21′W. Elev. 1,968 ft/600 m. Temperate climate. Agr. (coffee, sugarcane, corn, beans, fruits); woods. Lacks paved roads but is not far from Mexico Highway 185.

Gueydan (gai-DAN), town (1990 pop. 1,611), Vermilion parish, S La., 22 mi/35 km W of Abbeville, near Queue De Tortue; 30°02′N 92°31′W. Elev. 9 ft/3 m. Rice, sugarcane. Hosts Gueydan Duck Festival. Inc. 1899.

Guffey, town, Park co., central Colo., on Currant Creek, in Rocky Mts., and 40 mi/64 km W of Colorado Springs. Elev. 8,680 ft/2,646 m. Tourism, timber. Pike Natl. Forest, Eleven Mile Canyon Reservoir, and Eleven Mile State Park to N. Currant Creek pass to NW (9,654 ft/2,943 m). Formerly Freshwater.

Guide Rock, village (1990 pop. 290), Webster co., S Nebr., 10 mi/16 km E of Red Cloud and on Republican R., near Kansas line; 40°04′N 98°19′W. Livestock; grain. Superior-Courtland Diversion Dam upstream (W).

Guigues (geeg), village, W Que., Canada, near L. Timiskaming, 9 mi/14 km E of Haileybury; 47°27′N 79°26′W. Quartz, silica mining.

Guilarte, Mount (gee-LAHR-te) (3,953 ft/1,205 m), SW central P.R., in Cordillera Central, 13 mi/21 km NW of Ponce, in Guilarte Forest.

Guild, N.H.: see NEWPORT.

Guildhall, town, ⊙ Essex co., NE Vt., on the Connecticut and 24 mi/39 km NE of St. Johnsbury in wilderness recreation area. Town had dates from 1795. Settled 1764.

Guilford (GIL-fuhrd), county (□ 657 sq mi/1,702 sq km; 1990 pop. 347,420), N central N.C.; ⊙ Greensboro; 36°04′N 79°47′W. In Piedmont region; drained by Haw and Deep rivers. Agr. (tobacco, corn, wheat, oats, soybeans, sorghum, hay; dairying; chickens, cattle, hogs); timber (pine, oak). Mfg. at Greensboro and High Point (major furniture mfg. center). Granite quarrying. L. Brandt reservoir to NW. Formed 1770.

Guilford 1 town (1990 pop. 19,848), New Haven co., S Conn., on L.I. Sound; 41°19′N 72°42′W. Fishing, agr. (fruits and vegetables), and tourism are economically important. Guilford lies in an area that includes several summer shore communities. Some of the oldest houses in Conn. are here; the stone Whitfield House (1639–1640), restored in 1936, is a state historical museum. Also of interest are the Hyland House (1660) and the Thomas Griswold House Mus. (1735). Founded 1639. **2** (GIL-fuhrd), industrial town (1990 pop. 1,710), including Guilford village, Piscataquis co., central Maine, on the Piscataquis and 8 mi/12.9 km W of Dover-Foxcroft; 45°12′N 69°20′W. Wood prods.; textiles. Settled 1803; inc. 1816. **3** town (1990 pop. 93), Nodaway co., NW Mo., on Platte R., and 14 mi/23 km SSE of Maryville; 40°10′N 94°44′W. **4** (GIL-fuhrd), uninc. town (1990 pop. 1,618), Franklin co., S Pa., residential suburb 3 mi/4.8 km E of Chambersburg and includes the community of Guilford Heights; 39°55′N 77°35′W. **5** town (1990 pop. 1,941), Windham co., SE Vt., just SE of Brattleboro; 42°47′N 72°37′W. Agr.; resorts.

Guilford, village (1990 pop. 300), Chenango co., S central N.Y., 30 mi/48 km NE of Binghamton; 42°23′N 75°27′W.

Guilford College (GIL-fuhrd), village, Guilford co., N central N.C., 5 mi/8 km W of downtown Greensboro.

Seat of Guilford Col. (Friends; coed.; 1834). To NE is Guilford Courthouse Natl. Military Park. Piedmont Triad International Airport to W.

Guilford Courthouse National Military Park (GIL-fuhrd), Guilford co., N N.C., 4 mi/6.4 km NW of downtown Greensboro. Important Revolutionary War battle fought here March 15, 1781, which led to ultimate defeat of British at Yorktown and end of war. Authorized 1917.

Guin (GWIN), town (1990 pop. 2,464), Marion co., NW Ala., 13 mi/21 km SSE of Hamilton. Lumber; clothing and mobile home mfg.

Guinea, uninc. village, Caroline co., NE Va., 11 mi/18 km S of Fredericksburg. Jackson House (where Stonewall Jackson died). Formerly called Guinea Station.

Guinea Station, Va.: see GUINEA.

Güines (GWEE-naiz), city (1994 est. pop. 46,000), La Habana prov., W Cuba; 22°50′N 82°02′W. It is located in one of the isl.'s most heavily farmed areas. Güines was founded in 1737 as the commercial and financial center of the rich surrounding farm region.

Güinía de Miranda (gwee-NEE-uh dai mee-RAHN-duh), small town, Villa Clara prov., central Cuba, 10 mi/16 km SE of Manicaragua; 20°04′N 79°52′W. Bet. tropical forests to S and tobacco production to N.

Guion (GEI-uhn), village (1990 pop. 93), Izard co., N Ark., 19 mi/31 km WNW of Batesville and on White R.; 35°55′N 91°56′W. Mfg. (industrial sand).

Güira (GWEE-ruh) or **Güira de Macurijes**, town, Matanzas prov., N Cuba, 23 mi/37 km SE of Matanzas; 22°45′N 81°23′W. RR junction and spa in agr. region (sugarcane, fruit).

Güira de Melena (GWEE-ruh dai mai-LAI-nuh), town, La Habana prov., W Cuba, on RR, 25 mi/40 km SSW of Havana; 22°49′N 82°31′W. In agr. region (sugarcane, bananas, potatoes, pineapples; livestock); mfg. of cigars; dairying.

Guisa (GWEE-suh), town (1994 est. pop. 20,000), Granma prov., E Cuba, at N foot of the Sierra Maestra, 10 mi/16 km SE of Bayamo; 20°15′N 76°32′W. Cattle raising; dairying; coffee.

Gulf, county (□ 775 sq mi/1,955 sq km; 1990 pop. 11,504), ⊙ Port St. Joe, NW Fla., in the Fla. Panhandle, bordered by the Gulf of Mexico to the S, Bay co. to the W, Calhoun co. to the N, and Apalachicola R. to the E; 29°53′N 85°14′W. Swampy lowland area, bordered by long sandspits enclosing St. Joseph Bay; contains L. Wimico and part of Dead L. Est. in 1925 when Calhoun co. split in two, it was named for the Gulf of Mexico. Harvesting of pulp and fishing are prominent economic activities. St. Joseph State Park, Billy Joe Rish State Park, and St. Vincent Natl. Wildlife Refuge located on peninsula separated from mainland by St. Joseph Bay. St. Joseph Aquatic Preserve is in St. Joseph Bay. Co. divided by time zone boundary: Central time zone in N, and Eastern time zone in S.

Gulf Breeze, town (□ 23 sq mi/60 sq km; 1990 pop. 5,530), Santa Rosa co., NW Fla., 6 mi/9.7 km SE of Pensacola; 30°22′N 87°10′W. Major beach suburb of Pensacola, to which it is connected by bridge and causeway.

Gulf Hills, uninc. town (1990 pop. 5,004), Jackson co., SE Miss., residential suburb 3 mi/4.8 km NNW of Ocean Springs, near Biloxi Bay; 30°26′N 88°49′W. Resort area.

Gulf Islands, SW B.C., Canada, populated group in Strait of Georgia, bet. mainland and SE Vancouver Isl. Includes Saltspring, Galiano, Valdes, Gabriola, Mayne, Saturna, and Pender isls. Lumbering; mixed farming; fishing; tourism.

Gulf Islands National Seashore (□ 102 sq mi/264 sq km), Harrison and Jackson cos., SE Miss. and Escambia, Santa Rosa, and Okaloosa cos., NW Fla. Historic forts and white sand beaches near Pensacola, Fla.; Fort Massachusetts (on Ship Isl.) and offshore isls. in SE Miss. Includes Ship, Horn, and Petit Bois isls., also Perdido Key and W part of Santa Rosa Isl., Fla. Fort Dickens is located on Santa Rosa. Mainland visitor's center E of Ocean Springs, Miss.; also at Pensacola Beach, Fla., on Santa Rosa. Authorized 1971.

Gulf Park Estates, uninc. town (1990 pop. 2,314), Jackson co., SE Miss., residential suburb 4 mi/6.4 km ESE of Ocean Springs, near Gulf of Mexico (Mississippi Sound); 30°22′N 88°45′W. Resort area.

Gulf Shores, city (1990 pop. 3,261), Baldwin co., SW Ala., 38 mi/61 km SE of Mobile; 30°16′N 87°42′W. Mfg. includes boat parts and repair, wood prods. Resort town with white sand beaches. Hosts a 4-day National Shrimp Festival every Oct. Fort Morgan historic site 21 mi/34 km W.

Gulf Stream, warm ocean current of the N Atlantic Ocean, off E North America, bet. c.24°00′N and 42°00′N. It was first described (1513) by Spanish explorer Ponce de León. The Gulf Stream originates in the Gulf of Mexico, and as the Florida Current, it passes through the Straits of Florida and along the coast of SE U.S., with a breadth of c.50 mi/80 km. North of Cape Hatteras, it is separated from the coast by a narrow southern extension of the cold Lab. Current and flows NE into the Atlantic Ocean. Where the warm surface waters of the Gulf Stream meet the cold winds accompanying the Lab. Current, one of the densest concentrations of fog in the world occurs. Parts of the Gulf Stream current are diverted SE, forming the Canary Currents, which carry cooler waters to the Iberian peninsula and NW Africa. An ensuing current, known as the NORTH ATLANTIC DRIFT, flows NW and provides temperate, relatively warm waters to W Europe. The Gulf Stream has an average speed of 4 mi/6.4 km per hour but slows down as it widens to the north. At the beginning of the Gulf Stream the water temp. is 80°F/27°C; the temp. decreases as the current moves north.

Gulfport, city (1990 pop. 40,775), a ⊙ Harrison co. (seat shared with Biloxi), SE Miss., 65 mi/105 km ENE of New Orleans, La., and 12 mi/19 km W of Biloxi, a port on Mississippi Sound, Gulf of Mexico; bounded N by Bernard Bayou; Biloxi Bay to NE; 30°23′N 89°04′W. A beach resort area, a port of entry (Miss. State Port; man-made port extends into Gulf), and a RR junction, it receives large shipments of bananas. The city's mfg. includes: ink and petroleum resins, steel, appliances, concrete, furniture, lumber, cleaning prods., tungsten carbide, apparel, asphalt, metal bldg. components, transport tanks, plastics, pharmaceuticals, boats, barges. Gulfport was settled (1891) as the site for a RR terminus. In 1902 its harbor was opened, and the city developed as an important lumber-shipping center. With the depletion of timber resources, Gulfport extended its shipping facilities and shipyards, and turned to mfg. and a growing tourist trade. Gambling casinos and several military installations are in Gulfport. A number of antebellum houses remain, and the city has one of the longest artificial sand beaches (28 mi/45 km) in the world, with tourists year-round. Seat of William Carry Col. Gulfport-Biloxi Regional Airport in N; Gulfport Naval Construction Batallion center in W. De Soto Natl. Forest is to the N; Ship Isl., with its Civil War Fort Massachusetts, is 12 mi/19 km out in the sound; passenger ferry to Ship Isl.; Copa and Grand Casinos. Inc. 1898.

Gulfport, town (☐ 3 sq mi/7.8 sq km; 1990 pop. 11,727), Pinellas co., W central Fla., 5 mi/8 km SW of St. Petersburg; 27°45′N 82°42′W. Settled 1843; inc. 1913.

Gulfport, village (1990 pop. 209), Henderson co., W Ill., on the Mississippi (bridged here), 11 mi/18 km SW of Oquawka, opposite Burlington, Iowa; 40°48′N 91°04′W. Agr. (cattle, hogs; corn, soybeans).

Gulkana, village (1990 pop. 103), S Alaska, on Copper R., and 50 mi/80 km NNE of Valdez, on Richardson Highway, just S of Junction with Tok Cut-off; 62°15′N 145°24′W. Tourism.

Gulkana River, S Alaska; rises in foothills of Alaska Range near 62°49′N 145°50′W; flows 70 mi/113 km S to enter Copper R. 3 mi/4.8 km S of Gulkana.

Gull Island, Mich.: see BEAVER ISLANDS.

Gull Islands, 2 small isls. in E entrance to L.I. Sound, SE N.Y., 10 mi/16 km S of New London, Conn. U.S. Fort Michie is on Great Gull Isl. (c.½ mi/⁹⁄₁₀ km long).

Little Gull Isl. (just NE) has lighthouse (41°12′N 72°06′W).

Gull Lake, town (1991 pop. 1,050), SW Sask., Canada, in the Cypress Hills, 35 mi/56 km WSW of Swift Current. Elev. 2,568 ft/783 m. Grain elevators; lumber; livestock.

Gull Lake, S central Alta., Canada, 15 mi/24 km NNW of Red Deer; 15 mi/24 km long, 4 mi/6 km wide. Drains SW into Red Deer R. through Blindman R.

Gull Lake, Canada: see GULLFOOT LAKE, Ont.

Gull Lake, mostly in Kalamazoo co., N end in Barry co., SW Mich., c.12 mi/19 km NE of Kalamazoo; c.4.5 mi/7 km long, 1 mi/1.6 km wide; 42°23′N 85°24′W. Yorkville near S end.

Gull Lake Reservoir (☐ 21 sq mi/54 sq km), Cass and Crow Wing cos., central Minn., on Gull R., 8 mi/12.9 km WNW of Brainerd; 9 mi/14.5 km long, 3 mi/4.8 km wide; 46°25′N 95°21′W. Elev. 1,196 ft/365 m; max. capacity 75,300 acre-ft. Gull R. drains S to Crow Wing R. Fed in N by small stream from Mayo and Upper Gull lakes, fed from W by Home, Cory, and Stony brooks. Formed by dam (16 ft/5 m high) at E outlet, built (1912) by Army Corps of Engineers for flood control; also used for water supply and recreation. Pillsbury State Forest on SW shore; Wilson Bay (SW), Steamboat Bay (SE). Resort area. Lumbertown USA nearby.

Gullfoot Lake or **Gull Lake** (6 mi /10 km long, 1 mi/2 km wide), S Ont., Canada, 45 mi/72 km NW of Peterborough; drains S by Gull R. into Balsam L. and Trent R. Minden is near N end.

Gully, village (1990 pop. 128), Polk co., NW Minn., c.40 mi/64 km NW of Bemidji; 47°46′N 95°37′W. Grain, sunflowers; dairying; mfg. (fertilizers).

GumBranch, town (1990 pop. 291), Liberty co., Ga., 5 mi/8 km W of Hinesville.

Gun Barrel City, town (1990 pop. 3,526), Henderson co., E Texas, 47 mi/76 km SE of Dallas, on E shore of Cedar Creek Reservoir; 32°19′N 96°08′W. Residential and recreational community.

Gun Cay, islet (1990 pop. 1,219), NW Bahama Isls., in Cat Cays (S Biminis); 24°34′N 79°18′W. Lighthouse.

Gun Lake, in Barry co., touches Allegan co. on W, SW Mich., 10 mi/16 km WSW of Hastings; c.3 mi/4.8 km long, 2 mi/3.2 km wide; 42°36′N 85°31′W. Drained by Gun R., which flows c.15 mi/24 km SW to Kalamazoo R. at Otsego. Mfg. (wood furniture). Yankee Springs State Recreational Area on N end.

Gun River, Mich.: see GUN LAKE.

Gunflint Lake, Cook co., NE Minn., and Thunder Bay dist., W Ont., in chain of lakes on Can.-U.S. border, 30 mi/48 km NW of Grand Marais; 8 mi/12.9 km long, 1 mi/1.6 km wide; elev. 1,543 ft/470 m. Drained by Pine R. from W end, fed by short stream from North L. to E. Fishing resorts. U.S. part in Boundary Waters Canoe Area of Superior Natl. Forest. LaVerendrye R. Provincial Park on N shore.

Gunn, town (1990 pop. 65), Cass co., W Mo., 10 mi/16 km E of Harrisonville; 38°40′N 94°09′W.

Gunnison, county (☐ 3,260 sq mi/8,443 sq km; 1990 pop. 10,273) W central Colo.; ⊙ Gunnison; 38°40′N 107°00′W. Sheep-grazing and coal-mining region, drained by Gunnison R., forms Morrow Point and Blue Mesa reservoir in W, both comprise Curecanti Natl. Recreation Area. Taylor Park reservoir and dam are part of irrigation system in E. County includes ranges of Rocky Mts. and parts of Gunnison Natl. Forest in much of NW, NE, and E of co., and part of Uncompahgre Natl. Forests in SW corner. Granor Hill Ski Area in S center. Formed 1877.

Gunnison 1 town (1990 pop. 4,636), ⊙ Gunnison co., W central Colo., on Gunnison R., just N of San Juan Mts., and 95 mi/153 km SE of Grand Junction; 38°32′N 106°55′W. Elev. 7,703 ft/2,348 m. Resort and former trade center in well-irrigated valley; cattle. light mfg. Coal, gold, silver mines nearby. Western State Col. of Colo. is here. Hq. for Gunnison Natl. Forest, which surrounds region to NW, NE, and SE. Roaring Judy State Fish Hatchery to N. Curecanti Natl. Recreation Area to SW. State prisons. Laid out as silver-mining town 1879; inc. 1880. **2** town (1990 pop. 1,298), Sanpete

co., central Utah, on San Pitch R., E of its confluence with Sevier R. Wasatch Range to E in Manti–La Sal Natl. Forest, 13 mi/21 km SW of Manti; 39°09′N 111°48′W. Elev. 5,125 ft/1,562 m. Barley, alfalfa, wheat; dairying; cattle, poultry, sheep, hogs. Originally called Hogs Wallow. Sevier Bridge Reservoir to NW; Gunnison Reservoir to NE. Founded 1860; inc. 1893.

Gunnison, village (1990 pop. 611), Bolivar co., NW Miss., 8 mi/12.9 km NE of Rosedale near Mississippi R.; 33°56′N 90°57′W. In agr. area (cotton, corn, rice, soybeans; cattle).

Gunnison, river, 180 mi/290 km long; rises in E Gunnison co., W central Colo. at confluence of Taylor and Slate rivers at Almont, Crystal, Blue Mesa, and Morrow Point reservoirs (Curecanti Natl. Recreation Area); flows SW, W, and NW through Black Canyon of the Gunnison Natl. Monument, past Delta, to the Colorado R. at Grand Junction, Colo. Gunnison Tunnel, c.5 mi/8 km long, was built bet. 1905 and 1909 to divert the river's water to the Uncompahgre Valley for irrigation.

Gunnison, Mount (12,719 ft/3,877 m), Gunnison co., W Colo., in West Elk Mts., 12 mi/19 km ESE of Paonia.

Gunpowder Falls, stream, N Md.; rises in NE Carroll co., near Pa. line; flows c.60 mi/97 km generally SE, through Baltimore co., to Gunpowder R. c.15 mi/24 km ENE of Baltimore. Prettyboy Dam and Loch Raven Dam impound water-supply reservoirs.

Gunpowder River, N Md., estuary (c.9 mi/14.5 km long) receiving Gunpowder Falls and Little Gunpowder Falls (streams); flows through Hartford and Baltimore cos., enters Chesapeake Bay in Aberdeen Proving Ground, c.15 mi/24 km ENE of Baltimore. The 2 most popular explanations for the name are that Native Americans buried gunpowder along the banks thinking it would grow and a miller ground charcoal here for gunpowder.

Gunter, town (1990 pop. 898), Grayson co., N Texas, 16 mi/26 km SSW of Sherman; 33°27′N 96°44′W. In agr. area (cattle; cotton); mfg. (pressure vessels, wooden staircases).

Guntersville, city (1990 pop. 7,038), ⊙ Marshall co., NE Ala., on Guntersville L. (on Tennessee R.), and 27 mi/43 km NW of Gadsden; river port. Processing center for cotton area; tires, feed, steel pipe, surgical supplies, textiles, lumber. Settled c.1818; named Marshall 1838; renamed 1848. Industries stimulated by construction of Guntersville Dam (7 mi/11.3 km NW) and development of TVA.

Guntersville Lake (☐ 108 sq mi/280 sq km), Marshall and Jackson cos., NE Ala., on Tennessee R., 7 mi/11.3 km NW of Guntersville, 75 mi/121 km ESE (upstream) of Wheeler Dam; 82 mi/132 km long, 1 mi/1.6 km–4 mi/6.4 km wide; 34°25′N 86°23′W. Extends into Marion co., SE Tenn., to Nickajack Lock and Dam (Nickajack L.); max. capacity 1,018,700 acre-ft. Formed by Guntersville Lock and Dam, a major TVA dam (94 ft/29 m high; 3,979 ft/1,213 m long) completed 1939; built for navigation, flood control, and power generation. U.S. Highway 431/State Highway 1 crosses dam.

Guntown, village (1990 pop. 692), Lee co., NE Miss., 13 mi/21 km N of Tupelo; 34°26′N 88°39′W. In agr. (cotton, grain; poultry, cattle; dairying) and timber area; mfg. (asphalt, rope, metal fabrication, fiberboard building materials). Lake Lamar Bruce State Lake to SE.

Gurabo (goo-RAH-bo), town (1990 pop. 28,737), E P.R., on the Loíza R. basin and 17 mi/27 km SSE of San Juan. Industrial and commercial area; mfg. (clothing, electronics, candy, pharmaceuticals).

Gurdon (GUHRD-uhn), town (1990 pop. 2,199), Clark co., S central Ark., 15 mi/24 km SSW of Arkadelphia; 33°55′N 93°09′W. RR junction. Mfg. (furniture, grade lumber, charcoal, raftwood, lumber, marimbas, drumsticks).

Gurley (GUHR-lee), village (1990 pop. 198), Cheyenne co., W Nebr., 12 mi/19 km N of Sidney, and on branch of North Platte R.; 41°19′N 102°58′W. Mfg. (steel fabrication and cabs for tractors).

Gurnee (gur-NEE), village (1990 pop. 13,701), Lake co., extreme NE Ill., suburb 37 mi/60 km NW of downtown

Chicago, on Des Plaines R. (bridged here), just W of Waukegan; 42°22′N 87°56′W. Remnant agr.; mfg. (medical equipment, pharmaceuticals, digital controls, inks, lighting fixtures, lubricants, emulsifiers, pumps and compressors, packaging, video games). Site of Gurnee Mills, one of the largest shopping centers in U.S. Site of major amusement park (Six Flags Great America) and outlet mall.

Gurnet Point, Mass.: see PLYMOUTH BAY.

Gustavia (goo-STAH-vyah), town, W Saint-Barthélemy, Fr. West Indies, 150 mi/241 km NNW of Basse-Terre, Guadeloupe; 17°54′N 62°52′W. Agr. (cotton, tropical fruits, livestock); fishing. Has a good harbor.

Gustavo A. Madero or **Villa Gustavo A. Madero** (goos-TAH-vo ah mah-DE-ro), delegación (1990 pop. 1,268,068), Federal dist., central Mexico, 2.5 mi/4 km N of Mexico City. Mfg. center (flour and textile milling, soapmaking). The Basilica de Guadalupe is in Gustavo A. Madero. Mineral springs and stone quarries are nearby.

Gustavo Díaz Ordaz (goos-TAH-vo DEE-ahs or-DAHZ), city (1990 pop. 11,933), N Tamaulipas state, Mexico, 5 mi/8 km W of Reynosa near the Marte R. Gómez Dam (Presa Marte R. Gómez); 17°58′N 91°13′W. This town is named after the president of Mexico from 1964 to 1970. Formerly called San Miguel de Camargo.

Gustavus (guh-STAI-vuhs), village, SE Alaska, on Icy Strait, 50 mi/80 km W of Juneau, near Glacier Bay Natl. Monument. Tourism. School.

Gustine, city (1990 pop. 3,931), Merced co., central Calif., in San Joaquin Valley, 25 mi/40 km S of Modesto; 37°15′N 121°00′W. Irrigated farming (sweet potatoes, beans, tomatoes), fruit growing, melons, almonds, grain, alfalfa; poultry; dairying; mfg. plastic pipe. San Luis Reservoir and State Recreation Area to S; San Luis and Merced natl. wildlife refuges to SE; George J. Hatfield State Park to N; Delta Mendota Canal to W. Inc. 1915.

Gustine, village (1990 pop. 430), Comanche co., central Texas, near Leon R., 33 mi/53 km ENE of Brownwood; 31°51′N 98°24′W. In agr. area (dairying; cattle; peanuts, pecans); mfg. (burial garments); oil and gas.

Guthrie, county (□ 593 sq mi/1,536 sq km; 1990 pop. 10,935), W central Iowa; ⊙ Guthrie Center; 41°40′N 94°30′W. Prairie agr. area (cattle, poultry; corn, oats), drained by Middle Raccoon and South Raccoon rivers and by Middle R. and Brushy Creek. Sand and gravel pits. Springbrook State Park and Convention Center in N; Sheeder Prairie State Preserve in W. Widespread flooding in area in 1993. Formed 1851.

Guthrie (GUHTH-ree), city (1990 pop. 10,518), ⊙ Logan co., central Okla., 28 mi/45 km N of Oklahoma City, near Cimarron R.; 35°50′N 97°25′W. Elev. 977 ft/298 m. RR junction. Processing and commercial center for oil production, dairying, and agr. area. Mfg. (conveyors, wooden containers, oil-field and pollution control equipment); RR shops. Seat of Benedictine Heights Col.; Mineral Wells Park is nearby. Langston Univ., 10 mi/16 km NE at Langston. Founded 1889; inc. 1890; it was territorial capital until 1907, then state capital

until 1910. The city contains a large Victorian historical district.

Guthrie (GUHTH-ree), town (1990 pop. 1,504), Todd co., S Ky., at Tenn. line, 23 mi/37 km SE of Hopkinsville; 36°38′N 87°10′W. RR junction. Agr. (tobacco, grain; livestock; dairying; timber); mfg. (corrugated paper, lumber, uniforms, railroad ties). Settled 1860; inc. 1867.

Guthrie, uninc. village (1990 pop. 160), ⊙ King co., NW Texas, c.85 mi/137 km E of Lubbock. Elev. 1,754 ft/535 m. In ranching region (cattle, horses; cotton; vegetables); oil and gas.

Guthrie Center, town (1990 pop. 1,614), ⊙ Guthrie co., W central Iowa, on South Raccoon R. and c.45 mi/72 km WNW of Des Moines; 41°40′N 94°30′W. Milling (flour, cereals, feed). Coal mines nearby. Springbrook State Park and Convention Center is N; Sheeder Prairie State Preserve to W. Inc. 1880.

Gutiérrez Zamora (goo-tee-E-res sah-MO-rah), town (1990 pop. 13,662), Veracruz state, E Mexico, on Tecolutla R., 5 mi/8 km from its mouth on the Gulf, and 15 mi/24 km E of Papantla de Olarte. Tobacco-growing center.

Guttenberg 1 town (1990 pop. 2,257), Clayton co., NE Iowa, on the Mississippi (dam and locks here), and 10 mi/16 km E of Elkader; 42°47′N 91°05′W. Mfg. of boxes, farm tools, beverages. Lead and zinc deposits. First settled in 1834 as Prairie la Porte; colonized and named by German immigrants 1845; inc. 1851. **2** (GUH-tuhn-buhrg), town (1990 pop. 8,268), Hudson co., NE N.J., on Hudson R., 5 mi/8 km NNE of Jersey City; 40°47′N 74°00′W. Mfg. (textiles, clothing, knit goods, metal prods., vegetable oils). Inc. 1859.

Guyandotte River (GEI-uhn-daht), 166 mi/267 km long, SW W.Va.; rises in S Raleigh co. SSW of Beckley, near Sophia; flows SW, W (through R. D. Bailey L. reservoir), and NNW past Gilbert, Logan, and Barboursville, to Ohio R. at Huntington.

Guymon (GEI-muhn), city (1990 pop. 7,803), ⊙ Texas co., central Okla. panhandle, on high plains of the panhandle, near North Canadian R., c.105 mi/169 km N of Amarillo (Texas), and 100 mi/161 km WNW of Woodward, Okla.; 36°41′N 101°28′W. Elev. 3,126 ft/953 m. Trade center for wheat, livestock, and dairy area. Oil and gas wells. Mfg. (agr. tillage tools, pressure tanks, printing, formula feeds). Optima Natl. Wildlife Refuge and Optima L. (North Canadian R.) to E. U.S. soil conservation station is nearby. Inc. 1905.

Guyot Glacier (goi-YUHT), SE Alaska, W arm of Malaspina Glacier, in St. Elias Mts.; drains into Icy Bay c.70 mi/113 km E of Yakutat; 60°N 141°22′W.

Guyot, Mount 1 (13,370 ft/4,075 m) in Rocky Mts., Park and Summit cos., central Colo., 6 mi/9.7 km ESE of Breckenridge. **2** (GEE-o), peak (6,621 ft/2,018 m) in Great Smoky Mts., on Tenn.-N.C. line, 40 mi/64 km ESE of Knoxville.

Guy's Hill or **Guys Hill**, village (1991 pop. 3,165), St. Mary parish, E central Jamaica, 25 mi/40 km NW of Kingston; 18°15′N 77°00′W. Tropical fruits, coffee, spices.

Guysborough (GEIZ-buh-ruh), county (□ 1,611 sq mi/4,172 sq km; 1991 pop. 11,724), S central N.S., Canada, on the Atlantic; ⊙ Guysborough; 45°24′N 61°30′W.

Guysborough, village (1991 pop. 6,518), ⊙ Guysborough co., E central N.S., Canada, at head of Chedabucto Bay, 30 mi/48 km SE of Antigonish; fishing port; ships pulpwood. Site of French fort, established 1636.

Guyton (GEI-tuhn), town (1990 pop. 740), Effingham co., E Ga., 25 mi/40 km NW of Savannah; 32°20′N 81°23′W. Mfg. of go-cart parts.

Guzmán, Mexico: see CIUDAD GUZMÁN.

Guzmán, Lake (goos-MAHN) (□ 56 sq mi/145 sq km), Chihuahua state, N Mexico, 60 mi/97 km SW of Juárez. An intermittent lake, the basin is 12 mi/19 km long, 3 mi/4.8 km–6 mi/9.7 km wide. Receives Casas Grandes R.

G.W. Andrews, Lake, reservoir (□ 2 sq mi/5.2 sq km), extreme SE Ala. and partly on Ga. border, on Chattahoochee R., 18 mi/29 km NW of Dothan; 31°16′N 85°07′W. Max. capacity 18,180 acre-ft. Extends N into Houston and Henry cos. on W shore (Ala.) and Early and Clay cos. on E shore (Ga.). Formed by George W. Andrews Lock and Dam (59 ft/18 m high), built (1964) by Army Corps of Engineers for navigation. Dam also known as George W. Andrews L. Dam.

Gwinn, town (1990 pop. 2,370), Marquette co., NW Upper Peninsula, Mich., 19 mi/31 km SSW of Marquette, at junction of Middle and East branches of Escanaba R.; 46°17′N 87°26′W. Agr. area. Sheet metal fabrication. Co. park nearby. K.I. Sawyer Air Force Base to NE.

Gwinner (GWIN-uhr), village (1990 pop. 585), Sargent co., SE N.Dak., 15 mi/24 km S of Lisbon; 46°13′N 97°39′W. Mfg. (computer printing, farm machinery, construction equipment).

Gwinnett (gwin-ET), county (□ 437 sq mi/1,132 sq km; 1990 pop. 352,910), N central Ga.; ⊙ Lawrenceville; 33°58′N 84°02′W. Piedmont area bounded NW by Chattahoochee R. and drained by Apalachee and Yellow rivers. One of the fastest-growing cos. in the U.S. in the 1980s and 1990s, as it became a middle-class mecca for metropolitan Atlanta. While still a bedroom community known for affordable housing, it became an important center of high-tech manufacturing, business, and industrial parks. Largest retail mall in state under construction in the late 1990s. Formed 1818.

Gwynn Island, Mathews co., E Va., just offshore (causeway) in Chesapeake Bay, at entrance to Piankatank R. estuary, 5 mi/8 km N of Mathews; c.3 mi/4.8 km long. Fish, crabs, oysters. Gwynn village on E side.

Gwynneville, village, Shelby co., central Ind., 12 mi/19 km NW of Rushville, near Rush co. line. Agr. area. Mfg. (agricultural prods.).

Gypsum, town (1990 pop. 1,750), Eagle co., W central Colo., on Eagle R. at mouth of Gypsum Creek, just N of Sawatch Mts., and 6 mi/9.7 km W of Eagle; 39°38′N 106°57′W. Elev. 6,320 ft/1,926 m. Some sheep; timber; mfg. (wood prods., wallboard).

Gypsum 1 (JIP-suhm), village (1990 pop. 365) Saline co., central Kansas, 13 mi/21 km SE of Salina; 38°42′N 97°25′W. RR junction. In wheat and cattle region. **2** village, Ottawa co., N Ohio, 9 mi/14 km WNW of Sandusky, across Sandusky Bay.

Gypsumville, village, central Man., Canada, near NE end of L. Manitoba, 150 mi/241 km NNW of Winnipeg; 51°46′N 98°37′W. Gypsum quarrying.

H

H. Neely Henry Lake, Calhoun co., NE Ala., 17 mi/ 27 km SSW of Gadsden, on the Coosa R.; 33°47′N 86°03′E. Max. capacity 109,000 acre-ft. Formed by H. Neely Henry Dam (57 ft/17 m high), built (1966) by the Ala. Power Company for hydroelectric power and recreation; crossed by State Highway 144. Also called Neely Henry L. and Dam; commonly called Henry Neely L.

Ha Ha Bay, inlet of the Saguenay R., S central Que., E Canada, 12 mi/19 km ESE of Chicoutimi; 7 mi/11 km long, 3 mi/5 km wide. At its head are Bagotville, Port Alfred, and Grande Baie.

Haakon (HAW-kin), county (□ 1,827 sq mi/4,732 sq km; 1990 pop. 2,624), central S.Dak.; ☉ Philip; 44°17′N 101°31′W. Agr. and cattle-raising region drained in S by Bad R. and in N by Plum Creek; bounded N by Cheyenne R. Wheat; ranching; cattle, poultry. Cheyenne River Indian Reservation to N in Ziebach co. Formed 1914.

Habana, Cuba: see HAVANA.

Habana, La, Cuba: see HAVANA.

Habersham (HA-buhr-sham), county (□ 283 sq mi/ 733 sq km; 1990 pop. 27,621), NE Ga. on S.C. state line; ☉ Clarkesville; 34°38′N 83°32′W. Blue Ridge (N) and piedmont (S) area. Farming (cotton, hay, sweet potatoes, apples, peaches; poultry, cattle, hogs; timber). Textile mfg. Part of Chattahoochee Natl. Forest in N. Formed 1818.

Hachita (ah-CHEE-tuh), uninc. village, Grant co., SW N.Mex., 38 mi/61 km WSW of Deming, at crossroads just N of N.Mex. bootheel, 12 mi/19 km to NW of Mexico (Chihuahua) border. In desert area. Little Hatchet Mts. to W; Cedar Mt. Range to E; Continental Divide passes to N. Port of entry at Antelope Wells c.46 mi/74 km to SSW.

Hacienda Heights (hah-see-EN-dah), uninc. city (1990 pop. 52,354), Los Angeles co., S Calif., residential suburb 16 mi/26 km ESE of downtown Los Angeles, NE of Whittier, in Puente Hills; 34°00′N 117°58′W. Mfg. (electrical and electronic equip.).

Hackberry, uninc. town (1990 pop. 1,664), Cameron parish, La., 15 mi/24 km N of Cameron; 29°59′N 93°20′W. Storage facility of the Natl. Strategic Petroleum Reserve. A recreational fishing area, it claims to be the Crab Capital of the South.

Hackensack (HA-kin-sak), city (1990 pop. 37,049), ☉ Bergen co., NE N.J., on the Hackensack R., a residential and industrial suburb of N.Y. city; 40°53′N 74°02′W. Mfg. includes furniture, clothing, textiles, machinery, and processed foods. Trading post here est. 1647 by Du. settlers from Manhattan. During the Amer. Revolution the city served as camping ground for armies of both sides. Grew as a commercial and shipping center in the early 1800s. Of interest are the Church on the Green (First Du. Reformed; built 1696, rebuilt 1728) and the von Steuben House (1739), a state historic site and the hq. of the co. historical society. A campus of Fairleigh Dickinson Univ. is here. Settled 1647, inc. as a city 1921.

Hackensack (HA-kin-sak), village (1990 pop. 245), Cass co., central Minn., 12 mi/19 km SSE of Walker on E shore of Birch L.; 46°55′N 94°31′W. In wooded lakes region. Poultry; oats, wild rice; dairying; timber; mfg. (signs, septic tanks). Part of Foothills State Forest to W; Chippewa Natl. Forest to N.

Hackensack (HA-kin-sak), river, c.45 mi/72 km long, N.Y. and N.J.; rises in SE N.Y.; flows S through the Jersey Meadows, NE N.J., to Newark Bay. The lower Hackensack is heavily industrialized and economically tied to the ports on Newark Bay and to the industrial development on the nearby Passaic R. It is navigable by oceangoing vessels in N.J. to Kearny, and by tugs and barges to Hackensack. Upper course is dammed to form 3 reservoirs that supply water to Rockland (N.Y.) and Bergen (N.J.) cos.

Hackett, village (1990 pop. 490), Sebastian co., W Ark., 13 mi/21 km S of Fort Smith, near Okla. state line; 35°11′N 94°24′W.

Hackettstown, town (1990 pop. 8,120), Warren co., NW N.J., in fertile Musconetcong Valley, 14 mi/23 km W of Dover. Metal prods., machinery, plastics; vegetables, dairy prods. State fish hatcheries located here. Seat of Centenary Col. Inc. 1853.

Hackleburg, town (1990 pop. 1,161), Marion co., NW Ala., 13 mi/21 km NE of Hamilton. Apparel; mobile homes. William B. Bankhead Natl. Forest is E.

Hackletons Cliff, 1,000-ft/305-m limestone escarpment, c. 1 mi/1.6 km inland from E coast of Barbados; 1.5 mi/ 2.4 km long.

Hadar (HAI-duhr), village (1990 pop. 291), Pierce co., NE Nebr., 7 mi/11.3 km SSE of Pierce, and on branch of Elkhorn R.; 42°06′N 97°27′W.

Haddam, town (1990 pop. 6,769), Middlesex co., S Conn., bisected by the Connecticut R. (here bridged), just S of Middletown; 41°28′N 72°32′W. Includes the Higganum sect. of Haddam. Agr. Industries include lumberyards; mfg. of machinery, electronic equip., wire prods., plastics, molding; extruding and offset printing. Atomic energy plant. State forest. Settled 1662, inc. 1668.

Haddam (HAD-uhm), village (1990 pop. 195), Washington co., N Kansas, on small affluent of Little Blue R., and 13 mi/21 km WNW of Washington; 39°51′N 97°17′W. Grain; livestock.

Haddock (HAD-uhk), town (1990 pop. 750), Jones co., Ga., 17 mi/27 km NE of Macon; 33°02′N 83°25′W. Mfg. of canned food prods.

Haddon (HA-duhn), township (1990 pop. 14,837), Camden co., S N.J., 4 mi/6.4 km SE of Camden; 39°54′N 75°03′W. Suburban residential community. Inc. 1865.

Haddon Heights (HA-duhn), residential borough (1990 pop. 7,860), Camden co., SW N.J., 5 mi/8 km SE of Camden; 39°52′N 75°04′W. Laid out c.1891, inc. 1904.

Haddonfield (HA-duhn-feeld), borough (1990 pop. 11,628), Camden co., SE N.J., a residential suburb just SE of Camden; 39°53′N 75°01′W. Of interest are Indian King Tavern (1750), where the 1st state legislature met in 1777, and the Haddonfield historical society; downtown area is historic preservation dist. with many 19th- and some 18th-cent. structures. Site of first complete dinosaur fossil ever found, "Haddonfield Hadrosaur," made natl. historical landmark 1993. Settled c.1713, inc. 1875.

Hadley, town (1990 pop. 4,231), Hampshire co., W central Mass., on Connecticut R. opposite Northampton; 42°22′N 72°34′W. Paper mills. Settled 1659, inc. 1661.

Hadley, village (1990 pop. 94), Murray co., SW Minn., 5 mi/8 km W of Slayton, near Beaver Creek; 44°00′N 95°51′W. Dairying.

Hadleys Purchase, land purchase, Coos co., N central N.H., 25 mi/40 km SSW of Berlin. Wilderness area in White Mt. Natl. Forest.

Hadlock, uninc. town (1990 pop. 2,742), Jefferson co., NW Wash., 6 mi/9.7 km S of Port Townsend, on Port Townsend Bay, arm of Puget Sound; 48°03′N 122°46′W. Fish, crabs, oysters. Resort area. Old Fort Townsend State Park to N; Anderson L. State Park to W; Jefferson Co. Internatl. Airport to W. Bridge to Indian Isl. Naval Reservation 1 mi/1.6 km ESE. Also called Port Hadlock.

Hadlyme, village and postal section of East Haddam and Lyme, Conn., in N Lyme and S East Haddam. Gillette Castle State Park, with rock mansion of actor William Hooker Gillette (noted for creating role of Sherlock Holmes in 1899) overlooking Connecticut R. Seasonal ferry to Chester.

Hafford, town (1991 pop. 478), central Sask., W Canada, 50 mi/80 km NW of Saskatoon, near Redberry L. (9 mi/14 km long, 6 mi/10 km wide); 52°43′N 107°21′W. Wheat.

Hagaman, village (□ 1 sq mi/2.6 sq km; 1990 pop. 1,377), Montgomery co., E central N.Y., 2 mi/3.2 km N of Amsterdam; 42°58′N 74°09′W.

Hagan (HAI-guhn), city (1990 pop. 787), Evans co., E central Ga., 3 mi/4.8 km W of Claxton; 32°09′N 81°56′W.

Hagensborg, village, W central B.C., W Canada, at E end of Bella Coola Valley, 13 mi/21 km E of Bella Coola; 52°23′N 126°34′W. Settled by Norwegians from Minnesota (1874), attracted to area for its similarity to Norway. Mixed farming; fishing; timber.

Hager City (HAI-guhr), village, Pierce co., W Wis., 3 mi/ 4.8 km N (by bridge) of Red Wind (Minn.), on Mississippi R. Barley, soybeans; livestock. Mfg. (power transmission poles).

Hagerhill (HAI-guhr-hil), uninc. town (1990 pop. 850), Johnson co., E Ky., 3 mi/4.8 km SSE of Paintsville, near Levisa Fork R. Bituminous coal. Mfg. (machinery).

Hagerman, town (1990 pop. 961), Chaves co., SE N.Mex., near Pecos R., near mouth of Rio Felix, 23 mi/37 km SSE of Roswell; 33°06′N 104°19′W. In cotton and alfalfa region.

Hagerman 1 village (1990 pop. 600), Gooding co., S Idaho, 15 mi/24 km SW of Gooding, and on Snake R., near mouth of Big Wood R.; elev. 2,964 ft/903 m; 42°49′N 114°54′W. Watermelons; corn, wheat, alfalfa; winery. U.S. fish hatchery. Hagerman Valley Historical Society Mus. here. Bliss Dam (Snake R.) to N; Hagerman Fossil Beds Natl. Monument to S. **2** village (1990 pop. 1,450), Suffolk co., SE N.Y., just E of Patchogue; 40°46′N 72°59′W.

Hagerman Fossil Beds National Monument (□ 7 sq mi/18.1 sq km), Twin Falls co., S Idaho, 23 mi/ 37 km WNW of Twin Falls. Fossils dating from the Pliocene era, with over 125 prehistoric zebra-like horse skeletons excavated. Authorized 1988.

Hagerman Pass, Colo.: see SAWATCH MOUNTAINS.

Hagerstown (HAI-guhrz-toun), city (1990 pop. 35,445), ☉ Washington co., NW Md., on Antietam Creek, near its junction with the Potomac R., in the fertile Cumberland Valley; 39°38′N 77°43′W. Shipping and processing center for agr. prods. Its diverse mfg. includes pipe organs, aircraft, and furniture. The 1st settler was Jonathan Hager, a Westphalian German, who built a home here in 1737, which is now a mus. Most of the other settlers were also German. Occupied both by Northern and Southern troops during the Civil War; the bloody battle of Antietam (Sharpsburg) was fought nearby. The Baltimore and Ohio RR reached here in 1867, and for many decades the town was the junction of 4 RRs. Fort Ritchie, 13 mi/21 km NE on Pa. state line scheduled for closing. Was major center for Intelligence Training in World War II. Inc. 1791.

Hagerstown, town (1990 pop. 1,835), Wayne co., E Ind., on W Fork of Whitewater R., and 16 mi/26 km WNW of Richmond; 39°55′N 85°10′W. Trading center in livestock and grain area; mfg. (candy, consumer goods, wood prods.).

Hagerstown Valley, N Md. The valley and ridge extend approximately 65 mi/105 km W from South Mt. and Elk Ridge (E) to Dans (local name for the Allegheny front), Powell, and Fairview mts. (W). The 2 distinct subdivisions of the region are the Valley-Ridge sect. and the Great Appalachian Valley, also known as Hagerstown Valley in Md., Shenandoah Valley in Va., and Cumberland Valley in Pa. The 2 rivers draining into Hagerstown Valley are the Antietam to the E and Conococheague to the W.

Hagersville (HAI-guhrz-vil), village, S Ont., central Canada, 22 mi/35 km SW of Hamilton; 42°57′N 80°03′W. Dairying; grain and seed milling. Stone quarrying; natural-gas wells.

Hague, village (1991 pop. 655), central Sask., W Canada, 30 mi/48 km NNE of Saskatoon; 52°30′N 106°25′W. Mixed farming; dairying.

Hague 1 (HAIG), resort village (1990 pop. 450), Warren co., E N.Y., in the Adirondack Mts., on W shore of L. George, 8 mi/12.9 km SSW of Ticonderoga; 43°42′N 73°32′W. **2** village (1990 pop. 109), Emmons co., S N.Dak., 20 mi/32 km SSE of Linton; 46°01′N 100°00′W. Rice L. to W. **3** uninc. village, Westmoreland co., E Va., 50 mi/80 km ESE of Fredericksburg. Agr. (grain, soybeans; cattle. Nearby is Yeocomico Church, originally built 1655; rebuilt 1706.

Hague's Peak, Colo.: see MUMMY RANGE.

Hahira (hai-HEI-ruh), town (1990 pop. 1,353), Lowndes

co., S Ga., 12 mi/19 km NNW of Valdosta; 30°59′N 83°22′W. Tobacco market; logging, wood production; center of production for honey and beekeeping supplies.

Hahnville (HAHN-vil), uninc. town (1990 pop. 2,599), ⊙ St. Charles parish, SE La., on the Mississippi R., and 19 mi/31 km W of New Orleans; 29°58′N 90°25′W. Vegetables, sugarcane; cattle; alligators, catfish, crabs; mfg. (jambalaya and dirty rice). Petroleum refining nearby.

Haigler, village (1990 pop. 225), Dundy co., S Nebr., 20 mi/32 km W of Benkelman, and on Republican R., at Kansas state line, near Colo. state line; 40°00′N 101°56′W. Livestock; grain. Rock Creek State Recreation Area and fish hatchery to NE.

Haiku (HAH-ee-KOO), town (1990 pop. 3,500), on N coast of Maui Isl., Maui co., Hawaii, 9 mi/14.5 km E of Kahului, 3 mi/4.8 km inland from Pauwela Point. Sugarcane, pineapples; cattle. Hookipa Beach Park to NW, Koolau Forest Reserve to SE.

Hailey, city (1990 pop. 3,687), ⊙ Blaine co., S central Idaho, on Big Wood R., and c.100 mi/161 km E of Boise; 43°31′N 114°18′W. Elev. 5,342 ft/1,628 m. Trade center for mining (silver, lead) and livestock area; mfg. (printing and publishing); lumber milling. Summer resort, hq. for Sawtooth Natl. Forest (NW and NE). Friedman Memorial Airport. Clarendon Hot Springs to NW. Sawtooth Mts. are N. Inc. as village 1903, as city 1909.

Haileybury, town (1991 pop. 4,962), ⊙ Timiskaming dist., E Ont., central Canada, on L. Timiskaming, 80 mi/129 km N of North Bay. Distributing and residential center for rich mining region, with pulp, lumber milling. Ski resort. Airfield. Silver, gold, cobalt are mined in immediate vicinity. Site of mining school. Developed after discovery (1903) of silver at nearby Cobalt; inc. 1905. Town was almost wholly destroyed (1922) by fire.

Haileyville, town (1990 pop. 918), Pittsburg co., SE Okla., 12 mi/19 km ESE of McAlester and adjoining Hartshorne (E); 34°51′N 95°34′W. In cattle-raising area. Jack Fork Mts. to S; headwaters of L. Arrowhead reservoir to N. Settled c.1890.

Haines 1 village (1990 pop. 1,238), SE Alaska, on Chilkoot Inlet, arm of Lynn Canal, and 75 mi/121 km NNW of Juneau, 15 mi/24 km SSW of Skagway; 59°14′N 135°26′W. Tourism; fishing and fish processing. Site of state fair; Chilkoot dancers. During World War II a highway, the Haines Cut-off, was built connecting Haines with the Alaska Highway at Haines Junction (B.C.). N terminus of Alaska ferry system. Docks near former Chilkoot Barracks, previously site of Fort William H. Seward, U.S. army post. **2** village (1990 pop. 405), Baker co., NE Oregon, 10 mi/16 km NNW of Baker City, on Powder R., at mouth of Rock Creek; 44°54′N 117°56′W. Elev. 3,333 ft/1,016 m. Dairy prods.; wheat, potatoes; sheep, cattle. Timber. Site of Eastern Oregon Mus. Anthony Lakes Ski Area to W. Wallowa-Whitman Natl. Forest to W.

Haines, borough (□ 2,357 sq mi/6,105 sq km; 1990 pop. 2,117), SE Alaska, on Canada (B.C.; E and NW) border, at head of Long Canal inlet (which forms part of E boundary). Main towns are Haines and Skagway. Chilkat Range to S; part of the Coast Mts. to NE; Takhinsah Mts. to W. Drained by Chilkat and Klehini rivers. Part of Tongass Natl. Forest in S and E. Haines State Forest and Chilkat State Park in center. Klondike Gold Rush Natl. Historical Site at Skagway. Tourism. Fishing; timber.

Haines City (HAINZ), town (□ 8 sq mi/20.7 sq km; 1990 pop. 11,683), Polk co., central Fla., c.50 mi/80 km ENE of Tampa; 28°06′N 81°37′W. Citrus-fruit shipping center, with packing houses and canneries; mfg. of fertilizer, citrus oil, and pulp feed. Seat of military institute.

Haines Cut-off, SE Alaska and NW Canada (NW B.C. and SW Yukon), branch (150 mi/241 km long) of the Alaska Highway; extends N from Haines (Alaska), via Chilkat Pass (B.C.), to junction with Alaska Highway at Haines Junction (Yukon Territory). Alaska Highway outlet to Gulf of Alaska and SE Alaska towns on the Alaska Panhandle.

Haines Falls, resort village (1990 pop. 700), Greene co., SE N.Y., in the Catskill Mts., at upper end of Kaaterskill Clove, 12 mi/19 km W of Catskill; 42°12′N 74°06′W. Scenic waterfall here. North L. is E.

Haines Junction, village (1991 pop. 477), SW Yukon, NW Canada, 120 mi/193 km NW of Skagway, and on Alaska Highway, at junction with Haines Cut-off (road to Haines, Alaska); 60°45′N 137°32′W.

Haines Landing, Maine: see RANGELEY.

Hainesport, township (1990 pop. 3,249), Burlington co., W N.J., 2 mi/3.2 km W of Mt. Holly; 39°58′N 74°50′W. Rancocas State Park to E.

Hainesville 1 village, Lake co., NE Ill., 10 mi/16 km W of Waukegan; 42°20′N 88°04′W. **2** village, Sussex co., NW N.J., 2 mi/3.2 km E of the Delaware R., and 14 mi/ 23 km N of Newton. In hilly recreation region; Delaware Water Gap Natl. Recreation Area just W.

Hairy Hill, village (1991 pop. 69), central Alta., W Canada, 19 mi/31 km NNE of Vegreville. Tanning, dairying; mixed farming; grain.

Haiti (HAI-tee), Fr. *Haïti* (ah-ee-TEE), independent republic (□ 10,700 sq mi/27,713 sq km; 1990 pop. 5,820,000), West Indies, on the W ⅓ of the isl. of Hispaniola, on the Atlantic Ocean (N) and the Caribbean Sea (S); ⊙ PORT-AU-PRINCE 19°00′N 72°25′W. Bordered E by the Dominican Republic. Jamaica lies to the W and Cuba to the NW. Important cities include Port-au-Prince, CAP-HAÏTIEN, and GONAÏVES. The offshore isls. of Tortuga and Gonâve also belong to Haiti. Agr. is the principal economic activity. Mostly mountainous; c.⅓ of the land is arable. Subsistence crops include cassava, rice, sugarcane, sorghum, yams, corn, and plantains. Most Haitians own and farm tiny plots of land, and great pop. density has caused rural poverty. Coffee is the major export; other exports include cotton, sugar, sisal, bauxite, and essences. Spiny lobsters constitute an important share of Haitian exports to the U.S., the country's leading trading partner. Industry in Haiti consists largely of light mfg.; products include foodstuffs, liquors, essential oils, leather goods, soap, and footwear. Some bauxite and copper are mined but other mineral deposits have barely been tapped. There is a cruise-ship port at Labadu. The most densely populated country in Lat. Amer. and has the lowest per capita income. Need for more farmland, fuel, and construction materials has led to serious deforestation. Prolonged economic inequality, political instability, and a near total lack of medical care continue to be serious problems in Haiti. About 95% of the inhabitants are descendants of Afr. slaves who still follow West Afr. cultural patterns. Since the mid-19th cent., however, Haiti has been dominated by the mulatto minority, which clings to Fr. cultural traditions; the official languages of Haiti are Haitian Creole and Fr., although the vast majority of the people speak the former. Roman Catholicism is the predominant religion, but Afr. nature gods are still worshipped and *vodun* (voodoo) rites are practiced. Economic hardship and political upheavals have caused numerous Haitians to emigrate, especially to the U.S. Despite the conditions here, the U.S. continued to maintain and enforce all immigration regulations into the early 1990s, which included sending back many Haitian emigres. The isl. of Hispaniola was inhabited by the Arawaks prior to the arrival of Columbus in 1492. Disease, ill treatment, and execution by the Spaniards decimated the Arawaks, who gave Haiti ("land of mountains") its name. While establishing plantations in E Hispaniola (now the Dominican Republic), however, the Span. largely ignored the W part of the isl., which by the 17th cent. became a base for Fr. and Eng. buccaneers. Gradually Fr. colonists, importing Afr. slaves, developed sugar plantations on the N coast. Spain ceded Haiti (then called Saint-Domingue) to France in 1697. It became France's most prosperous colony in the Americas and one of the world's chief coffee and sugar producers. Haitian society became stratified into Frenchmen, Creoles, freed blacks, and black slaves, with the mulattoes, whose social status was in-bet. When Creole planters sought to prevent mulatto representation in the Fr.

Natl. Assembly and in local assemblies, the mulattoes revolted, destroying the rigid structure of Haitian society. The blacks formed guerrilla bands led by Toussaint L'Ouverture, a former slave who had been made an officer of the Fr. forces on Hispaniola. In 1795, Spain ceded its part of the isl. to France, and in 1801 Toussaint conquered it, abolished slavery, and proclaimed himself governor general of an autonomous govt. over all Hispaniola. Napoleon sent his brother-in-law, Gen. Charles Leclerc, in an unsuccessful effort to reconquer the isl. Toussaint, taken by trickery, died in a Fr. prison; but the revolt continued and forced the Fr. troops, already ravaged by yellow fever, to withdraw. The rebels received unexpected aid from U.S. President Thomas Jefferson, who feared that Napoleon would use Saint-Domingue as a base to invade La. In 1804, Haiti became the 2d nation in the Western Hemisphere, after the U.S., to win complete independence. The remaining French and Creoles were expelled, and Jean-Jacques Dessalines, an ex-slave, proclaimed himself emperor. Haiti's last emperor (1847–1859) was Faustin Soulouque. Since the end of his reign, the country has been a republic. Political and social conflict persisted, intensified by the mulatto-black hostility, and Haiti's economy, which had never recovered from the violent struggle for independence, declined further. After the dictator Guillaume Sam was killed in a popular uprising in 1915, the U.S. took the opportunity to invade Port-au-Prince. Although financial and general material progress advanced under Amer. military occupation, Haiti protested, and a U.S. Senate investigation in 1921 found that the avowed purpose of preparing Haiti for responsible self-govt. had been ignored. In 1930 a U.S. presidential commission recommended that Haiti be allowed to elect a legislature that would, in turn, name a president. The marines were finally withdrawn in 1934, although U.S. fiscal control was maintained until 1947. Political instability persisted in Haiti after World War II. François ("Papa Doc") Duvalier, elected president in 1957, suppressed opposition and in 1964 he proclaimed himself president for life. When he died in 1971 he was succeeded by his 19-year-old son, Jean-Claude ("Baby Doc"), who also became president for life. In 1986, popular discontent became great enough to induce him to flee the country. In Dec. 1990, Jean-Bertrand Aristide was elected president but was exiled in a military coup led by Lt. Gen. Raoul Cedras. The U.S. and the OAS responded with economic sanctions. In Sept. 1994, Cedras agreed to a U.S.-backed plan for Aristide to return to power, after a show of U.S. military force. UN troops (mostly from the U.S.) landed unopposed in Haiti in Sept. 1994, U.S. sanctions were lifted, and Cedras resigned on Oct. 10, paving the way for Aristide's return on Oct. 15. Command of U.S. forces was turned over to the UN on March 31, 1995, and on Dec. 17, 1995, Haitians voted for Aristide's successor, Rene Preval, who took office Feb. 7, 1996.

Haiti, sugar-mill village, Camagüey prov., E Cuba, 45 mi/ 72 km SSE of Camagüey, 1.9 mi/3 km from Caribbean Sea; 20°46′N 77°52′W. Formerly Francisco.

Haiti, West Indies: see HISPANIOLA.

Hakalau (HAH-ka-LOU), village, E Hawaii isl., Hawaii co., Hawaii, 12 mi/19 km N of Hilo, near Hakalau Bay, on Hamakua Coast (NE). Hilo Forest Reserve to SW.

Halachó (ah-lah-CHO), town (1990 pop. 8,374), Halachó municipio, Yucatán, SE Mexico, on RR, and 45 mi/ 72 km SW of Mérida; 20°28′N 90°04′W. Agr. center (henequen, sugarcane, corn, fruit); tropical wood.

Halawa (HAH-LAH-vah), city (1990 pop. 13,408), near E end of Molokai isl., Maui co., Hawaii, 17 mi/27 km ENE of Kaunakakai, on Halawa Bay, at mouth of Halawa Stream; 21°22′N 157°55′W. Cattle. Landing strip. Halawa Point 2 mi/3.2 km E. Halawa Beach Park to N; Molokai Forest Reserve to W. Mokuhooniki Isl. Bird Refuge to SE.

Halawa Heights (HAH-LAH-vah), town (1990 pop. 7,000), S Oahu isl., Honolulu co., Hawaii, residential suburb 7 mi/11.3 km NW of downtown Honolulu, bet. South Halawa and Aiea streams. Pearl Harbor to SW;

Ewa Forest Reserve to NE. New Interstate Highway H3 crosses Koolau Mts., to NE, from here.

Halbur, town (1990 pop. 215), Carroll co., W central Iowa, 7 mi/11.3 km SW of Carroll; 42°00′N 94°58′W. In agr. area.

Halcott, Mount, 3,537 ft/1,078 m, Greene co., SE N.Y., in the Catskill Mts., 28 mi/45 km NW of Kingston; 42°11′N 74°26′W.

Haldeman (HAWL-duh-muhn), uninc. village (1990 pop. 200), Rowan co., NE Ky., 7 mi/11.3 km NE of Morehead, near source of Tygarts Creek, in Daniel Boone Natl. Forest. Agr. (tobacco; cattle; timber).

Haldimand (HOL-dim-uhnd), county (□ 488 sq mi/ 1,264 sq km), S Ont., central Canada, on L. Erie, and on Grand R.; ⊙ Cayuga; 42°55′N 79°50′W.

Hale 1 county (□ 656 sq mi/1,699 sq km; 1990 pop. 15,498), W central Ala.; ⊙ Greensboro. In Black Belt; bounded on W by Black Warrior R. Cattle; corn, soybeans, grain; catfish; timber. Formed 1867. **2** county (□ 1,004 sq mi/2,600 sq km; 1990 pop. 34,671), NW Texas; ⊙ Plainview; 34°04′N 101°49′W. On the Llano Estacado; elev. 3,250 ft/990 m–3,500 ft/1,070 m. Drained by White R., Running Water Draw (continuation of White R.) and Blackwater Draw. A leading Texas agr. co., with large irrigated acreage; grain sorghum, cotton, alfalfa, soybeans, corn, sunflowers, sugar beets, vegetables; beef cattle. Oil, clay, and natural gas deposits. Has small lakes (waterfowl hunting). Formed 1876.

Hale, city (1990 pop. 480), Carroll co., NW central Mo., near Grand R., 17 mi/27 km SE of Chillicothe; 39°36′N 93°20′W. Wheat, corn, soybeans; hogs, cattle; feed and fertilizer.

Hale Center, town (1990 pop. 2,067), Hale co., NW Texas, on the Llano Estacado, 10 mi/16 km SW of Plainview; 34°03′N 101°50′W. Elev. 3,423 ft/1,043 m. In cattle and irrigated agr. area (cotton; sunflowers, sugar beets, vegetables). Est. 1893, inc. 1921.

Haleakala National Park (HAH-lai-AH-ka-LAH) (□ 45 sq mi/117 sq km), on Maui isl., Maui co., Hawaii; park area extends SE through Kipahulu Valley to Puhilele Point on Haleakala Coast, including Waimoku Falls and the Seven Pools. Originally est. 1916 as part of Hawaii Natl. Park, which included unit on Hawaii isl., renamed Hawaii Volcanoes Natl. Park, 1960; separated in 1961 as Haleakala Natl. Park. Haleakala volcano, Puu Ulaula, 10,023 ft/3,055 m high, has been dormant since the mid-1700s. Its crater, 2,720 ft/829 m deep with an area of 19 sq mi/49 sq km, is one of the largest in the world. In 1976, 19,270 acres/7,799 ha were designated as a wilderness area. Main entrance and visitors center via Haleakala Crater Road from Pukalani. Rare silversword plants and many native and migratory birds are found here. Biosphere Reserve (1980).

Haleburg, town (1990 pop. 97), Henry co., SE Ala., near Chattahoochee R., 14 mi/23 km SE of Abbeville.

Haledon (HAIL-duhn), borough (1990 pop. 6,951), Passaic co., NE N.J., just NW of Paterson; 40°56′N 74°11′W. Mfg. (textiles, pharmaceuticals). Inc. 1908.

Haleiwa (HAH-lai-EE-vah), town (1990 pop. 2,442), on NW coast of Oahu, Honolulu co., Hawaii, 23 mi/37 km NW of Honolulu, at mouth of Anahulu Stream; 21°36′N 158°06′W. Coral gardens. Two beach parks (including Haleiwa Beach Park) and a harbor border Waialua Bay. Mfg. (clothing).

Halemaumau (HAH-lai-MAH-oo-MAH-oo), crater in W part of Kilauea Caldera, S central Hawaii, Hawaii co., Hawaii, 27 mi/43 km SSW of Hilo; 250 ft/76 m wide, 400 ft/122 m long, with floor covering 95 acres/ 38 ha; elev. of crater rim, 3,640 ft/1,109 m; elev. of crater floor 3,412 ft/1,040 m; rim of Kilauea Caldera, 4,078 ft/ 1,243 m. Periodic eruptions send lava over the rim.

Hales Bar Dam, Tenn.: see NICKAJACK LAKE.

Hales Corners, city (1990 pop. 7,623), Milwaukee co., SE Wis., a suburb 10 mi/16 km SW of downtown Milwaukee; 42°56′N 88°02′W. In dairy and farm area. Fox farm; mfg. (wood and fabricated metal prods.). Speedway. Jeremiah Curtin House State Historic Site and Experimental Aircraft Assn. Aviation Mus.

Hales Location, locality, Carroll co., E central N.H.,

7 mi/11.3 km NNW of Conway, in White Mt. Natl. Forest. Drained by Lucy Brook. Timber.

Halesite, village (1990 pop. 2,687), Suffolk co., SE N.Y., on Huntington Harbor, on N shore of W L.I., just N of Huntington; 40°53′N 73°24′W. In summer recreational and residential area.

Halethorpe, village, Baltimore co., N Md., 2 mi/3.2 km SW of Baltimore. The name meaning, "Healthy Town," was suggested by Baltimore and Ohio (B & O) RR officials, many of whom lived here.

Haley's Island, Maine: see ISLES OF SHOALS.

Haleyville, city (1990 pop. 4,452), Winston co., NW Ala., 15 mi/24 km WNW of Double Springs, in William B. Bankhead Natl. Forest. Furniture and mobile home mfg. During the Civil War, Haleyville seceded from Ala. and c.2,000 Haleyville and Winston co. residents joined the Union army.

Half Dome, Calif.: see YOSEMITE NATIONAL PARK.

Half Moon, uninc. town (1990 pop. 6,306), Onslow co., E N.C., residential suburb 5 mi/8 km N of downtown Jacksonville, near New R.; 34°49′N 77°28′W.

Half Moon Bay, city (1990 pop. 8,886), San Mateo co., W Calif., suburb 23 mi/37 km S of downtown San Francisco, on picturesque Half Moon Bay, of Pacific Ocean, at mouth of Pilarcitos Creek; 37°28′N 122°27′W. Sheltered on N by Pillar Point. Artichokes, brussel sprouts; grain; Christmas trees, ornamentals, flowers, nursery prods.; fishing; mfg. (musical instruments, light mfg.). Annual Pumpkin Festival. Half Moon Bay Airport to NW; Santa Cruz Mts. and San Francisco State Fish and Game Reserve to NE; part of Half Moon Bay State Beach is to N.

Half Way House, uninc. town (1990 pop. 1,415), Montgomery co., SE Pa., residential suburb 3 mi/4.8 km N of Pottstown; 40°17′N 75°38′W. Also spelled Halfway House.

Half Way Tree, N suburb of Kingston, ⊙ St. Andrew parish, SE Jamaica, in Liguanea Plain, c.3.5 mi/5.6 km N of Kingston; 18°00′N 76°48′W. Small agr. region (mangoes, vegetables, coffee; cattle); mfg. of cigars and cigarettes; dairying. Township of shopping plazas; historic clock tower as landmark. In N outskirts is King's House, since 1872 the official residence of governors and, beginning 1996, governor general of Jamaica. Historical St. Andrew parish church, burial place of governors.

Halfway 1 village (1990 pop. 8,873), Washington co., W Md., just SW of Hagerstown; 39°37′N 77°46′W. **2** village (1990 pop. 311), Baker co., NE Oregon, on W Fork Pine Creek, near Idaho state line, 36 mi/58 km ENE of Baker City; 44°52′N 117°06′W. Dairy prods.; wheat, potatoes; sheep, cattle. Oxbow Dam, on Snake R., 15 mi/24 km to NE. Brownlee Dam, on Snake R., 11 mi/18 km to E. Hells Canyon Natl. Recreation Area to NE. Umatilla Natl. Forest, including Eagle Cap Wilderness Area, to N.

Halfway Mountain (1,400 ft/427 m), W central N.F., E Canada, 8 mi/13 km SW of Buchans, near N shore of Red Indian L.

Halfway Rock Light, SW Maine, small lighthouse isl. midway bet. Portland Head and Seguin Isl. Light, Casco Bay, and 10 mi/16 km E of Portland. Completed 1871.

Haliburton, county (□ 1,486 sq mi/3,849 sq km; 1991 pop. 14,421), S Ont., central Canada, on Burnt R.; ⊙ Minden; 44°10′N 78°30′W.

Haliburton, village, S Ont., central Canada, near N end of Kashagawigamog L., 50 mi/80 km NNE of Lindsay; 45°03′N 78°03′W. Lumbering. Center of Haliburton Highlands lakes region (sport fishing, hunting; seasonal cabins).

Halibut Cove, fishing and tourist settlement, S Alaska, SW Kenai Peninsula, on Kachemak Bay, 19 mi/31 km NE of Seldovia. Artist colony reached by ferry from Homer.

Halifax, county (□ 2,063 sq mi/5,343 sq km; 1991 pop. 330,846), S N.S., E Canada, on the Atlantic Ocean; ⊙ Halifax. Largest co. of prov.

Halifax 1 (HA-luh-faks), county (□ 730 sq mi/ 1,891 sq km; 1990 pop. 55,516), NE N.C.; ⊙ Halifax; 36°15′N 77°39′W. Bounded N and E by Roanoke R.

(forms Roanoke Rapids and Gaston reservoirs in NW), S by Fishing Creek. In Piedmont region; agr. area (tobacco, peanuts, cotton, corn, wheat, oats, soybeans, sorghum, hay, potatoes, sweet potatoes; chickens, hogs; some dairying); timber. Mfg. at Weldon, some mfg. at Roanoke Rapids and Scotland Neck. Co. border in NW, within 3 mi/4.8 km of Va. state line. Medoc State Park in SW. Formed 1758. **2** county (□ 824 sq mi/ 2,134 sq km; 1990 pop. 29,033), S Va.; ⊙ Halifax; 36°46′N 78°56′W. Independent city of South Boston reverted to town status in 1995. Bounded S by N.C. state line, N and E by Roanoke (Staunton) R.; drained by Dan, Banister, and Hyco rivers (hydroelectric plants). Mfg. at South Boston and Halifax; agr. (a leading Va. tobacco-growing co.; also wheat, corn, hay, soybeans; cattle). Staunton R. State Park in E. Formed 1752.

Halifax, city (1991 pop. 114,455), ⊙ N.S., S central N.S., E Canada, on the Atlantic Ocean; 44°39′N 63°36′W. Largest city in the Maritime provs. and one of Canada's principal ice-free Atlantic ports. E terminus of Canada's 2 great RR systems and of its transcontinental highway. Its many industries include commercial fishing, fish processing, shipbuilding, oil refining, and the mfg. of motor vehicles, electronics, clothing, and furniture. Home port of the Can. Atlantic fleet and the hq. of its E army. Founded in 1749 as Chebucto; later renamed for the earl of Halifax, then president of the Board of Trade and Plantations. It was intended originally to be a Brit. naval stronghold comparable to that of France at Louisburg. It served as a naval base for the expedition against Louisburg in 1758, against the Amer. colonies in the Amer. Revolution, and against the U.S. in the War of 1812. The first transatlantic steamship service, from Halifax to Great Britain, began in 1840. During both world wars the port was an important naval and air base, convoy terminal, and embarkation center. In 1917 a Fr. munitions vessel carrying explosives was rammed in the harbor by a Belg. relief vessel, causing an explosion that killed about 1,800 people, injured about 9,000 more (20% of the pop.), and destroyed the N part of the city. Places of interest include the Citadel fortress (1856); Prov. House (1818); St. Paul's Church, the oldest (1750) Anglican church in Canada; and Point Pleasant Park. Seat of Dalhousie Univ. (1818), the Univ. of Kings Col., Mount St. Vincent Univ., St. Mary's Univ., and technical and art schools.

Halifax 1 rural town (1990 pop. 6,526), Plymouth co., SE Mass., 10 mi/16 km WNW of Plymouth; 42°00′N 70°52′W. Settled c.1670, inc. 1734. **2** town (1990 pop. 588), Windham co., SE Vt., on Mass. state line, 11 mi/ 18 km SW of Brattleboro; 42°46′N 72°45′W. **3** town (1990 pop. 688), ⊙ Halifax co., S Va., 5 mi/8 km N of South Boston, on Banister R. (Banister Dam and hydroelectric plant); 36°46′N 78°55′W. Mfg. (textiles, shoes, pet food); in agr. area (tobacco, corn, soybeans, wheat, hay; cattle). Inc. 1875.

Halifax (HA-luh-faks), village (1990 pop. 327), ⊙ Halifax co., NE N.C., 28 mi/45 km NNE of Rocky Mount, and on Roanoke R.; 36°19′N 77°35′W. Tobacco, cotton, peanuts, grain; poultry, livestock. Site of first N.C. constitutional convention (1776). Settled c.1750.

Halifax (HA-li-faks), borough (1990 pop. 911), Dauphin co., S central Pa., 14 mi/23 km NNW of Harrisburg, on Susquehanna R. Agr. (grain, soybeans, apples; livestock, poultry; dairying); mfg. (plastic prods., stoves and furnaces, leather prods.). Appalachian Trail passes to S on Peters Mt. ridge; Clemson Isl. to W.

Halifax Harbour, inlet of the Atlantic Ocean, S N.S., E Canada; 15 mi/24 km long, 6 mi/10 km wide at entrance; 44°35′N 63°31′W. On W shore is Halifax; on E is Dartmouth; 2 bridges and ferry link the 2 cities at the Narrows. N part of inlet is called Bedford Basin. One of largest natural harbors in N. Amer. Major container port facilities. Autoport receives 120,000 imported motor vehicles annually. Formerly called Chebucto Harbour.

Halifax River, narrow lagoon, c.25 mi/40 km long, in Volusia co., E central Fla., sheltered from the Atlantic Ocean by barrier beach (site of Daytona Beach and other resorts); extends N from Ponce de Leon Inlet (at

N end of Hillsborough R. lagoon). Followed by Intracoastal Waterway.

Haliimaile (HAH-LEE-ee-MEI-lai), town (1990 pop. 841), Maui isl., Maui co., Hawaii, 8 mi/12.9 km ESE of Kahului, 5 mi/8 km inland from N coast; 20°52′N 156°20′W. Sugarcane, pineapples; cattle. Maunaloa Col. 1.5 mi/2.4 km N.

Halkett, Cape, N Alaska, on Arctic Ocean, 110 mi/ 177 km ESE of Barrow; 70°47′N 152°05′W. Inuit trading post of Cape Halkett is 10 mi/16 km WNW.

Halkirk (HAL-kuhrk), village (1991 pop. 150), S central Alta., W Canada, 23 mi/37 km E of Stettler; 52°17′N 112°09′W. Coal mining. Mixed farming; wheat; cattle; dairying.

Hall 1 county (□ 426 sq mi/1,103 sq km; 1990 pop. 95,428), NE Ga.; ⊙ Gainesville; 34°19′N 83°49′W. Piedmont area drained by Chattahoochee and Oconee rivers. Prods. include soybeans, hay, sweet potatoes; cattle, hogs, poultry; eggs. Granite and marble. Formed 1818. **2** county (□ 552 sq mi/1,430 sq km; 1990 pop. 48,925), S central Nebr.; ⊙ Grand Island; 40°52′N 98°30′W. Irrigated agr. and industrial region drained by Platte, Wood, and South Loup rivers. Mfg. at Grand Island; corn, soybeans, wheat, sorghum, vegetables; cattle, hogs; dairy and poultry prods. In area are Cheyenne and War Axe (SW) and Mormon Isl. (SE) state waysides. Formed 1859. **3** county (□ 904 sq mi/2,341 sq km; 1990 pop. 3,905), NW Texas; ⊙ Memphis; 34°31′N 100°41′W. In plains region below Caprock escarpment of Llano Estacado; elev. 2,200 ft/670 m–3,300 ft/ 1,000 m. Crossed by Prairie Dog Town Fork of Red R. Agr., chiefly cotton; also grain and sweet sorghum, wheat, peanuts; beef and dairy cattle, hogs. Formed 1876.

Hall, village (1990 pop. 100), Granite co., W Mont., on Flint Creek, 55 mi/89 km W of Helena. Hay; cattle, horses. In area are Lolo (W) and Deerlodge (S and SE) natl. forests. Garnet Range to N.

Hall, Fort, Idaho: see FORT HALL.

Hall Island 1 SE Franklin dist., N.W.T., N Canada, in the Gulf of Boothia, near W entrance of Fury and Hecla Strait, off NW Baffin Isl.; 40 mi/64 km long, 6 mi/ 10 km wide; 70°00′N 87°00′W. **2** SE Franklin dist., N.W.T., N Canada, in the Atlantic Ocean, off Hall Peninsula, SE Baffin Isl.; 6 mi/10 km long; 62°32′N 64°10′W.

Hall Island, W Alaska, in Bering Sea, 3 mi/4.8 km NW of St. Matthew Isl., and 180 mi/290 km WNW of Nunivak Isl.; 6 mi/9.7 km long, 2 mi/3.2 km wide; 60°33′N 172°42′W. Rugged.

Hall Park, town (1990 pop. 1,090), Cleveland co., central Okla., residential suburb 17 mi/27 km SSE of downtown Oklahoma City, and 3 mi/4.8 km NE of downtown Norman; 35°11′N 97°24′W. Surrounded by city of Norman.

Hall Peninsula, SE Baffin Isl., SE Franklin dist., N.W.T., N Canada, extends 150 mi/241 km SE into Davis Strait, bet. Cumberland Sound and Frobisher Bay; 100 mi/ 161 km wide at base; 62°40′N 65°10′W. SE extremity is Blunt Peninsula. Frobisher Bay trading post on S shore.

Hall Summit, village (1990 pop. 227), Red River parish, NW La., 30 mi/48 km SE of Shreveport; 32°11′N 93°15′W. In agr. area (cotton, peaches, soybeans; cattle). Logging.

Hallam (HAWL-uhm), village (1990 pop. 309), Lancaster co., SE Nebr., area drainage of N Fork Big Nemaha R., 18 mi/29 km S of Lincoln; 40°32′N 96°47′W. Olive Creek L. State Recreation Area to NW.

Hallam (HA-lahm), borough (1990 pop. 1,375), York co., S Pa., 7 mi/11.3 km ENE of York. Post office name is Hellam; borough surrounded by Hellam township. Mfg. (apparel, paper prods.). Agr. area (apples, soybeans, grain; poultry, livestock; dairying). Samuel S. Lewis State Park to E.

Hallam Peak (10,560 ft/3,219 m), SE B.C., W Canada, near Hamber Provincial Park, 55 mi. SW of Jasper; 52°11′N 118°46′W.

Hallandale, city (□ 4 sq mi/10.4 sq km; 1990 pop. 30,996), extreme SE Broward co., SE Fla., on the Atlantic coast and the Intracoastal Waterway; 25°59′N

80°08′W. Retirement center, esp. for Fr. Canadians. Horse and greyhound racetracks are major sources of employment. A principal tourist attraction is Gulf Stream Park, site of the annual Fla. Derby. Settled 1897, inc. 1927.

Hallett (HA-let), village (1990 pop. 159), Pawnee co., N Okla., 14 mi/23 km ESE of Pawnee; 36°13′N 96°34′W. Agr. center.

Hallettsville, city (1990 pop. 2,718), ⊙ Lavaca co., S Texas, on Lavaca R., and 17 mi/27 km NE of Yoakum; elev. 232 ft/71 m; 29°26′N 96°56′W. In agr. area (cattle, hay; corn, rice, milo); mfg. (natural-gas processing, printing; canned and bottled beverages, livestock trailers).

Halley (HA-lee), village, Desha co., SE Ark., 6 mi/9.7 km E of Dermott, bet. Big Bayou and Boeuf R.

Halliday (HA-luh-dai), village (1990 pop. 288), Dunn co., W central N.Dak., 27 mi/43 km WNW of Beulah, and on Spring Creek; 47°21′N 102°20′W. Fort Berthold Indian Reservation to N.

Hallock (HA-luhk), town (1990 pop. 1,304), ⊙ Kittson co., extreme NW Minn., c.60 mi/97 km N of Grand Forks (N.Dak.), on South Branch Two Rivers, opposite mouth of Middle Branch Two Rivers, near Canada (Man.) border; elev. 827 ft/252 m; 48°46′N 96°56′W. Grain, potatoes, sunflowers, flax, sheep, alfalfa, sugar beets; livestock; mfg. (concrete prods.). Hunting and fishing in vicinity. Plotted 1879, inc. 1887.

Hallowell (HAH-luh-wel), city (1990 pop. 2,534), Kennebec co., S Maine, on the Kennebec R., just S of Augusta; 44°17′N 69°48′W. Boatbuilding. Hallowell granite used for state capitol. Settled c.1754; town inc. 1771, including present Augusta; city inc. 1850.

Halls, town (1990 pop. 2,431), Lauderdale co., W Tenn., 10 mi/16 km S of Dyersburg; 35°53′N 89°24′W. Timber and cotton-growing area. Mfg. plastics.

Hall's Stream, c.20 mi/32 km long, N.H., Vt., and Canada (Que.); rises in NW N.H.; flows SSW to the Connecticut R. at Canaan (Vt.); forms internatl. border above Beecher Falls (Vt.).

Hallsboro, uninc. village, Columbus co., SE N.C., 6 mi/ 9.7 km E of Whiteville. L. Waccamaw State Park to SE.

Hallstead (HAL-sted), borough (1990 pop. 1,274), Susquehanna co., NE Pa., 13 mi/21 km SE of Binghamton (N.Y.), on Susquehanna R. (bridged to Great Bend, 1 mi/1.6 km N), near N.Y. state line. Agr. (grain; livestock; dairying); mfg. (electronics). Salt Springs State Park to SW. Founded 1787, inc. 1874.

Hallsville 1 town (1990 pop. 917), Boone co., central Mo., 13 mi/21 km NNE of Columbia; 39°07′N 92°13′W. Corn, hay; cattle. **2** town (1990 pop. 2,288), Harrison co., E Texas, 12 mi/19 km W of Marshall, and 10 mi/ 16 km E of Longview, near Sabine R.; 32°30′N 94°34′W. In agr. area (cattle, hogs; nurseries); timber.

Halltown, town (1990 pop. 161), Lawrence co., SW Mo., 18 mi/29 km W of Mt. Vernon, 37°11′N 93°37′W. Plotted 1887.

Hallwood, village (1990 pop. 228), Accomack co., E Va., 12 mi/19 km N of Accomac; 37°52′N 75°35′W. Chesapeake Bay to W. Agr. (grain, vegetables; livestock, poultry).

Halma (HAL-muh), village (1990 pop. 73), Kittson co., NW Minn., 18 mi/29 km SE of Hallock, in Red R. valley; 48°39′N 96°35′W. Grain, sunflowers. Twin Lakes Wildlife Area to W.

Halsey (HAHL-zee), village (1990 pop. 667), Linn co., W Oregon, 17 mi/27 km S of Albany, 6 mi/9.7 km E of Willamette R.; 44°22′N 123°06′W. Dairy prods.; grain, fruit; cattle; timber; pulp mills.

Halstad (HAL-stuhd), village (1990 pop. 611), Norman co., NW Minn., on Red R., and 32 mi/51 km N of Fargo (N. Dak.); 47°21′N 96°49′W. Agr. area (grain, potatoes, sunflowers, sugar beets); mfg. (printing).

Halstead (HAWL-sted), town (1990 pop. 2,015), Harvey co., S central Kansas, on Little Arkansas R., and 10 mi/ 16 km WSW of Newton; 38°00′N 97°30′W. Market and shipping point for wheat and livestock region; flour milling. Mfg. (animal feeds, lumber, mobile homes). Health Mus. Inc. 1877.

Halten Hills, town (1986 pop. 35,570), Ont., central Canada, 12 mi/19 km W of metropolitan Toronto. Created by 1984 amalgamation of Acton, Georgetown, and Esquising township. Mfg. (paper prods., electric and electronic prods.; weather stripping).

Haltom City, city (1990 pop. 32,856), Tarrant co., N Texas, suburb 6 mi/9.7 km NE of downtown Fort Worth, near West Fork Trinity R. Drained by Big Fossil Creek. Mfg. (transportation equip., bldg. materials, light poles, foods). Inc. after 1940.

Halton, county (□ 363 sq mi/940 sq km), S Ont., central Canada, on L. Ontario; ⊙ Milton West; 43°30′N 79°53′W.

Ham Lake, town (1990 pop. 8,924), Anoka co., E Minn., suburb 17 mi/27 km N of downtown Minneapolis; 45°15′N 93°12′W. Drained by Coon Creek in S; Ham L. in center, L. Netta and part of Coon L. in N. Mfg. (commercial fixtures, bldg. materials, wood prods.; machining). Carlos Avery Wildlife Area to E.

Ham Sud (ham SYOOD), village, ⊙ Wolfe co., S Que., E Canada, at foot of Ham Mt. (2,325 ft/709 m), 30 mi/ 48 km NE of Sherbrooke. Dairying; cattle raising; potato growing.

Hamber Provincial Park (□ 3,800 sq mi/9,842 sq km), SE B.C., W Canada, on Alta. border, in the Rocky and Selkirk mts., NE of Revelstoke; extends along upper reaches of the Columbia R. and borders on Jasper and Banff natl. parks. Peaks over 10,000 ft/3,048 m high include Sir Sanford, Laussedat, Mummery, Bryce, Shackleton, Iconoclast, Adamant, Ghost mts. Numerous small headwaters of Columbia R. rise here.

Hamberg, village (1990 pop. 19), Wells co., central N.Dak., 10 mi/16 km NNE of Fessenden; 47°45′N 99°30′W. Near New Rockford Canal.

Hamblen (HAM-blin), county (□ 174 sq mi/451 sq km; 1990 pop. 50,480), NE Tenn.; ⊙ Morristown; 36°13′N 83°16′W. In Great Appalachian Valley region; Bays Mt. along SE border. Bounded N by Cherokee Reservoir (Holston R.), S by Nolichucky R. Agr. (tobacco, corn, potatoes, vegetables; poultry, livestock; dairy prods.). Mfg. at Morristown. Formed 1870.

Hambleton, village (1990 pop. 265), Tucker co., NE W.Va., on Laurel Fork R., in Monongahela Natl. Forest, 2 mi/3.2 km SE of Parsons; 39°04′N 79°39′W. Includes Fernow Experimental Forest to SW.

Hamburg, city (1990 pop. 1,248), Fremont co., extreme SW Iowa, on Nishnabotna R., near Mo. state line, and 18 mi/29 km SW of Shenandoah; 40°36′N 95°39′W. Mfg. (foods and beverages, feed, alcohol prods., bricks); has large nursery. Waubonsie State Park to NW. Inc. 1867.

Hamburg, town (1990 pop. 3,098), ⊙ Ashley co., SE Ark., c.48 mi/77 km E of El Dorado; 33°13′N 91°47′W. In lumbering (pine, oak) and agr. area (cotton, rice, hay). Mfg. (lumber, apparel, radio loudspeaker cones). Overflow Wildlife Refuge to SE.

Hamburg 1 village (1990 pop. 150), Calhoun co., W Ill., on the Mississippi R., and 7 mi/11.3 km NW of Hardin; 39°13′N 90°43′W. Apple growing. **2** village, Livingston co., SE Mich., 10 mi/16 km N of Ann Arbor; 42°26′N 83°48′W. Located in small lakes dist. Mfg. (electrical equip., fabricated metal prods.). Pinckney State Recreation Area to W. **3** village (1990 pop. 492), Carver co., S Minn., c.40 mi/64 km WSW of Minneapolis; 44°43′N 93°57′W. Poultry, livestock; soybeans, alfalfa; dairying; mfg. (feeds, fertilizers). **4** village, Franklin co., SW Miss., 20 mi/32 km E of Natchez. **5** village (□ 2 sq mi/5.2 sq km; 1990 pop. 10,442), Erie co., W N.Y., S of Buffalo; 42°43′N 78°49′W. Part of a township of 48,000 people, Hamburg is a residential and industrial suburb of Buffalo. Its mfg. includes rubber goods and optical prods. Seat of Hilbert Col. Settled 1808, inc. 1874. **6** village, Aiken co., W S.C., on Savannah R., opposite Augusta (Ga.) and now part of North Augusta (S.C.). Founded as W terminus of state's first RR, completed 1833 to Charleston. **7** village, Marathon co., central Wis., 14 mi/23 km NW of Wausau; 45°06′N 89°53′W.

Hamburg 1 borough (1990 pop. 2,566), Sussex co., NW N.J., on Wallkill R., 12 mi/19 km NE of Newton;

Cross references are shown in SMALL CAPITALS. The pronunciation key is on page xv. The dates of population figures are on page xii.

41°08′N 74°34′W. "Gingerbread Castle" here has scenes from various fairy tales. In suburbanizing area. Inc. 1920. **2** borough (1990 pop. 3,987), Berks co., E central Pa., 15 mi/24 km NNW of Reading, on Schuylkill R. Agr. area (grain, soybeans; livestock, poultry; dairying); mfg. (food prods., fabricated metal prods., apparel, machinery; printing and publishing; iron foundry). Pa. Du. Folk Culture Center to E at Lenhartsville. Weiser State Forest and Appalachian Trail, in Blue Mt. ridge to N. Founded 1779, inc. 1837.

Hamburg, Conn.: see LYME.

Hamden, town (1990 pop. 52,434), New Haven co., S Conn.; 41°23′N 72°55′W. The town was named for John Hampden, the Eng. Puritan patriot. A residential and mfg. suburb of New Haven, of which it was once a part, Hamden makes machinery, electrical prods., metal goods, computer prods., wire and cable, bldg. materials, fabricated metals and rolled steel; other industries are construction, business services, and retail trade. The town's industrial development dates back to 1798, when Eli Whitney set up an arms factory using techniques of mass production. A plaque marks the site. Has many early mill sites, pre-Revolutionary and Civil War houses, and a restored opera house. Seat of Quinnipiac Col. Settled c.1638, inc. 1786.

Hamden, village (1990 pop. 877), Vinton co., S Ohio, 27 mi/43 km ESE of Chillicothe; 39°10′N 82°31′W. In agr. area.

Hamel, village (1990 pop. 530), Madison co., SW Ill., 8 mi/12.9 km NE of Edwardsville, just beyond St. Louis urban fringe; 38°53′N 89°50′W. Corn, soybeans; mfg. (concrete, metal tools).

Hamel, Minn.: see MEDINA.

Hamer (HAI-mur), uninc. village, Dillon co., NE S.C., 6 mi/9.7 km NE of Dillon, at N.C. state line. "South of the Border," a large tourist attraction with a Mex. theme nearby; well-known landmark of Interstate 95.

Hamersville (HA-muhrz-vil), village (1990 pop. 586), Brown co., SW Ohio, 32 mi/51 km ESE of Cincinnati; 38°55′N 83°59′W. In agr. area.

Hamill Peak (10,640 ft/3,243 m), SE B.C., W Canada, in Selkirk Mts., 60 mi/97 km NE of Nelson; 50°13′N 116°38′W.

Hamilton, parish (1991 pop. 4,680), N Bermuda, S of St. George's parish; 32°20′N 64°43′W.

Hamilton 1 county (□ 519 sq mi/1,344 sq km; 1990 pop. 10,930), N central Fla., on Ga. state line (N), on Suwannee (S,E) and Withlacoochee (W) rivers; ⊙ Jasper; 30°29′N 82°57′W. Flatwoods area with swamps in E; drained by Alapaha R. Farming (corn, peanuts, cotton, tobacco, vegetables; livestock raising (hogs, cattle), and lumbering. Formed 1827. **2** county (□ 435 sq mi/1,127 sq km; 1990 pop. 8,499), SE Ill.; ⊙ McLeansboro; 38°04′N 88°33′W. Agr. (livestock; fruit, wheat, corn, redtop seed). Drained by North Fork of Saline R. Formed 1821. **3** county (□ 402 sq mi/1,041 sq km; 1990 pop. 108,936), central Ind.; ⊙ Noblesville; 40°04′N 86°03′W. Diversified mfg., including the processing of farm prods., at Noblesville and Sheridan; soybeans, corn, wheat; dairy prods.; cattle, hogs. Drained by West Fork of White R., and by Cicero (Morse Reservoir at center of co.), and small Prairie and Duck creeks. Part of Indianapolis metropolitan area (residential). Geist Reservoir, on Fall Creek, in SE. Formed 1823. **4** county (□ 577 sq mi/1,494 sq km; 1990 pop. 16,071), central Iowa; ⊙ Webster City, 42°22′N 93°43′W. Prairie agr. area (hogs, poultry, cattle; corn, soybeans, oats) drained by Boone and Skunk rivers; bituminous-coal deposits. Little Wall L. in S. Widespread flooding in 1993. Formed 1856. **5** county (□ 997 sq mi/2,582 sq km; 1990 pop. 2,388), SW Kansas, on Colo. (W) state line; ⊙ Syracuse; 38°01′N 101°40′W. Prairie region; drained by Arkansas R. Wheat, sorghum; cattle. One of 4 Kansas cos. in Mountain time zone; Central-Mountain time zone boundary follows S and E co. border. Formed 1886. **6** county (□ 546 sq mi/1,414 sq km; 1990 pop. 8,862), SE central Nebr.; ⊙ Aurora; 41°52′N 97°59′W. Irrigated agr. region bounded N and NW by Platte R.; drained by Big Blue and W Fork Big Blue rivers. Cattle, hogs; dairying; corn, soybeans, sorghum.

Formed 1870. **7** county (□ 1,807 sq mi/4,680 sq km; 1990 pop. 5,279), NE central N.Y.; ⊙ Lake Pleasant; 43°39′N 74°30′W. Situated entirely in the Adirondacks; drained by tributaries of the Hudson R. and by Raquette, Black, and Sacandaga rivers. Well-known resorts on Indian, Long, Raquette, Piseco, and Pleasant lakes, and Fulton Chain of Lakes; many skiing areas; hunting, fishing. Some agr. (dairy prods.; poultry, livestock; hay, grain). Formed 1816. **8** county (□ 414 sq mi/1,072 sq km; 1990 pop. 866,228), extreme SW Ohio; ⊙ CINCINNATI, 39°11′N 84°32′W. Bounded W by Ind. state line, S by Ohio R. (here forming Ky. state line); drained by Great Miami, Little Miami, and Whitewater rivers and by small Mill Creek. In the Till Plains physiographic region. Entirely within metropolitan dist. of Cincinnati. There is, however, coal mining and oil and gas extraction. Agr. prods. include vegetables, nursery and greenhouse crops; dairying; mfg. of food prods. and beverages, clothing, plastics, consumer goods, metal prods., electrical prods., transportation equip. Formed 1790. **9** county (□ 576 sq mi/1,492 sq km; 1990 pop. 285,536), SE Tenn., on Ga. (S) state line; ⊙ CHATTANOOGA; 35°11′N 85°10′W. Crossed N-S by Tennessee R. Includes parts of Hales Bar and Chickamauga reservoirs. Walden Ridge is in W and NW, parts of Lookout Mt. and of Chickamauga and Chattanooga Natl. Military Park in S. Fertile farm lands (livestock; corn, hay, fruit); coal and iron deposits, gravel, clay, timber tracts. Mfg. at Chattanooga. Nuclear power plants Sequoyah 1 (initial criticality July 5, 1980) and Sequoyah 2 (initial criticality Nov. 5, 1981) are 10 mi/16 km NE of Chattanooga. They use cooling water from Chickamauga L., and each has a max. dependable capacity of 1,122 MW. Formed 1819; absorbed James co. in 1919. **10** county (□ 836 sq mi/2,165 sq km; 1990 pop. 7,733), central Texas; ⊙ Hamilton; 31°41′N 98°06′W. Mainly prairies; drained by Leon, Bosque, and Lampasas rivers. Livestock, esp. cattle, also sheep, goats (wool, mohair marketed); dairying; agr. (wheat, oats, barley, corn; hay). Natural gas and oil fields; sand and gravel. Formed 1842.

Hamilton, city (1990 est. pop. 3,100), ⊙ Bermuda, in Pembroke parish, on Bermuda Isl.; 32°17′N 64°47′W. Port at the head of Great Sound, a huge lagoon and deep-water harbor protected by coral reefs. Focus of Bermuda's commercial and social life and a major tourist resort and port-of-call of cruise ships. Duty-free shopping center.

Hamilton, city (1991 pop. 318,499), S Ont., central Canada, at the W end of L. Ontario; 43°15′N 79°50′W. On a narrow plain bet. its harbor (connected by canal with the lake) and the Niagara escarpment. Important port, transportation center, and mfg. city. Canada's leading producer of iron and steel; other mfg. includes motor vehicles, heavy machinery, chemicals, and electrical, paper, and textile prods. Settled in 1778, it became an important port city with the opening (1830) of the Burlington Canal, which linked Hamilton Harbor with L. Ontario. Places of interest include the Royal Botanical Gardens, the open-air market, the historical mus. in Dundern Park, and the Can. Football Hall of Fame. Seat of McMaster Univ. (1887).

Hamilton 1 city (1990 pop. 3,281), Hancock co., W Ill., on the Mississippi R., opposite Keokuk (Iowa; connected by bridge), 12 mi/19 km W of Carthage; 40°23′N 91°21′W. Trade and shipping center in agr. area (corn, wheat, soybeans; livestock). Stone quarry. Nearby is L. Keokuk, or L. Cooper, formed by Keokuk Dam in Mississippi R., with recreational and resort facilities. Inc. 1859. **2** city (1990 pop. 1,737), Caldwell co., NW Mo., 24 mi/39 km W of Chillicothe; 39°44′N 94°00′W. Corn, soybeans, oats, wheat; cattle, hogs; mfg. (shoes); lumber. Founded 1855, inc. 1868. Boyhood home of James Cash (J.C.) Penney, retail merchant. **3** city (1990 pop. 61,368), ⊙ Butler co., SW Ohio, on the Great Miami R.; 39°23′N 84°34′W. An agr. trading and mfg. center, Hamilton has paper and pulp mills and many factories that make a variety of prods., including safes, machinery, chemicals, textiles, and motor vehicle parts. Major employment sectors are steel, insurance. Settled on the

site of Fort Hamilton, built in 1791. William Dean Howells was raised here. Points of interest include the Soldiers', Sailors', and Pioneers' Monument and the co. historical society. Miami Univ. of Ohio has a branch here. Inc. 1857.

Hamilton 1 town (1990 pop. 5,787), ⊙ Marion co., NW Ala., 45 mi/72 km NW of Jasper, near Miss. state line. Lumber; cotton. Mobile homes; textiles. Settled c.1818. **2** town (1990 pop. 684), Steuben co., NE Ind., on small Hamilton L., 8 mi/12.9 km SSE of Angola; 41°32′N 84°55′W. In agr. and resort area; mfg. (fabricated metal prods., electrical prods., tranportation equip., plastics). **3** town (1990 pop. 115), Marion co., S central Iowa, near Cedar Creek, 15 mi/24 km SE of Knoxville; 41°10′N 92°54′W. In bituminous-coal mining and agr. area. **4** rural upper-income residential town (1990 pop. 7,280), Essex co., NE Mass., 9 mi/14.5 km W of Gloucester; 42°38′N 70°52′W. Site of Myopia Hunt and Polo Clubs. Settled 1638, inc. 1793. **5** town (1990 pop. 2,737), ⊙ Ravalli co., W Mont., 45 mi/72 km S of Missoula, and on Bitterroot R., near Bitterroot Range and Idaho state line (to W); 46°15′N 114°10′W. Trading point for irrigated agr. and mining region; silver, lead, zinc mines; lumber mills; cattle, sheep, horses, llamas. Mfg. (apparel, animal feeds, log homes, wood prods.). Rocky Mt. Laboratory (focussing upon Rocky Mt. Spotted Fever); Private Biotechnology Laboratory, Fish hatchery to SE. Inc. 1894. Daly Mansion (1890), 42-room mansion of "Copper King" Marcus Daly, on 50 acres/20 ha N of town. **6** mining ghost town, White Pine co., E Nev., in White Pine Mts., 32 mi/51 km W of Ely, in Humboldt Natl. Forest. During its silver boom (c.1865–1873), its pop. reached c.10,000. Mt. Hamilton to W. **7** town (1990 pop. 2,937), ⊙ Hamilton co., central Texas, c.60 mi/97 km W of Waco; 31°42′N 98°07′W. Elev. 1,154 ft/352 m. In agr. area (cattle; wheat, sorghum); dairying. A natural gas field is W; sand and gravel; mfg. (wood prods.).

Hamilton 1 village, W Alaska, on arm of Yukon R. delta, 70 mi/113 km SW of St. Michael; 62°53′N 163°51′W. Fur-trading post, supply point, steamer landing. School. Sometimes called Old Hamilton. New Fort Hamilton village is 10 mi/16 km S. **2** village (1990 pop. 454), ⊙ Harris co., W Ga., 21 mi/34 km NNE of Columbus; 32°46′N 84°53′W. **3** village (1990 pop. 301), Greenwood co., SE Kansas, 12 mi/19 km NNE of Eureka; 37°58′N 96°09′W. In livestock-raising, dairying, and grain-growing region. **4** village (□ 1 sq mi/2.6 sq km; 1990 pop. 3,790), Madison co., central N.Y., 25 mi/40 km SW of Utica; 42°49′N 75°32′W. In dairying and farming region. Seat of Colgate Univ. Settled 1795, inc. 1816. **5** village (1990 pop. 544), Martin co., E N.C., on Roanoke R. (head of navigation), and 18 mi/29 km ENE of Tarboro. Tobacco, cotton, peanuts, grain, sweet potatoes; poultry, livestock. Mfg. (fabrics). Historic Hamilton Visitor Center; Fort Branch Battlefield State Historic Site. Inc. 1804. **6** village (1990 pop. 74), Pembina co., NE N.Dak., 9 mi/14.5 km E of Cavalier; 48°48′N 97°27′W. Seat of co. fair. **7** village (1990 pop. 700), Loudoun co., N Va., 6 mi/9.7 km W of Leesburg, in E foothills of the Blue Ridge Mts; 39°8′N 77°40′W. Light mfg.; agr. (dairying; livestock; grain, soybeans, apples). **8** village (1990 pop. 228), Skagit co., NW Wash., on Skagit R., and 18 mi/29 km ENE of Mt. Vernon; 48°31′N 122°60′W. Agr. and logging region. Mt. Baker–Snoqualmie Natl. Forest to NE and SE; Lower Baker Dam (forms L. Shannon); Mt. Baker (10,775 ft/3,284 m) to NE; Mt. Baker Natl. Recreation Area on S slopes.

Hamilton, township (1990 pop. 86,553), Mercer co., central N.J., 5 mi/8 km E of Trenton; 40°12′N 74°40′W. Inc. 1842.

Hamilton, Canada: see CHURCHILL.

Hamilton, R.I.: see NORTH KINGSTOWN.

Hamilton Air Force Base, Calif.: see SAN RAFAEL.

Hamilton Beach, village, S Ont., central Canada, W suburb of Hamilton, on narrow spit bet. Hamilton Bay and L. Ontario. Resort.

Hamilton, Cape, SW Victoria Isl., SW Franklin dist., N.W.T., N Canada, on W coast of Wollaston Peninsula; 69°31′N 116°25′W.

Hamilton City, uninc. town (1990 pop. 1,811), Glenn co., N central Calif., 10 mi/16 km W of Chico, on Sacramento R., near mouth of Stony Creek. Sugar beets, citrus, prunes, plums, olives, walnuts, pistachios, almonds, grain, rice, wheat; dairying. Tehama Colusa Canal passes to W.

Hamilton Cove or **Sainte Anne de Portneuf** (sant AHN duh por-NUHF), village (1991 pop. 1,032), E Que., E Canada, on the St. Lawrence R., and 30 mi/48 km WNW of Rimouski. Lumbering center.

Hamilton, Fort, N.Y.: see FORT HAMILTON.

Hamilton Grange, memorial, in Hamilton Heights sect. of W Harlem, Upper Manhattan, SE N.Y., on W 195th St. bet. Amsterdam Ave. and Broadway. The only home ever owned by Alexander Hamilton (and one of the few memorials to him), it is a rare example of John McComb residential architecture. Hamilton lived here until his 1804 death in duel with Aaron Burr. Memorial site also includes 7-ft/2.1-m bronze statue of Hamilton, resting atop 8-ft/2.4-m granite pier. Originally built for Hamilton Club in Brooklyn, the statue was moved here after the club's closure in 1936. Authorized 1962 as historic site.

Hamilton Inlet, Canada: see MELVILLE, LAKE.

Hamilton, Lake, Garland co., in W central Ark., on Ouachita R., 5 mi/8 km S of Hot Springs; c.25 mi/40 km long; 34°25′N 93°01′W. Extends N and to Blakely Mt. Dam (L. Ouachita). Formed by Carpenter Dam. Ouachita Natl. Forest on NW shore; fish hatchery on S shore.

Hamilton, Mount, peak (4,213 ft/1,284 m), Santa Clara co., W Calif., in Diablo Range, 15 mi/24 km E of San Jose. Site of Lick Observatory (built 1876–1888), directed by the Univ. of Calif. In 1959 a 120-in/305-cm telescope was installed by the Calif. Inst. of Technology.

Hamilton, Mount, Nev.: see WHITE PINE MOUNTAINS.

Hamilton Square, village, Mercer co., W N.J., 5 mi/8 km E of Trenton. Pottery, rubber prods. Largely residential.

Hamiota (ha-mi-O-tuh), village (1991 pop. 823), SW Man., central Canada, 36 mi/58 km NW of Brandon; 50°11′N 100°36′W. Lumbering; wheat.

Hamler, village (1990 pop. 623), Henry co., NW Ohio, 12 mi/19 km SSE of Napoleon; 41°14′N 84°02′W.

Hamlet 1 town (1990 pop. 789), Starke co., NW Ind., 6 mi/9.7 km N of Knox; 41°23′N 86°35′W. Ships farm produce. **2** town (1990 pop. 6,196), Richmond co., S N.C., 5 mi/8 km SE of Rockingham, near S.C. state line; 34°53′N 79°42′W. Agr. area (cotton, tobacco, grain, sweet potatoes; poultry, livestock. Mfg. (transportation equip., paper prods., apparel, plastic prods., fabricated metal prods., consumer goods; machining, poultry processing). RR junction; once had 42 passenger trains per day. Natl. RR Mus. Seat of Richmond Community Col.

Hamlet 1 village (1990 pop. 60), Hayes co., SW Nebr., 35 mi/56 km WNW of McCook, and on Frenchman Creek; 40°22′N 101°13′W. **2** village (1990 pop. 80), Chautauqua co., extreme W N.Y., 13 mi/21 km SE of Dunkirk; 43°19′N 77°55′W.

Hamletsburg, village (1990 pop. 85), Pope co., extreme SE Ill., on Ohio R., and 17 mi/27 km S of Golconda; 37°08′N 88°27′W.

Hamlin, county (□ 537 sq mi/1,391 sq km; 1990 pop. 4,974), E S.Dak.; ⊙ Hayti; 44°40′N 97°12′W. Dairying and livestock area drained by Big Sioux R. Several lakes in S, L. Poinsett (largest) on border with Brookings co. (has L. Poinsett State Recreation Area). Corn, wheat, soybeans, flax, potatoes; cattle, hogs, poultry. Formed 1873.

Hamlin 1 town (1990 pop. 2,791), on border bet. Fisher and Jones cos., W central Texas, 37 mi/60 km NNW of Abilene; 32°53′N 100°07′W. In cotton area; wheat; cattle. Oil, gypsum, sand and gravel. Mfg. (grain and feed, gasoline). Inc. 1907. **2** town (1990 pop. 1,030), ⊙ Lincoln co., W W.Va., on Mud R., 20 mi/32 km ESE of Huntington; 38°16′N 82°05′W. Coal, natural gas, and oil region. Agr. (corn, tobacco, potatoes); cattle. Light mfg.

Hamlin, village (1990 pop. 50), Brown co., NE Kansas,

6 mi/9.7 km NW of Hiawatha, near Nebr. state line; 39°55′N 95°37′W. Corn; livestock; poultry; dairying.

Hamlin, plantation (1990 pop. 204), Aroostook co., NE Maine, on St. John R., and 29 mi/47 km NE of Presque Isle; 47°05′N 67°52′W.

Hamlin Lake, Mich.: see BIG SABLE RIVER.

Hammels, a section of S Queens borough of N.Y. city, SE N.Y., on Rockaway Peninsula; 40°35′N 73°49′W. Also spelled Hammel.

Hammon (HA-muhn), village (1990 pop. 611), Roger Mills co., W Okla., 15 mi/24 km N of Elk City; 35°37′N 99°22′W. In cattle-raising, dairying, agr. area (wheat).

Hammonasset Point, S Conn., peninsula, on L.I. Sound near Madison; c.2 mi/3.2 km long. Here are Hammonasset Beach State Park and mouth of Hammonasset R. (c.20 mi/32 km. long), which rises S of Middletown, flows SSE to Clinton Harbor just E of Hammonasset Point.

Hammond 1 city (1990 pop. 84,236), Lake co., extreme NW Ind., bounded by L. Michigan, the Ill. state line, and the Little Calumet R., and traversed by the Grand Calumet R.; 41°37′N 87°29′W. Originally important as a slaughterhouse site, Hammond was a meatpacking town until its great packing house was destroyed by fire in 1901. Mfg. here include food prods., fabricated metal prods., chemicals, machinery, bldg. materials, transportation equip., foods, petroleum prods.; secondary steel processing; fire brick refractories. A campus of Purdue Univ. is here. Settled 1851. Laid out 1875. Inc. 1884. **2** city (1994 pop. 17,654), Tangipahoa parish, SE La., 43 mi/69 km NNW of New Orleans; 30°31′N 90°28′W. RR junction. In agr. area (vegetables; cattle, dairying); timber; mfg. (bldg. materials, consumer goods, paper prods., fabricated metal prods., machinery; meat processing). Seat of Southeastern La. Univ. Has major highway crossroads, I-55 (N-S) and I-12 (E-W). Zemurry Gardens and Global Wildlife Park. Home of the Black Heritage Festival. Inc. 1888.

Hammond, town (1990 pop. 1,097), St. Croix co., W Wis., 16 mi/26 km E of Hudson; 44°58′N 92°26′W. Dairying; mfg. (polyester film).

Hammond 1 village (1990 pop. 527), Piatt co., central Ill., 18 mi/29 km E of Decatur; 39°47′N 88°35′W. In grain area. **2** village (1990 pop. 205), Wabasha co., SE Minn., 15 mi/24 km NNE of Rochester, on Zumbro R., in Richard J. Dorer Memorial Hardwood State Forest; 44°13′N 92°22′W. Grain; livestock. **3** village (1990 pop. 270), St. Lawrence co., N N.Y., bet. Black L. and St. Lawrence R., 19 mi/31 km SW of Ogdensburg; 44°27′N 75°41′W. Timber; agr. (dairying; grain, hay). **4** village (1990 pop. 589), Clatsop co., NW Oregon, on Columbia R. estuary, 1 mi/1.6 km E of Pacific Ocean; 46°12′N 123°57′W. Terminus of RR spur from Warrenton. Smoked, fresh, frozen seafood. Fort Stevens State Park to W.

Hammond, plantation (1990 pop. 93), Aroostook co., E Maine, just NW of Houlton; 46°14′N 67°57′W. In agr. area.

Hammond, Canada: see PORT HAMMOND.

Hammond-Harwood House National Historic Site (c.1774), Annapolis, Anne Arundel co., central Md. The house exemplifies Amer. Georgian architecture in refinement of detail and excellence of design. The symmetrical brick bldg. has 2 wings with polygonal bays. The architect, William Buckland, one of few of the period who can be identified, designed it for Matthias Hammond, a young member of the Md. Assembly who played a role in events leading up to the Amer. Revolution. Ownership of the house eventually passed to William Harwood, a grandson of William Buckland. Preserved as a historical landmark since 1924, first by St. Johns Col., later by the Hammond-Harwood House Assn.

Hammondsport, village (1990 pop. 929), Steuben co., S N.Y., at S end of Keuka L., 20 mi/32 km NNW of Corning; 42°24′N 77°13′W. In grape-growing area; winemaking center; mfg. of metal prods. Summer residential and recreational area. Birthplace of Glenn Curtiss, who made aviation experiments in the village. Mus. Inc. 1871.

Hammondville, town (1990 pop. 420), De Kalb co., NE Ala., near Valley Head, c.10 mi/16 km NE of Fort Payne.

Hammonton, town (1990 pop. 12,208), Atlantic co., S N.J., a residential and mfg. suburb of Philadelphia; 39°38′N 74°46′W. Shipping and processing center for fruit and mfg. of wood prods., clothing, medical supplies and pharmaceuticals. Site of a winery. Inc. 1866.

Hampden, county (□ 634 sq mi/1,642 sq km; 1990 pop. 456,310), SW Mass., on Conn. state line; ⊙ Springfield; 42°07′N 72°40′W. Bisected by Connecticut R., which supplies power to its industrial cities. The Conn. Valley Lowland formed in middle of co. Varied mfg. (paper and paper prods., foods, rubber and plastic prods., metal prods., industrial machinery and equip., electronic equip., consumer goods; printing and publishing). Vegetables, fruit; livestock; dairying, nursery prods. Formed 1812.

Hampden 1 town (1990 pop. 5,974), Penobscot co., S Maine, on the Penobscot R., just S of Bangor; 44°43′N 68°53′W. Park commemorates Dorothea Dix (b. here). Settled 1767, inc. 1794. **2** town (1990 pop. 4,709), Hampden co., S Mass., near Scantic R., 8 mi/12.9 km ESE of Springfield; 42°04′N 72°25′W. Dairying; vegetables. Settled c.1740, inc. 1878.

Hampden, village (1990 pop. 89), Ramsey co., NE N.Dak., 21 mi/34 km NNE of Devils L.; 48°32′N 98°39′W.

Hampden Sydney, uninc. town (1990 pop. 1,240), Prince Edward co., central Va., 7 mi/11.3 km SSW of Farmville; 37°14′N 78°27′W. Mfg. (wine); agr. (tobacco, grain; hogs; dairying); timber. Seat of Hampden-Sydney Col.

Hampshire 1 county (□ 545 sq mi/1,412 sq km; 1990 pop. 146,568), W central Mass.; ⊙ Northampton; 42°20′N 72°40′W. Bisected by Connecticut R.; drained by Westfield R. and other small streams. Conn. Valley Lowland bisects co. The Berkshires touch W sect.; Mounts Tom and Holyoke are near the Connecticut. Generally forested and agr. (tobacco, hay, vegetables, fruit; poultry; livestock; dairying); mfg. (textile goods; paper, plastic, and metal prods.; machinery; photographic equip.; consumer goods). Formed 1662. **2** county (□ 645 sq mi/1,671 sq km; 1990 pop. 16,498), NE W.Va., in E Panhandle; ⊙ Romney; 39°18′N 78°36′W. Bounded N, in part, by Potomac R. (Md. state line), E by Va.; drained by South Branch of Potomac, Cacapon, and North rivers. Traversed by valleys and ridges of the Appalachian Mts. Agr. (corn, hay, alfalfa, grains, potatoes, sorghum, honey, fruit); livestock, poultry. Some mfg. at Romney. Timber. Small part of George Washington Natl. Forest in SE; Edwards Run Wildlife Management Area in E; Short Mt. and Nathanial Mt. wildlife areas in S; Fort Mill and Springfield wildlife management areas in W. Formed 1753.

Hampshire, village (1990 pop. 1,843), Kane co., NE Ill., 18 mi/29 km NNW of Geneva; 42°06′N 88°31′W. In agr. area (dairy prods.; livestock; grain).

Hampstead, city (1991 pop. 8,645), S central Que., E Canada, residential suburb 4 mi/6 km SW of downtown Montreal, on Montreal Isl.; 45°37′N 66°05′W. Bounded by city of Montreal on NE and SE.

Hampstead 1 (HAMP-sted), town (1990 pop. 2,608), Carroll co., N Md., 25 mi/40 km NW of Baltimore; 39°37′N 76°52′W. Power tool mfg. Laid out in 1786. **2** (HAMP-stuhd), town (1990 pop. 6,732), Rockingham co., SE N.H., 6 mi/9.7 km N of Salem; 42°52′N 71°10′W. Mfg. (plastic prods., computer equip., electronic equip.; printing and publishing); agr. (nursery crops, vegetables; poultry, cattle; dairying). Island Pond (2 mi/3.2 km long) in W; Angle and Wash ponds in N. Includes village of East Hampstead.

Hampstead (HAMP-stid), village (1991 pop. 339), S N.B., E Canada, on St. John R. (ferry), and 24 mi/39 km N of St. John. Granite quarrying.

Hampton, county (□ 562 sq mi/1,456 sq km; 1990 pop. 18,191), S S.C.; ⊙ Hampton; 32°46′N 81°08′W. Bounded SW by Savannah R.; drained by the Coosawhatchie R. Hunting. Timber. agr. includes hogs, cattle; corn, wheat, soybeans, peanuts, cotton, watermelons, peaches. Formed 1878.

Hampton 1 (HAMP-tuhn), city (1990 pop. 4,133), ⊙

Franklin co., N central Iowa, 29 mi/47 km S of Mason City; 42°45′N 93°12′W. RR junction. Agr. trade and processing center (corn, packed poultry, feed). Wood, metal, stone, and concrete prods.; fertilizers; motor home components; nursery. Limestone quarries, sand and gravel pits nearby. Beeds L. State Park is NW. Founded 1856, inc. 1870. **2** independent city (□ 57 sq mi/148 sq km; 1990 pop. 133,793), SE Va., 8 mi/12.9 km NNW of Norfolk, port on Hampton Roads, at mouth of James R., connected to Norfolk by Hampton Roads Bridge-Tunnel; 37°02′N 76°17′W. Separate from adjoining co.; bounded W by independent city of Newport News, N by independent city of Poquoson. RR terminus; mfg. (machinery, chemicals, lumber, bldg. materials, consumer goods, wood prods., foods, transportation equip.; machining, steel fabrication, electronic instrumentation); large seafood packing and shipping industry (fish, crabs, and oysters). Langley Air Force Base (est. 1917), which includes NASA's Langley Research Center, are in N; historic Ft. Monroe Military Reservation (built 1819–1834) in SE on Chesapeake Bay. One of the oldest continuous Eng. settlements in the country, Hampton was founded on the site of the Native Amer. village Kecoughtan. Attacked by pirates in late 17th cent. (Blackbeard captured off the coast), shelled in the Revolutionary War, sacked by British in 1813, and nearly burned to the ground by evacuating Confederates in 1861 to prevent Union possession. Seat of Hampton Univ., Thomas Nelson Community Col. St. John's Episcopal Church (1728; original church est. 1610), nearby reproduction of a Native Amer. village. Plum Tree Isl. Natl. Wildlife Reservation to N. Big Bethel Reservoir in NW corner. Formerly Elizabeth City co. Settled 1610 by colonists from Jamestown, inc. 1849.

Hampton 1 (HAMP-tuhn), town (1990 pop. 1,562), ⊙ Calhoun co., S Ark., on Champagnolle Creek, 21 mi/34 km E of Camden; 33°32′N 92°28′W. In agr. area. Mfg. (apparel). **2** town (1990 pop. 1,578), Windham co., E Conn., on Little R., and 9 mi/14.5 km NE of Willimantic; 41°47′N 72°03′W. In hilly region. Agr. Has 18th- and 19th-cent. houses; part of state forest. **3** town (1990 pop. 2,694), Henry co., N central Ga., 9 mi/14.5 km N of Griffin; 33°23′N 84°17′W. Mfg. includes bldg. materials, machinery parts, consumer goods, fabricated metal goods, electrical equip.; egg production. NASCAR racing at Atlanta Motor Speedway; Atlanta regional air-traffic control center. **4** town (1990 pop. 12,278), Rockingham co., SE N.H., on Atlantic Ocean (E) and Hampton Harbor (S), 9 mi/14.5 km S of Portsmouth; 42°56′N 70°49′W. Mfg. (chemicals, electronic equip., tools, aerospace prods., leather; architectural millwork; printing and publishing). Agr. (nursery crops, vegetables, apples; cattle, poultry; dairying). Henry Dearborn b. here. Hampton Beach and North Beach, on coast, are resort areas. Hampton Beach State Park and State Pier in SE. North Hampton and Hampton Falls were formerly in Hampton. Settled 1638, inc. 1639. **5** town (1990 pop. 2,997), ⊙ Hampton co., SW S.C., 55 mi/89 km N of Savannah; 32°52′N 81°06′W. Mfg. of wood prods., chemicals, plastics, and laminates. In agr. area producing cotton, corn, sweet potatoes, watermelons, peanuts, peaches; timber; livestock.

Hampton (HAMP-tuhn), village (1991 pop. 3,590), ⊙ Kings co., S N.B., E Canada, on Kennebecasis R., and 20 mi/32 km NE of St. John. In dairying and farming region. Popular summer residence for St. John residents.

Hampton 1 (HAMP-tuhn), village (1990 pop. 1,601), Rock Island co., NW Ill., suburb of Rock Isl. and Moline, on the Mississippi R.; 41°32′N 90°24′W. Metal electroplating. **2** village (1990 pop. 363), Dakota co., SE Minn., 24 mi/39 km S of St. Paul, and 11 mi/18 km SW of Hastings; 44°36′N 93°00′W. Grain, soybeans; livestock, poultry; dairying; mfg. (meat processing; fertilizers). **3** village (1990 pop. 432), Hamilton co., SE central Nebr., 5 mi/8 km E of Aurora; 40°52′N 97°53′W. **4** village, Carter co., NE Tenn., 5 mi/8 km SE of Elizabethton; 36°17′N 82°10′W.

Hampton, borough (1990 pop. 1,515), Hunterdon co., W N.J., near Musconetcong R., 13 mi/21 km E of Phillipsburg; 40°42′N 74°58′W.

Hampton, township (1990 pop. 15,568), Allegheny co., W Pa., residential suburb 9 mi/14.5 km NNW of Pittsburgh; 40°35′N 79°57′W. Mfg. includes tool and die and ornamental iron. Includes the communities of Allison Park, DeHaven, Wildwood, and Hardy.

Hampton, N.C.: see RUTH.

Hampton Bays, summer-resort village (□ 21 sq mi/54 sq km; 1990 pop. 7,893), Suffolk co., SE N.Y., on shore of SE L.I., 7 mi./11.3 km W of Southampton; 40°51′N 72°31′W. In diversified-farming area; boatyards. Until 1922 called Good Ground. Pop. figure includes Rampasture, Squiretown, and Tiana.

Hampton Beach, N.H.: see HAMPTON.

Hampton Falls, town (1990 pop. 1,503), Rockingham co., SE N.H., 5 mi/8 km SSW of Hampton; 42°55′N 70°53′W. Bounded on E by Hampton Harbor. Agr. (dairying; cattle, poultry; vegetables; nursery crops); mfg. (commercial printing). Set off from Hampton 1726.

Hampton Harbor, SE N.H., small bay (1 mi/1.6 km long, ½ mi/⅘ km wide) S of Hampton, near Mass. state line; receives 2 tidal streams.

Hampton National Historic Site, Baltimore co., NE Md. Late-18th-cent. Georgian mansion (1783–1790) with a portrait gallery and terraced gardens. Built by George Ridgely. Authorized 1948.

Hampton Roads, harbor, SE Va., in James R. estuary at its entrance to Chesapeake Bay, East Elizabeth R. estuary enters from S, Willoughby Bay on S, just within entrance; 4 mi/6.4 km long and 40 ft/12 m deep. One of the world's finest natural harbors, it has been a major anchorage point since colonial times and has extensive harbor facilities and shipyards; Newport News, Hampton on the N shore; Norfolk, Portsmouth on the S. The Port of Hampton Roads, est. 1926 under the State Port Authority of Va., is one of the busiest U.S. seaports. Hampton Roads has long been important to the U.S. Navy; Norfolk is hq. for the Atlantic Fleet. Norfolk Navy Base on SE side, Craney Isl. Army Corps of Engineers Base on S. A vehicular tunnel (7,479 ft/2,280 m) under the roads opened in 1957. Hampton Roads was the site of the Civil War battle (March 1862) bet. the ironclads *Monitor* and *Merrimack*.

Hams Fork, river, c.100 mi/161 km long, SW Wyo.; rises in S tip of Salt R. Range, central Lincoln co.; flows S through L. Viva Naughton Reservoir, past Kemmerer, then E, past Opal, and SE to Blacks Fork of Green R. at Granger.

Hamtramck (ham-TRA-mik), city (1990 pop. 18,372), Wayne co., SE Mich., suburb 4 mi/6.4 km N of downtown Detroit; 42°23′N 83°03′W. Mfg. (meat processing; machinery, foods, motor vehicles and transportation equip., chemicals, plastic prods.). The site was settled by Frenchmen in the late 18th cent. The city grew quickly after the coming of the automobile industry c.1910. Points of interest include St. Florian's Church (a prime example of Gothic architecture); and the memorial and grave of Col. John F. Hamtramck, 1st U.S. commander of the Detroit garrison. The city has a large Pol.-Amer. community and various Pol. cultural events. NW corner touches city of Highland Park; both cities are completely surrounded by city of Ontario. Inc. as a city 1922.

Hana (HAH-nah), village (1990 pop. 683), E Maui, Maui co., Hawaii, 32 mi/51 km ESE of Kahului, at E end of Maui, on Hana Bay; 20°46′N 155°59′W. Harbor; airport. Secluded and beautiful area. Charles A. Lindbergh buried nearby. Hana Airport to NW. Waianapanapa State Park to N, on coast. Extension to coast of Haleakala Natl. Park 7 mi/11.3 km to SW. Hana Forest Reserve to SW. Hana Cultural Center and Mus. Hana Bay Beach Park is here.

Hanábana River (ah-NAH-bah-nah), c.50 mi/111 km long, W Cuba; flows along border bet. Matanzas and Cienfuegos provs.; 22°28′N 80°34′W. Drains 406 sq mi/1,051 sq km of plains and foothills W of Alturas de Santa Clara, emptying into the Zapata marshes. Formerly called Amarillas R.

Hanabanilla River (ah-nah-bah-NEE-yuh), c.20 mi/32 km long, Villa Clara prov., central Cuba; small affluent of the Arimao R., which it joins at Arimao town, 15 mi/24 km E of Cienfuegos; 22°07′N 80°06′W. Known for its waterfall. Headwaters held in a dam of same name.

Hanaford, village (1990 pop. 380), Franklin co., S Ill., 5 mi/8 km SE of Benton; 37°57′N 88°50′W. In bituminous-coal and agr. area. Also called Logan.

Hanagita Peak (HA-nuh-GEE-duh) (8,504 ft/2,592 m), S Alaska, in Chugach Mts., 80 mi/129 km ENE of Cordova; 61°05′N 143°43′W.

Hanahan (HA-nuh-han), city (1990 pop. 13,176), Berkeley co., SE S.C. suburb 9 mi/14.5 km NNW of downtown Charleston; 32°55′N 80°00′W. Mfg. includes machining, metal fabricating, mfg. of plastic prods. Charleston Naval Base to NE; Charleston Air Force Base to W. Charleston Internatl. Airport to SW. Goose Creek Reservoir to N.

Hanalei (HAH-nah-LAI), village (1990 pop. 461), N Kauai, Kauai co., Hawaii, near head of Hanalei Bay and Hanalei R., 18 mi/29 km NW of Lihue, on Kuhio Highway, between Hanalei R. (N) and Waioli Stream (W); 22°12′N 159°30′W. Hanalei Mus. Hanalei Natl. Wildlife Refuge to E. Halelea Forest Reserve to S, including Mt. Kaliko (4,201 ft/1,280 m). Waioli Mission. Waioli Beach Park is here. Hanalei Beach Park at mouth of Hanalei R., to N.

Hanamaulu (HAH-nah-MAH-OO-loo), village (1990 pop. 3,611), SE Kauai, Kauai co., Hawaii, 2 mi/3.2 km N of Lihue, on Kuhiô Highway, and on Hanamaulu Bay, at mouth of Hanamaulu Stream; 22°00′N 159°20′W. Co. Correctional Facility to N. Kalepa Forest Reserve and Wailua R. State Park to N. Ahukini State Recreational Park to E on coast; mus.

Hanapepe (HAH-nah-PAI-PAI), town (1990 pop. 1,395), S Kauai, Kauai co., Hawaii, at head of Hanapepe Bay, at mouth of Hanapepe R., NW of Port Allen, on Kaumualii Highway; 21°55′N 159°35′W. Mfg. (ice cream); Port Allen Airport (Burns Field) at Puolo Point to S; Salt Pond Beach Park to SW. Hanapepe Stadium; Hoary Head Stadium to W.

Hanceville (HANS-vil), town (1990 pop. 2,246), Cullman co., N central Ala., 10 mi/16 km SSE of Cullman. Farm shipping center. Animal feeds, fertilizer, bldg. materials, wood prods. Seat of Wallace State Community Col.

Hancock 1 county (□ 485 sq mi/1,256 sq km), E central Ga.; ⊙ Sparta; 33°16′N 83°00′W. Bounded E by Ogeechee R., W by Oconee R. Intersected by fall line. Agr. includes cotton, corn, forage, pecans; cattle; lumber and wood prods. Formed 1793. **2** county (□ 814 sq mi/2,108 sq km; 1990 pop. 21,373), W Ill.; ⊙ Carthage; 40°31′N 91°09′W. Bounded W by the Mississippi R., here dammed into L. Keokuk; drained by La Moine R. and Bear Creek. Agr. area (corn, wheat, soybeans, fruit; cattle, hogs; dairying). Limestone quarries, sand pits. Some mfg. Formed 1825. **3** county (□ 306 sq mi/793 sq km; 1990 pop. 45,527), central Ind.; ⊙ Greenfield; 39°49′N 85°46′W. Drained by Sugar Creek, small Brandywine Creek, and Big Blue R. Agr. area (vegetables, corn, wheat; hogs, cattle; dairying). Part of Indianapolis metro area. Formed 1827. **4** county (□ 573 sq mi/1,484 sq km; 1990 pop. 12,638), N Iowa; ⊙ Garner, 43°05′N 93°43′W. Prairie agr. area (cattle, hogs, poultry; corn, oats) drained by branches of Iowa R. and Lime Creek. Contains small lakes (glacial origin); sand and gravel pits. Crystal L. State Park in NW; Pilot Knob L. and State Park in NE; Eagle L. in center; Twin Lakes in S. General flooding here in 1993. Formed 1851. **5** county (□ 198 sq mi/513 sq km; 1990 pop. 7,864), NW Ky.; ⊙ Hawesville; 37°51′N 86°46′W. Bounded N and NE by Ohio R. (Ind. state line); drained by Blackford Creek, forms part of W border. Agr. area (burley tobacco, corn, hay, alfalfa, soybeans, wheat; cattle, hogs). Cannelton Locks and Dam on Ohio R. in NE. Formed 1829. **6** county (□ 2,351 sq mi/6,089 sq km; 1990 pop. 46,948), S and SE Maine; ⊙ Ellsworth; 44°32′N 68°22′W. Gateway to Mt. Desert Isl. and Acadia Natl. Park. Mfg. (wood and paper prods., machinery). Agr.; dairying; granite quarrying; hunting and fishing. Bays, isls., and inland lakes are resort sites. Drained by Penobscot R. **7** county (□ 552 sq mi/1,430 sq km; 1990 pop. 31,760), SE Miss., on Mississippi Sound of Gulf of Mexico (S); ⊙ Bay St. Louis; 30°23′N 89°28′W. Pearl R. La. state line on W; drained by Jordan and Wolf rivers. Agr. (corn, cotton, pecans; timber); seafood. Beach resorts. Buccaneer State Park on coast in SE. Stennis Space Center (NASA) in W. Formed 1812. **8** county (□ 532 sq mi/1,378 sq km; 1990 pop. 65,536), NW Ohio; ⊙ Findlay; 41°01′N 83°40′W. Intersected by Blanchard R. In the Till Plains physiographic region, except for the NW portion (in the Lake Plains region). Hogs, sheep, corn, soybeans, vegetables. Diversified mfg., esp. at Findlay (food prods., plastic prods., household appliances, transportation equip.); limestone quarries. Includes Van Buren State Park. Formed 1820. **9** county (□ 231 sq mi/598 sq km; 1990 pop. 6,739), NE Tenn., on Va. (N) state line; ⊙ Sneedville; 36°32′N 83°13′W. Traversed by Powell Mt. and other ridges of the Appalachians; drained by Clinch and Powell rivers. Agr. (livestock; tobacco, tomatoes). Formed 1844. **10** county (□ 88 sq mi/228 sq km; 1990 pop. 35,233), N W.Va., at tip of N Panhandle; ⊙ New Cumberland; 40°31′N 80°34′W. Bounded N and W by Ohio R. (Ohio state line), E by Pa. Industrial region, esp. steel milling. Mfg. at Weirton, Newell, and Chester. Clay and glass-sand pits. Agr. (corn, wheat, oats, alfalfa, nursery crops). Includes Tomlinson Run State Park in NW; Hillcrest Wildlife Management Area in NE. Formed 1848.

Hancock, city (1990 pop. 4,547), Houghton co., NW Upper Peninsula, N Mich., opposite Houghton, on Keweenaw Waterway (port facilities); 47°07′N 88°35′W. Light mfg.; meat processing. Tourism; resort. Lift bridge connects it to Houghton. Houghton Co. Airport to NE. Seat of Suomi Col. Historic Arcadian Copper Mines (tours). F. J. McLain State Park to N. Plotted 1859; inc. as village 1875, as city 1903.

Hancock 1 town (1990 pop. 201), Pottawattamie co., SW Iowa, 26 mi/42 km ENE of Council Bluffs; 41°23′N 95°21′W. **2** resort town (1990 pop. 1,757), Hancock co., S Maine, on Frenchman Bay, N of Mt. Desert Isl., and 8 mi/12.9 km E of Ellsworth; 44°31′N 68°16′W. **3** town (1990 pop. 1,926), Washington co., W Md., on the Potomac R. (bridged), and 25 mi/40 km W of Hagerstown, at narrowest point of Md. (c.2 mi/3.2 km wide); 39°42′N 78°10′W. Center for agr. and timber. Hunting preserves nearby. Inc. 1853. **4** town (1990 pop. 628), Berkshire co., NW Mass., 7 mi/11.3 km NNW of Pittsfield, near N.Y. state line; 42°31′N 73°19′W. Resort; dairying. **5** town (1990 pop. 1,604), Hillsborough co., S N.H., 28 mi/45 km W of Manchester; 42°58′N 71°59′W. Drained by Contoocook R. Mfg. (wood prods.); timber; agr. (vegetables, fruit; livestock, poultry; dairying). Powder Mill Pond in E; Nubanusit L. on W border. **6** town (1990 pop. 340), Addison co., central Vt., on White R., and 18 mi/29 km ESE of Middlebury, in Green Mts.; 43°55′N 72°55′W. Winter sports. Forest prods.

Hancock 1 village (1990 pop. 723), Stevens co., W Minn., 9 mi/14.5 km SE of Morris; 45°30′N 95°47′W. Grain, sunflowers, soybeans; cattle, hogs; mfg. (concrete prods.). Page L. to N. **2** summer-resort village (□ 1 sq mi/2.6 sq km; 1990 pop. 1,330), Delaware co., S N.Y., in the Catskill Mts., at junction of East and West branches here forming the Delaware R., 35 mi/56 km ESE of Binghamton; 41°57′N 75°16′W. Mfg. (medical supplies, electrical equip., fabricated metal prods., wood prods., consumer goods, furniture). Inc. 1888. **3** village (1990 pop. 382), Waushara co., central Wis., 24 mi/39 km SE of Wisconsin Rapids; 44°07′N 89°31′W. In dairying and farming area, on Pine L. Agr. research station and wildlife area nearby.

Hancock, Fort, N.J.: see SANDY HOOK.

Hancock, Lake, Polk co., central Fla., 3 mi/4.8 km N of Bartow; c.4 mi/6.4 km long, 3 mi/4.8 km wide; source of Peace R.

Hancock, Mount 1 peak (4,430 ft/1,350 m), Grafton co., N central N.H., 9 mi/14.5 km NE of North Woodstock, in White Mts., in White Mt. Natl. Forest. **2** peak (10,214 ft/3,113 m), Rocky Mts., in S Yellowstone Natl. Park, Teton co., NW Wyo., 10 mi/16 km S of Yellowstone L.

Hancocks Bridge, village, Salem co., SW N.J., on Alloway Creek, and 5 mi/8 km S of Salem. Hancock House (1734), site of massacre of Revolutionary troops by Tories, here.

Hand, county (□ 1,440 sq mi/3,730 sq km; 1990 pop. 4,272), central S.Dak.; ⊙ Miller; 44°32′N 99°00′W. Level agr. region watered by Wolf, Turtle, and Sand creeks. Wheat, oats, rye, barley, corn; dairy prods.; cattle, hogs. L. Louise State Recreation Area at center. Formed 1873.

Handies Peak (14,048 ft/4,282 m), Hinsdale co., SW Colo., in San Juan Mts., 11 mi/18 km NE of Silverton.

Handley, village (1990 pop. 334), Kanawha co., W central W.Va., on Kanawha R., 17 mi/27 km SE of Charleston; 38°11′N 81°22′W.

Handsboro, village (1990 pop. 1,577), in E part of Gulfport, Harrison co., SE Miss., 8 mi/12.9 km W of Biloxi, on Mississippi Sound. In shore-resort area. Now part of city of Gulfport.

Hanford, city (1990 pop. 30,897), ⊙ Kings co., central Calif., 21 mi/34 km W of Visalia; 36°20′N 119°39′W. RR junction and an agr. trade and processing center of the San Joaquin Valley. Along with Fresno it has prospered from the commercial enterprises and agr.-related business. Rubber and oil companies here. Cotton; wheat, barley, pistachios, almonds, olives, cantaloupes, tomatoes, plums, peaches, nectarines; dairying; turkeys; flour mill. Lemoure Naval Air Station to W. Tulare L. irrigation reservoir to SW. Inc. 1891.

Hanford Works, Wash.: see RICHLAND.

Hanging Hills, S central Conn., small trap ridge just NW of Meriden, rising to 1,024 ft/312 m in West Peak. Area is state park, with recreational facilities.

Hanging Rock, village (1990 pop. 306), Lawrence co., S Ohio, on Ohio R., and 4 mi/6 km NW of Ironton; 38°33′N 82°43′W.

Hankins, resort village (1990 pop. 400), Sullivan co., SE N.Y., on the Delaware R. (here forming Pa. state line), and 17 mi/27 km W of Liberty; 41°49′N 75°05′W.

Hankinson, town (1990 pop. 1,038), Richland co., SE N.Dak., 20 mi/32 km SW of Wahpeton. Dairy prods.; livestock; grain; 46°04′N 96°53′W. RR junction. Site of convent and Acad. of Sisters of St. Francis. Willard and Grass lakes to SW. (Sisseton) Wahpeton Indian Reservation to S. Inc. 1912.

Hanks, village (1990 pop. 11), Williams co., NW N.Dak., 33 mi/53 km NNW of Williston; 48°36′N 103°47′W. Ranching in vicinity. L. Zahl Wildlife Refuge to E.

Hanksville, uninc. village (1990 pop. 487), Wayne co., S central Utah, 50 mi/80 km SSW of Green River town, and 50 mi/80 km W of Loa, on Fremont R. S of its junction with Muddy R., where the 2 form the Dirty Devil R.; elev. c.4,300 ft/1,310 m. Cattle; tourism. Settled 1882. Crossroads for natl. park area, with Capitol Reef (W) and Canyonlands (E) natl. parks in area, Glen Canyon Natl. Recreation Area to SE, and Goblin Valley State Park to N.

Hanley, town (1991 pop. 499), S central Sask., W Canada, 35 mi/56 km SSE of Saskatoon; 51°37′N 106°26′W. Grain elevators; dairying.

Hanley Falls, village (1990 pop. 246), Yellow Medicine co., SW Minn., 9 mi/14.5 km SW of Granite Falls, on Yellow Medicine R.; 44°41′N 95°37′W. RR junction. Corn, oats, soybeans; livestock. Wood L. to E.

Hanley Hills, town (1990 pop. 2,325), St. Louis co., E Mo., residential suburb 8 mi/12.9 km NW of downtown St. Louis; 38°40′N 90°19′W.

Hanlontown, town (1990 pop. 193), Worth co., N Iowa, near Lime Creek, 14 mi/23 km SW of Northwood; 43°16′N 93°22′W. Peat mining and processing.

Hanna, town (1991 pop. 2,996), SE central Alta., W Canada, 35 mi/56 km ENE of Drumheller; 51°38′N 111°55′W. Coal mining; dairying; mixed farming; flour milling; wheat, rye, oats.

Hanna, town (1990 pop. 1,076), Carbon co., S Wyo., 35 mi/56 km E of Rawlins; 41°52′N 106°33′W. Elev. c.6,777 ft/2,066 m. Coal mines, one of most productive in area. Nearby is site of Fort Halleck, military post est. 1862 on Overland stage route. Seminoe Reservoir to NW. Settled 1887, inc. 1936.

Hanna 1 village (1990 pop. 550), La Porte co., NW Ind., 13 mi/21 km SSW of LaPorte. RR junction. Dairying; fruit. Laid out 1858. **2** village (1990 pop. 99), McIntosh co., E Okla., 20 mi/32 km NNW of McAlester, on Canadian R. (upper reach of Eufaula L.); 35°12′N 95°53′W. In agr. area.

Hanna City, village (1990 pop. 1,205), Peoria co., central Ill., 11 mi/18 km W of Peoria; 40°41′N 89°47′W. In agr. (corn, soybeans; cattle) and bituminous-coal-mining area.

Hannaford, village (1990 pop. 204), Griggs co., E central N.Dak., 10 mi/16 km S of Cooperstown, and on Bald Hill Creek; 47°18′N 98°11′W. RR junction. L. Ashtabula Reservoir to SE.

Hannah, village (1990 pop. 49), Cavalier co., N N.Dak., port of entry 25 mi/40km NW of Langdon, near Can. (Man.) border; 48°58′N 98°41′W. RR terminus. Rush L. to S.

Hannastown (HA-nuhz-toun), uninc. village, Westmoreland co., SW Pa., 5 mi/8 km NNE of Greensburg, on Crabtree Creek; 40°21′N 79°29′W. Colonial-era co. seat and center of dispute bet. Pa. and Va. over possession of Westmoreland territory, resolved 1779 by extension of Mason-Dixon line W. Destroyed 1782 by Native Amer. raid. Old Hanna's Town historic site.

Hannibal (HAN-nuh-buhl), city (1990 pop. 18,004), Marion and Ralls cos., NE Mo., on the Mississippi R.; 39°42′N 91°22′W. River port and shipping center. Industries include meat canning, printing, and the mfg. of boats, electronics, and lumber and metal prods. Corn, soybeans; dairying; cattle, hogs. Major tourist destination. RR junction; RR and highway bridges. Famous as the boyhood home of Mark Twain; his house has been preserved, and a mus., statue, lighthouse, and a bridge across the Mississippi commemorate him; the famous Mark Twain cave is S of city. Seat of Hannibal–La Grange Col. City spared during 1993 floods. Plotted 1819, inc. 1845.

Hannibal, village (□ 1 sq mi/2.6 sq km; 1990 pop. 613), Oswego co., N central N.Y., 10 mi/16 km SW of Oswego; 43°19′N 76°34′W. In dairy and fruit area.

Hannibal Lock and Dam, Wetzel Co., N W.Va., and Monroe co., SE Ohio, on Ohio R., at Hannibal, Ohio, and 2 mi/3.2 km N (upstream) from New Martinsville, W.Va.; 42 ft/13 m high; the reservoir created has a max. water storage capacity of 130,000 acre-ft. Built (1974) by the Army Corps of Engineers for navigational purposes; originally called Lock and Dam No. 14.

Hano, Indian pueblo, Navajo co., NE Ariz., atop a mesa in Hopi Indian Reservation, 3 mi/4.8 km N of Polacca, on Wepo Wash, c.65 mi/105 km NNE of Winslow; elev. c.6,200 ft/1,890 m. Founded in 17th cent. by immigrant Tewa-speaking Native Americans who have since adopted Hopi customs.

Hanover, parish (□ 177 sq mi/458 sq km; 1991 pop. 65,389), Cornwall co., NW Jamaica, on W promontory of the isl.; ⊙ Lucea; 18°25′N 78°08′W. E boundary along Great R. Principal agr. crops (rice, bananas, lime, yams, breadfruit). Lucea and Green Isl. ship bananas. Near Lucea are phosphate deposits.

Hanover, county (□ 474 sq mi/1,228 sq km; 1990 pop. 63,306), E central Va.; ⊙ Hanover; 37°45′N 77°29′W. Partly in the Piedmont region (W), with coastal plain (E); bounded NE by North Anna and Pamunkey rivers, S by Chickahominy R.; drained by South Anna R. Agr. area (tobacco, soybeans, barley, wheat, corn, peanuts, hay; cattle, poultry; dairying). Many Civil War battle sites (at Cold Harbor, Gaines's Mill, Mechanicsville). Cold Harbor Natl. Cemetery, part of Richmond Natl. Battlefield Park in SE. Formed 1720.

Hanover, town (1991 pop. 6,711), S Ont., central Canada, on Saugeen R., and 28 mi/45 km S of Owen Sound; 44°09′N 81°02′W. Woodworking, light mfg. Dairying.

Hanover 1 town (1990 pop. 3,610), Jefferson co., SE Ind., near Ohio R., 5 mi/8 km WSW of Madison; 38°43′N 85°28′W. Agr. area. Mfg. (medical supplies), meat processing. Seat of Hanover Col. Laid out 1832. **2** town

(1990 pop. 272), Oxford co., W Maine, on the Androscoggin R., and 21 mi/34 km NNW of South Paris; 44°29′N 70°44′W. **3** town (1990 pop. 11,912), Plymouth co., E Mass., on North R., and 20 mi/32 km SE of Boston; 42°07′N 70°52′W. Mfg. rubber, tools, machinery; binding and publishing. Dairying; poultry. Settled 1649, inc. 1727. **4** town (1990 pop. 787), Hennepin and Wright cos., E Minn., suburb 24 mi/39 km NW of downtown Minneapolis, on Crow R.; 45°09′N 93°39′W. Grain; livestock, poultry; dairying; mfg. (fabricated metal and wood prods.). Crow Hassan Park Reserve to NE; several small natural lakes in area. **5** town (1990 pop. 9,212), Grafton co., SW N.H., 4 mi/6.4 km NW of Lebanon, bounded W by Connecticut R. (Vt. state line). Light mfg. Seat of Dartmouth Col. and a cultural and recreational center. Dartmouth Hitchcock Medical Center. North Peak (2,300 ft/701 m) in NE; Appalachian Trail crosses town NE to W center (crosses bridge to Vt.). Includes village of Etna, 3 mi/4.8 km E of town center, mfg. (mobile classrooms). Settled 1765, inc. 1769.

Hanover 1 village (1990 pop. 908), Jo Daviess co., NW Ill., on Apple R. (bridged here), and 13 mi/21 km SSE of Galena; 41°58′N 88°08′W. In agr. area (dairying; cattle, hogs, ducks; oats); mfg. (transportation equip.). Savanna Army Depot to SW on Mississippi R. **2** village (1990 pop. 696), Washington co., NE Kansas, on Little Blue R., and 11 mi/18 km NW of Marysville; 39°53′N 96°52′W. RR junction and Pony Express Station to E. **3** village (1990 pop. 481), Jackson co., S Mich., 13 mi/21 km SW of Jackson; 42°06′N 84°32′W. In diversified farming area. Machining. **4** village, Fergus co., central Mont., on Big Spring Creek, and 7 mi/11.3 km NW of Lewistown. Gypsum rock deposits. **5** uninc. village (1990 pop. 300), Grant co., SW N.Mex., in foothills of Pinos Altos Mts., 11 mi/18 km ENE of Silver City; elev. 6,340 ft/1,932 m. Gold, silver, copper mines in vicinity. Black Peak is 8 mi/12.9 km NNW, Gila Natl. Forest to N. Santa Rita Open Pit Copper Mine is here. **6** village (1990 pop. 803), Licking co., central Ohio, 8 mi/13 km E of Newark; 40°04′N 82°16′W. **7** uninc. village, ⊙ Hanover co., E central Va., near Pamunkey R., 15 mi/24 km N of Richmond. Agr. (grain, soybeans; poultry, cattle). Patrick Henry lived here and pleaded (1763) his 1st important case in the co. courthouse (c.1735; extant). Nearby hamlet of Hanovertown nearly became capital of Va. in 1751.

Hanover (HA-no-vuhr), borough (1990 pop. 14,399), York co., SE Pa., 17 mi/27 km SW of York; 39°48′N 76°59′W. RR junction. Large and varied industrial base includes food processing (esp. pretzels) and mfg. (apparel, machinery, tool and die, fabricated metal prods., food prods., plastics prods., chemicals, paper prods.; printing and publishing). Agr. (grain, apples, soybeans; livestock, poultry; dairying). Standardbred horses raised here (many famous trotters have "Hanover" in their names). A cavalry action preceding the battle of Gettysburg was fought here in June 1863. Nearby are Devener (N) and Hanover (W) airports. Codorus State Park, on L. Marburg reservoir, to E. Inc. 1815.

Hanover, rural municipality (1986 pop. 8,033), SE of Winnipeg, Man., central Canada. Land set aside in 1873 as East Reserve for Mennonite settlements. Diversified agr. Commuter community for Winnipeg.

Hanover 1 township (1990 pop. 11,538), Morris co., N N.J., 5 mi/8 km NE of Morristown; 40°49′N 74°25′W. Inc. 1798. **2** (HA-no-vuhr), township (1990 pop. 14,399), Luzerne co., NE central Pa., suburb 2 mi/3.2 km SW of downtown Wilkes-Barre, on Susquehanna R., in Wyoming Valley. In declining anthracite-coal-mining region. Surrounds boroughs of Warrior Run and Sugar Notch.

Hanover, Conn.: see SPRAGUE.

Hanover Park, village (1990 pop. 32,895), Cook and Du Page cos., NE Ill., suburb 27 mi/43 km WNW of downtown Chicago, 2 mi/3.2 km SW of Schaumburg; 41°59′N 88°08′W. Mfg. (fabricated metal prods., electrical and electronic equip., water softeners).

Hanoverton (ha-NO-vuhr-tuhn), village (1990 pop. 434), Columbiana co., E Ohio, 23 mi/37 km E of Canton; 40°45′N 80°56′W.

Hanovertown, Va.: see HANOVER.

Hans Lollik Islands (HANZ LAW-lik), 2 islets and several rocks just off N St. Thomas Isl., U.S.V.I., 4 mi/6.4 km NNE of Charlotte Amalie. Hans Lollik Isl. proper (489 acres/198 ha; elev. 713 ft/217 m) is at 18°24′N 64°54′W; Little Hans Lollik is just N.

Hansboro, village (1990 pop. 20), Towner co., N N.Dak., port of entry 33 mi/53 km N of Cando, near Can. (Man.) border; 48°57′N 99°22′W. U.S. custom house here. RR terminus.

Hansell, town (1990 pop. 83), Franklin co., N central Iowa, 5 mi/8 km E of Hampton; 42°45′N 93°05′W. Livestock; grain.

Hansen, town (1990 pop. 848), Twin Falls co., S Idaho, 8 mi/12.9 km E of Twin Falls, and on Snake R.; 42°32′N 114°18′W. Elev. 4,000 ft/1,220 m. Irrigated farming (sugar beets, potatoes, fruit, hay, grain; cattle).

Hansen Dam, Calif.: see TUJUNGA CREEK.

Hansford, county (□ 920 sq mi/2,383 sq km; 1990 pop. 5,848), extreme N Texas, on Okla. (N) state line; ⊙ Spearman; 36°16′N 101°20′W. In high grassy plains of the Panhandle; elev. 3,000 ft/914 m–3,800 ft/1,158 m. Drained by Coldwater and Palo Duro creeks. Wheat-producing area; also grain, sorghums, corn, wheat; beef cattle, some sheep. Natural gas wells, some oil; stone; helium. Palo Duro reservoir in E. Formed 1876.

Hanska (HAN-skuh), village (1990 pop. 443), Brown co., S Minn., 12 mi/19 km S of New Ulm; 44°08′N 94°29′W. Grain, soybeans, peas; livestock, poultry; dairying. Mfg. (fertilizers and feeds). L. Hanska to W, Linden L. to E.

Hanska, Lake (HAN-skuh), Brown co., S Minn., 13 mi/21 km SW of New Ulm; 7.5 mi/12.1 km long, ½ mi/⅘ km wide; 44°08′N 94°36′W. Dam at SE end raises lake level; drains 6 mi/9.7 km through channel to Butterfield Creek, then 2 mi/3.2 km, to Watonwan R. L. Hanska Co. Park at SE end.

Hanson, county (□ 435 sq mi/1,127 sq km; 1990 pop. 2,994), SE central S.Dak.; ⊙ Alexandria; 43°39′N 97°47′W. Agr. and livestock-raising region drained by James R. Dairy prods.; corn, wheat; poultry, cattle, hogs. Formed 1871.

Hanson 1 town (1990 pop. 450), Hopkins co., W Ky., 7 mi/11.3 km N of Madisonville; 37°25′N 87°28′W. Coal mining; agr. (tobacco, grain; livestock). **2** residential town (1990 pop. 9,028), Plymouth co., E Mass., 25 mi/40 km SSE of Boston; 42°03′N 70°53′W. Mfg. (flourescent lighting); cranberries. Settled 1632, set off from Pembroke 1820.

Hanston, village (1990 pop. 326), Hodgeman co., SW central Kansas, on Buckner Creek, and 31 mi/50 km W of Larned; 38°07′N 99°42′W. Grain; livestock.

Hants, county (□ 1,229 sq mi/3,183 sq km; 1991 pop. 37,843), central N.S., E Canada, on the Bay of Fundy; ⊙ Windsor.

Hantsport, town (1991 pop. 1,274), W central N.S., E Canada, on Avon R., near its mouth on the Minas Basin, and 5 mi/8 km NNW of Windsor; 45°04′N 64°11′W. Paper mfg., fruit packing; gypsum quarrying.

Hapeville (HAIP-vil), RR town and Atlanta suburb (1990 pop. 5,483), Fulton co., NW central Ga., 7 mi/11.3 km SSW of Atlanta; 33°40′N 84°25′W. Motor vehicle-assembly and airplane-rebuilding plants; printing; sawmilling. Adjacent to Atlanta Hartsfield Internatl. Airport, which has expanded into the community, acquiring many homes and businesses. Inc. 1891.

Happy, village (1990 pop. 588), Swisher co., NW Texas, on Llano Estacado, c.40 mi/64 km N of Plainview; 34°44′N 101°51′W. In wheat, corn, cotton, and cattle area.

Happy Valley, town (1991 pop. 8,610), S central Lab., NE Canada, 5 mi/8 km SE of Goose Bay, on N bank of Churchill R.; 53°18′N 60°18′W. Connected by road to Goose Bay and air base. Est. 1970 as residential support center for military base. Has also served to support hydro projects on Churchill R. Amalgamated as Happy Valley–Goose Bay, 1975.

Happy Valley, town (1990 pop. 1,519), Clackamas co., NW Oregon, residential suburb 7 mi/11.3 km SE of downtown Portland; 45°26′N 122°32′W. Agr. to E and SE. Dairying; poultry; fruit, grain; nurseries.

Harahan (HA-ruh-han), city (1990 pop. 9,927), Jefferson parish, SE La., a suburb 8 mi/13 km W of downtown New Orleans, on the Mississippi R.; 29°57′N 90°12′W. Agr. shipping center; mfg. (fabricated metal prods., bldg. materials, machinery, soft drinks, paper prods., foods, chemicals). Huey P. Long Bridge over the Mississippi is nearby.

Haralson (HER-uhl-suhn), county (□ 285 sq mi/738 sq km; 1990 pop. 21,966), NW Ga.; ⊙ Buchanan; 33°47′N 85°13′W. Bounded W by Ala. state line. Piedmont area drained by Tallapoosa R. Agr. includes corn; cattle, hogs, poultry. Textile mfg. and sawmilling. Formed 1856.

Haralson (HER-uhl-suhn), village (1990 pop. 139), Coweta co., W Ga., 16 mi/26 km SE of Newnan; 33°14′N 84°34′W. Mfg. of surveillance equip.

Harbine (HAHR-bein), village (1990 pop. 66), Jefferson co., SE Nebr., 13 mi/21 km WSW of Beatrice; 40°11′N 96°58′W.

Harbison Canyon, uninc. town (1990 pop. 2,122), San Diego co., S Calif., residential suburb 19 mi/31 km NE of downtown San Diego, 7 mi/11.3 km E of El Cajon; 32°49′N 116°50′W. Sequon Indian Reservation to S.

Harbor, uninc. town (1990 pop. 2,143), Curry co., SW Oregon, 53 mi/85 km SW of Grants Pass, and 1 mi/1.6 km E of Brookings, on Pacific Ocean, at mouth of Chetco R.; 42°02′N 124°15′W. Fish. Mfg. (seafood processing).

Harbor Beach, city (1990 pop. 2,089), Huron co., E Mich., 17 mi/27 km E of Bad Axe, on L. Huron; 43°51′N 82°39′W. RR terminus. Resort center; mfg. (food processing, motor vehicle wiring; harnesses, chemicals). Settled 1837; inc. as village 1882, as city 1909.

Harbor City, suburban section of Los Angeles city, Los Angeles co., S Calif., 18 mi/29 km S of downtown Los Angeles and W of Long Beach; San Pedro area to S, in harbor dist. Mfg. (consumer goods, fabricated rubber prods., dental equip., plastic prods., transportation equip., chemicals). Palos Verdes Peninsula to SW.

Harbor Country, term for a group of 8 small towns, SW Mich., including Grand Union, Michiana, New Buffalo (main center), Three Oaks, Union Pier, Lakeside, Harbert, and Sawyul. Upscale summer communities, marinas, hotels. Area was formerly a farming and logging community; today, there are still many working farms and orchards.

Harbor Island, Bahama Isls.: see HARBOUR ISLAND.

Harbor Island, Texas: see ARANSAS PASS.

Harbor Springs, town (1990 pop. 1,540), Emmet co., NW Mich., on Little Traverse Bay of L. Michigan, and 4 mi/6.4 km NNW of Petoskey; 45°25′N 84°59′W. Lumbering; boatyards, fisheries; agr. (potatoes, apples, grain; livestock); mfg. (electrical enclosures, fabricated metal prods.). Boyne Highlands Ski Area to N; Nubs Nob Ski Area to NE. Year-round resort. Inc. as village 1881, as city 1932.

Harbor View, village (1990 pop. 122), Lucas co., NW Ohio, on Maumee Bay, E of Toledo, across Maumee R.; 41°42′N 83°26′W.

Harborcreek, uninc. town (1990 pop. 1,500), Erie co., NW Pa., residential suburb 7 mi/11.3 km E of Erie, and 1 mi/1.6 km SE of L. Erie; 42°09′N 79°57′W. Mfg. includes plastic molding. Agr. includes dairying; livestock; hay, corn, apples, grapes. Presque Isle Wine Cellars and Moorhead Airport to NE.

Harbour au Bouche, Canada: see HAVRE BOUCHER.

Harbour Buffet (BUH-fit), fishing village, SE N.F., E Canada, on SE coast of Long Isl., in Placentia Bay, 17 mi/27 km NNW of Argentia; 47°32′N 54°04′W.

Harbour Grace, town (1991 pop. 3,419), E N.F., E Canada, on Conception Bay; 47°41′N 53°15′W. Leading fishing port with fish-processing plants. Settled c.1550, one of the oldest towns in the prov. Airport nearby.

Harbour Island, islet and district (□ 1.5 sq mi/3.9 sq km), central Bahama Isls., off NE tip of Eleuthera Isl., 33 mi/53 km NE of Nassau; 25°30′N 76°38′W. The small isl. is one of the most densely populated in the archipelago; produces tomatoes, pineapples, coconuts. The chief settlement, Dunmore Town, has a fine harbor. Harbour Isl. was one of the 1st in the Bahamas to be settled by buccaneers. Its fine beaches attract many tourists. Also spelled Harbor Isl.

Harbour Island, largest of Penguin Isls., just off S N.F., E Canada; 1 mi/2 km long; 47°23′N 56°59′W.

Harcourt, town (1990 pop. 306), Webster co., central Iowa, 16 mi/26 km S of Fort Dodge; 42°15′N 94°10′W. In agr. area.

Harcuvar Mountains, in La Paz and Yavapai cos., W Ariz., c.40 mi/64 km W of Wickenburg; rise to c.5,000 ft/1,525 m.

Hardburly (HAHR-buhr-lee), village (1990 pop. 340), Perry co., SE Ky., in Cumberland foothills, 5 mi/8 km NE of Hazard, and 2 mi/3.2 km E of Bulan. RR spur terminus. Bituminous coal.

Hardee (hahr-DEE), county (□ 638 sq mi/1,652 sq km; 1990 pop. 19,499), central Fla.; ⊙ Wauchula; 27°29′N 81°48′W. Rolling terrain, partly swampy, with many small lakes; drained by Peace R. Citrus and strawberry region, with cattle and poultry raising. Formed 1921.

Hardeeville (1990 pop. 1,583), Jasper co., S S.C., 18 mi/29 km W of Hilton Head, and 5 mi/8 km from Ga. state line; 32°16′N 81°04′W. Mfg. includes fabricated metal prods., lumber; sand processing. Agr. includes timber; livestock; grain, soybeans.

Hardeman 1 (HAHR-duh-muhn), county (□ 655 sq mi/1,696 sq km; 1990 pop. 23,377), SW Tenn., on Miss. (S) state line; ⊙ Bolivar; 35°12′N 89°00′W. Drained by Hatchie R. Cotton, corn, fruit; livestock; timber; some lumbering; fuller's clay. Formed 1823. **2** county (□ 697 sq mi/1,805 sq km, 1990 pop. 5,283), N Texas; ⊙ Quanah; 34°17′N 99°45′W. Bounded in part and drained in S by Pease R.; bounded by Red R. (here forming Okla. state line) on N. Wheat, cotton, peanuts; sheep, horses, angora goats, cattle; also grain. Gypsum mining; some oil and gas production. Drained by Wanderer's Creek, which forms L. Pauline at center of co. L. Copper Breaks and Copper Breaks State Park in S. Formed 1858.

Hardesty (HAHR-des-tee), village (1990 pop. 228), Texas co., central Okla. Panhandle, 16 mi/26 km ESE of Guymon; 36°36′N 101°11′W. Optima L. reservoir (on North Canadian, or Beaver, R.) and Optima Natl. Wildlife Refuge to N.

Hardin 1 county (□ 181 sq mi/469 sq km; 1990 pop. 5,189), extreme SE Ill.; ⊙ Elizabethtown; 37°31′N 88°31′W. Bounded S and E by Ohio R.; drained by short Big Creek. Agr. (wheat, corn, sorghum; livestock; timber). Mfg. (fluorspar prods. from imported fluorspars). About 90% of co. in Shawnee Natl. Forest, also part of Cave in Rock State Park. Toll ferry to Ky. at Cave in Rock. One of 17 Ill. cos. to retain Southern-style commission form of co. govt. The last Ill. fluorspar mine closed in 1996. Formed 1839. **2** county (□ 569 sq mi/ 1,474 sq km; 1990 pop. 19,094), central Iowa; ⊙ Eldora; 42°23′N 93°15′W. Prairie agr. area (hogs, cattle, poultry; corn, oats, soybeans) drained by Iowa R. Mfg. at Iowa Falls. Limestone quarries; sand, clay, and gravel pits. Pine L. and Steamboat Rock state parks in E. Widespread flooding of fields and rivers in 1993. Formed 1851. **3** county (□ 629 sq mi/1,629 sq km; 1990 pop. 89,240), central and N Ky., on Ind. (extreme N; across Ohio R.) state line; ⊙ Elizabethtown; 37°42′N 85°58′W. Bounded E by Salt R. and Rolling Fork; drained by Rough and Nolin rivers. Gently rolling agr. area (burley tobacco, corn, wheat, hay, alfalfa, soybeans; hogs, cattle, poultry; dairying; limestone quarries, sand pits, asphalt deposits. Mfg. at Elizabethtown. Part of Fort Knox Military Reservation in E, includes U.S. Gold Bullion Depository. Vernon-Douglas State Nature Preserve in E. Formed 1792. **4** county (□ 467 sq mi/ 1,210 sq km; 1990 pop. 31,111), W central Ohio; ⊙ Kenton, 40°39′N 83°40′W. Intersected by Scioto, Blanchard, and Ottawa rivers. In the Till Plains physiographic region. Agr. area (hogs, poultry; wheat, corn, soybeans); mfg. at Kenton, Ada, and Forest (paper prods., transportation equip.); limestone quarries, gravel pits. Formed 1833. **5** county (□ 595 sq mi/ 1,541 sq km; 1990 pop. 22,633), SW Tenn., on Miss. and Ala. (both S) state lines; ⊙ Savannah; 35°12′N 88°11′W.

Bounded NE by Tennessee R. Timber and agr. (livestock; cotton, corn, hay) area; iron ore, limestone deposits. Mfg. at Savannah. Includes Pickwick Landing Dam and part of Pickwick Landing Reservoir in S, Shiloh Natl. Military Park in SW. Formed 1819. **6** county (□ 897 sq mi/2,323 sq km; 1990 pop. 41,320), SE Texas; ⊙ Kountze; 30°20′N 94°23′W. Bounded E by Neches R. and drained by its tributaries. S part on Gulf coastal plains; rolling, wooded in N (lumbering). Agr. (forage crops); livestock raising (cattle, hogs; egg production). Oil, natural gas fields; sand and gravel; timber. Formed 1858.

Hardin (HAHR-din), city (1990 pop. 598), Ray co., NW Mo., near Missouri R., 8 mi/12.9 km E of Richmond; 39°16′N 93°49′W. Corn, wheat, soybeans; hogs; cattle; grain elevators. Town and surrounding farmland damaged in 1993 flood.

Hardin (HAHR-duhn), town (1990 pop. 2,940), ⊙ Big Horn co., S Mont., on Bighorn R., at mouth of Little Bighorn R., and 45 mi/72 km E of Billings; 45°44′N 107°37′W. Beet sugar; barley; livestock. Gas fields, coal mining; tourism. Trading point for Crow Indian Reservation to S and SE. Co. Fairgrounds, Bighorn Co. Historical Mus., Little Bighorn Battlefield Natl. Monument to SE; Big Horn Canyon Natl. Recreation Area to SW, Grant Marsh Wildlife Management Area to N. Inc. 1911.

Hardin 1 village (1990 pop. 1,071), ⊙ Calhoun co., W Ill., on Illinois R. (bridged to East Hardin), and 30 mi/ 48 km NW of Alton, 39°09′N 90°37′W. Center of apple- and grain-growing dist.; also sorghum; hogs; vinegar factory. Sustained heavy damage in floods of 1993. **2** (HAHR-duhn), village (1990 pop. 595), Marshall co., W Ky., 10 mi/16 km N of Murray, near East Fork Clarks R.; 36°45′N 88°17′W. RR terminus. Agr. (tobacco, grain, soybeans; hogs; cattle); mfg. (fertilizer, boat docks, meats). Kenlake State Resort park on Kentucky L., to E. **3** village (1990 pop. 563), Liberty co., SE Texas, 36 mi/ 58 km W of Beaumont, near Trinity R.; 30°08′N 94°44′W. Timber; oil and natural gas. Agr. (rice, soybeans). Big Thicket Natl. Preserve to NE.

Harding 1 county (□ 2,136 sq mi/5,532 sq km; 1990 pop. 987), NE N.Mex.; ⊙ Mosquero; 35°51′N 103°49′W. Hay, some alfalfa, wheat, oats, barley, millet; cattle, some sheep. Bounded W by Canadian R. (Canadian R. Canyon), drained by Ute, Tequesquite, and Carrizo creeks. Formed 1921. **2** county (□ 2,677 sq mi/6,933 sq km; 1990 pop. 1,669), NW S.Dak., on Mont. (W) and N.Dak. (N) state lines; ⊙ Buffalo; 45°35′N 103°30′W. Wheat; sheep-raising area watered by Little Missouri R. and branches of Grand and Moreau rivers. Petroleum and large deposits of lignite coal; numerous small ranches. Cave Hills; Crow Butte (3,385 ft/971 m) has limestone ridges in N, SW, and E; part of Custer Natl. Forest near each. Slim Buttes in SE (3,672 ft/1,119 m); site of Battle of Slim Buttes (18/6) in E, near Reva. Several units of Custer Natl. Forest in SW, E, and N (remainder mostly in S Mont.). Formed 1908.

Harding, village (1990 pop. 76), Morrison co., central Minn., near Platte R., 20 mi/32 km NE of Little Falls; 46°07′N 94°02′W. Agr. area (grain; livestock; dairying). Inc. 1938.

Hardinsburg 1 town (1990 pop. 322), Washington co., S Ind., 13 mi/21 km SW of Salem; 38°28′N 86°16′W. Agr. area. Wood furniture. Laid out 1838. **2** town (1990 pop. 1,906), ⊙ Breckinridge co., NW Ky., 35 mi/56 km E of Owensboro; 37°46′N 86°27′W. Agr. (burley tobacco, corn, wheat) and hardwood timber; mfg. (linens, apparel, bldg. materials, lumber, paper prods., crushed stone). Co. Airport to E. Broadmoor Gardens and Conservatory to NE, at Irvington. Rough R. L. reservoir and Rough R. Dam State Resort Park to S, Mt. Laurel L. to E.

Hardisty, town (1991 pop. 656), E Alta., W Canada, on Battle R., and 22 mi/35 km SW of Wainwright; 52°41′N 111°18′W. Grain elevators, stockyards; mixed farming.

Hardman, uninc. village, Morrow co., N Oregon, 15 mi/ 24 km SSW of Heppner. Wheat. Umatilla Natl. Forest to SE.

Hardtner (HAHRT-nuhr), village (1990 pop. 198), Barber co., S Kansas, 9 mi/14.5 km W of Kiowa, near Okla. state line; 37°00′N 98°39′W. Cattle; wheat.

Hardwick 1 town (1990 pop. 8,800), Baldwin co., central Ga., 29 mi/47 km NE of Macon; 33°04′N 83°13′W. Ga. Col. nearby. **2** town (1990 pop. 2,385), Worcester co., central Mass., on branch of Ware R., 21 mi/34 km WNW of Worcester, and near Quabbin Reservoir; 42°21′N 72°13′W. Dairying. Settled 1737, inc. 1739. Includes villages of Gilbertville and Wheelwright. **3** town (1990 pop. 2,964), including Hardwick village, Caledonia co., N central Vt., 19 mi/31 km WNW of St. Johnsbury, and on Lamoille R.; 44°31′N 72°20′W. Dairy prods. Settled before 1800.

Hardwick, village (1990 pop. 234), Rock co., extreme SW Minn., 8 mi/12.9 km N of Luverne; 43°46′N 96°12′W. Corn, soybeans, oats; livestock; poultry; dairying. Blue Mounds State Park to S.

Hardy, county (□ 585 sq mi/1,515 sq km; 1990 pop. 10,977), NE W.Va., in E Panhandle, on Va. (E and S) state line; ⊙ Moorefield; 39°00′N 78°51′W. Drained by South Branch of Potomac R. and its South Fork, and by Cacapon and Lost rivers. Traversed by ridges (including North and Shenandoah mts.) and valleys of the Allegheny Mts. Includes Lost R. State Park in S center, and part of George Washington Natl. Forest in E. Agr. (corn, oats, grains, soybeans, potatoes, alfalfa, sorghum); livestock, poultry; dairying. Limestone and marble quarrying. Mfg. at Moorefield (esp. poultry processing). Formed 1786.

Hardy 1 town (1990 pop. 538), N Ark., 28 mi/45 km W of Pocahontas, and on Spring R.; 36°19′N 91°28′W. Harold E. Alexander Wildlife Management Area to S. Growing retirement pop. Former county seat (shared with Evening Shade); later replaced by Ash Flat. **2** town (1990 pop. 47), Humboldt co., N central Iowa, 23 mi/ 37 km NNE of Fort Dodge; 42°48′N 94°02′W. In agr. area. **3** uninc. town (1990 pop. 900), Pike co., E Ky., in the Cumberland Mts., near Tug Fork R. (W.Va. state line), 5 mi/8 km SSE of Williamson (W.Va.). In bituminous-coal-mining area.

Hardy 1 village (1990 pop. 206), Nuckolls co., S Nebr., 7 mi/11.3 km E of Superior, at Kansas state line, near Republican R.; 40°00′N 97°55′W. Dairy and poultry prods., livestock; grain. **2** village, Kay co., N Okla., near Kansas state line, 25 mi/40 km NE of Ponca City. In agr. area.

Hardy Dam, Mich.: see MUSKEGON RIVER.

Hardy Dam Pond, reservoir, Newaygo co., central Mich., on Muskegon R., bet. Rogers Dam and Croton Dam ponds, in Manistee Natl. Forest, 16 mi/26 km SSW of Big Rapids; 43°29′N 85°38′W. Formed by Hardy Dam (100 ft/30 m high), built in 1931.

Hardy Lake, reservoir, Scott Co., SE Ind., on Quick Creek, in Hardy L. State Recreation Area, 8 mi/12.9 km NNE of Scottsburg; 3 mi/4.8 km long; 38°46′N 85°42′W. Max. capacity 14,700 acre ft. Formed by Hardy L. Dam (48 ft/15 m high), built (1970s) by the Ind. Dept. of Natural Resources for water supply. Also called Quick Creek Reservoir.

Hardyston, township (1990 pop. 5,275), Sussex co., NW N.J., 1 mi/1.6 km S of Hamburg; 41°07′N 74°33′W. Inc. 1798.

Hare Bay, inlet, NE N.F., E Canada; 20 mi/32 km long, 10 mi/16 km wide at entrance; 51°17′N 55°50′W.

Hare Hill 1 (1,958 ft/597 m), W N.F., E Canada, at SW end of Grand L., 22 mi/35 km SSW of Corner Brook. **2** (995 ft/303 m), S N.F., E Canada, on W side of Burin Peninsula, near E side of Fortune Bay; highest point of Burin Peninsula.

Hare Indian River, 120 mi/193 km long, NW Mackenzie dist., N.W.T., N Canada; rises W of Great Bear L.; flows W to Mackenzie R. at Fort Good Hope.

Hare Island or **Île aux Lièvres** (EEL o LYE-vruh), island, SE central Que., E Canada, in the St. Lawrence R., opposite Rivière du Loup; 8 mi/13 km long, 1 mi/ 2 km wide. Just E are the Brandypot islets.

Harford (HAHR-ford), county (□ 526 sq mi/1,362 sq km; 1990 pop. 182,132), NE Md., on Pa. (N) state line; ⊙

Bel Air; 39°32′N 76°18′W. Bounded NE by the Susquehanna R., SE and S by Chesapeake Bay. Piedmont agr. area (N) produces dairy prods., vegetables, fruit, grain; poultry. Stone quarries. Coastal plain (S fringe) occupied mostly by Federal reservations (Aberdeen Proving Ground, Army Chemical Center, and Edgewood Arsenal). Commercial fisheries, shore resorts, some industries (esp. vegetable canneries, clothing factories). Includes many large estates. Formed 1773.

Hargill, uninc. town (1990 pop. 1,349), Hidalgo co., S Texas, 22 mi/35 km NE of McAllen. Located in N margin of irrigated Rio Grande Valley; rich agr. area (citrus, vegetables, cotton, sugarcane; cattle).

Harker Heights, city (1990 pop. 12,841), Bell co., central Texas, residential suburb 4 mi/6.4 km E of Killeen, and 17 mi/27 km WSW of Temple; 31°03′N 97°39′W. Drained by Nolan Creek. Agr. to S (grains, cotton; cattle). Large Fort Hood Military Reservation to N. Stillhouse Hollow L. reservoir to SE.

Harkers Island, uninc. town (1990 pop. 1,759), Carteret co., E N.C., on Harkers Isl. in sheltered Core Sound, 4 mi/6.4 km E of Beaufort; 5 mi/8 km long, 1 mi/1.6 km wide; bridged to mainland; 34°42′N 76°33′W. Ferry to Cape Lookout Lighthouse, in Cape Lookout Natl. Seashore to SE. Mouth of North R. inlet to W. Mfg. (consumer goods).

Harkin, Mount (9,788 ft/2,983 m), SE B.C., W Canada, near Alta. border, in Rocky Mts., on SE edge of Kootenay Natl. Park, 30 mi/48 km SW of Banff; 50°47′N 115°52′W.

Harlan 1 (HAHR-luhn), county (□ 467 sq mi/1,210 sq km; 1990 pop. 36,574), SE Ky., on Va. (S and E) state line; ⊙ Harlan; 36°51′N 83°13′W. In the Cumberland Mts.; drained by Cumberland R. and its Poor and Clover forks; includes Kentenia State Forest in NW, Black Mt. (4,139 ft/1,262 m; highest point in Ky.) in E. One of leading coal-producing cos. of Ky. Hardwood timber; some agr. (burley tobacco; livestock). Labor conflicts bet. coal operators and miners here (nicknamed “Bloody Harlan”) have been frequent and bitter; after 20 years of strife, mines were unionized in 1941. Part of Daniel Boone Natl. Forest in N; Cranks Creek Wildlife Management Area in S; small part of Cumberland Gap Natl. Historical Park in SW corner; part of Kingdom Come State Park in NE. **2** county (□ 574 sq mi/1,487 sq km; 1990 pop. 3,810), S Nebr., on Kansas (S) state line; ⊙ Alma; 40°10′N 99°24′W. Agr. region in S; drained by Republican R., here impounded by Harlan Co. Dam. Cattle, hogs; corn, wheat, sorghum; dairy and poultry prods. Formed 1871.

Harlan, city (1990 pop. 5,148), ⊙ Shelby co., W Iowa, on West Nishnabotna R. (hydroelectric plant), and 37 mi/60 km NE of Council Bluffs; 41°38′N 95°19′W. Mfg. (plastic prods.; pallet and hammer milling, seed corn and soybean processing; rendering plant, cement works, machine shop). Prairie Rose State Park to SE. Settled 1858, inc. 1879.

Harlan (HAHR-luhn), town (1990 pop. 2,686), ⊙ Harlan co., SE Ky., in the Cumberland Mts., 27 mi/43 km NE of Middlesboro, at joining of Clover and Martin forks of Cumberland R.; 36°50′N 83°19′W. RR junction. Coal-mining center in one of Ky.'s largest coalfields. Some timber; some agr. (tobacco; livestock) in region; mfg. (coal processing; machinery, lumber, foods; printing and publishing). Kentenia State Forest and part of Daniel Boone Natl. Forest to N; Cranks Creek Wildlife Management Area to SE; Martins Fork L. reservoir in S. City settled 1819 as Mt. Pleasant; grew as coal-shipping point after coming of RR in 1911.

Harlan, village (1990 pop. 1,200), Allen co., NE Ind., 13 mi/21 km NE of Fort Wayne. Mfg. (cabinets). Corn, soybeans.

Harlan County Lake, reservoir, Harlan co., S Nebr., on Republican R., 40 mi/64 km SSW of Kearney, near Kansas state line; c.15 mi/24 km long; 40°03′N 99°12′W. Max. capacity 850,000 acre-ft. Prairie Dog Creek enters from SW. Formed by Harlan Co. Dam (100 ft/30 m high), built (1952) by the Army Corps of Engineers for flood control and irrigation.

Harlem 1 town (1990 pop. 2,826), Hendry co., central Fla., adjacent to Clewiston; 26°44′N 80°57′W. **2** town (1990 pop. 2,199), Columbia co., E Ga., 19 mi/31 km WSW of Augusta; 33°25′N 82°19′W. Mfg. of bldg. materials, fabricated metal prods.; printing and publishing. **3** town (1990 pop. 882), Blaine co., N Mont., on Milk R., and 43 mi/69 km E of Havre; 48°32′N 108°47′W. Cattle, sheep; sugar beets; gas, oil, and gold in area. Mfg (plastics prods.). Seat of Fort Belknap Col. Hq. of Fort Belknap Agency in Fort Belknap Indian Reservation, 3 mi/4.8 km SSE. Black Coulee Natl. Wildlife Refuge to NE. Inc. 1910.

Harlem, residential and business section of upper Manhattan, N.Y. city, bounded roughly by 110th St. (S), the East R. (E) and Harlem R. (NE), 168th St. (NW), Amsterdam Ave. (NW), and Morningside Park (SW). The Du. settlement of Nieuw Haarlem was est. 1658 by Peter Stuyvesant. To the W of Harlem, near the present site of Columbia Univ., Br. and Continental forces fought (Sept. 16, 1776) the Battle of Harlem Heights. Harlem remained rural until the 19th cent. when improved transportation facilities linked it with lower Manhattan. It then became a fashionable residential sect. of N.Y. city. By the turn of the cent. Harlem had a large Jewish pop.; starting around 1910 Harlem became the scene of increasing Afr.-Amer. migration from the South. It soon became the largest and most influential Afr.-Amer. community in the nation, one of the centers of innovation in jazz, and the home of such Harlem Renaissance authors as Langston Hughes, Countee Cullen, and Zora Neale Hurston. In East Harlem, a largely Ital. neighborhood—the home of Mayor Fiorello H. LaGuardia—many Puerto Ricans and other Hispanic-Americans settled after World War II. The intersection of 7th Ave. and 125th Street is generally considered the heart of Harlem; Lenox Ave., once internationally known for its entertainment spots, is now mainly lined with housing developments. Strivers' Row is a block of well-preserved turn-of-the-cent. townhouses. Site of the Abyssinian Baptist Church, headed for many years by Adam Clayton Powell, Jr., and the Apollo theater, noted for performances by Afr.-Amer. musicians and entertainers. An extensive scholarly collection is housed at the Schomburg Center for Research in Black Culture (part of the N.Y. Public Lib.), which is adjacent to the Countee Cullen branch of the lib. Harlem today has a mixture of poverty and some gentrification, in part due to a city policy favoring renovations of abandoned residential bldgs. Increasingly popular as a tourist destination. Designated (1996) as an Enterprise Zone.

Harlem River, navigable tidal channel, 8 mi./12.9 km long with Spuyten Duyvil Creek, in N.Y. city, SE N.Y., separating Manhattan from the Bronx. Connecting the Hudson and East rivers, it is a shipping shortcut bet. L.I. Sound and river ports N of N.Y. city. Several RR and many street bridges span the river.

Harleysville, uninc. town (1990 pop. 7,405), Montgomery co., SE Pa., 27 mi/43 km NW of Philadelphia; 40°16′N 75°23′W. Mfg. includes machinery, fabricated metal prods., food prods., medical supplies, electronic equip., chemicals. Agr. includes dairying; livestock; grain, soybeans, apples.

Harleyville, village (1990 pop. 633), Dorchester co., SE central S.C., 20 mi/32 km NW of Summerville; 33°12′N 80°27′W. Mfg. of portland cement. Agr. includes poultry; grain, soybeans, cotton.

Harlingen, city (1990 pop. 48,735), Cameron co., extreme S Texas, 23 mi/37 km NW of Brownsville; 26°11′N 97°41′W. RR junction,in a shipping and processing center in the lower Rio Grande valley, an irrigated farming area yielding citrus and other fruits, grain, vegetables, sugarcane, and cotton. The city, which is linked to the Intracoastal Waterway by a barge channel (Arroyo Colorado), has food processing, apparel mfg., and factories making various chemical, concrete and metal prods. Founded (c.1904) with the coming of the RR and grew with the agr. development of the surrounding area. Rio Grande campus of Texas Technical Col. and Marine Military Acad. are both at Harlingen Industrial Air Park; Rio Grande Valley Internatl. Airport (NE); Iwo Jima War Memorial. Inc. 1910.

Harlowton, town (1990 pop. 1,049), ⊙ Wheatland co., central Mont., on Musselshell R., at mouth of Antelope Creek, and 80 mi/129 km NW of Billings; 46°26′N 109°50′W. Stone quarries; flour mill; dairying; wheat, barley, oats, alfalfa; cattle, sheep, hogs. Inc. 1917. Upper Musselshell Historical Society Mus. Originally called Merino.

Harman, village (1990 pop. 128), Randolph co., E W.Va., on Gandy Creek, in Monongahela Natl. Forest, 17 mi/27 km E of Elkins; 38°55′N 79°31′W. Canaan Valley State Park to NE.

Harmarville (HAHR-mahr-vil), uninc. town (1990 pop. 1,200), Harmar township, Allegheny co., SW Pa., residential suburb 10 mi/16 km NE of downtown Pittsburgh, on Allegheny R., opposite (1 mi/1.6 km NW of) Oakmont; 40°31′N 79°50′W. Agr. (corn, hay; livestock; dairying) to N.

Harmon, county (□ 538 sq mi/1,393 sq km; 1990 pop. 3,793), SW Okla.; ⊙ Hollis; 34°44′N 99°50′W. Bounded SW (Red R.) and W by Texas; drained by the Salt and Prairie Dog Town forks of Red R. Hilly agr. area (peanuts, sorghum, cotton, wheat, vegetables, black-eyed peas; cattle); mesquite. Originally claimed by both Texas and Okla. territories. Formed 1909.

Harmon, village (1990 pop. 186), Lee co., N Ill., 9 mi/14.5 km SSW of Dixon; 41°43′N 89°33′W. In rich agr. area.

Harmon, section of Croton-on-Hudson, Westchester co., SE N.Y., on E bank of the Hudson R., just N of Ossining; an important stop on Amtrak and Metro-North RR, at N end of its electrified sect. Nearby is Croton Point Park (recreation).

Harmony 1 town (1990 pop. 645), Clay co., W Ind., suburb 3 mi/4.8 km E of Brazil; 39°32′N 87°04′W. Mfg. (industrial machinery). **2** town (1990 pop. 838), Somerset co., central Maine, 17 mi/27 km NE of Skowhegan; 44°58′N 69°32′W. Wood prods. **3** town (1990 pop. 1,081), Fillmore co., SE Minn., near Iowa state line, 9 mi/14.5 km SSE of Preston; 43°33′N 92°00′W. Grain, soybeans; livestock, poultry; dairying; mfg. (machinery, feeds, transportation equip.). Hammervold Landing Field to N. Area known for its karst topography. Niagara Cave is 4 mi/6.4 km SSW, with 60 ft/18 m waterfall 200 ft/61 m below surface of earth. **4** town (1990 pop. 431), Iredell co., W central N.C., 14 mi/23 km NNE of Statesville; 35°57′N 80°46′W. Tobacco, grain, soybeans; poultry, livestock. Mfg. (stained glass windows, poultry feed).

Harmony, borough (1990 pop. 1,054), Butler co., W Pa., 12 mi/19 km WSW of Butler, and 1 mi/1.6 km NE of Zelienople, on Connoquenessing Creek. Mfg. (medical supplies, consumer goods). Agr. (corn, hay; livestock; dairying). First settlement (1805) of Harmony Society.

Harmony, township (1990 pop. 3,694), Beaver co., W Pa., residential suburb 2 mi/3.2 km N of Ambridge on Ohio R.; 40°36′N 80°13′W. RR yards.

Harnett, county (□ 601 sq mi/1,557 sq km; 1990 pop. 67,822), central N.C.; ⊙ Lillington; 35°22′N 78°51′W. Forested sandhills area; drained by Cape Fear and South rivers; bounded S in part by Little R. Farming (esp. tobacco; cotton, corn, wheat, sorghum, hay, potatoes, sweet potatoes, peppers; chicken, cattle, hogs; catfish); textile mfg.; timber. Sand and gravel. Raven Rock State Park in N center. Averasboro Battleground State Historical Site on S border, in SE. Formed 1855.

Harney (HAHR-nee), county (□ 10,227 sq mi/26,488 sq km; 1990 pop. 7,060), SE central Oregon; ⊙ Burns; 43°04′N 118°58′W. Bounded S by Nev., drained by Silver R. and Donner und Blitzen R. Land area forms 9th-largest co. in U.S. Timber. Agr. (alfalfa, wheat, oats, barley; sheep, cattle). Part of Great Sandy Desert in W. Steens Mt., a ridge 40 mi/64 km long, is in SE. Malheur and Harney lakes in center. Burns Indian Reservation in N center, N of Burns. Units of Malheur Natl. Wildlife Refuge in center, at Harney and Malheur lakes and Donner und Blitzen R. Alvord Desert is SE of Steens Mt. Part of Malheur Natl. Forest in N; part of Ochoco Natl. Forest in NW. Squaw Butte Range Experimental

Area in NW. Frenchglen Hotel State Wayside in S center. Founded 1889.

Harney (HAHR-nee), locality, Harney co., E central Oregon, 11 mi/18 km ENE of Burns, near Rattlesnake Creek.

Harney, Lake, a shallow widening of St. Johns R., on border bet. Volusia and Seminole cos., E central Fla., 12 mi/19 km ESE of Sanford; c.4 mi/6.4 km long, 2 mi/3.2 km–3 mi/4.8 km wide.

Harney Lake (HAHR-nee), SE central Oregon, alkali lake, surrounded by part of Malheur Natl. Wildlife Refuge, linked by channel to Malheur L. to NE, 20 mi/32 km S of Burns; c.10 mi/16 km wide. No outlet for 2 lakes. Receives Silver Creek from NW.

Harney Peak, mountain peak (7,242 ft/2,207 m), in the Black Hills, SW S.Dak., highest point in state.

Haro Strait (HAI-ro), channel of the Pacific Ocean, off W Canada (SW B.C.) and U.S. (NW Wash.), at SE end of Vancouver Isl., joins straits of Georgia (N) and Juan de Fuca (S). Separates Vancouver and Saturna isls. (W) and San Juan and Stuart isls. (E). Internatl. border runs through center of strait.

Harold, village (1990 pop. 520), Floyd co., E Ky., in Cumberland foothills, on Levisa Fork R., and 8 mi/12.9 km WNW of Pikeville. Bituminous coal, oil, and gas; mfg. (commercial printing).

Harper 1 county (☐ 802 sq mi/2,077 sq km; 1990 pop. 7,124), S Kansas, on Okla. (S) state line, in Red Hills region; ⊙ Anthony; 37°12′N 98°04′W. Drained (NE) by Chikaskia R. Wheat, barley, oats; sheep, cattle. Food processing. Mfg. at Harper and Anthony. Formed 1873. **2** county (☐ 1,041 sq mi/2,696 sq km; 1990 pop. 4,063), NW Okla.; ⊙ Buffalo; 36°46′N 99°39′W. Bounded N by Kansas; intersected by North Canadian (Beaver) R. and Buffalo Creek. Cimarron R. forms NE border, also drains NW corner. Plains agr. area (livestock; wheat, barley). Formed 1907.

Harper 1 town (1990 pop. 147), Keokuk co., SE Iowa, 8 mi/12.9 km ENE of Sigourney; 41°21′N 92°02′W. Feed milling. **2** town (1990 pop. 1,735), Harper co., S Kansas, 45 mi/72 km SW of Wichita; 37°17′N 98°01′W. RR junction. In wheat area. Mfg. (farm machinery; meatpacking). Settled 1877, inc. 1880.

Harper Woods, city (1990 pop. 14,903), Wayne co., SE Mich., residential suburb 10 mi/16 km NE of downtown Detroit, 3 mi/4.8 km W of L. St. Clair; 42°26′N 82°55′W. Mfg. (fabricated metal prods.). Borders Macomb co. on N, city of Detroit on W and S.

Harpers Ferry, town (1990 pop. 284), Allamakee co., extreme NE Iowa, on Mississippi R., and 11 mi/18 km ESE of Waukon; 43°12′N 91°09′W. Dairy prods., concrete blocks.

Harpers Ferry, village (1990 pop. 308), Jefferson co., NE W.Va., 7 mi/11.3 km NE of Charles Town; 39°19′N 77°44′W. On Potomac R. (Md. state line), at mouth of the Shenandoah R.; Va state line to E. The town is a tourist attraction, known for its history and its scenic beauty. John Brown's seizure of the U.S. arsenal here on Oct. 16, 1859, and the town's subsequent strategic importance during the Civil War, when it was considered the key to the Shenandoah Valley, brought it into natl. prominence. In 1747, Robert Harper, a millwright, established a ferry at the junction of the 2 rivers—hence the town's name. The U.S. arsenal was located here in 1796, and by the mid–19th cent., Harpers Ferry was an important arms-producing center, with mills, numerous gun factories, and huge stores of weapons and ammunition. The development of the Chesapeake and Ohio Canal and of the Baltimore & Ohio RR increased its importance, making it a transportation link bet. the Ohio Valley and the E Coast. During the Civil War it was primarily held by Union soldiers, but changed hands a number of times. Its industrial plant was repeatedly destroyed by troops of both sides. Harpers Ferry never recovered economically, and a series of devastating floods in the late 19th cent. ended all hopes for revival. Despite continued flooding during the 20th cent., many old bldgs. remain. Of interest are the fire engine house in which John Brown was captured; the John Brown Mus.; and the old steps, hand-carved (early 1800s) into the natural stone, which lead to Robert Harper's house (1775–1782) and to Jefferson Rock. The Harpers Ferry Natl. Historical Park is here (☐ 4 sq mi/10.4 sq km; est. 1955). Appalachian Trail passes through town. Inc. 1763.

Harpers Ferry National Historical Park, W.Va., Md., Va.: see HARPERS FERRY.

Harpersville, town (1990 pop. 772), Shelby co., central Ala., 15 mi/24 km NE of Columbiana.

Harpeth River, 117 mi/188 km long, central Tenn.; rises 10 mi/16 km SW of Murfreesboro, in Rutherford co.; meanders generally NW, past Franklin, to Cumberland R. 5 mi/8 km WNW of Ashland City; 36°18′N 87°09′W. The sect. in Davidson co. is designated a state scenic river.

Harpster, village (1990 pop. 233), Wyandot co., N central Ohio, 11 mi/18 km NW of Marion; 40°44′N 83°15′W.

Harpswell, resort town (1990 pop. 5,012), Cumberland co., SW Maine, on peninsula (Harpswell Neck; W) and isls. (Orrs and Bailey isls., and Sebascodegan Isl., also called Great, or East Harpswell, Isl.; all bridge-linked), in Casco Bay, and 15 mi/24 km NE of Portland; 43°46′N 69°58′W. Includes Cundys Harbor, Orrs Island, and Harpswell Center villages, latter with church (1843) where Elijah Kellogg preached. Settled 1720, inc. 1758.

Harpswell Sound, SW Maine, arm of Casco Bay extending c.12 mi/19 km bet. Harpswell Neck and Orrs and Sebascodegan isls.

Harquahala Mountains, in La Paz and Maricopa cos., W Ariz., S of Harcuvar Mts., c.35 mi/56 km WSW of Wickenburg; rise to 5,672 ft/1,729 m.

Harrah (HA-ruh), town (1990 pop. 4,206), Oklahoma co., central Okla., suburb 20 mi/32 km E of downtown Oklahoma City, and on North Canadian R.; 35°29′N 97°10′W. In agr. area; mfg. (meat processing, poultry processing and prods.). John Miskelly State Park to W.

Harrah (HAHR-ruh), village (1990 pop. 341), Yakima co., S Wash., 15 mi/24 km S of Yakima, in NE part of Yakima Indian Reservation; 46°24′N 120°32′W. Wheat, spearmint, peppermint, fruits (apples, pears, peaches), vegetables; mfg. (fertilizers, peppermint extracts).

Harraseeket River (har-uh-SEE-ket), SW Maine, inlet of Casco Bay near Freeport, just NE of Portland; c.4 mi/6.4 km long.

Harrell (HAR-uhl), village (1990 pop. 258), Calhoun co., S Ark., 26 mi/42 km E of Camden; 33°30′N 92°24′W. Mfg. (bldg. materials). L. Poinsett State Park to SE.

Harrells (HER-uhls), village (1990 pop. 187), Sampson co., SE central N.C., 20 mi/32 km SSE of Clinton; 34°43′N 78°12′W. Tobacco, cotton, peanuts, sweet potatoes; poultry, livestock.

Harrellsville, village (1990 pop. 106), Hertford co., NE N.C., 10 mi/16 km E of Ahoskie, near Chowan R.; 36°17′N 76°47′W.

Harricanaw River (ha-ri-KAH-no), 250 mi/402 km long, W Que. and NE Ont., E Canada; rises near Val d'Or; flows NW to James Bay of Hudson Bay, 50 mi/80 km SW of Rupert House; crosses into Ont. near its mouth. Navigable for 50 mi/80 km.

Harrietta, village (1990 pop. 157), Wexford co., NW Mich., 15 mi/24 km WNW of Cadillac; 44°18′N 85°42′W. In farm area. Has state fish hatchery. In Manistee Natl. Forest.

Harriman, city (1990 pop. 7,119), Roane co., E Tenn., near Tennessee R., 35 mi/56 km W of Knoxville; 35°56′N 84°33′W. In rolling hills; in fruit-growing, timber, limestone, sand, and gravel area; lumber milling; mfg. of textiles, hosiery, canoes. Watts Bar Reservoir is S. Plotted 1889; inc. 1891.

Harriman, village (1990 pop. 2,288), Orange co., SE N.Y., 10 mi/16 km WSW of Highland Falls; 41°18′N 74°08′W. Harriman sect. of Palisades Interstate Park is just E.

Harriman Reservoir (HER-i-man), in towns of Whitingham and Wilmington, Windham co., S Vt., on Deerfield R., 17 mi/27 km WSW of Brattleboro; c.8 mi/12.9 km long; 42°52′N 72°52′W. Formed by Harriman Dam (earth-fill construction; 200 ft/61 m high), built (1924) for power generation. Green Mt. Natl. Forest to W. Also called Davis Bridge Dam.

Harrington 1 town (1990 pop. 2,311), Kent co., central Del., 16 mi/26 km S of Dover; 38°55′N 75°34′W. RR junction.Trading and shipping point in agr. area; mfg. (petroleum prods., plastics prods.; meatpacking; millwork). Del. State Fairgrounds and Raceway are here to S; Killen's Pond State Park to NE. Inc. 1869. **2** town (1990 pop. 893), Washington co., E Maine, on Pleasant Bay, and 19 mi/31 km SW of Machias; 44°31′N 67°47′W. Fishing; lumbering; canneries. Resorts.

Harrington, village (1990 pop. 449), Lincoln co., E Wash., 13 mi/21 km SSW of Davenport, on Coal Creek; 47°29′N 118°15′W. In Columbia basin agr. region; wheat, barley, oats, rye, alfalfa, potatoes; cattle. Coffeepot L. and Twin Lakes to W.

Harrington Harbour, village, E Que., E Canada, on largest of the Harrington Isls., a group of 12 islets in Gulf of St. Lawrence; 50°30′N 59°29′W. Magnesite mining.

Harrington Lake, reservoir, Piscataquis co., central Maine, on sidestream of Soper Brook, 30 mi/48 km/64 km NW of Millinocket; 4 mi/6.4 km long; 45°56′N 68°40′W. In wilderness recreational area.

Harrington Park, residential borough (1990 pop. 4,623), Bergen co., NE N.J., 11 mi/18 km NE of Paterson; 40°59′N 73°58′W. Inc. 1904.

Harrington Sound, landlocked lagoon, E Bermuda Isl.; 2.25 mi/3.7 km long, 1.5 mi/2.4 km wide; has narrow, 200-ft/61-m entrance in NW.

Harris 1 county (☐ 465 sq mi/1,204 sq km; 1990 pop. 17,788), W Ga.; ⊙ Hamilton; 32°44′N 84°55′W. Bounded W by Ala. state line (formed here by Chattahoochee R.). Piedmont livestock; agr. (cotton, wheat, vegetables, fruit); cattle, hogs; and sawmilling area. Franklin D. Roosevelt State Park (NE). Langdale, Riverview, Bartletts Ferry, and Goat Rock dams create reservoirs on the Chattahoochee here. Formed 1827. **2** county (☐ 1,777 sq mi/4,602 sq km; 1990 pop. 2,818,199), S Texas, on Gulf coast plains; ⊙ Houston; 29°51′N 95°23′W. Seaport, industrial center. Important cities include Houston, Pasadena, Baytown, and La Porte. Bounded on N by Spring Creek, on E in part by Cedar Creek, on S by Clear Creek and Clear L., on SE by Galveston Bay; drained by San Jacinto R. (forms L. Houston reservoir in NE) and its tributaries. Forested in N; highly urbanized S and E; agr. and timber in NW. Large oil, natural-gas production; also salt, sulphur, clay, lime, sand, and gravel; a leading cattle-raising co.; irrigated agr. (esp. rice, corn, peanuts, vegetables, hay; some nurseries); some timber. Bay resorts. Houston Intercontinental Airport in N. Includes San Jacinto Battlefield State Historic Site and Battleship Texas State Historic Site both in E, on San Jacinto R.; L. Houston State Park in NE; Sheldon State Wildlife Management Area in E. Formed 1836.

Harris 1 town (1990 pop. 170), Osceola co., NW Iowa, 15 mi/24 km E of Sibley; 43°27′N 95°25′W. In livestock and grain area. **2** town (1990 pop. 843), Chicago co., E Minn., 44 mi/71 km N of St. Paul, on Goose Creek; 45°36′N 92°59′W. Grain; cattle, poultry; dairying; light mfg. Small lakes in area. **3** town (1990 pop. 102), Sullivan co., N Mo., 14 mi/23 km WNW of Milan; 40°18′N 93°20′W.

Harris, village, E Montserrat, B.W.I., 4 mi/6.4 km E of Plymouth. Sea-isl. cotton, fruit.

Harris, village (1991 pop. 214), SE central Sask., W Canada, 45 mi/72 km SW of Saskatoon. Flour milling; mixed farming.

Harris 1 village, Routt co., NW Colo., on Yampa R., near Park Range, and 12 mi/19 km W of Steamboat Springs; elev. c.6,350 ft/1,935 m. Coal-mining point. Formerly Mount Harris. **2** village (1990 pop. 39), Anderson co., W Kansas, 11 mi/18 km E of Garnett; 38°19′N 95°26′W. Livestock; grain; dairying. **3** village, Coventry and West Warwick towns, R.I.; 41°43′N 71°32′W.

Harris, Lake, Lake co., central Fla.; c.11 mi/18 km long, 6 mi/9.7 km wide. Connected by canal with L. Eustis, it forms part of lake system drained by Oklawaha R.

Harris Nuclear Power Plant, N.C.: see WAKE.

Harrisburg 1 city (1990 pop. 9,289), ⊙ Saline co., SE Ill., 25 mi/40 km ESE of West Frankfort; 37°44′N 88°32′W. Center of bituminous-coal-mining and agr. area. Shawnee Natl. Forest is S. Inc. 1861. Annexed Dorrisville in 1923. Ill. Youth Center nearby. **2** city (1990 pop.

52,376), ⊙ Pa. and Dauphin co., SE Pa., 90 mi/145 km WNW of Philadelphia, on the Susquehanna R.; 40°16'N 76°52'W. Blue Mt. Ridge to N. Commercial, wholesale, administrative, and transportation center. Mfg. (fabricated metal prods., transportation equip., food prods., machinery, electrical and electronic equip., bldg. materials; steel fabricating, scrap metal processing, printing and publishing). Naval Ships Parts Center to W, Defense Distribution Center to SE. Harrisburg became the state capital in 1812 and grew as an inland transportation center with the opening of the Pa. Canal in 1827 and the arrival of the RR in 1836. Has numerous parks. Its sprawling Ital. Renaissance state capitol (completed 1906) has a 272-ft/83-m dome modeled after St. Peter's in Rome. Other notable structures are the Education Bldg., which contains the state lib.; the Pa. State Mus.; the William Penn Memorial Mus.; the John Harris Mansion (1766), founder of Harrisburg; and the Soldiers' and Sailors' Memorial Bridge. Seat of Harrisburg Area Community Col., Penn State Univ. Center; state hosp., co. prison; Art Assn. of Harrisburg (exhibitions); State Farm Show Bldg.; Pa. Natl. Race Course to NE; Harrisburg Internatl. Airport 8 mi/12.9 km SE at Middletown; Capitol City Airport 3 mi/4.8 km to SSE at New Cumberland; Olmstead Air Force Base to SE, at Middletown; Camp Hills State Correctional Institution to SW. Three Mile Isl. nuclear plant 10 mi/16 km to SE, site of a major nuclear accident in 1979. Appalachian Trail passes to N, on Peters Mt. ridge, and to W. Settled c.1710 by John Harris, who est. a trading post and operated a ferry here; inc. 1791.

Harrisburg 1 town (1990 pop. 1,943), ⊙ Poinsett co., NE Ark., 19 mi/31 km S of Jonesboro, on Crowley's Ridge; 35°33'N 90°43'W. In agr. area; lumber milling; mfg. (wood prods., shoes, aggregate materials). **2** town, Boone co., central Mo., 15 mi/24 km NNW of Columbia; 39°08'N 92°27'W. Coal mining. **3** town (1990 pop. 1,625), Cabarrus co., S central N.C., 13 mi/21 km NE of Charlotte, 7 mi/11.3 km SW of Concord, near Rocky R.; 35°19'N 80°40'W. Agr. area (grain, soybeans, sorghum; poultry, livestock; dairying). Mfg. (transportation equip., chemicals, bldg. materials, fabricated metal prods.; galvanizing). **4** town (1990 pop. 1,939), Linn co., W Oregon, on Willamette R. Mfg. (hides, tallow, concrete); 44°16'N 123°09'W. Agr. (fruit, vegetables, grain; cattle); dairy prods. Timber. Washburn Wayside State Park to NW.

Harrisburg 1 (HER-is-buhrg), village (1990 pop. 80), ⊙ Banner co., W Nebr., 20 mi/32 km S of Scottsbluff. Grain; cattle. Wildcat Hills State Recreation Area to N. **2** village (1990 pop. 340), on border bet. Franklin and Pickaway cos., central Ohio, 13 mi/21 km SW of Columbus; 39°49'N 83°10'W. **3** village (1990 pop. 727), Lincoln co., SE S.Dak., 8 mi/12.9 km S of Sioux Falls; 43°25'N 96°42'W. Mfg. of cabinets.

Harrison 1 county (□ 479 sq mi/1,241 sq km; 1990 pop. 29,890), S Ind.; ⊙ Corydon; 38°12'N 86°07'W. Bounded SE, S, and SW by Ohio R. (here forming Ky. state line), and W by Blue R.; drained by Indian Creek and small Buck Creek. Agr. (soybeans, corn, wheat; cattle, poultry); natural gas; limestone. Lumber milling; mfg. of furniture, glass, dairy prods. Stone quarries; timber. Corydon Capital State Memorial at Corydon. Part of Harrison Crawford State Forest in W. Formed 1808. **2** county (□ 700 sq mi/1,813 sq km; 1990 pop. 14,730), W Iowa, on Nebr. state line (W; formed here by Missouri R.); ⊙ Logan; 41°41'N 95°48'W. Prairie agr. area (cattle, hogs; corn, barley, oats) drained by Boyer, Soldier, and Little Sioux rivers. Wilson Isl. State Park in SW corner; Desoto Bend Natl. Wildlife Refuge and Visitors' Center in SW. Several rivers flooded in 1993. Formed 1851. **3** county (□ 309 sq mi/800 sq km; 1990 pop. 16,248), N Ky.; ⊙ Cynthiana; 38°26'N 84°19'W. Bounded NE by Licking R., S by Silas Creek; drained by South Fork of Licking R. and several creeks. Gently rolling upland agr. area, in Bluegrass region (burley tobacco, hay, alfalfa, soybeans, wheat, corn; hogs, cattle, poultry; dairying); timber; limestone quarries. Mfg. at Cynthiana. Quiet Trails State Nature Preserve in N. Formed 1793. **4** county (□ 976 sq mi/2,528 sq km; 1990 pop. 165,365), SE Miss.; ⊙ Gulfport and Biloxi, ports on Mississippi Sound (S); 30°25'N 89°05'W. Drained by Biloxi, Wolf, and Tchoutacabouffa rivers and Bernard Bayou rivers. Agr. (corn, pecans, citrus; cattle; timber); extensive seafood industries, esp. at Biloxi. Includes part of De Soto Natl. Forest in NW. Formed 1841. **5** county (□ 720 sq mi/1865 sq km; 1990 pop. 8,469), NW Mo.; ⊙ Bethany; 40°21'N 93°58'W. Borders Iowa on N. Corn, wheat, hay; sheep, cattle; limestone. Light mfg. at Bethany. Formed 1845. **6** county (□ 411 sq mi/1,064 sq km; 1990 pop. 16,085), E Ohio; ⊙ Cadiz, 40°17'N 81°04'W. Drained by Stillwater and small Conotton creeks. Includes Tappan and Clendening reservoirs. In the Unglaciated Plain physiographic region. Coal mining; agr. (nursery and greenhouse crops, hogs, grains, soybeans, vegetables); mfg. at Cadiz and Scio (printing and publishing); limestone quarries. Formed 1813. **7** county (□ 915 sq mi/2,370 sq km; 1990 pop. 57,483), E Texas; ⊙ Marshall; 32°32'N 94°22'W. Commercial, industrial center. Bounded E by La. state line, NE by Caddo L. (formed by Big Cypress Creek), SW by Sabine R.; drained by Little Cypress Bayou (forms part of N border). Hilly wooded region (extensive timber); agr. (nurseries, hay); dairying; livestock (cattle, hogs, horses). Large clay prods. industry; also oil, natural gas, coal; sand and gravel. Includes Caddo L. State Park (recreation) on S shore of Caddo L., in NE. Formed 1839. **8** county (□ 417 sq mi/1,080 sq km; 1990 pop. 69,371), N W.Va.; ⊙ Clarksburg; 39°17'N 80°22'W. On Allegheny Plateau; drained by the West Fork R., and Simpson and Tenmile creeks. Agr. (corn, alfalfa, hay, nursery crops); livestock, poultry; dairying. Natural gas and oil wells; bituminous-coal mines. Mfg. at Clarksburg and Bridgeport. Watters Smith Memorial State Park in S; E part of North Bend State Trail in W. Formed 1784.

Harrison 1 city (1990 pop. 9,922), ⊙ Boone co., N Ark., c.60 mi/97 km ENE of Fayetteville, in the Ozark Mts.; 36°14'N 93°07'W. Commercial center for farm area (fruit; cattle, hogs, poultry). Mfg. (wood prods., cheese, flour, clothing, fabricated metal prods., consumer goods, bldg. materials, transportation equip., paper prods., fiberglass prods.); die-casting plant, produce houses. Mystic Cave to S; Buffalo R. Natl. Park to S. Seat of Ark. Community Col. Growing retirement pop. Plotted c.1860, inc. 1876. **2** city (1990 pop. 7,518), Hamilton co., extreme SW Ohio, 19 mi/31 km WNW of Cincinnati, and on Whitewater R., at Ind. state line, contiguous to West Harrison (Ind.); 39°14'N 84°48'W. Laid out 1813.

Harrison 1 town (1990 pop. 414), Washington co., E central Ga., 12 mi/19 km SSE of Sandersville; 32°50'N 82°44'W. **2** resort town (1990 pop. 1,951), Cumberland co., SW Maine, 37 mi/60 km NW of Portland, at N end of Long L.; 44°06'N 70°38'W. Light mfg. (machinery, bldg. materials). Inc. 1805. **3** town (1990 pop. 1,835), ⊙ Clare co., central Mich., 18 mi/29 km N of Mt. Pleasant, on W side of Budd L.; 44°01'N 84°48'W. In agr. area (livestock; potatoes, beans; dairy prods.); mfg. (lumber, machinery). Resort area (lakes). Wilson State Park to E; Snowsnake Mt. Ski Area to S. Seat of Mid Mich. Community Col. Settled 1878, inc. as city 1891. **4** town (1990 pop. 13,425), Hudson co., NE N.J., an industrial suburb on the Passaic R., opposite Newark; 40°44'N 74°09'W. The town has several foundries. Mfg. includes plastics, paperboard, and metal prods. Inc. 1869.

Harrison 1 village (1990 pop. 226), Kootenai co., N Idaho, 15 mi/24 km NW of St. Maries, and on E shore of Coeur d'Alene L., at mouth of Coeur d'Alene R., 1 mi/1.6 km N of Coeur d'Alene Indian Reservation; 47°27'N 116°47'W. Agr.; recreation. Coeur d'Alene Natl. Forest to N. **2** village (1990 pop. 130), Madison co., SW Mont., 36 mi/58 km W of Bozeman, and on North Willow and South Willow creeks, which closely parallel each other forming Willow Creek to NE. Lewis and Clark Caverns State Park to N. Willow Creek Reservoir (Harrison L.) to E, just NE of Tobacco Root Mts., in ranching and mining (gold, tungsten) region. **3** village (1990 pop. 291), ⊙ Sioux co., NW Nebr., 45 mi/72 km WSW of Chadron, near Wyo. state line; 42°41'N 103°52'W. In ranching region; livestock; poultry prods.; grain, potatoes. Relics of prehistoric man found nearby. Near source of White R. Oglala Natl. Grasslands to N. **4** residential village and town (□ 17 sq mi/44 sq km; 1990 pop. 23,308), Westchester co., SE N.Y., bet. Mamaroneck (SW) and Rye (NE), near L.I. Sound; 41°01'N 73°43'W. Mfg. of industrial vacuums and polishers. Affluent community.

Harrison, township (1990 pop. 11,763), Allegheny co., W central Pa., suburb 20 mi/32 km NE of Pittsburgh; 40°37'N 79°43'W. Bounded E and S by Allegheny R. Includes Natrona and Natrona Heights in S; rural in N. Agr. (corn, hay; livestock; dairying).

Harrison Bay, N Alaska, shallow inlet of Beaufort Sea, bet. Cape Halkett (W) and Beechey Point (E), c.120 mi/193 km ESE of Barrow; 70°40'N 151°15'W. Receives Colville R.

Harrison, Cape, promontory on the Atlantic Ocean, SE Lab., NE Canada; 54°46'N 58°26'W. Site of navigation radio station, 130 mi/209 km NE of Happy Valley–Goose Bay. Offshore oil and gas exploration.

Harrison City, uninc. town (1990 pop. 900), Westmoreland co., SW Pa., suburb 2 mi/3.2 km NWS of Jeannette; 40°21'N 79°38'W. Mfg. of motor controls; agr. includes dairying; livestock; corn, hay. Bushy Run Battlefield Historical Site to E.

Harrison Hot Springs, village (1991 pop. 655), S B.C., W Canada, at S end of Harrison L., 12 mi/19 km NE of Chilliwack. Resort, with mineral springs.

Harrison Lake (□ 87 sq mi/225 sq km), S B.C., W Canada, 12 mi/19 km NE of Chilliwack; 30 mi/48 km long, 1 mi/2 km–5 mi/8 km wide. Contains Long Isl. (6 mi/10 km long). Receives Lillooet R. (NW); drains S into Fraser R.

Harrison Mills, village, S B.C., W Canada, on Fraser R., at mouth of Harrison R. (outlet of Harrison L.), 5 mi/8 km N of Chilliwack. Lumbering.

Harrisonburg, independent city (□ 17 sq mi/44 sq km; 1990 pop. 30,707), ⊙ surrounding Rockingham co., NW Va., in Shenandoah Valley; 38°26'N 78°52'W. RR junction. Mfg. (computers, clothing, paper prods., machinery, bldg. materials, fabricated metal prods., transportation equip., chemicals, furniture, animal feeds, fertilizers; sheet metal fabrication, printing and publishing). Processing center in an agr. area (poultry, livestock; dairying; also grain, apples, peaches, soybeans). Gen. T. J. (Stonewall) Jackson ended his Valley Campaign just E in 1862. Seat of James Madison Univ., Eastern Mennonite Col. Hq. of George Washington Natl. Forest. Limestone caverns in area: Endless Caverns to NE, Grand Caverns to S; Shenandoah Natl. Park to SE. Settled 1739, inc. 1916.

Harrisonburg, village (1990 pop. 453), ⊙ Catahoula parish, E La., on Ouachita R., and 30 mi/48 km NW of Natchez (Miss.); 31°46'N 91°49'W. In agr. area (cotton, corn, fruit, sorghum, sweet potatoes, peas; cattle, horses); catfish. Sicily Isl. Hills State Wildlife Area to NE.

Harrison's Cave, natural limestone and coral cavern, NE Bridgetown, St. Thomas parish, central Barbados. Said to be largest caverns in West Indies. Underground tours operated by Barbados Natl. Trust.

Harrisonville, city (1990 pop. 7,683), W Mo., ⊙ Cass co., 32 mi/51 km SSE of Kansas City; 38°39'N 94°20'W. Corn, wheat, sorghum; cattle. Mfg. (consumer goods, machinery). Laid out 1837.

Harriston, town (1991 pop. 1,995), S Ont., central Canada, on Maitland R., and 40 mi/64 km NW of Guelph; 43°55'N 80°53'W. Meatpacking, dairying, woodworking.

Harristown, town (1990 pop. 1,319), Macon co., central Ill., 7 mi/11.3 km W of Decatur; 39°50'N 89°03'W. Wheat, corn, soybeans. Lincoln Trail Homestead State Park to S.

Harrisville 1 town (1990 pop. 981), Cheshire co., SW N.H., 9 mi/14.5 km E of Keene; 42°56'N 72°05'W. Agr. (dairying; poultry, cattle, sheep; nursery crops); mfg. (textiles, water coolers). Skatutakee L. in S center; Silver L., Childs Bog in NW. **2** town (1990 pop. 3,004), Weber co., N Utah, residential suburb 4 mi/6.4 km NW of Ogden; 41°16′N 111°58′W. Elev. c.4,400 ft/1,341 m. Agr. area (vegetables, fruit, alfalfa, barley; dairying; cattle). Wasatch Range and Natl. Forest to E. Ogden Defense Depot to S. Settled 1850. **3** town (1990 pop. 1,839), ⊙ Ritchie co., NW W.Va., on North Fork of Hughes R., 27 mi/43 km E of Parkersburg; 39°12′N 81°02′W. Agr. (corn); livestock, poultry. Mfg. (clothing, bldg. materials, textiles). Oil production. North Bend State Park to W; North Bend State Trail to NW. Plotted 1822.

Harrisville 1 village (1990 pop. 470), ⊙ Alcona co., NE Mich., 30 mi/48 km SSE of Alpena, on L. Huron; 44°39′N 83°17′W. Summer resort; nurseries; mfg. (tool and die, concrete). Harrisville State Park on lake; Newegon State Park 21 mi/34 km N. **2** village (1990 pop. 703), Lewis co., N central N.Y., on West Branch of Oswegatchie R., and 33 mi/53 km ENE of Watertown; 44°08′N 75°19′W. **3** village (1990 pop. 308), Harrison co., E Ohio, 8 mi/13 km SE of Cadiz; 40°11′N 80°53′W. In agr. and coal-mining area. **4** village (1990 pop. 1,670), Burrillville town, Providence co., R.I., 15 mi/24 km NW of Providence; 41°58′N 71°41′W.

Harrisville (HER-is-vil), borough (1990 pop. 862), Butler co., W Pa., 4 mi/6.4 km ESE of Grove City. Mfg. (limestone processing; concrete); agr. (potatoes, corn, hay; livestock; dairying).

Harrod, village (1990 pop. 537), Allen co., W Ohio, 10 mi/16 km ESE of Lima; 40°42′N 83°55′W. In agr. area; wood prods.

Harrodsburg (HA-ruhdz-buhrg), town (1990 pop. 7,335), ⊙ Mercer co., central Ky., S of Frankfort; 37°46′N 84°50′W. Trade center in Bluegrass region producing livestock; grain and tobacco; dairying; mfg. (paper prods., optical lenses, shipping goods, textiles). Tourist and resort city, with mineral springs. The oldest settlement W of the Alleghenies, it was founded in 1774 by James Harrod. One of the settlement's early leaders was George Rogers Clark. Old Fort Harrod State Park to NE contains a replica of old fort (1775), site of state's first school, Historical Society Mus., Butaan War Memorial.

Harrodsburg Dam, Ky.: see DIX RIVER.

Harrogate (HA-ruh-gait), village, Claiborne co., NE Tenn., near Ky.-Va. state line, 5 mi/8 km S of Cumberland Gap; 36°35′N 83°40′W. Coal deposits. Seat of Lincoln Memorial Univ.

Harrold, village (1990 pop. 167), Hughes co., central S.Dak., 22 mi/35 km ENE of Pierre, and on Medicine Knoll Creek; 44°31′N 99°44′W.

Harrow, town (1991 pop. 2,584), S Ont., central Canada, near L. Erie, 17 mi/27 km S of Windsor; 42°02′N 82°55′W. In dairying, farming region.

Harrowsmith, village, SE Ont., central Canada, 15 mi/24 km NW of Kingston. Dairying, mixed farming.

Harry S. Truman Reservoir (□ 87 sq mi/225 sq km), W central Mo., on Osage R., 31 mi/50 km SSW of Sedalia; 38°16′N 93°24′W. Max. capacity 5,202,000 acre-ft. Star shaped; has 4 main arms radiating from dam area. Fed by Pomme de Terre, Horse, and South Grand rivers. Formed by Harry S. Truman Dam (98 ft/30 m high), built (1978) by Army Corps of Engineers for power generation; also used for flood control and recreation. Harry S. Truman State Park near dam.

Harry S. Truman Historic Site, Independence, Jackson co., W central Mo. Home of U.S. President Harry S. Truman from 1919 until 1972. Authorized 1983. Truman Mus. and Lib. nearby.

Harry Strunk Lake, reservoir (□ 9 sq mi/23.3 sq km), Frontier co., S central Nebr., on Medicine Creek, 24 mi/39 km ENE of McCook; 40°23′N 100°13′W. Max. capacity 194,080 acre-ft. Formed by Medicine Creek Dam (165 ft/50 m high), built (1949) by the Bureau of Reclamation for irrigation; also used for flood control. Medicine Creek Reservoir State Recreational Area to W.

Harsens Island, St. Clair co., SE Mich., in delta of St. Clair R., in L. St. Clair, opposite Walpole Isl. (Ont.); c.5 mi/8 km long, 3 mi/4.8 km wide. Summer resort, known for fishing. Sans Souci village (area noted for waterfowl) is on E shore. Settled c.1779.

Hart 1 county (□ 257 sq mi/666 sq km; 1990 pop. 19,712), NE Ga.; ⊙ Hartwell; 34°21′N 82°58′W. Bounded E and N by S.C. state line, formed here by Savannah and Tugaloo rivers. Piedmont agr. area (cotton, wheat, soybeans, corn, hay, sweet potatoes; cattle, hogs, poultry). Formed 1853. **2** county (□ 417 sq mi/1,080 sq km; 1990 pop. 14,890), central Ky.; ⊙ Munfordville; 37°17′N 85°53′W. Bounded NE by Nolin R. (including part of Nolin River L. reservoir); drained by Green R. Rolling agr. area (burley tobacco, corn, wheat, soybean). Includes part of Mammoth Cave Natl. Park in SW; many limestone caves in area; Kentucky, Mammoth Onyx, and Hidden River caves; Amer. Cave Mus. in S, at Horse Cave town. Formed 1819.

Hart 1 town (1990 pop. 1,942), ⊙ Oceana co., W Mich., 33 mi/53 km NNW of Muskegon, and on short Pentwater R.; 43°42′N 86°21′W. Potatoes, fruit, vegetables (esp. asparagus), beans; livestock, poultry; dairy; mfg. (food processing, confections, and cherry prods.); resort. Charles Mears State Park to NW; Silver L. State Park to SW; Manistee Natl. Forest to E and N. Inc. as village 1885, as city 1947. **2** town (1990 pop. 1,221), Castro co., NW Texas, 25 mi/40 km NW of Plainview; 34°23′N 102°06′W. Agr. area (cattle, sheep, hogs; corn, wheat, cotton). Mfg. (fertilizer).

Hart Island, N.Y.: see HARTS ISLAND.

Hart Lake Reservoir (□ 12 sq mi/31 sq km), Lake co., S central Oregon, in the Warner Valley, 25 mi/40 km NE of Lakeview; 42°27′N 119°50′W. Max. capacity 52,150 acre-ft. Formed by Hart L. Reservoir Dam (19 ft/6 m high), built (1963) for irrigation. Hart Mt. Natl. Antelope Refuge just E.

Hart Mountain (2,700 ft/823 m), W Man., central Canada, 27 mi/43 km NNW of Swan R.; highest point of Porcupine Mt.

Hart Mountain, peak (7,710 ft/2,134 m), Lake co., S Oregon, rising from high plateau of Harney Basin, in Great Basin, c.80 mi/129 km SSW of Burns. Hart L. (6 mi/9.7 km long, 2 mi/3.2 km wide; semi-dry), one of numerous intermittent lakes in Warner Valley, which has geysers and sub-surface thermal activity, to W. Hart Mt. Natl. Antelope Refuge in SW.

Hartford, county (□ 750 sq mi/1,943 sq km), central and N Conn., on Mass. state line, bisected by Connecticut R.; ⊙ Hartford; 41°48′N 72°43′W. Mfg. (airplanes, machinery, hardware, tools, bldg. materials, paper, clothing, food prods., rubber prods., leather prods., furniture, fabricated metal prods., textiles, wood prods., consumer goods, electronic goods, transportation equip., chemicals). Agr. (tobacco, dairy prods., poultry, vegetables, fruit, corn, potatoes, nursery prods., seeds). Includes several state parks and forests. Drained by Farmington, Quinnipiac, Pequabuck, Hockanum, and Scantic rivers. Constituted 1666.

Hartford, city (1990 pop. 139,739), ⊙ Conn. and Hartford co., central Conn., on the W bank of the Connecticut R.; 41°46′N 72°40′W. Settled as Newtown 1635–1636 on the site of a Du. trading post (1633; abandoned 1654). The 2d-largest city in the state, it is a port of entry and a world-famous insurance center. Its insurance business began in 1794, and the area remains home to the hq. of several major companies (although mergers and downsizing during the 1990s diminished the insurance industry's importance somewhat). During the 1970s and 1980s, however, many insurance companies branched out of the city into the growing suburban locations. Mfg. includes precision instruments, computers, transportation equip., firearms, and electric equip. One of the earliest and strongest colonial centers, Hartford and 2 other towns formed (1639) the Conn. Colony, adopting the Fundamental Orders. From 1701 to 1875 it was joint capital with New Haven. It was an important military supply depot during the Amer. Revolution, and in 1814–1815, it hosted the Hartford Convention. Landmarks include the Old State House (1796; designed by Charles Bulfinch), where the Hartford Convention met; the site of the Charter Oak; the capitol (completed 1878; designed by Richard M. Upjohn); and the famous Travelers Insurance tower. The Conn. state lib. includes the Colt collection of firearms. Has a noted art mus. (the Wadsworth Atheneum), a symphony orchestra, and an opera company. Other attractions are the Harriet Beecher Stowe House (1871), where Stowe lived 1873–1896, and the Mark Twain Memorial (1873–1874). Noah Webster, John Fiske, and the elder J. P. Morgan were b. here; the theologian Horace Bushnell, the author Charles Dudley Warner, and the poet Wallace Stevens lived here. The *Hartford Courant*, founded in 1764, is one of the country's oldest newspapers. The city's many parks include Elizabeth Park, scene of an annual rose festival, and Colt Park. Among Hartford's institutions of higher education are Trinity Col., Capital Community Technical Col., the Univ. of Hartford, Hartford Col. for Women, and a branch of the Univ. of Conn. There is also the Amer. School for the Deaf (in West Hartford) and the Conn. Inst. for the Blind. Constitution Plaza, a 15-acre/6-ha development project, was completed in 1964. Inc. 1784.

Hartford 1 town (1990 pop. 2,448), Geneva co., SE Ala., 12 mi/19 km ENE of Geneva, bet. Choctawhatchee R. and Fla. state line. Pecan shelling, cotton ginning, lumber milling. Founded 1894. **2** town (1990 pop. 768), Warren co., S central Iowa, 10 mi/16 km NE of Indianola; 41°27′N 93°24′W. Sorghum mill. **3** town (1990 pop. 2,532), ⊙ Ohio co., W Ky., on Rough R., and 25 mi/40 km SSE of Owensboro; "twin city" of Beaver Dam 4 mi/6.4 km to SSE; 37°27′N 86°53′W. In coal, timber, limestone, and agr. (corn, burley tobacco, hay; cattle, hogs) area; mfg. (crushed limestone; apparel; lumber). Founded 1782. **4** town (1990 pop. 722), Oxford co., W Maine, 14 mi/23 km NE of South Paris, and on branch of Nezinscot R.; 44°22′N 70°19′W. In farming, recreational area; wood prods. **5** town (1990 pop. 2,341), Van Buren co., SW Mich., 16 mi/26 km NE of Benton Harbor, and on Paw Paw R.; 42°12′N 86°10′W. In fruit-growing area; nurseries; vegetables; ships fruit; winery. Mfg. (fruit and vegetable processing; asphalt). Inc. 1877. **6** town (1990 pop. 1,262), Minnehaha co., E S.Dak., 12 mi/19 km WNW of Sioux Falls; 43°37′N 96°56′W. Mfg. (bulk conveyors); honey. Wild Game Farm. **7** town (1990 pop. 9,404), Windsor co., E Vt., on the Connecticut R., at mouth of White R., and 9 mi/14.5 km E of Woodstock; 43°39′N 72°23′W. Wood prods., woolen prods. Includes residential villages of Hartford and Wilder, industrial and transportation center White River Junction, and Quechee village (E of Quechee Gorge whose top is 162 ft/49 m above the Ottauquechee R.; has a small woolen mill). Gateway to resort area (W). Large hydroelectric dam in the Connecticut at Wilder. Settled 1765. **8** town (1990 pop. 8,188), Washington co., E Wis., on small Rubicon R. (tributary of Rock R.), near small Pike L. (resort), and 30 mi/48 km NW of Milwaukee; 43°19′N 88°23′W. In dairy and farm area. Cheese, canned vegetables; mfg. (consumer goods, wood prods., plastic prods., tool and die, electrostatic powder coating, transportation equip., furniture, fabricated metal prods., beverages; tanning, metal fabricating). Pike L. State Park to E. Settled c.1844, inc. 1883.

Hartford 1 village (1990 pop. 721), Sebastian co., W Ark., 24 mi/39 km S of Fort Smith; 35°01′N 94°22′W. In diversified agr. area. Ouachita Natl. Forest to S. **2** village (1990 pop. 1,676), Madison co., SW Ill., on the Mississippi R., industrial suburb 15 mi/24 km NNE of downtown St. Louis, within St. Louis metropolitan area; 38°49′N 90°05′W. Oil and copper refining. Lewis and Clark State Memorial on river, opposite confluence of Missouri R., starting point of Lewis and Clark Expedition to NW. Inc. 1920. **3** village (1990 pop. 541), Lyon co., E central Kansas, on Neosho R., and 14 mi/23 km SE of Emporia; 38°18′N 95°57′W. Grain; livestock. At W (upstream) end of John Redmond Reservoir. **4** village (1990 pop. 418), Licking co., Ohio; 40°14′N 82°41′W. **5** village (1990 pop. 487), Mason co., W W.Va., on Ohio R., 14 mi/23 km NNE of Point Pleasant, and 3 mi/4.8 km SE of Pomeroy (Ohio); 39°00′N 81°59′W. Agr. (grain, tobacco); livestock; dairying. Also known as Hartford City.

Hartford City, city (1990 pop. 6,960), ⊙ Blackford co., E Ind., 18 mi/29 km N of Muncie; 40°27′N 85°22′W. In rich agr. area (livestock; dairy prods.; soybeans, grain). Natural gas and oil fields nearby. Mfg. (glass, rubber prods., transportation equip., concrete prods., canned goods, consumer goods, lumber prods.). Settled 1832, laid out 1839.

Hartford City, W.Va.: see HARTFORD, village.

Hartington, town (1990 pop. 1,583), ⊙ Cedar co., NE Nebr., 30 mi/48 km SSE of Yankton (S.Dak.), near Missouri R.; 42°37′N 97°15′W. Grain; mfg. (machinery, cheese prods., printing). Inc. 1883.

Hartland, town (1991 pop. 890), W N.B., E Canada, on St. John R. (longest covered bridge in the world; 1,283 ft/391 m), and 10 mi/16 km N of Woodstock, near U.S. (Maine) border; 46°18′N 67°32′W. Agr. market in Irish potato region; woodworking.

Hartland 1 town (1990 pop. 1,866), Hartford co., N Conn., in hilly region, on Mass. state line, and 21 mi/34 km NW of Hartford; 42°00′N 72°57′W. Includes East Hartland village. Agr. and mfg. of wood prods. Part of Barkhamsted Reservoir (on East Branch Farmington R.), state forests here. **2** town (1990 pop. 1,806), Somerset co., central Maine, on the Sebasticook R., and 15 mi/24 km NE of Skowhegan; 44°53′N 69°30′W. In farming area; tannery. Settled c.1800, inc. 1820. **3** town (1990 pop. 2,988), Windsor co., E Vt., on the Connecticut R., 10 mi/16 km SE of Woodstock; 43°34′N 72°25′W. In dairying area. Includes villages of North Hartland, at mouth of Ottauquechee R., and Hartland Four Corners. Settled 1763. **4** town (1990 pop. 6,906), Waukesha co., SE Wis., on Bark R., and 22 mi/35 km W of Milwaukee; 43°06′N 88°20′W. In dairying and farming area with resort lakes nearby. Mfg. of dairy prods., wood prods., steel prods., medical equip., microfiche, fiberglass, plastic prods., teflon seals; machining.

Hartland 1 village, Livingston co., SE Mich., 10 mi/16 km NE of Howell; 42°39′N 83°45′W. In farm area. Numerous lakes in area. **2** village (1990 pop. 270), Freeborn co., S Minn., 13 mi/21 km NNW of Albert Lea; 43°47′N 93°29′W. Dairying; poultry; grain.

Hartleton (HAHR-tel-tuhn), borough (1990 pop. 246), Union co., central Pa., 15 mi/24 km WSW of Lewisburg. Corn, hay; dairying. Parts of Bald Eagle State Forest to N and S.

Hartley, county (□ 1,463 sq mi/3,789 sq km; 1990 pop. 3,634), extreme N Texas; ⊙ Channing; 35°50′N 102°36′W. Elev. 3,400 ft/1,036 m–4,400 ft/1,341 m. In high, grassy plains of the Panhandle, and bounded W by N.Mex. state line. Drained by Rita Blanca, Carrizo, and Punta de Agua creeks. Large-scale cattle-ranching area; extensively irrigated region, wheat, corn, sorghum; natural-gas wells. Includes Rita Blanca L. (recreational area) in N. Formed 1876.

Hartley, town (1990 pop. 1,632), O'Brien co., NW Iowa, 10 mi/16 km NE of Primghar; 43°10′N 95°28′W. Dairy, wood, and metal prods. Inc. 1888.

Hartline, village (1990 pop. 176), Grant co., E central Wash., 33 mi/53 km NE of Ephrata; 47°42′N 119°07′W. Alfalfa; cattle. Banks L. reservoir in Grand Coulee, to NW.

Hartly, village (1990 pop. 107), Kent co., W Del., 10 mi/16 km W of Dover; 39°10′N 75°42′W. In agr. area.

Hartman 1 village (1990 pop. 498), Johnson co., NW Ark., 8 mi/12.9 km WSW of Clarksville, near Arkansas R. (L. Dardanelle); 35°25′N 93°37′W. **2** village (1990 pop. 108), Prowers co., SE Colo., near Arkansas R., and Kansas state line, 22 mi/35 km E of Lamar; 38°07′N 102°13′W. Elev. c.3,600 ft/1,100 m. Terminus of RR spur from Lamar.

Hartney, town (1991 pop. 477), SW Man., central Canada, on Souris R., and 35 mi/56 km SW of Brandon; 49°29′N 100°31′W. Grain elevators; livestock.

Harts, uninc. town (1990 pop. 2,332), Lincoln co., W W.Va., 16 mi/26 km W of Madison, near Guyandotte R.; 38°01′N 82°07′W. Agr. (corn, tobacco); cattle. Timber. Mfg. (lumber). Big Ugly Wildlife Management Area to NE.

Harts Island, part of Bronx borough of NE N.Y. city, SE N.Y., in L.I. Sound, near City Isl. and Pelham Bay Park; c.1 mi/1.6 km long; 40°51′N 73°46′W. Mainland ferry to City Isl. The city's cemetery (potter's field) is here. Formerly site of city reformatory. Sometimes called Hart Isl. or Hart's Isl.

Harts Location, town (1990 pop. 36), Carroll co., N central N.H., 23 mi/37 km SSW of Berlin, in White Mts. Drained by Saco R. Tourism. White Mt. Natl. Forest in S ½; N part surrounded by White Mt. Natl. Forest. Crawford Notch State Park in N; Appalachian Trail crosses N; Silver Cascade Falls in N.

Hartsburg, town, (1990 pop. 131), Boone co., central Mo., on Missouri R., 10 mi/16 km NW of Jefferson City. Pumpkins, corn, soybeans; cattle. Flooding in 1993 severely damaged town. Access to Katy Trail State Park.

Hartsburg, village (1990 pop. 306), Logan co., central Ill., 8 mi/12.9 km NNW of Lincoln; 40°15′N 89°26′W. In agr. area (cattle, hogs; corn, soybeans).

Hartsdale, residential village (□ 3 sq mi/7.8 sq km; 1990 pop. 9,587), Westchester co., SE N.Y., just SW of White Plains; 41°01′N 73°48′W.

Hartsel, village, Park co., central Colo., in Rocky Mts., 55 mi/89 km WNW of Colorado Springs; elev. 8,864 ft/2,702 m. Hot springs and Antero Reservoir and Antero State Wildlife Area to W; Spinney Mt. Reservoir and State Park to E. Region nearly surrounded by Pike Natl. Forest.

Hartselle, city (1990 pop. 10,795), Morgan co., N Ala., 12 mi/19 km SSE of Decatur. In cotton, corn, and vegetable area. Copper wire and pipe, clothing mfg. William B. Bankhead Natl. Forest is SW. Founded 1870, inc. 1875.

Hartshorne (HAHRTS-horn), town (1990 pop. 2,120), Pittsburg co., SE Okla., 13 mi/21 km SE of McAlester, and contiguous to Haileyville (to W); 34°50′N 95°33′W. In mining, cattle-raising, and agr. area (grain); mfg. (wood prods., electronic equip.). Oil and natural-gas wells. Jack Fork Mts. to S; headwaters of L. Arrowhead reservoir to N. Settled c.1890.

Hartstene Island (HAHRT-steen), Mason co., W Wash., in Puget Sound, 9 mi/14.5 km N of Olympia. Bounded E by Case Inlet, S by Dana Passage (bridged to mainland). In area are Jarrell Cove (N) and McMicken Isl. (E; off E shore) state parks; Squaxin Isl. Indian Reservation and State Park to SW. Village of Hartstene at N end. Timber. Fishing.

Hartsville 1 town (1990 pop. 391), Bartholomew co., S central Ind., on small Clifty Creek, and 12 mi/19 km ENE of Columbus; 39°16′N 85°42′W. In agr. area. **2** town (1990 pop. 8,372), Darlington co., NE S.C., 21 mi/34 km NW of Florence; 34°22′N 80°04′W. Mfg. includes packaged foods, fertilizers, fabricated metal prods., fiberglass boats, textiles, paper and paper prods. Agr. includes livestock, poultry; dairying; grain, soybeans. Seat of Coker Col. H. B. Robinson 2 Nuclear Power Plant on L. Robinson immediately to NW. Experimental seed farm nearby. **3** town (1990 pop. 2,188), ⊙ Trousdale co., N Tenn., 15 mi/24 km NE of Lebanon; 36°24′N 86°10′W. In agr. area (tobacco, corn, wheat); mfg. of boots and steel fabrication. In Civil War, Federal garrison here was defeated (1862) by Gen. John H. Morgan. Settled in early 1800s; inc. 1913.

Hartsville, Mass.: see NEW MARLBORO.

Hartville, city (1990 pop. 539), S central Mo., ⊙ Wright co., in the Ozark Mts., on Gasconade R., and 43 mi/69 km E of Springfield; 38°25′N 93°55′W. Peaches, apples, hay; dairying; cattle; timber. Mfg. of livestock feed and fertilizer. Settled 1832. Destroyed during Civil War.

Hartville 1 industrial village (1990 pop. 2,031), Stark co., E central Ohio, 14 mi/23 km SE of Akron; 40°58′N 81°20′W. Rubber goods, plastic prods. **2** village (1990 pop. 78), Platte co., SE Wyo., on North Platte R. (Guernsey Reservoir), and 22 mi/35 km NE of Wheatland; elev. c.4,750 ft/1,448 m; 42°19′N 104°43′W. Terminus of RR spur from Guernsey. Region of prehistoric stone quarries to NE.

Hartwell, town (1990 pop. 4,555), ⊙ Hart co., NE Ga., 16 mi/26 km NNW of Elberton, near S.C. state line; 34°21′N 82°56′W. Mfg. of athletic equip., consumer goods, fabricated metal prods., clothes, machinery parts, transportation equip.; egg production, mica mining and production, printing and publishing. Named for Amer. Revolutionary heroine Nancy Hart. Adjacent to L. Hartwell on Savannah R. Inc. 1856.

Hartwell Lake, reservoir, NE Ga. and NW S.C., on Savannah R. (Ga.-S.C. state line), 13 mi/21 km SE of Anderson (S.C.); 34°20′N 82°49′W. Lower reservoir 10 mi/16 km long; Keowee (Seneca) R. enters from N, Tugaloo R. (Ga.-S.C. state line) enters from NW, both forming arms each c.25 mi/40 km long. Formed by Hartwell Dam (195 ft/59 m high), built (1960) by the Army Corps of Engineers for flood control, navigation, and power generation. Hartwell near SW shore. State parks on NE (S.C.) and SW (Ga.) shores.

Hartwick, town (1990 pop. 115), Poweshiek co., central Iowa, 12 mi/19 km NE of Montezuma; 41°46′N 92°20′W. In agr. area.

Harvard, city (1990 pop. 5,975), McHenry co., N Ill., near Wis. state line, 12 mi/19 km NW of Woodstock; 42°25′N 88°37′W. RR town (with repair shops); trade center in dairying and resort area; mfg. of dairy prods., hardware, telecommunications. Inc. 1867.

Harvard 1 residential town (1990 pop. 12,329), Worcester co., E central Mass., 19 mi/31 km NNE of Worcester; 42°31′N 71°35′W. Orchards. A Shaker house and cemetery, a Native Amer. mus., and a Harvard Univ. observatory are here. Nearby is a mus. on the site of Fruitlands, a cooperative vegetarian community founded by Bronson Alcott. Includes village of Still River. Inc. 1732. **2** town (1990 pop. 926), Clay co., S Nebr., 15 mi/24 km E of Hastings. Dairy and poultry prods., grain; livestock. Harvard Marsh, one of the declining number of Rainwater Basin ponds or lagoons remaining, protected as a wildlife preserve of U.S. Fish and Wildlife Service.

Harvard College Observatory, astronomical observatory located in Cambridge, Mass., operated by Harvard Univ. (Harvard Col. at the time of the observatory's founding in 1839). Its equip. includes a 61-in/155-cm reflecting telescope and 15-in/38-cm and 12-in/30-cm refracting telescopes. Programs of the Harvard Observatory include various aspects of solar physics, stellar and nebular spectroscopy and photometry, and theoretical cosmology. Among the noted directors of the observatory have been W. C. Bond, G. P. Bond, E. C. Pickering, and Harlow Shapley. In 1973 the research programs of the Harvard Col. Observatory were merged with those of the Smithsonian Astrophysical Observatory to form the Harvard-Smithsonian Center for Astrophysics; the observatory itself, however, maintains its separate status under the control of Harvard.

Harvard, Mount (14,420 ft/4,395 m), Chaffer co., central Colo., in Collegiate Range of Sawatch Mts., in San Isabel Natl. Forest, E of Continental Divide, 23 mi/37 km S of Leadville. Peak is 3d-highest in Rocky Mts. of U.S. Named in 1869 by a group of climbers from Harvard Col.

Harvel, village (1990 pop. 213), in Christian and Montgomery cos., S central Ill., 20 mi/32 km SW of Taylorville; 39°21′N 89°31′W.

Harvest, village (1990 pop. 1,922), Madison co., N Ala., 13 mi/21 km NW of Huntsville; 34°51′N 86°45′W.

Harvey, county (□ 540 sq mi/1,399 sq km; 1990 pop. 31,028), S central Kansas; ⊙ Newton; 38°02′N 97°25′W. Flat to gently rolling prairie, drained by Little Arkansas R. and Walnut Creek (E). Wheat, corn, oats, barley, soybeans, apples; cattle, poultry. Millwork; industrial machinery. Formed 1872.

Harvey 1 city (1990 pop. 29,771), Cook co., NE Ill., suburb 20 mi/32 km SSW of downtown Chicago; 41°36′N 87°39′W. Mfg. (steel forging; fabricated metal prods., chemicals, machinery, electronic equip.). Harvey has an oil research center. Founded by Turlington W. Harvey, a wealthy lumberman, in 1890. South Suburban Col. of Cook Co. in neighboring South Holland. Inc. 1891. **2** (HAHR-vee), uninc. city (1990 pop. 21,222), Jefferson parish, SE La., on W bank (levee) of the Mississippi R., suburb opposite and 2 mi/3 km S of downtown New Orleans; 29°54′N 90°04′W. Mfg. (bldg.

materials, paper prods., fabricated metal prods., mineral oil, chemicals, fiberglass fabrication, machinery; barge building, marine vessel repair); shrimp, crabmeat, oysters. Harvey Lock (425 ft/130 m long) links the Mississippi to Intracoastal Waterway here. Also Cosmopolite City.

Harvey 1 town (1990 pop. 235), Marion co., S central Iowa, 10 mi/16 km E of Knoxville, near Des Moines R.; 41°19′N 92°55′W. Brick and tile plant. Limestone quarries, sand and gravel pits nearby. **2** town (1990 pop. 2,263), Wells co., central N.Dak., on Sheyenne R., and 80 mi/129 km NNE of Bismarck; 47°46′N 99°55′W. Sunflowers, dairy prods., potatoes, wheat. Mfg. (concrete). Inc. 1906.

Harvey 1 village (1991 pop. 372), Albert co., SE N.B., E Canada, near Shepody Bay, 2 mi/3 km SSE of Riverside-Albert, 10 mi/16 km SW of Hopewell Cape; 45°42′N 64°43′W. Mining and fishing in region. **2** village, York co., SW N.B., E Canada, on SE end of Harvey L., 24 mi/39 km SW of Fredericton. Woolen mill; mixed agr.; dairying; potatoes, apples. Tourism. Formerly Harvey Station.

Harvey, village (1990 pop. 1,377), Marquette co., on L. Superior, NW Upper Peninsula, N Mich., 4 mi/6.4 km SE of Marquette; 46°29′N 87°20′W. Resort; fish hatchery. Cliffs Ridge Ski Area to W; Highland State Recreation Area to E.

Harvey Cedars, resort borough (1990 pop. 362), Ocean co., E N.J., on Long Beach isl., 17 mi/27 km SSE of Toms River, and 30 mi/48 km NNE of Atlantic City; 39°42′N 74°08′W. Artists' summer colony here.

Harvey Lake (□ 3 sq mi/8 sq km), SW N.B., E Canada, 23 mi/37 km SW of Fredericton; 3 mi/5 km long, 1 mi/2 km wide; 45°45′N 67°01′W. Village of Harvey (York co.) on SE end.

Harveys Lake, borough (1990 pop. 2,746), Luzerne co., NE central Pa., residential community 12 mi/19 km NW of Wilkes-Barre; 41°21′N 76°01′W. Town surrounds Harveys L.

Harveysburg, village (1990 pop. 437), Warren co., SW Ohio, 20 mi/32 km SSE of Dayton, and on small Caesar Creek; 39°30′N 84°00′W.

Harveyton, village, Perry co., SE Ky., in Cumberland foothills, 5 mi/8 km N of Hazard. Bituminous coal.

Harveyville, village (1990 pop. 267), Wabaunsee co., E central Kansas, 23 mi/37 km SW of Topeka; 38°47′N 95°57′W. In cattle, poultry, and grain region.

Harviell (hahr-vee-EL), uninc. town, Butler co., SE Mo., 8 mi/12.9 km NW of Poplar Bluff.

Harwich (HAHR-wich), town (1990 pop. 10,275), Barnstable co., SE Mass., on S coast of Cape Cod, 12 mi/19 km E of Barnstable; 41°41′N 70°04′W. Summer resort; cranberries (birthplace of the industry), vegetables. Once whaling and shipbuilding center. Includes resort villages of Harwich Port (yachting), North Harwich, East Harwich (1990 pop. 3,828), South Harwich, and West Harwich. Pleasant L. (c.1.5 mi/2.4 km long) is nearby. Historical mus. Settled c.1670, inc. 1694.

Harwinton, town (1990 pop. 5,228), Litchfield co., NW Conn., on Naugatuck R., and 4 mi/6.4 km SE of Torrington; 41°45′N 73°03′W. In hilly region; agr. Retail services, construction, landscaping; tool and die. Settled 1730, inc. 1737.

Harwood, town (1990 pop. 89), Vernon co., W Mo., near Osage R.,14 mi/23 km NE of Nevada; 37°57′N 94°09′W. Hay, sorghum; cattle.

Harwood, village, S Ont., central Canada, on Rice L., 13 mi/21 km SE of Peterborough; 44°08′N 78°11′W. Fruit; dairying; mixed farming.

Harwood, uninc. village (1990 pop. 112), Gonzales co., S central Texas, 9 mi/14.5 km E of Luling. RR spur junction. Cattle, poultry.

Harwood Heights, village (1990 pop. 7,680), Cook co., NE Ill., suburb 11 mi/18 km NW of downtown Chicago; 41°58′N 87°48′W. Mfg. (fabricated metal prods., machinery, tapes and adhesives, tools).

Hasbrouck Heights (HAZ-brook), borough (1990 pop. 11,488), Bergen co., NE N.J., a residential suburb adjoining Hackensack; 40°51′N 74°04′W. Settled c.1685, inc. 1894.

Haskell 1 (HAS-kuhl), county (□ 577 sq mi/1,494 sq km; 1990 pop. 3,886), SW Kansas; ☉ Sublette; 37°33′N 100°52′W. Flat to rolling prairie, with sand dunes in extreme N. Cimarron R. in extreme SW. Wheat, corn, sorghum; cattle. Small natural-gas fields. Formed 1887. **2** county (□ 625 sq mi/1,619 sq km; 1990 pop. 10,940), E Okla.; ☉ Stigler; 35°13′N 95°06′W. Bounded N by Canadian R. (Eufaula Dam and L. in far NW corner) and Robert S. Kerr L. SE corner in Ouachite Mts.; Sansbois Mts. on S border. Drained by Sansbois Creek and NE by Arkansas R. (Robert S. Kerr L.). Agr. (barley, hay, soybeans, corn; cattle; timber; coal mines. Part of Sequoyah Natl. Wildlife Refuge in N. Recreation. Formed 1907. **3** county (□ 910 sq mi/2,357 sq km; 1990 pop. 6,820), NW central Texas; ☉ Haskell; 33°10′N 99°43′W. Drained by Double Mt. Fork of Brazos R. and Paint Creek. Irrigated agr. (cotton, sorghum, wheat, oats, barley, peanuts); livestock (beef cattle). Oil, natural-gas wells. L. Stamford reservoir in SE corner. Formed 1858.

Haskell, city (1990 pop. 1,342), Saline co., central Ark., 5 mi/8 km SSW of Benton; 34°30′N 92°38′W. RR junction; mfg. (aluminum recycling).

Haskell 1 (HAS-kuhl), town (1990 pop. 2,143), Muskogee co., E Okla., 18 mi/29 km WNW of Muskogee, and 25 mi/40 km SE of Tulsa, near Arkansas R.; 35°49′N 95°40′W. Trade center in agr. area (corn, potatoes; livestock; dairying); mfg. (hazardous waste-derived fuels, fabricated metal prods., food prods.); oil and natural-gas wells. Founded 1903. **2** town (1990 pop. 3,362), ☉ Haskell co., NW central Texas, c.50 mi/80 km N of Abilene; 33°09′N 99°43′W. Elev. 1,553 ft/473 m. In cattle-ranching and agr. area (cotton, wheat, peanuts); light mfg.; oil and gas. L. Stamford reservoir to SE. Settled 1882, inc. 1907.

Haskell (HA-skuhl), village in Wanaque borough, Passaic co., NE N.J., on Wanaque R., and 10 mi/16 km NW of Paterson. Largely residential.

Haskins, village (1990 pop. 549), Wood co., NW Ohio, 6 mi/10 km NNW of Bowling Green, near Maumee R.; 41°28′N 83°42′W. In agr. area.

Haslet, town (1990 pop. 795), Tarrant co., N Texas, suburb 14 mi/23 km N of downtown Fort Worth; 32°57′N 97°20′W. Agr. area on fringe of Dallas–Fort Worth Metroplex. Mfg. (plastics; machining).

Haslett (HAS-let), village (1990 pop. 10,230), Ingham co., S central Mich., suburb 6 mi/9.7 km E of Lansing, near L. Lansing (c.1.5 mi/2.4 km long, 1 mi/1.6 km wide); 42°45′N 84°24′W. Mfg. (metal finishing). Part of inc. city of Meridian Township.

Hassayampa River, intermittent stream, c.60 mi/97 km long, W central Ariz.; rises S of Prescott, in Yavapai co., flows S, past Wickenburg, to Gila R., 8 mi/12.9 km WSW of Buckeye. Crossed by Hayden-Rhodes Aqueduct, c.25 mi/40 km N of its mouth.

Hasselborg, Lake (HA-suhl-borg), SE Alaska, central Admiralty Isl., 18 mi/29 km NE of Angoon; 4 mi/6.4 km long; 57°43′N 134°16′W. Fishing, hunting.

Hassell, village (1990 pop. 95), Martin co., E N.C., 14 mi/23 km WNW of Williamston; 35°54′N 77°16′W. Tobacco, grain, cotton; livestock; poultry.

Hasson Heights (HA-SUHN), uninc. town (1990 pop. 1,610), Venango co., NW Pa., residential suburb 1 mi/1.6 km NE of Oil City; 41°27′N 79°40′W. Oil fields in vicinity.

Hastings, county (□ 2,323 sq mi/6,017 sq km; 1991 pop. 116,434), SE Ont., central Canada, on L. Ontario; ☉ Belleville; 44°45′N 77°35′W.

Hastings 1 city (1990 pop. 15,445), ☉ Dakota co., SE Minn., suburb 18 mi/29 km SE of downtown St. Paul, on the Mississippi R., opposite and to W of its confluence with the St. Croix R; 44°43′N 92°50′W. Vermillion R. drains S part of city, and enters Mississippi R. to SE; Wis. state line follows St. Croix R. and Mississippi R, SE. Farm trade (poultry, livestock; grain, soybeans; dairying) and mfg. center (flour, computer equip., fertilizers and feeds; printing and publishing; other diversified light mfg.). Minn. Veterans Home is here. Afton State Park to N; Richard J. Dorer Memorial Hardwood State Forest to S; Gores Pool No.

3 Wildlife Area to SE, on Mississippi R.; Lower St. Croix Scenic Riverway to NE; Hastings Lock and Dam No. 2 are here, forms Spring L. on Mississippi R. Inc. 1857. **2** city (1990 pop. 6,549), ☉ Barry co., SW Mich., 29 mi/47 km SE of Grand Rapids, and on Thornapple R.; 42°38′N 85°17′W. In agr. area. Mfg. (transportation equip., machinery, rubber prods., fire-fighting apparatus, crossbows; publishing). Resort; several lakes nearby. Native Amer. mounds in vicinity. Airport to W. Settled c.1836, inc. as village 1855, as city 1871. **3** city (1990 pop. 22,837), ☉ Adams co., S central Nebr., 26 mi/42 km S of Grand Isl., near headwaters of W Fork Big Blue R.; 40°35′N 98°23′W. RR junction. Mfg. includes processed foods, construction materials; printing; RR shops. Seat of Hastings Col., Central Community Col.–Hastings Campus E of town. Has Hastings Mus., Co. Fairgrounds. Municipal Airport to W. D. L. D. State Wayside to E. Inc. 1874.

Hastings, town (1990 pop. 187), Mills co., SW Iowa, on West Nishnabotna R., and 13 mi/21 km E of Glenwood; 41°01′N 95°30′W. In agr. area.

Hastings, village (1991 pop. 1,148), SE Ont., central Canada, on Trent R., and 18 mi/29 km E of Peterborough; 44°18′N 77°57′W. Light mfg.

Hastings, village (1990 pop. 164), Jefferson co., S Okla., 8 mi/12.9 km W of Waurika; 34°13′N 98°06′W. In agr. area. Waurika L. reservoir to NE.

Hastings, SE residential suburb and seaside resort of Bridgetown, SW Barbados.

Hastings, borough (1990 pop. 1,431), Cambria co., W central Pa., 25 mi/40 km NNE of Johnstown. Light mfg.; bituminous coal; agr. area (potatoes, grain; livestock, dairying). Prince Gallitzin State Park to E. Inc. 1894.

Hastings-on-Hudson, upper-income residential and industrial village (□ 2 sq mi/5.2 sq km; 1990 pop. 8,000), Westchester co., SE N.Y., on E bank of the Hudson R., just N of Yonkers; 40°59′N 73°52′W. Mfg. of consumer goods; some light industry. Inc. 1879.

Haswell, village (1990 pop. 62), Kiowa co., E Colo., 20 mi/32 km W of Eads; elev. c.4,538 ft/1,383 m; 38°27′N 103°09′W. Cattle; wheat, sunflowers, sorghum. Adobe Creek Reservoir (Blue L.) to S.

Hatboro (HAT-buhr-o), borough (1990 pop. 7,382), Montgomery co., SE Pa., suburb 15 mi/24 km NNE of downtown Philadelphia, on Pennypack Creek. Mfg. (machinery, medical equip., machinery, fabricated metal prods., consumer goods, tool and die, foods, bldg. materials; commercial printing. Agr. (grain, soybeans, apples; livestock; dairying). U.S. Naval Air Station (Willow Grove) to NW. Settled in early 18th cent., inc. 1871.

Hatch, town (1990 pop. 1,136), Dona Ana co., SW N.Mex., on Rio Grande, and 39 mi/63 km NW of Las Cruces; 32°40′N 107°09′W. In irrigated agr. region (cattle, sheep; vegetables, grain, chilies, jalpenos, alfalfa); light mfg. RR junction to E. Leasburg Dam State Park and Fort Selden State Monument to SE; Percha Dam and Caballo L. state parks to NW. Sierra Caballo to N; Sierra de las Uvas to S.

Hatch, village (1990 pop. 103), Garfield co., SW Utah, 15 mi/24 km S of Panguitch; 37°38′N 112°25′W. Alfalfa; cattle. Units of Dixie Natl. Forest to E and W; Utah State Fish Hatchery is here.

Hatchet Bay, town, central Bahama Isls., on N Eleuthera Isl., 20 mi/32 km NW of Governor's Harbour, 55 mi/89 km ENE of Nassau; 25°20′N 76°28′W. Dairying; poultry farming.

Hatchie River (HACH-ee), c.175 mi/282 km long, in Miss. and Tenn.; rises in NE Union co., N Miss.; flows NNW into W Tenn., and WNW to Mississippi R. through Hatchis Natl. Wildlife Refuge, passes N of Covington, 30 mi/48 km N of Memphis. Receives Tuscumbia R. from SE, 6 mi/9.7 km E of Middleton.

Hatchineha Lake (ha-chuh-NEE-hah), Polk co., central Fla., 11 mi/18 km ESE of Haines City; c.7 mi/11.3 km long, 2 mi/3.2 km wide. Kissimmee R. connects it with L. Kissimmee (S) and with chain of lakes (including Tohopekaliga L.) to N.

Hatchville, Mass.: see FALMOUTH.

Hatfield 1 town (1990 pop. 3,184), Hampshire co., W Mass., on Connecticut R., just above Northampton; 42°23′N 72°37′W. Wood prods.; barium-sulphate mine; tobacco. Settled 1661, set off from Hadley 1670. **2** uninc. town (1990 pop. 1,900) Fayette co., SW Pa., residential suburb 2 mi/3.2 km S of Uniontown; 39°52′N 79°44′W.

Hatfield 1 village (1990 pop. 414), Polk co., W Ark., 10 mi/16 km SW of Mena, near Okla. state line, near Mountain Fork R.; 34°29′N 94°22′W. Sawmilling, mfg. (posts and poles, lumber, wood prods.). Ouachita Natl. Forest to E and NW. **2** village (1990 pop. 900), Spencer co., SW Ind., 18 mi/29 km ESE of Evansville. Livestock, poultry. **3** village (1990 pop. 66), Pipestone co., SW Minn., near Rock R., 7 mi/11.3 km ESE of Pipestone; 43°57′N 96°11′W. Grain; livestock; dairying.

Hatfield, borough (1990 pop. 2,650), Montgomery co., SE Pa., suburb 22 mi/35 km N of Philadelphia, on West Branch Neshaminy Creek. Mfg. (machinery, bldg. materials, fabricated metal prods., plastic prods., apparel, wood prods., food prods.; library bindery; printing). Settled 1860, inc. 1898.

Hatiguanico River (ah-tee-gwah-NEE-ko), sluggish stream in Matanzas prov., W Cuba; rises near L. Tesoro; flows W through mangrove swamps of Zapata to the Gulf of Batabanó; 22°31′N 81°36′W.

Hatillo (ah-TEE-yo), town (1990 pop. 32,703), NW P.R., on the coast, 7 mi/11.3 km W of Arecibo. Dairying center (⅓ of milk consumed in P.R. produced here). Coffee-growing area. Light mfg. (food, textiles, wood and cement prods.). Famous for its costume parade on Innocents' Day (Dec. 28).

Hatillo (ah-TEE-yo), village, Duarte prov., central Dominican Republic, on Yuna R., and 23 mi/37 km S of San Francisco de Marcorís. Iron and gold mining.

Hatley 1 (HAT-lee), village (1990 pop. 529), Monroe co., E Miss., 4 mi/6.4 km E of Amory; 33°58′N 88°25′W. Cotton, corn; cattle; dairying; timber. **2** village (1990 pop. 25), Marathon co., central Wis., 15 mi/24 km ESE of Wausau, on Placer R.; 44°53′N 89°20′W. In dairying region. Mfg. (hardwood veneers).

Hato (HAH-to), village and airport (Aeropuerto Internashonal Hato), E central Curaçao, Neth. Antilles, 5 mi/8 km N of Willemstad; 12°11′N 68°17′W.

Hato Mayor, province (□ 514 sq mi/1,330 sq km; 1993 pop. 76,761), E Dominican Republic, along S shore of Samana Bay; ⊙ Hato Mayor; 18°50′N 69°20′W. Agr. area (cocoa, rice, beans; cattle). Fishing along Samana Bay.

Hato Mayor (AH-to mei-YOR), town (1993 pop. 25,049), Seibo prov., E Dominican Republic, 22 mi/35 km N of San Pedro de Macorís; ⊙ Hato Mayor prov.; 18°42′N 69°20′W. Agr. center (sugarcane, coffee, cacao, rice, fruit). First settled 1520.

Hato Rey (AH-to RAI), N residential suburb of Central San Juan, N P.R., 5 mi/8 km SE of Old San Juan. Isl.'s main business dist., includes many financial institutions.

Hatteras (HA-tuh-ruhs), uninc. village, Dare co., E N.C., 48 mi/77 km S of Manteo, on Pamlico Sound, in Cape Hatteras Natl. Seashore, near SW end of Hatteras Isl., in N. C.'s Outer Banks sand barrier; Atlantic Ocean to S. Resort; boatbuilding, fishing. Mfg. (commercial boats). Free ferry to NE end of Ocracoke Isl., across Hatteras Inlet (passage). Cape Hatteras (lighthouse) 10 mi/16 km to E. Beach recreation area.

Hatteras, Cape (HA-tuh-ruhs), promontory, Dare co., E N.C., on Hatteras Isl., in Outer Banks, sand barrier bet. the Atlantic Ocean (E and S) and Pamlico Sound (NW), in Cape Hatteras Natl. Seashore. Called the Graveyard of the Atlantic, the cape experiences frequent storms that drive ships landward toward its dangerous shallow and changing depths. Cape Hatteras Lighthouse (built 1870) was removed in 1936 due to heavy beach erosion, but is again exposed to the ocean.

Hatteras Inlet (HA-tuh-ruhs), N.C., passage c.1 mi/1.6 km wide, connecting Pamlico Sound (NW) with the Atlantic Ocean (SE), between Hatteras (NE) and Ocracoke (SE) isls., in Cape Hatteras Natl. Seashore. Border bet. Dare and Hyde cos. passes through inlet. Free ferry carries State Highway 12 traffic across inlet on Pamlico Sound side.

Hatteras Island (HA-tuh-ruhs), Dare co., E N.C., section of the Outer Banks, extending S from New Inlet (now blocked; joined to Pea Isl. to N) to Cape Hatteras and then SW to Hatteras Inlet, lying bet. Pamlico Sound (W) and the Atlantic Ocean (E and S); 40 mi/64 km long, 1 mi/1.6 km–3 mi/4.8 km wide. Site of fishing, resort villages (including Hatteras, Avon, Buxton), several coast guard stations. In Cape Hatteras Natl. Seashore. Sect. of State Highway 12 extends length of isl. except SW end.

Hattiesburg (HA-teez-buhrg), city (1990 pop. 41,882), ⊙ Forrest co., Forrest and Lamar cos., SE Miss., 83 mi/134 km SE of Jackson, on the Leaf R., at mouth of Bowie R.; 31°18′N 89°18′W. Major RR, trade, and industrial center in an agr. area (cotton, corn; poultry; timber); mfg. (sand and gravel processing, steel fabrication; lumber, industrial machinery, signs, resins, furniture, apparel, rubber, consumer goods, bldg. materials, food and beverages, chemicals). Pine Belt Regional Airport to N; Municipal Airport to SE. Seat of the Univ. of Southern Miss. and of William Carey Col. Camp Shelby Natl. Guard base to SE (mus.); All-Amer. Rose Garden; Hattiesburg Area Historical Society Mus.; Hattiesburg Arts Council Gall.; zoo at Kamper Park. De Soto Natl. Forest to SE; Paul B. Johnson State Park to S. Inc. 1884.

Hatton (HA-tuhn), town (1990 pop. 800), Traill co., E N.Dak., 30 mi/48 km SW of Grand Forks; 47°38′N 97°27′W. Grain; livestock. Site of Carl Ben Eielson Memorial Arch.

Hatton, village (1990 pop. 71), Adams co., SE Wash., 32 mi/51 km SW of Ritzville, in Columbia basin agr. region; 46°47′N 118°50′W. Wheat; cattle.

Hatton Fields, village, Monterey co., W Calif., near Carmel.

Hatuey (ah-too-WAI), town, Camagüey prov., E Cuba, on RR, and 27 mi/43 km ESE of Camagüey; 21°12′N 77°32′W. Sugarcane; cattle; lumber. Alfredo Alvarez Mola sugar mill is 2 mi/3.2 km S. Named after valiant indigenous warrior who fought Spaniards.

Hatzic (HAT-sik), village, SW B.C., W Canada, on Fraser R., and 14 mi/23 km W of Chilliwack. Lumbering; dairying; fruit, vegetables.

Haubstadt, town (1990 pop. 1,455), Gibson co., SW Ind., 10 mi/16 km S of Princeton; 38°12′N 87°34′W. In grain-growing area. Mfg. (meatpacking; specialty machinery).

Haugen (HOU-gan), village (1990 pop. 305), Barron co., NW Wis., SE of Bear L., 8 mi/12.9 km N of Rice L.; 45°36′N 91°46′W. Dairying. W terminus of Tuscobia State Trail to S.

Haughton (HO-tuhn), town (1990 pop. 1,664), Bossier parish, NW La., 15 mi/24 km E of Shreveport; 32°30′N 93°31′W. Cotton; timber; mfg. (pulpwood, propane). L. Bistineau State Park to SE. Barksdale Air Force Base to W.

Hauppauge (HAW-pawg), village (□ 10 sq mi/26 sq km; 1990 pop. 19,750), Suffolk co., SE N.Y., on central L.I., 2 mi/3.2 km SW of Smithtown Branch; 40°49′N 73°12′W. Major central L.I. mfg.-industrial region. Long association with aircraft and aerospace industries has created a technologically sophisticated concentration of electronic, electrical, metals, machinery, and fabrication businesses. Mfg. of instruments, parts, and supplies; also telecommunications, computers, and software.

Hauser, village (1990 pop. 380), Kootenai co., N Idaho, 12 mi/19 km WNW of Coeur d'Alene, near Wash. state line; 47°46′N 117°01′W. Small Hauser L. is N.

Hauser Dam (HOU-suhr), on the Missouri R., Lewis and Clark co., W Mont., 13 mi/21 km NE of Helena; 125 ft/38 m high. Built (1911) by the Mont. Power Co. for hydroelectric power. Impounds reservoir (L. Hauser) with max. capacity 109,470 acre-ft.

Hauser, Lake (HOU-suhr), reservoir, Lewis and Clark co., W central Mont., on Missouri R., 10 mi/16 km NE of Helena; c.15 mi/24 km long; 46°43′N 111°43′W. Canyon Ferry Dam at SE end. Channel (4 mi/6.4 km long), widening of Silver Creek, connects with L. Helena (SW). Formed by Hauser Dam (125 ft/38 m high). Helena Natl. Forest on E side; Hauser L. State Park on W side.

Haute, Île (OT, eel), islet in the Bay of Fundy, off N N.S., E Canada, in entrance of Minas Channel, 6 mi/10 km SW of Cape Chignecto; 45°15′N 65°00′W.

Hauula (HOU-OO-lah), town (1990 pop. 3,479), N Oahu isl., Honolulu co., Hawaii, on NE coast, 20 mi/32 km N of Honolulu; 21°35′N 157°55′W. Hauula Beach Park here; Hauula Forest Reserve to SW, Sacred Falls State Park to S.

Havana, Span. *La Habana*, city (1997 est. pop. 2,200,000), ⊙ both Cuba and Ciudad de la Habana prov., W Cuba; c.100 mi/161 km SSW of Key West (Fla.); 23°08′N 82°21′W. The largest city and chief port of the West Indies, and the political, economic, and cultural center of Cuba. Havana's climate is humid and subtropical (mean annual temp. is 76°F/24.5°C and average rainfall is 43 in/109 cm) but moderated by seawinds. Subject to occasional hurricanes. With one of the best natural harbors in the Caribbean Sea, it has long been strategically and commercially important. An important hub of air and maritime transportation, it is also the focal point of Cuban commerce and tourism, exporting sugar, tobacco, and fruits. Imports passing through its port include consumer durables, foodstuffs, cotton, machinery, and technical equip. Local industries include shipbuilding, light industries (mostly food processing and canning), biotechnology; also, assembly plants, rum distilleries, and factories making the famous Havana cigars. One of few Lat. Amer. capitals with light industry (e.g., tobacco factories) so close to govt. bldgs. (here, near the *Capitolio*, former capitol bldg.). Tourism has been greatly revived in the 1990s as Cuba redirects its economic model from central planning toward a mixed economy. Havana and Varadero (56 mi/90 km E) are now major tourist destinations. The collapse of trade and aid from the Soviet bloc in the late 1980s led to a new, receptive attitude toward foreign (Western) investment. Founded 1st in 1516 on S coast of Cuba, then on N coast c.4.3 mi/7 km from current site near mouth of Almendares R., later re-established on W side of Havana Bay (1519). One of 7 original settlements (*villas*) of Diego Velázquez, Span. conquistador and 1st colonial governor of Cuba. Havana became capital in the late 16th cent. Span. galleons assembled in Havana's harbor for their return voyage to Spain, combining cargo from Mexico, Panama, and Colombia. Privateers from other Eur. countries preyed on these galleons and raided many Cuban towns during the 17th and 18th cent. Havana fell to Anglo-Amer. forces in 1762, but was returned to Spain the following year, partly in exchange for Florida. By the early 19th cent., Havana was among the wealthiest commercial centers in the Western Hemisphere. It benefited greatly from the out-migration of Haitian Fr. and Creole sugar barons fleeing the 1792 slave revolt. As the 19th cent. progressed, the city was caught up in the anti-Span. independence movement. The Span.-Amer. War was precipitated by the destruction of the U.S. battleship *Maine* in Havana harbor in 1898, and Amer. troops occupied the city. The U.S. set up administrative hq. here (1898–1902), modernizing ports, roads (including the W extension of the seaside promenade, the Malécon), public lighting, communications, and sanitary conditions (eliminating yellow fever). Until 1959, the close relations bet. the U.S. and Cuba were strongly reflected in the commercial and cultural life of the city and Havana's hotels and entertainment made it a popular winter resort for Amer. tourists until that year. Although almost entirely a city of hard-working merchants and civil servants, Havana was also part of an illicit triangle of gambling, prostitution, and political corruption that included Las Vegas (Nev.) and Miami (Fla.). After the govt. of Fidel Castro took control, the Amer. presence was replaced by that of the USSR, which provided favorable terms of trade and foreign aid through the late 1980s. Castro's policy of directing economic resources toward rural areas and smaller urban centers led to the deterioration of Havana, esp. the old city (Habana Vieja). Restoration efforts have been spotty, despite the fact that in 1982, UNESCO declared Habana Vieja and an adjacent network of fortresses (El Morro, La Punta, La Cabaña, La Fuerza Real, Príncipe) a World Heritage Site. In 1994, a joint-venture firm (*empresa mixta*) called Habanaguex, began controlling about a dozen restaurants and small hotels in and around Habana Vieja in an attempt to generate hard currency that, in turn, would be used for improvements to the old quarters. Havana harbor is one of the most polluted in the Americas due to the activities of oil refineries in the back bay dist. of Regla. The city has a diverse collection of colonial, baroque, neoclassical, Art Deco, and Modern bldgs. Most of the city's housing stock, however, reflects modest 20th-cent. bldgs., giving the city a remarkably uniform skyline. Although much in need of repair, Havana is expected to be refurbished through foreign investment and internatl. tourism. Since 1993, over 100 types of private-sector employment jobs have been approved by the govt., stimulating small-scale business growth both here and in the rest of the country.

Havana, city (1990 pop. 3,610), ⊙ Mason co., central Ill., on Illinois R. (shipping), opposite mouth of Spoon R., and 32 mi/51 km SW of Peoria; 40°17′N 90°03′W. Trade, shipping, and industrial center in agr. area; mfg. (food prods., metal prods.). Important river port in early 19th cent. Site of Lincoln-Douglas debate is marked. Nearby are resorts on lakes along Illinois R., Chautauqua Natl. Wildlife Refuge, and Dickson Mounds Mus. Founded 1827, inc. 1853.

Havana (huh-VAN-nah), town (☐ 1 sq mi/2.6 sq km; 1990 pop. 1,654), Gadsden co., NW Fla., near Ga. state line, 15 mi/24 km NW of Tallahassee; 30°37′N 84°25′W. Canned foods (fruit, vegetables); feed, fertilizer. Settled 1904, inc. 1906.

Havana 1 (huh-VA-nuh), village (1990 pop. 358), Yell co., W central Ark., 25 mi/40 km WSW of Russellville; 35°06′N 93°31′W. Magazine Mt., highest point in Ark. (2,753 ft/839 m), 4 mi/6.4 km N, in Logan co. Nearby are Ozark (N) and Ouachita (S) natl. forests. **2** village (1990 pop. 121), Montgomery co., SE Kansas, 15 mi/24 km SW of Independence; 37°05′N 95°56′W. In livestock and grain area. Oil field here. **3** village (1990 pop. 124), Sargent co., SE N.Dak., 11 mi/18 km S of Forman, at S.Dak. state line; 45°57′N 97°37′W. (Sisseton) Wahpeton Indian Reservation to E.

Havasu City, Ariz.: see LAKE HAVASU CITY.

Havasu Lake, on Colorado R., on the border bet. W Ariz. and SE Calif., formed by Parker Dam, 60 mi/97 km S of Kingman (Ariz.); c.45 mi/72 km long. Its headwaters extend c.50 mi/80 km from dam, to near Needles (Calif.). Maximum capacity 717,000 acre-ft. Formed by Parker Dam. Chemehueva Indian Reservation on W shore; parts of Havasu Natl. Wildlife Refuge on NE shore and E of dam. Lake Havasu City (Ariz.) on E shore. Bill Williams R. enters from E, near dam.

Havelock (HAV-lahk), city (1990 pop. 20,268), Craven co., E N.C., 18 mi/29 km SE of New Bern, near Neuse R. estuary (to N), in Croatan Natl. Forest; 34°54′N 76°53′W. RR junction. Mfg. (printing and publishing; apparel). Service center for Cherry Point Marine Corps Air Station, to N. Swampy area with several natural lakes to W, including Catfish, Long, Great, and Ellis Simon lakes.

Havelock, town (1990 pop. 217), Pocahontas co., N central Iowa, 6 mi/9.7 km N of Pocahontas; 42°49′N 94°42′W. Livestock; grain.

Havelock (HAV-lahk), village (1991 pop. 1,376), SE Ont., central Canada, 23 mi/37 km ENE of Peterborough. Dairying; mfg. of fishing tackle.

Havelock (HA-vuh-lawk), N suburb, 4 mi/6.4 km NE of downtown Lincoln, Lancaster co., SE Nebr. Industrial base. City annexed to Lincoln 1930.

Haven (HAI-ven), town (1990 pop. 1,198), Reno co., S central Kansas, 13 mi/21 km SE of Hutchinson, near Arkansas R.; 37°53′N 97°46′W. In wheat region. Mfg. (fabricated metal prods.). Cheney Reservoir and Cheney State Park to S.

Havensville (HAI-venz-vil), village (1990 pop. 135), Pottawatomie co., NE Kansas, 18 mi/29 km NE of Westmoreland; 39°30′N 96°04′W. Cattle; grain.

Haverford (HA-vuh-fuhrd), township (1990 pop. 49,848), Delaware co., SE Pa., W residential suburb 7 mi/11.3 km W of downtown Philadelphia; 40°00′N 75°17′W. Bounded E by Cobbs Creek. Some mfg. Includes villages of Havertown, Llanerch, Beechwood, Manoa, Preston, Penfield, Brookline, South Ardmore, Oakmont, and part of Drexel Hill (partly in Upper Darby township). Seat of Haverford Col. Arboretum in N. Village of Haverford is to E in Montgomery co.

Haverhill (HAI-vruhl), city (1990 pop. 51,418), Essex co., NE Mass., on the Merrimack R.; 42°47′N 71°05′W. Formerly one of the nation's leading shoe producers, Haverhill processes leather and makes leather, textile, and paper prods. High-technology computer industries in the area and the mfg. of electronic components add to the city's economic base. Skiing at Ward Hill. Points of interest are John Greenleaf Whittier's birthplace (the house dates from c.1688) and the home of Hannah Dustin. Seat of the Haverhill branch of Northeastern Univ., Bradford Col., and a community col. Includes sect. of Bradford. Inc. as a town 1641, as a city 1870.

Haverhill (HAI-vruhl), town (1990 pop. 4,164), Grafton co., W N.H., 22 mi/35 km W of Littleton; 44°04′N 72°00′W. Bounded by Connecticut R. (Vt. state line); drained by Oliverian and Clark brooks. RR terminus. Agr. (dairying; cattle, poultry; nursery crops; timber); mfg. (wood prods.). Includes Woodsville village in NW; site of Bedell Bridge State Park is here (covered bridge); Black Mt. State Forest in NE. Inc. 1763.

Haverhill, village (1990 pop. 144), Marshall co., central Iowa, 8 mi/12.9 km SSW of Marshalltown; 41°56′N 92°57′W. Agr. area (corn, oats; cattle, hogs).

Haverstraw (HA-vuhr-straw), village (☐ 5 sq mi/13 sq km; 1990 pop. 9,438), Rockland co., SE N.Y., on W bank of the Hudson R., and 6 mi/9.7 km NW of Ossining; 41°11′N 73°57′W. Mfg. (furniture, textiles, consumer goods, wire and cable); stone quarrying. Commuter suburb. Inc. 1854.

Havertown (HA-vuhr-toun), uninc. town, Delaware co., SE Pa., residential suburb 7 mi/11.3 km W of Philadelphia, near Cobbs Creek; 39°58′N 75°18′W. Mfg. includes printing and publishing, and light diversified mfg.

Haviland 1 (HA-vi-land), village (1990 pop. 624), Kiowa co., S Kansas, 20 mi/32 km W of Pratt; 37°37′N 99°06′W. In grain and livestock region. **2** village (1990 pop. 210), Paulding co., NW Ohio, 10 mi/16 km N of Van Wert; 41°01′N 84°35′W.

Havre (HAI-vuhr), city (1990 pop. 10,201), ⊙ Hill co., N Mont., on the Milk R. (forms Fresno Reservoir to NW); 48°32′N 109°41′W. Wheat, hay; cattle, sheep, hogs. Mfg. (agr. equip., bldg. materials); gas and oil field to SE (Blaine co.). Ft. Assinniboine (1879) and Agr. Research Center to SW. Rocky Boy's Indian Reservation to S. Wahkpa Chu'qn Archaeological Site and L. Thibadeau Natl. Wildlife Refuge to N. Earl H. Clack Memorial Mus. and units of Rookery Wildlife Management Area to W. Founded in 1891 with the coming of the RR. The area is served by the Milk R. project. Seat of Mont. State Univ.-Northern. Originally called Bull Hook Bottoms. Inc. 1892.

Havre Aubert (AH-vruh o-BER) or **Amherst**, village, E Que., E Canada, on E Amherst Isl., one of the Magdalen Isls.; 47°15′N 61°50′W. Fishing port.

Havre aux Maisons, Canada: see HOUSE HARBOUR.

Havre Boucher (AH-vruh boo-SHAI) or **Harbour au Bouche** (HAHR-buhr o BOOSH), village, E N.S., E Canada, on George Bay, 22 mi/35 km ENE of Antigonish; 45°39′N 61°31′W. Fishing.

Havre de Grace, city (1990 pop. 8,952), Harford co., NE Md., on Chesapeake Bay, at mouth of the Susquehanna R. (bridged 1940), and 33 mi/53 km NE of Baltimore; 39°33′N 76°06′W. Trade center for agr. area (vegetables, esp. tomatoes; fruit, corn; dairy prods.; poultry), with granite quarries. Canneries; commercial fisheries. Resort center; sport fishing, yachting (annual July regatta), duck hunting (on nearby Susquehanna Flats). Nearby are Federal reservations (Aberdeen Proving Ground, Army Chemical Center, Perry Point Veterans' Hosp.). First settled in 1650 and known as Susquehanna Lower Ferry, the town was est. 1785.

Havre Saint Pierre (AH-vruh sa PYER), village (1991 pop. 3,502), E Que., E Canada, on the St. Lawrence R., and 19 mi/31 km ESE of Mingan; 50°15′N 63°35′W. Titanium center; trading post.

Haw Knob, Tenn. and N.C.: see UNICOI MOUNTAINS.

Haw River, town (1990 pop. 1,855), Alamance co., N central N.C., on Haw R., and suburb 4 mi/6.4 km E of Burlington; 36°05′N 79°21′W. Tobacco, grain, potatoes, sweet potatoes; chickens, hogs; dairying. Mfg. (textiles, rubber prods.). Settled 1747.

Haw River, c.110 mi/177 km long, N central N.C.; rises NW of Greensboro in NW Guilford co.; flows E and SSE, past town of Haw River, E of Burlington, through Jordan L. reservoir, where New Hope R. joins it from N, forming larger part of reservoir, before joining Deep R. near Haywood to form Cape Fear R.

Hawaii (hah-WEI-ee), state (☐ 10,931 sq mi/28,311 sq km; 1995 est. pop. 1,186,815), central Pacific, admitted to the Union in 1959 as the 50th state; ⊙ HONOLULU (on OAHU); 21°13′N 156°56′W. Consists of a group of 8 major isls. and numerous islets in the Pacific Ocean, c.2,100 mi/3,380 km SW of San Francisco. Hawaii isl., referred to locally as "the Big Isl.," is the largest and geologically the youngest of the group, and Oahu is the most populous and economically important. The other principal isls. are KAHOOLAWE, KAUAI, LANAI, MAUI, MOLOKAI, and NIIHAU. The PALMYRA atoll and Kingman Reef, which were within the boundaries of Hawaii when it was a U.S. territory, were excluded when statehood was achieved. The Hawaiian Isls. are of volcanic origin and are edged with coral reefs. Generally fertile with a mild climate, they are sometimes called "the paradise of the Pacific" because of their spectacular beauty; abundant sunshine; acres of green plants and gaily colored flowers; coral beaches with rolling white surf and fringed with palms; and, rising with sober majesty to solitary heights, cloud-covered volcanic peaks. Some of the world's largest active and inactive volcanoes are found on Hawaii and Maui; eruptions of the active volcanoes have provided spectacular displays but their lava flows have occasionally caused great property damage. Mauna Kea and Mauna Loa are volcanic mts. on Hawaii isl.; Haleakala volcano is on Maui in HALEAKALA NATIONAL PARK. Vegetation is generally luxuriant below 6,500 ft/1,981 m elev. on windward NE exposures, with giant fern forests in HAWAII VOLCANOES NATIONAL PARK. Seasonally arid growth prevails on leeward SW slope and low-lying isls. Niihau, Kahoolawe, and W Molokai. Mt. slopes above 6,500 ft/1,981 m are very arid. Although many species of birds and domestic animals have been introduced on the isls., there are few wild animals other than feral boars and goats, and there are no snakes. The coastal waters abound with fish. Sugarcane and pineapples, grown chiefly on large company-owned plantations, have long been the major agr. prods. and the basis of the isls.' principal industry, food processing, but are declining from competition from other countries. Other prods. include macadamia nuts, bananas, avocados, and other fruits and vegetables, coffee, dairy prods.; cattle and calves. Commercial fishing is also prevalent; tuna is the principal species caught. U.S. military defense installations at PEARL HARBOR and elsewhere in the state are extremely important to Hawaii's economy. Tourism is the leading source of income. The 1st known settlers of the Hawaiian Isls. were Polynesian voyagers (the date of 1st migration is believed to be A.D. c.750). The isls. were 1st visited by Europeans in 1778 by the Eng. explorer Capt. James Cook, who named them the Sandwich Isls. for the Eng. earl of Sandwich. At that time the isls. were under the rule of warring native kings. In 1810, Kamehameha I became the sole sovereign of all the isls., and, in the peace that followed, agr. and commerce were promoted. As a result of Kamehameha's hospitality, Amer. traders were able to exploit the isls.' sandalwood, which was much valued in China at the time. Trade with

China reached its peak during this period. However, the period of Kamehameha's rule was also one of decline. Europeans and Americans brought with them devastating infectious diseases, and over the years the native pop. was greatly reduced. The adoption of Western ways contributed to the decline of native cultural tradition. This period also marked the breakdown of the traditional Hawaiian religion; years of religious unrest followed. When missionaries arrived from Boston in 1820 they found a less idyllic Hawaii than the one Captain Cook had discovered. Kamehameha III, who ruled 1825–1854, relied on the missionaries for advice and allowed them to preach Christianity. The missionaries established schools, developed the Hawaiian alphabet, and used it for translating the Bible into Hawaiian. In 1839, Kamehameha III issued a guarantee of religious freedom, and the following year a constitutional monarchy was established. From 1842 to 1854 an Amer., G. P. Judd, held the post of prime minister, and under his influence many reforms were carried out. In the following decades commercial ties bet. Hawaii and the U.S. increased. In 1848 the isls.' feudal land system was abolished, making private ownership possible and thereby encouraging capital investment in the land. By this time the sugar industry, which had been introduced in the 1830s, was well established. Hawaiian sugar gained a favored position in U.S. markets under a reciprocity treaty made with the U.S. in 1875. The treaty was renewed in 1884 but not ratified. Ratification came in 1887 when an amendment was added giving the U.S. exclusive rights to establish a naval base at Pearl Harbor. The amount of sugar exported to the U.S. increased greatly, and Amer. businessmen began to invest in the Hawaiian sugar industry. Along with the Hawaiians in the industry, they came to exert powerful influence over the isls.' economy and govt., a dominance that was to last until World War II. Toward the end of the 19th cent., agitation for constitutional reform in Hawaii led to the overthrow (1893) of Queen Liliuokalani, who had ruled since 1891. A provisional govt. was established and John L. Stevens, the U.S. minister to Hawaii, proclaimed the country a U.S. protectorate. President Grover Cleveland, however, refused to annex Hawaii since most Hawaiians did not support a revolution; the Hawaiians and Americans in the sugar industry had aggravated the overthrow of the monarchy to serve their business needs. The U.S. tried to bring about the restoration of Queen Liliuokalani, but the provisional govt. on the isls. refused to give up power and instead established (1894) a republic with Sanford B. Dole as president. Cleveland's successor, President William McKinley, favored annexation, which was finally accomplished in 1898. In 1900 the isls. were made a territory, with Dole as governor. In this period, Hawaii's pineapple industry expanded as pineapples were 1st grown for canning purposes. In 1937 statehood for Hawaii was proposed and refused by the U.S. Congress — the territory's mixed pop. and distance from the U.S. mainland were among the obstacles. On Dec. 7, 1941, Jap. aircraft made a surprise attack on Pearl Harbor, plunging the U.S. into World War II. During the war the Hawaiian Isls. were the chief Pacific base for U.S. forces and were under martial law (Dec. 7, 1941–March 1943). The post-war years ushered in important economic and social developments. There was a dramatic expansion of labor unionism, marked by major strikes in 1946, 1949, and 1958. The Internatl. Longshoremen's and Warehousemen's Union organized the waterfront, sugar, and pineapple workers. The tourist trade, which had grown to major proportions in the 1930s, expanded further with post-war advances in air travel and with further investment and development. The building boom brought about new construction of luxury hotels and housing developments; Hawaii is home to the world's most expensively built resort, the Hyatt Regency Waikoloa, which cost $360 million to construct. More ethnic and cultural groups are represented in Hawaii than in any other state. Chin. laborers, who came to work in the sugar industry, were the 1st of the large groups of immigrants to arrive (starting in 1852), and Filipinos and Koreans were the last (after 1900). Other immigrant groups — including Portuguese, Germans, Japanese, and Puerto Ricans — came in the latter part of the 19th cent. Intermarriage with other races has brought a further decrease in the number of pure-blooded Hawaiians, who comprise a very small percentage of the pop. After having sought statehood for many decades, Hawaii was finally admitted to the Union on Aug. 21, 1959. In 1969 the construction of a new state capitol was completed. Hawaii's constitution was drafted in 1950 and became effective in 1959 upon attainment of statehood. A governor elected every 4 years heads the executive. The legislature has a senate with 25 members elected for 4-year terms and a house of representatives with 51 members elected for 2-year terms. The state elects 2 representatives and 2 senators to the U.S. Congress and has 4 electoral votes. Hawaii has long been known as a Democratic state. John A. Burns, a Democrat, was elected governor in 1962 and reelected in 1966 and 1970. Daniel Inouye, a Democratic Hawaiian senator of Jap. descent elected in 1962, was the chairman of the Iran-Contra Committee 1987–1988. The Univ. of Hawaii is located at Honolulu. In 1961 the Center for Cultural and Technical Interchange bet. East and West was dedicated at the univ. and drew graduate students and technical trainees from Asia and the Pacific area.

Hawaii (hah-WEI-ee), county (□ 5,086 sq mi/ 13,173 sq km; 1990 pop. 120,317), coextensive with isl. of Hawaii, SE Hawaii; ⊙ Hilo; 19°36'N 155°30'W. Largest co. in Hawaii. Includes several small coastal islets, esp. along NE coast. Divided into 12 administrative dists.; there are no incorporated cities.

Hawaii (hah-WEI-ee), island (□ 4,034 sq mi/ 10,448 sq km; 1990 pop. 120,217), largest and southernmost isl. of the state of Hawaii and coextensive with Hawaii co. (which also includes a few coastal islets). Hamakua Coast on NE, Kona Coast on W, Kohala Coast on NW, Kohala Peninsula in N. Geologically the youngest of the Hawaiian group, Hawaii is made up of 5 volcanic mt. masses rising from the floor of the Pacific Ocean — Mauna Kea (13,800 ft/4,205 m above sea level, the highest point in the state); (N) Mauna Loa (13,677 ft/4,169 m), center of isl.; Hualalai (8,275 ft/ 2,522 m) in W; Kohala (5,489 ft/1,673 m) in NW; and Kilauea (4,090 ft/1,247 m) in SE. Ka Lae (South Point) is southernmost point in the U.S. Lava flows, some of which reach the sea, and volcanic ash cover parts of the isl. The N and NE coasts are rugged with high cliffs; the W and S coasts are generally low, with some good beaches. An unusual black-sand beach of volcanic origin lies on the SE coast at Punaluu. Has numerous (over 20) forest reserves, largest being Kohala (N); Mauna Kea, Mauna Loa, and Kapapala (center); Kau (S); Hilo, Upper Waiakea, and Puna (E). Short rivers radiate from the major summits; Wailuku R., the longest, flows into Hilo Bay. Many waterfalls are on the isl. Much of Hawaii has a tropical-rainy climate, with the N and E slopes receiving the most rain. The W and S slopes are much drier; the Kau Desert is in S Hawaii. Temperatures decrease with elevation; Mauna Loa and Mauna Kea are usually snow-covered in winter. Vegetation varies from tropical rain forest to grasslands to barren volcanic areas. Sugarcane, the isl.'s principal product, is no longer harvested. Macadamia nuts and other fruits, vegetables, flowers, coffee, and beef cattle remain important (Parker Ranch in N; □ 313 sq mi/ 811 sq km). The Kona dist. of W Hawaii is the coffee belt of the U.S. and is also known for its resorts and offshore deep-sea fishing. Hilo, on the E coast, is the isl.'s largest city, 2d-largest city in Hawaii, chief port, and is the co. seat. Hawaii Belt Road, a highway linking the coastal towns, encircles the isl. At Kealakekua Bay on W coast there is a monument to Capt. James Cook, the 1st Eng. explorer to visit (1778) the Hawaiian isls. HAWAII VOLCANOES NATIONAL PARK in the SE and City of Refuge (Pu'uhonua o Honaunau) Natl. Historical Park are on Hawaii. All over the isl. *heiaus* (anc. temples) are found. Puukohola Heiau Natl. Historic Site in NW. Wailuku R. and Wailoa R. state parks at Hilo, in E; Lapakahi State Historic Park in NW; Lava Tree State Monument in E; Kalopa State Recreational Area in N; Old Kona Airport State Park on W coast; Kealakekua State Underwater Park on W coast; Mauna Kea State Recreational Area in N center; Kilauea State Recreational Area in SE center; Kaloko-Honokokau Natl. Historic Park on W (Kona) coast; Pohakuloa Military Training Area in N center; the Puna Dist. 10 mi/16 km S of Hilo has several semirural residential developments, including Hawaiian Acres, Hawaiian Beaches, Orchid Land Estates, Hawaiian Paradise Parks.

Hawaii Ocean View Estates, village (1990 pop. 450), S Hawaii, 57 mi/92 km SW of Hilo, 6 mi/9.7 km inland from Ka Lae (SW) Coast, on Hawaii Belt Road, opposite Hawaiian Ranchos. Kapua-Manuka Forest Reserve to NW. Located on barren lava at S end of Southwest Rift Zone of Mauna Loa. Residential community.

Hawaii Volcanoes National Park (□ 355 sq mi/ 919 sq km), on Hawaii isl., Hawaii co., Hawaii, generally 20 mi/32 km–25 mi/40 km SW of Hilo, extending near center of isl. to SE coast; includes smaller unit 15 mi/24 km SW of Hilo. Est. 1916 as Hawaii Natl. Park. The NW extension of park includes Mauna Loa at W end, reached by trail from Hawaii Belt Road; SE coastal sect. includes Kilauea in N, the Great Crack, and Kau Desert in W, Chain of Craters in E. The park contains 2 of the most active volcanoes in the world — KILAUEA with Halemaumau Crater, and MAUNA LOA with the active Mokuaweoweo crater on its summit. Active lava flows just beyond park's E boundary have destroyed coastal access to park on Chain of Craters Road. The vegetation around Kilauea is varied — a few miles W of the arid Kau Desert is a lush fern jungle. Park renamed 1960. The Haleakala sect. (Maui Isl.) was made a separate park in 1961.

Hawaiian Gardens, city (1990 pop. 13,639), Los Angeles co., S Calif., residential suburb 16 mi/26 km SE of downtown Los Angeles, and 7 mi/11.3 km NE of downtown Long Beach, near San Gabriel R.; 33°50'N 118°04'W. Los Alamitos Naval Air Station to S. Mfg. (confections, aircraft parts). City finances depend largely on income from tax-free bingo parlor.

Hawarden (hai-WAHR-duhn), village (1991 pop. 102), S central Sask., W Canada, 50 mi/80 km S of Saskatoon; 51°25'N 106°36'W. Grain elevators.

Hawesville (HAWZ-vil), town (1990 pop. 998), ⊙ Hancock co., NW Ky., 23 mi/37 km ENE of Owensboro, on the Ohio R. (bridge to Cannelton, Ind.); 37°53'N 86°45'W. Shipping point for agr. area (burley and dark tobacco, corn, wheat); mfg. (primary aluminum production; fabricated metal prods., paper and pulp). Co. Mus. in historic depot (1903). Cannelton Locks and Dam to E, on Ohio R. Est. 1836.

Hawi (HAH-VEE), town (1990 pop. 924), N Hawaii isl., Hawaii co., Hawaii, near Upolu Point, NW tip of Kohala Peninsula, 59 mi/95 km NW of Hilo, 1.5 mi/2.4 km inland from N coast; 20°14'N 155°49'W. Upolu Airport, at Upolu Point, to NW. Mookini Heiau (Temple) State Monument and King Kamehameha I Birthplace State Memorial to W at Limukoko Point. Puuokumau Reservoir to S.

Hawk Peak (10,627 ft/3,239 m), Graham co., SE Ariz., in Pinaleno Mts., near Mt. Graham, 13 mi/21 km SW of Safford.

Hawk Point, town (1990 pop. 472), Lincoln co., E Mo., near West Fork of Cuivre R., 8 mi/12.9 km W of Troy; 38°58'N 91°07'W. Meat processing.

Hawk Run, uninc. town (1990 pop. 900), Clearfield co., central Pa., 2 mi/3.2 km NE of Phillipsburg, near Moshannon Creek; 40°55'N 78°12'W.

Hawke's Harbour, settlement, on Hawke Isl. (5 mi/8 km long, 5 mi/8 km wide), just off SE Lab., NE Canada; 53°01'N 55°50'W. Lumbering.

Hawkesbury, town (1991 pop. 9,706), SE Ont., central Canada, on the Ottawa R.; 45°37'N 74°36'W. Lumber and paper mills; mfg. of clothing, glass, and prefabricated homes.

Hawkesbury Island (□ 159 sq mi/412 sq km), W B.C., W Canada, in Douglas Channel (N arm of Hecate

Strait), just N of Gribbell Isl.; 27 mi/43 km long, 2 mi/ 3 km–12 mi/19 km wide.

Hawkeye, town (1990 pop. 460), Fayette co., NE Iowa, 7 mi/11.3 km WSW of West Union; 42°56′N 91°57′W. In agr. area.

Hawkins, county (□ 494 sq mi/1,279 sq km; 1990 pop. 44,565), NE Tenn.; ⊙ Rogersville; 36°27′N 82°57′W. Bordered N by Va.; traversed by Clinch and Bays mts., ridges of the Appalachians; drained by Holston R. Includes part of Cherokee Reservoir. Hardwood timber; agr. (tobacco, corn, fruit, hay); livestock; dairying; industrial sand. Dimension marble from here was used in the Washington Monument. Formed 1786.

Hawkins, town (1990 pop. 1,309), Wood co., NE Texas, on Sabine R., 17 mi/27 km N of Tyler; 32°35′N 95°12′W. In oil and agr. area; mfg. (gasoline). L. Hawkins to NW.

Hawkins, village (1990 pop. 375), Rusk co., N Wis., 19 mi/ 31 km ENE of Ladysmith; 45°30′N 90°42′W. Dairying; livestock raising; farming. Woodworking; mfg. (wood prods.). Flambeau R. State Forest to N.

Hawkins Peak (10,024 ft/3,055 m), Alpine co., E Calif., in the Sierra Nevada, c.15 mi/24 km S of L. Tahoe; flanks Ebbetts Pass on S.

Hawkinsville, town (1990 pop. 3,527), ⊙ Pulaski co., S central Ga., on Ocmulgee R., and 39 mi/63 km SSE of Macon; 32°17′N 83°28′W. Mfg. includes meatpacking; confections, textiles; lumber mills. Inc. 1830.

Hawks Nest State Park, W.Va.: see GAULEY BRIDGE.

Hawksbill Mountain, peak (4,049 ft/1,234 m) of the Blue Ridge Mts., N Va., 8 mi/12.9 km SSE of Luray; highest point in Shenandoah Natl. Park and of Blue Ridge (N of Waynesboro).

Hawley 1 town (1990 pop. 317), Franklin co., NW Mass., 15 mi/24 km W of Greenfield; 42°35′N 72°55′W. In hilly area. Fruit. Dubuque Memorial State Forest nearby. **2** town (1990 pop. 1,655), Clay co., W Minn., 20 mi/ 37 km E of Fargo, N.Dak., near Buffalo R.; 46°52′N 96°19′W. Mfg. (printing and publishing; foods, machinery). Barnsville Wildlife Area to S; Buffalo R. State Park to W; small lakes to E; state game refuge nearby. Settled c.1870.

Hawley, village (1990 pop. 606), Jones co., W central Texas, 14 mi/23 km NNW of Abilene, on Clear Fork of the Brazos R.; 32°36′N 99°48′W. Agr. area (grain, cotton, watermelons; cattle). L. Fort Phantom Hill to E.

Hawley, borough (1990 pop. 1,244), Wayne co., NE Pa., 8 mi/12.9 km SSE of Honesdale, on Lackawaxen R., at mouth of Middle Creek. Mfg. (printing and publishing; sheet metal fabricating; consumer goods). L. Wallenpaupack reservoir, resort area, to SW. Numerous residential developments in area, especially W and SW; Tanglewood Ski Area to S; part of Del. State Forest to SE. Settled 1803, inc. 1884.

Haworth (HAI-wuhrth), village (1990 pop. 293), McCurtain co., extreme SE Okla., 10 mi/16 km ESE of Idabel; 33°50′N 94°39′W. Located in unit of Ouachita Natl. Forest.

Haworth (HAW-wuhrth), borough (1990 pop. 3,384), Bergen co., NE N.J., 10 mi/16 km ENE of Paterson; 40°57′N 74°00′W. Inc. 1894.

Hawthorn (HAW-thorn), borough (1990 pop. 528), Clarion co., W central Pa., 14 mi/23 km SSE of Clarion, on Red Bank Creek. Agr. (corn, hay, potatoes; dairying).

Hawthorn Woods, village (1990 pop. 4,423), Lake co., NE Ill., residential suburb 33 mi/53 km NW of downtown Chicago, 4 mi/6.4 km NE of Lake Zurich town; 42°13′N 88°03′W.

Hawthorne, city (1990 pop. 71,349), Los Angeles co., S Calif., a suburb 10 mi/16 km SW of downtown Los Angeles, 4 mi/6.4 km E of Pacific Ocean coast (Manhattan State Beach); 33°55′N 118°21′W. In an oil- and gas-producing area. Has large-scale mfg. of navigation systems, solar panels, electronic components, silicon instruments, transportation equip. Hawthorne Municipal Airport, Los Angeles Internatl. Airport to NW. Inc. 1922.

Hawthorne 1 (HAW-thorn), town (1990 pop. 1,305), Alachua co., N central Fla., 12 mi/19 km SE of Gainesville; 29°35′N 82°05′W. **2** uninc. town (1990 pop. 4,162), ⊙ Mineral co., W Nev., near Walker L., 90 mi/145 km

SE of Reno; 38°31′N 118°37′W. Elev. 4,320 ft/1,317 m. U.S. naval arsenal and ammunition depot surrounds town, except on SW. Tourist center; gold, silver, sand and gravel; mfg. (drilling services); cattle. Old mining town of Aurora is c.40 mi/64 km SW. Wassuk Range W. Yosemite Natl. Park (Calif.) 50 mi/80 km to SW. Part of Toiyabe Natl. Forest and Wassuk Range to SW. Walker L. to NW; Walker L. State Recreational Area on W shore. Inc. c.1940.

Hawthorne, village (□ 1 sq mi/2.6 sq km; 1990 pop. 4,764), Westchester co., SE N.Y., 6 mi/9.7 km N of White Plains, near Kensico Reservoir (E); 41°06′N 73°47′W. Mfg. (jewelry, laboratory equip., electrical equip., chemicals, fabricated metal prods., ultraviolet absorbers).

Hawthorne (HAW-thorn), borough (1990 pop. 17,084), Passaic co., NE N.J.; 40°57′N 74°09′W. Residential suburb, with some light mfg. Settled 1850, inc. 1898.

Haxtun, town (1990 pop. 982), Phillips co., NE Colo., near South Platte R., 17 mi/27 km WNW of Holyoke; 40°38′N 102°37′W. Elev. 4,028 ft/1,228 m. Shipping point in irrigated grain, sugar beet, and cattle region. In Sand Hills area.

Hay, river, c.530 mi/850 km long, W Canada; rises in several headstreams in NE B.C. and NW Alta.; flows generally NE through NW Alta., over Alexander Falls, and into Great Slave L. Its valley, a principal N-S route, is followed by a highway and a RR.

Hay, Cape 1 N extremity of Baffin Isl., E Franklin dist., N.W.T., N Canada, on Lancaster Sound; 73°53′N 79°49′W. **2** S extremity of Melville Isl., W Franklin dist., N.W.T., N Canada, on McClure Strait; 74°24′N 113°08′W. **3** NW extremity of Bylot Isl., E Franklin dist., N.W.T., N Canada, at E entrance of Lancaster Sound; 73°53′N 79°49′W.

Hay Lakes, village (1991 pop. 327), central Alta., W Canada, on small Little Hay L., 30 mi/48 km SE of Edmonton; 53°12′N 113°03′W. Mixed farming, dairying.

Hay, Mount (8,870 ft/2,704 m), on U.S. (Alaska)–Canada (B.C.) border, St. Elias Mts., 75 mi/121 km ESE of Yakutak; 59°15′N 137°36′W.

Hay River, town (1991 pop. 3,206), S Mackenzie dist., N.W.T., N Canada, on SW shore of Great Slave L., at mouth of Hay R., 70 mi/113 km WSW of Fort Resolution; 60°51′N 118°44′W. Terminus of Great Slave RR (completed 1964) and of paved highway from Alta. Transfer point and lake port for supply barges that go to points on lake and Mackenzie R. Hudson Bay Co. fur trading post (est. 1868); transshipment point for Yellowknife region, at N end of road from railhead at Grimshaw (Alta.). Airfield, govt. radio, TV, and meteorological stations; site of Anglican and R.C. mission and hosp. Fishing, trapping; service industries; oats and vegetables are grown. Scheduled air service. Former lead-zinc mine at nearby Pine Point (closed 1987). Town has 17-story apartment bldg., tallest bldg. in N.W.T.

Hay River, river, c.50 mi/80 km long, NW Wis.; rises in Beaverdam L. (Barron co.); flows S to Red Cedar R. (Tainter L.), 8 mi/12.9 km N of Menomonie.

Hay Springs, village (1990 pop. 693), Sheridan co., NW Nebr., 20 mi/32 km SE of Chadron; 42°40′N 102°41′W. Livestock; dairy prods.; grain, potatoes in irrigated Mirage Flats. Collection of prehistoric bones is here. Pine Ridge unit of Nebr. Natl. Forest to W (in Butte co.); Walgren L. State Recreation Area to SE.

Haycock, village, W Alaska, SE Seward Peninsula, near Koyuk R., 18 mi/29 km N of Koyuk.

Hayden 1 town (1990 pop. 385), Blount co., N central Ala., 18 mi/29 km WNW of Oneonta. **2** town (1990 pop. 909), Gila and Pinal cos., SE central Ariz., on Gila R., 3 mi/4.8 km NW of confluence with San Pedro R., 55 mi/89 km NNE of Tucson; 33°00′N 110°46′W. Copper smelting; lime; cattle, sheep. San Carlos Indian Reservation to E; Ray Mine (open pit copper mine) to N. **3** town (1990 pop. 1,444), Routt co., NW Colo., on Yampa R., W of Park Range, and 22 mi/35 km W of Steamboat Springs; 40°29′N 107°15′W. Elev. 6,337 ft/ 1,932 m. Coal mining. Shipping point in sheep and cattle region. Parts of Routt Natl. Forest to N and S; Elkhead Reservoir to NW. **4** town (1990 pop. 3,744),

Kootenai co., N Idaho, suburb 4 mi/6.4 km N of Coeur d'Alene, near Hayden L.; 47°46′N 116°48′W. Mfg. (embroidered logos, electrical and electronic equip., fabricated metal prods., lumber.

Hayden Lake, village (1990 pop. 338), Kootenai co., N Idaho, 8 mi/12.9 km NNE of Coeur d'Alene; 47°46′N 116°45′W. Coeur d'Alene Natl. Forest to E.

Hayden Lake, reservoir, Kootenai co., N Idaho, on Spokane R. tributary, 4 mi/6.4 km NNE of Coeur d'Alene, and 6 mi/9.7 km N of Coeur d'Alene L.; 7 mi/11.3 km long, 2 mi/3.2 km wide; 47°45′N 116°47′W. Used for irrigation. Extends E into Coeur d'Alene Natl. Forest. Towns of Hayden and Dalton Gardens at SW end, Hayden Lake village on N shore.

Hayden Peak (12,479 ft/3,804 m), in Uinta Mts., on border bet. Summit and Duchesne cos., NE Utah, in High Uintas Wilderness Area, 45 mi/72 km NNW of Duchesne.

Hayden-Rhodes Aqueduct, c.210 mi/338 km long, W and central Ariz., in La Paz and Maricopa cos.; begins at L. Havasu Reservoir, near Parker Dam; flows SE then E, passing N of Phoenix to Salt R. at Granite Reef Dam, 22 mi/35 km E of Phoenix. Diverts water from Colorado R. to Salt R. and Gila R. valleys for irrigation and urban use. Salt-Gila Aqueduct continues S to Santa Cruz R.

Haydenville, Mass.: see WILLIAMSBURG.

Hayes, county (□ 713 sq mi/1,847 sq km; 1990 pop. 1,222), SW Nebr.; ⊙ Hayes Center; 40°31′N 101°03′W. Agr. area drained by Frenchman Creek and other branches of Republican R. Cattle, hogs; corn, wheat, beans. Central/Mountain time zone boundary follows W and NW co. line. Formed 1877.

Hayes, town (1991 pop. 8,447), Clarendon parish, S Jamaica, in irrigated Vere Plain, 4 mi/6.4 km S of May Pen; 17°53′N 77°15′W. Sugarcane.

Hayes, river, c.300 mi/480 km long, Man., central Canada; rises in a lake NE of L. Winnipeg, central Man.; flows NE to Hudson Bay. Chief route used by Hudson's Bay Co. traders from Hudson Bay to L. Winnipeg and the interior; York Factory, an important establishment of the company, is at its mouth.

Hayes Center, village (1990 pop. 259), ⊙ Hayes co., SW Nebr., 30 mi/48 km NW of McCook, and on branch of Republican R.; 40°30′N 101°01′W. Dairy and poultry prods.; livestock; grain, alfalfa pellets.

Hayes, Fort, Ohio: see COLUMBUS.

Hayes, Mount (13,832 ft/4,216 m), E Alaska, in Alaska Range, 90 mi/145 km SSE of Fairbanks; 63°38′N 146°43′W.

Hayesville, uninc. city (1990 pop. 14,318), Marion co., NW Oregon, residential suburb 3 mi/4.8 km NE of downtown Salem; 44°58′N 122°58′W. State Fairgrounds to SW.

Hayesville, town (1990 pop. 62), Keokuk co., SE Iowa, 10 mi/16 km SW of Sigourney; 41°15′N 92°15′W. Limestone quarries nearby.

Hayesville 1 village (1990 pop. 279), ⊙ Clay co., W N.C., 80 mi/129 km WSW of Asheville, on Hiwassee R. (forms Chatuga L. reservoir to SE); 35°02′N 83°49′W. Resort area. Corn, tobacco, apples, peaches; chickens, cattle. Mfg. (clothing, wire and cable; printing and publishing). Nantahala Natl. Forest to W, N, and E. Chattahoochee Natl. Forest (Ga.) to S. **2** village (1990 pop. 457), Ashland co., N central Ohio, 7 mi/11 km SE of Ashland; 40°46′N 82°16′W.

Hayfield 1 town (1990 pop. 1,283), Dodge co., SE Minn., 20 mi/32 km SW of Rochester; 43°53′N 92°50′W. Agr. area (poultry, livestock; grain, soybeans, peas; dairying); mfg. (windows and doors, feeds, fiber cans). **2** uninc. town, Fairfax co., NE Va., residential suburb 6 mi/9.7 km SW of Alexandria, 12 mi/19 km SSW of Washington, D.C.; 38°45′N 77°08′W. Fort Belvoir Military Reservation to S, U.S. Coast Guard Radio Station to E.

Hayfork, uninc. town (1990 pop. 2,605), Trinity co., NW Calif., 17 mi/27 km SW of Weaverville, on Hayfork Creek; 40°34′N 123°08′W. Area surrounded by Shasta-Trinity Natl. Forest. Cattle; hay, timber.

Haymarket, town (1990 pop. 483), Prince William co.,

NE Va., 10 mi/16 km WNW of Manassas; 38°48′N 77°38′W. In agr. area (grain, soybeans, nursery stock; livestock; dairying). Manassas Natl. Battlefield Park to E.

Haymock Lake (HA-muhk), Piscataquis co., N central Maine, 50 mi/80 km NNW of Millinocket, in wilderness recreational area; 2.5 mi/4 km long, 1 mi/1.6 km wide. Drains W into Eagle L.

Haynes, village, S central Alta., W Canada, 18 mi/29 km E of Red Deer. Coal mining; oil and gas. Cattle; wheat, oats.

Haynes (HAINZ), village (1990 pop. 37), Adams co., SW N.Dak., 8 mi/12.9 km E of Hettinger; 45°58′N 102°28′W.

Haynesville 1 (HAINZ-vil), town (1990 pop. 2,854), Claiborne parish, N La., 50 mi/80 km NE of Shreveport, near Ark. state line; 32°58′N 93°08′W. Oil and natural-gas wells, oil refineries; varied agr. (watermelons; cattle, hogs, poultry; dairying); timber; mfg. (consumer goods, apparel). Inc. 1861. **2** town (1990 pop. 243), Aroostook co., E Maine, on the Mattawamkeag R., and 22 mi/35 km SSW of Houlton; 45°49′N 67°58′W.

Hayneville, village (1990 pop. 969), ⊙ Lowndes co., S central Ala., 21 mi/34 km SW of Montgomery.

Hays, county (□ 679 sq mi/1,759 sq km; 1990 pop. 65,614), S central Texas; ⊙ San Marcos; 30°03′N 98°01′W. Crossed SW-NE by Balcones Escarpment, dividing prairies in SE from hilly N and W, part of Edwards Plateau; drained by San Marcos and Blanco rivers. Agr.; livestock (esp. in N); cotton, corn, wheat, grain sorghum, oats, hay, fruit, and vegetables; cattle, sheep, goats (wool, mohair marketed). Limestone, sand and gravel. Tourist trade; springs, scenic hills, hunting, fishing. Formed 1848.

Hays, city (1990 pop. 17,767), ⊙ Ellis co., W central Kansas; 38°52′N 99°19′W. Elev. 1,997 ft/609 m. RR, trade, and medical center in a grain, cattle, and oil area. Mfg. (electronic equip., bldg. materials, plastics prods., feeds, medical supplies, consumer goods, aircraft, motorcycles; meatpacking). Fort Hays est. 1865 14 mi/23 km SE of the city, on a stagecoach road to Denver. The fort was abandoned in 1889 and the land turned over to the state with the understanding that it be used for a school, an agr. experiment station. The school has grown into Fort Hays State Univ.; the agr. experiment station (laid out 1901) is one of the world's largest; and Frontier Historical Park, a state historic site, contains Old Fort Hays surviving bldgs. Inc. 1885.

Hays, uninc. town (1990 pop. 1,522), Wilkes co., NW N.C., 8 mi/12.9 km NNE of Wilkesboro; 36°15′N 81°07′W. Agr. area (tobacco, grain, soybeans; poultry; dairying).

Hays (HAIZ), village (1990 pop. 333), Blaine co., N Mont., 45 mi/72 km, SW of Malta, in S part of Fort Belknap Indian Reservation, on Little Peoples Creek; 48°00′N 108°39′W. Wheat, barley, oats, beans, alfalfa; cattle, sheep; gas, oil, and gold in area. Little Rocky Mts., an outline of Main Rocky Mts., to S. Old Mission; Natural Bridge State Monument. Upper Missouri Natl. Wild and Scenic R. to SW, Charles M. Russell Natl. Wildlife Refuge to S.

Haysi (HAI-sei), town (1990 pop. 222), Dickenson co., SW Va., on Russell Fork R., 10 mi/16 km NE of Clintwood; 37°12′N 82°17′W. Agr. (cattle; tobacco). Breaks Interstate Park (Ky. and Va.) to N; Flanagan Reservoir (Pound R.) to W.

Haystack, Mount (4,918 ft/1,499 m), Essex co., NE N.Y., a peak of the High Peaks sect. of the Adirondack Mts., just SE of Mt. Marcy, and 14 mi/23 km SSE of Lake Placid village; 44°06′N 73°54′W.

Haystack Mountain, ski area, Windham co., S. Vt., in Wilmington, and 15 mi/24 km W of Brattleboro.

Haystack Peak (12,020 ft/3,664 m), highest point in Deep Creek Mts., NW Juab co., W Utah, near Nev. state line.

Haysville, city (1990 pop. 8,364), Sedgwick co., S central Kansas, suburb 10 mi/16 km S of downtown Wichita, near Arkansas R.; 37°34′N 97°20′W. Agr. to S (wheat, sorghum; cattle). Mfg. (plastics prods.).

Haysville, village (1990 pop. 600), Dubois co., SW Ind., 7 mi/11.3 km N of Jasper, near East Fork White R. Cattle; soybeans.

Haysville (HAIZ-vil), borough (1990 pop. 100), Allegheny co., SW Pa., residential suburb 10 mi/16 km NW of downtown Pittsburgh, and 2 mi/3.2 km E of Sewickley, on Ohio R., opposite Coraopolis.

Hayti (HAI-TEI), city (1990 pop. 3,280), Pemiscot co., in bootheel of extreme SE Mo., near Mississippi R., 7 mi/ 11.3 km NW of Caruthersville; 36°13′N 89°45′W. RR junction. Cotton, rice, soybeans; mfg. (fabricated metal prods.; aircraft rebuilding).

Hayti (hai-TEI), village (1990 pop. 372), ⊙ Hamlin co., E S.Dak., 18 mi/29 km SSW of Watertown; 44°39′N 97°12′W. Dairy prods.; livestock, poultry; grain, potatoes.

Hayti Heights (HAI-TEI), town (1990 pop. 893), Pemiscot co., in the bootheel of extreme SE Mo., 1 mi/ 1.6 km E of Hayti; 36°13′N 89°46′W. Residential.

Hayward, city (1990 pop. 111,498), Alameda co., W Calif., suburb 13 mi/21 km SE of downtown Oakland, E of San Francisco Bay; 37°38′N 122°06′W. Bounded by San Lorenzo Creek on N. Important commercial and distributing center for farm prods.; mfg. (wire, plastics, and screw-machine prods., fabricated metal prods., paper prods., textiles, machinery, motor vehicles). The city has profited from development in the San Francisco Bay area, and in the 1970s–1980s, Hayward was the site of active middle-income housing growth that spurred a pop. increase. Hayward Municipal Airport. Seat of Calif. State Univ., Hayward and Chabot Col. (2-year). E terminus of the San Mateo Bridge (toll), to SW, across San Francisco Bay. Walpert ridge to E. Settled 1851, inc. 1876.

Hayward, town, ⊙ Sawyer co., N Wis., on Namekagon R., St. Croix Natl. Scenic Riverway, and 55 mi/89 km SE of Superior. In wooded lake region. Dairy plants, boatyards; mfg. (coffee, furniture, wood prods., consumer goods). RR terminus. Lac Courte Oreilles Indian Reservation to SE; Natl. Freshwater Fishing Hall of Fame. Settled c.1881, inc. 1915.

Hayward, village (1990 pop. 1,897), Freeborn co., S Minn., near Iowa state line, 6 mi/9.7 km E of Albert Lea; 46°00′N 91°28′W. Dairying; mfg. (steel fabrication; machine tools). Dodge Center Airport to SE. Myre Big Isl. State Park to W.

Haywood 1 county (□ 554 sq mi/1,435 sq km; 1990 pop. 46,942), W N.C.; ⊙ Waynesville; 35°32′N 82°58′W. Partly (SE) in the Blue Ridge Mts.; bounded NW by Tenn. state line, drained by Pigeon R. Largely forested; agr. area (tobacco, hay, corn, potatoes; dairying); cattle, hogs; timber. Resort area; some mfg. at Canton and Waynesville. Blue Ridge (Natl.) Parkway follows SW and SE co. borders. Parts of Pisgah Natl. Forest in N and SE; Waterville L. (Pigeon R.) reservoir in N; part of Great Smoky Mts. Natl. Park in NW. Formed 1808. **2** county (□ 519 sq mi/1,344 sq km; 1990 pop. 19,437), W Tenn.; ⊙ Brownsville; 35°35′N 89°17′W. Drained by Hatchie R. and South Fork of Forked Deer R. Leading cotton producer; also soybeans, sorghum, tomatoes, corn; livestock; timber. Formed 1823.

Haywood, uninc. village, Chatham co., central N.C., 27 mi/43 km SW of Raleigh, on Haw R., near its confluence with Deep R. to form Cape Fear R. RR junction. Jordan L. (N) and Harris L. (E) reservoirs nearby.

Hazard, city (1990 pop. 5,416), ⊙ Perry co., SE Ky., 90 mi/ 145 km SE of Lexington, in Cumberland foothills, on North Fork Kentucky R.; 37°15′N 83°12′W. Elev. 867 ft/ 264 m. Trade, shipping, and industrial center for bituminous-coal-mining area; agr. (tobacco); livestock; timber. Mfg. (machining, coal processing; machinery, lumber, bldg. materials, apparel). Wendel H. Ford Airport to N, Davis Park and Mus. Part of Daniel Boone Natl. Forest to SW.

Hazard, village (1990 pop. 78), Sherman co., central Nebr., 14 mi/23 km SSW of Loup City, and on Mud Creek; 41°05′N 99°04′W.

Hazardville, Conn.: see ENFIELD.

Hazel 1 village (1990 pop. 460), Calloway co., SW Ky., at Tenn. state line, 7 mi/11.3 km S of Murray, near East

Fork Clarks R.; 36°30′N 88°19′W. Agr. (tobacco, grain; livestock; dairying). **2** village (1990 pop. 103), Hamlin co., E S.Dak., 17 mi/27 km SW of Watertown; 44°45′N 97°22′W.

Hazel Crest, village (1990 pop. 13,334), Cook co., NE Ill., S suburb of Chicago; 41°34′N 87°41′W. Inc. 1911.

Hazel Green 1 uninc. town (1990 pop. 250), Wolfe co., E central Ky., on Red R., and 45 mi/72 km ESE of Winchester, in the Cumberland Mts. Mfg. (textiles). **2** town (1990 pop. 1,171), Grant co., extreme SW Wis., near Ill. state line, 12 mi/19 km E of Dubuque (Iowa); 42°31′N 90°26′W. In livestock area. Formerly an important lead-mining center.

Hazel Green, village (1990 pop. 2,208), Madison co., N Ala., near Flint R., and Tenn. state line, 15 mi/24 km N of Huntsville; 34°55′N 86°34′W.

Hazel Park, city (1990 pop. 20,051), Oakland co., SE Mich., a suburb 9 mi/14.5 km NNW of downtown Detroit; 42°27′N 83°05′W. Has varied light mfg. (machinery, metal prods.; metal plating) and Hazel Park Racetrack. Most of the early settlers were German. Ottawa chief Pontiac made his hq. here. Borders Detroit city and Wayne co. in S, Macomb co. on E. Inc. 1942.

Hazel Run, village (1990 pop. 81), Yellow Medicine co., SW Minn., 9 mi/14.5 km WSW of Granite Falls, near Yellow Medicine R.; 44°45′N 95°43′W. Grain; livestock.

Hazelhurst, village, Oneida co., N Wis., 19 mi/31 km NW of Rhinelander, in wooded lake region. Mfg. (electronic equip., concrete prods.). Amer. Legion State Forest to E; on Bearskin State Trail. Formerly a lumbering town.

Hazelton, village (1991 pop. 339), W central B.C., W Canada, on Skeena R., at mouth of Bulkley R., and 130 mi/ 209 km NE of Prince Rupert; 55°15′N 127°40′W. Silver, lead, zinc, uranium mining; logging; cattle. Est. 1868 as Hudson's Bay Co. trading post. Historic Indian Village at 'Ksan, 4.5 mi/7.2 km N. New Hazelton (1991 pop. 786) is 4 mi/6 km E. Riverboats once plied the Skeena R. to the coast.

Hazelton 1 village (1990 pop. 394), Jerome co., S Idaho, 15 mi/24 km WNW of Burley; 42°35′N 114°08′W. Elev. 4,068 ft/1,240 m. Beans, potatoes, sugar beets; barley, corn; fertilizers. Wilson L. reservoir to N; Miller Dam (Snake R.) to E. **2** village (1990 pop. 128), Barber co., S Kansas, 7 mi/11.3 km NE of Kiowa; 37°05′N 98°24′W. In cattle area. **3** village (1990 pop. 240), Emmons co., S N.Dak., 33 mi/53 km SE of Bismarck; 46°28′N 100°16′W.

Hazelton, Ind.: see HAZLETON.

Hazelwood, city (1990 pop. 15,324), St. Louis co., E. Mo., a residential, commercial, and industrial suburb 18 mi/ 29 km NW of downtown St. Louis; 38°46′N 90°21′W. On N side of Lambert–St. Louis Airport. Has a diverse mfg. base (aircraft, motor vehicles, microbiology instrumentation, plastic prods., utility receptacles, power tools, paper goods, foods and beverages, medical equip., chemicals; publishing). Inc. as a village 1949, city charter approved 1969.

Hazelwood, town (1990 pop. 1,678), Haywood co., W N.C., 1 mi/1.6 km SW of Waynesville; 35°28′N 83°00′W. RR terminus. In mt.-resort area. Grain; cattle; dairying; mfg. (machining; footwear, fertilizers). Part of Pisgah Natl. Forest to SW and SE.

Hazen 1 (HAIZ-uhn), town (1990 pop. 1,668), Prairie co., E central Ark., 19 mi/31 km N of Stuttgart; 34°47′N 91°34′W. Mfg. (powder metal parts). Wattensaw Wildlife Management Area to NE. **2** town (1990 pop. 2,818), Mercer co., central N.Dak., 52 mi/84 km NW of Bismarck, and on Knife R.; 47°17′N 101°37′W. Lignite mines; wheat. Sakakawea State Park and Reservoir to N.

Hazen, Lake, N Ellesmere Isl., NE Franklin dist., N.W.T., N Canada, at foot of United States Range, WNW of Lady Franklin Bay; 55 mi/89 km long, 3 mi/5 km– 12 mi/19 km wide; 81°50′N 70°W.

Hazen Strait, W Franklin dist., N.W.T., N Canada, arm of the Arctic Ocean, bet. South Borden and Melville isls.; 60 mi/97 km long, 50 mi/80 km wide; 76°N 110°W. Connects Prince Gustav Adolph Sea and Byam Martin Channel.

Hazlehurst 1 (HAI-zuhl-huhrst), town (1990 pop.

4,202), ⊙ Jeff Davis co., SE central Ga., c.45 mi/72 km NNW of Waycross, near Altamaha R.; 31°52′N 82°36′W. Tobacco market; mfg. of clothes, paper goods, machinery, textiles, lumber, consumer goods. Settled late 1850s, inc. 1891. **2** (HAI-zuhl-huhrst), town (1990 pop. 4,221), ⊙ Copiah co., SW Miss., 38 mi/61 km SSW of Jackson; 31°51′N 90°23′W. In agr. (cotton, corn, soybeans; poultry, cattle; dairying) and timber area; ships tomatoes, fruit; mfg. (fabricated metal prods., lumber, plastics; poultry processing). Homochitto Natl. Forest to SW. Founded 1857, inc. 1865.

Hazlet, township (1990 pop. 21,976), Monmouth co., NE N.J., 10 mi/16 km E of Perth Amboy; 40°25′N 74°10′W. Major industry is flavors and fragrance company. Inc. 1848.

Hazleton (HAI-zel-tuhn), city (1990 pop. 24,730), Luzerne co., E Pa., 20 mi/32 km SSW of Wilkes-Barre, near Black Creek; 40°57′N 75°58′W. RR junction. Once a major anthracite-coal-producing region, it now has a diverse economy. Mfg. (apparel, food prods., asphalt, fabricated metal prods., fiberglass windows, plastic prods.; printing and publishing). Agr. area (grain, potatoes; livestock; dairying). Settled c.1809. Its name derives from the hazel bushes that grew in the swamp called Haselschwamm by the early Ger. settlers. The settlement increased in size and development after coal was discovered nearby in 1826. Coal production reached its peak during the 1st ½ of the 20th cent., but declined afterward. Pa. State Univ. (Hazleton campus, 2-year). State hosp., with a school of nursing. Hazleton Municipal Airport to N; Eagle Rock Ski Area to E; Eckley Miners' Village, 19th-cent. mining town, to E. Inc. as a borough 1856, as a city 1892.

Hazleton 1 town (1990 pop. 357), Gibson co., SW Ind., on White R., and 9 mi/14.5 km N of Princeton; 38°29′N 87°32′W. Oil wells. Also spelled Hazelton. **2** town (1990 pop. 733), Buchanan co., E Iowa, 10 mi/16 km N of Independence; 42°37′N 91°54′W. Feed milling. Limestone quarries nearby.

He Devil Mountain, highest peak (9,393 ft/2,863 m) in Seven Devils Mts., SW Idaho co., W Idaho, in Nez Perce Natl. Forest, 35 mi/56 km NW of McCall. Rises above Hells Canyon Snake R. (W).

Head of Jeddore (je-DOR), village, S N.S., E Canada, at head of Jeddore Bay, 30 mi/48 km ENE of Halifax. Fishing port; lumbering.

Head of Passes, section of lower Mississippi R., 18 mi/29 km SE of Triumph, La.; 29°10′N 89°15′W. Area where the Mississippi R. branches into small channels, including North, South, and Southwest passes. Because of sedimentation, navigation was difficult. The 1st naval battle on the Mississippi R. during the Civil War occurred here.

Head of the Harbor, village (□ 3 sq mi/7.8 sq km; 1990 pop. 1,354), Suffolk co., SE N.Y., on Stony Brook Harbor on N shore of L.I., 14 mi/23 km E of Huntington; 40°53′N 73°09′W. In summer-resort area.

Head Tide, Maine: see ALNA.

Headland, town (1990 pop. 3,226), Henry co., SE Ala., 17 mi/27 km SSW of Abbeville. Peanut shelling; peanut and cottonseed prods., fertilizer, lumber. State agr. experiment station here.

Headquarters, uninc. village (1990 pop. 300), Clearwater co., N Idaho, 22 mi/35 km ENE of Orofino; elev. 3,136 ft/956 m. RR terminus. Timber; cattle. Clearwater Natl. Forest to E; Bald Mt. Ski Area to SW; Dworshak Reservoir to W.

Headrick, village (1990 pop. 183), Jackson co., SW Okla., 11 mi/18 km E of Altus, near North Fork of Red R.; 34°37′N 99°08′W. In cotton area.

Head-Smashed-In Buffalo Jump, historical Native Amer. hunting ground and World Heritage Site, SW Alta., W Canada, 15 mi/24 km W of Ft. McLeod; 36 ft/11 m cliff on N side of Oldman R. valley, 1 of 150 sites in valley where buffalo (bison) were stampeded in large herds and plunged to their deaths by Plains Indians. Spear points date to 7000 B.C.; horses were in use by 1830s; final drive mid-1800s. Mus. built into cliff face.

Healdsburg, city (1990 pop. 9,469), Sonoma co., W Calif., 13 mi/21 km NNW of Santa Rosa, on Russian R.; 38°37′N 122°52′W. Apples, grapes, grain, vegetables, nursery prods.; dairying; poultry. Mfg. (dehydrated fruits and vegetables; wineries, electronic components, machinery, motor vehicles).

Healdton (HEELD-tuhn), city (1990 pop. 2,872), Carter co., S Okla., 21 mi/34 km WNW of Ardmore; 34°13′N 97°29′W. In oil and natural-gas, agr., dairying, and livestock-raising area; mfg. (lingerie; printing); oil wells. Oil mus.

Healing Spring, uninc. village, Bath co., NW Va., in Allegheny Mts., 14 mi/23 km NNE of Covington, in George Washington Natl. Forest. Agr. (cattle); timber. Mineral springs.

Healy (HEE-lee), village (1990 pop. 47), S central Alaska, near Mt. McKinley Natl. Park, on Alaska RR, 50 mi/80 km S of Nenana; 63°58′N 144°43′W. Dall sheep. Major coal mine; thermal electric power plant; coal is exported to Korea and is main source of electricity in Fairbanks North Star borough.

Heard (HUHRD), county (□ 301 sq mi/780 sq km; 1990 pop. 8,628), W Ga., on Ala. state line; ⊙ Franklin; 33°18′N 85°08′W. Piedmont area intersected by Chattahoochee R. Agr. (hay, vegetables, fruit; cattle, poultry). Gravel; apparel and textiles. Formed 1830.

Hearne, town (1990 pop. 5,132), Robertson co., E central Texas, in the Brazos valley, c.50 mi/80 km SSE of Waco; 30°52′N 96°35′W. RR junction in rich agr. area (cotton, sorghum, grains, watermelons; cattle, hogs, poultry). Mfg. (vitreous china, fabricated metal prods., wood prods., machinery). Settled 1868, inc. 1871.

Hearst (HUHRST), town (1991 pop. 6,079), N central Ont., central Canada, 60 mi/97 km WNW of Kapuskasing; 49°42′N 83°40′W. Farming; lumbering.

Heart, river, 180 mi/290 km long, N.Dak.; rises in the low prairie country near the Little Missouri R., Billings co., SW N.Dak., near the S unit of the Theodore Roosevelt Natl. Park at 46°56′N 103°13′W; flows E through Patterson Reservoir, past Dickinson, through L. Tschida and Heart Butte Dam, to the Missouri R. at Mandan. The Heart Butte and Dickinson dams, irrigation and flood control units built by the U.S. Bureau of Reclamation as part of the Missouri R. Basin Project, have created the region's largest lakes, which are major recreation areas. Main tributaries are Antelope and Big Muddy creeks and Green R.

Heart Butte (BYOOT), village (1990 pop. 499), Pondera co., N Mont., on the S fork of Whitetail Creek, 33 mi/53 km SW of Cut Bank, in S part of Blackfeet Indian Reservation; 48°17′N 112°50′W. Hogs; wheat, barley, oats, alfalfa. Lewis and Clark Natl. Forest to SW.

Heart Butte Dam, N.Dak.: TSCHIDA, LAKE.

Heart Island, small isl., of the Thousand Isls., Jefferson co., N N.Y., in the St. Lawrence R., just NW of Alexandria Bay; 2 mi/3.2 km long; 44°21′N 75°55′W. Boldt Castle here attracts tourists.

Heart's Content, coast town (1991 pop. 567), SE N.F., E Canada, on NW coast of Avalon Peninsula, on inlet of Trinity Bay, 37 mi/60 km NW of St. John's; 47°53′N 53°22′W. Fishing. Hydroelectric plant. Lumbering region.

Heartwell, village (1990 pop. 69), Kearney co., S Nebr., 10 mi/16 km NE of Minden, near Platte R.; 40°34′N 98°47′W.

Heath, city (1990 pop. 7,231), Licking co., central Ohio, near Licking R., and 3 mi/5 km S of Newark; 40°01′N 82°26′W. Former Newark Air Force Base nearby that specialized in guidance of navigation systems; closed base scheduled for privatization.

Heath 1 town (1990 pop. 716), Franklin co., NW Mass., 12 mi/19 km WNW of Greenfield; 42°42′N 72°50′W. Agr. area. **2** town (1990 pop. 2,108), Rockwell co., N Texas, residential suburb 18 mi/29 km ENE of downtown Dallas, on E shore of L. Ray Hubbard (E Fork Trinity R.); 32°51′N 96°28′W. Agr. area (cattle, horses; wheat). Recreation.

Heath (HEETH), village, Fergus co., central Mont., on the E fork of Big Spring Creek, 8 mi/12.9 km ESE of Lewistown. Gypsum deposits and processing plants. Big Spring Trout Hatchery to W. Formerly called Gypsum.

Heath Springs, town (1990 pop. 907), Lancaster co., N S.C., 9 mi/14.5 km SE of Lancaster; 34°35′N 80°40′W. Fish hatcheries; mfg. of chemicals, machinery. Agr. includes turkeys, cattle; soybeans.

Heathrow, town, Seminole co., central Fla., 15 mi/24 km N of Orlando. Hq. of Amer. Automobile Assn. (AAA).

Heathsville, uninc. village, ⊙ Northumberland co., E Va., 65 mi/105 km SE of Fredericksburg. Mfg. (printing and publishing; oyster processing); agr. (tomatoes, grain, soybeans; poultry, cattle). Entrance to Potomac R. estuary to NE.

Heavener (HEEV-nuhr), town (1990 pop. 2,601), Le Flore co., SE Okla., 10 mi/16 km S of Poteau, just N of the Ouachita Mts. RR junction; 34°53′N 94°36′W. In farm and recreation area (corn, potatoes); mfg. (apparel, machinery). Heavener-Runestone State Park here. Ouachita Natl. Forest to S and E; L. Wister reservoir and State Park to W. A state fish hatchery is here.

Hebardville, village, Ware co., SE Ga., just NW of Waycross; 31°14′N 82°22′W. Also spelled Hebardsville.

Hebbronville, town (1990 pop. 4,465), ⊙ Jim Hogg co., extreme S Texas, c.55 mi/89 km E of Laredo; elev. 550 ft/168 m; 27°19′N 98°41′W. In oil- and gas-producing region; cattle ranching; sorghum; mfg. (lumber).

Heber 1 (HEE-buhr), uninc. town (1990 pop. 750), Navajo co., E central Ariz., 40 mi/64 km from Winslow, in Apache-Sitgreaves Natl. Forest, in Black Canyon; elev. 6,439 ft/1,963 m. Timber. Fort Apache Indian Reservation and Mogollon Rim escarpment to S. **2** uninc. town (1990 pop. 2,566), Imperial co., S Calif., 4 mi/6.4 km SE of El Centro, in irrigated Imperial Valley, 6 mi/9.7 km N of Mex. border; 32°44′N 115°31′W. Vegetables, tomatoes, sugar beets, melons, dates, corn, wheat, alfalfa; cotton; cattle, sheep.

Heber City (HEE-buhr), city (1990 pop. 4,782), ⊙ Wasatch co., N central Utah, 23 mi/37 km NE of Provo, near Provo R.; 40°30′N 111°24′W. In mt. region; elev. 5,595 ft/1,705 m. Trade center and cattle-shipping point; alfalfa, barley; dairying; sheep; mfg. (cheese, dehydrated foods; publishing). Lead, silver, zinc mines in vicinity; sand and gravel. Jordanelle Reservoir and State Park to N; parts of Uinta Natl. Forest to W, S, and E. Heber Valley RR, scenic RR to Provo Canyon (SW). City settled 1859 by Mormons. Hot-water pools of extinct geysers nearby.

Heber Springs (HEE-buhr), town (1990 pop. 5,628), ⊙ Cleburne co., N central Ark., c.55 mi/89 km NNE of Little Rock, in the Ozark Mts.; 35°30′N 92°02′W. Agr.; lumbering; mfg. (wood prods., machinery, bldg. materials, leather prods., medical equip., consumer goods, tools). Dam and fish hatchery to NE. Laid out 1881. Greers Ferry L. (reservoir) to N.

Hébertville (ai-BER-vil), village (1991 pop. 2,400), central Que., E Canada, 23 mi/37 km W of Jonquière. Lumbering; dairying.

Hebgen Lake (HEB-guhn), reservoir, Gallatin co., SW Mont., at S end of Madison Range, in Gallatin Natl. Forest, 19 mi/31 km NW of West Yellowstone; c.20 mi/32 km long, max. 6 mi/9.7 km wide; 44°52′N 111°18′W. Formed by Hebgen Dam, built shortly after Aug. 17, 1959, earthquake, to regulate water flow. Earthquake (Quake) L., natural reservoir formed by landslide during 1959 earthquake, is below dam. Idaho to SW, Wyo. to E.

Hebron 1 (HEE-bruhn), town (1990 pop. 7,079), Tolland co., E central Conn., on Salmon R., and 18 mi/29 km SE of Hartford; 41°38′N 72°23′W. In agr. area. Includes Gilead and Amston villages and Amston L. (c.1 mi/1.6 km long). Rev. Samuel Peters, Tory author of exaggerated account of Conn. "blue laws," lived here. Has 18th-cent. houses. Settled 1704, inc. 1708. **2** town (1990 pop. 3,183), Porter co., NW Ind., 13 mi/21 km SW of Valparaiso; 41°19′N 87°12′W. Agr. area. **3** uninc. town (1990 pop. 1,200), Boone co., N Ky., suburb 14 mi/23 km WSW of Cincinnati (Ohio), and 12 mi/19 km W of Covington. Agr. to W and SW (tobacco; livestock, poultry; dairying). Mfg. (sand and gravel processing, tool and die, chemicals, machinery, plastic prods., fabricated metal prods., transportation equip.). Internatl. airport to SE. **4** town (1990 pop. 878), Oxford co., W Maine, just E of South Paris; 44°12′N 70°23′W. Orchard center. **5** town (1990 pop. 665), Wicomico co., SE Md., 6 mi/9.7 km NW of Salisbury; 38°25′N 75°42′W. In vegetable-farm and timber area; lumber mill, clothing factories. A stone placed here in 1760 marks the town as exactly halfway between the Atlantic coast and Chesapeake Bay. **6** town (1990 pop. 1,765), ⊙ Thayer co., SE Nebr., 65 mi/105 km SW of Lincoln, and on Little Blue R.; 40°10′N 97°35′W. RR terminus. Grain; mfg. (cheese prods.; publishing). On old Oregon Trail. Founded 1869. **7** (HE-bruhn), town (1990 pop. 386), Grafton co., central N.H., 18 mi/29 km NNW of Franklin; 43°41′N 71°47′W. Drained by Cockermouth R., which flows into N end of Newfound L., on S border. Agr. (poultry, cattle; apples, vegetables; dairying; nursery crops); tourism. **8** (HEE-bruhn), town (1990 pop. 888), Morton co., SW central N.Dak., 55 mi/89 km W of Mandan; 46°53′N 102°02′W. Dairy produce; livestock; wheat, corn, barley; mfg. (bricks). Inc. 1916. **9** town (1990 pop. 1,128), Denton co., N Texas, small residential suburb 17 mi/27 km NNW of downtown Dallas, in urban fringe area; 33°02′N 96°54′W.

Hebron (HEE-bruhn), village, NE Lab., NE Canada, on N side of entrance of Hebron Fiord (30 mi/48 km-long inlet of the Atlantic Ocean); 58°12′N 62°37′W. Fishing port and seaplane anchorage.

Hebron 1 village (1990 pop. 809), McHenry co., NE Ill., near Wis. state line, 11 mi/18 km N of Woodstock; 42°28′N 88°25′W. In agr. area (corn; dairying); mfg. (plastic prods., garden tools). **2** village (1990 pop. 2,076), Licking co., central Ohio, 8 mi/13 km SW of Newark; 39°58′N 82°29′W. Dairy prods. Buckeye L. Park (resort) is nearby.

Hecate Island, Canada: see CALVERT ISLAND.

Hecate Strait (HE-kuht), W B.C., W Canada, separates Queen Charlotte Isls. from mainland; joins Dixon Entrance (NNW) and Queen Charlotte Sound (SSE); 160 mi/257 km long, 40 mi/64 km—80 mi/129 km wide. Salmon and halibut fisheries.

Hecelchakán (e-sel-chah-KAHN), city (1990 pop. 7,793) and township, ⊙ Hecelchakán municipio, Campeche, SE Mexico, on NW Yucatán peninsula, on RR, and 65 mi/105 km SW of Mérida; 20°10′N 90°09′W. Agr. center (corn, sugarcane, henequen, tobacco, tropical fruit; livestock).

Heceta Beach (huh-KEE-tuh), uninc. village, W Oregon, on the Pacific Ocean, 4 mi/6.4 km N of Florence, just N of mouth of Siuslaw R. Heceta Head Cape and lighthouse 7 mi/11.3 km to N. Siuslaw Natl. Forest to N and E; Washburns Memorial and Devils Elbow state parks to N.

Heceta Head (huh-KEE-tuh), Lane co., W Oregon, coastal promontory, c. 20 mi/32 km S of Waldport. Lighthouse.

Hecker, village (1990 pop. 534), Monroe co., SW Ill., 9 mi/14.5 km ESE of Waterloo; 38°17′N 89°59′W. In agr. area.

Heckscher State Park (HEK-shuhr), recreational area (□ 2 sq mi/5.2 sq km) on S L.I., SE N.Y., on peninsula extending into Great South Bay SE of Islip; 40°42′N 73°09′W. Swimming, picnicking, hiking, horseback riding.

Hecla, village (1990 pop. 398), Brown co., N S.Dak., 33 mi/53 km NNE of Aberdeen, near James R.; 45°52′N 98°09′W. Mfg. (machinery). Sand L. Natl. Wildlife Refuge to W; Mud L. Reservoir to SW.

Hecla and Griper Bay, inlet of the Arctic Ocean, N Melville Isl., W Franklin dist., N.W.T., N Canada; 85 mi/137 km long, 25 mi/40 km–60 mi/97 km wide; 76°00′N 113°00′W.

Hecla, Cape (HE-kluh), NE Ellesmere Isl., NE Franklin dist., N.W.T., N Canada, on Lincoln Sea of the Arctic Ocean; 82°54′N 64°40′W.

Hector, town (1990 pop. 1,145), Renville co., S central Minn., 14 mi/23 km E of Olivia; 44°44′N 94°42′W. Grain, sugar beets, soybeans, beans; livestock, poultry; dairying. Mfg. (electrical equip., tools, consumer goods; meat processing).

Hector, village, SE B.C., E Canada, near Alta. border, in Rocky Mts., in Yoho Natl. Park, 40 mi/64 km NW of Banff; elev. 5,213 ft/1,589 m. Bet. this point and Field

the Can. Pacific RR passes through the SPIRAL TUNNELS.

Hector Lake, SW Alta., W Canada, near B.C. border, in Rocky Mts., in Banff Natl. Park, at foot of Mt. Hector, 45 mi/72 km NW of Banff; 4 mi/6 km long, 1 mi/2 km wide; elev. 5,704 ft/1,739 m. Drains SE into Bow R.

Hector, Mount (11,135 ft/3,394 m), SW Alta., W Canada, near B.C. border, in Rocky Mts., in Banff Natl. Park, 40 mi/64 km NW of Banff; 51°39′N 116°16′W. At its foot is Hector L.

Hedgesville (HE-jez-vil), village (1990 pop. 227), Berkeley co., NE W.Va., in E Panhandle, 7 mi/11.3 km NNW of Martinsburg; 39°32′N 77°59′W. Agr. (grain, apples); livestock. Sleepy Creek Wildlife Management Area.

Hedley, village, S B.C., W Canada, in Cascade Mts., on Similkameen R., and 26 mi/42 km WSW of Penticton; elev. 4,500 ft/1,372 m; 49°21′N 120°04′W. Gold and silver mining.

Hedley, village (1990 pop. 391), Donley co., extreme N Texas, in the Panhandle, 15 mi/24 km SE of Clarendon; 34°52′N 100°39′W. In agr. area (cotton, peanuts; cattle).

Hedrick, town (1990 pop. 810), Keokuk co., SE Iowa, 12 mi/19 km SW of Sigourney; 41°10′N 92°18′W. Livestock; grain.

Hedwig Village, town (1990 pop. 2,616), Harris co., SE Texas, residential suburb 9 mi/14.5 km WNW of downtown Houston, surrounded by city of Houston; 29°46′N 95°31′W.

Heflin, town (1990 pop. 2,906), ⊙ Cleburne co., E Ala., near Tallapoosa R., 15 mi/24 km E of Anniston. Lumber milling, clothing mfg., poultry processing. Settled 1883, inc. 1892.

Heflin (HEF-len), village (1990 pop. 253), Webster parish, NW La., 10 mi/16 km S of Minden; 32°28′N 93°16′W. In agr. area (cotton, vegetables; cattle). L. Bistineau reservoir to W.

Hegeler, uninc. town (1990 pop. 1,853), Vermilion co., E central Ill., suburb 4 mi/6.4 km S of Danville, near Ind. state line; 40°04′N 87°38′W.

Heidelberg (HEI-duhl-buhrg), town (1990 pop. 981), Jasper co., E central Miss., 16 mi/26 km NNE of Laurel; 31°53′N 88°59′W. Agr. (corn, cotton; poultry, cattle; dairying; timber); mfg. (automotive armatures); oil refinery. Oil field nearby.

Heidelberg, village (1990 pop. 73), Le Sueur co., S Minn., 8 mi/12.9 km NE of Le Center; 44°29′N 93°37′W. Grain; livestock, poultry; dairying.

Heidelberg (HEI-duhl-buhrg), borough (1990 pop. 1,238), Allegheny co., SW Pa., residential suburb 6 mi/9.7 km SW of downtown Pittsburgh, on Chartiers Creek. Woodville State Hosp. to S.

Heidrick (HED-rik), village (1990 pop. 700), Knox co., SE Ky., 2 mi/3.2 km NE of Barbourville, in the Cumberland Mts., near Cumberland R. Agr. (tobacco); coal.

Heise, uninc. village (1990 pop. 84), Jefferson co., E Idaho, 20 mi/32 km NE of Idaho Falls, on Snake R. Irrigated agr. area. Targhee Natl. Forest and Kelly Canyon Ski Area to E.

Helderbergs, the, N-facing limestone escarpment (c.1,700 ft/518 m) of the Catskill Mts. (NE edge of Allegheny Plateau), E N.Y., along S side of Mohawk valley W of Albany; 42°39′N 74°01′W. Also known as the Helderberg Mts.

Helen or **Helen Mine**, village, central Ont., central Canada, near Wawa L., 110 mi/177 km NNW of Sault Ste. Marie. Iron-mining center.

Helen, village (1990 pop. 300), White co., NE Ga., 22 mi/35 km WNW of Toccoa, near Chattahoochee R.; 34°42′N 83°43′W. Resort community with a Bavarian alpine village theme. Also light mfg. and retail discount outlet malls.

Helena 1 (HE-luh-nuh), city (1990 pop. 3,918), Shelby co., central Ala., near Cahaba R., suburb 15 mi/24 km S of Birmingham. **2** city (1990 pop. 24,569), ⊙ Mont. and Lewis and Clark co., W central Mont., 48 mi/77 km NNE of Butte, on E slope of the Rocky Mts., just E of the Continental Divide; 46°36′N 112°01′W. Commercial, trading, and shipping center in a ranching and mining area. Mfg. includes concrete and sheet metal prods., dairy prods.; consumer goods; printing and

publishing. The state corporate offices of major electronics, engineering, communications, and healthcare organizations, as well as the Federal Reserve bank, are here. Increased tourism and expanding artists' colonies have strengthened Helena's economic base. Agr. area, including cattle, sheep; wheat, barley, oats. Founded after the discovery of gold (1864) in Last Chance Gulch (which has become Helena's main street) and grew rapidly. In 1875 a general election ratified the choice of Helena to replace Virginia City as territorial capital. In the 1890s it maintained its position as state capital against the rivalry of Anaconda. Original mining was principally for gold and silver. As these minerals were depleted, stores of copper, lead, and zinc were discovered and exploited. Seat of Carroll Col. Has numerous mus., landmarks, and monuments. Original Governors Mansion (1888), Holter Mus. of Art, Mus. of Gold, Masonic Grand Lodge, Reeder's Alley, Helena Civic Center, Archie Bray Foundation (school of pottery), Poindexter Collection of Abstract Art, F. Jay Haynes Photo Collection, Mont. Homeland Exhibit, Mackay Gal., Mont. Historical Society Mus., Myrna Loy Center for the Performing Arts. The capitol bldg. has noteworthy historical and artistic collections. The city is surrounded by scenic mts. and is the hq. of Helena Natl. Forest. L. Helena formed on sidestream of Missouri R. to NE, Hauser L. and Black Sandy State Park to NE, and Canyon Ferry L. and State Park to E, both formed by dams on Missouri R., units of Helena Natl. Forest to W, SE, and NE, Gates of the Mts. Wilderness to NE. Great Divide Ski Area to NW, Fort Harrison Military Reservation to W. Originally called Last Chance Gulch. Inc. 1870.

Helena 1 (HE-luh-nuh), town (1990 pop. 7,491), ⊙ Phillips co., E central Ark., on the Mississippi R., and at the S end of Crowley's Ridge; 34°31′N 90°35′W. Larger city of West Helena adjoins to W. RR center and river port with an economy based on cotton, lumber, and agr. processing. Mfg. (soybean meal, cottonseed prods.; printing). Occupied by Union troops in the Civil War; they were attacked unsuccessfully by Confederates in the Battle of Helena (July 4, 1863). Seat of Phillips Co. Community Col. Inc. 1833. **2** (he-LEE-nuh), town (1990 pop. 1,256), Telfair co., S central Ga., 32 mi/51 km S of Dublin, and on Little Ocmulgee R., adjacent to McRae (E); 32°05′N 82°55′W. Mfg. includes vegetable processing; machinery. **3** (HE-luh-nuh), town (1990 pop. 1,043), Alfalfa co., N Okla., 24 mi/39 km WNW of Enid; 36°32′N 98°16′W. In grain and livestock area; mfg. (concrete).

Helena 1 (HE-luh-nuh), village (1990 pop. 267), Sandusky co., N Ohio, 9 mi/14 km W of Fremont; 41°20′N 83°17′W. In agr. area. **2** (huh-LAI-nuh), uninc. village, Newberry co., NW central S.C., 1 mi/1.6 km W of Newberry.

Helena Island, Parry Isls., N Franklin dist., N.W.T., N Canada, just off N Bathurst Isl.; 23 mi/37 km long, 8 mi/13 km wide; 76°46′N 101°30′W.

Helena, Lake (HE-luh-nuh), reservoir, Lewis and Clark co., W central Mont., on Missouri R. (to NE), on backwater from Hauser Dam (L. Hauser; linked widened Silver Creek), 7 mi/11.3 km NNE of Helena; 3 mi/4.8 km long, 2 mi/3.2 km wide; 46°41′N 111°55′W. Receives Prickly Pear and Silver creeks.

Helix (HEE-liks), village (1990 pop. 150), Umatilla co., NE Oregon, 15 mi/24 km NNE of Pendleton; 45°51′N 118°39′W. Fruit, vegetables; cattle.

Hell, village, Livingston co., SE Mich., 15 mi/24 km NW of Ann Arbor; 42°26′N 83°59′W. In small lakes area. Resort; agr. (grain, apples; cattle). Pinckney State Recreation Area to S.

Hell Gate, narrow channel of the East R., SE N.Y., bet. Wards Isl. and Astoria, Queens, N.Y. city; 40°47′N 73°56′W. Named Hellegat by the Du. navigator Adriaen Block, who passed through it into L.I. Sound in 1614, it was dangerous to ships because of its strong tidal currents and rocks. Cleared of all obstacles, it allows oceangoing vessels to sail bet. N.Y. Harbor and L.I. Sound. It is crossed by the Triborough highway bridge and by the Hell Gate RR bridge.

Hell Hole Reservoir (□ 2 sq mi/5.2 sq km), Placer co., E central Calif., on Rubicon R., in Eldorado Natl. Forest, 12 mi/19 km W of L. Tahoe; 39°03′N 120°07′ W. Max. capacity 209,000 acre-ft. Formed by Hell Hole Reservoir Dam (410 ft/125 m high), built (1966) by the Bureau of Reclamation for irrigation; also used for power generation, water supply, and recreation. Desolation Valley Wilderness Area nearby.

Hellam, Pa.: see HALLAM.

Hellertown (HE-luhr-toun), borough (1990 pop. 5,662), Northampton co., E Pa., suburb 3 mi/4.8 km SSE of downtown Bethlehem, on Saucon Creek. Mfg. (apparel, bricks); sand quarry. Agr. (corn, hay, apples, soybeans; dairying). Campus of Lehigh Univ. to NW. Lost R. Caverns to SE. Settled c.1740, inc. 1872.

Hellier (HEL-uhr), uninc. village (1990 pop. 400), Pike co., E Ky., near Va. state line, in the Cumberland Mts., 13 mi/21 km SE of Pikeville. Bituminous-coal mining. Jefferson Natl. Forest to SE.

Hells Canyon, S Idaho, extends c.125 mi/201 km N along the Oregon state line, reaches a max. depth of c.7,900 ft/2,408 m. Sometimes called Grand Canyon of the Snake R.; the greatest of the Snake's many gorges and one of the deepest in the world.

Hells Canyon Reservoir, NE Oregon and W Idaho, on Snake R., at upper (S) end of Hells Canyon, 60 mi/97 km E of La Grande (Oregon); c.25 mi/40 km long; 45°10′N 116°16′W. Max. capacity 200,000 acre-ft. Oxbow Dam at SW tip. Formed by Hells Canyon Dam (218 ft/66 m high), built by the Idaho Power Co., for power generation. Hells Canyon Natl. Recreation Area N of dam.

Hell's Kitchen, N.Y.: see CLINTON.

Hellshire Hills (□ 45 sq mi/72 sq km), hills (800 ft/245 m) and Kingston suburb, St. Catherine parish, S Jamaica, 6 mi/9.7 km WSW of greater Portmore sect. of twin city of Kingston; 17°53′N 76°58′W. These rolling limestone hills occupy the S promontory of the parish. A varied coastline of white sandy beach and rugged cliffs borders the S and large sugarcane estates of Innswood and Bernard Lodge separate it by 5 mi/8 km from Spanish Town on the N. Further NE Portmore and Port Henderson housing estates link the area to Kingston via a causeway. West Point along the coastline at the mouth of Salt Isl. Creek emerges into Salt Isl. Lagoon at Galleon Harbor, and Old Harbor is to the W. Identified as an ideal development area with Manatee Bay and Central Highlands.

Helmetta, borough (1990 pop. 1,211), Middlesex co., E N.J., 8 mi/12.9 km S of New Brunswick; 40°22′N 74°25′W. Former snuff mfg. center in 19th cent. In rapidly suburbanizing area.

Helmville, village (1990 pop. 80), Powell co., W Mont., on Nevada Creek, near confluence with Blackfoot R., and 50 mi/80 km WNW of Helena. In agr. and ranching region. Site of well-known Labor Day Rodeo. Helena Natl. Forest to E, Nevada L. Reservoir to SE, Garnet Range to S.

Helotes (ai-LO-tes), town (1990 pop. 1,535), Bexar co., S central Texas, suburb 14 mi/23 km NW of downtown San Antonio; 29°34′N 98°41′W. Agr. area (cattle; wheat, corn, peanuts). Mfg. (nut processing; plastic prods., marble prods., bldg. materials, fabricated metal prods.).

Helper, town (1990 pop. 2,148), Carbon co., E central Utah, in canyon of Price R., 6 mi/9.7 km NNW of Price; elev. 5,840 ft/1,780 m; 39°41′N 110°51′W. Shipping center for coal-mining and agr. (fruit, hay, sugar beets) area. Known as Pratts Siding until 1892, renamed for locomotives called "helpers" that were stored here. Scofield Dam, nearby on Price R., is used for irrigation. Price Canyon Recreation Area to NW; part of Ashley Natl. Forest to NE. Uinta Natl. Forest to NW; Manti–La Sal Natl. Forest to W. Scofield Reservoir and State Park to NW. Western Mining and RR Mus. Junction of RR spur to Wattis. Settled 1883, inc. 1907.

Helvetia (hel-VEE-zhah), uninc. village, Brady township, Clearfield co., W central Pa., 5 mi/8 km S of Du Bois, on Stump Creek; 41°02′N 78°46′W. Bituminous-coal region.

Hemby Bridge (HEM-bee), uninc. town (1990 pop. 2,876), Union co., S N.C., residential suburb 13 mi/21 km SE of downtown Charlotte; 35°07′N 80°37′W.

Hemet, city (1990 pop. 36,094), Riverside co., S Calif., suburb 28 mi/45 km SE of Riverside, in the San Jacinto valley; 33°44′N 117°00′W. Citrus, avocados, vegetables, grain; nursery stock; poultry, eggs; dairying. Mfg. (carbon prods., furniture, motor vehicles). In a co. marked by fast growth during the 1970s and 1980s as a result of increased local agribusiness and the development of the aircraft industry in the area, much work has been provided, and Hemet is one of the many cities that has benefitted from these developments. Seat of Mt. San Jacinto Col. A special tourist attraction is the Ramona Outdoor Play, staged annually by residents of the twin cities of Hemet and San Jacinto. San Diego Aqueduct passes N-S to W, branches from Colorado R. Aqueduct to N; Soboba Indian Reservation to E, part of San Bernardino Natl. Forest to E. Inc. 1910.

Hemingford, village (1990 pop. 953), Box Butte co., NW Nebr., 18 mi/29 km NW of Alliance; elev. 4,259 ft/1,298 m; 42°19′N 103°04′W. Poultry prods., grain, sugar beets, potatoes; livestock. Fishing lures. Box Butte Reservoir State Recreation Area to N (Dawnes co.).

Hemingway, town (1990 pop. 829), Williamsburg co., E S.C., 33 mi/53 km SSE of Florence; 33°45′N 79°26′W. Mfg. includes wire, consumer goods, foods, textiles, apparel, plastic prods.; poultry processing. Agr. includes poultry, livestock; tobacco, grain, soybeans, cotton.

Hemlock 1 village (1990 pop. 1,601), Saginaw co., E central Mich., 14 mi/23 km W of Saginaw; 43°25′N 84°13′W. Farm area. Mfg. (medical equip., bldg. materials). **2** village (1990 pop. 203), Perry co., central Ohio, 9 mi/14 km S of New Lexington; 39°35′N 82°09′W.

Hemlock Lake, one of the Finger Lakes, Livingston co., W central N.Y., 28 mi/45 km S of Rochester; 7 mi/11.3 km. long; 42°44′N 77°37′W. In agr. area. Supplies water to Rochester.

Hemmingford, village (1991 pop. 729), S Que., E Canada, 32 mi/51 km S of Montreal, near U.S. (N.Y.) border; 45°03′N 73°36′W. Agr.

Hemp, N.C.: see ROBBINS.

Hemphill, county (□ 912 sq mi/2,362 sq km; 1990 pop. 3,720), extreme N Texas; ⊙ Canadian; elev. 2,500 ft/762 m–3,000 ft/914 m; 35°49′N 100°16′W. On high plains of the Panhandle, and bounded E by Okla. state line. Drained by Canadian and Washita rivers. Cattle-ranching region in N, producing also horses; some agr. in S (wheat, grain sorghum; hay); oil and natural gas. Hunting, fishing in L. Marvin and Canadian R. regions. Black Kettle Natl. Grassland in NE, includes small L. Marvin, on small tributary of Canadian R. Formed 1876. Acquired parts of Ellis and Roger Mills cos. (Okla.), in resurvey of 100th meridian (1930).

Hemphill, town (1990 pop. 1,182), ⊙ Sabine co., E Texas, near La. state line, c.50 mi/80 km E of Lufkin; elev. 267 ft/81 m; 31°20′N 93°50′W. Trade point in timber; cattle, poultry; vegetables, fruit area; mfg. (lumber). Recreation area. Located on W edge of Sabine Natl. Forest; large Toledo Bend Reservoir (Sabine R., La. state line) to E; Sam Rayburn Reservoir to SW. Inc. as city 1939.

Hempstead, county (□ 741 sq mi/1,919 sq km; 1990 pop. 21,621), SW Ark.; ⊙ Hope; 33°43′N 93°39′W. Bounded SW by Red and Little rivers and N by Little Missouri R. and Hickory Creek. Agr. area (soybeans; cattle, hogs, chickens); timber. Mfg. at Hope. Part of Millwood L. Reservoir (Little R.) in W; Hope Wildlife Management Area at center; Bais D'Arc Wildlife Management Area to SW; Old Washington Historic State Park at Washington at center of co. Formed 1818.

Hempstead 1 town (□ 144 sq mi/373 sq km; 1990 pop. 725,639), in township of Hempstead, Nassau co., SE N.Y., on W L.I.; 40°39′N 73°36′W. Nation's most populous town. Occupies the S ½ of Nassau co. The City of Hempstead (1990 pop. 49,453), located in the N central part of Hempstead township and having only 1% of the co.'s area, has 7% of the co.'s pop. It is a retail center for the area. Electronic equip., tools, chemicals, and metal prods. are made here. City pop. is largely Afr.-Amer. The town grew significantly in the 1970s with the construction of nearby freeways, large retail outlets, and the expansion of regional suburban industries. Settled in 1644 by Eng. colonists who named it for their old home in England, Hemel-Hempstead. Seat of Hofstra Univ. Has many colonial houses and monuments. Founded as a village, inc. 1853. **2** town (1990 pop. 3,551), ⊙ Waller co., SE Texas, near Brazos R., c.50 mi/80 km WNW of Houston; 30°05′N 96°04′W. In agr., oil-producing, cattle area; light mfg. Nearby is "Liendo," plantation of sculptor Elisabeth Ney (built 1853).

Hempstead Harbor, inlet of L.I. Sound indenting N shore of W L.I., SE N.Y., E of Manhasset Neck, and c.5 mi/8 km N of Hempstead; 4 mi/6.4 km wide at entrance bet. Matinicock (E) and Prospect (W) points; 5 mi/8 km long. Roslyn is at its head; Glen Cove, Sea Cliff, Glenwood Landing, and Glen Head are on or near its shores.

Hen and Chickens, S Ont., central Canada, group of islets at W end of L. Erie, 9 mi/14 km W of Pelee Isl.

Henager (HE-nuh-guhr), town (1990 pop. 1,934), DeKalb co., NE Ala., 13 mi/21 km NNW of Fort Payne; 34°38′N 85°44′W. Trucking business; textile mfg. Sequoyah Caverns located nearby.

Henderson 1 county (□ 395 sq mi/1,023 sq km; 1990 pop. 8,096), W Ill.; ⊙ Oquawka; 40°49′N 90°54′W. Bounded W by the Mississippi R.; drained by Henderson Creek. Agr. (cattle, hogs, poultry; corn, soybeans); limestone. Beaches, campsites along the Mississippi. Formed 1841. **2** county (□ 467 sq mi/1,210 sq km; 1990 pop. 43,044), NW Ky.; ⊙ Henderson; elev. 401 ft/122 m; 37°47′N 87°34′W. Bounded N by the Ohio (Ind. state line), SW by Highland Creek, E and SE by Green R.; drained by Green R. (NE). Rolling plateau agr. area (dark and burley tobacco, corn, wheat, soybeans, alfalfa, hay; hogs, cattle); bituminous-coal mines, oil wells; clay, sand and gravel. Mfg. at Henderson. Includes Diamond Isl. in Ohio R., in NW; John James Audubon State Park in N; Sauerheber Wildlife Management Area in NW; Newburgh Lock and Dam, on Ohio R., in NE. Ky., on Ind. side of Ohio R., 4 mi/6.4 km S of Evansville (Ind.), isolated by changing river course, includes Ellis Park Racecourse. Formed 1798. **3** county (□ 374 sq mi/969 sq km; 1990 pop. 69,285), SW N.C.; ⊙ Hendersonville; 35°20′N 82°28′W. E part in the Blue Ridge Mts.; bounded S by S.C.; drained by upper French Broad, Broad, and Green rivers. Resort area. Agr. area (dairying; cattle; soybeans, hay, tobacco, poultry, apples, corn); textile mfg.; stone quarrying. Mfg. at Fletcher and Hendersonville. Holmes Educational State Forest in W; Carl Sandburg Home Natl. Historical Site in S, at Flat Rock; L. Summit reservoir (Green R.) in S; part of Pisgah Natl. Forest in NW. Formed 1838. **4** county (□ 515 sq mi/1,334 sq km; 1990 pop. 21,844), W Tenn.; ⊙ Lexington; 35°39′N 88°23′W. Drained by Big Sandy R. Agr. (cotton, corn, soybeans, peaches, vegetables; livestock); lumbering. Includes Natchez Trace Forest and State Park. Formed 1821. **5** county (□ 949 sq mi/2,458 sq km; 1990 pop. 58,543), E Texas; ⊙ Athens; 32°12′N 95°50′W. Bounded W by Trinity R., E by Neches R. (forms L. Palestine); partly wooded (timber). Agr. (esp. vegetables, melons, nursery crops, black-eyed peas, legumes); cattle, hogs, horses, ratites (emus, ostriches, rheas). Oil, natural gas; lignite, sulfur; sand and gravel. Hunting; fishing. Purtis Creek State Park in N; Cedar Creek Reservoir in W; L. Athens reservoir near center. Formed 1846.

Henderson 1 city (1990 pop. 25,945), ⊙ Henderson co., NW Ky., 9 mi/14.5 km S of Evansville (Ind.), on the Ohio R.; 37°50′N 87°34′W. RR junction. Agr. (dark and burley tobacco, corn; livestock); oil, coal. Mfg. (transportation equip., plastic prods., furniture, consumer goods, chemicals, fabricated metal prods., bldg. materials, paper prods., lumber, machinery, flour; printing and publishing, denim processing, aluminum smelting). Henderson City-Co. Airport to W. Naturalist and painter John J. Audubon lived here 1810–1819. John James Audubon State Park, with a mus. and a bird sanctuary to NE. Ellis Park Racecourse (annual thoroughbred racing) 5 mi/8 km to NNE in sect. of Ky. on Ind. side of Ohio R., adjacent to Evansville. A branch of the Univ. of Ky. is here. Founded 1797, inc. as a city 1867. **2** (HEN-duhr-suhn), city (1990 pop. 64,942), Clark co., including suburb 12 mi/19 km of Las Vegas, SE Nev., in a desert area overlooking Las Vegas and surrounded by mts.; elev. 1,881 ft/573 m; 36°01′N 115°00′W. Limestone; mfg. (plastics prods., fabricated metal prods., lime prods., foods, transportation equip., consumer goods, chemicals, bldg. materials; printing and publishing); tourism, recreation. Center for defense-related industries, specializing in large-volume chemical mfg. Hydroelectric power is supplied by Hoover Dam. Founded (1942) to provide houses for employees of a magnesium plant. Southern Nevada Mus. and Heritage Mus. are here. L. Mead Recreational Area adjoins city to NE. Sunrise Mt. Natural Area to N. Highland Range, crucial bighorn habitat area to S. Inc. 1953. **3** city (1990 pop. 15,655), ⊙ Vance co., N N.C., 41 mi/66 km NNW of Raleigh; 36°19′N 78°24′W. RR junction. Agr. area (grain, soybeans, tobacco; poultry, livestock). Mfg. (apparel, textiles, furniture, fabricated metal prods., industrial minerals, bldg. materials, mobile homes, consumer goods, machinery, foods; printing). Seat of Vance-Granville Community Col. Kerr L. State Recreation Area to N; large S arm of Kerr Reservoir (Roanoke R.) to N. Settled c.1811, inc. 1841. **4** city (1990 pop. 4,760), ⊙ Chester co., SW Tenn., 16 mi/26 km SE of Jackson; 35°26′N 88°38′W. In timber and farm area; mfg. of clothing, fabricated metal prods. Seat of Freed-Hardeman Col. Chickasaw State Park, with Native Amer. burial mounds, is nearby. **5** city (1990 pop. 11,139), ⊙ Rusk co., NE Texas, 25 mi/40 km S of Longview; 32°09′N 94°47′W. Elev. 505 ft/154 m. Prosperous oil and natural-gas city. RR terminus; dairying; cattle, horses; vegetables, watermelons; nursery crops; timber. Mfg. (furniture, machinery, bldg. materials, wood prods.; meat processing). Originally a pinewoods lumbering town, then a cotton center, the city was transformed in 1930 when C. M. Joiner struck the 1st gusher of the fabulously rich East Texas Oil Field nearby. Site of an Old Shawnee village in the area. Seat of Texas Baptist Inst. Inc. 1877.

Henderson 1 uninc. town, Adams co., N central Colo., suburb 15 mi/24 km NE of downtown Denver, on South Platte R.; elev. 5,020 ft/1,530 m. Mfg. (machinery, transportation equip., fabricated metal prods., bldg. materials). **2** town (1990 pop. 206), Mills co., SW Iowa, near West Nishnabotna R., 25 mi/40 km ESE of Council Bluffs; 41°08′N 95°25′W. In grain and livestock region. **3** (HEN-duhr-suhn), town (1990 pop. 1,543), St. Martin parish, La., 12 mi/19 km E of Lafayette; 30°18′N 91°47′W. Located at the edge of Atchafalaya Swamp. Crawfish ponds in area. Known for its seafood restaurants. Inc. 1971. **4** town (1990 pop. 66), Caroline co., E Md., near Del. state line, 14 mi/23 km WSW of Dover (Del.); 39°04′N 75°46′W. Originally named Meredith's Crossing or River Bridges, but in 1868, when the RR arrived, it was named for one of the Baltimore and Ohio directors. **5** town (1990 pop. 746), Sibley co., S Minn., 45 mi/72 km SW of Minneapolis, on Minnesota R., at mouth of Rush R.; 44°31′N 93°54′W. Grain; livestock, poultry; dairying; mfg. (displays). Rush R. State Park to W.

Henderson 1 village (1990 pop. 290), Knox co., NW central Ill., near Henderson Creek, 4 mi/6.4 km N of Galesburg; 41°01′N 90°20′W. In agr. area (cattle, hogs; corn, soybeans, sorghum; dairying). **2** village (1990 pop. 999), York co., SE central Nebr., 12 mi/19 km SW of York; 40°46′N 97°48′W. Irrigation equip.; printing, light mfg. **3** village (1990 pop. 549), Mason co., W W.Va., 4 mi/6.4 km E of Gallipolis (Ohio), and 2 mi/3.2 km S of Point Pleasant, on Ohio R. (bridged to Galliopolis), at mouth of Kanawha R. (bridged to Point Pleasant); 38°49′N 82°08′W. Grain; poultry, livestock. Chief Cornstalk Wildlife Management Area to SE.

Henderson Creek, c.75 mi/121 km long, W Ill.; rises in branches near Galesburg; flows W and SW, to the Mississippi R. 5 mi/8 km above Burlington (Iowa); 41°01′N 90°18′W.

Henderson Harbor, resort village (1990 pop. 350), Jefferson co., N N.Y., on Henderson Bay (an inlet of L. Ontario), 16 mi/26 km SW of Watertown; 43°52′N 76°11′W. Fishing.

Henderson Lake, reservoir, Essex co., NE N.Y., on Hudson R., in the Adirondack Mts., in Adirondack Park, 17 mi/27 km S of Saranac; c.1.5 mi/2.4 km long; 44°05′N 74°04′W. Drains S into Sanford L. Formed by dam 5 mi/8 km S of source of Hudson R.

Hendersonville, city (1990 pop. 32,188), Sumner co., N central Tenn., on Old Hickory Reservoir (Cumberland R.), 14 mi/23 km NE of Nashville, 36°18′N 86°37′W. In area of limestone and phosphate deposits; agr. (tobacco, soybeans); livestock raising. Mfg. (furniture, tooling, machinery). Home to a number of country music singers. Inc. 1968.

Hendersonville, town (1990 pop. 7,284), ⊙ Henderson co., SW N.C., 20 mi/32 km SSE of Asheville, in the Blue Ridge Mts.; 35°19′N 82°27′W. RR junction. Resort center; agr. trade (dairying; livestock; corn, tobacco, soybeans); mfg. (clothing, electrical equip., consumer goods, textiles, ceramic and foam filters, crushed stone; sheet metal fabricating). Carl Sandburg Home Natl. Historical Site to S at Flat Rock. Pisgah Natl. Forest to W; Holmes Educational State Forest to SW.

Hendley, village (1990 pop. 42), Furnas co., S Nebr., 7 mi/11.3 km W of Beaver City, and on Beaver Creek; 40°07′N 99°58′W.

Hendricks, county (□ 408 sq mi/1,057 sq km; 1990 pop. 75,717), central Ind.; ⊙ Danville; 39°46′N 86°31′W. Drained by Big Walnut, Mill, and Whitelick creeks. Part of Indianapolis metro area; includes satellite communities of Brownsburg and Plainfield. Corn, soybeans, fruit; hogs, cattle, sheep; flour milling, processing of dairy prods. and lumber; timber. Formed 1823.

Hendricks 1 village (1990 pop. 684), Lincoln co., SW Minn., near S.Dak. state line, and 9 mi/14.5 km WNW of Ivanhoe, at E end of L. Hendricks (extends into S.Dak.), at exit of Lac qui Parle R.; 44°30′N 96°25′W. Grain; poultry, livestock; dairying. **2** village (1990 pop. 303), Tucker co., NE W.Va., 3 mi/4.8 km ESE of Parsons, on Laurel Fork R., at mouth of Blackwater R.; 39°04′N 79°37′W. Coal-mining and agr. area. Mfg. (wood prods.). In Monongahela Natl. Forest; Fernow Experimental Forest to SW.

Hendrix, village (1990 pop. 108), Bryan co., S Okla., 15 mi/24 km S of Durant, and on Red R.; 33°46′N 96°24′W.

Hendrum (HEN-druhm), village (1990 pop. 309), Norman co., W Minn., on Red R., near mouth of Wild Rice R., 26 mi/42 km N of Fargo (N.Dak.); 47°15′N 96°48′W. Wheat, potatoes, sunflowers, sugar beets, soybeans.

Hendry (HEN-dree), county (□ 1,189 sq mi/3,080 sq km; 1990 pop. 25,773), S central Fla.; ⊙ La Belle; 28°54′N 82°22′W. Everglades sugarcane-growing and cattle-raising area, crossed in NW corner by Caloosahatchee R.; touches L. Okeechobee (NE). Has Seminole Indian Reservation in SE. Formed 1923.

Henefer, village (1990 pop. 554), Summit co., N Utah, 27 mi/43 km SE of Ogden, and 25 mi/40 km NE of Salt Lake City, on Weber R.; elev. 5,280 ft/1,609 m; 41°01′N 111°29′W. Alfalfa; dairying; sheep, cattle. Wasatch Natl. Forest to N and W; East Canyon Reservoir and State Park to SW. Lost Creek Reservoir and State Park to NE. Echo Reservoir to SE. Settled 1860s.

Henik Lakes (HE-nik), S Keewatin dist., N.W.T., N Canada, group of 2 lakes S of Yathkyed L. South Henik L. (50 mi/80 km long, 1 mi/2 km–12 mi/19 km wide) is at 61°30′N 97°35′W; just N is North Henik L. (18 mi/29 km long, 10 mi/16 km wide). Both drain E into Hudson Bay through Kaminak L.

Henlawson (hen-LAW-suhn), uninc. town (1990 pop. 950), Logan co., SW W.Va., 4 mi/6.4 km NNE of Logan, near Guyandotte R. Coal-mining and agr. area. Chief Logan State Park to W.

Henley, uninc. town, Cole co., central Mo., on Osage R., and 18 mi/29 km SSW of Jefferson City. Former RR bridge over Osage R.

Henley Harbour, village, SE Lab., NE Canada, on inlet of the Atlantic Ocean, 20 mi/32 km SW of Battle Harbour; 52°01′N 55°51′W. Fishing port; lumbering.

Henlopen Acres, resort town (1990 pop. 107), Sussex co., SE Del., on Atlantic Ocean, 1 mi/1.6 km N of Rehoboth Beach; 38°44′N 75°05′W.

Henlopen, Cape (hen-LO-pen), E Sussex co., SE Del., at S side of entrance of Delaware Bay, opposite Cape May (N.J.), 12 mi/19 km to NNE; 38°48′N 75°06′W. Ferry carries RR and U.S. Highway 9 to Cape May. Site of U.S. Fort Miles, now Cape Henlopen State Park. Lewes and Rehoboth Canal parallels coast SW of cape.

Hennepin (HE-ne-pin), county (□ 606 sq mi/1,570 sq km; 1990 pop. 1,032,431), E Minn.; ⊙ Minneapolis, twin city to St. Paul (Ramsey co.) to E; 45°00′N 93°28′W. Urbanized area in Minneapolis–St. Paul metro region. Bounded NE and SE by Mississippi R., NW by Crow R., S by Minnesota R. Mfg. and commerce at Minneapolis, also Bloomington, Minnetonka, Plymouth, Maple Grove, and other municipalities; agr. (corn, soybeans, oats, alfalfa; cattle, sheep, poultry; dairying; nursery stock). Minneapolis–St. Paul Internatl. Airport in SE. Minnesota Valley Natl. Wildlife Refuge along S border; Fort Snelling Natl. Cemetery and State Park in SE; Minnehaha Falls, on Mississippi R., in E; L. Minnetonka in SW; numerous natural lakes in co. Formed 1852.

Hennepin, village (1990 pop. 669), ⊙ Putnam co., N central Ill., on Illinois R. (bridged) near its great bend, and 8 mi/12.9 km SW of Spring Valley; 41°15′N 89°19′W. Grain elevator. Fishing in Senachwine and Sawmill lakes. Oldest functional courthouse in Ill.

Hennessey, town (1990 pop. 1,902), Kingsfisher co., central Okla., 21 mi/34 km S of Enid, near Turkey Creek; 36°06′N 97°54′W. In grain and livestock area; mfg. (metal bldgs.). Laid out 1889.

Henniker (HE-ni-kuhr), town (1990 pop. 4,151), Merrimack co., S central N.H., 14 mi/23 km W of Concord; 43°10′N 71°49′W. Drained by Contoocook R. and Amey Brook. Agr. (dairying; livestock, poultry; apples, vegetables; timber); mfg. (medical supplies, lumber, bldg. materials); summer resort. Seat of New England Col. Craney Hill (1,402 ft/427 m) and Pat's Peak Ski Area in S; covered bridge. Settled 1763–1764, inc. 1768.

Henning, town (1990 pop. 802), Lauderdale co., W Tenn., 27 mi/43 km SSW of Dyersburg; 35°41′N 89°34′W. In cotton-growing area. Alex Haley House Mus. here.

Henning 1 village (1990 pop. 273), Vermilion co., E Ill., 12 mi/19 km NNW of Danville; 40°18′N 87°42′W. In agr. and bituminous-coal area. **2** village (1990 pop. 738), Otter Tail co., W Minn., 30 mi/48 km E of Fergus Falls; 46°19′N 95°26′W. Grain, sunflowers; livestock, poultry; dairying. Resort area. East Battle L to W, Otter Tail L. to NW; Inspiration Peak State Park to SW.

Henrico (hen-REI-ko), county (□ 243 sq mi/629 sq km; 1990 pop. 217,881), E central Va.; seat is Richmond (independent city separate from adjacent cos.); 37°32′N 77°24′W. W part of co. is in Piedmont region, E part on coastal plain; bounded S in part by James R. N and NE by the Chickahominy R. Agr. (hay, barley, wheat, corn, soybeans; poultry, beef cattle). Most of co. is urbanized, esp. in center, around Richmond. Civil War battlefields in co. are included in sects. of Richmond Natl. Battlefield Park in S. Glendale Natl. Cemetery in SE. Formed 1634.

Henrietta, city (1990 pop. 412), Ray co., NW Mo., near Missouri R., 4 mi/6.4 km SE of Richmond; 39°14′N 93°56′W. Soybeans, corn; livestock. Mfg. (aluminum granules). Damaged during 1993 flood.

Henrietta, town (1990 pop. 2,896), ⊙ Clay co., N Texas, 18 mi/29 km ESE of Wichita Falls, and on Little Wichita R; elev. 915 ft/279 m. In cattle, cotton, oil and gas area; agr. business; dairying; mfg. (sheet metal fabrication, trophies, transportation equip.). L. Arrowhead State Park (formed by Wichita R.) to SW. Founded 1857, resettled 1873, inc. 1882.

Henrietta, uninc. village, Rutherford co., SW N.C., 15 mi/24 km W of Shelby. Grain, soybeans; poultry, livestock. Mfg. (apparel).

Henrietta Maria, Cape, NE Ont., central Canada, on

Hudson Bay, on W side of entrance of James Bay; 55°09′N 82°20′W.

Henriette (HEN-ree-YET), village (1990 pop. 78), Pine co., E Minn., 8 mi/12.9 km WNW of Pine City; 45°52′N 93°07′W. Grain; livestock; dairying.

Henrieville, village (1990 pop. 163), Garfield co., S Utah, 30 mi/48 km SE of Panguitch; 37°33′N 111°59′W. Alfalfa, barley; cattle. Kodachrome Basin State Park to S. Old schoolhouse (1881) serves as town hall. Settled 1870s.

Henry 1 county (☐ 568 sq mi/1,471 sq km; 1990 pop. 15,374), SE Ala.; ⊙ Abbeville; 31°30′N 85°15′W. Coastal plain bounded on E by Chattahoochee R. (Ga. state line), drained (W) by Choctawhatchee R. Peanuts, corn; hogs; bauxite; lumber. Formed 1819. **2** county (☐ 331 sq mi/857 sq km; 1990 pop. 58,741), N central Ga.; ⊙ McDonough; 33°28′N 84°10′W. Rapidly urbanizing co. on Atlanta's S side. Bisected by I-75 which has become a major force in economic growth. Ga. Natl. Golf Club in McDonough. Formed 1821. **3** county (☐ 825 sq mi/2,137 sq km; 1990 pop. 51,159), NW Ill.; ⊙ Cambridge; 41°21′N 90°09′W. Bounded NW by Rock R.; drained by Green and Edwards rivers; old Illinois and Mississippi Canal crosses co. Agr. (corn, soybeans, vegetables; cattle, hogs; dairy prods.). Mfg. (food prods., machinery; metal industries). Formed 1825. **4** county (☐ 394 sq mi/1,020 sq km; 1990 pop. 48,139), E Ind.; ⊙ New Castle; 39°56′N 85°24′W. Corn, soybeans; hogs, poultry. Mfg. (esp. transportation equip.) at New Castle and Knightstown. Drained by Big Blue R., Flatrock R., and small Fall Creek. Wilbur Wright State Fish and Wildlife Area N of New Castle. Wilbur Wright Birthplace State Memorial in E. Formed 1821. **5** county (☐ 436 sq mi/1,129 sq km; 1990 pop. 19,226), SE Iowa; ⊙ Mount Pleasant; 40°59′N 91°33′W. Prairie agr. area (sheep, cattle; corn, soybeans) drained by Skunk R.; limestone quarries. Oakland Mills State Park in SW; Geode State Park in SE, known for its quartzite geodes. Flooding along Skunk R. in 1993. Formed 1836. **6** county (☐ 291 sq mi/754 sq km; 1990 pop. 12,823), N Ky.; ⊙ New Castle, 38°27′N 85°09′W. Bounded E by Kentucky R.; drained by Little Kentucky R. and Floyds Fork. Gently rolling upland agr. area (burley tobacco, corn, hay, alfalfa, soybeans, wheat; cattle, hogs, horses, poultry; dairying; timber), in Bluegrass region. Primary metals industries, electronics. Zinc and lead mines in S were productive during World Wars I and II. Formed 1798. **7** county (☐ 737 sq mi/1909 sq km; 1990 pop. 20,044), W central Mo.; ⊙ Clinton; 38°23′N 93°47′W. Drained by South Grand R. Corn, wheat, soybeans; sorghum, sweet corn; cattle. Strip coal mines in SW. Some mfg. at Clinton and Windsor. S Grand and Tebo Arms of Truman L. enter co. from E. Fishing, boating. Montrose Conservation Area in SW. Formed 1834. **8** county (☐ 416 sq mi/1,077 sq km; 1990 pop. 29,108), NW Ohio; ⊙ Napoleon; 41°21′N 84°06′W. Intersected by Maumee R. In the Lake Plains physiographic region. Diversified farming (corn, wheat, oats, sugar beets, vegetables); mfg. (preserved fruits and vegetables, fabricated metal prods., cutlery and tools, transportation equip.). Formed 1824. **9** county (☐ 599 sq mi/1,551 sq km; 1990 pop. 27,888), NW Tenn.; ⊙ Paris; 36°20′N 88°18′W. Bounded N by Ky., E by Kentucky Reservoir (Tennessee R.; here receives the Big Sandy); drained by East Fork Clarks R. and forks of the Obion. Agr. area (corn, cotton, tobacco, sweet potatoes, soybeans; livestock); dairy prods., some mfg. at Paris. Timber; clay pits. Formed 1821. **10** county (☐ 384 sq mi/995 sq km; 1990 pop. 56,942), S Va.; ⊙ Martinsville (independent city, separate from co.); 36°40′N 79°52′W. In Piedmont region, bounded S by N.C. state line; drained by Smith and North and South Mayo rivers. Mfg. at Bassett (noted for its furniture prods.), Fieldale, Collinsville, and Ridgeway; agr. (esp. tobacco; also hay; cattle, poultry; honey); timber. Part of Fairy Stone State Park, Philpott Reservoir in NW. Formed 1777.

Henry, city (1990 pop. 2,591), Marshall co., N central Ill., on Illinois R. (bridged here), and 7 mi/11.3 km N of Lacon; 41°06′N 89°21′W. In agr. area (corn, soybeans, fruit; cattle); ships grain; mfg. (chemicals). Nurseries. Nearby is Senachwine L. Founded in early 1840s; inc. 1854.

Henry, town (1990 pop. 317), Henry co., NW Tenn., 8 mi/13 km SW of Paris; 36°12′N 88°25′W.

Henry 1 village (1990 pop. 145), Scotts Bluff co., extreme W Nebr., 20 mi/32 km WNW of Scottsbluff, and on North Platte R. at Wyo. state line; 42°00′N 104°02′W. Oregon Trail follows S side of river. **2** village (1990 pop. 215), Codington co., E S.Dak., 18 mi/29 km W of Watertown; 44°52′N 97°27′W. Potatoes, corn; pheasant hunting.

Henry, Cape, Virginia Beach (independent city), SE Va., promontory at entrance to Chesapeake Bay, 18 mi/29 km ENE of Norfolk. Cape Henry Memorial marks the approximate 1st landing site of Eng. settlers of Jamestown in 1607. In 1939 the site became a separate unit of Colonial Natl. Historical Park (which also includes historic towns of Yorktown and Jamestown). Old Cape Henry Lighthouse, Ft. Story Military Reservation, Seashore State Park. Atlantic Univ. to S.

Henry, Fort, provincial historic park, fortification, SE Ont., E Canada, on the St. Lawrence R., near L. Ontario, at SW end of Rideau Canal, overlooking Kingston harbor; 44°14′N 76°28′W. Built 1812, original fort was demolished 1832 and replaced by present structure. Later a mus., it was camp for prisoners of war in World Wars I and II. Commonly referred to as Old Fort Henry. Can. Forces Base Kingston is 1 mi/2 km E.

Henry, Fort, Tenn.: see FORT HENRY.

Henry Hudson Bridge, N.Y. city, SE N.Y., over Spuyten Duyvil, connects N tip of Manhattan with the Riverdale sect. of the Bronx; 40°53′N 73°56′W. A double-deck vehicular structure, it is 2,000 ft/610 m long overall and 142 ft/43 m above the water.

Henry Island, islet, in Gulf of St. Lawerence, NE N.S., E Canada, off W Cape Breton Isl., 5 mi/8 km SW of Port Hood; 45°58′N 61°36′W.

Henry Kater, Cape, E Baffin Isl., E Franklin dist., N.W.T., N Canada, on Davis Strait, E extremity of Henry Kater Peninsula (55 mi/89 km long, 7 mi/11 km–23 mi/37 km wide), forming N shore of Home Bay; 69°04′N 66°46′W.

Henry Mountains, in E Garfield co. (extends into Wayne co.), S Utah, W of Dirty Devil R., E of Escalante. Chief peaks are Mts. Hillers (10,723 ft/3,268 m), Pennell (11,371 ft/3,466 m), and Ellen (11,522 ft/3,512 m). Laccolith intrusive formations. Recreation area.

Henryetta, town (1990 pop. 5,872), Okmulgee co., E central Okla., 12 mi/19 km S of Okmulgee; 35°26′N 95°58′W. In diversified agr. area; mfg. (glass prods., chemicals, consumer goods, machinery; sawmill). Coal mines; oil and natural-gas wells. L. Eufaula reservoir to E. Founded c.1900.

Henrys Fork, river, c.110 mi/177 km long, SE Idaho; rises in Henrys L. (☐ 8 sq mi/20.7 sq km; 4 mi/6.4 km long, 2 mi/3.2 km wide), near Mont. state line and Continental Divide, N Fremont co., in Targhee Natl. Forest; flows S through Island Park Reservoir, over Upper Mesa and Lower Mesa Falls (114 ft/35 m) and SW, past St. Anthony, to Snake R. 10 mi/16 km SW of Rexburg. Island Park Dam (91 ft/28 m high, 9,448 ft/2,880 m long; completed 1938) is in upper course near Island Park. Used in irrigation of upper Snake R. valley; impounds Island Park L. (12 mi/19 km long).

Henryville, village (1991 pop. 677), S Que., E Canada, 12 mi/19 km SSE of St. Jean. Dairying.

Henryville, village (1990 pop. 1,132), Clark co., S Ind., 7 mi/11.3 km NW of Charlestown. Clark State Forest to W. Cattle; corn.

Hensall (HEN-sol), village (1991 pop. 1,238), S Ont., central Canada, 24 mi/39 km SSE of Goderich; 43°26′N 81°30′W. Dairying, mixed farming.

Hensel, village (1990 pop. 64), Pembina co., NE N.Dak., 8 mi/12.9 km SSW of Cavalier; 48°41′N 97°39′W. Formerly called Canton.

Henshaw, Lake, Calif.: see SAN LUIS REY RIVER.

Hensley, village, Pulaski co., central Ark., 16 mi/26 km SSE of Little Rock.

Hepburn, town (1990 pop. 41), Page co., SW Iowa, near Nodaway R., 8 mi/12.9 km N of Clarinda; 40°51′N 95°01′W.

Hepburn, village (1991 pop. 463), central Sask., W Canada, 28 mi/45 km N of Saskatoon. Mixed farming, dairying.

Hephzibah (HEP-zuh-buh), town (1990 pop. 2,466), Richmond co., E Ga., 12 mi/19 km SSW of Augusta; 33°17′N 82°07′W. Clay and wood prods.

Hepler, village (1990 pop. 150), Crawford co., SE Kansas, 23 mi/37 km NW of Pittsburg; 37°39′N 94°58′W. Agr.

Heppner, town (1990 pop. 1,412), ⊙ Morrow co., N Oregon, on Willow Creek (forms Willow Creek Reservoir to E), c.41 mi/66 km SW of Pendleton; elev. 1,955 ft/596 m; 45°21′N 119°32′W. RR terminus. Potatoes, onions; sheep, cattle. Umatilla Natl. Forest to SE.

Hepworth, village (1991 pop. 453), S Ont., central Canada, 12 mi/19 km NW of Owen Sound. Dairying, mixed farming.

Herald Harbor, summer resort (1990 pop. 1,707), Anne Arundel co., central Md., on Severn R., 7 mi/11.3 km NW of Annapolis; 39°03′N 76°34′W. The name of this beach resort is attributed to promotional efforts made by the *Washington Herald* in 1924. One article was headlined, "Herald Harbor Plans Announced." One thousand lots were presumably sold on 1 day.

Herald Square, in Midtown sect. of Manhattan borough of N.Y. city, SE N.Y., intersection of 6th Ave., 34th St., and Broadway. Major commercial center; formerly called Greeley Sq., it was renamed after the N.Y. *Herald*. In 1902, Macy's built what was then the world's largest dept. store, and other retailers soon followed, including Gimbel's, Ohrbach, and Saks 5th Ave. Although the latter 3 stores closed in the 1980s, Macy's remains, and other shops also ring the area. Pennsylvania RR station to SE, Empire State Bldg. to SW.

Herb Lake, village, N central Man., central Canada, on Wekusko L., 85 mi/137 km E of Flin Flon; 54°47′N 99°47′W. Former mining area.

Herbert, town (1991 pop. 941), S Sask., W Canada, near Rush L., 27 mi/43 km ENE of Swift Current; 50°26′N 107°13′W. Grain elevators, lumber and flour mills.

Herbert G. West, Lake, reservoir (☐ 10 sq mi/26 sq km), Franklin co., SE Wash., on Snake R., 33 mi/53 km NE of Pasco; 46°34′N 118°32′W. Max. capacity 432,000 acre-ft. Formed by Lower Monumental Dam (226 ft/69 m high) built (1969) by Army Corps of Engineers for navigation; also used for power generation, flood control, and recreation and as a fish and wildlife pond. L. Sacajewea downstream.

Herbert Hoover National Historic Site, E Iowa; extends over 187 acres/76 ha. Birthplace, childhood home, and gravesite of President Herbert Hoover; lib., mus. Authorized 1965.

Herculaneum (HUHR-kyoo-LAI-nee-uhm), town (1990 pop. 2,263), Jefferson co., E Mo., on Mississippi R., satellite town 25 mi/40 km S of St. Louis; 38°15′N 90°23′W. Limestone quarries; largest lead smelter in the U.S. Historic lead shot tower of 1809. Plotted 1808.

Hercules, city (1990 pop. 16,829), Contra Costa co., W Calif., suburb 13 mi/21 km N of downtown Oakland, on San Pablo Bay, 7 mi/11.3 km NE of Richmond, at mouth of Refugio Creek; 38°01′N 122°18′W. Mfg. (computer equip., laboratory instruments; petroleum refining).

Hércules, Mexico: see CAYETANO RUBIO.

Hereford, city (1990 pop. 14,745), ⊙ Deaf Smith co., N Texas, 40 mi/64 km SW of Amarillo, in the Panhandle; elev. 3,806 ft/1,160 m; 34°49′N 102°24′W. Livestock; cattle feeding is an important industry, along with meatpacking and sugar refining. Vegetables (esp. onions), sugar beets, sunflowers, and grains are grown on irrigated farms in the semiarid plains. Former site of Natl. Cowgirl Hall of Fame (1975–1996). Buffalo L. Natl. Wildlife Refuge to E. Inc. 1906.

Hereford (HE-re-ford), village, Baltimore co., N Md., 20 mi/32 km N of Baltimore. Takes its name from the abandoned Hereford Farmhouse built (1714) by the Merryman family of Hereford, England. Site of cross-country races for Grand Natl. Steeplechase and My Lady's Manor race. Eighteen fences and 2 water

Cross references are shown in SMALL CAPITALS. The pronunciation key is on page xv. The dates of population figures are on page xii.

jumps make the course one on the most dangerous in America.

Hereford Inlet (HIR-fuhrd), S N.J., passage (c.2 mi/ 3.2 km wide) connecting the Atlantic Ocean and Intracoastal Waterway channel, bet. North Wildwood and S tip of Seven Mile Beach.

Herendeen Bay (HE-ren-deen), village, SW Alaska, on Alaska Peninsula, at head of Herendeen Bay, inlet (20 mi/32 km long) of Bristol Bay of Bering Sea; 55°46'N 160°43'W. Fishing. Surface coal veins in vicinity.

Herington (HER-ing-tuhn), town (1990 pop. 2,685), Dickinson co., central Kansas, 22 mi/35 km SE of Abilene; 38°40'N 96°57'W. RR junction. Shipping and trade center, with RR repair shops, for livestock and grain area. Mfg. (industrial machinery). Monument to the missionary Juan de Padilla is here. Inc. 1887.

Heritage Hills, inc. village within the town of Southbury, New Haven co., SW Conn. Retirement center with 2,500 homes.

Herkimer (HUHR-ki-muhr), county (☐ 1,458 sq mi/ 3,776 sq km; 1990 pop. 65,797), N central N.Y.; ⊙ Herkimer; 43°24'N 74°57'W. Long, narrow area, with N part extending into the Adirondack Mts., and S part in fertile Mohawk valley, which contains virtually all of the co.'s pop. Drained by Mohawk R., and by Unadilla, Black, and Moose rivers. Mfg., farming, and dairying in S. Many mt. and lake resorts in N. Formed 1791.

Herkimer (HUHR-ki-muhr), industrial village (☐ 2 sq mi/5.2 sq km; 1990 pop. 7,945), ⊙ Herkimer co., central N.Y., on Mohawk R., at mouth of W. Canada Creek, and 13 mi/21 km ESE of Utica; 43°01'N 74°59'W. Formerly shipping, commercial, and trade center for surrounding Mohawk valley agr. and industrial area that stretched W through village of Mohawk to Ilion and Frankfort. Today, however, the industrial center of the Mohawk Valley has greatly declined. Mfg. includes machinery, consumer goods, wood prods., and firearms. Herkimer Co. Historical Society has important documents and exhibits here. World-renowned "Herkimer diamonds" (actually a clear quartz) are to be found along West Canada Creek Valley N of the village. Settled c.1725, inc. 1807.

Herman 1 village (1990 pop. 485), Grant co., W Minn., 15 mi/24 km SW of Elbow Lake town; 45°48'N 96°08'W. Grain; livestock, poultry; dairying; mfg. (wire harnesses; light mfg.). Several small lakes to E and SE. **2** village (1990 pop. 186), Washington co., E Nebr., 10 mi/16 km NNW of Blair, near Missouri R.; 41°40'N 96°13'W. Grain; livestock. Mfg. (portable grain augers).

Hermann (HUHR-muhn), city (1990 pop. 2,754), E central Mo., ⊙ Gasconade co., on Missouri R., 41 mi/ 66 km E of Jefferson City; 38°42'N 91°26'W. Dairying; cattle, poultry, hogs; mfg. (plastic prods., transportation equip., consumer goods, wine; meat processing); clay. Wineries; tourism. Has annual Maifest and Oktoberfest celebrations. Settled 1837 by Ger. immigrants. Deutschherr State Historic Site. Over 100 structures are on the Register of Historic Places. Inc. 1839.

Hermansville, village, Menominee co., SW Upper Peninsula, N Mich., 24 mi/39 km SE of Iron Mountain city, and on Little Cedar R.; 45°42'N 87°36'W. Lumber milling.

Hermantown, town (1990 pop. 6,761), St. Louis co., NE Minn., residential suburb 6 mi/9.7 km W of downtown Duluth, on Midway R.; 46°48'N 92°14'W. Mfg. (sheet metal fabrication); agr. (dairying; poultry; hay). Duluth Municipal Airport to NE.

Hermanville, village, Claiborne co., SW Miss., 8 mi/ 12.9 km E of Port Gibson. Agr. (cattle; corn, cotton; timber); mfg. (lumber).

Hermenegildo Galeana, Mexico: see BIENVENIDO.

Herminie (HER-mi-nee), uninc. town (1990 est. pop. 2,000), Westmoreland co., SW Pa., 19 mi/31 km SE of Pittsburgh, on Little Sewickley Creek; 40°15'N 74°43'W. Agr. (corn, hay; dairying). Light mfg. Shuster Cellars Winery to N.

Hermiston (HUHR-muhs-stuhn), city (1990 pop. 10,040), Umatilla co., N Oregon, 27 mi/43 km NW of

Pendleton, near Umatilla R., 5 mi/8 km S of its confluence with the Columbia R.; 45°49'N 119°16'W. RR junction to S. Mfg. (frozen vegetables, mobile homes, bldg. materials; printing and publishing). Grains; cattle. Umatilla Ordnance Depot (chemical weapons) to W. Cold Springs Natl. Wildlife Refuge and Hot Rock State Park to NE. McNary Dam (Columbia R.) to N. Inc. 1910.

Hermitage (HUHR-mah-tuhj), city (1990 pop 15,300), Mercer co., W Pa., suburb 3 mi/4.8 km E of Sharon; 41°13'N 80°26'W. Mfg. of fabricated metal prods., machinery, food prods., chemicals. Agr. includes dairying; livestock; grain, potatoes, soybeans. Hermitage and Sharon airports in S. Shenango R. L. reservoir to N. Formerly a township.

Hermitage 1 (HUHR-mi-tij), town (1990 pop. 512), ⊙ Hickory co., central Mo., in the Ozark Mts., on Pomme de Terre R., and 50 mi/80 km N of Springfield; 37°56'N 93°19'W. Wheat, soybeans; dairying; cattle; mfg. (apparel). Tourism and lake region. Pomme de Terre L. to S; extension of Harry S. Truman L. to N; Pomme de Terre State Park. Plotted 1847. **2** town, Davidson co., central Tenn., 10 mi/16 km E of Nashville, 36°11'N 86°37'W. The Hermitage, home of Andrew Jackson, is just N.

Hermitage, village (1991 pop. 756), S N.F., E Canada, on SE shore of Hermitage Bay, 80 mi/129 km E of Burgeo; 47°33'N 55°56'W. Fishing.

Hermitage (HUHR-muh-tij), village (1990 pop. 639), Bradley co., S Ark., 32 mi/51 km ENE of El Dorado in L'Aigle co.; 33°27'N 92°10'W. RR junction to N. Known for production of tomatoes.

Hermitage (HUHR-mi-tej), historic site, home of President Andrew Jackson, Davidson co., central Tenn., 12 mi/19 km E of Nashville. The house, in a fine formal garden, was built 1819–1831; a church on the grounds was built 1823. Jackson and his wife are buried in the plantation graveyard.

Hermitage Bay, inlet of the Atlantic Ocean, S N.F., E Canada; 30 mi/48 km long, 10 mi/16 km wide at entrance; 47°35'N 55°50'W. Many fishing settlements on its shores. N arm of Hermitage Bay is the Bay d'Espoir. Bay contains several isls.

Hermleigh (HUHR-mah-lee), uninc. town (1990 pop. 200), Scurry co., NW central Texas, 10 mi/16 km SE of Snyder. In agr. and cattle-ranching area.

Hermon (HUHR-muhn), town (1990 pop. 3,755), Penobscot co., S Maine, 7 mi/11.3 km W of Bangor; 44°49'N 68°55'W. In agr. area. Settled c.1790.

Hermon, village (1990 pop. 407), St. Lawrence co., N N.Y., 20 mi./32 km SE of Ogdensburg; 44°28'N 75°13'W.

Hermosa, village (1990 pop. 242), Custer co., SW S.Dak., 17 mi/27 km S of Rapid City, and on Battle Creek; 43°50'N 103°11'W. Near E entrance to Custer State Park. Tourism at E edge of Black Hills.

Hermosa Beach, city (1990 pop. 18,219), Los Angeles co., S Calif., residential suburb 14 mi/23 km SW of downtown Los Angeles, on Santa Monica Bay, Pacific Ocean; 33°56'N 118°25'W. Beach resort and recreation area. Nearby are Manhattan (N) and Redondo (S) state beaches. Inc. 1907.

Hermosillo (er-mo-SEE-yo), city (1990 pop. 406,417) and township, ⊙ Sonora state, NW Mexico, on Mexico Highway 15; 29°15'N 110°59'W. At the entrance to the gorge of the Sonora R. Hermosillo is a transportation, mfg. (motor vehicles), and agr. center in an irrigated area where cereals and cotton are grown and cattle are raised. Est. 1700 as a Native Amer. town with a Jesuit missionary, the city was later renamed in honor of the Span. general José María González de Hermosillo. Airport.

Hernando (her-NAN-do), county (☐ 589 sq mi/ 1,526 sq km; 1990 pop. 101,115), W central Fla., bet. Withlacoochee R. (E) and Gulf of Mexico (W); ⊙ Brooksville; 28°33'N 82°28'W. Lowland area with marshy coast and small scattered lakes. Agr. (poultry, cattle, hogs; corn, citrus fruit, peanuts); sawmilling; limestone quarrying. Formed 1843.

Hernando 1 (her-NAN-do), town (☐ 3 sq mi/7.8 sq km; 1990 pop. 2,103), Citrus co., W central Fla., 25 mi/40 km

SW of Ocala, on Tsala Apopka L.; 28°54'N 82°22'W. Fishing; phosphate quarrying. **2** town (1990 pop. 3,125), ⊙ De Soto co., extreme NW Miss., 22 mi/35 km S of Memphis (Tenn.); 34°49'N 89°59'W. Trade center for agr. region (soybeans, cotton, corn; cattle; dairying); mfg. (aluminum and paper prods., crushed stone, electrical goods, wood prods.; beef processing). Arkabutla L. reservoir to SW; Hernando de Soto Memorial Trail. Inc. 1837.

Herndon, town (1990 pop. 16,139), Fairfax co., N Va., suburb 20 mi/32 km WNW of Washington, D.C.; 38°58'N 77°23'W. Mfg. (printing and publishing; electronic equip., machinery, computer equip., biological solutions, text encryption devices); some agr. to NW (dairying; poultry, cattle; nursery stock). Dulles Internatl. Airport to W. Natl. Weather Service to W. Inc. 1874; recharted 1938.

Herndon (HUHRN-duhn), village (1990 pop. 170), Rawlins co., NW Kansas, on Beaver Creek, and 16 mi/26 km ENE of Atwood, near Nebr. state line; 39°54'N 100°47'W. Grain; livestock.

Herndon, borough (1990 pop. 422), Northumberland co., E central Pa., 11 mi/18 km SSW of Sunbury, on Susquehanna R. Mfg. (wood prods., crushed limestone); agr. (corn, hay; poultry; dairying).

Herod (HER-uhd), town, Terrell co., SW Ga., 6 mi/ 9.7 km S of Dawson; 31°41'N 84°26'W.

Heroica Caborca (e-ro-EE-kah kah-BOR-kah), city (1990 pop. 8,574) and township, Sonora, NW Mexico, on Magdalena R. (irrigation), and 80 mi/129 km SW of Nogales; 30°42'N 112°10'W. Agr. center (wheat, corn, cotton, beans). Silver, copper deposits nearby.

Heroica Ciudad de Tlaxiaco (he-RO-ee-kah see-OO-dahd dai tlahk-see-AH-ko), town (1990 pop. 9,555), W central Oaxaca, Mexico, 65 mi/105 km WNW of Oaxaca de Juárez, and on Mexico Highway 125, bet. Putla de Guerrero and San Pedro y San Pablo Teposcolula; elev. 6,555 ft/1,998 m; 17°15'N 97°40'W. On the banks of the Tlaxiaco R. The Los Tejocotes Antimony Mining Dist. is a short distance W of Tlaxiaco in San Juan Mixtepec municipio. Agr. (corn, beans); cattle raising; forestry (pine, oak). An important commercial center that serves the surrounding rural pop. Formerly Santa María Asunción Tlaxiaco.

Heroica Guaymas (e-RO-ee-kah goo-AI-mas), city (1990 pop. 87,484) and township, Sonora state, NW Mexico, on the bay of Guaymas, on Mexico Highway 15; 27°59'N 110°54'W. A port on the Gulf of California, it is the outlet for Hermosillo. On a scenic inlet girt by desert mts. Its fine beaches, excellent deep-sea fishing, and transportation facilities have made it a popular tourist resort. In addition to its role as a commercial center for the surrounding region, Guaymas has a substantial fishing industry. Although the surrounding area was explored as early as 1539, the city was not established until the early 18th cent. by Jesuit missionaries. U.S. forces occupied Guaymas in 1846, during the Mex. War, and it was held by the French in 1865–1866.

Heroica Matamoros (e-RO-ee-kah mah-tah-MO-ros), city (1990 pop. 266,055) and township, ⊙ Matamoros municipio, Tamaulipas state, NE Mexico, near the mouth of the Rio Grande, opposite Brownsville (Texas), and on Mexico Highways 2 and 180; 25°53'N 97°30'W. Linked by RR and highway with the U.S.; internatl. trading center and point of entry. Center of an agr. region that has become increasingly industrialized. Foreign-owned mfg. plants (motor vehicle parts), known as maquiladoras, proliferated in the area and constitute a dominant part of the economy. Founded in 1700 as San Juan de los Esteros, the city was renamed in 1851 in honor of the leader for Mex. independence Mariano Matamoros.

Heroica Nogales (e-RO-ee-kah no-GAH-les), city (1990 pop. 105,873) and township, Sonora, NW Mexico, on U.S. border, adjoining Nogales (Ariz.), 160 mi/257 km N of Hermosillo, on Mexico Highway 15; 31°20'N 111°00'W. RR junction at terminus of Mexico's W coast RR; internatl. trading point in cattle-raising and mining area (graphite, manganese, silver, gold, lead, antimony). Exports winter vegetables of S Sonora and Sinaloa.

Heróica Puebla de Zaragoza (e-RO-ee-kah poo-EB-lah dai sah-rah-GO-sah) or **Puebla** (poo-EB-lah), city (1990 pop. 1,007,170), ⊙ Puebla state, E central Mexico; elev. 7,093 ft/2,162 m; 19°03′N 98°10′W. Named Heróica Puebla de Zaragoza, in honor of Gen. Ignacio Zaragoza, who defeated the Fr. forces here in 1862. Located in a highland valley, it is an important agr., commercial, and mfg. center, as well as a popular tourist spot. The site of Mexico's 1st textile-producing factory, Puebla has cotton mills, a motor vehicle factory, onyx quarries, and pottery and food industries. Noted for the colored tiles that decorate its bldgs. and numerous churches, as well as those of nearby Cholula. The cathedral, built 1552–1649, is one of the finest in Mexico; the theater, constructed in 1790, is said to be the oldest on the continent. Founded c.1535 as Puebla de los Ángeles, the city was historically a link bet. the coast and Mexico city. Taken (1847) by U.S. Gen. Winfield Scott during the Mex. War. Fr. troops captured Puebla in 1863 but were ousted by Porfirio Díaz in 1867. Puebla was the center of a large earthquake in 1973 that caused intense damage to the city and its surrounding region.

Heroica Zitácuaro (e-RO-ee-kah see-TAH-kwah-ro), city (1990 pop. 66,983) and township, ⊙ Zitácuaro municipio, Michoacán, central Mexico, in valley of central plateau, on RR, and 50 mi/80 km SE of Morelia, on Mexico Highway 15; 19°28′N 100°21′W. Lumbering and agr. center (cereals, vegetables, fruit livestock); sawmilling, tanning, soapmaking, vegetable oil extracting, resin processing. Tourism. The spa of Purúa or San José Purúa, with mineral waters, is 9 mi/14.5 km WNW.

Heron Lake, village (1990 pop. 730), Jackson co., SW Minn., NW of Heron L., near Jack Creek, 21 mi/34 km NW of Jackson; 43°47′N 95°19′W. Grain, soybeans; livestock.

Heron Lake (□ 13 sq mi/34 sq km), Jackson co., SW Minn., 20 mi/32 km NE of Worthington; 12 mi/19 km long (including S Heron L.), 3 mi/4.8 km wide; elev. 1,400 ft/427 m. Has N outlet into Des Moines R.; Jack Creek enters lake from W. Short channel connects lake with South Heron L., to SE. Abundance of game here.

Heron Lake (HE-ruhn), reservoir, Rio Arriba co., N N.Mex., on Willow Creek, in Heron L. State Park, 7 mi/11.3 km W of Tierra Amarilla; 3 mi/4.8 km long; 36°40′N 106°40′W. Max. capacity 430,000 acre-ft. Formed by Heron Dam (254 ft/77 m high), built by the U.S. govt. for irrigation, water supply, and recreation.

Herreid, village (1990 pop. 488), Campbell co., N S.Dak., 28 mi/45 km NE of Mobridge, and on Spring Creek; 45°50′N 100°04′W. Pocasse Natl. Wildlife Refuge to W.

Herreras, Los, Mexico: see LOS HERRERAS.

Herrick 1 village (1990 pop. 466), Shelby co., central Ill., 17 mi/27 km SSW of Shelbyville; 39°13′N 88°59′W. In agr. area. **2** village (1990 pop. 139), Gregory co., S S.Dak., 7 mi/11.3 km SE of Burke, 43°07′N 99°11′W. Small trading point for agr. area. Burke L. State Rec. Area to NW.

Herrin, city (1990 pop. 10,857), Williamson co., S Ill., 8 mi/12.9 km NNW of Marion; 37°47′N 89°01′W. Trade center of an extensive coal-mining area. Mfg. includes consumer goods, electrical goods, and clothing. The city was the site of the Herrin Massacre; in 1922 during a co.-wide coal strike, clashes bet. unionized strikers and nonunion miners, who had been imported by the coal company, resulted in nearly 25 deaths. Settled 1818, inc. 1898.

Herrings, village (1990 pop. 140), Jefferson co., N N.Y., near Black R., 13 mi/21 km E of Watertown; 44°01′N 39°75′W.

Herrington Lake, reservoir (□ 5 sq mi/13 sq km), Mercer co., central Ky., on Dix R., 22 mi/35 km SSW of Lexington; 37°47′N 84°43′W. Max. capacity 300,000 acre-ft. Formed by Dix Dam (287 ft/87 m high), built (1925) for power generation.

Herschel Island, N Yukon, Canada, in Beaufort Sea of the Arctic Ocean, on W side of entrance of Mackenzie Bay; 11 mi/18 km long, 2 mi/3 km–7 mi/11 km wide; 69°35′N 139°05′W. Herschel village, on E coast, has Royal Can. Mounted Police post.

Herscher (HUHR-schuhr), village (1990 pop. 1,278), Kankakee co., NE Ill., 13 mi/21 km WSW of Kankakee; 41°02′N 88°05′W. In agr. area.

Hersey, town (1990 pop. 69), Aroostook co., E Maine, 28 mi/45 km W of Houlton; 46°04′N 68°22′W.

Hersey, village (1990 pop. 354), Osceola co., central Mich., 3 mi/4.8 km SE of Reed City, and on Muskegon R.; 43°51′N 85°26′W. In lake and agr. area.

Hershey, uninc. city (1990 pop. 11,860, with adjacent Swatara Station), Derry township, Dauphin co., S central Pa., 12 mi/19 km E of Harrisburg. Company town owned by Hershey Corp. Mfg. (tool and die, machinery, explosives, food prods.). Agr. area (apples, soybeans, grain; poultry, livestock; dairying). Hershey Park (□ 2 sq mi/5.2 sq km), theme park; Hershey's Chocolate World; Hershey Mus.; ZooAmerica (N. Amer. wildlife); Hershey Medical Center; Indian Echo Caverns to SW. Founded 1903.

Hershey, village (1990 pop. 579), Lincoln co., SW central Nebr., 12 mi/19 km W of North Platte city, bet. North and South Platte rivers; 41°09′N 101°00′W. Livestock; grain; mfg. (light aircraft). RR junction to W.

Hertford (HUHRT-fuhrd), county (□ 360 sq mi/932 sq km; 1990 pop. 22,523), NE N.C.; ⊙ Winton; 36°21′N 76°58′W. Bounded N by Va. state line, E by Chowan R., drained by Meherrin R., forms NW boundary; coastal plain (W) and tidewater (E). Agr. (peanuts, tobacco, cotton, corn, wheat, sorghum, soybeans, potatoes; chickens, hogs); timber (pine, gum, oak). Formed 1759.

Hertford (HUHRT-fuhrd), town (1990 pop. 2,244), ⊙ Perquimans co., NE N.C., 16 mi/26 km SW of Elizabeth City, and on Perquimans R.; 36°10′N 76°28′W. Fish, crabs. Peanuts, cotton, grain, soybeans, potatoes; chickens, livestock. Mfg. (clothing). Newberg-White House (c. 1730). Settled before 1700; inc. 1758.

Hespeler, Canada: see CAMBRIDGE.

Hesperia, city (1990 pop. 50,418), San Bernardino co., S Calif., 21 mi/34 km N of San Bernardino, near Mojave R., in SW part of Mojave Desert; 34°25′N 117°18′W. Mojave R. Forks Reservoir to S; San Bernardino Mts. and San Bernardino Natl. Forest to S; Sherwood L. State Recreation Area to S. Cattle; fruit, alfalfa, grain. Mfg. (fabricated metal prods., trusses, concrete prods., electronic equip., wood prods.; printing and publishing). Limestone quarrying in area.

Hesperia (he-SPIR-ee-uh), village (1990 pop. 846), Oceana and Newaygo co., W Mich., 26 mi/42 km NNE of Muskegon, and on White R.; 43°34′N 86°02′W. In resort and fruit-growing area. Manistee Natl. Forest to W and N.

Hesperus, village, La Plata co., SW Colo., on La Plata R., and 12 mi/19 km W of Durango; elev. 8,110 ft/2,472 m.

Hesperus Mountain (13,232 ft/4,033 m), in La Plata Mts., SW Colo., 16 mi/26 km NW of Durango.

Hess, Mount (11,940 ft/3,639 m), E Alaska, in Alaska Range, 80 mi/129 km S of Fairbanks; 63°37′N 147°06′W.

Hessel, village, Mackinac co., SE Upper Peninsula, N Mich., 17 mi/27 km NE of St. Ignace, on L. Huron; 46°00′N 84°25′W. Airport. Les Cheneaux Isls. to SE. Hiawatha Natl. Forest to W.

Hessmer (HE-se-muhr), village (1990 pop. 578), Avoyelles parish, E central La., 21 mi/34 km SE of Alexandria, near Red R.; 31°03′N 92°07′W. Grand Cote Natl. Wildlife Refuge to NW. In agr. area (cotton, rice, sugarcane); logging; catfish; mfg. (canned vegetables, cypress lumber).

Hesston, town (1990 pop. 3,012), Harvey co., S central Kansas, 8 mi/12.9 km NW of Newton; 38°08′N 97°25′W. In wheat region; farm equip. Bethel Col. 6 mi/9.7 km SE near North Newton.

Hester, village, Greer co., SW Okla., 6 mi/9.7 km SSE of Mangum, near North Fork of Red R.

Hetch Hetchy Aqueduct, 156 mi/251 km long, Tuolumne co., central Calif.; runs from Hetch Hetchy Reservoir W, roughly paralleling Tuolumne R., runs past Groveland, Oakdale and Modesto, crosses San Joaquin R., 10 mi/16 km W of Modesto, continues across Diablo Range, past Fremont and Newark, crosses lower end of San Francisco Bay S of Dumbarton Bridge, continues past E Palo Alto, N Fair Oaks and Redwood City, ending up at Upper Crystal Springs Reservoir (in San Andreas Rift Zone), 20 mi/32 km S of downtown San Francisco, in San Mateo co.

Hetch Hetchy Reservoir (□ 3 sq mi/7.8 sq km), Tuolumne co., E central Calif., on Tuolumne R., in N part of Yosemite Natl. Park, 65 mi/105 km ESE of Merced; 37°57′N 119°47′W. Max. capacity 372,000 acre-ft. Formed by O'Shaughnessy Dam (430 ft/131 m), built (1923) for power generation and water supply for City and Co. of San Francisco. Enlarged 1938.

Hetch Hetchy Valley, in Yosemite Natl. Park, Tuolumne co., central Calif., on the Tuolumne R., 12 mi/19 km N of Yosemite village. O'Shaughnessy Dam (forms Hetch Hetchy Reservoir in lower 10 mi/16 km of valley) turned the valley into a lake 10 mi/16 km long, which is used for generating power and for supplying water to San Francisco by Hetch Hetchy Aqueduct. Also called the Grand Canyon of the Tuolumne.

Hetland, village (1990 pop. 53), Kingsbury co., E S.Dak., 5 mi/8 km W of Arlington; 44°22′N 97°13′W.

Hettick, village (1990 pop. 211), Macoupin co., SW Ill., 10 mi/16 km WNW of Carlinville; 39°21′N 90°02′W. In agr. and bituminous-coal area.

Hettinger (HE-ting-guhr), county (□ 1,133 sq mi/2,934 sq km; 1990 pop. 3,445), SW N.Dak.; ⊙ Mott; 46°25′N 102°27′W. Agr. area drained by Cannonball R. and Thirtymile Creek. Dairy prods.; wheat, rye; cattle. Formed 1883.

Hettinger (HE-ting-guhr), town (1990 pop. 1,574), ⊙ Adams co., SW N.Dak., 62 mi/100 km SSE of Dickinson, near S.Dak. state line; 46°00′N 102°37′W. Agr.; dairying. Inc. 1916. Grand R. Natl. Grassland to S.

Heuvelton (HUH-vuhl-tuhn), village (1990 pop. 771), St. Lawrence co., N N.Y., on Oswegatchie R., and 6 mi/9.7 km SE of Ogdensburg; 44°37′N 75°24′W.

Hewanorra International Airport, St. Lucia: see VIEUX FORT.

Hewitt 1 village (1990 pop. 269), Todd co., W central Minn., 8 mi/12.9 km SSE of Wadena, on Wing R.; 46°19′N 95°05′W. Poultry, livestock; grain, potatoes; dairying; mfg. (wood prods.). **2** village (1990 pop. 595), Wood Co., central Wis., 4 mi/6.4 km SE of Marshfield; 44°38′N 90°06′W. Dairying; livestock; general farming. Agr. research station to W.

Hewlett, village (1990 pop. 6,620), Nassau co., SE N.Y., near S shore of W L.I., 6 mi/9.7 km SE of Jamaica; 40°38′N 73°41′W. It is 1 of "Five Towns" of L.I.; affluent residential area, with small light industry.

Hewlett Bay Park, residential village (1990 pop. 440), Nassau co., SE N.Y., on S shore of W L.I., on small Hewlett Bay, just S of Valley Stream; 40°38′N 73°42′W.

Hewlett Neck, residential village (1990 pop. 547), Nassau co., SE N.Y., on S shore of W L.I., just S of Valley Stream; 40°37′N 73°42′W.

Hewlett Point, N.Y.: see MANHASSET BAY.

Hewitt, town (1990 pop. 8,983), McLennan co., E central Texas, suburb 9 mi/14.5 km S of downtown Waco. Agr. area (cattle; dairying; cotton). Mfg. (cultured marble, wood and gypsum prods.; steel fabricating, diversified light mfg.).

Heyburn, town (1990 pop. 2,714), Minidoka co., S Idaho, 2 mi/3.2 km NE of Burley, and on Snake R.; elev. 4,342 ft/1,323 m; 42°34′N 113°46′W. Ships grain, sheep, cattle; dairying; potatoes, beans, sugar beets.

Heyburn, Lake, reservoir, Creek co., E central Okla., on Polecat Creek, 23 mi/37 km SW of Tulsa; c.11 mi/18 km long; 35°56′N 96°17′W. Formed by Heyburn Dam. Heyburn State Park is here.

Heywoods Resort, large luxury hotel complex set amid extensive gardens, just N of Speightstown, Barbados.

Heyworth, village (1990 pop. 1,627), McLean co., central Ill., 10 mi/16 km S of Bloomington; 40°18′N 88°58′W. Trade center in agr. area (corn, soybeans; livestock).

Hialeah (hei-uh-LEE-uh), city (□ 19 sq mi/49 sq km; 1990 pop. 188,004), Dade co., SE Fla., 10 mi/16 km NW of Miami; 25°51′N 80°17′W. Printing; mfg. of metal and plastic goods. Nearby Miami Internatl. Airport is a major employer. A vibrant Cuban community dominates the city's pop. and adds to Hialeah's work force and housing developments. Inc. 1925.

Hialeah Gardens (hei-uh-LEE-uh), town (□ 2 sq mi/ 5.2 sq km; 1990 pop. 7,713), Dade co., SE Fla., 9 mi/ 14.5 km WNW of Miami; 25°52′N 80°20′W. Mfg. includes figurines, wood prods., bldg. materials, apparel, marble prods.; textile printing.

Hiawassee (hei-uh-WAH-see), village (1990 pop. 547), ⊙ Towns co., NE Ga., near N.C. state line, 34 mi/55 km NW of Toccoa, on Chatuge Reservoir; 34°57′N 83°45′W. Retirement and recreation area along L. Chatuge in N Ga. Mts. Annual Ga. Mt. fair near Brasstown Bald. Annual bluegrass music festival held here. Mfg. includes clothing, machinery, boat docks; fish processing.

Hiawatha (HEI-uh-WAH-thuh), city (1990 pop. 4986), Linn co., E central Iowa, suburb 4 mi/6.4 km N of Cedar Rapids; 42°02′N 91°40′W. Mfg. (concrete, fabricated metal prods.). Agr. to N and W (corn; cattle, hogs).

Hiawatha (hei-uh-WAH-thuh), town (1990 pop. 3,603), ⊙ Brown co., NE Kansas, 37 mi/60 km W of St. Joseph (Mo.); 39°51′N 95°32′W. RR junction. Trade center for livestock-raising and agr. area (grain, apples); dairying. Mfg. (lumber, hand tools, feeds). Davis Memorial, with 11 statues of John Davis and wife, are in cemetery. Brown State Fishing L. to E; Iowa Sac and Fox Indian Reservation to NE. Inc. 1859.

Hiawatha, village (1990 pop. 43), Carbon co., E central Utah, 15 mi/24 km SW of Price; 39°30′N 111°01′W. Cattle; coal mining. RR spur terminus at Wattis to N. Manti–La Sal Natl. Forest to W.

Hibbing (HI-beeng), city (1990 pop. 18,046), St. Louis co., NE Minn., 58 mi/93 km NW of Duluth, in the Mesabi Iron Range, 90 mi/145 km S of the Can. (Ont.) border; elev. 1,489 ft/454 m; 47°23′N 92°57′W. Iron mining, formerly the major industry, has declined. Mfg. (paper and metal prods., electronic equip., chemicals, candy, storage tanks, mining equip., explosives); poultry; alfalfa, oats; dairying; timber; tourism, recreation. In 1917, Hibbing was moved 2 mi/3.2 km S to make room for one of the world's largest open-pit iron mines. Mine viewing point located in densely forested region rich with wildlife. Hunting and camping are popular activities in the area. Hibbing Airport 5 mi/ 8 km to SE, Palucci Space Theater (astronomy and space programs), St. Louis Co. Fairgrounds. Seat of Hibbing Area Technical and Hibbing Community cols. In area are George Washington (NW) and Superior (NE) natl. forests; McCarthy Beach State Park to N; numerous small natural lakes, esp. to W. Inc. 1893.

Hibernia (hei-BUHR-nee-uh), village, Morris co., N N.J., 10 mi/16 km N of Morristown. Largely residential. Until c.1912 was thriving iron-mining town; Hibernia Furnace here furnished munitions in Amer. Revolution.

Hicacos Peninsula (hee-KAH-koz), narrow spit, Matanzas prov., NW Cuba, 20 mi/32 km ENE of Matanzas, flanking NW Cárdenas Bay; 11 mi/18 km long NE-SW; 23°12′N 81°12′W. Terminates in Hicacos Cape. Has saltworks. Varadero beach resort along N shore is a major internatl. tourist destination.

Hickam Field, U.S. Air Force base (1990 pop. 6,553), S Oahu, Hawaii, 12 mi/19 km NW of Honolulu, near Pearl Harbor; 21°20′N 157°57′W. Completed 1935, it was bombed (Dec. 7, 1941) by the Japanese.

Hickman 1 county (□ 252 sq mi/653 sq km; 1990 pop. 5,566), W Ky.; ⊙ Clinton, 36°40′N 88°59′W. Bounded W by the Mississippi R. (Mo. state line), SE corner by Tenn. state line; drained by Obion Creek and Bayou de Chien. Gently rolling agr. area (dark and burley tobacco, soybeans, wheat, corn, hay; hogs, cattle, poultry; dairying); mfg. at Clinton. Includes Columbus Belmont Battlefield State Park in NW; Obion Creek Wildlife Management Area in NE. Includes Wolf Isl. on Mo. side of Mississippi R., road access from Mo. across old channel of river. Formed 1821. **2** county (□ 613 sq mi/ 1,588 sq km; 1990 pop. 16,754), central Tenn.; ⊙ Centerville; 35°48′N 87°28′W. Drained by Duck R. and tributaries. Livestock raising; dairying; general agr.; phosphate mining; lumbering. Some mfg. at Centerville. Formed 1807.

Hickman 1 town (1990 pop. 2,689), ⊙ Fulton co., extreme W Ky., 36 mi/58 km WSW of Mayfield; 36°33′N 89°11′W. Trade and shipping center for agr. area (cotton, tobacco, grain, hay), with timber; mfg. (fabricated metal prods., electronic equip.). Flood wall (1934). Reelfoot L. is 10 mi/16 km SW, in Tenn. Reelfoot Natl. Wildlife Refuge in Ky. and Tenn. Settled 1819; inc. 1834. **2** town (1990 pop. 1,081), Lancaster co., SE Nebr., 12 mi/ 19 km S of Lincoln; 40°37′N 96°37′W. Dairy and poultry prods., grain; livestock. Satellite community of Lincoln. In area are Wagon Train L. (E) and Stagecoach L. (S) state recreation areas.

Hickman, Mount (9,700 ft/2,957 m), NW B.C., W Canada, near U.S. (Alaska) border, in Coast Mts., 70 mi/ 113 km NE of Wrangell; 57°16′N 131°07′W.

Hickory, county (□ 410 sq mi/1062 sq km; 1990 pop. 7,335), central Mo., in the Ozark Mts.; ⊙ Hermitage; 37°56′N 93°19′W. Drained by Pomme de Terre and Little Niangua rivers. Corn, wheat, soybeans, hay; dairying; cattle. Recreation around lakes. Pomme de Terre State Park, Pomme de Terre L. in S, arm of Harry S. Truman L. in N. Formed 1845.

Hickory, city (1990 pop. 28,474), Burke and Catawba cos., W N.C., 50 mi/80 km NW of Charlotte, near Catawba R., forms L. Hickory reservoir to N, L. Rhodhiss reservoir to NW, at E edge of the Blue Ridge Mts.; 35°44′N 81°19′W. RR junction. Processing and trade center for an abundant agr. region (grain, soybeans; poultry, hogs, cattle; dairying), with related industries. Mfg. (textiles and apparel; stone and plastic prods. and construction materials; electric and electronic equip., furniture, optical fibres, fabricated metal prods., consumer goods; printing). Hickory's location in the Blue Ridge Mts. has led to developing tourism. Seat of Lenoir Rhyne Col. Arts center of Catawba Valley, includes Hickory Mus. of Art and Catawba Science Center. Catawba Valley Community Col. to SE, between Hickory and Newton. Hickory Motor Speedway to E. Inc. 1870.

Hickory 1 uninc. town (1990 pop. 900), Washington co., SW Pa., 9 mi/14.5 km N of Washington; 40°17′N 80°18′W. Mfg. of lumber, machinery. Agr. includes dairying; livestock; corn, hay. **2** town, York co., N S.C., 10 mi/16 km W of York.

Hickory 1 village (1990 pop. 152), Graves co., W Ky., on Mayfield Creek, and 5 mi/8 km N of Mayfield. Agr. (tobacco, grain; livestock, poultry); clay; mfg. (lumber; clay processing, poultry processing). Also known as Hickory Grove. **2** village (1990 pop. 493), Newton co., E central Miss., 19 mi/31 km W of Meridian, on Potterchitto Creek; 32°19′N 89°01′W. Agr. (cotton, corn; poultry, cattle; dairying). **3** village (1990 pop. 77), Murray co., S Okla., 17 mi/27 km SSW of Ada; 34°33′N 96°51′W. In agr. area.

Hickory Flat, village (1990 pop. 535), Benton co., N Miss., 13 mi/21 km NW of New Albany, in Holly Springs Natl. Forest; 34°37′N 89°11′W. Agr. (cattle; timber); mfg. (furniture, wood prods.).

Hickory Grove, village, (1990 pop. 287), York co., SE S.C., 10 mi/16 km W of York; 34°58′N 81°25′W. Mfg. includes meat processing; chemicals, apparel. Agr. includes cotton, grain, soybeans, peaches; livestock, poultry; dairying.

Hickory Hills, city (1990 pop. 13,021), Cook co., NE Ill., suburb 15 mi/24 km SW of downtown Chicago; 41°43′N 87°49′W. Mfg. (fabricated metal prods., machinery, electronic goods); sheet metal fabricating, diverse light mfg.

Hickory Lake, N.C.: see CATAWBA RIVER.

Hickory Ridge, village (1990 pop. 436), Cross co., E Ark., 27 mi/43 km NW of Wynne, near Bayou DeView; 35°23′N 90°59′W. Rice processing.

Hickox (HI-kahks), town, Brantley co., SE Ga., 22 mi/ 35 km E of Waycross; 31°09′N 81°59′W.

Hicksville, uninc. city (□ 6 sq mi/15.5 sq km; 1990 pop. 40,174), Nassau co., SE N.Y., on L.I.; 40°45′N 73°31′W. It is chiefly residential, with electronic and metal prods. mfg. and some nearby vegetable farming. Site of the Broadway Mall, one of the largest shopping centers in U.S. Founded 1648.

Hicksville, village (1990 pop. 3,664), Defiance co., NW Ohio, near Ind. state line, 20 mi/32 km W of Defiance; 41°17′N 84°46′W. Shipping and processing center in farming and dairying area; mfg. (wood prods., food prods.). Founded 1836.

Hico (HI-ko), town (1990 pop. 1,342), Hamilton co., central Texas, on Bosque R., and c.60 mi/97 km NW of Waco; 31°58′N 98°01′W. In agr. area (dairying; cattle; grain); mfg. (machining).

Hidalgo (ee-DAHL-go), state (□ 8,058 sq mi/ 20,870 sq km; 1990 pop. 1,888,366), central Mexico; ⊙ PACHUCA DE SOTO. Crossed by the Sierra Madre Oriental, the state is extremely mountainous; in the S and W areas, however, are plains and fertile valleys lying within Mexico's central plateau. The climate is warm in the lower valleys, temperate on the plateau, and cold in the mts. One of Hidalgo's chief crops is maguey, grown on the central plateau. Alfalfa, corn, sugarcane, and coffee are also cultivated. The state's main industry is mining (esp. around Pachuca de Soto), and Hidalgo is a leading natl. producer of silver, gold, copper, lead, iron, and sulfur. Cement, textile, motor vehicle mfg. and esp. oil refining are other major industries. The territory was occupied successively by the Toltec (whose capital was Tollán – now Tula) and the Aztecs. Conquered by the Spanish in 1530, it was part of the prov. and state of Mexico until it became the separate state of Hidalgo in 1869.

Hidalgo 1 (hi-DAHL-go), county (□ 3,447 sq mi/ 8,928 sq km; 1990 pop. 5,958), extreme SW N.Mex.; ⊙ Lordsburg; 31°55′N 108°42′W. Watered N by Gila R.; bounded by Ariz. (W) and Mexico (Sonora and Chihuahua states; S, SE). Cattle, some sheep; chilies, cotton, hay, alfalfa, some sorghum, wheat, oats, barley, Christmas trees. Mining (clay, gold, silver, silica) near Lordsburg. Includes parts of Coronado (SW) and Gila (NE) natl. forests. Continental Divide in S passes through Animas Mts. and part of Pyramid Mts. Formed 1919. **2** county (□ 1,582 sq mi/4,097 sq km; 1990 pop. 383,545), extreme S Texas; ⊙ Edinburg; 26°23′N 98°10′W. S part is in rich irrigated valley of the Rio Grande (Mex. border), producing large part of Texas citrus crop, huge vegetable crops, sugarcane, grain; cotton; N part has ranches (beef and dairy cattle). Agribusiness important; oil, natural gas production and refining; stone, sand and gravel. Winter resort area. Santa Ana Natl. Wildlife Refuge and Bentsen–Rio Grande Valley State Park in S, both on Rio Grande. Formed 1852.

Hidalgo 1 (ee-DAHL-go), town (1990 pop. 721), Coahuila, N Mexico, on the Rio Grande (Texas border), and 75 mi/121 km SE of Piedras Negras; 27°49′N 99°50′W. Cattle grazing. Also Villa Hidalgo. **2** (ee-DAHL-go), town (1990 pop. 4,272), Tamaulipas, N Mexico, at E foot of Sierra Madre Oriental, near Nuevo León border, 40 mi/64 km NNW of Ciudad Victoria; 24°16′N 99°28′W. Sugarcane, beans; livestock.

Hidalgo, town (1990 pop. 3,292), Hidalgo co., extreme S Texas, port of entry on the Rio Grande (Mex. border; bridged) opposite Reynosa (Mexico), and c.7 mi/ 11.3 km S of McAllen; 26°06′N 98°15′W. In irrigated agr. area (citrus, vegetables; cotton); mfg. (water filters). Santa Ana Natl. Wildlife Refuge to E, Bentsen–Rio Grande Valley State Park to NW.

Hidalgo, village (1990 pop. 122), Jasper co., SE Ill., 13 mi/ 21 km N of Newton; 39°09′N 88°09′W. In agr. area.

Hidalgo, Mexico: see CIUDAD HIDALGO.

Hidalgo, Mexico: see MESONES HIDALGO.

Hidalgo del Parral (ee-DAHL-go del pah-RAHL) or **Parral** (pah-RAHL), city (1990 pop. 88,197) and township, Chihuahua state, N Mexico, on the Parral R., on Mexico Highway 45; 26°58′N 105°40′W. RR and highway junction. One of Mexico's large mining centers, esp. for silver, which has been mined in the region since the 16th cent. From 1640 to 1731, the city was the capital of the colonial prov. of Nueva Vizcaya. One of the 1st cities to take up arms during Francisco Madero's revolution of 1917, it was later (1923) the site of the assassination of Pancho Villa.

Hidalgo, Villa, Mexico: see VILLA HIDALGO.

Hidalgo Yalalag, Mexico: see VILLA HIDALGO.

Hidalgotitlán (ee-dahl-go-teet-LAHN), town (1990 pop. 3,738), Veracruz, SE Mexico, on Isthmus of Tehuantepec, on Coatzacoalcos R., and 17 mi/27 km SSW of Minatitlán; 17°46′N 94°39′W. Fruit; livestock.

Hidden Hills, city (1990 pop. 1,729), Los Angeles co., S Calif., residential suburb 24 mi/39 km WNW of downtown Los Angeles, at extreme W end of San Fernando Valley; 34°10′N 118°40′W. Santa Monica Mts. Natl. Recreation Area to S.

Hidden Inlet, fishing village, extreme SE Alaska, on Pearse Canal, 60 mi/97 km SE of Ketchikan; 54°59′N 130°21′W.

Hidden Meadows, uninc. town (1990 pop. 2,371), San Diego co., S Calif., residential suburb 3 mi/4.8 km NW of Escondido. Merriam Mts. to N. Citrus, avocados, nursery stock.

Hidden River Cave, Ky.: see HORSE CAVE.

Hidden Valley, Colo.: see ROCKY MOUNTAIN NATIONAL PARK.

Hidden Valley Lake, uninc. town (1990 pop. 1,961), Lake co., NW Calif., 19 mi/31 km NE of Healdsburg, on Putah Creek, in Coyote Valley. Residential community.

Hiddenite (HID-neit), uninc. town (1990 pop. 800), Alexander co., W central N.C., 6 mi/9.7 km ESE of Taylorsville. Tobacco, grain; poultry, livestock; dairying. Mfg. (furniture, lumber, polyurethane foam). Named for gem hiddenite discovered here (c.1879) and mined for a time.

Higbee, city (1990 pop. 639), Randolph co., N central Mo., 9 mi/14.5 km SSW of Moberly; 39°18′N 92°30′W. Corn, wheat, soybeans; cattle; mfg. (wine barrels). Former coal-mining area.

Higden, village (1990 pop. 92), Cleburne co., N central Ark., 11 mi/18 km WNW of Heber Springs, in the Ozark Mts., on Greers Ferry L. Reservoir (Little Red R.); 35°34′N 92°12′W.

Higganum, village (1990 pop. 1,672), Middlesex co., S Conn., just S of Middletown; 41°29′N 72°33′W. Postal sect. of the town of Haddam that lies entirely to the W of the Connecticut R. with part of Haddam. Publishing.

Higgins, village (1990 pop. 464), Lipscomb co., extreme N Texas, in the Panhandle, c.40 mi/64 km SW of Woodward (Okla.); 36°07′N 100°01′W. In wheat and cattle region. Black Kettle Natl. Grassland to SW.

Higgins Bay, village (1990 pop. 50), Hamilton co., E central N.Y., in the Adirondack Mts., on Piseco L., c.40 mi/64 km NE of Utica; 43°25′N 74°32′W.

Higgins Lake, Roscommon co., N central Mich., 5 mi/8 km W of Roscommon; .7 mi/11.3 km long, 4 mi/6.4 km wide; 44°43′N 85°40′W. Touches Crawford co. border on N. Resorts; fishing. South Higgins L. State Park at SE end; North Higgins L. State Park on N end. Joined to Houghton L. (S) by small passage.

Higginson, village (1990 pop. 255), White co., central Ark., 4 mi/6.4 km SSE of Searcy; 35°12′N 91°42′W.

Higginsport, village (1990 pop. 298), Brown co., SW Ohio, on the Ohio R., and 6 mi/10 km SSW of Georgetown; 38°48′N 83°58′W.

Higginsville, city (1990 pop. 4,693), Lafayette co., W central Mo., near Missouri R., 12 mi/19 km SE of Lexington; 39°03′N 93°43′W. Wheat, corn, soybeans; cattle, hogs. Limestone quarry. Mfg. (electronic equip., plastic prods.). Laid out 1869. Confederate Memorial State Historic Site with cemetery.

Higgston, town (1990 pop. 274), Montgomery co., E central Ga., 3 mi/4.8 km W of Vidalia; 32°13′N 82°28′W.

High Bridge, uninc. village (1990 pop. 300), Jessamine co., central Ky., 8 mi/12.9 km SW of Nicholasville, on Kentucky R. (Palisades of the Ky. gorge), at Dix R. mouth, and 20 mi/32 km SW of Lexington, in Bluegrass region. Limestone quarrying. Historic Shaker settlement of Pleasant Hill (or Shakertown) to SW. High Bridge, a 317-ft/97-m-high RR bridge across Kentucky R., is here. Dix Dam (Herrington L. reservoir) on Dix R., to S.

High Bridge, borough (1990 pop. 3,886), Hunterdon co., W N.J., on South Branch of Raritan R., and 15 mi/24 km E of Phillipsburg; 40°40′N 74°54′W. Metal

prods.; grain, vegetables. State park nearby. Settled before 1750, inc. 1898.

High Falls, village (1990 pop. 700), Ulster co., SE N.Y., on Rondout Creek, and 10 mi/16 km SW of Kingston; 41°50′N 74°08′W. In resort and agr. area.

High Hill, town (1990 pop. 204), Montgomery co., E central Mo., 9 mi/14.5 km SE of Montgomery City; 38°52′N 91°22′W. Fire-clay.

High Island, uninc. village (1990 pop. 500), Galveston co., S Texas, 32 mi/51 km NE of Galveston, bet. Gulf coast (S) and Gulf Intracoastal Waterway, at base of Bolivar Peninsula. Oil field center, on salt dome in marshland. Resort area. Nearby are Anahuac (NW) and McFadden (NE) natl. wildlife refuges.

High Island, Mich.: see BEAVER ISLANDS.

High Level, town (1991 pop. 2,849), NW Alta., W Canada, 150 mi/241 km N of Peace River, on Mackenzie Highway, and on RR to Hay River (N.W.T.); 58°31′N 117°08′W. Est. 1940s; grew in 1960s with regional oil boom. Has strong agr. economy; grain elevators, sawmill; timber. Scheduled air service.

High Plains, Texas and N.Mex.: see LLANO ESTACADO.

High Point, city (1990 pop. 69,496), Davidson, Guilford, and Randolph cos., N N.C., suburb 16 mi/26 km SW of Greensboro; 35°58′N 80°00′W. Deep R. passes to NE, in a heavily forested Piedmont region. RR junction. Trade, industrial, and commercial center for an agr. area, noted for the production of furniture and hosiery. Mfg. (printing; wood, plastic, metal, and rubber prods.; furniture, chemicals, sandpaper, electronic equip., apparel, textiles, embroidery, motor vehicles, consumer goods). Four annual furniture expositions are held here. Of interest is the restored home of a blacksmith (1786). Seat of High Point Univ. and N.C. School of the Arts. Internatl. Home Furnishings Center; Furniture Discovery Center, mus. on furniture mfg. High Point Mus. and Historical Park. Angela Peterson Doll Mus. Emerald Point theme park. Settled before 1750, inc. 1859.

High Point 1 summit (1,803 ft/550 m) of Kittatinny Mt. ridge, extreme NW N.J.; highest point in state, with view of 3 states. Has war memorial tower (225 ft/69 m high). Surrounding region included in High Point State Park (□ 3 sq mi/7.8 sq km), year-round forest recreational area. **2** summit (3,075 ft/937 m) in the Catskill Mts., Ulster co., SE N.Y., 15 mi/24 km W of Kingston; 41°56′N 74°17′W.

High Prairie, town (1991 pop. 2,932), W Alta., W Canada, 65 mi/105 km SE of Peace R., and 15 mi/24 km W of Lesser Slave L.; 55°26′N 116°29′W. Lumbering; mixed farming; wheat, oats.

High Ridge, uninc. city, Jefferson co., E Mo., 20 mi/32 km SW of St. Louis; 38°27′N 90°31′W. Residential and mfg. suburb. Mfg. (fabricated metal prods., electronic equip., machinery).

High River, town (1991 pop. 6,269), S Alta., W Canada, at foot of Rocky Mts., 35 mi/56 km SSE of Calgary; 50°35′N 113°52′W. Coal mining; grain, wheat; cattle; dairying. In oil-producing region.

High Rock Lake, reservoir (□ 24 sq mi/62 sq km), on border bet. Rowen and Davidson cos., central N.C., on Yadkin (Pee Dee) R., 32 mi/51 km S of Winston-Salem; c.15 mi/24 km long; 35°36′N 80°14′W. Max. capacity 248,800 acre-ft. Has several long arms. Formed by High Rock Dam (70 ft/21 m high), built (1927) by Army Corps of Engineers for power generation. Tuckertown L. downstream.

High Shoals, town, Oconee, Walton, and Morgan cos., NE central Ga., 12 mi/19 km SW of Athens, and on Apalachee R.; 33°49′N 83°30′W.

High Shoals, village (1990 pop. 605), Gaston co., S N.C., 9 mi/14.5 km N of Gastonia, on South Fork Catawba R.; 35°23′N 81°12′W. Agr. area (grain, cotton, tobacco; poultry, livestock; dairying).

High Sierra, Calif.: see SIERRA NEVADA.

High Springs, town (□ 9 sq mi/23.3 sq km; 1990 pop. 3,144), Alachua co., N central Fla., near Santa Fe R., 21 mi/34 km NW of Gainesville; 29°49′N 82°35′W. Agr. trade and shipping point; RR shops. Quarries (phosphate, flint) nearby. Founded c.1885.

Highbridge, a residential section of SW Bronx borough of N.Y. city, SE N.Y.; 40°50′N 73°56′W.

Highfield, uninc. village, Butler township, Butler co., W Pa., suburb 1 mi/1.6 km W of Butler; 40°51′N 79°55′W.

Highgate, town (1991 pop. 5,418), St. Mary parish, N Jamaica, in uplands, on RR, and 23 mi/37 km NNW of Kingston; 18°19′N 76°52′W. Fruit growing; livestock grazing. Busy agr. and commercial center.

Highgate, town (1990 pop. 3,020), Franklin co., NW Vt., on L. Champlain, at Can. (Que.) border, at mouth of Missisquoi R., and 8 mi/12.9 km N of St. Albans; 44°57′N 73°02′W. Metal prods.; lime, lumber. Port of entry. Highgate Springs is family-style resort village.

Highgate, village (1991 pop. 488), S Ont., central Canada, 20 mi/32 km ENE of Chatham; 52°52′N 108°27′W. Dairying; mixed farming; lumbering.

Highgrove, uninc. town (1990 pop. 3,175), Riverside co., S Calif., residential suburb 5 mi/8 km NNE of Riverside, and 8 mi/12.9 km SSW of San Bernardino. Citrus, nursery stock; dairying.

Highland 1 county (□ 554 sq mi/1,435 sq km; 1990 pop. 35,728), SW Ohio; ⊙ Hillsboro, 39°11′N 83°37′W. Drained by East Fork of Little Miami R., Paint, Small White Oak, and Rattlesnake creeks. In the Till Plains physiographic region, except for the SE portion which is in the Lexington Plain region. Agr. (nursery and greenhouse crops, tobacco, grains; dairying; hogs); mfg. at Hillsboro and Greenfield (textiles, plastic prods., transportation equip.); limestone quarries. Formed 1805. **2** county (□ 416 sq mi/1,077 sq km; 1990 pop. 2,635), NW Va.; ⊙ Monterey; 38°21′N 79°33′W. In Alleghany Mts., bounded (W, N) by W.Va. state line; drained by Jackson, Bullpasture, Cowpasture, South Branch Potomac rivers and Back Creek. Some agr. (hay, alfalfa, potatoes, sugar maples; cattle- and sheep-raising area); timber; freshwater fish (trout). Formed 1847.

Highland 1 city (1990 pop. 34,439), San Bernardino co., SE Calif., suburb 4 mi/6.4 km E of San Bernardino, 59 mi/95 km E of downtown Los Angeles. Drained S by Santa Ana Wash. R. In a citrus-grove area at the foot of the San Bernardino Mts.; also light mfg. Developed along with the S Calif. area in the growth of agribusiness and aircraft industries. Patton State Hospital is here, and Norton Air Force Base to S. San Bernardino Mts., in San Bernardino Natl. Forest, to N. San Manuel Indian Reservation to N. **2** city (1990 pop. 7,525), Madison co., SW Ill., 16 mi/26 km ESE of Edwardsville; 38°44′N 89°40′W. In dairying and agr. area (corn, wheat; poultry, livestock; mfg. (food prods., machinery, transportation equip.). Founded 1831 by Swiss; inc. 1863.

Highland 1 town (1990 pop. 23,696), Lake co., extreme NW Ind., in the Chicago metropolitan area; 41°33′N 87°28′W. Mfg. (dairy prods., mineral granules for sand-blasting). Settled 1883 as Clough Postal Station, name changed to Highland in 1888. Inc. 1910. **2** town (1990 pop. 5,002), Utah co., N central Utah, suburb 15 mi/24 km NNW of Provo, and 25 mi/40 km SSE of Salt Lake City, on American Fork R.; 40°25′N 111°47′W. Dairying; cattle; fruit, vegetables, sugar beets. Timpanogos Cave Natl. Forest, in Wasatch Range, to E. Settled 1875.

Highland 1 village (1990 pop. 942), Doniphan co., extreme NE Kansas, 10 mi/16 km WNW of Troy; 39°51′N 95°16′W. In agr. region (apples, grain; livestock, poultry). Seat of Highland Community Col. Brown State Fishing L. to W. **2** village (□ 4 sq mi/10.4 sq km; 1990 pop. 4,492), Ulster co., SE N.Y., on W bank of the Hudson R. (here crossed by Mid-Hudson Bridge), opposite Poughkeepsie; 41°43′N 73°58′W. Summer residential area; mfg. (computer equip., apparel, wine and other beverages, electrical goods). Center of mid-Hudson apple-growing region, largest in state after Wayne co. region. **3** village (1990 pop. 275), Highland co., SW Ohio, 10 mi/16 km N of Hillsboro, and on small Rattlesnake Creek; 39°20′N 83°35′W. **4** uninc. village, McCandless township, Allegheny co., SW Pa., residential suburb 8 mi/12.9 km NNW of downtown Pittsburgh; 40°28′N 79°55′W–40°33′N 80°02′W. **5** village (1990 pop. 799), Iowa co., SW Wis., 14 mi/23 km NW of Dodgeville;

43°02′N 90°22′W. Makes cheese; timber; stoneware pottery; winery. Black Hawk L. Reservoir to SE; on Pecatonica State Trail.

Highland, plantation (1990 pop. 38), Somerset co., central Maine, 10 mi/16 km WNW of Bingham; 45°05′N 70°04′W.

Highland Acres, uninc. town (1990 est. pop. 3,151), Kent co., central Del., 2 mi/3.2 km S of Dover; 39°07′N 75°31′W. Largely a residential suburb of Dover.

Highland Beach, town (1990 pop. 102), Anne Arundel co., central Md., 3 mi/4.8 km SE of Annapolis, on Chesapeake Bay; 38°56′N 76°28′W. In shore-resort area. Charles Douglass, son of Frederick Douglass, the Afr.-Amer. abolitionist, bought land here in 1892 and built the 1st house in 1894 as part of a summer community for Afr.-Amer. intellectuals. It is still a private community with private beaches and homes. Inc. 1922.

Highland City, town (1990 pop. 1,919), Polk co., central Fla., 8 mi/12.9 km SE of Lakeland; 27°57′N 81°52′W. Mfg. includes metal fabrication, fresh fruit processing; mailboxes, powder coatings.

Highland Falls, summer residential-recreational village (□ 1 sq mi/2.6 sq km; 1990 pop. 3,937), Orange co., SE N.Y., on W bank of the Hudson R., and 10 mi/16 km S of Newburgh, just S of West Point military acad.; 41°21′N 73°58′W. Settled 1800, inc. 1906.

Highland Heights, city (1990 pop. 6,249), Cuyahoga co., N Ohio, an E suburb of Cleveland; 41°32′N 81°28′W.

Highland Heights, town (1990 pop. 4,223), Campbell co., N Ky., a suburb 5 mi/8 km SSE of downtown Cincinnati (Ohio), near Ohio R.; 39°02′N 84°27′W. Light mfg. Seat of Northern Ky. Univ.

Highland Hills, uninc. village (1990 pop. 1,600), Du Page co., NE Ill., suburb 19 mi/31 km W of downtown Chicago, S of Lombard; 41°50′N 88°00′W.

Highland Lake 1 village, Cumberland co., Maine, suburb of Portland. **2** resort village (1990 pop. 450), Sullivan co., SE N.Y., on small Highland L., 13 mi/21 km SW of Monticello; 41°32′N 74°51′W.

Highland Lake 1 reservoir, Winchester town, Litchfield co., NW Conn., on small branch of Mad Still R., 9 mi/14.5 km NNE of Torrington; 2 mi/3.2 km long; 41°55′N 73°05′W. Plat Hill State Park on SW shore. **2** reservoir and resort lake, Stoddard and Washington towns, Cheshire and Sullivan cos., SW N.H., on North Branch Conticook R., 16 mi/26 km NNE of Keene; 6 mi/9.7 km long; 43°06′N 72°04′W.

Highland Mills, village (□ 1 sq mi/2.6 sq km; 1990 pop. 2,576), Orange co., SE N.Y., 8 mi/12.9 km W of Highland Falls; 41°21′N 74°07′W.

Highland Park 1 city (1990 pop. 30,575), Lake co., NE Ill., a suburb of Chicago on L. Michigan; 42°10′N 87°48′W. Retail and medical center for the North Shore area. Nearby Ravinia Park is the summer home to the Chicago Symphony Orchestra; the park also hosts a well-known music festival. Sheridan Reserve Center (formerly Fort Sheridan) is adjacent to the city. Inc. 1869. **2** city (1990 pop. 20,121), Wayne co., SE Mich., suburb 6 mi/9.7 km NNW of and completely surrounded by Detroit; 42°23′N 83°05′W. SE corner touches city of Hamtramck. Tractor and motor vehicle assembly are the city's main industries; mfg. (coffee processing, printing; decorative chrome plates). Former hq. (designed by Minoru Yamasaki) of the Chrysler Corp. Grew mainly after Henry Ford established his 1st Model T auto plant here in 1910; it was here that assembly-line production was 1st based. Seat of Wayne Co. Community Col. Laid out 1818, inc. as a city 1917.

Highland Park 1 uninc. town (1990 pop. 1,583), Derry township, Mifflin co., central Pa., residential suburb 2 mi/3.2 km N of Lewistown, on Kishacoquillas Creek; 40°37′N 77°34′W. **2** uninc. town (1990 pop. 1,800), Cumberland co., S Pa., residential suburb 2 mi/3.2 km SW of Harrisburg; 40°13′N 76°54′W. **3** town (1990 pop. 8,739), Dallas co., N Texas, residential suburb 4 mi/6.4 km N of downtown Dallas; 32°49′N 96°47′W. Surrounded by city of Dallas, as is neighboring University Park (N). Dallas Love Field airport to W. In 1916 V. C. Prather set aside land to build one of the 1st planned

shopping centers; construction actually began in 1931 (Span. architectural style). Settled 1907, inc. 1913.

Highland Park, village, Sullivan co., NE Tenn., suburb just E of Kingsport.

Highland Park, residential borough (1990 pop. 13,279), Middlesex co., N central N.J., on the Raritan R., opposite New Brunswick. Inc. 1905.

Highland Park, N residential section of Los Angeles city, Los Angeles co., S Calif., 4 mi/6.4 km NE of downtown Los Angeles, and SW of Pasadena. Founded 1887; annexed 1895 by Los Angeles.

Highland Park, Pa.: see UPPER DARBY.

Highland Peak (10,935 ft/3,333 m), Alpine co., E Calif., in the Sierra Nevada, c.30 mi/48 km SSE of L. Tahoe, in Eldorado Natl. Forest.

Highland Springs, uninc. city (1990 pop. 13,823), Henrico co., E central Va., residential suburb 6 mi/9.7 km E of downtown Richmond, near Chickahominy R.; 37°32′N 77°19′W. Mfg. (wood prods., awards). Seven Pines Natl. Cemetery to SE; Richmond Internatl. Airport, Va. Aviation Mus. to S.

Highlands, county (□ 1,106 sq mi/2,865 sq km; 1990 pop. 68,432), central Fla., bounded E by Kissimmee R.; ⊙ Sebring; 27°20′N 81°20′W. Rolling terrain with many lakes, notably L. Istokpoga; SE corner of co. in Everglades. Citrus-fruit and cattle area; also vegetable and poultry farming. Formed 1921.

Highlands 1 uninc. town (1990 pop. 2,644), San Mateo co., W Calif., residential suburb 17 mi/27 km S of downtown San Francisco, on San Mateo Creek. Lower Crystal Springs Reservoir, in San Francisco State Fish and Game Refuge, to SW. **2** town (1990 pop. 948), Macon co., W N.C., 13 mi/21 km SE of Franklin, near Ga. state line; 35°02′N 83°12′W. Mt. resort in Nantahala Natl. Forest; Chattahoochee Natl. Forest (Ga.) to S, Sumter Natl. Forest (S.C.) to SE. Common corner of Ga., N.C., and S.C. 7 mi/11.3 km to SE. Tobacco, corn; cattle. Mfg. (printing and publishing). Bridal Veil Falls (120 ft/37 m) to NW. L. Sequayah reservoir to NW. Scaly Mt. Ski Area to NW. **3** uninc. town (1990 pop. 6,632), Harris co., S Texas, suburb 18 mi/29 km E of downtown Houston, and 7 mi/11.3 km NW of Baytown, on San Jacinto R. (Winters L.); 29°48′N 95°03′W. In agr. area; mfg. (chemicals, plastic prods.; sheet metal fabrication, sand and clay processing). Highlands Reservoir to E.

Highlands, resort borough (1990 pop. 4,849), Monmouth co., E N.J., bet. Navesink R. and Sandy Hook Bay, 5 mi/8 km NE of Red Bank; 40°23′N 73°59′W. Seafood. Largely residential. On nearby Navesink Highlands is the Twin Towers, one of most powerful lighthouse systems in U.S. First U.S. Navy wireless station (1903) nearby, and U.S. Army reservation just S. Inc. 1900.

Highlands Forge Lake, Essex co., NE N.Y., in Adirondack Mts., 3 mi/4.8 km N of Willsboro; 1.5 mi/2.4 km long; 44°30′N 73°26′W. Receives drainage from Long Pond, located immediately S. Drains NE to L. Champlain's Willsboro Bay. Dam at N end. Surface elev. 567 ft/173 m above mean sea level. Rattlesnake Mt. (elev. 1,316 ft/401 m) immediately SE.

Highlands of Navesink, N.J.: see NAVESINK HIGHLANDS.

Highlandville, town (1990 pop. 722), Christian co., SW Mo., in the Ozark Mts., near James R., 6 mi/9.7 km SSW of Ozark.

Highmore, town (1990 pop. 835), ⊙ Hyde co., central S.Dak., 45 mi/72 km ENE of Pierre; 44°31′N 99°26′W. Trading center for farming region; dairy prods.; livestock; grain. State experiment farm nearby.

Highmount, resort village (1990 pop. 300), Ulster co., SE N.Y., in the Catskill Mts., NW of Kingston, and near Belle Ayr Mt. (skiing); 42°08′N 74°29′W.

Highspire (HEI-SPEI-uhr), borough (1990 pop. 2,668), Dauphin co., S Pa., residential suburb 6 mi/9.7 km SE of Harrisburg, on Susquehanna R. (bridged). Mfg. (food prods.). Some agr. in area (corn; poultry; dairying). Harrisburg Internatl. Airport to SE, on Susquehanna R. Settled 1775, laid out 1814, inc. 1867.

Highsplint, Ky., see LEJUNIOR.

Hightstown, borough (1990 pop. 5,126), Mercer co., central N.J., near Millstone R., 12 mi/19 km ENE of Trenton; 40°16′N 74°31′W. Trade center in agr. area (vegetables, nursery prods.) in the process of suburbanizing; mfg. (textiles). Seat of Peddie Preparatory School. Nearby (4 mi/6.4 km SE) is former Jersey Homesteads, now Roosevelt borough. Settled 1721, inc. 1853.

Highview, uninc. city (1990 pop. 14,814), Jefferson co., N Ky., residential suburb 9 mi/14.5 km SE of dowtown Louisville; 38°08′N 85°38′W. Agr. to S (tobacco, grain; livestock).

Highway City, uninc. town (1990 pop. 1,200), Fresno co., S central Calif., suburb 8 mi/12.9 km NW of downtown Fresno, near King R. Citrus, grain, cotton; dairying; cattle, poultry.

Highwood, city (1990 pop. 5,331), Lake co., NE Ill., suburb 24 mi/39 km NNW of Chicago, on L. Michigan, 12 mi/19 km NNW of Evanston; 42°12′N 87°48′W. Site of Sheridan U.S. Army Reserve Center. Fort Sheridan decommissioned in 1990s. Inc. 1886.

Highwoods, village, Marion co., central Ind., NW suburb of Indianapolis. Part of Indianapolis.

Higley, uninc. town (1990 pop. 500), Maricopa co., central Ariz., residential suburb 22 mi/35 km SE of downtown Phoenix, surrounded by extensions of Gilbert city limits, which adjoins it to NW. Williams Air Force Base to E; Ariz. Boys Ranch to SE; Chandler Municipal Airport to SW.

Higueras (ee-GWE-rahs), town (1990 pop. 918), Nuevo León, N Mexico, 27 mi/43 km NE of Monterrey. Grain, cactus fibers; livestock.

Higüero, Point (hee-GWE-ro), on NW coast of P.R., 9 mi/14.5 km SW of Aguadilla; 18°22′N 67°16′W. Former Bonus Thermoelectric Nuclear Plant nearby.

Hiland Park (HEI-luhnd), town (□ 5 sq mi/13 sq km; 1990 pop. 3,865), Bay co., NW Fla., 5 mi/8 km NE of Panama City; 30°11′N 85°37′W.

Hilbert, town (1990 pop. 1,211), Calumet co., E Wis., 14 mi/23 km SE of Appleton; 44°08′N 88°09′W. Mfg. (cheese, animal feed). RR junction.

Hilda, village (1990 pop. 342), Barnwell co., W S.C., c.7 mi/11.3 km ENE of Barnwell; 33°16′N 81°15′W. Agr. includes livestock, poultry; dairying; grain, cotton, peanuts.

Hildale, town (1990 pop. 1,325), Washington co., SW Utah, 32 mi/51 km ESE of St. George, on Ariz. state line adjacent to Colorado City (Ariz.); 37°00′N 112°58′W. Mfg. (cabinets). Cattle. Zion Natl. Park to N. Cottonwood Point Wilderness Area, Kaibab Indian Reservation, and Pipe Spring Natl. Monument (all in Ariz.) to SE.

Hildebran (HIL-duh-bran), town (1990 pop. 790), Burke co., W central N.C., 4 mi/6.4 km WSW of Hickory; 35°43′N 81°25′W. Grain, soybeans; chickens, hogs. Mfg. (apparel, lumber, furniture, wood prods.; fabricated metal prods.).

Hildreth, village (1990 pop. 364), Franklin co., S Nebr., 23 mi/37 km S of Kearney; 40°20′N 99°02′W. RR terminus. Dairying; grain; livestock.

Hilgard, Mount, peak (11,533 ft/3,515 m) in Fish L. Plateau, Sevier co., S central Utah, 30 mi/48 km ESE of Richfield, in Fishlake Natl. Forest.

Hilham (HI-luhm), town, Overton co., N Tenn., 30 mi/48 km N of Cookeville.

Hill 1 county (□ 2,916 sq mi/7,552 sq km; 1990 pop. 17,654), N Mont., on Can. (Sask. and Alta.) border; ⊙ Havre; 48°38′N 110°07′W. Agr. area drained by Milk R., forms Fresno Reservoir in center of co. Drained also by Lodge, Big Sandy, and Sage creeks. Cattle, sheep, hogs; wheat, barley, oats, and hay. Part of Rocky Boy's Indian Reservation in SE. Formed 1912. **2** county (□ 985 sq mi/2,551 sq km; 1990 pop. 27,146), N central Texas; ⊙ Hillsboro; 31°59′N 97°07′W. Rich blackland prairies; bounded W by Brazos R.; drained by Aquilla and Nolan creeks. Agr. (esp. cotton; also corn, wheat, sorghum; hay); cattle, horses, hogs; limestone; oil and gas. Mfg. at Hillsboro. In W is Whitney Dam in Brazos R. Aquilla L. reservoir in S center; L. Whitney reservoir and State Park on W border (Brazos R.). Formed 1853.

Hill, town (1990 pop. 814), Merrimack co., S central N.H.,

5 mi/8 km NW of Franklin; 43°31′N 71°46′W. Bounded E by Pemiqewasset R. (Franklin Falls Reservoir). Agr. (poultry, livestock; apples, vegetables; dairying; nursery crops); mfg. (machining). Flood-control dam on Pemigewasset R. caused village to be moved to new site and rebuilt as model town, 1940–1941. Original town settled 1768.

Hill Air Force Base, Utah: see OGDEN.

Hill City, town (1990 pop. 1,835), ⊙ Graham co., NW Kansas, on South Fork Solomon R., and 45 mi/72 km NW of Hays; 39°22′N 99°50′W. Wheat. Oil mus. Laid out 1880, inc. 1888.

Hill City 1 village (1990 pop. 469), Aitkin co., N central Minn., 32 mi/51 km N of Aitkin, on W shore of Hill L., near Hill R.; 46°59′N 93°35′W. Alfalfa, hay, wild rice; mfg. (machinery, bldg. materials). Hill R. State Forest to W, S, and E, including Moose-Willow Wildlife Area to SE. **2** village (1990 pop. 650), Pennington co., W S.Dak., 20 mi/32 km SW of Rapid City, in Black Hills Natl. Forest; elev. 4,976 ft/1,517 m; 43°55′N 103°34′W. Agr.; gold, tungsten mines; timber. Nearby Sheridan L. used for recreation. Harney Peak (7,242 ft/2,207 m) to S.

Hill Country Village, town (1990 pop. 1,038), Bexar co., S central Texas, residential suburb 10 mi/16 km N of downtown San Antonio; 29°34′N 98°29′W.

Hill Island, SE Ont., E Canada, on U.S. (N.Y.) border, in the St. Lawrence R., in Thousand Isls., 25 mi/40 km ENE of Kingston; connected with Wellesley Isl. (N.Y.), and with Ont. mainland by Thousand Isls. Internatl. Bridge.

Hill Military Reservation, Va.: see FREDERICKSBURG.

Hillaby, Mount, hill (1,104 ft/336 m), highest in Barbados, 7 mi/11.3 km NNE of Bridgetown. Potteries are nearby.

Hillburn, village (□ 2 sq mi/5.2 sq km; 1990 pop. 892), Rockland co., SE N.Y., in the Ramapos, at N.J. state line, just W of Suffern; 41°07′N 74°10′W. In resort area. Inc. 1893.

Hillcrest, village (1990 pop. 828), Ogle co., N central Ill., 2 mi/3.2 km N of Rochelle; 41°57′N 89°04′W. Agr. area.

Hillcrest, residential suburb (□ 1 sq mi/2.6 sq km; 1990 pop. 6,447), Rockland co., S N.Y.; 41°07′N 74°02′W. Part of dense cluster of residential commuter communities off Palisades Interstate Parkway at E foot of Ramapo Mts.

Hillcrest Center, residential suburb, Kern co., central Calif., 2 mi/3.2 km E of downtown Bakersfield. In irrigated agr. area.

Hillcrest Heights, uninc. residential town (1990 pop. 17,136), Prince Georges co., W central Md., suburb of Washington, D.C.; 38°50′N 76°58′W. In a fast-growing, moderate-income area.

Hillcrest Village, village (1990 pop. 695), Brazoria co., SE Texas, residential suburb 24 mi/39 km SSE of Houston, and 2 mi/3.2 km SSE of Alvin, on Mustang Bayou; 29°23′N 95°13′W.

Hiller, uninc. town (1990 pop. 1,401), Redstone township, Fayette co., SW Pa., 30 mi/48 km S of Pittsburgh, and 1 mi/1.6 km SW of Brownsville, near Monongahela R. Agr. area (corn, hay; dairying).

Hillers, Mount, 10,723 ft/3,268 m, E Garfield co., S Utah, in Henry Mts., 32 mi/51 km S of Hanksville.

Hilliard, city (1990 pop. 11,796), Franklin co., central Ohio, suburb 10 mi/16 km WNW of Columbus; 40°02′N 83°08′W. In agr. area.

Hilliard (HIL-yuhrd), town (□ 3 sq mi/7.8 sq km; 1990 pop. 1,751), Nassau co., extreme NE Fla., 28 mi/45 km NW of Jacksonville; 30°41′N 81°55′W.

Hillman 1 village (1990 pop. 643), Montmorency co., N Mich., 22 mi/35 km W of Alpena, and on Thunder Bay R.; 45°04′N 83°54′W. Mfg. (wire cloth and filters). **2** village (1990 pop. 45), Morrison co., central Minn., 24 mi/39 km E of Little Falls, near Hillman Creek; 46°00′N 93°53′W. Dairying. Inc. 1938.

Hillrose, village (1990 pop. 169), Morgan co., NE Colo., on South Platte R., at mouth of Beaver Creek, and 16 mi/26 km ENE of Fort Morgan; elev. c.4,165 ft/1,269 m; 40°19′N 103°31′W. RR junction to N. Sand Hills nearby. Prewitt Reservoir to NE.

Hills, town (1990 pop. 662), Johnson co., E Iowa, 7 mi/11.3 km S of Iowa City, near Iowa R.; 41°34′N 91°32′W.

Hills, village (1990 pop. 607), Rock co., extreme SW Minn., on Iowa (S) and S.Dak. (W) state lines, 19 mi/31 km W of Sioux Falls (S.Dak.), and 12 mi/19 km SW of Luverne on Mud Creek; 43°31′N 96°21′W. Corn, oats, soybeans; hogs, cattle; dairying; mfg. (fertilizer). RR junction to W.

Hills and Dales, village (1990 pop. 297), Stark co., E central Ohio, 4 mi/6 km NW of Canton; 40°49′N 81°26′W.

Hills Creek Lake, reservoir (□ 4 sq mi/10.4 sq km), Lane co., W central Oregon, on Middle Fork of Willamette R., in Willamette Natl. Forest, on W slope of Cascade Range, 40 mi/64 km SE of Eugene; 43°25′N 122°28′W. Max. capacity 356,000 acre-ft. Formed by Hills Creek Dam (341 ft/104 m high), built (1962) by Army Corps of Engineers and U.S. Dept. Agr. Forest Service for flood control; also used for power generation, irrigation, water supply, recreation, and navigation.

Hillsboro 1 city (1990 pop. 4,400), ⊙ Montgomery co., S central Ill., 8 mi/12.9 km E of Litchfield; 39°09′N 89°28′W. In agr. area (soybeans, corn, wheat, hay; cattle); mfg. (zinc oxide, glass prods.). Inc. 1855. Several recreational reservoirs in area include L. Glenn Shoals to N, L. Lou Yaeger to W, and Coffeen L. to SE. **2** city (1990 pop. 6,235), ⊙ Highland co., SW Ohio, 34 mi/55 km WSW of Chillicothe; 39°12′N 83°37′W. Trade center for livestock-raising, farming, and limestone quarrying area; mfg. In 1873, Women's Temperance Crusade was founded here. Several mound builders' forts are nearby. Plotted 1807. **3** city (1990 pop. 37,520), ⊙ Washington co., NW Oregon, suburb 14 mi/23 km W of Portland, on the Tualatin R., at mouth of Dairy Creek; 45°31′N 122°56′W. RR junction. Mfg. (foods, wood prods., furniture, plastics, sheet metal, electronic goods, computer equip., harnesses, quartz crucibles, medical equip., consumer goods; meat processing, printing, publishing). Agr. (fruit, nuts, vegetables, grain; poultry, cattle); dairy prods.; wineries. Points of interest include pioneer mus. and cemetery, notable old Scottish church. Portland Hillsboro Airport to NE. Bald Peak State Park to S. Settled c. 1845.

Hillsboro 1 town (1990 pop. 587), Lawrence co., NW Ala., near Wheeler Reservoir (in Tennessee R.), 12 mi/19 km WNW of Decatur. **2** town (1990 pop. 499), Fountain co., W Ind., 13 mi/21 km ESE of Covington; 40°07′N 87°10′W. In agr. area. **3** town (1990 pop. 151), Henry co., SE Iowa, 12 mi/19 km SW of Mount Pleasant; 40°50′N 91°42′W. Limestone quarries. **4** town (1990 pop. 2,704), Marion co., central Kansas, 10 mi/16 km W of Marion, near Cottonwood R.; 38°21′N 97°12′W. In agr. area (winter wheat, corn; poultry, livestock); bookbinding. Mfg. (dairy prods., feeds, transportation equip.). Seat of Tabor Col. Marion L. Reservoir to NE. Mennonite Heritage Center to SW at Goessel. Founded 1879, inc. 1884. **5** town (1990 pop. 164), Caroline co., E Md., on Tuckahoe Creek, and 6 mi/9.7 km WNW of Denton; 38°55′N 75°56′W. Named for Lord Hillsboro, a relative of Lord Baltimore, it was previously called Tuckahoe Bridge because of the span over the river here. Charles Wilson Peale, a noted Md. artist, used to live here. A stone monument marks the site of an early Methodist chapel. **6** town (1990 pop. 1,625), ⊙ Jefferson co., E Mo., 35 mi/56 km SW of St. Louis; 38°13′N 90°34′W. Light mfg. Semi-urban development in area; satellite community of St. Louis. Seat of Jefferson Col. Plotted 1839. **7** town (1990 pop. 1,826), Hillsborough co., S N.H., 18 mi/29 km WSW of Concord. Drained by Contoocook R. and Beards and Sand brooks. Mfg. (transportation equip., grinding wheels; printing and publishing); agr. (vegetables, apples, nursery crops; livestock, poultry; dairying). President Franklin Pierce Homestead, in SW, was built 1804 by president's father, restored 1925. Fox Forest in E; part of Low State Forest in N; part of Franklin Pierce L. in SW. Settled 1741, inc. 1772. Also spelled Hillsborough. **8** town (1990 pop. 1,488), ⊙ Traill co., E N.Dak., 39 mi/63 km N of Fargo, and on Goose R.; 47°23′N 97°03′W. Grain, potatoes; livestock. Inc. 1880. **9** town (1990 pop. 7,072), ⊙ Hill co., N central Texas, 32 mi/51 km N of Waco; elev. 634 ft/193 m; 32°00′N 97°07′W. RR junction in rich blackland agr. area (cotton, corn, sorghum; also cattle, horses); mfg. (apparel, fabricated metal prods., furniture, bldg. materials); gas and oil. Seat of Hill Jr. Col. Aquilla L. reservoir to SW; Confederate Research Center and Gun Mus. Inc. 1853. **10** town (1990 pop. 72), Loudoun co., N Va., 10 mi/16 km NW of Leesburg; 39°12′N 77°43′W. Agr. (livestock; grain, apples). **11** town (1990 pop. 1,288), Vernon co., SW Wis., on tributary of Baraboo R., and 45 mi/72 km ESE of La Crosse; 43°38′N 90°20′W. In timber and farm area. Dairy prods., flour, lumber; mfg. (textiles, footwear). Hosp. and airfield here. Settled 1854; inc. as village in 1885, as city in 1939.

Hillsboro 1 uninc. village, Fleming co., NE Ky., 13 mi/21 km NW of Moreland. In agr. area (tobacco, grain; livestock). Hillsboro Covered Bridge is here. **2** village (1990 pop. 175), Sierra co., SW N.Mex., in SE foothills of Mimbres Mts., extension of Black Range, near Rio Grande, 24 mi/39 km SW of Truth or Consequences; elev. 5,236 ft/1,596 m. Cattle, sheep. Once a busy silver-mining point with pop. (1886) of 5,000. Gila Natl. Forest to W. **3** village (1990 pop. 188), Pocahontas co., E W.Va., 9 mi/14.5 km SW of Marlinton, near Greenbrier R.; 38°8′N 80°12′W. Droop Mt. Battlefield State Park is 3 mi/4.8 km SW, at Droop village. Pearl Buck Mus. (author, 1892–1973). Part of Monongahela Natl. Forest to NW and SE; Watoga State Park to SE; Greenbrier R. State Trail passes to E.

Hillsboro Beach (HILZ-buh-ruh), town (□ 1 sq mi/2.6 sq km; 1990 pop. 1,748), Broward co., SE Fla., 2 mi/3.2 km N of Pompano Beach; 26°16′N 80°04′W.

Hillsboro River (HILZ-buh-ruh), c.55 mi/89 km long, central and W central Fla.; rises N of Lakeland; flows NW and then SW to Hillsboro Bay (an arm of Tampa Bay), at Tampa.

Hillsborough, village (1991 pop. 1,239), SE N.B., E Canada, on Petitcodiac R. estuary, and 13 mi/21 km SE of Moncton; 45°56′N 64°39′W. Ships oil shale, albertite, manganese, coal, gypsum from Albert Mines. Fishing (cod, lobster, clams, oysters). Settled 1765.

Hillsborough, town, W Carriacou, Grenadines, Grenada, West Indies, 35 mi/56 km NE of St. George's, Grenada; 12°28′N 61°27′W. Administrative and commercial center. Has fine harbor. Cotton, limes.

Hillsborough 1 (HILZ-buh-ruh), county (□ 1,266 sq mi/3,279 sq km; 1990 pop. 834,054), W central Fla., on Gulf coast and bounded S and partly W by Tampa Bay; ⊙ Tampa; 27°54′N 82°20′W. Rolling and level terrain with many small lakes; drained by Hillsboro R. Agr. (citrus fruit, tomatoes, strawberries, peanuts, corn); dairying, poultry raising; fishing. Mfg. (food, tobacco, and wood prods.). Some quarrying (phosphate, sand, shells). Massive urban growth since 1975 as metropolitan Tampa has expanded rapidly. Formed 1834. **2** (HILZ-buh-ro), county (□ 892 sq mi/2,310 sq km; 1990 pop. 336,073), S N.H., on Mass. (S) state line; ⊙ Nashua; 42°54′N 71°43′W. Mfg. center of N.H., one of leading industrial cos. of U.S., with mfg. at Manchester, Nashua, Bedford, Hudson, Merrimack, and Milford. Granite quarrying; timber; agr. (vegetables, corn, beans, hay, apples; cattle, hogs, poultry; dairying). Resorts. Drained by Contoocook, Piscataquog, Souhegan, Merrimack, and Nashua rivers. Franklin Pierce Homestead in NW, at Hillsborough; Silver L. State Park in SE; Miller and Greenfield state parks and Sheiling Forest in W center; Clough State Park in NE; Fox Forest and part of Low State Park in NW. Formed 1769.

Hillsborough, city (1990 pop. 10,667), San Mateo co., W Calif., residential suburb 14 mi/23 km S of downtown San Francisco, 3 mi/4.8 km NW of San Mateo, on San Francisco Bay. Software development. San Francisco Internatl. Airport to NW. Coyote Point to E; San Francisco State Fish and Game Refuge to SW, including San Andreas Fault (Lower Crystal Springs Reservoir). Inc. 1910.

Hillsborough, town (1990 pop. 4,263), ⊙ Orange co., N central N.C., 11 mi/18 km NW of Durham, on Eno R.;

36°04′N 79°05′W. Mfg. (machinery, plastic prods., medical equip., paper goods, packaging, salon equip., power supplies). Agr. area (tobacco, grain, soybeans, sorghum; poultry, livestock; dairying). Eno R. State Park to E. An early provincial capital of N.C.; in 1768, scene of disturbances by the Regulators. Thomas Hart Benton b. here. Settled before 1700; plotted 1754.

Hillsborough, township (1990 pop. 28,808), Somerset co., N N.J., 5 mi/8 km S of Somerville; 40°30′N 74°40′W. Brick mfg. Inc. 1798.

Hillsborough Bay, inlet of Northumberland Strait, S central P.E.I., E Canada; 10 mi/16 km long, 10 mi/16 km wide at entrance. Receives Hillsborough R. at its head at Charlottetown. St. Peters Isl. is in entrance of bay.

Hillsborough Dam, lake, Tobago, Rep. of Trinidad and Tobago, in S central area. Supplies drinking water for the isl.

Hillsborough River (HILZ-buh-ruh), narrow lagoon, c.18 mi/29 km long, in Volusia co., E central Fla., sheltered from the Atlantic Ocean by barrier beach; extends S from Ponce de Leon Inlet (at S end of Halifax R. lagoon) to N end of Mosquito Lagoon. Followed by Intracoastal Waterway.

Hillsborough River, 30 mi/48 km long, central P.E.I., E Canada; rises 18 mi/29 km ENE of Charlottetown; flows W and SW, past Charlottetown, to Hillsborough Bay at Charlottetown.

Hillsburgh, village, S Ont., central Canada, 18 mi/29 km NNE of Guelph. Dairying, mixed farming.

Hillsdale, village, S Ont., central Canada, 17 mi/27 km W of Orillia. Dairying, mixed farming.

Hillsdale, county (☐ 607 sq mi/1,572 sq km; 1990 pop. 43,431), S Mich., on Ohio (S) and Ind. (SW) state lines; ⊙ Hillsdale; 41°53′N 84°35′W. Drained by headstreams of the Kalamazoo R. and by St. Joseph R. Agr. (forage crops, corn, wheat, oats, apples, soybeans; cattle, hogs, sheep; dairy prods.). Mfg. (consumer goods, plastic prods., bakery prods., playground equip., transportation equip.; machining) at Hillsdale, Jonesville, and Reading. Many small lakes. Organized 1835.

Hillsdale 1 town (1990 pop. 8,170), ⊙ Hillsdale co., S Mich., 25 mi/40 km SSW of Jackson, and on St. Joseph R.; 41°55′N 84°38′W. Trade and mfg. center (transportation equip., textiles; food processing). Seat of Hillsdale Col., with 60-acre/24-ha Slayton Arboretum. Native Amer. mounds nearby. Settled 1834; inc. as village 1847, as city 1869. **2** town (1990 pop. 1,948), St. Louis co., E Mo., residential suburb 6 mi/9.7 km NW of downtown St. Louis; 38°41′N 90°17′W.

Hillsdale 1 village (1990 pop. 489), Rock Island co., NW Ill., 19 mi/31 km ENE of Moline, on Rock R.; 41°36′N 90°10′W. Corn, soybeans; cattle, hogs; dairying; mfg. (firearms, wood prods.), meatpacking. Anc. Mississippi R. flowed across this site, toward SE. **2** village (1990 pop. 500), Vermillion co., W Ind., 8 mi/12.9 km N of Clinton, on Wabash R. Corn, wheat; cattle. **3** village, Miami co., E Kansas, 7 mi/11.3 km N of Paola. Cattle raising, farming. Hillsdale L. Reservation to W. **4** village (1990 pop. 150), Columbia co., SE N.Y., near Mass. state line, 8 mi/12.9 km W of Great Barrington (Mass.); 42°13′N 73°32′W. Skiing at nearby Catamount Mt. in the Berkshires. **5** village (1990 pop. 96), Garfield co., N Okla., 13 mi/21 km NW of Enid; 36°33′N 97°59′W. In agr. area.

Hillsdale, borough (1990 pop. 9,750), Bergen co., NE N.J., 8 mi/12.9 km N of Hackensack; 41°00′N 74°02′W. Primarily residential. Inc. 1923.

Hillsgrove, neighborhood, in Warwick city, Kent co., E central R.I., 7 mi/11.3 km SSW of Providence. Theodore F. Green State Airport (Providence) here.

Hillshire Village, village (1990 pop. 617), Harris co., SE Texas, residential suburb 8 mi/12.9 km WNW of downtown Houston, surrounded by city of Houston.

Hillside 1 village (1990 pop. 7,672), Cook co., NE Ill., W suburb of Chicago, 10 mi/16 km E of Wheaton; 41°52′N 87°54′W. Computer services. Inc. 1905. **2** village, Prince Georges co., central Md., ESE suburb of Washington, D.C.

Hillside, township (1990 pop. 21,044), Union co., NE N.J., 2 mi/3.2 km SW of Newark; 40°42′N 74°13′W. Mixed industry, including metal prods. and frozen juices. Inc. 1913.

Hillside Gardens, village and uninc. suburb, Jackson co., S Mich., 5 mi/8 km NW of Jackson.

Hillsview, village (1990 pop. 4), McPherson co., N S.Dak., 55 mi/89 km WNW of Aberdeen; 45°40′N 99°33′W.

Hillsville, town (1990 pop. 2,008). ⊙ Carroll co., SW Va., in the Blue Ridge, 12 mi/19 km NE of Galax; 36°46′N 80°44′W. Mfg. (machinery, clothing and textiles, lumber, crushed stone); agr. (grain, cabbage, apples; cattle); dairying.

Hilltonia (hil-TO-nee-uh), city (1990 pop. 402), Screven co., E Ga., 10 mi/16 km NNW of Sylvania; 32°53′N 81°40′W.

Hilltop, town (1990 pop. 749), Anoka co., E Minn., residential suburb 5 mi/8 km N of downtown Minneapolis, E of Mississippi R., surrounded by Columbia Heights city; 45°03′N 93°14′W.

Hilltop, uninc. village (1990 pop. 250), Fayette co., S central W.Va., 11 mi/18 km N of Beckley, near Dunloup Creek. In coal region. New R. Gorge Natl. R. to E.

Hillview, town (1990 pop. 6,119), Bullitt and Jefferson cos., NW Ky., residential suburb 13 mi/21 km SSE of downtown Louisville; 38°04′N 85°41′W. Agr. area (burley tobacco, grain; livestock, poultry; dairying).

Hillview, village, (1990 pop. 271), Greene co., W Ill., near Illinois R., 13 mi/21 km NW of Carrollton; 39°27′N 90°32′W. In agr. area.

Hillview Reservoir, in Yonkers, Westchester co., SE N.Y., in Yonkers; covers 90 acres/36 ha; 40°55′N 73°53′W. Part of N.Y. city water-supply system; completed 1915. Terminus of Catskill and Delaware aqueducts, and head of tunnel system delivering water to boroughs of N.Y. city.

Hillwood, uninc. town, Fairfax co., NE Va., residential suburb 7 mi/11.3 km W of Washington, D.C.; 38°52′N 77°10′W.

Hilmar-Irwin, uninc. town (1990 pop. 3,392), Merced co., central Calif., 4 mi/6.4 km S of Turlock, near Merced R. Dairying; poultry; fruit, sweet potatoes, beans, tomatoes, grain, cotton, almonds. Mfg. (cheese).

Hilo (HEE-lo), city (1990 pop. 37,808), ⊙ Hawaii co., Hawaii, on Hilo Bay of Hawaii isl. (the Big Isl.), 200 mi/322 km SE of Honolulu, at mouth of Wailuku R.; 19°41′N 155°05′W. The 2d-largest city of Hawaii, a port of entry, and the only metropolitan area on the isl., Hilo is the trade and shipping center for an orchid, papaya, and macadamia nut region; fish, prawns, and until 1996, sugar. Mfg. (chemicals, machinery, dairy prods., machinery, food and beverages; printing and publishing). With the demise of sugar, the economy became based heavily on tourism, which was spurred by the inauguration in 1967 of direct air service to the U.S. mainland; Hilo Internatl. Airport (General Lyman Field) on E side of city. Among Hilo's points of interest are the peaks of Mauna Kea and Mauna Loa, which rise behind the city; waterfalls on the Wailuku R.; the Lyman Mission House (c.1839) and Mus.; East Hawaii Cultural Center; Wailoa R. State Park includes Waiakea Pond, near center of city, near bay front; and an isl.-park in Hilo Bay. Seat of Hilo Col., the Univ. of Hawaii at Hilo, and Hilo Community Col. Badly damaged by tidal waves in 1946 and 1960; after the latter tidal wave, the lowland area was drained and a hill 26 ft/8 m above sea level was constructed. Akaka Falls State Park to N; Wailuku R. State Parks to W (includes Rainbow Falls); Keaukaha Military Reserve to SE. S of airport (Natl Guard); Bayfront Beach Park, includes Lilioukalani Gardens, Coconut (linked by footbridge) and Kaulainaiwi Isls., E of city center; Hilo Breakwater, on E side of bay, creates harbor and protects ships from Blonde Reef, immediately to E. Panaewa and Waiakea Forest Reserves to S, including Panaewa Zoo; Hilo Forest Reserve to W; Kaumana Caves to SW. Starting point of Hawaii Belt Road, which encircles the Big Isl. Settled by missionaries c.1822, inc. as a city 1911.

Hilo Bay, crescent-shaped indention, Pacific Ocean, only anchorage on E coast, Hawaii co, Hawaii Isl., Hawaii. Exposed to NE trade wind, vulnerable to tidal waves, protected on E by Hilo Breakwater, Blonde Reef lies beyond it. Coconut Isl., connected to mainland by footbridge, and Kaulainaiwi Isl., in the bay, both part of Bayfront Beach Park.

Hilton, village (☐ 1 sq mi/2.6 sq km; 1990 pop. 5,216), Monroe co., W N.Y. 13 mi/21 km NW of Rochester; 43°17′N 77°47′W. Milling; metalworking fluids; agr. (fruit, wheat).

Hilton Head, city (1990 pop. 23,694), Beaufort co., 17 mi/27 km ENE of Savannah (Ga.), on Hilton Head Isl.; 32°12′N 80°45′W. Tourism is the main industry.

Hilton Head Island, S S.C., 1 of Sea Isls., SW of Port Royal Sound, 17 mi/27 km ENE of Savannah (Ga.): c.12 mi/19 km long, 1 mi/1.6 km–5 mi/8 km wide. Hilton Head village on W shore. Major resort and convention center. Airport.

Hiltonbeach, village (1991 pop. 217), S central Ont., central Canada, on St. Joseph Isl., on St. Joseph Channel of L. Huron, 28 mi/45 km SE of Sault Ste. Marie. Lumbering. Also written Hilton Beach.

Hima (HEI-muh), uninc. village (1990 pop. 600), Clay co., SE Ky., 17 mi/27 km E of London, and 2 mi/3.2 km S of Manchester, near Gross Creek, in Cumberland foothills, in Daniel Boone Natl. Forest. Coal, timber, and agr. (tobacco; livestock).

Himlerville (HEIM-luhr-vil) or **Beauty**, locality, Martin co., E Ky., 3 mi/4.8 km ESE of Inez, in Cumberland Mts. Historic Hung. camp of immigrant coal miners. Has 13-room mansion of Marton Himler.

Hinche (ANGSH), town (1982 pop. 10,070), ⊙ Centre dept., E central Haiti, 45 mi/72 km NE of Port-au-Prince; 19°01′N 72°01′W. On fertile plain. Coffee, sugarcane, sisal, cotton, fruit; cattle; beekeeping; cotton processing.

Hinchinbrook, Cape, S Alaska, S tip of Hinchinbrook Isl.; 60°16′N 146°37′W.

Hinchinbrook Entrance (HIN-chin-bruk), S Alaska, bet. Hinchinbrook (E) and Montague isls. (W), joins Gulf of Alaska and Prince William Sound.

Hinchinbrook Island, S Alaska, in Gulf of Alaska, at mouth of Prince William Sound, 20 mi/32 km SW of Cordova; 22 mi/35 km long, 4 mi/6.4 km–13 mi/21 km wide; 60°23′N 146°25′W. Nuchek village is in W.

Hinckley, town (1990 pop. 946), Pine co., E Minn., on Grindstone R., 14 mi/23 km N of Pine City; 46°00′N 92°56′W. RR junction. Oats; cattle, sheep, poultry; dairying. Mfg. (machinery; meat processing); timber. Nearly destroyed in Great Fire of 1894, later rebuilt and became center for lumbering. Chengwatana State Forest to SE; Sandstone Natl. Wildlife Refuge to NE; large St. Croix State Park to E.

Hinckley 1 village (1990 pop. 1,682), De Kalb co., N Ill., 16 mi/26 km S of Sycamore; 41°46′N 88°38′W. In rich agr. area. **2** village (1990 pop. 658), Millard co., W Utah, at S margin of Sevier desert, 5 mi/8 km SW of Delta, near Sevier R.; elev. 4,600 ft/1,402 m; 39°19′N 112°40′W. Alfalfa, wheat, barley, sugar beets; dairying; cattle. Precious metals mining. Fort Deseret State Historical Park to S. Gunnison Massacre Monument to SW. Topaz War Relocation Center Historical Site to NW.

Hinckley Reservoir, N.Y.: see WEST CANADA CREEK.

Hindman (HEIND-muhn), town (1990 pop. 798), ⊙ Knott co., E Ky., in Cumberland foothills, 13 mi/21 km ENE of Hazard; 37°19′N 82°58′W. In coal-mining and agr. area; light mfg. Seat of Hindman Settlement School (founded 1902). Carr Fork L. reservoir to S.

Hinds (HEINDZ), county (☐ 877 mi/1,411 km; 1990 pop. 254,441), W Miss.; ⊙ JACKSON (⊙ Miss.) and Raymond; 32°15′N 90°26′W. Bounded E by Pearl R., NW and partly W by Big Black R. Agr. (cotton, corn, soybeans, vegetables, potatoes; cattle, poultry; timber); natural gas, paper and pulp. Mfg. at Jackson and Clinton. Co. is urbanized in E, including Jackson, state's largest city. LeFleur's Bluff State Park in E, in city of Jackson; L. Dockery State L. in E, S of Jackson. Natchez Trace (Natl.) Parkway, crosses co. includes incomplete sect. Formed 1821.

Hind's Hill (2,158 ft/658 m), W central N.F., E Canada, 45 mi/72 km E of Corner Brook, overlooking Hind's L.

Hind's Lake (☐ 14 sq mi/36 sq km), W central N.F., E Canada, 40 mi/64 km E of Corner Brook, at foot of Hind's Hill; 7 mi/11 km long, 3 mi/5 km wide.

Hindsboro, village (1990 pop. 346), Douglas co., E central Ill., 10 mi/16 km SE of Tuscola; 39°40'N 88°07'W. In agr. area.

Hindsdale (HEINDS-dail), village (1990 pop. 225), Valley co., NE Mont., 24 mi/39 km NW of Glasgow, on Milk R. at its confluence with Rock Creek. Wheat, barley, oats; cattle, sheep, hogs. Larb Hills to SW.

Hi-Nella (HEI-NE-luh), residential borough (1990 pop. 1,045), Camden co., SW N.J., 8 mi/12.9 km SE of Camden; 39°50'N 75°01'W.

Hines, town (1990 pop. 1,452), Harney co., E central Oregon, 2 mi/3.2 km S of Burns, near Silvies R.; elev. 4,155 ft/1,266 m; 43°34'N 119°04'W. Lumber; millwork.

Hines Creek, village (1991 pop. 423), W Alta., W Canada, near Peace R., 50 mi/80 km W of Peace River town; 56°14'N 118°36'W. Lumbering; mixed farming; wheat.

Hinesburg (HINS-buhrg), town (1990 pop. 3,780), Chittenden co., NW Vt., 12 mi/19 km SSE of Burlington. Settled just after Amer. Revolution.

Hinesville (HEINZ-vil), city (1990 pop. 21,603), ⊙ Liberty co., SE Ga., 33 mi/53 km WSW of Savannah; 31°50'N 81°36'W. In farm area. Fort Stewart nearby is responsible for much of the city's growth. Mfg. includes printing and publishing; concrete.

Hingham (HEENG-uhm), town (1990 pop. 19,821), Plymouth co., E Mass., S of Boston, on the S shore of Hingham Bay; 42°13'N 70°54'W. Hingham is primarily residential with some diverse light industry (metals, scientific instruments). Once a fishing and shipbuilding center, its bay shore draws annual visitors. The Old Ship Church (1681), a fine example of Amer. Gothic architecture, is one of the oldest houses of worship in the U.S. and has been in continuous use since it was built. Wompatuch State Park is here. Includes village of South Hingham. Inc. 1635.

Hingham (HING-uhm), village (1990 pop. 181), Hill co., N Mont., 33 mi/53 km W of Havre; 48°34'N 110°25'W. Storage and shipping center for grain and livestock.

Hinsdale, county (☐ 1,123 sq mi/2,909 sq km; 1990 pop. 467), SW central Colo.; ⊙ Lake City; 37°49'N 107°16'W. Tourist and timber area, some livestock (sheep). Continental Divide crosses twice, heading SW across N (also forming small E-W section of E boundary), turns to SE in neighboring San Juan co., to W, and crosses S part of co., about 80% of co. is natl. forest. S of Divide, source of Rio Grande immediately W in San Juan, headwaters flow E across center of co., through Rio Grande Reservoir; N part drained by Lake Fork of Gunnison and Cobolla Creek; S drained by Los Pinos (source) and Pindra rivers, both branches of San Juan. Includes parts of San Juan Mts. Part of Uncompahgre Natl. Forest in NW corner; parts of Gunnison Natl. Forest N of Divide in NE and N center; Rio Grande Natl. Forest in center, bet. Divide sections; San Juan Natl. Forest in S. Williams Creek Reservoir in SE; L. San Cristobal Reservoir in N center. Formed 1874.

Hinsdale 1 town (1990 pop. 1,959), Berkshire co., W Mass., in the Berkshires, 7 mi/11.3 km E of Pittsfield; 42°26'N 73°07'W. Resort; agr. Settled 1763; inc. 1804. Peru State Forest nearby. **2** town (1990 pop. 3,936), Cheshire co., SW N.H., 14 mi/23 km SE of Keene; 42°48'N 72°30'W. Bounded S (for 1 mi/1.6 km) by Mass. state line, W by Connecticut R. (Vt. state line); drained by Ashuelot R. Agr. (dairying; cattle, poultry; apples, vegetables; timber); mfg. (wire rope and cable, flashlights, paper prods.). Part of Pisgah State Park in NE, part of Wantastiquet Mt. State Forest in NW. Settled c.1742; inc. 1753.

Hinsdale, village (1990 pop. 16,029), Cook and Du Page cos., NE Ill., part of the greater Chicago metropolitan area; 41°48'N 87°56'W. Computer systems software. Inc. 1873.

Hinton, town (1986 pop. 8,629), Alta., Canada, in Alta. foothills, 177 mi/285 km W of Edmonton; 53°24'N 117°35'W. Coal mining service center; winter recreation.

Hinton 1 town (1990 pop. 697), Plymouth co., NW Iowa, 13 mi/21 km SSE of Le Mars; 42°37'N 96°17'W. Livestock; grain. **2** town (1990 pop. 1,233), Caddo co., W central Okla., 22 mi/35 km WSW of El Reno; 35°30'N 98°21'W. In agr. area (cotton, wheat, corn; cattle). Red Rock Canyon State Park to S. **3** town (1990 pop. 3,433), ⊙ Summers co., S W.Va., 18 mi/29 km SE of Beckley, on New R., 1 mi/1.6 km N of mouth of Greenbrier R., and 4 mi/6.4 km NNE of mouth of Bluestone R.; 37°39'N 80°52'W. RR shops; shipping point for agr. area (grain; livestock; dairy prods.); processes lumber, beverages. Mfg. (concrete; printing and publishing). Hinton Visitor Center is here. Bluestone Dam (New R.), in Bluestone State Park and Wildlife Management Area, to S; New R. Gorge Natl. R. to N; Pipestem State Park and Bluestone Natl. Scenic R. to SW. Settled 1831; inc. 1880.

Hinton, uninc. village, Rockingham co., NW Va., 4 mi/6.4 km W of Harrisonburg; 38°27'N 78°58'W. Mfg. (furniture, poultry processing); agr. (grain; poultry, livestock; dairying).

Hiram 1 (HEI-ruhm), town (1990 pop. 1,389), Paulding co., NW Ga., 23 mi/37 km WNW of Atlanta; 33°52'N 84°46'W. Mfg. (apparel, concrete); printing and publishing. **2** (HEI-ruhm), town (1990 pop. 1,260), Oxford co., W Maine, on Saco R. and 27 mi/43 km SW of South Paris; 43°52'N 70°49'W. Wood prods.

Hiram 1 (HEI-ruhm), uninc. village (1990 pop. 400), Harlan co., SE Ky., 3 mi/4.8 km WSW of Cumberland, on Poor Fork of Cumberland R. Bituminous coal; timber. Daniel Boone Natl. Forest to NW. **2** village (1990 pop. 1,330), Portage co., NE Ohio, 23 mi/37 km NE of Akron; seat of Hiram Col.; 41°19'N 81°08'W.

Hiseville (HEIZ-vil), village (1990 pop. 220), Barren co., S Ky., 10 mi/16 km NE of Glasgow; 37°06'N 85°49'W. Agr. (burley tobacco, grain; livestock). Caves in area.

Hispaniola (ees-pah-nee-O-lah), Span. *Española*, second largest island of the West Indies (☐ 29,530 sq mi/76,483 sq km), bet. Cuba and Puerto Rico; 19°00'N 71°00'W. HAITI occupies the W ⅓ of the isl. and the DOMINICAN REPUBLIC the remainder. Largest cities include Port-au-Prince, Haiti, and Santo Domingo, the Dominican Republic. Visited by Columbus in 1492, the isl. was called Española. The later Fr. colony was called Saint-Domingue, after Santo Domingo, the Span. colony in the E part of the isl. The terrain, dominated by the Cordillera Central, is high and rugged; Pico Duarte (10,417 ft/3,175 m high) is the tallest peak. Extending far W, like the claws of a crab, 2 mt. ranges form the scenic Gulf of Gonâve. The climate is subtropical, and agr. (coffee, cocoa, sugarcane, and tobacco) flourishes in the abundant rainfall. In some areas of the isl. (esp. Haiti), increased pop. has caused significant deforestation for cultivation.

Historic Camden National Affiliated Area, Kershaw co., N central S.C., authorized 1982. Colonial village. Est. 1730; occupied by the British 1780–1781.

Hitchcock, county (☐ 718 sq mi/1,860 sq km; 1990 pop. 3,750), S Nebr.; ⊙ Trenton; 40°10'N 101°02'W. Agr. area bounded S by Kansas; drained by Republican R. and Fredmen Creek. Corn, wheat, sorghum, sunflower seed; cattle, hogs. Petroleum. Central/Mountain time zone boundary follows W boundary. Swanson Reservoir and State Recreation Area in W center; Massacre Canyon Monument in E center. Formed 1873.

Hitchcock, town (1990 pop. 5,868), Galveston co., S Texas, suburb 7 mi/11.3 km SW of Texas City, on Highland Bayou; 29°19'N 95°01'W. Oil and gas; cattle; rice, soybeans; mfg. (industrial chemicals).

Hitchcock 1 village (1990 pop. 139), Blaine co., W central Okla., 9 mi/14.5 km NNE of Watonga; 35°58'N 98°20'W. In agr. area. Roman Nose State Park to SW. **2** village (1990 pop. 95), Beadle co., E central S.Dak., 20 mi/32 km NNW of Huron; 44°37'N 98°28'W.

Hitchins (HICH-uhns), uninc. village (1990 pop. 400), Carter co., NE Ky., 21 mi/34 km SW of Ashland. In agr. and clay-producing area; agr. (tobacco, corn; cattle). Grayson L. reservoir and State Park to SW.

Hitchita (hich-EET-uh), village (1990 pop. 118), McIntosh co., E Okla., 14 mi/23 km ESE of Okmulgee, on Deep Fork (Canadian R.) arm of Eufaula L. (to S); 35°31'N 95°45'W. In agr. area. Eufaula L. nearby.

Hitterdal (HI-tuhr-dawl), village (1990 pop. 242), Clay co., W Minn., 26 mi/42 km ENE of Fargo N.Dak.; 46°58'N 96°15'W. Grain, beans, sugar beets; dairying. White Earth Indian Reservation to E; small lakes to E and SE.

Hiwassee Lake (hei-WAW-see), reservoir (☐ 3 sq mi/7.8 sq km), Cherokee co., extreme W N.C., in Nantahala Natl. Forest, on Hiwassee R., 70 m/112 km SW of Waynseville and near Ga. and Tenn. borders; 35°09'N 84°11'W. Formed by Hiwassee Dam (307 ft/97 m high), built (1940) by TVA for flood control.

Hiwassee River, c.140 mi/225 km long, Ga., N.C., and Tenn.; rises in the Blue Ridge in Towns co., N Ga.; flows NW through SW corner of N.C., past Hayesville, and NW, past Murphy, into Cherokee Natl. Forest, into SE Tenn., joins Tennessee R. (Chickamauga Reservoir) 13 mi/21 km N of Cleveland, Tenn., in Polk co.; 35°24'N 85°00'W. Drains 2,700 sq mi/6,993 sq km, including entire drainage basin of the Ocoee R., a tributary. In N.C., Apalachia, Hiwassee, and Chatuge dams are major TVA units. Hiwassee Dam (307 ft/94 m high, 1,287 ft/392 m long; completed 1940) is 10 mi/16 km WNW of Murphy; concrete, straight gravity, overflow construction; used for hydroelectric power and flood control. Impounds Hiwassee Reservoir (☐ c. 10 sq mi/26 sq km; 22 mi/35 km long, capacity 438,000 acre-ft.) in Cherokee co., N.C. Designated a Tenn. Scenic R. in 1968. Whitewater rafting, canoeing.

Hixton, village (1990 pop. 345), Jackson co., W central Wis., on Trempealeau R. and 38 mi/61 km SE of Eau Claire; 44°22'N 91°00'W. In dairying region. Timber.

Hoagland, village (1990 pop. 600), Allen co., NE Ind., 11 mi/18 km SE of Fort Wayne. Corn, oats, soybeans. Mfg. (wooden cabinets). Laid out 1872.

Hoback River (HO-bak), c.30 mi/48 km long, W Wyo.; rises in NW Sublette co.; flows NW, through picturesque Hoback Canyon, past N Wyoming Range, to Snake R. 10 mi/16 km S of Jackson.

Hobart, city (1990 pop. 21,822), Lake co., extreme NW Ind.; 41°32'N 87°16'W. Metal prods., electric coils and transformers, herbal prods., tools and castings, and food products are made in Hobart. Part of the Calumet region. Laid out c.1849, inc. 1921.

Hobart (HO-buhrt), town (1990 pop. 4,305), ⊙ Kiowa co., SW Okla., c.45 mi/72 km NW of Lawton; 35°01'N 99°05'W. Elev. 1,547 ft/472 m. Trade center for rich agr. area (cotton, grain, alfalfa, sorghum; cattle, sheep); mfg. (oil seals, flexible aluminum packaging); cold-storage plants. Altus L. to SW. Inc. 1901.

Hobart, village (1990 pop. 385), Delaware co., S N.Y., in the Catskills, on West Branch of Delaware R. and 20 mi/32 km ESE of Oneonta; 42°22'N 74°40'W. Feed and pharmaceuticals.

Hobbs, city (1990 pop. 29,115), Lea co., SE N.Mex., 95 mi/153 km SE of Roswell; 32°43'N 103°09'W. Elev. 3,625 ft/1,105 m. Inc. 1929. With the discovery (c.1928) of oil and natural gas in the area, Hobbs became one of the last great oil-boom towns in the U.S. It still remains a major shipping and trading center for oil-well supplies. Chemical production is of increasing importance, as are feedlots for livestock (sheep, cattle, dairying) and the raising of thoroughbred horses. Cotton, wheat, peanuts, vegetables, and melons are grown on irrigated farms in the area. Beef cattle have long been important in Hobbs; dairy farming is growing. Mfg. (concrete, machinery, fabricated metal prods., chemicals); mining. N. Mex. Junior Col. and the Col. of the Southwest are in the city. Lea Co. Hobbs Airport to SW. Harry McAdams State Park is here.

Hobe Sound, resort town (☐ 5 sq mi/13 sq km; 1990 pop. 11,507), Martin co., E central Fla., 12 mi/19 km N of W. Palm Beach, near Jupiter Isl.; 27°04'N 80°08'W.

Hobgood (HAHB-gud), village (1990 pop. 435), Halifax co., NE N.C., 12 mi/19 km NE of Tarboro near Fishing Creek; 36°01'N 77°24'W. Tobacco, cotton, soybeans, grain, poultry, hogs.

Hobkirks Hill, S.C.: see CAMDEN.

Hoboken (HO-BO-kin), city (1990 pop. 33,397), Hudson

Cross references are shown in SMALL CAPITALS. The pronunciation key is on page xv. The dates of population figures are on page xii.

co., NE N.J., on the Hudson R. adjoining Jersey City and opposite Manhattan; 40°44′N 74°01′W. Settled by the Dutch c.1640, inc. as a city 1855. It is a port of entry and a RR terminal. The city has food-processing industries and factories that make electronic, chemical, and metal prods. The site changed title many times before John Stevens gained possession in 1784. He built his home at Castle Point (an unusual rock formation overlooking the river) and laid out the town in 1804. Stevens built (c.1825) and ran on his estate the 1st locomotive to pull a train on tracks in the U.S. Hoboken became an important industrial and commercial center in the late 19th cent. with a major port, shipyards, and warehouses. In the 1970s and 1980s, professionals, artists, and students flocked to the city for its affordable, renovated housing and easy access to N.Y. city. Hoboken's reputation has grown accordingly, and it has become a cultural community with art galleries, musical events, entertainment, and developing businesses. Higher rents brought by the arrival of these new Hobokenites have made it harder for poorer residents to remain in the community, though. John Jacob Astor lived here; his home was a gathering place for authors, including Fitz-Greene Halleck, Washington Irving, and William Cullen Bryant. Hoboken is the seat of Stevens Inst. of Technology. Frank Sinatra b. here.

Hoboken (HO-bo-kihn), village (1990 pop. 440), Brantley co., SE Ga., 13 mi/21 km E of Waycross; 31°11′N 82°08′W. Mfg. of lumber.

Hobson, village (1990 pop. 226), Judith Basin co., central Mont., on Judith R. and 21 mi/34 km W of Lewistown; 47°00′N 109°52′W. Wheat, barley, alfalfa, cattle, sheep; sapphires. Sapphire Village and Mine 19 mi/31 km to WSW. Ackley L. State Park to SW.

Hobson City, residential suburb (1990 pop. 794), Calhoun co., E Ala., a town just SW of Anniston. Sportswear mfg.

Hobson Lake, E B.C., Canada, in Cariboo Mts., in Wells Gray Provincial Park, 120 mi/193 km N of Kamloops; 20 mi/32 km long, 1 mi/2 km–2 mi/3 km wide. Elev. 2,735 ft/834 m. Drains S into North Thompson R. through Clearwater L.

Hocabá (o-kah-BAH), town (1990 pop. 3,648), ⊙ Hocabá municipio, Yucatán, SE Mexico, 26 mi/42 km ESE of Mérida; 20°49′N 89°29′W. On RR. Henequen, tropical fruit, corn, beans, livestock.

Hochelaga 1 Canada: see MONTREAL ISLAND. **2** Canada: see MONTREAL.

Hockanum River, c.25 mi/40 km long, central Conn.; rises in Shenipsit L.; flows SW, past Rockville, to the Connecticut at East Hartford. Many early mill sites.

Hocking, county (□ 421 sq mi/1,090 sq km; 1990 pop. 25,533), S central Ohio; ⊙ Logan; 39°31′N 82°28′W. Intersected by Hocking R. and small Rush, Salt, and Monday creeks. Primarily in the Unglaciated Plain physiographic region. Agr. (nursery and greenhouse crops; beef cows, poultry; corn); mfg. at Logan (rubber prods., plastics, electrical goods); coal mining; clay, sand, and gravel pits. Formed 1805.

Hocking, village, Athens co., SE Ohio, on Hocking R., just N of Athens, 39°44′N 82°28′W.

Hocking River, c.100 mi/161 km long, SE Ohio; rises in Fairfield co.; flows SW, past Lancaster, Logan, Nelsonville, and Athens, to the Ohio 22 mi/35 km SW of Marietta; 39°11′N 81°45′W.

Hockley, county (□ 908 sq mi/2,352 sq km; 1990 pop. 24,199), NW Texas; ⊙ Levelland; 33°36′N 102°20′W. Drained in N by intermittent Yellow House Draw creek. Rich agr. region, with extensive irrigated areas; cotton, grain sorghum; livestock (beef cattle, hogs; some sheep, horses, mules). Large oil and gas production. Formed 1876.

Hockley, uninc village (1990 pop. 300), Harris co., SE Texas, 35 mi/56 km NW of downtown Houston. Agr. area (cattle, dairying, horses, rice, vegetables). Oil and natural gas, salt mines. Mfg. (aggregated salt).

Hoctún (ok-TOON), town (1990 pop. 4,623), Yucatán, SE Mexico, 28 mi/45 km ESE of Mérida; 20°48′N 89°14′W. Henequen, sugarcane, corn.

Hodgdon (HAHJ-duhn), town (1990 pop. 1,257), Aroostook co., E Maine, 5 mi/8 km S of Houlton. In agr., lumbering area. Inc. 1832.

Hodge, village (1990 pop. 562), Jackson parish, N central La., on Dugdemona R., and 40 mi/64 km WSW of Monroe; 32°16′N 92°44′W. RR junction; in agr. area; mfg. (paper grocery bags, kraft paper). Caney Creek reservoir to E. Jackson Bienville State Wildlife Area to N.

Hodgeman (HAHJ-muhn), county (□ 860 sq mi/2,227 sq km; 1990 pop. 2,177), SW central Kansas; ⊙ Jetmore; 38°05′N 99°54′W. Rolling prairie region, watered by Pawnee R. and Buckner Creek. Wheat, sorghum, cattle. Hodgeman State Fishing L. at center. Formed 1879.

Hodgenville (HAHJ-uhn-vil), town (1990 pop. 2,721), ⊙ Larue co., central Ky., on Nolin R. and 45 mi/72 km S of Louisville; 37°34′N 85°44′W. In agr. (burley tobacco, corn; livestock), limestone quarries, and timber area; mfg. (furniture, apparel, wooden prods.; lumber). Abraham Lincoln Natl. Historic Site to S; Lincoln's boyhood home (Knob Creek Farm) to NE; The Lincoln Mus., Lincoln Statue on Lincoln Square. S boundary is Central/Eastern time zone boundary, co. is in Eastern. Settled c.1789; est. 1818.

Hodges (HAH-juhs), town (1990 pop. 272), Franklin co., NW Ala., 17 mi/27 km SSW of Russellville.

Hodges, village (1990 pop. 125), Greenwood co., W S.C., 8 mi/12.9 km NW of Greenwood; 34°17′N 82°15′W. Mfg. of windows and door stock, textiles.

Hodges Hill (1,868 ft/569 m), central N.F., Canada, 14 mi/23 km NW of Grand Falls.

Hodgeville, village (1991 pop. 258), S Sask., Canada, on Wiwa Creek and 40 mi/64 km ESE of Swift Current; 50°07′N 106°59′W. Grain elevators, dairying.

Hodgkins, village (1990 pop. 1,963), Cook co., NE Ill., W suburb of Chicago; 41°46′N 87°51′W. On the Sanitary and Ship Canal.

Hoehne, village, Las Animas co., S Colo., on Purgatoire R. and 10 mi/16 km NE of Trinidad. Elev. c.5,728 ft/1,746 m. In irrigated agr. region; wheat, hay, sorghum, cattle. Rail junction to S.

Hoffman 1 village (1990 pop. 492), Clinton co., SW central Ill., 8 mi/12.9 km W of Centralia; 38°32′N 89°15′W. Sorghum, wheat; dairying; coal; mfg. of mobile power units, metal stamping. Centralia Correctional Center to E. **2** village (1990 pop. 576), Grant co., W Minn., 14 mi/23 km SE of Elbow Lake town, bet. Pomme de Terre R. (W) and Chippewa R. (E); 45°49′N 95°47′W. Agr. area (grain, sunflowers, sugar beets; livestock, poultry; dairying); mfg. (aseptic food prods.). **3** village (1990 pop. 348), Richmond co., S N.C., 13 mi/21 km NE of Rockingham near Drowning Creek; 35°01′N 79°32′W. Grain, tobacco, cotton, soybeans, poultry, livestock. Mfg. (window frame parts, wooden moldings, sand and gravel processing). Sandhills Recreation Area to SW. **4** village (1990 pop. 175), Okmulgee co., E central Okla., 6 mi/9.7 km ENE of Henryetta, on Deep Fork of Canadian R., arm of Eufaula L. reservoir to E; 35°29′N 95°50′W. In agr. area.

Hoffman Estates, village (1990 pop. 46,561), Cook co., NE Ill., suburb 30 mi/48 km NW of downtown Chicago, 6 mi/9.7 km E of Elgin; 42°03′N 88°08′W. Residential area. Poplar Creek Theatre in W part.

Hoffman Island, artificial isl., part of Richmond borough of N.Y. city, SE N.Y., in Lower N.Y. Bay, just off E Staten Isl.; 40°35′N 74°03′W. Covers an area of c.10 acres/4 ha. Created 1872, it was formerly a quarantine station.

Hoffman Mountain (elev. 3,715 ft/1,132 m), Essex co., NE N.Y., in the High Peaks sect. of the Adirondacks, 15 mi/24 km SSE of Mt. Marcy and just NW of Schroon L. village; 43°55′N 73°50′W.

Hog Hammock, village, McIntosh co., SE Ga. on Sapelo Isl., 8 mi/12.9 km ESE of Eulonia; 31°23′N 81°16′W. Hog Hammock is home to the decendents of former slaves, who developed their own way of speaking, called Gullah.

Hog Island, Bahamas: see PARADISE ISLAND.

Hog Island 1 in city of Philadelphia, Philadelphia co., on W shore of Delaware R., at W side of mouth of Schuylkill R. Separated from mainland by Mingo Creek, merged with Tinicum Isl. to W by Philadelphia Internatl. Airport. In World War I, important govt. shipyard here; now an industrial and shipping area. Fort Mifflin Historical Site on Delaware R., in S. **2** Northampton co., E Va., barrier isl. bet. the Atlantic Ocean (E) and Hog Isl. Bay (W), 18 mi/29 km NE of Cape Charles city; 9 mi/14.5 km long N–S, 6 mi/9.7 km wide. Great Machipongo Inlet, at S end, links bay and ocean; Little Machipongo Inlet is at N end; Parramore Isl. to N, Cobb Isl. to S. Lighthouse.

Hog Island, Mich.: see BEAVER ISLANDS.

Hogansburg, village (1990 pop. 100), Franklin co., N N.Y., on St. Regis R. near its mouth on the St. Lawrence, and 11 mi./18 km ENE of Massena; 44°58′N 74°41′W. Awakesasne (Mohawk Indian) Mus. here. Nearby is St. Regis Indian Reservation (partly in Canada).

Hogansville, town (1990 pop. 2,976), Troup co., W Ga., 11 mi/18 km NE of La Grange; 33°10′N 84°54′W. Mfg. includes coated mesh fabrics, clothing, fabric chemicals, maps. Inc. 1870.

Hogatza River (ho-GAT-suh), 130 mi/209 km long, W central Alaska; rises in S foothills of Brooks Range near 66°55′N 153°50′W; flows SSW to Koyukuk R. at 66°N 155°23′W.

Hogback Mountain, peak (3,240 ft/988 m) in the Blue Ridge, Greenville co., NW S.C., 6 mi/9.7 km W of Landrum, near N.C. state line.

Hogback Mountain, Mont.: see SNOWCREST MOUNTAINS.

Hogsty Reef, central Bahama Isls., 40 mi/64 km NW of Great Inagua Isl., 310 mi/499 km SE of Nassau; 21°40′N 73°50′W. The reef is c.6 mi/9.7 km long (W-E), 3 mi/4.8 km wide. Off it are 2 small cays. Called Les Etoiles on early Fr. charts.

Hoh River (HO), c.30 mi/48 km long, mainly Jefferson co., NW Wash.; formed at W end of Olympic Natl. Park by N and S forks (S fork c.20 mi/32 km long, N fork c.30 mi/48 km long) rising N and S of Mt. Olympus; main stream flows SW from junction to Pacific Ocean at Hoh Indian Reservation, 15 mi/24 km S of Forks.

Hohenwald (HO-uhn-wohld), city (1990 pop. 3,760), ⊙ Lewis co., central Tenn., 30 mi/48 km W of Columbia; 35°33′N 87°33′W. In forest and farm region; mfg. (apparel, shoes). Center for used clothing stores. Meriwether Lewis Natl. Monument is SE.

Hohokam Pima National Monument (□ 2 sq mi/5.2 sq km), Pinal co., S central Ariz., 22 mi/35 km SSE of Phoenix, in Gila R. Indian Reservation, NW of Coolidge. Archaeological remains of a large Hohokam Indian village of Sackstown culture, 300 B.C.–A.D. 1100. Authorized 1972; not yet established and not open to public as of 1996.

Ho-Ho-Kus (HO-HO-kuhs), borough (1990 pop. 3,935), Bergen co., NE N.J., on small Hohokus R., 7 mi/11.3 km NNW of Hackensack; 41°00′N 74°05′W. Largely residential. Has 2 notable 18th-cent. houses. Inc. 1908.

Hoisington (HOI-zing-tuhn), town (1990 pop. 3,182), Barton co., central Kansas, 11 mi/18 km N of Great Bend; 38°31′N 98°46′W. In wheat, livestock, and poultry area; dairying; RR maintenance. Mfg. (wire drawing, feed mixers). Cheyenne Bottoms L. to SE. Inc. 1886.

Hokah (HO-kah), village (1990 pop. 687), Houston co., extreme SE Minn., 8 mi/12.9 km WSW of La Crosse, Wis., on Root R., W of its entrance to Mississippi R.; 43°45′N 91°20′W. Grain, soybeans; livestock, poultry; dairying; timber; mfg. (lumber). Richard J. Dorer Memorial Hardwood State Forest to W, S, and E.

Hoke, county (□ 392 sq mi/1,015 sq km; 1990 pop. 22,856), S central N.C.; ⊙ Raeford; 35°01′N 79°13′W. Bounded W by Drowning Creek, N by Little R.; source of Big Swamp R. in SE. Forested sand hills. Agr. area (cotton, tobacco, corn, peaches, wheat, soybeans, hay, peanuts, cattle); timber. Part of large Fort Bragg Military Reserve in N. Formed 1911.

Hokendauqua (HO-ken-DAW-kwah), uninc. town (1990 pop. 3,413), Lehigh co., E Pa., residential suburb 4 mi/6.4 km N of downtown Allentown, on Lehigh R., opposite North Catasauqua.

Hokes Bluff, city (1990 pop. 3,739), Etowah co., NE Ala., a suburb 8 mi/12.9 km E of Gadsden. Inc. since 1946.

Holberg Inlet (HOL-buhrg), SW B.C., Canada, N arm of Quatsino Sound, N Vancouver Isl., in lumbering, fishing area; 21 mi/34 km long, 1 mi/2 km wide. Holberg village is at W end.

Holbrook 1 town (1990 pop. 4,686), ⊙ Navajo co., E central Ariz., on Little Colorado R., near mouth of Siver Creek and c.90 mi/145 km ESE of Flagstaff; 34°54′N 110°09′W. Trade and tourist center in agr. area (cattle, sheep, hogs and poultry raising; corn, alfalfa, hay); mfg. (printing and publishing); junction of logging RR spur to Apache-Sitgreaves Natl. Forest to S. Petrified Forest Natl. Park is 15 mi/24 km E; Hopi and Navajo Indian reservations are N. Northland Pioneer col. (2 year). Settled in 1870s, inc. 1917. **2** town (1990 pop. 11,041), Norfolk co., E Mass. Settled 1710, set off from Randolph and inc. 1872; 42°09′N 71°01′W. It has both agr. and mfg. (paper, chemicals, metal prods.).

Holbrook 1 village (1990 pop. 233), Furnas co., S Nebr., 33 mi/53 km ENE of McCook and on Republican R; 40°17′N 100°00′W. Grain, livestock. **2** uninc. village, census-designated place (□ 6 sq mi/15.5 sq km; 1990 pop. 25,273), Suffolk co., SE N.Y.; abuts L.I.-MacArthur Islip Airport on N; 40°47′N 73°04′W. Diverse mfg. (knitted outerwear, welding equip. and supplies, plastic molding, auto and industrial fasteners, ironwork, precision machining, corrugated cardboard containers, electronic and electrical prods.).

Holcomb 1 (HOL-kuhm), town (1990 pop. 1,400), Finney co., SW Kansas, 7 mi/11.3 km WNW of Garden City, on Arkansas R.; 37°59′N 100°59′W. Wheat, cattle; mfg. (beef processing). **2** (HAW-kuhm), town (1990 pop. 531), Dunklin co., in boot heel of extreme SE Mo., near St. Francis R., 12 mi/19 km N of Kennett; 36°23′N 90°01′W. Cotton, soybeans.

Holcomb 1 (HOL-kuhm), village, Grenada co., N central Miss., 20 mi/32 km NNE of Greenwood, near Yalobusha R. Agr. (cotton, corn; cattle). **2** village (1990 pop. 790), Ontario co., W central N.Y., 20 mi/32 km SE of Rochester, 7 mi/11.3 km W of Canandaigua; 42°53′N 77°25′W. In farming area; mfg. (communications equip., agr. chemicals).

Holden, city (1990 pop. 2,389), Johnson co., W central Mo., 14 mi/23 km W of Warrensburg; 38°42′N 93°59′W. Soybeans, corn; cattle; mfg. (agr. equip.). Laid out 1857.

Holden 1 town (1990 pop. 2,952), Penobscot co., S Maine, just SE of Bangor; 44°45′N 68°40′W. Natl. Grange of Patrons of Husbandry founded here 1867. **2** town (1990 pop. 14,628), Worcester co., central Mass., a residential suburb 6 mi/9.7 km NNW of Worcester; settled 1723, set off and inc. 1741; 42°22′N 71°52′W. Mfg. (electric and metal prods., plastics, and machinery). Includes village of Jefferson. **3** uninc. town (1990 pop. 1,246), Logan co., SW W.Va., 5 mi/8 km WSW of Logan; 37°48′N 82°0′W. Coal-mining area. Mfg. (coal processing, mining machinery).

Holden, village (1991 pop. 411), central Alta., Canada, 30 mi/48 km NE of Camrose; 53°14′N 112°14′W. Dairying, mixed farming.

Holden, village (1990 pop. 402), Millard co., W central Utah, 10 mi/16 km NNE of Fillmore; 39°06′N 112°16′W. Elev. 5,115 ft/1,559 m. Alfalfa; dairying; cattle. Pavant Range to the E. Parts of Fishlake Natl. Forest to N and E. Pavant Range to E; Pavant Butte (5,771 ft/1,759 m) to W.

Holden Beach, village (1990 pop. 626), Brunswick co., SE N.C., 30 mi/48 km SW of Wilmington, on Atlantic Ocean; 33°54′N 78°18′W. Entrance to Lockwood Folly Inlet to E; Intracoastal Waterway canal passes to N. Beach resort area.

Holdenville, town (1990 pop. 4,792), ⊙ Hughes co., central Okla., 25 mi/40 km NE of Ada; 35°04′N 96°24′W. Elev. 903 ft/275 m. RR junction. Trade center for oil and agr. area (corn, peanuts, watermelons); grain elevators, oil wells; mfg. (catfish processing, sweaters, hardware); catfish farming. L. Holdenville (c.3 mi/4.8 km long; fishing), with fish hatchery to SE, and site of old Fort Holmes are nearby. Inc. 1898.

Holderness (HOL-duhr-ness), town (1990 pop. 1,694), Grafton co., central N.H., 14 mi/23 km NNW of Laconia; 43°44′N 71°35′W. Bounded in NW by Pemiqewasset R.; drained by Owl Brook. Agr. (poultry, cattle; vegetables; nursery crops; timber); resort area. Science Center of N.H. is here. Part of Squam L. in E, Little Squam L. in center; Mt. Prospect (2,072 ft/632 m) in N.

Holdfast, village (1991 pop. 239), S central Sask., Canada, near Last Mountain L., 50 mi/80 km NW of Regina. Wheat.

Holdingford, village (1990 pop. 561), Stearns co., central Minn., 18 mi/29 km NW of St. Cloud, on South Branch Two Rivers; 45°43′N 94°28′W. Grain; livestock, poultry; dairying; light mfg.

Holdrege, city (1990 pop. 5,671), ⊙ Phelps co., S Nebr., located in Platte River valley, 24 mi/39 km SW of Kearney; 40°26′N 99°22′W. RR junction. Flour; livestock; grain, dairy prods. Mfg. (feed and fertilizer, woven labels, diposable syringes, excavating equip., agri. equip.). Co. historical mus. here. Settled 1883, inc. 1884.

Hole in the Wall, Bahama Isls.: see GREAT ABACO ISLAND.

Holetown, town, W Barbados, B.W.I., 6 mi/9.7 km N of Bridgetown. Surrounded by hotels and vacation cottages. Has an old fort. Site where English made their 1st landing, in 1625, is commemorated by a column. Formerly called St. James Town.

Holgate (HOL-gait), village (1990 pop. 1,290), Henry co., NW Ohio, 10 mi/16 km S of Napoleon; 41°14′N 84°08′W. In dairying, poultry raising, and grain producing dist.

Holguín (ol-GEEN), province, (1994 pop 1,086,000), E Cuba; ⊙ Holguín. Bordered N by Atlantic Ocean, SE by Guantánamo prov., SW by Granma prov., and W by Las Tunas prov. (□ 3,440 sq mi/8,910 sq km). One of 5 provs. created in 1976 jurisdictional reorganization, from old Oriente prov. Important cities: Holguín (1994 pop. est. 246,000), Banes (1994 pop. est. 35,000). Drained by Nipe, Mayarí, Tacajó, Gibara, and Moa rivers. Plantains, sugarcane, and other vegetables are grown in lowlands, whereas uplands and mts. constitute important ecological reserves and are covered with thick, tropical forests and pines. Important nickel concentrations are found in these mountainous areas and elsewhere in prov., forming a key export mineral for the nation. By 1994, 10 sugar mills operated in prov., processing cane produced on the nearly 700,000 acres/285,000 ha devoted to sugarcane. Tubers, greens, and plantains make it a major vegetable producer.

Holguín (ol-GEEN), city, (1994 est. pop. 246,000), ⊙ Holguín prov., E Cuba; 20°53′N 76°46′W. Cuba's 4th largest city, it is a prosperous commercial center and transportation hub in a fertile region of diversified agr. and the center of nickel production. Often called "Cuba's granary," Holguín is located in a region where corn, beans, sugarcane, tobacco, and cattle are raised. Mfg. includes agr. machinery. Most exports are handled by its port, Gibara, c.16 mi/25 km N (though Banes and Nipes Bays, c.25 mi/40 km E, are among Cuba's finest ports); Calixto García Internatl. Airport is 10 mi/16 km SSW. The city, founded in 1523, was named for Garcia Holguín, a 16th-cent. conquistador in Mexico. It was moved to its present site in the 18th cent.

Holiday, city (□ 5 sq mi/13 sq km; 1990 pop. 19,360), Pasco co., W central Fla., 25 mi/40 km NW of Tampa; 28°11′N 82°44′W. Mfg. includes women's swimwear, kitchen cabinets, commercial printing, and industrial tools.

Holiday Hills, village (1990 pop. 807), McHenry co., NE Ill., residential suburb 5 mi/8 km SE of McHenry, on Fox R.; 42°17′N 88°13′W. Moraine Hills State Park to N.

Holiday Shores, uninc. village (1990 pop. 350), Madison co., SW Ill., suburb 25 mi/40 km NNE of downtown St. Louis, Mo., 6 mi/9.7 km ENE of Behalto; 38°55′N 89°56′W. Centered on L. Holiday.

Holikachuk (HO-lee-KA-chuhk), Indian village, W Alaska, on Innoko R., and 50 mi/80 km N of Holy Cross. Salmon fishing; fur-trading post. Formerly spelled Holocachaket or Hologachaket.

Holin Hall Village, uninc. town, residential suburb 5 mi/8 km S of Alexandria, 12 mi/19 km S of Washington, D.C., near Potomac R.

Holland, village, S Man., Canada, 50 mi/80 km ESE of Brandon. Lumbering, grain elevators.

Holland, city (1990 pop. 30,745), Ottawa and Allegan cos., SW Mich., near L. Michigan, on L. Macatawa, in a dairy and poultry area; 42°46′N 86°05′W. Elev. 610 ft/186 m. Mfg. (food and beverage, printing, machining, fabricated metal prods., electronic equip., furniture); 2 wooden shoe factories; delftware (earthenware) factory, only delft factory in U.S. Furnaces have been made there since 1906. Other prods. include chemicals and boats. RR junction. Tulip growing is an important industry, and the city's many Du. descendants hold a week-long tulip festival each spring. Dutch Village, to N, has full scale bldgs. of Du. architecture, windmills, canals, gardens. The Dutch Reformed Church operates Hope Col. and Western Theological Seminary. Coast guard station is on L. Macatawa; Holland State Park to W on L. Mich; Saugatuck State Park to SW, also on L. Mich.; Municipal airport to S. Baker Furniture Mus. The city is a popular summer resort. Founded 1847 by Du. settlers, inc. 1867.

Holland 1 town (1990 pop. 675), Dubois co., SW Ind., 10 mi/16 km SSW of Jasper. In agr. area. Mfg. (ice cream). **2** town (1990 pop. 215), Grundy co., central Iowa, 4 mi/6.4 km NNW of Grundy Center; 42°23′N 92°47′W. In agr. area. **3** agr. town (1990 pop. 2,185), Hampden co., S Mass., on headstream of Quinebaug R. and 22 mi/35 km E of Springfield. Hamilton Reservoir. **4** agr. town (1990 pop. 237), Pemiscot co., in bootheel of extreme SE Mo., in Mississippi alluvial plain, 15 mi/24 km SW of Caruthersville; 36°03′N 89°52′W. Cotton, rice, soybeans; mfg. (typewriter ribbons). **5** uninc. town (1990 pop. 5,250), Bucks co., SE Pa., suburb 17 mi/27 km NNE of Philadelphia and 12 mi/19 km WSW of Trenton N.J. on Mill Creek; 40°10′N 74°59′W. Mfg. includes metal castings. Springfield L. reservoir in NW. **6** town (1990 pop. 1,118), Bell co., central Texas, 22 mi/35 km W of Temple, near Little R.; 30°52′N 97°24′W. In cotton; corn, wheat, sorghum; cattle area; mfg. (fertilizers). **7** (HAW-lind), town (1990 pop. 423), Orleans co., N Vt., on Que. (Canada) line, 10 mi/16 km E of Newport; 44°57′N 72°00′W.

Holland 1 village (1990 pop. 216), Pipestone co., SW Minn., 9 mi/14.5 km NE of Pipestone, on Rock R.; 44°05′N 96°11′W. Agr. area (grain, soybeans, peas, potatoes; poultry, livestock; dairying). **2** residential village (□ 3 sq mi/7.8 sq km; 1990 pop. 1,288), Erie co., W N.Y., on East Branch of Cazenovia Creek and 25 mi/40 km SE of Buffalo; 42°38′N 78°32′W. Farm community; dairy prods., vegetables, field corn, hay. **3** village (1990 pop. 1,210), Lucas co., NW Ohio, 9 mi/14 km W of Toledo; 41°37′N 83°42′W.

Holland Bay, small inlet of the Caribbean in St. Thomas parish, on E Jamaica coast, on Jamaica Channel, 38 mi/61 km E of Kingston; 17°56′N 76°13′W. Receives Plantain Garden R. Adjoining is village of Holland. Tourist attraction.

Holland Patent, village (1990 pop. 411), Oneida co., central N.Y., 10 mi/16 km N of Utica; 43°14′N 75°15′W.

Holland Tunnel, vehicular tunnel (2 tubes) under the Hudson R. bet. Manhattan borough of N.Y. city, SE N.Y., and Jersey City, N.J.; 40°43′N 74°01′W. Completed 1927, it is 9,250 ft/2,819 m long.

Hollandale (HAHL-uhn-dail), town (1990 pop. 3,576), Washington co., W Miss., 20 mi/32 km SSE of Greenville, and on Deer Creek; 33°10′N 90°50′W. In agr. area (cotton, grain, soybeans, sorghum; cattle, catfish; timber); mfg. (catfish processing, metal fabrication).

Hollandale 1 village (1990 pop. 289), Freeborn co., S Minn., 12 mi/19 km NE of Albert Lea; 43°45′N 93°12′W. Grain, soybeans; livestock, poultry; dairying; light mfg. **2** village (1990 pop. 256), Iowa co., S Wis., 11 mi/18 km SE of Dodgeville; 42°52′N 89°55′W. In agr. area. Septic tanks. Yellowstone L. State Park to S.

Hollansburg, village (1990 pop. 300), Darke co., W Ohio, 11 mi/18 km SW of Greenville, at Ind. state line; 39°59′N 84°48′W. Cheese.

Cross references are shown in SMALL CAPITALS. The pronunciation key is on page xv. The dates of population figures are on page xii.

Hollenberg (HAHL-en-buhrg), village (1990 pop. 28), Washington co., NE Kansas, on Little Blue R., near Nebr. line, and 12 mi/19 km NNE of Washington; 39°58′N 96°59′W. Grain, cattle. Washington State Fishing L. to SW. Inc. 1937.

Holley, village (□ 1 sq mi/2.6 sq km; 1990 pop. 1,890), Orleans co., W N.Y., on the Barge Canal, and 22 mi/35 km WNW of Rochester; 43°13′N 78°01′W. Mfg. of pallets and boxes, hardwood lumber, metal fabrications. Agr. (fruit, grain). Inc. 1867.

Holliday 1 town (1990 pop. 139), Monroe co., NE central Mo., 6 mi/9.7 km W of Paris; 39°29′N 92°07′W. **2** town (1990 pop. 1,475), Archer co., N Texas, 12 mi/19 km SSW of Wichita Falls; 33°48′N 98°41′W. In oil-producing and irrigated farm area (cattle; dairying; wheat). L. Wichita is just E.

Holliday Lakes, town (1990 pop. 1,039), Brazoria co., SE Texas, residential suburb 7 mi/11.3 km NW of Angelton, in Brazosport Area, on Oyster Creek. Agr. area.

Hollidaysburg, borough (1990 pop. 5,624), ⊙ Blair co., S central Pa., 6 mi/9.7 km S of Altoona, near Frankstown Branch Juniata R. Mfg. (crystal oscillators, metal coil toys, steel fabricating); agr. (apples, corn, hay; dairying). Blue Knob Valley Airport to SW. Holidaysburg State Hosp. to NW. Allegheny Portage RR Natl. Historic Site to W, carried canal boats over Allegheny Mts. to Johnstown in mid–19th cent; Canoe Creek State Park to NE. Settled 1768, laid out 1820.

Hollinger Mines, Canada: see PORCUPINE.

Hollins, uninc. city (1990 pop. 13,057), Roanoke co., SW Va., residential suburb 5 mi/8 km NNE of downtown Roanoke; 37°20′N 79°57′W. Mfg. (metal tubes). Hollins Col. (women). Carvin Cove Reservoir to NW.

Hollis 1 town (1990 pop. 5,705), Hillsborough co., S N.H., 6 mi/9.7 km W of Nashua; 42°45′N 71°34′W. Bounded S by Mass. state line. Mfg. (machining, commercial printing, mechanical equip., computer software); agr. (pumpkins, fruit, vegetables, nursery crops, corn; poultry, cattle, hogs; dairying). Silver L. State Park in center. **2** town (1990 pop. 2,584), ⊙ Harmon co., extreme SW Okla., 33 mi/53 km W of Altus, near Texas state line (to S and W); 34°41′N 99°55′W. Elev. 1,615 ft/492 m. In livestock, cotton, and wheat area; peanuts, vegetables; mfg. (meat processing); mesquite. Inc. as town 1905, as city 1929.

Hollis, a residential sect. of E central Queens borough of N.Y. city, ESE N.Y.; 40°43′N 73°46′W.

Hollis Center, town, York co., SW Maine, 10 mi/16 km NNE of Alfred and on the Saco. Wood prods. Inc. 1798.

Hollister 1 city (1990 pop. 19,212), ⊙ San Benito co., W Calif., 38 mi/61 km SE of San Jose, in San Benito valley, on San Benito R, 18 mi/29 km E of Monterey Bay, Pacific Ocean. Elev. 291 ft/89 m. Nursery prods., flower-seed growing; vegetables; poultry, eggs; grapes, grain, nuts. Mfg. (nut processing, metal stampings, wet process systems). Has a community col. Holds annual rodeo. Diablo Range to E; Hollister Hills State Park to S, San Juan Bautista State Historical Park to W. Settled 1868, inc. 1874. **2** resort city (1990 pop. 2,628), Taney co., S Mo., in the Ozarks, on L. Taneycomo (formed by White R.), across the lake from Branson; 36°37′N 93°13′W. Downtown business dist. built in Tudor style in early 20th century. Tourist and recreation area.

Hollister 1 village (1990 pop. 144), Twin Falls co., S Idaho, 15 mi/24 km SW of Twin Falls, near Demp Creek; 42°21′N 114°35′W. Elev. 4,500 ft/1,372 m. Mud L. to NW; Magic Mt. Ski Area to SE; part of Sawtooth Natl. Forest to SE. **2** village (1990 pop. 59), Tillman co., SW Okla., 9 mi/14.5 km ESE of Frederick; 34°20′N 98°52′W. In cotton and grain area.

Holliston, town (1990 pop. 12,926), Middlesex co., E Mass., residential suburb 20 mi/32 km SW of Boston; 42°12′N 71°27′W. Settled c.1659, inc. 1724. Mfg. include plastics, glass, wood, paper prods., and computer-related prods.

Holloman Air Force Base, N.Mex.: see ALAMOGORDO.

Hollow Creek, town (1990 pop. 991), Jefferson co., N Ky., residential suburb 8 mi/12.9 km SE of downtown Louisville, near Fern Creek; 38°08′N 85°37′W. General Electric Appliance park (industrial) to NW.

Hollow Rock, town (1990 pop. 902), Carroll co., NW Tenn., 9 mi/14 km ENE of Huntingdon; 36°02′N 88°16′W.

Holloway 1 village (1990 pop. 123), Swift co., W central Minn., near Pomme de Terre R. and Cottonwood Creek, 16 mi/26 km WSW of Benson; 45°15′N 95°54′W. Grain; livestock; dairying; mfg. (fertilizers). **2** village (1990 pop. 354), Belmont co., E Ohio, 11 mi/18 km SW of Cadiz, near Piedmont L.; 40°10′N 81°07′W. In coal mining area.

Hollsopple (hol-SAH-puhl), uninc. village, Somerset co., SW Pa., 8 mi/12.9 km S of Johnstown on Stonycreek R.; 40°12′N 78°55′W. Mfg. includes steel ingots and billets, wood prods. Quemahoning Reservoir on Quemahoning Creek.

Holly 1 town (1990 pop. 877), Prowers co., SE Colo., on Arkansas R., at mouth of Wild Horeses Creek, near Kansas state line, and 24 mi/39 km E of Lamar; 38°03′N 102°07′W. Elev. 3,367 ft/1,026 m. In wheat, cattle, corn, barley, sorghum region; mfg. (dog and cat food). **2** town (1990 pop. 5,595) Oakland co., SE Mich., 15 mi/24 km S of Flint and 20 mi/32 km NW of Pontiac and on Shiawassee R., in an area of many lakes; 42°47′N 83°37′W. Mfg. (auto parts, winery, foundry, machinery, automotive tubing, apple cider). Seven Lakes State Park to W; Holly State Recreation Area to NE; Mt. Holly and Pine Knob Ski Areas to E. Settled 1836, inc. 1865.

Holly Beach, La.: see CAMERON.

Holly Grove, village (1990 pop. 675), Monroe co., E central Ark., 21 mi/34 km ENE of Stuttgart; 34°36′N 91°12′W. In agr. area.

Holly Hill 1 town (□ 4 sq mi/10.4 sq km; 1990 pop. 11,141), Volusia co., E central Fla., 3 mi/4.8 km N of Daytona Beach on the Atlantic Ocean; 29°14′N 81°02′W. Area noted for its flowers; coquina quarries. **2** town (1990 pop. 1,478), Orangeburg co., S central S.C., 27 mi/43 km ESE of Orangeburg; 33°19′N 80°24′W. Mfg. includes wood chairs, fiberboard, lumber, cement, printing and publishing, sportcoats, toys. Agr. includes watermelons, tobacco and grains, livestock, cotton area. Santee-Cooper hydroelectric and navigation development is E. Inc. 1887.

Holly Pond, town (1990 pop. 602), Cullman co., N Ala., 13 mi/21 km E of Cullman, near Mulberry Fork.

Holly Ridge, town (1990 pop. 728), Onslow co., E N.C., 20 mi/32 km SSW of Jacksonville; 34°29′N 77°33′W. Agr. area (tobacco, cotton, peanuts, corn, soybeans, poultry, livestock). Atlantic Ocean and Intracoastal Waterway separated by Topsail Isl. (sand-barrier isl.) to SE. Inc. after 1940.

Holly River State Park (□ 13 sq mi/34 sq km), Webster co., central W.Va., in the Allegheny Mts., 21 mi/34 km S of Buckhannon, drained by Holly R. Wooded recreational area; facilities for fishing, swimming, other sports. Est. 1938.

Holly Shelter Swamp (□ c.100 sq mi/259 sq km), SE N.C., NE of Wilmington, and bordering Northeast Cape Fear R. on E. Includes Holly Shelter Game Refuge (c.30,000 acres/12,141 ha), E of Burgaw. Angola Swamp is N.

Holly Springs 1 town (1990 pop. 2,406), Cherokee co., NW Ga., 4 mi/6.4 km S of Canton; 34°10′N 84°30′W. Mfg. of hydrogen gas producing systems. **2** town (1990 pop. 7,261), ⊙ Marshall co., N Miss., 41 mi/66 km SE of Memphis, Tenn.; 34°46′N 89°26′W. RR junction. Trade and market center for cotton-growing and dairying region; mfg. (wall paneling, steel and alloy fabrication, industrial machinery, printing and publishing, kitchen appliances, bricks, metal stampings); clay deposits. Rust Col. is here. Has many fine antebellum homes. Montrose Mansion (1858). In Civil War, town was captured (1862) by Confederates, thus delaying Grant's advance against Vicksburg. Clark Art Gall.; Marshall County Historical Mus. Wall Doxey State Park to S; Holly Springs Natl. Forest to E. Inc. 1837. **3** town (1990 pop. 908), Wake co., central N.C., 14 mi/23 km SW of Raleigh; 35°39′N 78°50′W. Cotton, tobacco, grain; poultry, livestock. Mfg. (electronic equip., synthetic yarns, upholstered furniture). Harris L. reservoir to SW.

Hollymead, uninc. town, Albermarle co., central Va., residential suburb 7 mi/16 km NNE of Charlottesville; 38°07′N 78°26′W.

Hollyville, village (1990 pop. 649), Jefferson co., N Ky., residential suburb 12 mi/19 km S of downtown Louisville; 38°05′N 85°45′W. Agr. area (tobacco, grain; livestock).

Hollywood, city (□ 30 sq mi/78 sq km; 1990 pop. 121,697), extreme SE Broward co., SE Fla., on the Atlantic Ocean; 26°01′N 80°09′W. A popular retirement center and part of the Miami/Ft. Lauderdale metropolitan area, Hollywood produces electronic equip. and bldg. materials and has a number of office parks. Most of Port Everglades, the county's largest port with an extensive warehouse complex, is within the city limits. Inc. 1925.

Hollywood 1 town (1990 pop. 916), Jackson co., NE Ala., near Tennessee R., 5 mi/8 km NE of Scottsboro; 34°43′N 85°58′W. **2** town (1990 pop. 2,094), Charleston co., SE S.C., 17 mi/27 km W of Charleston; 32°45′N 80°12′W. Mfg. of meat prods. and septic tanks.

Hollywood, village, St. Marys co., S Md., 5 mi/8 km NE of Leonardtown, near Patuxent R. Resorts nearby (Sam Abell Cove, Clarks Landing; swimming, fishing, duck hunting, boating). Sotterly, begun in 1717, is still a working plantation with a house built in 1730. Nearby are St. Mary's Airport and Greenwell State Park.

Hollywood, uninc. community, Dunklin co., in boot heel of extreme SE Mo., near St. Francis R., 15 mi/24 km SSW of Kennett.

Hollywood, suburban section of the city of Los Angeles (1985 est. pop. 250,000), S Calif., on the E slopes of the Santa Monica Mts. Often referred to as "Tinsel Town" for its glitter and high lifestyle (now fading). Mfg. (broadcasting equip., photographic equip., electric light bulbs, motion picture industry). Noted for its major film and television studios and their executive offices, many have relocated to nearby suburbs such as Burbank and Glendale due to deterioration of community and increasing crime. Although many films are shot on location in cities and countries throughout the world, Hollywood remains the symbolic center of the U.S. motion-picture industry. Since the first film was made there c.1911, the community has come to signify the film industry in general — its morals, manners, and characteristics. Hollywood attracts large numbers of tourists. Points of interest include Hollywood Blvd., Hollywood Bowl, and Grauman's Chinese Theatre and its Walk of Fame. La Brea Tar Pits and Los Angeles County Art Mus. to W. In surrounding hills is Griffith Park (with an observatory and planetarium) to NE, and the homes of film celebrities in Beverly Hills and Malibu, to W. The Univ. of Judaism and a 2-year col. are in Hollywood. Inc. 1903, consolidated with Los Angeles 1910.

Hollywood Beach, Md.: see CHESAPEAKE CITY.

Hollywood by the Sea, village, Ventura co., S Calif.

Hollywood Park, city (1990 pop. 2,841), Bexar co., S central Texas, residential suburb 11 mi/18 km N of downtown San Antonio; 29°36′N 98°28′W.

Holman Island (HOL-muhn), trading post, W Victoria Isl., SW Franklin dist., N.W.T., Canada, on Amundsen Gulf at entrance of Prince Albert Sound; 70°44′N 117°45′W. Radio station; site of R.C. mission.

Holmdel (HOLM-del), township (1990 pop. 11,532), Monmouth co., E N.J., 7 mi/11.3 km NE of Freehold, in suburban area; 40°22′N 74°10′W. AT&T Bell Laboratories here.

Holmen (HOL-men), town (1990 pop. 3,220), La Crosse co., W Wis., 10 mi/16 km N of La Crosse, near Mississippi R.; 43°57′N 91°15′W. In farm and dairy region. Mfg. (custom casework, silk screening, feather processing, concrete prods.). On Great River State Trail.

Holmes 1 county (□ 483 sq mi/1,251 sq km; 1990 pop. 15,778), NW Fla., on Ala. line (N) and bounded E by Holmes Creek; ⊙ Bonifay; 30°52′N 85°48′W. Rolling agr. area (corn, peanuts, cotton, vegetables, livestock) drained by Choctawhatchee R.; has forest industries (lumber, naval stores). Formed 1848. **2** (HOMZ), county (□ 764 sq mi/1,979 sq km; 1990 pop. 21,604), central Miss.; ⊙ Lexington; 33°07′N 90°05′W. Bounded E by Big Black R., NW and SW corners by Yazoo R.; drained by Tchula L. slough, forms part of W boundary. Agr. (cotton, corn, soybeans, sorghum; cattle; timber); clay deposits. Bee L., oxbow lake of Yazoo R., in SW corner. Morgan Brake Natl. Wildlife Refuge in W, Hillside Natl. Wildlife Refuge in SW; Holmes County State Park in E. Formed 1833. **3** county (□ 424 sq mi/1,098 sq km; 1990 pop. 32,849), central Ohio; ⊙ Millersburg; 40°33′N 81°54′W. Intersected by Killbuck Creek and Walhonding R. In the Glaciated Plain physiographic region. Agr. (livestock; dairy prods.; grain, nursery crops); mfg. at Millersburg (rubber, plastic, and wood prods.); coal mines, sandstone quarries, gravel pits. Formed 1825.

Holmes Beach, town (□ 1 sq mi/2.6 sq km; 1990 pop. 4,810), Manatee co., W central Fla., located on Anna Maria Key, 11 mi/18 km W of Brandenton; 27°30′N 82°43′W.

Holmes Creek, c.60 mi/97 km long, NW Fla.; rises in SE Ala.; flows SW into Fla., to Choctawhatchee R. 21 mi/34 km SE of De Funiak Springs; navigable below Vernon.

Holmesville, village (1990 pop. 419), Holmes co., central Ohio, 33 mi/53 km ESE of Mansfield, and on Killbuck Creek; 40°37′N 81°55′W.

Holmfield, village, SW Man., Canada, on Whitemud R. and 9 mi/14 km ESE of Killarney; 49°08′N 99°28′W. Grain, stock.

Holocachaket, Alaska: see HOLIKACHUK.

Hologachaket, Alaska: see HOLIKACHUK.

Holstein, town (1990 pop. 1,449), Ida co., W Iowa, 10 mi/16 km NNW of Ida Grove; 42°29′N 95°32′W. In livestock and grain area. Settled 1882.

Holstein, village (1990 pop. 207), Adams co., S Nebr., 15 mi/24 km SW of Hastings and on branch of Little Blue R; 40°27′N 98°39′W.

Holston, river, c.120 mi/193 km long, NE Tenn.; formed by the uniting of its N and S forks; flowing SW through the Great Appalachian Valley, joining the French Broad R. at Knoxville to form the Tennessee R.; 35°57′N 83°51′W. Settlement along the Holston began before the Amer. Revolution, and it was a major route of westward migration. On the river is Cherokee Dam, a flood control unit of the Tenn. Valley Authority that impounds Cherokee L.; there are several smaller dams on the Holston's S fork.

Holston Mountain (HOL-stuhn), ridge (2,500 ft/762 m–4,000 ft/1,219 m) of the Appalachians bet. South Fork Holston R. (N) and Iron Mts. (SE), NE Tenn. and SW Va., from Elizabethton, Tenn., extends c.30 mi/48 km NE to Damascus, Va. Highest point (c.4,300 ft/1,311 m) is 7 mi/11 km NE of Elizabethton. Included in Cherokee and Jefferson natl. forests. Sometimes considered a range of Unaka Mts. The Appalachian Trail runs along part of its length. Summit, 36°30′N 82°38′W.

Holt 1 county (□ 456 sq mi/1181 sq km; 1990 pop. 6,034), NW Mo.; ⊙ Oregon; 40°05′N 95°12′W. Bet. Missouri (W and S) and Nodaway (E) rivers; drained by Tarkio R. Corn, wheat, apples; cattle, hogs. Squaw Creek National Wildlife Refuge, Big Lake State Park. Areas along river were flooded in 1993. Formed 1841. **2** county (□ 2,417 sq mi/6,260 sq km; 1990 pop. 12,599), N Nebr.; ⊙ O'Neill; 42°27′N 98°46′W. Grazing region with well irrigation, partly in Sand Hills bounded N by Niobrara R.; drained by Elkhorn R. Cattle, hogs, corn, alfalfa, wild hay, soybeans, dairy and poultry prods. Atkinson L. State Recreation Area in W; Small Swan L. in SW; Goose L. in S. Formed 1876.

Holt 1 town (1990 pop. 11,744), Ingham co., S central Mich., suburb 7 mi/11.3 km S of Lansing; 42°38′N 84°31′W. In agr. area (livestock; grain, vegetables, apples; dairy prods.); mfg. (food processing, hydraulic hose fittings, fiberglass prods.). **2** town (1990 pop. 311), Clay and Clinton cos., W Mo., on Fishing R. and 15 mi/24 km NNE of Liberty; 39°27′N 94°20′W. Corn, cattle.

Holt 1 village (1990 pop. 4,125), Tuscaloosa co., W Ala., on Black Warrior R. and 5 mi/8 km NE of Tuscaloosa; near Holt Lock and Dam. **2** village (1990 pop. 88), Marshall co., NW Minn., 12 mi/19 km N of Thief R. Falls; 48°17′N 96°11′W. Agr. area (grain, beans, potatoes; livestock). Agassiz Natl. Wildlife Refuge to E.

Holt Lock and Dam, Tuscaloosa co., W Ala., on Black Warrior R. 7 mi/11.3 km ENE of Tuscaloosa and 2 mi/3.2 km E of Holt; 33°15′N 87°26′W. Dam (108 ft/33 m high) built by the Army Corps of Engineers (1968) for navigation and hydroelectric generation; max. capacity c.117,990 acre-ft.

Holt Mine, Ky.: see HOLT.

Holter Lake (HOL-tuhr), reservoir, Lewis and Clark co., W central Mont., on Missouri R., 30 mi/48 km N of Helena; c.30 mi/48 km long; 47°00′N 112°00′W. Max. capacity 265,000 acre-ft. Hauser Dam at S end. Formed by Holter Dam (gravity; 125 ft/38 m high), built (1918) by the Mont. Power Company for power generation. Upper Holter L. separated from main reservoir by narrow sect. in Gates of the Rock Mtns. canyon.

Holton 1 town (1990 pop. 451), Ripley co., SE Ind., 14 mi/23 km ENE of North Vernon, near Otter Creek; 39°05′N 85°23′W. Versailles State Park to E; Jefferson Proving Ground to S. Cattle, poultry, corn. **2** (HOL-tuhn), town (1990 pop. 3,196), ⊙ Jackson co., NE Kansas, 29 mi/47 km N of Topeka; 39°28′N 95°43′W. In livestock and grain region. Mfg. (rotary mowers, feed, sausage and prepared meat). Potawatomi Indian Reservation is nearby. Laid out 1857 by Free Staters; inc. 1870.

Holton, village, SE Lab., Canada, on coast of Labrador Sea, 5 mi/8 km N of Man of War Point. Fishing village in area.

Holts Summit, town (1990 pop. 2,292), Callaway co., central Mo., 5 mi/8 km NE of Jefferson City; 38°38′N 92°07′W. Residential suburb of Jefferson City. Mfg. (utility trailers, light mfg.).

Holtville, city (1990 pop. 4,820), Imperial co., S Calif., 10 mi/16 km E of El Centro, in irrigated Imperial Valley, on Alamo R. RR terminus. Tomatoes, vegetables, melons, dates, wheat, alfalfa, corn, sugar beets; cattle, sheep. 10 mi/16 km N of Mex. border. Inc. 1908.

Holtz Bay, Alaska: see ATTU ISLAND.

Holualoa (HO-LOO-ah-LO-ah), town (1990 pop. 3,834), W Hawaii Isl., Hawaii co., Hawaii, near Kailua Bay, in the Kona dist., 53 mi/85 km W of Hilo, 2 mi/3.2 km inland from Kona (W) coast, on Mamalahoa Highway; 19°38′N 155°55′W. Produces coffee, but this production has been declining since the early 1980s. Waiaka Forest Reserve to E, Kakaluu Forest Reserve to SE.

Holy Cross, town (1990 pop. 304), Dubuque; co., E Iowa, 17 mi/27 km WNW of Dubuque; 42°36′N 91°00′W. Limestone quarry.

Holy Cross, village (1990 pop. 277), W Alaska, on Yukon R. at mouth of Innoko R. and Reindeer R. and 120 mi/193 km NE of Bethel; 62°12′N 159°47′W. Est. 1887.

Holy Cross, Mount of the, peak (14,005 ft/4,269 m) in Sawatch Mts., Eagle co., W central Colo., 18 mi/29 km NW of Leadville. Near its summit, snow-filled crevices c.50 ft/15 m wide form a huge cross more than 1,000 ft/305 m long, with 750-ft/229-m-long arms. Formerly (1929–1950) Holy Cross Natl. Monument; site now administered by U.S. Forest Service (White River Natl. Forest).

Holyoke (HOL-yok), city (1990 pop. 43,704), Hampden co., S central Mass., on the Connecticut R.; 42°13′N 72°38′W. The city has varied mfg. including printed materials, medical supplies, consumer goods, metal prods., electronic goods, and chemicals. Holyoke Community Col. is here. Mt. Holyoke Col. and a U.S. air force base are nearby. Ski resort, amusement park. Holyoke Mall at Ingelside, one of the largest shopping centers in U.S. Largest planned industrial city of U.S. Industrial Revolution. Largest dam in world in 1848 across Connecticut R. Dinosaur Footprints Park and Hampton Pond State Park. Settled 1745, inc. 1873.

Holyoke, town (1990 pop. 1,931), ⊙ Phillips co., NE Colo., on Frenchman Creek, near Nebr. line, and 45 mi/72 km E of Sterling; 40°34′N 102°17′W. Elev. 3,746 ft/1,142 m. Cattle, sunflowers, beans; light mfg. Inc. 1888.

Holyoke, Mount, Mass.: see HOLYOKE RANGE.

Holyoke Range (HOL-yok), W central Mass., E–W range just N of South Hadley; c.8 mi/12.9 km long. Rises to 1,106 ft/337 m in Mt. Norwottock. Mt. Holyoke (878 ft/268 m), at W end, has road to summit. Volcanic basalt ridges within Connecticut R. valley.

Holyrood (HAHL-ee-rood), village (1990 pop. 492), Ellsworth co., central Kans., 10 mi/16 km SW of Ellsworth; 38°35′N 98°24′W. Shipping point in wheat region.

Homathko River (ho-MATH-ko), 80 mi/129 km long, SW B.C., Canada; rises in Coast Mts. near 51°50′N 124°45′W; flows generally S to head of Bute Inlet.

Home Bay, E Baffin Isl., E Franklin dist., N.W.T., Canada, inlet of Davis Strait; 40 mi/64 km long, 50 mi/80 km wide at mouth; 68°40′N 67°30′W. Bounded N by Henry Kater Peninsula.

Home Corner, village, Grant co., NE central Ind., suburb of Marion (SE).

Home Garden, uninc. town (1990 pop. 1,549), Kings co., central Calif., residential suburb 2 mi/3.2 km SSE of Hanford. Hanford Municipal Airport to N. Fruit, nuts, melons, tomatoes, grain, dairying, cattle, poultry.

Home Gardens, uninc. town (1990 pop. 7,780), Riverside co., S Calif., residential suburb 11 mi/18 km WSW of Riverside and 3 mi/4.8 km E of Corona. L. Mathews reservoir to SE. Fruit, grain, nursery prods., grain, poultry, cattle, dairying.

Homeacre (HOM-ai-kuhr), uninc. town (1990 pop. 4,500), Butler co., W Pa., residential suburb 2 mi/3.2 km W of Butler; 40°51′N 79°56′W.

Homecroft, town (1990 pop. 758), Marion co., central Ind.; 39°40′N 86°08′W.

Homedale, town (1990 pop. 1,963), Owyhee co., SW Idaho, on Snake R., at mouths of Jump Creek and Succor Creek, and 15 mi/24 km W of Caldwell, near Oregon line; 43°37′N 116°57′W. In Idaho sect. of Owyhee irrigation project. Cattle; alfalfa, oats, grain; potatoes, sugar beets; mfg. Succor Creek State Recreation Area to SW (Oregon).

Homeland, city (1990 pop. 981), Charlton co., SE Ga., 2 mi/3.2 km NNW of Folkston; 30°51′N 82°01′W.

Homeland, uninc. town (1990 pop. 3,312), Riverside co., S Calif., residential suburb 21 mi/34 km SE of Riverside. Lakeview Mts. to N; Double Butte to S. San Diego Aqueduct passes to E. Cattle, dairying, poultry, nursery prods., grain.

Homer 1 town (1990 pop. 742), ⊙ Banks co., NE Ga., 18 mi/29 km E of Gainesville; 34°20′N 83°30′W. Mfg. of clothing; lumber. **2** town (1990 pop. 4,152), ⊙ Claiborne parish, N La., 45 mi/72 km NE of Shreveport; 32°48′N 93°04′W. Trade center in oil and natural gas, timber area; lumber milling; mfg. (plastic molding, wood prods., packaging prods., wood paneling); dairying. Unit of Kisatchie Natl. Forest to NE, L. Claiborne reservoir to SE with L. Claiborne State Park at SE end of lake. Hosts Louisiana Wildlife Festival. Gr. Revival Courthouse. Prior to Civil War a newspaper called the Homer Iliad was published here. Settled 1830, inc. 1850. **3** town (1990 pop. 1,758), Calhoun co., S Mich., 7 mi/11.3 km SSW of Albion and on a branch of Kalamazoo R.; 42°08′N 84°48′W. Agr. (wheat, corn, and hay); poultry; mfg. (iron foundry, plastic foam molding, machining). Settled 1832, inc. 1871.

Homer 1 village (1990 pop. 3,660), S Alaska, on Kachemak Bay, SW Kenai Peninsula, 75 mi/121 km WSW of Seward; 59°36′N 151°25′W. Connected by highway with Seward, Kenai, Soldatna, and Anchorage. Tourism; fishing, fish processing. Site of old Eskimo and Rus. settlements. **2** village (1990 pop. 1,264), Champaign co., E Ill., 16 mi/26 km ESE of Champaign; 40°01′N 87°57′W. In agr. area; corn, wheat, soybeans, livestock. Village formerly on Salt Creek to N but moved in 19th cent. to be on RR. **3** village (1990 pop. 553), Dakota co., NE Nebr., 12 mi/19 km S of Sioux City, Iowa, near Missouri R; 42°19′N 96°29′W. Farm trading center. Site of 18th-cent. Omaha Indian village nearby. Winnebago and Omaha Indian Reservations to S (both in Thurston co.). **4** village (□ 1 sq mi/2.6 sq km; 1990 pop. 3,476), Cortland co., central N.Y., in the Tioughnioga valley, just N of Cortland; 42°38′N 76°10′W. Farm trade center, with mfg. of industrial filament; prefabricated houses, metalworking compounds, wood handles and spindles, specialized production and automation equip., sand and gravel pits. Old Homer Village Historic Dist. here. Settled 1791, inc. 1835.

Homer City, borough (1990 pop. 1,809), Indiana co., SW central Pa., 5 mi/8 km S of Indiana, on Two Lick Creek. Mfg. (bulk materials handling equip.); surface bituminous coal; agr. (soybeans; grain; livestock, dairying). Inc. 1872.

Homerville, city (1990 pop. 2,560), ⊙ Clinch co., S Ga., 25 mi/40 km WSW of Waycross, near Okefenokee Swamp; 31°02′N 82°45′W. Mfg. of metal containers, modular bldgs., clothing, plastics; pulpwood, lumber, wood prods. Founded on the RR 1859, inc. as town 1869, as city 1931.

Homes Run Acres, uninc. town, Fairfax co., NE Va., residential suburb 10 mi/16 km W of Washington, D.C.

Homestead, city (☐ 11 sq mi/28 sq km; 1990 pop. 26,866), Dade co., SE Fla.; inc. 1913. A satellite town 25 mi/40 km S of Miami; 25°27′N 80°27′W. Homestead is a trade center for the Redland dist. to its N, known for its many varieties of citrus and other fruits and vegetables. Nearby Homestead Air Force Base, though sharply cut back during the 1990s, is still important to the economy. The city is adjacent to Everglades Natl. Park and lies astride the gateway to the Fla. Keys. Local attractions include several tropical gardens, a pioneer mus., and a castlelike bldg. furnished with coral items. A state subtropical experiment station is there, and a nuclear power plant is nearby. In 1992, Hurricane Andrew swept through the city, leveling much of it. Homestead Air Force Base suffered serious hail damage. A massive, nationwide relief effort followed, and the city was rebuilt during the mid-1990s. The Turkey Point nuclear power facility is located on the shore of Biscayne Bay c.3 mi/4.8 km E.

Homestead 1 village, Iowa co., E Iowa, 7 Amana Colony villages, located S of Iowa R. Agr. (corn; cattle, hogs); winery; home industries. **2** village, Portsmouth town, Prudence Isl., R.I.; 41°37′N 71°18′W. Summer resort.

Homestead, borough (1990 pop. 4,179), Allegheny co., SW Pa., suburb 5 mi/8 km SE of downtown Pittsburgh, on the Monongahela R. (bridged); 40°24′N 79°54′W. Mfg. (babbitt bearings, carbide machinery, cleaning chemicals, cylindrical grinders). Once a foremost U.S. steel producer. In 1892 the famous outbreak of the Homestead Strike, one of the most bitterly fought industrial disputes in U.S. labor history, occurred here. Inc. 1880.

Homestead Monument, Gage co., SE Nebr., 5 mi/8 km W of Beatrice. Site of the first farm claimed under the Homestead Act of 1862. Has an area of 195 acres/79 ha. Freeman Schoolhouse; over 100 acres/40 ha of tall grass prairie and wooded stream. Authorized 1936.

Homestead Valley, uninc. town (1990 pop. 3,840), Marin co., W Calif., residential suburb 10 mi/16 km NW of downtown San Francisco. Mt. Tamalpais Game Refuge, in Richardson Bay, arm of San Francisco Bay, to SE; Mt. Tamalpais State Park and Muir Woods Natl. Monument to W. Statistically reported as Tamalpais-Homestead Valley (1990 pop. 9,601). Tamalpais Valley is 2 mi/3.2 km to S.

Hometown, city (1990 pop. 4,769), Cook co., NE Ill., 14 mi/23 km SW of downtown Chicago, NE of Oak Lawn; 41°43′N 87°43′W. Residential suburb.

Hometown, uninc. town (1990 pop. 1,545), Schuylkill co., E central Pa., 9 mi/14.5 km S of Hazleton; 40°49′N 75°59′W. Anthracite coal mining. Tuscarora L. and State Park to W.

Homewood, city (1990 pop. 22,922), Jefferson co., N central Ala., a residential suburb S of Birmingham. Shades Mountain and Oak Mountain state parks nearby. Inc. 1921.

Homewood, village (1990 pop. 19,278), Cook co., NE Ill., a residential suburb S of Chicago; 41°33′N 87°39′W. Plotted 1852, inc. 1893.

Homewood, borough (1990 pop. 162), Beaver co., W Pa., 4 mi/6.4 km N of Beaver Falls, near Beaver R. corn, hay, dairying.

Homewood, suburb of Annapolis, Anne Arundel co., central Md.

Hominy (HAHM-in-ee), town (1990 pop. 2,342), Osage

co., N Okla., 29 mi/47 km NW of Tulsa; 36°25′N 96°23′W. In agr. and oil- and natural gas-producing area; mfg. (oil field equip., T-shirts, lingerie). In Osage Indian Reservation. Skiatook L. reservoir to E. Est. as an Indian agency in 1874; laid out 1905, inc. 1908.

Homochitto River (ho-muh-CHIT-uh), c.90 mi/145 km long, SW Miss.; rises in SW Copiah co.; flows SW and W, through Homochitto Natl. Forest, past Bude, enters the Mississippi R. through 2 main channels, one 17 mi/27 km SSW of Natchez, the other 25 mi/40 km SSW of Natchez, through Old River L.

Homosassa (ho-mo-SAS-uh), fishing port (☐ 5 sq mi/13 sq km; 1990 pop. 2,113), Citrus co., W central Fla., 18 mi/29 km W of Inverness, on Gulf coast; 28°46′N 82°37′W. The Homosassa Isls., a group of many small mangrove isls., are just offshore. Homosassa Springs, a resort, is 2 mi/3.2 km ENE.

Homosassa Springs (ho-mo-SAS-uh), town (☐ 13 sq mi/34 sq km; 1990 pop. 6,271), Citrus co., W central Fla., 25 mi/40 km NW of Brooksville; 28°48′N 82°32′W.

Homún (o-MOON), town (1990 pop. 4,514), Yucatán, SE Mexico, 27 mi/43 km SE of Mérida. Henequen, tropical fruit, sugarcane, corn.

Honaker (HON-aik-uhr), town (1990 pop. 950), Russell co., SW Va., in Allegheny Mts., near Clinch R., 10 mi/16 km NE of Lebanon; 37°01′N 81°58′W. Mfg. (lumber, clothing); agr. (corn, soybeans; livestock; dairying); timber.

Honalo (HO-nah-LO), town (1990 pop. 1,926), W Hawaii isl., Hawaii co., Hawaii, 52 mi/84 km WSW of Hilo, 3 mi/4.8 km N of Captain Cook, 2 mi/3.2 km inland from Kona (W) coast; 19°34′N 155°54′W. Coffee, fruit. Daifukuji Buddhist Temple. Kahaluu Forest Reserve to NE.

Honaunau (HO-NOU-NOU), town (1990 pop. 2,000), W Hawaii isl., Hawaii co., Hawaii, 53 mi/4.8 km WSW of Hilo, 3 mi/4.8 km S of Captain Cook. Tourism. Coffee, cattle; fish. Honaunau Forest Reserve to E; Puu O Honaunau Natl. Historical Park to W on Kiilae and Honaunau bays. Honaunau Rodeo Arena to W.

Honda Bay (ON-duh), sheltered inlet, Pinar del Río prov., NW Cuba, just N of town of Bahía Honda, 50 mi/80 km WSW of Havana; 22°57′N 83°11′W. Near shark, lobster, and red snapper fishing grounds.

Honda, Ensenada, P.R.: see ENSENADA HONDA.

Hondo, town (1990 pop. 6,018), ⊙ Medina co., SW Texas, W of San Antonio; 29°21′N 99°09′W. Elev. 905 ft/276 m. In ranching and irrigated farm area (cattle, sheep, goats; grain, peanuts, cotton, vegetables); mfg. (grain processing, rebuilt aircraft engines, feeds, bathroom fixtures). Medina L. (irrigation, recreation) is 17 mi/27 km NE. Inc. after 1940.

Hondo (ON-do), uninc. village (1990 pop. 425), Lincoln co., central N.Mex., 47 mi/76 km W of Roswell, at confluence of Rio Ruidoso and Rio Bonito, which form Rio Hondo. Cattle, sheep, alfalfa. Timber. Parts of Lincoln Natl. Forest to N and W; Mescalero Apache Indian Reservation to SW. Sacramento Mts. to W. Lincoln State Monument to NW.

Hondo, Río or **Hondo River** (ON-do), c.130 mi/209 km long, Yucatán Peninsula, SE Mexico (Campeche and Quintana Roo states), NE Guatemala, and N Belize, on Belize-Mexico border; rises as Río Azul NE of Uaxactún (Guatemala); flows NE, along internatl. border, to Chetumal Bay (Caribbean Sea) at Chetumal, Mexico. Receives Booth's R. at Dos Bocas, Belize, and from there until it exits Belize, it is called Blue Creek.

Hondo, Río (ON-do), 106 mi/171 km long, 11th longest river in Cuba; flows through Pinar del Río prov., emptying into Caribbean Sea. Drains 578 sq mi/1,497 sq km.

Honea Path (HUH-nee), town (1990 pop. 3,841), Anderson and Abbeville cos., NW S.C., 16 mi/26 km ESE of Anderson; 34°27′N 82°23′W. Mfg. of cotton and synthetic textiles, clothing, rubber gloves; agr. includes poultry, dairying, grain, soybeans, livestock.

Honeoye (HUHN-ee-oi), resort village, Ontario co., W central N.Y., at N end of Honeoye L., 27 mi/43 km S of Rochester; 42°47′N 77°31′W.

Honeoye Creek, N.Y.: see HONEOYE LAKE.

Honeoye Falls (HUHN-ee-oi), residential village (☐ 2 sq mi/5.2 sq km; 1990 pop. 2,340), Monroe co., W N.Y., on Honeoye Creek and 15 mi/24 km S of Rochester; 42°57′N 77°35′W. Mfg. (air, gas, and liquid filtration equip.; safety flashers, RR lanterns, reflectors, terminal boards and strips); agr. (grain, vegetables; dairying). Inc. 1838. Honeoye village is 12 mi/19 km S, on Honeoye L.

Honeoye Lake (HUIIN-ee-oi), one of the Finger Lakes, Ontario co., W central N.Y., W of Canandaigua L. and 25 mi/40 km S of Rochester; 4 mi/6.4 km long, up to ¾ mi/1.21 km wide; 42°45′N 77°31′W. Resorts. Drained by Honeoye Creek, which flows c.35 mi/56 km NW and W, past Honeoye Falls, to Genesee R. 5 mi/8 km N of Avon.

Honesdale, borough (1990 pop. 4,972), ⊙ Wayne co., NE Pa., 24 mi/39 km ENE of Scranton, on Lackawaxen R. at mouth of Dyberry Creek. Mfg. (furniture, food processing, sand and gravel processing, printing and publishing, concrete). First trial run of a locomotive in U.S. made here (1829). Was W terminus of Delaware and Hudson Canal. Cherry Ridge Airport to S; Dorflinger Glass Mus.; Stourbridge Line Rail Excursion; Wayne Co. Historical Society Mus.; Cadjaw Pond to SW; Prompton L. reservoir to NW. Settled 1803, inc. 1831.

Honey (ON-ei), town (1990 pop. 943), ⊙ Chila Honey municipio, Puebla, central Mexico, in Sierra Madre Oriental, on Hidalgo border, 12 mi/19 km WNW of Huauchinango; 20°16′N 98°11′W. RR terminus.

Honey Brook, borough (1990 pop. 1,184), Chester co., SE Pa., 22 mi/35 km E of Lancaster, near West Branch Brandywine Creek (source 1 mi/1.6 km to N). Mfg. (apparel, food processing, metal fabricated prods., truck trailers); rock quarries. Agr. area (apples, grain; livestock, poultry, dairying). Struble L. reservoir to NE.

Honey Grove, town (1990 pop. 1,681), Fannin co., NE Texas, 21 mi/34 km WSW of Paris; 33°34′N 95°54′W. Elev. 668 ft/204 m. In cotton, sorghum, soybeans; cattle; mfg. (fertilizers, burial vaults). Nearby is large game and reforestation preserve; Caddo Natl. Grassland to N. Inc. 1872.

Honey Island, uninc. village (1990 pop. 401), Hardin co., SE Texas, 30 mi/48 km NW of Beaumont. In agr. area. Units of Big Thicket Natl. Preserve to S and N.

Honey Lake, Lassen co., NE Calif., at E base of the Sierra Nevada, near Nev. state line; 5 mi/8 km–10 mi/16 km wide. Elev. 3,949 ft/1,204 m. Intermittently dry bed. Receives Susan R. from NW, Receives Honey Valley Creek from SE. Its valley has irrigated agr. Honey L. State Wildlife Area on N shore; Plumas Natl. Forest to SW; Sierra Army Depot to SE.

Honeyville, town (1990 pop. 112), Box Elder co., N Utah, 10 mi/16 km NNW of Brigham City; 41°37′N 112°04′W. Fruit, sugar beets, barley, wheat, alfalfa; dairying; cattle, sheep. Wasatch Range and Natl. Forest, including Wellsville Mt. Wilderness Area, to E. Crystal Hot Springs here. Elev. 4,268 ft/1,301 m. Settled 1862.

Honga, Md.: see HOOPER ISLANDS.

Honga River (HON-ga), E Md., wide arm of Chesapeake Bay, bet. Hooper Isls. (W) and the Eastern Shore (E), in Dorchester co.; c.15 mi/24 km long.

Honnedaga Lake, Herkimer co., N central N.Y., in the Adirondacks, 35 mi/56 km NE of Utica; c.4 mi/6.4 km long; 43°31′N 74°49′W. Recreational fishing.

Honokaa (HO-no-KAH-ah), town (1990 pop. 2,186), NE Hawaii isl., Hawaii co., Hawaii, 35 mi/56 km NW of Hilo, centered 1 mi/1.6 km from Hamakua Coast, on elevated coast; 20°04′N 155°28′W. Macadamia nuts; Macadamia nuts factory to N, near coast; mfg.; rodeo. Parts of Hamakua Forest Reserve to W, SW, and SE; Kalopa State Recreational Area to S.

Honokahua (HO-no-kah-HOO-ah), village (1990 pop. 477), W Maui, Maui co., Hawaii, 14 mi/23 km NW of Kahului, and 8 mi/12.9 km N of Lahaina, at mouth of Honokahua Stream. Cattle; resorts. Honolua Bay Marine Conservation Dist. to NE; D. T. Fleming Beach Park is here; Honokahua Bay (NE); Oneloa Bay (NW); West Maui Forest Reserve to SE.

Honokowai (HO-no-ko-WEI), town (1990 pop. 2,000),

Maui isl., Maui co., Hawaii, 14 mi/23 km WNW of Kahului, 5 mi/8 km N of Lahaina. Pineapples. Honokowai Beach Park here; Kaanapali Airport to S; gateway to W Maui resort areas.

Honolulu, county (□ 2,126 sq mi/5,506 sq km; 1990 pop. 836,231), central Hawaii; ⊙ Honolulu; 23°34′N 164°41′W. Most populous co. in Hawaii; includes Oahu isl. and all NW Hawaiian isls. W of Kaula and Niihau, except for Midway, uninhabited; Midway administered by U.S. Navy. Honolulu city is on S coast of Oahu isl. Locally administered by 7 dists.

Honolulu (HO-no-LOO-loo), city (1990 pop. 365,272), ⊙ the state of Hawaii and ⊙ Honolulu co., on the S coast of the isl. of OAHU; 21°19′N 157°48′W. With cruise ship and air connections to the U.S. mainland, Asia, Australia, and N.Z., Honolulu is the crossroads of the Pacific, as well as the economic center and principal port of the Hawaiian Isls. The city is famous for its beauty and the variety of its ethnic groups. It lies on a narrow plain bet. the sea and the Koolau Range and climbs the slopes of Punchbowl. Bypassed by Capt. James Cook when he explored the isls. in 1778, Honolulu's harbor was entered and praised in 1794 by William Brown, an Eng. captain. Honolulu's history from 1820, when missionaries arrived on the isls, is much the same as that of Hawaii. Growing from a settlement of thatched grass huts into the main residence of Hawaiian royalty and later of foreign consuls, Honolulu became the permanent capital of the kingdom of Hawaii in 1845. In the 19th cent., Amer. and Eur. whalers and sandalwood traders visited its port. It remained Hawaii's capital when the isls. were annexed by the U.S. in 1898 and achieved statehood in 1959. The Japanese bombed Pearl Harbor, the naval base W of Honolulu, on Dec. 7, 1941, and during World War II the port became a strategic naval base and a staging area for U.S. forces in the Pacific. Since the war, a rise in tourism, diversification of industry, and construction of luxury hotels and housing developments have made Honolulu the business and pop. center of Hawaii. Sugar processing and pineapple canning are no longer Honolulu's major industries. Increased peacetime defense activity at the many military installations in the area (Pearl Harbor Naval Shipyard, Schofield Barracks, Fort Shafter, Camp H. M. Smith, Hickam Field), expansion of harbor facilities, and the completion of an internatl. airport further aided the city's growth. Honolulu Harbor near downtown; Pearl Harbor 5 mi/8 km NW of downtown. Mfg. (jewelry, printing and publishing, apparel, food and beverages, rubber prods., construction materials, consumer goods, electronics and computer equip., machinery, metal prods.). The largest of Honolulu's parks is Kapiolani, containing a zoo, an aquarium, and Waikiki Shell, where the Honolulu Symphony gives concerts. Also in Honolulu is the Arizona Memorial for the 1,100 who died during the bombing of Pearl Harbor. Notable institutions are the Univ. of Hawaii at Manoa; Kapiolani Community Col.; Honolulu Community Col.; Chaminade Univ.; Hawaii Pacific Univ.; Hawaiian Baptitst Acad.; the Bishop Mus., noted for its studies of Polynesia; the Honolulu Acad. of Arts; and Kawaiahao Church (1841), where funerals for Hawaiian monarchs and nobility were held. Iolani Palace, the former home of Hawaii's kings, is the only royal palace in the U.S. Neal Blaisdell Concert Hall and Convention Center; Foreign Trade Zone; Quarantine Station at Honolulu Harbor; Ala Moana Center, one of the largest shopping centers in the U.S.; Waikiki Beach, especially noted for bathing and surfing, and famous Diamond Head crater are both in E part of the city; Natl. Cemetery of the Pacific (at Punchbowl Crater) N of Downtown; Honolulu Watershed Forest Reserve to NE; Kewalo Basin State Park on waterfront;

Honomu (HO-no-MOO), village (1990 pop. 532), E Hawaii isl., Hawaii co., Hawaii, on the Hamakua Coast (NE) at Kohola Point, 10 mi/16 km N of Hilo, near mouth of Kolekole Stream; 19°52′N 155°06′W. Hilo Forest Reserve and Akaka Falls State Park to W; Kolekole Beach Park to N.

Honor, village (1990 pop. 292), Benzie co., NW Mich., 4 mi/6.4 km NE of Beulah, on Platte R., SE of Platte L.; 44°40′N 86°01′W.

Hood, county (□ 436 sq mi/1,129 sq km; 1990 pop. 28,981), N central Texas; ⊙ Granbury; 32°25′N 97°49′W. Drained by Brazos R. Agr. (mainly peanuts, hay, pecans); cattle. Oil and gas. Part of Squaw Creek L. reservoir in S; L. Granbury reservoir and Acton State Historic Site in E. Formed 1866.

Hood Bay, SE Alaska, inlet of Chatham Strait, on W coast of Admiralty isl., just S of Angoon; 13 mi/21 km long, 5 mi/8 km wide at mouth. Hood Bay or Killisnoo fishing village is on N shore.

Hood Canal, inlet, W Wash., narrow arm extending SSW from entrance of PUGET SOUND channel hooks NE at S end, c.15 mi/24 km, coming within 1 mi/1.6 km of Case Inlet of Puget Sound, creating narrow isthmus of Kitsap Peninsula; on Admiralty Inlet c.50 mi/80 km along E side of Olympic Peninsula. Dabob Bay, arm in N part of inlet; highway bridge crosses inlet near its mouth.

Hood, Mount (11,235 ft/3,424 m), on Hood River and Clackamus co. lines, NW Oregon, in the Cascade Range, E of Portland. Highest point in the state and the center of Mt. Hood Natl. Forest and Mt. Hood Wildernes Area. A symmetrical, cone-shaped, dormant volcano, with glaciers and forested lower slopes, it rises high above the surrounding range and is a favorite mt.-climbing and skiing center. Timberline Lodge at S boundary. Several ski areas to S and SE.

Hood River, county (□ 533 sq mi/1,380 sq km; 1990 pop. 16,903), N Oregon; ⊙ Hood River; 45°31′N 121°38′W. Mt. Hood (highest point in state) is in Cascade Range on SW boundary. Columbia R. (Bonneville Reservoir) forms N boundary. Agr. (apples, cherries, pears, grapes, peaches; cattle); timber; wineries. Recreation. Mt. Hood Natl. Forest occupies most of co., in W, S, and SE. Eight state parks in W, all on Columbia R.; they include Viento, Wygant, and Starvation Creek State Parks. Parts of Columbia and Mt. Hood Wilderness Areas in W and S. Ski area in S. Steady winds through Hood R. Gorge make it the "Sailboard Capital of the World." Formed 1908.

Hood River, town (1990 pop. 4,632), ⊙ Hood River co., N Oregon, on Columbia R. (Bonneville Reservoir) at mouth of Hood R., c.55 mi/89 km ENE of Portland; 45°42′N 121°31′W. Elev. 54 ft/16 m. Highway bridge to White Salmon, Wash. 2 mi/3.2 km to NE. Trade, packing, shipping center for irrigated orchards (pears, apples, cherries, grapes) of Hood R. Valley, stretching to base of Mt. Hood, 25 mi/40 km S, whose glaciers feed the river. Mfg. (beer, bakery goods, lumber, millwork, concrete, utility substations). Wineries. Tourism. Annual internatl. sailboarding events and music festival. Settled 1854, inc. 1895.

Hoodsport, uninc. town (1990 pop. 1,100), Mason co., W Wash., 13 mi/21 km N of Shelton, on Hood Canal inlet, N of the Great Bend of inlet. Fish hatchery. Winery. Junction of road to SE corner of Olympic Natl. Park (park is NW). Potlatch State Park and Skokomich Indian Reservation to S; Olympic Natl. Forest and L. Cushman reservoir to W.

Hook Mountain Park, N.Y.: see NYACK.

Hooker, county (□ 721 sq mi/1,867 sq km; 1990 pop. 793), central Nebr.; ⊙ Mullen, located in the Sand Hills region; 41°53′N 101°08′W. Agr. area drained by Middle Loup and Dismal rivers. Cattle, hogs. Central/Mountain time zone boundary follows E and S boundaries. Formed 1889.

Hooker, town (1990 pop. 1,551), Texas co., central Okla. Panhandle, on high plains, 20 mi/32 km NE of Guymon; 36°51′N 101°12′W. Shipping and trading point in wheat-growing area; cattle; mfg. (liquid hydrocarbons); natural gas. Inc. 1907.

Hooker, Mount, Wyo.: see WIND RIVER RANGE.

Hookerton, village (1990 pop. 422), Greene co., E central N.C., 11 mi/18 km N of Kinston, on Contentace Creek; 35°25′N 77°35′W. In agr. area (tobacco, cotton, peanuts, grain, poultry, livestock).

Hooks, town (1990 pop. 2,684), Bowie co., NE Texas, 15 mi/24 km W of Texarkana; 33°28′N 94°16′W. In agr. area (vegetables, rice; cotton; cattle; dairying). Oil and gas; mfg. (jams and jellies). Inc. after 1940.

Hooksett (HUK-suht), town (1990 pop. 8,767), Merrimack co., S N.H., at falls of the Merrimack, 6 mi/9.7 km N of Manchester, on both sides of Merrimack R.; 43°03′N 71°26′W. Mfg. (machinery, electronic assembly, food prods., construction materials; printing); agr. (apples, vegetables, nursery crops; poultry, livestock; dairying). Part of Bear Brook State Park in NE. Includes village of South Hookset. Inc. 1822.

Hookstown, borough (1990 pop. 169), Beaver co., W Pa. 5 mi/8 km ESE of East Liverpool, Ohio, on Mill Creek. Mfg. (metal fabricating); agr. (corn, hay; dairying). Raccoon Creek State Park to S.

Hoolehua (HO-o-lai-HOO-ah), village, W central Molokai, Maui co., Hawaii, 6 mi/9.7 km NW of Kaunakakai, 1 mi/1.6 km N of Maunaloa Highway, near N coast. Hoolehua Airport to SW.

Hoonah, village (1990 pop. 795), SE Alaska, on N shore of Chichagof Isl., on Icy Strait 40 mi/64 km WSW of Juneau; 58°06′N 135°25′W. Fishing, fish processing. Harbor is called Port Frederick.

Hoopa, uninc. village, Humboldt co., NW Calif., on Trinity R., 30 mi/48 km NE of Eureka. Hq. Hoopa Indian Reservation in S part. Sheep, cattle, lambs; timber. Six Rivers Natl. Forest to S, E and N.

Hooper 1 village (1990 pop. 112), Alamosa co., S Colo. in San Luis Valley, 20 mi/32 km N of Alamosa; 37°45′N 105°52′W. Elev. 7,553 ft/2,302 m. Great Sand Dunes Natl. Monument to E; San Luis Lakes State Park to SE. **2** village (1990 pop. 850), Dodge co., E Nebr., 12 mi/19 km NNW of Fremont and on Elkhorn R; 41°36′N 96°32′W. Grain, livestock, poultry and dairy prods. Mfg. (classic car parts).

Hooper, N.Y.: see ENDWELL.

Hooper Bald, N.C.: see UNICOI MOUNTAINS.

Hooper Bay, Inuit village (1990 pop. 845), W Alaska, on Hooper Bay (15 mi/24 km long) of Bering Sea, 4 mi/6.4 km ESE of Point Dall; 61°33′N 165°48′W.

Hooper Islands, Dorchester co., E Md., 3 low marshy islands extending c.12 mi/19 km N-S in Chesapeake Bay, N of Hooper Strait; separated from mainland by Honga R. Bridged to mainland (N). Named after Henry Hooper, who owned much of the land on Upper Hooper Isl. The 4 isls. which form a chain 14 mi/23 km long were settled around 1660 by colonists from St. Mary's across the bay. A church built in 1872 stands on the site of St. Mary, Star of the Sea (R.C.). One of the greatest concentrated areas of migrating geese and ducks in Amer., iron bars are placed over larger windows to prevent wild fowl, attracted by lights, from breaking panes. Bridge connects N and middle isls. Fisheries (fish, crabs, oysters) seafood packing houses, vegetable canneries. Excellent sport fishing, duck and goose hunting. Villages are Honga and Fishing Creek on N Island; Hoopersville on middle isl. Lower isl. is uninhabited hunting grounds. John Smith, when caught in a storm here in 1608, called the area "Limbo."

Hooper Strait, E Md., narrow channel of Chesapeake Bay, Md., bet. Bloodsworth Isl. (S) and Dorchester co. shore and Hooper Isls. (N).

Hoopersville, Md.: see HOOPER ISLANDS.

Hoopeston (HUPE-stun), city (1990 pop. 5,871), Vermilion co., E Ill., 23 mi/37 km N of Danville; 40°28′N 87°40′W. Canning center; mfg. of packaging machinery, castings; agr. (vegetables, livestock). Plotted 1871, inc. 1877.

Hoople (HOOP-uhl), village (1990 pop. 310), Walsh co., NE N.Dak., 13 mi/21 km NW of Grafton and on N branch of Park R; 48°32′N 97°38′W. Ships potatoes.

Hooppole, village (1990 pop. 196), Henry co., NW Ill., 22 mi/35 km NNE of Cambridge; 41°31′N 89°54′W. In agr. area.

Hoosac Range (HOO-zuhk), S continuation of the Green Mts., NW Mass. and SW Vt., running from N to S. Rises to c.3,000 ft/910 m. The Hoosac RR tunnel, c.5 mi/8 km long, built from 1852 to 1873, at the cost of nearly 200 lives, cuts beneath the range from E to W.

Hoosac Tunnel (HOO-zuhk), village in Florida town,

Berkshire co., NW Mass., 6 mi/9.7 km E of North Adams, at E end of Hoosac Tunnel (c.25,000 ft/7,620 m long; completed 1873), which carries RR under Hoosac Range.

Hoosic River (HOO-zuhk), c.70 mi/113 km long, Mass. and N.Y.; rises in Hoosac Range in NW Mass.; flows N, NW, and W, past Adams, North Adams, and Williamstown, Mass., across SW corner of Vt., and past Hoosick Falls, N.Y. (water power), to the Hudson R. c.14 mi/23 km above Troy.

Hoosick Falls, industrial village (□ 1 sq mi/2.6 sq km; 1990 pop. 3,490), Rensselaer co., E N.Y., on Hoosic R. (water power from falls), near Vt. border, and 27 mi/43 km NE of Albany; 42°53'N 73°20'W. In dairying area; diversified mfg. Bennington Battlefield Park is NE. Small lakes (resorts) are nearby. Hoosick Falls Historic Dist. Inc. 1827.

Hoosier Pass (11,539 ft/3,517 m), central Colo., in Rocky Mts., on Park and Summit co. line. Crossed by State Highway 9. Crosses Continental Divide N-S. Arapaho Natl. Forest (N); Pike Natl. Forest (S). Mt. Lincoln is nearby.

Hoover, city (1990 pop. 39,788), Jefferson and Shelby cos., N central Ala., residential suburb on S of Birmingham; 33°45'N 86°49'W.

Hoover Dam (HOO-vuhr), on the Colorado R. bet. Clark co., S Nev. and Mohave co., NW Ariz.; 726 ft/ 221 m high, 1,244 ft/379 m long; 36°01'N 114°46'W. One of the world's largest dams. Built 1931–1936 by the U.S. Bureau of Reclamation; named for President Herbert Hoover; known as Boulder Dam 1933–1947. A key unit on the Colorado R., the dam is a major supplier of hydroelectric power and provides for flood control, river regulation, and improved navigation. Impounds L. Mead, the largest man-made reservoir in the U.S. at 32,501 cu yd/24,850 cu m (but does not rank among top 25 in world). Dam is focal point of Lake Mead Natl. Recreational Area, which extends N and E around lake, and S around L. Mohave (Davis Dam). Boulder City, Nev., was built to house workers on the project.

Hoover Memorial Reservoir (□ 5 sq mi/13 sq km), Franklin and Delaware cos., central Ohio, on Big Walnut Creek, 5 mi/8 km NE of Columbus; 40°06'N 82°53'W. Max. capacity 144,079 acre-ft. Formed by Hoover Dam (67 ft/20 m high), built for water supply; also used for recreation.

Hooverson Heights, uninc. town (1990 pop. 3,056), Brooke co., N W.Va., residential community 6 mi/ 9.7 km S of Weirton and 1 mi/1.6 km E of Follansbee, near Ohio R.; 40°19'N 80°34'W.

Hooversville, borough (1990 pop. 731), Somerset co., SW Pa., 10 mi/16 km S of Johnstown, on Stonycreek R. Agr. includes corn, oats, potatoes; livestock; dairying. Quemahoning Reservoir to W. Inc. 1896.

Hooverville, Pa.: see SEWARD.

Hop Bottom, borough (1990 pop. 345), Susquehanna co., NE Pa., 11 mi/18 km SSE of Montrose, on Martins Creek. Resort area. Agr. (corn, hay; dairying).

Hop River, small stream, c.15 mi/24 km long, E central Conn.; formed by several branches near Andover; flows SE and E to Willimantic R. just NW of Willimantic. Site of Andover Dam (for flood control) and L., 8 mi/ 12.9 km W of Willimantic.

Hop River, Conn.: see COLUMBIA.

Hopatcong (ho-PAT-kuhng), borough (1990 pop. 15,586), Sussex co., N N.J., 10 mi/16 km SE of Newton and on L. Hopatcong (c.7 mi/11.3 km long), in hilly region NW of Dover; 40°57'N 74°39'W. Resorts include Landing, Mt. Arlington, L. Hopatcong.

Hopatcong, Lake, reservoir (□ 4 sq mi/10.4 sq km), Morris co., N N.J., on Muscontcong R., 12 mi/19 km WNW of Parsippany; 40°55'N 74°40'W. Max. capacity 48,209 acre-ft. Formed by L. Hopatcong Dam (17 ft/ 5 m high), built for flood control.

Hope, agr. station, St. Andrew parish, SE Jamaica, on Hope R., and 3 mi/4.8 km NE of Kingston; 18°2'N 76°45'W. Comprises Jamaica School of Agr., research laboratories, and botanical gardens. Also a tourist site. Was once part of large Hope sugar estate, which prospered in 18th cent. Bought by govt. in 1913. Also called Hope Gardens.

Hope, city (1990 pop. 9,643), ☉ Hempstead co., SW Ark.; 33°40'N 93°35'W. RR junction. Commercial center. Agr. (watermelons); mfg. (food prods. and processing, machinery, apparel, printing, bakery prods.). The city is the birthplace and boyhood home of President Bill Clinton. Hope Wildlife Management Area to N; Bais D'Arc Wildlife Management Area to SW.

Hope, town (1991 pop. 3,147), SW B.C., Canada, on Fraser R., at mouth of Coquihalla R., and 27 mi/43 km NE of Chilliwack; 49°23'N 121°26'W. In mining (gold, silver) and lumbering region.

Hope 1 town (1990 pop. 2,171), Bartholomew co., S central Ind., 11 mi/18 km NE of Columbus; 39°18'N 85°46'W. In agr. area. Mfg. (meat processing, special machinery, plastics, lumber, steel fabricating). **2** town (1990 pop. 1,017), Knox co., S Maine, 10 mi/16 km N of Rockland; 44°15'N 69°11'W. In agr., resort region. Wood prods.

Hope 1 village, S Alaska, on N shore of Kenai Peninsula, on Turnagain Arm, 23 mi/37 km SSE of Anchorage, on highway from Anchorage. Tourism. Scene (1896) of gold rush. **2** village (1990 pop. 99), Bonner co., N Idaho, on E shore of Pend Oreille L., 14 mi/23 km E of Sandpoint. Site of Thompson's Trading Post (1809) to SE; 48°15'N 116°19'W. Kaniksu Natl. Forest to NE. **3** village (1990 pop. 404), Dickinson co., central Kansas, 17 mi/27 km SSE of Abilene; 38°41'N 97°04'W. RR junction. In wheat, cattle, sheep, and poultry area; dairy prods. **4** village and township (1990 pop. 1,719), Warren co., NW N.J., on small Beaver Brook, near Jenny Jump Mt., and 8 mi/12.9 km NE of Belvedere; 40°54'N 74°58'W. Has 18th-cent. bldgs., including stone mill built 1768 by Moravian settlers. Amusement park. **5** village (1990 pop. 101), Eddy co., SE N.Mex., on Rio Peñasco and 57 mi/92 km NW of Carlsbad; 32°49'N 104°44'W. Corn, alfalfa; cattle, sheep. **6** village (1990 pop. 281), Steele co., E N.Dak., 15 mi/24 km SSE of Finley; 47°19'N 97°43'W. Dairy prods., grain.

Hope, R.I.: see SCITUATE.

Hope Bay, town (1991 pop. 1,569), Portland parish, NE Jamaica, on the coast, on RR, and 7 mi/11.3 km W of Port Antonio; 18°12'N 76°34'W. In fruit-growing region (bananas, coconuts, cacao).

Hope Creek Nuclear Power Plant, New Jersey: see SALEM CO.

Hope Gardens, Jamaica: see HOPE.

Hope Mills, town (1990 pop. 8,184), Cumberland co., S central N.C., suburb 7 mi/11.3 km SSW of Fayetteville, on Rockfish Creek; 34°58'N 78°57'W. Ft. Bragg Army base and Pope Air Force base are adjacent. Mfg. (polyester yarn, embroidered fabric, gift items, machining). Agr. area (cotton, tobacco, grain, poultry, peanuts, soybeans, sweet potatoes; livestock). Fayetteville Regional Airport to E.

Hope, Mount, R.I.: see BRISTOL.

Hope, Point, headland, NW Alaska, on Chukchi Sea; 68°20'N 166°45'W. Site of Point Hope Inuit village. Whaling.

Hope River, c.15 mi/24 km long, St. Andrew parish, SE Jamaica; flows S, entering the Caribbean 5 mi/8 km ESE of Kingston; 18°2'N 76°44'W. Used for water supply of Kingston and suburbs.

Hope Town, town, N Bahama Isls., on cay just off E central Great Abaco Isl., 115 mi/185 km NNE of Nassau; 26°32'N 76°58'W. Fishing and trading. Lighthouse.

Hope Valley, village (1990 pop. 1,445) in Hopkinton town, Washington co., SW R.I., on Wood R. (bridged here) and 11 mi/18 km NNE of Westerly; 41°31'N 71°43'W. Abolitionist and teacher Prudence Crandall b. here, 1803.

Hopedale, town (1990 pop. 5,666), including Hopedale village, Worcester co., S Mass., 17 mi/27 km SE of Worcester; 42°08'N 71°32'W. Once a Christian communistic community (1841–c.1857); later developed as textile "company town." Textile loom factory now closed but was once the largest loom factory in U.S. Settled 1660, inc. 1886.

Hopedale, village (1991 pop. 515), E Lab., Canada, on the Atlantic; 55°28'N 60°12'W. Fishing port and seaplane anchorage.

Hopedale 1 village (1990 pop. 805), Tazewell co., central Ill., 14 mi/23 km SE of Pekin; 40°25'N 89°25'W. In agr. area. **2** village (1990 pop. 685), Harrison co., E Ohio, 6 mi/10 km NE of Cadiz, in coal mining area; 40°19'N 80°54'W.

Hopelawn, N.J.: see WOODBRIDGE.

Hopelchén (o-pel-CHEN), city (1990 pop. 6,186) and township, Campeche, SE Mexico, on Yucatán Peninsula, 45 mi/72 km E of Campeche; 19°46'N 89°50'W. Timber, sugar, chicle, fruit, henequen.

Hopes Advance, Cape, N Que., Canada, on Hudson Strait, on W side of entrance of Ungava Bay; 61°02'N 69°30'W.

Hopeville, town, Clarke co., S Iowa, 13 mi/21 km WSW of Osceola.

Hopewell, independent city (□ 11 sq mi/28 sq km; 1990 pop. 23,101), SE Va., 18 mi/29 km SSE of Richmond, on James R., at mouth of Appomattox R.; 37°17'N 77°17'W. RR junction; a deep-water port; mfg. (chemicals, polyester fibers, printing and publishing, paperboard). Founded as a munitions center. In 1926, Hopewell annexed City Point, General U.S. Grant's base of operations in 1864–1865, now part of Petersburg Natl. Battlefield. Historic Weston Plantation on Appomattox R. Benjamin Harrison Bridge (James R.) to E. Ft. Lee Military Reservation to N. Founded 1913, inc. 1916.

Hopewell, town (1991 pop. 4,268), Hanover parish, NW Jamaica, on coast, 6 mi/9.7 km W of Montego Bay; 18°15'N 78°18'W. Rice, bananas, yams.

Hopewell, village, NE N.S., Canada, 8 mi/13 km SSW of New Glasgow; 45°28'N 62°42'W. Dairying, farming.

Hopewell 1 village (1990 pop. 343), Marshall co., central Ill., 20 mi/32 km NNE of Peoria, on Illinois R.; 40°58'N 89°27'W. Corn, soybeans. **2** village (1990 pop. 2,569), Bradley co., SE Tenn., 4 mi/6 km N of Cleveland.

Hopewell 1 borough (1990 pop. 1,968), Mercer co., W N.J., 11 mi/18 km N of Trenton; 40°23'N 74°45'W. In agr. region (produce, dairy prods.); mfg. (metal prods., telecommunications, engineering research, and canned goods). Has Baptist Church (1748); monument (1865) to John Hart, who lived here; historical mus. State children's home — the former Lindbergh estate deeded (1941) to state. Settled before 1700, inc. 1891. **2** borough (1990 pop. 194), Bedford co., S Pa., 15 mi/24 km NE of Bedford, on Raystown Branch of Juniata R.

Hopewell Cape, village, ☉ Albert co., SE N.B., Canada, at head of Shepody Bay, at mouth of Petitcodiac R., and 19 mi/31 km SE of Moncton; 45°48'N 64°35'W. Lumbering.

Hopewell Furnace National Historic Site, Berks and Chester cos., SE Pa., 6 mi/9.7 km SW of Pottstown; 40°12'N 75°46'W. Has an area of 848 acres/343 ha. Iron-making site from 19th cent. with reconstructed blast furnace, ironmaster's mansion, auxilliary structures. French Creek State Park adjoins it to NW. Authorized 1938.

Hopkins 1 county (□ 554 sq mi/1,435 sq km; 1990 pop. 46,126), W Ky.; ☉ Madisonville; 37°18'N 87°32'W. Bounded E by Pond R., W by Tradewater R. Rolling agr. area (burley and dark tobacco, hay, alfalfa, soybeans, wheat, corn; hogs, cattle); important bituminous coal mines; oil wells, hardwood timber; some mfg. Tradewater Wildlife Management Area in SW, White City Wildlife Management Area in E. Formed 1806. **2** county (□ 792 sq mi/2,051 sq km; 1990 pop. 28,833), NE Texas; ☉ Sulphur Springs. Bounded N by South Fork of Sulphur R. (forms Cooper L. in NW); drained by White Oak and Lake Fork creeks; 33°08'N 95°33'W. Prairies in W; hilly in E. Dairying (a leading Texas co.); agr. (hay, silage; wheat, corn, rice, soybeans); cattle; timber. Oil and natural gas wells; clay mining; lignite. Milk processing. Mfg., processing of farm prods. at Sulphur Springs. Formed 1846.

Hopkins 1 city (1990 pop. 16,534), Hennepin co., SE Minn., a suburb 7 mi/11.3 km WSW of downtown Minneapolis; 44°55'N 93°24'W. RR junction. Mfg. (machinery; computer and electronic parts, printing and publishing, steel siding, wall murals, air pollution equip., gun drilling, packaging, labels, opthamalic lenses, tools, jellies and candy, lumber, bakery prods., software). An annual raspberry festival is held in Hopkins. Small lakes in area, especially SW. Inc. as West Minneapolis 1893, name changed 1928. **2** city (1990 pop. 575), Nodaway co., NW Mo., near One Hundred and Two R., 14 mi/23 km N of Maryville, near Iowa State Univ.; 40°32′N 94°49′W. Corn, wheat, soybeans; hogs, cattle; mfg. (corrugated metal pipe).

Hopkins, village (1990 pop. 546), Allegan co., SW Mich., 8 mi/12.9 km NNE of Allegan; 42°37′N 85°45′W. In farm area. Mfg. (trash compactors).

Hopkins Landing, village, SW B.C., Canada, on Thornbrough Channel of Howe Sound, 20 mi/32 km NW of Vancouver; 49°26′N 123°29′W. Lumber-shipping port.

Hopkins Park, village (1990 pop. 601), Kankakee co., E central Ill., 14 mi/23 km ESE of Kankakee, near Ind. state line; 41°04′N 87°36′W. Corn, soybeans; mfg. liquid food supplements.

Hopkinsville, city (1990 pop. 29,809), ⊙ Christian co., SW Ky., 60 mi/97 km WSW of Bowling Green, on South Fork Little R.; 36°51′N 87°29′W. Elev. 548 ft/167 m. RR junction. Fertile agr. lands surround Hopkinsville, which is a leading dark and burley tobacco and livestock market; also grain; poultry; dairying; heavy mfg. Hopkinsville Community Col., part of the Univ. of Ky., is in the city. Hopkinsville–Christian County Airport to E. Fort Campbell Military Reservation (Ky./Tenn.) to SW. Pennyrile Forest State Resort Park to NW. Inc. 1804.

Hopkinton 1 town (1990 pop. 695), Delaware co., E Iowa, on Maquoketa R., and 15 mi/24 km SE of Manchester; 42°20′N 91°15′W. **2** town (1990 pop. 9,191), including Hopkinton village, Middlesex co., E central Mass., 26 mi/42 km WSW of Boston; 42°14′N 71°32′W. Mfg. (electronic and computer equip., machinery). Annual Boston Marathon starts here. State Park. Settled c.1715, inc. 1744. **3** town (1990 pop. 4,806), Merrimack co., S N.H., 6 mi/9.7 km W of Concord; 43°11′N 71°41′W. Drained by Contoocook and Warner rivers. Mfg. (construction materials, sawmill machinery); agr. (nursery crops, vegetables, apples; livestock, poultry; dairying). Legislature met here occasionally, 1798–1807. Congregational church (1789) has Revere bell; Long Memorial Lib. has N.H. Antiquarian Society collection. Settled 1736, inc. 1765. Includes Contoocook village (1990 pop. 1,334; covered bridge is here) on Contoocook R., in N. **4** town (1990 pop. 6,873), Washington co., SW R.I., 30 mi/48 km SSW of Providence; 41°29′N 71°45′W. In agr. area; mfg. (textiles, yarn, twine). Includes villages of Ashaway, Canonchet, Hope Valley, Hopkinton, and Rockville, and part of Potter Hill village. Set off from Westerly and inc. 1757. Named in 1757 for Gov. Stephen Hopkins.

Hopland, uninc. town (1990 pop. 900), Mendocino co., NW Calif., 11 mi/18 km S of Ukiah, on Russian R. Fruit, grapes, hops, beans, nursery prods.; dairying; cattle. Mfg. (beer, winery).

Hopland, village, Mendocino co., NW Calif., in Russian R. valley, 13 mi/21 km S of Ukiah.

Hopwood, uninc. town (1990 pop. 2,021), South Union and North Union townships, Fayette co., SW Pa., suburb 2 mi/3.2 km SE of Uniontown. Mfg. (concrete blocks, machinery). Chestnut Ridge and Forbes State Forest to SE. Hutchinson reservoirs (Nos. 1,2, and 3) to S. Founded 1791.

Hoquiam (HO-kwee-uhm), town (1990 pop. 8,972), Grays Harbor co., W Wash., 4 mi/6.4 km W of Aberdeen, at mouth of Hoquiam R., on Grays Harbor; 46°59′N 123°54′W. RR junction. With its twin city, Aberdeen, it has fishing (including shellfish), lumbering, paper, cranberry, and tourist industries; mfg. (cedar prods., lumber, veneer, plywood, paper industry machinery). Bowerman Airport on peninsula in harbor, to SW. Olympic Natl. Park and Olympic Natl. Forest are to the N. Inc. 1890.

Horace 1 village (1990 pop. 168), Greeley co., W Kansas, 2 mi/3.2 km W of Tribune; 38°28′N 101°47′W. In agr. and cattle area. **2** village (1990 pop. 662), Cass co., E N.Dak., 10 mi/16 km SW of Fargo; 46°45′N 96°54′W. RR terminus.

Horatio (hor-AISH-ee-o), town (1990 pop. 793), Sevier co., SW Ark., 7 mi/11.3 km S of De Queen, near Little R.; 33°56′N 94°21′W. RR junction to SW. Mfg. (lumber).

Horatio, village, Sumter co., central S.C.,17 mi/27 km NE of Sumter near Wateree R. Agr. includes cotton, soybeans, corn; broilers; cattle.

Horcasitas, Mexico: see SAN MIGUEL DE HORCASITAS.

Hords Creek Lake, reservoir, Coleman co., central Texas, on Hords Creek (tributary of Pecan Bayou), 10 mi/16 km W of Coleman; 7 mi/11.3 km long; 31°50′N 99°34′W. Max. capacity, c.49,000 acre-ft. Formed by dam (91 ft/28 m high), a unit of Colorado R. flood-control project.

Hordville, village (1990 pop. 164), Hamilton co., SE central Neb., 16 mi/26 km NNE of Aurora and near Platte R; 41°04′N 97°53′W.

Horicon (HOR-i-kahn), town (1990 pop. 3,873), Dodge co., S central Wis., on Rock R., and 10 mi/16 km E of Beaver Dam; 43°26′N 88°38′W. In farm area. Agr. (dairy; livestock, poultry; grain); mfg. (plastics, machinery, furniture, wood, iron and steel prods., foods). RR junction. Horicon Marsh Wildlife Area and Horicon Natl. Wildlife Refuge to N. Sinissippi L. to S. Inc. 1897.

Horicon, N.Y.: see BRANT LAKE.

Horizon City, town (1990 pop. 2,308), El Paso co., extreme W Texas, residential suburb 17 mi/27 km ESE of downtown El Paso, in irrigated agr. area; 31°40′N 106°11′W.

Hormigueros (or-mee-GAI ros), town (1990 pop. 15,212), W P.R., 4 mi/6.4 km S of Mayagüez. Satellite of Mayagüez, which is practically taken up Hormigueros; most industry oriented toward Mayagüez. Industrial and commercial area; light mfg. Famed for its shrine of Our Lady of Montserrate (1775).

Horn Island, Jackson co., SE Miss., part of coastal isl. chain in the Gulf of Mexico, partly sheltering Mississippi Sound (N), 10 mi/16 km SSW of Pascagoula; c.14 mi/23 km long. Lighthouse (30°14′N 88°29′W). To E is deepwater channel (Horn Island Pass) leading from the Gulf to Pascagoula Bay. Part of Gulf Isls. Natl. Seashore. Petit Bois Isl. to E, Ship Isl. to W.

Horn Lake, town (1990 pop. 9,069), De Soto co., NW Miss., suburb 12 mi/19 km S of downtown Memphis, Tenn., and 2 mi/3.2 km S of Southampton; 34°57′N 90°02′W. Mfg. (cast metal prods., elevators, lumber, food seasonings, sheet metal prods.). Horn L. to W.

Horn Peak, Colo.: see SANGRE DE CRISTO MOUNTAINS.

Hornbeak, town (1990 pop. 445), Obion co., NW Tenn., 17 mi/27 km SW of Union City; 36°19′N 89°17′W.

Hornbeck (HOORN-bek), town (1990 pop. 427), Vernon parish, W La., 56 mi/90 km W of Alexandria, near Texas state line; 31°20′N 93°24′W. Agr.; mfg. of wood prods. State Wildlife Area to E.

Hornby Island (□ 11 sq mi/28 sq km), SW B.C., Canada, in Strait of Georgia off Vancouver Isl., just E of Denman Isl. and 16 mi/26 km SE of Courtenay; 6 mi/10 km long, 4 mi/6 km wide. Fishing, logging. Ferry from S end of Denman Isl.

Hornell, city (□ 2 sq mi/5.2 sq km; 1990 pop. 9,877), Steuben co., SW N.Y., on the Canisteo R.; 42°19′N 77°39′W. Settled 1790, inc. 1906. Hornell also has light mfg., including electric equip. and electronics, woven synthetic fabrics.

Hornepayne, town (1991 pop. 1,610), N central Ont., Canada, 200 mi/322 km N of Sault Ste. Marie. Elev. 1,074 ft/327 m. Gold mining, lumbering.

Hornersville, town (1990 pop. 629), Dunklin co., extreme SE Mo., on Little R. drainage channel in Mississippi alluvial plain, 14 mi/23 km S of Kennett; 36°02′N 90°06′W. Soybeans, cotton, corn. Mfg. (barbecue sauce).

Hornick, town (1990 pop. 222), Woodbury co., W Iowa, on West Fork Little Sioux R., and 25 mi/40 km SE of Sioux City; 42°13′N 96°05′W. In agr. area.

Hornitos, uninc. village, Mariposa co., central Calif., 18 mi/29 km NE of Merced. Cattle. Has bldgs. dating from gold rush days. New Exchequer Dam (L. McClure) to N.

Hornsby, town (1990 pop. 313), Hardeman co., SW Tenn.,

30 mi/48 km S of Jackson; 35°14′N 88°50′W. In farm area; lumber.

Horry (OR-ree), county (□ 1,255 sq mi/3,250 sq km; 1990 pop. 144,053), E S.C.; ⊙ Conway; 33°54′N 78°58′W. Bounded W and NW by Little Pee Dee R., SE by the Atlantic, NE by N.C. state line, and SW by the Great Pee Dee R.; drained by Waccamaw R. Intracoastal Waterway canal passes near coast. Summer resort area; includes Myrtle Beach (state park here). Agr. interests include timber, tobacco; also cotton, corn, hogs, cattle, soybeans, oats, wheat. Hunting and fishing attract tourists. Formed 1785 as Kingston, renamed 1801.

Horse Cave, town (1990 pop. 2,284), Hart co., central Ky., 32 mi/51 km ENE of Bowling Green; 37°10′N 85°54′W. Tourist resort for Ky. limestone cave region and an E gateway to MAMMOTH CAVE NATIONAL PARK. Agr. (livestock, poultry); dairying; burley tobacco, corn, wheat); mfg. (benches, lumber, commercial printing, plastic cups, crushed stone, concrete, truck seats). Hidden R. Cave, with an underground river containing blind fish, is here, also Kentucky Cave and Mammoth Onyx Cave. Horse Cave Theatre (1911).

Horse Creek, 136 mi/219 km long, in SE Wyo. and W Nebr.; rises in Laramie Mts. near Laramie, Wyo., SW Albany co.; flows E, N, and E, past La Grange, to North Platte R. near Morrill, Nebr., just E of Nebr. state line. Hawk Springs Reservoir formed on small tributary 6 mi/9.7 km N of La Grange.

Horse Creek Reservoir, SE Colo., on side channel of Horse Creek, on Bent-Otero co. border, 11 mi/18 km NW of Las Animas; 3 mi/4.8 km long; 38°09′N 103°23′W. Extends N. Max. capacity of 43,125 acre-ft. formed by Horse Creek Dam (31 ft/9 m high), built (1971) for irrigation. Formerly Timber L.

Horse Islands, Canada: see SAINT BARBE ISLANDS.

Horse Mesa Dam, Ariz., see APACHE LAKE.

Horse Pasture, uninc. town, Henry co., S Va., 6 mi/9.7 km SW of Martinsville; 36°37′N 79°57′W. Agr. (tobacco; cattle, poultry).

Horsefly Lake, S central B.C., Canada, in Cariboo Mts., 120 mi/193 km SE of Prince George, S of Quesnel L. Drained W into Fraser R. by Quesnel R.; 28 mi/45 km long, 1 mi/2 km–2 mi/3 km wide; 52°25′N 121°00′W.

Horsehead Lake, Kidder co., central N.Dak., 14 mi/23 km NNE of Steele; 6 mi/9.7 km long; 47°02′N 99°47′W.

Horseheads, village (□ 3 sq mi/7.8 sq km; 1990 pop. 6,802), Chemung co., S N.Y., 5 mi/8 km N of Elmira; 42°10′N 76°49′W. Mfg. (coil and precision springs, cable TV connectors, plastic prods., electronic tubes, power amplifiers, TV camera systems, image and storage tubes); sand, gravel pits. Agr. (dairy prods.; poultry, apples). Settled 1789, inc. 1837.

Horseneck Beach, Mass.: see WESTPORT.

Horseshoe Bend, village (1990 pop. 643), Boise co., W Idaho, 21 mi/34 km N of Boise, in bend of Payette R.; Black Canyon Dam downstream (W), 43°55′N 1116°11′W. Logging, sawmill prods.; cattle; alfalfa. Bogus Basin Ski Area to S.

Horseshoe Bend, a turn on the Tallapoosa R., near Dadeville, E central Ala. Site of a battle on March 27, 1814, in which the Creeks, led by chief William Weatherford, were significantly defeated by a militia under the command of Andrew Jackson. Horseshoe Bend Natl. Military Park is here.

Horseshoe Bend Military Park (□ 3 sq mi/7.8 sq km), E central Ala., 13 mi/21 km E of Alexander City. Authorized 1956.

Horseshoe Lake Conservation Area, Alexander co., extreme S Ill., c.12 mi/19 km NW of Cairo; c.7 mi/11.3 km long; 37°08′N 89°21′W. State game preserve. The lake is a remnant of the Mississippi R.

Horseshoe Mountain, peak (13,898 ft/4,236 m) in Rocky Mts., bet. Park and Lake cos., central Colo., 7 mi/11.3 km ESE of Leadville, and S of Mosquito Pass.

Horsetooth, reservoir (□ 3 sq mi/7.8 sq km), Larimer co., N central Colo., on Cache La Poudre R., 3 mi/5 km W of Fort Collins; 40°36′N 105°10′W. Formed by Horsetooth Dam (155 ft/47 m high), built (1949) by the

Bureau of Reclamation for irrigation. Roosevelt Natl. Forest just W.

Horsham (HOR-shuhm), uninc. city (1990 pop. 15,051), Montgomery co., SE Pa., 12 mi/19 km NE of Norristown. Mfg. (electronic equip., apparel, computers, chemicals, construction equip., level controls, consumer goods). U.S. Naval Air Station (Willow Grove) to NW.

Horton, town (1990 pop. 1,885), Brown co., NE Kansas, 23 mi/37 km WNW of Atchison; 39°39′N 95°31′W. Trading point in grain, livestock, and fruit area; dairy prods. Mfg. (industrial machinery). Mission L., just NE, is source of city's water supply. Kickapoo Indian Reservation to W. Inc. 1887.

Horton 1 village, Jackson co., S Mich., 9 mi/14.5 km SW of Jackson; 42°09′N 84°31′W. In farm and lake-resort area; mfg. of specialty machinery. **2** resort village, Delaware co., S N.Y., in the Catskills, on Beaver Kill, and c.50 mi/80 km W of Kingston; 41°58′N 75°01′W.

Horton, river, c.275 mi/440 km long, Canada; rising in a lake N of Great Bear L., Inuvik Region, N.W.T.; flowing NW to Franklin Bay, a part of the Beaufort Sea.

Hortonia, Lake, in towns of Sudbury and Hubbardton, Rutland co., W Vt., on Hubbardton R., 15 mi/24 km NW of Rutland; c.2 mi/3.2 km long; 43°43′N 73°12′W. River drains SW. Resort.

Hortonville, town (1990 pop. 2,029), Outagamie co., E Wis., 11 mi/18 km NW of Appleton; 44°20′N 88°37′W. In dairying and fruit-growing area. Mfg. (toys, juvenile furniture, vegetable canning, concrete pavers, nails, and wire prods.).

Hoschton (HUHSH-tuhn), village (1990 pop. 642), Jackson co., NE central Ga.,22 mi/35 km WNW of Athens; 34°05′N 83°46′W. Mfg. includes industrial threads, nursery bottles, sports car assembly.

Hoskins, village (1990 pop. 307), Wayne co., NE Nebr., 16 mi/26 km SW of Wayne, and on branch of Elkhorn R.; 42°06′N 97°17′W. Machinery.

Hosmer, village (1990 pop. 310), Edmunds co., N S.Dak., 23 mi/37 km WNW of Ipswich; 45°34′N 99°28′W. In agr. area.

Hospers, town (1990 pop. 643), Sioux co., NW Iowa, 9 mi/14.5 km SSW of Sheldon; 43°04′N 95°54′W. Agr. (livestock; grain; beef prods.); plastic injection moldings.

Hosston (HAHS-tuhn), village (1990 pop. 417), Caddo parish, extreme NW La., near Red R., 25 mi/40 km N of Shreveport, at E end of Black Bayou L. reservoir; 32°53′N 93°53′W. Oil and natural gas field in vicinity. Black Bayou State Game and Fish Preserve.

Hostos (OS-tos), village (1993 pop. 1,621), Duarte prov., E central Dominican Republic, in fertile La Vega Real valley, on RR and 33 mi/53 km E of La Vega. Cacao, rice. Until 1928, La Ceiba.

Hostotipaquillo (os-to-tee-pah-KEE-yo), town (1990 pop. 2,790), ⊙ Hostotipaquillo municipio, Jalisco, W Mexico, 55 mi/89 km NW of Guadalajara. Elev. 3,507 ft/1,069 m. Silver, gold, and copper mining; agr. (beans, corn, wheat, alfalfa; livestock); commerce.

Hot Spring, county (□ 622 sq mi/1,611 sq km; 1990 pop. 26,115), central Ark.; ⊙ Malvern; 34°19′N 92°57′W. Drained by Ouachita R. and small Caddo R. Agr. (cattle, hogs). Mfg. at Malvern and Jones Mill. Barite and rutile clay mining; bentonite, sand, gravel deposits; timber. Remmel Dam forms L. Catherine in N. co.; L. Catherine State Park is on S shore; part of DeGray L. reservoir (Caddo R.) on S boundary; small part of Ouachita Natl. Forest in far NW corner. Formed 1829.

Hot Springs, county (□ 2,006 sq mi/5,196 sq km; 1990 pop. 4,809), N central Wyo.; ⊙ Thermopolis; 43°42′N 108°26′W. Mining, natural gas and oil, and some agr. in N (alfalfa, sugar beets; some cattle); drained by Bighorn R. Coal. Part of Absaroka Range in W; small part of Shoshone Natl. Forest in extreme W. Hot Springs State Park in E center. Part of Wind R. Indian Reservation in S; Owl Creek Mts. in S. Formed 1911.

Hot Springs, town (1990 pop. 4,235), ⊙ Fall River co., SW S.Dak., 45 mi/72 km SSW of Rapid City, just S of Black Hills, and on Fall R.; 43°25′N 103°28′W. Health

resort; sulphur hot springs; dairy prods., timber, sandstone, alfalfa seed. Wind Cave Natl. Park, and Custer State Park to N. Mfg. (boots and saddles). Black Hills Natl. Forest to W and S. Cold Brook Reservoir Recreation Area to S. First settled 1879, inc. 1882.

Hot Springs 1 village (1990 pop. 411), Sanders co., NW Mont., 46 mi/74 km SSW of Kalispell, in W part of Flathead Indian Reservation; 47°37′N 114°40′W. Mineral waters resort. Lolo Natl. Forest to W. **2** village (1990 pop. 478), Madison co., W N.C., 25 mi/40 km NW of Asheville, on French Broad R., near Tenn. state line, in Pisgah Natl. Forest; 35°53′N 82°49′W. Tobacco, corn; cattle. Mfg. (nylon carrying cases). Appalachian Trail passes NE-SW through village. **3** uninc. village, Bath co., W Va., in Allegheny Mts., 17 mi/27 km NE of Covington, in George Washington Natl. Forest. Mfg. (beer). Mineral springs. Homestead Resort. Douthat State Park to SE, L. Moomaw Recreation Area to W.

Hot Springs, N.Mex.: see TRUTH OR CONSEQUENCES.

Hot Springs National Park 1 or **Hot Springs**, city (1990 pop. 32,462), ⊙ Garland co., W central Ark.; 47 mi/76 km WSW of Little Rock; 34°29′N 93°02′W. Settled 1807, inc. 1876. The city's N side is nearly surrounded by Hot Springs Natl. Park, noted for its hot mineral springs that have made the city a famous health resort. Central Ave., which runs N-S bet. sects. of the park, is known as Bath House Row. Situated in the Ouachita Mts., the city is at the center of the reservoir system of the Ouachita R., L. Catherine to E, L. Hamilton in S, and L. Ouachita to NW. Diversified mfg. Fish hatchery to S on L. Hamilton. The area was visited by the Span. explorer Hernando De Soto in 1541. The properties of the waters were investigated in 1804 under the authorization of President Thomas Jefferson. Garland Co. Community Col. here. Ouachita Natl. Forest to W. **2** (□ 9.12 sq mi/23.62 sq km), W central Ark. Dominates the N part of the city of Hot Springs Natl. Park (Hot Springs). Visited by Span. explorer Hernando De Soto in 1541. The springs, long used by Native Americans for medicinal purposes, became a Federal Reservation in 1832. From 750,000 gals/2,838,975 liters to 950,000 gals/3,596,035 liters of water per day, with an average temp. of 143°F/62°C, flow from 47 springs. The Natl. Park Service collects, cools, and supplies water to bathhouses in and out of the park. Camping, hiking. Est. 1921.

Hot Sulphur Springs, village (1990 pop. 347), ⊙ Grand co., N Colo., on Colorado R., in W foothills of Front Range, and 65 mi/105 km WNW of Denver; 40°04′N 106°05′W. Elev. 7,670 ft/2,338 m. Resort; hq. of Arapaho Natl. Forest. Williams Fork Reservoir to SW; Windy Gap Reservoir to E; parts of forest located to N and S, and Williams Fork game preserve. Mineral springs here. County mus. here with preserved bldgs. and Native Amer. artifacts.

Hotchkiss, town (1990 pop. 744), Delta co., W Colo., on North Fork of Gunnison R., at mouth of Leroux Creek, just W of West Elk Mts., and 20 mi/32 km ENE of Delta; 38°47′N 107°43′W. Elev. 5,351 ft/1,631 m. In fruit-growing region. Hotchkiss Natl. Fish Hatchery to SW. Gunnison Natl. Forest to E

Hotevilla (ho-tay-villa), uninc. town, NE Ariz., atop a mesa c.65 mi/105 km W of Winslow, in Hopi Indian Reservation. Elev. c.5,900 ft/1,798 m. Sheep, cattle, hogs; crafts. Founded 1906 by dissenting residents of Oraibi.

Hotham Inlet, NW Alaska, arm of Kotzebue Sound, extending SE from Kotzebue, forms E side of Baldwin Peninsula; 50 mi/80 km long, 5 mi/8 km–20 mi/32 km wide. Receives Kobuk R. At head of inlet is Selawik L.

Hottah Lake (□ 377 sq mi/976 sq km), W central Mackenzie dist., N.W.T., Canada, 60 mi/97 km S of Port Radium; 40 mi/64 km long, 1 mi/2 km–20 mi/32 km wide; 65°5′N 118°30′W. Drained N into Great Bear L. by Camsell R. (50 mi/80 km long).

Hotte, Massif de la (mah-SEEF duh lah OT), range in SW Haiti, stretches through Jacmel Peninsula for c.130 mi/209 km to Jacmel; 18°24′N 74°02′W. Rises to over 7,500 ft/2,286 m. Lignite, bauxite, and manganese deposits.

Houck, uninc. town (1990 pop. 900), Apache co., E. Ariz., 30 mi/48 km SW of Gallup, N.Mex., on Puerco R. (Span., *Rio Puerco*), in S part of Navajo Indian Reservation. Sheep, cattle, crafts. Zuni Indian Reservation (N.Mex.) to SE.

Houghton, county (□ 1,501 sq mi/3,888 sq km; 1990 pop. 35,446), ⊙ Houghton, NW Upper Peninsula, Mich., includes S part of Keweenaw Peninsula, extending into L. Superior. Partly bounded SE by Keweenaw Bay; drained by Ontonagon and Sturgeon rivers. Intersected NE by KEWEENAW WATERWAY and traversed by Copper Range; 46°58′N 88°39′W. Some mfg. at Hancock and Houghton. Cattle, poultry; agr. (forage crops, oats), dairying, lumbering; tourism, resorts. F.J. McLain State Park in N; Mt. Ripley Ski Area NW of Houghton; Twin Lakes State Park at center; several lakes are in co.; S ⅓ of co. is in Ottawa Natl. Forest; S boundary coincides with Central/Eastern time zone boundary (co. is in Eastern). Region settled by Finn. immigrants. Organized 1846.

Houghton, city (1990 pop. 7,498), ⊙ Houghton co., NW Upper Peninsula, Mich., opposite Hancock, on Keweenaw Waterway (port facilities); 47°06′N 88°33′W. Shipping, distribution, and industrial center for Keweenaw Peninsula. Mfg. (wood prods., publishing), lumbering; tourism; farming. Seat of Mich. Technological Univ.; mineralogical mus.; has mainland hq. of Isle Royale Natl. Park; passenger ferry to Rock Harbor lodge, Isle Royale; vertical lift bridge to Hancock and rest of Keweenaw Peninsula. Mt. Ripley Ski Area to NW. Settled 1851, inc. 1867.

Houghton (HO-tuhn), town (1990 pop. 1,005), King co., W Wash., on E shore of L. Washington, just S of Kirkland.

Houghton 1 village (1990 pop. 127), Lee co., SE Iowa, 19 mi/31 km NW of Ft. Madison; 40°46′N 91°36′W. Mfg. (prefabricated metal bldgs., farm machinery). Corn, oats; cattle, hogs. **2** (HOT-uhn), village (□ 2 sq mi/5.2 sq km; 1990 pop. 1,740), Allegany co., W N.Y., on Genesee R., and 22 mi/35 km S of Warsaw; 42°25′N 78°09′W. Agr. (dairy prods.; fruit, grain). Seat of Houghton Col. (1923).

Houghton Heights or **Houghton Lake Heights**, town, Roscommon co., N central Mich., residential and resort community on SW shore of Houghton L.; 44°19′N 84°46′W.

Houghton Lake, Roscommon co., N central Mich., c.20 mi/32 km WNW of West Branch; 44°21′N 84°43′W. Largest lake of state (c.16 mi/26 km long, 7 mi/11.3 km. wide). Source of Muskegon R. Houghton L.; resort village, is on SW shore. Light mfg. Year-round fishing; winter sports; waterfowl feeding grounds. Villages of Prudenville, Houghton Lake, and Houghton Heights on S shore.

Houghton, Port (HOO-tuhn), SE Alaska, arm of Stephens Passage, 75 mi/121 km SE of Juneau; 20 mi/32 km long, 57°19′N 133°27′W.

Houlka, Miss.: see NEW HOULKA.

Houlton (HOLT-uhn), town (1990 pop. 6,613), including Houlton village, ⊙ Aroostook co., E Maine, on Meduxnekeag R., and 100 mi/161 km NNE of Bangor, near N.B. border; 46°08′N 67°50′W. Port of entry. Trade, RR, shipping center for large potato-growing area; commercial center for tourist region (hunting, fishing, canoeing). Light mfg. Airport is E of town.

Houma (HO-muh), city (1990 pop. 30,495), ⊙ Terrebonne parish, SE La., 44 mi/71 km SW of New Orleans, on Bayou Terrebonne; 29°35′N 90°43′W. Port on the Intracoastal Waterway; junction with Houma Navigation Canal to Gulf of Mexico. Pontoon bridge crosses canal; also 55 other bridges in area. Leading industries include mfg. (motor vehicles, oil field equip. and machinery, pneumatic relays, chemical tanks, valve parts, process control systems, slings, wire rope, drilling tools, sign brackets, tugboats); shipbuilding; printing and publishing; shrimp processing. Hosts Freedom Festival. Many fine antebellum homes. South La. Trade School is here; nearby is a U.S. sugarcane experiment station. Founded in 1834; inc. 1848.

Houma Navigation Channel (HO-muh), canal,

c.30 mi/48 km long, Terrebonne parish, SE La., S extension of Gulf Intracoastal Waterway. Intersects Waterway S of Houma, goes S and SSE to Terrebonne Bay, Gulf of Mexico. Provides direct barge transport of offshore oil and natural gas to processing facilities in the Houma area and other parts of La.

Housatonic, village, Mass.: see GREAT BARRINGTON.

Housatonic (HOO-zuh-TAW-nik), river, c.130 mi/210 km long, W Mass.; rising in the Berkshires; flows generally S through W Connecticut to L.I. Sound at Stratford. The river has long been used as a source of power, with various hydroelectric plants in Connecticut.

House, uninc. village (1990 pop. 85), Quay co., E N.Mex., 44 mi/71 km SSW of Tucamcari; 34°38′N 103°54′W. Livestock, cotton, grain, alfalfa, vegetables.

House Harbour or **Havre aux Maisons** (AH-vr o mai-ZOH), village, E Que., Canada, on Alright Isl., one of the Magdalen Isls.; 47°24′N 61°49′W. Fishing port.

House Island, SW Maine, small isl. off South Portland; one of 1st settlements in Casco Bay area; fortified since 17th cent. Fort Scammel built 1808; rebuilt 1862; now abandoned.

House Springs, uninc. town, Jefferson co., E Mo., suburb 24 mi/39 km SW of downtown St. Louis, on Big R. Light mfg.

Houston 1 (HYOO-stuhn), county (□ 581 sq mi/1,505 sq km; 1990 pop. 81,331), extreme SE Ala.; ⊙ Dothan, 31°09′N 85°19′W. Bounded E by Chattahoochee R. and Ga., S by Fla. Rich agr. region (peanuts, corn, soybeans; hogs, beef cattle). Nuclear power plants Farley 1 (initial criticality Aug. 9, 1977; max. dependable capacity of 814 MWe) and Farley 2 (initial criticality May 8, 1981; max. dependable capacity of 824 MWe) are 18 mi/29 km SE of Dothan. Uses cooling water from the Chatahoochee R. Formed 1903. **2** (HOUS-tuhn), county (□ 379 sq mi/982 sq km; 1990 pop. 89,208), central Ga.; ⊙ Perry; 32°28′N 83°40′W. Bounded E by Ocmulgee R. Coastal plain agr. (cotton, corn, melons, soybeans, wheat, peanuts, pecans, peaches; cattle, hogs, poultry); timber area. Formed 1821. **3** (HYOOS-tuhn), county (□ 568 sq mi/1,471 sq km; 1990 pop. 18,497), extreme SE Minn.; ⊙ Caledonia; 43°40′N 91°30′W. Drained by Root R.; bounded E by Mississippi R. (forms Wis. state line), S by Iowa state boundary. Agr. area (corn, oats, soybeans, hay, alfalfa; hogs, cattle, poultry; dairying); timber; sand and gravel; limestone. Beaver Creek Valley State Park in center; part of Richard J. Dorer Memorial Hardwood State Forest covers NW, center, and SE parts of co.; parts of Upper Mississippi R. Natl. Wildlife Refuge in NE and SE. Winnebago Indian Reservation in NE. Formed 1854. **4** county (□ 207 sq mi/536 sq km; 1990 pop. 7,018), NW Tenn.; ⊙ Erin; 36°17′N 87°43′W. Bounded W by Kentucky Reservoir (Tennessee R.). Livestock raising; dairying; agr. (corn, tobacco, sweet potatoes). Formed 1871. **5** county (□ 1,236 sq mi/3,201 sq km; 1990 pop. 21,375), E Texas; ⊙ Crockett; 31°19′N 95°25′W. Bounded W by Trinity R., E by Neches R.; includes part of Davy Crockett Natl. Forest. Rolling wooded area (much timber); agr. (hay; cotton; peanuts, pecans, grains, watermelons); cattle, hogs, horses. Some oil, natural gas; sand and gravel. Lumber milling, oil refining, mfg., produce processing. Houston Co. L. reservoir to NW; Davy Crocket Natl. Forest in E; Mission Tejas State Historical Park in NE. Formed 1837.

Houston 1 city (1990 pop. 2,118), S central Mo., ⊙ Texas co., near Big Piney R. in the Ozarks, 32 mi/51 km SW of Salem; 37°19′N 91°57′W. Cattle, recreational center for the region; lumber and stave factory. Mfg. (apparel). **2** city (1990 pop. 1,630,553), ⊙ Harris co., corporate limits extend SW into Fort Bend co. and N into Montgomery co., SE Texas; 29°46′N 95°23′W. Elev. 55 ft/17 m. A deepwater port on the Houston Ship Channel, it is the 4th-largest city in the nation, largest city in Texas and the largest city in the entire South and Southwest, U.S. port of entry; a great industrial, commercial, and financial hub; one of the world's major oil centers; and the 3rd busiest tonnage-handling port in the U.S. (after New York and S La.). Numerous space and science research firms; electronics plants; giant oil refineries; high-tech industries; computer technology; one of the world's greatest concentrations of petrochemical works; steel and paper mills; shipyards; breweries; meatpacking houses; and mfg. (oil drilling equipment, clothing, glass, household items, seismic instruments). Major center of finance with a large number of banks, many of them foreign. The Texas Medical Center is the world's largest hosp. complex and a leading medical research facility. Founded in 1836 by J. K. and A. C. Allen, it was named for Sam Houston, and served (1837–1839) as capital of the Texas Republic. In the course of the 19th cent. it grew to a prosperous RR center. The digging (1912–1914) of the Houston Ship Channel made it a deepwater port and led to its expansion. Coastal oil fields, natural gas, sulfur, salt, and limestone deposits, and shipbuilding during World War II, poured quick wealth into the city. NASA Manned Spacecraft Center (1961; renamed the Lyndon B. Johnson Space Center in 1973) in SE brought the aerospace industry. It is the seat of Rice Univ., Texas Southern Univ., the Univ. of Houston, the Univ. of St. Thomas, Dominican Col., Houston Baptist Univ., Sam Houston Col., and 2-year community cols. Its many parks include the large Hermann Park, which has a zoo, a mus. of natural science, and a planetarium. Houston has several notable art museums, an arboretum, and a botanical garden. The civic center includes the Sam Houston Coliseum and Music Hall and the massive George R. Brown Convention Center (1987), one of the nation's largest; the Jesse H. Jones Hall for the Performing Arts, home of the symphony orchestra; and a convention and exhibit center, featuring the Natl. Space Hall of Fame. Other tourist attractions include the Galleria and the Greenspoint Mall, two of the largest shopping centers in the U.S.; Old Market Square; Sam Houston Historical Park, which contains restored homes (built 1824–1868) and reconstructed bldgs.; the Astrodome (opened 1965, officially the Harris Co. Domed Stadium, part of convention center complex, and includes Astrohall and Astroarena) and its adjacent "Astroworld," an amusement center. San Jacinto Battleground is in nearby Pasadena. Houston L. to NE; large Addicks and Barker flood control reservoirs in W part of city, are generally dry except during heavy rains and hurricanes. Sheldon State Wildlife Management Area to NE. Served by Houston Intercontinental Airport (N), Ellington Field and William P. Hobby Airport., both in SE part of city. Inc. 1837.

Houston 1 (HYOOS-tuhn), town (1990 pop. 697), S Alaska, 30 mi/48 km N of Anchorage, 25 mi/40 km W of Palmer, on Little Sustina R.; 61°37′N 149°46′W. Town is located on George Parks Highway (Rt. 3) and Alaska RR, 12 mi/19 km NW of Knik Arm of Cook Inlet. Salmon fishing center. **2** town (1990 pop. 1,013), Houston co., extreme SE Minn., 17 mi/27 km W of La Crosse Wis., on Root R., W of confluence of South Fork Root R., in Richard J. Dorer Memorial Hardwood State Forest; 43°45′N 91°34′W. Grain, soybeans; livestock, poultry; dairying; mfg. (button parts and button machines, feeds). **3** town (1990 pop. 3,903), a ⊙ Chickasaw co. (seat shared with Okolona), NE central Miss., 32 mi/51 km SSW of Tupelo; 33°53′N 89°00′W. RR terminus. In agr. (cotton, corn; dairying; timber) area; mfg. (fiber optics, furniture, apparel, cotton batting, paper prods., carpet padding, lumber). Nearby are Indian mounds and Geology Hill. Part of Tombigbee Natl. Forest in N and center. Inc. 1837.

Houston 1 (YOO-stuhn), village (1990 pop. 149), Perry co., central Ark., 15 mi/24 km WSW of Conway, near Arkansas R. (N) and Fourche La Fave R. (S); 35°01′N 92°41′W. **2** village (1990 pop. 487), Kent co., central Del., 16 mi/26 km S of Dover and 4 mi/6.4 km W of Milford; 38°55′N 75°30′W. In agr. area (fruit, vegetables; livestock, poultry; dairying).

Houston (HYOOS-tuhn), borough (1990 pop. 1,445), Washington co., SW Pa., suburb 2 mi/3.2 km SW of Canonsburg and 5 mi/8 km N of Washington, on Chartiers Creek. Mfg. (cement blocks, plastic prods., steel). Laid out 1871, inc. 1901.

Houston, district municipality (1986 pop. 3,905), B.C., Canada, on Yellowhead Highway, at confluence of Bulkley and Morice rivers. Lumber; mining; cattle ranching.

Houston Acres (YOO-stuhn), village (1990 pop. 496), Jefferson co., N Ky., residential suburb 7 mi/11.3 km ESE of downtown Louisville; 38°12′N 85°36′W.

Houston Lake, village (1990 pop. 303), Platte co., E Mo., residential suburb 7 mi/11.3 km NNW of downtown Kansas City, just N of Riverside; 39°11′N 94°37′W.

Houston, Lake, reservoir (□ 19 sq mi/49 sq km), Harris co., SE Texas, on San Jacinto R., 25 mi/40 km ENE of Houston; 29°55′N 95°08′W. Max. capacity 281,800 acre-ft. Formed by L. Houston Dam (66 ft/20 m high), built (1964) for water supply; also used for irrigation and recreation. L. Houston State Park at N end of reservoir.

Houston Ship Channel, S Texas, dredged deepwater channel c.50 mi/80 km long, connecting port of Houston with the Gulf of Mexico via Buffalo Bayou, San Jacinto R., and Galveston Bay. Vehicular tunnels under Buffalo Bayou bet. Pasadena (just E of Houston) and Salena Park and under San Jacinto R. sect., bet. Baytown and La Porte. Development began 1912; channel has since been deepened and widened to accommodate large vessels. San Jacinto Monument and Battleship Texas on S shore.

Houstonia, town (1990 pop. 283), Pettis co., central Mo., 15 mi/24 km NNW of Sedalia; 38°53′N 93°21′W.

Houtzdale (HOUTS-dail), borough (1990 pop. 1,204), Clearfield co., central Pa., 22 mi/35 km N of Altoona. Logging; surface bituminous coal mining, clay. Laid out 1870, inc. 1872.

Hoven, village (1990 pop. 522), Potter co., N central S.Dak., 18 mi/29 km NNE of Gettysburg; 45°14′N 99°46′W. Mfg. (cheese (?is)& cream).

Hovenweep National Monument (□ 1 sq mi/2.6 sq km), San Juan co., SE Utah and Montezuma co., SW Colo. Six groups of pre-Columbian cliff dwellings, towns and pueblos. Utah contains 440 acres/178 ha of the cliffs, comprising 1 unit; Colo. contains the other unit, with an area 345 acres/140 ha. Authorized 1923.

Hovey Lake (HUH-vee), Posey co., extreme SW Ind., in Hovey L. State Fish and Wildlife Area, 9 mi/14.5 km SSW of Mt. Vernon; 37°48′N 87°56′W. Natural backwater lake of Ohio R. (1 mi/1.6 km E and S).

Howard 1 county (□ 595 sq mi/1,541 sq km; 1990 pop. 13,569), SW Ark.; ⊙ Nashville; 34°05′N 93°59′W. Drained by Saline (forms most of W boundary) and Cassatot rivers. Agr. (cattle, hogs, chickens). Cotton ginning, sawmilling; mfg. of wood and cement prods. Timber; cinnabar mines. Part of Millwood L. Reservoir in extreme SW corner; part of L. Greerson Wildlife Management Area in NE; Dierks L. Reservoir (Saline R.) on W boundary; Gillham L. Reservoir (Cassatat R.) in NW; Howard Co. Wildlife Management Area in NW. Formed 1873. **2** county (□ 293 sq mi/759 sq km; 1990 pop. 80,827), central Ind.; ⊙ KOKOMO; 40°29′N 86°07′W. Rich agr. area (corn, soybeans, wheat, hogs, cattle, poultry); diversified mfg. Drained by Wildcat Creek. Formed 1844. **3** county (□ 473 sq mi/1,225 sq km; 1990 pop. 9,809), NE Iowa, on Minn. line (N); ⊙ Cresco, located at E end of co.; 43°21′N 92°19′W. Rolling prairie agr. area (hogs, cattle, poultry; corn, oats; dairying) drained by Upper Iowa, Wapsipinicon, and Turkey rivers. Limestone quarries, sand and gravel pits. Hayden Prairie State Preserve in NW; Lidtke Mill in N, near Lime Springs. Formed 1851. **4** county (□ 253 sq mi/655 sq km; 1990 pop. 187,328), central Md.; ⊙ Ellicott City; 39°15′N 76°56′W. Bounded NE by Patapsco R., W and SW by Patuxent R. Mostly rolling piedmont, with SE part in coastal plain. Agr. produce (dairy prods., poultry, vegetables, apples, some grain) marketed in metropolitan dist. of Baltimore (E). Also mfg., furniture, chemicals, fabricated metals, electronics. Named after Col. John Edgar Howard, Revolutionary War hero and governor of Md. from 1788 to 1791. Until the appearance of the planned community of Columbia, the co. was almost entirely agr. It is the only Md. co. that borders near the Chesapeake Bay for the state boundaries. Located entirely on the Piedmont

Plateau. Formed in 1851. **5** county (□ 469 sq mi/ 1,215 sq km; 1990 pop. 9,631), central Mo.; ⊙ Fayette; 39°08′N 92°42′W. Borders Missouri R. on W and S. Corn, wheat, apples, soybeans; cattle, hogs, poultry; mfg. at Glasgow and Fayette. Floods of 1993 caused damage in Glasgow and New Franklin. Formed 1816. Known as "Mother of Missouri counties" for its original large size and for so many cos. having been formed from it. Center of the highest Boonslick region. Boonslick State Park in SW. Original E terminus of the Santa Fe Trail in the 1820s. **6** county (□ 575 sq mi/1,489 sq km; 1990 pop. 6,055), E central Nebr.; ⊙ St. Paul; 41°13′N 98°31′W. Agr. region drained by North Loup and Middle Loup rivers, the 2 merge NW of S Canal to become Loup Reservoir. Cattle, hogs, corn, alfalfa, soybeans, dairy, and poultry prods. North Loup State Wayside Area at center of co. Formed 1871. **7** county (□ 904 sq mi/2,341 sq km; 1990 pop. 32,343), NW Texas; ⊙ Big Spring; 32°18′N 101°26′W. Rolling plains, drained by Beals Creek, Morgan Creek, and Mustang Draw. Elev. 2,200 ft/671 m–2,800 ft/853 m. Livestock (beef cattle); agr. in E (cotton, wheat, vegetables, black-eyed peas, sesame). Oil, natural gas fields; oil and gas refining, stone, sand and gravel. Includes Big Spring State Park. Formed 1876.

Howard, city (1990 pop. 9,874), Brown Co., E Wis., suburb 4 mi/6.4 km NW of Green Bay city, on Green Bay, arm of L. Michigan; 44°34′N 88°04′W. RR junction. Oneida Indian Reservation to SW.

Howard 1 town (1990 pop. 815), ⊙ Elk co., SE Kansas, on headstream of Elk R. and 55 mi/89 km ESE of Wichita; 37°28′N 96°15′W. Elev 1,000 ft/305 m. Trade center for livestock region. Mfg. (lumber and wood prods.). County mus. Founded 1870, inc. 1877. **2** town (1990 pop. 1,156), ⊙ Miner co., SE central S.Dak., 45 mi/ 72 km NW of Sioux Falls; 44°00′N 97°31′W. Near W Fork Vermillion R. Plotted 1881.

Howard, borough (1990 pop. 749), Centre co., central Pa., 9 mi/14.5 km NE of Bellefonte, on SE shore of Sayer (Blanchard) L. reservoir (Bald Eagle Creek). Mfg. (apparel). Bald Eagle State Park to NE and NW; Howard State Nursery to SW.

Howard A. Hanson Reservoir (□ 31 sq mi/80 sq km), King co., W central Wash., on Green R., in Cascade Mts., in Mt. Baker–Snoqualmie Natl. Forest, 35 mi/ 56 km SE of Seattle; 47°17′N 121°47′W. Max. capacity 136,700 acre-ft. Formed by Howard A. Hanson Dam (235 ft/72 m high), built (1962) by Army Corps of Engineers for flood control.

Howard Beach, a residential neighborhood of S Queens borough of N.Y. city, SE N.Y., on N shore of Jamaica Bay; 40°39′N 73°51′W. Many houses here are located along the water. Pop. mostly Ital. In 1986, an assault by white teenagers upon 3 passing Afr.-Americans (1 of whom died) resulted in what became known as the Howard Beach case; the teens were convicted of manslaughter.

Howard City, town (1990 pop. 1,351), Montcalm co., central Mich., 32 mi/51 km NNE of Grand Rapids and on short Tamarack R.; 43°23′N 85°28′W. In agr. and lake-resort area. Agr. (grain, potatoes, beans, vegetables, apples); livestock; dairy prods.; mfg. (paper roller headers).

Howard City, Nebr.: see BOELUS.

Howard Lake, town (1990 pop. 1,343), Wright co., S central Minn., 12 mi/19 km SW of Buffalo, at S end of Howard L.; 45°03′N 94°04′W. Diversified-farming area (poultry; grain, soybeans; dairying); mfg. (feeds, kitchen cabinets, pewter awards, egg processing, wooden wagon wheels). Dutch L. to SE.

Howard Mountain, Colo.: see NEVER SUMMER MOUNTAINS.

Howard Prairie Lake, reservoir, Jackson co., SW Oregon, on Jenny Creek, in Howard Prairie Recreation Area, 25 mi/40 km ESE of Medford; 5 mi/8 km long; 42°12′N 122°22′W. Max. capacity 76,700 acre-ft. Formed by Howard Prairie Dam (82 ft/25 m high), built (1958) for irrigation, power generation, and flood control.

Howards Grove, town (1990 pop. 2,329), Sheboygan Co., E Wis., 8 mi/12.9 km NW of Sheboygan; 43°49′N

87°49′W. Dairying, grain, fruit, vegetables. Mfg. (wood pallets).

Howardville, village (1990 pop. 440), New Madrid co., SE Mo., 3 mi/4.8 km WSW of New Madrid in the Mississippi alluvial plain; 36°34′N 89°35′W. Residential and commercial area.

Howe, town (1990 pop. 2,173), Grayson co., N Texas, 9 mi/14.5 km S of Sherman; 33°30′N 96°36′W. In agr. area (cattle; peanuts); mfg. (sheet metal fabrication).

Howe 1 village (1990 pop. 550), Lagrange co., NE Ind., 5 mi/8 km N of Lagrange, on Pigeon R. Pigeon R. State Fish and Wildlife Area to E. Mfg. (metal stamping, food prods., mobile homes). Cattle, poultry; corn, wheat. **2** village (1990 pop. 510), Le Flore co., E Okla., suburb 7 mi/11.3 km SE of Poteau; 34°57′N 94°38′W. RR junction. In agr. area.

Howe Caverns, N.Y.: see HOWES CAVE.

Howe Island (□ 12 sq mi/31 sq km), SE Ont., Canada, one of the Thousand Isls., in the St. Lawrence, near its outlet from L. Ontario, 8 mi/13 km E of Kingston; 8 mi/ 13 km long, 3 mi/5 km wide. Separated from mainland by narrow Bateau Channel.

Howe Sound, inlet of Strait of Georgia, SW B.C., Canada, 10 mi/km NW of Vancouver; 26 mi/42 km long, 1 mi/2 km–10 mi/16 km wide; 49°22′N 123°18′W. Receives Squamish R. at head; contains Gambier, Bowen, Anvil, and Keats isls. Fishing and lumbering area. Copper mining at Brittania Beach on E shore, now closed. Recreation all season. Port Mellon, Langdale, Gibsons on W shore; Squamish, Brittania Beach, and Horseshoe Bay on E shore.

Howell, county (□ 920 sq mi/2383 sq km; 1990 pop. 31,447), S Mo., ⊙ West Plains; 36°46′N 91°53′W. In the Ozarks; drained by Eleven Point R. Livestock, cattle, goats, horses, and agr. region (corn, hay); oak, cedar, pine timber; stone quarries. Mfg. at West Plains Willow Springs, and Mt. View. Mark Twain Natl. Forest in NW part. Tourism, canoeing. Formed 1857.

Howell 1 town, Echols co., S Ga., 13 mi/21 km E of Valdosta, near Alapaha R.; 30°49′N 83°03′W. **2** town (1990 pop. 8,184), ⊙ Livingston co., SE Mich., 33 mi/53 km ESE of Lansing, on small Thompson L.; 42°36′N 83°56′W. RR junction. In agr. and dairying area. Mfg. (electronic equip., chemicals, metal prods., lubricants and hydarulic fluids, metal plating, plastic molding, transformers, soft drinks, baking containers, electric breakers, hospital supplies, aluminum wheels); summer resort. Airport. Numerous lakes to SE; Mt. Brighton Ski Area to SE. Settled 1834; inc. as village 1863, as city 1915.

Howell, village (1990 pop. 237), Box Elder co., NW Utah, 30 mi/48 km NW of Brigham City; 41°46′N 112°26′W. Alfalfa, wheat, barley; dairying; cattle, sheep. Golden Spike Natl. Historical Site 15 mi/24 km SSW.

Howell, township (1990 pop. 38,987), Monmouth co., NE N.J., 8 mi/12.9 km W of Asbury Park; 40°10′N 74°11′W. Light industry. Inc. 1801.

Howells, village (1990 pop. 615), Colfax co., E Nebr., 20 mi/32 km NNE of Schuyler, and on branch of Elkhorn R; 41°43′N 97°00′W. Grain; cheese.

Howes Cave, village (1990 pop. 200), Schoharie co., E central N.Y., 32 mi/51 km W of Albany; 42°41′N 74°23′W. Tourist trade attracted by Howe Caverns, among largest in NE U.S., with underground stream and lake. Nearby are Secret Caverns.

Howey-in-the-Hills (HOU-ee), village (□ 1 sq mi/ 2.6 sq km; 1990 pop. 724), Lake co., central Fla., 10 mi/ 16 km SE of Leesburg, on L. Harris; 28°43′N 81°46′W. Citrus-fruit packing and canning. Conference center.

Howick (HOU-ik), village (1991 pop. 636), SW Que., Canada, near Châteauguay R., 15 mi/24 km ESE of Valleyfield; 45°11′N 73°51′W. Dairying.

Howkan Island, Alaska: see LONG ISLAND.

Howland (HOW-lund), town (1990 pop. 1,435), Penobscot co., central Maine, 30 mi/48 km N of Bangor and on Penobscot R., at mouth of the Piscataquis; 45°15′N 68°42′W. Plywood, paper mills. Inc. 1826.

Howland, uninc. village (1990 pop. 6,732), Trumbull co., NE Ohio, 3 mi/5 km E of Warren; 41°15′N 80°45′W. Often called Howland Corners or Howland Center.

Howson Peak (HOU-suhn) (9,000 ft/2,743 m), W central B.C., Canada, in Coast Mts., 30 mi/48 km SW of Smithers; 54°25′N 127°45′W.

Hoxie 1 (HAHK-see), town (1990 pop. 2,676), Lawrence co., NE Ark., 20 mi/32 km NW of Jonesboro, bet. Black and Cache rivers; 36°02′N 90°58′W. RR junction; mfg. (machinery). **2** town (1990 pop. 1,342), ⊙ Sheridan co., NW Kansas, 30 mi/48 km E of Colby; 39°21′N 100°26′W. Shipping and trading point in grain and livestock region.

Hoxsie, R.I.: see WARWICK.

Hoyleton, village (1990 pop. 508), Washington co., SW Ill., 13 mi/21 km SSE of Carlyle; 38°27′N 89°16′W. In agr. area.

Hoyt, village (1990 pop. 489), Jackson co., NE Kansas, 13 mi/21 km N of Topeka; 39°15′N 95°42′W. In livestock and grain region.

Hoyt Lakes, town (1990 pop. 2,348), St. Louis co., NE Minn., 17 mi/27 km E of Virginia, on S shore of Colby L., formed on Partridge R., in part of Superior Natl. Forest; 47°33′N 92°07′W. RR junction to NE. Mfg. of hardwood prods.; agr. (timber, dairying; cattle; oats, alfalfa). Recreation area.

Hoytville, village (1990 pop. 301), Wood co., NW Ohio, 14 mi/23 km SSW of Bowling Green; 41°11′N 83°47′W.

Huacana, La, Mexico: see LA HUACANA.

Huachinera (wah-chee-NE-rah), town (1990 pop. 928), NW Sonora, Mexico, 85 mi/137 km SSE of Agua Prieta; 30°12′N 108°57′W. Elev. 3,320 ft/1,012 m. Hot dry climate. On Babidanchic R., tributary of Bavispe R., in outlier ranges of Sierra Madre Occidental. On unpaved road.

Huachuca City, town (1990 pop. 1,782), Cochise co., SE Ariz., suburb 5 mi/8 km N of Sierra Vista; 31°37′N 110°20′W. Cattle; cotton, grain, alfalfa; mfg. (concrete). San Pedro Riparian Natl. Conservation Area to E.

Huachuca Mountains, in SW Cochise co., SE Ariz., in SW part of Sierra Vista city, near Mex. border. Miller Peak (9,466 ft/2,885 m) is highest point. Huachuca Peak (8,406 ft/2,562 m), also in range, is 5 mi/8 km SW of Sierra Vista. S part lies in Coronado Natl. Forest.

Huajicori (wah-hee-KO-ree), town (1990 pop. 2,060), Nayarit, W Mexico, on Acaponeta R. and 12 mi/19 km N of Acaponeta. Corn, sugarcane, beans; cattle; silver and gold deposits.

Huajuapam de León (wah-hoo-ah-PAHM de le-ON), city (1990 pop. 32,097) and township, ⊙ Huajuapan de Leon, Oaxaca, S Mexico, in Sierra Madre del Sur, on Inter-Amer. Highway, and 105 mi/169 km NW of Oaxaca de Juárez; 17°48′N 97°46′E. Elev. 5,249 ft/1,600 m. Agr. center (cereals, coffee, sugarcane, fruit); mfg. straw hats. Formerly Huajuapan de León.

Huajuapan de León, Mexico: see HUAJUAPAM DE LEÓN.

Hualahuises (wah-lah-WEE-ses), town (1990 pop. 4,858), ⊙ Hualahuises municipio, Nuevo León, N Mexico, in foothills of Sierra Madre Oriental, 8 mi/12.9 km W of Linares; 24°56′N 99°42′W. Grain; livestock.

Hualalai (HOO-ah-LAH-LEI), mountain (8,275 ft/ 2,522 m), near W coast, Hawaii isl., Hawaii co., Hawaii.

Hualapai Mountains (hua-la-pi), range in S central Mohave co., W Ariz., extends c.50 mi/80 km S from point near Kingman. Hualapai Peak (8,417 ft/2,566 m), 12 mi/19 km SE of Kingman, is highest point. NE extension, Peacock Mts., rise to 6,292 ft/1,918 m in Peacock Peak, 17 mi/27 km ENE of Kingman. Wabayuma Peak Wilderness Area in W center of Hualapai range.

Huamantla (wah-MAHN-tlah), city (1990 pop. 32,195) and township, Tlaxcala, central Mexico, at E foot of Malinche volcano, on RR, and 25 mi/40 km NE of Puebla; 19°18′N 97°55′W. Elev. 8,376 ft/2,553 m. Agr. center (corn, wheat, barley, alfalfa, beans, maguey; livestock); flour milling, pulque distilling. Many churches. Also known as Heroica Ciudad de Huamantla.

Huamuxtitlán (wah-moosh-tee-TLAHN), city (1990 pop. 4,769) and township, ⊙ Huamuxtitlán municipio, Guerrero, SW Mexico, in Sierra Madre del Sur, 50 mi/ 80 km ENE of Chilapa de Álvarez; 17°48′N 98°34′W. Elev. 3,691 ft/1,125 m. Cereals, sugarcane, fruit.

Huandacareo (wahn-dah-KAR-ee-o), town (1990 pop. 7,319), Michoacán, central Mexico, on NW shore of L.

Cuitzeo, 22 mi/35 km NW of Morelia. Elev. 6,047 ft/1,843 m. Agr. center (cereals, fruit; livestock).

Huanímaro (wah-NEE-mah-ro), city (1990 pop. 4,087), ⊙ Huanímaro municipio, Guanajuato, central Mexico, on central plateau, 22 mi/35 km SSW of Irapuato; 20°22′N 101°29′W. Elev. 8,068 ft/2,459 m. Cereals, alfalfa, beans, sugarcane, fruit. also Guanímaro.

Huaniqueo de Morales (wah-nee-KAI-o de mo-RAH-les), town (1990 pop. 3,302), ⊙ Huaniqueo municipio, Michoacán, central Mexico, 30 mi/48 km NW of Morelia. Elev. 6,775 ft/2,065 m. Cereals, fruit; livestock.

Huanusco (wah-NOOS-ko), town (1990 pop. 1,766), Zacatecas, N central Mexico, 22 mi/35 km E of Tlaltenango de Sánchez Román, on Mexico Highway 54. Also San Pedro Huanusco.

Huapango, Lake (wah-PAHN-go), artificial lake in Mexico state, central Mexico, 51 mi/82 km NW of Mexico City; c.12 mi/19 km long.

Huaquechula (wah-kai-CHOO-lah), town (1990 pop. 2,966), Puebla, central Mexico, 12 mi/19 km SW of Atlixco. Cereals, sugarcane, vegetables, livestock.

Huásabas (WAH-sah-bas), town (1990 pop. 1,060), Sonora, NW Mexico, on Bavispe R. and 115 mi/185 km NE of Hermosillo. Livestock, wheat.

Huasca de Ocampo (WAS-kah de o-KAM-po), town (1990 pop. 840), Hidalgo, central Mexico, 12 mi/19 km NE of Pachuca de Soto. Corn, maguey, beans, livestock.

Huasteca, La (was-TEK-ah), Gulf lowlands in NE Mexico, comprise central and lower Pánuco R. basin of Veracruz and Tamaulipas; rise near slopes of Sierra Madre Oriental in Hidalgo and San Luis Potosí. Fertile region with abundant rain, tropical in the plains. Excellent pastures for livestock raising; large-scale sugarcane prod., cereals, fruit. Formerly center of Mexico's petroleum industry. Named for Huastec Indians, some 90,000 of whom still live in the W margins of the region.

Huatabampo (wah-tah-BAHM-po), city (1990 pop. 26,037) and township, Sonora, NW Mexico, on the Gulf of California, near Mayo R. mouth (Río Mayo Irrigation District), 21 mi/34 km SW of Navojoa; 26°49′N 109°40′W. Agr. center (chickpeas, cereals, vegetables, fruit). Many agr. prods. for export.

Huatlatlauca (wah-tla-tla-OO-kah), town (1990 pop. 1,464), Puebla, central Mexico, near Atoyac R., 27 mi/43 km SSE of Puebla. Corn, sugarcane, fruit, livestock.

Huatulco (wah-TOOL-ko), village, Oaxaca, Mexico. Fashionable resort village surrounded by coffee plantations along the Pacific coast.

Huatulco Bays (wah-TOOL-ko), region, Oaxaca, Mexico. A series of 9 small bays on the Pacific coast of Oaxaca, 24 mi/40 km E of Puerto Angel. Developed in the early 1990s as a new luxury beach resort area. Served by Mexico Highway 200 and commercial air service.

Huatusco, Mexico: see HUATUSCO DE CHICUELLAR.

Huatusco de Chicuellar (wah-TOOS-ko de chee-KWAI-yar), city (1990 pop. 21,286) and township, ⊙ Huatusco municipio, Veracruz, E Mexico, in Sierra Madre Oriental, 50 mi/80 km W of Veracruz on Mexico Highway 125; 19°12′N 96°08′W. Agr. center (bananas, corn, coffee, sugarcane).

Huauchinango (wou-chee-NAN-go), city (1990 pop. 38,708) and township, Puebla, central Mexico, in SE Sierra Madre Oriental, 45 mi/72 km E of Pachuca de Soto on Mexico Highway 130; 20°11′N 98°04′W. Processing and agr. center (corn, coffee, sugarcane, tobacco, vegetables, fruit); floriculture; tanning, lumbering, shoe mfg. Necaxa dam and hydroelectric plant are nearby. Also known as Huauchinango de Degollado.

Huautepec (WOU-te-pek), town (1990 pop. 1,595), in N central Oaxaca, Mexico, 17 mi/27 km E of Teotitlán de Flores Magón. Elev. 8,104 ft/2,470 m. Steep terrain in the Papaloapan R. basin. Cold to temperate climate. Agr. (corn, beans, wheat, potatoes, fruits). Connected by unpaved road to Huatla de Jiménez. Also Santa María Asunción Huautepec.

Huautla (WOU-tlah), town (1990 pop. 2,766), Hidalgo, central Mexico, in Sierra Madre Oriental foothills, 12 mi/19 km SE of Huejutla. Agr. center (corn, rice, sugarcane, tobacco, fruit; livestock).

Huautla de Jiménez (WOU-tlah de hee-ME-nes), city (1990 pop. 8,232) and township, Oaxaca, S Mexico, in Sierra Mazateca 15 mi/24 km E of Teotitlán de Flores Magón in Petlapa R. drainage (to Papaloapan R.); 18°10′N 96°51′W. Elev. 7,218 ft/2,200 m. Agr. center (cereals, fruit). In Mazatec-speaking area. Also Huautla.

Huayacocotla (wah-yah-ko-KO-tlah), town (1990 pop. 3,210), Veracruz, E Mexico, in Sierra Madre Oriental, 33 mi/53 km NNE of Pachuca de Soto (Hidalgo); 20°34′N 98°27′W. Cereals, sugarcane, coffee.

Huazalingo (wah-sah-LEEN-go), town (1990 pop. 625), Hidalgo, central Mexico, 14 mi/23 km SW of Huejutla de Reyes. Corn, rice, sugarcane, tobacco; livestock.

Hubbard, county (☐ 999 sq mi/2,587 sq km; 1990 pop. 14,939), NW central Minn.; ⊙ Park Rapids; 47°06′N 94°54′W. Mississippi R. drains NW corner (source at L. Itasca to W of co.). Alfalfa, oats, barley, rye, potatoes, beans; timber; peat deposits. Parts of Paul Bunyan State Forest in N and center; Badoura State Forest in SE; part of L. Itasca State Park in W; numerous small natural lakes throughout co., esp. in S. Formed 1883.

Hubbard, city (1990 pop. 8,248), Trumbull co., NE Ohio, 5 mi/8 km NE of Youngstown, near Pa. state line; 41°09′N 80°34′W. Inc. 1869.

Hubbard 1 town (1990 pop. 814), Hardin co., central Iowa, 11 mi/18 km WSW of Eldora; 42°18′N 93°17′W. Feed, concrete blocks. **2** town (1990 pop. 1,881), Marion co., NW Oregon, 20 mi/32 km NW of Salem and 25 mi/40 km SSW of Portland, near Pudding R.; 45°10′N 122°48′W. Mfg. (apparel, metal forgings). Nuts, fruits. Dairy prods.; poultry. **3** town (1990 pop. 1,589), Hill co., N central Texas, 29 mi/47 km NE of Waco; 31°51′N 96°47′W. In cotton-growing area; oil and natural gas. Navarro Hills L. reservoir to NE.

Hubbard, village (1990 pop. 199), Dakota co., NE Nebr., 9 mi/14.5 km W of Dakota City; 42°23′N 96°35′W.

Hubbard Creek Lake, reservoir (☐ 24 sq mi/62 sq km), Stephens co., N central Texas, on Hubbard Creek, 55 mi/88 km NE of Abilene; 32°50′N 98°58′W. Max. capacity 720,000 acre-ft. Formed by Hubbard Creek L. Dam (112 ft/ 34 m high), built (1962) for water supply.

Hubbard Glacier, SE Alaska, on Disenchantment Bay at head of Yakutat Bay; 50 mi/80 km long; 60°02′N 139°25′W. Part of St. Elias Mts. glacier system.

Hubbard Lake, Alcona co., NE Mich., 15 mi/24 km SSW of Alpena; c.7 mi/11.3 km long, 3 mi/4.8 km wide; 44°48′N 83°33′W. Fishing. Source of a branch of Thunder Bay R. Hubbard L., resort village, is near N end in Alpena co. (light mfg.).

Hubbard, Mount (14,950 ft/4,557 m), on Yukon-Alaska border in St. Elias Mts., 140 mi/225 km W of Whitehorse, 60 mi/97 km NNE of Yakutat; 60°19′N 139°04′W.

Hubbardston, agr. town (1990 pop. 2,797), Worcester co., N central Mass., 18 mi/29 km NNW of Worcester, near Wachusett Mt.; 42°29′N 72°00′W. Settled 1737, inc. 1767. Mfg. (backhoe attachments).

Hubbardston, village (1990 pop. 404), on Ionia-Clinton co. line, S central Mich., 14 mi/23 km NE of Ionia and on Fish Creek; 43°05′N 84°50′W. In farm area.

Hubbardton, town (1990 pop. 576), Rutland co., W Vt., 12 mi/19 km NW of Rutland, at N end of L. Bomoseen; 43°42′N 73°10′W. Scene (July 7, 1777) of Br. victory over Seth Warner.

Hubbell, town (1990 pop. 1,174), Houghton co., NW Upper Peninsula, Mich., 8 mi/12.9 km NE of Houghton, on Torch L. (connected by deepwater channel to Keweenaw Waterway); 47°10′N 88°26′W. Copper mining area; copper refining; mfg. (copper oxides). Houghton Airport to W.

Hubbell, village (1990 pop. 55), Thayer co., SE Nebr., 12 mi/19 km SSE of Hebron, at Kansas line, and on branch of Little Blue R; 40°00′N 97°30′W.

Hubbell Trading Post National Historic Site, Apache co., NE Ariz., in Navajo Indian Reservation, at Ganado, 47 mi/76 km WNW of Gallup N.Mex.; 160 acres/65 h. Example of a late-19th-cent. trading post in the Southwest, still active. Authorized 1965.

Huber Ridge, uninc. village (1990 pop. 5,255), Franklin co., central Ohio, a NE suburb of Columbus; 40°05′N 82°55′W.

Hudson, county (☐ 62 sq mi/161 sq km; 1990 pop. 553,099), NE N.J., bounded by Passaic R. and Newark Bay (W), and Hudson R. and Upper New York Bay (E); ⊙ JERSEY CITY; 40°43′N 74°04′W. Heavily industrialized, with varied mfg., oil refining, shipbuilding, RR and ocean shipping. Jersey City is a commercial and transportation center of N.Y. city metropolitan area. Site of Liberty State Park which includes the N.J. State Science Center. Drained by Hackensack R. Formed 1840.

Hudson 1 city (1990 pop. 19,530), Hillsborough co., S N.H. Bounded S by Mass. state line; W by Merrimack R. opposite (1 mi/1.6 km E of) Nashua; 42°46′N 71°24′W. Mfg. (apparel, computer and electronic equip., textiles, printing, sheet metal fabrication); agr. (fruit, vegetables, corn, nursery crops; poultry, livestock; dairying). The city's main growth is due to the establishment of high-technology computer industries and added housing developments in the area. Est. 1673 as part of Dunstable, Mass., included in N.H. as Nottingham West in 1746; name changed to Hudson in 1830. **2** city (☐ 2 sq mi/5.2 sq km; 1990 pop. 8,034), Columbia co., SE N.Y. on the Hudson R.; 42°15′N 73°47′W. The city was a whaling and trading port until 1812. Its industries included textiles, furniture, cement, and metal prods., but these are largely gone. Many colonial and Revolutionary era homes are in the area. Olana, estate of Frederic E. Church, 2.5 mi/4 km S of city. Settled c.1622 by the Dutch and later in 1783 by Eng. whalers; inc. 1785.

Hudson 1 town (1991 pop. 488), NW Ont., Canada, on inlet of L. Seul, 12 mi/19 km W of Sioux Lookout, in gold mining, dairying, grain-growing region. **2** town (1991 pop. 4,829), S Que., Canada, on L. of the Two Mountains, 8 mi/13 km E of Rigaud. Dairying, potato growing; resort.

Hudson 1 town (1990 pop. 918), Weld co., N Colo., 30 mi/48 km NE of Denver; 40°04′N 104°38′W. Elev. 5,024 ft/1,531 m. In agr. region, fruit, sugar beets, beans, wheat, cattle, horeses; mfg. (plastic injection molding). **2** town (☐ 3 sq mi/7.8 sq km; 1990 pop. 7,344), Pasco co., W central Fla., 30 mi/48 km NW of Tampa; 28°21′N 82°42′W. Mfg. includes construction materials, furniture, lime rock processing. **3** town (1990 pop. 438), Steuben co., NE Ind., 9 mi/14.5 km SSW of Angola; 41°32′N 85°05′W. Potatoes, onions; mfg. (metal furniture, extruded plastics, metal stampings). **4** town (1990 pop. 2,037), Black Hawk co., E central Iowa, 8 mi/12.9 km SW of Waterloo; 42°25′N 92°27′W. In agr. area. **5** town (1990 pop. 1,048), Penobscot co., S central Maine, 15 mi/24 km NNW of Bangor; 45°00′N 68°52′W. **6** industrial and residential town (1990 pop. 17,233), Middlesex co., E central Mass., on the Assabet R.; 42°23′N 71°33′W. In an apple-growing region. Mfg. includes communications equip., locks, chemicals, plastics, electronic and metal prods., and semiconductors. Settled c.1699, inc. 1866 **7** town (1990 pop. 2,580), Lenawee co., SE Mich., on Tiffin R. and 16 mi/26 km WSW of Adrian; 41°51′N 84°20′W. Shipping point for rich farm area; mfg. (wire forms, aluminum and sand castings, screw machine prods.). Native Amer. mounds nearby. L. Hudson State Recreation Area to E. Settled 1834; inc. as village 1853, as city 1893. **8** town (1990 pop. 2,819), Caldwell co., W central N.C., 5 mi/8 km SE of Lenoir; 35°51′N 81°29′W. Timber; tobacco, grain; poultry, livestock. Mfg. (leather prods., industrial packaging, curved plywood, lumber handling systems, dining room chairs, clothing, woven cloth, yarn). L. Rhodhiss reservoir to S. **9** town (1990 pop. 2,374), Angelina co., E Texas, suburb 2 mi/3.2 km WSW of Lufkin; 31°19′N 94°47′W. Timber area. Davy Crocket Natl. Forest to SW. **10** town (1990 pop. 6,378), ⊙ St. Croix co., W Wis., on St. Croix R. and 15 mi/24 km E of St. Paul, Minn.; 44°58′N 92°44′W. In dairying and grain-growing area. RR workshops; mfg. (dairy prods., furniture, refrigerators). A nearby park has Indian mounds. Lower St. Croix Natl. Scenic Riverway; Willow R. State Park to NE. Inc. 1856.

Cross references are shown in SMALL CAPITALS. The pronunciation key is on page xv. The dates of population figures are on page xii.

Hudson 1 village (1990 pop. 1,006), McLean co., central Ill., 8 mi/12.9 km N of Bloomington; 40°36'N 88°59'W. In rich agr. area. L. Bloomington and Evergreen L. are nearby. **2** village (1990 pop. 159), Stafford co., S central Kansas, 19 mi/31 km SSE of Great Bend, near Rattlesnake Creek; 38°06'N 98°39'W. In wheat area. Quivira Natl. Wildlife Refuge, with extensive salt marshes, is to E. **3** village (1990 pop. 332), Lincoln co., SE S.Dak., 14 mi/23 km SSE of Canton and on Big Sioux R., near Iowa state line; 43°07'N 96°27'W. Honey; meat processing. **4** village (1990 pop. 392), Fremont co., W central Wyo., on Popo Agie R. and 9 mi/14.5 km NE of Lander, on S boundary of Wind R. Indian Reservation; 42°53'N 108°34'W. Elev. 5,094 ft/1,553 m.Trading and cattle-shipping point in vegetable (corn, beans, sugar beets) region; coal mines.

Hudson Bay, village, E Sask., Canada, 80 mi/129 km SW of the Pas; 52°51'N 102°23'W. RR junction for the Pas–Flin Flon mining region; lumbering, clay quarrying, mixed farming.

Hudson Bay, inland sea (□ c.475,000 sq mi/1,230,000 sq km), of N. Amer., E central Canada; c.850 mi/1,370 km long and c.650 mi/1,050 km wide. Hudson Bay and James Bay (its S extension) and all their isls. border the N.W.T., Man., Ont., and Que. Hudson Strait (c.450 mi/720 km long) connects Hudson Bay with the Atlantic Ocean, and Foxe Channel leads to the Arctic Ocean. Mansel, Coats, and Southampton isls. are at the N end of the bay. Hudson Bay occupies the southernmost portion of the Hudson Bay Lowlands, a depression in the Can. Shield formed during the Pleistocene epoch by the weight of the continental ice sheet. As the ice retreated, the region was flooded by the sea, and sediments were deposited in it. With the burden of ice removed, the floor of the lowlands has been slowly rising and the bay is gradually becoming shallower. The W shores are generally low and marshy and covered by tundra, while the E coast is barren and rocky, with the Ottawa and Belcher isl. groups offshore. Many rivers, including the Churchill and Nelson, drain into the bay. Hudson Bay moderates the local climate; it is ice-free and open to navigation from mid-July to Oct. The bay was explored and named (1610) by Henry Hudson in his search for the Northwest Passage. The surrounding region was a rich source of furs, and France and England struggled for its possession until 1713, when France ceded its claim by the Peace of Utrecht. Hudson's Bay Company set up many trading posts there, esp. at river mouths; some of the posts have operated continuously since 1670. The Hudson Bay RR (opened 1929) links the prairie provs. with Churchill, Man., a port for oceangoing freighters.

Hudson Falls, village (□ 1 sq mi/2.6 sq km; 1990 pop. 7,651), ⊙ Washington co., E N.Y., on E bank of the Hudson and 3 mi/4.8 km E of Glens Falls; 43°17'N 73°34'W. In diversified farming area; lumber and paper milling; mfg. of pulp and paper milling machinery, flexible couplings. Hudson Falls Historic Dist. Settled 1761, inc. 1810.

Hudson Heights, village, S Que., Canada, on L. of the Two Mountains, 7 mi/11 km E of Rigaud; 45°27'N 74°10'W. Dairying, potato growing.

Hudson Lake, village (1990 pop. 1,347), LaPorte co., NW Ind., 12 mi/19 km NE of LaPorte, at E end of Hudson L. RR junction. Dairying, fruit. Laid out c.1831.

Hudson Oaks, village (1990 pop. 711), Parker co., N central Texas, 20 mi/32 km W of Fort Worth, on SW shore of L. Weatherford reservoir; 32°45'N 97°42'W. Residential satellite community W of Dallas–Fort Worth urbanized area. Agr. area.

Hudson River, c.315 mi/507 km long, N.Y.; rising in L. Tear of the Clouds, on Mt. Marcy in the Adirondack Mts., NE N.Y.; flowing generally S to Upper N.Y. Bay at N.Y. city; the Mohawk R. is its chief tributary. The Hudson is navigable by ocean vessels to Albany and by smaller vessels to Troy; leisure boats and self-propelled barges use the canalized sect. bet. Troy and Fort Edward, the head of navigation. Divisions of the N.Y. State Barge Canal connect the Hudson with the Great Lakes and with L. Champlain and the St. Lawrence R. The Hudson is tidal to Troy (c.150 mi/240 km upstream); this sect. is considered to be an estuary. The main headstream of the Hudson is Feldspar Creek–Opalescent R. The upper course of the river has many waterfalls and rapids. The middle course, bet. Albany and Newburgh, is noted for the Catskill and Shawangunk Mts. on the W and by the large estates (the Roosevelt home at Hyde Park is the most famous) on the E bank. From Newburgh to Peekskill the river crosses the mountainous and forested Hudson Highlands in a deep, scenic gorge. West Point Military Acad. overlooks the river there, and Bear Mt. Bridge spans this sect. Near Tarrytown the river widens to form the N.Y. State Thruway and the Tappan Zee Bridge; from there to its mouth the Hudson is flanked on the W by the sheer cliffs of the Palisades. At the mouth are the ports of N.Y. and N.J. The Hudson forms part of the N.Y.-N.J. border, and the 2 states are linked by the George Washington Bridge, the Holland and Lincoln vehicular tunnels, and RR tubes. Sighted 1st by Verrazano in 1524, the river was explored by Henry Hudson in 1609. It was a major route for Native Americans and later for the Du. and Eng. traders and settlers. During the Amer. Revolution both sides fought for control of the Hudson; many battles were fought along its banks. In 1825 the Erie Canal linked the river with the Great Lakes, providing the 1st all-water trans-Appalachian route. Many industries are located on the Hudson's banks, and pollution by raw sewage and industrial wastes became a serious problem in the 1900s; anti-pollution legislation passed in 1965 has sought to protect the river from further contamination. Although pollution continued throughout the 1970s, 1980s, and 1990s, the state and municipal govts. and environmental groups have contributed a significant clean-up effort, including more anti-pollution regulation. A major sewage treatment plant was constructed in the 1980s along the river. The Hudson is featured in the legend of Rip Van Winkle and other stories by Washington Irving.

Hudson River Greenway, park, E N.Y., extending eventually along E shore of Hudson R. from N.Y. city line to the Troy dam in Renssalaer co., and from the N.J. state line to the mouth of the Mohawk R., N of Albany, along the W shore. Length will be c.130 mi/209 km on each side. Purpose of plan is to link urban, suburban, rural, historical, cultural, and recreational resources of the Hudson Valley, as well as to preserve open land and develop Hudson Valley trails. Idea proposed in early 1980s; State Greenway Act of 1991 began implementation; intended to be completed in 2005.

Hudson Strait, N Que. and SE Franklin dist., N.W.T., Canada, arm of the Atlantic, extending from N extremity of Lab. to Hudson Bay at NW extremity of Ungava Peninsula, opposite Southampton Isl.; 450 mi/724 km long, 40 mi/64 km–150 mi/241 km wide; 60°30'–64°30'–78°00'W. Ungava Bay, N Que., is S arm. At E entrance of strait are Killinek and Resolution isls.; at W entrance are Salisbury and Nottingham isls. Foxe Channel connects strait with Foxe Basin and thence with other arms of the Arctic Ocean. Trading posts on strait include Lake Harbour on Baffin Isl. and Sugluk on Ungava Peninsula. Ice-free from mid-July until Oct., strait is navigable with ice breakers during greater part of the year. Reputedly entered by Sebastian Cabot, 1498, E end of Hudson Strait was explored by Sir Martin Frobisher, 1576–1578, and by John Davis, 1585–1587; in 1610 Henry Hudson 1st navigated its full length. It later became main route of Hudson's Bay Co. vessels and, since 1931, of grain ships from Churchill.

Hudson Village, city (1990 pop. 5,159), Summit co., NE Ohio, 11 mi/18 km NE of Akron; 41°14'N 81°27'W. Photographic equip., sheet metal, fireworks, textiles. Western Reserve Acad. (1826) is here. Settled 1799, inc. 1837.

Hudsonville, town (1990 pop. 6,170), Ottawa co., SW Mich., suburb 11 mi/18 km SW of downtown Grand Rapids; 42°52'N 85°51'W. In orchard, dairy, and farm area. Mfg. (routers and welders, plastic molding, screw machine prods., wood prods.). Inc. 1926.

Hudspeth, county (□ 4,572 sq mi/11,841 sq km; 1990 pop. 2,915), extreme W Texas; ⊙ Sierra Blanca; 31°26'N 105°22'W. Bounded N by N.Mex. line, S by the Rio Grande (Mex. border); 3d largest co. in state. High plateau region (elev. c.3,500 ft/1,067 m) with mts. (up to c.7,500 ft/2,286 m) surrounding a central bolson with intermittent drainage into large playas (saltworks; figured in Salt War, 1877) in NE. Irrigated agr. (water from Elephant Butte Reservoir, N.Mex.) in Rio Grande valley (cotton, alfalfa; vegetables); cattle, hogs; minerals (talc, gypsum). Part of Sierra Diablo is in E, Eagle Peak in SE, Quitman Mts. in S, Sierra Blanca Mt. in S center, Finlay Mts. in W center, Hueco Mts. in NW, scattered mts. in N; part of Guadalupe Mts. Natl. Park in NE corner; small part of Fort Bliss Military Reservation in NW corner; one of 2 W Texas cos. wholly in Mountain time zone (also El Paso co. and part of Culberson co.). Formed 1917.

Hueco Mountains, extreme W Texas and S N.Mex., N–S range c.55 mi/89 km long, NE of El Paso. Rise to 6,767 ft. in Cerro Alto Peak, Texas. At Hueco Tanks (c.25 mi/40 km ENE of El Paso) are caves, natural rock reservoirs, and pictographs left by tribes whose stronghold this was; camp grounds here. Diablo Bolson is E.

Huehuetán (we-we-TAHN), town (1990 pop. 5,511), Chiapas, S Mexico, in Pacific lowland, near highway, on RR, and 10 mi/16 km SE of Huixtla. Coffee, sugarcane, fruit; livestock.

Huehuetla 1 (we-WE-tlah), town (1990 pop. 2,362), ⊙ Huehuetla municipio, Hidalgo, central Mexico, in E foothills of Sierra Madre Oriental, 50 mi/80 km NE of Pachuca de Soto; 20°35'N 98°4'W. Elev. 984 ft/300 m. Corn, sugarcane, coffee, fruit, beans; livestock. **2** town (1990 pop. 2,022), Puebla, central Mexico, in SE foothills of Sierra Madre Oriental, 28 mi/45 km ESE of Huauchinango. Sugarcane, coffee, tobacco, fruit. In Totonac Indian area.

Huehuetlán (we-we-TLAHN), town (1990 pop. 485), SE San Luis Potosí, Mexico, 30 mi/49 km S of Ciudad Valles in the Tancanhuitz sierra. Water sources are from the Esperanza and Huichihuan rivers. Agr. (sugarcane, coffee), cattle.

Huehuetlán, Mexico: see SANTO DOMINGO HUEHUETLÁN.

Huehuetlán El Chico (we-we-TLAHN el CHEE-ko), town (1990 pop. 4,711), Puebla, central Mexico, 21 mi/34 km SW of Izúcar de Matamoros. Agr. center (corn, rice, sugarcane, fruit; livestock).

Huehuetlán el Grande, Mexico: see SANTO DOMINGO HUEHUETLÁN.

Huehuetoca (we-we-TO-kah), town (1990 pop. 3,011), ⊙ Huehuetoca municipio, Mexico state, central Mexico, on RR and 28 mi/45 km N of Mexico City, within the Zona Metropolitana de la Ciudad de México; 19°49'N 99°9'W. Elev. 7,536 ft/2,297 m. Corn, maguey; livestock.

Huejotitán (we-ho-tee-TAHN), town (1990 pop. 334), Chihuahua, N Mexico, 30 mi/48 km WNW of Hidalgo del Parral. Corn, cotton, beans, sugarcane, tobacco.

Huejotzingo (we-hot-SEEN-go), city (1990 pop. 16,869) and township, Puebla, central Mexico, on central plateau, 15 mi/24 km NW of Puebla on Mexico Highway 190; 19°10'N 98°23'W. RR terminus; fruit-growing center (apples, pears, plums, figs, nuts); cider mfg.; handwoven serapes. Has 17th-cent. church and a monastery of San Francisco.

Huejúcar (we-HOO-kar), town (1990 pop. 3,520), ⊙ Huejúcar municipio, Jalisco, N central Mexico, on Zacatecas border, 19 mi/31 km N of Colotlán. Cereals, vegetables; livestock.

Huejuquilla el Alto (we-hoo-KEE-yah el AHL-to), town (1990 pop. 3,689), Jalisco, W Mexico, near Zacatecas border, 50 mi/80 km NW of Colotlán; 22°40'N 103°52'W. Elev. 5,577 ft/1,700 m. Cereals, alfalfa, beans; livestock.

Huejutla de Reyes (we-HOO-tlah de RAI-yes), city (1990 pop. 24,747) and township, ⊙ Huejutla de Reyes municipio, Hidalgo, central Mexico, in E foothills of Sierra Madre Oriental, near Veracruz border, 75 mi/121 km NNE of Pachuca de Soto; 21°08'N 98°24'W. Elev. 564 ft/172 m. Agr. center (corn, rice, sugarcane, tobacco, coffee, fruit; cattle); cigars.

Hueneme, Calif.: see PORT HUENEME.

Huépac (WE-pak), town (1990 pop. 905), ⊙ Huépac municipio, Sonora, NW Mexico, on Sonora R. (irrigation) and 75 mi/121 km NE of Hermosillo; 29°54′N 110°10′W. Elev. 1,588 ft/484 m. Farming where irrigation water available. Livestock; wheat, corn, vegetables, sugarcane.

Huerfano, county (□ 1,593 sq mi/4,126 sq km; 1990 pop. 6,009), S Colo.; ⊙ Walsenburg; 37°41′N 104°57′W. Coal-mining and livestock grazing area, bounded W by Sangre de Cristo Mts.; drained by Cucharas (forms Cucharas Reservoir in NE) and Huerfano rivers. Part of San Isabel Natl. Forest in NW, W, and S; S end of Wet Mts. in NW. Orlando Reservoir in NE; Lathrop State Park at center. Cucharas Ski Area in S. Formed 1861.

Huerfano River, 99 mi/159 km long, S Colo., in Sierra Blanca, in W Huertano co., at Gardner; confluence of Huerfano, Muddy, and (in downstream) Williams creeks; flows E and NE to Arkansas R. E of Pueblo. Source Lily L.

Huetamo de Núñez (we-TAH-mo de NOON-yez), city (1990 pop. 17,711), ⊙ Huetamo municipio, Michoacán, central Mexico, in Río Balsas valley, 24 mi/39 km NW of Ciudad Altamirano (Guerrero); 18°36′N 100°54′W. Agr. center (sugar, coffee, fruit, cereals); tanning.

Huetter, village (1990 pop. 82), Kootenai co., N Idaho, 6 mi/9.7 km W of Coeure d'Alene and 2 mi/3.2 km E of Post Falls, on Spokane R; 47°42′N 116°51′W.

Huevos Island (HWAI-vos), off NW Trinidad, Trinidad and Tobago, in the Dragon's Mouth, bet. Chacachacare isl. (W) and Monos Isl. (E); 253 acres/102 ha; 10°42′N 61°43′W. Elev. 680 ft/207 m. Bathing resort.

Huexotla (we-HO-tlah), village, Mexico state, central Mexico, 4 mi/6.4 km SSW of Texcoco de Mora; 19°30′N 98°50′W. Site of many archaeological remains (temples, pyramids, etc.). Also San Luis Huexora.

Huey, village (1990 pop. 210), Clinton co., SW Ill., 4 mi/6.4 km E of Carlyle; 38°36′N 89°17′W. In agr. and oil-producing area. Near Rend L.

Hueyapan (we-YAH-pahn), town (1990 pop. 3,388), Hueyapan municipio, Puebla, central Mexico, in Sierra Madre Oriental, 6 mi/9.7 km SE of Tulancingo. Cereals, sugarcane, vegetables, coffee; wood, resins.

Hueyapan de Ocampo (we-YAH-pahn de o-KAM-po), town (1990 pop. 3,561), Veracruz, SE Mexico, in Gulf lowland, 17 mi/27 km NW of Acayucan. Sugarcane, fruit.

Hueyotlipan (wai-o-TLEE-pahn), town (1990 pop. 3,701), Tlaxcala, central Mexico, 13 mi/21 km NW of Tlaxcala. Maguey, corn, wheat, beans; livestock.

Hueyotlipan, Mexico: see SANTO TOMÁS HUEYOTLIPAN.

Hueypoxtla (wai-POSH-tlah), town (1990 pop. 2,659), Mexico state, central Mexico, 33 mi/53 km N of Mexico city. Grain, maguey, stock.

Hueytamalco (wai-tah-MAHL-ko), town (1990 pop. 3,553), Puebla, E Mexico, in foothills of Sierra Madre Oriental, 10 mi/16 km NE of Teziutlán. Sugarcane, fruit.

Hueytepec, Sierra de (WAI-te-pek), range in Chiapas, S Mexico, a N spur of Sierra Madre, E of Tuxtla Gutiérrez; extends c.60 mi/97 km NW-SE, forming E water-shed of upper Grijalva R. The Cerro Hueytepec rises to 8,946 ft/2,727 m. San Cristóbal de las Casas is its center. Sometimes spelled Huitepec; also known as Sierra Los Altos de Chiapas.

Hueytlalpan (wai-TLAL-pahn), town (1990 pop. 1,867), Puebla, central Mexico, in foothills of Sierra Madre Oriental, 25 mi/40 km ESE of Huauchinango. Coffee, tobacco, sugarcane, fruit.

Hueytown (HYOO-ee-TOUN), city (1990 pop. 15,280), Jefferson co., N. central Ala., just SW of Birmingham. Fishing lures mfg. here.

Huffman Dam, Greene co., SW Ohio, on Mad R., 5 mi/8 km ENE of downtown Dayton; 73 ft/22 m high; 39°48′N 84°05′W. Built in 1922 for flood control. Reservoir is dry except during flood periods; max. potential capacity 297,000 acre-ft.; extends into Montgomery and Clark cos.

Hugh Butler Lake, reservoir, in Frontier co. and on Red

Willow co. border, SW Nebr., on Red Willow Creek; c.10 mi/16 km long; 40°22′N 100°39′W. Max. capacity 163,500 acre-ft. Formed by Red Willow Dam (117 ft/36 m high), built (1962) by the Bureau of Reclamation for irrigation, flood control and recreation.

Hughenden, village (1991 pop. 285), E Alta., Canada, near small Hughenden L., 23 mi/37 km S of Wainwright. Grain elevators, lumbering, mixed farming.

Hughes 1 county (□ 814 sq mi/2,108 sq km; 1990 pop. 13,023), central Okla.; ⊙ Holdenville; 35°02′N 96°15′W. Intersected by Canadian and North Canadian, and Little rivers; includes L. Holdenville in SW center. Agr. (corn, peanuts, hay, watermelons, peanuts; cattle, hogs). Some mfg. at Holdenville. Oil and natural gas wells; catfish farming; mfg. of apparel. Formed 1907. **2** county (□ 800 sq mi/2,072 sq km; 1990 pop. 14,817), central S.Dak.; ⊙ Pierre; 44°23′N 99°59′W. Agr. region bounded S and SW by Missouri R., and watered by Medicine Knoll Creek and other intermittent streams (L. Oahe reservoir formed by Oahe Dam upstream from Pierre). Part of Crow Creek Indian Reservation in SE. Wheat, corn, barley; hogs, cattle. Formed 1873.

Hughes, town (1990 pop. 1,810), St. Francis co., E Ark., 27 mi/43 km WSW of Memphis (Tenn.), near Mississippi R.; 34°57′N 90°28′W. Mud L. to SW. In agr. area (cotton, rice, soybeans); lumber milling. Mfg. (picture frames and bulletin boards). Hunting, fishing. Founded 1913.

Hughes, Indian village (1990 pop. 54), central Alaska; on Koyukuk R. and 80 mi/129 km NW of Tanana; 66°03′N 154°13′W. Airfield.

Hughes River (HYOOS), 18 mi/29 km long, NW W.Va.; formed in E Ritchie co. by junction of North Fork (c.50 mi/80 km long; flows generally SW) and South Fork (c.40 mi/64 km long; flows generally W); flows W, through Hughes R. Wildlife Management Area, to Little Kanawha R., 12 mi/19 km SE of Parkersburg.

Hughes Springs, town (1990 pop. 1,938), Cass co., NE Texas, 35 mi/56 km NNW of Marshall. Resort, with mineral springs; lumber milling; nursery; mfg. (oil field pipe couplings, consumer displays); 33°00′N 94°37′W. Daingerfield State Park to W.

Hugheston (HYOOS-tuhn), uninc. town (1990 pop. 950), Kanawha co., W central W.Va., on Kanawha R., c.18 mi/29 km SE of Charleston. Mfg (mining equip.).

Hughestown (HYOOS-toun), borough (1990 pop. 1,734), Luzerne co., NE central Pa., residential suburb 8 mi/12.9 km NE of Wilkes-Barre and 8 mi/12.9 km SW of Scranton, near Susquehanna R. Inc. 1879.

Hughesville, village (1990 pop. 1,319), Charles co., S Md., 28 mi/45 km SSE of Washington; 38°32′N 76°47′W. Tobacco market and farm trade center.

Hughesville, borough (1990 pop. 2,049), Lycoming co., N central Pa., on Muncy Creek, 17 mi/27 km E of Williamsport. Light mfg. Agr. area (potatoes, soybeans, corn, hay, dairying). Part of Tiadaghton State Forest to N. Laid out 1816, inc. 1852.

Hughson, city (1990 pop. 3,259), Stanislaus co., central Calif., in San Joaquin Valley, 7 mi/11.3 km SE of Modesto, near Tuolumne R. Dairying; polutry; irrigated farming (nuts, vegetables, melons, pumpkins); fruit-growing; mfg. (almond processing, cabinets, machining).

Hughsonville, resort village (1990 pop. 1,400), Dutchess co., SE N.Y., near the Hudson R., 13 mi/21 km S of Poughkeepsie; 41°35′N 73°45′W.

Hugo 1 town (1990 pop. 4,417), Washington co., E Minn., residential suburb 16 mi/26 km NNE of downtown St. Paul; 45°09′N 92°57′W. Mfg. (boring equip., wire forms, plastic molds). White Beard L. to S, numerous small natural lakes in Hugo and vicinity. **2** town (1990 pop. 5,978), ⊙ Choctaw co., SE Okla., c.45 mi/72 km E of Durant, near Red R.; 34°00′N 95°31′W. RR junction; trade center for agr. area (grain, livestock, peanuts). Mfg. (vegetable processing, onions, sportswear); RR shops. Hugo L. reservoir is NE. Inc. 1908.

Hugo, village (1990 pop. 660), ⊙ Lincoln co., E Colo., on Big Sandy Creek and 90 mi/145 km SE of Denver; 39°07′N 103°28′W. Elev. 5,046 ft/1,538 m. Cattle, wheat, sunflowers.

Hugo Lake, reservoir (□ 21 sq mi/54 sq km), Choctaw co., SE Okla., on Kiamichi R., 5 mi/8 km ENE of Hugo; 34°01′N 95°23′W. Max. capacity 1,249,800 acre-ft. Formed by Hugo Dam (101 ft/31 m high), built (1974) by Army Corps of Engineers for flood control; also used for water supply and recreation. Indian Natl. Turnpike just W.

Hugoton (YOO-go-tuhn), town (1990 pop. 3,179), ⊙ Stevens co., SW Kansas, 22 mi/35 km WNW of Liberal; 37°10′N 101°20′W. Elev. 3,107 ft/947 m. Shipping point in Great Plains wheat area; center of a major natural-gas field, with pipelines to NE U.S. Gas distribution. Co. mus. Founded 1885, inc. 1910.

Huguenot Park, a sect. of Staten Isl. borough of N.Y. city, on S Staten Isl., SE N.Y.; 40°32′N 74°12′W.

Huhi (oo-EE), town (1990 pop. 3,666), Yucatán, SE Mexico, 33 mi/53 km SE of Mérida. Henequen, tropical fruit, sugarcane, corn.

Huichapan (wee-CHA-pahn), city (1990 pop. 6,212) and township, ⊙ Huichapan municipio, Hidalgo, central Mexico, on central plateau, 60 mi/97 km WNW of Pachuca de Soto on Mexico Highway 45; 20°22′N 99°38′W. Elev. 6,896 ft/2,102 m. Wine producing. Thermal springs nearby.

Huiloapan, Mexico: see HUILOAPAN DE CUAUHTÉMOC.

Huiloapan de Cuauhtémoc (wee-LO-ah-pahn dai kwou-TE-mok), town (1990 pop. 3,342), W Veracruz, Mexico, 3.1 mi/5 km S of Orizaba. Elev. 4,265 ft/1,300 m. Temperate climate. Agr. (corn, beans, chile, coffee, fruits), woods, cattle and poultry raising.

Huimanguillo (wee-mahn-GWEE-yo), city (1990 pop. 21,536) and township, ⊙ Huimanguillo municipio, Tabasco, SE Mexico, on Grijalva R. (Chiapas border) and 33 mi/53 km WSW of Villahermosa; 17°50′N 93°23′W. Elev. 98 ft/30 m. Important oil production. Agr. center (bananas, tobacco, mangoes, rice, coffee, beans). La Venta archaeological site is nearby.

Huimilpan (wee-MEEL-pahn), town (1990 pop. 2,632), Querétaro, central Mexico, 15 mi/24 km SSE of Querétaro. Elev. 7,382 ft/2,250 m. Grain, sugarcane, alfalfa, vegetables; livestock.

Huiramba (hoo-ee-RAHM-bah), town (1990 pop. 2,402), in central Michoacán, Mexico, 16 mi/25 km from Pátzcuaro. Mountainous with cold climate. Inhabitants are laborers dedicated to forestry and some local crafts. Poor roads.

Huistán, Mexico: see HUIXTÁN.

Huitiupan (wee-tee-OU-pahn), town (1990 pop. 1,875), Chiapas, S Mexico, in N outliers of Sierra Madre, 8 mi/12.9 km NE of Simojovel. A Tzotzil Indian community. Corn, fruit.

Huitzilac (weet-SEE-lak), town (1990 pop. 3,235), Morelos, central Mexico, 8 mi/12.9 km N of Cuernavaca. Wheat, fruit; livestock.

Huitzilan (weet-SEE-lahn), town, (1990 pop. 3,293), ⊙ Huitzilan de Serdán municipio, Puebla, central Mexico, in foothills of Sierra Madre Oriental, 17 mi/27 km E of Zacatlán. Corn, tobacco, sugarcane, fruit. In Totonac Indian area.

Huitzilan de Serdan, Mexico: see HUITZILAN.

Huitziltepec, Mexico: see SANTA CLARA HUITZILTEPEC.

Huitzuco de los Figueroa, Mexico: see CIUDAD HUITZUCO.

Huixquilucan de Degollado (weesh-kee-LOO-kahn de dai-go-YAH-do), town (1990 pop. 6,510), ⊙ Huixquilucan municipio, Mexico state, central Mexico, 14 mi/23 km WSW of Mexico city, and in the Zona Metropolitana de la Ciudad de México.

Huixtán (weesh-TAN), town (1990 pop. 1,447), Chiapas, S Mexico, in Sierra de Hueytepec, 11 mi/18 km E of San Cristóbal de las Casas; 16°43′N 92°03′W. Elev. 6,562 ft/2,000 m. Wheat, fruit. In Tzotzil Maya-speaking area. Formerly Huistán.

Huixtla (WEESH-tlah), city (1990 pop. 24,980) and township, Chiapas, S Mexico, in Pacific lowland, on RR and 23 mi/37 km NW of Tapachula. At junction of Mexico Highways 190 and 200. Trading, processing, and agr. center (coffee, sugarcane, cacao, cotton, fruit; livestock); mfg. (furniture, shoes).

Huizcolotla, Mexico: see SAN SALVADOR HUIXCOLOTLA.

Cross references are shown in SMALL CAPITALS. The pronunciation key is on page xv. The dates of population figures are on page xii.

Hulbert, village (1990 pop. 499), Cherokee co., E Okla., 10 mi/16 km W of Tahlequah, near Neosho R. (Ft. Gibson L. to W); 35°55'N 95°08'W. Mfg. (oil field parts). Sequoyah State Park to W.

Hulett (HYOO-let), village (1990 pop. 429), Crook co., NE Wyo., 22 mi/35 km NW of Sundance, on Belle Fourche R.; 44°41'N 104°35'W. Elev. 3,755 ft/1,145 m. Cattle, sheep; sugar beets, wheat; timber; mfg. (lumber). Bear Lodge Mts. and unit of Black Hills Natl. Forest to SE; Devils Tower Natl. Monument to S; Missouri Buttes to SW.

Huletts Landing, resort village (1990 pop. 200), Washington co., E N.Y., on L. George, 8 mi/12.9 km NW of Whitehall; 43°39'N 73°30'W.

Hull, county (□ 139 sq mi/360 sq km), SW Que., Canada, on Ont. border, on Ottawa R.; ⊙ Hull; 45°40'N 75°35'W.

Hull, city (1991 pop. 60,707), SW Que., Canada, at the confluence of the Ottawa and Gatineau rivers, opposite the city of Ottawa; 45°26'N 75°44'W. Hydroelectric power station; paper, pulp, textile, steel, and lumber mills; iron foundries; cement and meatpacking plants. Hull is a center for service industries and for federal govt. offices. Civil servants form the largest bloc of workers in Hull. Fr. speaking part of Natl. Capital Region. The Can. Mus. of Civilization is in the city. Nearby is Gatineau Park, a large recreation area. Inc. 1875.

Hull 1 town (1990 pop. 156), Madison co., NE Ga., 6 mi/9.7 km NE of Athens; 34°01'N 83°17'W. **2** town (1990 pop. 1,724), Sioux co., NW Iowa, 27 mi/43 km N of Le Mars; 43°11'N 96°07'W. Livestock, grain. Inc. 1888. **3** town (1990 pop. 10,466), Plymouth co., E Mass., on narrow Nantasket Peninsula in Massachusetts Bay, and 10 mi/16 km ESE of Boston; 42°18'N 70°53'W. Summer resort. Settled 1624, inc. 1644. Resort villages include Allerton, Kenberma, NANTASKET BEACH. **4** uninc. town (1990 pop. 1,800), Liberty co., SE Texas, 32 mi/51 km W of Beaumont. In oil, timber, farm area (cattle; rice, soybeans). Big Thicket Natl. Preserve to N and NE.

Hull Mountain (6,873 ft/2,095 m), Lake/Mendocino co. line, NW Calif., 34 mi/55 km N of Lakeport, in the Coast Ranges. In Mendocino Natl. Forest.

Hulmeville (HUHLM-vil), borough (1990 pop. 916), Bucks co., SE Pa., residential suburb 17 mi/27 km NE of downtown Philadelphia and 3 mi/4.8 km WSW of Levittown, on Neshaminy Creek. Light mfg.

Humacao (oo-mah-KOU), town (1990 pop. 55,203), E P.R., 28 mi/45 km SE of San Juan, near the coast. Its port, Playa de Humacao or Punta Santiago is 5 mi/8 km ENE; 18°9'N 65°49'W. Port of entry. Commercial, industrial, tourism center. Sugarcane; mfg. (plastic prods., chemicals, electronics). Resort (Palmas del Mar). Has district and municipal courts. Small airport. Mus. and cultural center here. Univ. of P.R.–Humacao located here.

Humansville, city (1990 pop. 1,084), Polk co., SW central Mo., in the Ozarks. bet. Sac R. and Pomme de Terre R., 15 mi/24 km NW of Bolivar; 37°47'N 93°34'W. Corn, soybeans; cattle; mfg. (boxes).

Humarock, Mass.: see MARSHFIELD.

Humber, river, c.75 mi/120 km long, W N.F., Canada; rising in the Long Mts.; flowing SE then SW, through Deer L., to the Bay of Islands at Corner Brook.

Humbermouth (HUHM-buhr-muhth), village, W N.F., Canada, on Humber R. estuary; 48°58'N 57°55'W. On RR, and 3 mi/5 km E of Corner Brook; lumbering center, agr. market (dairying, cattle raising; potatoes, vegetables).

Humberstone (HUHM-buhr-stuhn), village, S Ont., Canada, on L. Erie, at S end of Welland Ship Canal, opposite Port Colborne. Humberstone Lock, on the canal, is one of world's largest lift locks.

Humbird, village, Clark co., central Wis., 36 mi/58 km SE of Eau Claire, in dairying and farming area. Hay, cheese.

Humble, city (1990 pop. 12,060), Harris co., SE Texas, suburb 17 mi/27 km N of downtown Houston; 29°59'N 95°15'W. Elev. 96 ft/29 m. Bounded N by W Fork San Jacinto R., nearly surrounded by extended Houston city limits. In oil and gas field; mfg. (rubber and plastic components, oil field parts, golf equip., diversified light mfg.). Houston Intercontinental Airport to W; L. Houston reservoir (San Jacinto R.) to E. Founded 1888, inc. 1933. Had oil boom, 1904.

Humboldt 1 county (□ 3,573 sq mi/9,254 sq km; 1990 pop. 119,118), NW Calif., on Pacific coast; ⊙ Eureka; 40°42'N 123°55'W. Humbodlt Bay indents central coastline, bay parallels coast for 18 mi/29 km. Cape Mendocino is westernmost point of Calif. Drained by Klamath, Trinity, Mad, Eel, and Mattole rivers. Mainly in Coast Ranges; includes part of Klamath Mts. in E and NE, King Mt. Range in SW, Rainbow Ridge in W. Six Rivers Natl. Forest in E and NE; Hoopa Valley Indian Reservation in N; Humboldt Bay Natl. Wildlife Refuge in W; part of Redwood Natl. Park in NW; Prairie Creek Redwoods, Dry Lagoon, and Patrick's Point state parks and Trinidad State Beach in NW; Grizzly Creek Redwoods and Humboldt Redwoods state parks in S center; Benbow L. State Recreation Area in S. World's tallest tree (364 ft/111 m) is near Dyerville. Logging (redwood, Douglas fir, cedar, spruce), timber; dairying; cattle, lambs, sheep raising (for Merino wool). Noted recreational area (fishing, camping, hiking, bathing). Salmon; crabs. Some quarrying and mining (sand, gravel, clay, gold, silver). Formed 1853. **2** county (□ 435 sq mi/1,127 sq km; 1990 pop. 10,756), N central Iowa; ⊙ Dakota City; 42°46'N 94°12'W. Prairie agr. area (hogs, cattle, corn, oats, soybeans) drained by Des Moines and East Des Moines rivers. Bituminous-coal deposits, limestone quarries. Winter World ski area to E. Widespread flooding occurred in 1993. Formed 1857. **3** (HUHM-buhlt), county (□ 9,658 sq mi/25,014 sq km; 1990 pop. 12,844), NW Nev.; ⊙ Winnemucca; 41°24'N 118°07'W. Ranching and mining area watered by Quinn, Little Humboldt, and Humboldt rivers and bordering on Oregon, on N; borders Idaho for 1 mi/1.6 km in NE corner. Cattle, sheep; hay, potatoes; silver, copper, gold; sand and gravel, clay. Santa Rosa Range is in NE, in part of Humboldt Natl. Forest. Summit L. Indian Reservation and Lahontan Cutthroat Trout Natural Area are in W part of Black Rock Desert in SW. Formed 1861. Part of Fort Mcdermitt Indian Reservation on Oregon boundary in NE; smaller section in N center of co. Part of Sheldon Natl. Wildlife Refuge in NW. Chimney Dam Reservoir in E.

Humboldt 1 city (1990 pop. 4,438), Humboldt co., N central Iowa, on Des Moines R., near mouth of the East Des Moines, and 15 mi/24 km N of Fort Dodge; 42°43'N 94°13'W. Mfg. (belt conveyors, heating equip., meat prods., steel and plastic fabr., concrete and wood prods., beverages). Limestone quarries, sand pits nearby. Settled 1863, inc. 1869. **2** (HUHM-bolt), city (1990 pop. 9,651), Gibson co., W central Tenn., 75 mi/121 km NW of Memphis; 35°50'N 88°58'W. Livestock, agr. (strawberries, cotton, corn, cabbage). Humboldt also has a nearby state fish hatchery, several granite and marble works, and diverse mfg. including golf balls, yarns, and electric motors. Inc. 1865.

Humboldt (HUHM-bolt), town (1991 pop. 4,989), central Sask., Canada, 65 mi/105 km E of Saskatoon; 52°12'N 105°07'W. Grain elevators. Service center for region. Resort with medicinal springs.

Humboldt 1 (HUHM-bolt), town (1990 pop. 2,178), Allen co., SE Kansas, on Neosho R., and 9 mi/14.5 km N of Chanute; 37°48'N 95°26'W. RR junction. Shipping point in oil and grain region; mfg. of cement prods.; special machinery. Laid out 1857; inc. as village 1866, as city 1870. **2** town (1990 pop. 1,003), Richardson co., extreme SE Nebr., 19 mi/31 km WNW of Falls City and on North Fork of Nemaha R; 40°10'N 95°56'W. Grain; mfg. (apparel, flour, feed). Settled c.1856.

Humboldt 1 village (1990 pop. 470), Coles co., E central Ill., 12 mi/19 km NW of Charleston; 39°36'N 88°19'W. In rich agr. area. **2** village (1990 pop. 74), Kittson co., 12 mi/19 km NW of Hallock, 5 mi/8 km S of Canada (Man.) border, Red R. (N.Dak. state line) 5 mi/8 km to W; 48°55'N 97°05'W. Mfg. (feeds). **3** village (1990 pop. 468), Minnehaha co., E S.Dak., 20 mi/32 km WNW of Sioux Falls; 43°38'N 97°04'W. Chemicals; grain; hogs. L. Vermillion State Rec. Area to SW.

Humboldt (HUHM-buhlt), river, c.300 mi/483 km long, W U.S.; begins at confluences of Mary's and Bishop Creek, c.15 mi/24 km W of Wells, NE Nev.; flows generally WSW, receives North Fork Humboldt from N, flows past Elko, receives South Fork Humboldt from S, then flows past Carlin, Battle Mountain, receives Little Humboldt R. from NE before passing Winnemucca, continues through Rye Patch Reservoir, finally flowing past Lovelock before entering Humboldt Sink; intermittent Humboldt L. in sink; no ocean outlet. Along with its tributaries, the Humboldt drains most of N Nevada. Known to early explorers and named by J. C. Frémont, the river was an important route followed by many of the emigrants from Salt Lake City to central Calif. Its course supplied wagon trains with water and grass. Its length varies with the season, and its volume decreases downstream. It is the longest river in Great Basin, and served to open the way for the 1849 Calif. gold rush. Most of the towns of N Nev. are located on the river in a valley used by Union Pacific and Southern Pacific RRs and interstate highway 80 (replaced U.S. highway 40 in 1970s) as an E-W route. Near Lovelock the Humboldt project of the U.S. Bureau of Reclamation is served by the Rye Patch Dam (completed 1936), which impounds water for irrigation. Forage crops are raised along the river. Upper course, to North Fork, sometimes called East Fork Humboldt. North Fork Humboldt R. rises in N Elko co., joins Humboldt 14 mi/23 km ENE of Elko, flows c.70 mi/113 km SSE. South Fork Humboldt R. rises in NW White Pine co., flows N c.65 mi/105 km through South Fork Reservoir, joins Humboldt 7 mi/11.3 km WSW of Elko.

Humboldt Hill, uninc. town (1990 pop. 2,865), Humboldt co., NW Calif., residential suburb 6 mi/9.7 km SSW of Eureka, at Humboldt Hill, 1 mi/1.6 km E of South Bay of Humboldt Bay. Col. of the Redwoods to S.

Humboldt House, a natl. park, in Taxco de Alarcón, Guerrero, Mexico, on Juan Ruíz de Alarcón. Dating from the 16th cent. While on a scientific journey to S. Amer. and Cuba, Baron von Humboldt spent the night here in April 1803. The Moorish style house has been a convent, hosp., and Taxco's 1st movie theater. It is now the Museo de Arte Virreinal.

Humboldt Peak (14,064 ft/4,287 m), in Sangre de Cristo Mts., Custer co., S Colo.

Humboldt Range (HUHM-buhlt), NW Nev., in Pershing co., extending generally N-S along E Humboldt R., forms Rye Patch Reservoir to NW. Rises to 9,834 ft/2,997 m in Star Peak, at N end. Humboldt Sink is to SW. Gold, silver, diatomite.

Humboldt Salt Marsh (HUHM-buhlt), W Nev., in Churchill co., 45 mi/72 km NE of Fallon; 15 mi/24 km long, 6 mi/9.7 km wide. Fed by Spring Creek from NE and intermittent affluents from Clan Alpine Mts. (E). Carson Sink to W. Separated by Stillwater Range.

Humboldt Sink, Pershing and Churchill cos., W Nev., N of Carson Sink, c.30 mi/48 km N of Fallon; 11 mi/18 km long, max. width 4 mi/6.4 km. Intermittently dry lake bed fed by Humboldt R. from NE; has no outlet. Humboldt L. is body of water at center of sink. Trinity Range to NW. Area protected by Humboldt Wildlife Management Area.

Humbolt, uninc. town (1990 pop. 787), Yavapai co., W central Ariz., 13 mi/21 km ESE of Prescott, on headstream of Aqua Fria R. Elev. 4,980 ft/1,518 m. Cattle, sheep, hay, alfalfa; mfg. (pesticides). Parts of Prescott Natl. Forest to E and W.

Hume, town (1990 pop. 287), Bates co., W Mo., 20 mi/32 km SW of Butler; 38°05'N 94°34'W. Agr.

Hume, village (1990 pop. 406), Edgar co., E Ill., 15 mi/24 km NNW of Paris; 39°47'N 87°52'W. In agr. area; ships grain.

Humeston, town (1990 pop. 553), Wayne co., S Iowa, 11 mi/18 km NW of Corydon; 40°51'N 93°30'W. Livestock, grain.

Hummels Wharf, uninc. town (1990 pop. 1,069), Snyder co., central Pa., residential suburb 3 mi/4.8 km SW of Sunbury on Susquehanna R.; 40°49'N 76°50'W.

Hummelstown (HUH-muhls-toun), borough (1990 pop. 3,981), Dauphin co., S central Pa., 9 mi/14.5 km E of Harrisburg and 3 mi/4.8 km W of Hershey, on Swatara Creek. Mfg. (food prods., asphalt, machinery). Agr. area (apples, soybeans, grain; poultry, livestock, dairying). Indian Echo Caverns to S. Founded c.1740, laid out 1762, inc. 1874.

Humnoke (HUHM-nok), village (1990 pop. 311), Lonoke co., central Ark., 12 mi/19 km WNW of Stuttgart; 34°32′N 91°45′W.

Humphrey, town (1990 pop. 743), Jefferson and Arkansas cos., central Ark., 21 mi/34 km NE of Pine Bluff; 34°25′N 91°42′W. Bayou Meto Wildlife Management Area to S.

Humphrey, village (1990 pop. 741), Platte co., E Nebr., 19 mi/31 km NNW of Columbus and on branch of Elkhorn R; 41°41′N 97°29′W. Grain.

Humphreys 1 (HUHM-freez), county (□ 431 sq mi/ 1,116 sq km; 1990 pop. 12,134), W Miss.; ☉ Belzoni, 33°07′N 90°31′W. Bounded partly W in part by Sunflower R., Tchula Lake Creek forms part of E boundary; drained by Yazoo R. (forms part of boundary in NE and SE) and tributaries. Agr. (cotton, corn, rice, soybeans, wheat; cattle, catfish; timber). Formed 1918. **2** county (□ 555 sq mi/1,437 sq km; 1990 pop. 15,795), central Tenn.; ☉ Waverly; 36°02′N 87°46′W. Bounded W by Tennessee R.; drained by Duck and Buffalo rivers. Includes part of Kentucky Reservoir Timber; livestock raising, dairying, agr. (corn, soybeans, tomatoes). Formed 1809.

Humphreys, town (1990 pop. 98), Sullivan co., N Mo., 12 mi/19 km SW of Milan; 40°07′N 93°19′W. Cattle; corn, soybeans.

Humphreys, Fort, Va.: see BELVOIR, FORT.

Humphreys, Mount (13,986 ft/4,263 m), E Calif., in the Sierra Nevada, on Fresno-Inyo co. line, 17 mi/27 km WSW of Bishop.

Humphreys Peak (12,643 ft/3,854 m), Coconino co., N Ariz., 10 mi/16 km N of Flagstaff, in San Francisco Mts., in Coconino Natl. Forest. On rim of eroded volcano; highest point in Ariz. Ariz. Snowbowl Ski Area to SW.

Humptulips River (huhmp-TOO-lips), SW Wash.; formed 18 mi/29 km N of Hoquiam by W (c.30 mi/ 48 km long) and E forks (c.20 mi/32 km long) both rising in Olympic Natl. Forest; flows c.20 mi/32 km SW to Grays Harbor, 8 mi/12.9 km NW of Hoquiam.

Hundred, village (1990 pop. 386), Wetzel co., N W.Va., 22 mi/35 km E of New Martinsville, near Pa. state line; 39°40′N 80°27′W. Oil, natural gas, and agr. area. Fish Creek Covered Bridge (1881).

Hundred and Two River, Iowa and Mo.: see ONE HUNDRED AND TWO RIVER.

Hungry Horse, town (1990 pop. 940), Flathead co., NW Mont., on Flathead R. at mouth of South Fork Flathead R. Tourism, mfg. (jams and jellies). Hungry Horse Dam and Reservoir to SE (on South Fork), and 17 mi/ 27 km NE of Kalispell.

Hungry Horse Reservoir, Flathead co., NW Mont., on S. Fork Flathead R., in Flathead Natl. Forest, 20 mi/ 32 km NE of Kalispell; c.35 mi/56 km long; 48°21′N 114°01′W. Formed by Hungry Horse Dam (564 ft/172 m high, 2,115 ft/645 m long), built (1948–1953) as unit in Columbia River Basin project for power generation, flood control, and irrigation.

Hunker, borough (1990 pop. 328), Westmoreland co., SW central Pa., 8 mi/12.9 km SSW of Greensburg, on Sewickley Creek. Agr. (apples, corn, dairying).

Hunnewell (HUHN-nee-wel), city (1990 pop. 219), Shelby co., NE Mo., near Salt R., 7 mi/11.3 km W of Monroe City; 39°40′N 91°51′W. Soybeans, corn; cattle, hogs. Hunnewell L. to NW.

Hunnewell (HUHN-ee-wel), village (1990 pop. 87), Sumner co., S Kansas, at Okla. state line, 16 mi/26 km S of Wellington; 37°00′N 97°24′W. In wheat area.

Hunt, county (□ 882 sq mi/2,284 sq km; 1990 pop. 64,343), NE Texas; ☉ Greenville;33°07′N 96°05′W. Rich blackland prairie in W and NW; timbered in E; drained by Sabine R. (forms L. Tawakoni in SE corner) and S Fork of Sulphur R. Agr. (especially cotton; hay, nursery crops; wheat); dairying; cattle, horses. Some oil and gas production; sand and rock. Mfg., processing at Greenville and Commerce. Part of L. Tawakoni State Park on S boundary. Formed 1846.

Hunt, uninc. village (1990 pop. 708), Kerr co., SW Texas, 14 mi/23 km WNW of Kerrville, on Guadalupe R. (source to W). Ranching area (cattle, sheep, goats); wheat, pecans.

Hunt, Mount (9,000 ft/2,743 m), SE Yukon, Canada, near N.W.T. border, in Mackenzie Mts.; 61°28′N 129°14′W.

Hunt River, c.8 mi/12.9 km long, S central R.I.; rises NE of Exeter; flows SE, then NE, bet. East Greenwich and North Kingstown towns, to Narragansett Bay SE of East Greenwich village. Called Potowomut R. in lower course, where it is S boundary of Potowomut Peninsula.

Hunter 1 village (1990 pop. 137), Woodruff co., E central Ark., 20 mi/32 km W of Forrest City; 35°02′N 91°07′W. **2** village (1990 pop. 116), Mitchell co., N central Kansas, 18 mi/29 km SW of Beloit; 39°14′N 98°24′W. Home of Veras. Grain, livestock. Oil. **3** resort village (□ 1 sq mi/ 2.6 sq km; 1990 pop. 429), Greene co., SE N.Y., in the Catskills, on Schoharie Creek and 17 mi/27 km W of Catskill; 42°12′N 74°13′W. **4** village (1990 pop. 218), Garfield co., N Okla., 16 mi/26 km NE of Enid; 36°33′N 97°39′W. In grain and livestock area.

Hunter, uninc. community, Carter co., S Mo., in the Ozarks, near Current R., c.12 mi/19 km SE of Van Buren, Ozark Natl. Scenic Riverways canoe access to W.

Hunter Air Field, Ga., in Savannah, Chatham co. Home of Natl. Guard air unit, adjacent to the Savannah airport.

Hunter Island 1 tract of land in NW Ont., Canada, extending N from Minn. border, 100 mi/161 km W of Fort William; 50 mi/80 km long, 30 mi/48 km wide. Region of small lakes and streams, flowing into Rainy R. **2** (□ 129 sq mi/334 sq km), SW B.C., Canada, in NE part of Queen Charlotte Sound, 6 mi/10 km S of Bella Bella; 21 mi/34 km long, 3 mi/5 km–10 mi/16 km wide; 51°55′N 128°05′W. Rises to 2,950 ft/899 m.

Hunter Liggett Military Reservation, Calif.: see JOLON.

Hunter, Mount (14,573 ft/4,442 m), S central Alaska, in Alaska Range, in Mt. McKinley Natl. Park, 130 mi/ 209 km NNW of Anchorage; 62°57′N 151°05′W.

Hunter Mountain (4,025 ft/1,227 m), Greene co., SE N.Y., in Catskill Mts., 19 mi/31 km W of Catskill; 42°10′N 74°14′W. Skiing resort.

Hunter River, village (1991 pop. 356), central P.E.I., Canada, on Hunter R. and 15 mi/24 km WNW of Charlottetown; 46°21′N 63°21′W. Mixed farming, dairying; potatoes.

Hunterdon, county (□ 437 sq mi/1,132 sq km; 1990 pop. 107,776), W N.J., bounded W by Delaware R.; ☉ Flemington; 40°34′N 74°52′W. Agr. area (poultry, produce, corn, grain, fruit, dairy prods.) that is rapidly suburbanizing as an outer suburb; mfg. (food prods., paper, printing, publishing, chemicals, plastics prods., metal prods., electronic equip., measuring and controlling devices). Includes Voorhees State Park. Drained by the Musconetcong R. and by South Branch of Raritan R. Musconetcong Mt. is in W. Co. formed 1714.

Hunter's Creek Village, town (1990 pop. 3,954), Harris co., SE Texas, residential suburb 8 mi/12.9 km W of downtown Houston, bounded S by Buffalo Bayou. Surrounded by city of Houston.

Hunter's Island, N.Y.: see PELHAM BAY PARK.

Huntersville, town (1990 pop. 3,014), Mecklenburg co., S N.C., 12 mi/19 km N of Charlotte; 35°25′N 80°50′W. Tobacco, grain, soybeans; livestock. Mfg. (materials handling equip., surgical blades, robotic machinery, hardwood prods., electronic control panels). Energy Explorium, hands-on mus. at dam. Cowans Ford Dam, on Catawba R., to W, forms L. Norman reservoir to NW, Mountain Island L. reservoir (Catawba R.) to SW.

Huntertown, town (1990 pop. 1,330), Allen co., NE Ind., 9 mi/14.5 km N of Fort Wayne, near source of Eel R.; 41°14′N 85°10′W. Mfg. (machinery, asphalt). Corn, soybeans. Settled 1830s.

Hunting Island, Beaufort co., S S.C., one of Sea Isls., just E of St. Helena Isl., to which it is connected by highway bridge; c.5 mi/8 km long. Huntington Isl. State Park (c.5,000 acres/2,024 ha), resort colony, and wildlife sanctuary here.

Hunting Valley, village (1990 pop. 799), on Cuyahoga-Geauga co. line, N Ohio, an E suburb of Cleveland; 41°28′N 81°24′W.

Huntingburg, city (1990 pop. 5,242), Dubois co., SW Ind., 6 mi/9.7 km S of Jasper; 38°18′N 86°58′W. Agr. area (grain, poultry, strawberries; livestock; dairy prods.); mfg. (carbide cutting tools, furniture and wood prods., packed meat, turkey prods.); clay and limestone. RR junction. Founded 1839.

Huntingdon, county (□ 361 sq mi/935 sq km; pop.), S Que., Canada, on Ont. and N.Y. borders, on the St. Lawrence; ☉ Huntingdon; 45°02′N 74°05′W.

Huntingdon, county (□ 890 sq mi/2,305 sq km; 1990 pop. 44,164), S central Pa.; ☉ Huntingdon. Hilly region, drained by Juniata R. and Raystown Branch Juniata R. (forms large Raystown L. reservoir in SW). Crossed by several ridges (NNE-SSW angles): Bald Eagle Mt. (NW boundary); Tussey Mt. (SW boundary); Jacks Mt. (partly on NE boundary); Blacklog Mt., Shade Mt., Tuscarora Mt. (SE boundary). Clay, bituminous coal, glass sand; mfg. at Huntingdon and Mt. Union. Agr. (corn, wheat, oats, hay, alfalfa; poultry, hogs, cattle, dairying). Parts of Rothrock State Forest in NE, N, and center; Lincoln Caverns in W; Trough Creek State Park in SW; Greenwood Furnace and Whipple Dam State Parks in NE. Formed 1787.

Huntingdon, town (1991 pop. 2,859), ☉ Huntingdon co., S Que., Canada, on Châteauguay R. and 40 mi/64 km SW of Montreal, near N.Y. border; 45°05′N 74°11′W. Milling, lumbering, dairying.

Huntingdon, town (1990 pop. 4,180), ☉ Carroll co., NW Tenn., 34 mi/55 km NE of Jackson; 36°00′N 88°24′W. In agr. area (cotton, grain, sweet potatoes, tomatoes); lumber and clay area. Settled and inc. 1821.

Huntingdon, village, SW B.C., Canada, on Wash. border, 1 mi/1.6 km S of Abbotsford, and 10 mi/16 km S of Mission; 49°00′N 122°16′W. Dairying; cattle, fruit, hops.

Huntingdon, borough (1990 pop. 6,843), ☉ Huntingdon co., S central Pa., 21 mi/34 km E of Altoona, on Juniata R. Mfg. (fabricated metal prods., electronic connectors, printing and publishing, wood prods., vinyl wallets, glass fiber yarns, canvas footwear); glass sand; timber. Juniata Col.; Lincoln Caverns are W; Trough Creek State Park to S; large Raystown Reservoir to S, on Raystown Branch Juniata R.; parts of Rothrock State Forest to N and S, including Pa. State Univ. Experimental Forest to NE; Whipple Dam and Greenwood Furnace state parks to NE. Settled c.1755, laid out 1767, inc. 1796.

Huntingdon Valley, uninc. village, Montgomery co., SE Pa., industrial suburb 12 mi/19 km NNE of Philadelphia; 40°07′N 75°03′W. Mfg. includes industrial equip., machinery, chemicals, tool and die, apparel, commercial printing.

Huntington, county (□ 387 sq mi/1,002 sq km; 1990 pop. 35,427), NE central Ind.; ☉ Huntington. Agr. area (corn, soybeans, vegetables; poultry, hogs, cattle; dairy prods.). Diversified mfg. at Huntington. Limestone quarrying; timber. Drained by Wabash, Salamonie, and Little Wabash rivers, and by small Clear Creek. Huntington Reservoir and Little Turtle State Recreation Area SE of Huntington; Salamonie Reservoir, with Lost Bridge State Recreation Area in SE. Formed 1832.

Huntington 1 city (1990 pop. 16,389), ☉ Huntington co., NE Ind.; 40°53′N 85°31′W. It is a farm trade center and an industrial city. Mfg. (automotive parts, machinery, construction material, food and beverages, cleaning agents, fireplaces, electrical equip., rubber, plastic; printing, packaging). The city is the seat of Huntington Col. The Wabash R. and its forks were a Native Amer. gathering place and early trade center. Settled 1831, inc. 1848. **2** city (1990 pop. 1,875), Emery co., central Utah, 20 mi/32 km SSW of Price, on Huntington Creek; 39°19′N 110°57′W. Elev. 5,791 ft/1,765 m. Alfalfa; cattle; coal mining. Power plant. Huntington L. (not on creek) and State Park to NE. Manti–La Sal Natl. Forest to W; Electric L. to NW. Settled 1878, inc. 1891. **3** city (1990 pop. 54,844), ⊙ Cabell co., in Cabell and Wayne cos., W W.Va., 45 mi/72 km W of Charleston, 10 mi/16 km ESE of Ashland Ky., on the Ohio R. (bridged to Ohio), at mouth of Guyandotte R.; 38°24′N 82°25′W. Elev. c.550 ft/168 m. The 2d-largest city in state (pop. over 70,000 in 1970, city has lost pop. at a faster rate than Charleston, falling to 2d place). Commercial (wholesale and market) and mfg. center for deep and surface bituminous coal; oil; natural gas. Farm (esp. tobacco, fruit) region. Important RR city (huge repair shops); river port (ships coal). Tri-State Airport (Walker Long Field) to W. Industries include reduction and fabrication of nickel alloys; mfg. (transportation equip., glass, furniture, wood prods., chemicals (dyes), plastics, lubricating oils, electrical goods, metal goods, industrial machine parts, flour and other foods, beverages, packaging, printing and publishing). Marshall Univ. State institutions here include industrial school for girls, hosp. for the insane, children's home. RR mus.; Antique Radio Mus.; Huntington Mus. of Art; Camden Park, turn-of-cent. amusement park with wooden roller coaster, to W. Along river here is 11 mi/18 km flood wall. Wayne Natl. Forest (Ohio) to N; Beech Fork State Park and Beech Fork L. Wildlife Management Area to S. City founded 1871 as W terminus of Chesapeake & Ohio RR.

Huntington 1 town (□ 137 sq mi/355 sq km; 1990 pop. 191,474), Suffolk co., SE N.Y., on N shore of L.I.; 40°53′N 73°22′W. Chiefly residential heart of township containing 17 contiguous communities, noted for their precision mfg. Numerous harbors and boatyards; major retailing center. Seat of Immaculate Conception Col., World Friends Col. Settled 1653. **2** town (1990 pop. 1,794), Angelina co., E Texas, 10 mi/16 km ESE of Lufkin, near Angelina R.; 31°16′N 94°34′W. In pine timber; poultry, cattle area. Recreation. Inc. 1938. **3** town (1990 pop. 1,069), Chittenden co., NW Vt., on small Huntington R. and 17 mi/27 km SE of Burlington; woodworking, dairy prods.; 44°17′N 72°57′W. Includes part of Camels Hump State Forest, with cross-country ski centers. **4** uninc. town, Fairfax co., NE Va., residential suburb, 1 mi/1.6 km SW of Alexandria, 7 mi/11.3 km S of Washington, D.C., on Cameron Run creek at its entrance to Potomac R.; 38°47′N 77°04′W. Woodrow Wilson Memorial Bridge to E. S terminus of Washington Metro (subway) yellow line.

Huntington 1 village (1990 pop. 715), Sebastian co., W Ark., 22 mi/35 km SSE of Fort Smith; 35°04′N 94°16′W. In agr. area; mfg. (concrete septic tanks). **2** village (1990 pop. 522), Baker co., E Oregon, 25 mi/40 km N of Vale, on Burnt R., near its confluence with the Snake R. to E; 44°21′N 117°16′W. Elev. 2,113 ft/644 m. Agr. (wheat, barley, oats, potatoes; sheep, cattle); dairy prods. Farewell Bend State Park to SE.

Huntington Bay, residential village, Suffolk co. (□ 2 sq mi/5.2 sq km; 1990 pop. 1,521), SE N.Y., on N shore of L.I., on inlet of Huntington Bay, just NE of Huntington; 40°54′N 73°25′W. Site of capture of Nathan Hale by Br. forces during Amer. Revolution.

Huntington Bay, an arm of L.I. Sound, SE N.Y., indenting N shore of L.I. N of Huntington, which is at head of Huntington Harbor (c.2 mi/3.2 km long), bay's S arm; 40°55′N 73°25′W. It is c.4.5 mi/7.2 km wide at entrance bet. Lloyd Point (W) and Eatons Neck Point (E); 3.5 mi/5.6 km long. Northport Bay and Centerport Harbor connect with Huntington Bay on SE, Lloyd Harbor adjoins on W.

Huntington Beach, city (1990 pop. 181,519), Orange co., S Calif., suburb 26 mi/42 km SSE of downtown Los Angeles and 10 mi/16 km ESE of Long Beach, on the Pacific Ocean coast. In an oil producing area. It has aerospace vehicles, aircraft parts, optical instruments, and heat transfer equipment industries. The city's pop. increased 3,366% bet. 1950 and 1990 and is still rapidly climbing. Such growth is due to migration from central city and to the major high-technology, aircraft, and oil industries that have continued to develop in the area. The city has long been known for its fine beaches and has become one of the surfing capitals of S California. Golden West Col. (2-year) is located in Huntington Beach. Meadowland Airport in W. Sunset Bay (Huntington Harbor) in W, marina with man-made residential islands and coves (former marsh); Sunset Beach bet. bay and ocean; Bolsa Chica State Beach in SW, with Bolsa Bay marsh behind beach, Huntington State Beach in Costa Mesa to S. Seal beach U.S. Naval Weapons Station to NW, Los Alamitos Naval Air Station to N. Inc. 1909.

Huntington Harbor, N.Y.: see HUNTINGTON BAY, inlet.

Huntington Lake, reservoir, Fresno co., E central Calif., on Big Creek, in the Sierra Nevada Mts., 45 mi/72 km NE of Fresno; 6 mi/9.7 km long; 37°14′N 119°11′W. Formed by Huntington L. Dam (165 ft/50 m high, 1,310 ft/399 m long), built (1917) for power generation. Receives water through tunnel from Florence L. (12 mi/19 km E); tunnel diverts water to Shaver L. (7 mi/11.3 km SSW). Lakeshore village on NE shore.

Huntington Lake, Huntington Co., NE central Ind., on Wabash R., in Little Turtle State Recreation Area, 3 mi/4.8 km SE of Huntington; 6 mi/9.7 km long; 40°50′N 85°28′W. Max. capacity 153,100 acre-ft. Formed by Huntington Dam (89 ft/27 m high), built (1968) by the Army Corps of Engineers for flood control.

Huntington Park, city (1990 pop. 56,065), Los Angeles co., S Calif., a residential and industrial suburb 4 mi/6.4 km S of downtown Los Angeles. Varied mfg. includes metal fabrication and processing, glass, rubber prods., industrial equip.). Los Angeles R. to E and N. Founded 1856, inc. 1906.

Huntington Station, uninc. town (□ 5 sq mi/13 sq km; 1990 pop. 28,247), Suffolk co., SE N.Y., on N shore of L.I.; 40°50′N 73°24′W. Diverse mfg. base. Popular vacation and fishing area on L.I.'s N shore nearby. Walt Whitman b. here.

Huntington Woods, city (1990 pop. 6,419), Oakland co., SE Mich., residential suburb 12 mi/19 km NW of downtown Detroit; 42°28′N 83°10′W. Detroit Zoological Park in SE part of city. Inc. as village 1926, as city 1932.

Huntland, town (1990 pop. 885), Franklin co., S Tenn., near Ala. line, 13 mi/21 km, SW of Winchester; 35°03′N 86°16′W.

Huntleigh (HUHNT-lee), village (1990 pop. 392), St. Louis co., E Mo., residential suburb 12 mi/19 km W of downtown St. Louis; 38°36′N 90°24′W.

Huntley 1 village (1990 pop. 2,453), McHenry and Kane cos., NE Ill., 11 mi/18 km NW of Elgin; 42°10′N 88°25′W. In dairying area. Summer resorts nearby. **2** village (1990 pop. 300), Yellowstone co., S Mont., on Yellowstone R at mouth of Pryor Creek, and 12 mi/19 km NE of Billings. RR junction. Huntley Irrigation Project was the first one completed in Montana, 1907. Huntley Project Mus. of Irrigated Agr. Agr. research center to E. **3** village (1990 pop. 58), Harlan co., S Nebr., 9 mi/14.5 km NNE of Alma and on branch of Republican R; 40°12′N 99°17′W.

Hunts Peak (13,067 ft/3,983 m), S central Colo., in N tip of Sangre de Cristo Mts., bet. Fremont and Saguache cos.

Hunt's Point, a residential, wholesale, and industrial sect. of S Bronx borough of N.Y. city, SE N.Y., at confluence of Bronx and East rivers; 40°49′N 73°54′W. Site of N.Y. city's major produce market.

Huntsdale, uninc. town, Boone co., central Mo., on Missouri R. and 8 mi/12.9 km W of Columbia.

Huntsville 1 city (1990 pop. 159,789), seat of Madison co., N Ala. A major center for U.S. space research, Huntsville is the site of the Redstone Arsenal, the U.S. army's control and procurement center for guided missiles and rockets, NASA's George C. Marshall Space Flight Center (est. 1960), and the U.S. Space and Rocket Center (home of Space Camp). Although Huntsville's economy centers around the aerospace and high-technology industries, tires, glass, machinery, electrical, copper tubing, and computer equip. are also produced. The constitutional convention of the Ala. Territory was held in 1819 in Huntsville, where the 1st state legislature met. Numerous antebellum buildings remain. Huntsville is the seat of Oakwood Col., Ala. Agricultural and Mechanical Univ., and the Univ. of Ala. at Huntsville. Monte Sano State Park nearby. Inc. 1811. **2** city (1990 pop. 1,567), ⊙ Randolph co., N central Mo., 5 mi/8 km W of Moberly; 39°26′N 92°32′W. Corn, soybeans; crushed stone; limestone quarries; former extensive coal mines. Founded c.1830. **3** city (1990 pop. 27,925), ⊙ Walker co., E central Texas; 30°42′N 95°32′W. Elev. 401 ft/122 m. Located in a pine area, with sawmills. Farming along with agr. and livestock trading add to the city's economic base; mfg. (mirrors, signs, printing, oil and gas field equip., lumber). Huntsville, the home of Samuel Houston, contains his grave (with an impressive monument; tallest free-standing statue in U.S.), his restored home, and other memorials. Also in the city are Sam Houston State Univ. and the Texas Dept. of Criminal Justice, Institutional Division; hq. and prison (U.S. most active execution chamber). An annual rodeo held by the prisoners draws many spectators. Sam Houston Natl. Forest to S and E; Huntsville State Park to S. Inc. 1845.

Huntsville, town (1991 pop. 14,997), SE Ont., Canada, on the Muskoka R.; 45°20′N 79°13′W. Lumber mills and a woodworking plant; main economic base is year-round tourist trade.

Huntsville 1 town (1990 pop. 159,789), ⊙ Madison co., NW Ark., 24 mi/39 km E of Fayetteville, in the Ozarks; 34°42′N 86°37′W. Mfg. (processed turkey, printed circuit assemblies). Withrow State Park and Madison Co. Wildlife Management Area to N. **2** town (1990 pop. 660), ⊙ Scott co., N Tenn., 45 mi/72 km NW of Knoxville; 36°25′N 84°29′W. Lumbering; oil deposits.

Huntsville 1 village (1990 pop. 343), Logan co., W central Ohio, 6 mi/10 km NNW of Bellefontaine, in agr. area; 40°26′N 83°48′W. **2** village (1990 pop. 561), Weber co., N Utah, 9 mi/14.5 km E of Ogden, in Wasatch Range; 41°15′N 111°46′W. Elev. 4,920 ft/1,500 m. Ogden R. Canyon to W. Wasatch Natl. Forest surrounds area except NW. Located on East Fork Arm of Pineview Reservoir. Ski resort area: Snow Basin to SW, Nordic Valley to NW, Powder Mt. to N. Trappist Monastery to SE. Tourism.

Hunucmá (oo-nook-MAH), town (1990 pop. 17,459), ⊙ Hunucmá municipio, Yucatán, SE Mexico, 16 mi/26 km W of Mérida; elev. 16 ft/5 m; 21°01′N 89°52′W. Henequen, tropical fruit, citrus, corn, beans; livestock.

Hurdland, town (1990 pop. 212), Knox co., NE Mo., near North Fork of Salt R., 7 mi/11.3 km W of Edina; 40°08′N 92°17′W. Agr.

Hurdsfield, village (1990 pop. 92), Wells co., central N. Dak., 20 mi/32 km SW of Fessenden; 47°27′N 99°55′W.

Hurley 1 town (1990 pop. 1,534), Grant co., SW N.Mex., in W foothills of Pinos Altos Mts., 15 mi/24 km SE of Silver City; 32°42′N 108°07′W. Elev. 5,720 ft/1,743 m. Cattle, some sheep, alfalfa, grain. Silver City–Grant Airport to S; Gila Natl. Forest is N; City of Rocks State Park to SE; Santa Rita Open Pit Copper Mine to NE. **2** town (1990 pop. 1,782), ⊙ Iron co., N Wis., on Montreal R., opposite Ironwood, Mich., in Gogebic Range; 46°26′N 90°12′W. Mfg. (carbonated beverages). It was a boom town (mining, lumbering) until c.1910. Founded 1885, inc. 1918.

Hurley 1 village (□ 5 sq mi/13 sq km; 1990 pop. 4,644), Ulster co., SE N.Y., just W of Kingston; 41°54′N 74°03′W. In agr. and summer-resort area. **2** village (1990 pop. 372), Turner co., SE S.Dak., 8 mi/12.9 km S of Parker; 43°16′N 97°05′W.

Hurleyville, resort village (1990 pop. 750), Sullivan co., SE N.Y., 6 mi/9.7 km N of Monticello; 41°45′N 74°40′W.

Hurlock (HER-lok), town (1990 pop. 1,706), Dorchester co., E Md., on Delmarva Peninsula, 13 mi/21 km ENE of Cambridge; 38°38′N 75°52′W. Vegetable processing center, but also has tin can and shirt factories. Named after John M. Hurlock, who erected the 1st store in 1869 and 1st home in 1872. Hurlock is said to have won the right to name the town after himself in a tree-felling contest with another land owner.

Huron (HYOO-ruhn), county (□ 1,245 sq mi/3,225 sq km; 1991 pop. 59,065), S Ont., Canada, on L. Huron; ⊙ Goderich; 43°40′N 81°30′W.

Huron 1 county (□ 2,136 sq mi/5,532 sq km; 1990 pop.

34,951), E Mich.; ⊙ Bad Axe; 43°57′N 82°50′W; at tip of the "thumb," in S L. Huron. Bounded E and N by L. Huron; W by Saginaw Bay (numerous isls. off Saginaw Bay shores). Drained by headwaters of the Cass and by small Pigeon and Willow rivers. Poultry; cattle, hogs; dairy prods.; agr. (beans, sugar beets, corn, wheat); mfg. (plastics prods., metal prods., industrial machinery); resorts on L. Anson. Albert E. Sleeper State Park and Port Crescent State Park in N. Organized 1859. **2** county (□ 497 sq mi/1,287 sq km; 1990 pop. 56,240), N Ohio; ⊙ Norwalk, 41°09′N 82°33′W. Drained by Huron and Vermilion rivers. In the Lake and Till Plains physiographic region. Agr. area (nursery and greenhouse crops, sheep, corn, vegetables); mfg. at Bellevue, Norwalk, New London (bakery prods., household furniture, farm and garden machinery); gravel pits. Formed 1815.

Huron 1 city (1990 pop. 4,766), Fresno co., central Calif., 40 mi/64 km SSW of Fresno, in San Joaquin Valley. Kettleman Hills to S; Black Mt. to W. California Aqueduct passes to E. Irrigated agr. area (cotton, grain, fruit, vegetables, dairying, cattle). Lemoore naval air station to E. **2** city (1990 pop. 7,030), Erie co., N Ohio, on harbor on L. Erie, at mouth of Huron R., 10 mi/16 km ESE of Sandusky; 41°23′N 82°34′W. Fishing; coal and iron ore transshipping; tourist resort. Makes cement blocks, boats, sauerkraut, pickles. Settled c.1805. **3** city (1990 pop. 12,448), ⊙ Beadle co., E central S.Dak., on the James R.; inc. 1883. A shipping and trade center for a large livestock and grain area, it has meatpacking, lumbering, and tourism industries. It is also the administrative center for a number of state and Federal agencies. Huron was the hometown of Hubert Humphrey. The city is the seat of Huron Univ. The S.Dak. State Fair is held annually in Huron. Mfg. (asphalt, pork processing, mining equip., concrete, capacitor banks, security doors). James R. and Lake Byron State Lakeside Use Areas to N; state fairgrounds; Pioneer Mus.; RR junction.

Huron (HYOR-ahn), village (1990 pop. 75), Atchison co., extreme NE Kansas, 13 mi/21 km WNW of Atchison, in corn belt; 39°38′N 95°20′W. RR junction to N. Atchison State Fishing L. to E.

Huron Bay, Mich., narrow inlet of L. Superior indenting N shore of Upper Peninsula, c.20 mi/32 km SE of Houghton and just E of Keweenaw Bay, from which it is separated by narrow peninsula (c.18 mi/29 km long) terminating in Point Abbaye; 46°53′N 88°13′W.

Huron, Lake (□ 23,010 sq mi/59,596 sq km), bet. Ont., Canada, and Mich.; 206 mi/332 km long and 183 mi/295 km at its greatest width; 2d-largest of the GREAT LAKES. It has a surface elev. of 580 ft/177 m (177 m) above sea level and a max. depth of 750 ft/229 m. Centrally located bet. the upper and lower Great Lakes, L. Huron receives the waters of L. Superior through the St. Marys R. and those of L. Michigan through the Straits of Mackinac; it drains into L. Erie through the St. Clair R.–L. St. Clair–Detroit R. system. Large tributaries flowing into the lake include the Mississagi, Wanapitei, Spanish, and French rivers from Ont., and the Au Sable and Saginaw rivers from Mich. The N shoreline is irregular, with many bays and inlets; the largest are Georgian Bay and North Channel, which indent the Ont. shore and are nearly landlocked by Manitoulin Isl. and the Bruce Peninsula. Saginaw Bay is the principal indentation on the S shores. L. Huron is part of the Great Lakes–St. Lawrence Seaway system and is navigated by oceangoing and lake vessels that carry cargoes of iron ore, grain, coal, limestone, and other goods. Navigation is impeded by ice in the shallower sections from mid-Dec. to early April. The lake is subject to occasional violent storms. The principal lakeshore cities are Port Huron, Mich., and Sarnia, Ont., at the lake's outlet; Owen Sound, Midland, and Parry Sound, Ont.; and Bay City, Alpena, and Cheboygan, Mich. The waters of the lake are relatively unpolluted; commercial and sport fishing is important, and several resorts are located along the lake shore. Major salt deposits are worked at the S end of the lake. Georgian Bay, an arm of the lake, is a popular resort area, and recreational facilities are provided at Georgian Bay Isls. Natl. Park (Canada), on the isl. in Mackinac Strait, and at numerous state and provincial parks along the lake's scenic shores. Samuel de Champlain visited L. Huron in 1615.

Huron Mountains (c.1,500 ft/457 m–1,800 ft/549 m), granitic range in NW Marquette and NE Baraga cos., Upper Peninsula, Mich., extending c.20 mi/32 km NW-SE near S shore of L. Superior; 46°50′N 87°55′W. Wilderness recreational region, with lakes (Independence; Ives, Mountain). Mt. Avron (1,979 ft/603 m), highest point in Mich., in W in Avron Hills.

Huron River 1 c.97 mi/156 km long, SE Mich.; rises in small lakes in Oakland and Livingston cos.; flows SW and S to Dexter, then SE, past Ann Arbor and Ypsilanti, through Ford and Belleville lakes, then past Belleville and Flat Rock to L. Erie, SE of Rockwood; 46°51′N 88°04′W. Utilized for power. In SW part of Detroit metropolitan area. **2** c.11 mi/18 km long, N Ohio, formed by East and West branches in S Erie co.; flows N to L. Erie at Huron. East Branch rises in Huron co., flows c.32 mi/51 km N. West Branch rises near Shiloh, flows c.38 mi/61 km N, past Monroeville, to union with East Branch.

Hurricane 1 (HUHR-i-kuhn), town (1990 pop. 3,915), Washington co., SW Utah, near Virgin R., 17 mi/27 km ENE of St. George; 37°09′N 113°20′W. In fruit area; mfg. (apparel). Copper mining. Settled 1906. Dixie Natl. Forest to NW; Quail Creek Reservoir and State Park to W; Zion Natl. Park to E. **2** town (1990 pop. 4,461), Putnam co., W central W.Va., 22 mi/35 km W of Charleston; 38°26′N 82°01′W. Coal-mining area. Agr. (corn, tobacco); livestock; poultry. Mfg. (truck equip. parts, clothing, machining). Inc. 1888.

Hurricane Creek, Ark.: see BAUXITE.

Hurricane Island, Knox co., S Maine, in Penobscot Bay, 3 mi/4.8 km WSW of Vinalhaven village, Vinalhaven Isl.; 8/10 mi/1.2 km long.

Hurricane Mountain (3,687 ft/1,124 m), Essex co., NE N.Y., in High Peaks sect. of Adirondack Mts., 12 mi/19 km NE of Mt. Marcy and 13 mi/21 km ESE of L. Placid village; 44°14′N 73°44′W.

Hurst 1 city (1990 pop. 842), Williamson co., S Ill., 14 mi/23 km NW of Marion; 37°50′N 89°08′W. In bituminous coal-mining and agr. area. **2** city (1990 pop. 33,574), Tarrant co., N Texas, suburb 8 mi/12.9 km NE of downtown Fort Worth; 32°50′N 97°10′W. Mfg. (helicopters, helicopter components, aviation parts, draperies and bedspreads). Seat of Tarrant Co. Junior Col. NE Campus. Dallas–Fort Worth Internatl. Airport to NE.

Hurstbourne (HUHRST-born), town (1990 pop. 4,420), Jefferson co., N Ky., residential suburb 9 mi/14.5 km E of downtown Louisville.

Hurstville, town, Jackson co., E Iowa, 2 mi/3.2 km N of Maquoketa. Hybrid seed corn.

Hurt, town, Pittsylvania co., S Va., 22 mi/35 km S of Lynchburg, 1 mi/1.6 km SW of Altavista, on Roanoke R.; 37°05′N 79°17′W. RR junction. Mfg. (textile dyeing and finishing, millwork, machining); agr. (tobacco, grain, soybeans; cattle, dairying). Leesville L. reservoir to SW.

Hurtsboro, town (1990 pop. 707), Russell co., E Ala., 28 mi/45 km SW of Phenix City. Lumber.

Hussar (hoo-ZAHR), village (1991 pop. 146), S Alta., Canada, 30 mi/48 km S of Drumheller; 51°02′N 112°41′W. Wheat.

Hustisford (HUHS-tis-fuhrd), town (1990 pop. 979), Dodge co., S central Wis., 14 mi/23 km SE of Beaver Dam and on Rock R.; 43°21′N 88°35′W. Here dammed to form Sinissippi L. to N (c.3 mi/4.8 km long). Dairy prods.; mfg. (air compressors, hardware).

Hustler, village (1990 pop. 156), Juneau co., central Wis., c.46 mi/74 km E of La Crosse; 43°52′N 90°16′W. In farming area. Butter and cheese.

Hustonville (YOO-stuhn-vil), village (1990 pop. 313), Lincoln co., central Ky., 13 mi/21 km S of Danville; 37°28′N 84°49′W. In agr. area (burley tobacco, grain; livestock; dairying); mfg. (farm equip., raw lumber). Isaac Shelby State Historic Site to N.

Hutch Mountain, peak (8,532 ft/2,601 m) in high plateau (c.7,000 ft/2,134 m), Coconino co., central Ariz., c.30 mi/48 km SE of Flagstaff, SE of Mormon L., in Coconino Natl. Forest.

Hutchins, town (1990 pop. 2,719), Dallas co., N Texas, suburb 10 mi/16 km SSE of downtown Dallas, on Trinity R.; 32°38′N 96°42′W. Mfg. (plastic moldings, business forms).

Hutchinson 1 county (□ 814 sq mi/2,108 sq km; 1990 pop. 8,262), SE S.Dak.; ⊙ Olivet; 43°20′N 97°45′W. Agr. and cattle-raising area drained by James R. and Wolf Creek. Dairy prods.; corn, wheat, barley, soybeans, oats; cattle, hogs, poultry. Formed 1862. **2** county (□ 895 sq mi/2,318 sq km; 1990 pop. 25,689), extreme N Texas; ⊙ Stinnett; 35°50′N 101°21′W. On high treeless plains of the Texas Panhandle, here broken by gorge of Canadian R.; elev. 3,000 ft/914 m–3,500 ft/1,067 m. Much of co. underlaid by huge Panhandle natural gas and oil field; here is one of world's largest natural gas pumping stations, and large carbon black and oil refining industries; mfg. of petroleum prods.; some irrigated agr. (corn, wheat, sorghum); livestock (beef cattle). Part of L. Meredith Natl. Recreation Area in SW corner, including Sanford Dam which forms the lake in the Canadian R. Formed 1876.

Hutchinson 1 (HUHCH-in-suhn), city (1990 pop. 39,308), ⊙ Reno co., S central Kansas, on the Arkansas R.; 38°04′N 97°54′W. Elev. 1,538 ft/469 m. RR junction. It is a commercial and industrial center in a grain (especially wheat), livestock, and oil region. Mfg. (grain milling, vehicle parts, fuel tanks, bakery prods., textile bags, industrial valves, welding supplies, signs, food prods., asphalt, ambulances). Its many facilities include a giant grain elevator, over ½ a mile long. Salt is extracted from great beds beneath the city. Hutchinson Community Col., a planetarium, and the Kansas state fairgrounds here. Kansas Cosmosphere and Space Center. Inc. 1872. **2** city (1990 pop. 11,523), McLeod co., S central Minn., 55 mi/89 km W of Minneapolis, on South Fork Crow R.; 44°53′N 94°22′W. Mfg. (agr. equip., concrete blocks, wood furniture, fertilizer, sheet metal, dry yeast, wood boxes, magnetic tapes, machining); grain, soybeans, peas; livestock, poultry; dairying. Part of settlement burned in Sioux uprising of 1862. Several small lakes in area, Otter L. to W. Founded 1855, inc. 1881.

Hutchinson River, 5 mi/8 km long, small stream in SE N.Y.; rises in S Westchester co., just E of Scarsdale; flows generally S through the Bronx to Eastchester Bay in Pelham Bay Park. Impounded to created 3 reservoirs along its modes and length. Paralleled by landscaped Hutchingson R. Parkway. Named for Anne Hutchinson.

Hutsonville, village (1990 pop. 622), Crawford co., SE Ill., on the Wabash (bridged here) and 8 mi/12.9 km NNE of Robinson; 39°06′N 87°39′W. In agr. area (wheat, corn, livestock, hay).

Huttig (HUHT-ig), town (1990 pop. 831), Union co., S Ark., 30 mi/48 km ESE of El Dorado, near La. line; 33°02′N 92°10′W. Mfg. (softwood lumber); woodworking. Lower Ouachita Wildlife Management Area to E; Felsenthat Natl. Wildlife Refuge and Felsenthal Lock and Dam (impounds L. Jack Lee) to NE Ouachita R. Inc. 1904.

Hutto, village (1990 pop. 630), Williamson co., central Texas, 22 mi/35 km NNE of Austin, on Bushy Creek; 30°33′N 97°32′W. Cotton, corn, wheat; cattle; mfg. (machine parts).

Huttonsville, village (1990 pop. 211), Randolph co., E central W.Va., 16 mi/26 km SSW of Elkins, on Tygart R.; 38°42′N 79°58′W. Monongahela Natl. Forest to E; Kumbrabow State Forest to SW.

Huxley, town (1990 pop. 2,047), Story co., central Iowa, 20 mi/32 km N of Des Moines, 8 mi/12.9 km S of Ames; 41°53′N 93°35′W. Livestock; grain; apparel.

Huxley, village, S central Alta., Canada, 70 mi/113 km NE of Calgary. Coal mining; oil and gas; wheat, oats.

Huxley, Mount (12,216 ft/3,723 m), SE Alaska, in St. Elias Mts., 20 mi/32 km N of Icy Bay; 60°20′N 141°10′W.

Hyannis (hei-YAN-uhs), resort town (1990 pop. 14,120), Barnstable co., SE Mass., on Cape Cod, seat of town of

Barnstable offices; 41°39′N 70°18′W. It is the business center and shipping point of the area; major industries are tourism and home construction; large retail malls. Other industry includes recreational prods., candles, foams (polyethylene). Hyannis provides ferry transportation to Martha's Vineyard and Nantucket isl. Barnstable Municipal Airport. A community col. and a conservatory of music and arts are located there. Nearby Hyannisport is famous as the site of a compound of houses owned by the Kennedy family. Inc. 1639.

Hyannis (hei-AN-is), village (1990 pop. 210), ⊙ Grant co., W central Nebr. in Sand Hills, 60 mi/97 km E of Alliance and 62 mi/100 km N of Ogallala; 42°00′N 101°45′W. Livestock; wild hay. Numerous small natural lakes including Raymond and Collins to NE, George I. to SW, Home and Big Buckboard to S.

Hyatt Regency Resort, tourist complex, St. Kitts, Federation of St. Kitts and Nevis, West Indies. A 250-room all-inclusive resort at South Friar's Bay on SE peninsula; opened in 1995 as part of tourism development program.

Hyattstown (HI-ats-town), town, Montgomery co., central Md., 17 mi/27 km NW of Rockville. A commuter suburb of Washington, the first house here was built by Seth Hyatt about 1800. A relative, Jesse (1763–1813) ran a hotel behind the Methodist Church. Union and Confederate forces skirmished here in 1862. An abandoned grist mill is on Hyattsville Mill Rd.

Hyattsville, city (1990 pop. 13,864), Prince Georges co., W central Md., a suburb of Washington, D.C.; 38°58′N 76°57′W. A residential community with some light industry and commercial activity, Hyattsville is named after Christopher Hyatt. Christopher, who settled here in 1860, was a close relative of Seth Hyatt, the founder of Hyattstown. It is located in an area of major housing development and service industries, particularly for middle-income families who work in Washington, D.C. The Marquis de Lafayette stayed at Bothwick Hall, and the inventor, James Harrison Rogers, was a resident. Since it is closer to the centers of pop. than the co. seat, Upper Marlboro, the Co. Lib. and many co. offices are located here. Inc. 1886.

Hyattville (HEI-uht-vil), village, Big Horn co., N Wyo., on Paintrock Creek branch of Big Horn R., located in W foothills of Bighorn Mts. and 24 mi/39 km ESE of Basin. Elev. c.4,457 ft/1,358 m. In bean- and sugar beet-growing area. Medicine Lodge State Archaeological Site is here. Bighorn Natl. Forest to E.

Hybla Valley, uninc. city, Fairfax co., NE Va., residential suburb 4 mi/6.4 km SSW of Alexandria, 11 mi/18 km SSW of Washington, D.C.; 38°45′N 77°04′W. Huntley Meadows Park to W.

Hydaburg (HEI-duh-buhrg), town (1990 pop. 384), SE Alaska, on W coast of Prince of Wales Isl., 23 mi/37 km SE of Craig; 55°12′N 132°49′W. Fishing, fish processing, some timber. Connected by road network to N parts of isl. Totem park. Founded 1911, combined 3 Haida settlements: Sukkwan, Howkan, and Klinkwan. Inc. 1927.

Hyde 1 (HEID), county (☐ 1,424 sq mi/3,688 sq km; 1990 pop. 5,411), E N.C.; ⊙ Swan Quarter; 35°24′N 76°09′W. Forested and swampy tidewater area; bounded SE by Atlantic Ocean, bounded N in part (NE) by Alligator R. estuary, W in part by Pungo R. estuary, E by Long Shal R. estuary; crossed by Alligator-Pungo Canal; includes Ocracoke Isl. sand barrier isl., part of Outer Banks and Cape Hatteras Natl. Seashore 20 mi/32 km SE of mainland across Pamlico Sound (ferry from Swan Quarter to Ocracoke village). Agr. area (cotton, corn, wheat, soybeans; hogs); timber; fish, crabs, oysters. L. Mattamuskert Natl. Wildlife Refuge in center; Swanquarter Natl. Wildlife Refuge in SW; Alligator L. in N; part of Pungo L. in NW; large L. Mattamuskert in center (natural lakes). Formed 1705. **2** county (☐ 866 sq mi/2,243 sq km; 1990 pop. 1,696), central S.Dak.; ⊙ Highmore; 44°32′N 99°28′W. Agr. area drained by Medicine Knoll and Wolf creeks; Missouri R. and Crow Creek Indian Reservation in SW corner. Wheat; dairy prods.; cattle. Part of Crow Creek Indian Reservation in SW corner; SW corner borders Miss. R. Formed 1873.

Hyde, uninc. town (1990 pop. 1,643), Clearfield co., central Pa., residential suburb 2 mi/3.2 km SW of Clearfield on West Branch Susquehanna R.; 41°00′N 78°28′W. Agr. includes dairying.

Hyde Park 1 town (☐ 39 sq mi/101 sq km; 1990 pop. 21,230), Dutchess co., SE N.Y., on Hudson R.; 41°47′N 73°56′W. It is famous as the site of the Roosevelt estate, part of the 264-acre/107-ha FDR Natl. Historic Site where President Franklin D. Roosevelt was born and is buried. The Roosevelt Lib. (1941) contains historical material dating from 1910 until Roosevelt's death in 1945. The adjacent 180-acre/73-ha Eleanor Roosevelt Natl. Historic Site (Val-Kill), an estate used by Mrs. Roosevelt as her personal retreat, was built for her by her husband, in 1925. Hyde Park is also the site of the Frederick W. Vanderbilt mansion and 2 state parks. All 3 homes are natl. historic sites. Seat of Culinary Inst. of Amer. Settled c.1740. **2** uninc. town (1990 pop. 2,700), Berks co., SE central Pa., residential suburb 3 mi/4.8 km N of Reading; 40°22′N 75°55′W. RR junction. **3** town (1990 pop. 2190), Cache co., N Utah, 8 mi/12.9 km N of Logan; 41°47′N 111°48′W. Wasatch Natl. Forest and Mt. Naomi Wilderness Area to E. Elev. 4,560 ft/1,390 m. Settled 1860s. **4** town (1990 pop. 2,344), including Hyde Park village, ⊙ Lamoille co., N central Vt., 23 mi/37 km N of Montpelier. Lumber; wood prods.; dairying; 44°37′N 72°33′W. Settled 1787. North Hyde Park village is a woodworking center.

Hyde Park, borough (1990 pop. 542), Westmoreland co., SW central Pa., on Kiskiminetas R. 1 mi/1.6 km E of Leechburg. Mfg. (cast iron rolls); agr. (corn, hay; livestock, dairying).

Hyden (HEID-uhn), village (1990 pop. 375), ⊙ Leslie co., SE Ky., 12 mi/19 km WSW of Hazard, in Cumberland Mts., on Middle Fork Kentucky R., surrounded by Daniel Boone Natl. Forest; 37°09′N 83°22′W. Light mfg. Seat of Frontier Nursing Service Hosp., including Wendover Big House (1925), to W. Buckhorn L. reservoir and State Resort Park to N. Est. 1882.

Hyder (HEI-duhr), village (1990 pop. 85), SE Alaska, on B.C. border, at head of Portland Canal, 2 mi/3.2 km S of Stewart, B.C. Supply point; port of entry; small-scale mining (gold, silver, lead, tungsten). Originally named Portland City; renamed for geologist F.B. Hyder. Town destroyed by great fire of 1948. Most mining ceased 1956. Granduc copper mine closed 1984; Westmin gold and silver mine continues to operate. Air service, road connection through Canada, ferry connections. Popular for tourist nightlife (2 bars). "Friendliest Ghost Town in Alaska." In Misty Fiords Natl. Monument.

Hydesville, uninc. town (1990 pop. 1,131), Humboldt co., NW Calif., 17 mi/27 km SSE of Eureka, near Van Duzen R. Humboldt Redwoods State Park to S; Grizzly Creek Redwoods State Park to E. Timber, cattle, sheep.

Hydetown (HEID-toun), borough (1990 pop. 681), Crawford co., NW Pa., 3 mi/4.8 km NW of Titusville, on Thompson Creek, near its mouth on Oil Creek to SW. Dairying.

Hydeville, Vt.: see CASTLETON.

Hydro, town (1990 pop. 977), Caddo co., W central Okla., 8 mi/12.9 km E of Weatherford, on Deer Creek; 35°32′N 98°34′W. In agr. area (cotton, grain); mfg. (peanut processing, peanut butter, sand and gravel).

Hygiene, uninc. village, Boulder co., N central Colo., 4 mi/6.4 km W of Longmont, on St. Vrain Creek. Elev. 5,090 ft/1,551 m. Cattle; fruit, vegetables, wheat; mfg. of feeds.

Hymera, town (1990 pop. 771), Sullivan co., SW Ind., 9 mi/14.5 km NNE of Sullivan; 39°11′N 87°18′W. In agr. area; bituminous-coal mining. Shakamak State Park is nearby. Plotted 1870.

Hyndman (HIND-muhn), borough (1990 pop. 1,019), Bedford co., S Pa., on Wills Creek, 22 mi/35 km SW of Bedford. Mfg. (sawmill, lumber); Agr. (corn, oats, hay; livestock; dairying). Leap Airport to N. Little Allegheny Mt. ridge to W; Wills Mt. ridge to E. Severely damaged by fire, 1949. Laid out 1840, inc. 1877.

Hyndman, Peak, highest (12,078 ft/3,681 m) of Pioneer Mts., on Custer-Blaine co. line, central Idaho, 11 mi/18 km ENE of Sun Valley. On boundary of Challis (NE) and Sawtooth (SW) natl. forests.

Hyrum, town (1990 pop. 4,829), Cache co., N Utah, 7 mi/11.3 km S of Logan, and near Wasatch Range; 41°37′N 111°50′W. Vegetables, wheat, barley; dairying; cattle; mfg. (meat packing). Elev. 4,750 ft/1,448 m. Hyrum Reservoir and Hyrum State Park on SW end of town, impounds water for irrigation of surrounding region. Settled 1860.

Hyrum Reservoir, at Hyrum, Cache co., N Utah, on Little Bear R., in Hyman State Park, 11 mi/18 km NE of Brigham City; 2 mi/3.2 km long; 41°29′N 111°53′W.

Hysham (HI-shuhm), village (1990 pop. 361), ⊙ Treasure co., S central Mont., on Yellowstone R., 74 mi/119 km NE of Billings; 46°17′N 107°13′W. RR junction to E; shipping point for cattle, corn, hay, sugar beets.

Hythe (HEITH), village (1991 pop. 623), W Alta., Canada, near B.C. border, on Beaverlodge R., and 32 mi/51 km WNW of Grande Prairie; 55°19′N 119°34′W. Lumbering, mixed farming.

I

Iaeger (EI-guhr), town (1990 pop. 551), McDowell co., S W.Va., on Tug Fork R., 13 mi/21 km W of Welch; 37°27′N 81°48′W. Semibituminous-coal field. Mfg. (coal processing). RR junction. Panther State Forest to W.

Iatt, Lake (EI-uht), reservoir, Grant parish, central La., on Iatt Creek, 3 mi/5 km NE of Colfax; c.7 mi/11 km long; 31°33′N 92°39′W. Natural marshy lake now impounded by dam. L. Iatt State Game and Fish Preserve here. Kisatchie Natl. Forest to E.

Ibapah (ei-BUH-pah), uninc. village (1990 pop. 10), Tooele co., W Utah, 48 mi/77 km S of Wendover, near Nev. state line. Cattle; gold mining. Goshute Indian Reservation to S and SW; Deseret Military Test Center to E. Deep Creek Range to E. Highway access to rest of Utah via Nev.

Iberia (EI-bir-ee-uh), parish (□ 588 sq mi/1,523 sq km; 1990 pop. 68,297), S La., on Gulf of Mexico; ⊙ New Iberia; 30°01′N 91°49′W. Bounded SW by Vermilion Bay, E by Belle R.; intersected by Bayou Teche, Big Bayou Pigeon, and Atchafalaya Main Channel. Includes Avery, Jefferson, and Weeks isls. (salt domes). Oil and gas wells, huge salt mines, sulphur mines; fisheries (crawfish, catfish, shrimp, crabs, finfish). Rich agr. area (sugarcane, soybeans, rice, vegetables, nursery crops; home gardens; cattle; dairying). Varied mfg. includes food (esp. pepper) prods., apparel, metal prods., industrial machinery; shipbuilding. Hunting, fur trapping. Crossed by Intracoastal Waterway. First settled by Span. colonists. Named after the Iberian Peninsula. L. Peigneur in W. Part of Allakanas State Wildlife Area in E. L. Fausse Pointe, including state park, in E center. Part of Cypremort Point State Park in S. Beyond Vermilion Bay, to S, lies large Marsh Isl. (entirely in Russell Sage State Wildlife Refuge); 3 mi/5 km S of Marsh Isl., in Gulf, are the Shell Keys (Natl. Wildlife Refuge). Both Marsh Isl. and Shell Keys are parts of Iberia parish. Formed 1868.

Iberia, town (1990 pop. 650), Miller co., central Mo., 14 mi/23 km SE of Tuscumbia; 38°05′N 92°17′W. Hay; cattle, turkeys; mfg. (apparel, wood prods.).

Iberville (ee-ber-VEEL), county (□ 198 sq mi/513 sq km), S Que., E Canada, near U.S. (N.Y.) border, on Richelieu R.; ⊙ Iberville; 45°15′N 73°01′W.

Iberville (IB-uhr-vil), parish (□ 611 sq mi/1,582 sq km; 1990 pop. 31,049), SE central La.; ⊙ Plaquemine; 30°17′N 91°14′W. Bounded W by Atchafalaya R.; intersected by Mississippi R. in E. Agr. (corn, hay, soybeans, nursery crops, sugarcane; home gardens; cattle, horses, exotic fowl; crawfish, catfish, alligators; logging; mfg. (chemicals, plastics, lumber, metal prods., industrial machinery); oil and gas fields. Drained by Grand R.; intersected by Bayou Maringouin and Bayou des Glaises. Locks connect Mississippi R. to the Plaquemine branch of Port Allen–Morgan City canal. Part of Atchafalaya Natl. Wildlife Refuge in NW corner. Named after Pierre Le Moyne, sieur d'Iberville, brother of sieur de Bienville. Occupied by Union forces during Civil War. Formed 1807.

Iberville (ee-ber-VEEL), town (1991 pop. 9,352), ⊙ Iberville co., S Que., E Canada, on Richelieu R., and 22 mi/35 km SE of Montreal; 45°19′N 73°14′W. Mfg. of chemicals, pottery; iron founding, woodworking; market in dairying region. Site of Amer. mother-house of the Marist Brothers.

Icacos Point (ee-KAH-kos), SW Trinidad, Trinidad and Tobago, W sect. of the SW peninsula, on the Serpent's Mouth, and 10 mi/16 km off Venezuela coast, terminating in Icacos Point headland at 10°02′N 61°55′W.

Icard (EI-kahrd), uninc. town (1990 pop. 2,553), Burke co., W central N.C., 7 mi/11.3 km W of Hickory L.; 35°43′N 81°27′W. Rhodhiss reservoir (Catawba R.) to

N. Grain, soybeans; chickens, hogs. Mfg. (packaging, apparel, fabricated metal prods.).

Icaria, Lake, reservoir, Adams co., SW Iowa, on Kemp Creek, 7 mi/11.3 km N of Corning; 5 mi/8 km long; 41°04′N 94°44′W. Max. capacity 25,310 acre-ft. Formed by dam (49 ft/15 m high), built (1974) by the Soil Conservation Dist. for flood control.

Ice Age National Reserve (□ 50 sq mi/130 sq km), Wis. Contains kettles, drumlins, eskers. First natl. scientific reserve in Wis. Scattered across Wis.; 9 units include Horicon Marsh Wildlife Area, Interstate Park, Kettle Moraine State Park (N unit), Mill Bluff and Devil's L. state parks. Est. 1971.

Ice Caves Mountain, natl. natural landmark (□ 6 sq mi/15.5 sq km), Ulster co., SE N.Y., 26 mi/42 km SE of Kingston, and 20 mi/32 km NW of Newburgh; 41°40′N 74°22′W. Access to the site by road is via N.Y. Route 52E from Ellenville (4 mi/6.4 km). Features include Sam's Point (elev. 2,255 ft/687 m), glacially scoured L. Maratanza, and 2 large ice caves, with enormous fissures and cracks where drifts of snow often linger even in summer. In the bottom "galleries" (c.100 ft/30 m below the surface), there are walls of ice and huge icicles as well.

Ice House Reservoir, El Dorado co., central Calif., on South Fork of Silver Creek, in Eldorado Natl. Forest, 22 mi/35 km WSW of South Lake Tahoe; 3 mi/4.8 km long; 38°52′N 120°22′W. Elev. 5,433 ft/1,656 m. Extends E. Max. capacity 45,960 acre-ft. Formed by Ice House Dam (132 ft/40 m high), built (1959) for water supply of Sacramento.

Ice Mountain, W.Va.: see ROMNEY.

Icemorelee (EIS-more lee), town, Union co., S N.C., just NW of Monroe. In large annexation area of Monroe.

Ichawaynochaway Creek (i-chuh-wai-NAH-chuh-wai), c.65 mi/105 km long, SW Ga.; rises NE of Cuthbert; flows SSE, past Morgan, to Flint R. 13 mi/21 km SW of Newton; 31°58′N 84°37′W.

Iconoclast Mountain (10,630 ft/3,240 m), SE B.C., W Canada, in Selkirk Mts., on E edge of Hamber Provincial Park, 35 mi/56 km NE of Revelstoke; 51°27′N 117°45′W.

Icpic, Alaska: see IKPEK.

Icy Bay, SE Alaska, at head of the Panhandle, on Gulf of Alaska, 70 mi/113 km WNW of Yakutat; 12 mi/19 km long, 8 mi/12.9 km wide; 59°55′N 141°33′W; receives Guyot and Malaspina glaciers.

Icy Cape 1 in S Alaska, on Gulf of Alaska at W entrance to Icy Bay, 75 mi/121 km WNW of Yakutat; 59°55′N 141°38′W. **2** in NW Alaska, on Chukchi Sea, at W edge of Natl. Petroleum Reserve–Alaska; 70°20′N 161°50′W. Akeonik settlement here.

Icy Strait, SE Alaska, bet. Chichagof Isl. and the mainland, extends 40 mi/64 km NW from Chatham Strait (58°07′N 135°00′W) to Glacier Bay (58°22′N 136°00′W) and Cross Sound.

Ida, county (□ 432 sq mi/1,119 sq km; 1990 pop. 8,365), W Iowa; ⊙ Ida Grove; 42°22′N 95°30′W. Prairie agr. area (cattle, hogs, poultry; corn, oats, soybeans) drained by Maple and Soldier rivers; sand and gravel pits (N), bituminous-coal deposits (S). General flooding here in 1993. Formed 1851.

Ida 1 (EI-duh), village (1990 pop. 250), Caddo parish, NW La., 32 mi/51 km NNW of Shreveport, at Ark. state line; 33°00′N 93°54′W. In agr. and timber area. Oil and natural-gas production. **2** village, Monroe co., extreme SE Mich., 9 mi/14.5 km W of Monroe; 41°54′N 83°34′W. In farm area. Feed and fertilizer.

Ida Grove, city (1990 pop. 2,357), ⊙ Ida co., W Iowa, on Maple R., and 50 mi/80 km ESE of Sioux City; 42°20′N 95°28′W. In livestock and grain area. Mfg. (consumer goods, construction materials, transportation equip.). Settled 1856, inc. 1887.

Ida, Lake, Douglas co., W Minn., 5 mi/8 km N of Alexandria; 14 mi/8 km long, 2 mi/3.2 km wide; 45°59′N 95°24′W. Fed N from L. Miltona; drained from S. Resort area. L. Carlos to E.

Ida, Mount (10,472 ft/3,192 m), E B.C., W Canada, in Rocky Mts., 100 mi/161 km E of Prince George; 54°03′N 120°20′W.

Idabel (EI-duh-bel), town (1990 pop. 6,957), ⊙ McCurtain co., extreme SE Okla., 38 mi/61 km ESE of Hugo, bet. Little (N) and Red (SW) rivers; 33°53′N 94°49′W. In farming and lumbering region; sawmills; mfg. (apparel, lumber, transportation equip., millwork, paper prods.; meat processing). Red River Mus. here. Unit of Ouachita Natl. Forest to E. Inc. 1906.

Idaho, state (□ 83,573 sq mi/216,456 sq km; 1995 est. pop. 1,163,261), NW U.S., one of the Rocky Mt. states, admitted as the 43d state of the Union in 1890; ⊙ and largest city BOISE 44°14 114°17′W. Bounded N by Canada (B.C.), E by Mont. and Wyo., S by Utah and Nev., and W by Oregon and Wash. From the N Panhandle, where Idaho is about 45 mi/72 km wide, the state broadens S of the Bitterroot Range to 310 mi/499 km in width. Much of Idaho has a primitive and unspoiled natural beauty, with rugged slopes and towering peaks, a vast expanse of timberland, scenic lakes, wild rivers, cascades, and spectacular gorges. Hells Canyon (Grand Canyon of the Snake R.) on the W border, which at one point is 7,900 ft/2,408 m below the mountaintops, is the deepest gorge (5,500 ft/1,676 m deep) in N. Amer. The climate of the state ranges from hot summers in the arid volcanic plains of S to cold, snowy winters in the high wilderness areas of central and N Idaho. The Snake R. flows in a great arc across S Idaho; with its tributaries the river has been harnessed to produce hydroelectric power and to irrigate vast areas of dry, fertile volcanic soil. To the N of the Snake R. valley, in central and N central Idaho, are the massive Sawtooth and the Salmon R. mts., which shelter some of the most magnificent wilderness areas remaining in the U.S., including the Selway-Bitterroot Wilderness Area and the Frank Church–R. of No Return Wilderness Area. In the central and N central regions and in the Panhandle there are tremendous expanses of natl. forests covering approximately 40% of the state and constituting one of the largest gross areas of natl. forests in the nation, notably, in N, Kamiksu, St. Joe, Coeur d'Alene, Clearwater and Nez Perce natl. forests; in S center, Payette, Salmon, Challis, and Boise natl. forests; in E and SE, Targhee, Caribou, Cache, and Sawtooth natl. forests. The state's jagged granite peaks include Mt. Borah, in Custer co., S center of state, which reaches an elev. of 12,662 ft/3,859 m. Rushing rivers such as the Salmon and the Clearwater, and many lakes, notably L. Pend Oreille, Couer d'Alene L. (often described as one of the world's loveliest), and Priest L., as well as the state's mt. areas, make Idaho a superb fish and game preserve and vacation land; white-water rafting, esp. on Salmon R., also known as the R. of No Return (so named by Lewis and Clark expedition). The state is esp. inviting to campers, anglers, and hunters (Idaho has one of the largest elk herds in the nation. Agr. is still the most important sector of the state's economy. Cattle and calves are among the leading agr. prods.; dairy prods. are also important. Irrigated Snake Valley produces nearly all of Idaho's famous potato crop, with greatest concentration in the upper valley (E), around Pocatello; also produces most of Idaho's other crops. Idaho's chief crops are potatoes (for which the state is nationally famous and by far the nation's largest producer), hay, wheat, fruits and vegetables and sugar beets. Food processing is the chief industry; lumber and wood prods., chemicals, and electronic components are other major manufactured items. The growth of the winter sports industry has helped make Idaho a leading tourist state. Mining, once a major source of income, and still important, but has been surpassed by agr., mfg., and tourism in annual income earned. Silver, antimony, phosphate rock, gold, lead, and zinc are the principal minerals produced. The most important cities are Boise, Pocatello, and Idaho Falls. Probably the 1st non-Native Americans to enter the area that is now Idaho were members of the Lewis and Clark expedition in 1805. They were not far ahead of the fur traders who came to the region shortly thereafter. Can. trader David Thompson of the North West Co., established the 1st trading post here in 1809. The next year traders from

St. Louis penetrated the mts., and Andrew Henry of the Missouri Fur Co. established a post near present-day Rexburg, the 1st Amer. trading post in the area. In this period the fortunes of the Idaho region were wrapped up with those of the Columbia R. region, and the area encompassed by what is now the state of Idaho was part of Oregon country, held jointly by the U.S. and Great Britain 1818–1846. Fur traders in an expedition sent out by John Jacob Astor came to the Snake R. region to trap for furs after having established (1811) a trading post at Astoria on the Columbia R. In 1821, 2 Br. trading companies operating in the Idaho region, the North West and the Hudson's Bay companies, were joined together as the Hudson's Bay Co. which, after 1824, came into competition with Amer. mt. men also trapping in the area. By the 1840s the 2 groups had severely depleted the region's fur supply. In 1846 the U.S. gained sole claim to Oregon country S of the 49th parallel by the Oregon Treaty with Great Britain. The area was established as a territory in 1848. Idaho still had no permanent settlement when Oregon Territory became a state in 1859 and the E part of Idaho was added to Washington Territory. A Mormon outpost founded at Franklin in 1860 is considered the 1st permanent settlement, but it was not until the discovery of gold that settlers poured into Idaho. Gold was discovered on the Clearwater R. in 1860, on the Salmon in 1861, in the Boise R. basin in 1862, and gold and silver were found in the Owyhee R. country in 1863. The usual rush of settlers followed, along with the spectacular but ephemeral growth of towns. Most of these settlements are only ghost towns now, but the many settlers who poured in during the gold rush—mainly from Wash., Oregon, and Calif., with smaller numbers from the E—formed a pop. large enough to demand new govt. administration, and Idaho Territory was set up in 1863. Native Americans, mostly Kootenai, Nez Percé, Western Shoshone, Bannock, Coeur d'Alene, and Pend d'Oreille, became upset by the incursion of settlers and some resisted violently. The Federal govt. had subdued many of these ethnic groups by 1858, placing them on Native Amer. reservations. The Bannock were defeated in 1863 and again in 1878. In 1876–1877 the Nez Percé, led by Chief Joseph, made their heroic but unsuccessful attempt to flee to Canada while being pursued by U.S. troops. The late 19th cent. also witnessed the growth of cattle and sheep ranching, along with the strife that developed bet. the 2 groups of ranchers over grazing areas. A new mining boom started in 1882 with the discovery of gold in the Coeur d'Alenes, and although the gold strike ended in disappointment, it prefaced the discovery there of some of the richest silver mines in the world. Wallace and Kellogg became notable mining centers, and the Bunker Hill and Sullivan (a lead mine) became one of the most famous of mines. Severe labor troubles there at the end of the cent. led to political uprisings. Frank Steunenberg, who as governor, had used Federal troops to put down the uprisings, was assassinated in 1905. The trial of William Haywood and others accused of involvement in the murder drew natl. attention and marked the beginning of the long career of William E. Borah (who had prosecuted the mine leaders) as an outstanding Republican party leader in the state and nation. The coming of the RRs (notably the Northern Pacific) through here in the 1880s–1890s brought new settlers and aided in the founding of such cities as Idaho Falls, Pocatello, and American Falls. Farming expanded in the state and private interests developed irrigation projects. Some of these aroused public opposition, which led to establishment of state irrigation dists. under the Carey Land Act of 1894. The Reclamation Act of 1902 brought direct Federal aid, and furthered reclamation work in Idaho. Notable among public reclamation projects are the Boise and Minidoka projects. The projects, both public and private, have also helped to increase the development of Idaho's enormous potential of hydroelectric power. Three new private hydroelectric projects along the Snake R. were put into operation bet. 1959 and 1968. The unspoiled quality of much of Idaho's land has nourished one of the newest and most profitable of Idaho's businesses—the tourist trade. SUN VALLEY, one of the nation's notable year-round vacation spots, is an example of the development of resorts in Idaho. The state also contains the Craters of the Moon Natl. Monument in SE, a volcanic area, dormant only 2,100 years, a major contributor, along with Yellowstone, to the basaltic layers that underlie the Snake R. Plain; a small sect. of Yellowstone Natl. Park on Wyo. state line; Sawtooth Natl. Recreation Area in S center. Indian Reservations include, Coeur d'Alene and Nez Perce in N, Fort Hall in SE, part of Duck Valley is on Nev. state line in SW. In 1949 a large Atomic Energy Commission project was begun here. The Natl. Reactor Testing Station is situated near Arco, the 1st Amer. town to be lighted by electricity obtained from atomic-power plants. EBR-1 (Experimental Breeding Reactor), 1st nuclear reactor in world, is now a Natl. Historic Landmark, on grounds of Idaho (Lost River) Natl. Engineering Laboratory, U.S. Dept. of Energy, SE Idaho. Idaho suffered during the recession of the early 1980s, largely due to the drop in energy prices. The state, however, was able to rebound later in the decade through the attraction of new business, including high-technology firms, notably at Boise and Coeur d'Alene. Idaho's constitution was adopted in 1889 and became effective in 1890 upon statehood. The state's chief executive is a governor elected for a term of 4 years. The legislature consists of an 84-member house of representatives and a 42-member senate. State representatives and senators are elected every 2 years. The state also elects 2 Representatives and 2 Senators to the U.S. Congress and has 4 electoral votes. Idaho is a Republican state in natl. politics but, until 1994, had Democratic governors since 1970. Outstanding among Idaho's institutions of higher learning is the Univ. of Idaho, at Moscow; Idaho State Univ., at Pocatello; and Boise State Univ., at Boise. E-W sect. of Salmon R. in N central Idaho Serves as time-zone boundary splitting the state bet. Mountain (S) and Pacific (N). Idaho has 44 cos.: ADA, ADAMS, BANNOCK, BEAR LAKE, BENEWAH, BINGHAM, BLAINE, BOISE, BONNER, BONNEVILLE, BOUNDARY, BUTTE, CAMAS, CANYON, CARIBOU, CASSIA, CLARK, CLEARWATER, CUSTER, ELMORE, FRANKLIN, FREMONT, GEM, GOODING, IDAHO, JEFFERSON, JEROME, KOOTENAI, LATAH, LEMHI, LEWIS, LINCOLN, MADISON, MINIDOKA, NEZ PERCE, ONEIDA, OWYHEE, PAYETTE, POWER, SHOSHONE, TETON, TWIN FALLS, VALLEY, and WASHINGTON.

Idaho, county (☐ 8,502 sq mi/22,020 sq km; 1990 pop. 13,783), central Idaho; ⊙ Grangeville; 45°51'N 115°28'W. Agr. and mining area bounded E by Bitterroot Range and Mont., W by Hells Canyon of the Snake R. and Oregon; drained by the South and Middle forks of Clearwater and Salmon rivers. Wheat, barley; alfalfa, hay; sheep, cattle; copper, gold, silver, lead. In Bitterroot Mt. Region. Large part of Nez Perce Natl. Forest throughout co., except NW; part of Salmon R. primitive area. In area are Seven Devils (W), Salmon R. (SE), and Clearwater (NE) mts.; part of Clearwater Natl. Forest in N; part of Nez Perce Indian Reservation in NW; small part of Hells Canyon Natl. Recreation Area in SW corner; units of Nez Perce Natl. Historical Park in NW at East Kamish and Grangerville; Gospel Hump Wilderness Area in center; part of Selway-Bitteroot Wilderness Area in E, part of Frank Church–River of No Return Wilderness Area in SE. Pacific/Mountain time zone border follows Snake R., N on W side, then follows Salmon R. back S and E, across co., then N on E border, putting S and far W in Mountain time zone, N center and E in Pacific time zone. Largest co. in land area in Idaho, 17th-largest in U.S. Formed 1861.

Idaho City, village (1990 pop. 322), ⊙ Boise co., SW Idaho, on Morse Creek, and 24 mi/39 km NE of Boise; 43°51'N 115°51'W. Elev. 3,906 ft/1,191 m. In mt. area. Lumber milling, placer mining for gold; tourism. Important gold-mining center in 1860s (est. pop. 30,000); classic gold-mining town with saloon and Boot Hill cemetery (of 200 people buried here, only 28 are said to have died of natural causes). Boise Basin Mus. In Boise Natl. Forest.

Idaho Falls, city (1990 pop. 43,929), ⊙ Bonneville co., SE Idaho, 46 mi/74 km NNE of Pocatello, traversed by the Snake R.; 43°29'N 112°02'W. Elev. 4,710 ft/1,436 m. The chief city of the extensively irrigated upper Snake valley, Idaho Falls is the prosperous commercial and processing center of a cattle, dairy, and farm region that produces potatoes, wheat, sugar beets, and alfalfa. Mfg. includes bldg. materials, consumer goods, food prods., leather goods, electronic equip., satellite antennas. Tourism is important since the city lies near several natl. parks and major recreational areas. Idaho Natl. Engineering Laboratory, including EBR-1 Natl. Historic Landmark, 1st nuclear reactor in world, is 45 mi/72 km W. Originally a miner's fording point over the Snake R., first settled by Mormons. Municipal Airport to NW. The impressive Idaho Falls Mormon Temple (opened 1944) is a prominent landmark. Idaho Vietnam Memorial is at Freeman Park. Seat of Eastern Idaho Technical Col. Ririe Reservoir to E; Several annual rodeos are held here. Inc. 1900.

Idaho Springs, town (1990 pop. 1,834), Clear Creek co., N central Colo., on Clear Creek, in Front Range, and 26 mi/42 km W of Denver; 39°44'N 105°30'W. Elev. 7,540 ft/2,298 m. Trade center, resort with hot mineral springs. Mfg. Gold, silver, lead, and copper mines in vicinity. Nearby are site of 1st important gold strike (1859) in Colo. and Edgar mine, operated by Colo. School of Mines for instruction of students. Parts of Arapaho Natl. Forest to S and NW; Mt. Evans State Wildlife Area to S. Settled 1859–1860, inc. 1885.

Idalou, town (1990 pop. 2,074), Lubbock co., NW Texas, on the Llano Estacado, 11 mi/18 km NE of Lubbock; 33°39'N 101°40'W. Mfg. (small agr. equip.).

Idanha (ee-DAN-uh), village (1990 pop. 289), Marion co., NW Oregon, on North Santiam R., c. 50 mi/80 km ESE of Salem, surrounded by Willamette Natl. Forest; 44°42'N 122°04'W. Timber. Fish hatchery to SE. Detroit L. Reservoir and State Park to W; Mt. Jefferson Wilderness Area to E.

Idaville, village (1990 pop. 700), White co., N central Ind., 6 mi/9.7 km E of Monticello. Dairying; soybeans, corn; hogs.

Ideal, town (1990 pop. 554), Macon co., central Ga., 9 mi/14.5 km NW of Oglethorpe; 32°22'N 84°11'W.

Iditarod (ei-DI-tah-rawd), village, W Alaska, on Iditarod R., and 118 mi/190 km SE of Unalakleet; 62°28'N 158°02'W. Placer gold mining. Scene (1908) of gold rush.

Iditarod (ei-DI-tah-rawd), affiliated area and former Alaska Gold Rush trail, Alaska. extending 1,049 mi/1,688 km from Anchorage to Nome. Annual 1,049-mi/1,688-km sled-dog race in late Feb. starts at Mulcahy Park, Anchorage, follows Glenn Highway through Knik before entering wilderness and ending at Nome. Dog Mushers' Hall of Fame at Knik. Authorized 1980

Iditarod River (ei-DI-tah-rawd), 150 mi/241 km long, W Alaska; rises N of Chuathbaluk; flows in an arc NE, N, and finally W, to Innoko R. at 63°02'N 158°45'W. Placer gold mining in valley.

Idlewild Airport, N.Y.: see JFK (JOHN F. KENNEDY) INTERNATIONAL AIRPORT.

Idyllwild, Calif.: see SAN JACINTO MOUNTAINS.

Idyllwild–Pine Cove, uninc. town (1990 pop. 2,853), Riverside co., S Calif., residential suburb 10 mi/16 km SW of Palm Springs, in San Jacinto Mts. Mt. San Jacinto State Park to N. Idyllwild sect. in Strawberry Valley; Pine Cove extends 2 mi/3.2 km NW. Mfg. (wire drawing).

Idylwood, uninc. city, Fairfax co., NE Va., residential suburb 9 mi/14.5 km W of Washington, D.C., 2 mi/3.2 km W of Falls Church; 38°53'N 77°12'W.

Igiugig (i-GYOO-gik), village (1990 pop. 33), S Alaska, on Kvichak R., at SW end of Iliamna L., 40 mi/64 km SW of Newhalen; 59°20'N 155°54'W. Fishing; supply point for sportsmen.

Igloo, village, NW Alaska, on Seward Peninsula, 45 mi/72 km N of Nome. Also called Marys Igloo.

Igloolik, village (1991 pop. 936), NE N.W.T., N Canada,

on Igloolik Isl., in Foxe Basin, NE of Melville Peninsula; 69°24′N 81°48′W. Site has been continuously occupied by Inuit people since 2000 B.C. Governmental anthropological research center. Co-op mfg. of handicrafts, clothing. Hunting, fishing, sealing. Radio station; Royal Can. Mounted Police post. Scheduled air service.

Igloolik Island (ig-LOO-lik), SE Franklin dist., N.W.T., N Canada, in Foxe Basin, just off NE Melville Peninsula; 10 mi/16 km long, 1 mi/2 km–7 mi/11 km wide; 69°24′N 81°49′W. Formerly site of trading post, radio station, and R.C. mission.

Ignace (ig-NUHS), town (1991 pop. 1,935), W Ont., central Canada, on Agimak L. (5 mi/8 km long), 50 mi/80 km SSE of Sioux Lookout; 49°25′N 91°40′W. In gold-mining, lumbering region.

Ignacio, village (1990 pop. 720), La Plata co., SW Colo., on Los Pinos R., in foothills of San Juan Mts., and 17 mi/27 km SE of Durango; 37°07′N 107°37′W. Elev. c.6,432 ft/1,960 m. Cattle, sheep; hay, oats. Hq. of Southern Ute Indian Reservation, located to E and SW. U.S. Southern Ute Agency school and hosp. for Native Americans here. Navajo State Park to SE; San Juan Natl. Forest to NE.

Ignacio Allende, Mexico: see ATLEQUIZAYAN.

Ignacio de la Llave (eeg-NAH-see-o dai lah YAH-vai), town, central E Veracruz, Mexico, on the plains of Sotavento, at edge of Papaloapan Delta, 12 mi/20 km S of Veracruz. Hot climate. Agr. (corn, beans, sesame, fruits, sugarcane). Sugar and alcohol industry; cattle and poultry industries.

Ignacio Zaragoza (eeg-NAH-see-o zah-rah-GO-sah), town (1990 pop. 2,997), in N central Chihuahua, Mexico, on Piedras Verdes R., 25 mi/40 km W of Nuevo Casas Grandes; elev. 4,921 ft/1,500 m. Partly mountainous near Sierra Madre Occidental. Temperate climate. Agr. (corn, wheat, fruit); cattle raising. Wood prods. Road connects with Mexico Highway 2 and Juárez.

Ignaluk, Alaska: see LITTLE DIOMEDE ISLAND.

Iguak, Alaska: see OHOGAMIUT.

Iguala de la Independencia (ee-GWAH-lah dai lah een-dai-pen-DEN-see-ah), city (1990 pop. 83,412) and township, Guerrero state, S Mexico, on the Cocula R. (Balsas R. tributary); 18°21′N 99°31′W. Communications, distribution, and processing center of the surrounding mining and agr. region. Famous historically as the place where Agustín de Iturbide proclaimed the Plan of Iguala, which contained the guarantees of independence, on Feb. 24, 1821.

Igualapa (ee-gwah-LAH-pah), town (1990 pop. 2,197), Guerrero, SW Mexico, in Pacific lowland, 8 mi/12.9 km WNW of Ometepec. Fruit, sugarcane; livestock.

Igushik (I-goo-shik), village, SW Alaska, on W shore of Nushagak Bay, at mouth of small Igushik R., 30 mi/48 km SW of Dillingham.

Ihlen (EE-lahn), village (1990 pop. 101), Pipestone co., SE Minn., near S.Dak. state line, 7 mi/11.3 km SSW of Pipestone; 43°54′N 96°22′W. Grain; livestock. Split Rock Creek State Park, on Split Rock L. reservoir to SE.

Ikatan, village, on SE Unimak Isl., SW Alaska, on Ikatan Bay; 54°45′N 163°19′W.

Ikpek, village, W Alaska, on Nome Bay. Sometimes spelled Icpic.

Ila (EI-luh), town (1990 pop. 297), Madison co., NE Ga., 15 mi/24 km NNE of Athens; 34°10′N 83°17′W.

Ilamatlán (ee-lah-mah-TLAN), town (1990 pop. 779), Veracruz, E Mexico, in Sierra Madre Oriental, on Puebla border, 22 mi/35 km SW of Chicontepec de Tejeda. Corn, sugarcane, coffee.

Ilchester (IL-ches-tuhr), village, Howard co., central Md., on Patapsco R., and 9 mi/14.5 km WSW of downtown Baltimore. The Thistle Factory, turning out cotton printed cloth, was established here by George and William Morris; now turns out recycled paper prods. in a big stone factory surrounded by stone homes of the workers. St. Mary's Col. (c.1868), on 170 acres/69 ha of ground belonging to the Redemptorist Fathers, has been vacant since 1972.

Île de l'Est, in Gulf of St. Lawrence, E Que., Canada, one of Magdalen Isls., bet. Grosse Isl. and Coffin Isl.,

85 mi/137 km NNE of Prince Edward Isl.; 5 mi/8 km long, 2 mi/3 km wide; 47°37′N 61°27′W.

Île d'Entrée, island, in Gulf of St. Lawrence, E Que., one of Magdalen Isls., 60 mi/97 km NNE of Prince Edward Isl.; 2 mi/3 km long, 2 mi/3 km wide; 47°17′N 61°42′W.

Île Jésus, Canada: see LAVAL.

Île Maligne (eel muh-LEEN), town, central Que., Canada, on Île d'Alma, on Saguenay R., and 2 mi/3 km NE of St. Joseph d'Alma. Aluminum mill; hydroelectric plant.

Île Royale, Canada: see CAPE BRETON ISLAND.

Île Saint Jean, Canada: see PRINCE EDWARD ISLAND.

Île-aux-Noix (eel-o-nwah), island, covering 210 acres/85 hectares, in the Richelieu R. near St. Jean, S Que., Canada; 45°08′N 73°17′W. During the Fr. and Indian War (1759) the French built a fort here to delay the British advance on Montreal but were forced to surrender it in 1760. Named Fort Lennox and occupied by a Br. garrison, the isl. fell (1775) to Amer. forces and was used as a base by the Amer. generals Schuyler and Montgomery for attacks on Montreal and Que. until abandoned in 1776. The British then used the isl. to supply their operations against the Amer. fleet on L. Champlain. The present Fort Lennox dates from the 1820s, when the old fortifications were repaired and additions were built. It was a military post until 1870. Site of Fort Lennox Natl. Historic Park (est. 1921).

Iliamna (i-lee-YAM-nuh), village (1990 pop. 94), S Alaska, on N shore of Iliamna L., 120 mi/193 km W of Homer, 59°45′N 153°53′W. Sport fishing on Iliamna L. Newhalen village (1990 pop. 160) is 3 mi/4.8 km WSW.

Iliamna (i-lee-YAM-nuh), lake (□ c.1,000 sq mi/2,590 sq km), SW Alaska, at the base of the Alaska Peninsula; 75 mi/120 km long and up to 22 mi/35 km wide. Largest lake in Alaska and the 2d-largest freshwater lake wholly within the U.S. Fed by many lakes and streams; the Kvichak R. drains it SW into Bristol Bay. Noted for sport fishing. Iliamna, Newhalen, and Kakhonak are the chief lakeside villages.

Iliamna Volcano (10,016 ft/3,053 m), active volcano, S Alaska, W of Cook Inlet, 150 mi/241 km SW of Anchorage; 60°02′N 153°06′W.

Iliff, village (1990 pop. 174), Logan co., NE Colo., on South Platte R., near Nebr. state line, and 11 mi/18 km NE of Sterling; 40°45′N 103°04′W. Elev. 3,833 ft/1,168 m. In sugar beet, sunflowers region.

Ilion (IL-ee-uhn), industrial village (□ 2 sq mi/5.2 sq km; 1990 pop. 8,888), Herkimer co., central N.Y., on Mohawk R. and Barge Canal, 11 mi/18 km SE of Utica; 43°00′N 75°02′W. Mfg. (consumer goods, powder, metal prods., lumber); in dairying area. Part of the former Herkimer (village). In Mohawk-Ilion-Frankfort industrial region. Remington Arms Mus. Inc. 1852.

Illecillewaet (il-uh-SIL-uh-wet), mountain stream, c.50 mi/80 km long, SE B.C., W Canada; rises in Illecillewaet glacier, on the W slope of the Selkirk Mts.; flows SW in a mt. valley to join the Columbia R. near Revelstoke. For almost its entire distance it is followed by the Can. Pacific RR and is well known to travelers for its exceptional beauty.

Illilovette Fall, Calif.: see YOSEMITE NATIONAL PARK.

Illinois, state (57,918 sq mi/150,007 sq km; 1995 est. pop. 11,829,940), N central U.S., in the Midwest, admitted as the 21st state of the Union in 1818; ⊙ SPRINGFIELD; 40°07′N 89°21′W. Bounded N by Wis., E by Ind., SE and S by Ky. (where the Ohio R. forms the state line), and W by Mo. and Iowa (where the Mississippi R. forms the state line). L. Michigan is on the NE. The broad level lands that gave Ill. the nickname Prairie State were fashioned by late Cenozoic glaciation, which leveled rugged ridges and filled valleys in over 90% of the state. Cluster of about 60 small glacial lakes in NE, esp. Lake, McHenry, and Cook cos. The fertile prairies are drained by over 275 rivers, most of which flow to the Mississippi-Ohio systems; the Illinois is the state's largest river. These rivers provided early explorers a way SW from L. Michigan into the interior of the continent and later, in the days of canal building, played a big part in hastening settlement of the prairies. The completion of the Erie Canal linked Ill., through the Great

Lakes, to the E seaboard of the U.S. The Illinois Waterway, which includes the Chicago Sanitary and Ship Canal deepened for the waterway, links Chicago to the Mississippi basin as the old Chicago and Ill. and Mich. canals once did, and the St. Lawrence Seaway provides access for oceangoing vessels. The waterways are but a part of a transportation complex that includes RRs, airlines, and a very extensive modern highway system. Although the area's climate varies, with extreme temperatures in parts of the state, the rich land, adequate rainfall (32 in/81 cm–46 in/116 cm annually), and a long growing season make Ill. an important agr. state. It consistently ranks near the top in the production of corn and soybeans. Hogs and cattle are also principal sources of farm income. Other major crops include hay and wheat. Beneath the fertile topsoil lies mineral wealth, and the state is a leading producer of fluorspar. Bituminous-coal fields and oil deposits make S Ill. a major source of fuel; Ill. ranks high among the states in the production of coal, and its reserves are greater than any other state E of the Rocky Mts. These agr. and mineral resources encouraged the establishment of abundant industries along the state's excellent lines of communication and transportation, and by 1880 income from industry was almost double that from agr. Major industries include the mfg. of electrical and nonelectrical machinery, food prods., fabricated and primary metal prods., and chemicals; and printing and publishing. CHICAGO, ROCKFORD, and PEORIA are the 3 largest cities. Metropolitan Chicago, the country's leading RR center, is also a major industrial center, famous for its huge grain mills and elevators. Outside Chicago is the Argonne Natl. Laboratory, a major research and development installation of the Atomic Energy Commission. Suburbs of Chicago such as Schaumburg and Oak Brook have become important business centers. Scattered across the N ½ of the state are cities with specialized industries — Elgin, Peoria, Rock Island, Moline, and Rockford. Industrially important cities in central Ill. include Joliet, Springfield, and Decatur. At the end of the 18th cent. the Illinois, Sac, Fox, and other Native Amer. groups were living in the river forests, where many cents. before them the prehistoric Mound Builders had dwelt. Fr. explorers and missionaries came to the region early. Father Marquette and Louis Joliet, on their return from a trip down the Mississippi, paddled up the Illinois in 1673, and 2 years later Marquette returned to establish a mission in the Ill. country. In 1679 the Fr. explorer Robert Cavelier, sieur de La Salle, went from L. Michigan to the Illinois, where he founded (1680) Fort Creve Coeur and with his lieutenant, Henri de Tonti, completed (1682–1683) Fort St. Louis on Starved Rock cliff. Fr. occupation of the area was sparse, but the settlements of Cahokia and Kaskaskia achieved a minor importance in the 18th cent., and the area was valued for fur trading. By the Treaty of Paris of 1763, ending the Fr. and Indian Wars, France ceded all of the Ill. country to Great Britain. However, the British did not take possession until resistance, led by the Ottawa chief, Pontiac, was quelled (1766). In the Amer. Revolution, George Rogers Clark and his expedition captured (1778) the Br. posts of Cahokia and Kaskaskia before going on to take Vincennes. The Ill. region was an integral part of the Old Northwest that came within U.S. borders by the 1783 Treaty of Paris ending the Revolution. Under the Ordinance of 1787 the area became the Northwest Territory. Made part of Ind. Territory in 1800, Ill. became a separate territory in 1809. The fur trade was still flourishing throughout most of Ill. when it became a state in 1818, but already settlers were pouring down the Ohio R. by flatboat and barge and across the Genesee wagon road. In 1820 the capital was moved from Kaskaskia to Vandalia. The Black Hawk War (1832) practically ended the tenure of the Native Americans here and drove them W of the Mississippi. In the 1830s there was heavy and uncontrolled land speculation. Mob fury broke out with the murder (1837) of the abolitionist Elijah P. Lovejoy at Alton and in the lynching (1844) of the Mormon leader Joseph Smith and his brother Hyrum at Carthage. Industrial development came with the opening of an agr. implements factory by Cyrus H. McCormick at Chicago and John Deere at Moline in 1847 and the building of the RRs in the 1850s. During this period the career of Abraham Lincoln began. In the state legislature, Lincoln and his colleagues from Sangamon co. had worked hard and successfully to bring the capital to Springfield in 1839. As Ill. moved toward a wider role in the country's affairs, Lincoln and another Ill. lawyer, Stephen A. Douglas, won natl. attention with their debates on the slavery issue in the senatorial race of 1858. In 1861, Lincoln became President and fought to preserve the Union in the face of the South's secession. During the Civil War, Ill. supported the Union, but there was much proslavery sentiment in the S part of the state. By the 1860s industry was well established, and many immigrants from Europe had already settled here, foreshadowing the influx still to come. Immediately after the war, industry expanded to tremendous proportions, and the Ill. legislature, by setting aside acreage for stockyards, prepared the way for the development of the meatpacking industry. Economic development had outrun the construction of facilities, and Chicago, which had grown dramatically since the 1830s, was a mass of flimsy wooden structures when the fire of 1871 destroyed most of the city. In the latter part of the 19th cent. farmers in the state revolted against exorbitant freight rates, tariff discrimination, and the high price of manufactured goods. Ill. farmers enthusiastically joined the Granger movement. Laborers in factories, RRs, and mines also became restive, and from 1870 to 1900 Ill. was the scene of such violent labor incidents as the Haymarket Square riot of 1886 and the Pullman strike of 1894. In the 20th cent. labor conditions improved, but violent labor disputes persisted, notably the massacre at Herrin in 1922 during a coal-miners' strike and the bloody riot during a steel strike at Chicago in 1937. State politics became divided by the conflicting forces of farmers, laborers, and corporations, and opposing political machines came into being downstate and upstate. In 1937 new oil fields were discovered in S Ill., further enhancing the state's industrial development. During World War II the nation's 1st controlled nuclear reaction was executed at the Univ. of Chicago, paving the way for development of nuclear weapons during the war. World War II spurred the growth of the Chicago metropolitan area. Adlai E. Stevenson, governor of Ill. (1949–1953), achieved natl. prominence in winning the Democratic presidential nomination in 1952 and 1956. Also during the 1950s the "gateway amendment" to the Ill. constitution simplified the state's constitutional amendment process. S Ill. experienced pop. declines in the 1950s and 1960s as farms in the S became more mechanized, providing fewer jobs in the area. Civil rights demonstrations were held in Cicero in 1967; Democratic convention riots occurred in Grant Park, Chicago in 1968. The area was hard hit again in the 1980s as farm prices fell and farm machinery, the major industrial product of S Ill., was no longer in high demand. The N portion of the state saw a major decline in mfg. in the 1970s and 1980s, which was partially offset by an increase in the service and trade industry and Chicago's continued strength as a financial center. In the 1990s decline leveled off with opening of new foreign markets, such as E Europe. Flood of 1993 affected all cos. bordering Mississippi R., esp. Monroe and Jersey cos. The Illinois (below Beardstown) and the Wabash rivers (in separate flooding) were also affected. In 1970, Ill. adopted a new state constitution that, among other reforms, banned discrimination in employment and housing. The governor of Ill. is elected for a term of 4 years. The state legislature, called the general assembly, consists of a house of representatives with 118 members elected to serve for 2 years and a senate with 59 members elected for 2 or 4 years. Ill. elects 20 Representatives and 2 Senators to the U.S. Congress and has 22 electoral votes. Institutions of higher learning in Ill. include the Univ. of Ill., at Urbana-Champaign, Chicago, and Springfield; DePaul Univ., at Chicago; Northwestern Univ., at Evanston; the Univ. of Chicago and the Ill. Inst. of Technology, in Chicago; Ill. State Univ., at Normal; Southern Ill. Univ., at Carbondale and Edwardsville; Eastern Ill. Univ. at Charleston; Western Ill. Univ. at Macomb; and Governors State Univ. at University Park. Among the state's many tourist attractions are Shawnee Natl. Forest, with recreational facilities; the Cahokia Mounds; and many state parks and historical sites, including New Salem and Lincoln's home and burial place in Springfield. An additional summer attraction is the Ill. State Fair in Springfield and the Du Quoin State Fair. Ill. has 102 cos.: ADAMS, ALEXANDER, BOND, BOONE, BROWN, BUREAU, CALHOUN, CARROLL, CASS, CHAMPAIGN, CHRISTIAN, CLARK, CLAY, CLINTON, COLES, COOK, CRAWFORD, CUMBERLAND, DE KALB, DE WITT, DOUGLAS, DU PAGE, EDGAR, EDWARDS, EFFINGHAM, FAYETTE, FORD, FRANKLIN, FULTON, GALLATIN, GREENE, GRUNDY, HAMILTON, HANCOCK, HARDIN, HENDERSON, HENRY, IROQUOIS, JACKSON, JASPER, JEFFERSON, JERSEY, JO DAVIESS, JOHNSON, KANE, KANKAKEE, KENDALL, KNOX, LAKE, LA SALLE, LAWRENCE, LEE, LIVINGSTON, LOGAN, MCDONOUGH, MCHENRY, MCLEAN, MACON, MACOUPIN, MADISON, MARION, MARSHALL, MASON, MASSAC, MENARD, MERCER, MONROE, MONTGOMERY, MORGAN, MOULTRIE, OGLE, PEORIA, PERRY, PIATT, PIKE, POPE, PULASKI, PUTNAM, RANDOLPH, RICHLAND, ROCK ISLAND, ST. CLAIR, SALINE, SANGAMON, SCHUYLER, SCOTT, SHELBY, STARK, STEPHENSON, TAZEWELL, UNION, VERMILION, WABASH, WARREN, WASHINGTON, WAYNE, WHITE, WHITESIDE, WILL, WILLIAMSON, WINNEBAGO, and WOODFORD.

Illinois and Michigan Canal, Ill.: see ILLINOIS WATERWAY.

Illinois and Michigan Canal National Heritage Corridor, Affiliated Area (□ 503 sq mi/1,303 sq km), NE Ill. Canal vital to W expansion and growth of Chicago. Corridor authorized 1984.

Illinois and Mississippi Canal, NW Ill., abandoned waterway (75 mi/121 km long) bet. the Mississippi R. at Rock Island and Illinois R. near Hennepin; 41°28'N 90°11'W. Opened 1907; soon abandoned because of RR competition. Resurrected in late 20th cent. as a recreational waterway. Often called Hennepin Canal.

Illinois River, 273 mi/439 km long, NE Ill.; formed by the confluence of the Des Plaines and Kankakee rivers; flows SW to the Mississippi R. at Grafton; 41°23'N 88°15'W. Important commercial and recreational waterway. Forms the greater part of the Illinois Waterway, which links the Great Lakes with the Mississippi. The chief city on the river is Peoria. Water quality has improved after decline in early 20th cent.

Illinois Waterway, 336 mi/541 km long, linking L. Michigan with the Mississippi R., N Ill. An important part of the waterway connecting the Great Lakes with the Gulf of Mexico. The Illinois Waterway extends from the mouth of the Chicago R., on L. Michigan, following the Chicago Sanitary and Ship Canal, the lower Des Plaines R., and the Illinois R. to the Mississippi at Grafton. The Calumet channels branch SE from the waterway and link it with the Calumet industrial region along the Ill.-Ind. state line. Principal cargoes, carried chiefly by barges, are coal, petroleum, and grain prods. Recreational areas, including the Illinois and Michigan Canal Natl. Heritage Corridor, have been developed along the waterway. Also known as the Illinois and Michigan Canal.

Illiopolis (il-lee-AW-po-lis), village (1990 pop. 934), Sangamon co., central Ill., 15 mi/24 km W of Decatur; 39°51'N 89°15'W. In agr. area; ships grain.

Illmo, Mo.: see SCOTT CITY.

Ilwaco (il-WAH-ko), town (1990 pop. 815), Pacific co., SW Wash., at mouth of the Columbia, 12 mi/19 km NW of Astoria (Oregon); 46°19'N 124°02'W. Cranberries; salmon, halibut, oysters; mfg. (shipbuilding). Tourism, recreation. Willapa Natl. Wildlife Refuge to NE; Cape Disappointment (N side of entrance to Columbia R. estuary) and Fort Canby State Park to S; Fort Columbia State Park to SE.

Imbert (eem-BERT), town (1993 pop. 6,504), Puerto Plata prov., N Dominican Republic, 10 mi/16 km W of Puerto Plata; 19°45'N 70°52'W. Agr. center (cacao, coffee, sugar). Sugar mill nearby. Until 1925, called Bajabonico.

Imbler (IM-bluhr), village (1990 pop. 299), Union co., NE Oregon, 12 mi/19 km NE of La Grande, on Grande Ronde R.; 45°27'N 117°57'W. Grain, potatoes; cattle. In area are Umatilla (W) and Wallowa-Whitman (E) natl. forests.

Imboden (im-BO-duhn), village (1990 pop. 616), Lawrence co., NE Ark., 13 mi/21 km W of Pocahontas, and on Spring R.; 36°12'N 91°10'W. Mfg. (silk trees and florals).

Imías (ee-MEE-ahs), small town, in Guantánamo prov., SE Cuba, on lee side of El Plurial range, 2 mi/3.2 km from Caribbean Sea, on river of same name; 20°04'N 74°37'W. Small beach resort.

Imlay (IM-lai), uninc. town (1990 pop. c.1,000), Pershing co., W central Nev., 30 mi/48 km SW of Winnemucca, near Humboldt R. (forms Rye Patch Reservoir; Rye Patch State Recreation Area on its shores, to W and SW). Tungsten. Cattle, sheep, barley, alfalfa. Humbolt Range to S.

Imlay City (im-LAI), town (1990 pop. 2,921), Lapeer co., E Mich., near source of Belle R., 11 mi/18 km ESE of Lapeer; 43°01'N 83°04'W. Agr. (potatoes, carrots, beans grain); mfg. (motor vehicles and transportation equip., tool and die, plastic prods., potting soil, pickles). Native Amer. mounds nearby. Inc. 1873.

Immokalee (i-MOK-uh-lee), town (□ 7 sq mi/18.1 sq km; 1990 pop. 14,120), Collier co., SW Fla., 32 mi/51 km ESE of Fort Myers, in the Everglades; 26°25'N 81°25'W. Vegetable farming.

Imogene, town (1990 pop. 88), Fremont co., SW Iowa, 8 mi/12.9 km NNW of Shenandoah; 40°52'N 95°25'W. Livestock; grain.

Imp Mountain, N.H.: see CARTER-MORIAH RANGE.

Imperial, county (□ 4,175 sq mi/10,813 sq km; 1990 pop. 109,303), S Calif., on Mex. (Baja California Norte state; S) border; ⊙ El Centro; 33°02'N 115°21'W. Bordered E by Colorado R. (Ariz. state line). In Colorado Desert; desert ranges (low Superstition Mts., W; Chocolate Mts., E), enclose IMPERIAL VALLEY. Drainage channels (New and Alamo rivers) carry wastewater to Salton Sea (NW). Winter garden agr. region irrigated by ALL-AMERICAN CANAL, which closely parallels internatl. border; asparagus, broccoli, cauliflower, carrots, tomatoes, onions, melons, dates, corn, sugar beets, wheat; cotton; alfalfa, hay; cattle, sheep. Quarrying and mining (gypsum, sand, gravel). Part of PALO VERDE VALLEY in NE. Fort Yuma Indian Reservation is in SE; part of Torres Martinez Indian Reservation in NW corner, on Salton Sea; parts of large Anza-Borrego Desert State Park in W; Salton Sea (salt lake) in NW, extends N into Riverside co., part of Salton Sea State Recreation Area in N, on NE shore, Salton Sea Natl. Wildlife Refuge in S part of lake, part of Cibola Natl. Wildlife Refuge in E; Picacho State Recreation Area in E, on Colorado R. Chief communities are Brawley, Calexico, Calipatria, El Centro. Formed 1866; irrigation development was begun in 1900.

Imperial 1 city (1990 pop. 4,113), Imperial co., S Calif., 3 mi/4.8 km N of El Centro. Oldest community in the irrigated Imperial Valley. Hq. of Imperial Irrigation Dist. and seat of co. fair. Stockyards; vegetables, tomatoes, melons, sugar beets, wheat, corn, alfalfa; cattle, sheep. Seat of Imperial Valley Col. (2-year). Founded 1902, inc. 1904. **2** uninc. city, Jefferson co., E Mo., mfg., commercial, and residential suburb 21 mi/34 km SSW of downtown St. Louis, on Mississippi R.; 38°22'N 90°22'W. Mastodon State Park. Mfg. (chemicals, transportation equip.).

Imperial, town (1991 pop. 364), S central Sask., W Canada, 70 mi/113 km NNW of Regina. Wheat; livestock.

Imperial 1 town (1990 pop. 2,007), ⊙ Chase co., S Nebr., 32 mi/51 km S of Ogallala, N of Frenchman Creek, in Great Plains region; 40°31'N 101°38'W. Grain, potatoes, beans, sunflower seeds, popcorn, potatoes; livestock; poultry prods. Champion Mill State Historical Park and Champion L. State Recreation Area to SW; Enders Reservoir State Recreation Area to SE. Settled c.1885

2 uninc. town (1990 pop. 3,200), Allegheny co., W Pa., suburb 13 mi/21 km W of downtown Pittsburgh; 40°26′N 80°14′W. Mfg. (paper prods., metal coatings; light mfg.). Agr. (dairying) to S. Pittsburgh Internatl. Airport immediately to N.

Imperial, uninc. village (1990 pop. 720), Pecos co., extreme W Texas, 29 mi/47 km NNE of Fort Stockton. Irrigated area of Pecos valley. Cattle, sheep, goats; cotton; vegetables, pecans.

Imperial Beach, city (1990 pop. 26,512), San Diego co., S Calif., residential suburb 9 mi/14.5 km S of downtown San Diego, on the Mex. (Baja Calif. Norte state) border, 6 mi/9.7 km NW of Tijuana (Mexico), on Pacific Ocean, at base of Coronado Peninsula. San Diego Bay to NE. Drained by Tijuana and Otay rivers. Mfg. (cabinets). The southwesternmost city in the continental U.S. Coronado Naval Air Station and Amphibious Base to N, Imperial Beach Naval Radio Station in N, Ream Field Auxiliary Naval Air Station in S. Border Field State Park in SW; Silver Strand State Beach to N. Inc. 1956.

Imperial Dam, on Colorado R., on Ariz.-Calif. state line), 15 mi/24 km NE of Yuma (Ariz.); 3,475 ft/1,059 m long, including diversion structures and dike; 31 ft/9 m high; 32°52′N 114°26′W. Completed 1938 by Bureau of Reclamation; water diverted into All-Amer. Canal to Imperial Valley. Highly silted Imperial Reservoir includes 2 backwater lakes 7 mi/11.3 km N of dam: Martinez (Ariz.) and Ferguson (Calif.) lakes.

Imperial Reservoir (□ 15 sq mi/39 sq km), SE Calif., on Colorado R., bet. SE Calif. (Imperial co.) and SW Ariz. (Yuma co.), in Imperial Natl. Reserve, 9 mi/14.5 km NE of Yuma (Ariz.); 32°53′N 114°28′W. Max. capacity 160,000 acre-ft. Formed in Ariz. by Imperial Diversion (also known as Imperial Dam; 85 ft/26 m high), built (1938) by the Bureau of Reclamation for irrigation. Also known as Ferguson and Martinez lakes.

Imperial Valley, fertile region in the Colorado Desert, Imperial and Riverside cos., SE Calif., extending S into Baja California Norte state, NW Mexico. At various times has either been part of the Gulf of California or part of a river system that flowed into the gulf, now having no outlet; most of the region is below sea level; its lowest point is 235 ft/72 m at the S shore of the Salton Sea. Receiving only c.3 in/7.6 cm of rain annually, the valley experiences extremely high temperatures (max. temp. 115°F/46°C) and has a great daily temp. range. Having one of the longest growing seasons in the U.S. (over 300 days), supports 2 crops a year with extensive irrigation, with the Colorado R. being the primary source of water; it was first irrigated in 1901. Several disastrous floods on the Colorado R. in 1905–1906 inundated the area; not until 1935, with the completion of Hoover Dam, was the valley safe from floods. Approximately 1,563 sq mi/4,048 sq km have been irrigated, chiefly by the All-Amer. Canal, also Coachella and Westside Main canals. The valley is an important source of winter fruits and vegetables for the N areas of the U.S.; cotton, dates, grains, and poultry and dairy prods. are also important. Brawley, Calexico, and El Centro (all in Calif.) are the main U.S. cities in the valley; Coachella and Indio are at NW end of Salton Sea; Mexicali (Mexico), also in the valley, is the center of Mexico's important cotton-growing dist.

Imperoyal (im-puh-ROI-uhl), locality, S N.S., E Canada, on Halifax Harbour, near its mouth on the Atlantic Ocean, 6 mi/10 km SE of Halifax. Petroleum-refining center.

Imuris (ee-MOO-rees), town (1990 pop. 4,086), Sonora, NW Mexico, on Magdalena R. (irrigation), on RR, and 40 mi/64 km S of Nogales at intersection of Mexico Highways 2 and 15; 30°48′N 110°52′W. Wheat, corn, cotton, alfalfa, sugarcane.

Ina (EI-nah), village (1990 pop. 489), Jefferson co., S Ill., 12 mi/19 km S of Mount Vernon; 38°08′N 88°54′W. Agr. Big Muddy R. Correctional Center and Rend L. nearby.

Inagua, island group (1990 pop. 985) of the Bahamas. A virtually isolated cluster at the S end of the archipelago; includes Great Inagua, Little Inagua, and some islets; 21°22′N 73°24′W. Matthew Town is the chief settlement. Salt production is the primary economic activity. Also known for its flamingos.

Inchelium (in-chuh-LEE-uhm), uninc. village (1990 pop. 393), Ferry co., NE Wash., 40 mi/64 km NE of Coulee Dam, on Columbia R. (Franklin D. Roosevelt L. reservoir; Coulee Dam Natl. Recreation Area follows shore), in E part of Colville Indian Reservation; 48°20′N 118°15′W. Gifford Ferry, Columbia R., 4 mi/6.4 km to SE. Mfg. (wood preserving).

Incline Village, uninc. town (1990 pop. 7,119), Washoe co., W Nev., 11 mi/18 km WNW of Carson City, 2 mi/3.2 km E of Calif. state line, on Crystal Bay, NE end of L. Tahoe, in Sierra Nevada; 39°16′N 119°57′W. Gambling resort; tourism; mfg. (wood prods.). Toiyabe Natl. Forest to N; L. Tahoe Nev. State Park to SE. Diamond Peak, Mt. Rose, and Slide Mt. ski areas to NE. Ponderosa Ranch, site of "Bonanza" TV series, is here.

Indaparapeo (een-dah-pah-RAH-pee-o), town (1990 pop. 6,498), Michoacán, central Mexico, 15 mi/24 km NE of Morelia. Cereals, vegetables, fruit; livestock.

Indé (en-DAI), town (1990 pop. 851), Durango, N Mexico, 60 mi/97 km NNE of Santiago Papasquiaro; 25°53′N 105°10′W. Elev. 6,102 ft/1,860 m. Silver, gold, copper deposits, mined in the past.

Independence, county (□ 771 sq mi/1,997 sq km; 1990 pop. 31,192), NE central Ark.; ⊙ Batesville; 35°44′N 91°34′W. Bounded E by Black R.; drained by White R. and Departee Creek. Agr. (rice, soybeans, wheat; cattle, hogs). Mfg. at Batesville; black marble and limestone quarries; timber. Part of Ozark Mts. in W. Founded 1820.

Independence 1 city (1990 pop. 5,972), ⊙ Buchanan co., E Iowa, on Wapsipinicon R., and 23 mi/37 km E of Waterloo; 42°28′N 91°53′W. Mfg. (sheet-metal fabrication; corn milling; dressed poultry, feed, dairy and metal prods.). Limestone quarries, sand and gravel pits nearby. Mental health inst. W of town (1873). **2** city (1990 pop. 9,942), ⊙ Montgomery co., SE Kansas, on the Verdigris R., near the Okla. state line; 37°13′N 95°42′W. In an important oil-producing area where corn and wheat are also grown. Mfg. (machinery, transportation equip., fabricated metal prods.; natural-gas distribution). Founded (1869) on a former Osage reservation. Boomed with the discovery of natural gas in 1881 and oil in 1903. Seast of Independence Community Col. Hometown of playwright William Inge and oil magnate Harry Sinclair. **3** city (1990 pop. 10,444), ⊙ Kenton co., N Ky., a residential suburb 11 mi/18 km S of Cincinnati, Ohio, and 9 mi/14.5 km S of Covington; 38°57′N 84°32′W. Agr. area (burley tobacco; cattle; dairying); mfg. (sheet-metal fabricating; machine tools). **4** city (1990 pop. 112,301), ⊙ Jackson co., W Mo., suburb 7 mi/11.3 km E of downtown Kansas City; 39°05′N 94°20′W. Considered by residents as sister city to Kansas City (predates Kansas City). Agr. to E (soybeans, corn, sorghum; dairying), mfg. (machinery, bldg. materials, apparel, foods, paper prods., ordnance; printing). Natural gas in the area contributes to the city's industries and economy. In the 1830s and 1840s, Independence was the starting point for expeditions over the Santa Fe, Oregon, and Calif. trails. A group of Mormons settled here in 1831 after the Mormon leader Joseph Smith declared Jackson Co. as the original Garden of Eden. World hq. of the Reorganized Church of Jesus Christ of Latter Day Saints (a break away from the Mormon Church) and a new temple was built in 1994. A major mus. of the Church of Jesus Christ of Latter Day Saints (based in Utah) is also located here. Home of President Harry S. Truman (preserved as Natl. Historical Site) and seat of the Harry S. Truman Lib. and Mus., on whose grounds the former president is buried. Other points of interest include the old co. jail and mus. (1859; restored); the old co. courthouse (1825; restored); and nearby Fort Osage on the Missouri R. (1808; reconstructed). Central Missouri State Col. has a residence center here. Inc. 1849. **5** city (1990 pop. 6,500), Cuyahoga co., NE Ohio, S suburb of Cleveland, on State Highway 21; 41°23′N 81°38′W. Chemicals mfg. hq.

Independence 1 town (1990 pop. 1,632), Tangipahoa parish, SE La., 13 mi/21 km N of Ponchatoula, on Tangipahoa R.; 30°39′N 90°31′W. Strawberries, vegetables; catfish, crawfish; mfg. (furniture, chemicals). Inc. 1903. **2** town (1990 pop. 2,822), Hennepin co., E Minn., residential suburb 19 mi/31 km W of downtown Minneapolis; 45°01′N 93°42′W. L. Independence on E border, Sarah L. on N border, in NE; L. Minnetonka to SE. Morris T. Baker Park Reserve to E. **3** town (1990 pop. 4,425), Polk co., NW Oregon, on Willamette R., 8 mi/12.9 km SE of Dallas; 44°51′N 123°11′W. RR junction. Agr. (grapes, hops, corn, beans, grain; poultry, hogs, sheep, cattle); dairy prods.; nurseries. Ankeny Natl. Wildlife Refuge to SE; Helnick State Park to SW. Inc. 1874. **4** town (1990 pop. 988), ⊙ Grayson co., SW Va., in the Blue Ridge, 13 mi/21 km WSW of Galax, near N.C. state line; 36°37′N 81°09′W. Mfg. (machinery, clothing, bottled water, consumer goods, fabricated metal prods., electronic equip.; printing and publishing); agr. (tobacco, corn; livestock; dairying). Point Lookout Mt. (4,554 ft/1,388 m) to N. **5** town (1990 pop. 1,041), Trempealeau co., W Wis., on Trempealeau R., and 23 mi/37 km NE of Winona (Minn.); 44°21′N 91°25′W. Dairy and farm area (grain); dairy prods.; mfg. (wood prods., concrete prods.). Settled 1856; inc. as village in 1876, as city in 1942.

Independence 1 uninc. village, ⊙ Inyo co., E Calif., in Owens Valley, 35 mi/56 km S of Bishop. Mining (gold, salt, lead, mercury); livestock raising (cattle). Winter sports center. Eastern Calif. Mus. Mt. Whitney is S. Large fish hatchery to NW and old Fort Independence are nearby. Fort Independence Indian Reservation to N. Nearby are Kings Canyon (W) and Sequoia (SW) natl. parks; part of Inyo Natl. Forest to E and W. Owens R. to E, Los Angeles Aqueduct passes to E (branches form Owens R. c.15 mi/24 km to N). **2** village, Tate co., NW Miss., 28 mi/45 km SSE of Memphis (Tenn.). Agr. (cotton, grain; cattle).

Independence, Fort, Mass.: see CASTLE ISLAND.

Independence, Lake, Marquette co., NW Upper Peninsula, N Mich., 22 mi/35 km NW of Marquette, bet. Huron Mts. (W and SW) and L. Superior (1 mi/1.6 km away); c.2 mi/3.2 km long, 1.5 mi/2.4 km wide. Village of Big Bay on W end; 46°48′N 87°42′W.

Independence, Mount, W Vt., hill in Orwell town, near L. Champlain, opposite Ticonderoga (N.Y.); site of Amer. Revolutionary defenses.

Independence Mountains, NE Nev., in Elko co.; extends N from Humboldt R., NW of Elko. Rises to McAfee (10,438 ft/3,182 m) and Jacks (10,198 ft/3,108 m) peaks. N point in Humboldt Natl Forest.

Independence National Historical Park, city of Philadelphia, Philadelphia co., SE Pa., in E central Center City; covers 45 acres/18 ha; 39°56′N 75°08′W. Historic points of interest include Independence Hall, Congress Hall, Old City Hall, Franklin Court. Independence Hall is the site of the signing of the Declaration of Independence. Authorized 1948.

Independence Pass, Colo.: see SAWATCH MOUNTAINS.

Independencia (een-dai-pen-DEN-see-ah), province (1993 pop. 38,185), SW Dominican Republic, bet. L. Enriquillo and Haiti border; ⊙ Jimaní; 18°15′N 71°30′W. Formed 1949 out of W Bahoruco prov.

Independencia, La, Mexico: see LA INDEPENDENCIA.

Index, village (1990 pop. 139), Snohomish co., NW Wash., 32 mi/51 km ESE of Everett, and on Skykomish R., at junction of North and South forks, in Cascade Range; 47°49′N 121°33′W. Gold, silver; granite quarries; salmon; timber. Area surrounded by mts. Baker-Snoqualmie Natl. Forest, including Henry M. Jackson Wilderness Area to NE and Alpine Lakes Wilderness to S. Sunset Falls (on South Fork) to S; Mt. Index (5,979 ft/1,822 m) to S.

India Hook, uninc. town (1990 pop. 1,506), York co., N S.C., residential suburb 4 mi/6.4 km NW of Rock Hill; 35°00′N 81°02′W.

Indiahoma (in-dee-uh-HO-muh), village (1990 pop. 337), Comanche co., SW Okla., 20 mi/32 km W of Lawton, on West Cache Creek, S of the Wichita Mts; 34°37′N 98°45′W. Trade center for agr. area. Fort Sill

Military Reservation to NE; Wichita Mts. Natl. Wildlife Refuge to N.

Indialantic (in-dee-uh-LAN-tik), town (□ 1 sq mi/ 2.6 sq km; 1990 pop. 2,844), Brevard co., E central Fla., 3 mi/4.8 km E of Melbourne; 28°05′N 80°34′W. Mfg. includes medical equip., baked goods.

Indian Arm, N arm of Burrard Inlet, SW B.C., Canada, 8 mi/13 km NE of Vancouver; 13 mi/21 km long, 1 mi/ 2 km wide. Receives small Indian R. at head. On both shores mts. rise to 3,000 ft/914 m–5,000 ft/1,524 m.

Indian Beach, village (1990 pop. 153), Carteret co., E N.C., 12 mi/19 km WSW of Morehead City, on Atlantic Ocean, on Bogue Isl.; 34°41′N 76°53′W. Beach resort area. Theodore Roosevelt State Natural Area and N.C. Aquarium to E.

Indian Creek, village (1990 pop. 247), Lake co., NE Ill., residential suburb 27 mi/43 km NNW of Chicago, 8 mi/12.9 km W of Lake Forest; 42°13′N 87°58′W.

Indian Creek, c.60 mi/97 km long, S Ind.; rises in SW Clark co., flows SW to the Ohio R. 11 mi/18 km SW of Corydon.

Indian Harbour Beach, town (□ 2 sq mi/5.2 sq km; 1990 pop. 6,933), Brevard co., E central Fla., 20 mi/32 km S of Cape Canaveral; 28°08′N 80°35′W. Mfg. includes water and waste systems, communications equip., and cosmetics.

Indian Head, town (1991 pop. 1,827), SE Sask., Canada, E of Regina; 50°32′N 103°40′W. In wheat-growing region. Flour mills and grain elevators. Agr.

Indian Head, town (1990 pop. 3,531), Charles co., S Md., on the Potomac c.28 mi/45 km below Washington; 38°36′N 77°10′W. The U.S. Naval Ordnance Station, sometimes called the U.S. Naval Propellant Plant, a facility covering 2,072 acres/839 ha and with 1,347 bldgs., has been located here since 1890. Producing solid rocket fuel, it is the largest employer in Carroll co., with 2,200 civilian workers. Original houses built by the Navy as residences for its workers have been privately sold.

Indian Head Park, village (1990 pop. 3,503), Cook co., NE Ill., residential suburb 15 mi/24 km WSW of Chicago, near Des Plaines R.; 41°46′N 87°54′W.

Indian Hill, village, Hamilton co., extreme SW Ohio, suburb c.10 mi/16 km NE of Cincinnati; 39°11′N 84°20′W. Inc. 1941.

Indian Hills, town (1990 pop. 10,740), Jefferson co., N Ky., residential suburb 5 mi/8 km ENE of Louisville, near Ohio R. Zachary Taylor Natl. Cemetery to NE.

Indian Hills Cherokee Section (CHER-uh-kee), town (1990 pop. 1,005), Jefferson co., N Ky., residential suburb 7 mi/11.3 km ENE of Louisville. Zachary Taylor Natl. Cemetery is here, including grave of President Taylor.

Indian House Lake (□ 125 sq mi/324 sq km), NE Que., Canada, on George R.; 56°N 64°30′W; 35 mi/56 km long, 2 mi/3 km wide. On E shore hills rise to c.1,800 ft/ 549 m.

Indian Island, Knox co., S Maine, small lighthouse isl. off harbor of Rockport.

Indian Islands, Canada: see EAST INDIAN ISLAND and WEST INDIAN ISLAND.

Indian Lake 1 resort village (1990 pop. 600), Hamilton co., NE central N.Y., in Adirondack Mts., near N end of Indian L. (□ c.7 sq mi/18.1 sq km; c.7 mi/11.3 km long), c.45 mi/72 km NW of Glens Falls; 43°47′N 74°18′W. Lumber and wood prods. **2** village (1990 pop. 390), Cameron co., extreme S Texas, residential community 12 mi/19 km N of Brownsville, W of Los Fresnos; 26°05′N 97°30′W. Irrigated agr. area of Rio Grande Valley.

Indian Lake, borough (1990 pop. 388), Somerset co., SW Pa., residential community 11 mi/18 km E of Somerset; 40°02′N 78°51′W. Town surrounds Indian L. reservoir. L. Stonycreek reservoir immediately to S.

Indian Lake, reservoir, Logan co., W central Ohio, at source of Great Miami R., 10 mi/16 km NW of Bellefontaine; c.4 mi/6 km wide; 40°28′N 83°53′W. Formed by Indian L. Dam. Indian L. State Park on S shore.

Indian Lake, Mich.: see INDIAN RIVER.

Indian Lake, N.J.: see DENVILLE.

Indian Lorette, Canada: see LORETTEVILLE.

Indian Orchard, Mass.: see SPRINGFIELD.

Indian Pass, gorge in Adirondack Mts., Essex co., NE N.Y., bet. Wallface Mt. (W) and Mt. MacIntyre (E), c.6 mi/9.7 km WNW of Mt. Marcy, c.1,300 ft/396 m deep, c.1 mi/1.6 km long; 44°08′N 74°02′W. Hiking trails.

Indian Peak (9,817 ft/2,992 m), SE B.C., Canada, near Alta. border, in Rocky Mts., near SE side of Kootenay Natl. Park, 20 mi/32 km SSW of Banff; 50°55′N 115°45′W.

Indian Point Nuclear Power Plants, 2 nuclear power–generating stations, Westchester co., at Buchanan on E side of Hudson R., 35 mi/56 km N of N.Y. city; 41°16′N 73°56′W. Con Edison Company of N.Y. owns and operates Indian Point Unit 2, a 975-MW reactor that began operating in 1974; and the N.Y. Power Authority owns Indian Point Unit 3, a 960-MW generator that began operating in 1976. Indian Pt. Unit 3 was shut down from Feb. 1993–July 1995 due to acute operational and management problems (formerly run by the N.Y. Power Authority, it is now privately managed). Indian Point Unit 1, halted operations in 1974; its nuclear fuel was removed from the reactor and its facilities now support the operation of Indian Point Unit 2. Indian Point's nuclear facilities are surrounded by more people than any other nuclear power site in the country; 10% of U.S. pop. lives within 60 mi/97 km of the site.

Indian Pond, Somerset co., central Maine, in St. Albans town, 18 mi/29 km NE of Skowhegan; 3.5 mi/5.6 km long.

Indian Pond, reservoir, Somerset co., W central Maine, on Kennebec R., 15 mi/24 km W of Greenville; 8 mi/ 12.9 km long; 45°30′N 69°50′W. Receives old and new channels of Kennebec R. from Moosehead L. reservoir (NE).

Indian River, county (□ 616 sq mi/1,595 sq km; 1990 pop. 90,208), E central Fla., on the Atlantic (E); ⊙ Vero Beach; 27°41′N 80°34′W. Coastal lowland bordered by barrier beach enclosing Indian R. lagoon; interior is a marshy peat area containing L. Wilmington. Co. forms part of Indian R. dist. noted for its citrus fruit, especially oranges; also a farming and tourist region; sugarcane grown around Fellsmere. Formed 1925.

Indian River 1 village, E Alaska, on Copper R., 120 mi/ 193 km NE of Valdez, on Tok Cut-off. **2** village, Cheboygan co., N Mich., 18 mi/29 km SSW of Cheboygan, on SE shore of Burt L.; 45°24′N 84°36′W. In resort and forest area. Light mfg. Burt L. State Park to W.

Indian River, lagoon, c.100 mi/161 km long, E central Fla.; parallel to the Atlantic coast from N of Titusville S to Stuart. Along the lagoon a variety of citrus and vegetable prods. are grown and transported by small boats to towns on its waterway and those farther inland. The river's coasts have been marked by housing developments, especially for retired communities and for vacationers. Notable resort towns along its shores include Titusville, Vero Beach, Sebastian, and Fort Pierce.

Indian River 1 10 mi/16 km long, Sussex co., SE Del., tidal estuary formed by small streams just W of Millsboro (dam here); flows E, widens into Indian R. Bay before entering Atlantic Ocean through narrow passage in Del. Seashore State Park 5 mi/8 km N of Bethany Beach. **2** c.40 mi/64 km long, in S Upper Peninsula, Mich.; rises in NW Schoolcraft co., flows SE to Indian L. (c.6 mi/9.7 km long, 4 mi/6.4 km wide) just NW of Manistique, then short distance E to Manistique R.; 45°59′N 86°17′W. Palms Book State Park on NW end; 2 units of Indian L. State Park on E and W sides; Big Spring on W side. Sometimes called Big Indian R. **3** c.80 mi/129 km long, in N N.Y.; rises in N Lewis co., flows NW to Antwerp, and SW, past Philadelphia, then generally N, past Theresa, to S end of Black L. in St. Lawrence co. At Natural Bridge, river has cut limestone bridge and caverns.

Indian River Bay, estuary, SE Del., widening of Indian R., which enters from West Rehoboth Bay and forms large N arm of bay, c.6 mi/9.7 km long, 4 mi/6.4 km

wide; 38°36′N 75°06′W. Barrier beach (Del. Seashore State Park), cut by dredged passage, protects bay from the Atlantic.

Indian River Shores, town (□ 7 sq mi/18.1 sq km; 1990 pop. 2,278), Indian River co., E central Fla., 5 mi/8 km NE of Vero Beach; 27°42′N 80°22′W.

Indian Rocks Beach, town (1990 pop. 3,963), Pinellas co., W central Fla., 10 mi/16 km S of Clearwater; 27°53′N 82°50′W.

Indian Shores, town (1990 pop. 1,405), Pinellas co., W central Fla., 12 mi/19 km S of Clearwater; 27°51′N 82°50′W.

Indian Springs, uninc. village (1990 pop. 1,164), Clark co., S Nev., 40 mi/64 km NW of Las Vegas; 36°34′N 115°40′W. Indian Springs Air Force Base is here (N). Hq. for Nellis Air Force Bombing and Gunnery Range (□ c.5,000 sq mi/12,950 sq km), which includes Nevada Test Site (U.S. Atomic Energy Commission) to NW, and Frenchman Flat, desert basin which was site (Jan. 1951) of experimental atomic explosions. Part of Toiyabe Natl. Forest, including Mt. Charleston to S. Desert Natl. Wildlife Range to N. Desert View Natl Area to SE.

Indian Stream, c.25 mi/40 km long, Coos co., N N.H.; rises near Que. border, flows S to the Connecticut R. below Pittsburg.

Indian Stream Republic, short-lived independent territory at headwaters of Connecticut R., over which neither U.S. nor Can. jurisdiction was established. Set up 1832 by local inhabitants; annexed 1835 by N.H.; awarded to U.S. by Webster-Ashburton Treaty of 1842.

Indian Territory, in U.S. history, name applied to the region in U.S. Great Plains set aside for Native Americans by the Indian Intercourse Act (1834). In the 1820s, the Federal govt. began moving the Five Civilized Tribes of the Southeast (Cherokee, Creek, Seminole, Choctaw, and Chickasaw) to lands W of the Mississippi R. The Indian Removal Act of 1830 gave the president authority to designate specific lands for them, and in 1834 Congress formally approved the choice. The Indian Territory included present-day Okla. N and E of the Red R., as well as parts of Kansas and Nebr.; the lands were delimited in 1854, however, by the creation of the Kansas and Nebr. territories. Tribes other than the original 5 also moved there, but each one maintained its own govt. As white settlers continued to move W, pressure to abolish the Indian Territory mounted. With the opening of W Okla. to whites in 1889 the way was prepared for the extinction of the territory, achieved in 1907 with the entrance of Okla. into the Union. Oklahoma Territory est. 1890; opened the region to white settlement. The Indian Removal Act of 1830 exchanged Indian lands in SE U.S. for land W of Miss. The 5 civilized tribes functioned as nations. The relocation of the tribes, known as the Trail of Tears, in the winter of 1838–1839 caused many deaths. See OKLAHOMA.

Indian Trail, town (1990 pop. 1,942), Union co., S N.C., suburb 14 mi/23 km SE of Charlotte; 35°04′N 80°40′W. In agr. area (cotton, grain; livestock; dairying); mfg. (transformers, paper prods., metal fabrication).

Indian Village, town (1990 pop. 142), St. Joseph co., N Ind., suburb of South Bend; 41°43′N 86°14′W.

Indian Wells, city (1990 pop. 2,647), Kern co., S central Calif., 11 mi/18 km WNW of Ridgecrest, in Mojave Desert. Cattle. Los Angeles Aqueduct passes to W. Kern County Airport No. 8 to SE.

Indiana, state (□ 36,420 sq mi/94,328 sq km; 1995 est. pop. 5,803,471), N central U.S., in the Midwest, admitted as the 19th state of the Union in 1816; 39°47′N 86°08′W; ⊙ INDIANAPOLIS, in the central part of the state. Indianapolis is the largest city; other major cities are FORT WAYNE, EVANSVILLE, and GARY. Ind. is bounded on the N by Mich. and L. Michigan, on the E by Ohio, on the S by Ky. (from which it is separated by the Ohio R.), and on the W by Ill. Northern Ind. is a glaciated lake area, separated by the Wabash R. from the central agr. plain, which is rich with deep glacial drift. The S portion of the state is a succession of bottomlands interspersed with knolls and ridges, gorges and valleys. Limestone caves, such as the big Wyandotte Cave, and mineral springs, as at French Lick and West Baden Springs, are found there. The unglaciated soil is shallow in S Ind., and the cutting of timber has caused erosion, but there is still extensive farming. Although Ind. as a whole is a mfg. state, about ¾ of the land is utilized for agr. With a growing season of about 170 days and an average rainfall of 40 in/102 cm per year, Ind. farms have rich yields. Grain crops, mainly corn and wheat, are important and also support the livestock and dairying industries. Indiana is the nation's leading producer of popcorn, and soybeans and hay are also principal crops. Vegetables and fruits are produced in great quantity and variety as well. Livestock, esp. hogs, cattle, and poultry, is another major agr. prod. Meat packing is chief among the many industries related to agr. Although the urban pop. exceeds the rural, many towns are primarily service centers for agr. communities. There are, however, cities with varied, heavy industries; prominent, besides Indianapolis, Evansville, Fort Wayne, and Gary, are KOKOMO, SOUTH BEND, ELKHART, and TERRE HAUTE. These cities were among the highest in the nation in unemployment during the recession of the early 1980s. In the Calumet region along Indiana's L. Michigan shoreline, marshy wastelands were drained and transformed into an area supporting a complex of factories and refineries. In the mid-1990s, Indiana led the nation in the production of steel. Other leading mfg. includes electrical equip., transportation equip., mobile homes, nonelectrical machinery, chemicals, food prods., and fabricated metals. Rich mineral deposits of coal and stone (the S central Ind. area is the nation's leading producer of bldg. limestone) have encouraged construction and industry. Throughout the state the prods. of farms and factories are transported by truck and by RR. Ind. calls itself the crossroads of America, and its extreme NW corner—where transportation lines head E after converging on nearby Chicago from all directions—is one of the most heavily traveled areas in the world in terms of RR, road, and air traffic. Waterborne traffic is also important to Ind. Improvements on the Ohio R. and the opening (1959) of the St. Lawrence Seaway, linking the Great Lakes with the Atlantic Ocean, have benefited the state. With the opening in 1970 of the Burns Waterway Harbor on L. Michigan, Ind. gained its 1st public port and enhanced its shipping facilities. The Mound Builders were some of Indiana's earliest known inhabitants; their cultural remains have been found along Indiana's rivers and bottomlands. The region was first explored by Europeans, notably the French, in the late 17th cent. The leading Fr. explorer was Robert Cavalier, sieur de La Salle, who came to the area in 1679. At the time of exploration, the area was occupied mainly by Native Amer. groups of the Miami, Delaware, Potawato, and Shawnee descents. Vincennes, the 1st permanent settlement, was fortified in 1732, but for the early 1700s, most of the settlers in the area were Jesuit missionaries or fur traders. By the Treaty of Paris of 1763 ending the Fr. and Indian Wars, Ind., then part of the area known as the Old Northwest, passed from Fr. to Br. control. Along with the rest of the Old Northwest, Ind. was united with Canada under the Quebec Act of 1774. During the Amer. Revolution an expedition led by George Rogers Clark captured, lost, and then recaptured Vincennes from the British. By the Treaty of Paris of 1783 ending the Revolutionary War, Great Britain ceded the Old Northwest to the U.S. Ind. was still largely unsettled when the Northwest Territory, of which it formed a part, was est. in 1787. Native Americans in the territory resisted settlement, but Gen. Anthony Wayne's victory at Fallen Timbers in 1794 effectively ended Native Amer. resistance in the Old Northwest. U.S. forces led by Gen. William Henry Harrison also defeated the Native Amer. forces in the battle of TIPPECANOE RIVER (1811) in the Wabash country. In 1800, Indiana Territory was formed and included the states of Ind., Ill., and Wis., and parts of Mich. and Minn. Vincennes was made the capital, which in 1813 was moved to Corydon. A constitutional convention met in 1816, and Ind. achieved statehood. Jonathan Jennings, an opponent of slavery, was elected governor. Indianapolis was laid out as the state capital, and the govt. moved there in 1824–1825. Ind. was the site of several experimental communities in the early 19th cent., notably the Rappite (1815) and Owenite (1825) settlements at New Harmony. In the 1840s the Wabash and Erie Canal opened bet. Lafayette and Toledo (Ohio), giving Ind. a water route via L. Erie to markets in the E. Also in the 1840s the state's 1st RR line was completed bet. Indianapolis and Madison. The Hoosier spirit of simplicity and forthrightness that developed during Indiana's early years of statehood figured in the writings of Edward Eggleston in *The Hoosier Schoolmaster* and was represented much later in works by James Whitcomb Riley, George Ade, and Gene Stratton Porter. The Civil War brought great changes in the state. In the elections of 1860, Ind. voted for Lincoln, who had spent his boyhood here. Although there was some proslavery sentiment in the state, represented by the Knights of the Golden Circle, Oliver P. Morton, governor during the war, held the state unswervingly to the Union cause even after the constitutional govt. broke down in 1862. Confederate general John Hunt Morgan led a raid into Ind. in 1863, but otherwise little action occurred in the state. Mfg., which had been stimulated in Ind. by the needs of the war, developed rapidly after the war. Factories sprang up, and the old rustic pattern was broken. However, Indiana's farmers continued to be an important force in the state, and in the hard times following the Panic of 1873 indebted farmers expressed their discontent by supporting the Granger movement and later the Greenback party in 1876 and the Populist party in the 1890s. Industrial development came to the Calumet region in the late 19th cent. with the establishment of an oil refinery at Whiting. As the 19th cent. drew to a close, industry continued to expand and the growing numbers of industrial workers in the state sought to organize through labor unions. Eugene V. Debs, one of the great early labor leaders, was from Ind., and the labor movement at Gary in the Calumet area figured prominently in the nationwide steel strike just after World War I. Ind. was an early leader in the production of automobiles. Before Detroit took control of the industry in the 1920s, Ind. boasted over 300 automobile companies. Ind. industries contributed heavily to the war effort. Ind. society in the early 20th cent. has been described in a number of studies and books. The classic sociological study by Robert S. Lynd and Helen M. Lynd of an Amer. mfg. town, *Middletown* (1929), was based on data from Muncie, Ind. In the 1920s religious and racial intolerance was exploited in Ind. by the Ku Klux Klan. In the 1930s and 1940s, Wendell Willkie and Ernie Pyle, both natives of Ind., became nationally prominent figures in politics and journalism, respectively. In the 1980s, Indianapolis experienced significant growth with a diversified economy, something the N industrial portion of the state has been unable to achieve. Concern for education has long been manifest in the state. Robert Dale Owen, son of the Eng. reformer Robert Owen (who founded an idealistic community at New Harmony), promoted tax support of public schools, and this policy was incorporated into the state constitution of 1851. Among the institutions of higher learning in Ind. are Ind. Univ., at Bloomington; Purdue Univ., at West Lafayette; the Univ. of Notre Dame, at South Bend; Ind. Univ./Purdue Univ. at Indianapolis (IUPUI); Ind. State Univ., at Terre Haute; DePauw Univ., at Greencastle; Butler Univ., at Indianapolis; Valparaiso Univ., at Valparaiso; Wabash Col., at Crawfordsville; Earlham Col., at Richmond; and Goshen Col., at Goshen. In 1962, the U.S. Congress authorized the establishment of the Lincoln Boyhood Natl. Memorial in S Ind. Ind. Dunes Natl. Lakeshore, with a 3-mi/4.8-km frontage on L. Michigan, is noted for its beautiful shifting sand dunes. Formerly a state park, the area was made a Natl. Lakeshore in 1966. The Indianapolis Motor Speedway is the site of the famous annual 500-mi/805-km auto race. Indiana's constitution dates from 1851 and provides for an elected executive and legislature. A governor serves as the chief executive for a term of 4 years. The legislature, called the General Assembly, has a senate with 50 members elected for 4 years and a house of representatives with 100 members elected for 2 years. Ind. elects 10 Representatives and 2 Senators to the U.S. Congress and has 12 electoral votes. Although Ind. in the late 19th cent. was regarded as a "swing state" electorally, in the 20th cent. its voting pattern has been generally conservative and Republican. Republican J. Danforth Quayle, elected to the U.S. Senate in 1980 and 1986, was elected Vice-President of the U.S. in 1988. However, Democrats have had some successes in gubernatorial and congressional elections. Ind. has 92 cos.: ADAMS, ALLEN, BARTHOLOMEW, BENTON, BLACKFORD, BOONE, BROWN, CARROLL, CASS, CLARK, CLAY, CLINTON, CRAWFORD, DAVIESS, DEARBORN, DECATUR, DEKALB, DELAWARE, DUBOIS, ELKHART, FAYETTE, FLOYD, FOUNTAIN, FRANKLIN, FULTON, GIBSON, GRANT, GREENE, HAMILTON, HANCOCK, HARRISON, HENDRICKS, HENRY, HOWARD, HUNTINGTON, JACKSON, JASPER, JAY, JEFFERSON, JENNINGS, JOHNSON, KNOX, KOSCIUSKO, LAGRANGE, LAKE, LA PORTE, LAWRENCE, MADISON, MARION, MARSHALL, MARTIN, MIAMI, MONROE, MONTGOMERY, MORGAN, NEWTON, NOBLE, OHIO, ORANGE, OWEN, PARKE, PERRY, PIKE, PORTER, POSEY, PULASKI, PUTNAM, RANDOLPH, RIPLEY, RUSH, SAINT JOSEPH, SCOTT, SHELBY, SPENCER, STARKE, STEUBEN, SULLIVAN, SWITZERLAND, TIPPECANOE, TIPTON, UNION, VANDERBURGH, VERMILLION, VIGO, WABASH, WARREN, WARRICK, WASHINGTON, WAYNE, WELLS, WHITE, and WHITLEY.

Indiana, county (☐ 834 sq mi/2,160 sq km; 1990 pop. 89,994), W central Pa.; ⊙ Indiana. Bounded S by Conemaugh R.; drained by Blacklick, Two Lick, Mahoning, and Little Mahoning creeks. Coal-mining, mfg., agr. region. Bituminous coal, limestone; mfg. at Indiana and Blairsville. Agr. (corn, wheat, oats, hay, alfalfa, potatoes; poultry, sheep, hogs, cattle; dairying). Small part of Gallitzin State Forest in SE corner; Yellow Creek State Park in E center; Yellow Creek L. and Two Lick reservoirs in E center. Formed 1803.

Indiana, borough (1990 pop. 15,174), ⊙ Indiana co., W central Pa. RR terminus and principal supply and trading center for a bituminous-coal mining area in the Allegheny Mts.; 40°37'N 79°09'W. Mfg. (diesel engines, medical prods., food, printing and publishing, lab equip., rubber prods.); surface coal mining. Agr. area (corn, hay; livestock, dairying). Actor Jimmy Stewart b. here 1908. Seat of Indiana Univ. of Pa. County. Jimmy Stewart Field (public airport) to E; Jimmy Stewart Mus.; County Historical Society; Two Lick Reservoir to E; Yellow Creek Reservoir and State Park to SE. Inc. 1816.

Indiana Dunes (☐ 20 sq mi/52 sq km), NW Ind., 200-ft/60-m sand dunes, beaches, and marshes along the S shore of L. Michigan. Natl. Lakeshore, authorized 1966.

Indiana Harbor, Ind.: see EAST CHICAGO.

Indianapolis, city (1990 pop. 741,952), ⊙ Indiana and Marion co., central Ind., on the White R.; 39°47'N 86°09'W. Selected 1820 as the site of the state capital (which was moved here 1824–1825). The largest city in Ind., it is the chief processing point in a rich agr. region and is a major grain market. It is also the commercial, transportation, and industrial center for a large area and is Indiana's leading mfg. city (printing and publishing, flour milling, construction equip., clay prods., electronics, paper prods., chemicals, auto parts, food prods., feeds and fertilizers, lumber prods., agr. equip., crushed limestone, dairy prods., apparel, pharmaceuticals). The site for the city was deliberately located at a point equidistant from the 4 corners of Ind.; largest metropolitan area in U.S. not situated on a navigable river. On Jan. 1, 1970, Indianapolis consolidated with all of Marion co., except for the municipalities of Beech Grove, Southport, Speedway, and Lawrence. The city is the seat of Butler Univ., Marian Col., Univ. of Indianapolis, Christian Theological Seminary, and Indiana Univ.–Purdue Univ. at Indianapolis (IUPUI), with many units, including the Medical Center and the Herron School of Art. The Amer. Legion has its natl. hq. here in a bldg. erected as a war memorial. Landmarks are the state capitol (1878–1888); the state lib. and historical bldg.; the home and burial place of James Whitcomb Riley; the home and burial place of Benjamin Harrison (23d president of the U.S.); a Carmelite monastery; the Soldiers and Sailors Monument (1902); the Bank One Tower, tallest building in the state; and the Indianapolis Motor Speedway, site of the world-famous annual 500-mi/805-km automobile race (Indy 500). In the city's downtown sect. is the RCA Dome (formerly Hoosierdome), a massive indoor sports facility and convention center. In the 1980s, Indianapolis acquired a Natl. Football League team, the Colts, and Market Sq. Arena is the home of the Indiana Pacers. The city hosts numerous cultural events and has noteworthy mus., a symphony orchestra, and a zoo. Indianapolis Internatl. Airport is on the W edge of the city. Fort Benjamin Harrison (to the NE) has been closed; part of its area has been converted to a state park, and the rest is being developed as residential and commercial property. The Naval Air Warfare Center (NAWC) was privatized in 1996 and is now devoted to the design and production of advanced electronics; this was the largest privatization of an Amer. military base in history. Inc. 1847.

Indianola 1 (in-dee-uh-NO-luh), city (1990 pop. 11,340), ⊙ Warren co., S central Iowa, 16 mi/26 km S of Des Moines, N of South R.; 41°21′N 93°34′W. Mfg. (bldg. equip., agr. machinery, plastic and metal prods., consumer goods, animal feed). Seat of Simpson Col. (1860). L. Ahquabi State Park to S. Inc. 1863. **2** city (1990 pop. 11,809), ⊙ Sunflower co., W Miss., 24 mi/ 39 km E of Greenville, near Sunflower R.; 33°27′N 90°38′W. In rich agr. area (cotton, corn, alfalfa, rice, soybeans, pecans; catfish); mfg. (catfish, meat, and pecan processing; paper prods.). Settled in mid–19th cent.; inc. 1886.

Indianola 1 (IN-dee-ah-NO-lah), uninc. town (1990 pop. 900), Allegheny co., W Pa., on Deer Creek, suburb 11 mi/18 km NW of Pittsburgh; 40°34′N 79°51′W. Mfg. of medical equip. and plastic prods. **2** uninc. town (1990 pop. 1,729), Kitsap co., NW Wash., 7 mi/11.3 km SW of Edmonds, on Port Madison bay, arm of Puget Sound; 47°45′N 122°31′W. Mfg. (consumer goods). Port Madison Indian Reservation to E.

Indianola 1 (en-de-an-OH-la), village (1990 pop. 336), Vermilion co., E Ill., 14 mi/23 km SSW of Danville; 39°55′N 87°44′W. In agr. and bituminous-coal area. Near Little Vermilion R. **2** village (1990 pop. 672), Red Willow co., S Nebr., 10 mi/16 km E of McCook, on Republican R.; 40°13′N 100°25′W. Grain, livestock; butchering. **3** village (1990 pop. 171), Pittsburg co., SE Okla., 16 mi/26 km N of McAlester, near Canadian R. (Eufaula L.); 35°10′N 95°46′W. **4** uninc. village (1990 pop. 125), Calhoun co., S Texas, on Matagorda Bay, c.11 mi/18 km SE of Port Lavaca. Founded 1844, it was once most active port in state and port of entry for many immigrants; destroyed by hurricanes of 1875 and 1886. Myrtle Foester Whitmire Division, Aransas Natl. Wildlife Refuge to W.

Indiantown, town (□ 5 sq mi/13 sq km; 1990 pop. 4,794), Martin co., E central Fla., 35 mi/56 km NW of West Palm Beach; 27°02′N 80°28′W. Mfg. includes flour, concrete, beverages, and bldg. equip.

Indiantown Gap Military Reservation, Pa.: see ANNVILLE.

Indin Lake, S central Mackenzie dist., N.W.T., Canada, 120 mi/193 km NNW of Yellowknife, 25 mi/40 km long, 1 mi/2 km–8 mi/13 km wide; 64°15′N 115°15′W. Drains S into Great Slave L. by Snare R. Gold deposits discovered here 1945.

Indio, city (1990 pop. 36,793), Riverside co., SE Calif., 65 mi/105 km ESE of Riverside, 23 mi/37 km SE of Palm Springs, in the Coachella Valley of the Colorado Desert, 22 ft/7 m below sea level. It is the trade and administrative center for a citrus, grape, and date area; also cotton; grain; poultry. Indio has become the center of one of the largest date-producing areas in the U.S. Mfg.

(machinery). The Natl. Date Festival is held on the Indio county fairgrounds. The area has also benefited from the regional growth of it becoming a resort and retirement community. Date Gardens; Joshua Tree Natl. Monument to NE; San Bernardino Natl. Forest and Santa Rosa Mts. to SW; Salton Sea 15 mi/24 km to SE, inland saltwater lake; Cabazon Indian Reservation to SE. Founded 1876, inc. 1930.

Industrial Airport, industrial area, Johnson co., Kansas, 4 mi/6.4 km SW of Olathe, in urban-growth fringe of Kansas City, Kansas, and Kansas City, Mo. Mfg. (consumer goods, printing, food emulsifiers, wood prods., communications equip., farm machinery, fats and oils). Agr. to S and W. Airport.

Industry, town (1990 pop. 685), Franklin co., W central Maine, 7 mi/11.3 km NE of Farmington; 44°45′N 70°03′W. Contains villages of Allen Mills and West Mills.

Industry 1 village (1990 pop. 571), McDonough co., W Ill., 9 mi/14.5 km SSE of Macomb; 40°19′N 90°36′W. Agr. (corn, sorghum; cattle, hogs); coal processing. **2** uninc. village (1990 pop. 475), Austin co., S Texas, 68 mi/109 km WNW of Houston. Oil and natural gas. Agr. (livestock; cotton, peanuts). Timber. Mfg. (lumber, concrete).

Industry, borough (1990 pop. 2,124), Beaver co., W Pa., 7 mi/11.3 km WSW of Beaver, on Ohio R.; 40°39′N 80°24′W. Mfg. includes steel beams. Agr. includes dairying; livestock. Nuclear-power plant at Shippingport across the river to S.

Industry, City of (1990 pop. 631), Los Angeles co., S Calif., industrial suburb 17 mi/27 km E of Los Angeles, near San Jose Creek. Mfg. (consumer goods, dairy prods., plastic prods., carpeting, fabricated metal prods., lumber, chemicals, industrial equip., food, ground minerals, leather prods., resins, rubber prods., paper prods., motors, printing).

Inez, town (1990 pop. 1,371), Victoria co., S Texas, 13 mi/ 21 km NE of Victoria, near Arenosa Creek; 28°52′N 96°47′W. Oil and natural gas. Agr. (cotton, rice; cattle; dairying).

Inez (ei-NEZ), village (1990 pop. 511), ⊙ Martin co., E Ky., in Cumberland Mts., 26 mi/42 km N of Pikeville; 37°52′N 82°32′W. Coal; agr. (livestock; tobacco); coal processing, light mfg. Big Sandy Regional Airport to N. Martin County Reservoir to N.

Ingalls, town (1990 pop. 889), Madison co., E central Ind., on small Fall Creek, 24 mi/39 km NE of Indianapolis; 39°58′N 85°48′W. In agr. area.

Ingalls (ING-guhls), village (1990 pop. 301), Gray co., SW Kansas, on Arkansas R., 6 mi/9.7 km WNW of Cimarron; 37°49′N 100°27′W. Grain; cattle.

Ingalls, Mount (8,377 ft/2,553 m), Plumas co., NE Calif., in the Sierra Nevada, 17 mi/27 km E of Quincy. In Plumas Natl. Forest. Copper mine on its slopes.

Ingersoll, town (1991 pop. 9,378), S Ont., Canada, on the Thames R., E of London; 43°02′N 80°53′W. Large dairy-processing industry and light mfg.

Ingersoll (ING-uhr-sahl), village, Alfalfa co., N Okla., 3 mi/4.8 km NW of Cherokee. In grain-growing area.

Ingham (ING-uhm), county (□ 560 sq mi/1,450 sq km; 1990 pop. 281,912), S central Mich.; 42°36′N 84°22′W; ⊙ Mason. Lansing, the state capital, is in NW corner. Drained by Grand and Red Cedar rivers, and small Sycamore Creek. Agr. (apples, wheat, soybeans, corn, hay, beans, onions, cucumbers, carrots); hogs, cattle, sheep, poultry; dairy prods. Mfg. at Lansing. Oil and gas extraction. Also includes suburbs of E. Lansing and Meridian township. Formed 1838.

Ingleside, town (1990 pop. 5,696), San Patricio co., S Texas, suburb 12 mi/19 km ENE of Corpus Christi, across Corpus Christi Bay; 27°52′N 97°12′W. Oil refining. Corpus Christi Bay to SW, Redfish Bay and Intracoastal Waterway to E; Ingleside Naval Station at cape to S.

Inglestat, Alaska: see KOYUK.

Inglewood, city (1990 pop. 109,602), Los Angeles co., S Calif., residential and industrial suburb 7 mi/11.3 km SW of Los Angeles. The city grew substantially during 1950s and 1960s and is bounded by Los Angeles on the

E, N, and W, and by Hawthorne and El Segundo on the S. In an oil-producing area. Its mfg. includes motor-vehicle parts, furniture, processed food, plastics prods., and electronic equip. The city has greatly benefited from the regional advancement, extension, and development of these industries. Inglewood's pop. has grown accordingly. Los Angeles Internatl. Airport to W. Northrop Univ., the Hollywood Park and the (Los Angeles) Great Western Forum, a massive arena that hosts Los Angeles Lakers basketball games as well as concerts. Dockweiler State Beach, on Pacific Ocean, 5 mi/8 km W. Founded 1873, inc. 1908.

Inglewood, uninc. town (1990 pop. 6,500), King co., W Wash., residential suburb 11 mi/18 km NNE of Seattle, on E shore of L. Washington, near its N end, at mouth of Sammamish R. St. Edward State Park to SW, on lake shore.

Inglis (ING-gliss), town (□ 3 sq mi/7.8 sq km; 1990 pop. 1,241), Levy co., W central Fla., 35 mi/56 km WSW of Ocala; 29°01′N 82°39′W. Mfg. (machine parts).

Ingomar 1 (ING-guh-mahr), village, Union co., N Miss., 6 mi/9.7 km SSW of New Albany. In agr. and dairying area. **2** village (1990 pop. 60), Rosebud co., SE central Mont., 41 mi/66 km NW of Forsyth, near source of East Fork Froze to Death Creek. Sheep and cattle. Black Sea Reservoir to NE. One of the largest sheep-shearing plants in the state.

Ingonish (ing-guh-NISH), village, NE N.S., Canada, on NE coast of Cape Breton Isl., 40 mi/64 km NNW of Sydney; 46°41′N 60°22′W. Fishing port, tourist resort. Extending W is Cape Breton Highland Natl. Park.

Ingram, town (1990 pop. 1,408), Kerr co., SW Texas, on Guadalupe R., c.60 mi/97 km NW of San Antonio; 30°04′N 99°14′W. Elev. 1,600 ft/488 m. Trading point in ranching area (cattle, sheep, goats; wheat, pecan, apples). Est. 1883; new section built after flood of 1936.

Ingram, village (1990 pop. 91), Rusk co., N Wis., 14 mi/ 23 km ENE of Ladysmith; 45°30′N 90°48′W. In dairying and stock-raising area.

Ingram (ING-rahm), borough (1990 pop. 3,901), Allegheny co., SW Pa., residential suburb 3 mi/4.8 km W of Pittsburgh, near Ohio R. Inc. 1902.

Ingram Beach, village, Horry co., E S.C., 14 mi/23 km NE of Myrtle Beach, on Atlantic Ocean, in Grand Strand beach resort area.

Inkom, town (1990 pop. 769), Bannock co., SE Idaho, 12 mi/19 km SE of Pocatello, on Portneuf R.; 42°48′N 112°15′W. Mfg. (portland cement). Parts of Caribou Natl. Forest to SW and E; Pebble Creek Ski Area to E; Fort Hall Indian Reservation to N (port of entry).

Inks Lake, reservoir (□ 1 sq mi/2.6 sq km), Burnet-Llano co. line, S central Texas, on Colorado R., 3 mi/ 4.8 km below Buchanan Dam, c.10 mi/16 km WSW of Burnet; 30°43′N 98°22′W. Formed by Roy Inks Dam. Natl. Fish Hatchery. Inks L. State Park on E shore.

Inkster, city (1990 pop. 30,772), Wayne co., SE Mich., suburb 14 mi/23 km WSW of Dearborn, on the Rouge R.; 42°17′N 83°19′W. Mfg. (fabricated metal prods., storage tanks, chemicals, gaskets and seals). Nearby auto plants suffer from the decline of the auto industry in the 1970s and 1980s. Drained by Lower R. Rouge. Settled 1825 as Moulin Rouge, renamed 1863, inc. as a city 1964.

Inkster, village (1990 pop. 95), Grand Forks co., E N.Dak., 33 mi/53 km NW of Grand Forks, near Forest R.; 48°08′N 97°38′W.

Inland Empire, name given to vast region of Columbia R. basin in E Wash., N Oregon E of the Cascades, and N Idaho, and sometimes including NW Mont.; Spokane (Wash.) is chief center. Dry farming (wheat) and livestock grazing have long predominated, but large-scale irrigation is contemplated through the Columbia R. project, so as to increase the variety of the region's agr. produce. Mining and lumbering are important in Idaho and Mont. portions.

Inlet, resort village (1990 pop. 400), Hamilton co., NE central N.Y., in Adirondack Mts., bet. 2 lakes of Fulton Chain of Lakes, c.50 mi/80 km NNE of Utica; 43°44′N 74°44′W.

Inman, town (1990 pop. 1,742), Spartanburg co., NW

S.C., 12 mi/19 km NW of Spartanburg; 35°02′N 82°05′W. Mfg. (textiles, paper, chemicals, copper wire). Agr. includes soybeans, apples; poultry, hogs; dairying. Painter Henry Inman and others in S.C. created some of the earliest genre painting done in the U.S. (1825–1850).

Inman 1 village (1990 pop. 1,035), McPherson co., S central Kansas, 15 mi/24 km NE of Hutchinson; 38°13′N 97°46′W. In wheat region; flour milling. Mfg. (lumber). Oil wells nearby. **2** village (1990 pop. 159), Holt co., N Nebr., 8 mi/12.9 km SE of O'Neill, on Elkhorn R; 42°22′N 98°31′W. **3** uninc. village, Wise co., SW Va., 9 mi/14.5 km W of Norton, 2 mi/3.2 km NW of Appalachia, in Jefferson Natl. Forest. Coal mining.

Inman Mills, uninc. village (1990 pop. 1,571), Spartanburg co., NW S.C., 12 mi/19 km NW of Spartanburg, 1 mi/1.6 km SW of Inman; 35°02′N 82°05′W. Textiles and paper mills in area.

Innisfail (I-nis-fail), town (1991 pop. 5,700), S central Alta., Canada, near Red Deer R., 18 mi/29 km SSW of Red Deer; 52°02′N 113°57′W. Grain elevators; dairying; ranching.

Innisfree, village (1991 pop. 254), E Alta., Canada, 28 mi/45 km W of Vermilion. Dairying; grain; stock.

Innoko River, c.450 mi/724 km long, W Alaska; rises near 63°00′N 156°30′W, flows first N, then in a winding course generally SW, to Yukon R. opposite Holy Cross.

Innuit, Mount (4,554 ft/1,388 m), E Lab., Canada, at head of Nachvak Fiord; 59°02′N 64°09′W.

Inola (ei-NO-luh), town (1990 pop. 1,444), Rogers co., NE Okla., 25 mi/40 km E of Tulsa. In livestock-raising and agr. area; mfg. (machine parts, figurines, lead, medical equip.).

Inside Passage, natural, protected waterway, c.950 mi/1,530 km long, threading through the Alexander Archipelago off the coast of B.C. (Canada) and SE Alaska. From Seattle, Wash., to Skagway, Alaska, or via Cross Sound to the Gulf of Alaska, the route uses channels and straits bet. isls. and the mainland that afford protection from the storms and open waters of the Pacific Ocean. Snow-capped mts., forests, waterfalls, glaciers, and deep, narrow channels give the Inside Passage great scenic beauty. It was known to Span., Rus., Eng., and Amer. explorers. Important coastal route for Can. shipping as well as the route generally used by ships sailing bet. the continental U.S. and Alaska.

Inspiration, uninc. village, Gila co., SE central Ariz., in Pinal Mts., 2 mi/3.2 km N of Miami. Copper mining.

Institute, uninc. town, Kanawha co., W central W.Va., suburb 8 mi/12.9 km WNW of Charleston, on Kanawha R. Mfg. (asphalt prods., industrial and agr. chemicals). W.Va. State Col.

Insull (IN-suhl), village, Harlan co., SE Ky., in the Cumberlands, 16 mi/26 km NE of Middlesboro, 3 mi/4.8 km NW of Alva. Bituminous coal.

Insurgente José María Morelos y Pavón (een-soor-HEN-tai ho-SAI mah-REE-ah mo-RE-los ee pah-VON), natl. park, in central Michoacán, Mexico, 16 mi/26 km E of Morelia. Mexico Highway 15 leads to the park known for its scenic views.

Insurgente Miguel Hidalgo Y Costilla (een-soor-HEN-tai mee-GEL ee-DAHL-go ee ko-STEE-yah), natl. park (□ 7 sq mi/18.1 sq km), W of San Ángel (Álvaro Obregón), Mexico, suburb of México City on Mexico Highway 15. This park is locally called La Marquesa. The battle of Monte de las Cruces took place here in the 19th cent. It was an important battle in the War of Independence. There are picnic sites, a trout hatchery, and a lake here.

Inter-American Highway, section of the Pan-Amer. Highway system from Nuevo Laredo (Mexico) to Yaviza (Panama); c.3,400 mi/5,472 km long. The principal highway connecting the countries of Central Amer. In Mexico, N of Mexico city, it is designated Highway 85; from Mexico city to Guatemalan border, Highway 90. In Central Amer., it is usually called Highway C.A.1.

Interborough (Interboro) Parkway, Queens and Brooklyn boroughs of N.Y. city, SE N.Y., at extreme W end of Long Isl. Short parkway (4.7 mi/7.6 km long) snakes its way from the East N.Y.–Highland Park area of Brooklyn E to the Grand Central Parkway in Kew Gardens, Queens. Completed Aug. 1935, its lack of breakdown lanes, narrow, winding character, difficult lane changes, and low median barrier made it one of the most hazardous thoroughfares in the metropolitan area until 1973, when its safety was improved to meet modern standards. Renamed Jackie Robinson Parkway in 1997.

Intercourse, uninc. town (1990 pop. 1,200), Lancaster co., SE Pa., 10 mi/16 km E of Lancaster; 40°02′N 76°06′W. In rich agr. area. Mfg. (furniture, food prods.). Agr. (grain, potatoes, soybeans, apples; livestock; dairying). Pennsylvania Dutch region. People's Place Quilt Mus.

Interior, village (1990 pop. 67), Jackson co., SW central S.Dak., 25 mi/40 km WSW of Kadoka, just E of Badlands Natl. Park; on White R.; 43°43′N 101°58′W. Located S of park hq. Pine Ridge Indian Reservation S of river; Buffalo Gap Natl. Grassland N of river. Center of tourist trade.

Interlachen (IN-tuhr-LAH-kuhn), town (□ 6 sq mi/15.5 sq km; 1990 pop. 1,160), Putnam co., N central Fla., 15 mi/24 km W of Palatka; 29°37′N 81°54′W.

Interlaken, uninc. town (1990 pop. 6,404), Santa Cruz co., W Calif., residential suburb 2 mi/3.2 km NE of Watsonville, in Pajaro Valley, between Kelly, Dew, and Tynan lakes. Santa Cruz Mts. to NE. Fruit, nuts, vegetables, grain, flowers, nursery prods.

Interlaken, village (1990 pop. 680), Seneca co., W central N.Y., in Finger Lakes region, near Cayuga L., 18 mi/29 km NW of Ithaca; 42°37′N 76°43′W. Agr. (sweet corn; field corn; vineyards, wineries).

Interlaken (IN-tuhr-LAH-kuhn), borough (1990 pop. 910), Monmouth co., E N.J., near coast, 13 mi/21 km E of Freehold and just N of Asbury Park; 40°13′N 74°01′W.

Interlaken, Mass.: see STOCKBRIDGE.

Interlochen (IN-tur-LAH-kun), village, Grand Traverse co., NW Mich., 10 mi/16 km SSW of Traverse City; 44°38′N 85°46′W. In fruit-growing and resort area. Hq. for Interlochen Center for the Arts (formerly Natl. Music Camp). The 8-week Interlochen Arts festival takes place every summer, with performances of more than 360 concerts. Interlochen State Park to S bet. Duck and Green lakes.

International Amistad Reservoir, in Texas and Coahuila (Mexico), on Rio Grande, 10 mi/16 km WNW of Del Rio (Texas); c.60 mi/97 km long; 29°27′N 101°01′W. Max. capacity 5,658,600 acre-ft. Devil's R. forms 30-mi/48-km N arm. Formed by Internatl. Amistad Dam (247 ft/75 m high), built (1969) by the U.S. and Mexico for flood control and irrigation. Amistad Natl. Recreation Area (Texas) on NE shore, Parque Nacional los Novillos (Mexico) on SW shore.

International Falcon Reservoir (□ 180 sq mi/466 sq km), on S Texas–NW Tamaulipas (Mexico) border, on Rio Grande, 70 mi/113 km SSE of Laredo (Texas); 25°34′N 99°10′W. Max. capacity 3,177,000 acre-ft. Formed by Internatl. Falcon L. Dam (also known as Falcon Dam; 175 ft/53 m high), built (1953) by Internatl. Boundary and Water Commission for flood control; also used for irrigation and power generation. Falcon State Park near dam.

International Falls, town (1990 pop. 8,325), ⊙ Koochiching co., N Minn., 140 mi/225 km NW of Duluth, on Rainy R. below its outlet from Rainy L., opposite Fort Frances, Ont. (Canada); 48°35′N 93°24′W. Port of entry; toll bridge to Fort Frances. Mfg. (pulpwood, wood prods., paper, beverages, printing and publishing); timber; cattle; alfalfa; dairying. Tourism. Growth followed construction of paper mill (1904) at falls in Rainy R. Recognized on natl. weather reports for its frequent coldest daily temperature readings for U.S. (outside Alaska); sometimes referred to as "Frostbite Falls" and the "Icebox of the Nation." Voyageurs Natl. Park to E.

International Peace Garden, affiliated area (□ 4 sq mi/10.4 sq km) of U.S. and Can. natl. park systems, N N.Dak. and SW Man. (Canada), where U.S. Highway 281 meets Man. Highway 10; 15 mi/24 km N of Dunseith (N.Dak.), 16 mi/26 km S of Boissevain (Man.); 48°59′N 100°03′W. A total of 1.4 sq mi/3.6 sq km is in N.Dak.; 2.6 sq mi/6.7 sq km in Man. Dedicated 1932. Commemorates peaceful relations between Canada and the U.S. Includes the 120-ft/37-m-tall Peace Tower. Camping facilities.

Interstate State Park (□ 2 sq mi/5.2 sq km), Polk co., Wis.; located SW of St. Croix Falls (town on St. Croix R.). Its central feature is the scenic gorge called the Dalles of the St. Croix, with rock walls c.200 ft/61 m high; there are curious rock formations and potholes. There is also another Interstate State Park (□ 293 acres/119 ha) in Chicago co., Minn., across St. Croix R.; administered separately.

Intracoastal Waterway, partly natural, partly artificial waterway providing sheltered passage for commercial and leisure boats along the U.S. Atlantic coast from Boston (Mass.) S to Key West (Fla.), where it wraps along the Gulf of Mexico coast to Brownsville (Texas) at the mouth of the Rio Grande; c.3,000 mi/4,828 km long. The toll-free waterway, authorized by Congress in 1919, is maintained by the Army Corps of Engineers at a min. depth of 12 ft/4 m for most of its length; some parts have 7 ft/2.1 m and 9 ft/2.7 m depths. Among some of the waterway's most often used canals along the Atlantic route are the Chesapeake and Delaware, and Albemarle; along the Gulf route the most used are the New Orleans Rigolets Cut, the Port Arthur–Corpus Christi Channel, and the Inner Harbor Navigational Canal at New Orleans. It runs along the entire coastline of Fla. The separate Okeechobee Waterway in E central and SW Fla. crosses the Fla. peninsula. Plans to build a canal across N Fla. to link the Atlantic and Gulf sects. were blocked in 1971 by a presidential order to prevent potential environmental damage. Many miles of navigable waterways connect with the coastal system, including the Hudson R., N.Y. State Barge Canal, Chesapeake Bay, the Savannah R., the Apalachicola R., and the entire Mississippi R. system. The Intercoastal Waterway has a good deal of commercial activity; barges haul petroleum prods., foodstuffs, bldg. materials, and manufactured goods.

Inukjuak or **Port-Harrison**, village (1991 pop. 1,044), NW Que., Canada, on E shore of Hudson Bay, W side of Ungava Peninsula, at mouth of Innuksuak R. Populated by Inuit people. Scheduled air service. Hunting, fishing, trapping.

Inuvik (IN-oo-vik), NW region (□ 152,089 sq mi/393,911 sq km; 1991 pop. 8,491), N.W.T., Canada, extending E from the Yukon to the Hornaday R. and N from Wrigley to include Banks Isl. The town of Inuvik, built in the 1950s and 1960s, is the regional hq. Inuvik is the largest community N of the Arctic Circle. The N Mackenzie R. forms the heart of the region, which is steadily developing its oil and natural-gas resources. Native hunting, sealing, and crafts. The region is a mix of subarctic coniferous forest and arctic tundra.

Inuvik (IN-oo-vik), town (1991 pop. 3,206), Inuvik region, N.W.T., Canada, on the E channel of the Mackenzie R.; 68°21′N 133°42′W. It was built (1954–1962) as a new townsite for Aklavik and was the 1st model town in the Can. Arctic. Inuvik has an airport.

Inver Grove Heights, city (1990 pop. 22,477), Dakota co., SE Minn., suburb 7 mi/11.3 km S of St. Paul, on Mississippi R. (bridged); 44°49′N 93°03′W. It has benefited from the industrial and cultural growth of the greater Minneapolis–St. Paul area. Mfg. (motor-vehicle and aircraft parts, asphalt, feeds, consumer goods, bldg. materials, paper prods., medical equip.). South St. Paul Airport to NE. Seat of Inver Hills Community Col. Several small lakes in city.

Invermay, village (1991 pop. 328), SE Sask., Canada, near small Saline and Stonewall lakes, 33 mi/53 km WNW of Canora. Mixed farming.

Invermere, resort village (1991 pop. 2,207), SE B.C., Canada, on slope of Rocky Mts., on Windermere L., 50 mi/80 km SSW of Banff; 50°30′N 116°02′W. Elev. 2,863 ft/859 m. Logging; tourism, ski-resort area.

Inverness (IN-vuhr-NES), county (□ 1,409 sq mi/3,649 sq km; 1991 pop. 21,620), NE N.S., Canada, in E part of Cape Breton Isl., on Gulf of St. Lawrence; ⊙ Port Hood.

Inverness, town, E N.S., Canada, on W coast of Cape Breton Isl., on Northumberland Strait, 55 mi/89 km W of Sydney. Formerly coal-mining center and coal-shipping port.

Inverness, village (1991 pop. 276), ⊙ Megantic co., S Que., Canada, 16 mi/26 km NW of Thetford Mines. Copper and magnesite mining; dairying; cattle and pig raising; lumbering.

Inverness 1 (IN-vuhr-NES), uninc. town (1990 pop. 1,422), Marin co., W Calif., 20 mi/32 km NW of San Rafael, on W side of Tomales Bay, on Point Reyes Peninsula, bounded N, W, and S by Point Reyes Natl. Seashore. Tomales Bay lies in San Andreas Fault. Clams, oysters, mussels. Tourism. **2** town (□ 8 sq mi/20.7 sq km; 1990 pop. 5,797), Citrus co., W central Fla., c.60 mi/97 km NNE of Tampa, on Tsala Apopka L.; 28°50′N 82°20′W. Agr. trade center; vegetable packing; fishing; phosphate quarrying. **3** (in-VUHR-nes), town (1990 pop. 1,174), Sunflower co., W Miss., 8 mi/12.9 km SSE of Indianola; 33°21′N 90°35′W. In rich agr. area (cotton, corn, rice, soybeans; cattle); mfg. (catfish processing, agr. equip.).

Inverness 1 (IN-vuhr-NES), village (1990 pop. 6,503), Cook co., NE Ill., residential suburb 30 mi/48 km NW of Chicago; 42°07′N 88°05′W. Some remnant agr. Inc. 1962. **2** village (1990 pop. 220), Hill co., N Mont., 47 mi/76 km W of Havre. Cattle, sheep, hogs; wheat, barley, oats, hay.

Inverness (IN-vuhr-NES), residential suburb (1990 pop. 2,528) of Birmingham, Shelby co., N. central Ala.; 33°24′N 86°43′W.

Invisible Mountain, Idaho: see LOST RIVER RANGE.

Inwood 1 town (□ 2 sq mi/5.2 sq km; 1990 pop. 6,824), Polk co., central Fla., 10 mi/16 km E of Lakeland; 28°02′N 81°46′W. **2** town (1990 pop. 824), Lyon co, NW Iowa, 15 mi/24 km SW of Rock Rapids; 43°17′N 96°26′W. In livestock and grain area. **3** uninc. town (1990 pop. 1,360), Berkeley co., NE W.Va., 7 mi/11.3 km SSW of Martinsburg; 39°21′N 78°02′W. Agr. (grain, apples); livestock; dairying. Limestone quarrying. Mfg. (food and beverages, crushed limestone).

Inwood, village, S Ont., Canada, 10 mi/16 mi ESE of Petrolia; 50°30′N 97°30′W. Dairying; mixed farming.

Inwood, residential village (□ 2 sq mi/5.2 sq km; 1990 pop. 7,767), Nassau co., SE N.Y., on W L.I., near E shore of Jamaica Bay, one of the "5 Towns of L.I.," 9 mi/14.5 km SW of Hempstead; 40°37′N 73°45′W. Affluent residential area; some light mfg.

Inwood, residential district, NW Manhattan borough, N.Y. city, SE N.Y., along the Hudson and Harlem rivers; 40°52′N 73°56′W. Northernmost part of Manhattan isl. Pop. largely Hispanic and Afr.-Amer. Contains Inwood Hill and Fort Tryon parks; site of the Cloisters, noted mus. of medieval art. Also here is Dyckman House (built 1783), the last 18th-cent. farmhouse in Manhattan.

Inyan Kara Creek (IN-yuhn KAR-uh), 43 mi/69 km long, NE Wyo.; rises in NE corner of Weston co. in Black Hills near Inyan Kara Mt., flows NW to Belle Fourche R. 16 mi/26 km NE of Moorcroft.

Inyan Kara Mountain (IN-yuhn KAR-uh), peak (6,368 ft/1,941 m) in W part of Black Hills, Crook co., NE Wyo., 14 mi/23 km S of Sundance.

Inyo, county (□ 10,192 sq mi/26,397 sq km; 1990 pop. 18,281), E Calif.; ⊙ Independence; 36°36′N 117°30′W. Crest of Sierra Nevada (High Sierras) along W boundary, also forms E boundary of Kings Canyon and Sequoia natl. parks. Co. is leading producer in state of lead, tungsten, and talc; also mining of molybdenum, zinc, silver; and extraction of borax, potash, salt, and soda. Some irrigated farming (in Owens Valley); stock raising; dairying. Camping, hunting, fishing, and winter sports in mts.; winter resorts in Death Valley. Includes Mt. Whitney (14,495 ft/4,418 m), highest peak in U.S., outside Alaska, and 9 other peaks over 14,000 ft/4,267 m. In E, bounded by Nev. state line, includes large part of Death Valley Natl. Monument, which has lowest point (282 ft/86 m below sea level) in Western Hemisphere. Bet. the Sierra Nevada and Panamint Range (W wall of Death Valley) are arid basins (notably Owens Valley), Inyo Mts., and other ranges. E of Death Valley is Amargosa Range. Owens R. supplies water to Los Angeles Aqueduct (begins in NW part of co., runs S at base of Sierra Nevada, to Los Angeles); Amargosa R., Furnace Creek vanish in Death Valley. Includes Big Pine, Fort Independence, and Lone Pine Indian reservations, all in NW in Owens Valley. Partly in Inyo Natl. Forest. Owens L. (dry) in W; part of large China L. Naval Weapons Center in SW. Formed 1866.

Inyo Mountains, Inyo co., E Calif., range bet. Owens Valley (W) and Saline Valley (E), extending 70 mi/113 km SSE from S end of White Mts., SE of Bishop, to point just SE of Owens L., on E side of Sierra Nevadas. Rise to 11,123 ft/3,390 m at Waucoba Mt., 18 mi/29 km SE of Big Pine. Crossed by Westgard Pass (State Highway 168; 7,313 ft/2,229 m) just NE of Big Pine. N part in Inyo Natl. Forest.

Inyokern, uninc. village, Kern co., S central Calif., in Mojave Desert, 62 mi/100 km ENE of Bakersfield. RR junction. China L. Naval Weapons Center (one of 2 large sections to NE); China L. (dry) to NE; Sequoia Natl. Forest and Pacific Crest Trail to W; Los Angeles Aqueduct passes to W.

Ioco (ei-O-ko), town, SW B.C., Canada, at W end of Burrard Inlet of the Strait of Georgia, 10 mi/16 km ENE of Vancouver, opposite Port Moody; 49°18′N 122°52′W. Oil refinery.

Iola (ei-O-luh), city (1990 pop. 6,351), ⊙ Allen co., SE Kansas, on Neosho R., 35 mi/56 km W of Fort Scott; 37°55′N 95°24′W. Elev. 1,040 ft/317 m. RR junction. Trade center for wheat, cattle, and hog region; dairying; mfg. of cement, rubber prods., clothing, bldg. materials, consumer goods, motor-vehicle parts, honey. County fair takes place here annually in Aug. Allen County Community Col. Founded 1859, inc. 1870.

Iola (ei-O-luh), town (1990 pop. 1,125), Waupaca co., central Wis., 22 mi/35 km E of Stevens Point; 44°30′N 89°07′W. In agr. area (dairy prods.; oxen); mfg. (book publishing).

Iola (ei-O-lah), village (1990 pop. 163), Clay co., S central Ill., 8 mi/12.9 km NW of Louisville; 38°49′N 88°37′W. In agr. (wheat, corn, soybeans, cattle), oil, and natural-gas area. Inc. 1914.

Iona 1 (ei-O-nuh), town (□ 10 sq mi/26 sq km; 1990 pop. 9,565), Walton co., NW Fla., 5 mi/8 km E of De Funiak Springs; 26°30′N 81°57′W. **2** town (1990 pop. 1,049), Bonneville co., SE Idaho, near Snake R., residential suburb 5 mi/8 km ENE of Idaho Falls; 43°32′N 111°56′W. Elev. 4,788 ft/1,459 m. Junction of RR terminus to Ammon. In irrigated region (cattle, sheep; dairying; grains, alfalfa; potatoes). Ririe Reservoir to E.

Iona (ei-O-nuh), village (1990 pop. 158), Murray co., SW Minn., 5 mi/8 km SSW of Slayton; 43°54′N 95°47′W. Grain; livestock; dairying. Lakes to E.

Ione, city (1990 pop. 6,516), Amador co., central Calif., 33 mi/53 km SE of Sacramento, on Sutter Creek; 38°22′N 120°57′W. Grain, grapes, walnuts; cattle. Clay refractory. Preston School of Industry. Camanche Reservation to S; Pardee Reservoir to SE.

Ione 1 (ei-ON), village (1990 pop. 255), Morrow co., N Oregon, 16 mi/26 km NW of Heppner, on Willow Creek; 45°30′N 119°49′W. Agr. (wheat, alfalfa, potatoes; sheep, cattle). **2** village (1990 pop. 507), Pend Oreille co., NE Wash., 25 mi/40 km NE of Colville, on Pond Oreille R.; 48°45′N 117°25′W. Mfg. (lumber). Parts of Colville Natl. Forest to E and W; Selkirk Mts. to W. Box Canyon Dam 2 mi/3.2 km N (downstream).

Ionia (ei-O-nee-uh), county (□ 580 sq mi/1,502 sq km; 1990 pop. 57,024), S central Mich.; ⊙ Ionia; 42°56′N 85°04′W. Intersected by Grand R., and drained by Flat, Looking Glass, and Maple rivers. Poultry, cattle, hogs; forage crops, wheat, oats, barley, corn, green beans, beans, peas, dry strawberries, apples, peaches. Mfg. at Ionia, Belding, and Portland; lake resorts. Ionia State Park in W center of co. Organized 1837.

Ionia 1 town (1990 pop. 304), Chickasaw co., NE Iowa, 7 mi/11.3 km W of New Hampton; 43°02′N 92°27′W. In livestock and grain area. **2** town (1990 pop. 5,935), ⊙ Ionia co., S central Mich., 30 mi/48 km E of Grand Rapids, on Grand R.; 42°59′N 85°03′W. Poultry; agr. (grain, fruit); mfg. (furniture, food processing, motor-vehicle parts, fabricated metal prods., printing); ships beans. Airport. Has a state reformatory and a state mental hosp. Ionia State Park to SW. Settled 1833; inc. as village 1865, as city 1873. **3** (ei-ON-yah), town (1990 pop. 126), Benton co., central Mo., 15 mi/24 km S of Sedalia; 38°30′N 93°19′W.

Iosco, county (□ 1,890 sq mi/4,895 sq km; 1990 pop. 30,209), NE Mich.; 44°16′N 83°20′W; ⊙ Tawas City. Port on Tawas Bay. Bounded E by L. Huron; drained by Au Sable and Au Gres rivers and small Tawas R. Cattle, hogs; agr. (corn, wheat, oats, barley); mfg. (metal forgings, industrial machinery, gypsum prods., dairy prods., lumber milling, woodworking); cement plants; resorts. Includes part of Huron Natl. Forest, in N ½ of co., also Tawas and Van Ettan lakes; Tawas Point State Park in E; Paul B. Wurtsmith Air Force Base in NE. Organized 1857.

Iota (ei-O-tuh), town (1990 pop. 1,256), Acadia parish, S La., 11 mi/18 km NW of Crowley, near Bayou des Cannes; 30°20′N 92°30′W. In rice-growing area; mfg. of plastic pipe. Inc. 1902.

Iowa, state (□ 56,276 sq mi/145,755 sq km; 1995 est. pop. 2,841,764), N central U.S., in the Midwest, admitted to the Union in 1846 as the 29th state; ⊙ DES MOINES; 42°02′N 93°28′W. Des Moines is the largest city; other major cities are CEDAR RAPIDS, DAVENPORT, and SIOUX CITY. Nicknamed the Hawkeye State, Iowa is bordered on 2 sides by rivers; the Mississippi separates it on the E from Wis. and Ill., and the Missouri and the Big Sioux separate it on the W from Nebr. and S.Dak. The state is bounded on the N by Minn. and on the S by Mo.; 22 mi/35 km of border with Mo. formed by Des Moines R., in SE. Iowa is an area of rich, rolling plains, interrupted by many rivers. The terrain is low and gently sloping, except for the hills in the unglaciated area of NE Iowa, the steeply sloping bluffs on the banks of the Mississippi, and the moundlike bluffs on the banks of the Missouri. The rivers of the E ⅔ of Iowa flow to the Mississippi; those of the remaining ⅓ flow to the Missouri. The original woodlands, which included black walnut and hickory, were destroyed by lumbering and land clearing in the 19th cent., and the present wooded sects. are covered only with a 2d or 3d growth of timber. Typical of Iowa is the prairie. The Iowa lakes dist., extending S from Minn., has over 40 small natural lakes of glacial origin, most generally NE of Spencer, and a smaller group generally W of Mason City; a regional recreation area. Covered a little more than a cent. ago with grass higher than the wheels of the pioneers' prairie schooners (covered wagons), the prairies are now covered with fields of corn and other grains. The wildflowers that once blossomed among the prairie grass still brighten the roadsides; however, few areas of the original grassland remain, and prairie grass preserves have been established. The cornfields have replaced the grasslands as the habitat of wild turkeys, prairie chickens, and quail. Iowa abounds with migratory geese and ducks and the imported ring-necked pheasant and Eur. partridge, all of which are hunted in the autumn. The climate is continental: NW winds drive the mercury down to below 0°F/−18°C in winter, and in the summer hot air masses bring oppressive heat; violent thunderstorms, hail, and occasional droughts vex the farmer. The average annual rainfall is 31 in/78.7 cm, and, since most of the rain falls in summer, the soil is often washed away. Iowans have had to fight erosion with modern plowing and planting practices, control of water flow, and reforestation. In addition, floods have inflicted great loss of life and property damage on cities and countryside alike; therefore, flood-control projects are vitally important to Iowa. The state was at the center of the catastrophic floods of 1993, and suffered greatly as a result. Des Moines and Davenport were hit especially hard. Yet Iowa has some of the most fertile agr. land in the world. The deep, porous soil yields corn and other grains in tremendous quantities, and the corn-fed hogs and cattle are nationally known. In 1990, Iowa led the nation in the production of corn and hogs, and ranked in the top 10 in the raising of cattle. In addition to corn, Iowa's other major crops are soybeans, hay, and oats. Iowans have used the rich earth and its bounty to gain the nation's 2d-highest total cash receipts from farm marketing. Agr. in Iowa also benefits the state's chief industry, food processing, and in Sioux City and Cedar Rapids many factories process farm prods. Machinery, tires, appliances, electronic equip., and chemicals are among the other mfg. Cement is the most important mineral prod.; others are stone, sand, gravel, lead, zinc, and gypsum. Mineral production is small, however. In prehistoric times, the Mound Builders, a farming people, lived in the Iowa area. When Europeans 1st came to explore the region in the 17th cent., various Native Amer. groups, including the Iowa (reputedly the source of the state's name), occupied the land. The Sac and Fox also ranged over the land, but it was the combative Sioux who dominated the area. In 1673 the Fr. explorers Father Jacques Marquette and Louis Jolliet traveled down the Mississippi R. and touched upon the Iowa shores, as did Robert Cavelier, sieur de La Salle, in 1681–1682. The areas surrounding the Des Moines and Mississippi rivers were profitable for fur traders, and a number of Iowa towns developed from trading posts. Late in the 18th cent. a Fr. Canadian, Julien Dubuque, leased land from Native Americans around the Dubuque area and opened lead mines there. After his death they refused to permit others to work the mines, and U.S. troops under Lt. Jefferson Davis protected Native Amer. rights to the land as late as 1830. However, their hold was doomed after the U.S. acquired Iowa as part of the Louisiana Purchase of 1803. In 1832 the Black Hawk War broke out as the Sac and Fox, led by their chief, Black Hawk, fought to regain their former lands in Ill. along the Mississippi R. They were defeated by U.S. troops and were forced to leave the Ill. lands and cede to the U.S. much of their land along the river on the Iowa side. Within 2 decades after the Black Hawk War, all Native Amer. lands had been ceded to the U.S. Meanwhile, a great rush of frontiersmen came to settle the prairies and take the mines. Slavery was prohibited in Iowa under the Missouri Compromise of 1820, which excluded it from the lands of the Louisiana Purchase N of lat. 36°30′N. Part of Missouri Territory prior to 1821, Iowa was subsequently part of both the Michigan and Wisconsin territories. By 1838, Iowa Territory was organized, with Burlington as the temporary capital. In the following year, Iowa City became the capital. The Iowans quickly built a rural civilization like that of New England, where many of them had lived. Later, immigrants from Europe, notably Germans, Czechs, Dutch, and Scandinavians, brought their agr. skills and their own customs to enrich Iowa's rural life, and a group of Ger. Pietists established the Amana Church Society, a successful attempt at communal social organization. A system of public schools was set up in 1839, and successful efforts soon were made to establish colleges and univs. Iowa became a state in 1846, and Ansel Briggs was elected as the 1st governor. In 1857 the capital was moved from Iowa City to Des Moines. In that same year the state adopted its 2d constitution. Iowa prospered greatly with the beginning of RR construction, and the rivalry bet. towns to get the lines was so fierce that the grant of big land tracts to RR companies was curtailed by legislative act in 1857. In 1855 the state's 1st RR line was completed bet. Davenport and Muscatine along the E border. Before and during the Civil War, Iowans, generally owners of small, independent farms, were naturally sympathetic to the antislavery side, and many fought for the Union. The Underground Railroad, which helped many fugitive slaves escape to free states, was active in Iowa, and the abolitionist John Brown made his hq. there for a time. Iowa's farmers prospered after the Civil War, but during the hard times that afflicted the country in the 1870s they found themselves burdened with debts. Feeling oppressed by the currency system, corporations, and

high RR and grain-storage rates, many of Iowa's farmers supported the Granger movement, the Greenback Party, and the Populist Party. The reform movements had some success in the state. Granger laws were enacted in 1874 and 1876 regulating RR rates, but these laws were repealed in 1877 under pressure from the RR companies. By the end of the 19th cent., times improved, and the agr. movements declined. Farm units grew larger, and mechanization brought great increases in productivity. Much of the state's society may still resemble that depicted in the paintings of Iowan artist Grant Wood, but the state's industrial economy as well as other elements of modernization has altered this image. The volatile nature of agr. prices combined with a steady decline in mfg. has made Iowa susceptible to economic recession. This was esp. true in the 1980s, when Iowa was 2d in the U.S. in outmigration with a 4.7% decline in pop. Among Iowa's colorful figures were Buffalo Bill, John Wayne, Bix Beiderbecke, Glenn Miller, and Billy Sunday. Other public figures associated with the state are James Wilson, U.S. Secretary of Agr. for 16 years (1897–1913), and the noted members of the Wallace family — Henry Wallace, Henry Cantwell Wallace, and Henry Agard Wallace. Herbert C. Hoover and Harry L. Hopkins were born in Iowa. Herbert Hoover Natl. Historic Site, which contains Hoover's birthplace, childhood home, and grave, and the Herbert Hoover Presidential Lib. are at West Branch. On July 19, 1989, United Airlines DC-10 crashed at Sioux City, killing 111. N of Marquette is Effigy Mounds Natl. Monument, site of Native Amer. mounds built by the area's earliest inhabitants. Many state parks and forests provide recreational facilities. Iowa's constitution was adopted in 1857. The governor is elected for a term of 4 years and may be reelected. The general assembly, or legislature, has a senate with 50 members elected for 4-year terms and a house of representatives with 100 members elected for 2-year terms. Iowa is represented in the U.S. Congress by 2 senators and 5 representatives. The state has 7 electoral votes. Terry Branstad, a Republican, was elected governor in 1982 and was reelected in 1986, and 1990. Among the educational institutions in Iowa are Iowa State Univ. of Science and Technology, at Ames; the Univ. of Iowa, at Iowa City; Grinnell Col., at Grinnell; Cornell Col., at Mount Vernon; Drake Univ., at Des Moines; Univ. of Northern Iowa, at Cedar Falls; and the Univ. of Dubuque, Loras Col., and Clarke Col., at Dubuque. Iowa has 99 cos.: ADAIR, ADAMS, ALLAMAKEE, APPANOOSE, AUDUBON, BENTON, BLACK HAWK, BOONE, BREMER, BUCHANAN, BUENA VISTA, BUTLER, CALHOUN, CARROLL, CASS, CEDAR, CERRO GORDO, CHEROKEE, CHICKASAW, CLARKE, CLAY, CLAYTON, CLINTON, CRAWFORD, DALLAS, DAVIS, DECATUR, DELAWARE, DES MOINES, DICKINSON, DUBUQUE, EMMET, FAYETTE, FLOYD, FRANKLIN, FREMONT, GREENE, GRUNDY, GUTHRIE, HAMILTON, HANCOCK, HARDIN, HARRISON, HENRY, HOWARD, HUMBOLDT, IDA, IOWA, JACKSON, JASPER, JEFFERSON, JOHNSON, JONES, KEOKUK, KOSSUTH, LEE, LINN, LOUISA, LUCAS, LYON, MADISON, MAHASKA, MARION, MARSHALL, MILLS, MITCHELL, MONONA, MONROE, MONTGOMERY, MUSCATINE, O'BRIEN, OSCEOLA, PAGE, PALO ALTO, PLYMOUTH, POCAHONTAS, POLK, POTTAWATTAMIE, POWESHIEK, RINGGOLD, SAC, SCOTT, SHELBY, SIOUX, STORY, TAMA, TAYLOR, UNION, VAN BUREN, WAPELLO, WARREN, WASHINGTON, WAYNE, WEBSTER, WINNEBAGO, WINNESHIEK, WOODBURY, WORTH, and WRIGHT.

Iowa 1 county (□ 587 sq mi/1,520 sq km; 1990 pop. 14,630), E central Iowa; ⊙ Marengo; 41°41′N 92°04′W. Rolling prairie agr. area (cattle, hogs, sheep, poultry; corn, oats) drained by Iowa and English rivers. In NE are 7 villages of the Amana colonies. Formed 1843. **2** county (□ 768 sq mi/1,989 sq km; 1990 pop. 20,150), S Wis.; ⊙ Dodgeville; 43°00′N 90°07′W. Dairy-prods. processing is chief industry; agr. (barley, oats, corn, soybeans; cattle, hogs, sheep, poultry); lead and zinc deposits. Bordered N by Wisconsin R.; drained by Pecatonica and Blue rivers. Tower Hill State Park in N; Governor Dodge State Park in center; Wintergreen Ski

Area in N; Timberline Ski Area in NE; W part of Military Ridge State Trail runs through center of co., terminating at Dodgeville. Frank Lloyd Wright–designed homes Taliesin and House on the Rock (both open to visitors) are in N. Formed 1829.

Iowa, town (1990 pop. 2,588), Calcasieu parish, SW La., 11 mi/18 km E of Lake Charles; 30°14′N 93°01′W. RR junction to E. Soybeans, sorghum; cattle, horses, hogs.

Iowa, river, 329 mi/529 km long, rising in the lakes of N Iowa and flowing SE to the Mississippi R., SE Iowa; Cedar R. (300 mi/483 km long) is its chief tributary. A power dam crosses the gorge at Iowa Falls. The Iowa R. has an extensive flood-control system; Coralville Dam and reservoir, N of Iowa City, is the largest unit.

Iowa City, city (1990 pop. 59,738), ⊙ Johnson co., E Iowa, on both sides of the Iowa R.; 41°39′N 91°32′W. Mfg. (foam rubber, animal feed, paper, food prods.). Founded 1839 as the capital of Iowa Territory. The old stone capitol in the city was begun in 1840; the legislature sat there until the seat of govt. was moved to Des Moines in 1857. With the arrival of the RR (1855), Iowa City became an important outfitting center for the westward trails. The seat of the Univ. of Iowa (1855), the city is a major center of medical treatment and research. The univ. sponsors the Iowa Writers' Workshop, one of the most prestigious of U.S. creative writing programs, attracting teachers and students from all over the world. The city's activities center greatly around the univ. The lib. of the state historical society is in Iowa City. Nearby are the villages of the Amana Society, Coralville dam and reservoir, and the Herbert Hoover Presidential Lib., as well as his birthplace (in West Branch). Inc. 1853.

Iowa Falls, city (1990 pop. 5,424), Hardin co., central Iowa, on Iowa R., 38 mi/61 km NNW of Marshalltown; 42°31′N 93°16′W. RR junction. Agr.-processing center (packed poultry and eggs, dairy prods.; feeds; soybean meal and oil; tankage); mfg. (concrete blocks, luggage, plastic prods.). Limestone quarries nearby. Has Ellsworth Community Col. and mus. of pioneer relics. Annual state Baptist convention held here. Settled 1853, inc. 1889.

Iowa Park, town (1990 pop. 6,072), Wichita co., N Texas, suburb 11 mi/18 km W of Wichita Falls, near Wichita R; 33°57′N 98°40′W. In oil, agr. area (cotton, cattle, wheat); mfg. of oil-field supplies. Texas-Okla. Fair, Southwestern Oil Exposition held here. Seat of agr. experiment station.

Ipava (ei-PAI-vah), village (1990 pop. 483), Fulton co., W central Ill., 9 mi/14.5 km SW of Lewiston; 40°21′N 90°19′W. In agr. (corn, wheat, sorghum, soybeans, cattle) and bituminous-coal-mining area; ships grain. Vestiges of Camp Ellis, a World War II prisoner-of-war camp, nearby.

Ipperwash, military reservation, 25 mi/40 km NE of L. Huron, Ont., Canada. Land scheduled to be given back to the Chippewa tribe, who seized part of the base in 1995 in order to demand its return.

Ipswich, town, St. Elizabeth parish, W Jamaica, on Jamaica RR, 21 mi/34 km SSE of Montego Bay; 18°13′N 76°42′W. In agr. region (corn, vegetables; livestock).

Ipswich 1 town (1990 pop. 11,873), Essex co., NE Mass., on the Ipswich R. and Ipswich Bay, 11 mi/18 km NNE of Beverly; 42°42′N 70°50′W. Ipswich clams are found here. Tourism and the production of electronic and wood prods. are important; also fishing and shellfish. Crane's Beach, one of the country's most beautiful beaches, is in Ipswich. Of interest are the many well-preserved colonial and historic bldgs.; Choate Bridge, the 1st stone bridge in the U.S. (1764); and the John Whipple House (c.1640), with the Ipswich Historical Society collection. An Air Force radar experimental station is also here. Plum Island State Park. Inc. 1634. **2** town (1990 pop. 965), ⊙ Edmunds co., N S.Dak., 25 mi/40 km W of Aberdeen; 45°26′N 99°01′W. In farming and cattle-raising region. Prayer Rock E of town; Mina State Recreational Area to E.

Ipswich Bay, bight (c.6 mi/9.7 km wide) of the Atlantic, E Mass., E of Ipswich; sheltered on S and E by Cape Ann.

Cross references are shown in SMALL CAPITALS. The pronunciation key is on page xv. The dates of population figures are on page xii.

Ipswich River, c.35 mi/56 km long, NE Mass.; rises in NE Middlesex co., flows generally NE, past Ipswich, to Ipswich Bay. Includes wildlife sanctuary.

Iqaluit (ee-KAH-loo-it), town (1991 pop. 3,552), E N.W.T., Canada, Franklin dist., S Baffin Isl., at head of Frobisher Bay; 63°44′N 68°30′W. Sir Martin Frobisher explored the area in 1576 and celebrated Thanksgiving at this site in 1577. Became part of D.E.W. Line warning system in 1953 (Crystal II). Administrative, transportation, commercial, and service center for Canadian Arctic. Probably site of capital for new Nunavut Territory, April 1, 1999. Trapping, hunting, fishing, sealing. Mfg. (jewelry, apparel, crafts). Tourism. Inuit Cultural Mus. Hosp., radio and TV stations, scheduled air service. Qaummaarviit Historic Park. Formerly Frobisher Bay. Town est. 1942 with installation of U.S. Army Air Force station.

Ira, town (1990 pop. 426), Rutland co., W central Vt., 6 mi/9.7 km SW of Rutland; 43°32′N 73°04′W. Lumber, dairy prods.

Iraan (I-ruh-an), town (1990 pop. 1,322), Pecos co., extreme W Texas, on Pecos R., c.55 mi/89 km E of Fort Stockton; 30°54′N 101°54′W. Elev. 2,200 ft/671 m. Oil field; agr. (livestock; cotton; vegetables, pecans, grain); mfg. (gas processing). Archaeological mus.

Irapuato (ee-ra-PWAH-to), city (1990 pop. 265,042) and township, ⊙ Irapuato municipio, Guanajuato state, W central Mexico, on the Irapuato R., on Mexico Highway 45-110; 20°40′N 101°20′W. Elev. 5,656 ft/1,724 m. It is the commercial and communications center of the surrounding mining and agr. (cereals and cattle) region. The fruits and flowers of Irapuato's luxurious gardens are famous throughout Mexico.

Irasburg, town (1990 pop. 907), Orleans co., N Vt., on Black R., 10 mi/16 km SSW of Newport; 44°49′N 72°16′W. Dairying. Settled 1798 on Ira Allen's 1781 grant.

Iredell (EIR-del), county (□ 593 sq mi/1,536 sq km; 1990 pop. 92,935), W central N.C.; ⊙ Statesville; 35°48′N 80°52′W. In Piedmont region; bounded SW by Catawba R. (forms L. Norman reservoir in SW corner); drained by South Fork of Yadkin R. Agr. area (tobacco, corn, wheat, hay, barley, soybeans); mfg. (rubber, plastics, metal prods.); timber. Mfg. at Statesboro, Mooresville, Troutman. Duke Power State Park in SW on L. Norman. Fort Dobbs State Historical Site in center. Formed 1788.

Iredell, village (1990 pop. 339), Bosque co., central Texas, on Bosque R., c.50 mi/80 km NW of Waco; 31°59′N 97°52′W. In farm area. Mfg. (apparel).

Ireland, village (1990 pop. 600), Dubois co., SW Ind., 4 mi/6.4 km NW of Jasper. Mfg. (luggage). Wheat, corn, soybeans; cattle, hogs. Flat land.

Ireland Island, northwesternmost part of Bermuda, at entrance to Great Sound, W of Hamilton; 1.5 mi/2.4 km long, ¼ mi/⅖ km wide; 32°19′N 64°50′W. A narrow channel divides it into 2 parts. Has Br. naval base.

Ireland's Eye Island (□ 2 sq mi/5 sq km), SE N.F., Canada, on NW side of Trinity Bay, 35 mi/56 km NNW of Carbonear; 48°13′N 53°30′W. Fishing.

Irene, village (1990 pop. 464), Turner, Clay, and Yankton cos., SE S.Dak., 20 mi/32 km NE of Yankton; 43°04′N 97°09′W.

Ireton, town (1990 pop. 597), Sioux co., NW Iowa, 14 mi/23 km W of Orange City; 42°58′N 96°19′W. In livestock and grain area; feeds; meat processing.

Irimbo (ee-REEM-bo), town (1990 pop. 2,355), Michoacán, central Mexico, 6 mi/9.7 km E of Ciudad Hidalgo. Elev. 6,906 ft/2,105 m. Corn; livestock.

Irion, county (□ 1,051 sq mi/2,722 sq km; 1990 pop. 1,629), W Texas; ⊙ Mertzon; 31°18′N 100°58′W. Elev. c.2,000 ft/610 m–2,500 ft/762 m. Broken prairie, drained by Middle Concho R. and spring-fed small streams. Ranching region (sheep, Angora goats, cattle), wool and mohair; some agr. (milo, cotton). Oil and gas. Formed 1889.

Irma, village (1991 pop. 442), E Alta., Canada, near Sask. border, 17 mi/27 km WNW of Wainwright; 52°55′N 111°14′W. Dairying; grain, mixed farming.

Irmo (UHR-mo), city (1990 pop. 11,280), Lexington co., central S.C., residential suburb 9 mi/14.5 km WNW of Columbia, near L. Murray; 34°05′N 81°11′W. Mfg. of nylon filament and log homes.

Irois, Cape (ee-RWAH), on westernmost headland of Jacmel Peninsula, Haiti, 5 mi/8 km SSW of Anse-d'Hainault; 18°26′N 74°28′W.

Irois, Les (ee-RWAH, laiz), town (1982 pop. 1,621), Grande-Anse dept., Haiti, on the far W end of Jacmel Peninsula; 18°24′N 74°27′W. Cocoa growing.

Iron 1 county (□ 1,211 sq mi/3,136 sq km; 1990 pop. 13,175), SW Upper Peninsula, Mich.; ⊙ Crystal Falls; 46°12′N 88°30′W. Bounded S by Wis. line. Drained by Brule, Michigamme, Paint, and Iron rivers. Lumbering; cattle, sheep; agr. (potatoes, oats, forage crops); dairy prods.; some mfg. at Crystal Falls; lake resorts. Many small lakes and streams. Part of Ottawa Natl. Forest in W; Bewabic State Park in S; Brule Mt. Ski Area in S. Includes part of Menominee iron range. Univ. of Mich. forestry school's summer camp is here. One of 4 cos. in Mich. in Central time zone (N boundary and N part of E and W boundaries coincide with Eastern/Central time zone boundary). Formed and organized 1885. **2** county (□ 554 sq mi/1,435 sq km; 1990 pop. 10,726), SE central Mo.; ⊙ Ironton; 37°32′N 90°45′W. In the Ozarks, in St. Francois Mts.; includes Taum Sauk Mt. (1,772 ft/540 m), highest point in state. Agr. (cattle, hogs, mixed farming), mining (manganese, lead, iron, granite, zinc); oak, pine timber; recreation; resorts. Units of Mark Twain Natl. Forest in SE and W; Elephant Rocks State Park in NE. Formed 1857. **3** county (□ 3,302 sq mi/8,552 sq km; 1990 pop. 20,789), SW Utah; ⊙ Parowan; 37°51′N 113°16′W. Mt. and plateau region bordering on Nev. Alfalfa, barley; dairying; cattle; iron ore in Iron Mts. (Columbia Mine, S). Cedar Breaks Natl. Monument in SE; parts of Dixie Natl. Forest in Markagunt Plateau in S, SE and SW. Kolob Terrace S of Cedar City; desert area in N. Iron Mission State Historical Park in E center. Small part of Fishlake Natl. Forest in NE corner; small part of Zion Natl. Park in S. Formed 1850. **4** county (□ 918 sq mi/2,378 sq km: 1990 pop. 6,153), N Wis.; ⊙ Hurley; 46°19′N 90°15′W. Near Hurley, iron mining is principal industry. Bounded partly N by L. Superior and Montreal R. (here forming Mich. border); drained by tributaries of Bad R. and by Montreal R. Gogebic Range (valuable source of iron ore) extends across co. S half of Iron co. is largely wooded, with many lakes, and forms a large resort area. Whitecap Mt. Ski Area in N; large Turtle-Flambeau Flowage Reservoir in S; Flambeau R. State Forest extends downstream from dam; part of Lac du Flambeau Indian Reservation in SE corner; small part of Bad R. Indian Reservation in NW corner; part of Northern Highlands State Forest in E. Formed 1893.

Iron, Minn.: see IRON JUNCTION.

Iron Belt, village, Iron co., N Wis., 6 mi/9.7 km WSW of Hurley. Mfg. (paving prods.).

Iron Bridge Dam, Texas: see TAWAKONI, LAKE.

Iron City, village (1990 pop. 503), Seminole co., extreme SW Ga., 16 mi/26 km WNW of Bainbridge; 31°01′N 84°49′W.

Iron Gate, village (1990 pop. 417), Alleghany co., NW Va., 3 mi/4.8 km SE of Clifton Forge, on Jackson R., in George Washington Natl. Forest; 37°47′N 79°47′W. Cowpasture R. joins Jackson R. 2 mi/3.2 km SE to form James R. Mfg. (molded rubber parts); agr. (corn, alfalfa, apples; cattle).

Iron Junction, village (1990 pop. 133), St. Louis co., NE Minn., just S of Mesabi Iron Range, 8 mi/12.9 km SSW of Virginia; 47°25′N 92°36′W. RR junction. Oats, alfalfa; dairying; mfg. (electronic ice fishing equip.); iron mines in area.

Iron Mountain, town (1990 pop. 8,525), ⊙ Dickinson co., SW Upper Peninsula, Mich., c.50 mi/80 km W of Escanaba, near Wis. state line; 45°49′N 88°03′W. Distribution point for region. Mfg. (wood prods., auto parts, food processing, machining, wood furniture); livestock; hay; timber; dairying; resort (winter sports). Veterans' hosp. nearby. Mining mus. Pine Mt. Ski Area to N; Ford Airport to SW; Iron Mt. Iron Mine (tourist attraction) to E, at Norway. Settled 1879, inc. 1889.

Iron Mountains 1 Iron and Washington cos., SW Utah. Rise to 7,831 ft/2,387 m in Iron Mt., 17 mi/27 km W of Cedar City. S end in Dixie Natl. Forest. Iron mining. **2** range, in NE Tenn. and SW Va., ridge (2,500 ft/762 m–4,500 ft/1,372 m) of the Appalachians bet. Holston (SW) and Stone (E) mts., from Doe R. near Elizabethton, Tenn., extending c.80 mi/129 km NE to New R. SE of Wytheville, Va. A spur in Va., just NE of Tenn.-N.C. state line, includes Mt. Rogers (5,729 ft/1,746 m) and Whitetop Mt. (5,520 ft/1,682 m). Included in Cherokee and Jefferson natl. forests. Sometimes considered a range of Unaka Mts.

Iron Ridge, town (1990 pop. 887), Dodge co., S central Wis., near Rock R., 15 mi/24 km ESE of Beaver Dam; 43°23′N 88°31′W. In dairying region. Mfg. (custom tools). RR junction. Horicon Marsh Wildlife Area to NW.

Iron River, town (1990 pop. 2,095), Iron co., SW Upper Peninsula, Mich., 33 mi/53 km NW of Iron, and on Iron R.; 46°06′N 88°38′W. In lumbering region. Livestock; potatoes; dairy prods.; mfg. (machining, naval equip. and cranes); lake resort. Ottawa Natl. Forest to NW; Brule Mt. Ski Area to SW; Bewabic State Park to E. Settled by iron-ore prospectors c.1881; inc. as village 1885, as city 1926.

Iron River, village (1990 pop. 901), Bayfield co., extreme N Wis., 25 mi/40 km W of Ashland; 46°32′N 91°21′W. In lake-resort region. Lumbering, dairying, farming; mfg. (logging machinery, precision machining). Chequamegon Natl. Forest to E and SE; Brule R. State Forest to W.

Iron River, c.25 mi/40 km long, SW Upper Peninsula, Mich.; rises in small lakes in SW Iron co.; flows SE, past Stambaugh, to Brule R. 5 mi/8 km SE of Caspian; 46°07′N 88°43′W.

Iron Station, uninc. village, Lincoln co., W central N.C., 6 mi/9.7 km SE of Lincolnton. Cotton, grain, poultry, livestock. Mfg. (store fixtures, lumber roller bearings, printing inks).

Irondale (EI-ruh-dail), city (1990 pop. 9,454), Jefferson co., N central Ala., suburb E of Birmingham.

Irondale 1 uninc. town, Adams co., N central Colo., near South Platte R., residential suburb 7 mi/11.3 km NE of Denver and NE of Commerce City, at NW boundary of Rocky Mt. Arsenal. Elev. c.5,115 ft/1,559 m. **2** town (1990 pop. 474), Washington co., E central Mo., in the St. Francois Mts., on Big R., and 10 mi/16 km SSE of Potosi; 37°49′N 90°40′W.

Irondale, village (1990 pop. 382), Jefferson co., E Ohio, 15 mi/24 km NNW of Steubenville, near the Ohio R.; 40°34′N 80°43′W. Clay prods., lumber.

Irondequoit (eer-AHN-duh-koit), town (□ 16 sq mi/41 sq km; 1990 pop. 52,377), Monroe co., W N.Y., on L. Ontario and Irondequoit Bay, 5 mi/8 km NNE of downtown Rochester; 43°12′N 77°34′W. Partly enclosed by the city. Settled 1791, organized 1839.

Irondequoit Bay (eer-AHN-duh-koit), Monroe co., W N.Y., inlet of L. Ontario just NE of Rochester; c.4 mi/6.4 km long, ½ mi/⁸⁄₁₀ km–1 mi/1.6 km wide; 43°13′N 77°52′W. Receives small Irondequoit Creek from S.

Ironton 1 (EI-uhrn-tuhng), city (1990 pop. 1,539), SE central Mo., ⊙ Iron co., in St. Francois Mts., 17 mi/27 km SW of Farmington; 37°36′N 90°38′W. Tourism, resorts, timber and wood prods., mixed farming; former major iron mines. Historic court house (1858–1860). Civil War battle of Pilot Knob, fought nearby on Sept. 27, 1864 (Fort Davidson State Historic Site), resulted in reverse for Confederates under Sterling Price. Mark Twain Natl. Forest nearby; Taum Sauk Mt., highest point in Mo., to W. Founded 1857. **2** industrial city (1990 pop. 12,751), ⊙ Lawrence co., S Ohio, on the Ohio R. Mfg. (chemicals, dyes, metal pipes, plastics, and iron prods.); some coal is mined. Ironton was a great iron-producing center during the Civil War. From c.1900 to 1910 the city had the largest blast furnace in the world, Big Etna, with a capacity of 100 tons per day. However, the development of the N iron-ore ranges and improved transportation by RR and on the Great Lakes led to the decline of its iron industry by the early 20th cent. The remains of many giant charcoal iron furnaces are local landmarks. Inc. as a city 1865.

Ironton 1 village, Ouray co., SW Colo., S of Ouray on Red Mountain Creek, 12 mi/19 km N of Silverton. Elev. c.9,800 ft/2,987 m. In mining area. **2** village (1990 pop. 553), Crow Wing co., central Minn., 14 mi/23 km NE of Brainerd and 1 mi/1.6 km W of Crosby, in Cuyuna Iron Range; 46°28'N 94°00'W. Grain, oats, alfalfa; dairying; poultry; mfg. (machining, signs); iron-mining dist. In lake and forest area, Crow Wing State Forest to N. **3** village (1990 pop. 200), Sauk co., S central Wis., on Baraboo R. and 21 mi/34 km WNW of Baraboo; 43°32'N 90°08'W. In dairy and livestock region.

Ironville, uninc. village (1990 pop. 400), Boyd co., NE Ky., residential suburb 3 mi/4.8 km SW of Ashland. Tobacco, alfalfa, cattle.

Ironwood, town (1990 pop. 6,849), Gogebic co., W Upper Peninsula, Mich., on Montreal R., 95 mi/153 km ESE of Duluth, Minn., 12 mi/19 km SE of L. Superior shore, opposite Hurley, Wis.; 46°27'N 90°09'W. Elev. 1,503 ft/458 m. Trade center for Gogebic Range region; mfg. (sportswear, publishing, plastic molding, concrete blocks, canvas prods.); lumbering, dairy and vegetable farming; resort (winter sports). Gogebic Community Col. Ottawa Natl. Forest to NE; Mt. Zion Ski Area to NW, Big Powderhorn Ski Area to E; Gogebic Municipal Airport to N. Founded 1885, inc. 1889.

Iroquois (EE-rah-kwoi), county (□ 1,118 sq mi/2,896 sq km; 1990 pop. 30,787), E Ill., on Ind. line (E); ⊙ Watseka; 40°44'N 87°49'W. Agr. (corn, sorghum, soybeans, cattle, hogs; dairying). Mfg. (food prods., wood prods., industrial machinery). Drained by Iroquois R. and small Sugar Creek. Formed 1833.

Iroquois (EE-ruh-kwoi), village (1991 pop. 1,211), SE Ont., Canada, on the St. Lawrence, and 15 mi/24 km NE of Prescott; 44°51'N 75°19'W. Milling, mfg., dairying.

Iroquois 1 village (1990 pop. 199), Iroquois co., E Ill., on Iroquois R. (bridged here), and 9 mi/14.5 km ENE of Watseka; 40°49'N 87°34'W. In agr. area (corn, sorghum, soybeans, cattle, hogs). **2** village (1990 pop. 328), Kingsbury and Beadle cos., E central S.Dak., 15 mi/24 km W of De Smet; 44°22'N 97°50'W.

Iroquois Falls, town (1991 pop. 5,999), E central Ont., Canada, on Abitibi R., and 27 mi/43 km SE of Cochrane; 48°46'N 80°40'W. Pulp, paper, and sulphite milling center. Nearby are waterfalls and hydroelectric station.

Iroquois River, c.85 mi/137 km long, in NW Ind. and NE Ill.; rises in Jasper co., NW Ind.; flows WSW to Watseka, Ill., then generally N to Kankakee R. c.4 mi/6.4 km above Kankakee.

Irricana (i-ruh-KAH-nuh), village (1991 pop. 812), S central Alta., near Rosebud R., 28 mi/45 km NE of Calgary; 51°19'N 113°37'W. RR junction in irrigated area.

Irrigon (IR-uh-gahn), village (1990 pop. 737), Morrow co., N Oregon, 10 mi/16 km WNW of Hermiston, on Columbia R. (L. Umatilla reservoir); 45°53'N 119°29'W. RR terminus. Corn, alfalfa, wheat, potatoes cattle. Mfg. (dried corn, alfalfa pellets). Umatilla Natl. Wildlife Refuge to W. Umatilla Ordnance Depot to S.

Irvine, city (1990 pop. 110,330), Orange co., SW Calif., suburb 36 mi/58 km SE of downtown Los Angeles and 10 mi/16 km SSE of Anaheim; 33°40'N 117°48'W. Its industries include the research and development of high-technology electronics, esp. computer prods., as well as service and retailing; also mfg. of motor vehicles, pharmaceuticals, aerospace vehicles and aircraft parts, and medical instruments. However, Irvine is best known as an educational center and the seat of Univ. of California, Irvine (est. 1965). City was built in the 1970s as a planned community on farmland that was part of the Irvine Ranch (which had been carved out of 3 Span. and Mex. land grants in 1876). It is one of the fastest-growing cities in the U.S., marked by a pop. increase of nearly 78% bet. 1980 and 1990. Irvine Valley Col. (2-year). Of interest are several old preserved bldgs. John Wayne (Orange co.) Airport to W. Santa Ana Mts. and Cleveland Natl. Forest to NE; Lion Country safari theme park in E; Corona del Mar State Beach in SW; San Joaquin Hills to S. Santa Ana Marine Corps Air Base (helicopter station) to N, El Toro Marine Corps Air Station to E. Inc. 1971.

Irvine (EER-vin), town (1991 pop. 326), SE Alta., Canada, near Sask. border, 19 mi/31 km ESE of Medicine Hat; 49°57'N 110°16'W. Grain elevators. Coal and gas deposits near by.

Irvine (UHR-vuhn), town (1990 pop. 2,836), ⊙ Estill co., E central Ky., 38 mi/61 km SE of Lexington, on Kentucky R., N of Station Camp Creek mouth; 37°42'N 83°58'W. In agr. (burley tobacco, soybeans, corn; hogs, cattle; timber); mfg. (overalls and jackets, printing and publishing, lumber). Mt. Mushroom Festival (April). Daniel Boone Natl. Forest is to E and S; Lexington-Bluegrass Army Depot (Madison co.) to W.

Irvine, uninc. village, Warren co., NW Pa., 7 mi/11.3 km W of Warren on Brokenstraw Creek just W of its mouth on Allegheny R.; 41°50'N 79°16'W. Mfg. includes iron and steel forgings.

Irvines Landing, village, SW B.C., Canada, on Malaspina Strait of Strait of Georgia, at mouth of Jervis Inlet, 30 mi/48 km N of Nanaimo; 49°37'N 124°02'W. Lumber shipping port.

Irving, city (1990 pop. 155,037), Dallas co., N Texas, a growing suburb 9 mi/14.5 km NW of downtown Dallas and 21 mi/34 km ENE of downtown Fort Worth; 32°51'N 96°58'W. Elev. 470 ft/143 m. Bounds city of Dallas (E) and extension of city of Fort Worth (W). Bounded on E by Elm Fork Trinity R. and S in part by W Fork Trinity R. Mfg. (bldg. supplies, chemicals, electronic equip., and airplane parts). The city has grown rapidly along with the expanding business community of the Dallas–Fort Worth metropolitan area, and the city pop. increased by more than 40% bet. 1980 and 1990. City is now hemmed in by neighboring municipalities. Irving has profited from the nearby oil, aerospace, electronic, engineering, and auto industries. The prosperous business center, Las Colinas, which is hq. to the Exxon Oil Co., is nearby. The Texas Stadium, home of the Dallas Cowboys professional football team; the Univ. of Dallas, North Lake Col. (2-year); and the Dallas–Fort Worth Regional Airport (opened 1974) are partly within city on W, on Dallas-Tarrant co. boundary. North L. Park in N. Inc. as a city 1952.

Irving, village (1990 pop. 516), Montgomery co., S central Ill., 5 mi/8 km NE of Hillsboro; 39°12'N 89°24'W. In agr. and bituminous coal area.

Irvington 1 town (1990 pop. 1,180), Breckinridge co., NW Ky., 40 mi/64 km SW of Louisville; 37°52'N 86°16'W. Trade center in agr. area (burley tobacco, corn, wheat, hay; livestock); mfg. (crushed stone). **2** town (1990 pop. 59,774), Essex co., NE N.J., an industrial suburb just to the W of Newark; 40°43'N 74°13'W. Settled 1692 as Camptown, renamed 1852, inc. 1898. Mfg. (tools, castings, photographic equip., paints, bldg. materials, and plastic and paper prods.). **3** town (1990 pop. 496), Lancaster co., E Va., 18 mi/29 km NNE of Gloucester, on Rappahannock R. (bridged to SE), arm of Chesapeake Bay; 37°39'N 76°25'W. Mfg. (valves, sailboat masts, seafood packing and canning). Tides Inn (resort). Christ Church (1732) to N.

Irvington 1 uninc. village, Alameda co., W Calif., suburb 25 mi/40 km SE of Oakland. In orchard and vineyard region. Mfg. (electronic components, motor-vehicle parts, candies, lumber, wire prods.). Hetch Hetchy Aqueduct runs E-W to N. San Jose Mission to E. **2** village (1990 pop. 827), Washington co., SW Ill., 9 mi/14.5 km NE of Nashville; 38°26'N 89°09'W. In fruit-growing area. **3** residential village (□ 4 sq mi/10.4 sq km; 1990 pop. 6,348), Westchester co., SE N.Y., on E bank of the Hudson R., bet. Dobbs Ferry (S) and Tarrytown; 41°02'N 73°52'W. Mfg. (greenhouses, pool enclosures, elastic webbing for apparel, photographic accessories, adhesives, apparel); agr. (horticultural crops, vegetables). Here at "Nevis," once the estate of Alexander Hamilton's son, are a Columbia Univ. arboretum and a children's mus. Home for cardiac children here. Originally called Dearman; renamed (1857) for Washington Irving, who bought the estate "Sunnyside" (extant) here in 1835. Settled c.1655, inc. 1872.

Irvington, neighborhood, Marion co., central Ind., c.4 mi/6.4 km ESE of downtown Indianapolis. Historic dist., noteworthy architecture. Laid out 1870. Annexed to Indianapolis 1902.

Irvona (uhr-VO-nah), borough (1990 pop. 666), Clearfield co., central Pa., 20 mi/32 km NNW of Altoona, on Clearfield Creek. Mfg. (refractory specialties); agr. (dairying).

Irwin, county (□ 372 sq mi/963 sq km; 1990 pop. 8,649), S central Ga.; ⊙ Ocilla; 31°36'N 83°16'W. Coastal plain agr. wheat, cotton, corn, tobacco, peanuts, peaches; cattle, hogs, poultry; and timber area drained by Alapaha and Satilla rivers. Jefferson Davis Memorial State Park (W). Formed 1818.

Irwin 1 town (1990 pop. 394), Shelby co., W Iowa, on West Nishnabotna R., and 11 mi/18 km NE of Harlan; 41°47'N 95°12'W. Mfg. (steel grain boxes). **2** uninc. town (1990 pop. 1,296), Lancaster co., N S.C., residential suburb 2 mi/3.2 km SW of Lancaster; 34°41'N 80°49'W.

Irwin 1 village (1990 pop. 108), Bonneville co., SE Idaho, on Snake R., and 38 mi/61 km E of Idaho Falls, near Wyo. Caribou Natl. Forest to SW, Targhee Natl. Forest to NE, Palisades Dam and Reservoir to SE (Snake R.); 43°24'N 111°16'W. **2** village (1990 pop. 50), Kankakee co., NE Ill., 7 mi/11.3 km SW of Kankakee; 41°02'N 87°58'W. In agr. area (corn, soybeans; dairying).

Irwin, borough (1990 pop. 4,604), Westmoreland co., SW Pa., suburb 16 mi/26 km SE of downtown Pittsburgh. Coal, limestone; mfg. (metal prods., computer and electronic equip., machinery, motor vehicle parts). Agr. (grain; livestock, dairying). Laid out 1853, inc. 1864.

Irwindale, city (1990 pop. 1,050), Los Angeles co., S Calif., residential suburb 18 mi/29 km ENE of downtown Los Angeles, S of Azusa, near San Gabriel R.; 34°07'N 117°58'W.

Irwinton, village (1990 pop. 641), ⊙ Wilkinson co., central Ga., 27 mi/43 km E of Macon; 32°49'N 83°10'W. Mfg. of lumber, wooden pallets. Major center for Kaolin mining and processing.

Isaac Lake, E B.C., Canada, in Cariboo Mts., 70 mi/113 km ENE of Quesnel; 28 mi/45 km long, 1 mi/2 km–2 mi/3 km wide. Elev. 3,200 ft/975 m. Drains SE through Lanezi L. and Cariboo R. into Quesnel R.

Isaacs Harbour, village, E N.S., Canada, on Isaacs Harbour R., near its mouth on the Atlantic, 17 mi/27 km SSW of Guysborough; 45°11'N 61°40'W. Fishing. In gold mining region.

Isabel 1 (IZ-uh-bel), village (1990 pop. 104), Barber co., S Kansas, 14 mi/23 km SE of Pratt; 37°28'N 98°32'W. In cattle and wheat region; feeds. **2** village (1990 pop. 319), Dewey co., N central S.Dak., 17 mi/27 km W of Timber L.; 45°23'N 101°25'W. Lignite mines nearby; in N part of Cheyenne R. Indian Reservation.

Isabel Segunda (ee-sah-BEL se-GOON-dah) or **Isabela II**, town, on N shore of Vieques Isl., off E P.R., 50 mi/80 km ESE of San Juan; 18°09'N 65°26'W. Main town and landing of the isl. Tourism. U.S. naval base. Has last fort built by Spain in New World. Lighthouse. Mus.

Isabela (ee-sah-BAI-lah), ruins of a town on the N shore of Hispaniola, in Dominican Republic, at the base of Cape Isabela. Believed to have been founded by Columbus (c.1494), it was one of the first Span. settlements in the New World.

Isabela (ee-sah-BAE-lah), town (1990 pop. 39,147), NW P.R., near the Atlantic, 9 mi/14.5 km NE of Aguadilla. Mfg. (shoes, women's clothing, electric transformers, water meters, tiles); horse raising, cattle. Fishing; tourism. Site of experimental agr. station and branch of Univ. of P.R.-Mayaguez. Large sand dune reserves have been exploited for the construction industry.

Isabela, Cape (ee-sah-BAI-lah), headland on N coast of Dominican Republic, 23 mi/37 km WNW of Puerto Plata; 19°58'N 71°W. The ruined town of ISABELA, reputedly the 1st town settled by Spanish in America, is nearby.

Isabela de Sagua (ee-sah-BAI-luh dai SAH-gwah) or **La Isabela**, town, Villa Clara prov., central Cuba, port for Sagua la Grande, on Nicholas Channel, 37 mi/60 km N of Santa Clara; 22°56′N 80°01′W. RR terminus; sugar-shipping and fishing (sharks, oysters, crabs) center. Also a seaside resort.

Isabela, La, Cuba: see ISABELA DE SAGUA.

Isabella, county (□ 577 sq mi/1,494 sq km; 1990 pop. 54,624), central Mich.; ⊙ Mt. Pleasant; 43°38′N 84°50′W. Drained by Chippewa and Pine rivers. Cattle, hogs, poultry, sheep; dairying; agr. (sugar beets, beans, wheat, oats, soybeans, hay, asparagus); mfg. at Mt. Pleasant; oil wells, refineries. The large Isabella Indian Reservation dominates center of co. (c.100 sq mi/259 sq km), includes city of Mt. Pleasant. Organized 1859.

Isabella, village, Polk co., SE Tenn., near Ga.-N.C.-Tenn. border, 50 mi/80 km E of Chattanooga.

Isabella, Cape, SE Ellesmere Isl., NE Franklin dist., N.W.T., Canada, on Smith Sound; 78°21′N 75°W. Named (1818) by John Ross after one of his expedition vessels.

Isabella Dam, Calif.: see KERN RIVER.

Isabella River, 30 mi/48 km long, Lake co., NE Minn.; rises in L. Isabella (3 mi/4.8 km long, 2 mi/3.2 km wide; 47°47′N 91°31′W), fed by Perent R from E; flows NW, through Superior Natl. Forest; receives Island R. from SE below Isabella L.; receives Snake R. from S in Bald Eagle L. where it turns NW, passes through Gabbro L. reservoir before it enters South Fork Kawishiwi R.

Isabelle, Lake, reservoir (□ 18 sq mi/47 sq km), Kern co., S central Calif., on Kern R., in S part of Sequoia Natl. Forest, 33 mi/53 km ENE of Bakersfield; 35°37′N 118°28′W. Max. capacity 568,000 acre-ft. Formed by Isabelle Dam (185 ft/56 m high), built (1953) by Army Corps of Engineers for flood control, irrigation, recreation, and power generation.

Isachsen, Cape, NW extremity of Ellef Ringnes Isl., N Franklin dist., N.W.T., Canada, on the Arctic Ocean; 79°25′N 105°30′W.

Isachsen Peninsula, Canada: see ELLEF RINGNES ISLAND.

Isanti (ei-SAN-tee), county (□ 451 sq mi/1,168 sq km; 1990 pop. 25,921), E Minn.; ⊙ Cambridge; 45°33′N 93°17′W. Agr. area drained by Rum R. Corn, soybeans, oats, rye, alfalfa; hogs, sheep, poultry; dairying. Numerous small lakes throughout co.; Green L. in W, L. Fannie in E. Formed 1849.

Isanti (ei-SAN-tee), town (1990 pop. 1,228), Isanti co., E Minn., 5 mi/8 km S of Cambridge on Rum R.; 45°29′N 93°15′W. Poultry; grain, soybeans; dairying; mfg. (machine prods., food processing, metal fabrication, trusses, consumer goods).

Ischua (ISH-yoo-ai), village (1990 pop. 200), Cattaraugus co., W. N.Y., on Ischua Creek, 12 mi/19 km N of Olean; on RR.

Ischua Creek (ISH-yoo-ai), c.30 mi/48 km long, W N.Y.; rises W of Machias; flows S to Allegheny R. at Olean. Called Olean Creek below junction with small Oil Creek.

Ishpeming (ish-PEM-ing), town (1990 pop. 7,200), Marquette co., NW Upper Peninsula, Mich., 14 mi/23 km SW of Marquette, in Marquette Iron range; 46°29′N 87°39′W. RR junction. Lumbering; cattle; mfg. (logging, construction, sand and gravel, hardwood parquet); iron mining. U.S. Natl. Ski Hall of Fame; birthplace of skiing in Amer.; ski tournaments held here since 1888. Inc. as village 1871, as city 1873.

Ishuatán, Mexico: see IXHUATÁN.

Isidro Fabela (ee-SEED-ro fah-BE-lah), town (1990 pop. 5,190), ⊙ Isidro Fabela municipio, Mexico, 20 mi/33 km WNW of Mexico City on E slopes of Cerro Monte Alto, included within the Zona Metropolitana de la Ciudad de México; 19°34′N 99°26′W. Elev. 9,186 ft/2,800 m. Cool climate, in wooded area on W slopes bordering the Basin of Mexico; agr. (small farming). Town formerly Tlazala de Fabela, municipio formerly Iturbide.

Isinglass River (EI-zin-glas), c.15 mi/24 km long, SE N.H.; rises at Bow L. in W Strafford co.; flows E to the Cocheco below Rochester.

Isla (EES-lah), town (1990 pop. 18,484), SE Veracruz, Mexico, 40 mi/58 km SSW of San Andrés Tuxtla; on RR and 3 mi/5 km S of Mexico Highway 145.

Isla Angel de la Guarda National Park (EES-lah AHN-hel dai la GWAHR-dah), a biological reserve in Baja California, Mexico. It is an isl. located in the Gulf of California separated from the Peninsula by the Canal of Whales (Canal de Ballenas). A chain of mts. reaching 3,281 ft/1,000 m cover the area. The W coast is inaccessible. The isl. is uninhabited.

Isla Cancún, Mexico: see CANCÚN.

Isla de Pinos, Cuba: see JUVENTUD, ISLA DE LA.

Isla Grande (EES-lah GRAHN-de), airport, NE P.R., just SE of Old San Juan, across San Antonio Channel and W of Miramar sector of Santurce. Artificially built from sediment dredged from San Juan Bay.

Isla Guadalupe Biosphere Reserve (EES-lah wah-dah-LOO-pe), biosphere reserve in Baja California, Mexico, in the Pacific Ocean, 168 mi/270 km from the W coast of Baja California; 28°45′N 118°10′W–29°15′N 118°30′W. It measures 21 mi/33 km from the N to the S and is only 6 mi/10 km wide. It is of volcanic origin and a mt. range in the N reaches 4,593 ft/1,400 m. The isl. is covered with desert vegetation and is home to herds of sea lions.

Isla, La, Mexico: see SAN ANTONIO LA ISLA.

Isla Mujeres (EES-lah moo-HE-res), town (1990 pop. 6,708), Quintana Roo, SE Mexico, on small Mujeres Isl. (□ 1.3 sq mi/3.4 km²), 5 mi/8 km off NE Yucatán Peninsula, 16 mi/25 km NE of Cancún. Tourist resort. Formerly belonging to great Maya federation, isl. has many archaeological remains.

Isla Tiburón Biosphere Reserve (EES-lah tee-boo-RON), a biological reserve off the W central coast of Sonora, Mexico. This is the largest isl. in the Gulf of California and it is a reserve for flora and fauna, such as cormorants, seagulls, pelicans, and sea lions. A permit is required to visit this isl.

Isla Verde (EES-lah VER-de), beach and residential sector, NE P.R., 5.5 mi/8.9 km E of Old San Juan. Tourist hotels; residential condominiums. Luiz Muñoz Marin Internatl. Airport.

Isla Vista, uninc. city (1990 pop. 20,395), Santa Barbara co., SW Calif., 10 mi/16 km W of Santa Barbara on Pacific Ocean; 34°25′N 119°52′W. Univ. of Calif. (Santa Barbara) to E; Santa Barbara Airport to NE. El Capitan State Park to W; Los Padres Natl. Forest to N. Residential and resort community. Fruit, vegetables, avocados, grain, cattle.

Islamorada (ei-luh-muh-RUH-dah), town (□ 1 sq mi/2.6 sq km; 1990 pop. 1,220), Monroe co., upper Fla. Keys, 20 mi/32 km SW of Key Largo; 24°55′N 80°38′W. Mfg. includes printing and publishing.

Island, county (□ 517 sq mi/1,339 sq km; 1990 pop. 60,195), NW Wash.; ⊙ Coupeville, Whidbey Isl. Co. consists of Whidbey Isl. and Camano Isl. in Puget Sound, NW of Everett, also Smith Isl. in Strait of Juan de Fuca (W); 48°09′N 122°35′W. Alfalfa, hay, berries, vegetables; fishing and summer resorts. County bounded by Skagit Bay, Davis Slough and Port Susan Bay (arm of Puget Sound) on E, by main channel of Puget Sound, on SW. Saratoga Passage separates N 2 isls. Main town is Oak Harbor, on Whidbey Isl. Ebey's Landing Natl. Historical Reserve at Coupville; Camano Isl. State Park in E; Deception Pass and Joseph Whidbey state parks in N; South Whidbey State Park in S. Formed 1853.

Island, village (1990 pop. 446), McLean co., W Ky., 22 mi/35 km S of Owensboro; 37°26′N 87°09′W. In agr. area (tobacco, grain; livestock; timber); mfg. (wooden pallets).

Island Beach, borough and beach, Ocean co., E N.J., on lower 8 mi/12.9 km of peninsula bet. Barnegat Bay and the Atlantic, S of Seaside Park and N of Barnegat Inlet. It is a state park, opened in 1959, noted for plant life and wildlife. Borough set off from Berkeley township and inc. 1933.

Island City, village (1990 pop. 696), Union co., NE Oregon, on Grande Ronde R., 4 mi/6.4 km E of La

Grande; 45°20′N 118°02′W. Elev. 2,750 ft/838 m. Agr. (cherries, apples, grain, potatoes; cattle). Part of Wallowa-Whitman Natl. Forest to NW.

Island Falls, town (1990 pop. 897), Aroostook co., central Maine, 22 mi/35 km SW of Houlton, and on Matawamkeag L.; 45°59′N 68°14′W. Trade center for agr., lumbering, recreation (hunting, fishing) area. Settled 1843, inc. 1872.

Island Falls 1 village, NE Ont., Canada, on Abitibi R. (66-ft/20-m falls), and 40 mi/64 km NNW of Cochrane. Hydroelectric power center, supplying Cochrane mining region. **2** village, E Sask., Canada, on Churchill R. (falls), and 55 mi/89 km NNW of Flin Flon. Hydroelectric power center, supplying Flin Flon and Sherridon mining region.

Island Heights, resort borough (1990 pop. 1,470), Ocean co., E N.J., on Toms R., near Barnegat Bay, just E of Toms River; 39°56′N 74°09′W.

Island Lake, city (1990 pop. 4,449), McHenry and Lake cos., NE Ill., suburb 34 mi/55 km NW of downtown Chicago, 6 mi/9.7 km SE of McHenry; 42°16′N 88°12′W. Small lakes in area. Mfg. (printing, oil field valves and fittings). Moraine Hills State Park to NW.

Island Lake (□ 550 sq mi/1,425 sq km), E Man., Canada, on Ont. border; 55 mi/89 km long, 20 mi/32 km wide. Drains into Hudson Bay.

Island Lake, reservoir (□ 18 sq mi/47 sq km), St. Louis co., NE Minn., on Cloquet R., 20 mi/32 km N of Duluth; 47°00′N 92°14′W. Max. capacity 171,520 acre-ft. Formed by Island Lake Dam (45ft/14 m high), built (1915) for power generation; also used for recreation. Cloquet Valley State Forest to N.

Island No. 10, former island in the Mississippi R., bet. NW Tenn. and SE Mo. Site of an important W campaign of the Civil War.

Island Park 1 village (1990 pop. 159), Fremont co., E Idaho, 35 mi/56 km NE of St. Anthony, on Henry's Fork R.; 44°34′N 111°20′W. In Targhee Natl. Forest; Island Park Dam and Reservoir on Henrys Fork is 1 mi/1.6 km to W, Harriman State Park is on its S shore; Yellowstone Natl. Park to E; Henry's L. reservoir and State Park to N. **2** residential village (1990 pop. 4,860), Nassau co., SE N.Y., on isl. off S shore of W L.I., 7 mi/11.3 km S of Hempstead; 40°36′N 73°39′W. Connected by causeways to Long Beach (S) and L.I. Inc. 1926. **3** village, Portsmouth town, Newport co., SE R.I., on Rhode Isl., 2 mi/3.2 km E of Portsmouth village. Yacht club, harbor, and numerous beaches located here.

Island Park, locality, Hennepin co., E Minn., residential sect. in S part of town of Mound, on Phelps isl. in L. Minnetonka, 20 mi/32 km W of Minneapolis; 44°55′N 93°38′W. Cooks Bay to W.

Island Park Dam, Idaho: see HENRYS FORK.

Island Park Reservoir (□ 14 sq mi/36 sq km), Fremont co., E Idaho, on Henry's Fork Snake R., abutting Targhee Natl. Forest; 45 mi/72 km NNE of Rexburg; 44°25′N 111°24′W. Max. capacity 169,646 acre-ft. Formed by Island Park Dam (94 ft/29 m high), built (1938) by the Bureau of Reclamation for irrigation; also used for recreation.

Island Pond 1 Vt.: see BRIGHTON. **2** N.H.: see HAMPSTEAD.

Island View, village (1990 pop. 150), Koochiching co., N Minn., 9 mi/14.5 km E of International Falls, on peninsula in Rainy L. Black Bay to S, Black Bay Narrows to E; Voyageurs Natl. Park to E; 48°36′N 93°11′W.

Islandia, village (1990 pop. 2,799), Suffolk co., SE N.Y., 5 mi/8 km N of central Islip; 40°49′N 73°10′W. Mfg.

Islands, Bay of, inlet (20 mi/32 km long, 10 mi/16 km wide at entrance) of the Gulf of St. Lawrence, W N.F., Canada, 20 mi/32 km N of Corner Brook; 49°10′N 58°15′W. Contains Tweed, Pearl, Woods, Guernsey, and Governors isls. E shore is deeply indented by 3 arms; S arm receives Humber R. estuary. On shore are several fishing settlements.

Islas de Golfo de California, a special biological reserve in S Baja California Sur, Mexico. This is a multi-isl. reserve including Ángel de la Guarda, San Marcos, Coronado, Carmen, Monserrate, Santa Catarina, Santa

Cruz, San José Espíritu Santo, Cerralvo (in front of the E coast of the Baja California peninsula), and La Tiburón, the largest isl. in the country.

Isle (EIL), village (1990 pop. 566), Mille Lacs co., E Minn., 36 mi/58 km SE of Brainerd, on SE shore of Mille Lacs L. on Isle Harbor; 46°08′N 93°27′W. Grain; livestock, poultry; dairying; mfg. (fishing tackle, electroplating, printing and publishing); timber; sand and gravel. Granite quarries nearby. Mille Lacs Wildlife Area to SW; Father Hennepin State Park to NW, at Pope Point; Mille Lacs L.; small part of Mille Lacs Indian Reservation to NE.

Isle au Haut (EI-luh HO), town (1990 pop. 46), Knox co., S Maine, on Isle au Haut (□ c.9 sq mi/23.3 sq km) and adjacent isls., 25 mi/40 km ESE of Rockland in Isle au Haut Bay; 44°00′N 68°34′W. Part of the isl. is in Acadia Natl. Park.

Île du Cap aux Meules, in the Gulf of St. Lawrence, E Que., Canada, one of the Magdalen Isls., 60 mi/97 km N of Prince Edward Isl.; 5 mi/8 km long, 4 mi/6 km wide; 47°23′N 61°55′W. Étang du Nord (W) is chief town. Fisheries. Wolf Isl., narrow spit of land, extends NE to Grosse Isl.

Isle La Motte, island and town (1990 pop. 408), 6 mi/9.7 km long and 2 mi/3.2 km wide, in L. Champlain, NW Vt.; 44°52′N 73°19′W. The French chose the isl. as the site for Fort Ste. Anne (built 1666), the first recorded Eur. settlement in Vermont. Ste. Anne's shrine is here. Limestone quarries.

Isle La Ronde (EIL luh-ROON), islet, Grenada, West Indies, NNE of Sauteurs. Home to a few fishing families, sea bird pops.

Isle of Hope, resort town (1990 pop. 1,400), Chatham co., E Ga., 6 mi/9.7 km SSE of Savannah, near the Atlantic; 31°58′N 81°03′W.

Isle of Palms, town (1990 pop. 3,680), Charleston co., SE S.C., on Isle of Palms isl. (5.5 mi/8.9 km long), 8 mi/12.9 km E of Charleston; 32°47′N 79°45′W. Suburb of Charleston and resort center. Bridged to Sullivans Isl. (SW). Intracoastal Waterway passes to W. Destroyed by Hurricane Hugo (1989); since rebuilt.

Isle of Springs, island, Lincoln co., S Maine, in Sheepscot R. just W of Boothbay Harbor town; c.½ mi/⅘ km in diameter. Formerly called Sweet Isl.

Isle of Wight, county (□ 362 sq mi/938 sq km; 1990 pop. 25,053), SE Va.; ⊙ Isle of Wight; 36°54′N 76°42′W. In the Tidewater region; bounded W by Blackwater R., NE by the James estuary. Agr. (sandy soils produce peanuts, corn, hay, soybeans, melons, barley, wheat, cotton; hogs; cattle); some timber. Historic bldgs. include St. Luke's Church, one of the oldest churches in Amer., at Benn's Church in NE. L. Burnt Mills reservoir in NE, on Western Branch Nansemond R. Formed 1634.

Isle of Wight, uninc. village, ⊙ Isle of Wight co., SE Va., 12 mi/19 km NNW of Suffolk. Agr. (grain, soybeans, melons, cotton, peanuts; livestock).

Isle Royale National Park (EIL roi-AL) (□ 210 sq mi/544 sq km), comprising Isle Royale and about 200 smaller islands, in L. Superior, NW Mich. Isle Royale—210 sq mi/544 sq km, 45 mi/72 km long, max. 8 mi/12.9 km wide—is the largest isl. in L. Superior; Greenstone Ridge and Trail extend along its entire length. It includes L. Siskiwit. Ryan Isl., in L. Siskiwit, is the largest isl. in the largest lake, on the largest isl. in the world's largest fresh-water lake. Glaciated, the isl. has about 50 lakes, also streams and inlets. It remains a roadless (does have trails and portage system) forested wilderness. Campgrounds located throughout inland; canoeing, fishing, hiking. Its abundant wildlife includes squirrels, beaver, fox, moose, wolves, and many birds. The French, lured by the fur trade, named the isl. in 1671. Isle Royale became U.S. territory in 1783 and was ceded to the U.S. by the Chippewa in 1843. It was mined for copper from 1843 to 1899; large areas of forest were burned to expose the ore and to build settlements. Has pre-Columbian copper-mine sites. In the early 1900s the isl. was a popular vacation retreat; still has a few private cabins. Season mid-May to Oct 1. 40 mi/64 km from Mich.'s Upper Peninsula, 15 mi/24 km from Ont. shore, and 20 mi/32 km from Minn. Acreage includes park office and ranger ferry terminal at Houghton. Accommodations and services at Rock Harbor Lodge area (NE); reached by ferries from Copper Harbor and Houghton. Ferry from Grand Portage, Minn., to Windigo ranger station at SW end; shuttle service encircles isl. Est. 1940.

Isle Saint George, Ohio: see BASS ISLANDS.

Isle Verte (eel VERT), village, S Que., Canada, on the St. Lawrence and 16 mi/26 km NE of Rivière du Loup; dairying, lumbering, peat moss mfg. Opposite is Île Verte.

Île-aux-Coudres (eel-o-KOO-druh), island, in the St. Lawrence R., SE Que., Canada; c.6 mi/10 km long and 3 mi/5 km wide. Named by Jacques Cartier in 1535 for the hazelnuts growing here. The 1st R.C. mass in Canada was celebrated on the isl. the same year. Because it preserves traditional Que. rural life, the isl. is a tourist attraction.

Isles Dernieres (EEL dern-YER), S La., uninhabited island chain (c.18.5 mi/31 km long), 38 mi/61 km S of Houma, bet. Caillou Bay and L. Pelto (N) and Gulf of Mexico (S); 29°02′N 90°48′W. Once a continuous barrier beach; fashionable mid-19th-cent. resorts here were destroyed by hurricane (1856), which took many lives.

Isles of Shoals, Maine and N.H., islands 10 mi/16 km SE of Portsmouth, N.H. Appledore, Cedar, Duck, and Smuttynose (or Haley's) isls. are in Maine; Lunging, White (lighthouse), and Star isls. are in N.H. Resorts on Appledore and Star isls.

Islesboro (EILZ-buhr-o), island and town (1990 pop. 579), Waldo co., S Maine, in Penobscot Bay SE of Belfast; c.11.5 mi/19 km long, ½ mi/⅘ km–1.5 mi/2.4 km wide; 44°17′N 68°55′W. Includes resort villages of Dark Harbor, Pripet, North Islesboro. Sometimes Islesborough.

Islesford, Maine: see CRANBERRY ISLES.

Isleta (iz-LET-ah), pueblo (1990 pop. 1,703), Bernalillo co., central N.Mex., 12 mi/19 km S of downtown Albuquerque, on the E bank of the Rio Grande, in Isleta Indian Reservation (1990 pop. 2,915); 34°52′N 106°40′W. Confluence of Rio Puerco and Rio San Juan in W part of reservation. It is a tourist attraction. According to many experts, the pueblo stands on the site it occupied when discovered in 1540. It was the seat of the Franciscan mission of San Antonio de Isleta from c.1621 until the Pueblo revolt of 1680. The Spanish captured the pueblo in 1681, and most of the captives were ultimately settled at Ysleta, Texas. In the early 18th cent., when N Isleta was either rebuilt or repopulated, it became the mission of San Agustín de Isleta. The Pueblo in Isleta are mainly farmers; the language there is Tanoan.

Isleton, city (1990 pop. 833), Sacramento co., central Calif., 28 mi/45 km S of Sacramento and 13 mi/21 km NE of Antioch, in San Joaquin/Sacramento Delta; San Joaquin R. 4 mi/6.4 km to S, Sacramento R. 3 mi/4.8 km to NW; 38°10′N 121°36′W. Vegetables, corn, tomatoes, beans, sugar beets, rice; cattle. Founded 1874, inc. 1923.

Islington, town (1991 pop. 2,868), St. Mary parish, NE Jamaica, 23 mi/37 km NNW of Kingston; 18°19′N 76°51′W. Road junction.

Islington, Mass.: see WESTWOOD.

Islip, suburban residential village (1990 pop. 18,924), Suffolk co., SE N.Y., on S shore of L.I., on Great South Bay, just E of Bay Shore; 40°43′N 73°11′W. Mfg. (mixers for food and chemical industries, telecommunications and aerospace instrumentation; aircraft parts); in recreational and duck-farming area; horticultural crops. Heckscher State Park (recreation facilities) is SE of Islip and Seatuck Natl. Wildlife Refuge is immediately S. S terminus of L.I. Greenbelt trail, which runs N from Great South Bay to Sunken Meadows State Park on N shore of L.I., N of Kings Park, on Smithtown Bay.

Islip Terrace, suburban residential village (□ 1 sq mi/2.6 sq km; 1990 pop. 5,530), Suffolk co., SE N.Y., on central L.I., 2 mi/3.2 km NE of Islip; 40°45′N 73°11′W.

Ismay (IS-mai), village (1990 pop. 19), Custer co., E Mont., on O'Fallon Creek at mouth of Sandstone Creek, and 52 mi/84 km E of Miles City; 46°30′N 104°48′W. Cattle, sheep, hay. Also called Joe.

Isola (ei-SO-luh), town (1990 pop. 732), Humphreys co., W Miss., 8 mi/12.9 km NW of Belzoni; 33°15′N 90°35′W. In rich agr. area (cotton, corn, rice; cattle); mfg. (catfish processing, catfish feed).

Israel River, c.25 mi/40 km long, Coos co., N N.H.; rises in Presidential Range; flows NW to the Connecticut R. near Lancaster.

Issaquah (I-suh-kwah), town (1990 pop. 7,786), King co., W central Wash., suburb 15 mi/24 km ESE of downtown Seattle, on Sammamish R.; 47°32′N 122°02′W. RR terminus. Dairy prods.; poultry; timber; mfg. (in vitro diagnostic substances, printed circuit boards, X-ray apparatus, metal prods., electromedical apparatus, printing, wiring devices, refrigeration equip., measurement equip.). Lake Sammamish State Park to NW.

Issaquena (is-uh-KWEE-nuh), county (□ 441 sq mi/1,142 sq km; 1990 pop. 1,909), W Miss.; ⊙ Mayersville; 32°44′N 90°59′W. Bounded W by the Mississippi R. (La. state line), NW corner of co. touches SW corner of Ark., Yazoo R. forms parts of S and E boundaries; state boundary follows old channel of Mississippi R., including Albermarle L. and other oxbow lakes on either side of river. Agr. (cotton, corn, oats, sorghum, soybeans, wheat; cattle; timber). Includes part of Delta Natl. Forest in SE. Has oxbow lakes along the Mississippi. Mahannah Wildlife Management Area in S, Anderson-Tully Wildlife Management Area in center, Shipland Wildlife Management Area in W. Formed 1844.

Istokpoga, Lake (iz-stock-PO-guh), Highlands co., central Fla., 25 mi/40 km NW of L. Okeechobee; c.10 mi/16 km long, 5 mi/8 km wide; connected by channel (N) with Lakes Weohyakapka and Kissimmee; has short outlet (dredged) at E end to Kissimmee R.

Istrouma (is-TROO-muh), suburb, East Baton Rouge parish, SE central La., part of Baton Rouge.

Italian Mountain, peak (13,378 ft/4,078 m) in Rocky Mts., Gunnison co., W central Colo., 13 mi/21 km ENE of Crested Butte, in Gunnison Natl. Forest.

Italy, town (1990 pop. 1,699), Ellis co., N central Texas, 13 mi/21 km SSW of Waxahachie and 38 mi/61 km S of Dallas, near Chambers creek; 32°10′N 96°52′W. In rich blackland agr. area (cotton, corn, grain; cattle; dairying). Mfg. (disposable protective clothing, chain-link fence hardware, industrial aprons).

Itasca (ei-TAS-kuh), county (□ 2,927 sq mi/7,581 sq km; 1990 pop. 40,863), N Minn.; ⊙ Grand Rapids; 47°30′N 93°37′W. Drained by Mississippi R. (forms part of SW boundary, including L. Winnibigoshish reservoir). Agr. area (hay, alfalfa; cattle; some dairying); timber; peat deposits; iron mining in W part of Mesabi Iron Range. Parts of Leech L. Indian Reservation in SW; part of Chippewa Natl. Forest in W; Big Fork and George Washington state forests in N; Golden Anniversary State Forest in S; Scenic State Park in N; Hill Annex Mine State Park in E; Schoolcraft State Park on SW boundary. Numerous lakes, including Bowstring L., in W, and Pokegama L. Formed 1849.

Itasca, town (1990 pop. 1,523), Hill co., N central Texas, 42 mi/68 km SSE of Fort Worth; 32°09′N 97°09′W. In cotton, grain; cattle area; mfg. (fertilizer). Settled 1882; inc. as city 1910.

Itasca (i-TAS-kuh), village (1990 pop. 6,947), Du Page co., NE Ill., residential suburb 18 mi/29 km WNW of downtown Chicago and 15 mi/24 km ESE of Elgin; 41°58′N 88°01′W. Some agr. (corn, oats).

Itasca, Lake (ei-TAS-kuh) (□ 2 sq mi/5.2 sq km), Clearwater co. (SE arm extends into Hubbard co.), NW central Minn., shallow lake, in a pine-wooded swampy region; 47°13′N 95°12′W. It is the source of the Mississippi R., which drains N from lake before turning E and S; stepping stones cross river at its exit point. Henry R. Schoolcraft identified it (1832) as the source of the Mississippi. Although unarguably the source of the named river, the river's true physical course has been disputed by geographers. In 1891 the lake was included in Itasca State Park, which has a historical and natural-history mus. A school of forestry and a biological-research station are nearby.

Itawamba (it-uh-WAHM-buh), county (□ 540 sq mi/ 1,399 sq km; 1990 pop. 20,017), NE Miss., borders E on Ala.; ⊙ Fulton; 34°16′N 88°21′W. Drained by East Fork of Tombigbee R. Agr. (cotton, corn, soybeans; poultry, cattle; timber). Natchez Trace (Natl.) Parkway passes through NW corner. Part of John Bell Williams Wildlife Management Area (canal section) in N. Formed 1836.

Ithaca, city (□ 6 sq mi/15.5 sq km; 1990 pop. 29,541), ⊙ Tompkins co., S central N.Y., at S end of Cayuga L., in the Finger Lakes region; 42°26′N 76°30′W. It is important chiefly as an educational center, the seat of Cornell Univ., Ithaca Col., and State Univ. of N.Y.'s Cornell campus. Mfg. includes computer-controlled valves and pumps, logic analyzers and performance-board testers, computer hardware and software, vibration isolators, steel fabrication, precision machining, chains, sprockets, and timing belts. Subsurface salt mines and brine wells NE and NW of Ithaca. City has access to the N.Y. State Barge Canal. Tourism in the Finger Lakes area is important to the city's economy. A state hosp. is also in Ithaca. Settled 1789, inc. as a city 1888.

Ithaca (I-thuh-kuh), town (1990 pop. 3,009), ⊙ Gratiot co., central Mich., 34 mi/55 km WSW of Saginaw; 43°17′N 84°35′W. In agr. area (livestock; beans, sugar beets, dairy prods.); mfg. (aircraft-engine components, die sets, printing, molded plastics). Inc. 1869.

Ithaca 1 village (1990 pop. 133), Saunders co., E Nebr., 5 mi/8 km SE of Wahoo and on branch of Platte R.; 41°09′N 96°32′W. Pioneer State Wayside Area to SW. **2** village (1990 pop. 119), Darke co., W Ohio, 12 mi/ 19 km SSE of Greenville, in agr. area; 39°56′N 84°33′W.

Itkillik River (IT-ki-lik), c.180 mi/290 km long, N Alaska; rises in N Brooks Range near 68°10′N 150°W; flows to Colville R. near its mouth at 70°03′N 151°02′W.

Itta Bena (it-uh BEEN-uh), town (1990 pop. 2,377), Leflore co., W central Miss., 8 mi/12.9 km WSW of Greenwood; 33°30′N 90°19′W. In cotton-growing area, agr. (cattle; corn, rice, sorghum, soybeans); mfg. (catfish processing). Seat of Mississippi Valley State Univ. (to N).

Ituna (ei-TOO-nuh), town (1991 pop. 803), SE Sask., Canada, in the Beaver Hills, 45 mi/72 km W of Yorkton; 51°10′N 103°30′W.

Iturbide (ee-tor-BEE-de), town (1990 pop. 1,808), Nuevo León, N Mexico, in Sierra Madre Oriental, 23 mi/37 km WSW of Linares on Mexico Highway 60; 24°45′N 99°53′W. Grain, livestock.

Iturbide, Mexico: see VILLA HIDALGO, San Luis Potosí.

Iuka (ei-YOO-kuh), town (1990 pop. 3,122), ⊙ Tishomingo co., extreme NE Miss., 20 mi/32 km ESE of Corinth; 34°48′N 88°12′W. Agr. (grain, soybeans; hogs); mfg. (apparel, consumer goods, shoes, limestone); sandstone, clay deposits; mineral spring. A Civil War battle was fought here in 1862. Fine antebellum houses survive. Old Courthouse (1870). Woodall Mt. (806 ft/ 246 m), highest point in Miss., 3 mi/4.8 km to W; Pickwick L. reservoir (Tennessee R.) to NE, Bear R. Arm to E; J. P. Coleman State Park, on SW shore of Pickwick L., to N. Inc. 1857.

Iuka 1 (ei-YOO-kah), village (1990 pop. 388), Marion co., S Ill., 8 mi/12.9 km E of Salem; 38°36′N 88°47′W. In agr. (grain, cattle) and oil area. **2** (ei-YOO-kuh), village (1990 pop. 197), Pratt co., S Kansas, 6 mi/9.7 km N of Pratt; 37°43′N 98°43′W. In wheat area.

Iva (EI-vuh), town (1990 pop. 1,174), Anderson co., NW S.C., 14 mi/23 km S of Anderson; 34°18′N 82°39′W. Mfg. includes clothing, cotton and polyester cloth; agr. area that produces poultry, cattle, hogs, dairying, grain, soybeans. Founded c.1885.

Ivanhoe 1 town (1990 pop. 3,293), Tulare co., central Calif., 5 mi/8 km NE of Visalia; 36°23′N 119°13′W. Orchards, citrus groves, grapes, nuts, grain; cattle; nursery prods. **2** town (1990 pop. 751), ⊙ Lincoln co., SW Minn., near S.Dak. state line, 23 mi/37 km W of Marshall; 44°27′N 96°15′W. Elev. 1,658 ft/505 m. Grain, soybeans, alfalfa; livestock, poultry; dairying; light mfg.

Ivanhoe, uninc. village, Wythe co., SW Va., near New R.,

10 mi/16 km SSE of Wytheville. Agr. (livestock; grain, cotton, peanuts). New River Trail passes to E.

Ivesdale, village (1990 pop. 339), Champaign co., E central Ill., 15 mi/24 km SW of Champaign; 39°57′N 88°27′W. In agr. area (corn, soybeans).

Ivey, town (1990 pop. 1,053), Wilkinson co., central Ga., 11 mi/18 km SSW of Milledgeville; 32°55′N 83°18′W. Mfg. of steel tanks.

Ivins (EI-vihnz), town (1990 pop. 1,630), Washington co., SW Utah, 5 mi/8 km NW of St. George, near Santa Clara R.; 37°10′N 113°40′W. Snow Canyon State Park to NE; Gunlock State Park to NW.

Ivor (EI-vor), town (1990 pop. 324), Southampton co., SE Va., 17 mi/27 km N of Franklin, near Blackwater R.; 36°53′N 76°54′W. Mfg. (meat packing, fertilizer).

Ivoryton, Conn.: see ESSEX.

Ivujivik or **Notre-Dame-d'Ivugivic,** village (1991 pop. 263), N Que., Canada, at NW tip of Ungava Peninsula, where Hudson Strait enters Hudson Bay; 62°25′N 77°54′W. Pop. is Inuit. Scheduled air service. Hunting, fishing, trapping.

Ivy, uninc. village, Albemarle co., central Va., 5 mi/8 km W of Charlottesville. Mfg. (clothing, wall clocks); agr. (dairying; livestock; grain, apples). Meriwether Lewis b. here, 1774. Also called Ivy Depot.

Ivyland, borough (1990 pop. 490), Bucks co., SE Pa., industrial suburb 16 mi/26 km NNE of Philadelphia. Mfg. (machinery, pressure vessels, laboratory equip., electronic components, canvas prods., windows, graphic-arts equip., food preparations, flavors). Agr. to NE (grain; livestock; dairying). U.S. Naval Air Development Center to S.

Ivywild, village, El Paso co., E central Colo., 2 mi/3.2 km SSW of, and part of, Colorado Springs.

Ixcamilpa (eesh-kam-MEEL-pah), town (1990 pop. 1,456), ⊙ Ixcamilpa de Guerrero municipio, Puebla, central Mexico, 40 mi/64 km SSW of Izúcar de Matamoros (on the Guerrero border); 18°00′N 98°42′W. Corn, sugarcane; livestock.

Ixcamilpa de Guerrero, Mexico: see IXCAMILPA.

Ixcapuzalco (eesh-kah-poo-SAHL-ko), town (1990 pop. 578), ⊙ Pedro Ascencio Alquisiras municipio, Guerrero, SW Mexico, on S slope of central plateau, 21 mi/ 34 km WSW of Taxco de Alarcón. Cereals, sugarcane, fruit.

Ixcateopan de Cuauhtémoc (ish-kah-te-O-pan de kwou-TE-mok), town (1990 pop. 2,064), Guerrero, SW Mexico, 17 mi/27 km WSW of Taxco de Alarcón. Cereals, sugarcane, fruit, timber.

Ixcatepec (eesh-KA-te-pek), town (1990 pop. 2,909), Veracruz, E Mexico, in Sierra Madre Oriental foothills, 40 mi/64 km NW of Túxpam de Rodríguez Cano. Cereals, sugarcane, coffee, fruit.

Ixhuacán de los Reyes (eesh-wah-KAN de los RE-yes), town (1990 pop. 2,253), Veracruz, E Mexico, in Sierra Madre Oriental, 17 mi/27 km SW of Xalapa Enríquez. Corn, fruit. Formerly Ixhuacán.

Ixhuatán (eesh-wah-TAHN), town (1990 pop. 1,797), in NW Chiapas, Mexico, 37 mi/60 km NW of San Cristóbal de las Casas, on Mexico Highway 195; 17°17′N 93°02′W. Elev. 1,640 ft/500 m. A Zoque Indian community. Formerly Ishuatán.

Ixhuatlán de Madero (eesh-wat-LAHN de ma-DAI-ro), town (1990 pop. 1,295), Veracruz, E Mexico, in Sierra Madre Oriental foothills, 40 mi/64 km SE of Túxpam de Rodríguez Cano; 20°42′N 98°00′W. Corn, sugarcane, fruit.

Ixhuatlán del Café (eex-waht-LAHN del ka-FE), town (1990 pop. 5,952), Veracruz, E Mexico, in Sierra Madre Oriental, 12 mi/19 km N of Córdoba; 20°42′N 98°00′W. Coffee, corn, fruit. Formerly Ixhuatlán.

Ixhuatlán del Sureste (eesh-wat-LAHN del soor-ES-te), town (1990 pop. 7,652), Veracruz, SE Mexico, on Isthmus of Tehuantepec, 11 mi/18 km ENE of Minatitlán; 20°42′N 98°00′W. Tropical fruit, livestock. Petroleum production. Sometimes Chapopotla.

Ixhuatlancillo (eesh-wah-tlahn-SEE-yo), town (1990 pop. 3,484), ⊙ Ixhuatlancillo municipio, Veracruz, E Mexico, in Sierra Madre Oriental, 4 mi/6.4 km NW of Orizaba. Coffee, sugarcane, tobacco, fruit.

Ixil (eesh-EEL), town (1990 pop. 2,548), Yucatán, SE Mexico, 16 mi/26 km NE of Mérida. Henequen.

Ixmatlahuacán (eesh-mah-tlah-wah-KAHN), town (1990 pop. 1,431), Veracruz, SE Mexico, in Sotavento lowlands, 6 mi/9.7 km NNW of Cosamaloapan. Sugarcane, bananas.

Ixmiquilpan (eesh-mee-KEEL-pahn), city (1990 pop. 26,967) and township, Hidalgo, central Mexico, on Tula R., on Inter-American Highway, and 40 mi/64 km NW of Pachuca de Soto; 20°29′N 99°14′W. Elev. 5,577 ft/ 1,700 m. Cereals, maguey; livestock; native textiles. Anc. Otomí Indian capital.

Ixonia (iks-O-nee-ah), village, Jefferson co., S Wis., 8 mi/ 12.9 km SE of Watertown. Dairying, wheat. Transitional urban area. Mfg. (tool and die, metal prods., feeds, furniture).

Ixpantepec Nieves (eesh-PAHN-te-pek nee-E-ves), town (1990 pop. 1,241), in far NW Oaxaca, Mexico, 19 mi/30 km SW of Huajuapam de León. Elev. 7,677 ft/ 2,340 m. Steep terrain with cold climate. Corn, wheat, beans; mescal; local straw textiles. On unpaved road with connections to Huajuapam de León and Silacayoapam.

Ixtacamaxtitlán (eesh-tah-ka-mash-teet-LAHN), town (1990 pop. 266), Puebla, central Mexico, 27 mi/43 km SSE of Zacatlán. Corn, maguey. Silver, gold, copper deposits nearby.

Ixtaccihuatl, Mexico: see IZTACCIHUATL.

Ixtacomitán (eesh-tah-ko-mee-TAHN), town (1990 pop. 2,968), Chiapas, S Mexico, 45 mi/72 km N of Tuxtla Gutiérrez, on Mexico Highway 195; 17°26′N 93°05′W. Rice, fruit. A Zoque Indian community.

Ixtacuixtla, Mexico: see VILLA MARIANO MATAMOROS.

Ixtacuixtla de Mariano Matamoros, Mexico: see VILLA MARIANO MATAMOROS.

Ixtaczoquitlán (eeks-tak-zo-keet-LAHN), town (1990 pop. 12,153), Veracruz, E Mexico, in Sierra Madre Oriental, 3 mi/4.8 km NE of Orizaba. Elev. 3,891 ft/1,186 m. Coffee, sugarcane, fruit.

Ixtapa (eesh-TAH-pah), town (1990 pop. 3,462), Chiapas, S Mexico, in N spur of Sierra Madre, 13 mi/21 km E of Tuxtla Gutiérrez. Elev. 3,625 ft/1,105 m. Cereals, fruit; livestock. A Tzotzil Maya community.

Ixtapa Point (eesh-TAH-pah), cape on Pacific coast of Guerrero, SW Mexico, 6 mi/10 km W of Zinuatanejo; 17°40′N 101°40′W.

Ixtapaluca (eeks-tah-pah-LOO-kah), town (1990 pop. 115,711), Mexico state, central Mexico, 19 mi/31 km SE of Mexico city, and part of the Zona Metropolitana de la Ciudad de México. Cereals, maguey, livestock.

Ixtapan de la Sal (eesh-TAH-pahn de lah SAHL), town (1990 pop. 13,259), Mexico state, central Mexico, 32 mi/ 51 km S of Toluca de Lerdo. Sugarcane, coffee, cereals, fruit. Thermal springs.

Ixtapan del Oro (eeks-TAH-pahn del O-ro), town (1990 pop. 1,273), Mexico state, central Mexico, 40 mi/64 km W of Toluca de Lerdo. Grain, fruit; livestock.

Ixtapangajoya (eeks-tah-pahn-gah-HO-yah), town (1990 pop. 627), Chiapas, S Mexico, in Gulf lowland, 37 mi/60 km S of Villahermosa; 17°30′N 92°02′W. Fruit. A Zoque Indian community.

Ixtenco or **San Juan Ixtenco,** (eeks-TEN-ko), town (1990 pop. 5,356), Tlaxcala, central Mexico, at E foot of Malinche volcano, 25 mi/40 km NE of Puebla. Agr. center (corn, wheat, barley, alfalfa, beans; livestock).

Ixtepec (EEKS-te-pek), town (1990 pop. 3,848), ⊙ Ixtepec municipio, Puebla, central Mexico, in E foothills of Sierra Madre Oriental, 25 mi/40 km SE of Huauchinango; 18°26′N 100°09′W. Sugarcane, coffee, tobacco, fruit.

Ixtlahuaca de Rayón (eesh-tlah-WAH-kah de rah-YON), town (1990 pop. 4,428), ⊙ Ixtlahuaca municipio, Mexico state, central Mexico, on Lerma R., and 40 mi/64 km WNW of Mexico city. Cereals, fruit; livestock. Silver deposits nearby.

Ixtlahuacán (eesh-tlah-wah-KAHN), town (1990 pop. 2,244), Colima, W Mexico, on coastal plain, 16 mi/ 26 km S of Colima; 19°00′N 103°40′W. Rice, corn, sugarcane, coffee, tobacco, fruit.

Ixtlahuacán de los Membrillos (eesh-tlah-wah-KAHN

de los mem-BREE-yos), town (1990 pop. 4,503), ⊙ Ixtlahuacán de los Membrillos municipio, Jalisco, central Mexico, near L. Chapala, on RR, and 25 mi/40 km SSE of Guadalajara. Wheat-growing center.

Ixtlahuacán del Río (eesh-tlah-wah-KAHN del REE-o), town (1990 pop. 4,807), Jalisco, central Mexico, on affluent of Santiago R., and 14 mi/23 km NE of Guadalajara; 20°50′N 103°20′W. Grain, sugarcane, fruit; livestock.

Ixtlán de Juárez (eesh-TLAHN de HWAH-res), town (1990 pop. 1,894), Oaxaca, S Mexico, surrounded by spurs of Sierra Madre del Sur, 25 mi/40 km NE of Oaxaca de Juárez, on Mexico Highway 175; 17°22′N 96°20′W. Elev. 5,577 ft/1,700 m. Corn, beans, wheat, fruits; livestock; mfg. serapes.

Ixtlán de los Hervores (eesh-TLAHN de los er-VO-res), town (1990 pop. 5,352), ⊙ Ixtlán municipio, Michoacán, central Mexico, on central plateau, 18 mi/29 km NW of Zamora de Hidalgo, on Mexico Highway 35. Agr. center (cereals, fruit, vegetables; livestock). Geysers and springs nearby. Formerly Ixtlán.

Ixtlán del Río (eesh-TLAHN del REE-o), city (1990 pop. 19,645), Nayarit, W Mexico, amid W outliers of Sierra Madre Occidental, 50 mi/80 km SE of Tepic, on RR, and on Mexico Highway 15; 21°02′N 104°22′W. Elev. 3,419 ft/1,042 m. Silver, gold, lead deposits. Agr. center (corn, beans, sugarcane, bananas); sugar refineries, tanneries. Formerly Ixtlán.

Izamal (ee-SAH-mal), city (1990 pop. 13,413) and township, Yucatán, SE Mexico, 39 mi/63 km E of Mérida; 20°56′N 89°01′W. On RR. Agr. center (henequen, sugarcane, corn). Site of anc. Maya town (believed to be older than Chichén Itzá), an aboriginal pilgrimage site. Many religious remains, pyramids, mausoleum. Monastery and cathedral were erected 1553 on site of Maya temples.

Izard (IZ-uhrd), county (□ 584 sq mi/1,513 sq km; 1990 pop. 11,364), N Ark.; ⊙ Melbourne; 36°05′N 91°54′W. Bounded SW by White R.; drained by Strawberry R. Agr. (cattle, hogs, chickens; hay; dairying); lumber milling, cotton ginning; glass sand, gravel pits. North Central Correctional Unit in W. Formed 1825.

Iztacalco (eez-ta-KAHL-ko), city (1990 pop. 448,322) and delegación, Federal dist., S central Mexico; 19°23′N 99°07′W. It is an industrial center, now a part of greater Mexico city, SE of city center. Several historic landmarks have been preserved. La Calzada de la Viga built on site occupied by anc. National Canal de la Viga. It was a trade route to Mexico city for cargoes of flowers, vegetables, and fruits.

Iztaccihuatl or **Ixtaccihuatl** (eez-tah-SEE-watl) [Aztec=white woman], dormant volcano (17,342 ft/ 5,286 m), central Mexico, on the border bet. Puebla and Mexico states; 19°11′N 98°38′W. Irregular in outline, and snow-capped, it is also popularly known as the Sleeping Woman. Also Ixtacihuatl.

Iztaccihuatl-Popocatépetl (eez-tah-SEE-watl–po-po-kah-TE-petl), national park (□ 100 sq mi/ 259 sq km), in SE Mexico state, Mexico. These are snow covered twin volcanoes, Popocatépetl (17,890 ft/5,453 m), called "smoking mountain" and Iztaccihuatl (17,346 ft/ 5,287 m), called "sleeping woman." The peak of Popocatépetl, 55 mi/88 km SE of Mexico city, lies on the borders of the states of Mexico, Morelos, and Puebla. It is the 2d highest mountain in Mexico after Pico de Orizaba. A saddle valley separates the 2 volcanoes, which can be reached by a paved road branching off Mexico route 115, 1 mi/1.6 km S of the town of Amecameca. Cold climate. Rough terrain. It is a 2-day climb to the summit of these volcanoes. Also known as Izta-Popo.

Iztapalapa (ees-tah-pah-LAH-pah), delegación (1990 pop. 1,490,499), Federal dist., S central Mexico. Part of greater Mexico city, SE of city center. It is a commercial and industrial center; the city's main wholesale market is here. Founded on the site of an important pre-Columbian city.

Izúcar de Matamoros (ee-SOO-kar de ma-tah-MO-ros), city (1990 pop. 32,559) and township, Puebla, central Mexico, on RR, on Inter-American Highway (Mexico Highway 190), and 35 mi/56 km SW of Puebla; 18°38′N 98°30′W. Center for growing and refining sugar; rice, fruit; livestock. Site of battle in revolution against Spain. Sometimes Matamoros.

J

J. Percy Priest Lake, reservoir (c.20 mi/32 km long), Davidson and Rutherford cos., N Tenn., on Stones R., 10 mi/16 km E of downtown Nashville; 36°08′N 86°36′W. Max. capacity 652,000 acre-ft. Formed by J. Percy Priest Dam (129 ft/39 m high), built (1967) by the Army Corps of Engineers for flood control and power generation. Long Hunter State Park on NE shore, near dam.

J. Strom Thurmond Lake or **Clark Hill Lake**, reservoir (36 mi/58 km long), Ga. and S.C., on Savannah R. (Ga.-S.C. border), 20 mi/32 km NNW of Augusta, Ga.; 33°39′N 82°11′W. Max. capacity 2,900,000 acre-ft. Formed by J. Strom Thurmond Dam (or Clarks Hill Dam; 200 ft/61 m high, 5,660 ft/1,725 m long) for flood control, navigation, power generation, and recreation. Several state parks on both sides; Sumter Natl. Forest (S.C.) on NE shore. Wealthy coastal residents established summer homes here in early 19th cent. to escape oppressive weather in S Georgia. One of the largest inland man-made lakes in the S.

Jacala (hah-KAH-lah), town (1990 pop. 3,194), Hidalgo, central Mexico, in Sierra Madre Oriental, on Inter-American Highway (Mexico Highway 85), and 70 mi/113 km NNW of Pachuca de Soto; ⊙ Jacala de Ledesma municipio; 21°01′N 99°12′W. Small farming.

Jacinto City, town (1990 pop. 9,343), Harris co., SE Texas, residential suburb 6 mi/9.7 km E of downtown Houston, on Hunting Bayou; 29°46′N 95°14′W. Inc. since 1940.

Jack, county (□ 920 sq mi/2,383 sq km; 1990 pop. 6,981), N Texas; ⊙ Jacksboro; 33°14′N 98°10′W. Drained by W Fork of Trinity R. Livestock (cattle, horses, ostriches); wheat, pecans; wool, mohair marketed. Oil and natural-gas wells; gravel; tourism; timber. Fort Richardson State Historical Park at Jacksboro (center of co.). Formed 1856.

Jack Lee, Lake, reservoir (□ 36 sq mi/93 sq km), extreme S central Ark., near La. border, on Ouachita R., in Felsenthal Natl. Wildlife Refuge, 7 mi/11.3 km W of Crossett; 33°03′N 92°12′W. Max. capacity 76,700 acre-ft. Fed by Saline R. Formed by Felsenthal Lock and Dam (105 ft/32 m high), built (1978) by Army Corps of Engineers for navigation and recreation. Dam also known as Lock and Dam #6; reservoir also known as Ouachita Reservoir.

Jack Wade, village, E Alaska, near Yukon border, 65 mi/105 km W of Dawson, on Taylor "Top of the World" Highway. Gold placers; tourism.

Jackfish, village, central Ont., Canada, on Jackfish Bay of L. Superior, 14 mi/23 km E of Schreiber; 48°48′N 86°58′W. Gold mining.

Jackfish Bay (5 mi/8 km long, 1 mi/1.6 km wide), Lake co., NE Minn., near Can. (Ont.) border, 10 mi/16 km NNE of Ely, SW extension of Basswood L. (connected by narrow passage), in Boundary Waters Canoe Area of Superior Natl. Forest; 48°02′N 91°44′W. Pipestone Bay extends SW from near entrance to Jackfish Bay. Also known as Jackfish L.

Jackfish Lake (10 mi/16 km long, 6 mi/10 km wide), W Sask., Canada, 17 mi/27 km N of North Battleford. Drains S into North Saskatchewan R. Just E is Murray L. (6 mi/10 km long, 3 mi/5 km wide).

Jackie Robinson Parkway, N.Y.: see INTERBOROUGH (INTERBORO) PARKWAY.

Jackman, town (1990 pop. 920), Somerset co., W Maine, 25 mi/40 km W of Moosehead L., 15 mi/24 km E of Que. line, 33 mi/53 km NW of Greenville; 45°36′N 70°12′W. Port of entry; center of wilderness hunting, fishing, camping region; lumbering.

Jackpot, uninc. village (1990 pop. 400), Elko co., NE Nev., 60 mi/97 km NNE of Wells and 40 mi/64 km SSW of Twin Falls, Idaho, on Idaho state line, on Salmon Falls Creek. Jackpot has become one of several gambling resorts on that have been developed at the Nev./Idaho border. Part of Humboldt Natl. Forest to W. Estab. in 1959.

Jacks Mountain, ridge (c.2,000 ft/610 m), central Pa., 2 mi/3.2 km wide (SW-NE), runs c.70 mi/113 km from central part of Huntingdon co. to NW part of Snyder co., where it merges with Creek Mt. ridge; 40°37′N 77°37′W–40°51′N 77°06′W. Juniata R. flows through gap W of Mount Union. Sandstone, silica.

Jacksboro 1 coal-mining town (1990 pop. 1,568), NE Tenn., 28 mi/45 km NW of Knoxville; ⊙ Campbell co.; 36°20′N 84°11′W. **2** town (1990 pop. 3,350), N Texas, 50 mi/80 km SSE of Wichita Falls; ⊙ Jack co. Elev. 1,074 ft/327 m. In cattle ranching; oil and natural gas; timber area; light mfg. Fort Richardson State Historic Site (founded 1867; extant). Settled 1855; inc. 1899.

Jackson 1 county (□ 1,126 sq mi/2,916 sq km; 1990 pop. 47,796), NE Ala.; ⊙ Scottsboro; 34°46′N 86°00′W. Agr. region bordering on Ga. and Tenn., drained by Tennessee and Paint Rock rivers and Guntersville Reservoir. Soybeans, hay, corn; cattle, poultry; timber; deposits of coal and limestone. Formed 1819. **2** county (□ 641 sq mi/1,660 sq km; 1990 pop. 18,944), NE Ark.; ⊙ Newport, Black R. forms NW boundary; 35°36′N 91°12′W. Drained by White and Cache rivers, and by Departee Creek. Agr. (wheat, sorghum, soybeans, rice, hogs). Mfg. at Newport. Sand and gravel pits. Formed 1829. Jacksonport State Park in NW. **3** county (□ 1,621 sq mi/4,198 sq km; 1990 pop. 1,605), N Colo.; ⊙ Walden; 40°40′N 106°20′W. Continental Divide forms S boundary. Agr. area, bordering on Wyo.; drained by headwaters of North Platte R. Livestock, lumber. Walden L., L. John and Delany Butte Lakes at co. center. Most of Colorado State Forest in E. Includes part of Routt Natl. Forest in W and SE, small part of Arapaho Natl. Forest on S boundary. Part of Park Range in W and Medicine Bow Mts. in E. Formed 1909. **4** county (□ 942 sq mi/2,440 sq km; 1990 pop. 41,375), NW Fla., on Ala. (N) and Ga. (E; Chattahoochee R.) state lines; ⊙ Marianna; 30°48′N 85°12′W. Rolling agr. area (peanuts, corn, cotton, vegetables, hogs) with many small lakes; drained by Chipola R. Some mfg. (food prods.; lumber), and limestone quarrying. Formed 1822. **5** county (□ 337 sq mi/873 sq km; 1990 pop. 30,005), NE central Ga.; ⊙ Jefferson; 34°08′N 83°34′W. Piedmont area drained by Oconee R. Agr. (hay, sweet potatoes, apples, peaches; cattle, hogs, poultry); textile mfg. Formed 1796. **6** county (□ 602 sq mi/1,559 sq km; 1990 pop. 61,067), SW Ill.; ⊙ Murphysboro; 37°46′N 89°21′W. Bounded SW by Mississippi R.; drained by Big Muddy and Little Muddy rivers and Beaucoup Creek. Carbondale (with Southern Illinois Univ.) is dominant city, in E part. Agr. area (wheat, sorghum, fruit, cattle; dairying), with some mfg. (wood prods., paper prods., fabricated metal prods.). Bituminous coal mining. Includes part of Shawnee Natl. Forest and Lake Murphysboro and Grant City State Parks, also L. Kincaid and Ceder L. reservoirs. Formed 1816. **7** county (□ 513 sq mi/1,329 sq km; 1990 pop. 37,730), S Ind.; ⊙ Brownstown; 38°55′N 86°02′W. Bounded S by Muscatatuck R.; drained by East Fork by White R. and tributaries of the Muscatatuck. Agr. area (corn, wheat, vegetables, cattle, hogs, truck, poultry), with diversified mfg.; timber. Hoosier Natl. Forest in NW corner; Cypress Lake State Fishing Area in NE. Brownstown State Fishing Area W of Brownstown; Muscatuck Natl. Wildlife Refuge on E boundary. Starve Hollow State Beach and part of Jackson-Washington State Forest in S, includes Driftwood State Fish Hatchery. Formed 1816. **8** county (□ 649 sq mi/1,681 sq km; 1990 pop. 19,950), E Iowa, on Ill. line (E; formed here by Mississippi R.); ⊙ Maquoketa; 42°10′N 90°35′W. Prairie agr. area (hogs, cattle, poultry; corn, oats, soybeans) drained by Maquoketa and North Fork Maquoketa rivers; limestone quarries. Maquoketa Caves State Park in SW; Bellevue State Park in E on Miss. R., below Lock and Dam No. 12. St. Donatus, located in NE corner near Miss. R., is a picturesque Luxembourger village, that was settled by Luxembourg immigrants. General river flooding occurred in 1993. Formed 1837. **9** county (□ 657 sq mi/1,702 sq km; 1990 pop. 11,525), NE Kansas; ⊙ Holton; 39°24′N 95°50′W. Rolling prairie, watered by Delaware R. Wheat, sorghum, soybeans, cattle, hogs. Potawatomi Indian Reservation, dominant feature of co., is W of Mayetta. Formed 1857. **10** county (□ 346 sq mi/896 sq km; 1990 pop. 11,955), SE central Ky., in Cumberland foothills; ⊙ McKee; 37°25′N 84°00′W. Bounded SW by Rockcastle R; drained by Middle Fork Rockcastle R. and by Station Camp Creek. Large part of co. in Daniel Boone Natl. Forest in NE, center, and SW. Mt. agr. area (burley tobacco, hay, alfalfa, corn; cattle, poultry; dairying); timber; limestone. Formed 1858. **11** county (□ 723 sq mi/1,873 sq km; 1990 pop. 149,756), S Mich.; ⊙ Jackson; 42°15′N 84°25′W. Drained by Grand and Raisin rivers and headstreams of the Kalamazoo. Agr. (forage crops, corn, hay, apples, soybean, wheat, oats; cattle, hogs, sheep, dairy prods.); mfg. at Jackson. Contains many small lakes (fishing, swimming), in E ½ of co. Organized 1832. **12** county (□ 719 sq mi/1,862 sq km; 1990 pop. 11,677), SW Minn.; ⊙ Jackson; 43°40′N 95°09′W. Bordering Iowa (S) and watered by Des Moines R. and headwaters of Little Sioux R. Agr. area (corn, oats, soybeans, alfalfa; sheep, hogs, cattle). Includes part of Coteau des Prairies; Kilen Woods State Park in NE center; Heron L. and South Heron L. are in NW center. Several small natural lakes, especially near S boundary. Formed 1857. **13** county (□ 1,043 sq mi/2,701 sq km; 1990 pop. 115,243), extreme SE Miss.; ⊙ Pascagoula; 30°27′N 88°37′W. Bounded E by Ala. state line, S on Mississippi Sound, Gulf of Mexico; drained by Pascagoula and Escatawpa rivers. Cotton, corn, pecans, honey; timber; fish, shrimp, crab; catfish farming. Includes part of De Soto Natl. Forest in NW; Grand Bay Natl. Wildlife Refuge in SE, Mississippi Sandhill Crane Natl. Wildlife Refuge in SW, Shepard State Park in S, Gulf Marine State Park in SW, Ward Bayou Wildlife Management Area in center, part of Pascagoula River Wildlife Management Area in N, included Horn and Petit Bois Isls. in Gulf of Mexico, part of Gulf Isls. Natl. Seashore, visitors center on mainland in SW part of co. Formed 1812. **14** county (□ 603 sq mi/1,562 sq km; 1990 pop. 633,232), W Mo.; ⊙ Independence; 39°01′N 94°21′W. Bounded N by Missouri R.; Kansas R. enters the Missouri at NW corner. Has the downtown and major part of city of Kansas City, (also goes in to Clay and Platte cos.). Other major cities include Independence, Raytown, Lee's Summit, Blue Springs, and Grandview. Agr. (wheat, corn, soybeans, dairy prods.); mfg. grain, and livestock industries centered at Kansas City. County was designated as the original Garden of Eden by Mormon prophet Joseph Smith. James A. Reed Wildlife Area in S; Burr Oak Woods Wildlife Area at Blue Springs; Lake Jacomo, Longview Lake, and Blue Springs Lake are Army Corps of Engineers reservoirs, Lake Sacamo Park at Lee's Summit. Professional football and baseball stadiums at intersection of I-70 and I-435. Formed 1826. **15** county (□ 494 sq mi/1,279 sq km; 1990 pop. 26,846), W N.C.; ⊙ Sylva; 35°17′N 83°08′W. Partly in the Blue Ridge Mts. (SE); bounded S by S.C. state line; Balsam Mt. in E, Cowee Mts. in W; drained by Tuckasegee R. All but N end of co. in Nantahala Natl. Forest (Glenville). Thorpe L. reservoir in S center. Farming (cattle, apples, tobacco, hay, corn); timber; mica and talc mining; resort region. Mfg. at Sylva. Blue Ridge (Natl.) Parkway follows NE co. line. Part of Eastern Cherokee (Qualla Boundary) Indian Reservation in N. Formed 1851. **16** county (□ 420 sq mi/1,088 sq km; 1990 pop. 30,230), S Ohio; ⊙ Jackson; 39°02′N 82°37′W. Drained by Little Scioto R. and small Symmes and Little Raccoon creeks. Includes Buckeye Furnace and Leo Petroglyph state parks, and Canter's Cave. In the Unglaciated Plain physiographic region. Agr. area (poultry, corn); mfg. at Jackson, Oak Hill, Wellston (food, wood prods.); coal mining. Formed 1816. **17** county (□ 804 sq mi/2,082 sq km; 1990 pop. 28,764), extreme SW Okla.; ⊙ Altus; 34°35′N 99°24′W. Bounded S by Texas (Red R.), on E by N Fork Red R.; drained by Salt Fork of Red R. Agr. (cotton, wheat, sorghum, alfalfa); cattle; light mfg. Greyhound breeding. Irrigation from Altus Dam to N (not in co.). Formed 1907. **18** county (□ 2,801 sq mi/ 7,255 sq km; 1990 pop. 146,389), SW Oregon; ⊙ Medford; 42°25′N 122°44′W. Mt. area bordering Calif. on S, crossed by Rogue R. Agr. (pears, plums, peaches, grapes, cherries, apples, wheat, oats, barley, hops, nuts; poultry, hogs, sheep, cattle); wineries, nurseries. Includes part of Siskiyou Mts. in SW and parts of Rogue R. Natl. Forest, including part of Sky Lakes Wilderness Area on E boundary, in S, N, and E. Small part of Klamath Natl. Forest in S; part of Crater Lake Natl. Park on NE boundary; Stewart and Casey State Parks in NE; TouVelle State Park in center; Tub Springs State Wayside in SE; Ben Hur Lampman State Wayside and Valley of the Rogue State Park in W. Formed 1852. **19** county (□ 1,871 sq mi/4,846 sq km; 1990 pop. 2,811), SW central S.Dak.; ⊙ Kadoka; 43°42′N 101°38′W. Agr. area watered by intermittent streams; also Pass and Bear-in-the-Lodge creeks. Hay, soybeans; cattle. Extreme NE part of Badlands Natl. Park in W (including park hq.). Buffalo Gap Natl. Grassland in NW. Area S of White R. former Washabaugh co. All of co. S of White R. (over ½ of co.) is part of the large Pine Ridge Indian Reservation. Formed 1883 and later absorbed into other cos.; reconstituted 1914. **20** county (□ 327 sq mi/847 sq km; 1990 pop. 9,297), N central Tenn.; ⊙ Gainesboro; 36°22′N 85°40′W. Crossed by Cumberland R. Agr. (tobacco, livestock, corn, fruit); oil wells; timber. Formed 1801. **21** county (□ 857 sq mi/ 2,220 sq km; 1990 pop. 13,039), S Texas; ⊙ Edna; 28°56′N 96°34′W. On Gulf of Mexico coastal plain; indented by Lavaca Bay in S. Bounded SW by Arenosa Creek; drained by Lavaca and Navidad rivers. Oil, natural-gas wells; cattle ranching; agr. (cotton, rice, grain sorghum); livestock raising. L. Texana reservoir (Navidad R.) and State Park in center of co. Formed as municipality 1835, as co. 1836. **22** county (□ 472 sq mi/ 1,222 sq km; 1990 pop. 25,938), W W.Va.; ⊙ Ripley; 38°49′N 81°40′W. Bounded NW by Ohio R. (Ohio state line); drained by Mill Creek. Natural-gas and oil wells; some coal. Agr. (corn, wheat, oats, tobacco, potatoes, alfalfa, hay, nursery crops); cattle; some dairying. Some mfg. at Ripley, Ravenswood. Frozen Camp Wildlife Management Area in E; Woodrum Wildlife Management Area in S; Cedar L. State Camp (FFA-FHA) in center. Formed 1831. **23** county (□ 1,000 sq mi/ 2,590 sq km; 1990 pop. 16,588), W central Wis.; ⊙ Black R. Falls, 44°20′N 90°52′W. Dairying area. Agr. (potatoes, barley, corn, soybeans, peas, brans, cranberries; cattle, hogs, sheep, poultry); some mfg. Intersected by Black, Buffalo, and Trempealeau rivers. Winnebago Indian Reservation at center; Arbutus L. on N boundary; Black R. State Forest in E center, crosses co. N-S; smaller units of Black R. Falls, includes Castle Mound. Formed 1853

Jackson, parish (□ 583 sq mi/1,510 sq km; 1990 pop. 15,705), N central La.; ⊙ Jonesboro; 32°14′N 92°43′W. Agr. (hay, vegetables, cattle, poultry). Mfg. of paper prods.; logging; timber. Drained by Dugdemona R. and Castor Creek. Caney Creek reservoir in S. Part of Jackson-Bienville State Wildlife Area in NW. Named after President Andrew Jackson. Formed 1845.

Jackson 1 city (1990 pop. 3,545), central Calif., 40 mi/ 64 km ESE of Sacramento, on Jackson Creek; ⊙ Amador co.; 38°21′N 120°46′W. RR terminus. Trade and mining center in 1849 Calif. Gold Rush region. Gold mines, marble quarries, clay pits, farms (grapes, walnuts, grain; cattle), vineyards nearby; mfg. (printing and publishing). Argonaut and Kennedy quartz mines, operating since early 1850s, are more than 1 mi/1.6 km deep. Pardee Reservoir to SW (Mokelumne R.); Jackson Butte to E (2,310 ft/704 m). Founded during gold rush; made ⊙ in 1851; inc. 1905. **2** city (1990 pop. 37,446), S Mich., on the Grand R.; ⊙ Jackson co.; 42°14′N 84°24′W. Elev. 960 ft/293 m. It is an industrial and commercial center in a farm region. Mfg. (machinery, aerospace components, transportation equip., food, fabricated metal prods., electronic equip., construction materials). RR junction. Several automobile models were pioneered in Jackson in the early 20th cent. The first Republican convention was held in the

city on July 6, 1854; a tablet marks the site. Jackson Community Col. to S; Michigan Space Center to S; Reynolds Field Airport to W. Nearby are Spring Arbor Col. and a state prison. Inc. 1857. **3** city (1990 pop. 196,637), Hinds and Madison cos., W central Miss., ⊙ of state and of Hinds co. (shares co. seat with Raymond), on the Pearl R. (forms large Ross Barnett Reservoir to NE); 32°19′N 90°12′W. RR junction. It is the state's largest city and commercial center, with important RR, warehouse, and distributing operations. Mfg. (food, construction materials, glass, paper prods., printing and publishing, lumber, machinery, consumer goods, furniture, concrete, fabricated metal prods.). The site of the city, a trading post known as Le Fleur's Bluff near the Natchez Trace, was chosen and laid out as the state capital in 1821 and named for Andrew Jackson. The first U.S. law giving property rights to married women was passed here in 1839. During the Civil War, Jackson was a military center for the Vicksburg Campaign and was largely destroyed by Sherman's forces in 1863. The old capitol (1839) is preserved as a mus.; the new capitol was completed in 1903. Among the many points of interest are the governor's mansion (erected 1839); city hall, which was used as a hosp. during the Civil War; a 220-acres/89-ha scale model of the Mississippi R. flood control system; Mynelle's Gardens; a Jackson Zoological Park; Municipal Art Gall.; a notable Confederate monument; and many antebellum homes; Miss. Agr. and Forestry Mus.; Miss. Mus. of Natural History; Miss. State Historical Mus.; Dizzy Dean Mus.; Davis Planetarium/McNair Space Theater; Smith Robertson Mus. (Afr.-Amer. culture). Belhaven Col., Jackson State Univ., Millsaps Col., the Univ. of Mississippi Medical Center, and several state institutions for the physically and mentally handicapped are here. Nearby are Tougaloo Col. (Ridgeland) and Mississippi Col. (Clinton). During the 1960s, Jackson was the scene of considerable racial unrest. In May 1970, demonstrations at the predominantly black Jackson State Col. resulted in the deaths of 2 students. Allen C. Thompson Airport to E; Hawkins Field Airport in NW. LeFleurs Bluff State Park in city, NE of downtown. Inc. 1833. **4** city (1990 pop. 9,256), SE Mo., 10 mi/16 km NW of Cape Girardeau; ⊙ Cape Girardeau co.; 37°22′N 89°39′W. Corn, lumber, cattle, dairy prods.; mfg. (transportation equip., machinery, fabricated metal prods., construction materials). Founded c.1815. **5** city (1990 pop. 6,144), S Ohio, 28 mi/45 km NE of Portsmouth; ⊙ Jackson co.; 39°38′N 82°37′W. Steel mills, foundries; also produces clay prods., lumber. Coal mines; clay, sand, gravel, and silica pits. Buckeye Furnace and Leo Petroglyph state parks, and Canter's Cave are nearby. Founded 1817. **6** city (1990 pop. 48,949), W Tenn., on the South Fork of the Forked Deer R., c. 81 mi. ENE of Memphis; ⊙ Madison co.; 35°37′N 88°50′W. RR shipping point for extensive farm area. Food packaging; mfg. (textiles, consumer goods). Jackson experienced development as a trucking center. It is the seat of Lane Col., Lambuth Col., Union Univ., and a community col. Nearby is a state park with Native Amer. mounds. Home and burial site of Casey Jones; Casey Jones RR mus. is here. Founded by a nephew of Andrew Jackson, inc. 1823.

Jackson 1 town (1990 pop. 5,819), Clarke co., SW Ala., on Tombigbee R. (RR bridge), and 16 mi/26 km SSW of Grove Hill. Lumber, apparel. Artesian mineral wells and Salt Springs State Park nearby. Inc. 1816. **2** town (1990 pop. 4,076), central Ga., c.40 mi/64 km SE of Atlanta; ⊙ Butts co.; 33°17′N 83°58′W. Mfg. includes fixtures, apparel, concrete, fabricated metal prods. Indian Springs State Park nearby, where Creek nation and the U.S. govt. signed treaty ceding territory to the U.S. L. Jackson and Dauset Trails Nature Center. Once a thriving resort area. Inc. 1826. **3** town (1990 pop. 2,466), E central Ky., in the Cumberland Mts., on North Fork Kentucky R., and 24 mi/39 km NNW of Hazard; ⊙ Breathitt co.; 37°33′N 83°22′W. Trade center for coal mining and agr. (cattle, poultry; corn, fruit, potatoes, tobacco; honey) area; mfg. (computer equip.). Juliann Carroll Airport to SE. Seat of Lees Col. (1864; 2-year).

County Mus. Parts of Robinson Forest, Univ. of Ky., research tract, to SE; Pan Bowl L. to N, natural oxbow lake. Estab. 1883. **4** town (1990 pop. 3,891), East Feliciana parish, SE central La., on Thompson Creek, 27 mi/ 43 km N of Baton Rouge; 30°50′N 91°13′W. Rolling hill country. In agr. area; mfg. (concrete, lumber); winery. State mental hosp. here. Audubon State Commemorative Area to SW, site of antebellum home of John James Audubon. Centenary State Commemorative Area to E, site of former Centenary Col. (1800s). **5** town (1990 pop. 415), Waldo co., S Maine, 14 mi/ 23 km NNW of Belfast; 44°36′N 69°09′W. Agr., lumbering. **6** town (1990 pop. 3,559), SW Minn., 27 mi/ 43 km W of Fairmont, on Des Moines R., near Iowa state line; ⊙ Jackson co.; 43°37′N 94°59′W. Elev. 1,459 ft/445 m. Trade and shipping point; grain, soybeans, alfalfa; livestock; light mfg. Kilen Woods State Park to NW; Spirit L. (Iowa) to SW. Settled before 1857, scene of Sioux uprising 1862, inc. 1881. **7** town (1990 pop. 678), Carroll co., E N.H., 22 mi/35 km S of Berlin; 44°11′N 71°12′W. Drained by Ellis R. Agr. (livestock; dairying); timber; resort area. Parts of White Mt. Natl. Forest in W, N, and E; Black Mt. ski area and Nestlenook Farm cross-country ski area in center; covered bridge. **8** town (1990 pop. 1,681), Aiken co., W S.C., near Savannah R., 18 mi/29 km SSW of Aiken; 33°19′N 81°47′W. Grew with establishment nearby (1951) of Savannah R. Nuclear Power Plant of Atomic Energy Commission. Redcliffe Plantation State Park N and E. Mfg. of concrete, ordnance, transportation equip. Agr. includes cotton, peanuts, grains, livestock, poultry. **9** town (1990 pop. 2,486), Washington co., E Wis., 23 mi/37 km. NNW of Milwaukee; 43°19′N 88°09′W. In dairying and farming area; mfg. (fabricated metal prods., pharmaceuticals). **10** town (1990 pop. 4,472), NW Wyo., on Gros Ventre R. near its confluence with Snake R., just S of Grand Teton Natl. Park, and 65 mi/ 105 km E of Idaho Falls, Idaho; ⊙ Teton co.; 43°28′N 110°45′W. Elev. c.6,209 ft/1,893 m. Resort and trading point in JACKSON HOLE; agr., livestock; mfg. (food, apparel, construction materials, printing and publishing). A very popular tourist community and a haven for artists and writers. Hq. of Bridger-Teton Natl. Forest (to E and S). Rodeo takes place annually. Hunting and dude ranches in vicinity. Daily gunfight enactment takes place on town square during the summer. Natl. Wildlife Art Mus. (1994) is here. Natl. Elk Refuge to NE; Targhee Natl. Forest to W.

Jackson 1 village (1990 pop. 230), Dakota co., NE Nebr., 7 mi/11.3 km W of Dakota City, near Missouri R. and S.Dak. state line; 42°27′N 96°34′W. **2** village (1990 pop. 592), NE N.C., 14 mi/23 km SE of Roanoke Rapids; ⊙ Northampton co.; 36°23′N 77°25′W. Agr. area (peanuts, cotton, tobacco, grain, poultry, livestock).

Jackson, borough (1990 pop. 33,233), Ocean Co., E N.J., 40°06′N 74°21′W. Site of Six Flags Great Adventure Theme Park with looping roller coasters and drive-through animal safari park.

Jackson Center, village (1990 pop. 1,398), Shelby co., W Ohio, 12 mi/19 km NE of Sidney; 40°26′N 84°02′W.

Jackson Center, borough (1990 pop. 244), Mercer co., W Pa., 6 mi/9.7 km NE of Mercer, on Yellow Creek. Light mfg.; dairying. L. Latonka reservoir to W.

Jackson, Fort 1 fort in La.: see TRIUMPH. **2** fort in S.C.: see COLUMBIA.

Jackson Gulch Dam, Colo.: see MANCOS RIVER.

Jackson Heights, section of borough of Queens, N.Y. city, SE N.Y.; 40°45′N 73°53′W. Just S of LaGuardia Airport, Flushing Meadow to E, Brooklyn-Queens Expressway to W. Its main commercial thoroughfare is 37th Ave. Once a mix of Italians, Jews, Irish, Poles, and later Colombians, the neighborhood saw a major influx of Asian Indians, Koreans, Thais, and Chinese in the early 1980s which has given it a remarkable ethnic diversity. Begun in 1910s as a project by the Queensboro Corp., most of the apartment bldgs. and homes were built in Georgian and Tudor style. The purpose was to create a unified community modeled on the garden suburbs in England and Germany. With their architectural flourishes, luxurious gardens, and arboreal sidewalks, the structures here coined the term "garden apartments." The 30-block historic dist. here is 1 of only 2 in Queens.

Jackson Hole, valley (c.50 mi/80 km long and 6 mi/ 9.7 km to 8 mi/12.9 km wide), Teton co., NW Wyo. Grand Teton Natl. Park protects all but S end of valley. The valley is hemmed in — hence the term "hole" — by mts., the Teton Range (W), Snake R. Range (SW), Gros Ventre Range (SE), and lesser ranges (NE). Jackson L. in N, 39 sq mi/101 sq km, originally a natural lake on the Snake R., was dammed in 1911 and 1916 to control the river's flow. Popular with hunters and trappers from the time U.S. trapper David Jackson, for whom it was named, wintered there 1828–1829, the valley is now a major tourist destination, with the only airport in a U.S. natl. park. The Natl. Elk Refuge, SE of Grand Teton Natl. Park (1,500 acres/607 ha), is the winter home of the largest elk herd in N. America. Bald eagles and the rare trumpeter swan inhabit the area. Jackson Hole and Snow King Ski Areas in S. Jackson Hole was first settled in 1880s.

Jackson Junction, town (1990 pop. 87), Winneshiek co., NE Iowa, 18 mi/29 km SW of Decorah; 43°06′N 92°02′W. Limestone quarries.

Jackson Lake 1 reservoir (c.10 mi/16 km long, 1 mi/ 1.6 km wide), on Butts-Jasper co. border, central Ga., on Ocmulgee R., 7 mi/11.3 km E of Jackson; 33°19′N 83°50′W. Receives (N) Alcovy, Yellow, and South rivers, which form Ocmulgee R. here. Formed by Lloyd Shoals Dam (c.100 ft/30 m high, 500 ft/152 m long), built (1910) for power generation. Popular recreation area. Also called Lloyd Shoals Reservoir. **2** reservoir (c.2 mi/ 3.2 km long), Prince William co., NE Va., at confluence of Cedar Run and Broad Run forming Occoquan Creek, 4 mi/6.4 km SSE of Manassas; 38°42′N 77°24′W. Village of Lake Jackson near dam.

Jackson Lake (☐ 40 sq mi/104 sq km; 18 mi/29 km long, average 4 mi/6.4 km wide), Teton co., NW Wyo., on Snake R., in Jackson Hole valley, in Grand Teton Natl. Park, 28 mi/45 km NNE of Jackson; 43°51′N 110°36′W. Elev. c.6,750 ft/2,057 m. Natural lake with level raised by Jackson Lake Dam (70 ft/21 m high), at SE corner, built (1916) for irrigation and flood control. R. enters from N. Teton Range Mts. bound lake on W.

Jackson, Mount 1 peak in N.H.: see PRESIDENTIAL RANGE. **2** peak in Mont.: see LEWIS RANGE.

Jackson Mountains, (8,923 ft/2,720 m at King Lear peak), NW Nev., in Humboldt co., E of Black Rock Desert. Quinn R. to W.

Jackson Reservoir (☐ 4 sq mi/10.4 sq km), Morgan co., NE Colo., on tributary of S. Platte R., 30 mi/48 km E of Greeley; 40°22′N 104°05′W. Max. capacity 47,000 acre-ft. Formed by Jackson Lake Dam (38 ft/ 12 m high), built (1900) for irrigation. Jackson Lake State Park at N end of reservoir.

Jackson River, c.75 mi/1,221 km long, W Va.; rises in Allegheny Mts. in central Highland co., flows SSW, through L. Moomaw reservoir (formed by Gathright Dam), past Covington, and ENE, past Clifton Forge, joins Cowpasture R. SE of Iron Gate to form James R.

Jackson Springs, uninc. village, Moore co., central N.C., 13 mi/21 km WNW of Southern Pines near Drowning Creek. Tobacco, grain. livestock.

Jacksonboro, village, Colleton co., S S.C., near Edisto R., 15 mi/24 km SE of Walterboro. Site of State legislature in 1781 when the British occupied Charleston; timber.

Jacksonburg, village (1990 pop. 50), Butler co., extreme SW Ohio, 7 mi/11 km W of Middletown; 39°32′N 84°30′W. Sometimes spelled Jacksonburgh.

Jacksonport 1 village (1990 pop. 264), Jackson co., NE Ark., 3 mi/4.8 km NW of Newport, and on White R.; 35°38′N 91°18′W. Jacksonport State Park is here. **2** village, Door co., NE Wis., on Door Peninsula, on L. Michigan, 13 mi/21 km NE of Sturgeon Bay. Formerly a lumber port. Whitefish Dunes State Park to S.

Jacksonville 1 city (1990 pop. 10,283), Calhoun co., E Ala., 12 mi/19 km NNE of Anniston; in dairying area; textiles, lumber, fabricated metal prods., furniture. Jacksonville State Univ. here. Fort McClellan nearby. **2** city (1990 pop. 29,101), Pulaski co., central Ark.;

34°52′N 92°07′W. RR junction. Mfg. (printing and publishing, electronic equip., ordnance, plastic prods., fabricated metal prods., fixtures). The nearby Little Rock Air Force Base to N, a tactical air command installation; defense-related industries and missile bases are also important to Jacksonville's economy. Inc. 1941. **3** city (☐ 918 sq mi/2,378 sq km; 1990 pop. 672,971), coextensive (since 1968) with Duval co., extreme NE Fla., on the St. Johns R. near its mouth on the Atlantic Ocean; 30°19′N 81°39′W. The largest city in the state (and in the U.S. in total area), it is a RR, air, and highway focal point and a busy port of entry, with ship repair yards and extensive freight-handling facilities. Lumber, phosphate, paper, and wood pulp are the principal exports. The city has a large and diverse mfg. base. Jacksonville is one of the most important Southern centers of commerce, finance, and insurance on the Atlantic coast. It is also a major E. Coast center of U.S. navy operations; 3 important naval installations are in the area, including Jacksonville Naval Air Station and the large Mayport base at the mouth of the St. Johns R. Jacksonville is also a tourist resort, with ocean beaches, fishing and yachting facilities, and inland hunting areas. Educational facilities include the Univ. of N Fla., Edward Waters Col., Jones Col., and a junior col. Inc. 1832. **4** city (1990 pop. 19,324), W central Ill., 31 mi/50 km W of Springfield; ☉ Morgan co.; 39°44′N 90°13′W. Its industries include bookbinding and mfg. of plastics, fabricated metal prods. It is the seat of Illinois Col., MacMurray Col., Jacksonville Correctional Center, a state mental hosp., and schools for the deaf and blind. Stephen A. Douglas and William Jennings Bryan lived there. Jacksonville was a station on the Underground Railroad and on Illinois's first true RR, the Northern Cross. Laid out 1825, inc. 1840. **5** city (1990 pop. 30,398), E N.C., c.105 mi/169 km SE of Raleigh on the New R.; ☉ Onslow co.; 34°45′N 77°24′W. Mfg. (food, printing and publishing, machinery). It is also a summer resort. Camp Lejeune U.S. Marine Corps training base, is adjacent to the city, to S and SE; New R., a Marine Air Station, to S; both installations play a major role in Jacksonville's economy. A Coastal Carolina Community Col. is here. Hoffmann Forest to NE; Hammocks Beach State Park to SE; Topsail Isl. beach resort to S. Settled c.1757. **6** city (1990 pop. 12,765), Cherokee co., E Texas, 27 mi/43 km S of Tyler; 31°58′N 95°15′W. Elev. 516 ft/157 m. RR junction; tomato-shipping center in rich vegetable-growing region; canneries; timber, nursery plants; mfg. (furniture, wood prods., apparel); oil and gas. Baptist Missionary Theologogian Col., Jacksonville Col. (2-year), Lon Morris Col. (2-year). L. Jacksonville to SW; L. Palestine to NW. Founded nearby 1847; moved to present site 1872.

Jacksonville 1 town (1990 pop. 128), Telfair co., Ga., 22 mi/35 km NNW of Douglas; 31°49′N 82°59′W. **2** town (1990 pop. 115), Randolph co., N central Mo., 11 mi/18 km N of Moberly; 39°35′N 92°28′W. Corn, soybeans, cattle. **3** town (1990 pop. 1,896), Jackson co., SW Oregon, 5 mi/8 km WSW of Medford; 42°18′N 122°58′W. Timber. Wineries. Historic gold rush town. Site of Mus. of Southern Oregon History. Music festivals.

Jacksonville 1 village (1990 pop. 544), Athens co., SE Ohio, 9 mi/14 km N of Athens, and on small Sunday Creek, in coal mining area; 39°28′N 82°05′W. **2** village (1990 pop. 244), Windham co., Vt.; part of WHITINGHAM, town.

Jacksonville, borough (1990 pop. 89), Indiana co., SW central Pa., 9 mi/14.5 km SW of Indiana, on Aultmans Run. Dairying.

Jacksonville Beach, city (☐ 21 sq mi/54 sq km; 1990 pop. 17,839), Duval co., extreme NE Fla., 17 mi/27 km ESE of Jacksonville, on the Atlantic; 30°16′N 81°22′W. Inc. 1907.

Jacmel (zhak-MEL), city (1989 est. pop. 217,000), S Haiti, c.25 mi/40 km S of Port-au-Prince; ☉ Sud-Est dept.; 18°14′N 72°32′W. Jacmel is an important fishing

port on the Caribbean Sea. Agr. (cacao, cotton, tobacco, coffee growing and processing); essential-oils and pectin distilleries, cotton-seed oil extraction, cigar mfg.; bauxite, manganese deposits nearby. Also spelled Jaquemel.

Jacmel Peninsula (zhak-MEL), (140 mi/225 km long), SW Haiti, bet. Gulf of Gonaïves (N) and the Caribbean (S); traversed by the Massif de la Hotte. Port-au-Prince is at its base. Along its coast are a number of ports: Jérémie, Les Cayes, and Jacmel, Petit-Goâve, which ship the prods. of the fertile region (sugarcane, coffee, cacao, cotton, tropical fruit, tobacco, sisal) and are home to fishing fleets. Manganese, lignite, bauxite deposits. Sometimes called Tiburon Peninsula.

Jacob Riis, a municipal park of N.Y. city, SE N.Y., on Rockaway Peninsula in S Queens borough; 40°34′N 73°53′W. Ocean bathing; recreational facilities. Marine Parkway bridge across Rockaway Inlet is here.

Jacobi Island, Alaska: see YAKOBI ISLAND.

Jacobs Pillow, Mass.: see LEE.

Jacobus (JA-kuh-bus), borough (1990 pop. 1,370), York co., S Pa., 6 mi/9.7 km S of York. Mfg. (electronic prods.). Agr. area (grain, soybeans, apples; poultry, livestock, dairying). Richard M. Nixon Co. Park to W. Lakes William and Redman (both on East Fork Codorus Creek) to N.

Jacomino (hah-ko-MEE-no), town, Ciudad de La Habana prov., W Cuba, 3 mi/4.8 km SE of Havana in suburbs.

Jacona de Plancarte (hah-KO-nah de plan-KAHR-tai), town (1990 pop. 35,846), Michoacán, central Mexico, on central plateau, 2 mi/3.2 km SSW of Zamora de Hidalgo on Mexico Highway 40; ☉ Jacona municipio; 19°58′N 102°19′W. Agr. center (cereals, sugarcane, fruit; livestock).

Jacque Peak (13,205 ft/4,025 m), in Rocky Mts., Summit co., NW central Colo., 8 mi/12.9 km WSW of Breckenridge, in Arapaho Natl. Forest. Also known as Eagle R. Peak.

Jacques Cartier, Mount or **Tabletop**, peak (4,160 ft/ 1,268 m), E Que., Canada, on N side of Gaspé Peninsula, 70 mi/113 km W of Gaspé; 48°59′N 65°57′W. Highest peak of Shickshock Mts., in Gaspesian Provincial Park.

Jacumba (ha-koom-bah) uninc. village, San Diego co., S Calif., at Mexico (Baja Calif. Norte) border, opposite Rumerosa, Mexico (no crossing), c.55 mi/89 km ESE of San Diego. Hot springs. Carrizo Gorge is nearby. Anza-Borrego Desert State Park to N.

Jaffrey, town (1990 pop. 5,361), Cheshire co., SW N.H., 15 mi/24 km SE of Keene; 42°49′N 72°03′W. RR terminus. Agr. (cattle, sheep, poultry; vegetables; dairying; nursery crops; mfg. (fabricated metal prods., printing and publishing, electronic equip.). Thorndike Pond in N, Contoocook L. on S boundary; Monadnock Mt. (3,165 ft/965 m), in Monadnock State Park, in NW. Settled c.1758, inc. 1773.

Jagüey Grande (hah-GWAI GRAHN-dai), town, Matanzas prov., W Cuba, on RR and Natl. Highway, 45 mi/72 km SE of Matanzas; 22°32′N 81°08′W. Agr. center (sugarcane, honey, poultry, cattle); lumbering and charcoal burning. The Australia sugar central is 2 mi/3.2 km S.

Jájome Alto, resort, SE central P.R., in Cordillera Central, 6 mi/9.7 km NNW of Guayama. Governor's summer residence. SE is a replica of the Grotto of Our Lady of Lourdes.

Jakin (JAI-kuhn), village (1990 pop. 137), Early co., SW Ga., 7 mi/11.3 km WNW of Donalsonville, near the Chattahoochee R.; 31°05′N 84°59′W.

Jal, town (1990 pop. 2,156), Lea co., extreme SE N.Mex., on Llano Estacado, near SE corner of N.Mex., Texas state boundary to E and S; 40 mi/64 km S of Hobbs; 32°06′N 103°11′W. Oil fields; cattle, sheep, cotton, wheat, alfalfa. The name is derived from a cattle brand and the Jal Ranch. The origins of the initials are unclear. Settled c.1916, inc. 1928. Developed with discovery of oil (1927) in vicinity.

Jala (HAH-lah), town (1990 pop. 9,329), Nayarit, W

Mexico, at E foot of Ceboruco volcano, 45 mi/72 km SE of Tepic. Corn, beans, sugarcane, fruit; cattle.

Jalacingo (hah-lah-SEEN-go), city (1990 pop. 6,240) and township, Veracruz, E Mexico, in Sierra Madre Oriental, 33 mi/53 km NW of Xalapa Enríquez on Mexico Highway 129; 19°48′N 97°19′W. Agr. center (corn, sugarcane, coffee, tobacco, fruit).

Jalapa, Mexico: see XALAPA ENRÍQUEZ.

Jalapa de Méndez (hah-LAH-pah dai MEN-dez), city (1990 pop. 3,855) and township, Tabasco, SE Mexico, on affluent of Grijalva R., and 20 mi/32 km SSE of Villahermosa; 18°45′N 92°48′W. Rice, coffee, beans, fruit.

Jalatlaco (hah-lah-TLAH-ko), town (1990 pop. 8,646), Mexico state, central Mexico, 25 mi/40 km SW of Mexico city. Agr. center (cereals, vegetables, livestock; dairying). Also Xalatlaco.

Jalcomulco (hahl-ko-MOOL-ko), town (1990 pop. 2,325), Veracruz, E Mexico, in Sierra Madre Oriental, 17 mi/27 km SE of Xalapa Enríquez; 19°20′N 96°33′W. Corn, coffee, fruit.

Jalisco (hah-LEES-ko), state (31,152 sq mi/80,684 sq km; 1990 pop. 5,302,689), W Mexico; ⊙ GUADALAJARA; 18°58′N 101°28′W. Bounded on the W by the Pacific, Jalisco is dominated by the S end of the Sierra Madre Occidental and the W extremity of the Transverse Volcanic Axis, extending across central Mexico. The hot, tropical plains of the coast are broken by spurs of the Sierra, and most of the E part of the state lies within the central plateau. In the central part of Jalisco is an intermontane basin containing L. Chapala, Mexico's largest lake; it is drained by the Lerma-Santiago system. Because of the variety of climate, landform, and elev., nearly every kind of fruit and vegetable grows somewhere in Jalisco. Corn and wheat from the central plateau make it known as the "granary of Mexico"; rice and wheat are grown in the S; and the mts. yield timber and minerals (especially iron, silver, some gold, and precious stones). The raising of livestock and the processing of food prods. are also important. Although Jalisco was explored as early as 1522, a serious invasion of the area, later included in Nueva Galicia, was not undertaken until 1529 by Nuño de Guzmán. Shortly before the War of the Reform (1858–1861), Jalisco became a leading state in the great liberal revolution of Benito Juárez. It was occupied by the Fr. in the wars of intervention but was recaptured in 1866. In 1884 the territory of Nayarit was separated from Jalisco.

Jalisco, Mexico: see XALISCO.

Jalostotitlán (hah-lo-sto-tee-TLAHN), city (1990 pop. 18,089) and township, Jalisco, central Mexico, on interior plateau, 65 mi/105 km NE of Guadalajara on Mexico Highway 80; ⊙ Jalostotitlán municipio; 21°11′N 102°29′W. Elev. 5,686 ft/1,733 m. Agr. center (corn, wheat, beans, chickpeas; livestock).

Jalpa (HAHL-pah), town (1990 pop. 12,731), Zacatecas, N central Mexico, on Juchipila R., and 27 mi/43 km SE of Tlaltenango de Sánchez, near junction of Mexico Highways 70 and 54; ⊙ Jalpa municipio; 21°40′N 103°00′W. Elev. 5,906 ft/1,800 m. Agr. center (grain, beans, sugarcane; livestock).

Jalpa de Méndez (HAHL-pah dai MEN-dez), town (1990 pop. 11,789), Tabasco, SE Mexico, at W edge of Grijalva R. delta, and 17 mi/27 km NW of Villahermosa; ⊙ Jalpa de Méndez municipio. Elev. 131 ft/40 m. Corn, rice, beans, tobacco, fruit; livestock.

Jalpan (HAHL-pahn), town (1990 pop. 540), Puebla, central Mexico, 22 mi/35 km NNE of Huauchinango. Sugarcane, coffee, fruit. In Totonac Indian area.

Jalpan de Serra (HAHL-pahn dai SE-rah), city (1990 pop. 5,042) and township, Querétaro, central Mexico, in a valley of Sierra Madre, 75 mi/121 km NE of Querétaro on Mexico Highway 120. Elev. 2,526 ft/770 m. Grain, sugarcane, bananas, dates, pineapples, pomegranates, limes, sweet potatoes, coffee, maguey.

Jaltenango de la Paz (hahl-te-NAHN-go dai la pahz), town, Chiapas, SE Mexico, in a valley of the Sierra de Chiapas, on Jaltenango R., 60 mi/96 km S of San Cristobal de las Casas; ⊙ Jaltenango municipio; 15°51′N 92°43′W. Elev. 2,133 ft/650 m. Agr. (small farming).

Jaltenco (hahl-TEN-ko), town (1990 pop. 5,661), Mexico state, central Mexico, 23 mi/37 km N of Mexico City and in the Zona Metropolitana de la Ciudad de México. Cereals, fruit; livestock. Also San Andrés Jaltenco.

Jáltipan, Mexico: see JÁLTIPAN DE MORELOS.

Jáltipan de Morelos (HAHL-te-pahn dai mo-RE-los), city (1990 pop. 32,055) and township, Veracruz, SE Mexico, on Isthmus of Tehuantepec, 12 mi/19 km W of Minatitlán on Mexico Highway 180; 17°58′N 94°42′W. Agr. center (rice, fruit, coffee; livestock).

Jaltocán (hahl-to-KAN), town (1990 pop. 4,552), Hidalgo, N Mexico, in foothills of Sierra Madre Oriental, 8 mi/12.9 km W of Huejutla de Reyes. Rice, corn, sugarcane, tobacco, coffee, fruit.

Jamaica, republic (☐ 4,411 sq mi/11,424 sq km; 1991 pop. 2,314,479), coextensive with the isl. of Jamaica, 146 mi/235 km long, 22 mi/35 km–51 mi/82 km wide, West Indies, 90 mi/145 km S of Cuba and 100 mi/161 km W of Haiti; ⊙ KINGSTON; 17°43′N–18°32′N 76°05′W–78°26′W. Jamaica is the 3d-largest isl. in the Caribbean. Besides Kingston, other important cities are SPANISH TOWN and MONTEGO BAY. The Jamaica RR connects Kingston and Montego Bay and links inland settlements to Port Antonio. The 2 internatl. airports — the Norman Manley Palisadoes Internatl. Airport in Kingston and the Donald Sangster Internatl. Airport in Montego Bay — facilitate travel with the rest of world. Although largely a limestone plateau more than 3,000 ft/914 m above sea level, Jamaica has a mountainous backbone that extends across the isl. from the W and rises to the Blue Mts. in the E; Blue Mt. (7,402 ft/2,256 m) is the highest point. Rainfall is heavy in this region (where there are extensive timber reserves) but diminishes westward across the plateau, which is a rugged area deeply dissected by streams and underlain by subterranean rivers. The heart of the plateau, known as the Cockpit Country or Cockpits, is used mostly for livestock grazing. A narrow plain along the N coast and several larger plains near the S shore are Jamaica's major agr. zones. The N coast also has fine beaches and is the focus of tourism. The Rio Grande and the Black R. are the country's chief waterways, but neither is navigable for long distances. The coastal bands widened by broad river valleys, as well as the mountain slopes, support the bulk of Jamaica's export crops: the famed Blue Mt. coffee, sugarcane — from which rum and molasses are also made — bananas, ginger, citrus fruits, cocoa, pimento, and tobacco. Most of these crops are grown on large plantations. Small peasant farms produce some ginger, bananas, and sugarcane for export but mainly raise such subsistence crops as yams, breadfruit, and cassava. Mining is a major source of wealth; since large, easily accessible deposits of bauxite were discovered in 1942, Jamaica has become one of the world's leading suppliers of this ore. Along with the alumina made from it, bauxite accounts for almost ½ of Jamaica's foreign exchange. Tourism is the biggest earner of exchange. Among Jamaica's internationally known resort areas are Montego Bay, Ocho Rios, and Negril. Apparel constitutes the chief export item of the mfg. sector. Jamaica's other industries (mainly concentrated in the Kingston area) include oil refining, tobacco processing, flour milling, and the production of cement, textiles, and processed foods. Since the late 1960s industry has generated a greater share of the natl. income than agr., which, however, still employs the largest percentage of the work force. The U.K., U.S., and Canada, Jamaica's top trading partners, also provide much needed capital for economic development. The country is divided into 3 cos. and subdivided into 14 parishes. On the E is Surrey co., with parishes of Kingston, St. Andrew and St. Thomas to the S and Portland to the N. Middlesex, the central co., has St. Mary and St. Ann parishes to the N, bordered by St Catherine, Clarendon, and Manchester to the S. On the W is Cornwall co., with Trelawny, St. James and Hanover to the N and bounded to the S by St. Elizabeth and Westmoreland. English is the official language, but many Jamaicans also speak a Jamaican creole dialect. The unit of currency is the Jamaican dollar of 100 cents. About ½ of the pop. is rural, but migration to the cities continues; the greatest urban concentration is around Kingston. Adequate health facilities and islandwide education from the early childhood to the univ. level are available to all Jamaicans. People of Afr. descent predominate in Jamaica, making up approximately 90% of the pop. A small upper class is largely of European descent. Afro-Europeans and such Middle Eastern and Asian groups as Lebanese, Syrians, Chinese, and Indians, make up the rest of the pop. The chief religion is Protestantism, although there is considerable religious variety. Sighted by Christopher Columbus in 1494, Jamaica was conquered and settled in 1509 by Spaniards under a license from Columbus's son. Spanish exploitation decimated the native Arawaks. The isl. remained Spanish until 1655, when Admiral William Penn and Robert Venables captured it; it was formally ceded to England in 1670, but the local European pop. obtained a degree of autonomy. Jamaica prospered from the wealth brought by buccaneers, notably Sir Henry Morgan, to Port Royal, the capital; in 1692, however, much of the city sank into the sea during an earthquake, and Spanish Town became the new capital. A huge, mostly Afr., slave pop. grew up around the sugarcane plantations in the 18th cent., when Jamaica was a leading world sugar producer. Freed and escaped slaves, sometimes aided by the maroons (slaves who had escaped to remote areas after Spain lost control of Jamaica), succeeded in organizing frequent uprisings against the European landowners. The sugar industry declined in the 19th cent., partly because of the abolition of slavery in 1833 (effective 1838) and partly because of the elimination in 1846 of the imperial preference tariff for colonial prods. entering the Br. market. Economic hardship was the prime motive behind the Morant Bay rebellion by freedmen in 1865. The British ruthlessly quelled the uprising and also forced the frightened legislature to surrender its powers; Jamaica became a crown colony. Poverty and economic decline led many blacks to seek temporary work in neighboring Caribbean areas and in the United States; many left the isl. permanently, emigrating to England, Canada, and the U.S. Indians were imported to meet the labor shortage on the plantations after the slaves were freed, and agr. was diversified to lessen dependence on sugar exports. A new constitution in 1884 marked the initial revival of local autonomy for Jamaica. Despite labor and other reforms, black riots recurred, notably those of 1938, which were caused mainly by unemployment and resentment against Br. racial policies. Jamaican blacks had been considerably influenced by the theories of black nationalism promulgated by the Amer. expatriate Marcus Garvey. A royal commission investigating the 1938 riots recommended an increase of economic development funds and a faster restoration of representative govt. for Jamaica. In 1944 universal adult suffrage was introduced, and a new constitution provided for a popularly elected house of representatives. By 1958, Jamaica became a key member of the Br.-sponsored West Indies Federation. The fact that Jamaica received only ⅓ of the representation in the federation, despite its having more than ½ the land area and pop. of the grouping, bred resentment; a campaign by the nationalist labor leader Sir Alexander Bustamante led to a 1961 decision, by popular referendum, to withdraw from the federation. The following year Jamaica won complete independence from Great Britain. The country has a 2-party system: the Jamaica Labor Party (JLP) favors private enterprise, while the People's Natl. Party (PNP) advocates moderate socialism. Bustamante, leader of the JLP, became the 1st prime minister of independent Jamaica. The party continued in power until 1972, when the PNP won an impressive victory. Although the PNP administration worked effectively to promote civil liberties and reduce illiteracy, economic problems proved more difficult. In 1976 the PNP won decisively after a violent election contest bet. the 2 parties. The PNP continued to promote socialist policies, nationalizing businesses and strengthening ties to Cuba. Lack of foreign investment and aid continued to hurt the economy. In 1980 the JLP was elected to power, with the administration favoring privatization, distancing itself from Cuba, attracting foreign investment, stimulating tourism, and finding the U.S. willing to provide substantial aid. Nonetheless, 2 major hurricanes (1980, 1988) hit Jamaica, setting back prospects for substantial economic progress. Jamaica is internationally known as the home of "reggae" music developed by Bob Marley.

Jamaica (huh-MEI-kuh), town, Guantánamo prov., E Cuba, on RR, and 5 mi/8 km NE of Guantánamo; 20°11'N 75°08'W. Agr. center (cacao, coffee, fruit, sugarcane). There are 4 sugar mills within a 10 mi/16 km radius.

Jamaica 1 town (1990 pop. 232), Guthrie co., W central Iowa, 15 mi/24 km NE of Guthrie Center; 41°51'N 94°18'W. In agr. area. **2** town (1990 pop. 754), Windham co., SE Vt., on West R., and 10 mi/16 km NW of Newfane; 43°06'N 72°47'W. Partly in Green Mtn. Natl. Forest. In hunting, fishing region; lumber

Jamaica, a commercial, industrial, and administrative center in central Queens borough of N.Y. city, SE N.Y.; 40°41'N 73°49'W. Chief transfer station of L.I. RR, subway terminus, highway hub. Diversified mfg.; extensive residential sects.; has declined as retailing center. Co. courthouse. Points of interest include King Mansion (c.1750) and edifice (1813) of 1st Presbyterian Church, organized 1662. Federal Social Security Admministration hq. Main bldg. of Queens Borough Public Lib. and Jamaica Race Track are here. Settled in mid–17th cent, it was 1st capital of Queens co.

Jamaica Bay (□ c.20 sq mi/52 sq km), SW L.I., SE N.Y., separated from the Atlantic Ocean by Rockaway Peninsula; 40°37'N 73°51'W. The Rockaway Inlet links it to the sea. The shallow bay has many isls., and its shores are generally marshy. There is a min. of water movement and pollution is a problem. Nearly all of the bay is in the boroughs of Brooklyn and Queens in N.Y. city; since 1950 much of the adjacent area has been reclaimed for housing. JFK Internatl. Airport extends into the bay. Part of Gateway Natl. Recreation Area, the bay is used for boating and fishing and is a wildlife refuge.

Jamaica Beach, village (1990 pop. 624), Galveston co., SE Texas, on Galveston Isl., suburb 11 mi/18 km SW of downtown Galveston, on Gulf of Mexico, surrounded by city of Galveston; 29°11'N 94°58'W. Residential and recreational beach community. Galveston Isl. State Park to SW.

Jamaica Channel, channel in the Caribbean Sea, separating Jamaica (W) from Hispaniola isl. (E) and forming SW continuation of Windward Passage, 120 mi/193 km wide bet. 18°N 74°30'W and 18°N 76°1'W. In the channel are Navassa Isl. (N) and Morant Cays (at its S entrance).

Jamaica Estates, S section of E central Queens borough, N.Y. city, SE N.Y., bounded on E by 188th St., S by Hillside Ave., W by Home Lawn St., and N by Union Turnpike; 40°44'N 73°46'W. Affluent residential neighborhood. Began with purchase of 507-acre/205-ha tract by Jamaica Estates Co. in 1907; layout of residential park of 1- and 2-story houses, some occupying 3 lots, was designed to conform to the contour of the land. Today there are 1,700 houses on 80 blocks of tree-lined streets. When initial deed restrictions expired in 1929, Jamaica Estates Association was formed to preserve the neighborhood's character; the only place apartment bldgs. were permitted was along Hillside Ave.

Jamaica Plain, Mass.: see BOSTON.

Jamal (hah-mahl), uninc. town (1990 pop. 2,258), San Diego co., S Calif., residential suburb 17 mi/27 km E of downtown San Diego, Sequan Indian Reservation to N; Cleveland Natl. Forest to E. Dairying, poultry, fruit, flowers.

Jamapa (hah-MAH-pah), town (1990 pop. 3,209), Veracruz, E Mexico, in Gulf lowland, 13 mi/21 km SW of Veracruz; 19°02'N 96°08'W. Fruit.

Jamay (HAH-mai), town (1990 pop. 13,954), Jalisco, central Mexico, on E shore of L. Chapala, 50 mi/80 km SE of Guadalajara; 20°20'N 102°41'W. Agr. center (wheat, corn, oranges, beans, alfalfa, livestock).

James, former co., E Tenn.: see HAMILTON, co.

James A. FitzPatrick Nuclear Power Plant, Oswego co., central N.Y., on S shore of L. Ontario, 7 mi/11.3 km NE of Oswego; 43°31'N 76°25'W. Began commercial operation July 1975; has generating capacity of 800 MW. Lake water is used to cool the reactor. Owned by the N.Y. Power Authority; now operated by private management. The plant generates power for municipal electric systems, rural cooperatives, N.Y. state's major private utilities, N.Y. city's public agencies, Westchester co., govt. agencies, and industries. Closed by Nuclear Regulatory Commission due to mechanical and safety inadequacies in Nov. 1991; reopened Jan. 1993.

James A. Garfield Historic Site, NE Ohio, authorized 1980, home of the 20th President and site of the first presidential memorial library.

James Bay, shallow S arm of Hudson Bay, c.300 mi/480 km long and 140 mi/230 km wide, E central Canada, in the N.W.T. bet. Ont. and Que. Numerous rivers flow into the bay. Of its many isls., the largest is Akimiski (1,158 sq mi/3,000 sq km). The bay was discovered (1610) by Henry Hudson but was named for Capt. Thomas James, an Englishman who explored much of it in 1631. An early fur-trading post established by Groseilliers and Radisson became (1670) Rupert House, the 1st post estabalished here by the Hudson's Bay Co. Other important posts on James Bay are Fort Albany, Fort George, and Eastmain. The shores of the bay and some of its isls. are wildlife reserves. Akimiski Island Bird Sanctuary; game sanctuaries at Twin Isls., Trodely Isl., Charlton Isl.; bird sanctuaries also at Hannah Bay, Ont. and Boatswain Bay, Que. Entire bay is set aside as James Bay Preserve. The JAMES BAY PROJECT, a colossal hydroelectric development on the E coast of James Bay, has evoked a tremendous negative response from environmentalists and Cree Indians, who claim that the project is disrupting the lives of the natives and destroying the region. Rivers have been diverted, forests have been incinerated, and wilderness areas have been inundated. Phase I, finished in 1984, created the world's largest underground powerhouse, a tiered spillway on GRAND RIVER 3 times the height of NIAGARA FALLS, and 5 reservoirs that total ½ the volume of L. Ontario. The completion of the project was threatened in 1992 when the N.Y. State Power Authority refused to sign a purchase contract. Includes Great Whale R. (Hudson Bay), La Grande R., and Nottaway/Broadback R. Basins. The isls. within James Bay, Hudson Bay, and Ungava Bay belong to N.W.T.

James Bay Project, hydroelectric scheme, central Que., Canada; partially completed project of Hydro-Quebec and Que. government. Extends from Jarvis and Hudson Bays on W to Lab. border on E; from NE of Val d'Or on S to Nastapoca R. on N. Since its inception in 1975, numerous dams, diversion channels, and power houses have been planned or built. There are 4 planned stages within the scheme: La Grande Phase One, completed 1985, involved construction of reservoirs on La Grande R.; La Grande Phase Two, involves redirection of flow from Eastmain, Laforge, and Caniapiscau rivers (the latter flows N to Ungava Bay) into La Grande R., to be completed 1996; Great Whale Project, diversion of Little Whale and Nastapoca rivers to Great Whale R., to be completed in 2001. NBR Project, diversion of Rupert and Nottaway rivers to Broadback R. basin, to be completed in 2004. Phase One is already generating more power than all of Quebec's 25 coal and 1 nuclear power plants combined. General concern over environmental and social impact on Cree and Inuit people. Wildlife and fish pops. have been affected; possible effect on beluga whale pops. off coast, deprived of ice-free channels at mouths of diverted rivers. In 1984, 10,000 caribou were drowned in flood waters on lower Caniapiscau R. attributed to release from dam; Hydro-Quebec blamed heavy rains. Sale of energy to U.S. and other parts of Canada could go to mfg. development of those areas instead of Que. Although financially native peoples have benefitted from agreements relating to project, they have objected to its expansion.

James City, county (□ 179 sq mi/464 sq km; 1990 pop. 34,859), SE Va.; ⊙ Williamsburg (independent city separated from adjoining James City, York cos.); 37°18'N 76°46'W. In Tidewater region, bounded NE by York R., W by Chickahominy R., S by James R. Includes Jamestown Island, site of 1st permanent Eng. settlement in Amer. (1607); both part of Colonial Natl. Historical Park and Colonial Parkway. Agr. (hay, barley, wheat, soybeans, tobacco, corn, potatoes, fruit; cattle; dairying); fish, oysters, crabs. York R. State Park in NE. Formed 1634.

James City, uninc. town (1990 pop. 4,279), Craven co., E N.C., residential suburb 1 mi/1.6 km S of and opposite New Bern, on Trent R. (bridged), at its entrance to Nuese R.; 35°04'N 77°01'W. Croatan Natl. Forest to S.

James Creek, Pa.: see MARKLESBURG.

James H. Turner Dam, Calif., see SAN ANTONIO RESERVOIR.

James Island, uninc. town (1990 pop. 4,400), Charleston co., SE S.C., suburb 3 mi/4.8 km SW of downtown Charleston, in N center of James Isl. One of the Sea Islands, 8 mi/12.9 km long and 6 mi/9.7 km wide.

James Island, village, SW B.C., Canada, on James Isl. (2 mi/3 km long, 1 mi/2 km wide), in Haro Strait, off SE Vancouver Isl., 14 mi/23 km N of Victoria. Fishing, lumbering.

James Island, S.C.: see CHARLESTON.

James, Lake, natural lake, in central Steuben co., NE Ind. Indiana's 4th largest natural lake. Glacially formed. Average depth 86 ft/26 m.

James, Lake, reservoir (□ 10 sq mi/26 sq km), Burke co., W N.C., on Catawba R., 40 mi/64 km ENE of Asheville; 35°44'N 81°53'W. Max. capacity 277,960 acre-ft. Formed by Bridgewater Dam (100 ft/30 m high), built (1919) for power generation. Lake James State Park on W end of reservoir.

James Peak (13,294 ft/4,052 m), in Front Range, Grand and Boulder cos., N central Colo., c.35 mi/56 km WNW of Denver, on Continental Divide, E of Winter Rock. Moffat Tunnel passes through part of mt.

James River 1 flows c.80 mi/129 km SW, S central Mo.; rises in the Ozarks in Webster Co., to Table Rock L. (White R.) S of Galena. Fishing, canoeing. Lake Springfield on it on S side of Springfield. **2** 710 mi/1,143 km long, in N.Dak. and S.Dak.; rises in Wells co. in central N.Dak.; flows across S.Dak. to the Missouri R. at Yankton, S.Dak.; 47°28'N 99°51'W. Jamestown Dam, forming Jim L. (1,500 acres/607 ha), on the river is an irrigation and flood control unit of the Missouri River Basin Project of the U.S. Bureau of Reclamation. New Rockford Canal connects upper James R. with upper Sheyenne R. in Wells co. irrigation canal. In N. Dak., James R. flows E past Fessenden and New Rockford, then S through Arrowwood L. and Jim L. reservoirs, past La Moure and Oakes. In S. Dak., the river continues through Mud L. and Columbia Road reservoirs, both of which are in Sand L. Natl. Wildlife Refuge, past Redfield, Huron, and Mitchell. The James is also known as the Jim R. or the Dakota R. **3** 340 mi/547 km long, formed in W central Va. by Jackson and Cowpasture rivers; 37°47'N 79°46'W. Flows generally E past Glasgow, where it receives Maury (North) R. from N, cuts through Blue Ridge at Balcony Falls, past Lynchburg, Goochland, Richmond, overfalls and around isl. includ. Williams Island and Belle Isle, past Hopewell, where it becomes a tidal river, continues ESE through series of historic plantations, widens into estuary c.12 mi/19 km W of Williamsburg and receives Chickahominy R. from NW. Continues past Jamestown and Newport News, forms Hampton Roads, harbor for Newport News, Hampton, Portsmouth, and Norfolk, before entering Chesapeake Bay, c.20 mi/32 km W of mouth of the bay.

James Ross Strait, arm (110 mi. long, 30–40 mi. wide) of the Arctic Ocean, S Franklin dist., N.W.T., Canada, bet. King William Isl. (SW) and Boothia Peninsula (NE); 70°N 96°W. Connects N with sea area leading to McClintock Channel and Franklin Strait.

James W. Dalton Highway, dirt and gravel road

(257 mi/414 km long), Alaska, running parallel to Trans-Alaska pipeline from Livengood (84 mi/135 km N of Fairbanks) to Deadhorse, just S of Prudhoe Bay. Cuts across 3 wilderness preserves and Gates of the Arctic National Park.

James W. Trimble Lock and Dam (39 ft/12 m high), on border of Sebastian and Crawford cos., W Ark., on Arkansas R., 8 mi/12.9 km ESE of Ft. Smith, at city limits; 35°22′N 94°20′W. Built (1969) by the Army Corps of Engineers for navigation. The raised channel has a max. capacity of 59,100 acre-ft.; extends W past downtown Ft. Smith into Oklahoma. Originally called Lock and Dam #13.

Jamesburg, borough (1990 pop. 5,294), Middlesex co., E N.J., 10 mi/16 km S of New Brunswick; 40°21′N 74°26′W. Some light industry. Inc. 1887.

Jameson (JAI-muh-suhn), town (1990 pop. 149), Daviess co., NW Mo., near the Grand R., and 9 mi/14.5 km N of Gallatin; 40°00′N 93°59′W. Mormon Shrine of Adam-ondi-Ahman to S.

Jameson Point, Knox co., S Maine, forms N side of Rockland harbor. Has breakwater, lighthouse.

Jamesport, city (1990 pop. 570), Daviess co., NW Mo., 18 mi/29 km NW of Chillicothe; 39°58′N 93°47′W. Corn, soybeans, wheat; cattle, hogs; concrete. Large Amish community established 1953. Numerous antique shops. Platted 1857.

Jamesport, village (□ 7 sq mi/18.1 sq km; 1990 pop. including S. Jamesport 1,532), Suffolk co., SE N.Y., on NE L.I., near Great Peconic Bay, 4 mi/6.4 km ENE of Riverhead; 40°57′N 72°34′W. In summer resort area.

Jamestown 1 city (□ 8 sq mi/20.7 sq km; 1990 pop. 34,681), Chautauqua co., W N.Y., on Chautauqua L.; 42°06′N 79°14′W. It is the business and financial center of a dairy, livestock, and vineyard area. The chief industries are food processing; mfg. of furniture, machinery. Seat of Jamestown Community Col. Nearby are Allegany State Park and the Chautauqua Inst., a cultural and recreational center on the lake. Founded c.1806, inc. as a city 1886. **2** city (1990 pop. 15,571), seat of Stutsman co., SE N.Dak., on the James R., in a farm area, 85 mi/137 km W of Fargo; 46°54′N 98°42′W. It is the trade and processing center for an agr. area where sunflowers, grain and flour are produced and livestock is raised, mfg. (food, printing and publishing, ordnance, construction materials). Jamestown Col., a state home for handicapped children, and a state mental hosp. are in the city. Fort Seward Historic Site to W, and a restored frontier village lie to S on the outskirts. Fish hatchery to NE. Municipal Airport in NE part of city. Jamestown Reservoir (Jim L.) to N. Pipestone L. to NW. Founded 1871 when Fort Seward was established to protect RR workers, inc. 1881. **3** city (1990 pop. 1,862), N Tenn., 37 mi/60 km NE of Cookeville; ⊙ Fentress co.; 36°26′N 84°56′W. In hilly coal, oil, gas, and timber area; lumbering; livestock raising; mfg. of apparel. Alvin C. York State Historic Site and Big South Fork National River and Recreation Area nearby. Settled 1827; inc. 1837.

Jamestown 1 uninc. town (1990 pop. 2,178), Tuolumne co., central Calif., 3 mi/4.8 km SW of Sonora; 37°58′N 120°25′W. Timber; cattle; hay; apples. Gold-mining center in 1849 Calif. Gold Rush region; received its nickname "Jimtown" in gold rush. Table Mountain is nearby. **2** town (1990 pop. 764), Boone co., central Ind., 13 mi/21 km SW of Lebanon; 39°56′N 86°38′W. In agr. area; lumber. **3** town (1990 pop. 1,641), S Ky., in Cumberland foothills, 27 mi/43 km WSW of Somerset, Wolf Creek Dam in Cumberland R. is SW; ⊙ Russell co.; 36°59′N 85°04′W. Light mfg. Russell Co. Airport to NW. L. Cumberland reservoir to S and SE; L. Cumberland State Resort Park to S; Wolf Creek Dam Natl. Fish Hatchery to SW. Estab. 1827. **4** town (1990 pop. 148), Bienville parish, 4 mi/6.4 km NE of Ringgold; 32°10′N 93°12′W. Gas field. Named in honor of Jamestown, Va. **5** town (1990 pop. 298), Moniteau co., central Mo., near Missouri R., 11 mi/18 km NNE of California; 38°46′N 92°28′W. Cattle, hogs, corn. **6** town (1990 pop. 2,662), Guilford co., N central N.C., suburb 5 mi/8 km NE of High Point and 11 mi/18 km SW of Greensboro, on Deep R.; 36°00′N 79°55′W. Mfg. (food, electronic equip., textiles, chemicals). **7** suburb and resort town (1990 pop. 4,999), including Jamestown village, Newport co., S R.I., coextensive with Conanicut Isl. (c.9 mi/14.5 km long, 1 mi/1.6 km–2 mi/3.2 km wide), in Narragansett Bay W of Newport; 41°31′N 71°22′W. Farming. Jamestown Bridge (1940) connected with North Kingstown (W), replaced by Jamestown-Verrazano Bridge, 1992. Pell Bridge (1969) connects isl. and Newport; longest New England bridge. Beavertail Light, at S tip of isl., was estab. before 1750. Several pre-Revolutionary bldgs. remain. Named in honor of James II, Duke of York and Albany. Inc. 1678.

Jamestown 1 village, Independence co., NE central Ark., 6 mi/9.7 km SW of Batesville. **2** village (1990 pop. 251), Boulder co., N Colo., in foothills of Front Range, 8 mi/12.9 km NW of Boulder; 40°07′N 105°23′W. Elev. c.6,920 ft/2,109 m. Supply point in gold-mining region. Rocky Mt. Natl. Park to NW. Surrounded by Roosevelt Natl. Forest. **3** village (1990 pop. 325), Cloud co., N Kansas, 11 mi/18 km W of Concordia; 39°36′N 97°51′W. RR junction. In wheat region. **4** village (1990 pop. 1,794), Greene co., S central Ohio, 10 mi/16 km ESE of Xenia, and on small Caesar Creek; 39°39′N 83°44′W. Settled 1806, laid out 1815. **5** village (1990 pop. 84), Berkeley co., SE S.C., 35 mi/56 km NNE of Charleston, near Santee R., in Francis Marion National Forest; 33°17′N 79°42′W. Light mfg. Agr. includes timber; livestock, poultry; cotton, grain.

Jamestown, borough (1990 pop. 761), Mercer co., NW Pa., 22 mi/35 km SW of Meadville, on Shenango R. (forms Pymatuning Reservoir to NW). Light mfg.; agr. (grain, potatoes; dairying). Greenville Airport to SE.

Jamestown, locality, James City co., SE Va., 5 mi/8 km SW of Williamsburg, on Jamestown Isl., on James R., part of Colonial Natl. Historic Park, connected with Williamsburg and Yorktown by Colonial Parkway; 37°19′N 78°17′W. First permanent Eng. settlement in Amer.; est. May 14, 1607, by the London Co. on a marshy peninsula (now an isl.) in the James R. and named for the reigning Eng. monarch, James I. Disease, starvation, and Native Amer. attacks wiped out most of the colony, but the London Co. continually sent more men and supplies. John Rolfe cultivated the 1st tobacco here in 1612, introducing a successful source of livelihood; in 1619 the 1st representative govt. in the New World met at Jamestown, which remained the capital of Va. throughout the 17th cent. The village was almost entirely destroyed during Bacon's Rebellion; it was partially rebuilt but fell into decay with the removal of the capital to Williamsburg (1698–1700). Of the 17th-cent. settlement, only the old church tower (built c.1639) and a few gravestones remain. It is included in Colonial Natl. Historical Park.

Jamestown Bay, district, SE Alaska, on W shore of Baranof Isl., 4 mi/6.4 km E of Sitka; 57°03′N 135°17′W. Fishing.

Jamestown National Historic Site, 21 acres/8 ha, James City co., SE Va., an affiliated area of Natl. Park system, on upper part of Jamestown Isl., 5 mi/8 km SW of Williamsburg; 37°19′N 78°10′W. Site of the 1st permanent Eng. settlement in Amer. Authorized 1940. See JAMESTOWN, Va.

Jamesville, village (1990 pop. 612), Martin co., NE N.C., on Roanoke R., and 9 mi/14.5 km SE of Williamston; 35°48′N 76°54′W. Agr. area (tobacco, peanuts, cotton, grain, chickens, hogs). Mfg. (plastic prods.).

Jamesville, suburb (1990 pop. 700) of Syracuse, Onondaga co., central N.Y., 5 mi/8 km SE of city center; 42°59′N 76°04′W. Light mfg.

Jan Tiel (yahn TEEL), village, S Curaçao, Neth. Antilles; beach resort on coastal lagoon, 3 mi/4.8 km ESE of Willemstad.

Jane Franklin, Cape, NW King William Isl., S Franklin dist., N.W.T., Canada, on Victoria Strait; 69°36′N 98°20′W. Remains of camp, graves, and other relics of Franklin expedition, 1847–1848, were found here by McClintock (1859) and Hall (1861–1865).

Jane Lew, village (1990 pop. 439), Lewis co., central W.Va., 12 mi/19 km S of Clarksburg; 39°06′N 80°24′W. Coal-mining. Mfg. (hand-blown glassware, steel tubing, coal processing). Agr. (corn, potatoes); livestock. Jacksons Mill State 4-H Camp to SW.

Janesville, city (1990 pop. 52,133), ⊙ Rock co., S central Wis., on the Rock R., 30 mi/48 km SE of Madison; twin city with Beloit, 13 mi/21 km S; 42°40′N 89°01′W. Industrial and commercial center in a grain, dairy farm, and tobacco area. Mfg. (agr. equipment, machinery, consumer goods, metal prods., feeds, printing and publishing, concrete, transportation equipment, plastic prods., prepared food). Major RR junction. Wis. School for visually handicapped, Univ. of Wis. (Janesville campus), and Blackhawk Technical Col. (to S) are located here. Points of interest include the 26-room Tallman House, where Lincoln spent a weekend in 1859; the Stone House (1842), of Greek Revival style; and the Milton House (1844), which is connected to a log cabin by a tunnel used by runaway slaves as a stop on the Underground RR. Rock Co. Airport to S. Inc. 1853.

Janesville 1 town (1990 pop. 822), on Black Hawk-Bremer co. line, E central Iowa, on Cedar R., and 12 mi/19 km NNW of Waterloo; 42°38′N 92°27′W. Feed milling. Limestone quarries, sand and gravel pits nearby. **2** town (1990 pop. 1,969), Waseca co., S Minn., 10 mi/16 km WNW of Waseca, and 14 mi/23 km E of Mankato; 44°07′N 93°42′W. Agr. (grain, soybeans; livestock, poultry; dairying). Mfg. (feeds and fertilizers). L. Elysian reservoir to N; Buffalo L. to S. Plotted 1855, deserted in Sioux outbreak of 1862, inc. 1870.

Janicho, Mexico: see JANITZIO.

Jánico (HAH-nee-ko), officially Santo Tomás de Jánico, town (1993 pop. 1,264), Santiago prov., N central Dominican Republic, 11 mi/18 km SW of Santiago; 19°24′N 70°48′W. In agr. region (tobacco, cacao, coffee).

Janitzio (hah-NEET-see-o), island, in L. Pátzcuaro, Michoacán, central Mexico, 7 mi/11.3 km NNW of Pátzcuaro; c.1 mi/1.6 km long. Fishing village. Sometimes Janicho.

Janos (HAH-nos), town (1990 pop. 2,154), Chihuahua, N Mexico, on affluent of Casas Grandes R., and 90 mi/145 km SE of Douglas, Ariz., on Mexico Highway 2; 30°50′N 108°10′W. Elev. 4,452 ft/1,357 m. Cotton, cereals; cattle.

Jansen, village (1990 pop. 140), Jefferson co., SE Nebr., 5 mi/8 km NE of Fairbury; 40°11′N 97°04′W.

Jantetelco (hahn-te-TEL-ko), town (1990 pop. 3,474), Morelos, central Mexico, 13 mi/21 km SE of Cuautla; 18°42′N 98°45′W. Elev. 3,806 ft/1,160 m. Rice, sugarcane, fruit. Also known as San Pedro.

Janvrin Island, in the Atlantic, E N.S., Canada, off S Cape Breton Isl., just E of Madame Isl., at entrance of the Strait of Canso; 3 mi/5 km long, 2 mi/3 km wide; 45°32′N 61°10′W.

Japonski Island (juh-PAWN-skee), SE Alaska, in Alexander Archipelago, in Sitka Sound, just W of Sitka; 57°03′N 135°22′W. At Edgecumbe, site of U.S. naval base in World War II; installations now occupied by state boarding school. Russians had magnetic observatory here. Site of Sitka airport; connected to Sitka by bridge.

Jara, Villa, Mexico: see PASO DEL MACHO.

Jarabacoa (hah-rah-bah-KO-ah), town (1993 pop. 18,586), La Vega prov., central Dominican Republic, in the Cordillera Central, on Yaque del Norte, and 10 mi/16 km SW of La Vega; 19°08′N 70°40′W. Resort in fruit-growing valley. Has fine mt. climate. Just E are Jimenoa falls, a tourist site and hydroelectric project. Nickel deposit nearby.

Jarácuaro (ha-RAH-kwah-ro), small island and town (1990 pop. 1,871), Erongaricuaro municipio, Michoacán, central Mexico, in L. Pátzcuaro, 6 mi/9.7 km NW of Pátzcuaro. Fruit growing; fishing.

Jarahueca (hahr-uh-WAI-kuh), village, Sancti Spíritus prov., central Cuba, on RR, and 23 mi/37 km SE of Caibarién; 22°14′N 79°21′W. In agr. region (sugarcane; cattle). Has deposits of light oil.

Jaral del Progreso (hah-RAHL del pro-GRE-so), city (1990 pop. 14,545), in the S part of Guanajuato, Mexico, 22 mi/35 km SE of Salamanca, NE of Yuriria L., and on the Lerma River; 20°22'N 101°04'W. Elev. 6,204 ft/ 1,891 m. Terminus of branch RR line. Agr. (corn, beans, wheat, peaches); livestock.

Jarales (huh-RAH-les), uninc. village (1990 pop. 700), Valencia co., W central N.Mex., on Rio Grande, and 33 mi/53 km S of Albuquerque. Trading point in irrigated region. Cattle, sheep; dairying; corn, grain, alfalfa, fruit. Manzano Range and part of Cibola Natl. Forest E.

Jarboesville, Md.: see LEXINGTON PARK.

Jarbridge, uninc. village, Elko co., NE Nev., 57 mi/92 km NNW of Wells, 8 mi/12.9 km S of Idaho state line, in Humboldt Natl Forest. Gold.

Jardine (JAHR-deen), village (1990 pop. 35), Park co., S Mont., on Bear Creek near Yellowstone R., just W of Buffalo Plateau, 43 mi/69 km S of Livingston. Elev. c.7,000 ft/2,134 m. Mining; ski basin. Yellowstone Natl. Park just S; Absaroka-Beartooth Wilderness Area of Gallatin Natl. Forest to W, N, and E.

Jardines de la Reina (hahr-DEE-naiz dai luh REI-nuh), archipelago of coral reefs, off Caribbean coast of Ciego de Ávila prov., E Cuba, 70 mi/113 km SW of Camagüey; c.85 mi/137 km long NW–SE; 21°03'N 79°17'W. More than 400 keys, consisting of Cayos de las Doce Leguas (NW) and Laberinto de las Doce Leguas (SE), separated by the Canal de Caballones; bounded by the Gran Banco de Buena Esperanza (NE), sometimes considered to be a part of the Jardines de la Reina.

Jardines del Rey, Cuba: see CAMAGÜEY ARCHIPELAGO.

Jaronú (hahr-o-NOO), village, Camagüey prov., E Cuba, on RR, and 29 mi/47 km N of Camagüey; 21°49'N 77°57'W. Adjacent to modern sugar-mill village of Brasil, one of nation's largest.

Jarratt, town (1990 pop. 556), Greensville and Sussex cos., S Va., 10 mi NNE of Emporia, near Nottoway R.; 36°49'N 77°28'W. Mfg. (food prods., wood fiber sheathing). Agr. (livestock, poultry; cotton, tobacco; peanuts, grain).

Jarrell, uninc. village (1990 pop. 410), Williamson co., central Texas, 22 mi/35 km SSW of Temple. Agr. (cattle; cotton, corn, wheat). Limestone. Mfg. (fertilizer, flagstone).

Jaruco (hahr-OO-ko), town, La Habana prov., W Cuba, on small Jaruco R., and 23 mi/37 km ESE of Havana; 23°04'N 82°01'W. RR junction and agr. center (sugarcane, fruit, vegetables). Copper deposits nearby. Adjoining (W) are the Escaleras de Jaruco, a picturesque hilly range.

Jarvis, village, S Ont., Canada, 11 mi/18 km E of Simcoe. Grist milling, dairying; bees, poultry.

Jarvis Sound, S N.J., inlet (1.5 mi/2.4 km long, 0.75 mi/ 1.2km wide) just N of Cape May Harbor, to which it is joined by Intracoastal Waterway channel, which enters from Richardson Sound (N).

Jasonville, city (1990 pop. 2,200), Greene co., SW Ind., 16 mi/26 km NW of Bloomfield; 39°10'N 87°12'W. In agr. area (grain, fruit). Mfg. (electrical equipment, telephone line coils, wood prods.); bituminous-coal mines. Shakamak State Park nearby to W. Laid out 1859.

Jasper 1 county (□ 373 sq mi/966 sq km; 1990 pop. 8,453), central Ga.; ⊙ Monticello; 33°19'N 83°41'W. Bounded W by Ocmulgee R. (forms Lloyd Shoals Reservoir here); drained by Little R. Piedmont agr.; cattle, poultry; and timber area. Feldspar mining. Formed 1807. **2** county (□ 498 sq mi/1,290 sq km; 1990 pop. 10,609), SE central Ill.; ⊙ Newton; 39°00'N 88°09'W. Agr. (soybeans, corn, sorghum, wheat; cattle, hogs; dairy prods.). Oil. Some mfg. (auto parts). Drained by Embarras R. In SW of co. is Newton L.; Sam Parr State Park at center. Formed 1831. **3** county (□ 561 sq mi/ 1,453 sq km; 1990 pop. 24,960), NW Ind.; ⊙ Rensselaer; 41°02'N 87°07'W. Bounded N by Kankakee R.; drained by Iroquois R. Corn, soybeans; cattle, hogs; dairying. Jasper-Pulaski State Fish and Wildlife Area and Nursery in NE. Formed 1835. **4** county (□ 732 sq mi/ 1,896 sq km; 1990 pop. 34,795), central Iowa; ⊙ Newton; 41°41'N 93°02'W. Prairie agr. area (hogs, cattle, poultry; corn, oats), drained by Skunk and North Skunk rivers, and with bituminous-coal deposits. Rock Creek L. and Rock Creek State Park in E. Widespread flooding in 1993. Formed 1846. **5** county (□ 677 sq mi/ 1,753 sq km; 1990 pop. 17,114), E central Miss.; ⊙ Paulding and Bay Springs; 32°01'N 89°07'W. Drained by Tallahala Creek and short Tallahoma and Souinlovey creeks. Agr. (corn, cotton; poultry, cattle; dairying); timber. Oil fields. Includes part of Bienville Natl. Forest in NW. L. Claude Bennett State Lake in NE. Formed 1833. **6** county (□ 642 sq mi/1,663 sq km; 1990 pop. 90,465), SW Mo.; ⊙ Carthage; 37°12'N 94°20'W. Borders Kansas on W; drained by Spring R. Agr. (grain, soybeans; poultry, cattle, dairying). Mfg. at Joplin, Carthage, Webb City; former major lead, zinc mines; numerous abandoned surface and underground mines; limestone (marketed as marble) quarries; oak timber. Formed 1841. **7** county (□ 685 sq mi/1,774 sq km; 1990 pop. 15,487), extreme S S.C.; ⊙ Ridgeland; 32°26'N 81°01'W. Bounded W by Savannah R., NE by Coosawhatchie R., SE by New R. Agr. area (cattle, hogs; wheat, soybeans, hay, corn). Formed 1912. **8** county (□ 969 sq mi/2,510 sq km; 1990 pop. 31,102), E Texas; ⊙ Jasper; 30°44'N 94°01'W. Bounded W by Neches R. (forms B. A. Steinhagen L. [State Park] in NW). Heavily wooded; lumbering chief industry. Diversified agr. (cattle, hogs, horses, poultry; vegetables, pecans, fruit); oil and gas. Part of Big Thicket Natl. Preserve follows course of Neches R. downstream from Steinhagen L.; part of large Sam Rayburn Reservoir (Angelina R.) on N boundary; part of Angelina Natl. Forest in NW. Formed 1836.

Jasper 1 city (1990 pop. 13,553), ⊙ Walker co., NW central Ala.; 33°51'N87 °16'W. Jasper is a trade and processing center in a coal and timber area. Abundant agr., coal mining, and varied light mfg. (sporting goods, furniture, bottling; poultry processing). Walker Col. of the Univ. of Ala. at Birmingham is here. Inc. 1889. **2** city (1990 pop. 10,030), ⊙ Dubois co., SW Ind., on Patoka R., and 45 mi/72 km NE of Evansville; 38°23'N 86°56'W. Agr. area (grain, strawberries; livestock, poultry). Mfg. (wood prods., machinery, rubber prods., furniture, plastic products, electronic equip.); timber. Founded 1818, laid out 1830. **3** city (1990 pop. 994), Jasper co., SW Mo., 11 mi/18 km N of Carthage; 37°19'N 94°17'W. Agr. (wheat, soybeans; dairying; cattle), Mfg. (popcorn, auto parts). **4** city (1990 pop. 6,959), ⊙ Jasper co., E Texas, c.60 mi/97 km NNE of Beaumont; 30°55'N 94°00'W. Elev. 221 ft/67 m. In pine woods area; lumber milling, oil and gas. Agr. (cattle, horses, hogs; vegetables, fruit, pecans). Diversified light mfg. Angelina Natl. Forest to NW; Sabine Natl. Forest to NE; Sam Rayburn Reservoir to N; Martin Dies Jr. State Park, on Steinhagen L., to W. Settled 1824, inc. 1926.

Jasper, town, W Alta., Canada, near B.C. border, in Rocky Mts., on Athabaska R., and 200 mi/322 km WSW of Edmonton; 52°53'N 118°05'W. Elev. 3,470 ft/ 1,058 m. Tourist center in Jasper Natl. Park. Overlooked by peaks over 10,000 ft/3,048 m high.

Jasper 1 town (□ 1 sq mi/2.6 sq km; 1990 pop. 2,099), ⊙ Hamilton co., NE Fla., near Ga. line, 15 mi/24 km N of Live Oak; 30°31'N 82°57'W. Trade and processing center, in tobacco and timber region. Settled c.1825. **2** town (1990 pop. 1,772), ⊙ Pickens co., N Ga., c.50 mi/ 80 km N of Atlanta; 34°28'N 84°26'W. Mfg. (metal prods., yarn dying, apparel, molded rubber prods., printing and publishing). Several marble-clad, older bldgs. Inc. 1857. **3** town (1990 pop. 2,780), ⊙ Marion co., SE Tenn., near Ala. and Ga. state lines, 18 mi/29 km W of Chattanooga; 35°05'N 85°38'W. In fertile Sequatchie R. valley (dairying; tobacco, cotton). Coal deposits. Mfg. (vinyl siding, apparel).

Jasper 1 village (1990 pop. 332), ⊙ Newton co., NW Ark., 15 mi/24 km SSW of Harrison, in the Ozarks, near Ozark Natl. Forest and Buffalo Natl. R.; 36°00'N 93°11'W. Gene Bush–Buffalo R. Wildlife Management Area to SE; small unit of Ozark Natl. Forest to N, main unit to S. Tourism. **2** village (1990 pop. 599), Pipestone and Rock cos., SW Minn., near S. Dak. state line, 11 mi/ 18 km SSW of Pipestone, on Split Rock Creek; 43°51'N 96°24'W. Agr. area (grain, soybeans; livestock, poultry; dairying). Mfg. (feeds and fertilizers); silica quarries nearby. Split Rock Creek State Park to NE.

Jasper Lake, expansion of Athabaska R., W Alta., Canada, in Rocky Mts., in Jasper Natl. Park, 13 mi/21 km N of Jasper; 8 mi/13 km long, 1 mi/2 km wide. N end of lake was last site of Jasper House, Hudson's Bay Co. trading post, moved here 1801 from Brûlé L., abandoned 1875.

Jataté River (hah-tah-TE), c.150 mi/241 km long, in Chiapas, S Mexico; rises in Sierra de Hueytepec S of Ocosingo, flows SE to join Lacantún R. (Usumacinta system) near Guatemala border; 16°15'N 91°17'W.

Jatibonico (huh-tee-bo-NEE-ko), town, Sancti Spíritus prov., E Cuba, on Río Jatibonico del Sur, on Central Highway, on RR, and 27 mi/43 km W of Ciego de Ávila; 21°56'N 79°10'W. In agr. region (sugarcane, tobacco, livestock). Mfg. (pottery and cigars). The sugar mill of Uruguay is just SW.

Jatibonico del Norte, Río (huh-tee-bo-NEE-ko dail NOR-te, REE-o), 43 mi/70 km long, central Cuba; rises in the Sierra de Jatibonico 8 mi/12.9 km SSE of Caibarién, flows along Sancti Spíritus–Ciego de Ávila prov. border to N coast; 21°15'N 78°58'W. Has irregular course, obstructed by cataracts, and flowing partly through subterranean trench (2.5 mi/4 km long).

Jatibonico del Sur, Río (huh-tee-bo-NEE-ko dail sur), 73 mi/117 km long, 7th longest river in Cuba; flows through Sancti Spíritus prov. Drains 322 sq mi/ 835 sq km area and empties into Caribbean Sea.

Jaumave (hwah-MAH-ve), town (1990 pop. 3,875), Tamaulipas, NE Mexico, in a valley of E Sierra Madre Occidental outliers, 28 mi/45 km SW of Ciudad Victoria; 23°28'N 99°22'W. Small farming and ranching.

Java 1 village (1990 pop. 161), Walworth co., N S.Dak., 8 mi/12.9 km E of Selby; 45°30'N 99°52'W. In cattle-raising region. Lake Hiddenwood State Park to NW. **2** uninc. village, Pittsylvania co., S Va., 20 mi/32 km NNE of Danville. Mfg. (lumber, hickory chips). Agr. (dairying; cattle; grain, soybeans); timber.

Jay, county (□ 383 sq mi/992 sq km; 1990 pop. 21,512), E Ind., bounded E by Ohio state line; ⊙ Portland; 40°26'N 85°01'W. Agr. area (corn, oats, vegetables, soybeans; hogs, cattle, poultry). Diversified mfg. at Portland; lumber milling. Natural-gas and oil wells; timber. Drained by Salamonie R. Formed 1836.

Jay 1 town (1990 pop. 5,080), Franklin co., W central Maine, on the Androscoggin R., 13 mi/21 km SSE of Farmington. Village of Chisholm (1990 pop. 1,653) has pulp and paper mills; 44°31'N 70°13'W. Includes villages of Jay and North Jay. Inc. 1795. **2** town (1990 pop. 2,220), ⊙ Delaware co., NE Okla., near Ark. state line, 25 mi/40 km SE of Vinita; 36°25'N 94°47'W. Elev. 1,032 ft/315 m. Trade center for agr. and recreation area (fruit, berries; livestock, poultry). Mfg. (concrete, electronic equip., poultry processing). L. Eucha (formerly Upper Spavinaw L.) and Upper Spavinaw State Park to S; L. of the Cherokees to NW. **3** town (1990 pop. 381), Orleans co., N Vt., on Que. (Canada) border, 11 mi/ 18 km W of Newport; 44°58'N 72°28'W. Jay Peak is W, with ski resort.

Jay, resort village (1990 pop. 500), Essex co., NE N.Y., in Adirondack Mts., on East Branch of Ausable R., 26 mi/ 42 km SSW of Plattsburgh; 44°22'N 73°42'W.

Jay Peak (3,861 ft/1,177 m), in Green Mts., N Vt., near Que. (Canada) border, 15 mi/24 km W of Newport. N terminus of Long Trail. Downhill ski area.

Jayton, village (1990 pop. 608), Kent co., NW Texas, 40 mi/64 km NNE of Snyder, near Salt Fork Brazos R.; 33°15'N 100°34'W. Elev. 2,015 ft/614 m. In cattle and agr. (cotton; wheat, sorghum) region.

Jayuya (hah-YOO-yah), town (1990 pop. 15,527), central P.R., in Toro Negro Forest, 14 mi/23 km N of Ponce. Coffee-growing and production center. Agr. (tomatoes, citrus fruits, plantains); light mfg. Traditional woodcarving. Starting point for ascent of Tres Picachos peak, 3 mi/4.8 km E.

Jean, uninc. village (1990 pop. 125), Clark co., S Nev., 25 mi/40 km SSW of Las Vegas, 11 mi/18 km NE of Calif. state line. Cattle. Mfg. (plastics prods.). Toiyabe Natl. Forest to NW.

Jean Lafitte (ZHAWN lah-FEET), town (1990 pop. 1,469), elev. 2 ft/1 m, Jefferson parish, SE La., 14 mi/-

23 km S of New Orleans, on Dupre Cut-Off Canal; 29°45′N 90°07′W. Agr. (home gardens, nursery crops). Jean Lafitte Natl. Historical Park, Barataria Unit, to N; swamp tours. Village of Lafitte 4 mi/6 km S.

Jean Lafitte National Historical Park and Preserve (ZHAWN lah-FEET), SE La. This park includes 4 units, total acreage 20,020 acres/8,108 ha. Part of the New Orleans' French Quarter (18.6 acres/7.5 ha) is in Orleans parish, in the French Quarter of downtown New Orleans. Depicts life and Fr. heritage of La. delta region. Includes park visitor center. The Chalmette Battlefield (143 acres/58 ha) is in St. Bernard parish, 7 mi/11 km E of New Orleans. Est. 1907; site of Battle of New Orleans (1812) and Chalmette Natl. Cemetery. The Barataria unit (19,851 acres/8,040 ha) is in Jefferson and Lafourche parishes, 15 mi/24 km S of New Orleans. Sample of Mississippi R. delta ecology, including cypress swamps, marshes, bayous. Smuggling site provided to U.S. forces by Jean Lafitte's band during War of 1812. Lafitte helped Andrew Jackson defeat British in 1815 Battle of New Orleans. Isleno or Acadian unit (7.4 acres/3 ha) includes 3 small sites in Lafayette and St. Landry parishes. Hq. and cultural resources center in Lafayette.

Jeanerette (jen-uh-RET), city (1994 pop. 6,750), Iberia parish, S La., on navigable Bayou Teche, and 10 mi/16 km SE of New Iberia; 29°55′N 91°41′W. Market center for oil, natural gas. Agr. area (sugarcane, rice, soybeans); crawfish, catfish. Mfg. (boats, sugar-mill machinery, apparel); sugar milling. Jeanerette Mus. features sugarcane industry. Antebellum homes in area. Lake Fausse Pointe (State Park on E shore to NE).

Jeannette (juh-NET), city (1990 pop. 11,221), Westmoreland co., SW Pa., suburb 20 mi/32 km SE of Pittsburgh, on Brush Creek; 40°19′N 79°36′W. Located in a coal and natural-gas area. Mfg. (machinery, plastic prods., specialty glass, printing). Agr. (corn; livestock; dairying). Its glassworks date from 1889. Bushy Run Battleground historic site to N. Laid out 1888, inc. as a city 1937.

Jeannette, Mount (11,700 ft/3,566 m), SW Yukon, Canada, near Alaska border, in St. Elias Mts., 200 mi/322 km W of Whitehorse; 60°31′N 140°57′W.

Jean-Rabel (ZHAWNG–rah BEL), town (1982 pop. 3,294), Nord-Ouest dept., NW Haiti, near NW tip of Hispaniola isl., 23 mi/37 km WSW of Port-de-Paix; 19°52′N 73°11′W. Agr. center (sugarcane, sisal, fruit); bee-keeping; sugar processing. Copper deposits nearby. Its port, Bord-de-Mer-Jean-Rabel, is 4 mi/6.4 km NNW.

Jeddo, borough (1990 pop. 124), Luzerne co., E central Pa., 5 mi/8 km NE of Hazleton; 40°59′N 75°54′W. Former anthracite coal-mining area.

Jeddore Harbour (jeh-DOR), inlet (7 mi/11 km long, 3 mi/5 km wide) of the Atlantic, S N.S., Canada, 30 mi/48 km ENE of Halifax; 44°45′N 63°01′W. At head of bay is Head of Jeddore.

Jeff, village (1990 pop. 550), Perry co., SE Ky., 4 mi/6.4 km SE of Hazard, in Cumberland foothills, on North Fork Kentucky R. opposite mouth of Carr Fork Kentucky R. Bituminous coal. Agr. (tobacco; livestock). Mfg. (coal processing). Daniel Boone Natl. Forest to SW.

Jeff Davis 1 county (□ 331 sq mi/857 sq km; 1990 pop. 12,032), SE central Ga.; ⊙ Hazlehurst; 31°48′N 82°38′W. Bounded NW by Ocmulgee R., N by Altamaha R.; drained by Little Satilla R. Coastal plain agr. (cotton, soybeans, tobacco, corn, sugarcane, peanuts, pecans; cattle, hogs, poultry). Textile mfg. at Hazlehurst. Formed 1905. **2** county (□ 2,264 sq mi/5,864 sq km; 1990 pop. 1,946), extreme W Texas; ⊙ Fort Davis; 30°43′N 104°07′W. Primarily a high plateau (c.4,500 ft/1,372 m–8,382 ft/2,555 m), diamond-shaped co. extending W, touching the Rio Grande (Mex. border); rises to scenic Davis Mts. in center of co., including Mt. Livermore (8,382 ft/2,555 m; 2d-highest peak in state) and Mt. Locke, with McDonald Observatory in center. Part of Sierra Vieja Mts. is in W. Cattle-ranching area; dairying; goats, hogs; sorghum, cotton, melons, corn, hay, wheat; wine grapes. Davis Mts. State Park and Fort Davis Natl. Historic Site both in SE center. Formed 1887.

Jeffers, village (1990 pop. 443), Cottonwood co., SW Minn., 14 mi/23 km NNW of Windom; 44°03′N 95°12′W. Agr. (grain, soybeans; livestock). Mfg. (hydraulic cylinders, carts).

Jefferson 1 county (□ 1,123 sq mi/2,909 sq km; 1990 pop. 651,525), N central Ala.; ⊙ Birmingham; 33°35′N 86°52′W. Industrial area crossed by Locust Fork; and drained by the Black Warrior R. (W) and the Cahaba R. (E). Coal and iron mining, limestone quarrying, natural-gas production. The co., along with Walker co., once accounted for 60% of Ala.'s coal production, but now the industry is declining. Iron and steel prods. are made at Birmingham, Bessemer, Fairfield, Tarrant, and Leeds. Formed 1819. **2** county (□ 913 sq mi/2,365 sq km; 1990 pop. 85,487), central Ark.; ⊙ PINE BLUFF; 34°14′N 91°54′W. Intersected by Arkansas R. NW to SE; drained by Wabbaseka R. in NE, by Bayou Bartholomew in SW; Bayou Meto forms extreme E boundary. Agr. (cotton, hay, wheat, rice, soybeans; hogs, turkeys); timber. Mfg. at Pine Bluff. Lock and Dam No. 5 in NW, Emmett Sanders Lock and Dam near center. Pine Bluff Arsenal in NW; part of Bayou Meto Wildlife Management Area in E. Formed 1829. **3** county (□ 778 sq mi/2,015 sq km; 1990 pop. 438,430), central Colo.; ⊙ Golden; 39°38′N 105°16′W. Coal-mining and irrigated agr. region, bounded SE by South Platte R. (forms Chatfield and Cheesman reservoirs); drained by Clear Creek. Remnant agr. in NE part, most agr. replaced by urban growth from Denver in NE and growth of Lakewood, Golden, Arvada, and other Jefferson co. communities (sugar beets, beans; livestock). Fur farms. All but NE part of co. is in Front Range of Rocky Mts. and its foothills. Includes parts of Pike Natl. Forest in W and S; part of Chatfield State Park on SE boundary; part of Golden Gate State Park in NW. Land area was 785 sq mi/2,033 sq km in 1960, reduced by the encroachment of Denver co. in NE, which adjusts its boundaries every decennial year to absorb city of Denver's annexations into neighboring counties. Formed 1861. **4** county (□ 598 sq mi/1,549 sq km; 1990 pop. 11,296), NW Fla.; ⊙ Monticello, 30°25′N 83°54′W. Bounded by Ga. line (N), Gulf of Mexico (S), and Aucilla R. (E). Lowland area, partly swampy, with rolling terrain and L. Miccosukee in N. Agr. (corn, peanuts, cotton, vegetables, tung nuts; hogs, cattle) and some forestry (lumber, naval stores). Formed 1827. **5** county (□ 532 sq mi/1,378 sq km; 1990 pop. 17,408), E Ga.; ⊙ Louisville; 33°03′N 82°25′W. Coastal-plain agr. (cotton, corn, peanuts) and sawmilling area drained by Ogeechee R. Mfg. (trusses, textiles, apparel, consumer goods); printing and publishing. Formed 1796. **6** county (□ 1,105 sq mi/2,862 sq km; 1990 pop. 16,543), E Idaho; ⊙ Rigby; 43°49′N 112°19′W. Drained and irrigated by Snake R. in SE, forms part of NE boundary. Livestock-raising and irrigated agr. area in Snake R. plain. Clover, legumes, sugar beets, potatoes, alfalfa, orchards; wheat, barley, oats; sheep, cattle; poultry. Part of Idaho Natl. Engineering Laboratory (U.S. Department of Energy) on W boundary; Jefferson Rays L. and Mud L. reservoirs at center of co.; Camas Natl. Wildlife Refuge in N center. Formed 1913. **7** county (□ 583 sq mi/1,510 sq km; 1990 pop. 37,020), S Ill.; ⊙ Mount Vernon; 38°18′N 88°56′W. Major RR and road junction at Mt. Vernon. Agr. (cattle; sorghum, wheat). Mfg. (RR cars, rubber prods., machinery, electronic equip.). Bituminous-coal mining, oil. Drained by Big Muddy R. Formed 1819. Rend L. on S boundary. **8** county (□ 362 sq mi/938 sq km; 1990 pop. 29,797), SE Ind.; ⊙ Madison; 38°47′N 85°26′W. Bounded partly S by Ohio R. (here forming Ky. line); drained by Big Creek, Clifty Creek, and Indian-Kentuck Creek. Corn; cattle, poultry, hogs; diversified mfg.; timber. Contains Clifty Falls State Park on W edge of Madison; Hardy Lake State Recreation Area on W co. line. Part of Jefferson Proving Ground in N part. Formed 1811. **9** county (□ 436 sq mi/1,129 sq km; 1990 pop. 16,310), SE Iowa; ⊙ Fairfield; 41°02′N 91°57′W. Prairie agr. area (hogs, cattle, poultry; corn, soybeans, hay) drained by Skunk R.; coal mines, limestone quarries. Skunk R. flooded in 1993. Formed 1839. **10** county (□ 556 sq mi/1,440 sq km; 1990 pop. 15,905), NE Kansas; ⊙ Oskaloosa; 39°13′N 95°24′W. Hilly area, crossed by Delaware R.; bounded S by Kansas R. Corn, hogs, cattle, sorghum, hay, wheat; dairying. Limestone mining. Perry L. Reservoir at center of co., Perry State Park at dam. Formed 1855. **11** county (□ 398 sq mi/1,031 sq km; 1990 pop. 664,937), N Ky.; ⊙ LOUISVILLE, state's largest city and major transportation, commerce, and mfg. center for the South and Midwest; 38°11′N 85°39′W. Bounded W and N by Ohio R. (Ind. state line), drained by Floyds Fork river. Majority of the city is urbanized, while S and E margins remain agr. Agr. (vegetables, burley tobacco, hay, alfalfa, soybeans, wheat, corn; some livestock); quarrying (limestone, clay, sand, gravel); mfg. remains centered in Louisville. F.P. "Tom" Sawyer State Park is in NE; also numerous other city and co. parks. Formed in 1780 from old Kentucky co., Va., becoming one of 3 cos. of Ky. dist., then part of Va. **12** county (□ 527 sq mi/1,365 sq km; 1990 pop. 8,653), SW Miss.; ⊙ Fayette; 31°44′N 91°02′W. Bounded W by the Mississippi R., including Rodney L. in NW, Oxbow lake and former channel of Mississippi R. forms part of La.-Miss. state line. Includes part of Homochitto Natl. Forest in E and SE. Agr. (cotton, corn, soybeans; cattle); timber. Natchez Trace (Natl.) Parkway passes N-S through co. Formed 1802. **13** county (□ 667 sq mi/1,728 sq km; 1990 pop. 171,380), E Mo.; ⊙ Hillsboro; 38°16′N 90°35′W. On Mississippi R. (E) and Meramec R. (NE and NW); drained by Big R. Agr. (corn, hay; livestock); silica (sand), barite mines. Very hilly area experiencing urban growth, esp. in N and E. Part of St. Louis metropolitan area; major towns with mfg. include Arnold, Pevely, Herculaneum (lead smelter), Festus–Crystal City, and De Soto. Major uninc. residential areas include Imperial, Barnhart, High Ridge, House Springs, Fenton (city of Fenton is in St. Louis co.). Mastodon State Park archaeological site and mus. at Imperial. Sandy Creek Covered Bridge State Historic Site. Formed 1818. **14** county (□ 1,658 sq mi/4,294 sq km; 1990 pop. 7,939), SW central Mont.; ⊙ Boulder; 46°11′N 112°07′W. Agr. and mining region drained by Boulder R.; bounded S by Jefferson R., W by Continental Divide. Cattle, sheep, hogs; gold, silver, lead, zinc; hay, wheat, oats. Lewis and Clark Caverns State Park in SE; part of Deerlodge Natl. Forest in W and E; part of Helena Natl. Forest in NE and NW. Formed 1865. **15** county (□ 575 sq mi/1,489 sq km; 1990 pop. 8,759), SE Nebr.; ⊙ Fairbury; 40°10′N 97°09′W. Agr. region bounded S by Kansas; drained by Little Blue R. Cattle, hogs, corn, wheat, soybeans, sorghum, alfalfa; dairying. Clay quarry. Old Oregon Trail crosses co. from SE to NW with Historic Rock Creek Station SE of Fairbury. Alexandria Lakes State Recreation Area in W. Formed 1871. **16** county (□ 1,293 sq mi/3,349 sq km; 1990 pop. 110,943), N N.Y.; ⊙ Watertown; 43°59′N 76°02′W. Bounded W by L. Ontario and NW by St. Lawrence R.; drained by Black and Indian rivers (water power). Mfg., esp. at Watertown and Carthage; major dairying region; metallic and nonmetallic minerals mined. Over 188 sq mi/487 sq km of military installations, including Fort Drum. Named for Thomas Jefferson, who was president at time of co.'s creation. New Englanders, attracted by water power at Watertown, led movement to establish co. from large tract from Macomb Purchase that had been bought by Fr. nobleman Le Ray de Chaumont and refugees from the Fr. Revolution, who returned to France unable to accept the rigorous difficulties of pioneer life. Winter and summer recreational areas and state parks on L. Ontario and in Thousand Isls. region of St. Lawrence R. Formed 1805. **17** county (□ 411 sq mi/1,064 sq km; 1990 pop. 80,298), E Ohio; ⊙ STEUBENVILLE; 40°22′N 80°45′W. Bounded E by Ohio R., here forming W.Va. state line; drained by small Yellow and Cross creeks. In the Unglaciated Plain physiographic region. Coal mining; mfg. (lumber, wood, and metal prods., and steel mills); agr. (cattle, corn); ceramics plants. Formed 1797. **18** county (□ 773 sq mi/2,002 sq km; 1990 pop. 7,010), S Okla.; ⊙

Waurika; 34°06′N 97°50′W. Bounded S by Red R., here forming Texas line; and drained by Beaver and Mud creeks. Agr. (grain, corn); sheep, cattle. Mfg. at Waurika. Oil. Part of Waurika L. in NW. Formed 1907. **19** county (□ 1,791 sq mi/4,639 sq km; 1990 pop. 13,676), central Oregon; ⊙ Madras; 44°37′N 121°10′W. Mt. Jefferson, in Cascade Range, on W boundary. Drained by Deschutes R. Part of Warm Springs Indian Reservation in NW. Agr. (wheat, barley, oats, potatoes; poultry, sheep, cattle); lumber milling; mercury mining. Crooked River Natl. Grassland in S; part of Deschutes Natl. Forest in SW; Corbett State Park in SW corner; Cove Palisades State Park on L. Chinook Reservoir in W center. Formed 1914. **20** county (□ 656 sq mi/1,699 sq km; 1990 pop. 46,083), W central Pa.; ⊙ Brookville; 41°07′N 79°00′W. RR junction. Bounded N by Clarion R.; drained by Mahoning and Red Bank creeks. Agr. and mfg. area. Bituminous coal; mfg. at Punxatawney and Brookville; clay, sand, and gravel. Agr. (corn, wheat, oats, barley, hay, alfalfa, soybeans; sheep, hogs, cattle, poultry; dairying). Clear Creek State Park and State Forest in N. Formed 1804. **21** county (□ 318 sq mi/824 sq km; 1990 pop. 33,016), E Tenn.; ⊙ Dandridge; 36°03′N 83°27′W. In Great Appalachian Valley; traversed by Bays Mtn.; bounded NW by Holston R.; drained by French Broad R. Includes parts of Cherokee and Douglas reservoirs. Livestock raising, dairying, agr. (tobacco, fruit, corn, hay). Zinc mines, limestone quarries. Formed 1792. **22** county (□ 1,111 sq mi/2,877 sq km; 1990 pop. 239,397), SE Texas; ⊙ BEAUMONT; 29°53′N 94°09′W. On Gulf coastal plain; bounded E by Sabine L. (here forming La. state line); NE by Neches R., N by Pine Isl. Bayou, S by Gulf of Mexico; crossed by Gulf Intracoastal Waterway (to parallel Gulf Coast, also NE along Texas shore of Sabine L.). Sabine-Neches Waterway gives access from Gulf to deep-water ports of Beaumont and Port Arthur, important oil-shipping, oil-refining, and industrial centers. Oil, natural-gas fields. Cattle raising, agr. (rice, soybeans). Fishing, duck hunting. Small part of Big Thicket Natl. Preserve in N; Texas Point Natl. Wildlife Refuge, Sea Rim State Park, Sabine Pass Battleground State Historical Park in SE; McFadden Natl. Wildlife Refuge in S, on coast. Formed 1836. **23** county (□ 2,177 sq mi/5,638 sq km; 1990 pop. 20,146), W Wash.; ⊙ Port Townsend; 47°51′N 123°35′W. Bounded W by Pacific Ocean, E by Hood Canal and Puget Sound, far NE by Strait of Juan de Fuca; peaks of Olympic Mts. in interior. Timber, wood pulp; fish; cattle; dairying. Includes Hoh Indian Reservation in W and part of Quinault Indian Reservation in SW. Central part of Olympic Natl. Park and Olympic Mts., including Mt. Olympus (7,965 ft/2,428 m), crosses co. N-S in center, isolating W part of co., along Pacific Coast, from E part, on Puget Sound. Protection Isl. Natl. Wildlife Refuge in NE; Quillayute Natl. Wildlife Refuge off W coast; S part of coastal section of Olympic Natl. Park in W; Dosewallips and Pleasant Harbor state parks in SE; Anderson Lake, Fort Worden, Fort Flagler, Old Fort Townsend, and Mystery Bay state parks in NE; parts of Olympic Natl. Forest in SW and E, including the Brothers Wilderness Area and part of Buckhorn Wilderness Area, both in E. Includes Marrowstone and Indian isls. in NE (Puget Sound), latter is U.S. Naval Reservation. Formed 1852. **24** county (□ 211 sq mi/546 sq km; 1990 pop. 35,926), NE W.Va., at end of E Panhandle; ⊙ Charles Town, 39°18′N 77°51′W. In S part of Great Appalachian Valley; Blue Ridge is along SE border. Bounded NE by Potomac R. (Md. state line), SE and SW by Va.; drained by Shenandoah R., which joins the Potomac R. at Harpers Ferry, and by short Opequon Creek. Scenic resort region. Agr. (corn, wheat, oats, barley, soybeans, potatoes, alfalfa, hay, sorghum, apples; livestock; poultry; dairying); limestone and dolomite quarrying. Industry at Ranson, Charles Town. Part of Harpers Ferry Natl. Historic Park in NE (1,102 acres/446 ha); James Rumsey State Historic Monument in N; Shannondale Springs Wildlife Management Area in SE. Formed 1801. **25** county (□ 582 sq mi/1,507 sq km; 1990 pop. 67,783), S Wis.; ⊙ Jefferson, 43°02′N 88°46′W. Dairying is chief industry; agr. (wheat, corn, soybeans, potatoes; cattle, hogs, sheep, poultry); some mfg. at Lake Mills, Watertown, Jefferson, and Whitewater. Aztalan State Park in W; larger L. Koshkonong in SW; Glacial Drumlin State Trail passes E-W through center of co.; small part of Kettle Moraine State Forest in SE corner. Drained by Rock, Bark, and Crawfish rivers. Has lake resorts. Formed 1836.

Jefferson, parish (□ 409 sq mi/1,059 sq km; 1990 pop. 448,306), extreme SE La.; ⊙ Gretna; 29°55′N 90°03′W. Situated in the delta of the Mississippi R., which intersects parish in N; bounded S by Gulf of Mexico (Barataria Bay), N by L. Pontchartrain, W by Cataouatche, Salvador, and Little lakes. Important industrial parish, adjoining (in N) New Orleans. Widely varied mfg. in N. Home gardens, nursery crops, horses; oysters, shrimp, crabs, finfish, alligators, exotic fowl; oil and natural-gas wells. New Orleans Internatl. Airport in NW at Kenner. Traversed by Intracoastal Waterway. Grand Isle, 15 mi/24 km S of mainland at entrance to Barataria Bay, is part of parish, connected by bridge to Lafourche parish (W); includes Grand Isle State Park. City of New Orleans, to NE of parish, urbanized in N. Bayou Segnette State Park in N. Named after Thomas Jefferson. Formed 1825.

Jefferson 1 city (1990 pop. 4,292), ⊙ Greene co., central Iowa, on Raccoon R., and 43 mi/69 km W of Ames; 42°01′N 94°22′W. RR junction. Agr. trade center with dairy prods., feed, tankage; mfg. (consumer goods, fabricated metal prods., paper prods.). Sand and gravel pits nearby. Mahaney Memorial Carillon Tower here; Spring L. State Park to NE. Settled c.1854, inc. 1871. **2** uninc. city (1990 pop. 14,521), Jefferson parish, SE La., suburb 4 mi/6 km E of downtown New Orleans, on Mississippi R.; 29°58′N 90°10′W. Mfg. (paper prods., bldg. materials, food processing, fabricated steel, spirits and cordials, lubricating oils, pulp-mill equip.); printing and publishing. **3** uninc. city (1990 pop. 25,782), Fairfax co., N Va, residential suburb 8 mi/12.9 km W of Washington, D.C., includes communities of JEFFERSON VILLAGE and HILLWOOD.

Jefferson 1 town (□ 15 sq mi/39 sq km; 1990 pop. 2,763), ⊙ Jackson co., NE central Ga., 15 mi/24 km NW of Athens; 34°08′N 83°36′W. Mfg. (textiles, plastics, apparel; printing and publishing). Dr. Crawford W. Long performed an operation here in 1842 using ether as an anesthetic; commemorated in a mus. Many 19th-cent. homes. Inc. 1806. **2** town (1990 pop. 2,111), Lincoln co., S Maine, on Damariscotta L., and 18 mi/29 km NE of Wiscasset; 44°11′N 69°30′W. **3** town (1990 pop. 965), Coos co., N central N.H., 14 mi/23 km WSW of Berlin; 44°23′N 71°28′W. Drained by Israel R. Agr. (cattle, poultry; dairying; timber); mfg. (lumber, furniture, computer software). Santa's Village and Six Gun City theme parks are here. Parts of White Mt. Natl. Forest in S and NE; Agnew State Forest in S. **4** town (1990 pop. 1,300), ⊙ Ashe co., NW N.C., 20 mi/32 km NE of Boone, in the Blue Ridge Mts.; 36°25′N 81°28′W. Tobacco, corn; cattle; dairying. Mfg. (lumber; printing and publishing). Mt. Jefferson State Park to SE, New River State Park to E. Blue Ridge Parkway passes to SE. **5** town (1990 pop.1,805), Marion co., W Oregon, 8 mi/12.9 km NNE of Albany, on Santiam R.; 44°43′N 123°00′W. Agr. (fruit, nuts, berries, hops; poultry; dairy prods.); fabrics. Ankeny Natl. Wildlife Refuge to NW. **6** town (1990 pop. 745), Chesterfield co., N S.C., 21 mi/34 km ESE of Lancaster; 34°38′N 80°23′W. Mfg. (construction materials, textiles, gold bullion); agr. (livestock, poultry; grain, watermelons, tobacco, peaches). **7** town (1990 pop. 2,199), ⊙ Marion co., NE Texas, on Big Cypress Creek, and 14 mi/23 km N of Marshall; 32°45′N 94°20′W. Elev. 200 ft/61 m. RR junction. In oil, vegetables, timber (pine, cypress) area. Lumber milling; mfg. (fabricated metal prods., food processing, wood and flat-glass prods.). Tourism. Caddo L. (hunting, fishing) is to E, Caddo L. State Park to SE. Grew as a river port and lumbering center in area settled in 1830s; reached pop. of c.30,000 in 1875, later declined. Lake O' the Pines to W. **8** town (1990 pop. 6,078), ⊙ Jefferson co., S Wis. on Rock R., at confluence of Crawfish R., 30 mi/48 km ESE of Madison; 43°00′N 88°48′W. In dairying and farming region. Mfg. (furniture, shoes, textiles, wood prods., food and meat prods., vegetable processing; printing). Glacial Drumlin State Trail passes to N. Settled c.1836, inc. 1878.

Jefferson 1 village, Park co., central Colo., on Tarryall Creek, in Rocky Mts., and 50 mi/80 km SW of Denver; elev. c.9,500 ft/2,896 m. Shipping point for livestock and timber below Kenosha Pass (to NE, 10,001 ft/3,048 m). Pike Natl. Forest to W, N, and E. Jefferson L. to NW. Tarryall State Wildlife Area to SE. **2** village (1990 pop. 3,331), ⊙ Ashtabula co., extreme NE Ohio, 9 mi/14 km S of Ashtabula. Livestock and dairying area. Founded c.1804. **3** village (1990 pop. 36), Grant co., N Okla., 8 mi/12.9 km SSW of Medford; 36°43′N 97°47′W. In agr. area. **4** village (1990 pop. 527), Union co., SE S.Dak., 10 mi/16 km, SE of Elk Point, near Big Sioux R., 13 mi/21 km NW of Sioux City, Iowa; 42°36′N 96°33′W.

Jefferson 1 borough (1990 pop. 355), Greene co., SW Pa., 7 mi/11.3 km ENE of Waynesburg, near South Fork Tenmile Creek. Mfg. (apparel, lumber, wood prods.); agr. (sheep; dairying). **2** borough (1990 pop. 675), York co., S Pa., 12 mi/19 km SSW of York. Agr. (apples, soybeans, grain; livestock, poultry; dairying). Codorus State Park and L. Marburg reservoir to SW. **3** borough (1990 pop. 9,533), Allegheny co., W Pa., residential suburb 11 mi/18 km SSE of downtown Pittsburgh, and 2 mi/3.2 km W of Clairton on Peters Creek; 40°17′N 79°55′W.

Jefferson, township (1990 pop. 17,825), Morris co., N N.J., 10 mi/16 km W of Paterson; 41°00′N 74°32′W. Inc. 1809.

Jefferson, Mass.: see HOLDEN.

Jefferson Barracks, former military base, Mo., 10 mi/16 km S of downtown SAINT LOUIS, on Miss. R. Supply depot and training center for deployment of troops in the Amer. West (est. 1826), prominent in Amer. Civil War; now a co. park. Has natl. cemetery, veterans' hosp.

Jefferson City 1 city (1990 pop. 35,481), Cole and Callaway cos., central Mo., on the S bank of the Missouri R., W of mouth of the Osage; ⊙ Mo. and ⊙ Cole co.; 38°34′N 92°11′W. The state govt. is the major employer, but the city, with RR and river facilities, is also the commercial and processing center of an agr. area. It was chosen (1821) for the state capital; the legislature moved there from St. Charles in 1826. Because of divided loyalties and the difficulties of holding the state in the Union, Jefferson City was occupied by Federal troops during the Civil War. The Ital.-Renaissance capitol of Carthage marble (completed 1917) contains murals by Thomas Hart Benton and N. C. Wyeth, and is the site of the Mo. state mus. Mfg. (machinery, construction materials, dairy prods, consumer goods, bldg. materials, furniture, transportation equip., printing). In or near the city are Lincoln Univ. (a historic black state univ.), the state penitentiary and three other facilities, and a natl. cemetery. Regional shopping mall on W side. Major highway and property damage in 1993 floods, esp, in areas to N. Cedar City on N annexed in 1989. Inc. 1825. Commonly referred to as Jeff City. **2** city (1990 pop. 5,494), Jefferson co., E Tenn., near Cherokee Dam (Holston R.), 26 mi/42 km ENE of Knoxville; 36°07′N 83°30′W. Mfg. of springs, canned foods. Seat of Carson-Newman Col. Zinc mines nearby. Settled c.1810; inc. 1900.

Jefferson City, village (1990 pop. 100), Jefferson co., SW central Mont., on Prickly Pear Creek at mouth of Spring Creek, and 15 mi/24 km S of Helena. Gold and silver mines nearby. Helena Natl. Forest to E and W.

Jefferson Davis, county (□ 409 sq mi/1,059 sq km; 1990 pop. 14,051), S central Miss.; ⊙ Prentiss; 31°33′N 89°49′W. Drained by Bowie Creek (forms part of E boundary), other creeks. Agr. (cotton, corn; poultry, cattle, hogs); timber. Formed 1906.

Jefferson Davis, parish (□ 658 sq mi/1,704 sq km; 1990 pop. 30,722), SW La.; ⊙ Jennings; 30°16′N 92°49′W. Bounded E by Bayou Nezpique, SE by Mermentau R.

and Lake Arthur, and Bayou Lacassine forms part of W boundary. Drained in far NW by Calcasieu R. Oil, natural gas; agr. (sorghum, cotton, rice, soybeans, sweet potatoes, sod production; cattle, exotic fowl); fishing (crawfish, catfish); mfg. (apparel; shipbuilding; logging). First oil in La. discovered here (1901). Includes L. Arthur (recreation). Named after the President of the Confederacy. Formed 1910.

Jefferson Island, uninc. village, on one of the FIVE ISLANDS, in Iberia parish, S La., a salt dome rising from prairies just E of L. Peigneur, 9 mi/14 km W of New Iberia; 29°58′N 91°58′W. Low-draft port; fishing (shrimp, crawfish, crabs, fish, catfish); oil and natural-gas deposits. Large rock-salt mine to SE. Scenic gardens to N.

Jefferson, Mount, peak (10,495 ft/3,199 m), at joining of Jefferson (E), Marion (NW), and Linn (SW) co. boundary, NW central Oregon, in Cascade Range, 65 mi/105 km ESE of Salem at center of Mt. Jefferson Wilderness Area.

Jefferson, Mount 1 Nev.: see TOQUIMA RANGE. **2** N.H.: see PRESIDENTIAL RANGE.

Jefferson National Expansion Memorial Park, on the riverfront in downtown St. Louis, E Mo. A natl. park commemorating westward exploration and settlement; includes Gateway Arch and Mus. of Westward Expansion. Authorized 1935. See also SAINT LOUIS, Mo.

Jefferson River, 207 mi/333 km long, SW Mont.; rises in Centennial Mts. as Red Rock R. near Contentintal Divide (Mont.-Idaho state line); flows W through Upper and Lower Red Rock lakes, then NNW past Lima, to Clark Canyon Reservoir where it becomes Beaverhead R.; then flows NNE past Dillon joined by Big Hole and Ruby rivers near Twin Bridges; continues as Jefferson R. N and E to point just NE of Three Forks, where it joins Madison and Gallatin rivers to form the Missouri R. (28 mi/45 km WNW of Bozeman).

Jefferson Springs, resort village, Rutherford co., central Tenn., on Stones R., and 24 mi/39 km SE of Nashville.

Jefferson, Territory of, in U.S. history, region that roughly encompassed the present-day state of Colo., although extending 2° farther S and 1° farther N, organized by its inhabitants (1859–1861), but never given congressional sanction. After a great increase in emigration in the 1850s, settlers in Arapahoe co., Kansas Territory, felt the need to be closer to the seat of govt. They met in convention in Denver on Aug. 1, 1859, to discuss alternatives to the region's status. The 166 delegates present debated the benefits of reorganization as a state or as a territory and submitted the question on Sept. 5 to the public, which voted overwhelmingly for territorial status. Subsequently, Beverly D. Williams was sent as a representative to Congress, which, however, refused his petition. Nevertheless, the constitution of the Territory of Jefferson was adopted on Oct. 24, and the first session of its legislature met on Nov. 7. Robert W. Steele was elected provisional governor. Although illegal, the new govt. coexisted peacefully with the official co. institutions. Laws were passed regarding taxation, and the franchise was denied Native and Afri.-Americans. On Feb. 28, 1861, Congress passed the Organic Act, which created the Territory of Colo. The provisional govt. quickly dismantled, and William Gilpin replaced Steele as governor.

Jefferson Village, uninc. town, Fairfax co., NE Va., residential suburb 8 mi/12.9 km W of Washington, D.C.; 38°52′N 77°10′W.

Jeffersontown, city (1990 pop. 23,221), Jefferson co., N Ky., suburb 12 mi/19 km ESE of downtown Louisville; 38°12′N 85°34′W. Some agr. (potatoes, corn, apples, peaches); nursery prods.; mfg. (plastic prods., consumer goods, food and pharmaceutical processing equip., machinery, restaurant equip.).

Jeffersonville, city (1990 pop. 21,841), ⊙ Clark co., S Ind., at the falls of the Ohio R. opposite Louisville, Ky.; 38°18′N 85°44′W. Together with Clarksville and New Albany (Ind.) and Louisville (Ky.), referred to as Falls City Area. Located in a rich agr. area, the city is a shipping point for farm prods. Mfg. (chemicals, steel and wood prods., oil lubricants, electronic and transportation equip., textiles, construction materials, furniture, consumer goods, agr. machinery); food processing. The city was founded (1802) on the site of Fort Steuben (formerly Fort Finney) by veterans of George Rogers Clark's NW expedition, who were given the land in gratitude for their services. The original town was built according to plans suggested by Thomas Jefferson, after whom it is named. A branch of Ind. Vocational Technical Col. (Ivy Tech) and a U.S. Census Bureau Mapping Center are located here. Inc. 1817.

Jeffersonville 1 town (1990 pop. 1,545), ⊙ Twiggs co., central Ga., 19 mi/31 km SE of Macon; 32°41′N 83°20′W. Mfg. includes lumber, kaolin-clay processing. **2** town (1990 pop. 1,854), Montgomery co., NE central Ky., 7 mi/11.3 km SE of Mt. Sterling, near Slate Creek; 37°58′N 83°49′W. Agr. area (burley tobacco, corn; cattle, poultry; dairying). Mfg. (lumber).

Jeffersonville 1 village (1990 pop. 311), Wayne co., SE Ill., 5 mi/8 km NNW of Fairfield; 38°26′N 88°24′W. In agr. area. Also known as Geff. **2** village (1990 pop. 484), Sullivan co., SE N.Y., 10 mi/16 km W of Liberty; 41°46′N 74°55′W. Mfg. (lumber, wood prods., and machinery). In resort area. **3** village (1990 pop. 1,281), Fayette co., S central Ohio, 10 mi/16 km NW of Washington Court House, in livestock raising and farming area; 39°39′N 83°33′W. **4** uninc. village, West Norriton township, Montgomery co., SE Pa., 16 mi/26 km NW of downtown Philadelphia, and 2 mi/3.2 km NW of Norristown, near Schuylkill R.; 40°07′N 75°22′W. Mfg. (transportation equip.). **5** village (1990 pop. 462), Lamoille co., Vt.: 44°38′N 72°49′W. See CAMBRIDGE.

Jekyll Island, one of the Sea Isls., in Glynn co., SE Ga., just off the S coast of Brunswick, 2 mi/3.2 km to the SE (reached by crossing a causeway); c.7 mi/11.3 km long, 1 mi/1.6 km–2 mi/3.2 km wide; 31°04′N 81°24′W. Georgia's 1st brewery was once located here; hops, barley, and cotton once grown. The isl. residents own their homes but lease the land from the state. Made a state park in 1947, it was formerly a winter-resort colony of large estates, known as Millionaire's Village. The Jekyll Isl. club was once among the most exclusive clubs in the U.S. Famous luminaries living here included the Rockefellers, Pulitzers, Astors, Vanderbilts, Goulds, Morgans, and Jennings. First transcontinental telephone call made here in 1915. The Jekyll Isl. Authority now operates the 240-acre/97-ha historic dist.

Jellico (JEH-li-koh), city (1990 pop. 2,447), Campbell co., NE Tenn., at Ky. line, 45 mi/72 km NNW of Knoxville, in foothills of the Cumberlands; 36°35′N 84°08′W. Coal-mining center; mfg. of brass bearings, apparel; lumbering. U.S. mine-rescue station here. Settled 1795. Indian Mt. State Park just W.

Jellico Creek (JEL-uh-ko), uninc. village (1990 pop. 350), Whitley co., SE Ky., in the Cumberland Mts., 6 mi/9.7 km SW of Williamsburg, on Tenn. state line, opposite Jellico Tenn. In coal-mining area.

Jellicoe (JE-li-ko), village, N central Ont., Canada, near L. Nipigon, 110 mi/177 km NE of Thunder Bay; 49°41′N 87°31′W. Elev. 1,087 ft/331 m. Gold mining.

Jellison, Cape (JEL-uh-suhn), Hancock co., S Maine, peninsula on W shore of Penobscot Bay, and 8 mi/12.9 km NE of Belfast. Fort Point has lighthouse.

Jemez (HAI-mez), pueblo (1990 pop. 1,301), Sandoval co., central N.Mex., in Jemez Indian Reservation (1990 pop. 1,750), 31 mi/50 km NW of Bernalillo on the East Fork of the Jemez R.; 35°38′N 106°47′W. In the 16th cent. there were seven Jemez pueblos; by 1622 there were only two. One of the remaining pueblos was abandoned prior to the Pueblo revolt of 1680. The other took a prominent part in the revolt; the Jemez Native Americans attacked the Spanish repeatedly. In 1694 the pueblo was stormed and captured by the Spanish. Although the Jemez promised to remain at peace, they revolted in 1696, killed the missionaries there, and then fled into Navajo country, where they remained for several years. Some later returned to build (c.1700) the present village. The inhabitants are Pueblos of the Tanoan linguistic stock.

Jemez Canyon Reservoir (HAI-mez), Bernalillo co., N central N.Mex., on Jemez R., near its mouth on the Rio Grande, 20 mi/32 km N of Albuquerque; c.23 mi/37 km long; 35°22′N 106°29′W. Max. capacity 118,818 acre-ft. Intermittent. Formed by Jemez Canyon Dam (131 ft/40 m), built (1953) by the Federal govt. for flood and debris control. Extends into Santa Ana and Zia Indian reservations.

Jemez Mountain, N.Mex.: see VALLE GRANDE MOUNTAINS.

Jemez River (HAI-mez), Sandoval co., N central N.Mex.; rises in several branches near Redondo Peak; flows S, past Jemez Springs village, through Jemez and Zia Indian reservations, and SE to Rio Grande 5 mi/8 km N of Bernalillo; c.60 mi/97 km long.

Jemez Springs (HAI-mez), village (1990 pop. 413), Sandoval co., N central N.Mex., on Jemez R., in Valle Grande Mts., and 45 mi/72 km N of Albuquerque; 35°46′N 106°41′W. Agr. and livestock area. Jemez Pueblo to S and parts of Indian Reservation to S and W; fish hatchery and Fenton L. State Park to NW; Jemez State Monument is here.

Jemison (JE-mi-suhn), town (1990 pop. 1,898), Chilton co., central Ala., 11 mi/18 km NW of Clanton. Lumber; clothing.

Jemseg (JEHM-sehg), village, S N.B., Canada, on short Jemseg stream (connecting Grand L. with St. John R.), and 40 mi/64 km N of St. John.

Jena (JEN-uh), town (1990 pop. 2,626), ⊙ La Salle parish, central La., 34 mi/55 km NE of Alexandria; 31°42′N 92°08′W. In agr. area (cotton, soybeans; cattle, hogs); sawmills; metal industry; mfg. (concrete, fabricated metal prods,, lumber, pulpwood); publishing; oil fields nearby. Inc. 1927.

Jenera (JE-ni-ruh), village (1990 pop. 285), Hancock co., NW Ohio, 11 mi/18 km SSW of Findlay; 40°54′N 83°43′W.

Jenkinjones (JENK-in-jonz), uninc. village (1990 pop. 600), McDowell co., S W.Va., at Va. state line, 10 mi/16 km W of Bluefield, in bituminous-coal region.

Jenkins, county (□ 351 sq mi/909 sq km; 1990 pop. 8,247), E Ga.; ⊙ Millen; 32°47′N 81°58′W. Coastal plain agr. (cotton, corn, soybeans, peanuts, tobacco, wheat); cattle, hogs; lumber and wood prods., and timber area intersected by Ogeechee R. Formed 1905.

Jenkins 1 town (1990 pop. 2,751), Letcher co., SE Ky., 21 mi/34 km SSW of Pikesville, in the Cumberlands, at Va. state line; 37°10′N 82°37′W. Center of important bituminous-coal region. POUND GAP is 2 mi/3.2 km SW, pass through Pine Mt. ridge (2,380 ft/725 m). Mfg. (concrete, crushed stone). **2** uninc. town, Barry co., SW Mo., in the Ozarks, 14 mi/23 km NE of Cassville.

Jenkins, village (1990 pop. 262), Crow Wing co., central Minn., 21 mi/34 km NNW of Brainerd, in lakes and woods region; 46°38′N 94°19′W. Dairying; poultry; oats, alfalfa. Hay L. to E, Whitefish L. to NE.

Jenkinsburg, town (1990 pop. 213), Butts co., central Ga., 4 mi/6.4 km WNW of Jackson; 33°19′N 84°02′W.

Jenkintown (JAIN-kuhn-toun), borough (1990 pop. 4,574), Montgomery co., SE Pa., suburb 10 mi/16 km N of downtown Philadelphia. RR junction. Mfg. (machinery, commercial graphics, packaging, hardware). Seat of Beaver Col. to W (Glenside). Only synagogue designed by Frank Lloyd Wright is here. Settled 1750, inc. 1874.

Jenks, town (1990 pop. 7,493), Tulsa co., NE Okla., residential suburb 10 mi/16 km S of downtown Tulsa, and on Arkansas R.; 36°00′N 95°58′W. Mfg. (asphalt, paper prods.). Oral Roberts Univ. to NE; Jones Airport to N.

Jenner, uninc. village, Sonoma co., W Calif., at mouth of Russian R. on the Pacific Ocean, 22 mi/35 km W of Santa Rosa. Resort area. Dairying; fish, sheep, poultry; nursery prods.; fruit, grain. Sonoma Coast State Beach to S; Armstrong Redwoods State Park and Austin Creek State Recreation Area to NE; Fort Ross and Salt Point state parks, on coast, to NW. Also called Jenner-by-the-Sea.

Jennerstown (JE-nuhrs-toun), borough (1990 pop. 635), Somerset co., SW Pa., 12 mi/19 km SW of Johnstown. Agr. (corn, hay; livestock; dairying). Laurel Mt. village and ski resort to W; Stoughton L. reservoir to NE.

Jennings, county (□ 378 sq mi/979 sq km; 1990 pop. 23,661), SE Ind.; ⊙ Vernon; 39°00′N 85°38′W. Agr. area (corn, wheat, tobacco; cattle, hogs). Mfg. at North Vernon. Timber; limestone quarries. Drained by small Muscatatuck River and by Vernon, Graham, and Sand creeks. Brush Creek State Fish and Wildlife Area, Purdue Southeast Agr. Center, and Selmier State Forest NE of North Vernon. Crosley State Fish and Wildlife Area S of Vernon; part of Muscatatuck Natl. Wildlife Refuge in W. Formed 1816.

Jennings 1 (JEN-eengz), city (1990 pop. 11,305), ⊙ Jefferson Davis parish, SW La., 34 mi/55 km W of Lafayette, near Bayou Nezpique and its entrance to Mermentau R.; 30°13′N 92°40′W. In agr. area (cotton, rice, and small crops); bottling plant; mfg. (drugs, machinery, apparel, water-treatment systems, fabricated metal prods.); transportation equip.; oil field nearby. Barge port on Mermentau R., 5 mi/8 km SE. Inc. 1888. **2** city (1990 pop. 15,905), St. Louis co., E Mo., near Mississippi R., a residential and industrial suburb 7 mi/11.3 km NW of downtown St. Louis; 38°43′N 90°15′W. Mfg. (signs, blowpipes); food prods.

Jennings 1 village (1990 pop. 188), Decatur co., NW Kansas, on Prairie Dog Creek, and 23 mi/37 km SW of Norton; 39°40′N 100°17′W. Agr. and livestock raising. **2** village (1990 pop. 381), Pawnee co., N Okla., 17 mi/27 km SE of Pawnee; 36°10′N 96°34′W. In agr. area; mfg. (food processing, reclamation of lead prods.).

Jennings Lodge, uninc. town (1990 pop. 6,530), Clackamas co., NW Oregon, residential suburb 8 mi/12.9 km SSE of downtown Portland, and 1 mi/1.6 km NW of Gladstone, on Willamette R.; 45°23′N 122°36′W.

Jenny Jump Mountain (c.1,100 ft/335 m), ridge of Appalachians in NW N.J., NW of Belvidere. State forest here.

Jenny Lind Island or **Lind Island**, S Franklin dist., N.W.T., Canada, in Queen Maud Gulf, at SW end of Victoria Strait, off SE Victoria Isl.; 17 mi/27 km long, 10 mi/16 km wide; 68°52′N 101°30′W.

Jens Munk Island, SE Franklin dist., N.W.T., Canada, at head of Foxe Basin, off NW Baffin Isl.; 45 mi/72 km long, 17 mi/27 km wide; 69°42′N 79°40′W.

Jensen, village, Uintah co., NE Utah, on Green R., and 12 mi/19 km SE of Vernal. Oil and natural gas. Hq. for Dinosaur Natl. Monument (N). Stewart Lake Waterfowl Management Area to S (small lake 1 mi/1.6 km W of Green R.).

Jensen Beach (JEN-suhn), town (□ 5 sq mi/13 sq km; 1990 pop. 9,884), St. Lucie co., E central Fla., 7 mi/11.3 km SE of Port St. Lucie; 27°14′N 80°13′W. Mfg includes steel fabrication, stone processing, and metal doors.

Jerauld, county (□ 532 sq mi/1,378 sq km; 1990 pop. 2,425), SE central S.Dak.; ⊙ Wessington Springs; 44°03′N 98°37′W. Agr. area watered by intermittent streams; drained by Firesteel, Sand, and Smith creeks. Corn, wheat; cattle. Formed 1883.

Jerécuaro (he-RE-kwah-ro), city (1990 pop. 5,705) and township, Guanajuato, central Mexico, on affluent of Lerma R., and 20 mi/33 km NE of Acambaro, on RR; 20°09′N 100°31′W. Grain, sugarcane, alfalfa, fruit, vegetables.

Jérémie (zhai-rai-MEE), town (1982 pop. 18,493), ⊙ Grande-Anse dept., SW Haiti, port on NW coast of Jacmel Peninsula, on Gulf of Gonaïves, 120 mi/193 km W of Port-au-Prince; 18°39′N 74°08′W. Port ships produce of fertile region (cacao, coffee, sugarcane, mangoes, logwood, hides); bee-keeping. Fishing; mfg. of soap, cigars; bauxite deposits nearby.

Jérez, Mexico: see JÉREZ DE GARCÍA SALINAS, Zacatecas.

Jérez de García Salinas (HE-res de gar-SEE-ah sah-LEE-nahs), city (1990 pop. 34,319), Zacatecas, N central Mexico, on interior plateau, 30 mi/48 km WSW of Zacatecas; 22°39′N 103°00′W. Mining (tin, mercury) and agr. center (cereals, vegetables, sugarcane, livestock); tanning.

Jericho 1 (JER-i-ko), uninc. town (□ 3 sq mi/7.8 sq km; 1990 pop. 13,141), Nassau co., SE N.Y., on L.I.; 40°47′N 73°32′W. Chiefly residential; some light mfg. **2** town (1990 pop. 4,302), including Jericho village, Chittenden co., NW Vt., 10 mi/16 km E of Burlington; 44°28′N 72°57′W. Settled in late 18th cent.

Jericho, uninc. village (1990 pop. 5), Juab co., central Utah, 20 mi/32 km WNW of Nephi, near Tanner Creek. On RR; sheep and cattle center for wide region. Little Sahara Recreation Area to SW.

Jericho Bay (JER-i-ko), Hancock co., S Maine, bounded W, S, and E by Deer Isl., Isle au Haut, and Swans Isl.; opens NE into Blue Hill Bay.

Jerico Springs, city (1990 pop. 247), Cedar co., W Mo., 24 mi/39 km SE of Nevada; 37°37′N 94°00′W. Soybeans, corn, wheat; cattle. Former health springs resort. Plotted 1882.

Jerimoth Hill (je-REI-moth) (812 ft/247 m), highest point in R.I., in Foster town, near Conn. state line, c.20 mi/32 km W of Providence.

Jermyn (JUHR-min), borough (1990 pop. 2,263), Lackawanna co., NE Pa., 10 mi/16 km NE of Scranton, on Lackawanna R; 41°31′N 75°32′W. Former anthracite-coal center. Mfg. (machinery, burial caskets). Includes community of Nebraska to E. Inc. 1870.

Jerome, county (□ 601 sq mi/1,557 sq km; 1990 pop. 15,138), S Idaho; ⊙ Jerome; 42°42′N 114°16′W. County is opposite Twin Falls. Livestock-raising and irrigated agr. area (sheep, cattle; dairying; corn, barley, wheat; alfalfa, hay; potatoes, apples, sugar beets) bounded S by Snake R. and in Snake R. plain. Shoshone Falls to W (212 ft/65 m); Wilson L. reservoir in E. Formed 1919.

Jerome 1 town (1990 pop. 6,529), ⊙ Jerome co., S Idaho, near Snake R., 12 mi/19 km NNW of Twin Falls; 42°44′N 114°31′W. Elev. 3,600 ft/1,097 m. In irrigated agr. area (grain, vegetables, melons; poultry); dairying; mfg. (paper prods., concrete blocks, wooden trusses, fertilizers). On Snake R. Plain. Laid out 1907, inc. 1909. **2** uninc. town (1990 pop. 1,074), Somerset co., SW Pa., 9 mi/14.5 km SSW of Johnstown; 40°12′N 78°58′W. Agr. includes dairying; livestock; corn, oats, hay, potatoes. Quemahoning Reservoir to SE; Laurel Ridge State Park to NW.

Jerome 1 village, Yavapai co., central Ariz., in Black Hills, 25 mi/40 km NE of Prescott; elev. 5,354 ft/1,632 m. Former copper-mining center; RR terminus. Grew in 1880s after discovery of copper in 1870s; once had 13,000 people; inc. 1899. Jerome State Historic Park is here; located in Prescott Natl. Forest; Mingus Mt. (7,743 ft/2,360 m) to S. **2** village (1990 pop. 47), Drew co., SE Ark., 9 mi/14.5 km S of Dermott, near Bayou Bartholomew; 33°23′N 91°28′W. Cut-off Creek Wildlife Management Area to W. **3** village (1990 pop. 1,206), Sangamon co., central Ill., residential suburb 3 mi/4.8 km SW of downtown Springfield; 39°46′N 89°40′W. In agr. and oil area.

Jeromesville, village (1990 pop. 582), Ashland co., N central Ohio, 8 mi/13 km SE of Ashland, and on Jerome Fork of Mohican R.; 40°48′N 82°11′W. Formerly called Jeromeville.

Jerry City, village (1990 pop. 517), Wood co., NW Ohio, 8 mi/13 km SSE of Bowling Green, in agr. area; 41°15′N 83°36′W.

Jersey, county (□ 377 sq mi/976 sq km; 1990 pop. 20,539), W Ill.; ⊙ Jerseyville; 39°05′N 90°21′W. Bounded S by the Mississippi and W by Illinois R.; drained by Macoupin Creek. Agr. (soybeans, sorghum, apples, corn, wheat; cattle, hogs; dairying); mfg. Resorts on Illinois R. Free ferry across Illinois R. to Calhoun co. Pere Marquette State Park; towns of Elsah and Grafton, on Great R. Road, popular tourist areas; Great R. Road bicycle trail; limestone cliffs noted for bald eagle nesting. Formed 1839.

Jersey, town (1990 pop. 149), Walton co., N central Ga., 7 mi/11.3 km SW of Monroe; 33°43′N 83°48′W.

Jersey City, city (1990 pop. 228,537), ⊙ Hudson co., NE N.J., a port on a peninsula formed by the Hudson and Hackensack rivers and Upper New York Bay, opposite the lower area of Manhattan isl.; 40°42′N 74°03′W. Settled before 1650, inc. as Jersey City 1836. The 2d-largest city in the state and a commercial and industrial center surpassed only by Newark. It is a port of entry and a mfg. center. With 11 mi/18 km of waterfront and significant RR connections, Jersey City is an important transportation terminal point and distribution center. It has RR shops, oil refineries, warehouses, and plants mfg. a diverse assortment of prods., such as chemicals, petroleum and electrical goods, newspapers, textiles, and cosmetics. The city has benefited from its position across from Manhattan, and many Jersey City companies are extensions of those originating in N.Y. city. Further developments have included housing and shopping areas and marinas along the waterfront; other parts of the city, however, remain run-down after years of commercial activity. A large number of ethnic groups throughout U.S. history have settled in Jersey City before venturing out across the country. The area was acquired by Michiel Pauw c.1629. The Dutch soon set up the trading posts of Paulus Hook, Communipaw, and Horsimus. In 1674 the site fell permanently under Br. rule. The fort at Paulus Hook was captured by Light-Horse Harry Lee under Washington's plan, Aug. 19, 1779. Nearby Bergen was a stockaded Du. village dating from before 1620 and had N.J.'s 1st municipal govt., church (Dutch Reformed), and school (1662). Jersey City was consolidated with Bergen and Hudson City in 1869; the town of Greenville was added in 1873. The city's industrial growth began in the 1840s with the arrival of the RR and the improvement of its water transport system. In 1916, Jersey City docks were the scene of the "Black Tom" explosion that caused widespread property damage. The city has a modern medical center and is the seat of Jersey City State Col., Hudson Co. Community Col, and St. Peter's Col. Site of waterfront-renewal project. In Lincoln Park is a statue of Lincoln, built in 1929.

Jersey Homesteads, N.J.: see ROOSEVELT.

Jersey Shore, borough (1990 pop. 4,353), Lycoming co., N central Pa., 7 mi/11.3 km WSW of Williamsport, on West Branch of Susquehanna R. (bridged). Mfg. (tool and die, seed hybridization, fabricated metal prods., machinery, construction materials, corrugated containers, medical supplies, apparel); agr. (grain, potatoes; livestock; dairying). Jersey Shore Airport to E. Little Pine State Park to N; parts of Tiadaghton State Forest to N and S; Pine Creek to W. Settled 1785, inc. 1826.

Jersey Village, town (1990 pop. 4,826), Harris co., SE Texas, residential suburb 14 mi/23 km NW of downtown Houston; 29°53′N 95°34′W. Drained by White Oak Bayou. Oil and natural gas; agr. (cattle, horses; dairying; nurseries, vegetables).

Jerseyville, city (1990 pop. 7,382), ⊙ Jersey co., W Ill., 17 mi/27 km NNW of Alton; 39°07′N 90°19′W. Trade and shipping center in agr. area (apples, corn, wheat; livestock). Plotted 1834, inc. 1855.

Jerusalem 1 village (1990 pop. 144), Monroe co., E Ohio, 11 mi/18 km SSE of Barnesville, in agr. area; 39°51′N 81°05′W. **2** village, Narragansett town, R.I.; 41°22′N 71°31′W. Summer resort.

Jerusalem Mills, Md.: see KINGSVILLE.

Jervis Inlet (JAHR-vis), SW B.C., Canada, NE arm of Malaspina Strait of Strait of Georgia; 51 mi/82 km long, 1 mi/2 km–8 mi/13 km wide; mouth opposite Texada Isl., head near 50°13′N 123°58′W. At mouth is Nelson Isl.; 12 mi/19 km long, 5 mi/8 km wide.

Jessamine (JEZ-uh-muhn), county (□ 174 sq mi/451 sq km; 1990 pop. 30,508), central Ky.; ⊙ Nicholasville; 37°52′N 84°34′W. Bounded SW, S, and SE by Kentucky R; drained by Hickman Creek. Gently rolling upland agr. area in Bluegrass region (burley tobacco, corn, hay, alfalfa, soybeans; cattle, horses, poultry; dairying). Palisades of Kentucky R. (gorge) in SW; Jim Beam Nature Preserve; Daniel Boone's Cave and Camp Nelson Natl. Cemetery in S. Formed 1798.

Jessup (JESS-up), village (1990 pop. 6,537), Howard co., central Md., 14 mi/23 km SW of downtown Baltimore; 39°09′N 76°46′W. Originally named Jessup's Cut in the mid-18th century, shortened to Jessup in 1863. Original site of the Md. House of Correction, medium-security prison est. in 1878. Also site of the Md. State Reformatory for Women and the Perkins Hosp. for male prisoners. Famous for the Baltimore Produce Terminal, housing all the city's produce markets under one roof.

Jessup, borough (1990 pop. 4,605), Lackawanna co., NE Pa., suburb 7 mi/11.3 km NE of Scranton on Lackawanna R.; 41°27′N 75°32′W. Mfg. includes security printing, artificial Christmas trees, fabricated metal prods., apparel, consumer goods. Moosic Mts. to SE; Archbald Pothole State Park to NE. Includes the community of Winton.

Jessup, Lake (JES-uhp), Seminole co., central Fla., 13 mi/21 km NE of Orlando, N end connected with St. Johns R.; c.10 mi/16 km long, 1 mi/1.6 km–3 mi/4.8 km wide.

Jesup 1 (JES-uhp), town (1990 pop. 8,958), ⊙ Wayne co., SE Ga., c.55 mi/89 km SW of Savannah, near Altamaha R.; 31°36′N 81°53′W. Trade and processing center for agr. and timber area; mfg. (apparel, furniture, lumber and pulp, machinery, consumer goods, food processing, plastics, printing and publishing); RR responsible for town's growth. Inc. 1870. **2** town (1990 pop. 2,121), Buchanan co., E Iowa, 10 mi/16 km W of Waterloo; 42°28′N 92°04′W.

Jesup, Fort, La.: see MANY.

Jesús Carranza (hai-SOOS kah-RAHN-zah), town (1990 pop. 3,943), SE Veracruz, Mexico, 6 mi/9 km N of the Chiapas state border, 50 mi/80 km SW of Minatitlán, on RR, and 4 mi/6 km E of Mexico Highway 185 (Trans-Isthmian Highway). Agr. (corn, beans, rice, sesame, chiles, fruits); petroleum resources, precious woods, construction lumber, and cattle. Formerly Santa Lucrecia.

Jesus Island, Canada: see LAVAL.

Jesús María (hai-SOOS mah-REE-ah), city (1990 pop. 14,809) and township, Aguascalientes, N central Mexico, on San Pedro R., and 11 mi/16 km NW of Aguascalientes; 22°00′N 102°20′W. Cereals, fruit, vegetables, tobacco; livestock.

Jesús María 1 (hai-SOOS mah-REE-ah), town (1990 pop. 6,527), Jalisco, central Mexico, 21 mi/32 km E of Atotonilco el Alto. Grain, beans; livestock. **2** town (1990 pop. 1,656), ⊙ El Nayar municipio, in NW Nayarit, Mexico, 16 mi/25 km NW of Arteaga. In Cora Indian–occupied area. Formerly named Nayar.

Jesús Menéndez (ai-SUS men-AIN-daiz), sugar-mill town, Las Tunas prov., E Cuba, near Chaparra Bay (N), 23 mi/37 km NW of Holguín; 21°10′N 76°28′W. Has Cuba's largest sugar central. Formerly called Chaparra.

Jet, village (1990 pop. 272), Alfalfa co., N Okla., 25 mi/40 km NW of Enid; 36°40′N 98°10′W. In agr. area (wheat; livestock, poultry). Great Salt Plains L. reservoir, including Great Salt Plains State Park and Natl. Wildlife Refuge, to N.

Jetmore, town (1990 pop. 850), ⊙ Hodgeman co., SW central Kansas, on Buckner Creek of Pawnee R., and 24 mi/39 km NNE of Dodge City; 38°04′N 99°53′W. Grain; livestock. Co. mus. here; state park nearby. Hodgeman State Fishing L. to SE.

Jewel Cave, monument (☐ 1 sq mi/2.6 sq km), SW S.Dak., authorized 1908, in the Black Hills; 43°44′N 103°51′W. Limestone caves with chambers connected by narrow passages.

Jewell (JOO-uhl), county (☐ 914 sq mi/2,367 sq km; 1990 pop. 4,251), N Kansas, ⊙ Mankato; 39°47′N 98°13′W. Rolling plain area, bordering N on Nebr. Drained by Republican R. in extreme NE and its tributaries; White Rock Creek in N. Wheat, corn, sorghum, alfalfa; hogs, sheep, cattle. Formed 1870.

Jewell, town, Hamilton co., central Iowa, 19 mi/31 km N of Ames. In livestock and grain area; pork processing. Plotted 1880.

Jewell (JOO-uhl), village (1990 pop. 529), Jewell co., N Kansas, 9 mi/14.5 km SSE of Mankato; 39°40′N 98°09′W. In grain and livestock area.

Jewett 1 village (1990 pop. 194), Cumberland co., SE central Ill., 5 mi/8 km S of Toledo; 39°12′N 88°14′W. In agr. area. **2** resort village (1990 pop. 200), Greene co., SE N.Y., in Catskill Mts., 23 mi/37 km E of Catskill; 42°15′N 74°13′W. **3** village (1990 pop. 778), Harrison co., E Ohio, 6 mi/10 km N of Cadiz, and on small Conotton Creek; 40°22′N 81°00′W. Coal mining; sawmilling. Laid out 1851, inc. 1886. **4** village (1990 pop. 668), Leon co., E central Texas, c.60 mi/97 km ESE of Waco; 31°21′N

96°09′W. RR junction in agr. area. Oil and gas; mfg. (industrial glass, steel bars). L. Limestone reservoir to W.

Jewett City, Conn.: see GRISWOLD.

JFK (John F. Kennedy) International Airport (☐ 8 sq mi/20.7 sq km), S Queens borough of N.Y. city, SE N.Y., on NE side of Jamaica Bay; 40°34′N 73°48′W. This is 1 of 3 major airports serving metropolitan N.Y. city. Part of the Port Authority of N.Y. and N.J.'s facilities and operations. Opened in 1948 as Idlewild Airport, much of it was built on filled marshland of Jamaica Bay. A major employer in the area, generating roughly 78,000 on-site and another 98,000 off-site jobs. Has largest U.S. Customs facility in nation. In 1994, together with the Port Authority's La Guardia and Newark Internatl. Airports, handled over 25% (by value) of the country's internatl. air-cargo traffic. Major exports include machinery, fish and fish prods., and printed materials; major imports include apparel, footwear, fresh and frozen vegetables, and machinery. Exports are shipped mostly to the U.K., Japan, and Germany. In 1994, airport served 9.7 million passengers (2.2% of nation's total); nationally ranked 11th in passenger volume.

Jibacoa del Norte (hee-buh-KO-uh dail NOR-tai), town, La Habana prov., W Cuba, on RR, and 30 mi/48 km E of Havana; 23°09′N 81°53′W. In sugar-growing region.

Jicarilla Mountains (hi-kuh-REE-uh), S central N.Mex., N range of Sacramento Mts., in Lincoln co., NE of Carrizozo; lies in part of Lincoln Natl. Forest. Highest peak is Carrizo Peak (9,650 ft/2,941 m). Gold is mined.

Jico, Mexico: see XICO.

Jiguaní (hee-gwah-NEE), town, Granma prov., E Cuba, on Central Highway, on RR, and 13 mi/21 km E of Bayamo; 20°22′N 76°26′W. Dairying center. Also produces sugarcane, fruit, coffee, cacao. Granite quarrying. In its picturesque surroundings are ruins of a colonial castle and the Pepú caves.

Jigüey Bay (hee-GWAI), shallow inlet of Old Bahama Channel, off Camagüey prov., E Cuba, bet. Cayo Romano (isl.) and Cuba, 30 mi/48 km E of Morón; c.30 mi/48 km long NW–SE, 6 mi/9.7 km wide; 22°05′N 78°00′W. Receives Caonao R. and small Jigüey R.

Jilotepec (hee-LO-te-pek), town (1990 pop. 2,826), Veracruz, E Mexico, in Sierra Madre Oriental, 6 mi/9.7 km N of Xalapa Enríquez; 19°55′N 99°30′W. Elev. 6,201 ft/1,890 m. Corn, coffee, fruit.

Jilotepec, Mexico: see JILOTEPEC DE MOLINA ENRÍQUEZ.

Jilotepec de Abasolo, Mexico: see JILOTEPEC DE MOLINA ENRÍQUEZ.

Jilotepec de Molina Enríquez (hee-LO-te-pek dai mo-LEE-nah en-REE-kez), city (1990 pop. 8,209) and township, ⊙ Jilotepec municipio, Mexico state, central Mexico, 40 mi/64 km NW of Mexico city. Cereals, fruit, livestock. Formerly Jilotepec de Abasolo.

Jilotlán de los Dolores (hee-lo-TLAWN dai los do-LO-res), town (1990 pop. 1,205), Jalisco, central Mexico, 45 mi/72 km E of Colima. Isolated small farming community in the Transverse Volcanic Axis. Sugarcane, corn, fruit.

Jilotzingo, Mexico: see SANTA ANA JILOTZINGO.

Jim Hogg, county (☐ 1,136 sq mi/2,942 sq km; 1990 pop. 5,109), extreme S Texas; ⊙ Hebbronville; 27°03′N 98°40′W. Oil and natural gas; mainly cattle and ranching; some agr. (sorghum). Formed 1913.

Jim Lake, reservoir (☐ 27 sq mi/70 sq km), Stutsman co., E central N.Dak., on James R., 3 mi/5 km N of Jamestown; 46°56′N 98°43′W. Max. capacity 379,636 acre-ft. Formed by dam (110 ft/33 m high), built (1953) by the Bureau of Reclamation for irrigation; also used for flood control, recreation, and water supply. N part of reservoir within Arrowroot Natl. Wildlife Refuge.

Jim Thorpe, borough (1990 pop. 5,048), ⊙ Carbon co., E Pa., 22 mi/35 km NW of Allentown on Lehigh R.; 40°52′N 75°44′W. Agr. includes dairying. Borough created in the late 1950s by merging Mauch Chunk (the

former co. seat) and East Mauch Chunk boroughs. Borough named for Okla. football legend Jim Thorpe (1888–1953). State parks and reservoirs nearby.

Jim Wells, county (☐ 868 sq mi/2,248 sq km; 1990 pop. 37,679), S Texas; ⊙ Alice; 27°43′N 98°05′W. Bounded NE by Nueces R. (including dam of L. Corpus Christi) and drained by small Los Olmos, Agua Dulce and San Diego creeks. Large oil, natural gas production; caliche. Agr. includes grain sorghum, wheat, corn, vegetables; cotton; cattle, hogs; dairying. Lipantitlan State Park in NE corner. Formed 1911.

Jim Woodruff Dam, Ga. and Fla.: see SEMINOLE, LAKE.

Jimaguayú (hee-mah-gwah-YOO), small agr. town, Camagüey prov., E central Cuba, 2 mi/3.2 km from Central Highway, and 9 mi/14.5 km SE of Camagüey city; 21°18′N 77°52′W.

Jimaní (hee-mah-nee), town (1993 pop. 3,904), Bahoruco prov., SW Dominican Republic, bet. L. Enriquillo and Haiti border, 30 mi/48 km W of Neiba; 18°28′N 71°50′W. Coffee, fruit, timber. In 1949, became capital of newly formed Independencia prov.

Jiménez (hee-ME-nes), city (1990 pop. 28,773) and township, Chihuahua, N Mexico, on plateau E of Sierra Madre Occidental, on Florido R., and 125 mi/201 km SE of Chihuahua on Mexico Highway 49; 27°09′N 104°54′W. Elev. 4,531 ft/1,381 m. Mining center (fluorspar, mercury); silver, gold, lead, copper deposits; cotton gins. The region nearby is known for large number of meteorites, some of them discovered by the Spaniards in 16th and 17th cent., and now exhibited in School of Mines in Mexico city. Also Ciudad Jimenez.

Jiménez (hee-ME-nes), town (1990 pop. 963), Coahuila, N Mexico, near the Rio Grande (Texas border), 27 mi/43 km NW of Piedras Negras on Mexico Highway 2; 29°05′N 100°40′W. Elev. 755 ft/230 m. Wheat, bran; cattle. Istle fibers, candelilla wax.

Jiménez 1 Mexico: see VILLA JIMÉNEZ. **2** Mexico: see SANTANDER JIMÉNEZ.

Jiménez del Teul (hee-ME-nes del TE-ool), town (1990 pop. 1,555), Zacatecas, N central Mexico, near Durango border, 59 mi/95 km W of Fresnillo. An isolated town S of Chalchihuites Mining Dist. Maguey, corn; livestock raising.

Jiménez, Villa, Mexico: see VILLA JIMÉNEZ.

Jimenoa (hee-mai-NO-ah), falls and hydroelectric project, La Vega prov., central Dominican Republic, on affluent of the Yaque del Norte, just E of Jarabacoa, 10 mi/16 km SW of La Vega.

Jimmy Carter National Historic Site, SW Ga., in Plains. Carter home and other bldgs. and exhibits associated with the 39th President's life are showcased here. Visitor center. Authorized 1987.

Jiquilpan de Járez (hee-KEEL-pahn dai HWAH-res), city (1990 pop. 24,731) and township, Michoacán, central Mexico, on central plateau, 60 mi/97 km SE of Guadalajara; 19°57′N 102°42′W. Agr. center (cereals, sugarcane, tobacco, beans, fruit; livestock); flour milling.

Jiquipilas (hee-kee-PEE-las), town (1990 pop. 7,731), Chiapas, S Mexico, on N slopes of Sierra Madre, 36 mi/58 km W of Tuxtla Gutierrez and just S of Mexico Highway 190 (Inter-Amer. Highway). Corn, beans, sugarcane; fruit.

Jiquipilco (hee-kee-PEEL-ko), town (1990 pop. 1,232), Mexico state, central Mexico, 20 mi/32 km N of Tolca de Lerdo. Agr. center (cereals, fruit; livestock).

Jitotol de Zaragoza (hee-TO-tol dai sah-rah-GO-sah), town (1990 pop. 2,400), ⊙ Jitotol municipio, Chiapas, S Mexico, in N spur of Sierra Madre del Sur, 27 mi/43 km NE of Tuxtla Gutiérrez on Mexico Highway 195; 18°01′N 92°52′W. Cereals, tobacco, fruit. Zoque and Tzotzil Maya speakers in rural areas.

Jiutepec (hee-DU-te-pek), town (1990 pop. 82,845), Morelos, central Mexico, 5 mi/8 km SE of Cuernavaca. Sugarcane, rice, fruit; livestock.

Jo Daviess (jo-DAI-viss), county (☐ 618 sq mi/1,601 sq km; 1990 pop. 21,821), extreme NW Ill., bounded N by Wis. state line and W by the Mississippi (here forming Iowa state line); ⊙ Galena; 42°21′N 90°12′W. Drained by Apple, Plum, and Galena rivers.

Agr. (cattle, hogs, sheep, oats, alfalfa; dairying). Lead and zinc mines. Mfg.: dairy prods., metal prods., fertilizer, iron. Includes hilly area near Wis. line; Charles Mound (1,235 ft/376 m), highest point in Ill., is here. Contains Apple R. Canyon State Park, portion of Upper Mississippi R. Natl. Wildlife Refuge and U.S. Grant Home State Historical Site. Formed 1827. Savanna Army Depot in SW on Mississippi R. Tourism a major industry.

Joanna, uninc. town (1990 pop. 1,735), Lauren co., at SW edge of section of Sumter National Forest; 34°25′N 81°48′W. Mfg. includes cotton insulation prods. Agr. includes timber, dairying, poultry, livestock, grain.

Joannès (zho-ah-NEHS), village, W Que., Canada, 15 mi/24 km E of Rouyn; gold mining.

Joaquin, town (1990 pop. 805), Shelby co., E Texas, near the Sabine R. (La. boundary), headwaters of Toledo Bend Reservoir, opposite Logansport, La. (bridge), 45 mi/72 km SSE of Marshall; 31°58′N 94°02′W. Timber; oil and gas; poultry, cattle; vegetables. Sabine Natl. Forest to SE.

Job (JAHB), uninc. village (1990 pop. 40), Randolph co., E central W.Va., 15 mi/24 km ESE of Elkins, on Gandy Creek, in Monongahela Natl. Forest.

Jobabo (ho-BAH-bo), town, Las Tunas prov., E Cuba, near Jobabo R., 22 mi/35 km WSW of Victoria de las Tunas; 20°55′N 77°17′W. Home of Peru sugar mill.

Jobabo River (ho-BAH-bo), 48 mi/77 km long, in Las Tunas prov., E Cuba; flows S to the swamps at head of the Gulf of Guacanayabo; 20°50′N 77°15′W.

Jobos (HO-bos), village, S P.R., 3 mi/4.8 km SW of Guayama. Port of entry. Former sugar milling village. Puerto Jobos is 1.5 mi/2.4 km W.

Jocassee (jo-KAS-ee), village, Oconee co., NW S.C., in Blue Ridge Mts., 33 mi/53 km WNW of Greenville. Jocassee Dam is E.

Jocassee, Lake, reservoir, on Pickens-Oconee co. border, NW S.C., on Seneca (Keowee) R., 30 mi/48 km WNW of Greenville; 8 mi/12.9 km long, 3 mi/4.8 km wide; 34°58′N 82°55′W. Max. capacity 1,315,670 acre-ft. Formed by Jocassee Dam (385 ft/117 m high), built (1973) by the Duke Power Co. for power generation. Bounded W by Sumter Natl. Forest; Devils Fork State Park on SW shore.

Jocotepec (ho-KO-te-pek), town (1990 pop. 13,143), Jalisco, W Mexico, near W shore of L. Chapala, 27 mi/43 km SSW of Guadalajara, and just off Mexico Highway 15. Beans, grain, fruit; livestock.

Jocotitlán (ho-ko-teet-LAHN), town (1990 pop. 5,257), Mexico state, central Mexico, 30 mi/48 km N of Toluca de Lerdo. Cereals; livestock.

Joe B. Hoggsett Dam, Texas: see CEDAR CREEK RESERVOIR.

Joffre, Mount (JAH-fuhr) (11,316 ft/3,449 m), SE B.C., Canada, on Alta. border, in Rocky Mts., 50 mi/80 km SSE of Banff; 50°31′N 115°14′W.

Joggins (JAH-ginz), town, N N.S., Canada, on Chignecto Bay, 16 mi/26 km SW of Amherst; 45°42′N 64°26′W. Coal mining.

Johannesburg, uninc. village, Kern co., S central Calif., 50 mi/80 km NW of Barstow, in Rand Mts., Mojave Desert. Silver, tungsten, gold mines. Part of China Lake Naval Weapons Center to E; Cuddeback L. (dry) to SE.

John D. Rockefeller, Jr. Memorial Parkway, Teton co., NW Wyo., scenic 8.2 mi/13.2 km corridor between Yellowstone (N) and Grand Teton (S) natl. parks, commemorating Rockefeller's role in the creation of many natl. parks, including Grand Teton. Authorized 1972.

John Day, town (1990 pop. 1,836), Grant co., NE central Oregon, on John Day R., at mouth of Canyon Creek, 90 mi/145 km S of Pendleton; 44°25′N 118°57′W. Chromite deposits nearby. Site of Kam Wah Chung Mus. Parts of Malheur Natl. Forest to N and S, including Strawberry Mt. Wilderness Area to SE (Strawberry Range). John Day Fossil Beds Natl. Monument (Sheep Rock Unit) 35 mi/56 km WNW. Clyde Holliday State Park to W.

John Day, river, 281 mi/452 km long, rising in E Grant co., in Blue Mts., NE Oregon, flows W past the town of John Day, N to the Columbia R., past John Day

Fossil Beds Natl. Monument, 27 mi/43 km ENE of The Dalles, just upstream (E) of John Day Dam. The lower ½ of the river is in John Day River State Scenic Waterway. Unnavigable, the river is used to irrigate vegetable farms.

John Day Fossil Beds National Monument (□ 14,014 sq mi/36,296 sq km), Grant and Wheeler cos., N central Oregon. Consists of Sheep Rock, Painted Hills, and Clarno units. Sheep Rock Unit on John Day R., 35 mi/56 km WNW of John Day. Clarno Unit on John Day R., 10 mi/16 km SW of Fossil Beds. Painted Hills Unit on Ridge Creek, 65 mi/105 km WNW of John Day. Rich fossil remains extend over 5 geological epochs, Eocene through Pleistocene. Authorized 1974.

John Day Lock and Dam oregon/washington: see UMATILLA, LAKE.

John F. Kennedy Center for the Performing Arts Memorial, Washington, D.C., opened 1971. Site of cultural performances in its theater, concert hall, and opera house.

John Fitzgerald Kennedy Historic Site, Brookline, E Mass., birthplace and early boyhood home of President John F. Kennedy. Authorized 1967.

John H. Kerr Reservoir (□ 78 sq mi/202 sq km), S central Va. (Halifax and Mecklenburg cos.) and N central N.C. (Vance co.), on Roanoke R., 64 mi/103 km SW of Petersburg (Va.); 36°36′N 78°18′W. Max. capacity 3,363,500 acre-ft. Has 2 main branches. Formed by John H. Kerr Dam (144 ft/44 m high), built (1953) by Army Corps of Engineers for power generation; also used for water supply, recreation, and as a fish and wildlife pond. Kerr Lake State Recreational Area (N.C.) and 2 Va. state parks here.

John James Audubon State Park (□ 1 sq mi/ 2.6 sq km), Henderson co., W Ky., near the Ohio R., 3 mi/4.8 km NE of downtown Henderson, in city of Henderson. Memorial to famed naturalist and painter; includes migratory-bird refuge, mus., camping facilities, nature center.

John Martin Reservoir (□ 27.5 sq mi/71.2 sq km), Bent co., SE Colo., on Arkansas R., in John Martin Reservoir State Wildlife Area, 15 mi/24 km E of Las Animas; 12 mi/19 km long, 2 mi/3.2 km wide; 39°35′N 104°54′W. Formed by John Martin Dam (153 ft/47 m high, 2.6 mi/ 4.2 km long), built (1948) of concrete and earthfill for flood control and irrigation. Formerly Caddoa Reservoir.

John Muir National Historic Site, Contra Costa co., W Calif.; 339 acres/137 ha. John Muir House and Martinez Adobe, 1 mi/1.6 km S of Contra Costa, at Martinez, on Alhambra Avenue, commemorating contributions of John Muir to conservation and literature. Authorized 1964.

John Muir Trail, Calif., mountain footpath, c.200 mi/ 322 km long, follows crest of the Sierra Nevada from Yosemite Natl. Park (N) to Mt. Whitney in Sequoia Natl. Park (S). Now coincides with portion of Pacific Crest Natl. Scenic Trail.

John Redmond Lake, reservoir (□ 15 sq mi/39 sq km), Coffey co., E central Kansas, on Grand Neosho R., in Flint Hills Natl. Wildlife Refuge, 23 mi/37 km SE of Emporia; 38°15′N 95°46′W. Max. capacity 630,250 acre-ft. Formed by John Redmond Lake Dam (74 ft/23 m high), built (1964) by Army Corps of Engineers for flood control; also used for water supply and recreation. John Redmond State Park near dam. Also known as John Redmond Reservoir.

John W. Flannagan Reservoir, Dickenson co., extreme SW Va., in Pound R., 25 mi N of Norton, near Ky. state line, on boundary of Jefferson Natl. Forest; 37°14′N 82°20′W. Dam is 216 ft/66 m high, built in 1971 by the Army Corps of Engineers for flood control. Reservoir used for recreational purposes; has a max. water storage capacity of 145,700 acre-ft.

Johns, Ala.: see NORTH JOHNS.

Johns Island, Charleston co., S S.C., one of Sea Isls., c.5 mi/8 km WSW of Charleston; c.11 mi/18 km long, 5 mi/8 km–10 mi/16 km wide. Mfg. of neon signs and agr. chemicals; agr. includes vegetables, sweet potatoes, watermelons.

Johnsburg 1 village (1990 pop. 4,631), McHenry co., NE Ill., suburb 40 mi/64 km NW of downtown Chicago, 4 mi/6.4 km NE of McHenry; 42°22′N 88°14′W. Located on Fox R. at its outflow from L. Pistakee. **2** village (1990 pop. 300), Warren co., E N.Y., in Adirondack Mts., 26 mi/42 km NW of Glen Falls; 43°38′N 74°02′W. Resort. Lumbering.

Johnson 1 county (□ 682 sq mi/1,766 sq km; 1990 pop. 18,221), NW Ark.; ⊙ Clarksville, 35°34′N 93°27′W. Bounded S by Arkansas R. (L. Dardanelle in E part); drained by small Mulberry R. and Piney Creek. Agr. (soybeans; cattle, hogs, poultry [turkeys, chickens]). Coal mines; timber. Part of Ozark Natl. Forest is in N ½ of co. Formed 1833. **2** county (□ 313 sq mi/811 sq km; 1990 pop. 8,329), E central Ga.; ⊙ Wrightsville; 32°42′N 82°40′W. Bounded W by Oconee R.; drained by Ohoopee R. Coastal plain agr. area (cotton, corn, potatoes, soybeans, peanuts, fruit); mfg. of apparel, textiles; lumber and millwork, wholesale trade. Formed 1858. **3** county (□ 348 sq mi/901 sq km; 1990 pop. 11,347), S Ill.; ⊙ Vienna; 37°27′N 88°52′W. Agr. area (fruit, sorghum, wheat; cattle; dairy prods.). Lumbering; wood prods. Drained by Cache R.; includes part of Shawnee Natl. Forest (N); Ferne Clyffe State Park in NW; L. Egypt Recreational Area in N. Formed 1812. One of 17 Ill. counties to retain southern-style commission form of co. govt. **4** county (□ 321 sq mi/831 sq km; 1990 pop. 88,109), central Ind.; ⊙ Franklin; 39°29′N 86°06′W. Drained by West Fork of White R. and tributaries of the East Fork of White R. Part of Indianapolis metropolitan area; urban growth in N, esp. around Greenwood. Agr. (wheat, corn, soybeans, vegetables; dairy prods.; hogs, cattle; mfg. at Franklin, Greenwood, Edinburgh. Atterbury State Fish and Wildlife Area and part of Camp Atterbury military reservation in S. Formed 1822. **5** county (□ 623 sq mi/1,614 sq km; 1990 pop. 96,119), E Iowa; ⊙ Iowa City; 41°40′N 91°32′W. Prairie agr. area (corn; hogs, cattle, poultry) drained by Iowa R.; limestone quarries. Mfg. at Iowa City and Coralville. Includes L. Macbride State Park in N; Coralville Reservoir (Iowa R.), N of Iowa City. Formed 1839. **6** county (□ 480 sq mi/1,243 sq km; 1990 pop. 355,054), E Kansas; ⊙ Olathe; 38°52′N 94°52′W. Rolling plain area with low hills; bounded N by Kansas R., E by Mo. Agr. in far S and W (wheat, soybeans, hay; cattle). Mfg. (sand and gravel, oil and gas, paper prods., printing, chemicals, plastics prods., glass prods., electronic equip.). Scattered oil and gas fields. Fast-growing suburban area in NE, adjacent to Kansas City, Kansas and Kansas City, Mo. Formed 1855. **7** county (□ 263 sq mi/ 681 sq km; 1990 pop. 23,248), E Ky.; ⊙ Paintsville, 37°51′N 82°51′W. Drained by Levisa Fork. Agr. area in foothills of the Cumberland Mts. (burley tobacco, hay; some cattle and hogs). Coal mines, oil wells. Part of Paintsville L. reservoir in W; Paintsville L. State Park in W center. Formed 1843. **8** county (□ 826 sq mi/ 2,139 sq km; 1990 pop. 42,514), W central Mo.; ⊙ Warrensburg; 38°45′N 93°48′W. Drained by Blackwater R. Corn, wheat, sorghum, soybeans, hay, grapes; cattle, horses. Former coal mines, stone quarries, clay pits. Mfg. at Warrensburg, Holden, Kingsville. Knob Noster State Park and Whiteman Air Base in E. Formed 1834. **9** county (□ 376 sq mi/974 sq km; 1990 pop. 4,673), SE Nebr.; ⊙ Tecumseh; 40°24′N 96°16′W. Agr. area drained by branches of North Fork Big Nemaha R. Cattle, hogs, poultry; corn, sorghum, soybean, wheat; dairying; poultry prods., feed. Formed 1856. **10** county (□ 299 sq mi/774 sq km; 1990 pop. 13,766), extreme NE Tenn.; ⊙ Mountain City; 36°28′N 81°52′W. Bounded N by Va., E and SE by N.C.; Stone Mts. lie along N.C. state line; traversed by Iron Mts.; drained by Watauga R. Includes parts of Watauga Reservoir and Cherokee Natl. Forest. Lumbering, agr. (tobacco, vegetables, fruit); livestock; granite quarries. Formed 1836. **11** county (□ 734 sq mi/1,901 sq km; 1990 pop. 97,165), N central Texas; ⊙ Cleburne; 32°22′N 97°21′W. Bounded SW by Brazos R.; drained by tributaries of the Brazos (in W), including Nolan Creek, and the Trinity (in E). Shipping, processing center. Rich agr. area: cotton, wheat, grain sorghum, corn, silage, hay;

extensive dairying; cattle, hogs, horses. Limestone, sand and gravel. Mfg., processing at Cleburne. Cleburne State Park in SW; L. Pat Cleburne in SW center. Formed 1854. **12** county (□ 4,174 sq mi/10,811 sq km; 1990 pop. 6,145), N central Wyo.; ⊙ Buffalo; 44°02′N 106°34′W. Agr. and coal-mining region; watered by Powder R. and Clear and Crazy Woman creeks. Sugar beets, hay, alfalfa; sheep, cattle; timber; sand and gravel; oil, uranium, coal). Part of Bighorn Natl. Forest in NW, including part of Cloud Peak Wilderness Area; part of Bighorn Mts. in W ⅓ of co. Small L. De Smet Reservoir in N. Formed 1875.

Johnson (JAWN-son), town (1990 pop. 3,156), including Johnson village, Lamoille co., N central Vt., on Lamoille R. and 5 mi/8 km NW of Hyde Park; 44°38′N 72°40′W. Wood prods., woolens, sand and gravel; talc mills. Johnson State Col. here. Settled 1784.

Johnson 1 village (1990 pop. 46), Big Stone co., W Minn., 20 mi/32 km NNE of Ortonville; 45°34′N 96°17′W. Grain; mfg. (feeds). **2** village (1990 pop. 323), Nemaha co., SE Nebr., 8 mi/12.9 km W of Auburn; 40°24′N 96°00′W. In agr. region. **3** village (1990 pop. 196), Pottawatomie co., central Okla., 5 mi/8 km NE of Shawnee, on North Canadian R.; 35°24′N 96°50′W. Agr. area.

Johnson City, city (1990 pop. 49,381), Wash. and Carter cos., extreme NE Tenn., 20 mi/32 km SE of Kingsport, 36°20′N 82°23′W. In rich hardwood, mineral (zinc and iron ore deposits), and agr. (strawberries, tobacco, corn) area. Diverse mfg. includes fabricated metal prods., textiles, furniture, wood prods. East Tenn. State Univ. is here. Inc. 1869.

Johnson City 1 town (1990 pop. 1,348), ⊙ Stanton co., SW Kansas, 50 mi/80 km SW of Garden City; 37°34′N 101°45′W. Elev. 3,330 ft/1,015 m. In wheat area; feeds, fertilizers. **2** town (1990 pop. 932), ⊙ Blanco co., central Texas, 40 mi/64 km W of Austin, on Pedernales R.; 30°16′N 98°24′W. Elev. 1,197 ft/365 m. Mfg. The Lyndon B. Johnson National Historic Site includes Johnson's boyhood home and an information center. His birthplace and the family cemetery where he is buried are 15 mi/24 km W at Stonewall, at the LBJ ranch. Pedernales Falls State Park to E.

Johnson City 1 village (□ 4 sq mi/10.4 sq km; 1990 pop. 16,890), Broome co., S N.Y., in tri-city area including Endicott and Binghamton; 42°07′N 75°57′W. Noted for its Endicott-Johnson shoes; mfg. also includes computer equip., electrical equip., fabricated metal prods., and photographic equip. Originally called Lestershire, the area remained rural until a shoe company built a factory here in 1890. The name was changed in 1916. Inc. 1892. **2** village (1990 pop. 586), Clackamas co., NW Oregon, residential suburb, 8 mi/12.9 km SSE of downtown Portland and 1 mi/1.6 km NE of Gladstone, on Kellogg Creek; 45°23′N 122°34′W.

Johnson Creek, town (1990 pop. 1,259), Jefferson co., S Wis., on small Johnson Creek, and 8 mi/12.9 km S of Watertown; 43°04′N 88°46′W. In dairying region. Ships dairy prods., eggs; mfg. (grain processing, rubber prods., furniture, consumer goods). Aztalan State Park to W; Glacial Drumlin State Trail passes to S.

Johnsonburg, village, Warren co., NW N.J., 9 mi/14.5 km SW of Newton, in hilly region.

Johnsonburg, borough (1990 pop. 3,350), Elk co., N central Pa., 32 mi/51 km S of Bradford, on Clarion R.; 41°20′N 78°40′W. Mfg. (fabricated metal prods., paper prods.); natural gas; agr. (grain; livestock; dairying); timber. Allegheny Natl. Forest to W; Bendingo State Park to NE. Settled 1810, laid out 1888.

Johnsonville, town (1990 pop. 1,415), Florence co., E S.C., 30 mi/48 km SSE of Florence, near Lynches R; 33°49′N 79°27′W. Hogs, chickens; grain, cotton, tobacco; timber.

Johnsonville, village (1990 pop. 68), Wayne co., SE Ill., 14 mi/23 km NW of Fairfield; 38°31′N 88°32′W. In agr. area; oil wells.

Johnston 1 county (□ 795 sq mi/2,059 sq km; 1990 pop. 81,306), central N.C.; ⊙ Smithfield; 35°31′N 78°22′W. On coastal plain; drained by Neuse R.; source of South R. in SW. Agr. (tobacco, cotton, corn, wheat, oats, barley, soybeans, hay, potatoes, sweet potatoes; chickens, turkeys, cattle, hogs); timber (pine, gum). Cotton and lumber milling, tobacco processing. Mfg. at Smithfield, Selma and Clayton. Bentonville Battleground State Historical Site in S; Clemmons Educational State Forest in NW. Formed 1746. **2** county (□ 658 sq mi/1,704 sq km; 1990 pop. 10,032), S Okla.; ⊙ Tishomingo; 34°18′N 96°39′W. Bounded on S in part by L. Texoma (Washita R. arm); drained by Blue and Washita rivers. Cattle raising; dairying; peanuts. Sand and gravel pits. Part of Tishamingo Natl. Wildlife Refuge on arm of L. Texoma in S. Formed 1907.

Johnston 1 town (1990 pop. 4,702), Polk co., central Iowa, near Des Moines R., suburb, 7 mi/11.3 km NW of downtown Des Moines; 41°41′N 93°42′W. Mfg. (machinery, concrete; sand and gravel processing). Saylorville Dam to N; Margo Frankel Woods State Park to E. U.S. Camp Dodge nearby was active in World War II. **2** town (1990 pop. 26,542), Providence co., N central R.I., a suburb of Providence; 41°50′N 71°31′W. Among its manufactures are jewelry, textiles, and fabricated metals. Johnston is the home of several insurance companies. Its many historic landmarks include the Clemence-Irons House (c.1680). Named for Augustus Johnston, Attorney General for the county from 1758–1776. Set off from Providence and inc. 1759. **3** town (1990 pop. 2,688), Edgefield co., W S.C., 10 mi/16 km ENE of Edgefield; 33°49′N 81°48′W. Mfg. of cotton prods.; agr. includes livestock; dairying; grain, cotton, soybeans.

Johnston City, city (1990 pop. 3,706), Williamson co., S Ill., 7 mi/11.3 km N of Marion; 37°49′N 88°55′W. In bituminous-coal mining and agr. area (corn, wheat, hay). Inc. 1896.

Johnston Island, atoll, central Pacific, c.700 mi/1,100 km SW of Honolulu; c.3,000 ft/900 m long and c.600 ft/183 m wide. It was discovered by Americans in 1796 (or the British in 1807) and claimed by the U.S. in 1858. It was not, however, included in Hawaii statehood, but became an uninc. territory of the U.S. The U.S. Navy took over the atoll in 1934 and used it as a seaplane and submarine base during World War II. Operational control was given to the Defense Nuclear Agency in 1958, and the U.S. conducted a series of high altitude nuclear tests here during the 1950s and 1960s. It is still designated as a standby site should the U.S. resume testing. The Johnston Atoll Chemical Agent Disposal System (JACADS), a facility for the stockpiling and incineration of chemical weapons, is located here. The U.S. Army has used the island as a site for the destruction of chemical weapons since 1990. A bird reservation since 1923, the atoll was declared a Pacific Isls. Natl. Wildlife Refuge in 1974.

Johnston Station, Iowa: see JOHNSTON.

Johnstone Lake (□ 123 sq mi/319 sq km), S Sask., Canada, 22 mi/35 km SW of Moose Jaw; 20 mi/32 km long, 12 mi/19 km wide.

Johnstone Strait, SW B.C., Canada, joins Queen Charlotte Strait with Strait of Georgia, via Discovery Passage, separating Vancouver Isl. from mainland; 70 mi/113 km long, 2 mi/3 km–3 mi/5 km wide. Mainland shore deeply indented. Alert Bay is at W entrance.

Johnstons Station or **Johnston Station**, village, Pike co., SW Miss., on the Bogue Chitto, and 7 mi/11.3 km N of McComb.

Johnstown 1 city (□ 4 sq mi/10.4 sq km; 1990 pop. 9,058), ⊙ Fulton co., E central N.Y.; 43°00′N 74°22′W. Its leather-glove industry dates back to 1800; knitted goods, a variety of other leather goods, molded plastics, glue, and chemicals are also made. Notable bldgs. include the co. courthouse (1774) and Fort Johnstown (1771), the co. jail. The last Amer. Revolutionary battle in N.Y. state was fought in Johnstown on Oct. 25, 1781. Elizabeth Cady Stanton b. here. Seat of Fulton Montgomery Community Col. Founded 1772, inc. 1895. **2** city (1990 pop. 28,134), Cambria co., W central Pa., 55 mi/89 km E of Pittsburgh, at confluence of Little Conemaugh and Stonycreek rivers, which form Conemaugh R.; 40°19′N 78°55′W. Formerly one of the great centers of U.S. heavy industry, using coal from nearby Conemaugh Valley mines. Mfg. (fabricated metal prods., apparel, dairy prods., machinery, printing and publishing, consumer goods, construction materials, furniture, ice rinks). Branches of U.S. Steel and Bethlehem Steel were here before the decline of the steel industry in the 1970s and 1980s when thousands of jobs were lost. Part of abandoned Bethlehem Steel Plant used for Heritage Mus. The first Kelly pneumatic converter for the transformation of crude iron into steel was built here in 1862. On May 31, 1889, South Fork Dam with its large upriver reservoir c.12 mi/19 km above Johnstown broke as a result of heavy rains, and the city was flooded, with the devastating loss of nearly 2,200 lives; this was one of the greatest disasters of 19th-cent. industrialized America. The river was later channeled (completed 1943) for flood prevention, but the city continues to be subject to recurrent flooding. The Univ. of Pittsburgh at Johnstown 6 mi/9.7 km to SE; a state rehabilitation center to SW at Ferndale; Johnstown Flood Natl. Memorial 8 mi/12.9 km to E; Allegheny Portage RR Natl. Historic Site 20 mi/32 km to NE; Johnstown Flood Mus.; Johnstown-Cambria Co. Airport to E; Cambria Co. Arts Center, now a major tourist center; Johnstown Inclined Plane, Pa.'s steepest inclined RR; parts of Gallitzin State Forest to NW and SE; Laurel Ridge State Park to SW; Quemahoning Reservoir to S. Settled 1770, inc. as a city 1936.

Johnstown, town (1990 pop. 1,579), Weld co., N Colo., on Little Thompson R., 13 mi/21 km WSW of Greeley; 40°20′N 104°54′W. Elev. 4,818 ft/1,469 m. Grain, beans, and sugar beet region. Fertilizer.

Johnstown 1 village (1990 pop. 48), Brown co., N Nebr., 10 mi/16 km W of Ainsworth; 42°34′N 100°03′W. **2** village (1990 pop. 3,237), Licking co., central Ohio, 16 mi/26 km WNW of Newark, and on Raccoon Creek, in diversified farming area; 40°09′N 82°41′W.

Johnstown Flood National Memorial, Cambria co., W central Pa., 8 mi/12.9 km E of Johnstown, at South Fork Dam site, on South Fork of Little Conemaugh R; 164 acres/66 ha; 40°20′N 78°46′W. Memorializes the Johnstown flood of May 31, 1889, in which 2,200 people lost their lives, after dam collapsed during heavy rains. See JOHNSTOWN, Pa. Authorized 1964.

Joice, town (1990 pop. 245), Worth co., N Iowa, 19 mi/31 km NW of Mason City; 43°21′N 93°27′W. Livestock-shipping point; animal feeds. Rice L. State Park to NW.

Joiner, village (1990 pop. 645), Mississippi co., NE Ark., 27 mi/43 km NNW of Memphis, Tenn.; 35°30′N 90°09′W. Cotton, rice, soybeans. Mississippi R. to SE.

Joinerville, uninc. village, Rusk co., E Texas, 5 mi/8 km W of Henderson. In East Texas oil field.

Jojutla de Juárez (ho-HOOT-lah dai HWAH-res), city (1990 pop. 20,520) and township, ⊙ Jojutla municipio, Morelos, central Mexico, on S slope of central plateau, on RR, and 22 mi/35 km S of Cuernavaca; 18°36′N 99°10′W. Elev. 2,920 ft/890 m. Agr. center (rice, sugarcane, melons, tropical fruit; livestock). L. Tequesquitengo, popular fishing and hunting resort, is 4 mi/6.4 km W.

Jolalpan (ho-LAHL-pan), town (1990 pop. 4,505), Puebla, central Mexico, 30 mi/48 km SW of Izúcar de Matamoros. Elev. 2,690 ft/820 m. Corn, rice, fruit, sugar; livestock.

Joliet (JO-lee-EHT), city (1990 pop. 76,836), ⊙ Will co., NE Ill., on the Des Plaines R., satellite city of Chicago; 41°31′N 88°07′W. A river port and an industrial shipping center, with limestone quarries and coal mines in the area. Mfg. (machinery, electronic equip., chemicals, metal prods., paper prods., transportation equip., plastic prods., food prods., consumer goods); oil refineries. Riverboat gambling now primary industry. Joliet is the seat of the Col. of St. Francis and Joliet Junior Col. Joliet Army Ammunition Plant SW of city, now abandoned, to become a tall grass prairie, landfill, industrial park, and veterans' cemetary. New stockyards constructed early 1970s. Joliet Correctional Center here; Stateville Correctional Center, a max. security facility, nearby. Inc. 1845.

Joliet (jo-lee-ET), village (1990 pop. 522), Carbon co., S

Mont., on Rock Creek, and 31 mi/50 km SW of Billings; 45°29′N 108°58′W. In irrigated agr. region: barley, oats, corn, sugar beets, beans, garden crops; cattle, sheep. Cooney Reservoir State Park on Red Lodge Creek to WSW.

Joliette (zhol-YEHT), county (☐ 2,506 sq mi/ 6,491 sq km), S Que., Canada, on the St. Lawrence; ⊙ Joliette; 46°45′N 74°30′W.

Joliette (zho-LYEHT), city (1991 pop. 17,396), S Que., Canada, on L'Assomption R., NE of Montreal; 46°02′N 73°26′W. Industries include steel, paper, textile, and ceramic mfg., tobacco processing, and limestone quarrying. The Séminaire de Joliette, affiliated with the Univ. of Montreal, is here.

Jolivue, uninc. town, Augusta co., NW Va., 3 mi/4.8 km S of Staunton; 38°07′N 79°04′W. Agr. (apples, grain; livestock; dairying).

Jolley, town (1990 pop. 68), Calhoun co., central Iowa, 6 mi/9.7 km NW of Rockwell City; 42°28′N 94°43′W. In agr. area.

Jolly, village (1990 pop. 201), Clay co., N Texas, 9 mi/ 14.5 km E of Wichita Falls; 33°52′N 98°20′W. Oil and natural gas. Cattle; dairying; cotton, peaches. L. Arrowhead reservoir and State Park to S.

Jollyville, uninc. city (1990 pop. 15,206), Williamson co., S Texas, residential suburb 13 mi/21 km N of downtown Austin; 30°26′N 97°45′W. Located in growing N fringe of smaller urbanized area.

Jolo (JO-lo), uninc. town (1990 pop. 800), McDowell co., S W.Va., near Dry Fork, 14 mi/23 km SW of Welch near Va. state line. Bituminous-coal region. Panther State Forest to NW; Berwind L. Wildlife Management Area to SE.

Jolon (hoh-lone), village, Monterey co., W Calif., in valley of Coast Ranges, 35 mi/56 km NW of Paso Robles. In E edge of Hunter Liggett Military Reservation; restored Mission San Antonio de Padua (founded 1771) to NW.

Joly (zho-LEE), village, S Que., Canada, 30 mi/48 km SW of Quebec. Garnet mining.

Jo-Mary Lakes, central Maine, 10 mi/16 km W of Millinocket; chain of 3 lakes (Upper, Middle, and Lower), each c.3 mi/4.8 km long, joined to Pemadumcook L. to N.

Jonacatepec (ho-nah-KAH-te-pek), city (1990 pop. 6,269) and township, Morelos, central Mexico, 32 mi/ 51 km ESE of Cuernavaca; 18°41′N 98°48′W. Agr. center (rice, coffee, sugarcane, limes and other fruit).

Jones 1 county (☐ 402 sq mi/1,041 sq km; 1990 pop. 20,739), central Ga.; ⊙ Gray; 33°02′N 83°34′W. Bounded SW by Ocmulgee R. Intersected by fall line. Agr. (peaches, soybeans, pimientos; cattle, poultry, hogs); sawmilling. Part of Chattahoochee Natl. Forest in W. Formed 1807. **2** county (☐ 576 sq mi/1,492 sq km; 1990 pop. 19,444), E Iowa; ⊙ Anamosa; 42°07′N 91°07′W. Prairie agr. area (cattle, hogs, poultry; corn, oats) drained by Wapsipinicon and South and North Forks of Maquoketa rivers. Limestone quarries, sand and gravel pits. Wapsipinicon State Park to W. Formed 1837. **3** county (☐ 699 sq mi/1,810 sq km; 1990 pop. 62,031), SE Miss.; ⊙ Laurel and Ellisville; 31°37′N 89°10′W. Drained by Leaf R. and Tallahala Creek. Agr. (cotton, corn, sweet potatoes, honey; poultry, cattle; dairying); timber. Oil and natural gas. Includes part of De Soto Natl. Forest in SE. L. Bogue Homa State L. in NE. Formed 1826. **4** county (☐ 474 sq mi/1,228 sq km; 1990 pop. 9,414), E N.C.; ⊙ Trenton; 35°00′N 77°22′W. Forested and swampy tidewater area. Bounded S in part by White Oak R. White Oak Swamp (SE) including Catfish L. on E boundary; drained by Trent R. Agr. area (tobacco, corn, cotton, beans, wheat, soybeans, hay; hogs); timber (pine, gum). Stone quarrying. Includes part of Croatan Natl. Forest (SE), Wolf Swamp (S). Formed 1778. **5** county (☐ 971 sq mi/2,515 sq km; 1990 pop. 1,324), S central S.Dak.; ⊙ Murdo; 43°57′N 100°41′W. Agr. area drained by Bad R. and Dry and White Clay creeks; bounded S by White R. Wheat, cattle. Part of Fort Pierre Natl. Grassland in NE. Mt./ Central time zone boundary splits co. down middle, then follows White R. E; village of Draper is in Central (E of boundary), Murdo and Okaton in Mt. (W). Formed 1916. **6** county (☐ 937 sq mi/2,427 sq km; 1990 pop. 16,490), W central Texas; ⊙ Anson; 32°44′N 99°52′W. Rolling plains, drained by Clear Fork of Brazos R. Rich agr. co. (cotton, wheat, milo, hay, watermelons, peanuts); livestock (cattle). Oil and gas wells; gypsum, sand and gravel, stone. Formed 1858.

Jones, town (1990 pop. 2,424), Okla. co., central Okla., residential suburb 15 mi/24 km ENE of Okla. City, and on North Canadian R.; 35°34′N 97°17′W. In oil-producing and agr. area.

Jones Beach, state park (☐ 4 sq mi/10.4 sq km), on offshore bar, SW L.I., Nassau co., SE N.Y.; 40°36′N 73°30′W. Noted for its wide, white sand beaches, outdoor marine theater, and varied recreational facilities. Est. 1929 under Robert Moses's direction.

Jones Bluff Lake, reservoir (☐ 19 sq mi/49 sq km), central Ala., on Alabama R., bet. Autauga co. (N) and Montgomery and Lowndes cos. (S) 13 mi/21 km W of Montgomery; 32°19′N 86°47′W. Max. capacity 234,200 acre-ft. Formed by Robert F. Henry Lock and Dam (110 ft/34 m high), built (1971) by Army Corps of Engineers for navigation, power generation, and recreation. Extends along Alabama R in general E-W direction. Also known as R.E. (Bob) Woodruff L. and Jones Bluff L.

Jones Creek, town (1990 pop. 2,160), Brazoria co., SE Texas, residential suburb 7 mi/11.3 km WNW of Freeport, in Brazosport Area; 28°58′N 95°28′W. San Bernard Natl. Wildlife Refuge to SW.

Jones Mill, village, Hot Spring co., central Ark., near Remmel Dam and L. Catherine, 7 mi/11.3 km NW of Malvern. Mfg. (fabricated metal prods.).

Jones Pass (12,451 ft/3,795 m), N central Colo., in Front Range, on Contintental Divide, on Grand and Clear Creek co. line. Jones Pass Tunnel, ½ mi/⅘ km S (c.3 mi/ 4.8 km long; finished 1939), unit in Denver sewage-disposal system. Henderson tunnel, 8 mi/12.9 km long, runs beneath Jones Pass. Hiking trail crosses pass.

Jones Sound, NE Franklin dist., N.W.T., Canada, arm of Baffin Bay, bet. Ellesmere Isl. (N) and Devon Isl. (S); 250 mi/402 km long, 15 mi/24 km–60 mi/97 km wide; 76°N 85°W. At Baffin Bay end is Cobourg Isl. Discovered (1616) by William Baffin.

Jonesboro 1 city (1990 pop. 46,535), shares ⊙ functions with Lake City, Craighead co., NE Ark., on Crowley's Ridge; 35°49′N 90°41′W. Founded 1859, inc. 1883. RR junction and center. The city services a rich agr. area with many processing plants and much mfg. (construction materials, plastic prods., glass prods., food prods., transportation equip., apparel, consumer goods, machinery, paper prods.). Ark. State Univ. is here, and a state park is nearby. L. Frierson State Park to N. **2** city (1990 pop. 1,728), ⊙ Union co., S Ill., 30 mi/48 km N of Cairo, in Ill. Ozarks; 37°27′N 89°16′W. Agr. (fruit, wheat, sorghum, vegetables; dairying); limestone quarries; sawmill. A Lincoln-Douglas debate was held here in 1858. Shanee Natl. Forest nearby. Laid out 1816, inc. 1857. **3** city (1990 pop. 2,073), Grant co., E central Ind., on Mississinewa R., and 6 mi/9.7 km S of Marion; 40°29′N 85°38′W. Farm trading center in agr. area; mfg. (fabricted metal prods.). Plotted 1837.

Jonesboro 1 town (1990 pop. 3,635), ⊙ Clayton co., N central Ga., 17 mi/27 km S of Atlanta; 33°31′N 84°21′W. Suburb of Atlanta; once a major clothing and textile mfg. center. Historical mus. nearby on site of Civil War battle of Jonesboro in Sherman's Atlanta campaign (1864). The ancestors of Margaret Mitchell, author of *Gone with the Wind,* lived here. Confederate cemetary. Clayton State Col. and Univ., a unit of the Univ. system of Georgia, located nearby. Settled 1823, inc. 1859. **2** (JONZ-buhr-uh), town (1990 pop. 4,305), ⊙ Jackson parish, N central La., 40 mi/64 km WSW of Monroe; 32°14′N 92°43′W. RR junction to N. In agr. area (sweet potatoes, vegetables; cattle, poultry); concrete mfg., publishing. Caney Creek reservoir to E, Jackson Bienville State Wildlife Area to N. **3** town (1990 pop. 585), Wash. co., E Maine, at mouth of Chandler R., 7 mi/ 11.3 km SW of Machias; 44°40′N 67°34′W. Sometimes Jonesborough.

Jonesborough, formerly (until 1983) **Jonesboro**, town (1990 pop. 3,091), ⊙ Wash. co., NE Tenn., 6 mi/10 km WSW of Johnson City; 36°18′N 82°29′W. Laid out 1779; oldest town in Tenn.; was first capitol of State of FRANKLIN. Andrew Jackson admitted to law practice here in 1788. Among many old bldgs. is an inn built c.1798. Annual storytelling festival here.

Jonesburg, town (1990 pop. 630), Montgomery co., E central Mo., 13 mi/21 km SE of Montgomery City; 38°51′N 91°18′W. Mfg.

Jonesport, town (1990 pop. 1,525), Wash. co., E Maine, on peninsula W of Wohoa Bay and 15 mi/24 km SW of Machias; 44°32′N 67°30′W. Port of entry. Summer resort, fishing center. Settled 1763–1764; inc. 1832; included Beals until 1925.

Jonestown, town (1990 pop. 1,467), Coahoma co., NW Miss., 10 mi/16 km NE of Clarksdale, near Coldwater R.; 34°19′N 90°27′W. RR terminus. Agr. (cotton, corn, wheat, rice, soybeans; cattle); mfg. (cottonseed oil).

Jonestown, borough (1990 pop. 931), Lebanon co., SE central Pa., 6 mi/9.7 km NW of Lebanon, on Swatara Creek; 40°24′N 76°28′W. Mfg. (paper prods., transportation equip.); agr. (grain, soybeans, apples; poultry, livestock; dairying). Appalachian Trail passes to N on Blue Mt. ridge; Swatora State Park to N; Memorial L. State Park to W; Fort Indiantown Military Reserve to NW; Bellgrove Airport to NW.

Jonesville 1 town (1990 pop. 221), Bartholomew co., S central Ind., 10 mi/16 km S of Columbus; 39°04′N 85°53′W. In agr. area. Mfg. (furniture and wood prods.). Laid out 1851. **2** (JONZ-vil), town (1994 pop. 3,153), Catahoula parish, E La., on Ouachita R. (Black R.), at influx of Tensas and Little rivers, and 24 mi/39 km W of Natchez, Miss.; 31°37′N 91°50′W. In agr. area (corn, cotton); lumbering; mfg. (nylon twine, nets); fisheries. Built on site of anc. Native Amer. village. Catahoula Natl. Wildlife Reserve to SW (La Salle parish), Bayou Cocodrie Natl. Wildlife Refuge to SE (Concordia parish). Inc. 1904. **3** town (1990 pop. 2,283), Hillsdale co., S Mich., 4 mi/6.4 km NNW of Hillsdale, and on St. Joseph R.; 41°58′N 84°40′W. In diversified agr. area. Diversified mfg. Settled 1828, inc. 1855. **4** town (1990 pop. 1,549), Yadkin co., N N.C., on Yadkin R. opposite (2 mi/ 3.2 km SE of) Elkin; 36°13′N 80°50′W. In tobacco area, also grain; poultry, livestock; dairying. Mfg. (concrete, fabricated metal prods., apparel). **5** town (1990 pop. 1,205), Union co., N S.C., 14 mi/23 km ESE of Spartanburg; 34°50′N 81°40′W. Mfg. of cotton prods.; agr. includes poultry; grain, soybeans, peaches, and apples. Settled 1808, inc. 1876. **6** town (1990 pop. 927), ⊙ Lee co., extreme SW Va., near Powell R., 32 mi/51 km SW of Norton; 36°41′N 83°07′W. Ky. state line to NW, Tenn. state line to S. Mfg.; agr. (tobacco, corn, alfalfa; cattle).

Jonesville, village, S Alaska, in Matanuska Valley, 10 mi/ 16 km NE of Palmer; 61°48′N 148°51′W. Former coal mining center.

Jonotla (ho-NO-tlah), town (1990 pop. 1,403), Puebla, central Mexico, 28 mi/45 km E of Huauchinango. Sugar, coffee, tobacco, fruit. Also San Juan Jonotla.

Jonquière (zhohn-KYEHR), city (1991 pop. 57,933), S Que., Canada, on the Saguenay R., W of Chicoutimi; 48°25′N 71°15′W. Its chief industries produce paper, pulp, and aluminum. The city was reinc. in 1976, when it absorbed the surrounding cities of Arvida and Kénogami and the municipality of Saint-Dominique-de-Jonquière. Jonquière has a col. and a school of technology. Avrida was est. in 1925 as an Alcan company town around one of the (then) largest aluminum smelters in the world.

Jonuta (ho-NOO-tah), city (1990 pop. 4,576) and township, Tabasco, SE Mexico, on Usumacinta R., near Campeche border, and 45 mi/72 km SE of Frontera; 18°08′N 92°10′W. Rice, beans, tobacco, fruit.

Jopala (ho-PAH-lah), town (1990 pop. 2,553), Puebla, central Mexico, 24 mi/39 km E of Huauchinango. Sugar, coffee, fruit. In Totonal Indian area.

Joplin, city (1990 pop. 40,961), Jasper and Newton cos.,

SW Mo.; 37°04′N 94°30′W. It is a RR center, a major truck stop on I-44, a regional shopping center, the shipping and processing point of a grain and livestock region with dairy and fruit farms, and the industrial center of a former major lead and zinc area, the Tri-State Mining District. Mining has ceased in the Joplin area. Mfg. (transportation equip., plastic prods., food prods., fabricated metal prods., machinery, construction materials, paper prods., chemicals, leather prods.; machining, printing, meat packing). The city has a mineral mus. for the historic lead and zinc industry. It is the seat of Mo. Southern State Col. and Ozark Bible Col. The George Washington Carver Natl. Monument is nearby. Settled c.1839, inc. 1873.

Joppa (JAH-pa), village (1990 pop. 492), Massac co., extreme S Ill., on Ohio R., and 8 mi/12.9 km WNW of Metropolis; 37°12′N 88°50′W. Steam power plant here for Atomic Energy Commission plant near Paducah, Ky.

Joppa, Md.: see JOPPATOWNE.

Joppatowne, city (1990 pop. 11,084), Harford co., NE Md., near Little Gunpowder Falls (stream), 17 mi/27 km NE of Baltimore; 39°25′N 76°21′W. It is a large modern development, surrounding the mansion of Benjamin Rumsey (c.1773), which has been restored as the home of the Harford co. executive. Nearby is site of Joppa hamlet, capital of old Baltimore co. (1712–1768), which was a major Amer. tobacco market until c.1750.

Joquicingo (ho-kee-SEEN-go), town (1990 pop. 2,870), Mexico state, central Mexico, 21 mi/34 km SE of Toluca de Lerdo. Sugarcane, cereals; livestock.

Jordan, town (1990 pop. 2,909), Scott co., S Minn., near Minnesota R., 28 mi/45 km SW of Minneapolis; 44°40′N 93°37′W. Trading point in agr. area (grain; livestock, poultry; dairying); mfg. (fabricated metal prods., transportation equip., food prods., electronic equip., machinery); sawmill; sand and gravel pits nearby. Thompson Ferry State Wayside, on Minnesota Valley State Trail, to N. Plotted 1854, inc. as village 1872, as city 1891.

Jordan 1 village (1990 pop. 494), in Justun township, ⊙ Garfield co., E central Mont., 80 mi/129 km NW of Miles City on Big Dry Creek; 47°19′N 106°55′W. Trading point in irrigated ranching region; wheat, barley, hay; sheep, cattle. Hell Creek State Park and Hell Creek Bay of Fort Peck Reservoir to N; Charles M. Russell Natl. Wildlife Refuge to N. Site of FBI seizure of antigovt. militants in 1996. **2** village (☐ 1 sq mi/2.6 sq km; 1990 pop. 1,325), Onondaga co., central N.Y., 17 mi/27 km W of Syracuse; 43°04′N 76°28′W. Mfg.; in dairying area; onions, potatoes, sweet corn, beans. Inc. 1835.

Jordan, Lake (☐ 7.7 sq mi/19.9 sq km), on border of Coosa and Chilton cos., central Ala., on Coosa R., 17 mi/27 km NNE of Montgomery; 18 mi/29 km long; 32°36′N 86°15′W. Formed by Jordan Dam, privately built power dam (125 ft/38 m high, 2,066 ft/630 m long) completed 1929. New channel of Coosa R. exits L. Jordan S 1 mi/1.6 km WNW of dam and enters reservoir of Bouldin Dam.

Jordan Lake, N.C.: see B. EVERETT JORDAN LAKE.

Jordan River, 60 mi/97 km long, draining Utah L. N into Great Salt L., N central Utah, passing through Lehi, Sandy, West Valley City, and Salt L. City. Fed by numerous streams flowing off the Wasatch Range, the Jordan is used for irrigation and forms the heart of the Utah Oasis. Mormons settled along its banks in the mid-1800s. Named for Jordan R. in Middle East to which it bears an uncanny resemblance, flowing from a freshwater lake to a salt water lake and providing sustenance to a dry climate region.

Jordan River, Canada: see RIVER JORDAN.

Jordan Valley, village (1990 pop. 364), Malheur co., SE Oregon, on Jordan Creek, 70 mi/113 km S of Vale on Idaho boundary; 42°58′N 117°02′W. Elev. 4,389 ft/1,338 m.

Jordanville, village (1990 pop. 250), Herkimer co., central N.Y., 20 mi/32 km SE of Utica; 42°55′N 74°57′W. Agr. (dairying; field corn, hay). Site of Holy Trinity Rus.

Orthodox Seminary (largest Eastern Orthodox monastery in N. Amer.), with traditional Rus. architecture and gold-clad Byzantine domes that are visible for miles.

Jorullo (ho-ROO-yo), volcano (4,330 ft/1,320 m) in Michoacán, central Mexico, on SW slope of central plateau, 33 mi/53 km SE of Uruapan; crater is 1.2 mi/1.9 km wide; 19°0′N 101°35′W. Elev. 10,167 ft/3,099 m. One of 2 Mex. volcanoes to develop during historic time (the other is Parícutin), it 1st erupted in 1759, destroying what had been a rich agr. area. Has numerous craters and fumaroles; thermal waters. Last erupted 1958.

José Azueta 1 Mexico: see ZIHUATANEJO. **2** Mexico: see VILLA AZUETA.

José Cardel (ho-SAI kahr-DEL), town (1990 pop. 14,708), ⊙ La Antigua township, Veracruz, E Mexico, in Gulf lowland, on RR, on Mexico Highway 140, and 15 mi/24 km NW of Veracruz; 19°21′N 96°23′W. Coffee, fruit; livestock. Site of Mexico's only nuclear power plant, which began operation in 1989. Cortés landed here in April 1519. Also known as La Antigua; formerly San Francisco de las Peñas.

José María Morelos 1 (ho-SAI mah-REE-ah mo-RAI-los), town (1990 pop. 25,179), Quintana Roo, NE Mexico, 25 mi/40 km SW of Cancún; 20°42′N 97°32′W. Small farming; livestock. **2** town, N Tlaxcala, Mexico, 14 mi/23 km NW of Apizaco, near RR. Has good road connections. Temperate to cold climate. Agr. (cereals, fruits); woods; cattle and poultry raising.

José María Morelos, Mexico: see MAZATECOCHCO.

José Sixto Verduzco, Mexico: see PASTOR ORTIZ.

Joseph, town (1990 pop. 1,073), Wallowa co., NE Oregon, 6 mi/9.7 km SE of Enterprise, on Wallowa R.; 45°21′N 117°13′W. Elev. 4,191 ft/1,277 m. RR terminus. Mfg. (lumber, bronze and silver castings). Grain, potatoes; cattle. Part of Wallowa-Whitman Natl. Forest, including Eagle Cap Wilderness Area, to S; Hells Canyon Natl. Recreation Area (Snake R.) to E. Hells Canyon Dam 25 mi/40 km to E. Wallowa L. to S. Wallowa L. State Park at S end.

Joseph, village (1990 pop. 198), Sevier co., SW central Utah, 10 mi/16 km SW of Richfield, and on Sevier R.; 38°37′N 112°13′W. Elev. 5,435 ft/1,657 m. Alfalfa, barley; dairying; cattle. Parts of Fishlake Natl. Forest to E and NW. Fremont Indian State Park to SW; Big Rock Candy Mt. to S. Old Farm Mus. Settled 1864.

Joseph City, uninc. village (1990 pop. 650), Navajo co., E central Ariz., 10 mi/16 km WNW of Holbrook, on Little Colorado R. Timber. Navajo Indian Reservation to N.

Joseph Henry, Cape, NE Ellesmere Isl., NE Franklin dist., N.W.T., N Canada, on Lincoln Sea of the Arctic Ocean, NE extremity of Fielden Peninsula; 82°49′N 63°35′W.

Joseph, Lake, S Ont., central Canada, in Muskoka lake region, 16 mi/26 km SE of Parry Sound; 12 mi/19 km long, 4 mi/6 km wide.

Josephine, county (☐ 1,641 sq mi/4,250 sq km; 1990 pop. 62,649), SW Oregon; ⊙ Grants Pass; 42°21′N 123°33′W. Mt. area bordering on Calif. (S) and crossed by Rogue (N) and Illinois (SW) rivers; State Scenic Waterways in W. Agr. (wheat, oats, barley, apples, pears, plums, peaches, grapes; poultry, hogs, sheep, cattle); nurseries, wineries. Lumber. Gold. Parts of Siskiyou Natl. Forest, including Kalmiopsis Wilderness Area, in W; part of Rogue R. Natl. Forest in SE corner; parts of Siskiyou Mts. in W and S, including Oregon Caves Natl. Monument in SE; Illinois R. State Park in SW. Formed 1856.

Josephine, village (1990 pop. 503), Collin co., N Texas, 34 mi/55 km ENE of Dallas; 33°03′N 96°19′W. Agr. area just beyond urban fringe (cotton, sorghum, wheat; cattle, horses).

Joshua, town (1990 pop. 3,828), Johnson co., N central Texas, 20 mi/32 km S of Fort Worth; 32°27′N 97°22′W. Dairying; cotton; cattle; mfg. (transportation equip., machinery).

Joshua Tree, uninc. town (1990 pop. 3,898), San Bernardino co., S Calif., 54 mi/87 km E of San Bernardino,

and 25 mi/40 km NE of Palm Springs; 34°08′N 116°19′W. Twentynine Palms Marine Corps Base to NE, main entrance to E. Joshua Tree Natl. Monument to SE. Cattle.

Joshua Tree National Monument (☐ 875 sq mi/2,266 sq km), Riverside and San Bernardino cos., S Calif. Main (S) entrance c.40 mi/64 km ESE of Palm Springs, park road connects S entrance with Twentynine Palms to N. Rare Joshua trees (plentiful here), or "praying plant"; named by Mormons because of upstretched arms, includes wilderness area (1976). Variety of flora and fauna. Part of Little San Bernardino Mts. in W; Twentynine Palms Indian Reservation on N. Authorized 1936.

Jost Van Dyke, islet (1991 pop. 140), Br. Virgin Isls., 4 mi/6.4 km W of Tortola; 18°27′N 64°45′W. Rugged, mountainous, rising to 1,070 ft/326 m. Dr. William Thornton, a designer of the Washington capitol, b. here. Little Jost Van Dyke isl. is just E.

Jourdanton, town (1990 pop. 3,220), ⊙ Atascosa co., SW Texas, 35 mi/56 km S of San Antonio, near Atascosa R.; 28°54′N 98°32′W. In agr. area (peanuts, corn); dairying; mfg. (machinery).

Jourimain, Cape (JOOR-i-main), promontory on Northumberland Strait, SE N.B., E Canada, 32 mi/51 km ENE of Sackville; 46°10′N 63°49′W.

Jovellanos (ho-vai-YAHN-os), town (1994 est. pop. 25,000), Matanzas prov., W Cuba, on Central Highway, and 29 mi/47 km ESE of Matanzas; 22°48′N 81°13′W. RR junction and commercial center in sugar-growing region. Has foundries, machine shops, tobacco factories. Julio Reyes Cairo sugar mill is nearby (E).

Jovero, Dominican Republic: see MICHES.

Joy, village (1990 pop. 452), Mercer co., NW Ill., 7 mi/11.3 km W of Aledo; 41°12′N 90°52′W. In agr. area.

Juab (JOO-ab), county (☐ 3,406 sq mi/8,822 sq km; 1990 pop. 5,817), W Utah, on Nev. (W) state line; ⊙ Nephi; 39°42′N 112°47′W. Mining and agr. area watered in SE by Sevier R. Wheat, barley, alfalfa; cattle; silver. Part of Goshute Indian Reservation is in NW, on Nev. state line. Little Sahara Recreation Area (Bureau of Land Management) in SE, in White Sand Dunes; Fish Springs Natl. Wildlife Refuge in N center in Fish Springs Flats. Tintic Mining Dist. in NE, around Eureka (gold, silver, lead). Part of Fishlake Natl. Forest in SE, parts of Uinta Natl. Forest in E, including part of Mt. Nebo Wilderness Area in NE. N end of Sevier Bridge Reservoir in SE corner, including Yuba (W shore) and Painted Rock (E shore) state parks, on Sanpete co. border. Mona Reservoir in NE. Formed 1852.

Juan A. Escudero, Mexico: see TIERRA COLORADA.

Juan Aldama (hwan ahl-DAH-mah), town (1990 pop. 12,254), ⊙ Juan Aldama municipio, Zacatecas, N central Mexico, on interior plateau, near Durango border, 32 mi/51 km NW of Nieves on Mexico Highway 49; 24°17′N 103°23′W. Agr. (maguey, corn); livestock. Formerly San Juan de Mezquital.

Juan C. Bonilla, Mexico: see CUANALÁ.

Juan Cumatzi, Contla de, Mexico: see CONTLA.

Juan de Fuca, Strait of (HWAHN duh FYOO-kuh), inlet of the Pacific Ocean, bet. Vancouver Isl., B.C. (SW Canada; N) and Olympic Peninsula, Wash., (U.S.; S), linking the Strait of Georgia through Haro and Rosario straits, and Puget Sound with the Pacific; forms part of the U.S.-Canada border; 100 mi/161 km long, 11 mi/18 km–20 mi/32 km wide. Victoria (B.C.), the strait's largest city, is located on N side; ferries connect it with the U.S. mainland. It is the main shipping channel to Seattle, Tacoma, Vancouver (B.C.), Victoria, other parts. Cape Flattery (Wash.), at S side of Pacific entrance to strait; San Juan Isls. (Wash.), to NE; Whidbey Isl. at E end of strait. West Coast Trail Unit of Pacific Rim Natl. Park on NW coast. Port Angeles (Wash.), on S side. Discovered by the Eng. captain Charles W. Barkley in 1787, the strait was named for a sailor, Juan de Fuca, who reputedly had explored it for Spain in 1592.

Juan Dolio (HWAHN DO-lee-o), beach resort and residential community, Dominican Republic, 20 mi/32 km E of Santo Domingo airport.

Juan Galindo, Mexico: see NUEVO NECAXA.

Juan N. Méndez, Mexico: see ATENAYUCA.

Juan Rodríguez Clara (hwahn ro-DREE-gez KLAH-rah), town (1990 pop. 11,331), SE Veracruz, Mexico, 34 mi/55 km from San Andrés Tuxtla, on Mexico Highway 145, on RR; 17°59′N 95°24′W. Located on the plains of the Papaloapan R. basin. Hot climate. Agr. (corn, beans, plantains, rice, mangoes); cattle; forestry. Cooking oil.

Juan Vicente (HWAHN vee-SAIN-tai), beach resort, Holguín prov., E Cuba, on Nipe Bay (Atlantic Ocean), 2 mi/3.2 km NW of Mayarí, 50 mi/80 km N of Santiago de Cuba; 20°42′N /5°44′W.

Juana Díaz (HWAH-nah DEE ahz), town (1990 pop. 45,198), S central P.R., 8 mi/12.9 km ENE of Ponce. Some agr. including hogs, poultry; large mango growths (for export). Varied mfg. Marble, manganese deposits nearby. U.S. Navy Fort Allen is c.3 mi/4.8 km S.

Juanacatlán (hwah-nah-kah-TLAHN), town (1990 pop. 6,674), Jalisco, central Mexico, on Santiago (Lerma) R., and 16 mi/26 km SE of Guadalajara. Wheat, vegetables; livestock. El Salto hydroelectric plant (capacity 2,975 kw). The famous falls here, 2d in N. Amer. only to Niagara, are much reduced because of lowered water level in L. Chapala.

Juanita (hwahn-EE-tuh), uninc. town, King co., W Wash., residential suburb 8 mi/12.9 km NE of downtown Seattle, on E shore of L. Washington. Saint Edward State Park to NW.

Juárez (HWAH-rez), city (1990 pop. 789,522) and township, Chihuahua state, N Mexico, on the Rio Grande, opposite El Paso (Texas); 31°44′N 106°29′W. Elev. 3,734 ft/1,138 m. Connected with the U.S. by 3 internatl. bridges, it is a shipping point and highway and RR terminus. It is also the commercial and processing center for the surrounding cotton-growing area. Except for the river valley, under intense cultivation SE of the city, Juárez is surrounded by desert. It has experienced extremely rapid pop. growth and has been a favored location for maquiladoras, foreign-owned mfg. plants that finish goods, incl. computer and mechanical equip. parts. for sale in the U.S. It was originally called El Paso del Norte and included settlements on both sides of the river, until they were split by the Treaty of Guadalupe Hidalgo (1848). In 1888 the name of the Mex. town was changed to honor Benito Juárez, who made it his capital when exiled from central Mexico. Sometimes called Ciudad Juárez.

Juárez 1 (HWAH-rez), town (1990 pop. 5,571), Chiapas, S Mexico, in Gulf lowland, 27 mi/43 km SW of Villahermosa, on RR, in Zoque Indian area; 17°40′N 93°10′W. Cacao, rice. **2** town (1990 pop. 771), Coahuila, N Mexico, near Don Martín dam, in irrigated plain, 26 mi/42 km SE of Sabinas; 27°39′N 100°43′W. Elev. 984 ft/300 m. Cereals, fruit, istle fibers; cattle. **3** town (1990 pop. 678), ☉ Juárez Hidalgo municipio, Hidalgo, central Mexico, 50 mi/80 km NNW of Pachuca de Soto. Corn, wheat, beans, fruit; livestock. Also known as Juárez Hidalgo.

Juárez (HWAH-rez), settlement (1990 pop. 789,522), Nuevo Casas Grandes municipio, Chihuahua, NW Mexico, on Piedras Verdes R., 12 mi/20 km from Nuevo Casas Grandes, on Chihuahua State Highway 10; 30°18′N 108°04′W. Elev. 5,085 ft/1,550 m. Mixed farming and dairying. Agr. colony est. 1886 by Mormon immigrants from U.S. Was the principal center for the Mormon colonies, which still survive in the area. Also Colonia Juárez.

Juárez, Mexico: see BENITO JUÁREZ.

Juárez Hidalgo, Mexico: see JUÁREZ.

Juárez, Sierra (HWAH-rez, SYER-rah), range, in N Baja California, NW Mexico, extends c.90 mi/145 km SE from U.S. border, W of Laguna Salada; elev. 2,953 ft/900 m–6,562 ft/2,000 m. Gold placers. Sometimes Sierra de Juárez.

Juárez, Sierra de, Mexico: see OAXACA, SIERRA MADRE DE.

Juárez, Villa, Mexico: see CIUDAD MANTE.

Jubilee Lake, SE N.F., E Canada, 30 mi/48 km N of

Fortune Bay; 6 mi/10 km long, 4 mi/6 km wide; 48°03′N 55°10′W.

Júcaro (HOO-kah-ro), village, Ciego de Ávila prov., E Cuba, landing on the Caribbean Gulf of Ana María, 16 mi/26 km SSW of Ciego de Ávila (linked by RR); 21°36′N 78°52′W. Timber.

Juchipila (hoo-chee-PEE-lah), city (1990 pop. 7,750) and township, Zacatecas, N central Mexico, on Juchipila R., and 32 mi/51 km SSE of Tlaltenango De Sánchez Román on Mexico Highway 54; 21°25′N 103°07′W. Agr. center (grain, sugarcane, tobacco, fruit; livestock).

Juchipila River (hoo-chee-PEE-lah), c.120 mi/193 km long, in Zacatecas, N central Mexico; rises on interior plateau N of Villanueva; flows S, past Villanueva, Jalpa, and Juchipila, to Santiago (Lerma) R. 28 mi/45 km NNW of Guadalajara.

Juchique de Ferrer (hoo-CHEE-kai dai fe-RER), town (1990 pop. 2,998), Veracruz, E Mexico, 27 mi/43 km NE of Xalapa Enríquez; elev. 2,657 ft/810 m. Corn, coffee. Often Juchique.

Juchitán de Zaragoza (hoo-chee-TAHN dai zah-rah-GO-zah), city (1990 pop. 53,666), in SE Oaxaca, Mexico, on S part of isthmus of Tehuantepec, on banks of Rio de los Perros (flows to Mar Muerto Superior), on RR and Mexico Highways 190 (Inter-Amer. Highway) and 185 (Trans-Isthmian Highway), 25 mi/40 km NE of the port of Salina Cruz; 16°25′N 95°01′W. Very hot climate. Agr. (corn, beans); livestock. Important center for commerce and communications. Well known for straw-hat production. There is a creosote plant here. Export salt. Zapotec center; market and handicrafts attract tourists.

Juchitepec de Mariano Riva Palacio (hoo-CHEE-tai-pek dai mah-ree-AH-no REE-vah pah-LAH-see-o), town (1990 pop. 10,395), ☉ Juchitepec municipio, Mexico state, central Mexico, 29 mi/47 km SE of Mexico city, and in the Zona Metropolitana de la Ciudad de Mexico. Agr. center (cereals, vegetables; livestock). Formerly Xuchitepec and Juchitepec.

Juchitlán (hoo-chee-TLAHN), town (1990 pop. 3,617), Jalisco, W Mexico, 31 mi/50 km S of Ameca, on Mexico Highway 80. Agr. center (grain, sugarcane, flax, fruit, tobacco).

Jud, village (1990 pop. 84), La Moure co., SE central N.Dak., 32 mi/51 km WNW of La Moure; 46°31′N 98°54′W.

Juda, village, Green co., S Wis., 7 mi/11.3 km E of Monroe. In livestock, dairy, and grain region. Mfg. (cheese, whey prods.; meat processing).

Judge Daly Promontory (DAI-lee), NE Ellesmere Isl., NE Franklin dist., N.W.T., N Canada, peninsula, on Kennedy Channel; 100 mi/161 km long, 10 mi/16 km–48 mi/77 km wide; 81°00′N 67°00′W. Terminates NE at Cape Baird. Rises to c.6,000 ft/1,829 m near base of peninsula.

Judith Basin, county (☐ 2,282 sq mi/5,910 sq km; 1990 pop. 2,282), central Mont.; ☉ Stanford; 47°02′N 110°16′W. Agr. region drained by Judith R. and Arrow and Wolf creeks. Wheat, barley, hay; cattle, sheep, poultry. Sapphires, silver, and other metals. Part of Lewis and Clark Natl. Forest in SW and N, and Little Belt Mts. in SW. Ackley L. State Park in SE. Formed 1920.

Judith Gap, village (1990 pop. 133), Wheatland co., central Mont., on East Fork of Roberts Creek, 33 mi/53 km SSW of Lewistown; 46°41′N 109°45′W. Grain, hay; livestock. Parts of Lewis and Clark Natl. Forest to W and NE. Little Belt Mts. to W. Big Snowy Mts. to NE.

Judith, Point, R.I.: see POINT JUDITH.

Judith River, 124 mi/200 km long, central Mont.; rises in Little Belt Mts.; flows NE, past Utica and Hobson, to Missouri R. 18 mi/29 km NW of Winifred.

Judson 1 village (1990 pop. 61), Parke co., W Ind., 6 mi/9.7 km NNE of Rockville; 39°49′N 87°08′W. In agr. area. Laid out 1872. **2** village (1990 pop. 2,859), Greenville co., NW S.C., a residential suburb 2 mi/3.2 km W of downtown Greenville; 34°49′N 82°25′W.

Judsonia (juhd-SON-ee-uh), town (1990 pop. 1,915), White co., central Ark., 5 mi/8 km NE of Searcy, and on Little Red R.; 35°16′N 91°38′W. In strawberry-producing area. Mfg. (bronze casting; asphalt prods.).

Julesburg, town (1990 pop. 1,295), ☉ Sedgwick co., extreme NE Colo., on South Platte R., near Nebr. state line, and 55 mi/89 km NE of Sterling; 40°59′N 102°15′W. Elev. 3,477 ft/1,060 m. Trade center and RR division point in sugar beet region; cattle, poultry; wheat, corn, sunflowers. Founded 1881, inc. 1886.

Juliaetta, village (1990 pop. 488), Latah co., W Idaho, 18 mi/29 km SE of Moscow, and on Potlatch R.; 46°13′N 116°43′W. Grain, barley, oats; alfalfa; sheep, cattle; mfg. (sawmill prods., lumber). Nez Perce Indian Reservation to S.

Julian, uninc. town (1990 pop. 1,284), San Diego co., S Calif., 40 mi/64 km ENE of San Diego; 33°04′N 116°36′W. Nearby are Anza-Borrego Desert (E) and Cuyama Rancho (S) state parks; also, Santa Ysabel (N) and Inaja-Cosmit (SW) Indian reservations. Pacific Coast Trail passes to E. Cattle, poultry; grain ; dairying.

Julian, village (1990 pop. 71), Otoe and Nemaha cos., SE Nebr., 8 mi/12.9 km N of Auburn, near Missouri R.; 40°31′N 95°52′W.

Juliette, town (1990 pop. 600), Monroe co., Ga., on RR, 9 mi/14.5 km NE of Forsyth; 33°06′N 83°48′W. Mfg. includes textile finishing; crushed stone. Nearly abandoned when it was chosen in the early 1990s as the site for the filming of the motion picture *Fried Green Tomatoes*. Now a bustling tourist town with antique and craft stores, and the Whistle Stop Cafe. Near the Jarrell Plantation, L. Juliette, and the Rum Creek Wildlife Management Area.

Julimes (hoo-LEE-mes), town (1990 pop. 1,708), Chihuahua. N Mexico, on Conchos R. (irrigation), and 40 mi/64 km ESE of Chihuahua; 28°25′N 105°26′W. Elev. 3,839 ft/1,170 m. Grain, beans; cattle. Sulphur thermal springs.

Jumbo Mountain (11,217 ft/3,419 m), SE B.C., W Canada, in Selkirk Mts., 70 mi/113 km NNE of Nelson; 50°24′N 116°34′W.

Jumento Cays, Bahama Isls.: see RAGGED ISLAND AND CAYS.

Jump River, c.30 mi/48 km long, N central Wis.; formed by 2 forks rising in Price co. N Fork, rises in central Price co. and flows SW; S Fork, c.40 mi/64 km long, rises in E Price co., and flows SW, past Prentice, then W, where it joins N Fork. The Jump R. flows another 35 mi/56 km SW through wooded region, to Holcombe Flowage (reservoir) of Chippewa R., 13 mi/21 km S of Ladysmith. Main river is also called Big Jump R.

Jumpertown, village (1990 pop. 438), Prentiss co., NE Miss., 17 mi/27 km SSW of Corinth; 34°42′N 88°39′W. Cotton, corn, wheat, soybeans; cattle; dairying.

Juncos (HOON-kos), town (1990 pop. 30,612), E P.R., 21 mi/34 km SE of San Juan. Industrial and commercial area; varied mfg. Iron deposits nearby.

Junction, town (1990 pop. 2,654), ☉ Kimble co., W central Texas, on Edwards Plateau, c.100 mi/161 km NW of San Antonio; 30°29′N 99°46′W. Elev. 1,710 ft/521 m. At junction of North Llano and South Llano rivers to form Llano R. Important market and shipping center for wool, mohair, cattle, sheep, goats; pecans, sorghum; mfg. (bldg. materials, wood prods., cedar wood oil); sand and gravel; oil and natural gas. Scenery, hunting, fishing attract visitors. South Llano R. State Park to SW. Settled 1876, inc. 1928.

Junction 1 village (1990 pop. 201), Gallatin co., SE Ill., 3 mi/4.8 km WNW of Shawneetown; 37°43′N 88°14′W. In agr. area. **2** village (1990 pop. 132), ☉ Piute co., S Utah, 22 mi/35 km S of Beaver, and on Sevier R., near junction of East Fork Sevier R. (impounds water of Sevier R. for irrigation); 38°14′N 112°13′W. Elev. 6,250 ft/1,905 m. Alfalfa, vegetables; dairying; cattle, sheep; gold, silver. Parts of Fishlake Natl. Forest to W and NE; Dixie Natl. Forest to SE. Piute Reservoir and State Park to N. Co. Courthouse (1903).

Junction, Jamaica: see BULL SAVANNA / JUNCTION.

Junction City, city (1990 pop. 20,604), ☉ Geary co., NE Kansas, at the confluence of the Republican and Smoky Hill rivers, 22 mi/35 km E of Abilene, 18 mi/29 km SW of Manhattan; 39°01′N 96°50′W. The RR, trade, and processing center of an agr. and dairy area, it grew as the service center for Fort Riley Military Reserve 8 mi/

12.9 km N, which contributes to the city's economy. Mfg. (transportation equip.; foundry; gas distribution). Limestone quarries nearby. Milford L. Reservoir and Milford State Park to NW; Geary State Fishing L. to SW. Inc. 1859.

Junction City 1 town (1990 pop. 1,983), Boyle co., central Ky., 4 mi/6.4 km S of Danville, in Bluegrass region; 37°35'N 84°47'W. Agr. (burley tobacco, grain; livestock, poultry; dairying); mfg. (machinery, wood prods.). Isaac Shelby Cemetery State Historic Site to S. **2** town (1990 pop. 3,670), Lane co., W Oregon, 12 mi/19 km NNW of Eugene, near Willamette R.; 44°13'N 123°12'W. Shipping point for seeds and canned goods. Agr. (fruit, sweet corn, grain; poultry); dairy prods. Wood prods., chemicals. Nearby are Washburne (NW) and Alderwood (W) state waysides. Fern Ridge Reservoir to SW. Inc. 1872.

Junction City 1 village (1990 pop. 674), in Union co., S Ark., on La. state line, 14 mi/23 km S of El Dorado, and adjacent to Junction City (La.); 33°01'N 92°43'W. Mfg. (wood prods.), lumber milling; poultry. **2** village (1990 pop. 182), Talbot co., W Ga., 32 mi/51 km ENE of Columbus; 32°36'N 84°28'W. Furniture mfg.; crushed stone, sand processing. **3** village (1990 pop. 749), Union and Claiborne parishes, N. La., on Ark. state line, 4 mi/6 km S of El Dorado (Ark.), adjacent to Junction City (Ark.); 33°01'N 92°43'W. Lumber milling. Unit of Kisatchie Natl. Forest (including Corney L.) to SW. **4** village (1990 pop. 770), Perry co., central Ohio, 5 mi/8 km W of New Lexington; 39°43'N 82°18'W. **5** village (1990 pop 507), Portage co., central Wis., 14 mi/23 km NNE of Wisconsin Rapids; 44°35'N 89°46'W. Makes cheese. RR junction.

June Lake, uninc. village, Mono co., E Calif., on June L. (resort), c.10 mi/16 km S of Mono L. and 45 mi/72 km NW of Bishop; c.1.5 mi/2.4 km long. In Inyo Natl. Forest; Yosemite Natl. Park to W; June Mt. Ski Area to W; Mono Craters to N. Trout fishing.

June Park, town (□ 3 sq mi/7.8 sq km; 1990 pop. 4,080), Brevard co., E central Fla., 4 mi/6.4 km W of Melbourne; 28°04'N 80°41'W.

Juneau (JOO-no), county (□ 804 sq mi/2,082 sq km; 1990 pop. 21,650), central Wis.; ⊙ Mauston; 43°55'N 90°06'W. Predominantly agr. area (dairy prods., potatoes, beans, corn; soybeans; cattle, hogs, sheep, poultry). Processing of dairy prods. is principal industry. Bounded E by Wisconsin R.; drained by Yellow, Lemonweir, and Baraboo rivers. Wisconsin Dells (canyon area) are in SE. Includes part of Necedah Natl. Wildlife Refuge and central Wis. Conservation Area in N; Rocky Arbor State in SE corner; Buckhorn State Park in E; E end of La Crosse State Trail in SW corner. Formed 1856.

Juneau (JOO-no), city (1990 pop. 26,751), ⊙ Alaska, in the Alaska Panhandle, in SE corner of state, at the foot of 2 spectacular peaks, Mts. Juneau and Roberts; 61°48'N 134°27'W. A port on Gastineau Channel, Juneau is a trade center for the Panhandle area, with an ice-free harbor, and an airport. Surrounding road system extends max. of 40.5 mi/65.2 km NW; no road connections to outside. Ferry connections to other Panhandle communities; bridge to Douglas Isl. The state and Federal govt. are the major employers. Salmon and halibut fishing, mining, and tourism are important economic activities. Joseph Juneau and a partner discovered gold nearby in 1880, and the city developed as a gold rush town. Officially designated as capital of the Territory of Alaska in 1900 but did not function as such until the govt. offices were moved from Sitka in 1906. In 1959 it became state capital with the admission of Alaska to the Union. Douglas Isl., a part of the city, lies across the channel. The Alaska Historical Lib. and Mus. and Alaska State Mus. are here. Univ. of Alaska Southeast Campus serves the area. In 1970 city and borough govts. were united, including neighboring Douglas, making Juneau the largest city in area in the U.S., at 3,108 sq mi/8,050 sq km. Glacier Bay Natl. Park and Preserve to the NW. Alaskans voted in 1976 to move capital to Willow, W of Palmer, but defeated funding for it, 1982. Inc. 1900.

Juneau, town (1990 pop. 2,157), ⊙ Dodge co., S central Wis., 7 mi/11.3 km SE of Beaver Dam; 43°24'N 88°42'W. In dairying region. Mfg. (porcelain prods., machinery; food and dairy processing). Horicon Marsh Wildlife Area to NE. Inc. 1887.

Juneau (JOO-no), borough (□ 2,594 sq mi/6,718 sq km; 1990 pop. 26,751), SE Alaska, coterminous with Juneau city, which includes the former town of Douglas and all of Douglas Isl. Bounded on SW by Stephen's Passage, on W by Long Canal inlet, and on E by Can. (B.C.) border. Part of Coast Mts. and Tongass Natl. Forest to E. Point Bridget State Park to W. Tourism, fishing, timber.

Jungapeo de Juárez (hoon-GAH-pai-o dai HWAHR-res), town (1990 pop. 4,840), ⊙ Jungapeo municipio, Michoacán, central Mexico, 20 mi/32 km S of Hidalgo; 19°30'N 100°30'W. Cereals, fruit; livestock.

Juniata (JOO nee-A-tah), county (□ 393 sq mi/1,018 sq km; 1990 pop. 20,625), central Pa.; ⊙ Mifflintown. Agr. Area, drained by Juniata R. and Tuscarora Creek. Blacklog Mt. lies along SW, Shade Mt. along NW border; Tuscarora Mt. ridge forms SE border; bounded extreme E by Susquehanna R., NE by Mahantango and West Branch Mahantango creeks. Mfg. at Mifflintown. Agr. (corn, wheat, oats, hay, alfalfa, apples; poultry, sheep, hogs, cattle; dairying); timber. Parts of Tuscarora State Forest along SE and NW borders. Formed 1831.

Juniata (JOO-nee-tuh), village (1990 pop. 811), Adams co., S Nebr., 5 mi/8 km W of Hastings, and on branch of Little Blue R.; 40°35'N 98°30'W. Mfg. (aluminum foundry; irrigation supplies).

Juniata River (JOO-nee-A-tah), scenic stream, 90 mi/145 km long, central Pa.; formed 3 mi/4.8 km SE of Huntingdon by junction of Little Juniata R. (35 mi/56 km long) and Raystown Branch Juniata R.; flows generally E, past Mount Union, Lewistown, and Newport to Susquehanna R. 1 mi/1.6 km NE of Duncannon; passes through gaps in Jacks Mt. ridge at Mount Union and through Tuscarora Mt. ridge at Millerstown; 40°33'N 78°04'W. Raystown Branch rises in Alleghany Mts. in E Somerset co., flows E past Bedford and Everett, and NNE past Saxton and through large Raystown L. reservoir, joins Little Juniata R. 3 mi/4.8 km SE of Huntingdon to form Juniata R. Frankstown Branch; 105 mi/169 km long, rises in N edge of Bedford co., flows generally NE c.50 mi/80 km past Claysburg and Williamsburg to Little Juniata R., 6 mi/9.7 km NW of Huntingdon.

Juniata Terrace (JOO-nee-A-tah), borough (1990 pop. 556), Juniata co., central Pa., a residential suburb 1 mi/1.6 km S and across the Juniata R. from Lewistown; 40°34'N 77°34'W. Blue Ridge Mts. to SE.

Junior, village (1990 pop. 542), Barbour co., E W.Va., on Tygart R., 5 mi/8 km NW of Elkins; 38°58'N 79°57'W. Agr. (corn); livestock, poultry. Coal-mining area.

Junipero Serra Peak, Calif.: see SANTA LUCIA RANGE.

Junken, Cape (JUHN-kin), S Alaska, on S Kenai Peninsula, 30 mi/48 km ESE of Seward; 59°55'N 148°39'W.

Juno Beach (JOO-no), town (□ 1 sq mi/2.6 sq km; 1990 pop. 2,121), Palm Beach co., SE Fla., 13 mi/21 km N of West Palm Beach; 26°52'N 80°03'W.

Juntura (juhn-TUHR-uh), uninc. village, Malheur co., E Oregon, 45 mi/72 km WSW of Vale, on Malheur R. at mouth of North Fork.

Jupiter, city (□ 14 sq mi/36 sq km; 1990 pop. 24,986), Palm Beach co., SE Fla., 16 mi/26 km N of West Palm Beach, on Atlantic coast, near S end of Jupiter Isl.; 26°55'N 80°05'W. Resort city experiencing much growth since 1970.

Jupiter, uninc. village, Buncombe co., W N.C., 11 mi/18 km NNW of Asheville. Tobacco, corn; cattle, chickens.

Jupiter Island (□ 3 sq mi/7.8 sq km), Martin co., E central Fla., barrier beach on the Atlantic Ocean, separated from mainland by narrow channel 15 mi/24 km long; 27°02'N 80°06'W. At N end is St. Lucie Inlet, at S end Jupiter Inlet. Lighthouse at S tip.

Juquila, Mexico: see SANTA CATARINA JUQUILA.

Justice, village (1990 pop. 11,137), Cook co., NE Ill., W suburb of Chicago, on Illinois Waterway; 41°45'N 87°50'W.

Justin, town (1990 pop. 1,234), Denton co., N Texas, 13 mi/21 km SW of Denton; 33°05'N 97°17'W. Mfg. (bldg. materials).

Juventino Rosas, Mexico: see SANTA CRUZ DE JUVENTINO ROSAS.

Juventud, Isla de la (hoo-vain-TOOD, EE-sluh dai luh), Eng. *Isle of Youth*, island (□ 1,180 sq mi/3,056 sq km; 1989 est. pop. 71,500) and Special Municipality, off SW Cuba, from which it is separated by the Gulf of Batabanó; ⊙ Nueva Gerona. Until 1978 it was called Isla de Pinos (Eng. *Isle of Pines*). Pine forests cover much of the isl., and there are many mineral springs. Marble is quarried from low ridges in the N part; the S ¼ of the isl. is an elevated plain. The economy is based on fishing and agr. (primarily citrus fruits, some vegetables). Until the break in U.S.-Cuban relations in the early 1960s, much of the land was owned by Amer. citizens, and the climate and excellent fishing waters made the isl. an attractive resort. Bibijagua beach remains popular. Sighted by Columbus in 1494, Isla de la Juventud was later used as a penal colony and was a rendezvous for buccaneers. During the colonial period it was a summer resort and a rest area for the Span. military. Ceded to the U.S. after the Span.-Amer. War (1898) and later claimed by both the U.S. and Cuba because its name was omitted from the Platt Amendment, which defined Cuba's borders. Finally, in 1907, the U.S. Supreme Court declared that the isl. did not belong to the U.S.; a treaty was later signed (1925) confirming the isl. as Cuban. Near Nueva Gerona is a large prison, often used for political prisoners. During the govt. of Fidel Castro, himself jailed here in 1953, the isl. has been extensively beautified, but political prisoners are incarcerated here. The name change also reflects large numbers of schools and training programs for young people. Isla de la Juventud has suffered frequent damage from hurricanes.

Juxtlahuaca, Mexico: see SANTIAGO JUXTLAHUACA.

Cross references are shown in SMALL CAPITALS. The pronunciation key is on page xv. The dates of population figures are on page xii.

K

Ka Lae (kah LEI) [= south point], S extremity of Hawaii isl., Hawaii co., Hawaii, 65 mi/105 km SSW of Hilo, 220 mi/354 km SE of Honolulu; 18°54′N 155°41′W. Southernmost point in the U.S. Ka Lae Park at W side; Green Sand Beach on E side.

Kaaawa (KAH-ah-AH-VAH), town (1990 pop. 1,138), Oahu isl., Honolulu co., Hawaii, 16 mi/26 km N of Honolulu, on NE coast; 21°33′N 157°51′W. Pineapples, sugarcane; fish, prawns. Swanzy Beach Park to NW; Kaaawa Beach Park to SE; Waiahole Forest Reserve to SW; Kahana Valley State Park to W, including Crouching Lion rock formation.

Kaala (ka-AH-lah), peak (4,046 ft/1,233 m) of Waianae Range, W Oahu, Honolulu co., Hawaii, 20 mi/32 km NW of Honolulu. Highest point on Oahu.

Kaanapali (KAH-AH-nah-PAH-lee), village (1990 pop. 579), Maui isl., Maui co., Hawaii, 3 mi/4.8 km N of Lahaina, on W coast of West Maui Peninsula; 20°55′N 156°40′W. Tourism. Pineapples. Kaanapali Airport to N. N terminus of scenic train from Lahaina. Whalers Village Shopping Center and Mus. West Maui Forest Reserve to E.

Kaaterskill Clove, SE N.Y., in Catskill Mts., scenic gorge of small Kaaterskill Creek, extends c.5 mi/8 km bet. Haines Falls village (W; noted waterfall here) and Palenville (E); 42°11′N 74°04′W. Traversed by state highway.

Kabáh (kah-BAH), historic site, SW Yucatán, Mexico, 12 mi/19 km S of Mexico Highway 261 from Uxmal. This site is representative of Puuc architectural style and is dominated by a Palace of Masks, which is decorated with elaborate stone masks of Chac, the rain god. Across the road is a freestanding arch marking the spot where a Mayan road once connected Kabah from Uxmal.

Kabetogama, Lake (ka-buh-TO-guh-muh) (☐ 31 sq mi/80 sq km), in St. Louis co., extending W into Koochiching co., NE Minn., 16 mi/26 km ESE of International Falls, in Voyagers Natl. Park. Elev. 1,119 ft/341 m; 20 mi/32 km long, max. width 5 mi/8 km. Connected by channel to Namakan L. to E. Lake has numerous peninsulas, bays, and isls. Kettle Falls Dam at outlet (N) of Namakan L., has merged the lakes and evened their levels. Kabetogama State Forest to S; Rainy L. to N.

Kabinakagami Lake (ka-bin-uh-KA-guh-mee), central Ont., Canada, 150 mi/241 km W of Timmins; 16 mi/26 km long, 10 mi/16 km wide. Drains N into Kenogami R.

Kachemak Bay, arm (40 mi/64 km long, 20 mi/32 km wide) of Cook Inlet, S Alaska, SW Kenai Peninsula; 59°34′N 51°31′W. Haalibut Cove S; Seldovia village, S; Homer village, N.

Kadiak, Alaska: see KODIAK.

Kadoka, town (1990 pop. 736), ⊙ Jackson co., SW central S.Dak., 70 mi/113 km SW of Pierre, 25 mi/40 km ENE of Badlands Natl. Park (park hq.); at E end of Buffalo Gap Natl. Grassland; 43°49′N 101°30′W. Petrified Gardens near town; Pine Ridge Indian Reservation to S; tourist center; agr. (livestock).

Kaena Point (kah-AI-nah), NW tip of Oahu, Honolulu co., Hawaii, 30 mi/48 km NW of Honolulu; Kauai Channel to N. Kaena Military Reserve on N and SW shores of point.

Kagalaska Island (ka-guh-LAS-kah) (9 mi/14.5 km long, 7 mi/11.3 km wide), Andreanof Isls., Aleutian Isls., SW Alaska, just E of Adak.

Kagawong (KA-guh-wahng), village, S central Ont., Canada, on N Manitoulin Isl., on North Channel of L. Huron, 17 mi/27 km WSW of Little Current; 45°54′N 82°15′W. Fishing, lumbering.

Kaguyak 1 (ka-GEI-yak), fishing village, S Alaska, S Kodiak Isl., 80 mi/129 km SW of Kodiak; 56°52′N 153°46′W. **2** fishing village, S Alaska, on Shelikof Strait,

NE Alaska Peninsula, in Katmai Natl. Monument, 80 mi/129 km NW of Kodiak. Formerly spelled Kayuyak or Kayuyak.

Kahaluu 1 (KAH-hah-LOO-oo), town (1990 pop. 1,990), W Hawaii isl., Hawaii co., Hawaii, on Kahaluu Bay, Kona (W) Coast, 55 mi/89 km W of Hilo, 4 mi/6.4 km S of Kailua-Kona; 21°27′N 157°49′W. Tourism. White Sands (Disappearing Sands) Beach Park here; Farmer's Market. **2** town (1990 pop. 3,068), Oahu isl., Honolulu co., Hawaii, on E coast, 10 mi/16 km N of Honolulu, Kamehameha Highway. Laenani Beach Park here. Waiahole Forest Reserve and Koolau Range to W; Kahaluu Beach Park to S; Kahaluu Forest Reserve to SE.

Kahili (KAH-HEE-lee), peak (3,089 ft/942 m), NW Kauai, Hawaii.

Kahlotus (kah-LO-tuhs), village (1990 pop. 167), Franklin co., SE Wash., 35 mi/56 km NE of Pasco; 46°38′N 118°33′W. RR junction. In Columbia basin agr. region; wheat, vegetables, alfalfa, beans, potatoes. Palousa Falls and Lyons Ferry state parks to E; L. Kahlotus reservoir to E. Lower Monumental Dam, 6 mi/9.7 km S, forms L. Herbery on Snake R. Juniper Dunes Wilderness Area.

Kahoka (kuh-HO-kuh), city (1990 pop. 2,195), ⊙ Clark co., extreme NE Mo., 48 mi/77 km ENE of Kirksville; 40°25′N 91°43′W. Corn, soybeans. hogs; mfg. (candles). Laid out 1858. Battle of Athems State Park to N.

Kahoolawe (kah-HO-o-LAH-vai), uninhabited island (☐ 45 sq mi/117 sq km), Maui co., central Hawaii, 110 mi/177 km SE of Honolulu; separated from Maui isl. to the NE by Alalakeiki Channel and from Lanai isl. to NW by Kealaikahiki Channel. The isl., in the rain shadow of Haleakala, is low and unfertile; has served as a penal colony and as a U.S. military bombing range; now has been returned to the state for restoration. Kanapou Bay on E end; Kamohio Bay on S coast. Highest point is Lua Makika (1,477 ft/450 m) in E.

Kahuku (kah-HOO-koo), village (1990 pop. 2,063), Oahu, Honolulu co., Hawaii, about 1 mi/1.6 km off N coast, 26 mi/42 km NNW of Honolulu; 21°40′N 157°56′W. Comsat Earth Station to W; Makahoa Point to E; Kahuku Point to NW.

Kahuku Point, the N tip of Oahu, Honolulu co., Hawaii.; 21°42′N 157°59′W.

Kahului (KAH-hoo-LOO-ee), city (1990 pop. 16,889), N Maui, Maui co., Hawaii, 92 mi/148 km ESE of Honolulu, on Kahului Harbor, principal Maui port; 20°52′N 156°27′W. Twin city to the smaller Wailuku, to W; mfg. (meat packing, canned fruit, printing, service industry machines, lumber. Has Maui Community Col.; fairgrounds. The 2d-largest city (after Hilo), in Hawaii, outside of Oahu.

Kaibab Plateau, high tableland largely in Coconino co., N Ariz., extends N from Grand Canyon, past Marble Gorge, into S Utah. Elev. 7,500 ft/2,286 m–9,300 ft/2,835 m. Includes part of Kaibab Natl. Forest and N part of Grand Canyon Natl. Park; Kaibab Creek to W.

Kaieiewaho Channel, Hawaii: see KAUAI CHANNEL.

Kaien Island (kain), W B.C., Canada, in Chatham Sound, off Tsimpshian Peninsula, near mouth of Skeena R.; 6 mi/10 km long, 4 mi/6 km wide. On NW coast is Prince Rupert city. Isl. is linked with mainland (S) by RR and road bridges.

Kailua (kei-LOO-ah), uninc. city (1990 pop. 36,818), Honolulu co., Hawaii, 10 mi/16 km NE of Honolulu on the SE coast of Oahu, on Kailua Bay; 21°23′N 157°44′W. Bellows Air Force Base (inactive) to SE; Kaneohe Bay Marine Corps Base to N on Mokapu Peninsula. Kailua Beach County Park is here, to E; Ulu Po Heiau State Monument (temple) is here.

Kailua Bay 1 W Hawaii isl., Hawaii co., Hawaii. Historically, chief landing in Kona dist. for cattle shipment. The 1st missionaries in Hawaii landed here in 1820. Lighthouse at Kukailimoku Point. City of Kailua-Kona on shore. Mooring for pleasure cruise ships. **2** E Oahu isl., Honolulu co., Hawaii, near Mokapu Point, 9 mi/14.5 km NE of Honolulu. City of Kailua on shore; state seabird sanctuary, coral reef, beach.

Kailua-Kona (kei-LOO-ah-KO-nah), town (1990 pop. 9,126), W Hawaii isl., Hawaii co., Hawaii, on Kailua

Bay, Kona (W) Coast, 56 mi/90 km W of Hilo; 19°39′N 155°57′W. The 2d-largest town on the Big Isl. (Hawaii). Tourism. Coffee; fish, prawns. Mfg. (concrete prods., printing and publishing, brewing). Officially named Kailua, Kona is added to distinguish it from other Hawaiian towns of same name. Hulihee Palace, Univ. of the Nations here. Old Kona Airport State Park to NW. Honokohau Natl. Historical Park to N.

Kaiparowits Plateau (kuh-PAHR-o-witz), S Utah, mainly in Kane co., extends N into Garfield co. Elev. c.7,000 ft/2,134 m–8,000 ft/2438 m. Sparsely settled tableland W of Colorado R., bet. Escalante (to NE) and Paria (SW) rivers, SE end reaches Colorado R. (L. Powell); bordered on NE by the Straight Cliffs. Sheep and cattle grazing.

Kaiser Peak (10,320 ft/3,146 m), Fresno co., E central Calif., in Kaiser Ridge, in the Sierra Nevada, 50 mi/80 km NE of Fresno. Kaiser Pass (2,797 ft/853 m) to E.

Kaiwi Channel (kah-EE-vee), Pacific Ocean, bet. Molokai and Oahu isls., Hawaii, 26.5 mi/42.6 km wide.

Kakabeka Falls, village, W Ont., Canada, on Kaministikwia R. (with 130-ft/40-m falls), 17 mi/27 km W of Fort William; 48°25′N 89°37′W. Hydroelectric power center; dairying, grain growing.

Kakagi Lake, W Ont., Canada, 3 mi/5 km E of head of Whitefish Bay (L. of the Woods), 40 mi/64 km SE of Kenora; 20 mi/32 km long, 6 mi/10 km wide.

Kake, village (1990 pop. 700), SE Alaska, on N shore of Kupreanof Isl., 40 mi/64 km WNW of Petersburg; 56°58′N 133°55′W. Fishing, fish processing, lumbering.

Kakhonak, village, SW Alaska, on S shore of Iliamna L., at base of Alaska Peninsula; 59°26′N 154°54′W.

Kaktovik, village (1990 pop. 224), on Barter Isl., Alaska, E Beaufort Sea; 70°16′N 143°38′W. School; weather station. Only native settlement E of Colville R.; Inuits concentrated here in the 1950s when the now-abandoned DEW line was built.

Kalaheo (kah-LAH-HAI-o), town (1990 pop. 3,592), S Kauai, Kauai co., Hawaii, 10 mi/16 km WSW of Lihue, 2.5 mi/4 km N of S coast; 21°55′N 159°31′W. Sugarcane plantations to SE and S, referred to as the "Cane Coast"; Numila Cane Mill to SW, on Kaumualii Highway; Pohakea Mt. (1,429 ft/436 m) to NW; Ipuolono Reservoir to W; Elua Reservoir to N; Lihue-Koloa Forest Reserve to N.

Kalama (kuh-LAM-uh), town (1990 pop. 1,210), Cowlitz co., SW Wash., 10 mi/16 km N of Longview, on Columbia R. near mouth of Kalama R.; 46°01′N 122°51′W. River and RR shipping point, wheat export center; strawberries, vegetables; fish; mfg. (lumber, chemicals, beverages); logging. To NE are 2 state fish hatcheries on Kalama R. Founded 1870, was capital of Cowlitz co. until 1932.

Kalama River (kuh-LAM-uh), c.45 mi/72 km long, Cowlitz co., SW Wash.; rises SW of Mt. St. Helens, flows SW to Columbia R. 3 mi/4.8 km NW of Kalama. Lower river has 2 salmon hatcheries.

Kalamazoo (KAL-ah-muh-zoo), county (☐ 580 sq mi/1,502 sq km; 1990 pop. 223,411), SW Mich., 42°14′N 85°31′W; ⊙ Kalamazoo. Cattle, hogs, poultry, dairy prods.; apples, grapes, cherries, strawberries, corn, wheat, oats, soybeans; mfg. at Kalamazoo, Portage. Drained by Kalamazoo R. and short Portage R. Gull L. in NE; numerous small lakes in SW. Organized 1830.

Kalamazoo (KAL-ah-muh-zoo), city (1990 pop. 80,277), ⊙ Kalamazoo co., SW Mich., on the Kalamazoo R. at its confluence with Portage Creek; 42°16′N 85°35′W. Industrial and commercial center in a fertile farm area. Agr. (celery, peppermint, fruit); important paper industry; mfg. (paper prods., hydraulic equip., handling devices, meat prods., furniture, concrete, motor vehicle parts, printing plates, sheet metal prods., pharmeceuticals); winery. RR junction. Kalamazoo is the seat of Western Michigan Univ., Kalamazoo Col., Nazareth Col., Kalamazoo Valley Community Col., and a state mental hosp. The city has a natural history mus., an art institute, Kalamazoo Public Mus. and Planetarium, Aviation History Mus., and a symphony orchestra. Timber Ridge State Area to NW; numerous lakes to S

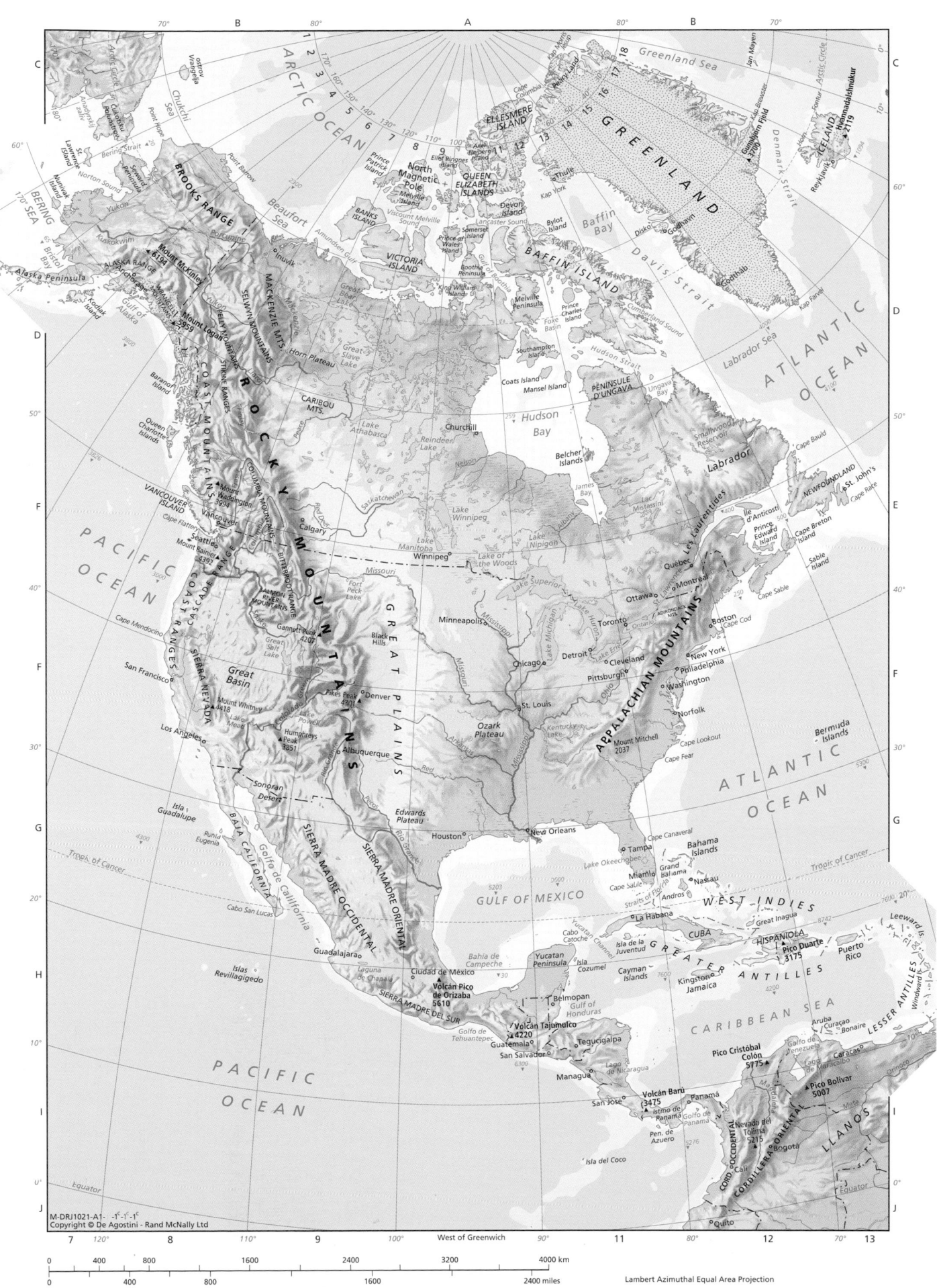

| 0 | 400 | 800 | 1600 | 2400 | 3200 | 4000 km |

| 0 | 400 | 800 | 1600 | 2400 miles |

Lambert Azimuthal Equal Area Projection

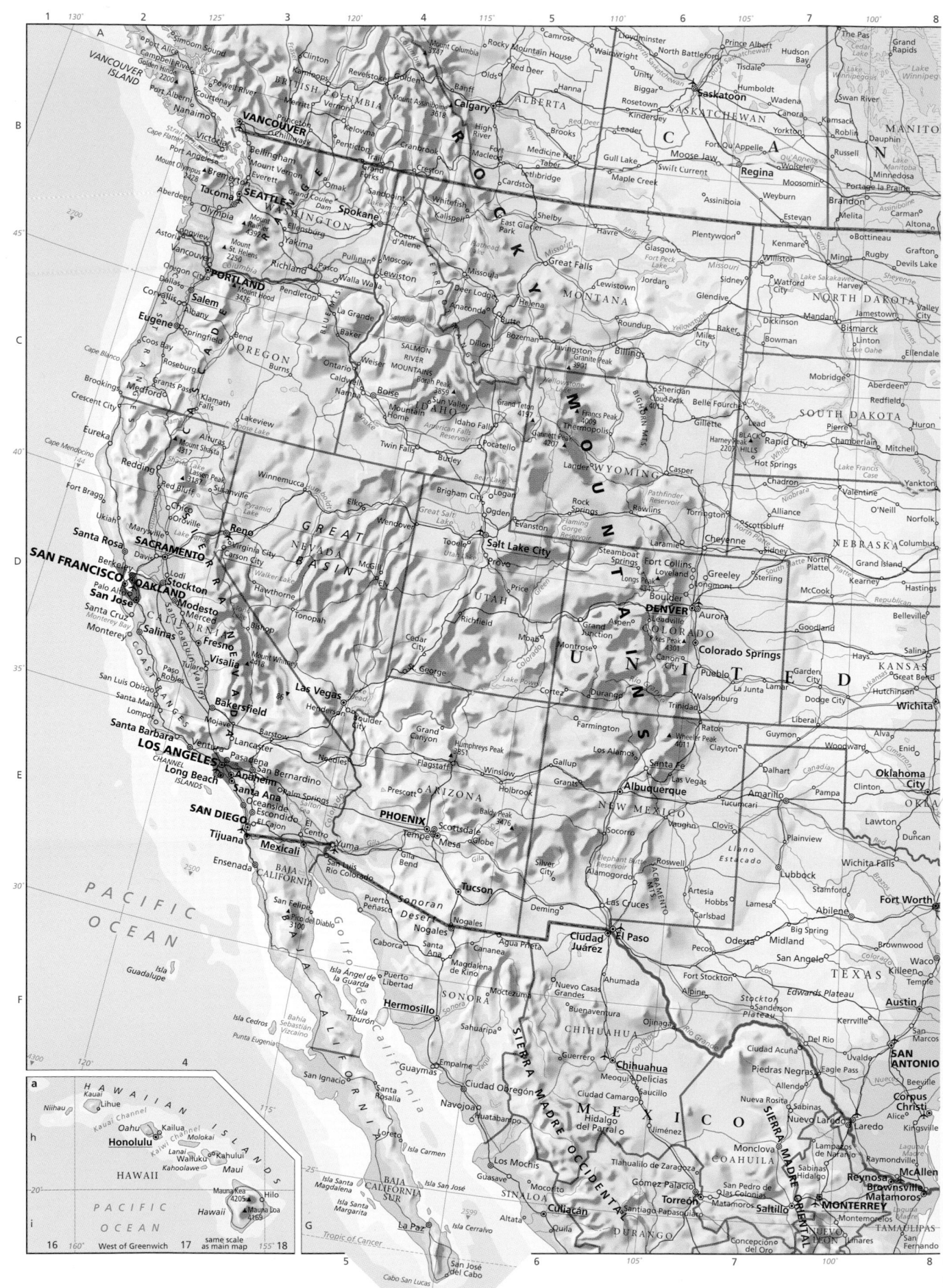

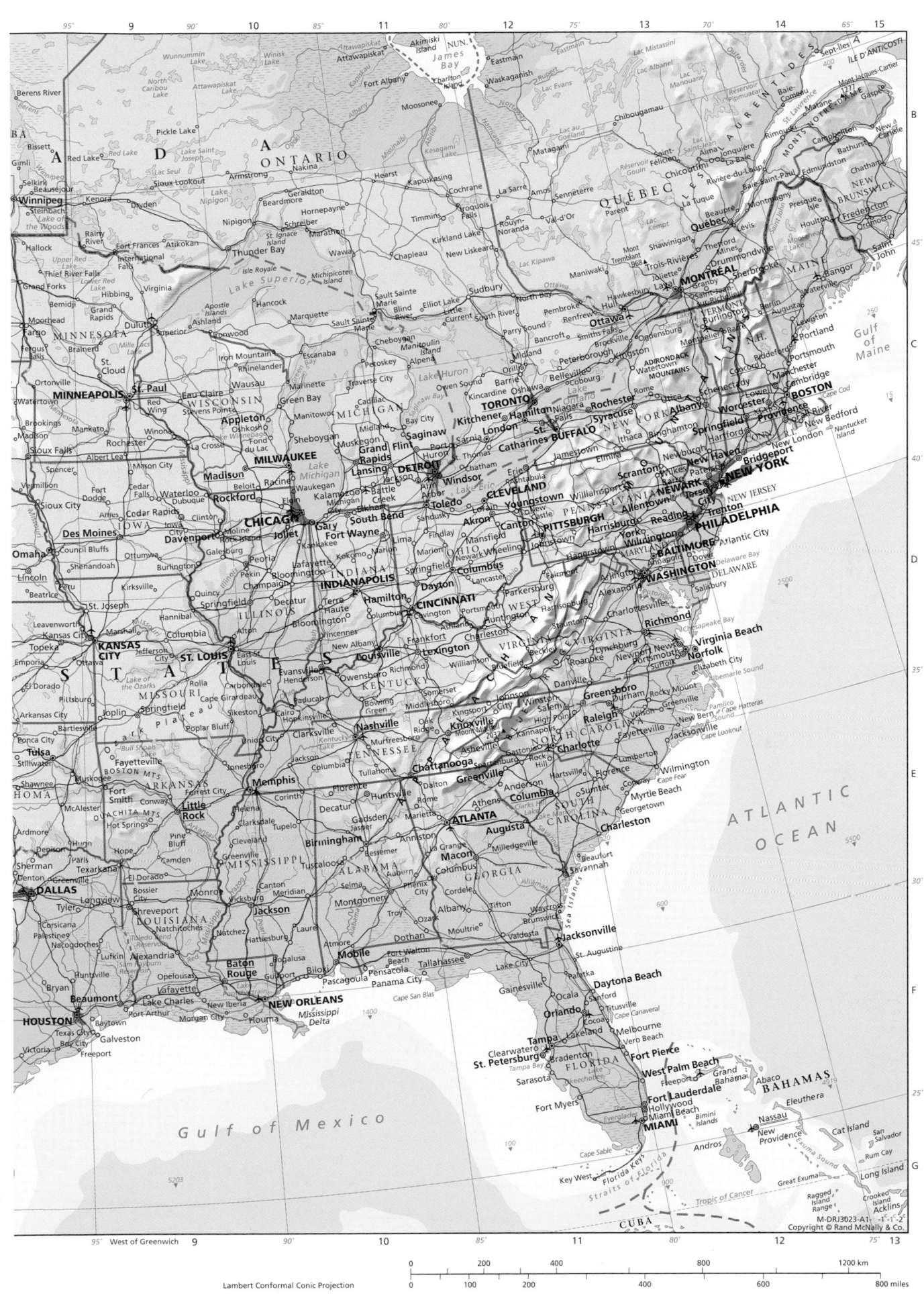

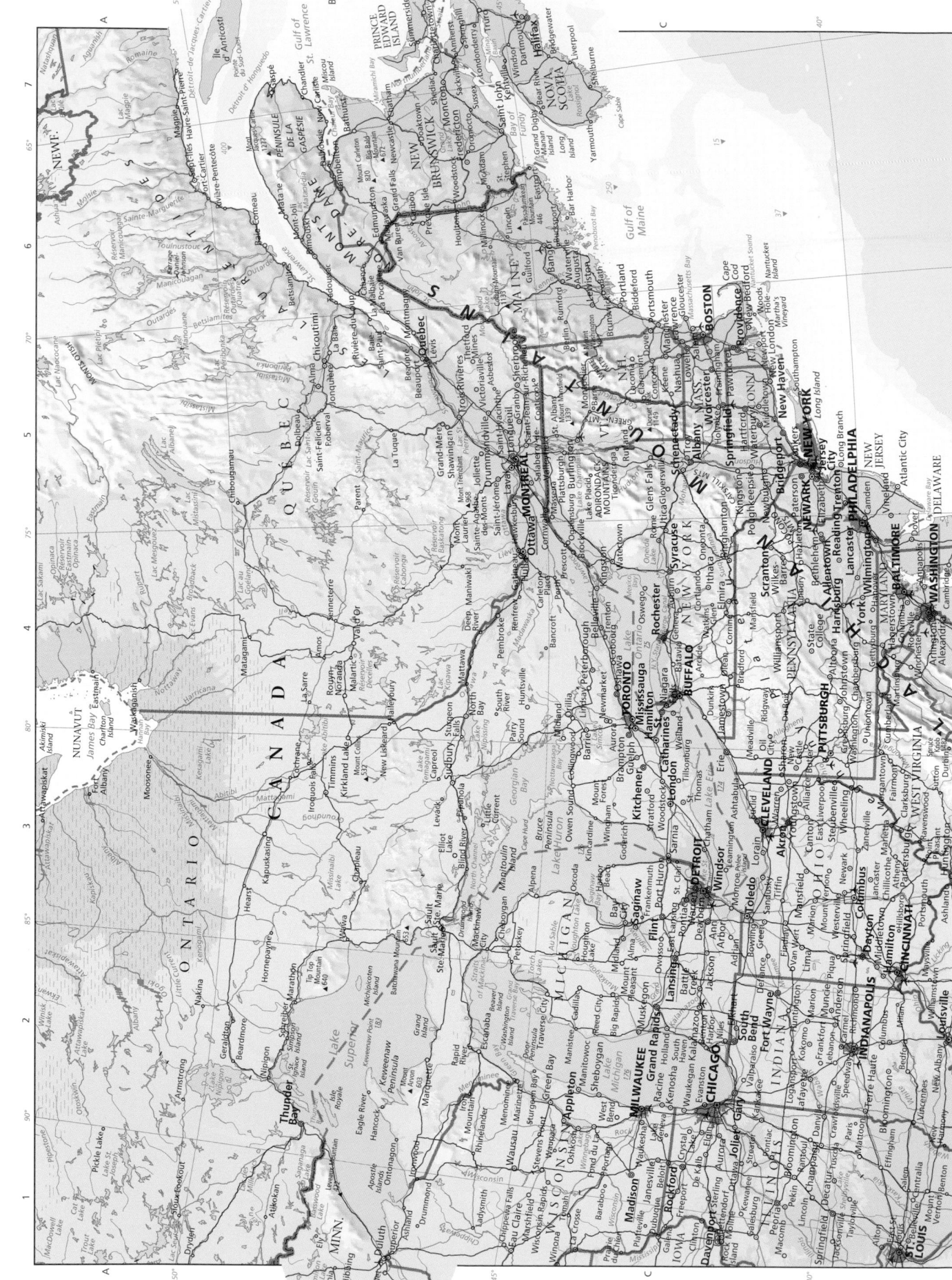

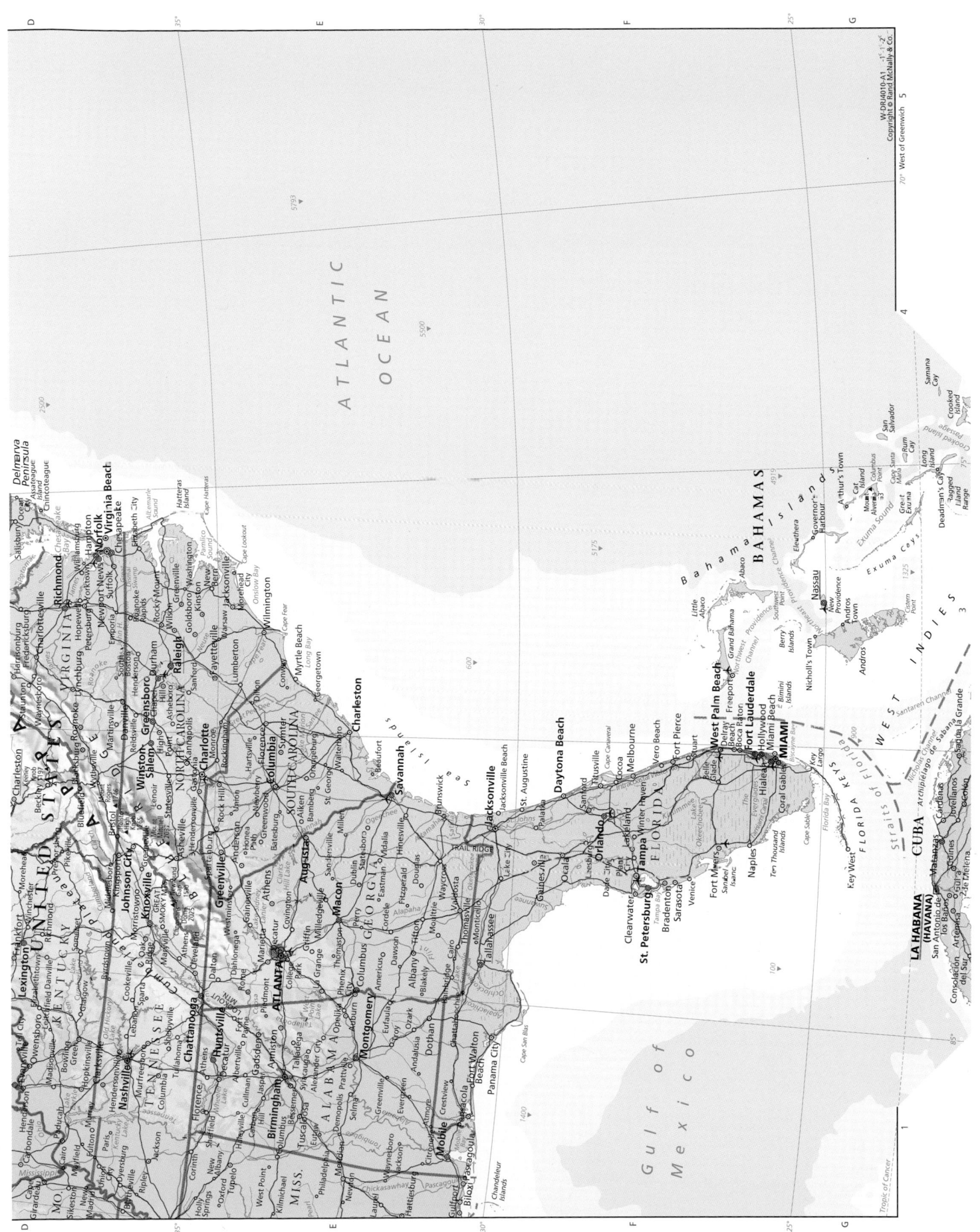

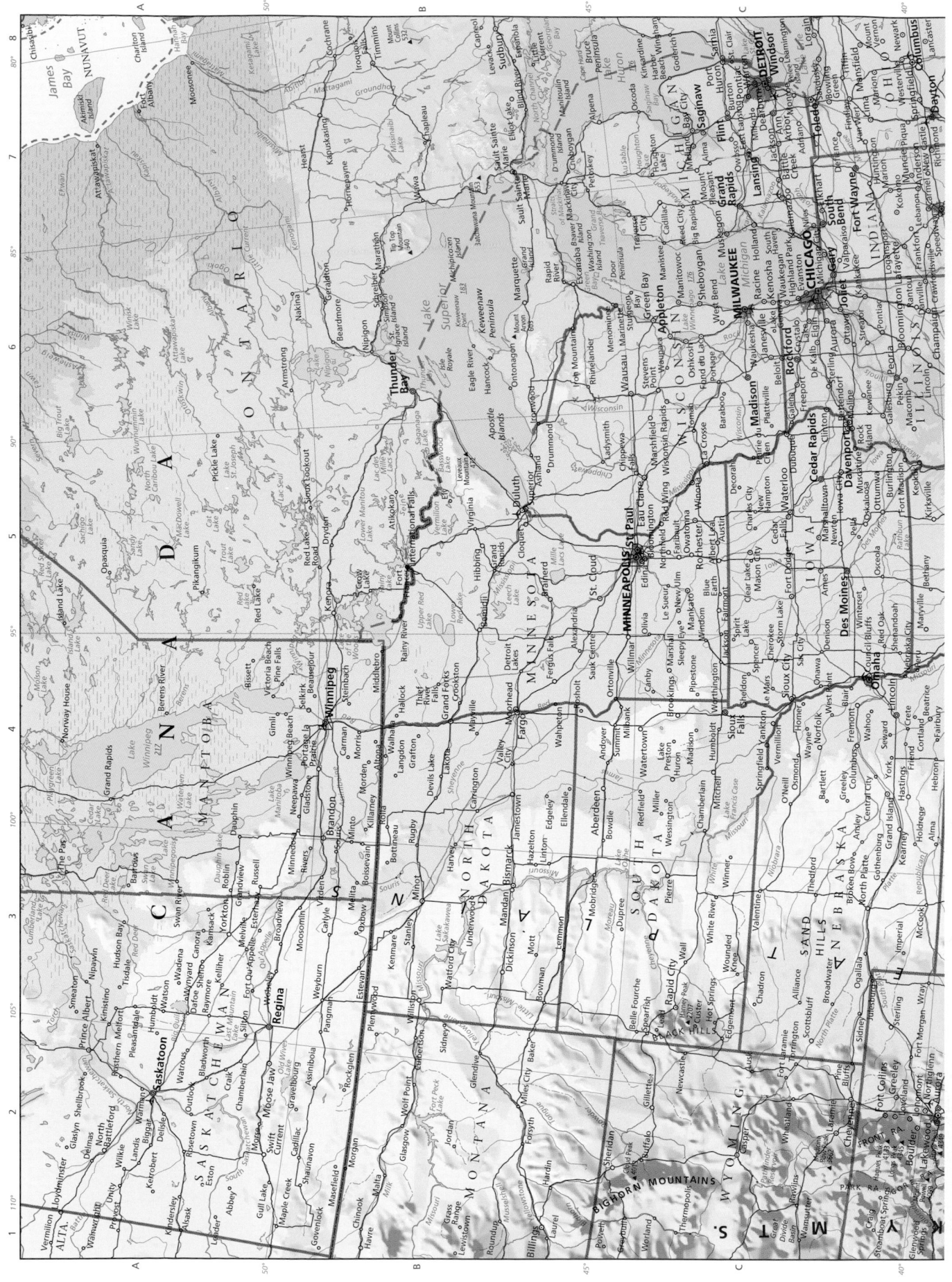

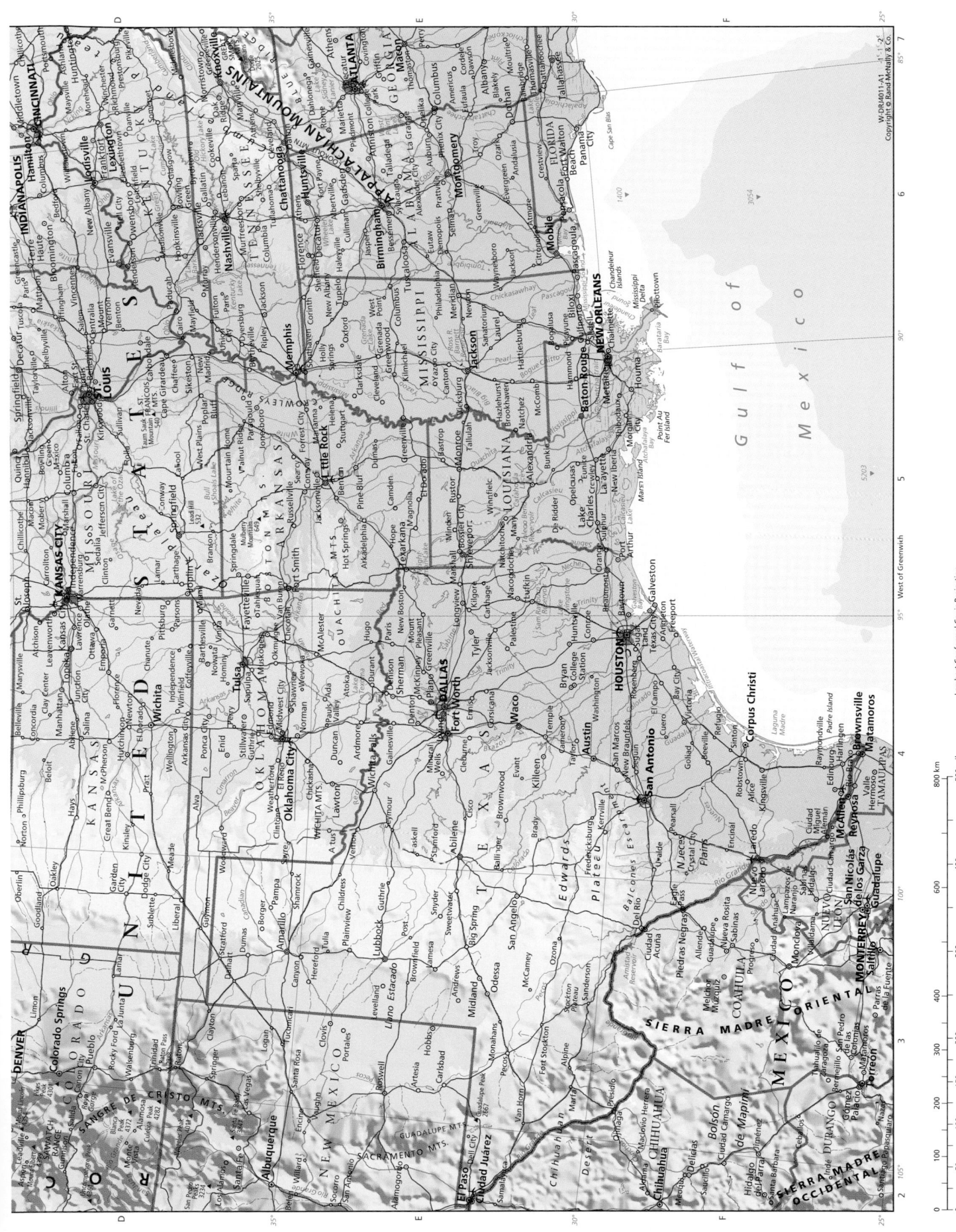

Lambert Conformal Conic Projection

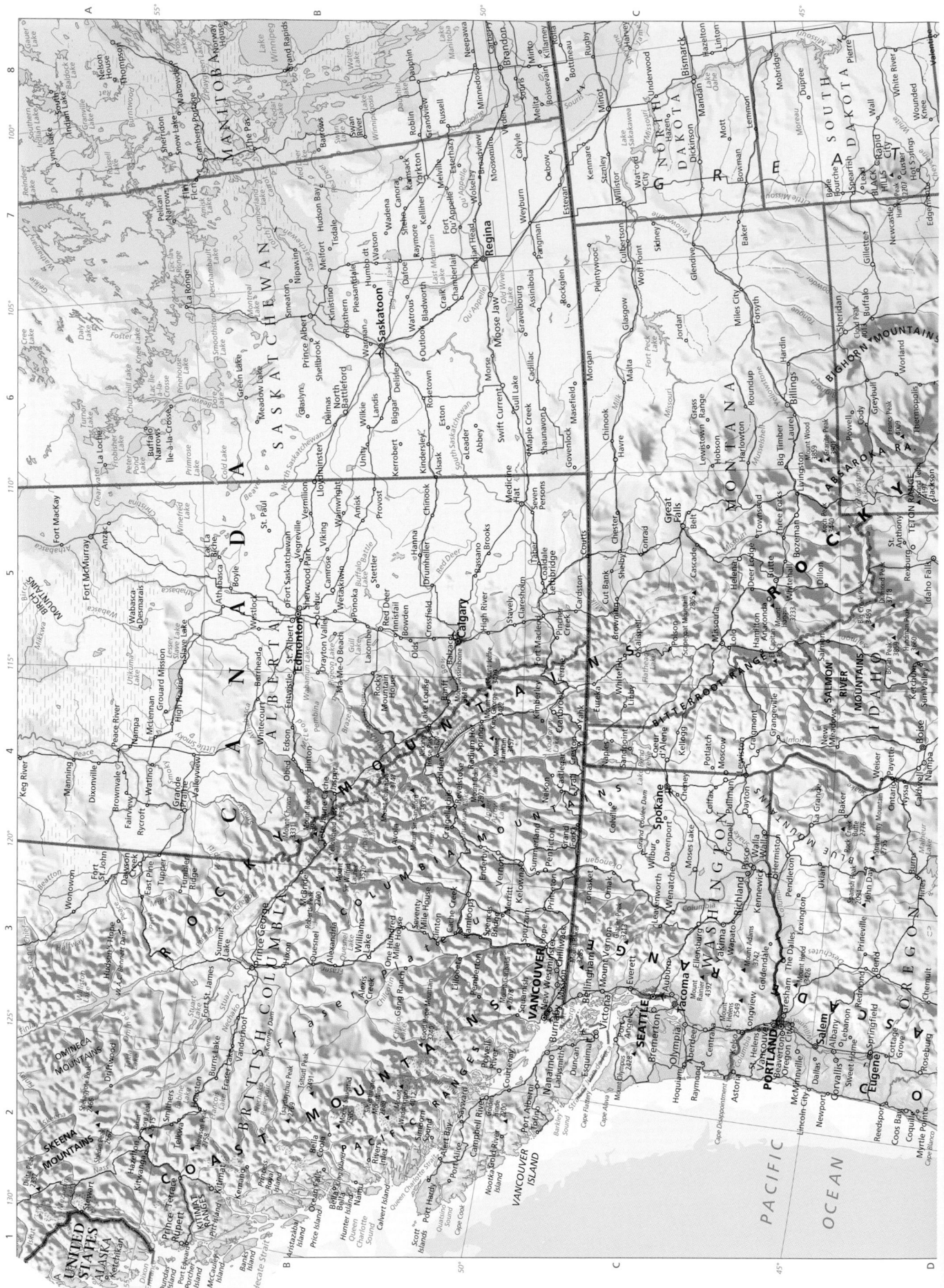

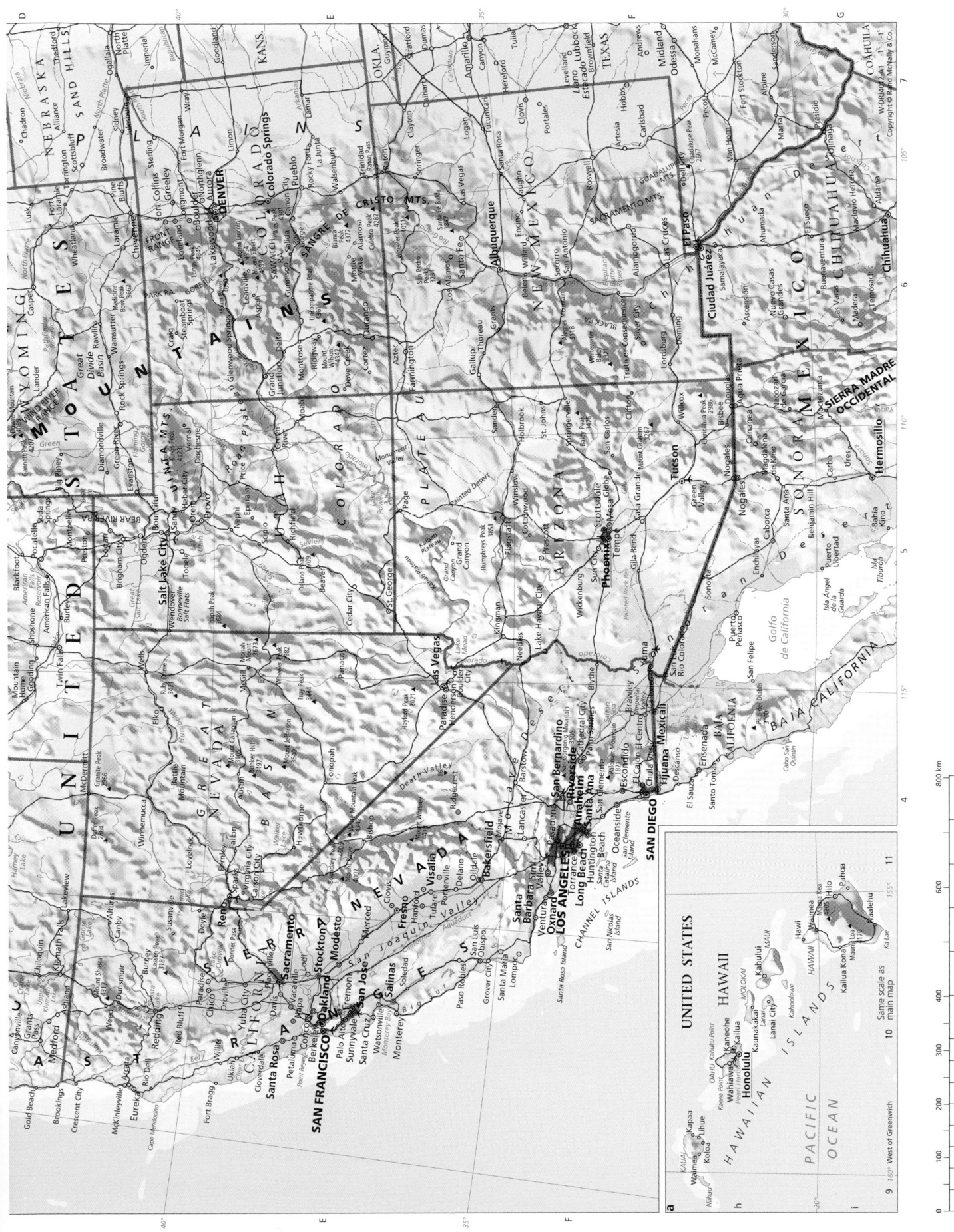

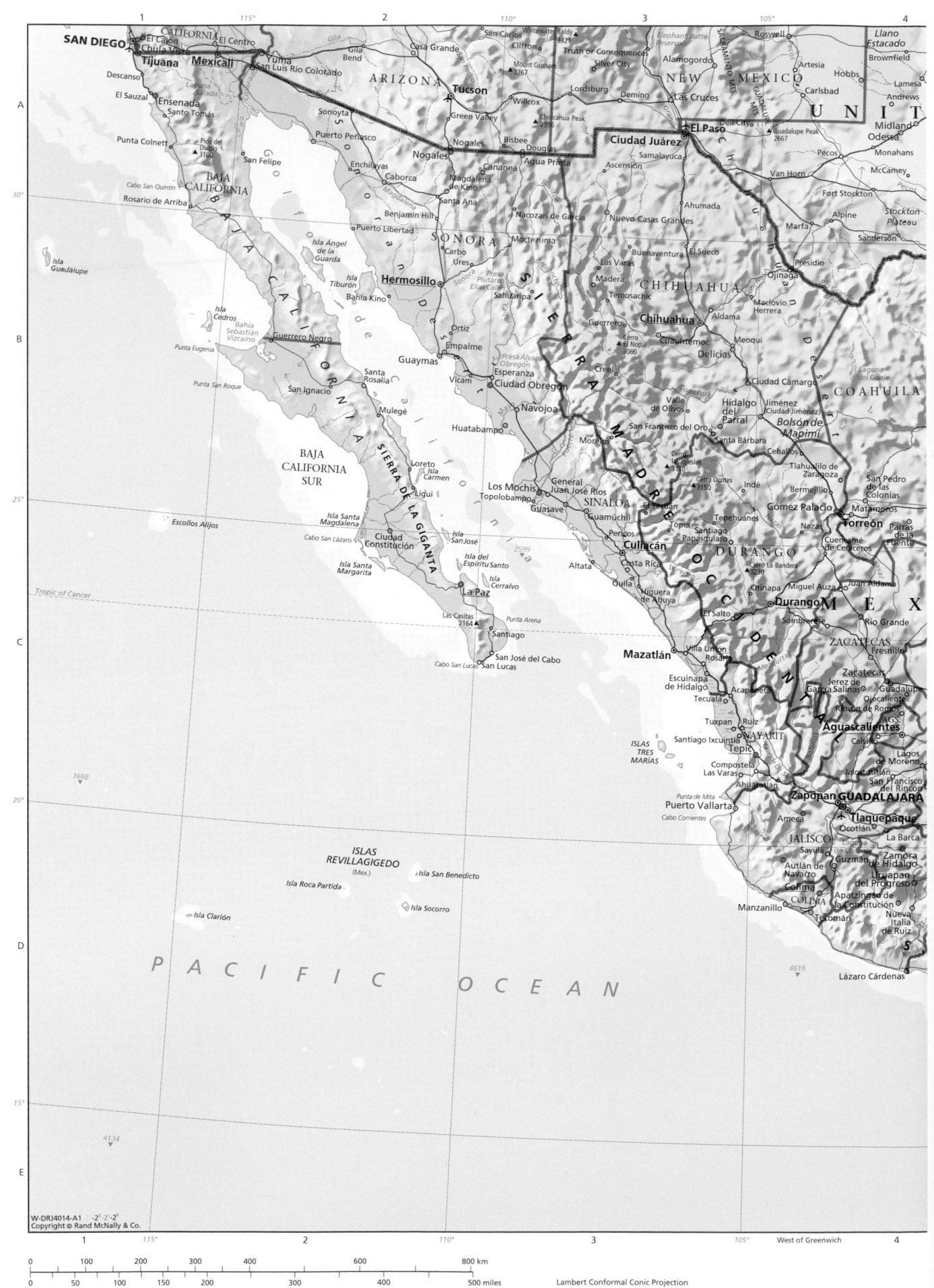

SAN DIEGO
Tijuana Mexicali
Descanso
El Sauzal
Ensenada
Santo Tomás
Punta Colnett
Pico del Diablo 3100
San Felipe

BAJA CALIFORNIA

Cabo San Quintín
Rosario de Arriba

Isla Guadalupe

Isla Ángel de la Guarda

Isla Cedros
Bahía Sebastián Vizcaíno

Guerrero Negro
Punta Eugenia
Punta San Roque

San Ignacio

Isla Tiburón
Bahía Kino

HERMOSILLO

Santa Rosalía
Mulegé

BAJA CALIFORNIA SUR

SIERRA DE LA GIGANTA

Loreto
Isla Carmen
Ligui

Isla Santa Magdalena

Ciudad Constitución

Cabo San Lázaro

Isla Santa Margarita

Isla San José

Isla del Espíritu Santo

La Paz

Isla Cerralvo

Las Casitas 2164

Santiago

Higuera de Abuya

Cabo San Lucas
San José del Cabo
San Lucas
Punta Arena

Escollos Alijos

Tropic of Cancer

ISLAS REVILLAGIGEDO
(Mex.)

Isla San Benedicto
Isla Roca Partida

Isla Socorro

Isla Clarión

1668

4134

P A C I F I C   O C E A N

CALIFORNIA El Centro
Yuma
San Luis Río Colorado
Laguna Salada
Gila
Gila Bend
Sonoyta
Puerto Peñasco
Enchilayas
Caborca
Santa Ana
Benjamín Hill
Puerto Libertad

ARIZONA

Casa Grande
San Carlos
Clifton
Mount Graham 3267
Green Valley
Willcox
Nogales
Nogales
Bisbee
Douglas
Cananea
Agua Prieta
Samalayuca

Whitewater Baldy 3327
Truth or Consequences
Silver City
Lordsburg
Deming
Las Cruces
El Paso
Ciudad Juárez
Ascensión

NEW MEXICO

Elephant Butte Reservoir
Alamogordo
Dell City
Guadalupe Peak 2667
Van Horn
Marfa

Roswell
Artesia
Carlsbad
Pecos
Fort Stockton
Alpine
Sanderson
Presidio
Ojinaga

Llano Estacado
Brownfield
Hobbs
Lamesa
Midland
Odessa
Monahans
McCamey
Stockton Plateau

UNIT
UNIT
MEX

Tucson

SONORA

Carbó
Ures
Sahuaripa
Ortiz
Empalme
Guaymas
Vicam
Ciudad Obregón
Navojoa
Huatabampo

Moctezuma
Nacozari de García

Presa Plutarco Elías Calles
Presa Álvaro Obregón

SIERRA MADRE

Temosachic
Cuauhtémoc
Creel

CHIHUAHUA

Buenaventura
El Sueco
Madera
Chihuahua
Aldama
Delicias
Meoqui
Ciudad Camargo

Nuevo Casas Grandes
Ahumada
Maclovio Herrera

COAHUILA

Laguna del Guaje

Guerrero
Cerro El Nopal 3060
Valle de Olivos
Hidalgo del Parral
Jiménez (Ciudad Jiménez)
Bolsón de Mapimí

San Francisco del Oro
Santa Bárbara
Morelos
Cerro Las Iglesias
Ceballos
Tlahualilo de Zaragoza

SINALOA

Los Mochis
Topolobampo
General Juan José Ríos
Guasave
Guamúchil
Pericos
Culiacán
Costa Rica
Altata
Quila

OCCIDENTAL

Cerro Ocotes 3150
Indé
Bermejillo
Gómez Palacio
Torreón
Matamoros
San Pedro de las Colonias

Topia
Tepehuanes
Santiago Papasquiaro
Nazas

DURANGO

Cerro La Bandera 3230
Otinapa
Miguel Auza
Juan Aldama
Durango
El Salto
Sombrerete
Río Grande

ZACATECAS

Mazatlán
Villa Unión
Rosario
Escuinapa de Hidalgo
Acaponeta
Tecuala
Ruiz

Zacatecas
Jerez de García Salinas
Fresnillo
Guadalupe
Calera
Aguascalientes

Tuxpan
Ojocaliente
Rincón de Romos

NAYARIT

Tepic
Santiago Ixcuintla
Las Varas
Compostela
Ahuacatlán

Lagos de Moreno
Jalostotitlán
San Francisco del Rincón

ISLAS TRES MARÍAS

Punta de Mita
Cabo Corrientes
Puerto Vallarta
Zapopan GUADALAJARA
Tlaquepaque
Ameca
Ocotlán
La Barca

JALISCO

Sayula
Autlán de Navarro
Colima

Zamora de Hidalgo
Guzmán
Uruapan
del Progreso

COLIMA

Manzanillo
Tecomán
Apatzingán de la Constitución
Nueva Italia de Ruiz

4616

Lázaro Cárdenas

2599

1
2
3
4
115°
110°
105°
West of Greenwich

30°
25°
20°
15°

W-DRJ4014-A1 -2°-2°-2°
Copyright © Rand McNally & Co.

0   100   200   300   400   600   800 km
0   50   100   150   200   300   400   500 miles

Lambert Conformal Conic Projection

Mexican State Abbreviations
AGS = AGUASCALIENTES
TLAX = TLAXCALA
D.F. = DISTRITO FEDERAL

GULF OF MEXICO

Tropic of Cancer

LA HABANA (HAVANA)

CUBA

MEXICO

YUCATAN PENINSULA

CAMPECHE

QUINTANA ROO

JAMAICA

Kingston

GUATEMALA

BELIZE

HONDURAS

Tegucigalpa

San Salvador

EL SALVADOR

NICARAGUA

Managua

CARIB

COSTA RICA

SAN JOSÉ

PANAMÁ

Panamá

PACIFIC

OCEAN

Cartagena

MEDELLÍN

CALI

W-DRJ4015-A1   -2°-2°-2°
Copyright © Rand McNally & Co.

West of Greenwich

Sinusoidal Projection

0   200   400   800   1200   1600 km

0   100   200   300   400   600   800   1000 miles

Map labels:

5 70° 6 65° 7 60° 8

A T L A N T I C   O C E A N

Tropic of Cancer

6900

A

B A H A M A S

Rum Cay
Samana Cay
Cape Verde
Crooked Island
Salina Point
Acklins
Mayaguana
Matthew Town
Great Inagua
Little Inagua

North Caicos
Middle Caicos
East Caicos
Caicos Islands
Grand Turk
Turks Islands

TURKS AND CAICOS ISLANDS
(U.K.)

7600

20°

Baracoa
Punta de Quemado
Île de la Tortue
Cap à Foux
Manzanillo Bay
Cabo Isabela
Puerto Plata
Cabo Frances Viejo

HISPANIOLA

8742

LESSER ANTILLES

BRITISH VIRGIN ISLANDS
Anegada
Virgin Gorda
Road Town
ANGUILLA
The Valley

L E S S E R

Limbé
Cap-Haïtien
Gonaïves
LA CITADELLE
Saint-Marc
Pico Duarte 3175
Mao
Moca
Santiago de los Caballeros
San Francisco de Macorís
Cabo Samaná
Sánchez
La Vega
Yuna

HAITI
Golfe de la Gonâve
Île de la Gonâve
Jérémie
Pointe Fanchon
San Juan de la Maguana
Alto Bandera 2630
Azua
Higüey
Cabo Engaño

PUERTO RICO
(U.S.)
Arecibo
SAN JUAN
Charlotte Amalie
St. Thomas
St. John
Virgin Islands (U.S.)
St. Christopher (St. Kitts)
ST. KITTS AND NEVIS
Basseterre
Nevis

A N T I L L E S

St. Martin (Fr.-Neth.)
Saba (Neth.)

ANTIGUA AND BARBUDA
St. John's
Antigua
Barbuda

Port-au-Prince
Pétion-Ville
Les Cayes
Jacmel
Île à Vache
Pointe Abacou
Canal du Sud
Morne La Selle 2674
Barahona
Enriquillo

SANTO DOMINGO
San Cristóbal
Pedro de Macorís
La Romana
Isla Saona
Bayamón
Caguas
Mayagüez
Cerro de Punta 1338
Ponce
Isla de Vieques
Cabo Rojo
Isla de Mona

MONTSERRAT (U.K.)
Plymouth

GUADELOUPE
Grande-Terre
Basse-Terre
Soufrière 1467
Pointe-à-Pitre (Fr.)
Marie Galante

DOMINICAN REPUBLIC

6000

Guadeloupe Passage

Morne Diablotins 1447

Roseau
DOMINICA

Isla Beata
Cabo Beata

Martinique Passage

Montagne Pelée 1397

Fort-de-France
MARTINIQUE (Fr.)

15°

C A R I B B E A N   S E A

4200

St. Lucia Channel
Mount Gimie 950
ST. LUCIA
Castries
Soufrière
St. Lucia Vincent Passage
ST. VINCENT AND THE GRENADINES
St. Vincent 1234
Kingstown
Grenadines

Mount Hillaby 340
Bridgetown
BARBADOS

C

ARUBA (Neth.)
Oranjestad
NETHERLANDS ANTILLES
Bonaire
Kralendijk
Curaçao
Willemstad

St. George's
GRENADA

W I N D W A R D   I S L A N D S

Punta Gallinas
Cabo de La Vela
Punta Espada
Cabo San Román
Punta Fijo
Puerto Bolívar
Uribia
Península de La Guajira
Península de Paraguaná

Golfo de Venezuela
Puerto Cumarebo

Islas Los Roques
Isla de Aves
Isla La Orchila
Isla Blanquilla
Isla La Tortuga

L E S S E R   A N T I L L E S

Tobago
Scarborough

Isla de Margarita
La Asunción
Porlamar

Pen. de Paria
Punta Pedras
Port of Spain
Arima
Trinidad

TRINIDAD AND TOBAGO

Santa Marta
Cabo de La Aguja
Riohacha
Maicao
Barranquilla
Soledad
Malambo
Sabanalarga
MARACAIBO
Pico Cristóbal Colón 5775
Valledupar
Agustín Codazzi
Campo de la Cruz
Plato

San Rafael
Dabajuro
Coro
Churuguara
Tucacas
Puerto Cabello
Maiquetía
CARACAS
Guarenas
Cumaná
Carúpano
Güiria
Gulf of Paria
San Fernando
Río Claro
Point Fortin
Boca de la Serpiente

10°

La Concepción
Santa Rita
Cabimas
Ciudad Ojeda
Machiques
Lago de Maracaibo
Cerro 1990
Carora
Barquisimeto
Tinaquillo
Chivacoa
San Felipe
Maracay
Valencia
La Victoria
Cúa
Ocumare del Tuy
Barcelona
Pozuelos
Maturín
Pedernales
Caripito
Carúpano

DELTA DEL ORINOCO
Tucupita
Temblador
Barrancas
Isla Tobejuba
Boca Grande
Corocoro Island

Mene Grande
Valera
Trujillo
Acarigua
San Carlos
San Juan de los Morros
Chaguaramas
Aragua de Barcelona
Anaco
Cantaura
El Tigre
Morawhanna

Ciénaga de Zapatosa
Cerro Mu 2610
Pailitas
Magangué
Mompós
El Banco
San Carlos del Zulia
Bocono
Guanare
El Sombrero
Valle de la Pascua
Parlaguan
San José de Guanipa
Ciudad Bolívar
Ciudad Guayana
Upata

GUYANA

Mérida
Pico Bolívar 5007
Barinas
Ciudad de Nutrias
Calabozo
Ciudad Bolívar

Embalse de Guri
Guasipati
Tumeremo
Matthews Ridge

Gamarra
Aguachica
Ocaña
San Juan de
Santa Bárbara
CÚCUTA
San Cristóbal
Pamplona

VENEZUELA

Caicara de Orinoco
Cerro Mato 1863
Cerro Bolívar 802
Ciudad Piar
El Callao

El Dorado

Simití
Puerto Wilches
Barrancabermeja

Bucaramanga
Floridablanca
Piedecuesta
San Gil
Málaga

Guasdualito
Elorza
Santa Rosa
La Urbana
La Paragua
Canaima
Salto Angel
Angel Falls

Puerto Berrío
Puerto Boyacá

Arauca
Arauquita
Cravo Norte
Guarico

Puerto Páez
Puerto Carreño
Auyán Tepuy 2950

La Gran Sabana

COLOMBIA

Nueva Antioquia

Tame
Yopal
Casanare
Ariporo
Trinidad

L L A N O S

Puerto Rondón
Puerto Nariño
Orocué

Cerro Yaví 2441

Iru Tepuy 2620
Mount Roraima 2875

La Dorada
Honda
Zipaquirá
Chiquinquirá
Barbosa
Duitama
Sogamoso
Tunja
Miraflores

Cerro Uquia 2500

Soacha
BOGOTÁ
Villavicencio
Puerto López
San Martín
Granada
Cerro Nevado 4560

Orocué
San Fernando de Atabapo

PAKARAIMA MOUNTAINS

5°

RORAIMA

B R A Z I L

Puerto Inírida

E

5 70° 6 65° 7

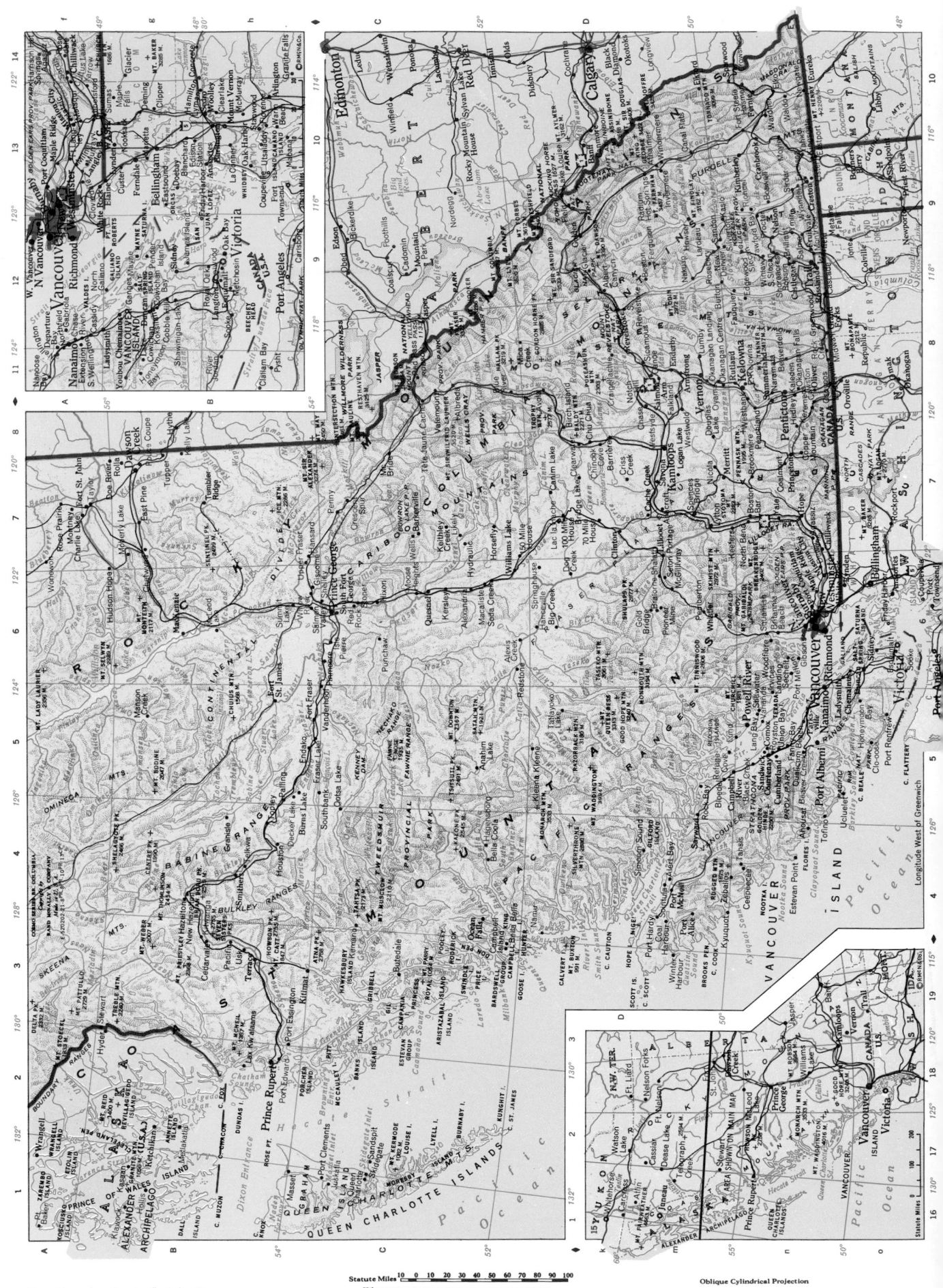

Note: Map colors do not reflect elevation.

Statute Miles 10 0 10 20 30 40 50 60 70 80 90 100

Kilometers 10 0 10 20   40   60   80   100 120 140

Oblique Cylindrical Projection

Note: Map colors do not reflect elevation.

Statute Miles 10 0 10 20 30 40 50 60 70
Kilometers 10 0 10 20 40   60   80   100

Oblique Cylindrical Projection

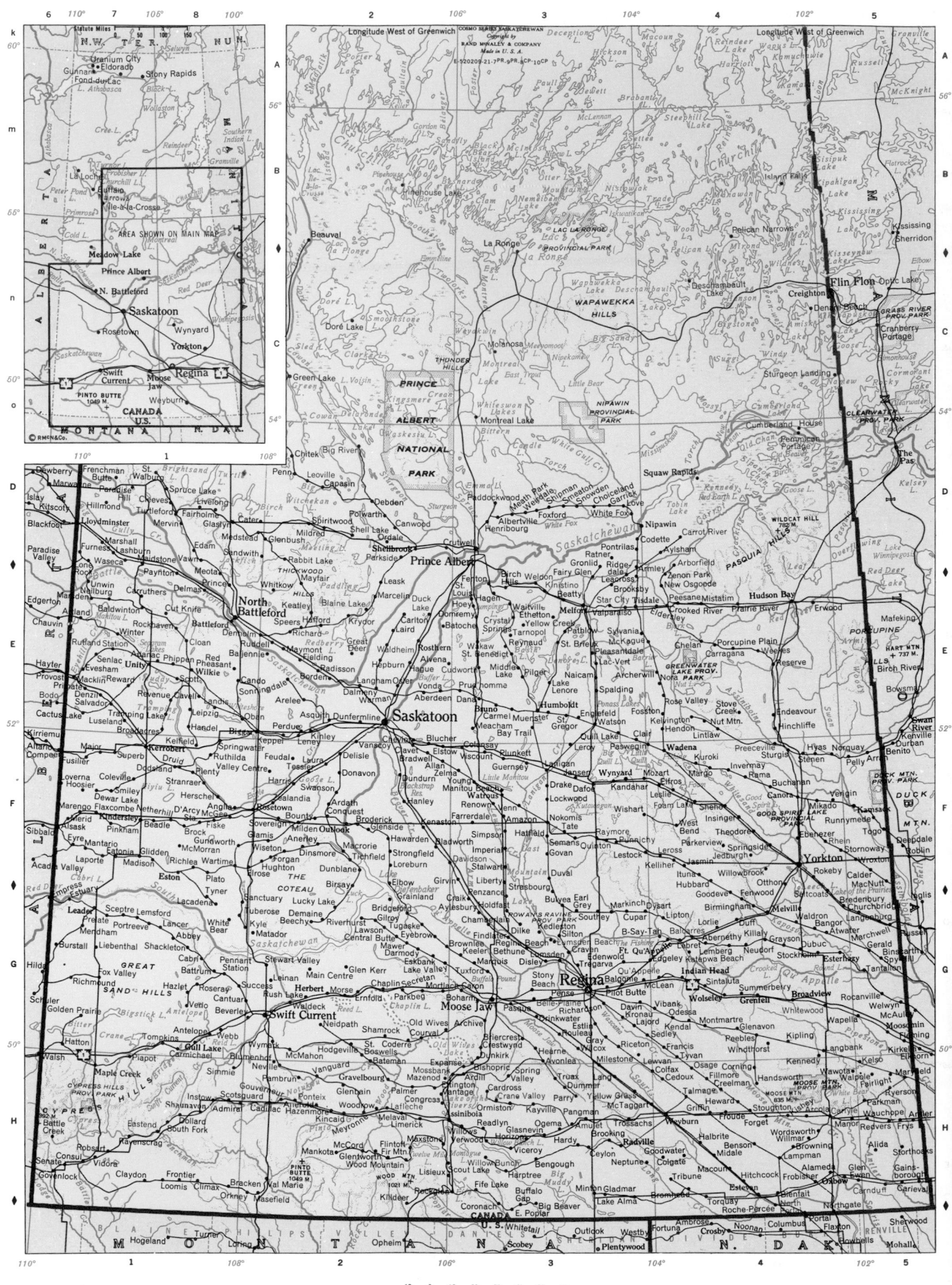

Note: Map colors do not reflect elevation.

Statute Miles
Kilometers

Oblique Cylindrical Projection

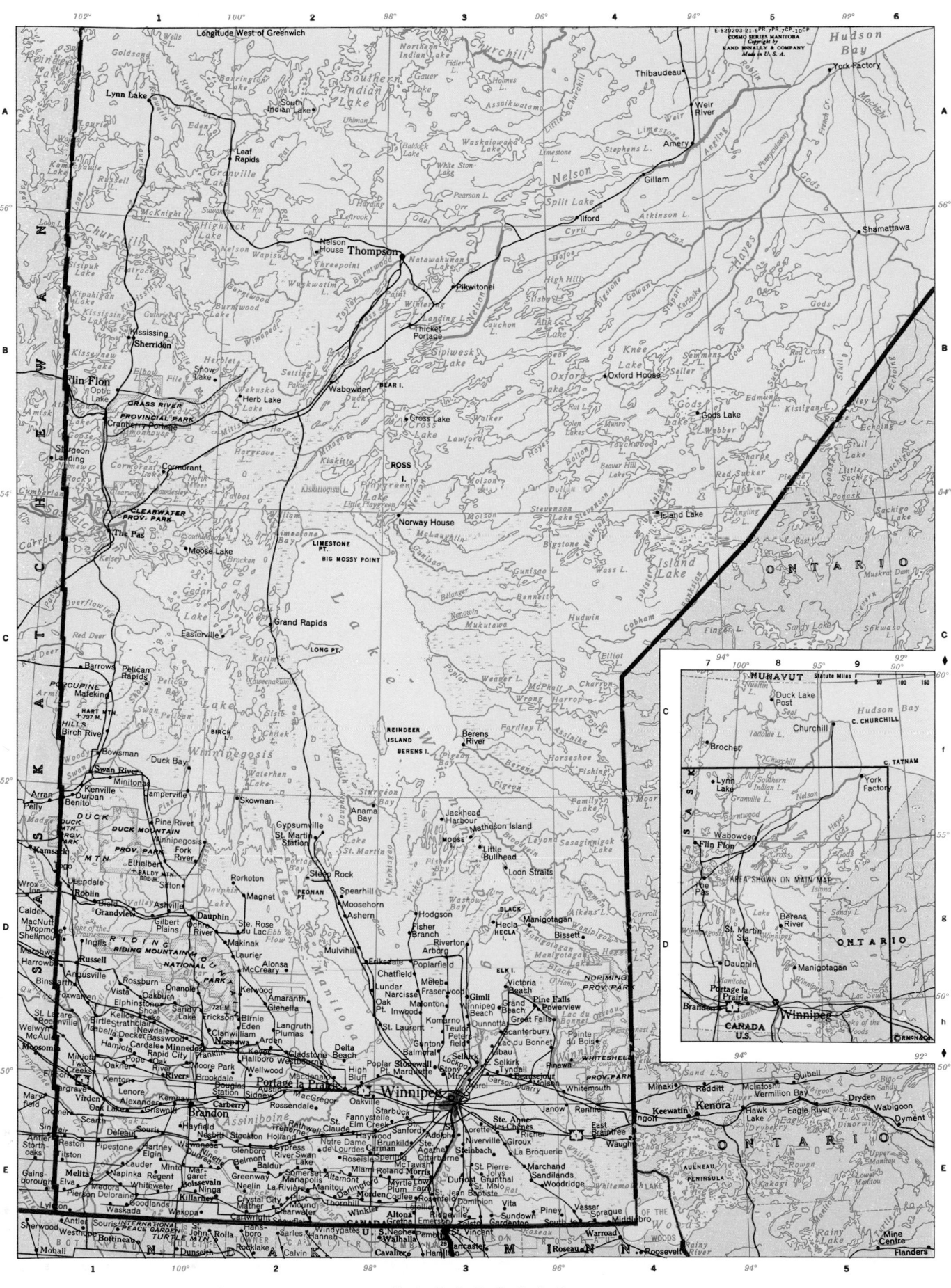

Note: Map colors do not reflect elevation.

Statute Miles
Kilometers

Oblique Cylindrical Projection

Note: Map colors do not reflect elevation.

Statute Miles
5 0 5 10 20 30 40 50

Kilometers
5 0 5 15 25 35 45 55 65 75

Oblique Cylindrical Projection

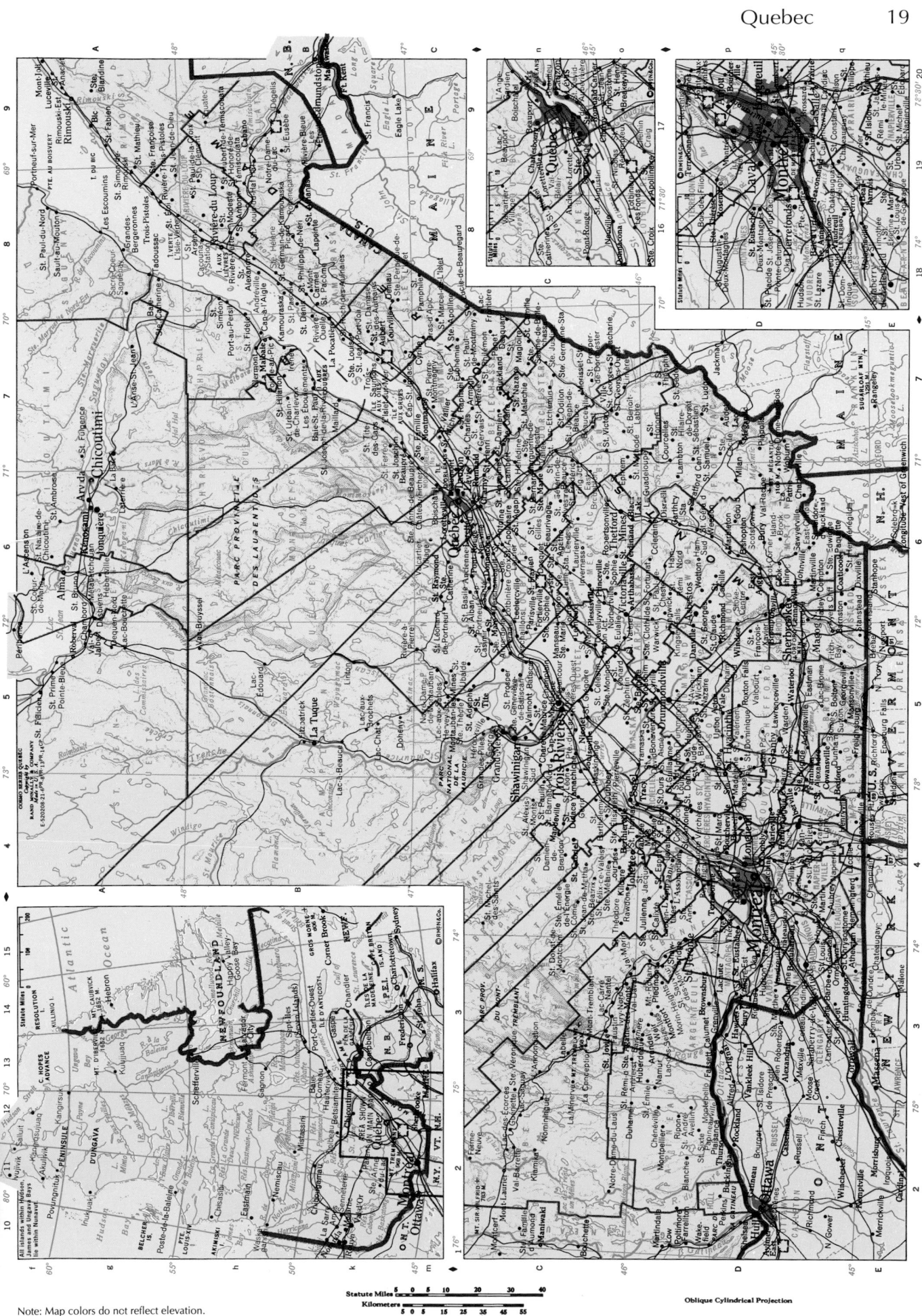

Note: Map colors do not reflect elevation.

Statute Miles 5 0 5 10 20 30 40
Kilometers 5 0 5 15 25 35 45 55

Oblique Cylindrical Projection

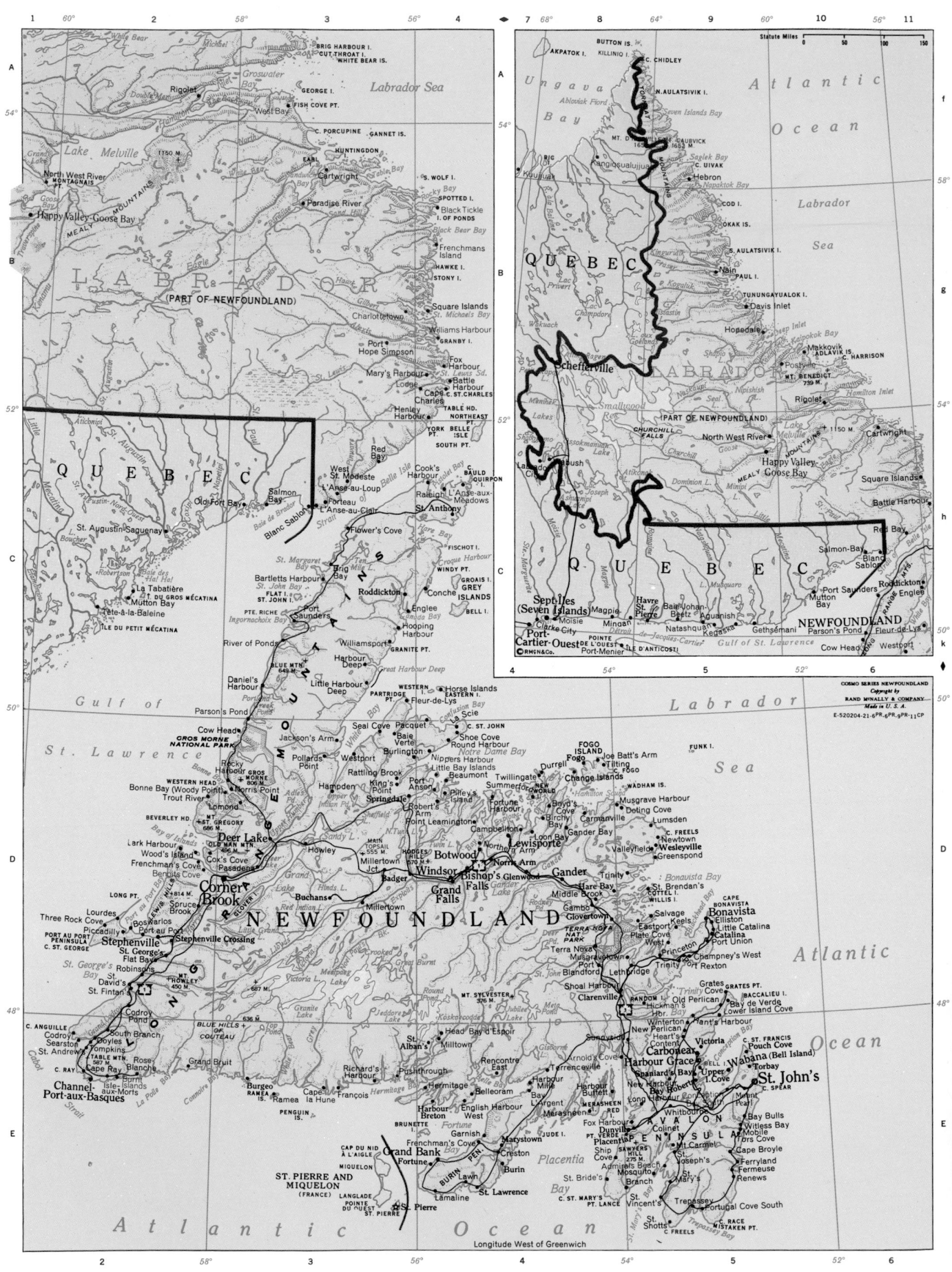

Note: Map colors do not reflect elevation.

Statute Miles
Kilometers

Lambert Conformal Conic Projection

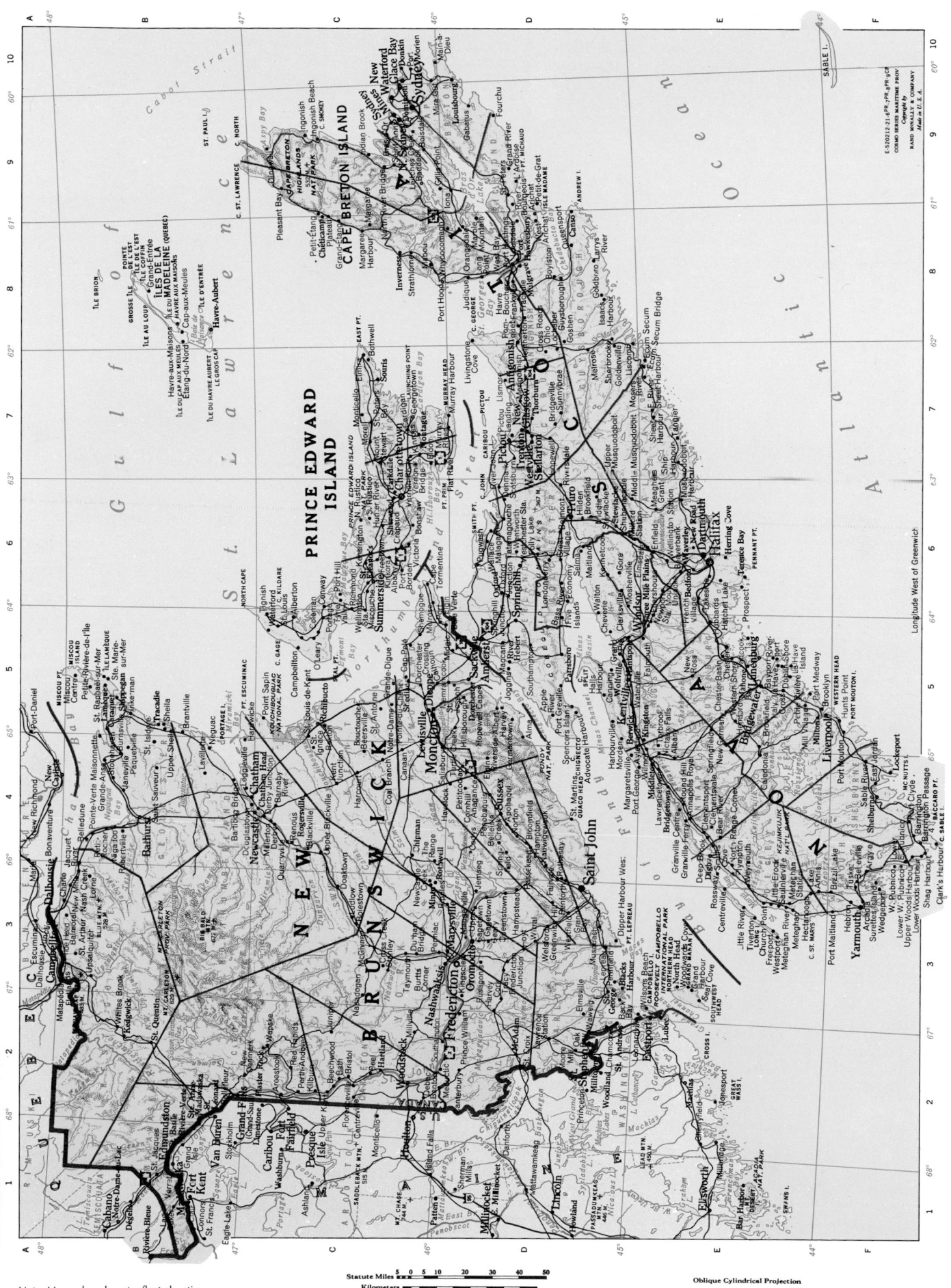

Note: Map colors do not reflect elevation.

Statute Miles 5 0 5 10   20   30   40   50

Kilometers 5 0 5   15   25   35   45   55   65   75

Oblique Cylindrical Projection

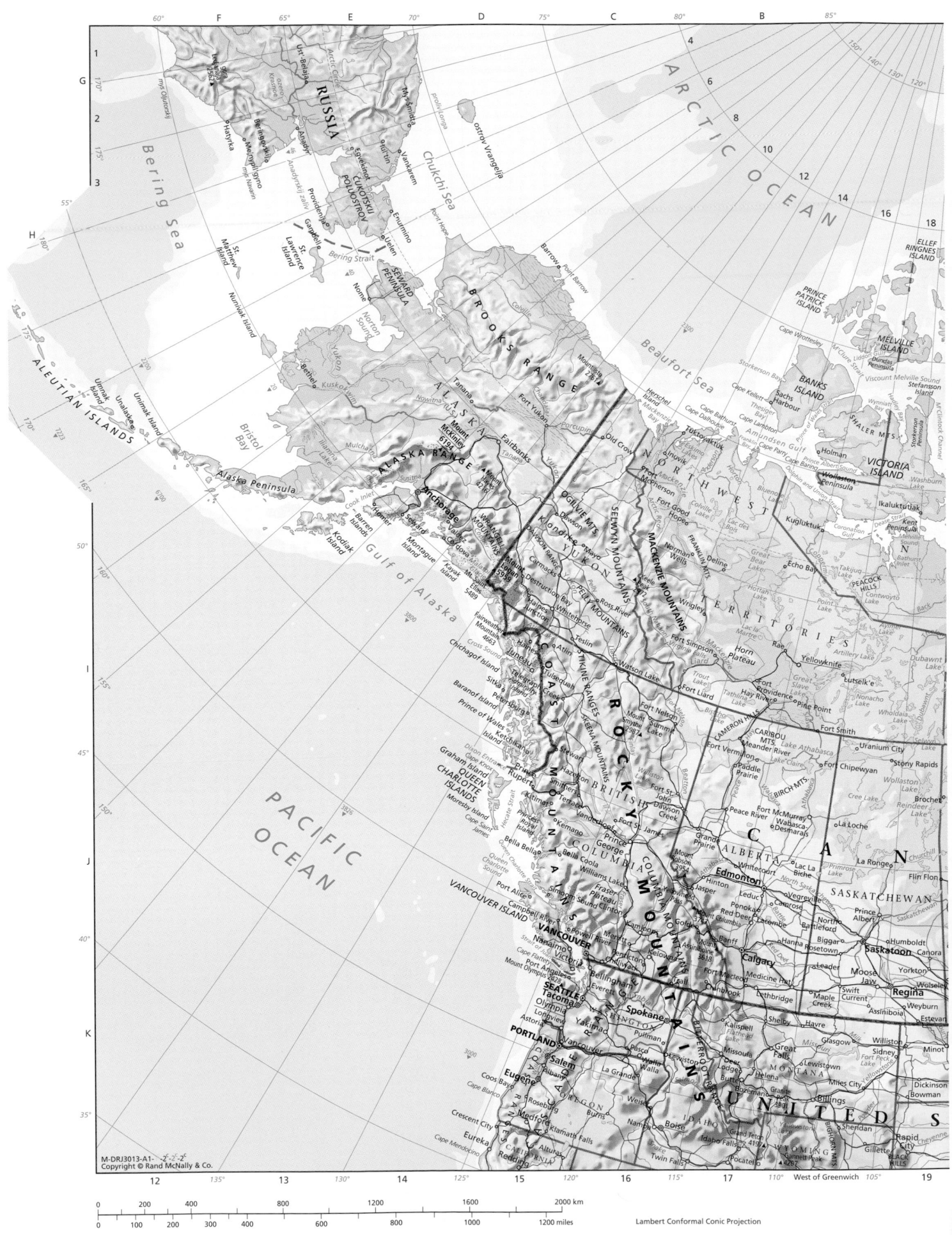

22

FAROE ISLANDS (Den.)
Tórshavn

ICELAND
Ísafjördur · Blönduós · Siglufjördur · Húsavík · Seydisfjördur · Neskaupstadur
Reykjavík · Þingvellir · Hvannadalshnúkur 2119
Keflavík · Selfoss · Vestmannaeyjar
Arctic Circle
Denmark Strait

Greenland Sea

GREENLAND (Den.)
Kap Morris Jesup
Peary Land
Lincoln Sea
Cape Columbia
Barbeau Peak 2616
Alert
Gunnbjørn Field 3700
Kap Brewster
Kap Gustav Holm
Angmagssalik
Ammassalik
Mont Forel 3360
Scoresbysund
Kap Dan
Kangerlussuaq
Uummannaq
Qaanaaq · Thule · Qaarsut
Kap York
Etah
Upernavik
Qeqertarsuaq
Disko
Godhavn
Ilulissat
Jakobshavn
Egedesminde
Christianshåb
Sukkertoppen
Holsteinsborg · Strømfjord
Godthåb (Nuuk)
Frederikshåb
Narssaq
Julianehåb
Qaqortoq
Kap Farvel
Greenland’s Høyeste Fjord
Jens Munks Ø

Baffin Bay
Davis Strait
Labrador Sea

ELLESMERE ISLAND
QUEEN ELIZABETH ISLANDS
AXEL HEIBERG ISLAND
BATHURST ISLAND
DEVON ISLAND
Coburg Island
Philpots Island
Jones Sound
Lady Ann Strait
Cape Parker
Cape Sherard
Lancaster Sound
Bylot Island
Mittimatalik
Pond Inlet
Cape Adair
Cape Craufurd
BAFFIN ISLAND
Kangiqtugaapik
Clyde River
Cape Dyer
Cumberland Sound
Pangnirtung
Cape Mercy
Lemieux Islands
Hoare Bay
Kimmirut
Meta Incognita Peninsula
Frobisher Bay
Iqaluit
Loks Land
Resolution Island
Killiniq

Penny Strait
Barrow Strait
Cornwallis Island
Qausuittuq
Russell Island
SOMERSET ISLAND
PRINCE OF WALES ISLAND
Prince Regent Inlet
Gulf of Boothia
Cape Swinburne
BOOTHIA PENINSULA
Cape Felix
Taloyoak
King William Island
Gjoa Haven
Oqsuqtooq
Pelly Bay
BRODEUR PENINSULA
Borden Peninsula
Eclipse Sound
Erichsen Lake

NUNAVUT
MELVILLE PENINSULA
Parry Bay
Igloolik
Hall Beach
Prince Charles Island
Air Force Island
FOXE PENINSULA
Foxe Basin
Cape Wilson
Naujaat
Repulse Bay
Vansittart Island
Cape Dorchester
Cape Dominion
Great Plain of the Koukdjuak
Nettilling Lake
Amadjuak Lake

FOXE CHANNEL
SOUTHAMPTON ISLAND
Salliq
Coral Harbour
Cape Kendall
Cape Low
Coats Island
Mansel Island
Nottingham Island
Salluit
Kangiqsujuaq
Ivujivik
Cape Wolstenholme
PÉNINSULE D’UNGAVA
Ungava Bay
Akpatok Island
Kangirsuk
Kuujjuaq
Kangiqsualujjuaq
Nain
Hopedale

Franklin Lake
Garry Lake
Aberdeen Lake
Baker Lake
Qamani’tuaq
Kangiqsliniq
Rankin Inlet
Yathkyed Lake
Kaminak Lake
Arviat
Nueltin Lake

NUNAVUT
Churchill
Cape Churchill
Tadoule Lake
Southern Indian Lake
Lynn Lake
South Indian Lake
Gillam
Thompson
Wabowden
York Factory
Fort Severn
Winisk
Cape Tatnam

MANITOBA
The Pas
Norway House
Lake Winnipeg
Grand Rapids
Berens River
Swan River
Dauphin
Russell
Portage la Prairie
Brandon
Melita
Bottineau
Gimli
Selkirk
WINNIPEG
Altona

Hudson Bay
Belcher Islands
Cape Henrietta Maria
Akimiski Island
James Bay
Charlton Island
Attawapiskat
Fort Albany
Moosonee
Big Trout Lake
Lansdowne House
Pickle Lake
Fort Severn

ONTARIO
Sioux Lookout
Red Lake
Lac Seul
Dryden
Kenora
Lake of the Woods
Fort Frances
International Falls
Atikokan
Thunder Bay
Nipigon
Lake Nipigon
Geraldton
Hearst
Kapuskasing
Cochrane
Timmins
Iroquois Falls
Hornepayne
Marathon
Wawa
Chapleau
Sault Sainte Marie
Elliot Lake
Sudbury
North Bay
Pembroke
Bancroft
Haliburton

QUÉBEC
Inukjuak
Povungnituk
Lac Payne
Lac Minto
Lac aux Feuilles
Kuujjuarapik
Whapmagoostui
Lac Bienville
Schefferville
Kuujjuaq
Lac Naococane
MONTS OTISH
Lac Mistassini
Chisasibi
Wemindji
Eastmain
Waskaganish
Matagami
Chibougamau
Lac Saint-Jean
Alma
Chicoutimi
Jonquière
Saint-Félicien
Roberval
Baie-Comeau
Sept-Îles
Havre-Saint-Pierre
ÎLE D’ANTICOSTI
Gaspé
LAURENTIDE MOUNTAINS
La Tuque
Shawinigan
Trois-Rivières
Maniwaki
Val-d’Or
Rouyn-Noranda
Amos
MONTRÉAL
QUÉBEC
Hull
Joliette
Rimouski
Matane

NEWFOUNDLAND
Labrador City
Wabush
Happy Valley–Goose Bay
Rigolet
Cartwright
Battle Harbour
Belle Isle
St. Anthony
Grey Islands
Fogo Island
Bonavista
St. John’s
Grand Bank
Corner Brook
Gander
Stephenville
Channel-Port aux Basques
APPALACHIAN MOUNTAINS

SAINT PIERRE AND MIQUELON (Fr.)
Saint-Pierre

Gulf of St. Lawrence
PRINCE EDWARD ISLAND
Charlottetown
CAPE BRETON ISLAND
Sydney
Glace Bay
Sable Island

NEW BRUNSWICK
Bathurst
Chatham
Moncton
Edmundston
Fredericton
Saint John

NOVA SCOTIA
Amherst
Truro
Halifax
Liverpool
Yarmouth
Digby
Cape Sable

MAINE
Bangor
Portland
Lewiston
Gulf of Maine

ATLANTIC OCEAN

UNITED STATES
NORTH DAKOTA
Bismarck
Devils Lake
Grand Forks
Fargo
Aberdeen
Pierre
Huron
Sioux Falls
SOUTH DAKOTA
Brookings

MINNESOTA
Bemidji
Moorhead
Duluth
St. Cloud
Brainerd
MINNEAPOLIS
St. Paul
Rochester
La Crosse
WISCONSIN
Superior
Ironwood
Marquette
Escanaba
Marinette
Green Bay
Wausau
Eau Claire
Appleton
Sheboygan
Madison
Milwaukee
Rockford
CHICAGO
Gary

MICHIGAN
Petoskey
Traverse City
Bay City
Saginaw
Flint
Grand Rapids
Lansing
DETROIT
Windsor
Lake Superior
Lake Michigan
Lake Huron
Lake Erie
Lake Ontario
Isle Royale

TORONTO
Kitchener
Hamilton
London
Chatham
Sarnia
Buffalo
Rochester
Syracuse
Watertown
Ottawa
Kingston
Belleville
Peterborough
Barrie
Orillia
Midland

NEW YORK
Albany
Binghamton
Scranton
Hartford
New Haven
NEW YORK
Newark
NEW JERSEY
Trenton
PHILADELPHIA
PENNSYLVANIA
BOSTON
Providence
Cape Cod

ATLANTIC OCEAN

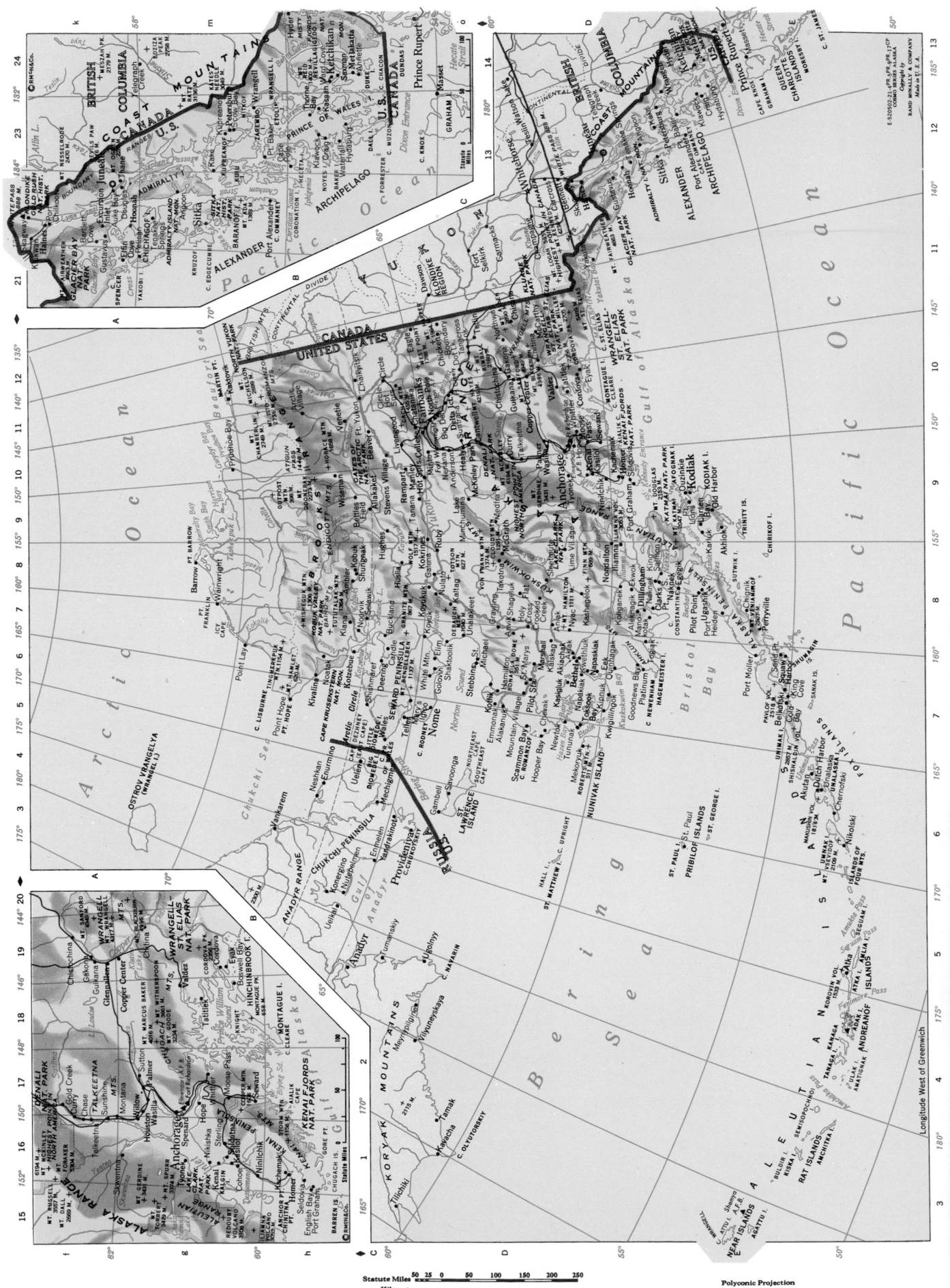

Note: Map colors do not reflect elevation.

Statute Miles 50 25 0   50   100   150   200   250
Kilometers 50 0   100   200   300

Polyconic Projection

and SW; municipal airport SE. County fairgrounds. Inc. 1883.

Kalamazoo River (KAL-ah-muh-zoo), c.138 mi/222 km long, S and SW Mich.; formed by junction of North and South branches at Albion. North Branch rises in S Jackson co. and flows c.25 mi/40 km NW; South Branch rises in NE Hillsdale co. and flows c.35 mi/56 km in a separate course, generally NNW. Main river continues NW, past Marshall, Battle Creek, Kalamazoo, Otsego, and Allegan, to L. Michigan at Saugatuck; 42°14′N 84°45′W. Power development at Winkler L., below Otsego, and Allegan Dam Pond below Allegan.

Kalaoa (KAH-lah-O-ah), town (1990 pop. 4,490), W Hawaii isl., Hawaii co., Hawaii, 6 mi/9.7 km N of Kailua-Kona, 55 mi/89 km W of Hilo, 5 mi/8 km inland from the Kona (W) Coast; 19°43′N 156°01′W. Cattle-ranching area. Coffee. Keahole Airport to W. Kaupulehu Forest Reserve to E; Honokohau Natl. Historical Park to SW.

Kalaupapa (kah-LOU-PAH-pah), peninsula, extending out from N Molokai isl., terminates at Kahiu Point, former leper colony, which is part of Maui co., Hawaii. Isolated by rock cliff (elev. 1,600 ft/488 m) to S; leper colony, open 1886–1969, now part of Kalaupapa Natl. Historical Park. Formerly known as Makanalua Peninsula.

Kalaupapa National Historic Park (□ 17 sq mi/44 sq km), N Molokai isl., Maui co., Hawaii, authorized 1980. Site of Kalaupapa colony for people suffering from leprosy (Hansen's disease), located at W base of peninsula of same name; separated from the isl. by 2,000-ft/610-m cliff. Park includes village of Kalawao, on E side of peninsula with monument to Belg. priest Father Damien (1886–1969), who organized the colony and gave spiritual comfort. Treatment has eliminated the need for isolation, but a few sufferers chose to remain. There are also ruins of 300 structures relating to early Hawaiian settlement. Extension 6 mi/9.7 km SE into isl. interior includes Waikolu Valley and Puu Kaeo (3,702 ft/1,128 m).

Kalawao (KAH-lah-WOU), county (□ 14 sq mi/36 sq km; 1990 pop. 130), officially dist. of Maui co., on Kalaupapa Peninsula, N Molokai isl., Hawaii. Kalaupapa leper settlement was on W side of peninsula; village of Kalawao in E side. Leper colony ended in 1969. Kalaupapa Natl. Historic Park authorized in 1980; co. continues to exist in name only, with Kalaupapa as its seat; Kalaupapa Airport and Molokai Lighthouse at Kahiu Point, N tip of peninsula.

Kaleva (kal-AI-vuh), village (1990 pop. 484), Manistee co., NW Mich., 18 mi/29 km NE of Manistee; 44°22′N 86°00′W. Apples, apple juice, and cider.

Kalgin Island, S Alaska, in Cook Inlet, 90 mi/145 km SW of Anchorage; 60°26′N 151°57′W. Isl. is 13 mi/21 km long, 2 mi/3.2 km–4 mi/6.4 km wide.

Kalida (kuh-LEI-duh), village (1990 pop. 947), Putnam co., NW Ohio, 17 mi/27 km NNW of Lima; 40°59′N 84°11′W. Livestock; grain.

Kalihiwai (kah-LEE-hee-WEI), village (1990 pop. 435), Kauai isl., Kauai co., Hawaii, on Kalihiwai Bay, N coast, 16 mi/26 km N of Lihue; 22°13′N 159°25′W. Sugarcane; fish. Princeville Airport to W; Kilauea Point Natl. Wildlife Refuge to NE; Anini Beach Park to W.

Kalinin Bay, bay, SE Alaska, on N shore of Kruzof Isl., on Salisbury Sound, 25 mi/40 km NW of Sitka.

Kalispell (KA-lis-pel), city (1990 pop. 11,917), ⊙ Flathead co., NW Mont., 95 mi/153 km N of Missoula, on Flathead R. and Ashley Creek, at mouths of Stillwater and Whitefish rivers; 48°12′N 114°19′W. Tourism; forestry (including Christmas-tree production); Agr. (fruit, wheat, barley, corn (maize), peas, garbanzo beans, lentils, rapeseed, mustard, mint, potatoes; cattle, horses, hogs, llamas, poultry); trade; mfg. (lumber, furniture; food processing; meat and dairy prods.; semiconductor equip., glass items; service industries. Flathead Valley Community Col., Conrad Mansion (1895), and Hockaday Center for the Arts here. The hq. of the Flathead Natl. Forest are in Kalispell, parts of forest to S, W, and E. Flathead L., 9 mi/14.5 km SSE, Glacier Natl. Park to NW. Creston Natl. Fish Hatchery to E; Lone Pine State

Park SW of city. Hungry Horse Dam and Reservoir to E. Inc. 1892.

Kalkaska (kal-KAS-kuh), county (□ 570 sq mi/1,476 sq km; 1990 pop. 13,497), NW central Mich.; 44°41′N 85°04′W; ⊙ Kalkaska. Drained by North Branch of Manistee and Boardman rivers. Agr. (potatoes, corn, wheat; cattle, hogs); logging, wood prods., esp. in NE; resorts. Several lakes. Includes a state forest and a state game refuge. Part of Camp Grayling Mich. Natl. Guard Reserve in SE; part of L. Skegemog in NW corner (S extension of Elk L.). Organized 1871.

Kalkaska (kal-KAS-kuh), town (1990 pop. 1,952), ⊙ Kalkaska co., NW central Mich., 22 mi/35 km ESE of Traverse City, on Boardman R.; 44°43′N 85°10′W. Supply center for farm and lake area; mfg. (steel parts, crafts, wire prods.). Inc. 1887.

Kallands, locality, central Alaska, on Yukon R., 30 mi/48 km W of Tanana.

Kalohi (kah-LO-hee), channel in Pacific Ocean bet. Lanai and Molokai isls., Maui co., Hawaii., 8 mi/12.9 km wide. Splits into Pailolo Channel (to NE) and Auau Channel (to SE).

Kaloko-Honokohau National Historic Park (kah-LO-ko HO-no-KO-HOU) (□ 1.81 sq mi/4.69 sq km), W Hawaii isl., Hawaii co., Hawaii, on Kona Coast, 3.5 mi/5.6 km NNW of Kailua-Kona on Honokohau Bay; authorized 1978. Site of important early pre-Eur. settlements; archaeological remains; petroglyphs; 3 fish ponds.

Kalona, town (1990 pop. 1,942), Washington co., SE Iowa, near English R., 14 mi/23 km N of Washington; 41°29′N 91°42′W. Feed, processed turkeys, dairy and metal prods. Large Amish settlement.

Kalskag, Inuit village (1990 pop. 172), W Alaska, on lower Kuskokwim R., 70 mi/113 km NE of Bethel; 61°32′N 160°22′W.

Kaltag, village (1990 pop. 240), W Alaska, on Yukon R., 60 mi/97 km SW of Galena; 64°19′N 158°44′W.

Kamakou, Mount (KAH-mah-KO-oo) (4,970 ft/1,515 m), E Molokai isl., Maui co., Hawaii, 9 mi/14.5 km E of Kaunakakai, in Molokai Forest Reserve. Highest peak on isl.

Kamas (KA-muhs), town (1990 pop. 1061), Summit co., N central Utah, on diversion canal, 12 mi/19 km E of Park City; 40°38′N 111°16′W. Sheep; logging, lumber. Part of Wasatch Natl. Forest (Uinta Range) to E. Kamas State Fish Hatchery to E; Jordanelle Reservoir and State Park to W. Elev. 6,473 ft/1,973 m. Settled 1857.

Kamay, uninc. village (1990 pop. 642), Wichita co., N Texas, 12 mi/29 km WSW of Wichita Falls, near Wichita R. Oil-field center. Cattle; cotton; light mfg. Formerly called Kemp City.

Kamehameha, Fort (kah-MAI-hah-MAI-hah), military reservation, on E side of entrance to Pearl Harbor, S Oahu, Honolulu co., Hawaii, 6 mi/9.7 km W of Honolulu. Honolulu Internatl. Airport to E; Hickam Air Force Base to N. Est. 1909.

Kamiah (KAM-e-ei), town (1990 pop. 1,157), Lewis co., W Idaho, 10 mi/16 km E of Nez Perce, on South Fork of Clearwater R., at mouth of Lawyer's Creek; 46°14′N 116°02′W. Mfg. (wood prods.). In E part of Nez Perce Indian Reservation; Nez Perce Natl. Historical Park (East Kamiah Site) to E; Nez Perce Natl. Forest to SE; Clearwater Natl. Forest to NE.

Kamiluk Lake (KA-mi-luhk) or **Kamilukuak Lake** (ka-mi-LUH-kwak), SW Keewatin dist., N.W.T., Canada, on Mackenzie dist. border; drains into Dubawnt L. (S); 62°25′N 101°40′W. Lake is 30 mi/48 km long, 20 mi/32 km wide; on S shore is trading post.

Kaminak Lake (KA-min-ak), SW Keewatin dist., N.W.T., Canada, 60 mi/97 km W of Tavani; 62°12′N 95°W. Lake is 40 mi/64 km long, 1 mi/2 km–22 mi/35 km wide; drains E into Hudson Bay.

Kaministikwia (kuh-min-is-TIK-wee-uh), river, c.60 mi/100 km long, Canada; rising in Dog L., W Ont., and flowing S, then E into L. Superior at Thunder Bay. In fur trading days it was the chief alternate to the Grand Portage–Pigeon R. route into the NW. After 1783, when the Pigeon R. formed part of the U.S. boundary, it became the main route used by the North

West Company to Fort William, their W hq. at the mouth of the river. Kakabeka Falls (130 ft/40 m high), W of Thunder Bay, is used to generate hydroelectricity.

Kaminuriak Lake (ka-min-YOO-ree-ak) (□ 360 sq mi/932 sq km), Keewatin dist., N.W.T., Canada, near 63°N 95°45′W.

Kamishak Bay, S Alaska, on W side of mouth of Cook Inlet, W of Seldovia, 45 mi/72 km wide at mouth, 20 mi/32 km long; 59°18′N 153°30′W. Contains Augustine Isl. and volcano.

Kamloops (KAM-loops), city (1991 pop. 67,057), S B.C., Canada, at the junction of the North Thompson and South Thompson rivers; 50°40′N 120°20′W. A trading post was 1st established on the site in 1812. A village grew up at the time of the Cariboo gold rush (1860), and in 1885 the main line of the Can. Pacific reached Kamloops. A transportation, finance, education, and administrative center, Kamloops supplies the surrounding mining, lumbering, and farming dists. It is also the center of B.C.'s cattle industry and a growing tourist site.

Kamloops Lake, S B.C., Canada, expansion of Thompson R., 6 mi/10 km W of Kamloops; 20 mi/32 km long, 20 mi/32 km wide.

Kamouraska (kam-oo-RA-skuh), county (□ 1,038 sq mi/2,688 sq km), SE Que., Canada, on Maine border, on the St. Lawrence R.; ⊙ St. Pascal; 47°30′N 69°30′W.

Kamouraska, village (1991 pop. 732), SE Que., Canada, on the St. Lawrence R., 15 mi/24 km ESE of La Malbaie. Dairying; resort.

Kampeska, village, Codington co., E S.Dak., 10 mi/16 km W of Watertown; 44°52′N 97°16′W. Just N is L. Kampeska (4 mi/6.4 km long, 3 mi/4.8 km wide), used for recreation. Shady Shore State Recreational Area on S side.

Kampsville, village (1990 pop. 399), Calhoun co., SW Ill., 9 mi/14.5 km N of Hardin, on Illinois R.; 39°17′N 90°36′W. Riprap Landing Conservation Area to N. Ferry across river.

Kamrar, town (1990 pop. 203), Hamilton co., central Iowa, 7 mi/11.3 km SE of Webster City; 42°23′N 93°43′W. In agr. area.

Kamsack (KAM-sak), town (1991 pop. 2,323), SE Sask., Canada, on Assiniboine R., at mouth of Whitesand R., 35 mi/56 km NE of Yorkton; 51°34′N 101°54′W. Distributing center; grain elevators; lumbering, dairying, livestock raising; natural gas production.

Kamuela, Hawaii: see WAIMEA.

Kanab (KUH-nab), town (1990 pop. 3289), ⊙ Kane co., S Utah, on Kanab Creek, and 60 mi/97 km S of St. George, near Ariz. state line; 37°01′N 112°31′W. Trade center for ranching and agr. area (alfalfa; cattle); lumbering; mfg. (rubber stamps), manganese mining. Elev. 4,925 ft/1,501 m. Coral Pink Sands State Park to W; Zion Natl. Park to NW. Kaibab Natl. Forest and Grand Canyon Natl. Park to SE, in Ariz. Kaibab Indian Reservation and Pipe Spring Natl. Monument to SW, both in Ariz. Settled 1864. Name means "willow" in Paiute.

Kanab Creek (KUH-nab), Utah and Arizona; rises in NW Kane co., S Utah, flows 90 mi/145 km S, past Kanab, Utah, and into Ariz., through Kaibab Indian Reservation, Kaibab Creek Wilderness Area and canyon in Kanab Plateau, to Colorado R. in N part of Grand Canyon Natl. Park. Artifacts of cliff dwellers have been found on its banks.

Kanab Plateau, tableland (c.6,000 ft/1,829 m) in NE Mohave co., NW Ariz., extends N from Colorado R. Bounded E by Kanab Creek, Kaibab Plateau is E of creek. Grand Canyon Natl. Park in S.

Kanabec (kuh-NAI-bek), county (□ 533 sq mi/1,380 sq km; 1990 pop. 12,082), E Minn.; ⊙ Mora; 45°57′N 93°17′W. Drained by Snake, Knife, Ann, and Groundhouse rivers. Agr. area (alfalfa, hay, oats, barley, potatoes; hogs, cattle, sheep, poultry; dairying). Ann L. Wildlife Area in W center; parts of Rum R. State Forest and Mille Lacs Wildlife Area on W boundary; Snake R. State Forest in NE; Knife L. in N; Fish L. in S. Formed 1858.

Kanaga Island (ka-NAW-guh), Andreanof Isls., Aleutian Isls., SW Alaska, 10 mi/16 km W of Adak Isl.; 30 mi/48 km long, 4 mi/6.4 km–8 mi/12.9 km wide; 51°47′N 177°15′W. Kanaga Volcano (N).

Kanakanak (kah-NUH-kah-nuhk), village, S Alaska, on W shore of Nushagak Bay, 6 mi/9.7 km SW of Dillingham.

Kananaskis Country, front range (□ 2,008 sq mi/ 5,201 sq km) of Rocky Mts. W of Calgary, Canada. From rolling sandstone foothills in E, the region grades to montane forest, alpine meadows, and rock and glacier peaks. Ranching, logging, coal mining, and hydroelectricity have made way to conservation and recreation pursuits. Site of 1988 Winter Olympic ski events.

Kanarraville (kuh-NAHR-uh-vil), village (1990 pop. 228), Iron co., SW Utah, just N of Zion Natl. Park, 10 mi/16 km SW of Cedar City; 37°32′N 113°10′W. Alfalfa, barley; dairying; cattle ranching. W of Cedar Mts. Elev. 5,541 ft/1,689 m. Dixie Natl. Forest to W; Zion Natl. Park (Kolob Canyons Area) to S. Settled 1861.

Kanasín (kah-nah-SEEN), town (1990 pop. 22,020), ⊙ Kanasín municipio, Yucatan, SE Mexico, on RR, and 5 mi/8 km SE of Mérida; 20°56′N 89°34′W. Henequen; corn, beans, tropical fruit.

Kanata, city (1991 pop. 37,344), SE Ont., Canada, suburb 12 mi/19 km SW of downtown Ottawa, part of Ottawa-Carleton Regional Municipality (1991 pop. 678,147); 45°20′N 75°54′W. Borders Ottawa R. on NE. Only E entremity is urbanized, remainder is rural. Mfg. (chemicals, electronic components, engineering instruments); mixed farming, dairying.

Kanawha (kuh-NAW-uh), county (□ 911 sq mi/ 2,359 sq km; 1990 pop. 207,619), W central W.Va.; ⊙ Charleston; 38°20′N 81°31′W. On Allegheny Plateau; bounded W, in part, by Big Coal R.; drained by Kanawha, Elk, and Pocatalico rivers. Bituminous-coal region; natural gas and oil wells. Mfg. at Charleston, South Charleston, Dunbar, Belle, and Nitro. Agr. (corn, tobacco, alfalfa, hay); cattle; poultry. Kanawha State Forest in SW; part of Wallback Wildlife Management Area in NE corner. Formed 1788.

Kanawha (kah-NAW-wah), town (1990 pop. 763), Hancock co., N Iowa, 15 mi/24 km SW of Garner; 42°55′N 93°47′W. In agr. area.

Kanawha (kah-NAW-wah), river, 97 mi/156 km long, W.Va., formed by the confluence of the New and Gauley rivers, NW Fayette co., S central W.Va., 35 mi/56 km ESE of Charleston. Flows NW past Smithers, Charleston, St. Albans, and Winfield, to the Ohio R. at Point Pleasant. There are rich coal, natural gas, and salt-brine deposits in the region, and numerous chemical plants along the river. There are navigation locks and power dams on the river, navigable to Charleston.

Kandiyohi (kan-dee-YO-hei), county (□ 862 sq mi/ 2,233 sq km; 1990 pop. 38,761), SW central Minn.; ⊙ Willmar; 45°08′N 95°00′W. Watered by several natural lakes, notably Green L. (NE), and Big Kandiyohi L. (S); drained by Crow R. Agr. area (oats, wheat, corn, alfalfa, hay, soybeans, sugar beets, beans, peas; hogs, sheep, cattle, poultry; dairying). Swed. settlement. Sibley State Park in N. Formed 1858.

Kandiyohi (kan-dee-YO-hei), village (1990 pop. 506), Kandiyohi co., S central Minn., 6 mi/9.7 km E of Willmar; 45°07′N 94°55′W. Livestock, poultry; grain, sugar beets, alfalfa; dairying. Little Kandiyohi L. to S, small natural lakes in area.

Kane 1 county (□ 524 sq mi/1,357 sq km; 1990 pop. 317,471), NE Ill.; ⊙ Geneva; 41°56′N 88°25′W. Agr. area (dairy prods.; corn, soybeans), with industrial centers along Fox R. producing varied manufactures. Limestone quarries. E margin of co. has experienced urban growth from Chicago. Major satellite communities include Carpentersville, Batavia, Elgin, Geneva, Aurora (mfg. centers). Drained by Fox R. and small Mill Creek. Formed 1836. **2** county (□ 4,108 sq mi/10,640 sq km; 1990 pop. 5,169), S Utah; ⊙ Kanab; 37°17′N 111°53′W. Grazing and agr. area bordering on Ariz., bounded on E and SE by Colorado R. (L. Powell, formed by Glen Canyon Dam, just S of Ariz. border), and drained, in W ½, by Paria and Virgin rivers. Agr. (apples; cattle); timber; terra-cotta; tourism. Part of Paria Canyon–Vermilion Cliffs Wilderness Area in S. Kaiparowits Plateau is in E, part of Paunsaugunt Plateau in NW. Large part of Glen Canyon Natl. Recreation Area in E; parts of Dixie Natl. Forest and part of Bryce Canyon Natl. Park in NW. Part of Zion Natl. Park on W state line. Coral Pink Sand Dunes State Park in SW; Kodachrome Basin State Park in N. Formed 1864.

Kane 1 village (1990 pop. 456), Greene co., W Ill., 8 mi/ 12.9 km SSE of Carrollton; 39°11′N 90°20′W. In agr. area (corn, soybeans). **2** village, Big Horn co., N Wyo., on Bighorn R. (Bighorn L.), at mouth of Shoshone R., near Mont. state line, and 9 mi/14.5 km E of Lovell. Bighorn Canyon Natl. Recreation Area immediately E.

Kane, borough (1990 pop. 4,590), McKean co., N Pa., 22 mi/35 km SSW of Bradford. Oil wells; mfg. (lumber, fabricated metal prods., consumer goods); agr. (dairying). Natural gas nearby. Health resort. Allegheny Natl. Forest to N, W, and S. Laid out 1860.

Kaneohe (KAH-nei-O-hei), uninc. city (1990 pop. 35,448), Honolulu co., Hawaii, on the E coast of Oahu, 8 mi/12.9 km NE of Honolulu, across Koolau Range, on Kaneohe Bay; 21°24′N 157°47′W. Once the site of a pineapple plantation and cannery, it is a residential seaside community. Mfg. (printing and publishing, jewelry). Windward Community Col.; Hawaii Loa campus of Hawaii Pacific Univ. The U.S. Kaneohe Marine Corps Base is nearby; it was attacked by the Japanese on Dec. 7, 1941. Many anc. fishponds built by Hawaiian chiefs are in the area. Kaneohe Bay Marine Corps Base to NE on Mokapu Peninsula; Haiku Naval Reserve to SW; Heeia State Park to N, on coast; Kaneohe Beach County Park to E; Valley of Temples to NW.

Kaneohe Bay (KAH-nai-O-hai), Hawaii, on the E coast of Oahu isl., Honolulu co., 10 mi/16 km NNE of Honolulu. Protected by coral reefs and dotted with isls. City of Kaneohe on SW end of bay. The shores of the bay are rimmed with anc. fishponds built by the Hawaiian chiefs. Univ. of Hawaii Marine Laboratory on Coconut Isl.; state park; Kaneohe U.S. Marine Corps Base is to E, at N end of Mokapu Peninsula.

Kangaroo Lake, Wis.: see BAILEYS HARBOR.

Kangiqsualajjuuq (KAN-je-SOO-yah-yuk), village (1991 pop. 529), NE Que., Canada, on SE shore of Ungava Bay, at mouth of George R. Replaced Port-Nouveau-Quebec village. Inuit community. Hunting, fishing, trapping. Scheduled air service.

Kangiqsujuaq (KAN-je-SOO-yak) or **Wakeham Bay**, village (1991 pop. 404), N Que., Canada, on S shore of Hudson Strait, NE end of Ungava Peninsula. Inuit community. Hunting, fishing, trapping. Scheduled air service.

Kangirsuk or **Payne Bay**, village (1991 pop. 351), N Que., Canada, W shore of Ungava Bay, E side of Ungava Peninsula, at mouth of Arnaud R. Inuit community. Hunting, fishing, trapping. Scheduled air service.

Kangirtuagaapik (KAN-jer-TOO-yah-pik), hamlet (1986 pop. 471), N.W.T., Canada, W shore of Patricia Bay, E coast of Baffin Isl., c.1,338 mi/2,153 km NE of Yellowknife. Hudson's Bay Co. post 1922–1987. U.S. Coast Guard weather station.

Kangley, village (1990 pop. 250), La Salle co., N Ill., on Vermilion R., 2 mi/3.2 km NW of Streator, and 16 mi/ 26 km S of Ottawa; 41°08′N 88°52′W. Agr. (dairying; corn, wheat, soybeans).

Kaniapiskau, Canada: see CANIAPISCAU.

Kaniapiskau, Lake (kan-yuh-PI-sko) (□ 375 sq mi/ 971 sq km), N central Que., Canada, on Hudson Bay–St. Lawrence watershed; 54°10′N 69°50′W; 20 mi/32 km long, 12 mi/19 km wide. Elev. 1,850 ft/564 m; drained by Kaniapiskau R.

Kankakee (KAN-ka-kee), county (□ 681 sq mi/ 1,764 sq km; 1990 pop. 96,255), NE Ill., on Ind. state line (E); ⊙ Kankakee; 41°08′N 87°51′W. Suburban communities of Bradley and Bourbonnais adjoin city of Kankakee on N. Agr. (corn, soybeans; livestock; dairying); mfg. (industrial machinery, wood prods., food prods., paper prods., chemicals, drugs, plastics prods., tile, industrial machinery, metal prods). Limestone deposits. Drained by Kankakee and Iroquois rivers. Kankakee R. State Park in NW. Formed 1853.

Kankakee, city (1990 pop. 27,575), ⊙ Kankakee co., E Ill., on the Kankakee R.; 41°07′N 87°51′W. It is a trade, processing, and shipping center for a rich agr. region (corn, soybeans; dairying). Mfg. (wire, vinyl tiles, consumer goods, printing, chemicals, pet food, polymers, corn milling, industrial metals). Limestone quarries are nearby. A state mental hosp., a state park, and Olivet Nazarene Col. are nearby. Kankakee Community Col. is in the city. Inc. 1855.

Kankakee River, c.135 mi/217 km long, in Ind. and Ill.; rises near South Bend, N Ind.; flows SW to a point near Kankakee, thence NW, joining Des Plaines R. SW of Joliet to form Illinois R.

Kannapolis (kuh-NAP-uh-lis), city (1990 pop. 29,696), Cabarrus and Rowan cos., W central N.C., 25 mi/ 40 km NNE of Charlotte; 35°29′N 80°37′W. Twin city to Concord 5 mi/8 km SSE. It is a planned residential company town once owned by Cannon Mills; known for its production of household linens and textiles in neighboring Concord. Mfg. (textiles, health and beauty prods., light mfg.). Rowan-Cabarras Community Col. to SW. Cannon Village includes Fieldcrest Cannon Textile Mus. and Exhibition Hall. Founded c.1905.

Kanopolis (kan-NAHP-uh-lis), village (1990 pop. 605), Ellsworth co., central Kansas, on Smoky Hill R., and 4 mi/6.4 km ESE of Ellsworth; 38°42′N 98°09′W. RR junction. In wheat and livestock area. Kanopolis Reservoir (□ 21.7 sq mi/56.2 sq km; 26 mi/42 km long) is formed by Kanopolis Dam, 12 mi/19 km SE on Smoky Hill R. Old Fort Harker here. Kanopolis State Park on lake. Mushroom Park to E, rock formations.

Kanopolis Lake, reservoir (□ 21.7 sq mi/56.2 sq km), Ellsworth co., central Kansas, on Smoky Hill R., 25 mi/ 40 km SW of Salinal; 26 mi/42 km long; 38°37′N 97°58′W. Max. capacity 433,000 acre-ft. Formed by Kanopolis Dam (131 ft/40 m high), built (1948) by Army Corps of Engineers for flood control; also used for irrigation, recreation, and water supply. Kanapolis State Park is near the dam; Smoky HIll Air Natl. Guard Range nearby.

Kanorado (kan-or-AID-o), village (1990 pop. 276), Sherman co., NW Kansas, 17 mi/27 km W of Goodland, at Colo. state line; 39°20′N 102°02′W. Shipping point in agr. area.

Kanosh (ka-NAWSH), village (1990 pop. 386), Millard co., W Utah, 15 mi/24 km SSW of Fillmore; 38°47′N 112°26′W. Alfalfa, barley, wheat; cattle; mfg. (apparel). Sevier L. (intermittent) 30 mi/48 km W. Paiute Indian Chief Kanosh buried at Kanosh Cemetery. Fishlake Natl. Forest to E and S, Kanosh Indian Reservation to NE. Elev. 5,125 ft/1,562 m.

Kansas, state (□ 82,282 sq mi/213,110 sq km; 1995 est. pop. 2,565,328), central U.S., admitted to the Union in 1861 as the 34th state; ⊙ TOPEKA; 38°21′N 98°12′W. Major cities include Topeka, WICHITA (the largest city in the state) and KANSAS CITY. Almost rectangular in shape, Kansas is bounded on the N by Nebr., on the E by Mo. (the Missouri R. forms the NE boundary for a short distance), on the S by Okla., and on the W by Colo. The geographical center of the U.S. (exclusive of Alaska and Hawaii) is located in Kansas bet. Smith Center and Lebanon. Mostly part of the GREAT PLAINS, Kansas is known for its massive wheat fields. The land rises gradually more than 3,000 ft/914 m from the E alluvial prairies of Kansas to its W semiarid high plains, which stretch toward the foothills of the Rocky Mts. The state is drained by the Kansas and Arkansas rivers, both of which generally run from W to E. The average annual rainfall of 27 in/69 cm is not evenly distributed: the E prairies receive up to 40 in/102 cm of rain, while the W plains average 17 in/43 cm. Occasional dust storms plague farmers and ranchers in the W. The climate is continental, with wide extremes — cold winters with blizzards and hot summers with tornadoes. Floods also wreak havoc in the state; hence, flood-control projects, such as dams, reservoirs, and levees, are a major undertaking. Kansas was once primarily an agr. state, but mfg. and services have surpassed agr. in economic importance. However, farming is still important to the state's economy, and Kansas is the nation's leading producer of wheat and one of the top producers of sorghum for grain. Corn and hay are also major crops. Cattle and calves are raised on the state's abundant grazing lands and constitute the single most valuable agr. item. Meat-packing and dairy industries are major economic activities, and the Kansas City stockyards are among the nation's largest. Food processing ranked as the state's 3d-largest industry in the early 1990s. The 2 leading industries are the manufacture of transportation equip. and industrial machines. Wichita is a leader in the aircraft industry, esp. in the production of private planes. Other important manufactured items are petroleum and coal prods. and nonelectrical machinery. The state is a major producer of crude petroleum and has large reserves of natural gas and helium. Kansas was once part of a great shallow sea, and salt deposits in commercially profitable quantities still remain. When the Span. explorer Francisco Vásquez de Coronado visited (1541) the Kansas area in his search for *Quivira* , a fabled kingdom of riches, the area was occupied by various Native Amer. groups of the Plains descent, notably the Kansa, the Wichita, and the Pawnee. In 1601, another Span. explorer, Juan de Oñate, penetrated the region, resulting in the introduction of the horse, which revolutionized the life of the Native Americans. While not actually exploring the Kansas area, Robert Cavelier, sieur de La Salle, claimed (c.1682) for France all territory drained by the Mississippi R., including Kansas. By the Treaty of Paris (1763), ending the Fr. and Indian Wars, France ceded the territory of W La. (including Kansas) to Spain. In 1800, Spain secretly retroceded the territory to France, from whom the U.S. acquired it in the Louisiana Purchase in 1803. The region was little known, however, and subsequent explorations include the Lewis and Clark expedition (1803–1806), the Arkansas R. journey of Zebulon M. Pike in 1806, and the scientific expedition of Stephen H. Long in 1819. Most of the territory that eventually became Kansas was in an area known as the "Great American Desert," considered unsuitable for U.S. settlement because of its apparent barrenness. In the 1830s the region was designated permanent Native Amer. country, and N and E tribes were relocated there. Forts were constructed for frontier defense and for the protection of the growing trade along the Santa Fe Trail, which crossed Kansas. Fort Leavenworth was est. in 1827, Fort Scott in 1842, and Fort Riley in 1853. Kansas, at this time mainly a region to be crossed on the way to Calif. and Oregon, was organized as a territory in 1854. Its settlement, however, was spurred not so much by natural westward expansion as by the determination of both proslavery and antislavery factions to achieve a majority pop. in the territory. The struggle bet. the factions was further complicated by conflict over the location of a transcontinental RR, with proponents of a central route (rather than a S route) eager to resolve the slavery issue in the area and promote settlement. The Kansas-Nebraska Act (1854), an attempted compromise on the extension of slavery, repealed the Missouri Compromise and reopened the issue of extending slavery N of lat. 36°30′ by providing for squatter sovereignty in Kansas and Nebr., allowing settlers of territories to decide the matter themselves. Meanwhile, the Emigrant Aid Co. was organized in Mass. to foster antislavery immigration to Kansas, and proslavery interests in Mo. and throughout the South took counteraction. Towns were established by each faction: Lawrence and Topeka by the free-staters, and Leavenworth and Atchison by the proslavery settlers. Soon all the problems attendant upon organizing a territory for statehood became subsidiary to the single issue of slavery. The first elections in 1854 and 1855 were won by the proslavery group; armed Missourians intimidated voters and election officials and stuffed the ballot boxes. Andrew H. Reeder was appointed the first territorial governor in 1854. The first territorial legislature ousted (1855) all free-state members, secured the removal of Gov. Reeder, moved the capital to Lecompton, and adopted proslavery statutes. In retaliation the abolitionists set up a rival govt. at Topeka in Oct., 1855. Violence soon came to the territory. The murder of a free-state man in Nov. 1855, led to the so-called Wakarusa War, a bloodless series of encounters along the Wakarusa R. The intervention of the new governor, Wilson Shannon, kept proslavery men from attacking Lawrence. However, civil war ultimately turned the territory into "bleeding Kansas." On May 21, 1856, proslavery groups and armed Missourians known as "Border Ruffians" raided Lawrence. A few days later a band led by the abolitionist crusader John Brown murdered 5 proslavery men in the Pottawatomie massacre. Guerrilla warfare bet. free-state men called Jayhawkers and proslavery bands—both sides abetted by desperadoes and opportunists—terrorized the land. After a new governor, John W. Geary, persuaded a large group of "Border Ruffians" to return to Mo., the violence subsided. The Lecompton legislature met in 1857 to make preparations for convening a constitutional convention. Gov. Geary resigned after it became clear that free elections would not be held to approve a new constitution. Robert J. Walker was appointed governor, and a convention held at Lecompton drafted a constitution. Only that part of the resulting proslavery constitution dealing with slavery was submitted to the electorate, and the question was drafted to favor the proslavery group. Free-state men refused to participate in the election with the result that the constitution was overwhelmingly approved. Despite the dubious validity of the Lecompton constitution, President James Buchanan recommended (1858) that Congress accept it and approve statehood for the territory. Instead, Congress returned it for another territorial vote. The proslavery group boycotted the election, and the constitution was rejected. Lawrence became de facto capital of the troubled territory until after the Wyandotte constitution (framed in 1859 and totally forbidding slavery) was accepted by Congress. The Kansas conflict and the issue of statehood for the territory became a natl. issue and figured in the 1860 Republican party platform. Kansas became a state in 1861, with the capital at Topeka. Charles Robinson was the first governor and James H. Lane, an active free-stater during the 1850s, one of the U.S. senators. In the Civil War, Kansas fought with the North and suffered the highest rate of fatal casualties of any state in the Union. The Confederate William C. Quantrill and his guerrilla band burned Lawrence in 1863. With peace came the development of the prairie lands. The construction of RRs made cowtowns such as ABILENE and DODGE CITY, with their cowboys, saloons, and frontier marshals, the shipping point for large herds of cattle driven overland from Texas. The buffalo herds disappeared (some buffalo still roam in state parks and game preserves), and cattle took their place. Pioneer homesteaders, adjusting to life on the timberless prairie and living in sod houses, suffered privation. In 1874, Mennonite emigrants from Russia brought the Turkey Red variety of winter wheat to Kansas. This wheat was instrumental in making Kansas the Wheat State as winter wheat soon came to replace spring wheat. Corn, too, soon became a major cash crop. Agr. production was periodically disrupted by natl. depressions and natural disasters. Repeated and prolonged droughts accompanied by dust storms, occasional grasshopper invasions, and floods caused severe economic dislocation. Mortgages weighed heavily on farmers, and discontent was expressed in farmer support of radical farm organizations and third-party movements, such as the Granger movement, Greenback party, and Populist party. Tax relief, better regulation of interest rates, and curbs on the power of RRs were sought by these organizations. Twice in the 1890s, Populist-Democrats were elected to the governorship. As conditions improved, Kansas returned largely to its allegiance to the Republican party and gained a reputation as a conservative stronghold with a bent for moral reform, indicated in the state's strong support of prohibition; laws against the sale of liquor remained on the books in Kansas from 1880 to 1949. Over the years improved agr. methods and machines increased crop yield. Irrigation proved practicable in some areas, and winter wheat and alfalfa were cultivated in dry regions. Wheat production greatly expanded during World War I, but the end of the war brought financial difficulties. During the 1920s and 1930s, Kansas was faced with labor unrest and the economic hardships of the depression. As part of the Dust Bowl, Kansas sustained serious land erosion during the long drought of the 1930s. Erosion led to the implementation of conservation and reclamation projects, particularly in the N and W parts of the state. In 1924 an effort of the Ku Klux Klan to gain political control was fought by William Allen White, editor of the Emporia *Gazette*, who supported many liberal causes. Alfred M. Landon, elected governor in 1932, was one of the few Republican candidates in the country to win election in the midst of the sweeping Democratic victory that year. He was nominated as the Republican presidential candidate in 1936. During World War II agr. thrived and industry expanded rapidly. The food-processing industry grew substantially, the cement industry enjoyed a major revival, and the aircraft industry boomed. After the war agr. prosperity once again declined when the state was hit by a severe drought and grasshopper invasion in 1948. Prosperity returned briefly during the Korean War, but afterward farm surpluses and insufficient world markets combined to make the state's tremendous agr. ability part of the natl. "farm problem." Kansas has become increasingly industrialized and urbanized, however, and industrial production has surpassed farm production in economic importance. Flood damage in the state, especially after a major flood in 1951, spurred the construction of dams (such as the Tuttle Creek, Milford, and Wilson dams) on major Kansas rivers, and their reservoirs have vastly increased water recreational facilities for Kansans. Since the 1970s, Kansas has become increasingly less rural. Accordingly, the economy has shifted its emphasis to finance and service industries located in and around major urban centers such as Wichita, Topeka, Lawrence, and Kansas City. Points of historical interest in Kansas include the boyhood home of President Dwight D. Eisenhower and the Eisenhower Lib. in Abilene; the home turned mus. of Carry Nation (in Medicine Lodge), who became convinced of her divine appointment to destroy the saloons; and Fort Leavenworth (a large Federal penitentiary). Govt. in Kansas is based on the constitution of 1859, adopted just before Kansas attained statehood. An elected governor heads the executive branch and serves a term of 4 years. The legislature has a house of representatives and a senate, with the 125 members of the house elected for 2-year terms and the 40 members of the senate elected for 4-year terms. Kansas is represented in the U.S. Congress by 4 representatives and 2 senators and has 6 electoral votes in presidential elections. Kansas has long been a Republican stronghold. Robert Dole, unsuccessful 1996 Republican presidential candidate, was a longtime senator for the state. Institutions of higher learning include the Univ. of Kansas (Lawrence), Kansas State Univ. (Manhattan), Wichita State Univ. (Wichita), and Washburn Univ. of Topeka (Topeka). Kansas has 105 cos.: ALLEN, ANDERSON, ATCHISON, BARBER, BARTON, BOURBON, BROWN, BUTLER, CHASE, CHAUTAUQUA, CHEROKEE, CHEYENNE, CLARK, CLAY, CLOUD, COFFEY, COMANCHE, COWLEY, CRAWFORD, DECATUR, DICKINSON, DONIPHAN, DOUGLAS, EDWARDS, ELK, ELLIS, ELLSWORTH, FINNEY, FORD, FRANKLIN, GEARY, GOVE, GRAHAM, GRANT, GRAY, GREELEY, GREENWOOD, HAMILTON, HARPER, HARVEY, HASKELL, HODGEMAN, JACKSON, JEFFERSON, JEWELL, JOHNSON, KEARNY, KINGMAN, KIOWA, LABETTE, LANE, LEAVENWORTH, LINCOLN, LINN, LOGAN, LYON, MCPHERSON, MARION, MARSHALL, MEADE, MIAMI, MITCHELL, MONTGOMERY, MORRIS, MORTON, NEMAHA, NEOSHO, NESS, NORTON, OSAGE, OSBORNE, OTTAWA, PAWNEE, PHILLIPS, POTTAWATOMIE, PRATT, RAWLINS, RENO, REPUBLIC, RICE, RILEY, ROOKS, RUSH, RUSSELL,

Cross references are shown in SMALL CAPITALS. The pronunciation key is on page xv. The dates of population figures are on page xii.

SALINE, SCOTT, SEDGWICK, SEWARD, SHAWNEE, SHERI-
DAN, SHERMAN, SMITH, STAFFORD, STANTON, STEVENS,
SUMNER, THOMAS, TREGO, WABAUNSEE, WALLACE,
WASHINGTON, WICHITA, WILSON, WOODSON, WYAN-
DOTTE.

Kansas 1 village (1990 pop. 887), Edgar co., E Ill., 13 mi/
21 km WSW of Paris; 39°32′N 87°56′W. Livestock,
grain. **2** village (1990 pop. 556), Delaware co., NE Okla.,
20 mi/32 km NNE of Tahelquah; 36°12′N 94°47′W.
Highway transportation center. Rocky Ford State Park
to SW.

Kansas, river, 170 mi/274 km long, Kansas; formed by
the junction of the Smoky Hill and Republican rivers
at Junction City, in E central Kansas; flows E past Manhattan, Topeka, Lawrence, and Shawnee to the Missouri R. at Kansas City, Kansas at Mo. border. The system drains parts of Kansas, Nebr., and Colo. Heavy
floods (esp. in 1951, 1977, and 1993) on the Kansas and
its tributaries caused great damage to the surrounding
farms and Kansas City area. Although itself freeflowing,
numerous dams and reservoirs have been built on its
tributaries to prevent flooding. Locally referred to as
Kaw R.

Kansas City, adjacent cities of the same name, one (1990
pop. 149,767) ⊙ Wyandotte co., NE Kansas (inc. 1859);
the other (1990 pop. 435,146) in Clay, Jackson, and
Platte cos., NW Mo. (inc. 1850); 39°07′N 94°43′W. They
are at the junction of the Missouri and Kansas (or Kaw)
rivers and together form a large commercial, industrial,
and cultural center. They are a port of entry, the focus
of many transportation lines, with markets for wheat,
hay, poultry, and seed. Both cities have meat, dairy, and
agr. processing and packaging plants. Among the chief
manufactures of the metropolitan area are auto bodies,
chemicals, petroleum and paper prods., machinery,
and transportation equip.; also printing and publishing. During the 1970s and 1980s the outlying towns and
cities that comprise Kansas City's suburban area developed their own industries, businesses, and corporate
bases for various companies. As a result, the pop. of
the 2 adjacent cities declined, and nearby suburban
communities and housing developments grew. The
area was the starting point of many Western expeditions; the Santa Fe and Oregon trails passed through
here. Several historic settlements of the early 19th cent.
(including Westport) have become full-fledged cities.
Kansas City, Kansas, is the seat of 2 junior cols., 2 theological seminaries, the Univ. of Kansas Medical Center,
and a state school for the blind (est. 1868). It has an
agr. hall of fame, a Shawnee mission (1839), and several
mus. A 19th-cent. Native Amer. cemetery is being incorporated into a unique center city mall. Kansas City,
Mo., is the site of the noted Nelson Art Gall., the Atkins
Mus. of Fine Arts, and the Country Club Plaza (finished in 1922; one of the 1st U.S. shopping malls).
Among its educational institutions are the Univ. of
Missouri–Kansas City, Avila Col., Park Col., Rockhurst
Col., Kansas City Art Inst., a col. of osteopathy and
surgery, a conservatory of music, 2 community cols.,
and a number of theological schools. The city has a
philharmonic orchestra and several theaters. The Kansas City *Star* has a distinguished history; it was founded
(1880) by William Rockhill Nelson and headed by him
until 1915. The Kansas City Royals (baseball) and the
Kansas City Chiefs (football) are the major sports
teams. The city has long been noted for its music history, particularly for jazz and swing, popular here since
the 1930s, when black musicians were attracted to the
city and made their music nationally famous. Kansas
City holds various jazz and blues festivals throughout
the year, and a Jazz Mus. opened in 1997. Richards-
Gebaur Air Force Base lies to the S.

Kantishna, village, S central Alaska, N of Mt. McKinley
Natl. Park, 100 mi/161 km SW of Nenana. Tourism;
gold mining. Rich mineral region, with lead, zinc, copper, gold, silver, antimony deposits.

Kantishna River, S tributary of Tanana R., 200 mi/
322 km long, central Alaska; rises on N slope of Mt.
McKinley; flows NE, past Toklat, to Tanana R. at

64°45′N 149°58′W. Upper course called McKinley R.
Receives Toklat R.

Kantunil (kahn-TOO-neel), town (1990 pop. 2,896), Yucatán, SE Mexico, 10 mi/16 km S of Izamal; 20°48′N
89°02′W. Henequen, sugarcane, corn.

Kantunilkin, city (1990 pop. 4,534), ⊙ Lázaro Cárdenas
municipio, Quintana Roo, SE Mexico, on E Yucatán
Peninsula, near Yucatán border, 42 mi/67 km W of
Cancún. Chicle, henequen, fruit. Archaeological remains nearby. Also called Kantunil-Kin.

Kapaa (ka-PAH-ah), town (1990 pop. 8,149), E Kauai,
Kauai co., Hawaii, 9 mi/14.5 km NNE of Lihue, on E
coast (Coconut Coast), on Kuhio Hwy, S of mouth
of Kapaa Stream; 22°06′N 159°20′W. Mfg. (printing
and publishing). Kapaa Beach Park is here; Nonou Forest Reserve to SW; Hoopii Falls to W (on Kapaa
Stream).

Kapaau (KAH-pah-OU), village (1990 pop. 1,083), N
Hawaii isl., Hawaii co., Hawaii, at N end of Kohala
Peninsula, 2 mi/3.2 km E of Hawi, 58 mi/93 km NW
of Hilo, 1 mi/1.6 km inland from N coast; 20°13′N
155°48′W. Sugarcane; cattle. King Kamehameha Statue.

Kapaau Halaula, town, N Hawaii isl., Hawaii co., Hawaii, on Kohala Peninsula, 1 mi/1.6 km inland from N.
coast. Kamehameha I b. nearby; his statue stands in
village. Also called Kohala.

Kapalaoa (kah-PAH-lah-O-ah), peak (3,310 ft/1,009 m),
central Kauai, Hawaii.

Kapalua (KAH-pah-LOO-ah), village (1990 pop. 408),
Maui isl., Maui co., Hawaii, 8 mi/12.9 km N of Lahaina,
on Oneloa Bay, NW coast, West Maui Peninsula;
21°00′N 156°39′W. Pineapples.

Kapapa (kah-PAH-pah), island, off E coast of Oahu isl.,
Honolulu co., Hawaii, 5 mi/8 km NW of Mokapu Peninsula, in Kaneohe Bay. Sea bird sanctuary.

Kaplan (KA-pluhn), city (1990 pop. 4,535), Vermilion
parish, S La., 8 mi/13 km W of Abbeville; 30°00′N
92°17′W. RR terminus (from Abbeville). Mfg. (shirts,
milled rice); oil field nearby. Holds Bastille Day Celebration. Inc. 1902.

Kapolei (KAH-po-LAI), town, S Oahu isl., Honolulu co.,
Hawaii, 11 mi/18 km WNW of Honolulu, 3 mi/4.8 km
inland from S coast, N of entrance to Barbers Point
Naval Air Station. Industrial area (concrete prods.,
chemicals, lumber, machinery, fabricated metal prods.;
wood preserving, petroleum refining, beverage processing, printing). Barbers Point and Barbers Point
Beach Park to SW.

Kappa, village (1990 pop. 134), Woodford co., central Ill.,
on Mackinaw R., and 12 mi/19 km N of Bloomington;
40°40′N 89°00′W. Agr. area.

Kapuskasing (ka-puhs-KAI-sing), town (1991 pop.
10,344), central Ont., Canada, on the Kapuskasing R.,
N of Timmins; 49°25′N 82°26′W. Lumbering and pulp
and paper mills; large tourism industry. Federal experimental farm nearby.

Kapuskasing River, 160 mi/257 km long, N Ont., Canada; rises near 48°N 83°05′W; flows NE, past Kapuskasing, to Mattagami R. at 49°50′N 82°W.

Karlsruhe (KAHRLZ-roo), village (1990 pop. 143), Mc-
Henry co., central N.Dak., 15 mi/24 km ENE of Velva,
on Wintering R.; 48°05′N 100°37′W.

Karlstad, town (1990 pop. 881), Kittson co., NW Minn.,
37 mi/60 km NNW of Thief River Falls; 48°34′N
96°31′W. Agr. (grain, potatoes, sugar beets, flax, sunflowers, beans; sheep); mfg. (meat processing; pastas).
Twin Lakes Wildlife Area to NE.

Karluck, Alaska: see KARLUK.

Karluk, uninc. townsite (1990 pop. 71), at mouth of Karluk R., S Alaska, W Kodiak Isl., on Shelikof Strait,
80 mi/129 km WSW of Kodiak; 57°35′N 154°24′W.
Salmon fishing (cannery at Uyak Bay); nearby is
salmon hatchery. Largest settlement in the Karluk Indian Reservation. Sometimes spelled Karluck.

Karnack, uninc. village (1990 pop. 775), Harrison co.,
NE Texas, 14 mi/23 km NE of Marshall. Mfg. (military
ammunition and explosives); timber; cattle. Pre–Civil
War structures SW of town; Claudia Taylor (Lady Bird
Johnson) b. here; Caddo L. State Park (hunting, fishing,
boating) is N, natural lakes formed by Big Cypress

Creek, rumored to have been formed by New Madrid
earthquake 1811–1812.

Karnak (KAHR-nack), village (1990 pop. 581), Pulaski
co., extreme S Ill., 18 mi/29 km NE of Mound City;
37°17′N 88°58′W. Adjacent to Cache R. State Natural
Area.

Karnes, county (□ 753 sq mi/1,950 sq km; 1990 pop.
12,455), S Texas; ⊙ Karnes City; 28°54′N 97°51′W.
Drained by San Antonio R. and Cibolo Creek, source
of Blanco and Medio creeks. Agr. (corn, wheat, grain
sorghum); livestock (cattle); dairying. Oil, natural gas
wells, uranium. Formed 1854.

Karnes City, town (1990 pop. 2,916), ⊙ Karnes co., S
Texas, c.50 mi/80 km SE of San Antonio, near San Antonio R; 28°53′N 97°54′W. Elev. 404 ft/123 m. In sorghum, corn, wheat, cattle area; dairying. Oil and gas,
uranium, stone; mfg. (fiberglass tanks and pipes, steel
trailers). Settled 1885, inc. 1914.

Karns City, borough (1990 pop. 226), Butler co., W Pa.,
12 mi/19 km NE of Butler. Mfg. (petroleum refining);
oil; agr. (dairying).

Kasaan (kuh-SAHN), village (1990 pop. 54), SE Alaska,
on Kasaan Bay, on E shore of Prince of Wales Isl.,
35 mi/56 km WNW of Ketchikan; 55°32′N 132°24′W.
Fishing; cannery. Haida Indian settlement.

Kasaan Bay (kuh-SAHN), SE Alaska, inlet of Clarence
Strait, E Prince of Wales Isl., 25 mi/40 km WNW of
Ketchikan; 35 mi/56 km long, 2 mi/3.2 km–8 mi/
12.9 km wide; near 55°31′N 132°25′W. Fishing. Sparsely
settled by Haida Indians. Kasaan village on N shore.

Kasba Lake, SW Keewatin dist., N.W.T., Canada, near
Mackenzie dist. and Man. borders; 43 mi/69 km long,
6 mi/10 km–23 mi/37 km wide; 60°20′N 102°15′W.
Drains N into Kazan R. through Ennadai L.

Kashagawigamog Lake, S Ont., Canada, extends SW
from Haliburton; 10 mi/16 km long, 1 mi/2 km wide.

Kashega (kuh-SHEE-guh), village, SW Unalaska Isl.,
Aleutian Isls., SW Alaska, 40 mi/64 km SW of Dutch
Harbor.

Kashegelok (kah-SHEE-ge-lok), Inuit village, SW
Alaska, on lower Holitna R., and 110 mi/177 km SE of
Holy Cross. Formerly spelled Kashegaluk.

Kasigluk (KAH-si-gluhk), village (1990 pop. 425), SW
Alaska, 32 mi/51 km NW of Bethel; 60°53′N 162°33′W.
Numerous small lakes in area. Fishing, hunting. Also
called Akolmiut.

Kasilof (KA-si-lof), fishing village, S Alaska, W Kenai
Peninsula, on Cook Inlet, 65 mi/105 km WNW of Seward. Site of Rus. settlement, est. 1786, called St. George.

Kaskaskia, small village (1990 pop. 32), Randolph co.,
SE Ill., on Kaskaskia isl. in the Mississippi R. where it
is joined by the Kaskaskia R., 5 mi/8 km W of Chester;
37°55′N 89°55′W. The settlement was est. 1703 by Jesuit
missionaries and named for a local Native Amer. group
of the Illinois. The French built a fort here in 1721,
which was destroyed when Kaskaskia was taken over
(1763) by the British. During the Amer. Revolution,
George Rogers Clark took (1778) U.S. possession of the
village. It thrived as the capital of Illinois Territory
(1809–1818) and state capital (1818–1820); the 1st Illinois
newspaper started here in 1814. The community declined after the capital was shifted (1820) to Vandalia.
Flooding from the Mississippi in the late 19th cent. further discouraged growth. Fort Kaskaskia State Park was
est. in 1927 across the Mississippi R. near Chester, Ill.
Frequent floods make permanent settlement difficult.

Kaskaskia River, c.320 mi/515 km long, central and SW
Ill.; rises near Urbana; flows generally SW across state
to the Mississippi just NW of Kaskaskia; 39°59′N
88°21′W. The river is dammed in Clinton co., forming
large Carlyle L., and Shelby co., forming large L. Shelbyville.

Kaslo (KAZ-lo), village (1991 pop. 863), SE B.C., Canada,
in Selkirk Mts., on Kootenay L., 35 mi/56 km NNE of
Nelson; 49°55′N 116°55′W. Elev. 1820 ft/546 m. Silver,
lead, zinc mining and smelting, logging (cedar), shipbuilding, fruit (cherries). Resort. Historical town. Oldest mineral claim in B.C.

Kasota (kuh-SO-duh), village (1990 pop. 655), LeSueur
co., S Minn., 9 mi/14.5 km N of Mankato, and 2 mi/

3.2 km S of St. Peter, on Shanaska Creek, S of its confluence with Minnesota R.; 44°17'N 93°58'W. Agr. area (corn, oats, soybeans; livestock, poultry); mfg. (bldg. materials, asphalt, injection molding, cut marble); limestone and marble quarries.

Kasson (KA-suhn), town (1990 pop. 3,514), Dodge co., SE Minn., 15 mi/24 km W of Rochester, near Middle Branch South Fork Zumbro R.; 44°01'N 92°45'W. Grain, soybeans, peas; livestock, poultry; dairying; mfg. (consumer goods, injection molds, concrete). Settled 1865, inc. 1870.

Katahdin (kuh-TAHD-uhn), mountain (5,268 ft/1,606 m), N central Maine, bet. branches of the Penobscot R. Highest point in Maine. The peak and the beautifully wooded, lake-dotted territory surrounding it constitute Baxter State Park, the gift of Gov. Percival P. Baxter in 1931. Mt. Katahdin is the N terminus of the Appalachian Trail.

Katahdin Iron Works (kuh-TAHD-uhn), Piscataquis co., central Maine, on Silver L., and 18 mi/29 km NNE of Dover-Foxcroft. In lumbering, recreational area. Site of abandoned iron mines.

Katalla (KA-duh-lah), village, S Alaska, 50 mi/80 km ESE of Cordova; 60°12'N 144°32'W. Center of abandoned Katalla oil field; had pop. of 5,000 in 1908.

Katepwa Beach (kuh-TEHP-wuh), village (1991 pop. 148), SE Sask., Canada, on the Fishing Lakes, 12 mi/19 km N of Indian Head. Resort.

Kater, Cape, NW extremity of Baffin Isl., E Franklin dist., N.W.T., Canada, on Prince Regent Inlet; 73°53'N 90°11'W.

Kates Needle, peak (10,002 ft/3,049 m), Alaska-B.C. (Canada) border, in Coast Range, 40 mi/64 km NE of Petersburg; 57°3'N 132°03'W.

Kathleen 1 town (□ 3 sq mi/7.8 sq km; 1990 pop. 2,743), Polk co., central Fla., 8 mi/12.9 km NW of Lakeland; 28°07'N 82°01'W. Mfg. includes cabinets. **2** town (1990 pop. 300), Houston co., Ga., 8 mi/12.9 km NE of Perry; 32°29'N 83°36'W. Mfg. includes food prods.; glass processing.

Kathryn, village (1990 pop. 72), Barnes co., SE N.Dak., 17 mi/27 km S of Valley City; 46°40'N 97°58'W. Clausen Springs to Fort Ransom Park to S.

Katmai National Park and Preserve (KAT-mei), park, preserve, wilderness, at the N end of the Alaska Peninsula on Shelikof Strait, S Alaska. Has one of the largest areas in the U.S. Natl. Park System; est. 1918 as a natl. monument; its borders were since expanded, and it was designated a park (3,716,000 acres/1,503,865 ha) and preserve (37,400 acres/15,136 ha) area in 1980; wilderness covers 3,473,000 acres/1,405,523 ha. Mt. Katmai and Novarupta volcanoes and the Valley of the Ten Thousand Smokes are located in this region, which is the site of one of the greatest volcanic eruptions in recorded history: Novarupta (1912). All plant and animal life in the area was destroyed by the ash and lava, although no people were reported killed. Kodiak Isl. (100 mi/160 km to the SE) was covered with c.1 ft/.3 m of ash. As lava beneath Mt. Katmai drained W to Novarupta, its top collapsed, forming a crater, 8 mi/12.8 km in circumference and 3,700 ft/1,128 m deep, in which a lake has formed. The Valley of the Ten Thousand Smokes (72 sq mi/186 sq km) has countless holes and cracks through which hot gases passed to the surface; all but a few have become extinct. The park also includes glacier-covered peaks, crater lakes, a coastline with dramatic fjords and waterfalls, dense marshlands, and heavy forests with a variety of wildlife, notably moose and grizzly bears.

Katmai Volcano (6,715 ft/2,047 m), S Alaska, in Katmai Natl. Monument, 100 mi/161 km WNW of Kodiak; 58°16'N 154°59'W. Active volcano with crater 8 mi/12.9 km in circumference and 3,700 ft/1,128 m deep. Within crater are lake, small isl., and glacier-covered walls. Erupted June 5, 1912, desolated Kodiak Isl., covered 53 sq mi/137 sq km with sand and lava, created VALLEY OF TEN THOUSAND SMOKES, a fumarole field. Investigated in 1915 by Natl. Geographic Society expedition.

Katonah (kuh-TO-nah), suburban residential village (1990 pop. 2,400), Westchester co., SE N.Y., 16 mi/26 km NNE of White Plains, on a reservoir of Croton R. system; 41°15'N 73°42'W. John Jay Homestead State Historic Site. Caramoor Music Festival each summer at Caramoor Center for Music and Arts.

Katy, town (1990 pop. 8,005), on Fort Bend–Harris-Waller co. line, S Texas, suburb 25 mi/40 km W of downtown Houston, on W fringe of large urbanized area; 29°48'N 95°49'W. Mfg. (signs, concrete roof tile, plastic prods.); agr. (cattle, rice, vegetables; nurseries).

Katzimo, N.Mex.: see ENCHANTED MESA.

Káua (KAH-wah), town (1990 pop. 1,369), Yucatán, Mexico, 13 mi/21 km WSW of Valladolid on the Mexico Highway 180; 20°37'N 88°25'W. Henequen, corn.

Kauai (kou-AH-ee), county (□ 1,266 sq mi/3,279 sq km; 1990 pop. 51,177), NW Hawaii, mainly KAUAI ISL, also NIIHAU ISL, KAULA ISL; ☉ Lihue, Kauai; 22°00'N 159°41'W. Locally administered by 10 dists., 9 on Kauai and 1 on Niihau; no incorporated cities.

Kauai (kou-AH-ee), island (1990 pop. 51,177), 549 sq mi/1,422 sq km, 32 mi/51 km in diameter, NW Hawaii, separated from Oahu isl. to the SE by Kauai Channel, from Niihau isl. to SW by Kumukahi Channel. Lihue (1990 pop. 5,536) is the largest town and ☉ Kauai co., and Nawiliwili Harbor the chief port. Administered by 9 dists. Geologically, Kauai is the oldest of the larger Hawaiian Isls. It was formed by volcanoes now extinct and deeply worn by heavy rainfall and by assault of surrounding ocean; Kawaikini (5,243 ft/1,598 m) and Waialeale (5,148 ft/1,569 m) are the tallest peaks. High annual rainfall has eroded deep valleys in Kauai's central mt. mass. Waimea Canyon (2,000 ft/610 m–3,000 ft/914 m deep; c.10 mi/16 km long), "Hawaii's Grand Canyon," in W, often compared with Arizona's Grand Canyon. The northeastern slopes of Waialeale, one of the wettest spots on earth, receive an annual average rainfall of 450 in/1,143 cm. Alakai Swamp occupies the isl.'s NW center, unusual in that it is located in upper elevs. and is source of isl.'s W streams, including headstreams of Waimea R. An independent kingdom when visited by English Capt. James Cook in 1778, Kauai became part of the Kingdom of Hawaii in 1810. The 1st major attempt at agr. development in Hawaii occurred there with the establishment of a sugar plantation in 1835. Most of the isl.'s people live along the coast. Agr. is a major industry with sugarcane, fruit, vegetables, and coffee the chief crops; tourism is central to the economy. Barking Sands Pacific Missile Range at W end of isl.; Forest reserves: Moloaa and Kealia (NE); Nonou and Kalepa (E); Lihue-Koloa, Haleea and NaPali-Kona (center); Pun Ka Pele (W). Hanalei Natl. Wildlife Refuge in N; Huleia Natl. Wildlife Refuge in SE; Kilauea Natl. Wildlife Refuge in NE; Natl. Tropical Botanical Gardens in S; Na Pali Coast State Park (NW); Waimea Canyon and Kokee State Park in W center; Polihale State Park on W coast; Russian Fort Elizabeth State Historic Park in SW; Wailua River and Lydgate State Parks in E; Ahukini State Recreaetional Park in E.

Kauai Channel, Pacific Ocean, bet. Kauai and Oahu isls., Hawaii, 63 naut. mi/116.6 km wide. Formerly called Kaieiewaho Channel.

Kaufman, county (□ 806 sq mi/2,088 sq km; 1990 pop. 52,220), NE Texas; ☉ Kaufman. Mainly rich blackland prairies, bounded W by Trinity R. and drained by its East Fork (forms L. Ray Hubbard in NW corner) and Cedar Creek. Agr. (cotton, corn, sorghum, wheat; hay; peaches; nursery prods.; cattle, horses). Mfg. at Terrell, Kaufman. Part of Cedar Creek Reservoir in SE. Formed 1848.

Kaufman, town (1990 pop. 5,238), NE Texas, 30 mi/48 km ESE of Dallas; ☉ Kaufman co.; 32°34'N 96°18'W. Elev. 438 ft/134 m. Market, shipping center in rich blackland agr. area (cotton; peaches, corn, wheat; cattle, horses); mfg. (textiles, fabricated metal prods.). Founded 1848, inc. 1873.

Kauiki Head (KAH-oo-EE-kee), point, E end of Maui isl., Maui co., Hawaii, 1 mi/1.6 km SE of Hana; 20°45'N 155°59'W. Extinct crater.

Kaukauna (ka-ka-HOO-nuh), city (1990 pop. 11,982), Outagamie co., E Wis., on the Fox R., a suburb 8 mi/12.9 km E of Appleton; 44°16'N 88°16'W. Mfg. (food, fabricated metal prods., paper); stone quarries nearby. A fur-trading post was established on the site by Pierre Grignon in 1760. The Grignon mansion (built 1836–1839 on the 1st land deeded in Wis., has been restored. Outagamie Co. Teachers Col. is in Kaukauna. Settled 1793, inc. 1885.

Kaula (ka-OO-lah), island, westernmost point of main (or Eastern) Hawaiian Isls., Kauai co., Hawaii, c.20 mi/32 km WSW of Niihau. Small, barren rock; light station (550 ft/168 m) for U.S. lighthouse service.

Kaulakahi Channel (kah-OO-lah-KAH-hee), 194 mi/312 km wide, Pacific Ocean, bet. Kauai and Niihau isls., Hawaii. Formerly Kumukahi Channel.

Kaumajet Mountains, Lab.: see COD ISLAND.

Kaumakani (KOU-mah-KAH-nee), town (1990 pop. 803), Kauai isl., Kauai co., Hawaii, 16 mi/26 km WSW of Lihue, 1 mi/1.6 km inland from S coast; 21°55'N 159°37'W. Sugarcane, fruit; cane sugar milling. Hoary Head Stadium to E. Salt Pond Beach Park to SE.

Kaumalapau (KOU-MAH-la-PAH-oo), port, W Lanai, Maui co., Hawaii, on Kaumalapau Harbor, 6 mi/9.7 km WSW of Lanai City, on W coast. Lanai airport to E; W terminus of Kaumalapau Highway.

Kaunakakai (KOU-nah-kah-KEI), town (1990 pop. 2,658), S Molokai isl., Maui co., Hawaii; 21°05'N 157°00'W. Port for Molokai isl.

Kauneonga Lake, N.Y.: see WHITE LAKE.

Kaw City, village (1990 pop. 314), Kay co., N Okla., within bend of Arkansas R. (Kaw L. reservoir), 11 mi/18 km E of Ponca City; 36°45'N 96°51'W. In agr. area; oil and gas wells; recreation.

Kaw Lake, reservoir (□ 27 sq mi/70 sq km), Kay co., NE Okla., on Arkansas R., 9 mi/14 km E of Ponca City; 36°42'N 96°45'W. Max. capacity 1,348,00 acre-ft. Extends N to Kansas state line. Formed by Kaw Dam (125 ft/38 m high), built (1976) by Army Corps of Engineers for flood control; also used for water supply and recreation. Borders on Osage Indian Reservation.

Kawaihae Bay (kah-WEI-HAH-ei), NW Hawaii, Hawaii, on S Kohala Coast. Kohala Peninsula to N. Harbor at Kawaihae is principal port for W Hawaii. Landing for cattle shipment; bathing beach.

Kawaikini (kah-WEI-KEE-nee), peak (5,243 ft/1,598 m), central Kauai, Kauai co., Hawaii, 9 mi/14.5 km NW of Lihue. Highest peak on isl.

Kawartha Lakes (kuh-WOR-thuh), group of 14 lakes, in a region c.50 mi/80 km long and c.25 mi/40 km wide, S Ont., Canada, near the towns of Lindsay and Peterborough. Balsam is the largest lake. They are popular as summer resorts. Many of the lakes form part of the Trent Canal system.

Kaweah, Lake, reservoir (□ 30 sq mi/78 sq km), Tulare co., central Calif., on Kaweah R., just W of Sequoia Natl. Park in Sequoia Natl. Forest, 15 mi/24 km ENE of Visalia; 36°25'N 119°00'W. Max. capacity 143,000 acre-ft. Formed by Terminus Dam (255 ft/78 m high), built (1962) by the Army Corps of Engineers for flood control, irrigation, recreation, and power generation.

Kaweah River (kah-wee-ah), c.40 mi/64 km SW, central Calif.; formed in Tulare co. at confluence of North and South forks in L. Kaweah reservoir, 20 mi/32 km ENE of Visalia; flows SW of Sequoia Natl. Park. past Farmersville (SE of Visalia) and S of Tulare to floor of San Joaquin Valley, where it divides into many channels, some of which reach Tulare L. reservoir; St. Johns R. (23 mi/37 km long) is a distributary. Used for irrigation. North Fork c.25 mi/40 km long flows SW, receives Kaweah Scout Fork (c.15 mi/24 km long, from E) and East Fork c.25 mi/40 km long, also from E, South Fork, c.25 mi/40 km long, flows W. All 4 branches rise in center of Sequoia Natl. Park, from N to S.

Kawela (kah-WAI-lah), village (1990 pop. 366), N Oahu isl., Honolulu co., Hawaii, in NE corner of isl., 28 mi/45 km NNW of Honolulu, 1 mi/1.6 km inland from Turtle Bay Resort, N coast; 21°41'N 158°00'W. Kawela Bay to NW; Kahuka Point to NE.

Kawishiwi River (kuh-WI-shi-wee), 60 mi/97 km long

(through North Fork), NE Minn.; rises in NE Lake co., in L. Polly; flows N through Koma and Malberg lakes, then W through Alice, Insula, and Hudson lakes and 4 reservoirs (lakes Three, Two, and One, and Carefree L.), below dam of Carefree L. river splits into 2 widely separate channels: North Fork flows c.10 mi/16 km W to Farm L.; South Fork flows c.20 mi/32 km first SW to NE end of Birch L., then from same end, through Birch L. Dam and White Iron L., joins North Fork at Farm L. (Birch L. extends 15 mi/24 km to SW of South Fork); 47°54′N 91°43′W. Kawichiwi R. continues N from Farm L. through Fall L. and Nenton L., and through Newton Falls (cataracts) to Pippstone Bay of Basswood L. (on U.S.-Can. border). Entire river is in Superior Natl. Forest; upper course is in Boundary Waters Canoe Area.

Kay, county (□ 945 sq mi/2,448 sq km; 1990 pop. 48,056), N Okla.; ⊙ Newkirk; 36°48′N 97°08′W. Bounded N by Kansas line, bounded in SE by Arkansas R. (Kaw L. reservoir in E); intersected by Arkansas and Chikaskia rivers and by the Salt Fork of Arkansas R. Includes L. Ponca in E. Agr. (wheat, barley, sorghum, alfalfa, soybeans); dairying; cattle, sheep. Mfg. at Ponca City, Blackwell, and Tonkawa. Oil and natural gas wells; extensive petroleum refining. Formed 1893.

Kayak Island (20 mi/32 km long, 1 mi/1.6 km–2 mi/3.2 km wide), S Alaska, in Gulf of Alaska, 65 mi/105 km SE of Cordova in Chugach Natl. Forest; 59°55′N 144°26′W. Cape St. Elias is S extremity. Bering anchored off shore, 1741. Isl. has shape of a kayak.

Kayayak, Alaska: see KAGUYAK.

Kaycee (KAI-see), village (1990 pop. 256), Johnson co., N central Wyo., on Red Fork of Powder R., 60 mi/97 km NNW of Casper; 43°42′N 106°38′W. Elev. 4,660 ft/1,420 m. Bighorn Mts. to W.

Kaye, Cape, NW Baffin Isl., E Franklin dist., N.W.T., Canada, on Prince Regent Inlet; 72°16′N 89°58′W.

Kayenta, uninc. town (1990 pop. 4,372), Navajo co., NE Ariz., 130 mi/209 km NE of Flagstaff, 18 mi/29 km S of Utah state line, in Navajo Indian Reservation, on Laguna Creek. Elev. 5,798 ft/1,767 m. Sheep, cattle, hogs; corn, alfalfa.

Kayford, uninc. village (1990 pop. 250), Kanawha co., W central W.Va., 25 mi/40 km SSE of Charleston.

Kayjay (KAI-jai), village (1990 pop. 225), Knox co., SE Ky., in the Cumberland Mts., 16 mi/26 km NNW of Middlesboro. In bituminous coal and timber area. Kentucky Ridge State Forest to SE.

Kaysville, city (1990 pop. 13,961), Davis co., N Utah, near Great Salt L., suburb 13 mi/21 km S of Ogden, 17 mi/27 km N of Salt Lake City; 41°01′N 111°56′W. Elev. 4,349 ft/1,326 m. Irrigated fruit and vegetable-raising area; dairynig; cattle, sheep; mfg. (food); coal mining. Wasatch Range and Natl. Forest to E. Originally called Kay's Fort. Settled 1849, inc. 1868.

Kayuyak, Alaska: see KAGUYAK.

Kazan River (kuh-ZAHN, -ZAN), 455 mi/732 km long, N.W.T., Canada; rises in SE corner of Mackenzie dist., flows NE into Keewatin Dist., through Ennadai and Yathkyed lakes, to Baker L. (which is drained by Chesterfield inlet).

Keaau (KAI-ah-OU), town (1990 pop. 1,584), E Hawaii, Hawaii co., Hawaii, 7 mi/11.3 km SSE of Hilo; in interior, 5 mi/8 km WSW of Haena Bay; 19°37′N 155°02′W. Mauna Loa Macadamia Nut Factory and Visitors Center to NE; Nani Mau Gardens to N; Panaewa Forest Reserve to N; Waiakea Forest Reserve to W. Also called Olaa.

Kealaikahiki Channel (kai-AH-lah-EE-kah-HEE-kee), 16 naut. mi/29.6 km wide, in Pacific Ocean, bet. Lanai and Kahoolawe isls., Maui co., Hawaii.

Kealakekua (kai-AH-lah-kai-KOO-ah), town (1990 pop. 1,453), W Hawaii isl., Hawaii co., Hawaii, 52 mi/84 km WSW of Hilo, 2 mi/3.2 km N of Captain Cook, 2 mi/3.2 km inland from Kona (W) Coast; 19°32′N 155°52′W. Coffee, fruit. Univ. of Hawaii Agr. Experimental Station, Kona Historical Society Mus. are here. Kealakekua Bay to SW.

Kealakekua Bay (kai-AH-lah-kai-KOO-ah), W Hawaii, Hawaii co., Hawaii. Capt. James Cook, 1st Eur. explorer

of the isls., was killed here 1779; Captain Cook Memorial at Cook Point, N end of bay; lighthouse at point. Kealakekua State Underwater Park along NE shore.

Kealia (ke-AH-LEE-ah), village, Kauai, Kauai co., Hawaii, on E coast, at mouth of Kapaa Stream on Kuhio Highway.

Keams Canyon, uninc. village, Navajo co., NE Ariz., in valley on high tableland (c.6,000 ft/1,829 m.), in Hopi Indian Reservation, 65 mi/105 km N of Holbrook. Agr. (sheep, cattle, hogs; corn, alfalfa). Reservation hq. here. Awatori ruins to SW.

Keansburg, resort borough (1990 pop. 11,069), Monmouth co., E N.J., on Raritan Bay and 9 mi/14.5 km ESE of Perth Amboy, on Point Comfort; 40°28′N 74°09′W. Fishing. Largely residential. Inc. 1917.

Kearney (KAHR-nee), county (□ 516 sq mi/1,336 sq km; 1990 pop. 6,629), S Nebr.; ⊙ Minden; 40°30′N 98°57′W. Agr. region bounded N by Platte R. Cattle, hogs; corn, soybean, wheat, sorghum, alfalfa, sunflower seed; dairy prods. Fort Kearny State Historical Park in NW; Pioneer Village at Minden. Formed 1860.

Kearney 1 (KAHR-nee), city (1990 pop. 1,790), Clay co., W Mo., 10 mi/16 km NE of Liberty, 23 mi/37 km NNE of Kansas City (satellite community); 39°21′N 94°21′W. Ships livestock, grain; coal mines; light mfg. A major center of mule breeding and raising in early 20th cent. Outlaw Jesse James' birthplace and farm on E side of town. Platted 1867. **2** city (1990 pop. 24,396), S central Nebr., on the Platte R; ⊙ Buffalo co.; 40°42′N 99°04′W. It is a commercial, industrial, and transportation center in an agr. area. Univ. of Nebr. at Kearney and Kearney State Col. located here. Mfg. (plastic prods., machinery, fabricated metal prods., printing and publishing, transportation equip., apparel). Fort Kearny State Historical Park to S (named for Gen. Stephen W. Kearny), est. 1848 to protect the Oregon Trail, was abandoned in 1871. Kearney Co. State Recreation Area to SE. Co. Fairgrounds, Municipal Airport, Union Pacific State Wayside Area to W. Inc. 1873.

Kearney (KEER-nee), town (1991 pop. 734), S Ont., Canada, 40 mi/64 km ENE of Parry Sound; lumbering.

Kearney, town (1990 pop. 2,262), Pinal co., S central Ariz., 55 mi/89 km N of Tucson, on Gila R. bet. Tortilla Mts. (SW) and Dripping Springs Mts. (NE). Cattle, sheep. Ray Copper Mine (open pit) to N.

Kearneysville (KAHRN-eez-vil), uninc. village, Jefferson co., NE W.Va., 6 mi/9.7 km SE of Martinsburg. Agr. (grain, apples); livestock; poultry. Light mfg. Leetown U.S. Fish Hatchery to SW. W. Va. Univ. horticultural farm.

Kearns (KUHRNZ), uninc. town (1990 pop. 28,874), Salt Lake co., N Utah, a suburb 9 mi/14.5 km SW of downtown Salt L. City; 40°38′N 112°00′W. Alfalfa, barley; cattle, sheep. Kennecott Bingham Copper Mine to SW. Salt Lake City Municipal Airport No. 2 to S. In spite of large pop. growth, Salt Lake co. remains an important agr. co.

Kearny (KAHR-nee), county (□ 871 sq mi/2,256 sq km; 1990 pop. 4,027), SW Kansas; ⊙ Lakin; 38°00′N 101°18′W. Gently rolling plain, drained by Arkansas R. Wheat; cattle; sorghum, sugar beets, alfalfa. Mountain/Central time zone boundary, follows W co. boundary. Kearny co. was on Mountain time zone, is now on Central. L. Mckinney Reservoir in E. Formed 1888.

Kearny (KAHR-nee), town (1990 pop. 34,874), Hudson co., NE N.J., 2 mi/3.2 km NNE of Newark; 40°45′N 74°07′W. The town is the site of shipyards (greatly enlarged in 1941) and dry docks. Mfg. includes chemicals, textiles, plastics, food, and electronic equip. Kearny contains many tidal wetlands bet. the Passaic and the Hackensack rivers that were filled for industrial and recreational purposes. One development project was the construction of the Meadowlands racetrack and arena, located near the town of Kearny. Inc. 1899

Kearsarge (KEER-sarj), village, Carroll co., E N.H., in town of Conway, 6 mi/9.7 km N of town center, at S edge of White Mt. Natl. Forest. Resort area. Mt. Cranmore Ski area is to E.

Kearsarge, Mount (KEER-sarj), peak (2,931 ft/893 m)

in Merrimack co., S central N.H., 11 mi/18 km WSW of Franklin, in Winslow State Park.

Kearsarge North Mountain (KEER-sarj), peak (3,268 ft/996 m) of White Mts., N Carroll co., N.H., 9 mi/14.5 km NNE of Conway; in White Mt. Natl. Forest.

Kearsarge Pass (11,823 ft/3,604 m), Inyo-Fresno co. line, E Calif., in the Sierra Nevada, c.10 mi/16 km W of Independence. E boundary of Kings Canyon Natl. Park.

Keasbey, N.J.: see WOODBRIDGE.

Keatchie (KEE-chee), village (1990 pop. 277), De Soto parish, NW La., 22 mi/35 km SSW of Shreveport, near Bayou Pierre; 32°11′N 93°54′W. Timber; cattle; oil and natural gas.

Keats Island (□ 3 sq mi/8 sq km), SW B.C., Canada, in Howe Sound, 18 mi/29 km WNW of Vancouver, opposite Gibsons Landing; mixed farming.

Keauhou (kai-OU-HO-oo, kai-O-oo-HO-oo), town (1990 pop. 1,000), W Hawaii isl., Hawaii co., Hawaii, on Kona (W) Coast, 55 mi/89 km W of Hilo, 6 mi/9.7 km S of Kailua-Kona. Tourism. Keauhou Bay to S. King Kamehameha III Birthplace State Monument to S. Kona Gardens here. Kahaluu Forest Reserve to E.

Kechi (KEECH-ei), village (1990 pop. 517), Sedgwick co., S central Kansas, suburb 7 mi/11.3 km NNE of downtown Wichita; 37°47′N 97°16′W. Residential. Agr. to N and E (wheat; cattle).

Kecoughtan, Va.: see HAMPTON.

Kedgwick, village (1986 pop. 1,129), N.B., Canada, francophone community 50 mi/80 km SW of Campellton; 47°38′N 67°20′W. Site of many 19th-cent. lumber camps on height of land in region. Sawmills, pulp shipment.

Keedysville (KEE-DEEZ-vill), town (1990 pop. 464), Washington co., W Md., near Antietam Creek, 11 mi/18 km S of Hagerstown, near Crystal Grottoes and Antietam Natl. Battlefield; 39°29′N 77°42′W. When residents asked the original name of Centerville be changed to avoid confusion with several other towns of the same name in the state, the petition had so many Keedy signatures on it the name Keedysville was decided on.

Keegan, Maine: see VAN BUREN.

Keego Harbor (KEE-go), village (1990 pop. 2,932), Oakland co., SE Mich., suburb 4 mi/6.4 km SW of Pontiac on E end of Cass L. and S end of Sylvan L.; 42°36′N 83°20′W.

Keel Peak (c.8,500 ft/2,591 m), W Mackenzie dist., N.W.T., Canada; 63°27′N 130°20′W.

Keeler, village, Inyo co., Calif., 12 mi/19 km S of Lone Pine on Ca. 136, on E side of Owens L. Former soda ash mining; served Cerro Gordo mine in Inyo Mts. (closed early 20th cent.).

Keeline (KEE-lein), village, Niobrara co., E Wyo., 15 mi/24 km W of Lusk, near Muddy Creek. Elev. 5,289 ft/1,612 m.

Keene (KEEN), city (1990 pop. 22,430), SW N.H., 40 mi/64 km W of Manchester; ⊙ Cheshire co.; 42°57′N 72°17′W. Drained by the Ashuelot R. It is a trade and mfg. center in a farming and resort area. Mfg. (printing and publishing, electronic equip., pet containment systems, fabricated metal prods., glass prods.); insurance. Seat of Keene State Col. Keene Muncipal Airport in S. Monadnock Mt. (3,165 ft/965 m), 10 mi/16 km to SE (state park), is a popular hiking site. Settled 1736, inc. as a city 1873.

Keene, town (1990 pop. 3,944), Johnson co., N central Texas, 23 mi/37 km S of Fort Worth; 32°23′N 97°19′W. In agr. (cotton; grain; dairying) area; light mfg. Grew up around Seventh Day Adventist Acad., now Southwestern Adventist Col.

Keene, resort village (1990 pop. 450), Essex co., NE N.Y., in Adirondack Mts., on E. Branch of Ausable R., 35 mi/56 km SSW of Plattsburgh; 44°11′N 73°48′W.

Keene Valley, resort village (1990 pop. 350), Essex co., NE N.Y., in scenic Keene Valley of Adirondack Mts., on E. Branch of Ausable R., 39 mi/63 km SSW of Plattsburgh.

Keeneland, Ky.: see LEXINGTON.

Keenesburg, village (1990 pop. 570), Weld co., NE Colo., 35 mi/56 km NE of Denver; 40°06′N 104°31′W. Elev. 4,958 ft/1,511 m. Sugar beets, beans, wheat, cattle. Horse Creek Reservoir to SW.

Keeney Knob, mountain (3,927 ft/1,197 m), Summers co., S W.Va., 11 mi/18 km NE of Hinton. Highest point of Keeney Mt., a ridge of the Allegheny Mts.

Keensburg, village (1990 pop. 238), Wabash co., SE Ill., 7 mi/11.3 km SW of Mount Carmel; 38°21′N 87°52′W. In agr. area.

Keeseville (KEEZ-vil), village (□ 1 sq mi/2.6 sq km; 1990 pop. 1,854), on Clinton-Essex co. line, NE N.Y., on Ausable R. (bridged), 13 mi/21 km S of Plattsburgh; 44°30′N 73°30′W. Some mfg.; in farm area (dairying; apples, potatoes, hay). Resort. Ausable Chasm is nearby. Settled 1806, inc. 1878.

Keesler Air Force Base, Miss.: see BILOXI.

Keewatin (kee-WAH-tin), S central region (□ 228,641 sq mi/592,334 sq km; 1991 pop. 5,834), N.W.T., Canada, N of Man. and W of Hudson Bay. Rankin Inlet is the regional hq. It was created in the early 1970s with the combining of Keewatin and E Mackenzie dists. Its boundaries, almost entirely within the Canadian Shield, include all of Hudson and James bays and all of the mainland of the N.W.T. E of Thelon R., except for the Boothia and Melville peninsulas. Fur trapping, sealing, and craft-making are important economic activities.

Keewatin, town (1991 pop. 2,059), W Ont., Canada, on L. of the Woods, 4 mi/6 km W of Kenora; 49°46′N 94°33′W. Hunting and fishing center, noted for its scenic beauty.

Keewatin (kee-WAW-duhn), town (1990 pop. 1,118), Itasca co., NE Minn., 7 mi/11.3 km WSW of Hibbing in Mesabi Iron Range; 47°23′N 93°05′W. Light mfg. Grew with exploitation of ore deposits after 1909.

Keg Creek, flows c.60 mi/97 km SW, SW Iowa; rises near Westphalia in Shelby co., past Glenwood, to Missouri R. 20 mi/32 km S of Council Bluffs.

Kegonsa, Lake, c.3 mi/4.8 km long, 2 mi/3.2 km wide, southernmost of the Four Lakes, Dane co., S Wis., 9 mi/14.5 km SE of Madison. Connected to L. Waubesa to NW by Yahara R., drained by Yahara R. on E. L. Kegonsa State Park on E shore.

Keiser (KEI-suhr), town (1990 pop. 805), Mississippi co., NE Ark., 22 mi/35 km SSW of Blytheville; 35°40′N 90°05′W. Cotton, rice. Inc. 1933.

Keith, county (□ 1,109 sq mi/2,872 sq km; 1990 pop. 8,584), SW central Nebr.; ⊙ Ogallala; 41°12′N 101°39′W. Agr. region drained by North Platte and South Platte rivers. Lake C.W. McConaughy (Kingsley Reservoir), on the North Platte, was created by KINGSLEY DAM. Cattle, hogs; wheat, corn, alfalfa, beans, sunflower seeds. Central/Mountain time zone boundary follows E boundary and E part of N boundary. L. Ogallala State Recreation Area N of North Platte, at center of co. (S of Kingsley Dam. L. McConaughy State Recreation Area at co. center and in NW; 7 units, 3 on S shore, 4 on N shore. Formed 1873.

Keithsburg (KEETHS-burgh), city (1990 pop. 747), Mercer co., NW Ill., on the Mississippi R. at mouth of Pope Creek, and 13 mi/21 km SW of Aledo; 41°06′N 90°56′W. In agr. area. Mark Twain Natl. Wildlife Refuge nearby. Inc. 1857.

Keithville (KEETH-vil), uninc. village, Caddo parish, NW La., 12 mi/19 km SSW of Shreveport; 32°19′N 93°50′W. In agr. and timber area; oil and natural gas; mfg. (construction equip., fabricated metal prods.).

Keizer (KEI-zuhr), city (1990 pop. 21,884), Marion co., NW Oregon, a residential suburb 3 mi/4.8 km N of Salem, on Willamette R.; 45°00′N 123°01′W. Agr. (fruit, nuts, vegetables; poultry; dairying). Willamette Mission and Maud Williamson State Parks to N.

Kejimkujik National Park, 140 sq mi/363 sq km, S central N.S., Canada, near Maitland Bridge. Rolling landscape with numerous lakes and streams. Micmac petroglyphs are found here. Est. 1968.

Kekaha (kai-KAH-hah), town (1990 pop. 3,506), SW Kauai, Kauai co., Hawaii, 25 mi/40 km W of Lihue, 5 mi/8 km W of Waimea Bay, on S coast, on Kaumualii

Highway; 21°58′N 159°43′W. Barking Sands Pacific Missile Range to W; Puu Ka Pele Forest Reserve to N: Waimea Canyon State Park to NE; Kokole Lighthouse and viewpoint of Niihau to W; Kekaha Beach Park.

Keku Strait (KAI-koo), 40 mi/64 km long, SE Alaska, in Alexander Archipelago; extends N to S bet. Kupreanof Isl. (E) and Kuiu Isl. (W), W of Kake.

Kelayres (kuh-LER-uhs), uninc. town (1990 pop. 950), Kline township, Schuylkill co., E central Pa., 6 mi/9.7 km SSW of Hazleton, and 1 mi/1.6 km W of McAdoo; 40°54′N 76°00′W. Anthracite coal. Tuscarora State Park to S.

Kelford, village (1990 pop. 204), Bertie co., NE N.C., 20 mi/32 km NW of Windsor, near source of Cashie R.; 36°10′N 77°13′W.

Kell, village (1990 pop. 213), Marion co., S Ill., 9 mi/14.5 km S of Salem; 38°29′N 88°54′W. In agr. and oil area.

Keller, city (1990 pop. 13,683), Tarrant co., N Texas, suburb 14 mi/23 km NNE of downtown Fort Worth; 32°55′N 97°13′W. Remnant agr. areas being replaced by urban growth. Mfg. (fabricated metal prods., concrete, electronic equip.).

Keller, town, Accomack co., E Va., 8 mi/12.9 km SSW of Accomac; 37°37′N 75°45′W. Agr. (grain vegetables; livestock, poultry; dairying).

Kellerton, town (1990 pop. 314), Ringgold co., S Iowa, 10 mi/16 km E of Mount Ayr; 40°42′N 94°02′W. In livestock and grain area.

Kellett Strait, N.W.T., Canada: see FITZWILLIAM STRAIT.

Kelley, town (1990 pop. 246), Story co., central Iowa, 11 mi/18 km WSW of Nevada; 41°57′N 93°39′W. Livestock; grain.

Kelleys Island, village (2,888 acres/1,169 ha; 1990 pop. 172), in L. Erie, Erie co., N Ohio; 41°35′N 82°42′W. Summer resort, fishing, wine growing; Glacial Grooves State Park is here. The name Wine Isls. is sometimes applied to Kelleys Isl. and neighboring isls.

Kelliher, village (1991 pop. 368), SE Sask., Canada, in the Beaver Hills, 55 mi/89 km W of Yorkton; 51°16′N 103°44′W. Mixed farming.

Kelliher (KE-li-yuhr), village (1990 pop. 348), Beltrami co., Minn., 38 mi/61 km NE of Bemidji, near South Branch Battle R.; 47°56′N 94°27′W. Grain, sunflowers; livestock; dairying; mfg. (hardwood lumber). Red Lake State Forest to N; Pine Island State Forest to E; Upper Red L. to NW; Lower Red L. to W.

Kellits (KEL-its), village (1991 pop. 2,291), Clarendon parish, central Jamaica, 15 mi/24 km N of May Pen; 18°10′N 77°14′W. Road junction town.

Kellnersville, village (1990 pop. 350), Manitowoc Co., E Wis., 12 mi/19 km NW of Manitowoc; 44°13′N 87°47′W. Dairying; grain, vegetables, fruit. Hidden Valley Ski Area to N.

Kellogg 1 town (1990 pop. 2,591), Shoshone co., N Idaho, on fork of Coeur d'Alene R. and 10 mi/16 km WSW of Wallace; 47°32′N 116°08′W. In mining dist. of Coeur d'Alene Mts.; former site of lead and zinc smelters and refineries, cadmium plant. Mfg. (fabricated metal prods., apparel). Grew with development of Bunker Hill and Sullivan lead mines (discovered 1885, now combined as one of world's leading producers). Mining Mus. Coeur d'Alene Natl. Forest to N; St. Joe Natl. Forest to S; Sunshine Miners Memorial to E; Silver Mt. Ski Area to S. Entire town has been transformed into Bavarian village. Founded as Milo 1893, renamed 1894, inc. 1913. **2** town (1990 pop. 626), Jasper co., central Iowa, on North Skunk R. and 7 mi/11.3 km E of Newton; 41°43′N 92°54′W. Light mfg.

Kellogg, village (1990 pop. 423), Wabasha co., SE Minn., near Mississippi R., 5 mi/8 km SSE of Wabasha; 44°18′N 92°00′W. Livestock; poultry; dairying; light mfg.; timber. Whitewater Wildlife Area to S; Richard J. Dorer Memorial Hardwood State Forest to SW; Lock and Dam No. 4 to NE.

Kelly Lake (40 mi/64 km long, 2 mi/3 km 4 mi/6 km wide), NW Mackenzie dist., N.W.T., Canada, 15 mi/24 km NE of Norman Wells; 65°25′N 126°15′W.

Kelly's Ford, on Rappahannock R., Fauquier co., N Va.,

20 mi/32 km NW of Fredericksburg. Scene of an indecisive Civil War cavalry engagement (March 17, 1863).

Kellyville, town (1990 pop. 984), Creek co., central Okla., 20 mi/32 km SW of Tulsa, 5 mi/8 km SW of Sapulpa; 35°56′N 96°13′W. In agr. and oil- and natural gas-producing area; light mfg.

Kelowna (kil-O-nuh), city (1991 pop. 75,950), S B.C., Canada, on Okanagan L.; 49°54′N 119°29′W. Now an extension of the Vancouver suburbs, Kelowna is a tourist resort and serves as a trade center for a fruit-growing and lumbering area. Mfg. of wine, machinery.

Kelseyville, uninc. town (1990 pop. 2,861), Lake co., NW Calif., near Clear L., 8 mi/12.9 km SE of Lakeport, 39 mi/63 km N of Santa Rosa; 38°58′N 122°49′W. Pears, grapes, walnuts, oats; cattle; winery. Large Clear L. State Park to N and E.

Kelso, city (1990 pop. 11,820), SW Wash., 45 mi/72 km NNW of Portland, Oregon, and 60 mi/97 km S of Olympia, on the Cowlitz R. near the Columbia R.; ⊙ Cowlitz co.; 46°08′N 122°54′W. Twin city with Longview, adjoins Kelso to SW. In a fertile farm area. Boatbuilding, fishing, and dairy farming are the major industries; mfg. (machinery, paper prods., wood prods.). Seaquest State Park, on Silver L. reservoir, to NE. Kelso Longview Airport to S. County Historical Mus. here. Settled in 1847, Kelso was an important stopping place for early steamboat travel along the Cowlitz R. Inc. 1889.

Kelso, town (1990 pop. 526), Scott co., SE Mo., near Mississippi R., 3 mi/4.8 km SE of Scott City; 37°11′N 89°32′W. Feeds.

Keltys, city (1990 pop. c.800), Angelina co., E Texas, just NW of Lufkin. Lumber milling.

Kelvington, town (1991 pop. 1,109), E Sask., Canada, 80 mi/129 km NW of Yorkton; 52°10′N 103°31′W. Dairying; lumbering; grain, livestock.

Kemah, town (1990 pop. 1,094), Galveston co., SE Texas, residential suburb 12 mi/19 km NNW of Texas City and 22 mi/35 km SE of Houston, on Galveston Bay, at mouth of Clear Creek, in area referred to as Clear Lake City. Mfg. (transportation equip., food, fabricated metal prods.).

Kemano Dam, Canada: see NECHAKO, river.

Kemmerer (KEM-uhr-uhr), town (1990 pop. 3,020), SW Wyo., on Hams Fork, near Utah state line, and 70 mi/113 km WNW of Rock Springs; ⊙ Lincoln co.; 41°46′N 110°32′W. Elev. c.6,927 ft/2,111 m. Shipping point for coal, cattle, sheep; some mfg. Fossil Butte Natl. Monument to W. The J.C. Penney Mother Store, first in nation-wide chain, 1902, is located here and is still open. Inc. 1899.

Kemp, town (1990 pop. 1,184), Kaufman co., NE Texas, c.40 mi/64 km SE of Dallas, near Cedar Creek and headwaters of Cedar Creek Reservoir (S). In cotton, corn, cattle area.

Kemp, village, Bryan co., S Okla., near Red R., 16 mi/26 km S of Durant. In agr. area.

Kemp City, village, Wichita co., Texas: see KAMAY.

Kemp, Lake, reservoir (□ 24 sq mi/62 sq km), Baylor co., N central Texas, on Big Wichita Creek, 40 mi/64 km W of Wichita Falls; 33°46′N 99°09′W. Max. capacity 502,900 acre-ft. Formed by Lake Kemp Dam (150 ft/35 m high), built (1923) by Army Corps of Engineers for water supply; also used for irrigation and recreation.

Kemper, county (□ 767 sq mi/1,987 sq km; 1990 pop. 10,356), E Miss., bordering E on Ala.; ⊙ De Kalb; 32°45′N 88°39′W. Drained by Sucarnoochee and Okatibbee creeks. Agr. (cotton, corn), cattle raising; catfish; timber. Kemper County L. (state lake) in center. Formed 1833.

Kemp's Bay, town, W Bahama Isls., on SE shore of Andros Isl., 75 mi/121 km S of Nassau; 24°01′N 77°33′W. Fishing, lumbering.

Kempt Lake (22 mi/35 km long, 15 mi/24 km wide), SW central Que., Canada, in the Laurentians, 120 mi/193 km NW of Montreal. Elev. 1,372 ft/418 m. Drained (W) by Lièvre R. Contains numerous isls.

Kempton, town (1990 pop. 362), Tipton co., central Ind., near Cicero Creek, 14 mi/23 km SSW of Kokomo; 40°17′N 86°14′W. In agr. area.

Kempton, village (1990 pop. 219), Ford co., E Ill., 22 mi/ 35 km WSW of Kankakee; 40°56′N 88°14′W. In rich agr. area (corn, soybeans, livestock).

Kemptville, town (1991 pop. 2,558), SE Ont., Canada, near Rideau R. and Rideau Canal, 28 mi/45 km S of Ottawa; 45°01′N 75°38′W. Dairying center, lumbering. Recreation.

Kenai (KEE-nai), locality (1990 pop. 6,327), S Alaska, W Kenai Peninsula, on Cook Inlet, at mouth of Kenai R., 65 mi/105 km SW of Anchorage; 60°32′N 151°12′W. Oil refineries, urea plant, offshore oil platforms; tourism; fishing, fish processing. Univ. of Alaska has Kenai community col. here. Has Rus. Orthodox church. U.S. garrison here, 1869. Estab. 1791 by Russians who built Fort St. Nicholas here.

Kenai Fjords National Park (KEE-nai) (1,046 sq mi/ 2,709 sq km), S Alaska; authorized 1980. Wilderness preserve, vast icefields, fjords, and outflowing glaciers.

Kenai Lake (KEE-nai) (25 mi/40 km long, 1 mi/1.6 km wide), S Alaska, 20 mi/32 km N of Seward, on Anchorage-Seward Highway. Tourism; fishing, hiking.

Kenai Mountains (KEE-nai), rise to c.7,000 ft/2,134 m 35 mi/56 km WSW of Seward, part of the Coast Ranges, S Alaska, extend 150 mi/241 km along SE side of Kenai Peninsula; slope steeply to Gulf of Alaska. Range has several glacier fields. Continued NE by Chugach Mts.

Kenai Peninsula, borough (☐ 16,079 sq mi/41,645 sq km, 1990 pop. 40,802), S Alaska, includes the Kenai Peninsula except for E section and part of W side of Cook Inlet. Bounded on the S by the Gulf of Alaska and the Kenai Mts. to S and E. Kenai Fjords Natl. Park to S; part of Katmai Natl. Park to S; Lake Clark Natl. Park and Preserve to W; part of Chugach Natl. Forest to E; Kenai National Wildlife Reserve to N and center; Kachemak Bay State Wilderness Park to S. Main towns are Seward, Soldotna, Kenai, and Homer. Tourism; fishing; timber.

Kenai Peninsula (KEE-nai), S Alaska, jutting c.150 mi/ 240 km into the Gulf of Alaska, bet. Prince William Sound and Cook Inlet. The Kenai Mts., c.7,000 ft/ 2,130 m high, occupy most of the peninsula. The coastal climate is mild, with abundant rainfall and a growing season adequate for many crops. There are forest, mineral, and fishing resources in the E and, in the W sect., petroleum, natural gas, coal, refineries; fishing; tourism; farmland. The Alaska RR crosses the peninsula from Seward. Highways connect Anchorage with Seward, Soldotna, Kenai, Homer, Hope. On the S coast of the peninsula is Kenai Fjords Natl. Park, which has striking glacial formations and contains the breeding areas for a variety of birds and sea mammals.

Kenansville (KEE-nuhnz-vil), town (1990 pop. 856), E N.C., 30 mi/48 km SW of Kinston; ⊙ Duplin co.; 34°57′N 77°58′W. Tobacco, cotton, grain, poultry, livestock. Light mfg. James Sprunt Community Col. Cowan Mus.

Kenaston (KE-nuhs-tuhn), village (1991 pop. 309), S central Sask., Canada, 36 mi/58 km WSW of Watrous; 51°30′N 106°17′W. Wheat, livestock.

Kenberma, Mass.: see HULL.

Kenbridge, town (1990 pop. 1,264), Lunenburg co., S Va., 27 mi/43 km SE of Farmville; 36°57′N 78°07′W. Light mfg.; agr. (tobacco, grain, soybeans; cattle); timber. Lunenburg Co. Airport to W.

Kendale Lakes (KEN-duhl), uninc. suburb (☐ 8 sq mi/ 20.7 sq km; 1990 pop. 48,524) of Miami, SW Dade co., SE Fla., 16 mi/26 km SW of Miami; 25°42′N 80°24′W.

Kendall 1 (KEN-duhl), county (☐ 322 sq mi/834 sq km; 1990 pop. 39,413), NE Ill.; ⊙ Yorkville; 41°35′N 88°25′W. Rich farming area (corn, soybeans, wheat). Mfg.: dairy prods., fabricated metal prods., electronic equip. Drained by Fox R. Includes Silver Springs State Park. Formed 1841. Initial stages of urban growth, influenced by Chicago, have started in extreme NE corner. **2** county (☐ 663 sq mi/1,717 sq km; 1990 pop. 14,589), S central Texas; ⊙ Boerne; 29°56′N 98°42′W. Elev. c.1,000 ft/305 m–2,000 ft/610 m. Generally broken area, on S edge of Edwards Plateau; drained by Guadalupe

and Blanco rivers; bounded by Cibolo Creek on S. Chiefly sheep, Angora-goat ranching region (wool, mohair marketed); also beef cattle, grain, wheat, oats. Natural gas deposits. Hunting, fishing, caves (Cascade Caverns, others) attract tourists. Formed 1862.

Kendall, village, Monroe co., W central Wis., 45 mi/ 72 km E of La Crosse, in dairying and livestock region. Sportswear. On La Crosse State Trail.

Kendall (KEN-duhl), uninc. suburb (☐ 23 sq mi/ 60 sq km; 1990 pop. 87,271) of Miami, Dade co., SE Fla., 11 mi/18 km SW of Miami; 25°40′N 80°20′W. Centered on North Kendall Drive, an E-W highway running from Biscayne Bay on E to Everglades about 15 mi/ 24 km to W. Residential communities predominate, but major retail and business complexes abound, particularly around Dadeland where North Kendall Drive intersects the Palmetto Expressway and U.S. 1.

Kendall Green, Mass.: see WESTON.

Kendall Mountain (13,068 ft/3,983 m), San Juan co., SW Colo., peak in San Juan Mts., 2 mi/3.2 km SE of Silverton.

Kendall Peak (13,338 ft/4,065 m), San Juan co., SW Colo., in San Juan Mts., 3 mi/4.8 km ESE of Silverton.

Kendallville, city (1990 pop. 7,773), Noble co., NE Ind., on Elkhart R., and 8 mi/12.9 km NE of Albion; 41°26′N 85°16′W. Shipping center in agr. area (especially onions); also dairy prods., livestock, soybeans, grain. Mfg. (transportation equip., paper prods., printing and publishing, machinery, fabricated metal prods., food). Mulholland Mus. has Indian and pioneer relics. Settled 1833.

Kendleton, village (1990 pop. 496), Fort Bend co., SE Texas, 44 mi/71 km SW of Houston, near San Bernard R; 29°26′N 00°96′W. Agr. area (rice, cotton, vegetables, corn, nurseries). Oil and natural gas.

Kendrick 1 village (1990 pop. 325), Latah co., W Idaho, 18 mi/29 km SE of Moscow, on Potlach R.; 46°37′N 116°39′W. Agr. center (cattle, sheep; alfalfa, barley, oats). Nez Perce Indian Reservation to S. **2** village (1990 pop. 171), Lincoln co., central Okla., 14 mi/23 km S of Cushing; 35°47′N 96°46′W. In agr. area.

Kendrick Peak (10,418 ft/3,175 m), rises from high plateau in Coconino co., N central Ariz., 18 mi/29 km NW of Flagstaff. On boundary of Kaibab (W) and Coconino (E) natl. forests.

Kenduskeag (ken-DUHS-keg), town (1990 pop. 1,234), Penobscot co., S Maine, lake area, 10 mi/16 km NW of Bangor; 44°55′N 68°55′W.

Kenduskeag Stream (ken-DUHS-keg), c.30 mi/48 km long, S Maine; rises in S Penobscot co., flows SE to the Penobscot at Bangor.

Kenedy, county (☐ 1,945 sq mi/5,038 sq km; 1990 pop. 460), extreme S Texas; ⊙ Sarita; 26°55′N 97°37′W. Flat coastal plain, bordering E on Gulf of Mexico; Padre Isl. (Natl. Seashore), a sand barrier isl., separated from mainland by Laguna Madre and Intracoastal Waterway. Large-scale ranching area (cattle, horses), most of co. is in huge King Ranch; some agr. (watermelons). Oil and gas. Co. has numerous small lakes. Formed 1921 from parts of Willacy, Hidalgo, and Cameron cos.

Kenedy, town (1990 pop. 3,763), Karnes co., S Texas, c.60 mi/97 km SE of San Antonio; 28°49′N 50°97′W. Oil and natural gas; cattle; dairying; wheat, corn, sorghum; mfg. (chemicals). Founded 1882, inc. 1910.

Kenefick (KEN-uh-fik), village (1990 pop. 147), Bryan co., S Okla., 11 mi/18 km N of Durant; 34°08′N 96°21′W. In agr. area.

Kenesaw (KE-nuh-saw), village (1990 pop. 818), Adams co., S Nebr., 14 mi/23 km WNW of Hastings; 40°37′N 98°39′W. Light mfg.

Kenhorst, borough (1990 pop. 2,918), Berks co., SE central Pa., residential suburb 2 mi/3.2 km S of Reading, on Angelica Creek. Mfg. (fabricated metal prods.). Inc. 1931.

Kenilworth (KE-nuhl-woorth), village (1990 pop. 2,402), Cook co., NE Ill., N suburb of Chicago, on L. Michigan, just N of Wilmette; 42°05′N 87°42′W. Eugene Field is buried here. Inc. 1896.

Kenilworth, borough (1990 pop. 7,574), Union co., NE N.J., 4 mi/6.4 km WNW of Elizabeth; 40°40′N

74°17′W. Mfg. (machinery, fabricated metal prods., paper prods., plastics). Inc. 1907.

Kenly, town (1990 pop. 1,549), Johnston co., central N.C., 15 mi/24 km NE of Smithfield; 35°35′N 78°07′W. Tobacco, cotton, peanuts, grain, potatoes, poultry, sweet potatoes, livestock. Light mfg. Tobacco Farm Life Mus. of N.C. is here.

Kenmar (KEN-mahr), uninc. town (1990 est. pop. 1,500), Loyalsock township, Lycoming co., N central Pa., residential suburb 2 mi/3.2 km E of Williamsport, on West Branch Susquehanna R.; 41°15′N 76°57′W.

Kenmare (KEN-mer), town (1990 pop. 1,214), Ward co., N N.Dak., 47 mi/76 km NW of Minot, and on Des Lacs R.; 48°40′N 102°04′W. Grain farms; dairy prods., livestock, potatoes. Lower Des Lacs L. to S, Upper Des Lacs L. to N. Des Lacs Natl. Wildlife Refuge on Des Lacs R. and lakes. RR junction. Inc. 1901.

Kenmore, uninc. town (1990 pop. 8,917), King co., W Wash., residential suburb 11 mi/18 km NNE of downtown Seattle, at N end of L. Washington, at mouth of Sammamish R.; 47°46′N 122°14′W. Saint Edward State Park to S.

Kenmore, residential suburb (☐ 1 sq mi/2.6 sq km; 1990 pop. 17,180) contiguous with N Buffalo, Erie co., NW N.Y.; 42°57′N 78°52′W. Inc. 1899.

Kennan, village (1990 pop. 169), Price co., N Wis., 25 mi/ 40 km ENE of Ladysmith; 45°31′N 90°35′W. Dairying. A unit of Chequamegon Natl. Forest to S; Flambeau R. State Forest to NW.

Kennard, town (1990 pop. 382), Henry co., E central Ind., 8 mi/12.9 km W of New Castle; 39°54′N 85°31′W. In agr. area.

Kennard 1 village (1990 pop. 371), Washington co., E Nebr., 6 mi/9.7 km SW of Blair, near Missouri R; 41°23′N 96°12′W. **2** village (1990 pop. 341), Houston co., E Texas, 15 mi/24 km ENE of Crockett, in Davy Crockett Natl. Forest; 31°21′N 95°10W. Timber area.

Kennebago Lake (ken-uh-BAI-go), Franklin co., W Maine, lake (5 mi/8 km long, 1 mi/1.6 km wide) 10 mi/ 16 km N of Rangeley L. Hunting, fishing.

Kennebec (KEN-uh-bek), county (☐ 951 sq mi/ 2,463 sq km; 1990 pop. 115,904), S Maine; ⊙ Augusta; 44°24′N 69°46′W. Mfg. (apparel, textiles, paper, wood and pulp prods.) at Hallowell, Waterville, and Gardiner on the Kennebec R.; dairying; canning and shipping of farm, orchard produce. Water power from Sebasticook and Kennebec rivers. Many resorts, notably in Belgrade and China lakes regions. Formed 1799.

Kennebec, village (1990 pop. 284), S central S.Dak., 40 mi/64 km SE of Pierre, and on Medicine Creek; ⊙ Lyman co.; 43°53′N 99°51′W. In farming region (dairy prods., livestock, poultry, grain). Dam and game preserve nearby. Lower Brule Indian Reservation to N.

Kennebec, river, 164 mi/264 km long, NW Maine; rising in Moosehead L. and flowing S to the Atlantic. The Androscoggin R. is its chief tributary. Samuel De Champlain explored the area in 1604–1605; in 1607, George Popham est. a short-lived colony, Fort St. George, at its mouth. Trading posts were est. shortly after 1625. In 1775, Amer. Gen. Benedict Arnold's expedition went up the Kennebec en route to Quebec. Lumber and, in the 19th cent., ice were shipped down the river to the coast, and shipbuilding flourished along its banks. Villages such as Augusta and Waterville, established near power sites, became industrial centers.

Kennebecasis River (ke-ne-buh-KA-sis), 60 mi/97 long, S N.B., Canada; rises NE of Sussex, flows km SW, past Sussex and Hampton, through 20-mi/32-km-long estuary called Kennebecasis Bay (4 mi/6 km wide) to St. John R. just above St. John.

Kennebunk (KEN-uh-buhnk), town (1990 pop. 8,004), York co., SW Maine, adjacent to Kennebunkport, and 10 mi/16 km SE of Alfred; 43°23′N 70°34′W. The first settlement (c.1650) grew as a trading and, later, a shipbuilding and shipping center with light mfg. The Wedding Cake House at Kennebunk is known for its scroll-saw architecture. Inc. 1820.

Kennebunk River (KEN-uh-buhnk), 15 mi/24 km long, SW Maine; rises in central York co., flows SE to the Atlantic at Kennebunkport.

Kennebunkport (KEN-uh-buhnk-port), town (1990 pop. 3,356), York co., SW Maine, on the Atlantic coast, and 15 mi/24 km SE of Alfred; 43°23'N 70°27'W. The early town, called Arundel, appears in Kenneth Roberts's books; the name was changed in 1821. The town is a summer resort, especially for authors, artists, and actors. It is also the vacation home of former President George Bush, dubbed the "summer White House" because of the frequent meetings there bet. Bush and his political advisers and other world leaders. Settled 1629, inc. 1653.

Kennecott, Alaska: see KENNICOTT.

Kennedale, town (1990 pop. 4,096), Tarrant co., N Texas, suburb 10 mi/16 km SE of downtown Fort Worth; 32°38'N 97°13'W. Drained by Village Creek (forms L. Arlington to N). Mfg. (rubber prods., explosives, concrete, ceramics). Inc. after 1940.

Kennedy, town (1990 pop. 523), Lamar co., W Ala., Canada c.14 mi/23 km SSE of Vernon. Apparel, lumber.

Kennedy, village (1991 pop. 296), SE Sask., Canada, 30 mi/48 km WSW of Moosomin; 50°01'N 102°21'W. Mixed farming.

Kennedy 1 village (1990 pop. 337), Kittson co., NW Minn., 9 mi/14.5 km S of Hallock, in Red R. valley; 48°38'N 96°54'W. Sunflowers, flax, sugar beets, beans; mfg. (food). **2** village, Chautauqua co., extreme W N.Y., on Conewango Creek, 8 mi/12.9 km NE of Jamestown; 42°09'N 79°06'W. In agr. area.

Kennedy, township (1990 pop. 7,152), Allegheny co., W Pa., residential suburb 7 mi/11.3 km NW of Pittsburgh on Ohio R.; 40°28'N 80°05'W.

Kennedy Lake (20 mi/32 km long, 1 mi/2 km–3 mi/5 km wide), SW B.C., Canada, on W Vancouver Isl., 30 mi/48 km WSW of Port Alberni. Drains W into Tofino Inlet of Clayoquot Sound.

Kennedy, Mount (13,095 ft/3,991 m), SW Yukon Territory, Canada, in the St. Elias Mts. near the Alaskan border. It was named in honor of U.S. President John F. Kennedy in 1965. Although visited in 1935, the mt. was climbed for the 1st time in 1965 by a team that included Robert F. Kennedy, the President's brother.

Kennedy Peak (7,456 ft/2,273 m), SW Graham co., SE Ariz., in Galiuro Mts., c.50 mi/80 km NE of Tucson, in section of Coronado Natl. Forest.

Kennedy Space Center, NASA's main U.S. launch facility, Orange co., E central Fla., 15 mi/24 km E of Titusville, on the peninsula just N of Cape Canaveral.

Kennedyville, village, Kent co., E Md., on the Eastern Shore, 7 mi/11.3 km NE of Chestertown. Originally settled by the Amish. Nearby is Shrewsbury Church, built 1832 on site of original church of the 1600s named for the Earl of Shewsbury. The grave of Gen. John Cadwalader bears an inscription written by Thomas Paine, the pamphleteer of both the American and French Revolutions.

Kenner (KEN-uhr), city (1990 pop. 72,033), Jefferson parish, SE La., a suburb 10 mi/16 km W of downtown New Orleans; 29°59'N 90°14'W. Bounds L. Pontchartrain on N, Mississippi R. on S. Kenner has grown rapidly since the 1970s into an area of moderate- to upper-income family housing developments in the New Orleans metropolitan region. Commercial activities; retail businesses; mfg. (electronics, food, chemicals, machinery, lumber, printing and publishing). New Orleans Internatl. Airport within the city limits, and Jefferson Downs racetrack nearby. Inc. 1952.

Kennesaw (KEN-uh-saw), town (1990 pop. 8,936), Cobb co., NW central Ga., 22 mi/35 km NW of Atlanta; 34°01'N 84°37'W. Suburb of Atlanta; major retail and service center along U.S. Highway 41 and I-75. Mfg. includes transportation equip., chemicals, concrete, printing and publishing, consumer goods. Kennesaw Mtn. Natl. Battlefield Park (civil war) nearby. Kennasaw State Univ., a unit of the Univ. System of Georgia. Big Shanty Mus. includes the General, a famous steam engine in Civil War lore.

Kennesaw Mountain (KEN-uh-saw), peak in Cobb co., NW Ga., 15 mi/24 km NW of Atlanta. Rises in 2 summits of 1,550 ft/472 m and 1,809 ft/551 m.; 33°58'N 84°34'W. Site of major Civil War battle.

Kenneth, village (1990 pop. 81), Rock co., SW Minn., 10 mi/16 km NE of Luverne; 43°45'N 96°04'W. Grain; livestock; dairying.

Kenneth City, town (1990 pop. 4,462), Pinellas co., W central Fla., 8 mi/12.9 km NW of St. Petersburg; 27°49'N 82°43'W.

Kennett, city (1990 pop. 10,941), in the boot heel of extreme SE Mo., near St. Francis R., 42 mi/68 km SE of Poplar Bluff; ⊙ Dunklin co.; 36°14'N 90°02'W. Rice, cotton, soybeans; mfg. (apparel, electronic equip., printing and publishing). Regional commercial and service center. Founded c.1845.

Kennett Square (KE-nuht), borough (1990 pop. 5,218), Chester co., SE Pa., 12 mi/19 km NW of Wilmington, Del., near Del. state line. Agr. area (corn, wheat, mushrooms, soybeans; poultry, livestock, dairying). Mfg. (apparel, food, concrete, electronic equip.). Major tourist center. Chaddsford Winery and Longwood Gardens to NE; White Clay Creek State Park to SW (Pa.-Del. border); Brandywine River Mus. nearby. Settled c.1750, inc. 1855.

Kennewick (KEN-uh-wik), city (1990 pop. 42,155), Benton co., SE Wash., 160 mi/257 km SE of Seattle, on the Columbia R. (L. Wallala reservoir) near the influx of the Snake R. (5 mi/8 km downstream, E); 46°12'N 119°10'W. RR junction. In an irrigated farm and vineyard region. One of the Tri-Cities (a fast-growing metropolis), along with Richland (9 mi/14.5 km WNW) and Pasco (2 mi/3.2 km NE); surpassed Richland c.1979 as largest of the three. Among the crops processed and packaged in the city are vegetables, potatoes, sugar beets, cherries, corn, and grapes; wheat; cattle; mfg. (machinery, fabricated metal prods., textiles, printing and publishing, fertilizers, food, electronics). The Department of Energy's nearby Hanford Works (established during World War II) and various hydroelectric dams and power plants on the Columbia R. are also important to the economy. Juniper Dunes Wilderness Area to NE; McNary Natl. Wildlife Refuge to E. Sacajawea State Park to E. Nuclear and other waste storage to N (large tract); has visitors' centers at Test Facility and Plant 2. Inc. 1904.

Kenney, village (1990 pop. 390), De Witt co., central Ill., 6 mi/9.7 km SW of Clinton; 40°06'N 89°05'W. In agr. area. On Salt Creek.

Kennicott (KE-ni-kaht), village, S Alaska, 4 mi/6.4 km NE of McCarthy, and 120 mi/193 km NE of Cordova, at foot of Wrangell Mts.; 61°28'N 142°54'W. Site of formerly important Kennecott copper mine, discovered 1898, closed down 1938. Village now practically deserted. Summer tourism; lodge located here.

Keno Hill or **Keno City** (KEE-no), village (1991 pop. 36), central Yukon, Canada, near Stewart R., 30 mi/48 km NE of Mayo Landing; 63°55'N 135°19'W. Silver and lead mining.

Kenogami, Lake (17 mi/27 km long, 1 mi/3 km–5 mi/8 km wide), central Que., Canada, on Chicoutimi R., and 10 mi/16 km SW of Chicoutimi. Water reservoir for Chicoutimi-Jonquière region.

Kenogami River, c.200 mi/322 km long, NW Ont., Canada; issues from N end of Long L., flows E and N to Albany R. at 51°06'N 84°30'W.

Kenora (kuh-NO-ruh), district (□ 153,220 sq mi/396,840 sq km; 1991 pop. 58,748), W Ont., Canada, on L. of the Woods and on Man. border; ⊙ Kenora; 51°00'N 90°00'W.

Kenora (kuh-NO-ruh), town (1991 pop. 9,782), W Ont., Canada, at the N end of the L. of the Woods; 49°46'N 94°28'W. Fish-processing plants and lumber, flour, pulp, and paper mills. Kenora contains an airport and serves as a base for fishing, hunting, and canoe trips.

Kenosha (ke-NO-shuh), county (□ 754 sq mi/1,953 sq km; 1990 pop. 128,181), extreme SE Wis.; ⊙ Kenosha; 42°34'N 87°48'W. Bordered E by L. Michigan, S by Ill. line. Dairying and farming area in W. Agr. (wheat, corn, soybeans, hogs, sheep); mfg. at Kenosha. Small lakes in SW. Bong State Recreation Area in NW. Drained by Des Plaines and Fox rivers. Formed 1850.

Kenosha (ke-NO-shuh), city (1990 pop. 80,352), seat of Kenosha co., SE Wis., a port of entry on L. Michigan, suburb for N Ill.; 42°34'N 87°50'W. Mfg. (transportation equip., apparel, printing and publishing, herbicides and fertilizers, electronics, food, machinery, fabricated metal prods.). The 1st public school in the state was begun here in 1849. A historical and art mus. and the co. courthouse (containing the co. historical mus.) are part of the civic center. Also in the city are Carthage Col., Gateway Technical Col., and a library designed by Daniel Burnham. Within the vicinity is the Univ. of Wisconsin at Parkside (to N). With Racine to N, forms urban link bet. Chicago, Ill., to S, and Milwaukee, Wis., to N. Inc. 1850.

Kenosha Mountains, Park co., central Colo., in Front Range, just N of Tarryall Mts., W of South Platte R. Kenosha Pass crosses hills in NW tip. North Twin Cone (12,319 ft/3,755 m), South Twin Cone (12,323 ft/3,756 m), and Mt. Blaine (12,306 ft/3,751 m) are 3 peaks of one mt., 4 mi/6.4 km E of Kenosha Pass.

Kenosha Pass (10,001 ft/3,048 m), Park co., central Colo., in Kenosha Hills, Park co., c.45 mi/72 km SW of Denver, and 18 mi/29 km NE of Fairplay. Crossed by U.S. Highway 285.

Kenova (kuh-NO-vuh), town (1990 pop. 3,748), Wayne co., W W.Va., suburb 8 mi/12.9 km W of Huntington, W.Va., and 6 mi/9.7 km SSE of Ashland, Ky., on the Ohio R. (Ohio state line) at mouth of Big Sandy R. (Ky. state line); 38°23'N 82°34'W. RR junction and trade center in bituminous-coal-mining area. Mfg. (food, chemicals, lumber); sand and gravel pits. Tri-State Airport (Walker Long Field) to SE. Inc. 1894.

Kenoza Lake, resort village (1990 pop. 400), Sullivan co., SE N.Y., on small Kenoza L., 12 mi/19 km WSW of Liberty; 41°44'N 74°57'W.

Kensal (KEN-sil), village (1990 pop. 191), Stutsman co., central N.Dak., 28 mi/45 km N of Jamestown; 47°17'N 98°43'W. Arrowwood Natl. Wildlife Refuge to W.

Kenscoff (KENS-kahf), town (1982 pop. 2,605), Ouest dept., S Haiti, mt. resort in the Massif de la Selle, 6 mi/9.7 km SSE of Port-au-Prince; 18°27'N 72°17'W. Elev. c.4,400 ft/1,341 m. Coffee growing; bauxite deposits nearby.

Kensett 1 (KEN-set), town (1990 pop. 1,741), White co., central Ark., 4 mi/6.4 km ESE of Searcy; 35°14'N 91°40'W. In agr. area; mfg. (hardwood lumber). **2** town (1990 pop. 298), Worth co., N Iowa, 6 mi/9.7 km S of Northwood; 43°21'N 93°12'W. Livestock, grain.

Kensico Reservoir (KEN-si-ko) (□ 3 sq mi/7.8 sq km), Westchester co., S N.Y. , on Bronx R., 15 mi/24 km N of Yonkers, and just W of N.Y.-Conn. border; 41°04'N 73°46'W. Max. capacity 116,560 acre-ft. Formed by Kensico Dam (168 ft/51m high), built (1916) for water supply.

Kensington (KEN-zing-tuhn), town (1991 pop. 1,332), W central P.E.I., Canada, near Malpeque Bay, 10 mi/16 km ENE of Summerside; 46°26'N 63°39'W. Agr. market in dairying, cattle-raising, potato-growing region.

Kensington 1 uninc. town (1990 pop. 4,974), Contra Costa co., W Calif., residential suburb 6 mi/9.7 km N of downtown Oakland, and 2 mi/3.2 km N of Berkeley, 2 mi/3.2 km E of San Francisco Bay; 37°55'N 122°17'W. Charles Lee Tilden Reg. Park and San Pablo Ridge to E. **2** town (1990 pop. 1,713), Montgomery co., central Md., NNW of Washington, on Rock Creek; 39°02'N 77°04'W. Originally known as Knowles Station, it was renamed in the 1890s by Brainard H. Warner, a landowner who admired the Kensington dist. of London. The town has spread out in recent years and the pop. of South and North Kensington are much larger than the center area. Site of very large Mormon temple. **3** town (1990 pop. 1,631), Rockingham co., SE N.H., and 3 mi/4.8 km S of Exeter; 42°55'N 70°57'W. Drained in NW by Exeter R. Light mfg.; agr. (nursery crops, vegetables; poultry, cattle; dairying).

Kensington 1 village, Hartford co., Conn.; postal section of BERLIN. **2** village (1990 pop. 553), Smith co., N Kansas, 13 mi/21 km W of Smith Center; 39°46'N 99°01'W. In corn belt; grain storage. **3** village (1990 pop. 295), Douglas co., W Minn., 18 mi/29 km WSW of Alexandria; 45°46'N 95°42'W. Dairying; poultry; alfalfa, soybeans, grain; mfg. (feeds). Kensington Rune Stone, with anc. inscription describing journey of Swedish and Norwegian explorers, was found nearby in 1989. Small natural lakes in area, especially to NE. **4** upper-income residential village (1990 pop. 1,104), Nassau co., SE N.Y., near N shore of W L.I., just SSE of Great Neck; 40°47′N 73°43′W.

Kent, district municipality (1986 pop. 3,394), B.C., Canada, 79 mi/127 km E of Vancouver, in upper Fraser R. valley. Dairy and mixed farming.

Kent 1 county (□ 1,734 sq mi/4,491 sq km; 1991 pop. 31,694), E N.B., Canada, on Northumberland Strait and Gulf of St. Lawrence; ⊙ Richibucto. **2** county (□ 918 sq mi/2,378 sq km; 1991 pop. 109,943), S Ont., Canada; ⊙ Chatham. Borders L. Erie to S, L. St. Clair to W; Thames R. bisects co. NE to SW, enters L. St. Clair at Lighthouse Court. Rondeau Prov. Park at Points aux Pins, L. Erie. Mixed farming; fruit, dairying, pumpkins.

Kent 1 county (□ 800 sq mi/2,072 sq km; 1990 pop. 110,993), central Del.; 39°"06N 75°33′W. Level coastal plain, with some marshland; bounded N in part by Smyrna R., W by Md. state line, S in part by Mispillion R., E by Delaware R. and Delaware Bay (both N.J. state line); drained by Leipsic, Choptank, Murderkill, and St. Jones rivers and Marshyhope Creek. Agr. (corn, vegetables, wheat, fruit; poultry; dairying); fishing; oysters; fruit and vegetable canning; processing of dairy prods.; mfg. at Dover. Dover Air Force Base is here. Killen's Pond State Park in S center. Woodland Beach Wildlife Area, Bombay Hook Natl. Wildlife Area, Little Creek Wildlife Area, Harvey Conservation Area, Milford Neck Widlife Area are all in E (N to S); Blackiston Wildlife Area in NW; N.G. Wilder Wildlife Area in SW. Formed 1683. **2** county (□ 414 sq mi/1,072 sq km; 1990 pop. 17,842), E Md.; ⊙ Chestertown; 39°14′N 76°06′W. Peninsula on Eastern Shore, bounded E by Del. state line, W by Chesapeake Bay. Coastal plain agr. area (vegetables, fruit, corn, wheat, livestock, dairy prods.); large seafood industry (esp. oysters); summer resorts; fishing, hunting. Once Kent co. took in all of the Eastern Shore; now it is the smallest co. in the area. Includes many old churches and houses as well as Washington Col., chartered in 1783 and named for George Washington with his express permission. Formed 1642. **3** county (□ 872 sq mi/2,258 sq km; 1990 pop. 500,631), SW Mich.; 43°01′N 85°32′W; ⊙ Grand Rapids. Intersected by Grand R. and drained by Flat, Rogue, and Thornapple rivers. Fruit growing (apples, peaches); also agr. (wheat, oats, barley, soybeans, cucumbers, onions, corn, potatoes, beans; cattle, hogs, sheep; dairy prods.); mfg. at Grand Rapids. Gypsum quarries, gravel pits. Numerous lakes in NE ¼. Has a state fish hatchery. Pando and Cannonsburg ski areas at co. center; SW quadrant of co. is highly urbanized by city of Grand Rapids and its suburbs. Organized 1836. **4** county (□ 190 sq mi/492 sq km; 1990 pop. 161,135), W and central R.I., bounded E by Narragansett Bay, W by Conn. state line; ⊙ East Greenwich; 41°40′N 71°35′W. Industrial, resort, and agr. area, producing chiefly textiles and textile machinery; also fabricated metal prods., chemicals; agr. (dairy prods., poultry, corn, potatoes, fruit, mushrooms); fisheries; lumbering; many printing and publishing establishments. Many coast recreation sites. Includes state forests and parks. Drained by Pawtuxet, Moosup, Flat, and Wood rivers. Inc. 1750. **5** county (□ 902 sq mi/2,336 sq km; 1990 pop. 1,010), NW Texas; ⊙ Clairemont; 33°11′N 100°46′W. Elev. 2,000 ft/610 m–2,800 ft/853 m. Rolling plains, with some broken areas; drained by Salt and Double Mt. forks of Brazos R., and White R. Cattle-ranching region; agr. (cotton, wheat, sorghum); beekeeping. Some oil and gas; sand and gravel. Formed 1876.

Kent 1 industrial city (1990 pop. 28,835), Portage co., NE Ohio; 41°08′N 81°22′W. Settled in 1805 as Franklin Mills, combined with Carthage and renamed as Kent 1863, inc. as a city 1920. Mfg. includes machinery and food. Main campus of Kent State Univ., where four young people were killed by Ohio Natl. Guardsmen during a 1970 protest of the Vietnam War. Liquid-crystal research center sponsored by Natl. Science Foundation and state of Ohio. **2** city (1990 pop. 37,960), King co., W central Wash., suburb 15 mi/24 km SSE of downtown Seattle, and 13 mi/21 km NE of downtown Tacoma, near Puget Sound; 47°23′N 122°14′W. Located in a fertile agr. area, the city has numerous food- and dairy-processing plants. Mfg. (chemicals, fabricated metal prods., electrical equip., fixtures, paper prods., transportation equip., apparel, aircraft, plastic prods., machinery, printing and publishing, furniture, food). Kent also has a large aerospace industry. The city and its pop. grew in the 1980s and early 1990s along with the developing Seattle metropolitan area. Puget Sound area 4 mi/6.4 km W. Inc. 1890.

Kent 1 resort town (1990 pop. 2,918), Litchfield co., W Conn., on Housatonic R. and N.Y. state line, 19 mi/31 km WSW of Torrington; 41°43′N 73°27′W. In hilly region; summer camps. Kent school (1906) here. Includes South Kent village, seat of South Kent school (1923); site of Bull's bridge-one of 2 covered bridges in Connecticut open to vehicular traffic. Industry includes agr. and mfg. of machinery and electronic equip.; 3 state parks. L. Waramaug is SE. Settled 1738, inc. 1739. **2** town (1990 pop. 65), Union co., S Iowa, near Little Platte R., 8 mi/12.9 km SW of Creston.

Kent, village (1990 pop. 131), Wilkin co., W Minn., 13 mi/21 km NNW of Breckenridge; 46°26′N 96°40′W. Grain, sunflowers; livestock.

Kent Acres, uninc. town (1990 est. pop. 1,807), Kent co., central Del., 1 mi/1.6 km S of Dover; 39°08′N 75°31′W. Suburb of Dover.

Kent City, village (1990 pop. 899), Kent co., SW Mich., 18 mi/29 km NNW of Grand Rapids; 43°13′N 85°45′W. In farm area. Fruit growing (apples, cherries, peaches); mfg. (frozen cherries, applesauce, juice).

Kent Island, E Md., largest (c.15 mi/24 km long, 1 mi/1.6 km–6 mi/9.7 km wide) and most historic of Chesapeake Bay isls., in Queen Annes co., at S side of mouth of Chester R., E of Annapolis. Separated from Eastern Shore mainland by narrow channel (bridged). Chester (seafood packing) and Stevensville are chief villages; others are Love Point (at N tip; lighthouse), Romancoke (S); Matapeake; Dominion; and Normans. Kent Point (S tip) has lighthouse. Isl. is E anchor of Chesapeake Bay Bridge. Large fishing and oystering fleet; seafood processing; tourist resort, with fishing (bluefish, rock and black bass), bathing, and duck hunting. William Claiborne est. here (1631) 1st permanent Eng. settlement in Md., claiming isl. for Va.; Lord Baltimore's grant of 1632 transferred it to Md., and his settlers landed at St. Mary's in 1634, but conflicting claims went unsettled until 1657. Near Stevensville is Kent Fort Manor (built c. 1638–1640).

Kent Peninsula, NE Mackenzie dist., N.W.T., Canada, on Dease Strait; 68°12′–68°56′N 104°55′–108°51′W. Extends 105 mi/169 km W from narrow isthmus into Coronation Gulf; 7 mi/11 km–29 mi/47 km wide.

Kent Point, Md.: see KENT ISLAND.

Kentfield, uninc. town (1990 pop. 6,030), Marin co., W Calif., a residential suburb 13 mi/21 km NNW of downtown San Francisco and 1 mi/1.6 km SW of San Rafael, on Corte Madera Creek; 37°57′N 122°33′W. Col. of Marin (2-year).

Kentland, town (1990 pop. 1,798), NW Ind., near Ill. state line, 38 mi/61 km NW of Lafayette; ⊙ Newton co.; 40°46′N 87°27′W. In grain and farming area. Corn, oats, soybeans, corn; light mfg. RR junction. Settled 1860. George Ade was b. here.

Kenton, county (□ 164 sq mi/425 sq km; 1990 pop. 142,031), extreme N Ky.; ⊙ Independence (formerly shared with Covington); 38°55′N 84°32′W. Bounded N by Ohio R. (Ohio state line), E by Licking R. Gently rolling upland area, in N part of Bluegrass region. Urbanized in N, part of Cincinnati Metropolitan area, remainder is agr. (cattle, poultry; corn, burley tobacco, hay, alfalfa; dairying). Mfg. in Covington and Erlanger. Formed 1840.

Kenton, city (1990 pop. 8,356), W central Ohio, 26 mi/42 km ESE of Lima, and on Scioto R.; ⊙ Hardin co.; 40°38′N 83°37′W. Trade center for agr. area; mfg. of food, machinery, transportation equip. Limestone quarries. Plotted 1833. Aircraft industries in area.

Kenton, town (1990 pop. 1,366), Gibson and Obion cos., NW Tenn., on Rutherford Fork of the Obion R., and 15 mi/24 km S of Union City; 36°12′N 89°01′W. In farm area. Near Gooch Wildlife Management Area.

Kenton 1 village (1990 pop. 232), Kent co., W central Del., 9 mi/14.5 km NW of Dover on Leipsic R. Md. state line is 5 mi/8 km to W; 39°13′N 75°40′W. **2** village, Cimarron co., Okla. Panhandle, on high plains, the westernmost village in Okla., near N.Mex. state line, 25 mi/40 km NW of Boise City, on Cimarron R. Just NW is Black Mesa (4,973 ft/1,516 m), highest point in Okla. Black Mesa State Park and L. Etling to SE.

Kenton Vale, village (1990 pop. 358), Kenton co., N Ky., residential suburb 4 mi/6.4 km S of Cincinnati, Ohio, 2 mi/3.2 km S of Covington, Ky; 39°02′N 84°31′W.

Kents Hill, Maine: see READFIELD.

Kentucky, state (1995 est. pop. 3,860,219), 40,411 sq mi/104,664 sq km, SE central U.S.; ⊙ FRANKFORT; 37°32′N 85°16′W. The commonwealth was admitted as the 15th state of the Union in 1792. LOUISVILLE and LEXINGTON the largest and 2d largest cities. The N boundary is formed by the Ohio R., separating Ky. from Ohio (NE), Ind. (N), and Ill. (NW); W boundary formed by the Mississippi R., forms Mo. state line. At the SW tip of the state, in Madrid Bend, c.5 sq mi/13 sq km of Ky. territory, created by a loop in the course of the Mississippi R., protrudes N from Tenn. into Mo. and is entirely separate from remainder of Ky. Tenn. borders Ky. on the S. In the E, the boundary with W.Va. is formed by the Big Sandy R. and its tributary, the Tug Fork; the Va. border runs NE-SW through the Cumberland Mts., part of the Appalachian Mt. chain. Many rapid creeks in the mts. feed the Kentucky, the Cumberland, and the Licking rivers, which together with the Tennessee and the Ohio are the chief rivers of the state. The Kentucky Dam on the Tennessee R. and Barkley Dam on the Cumberland R. (the 2 dams are only 3 mi/4.8 km apart) near Paducah, are a major part of the Tennessee Valley Authority (TVA) hydroelectric system. Land bet. the Lakes Recreation area, managed by the TVA, lies in neck of land 7 mi/11.3 km wide bet. Kentucky L. and L. Barkley, extends S into Tenn. Important reservoirs are Rough R., Nolin R., and Bannen R. reservoirs in center of state and L. Cumberland reservoir in S center. Central/Eastern time zone passes through center of state. From elevations of about 2,000 ft/610 m on the Cumberland Plateau in the SE, where Black Mt. (4,139 ft/1,262 m) marks the state's highest point, Ky. slopes to elevations of less than 800 ft/244 m along the W rim. The narrow valleys and sharp ridges of the mt. region are noted for forests of giant hardwoods and scented pine and for springtime blooms of laurel, magnolia, rhododendron, and dogwood. Unfortunately, these forests have suffered from the effects of acid rain. To the W, the plateau breaks in a series of escarpments, bordering a narrow plains region interrupted by many single conical peaks called knobs. Surrounded by the knobs region on the S, W, and E and extending as far W as Louisville is the Bluegrass country, the heart and trademark of the state. To the S and W lie the rolling plains and rocky hillsides of the Pennyroyal (Pennyrile) Plateau, a region that takes its name from a species of mint that grows abundantly in the area. There, underground streams have washed through limestone to form miles of caverns, some of the notable ones being in Mammoth Cave Natl. Park in SW central Ky. NW Ky. is generally rough, rolling terrain, with scattered but important coal deposits. The isolated far-western region, bounded by the Mississippi, Ohio, and Tennessee rivers, is referred to as the Purchase, or Jackson Purchase (for Andrew Jackson, who was a prominent member of the commission that bought it from the Chickasaw in 1818). Consisting of flood plains, some less than 250 ft/76 m above sea level, and rolling uplands, it is among the largest migratory-bird routes in the U.S. Little remains of Kentucky's great forests that once spread over ¾ of the state and were renowned for their size and density. Kentucky's climate is generally mild, with few extremes of heat and cold. The state is noted for the distilling of Bourbon whiskey, named for

Bourbon co., Va., of which N Ky. was once a part, and for the breeding of thoroughbred racehorses. In 1990 the state, esp. in W, N, and central Ky., was also the 2d-largest U.S. grower of tobacco, both dark and burley varieties, after N.C. Tobacco has long been the state's chief crop, and it is also the chief farm prod., followed by cattle, horses, and dairy prods. Hay, corn, and soybeans are other major crops raised in the state. Kentucky's economy derives by far the greatest share of its income from industry. Lexington is one of the world's largest loose-leaf tobacco markets. Louisville, Lexington, Bowling Green, Covington (in Cincinnati metro area), Owensboro, and Hopkinsville are major industrial centers. The state's chief industries manufacture electrical equip., food, automobiles, machinery, chemicals, and fabricated and primary metals. Printing and publishing, as well as tourism, have also become important industries. Ky. is one of the major U.S. producers of bituminous coal, the state's most valuable mineral, esp. in Appalachian cos. of E Ky. Other mineral prods. include stone, petroleum, and natural gas. When the Eastern seaboard of N. Amer. was being colonized in the 1600s, Ky. was part of the inaccessible country beyond the mts. After Robert Cavelier, sieur de La Salle, claimed all regions drained by the Mississippi and its tributaries for France, Br. interest in the area quickened. The 1st major expedition to the Tenn. region was led by Dr. Thomas Walker, who explored the E mt. region in 1750 for the Loyal Land Co. Walker was soon followed by hunters and scouts including Christopher Gist. Further exploration was interrupted by the last conflict (1754–1763) of the Fr. and Indian Wars bet. the Fr. and Br. for control of N. Amer., and Pontiac's Rebellion, a Native Amer. uprising (1763–1766). With the Br. victorious in both, settlers soon began to enter Ky. They came in defiance of a royal proclamation of 1763, which forbade settlement W of the Appalachians. Daniel Boone, the famous Amer. frontiersman, first came to Ky. in 1767; he returned in 1769 and spent 2 years in the area. A surveying party under James Harrod established the 1st permanent settlement at Harrodsburg in 1774, and the next year Boone, as agent for Richard Henderson and the Transylvania Co., a colonizing group of which Henderson was a member, blazed the Wilderness Road from Tenn. into the Ky. region and founded Boonesboro. Title to this land was challenged by Va., whose legislature voided (1778) the Transylvania Company's claims, although individual settlers were confirmed in their grants. Meanwhile, Ky. was made (1776) a co. of Va., and new settlers came through the Cumberland Gap and over the Wilderness Road or down the Ohio R. These early pioneers of Ky. and Tenn. were constantly in conflict with the Native Americans. The growing pop. of Kentuckians, feeling that Va. had failed to give them adequate protection, worked for statehood in a series of conventions held at Danville (1784–1791). Others, observing the weaknesses of the U.S. govt., considered forming an independent nation. Since trade down the Mississippi and out of Span.-held New Orleans was indispensable to Kentucky's economic development, an alliance with Spain was contemplated, and U.S. Gen. James Wilkinson, who lived in Ky. at the time, worked toward that end. However, in 1792 a constitution was finally framed and accepted, and in the same year the Commonwealth of Ky. (its official designation) was admitted to the Union, the 1st state W of the Appalachians. Isaac Shelby was elected the 1st governor, and Frankfort was chosen capital. U.S. Gen. Anthony Wayne's victory at the battle of Fallen Timbers in 1794 effectively ended Native Amer. resistance in Ky. In 1795, Pinckney's Treaty bet. the U.S. and Spain granted Americans the right to navigate the Mississippi, a right soon completely assured by the Louisiana Purchase of 1803. Enactment by the Federal govt. of the Alien and Sedition Acts (1798) promptly provoked a sharp protest in Ky. The state grew fast as trade and shipping centers developed and river traffic down the Ohio and Mississippi increased. The War of 1812 spurred economic prosperity in Ky., but financial difficulties after the war threatened many with ruin. The state responded to the situation by chartering in 1818 a number of new banks that were allowed to issue their own currency. These banks soon collapsed, and the state legislature passed measures for the relief of the banks' creditors. However, the relief measures were subsequently declared unconstitutional by a state court. The legislature then repealed legislation that had established the offending court and set up a new one. The state became divided bet. pro-relief and anti-relief factions, and the issue also figured in the division of the state politically bet. followers of the Tennesseean Andrew Jackson, then rising to natl. political prominence, and supporters of the Whig Party of Henry Clay, who was a leader in Ky. politics for almost ½ a cent. In the first ½ of the 19th cent., Ky. was primarily a state of small farms rather than large plantations and was not adaptable to extensive use of slave labor. Slavery thus declined after 1830, and for 17 years, beginning in 1833, the importation of slaves into the state was forbidden. In 1850, however, the legislature repealed this restriction, and Ky., where slave trading had begun to develop quietly in the 1840s, was converted into a huge slave market for the lower S. Anti-slavery agitation had begun in the state in the late 18th cent. within the churches, and abolitionists such as James G. Birney and Cassius M. Clay labored vigorously in Ky. for emancipation before the Civil War. Soon Ky., like other border states, was torn by conflict over the slavery issue. In addition to the radical anti-slavery element and the aggressive pro-slavery faction, there was also in the state a conciliatory group. At the outbreak of the Civil War, Ky. attempted to remain neutral. Gov. Beriah Magoffin refused to sanction President Lincoln's call for volunteers, but his warnings to both the Union and the Confederacy not to invade were ignored. Confederate forces invaded and occupied part of S Ky., including Columbus and Bowling Green. The state legislature voted (Sept. 1861) to oust the Confederates and Ulysses S. Grant crossed the Ohio and took Paducah, and the state was secured for the Union. After battles in Mill Springs, Richmond, and Perryville in 1862, there was no major fighting in the state, although the Confederate cavalryman John Hunt Morgan occasionally led raids into the state, and guerrilla warfare was constant. For Ky. it was truly a civil war as neighbors, friends, and even families became bitterly divided in their loyalties. Over 30,000 Kentuckians fought for the Confederacy, while about 64,000 served in the Union ranks. After the war many in the state opposed federal Reconstruction policies, and Ky. refused to ratify the Thirteenth and Fourteenth amendments to the U.S. Constitution. As in the South, an overwhelming majority of Kentuckians supported the Democratic party in the period of readjustment after the war, in many ways as bitter as the war itself. After the Civil War industrial and commercial recovery was aided by increased RR construction, but farmers were plagued by the liabilities of the one-crop (tobacco) system. After the turn of the cent., the depressed price of tobacco gave rise to a feud bet. buyers and growers, resulting in the Black Patch War. Night riders terrorized buyers and growers in an effort to stage an effective boycott against monopolistic practices of buyers. For more than a year general lawlessness prevailed until the state militia forced an agreement in 1908. Coal mining, which began on a large scale in the 1870s, was well established in mountainous E Ky. by the early 20th cent. The mines boomed during World War I, but after the war, when demand for coal lessened and production fell off, intense labor troubles developed. The attempt of the United Mine Workers of America (UMW) to organize the coal industry in Harlan co. in the 1930s resulted in outbreaks of violence, drawing natl. attention to "bloody" Harlan, and in 1937 a U.S. Senate subcommittee began an investigation into allegations that workers' civil rights were being violated. Further violence ensued, and it was not until 1939 that the UMW was finally recognized as a bargaining agent for most of the state's miners. Labor disputes and strikes have persisted in the state; some are still accompanied by violence. After World War I improvements of the state's highways were made, and a much-needed reorganization of the state govt. was carried out in the 1920s and 1930s. Since World War II, construction of turnpikes (toll highways), extensive development of state parks, especially state resort parks, with complete tourist facilities, and a marked rise in tourism have all contributed to the development of the state. Ky. benefitted from the energy crisis of the 1970s, when the state's large coal supply was in great demand. A mixture of strip, open-pit, and subsurface mining continues. In spite of hydroelectricity projects and tighter environmental controls, coal continues to be the primary (95%) type of fuel used in power plants in Ky. and surrounding states. However, a steady decline in mfg. has not been offset by a shift to service industries as in other states. As a result, Ky. has grown very little in the past few decades, and only 0.7% during the 1980s. Tourist attractions include the famous Kentucky Derby at Churchill Downs in Louisville and the celebrated horse farms surrounding Lexington in the heart of the Bluegrass region. The Abraham Lincoln Birthplace Natl. Historic Site, 45 mi/72 km S of Louisville and Cumberland Gap Natl. Historical Park (Ky., Tenn., Va.) in SE corner are historic landmarks. There are 2 natl. forests: Daniel Boone Natl. Forest, composed of 2 large sects. in SE center, and part of Jefferson Natl. Forest, on boundary of Va., in SE. Part of Big South Fork Natl. River and Recreation Area, on S boundary, extends into Ky. from Tenn. At Fort Knox Military Reservation is the U.S. Gold Depository. Ky. was renowned for its former family feuds, such as the notorious Hatfield-McCoy affair in the early 19th cent. Kentucky's state constitution was adopted in 1891. The governor of the state is elected for a term of 4 years. The general assembly, or legislature, is bicameral with a senate of 38 members and a house of representatives of 100 members. State senators are elected to serve for terms of 4 years, and representatives for 2 years. Ky. is represented in the U.S. Congress by 6 Representatives and 2 Senators and has 8 electoral votes in presidential elections. Institutions of higher learning include the Univ. of Ky. and Transylvania Univ., at Lexington; the Univ. of Louisville, at Louisville; Eastern Ky. Univ., at Richmond; Murray State Univ., at Murray; Western Ky. Univ., at Bowling Green; Ky. Wesleyan Col., at Owensboro; Union Col., at Barbourville, and Ky. State Univ., at Frankfort. Ky. has 120 cos.: ADAIR, ALLEN, ANDERSON, BALLARD, BARREN, BATH, BELL, BOONE, BOURBON, BOYD, BOYLE, BRACKEN, BREATHITT, BRECKINRIDGE, BULLITT, BUTLER, CALDWELL, CALLOWAY, CAMPBELL, CARLISLE, CARROLL, CARTER, CASEY, CHRISTIAN, CLARK, CLAY, CLINTON, CRITTENDEN, CUMBERLAND, DAVIESS, EDMONSON, ELLIOTT, ESTILL, FAYETTE, FLEMING, FLOYD, FRANKLIN, FULTON, GALLATIN, GARRARD, GRANT, GRAVES, GRAYSON, GREEN, GREENUP, HANCOCK, HARDIN, HARLAN, HARRISON, HART, HENDERSON, HENRY, HICKMAN, HOPKINS, JACKSON, JEFFERSON, JESSAMINE, JOHNSON, KENTON, KNOTT, KNOX, LARUE, LAUREL, LAWRENCE, LEE, LESLIE, LETCHER, LEWIS, LINCOLN, LIVINGSTON, LOGAN, LYON, MCCRACKEN, MCCREARY, MCLEAN, MADISON, MAGOFFIN, MARION, MARSHALL, MARTIN, MASON, MEADE, MENIFEE, MERCER, METCALFE, MONROE, MONTGOMERY, MORGAN, MUHLENBERG, NELSON, NICHOLAS, OHIO, OLDHAM, OWEN, OWSLEY, PENDLETON, PERRY, PIKE, POWELL, PULASKI, ROBERTSON, ROCKCASTLE, ROWAN, RUSSELL, SCOTT, SHELBY, SIMPSON, SPENCER, TAYLOR, TODD, TRIGG, TRIMBLE, UNION, WARREN, WASHINGTON, WAYNE, WEBSTER, WHITLEY, WOLFE, WOODFORD.

Kentucky, river, 259 mi/417 km long, formed by the junction of the North and South forks, at Beattyville, Lee co., central Ky., and flows NW past Irvine, Boonesboro, Frankfort to Ohio R. at Carrollton. The river is navigable by small craft for its entire length by means of locks. The Kentucky's upper course flows through a coal-mining region of Cumberland Mts. The lower course flows through the heart of Ky.'s Bluegrass region. North Fork Kentucky R., c.125 mi/201 km long, rises in E Letcher co., SE Ky., near Va. state line. Flows generally NW past Hazard and Jackson; receives Middle

Fork 1 mi/1.6 km E of confluence with South Fork. South Fork Kentucky R., c.30 mi/48 km long, formed by joining of Red Bird and Goose creeks in N Clay co., SE Ky., flows N to join North Fork. Middle Fork Kentucky R., c.85 mi/137 km rises in NE Harlan co., SE Ky. Flows generally NNW past Hayden and through Buckhorn L. reservoir to North Fork.

Kentucky Lake, reservoir, SW Ky. and NW Tenn., on Tennessee R., 8 mi/12.9 km W and parallel to L. Barkley (linked by channel), and 19 mi/31 km ESE of Paducah; c.185 mi/298 km long, max. 3 mi/4.8 km wide; 37°00′N 88°16′W. Max. capacity 6,002,600 acre-ft. Big Sandy R. enters from SSW, forms 14-mi/23-km arm; Duck R. enters from E 14 mi/23 km SW of Waverly, Tenn. Formed by Kentucky Lock and Dam (206 ft/63 m high, 8,422 ft/2,567 m long), built (1944) by as part of TVA system for flood control, navigation, and power generation. Pickwick Dam (Tenn.) at S tip. Surrounded by state parks and recreation areas, including Nathan B. Forrest State Historic Park (Tenn.). Partly in units of Tenn. Natl. Wildlife Refuge.

Kentucky Natural Bridge, Ky.: see NATURAL BRIDGE STATE RESORT PARK.

Kentville, town (1991 pop. 5,506), W N.S., Canada, on the Cornwallis R., NW of Halifax; 45°04′N 64°30′W. It is a tourist and trade center in the Annapolis valley, a fruit-growing region.

Kentwood, city (1990 pop. 37,826), Kent co., SW Mich., suburb 6 mi/9.7 km SE of Grand Rapids; 42°52′N 85°35′W. Mfg. (plastics, transportation equip., furniture). Drained by Plaster R. Kent Co. Internatl. Airport to SE.

Kentwood, town (1990 pop. 2,468), Tangipahoa parish, SE La., 42 mi/68 km N of Ponchatoula, on Tangipahoa R., near Miss. line; 30°56′N 90°31′W. Strawberries, vegetables; catfish; lumber milling; mfg. (feeds, apparel, food, bricks). Settled in mid-19th cent.; inc. 1893.

Kenvil, village, Morris co., N N.J., 9 mi/14.5 km NW of Morristown; mfg. (explosives, concrete prods., food). Large powder plant here (founded 1871) nearly destroyed in 1940 by explosions that took 48 lives.

Kenvir (KEN-vuhr), uninc. town (1990 pop. 800), Harlan co., SE Ky., in the Cumberland Mts., 9 mi/14.5 km E of Harlan. Bituminous coal; timber.

Kenwood, uninc. town, Sonoma co., W Calif., 10 mi/16 km NW of Sonoma, on Sonoma Creek. Los Guilicos Warm Springs to S; Annadel State Park to W; Sugarloaf Ridge State Park to NE. Grapes, apples, grain; dairying. Wineries (3).

Kenwood 1 uninc. village (1990 pop. 7,469), Hamilton co., extreme SW Ohio, a NE suburb of Cincinnati, off Interstate Highway 71; 39°12′N 84°22′W. **2** suburban village, Baltimore co., central Md., 5 mi/8 km WSW of downtown Baltimore, near Catonsville. Considered a part of Bethesda, it is noted for the flowering cherry trees on its curving streets in springtime.

Kenyon (KEN-yuhn), town (1990 pop. 1,552), Goodhue co., SE Minn., on North Fork Zumbro R., and 15 mi/24 km E of Faribault; 44°16′N 92°59′W. Grain, soybeans; livestock, poultry; dairying; light mfg. Nestrand Big Woods State Park to NW. Settled 1856, inc. 1885.

Kenyon, village, Washington co., R.I.: see CHARLESTOWN.

Keo (KEE-o), village (1990 pop. 154), Lonoke co., central Ark., 18 mi/29 km ESE of Little Rock; 34°36′N 92°00′W. Toltoc Mounds State Park to NW.

Keokuk, county (□ 579 sq mi/1,500 sq km; 1990 pop. 11,624), SE Iowa; ⊙ Sigourney; 41°20′N 92°10′W. Prairie agr. area (hogs, cattle, sheep, poultry; corn, oats) drained by Skunk, North and South Skunk, and South Fork English rivers. Limestone quarries, clay pits. Widespread river flooding occurred here in 1993. Formed 1837.

Keokuk, city (1990 pop. 12,451), seat of Lee co., extreme SE Iowa, on the Mississippi R. at the foot of the Des Moines R. rapids and in a farm area; 40°24′N 91°24′W. Its industries focus on food processing and packaging (turkeys, dairy items, wheat and corn prods.); mfg. (fabricated metal prods.). The city was named for Keokuk, a Sac tribal chief who ceded lands to settlers and who is buried beneath an impressive statue in Rand Park. Because of its location at the foot of the treacherous Des Moines R. rapids, Keokuk was a natural rest stop for boats ascending the Mississippi. During the Civil War 5 army hosps. there served the wounded; those who did not survive were buried in the city's natl. cemetery, where the Unknown Soldier Monument was erected. In 1877 a ship canal (9 mi/14.5 km long) was completed around the rapids; in 1910–1913 the river was dammed, Lock and Dam No. 19, creating L. Keokuk, and the dam along with a Miss. R. plant furnish hydroelectric power. Mark Twain worked as a printer in Keokuk; mementos of his stay are preserved. Also located here are Southeastern Community Col. and a Riverboat Mus. Serious flood damage occurred here and in adjacent parts of Mo. and Ill. in 1993. Inc. 1847.

Keomah Village, village (1990 pop. 99), Mahaska co., S central Iowa, 5 mi/8 km ESE of Oskaloosa, at E end of L. Keomah; 41°17′N 92°32′W. L. Keomah State Park nearby. Corn; cattle, hogs.

Keosauqua, town (1990 pop. 1,020), SE Iowa, on Des Moines R., and 30 mi/48 km SE of Ottumwa; ⊙ Van Buren co.; 40°43′N 91°57′W. Light mfg. Lacey Keosauqua State Park to S; W unit of Shimek State Forest to SW. The Des Moines R. flooded this area in 1993. Settled 1836, inc. 1851.

Keota, town (1990 pop. 1,000), Keokuk co., SE Iowa, 14 mi/23 km WNW of Washington; 41°22′N 91°57′W. Shipping point for livestock. Mfg. (machinery, food). Settled 1871, inc. 1873.

Keota 1 (kee-O-tuh), village (1990 pop. 5), Weld co., N Colo., 38 mi/61 km NE of Greeley; 40°42′N 104°04′W. Elev. 4,961 ft/1,512 m. Surrounded by units of Pawnee Natl. Grassland. Near Wild Horse Creek. **2** village (1990 pop. 625), Haskell co., E Okla., 21 mi/34 km NW of Poteau, on Sansbois Arm (Sansbois Creek) of Robert S. Kerr reservoir; 35°15′N 94°55′W. In agr. area; light mfg.

Keowee, Lake (KEE-uh-wee), reservoir, Oconee co. and on Pickens co. border, NW S.C., on Seneca (Keowee) and Little rivers, 28 mi/45 km W of Greenville. Formed by 2 dams, the Keowee Dam (70 ft/21 m high; built 1970; 34°48′N 82°53′W) on the Seneca (Keowee) R., and the Little R. Dam (135 ft high; built 1969; 34°44′N 82°54′W), on the Little R.; channel just W of Keowee Dam joins reservoirs. Max. capacity 500,000 acre-ft. Little R. sect. 10 mi/16 km long, extends NW, with 4-mi/6.4-km SW arm; Keowee sect. 12 mi/19 km long, extends N to Jocassee Dam. Both built by the Duke Power Co. for power generation.

Keowee River, NW S.C.; rises in Blue Ridge Mts. of SW N.C.; flows S where it joins Savannah R. WSW of Anderson, S.C.; two hydroelectric facilities created when Keowee Dam was completed forming L. Keowee in 1971 and Jocassee Dam completed in 1973 creating L. Jocassee.

Keowee River, S.C.: see SENECA RIVER.

Keremeos, village (1986 pop. 839), S B.C., Canada, on fertile bench of Similkameen R., 26 mi/42 km S of Penticton; 49°12′N 119°49′W. Former Hudson's Bay Company post. Mining; wine production.

Kerens, town (1990 pop. 1,702), Navarro co., E central Texas, 14 mi/23 km E of Corsicana; 32°07′N 96°13′W. Richland Chambers Reservoir to S. Settled 1881.

Kerhonkson, village (□ 5 sq mi/13 sq km; 1990 pop. 1,629), Ulster co., SE N.Y., on Rondout Creek, 19 mi/31 km SW of Kingston, just W of Shawangunk Mt. range; 41°46′N 74°17′W. Residential area, popular summer recreational spot.

Kerkhoven (kuhrk-HO-ven), village (1990 pop. 732), Swift co., SW central Minn., 14 mi/23 km WNW of Willmar, near Shakopee Creek; 45°11′N 95°19′W. Agr. (grain; livestock, poultry; dairying), Light mfg. Monson L. State Park to N.

Kerman, city (1990 pop. 5,448), Fresno co., central Calif., in San Joaquin Valley, 15 mi/24 km W of Fresno; 36°43′N 120°04′W. Agr. (cotton; grapes, nectarines, figs, raisins, almonds, vegetables, sugar beets, grain, alfalfa); winery. Mfg. (fertilizers, food prods., sanitary food containers). San Joaquin R. to N. Inc. 1946.

Kermit, town (1990 pop. 6,875), ⊙ Winkler co., W Texas, 38 mi/61 km NE of Pecos, near base of Caprock escarpment; 31°51′N 103°05′W. Elev. 2,890 ft/881 m. Supply center for oil, natural-gas area (Permian Basin), with cattle ranches. Mfg. (natural-gas processing, well hookups). Inc. 1938.

Kermit, village (1990 pop. 342), Mingo co., SW W.Va., on Tug Fork R. (bridged), opposite Warfield, Ky.; 37°50′N 82°24′W. Natural gas, bituminous coal. Mfg. (lumber). Cabwaylingo State Forest to NE, Laurel Creek Wildlife Management Area to E.

Kern, county (□ 8,142 sq mi/21,088 sq km; 1990 pop. 543,477), S central Calif.; ⊙ Bakersfield; 35°20′N 118°43′W. Includes S end of San Joaquin Valley, walled in by Tehachapi Mts. (S), S part of the Sierra Nevada (E), and Coast Ranges (W). Irrigated agr. (since 1880s); cotton; potatoes, grains, nuts, grapes, citrus, apples, plums, carrots, tomatoes, peppers; cattle; dairying. Limestone quarrying; gypsum, gold, clay mining; oil and natural gas. State's leading petroleum-producing co., with oil and natural-gas fields along W side of San Joaquin Valley and in Bakersfield dist. Part of Mojave Desert (borax, tungsten, silver, gold mines) in E and SE. Drained by Kern R., used for hydroelectric power; irrigation water supplied by Friant-Kern Canal of Central Valley Project. Los Angeles Aqueduct crosses co. N-S in E; Calif. Aqueduct crosses co. NW-SE in W. Part of Sequoia Natl. Forest in N; part of Los Padres Natl. Forest in S; Pacific Crest Natl. Scenic Trail crosses co. N-S in E center; Fort Tejon State Historical Park in S; Kern Natl. Wildlife Refuge in NW, Tule State Elk Reserve in W center; Red Rock Canyon State Recreation Area in E; Isabella L. reservoir in NE. Most of Edwards Air Force Base in SE corner, part of China L. Naval Weapons Center in NE corner. Elk Hills Naval Petroleum Reserve is in W. Formed 1893.

Kern River, 155 mi/249 km long, E Calif.; rises in the S Sierra Nevada, NE Tulare co., in NE corner of Sequoia Natl. Park, flows S through Inyo and Sequoia natl. forests, then SW through Isabella L. reservoir, and into S part of the San Joaquin valley, where it passes Bakersfield to N and enters Buena Vista L. irrigation reservoir. Town of Alta Sierra 5 mi/8 km W of Isabella L. The river has Isabella Dam as its chief facility. Kern R. is the S terminus of the Friant-Kern Canal, constructed bet. 1945 and 1951 to bring the waters of the San Joaquin R. to the region (see central valley project); irrigated agr. (alfalfa, fruit; cotton) and cattle grazing are practiced. U.S. explorer John Frémont named the river in honor of Edward M. Kern, the topographer of his 3d expedition. Gold was discovered along the river in 1853. Water from river's lower course and Buena Vista L. are used for irrigating Bakersfield area, also channeled into Calif. Aqueduct and other canals, leaving river with no natural outlet.

Kernersville (KUHR-nuhrs-vil), city (1990 pop. 10,836), Forsyth co., N central N.C., suburb 9 mi/14.5 km E of Winston-Salem and 15 mi/24 km W of Greensboro; 36°07′N 80°04′W. Mfg. (apparel, printing and publishing, electronic equip., paper and plastic prods., construction materials, textiles, transportation equip., metal and stone processing, machinery). High Point Reservoir to SE. Korners Falls, 7-level house built 1897. Settled before 1770 by Germans.

Kernville, uninc. town (1990 pop. 1,656), Kern co., S central Calif., 40 mi/64 km NE of Bakersfield, at N end of Isabella L. reservoir (Kern R.), in S part of Sierra Nevada; 35°46′N 118°26′W. Parts of Sequoia Natl. Forest surround area. Shirley Meadows Ski Area to S. Timber; cattle. Tourism.

Kerr, county (□ 1,107 sq mi/2,867 sq km; 1990 pop. 36,304), SW Texas; ⊙ Kerrville; 30°03′N 99°20′W. Elev. c.1,100 ft/335 m–2,400 ft/732 m. In scenic hill country of Edwards Plateau; drained by Guadalupe R., rising in springs here. Ranching (sheep, goats, cattle); agr. (hay, oats, wheat; pecans, apples) and vacation area, with camps, guest ranches, health resorts; hunting. Kerrville-Schreiner State Park in E center at Kerrville. Formed 1856.

Kerr Dam, Mont.: see POLSON.

Kerr, Lake (KUHR), reservoir, Marion co., N central Fla., in Ocala Natl. Forest, 23 mi/37 km ENE of Ocala; 3 mi/4.8 km long, 2 mi/3.2 km wide; 29°21′N 81°22′W.

Kerrick, village (1990 pop. 56), Pine co., E Minn., 38 mi/61 km SW of Duluth; 46°20′N 92°35′W. Dairying. Nemadji State Forest to E.

Kerrobert (kuh-RAH-buhrt), town (1991 pop. 1,143), W Sask., Canada, 30 mi/48 km N of Kindersley; 51°55′N 109°08′W. Grain elevators, lumbering, dairying.

Kerrville, city (1990 pop. 17,384), ⊙ Kerr co., S central Texas, 55 mi/89 km NW of San Antonio, on the Guadalupe R.; 30°02′N 99°08′W. Elev. 1,645 ft/501 m. Agr. (cattle, sheep, goats). Mfg. (transportation equip., computers, solar prods., food processing). Youth camps, dude ranches. It is also a vacation and health resort in the hill country on the edge of the Edwards Plateau. Schreiner Col. and a number of art galleries are in the city. Kerrville-Schreiner State Park on S edge of city. Settled 1846, inc. 1942.

Kersey 1 town (1990 pop. 980), Weld co., N Colo., on South Platte R., and 8 mi/12.9 km ESE of Greeley; 40°23′N 104°33′W. Elev. c.4,617 ft/1,407 m. In agr. region. Mfg. (agr. prods.). Lower Latham Reservoir to SW. **2** uninc. town (1990 pop. 900), Fox township, Elk co., N central Pa., 8 mi/12.9 km SE of Ridgway; 41°21′N 78°35′W. Mfg. (machinery; metal finishing). Agr. (grain; livestock, dairying). Moshannon State Forest to S.

Kershaw (kuhr-SHAW), county (□ 740 sq mi/1,917 sq km; 1990 pop. 43,599), N central S.C.; ⊙ Camden; 34°20′N 80°35′W. Contains L. Wateree and Wateree R; bounded E by Lynches R. Tourist area in Sand Hills; mining of mica, granite, sand, kaolin. Some agr. (peaches, pecans, sweet potatoes; poultry, cattle; corn, rye, hay, cotton), timber. Formed 1791.

Kershaw (kuhr-SHAW), town (1990 pop. 1,814), Lancaster co., N S.C., 20 mi/32 km N of Camden, near Little Lynches R; 34°32′N 80°35′W. Lumber mills. Mfg. (machinery, grain prods., mica processing, textiles, apparel).

Keshena (ke-SHEE-nuh), village (1990 pop. 685), ⊙ Menominee co., NE Wis., on Wolf R., and 9 mi/14.5 km WNW of Shawano, in the Menominee Indian Reservation; 44°52′N 88°38′W. The Indian Agency bldgs. and an R.C. mission are here. Oshkosh clan burial plot is nearby. Legend of Spirit lakes to E; Keshena Falls to N.

Keswick, town (1990 pop. 284), Keokuk co., SE Iowa, 9 mi/14.5 km N of Sigourney; 41°27′N 92°14′W. Livestock, grain.

Ketchikan (KE-chi-kan), city (1990 pop. 8,263), Gateway borough, SE Alaska, a port of entry on Revillagigedo Isl. in the Alexander Archipelago; 55°21′N 131°35′W. A supply point for miners in the gold rush of the 1890s, it has become a center of Alaska's fishing (especially salmon, halibut, and abalone), and the now-declining logging and pulp industries. Tourism and fish processing adds to the economy. Major molybdenum deposit nearby under sporadic development. Ferry connections to other panhandle communities and B.C., Canada. Its excellent ice-free harbor on Tongass Narrows makes it an important port on the Inside Passage and a distribution point for a large area. Continuance of pulp mill N of town problematic. Hq. for Tongas Natl. Forest; Dolly's House Mus., preserves some of 20 brothels that operated until 1954, in Creek Street red-light dist.

Ketchikan Gateway, borough (□ 13,828 sq mi/35,815 sq km; 1990 pop. 13,828), SE Alaska, includes Revillagigedo and Gravina Isls., as well as part of the Alaska Panhandle mainland. Most of the borough is located in the Tongass Natl. Forest. Misty Fjords Natl. Monument to E; Totem Bight State Historical Park to S. Main town is Ketchikan. Tourism; fishing; timber.

Ketchum, town (1990 pop. 2,523), Blaine co., S central Idaho, 13 mi/21 km NNW of Hailey, on Big Wood R.; 43°42′N 114°23′W. RR terminus. Mfg. (printing and publishing, sporting equip.). Summer and winter resort town; Sun Valley Ski Area to N; Sawtooth Natl. Recreation Area to NW; Sawtooth Natl. Forest to E, N, and W.

Ketchum, village (1990 pop. 263), Craig co., NE Okla., 10 mi/16 km SE of Vinita; L. of the Cherokees to SE; 36°31′N 95°01′W. Concrete. Inc. 1938.

Kettering, city (1990 pop. 60,569), Montgomery co., SW Ohio, a suburb of Dayton; 39°42′N 84°09′W. Mfg. (electric motors, transportation equip., machinery). Numerous testing laboratories for auto and electrical prods. The city is the seat of the Kettering Col. of Medical Arts and two major hosps. and research centers. Settled c.1812, inc. 1952.

Kettle Falls, town (1990 pop. 1,272), Stevens co., NE Wash., 8 mi/12.9 km. NE of Colville, bet. Colville R. (S) and a bay of Franklin D. Roosevelt L. reservoir (Columbia R.); 48°37′N 118°04′W. Junction of RR spur to Marcus (N), main line terminates at West Kettle Falls, to W. Agr. (alfalfa, wheat, barley, oats; hogs). Mfg. (wood prods.). Part of Colville Natl. Forest to W; Colville Indian Reservation to SW. Coulee Dam Natl. Recreation Area surrounds lake. Town moved (1938–1939) from site c.4 mi/6.4 km S, now covered by lake.

Kettle Island, village, Bell co., SE Ky., in the Cumberland Mts. near Pine Mt., 13 mi/21 km NNE of Middlesboro. Bituminous coal; timber.

Kettle Rapids Dam, Canada: see NELSON, river.

Kettle River, village (1990 pop. 190), Carlton co., E Minn., on Kettle R., and 40 mi/64 km SW of Duluth; 46°29′N 92°52′W. Agr. (poultry; oats, alfalfa; dairying). Mfg. (Indian pottery, feeds). Sandstone quarries in area.

Kettle River, 175 mi/282 km long, S B.C. (Canada) and N Wash. (U.S.); rises in Canada in Monashee Mts. W of Upper Arrow L., flows S to vicinity of Grand Forks, where it crosses Wash. state line twice, finally entering Columbia R. 13 mi/21 km NW of Colville. Fertile agr. valley (fruits, vegetables).

Kettle River, 80 mi/129 km long, E Minn.; rises in marshy area N of Carlton co., c.15 mi/24 km W of Cloquet, flows S, through Kettle L., and past villages of Kettle R. and Willow R., and town of Sandstone to St. Croix R., in Pine co., 10 mi/16 km ENE of Pine City, on W boundary of St. Croix State Park; 46°41′N 92°47′W.

Kettleman City, uninc. town (1990 pop. 1,411), Kings co., S central Calif., 26 mi/42 km SW of Hanford, on California Aqueduct; 36°01′N 119°58′W. Tulare L., irrigation reservoir, to NE. Agr. (pistachios, almonds, peaches, plums, nectarines, cantaloupes; grain; cattle, dairying, poultry). Mfg. (nut processing).

Kettleman Hills, mainly Kings and Fresno cos., S central Calif., low range (c.1,300 ft/396 m) along W side of San Joaquin Valley, 50 mi/80 km SW of Fresno. Important oil and natural-gas field here. Kettleman City to E.

Kettlersville, village (1990 pop. 194), Shelby co., W Ohio, 12 mi/19 km NNW of Sidney; 40°26′N 84°16′W. Also spelled Kettlerville.

Keuka (KYOO-kuh), resort village, Steuben co., W central N.Y., on E shore of Keuka L., 27 mi/43 km SSW of Geneva; 42°29′N 77°07′W.

Keuka Lake (KYOO-kuh), one of Finger Lakes, W central N.Y.; 42°28′N 77°10′W. Lake is 18 mi/29 km long and $\frac{1}{2}$ mi/$\frac{8}{10}$ km–2 mi/3.2 km wide; drains NE into Seneca L. Is the only Finger L. that still retains its distinctive, post-Pleistocene Y-shape. Penn Yan at N end and Hammondsport at S end are trade centers for surrounding resort, grape-growing, and wine-making region. The vineyard-cloaked slopes (esp. on W side) make this perhaps the loveliest of the Finger Lakes.

Keuka Park (KYOO-kuh), village (1990 pop. 1,200), Yates co., W central N.Y., on Keuka L., 19 mi/31 km SSW of Geneva; 42°37′N 77°05′W. Seat of Keuka Col.

Kevil (KEV-uhl), village (1990 pop. 337), Ballard co., W Ky., 16 mi/26 km W of Paducah; 37°04′N 88°53′W. In agr. area (tobacco, grain, soybeans; livestock; dairying). Mfg. (loudspeakers, machinery).

Kevin, village (1990 pop.185), Toole co., N Mont., 19 mi/31 km NNW of Shelby; 48°45′N 111°58′W. Located in Kevin-Sunburst oil and natural gas field. Cattle, sheep, hogs; wheat, barley, hay.

Kew, town (1990 pop. 328), Turks and Caicos Islands, North Caicos Isl.; 21°54′N 72°02′W.

Kew Gardens, residential sect. of central Queens borough of N.Y. city, SE N.Y.; 40°43′N 73°50′W. Upper-middle-class, mostly white neighborhood. Originally laid out as an Eng.-style planned community in early 20th cent. Contains Queens Borough Hall.

Kewagama Lake, W Que., Canada, 22 mi/35 km E of Rouyn; 10 mi/16 km long, 5 mi/8 km wide. Elev. 958 ft/292 m. Drains W into L. Timiskaming.

Kewanee (kee-WAH-nee), industrial city (1990 pop. 12,969), Henry co., NW Ill., 15 mi/24 km ESE of Cambridge; 41°14′N 89°55′W. A regional livestock, processing, trade, and shipping center. Mfg. (boilers, metal prods., farm machinery). The city holds an annual "Hog Capital Festival." The E campus of Black Hawk Col. is located 6 mi/9.7 km S of Kewanee. Inc. 1855.

Kewanna, town (1990 pop. 542), Fulton co., N Ind., 11 mi/18 km SW of Rochester; 41°01′N 86°25′W. Agr. area. Mfg. (metal prods.).

Kewaskum (kee-WAWS-kuhm), town (1990 pop. 2,515), Washington co., E Wis., on branch of Milwaukee R., and 7 mi/11.3 km NNW of West Branch; 43°31′N 88°13′W. In dairy and farm area. Mfg. (food-processing, machinery, cookware). Sunburst Ski Area to S; S end of Kettle Moraine State Forest (N unit) to E.

Kewaunee (kee-WAW-nee), county (□ 1,084 sq mi/2,808 sq km; 1990 pop. 18,878), E Wis.; ⊙ Kewaunee; situated near base of Door Peninsula; 44°35′N 87°26′W. Farming, dairying, lumbering, woodworking; agr. (barley, oats, wheat, corn, peas, beans; hay; cattle, hogs). Partly wooded, hilly terrain, drained by Kewaunee R. and several small streams. Bounded E by L. Michigan, NW by Green Bay. Kewaunee nuclear power plant, initial criticality March 7, 1974, is 27 mi/43 km of Green Bay, uses cooling water from L. Michigan, and has a max. dependable capacity of 511 MWe. Formed 1852.

Kewaunee, city (1990 pop. 2,750), ⊙ Kewaunee co., E Wis., on L. Michigan, on Door Peninsula, at mouth of small Kewaunee R., 25 mi/40 km E of Green Bay; 44°27′N 87°30′W. In dairying and stock-raising area. Mfg. (furniture, wood and aluminum prods., construction equip., pea and green-pea combines); dairy plants; breweries. RR terminus. A coast guard station is here. The North West Company set up a fur-trading post on site in 1795. Inc. 1883.

Kewaunee Nuclear Power Plant, Wisconsin: see KEWAUNEE county.

Keweenaw (KEE-WEE-naw), county (□ 5,959 sq mi/15,434 sq km; 1990 pop. 1,701), NW Upper Peninsula, Mich.; ⊙ Eagle R.; 47°28′N 88°09′W. On NE Keweenaw Peninsula in L. Superior. Resorts. About $\frac{2}{3}$ of residences in co. are seasonal. Includes Isle Royale Natl. Park (NW) and is traversed by the Copper Range. Several lakes. One of heaviest snowfall areas in U.S. Manitou Isl. off E end of peninsula (3 mi/4.8 km long, 1 mi/1.6 km wide). Fort Wilkins State Park, E of Copper Harbor. Formed and organized 1861.

Keweenaw (KEE-WEE-naw), peninsula, 60 mi/97 km long, projecting NE from the W Upper Peninsula, NW Mich., into L. Superior; 47°15′N 88°20′W. Portage L. and a connecting ship canal cut across the middle of the peninsula, converting its upper portion into an island and creating an important waterway. Consists mainly of parts of Houghton and Keweenaw cos. The canal is crossed by a highway bridge with one of the world's heaviest lift spans. Main towns are Houghton and Hancock.The area is popular with vacationers.

Keweenaw Bay (KEE-WEE-naw), NW Upper Peninsula, Mich., inlet of L. Superior (c.30 mi/48 km long, 15 mi/24 km wide at entrance, narrows to a point at S end) lying to E of curving Keweenaw Peninsula, 55 mi/89 km NW of Marquette; 46°55′N 88°19′W. It is E terminus of Keweenaw Waterway. Baraga, Keweenaw Bay village, and L'Anse, all resorts, are at its head.

Keweenaw National Historical Park (KEE-WEE-naw), Houghton, Keweenaw, and Ontonagon cos., Upper Peninsula, NW Mich. Commemorates copper mining heritage of Upper Michigan's Keweenaw Peninsula. Interim boundaries include village of Calumet, which has remained virtually unchanged from mining days (c.1900), and the old Quincy Mine N of Hancock.

There are also 8 cooperative sites, including Keweenaw and Houghton co. mus., Fort Wilkins and Porcupine Mts. state parks. Est. 1992; under development as of 1995.

Keweenaw Range, Mich.: see COPPER RANGE, Wis.

Keweenaw Waterway (KEE-WEE-naw), navigation channel (c.25 mi/40 km long), NW Upper Peninsula, Mich., intersecting Keweenaw Peninsula bet. Keweenaw Bay (SE) and L. Superior (NW). Consists of Portage L. (c.20 mi/32 km long, 2 mi/3.2 km wide), with a natural connection with Keweenaw Bay, and a land-cut ship canal (c.2 mi/3.2 km long) across former portage bet. Portage L. and L. Superior. U.S. lighthouse at L. Superior entrance. Hancock, Houghton are ports.

Key Biscayne (bis-KAIN), town (1990 pop. 8,854), E Dade co., SE Fla.; 25°41′N 80°10′W. Became independent from city of Miami in 1990. Site of annual Lipton tennis tournament.

Key Biscayne (bis-KAIN), island (□ 1 sq mi/2.6 sq km; 1990 pop. 8,854), Dade co., SE Fla., 5 mi/8 km SSE of Miami; 25°41′N 80°10′W. Isl. is 5 mi/8 km long. Partly shelters Biscayne Bay (W). At S end is Cape Florida, location of Bill Baggs State Park and Beach.

Key Colony Beach, island (1990 pop. 977), Monroe co., central Fla. Keys, 54 mi/87 km NE of Key West; 24°43′N 81°01′W.

Key Largo, town (1990 pop. 11,336), Monroe co., upper Fla. Keys, 60 mi/97 km S of Miami, northernmost island of Fla. Keys; 25°06′N 80°26′W. Diversified light mfg., especially marine equip.

Key Largo, narrow island (□ 22 sq mi/57 sq km), c.30 mi/48 km long, off SE Fla., northernmost and largest of the Fla. Keys; 25°06′N 80°26′W. Along with other Fla. Key isls., esp. Key West, it has become an increasingly popular tourist destination, noted for its scuba diving and beachside resorts. Housing developments and shopping complexes have been recently constructed. A major attraction is John Pennekamp Coral Reef State Park, the 1st underwater park in the U.S., containing c.78 sq mi/202 sq km of living coral and hundreds of varieties of marine life.

Key West, city (□ 6 sq mi/15.5 sq km; 1990 pop. 24,832), Monroe co., on an isl. at the SW extremity of the Fla. Keys, c.150 mi/240 km SW of Miami (but only 90 mi/145 km from Cuba). The southernmost city of the continental U.S., it is a port of entry (cruise ships), a popular resort with a tropical climate, a shrimping and fishing center, and an artists' colony.

Keya Paha (KEE-yah PAH-hah), county (□ 774 sq mi/2,005 sq km; 1990 pop. 1,029), N Nebr.; ☉ Springview, located N of Sand Hills region; 42°52′N 99°43′W. Grazing and mixed farming area bounded N by S.Dak., S by Niobrara R.; drained by Keya Paha R. Cattle, dairying, hogs; corn, alfalfa, wild hay. Formed 1884.

Keya Paha River (KEE-yah-PAH-hah), 101 mi/163 km long, S S. Dak. and N Nebr.; rises in Todd co., S.Dak.; flows ESE to Niobrara R. near Butte, Nebr.; 43°13′N 100°23′W.

Keyaluvik (kai-YAH-luh-vik), village, SW Alaska, on Bethel Bay.

Keyes, uninc. town (1990 pop. 2,878), Stanislaus co., central Calif., 7 mi/11.3 km SSE of Modesto, in San Joaquin Valley; 37°34′N 120°55′W. Fruit, nuts, vegetables, grapes, melons; grain; dairying, poultry.

Keyes (KEEZ), village (1990 pop. 454), Cimarron co., W Okla. Panhandle, 15 mi/24 km ENE of Boise City; 36°48′N 102°15′W. Livestock; grain.

Keyesport, village (1990 pop. 440), in Bond and Clinton cos., S central Ill., 12 mi/19 km NNE of Carlyle; 38°44′N 89°16′W. In agr. and oil area. On Carlyle L.

Keyhole Reservoir, Crook co., NE Wyo., on Belle Fourche R., 18 mi/29 km WSW of Sundance; 10 mi/16 km long; 44°22′N 104°42′W. Max. capacity 634,000 acre-ft. Has 5 mi/8 km S arm. Formed by Keyhole Dam (113 ft/34 m high), built (1952) by the Bureau of Reclamation for irrigation and flood control. Keyhole State Park at E end.

Keyport, uninc. village (1990 pop. 300), Kitsap co., NW Wash., 8 mi/12.9 km N of Bremerton, on Port Orchard, arm of Puget Sound, at entrance to Liberty Bay. Mfg.

(electronics; computers). U.S. Naval Reservation is here.

Keyport, borough (1990 pop. 7,586), Monmouth co., E N.J., 13 mi/21 km NNE of Freehold; 40°25′N 74°12′W. Resort and fishing center with harbor on Raritan Bay. Mfg. (rubber goods, clothing). Largely residential. Settled before 1700, inc. 1908.

Keyser (KEIZ-uhr), town (1990 pop. 5,870), ☉ Mineral co., NE W.Va., 20 mi/32 km SW of Cumberland, Md., in E Panhandle, on North Branch of the Potomac R.; 39°26′N 78°58′W. Mfg. (lumber, crushed limestone, glass, apparel, stainless-steel prods., air-conditioning prods., charcoal, coal processing). Agr. (grain, tobacco); livestock; poultry. Potomac State Col. of W. Va. Univ. (2 yr.). An important supply base in Civil War. Settled 1802.

Keystone, town (1990 pop. 568), Benton co., E central Iowa, 14 mi/23 km SW of Vinton; 42°00′N 92°12′W. In agr. area.

Keystone 1 village (1990 pop. 232), Pennington co., W S.Dak., 10 mi/16 km SW of Rapid City, in Black Hills, and Black Hills Natl. Forest; 43°53′N 103°25′W. Elev. 4,342 ft/1,323 m. Feldspar mill and pottery market. Mt. Rushmore Natl. Memorial nearby. Custer State Park to S. **2** village (1990 pop. 627), McDowell co., S W. Va., on Tug Fork R., 7 mi/11.3 km E of Welch; 37°25′N 81°27′W. Semi-bituminous-coal region. Inc. 1909.

Keystone Heights, town (1990 pop. 1,315), Clay co., NE Fla., c.45 mi/72 km W of St. Augustine; 29°46′N 82°01′W. Resort in lake region.

Keystone Lake 1 reservoir, Tulsa and Creek cos. and on Osage-Pawnee co. border, NE central Okla., on Arkansas R., 17 mi/27 km W of Tulsa; c.30 mi/48 km long; 36°08′N 96°14′W. Max. capacity 1,879,000 acre-ft. Cimarron R. forms c.25-mi/40-km W arm. Formed by Keystone Dam (104 ft/32 m high), built by the Army Corps of Engineers for flood control, water supply, and power generation. Keystone (S shore) and Walnut Creek (N shore) state parks are here. **2** reservoir, Armstrong co., W Pa., on North Branch Plum Creek, 10 mi/16 km NW of Indiana; 5 mi/8 km long; 40°13′N 79°18′W. Max. capacity 168,400 acre-ft. Formed by Keystone Dam (100 ft/30 m high), built (1965) for water supply. Also called Atwood Keystone L.

Keysville 1 town, Burke co., E Ga., 21 mi. SW of Augusta, and on Brier Creek; 33°14′N 82°14′W. **2** town (1990 pop. 606), Charlotte co., S Va., 45 mi/72 km SE of Lynchburg; 37°02′N 78°28′W. Mfg. (lumber, apparel, furniture). Agr. (tobacco, grain; dairying; cattle); timber. Southside Va. Community Col. (John H. Daniel campus).

Keytesville (KEETS-vil), city (1990 pop. 564), ☉ Chariton co., N central Mo., near Missouri R., 28 mi/45 km W of Moberly; 39°25′N 92°56′W. Corn, wheat, soybeans; hogs; cattle; lumber prods. Site of French Fort Orléans (est. 1723) nearby. Plotted 1830.

Kezar Falls, Maine: see PARSONSFIELD.

Kezar Lake, in Oxford co., W Maine, in summer resort area near N.H. state line; c.7.5 mi/12.1 km long. Drains S through Kezar Pond, to Saco R.

Kezar Lake, N.H.: see SUTTON.

Khantaak Island (KAN-tuhk), SE Alaska, 3 mi/4.8 km N of Yakutat; 6 mi/9.7 km long; 59°36′N 139°46′W.

Kiamichi River, c.165 mi/266 km long, SE Okla.; rises in E Le Flore co. near Ark. state line in the Ouachita Mts.; flows SW and S, past Muse and Clayton, to Antlers, then SE through Hugo L. reservoir to Red R. S of Fort Towson. Hugo L. (for flood control in Red R. basin) is 7 mi/11.3 km E of Hugo.

Kiana (kee-YAH-nuh), village (1990 pop. 385), NW Alaska, on lower Kobuk R., and 60 mi/97 km E of Kotzebue, N of Selawik L.; 66°58′N 160°27′W. Scene of gold rush, 1910.

Kiantone, village (1990 pop. 120), Chautauqua co., extreme W N.Y., 6 mi/9.7 km SSE of Jamestown; 42°01′N 79°12′W.

Kiawah Island (KEE-uh-wah) (1990 pop. 718), Charleston co., SE S.C., one of Sea Isls., 12 mi/19 km SW of

Charleston; c.10 mi/16 km long; 32°37′N 80°03′W. Resort center separated by narrow channel from Johns Isl. (N); Stono R. is E, Atlantic Ocean S.

Kibby Mountain (KIB-ee) (3,638 ft/1,109 m), W Maine, peak in extreme N Franklin co., 20 mi/32 km SW of Jackman.

Kick 'em Jenny, volcano, Grenada, West Indies. Underwater volcano, 663 ft/202 m below surface located N of Isle de Ronde.

Kickamuit River (KIK-ah-meyoo-it), c.4 mi/6.4 km long, E R.I.; rises in Swansea, Mass. town, near Mass.-R.I. state line; flows generally SE, bet. Bristol and Warren, to Mt. Hope Bay.

Kickapoo Creek 1 c.60 mi/97 km long, in central Ill.; rises in McLean co.; flows SW to Salt Creek SE of Lincoln; 40°27′N 88°46′W. **2** c.25 mi/40 km long, in N central Ill.; rises NW of Peoria; flows SE to Illinois R. just below Peoria; 40°57′N 89°38′W.

Kickapoo, Lake, Texas: see LITTLE WICHITA RIVER.

Kickapoo River (KI-kuh-poo), c.90 mi/145 km long, SW Wis.; rises S of Tomah; flows SSW though Wildcat Mt. State Park to Wisconsin R. 13 mi/21 km E of Prairie du Chien.

Kicking Horse, river, SE B.C., Canada; rising in the Rocky Mts.; flowing SW and NW to Golden, where it enters the Columbia R. Its course is rapid, with several high falls. Kicking Horse Pass, 5,339 ft/1,627 m high, NW of L. Louise, in Banff Natl. Park, connects the Bow R. with the Kicking Horse and is one of the principal RR and highway passes over the Continental Divide.

Kicking Horse Pass, Canada: see KICKING HORSE.

Kidder, county (□ 1,357 sq mi/3,515 sq km; 1990 pop. 3,332), central N.Dak.; ☉ Steele; 46°58′N 99°46′W. Agr. area watered by several small lakes, largest being E part of Long L. and Horsehead L. Diversified farming (cattle, wheat, barley, oats, hay, flax; dairying). Formed 1873. Long L. Natl. Wildlife refuge in SW. Slade Natl. Wildlife Refuge in S. L. George Natl. Wildlife Refuge and state park in SE.

Kidder, town (1990 pop. 241), Caldwell co., NW Mo., 8 mi/12.9 km N of Cameron; 39°46′N 94°05′W. Livestock area (cattle, hogs).

Kief (KEEF), village (1990 pop. 24), McHenry co., central N.Dak., 20 mi/32 km SE of Velva; 47°51′N 100°30′W. Kruger L. and other small lakes to S.

Kiefer (KEEF-uhr), town (1990 pop. 962), Creek and Tulsa cos., central Okla., residential suburb 15 mi/24 km SSW of Tulsa, 5 mi/8 km SE of Sapulpa; 35°56′N 96°02′W. In agr. and oil area. Bethesda Airport to S.

Kiel (KEEL), town (1990 pop. 2,910) on Manitowoc-/Calumet co. line, E Wis., on Sheboygan R., and 20 mi/32 km NW of Sheboygan; 43°55′N 88°01′W. Trade center for dairying area; woodworking; mfg. (cheese processing, cheesemaking equip., metal fabricating, wood tables, food-industry packaging equip., machinery, concrete pipe). Inc. 1920.

Kiester (KEES-tuhr), village (1990 pop. 606), Faribault co., S Minn., 18 mi/29 km SW of Albert Lea, on Brush Creek, near Iowa state line; 43°32′N 93°42′W. Agr. area (grain, soybeans; livestock); mfg. (feeds).

Kihei (KEE-HAI), city (1990 pop. 11,107), Maui isl., Maui co., Hawaii, 10 mi/16 km S of Kahului, on Maui's SW coast; 20°45′N 156°26′W. Tourism. Cattle, fish, prawns. Mfg. (communications equip., printing). Capt. Vancouver Monument.

Kilauea (KEE-LOU-AI-ah), town (1990 pop. 1,685), NE Kauai, Kauai co., Hawaii, 1 mi/1.6 km inland from N coast, on Kilauea Stream, on Kuhio Highway, 16 mi/26 km NNW of Lihue; Mokolea Point to NE; Kalihiwai Bay to NW. Princeville Airport to W; Kapinao Heiau (temple) to E, on Kilauea Bay; Kilauea Point Natl. Wildlife Refuge to N; Mokuaeae Isl. Seabird Sanctuary N of Point: Moloaa Forest Reserve to S; Anini Beach Park to NW.

Kilauea (KEE-LOU-AI-ah), caldera, 3,412 ft/1,040 m deep, SE Hawaii isl., Hawaii co., Hawaii, 22 mi/35 km SW of Hilo, 20 mi/32 km ESE of summit of Mauna Loa; in HAWAII VOLCANOES NATIONAL PARK; 22°12′N 159°24′W. Kilauea is at the volcanically active SE end of the Hawaiian chain, sitting atop the stationary Hawaiian vent. Halemaumau crater in W part of caldera. One of the largest active craters in the world, Kilauea has a circumference of c.8 mi/12.9 km and is surrounded by a wall of volcanic rock 200 ft/61 m to 500 ft/152 m high. Elev. at Hawaiian Volcano Observatory, 4,078 ft/1,243 m. Elev. of crater floor 3,412 ft/1,040 m; max. depth, 666 ft/203 m. Last erupted in Aug. 1997. Lava from the eruption destroyed a 700-year-old temple formerly used in human sacrifices.

Kilbourn, Wis.: see WISCONSIN DELLS.

Kilbourne 1 (KILL-born), village (1990 pop. 350), Mason co., central Ill., 14 mi/23 km NNW of Petersburg; 40°08′N 90°00′W. In agr. area. Near Sand Prairie-Scrub Oak State Natural Area. **2** (KIL-buhrn), village (1994 pop. 538), West Carroll parish, NW La., 12 mi/19 km NNW of Lake Providence town, on Ark. boundary; 33°00′N 91°19′W. In agr. area (cotton, rice, vegetables; cattle, hogs); timber.

Kildare, village (1990 pop. 94), Kay co., N Okla., 7 mi/11.3 km N of Ponca City; 36°48′N 97°02′W. In agr. area.

Kildare, Cape, NW P.E.I., Canada, on the Gulf of St. Lawrence, 6 mi/9.7 km S of Tignish; 46°53′N 63°58′W. Harvesting of Irish moss. Reputed landfall (1534) of Jacques Cartier. Named by Samuel Holland in 1765 after James, 20th earl of Kildare.

Kildeer, village (1990 pop. 2,257), Lake co., NE Ill., residential suburb 28 mi/45 km NW of downtown Chicago, 3 mi/4.8 km SE of Lake Zürich; 42°10′N 88°02′W.

Kildonan (kil-DO-nuhn), village, SW B.C., Canada, on S central Vancouver Isl., on an inlet of Barkley Sound, 18 mi/29 km SSW of Port Alberni; 49°00′N 125°00′W. Fishing (salmon, herring).

Kilgore, city (1990 pop. 11,066), on Gregg-Rusk co. line, E Texas, 24 mi/39 km E of Tyler; 32°23′N 94°52′W. Elev. 371 ft/113 m. Oil-producing and oil field supply center, in E Texas field. Mfg. (oil field equip., plastic prods., fiberglass boats, satellite antennas). Seat of Kilgore Col. (2 year). L. Cherokee reservoir to E. Settled 1872, inc. 1931. Rapid growth followed oil discovery, 1930.

Kilgore, village (1990 pop. 79), Cherry co., N Nebr., 20 mi/32 km W of Valentine, near S.Dak. line; 42°56′N 100°57′W. Mfg. (feed handling equip., flatbeds for pickups).

Kilkenny (kil-KE-nee), town, Coos co., N central N.H., 8 mi/12.9 km E of Lancaster. Wilderness area in White Mt. Natl. Forest; Mt. Cabot (4,160 ft/1,268 m) at center. Timber.

Kilkenny (kil-KE-nee), village (1990 pop. 167), Le Sueur co., S Minn., 15 mi/24 km W of Fairbault; 44°18′N 93°34′W. Dairying. Numerous small lakes in area; Diamond L. to NW.

Kill Devil Hills, town (1990 pop. 4,238), Dare co., NE N.C., 39 mi/63 km SE of Elizabeth City, on Atlantic Ocean, on Outer Banks; 36°01′N 75°40′W. Albermarle Sound to W. Town of Kitty Hawk 4 mi/6.4 km to NW. Beach resort area. Light mfg. Jockey's Ridge State Park to S. Site of Wright Brothers' flight experiments (1900–1903). Wright Brothers Natl. Memorial to W.

Kill Van Kull (KIL-van-KUHL), channel, 4 mi/6.4 km long and ½ mi/⁸⁄₁₀ km wide, connecting Upper New York Bay with Newark Bay, bet. Bayonne, N.J., and Staten Isl., N.Y. It is the main route for ships docking at the busy harbors of Port Elizabeth and Port Newark, N.J. Bayonne Bridge (1931; 1,652 ft/504 m long), the 2d-longest steel-arch bridge in the United States, spans the channel.

Killaloe (kil-uh-LOO), village (1991 pop. 707), SE Ont., Canada, near Golden L., 23 mi/37 km SW of Pembroke; dairying, lumbering. Formerly Killaloe Station.

Killam (KI-luhm), town (1991 pop. 1,053), E Alta., Canada, 40 mi/64 km ESE of Camrose; 52°47′N 111°51′W. Grain elevators.

Killarney (kil-AHR-nee), town (1991 pop. 2,163), SW Man., Canada, on Killarney L. (4 mi/6 km long), 50 mi/80 km SSE of Brandon; 49°11′N 99°40′W. Mfg. of agr. implements, cement; grain elevators; dairying, lumbering, livestock. Resort. Site of experimental fruit farm.

Killbuck, village (1990 pop. 809), Holmes co., central Ohio, on Killbuck Creek and 33 mi/53 km ESE of Mansfield; 40°29′N 81°59′W.

Killbuck Creek, N Ohio; rises in region W of Akron; flows c.75 mi/121 km S, past Wooster and Millersburg, to Walhonding R. 5 mi/8 km NW of Coshocton, and into the Muskingum R.; 40°19′N 81°56′W.

Killdeer, village (1990 pop. 722), Dunn co., W central N.Dak., 35 mi/56 km N of Dickinson and on Spring Creek; 47°22′N 102°45′W. Oil fields; livestock; dairy prods.; grain. Little Missouri State Primitive Park to N. Killdeer Battlefield Site to NW. L. Ilo to SE.

Killdeer Mountains, series of lofty buttes in Dunn co.W N.Dak., N of Killdeer; they extend 10 mi/16 km E-SW and rise 600 ft/183 m above surrounding countryside. S of Little Missouri R. Killdeer and Battlefield Historic Site; 47°26′N 102°55′W. Elev. 3,000 ft/914 m.

Killeen, city (1990 pop. 63,535), Bell co., central Texas, 21 mi/34 km W of Temple, half of Temple-Killeen metropolitan statistical area; 31°06′N 97°43′W. Elev. 833 ft/254 m. In a ranching and cotton region. The city has some mfg. (concrete, printing, wooden cabinets), but adjacent Fort Hood is the major source of employment. Founded in 1882 and named for a Santa Fe RR official, Killeen remained a small farming and ranching village until the establishment (1942) of Camp Hood, mainly to N, also to W of city. The camp's redesignation (1950) as a fort with a permanent status spurred a great pop. growth in the city. Fort Hood Army Airfield to N, Robert Gray Army Airfield to W, both in Fort Hood Military Reservation. Central Texas Col. (2 year) is in Killeen and Univ. of Central Texas and Amer. Educational Complex (Fort Hood) to W. Nearby Belton (NE) and Stillhouse Hollow (SE) lakes provide recreational facilities. Site of mass murder in Luby's Restaurant c.1990. Inc. 1893.

Killian (KIL-ee-an), town (1990 pop. 721), Livingston parish, La., 10 mi/16 km SW of Ponchatoula; 30°21′N 90°35′W.

Killik River, NW Alaska; rises in Brooks Range near 67°47′N 154°35′W; flows c.125 mi/201 km N to Colville R. at 69°N 153°55′W.

Killinek Island (20 mi/32 km long, 2 mi/3 km–9 mi/14 km wide), SE Franklin dist., N.W.T., Canada, at SE entrance of Hudson Strait, off N extremity of Lab. NE extremity is Cape Chidley (60°23′N 64°26′W), usually considered to be N tip of Lab. On W coast is Port Burwell trading post.

Killingly, town (1990 pop. 15,889), Windham co., NE Conn., on the Quinebaug R. and near the R.I. border, in a farm area; settled 1693, inc. 1708; 41°49′N 71°50′W. Dairy and livestock-trading center; fruits and vegetables; mfg. (textiles, machinery, and synthetic materials). Winter skiing.

Killington Peak (4,241 ft/1,293 m), S central Vt., E of Rutland, in recreational area with major downhill ski resort; one of highest summits of Green Mts.

Killingworth, town (1990 pop. 4,814), Middlesex co., S Conn., 20 mi/32 km ENE of New Haven; 41°22′N 72°34′W. Industry includes agr. and steel fabrication; summer camps. Mainly residential, has 18th-cent. houses, fine church (1817). State forest here.

Killiniq, former trading post, W Killiniq Isl. SE Franklin dist., N.W.T., Canada, on Ungava Bay; 60°25′N 64°49′W; Royal Can. Mounted Police post. Formerly Port Burwell.

Killisnoo, Alaska: see HOOD BAY.

Kilmarnock, town (1990 pop. 1,109), Lancaster and Northumberland cos., E Va., 22 mi/35 km NNE of Gloucester; Fleets Bay, arm of Chesapeake Bay, to SE; 37°42′N 76°22′W. Mfg. (printing and publishing, crab-meat processing); fish, oysters, crabs. Christ Church (1732) to SW.

Kilmer, Camp, N.J.: see NEW BRUNSWICK.

Kilmichael (KIL-mei-kuhl), town (1990 pop. 826), Montgomery co., central Miss., 10 mi/16 km ESE of Winona; 33°26′N 89°34′W. (cotton, corn, soybeans; cattle). Mfg. (men's and women's slacks).

Kiln, uninc. town (1990 pop. 1,262), Hancock co., SE Miss., 9 mi/14.5 km NW of Bay St. Louis, near Jordan R.; 30°25′N 89°25′W. Cotton, corn. Mfg. (signs, wooden reels). Stennis Space Center (NASA) to W.

Kim, village (1990 pop. 76), Las Animas co., SE Colo., 65 mi/105 km E of Trinidad, near N.Mex. line; 37°15′N 103°20′W. Elev. 5,686 ft/1,733 m. Livestock, wheat, sorghum, hay. Parts of Comanche Natl. Grassland to E and W.

Kimball, county (□ 952 sq mi/2,466 sq km; 1990 pop. 4,108), W Nebr. in High Plains; ⊙ Kimball; 41°12′N 103°42′W. Borders Colo. on S and Wyo. on W; drained by Lodgepole Creek. Agr. (cattle, hogs, wheat, potatoes, sunflower seed). Highest point (unnamed) in Nebr., in SW corner 5,426 ft/1,654 m. Oliver Reservoir State Recreation Area near co. center, W of Kimball. Formed 1888.

Kimball or **Kimball Prairie**, town (1990 pop. 2,574), ⊙ Kimball co., W Nebr., 42 mi/68 km S of Scottsbluff and on Lodgepole Creek; 41°13′N 103°39′W. Trade, grain-shipping center in Great Plains region; livestock, grain, beans, sunflower seed, potatoes, dried fruit and nuts. Mfg. (oil field machinery and bldgs., pipe threading, polyethylene pipe, burglar switches, printing, hay equip., computer keyboards). Oliver Reservoir and Lodgepark State Wayside Area to W; Pawnee Natl. Grassland to S (in Colo.). Inc. 1885.

Kimball 1, village (1990 pop. 690), Stearns co., S central Minn., 19 mi/31 km SSW of St. Cloud, near Clearwater R. Grain; livestock, poultry; dairying; mfg. (gravel-truck bodies and hoists, concrete prods., sausages); 45°18′N 94°18′W. Powder Ridge Ski Area to NW. Also called Kimball Prairie. **2** village (1990 pop. 743), Brule co., S central S.Dak., 20 mi/32 km ESE of Chamberlain; 43°45′N 98°57′W. **3** village (1990 pop. 550), McDowell co., S W.Va., on Tug Fork R., 4 mi/6.4 km E of Welch; 37°25′N 81°30′W. Semibituminous-coal mining. Agr. (fruit, tobacco); livestock. Mfg. (concrete). State mine rescue station here. Inc. 1911.

Kimball, Mount (c.9,500 ft/2,896 m), E Alaska, in Alaska Range, 40 mi/64 km W of Tanacross; 63°15′N 144°41′W.

Kimballton, town (1990 pop. 289), Audubon co., W central Iowa, 10 mi/16 km SW of Audubon; 41°37′N 95°04′W.

Kimberley (KIM-buhr-lee), town (1991 pop. 6,531), SE B.C., Canada; 49°41′N 115°59′W. Canada's highest city, (3,660 ft/1,115 m), it is the site of the Sullivan mine, where large quantities of silver, lead, and zinc are mined.

Kimberly 1 town (1990 pop. 2,367), Twin Falls co., S Idaho, 5 mi/8 km ESE of Twin Falls; 42°32′N 114°22′W. Livestock; wheat, beans, potatoes; mfg. (fertilizers). **2** town (1990 pop. 5,406), Outagamie co., E Wis., on Fox R., suburb 4 mi/6 km E of Appleton; 44°16′N 88°20′W. Mfg. (paper milling, coated paper, paper machine components, gumball vending machines). Inc. 1910.

Kimberly, uninc. village (1990 pop. 700), Fayette co., S central W.Va., near Kanawha R., 24 mi/39 km SE of Charleston. Coal-mining region. Agr. (grain); livestock. Mfg. (machining).

Kimble, county (□ 1,251 sq mi/3,240 sq km; 1990 pop. 4,122), W central Texas; ⊙ Junction; 30°29′N 99°45′W. In scenic Edwards Plateau. Elev. 1,800 ft/549 m–2,400 ft/732 m. Drained by N Llano and S Llano rivers, which join to form Llano R. at Junction, in center of co. Ranching (especially goats; also sheep, cattle); a leading U.S. co. in wool, mohair production. Sorghum, pecan growing. Sand and gravel; oil and gas. Scenery, hunting, fishing attract tourist trade. Formed 1858.

Kimbolton (KIM-buhl-tuhn), village (1990 pop. 134), Guernsey co., E Ohio, 9 mi/14 km N of Cambridge; 40°09′N 81°34′W.

Kimmswick, town (1990 pop. 135), Jefferson co., E Mo., on Mississippi R., S of mouth of the Meramec, residential suburb 18 mi/29 km S of St. Louis; 38°22′N 90°22′W. Nineteenth-cent. summer resort. Historical town; tourism. Mastodon State Park nearby.

Kinak (KEE-nak), Inuit village, W Alaska, on Kuskokwim R., near its mouth on Kuskokwim Bay, 40 mi/64 km SW of Bethel.

Kinards (KEI-nuhrds), uninc. town, Newberry and Laurens cos., NW central S.C., 11 mi/18 km NW of Newberry. Mfg. of wood chips, timber. Agr includes livestock, poultry, grain.

Kinbrae (KIN-buh-ree), village (1990 pop. 18), Nobles co., SW Minn., 16 mi/26 km NNE of Worthington; 43°49′N 95°28′W. Grain; livestock; dairying. Small natural lakes in area.

Kincaid (kin-KAID), village (1991 pop. 197), SW Sask., Canada, 45 mi/72 km W of Assiniboia; 49°40′N 107°00′W. Wheat.

Kincaid 1 village (1990 pop. 1,353), Christian co., central Ill., on South Fork of Sangamon R. (bridged here) and 19 mi/31 km SE of Springfield; 39°35′N 89°24′W. In agr. and bituminous-coal area. Inc. 1915. Near Sangchris L. State Park. **2** (kin-KAID), village (1990 pop. 170), Anderson co., E Kansas, 14 mi/23 km S of Garnett; 38°04′N 95°09′W. In livestock, grain, and dairy region. **3** uninc. village (1990 pop. 725), Fayette co., S central W.Va., 9 mi/14.5 km W of Fayetteville. Agr. (grain); livestock.

Kincardine (kin-KAHR-din), town (1991 pop. 6,585), S Ont., Canada, on L. Huron, W of Walkerton; 44°10′N 81°38′W. Resort that depends largely on jobs provided by the Bruce Nuclear Power Development to the N.

Kinchafoonee River (kinch-uh-FOO-nee), SW Ga.; rises near Buena Vista; flows S and SE c.75 mi/121 km, past Preston, to Flint R. at Albany.

Kinchil (KEEN-cheel), town (1990 pop. 4,371), Yucatán, SE Mexico, an mi/35 km W of Mérida; 20°55′N 89°57′W. Tropical fruit, corn, henequen.

Kinde (KEIND), village (1990 pop. 473), Huron co., E Mich., 10 mi/16 km N of Bad Axe; 43°56′N 82°59′W. In farm area.

Kinder (KIN-duhr), town (1990 pop. 2,246), Allen parish, SW La., near Calcasieu R., 28 mi/45 km NE of Lake Charles city; 30°30′N 92°51′W. RR junction; in rice, dairying, and cattle-raising area. Agr. (peaches, soybeans, pecans). Mfg. (life ring buoys; lumber); oilfield nearby. Large casino complex (Grand Casino Coushatta).

Kinderhook 1 (KIN-der-huk), village (1990 pop. 257), Pike co., W Ill., 20 mi/32 km WNW of Pittsfield; 39°42′N 91°09′W. In agr. area. **2** village, Branch co., S Mich., 10 mi/16 km S of Coldwater, near Ind. line, in lake area; 41°47′N 85°00′W. Large Coldwater L to NE. **3** village (□ 1 sq mi/2.6 sq km; 1990 pop. 1,293), Columbia co., SE N.Y.; 42°23′N 73°42′W. Mfg. of mechanical and hydraulic presses. Settled before the Amer. Revolution. Richard Upjohn designed St. Paul's Church (1851) here. President Martin Van Buren was born and is buried in Kinderhook; the Van Buren homestead, "Lindenwald," is S of the village. The House of History, maintained by the co. historical society, occupies an early-19th-cent. mansion. Inc. 1838.

Kinderhook Creek, c.45 mi/72 km long, SE N.Y.; rises in S Rensselaer co. in the Taconic Mts.; flows generally SW, past Valatie and Kinderhook, to the Hudson R. 4 mi/6.4 km N of Hudson.

Kindersley, town (1991 pop. 4,572), W Sask., Canada, 100 mi/161 km NW of Swift Current; 51°28′N 109°08′W. grain elevators, lumbering, livestock industry.

Kindred, village (1990 pop. 569), Cass co., SE N.Dak., 19 mi/31 km SSW of Fargo, near Sheyenne R.; 46°38′N 97°01′W. Grain, livestock, dairy.

Kineo, Mount 1 (kin-EE-o), peak (1,789 ft/545 m), Piscataquis co., central Maine, on peninsula extending W into Moosehead L. and 17 mi/27 km NNW of Greenville. Summer resort. **2** (KI-nee-yo), peak (3,320 ft/ 1,012 m) of White Mts., Grafton co., central N.H., 11 mi/18 km N of Plymouth, in White Mt. Natl. Forest.

King 1 county (□ 913 sq mi/2,365 sq km; 1990 pop. 354), NW Texas; ⊙ Guthrie; 33°36′N 100°15′W. Rolling plains area. Elev. 2,000 ft/610 m–2,500 ft/762 m. Drained by tributaries of S and Middle Wichita rivers, and Brazos R. in extreme SE. Large-scale cattle ranching co.; horses, also some agr. (vegetables). Oil and natural-gas wells; lime, copper deposits. Formed 1876. **2** county (□ 2,306 sq mi/5,973 sq km; 1990 pop. 1,507,319), W central Wash.; ⊙ SEATTLE; 47°28′N 121°51′W. Snoqualmie R.

rises in Cascade Range in E. Bounded on W by Puget Sound and Colvos Passage, on E by crest of Cascade Range, on S in part by White R. Strawberries, lettuce, hay; dairying; cattle, poultry; lumber, clays, coal (at Black Diamond). Muckleshoot Indian Reservation in S, SE of Auburn; rapidly growing urban area in W, bet. mts. and sound, around Seattle and S toward Tacoma (just SW of co. line). Includes part of Mt. Baker– Snoqualmie Natl. Forest and Alpine Lake Wilderness. Federation Forest, Olallie, Nolte and Kanaskat-Palmer state parks in S; Lake Sammamish, St. Edward, and Bridle Trails state parks in W; Salt Water and Dash Point state parks in SW. Co. includes Vashon and Maury isls., near Kitsap Peninsula, in W in Puget Sound. Formed 1852.

King, town (1990 pop. 4,059), Stokes co., N N.C., 15 mi/ 24 km NNW of Winston-Salem; 36°16′N 80°21′W. Tobacco, grain, soybeans, poultry, livestock. Mfg. (printing and publishing, blood flow meters, automotive parts, burial vaults, wooden store fixtures, oak furniture). Pilot Mt. State Park to NW; Hanging Rock State Park to NE.

King and Queen, county (□ 326 sq mi/844 sq km; 1990 pop. 6,289), E Va.; ⊙ King and Queen Court House; 37°43′N 76°54′W. In Tidewater region; bounded SW by Mattaponi and York rivers. Agr. (especially tomatoes; also barley, hay, soybeans, corn, wheat, legumes); cattle; oysters. Formed 1691.

King and Queen Court House, uninc. village, ⊙ King and Queen co., E Va., near Mattaponi R., 24 mi/55 km ENE of Richmond. Agr. (grain, soybeans, tomatoes; cattle). Mattaponi Indian Reservation to S. Sometimes called King and Queen.

King Christian Island (17 mi/27 km long, 9 mi/14 km wide), N Franklin dist., N.W.T., in Maclean Strait, off Ellef Ringnes Isl.; 77°45′N 102°10′W.

King City 1 city (1990 pop. 7,634), Monterey co., W Calif., on Salinas R., and 45 mi/72 km SE of Salinas; 36°13′N 121°08′W. Trade and shipping center near S end of rich irrigated Salinas valley. Agr. (beans, grain, some sugar beets, vegetables); dairying; cattle. Mfg. (dehydrated vegetables); asbestos mining and milling; printing and publishing. Hunter Liggett Military Reservation to SW. Los Padres Natl. Forest to W. Founded 1868, inc. 1911. **2** city (1990 pop. 986), Gentry co., NW Mo., 26 mi/42 km NE of St. Joseph; 40°02′N 94°31′W. Corn, soybeans, wheat; cattle, hogs; native bluestem prairie sod and seed. Plotted 1869.

King City, town (1990 pop. 2,060), Washington co., NW Oregon, suburb 10 mi/16 km SW of downtown Portland, on Tualatin R.; 45°24′N 122°47′W. Dairying, poultry, fruit, vegetables, grapes, berries. Retirement center. Bald Peak State Park to W.

King City, community, S central Ont., Canada, suburb 22 mi/35 km NNW of downtown Toronto, situated within Regional Municipality (former co.) of York, E of Highway 400 Freeway. Urban growth area, primarily rural. Mixed farming, dairying.

King Cove, village (1990 pop. 451), SW Alaska, near SW extremity of Alaska Peninsula, 10 mi/16 km WSW of Belkofski; 55°03′N 162°18′W. Fish canneries.

King Edward, Mount (11,400 ft/3,475 m), on Alta.-B.C., Canada, border, in Rocky Mts., on S edge of Jasper Natl. Park, 55 mi/89 km SSE of Jasper; 52°9′N 117°31′W.

King Edward VII Point, SE extremity of Ellesmere Isl., NE Franklin dist., N.W.T., Canada, on Jones Sound; 76°08′N 81°09′W.

King George, county (□ 187 sq mi/484 sq km; 1990 pop. 13,527), E Va.; ⊙ King George; 38°15′N 77°09′W. At base of Northern Neck peninsula; bounded by Potomac R. (shore forms Va.-Md. state line), Rappahannock R. on S. Rolling dairying and agr. region (corn, barley, wheat, hay, soybeans, alfalfa; cattle, hogs); hunting; commercial fishing. Includes DAHLGREN Naval Surface Weapons Center in NE. Caledon Natural Area in N. Formed 1720.

King George, uninc. village, ⊙ King George co., E Va., 16 mi/26 km E of Fredericksburg. Mfg. (concrete, bacon processing); in agr. area (grain, soybeans; cattle; hogs; dairying).

King George Islands, SE Keewatin dist., N.W.T., Canada, group of 15 small isls. and islets in Hudson Bay off W Ungava Peninsula; 57°20′N 78°30′W. Covers area c.30 mi/48 km long, 20 mi/32 km wide.

King George IV Lake (6 mi/10 km long, 5 mi/8 km wide), SW N.F., Canada, on Lloyds R. and 55 mi/89 km S of Corner Brook, at SW end of the Annieopsquotch Mts.

King George, Mount (11,226 ft/3,422 m), SE B.C., Canada, near Alta. border, 40 mi/64 km S of Banff; 50°36′N 115°24′W.

King Island (2.5 mi/4 km long, 1.5 mi/2.4 km wide), NW Alaska, in Bering Sea, SW of Seward Peninsula, 90 mi/ 145 km WNW of Nome; 64°59′N 168°3′W. Rises to 700 ft/213 m. Ukivok, an Inuit village on S shore, was abandoned; people moved to Nome.

King Kirkland, village, NE Ont., Canada, 4 mi/6 km E of Kirkland L.; 48°09′N 79°52′W. Gold mining.

King Lear, Nev.: see JACKSON MOUNTAINS.

King, Mount (17,130 ft/5,221 m), SW Yukon, Canada, near Alaska border, in St. Elias Mts., 190 mi/306 km W of Whitehorse; 60°35′N 140°40′W.

King, Mount Clarence, E Fresno co., E Calif., peak (12,909 ft/3,935 m) of the Sierra Nevada, in Kings Canyon Natl. Park, 14 mi/23 km W of Independence. Mt. STARR KING is in Yosemite Natl. Park.

King Mountain (3,141 ft/957 m), W Texas, near Pecos R., 5 mi/8 km N of McCamey. A landmark for pioneers.

King of Prussia, uninc. city (1990 pop. 18,406), Upper Merion township, Montgomery co., SE Pa.; 40°06′N 75°22′W. Mfg. (glass and steel fabricating, food, linen textiles, printing and publishing, liquified petroleum gas, water treatment equip., electrical equip., motors and gears, roller bearings, security systems, concrete reinforcing). Site of King of Prussia Plaza, one of the largest shopping malls in U.S. Villanova Univ. is nearby. Valley Forge Natl. Park, to NW, contains the Freedom Foundation natl. shrine that honors medal recipients from U.S. wars. Revolutionary War Mus. to SE.

King Oscar Land, NE Franklin dist., N.W.T., Canada, SW part of Ellesmere Isl.

King Ranch (c.825,000 acres/333,878 ha), S Texas, bet. Corpus Christi and Harlingen, headquarted and centered around Kingsville, Texas. Located mainly in Kleberg and Kenedy cos., occupying most of their land area, ranch extends N into Nueces co. and S into Willacy co. One of the largest ranches in the world, largest ranch in continental U.S. (ranch on isl. of Hawaii is larger). It has several divisions, of which the best known is Santa Gertrudis, the "home" ranch. The Santa Gertrudis, the only true cattle breed developed in N. America, was developed here. Thoroughbred racehorses are also raised. The ranch was founded in 1853 by Richard King, a steamboat captain. After King's death, the giant holdings were managed by his son-in-law, Robert Kleberg; later, Kleberg's son succeeded to the management. The property was divided in 1935, but the central ranches are still large enough to resemble a semifeudal domain. Profits from oil and natural gas rights and farming have been added to income gained from the great beef herds. King Ranch Mus. at Kingsville.

King Salmon, village (1990 pop. 696), SW Alaska, 320 mi/515 km SW of Anchorage, 15 mi/24 km E (by road) from Naknek R.; 58°44′N 156°32′W. Gateway to Katmai Natl. Park and Preserve, to E. Outfitting center. Salmon fishing.

King Salmon River, S Alaska, on Alaska Peninsula; rises in SW part of Katmai Natl. Monument near 58°09′N 155°25′W; flows 90 mi/145 km W to Bristol Bay at Egegik.

King William, county (□ 285 sq mi/738 sq km; 1990 pop. 10,913), E Va.; ⊙ King William; 37°42′N 77°5′W. In Tidewater region; bounded SW by Pamunkey R., NE by Mattaponi R., which join at SE tip of co. to form York R. estuary, arm of Chesapeake Bay. Mfg. (pulp and paper) at West Point; agr. (corn, barley, wheat, soybeans, hay, legumes; cattle; dairying; timber; fish and shellfish industries. Pamunkey Indian Reservation in S;

Mattaponi Indian Reservation in SE. Zoar State Forest in NW. Formed 1702.

King William, uninc. village, ⊙ King William co., E Va., 27 mi/43 km ENE of Richmond. Agr. (grain, soybeans; cattle; dairying). Zoar State Forest to NW. Mattaponi Indian Reservation to SE; Pamunkey Indian Reservation to S.

King William Island (□ 5,062 sq mi/13,111 sq km), Canada, in Arctic Archipelago, bet. Victoria Isl. and Boothia Peninsula. Lakes abound on the low (max. elev. 449 ft/137 m), rolling plain. Caribou summer range. Remains of Franklin expedition found here.

Kingait, N.W.T., Canada: see META INCOGNITA.

Kingdom City, village (1990 pop. 112), Callaway co., central Mo., 7 mi/11.3 km N of Fulton; 38°57′N 91°56′W. Important highway service and trucking center.

Kingfield, town (1990 pop. 1,114), Franklin co., W central Maine, on the Carrabassett, and 20 mi/32 km N of Farmington; 45°00′N 70°10′W. Wood prods. Sugar Loaf Ski resort is NW. Settled 1805, inc. 1816.

Kingfisher, county (□ 906 sq mi/2,347 sq km; 1990 pop. 13,212), central Okla.; ⊙ Kingfisher; 35°56′N 97°56′W. Intersected by Cimarron R. and Turkey Creek. Diversified agr. (wheat, alfalfa, barley, oats; cattle, sheep; dairying). Mfg. of industrial machinery is chief industry. Oil and natural gas deposits. Oil field. Formed 1890.

Kingfisher, town (1990 pop. 4,095), ⊙ Kingfisher co., central Okla., 35 mi/56 km NW of Oklahoma City; 35°50′N 97°56′W. Elev. 1,056 ft/322 m. In rich agr. area (mainly wheat; also alfalfa, livestock), oil and natural gas; dairying; light mfg. Chisholm Trail Mus.; Seay Mansion here. Founded 1889.

Kingman, county (□ 866 sq mi/2,243 sq km; 1990 pop. 8,292), S Kansas; ⊙ Kingman; 37°33′N 98°08′W. Plains region, watered by Chikaskia R. and South Fork of Ninnescah R. Wheat, sheep, cattle, hogs, rye, sorghum, strawberries. Kingman State Fishing L. in NW; Cheney Reservoir and Dam on NE corner, also Cherry State Park. Formed 1874.

Kingman, city (1990 pop. 12,722), ⊙ Mohave co., W Ariz., E of Black Mts., 88 mi/142 km SE of Las Vegas, Nev., and 163 mi/262 km NW of Phoenix; 35°12′N 114°01′W. Elev. 3,325 ft/1,013 m. Road and RR hub. Agr. (cattle; grain, alfalfa; melons); mfg. (fishing lures, metal prods., boat construction, aquarium supplies). Silver and copper mines nearby. Hualapai Mts. extend SE from Kingman, Corbat Mts. extend NW; Wabayuma Peak Wilderness Area to S; Mt. Nuttf and Warm Springs wilderness areas to SW; Hualapai Peak (8,417 ft/2,566 m), in Hualapai Mts. Park to SE; large main section of Hualapai Indian Reservation to NE. L. Mead Natl. Recreation Area to W and N; Davis Dam, on Colo. R., (forms L. Mohave) 30 mi/48 km W; Hoover Dam, also on Colorado R., 67 mi/108 km NW, (forms L. Mead). Founded 1882.

Kingman 1 town (1990 pop. 561), Fountain co., W Ind., 14 mi/23 km SSE of Covington; 39°58′N 87°17′W. Agr.; mfg. (fiberglass gloves, steel prods., and safety clothing). **2** town (1990 pop. 3,196), ⊙ Kingman co., S Kansas, on South Fork of Ninnescah R. and 40 mi/64 km W of Wichita; 37°38′N 98°06′W. RR junction. Market center for wheat region. Mfg. (metal stampings, meat packing, auto accessories). Kingman State Fishing L. to W. Founded c.1872, inc. 1883.

Kings 1 county (□ 1,374 sq mi/3,559 sq km; 1991 pop. 62,122), S N.B., Canada, extending N from St. John, drained by St. John R.; ⊙ Hampton. **2** county (□ 842 sq mi/2,181 sq km; 1991 pop. 56,317), NW N.S., Canada, on the Bay of Fundy; ⊙ Kentville. **3** county (□ 641 sq mi/1,660 sq km; 1991 pop. 19,328), in E P.E.I., Canada; ⊙ Georgetown.

Kings, county (□ 1,391 sq mi/3,603 sq km; 1990 pop. 101,469), S central Calif.; ⊙ Hanford; 36°04′N 119°49′W. Level irrigated farm land of San Joaquin Valley, drained by Kings and Tule rivers. Tulare L. irrigation reservoir is in central part. Kettleman Hills (rich oil and natural gas field here) are in SW. Cotton, oats, wheat, barley; fruits and vegetables; dairying; turkeys. Farm prods. processing and oil refining are chief industries. Gypsum quarrying. Part of Lemoure Naval Air Station in NW. Part of Diablo Range in far SW. Formed 1893.

Kings, N.Y.: see BROOKLYN.

Kings Beach, uninc. town (1990 pop. 2,796), Placer co., E Calif., 20 mi/32 km SSW of Reno, at end of L. Tahoe, on Nevada state boundry, opposite Crystal Bay, Nev.; 39°15′N 120°01′W. Tahoe Natl. Forest to W; Toiyabe Natl. Forest (Nev.) to E. Tourism.

Kings Canyon National Park (□ 72 sq mi/186 sq km), Fresno and Tulare cos., E Calif., c.60 mi/97 km E of Fresno; park covers 46,101 acres/18,657 ha. General Grant Grove sect. detached from park, adjoins Sequoia Natl. Park. Two large canyons of Kings R., numerous peaks of Sierra Nevada, giant sequoia trees. Sequoia Natl. Park adjoins to S. Authorized 1890. Originally called General Grant Natl. Park, name changed 1940.

Kings Creek, uninc. village, Cherokee co., N S.C., 12 mi/19 km E of Gaffney. Kings Mt. Natl. Military Park is NE. Mfg. of industrial minerals.

King's Landing, village, SW N.B., Canada, 17 mi/27 km WSW of Fredericton, on SW bank of St. John R. Construction of dam at Mactaquac, 1967, flooded pioneer farms in valley. Historical settlement built in mid-1970s has 60 bldgs. depicting period 1783–1900. Mixed farming, potatoes, dairying, apples, timber. Sport fishing, tourism. Formerly Lower Prince William.

Kings Manor, uninc. village, Upper Merion township, Montgomery co., SE Pa., suburb 14 mi/23 km NW of downtown Philadelphia, and 2 mi/3.2 km S of Norristown, near Schuylkill R.; 40°05′N 75°20′W. Light mfg.

Kings Mills, village, Warren co., SW Ohio, 22 mi/35 km NE of Cincinnati and on Little Miami R. Produces communications equip., chemicals, electrical equip. Major theme park.

Kings Mountain, city (1990 pop. 8,763), Cleveland co., SW N.C., 10 mi/16 km W of Gastonia near S.C. state line; 35°14′N 81°20′W. Agr. area (cotton, grain, hay, tobacco, poultry, livestock). Mfg. (textiles and apparel, heat-recovery modules, roof and floor trusses, fire extinguishers, tire cords, welding materials, swimming pool filters, mica processing, bricks, truck cabs, textile machinery). Kings Mt. Natl. Military Park (S.C.) 8 mi/12.9 km to SSW, Crowders Mt. State Park to SE. Inc. 1874.

Kings Mountain, isolated ridge (1,040 ft/317 m) in York co., N S.C., near N.C. state line, 30 mi/48 km WSW of Charlotte, N.C. in Kings Mt. Natl. Park and state park.

Kings Mountain National Military Park, York and Cherokee cos., N S.C., authorized 1931, 6 sq mi/15.5 sq km. Site of a crucial Amer. victory over the Br. during the Amer. Revolution (Oct. 7, 1780). Marked battlefield trail.

Kings Park, uninc. town, Fairfax co., NE Va., residential suburb 12 mi/19 km WSW of Washington, D.C.; 38°48′N 77°14′W. Lake Accotink Park to S.

Kings Park, village (□ 6 sq mi/15.5 sq km; 1990 pop. including San Reno 17,773), Suffolk co., SE N.Y., near N shore of W L.I., 9 mi/14.5 km E of Huntington; 40°53′N 73°15′W. Developed as utopian community in 1872; became farm for insane in 1885. State psychiatric center opened 1892 (is scheduled to be closed). Nearby is Sunken Meadow State Park (□ 520 acres/210 ha; bathing, hiking, picnicking). N terminus of the L.I. Greenbelt trail; S terminus is at Heckscher State Park. Trail follows Connetquot and Nissequogue R. valleys for 34 mi/55 km.

Kings Park West, uninc. town, Fairfax co., NE Va., residential suburb 14 mi/23 km WSW of Washington, D.C., 3 mi/4.8 km S of Fairfax, near Pohick Creek.

Kings Peak, Duchesne co., NE Utah, 45 mi/72 km N of Duchesne: see UINTA MOUNTAINS. In Uinta Mts., High Uinta Wilderness Area of Ashley Natl. Forest. 13,528 ft/4,123 m, highest point in Utah.

Kings Point, upper-income residential village (1990 pop. 4,843), Nassau co., SE N.Y., on NW L. I., on Great Neck peninsula, 8 mi/12.9 km N of Jamaica; 40°49′N 73°44′W. Seat of U.S. Merchant Marine Acad. (est. 1942). Inc. 1924.

Kings River 1 125 mi/201 km long, Calif.; begins with joining of Middle and South forks, 50 mi/80 km E of Fresno, W of Kings Canyon Natl. Park, in Fresno co.; flows W, receives North fork from NE, 35 mi/56 km E of Fresno; flows through Pine Flat Reservoir, then SW, crossed by Friant-Kern Canal as it enters San Joaquin Valley, where it passes through a network of irrigation canals before entering Tulare irrigation reservoir. **2** in NW Ark. and SW Mo.; rises in the Ozarks in SE Madison co. (Ark.); flows c.115 mi/185 km N to White R., lower 10 mi/16 km is arm of Table Rock L. reservoir; 15 mi/24 km SE of Cassville, Mo. **3** in NW Nev.; rises in N Humboldt co. near Oregon line; flows c.40 mi/64 km S to Quinn R. NE of Jackson Mts.

Kingsbridge, sect. of W Bronx borough of N.Y. city, SE N.Y., along Harlem R. opposite N Manhattan; 40°52′N 73°55′W.

Kingsburg, city (1990 pop. 7,205), Fresno co., central Calif., in San Joaquin Valley, near Kings R., 20 mi/32 km SE of Fresno; 36°31′N 119°33′W. Cantaloupes, citrus, nectarines, grain, sugar beets, almonds, vegetables; cotton; mfg. (dehydrated as well as canned fruits and vegetables; animal feeds, glass containers). Settled in 1870s, inc. 1908.

Kingsbury, county (□ 863 sq mi/2,235 sq km; 1990 pop. 5,925), E central S.Dak., ⊙ De Smet; 44°22′N 97°29′W. Agr. area watered by several lakes in E half of co., including L. Whitewood, L. Henry, L. Preston, and L. Thompson. Corn, wheat, flax, soybeans; dairy produce; cattle; abundance of ducks and pheasants. Formed 1873.

Kingsbury, town (1990 pop. 258), La Porte co., NW Ind., 5 mi/8 km S of La Porte; 41°32′N 86°42′W. Mfg. (chemicals, desulfurization prods., fireworks, plastic moldings, metal coatings).

Kingsbury, uninc. village (1990 pop. 200), Guadalupe co., S central Texas, c.45 mi/72 km ENE of San Antonio. Mfg. (zinc electroplating); agr. diverse area; cattle.

Kingsbury, plantation (1990 pop. 13), Piscataquis co., central Maine, 20 mi/32 km W of Dover-Foxcroft; 45°08′N 69°35′W. Lumbering, recreational area.

Kingsey Falls, village (1991 pop. 1,182), S Que., Canada, on Nicolet R. and 18 mi/29 km E of Drummondville; paper milling, dairying; cattle, pigs.

Kingsford, town (1990 pop. 5,480), Dickinson co., SW Upper Peninsula, Mich., suburb 2 mi/3.2 km SW of Iron Mountain city, and on the Menominee R.; 45°48′N 88°05′W. Mfg. (wood prods., iron castings, cutting tools, truck mounted loaders, concrete, furniture). Ford Airport nearby. Inc. as city 1947.

Kingsford Heights, town (1990 pop. 1,486), La Porte co., NW Ind., 10 mi/16 km S of La Porte; 41°29′N 86°41′W.

Kingsland 1 town (1990 pop. 4,699), Camden co., extreme SE Ga., 27 mi/43 km SSW of Brunswick, near Fla. line; 30°47′N 81°40′W. Originally a RR town and the site of a rice plantation. Mfg. includes trusses, missile parts, chemical plant, sawmilling. Crooked River State Park nearby. Growth of the town has been affected by the construction of Kings Bay submarine base in St. Mary's, Ga., just to the E of Kingsland. Founded 1894. **2** town (1990 pop. 2,725), Llano co., S central Texas, 50 mi/80 km WNW of Austin, on Colorado R., at head of L. Lyndon B. Johnson reservoir and at mouth of Llano R.; 30°39′N 98°27′W. Elev. 856 ft/261 m. Agr. (cattle, peaches, grain). Mfg. (chalk and tack boards). Recreation. Longhorn Caverns State Park to E; Inks Dam Natl. Fish Hatchery to NE.

Kingsland, village (1990 pop. 395), Cleveland co., S central Ark., 29 mi/47 km SW of Pine Bluff; 33°51′N 92°17′W. In agr. area; mfg. (hardwood lumber). Marks Mills Battleground State Historical Monument to SE.

Kingsley, town (1990 pop. 1,129), Plymouth co., NW Iowa, near West Fork Little Sioux R., 17 mi/27 km SW of Le Mars; 42°35′N 95°58′W. Mfg. (livestock remedies, troughs, millwork prods.). Inc. 1884.

Kingsley 1 village (1990 pop. 399), Jefferson co., N Ky., a suburb 4 mi/6.4 km E of downtown Louisville; 38°13′N 85°40′W. Bownan Field airport to NE. Farmington Historical Home (1810) to S. **2** village (1990 pop. 738), Grand Traverse co., NW Mich., 13 mi/21 km SSE of Traverse City; 44°34′N 85°32′W.

Kingsley Dam, Nebr.: see C. W. MCCONAUGHY, LAKE.

Kingsport, city (1990 pop. 36,365), Hawkins and Sullivan cos., NE Tenn., on the Holston R. near the Va. line, 21 mi/34 km NNW of Johnson City; 36°33′N 82°34′W. Industries include one of the largest printing and bookbinding plants in the U.S. Chemicals, plastics, paper, concrete, and glass are also produced. The city, encircled by mountains, stands on the site of forts Robinson (1761) and Patrick Henry (1775) on the old Wilderness Road. Warriors Path State Park is nearby. Inc. 1917.

Kingston, city (1991 pop. 56,597), S Ont., Canada, on L. Ontario, near the head of the St. Lawrence R. and at the end of Rideau Canal from Ottawa; 44°14′N 76°30′W. Kingston has probably the best harbor on the lake. Industries include the mfg. of locomotives, ships, vehicle parts, mining equip., textiles, aluminum prods., synthetic yarn, and ceramics. On the site stood Fort Frontenac, which was of great importance in the Fr. and Indian Wars. The present city was founded by United Empire Loyalists in 1783 and prospered during the War of 1812 as the Can. naval base for operations against the Americans. From 1841 to 1844 it served as the capital of Canada. Fort Henry, built during the War of 1812 and rebuilt from 1832 to 1836, is now a mus. Kingston is the seat of Queen's Univ. (1841), of the Royal Military Col., of Can. National Defense Col., and of Anglican and R.C. bishoprics and cathedrals.

Kingston, city (1991 city pop. 97,424) and parish, SE Jamaica, ⊙ of Jamaica and its largest city; 17°57′N 76°44′W. Bounded on S by Kingston Harbor Waterfront, it spreads N from the harbor over Liguanea Plain, bounded W and NW by St. Andrew parish, N by Lower St Andrew, NE by St. Andrew along the Long Mt. range, continuing from the Fort Nugent Tower S through Harbor View toward the Caribbean Sea. This chief port was founded in 1693 on a land-locked harbor as the finest harbor in the West Indies and the 7th-largest natural harbor in the world. In 1692 the former capital, Port Royal, at the tip of the long narrow peninsular forming the harbor, was inundated by an earthquake. The capital moved 1st to Spanish Town, 13 mi/21 km to the W and then in 1872 to Kingston, now the isl.'s leading commercial city. During this cent., the city was ravaged by hurricanes and a 1907 earthquake, as well as periods of severe urban unrest. By 1968 the Urban Development Corporation modernized the entire waterfront and commercial areas. Historic sites include the Cenotaph within the Natl. Heroes Park, burial place of Prime Ministers and National Heroes of the isl. including Marcus Garvey, Norman Manley and Sir Alexander Bustamante, the Inst. of Jamaica and the Jamaica Conference Center. RR terminus Kingston to Montego Bay Station. Served by Norman Manley Internatl. Airport at Palisadoes. Lighthouse at Great Plumb Point entrance to Kingston Harbor at 17°44′N 77°10′W. Exports include sugar, rum, molasses, bananas. Major industries include tourism, clothing mfg., tobacco processing, oil refining, flour milling, cement mfg. plants at Rockfort.

Kingston 1 city (1990 pop. 279), NW Mo., ⊙ Caldwell co., 48 mi/77 km NE of Kansas City; 39°38′N 94°02′W. Corn; cattle, hogs. Plotted 1843. **2** city (□ 8 sq mi/20.7 sq km; 1990 pop. 23,095), ⊙ Ulster co., SE N.Y., on the Hudson R. at the mouth of Rondout Creek; 41°55′N 74°00′W. A tourist hub for the Catskill-Shawangunk resort area; it has plants that make a variety of mfg. goods, including data acquisition and control systems, ships, conveyors and separators for sand and gravel, hydraulic systems, electronic and mechanical assemblies, filters and filter systems, machines, boilers, and draperies and textiles). The city is also a market for nearby fruit and vegetable farms (esp. apples). The 1st permanent settlement (called Wiltwyck) was est. in 1652. Kingston served as the 1st capital of N.Y. state until it was burned by the British in Oct. 1777. Its growth in the early 19th cent. was stimulated by the construction of the Delaware and Hudson Canal. It has undergone major economic changes: once a major producer of sandstone, then cigars, then shirts, and then computer mainframes (IBM closed in 1985). Among notable landmarks are many old Du. stone houses; the Senate house (1676), meeting place of the 1st N.Y. state legislature; the old Du. church (1659) and cemetery (1661); the burial place of James Clinton; and "Slabsides," former cottage of John Burroughs, located 9 mi/14.5 km S at West Park. Inc. as a village 1805, and as a city through the union (1872) of Kingston and Rondout. **3** city (1990 pop. 4,552), ⊙ Roane co., E Tenn., on arm of Watts Bar Reservoir of Clinch R. and 34 mi/55 km WSW of Knoxville; 35°52′N 84°31′W. Large coal-fired steam plant built by TVA (1955) generates elcctricity. Mfg. (chemicals).

Kingston 1 town (1990 pop. 9,045), including Kingston village, Plymouth co., SE Mass., on Plymouth Bay and 5 mi/8 km NW of Plymouth; 41°59′N 70°45′W. Publishing. Settled 1620, inc. 1726. **2** town (1990 pop. 5,591), Rockingham co., SE N.H., 6 mi/9.7 km SW of Exeter; 42°54′N 71°04′W. Mfg. (kitchen cabinets, lumber); timber; agr. (nursery crops, vegetables; cattle, poultry; dairying). Josiah Bartlett's 18th-cent. home (remodeled). Kingston State Park, bet. Great Pond (W) and Powwow Pond (SE) in S. Country Pond in S. Inc. 1694. **3** town (1990 pop. 1,237), Marshall co., S Okla., 8 mi/12.9 km SSE of Madill. L. Texoma to S and E (Red R. is S; Washita R. is E); 34°00′N 96°43′W. L. Texoma State Park to E. **4** uninc. town (1990 pop. 1,270), Kitsap co., W Wash., 5 mi/8 km W of Edmonds, on Appletree Cove of Puget Sound, at NE end of Kitsap Peninsula; 47°48′N 122°30′W. W terminus of ferry from Edmonds. Fishing; fruit, dairying. City of Seattle to SE. Port Madison Indian Reservation to S.

Kingston 1 village (1990 pop. 616), Bartow co., NW Ga.,13 mi/21 km E of Rome, near Etowah R.; 34°14′N 84°57′W. Mfg. of bird baths. Confederate cemetary. **2** village, De Kalb co., N Ill., on South Branch of Kishwaukee R. (bridged here) and 9 mi/14.5 km NNW of Sycamore; 42°05′N 88°45′W. In rich agr. area. **3** village, Somerset co., SE Md., 22 mi/35 km SSW of Salisbury. In vegetable farm area; lumber. Notable for Kingstown Hall, built in the early 1800s and the birthplace in 1815 of Anna Ella Carroll, daughter of Thomas King Carroll, governor of Md. (1830–1831). **4** village (1990 pop. 439), Tuscola co., E Mich., 12 mi/19 km SE of Caro; 43°24′N 83°11′W. In agr. area. Shay L. to S; Evergreen and Cat lakes to SW. **5** village (1990 pop. 131), Meeker co., S central Minn., 25 mi/40 km S of St. Cloud, on North Fork Crow R.; 45°11′N 94°18′W. Fish processing; agr. (grain, livestock, dairying). L. Francis to NE. **6** village (1990 pop. 1,153), Ross co., S Ohio, 10 mi/16 km NNE of Chillicothe; 39°28′N 82°55′W. Grain prods.; gas wells. **7** residential village (1990 pop. 6,504) in S. Kingston town, Washington co., S R.I., 24 mi/39 km S of Providence; 41°28′N 71°31′W. In agr. area. Univ. of R.I. here. Has many historic 18th- and 19th-cent. houses. **8** village (1990 pop. 134), Piute co., S Utah, 2 mi/3.2 km S of Junction, just E of confluence with Sevier R., on E Fork; 38°12′N 112°10′W. Dairying. Puinte Reservoir to N; parts of Fishlake Natl. Forest to N and NW, Dixie Natl. Forest to S. **9** uninc. village (1990 pop. 50), Fayette co., S central W. Va., 31 mi/50 km SE of Charleston, in coal-mining region. **10** village (1990 pop. 346), Green L. co., central Wis., on Grand R. and 35 mi/56 km W of Fond du Lac; 43°41′N 89°07′W. In lake, wildlife, dairy and farm area.

Kingston, borough (1990 pop. 14,507), Luzerne co., NE Pa., suburb 1 mi/1.6 km NW of Wilkes-Barre, on the Susquehanna R.; 41°15′N 75°53′W. Although chiefly residential, it has varied manufactures (food prods., textiles, machinery, upholstered furniture, apparel, conveyors). Settled 1769, inc. 1857.

Kingston Mines, village (1990 pop. 562), Peoria co., central Ill., on Illinois R. and 12 mi/19 km SW of Peoria; 42°06′N 88°45′W. In agr. and bituminous-coal-mining area; gravel pits.

Kingstown, town (1989 est. pop. 19,345), ⊙ St. Vincent and the Grenadines, West Indies; 13°08′N 61°13′W. The chief port of St. Vincent, Kingstown is an export center for the isl.'s agr. industry as well as a port of entry for tourists. Airport.

Kingstown R.I. see NORTH KINGSTOWN and SOUTH KINGSTOWN-

Kingstree, town (1990 pop. 3,858), ⊙ Williamsburg co., E central S.C., on Black R. and 38 mi/61 km S of Florence; 33°40′N 79°49′W. Mfg. includes ethyl alcohol, sportswear and other fabric clothing, hardwood veneers, enzymes, processed meats, rubber and plastic prods. Trade center for agr prods. such as tobacco, soybeans, grains, livestock, timber, cotton. Hunting and fishing resort. Settled 1732.

Kingsville, city (1990 pop. 25,276), ⊙ Kleberg co., S Texas, 35 mi/56 km SW of Corpus Christi; 27°30′N 97°51′W. Elev. 66 ft/20 m. It is hq. of the gigantic King Ranch; city is located in middle of ranch. The city is a processing center for cotton, cattle, hogs, horses, poultry, sorghum, vegetables and dairy prods. in a farm, oil, uranium, stone, and gas area; mfg. (tortillas, horseback riding equip., printing). Large petrochemical and gas plants are in the vicinity. Seat of Texas A&M Univ.–Kingsville. Head of Cayo del Grullo, arm of Baffin Bay to SE. Inc. 1911.

Kingsville, town (1991 pop. 5,716), S Ont., Canada, on L. Erie, 25 mi/40 km SE of Windsor; 42°02′N 82°45′W. Food processing. Nearby is large bird sanctuary.

Kingsville, town (1990 pop. 279), Johnson co., W central Mo., 18 mi/29 km W of Warrensburg; 38°44′N 94°04′W. Mfg. (alum. mold castings, casting machines).

Kingsville, hamlet (1990 pop. 3,550), Baltimore co., N Md., 15 mi/24 km NE of downtown Baltimore; 39°27′N 76°25′W. Nearby Jerusalem Mill (begun 1772), where guns were made during the Revolutionary War, is a part of Gunpowder State Park. The Kingsville Inn, encompassing a small house believed to have been built before 1740, is now incorporated into a funeral home.

Kingwood, town (1990 pop. 3,243), ⊙ Preston co., N W.Va., 19 mi/31 km SE of Morgantown; 39°28′N 79°40′W. Coal-mining, timber, and agr. area (grain, apples, grapes; livestock; poultry; dairying). Mfg. (lumber, bronze prods., coal processing). W.Va. Northern RR excursion trains to Tunnelton. Brieny Mt. Wildlife Management Area to SE; Alpine L. Ski Resort to E. Founded 1811.

Kingwood, uninc village (1990 pop. c.38,000) , Harris co., SE Texas, industrial suburb 25 mi/40 km NNE of downtown Houston, on N shore of W arm of L. Houston (West Fork of San Jacinto R.). Mfg. (calibration equip., atmospheric sensors, chart recorders).

Kinistino (ki-NI-sti-no), town (1991 pop. 701), central Sask., Canada, 35 mi/56 km ESE of Prince Albert; 52°57′N 105°02′W. Grain elevators, mixed farming.

Kinkaid Lake, reservoir, Jackson co., S Ill., on Kincaid Creek, 7 mi/11.3 km W of Murphysboro; 10 mi/16 km long; 37°47′N 89°27′W. Max. capacity 79,000 acre-ft. Formed by Crisenberry Dam (87 ft/27 m high), built (1970) for water supply. Partly in Shawnee Natl. Forest.

Kinloch (KIN-lahk), town (1990 pop. 2,702), residential suburb, E Mo., 12 mi/19 km NW of downtown St. Louis; 38°44′N 90°19′W. An Afr.-Amer. suburb that was a resettlement area for victims of the race riots in East St. Louis in the 1920s.

Kinmount, village, S Ont., Canada, 40 mi/64 km NNW of Peterborough; 44°47′N 78°39′W. Dairying, farming.

Kinmundy (KIN-mun-dee), city (1990 pop. 879), Marion co., S central Ill., 13 mi/21 km NNE of Salem; 38°46′N 88°50′W. In oil-producing area; food processing. Agr. (corn, wheat, livestock).

Kinnelon (KE-nuh-luhn), borough (1990 pop. 8,470), Morris co., N N.J., 12 mi/19 km NW of Paterson and 14 mi/23 km NNE of Morristown; 40°58′N 74°23′W. In suburban area.

Kinney, county (□ 1,365 sq mi/3,535 sq km; 1990 pop. 3,119), SW Texas; ⊙ Brackettville; 29°21′N 100°25′W. On S edge of Edwards Plateau and crossed E-W by Balcones Escarpment; Rio Grande (Mex. border) is SW boundary. Drained by Nueces R. and Sycamore (forms part of W boundary). Ranching area (cattle, sheep, goats; cotton; oats, sorghum); wool, mohair marketed; hunting. Formed 1850.

Kinney, village (1990 pop. 257), St. Louis co., NE Minn., in Mesabi Iron Range, 9 mi/14.5 km W of Virginia;

47°31′N 92°43′W. Large open-pit iron mine nearby. Superior Natl. Forest to N.

Kinross, town (1990 pop. 89), Keokuk co., SE Iowa, 14 mi/23 km NE of Sigourney; 41°27′N 91°59′W. Livestock; grain.

Kinsale (KIN-sail), village, W Montserrat, B.W.I., just SE of Plymouth. Sea-island cotton, fruit.

Kinsale (KIN-sail), uninc. village, Westmoreland co., E Va., 50 mi/80 km ESE of Fredericksburg, on Yeocomico R., inlet of Potomac R. estuary. Mfg. (oyster processing, lumber, fertilizer); agr. (grain, soybeans; cattle).

Kinsey, town (1990 pop. 1,679), Houston co., SE Ala., 6 mi/9.7 km NNE of Dothan; 31°17′N 85°20′W. In peanut-growing region.

Kinsley, town (1990 pop. 1,875), ⊙ Edwards co., SW central Kansas, on Arkansas R., and 35 mi/56 km ENE of Dodge City; 37°55′N 99°24′W. Elev. 2,160 ft/658 m. RR junction. Trade center for wheat and cattle region. Mfg. (power cylinders, concrete). Santa Fe Trail passed through here. Inc. 1878.

Kinsman 1 village (1990 pop. 112), Grundy co., NE Ill., 15 mi/24 km SSW of Morris; 41°11′N 88°34′W. In agr. area. **2** village, Trumbull co., NE Ohio, 18 mi/29 km NE of Warren, near Pa. line. Brass prods., lumber, animal feed.

Kinsman Mountain, peak (4,363 ft/1,330 m) of White Mts., W N.H., just N of Kinsman Notch and 8 mi/12.9 km NW of North Woodstock village, in White Mt. Natl. Forest. Appalachian Trail crosses summit.

Kinsman Notch, pass in White Mts., Grafton co., W N.H., 5 mi/8 km W of North Woodstock, in White Mt. Natl. Forest. Lost R. (Tributary of Moosilauke R.), running through caverns, is scenic feature. Source of Wild Ammonoosuc R. flows NW. Appalachian Trail crosses notch. State Highway 112 passes through.

Kinston (KIN-stuhn), city (1990 pop. 25,295), ⊙ Lenoir co., E N.C., 70 mi/113 km SE of Raleigh, on the Neuse R.; 35°16′N 77°35′W. It is a market for bright leaf tobacco and other agr. prods. Mfg. (concrete, boats, dairy prods., lumber, textiles and apparel, industrial chemicals, appliances, food processing). Lenoir Community Col. Harmony Hall (1772). Richard Caswell Memorial. CSS Neuse State Historical Site, Confederate gunboat. Settled c.1740, inc. 1849.

Kinston, town (1990 pop. 595), Coffee co., S Ala., 16 mi/26 km SSW of Elba, near Pea R.

Kinta, village (1990 pop. 233), Haskell co., E Okla., 12 mi/19 km SSW of Stigler, on Sanbois Creek; 35°07′N 95°14′W. In farm area. Sansbois Mts. to S.

Kintla Peak, Mont.: see LEWIS RANGE.

Kinzua Dam, Pa.: see ALLEGHENY RESERVOIR.

Kiowa 1 county (□ 1,785 sq mi/4,623 sq km; 1990 pop. 1,688), E Colo.; ⊙ Eads; 38°25′N 102°44′W. Borders on Kansas; watered by Big Sandy and Adobe creeks and reservoirs in S. Cattle; wheat, sunflowers, sorghum. Sand Creek Massacre site in N; Adobe Creek Reservoir (Blue L.) on S boundary, in SW. Group of reservoirs in S center; Nee So Pah, Nee Nashe, Nee Grande, Nee Shah (the Nee Reservoirs); others extend into Prowers co. to S, formed from Kicking Bend, Santanta, and other irrigation canals of Arkansas R. Formed 1889. **2** (KEE-uh-wah), county (□ 722 sq mi/1,870 sq km; 1990 pop. 3,660), S Kansas; ⊙ Greensburg; 37°33′N 99°17′W. Rolling plain, located in Red Hills region, watered by Rattlesnake and Mule creeks and Medicine Lodge R. Wheat, cattle, sorghum, corn, hay, soybeans. Formed 1886. **3** (KEE-uh-wah), county (□ 1,030 sq mi/2,668 sq km; 1990 pop. 11,347), SW Okla.; ⊙ Hobart; 34°55′N 98°58′W. Bounded W by North Fork of Red R.; drained by Elk Creek; Washita R. forms far E part of N boundary. Part of low Wichita Mts. in E. Agr. (wheat, cotton, oats, sorghum; cattle, sheep). Mfg. (rubber and plastic prods.) at Hobart. Granite and marble quarrying; oil wells. Great Plains State Park and Tom Steed L. reservoir in S; Altus L. reservoir on W boundary. Formed 1901.

Kiowa (KEE-uh-wah), town (1990 pop. 1,160), Barber co., S Kansas, near Okla. border, 18 mi/29 km S of Medicine Lodge; 37°01′N 98°28′W. In cattle region. In 1900, Carry Nation damaged saloon here. Inc. 1885.

Kiowa 1 village (1990 pop. 275), ⊙ Elbert co., central Colo., on Kiowa Creek, 40 mi/64 km SE of Denver; 39°21′N 104°27′W. Elev. 6,363 ft/1,939 m. Dairy prods.; cattle; wheat, oats, sunflowers. **2** (KEE-uh-wah), village (1990 pop. 718), Pittsburg co., SE Okla., 17 mi/27 km SSW of McAlester; 34°43′N 95°54′W. In agr. area (corn, oats); mfg. of metal prods. McAlester U.S. Army Ammunition Plant to N.

Kiowa Creek, central Colo., rises in N El Paso co., flows intermittently 111 mi/179 km N past Kiowa and Bennett, then NNE to South Platte R. 4 mi/6.4 km WNW of Fort Morgan.

Kipling, town (1991 pop. 1,005), SE Sask., Canada, 65 mi/105 km NE of Weyburn; lumbering, mixed farming.

Kipnuk, village (1990 pop. 470), W Alaska, near Bering Sea and Etolin Stait, 100 mi/161 km SW of Bethel; 59°55′N 164°05′W.

Kip's Bay, dist. of Manhattan borough of N.Y. city, SE N.Y., along East R. S of 42d St.

Kirby 1 town (1990 pop. 8,326), Bexar co., S central Texas, residential suburb 6 mi/9.7 km ENE of San Antonio; 29°27′N 98°23′W. Fort Sam Houston Military Reservation to W. **2** town (1990 pop. 347), Caledonia co., NE Vt., just NE of St. Johnsbury. In agr. area.

Kirby 1 village, Pike co., SW Ark., 38 mi/61 km WSW of Hot Springs. Cinnabar mine. L. Greerson reservoir to SW; Daily State Park on N shores to W. **2** village (1990 pop. 155), Wyandot co., N central Ohio, 21 mi/34 km NW of Marion; 40°49′N 83°25′W. **3** village (1990 pop. 59), Hot Springs co., N central Wyo., on Bighorn R., and 12 mi/19 km N of Thermopolis; 43°47′N 108°10′W. Elev. 4,270 ft/1,301 m. Coal-shipping point.

Kirby, Lake, in S part of Abilene, Taylor co., W central Texas, impounded by dam in small Cedar Creek (a S tributary of Clear Fork of Brazos R.); c.2.5 mi/4 km long; capacity 8,500 acre-ft.

Kirbyville, town (1990 pop. 1,871), Jasper co., E Texas, near Neches R., c.40 mi/64 km NNE of Beaumont; 30°39′N 93°54′W. RR junction; lumbering; cattle, horses; vegetables; light mfg. Founded 1895, inc. 1926.

Kirkersville, village (1990 pop. 563), Licking co., central Ohio, 12 mi/19 km SW of Newark; 39°57′N 82°35′W.

Kirkfield, village, S Ont., Canada, 20 mi/32 km NW of Lindsay. Dairying; mixed farming.

Kirkland, city (1990 pop. 40,052), King co., W Wash., a suburb 6 mi/9.7 km ENE of Seattle, on E shore of L. Washington; 47°41′N 122°11′W. Mfg. (semiconductors, transformers, prefabricated metal buildings, heating equip., computer peripherals, motor vehicles, apparel, navigation equip., aircraft parts, medical prods., machinery parts, molded plastics, petroleum refining, plywood). In the 1980s and early 1990s, Kirkland grew rapidly along with the Seattle metropolitan area. It is the seat of Northwest Col. (Assemblies of God). Bridle Trails State Park on S side of city. Inc. 1905.

Kirkland 1 village (1990 pop. 1,011), De Kalb co., N Ill., on South Branch of Kishwaukee R. (bridged here), and 12 mi/19 km NW of Sycamore; 42°05′N 88°50′W. In rich agr. area. **2** uninc. village (1990 pop. 102), Childress co., extreme N Texas, 10 mi/16 km ESE of Childress. In cotton, wheat, livestock region.

Kirkland Lake, mining town, E Ont., Canada; 48°09′N 80°02′W. An important gold-mining center. Gold was discovered here in 1911 and again in the 1980s at Harker. Iron ore mining; tourism.

Kirklin, town (1990 pop. 707), Clinton co., central Ind., near Sugar Creek, 10 mi/16 km SE of Frankfort; 40°11′N 86°22′W. In agr. area.

Kirkman, town (1990 pop. 98), Shelby co., W Iowa, on West Nishnabotna R., and 6 mi/9.7 km NE of Harlan; 41°43′N 95°16′W.

Kirkmansville, village, Todd co., S Ky., on Pond R., and 17 mi/27 km NE of Hopkinsville.

Kirkpatrick, locality, S Alta., Canada, on Red Deer R., and 6 mi/10 km WNW of Drumheller. Coal mining.

Kirksville, city (1990 pop. 17,152), ⊙ Adair co., N Mo.; 40°12′N 92°34′W. A processing, trade, and shipping center for a large agr. area. Corn, soybeans; sheep, cattle, hogs; light mfg. Andrew Taylor Still founded the 1st school of osteopathy here in 1892; it is now the Kirksville Col. of Osteopathic Medicine. Truman State Univ. Thousand Hills State Park is nearby. Inc. 1857.

Kirkville, town (1990 pop. 177), Wapello co., SE Iowa, 10 mi/16 km NNW of Ottumwa; 41°08′N 92°30′W. Livestock; grain.

Kirkwood, city (1990 pop. 27,291), St. Louis co., E Mo., a suburb 15 mi/24 km of St. Louis; on Meramec R.; 38°34′N 90°25′W. Primarily residential, it has some light mfg. Meramec Community Col. Inc. 1865.

Kirkwood, village (1990 pop. 884), Warren co., W Ill., 6 mi/9.7 km SW of Monmouth; 40°52′N 90°45′W. In agr. area.

Kiron, town (1990 pop. 301), Crawford co., W Iowa, 13 mi/21 km N of Denison; 42°11′N 95°19′W. In agr. area.

Kirtland, uninc. town (1990 pop. 3,552), San Juan co., NW N.Mex., 8 mi/12.9 km W of Farmington, on San Juan R.; 36°44′N 108°20′W. Cattle, sheep; dairying; grain, blue corn, alfalfa, potatoes, pumpkins. Navajo Indian Reservation to S and N; Ute Mt. Indian Reservation (N.Mex./Colo.) to N.

Kirtland Air Force Base, N.Mex.: see ALBUQUERQUE.

Kirtland Hills, village (1990 pop. 628), Lake co., NE Ohio, 20 mi/32 km ENE of Cleveland; 41°38′N 81°20′W. The 1st Mormon temple was built here (1833–1836) by Joseph Smith and his followers. Settled 1808, inc. 1926.

Kirvin, village (1990 pop. 107), Freestone co., E central Texas, 23 mi/37 km SSE of Corsicana; 31°46′N 96°19′W. Vegetables, peaches, melons; cattle.

Kirwin, village (1990 pop. 269), Phillips co., N Kansas, on North Fork Solomon R. and 12 mi/19 km ESE of Phillipsburg; 39°40′N 99°07′W. RR junction. Corn, livestock. Kirwin Reservoir and National Wildlife Reserve to SW; dam just S of town.

Kirwin Reservoir (□ 17 sq mi/44 sq km), Phillips co., N central Kansas, on North Fork of Solomon and Bow rivers, in Kirwin Natl. Wildlife Refuge, 54 mi/87 km N of Hays; 39°39′N 99°07′W. Max. capacity 513,020 acre-ft. Formed by Kirwin Dam (169 ft/52 m high), built (1955) by the Bureau of Reclamation for irrigation; also used for flood control.

Kiryas Joel, inc. village (□ 1 sq mi/2.6 sq km; 1990 pop. 7,437) within Monroe, Orange co., SE N.Y., 50 mi/80 km NW of N.Y. city; 41°20′N 74°10′W. Founded in 1974 by the Satmar sect of Hasidic Jews to accommodate, in part, their burgeoning pop. in the Williamsburg sect. of Brooklyn. In 1990, this insular religious community sought to establish the nation's 1st public school dist. for handicapped Hasidic Jewish children, to be partially supported by Federal tax dollars. When the U.S. Supreme Court declared the dist. unconstitutional in March 1995, the N.Y. state legislature passed a law supporting the legal integrity of the school dist.; this law was struck down by the Supreme Court in 1996. The legislature passed a new law in 1997 in another attempt to establish the dist., and the issue continues to be litigated in the courts.

Kisbey (KIZ-bee), village (1991 pop. 219), SE Sask., Canada, near Moose Mountain Creek, 40 mi/64 km NNE of Estevan; 49°38′N 102°40′W. Mixed farming.

Kishwaukee River (kish-WAH-kee), N Ill., c.60 mi/97 km long, rises in McHenry co., flows generally W and SW, past Belvidere, to Rock R. 6 mi/9.7 km below Rockford; 42°17′N 88°26′W. Its South Branch rises near Shabbona in De Kalb co., flows c.56 mi/90 km generally N and NW to Kishwaukee R., SE of Rockford.

Kiskatom, resort village, Greene co., SE N.Y., in the Catskill foothills, 5 mi/8 km WSW of Catskill; 42°12′N 73°58′W. Post office in Catskill.

Kiskiminetas River (KIS-kuh-MEH-nuh-tus), 27 mi/43 km long, in SW Pa., formed at Saltsburg by confluence of Conemaugh R. and Loyalhanna Creek; flows NW past Avonmore, Vandergrift, and Leechburg to Allegheny R. 1 mi/1.6 km E of Freeport; 40°29′N 79°27′W.

Kiskitto Lake (□ 65 sq mi/168 sq km), central Man., Canada, 26 mi/42 km N of L. Winnipeg; 20 mi/32 km long, 6 mi/10 km wide. Drains N into Nelson R.

Kiskittogisu Lake (□ 99 sq mi/256 sq km), central Man., Canada, 18 mi/29 km N of L. Winnipeg; 30 mi/

48 km long, 8 mi/13 km wide. Drains N into Nelson R.

Kismet (KIZ-met), village (1990 pop. 421), Seward co., SW Kansas, 15 mi/24 km NE of Liberal; 37°12′N 100°42′W. In grain region.

Kissimmee (kuh-SIM-ee), city (□ 13 sq mi/34 sq km; 1990 pop. 30,050), Osceola co., central Fla., on L. Tohopekaliga; 28°18′N 81°24′W. Located in an important agr. area, it is a major processing, packaging, and shipping center for the surrounding Kissimmee river basin, where citrus prods. (especially oranges) and beef are raised. The city also lies in a popular vacation area. Among the largest contributors to Kissimmee's economic development is nearby Walt Disney World (12 mi/19 km NW), the theme park and entertainment complex that draws millions of visitors each year. Kissimmee has motels and restaurants that serve many of the park's visitors.

Kissimmee, Lake (kuh-SIM-ee), Osceola co., central Fla., c.40 mi/64 km S of Orlando; c.15 mi/24 km long, 5 mi/8 km wide. Entered (NW) and drained (S) by Kissimmee R. Contains several small isls.

Kissimmee River (kuh-SIM-ee), c.140 mi/225 km long, central Fla., rises in Tohopekaliga L. in Osceola co., flows SSE to N end of L. Okeechobee 7 mi/11.3 km SW of Okeechobee. In upper course, connects chain of lakes (Tohopekaliga, Hatchineha, Kissimmee). River basin has large cattle range (Kissimmee Prairies), some citrus-fruit growing, and large wilderness tracts. River was channelized by the U.S. Army Corps of Engineers in 1970s and is now being restored.

Kississing Lake (□ 141 sq mi/365 sq km), W Man., Canada, near Sask. border, 24 mi/39 km NE of Flin Flon; 17 mi/27 km long, 16 mi/26 km wide. Drains into Churchill R.

Kistler (KIST-luhr), borough (1990 pop. 314), Mifflin co., central Pa., 1 mi/1.6 km E of Mount Union, on Juniata R. opposite Allenport (to SW). There is an uninc. village of Kistler 24 mi/39 km to E, in Northeast Madison township, Perry co., Pa.

Kistler (KIS-luhr), village (1990 pop. 700), Logan co., SW W.Va., 9 mi/14.5 km SE of Logan. RR junction. Coal mining area.

Kit Carson, county (□ 2,161 sq mi/5,597 sq km; 1990 pop. 7,140), E Colo.; ⊙ Burlington; 39°18′N 102°35′W. Grain and livestock area bordering on Kansas. Drained by South Fork of Republican and North Fork of Smoky Hill rivers and Spring, Sand, Landsman, and Beaver creeks. Cattle; wheat, hay, sunflowers, beans, sorghum, oats, corn. Flagler Reservoir and Flagler State Wildlife Area in W. Formed 1889.

Kit Carson, village (1990 pop. 305), Cheyenne co., E Colo., on Big Sandy Creek, and 24 mi/39 km W of Cheyenne Wells; 38°45′N 102°47′W. Elev. c.4,285 ft/ 1,306 m. Cattle; wheat, sunflowers, sorghum, corn. Sand Creek Massacre Site to SE. Inc. 1931.

Kit Carson Pass, Calif.: see CARSON PASS.

Kit Carson Peak (14,165 ft/4,317 m), in Sangre de Cristo Mts., E Saguache co., S Colo.; summit is just W of Custer co. line, in Rio Grande Natl. Forest.

Kitchener, city (1991 pop. 168,282), regional municipality of Waterloo, S Ont., Canada, in the Grand R. valley; 43°27′N 80°30′W. Packaged meats, metal and leather goods, spirits, appliances, furniture, and rubber prods. Because of the close ties bet. Kitchener and the city of Waterloo, the area is commonly known as Kitchener-Waterloo. Woodside Natl. Historic Park commemorates the birthplace of W. L. MacKenzie King. Settled largely by Mennonites from Pa. in 1806, it was known as Berlin until 1916, when it was renamed in memory of Lord Kitchener.

Kitchener, Mount (11,500 ft/3,505 m), SW Alta., Canada, near B.C. border, in Rocky Mts., on S edge of Jasper Natl. Park, 55 mi/89 km SE of Jasper; 52°13′N 117°20′W.

Kitchi, Mount (9,352 ft/2,850 m), E B.C., Canada, in Rocky Mts., 100 mi/161 km E of Prince George; 53°58′N 120°24′W.

Kite 1 village (1990 pop. 297), Johnson co., E central Ga., 12 mi/19 km WNW of Swainsboro, and on Ohoopee R.; 32°41′N 82°31′W. Light mfg. **2** uninc. village (1990

pop. 300), Knott co., E Ky., 9 mi/14.5 km E of Hindman, on right fork of Beaver Creek, in Cumbeland Mts. Bituminous coal. Mfg. (machinery).

Kitikmeot (ki-TIC-mee-aht), region (□ 228,641 sq mi/ 592,334 sq km; 1991 pop. 4,386), central N.W.T., Canada. Cambridge Bay on Victoria Isl. is the regional hq. The region extends E from the Great Bear L. to include the Boothia Peninsula, and N from the Fort Smith and Keewatin regions to include Victoria Isl. and the lower ½ of Prince of Wales Isl. Created in 1981 by the territorial govt., the region is inhabited mostly by Inuit people who rely on traditional activities such as fishing, sealing, and crafts.

Kitimat (KIT-i-mat), town (1991 pop. 11,305), W B.C., Canada, at the head of Douglas Channel; 54°00′N 128°42′W. Huge aluminum smelter (opened 1954), pulp and paper mills, and a petrochemical plant. Deep-water anchorage.

Kitsap (KIT-suhp), county (□ 565 sq mi/1,463 sq km; 1990 pop. 189,731), W Wash.; ⊙ Port Orchard; 47°38′N 122°39′W. Occupies N part of Kitsap peninsula, bounded W by Hood Canal and E by Puget Sound, deeply indented on E by Sinclair and Dyes inlets and Liberty Bay; Bainbridge Isl. separated from mainland by Port Orchard passage. Bremerton is important seaport and site of Puget Sound Navy Yard. County directly opposite city of Seattle, ferry service to Seattle and Edmonds. Illahee State Park in center; Scenic Beach State Beach in W; Blake Isl., Fay Bainbridge, and Fort Ward state parks in E, on Bainbridge Isl. U.S. Naval Station at Bangor, in W on Hood Canal, has Trident ballistic missile submarine base with ½ of all U.S. long-defense missiles. Includes Port Gamble and Port Madison Indian reservations in N. Fruits, nuts, poultry; fish, crabs, oysters, clams. Formed 1857.

Kitscoty, village (1991 pop. 625), E Alta., Canada, near Sask. border, 21 mi/34 km E of Vermilion; 53°20′N 110°20′W. Dairying; grain.

Kitt Peak (6,875 ft/2,096 m), in E edge of Tohono O'odham (Papago) Indian Reservation in the N end of Baboquivari Mts., central Pima Co., S Ariz., 40 mi/ 64 km WSW of Tucson. It is the site of Kitt Peak Natl. Observatory. Mex. border 29 mi/47 km SSW.

Kitt Peak National Observatory, central Pima co., S Ariz., astronomical observatory located 40 mi/64 km WSW of Tucson, Ariz., at summit of Kitt Peak (6,875 ft/ 2,096 m). It was founded in 1958 under contract with the Natl. Science Foundation and is administered by the Assn. of Univs. for Research in Astronomy. Its principal instrument is the Mayall 158 in/4 m reflector. The observatory's equip. also includes 84 in/2.1 m, 50 in/ 1.3 m, 36 in/0.9 m, and 16 in/0.4 m reflecting telescopes as well as a planned 138-in/3.5-m telescope. Used for wide angle photographs and electronic images of the sky, the Burrell Schmidt telescope is operated jointly with Case Western Reserve Univ. The 60-in/1.5-m Robert McMath Solar Telescope is the largest instrument of its kind in the world. Stellar research, now part of the Natl. Optical Astronomy Observatories, includes basic research on galaxies, stars, nebulae, and the solar system. The solar division, now part of the Natl. Solar Observatory, using the solar telescope in coordination with a vacuum spectrograph, analyzes the composition, magnetic field strength, motion, and physical nature of the sun. Other telescopes are located on Kitt Peak, notably those of the Natl. Radio Astronomy Observatory and Steward Observatory. Any astronomer can apply for time on the telescopes. A telescope allocation committee of astronomers selects the best proposals and time is assigned every 6 months.

Kittanning (KI-tah-ning), borough (1990 pop. 5,120), ⊙ Armstrong co., W central Pa., 35 mi/56 km NE of Pittsburgh, on Allegheny R. (bridged). Mfg. (agr. chemicals, fabricated metal prods., construction materials, apparel, sand and gravel processing). Agr. (corn, hay; livestock; dairying); bituminous coal; limestone; sand and gravel. Original site was an Indian village. Lock and Dam No. 7 here. Settled 1796; laid out 1804; inc. 1821.

Kittatinny Mountain (KI-tuh-TI-nee), ridge of the Appalachian system, extending across NW N.J. from

Shawangunk Mt., SE N.Y., to Blue Mt., S central Pa.; rises to High Point (1,803 ft/550 m), the highest peak in New Jersey. Kittatinny Mt. is a major resort and recreation area; the Appalachian Trail lies atop the ridge. The Delaware R. cuts through the E part of the ridge forming the Delaware Water Gap.

Kittery (KIT-uhr-ee), town (1990 pop. 9,372), York co., extreme SW Maine, at the mouth of the Piscataqua R., 27 mi/43 km S of Alfred; 43°06′N 70°42′W. Its economy centers around tourism and the Portsmouth Naval Shipyard, which services nuclear-powered submarines and is located on 2 isls. owned by the Federal govt. and connected with Kittery by 2 bridges. N.H. also lays claim to these 2 isls. Shipyard was 1st public shipyard in U.S. est. in 1800 as colonial shipyard, built 1st warship in Amer., HMS *Falkland*. In 1917, 1st U.S. submarine built. Yard built submarines (1st public shipyard to build nuclear submarine) until 1971. The oldest town in Maine (settled c.1623), it grew as a trading, fishing, lumber-shipping, and shipbuilding center. John Paul Jones's ship *Ranger* (1777) and the *Kearsarge* of Civil War fame were both built there. Several 18th-cent. houses remain. William Whipple, a signer of the Declaration of Independence, was born in Kittery. Inc. 1647.

Kittigazuit, locality, NW Mackenzie dist., N.W.T., Canada, on Refuge Cove, bay of the Beaufort Sea, at mouth of E channel of Mackenzie R. delta, 90 mi/145 km NE of Aklavik; 69°21′N 133°43′W. Site of Hudson's Bay Co. post, 1915–1929.

Kittitas (KIT-i-tuhs), county (□ 2,332 sq mi/ 6,040 sq km; 1990 pop. 26,725), central Wash.; ⊙ Ellensburg; 47°07′N 120°41′W. Naches and Little Naches rivers form SW boundary; bounded on E by Columbia R. (Wanapum L. reservoir). Mt. area drained by Yakima R. Potatoes, alfalfa, hay, wheat, barley, oats, peas; cattle, sheep; lumber; coal, gold, silica; dairying. Parts of Wenatchee Natl. Forest in NW, including part of Alpine Lakes Wilderness Area; part of Gifford Pinchot Natl. Forest in SW; Olmstead Place State Park in center; Gingko Petrified Forest and Wanapum state parks in E; L. Easton and Iron Horse state parks in W. Kencholus, Haches, and Clo Elum reservoirs in W; Priest Rapids L. reservoir, SE. Part of U.S. Military Reservation Yakima Training Center, in SE. Formed 1883.

Kittitas (KIT-i-tuhs), town (1990 pop. 843), Kittitas co., central Wash., 6 mi/9.7 km E of Ellensburg; 47°00′N 120°25′W. Wheat, barley, oats, potatoes, peas, hay. Olmstead Place State Park to W; Gingko Petrified Forest and Wanapum state parks to E. U.S. Military Reservation Yakima Training Center to SE.

Kittrell (ki-TRELL), village (1990 pop. 228), Vance co., N N.C., 8 mi/12.9 km SSW of Henderson; 36°13′N 78°26′W. Grain, tobacco; poultry, livestock. Mfg. (corn feed).

Kitts, uninc. village (1990 pop. 800), Harlan co., SE Ky., 3 mi/4.8 km E of Harlan, in the Cumberland Mts., on Clover Fork of Cumberland R. In coal mining area.

Kittson, county (□ 1,103 sq mi/2,857 sq km; 1990 pop. 5,767), extreme NW Minn.; ⊙ Hallock; 48°46′N 96°46′W. Drained by Two Rivers and its North, Middle, and South branches; bounded W by Red R. (N.Dak. state line), N by Can. (Man.). Agr. area (wheat, alfalfa, hay, flax, oats, barley, sugar beets, beans, sunflowers; sheep). Lake Bronson State Park in E center, on L. Bronson reservoir; Twin Lakes Wildlife Area in SE; Skull Lake Wildlife Area in NE. Formed 1878.

Kitty Hawk or **Kittyhawk**, town (1990 pop. 1,937), Dare co., NE N.C., 35 mi/56 km SE of Elizabeth City, on Albermarle Sound, at entrance to Curritick Sound (N); 36°04′N 75°43′W. Atlantic Ocean 3 mi/4.8 km to E. Bridge to mainland to NW. Light mfg. Residential developments in area. To SE is Kill Devil Hill and Wright Brothers Natl. Memorial, where the Wright brothers experimented successfully (1900–1903) with gliders and airplanes. First successful flight Dec. 17, 1903.

Kitzmiller, town (1990 pop. 275), Garrett co., W Md., in the Alleghenies, on North Branch of the Potomac (bridged to W.Va.), and 30 mi/48 km SW of Cumberland; 39°23′N 79°11′W. Bituminous-coal mining.

Named for Ebenezer Kitzmiller, an early settler in what was orginally a logging and later a mining area. Bloomington Dam and reservoir have recently been constructed here. Nearby are Potomac State Park and Backbone Mt. Sometimes called Kitzmillersville.

Kivalina (ki-vuh-LEE-nuh), Inuit village (1990 pop. 317), NW Alaska, on Chukchi Sea, 80 mi/129 km NW of Kotzebue; 67°43′N 164°31′W. Reindeer herding.

Kiwalik (ki-WAH-lik), village, NW Alaska, on SE shore of Kotzebue Sound, N Seward Peninsula, at mouth of Kiwalik R. and 60 mi/97 km SSE of Kotzebue. Port and transfer point for Candle and Kiwalik R. valley. Sometimes spelled Keewalik.

Kiwalik River (ki-WAH-lik), NW Alaska, on N side of Seward Peninsula; rises near 65°20′N 161°30′W; flows c.60 mi/97 km N, past Candle, to Kotzebue Sound at Kiwalik.

Klamath (KLAM-uhth), county (□ 6,136 sq mi/ 15,892 sq km; 1990 pop. 57,702), S Oregon, in Cascade foothills; ⊙ Klamath Falls; 42°40′N 121°39′W. Borders on Calif. to S. Drained by Klamath, Williamson, Sprague, and Lost rivers. Livestock raised in Klamath irrigation project, which extends S from Lost R. into Siskiyou co., N Calif. Agr. (wheat, oats, barley, alfalfa, potatoes; poultry, hogs, sheep, cattle); dairy prods. Millwork. Recreation. Bear Valley Natl. Wildlife Refuge in S; parts of Winema Natl. Forest in center and W; part of Deschutes Natl. Forest in N; parts of Fremont Natl. Forest in E; part of Rogue River Natl. Forest in SW; Klamath Forest Natl. Wildlife Refuge in N center, including Klamath Marsh; Upper Klamath Natl. Wildlife Refuge, on Upper Klamath L., in SW center; part of Lower Klamath Natl. Wildlife Refuge on S boundary; Collier Memorial and Kimball state parks in W center; Crater Lake Natl. Park in W. Formed 1882.

Klamath, town (1990 pop. 827), Del Norte co., NW Calif., 18 mi/29 km SE of Crescent City, 2 mi/3.2 km E of Pacific Ocean and on Klamath R. (here crossed by Douglas Memorial Bridge) near its mouth on the Pacific; 41°31′N 124°00′W. Game fishing; timber; cattle; dairying. Hoopa Valley Indian Reservation to SE. Prairie Creek Redwoods State Park to S; Six Rivers Natl. Forest to E; Redwoods Natl. Park to W; Rattlesnake Mts. to N (3,568 ft/1,088 m).

Klamath Agency (KLAM-uhth), uninc. village, Klamath co., S Oregon, 30 mi/48 km NNW of Klamath Falls; elev.4,170 ft/1,271 m. Collier Memorial State Park to E, located in small unit of Winema Natl. Forest. Fish hatchery to NW.

Klamath Falls (KLAM-uhth), city (1990 pop. 17,737), ⊙ Klamath co., SW Oregon, 55 mi/89 km ESE of Medford and 17 mi/27 km N of Calif. boundary, at the southern tip of Upper Klamath L., at exit of Klamath R.; 42°13′N 121°46′W. Elev. 4,105 ft/1,251 m. A processing and distributing center of a lumber, livestock, and farm area. Timber, dairy prods., and tourism are central to the city's economy. Agr. (grain, potatoes; poultry; dairy prods.; nurseries); mfg. (wood chips, millwork, plywood, furniture, printing, publishing, concrete, horse-drawn carriages, ice cream carts); geothermal energy for heating. Klamath Falls was settled in 1867 as Linkville. The Klamath Irrigation Project (1900) and the coming of the railroad (1909) stimulated its growth from a hamlet to a thriving city. Site of Oregon Inst. of Technology and Farell Mus. of Western Art and Indian Artifacts. Kingsley Field airport to S. Crater L. Natl. Park is 55 mi/89 km to NNW; Lava Beds Natl. Monument is 32 mi/51 km SSE (Calif.); parts of Winema Natl. Forest to N and NW, including Mt. Lakes Wilderness Area to NW; Lower Klamath Natl. Wildlife Refuge to S; Upper Klamath Natl. Wildlife Refuge to NW; Bear Valley Natl. Wildlife Refuge to SW. Inc. 1905.

Klamath Lake 1 Calif.: see LOWER KLAMATH LAKE. **2** Oregon: see UPPER KLAMATH LAKE.

Klamath Mountains (KLAM-uhth), part of Pacific Coast Range extending c.240 mi/386 km from SW Oregon, above the Trinity R., to NW Calif. The range is covered by 4 natl. forests: Siskiyou in Oregon, Six Rivers, Klamath, and Shasta-Trinity in Calif., and contains wildlife preserves and scenic portions of the Klamath R., rising in Upper Klamath L., and the Sacramento R. Tourism and timber industries are chief economic activity of the region. Hiking, camping.

Klamath River (KLAM-uhth), 263 mi/423 km long, in S Oregon and N Calif.; rises in small L. Ewauna connected to Upper Klamath L. by Link R., 2 mi/3.2 km long, at Klamath Falls; flows generally SW through John Boyle Reservoir, Oregon, and Capco L. Reservoir, Calif., receives Shartin R. from E, then flows through Klamath Mts. Receives Trinity R. from SE, then turns NW through Klamath Mts., Calif., turning NW in Humboldt co., and emptying into the Pacific NW of Klamath, Calif., 50 mi/80 km N of Eureka, at Redwood Natl. Park. The river is connected by Klamath Strait, 7 mi/11.3 km long, (largely in Oregon) with Lower Klamath L., in Calif. Supplies water for Klamath Irrigation Project, serving agr. area in Klamath co., Oregon, and Siskiyou co., Calif. Capco No. 1 Dam, completed in 1922 (227 ft/69 m high, 415 ft/126 m long), in Calif. sect. of stream, just S of Oregon line, is used for power. Trinity R., in Calif., is chief tributary.

Klawak or **Klawock** (KLAH-wahk), village (1990 pop. 722), SE Alaska, on W coast of Prince of Wales Isl., 5 mi/8 km N of Craig. Fishing, fish processing. First salmon cannery in Alaska was located here.

Klawak Island (KLAH-wahk) (4 mi/6.4 km long, 1 mi/ 1.6 km wide), SE Alaska, in Alexander Archipelago, W of Klawak village on Prince of Wales Isl.; 55°33′N 133°06′W.

Klawock, village, Alaska: see KLAWAK.

Kleberg, county (□ 1,090 sq mi/2,823 sq km; 1990 pop. 30,274), S Texas; ⊙ Kingsville; 27°25′N 97°39′W. Bounded on E by Gulf of Mexico, S by Baffin Bay and Los Olmos Creek. N part of Padre Isl. (Natl. Seashore) separated from mainland by Laguna Madre, park hq. and road access from N. Ranching area, including part of huge King Ranch, hq. at Kingsville; beef cattle, horses, also hogs, poultry, some agr. (cotton, sorghum; vegetables); oil, natural gas; uranium; stone. Coast resorts, fishing, wildlife sanctuary. Kingsville Naval Air Station Arms of Baffin Bay, Alazan Bay (NE), and Cayo del Grullo (NW) almost divide co. into 3 sections. Inland lake, Laguna Largo, is in NE. Formed 1913.

Klein, village, Musselshell co., central Mont., on Halfbreed Creek, 3 mi/4.8 km S of Roundup. Coal; sheep, cattle.

Klein Bonaire, Du. West Indies: see LITTLE BONAIRE.

Klein Curaçao, Neth. Antilles: see LITTLE CURAÇAO.

Klemme, town (1990 pop. 587), Hancock co., N Iowa, 6 mi/9.7 km S of Garner; 43°00′N 93°35′W. Animal feed.

Klickitat (KLIK-uh-tat), county (□ 1,904 sq mi/ 4,931 sq km; 1990 pop. 16,616), S Wash.; ⊙ Goldendale; 45°52′N 120°48′W. Agr., lumbering area, rising toward Cascade Range in N. Carrots, potatoes, alfalfa, hay, wheat, oats, grapes, pears, apples; cattle. Bounded by Columbia R. (S boundary and Oregon state boundary), drained by Klickitat and White Salmon (part of W boundary) rivers. Includes part of Yakima Indian Reservation along N boundary; Conboy Lake Natl. Wildlife Refuge in NW; Brooks Memorial and Goldendale Observatory state parks, at center; Maryhill and Horse Thief L. state parks in S. Formed 1860.

Klickitat (KLIK-uh-tat), uninc. town (1990 pop. 820), Klickitat co., S Wash., 16 mi/26 km W of Goldendale, on Klickitat R. Cattle; wheat, vegetables. Klickitat Springs to E. Klickitat Wildlife Area to N.

Klickitat River (KLIK-uh-tat), S Wash., rises in Cascade Range in Yakima Indian Reservation in W Yakima co., flows c.85 mi/137 km generally S to Columbia R. 10 mi/ 16 km NW of the Dalles, Oregon. Receives West Fork (15 mi/24 km long) from slopes of Mt. Adams; receives Little Klickitat R. (c.30 mi/48 km long) from E, rises in N central Klickitat co., flows SW and W, past Goldendale, joins Klickitat R. 11 mi W of Goldendale.

Klinaklini River, SW B.C., Canada; rises in Coast Mts. near 51°50′N 125°W; flows 120 mi/193 km in a wide arc SW and S to head of Knight Inlet.

Kline, village (1990 pop. 285), Barnwell co., SW S.C., 8 mi/12.9 km S of Barnwell; 33°07′N 81°20′W. Industry includes poultry, livestock; grain, cotton, peanuts.

Klondike (KLAHN-deik), region of YUKON TERRITORY, Canada, just E of the Alaska border. It lies around Klondike R., a small stream that enters the Yukon R. from the E at Dawson. The discovery in 1896 of rich placer gold deposits in Bonanza (Rabbit) Creek, a tributary of the Klondike, caused the Klondike stampede of 1897–1898. News of the discovery reached the U.S. in July 1897, and within a month thousands of people were rushing N. Most landed at Skagway at the head of Lynn Canal and crossed by Chilkoot or White Pass to the Upper Yukon, which they descended to Dawson. Others went in by the Copper R. Trail or over the Teslin Trail by Stikine R. and Teslin L., and some by the all-Canadian Ashcroft and Edmonton trails. The rush continued by these passes all the following winter. The other main access route was up the Yukon R., c.1,600 mi/2,575 km, by steamer. Many of those using this route late in 1897 were caught by winter ice below Fort Yukon and had to be rescued. With unexpected thousands coming in, the region was threatened by a food famine, and supplies were commandeered and rationed. The number in the Klondike in 1898 was c.25,000. Thousands of others who did not find claims drifted down the Yukon and found placer gold in Alaskan streams, notably at Nome, to which there was a new rush. Others went back to the U.S. Gold is still mined in the area.

Klondike Gold Rush Historical Park (KLAWN-deik) (20 sq mi/52 sq km; 13,195 acres/5,340 ha), SW Alaska and N Wash.; 59°28′N 135°19′W (Skagway portion). Authorized 1976. Site of the historic goldfields including Visitors' Center in Seattle's Pioneer Square, which served as the miners point of departure. Historic bldgs. in Skagway; goldfields along Chilkoot and White Pass Trail.

Klondike River (KLAHN-deik), W Yukon, Canada; rises E of Dawson; flows 100 mi/161 km W to Yukon R. at Dawson. Receives Bonanza Creek just SE of Dawson. Noted by Indians for its salmon. It gives its name to surrounding region.

Kluane, Indian village, SW Yukon, Canada, near Alaska border, on Kluane L., at foot of St. Elias Mts., 120 mi/ 193 km W of Whitehorse, and on Alaska Highway; 61°02′N 138°24′W. Center of Kluane Game Sanctuary (est. 1943).

Kluane Lake (□ 184 sq mi/477 sq km), SW Yukon, Canada, near Alaska border, at foot of St. Elias Mts., 120 mi/ 193 km W of Whitehorse; 61°15′N 138°44′W. It is 60 mi/ 97 km long, 1 mi/2 km–6 mi/10 km wide; drains N into Yukon R.

Kluane National Park (kloo-AIN), c.8,500 sq mi/ 22,000 sq km, SW Yukon Territory, Canada, bet. Kluane L. and the B.C. and Alaska borders; est. 1972. Located in the St. Elias Mts., the park contains some of Canada's highest mts. (including Mt. Logan, the nation's highest peak) and one of the world's largest non-polar systems of ice fields. Great variety of wildlife.

Klukwan (KLOOK-wahn), village, SE Alaska, on Chilkat R. and 20 mi/32 km NW of Haines, on Haines Highway; 59°24′N 135°54′W. Area contains iron ore.

Klutina River (KLOO-tuh-nuh), S Alaska; rises in Chugach Mts. near 61°44′N 145°45′W; flows 60 mi/97 km NE, through Klutina L. (17 mi/27 km long), to Copper R. at Cooper Center.

Knapp, village (1990 pop. 419), Dunn co., W Wis., 12 mi/ 19 km WNW of Menomonie; 44°57′N 92°04′W. In dairying area. Creamery; cheese.

Knapp Creek, village (1990 pop. 150), Cattaraugus co., W N.Y., 7 mi/11.3 km SW of Olean. In oil-producing area on Pa. line.

Knee Lake, NE Man., Canada, on Hayes R., 50 mi/ 80 km long, 5 mi/8 km wide; 55°N 94°40′W.

Knierim (NEAR-um), town (1990 pop. 71), Calhoun co., central Iowa, 10 mi/16 km ENE of Rockwell City; 42°27′N 94°27′W.

Knife Lake, Lake co., NE Minn. and Rainy Lake dist., W Ont., 35 mi/56 km NE of Ely, in chain of lakes on Can.-U.S. border; U.S. part is in Superior Natl. Forest

(Boundary Waters Canoe Area); Can. part is in Quetico Provincial Park; 10 mi/16 km long, average width 1 mi/ 1.6 km; 48°06′N 91°13′W. Fed from Ottertrack L. to NE through short stream; drains into Seed L. to SW through short stream.

Knife River, N.Dak.; rises in Killdeer Mts., Dunn co.,W central N.Dak.; flows E 120 mi/193 km to Missouri R. near Stanton; 47°20′N 103°10′W.

Knife River Indian Villages National Historic Site, at Stanton, Mercer co., central N.Dak., on Missouri R. Authorized 1974, 2 sq mi/5.2 sq km. Ruins of villages of Hidasta and Mandan Native Americans; last occupied, 1845.

Knight Inlet, SW B.C., Canada, arm (75 mi/121 km long, 1 mi/2km–4 mi/6 km wide) of Queen Charlotte Strait, opposite Vancouver Isl.; receives Klinaklini R. at head.

Knight Island 1 S Alaska, in Prince William Sound, E of Kenai Peninsula, 40 mi/64 km SE of Whittier (25 mi/ 40 km long, 2 mi/3.2 km–9 mi/14.5 km wide); 60°20′N 147°44′W. **2** (4 mi/6.4 km long), SE Alaska, in Yakutat Bay, 10 mi/16 km NW of Yakutat; 59°43′N 139°34′W.

Knight Island Passage, S Alaska, SW entrance to Prince William Sound, bet. Knight Isl. (E) and Kenai Peninsula and Chenega Isl. (W); 20 mi/32 km long, 3 mi/4.8 km–5 mi/8 km wide; 60°18′N 148°00′W.

Knightdale, town (1990 pop. 1,884), Wake co., central N.C., suburb 8 mi/12.9 km E of Raleigh, near Nuese R.; 35°47′N 78°29′W. Agr. area (cotton, tobacco, grain; poultry, livestock). Mfg. (sheet metal fabricating, motor controls, transformers, crushed granite).

Knights Landing, uninc. village, Yolo co., central Calif., 18 mi/29 km NW of Sacramento and on Sacramento R. (bridged here). Fruits, nuts, grain, sugar beets.

Knightstown, town (1990 pop. 2,048), Henry co., E central Ind., on Big Blue R. and 34 mi/55 km E of Indianapolis; 39°48′N 85°32′W. In livestock and grain area; mfg. Laid out 1827.

Knightsville, town (1990 pop. 740), Clay co., W Ind., just E of Brazil; 39°32′N 87°05′W. In agr. and bituminous-coal area. Residential community.

Knightville Reservoir, Hampshire co., W central Mass., on Westfield R., 11 mi/18 km W of Northampton; 43°18′N 72°52′W. Max. capacity 64,000 acre-ft. Formed by Knightville Dam (145 ft/44 m high), built (1941) by Army Corps of Engineers for flood control. Also known as Dry Reservoir.

Knik (kuh-NIK), village (1990 pop. 272), S Alaska, on W side of Knik Arm, 18 mi/29 km N of Anchorage; 61°27′N 149°44′W. Tourism.

Knik Arm (kuh-NIK), N arm (30 mi/48 km long, 2 mi/ 3.2 km–6 mi/9.7 km wide) of Cook Inlet, S Alaska; extends NE from Cook Inlet, just N of Anchorage.

Knippa (KAH-nip-pah), uninc. village (1990 pop. 360), Uvalde co., SW Texas, 10 mi/16 km NE of Uvalde, on Frio R. Cattle ranching, also sheep, goats; cotton, vegetables. Crushed stone, sand and gravel.

Knob Hill, village, El Paso co., E central Colo., 2 mi/ 3.2 km E of downtown Colorado Springs. Part of Colorado Springs.

Knob Noster (nahb NAHS-tuhr), city (1990 pop. 2,261), Johnson co., W central Mo., 10 mi/16 km E of Warrensburg; 38°46′N 93°34′W. Grain; livestock, egg processing. Whiteman Air Force Base (former Minuteman missile site, now bomber base) 3 mi/4.8 km S. Knob Noster State Park to SW.

Knobel (NO-buhl), village (1990 pop. 317), Clay co., extreme NE Ark., 19 mi/31 km NNW of Paragould; 36°19′N 90°35′W. Mfg. (hardwood, lumber). Dave Donaldson-Black R. Wildlife management area to NW.

Knobly Mountain (NAHB-lee), c.50 mi/80 km, Mineral and Grant cos., NE W.Va., a ridge of the Appalachian Mts., in E Panhandle; from North Branch of the Potomac R., opposite Cumberland, Md., extends SW to a point W of Petersburg, Va., rising to 2,000 ft/610 m–3,000 ft/914 m, with knoblike summits to over 3,000 ft/ 914 m.

Knott, county (☐ 353 sq mi/914 sq km; 1990 pop. 17,906), E Ky.; ⊙ Hindman; 37°21′N 82°57′W. Drained by Carr Fork of Kentucky R. and Troublesome and Buckhorn creeks. Bituminous-coal mining and agr. (livestock; some tobacco) area, in Cumberland foothills. Part of Robinson Forest Preserve (Univ. of Ky.) in NW. Carr Fork L. reservoir in S. Formed 1884.

Knott, uninc. village (1990 pop. 685), Howard co., W central Texas, 14 mi/23 km NW of Big Spring. Oil and natural gas. Agr. area (cattle; cotton, vegetables, black-eyed peas).

Knowles (NOLZ), village (1990 pop. 18), Beaver co., E Okla. Panhandle, 19 mi/31 km ENE of Beaver, midway bet. Cimarron R. (N) and Canadian R. (S); 36°52′N 100°11′W. In wheat and livestock area; mfg. (steel fabrication).

Knowlton, village, ⊙ Brome co., S Que., Canada, at S end of Brome L., 16 mi/26 km SE of Granby; 45°13′N 72°31′W. Dairying center; resort.

Knox 1 county (☐ 719 sq mi/1,862 sq km; 1990 pop. 56,393), NW central Ill.; ⊙ Galesburg; 40°56′N 90°12′W. Agr. (corn, wheat, soybeans; livestock; dairy prods.). Clay, gravel. Diversified mfg., chiefly at Galesburg. Drained by Spoon R. and Pope and Henderson creeks. Formed 1825. **2** county (☐ 524 sq mi/ 1,357 sq km; 1990 pop. 39,884), SW Ind.; ⊙ Vincennes; 38°41′N 87°25′W. Bounded W by Wabash R. (here forming Ill. boundary), E by West Fork of White R., and S by White R. Drained by Maria Creek, Deschee R., and Pond Creek. Agr. area (fruits, vegetables, watermelons, grain); also produces oil, natural gas, bituminous coal, sand and gravel. Mfg. at Vincennes; fruit-packing plants, nurseries, creameries. Indiana Territory State Memorial and George Rogers Clark Natl. Memorial (25.5 acres/10.3 ha) at Vincennes. Purdue U. Southwest Agr. Center near Emison; White Oak State Fishing Area near center of co. Cypress Pond, oxbow lake of Wabash R., in SW corner. Indiana's first county, formed 1790. **3** county (☐ 387 sq mi/1,002 sq km; 1990 pop. 29,676), SE Ky.; ⊙ Barbourville; 36°53′N 83°51′W. In the Cumberland Mts.; drained by Cumberland R. and Stinking Creek. Includes Dr. Thomas Walker State Historic Site in SW. Bituminous-coal mining; agr. (corn, hay, burley tobacco; cattle); timber, oil wells. Mfg. at Corbin and Barbourville. Formed 1799. **4** county (☐ 1,142 sq mi/2,958 sq km; 1990 pop. 36,310), S Maine, on Penobscot Bay; ⊙ Rockland; 44°06′N 69°07′W. Drained by St. George R. Coastal and isl. area has resorts, fishing, shipping of seafood, cement, and lime. Inland agr. and lake area produces poultry; apples. Resorts. L. St. George State Park. Formed 1860. **5** county (☐ 512 sq mi/1,326 sq km; 1990 pop. 4,482), NE Mo.; ⊙ Edina; 40°08′N 92°09′W. Drained by North Fork of Salt R. and Middle and South Fabius rivers. Corn, wheat, hay, soybeans; hogs; lumber; limestone quarry. Formed 1845. **6** county (☐ 1,139 sq mi/ 2,950 sq km; 1990 pop. 9,534) NE Nebr.; ⊙ Center; 42°38′N 97°53′W. Agr. area bounded N by Missouri R. (dammed [Gavins Point Dam] in NE corner of co. to form Lewis and Clark L.) and S.Dak.; drained by Niobrara R. Cattle, hogs; corn, wild hay, alfalfa, soybeans; dairying. Nivbrara State Park in NW; Lewis and Clark L. State Recreation Area in NE; Santer Indian Reservation in N central part of co. **7** county (☐ 532 sq mi/ 1,378 sq km; 1990 pop. 47,473), central Ohio; ⊙ Mount Vernon; 40°24′N 82°22′W. Drained by Kokosing and Mohican rivers and North Fork of Licking R. Mostly in the Glaciated Plain physiographic region, the NE portion in the Unglaciated Plain region. Agr. area (sheep, hogs, poultry; corn); mfg. at Mount Vernon (engines, air and gas compressors); also millwork, motor vehicle equipment and parts, metal foil and leaf. Formed 1808. **8** county (☐ 517 sq mi/1,339 sq km; 1990 pop. 335,749), E Tenn.; ⊙ Knoxville; 36°00′N 83°57′W. In Great Appalachian Valley; drained by Tennessee R. (here formed by junction of Holston and French Broad rivers); bounded SW by Clinch R. Includes part of Fort Loudoun Reservoir. Livestock; dairying; agr. (corn, hay, tobacco, fruits). Coal mines, limestone and marble quarries, clay pits. Industry at Knoxville. Formed 1792. **9** county (☐ 855 sq mi/2,214 sq km; 1990 pop. 4,837), N Texas; ⊙ Benjamin; 33°36′N 99°44′W. Plains area, bounded N in part by N Wichita R., drained by Brazos R., North and South forks of the Wichita. Irrigated agr. and livestock-raising (cotton, grain, sorghum, wheat, vegetables; cattle). Oil and gas. Formed 1858.

Knox, city (1990 pop. 3,705), ⊙ Starke co., NW Ind., on Yellow R. and 33 mi/53 km SW of South Bend; 41°17′N 86°37′W. In agr. area producing chiefly mint and onions; mfg. (automotive stampings, paper containers, molded plastics, timber prods., wood and aluminum windows). Bass Lake State Fish Hatchery nearby to SE. Laid out 1851.

Knox, village (1990 pop. 45), Benson co., N central N.Dak., 15 mi/24 km E of Rugby; 48°20′N 99°41′W. Dairy; livestock; wheat, oats. RR junction of spur to Wolford to E (at York).

Knox, borough (1990 pop. 1,182), Clarion co., W central Pa., 8 mi/12.9 km WNW of Clarion. Agr. (corn, hay, potatoes; livestock; dairying); mfg. (corrugated boxes); bituminous coal; timber. Name changed from Edenburg to its post office name in 1933.

Knox, Cape, W B.C., Canada, NW extremity of Graham Isl., on the Pacific, at SW end of Dixon Entrance; 54°11′N 132°54′W.

Knox City 1 town (1990 pop. 262), Knox co., NE Mo., bet. Middle and South Fabius rivers, 9 mi/14.5 km E of Edina; 40°08′N 92°00′W. Grain; livestock; lumber. **2** town (1990 pop. 1,440), Knox co., N Texas, c.80 mi/ 129 km WSW of Wichita Falls, near Brazos R.; 33°25′N 99°49′W. In cotton, grain; cattle area. Inc. 1916.

Knox, Fort, Ky.: see FORT KNOX.

Knoxville 1 city (1990 pop. 3,243), Knox co., NW central Ill., 4 mi/6.4 km SE of Galesburg; 40°54′N 90°17′W. In agr. area; dairy prods. Inc. 1832. Formerly the county seat. **2** city (1990 pop. 8,232), ⊙ Marion co., S central Iowa, 33 mi/53 km ESE of Des Moines, near Whitebreast Creek; 41°19′N 93°05′W. Ships coal and livestock; mfg. (clothing, dairy and meat prods., printing, industrial tapes, feed, concrete blocks). Limestone quarries nearby. Has large U.S. veterans hosp. Red Rock Reservoir (Des Moines R.) to N and NE. Settled 1845; inc. 1854. **3** city (1990 pop. 165,121), ⊙ Knox co., E Tenn., on the Tennessee R., 100 mi/161 km NE of Chattanooga, in the Great Smoky Mountains; 36°00′N 83°57′W. A port of entry, it is a trade and shipping center for a farm, bituminous-coal, limestone, and marble area. Its industries include meatpacking, tobacco marketing, and the mfg. of seat belts, clothing, electronics, mobile homes, chemicals, textiles, and marble, wood, and metal prods. Tourism adds to the economy. The city is surrounded by mountains and lakes, and the Great Smoky Mts. Natl. Park and several state parks are nearby. A house was built on this site c.1785, followed by a fort and then a town, named for Gen. Henry Knox. Knoxville was the capital of the Territory of the United States South of the R. Ohio from 1792 to 1796 and twice (1796–1812, 1817–1818) served as the state capital. During the Civil War the area was torn by divided loyalties; Federals occupied the city in Sept. 1863, and successfully withstood a Confederate siege (Nov.–Dec., 1863). The city is the seat of the Univ. of Tennessee, Knoxville Col., and the Tennessee School for the Deaf. It was also the site of the 1982 World's Fair, which introduced permanent new structures, such as the Sunsphere and the Tennessee Amphitheatre. Knoxville is hq. of the Tennessee Valley Authority. Norris Dam, from which the city procures its power, is nearby. Confederate Memorial Hall, the William Blount Mansion (1792), a replica of the old fort, Chisholm's Tavern (1792), and many other historic bldgs. Inc. 1876.

Knoxville 1 agr. village, ⊙ Crawford co., central Ga., 20 mi/32 km WSW of Macon; 32°43′N 83°59′W. **2** village, Frederick co., W Md., on the Potomac, 15 mi/ 24 km WSW of Frederick. Boasting of a select school for young ladies from 1864 to 1879, Knoxville's greatest claim to fame is being the only place in the local polling district where liquor was allowed in the election of 1904.

Knoxville, borough (1990 pop. 589), Tioga co., N Pa., 15 mi/24 km NNW of Wellsboro, on Cowanesque R., at mouth of Troups Creek, near N.Y. state line. Agr. (corn, hay; dairying); mfg. (feeds, ornamental irons, magnet assembly).

Kobuk (KO-buhk), village (1990 pop. 69), NW Alaska, on Kobuk R. and 6 mi/9.7 km E of Shungnak; 66°54′N 156°54′W.

Kobuk River (KO-buhk), NW Alaska; rises in Brooks Range near 67°05′N 154°15′W; flows c.300 mi/483 km W, past Kobuk, Shungnak, Kiana, and Noorvik, to Hotham Inlet 30 mi/48 km ESE of Kotzebue.

Kobuk Valley National Park (KO-buhk) (2,735 sq mi/7,084 sq km), NW Alaska; authorized 1980. A wildlife preserve N of the Arctic Circle; archaeological remnants of 10,000 years of human habitation.

Kobuta Station, uninc. village, Beaver co., W Pa., 4 mi/6.4 km WSW of Monaca, on Ohio R., at mouth of Raccoon Creek; 40°39′N 80°21′W. Synthetic rubber. Nuclear power plant to W.

Koch Peak, Mont.: see MADISON RANGE.

Kodiak, city (1990 pop. 6,365), NE Kodiak Isl., S Alaska, on Chiniak Bay of Gulf of Alaska; 57°47′N 152°24′W. Major fishing port; beef cattle; hunting; numerous canneries. Connected to Seward and Homer by Alaska Ferry system. St. Herman's Orthodox seminary. Russians under Shelekhov here moved (1792) their main settlement, originally established at Three Saints Bay, named it St. Paul's Harbor and later Kadiak or Kodiak. Hq. of Rus.-Amer. Company before it was moved to Sitka. In World War II Fort Greeley, major army supply base, was built nearby. Women's Bay coast guard base is 10 mi/16 km SW.

Kodiak Island, borough (□ 6,463 sq mi/16,739 sq km; 1990 pop. 13,309), S Alaska, includes the E part of the Alaska Peninsula, Kodiak Isl., and adjacent isls. (notably Afognak and Shuyak isls. to the NE and the Trinity Isls. to the S). Main town is Kodiak. Part of Katmai Natl. Park and parts of Becharof and Alaska Peninsula Natl. Wildlife Reserves to W; Kodiak Natl. Wildlife Reserve in center of Kodiak Isl., part of Chugach Natl. Forest on Afognak Isl.; Fort Abercrombie State Historical Park at Kodiak. Kodiak Indian Reservation in W part of Kodiak. Fishing; timber; furs.

Kodiak Island (□ 11,845 sq mi/30,679 sq km; 1990 pop. 13,309), off S Alaska, separated from the Alaska Peninsula by Shelikof Strait; 57°42′N 153°46′W. Alaska's largest isl. (c.100 mi/160 km long and 10 mi/16 km–60 mi/97 km wide), Kodiak is mountainous and heavily forested in the N and E; the native grasses in the S offer good pasturage for beef cattle and sheep. The isl. has many ice-free, deeply penetrating bays that provide sheltered anchorages and transportation routes. The Kodiak bear and the Kodiak king crab are native to the isl. Most of the isl. is a natl. wildlife refuge. In 1912 the eruption of Mt. Katmai on the mainland blanketed the isl. with volcanic ash, causing widespread destruction and loss of life. Explored in 1763 by Rus. fur trader Stepan Glotov, the isl. was the scene of the 1st permanent Rus. settlement in Alaska, founded by Grigori Shelekhov, a fur trader, on Three Saints Bay in 1784. The settlement was moved to Kodiak village in 1792 and became the center of Rus. fur trading. The largest town on the isl. is Kodiak (1990 pop. 6,365). Salmon fishing is a major occupation. Livestock farms, numerous canneries, and hunting. Many Aleut settlements and Orthodox churches.

Kofa Mountains (KO-fah) (4,828 ft/1,472 m), Yuma and La Paz cos., SW Ariz., N of Gila R.; extend c.20 mi/32 km NE from Castle Dome Mts.; rise to their highest point in W tip. In Kofa Natl. Wildlife Refuge.

Kohala Peninsula (ko-HAH-lah), N Hawaii isl., Hawaii co., Hawaii. Flanked by Pacific Ocean to NE and SW; Alenuihaha Channel, separating Hawaii and Maui, off NW tip. Rich in relics of anc. Hawaii. Kohala Mts. rise to 5,489 ft/1,673 m; large Kohala Forest Reserve occupies lower E quarter of peninsula; includes small Paoakalani Mokupuku and Paalaea isls., seabird sanctuaries; main town is Hawi, near N end.

Kohler, town (1990 pop. 1,817), Sheboygan co., E Wis., suburb 2 mi/3.2 km W of Sheboygan, on the Sheboygan R.; 43°44′N 87°46′W. Mfg. (plumbing fixtures). The Kohler plumbing-fixtures plant here, which still produces its famous stainless steel and porcelain prods., has been the scene of some of the longest and most

bitter labor disputes in U.S. history. The last strike began in 1954 and ended in 1962. Inc. 1912.

Kokadjo (kah-KAHJ-o), resort village, Piscataquis co., central Maine, on First Roach Pond (formerly Kokadjo L.), 37 mi/60 km NNW of Dover-Foxcroft. Hunting, fishing.

Kokanee Peak (ko-KA-nee) (9,400 ft/2,865 m), SE B.C., Canada, in Selkirk Mts., 18 mi/29 km NNE of Nelson; 49°45′N 117°08′W.

Koko Head, promontory and peak (642 ft/196 m), SE Oahu isl., Honolulu co., Hawaii, 9 mi/14.5 km ESE of Honolulu, E of Maunalua Bay; Nonoula and Ihehelauakea craters to NE and E; Koko Crater is 2.5 mi/4 km to NE (botanic garden to N of crater) and Kohelepelepe peak (1,208 ft/368 m) is 2 mi/3.2 km to NE. Both overlook Halona Blowhole, water spout formed by incoming ocean waves. All of these features are within Koko Head Regional Park.

Kokolik River (ko-KO-lik), c.150 mi/241 km long, NW Alaska; rises in NW Brooks Range near 68°35′N 162°W, flows N to Chukchi Sea at 69°52′N 162°43′W.

Kokomo, city (1990 pop. 44,962), ⊙ Howard co., N central Ind., on Wildcat Creek; 40°29′N 86°08′W. Mfg. (glass, motor vehicle parts, metal prods., plastics, food and beverages, plumbing fixtures). The 1st commercially built automobile was invented and tested in Kokomo in 1894 by Elwood Haynes. Of interest is the Elwood Haynes Mus. Indiana Univ. has a campus at Kokomo; branch of Ind. Vocational and Technical Col. (Ivy Tech). Grissom Air Base is nearby to N. RR junction. Inc. 1865.

Kokosing River (ko-KO-sing), c.50 mi/80 km long, cen tral Ohio; rises in Morrow co., flows generally SE, past Chesterville, Mt. Vernon, and Gambier, joining Mohican R. to form Walhonding R. 16 mi/26 km NW of Coshocton; 40°21′N 82°09′W.

Kokrines (KAHK-rins), village, W Alaska, on Yukon R., 80 mi/129 km WSW of Tanana, in Kokrines Hills.

Koksoak River (KAHK-so-ahk), 90 mi/145 km long, N Que., Canada; formed by Kaniapiskau and Larch rivers, 50 mi/80 km SW of Kuujjuaq (Fort Chimo), flows NE and N, past Kuujjuaq, to Ungava Bay 30 mi/48 km N of Fort Chimo; 3 mi/5 km wide at mouth.

Koliganek (ko-li-GAH-nek), village (1990 pop. 181), SW Alaska, on Nushagak R., 65 mi/105 km NE of Dillingham; 59°49′N 157°26′W.

Koloa (KO-LO-ah), town (1990 pop. 1,791), SE Kauai, Kauai co., Hawaii, 7 mi/11.3 km WSW of Lihue, 1.5 mi/2.4 km N of S coast at point where Waihohonu and Omao streams join to form Waikomo Stream; 21°54′N 159°27′W. Koloa Landing at coast at mouth of Waikomo; Koloa Mill, Hawaii's oldest (1837) sugar plantation, 1 mi/1.6 km to E; Lihue-Koloa Forest Reserve to NW; Natl. Tropical Botanical Garden to W at Lawai; Waita Reservoir to NE; Mauka Reservoir to N; Poipa Beach Park at Poipu and SE; Spouting Horn, a coastal water spout, is at Spouting Horn Beach Park to SW. Oldest Catholic church in Hawaii.

Kolob Canyon, Utah: see KOLOB TERRACE.

Kolob Terrace (KO-lahb), deeply dissected plateau, primarily in NE Washington co., SW Utah, extends N into Iron co., extending W from Markagunt Plateau and S from Cedar City; bounded W by jagged 3,000-ft/914-m escarpment. Rises to max. elev. of 9,000 ft/2,743 m in N; includes colorful Kolob Canyon (1,500 ft/457 m–2,500 ft/762m) and Horse Pasture Plateau in S, both part of Zion Natl. Park. Also called Kolob Plateau.

Kona (KO-nah), district, S and central part of Hawaii isl.'s W coast, Hawaii co., Hawaii; c.50 mi/80 km long. Includes Hawaii's coffee belt. The Kona coast, with fine deep-sea fishing offshore, is a favorite tourist spot. Growth of tourism has led to development of formerly agr.-oriented towns of Kailua-Kona, Captain Cook, Holualoa, Honaunau, among others. On Kealakelua Bay stands a monument to Eng. explorer Capt. James Cook, killed here by natives in 1779. Kailua Bay to the N was the landing site in 1820 of the 1st U.S. missionaries to Hawaii.

Konahuanui (KO-NAH-HOO-ah-NOO-ee), peak

(3,105 ft/946 m), E Oahu, Hawaii, of Koolau Range. Unnamed point nearby reaches 3,150 ft/960 m.

Konawa (KAHN-uh-wah), town (1990 pop. 1,508), Seminole co., central Okla., 15 mi/24 km NNW of Ada; 34°57′N 96°45′W. Trade center and shipping point for agr. (corn, alfalfa, peanuts; livestock) and oil and natural gas area; mfg. (orthopedic devices). L. Konawa reservoir to NE.

Konganevik Point (kon-gah-NAI-vik), NE Alaska, on Camden Bay of Beaufort Sea, 100 mi/161 km ESE of Beechey Point; 70°02′N 145°11′W. Inuit settlement here.

Konocti, Mount, Lake co., NW Calif., peak (3,967 ft/1,209 m) on W shore of Clear L., c.80 mi/129 km N of San Francisco.

Koocanusa Lake (koo-kuh-NOO-suh), reservoir, Kootenai R. (*Kootenay* in Canada), NW Mont., and SE B.C., largely within Kootenai Natl. Forest in Mont.; c.85 mi/137 km long, including 40 mi/64 km N extension into Canada, 1 mi/1.6 km–2 mi/3.2 km wide. Formed by multipurpose Libby Dam (420 ft/128 m high) in Lincoln co. (Mont.), 10 mi/16 km E of Libby. Tobacco R. enters from E in Mont.; Elk R. enters from NE in B.C. Bounded by the Purcell Range to the W, and the Salish Mts. to the E.

Koochiching (KOO-chi-cheeng), county (□ 3,154 sq mi/8,169 sq km; 1990 pop. 16,299), N Minn.; ⊙ International Falls; 48°15′N 93°46′W. Bounded N by Can. (Ont.) border, formed mainly by Rainy R. and Rainy L., in NE; drained by Big Fork and Little Fork rivers. Agr. area (alfalfa; cattle; some dairying); timber; some resorts in NE. Lumber and paper milling at International Falls. Area is noted for its record cold temp. Includes much of Nett L. and Nett L. Indian Reservation in SE. Large Koochiching State Forest covers much of SE part of co.; Pine Isl. State Forest covers most of W part; Smokey Bear State Forest is in N; part of Voyageurs Natl. Park in NE corner. Formed 1906.

Koolau Range (KO-o-LOU), mountain chain, extending c.30 mi/48 km NW-SE, nearly the length of Oahu isl., Honolulu co., Hawaii; rises to 3,105 ft/946 m in Konahuanui. It is cut by 2 scenic passes, Nuuanu Pali (State Highway 61, Pali Highway to Kailua) and another at the head of Kaliki Valley (State Highway 63, Likelike Highway to Kaneohe), which shorten the route bet. E and W Oahu; a 3d route across range is Interstate H3, under construction to NW of Honolulu; protected by Kahuka and Kawailoa forest reserves (N), Ewa Forest Reserve (center), Honolulu Watershed Forest Reserve (S), others; Kahana Valley and Sacred Falls State Parks to NE. Also known as Koolau Mts.

Koontz Lake, village (1990 pop. 1,615), Starke co., N central Ind., 10 mi/16 km NW of Plymouth, on Koontz L.; 41°25′N 86°29′W. Recreation.

Koosharem, village (1990 pop. 266), Sevier co., central Utah, 19 mi/32 km SE of Richfield, on Otter Creek; 38°30′N 111°52′W. Agr. (cattle). Elev. 6,914 ft/2,107 m. Site of treaty conference bet. Native Americans and settlers, 1873. Fish L. and Johnson reservoirs to NE; parts of Fishlake Natl. Forest to W and NE. Koosharem Reservoir (Cutter Creek) to N. Sevier Plateau SSW.

Kooskia (KOOS-kee-uh), village (1990 pop. 692), Idaho co., W central Idaho, 12 mi/19 km SE of Nezperce, at junction of Middle Fork and South Fork of Clearwater R., forming Clearwater R., in SE part of Nez Perce Indian Reservation; 46°08′N 115°58′W. Agr.; lumber; sheep, cattle; mfg. (lumber prods.). Loscha Historic Ranger Station 47 mi/76 km ENE. Nearby are Clearwater (NE) and Nez Perce (SE) natl. forests. Clearwater Mts. to SE; Nez Perce Natl. Historical Park (East Kamiah Site) to N.

Kootenai, county (□ 1,315 sq mi/3,406 sq km; 1990 pop. 69,795), N Idaho, in Panhandle Region; ⊙ Coeur d'Alene; 47°41′N 116°31′W. Rolling, wooded area bordering on Wash. (W), watered by Coeur d'Alene L. and Spokane and Coeur d'Alene rivers. Spokane (Wash.), 15 mi/24 km W of state line, has partially influenced co.'s growth. Lumbering, agr. (wheat, oats, alfalfa; cattle); mfg. (furniture). Old Mission at Gataldo (1853) Historical State Park in SE. Includes part of Coeur d'Alene Mts., in Coeur d'Alene Natl. Forest in E, including Fourth of July Canyon (Coeur d'Alene R.). Part of Coeur d'Alene Indian Reservation in S. Farragut State Park, at S end of L. Pend Oreille in NE corner; several small lakes in co. Formed 1864.

Kootenai (KOOT-en-ee), village (1990 pop. 327), Bonner co., N Idaho, 3 mi/4.8 km NE of Sandpoint, 1 mi/1.6 km E of Penderay, and on N shore of L. Pend Oreille; 48°19′N 116°31′W. Schweitzer Basin Ski Area to NW; Kaniksu Natl. Forest to E.

Kootenai (KOO-tin-ai), river, 407 mi/655 km long, NW U.S. and SW Canada; rises in the Rocky Mts., SE B.C.; flows S into NW Mont., NW through N Idaho, then N back into Canada, through Kootenay L. (64 mi/103 km long; 191 sq mi/495 sq km), an expansion of the river, before joining the Columbia R. at Castlegar. The river is used to generate hydroelectricity. The Can. name is spelled Kootenay.

Kootenay Lake, Canada: see KOOTENAI.

Kootenay National Park (□ 543 sq mi/1,406 sq km), SE B.C., SW Canada, in the Rocky Mts. near Kootenay L. Contains high peaks, glaciers, deep canyons, and hot springs. The Banff-Windermere Highway crosses the park. Est. 1920.

Kootenay River, U.S. and Canada: see KOOTENAI.

Kopomá (ko-po-MAH), town (1990 pop. 1,433), Yucatán, SE Mexico, 28 mi/45 km SW of Mérida; 20°39′N 89°54′W. Henequen, corn, tropical fruit.

Koppel (KAH-puhl), borough (1990 pop. 1,024), Beaver co., W Pa., 3 mi/4.8 km SW of Ellwood City, near Beaver R. Agr. (corn, hay, alfalfa; dairying); mfg. (fabricated metal prods., wood prods.).

Kopperston, uninc. village (1990 pop. 500), Wyoming co., S W.Va., 19 mi/31 km W of Beckley. In coal and gas region. RR terminus. Mfg. (coal processing).

Koronis, Lake (kuh-RO-nis), Stearns co., SE central Minn., extends S into Meeker co., 2 mi/3.2 km S of Paynesville, 21 mi/34 km NE of Willmar; 4 mi/6.4 km long, 3 mi/4.8 km wide. Boating and fishing resorts. Fed (from NE and Rice L.) and drained (SE, through dam) by North Fork Crow R.; both inflow and outflow are at SE end. Paynesville Municipal Park on N shore. Sometimes known as Cedar L.

Korovin Volcano (KOR-ro-vin) (5,030 ft/1,533 m), on E Atka Isl., Aleutian Isls., SW Alaska; 52°23′N 174°11′W. Active.

Kortes Dam (kor-TEZ), Carbon co., S central Wyo., on N. Platte R., 35 mi/56 km NE of Rawlins; 42°11′N 106°52′W. Minor reservoir extends 4 mi/6.4 km S to Seminoe Dam: headwaters of Pathfinder Reservoir below dam (N). Completed 1950.

Kosciusko (kuh-see-UH-sko), county (□ 554 sq mi/1,435 sq km; 1990 pop. 65,294), N Ind.; ⊙ Warsaw; 41°14′N 85°52′W. Center of NE Ind.'s lake region; includes lakes Wawasee and Winona. More than 20 natural lakes, glacial in origin, distributed across co. from NE corner to SW corner; largest is L. Wawasee. Drained by Tippecanoe and Eel rivers and small Turkey Creek. Agr. (poultry, hogs, cattle; dairy prods.; corn, soybeans, vegetables); timber. Mfg. at Warsaw. Wawasee State Fishing Area and Tri-County State Fish and Wildlife Area in NE. Formed 1835.

Kosciusko, town (1990 pop. 6,986), ⊙ Attala co., central Miss., 58 mi/93 km NE of Jackson, near Yockanookany R.; 33°03′N 89°35′W. RR spur terminus. Cotton, corn, soybeans; cattle; dairying; timber; light mfg. Kosciusko Mus. Natchez Trace (Natl.) Parkway passes to SE. Settled in early 1830s on old Natchez Trace; inc. 1836.

Kosciusko Island (kah-zee-UH-sko), SE Alaska, in Alexander Archipelago, W of Prince of Wales Isl., c.40 mi/64 km NW of Craig; 25 mi/40 km long, 5 mi/8 km–12 mi/19 km wide; 56°03′N 133°30′W.

Koshkonong (kosh-kuh-NAWNG), town (1990 pop. 198), Oregon co., S Mo., in the Ozarks near Spring R., 15 mi/24 km SW of Alton; 36°35′N 91°39′W. Grain; livestock. Wood pallets, ties, lumber. Grand Gulf State Park to S.

Koshkonong (KAHSH-kah-nahng), village, Jefferson

co., S Wis., 12 mi/19 km NNE of Janesville, on S shore of L. Koshkonong.

Koshkonong, Lake, reservoir, Rock co., SE Wis., on Rock R., 27 mi/43 km SE of Madison; 42°49′N 89°05′W. Max. capacity 107,000 acre-ft. Formed by Indian Lake Dam (13 ft/4 m high), built (1932) for recreation.

Kosse, village (1990 pop. 505), Limestone co., E central Texas, 35 mi/56 km SE of Waco; 31°18′N 96°37′W. In farm area (cotton, corn; cattle); silica sand and kaolin clay. Twin Oak Reservoir to SE.

Kossuth, county (□ 974 sq mi/2,523 sq km; 1990 pop. 18,591), N Iowa, on Minn. line; ⊙ Algona; 43°12′N 94°12′W. Largest co. in land area in Iowa; part of Iowa lakes district. Rolling prairie agr. area (cattle, hogs, poultry; corn, oats, soybeans) drained by East Des Moines R., Middle Branch Blue Earth R., and Union Slough. Has sand and gravel pits. Ambrose A. Call State Park SW of Algona; Union Slough Natl. Wildlife Refuge at center. Widespread flooding in 1993. Formed 1851.

Kossuth (kah-SOOTH), village (1990 pop. 245), Alcorn co., NE Miss., 8 mi/12.9 km WSW of Corinth; 34°52′N 88°38′W. In agr. area (cotton, corn, soybeans; cattle).

Kotcho Lake (□ 90 sq mi/233 sq km; 15 mi/24 km long, 1 mi/2km–7 mi/11 km wide), NE B.C., Canada, near Alta. border; 59°04′N 121°09′W. Drains S into Hay R.

Kotlik (KOT-lik), village (1990 pop. 461), W Alaska, on SW shore of Norton Sound, 55 mi/89 km SW of St. Michael, at edge of Yukon R. delta; 63°02′N 163°33′W.

Kotzebue (KAHT-se-boo), city (1990 pop. 2,751), NW Alaska, on Kotzebue Sound at the tip of Baldwin Peninsula; 66°53′N 162°39′W. It is one of the largest settlements of Inuit (Eskimos) in Alaska. A regional trade and supply center with local govt. offices, Kotzebue has a tourist industry. Fishing is economically important. The city, set on a tundra, began in the 18th cent. as an Eskimo trading post for arctic Alaska and part of Siberia; reindeer station est. 1897. Regional center for Noatak, Kobuk, and Selawik river valleys. Univ. of Alaska Extension Center. NANA Mus. of the Arctic, owned by native Inuit corporation. Red Dog Zinc Mine to N. Inc. 1958.

Kotzebue Sound (KAHT-se-boo), NW Alaska, arm of Chukchi Sea, on N side of Seward Peninsula, bounded E by Baldwin Peninsula; 100 mi/161 km long, 70 mi/113 km wide; 66°40′N 163° W. Kotzebue, Kiwalik, and Deering villages on shores. Eschscholtz Bay is SE arm. Discovered and named 1816 by Count Otto von Kotzebue while searching for Northwest Passage. Knud Rasmussen here completed (1924) overland crossing from Repulse Bay, N.W.T.

Kouchibouguac (koo-shee-buh-KWAK), village, E N.B., Canada, on Kouchibouguac R., near its mouth on Northumberland Strait, 10 mi/16 km NW of Richibucto. Lumbering.

Kouchibouguac National Park (koo-shee-buh-KWAK) (□ 87 sq mi/225 sq km), on Kouchibouguac Bay, E N.B., Canada, near Richibucto; est. 1969. The park's scenic features include lagoons, bays, and offshore sandbars.

Kouchibouguac River, 45 mi/72 km long, in E N.B., Canada; rises 30 mi/48 km S of Newcastle; flows ENE to Northumberland Strait 12 mi/19 km NNW of Richibucto.

Koukdjuak, Great Plain of the, tundra region of SW Baffin Isl., SE Franklin dist., N.W.T., Canada; c.120 mi/193 km long, 60 mi/97 km–90 mi/145 km wide. N boundary is Koukdjuak R. (50 mi/80 km long), which drains Nettilling L. into Foxe Basin.

Kountze, town (1990 pop. 2,056), ⊙ Hardin co., SE Texas, 25 mi/40 km NNW of Beaumont; 30°22′N 94°19′W. Elev. 85 ft/26 m. RR junction; timber area; cattle, hogs, forage crops; egg prods.; mfg. (hardwood lumber, paper cores and shorting). Calls itself (referred to as) the Big Lights in the Big Thicket, surrounded by several units of Big Thicket Natl. Preserve, visitor information station to N. Inc. after 1940.

Kouts, town (1990 pop. 1,603), Porter co., NW Ind.,

11 mi/18 km S of Valparaiso; 41°19′N 87°02′W. Mfg. (animal feed, spring wire). Laid out 1864.

Koyuk (KOI-yuhk), Inuit village (1990 pop. 231), W Alaska, on SE Seward Peninsula, at head of Norton Bay, at mouth of Koyuk R., 130 mi/209 km ENE of Nome; 64°55′N 161°09′W. Sometimes called Inglestat.

Koyuk River (KOI-yuhk), 120 mi/193 km long, W Alaska; rises on Seward Peninsula near 65°25′N 163°00′W; flows SE to Norton Bay at Koyuk.

Koyukuk (KOI-yuh-kuhk), Native Amer. village (1990 pop. 126), W Alaska, on Yukon R. at mouth of Koyukuk R., and 170 mi/274 km W of Tanana; 64°53′N 157°43′W. Airfield.

Koyukuk River (KOI-yuh-kuhk), c.500 mi/805 km long, N central Alaska; rises on S slope of Brooks Range near 67°58′N 151°15′W; flows generally SW, past Bettles, to Yukon R. at Koyukuk. Principal tributaries are Alatna and John rivers. Placer gold deposits on upper course. Partially explored (1855) by H. T. Allen.

Kralendijk (KRAH-luhn-DEIK), chief town of Bonaire, Neth. Antilles, on W inlet of the isl., guarded by Little Bonaire isl., 45 mi/72 km E of Willemstad, Curaçao; 12°09′N 68°16′W. Beachfront harbor. Fishing; shipbuilding; salt, aloe. The region has a desalinization plant, petroleum storage, and a wildlife sanctuary established on former plantations.

Kramer, village (1990 pop. 51), Bottineau co., N N.Dak., near Souris, or Mouse, R., 15 mi/24 km SW of Bottineau; 48°41′N 100°42′W. Large cooperative grain elevator. J. Clark Salyer Natl. Wildlife Refuge to W and S.

Kreamer (KREE-muhr), uninc. village, Snyder co., central Pa., 5 mi/8 km W of Selinsgrove on Middle Creek; 40°48′N 76°57′W. Mfg. of lumber, wood prods.; agr. includes dairying; timber.

Krebs, town (1990 pop. 1,955), Pittsburg co., SE Okla., 3 mi/4.8 km E of McAlester; 34°55′N 95°43′W. In agr. area. Once a coal mine boom town, coal mining has now declined. L. Arrowhead reservoir to E. Settled c.1880, inc. 1903.

Kremlin, village (1990 pop. 243), Garfield co., N Okla., 10 mi/16 km N of Enid; 36°32′N 97°49′W. In agr. area; oil and gas.

Kremmling, town (1990 pop. 1,166), Grand co., N central Colo., on Colorado R., just N of Gore Range, and 80 mi/129 km. WNW of Denver; 40°03′N 106°22′W. Elev. 7,362 ft/2,244 m. Market center for lumber and livestock region; sawmill; mfg. (lumber, food). Routt Natl. Forest nearby; parts of Arapaho Natl. Forest to W, NE, and SE; Williams Fork Reservoir to E.

Krenitzin Islands (kre-NIT-sin), group of 5 islands of the Fox Isls., E Aleutian Isls., SW Alaska, bet. Unalaska (SW) and Unimak (ENE); 54°01′N 165°23′W. Main isls. are Akutan and Akun.

Kress, village (1990 pop. 739), Swisher co., NW Texas, on Llano Estacado, 12 mi/19 km N of Plainview; 34°22′N 101°45′W. Agr. (wheat, cotton, corn, sorghum; cattle).

Krotz Springs, town (1990 pop. 1,285), St. Landry parish, S central La., 20 mi/32 km E of Opelousas, and on Atchafalaya R.; 30°32′N 91°45′W. Shallow-draft port; in oil and natural gas area; gasoline processing. Sherburne State Wildlife Area and Atchafalaya Natl. Wildlife Refuge to SE.

Krum, town (1990 pop. 1,542), Denton co., N Texas, 5 mi/8 km WNW of Denton; 33°16′N 97°13′W. Agr. area (cotton, wheat, sorghum, peanuts; cattle, horses). Light mfg.

Krupp, town (1990 pop. 53), Grant co., E central Wash., 25 mi/40 km ENE of Ephrata, on Crab Creek; 47°25′N 119°00′W. In Columbia basin agr. region.

Krusenstern, Cape (KROO-zuhn-stuhrn), N Mackenzie dist., N.W.T., Canada, on Coronation Gulf, at E end of Dolphin and Union Strait; 68°23′N 113°55′W. Trading post.

Krusenstern Island, Alaska: see LITTLE DIOMEDE ISLAND.

Kruzenshtern Island, Alaska: see LITTLE DIOMEDE ISLAND.

Kruzof Island (KROO-zawf), SE Alaska, in Alexander Archipelago, 10 mi/16 km W of Sitka; 23 mi/37 km long, 8 mi/12.9 km wide; 57°10′N 135°42′W. Mt. Edge-cumbe (S); fishing.

Krypton (KRIP-tahn), village (1990 pop. 300), Perry co., SE Ky., 8 mi/12.9 km NW of Hazard, in Cumberland foothills on North Fork Kentucky R. Bituminous coal–mining. Daniel Boone Natl. Forest to SW.

Kualapuu (koo-AH-lah-POO-oo), town (1990 pop. 1,661), N Molokai, Maui co., Hawaii, in interior, 2 mi/3.2 km from N coast and 4 mi/6.4 km NNW of Kaunakakai; 21°09′N 157°03′W. Kalaupapa Natl. Historical Park; pineapples formerly grown here; coffee. Kualapuu Reservoir to W; Molokai Forest Reserve to E; Palaau State Park to NE.

Kuiu Island (KOO-wee-yoo), SE Alaska, in Alexander Archipelago, bet. Kupreanof Isl. (E) of Baranof Isl. (W), 30 mi/48 km W of Petersburg; 65 mi/105 km long, 6 mi/9.7 km–23 mi/37 km wide; 56°28′N 134°1′W. Rises to c.3,000 ft/914 m. Fishing.

Kukuihaele (koo-KOO-ee-hah-AI-lai), village (1990 pop. 316), N Hawaii isl., Hawaii co., Hawaii, on Waipio Bay, 45 mi/72 km NW of Hilo, on Hamakua (NE) Coast; 20°07′N 155°34′W. Macadamia nuts; fish. Hamakua Forest Reserve to S.

Kulm (KUHLM), village (1990 pop. 514), La Moure co., S N.Dak., 32 mi/51 km W of La Moure; 46°17′N 98°57′W. Livestock, grain, dairy prods. Whitestone Battlefield Historic Site to SE.

Kulpmont, borough (1990 pop. 3,233), Northumberland co., E central Pa., 4 mi/6.4 km E of Shamokin. Mfg. (textiles, apparel); anthracite coal. Settled 1905, inc. 1916.

Kulpsville, uninc. town (1990 pop. 5,183), Montgomery co., SE Pa., 20 mi/32 km NW of Philadelphia on Towamencin Creek; 40°14′N 75°20′W. Mfg. includes fabricated metal prods., sealing devices, bearings, machinery; agr. includes dairying, livestock; grain.

Kulukak (KOO-loo-kak), Inuit village, SW Alaska, on Kulukak Bay, N arm (7 mi/11.3 km long, 4 mi/6.4 km–6 mi/9.7 km wide) of Bristol Bay, 50 mi/80 km W of Dillingham. Fishing.

Kumukahi, Cape (KOO-moo-KAH-hee), E extremity of Hawaii isl., Hawaii co., Hawaii; 19°31′N 154°48′W. Easternmost point in Hawaii and Hawaiian Isl. chain.

Kumukahi Channel, Hawaii: see KAULAKAHI CHANNEL.

Kuna, town (1990 pop. 1,955), Ada co., SW Idaho, suburb 15 mi/24 km SW of Boise; 43°29′N 116°25′W. In grain and livestock area (dairying; fruit, vegetables). Boise Municipal Airport (Gowen Field) to NE. L. Lowell reservoir (Deer Flat Natl. Wildlife Refuge to W).

Kunghit Island (KUHNG-git) (□ 83 sq mi/215 sq km), W B.C., SW Canada, southernmost of the Queen Charlotte Isls., 140 mi/225 km NW of Vancouver Isl., separated from Moresby Isl. (N) by Houston Stewart Channel (1 mi/2km–2 mi/3 km wide); 15 mi/24 km long, 1 mi/2 km–8 mi/13 km wide; 52°06′N 131°04′W. At S extremity is Cape St. James (51°56′N 131°01′W).

Kuparuk River (KOO-pah-ruhk), c.140 mi/225 km long, N Alaska; rises in N Brooks Range, near 68°40′N 149°00′W, flows N to Beaufort Sea of Arctic Ocean at 70°23′N 148°47′W.

Kupreanof Island (KOO-pree-yuh-nawf), SE Alaska, in Alexander Archipelago, W of Petersburg; 52 mi/84 km long, 20 mi/32 km–30 mi/48 km wide; 56°48′N 133°25′W. Rises to c.4,000 ft/1,219 m (NE). Lindenberg Peninsula (30 mi/48 km long, 12 mi/19 km wide) is separated from SE side of isl. by Duncan Canal. Fishing, fish processing. Kake village is in NW. Isl. named after Capt. Kupreanov, governor of Rus. Amer. who succeeded (1836) Baron Wrangell.

Kupreanof Point (KOO-pree-yuh-nawf), promontory, SW Alaska, on SW Alaska Peninsula, on E side of Stepovak Bay; 55°34′N 159°37′W.

Kupreanof Strait (KOO-pree-yuh-nawf), S Alaska, bet. Kodiak (S) and Afognak (N) isls., connects Gulf of Alaska (E) and Shelikof Strait (W), 25 mi/40 km WNW of Kodiak; 20 mi/32 km long, 2 mi/3.2 km–3 mi/4.8 km wide.

Kure Atoll or **Kure Island**, circular coral atoll with 2 small isls., N Pacific, in NW part of Hawaiian Isls., Hawaii co., Hawaii, c.60 mi/97 km NW of Midway, Internatl. Date Line c.100 mi/161 km to W, c.350 mi/563 km N of Tropic of Cancer; northernmost and westernmost point in Hawaii and Hawaiian chain. Elev. 20 ft/6 m. Annexed 1886 by Hawaii and worked for bird guano, placed (1936) under U.S. navy, coast guard base. Sometimes written Cure; formerly Ocean Isl.

Kure Beach (KYUHR-ee), village (1990 pop. 619), New Hanover co., SE N.C., 17 mi/27 km S of Wilmington, on Pleasure Isl., W of Atlantic Ocean, amd E of Cape Fear R. estuary; 34°00′N 77°54′W. Swimming resort. Bromine-extracting plant nearby. Ft. Fisher State Recreation Area and State Historical Site and N.C. State Aquarium to S. Toll ferry across Cape Fear R. to Southport 3 mi/4.8 km SSW.

Kurtistown, town (1990 pop. 910), E Hawaii isl., Hawaii co., Hawaii, 8 mi/12.9 km S of Hilo, 1 mi/1.6 km S of Keaau, 5 mi/8 km inland from E coast; 19°35′N 155°04′W. Fruit, macadamia nuts. Walakea Forest Reserve to NW. Kulani Honor Camp to W. Several residential and vacation home developments to S and E.

Kuskokwim, river, c.650 mi/1,046 km long; rises on the NW slopes of the Alaska Range, central Alaska; flows SW to the Bering Sea. The shores of the river are mostly forested or uninhabited. Bethel is major settlement near mouth of the river.

Kuskokwim Bay, SW Alaska, NW of Bristol Bay; 100 mi/161 km long, 100 mi/161 km wide at mouth; center near 59°30′N 162°30′W. Receives Kuskokwim R.

Kuskokwim Mountains, SW Alaska, W of Alaska Range, SE of Yukon R.; extend 250 mi/402 km NE-SW; 61°00′–64°00′N 155°00′–159°00′W. Rise to c.5,000 ft/1,524 m.

Kuttawa (KUHT-uh-wai), village (1990 pop. 535), Lyon co., W Ky., 25 mi/40 km E of Paducah, and 3 mi/4.8 km WSW of Eddyville, on Cumberland R. (L. Barkley reservoir); 37°03′N 88°06′W. In agr.; mfg. (catfish processing; plastic parts, plastic molding); limestone

quarry; hardwood timber area. Recreation and tourism. Town was relocated 2 mi/3.2 km to W from original site of c.1960 with construction of Barkley Dam (3 mi/4.8 km to W). Kentucky Dam (Tennessee R.) 6 mi/9.7 km to W.

Kutztown (KUHTS-toun), borough (1990 pop. 4,704), Berks co., E central Pa., 14 mi/23 km NNE of Reading. Agr. (livestock, poultry; grain, apples; dairying); mfg. (printing and publishing, trusses, apparel, food, bottled water; RR steel foundry); limestone. Seat of Kutztown Univ. of Pa. Crystal Cave to W. Two covered bridges to NW. Doe Mt. Ski Area to E. Settled 1733 by Germans, inc. 1815.

Kuujjuaq (KOOJ-jwak), village (1991 pop. 1,405), N Que., E Canada, on the Koksoak R. near its mouth at Ungava Bay; 58°06′N 68°24′W. Hudson's Bay Co. post, est. 1830.

Kuujjuarapik or **Great Whale River**, village (1991 pop. 605), NW Que., E Canada, on SE shore of Hudson Bay, at mouth of Grande R. de la Baleine (Great Whale R.). James Bay Hydro Project to E. Populated by Cree and Inuit peoples. Hunting, fishing, trapping. Scheduled air service.

Kvichak Bay (kah-VI-chak), S Alaska, NE arm of Bristol Bay, on E side of base of Alaska Peninsula; 50 mi/80 km long, 30 mi/48 km wide; 58°40′N 157°34′W. Base for Bristol Bay salmon fleet. Receives Kvichak R.

Kvichak River (kah-VI-chak), 65 mi/105 km long, S Alaska, at base of Alaska Peninsula; issues from Iliamna L.; flows SW to head of Kvichak Bay.

Kwethluk, Inuit village (1990 pop. 558), SW Alaska, near Kuskokwim R., on Kwethluk R., and 12 mi/19 km E of Bethel; 60°46′N 161°23′W. Formerly spelled Quithlook.

Kwigamiut (KWI-ga-mee-yoot), village, W Alaska, at S end of Nunivak Isl.; 59°48′N 166°05′W. Traditional Native culture maintained; carving, fishing.

Kwigillingok (kwi-GI-leeng-gok), village (1990 pop. 278), SW Alaska, on N side of Kuskokwim Bay, 65 mi/105 km NW of Platinum; 59°43′N 162°52′W. Formerly sometimes spelled Quillingok.

Kwiguk (KWI-guhk), village, W Alaska, on Yukon R., 30 mi/48 km NE of its mouth, 120 mi/193 km SSE of Nome.

Kwinhagak (KWI-nuh-gak), Inuit village (1990 pop. 501), SW Alaska, on E shore of Kuskokwim Bay, 50 mi/80 km N of Platinum; 59°45′N 161°52′W. Site of Moravian mission. Also spelled Quinhagak.

Kyle, town (1991 pop. 533), SW Sask., W Canada, 40 mi/64 km NNW of Swift Current. Wheat.

Kyle, town (1990 pop. 2,225), Hays co., S central Texas, near Blanco R., 21 mi/34 km SSE of Austin; 29°59′N 97°52′W. Agr. (cattle, sheep; cotton; fruit, vegetables); mfg. (steel foraging, steel fabrication).

Kyserike, resort village (1990 pop. 80), Ulster co., SE N.Y., on Rondout Creek, 12 mi/19 km SW of Kingston; 41°48′N 74°10′W. Also called Alligerville.

Kyte River, c.40 mi/64 km long, N Ill.; rises in E Lee co.; flows generally NW to Rock R. 3 mi/4.8 km S of Oregon; 42°00′N 89°04′W.

L

La Altagracia (lah ahl-tah-grah-SEE-ah), province (□ 1,191 sq mi/3,084 sq km; 1993 pop. 112,396), SE Dominican Republic; ⊙ Higuey; 18°35′N 68°38′W. At E tip of Hispaniola isl. Off S coast is Saona isl. Tropical lowlands with some outliers of Cordillera Central. Sugarcane is grown extensively in SW. Cattle raising. Prods. include bananas, coffee, rice, cacao, corn, hides, timber. Higuey is known for its shrine. Prov. was set up 1944; formerly part of Seibo prov.

La Antigua, Mexico: see JOSÉ CARDEL.

La Baie, city (1991 pop. 20,995), S Que., Canada, on Ha Ha Bay, an arm of the Saguenay R.; 48°20′N 70°52′W. Formed by the amalgamation of Bagotville, Port Alfred, and the parishes of Grande-Baie and Bagotville, La Baie has a natural harbor that services its paper and aluminum industries. It is the oldest municipality of the Saguenay–Lac Saint-Jean region.

La Bajada (lah bah-HAH-duh), town, SW Pinar del Río prov., extreme W Cuba, on Corrientes Bay; 21°55′N 84°28′W. Marks W limit of highway, although minor road continues W.

La Bajada (LAH buh-HAH-duh), uninc. village, Santa Fe co., N central N.Mex., suburb 13 mi/21 km WSW of Santa Fe, W of La Cienega, on Santa Fe R. Cattle, sheep; grain, corn, alfalfa. Part of Santa Fe Natl. Forest to NW.

La Barca (lah BAHR-kah), city (1990 pop. 25,006) and township, Jalisco, central Mexico, E of L. Chapala, on Lerma R., and 60 mi/97 km SE of Guadalajara; 20°20′N 102°33′W. Agr. center (grain, vegetables, oranges; livestock; dairying); tanning, beverage processing.

La Baye, Grenada: see GRENVILLE.

La Belle, city (1990 pop. 745), Lewis co., NE Mo., near Middle Fabius R., 12 mi/19 km W of Monticello; 40°07′N 91°54′W. Corn, soybeans; hogs; lumber.

La Belle, town (□ 2 sq mi/5.2 sq km; 1990 pop. 2,703), ⊙ Hendry co., SW Fla., on Caloosahatchee R., and 27 mi/43 km ENE of Fort Myers; 26°45′N 81°26′W. Shipping center for sugarcane, cattle, and watermelons.

La Belle Lake, Wis.: see LAC LA BELLE.

La Blanca, Mexico: see GENERAL PÁNFILO NATERA.

La Bolt, village (1990 pop. 91), Grant co., E S.Dak., 12 mi/19 km S of Milbank; 45°02′N 96°40′W.

La Brea, village, SW Trinidad, Trinidad and Tobago, on the Gulf of Paria, 10 mi/16 km WSW of San Fernando. Adjoins famous Pitch L., where asphalt is worked and then exported through La Brea pier at Pitch Point (10°15′N 61°37′W). Petroleum deposits nearby. Sir Walter Raleigh caulked his ships with asphalt here (1595).

La Brea, locality, Los Angeles co., S Calif. The La Brea asphalt pits (commonly referred to as La Brea Tar Pits), which yielded prehistoric animal and plant remains, are in SE corner of Hancock Park, on Wilshire Blvd., Los Angeles city, 6 mi/9.7 km W of downtown. The first fossils were found in 1875, and since 1906 the pits have been extensively researched. Formerly in Rancho La Brea.

La Cañada (kahn-YAH-dah), town (1990 pop. 7,815), ⊙ El Marqués municipio, Querétaro, central Mexico, on Querétaro R. (affluent of Apaseo R.), and 4 mi/6.5 km E of Querétaro. Produces flowers, fruit. Resort noted for thermal springs. Also known as Villa de Marqués.

La Cañada Flintridge (lah kahn-YAH-dah), city (1990 pop. 19,378), Los Angeles co., S Calif., in S foothills of San Gabriel Mts., a residential suburb 11 mi/18 km NNE of downtown Los Angeles, and NE of Glendale; 34°13′N 118°12′W. Printing and publishing. Descanso Gardens; Angeles Natl. Forest to NE.

La Carrière, Trinidad and Tobago: see POINTE-À-PIERRE.

La Ceiba, Dominican Republic: see HOSTOS.

La Center, town (1990 pop. 1,040), Ballard co., W Ky., 21 mi/34 km W of Paducah; 37°04′N 88°58′W. In agr. area (tobacco, grain, soybeans; hogs, cattle, poultry; dairying); light mfg.

La Center, village (1990 pop. 451), Clark co., SW Wash., on East Fork of Lewis R., and 15 mi/24 km N of Vancouver; 45°52′N 122°40′W. In agr. region; lettuce, berries, potatoes, oats. Paradise Point State Park to SW; Columbia R. 6 mi/9.7 km W.

La Cienega (LAH see-EN-i-guh), uninc. town (1990 pop. 1,066), Santa Fe co., N central N.Mex., residential suburb 12 mi/19 km WSW of Santa Fe, on Santa Fe R.; 35°34′N 106°06′W. Cattle, sheep; corn, grain. Santa Fe County Municipal Airport and Santa Fe Downs Racetrack to E. Part of Santa Fe Natl. Forest to NE.

La Ciénega, Mexico: see CIÉNEGA DE ZIMATLÁN.

La Coloma, Cuba: see COLOMA.

La Colorada (lah ko-lo-RAH-dah), town (1990 pop. 285), Sonora, NW Mexico, 32 mi/51 km SE of Hermosillo; 28°41′N 110°15′W. Elev. 1,270 ft/387 m. Copper mining; silver, lead, zinc, graphite.

La Compañía (lah kom-pahn-YEE-ah), town (1990 pop. 990), in the S central part of the state of Oaxaca, Mexico, 31 mi/50 km S of Oaxaca de Juárez, 6 mi/10 km W of Ejutia de Crespo. Agr. Zapotec Indian area.

La Concordia (lah kon-KOR-dee-ah), town (1990 pop. 6,675), Chiapas, S Mexico, in Grijualva R. valley S of Belisaria Domínguez Reservoir; 16°08′N 92°38′W. Elev. 1,805 ft/550 m. Cereals, sugarcane, fruit; livestock.

La Conner, village (1990 pop. 656), Skagit co., NW Wash., 7 mi/11.3 km WSW of Mt. Vernon, and on Swinomish Channel, slough bet. mainland and Fidalgo, near Skagit Bay, arm of Puget Sound; 48°23′N 122°29′W. Agr. (vegetables, grain, berries; dairying); fish, oysters; mfg. (boatbuilding, hardware, wood prods.). Bridges (2) to Fidalgo Isl. Swinomish Indian Reservation to W.

La Corne (luh KORN), village (1991 pop. 616), W Que., Canada, 18 mi/29 km SE of Amos. Molybdenum, lithium mining. Sometimes called Lacorne.

La Coste, town (1990 pop. 1,021), Medina co., SW Texas, 20 mi/32 km WSW of San Antonio, on Medina R. Oil and natural gas, sand and gravel. Agr. (cattle, sheep, goats; cotton, vegetables, peanuts). Mfg. (animal feeds).

La Crescent, town (1990 pop. 4,311), Houston co., extreme SE Minn., on Mississippi R. opposite La Crosse, Wis. (4 mi/6.4 km WNW of La Crosse; 2 highway bridges); 43°49′N 91°17′W. Agr. area (grain, soybeans; livestock, poultry; dairying); mfg. (burial vaults, septic tanks, concrete, wood trusses). Richard J. Dorer Memorial Hardwood State Forest to S; Lock and Dam No. 7 to N; small Winnebago Indian Reservation to S.

La Crescenta, uninc. city (1990 pop. 16,968), Los Angeles co., S Calif., in La Crescenta Valley, in S foothills of San Gabriel Mts., a residential suburb 12 mi/19 km N of downtown Los Angeles, NE of Glendale; 34°14′N 118°14′W. Light mfg. Site of Mt. Waterman Ski Area; Angeles Natl. Forest to NE.

La Croix, Lac (lak luh-KROI), long lake on U.S.-Can. border, St. Louis co., NE Minn. and Rainy Lake dist., W Ont. (Canada); 30 mi/48 km N of Ely; c.30 mi/48 km long, max. width 4 mi/6.4 km; 48°21′N 92°10′W. Elev. 1,184 ft/361 m. U.S. portion is in Superior Natl. Forest (Boundary Waters Canoe Area); E part of Can. portion in Quetico Provincial Park. Lake is fed from Iron L. to SE, through 2 widely separate channels, the 1st flows NW through Bottle L. (on U.S./Can. border), the 2d flows N through McAree L. in Ont., then W to Lac St. Croix; 2 channels form large Irving Isl. (Ont., Canada), 5 mi/8 km long, 4 mi/6.4 km wide. Lake is also drained by 2 separate rivers. The Namakan R. (c.30 mi/48 km long) flows NW and W through Ont. to Namakan L.; it is also drained through Loon R. (on U.S.-Can. border), first S through Loon L., then W and NW through Little Vermilion and Sand Point lakes, passing from Sand Point to Namakan lakes through Namakan Narrows. Resort area.

La Crosse, county (□ 479 sq mi/1,241 sq km; 1990 pop. 97,904), W Wis.; ⊙ La Crosse; 43°54′N 91°06′W. Agr. (corn, soybeans; cattle, hogs, sheep; dairying); lumber milling; other mfg. at La Crosse. Drained by La Crosse and Black rivers. Mt. La Crosse Ski Area in SW; La Crosse State Trail and Great River State Trail traverse co. Formed 1851.

La Crosse, city (1990 pop. 51,003), seat of La Crosse co., W Wis., c.100 mi/161 km NW of Madison, at the foot of high bluffs on the Mississippi R., where the La Crosse and Black rivers meet; 43°49′N 91°13′W. Mfg. (fabricated metal prods., machinery, bldg. materials, apparel, dairy prods., transportation equip., consumer goods; food and beverage processing, printing). A Fr. furtrading post was there in the late 18th cent. Later, the city contained a thriving lumber industry. The Univ. of Wisconsin at La Crosse, Viterbo Col., Western Wisconsin Technical Inst., and a U.S. fish hatchery and experimental farm are in La Crosse. The city also has a zoo, an aquarium, a historical mus., and a wildlife project. Terminus (E) of La Crosse State Trail and S terminus of Great River State Trail are here. Part of Upper Mississippi R. Natl. Wildlife Refuge is along the river here. Mt. La Crosse Ski Area to S; Lock and Dam No. 7 to NW. Inc. 1856.

La Crosse 1 (luh KRAWS), town (1990 pop. 677), La Porte co., NW Ind., 30 mi/48 km SSW of La Porte; 41°19′N 86°53′W. Agr. area. **2** town (1990 pop. 1,427), ⊙ Rush co., W central Kansas, 30 mi/48 km WNW of Great Bend; 38°31′N 99°18′W. Shipping point for wheat and cattle. Barbed Wire Mus. here, over 500 examples of barbed wire fencing. Founded 1876, inc. 1886. **3** town (1990 pop. 549), Mecklenburg co., S Va., suburb 2 mi/ 3.2 km SE of South Hill; 36°42′N 78°05′W. Mfg. (prefabricated steel bldgs., textiles); in agr. area (tobacco, peanuts, cotton, grain; livestock); timber. Mechlenburg Brunswick Regional Airport to E.

La Crosse (lah KRAWS), village (1990 pop. 336), Whitman co., SE Wash., 32 mi/51 km WNW of Pullman; 46°49′N 117°53′W. Ships wheat, barley, oats, rye; cattle, sheep. Palouse Falls State Park and Lyons Ferry State Park to SW.

La Crosse River, c.50 mi/80 km long, W Wis.; rises in Monroe co.; flows generally SW, past Sparta, to the Mississippi R. at La Crosse.

La Cruz 1 (lah KROOS), town (1990 pop. 1,400), Chihuahua, N Mexico, on Conchos R., on RR and Mexico Highway 45, and 75 mi/121 km SE of Chihuahua; 27°50′N 105°11′W. Elev. 4,062 ft/1,238 m. Cotton, corn, beans; cattle. **2** town (1990 pop. 8,537), ⊙ Elota municipio, Sinaloa, NW Mexico, on Elota R., in coastal lowland, on RR, and 70 mi/113 km SE of Culiacán Rosales; 23°53′N 106°53′W. Lumbering and agr. center (corn, chick peas, fruit); dye-extract factory. Also called La Cruz de Elota.

La Cruz de Elota, Mexico: see LA CRUZ.

La Cueva (lah KWE-vah), uninc. village (1990 pop. 200), Mora co., N N.Mex., on Mora R., and 5 mi/8 km SE of Mora, E of Sangre de Cristo Mts. Elev. 7,070 ft/ 2,155 m. In irrigated agr. region; livestock, fruit, grain, alfalfa.

La Cygne (luh SEEN), city (1990 pop. 1,066), Linn co., E Kansas, on Marais des Cygnes R., and 18 mi/29 km SSE of Paola; 38°21′N 94°45′W. Livestock and poultry raising, general agr. Limestone quarries. Marais des Cygnes Massacre Park to SE; Marais des Cygnes Waterfowl Refuge to W; La Cygne L. reservoir to E.

La Cygne Lake (luh SEEN), Linn and Miami cos., E Kansas, on North Sugar Creek, 11 mi/18 km NNE of Pleasanton, and 1 mi/1.6 km W of Mo. state line; 4 mi/ 6.4 km long; 38°18′N 94°39′W. Max. storage capacity 60,000 acre-ft. Formed by dam (37 ft/11 m high), built (1971) for flood control and water supply. La Cygne State Park is here.

La Descubierta (lah des-koo-bee-ER-tah), town (1993 pop. 4,086), Bahoruco prov., SW Dominican Republic, on N shore of L. Enriquillo, 15 mi/24 km W of Neiba; 18°37′N 71°41′W. Agr. (coffee, grapes, fruit); timber.

La Due, uninc. community, Henry co., W central Mo., 7 mi/11.3 km SW of Clinton. Strip coal mines.

La Esmeralda, Cuba: see ESMERALDA.

La Esperanza, Cuba: see PUERTO ESPERANZA.

La Estanzuela, Mexico: see GARCÍA DE LA CADENA.

La Estrelleta, Dominican Republic: see ELÍAS PIÑA prov.

La Farge, village (1990 pop. 766), Vernon co., SW Wis., on Kickapoo R., and 35 mi/56 km SE of La Crosse;

43°34′N 90°38′W. In dairying and tobacco-growing area. Timber; cheese, wood pallets.

La Fargeville, village (1990 pop. 600), Jefferson co., N N.Y., 16 mi/26 km N of Watertown; 44°12′N 75°58′W. In timber and lumbering area.

La Fayette (luh FAI-it), city (1990 pop. 6,313), ⊙ Walker co., NW Ga., 31 mi/50 km NNW of Rome; 34°43′N 85°17′W. Mfg. includes textiles, apparel, machinery and equip., wire harnesses, transportation equip., plastic prods., limestone processing. Old courthouse now restored as mus. Confederate General Braxton Bragg planned Battle of Chickamauga here. Chattahoochee Natl. Forest nearby. Founded 1835.

La Fayette 1 (LAH-fai-ET), village (1990 pop. 231), Stark co., N central Ill., 6 mi/9.7 km W of Toulon; 41°06′N 89°58′W. In agr. and bituminous-coal area. **2** (lah-FAI-it), village (1990 pop. 106), Christian co., SW Ky., near Tenn. state line, 17 mi/27 km SW of Hopkinsville. Agr. (tobacco; livestock). Fort Campbell Military Reservation to S and W. Also spelled Lafayette.

La Fé 1 (lah FAI), town, Isla de la Juventud, SW Cuba, 10 mi/16 km SSE of Nueva Gerona; 21°45′N 82°45′W. At major crossroads. Resort with mineral springs. Kaolin quarries to E and W. Small airstrip S. **2** town, Pinar del Río prov., W Cuba, on Palencia Bay; 22°03′N 84°17′W. Citrus production and ranching. Fishing.

La Feria, town (1990 pop. 4,360), Cameron co., extreme S Texas, 27 mi/43 km NW of Brownsville, and 9 mi/ 14.5 km W of Harlingen, in lower Rio Grande valley; 26°09′N 97°49′W. Near Arroyo Colorado and Willacy Canal. In rich irrigated area (cotton; vegetables; citrus); mfg. (Mex. herbs and spices, plastic molding, maps).

La Florida (lah flo-REE-dah), town, ⊙ La Florida municipio, Nariño dept., SW Colombia, 9 mi/14.5 km NW of Pasto. Wheat, sugarcane, vegetables; livestock.

La Follette (luh FAW-lit), city (1990 pop. 7,192), Campbell co., NE Tenn., near Norris Reservoir, 30 mi/48 km NNW of Knoxville, in E foothills of the Cumberlands; 36°23′N 84°07′W. Coal-mining center; mfg. (apparel). Inc. 1897.

La Fontaine, town (1990 pop. 909), Wabash co., NE central Ind., near Mississinewa R., 10 mi/16 km SSE of Wabash; 40°40′N 85°43′W. In agr. area.

La France, uninc. town, Anderson co., NW S.C. 10 mi/ 16 km NNW of Anderson. Hartwell L. reservoir to SW. Light mfg.; agr. (poultry, livestock; dairying; grain, soybeans).

La Gloria, uninc. village (1990 pop. 102), Starr co., extreme S Texas, 40 mi/64 km NNW of McAllen. Cattle; cotton; oil and natural gas.

La Grande, town, NW Que., Canada, 50 mi/80 km E of James Bay, 10 mi/16 km S of La Grande R., bet. L. Duncan (W) and La Grande Reservoir #2 (E). Est. c.1980 as staging center for James Bay Hydroelectric Project. Road connection from S. Scheduled air service.

La Grande, city (1990 pop. 11,766), ⊙ Union co., NE Oregon, 40 mi/64 km SE of Pendleton, on Grande Ronde R., E of Blue Mts., W of Wallowa Mts.; 45°19′N 118°05′W. Elev. 2,788 ft/850 m. RR junction; trade and shipping point for livestock, fruit, timber. Mfg. (particleboard; printing, publishing); agr. (potatoes; grain). Site of Eastern Oregon State Col., Hilgard Junction, and Red Bridge State Parks to W; parts of Wallowa-Whitman Natl. Forest to NW, SW, and E. Founded 1861; inc. 1886.

La Grande Dam, Wash.: see NISQUALLY RIVER.

La Grandeza (lah grahn-DAI-sah), town (1990 pop. 567), ⊙ La Grandeza municipio, Chiapas, S Mexico, in Sierra Madre, 11 mi/18 km N of Motozintla de Mendoza; 15°32′N 92°14′W. Elev. 6,201 ft/1,890 m. Sugarcane, fruit. Formerly called San Antonio La Grandeza.

La Grange 1 (luh GRAINJ), city (1990 pop. 25,597), ⊙ Troup co., W central Ga.; 33°02′N 85°02′W. Former cotton mill town, now an industrial center; mfg. (lumber, plastics, textiles, bldg. materials, transportation equip.; printing and publishing). The city is also a processing and shipping center for a rich agr. area. Many classic Gr. revival houses and restored historic bldgs.; seat of La Grange Col., including the Lamar Dodd Art

Center. Named for the Fr. estate of Marquis de Lafayette, whose statue, along with a fountain in Lafayette Park, is the focal point of the town. Important retail hub. The Troup Co. Archive and Historical Society; Chattahoochee Valley Art Mus.; West Ga. Technical Col. Inc. 1828. **2** city (1990 pop. 1,102), Lewis co., NE Mo., on the Mississippi, at mouth of Wyaconda R., and 6 mi/9.7 km S of Canton; 40°02′N 91°30′W. Grain; hogs; mfg. (iron castings). Plotted 1830. Wakona State Park on S side of town.

La Grange 1 (luh GRAINJ), town (1990 pop. 3,853), ⊙ Oldham co., N Ky., 25 mi/40 km ENE of Louisville; 38°23′N 85°22′W. In agr. area (burley tobacco, grain; dairying); mfg. (magnet wire, crushed limestone, stationery; steel fabricating). Rob Morris Home (1830); County Historical Society. **2** town (1990 pop. 2,805), Lenoir co., E central N.C., 12 mi/19 km SE of Goldsboro; 35°18′N 77°47′W. Agr. area (tobacco, cotton, grain, soybeans, sweet potatoes, poultry; livestock). Mfg. (apparel, electrical equip., meat processing, metal containers). Cliffs of the Neuse State Park to SW. Inc. 1869. **3** town (1990 pop. 167), Fayette co., SW Tenn., near Wolf R., 45 mi/72 km E of Memphis; 35°03′N 89°15′W. Antebellum plantation homes in area. **4** town (1990 pop. 3,951), ⊙ Fayette co., S central Texas, on Colorado R. and c.55 mi/89 km ESE of Austin; 29°54′N 96°52′W. Elev. 272 ft/83 m. Agr. (dairying; cattle; cotton, peanuts, pecans, corn, sorghum); mfg. (food processing, safety signs, wood prods.); oil and natural gas; sand and gravel. L. Fayette reservoir to E; Monument Hill State Park to SW and Kreische State Historic Site, both to SW. Est. 1831; became co. seat 1837. **5** town (1990 pop. 224), Goshen co., SE Wyo., on Horse Creek, near Nebr. state line, and 48 mi/77 km NE of Cheyenne; 41°38′N 104°09′W. Elev. 4,587 ft/1,398 m. Hawk Springs Reservoir and State Recreation Area to NW.

La Grange (luh GRAINJ), village (1990 pop. 15,362), Cook co., NE Ill., a W suburb of Chicago; 41°48′N 87°52′W. Settled 1830s, inc. 1879. It is primarily residential with some mfg. Limestone quarries are nearby.

La Grange Park, village (1990 pop. 12,861), Cook co., NE Ill., a W suburb of Chicago; 41°49′N 87°52′W. Mfg. (pens). Inc. 1892.

La Grulla, town (1990 pop. 1,335), Starr co., extreme S Texas, 25 mi/40 km W of McAllen, and on the Rio Grande (Mex. border). In rich irrigated agr. area (vegetables; cotton; cattle). Also called Grulla.

La Guadalupe, village (1991 pop. 1,721), S Que., Canada, 27 mi/43 km N of Megantic; 45°57′N 70°56′W. Dairying; lumbering; mfg. (food preparations, apparel).

La Habana (lah-ah-BAH-nuh), province, (1994 est. pop. 2,400,000; □ 2,197 sq mi/5,691 sq km), W Cuba; ⊙ Havana. Coastal plains average 31 mi/50 km in width bet. the Caribbean Sea and Atlantic Ocean; beaches and some low mts. in the N. Drained by the Almendares and the Jaruco rivers; several large aquifers (Vento, Sur, Gato) provide Havana with freshwater even though they suffer from saltwater intrusion along the Caribbean. Principal crops include tobacco, sugarcane, and vegetables; food processing is the leading industry. The majority of the pop. and industry is concentrated in and around Havana; about ¼ of the pop. resides in cities with over 20,000 people. After Havana, the largest towns include Güines, Artemisa, San José de Lajas, Guanajay, and Guira de Melena. Internatl. tourism was economically important until the U.S. and Cuba severed relations in 1960; tourism with countries besides the U.S. has been encouraged again since 1990.

La Habra, city (1990 pop. 51,266), Orange co., S Calif., suburb 18 mi/29 km SE of downtown Los Angeles, 6 mi/9.7 km N of Anaheim; 33°56′N 117°57′W. La Habra was settled in the 1860s by Basque sheepherders. Mfg. (computer equip., fabricated metal prods., plumbing fixtures, rubber prods., flavoring extracts; printing). Oil research center nearby. The city has grown along with the surrounding Los Angeles metropolitan area. Major housing developments have been constructed for the increasing pop., and the city's economic base has been strengthened by high-technology and electronic mfg. in the area. Inc. 1925.

La Habra Heights, city (1990 pop. 6,226), Los Angeles co., S Calif., residential suburb 17 mi/27 km ESE of downtown Los Angeles, E of Whittier; 33°58′N 117°57′W. Puente Hills to N.

La Harpe (luh HARP), city (1990 pop. 1,407), Hancock co., W Ill., 16 mi/26 km NNE of Carthage; 40°34′N 90°58′W. In agr. area (corn, soybeans, livestock; dairy prods.). RR junction. Inc. 1859.

La Harpe (luh HAHRP), village (1990 pop. 650), Allen co., SE Kansas, 6 mi/9.7 km E of Iola; 37°55′N 95°17′W. Livestock, grain; limestone quarry.

La Honda, uninc. village, San Mateo co., W Calif., 11 mi/ 18 km SSW of Redwood City, 21 mi/34 km W of San Jose, and 7 mi/11.3 km E of Pacific Ocean, on W side of Santa Cruz Mts., on La Honda Creek, in a canyon among redwood groves. San Mateo State Beaches to W; Portola and Castle Rock state parks to SE.

La Huacana (lah wah-KAH-nah), town (1990 pop. 9,168), Michoacán, W Mexico, 35 mi/56 km S of Uruapan; 18°58′N 101°49′W. Cereals, sugarcane, fruit; silver deposits.

La Huerta (lah WER-tah), town (1990 pop. 5,892), in SW Jalisco, Mexico on Pacific coast of Sierra Cacoma, 36 mi/58 km SW of Autlán de Navarro, on Mexico Highway 80. Irrigated by the Purificación R. The name reflects great agr. production (rice, sugarcane, tobacco, beans, peanuts, corn, fruit, plantains, watermelon, coconuts; fine woods and lumber).

La Hune, Cape (luh HOON), S N.F., Canada, on E side of La Hune Bay (extending 7 mi/11 km inland), 40 mi/ 64 km E of Burgeo; 47°32′N 56°02′W. Opposite is fishing village of La Hune.

La Independencia (lah een-de-pen-DEN-see-yah), town (1990 pop. 2,095), Chiapas, S Mexico, in Sierra Madre, 8 mi/12 km E of Comitán de Domínguez. Corn, fruit. Tojolabal-speaking Mayan Indians live in rural areas.

La Isabela, Cuba: see ISABELA DE SAGUA.

La Isabela, Dominican Republic: see ISABELA.

La Isabela1, town (1993 pop. 3,385), Monte Cristi prov., NW Dominican Republic, on highway, and 13 mi/21 km SE of Monte Cristi; 19°48′N 71°05′W. Agr. (rice, onions, potatoes). Until 1938, Villa Vásquez. Also called Villa Isabel.

La Isla, Mexico: see SAN ANTONIO LA ISLA.

La Jara, town (1990 pop. 725), Conejos co., S Colo., on La Jara Arroyo, near La Jara Creek, E of San Juan Mts., and 14 mi/23 km SSW of Alamosa, in San Luis Valley; 37°16′N 105°57′W. Elev. 7,602 ft/2,317 m. Cattle, sheep; wheat, oats, barley, hay prods. Rio Grand Natl. Forest to W.

La Jolla (lah HOI-yah), suburban sect. of SAN DIEGO city, San Diego co., S Calif., 12 mi/19 km NW of downtown San Diego. Mfg. (measuring devices, cereals, medical instruments); printing and publishing. Ocean beaches, in particular La Jolla shores and Black's Beach, and seawashed caves; tourism. The city has become a favorite retirement center as well as a prestigious residential and recreational area for San Diego professionals. The Scripps Inst. of Oceanography to NE, the Univ. of Calif. at San Diego to NE, and La Jolla Mus. of Contemporary Art are in La Jolla, Salk Inst. to NE. Torrey Pines State Reservoir to N; Mission Bay to S. Founded 1869.

La Joya (lah HOI-yah), town (1990 pop. 2,604), Hidalgo co., S Texas, 15 mi/24 km W of McAllen, on Rio Grande (Mex. border); 26°15′N 98°28′W. Rich irrigated agr. area (citrus, vegetables, cotton). Bentsen-Rio Grande Valley State Park to SE.

La Junta (lah HUHN-tah), town (1990 pop. 7,637), ⊙ Otero co., SE Colo., on Arkansas R., and 60 mi/97 km ESE of Pueblo; 37°58′N 103°32′W. Elev. c.4,066 ft/ 1,239 m. Trade and RR center, with repair shops, in grain and sugar-beet region; agr. (vegetables, wheat, corn; cattle, poultry); mfg. (consumer goods, food processing; publishing and printing, milling). Fort Bent Mus. has fossils and scale model of Bent's Fort, noted trading post that flourished nearby on the Arkansas R. from 1820s to 1850s. Otero Junior Col. here. Bent's Old Fort Natl. Historic Site to NE; Comanche Natl. Grassland to S. City founded 1875, inc. 1881.

La Libertad (lah lee-ber-TAHD), town (1990 pop. 1,480), Chiapas, S Mexico, in Usumacinta R. lowland, and 4 mi/6.4 km SSE of Emiliano Zapata. Elev. 177 ft/54 m. Rubber; fruit.

La Loma, Dominican Republic: see LOMA DE CABRERA.

La Luz (lah LOOS), mining settlement (1990 pop. 1,364), Guanajuato, central Mexico, in Sierra Madre Occidental, 7 mi/11.3 km WNW of Guanajuato; 23°04′N 102°52′W. Elev. 7,644 ft/2,330 m. Some mercury mining. Also called Mineral de la Luz.

La Luz (lah LOOS), uninc. town (1990 pop. 1,625), Otero co., S central N.Mex., residential suburb 5 mi/8 km N of Alamogordo; 32°58′N 105°56′W. Cattle, sheep; pecans, fruit, alfalfa. Sacramento Mts. and Lincoln Natl. Forest to E; Mescalero Apache Indian Reservation to NE.

La Magdalena Contreras (LAH mahg-dah-LAI-nah), delegación, (1990 pop. 195,041), in SW of Federal Dist., Mexico, 5.6 mi/9 km W of Tlalpan. Includes Sierra de las Cruces and Sierra de Ajusco. Site of some of Mexico city's most exclusive residential areas, along with middle-class housing developments. Conflicts have developed bet. real estate promoters and conservationists over preservation of forested areas, of which few remain in the Federal Dist., Site of an important battle (Aug. 19–20, 1847) of the Mex.-Amer. War.

La Magdalena Tlatlauquitepec (lah mahg-dah-LAI-nah tlah-tlah-oo-KEE-te-pek), town (1990 pop. 756), Puebla, central Mexico, 21 mi/34 km SSE of Puebla; 18°45′N 98°06′W. Cereals; livestock. Also La Magdalena.

La Malbaie (lah mahl-BAI) or **Murray Bay,** village (1991 pop. 3,968), S central Que., Canada, at the confluence of the Malbaie (or Murray) R. with the St. Lawrence; 47°39′N 70°10′W. Well-known resort in dairy-farming country.

La Malinche National Park (lah mah-LEEN-che), on the border bet. the states of Puebla and Tlaxcala, Mexico, 9 mi/14 km E of Apizaco then 8 mi/13 km S to Albergue La Malintzin in SE Tlaxcala. The park is located at the foot of the huge Malinche Volcano. (elev. 14,636 ft/4,461 m) within the Mexical Volcanic Axis; covers 114,277 acres/46,248 ha.

La Manzanilla de la Paz (lah mahn-sahn-EE-yah dai la pahs), town (1990 pop. 2,356), ⊙ La Manzanilla de la Paz municipio, Jalisco, central Mexico, in Sierra Madre Occidental, 30 mi/48 km ENE of Sayula, and 10 mi/16 km S of L. Chapala; 20°00′N 103°09′W. Grain, beans, fruit; livestock.

La Marque (luh-MAHRK), city (1990 pop. 14,120), Galveston co., SE Texas, suburb 5 mi/8 km SW of Texas City, on Highland Bayou; 29°22′N 94°59′W. In an agr. and oil area; mfg. (machining, machinery, electronic equip., cable wire). Originally a farm settlement, it later became a RR shipping point bet. Houston and Galveston. Modern La Marque is primarily a residential suburb for workers in Texas City and other nearby industrial centers. It is also an oil refining center. Settled c.1860, inc. 1953.

La Mata (lah MAH-tah), town (1993 pop. 8,660), 15 mi/23 km SE of San Francisco de Macorís, Sánchez Ramírez prov., central Dominican Republic; 19°06′N 70°10′W.

La Maurice National Park (□ 210 sq mi/544 sq km), S Que., Canada, near Trois-Rivières. In heavily wooded part of the Laurentian Mts. Est. 1970.

La Maya (lah MEI-yuh), town, Santiago de Cuba prov., E Cuba, on RR, and 17 mi/27 km NE of Santiago de Cuba; 20°10′N 75°39′W. Fruit; cattle.

La Mesa, city (1990 pop. 52,931), San Diego co., S Calif., a residential suburb 8 mi/12.9 km ENE of downtown San Diego; 32°46′N 117°01′W. It is a retail-trade center in suburban San Diego. Mfg. (machinery, diversified light mfg.). La Mesa has become a popular residence for upper- and middle-income professionals in the San Diego area. Points of interest include the McKinney House, the Pacific Southwest Railway Mus., and nearby Mt. Helix, with its impressive view of the surrounding region. Murray Reservoir to N. Inc. 1912.

La Mesa (lah MAI-sah), uninc. town (1990 pop. 900),

Dona Ana co., S N.Mex., 13 mi/21 km S of Las Cruces, on Rio Grande. In irrigated agr. area (cattle, sheep; vegetables, fruit, nuts).

La Mesilla (LAH muh-SEE-yuh), town (1990 pop. 1,975), Dona Ana co., S N.Mex., suburb 2 mi/3.2 km SW of downtown Las Cruces, on the Rio Grande; 32°16′N 106°48′W. Gadsden Purchase was signed here in 1853. The whole Mesilla Valley became part of the U.S. under the agreement. Mesilla was a central station on the overland mail route. From July 1861, to Aug. 1862, it was hq. for Col. John R. Baylor of the Confederate army, who proclaimed Mesilla the capital of the new Confederate territory. A mus. commemorates Billy the Kid, who once stood trial here. Las Cruces Airport to W; La Mesilla State Historical Park is here. Settled c.1850.

La Mirada, city (1990 pop. 40,452), Los Angeles co., S Calif., suburb 15 mi/24 km SE of downtown Los Angeles, and 12 mi/19 km NE of Long Beach; 33°54′N 118°01′W. Mfg. (metal, plastic, paper, and concrete prods., machinery). La Mirada derives from the Span. for "the view," referring to the panoramic view of the surrounding valleys from atop the city's hills. It was the original site of Calif.'s olive industry. The city is the seat of Biola Col. Inc. 1960.

La Misión or **Misión** (mee-SYON), town (1990 pop. 452), Hidalgo, central Mexico, 7 mi/11.3 km NNE of Jacala, and on the Querrétaro border. Grain, beans; livestock.

La Moille 1 (luh MOIL), village (1990 pop. 654), Bureau co., N Ill., near Bureau Creek, and 15 mi/24 km NE of Princeton; 41°31′N 89°16′W. In agr. area. **2** village, Marshall co., central Iowa, 7 mi/11.3 km W of Marshalltown. Feed.

La Moine River (luh MOIN), W Ill.; rises in SW Warren co.; flows c.100 mi/161 km SW, S, and SE, to Illinois R. below Beardstown; 40°38′N 90°45′W.

La Monte, city (1990 pop. 995), Pettis co., central Mo., 11 mi/18 km WNW of Sedalia; 38°46′N 93°25′W. Soybeans, corn; cattle; wood prods.

La Mott, Pa.: see CHELTENHAM.

La Motte, village (1991 pop. 415), W Que., Canada, on L. La Motte, 16 mi/26 km S of Amos; 48°23′N 78°07′W. Gold, copper, zinc, lead; logging.

La Motte, town (1990 pop. 219), Jackson co., E Iowa, 15 mi/24 km S of Dubuque; 42°17′N 90°37′W. In agr. area.

La Motte, Isle, Vt.: see ISLE LA MOTTE.

La Moure (luh MOR), county (□ 1,150 sq mi/2,979 sq km; 1990 pop. 5,383), SE central N.Dak.; ⊙ La Moure. Rich agr. area drained by James and Maple rivers and Cottonwood Creek. Wheat, corn, barley, rye; cattle, hogs; dairy prods. Formed 1873. L. Lanoar in S.

La Moure (luh MOR), town (1990 pop. 970), ⊙ La Moure co., SE central N.Dak., 45 mi/72 km SSE of Jamestown, and on James R.; 46°21′N 98°17′W. Trade center; livestock, dairying. Junction of RR spur to Edgeley. L. La Moure to S. Settled 1882; inc. 1905.

La Palma (lah PAHL-mah), town, Pinar del Río prov., W Cuba, 25 mi/40 km NNE of Pinar del Río; 22°45′N 83°33′W. In agr. region (sugarcane, tobacco); mfg. of cigars; lumbering. The Manuel Sanguily sugar mill is 5 mi/8 km NE.

La Palma, city (1990 pop. 15,392), Orange co., S Calif., suburb 19 mi/31 km SE of downtown Los Angeles, 5 mi/8 km W of Anaheim; 33°51′N 118°02′W. Knots Berry Farm, at Buena Park, to E. Mfg. (aircraft parts, chemicals, metal, paper and plastic prods.; printing).

La Panza Range, San Luis Obispo co., SW Calif., one of the Coast Ranges, extends c.30 mi/48 km NW-SE bet. Santa Lucia Range (W) and Temblor Range (E); rises to 4,054 ft/1,236 m, 24 mi/39 km E of San Luis Obispo. A N extension of the Sierra Madre; in Los Padres Natl. Forest.

La Parguera (lah pahr-GAI-rah), fishing village, SW coast of P.R., in E branch of Boquerón State Park (also known as La Parguera Park). Tourism; on Phosphorescent Bay where trillions of sea micro-organisms breed and illuminate the water. Univ. of P.R. Marine Sciences research facilities located on Magueyes Isl. nearby (S).

La Paz (lah PAHS), city (1990 pop. 137,641) and township, ⊙ and largest city of Baja California Sur state, W Mexico; 24°10′N 110°17′W. A tourist spot and transportation hub for the S Baja California peninsula, La Paz was first settled in 1811. The city was known for its pearl fishing until the middle of the 20th cent. when the oyster beds were destroyed by disease. It is known for its water sports, as well as being an entry point for the Los Cabos resort area to the S. La Paz is linked to MAZATLÁN and LOS MOCHIS by ferry, and to TIJUANA and MEXICALI by Mexico Highway 1. Internatl. airport to SE.

La Paz 1 Mexico: see LOS REYES ACAQUILPAN. **2** Mexico: see VILLA DE LA PAZ.

La Paz, county (4,513 sq mi/11,689 sq km; 1990 pop. 13,844), W Ariz.; ⊙ Parker; 33°43′N 113°58′W. Colorado R. (Calif. state line and Pacific/Mountain time zone boundary) bounds co. on W. Bill Williams and Santa Maria rivers form N co. line. Cattle; alfalfa, hay. Mt. ranges include Trigo Mts. (SW), Dome Rock Mts. (W), Harcuvar Mts. (E), and part of Kofa Mts. (S). Part of Colorado Indian Reservation in W; parts of Cibola and Imperial Natl. Wildlife Areas in SW; part of Kofa Natl. Wildlife Refuge in S; part of Havasu Natl. Wildlife Refuge in NW; part of Eagletail Mts. Wilderness Area in SE; part of Harquahala Mts. Wilderness Area on E boundary. Alamo State Park in NE. Part of large Yuma Proving Ground (U.S. Army) in SW. Co. formed in 1983 from Yuma co.

La Paz Bay (lah PAHS), large sheltered, deep-water inlet of Gulf of California, on SE coast of Baja California Sur, NW Mexico, bordered E by Espíritu Santo Isl.; 50 mi/80 km long NW-SE, c.20 mi/32 km wide. City of La Paz is at its head.

La Pe (lah PAHS), town (1990 pop. 1,389), in S central Oaxaca, Mexico, 34 mi/55 km S of Oaxaca de Juárez, and 7 mi/11km NW of Ejotga de Erespo. Elev. 4,856 ft/1,480 m. In the upper Miahuatlán R. valley. Temperate climate. Agr.

La Pérade, Canada: see SAINTE ANNE DE LA PÉRADE.

La Perla (lah PER-lah), town (1990 pop. 2,189), Veracruz, E Mexico, at SE foot of Pico de Orizaba, 6 mi/10 km N of Orizaba. Fruit.

La Perouse, Mount (per-ROOS) (10,728 ft/3,270 m), SE Alaska, in Fairweather Range, near Gulf of Alaska, 100 mi/161 km W of Juneau, in Glacier Bay Natl. Monument; 58°34′N 137°05′W.

La Perouse Pinnacle, Hawaii: see FRENCH FRIGATE SHOAL.

La Piedad de Cabadas (lah pee-ai-DAHD dai kah-BAH-dahs), city (1990 pop. 62,625), ⊙ La Piedad municipio, Michoacán, central Mexico, on central plateau, on Lerma R. (Guanajuato border), and 90 mi/145 km ESE of Guadalajara; 20°20′N 102°01′W. Mfg. and agr. center (cereals, sugarcane, fruit, vegetables; livestock); tanneries, rayon mills; mfg. (native shawls, sweets). Formerly called La Piedad de Cavadas.

La Place (luh PLAHS), uninc. city (1990 pop. 24,194), St. John the Baptist parish, SE La., on E bank (levee) of the Mississippi R., and 25 mi/40 km WNW of New Orleans; 30°21′N 91°51′W. In sugarcane and farming (vegetables; cattle) area; fishing (catfish, crawfish, alligators); mfg. (structural steel, synthetic rubber; printing and publishing). L. Pontchartrain shore, 4 mi/6 km NE. Manchac State Wildlife Area to N. Bonnet Carre Spillway to SE.

La Plaine, village (1991 pop. 1,331), SE Dominica, B.W.I., 10 mi/16 km ENE of Roseau; 15°20′N 61°15′W. Limes. Agr. demonstration center.

La Plata, county (□ 1,699 sq mi/4,400 sq km; 1990 pop. 32,284), SW Colo.; ⊙ Durango; 37°17′N 107°50′W. Cattle, sheep, grazing area, bordering on N.Mex. (S); bounded W by La Plata Mts.; drained by Animas, Florida (forms Lemon Reservoir), and Los Pinas (forms Vallecito Reservoir in E) rivers. Gold, silver, lead, and coal mines near Durango. Includes part of San Juan Natl. Forest in much of N ½. Part of Southern Ute Indian Reservation (S); Purgatory Ski Area (N). Formed 1874.

La Plata (lah-PLAI-tuh), city (1990 pop. 1,401), Macon co., N central Mo., 20 mi/32 km N of Macon; 40°01′N

92°29′W. RR junction. Agr. (corn, wheat, soybeans; cattle, hogs); mfg. (wood cabinets). Laid out 1855.

La Plata (luh PLAH-tah), town (1990 pop. 5,841), ⊙ Charles co. (since 1895), S Md., 25 mi/40 km S of Washington, D.C.; 38°32′N 76°58′W. Tobacco market; large warehouses. Arose in 1872 as a result of the coming of the RR, and replaced Port Tobacco as co. seat in 1895. U.S. Army Radio Receiving Station on 500 acres/2,020 ha is (1943) 2 mi/3.2 km NE.

La Plata Mountains, SW Colo. and NW N.Mex., spur of San Juan Mts. extending N-S bet. La Plata and Animas rivers. Highest point is Hesperus Peak (13,232 ft/4,033 m). Gold, silver, coal mined.

La Plata Peak (14,361 ft/4,377 m), Chaffe co., central Colo., in Sawatch Mts., 18 mi/29 km SW of Leadville, in San Isabel Natl. Forest.

La Plata River, c.70 mi/113 km long, in SW Colo. and NW N.Mex.; rises in La Plata Mts., W La Plata co., Colo.; flows S to San Juan R. just W of Farmington, N.Mex.

La Plume, township (1990 pop. 647), Lackawanna co., NE Pa., 12 mi/19 km NNW of Scranton; 41°33′N 75°45′W. Agr. includes livestock, vegetables; dairying. Seat of Keystone Jr. Col.; Lackawanna State Park to NE.

La Pointe, village (1990 pop. 147), SW Madeline Isl., in APOSTLE ISLANDS, Ashland co., N Wis., on narrow channel of L. Superior, on W side of entrance to Chequamegon Bay; 46°55′N 90°38′W. Fishing; mustard, coffee. A Fr. fortified trading post was built here in 1693, evacuated in 1698, and reoccupied 1718–1759. In early-19th cent., site of an Amer. Fur Company post. Ferry from Bayfield; tourism and historical mus. Apostle Isls. Natl. Lakeshore on adjacent isl.; Big Bay State Park to E.

La Porte, county (□ 613 sq mi/1,588 sq km; 1990 pop. 107,066), NW Ind., bounded NW by L. Michigan, N by Mich. state line, partly S by Kankakee R.; ⊙ La Porte; 41°33′N 86°44′W. Resorts on L. Michigan. Mfg., esp. at Michigan City and La Porte. Fruit, corn, soybeans; hogs, cattle; lake shipping; fisheries; timber. Natural lakes, glacially formed. Kingsbury State Fish and Wildlife Area in SE, part of Kankakee State Fish and Wildlife Area in S. Formed 1832.

La Porte 1 city (1990 pop. 21,507), ⊙ La Porte co., NW Ind.; 41°37′N 86°43′W. It is a mfg. center in a fertile farmland on the edge of the Calumet industrial region. Mfg. (machinery, plastic containers, agr., paper, wood, and rubber prods., furniture, chemicals, metals, transportation equip., fabricated metal prods., and baked goods). Pine L. is on the NW edge of the city. Laid out 1833; inc. 1835. **2** city (1990 pop. 27,910), Harris co., SE Texas, suburb 18 mi/29 km ESE of downtown Houston on Galveston Bay near Houston Ship Channel (San Jacinto R.); 29°40′N 95°02′W. Oil wells, refineries; mfg. (chemicals, plastics, agr. prods., marine cargo containers). La Porte Municipal Airport in city. Bridge and tunnel to Baytown across ship channel; Sylvan Beach County Park; San Jacinto Battleground and Battleship Texas State Historic Site to N. Settled 1889, inc. 1892.

La Porte City, town (1990 pop. 2,128), Black Hawk co., E central Iowa, on Wolf Creek near its mouth on Cedar R., and 15 mi/24 km SSE of Waterloo; 42°18′N 92°11′W. Mfg. (meat processing, dairy prods., feed, concrete blocks); limestone quarry nearby. Inc. 1871.

La Prairie, town (1990 pop. 68), Adams co., W Ill., 26 mi/42 km ENE of Quincy; 40°08′N 91°00′W. In agr. area.

La Prairie, village (1990 pop. 438), Itasca co., N central Minn., 2 mi/3.2 km E of Grand Rapids on Mississippi R., at mouth of Prairie R.; 47°13′N 93°29′W. Agr. (alfalfa; cattle; dairying); timber. Golden Anniversary State Forest to SE.

La Prenza, uninc. town, San Diego co., S Calif., residential suburb 8 mi/12.9 km E of downtown San Diego. Sweetwater Reservoir to S.

La Pryor, town (1990 pop. 1,343), Zavala co., SW Texas, 18 mi/29 km N of Crystal City, near Nueces R.; 28°56′N 99°50′W. Irrigated area (spinach, vegetables, corn, pecans; cotton).

La Puente, city (1990 pop. 36,955), Los Angeles co., S Calif., a growing suburb 16 mi/26 km E of downtown Los Angeles; 34°02′N 117°57′W. Primarily residential, it has some diverse light mfg. (hardware, electronics, paper prods., metal plating, scew machine prods.). Laid out 1841, inc. 1956.

La Purísima (lah poo-REE-see-mah), settlement (1990 pop. 391), Baja California Sur, Comondú municipio, NW Mexico, in valley, 180 mi/290 km NW of La Paz; 26°10′N 112°05′W. Some agr. (grain; livestock).

La Purisima Concepcion, Mission, Calif.: see LOMPOC.

La Push, uninc. village (1990 pop. 600), Clallam co., NW Wash., on Pacific coast, at mouth of Quillayute R., and 25 mi/40 km S of Cape Flattery. Hq. of Quillayute (Quilleute) Indian Reservation; located in reservation. Fish; timber. Flattery Rocks Natl. Wildlife Refuge to N; Quillayute Natl. Wildlife Refuge to S, both offshore. Reservation bounded N, E, and S by coastal unit of Olympic Natl. Park, including L. Ozette to N. Quillayute State Airport to NE.

La Quemada, Mexico: see QUEMADA.

La Quinta, city (1990 pop. 11,215), Riverside co., S Calif., suburb 17 mi/27 km SE of Palm Springs, 5 mi/8 km SW of Indio, in N foothills of Santa Rosa Mts.; 33°40′N 116°17′W. San Bernardino Natl. Forest to SW. Rapidly growing urban fringe in irrigated agr. area (citrus, dates, cotton, grain; nursery livestock, poultry).

La Reforma (lah re-FOR-mah), town (1990 pop. 1,185) in far SW Oaxaca, Mexico, 24 mi/39 km NE of Santiago Pinotepa Natl. A mountainous region; little fertile soil, hot climate. Agr. (cereals, fruits); woods. No roads. Connected to Mexico Highway 125 by unpaved road (12 mi/20 km). Elev. 3,117 ft/950 m.

La Reforma, Mexico: see REFORMA, town.

La Resolana, Mexico: see CASIMIRO CASTILLO.

La Riviera, uninc. city (1990 pop. 10,986), Sacramento co., central Calif., residential suburb 6 mi/9.7 km E of downtown Sacramento, on American R.; 38°34′N 121°22′W. Sacramento State Univ. and Goethe Arboretum to W.

La Roche, town, NW Sask., Canada, on E side of Lac La Loche, 260 mi/418 km NW of Saskatoon, 25 mi/40 km E of Alta. border. Sport fishing and hunting area. Timber, furs. Airstrip; hwy. from SE. Clearwater Prov. Park is 25 mi/40 km N.

La Romana (lah ro-MAH-nah), province (□ 209 sq mi/541 sq km; 1993 pop. 158,132), SE Dominican Republic, along the Caribbean coast; ⊙ LA ROMANA; 18°30′N 68°58′W. Agr. (sugarcane; sugarcane milling). The prov. lies in the coastal plain.

La Romana (lah ro-MAH-nah), city (1993 pop. 132,834), SE Dominican Republic, on the Caribbean Sea; ⊙ of La Romana prov. (1981 pop. 109,769); 18°30′N 69°00′W. Major port of La Romana prov.; airport; site of several resort hotels.

La Ronge, town (1986 pop. 2,696), Sask., Canada, W shore of Lac La Ronge; 55°06′N 105°18′W. Former site of Indian residential school and Hudson's Bay Company posts in area. Native community doubled since 1971. Tourist, administrative center, and prospecting departure point.

La Rose, village (1990 pop. 130), Marshall co., N central Ill., near Crow Creek, 10 mi/16 km ESE of Lacon; 40°58′N 89°13′W. In agr. area.

La Rue, village (1990 pop. 802), Marion co., central Ohio, 13 mi/21 km W of Marion, and on Scioto R.; 40°34′N 83°23′W.

La Russell, city (1990 pop. 114), Jasper co., SW Mo., on Spring R., and 14 mi/23 km E of Carthage; 37°08′N 94°03′W. Wheat, hay, sorghum; cattle.

La Sal, uninc. village, San Juan co., SE Utah. near Colo. state line, 25 mi/40 km SE of Moab, in La Sal Mts., in Lisbon Valley. Wheat; oil and natural gas; lumber. Elev. 7,125 ft/2,172 m. Part of Manti-La Sal Natl. Forest to N.

La Sal Mountains, range, La Sal Natl. Forest, San Juan and Grand cos., E Utah, bet. Colorado R. and Colo. state line. Chief peaks are Mt. Tomasaki (12,230 ft/3,728 m), Mt. Waas (12,311 ft/3,752 m), and Mt. Peale (12,721 ft//3,877 m). Copper deposits. Partly in Manti-La Sal Natl. Forest.

La Salle (luh SAHL), city (1991 pop. 73,804), S central Que., Canada, residential suburb 6 mi/10 km SSW of downtown Montreal, on Montreal Isl., on bend on NE side of St. Lawrence R., N of Mercier Bridge; 49°41′N 97°16′W. Canal Lachine to NW.

La Salle (luh SAHL), residential town, S Ont., Canada, on Detroit R., and 8 mi/12.9 km SW of Windsor.

La Salle 1 (luh SAL), county (□ 1,148 sq mi/2,973 sq km; 1990 pop. 106,913), N Ill.; ⊙ Ottawa; 41°20′N 88°52′W. Drained by Illinois, Fox, Vermilion, and Little Vermilion rivers. Includes part of Illinois and Michigan Canal Parkway. Agr. (corn, soybeans, wheat, cattle, hogs; dairy prods.); clay. Diversified mfg., chiefly at La Salle, Peru, Ottawa, and Streator. Includes Starved Rock, Buffalo Rock, Illini, and Mathieson state parks. Nuclear power plants: La Salle 1 (initial criticality June 21, 1982) and La Salle 2 (initial criticality March 10, 1984) are 11 mi/18 km SE of Ottawa. Use cooling water from a reservoir, and each has a max. dependable capacity of 1,036 MWe. Morseilles Natl. Guard Training Area near E side. Formed 1831. **2** (luh SAL), county (□ 1,494 sq mi/3,869 sq km; 1990 pop. 5,254), S Texas; ⊙ Cotulla. Drained by Nueces and Frio rivers. Mainly cattle-ranching area; partly in irrigated Winter Garden agr. (peanuts, watermelons, sorghum, corn) region. Oil and natural gas wells. Formed 1858.

La Salle (luh SAL), parish (□ 638 sq mi/1,652 sq km; 1990 pop. 13,662), central La.; ⊙ Jena; 31°42′N 92°08′W. Bounded W by Little R., Castor Creek, and Big Saline Bayou. Includes Catahoula L. in S center, and Saline L. on S boundary (fishing, waterfowl hunting). Oil and natural-gas fields; agr. (cotton, sugarcane, home gardens, soybeans, hay; cattle, hogs); logging, timber, lumber milling. Catahoula L. Diversion Canal crosses S part. Includes Catahoula Natl. Wildlife Refuge at E end of Catahoula L., in SE, part of Saline State Wildlife Area in S. Named after the Fr. explorer. Formed 1908.

La Salle (luh SAL), city (1990 pop. 9,717), La Salle co., N Ill., on the Illinois R. (bridged here); 41°20′N 89°05′W. It forms a tri-city unit with Peru and Oglesby. Agr. (corn, wheat, soybeans; cattle, hogs); mfg. (chemicals, cement, circuit boards, non-ferrous metal prods.). The city developed as an important water transportation center after the opening of the Illinois and Michigan Canal in 1848. Illinois Valley Community Col. across river. Settled 1830; inc. 1852.

La Salle (luh SAL), town (1990 pop. 1,783), Weld co., N Colo., on South Platte R., and suburb 5 mi/8 km S of Greeley; 40°21′N 104°42′W. Elev. 4,676 ft/1,425 m. RR junction. In irrigated wheat, beans, vegetable, cattle and sugar beet region. Light mfg. (feeds). Lower Latham Reservoir to E.

La Salle (luh SAL), village (1990 pop. 98), Watonwan co., S Minn., 7 mi/11.3 km NNE of St. James on Watonwan R.; 44°04′N 94°34′W. Grain, soybeans; livestock; mfg. (feeds). L. Hanska to N.

La Salle 1 and 2 Nuclear Power Plants, Illinois: see LA SALLE, CO.

La Salud (lah sah-LOOD), town, La Habana prov., W Cuba, on RR, and 18 mi/29 km SSW of Havana; 22°42′N 82°26′W. Tobacco, oranges, vegetables.

La Sarre, Canada: see SARRE, LA.

La Sierpe (lah see-ER-pai), town, SE Sancti Spíritus prov., central Cuba, 9 mi/14.5 km ESE of Zaza Reservoir; 21°46′N 79°14′W.

La Sierra (lah see-E-ruh), suburban sect. of Riverside city, Riverside co., S Calif., 6 mi/9.7 km SW of downtown Riverside, at La Sierra and Magnolia avenues. L. Mathews reservoir to S; Site of Loma Linda Univ.

La Station-du-Coteau, village (1991 pop. 1,061), SW Que., Canada, 5 mi/8 km WNW of Valleyfield; 45°17′N 74°14′W.

La Toma (lah TO-mah), resort, Peravia prov., S Dominican Republic, 15 mi/24 km W of Santo Domingo.

La Tour (luh TOOR), uninc. town, Johnson co., W central Mo., 12 mi/19 km E of Harrisonville.

La Trinidad Vista Hermosa (lah tree-nee-DAHD VEES-tah er-MO-sah), town (1990 pop. 167), NW Oaxaca, Mexico, 20 mi/32 km E of Huajuapam de León; 17°42′N 97°32′W. Elev. 7,152 ft/2,180 m. Agr. resources. Cold climate. A Mixtec community.

La Trinitaria, Mexico: see VILLA LA TRINITARIA.

La Tuque (lah tuhk), town (1991 pop. 10,003), S Que., Canada, on the St. Maurice R., NW of Quebec; 47°27′N 72°47′W. La Tuque, in a lumbering and farming region, was established as a trading post in the Fr. period; it grew after the coming of the RR in 1908. Pulp and paper center with a hydroelectric power station.

La Unión (lah oon-YON), town (1990 pop. 2,630), Guerrero, SW Mexico, in Pacific lowland, on La Unión R., 31 mi/50 km NW of Zihuatanejo, 4 mi/6km N of Mexico Highway 200. Rice, sugarcane, fruit. Silver deposits nearby.

La Union, community, Dona Ana co., N.Mex., 17 mi/ 27 km NNW of El Paso central business dist. One of the older communities in the Mesilla Valley. It was founded in 1853 near the banks of the Rio Grande. It was constantly in danger of being in a flood until the construction of Elephant Butte Dam.

La Valle (luh VAL), village (1990 pop. 446), Sauk co., S central Wis., on Baraboo R., 21 mi/34 km WNW of Baraboo; 43°34′N 90°07′W. In dairy and livestock region, on a mill pond. Cheese. Dutch Hollow L. to W; Redstone L. to NE.

La Vega (lah VAI-gah), province (□ 916 sq mi/ 2,373 sq km; 1990 pop. 335,140), central Dominican Republic; ⊙ La Vega; 19°07′N 70°37′W. A mountainous interior prov., bounded by Cordillera Central (S) and Cordillera Septentrional (N); drained by the Yaque del Norte and Camú R., which here forms La Vega Real valley, part of the republic's most fertile and densely populated Cibao region. Main crops include tobacco, cacao; also coffee, rice, corn; cattle; wheat in the uplands. Constanza and Jarabacoa, with nearby Jimenoa Falls, are mt. resorts. The region was visited in 1492 by Columbus, who built a fort. Became a prov. 1845.

La Vega (lah VAI-gah), city (1993 pop. 73,387), central Dominican Republic, on the Camú R.; ⊙ La Vega prov.; 19°15′N 70°30′W. La Vega is the commercial and processing center of a rich agr. region. A religious sanctuary erected on the site of an important battle in the colonial period is nearby. The city was founded in 1495.

La Vega Real (lah VAI-gah re-AHL), valley, NE Dominican Republic, fertile lowland, E sect. of the Cibao along Camú and Yuna rivers, extending c.60 mi/97 km E from La Vega city to Sánchez. Main crops are cacao, coffee, rice, corn, tropical fruit.

La Venta (lah VEN-tah), village (1990 pop. 439), Huimanguillo municipio, W Tabasco, Mexico, in coastal mangrove swamps, 30 mi/48 km E of Coatzacoalcos, near Tonalá R. (Veracruz border); 18°07′N 94°03′W. One of the most important Olmec archaeological sites in Mexico, colossal stone heads discovered here have been moved to Villahermosa, but largest pyramid in Olmec region remains. Site is now adjacent to a petroleum complex.

La Vergne, city (1990 pop. 7,499), Rutherford co., central Tenn., 15 mi/24 km SE of Nashville, near Percy Priest Reservoir (Stones R.), 36°00′N 86°34′W. Mfg. of tires, appliances, metal prods., plastics. Inc. 1972.

La Verkin, town (1990 pop. 1,771), Washington co., SW Utah, 20 mi/32 km NE of St. George, and on Virgin R.; 37°12′N 113°16′W. Fruit; cattle. Zion Natl. Park to E; Dixie Natl. Forest to NW. Quail Creek reservoir and State Park to W.

La Verne, city (1990 pop. 30,897), Los Angeles co., S Calif., suburb 26 mi/42 km ENE of downtown Los Angeles; 34°07′N 117°46′W. La Verne has expanded from a citrus growing town to a city with significant residential developments and light mfg. (electronic components, apparel, hand tools, ceramics, stone prods., plastics prods., synthetic rubber). Oil refining, high technology computers, and aerospace and defense-related indutries are in adjacent areas. La Verne Col. and a water filtration plant that serves much of the S Calif. region are in the city. Marshall Canyon Regional Park to NE, Bonelli Regional Park to SW; Angeles Natl. Forest to N. Inc. 1906.

La Vernia, village (1990 pop. 639), Wilson co., S Texas, 24 mi/39 km ESE of San Antonio, on Cibolo Creek; 29°21′N 98°06′W. Agr. (poultry; peanuts, vegetables, melons); mfg. (steel storage tanks).

La Veta, village (1990 pop. 726), Huerfano co., S Colo., on Cucharas R., in E foothills of Sangre de Cristo Mts., 15 mi/24 km WSW of Walsenburg; 37°30′N 105°00′W. Elev. c.7,013 ft/2,138 m. Resort and trading point in agr. and coal-mining region; livestock and grain prods. La Veta Pass (9,382 ft/2,860 m), W of La Veta, crossed by RR, in Sangre de Cristo Mts., is crossed by U.S. Highway 160. Cuchara Valley Ski Area to SW. Lathrop State Park to NE; part of San Isabel Natl. Forest to SW; part of San Isabel Natl. Forest with the Great Dikes of the Span. Peaks rock formations nearby.

La Villa, town (1990 pop. 1,388), Hidalgo co., S Texas, 14 mi/23 km E of Edinburg; 26°18′N 97°55′W. Irrigated agr. area in Rio Grande Valley (cotton, citrus, vegetables); mfg. (pickles).

La Villita, Mexico: see NOMBRE DE DIOS.

La Virginia, town, ⊙ La Virginia municipio, Risaralda dept., W central Colombia, on the Cauca R., 12 mi/ 19 km NW of Pereira. Sugarcane, plantains, coffee; livestock.

La Yesca (lah YES-kah), town (1990 pop 710), Nayarit, W Mexico, on Jalisco border, 55 mi/89 km ESE of Tepic, in an isolated part of Sierra Madre Occidental. Agr.; mining.

Labadieville (la-buh-DEE-vil), uninc. town (1990 pop. 1,821), Assumption parish, SE La., 20 mi/32 km NW of Houma, on Bayou Lafourche; 29°49′N 90°58′W. Agr. (sugarcane, rice; cattle); crawfish, alligators; mfg. (towboats, electronic instruments).

Labelle (lah-BEL), county (□ 2,392 sq mi/6,195 sq km), SW Que., Canada, on L. Baskatong; ⊙ Mont Laurier; 46°30′N 75°10′W.

Labelle, village (1991 pop. 2,103), S Que., Canada, in the Laurentians, 27 mi/43 km NW of Ste. Agathe des Monts; 46°17′N 74°44′W. In garnet-mining region; dairying.

Laberge, Lake (□ 87 sq mi/225 sq km), S Yukon, Canada, expansion of Lewes R., 20 mi/32 km N of Whitehorse; 30 mi/48 km long, 1 mi/2 km–4 mi/6 km wide.

Laberinto de las Doce Leguas, Cuba: see DOCE LEGUAS and CAYOS DE LAS.

Labette (luh-BET), county (□ 653 sq mi/1,691 sq km; 1990 pop. 23,693), SE Kansas; ⊙ Oswego; 37°11′N 95°17′W. Level area located in the Prairie region, bordering S on Okla.; drained in E by Neosho R. Agr. (cattle, hogs; strawberries, wheat, sorghum, soybeans, hay; dairying). Oil and gas fields; coal deposits. Tri-city airport in NW corner, serves region bet. Independence, Parsons, and Chanute. Big Hill L. reservoir in NW. Formed 1867.

Labette (luh-BET), village (1990 pop. 74), Labette co., SE Kansas, 9 mi/14.5 km SSE of Parsons; 37°13′N 95°10′W. Dairying, agr.

Labná (lahb-NAH), historic site, Tekax municipio, Yucatan, SE Mexico, 7 mi/11.3 km SW of Oxkutzcab; 20°13′N 89°34′W. Anc. Mayan city; one of best examples of Puuc style architecture. Most famous structure is an arch. The site is partly restored.

Laborie (lah-buhr-EE), village (1991 pop. 1,304), S St. Lucia, 17 mi/27 km S of Castries. Fishing.

Labrador, Canada: see LABRADOR-UNGAVA; NEWFOUNDLAND.

Labrador City, town (1991 pop. 9,061), Que., W Lab., Canada, 185 mi/298 km N of Sept-Iles, at S end of Wabash L. W terminus of spur of Que. N. Shore and Labrador RR. Connected to Wabush by project road from Happy Valley-Goose Bay via Churchill Falls. Iron mining dist. developed in early 1960s.

Labrador Current, cold ocean current formed off Lab. coast (Canada) by currents descending from Baffin Bay and W Greenland, bet. 45°N to 58°N; flows S along Lab. coast and E N.F., meets Gulf Stream off the Grand Banks; meeting of cold and warm streams results in the fogs for which this region is noted. Lab. Current carries ice into main shipping lanes bet. Amer. and Europe. The famous ocean liner *Titanic*, sailing from Liverpool to New York on her maiden voyage, struck an iceberg at 41°46′N 50°14′W and sank on the night of April 14-15, 1912. Also called Arctic Current or Arctic Stream.

Labrador Sea, part of North Atlantic Ocean, bet. Lab.

and SW Greenland, linked by Davis Strait with Baffin Bay. The West Greenland current flows N along the Greenland coast, and the Lab. current S along the Lab. coast.

Labrador-Ungava, peninsular region of E Canada (□ c.550,000 sq mi/1,424,500 sq km), bounded on the W by Hudson Bay, on the N by Hudson Strait and Ungava Bay, on the E by the Atlantic Ocean, and on the S by the St. Lawrence R. It is almost completely unpopulated. The W 80% of the peninsula belongs to Nouveau Québec (Ungava) and Saguenay cos. of Que. prov. The E 20%, called simply Lab., is part of N.F. Inuit communities who have lived along the coastline for centuries. The region S of Ungava Bay, originally a possession of the Hudson's Bay Co., was made a part of the N.W.T. in 1869, and later (1895) became a separate dist. In 1912 it was added to Que. prov., but in 1927 the E coast was awarded to N.F. by the Br. Privy Council. The N part of the region is a cold, barren tundra, the S part is covered by coniferous forests. Geologically part of the Can. Shield, the glaciated peninsula has many lakes and streams. There are vast and largely untapped mineral, hydroelectric, and timber resources on the peninsula. Since the mid-1950s the region's development has been aided by the construction of new ports and railheads at Sept-Iles and Port Cartier on the St. Lawrence R., which provide outlets for rich, new iron ore–mines in the interior; other mining includes asbestos, titanium, and copper.

Lac a l'Eau Claire (□ 410 sq mi/1,062 sq km), N Que., Canada; 56°00′N 74°30′W; 45 mi/72 km long, 20 mi/32 km wide. Elev. 790 ft/241 m; contains several isls. Drains into Hudson Bay.

Lac au Saumon (lahk o so-MO), village (1991 pop. 1,310), E Que., Canada, on Salmon L., 30 mi/48 km SSE of Matane; 48°25′N 67°20′W. Lumbering; dairying. Lake was formerly salmon spawning ground.

Lac aux Sables (lahk o SAH-bluh), village (1991 pop. 1,428), S central Que., Canada, on Batiscan R., at S end of L. aux Sables (3 mi/5 km long), 22 mi/35 km NE of Grand'Mère; 46°52′N 72°23′W. Agr.

Lac Beauport (lahk bo-POR), resort village (1991 pop. 4,462), S Que., Canada, on small L. Beauport, 10 mi/ 16 km NNW of Que.

Lac Bouchette (lahk boo-SHET), village (1991 pop. 1,485), S central Que., Canada, on Bouchette L. (5 mi/ 8 km long), on Quiatchouanish R., and 17 mi/27 km SSE of Roberval; 48°16′N 72°10′W. Elev. 1,135 ft/346 m. Quartz mining.

Lac du Flambeau (lak de FLAM-bo), village (1990 pop. 1,423), Vilas co., N Wis., on small Lac du Flambeau, 33 mi/53 km NW of Rhinelander; 45°58′N 89°54′W. Mfg. (electrical measuring instruments). Art center of the Lac du Flambeau Indian Reservation. Fish hatchery nearby; surrounded by numerous lakes.

Lac Etchemin (lahk eech-ME), town (1991 pop. 2,661), S Que., Canada, on L. Etchemin (3 mi/5 km long), 45 mi/72 km SE of Quebec city. Dairying; lumbering; pig raising.

Lac Ile-à-la-Crosse (lahk-eel–ah–lah–KROS), NW central Sask., Canada, expansion of Churchill R., 180 mi/ 290 km NW of Prince Albert; 60 mi/97 km long, 5 mi/ 8 km wide.

Lac La Belle, village (1990 pop. 258), Waukesha co., SE Wis., 10 mi/16 km ESE of Watertown on N end of La Belle L., near Oconomowoc; 43°08′N 88°31′W.

Lac la Biche (lahk lah BEESH), town (1991 pop. 2,549), E Alta., on Lac la Biche, 50 mi/80 km E of Athabaska; 54°46′N 111°58′W. Tanning, lumber and flour milling; dairying.

Lac La Ronge, Canada: see RONGE, LAC LA.

Lac Masson, Canada: see SAINTE MARGUERITE.

Lac qui Parle (LA kee PAHRL), county (□ 778 sq mi/ 2,015 sq km; 1990 pop. 8,924), SW Minn.; ⊙ Madison; 45°00′N 96°10′W. Bounded by S.Dak. on W, bounded N and NE by Minnesota R. (flows through Marsh and Lac qui Parle reservoirs; both in Lac qui Parle Wildlife Area), and drained by Lac qui Parle R. and its West Fork and by Yellow Bank R. Agr. area (corn, oats, wheat, soybeans, hay, alfalfa; hogs, cattle, sheep). Formed 1871.

Lac qui Parle Lake (LA kee PAHRL), reservoir, on boundary of Lac qui Parle and Chippewa cos., extends N into Swift co., SW Minn, on Minnesota R., 10 mi/ 16 km NW of Montevideo; 8 mi/12.9 km long, 1 mi/ 1.6 km wide; 45°02′N 95°53′W. Elev. 934 ft/285 m. Receives Lac qui Parle R., from SW at SE end (dam), in Lac qui Parle State Park. Remainder of lake and Marsh L. (upstream) are in Lac qui Parle Wildlife Area.

Lac qui Parle River (LA kee PAHRL), c.70 mi/113 km long; rises in small lake in Deuel co., E S.Dak., enters SW Minn. near Canby; flows NE, past Dawson, to Minnesota R. at SE end of Lac qui Parle; 44°45′N 96°32′W.

Lac Saint Jean Est (lahk se zhahn EST), county (□ 905 sq mi/2,344 sq km; 1991 pop. 51,963), S central Que., Canada, on L. St. John; ⊙ St. Joseph d'Alma; 48°30′N 71°40′W.

Lac Saint Jean Ouest (lahk se zhah WEST), county (□ 22,818 sq mi/59,099 sq km), central Que., Canada, on L. St. John; ⊙ Roberval; 49°00′N 73°00′W.

Lac Simard (lahk see-MAHR), (□ 59 sq mi/153 sq km), SW Que., Canada, 90 mi/145 km NNE of North Bay; 13 mi/21 km long, 10 mi/16 km wide; drained W by Ottawa R.; 47°38′N 78°40′W. Formerly known as L. Expanse.

Lac Vieux Desert, lake (□ c.10 sq mi/26 sq km) on Wis.-Mich. state line, largely in Vilas co. (Nicolet Natl. Forest), N Wis., and partly in Gogebic co. (Ottoawa Natl. Forest), W Upper Peninsula, Mich., in forested area. Muskellunge fishing; drained by Wisconsin R.

L'Acadie (lah-kah-DEE), village (1991 pop. 5,074), S Que., Canada, on Richelieu R., and 5 mi/8 km W of St. Jean. Dairying; grain, cattle.

Lacantún River (lah-kahn-TOON), Mexico; c.100 mi/ 161 km long, rises in several branches in Cuchumatanes Mts. of Guatemala; flows NW to Usumacinta R., receives Jataté R. in Chiapas.

Lacarne, Ohio: see PORT CLINTON.

Lacey, city (1990 pop. 19,279), Thurston co., W Wash., suburb 5 mi/8 km E of Olympia, near Puget Sound; 47°02′N 122°49′W. Agr. area (poultry; dairying; vegetables, fruit). Mfg. (paper prods., mobile homes, structural wood and sheet metal prods.). Seat of St. Martins Col. Fort Lewis Military Reservation to E and SE; Nisqually Indian Reservation to E; Nisqually Natl. Wildlife Refuge and Tolmie State Park to NE, on Puget Sound.

Lacey, township (□ 80 sq mi/207 sq km; 1990 pop. 22,141), Ocean co., E central N.J., 5 mi/8 km S of Lakehurst; 39°51′N 74°16′W. Inc. 1871.

Lacey-Lakeview, town (1990 pop. 3,617), McLennan co., E central Texas, residential suburb 4 mi/6.4 km NNE of downtown Waco, near Brazos R. Texas State Technical Col. and T.S.T.C. Airport to NE.

Laceyville, borough (1990 pop. 436), Wyoming co., NE Pa., 31 mi/50 km WNW of Scranton, on Susquehanna R. (bridged). Agr. (hay; dairying; timber); mfg. (wooden prods.).

Lachine (luh-SHEEN), city (1991 pop. 35,266), S Que., Canada, on Montreal isl., at the E end of L. St. Louis just SW of Montreal; 45°25′N 73°40′W. Industries include iron and steel foundries; mfg. (tires, electrical appliances, and electronics). Lachine was settled in 1675 and in 1689 was the scene of a battle bet. the French and the Iroquois. The city is the SW terminal of the Lachine Canal, connecting L. St. Louis with the St. Lawrence R. at Montreal. Constructed bet. 1821 and 1825 (later enlarged) to bypass the Lachine Rapids of the St. Lawrence, the canal has been superceded by the St. Lawrence Seaway canals.

Lachine Canal, on the St. Lawrence, S Que., Canada, extends SW-NE bet. the St. Lawrence at Montreal and L. St. Louis at Lachine, bypassing Lachine Rapids; 9 mi/ 14 km long. Opened c.1825, later enlarged; there are 5 locks.

Lachine Canal, Canada: see LACHINE, city.

Lachine Rapids, on the St. Lawrence, S Que., Canada, at S end of Montreal Isl., bet. S part of Montreal and Lasalle; 3 mi/5 km long, with total drop of 42 ft/13 m.

At E end of rapids is Heron islet. Rapids are bypassed by Lachine Canal. Hydroelectric power.

Lachute (luh-SHOOT), town (1991 pop. 11,730), S Que., Canada, on the North R., W of Montreal; 45°39′N 74°20′W. It is at the foot of the Laurentian Mts. Diverse mfg. includes textiles, lumber, wood and paper prods.

Lackawanna (LAK-ah-WAH-nah), county (□ 464 sq mi/1,202 sq km; 1990 pop. 219,039), NE Pa.; ⊙ Scranton. Bounded SW by Susquehanna R., SE by Lehigh R.; drained by Lackawanna R. Hilly upland rises in N, part of Pocono plateau in S, Lackawanna valley in center. Agr. (corn, oats, hay, alfalfa, vegetables; cattle; dairying); former major anthracite-coal-mining area. Mfg. at Scranton, Olyphant, Danmore, Carbondale, and Clark's Summit. Part of Lackawanna State Forest in SE; Lackawanna State Park in NW; Archbald Pothole State Park in NE center; Merli Sarnoski Park in NE. Formed 1878.

Lackawanna, city (□ 6 sq mi/15.5 sq km; 1990 pop. 20,585), Erie co., W N.Y., on L. Erie; 42°49′N 78°49′W. Mfg. (abrasives, chemicals, concrete). Formerly a major steel-making center, Lackawanna experienced the rapid and total decline of its foremost industry in the 1970s and 1980s. A distinguished city landmark is the elaborate Basilica of Our Lady of Victory, a R.C. shrine. Inc. 1909.

Lackawanna (LAK-ah-WAH-nah), river, 35 mi/56 km long, NE Pa.; rises on Susquehanna-Wayne co. line, c.15 mi/24 km N of Carbondale in West and East branches (both c.10 mi/16 km long and closely parallel each other, flowing S), which join at Stillwater L. reservoir; 41°41′N 75°29′W. Flows generally SW past Forest City, Carbondale, Olyphant, Scranton, and Old Forge to Susquehanna R. 8 mi/12.9 km WSW of Scranton. Former major anthracite-coal-mining area, now depleted.

Lackawaxen (LAK-uh-WAK-sen), uninc. village, Lackawaxen township, Pike co., NE Pa., 18 mi/29 km WNW of Post Services, N.Y., on the Delaware R. (N.Y. state line), at mouth of Lackawaxen R.; 41°28′N 74°59′W. Del. State Forest to SW.

Lackawaxen River (LAK-uh-WAK-sen), 25 mi/40 km long, NE Pa.; formed by joining of West Branch (c.15 mi/24 km long); flows through Belmont L. and Johnso Creek, 5 mi/8 km ENE of Forest City; flows SE, through Prompon L. reservoir, past Honesdale and Hawley, to Delaware R. at Lackawaxen (41°34′N 75°19′W); receives Wallenpaupack Creek, 2 mi/3.2 km E of Hawley.

Lackey (LAK-ee), uninc. village, Floyd co., E Ky., in Cumberland foothills, 17 mi/27 km W of Pikeville. In bituminous-coal area; mfg. (concrete).

Lackland Air Force Base, U.S. military installation, Bexar co., S Texas, in W part of San Antonio. Covers c.6,835 acres/2,766 ha; major air force training center. Est. 1941.

Laclede (luh-KLEED), county (□ 770 sq mi/1,994 sq km; 1990 pop. 27,158), S central Mo.; ⊙ Lebanon; 37°39′N 92°35′W. In the Ozarks; drained by Gasconade R. Cattle; wheat, corn, fruit growing, hay; oak timber; mfg. at Lebanon (pleasure boats). Part of Mark Twain Natl. Forest in E. Formed 1849.

Laclede (luh-KLEED), city (1990 pop. 410), Linn co., N central Mo., 5 mi/8 km W of Brookfield; 39°47′N 93°10′W. Corn, wheat, soybeans; cattle, hogs. Gen. John J. Pershing boyhood home state historic site. Pershing State Park in SW. Locust Creek Covered Bridge (1868) state historic site to W.

Laclede, uninc. village (1990 pop. 200), Bonner co., N Idaho, 12 mi/19 km SW of Sandpoint, on Pend Oreille R., Round L. State Park across river to E. Agr. (cattle); timber; mfg. (log homes, lumber).

Lacolle (lah-KOL), village (1991 pop. 1,392), S Que., Canada, S of Montreal and near the U.S. border; 45°05′N 73°22′W. During the War of 1812, the British defeated an invading Amer. army here on March 30, 1814.

Lacombe (luh-KOM), town (1991 pop. 6,934), S central Alta., Canada, near Gull L., 14 mi/23 km N of Red Deer; 52°28′N 113°44′W. RR junction. Grain elevators; lumber, flour, grist mills; dairying. Dominion experimental farm.

Lacombe (luh-KOM), uninc. city (1990 pop. 6,523), St. Tammany parish, La., 8 mi/12.9 km SE of Mandeville; 30°18′N 89°56′W. Bryon Lacombe Crab Festival held here. Originally settled by Fr. slave owners.

Lacon (LAI-kahn), city (1990 pop. 1,986), ⊙ Marshall co., N central Ill., on Illinois R. (bridged), and 24 mi/ 39 km NNE of Peoria; 41°01′N 89°24′W. In agr. area; grain elevator, textiles. Laid out as Columbia in 1826; inc. 1839.

Lacona, town (1990 pop. 357), Warren co., S central Iowa, 15 mi/24 km SE of Indianola; 41°11′N 93°22′W.

Lacona, village (□ 1 sq mi/2.6 sq km; 1990 pop. 593), Oswego co., N central N.Y., 25 mi/40 km NE of Oswego; 43°38′N 76°01′W. Mfg. of wooden architectural fabrications; sand, gravel pits.

Laconia (luh-KO-nee-yuh), city (1990 pop. 15,743), ⊙ Belknap co., central N.H., 22 mi/35 km N of Concord; 43°34′N 71°28′W. Bounded SW by Winnisquam L., NE by L. Winnipesaukee. City center in S on Winnipesaukee R., bet. Opeche Bay of L. Winnipesaukee (N) and Winnisquam L. (SW). It is a popular summer and winter resort, and the industrial and trade center of a lake resort and farming region. Mfg. (computer equip., machinery, bldg. materials, fabricated metal prods., transportation equip., paper prods., textiles, electronics, fabricated metal prods., medical equip.; printing and publishing, machining, aluminum foundry). N part is rural, some agr. (vegetables; cattle, poultry; dairying). Laconia Technical Col., N.H. Col. of Continued Education. Laconia Airport to NE. Large Paugus Bay of L. Winnipesaukee in N. Winnipesaukee Scenic RR follows lakeshore; cruise boat at Weirs Beach (N). Settled c.1761; inc. as a city 1893.

Laconia, town (1990 pop. 75), Harrison co., S Ind., near Ohio R., 12 mi/19 km S of Corydon; 38°02′N 86°05′W. In agr. area. Laid out 1816.

Lacoochee (lah-KOO-chee), town (□ 2 sq mi/5.2 sq km; 1990 pop. 2,072), Pasco co., W central Fla., 7 mi/11.3 km N of Dade City; 28°28′N 82°10′W.

Lacosta Island (luh-KOS-tuh), narrow barrier island, Gulf of Mexico, SW Fla., N of Captiva Pass, at entrance to Charlotte Harbor and Pine Isl. Sound; c.7 mi/11.3 km long. Sometimes called Cayo Costa.

Lacoste (luh-KAHST), village, SW Que., Canada, near L. Nominingue, 30 mi/48 km ESE of Mont Laurier. Mica mining.

Lacovia, town (1991 pop. 3,159), former capital of St. Elizabeth parish, SW Jamaica, stretches 2 mi/3.2 km along Black R., and 36 mi/58 km WNW of May Pen; 18°04′N 77°45′W. Used as an inland port for shipping sugar, logwood, and fustic down the river. In agr. region (cassava, corn, vegetables, spices; livestock).

Ladd, village (1990 pop. 1,283), Bureau co., N Ill., 14 mi/ 23 km E of Princeton; 41°22′N 89°12′W. In agr. area. RR junction. Inc. 1890.

Ladd Field, Alaska: see FORT WAINWRIGHT.

Laddonia, city (1990 pop. 581), Audrain co., NE central Mo., 13 mi/21 km ENE of Mexico; 39°14′N 91°38′W. Corn, wheat, soybeans; cattle, hogs; lumber.

Ladelle (luh-DEL), village, Drew co., SE Ark., 11 mi/ 18 km S of Monticello.

Ladera Heights, uninc. town (1990 pop. 6,316), San Mateo co., W Calif., residential suburb 30 mi/48 km SSE of downtown San Francisco, near San Francisquito Creek. Santa Cruz Mts. (SW); Portola and Castle Rock state parks (S). Sometimes called Ladera.

Ladera Heights, suburb of Los Angeles, Calif., 3 mi/ 4.8 km N of Inglewood in Baldwin Hills; 34°00′N 118°22′W.

Ladner, town, SW B.C., Canada, near mouth of S branch of Fraser R. delta on Strait of Georgia, 11 mi/18 km S of Vancouver; 49°05′N 123°05′W. Dairying; milk, fruit, vegetable, and fish canning; fishing, lumber shipping; flowers, nurseries. Urban enclave of Vancouver.

Ladoga (luh-DO-guh), town (1990 pop. 1,124), Montgomery co., W central Ind., on Raccoon Creek, and 11 mi/18 km SE of Crawfordsville; 39°55′N 86°48′W. Agr. area (corn, soybeans; livestock).

Ladonia 1 (luh-DON-yuh), village (1990 pop. 2,905), Russell co., E Ala., 3 mi/4.8 km W of Phenix City;

32°28′N 85°05′W. **2** village (1990 pop. 658), Fannin co., NE Texas, 27 mi/43 km SW of Paris; 33°25′N 95°57′W. Near North Sulphur R. Agr. (cotton, grain, peanuts, soybeans); mfg. (adhesive prods.). Historic downtown restored.

Ladora, town (1990 pop. 308), Iowa co., E central Iowa, 6 mi/9.7 km WSW of Marengo; 41°45′N 92°11′W. Livestock; grain.

Ladson, uninc. city (1990 pop. 13,540), Charleston and Berkeley cos., SE S.C., 16 mi/26 km NW of Charleston; 33°00′N 80°06′W. Mfg. (cabinets, power transformers; printing and publishing, steel fabricating); agr. (poultry, livestock; grain, cotton, soybeans).

Ladue, city (1990 pop. 8,847), St. Louis co., E Mo., a suburb 10 mi/16 km W of downtown St. Louis; 38°38′N 90°22′W. Exclusive residential area. Mfg. (vending machines); limestone quarry. Inc. 1936 as a consolidation of former towns of Ladue, Deer Creek, and McKnight.

Lady Evelyn Lake, SE central Ont., Canada, 16 mi/26 km W of Cobalt; 20 mi/32 km long, 4 mi/6 km wide. Elev. 930 ft/283 m. Drains S into L. Timagami; fishing resort.

Lady Franklin Bay, NE Ellesmere Isl., NE Franklin dist., N.W.T., Canada, inlet of Robeson Channel, at NW end of Hall Basin; 25 mi/40 km long, 6 mi/9.7 km–10 mi/16 km wide; 81°40′N 65°W. On N shore, near entrance of bay, is small inlet of DISCOVERY HARBOUR, site of FORT CONGER, both of importance in late-19th-cent. exploration of the Arctic.

Lady Franklin, Cape, NE extremity of Bathurst Isl., N central Franklin dist., N.W.T., Canada, at N end of Queens Channel; 76°40′N 98°42′W.

Lady Franklin Point, SW extremity of Victoria Isl., SW Franklin dist., N.W.T., Canada, on Coronation Gulf, at E entrance of Dolphin and Union Strait; 68°31′N 113°09′W.

Lady Lake, town (☐ 6 sq mi/15.5 sq km; 1990 pop. 8,071), Lake co., central Fla., c.20 mi/32 km SE of Ocala, in citrus-fruit and watermelon area; 28°55′N 81°55′W. Fruit packing.

Lady's Island, island, Beaufort co., S S.C., one of Sea Isls., c.35 mi/56 km NE of Savannah, Ga., connected by land to St. Helena Isl. (S) and Port Royal Isl. (W); c.10 mi/16 km long. Wilkins village on NE shore. Oyster and vegetable canning.

Ladysmith, town (1991 pop. 4,875), SW B.C., Canada, on SE Vancouver Isl., on inlet of Strait of Georgia, 13 mi/21 km SSE of Nanaimo; 48°58′N 123°49′W. Port and shipping point for nearby fishing, logging area; fruit-growing, vegetables, dairying.

Ladysmith, town (1990 pop. 3,938), ⊙ Rusk co., N Wis., on Flambeau R., and c.50 mi/80 km NE of Eau Claire; 45°27′N 91°05′W. In lake-resort area. Dairy prods.; mfg. (furniture, aluminum die parts, paper, wooden ware, canned vegetables). A large cooperative creamery is here; has hydroelectric plant. RR junction. Big Falls Flowage to NE. Inc. 1905.

Laeo Kailiu (LAH-ai-O KAH-ee-LEE-oo), on NW coast, Kauai isl., Kauai co., Hawaii, S of Kāhala Point, in Haena State Park, on Pacific Ocean.

Lafayette 1 (LAH-fai-ET), county (☐ 545 sq mi/1,412 sq km; 1990 pop. 9,643), SW Ark.; ⊙ Lewisville; 33°14′N 93°36′W. Bounded S by La. state line; W by Red R.; E, in part, by Dorcheat Bayou; drained by Bodeau Creek and Bayou. Oil and agr. area (wheat, soybeans; cattle, hogs, chickens). Timber; gravel; oil and gas. L. Erling Forest (Bodcau Bayou) in SE; Lafayette Wildlife Management Area in S, E of L. Erling; Conway Cemetery State Park in S. **2** county (☐ 547 sq mi/1,417 sq km; 1990 pop. 5,578), N central Fla., bounded E and NE by Suwannee R.; ⊙ Mayo; 28°46′N 81°43′W. Swampy flatwoods area, with many small lakes. Farming (corn, peanuts, tobacco), cattle raising, lumbering. Limestone and phosphate deposits. Formed 1856. **3** county (☐ 679 sq mi/1,759 sq km; 1990 pop. 31,826), N Miss.; ⊙ Oxford; 34°21′N 89°29′W. Drained by Yocona and Tallahatchie (forms part of N boundary) rivers; part of Sardis Reservoir (Tallahatchie R.) is in NW. Agr. (cotton, corn, soybeans; cattle; dairying); pine, hardwood timber. Part of Holly Springs Natl. Forest in NE. Formed 1836. **4** (LAH-fee-ET), county (☐ 634 sq mi/1,642 sq km; 1990 pop. 31,107), W central Mo.; ⊙ Lexington; 39°03′N 93°46′W. Bounded N by Missouri R. Agr. (wheat, soybeans, corn, apples, peaches, sorghum; cattle, hogs); limestone rock quarries; mfg. at Lexington, Odessa, Concordia, and Higginsville. Confederate Memorial State Park in center. Formed 1834. **5** county (☐ 634 mi/1,020 km; 1990 pop. 16), S Wis., bordered S by Ill.; ⊙ Darlington; 42°39′N 90°08′W. Dairying; agr. (barley, oats, wheat, corn, soybeans; cattle, hogs, sheep); zinc mining. Area formerly had important lead-mining industry. Drained by Pecatonica and Galena rivers. First Capitol State Park is in NW at Leslie; Yellowstone L. State Park in NE; E part of Pecatonica State Trail in NW. Formed 1846.

Lafayette (LAH-fai-ET), parish (☐ 283 sq mi/733 sq km; 1990 pop. 164,762), S La.; ⊙ Lafayette; 30°13′N 92°02′W. Bounded N by short Bayou Carenero, drained by Vermilion R. (navigable). Agr. (home gardens, corn, sorghum, hay, nursery crops, rice, sugarcane, sweet potatoes, cucumbers, other vegetables; honey; cattle, horses, exotic fowl; dairying); crawfish; lumber; oil, natural gas. Varied mfg. at Lafayette. Formed 1823.

Lafayette 1 (lah-FAI-it), city (1990 pop. 3,151), ⊙ Chambers co., E Ala., 18 mi/29 km N of Opelika. Mfg. (rubber, yarns, lumber milling, meat packing). Settled 1883. **2** (LAH-fai-ET), city (1990 pop. 23,501), Contra Costa co., NW Calif., a residential suburb 8 mi/12.9 km NE of downtown Oakland, in the San Francisco-Oakland area; 37°54′N 122°07′W. Diversified light mfg., including food processing and transportation equip. The city is a horse-raising and agr. trading center, esp. for walnuts. Mokelumne Aqueduct runs E-W through city. Las Trampas Regional Park to SE; Briones Regional park to N; Lafayette Reservoir in SW. Settled 1848, inc. 1968. **3** city (1990 pop. 14,548), Boulder co., N central Colo., suburb, 20 mi/32 km NNW of downtown Denver; 39°59′N 105°05′W. Elev. c.5,237 ft/1,596 m. In coal, poultry, dairy, grain, and sugar-beet area. Mfg. (roof trusses, computer ribbons). Inc. 1890. **4** city (1990 pop. 43,764), ⊙ Tippecanoe co., W central Ind., on the Wabash R.; 40°25′N 86°52′W. RR junction. A mfg. city in a grain, livestock, and dairy area. Mfg. (bldg. materials, electrical equip., fabricated metal prods., consumer goods, wire, food processing, transportation equip., heating equip., chemicals, animal health and feed prods., paperboard, pharmaceuticals, and rubber prods.; publishing). Motor vehicles are also assembled here. Tippecanoe Battlefield State Memorial (Nov. 1811) 5 mi/8 km N. Of interest is the rebuilt blockhouse of Fort Ouiatenon (1719), 4 mi/6.4 km W. Purdue Univ. located in adjacent West Lafayette. Laid out 1825. Inc. 1853. **5** city (1990 pop. 94,440), ⊙ Lafayette parish, S central La., 48 mi/77 km WSW of Baton Rouge, on the Vermilion R. (which is linked to the Intracoastal Waterway to S); 30°13′N 92°02′W. Known as the hub of cajun country. It is a commercial, shipping, and medical center for the area; agr. (sugarcane, rice, cotton; dairy cattle, livestock); mfg. (petroleum, apparel, jewelry, bldg. materials, and boxes); industries (oil equip. and service, printing and publishing, food processing). The area's oil and natural gas boom has contributed to a large increase and diversity of pop. and an influx of new businesses. The Heymann Oil Center is hq. for several oil companies. Of interest are St. John's Cathedral (site 1821; 3d structure 1916), a Carmelite monastery, a planetarium, Lafayette Natural History Mus., Children's Mus., and the Univ. Art Center. Cajun Dome stadium is here. Lafayette is the seat of the Univ. of Southwestern La., and the scene of an annual Mardi Gras, along with numerous other cultural festivals such as the Festival Acadiens. Evangeline Downs thoroughbred racetrack to N. Longfellow Evangeline State Commemorative Area to SE. Settled 1760s by Acadians; inc. 1836. **6** city (1990 pop. 3,641), ⊙ Macon co., N Tenn., 27 mi/43 km NNE of Lebanon; 36°31′N 86°02′W. Trade center for farm area; mfg. (transportation equip., apparel, greeting cards). Inc. since 1940.

Lafayette (LAH-fai-ET), town (1990 pop. 1,292), Yamhill co., NW Oregon, 5 mi/8 km NE of McMinnville, on Yamhill R.; 45°15′N 123°06′W. Agr. (vegetables, berries, grapes; poultry); mfg. (dairy prods.; bakery prods.); wineries. Maud Williamson State Park to S.

Lafayette 1 (LAH-fee-ET) village (1990 pop. 462), Nicollet co., S Minn., 9 mi/14.5 km NNE of New Ulm; 44°27′N 94°23′W. Agr. area (grain, soybeans, peas; livestock, poultry; dairying); mfg. (feeds, fertilizers, meat processing). **2** residential suburban village (1990 pop. 600), Onondaga co., central N.Y., 11 mi/18 km S of Syracuse; 42°54′N 76°06′W. Mfg. (hardwood lumber, rolling machinery, grinding and shaping tools, binders and folders); agr. (apples, vegetables, dairying, field corn, hay). **3** (LAH-fai-ET), village (1990 pop. 449), Allen co., W Ohio, 8 mi/13 km E of Lima, near Ottawa R.; 40°45′N 83°57′W. Limestone quarrying. **4** village, North Kingstown town, Washington co., S central R.I., 18 mi/29 km S of Providence, 2 mi/3.2 km E of Wickford. Residential and mfg. center. The Amer. Indian Federation owns a hall here and holds pow wows the first Saturday in Aug. Cocumscussoc State Park (undeveloped) is nearby.

Lafayette, Mount, N.H.: see FRANCONIA MOUNTAINS.

Lafayette Springs (LAH-fai-ET), village, Lafayette co., N Miss., 15 mi/24 km ESE of Oxford. In agr. and timber area (cotton, corn; cattle). Holly Springs Natl. Forest to N.

Lafitte (lah-FEET), uninc. village (1990 pop. 1,507), Jefferson parish, extreme SE La., on Intracoastal Waterway, and 18 mi/29 km S of New Orleans; 29°42′N 90°06′W. Shrimp fishing, seafood processing (shrimp, oysters, crab meat). Lafitte Village, on site of old settlement of Lafitte's 19th-cent. pirate band, is 5 mi/8 km SSE. Hosts the Jean Lafitte Seafood Festival. Hunting, fishing.

Laflèche or **La Flèche** (both: lah FLESH), town (1991 pop. 466), S Sask., Canada, 27 mi/43 km W of Assiniboia. Grain elevators, flour mills.

Laflin, borough (1990 pop. 1,498), Luzerne co., NE central Pa., residential suburb, 5 mi/8 km ENE of Wilkes-Barre, and 11 mi/18 km SW of Scranton.

Lafourche (lah-FOOSH), parish (☐ 1,157 sq mi/2,997 sq km; 1990 pop. 85,860), extreme SE La.; ⊙ Thibodaux; 29°48′N 90°49′W. Bounded S by Gulf of Mexico, SW by Bayou Pointe au Chien, E partly by Barataria Bay, N by Bayou Des Allemands and Lac Des Allemands; intersected by Bayou Lafourche (navigable); crossed by Intracoastal Waterway and Southwestern Louisiana Canal. Lake Boeuf in W, Lake Fields in center. Agr. (home gardens, sugarcane, cotton, vegetables; cattle, horses; quail and pheasants); crawfish, alligators, shrimp, crabs, finfish; natural gas, oil; logging; mfg., including food processing, paper prods., industrial machinery, shipbuilding. Part of Pointe au Chien State Wildlife Area in SW, Wisner State Wildlife Area in S. Formed 1805.

Lafourche, Bayou 1 (lah-FOOSH, BEI-yoo), c.75 mi/121 km long, NE La.; rises in Morehouse parish; flows generally S to Boeuf R. c.13 mi/21 km WSW of Winnsboro. Flows through Russell Sage State Wildlife Area. **2** 107 mi/172 km long, SE La., formerly a right bank distributary of the Mississippi R., from which it is now cut off by dam at Donaldsonville, Ascension parish; extends SE, through Assumption and Lafourche parishes, to Gulf of Mexico bet. Timbalier and Caminada bays. Called the longest line village in the world because of the 65 m/105 km of development on its levee. Navigable to Napoleonville. Crossed at Leeville by Southwestern Louisiana Canal, and intersected at Larose by Intracoastal Waterway.

Lafragua, Mexico: see SALTILLO, Puebla.

Lagartos Lagoon (lah-GAHR-tos), inlet of Gulf of Mexico on Yucatán-Quintana Roo border, N Yucatán Peninsula, 60 mi/97 km NE of Valladolid; linked with ocean by narrow, 12-mi/19-km channel. Also called Río Lagartos.

Lago de Camécuaro (LAH-go dai kah-MAI-kwah-ro), a national park, in S Michoacán, Mexico, 6 mi/10 km SE of Zamora de Hidalgo. Huge cypress trees in crystal clear water are the distinctive feature of the park. Swimming and boating are allowed.

Lago Vista, town (1990 pop. 2,199), Travis co., S Texas, suburb 19 mi/31 km NW of downtown Austin, lakeside development on 11 mi/18 km of N shore of L. Travis reservoir (Colorado R.). Elev. 1,230 ft/375 m. Agr. area; light mfg. Recreation. Airpower Mus.

Lagos de Moreno (lah-gos dai mo-RE-no), city (1990 pop. 63,646) and township, NE Jalisco, central Mexico, in Sierra Madre Occidental, on RR, and 23 mi/37 km NW of León; 21°21'N 101°55'W. Elev. 6,371 ft/1,942 m. Resort; silver-mining and agr. center (beans, chili, corn; livestock); dairy industry, shoe mfg. Colonial churches.

Lagrange, county (□ 386 sq mi/1,000 sq km; 1990 pop. 29,477), NE Ind.; ⊙ Lagrange; 41°38'N 85°26'W. Bounded N by Mich. state line; drained by Pigeon and short Little Elkhart rivers. Dairying; soybeans, oats, wheat, corn, grain; cattle, sheep, hogs; poultry hatcheries; processing of dairy prods. Pigeon R. State Fish and Wildlife Area (including Curtis Creek Trout Station) in NE. Scott Millpond State Fishing Area in NW. About 27 small natural lakes, glacial in origin, mostly concentrated in SE ¼ of co. Formed 1832.

Lagrange 1 (luh-GRAINJ), town (1990 pop. 2,382), ⊙ Lagrange co., NE Ind., on tributary of Pigeon R., and 28 mi/45 km E of Elkhart; 41°38'N 85°25'W. Mfg. (electrical equip., transportation equip., livestock feed, food prods. and processing). Plotted 1836; inc. 1855. **2** town (1990 pop. 557), Penobscot co., central Maine, 25 mi/40 km N of Bangor; 45°10'N 68°48'W. Agr.; lumbering.

Lagrange, village (1990 pop. 1,199), Lorain co., N Ohio, 8 mi/13 km S of Elyria, in agr. area; 41°14'N 82°07'W.

Lagro (LAI-gro), town (1990 pop. 496), Wabash co., NE central Ind., on Wabash R. opposite mouth of Salamonie R., and 5 mi/8 km ENE of Wabash; 40°50'N 85°44'W. Mfg. (ceiling tile). Salamonie R. State Forest nearby to SE. Laid out 1838.

LaGuardia Airport, borough of Queens, SE N.Y., along Flushing Bay; 40°47'N 73°53'W. This is 1 of 3 N.Y. city metropolitan area airports operated by the Port Authority of N.Y. and N.J. Opened in 1939 as North Beach Airport, it was N.Y. city's 2nd airport; 70% of its $22-million cost was paid for by the WPA. Only 8 mi/12.9 km from downtown Manhattan, it quickly became the city's main airport; even today it has a larger passenger volume than JFK Internatl. Primarily handles passenger traffic rather than cargo; it processes 900 domestic flights daily. The airport also had a marine terminal that was built to handle the internatl. "flying boats" of the 1930s; with its outstanding Art Deco architecture, the terminal continues to be used by land-based private aircraft.

Laguna, uninc. city (1990 pop. 9,828), Sacramento co., central Calif., residential suburb 9 mi/14.5 km SSE of downtown Sacramento, on Laguna Creek; 38°25'N 121°25'W. Agr. to S and E (grain, alfalfa, fruit, vegetables; dairying; poultry).

Laguna (luh-GOO-nuh), pueblo (1990 pop. 434), Cibola co., central N.Mex., at center of Laguna Indian Reservation (1990 pop. 3,731), 27 mi/43 km ESE of Grants, on Rio San Jose; 35°02'N 107°23'W. Est. on its present site 1699. Its inhabitants are Pueblo of the Keresan linguistic stock; many farms in outlying areas. Sheep, cattle. The pueblo is used essentially for ceremonial purposes. San Mateo Mts. to NW; Cañoncito Indian Reservation to E.

Laguna Beach, city (1990 pop. 23,170), Orange co., S Calif., suburb 40 mi/64 km SE of downtown Los Angeles, and 12 mi/19 km SSE of Santa Ana on Pacific Ocean, at mouth of Laguna Canyon Wash; 33°33'N 117°46'W. Irrigated agr. area. It is a residential and resort city with a noted art colony and many cultural attractions. Laguna Beach has profited from the rapid growth and prosperity of Orange co. Mfg. (navigation equip., pottery prods.). Laguna Beach Mus. of Art. San Joaquin Hills to NE. Founded 1887, inc. 1927.

Laguna Beach (luh-GOO-nuh), town (□ 2 sq mi/5.2 sq km; 1990 pop. 1,876), Bay co., NW Fla., 20 mi/32 km WNW of Panama City; 30°15'N 85°57'W.

Laguna de Catemaco National Park (lah-GOO-nah dai kah-te-MAH-ko) (□ 50 sq mi/130 sq km), in SE Veracruz, Mexico, 3.1 mi/5 km SE of San Andrés Tuxtla. This small park is located on the inside of Laguna Catemaco (3,959 mi/10,059 km), a volcanic caldera located in the Tuxtla Volcanoes. A popular weekend spot for visitors from the nearby Gulf Coastal Lowlands.

Laguna de Temazcal National Park (lah-GOO-nah dai te-MAHZ-kahl), N Oaxaca, Mexico, 3.1 mi/5 km NE of the President Miguel Aleman L. (Lago Presidente Miguel Alemán).

Laguna del Perro (luh-GOO-nuh del PE-ro), lake, Torrance co., central N.Mex., E of Manzano Range, just SE of Estancia; 12 mi/19 km long, 1 mi/1.6 km wide. Semi-dry; surrounded by numerous small, intermittent lakes.

Laguna District, [Span. = lake], irrigated area in E Durango and W Coahuila states, N central Mexico. Originally a 900,000 acres/364,230 ha tract, consisting of large estates, the land was reapportioned (1936) under President Lázaro Cárdenas and distributed to Mex. farmers under the Ejido system. It was a successful experiment in agrarian reform until 1952, when a severe drought scorched more than ½ the dist., turning 200,000 acres/80,940 ha of wheat and cotton fields into a dust bowl and obliging the govt. to take emergency measures to avert a famine. Settlement has continued there, but on a greatly reduced scale; water for irrigation comes from wells and from dams on the Nazas and Aguanaval rivers. Parts of the irrigated area have gone out of production because of salinization of soil.

Laguna Diversion, dam, on border of extreme SW Ariz. (Yuma co.) and SE Calif. (Imperial co.), on Colorado R., 7 mi/11.3 km NNE of Yuma, and c.14 mi/23 km from Mex. (Baja Calif.) border; 43 ft/13 m high; 32°52'N 114°29'W. Built (1909) by the Bureau of Reclamation for debris control and water supply. Forms Laguna Reservoir; extends N. Fort Yuma (Quechan) Indian Reservation at S end of reservoir. Also known as Laguna Dam.

Laguna Heights, uninc. town (1990 pop. 1,671), Cameron co., extreme S Texas, residential and resort community at S end of Laguna Madre, arm of Gulf of Mexico, 18 mi/29 km NE of Brownsville; 26°04'N 97°15'W.

Laguna Hills, uninc. city (1990 pop. 46,731), Orange co., S Calif., residential suburb 40 mi/64 km SE of downtown Los Angeles, and 6 mi/9.7 km NE of Laguna Beach; 33°36'N 117°43'W. El Toro Marine Corps Air Station to N which is scheduled by Pentagon for closure. Rapidly growing urban fringe area. Mfg. (electronic equip., measuring devices, diverse light mfg.).

Laguna Madre (lah-GOO-nah MAH-drai), NE Mexico and S Texas, narrow, shallow lagoon along Gulf coast; from Corpus Christi Bay, Texas, it extends c.120 mi/193 km S to mouth of the Rio Grande, whose delta interrupts it for c.40 mi/64 km, then continues c.100 mi/161 km to point 10 mi/16 km N of mouth of Soto la Marina R., Tamaulipas. Sheltered from the Gulf by narrow barrier isls. (notably Padre Isl., Texas). U.S. sect. is traversed by Gulf Intracoastal Waterway.

Laguna Mountains, S Calif., wooded range in central San Diego co., extends c.35 mi/56 km NW from Mexico border (N end of Sierra de Juárez). Max. elev. c.6,300 ft/1,920 m. Recreational region. Largely in Cleveland Natl. Forest. Carrizo Gorge is at SE end; Anza-Borrego Desert State Park to E, Cuyamaca Rancho State Park in center; several small Indian reservations in range.

Laguna Niguel (lah-GOO-nah nee-GEL), city (1990 pop. 44,400), Orange co., S Calif., residential suburb 43 mi/69 km SE of downtown Los Angeles, and 4 mi/6.4 km E of Laguna Beach, near Aliso Creek, in San Joaquin Hills; 33°32'N 117°42'W. Mfg. (plastics prods., irrigation equip.).

Laguna Park, uninc. village (1990 pop. 550), Bosque co., central Texas, 25 mi/40 km NW of Waco. Residential and recreational community at Whitney Dam, on Brazos R. Mfg. (sportswear); agr. area.

Laguna Vista, town (1990 pop. 1,166), Cameron co., extreme S Texas, 18 mi/29 km NE of Brownsville, on S end of Laguna Largo is to S. Recreation; 26°06'N 97°17'W. Laguna Atascosa Natl. Wildlife Refuge is to N.

Lagunas de Chacahua National Park (lah-GOO-nahs dai chah-KAH-wah), a national park, in S Oaxaca, Mexico, on the Pacific coast, 15 mi/24 km W of Puerto Escondido, and 14 mi/23 km SE of Santiago Pinotepa National. Covers 25,000 acres/10,118 ha. This park consists of numerous lagoons, bamboo groves, mangrove swamps, and a beach. There is varied plant and animal life. A dirt road off Mexico Highway 200 accesses the park.

Lagunas de Montebello (lah-GOO-nahs dai mon-te-BE-yo), a national park (□ 23 sq mi/60 sq km), in SE Chiapas, Mexico, 27 mi/44 km E of Mex. Highway 190 from La Trinitaria, on the Guatemala-Mexico border. Elev. 5,000 ft. Mountainous terrain with rain forest vegetation (ferns, pines, orchids, oakes, vanilla, cacao, and hule). The Chincultic archaeological zone is nearby with Mayan ruins.

Lagunas de Zempoala National Park (lah-GOO-nahs dai zem-po-AH-lah), in NW Morelos, Mexico, near the state of México. It is on the border S of the Sierra del Ajusco, 9 mi/15 km W of Tres Cumbres. Elev. 9,514 ft/2,900 m. Covers 11,673 acres/4,724 ha. There are 3 anc. volcanic craters filled with water. A branch of the Mexico-Cuernavaca road goes here. From the E to the W, they are the Laguna Zempoala, Compila, Tonatihua, Seca, Ocoyotongo, Quila, and Hueyapan. The last provides water to the towns of Huitzilac and Coajomulco. Cool humid climate surrounded by pine forests. Mexico Highway 95 provides access to this park.

Lagunillas 1 (lah-goo-NEE-yahs), town (1990 pop. 679), San Luis Potosí, N central Mexico, 37 mi/60 km SE of Río Verde. Grain, fruit; livestock. **2** town (1990 pop. 2,182), in E central Michoacán, Mexico, 16 mi/25 km E of Patzcuaro and N of Huiramba. On Grande de Morelia R. to SW. Agr. (wheat and corn). Connects with RR, on Mexico Highway 120. Acambaro-Morelia-Patzcuaro and Uruapan. Many small lagoons in the area.

Lagunitas, uninc. town (1990 pop. 1,821), Marin co., W Calif., 10 mi/16 km W of San Rafael, and on San Geronimo Creek, at its entrance to Lagunitas Creek, which rises on N slope of Mt. Tamalpais, flows generally NW c.30 mi/48 km to Tomales Bay; 38°01'N 122°42'W. Dam impounds Kent L. (c.2 mi/3.2 km long; for water supply) 5 mi/8 km W of San Rafael. Golden Gate Natl. Recreation Area to S, Point Reyes Natl. Seashore to W, both parks are on Pacific Ocean.

Lahaina (lah-HEI-nah), city (1990 pop. 9,073), Maui co., on the W coast of Maui isl., Maui co., Hawaii, on Auau Channel, 13 mi/21 km W of Kahului, 80 mi/129 km ESE of Honolulu; 20°53'N 156°40'W. In a sugarcane and pineapple region. Mfg. (sugarcane processing). Terminus (S) of scenic train roads from Kaanapali, 3.5 mi/5.6 km N. It was the scene of the first Eur. settlement in the isls. and served as capital from 1810 until the seat of govt. was moved (1845) to Honolulu. Hawaii's first newspaper was printed in Lahaina, and the isl.'s first school was est. here in 1831. A whaling port in the mid-19th cent., Lahaina was also an important anchorage for the U.S. Pacific Fleet in the 20th cent. Lahaina Cannery Mall; Seaman's Hosp. (Historical); Jodo Mission Buddhist Cultural Center; Wahikuli State Wayside Park to N; Puamana Beach Park and Launiupoko State Park to SE; West Maui Forest Reserve to E. Whale watching Dec.-April.

Lahave River (luh-HAIV), 60 mi/97 km long, W N.S., Canada; issues from small Lahave L., 30 mi/48 km ENE of Annapolis Royal; flows SE, through several small lakes, past Bridgewater, to the Atlantic 7 mi/11 km SSW of Lunenburg. Navigable below Bridgewater. Important salmon fisheries.

Lahoma (lah-HO-muh), village (1990 pop. 645), Garfield co., N Okla., 12 mi/19 km W of Enid; 36°23'N 98°05'W. In agr. area.

Lahontan Dam, Nev.: see CARSON RIVER.

Lahontan, Lake, extinct lake, W Nev. and NE Calif. Formed during wet periods coinciding with glacial surges during the Pleistocene epoch and, with L. Bonneville (Utah). Occupied a part of the Great Basin region. L. Lahontan retreated shortly after the Pleistocene epoch, but Pyramid, Winnemucca, and Walker lakes and Carson Sink are its remnants. Marine reptile fossils at Berlin-Ichthyosaur State Park, 70 mi/113 km SE of Fallon, (Nev.; archaeological dig). Lahontan Reservoir, on Carson R., in NW.

Lahontan Reservoir (luh-HAHN-tuhn), Churchill and Storey cos., W Nev., on Carson R., in Lahontan State Recreation Area, 13 mi/21 km W of Fallon; 39°27′N 119°04′W. Max. capacity 426,500 acre-ft.; 18 mi/29 km long. Carson R. enters on SW, drains NE to Carson Sink. Formed by Lahontan Dam (earth construction; 115 ft//35 m high), built (1915) by the Bureau of Reclamation for irrigation, power generation, and recreation.

Laidlaw, village, S B.C., Canada, on Fraser R., and 19 mi/ 31 km NE of Chilliwack; 49°18′N 121°36′W. Lumbering; dairying.

Laie (LAH-EE-ai), town (1990 pop. 5,577), Oahu, Honolulu co., Hawaii, on NNE coast, 24 mi/39 km NNW of Honolulu; 21°38′N 157°55′W. Laie Point to SE; Makahoa Point to N: Koolau Range to SW. Laie Temple, a large Mormon temple (1919), is Brigham Young Univ. Hawaii Campus; Polynesian Cultural Center; Malaekahana State Recreational Area.

Laingsburg, town (1990 pop. 1,148), Shiawassee co., S central Mich., 15 mi/24 km NE of Lansing; 42°53′N 84°20′W. In farm area (livestock; grain, soybeans, hay; dairy prods.). Sleepy Hollow State Park to NW (Clinton co.).

Laird (lerd), village (1991 pop. 221), central Sask., Canada, 40 mi/64 km N of Saskatoon; 52°43′N 106°35′W. Mixed farming; dairying.

Laja River, c.85 mi/137 km long, Guanajuato, central Mexico; rises near San Felipe in Sierra Madre Occidental; flows S, and past Comonfort, to Apaseo R. (affluent of Lerma R.) 3 mi/4.8 km SE of Celaya.

Lajas (LAH-huz), town, Cienfuegos prov., central Cuba, on RR, and 21 mi/34 km W of Santa Clara; 22°25′N 80°18′W. Agr. center (sugarcane, fruit). The sugar central of Caracas is 4 mi/6.4 km SE.

Lajas (LAH-hahs), town (1990 pop. 23,271), SW P.R., 11 mi/18 km SSE of Mayagüez, near the coast. Farmland; livestock, pineapples. Beach resort, tourism, fishing nearby (S) in La Parguera.

Lake 1 county (□ 1,259 sq mi/3,261 sq km; 1990 pop. 50,631), NW Calif.; ⊙ Lakeport; 39°05′N 122°46′W. Mt. and valley region, in the Coast Ranges; drained by Cache Creek and Eel R. Oats, pears, grapes, walnuts; cattle; timber. Anderson Springs 15 mi/24 km S of Clear L. Scenic recreational region; fishing, hunting, camping; mineral and hot springs (resorts). Mineral-water bottling; a leading quick-silver producing co. of Calif.; also sand and gravel quarrying. Hull Mt. (6,873 ft/ 2,095 m) on N boundary; part of Mendocino Natl. Forest in N; Clear L. State Park in center; L. Pillsbury in N. Several small Indian reservations (or rancherias). Formed 1961. **2** county (□ 383 sq mi/992 sq km; 1990 pop. 6,007), central Colo.; ⊙ Leadville; 39°13′N 106°20′W. Mining, dairying, and livestock-grazing area, drained by headwaters of Arkansas R. Gold, silver, lead, copper, zinc; molybdenum mines at Climax. Large part of co. in San Isabel Natl. Forest, except for Arkansas Valley (NE); extreme NE corner in Arapaho Natl. Forest. Sawatch Mts. extend N-S; includes Mt. Massive (14,421 ft/4,396 m; 2nd highest in U.S. Rocky Mts.) and Mt. Elbert (14,433 ft/4,399 m; highest point in Colo. and in U.S. Rocky Mts.). Turquois L. reservoir in NW. Formed 1861. **3** county (□1,156 sq mi/2,994 sq km; 1990 pop. 152,104), central Fla., bounded NE by St. Johns R.; ⊙ Tavares; 28°46′N 81°43′W. Rolling terrain with hundreds of lakes, including Harris, Griffin, Dora, Eustis, Yale, and part of Apopka. Ocala Natl. Forest extends into NE corner. Citrus fruit-growing area, with canneries and many packing houses; also watermelons, corn, peanuts, cotton, and poultry. Formed 1887. **4** county (□ 457 sq mi/1,184 sq km; 1990 pop. 516,418), extreme NE Ill., bounded E by L. Michigan and N by Wis. state line; ⊙ Waukegan; 42°20′N 88°00′W. Drained by Fox and Des Plaines rivers. Includes many N suburbs of Chicago; diversified mfg; rapid urban

growth area. Sand, gravel, stone deposits. Dairying, remnant agr. Two ski resorts, Illinois Beach State Park, and Chain O' Lakes State Park; fishing, duck hunting. Amusement park near Zion. Formed 1839. Nuclear power plants: Zion 1 (initial criticality June 19, 1973) and Zion 2 (initial criticality December 24, 1973) are 40 mi/64 km N of Chicago. Use cooling water from L. Michigan, and each has a max. dependable capacity of 1040 MWe. Major military presence at Great Lakes Naval Training Station and Philip Sheridan Arms Reserve Center. **5** county (□ 626 sq mi/1,621 sq km; 1990 pop. 475,594), extreme NW Ind.; ⊙ Crown Point; 41°29′N 87°23′W. Bounded N by L. Michigan, W by Ill. state line, S by Kankakee R.; traversed by Grand Calumet and Little Calumet rivers. Heavily industralized CALUMET region, part of metropolitan area of Chicago, is one of world's most important steel-mfg. centers. Harbors at Gary and East Chicago (Indiana Harbor). Agr. areas of co. produce vegetables, dairy prods., poultry, soybeans, corn. LaSalle State Fish and Wildlife Area in SW corner. Formed 1836. **6** county (□ 574 sq mi/ 1,487 sq km; 1990 pop. 8,583), W central Mich.; ⊙ Baldwin; 43°59′N 85°48′W. Cattle, dairy prods., forage crops; lumbering; resort and recreation area. Drained by Pere Marquette and Little Manistee rivers, and small South Branch of Manistee R. Part of Manistee Natl. Forest in W and S parts of co. and NE corner; numerous lakes, esp. NW and SW; Wood Hills Ski Area in W. Organized 1871. **7** county (□ 2,991 sq mi/7,747 sq km; 1990 pop. 10,415), NE Minn.; ⊙ Two Harbors; 47°38′N 91°25′W. Extensively watered area; bounded SE by L. Superior; N by chain of lakes (W-E: Crooked L., Basswood R., Basswood L., Knife L. and Ottertrack L., and other small lakes); along Can. (Ont.) border; S ½ of co. is drained by small streams, which feed into L. Superior, N half by many lakes, linked by rivers, notably Kawishiwi, Island and Cloquet (source) rivers. Timber; some dairying. Part of Superior Natl. Forest (including part of Boundary Waters Canoe Area) in N ⅔ of co. and is part of famous recreational region known as "Arrowhead Country." (Refers to triangular shape of NE Minn., area also called "North Shore"). State parks (N-S) on or near L. Superior shore include Caribou Falls State Park and George H. Crosby Manitou State Park (in E), Tettegouche State Park, Split Rock Lighthouse State Park, and Gooseberry Falls State Park (in SE), Flood Bay State Park, at Two Rivers (in S); Finland State Forest in E. Formed 1866. **8** county (□1,653 sq mi/ 4,281 sq km; 1990 pop. 21,041), NW Mont.; ⊙ Polson; 47°39′N 114°05′W. Mt. region drained by Flathead (forms part of W boundary) and Swan rivers. Wheat, barley, corn, oats, potatoes, rape seed, hay; cattle, sheep, hogs, horses, llamas, fruit (cherries); dairying. Five of 6 units of Flathead L. State Park in N, along shore of Flathead L.: West Shore Unit, Wild Horse Isl. Unit, Big Arm Unit, Finley Point Unit, and Yellow Bay Unit (E shore). L. Mary Ronan State Park in NW; Ninepipe and Pablo Natl. Wildlife refuges in center; Swan R. Natl. Wildlife Refuge and Swan L in NE; part of Natl. Bison Range in SW; part of Mission Mts. Tribal Wilderness in SE. Flathead Indian Reservation in all but N and NE margin of co. Flathead L. in N. Formed 1923. **9** county (□ 232 sq mi/601 sq km; 1990 pop. 215,499), NE Ohio; ⊙ Painesville; 41°42′N 81°15′W. Bounded N by L. Erie; drained by Grand and Chagrin rivers. In the Till Plains and Lake Plain physiographic regions. Fruit growing (apples, grapes); poultry. Mfg. at Painesville, Wickliffe, and Willoughby (paper prods., industrial organic chemicals, iron and steel foundries, metal forgings and stampings, precision measuring devices). Lake resorts. Formed 1840; smallest co. in Ohio. Perry nuclear power plant, initial criticality June 6, 1986, (7 mi/11 km NE of Painesville) uses cooling water from L. Erie, and has a max. dependable capacity of 1166 MWe. **10** county (□ 8,359 sq mi/21,650 sq km; 1990 pop. 7,186), S Oregon, mt. area containing Summer L. (W center), Abert L. in center, Silver L. and part of Goose L. (S boundary), borders Calif. and Nev.; ⊙ Lakeview; 42°47′N 120°23′W. Wheat, oats, barley; sheep, cattle. Clay; lumber. Hart Mt. Natl. Antelope

Refuge in SE. Warm Valley, a geyser basin with numerous dry lakes in SE (including Old Perpetual Geyser that spouts every 90 seconds). Parts of Fremont Natl. Forest in W; part of Great Sandy Desert in NE; Fort Rock State Monument in NW; Chandler and Booth State Waysides in S; Goose L. State Recreation Area on S boundary. **11** county (□ 575 sq mi/1,489 sq km; 1990 pop. 10,550), E S.Dak.; ⊙ Madison, 44°02′N 97°09′W. Agr. area. Madison L. in SE, L. Herman State Park in S. Agr. (corn, soybeans; dairy prods.); cattle, hogs, poultry; honey. Drained by E Fork Vermillion R. Formed 1873. **12** county (□ 164 sq mi/425 sq km; 1990 pop. 7,129), extreme NW Tenn.; ⊙ Tiptonville; 36°20′N 89°30′W. Bounded N by Ky.; W by the Mississippi (Mo. state line); NE by Reelfoot L. (hunting, fishing). Timber; agr. (corn, sorghum, soybeans, alfalfa, cotton; livestock). Formed 1870.

Lake, village (1990 pop. 369), Scott and Newton cos., central Miss., 35 mi/56 km W of Meridian; 32°20′N 89°19′W. Agr. (cotton, corn; poultry; cattle; dairying); mfg. (apparel). Bienville Natl. Forest to W and S.

Lake Alfred, town (□ 6 sq mi/15.5 sq km; 1990 pop. 3,622), Polk co., central Fla., 6 mi/9.7 km W of Haines City, in lake region; 28°05′N 81°43′W. Citrus fruit-shipping center, with packing houses, canneries, and experiment station; mfg. (citrus oil, pulp feed, and molasses; fertilizer, insecticides).

Lake Almanor Dam, Calif.: see ALMANOR, LAKE.

Lake Alpine, Calif.: see ALPINE, LAKE.

Lake Aluma (uh-LOOM-uh), village (1990 pop. 96), Oklahoma co., central Okla., residential suburb 7 mi/ 11.3 km NE of downtown Oklahoma City; 35°32′N 97°27′W.

Lake and Peninsula, borough (□ 23,632 sq mi/ 61,207 sq km; 1990 pop. 1,668), SW Alaska, includes the base of the Alaska Peninsula and several large lakes (L. Clark, Iliamna L., part of Naknek L., Becherof L., and Upper and Lower Ugaskik L.'s). Bounded on the NW by Bristol Bay, SE by Pacific Ocean, and Shelikof Strait. Part of L. Clark Natl. Park and Preserve and Katmai Natl. Park and Preserve to N; Becharof Natl. Wildlife Reserve in center and S; Aniakchak Natl. Monument and Preserve to SW. Fishing; crabs. Seals; pelts.

Lake Andes, town (1990 pop. 846), ⊙ Charles Mix co., S S.Dak., 47 mi/76 km SW of Mitchell, near L. Andes, in Yankton Indian Reservation; 43°09′N 98°32′W. L. Andes Natl. Wildlife Refuge at E end of lake. Fishing resort; trading point for agr. area; wheat, alfalfa, livestock.

Lake Angelus, village (1990 pop. 328), Oakland co., SE Mich., residential suburb 3 mi/4.8 km NW of Pontiac, suburb surrounds small L. Angelus; 42°41′N 83°19′W. Numerous lakes in area.

Lake Ann, village (1990 pop. 217), Benzie co., NW Mich., on NE end of Ann L., 12 mi/19 km SW of Traverse City; 44°43′N 85°50′W.

Lake Ariel, uninc. town (1990 pop. 950), Wayne co., NE Pa., 16 mi/26 km ENE of Scranton; 41°27′N 75°22′W. Mfg. (sand and gravel processing, poultry processing, asphalt, industrial power brushes, wood prods., printing, lumber, machinery); agr. (dairying, livestock; grain); timber.

Lake Arrowhead, uninc. town (1990 pop. 6,539), San Bernardino co., S Calif., residential suburb 11 mi/18 km NE of San Bernardino; 34°16′N 117°11′W. Surrounds L. Arrowhead reservoir, in San Bernardino Mts., San Bernardino Natl. Forest. Rim of the World Drive overlooks Los Angeles area. Mfg. (printing and publishing).

Lake Arrowhead, Calif.: see ARROWHEAD LAKE.

Lake Arthur, town (1990 pop. 3,194), Jefferson Davis parish, SW La., on L. Arthur (widening of navigable Mermentau R.), 34 mi/55 km ESE of Lake Charles city; 30°05′N 92°41′W. In rice and cattle area; also catfish, crawfish; oil and natural-gas fields. Recreation in vicinity. Inc. 1909.

Lake Arthur, village (1990 pop. 336), Chaves co., SE N.Mex., on Pecos R., and 32 mi/51 km SSE of Roswell; 33°00′N 104°21′W. Cattle, sheep, dairying; agr. (triticale, alfalfa, pecans, cotton, melons, hay).

Lake Barcroft, uninc. town, Fairfax co., NE Va., residential suburb 7 mi/11.3 km WSW of Washington, D.C., 6 mi/9.7 km NW of Alexandria, centered on L. Barcroft reservoir (Holmes Run creek); 38°51′N 77°09′W.

Lake Barrington, village (1990 pop. 3,855), Lake co., NE Ill., residential suburb 33 mi/53 km NW of downtown Chicago, 7 mi/11.3 km ESE of Crystal Lake (town); 42°12′N 88°10′W. Mfg. (printing equip).

Lake Bellaire, Mich.: see BELLAIRE.

Lake Benton, village (1990 pop. 693), Lincoln co., SW Minn., 15 mi/24 km S of Ivanhoe, near S.Dak. state line, at SW end of L. Benton; 44°15′N 96°17′W. Agr. (grain, soybeans; poultry; dairying); mfg. (printing, animal feeds). Resort area.

Lake Beulah (BYOO-lah), village, Walworth co., SE Wis., E of small L. Beulah (c.4 mi/6.4 km long), 10 mi/16 km NNW of Burlington.

Lake Bluff, village (1990 pop. 5,513), Lake co., extreme NE Ill., N residential suburb of Chicago, on L. Michigan, 17 mi/27 km NNW of Evanston; 42°16′N 87°50′W. Mfg. (steel and non-ferrous wool, industrial chemicals, metallurgical equip., furniture, paper prods., freight car components). Great Lakes Naval Training Station is just N. Inc. 1895.

Lake Bonaparte, N.Y.: see BONAPARTE, LAKE.

Lake Borgne Canal (born), SE La., joins L. Borgne with the Mississippi R. at Violet (lock here), 10 mi/16 km ESE of New Orleans; c.7 mi/11 km long. Eliminated by Mississippi R. Gulf Outlet, which parallels the lake's SW shore, linking Intracoastal Waterway (NW) with Breton Sound, Gulf of Mexico (SE). Also known as Ship Isl. Canal.

Lake Bronson, village (1990 pop. 272), Kittson co., NW Minn., 13 mi/21 km ESE of Hallock, on South Branch Two Rivers; 48°43′N 96°39′W. Agr. (grain, potatoes, sugar beets, beans, flax, sunflowers; livestock); mfg. (fertilizer). Twin Lakes Wildlife Area to SE; L. Bronson (State Park) to E.

Lake Buena Vista (BWAI-nuh VIS-tuh), town (□ 5 sq mi/13 sq km), Orange co., central Fla., 15 mi/24 km SW of Orlando; 28°23′N 81°31′W. Tourist center located adjacent to Walt Disney World.

Lake Butler, town (□ 1 sq mi/2.6 sq km; 1990 pop. 2,116), ⊙ Union co., N central Fla., 25 mi/40 km N of Gainesville; 30°01′N 82°20′W. Naval-stores center.

Lake Carmel, village (□ 5 sq mi/13 sq km; 1990 pop. 8,489), Putnam co., SE N.Y.; 41°27′N 73°40′W.

Lake Catherine, uninc. village (1990 pop. 1,515), Lake co., NE Ill., suburb 49 mi/79 km NW of downtown Chicago, 1 mi/1.6 km W of Antioch, 1 mi/1.6 km S of Wis. state line; 42°29′N 88°07′W. On narrow isthmus bet. L. Catherine (N) and Bluff L. (S).

Lake Charles, city (1990 pop. 70,580), ⊙ Calcasieu parish, SW La., 60 mi/97 km W of Lafayette; 30°13′N 93°12′W. RR junction. Located on L. Charles, a widening of the Calcasieu R., in a rice, timber, oil, and natural-gas region. Fishing (crawfish, shrimp, crabs); mfg. (machinery, petroleum prods., chemicals, concrete, transportation equip., food prods., fiberglass pipe lining, oil field equip.; barge and tugboat construction); printing and publishing; casinos. Lake Charles is an important ship and barge port and port of entry, connected with Gulf of Mexico and Intracoastal Waterway by Calcasieu Ship Channel. A 30-mi/48-km-long channel connects it with the Gulf of Mexico. Petroleum prods., chemicals, rice, and cotton shipped from the port. Cajun Music and Food Festival and Marshland Festival held here. Historical dist. has Victorian and Queen Anne houses. McNeese State Univ.; Creole Nature Trail. Sam Houston Jones State Park to N. Inc. 1867.

Lake Charles Canal, c.25 mi/40 km long, SW La., deep-water E-W land cut connecting Sabine R. just below Orange (Texas) with Calcasieu R. c.15 mi/24 km below Lake Charles city; section of Intracoastal Waterway.

Lake Chelan Dam, Wash.: see CHELAN, LAKE.

Lake Chelan National Recreation Area (shuh-LAN), N Wash., Stehekin Valley, and in N part of fjord-like L. Chelan; covers 61,883 acres/25,044 ha. Bounded by Wenatchee Natl. Forest on W and S, by Okanogan Natl. Forest on E (L. Chelan–Sawtooth Wilderness Area, E). North Cascades Natl. Park (S sect.) adjoins recreation area to NW. Road access from end of lake; passenger ferry from town of Chelan at SE end of lake (55 mi/89 km). Pacific Coast Trail passes through park's W corner; Rainbow Falls on Stenekin R. above its entrance to L. Chelan. Authorized 1968.

Lake City, city (1990 pop. 1,841), Calhoun co., central Iowa, 10 mi/16 km SSW of Rockwell City; 42°16′N 94°43′W. Mfg. (pipe organs, fiberglass prods.). Sand and gravel pits nearby. Inc. 1887.

Lake City 1 town (1990 pop. 7,153), Florence co., E central S.C., 25 mi/40 km S of Florence; 33°52′N 79°45′W. Mfg. (consumer goods, charcoal, textiles, apparel, bldg. materials); agr. (cotton, grain, vegetables; poultry, hogs). **2** town (1990 pop. 1,833), shares capital functions with Jonesboro, Craighead co., NE Ark., 12 mi/19 km E of Jonesboro, on St. Francis R.; 35°49′N 90°27′W. In area of sunken lands caused by 1811–1812 earthquakes. St. Francis Sunken Lands Wildlife Management Area on river. **3** town (□ 11 sq mi/28 sq km; 1990 pop. 10,005), ⊙ Columbia co., N central Fla.; 30°11′N 82°38′W. It was founded in the 1830s as a military post. Lake City is located in a farm and cattle area and produces tobacco, lumber prods., and naval stores. The city also has airplane repair centers and is the hq. to Ocala Natl. Forest. Key junction point in N Fla. where I-75 and I-10 intersect. Inc. 1921. **4** town (1990 pop. 4,391), Wabasha co., SE Minn., 15 mi/24 km SE of Red Wing on L. Pepin (natural lake on Mississippi R. bet. mouths of Miller and Gilbert creeks); 44°27′N 92°16′W. Milling point; agr. (grain; poultry, livestock; dairying); mfg. (chemical processing, wind tunnels, food processing, circuit boards, hand trucks, consumer goods; printing). Hydraulics Research Facility. Part of Richard J. Dorer Memorial Hardwood State Forest to NW; Frontenac State Park to NW; Upper Mississippi River Natl. Wildlife Refuge along river margins. Inc. 1872. **5** town (1990 pop. 2,166), Anderson co., E Tenn., 21 mi/34 km NW of Knoxville, near Norris Reservoir; 36°13′N 84°09′W. In coal-mining region. Until 1939, called Coal Creek.

Lake City 1 village (1990 pop. 223), ⊙ Hinsdale co., SW central Colo., on Lake Fork of Gunnison R., at mouth of Henson Creek, in San Juan Mts., and 45 mi/72 km SE of Montrose; 38°01′N 107°18′W. Elev. 8,671 ft/2,643 m. Uncompahgre Peak 8 mi/12.9 km WNW. L. San Cristobal reservoir to S (on Lake Fork); Uncompahgre Natl. Forest to NW; Gunnison Natl. Forest to E and S; Rio Grand Natl. Forest to S, beyond Continental Divide. **2** village (1990 pop. 858), ⊙ Missaukee co., N central Mich., 11 mi/18 km NE of Cadillac, on E end of L. Missaukee (c.3 mi/4.8 km long, 2 mi/3.2 km wide); 44°19′N 85°12′W. In resort and farm area. Mfg. (plastic prods., steel die forgings, lumber). Native Amer. earthworks and a state park are nearby. Inc. 1932. **3** village (1990 pop. 43), Marshall co., NE S.Dak., 17 mi/27 km ESE of Britton, just W of Lake Traverse (Sisseton Wahpeton) Indian Reservation; 45°43′N 97°24′W. Small lakes in area; supply point for hunters and fishermen. Roy L. State Park to SW; Clear L. State Lakeside Use Area to SE. L. Traverse (Sisseton) Indian Reservation to E.

Lake City, borough (1990 pop. 2,519), Erie co., NW Pa., 16 mi/26 km WSW of Erie, L. Erie 1 mi/1.6 km to NW; 42°01′N 80°20′W. Mfg. (transportation equip., machinery, steel molds, fabricated metal prods., food prods., wood prods.); agr. (dairying; livestock). Borough formally called North Girard.

Lake City, suburb (1990 pop. 2,733) of Atlanta, Clayton co., Ga., 1 mi/1.6 km SW of Forest Park; 33°37′N 84°20′W. Mfg. includes signs, tool and die, commercial printing, feeds.

Lake Clark Park and Preserve, park (□ 2,735 sq mi/7,084 sq km) and preserve (1,407,293 acres/569,531 ha), S Alaska. Covers 2,636,839 acres/1,067,129 ha. Authorized 1980, proclaimed Lake Clark Natl. Monument 1978. Waterfalls, tundra, and active volcanoes; grizzly and black bears, caribou, wolves, mink. Chigmit Range, red salmon spawning area. Redoubt Volcano, 10,197 ft/3,108 m.

Lake Clear, resort village (1990 pop. 400), Franklin co., NE N.Y., on L. Clear in the Adirondacks, 5 mi/8 km NW of Saranac L. village; c.2 mi/3.2 km long; 44°22′N 74°14′W.

Lake Cowichan (KOU-ich-uhn), village (1991 pop. 2,241), SW B.C., Canada, on S Vancouver Isl., on Cowichan L. at outlet of Cowichan R., 40 mi/64 km NW of Victoria; 48°49′N 124°02′W. In lumbering region.

Lake Crystal, town (1990 pop. 2,084), Blue Earth co., S Minn., 12 mi/19 km SW of Mankato; 44°06′N 94°13′W. Resort; agr. trading point (corn, oats, soybeans, peas, hogs; sheep, cattle); mfg. (fertilizers, dump bodies, metal fabricating). Minneopa State Park to NE; L. Crystal and Loon L. to E, Lily L. to N. Plotted 1857; inc. as village 1870; as city 1930.

Lake Dallas, town (1990 pop. 3,656), Denton co., N Texas, suburb 27 mi/43 km NW of downtown Dallas, and 30 mi/48 km NE of downtown Fort Worth, located on W shore of Lewisville L. reservoir (Elm Fork Trinity R.); 33°07′N 97°01′W. Agr. area (cotton, peanuts; cattle); mfg. (electronic assembly).

Lake Delton, town (1990 pop. 1,470), Sauk co., S central Wis., 9 mi/14.5 km. NNW of Baraboo, on L. Delton, near the Wisconsin Dells; 43°35′N 89°46′W. Mfg. (metal fabricating); resort area; tourism. Rocky Arbor State Park to N, Mirror L. State Park to SW.

Lake Elmo, town (1990 pop. 5,903), Washington co., E Minn., residential suburb 9 mi/14.5 km E of downtown St. Paul; 45°00′N 92°54′W. Corn, soybeans; cattle, sheep; mfg. (wood prods., sand and gravel, wood pallets, wood moldings). L. Elmo Airport to E. L. Elmo Regional Park at center of city. L. St. Croix (formed by St. Croix R.) to E, several small lakes in city, notably L. Elmo and Eagle Point L. at center, Olson L. and L. De Montreville in NW.

Lake Elmore, Vt.: see ELMORE.

Lake Elsinore, city (1990 pop. 18,285), Riverside co., S Calif., suburb 22 mi/35 km S of Riverside; 33°40′N 117°19′W. In rapidly growing SW Riverside co. Resort on NE shore of L. Elsinore reservoir (c.6 mi/9.7 km long), near hot mineral springs. Cattle, poultry; grain; mfg. (nuts and bolts, concrete, bricks); clay quarrying. Part of Cleveland Natl. Forest to SW, L. Elsinore State Recreation Area to W; RR Canyon Reservoir to E. Inc. 1888.

Lake Forest, city (1990 pop. 17,836), Lake co., NE Ill., residential suburb of Chicago, on L. Michigan; 42°14′N 87°51′W. The city is known for its scenic lakefront and impressive estates. It is the seat of L. Forest Col., Barat Col., and 2 preparatory schools. Settled 1835, inc. 1861.

Lake Forest, uninc. town, Greenville co., NW S.C., residential suburb 3 mi/4.8 km ENE of downtown Greenville. Greenville Downtown Airport to S. Bob Jones Univ. to NW.

Lake Forest, uninc. village, Placer co., E Calif., 2 mi/3.2 km NE of Tahoe City, on NW shore of L. Tahoe. Tourism; mfg. (industrial instruments, computer peripherals, sand and gravel processing).

Lake Forest Park, town (1990 pop. 4,031), King co., W Wash., residential suburb 11 mi/18 km NNE of downtown Seattle, at N end of L. Washington, at mouth of McAlee Creek; 47°46′N 122°17′W.

Lake Fork, stream, c.50 mi/80 km long; rising in Uinta Mts. near Tokewanna Peak, N Duchesne co., NE Utah, in High Uintas Wilderness Area of Ashley Natl. Forest; flows SE through Mona L. reservoir past Altamont to Duchesne R., 8 mi/12.9 km SW of Roosevelt. Moon L. Dam (110 ft/34 m high, 1,108 ft/338 m long; completed 1938) is chief unit in Moon L. irrigation project, which supplies water to c.70,000 acres/28,330 ha in NE Utah.

Lake Fork Reservoir, Rains, Wood, and Hopkins cos., NE Texas, on L. Fork Creek, 15 mi/24 km S of Sulphur Springs; 32°48′N 95°32′W. Max. capacity of 1,048,480 acre-ft. Formed by L. Fork Dam (82 ft/25 m high), built (1980) for water supply; also used for recreation.

Lake Fremont, Minn.: see ZIMMERMAN.

Lake Geneva (juh-NEE-vah), town (1990 pop. 5,979),

Walworth co., SE Wis., on NE shore of L. Geneva at its outlet (White R.), 38 mi/61 km SW of Milwaukee, and 55 mi/89 km NW of Chicago; 42°35′N 88°25′W. Recreation and resort area for both cities; year-round lake sports; mfg. (consumer goods, dies and stampings, metal spinnings, transportation equip., machinery, custom seals and moldings, screen printing). Has many estates of residents of Chicago, and a hotel designed by Frank Lloyd Wright. Bird sanctuary of Univ. of Chicago and Big Foot Beach State Park is to S. Settled before 1845, inc. 1883.

Lake George, village (1990 pop. 933), part of Lake George town (1990 pop. 3,211), ⊙ Warren co., E N.Y., on S tip of L. George in the foothills of the Adirondack Mts.; 43°25′N 73°43′W. It is a year-round tourist and sports center. Vestiges of Fort William Henry, built by Sir William Johnson, and Fort George are in the village. Inc. 1903.

Lake Grove, village (□ 2 sq mi/5.2 sq km; 1990 pop. 9,612) SE N.Y., Suffolk co., 7 mi/11.3 km NE of central Islip, 25 mi/40 km WSW of Riverhead; 40°51′N 73°07′W.

Lake Hamilton, town (1990 pop. 1,128), Polk co., central Fla., 4 mi/6.4 km S of Haines City, on L. Hamilton; 2 mi/3.2 km long; 28°03′N 81°37′W. Citrus-fruit-packing houses.

Lake Harbour, trading post (1991 pop. 365), S Baffin Isl., SE Franklin dist., N.W.T., Canada, at head of North Bay, inlet of Hudson Strait; 62°15′N 69°53′W. Mfg. (crafts; greenstone sculpting); fishing, sea mammal hunting. Scheduled air service. Royal Can. Mounted Police post. Site of Anglican mission. Fur trading post was est. 1911.

Lake Havasu City, city (1990 pop. 24,363), Mohave co., W Ariz., 145 mi/233 km WNW of Phoenix, and 51 mi/82 km SSW of Kingman, on Colorado R. (L. Havasu, formed by Parker Dam 18 mi/29 km SE); 34°30′N 114°18′W. Elev. 482 ft/147 m. Area referred to as Arizona's "West Coast." Mfg. (stationery, wood millwork, cotton finishing, electrical apparatus, concrete blocks, machine tools; boat building, printing and publishing). Warm Springs Wilderness Area to N. Separate sections of Havasu Natl. Wildlife Refuge to N and SE; Mohave Mts. to NE. Chemehuevi Indian Reservation across lake (W) in Calif. Original name Site Six. Planned retirement and recreational community developed in late 1960s. Pop. increased 6 times by 1990. London Bridge purchased and moved here 1969–1972, spans artificial lake (channel of L. Havasu called Little Thames R.) at Eng. village theme area. Lake Havasu State Park to S.

Lake Heights, uninc. town (1990 pop. 2,600), King co., W Wash., residential suburb 8 mi/12.9 km SE of downtown Seattle, on E shore of L. Washington, on East Channel, separating Mercer Isl. from mainland.

Lake Helen, town (□ 4 sq mi/10.4 sq km; 1990 pop. 2,344), Volusia co., E central Fla., 20 mi/32 km SW of Daytona Beach, in citrus-fruit-growing area; 28°58′N 81°13′W.

Lake Henry, village (1990 pop. 90), Stearns co., central Minn., 32 mi/51 km WSW of St. Cloud; 45°27′N 94°47′W. Grain; livestock, poultry; dairying.

Lake Hicpochee, Fla.: see CALOOSAHATCHEE RIVER.

Lake Hopatcong, N.J.: see HOPATCONG, LAKE.

Lake Huntington, resort village (1990 pop. 600), Sullivan co., SE N.Y., near Pa. state line, on small L. Huntington, 19 mi/24 km NW of Monticello; 41°41′N 74°59′W.

Lake in the Hills, village (1990 pop. 5,866), McHenry co., NE Ill., suburb 3 mi/4.8 km S of Crystal Lake; 42°11′N 88°19′W. Lake in the Hills Airport. Mfg. (protective clothing, warning signs).

Lake Isabella, uninc. town (1990 pop. 3,323), Kern co., S central Calif., 33 mi/53 km ENE of Bakersfield, at Isabella Dam (forms Isabella L. in Kern R.), in S part of Sierra Nevada; 35°37′N 118°28′W. Area surrounded by parts of Sequoia Natl. Forest. Shirley Meadows Ski Area to N; Miracle Hot Springs to SW. Timber, cattle, grain.

Lake Jackson, city (1990 pop. 22,776), Brazoria co., SE Texas, 9 mi/14.5 km NW of Freeport on the Brazos R.; 29°02′N 95°27′W. Near the Gulf of Mexico; drained by

Oyster Creek in N. It is a trading and shipping center for the many dairy and fruit farms in the area. Mfg. (loudspeakers). L. Jackson is the seat of Brazosport Col. (2-year). Brazoria Co. Airport to N; in Brazosport Area twin city to Freeport. Founded 1941.

Lake Junaluska (joon-uh-LUHS-kuh), uninc. town, (1990 pop. 2,482), Haywood co., W N.C., 3 mi/4.8 km NNE of Waynesville, on Pigeon R.; 35°31′N 82°58′W. Great Smoky Mts. Natl. Park to NW; parts of Pisgah Natl. Forest to N and SE.

Lake Landing, uninc. village, Hyde co., E N.C., 29 mi/47 km E of Belhaven on SE end of L. Mattamuskeet.

Lake Lansing, Mich.: see HASLETT.

Lake Lenore (luh-NOR), village (1991 pop. 336), central Sask., Canada, near Lenore L., 15 mi/24 km NE of Humboldt; 17 mi/27 km long, 4 mi/6 km wide; 52°24′N 104°59′W. Resort.

Lake Lillian, village (1990 pop. 229), Kandiyohi co., S central Minn., 15 mi/24 km SE of Willmar, on South Fork Crow R.; 44°57′N 94°52′W. Livestock; grain; dairying; mfg. (agr. equip.). L. Lillian to N, Big Kandiyohi L. to NW.

Lake Linden, town (1990 pop. 1,203), Houghton co., NW Upper Peninsula, Mich., 9 mi/14.5 km. NE of Houghton, on Torch L.; 47°12′N 88°24′W. Former copper region. Inc. 1885.

Lake Los Angeles, uninc. town (1990 pop. 7,977), Los Angeles co., S Calif., residential suburb 11 mi/18 km ESE of Lancaster, in Mojave Desert; 34°37′N 117°50′W. Small reservoir in S. Saddleback Butte State Park to NE. Antelope Valley Ind. Mus. is here. Fruit, vegetables, nuts, cotton, grain, cattle.

Lake Lotawana (lah-tuh-WAH-nuh), village (1990 pop. 2,141), Jackson co., E Mo., residential suburb 17 mi/27 km SE of downtown Kansas City; 38°55′N 94°15′W. Village surrounds L. Lotawana.

Lake Louise, village, SW Alta., Canada, near B.C. border, in Rocky Mts., in Banff Natl. Park, on Bow R., and 30 mi/48 km NW of Banff; 51°26′N 116°11′W. Elev. 5,050 ft/1,539 m. Famous tourist resort, with several large hotels, heated swimming pools, and extensive entertainment and sports facilities. Near foot of Mt. Victoria, 2 mi/3 km SW, is small L. Louise.

Lake Loveland Dam, Calif.: see SWEETWATER RIVER.

Lake Lure (LOOR), village (1990 pop. 691), Rutherford co., SW N.C., 23 mi/37 km SE of Asheville and on Broad R., forms L. Lure reservoir to N; hydroelectric plant; 35°26′N 82°12′W. Grain, soybeans, poultry; livestock.

Lake Luzerne, year-round resort village (1990 pop. 1,150), Warren co., E N.Y., in the Adirondacks, bet. the Hudson R., and small L. Luzerne; 43°19′N 73°48′W. Ski trails nearby. Also called Luzerne.

Lake Mahopac, N.Y.: see MAHOPAC.

Lake Manawa, resort village, Pottawattamie co., SW Iowa, on L. Manawa (c.2 mi/3.2 km long), just S of Council Bluffs. L. Manawa State Park is here.

Lake Mary, town (□ 9 sq mi/23.3 sq km; 1990 pop. 5,929), Seminole co., central Fla., 18 mi/29 km N of Orlando; 28°45′N 81°19′W. Mfg. includes electrical equip., computer peripherals, medical equip., plastic molding, telephone switching equip. Rapid growth since 1990.

Lake Mead National Recreation Area (□ 2,336 sq mi/6,050 sq km), Mohave co., NW Ariz., Clark co., SE Nev., includes all margins of L. Mead (Hoover Dam) and L. Mohave (Davis Dam) reservoirs on Colo. R. The first natl. recreation area of U.S. Natl. Park System. Adjoin W end of Grand Canyon Natl. Park on NE; separates NE, sections protect S part of Shivwits Plateau, N of Grand Canyon Natl. Park. Originally named Hoover Dam Natl. Recreation Area; name changed 1947. Authorized 1936.

Lake Meredith National Recreation Area, Hutchinson, Moore and Potter cos., NW Texas; covers 44,978 acres/18,203 ha. Includes L. Meredith reservoir, on the Canadian R., a popular water sports area in the Southwest. Was named Sanford Natl. Recreation Area (1965–1972); Alibates Flint Quarries Natl. Monument to SE. Authorized 1965.

Lake Mills 1 town (1990 pop. 2,143), Winnebago co., N

Iowa, near Minn. state line, 11 mi/18 km NNW of Forest City; 43°25′N 93°31′W. Vegetable cannery, feed mill. Inc. 1880. Rice L. State Park is SE. **2** town (1990 pop. 4,143), Jefferson co., S Wis., on Rock L., 24 mi/39 km E of Madison; 43°04′N 88°54′W. In dairying, farming, and resort region. Mfg. (dairy equip., food processing and refrigation equip., magnetic switches, liquid crystal displays, metal components; food processing). Lake Mills State Fish Hatchery to S. Aztalan State Park to E contains remains of 12th cent. Indian village, rare platform mounds, and a mus. with anc. Indian relics. Glacial Drumlin State Trail passes E-W to S. Settled c. 1836, inc. 1905.

Lake Milton, village, Mahoning co., NE Ohio, 16 mi/26 km W of Youngstown, on E shore of Milton Reservoir. Inc. 1930, disinc. 1947.

Lake Minchumina (min-CHOO-mi-nuh), village (1990 pop. 32), E central Alaska, on L. Minchumina, 150 mi/241 km SW of Fairbanks; 63°52′N 152°24′W. Airfield.

Lake Minnewaska, resort, Ulster co., SE N.Y., on small L. Minnewaska, in the Shawangunk Mt. range, 17 mi/27 km SW of Kingston; 41°44′N 74°13′W.

Lake Mohawk, N.J.: see MOHAWK.

Lake Monroe, town, Seminole co., central Fla., 22 mi/35 km N of Orlando. Light mfg. .

Lake Montezuma, uninc. town (1990 pop. 1,841), Yavapai co., central Ariz., 37 mi/60 km SSW of Flagstaff, on Wet Beaver Creek, in Prescott Natl. Forest. Timber; cattle, sheep. Units of Montezuma Castle Monument to NE and SW.

Lake Mykee Town (MEI-kee), village (1990 pop. 257), Callaway co., central Mo., 8 mi/12.9 km NE of Jefferson City; 38°40′N 92°05′W. Residential community surrounds L. Mykee.

Lake Nacimiento, uninc. town (1990 pop. 1,556), San Luis Obispo co., SW Calif., residential community 12 mi/19 km NW of Paso Robles, on SE arm of Nacimiento Reservoir, 2 mi/3.2 km S of Nacimiento Dam; 35°44′N 120°53′W. San Antonio Reservoir and Hunter-Liggett Mil. Reservation are to NW.

Lake Nebagamon (ne-BAG-uh-mawn), resort village (1990 pop. 900), Douglas co., NW Wis., on small L. Nebagamon, 22 mi/35 km SE of Superior; 46°30′N 91°41′W. Was lumbering center in late 1800s.

Lake Norden, village (1990 pop. 427), Hamlin co., E S.Dak., 23 mi/37 km S of Watertown, near L. Norden; 44°34′N 97°12′W. Dairy prods. L. Poinsett State Recreational Area to SE.

Lake o' the Cherokees, Okla.: see LAKE OF THE CHEROKEES.

Lake Odessa, town (1990 pop. 2,256), Ionia co., S central Mich., 30 mi/48 km W of Lansing; 42°46′N 85°08′W. In resort and agr. area; poultry. Mfg. (food processing, wire prods.). Settled c.1870, inc. 1889.

Lake of the Arbuckles, Okla.: see ARBUCKLE RESERVOIR.

Lake of the Cherokees, reservoir; Mayes, Delaware, and Ottawa cos.; NE Okla.; on Neosho (Grand) R.; 60 mi/97 km NE of Tulsa; c.45 mi/72 km long; 36°27′N 95°01′W. Elk R. enters from Mo. to form 8-mi/12.9-km E arm. Formed by Pensacola Dam (145 ft/44 m high, 6,500 ft/1,981 m long), built 1938–1941 by the state of Okla. for power generation, flood control, and water supply. State parks (4) on its shores.

Lake of the Ozarks (□ 93 sq mi/241 sq km); Miller, Gamden, Morgan, and Benton cos.; central Mo.; on Osage R.; 33 mi/53 km SW of Jefferson City; c.85 mi/137 km long, with shoreline of 1,375 mi/2,213 km; 38°12′N 92°36′W. Max. capacity 1,428,000 acre-ft. Extends W through Ozarks in serpentine course to Harry S. Truman Dam, near Warsaw. Three arms formed by Niangua R. (S), Grand Auglaize Creek (SE), and Gravoi (GRA-voi) Creek (N). Formed by Bagnell Dam (2,543 ft/775 m long; 148 ft/45 m high), built (1929–1931) for power generation and recreation by Union Electric Company L. of the Ozarks and Ha Ha Tonka state parks are here. Resort and residential communities of Osage Beach, Lake Ozark, Hurrican Deck, Sunrise Beach, Gravois Mills, Lakeland, and Lakeview Heights on the lake's shores.

Area in square miles is shown by the symbol □   capital city or county seat by ⊙

Lake of the Pines, uninc. town (1990 pop. 3,890), Nevada co., E central Calif., 12 mi/19 km S of Grass Valley, and 9 mi/14.5 km N of Auburn; 39°02′N 121°04′W. Surrounds L. of the Pines reservoir (Magnolia Creek), near Bear R.

Lake of the Woods, county (☐ 1,774 sq mi/4,595 sq km; 1990 pop. 4,076), NW Minn.; ⊙ Baudette; 48°46′N 94°54′W. Bounded NE by Rainy R., and N and NW by L. of the Woods, both form Can.-U.S. border (prov. of Man. to NW, prov. of Ont. to N and NE). Agr. region (oats, wheat, barley, alfalfa, potatoes, flax, sunflowers); timber. Northwest Angle State Forest in far N; part of Beltrami Isl. State Forest in S and SW; including part of Red L. Wildlife Management Area in S and SW. Widely scattered parts of Red Lake Indian Reservation in far N and in S; Zippel Bay State Park in N center, on S shore of L. of the Woods. Formed 1922.

Lake of the Woods, uninc. town (1990 pop. 2,748), Champaign co., E central Ill., 10 mi/16 km NW of Champaign, on Sangamon R.; 40°12′N 88°22′W. Residential area; covered bridge.

Lake of the Woods (☐ 1,485 sq mi/3,846 sq km), on the U.S.-Canada border in the pine forest region of N Minn. (U.S.), SE Man. (Canada), and SW Ont. (Canada); c.70 mi/110 km long. More than 66% of the lake is in Canada. A remnant of former glacial L. Agassiz, It is fed by the Rainy R., and drained to the NW by the Winnipeg R. It has a very irregular shoreline and approximately 14,000 isls. L. of the Woods separates the NW Angle, the northernmost land of the coterminous U.S., from the rest of Minn. Abundant in fish and game, the region is a resort area.

Lake Orange, village (1990 pop. 1,719), Orange co., SE N.Y., 6.5 mi/10.5 km SW of Newburgh on Beaverdam L.; 41°27′N 74°07′W. Pop. figure includes Salisbury Mills and Beaverdam L.

Lake Orion, town (1990 pop. 3,057), Oakland co., SE Mich., suburb 11 mi/18 km NNE of Pontiac, on E end of small L. Orion; 42°46′N 83°14′W. Agr. (grain; cattle); mfg. (tool and die, hydraulic and pneumatic components, rubber prods.). Satellite community of Detroit. Bald Mt. State Recreation Area to S; ski area to E. Inc. 1859.

Lake Orion Heights, village, Oakland co., SE Mich., residential suburb 8 mi/12.9 km N of Pontiac, near L. Orion; 42°46′N 83°15′W.

Lake Oswego (ah-SWEE-go), city (1990 pop. 30,576), Clackamas co., NW Oregon, suburb 6 mi/9.7 km S of downtown Portland on the Willamette R., 4 mi/6.4 km NW of Oregon City; 45°24′N 122°42′W. Oswego L. (2.5 mi/4 km long) runs E and W through the center of the city. RR junction. Mfg. (consumer goods, bakery prods., textiles, apparel, lumber, transportation equip.; printing and publishing). Marylhurst Col. to SE. Tryon Creek State Park to N; Mary S. Young State Park to S. Founded c. 1850; inc. 1909.

Lake o'the Pines, reservoir (☐ 29 sq mi/75 sq km), Camp, Upshur, and Marion cos., NE Texas, on Cypress Creek, 22 mi/51 km NE of Longview; 32°46′N 94°30′W. Max. capacity 1,998,740 acre-ft. Formed by Feprells Bridge Dam (97 ft/30 m high), built (1958) by Army Corps of Engineers for water supply; also used for recreation and power generation.

Lake Ozark, village (1990 pop. 681), Miller co., central Mo., 4 mi/6.4 km NNW of Osage Beach, on L. of the Ozarks (Osage R.); 38°11′N 92°37′W. Residential and recreation area. Bagnell Dam is 4 mi/4.8 km NE.

Lake Panasoffkee (pan-nah-SOF-kee), town (☐ 4 sq mi/10.4 sq km; 1990 pop. 2,705), Sumter co., central Fla., 30 mi/48 km S of Ocala; 28°47′N 82°07′W. Coleman Correctional Facility located here.

Lake Park 1 town (☐ 1 sq mi/2.6 sq km; 1990 pop. 6,704), Palm Beach co., SE Fla., 5 mi/8 km N of West Palm Beach, on L. Worth lagoon; 26°48′N 80°04′W. **2** town (1990 pop. 996), Dickinson co., NW Iowa, 11 mi/18 km WNW of Spirit L.; 43°27′N 95°19′W. In resort area; feed mill. State park, sand and gravel pits nearby.

Lake Park 1 village (1990 pop. 500), Lowndes co., S Ga., 11 mi/18 km SE of Valdosta, near Fla., state line; 30°41′N

83°11′W. Mfg. of paper bags; industrial sandblasting. Location of one of the 1st discount name-brands outlet malls located on Interstate 75; attracts tourists traveling in and out of Fla. **2** village (1990 pop. 638), Becker co., W Minn., 13 mi/21 km WNW of Detroit Lakes; 46°52′N 96°05′W. Agr. (grain, sugar beets, sunflowers; livestock, poultry; dairying); mfg. (fishing tackle). Numerous small natural lakes in area. White Earth Indian Reservation to NE.

Lake Peekskill, resort village (1990 pop. 2,150), Putnam co., SE N.Y., on Peekskill L. (c.½ mi/⁸⁄₁₀ km long), 5 mi/8 km NE of Peekskill; 41°21′N 73°53′W.

Lake Placid, town (☐ 1 sq mi/2.6 sq km; 1990 pop. 1,158), Highlands co., central Fla., 15 mi/24 km S of Sebring, in lake region; 27°18′N 81°22′W. Citrus fruit.

Lake Placid, village (☐ 1 sq mi/2.6 sq km; 1990 pop. 2,485), Essex co., NE N.Y., in the Adirondacks, surrounding Mirror L.; 44°16′N 73°59′W. Elev. 1,800 ft/549 m. Mfg. (foot supports, transportation equip.). Famous resort and sports center; Winter Olympics (1932, 1980) and the World Bobsled Championships (1969) were held here. Lake Placid has a summer theater and music festival, a figure-skating school, and annual winter sports competitions. The farm and burial place of the abolitionist John Brown are nearby. Terminus (N), at Old Military Rd., of 133-mi/214-km Northville–Lake Placid trail connecting Adirondack foothills and High Peaks region. Settled 1850, inc. 1900.

Lake Pleasant, village (1990 pop. 350), ⊙ Hamilton co., E central N.Y., on L. Pleasant (☐ c.2 sq mi/5.2 sq km; 3.5 mi/5.6 km long), 50 mi/80 km NE of Utica, in the Adirondacks; 43°28′N 74°25′W. Summer and winter recreation; summer residences.

Lake Pleasant 1 Ariz.: see PLEASANT LAKE, . **2** Mass.: see MONTAGUE.

Lake Preston, town (1990 pop. 663), Kingsbury co., E S.Dak., 9 mi/14.5 km E of De Smet, near L. Preston, L. Whitewood to SE; 44°21′N 97°22′W. In farming region (livestock, poultry; dairy prods.; grain); mfg. (cutting tools).

Lake Providence, town (1990 pop. 5,380), ⊙ East Carroll parish, extreme NE La., on Mississippi R., and 36 mi/58 km NNW of Vicksburg (Miss.); 32°49′N 91°11′W. In cotton-growing area; agr. (cattle; rice, pecans, soybeans, sorghum); mfg. (wood prods., pepper sauces). L. Providence (c.5 mi/8 km long; fishing), an oxbow lake, formed by the Mississippi, is just N. Bayou Macon State Wildlife Area to W. One of oldest towns in La.; settled c.1812, inc. 1876.

Lake Purdy, village (1990 pop. 1,840), Jefferson and Shelby cos., N central Ala., 7 mi/11.3 km E of Birmingham; 33°25′N 86°41′W.

Lake Quivira (kwuh-VER-uh), village (1990 pop. 983), Johnson co., E Kansas, residential suburb, 7 mi/11.3 km WSW of Kansas City, near Kansas R.; 39°02′N 94°46′W. Quivira L. reservoir at center of community.

Lake Range, Washoe co., W Nev., largely in Pyramid L. Indian Reservation, bet. Pyramid L. (W), and Winnemucca and Mud lakes (E). Rises to 8,182 ft/2,494 m in Tohakum Peak and to 7,608 ft/2,319 m in Pah-Rum Peak.

Lake Ridge, uninc. city, Prince William co., NE Va., residential suburb 21 mi/34 km SW of Washington, D.C., 12 mi/19 km SE of Manassas, near Occoquan River, Occoquan Dam to NE; 38°41′N 77°17′W.

Lake Ronkonkoma, village (☐ 4 sq mi/10.4 sq km; 1990 pop. 18,997), Suffolk co., SE N.Y., on central L.I., 7 mi/11.3 km NW of Patchogue, on L. Ronkonkoma (c.0.75 mi/1.21 km in diameter); 40°49′N 73°06′W. Residential-mfg. community.

Lake Rushford, N.Y.: see CANEADEA.

Lake Saint Croix Beach (KROI), town (1990 pop. 1,078), Washington co. E Minn., residential suburb 14 mi/23 km E of downtown St. Paul, on shore of L. St. Croix, natural lake on St. Croix R. (Wis. state line); 44°55′N 92°46′W. Lower St. Croix Natl. Scenic Riverway on the St. Croix R.

Lake Saint Louis, city (1990 pop. 7,400), St. Charles co., E Mo., suburb 14 mi/23 km W of St. Charles; 38°47′N

90°46′W. Residential area surrounds L. St. Louis. Light mfg.

Lake San Marcos, uninc. town (1990 pop. 3802), San Diego co., S Calif., residential suburb 30 mi/48 km N of downtown San Diego, 7 mi/11.3 km W of Escondido, 6 mi/9.7 km E of Pacific Ocean, on L. San Marcos reservoir, San Marcos R.; 33°08′N 117°13′W.

Lake Shore, village (1990 pop. 693), Cass co., central Minn., 15 mi/24 km NW of Brainerd, and 3 mi/4.8 km WSW of Nisswa at NE end of Gull L. reservoir; 46°30′N 94°21′W. Resorts. Dairying; poultry; oats, alfalfa. Pillsbury State Forest to SW.

Lake Spaulding Dam, Calif.: see YUBA RIVER.

Lake Station, city, Lake co., extreme NW Ind., just SE of Gary. In the Calumet industrial region; mfg. (surgical instruments, cement blocks).

Lake Stevens, town (1990 pop. 3,380), Snohomish co., NW Wash., on L. Stevens, residential suburb 5 mi/8 km E of Everett, and 30 mi/48 km NNE of Seattle; 48°01′N 122°04′W. Timber; mfg. (millwork, cedar prods., wood fencing); recreation. Mt. Baker-Snoqualmie Natl. Forest to E.

Lake Success, residential suburb (☐ 1 sq mi/2.6 sq km; 1990 pop. 2,484) of N.Y. city, Nassau co., SE N.Y., on NW L.I.; 40°46′N 73°42′W. L. Success was the temporary home of the UN from 1946 to 1950. Settled c.1730, inc. 1926.

Lake Tapawingo, village (1990 pop. 761), Jackson co., W Mo., suburb 13 mi/21 km ESE of downtown Kansas City, SE of Independence; 39°01′N 94°18′W. Residential.

Lake Tara, town, Clayton co., NW central Ga., N of Jonesboro; 33°32′N 84°21′W.

Lake View, plantation (1990 pop. 23), Piscataquis co., central Maine, on Schoodic L., and 19 mi/31 km ENE of Dover-Croft; 45°21′N 68°53′W. In recreational area.

Lake View 1 resort town (1990 pop. 1,303), Sac co., W Iowa, 8 mi/12.9 km SSW of Sac City, near Black Hawk L. (state park here); 42°18′N 95°02′W. Mfg. (popcorn; concrete). Gravel pits in vicinity. Settled 1875; inc. 1887. **2** town (1990 pop. 872), Dillon co., NE S.C., 35 mi/56 km ENE of Florence, near N.C. state line; 34°20′N 79°10′W. Mfg. of upholstery material; agr. (livestock; cotton, grain, soybeans). Formerly called Pages Mill.

Lake Villa, village (1990 pop. 2,857), Lake co., extreme NE Ill., 13 mi/21 km WNW of Waukegan; 42°25′N 88°04′W. In lake-resort area.

Lake Village, town (1990 pop. 2,791), ⊙ Chicot co., extreme SE Ark., 14 mi/23 km WSW of Greenville (Miss.), on L. Chicot; 33°19′N 91°16′W. Commercial fishing and fish farming; mfg. (processed catfish and *tilapia* [Afr. freshwater fish], hospital and industrial apparel). Founded in 1850s; inc. 1901.

Lake Village, village (1990 pop. 850), Newton co., NW Ind., 11 mi/18 km SSW of Lowell. La Salle State Fish and Wildlife Area to NW. Agr. area.

Lake Waccamaw (WAK-uh-maw), town (1990 pop. 954), Columbus co., SE N.C., 10 mi/16 km E of Whiteville, on N side of L. Waccamaw (c.5 mi/8 km long, 3 mi/4.8 km wide); 34°19′N 78°30′W. Hunting, fishing. Agr. (tobacco, peanuts, grain; livestock); mfg. (tobacco processing). L. Waccamaw State Park to SW.

Lake Wales, town (☐ 6 sq mi/15.5 sq km; 1990 pop. 9,670), Polk co., central Fla., 12 mi/19 km SE of Winter Haven; 27°53′N 81°35′W. Citrus fruit-shipping center; packing houses, large cannery, tannery; sand and gravel pits. Retirement community in the area. A once-noted resort that includes the Singing Tower (with a carillon of 71 bells) and bird sanctuary/park est. 1929 by Edward W. Bok. Plotted 1911.

Lake Wallula (wah-LAH-luh), reservoir (☐ 6 sq mi/15.5 sq km), in N central Oregon (Umatilla co.), and S central Wash. (Benson co.), on Columbia R., at E end of the Columbia Gorge, just N of Umatilla; 45°56′N 119°18′W. Max. capacity 1,350,000 acre-ft. Formed by McNary Dam (220 ft/67 m high), built (1954) by Army Corps of Engineers for navigation; also used for power generation, irrigation, flood control, and recreation.

Lake Washington Ship Canal, Wash.: see WASHINGTON LAKE.

Cross references are shown in SMALL CAPITALS. The pronunciation key is on page xv. The dates of population figures are on page xii.

Lake Waukomis (waw-KO-mis), village (1990 pop. 1,027), Platte co., W Mo., residential suburb, 12 mi/19 km NNW of downtown Kansas City; 39°13′N 94°38′W.

Lake Wilson, village (1990 pop. 319), Murray co., SW Minn., 10 mi/16 km W of Slayton, near Beaver Creek; 43°59′N 95°57′W. Agr. (grain; livestock, poultry; dairying); mfg. (feeds).

Lake Windermere, Canada: see ATHALMER.

Lake Winnebago (wi-nuh-BAI-go), village (1990 pop. 748), Cass co., W Mo., residential suburb 20 mi/32 km SSE of downtown Kansas City; 38°49′N 94°21′W.

Lake Wobegon, fictional lake and inc. town, Stolid co., central Minn. Based on the hometown of philosopher-raconteur Garrison Keillor and featured on his radio show *A Prairie Home Companion.* Elev. 1,418 ft/432 m. The 678-acre/274-ha spring-fed lake (1 mi/1.6 km in diameter, and 100 ft/30 m deep) flows into the Wobegon R., which in turn flows into the Sauk R. and then the Mississippi. Lake fills meteorite crater with high magnetic iron content, precluding the fixing of true geographical coordinates, and therefore appearing on no maps. Extreme continental climate, with icy-cold winters and cool summers. Settled in 1866 by immigrants from Lagebehynde co. in N central Norway, who were attracted to the "New Scandinavia" as homesteaders. Dairying supports patented cholesterol-rich ice cream. Ice-fishing, hunting, hiking, and contemplation are major activities and the economy is supplemented by a cent. of cash savings. Lutheran church and annual ice-fishing tournament are visitor attractions. Celebrated for its demographic uniqueness in that "all the women are strong, all the men are good-looking, and all the children are above average."

Lake Worth, city (☐ 6 sq mi/15.5 sq km; 1990 pop. 28,564), Palm Beach co., SE Fla., 7 mi/11.3 km S of West Palm Beach, on L. Worth (a lagoon); 26°37′N 80°03′W. It is a residential suburb and resort center popular for its bathing and fishing facilities. Mfg. includes sports equip., tents and awnings, apparel, and food prods. Palm Beach Community Col. is here. Inc. 1913.

Lake Worth, town (1990 pop. 4,591), Tarrant co., N Texas, residential suburb 7 mi/11.3 km NW of downtown Fort Worth, near L. Worth (W Fork Trinity R.); 32°48′N 97°25′W. Monroe Creek L. to SE; Fort Worth Nature Center and Refuge to NW. Inc. after 1940.

Lake Wylie, uninc. town (1990 pop. 2,599), York co., N S.C., 13 mi/21 km SW of Charlotte, N.C., and 13 mi/21 km N of Rock Hill, S.C.; 35°06′N 81°02′W. Residential community on W shore of L Wylie reservoir. N.C. state line to W and N. Catawba 1 and 2 Nuclear Power Plants adjoin.

Lake Wyonah, uninc. town (1990 pop. 1,055), Schuylkill co., E central Pa., residential community 6 mi/9.7 km SSE of Pottsville on Plum Creek; 40°35′N 76°10′W.

Lake Zurich (ZUHR-ick), village (1990 pop. 14,947), Lake co., NE Ill., suburb 31 mi/50 km NW of downtown Chicago, and 17 mi/27 km SW of Waukegan; 42°11′N 88°05′W. Rapid urban growth area; remnant agr.; mfg. (fabricated metal prods., appliances, textiles, food processing and equip., aluminum die, water treatment prods.).

Lakefield, village (1991 pop. 2,555), S Ont., Canada, on small Katchiwano L., at mouth of Otonabee R., 9 mi/14 km NNE of Peterborough; 44°26′N 78°16′W. Dairying; woodworking; resort.

Lakefield, town (1990 pop. 1,679), Jackson co., SW Minn., 10 mi/16 km WNW of Jackson, at SE tip of South Heron L., near Iowa state line; 43°40′N 95°10′W. Agr. trading point (grain; livestock); mfg. (gas fireplaces). Kilen Woods State Park to NE. Settled 1879; inc. 1887.

Lakefield-Wikiup, uninc. town (1990 pop. 6,779), Sonoma co., W Calif., residential suburb 7 mi/11.3 km NW of Santa Rosa, near Russian R. Sonoma Co. Fruit, grain; dairying; poultry. Airport.

Lakehills, town (1990 pop. 2,147), Bandera co., SW Texas, residential and recreational community, 28 mi/45 km WNW of San Antonio, in bend on N shore of Medina L. (Medina R.); 29°36′N 98°56′W.

Lakehurst, borough (1990 pop. 3,078), Ocean co., E central N.J., 6 mi/9.7 km NW of Toms River; 40°00′N 74°19′W. Early-20th-cent. resort area. It is important as the site of the Lakehurst Naval Air Station (est. 1919) and Air Warfare Center. The *Shenandoah* (1923) was the 1st airship to use the station, and transatlantic airships made it their U.S. terminal from 1924. The crash and burning of the *Hindenburg,* which took 36 lives, occurred here (May 6, 1937) as the hydrogen-filled Ger. zeppelin was being moored. Center for U.S. Navy blimps until 1940s. Inc. 1921.

Lakeland, city (1990 pop. 70,576), Polk co., central Fla., 30 mi/48 km E of Tampa; 28°02′N 81°57′W. It is an important processing and shipping center for a citrus-fruit-growing and phosphate-mining region and is a retail trade center that serves a large area. Mfg. (motor vehicle parts). The Fla. Citrus Commission, other state citrus organizations, and the Fla. Phosphate Council have their hq. in Lakeland, which is also a winter resort and recreation center. Points of interest include a major sports and convention complex and the Frank Lloyd Wright bldgs. at Fla. Southern Col. Inc. 1885.

Lakeland 1 town (1990 pop. 2,467), ⊙ Lanier co., S Ga., 19 mi/31 km NE of Valdosta, bet. Alapaha R. and Banks L.; 31°02′N 83°04′W. Agr. center; mfg. of lumber and wood prods. Nearby Banks L. Natl. Wildlife Refuge contains one of the best stands of pond cypress in the E U.S. **2** town (1990 pop. 2,000), Washington co., E Minn., suburb 14 mi/23 km E of downtown St. Paul, on St. Croix R. (L. St Croix; bridged), opposite Hudson, Wis.; 44°57′N 93°46′W. Mfg. (plastic prods., water agitators, sand and gravel processing, paving machines); agr. (cattle, sheep; corn, soybeans). Lower St. Croix Natl. Scenic Riverway on St. Croix R.

Lakeland, village, Jefferson co., N Ky., residential suburb 11 mi/18 km E of Louisville. Nearby is Ormsby Village.

Lakeland (1990 pop. 1,204), suburb NE of Memphis, Shelby co., SW Tenn. Inc. 1977.

Lakeland Shores, village (1990 pop. 291), Washington co., E Minn., residential suburb 14 mi/23 km E of downtown St. Paul, on shore of L. St. Croix; 44°57′N 92°45′W. Lower St. Croix Natl. Scenic Riverway on St. Croix R.

Lakeland Village, uninc. town (1990 pop. 5,159), Riverside co., S Calif., 23 mi/37 km. S of Riverside, on SW shore of L. Elsinore reservoir; 33°39′N 117°20′W. Part of Cleveland Natl. Forest to SW, includes the Elsinore Mts.; L. Elsinore State Recreation Area to NW.

Lakeline, village (1990 pop. 210), Lake co., NE Ohio, on L. Erie, 17 mi/27 km NE of Cleveland; 41°39′N 81°27′W.

Lakemont, town, Rabun co., extreme NE Ga., 6 mi/9.7 km S of Clayton, near L. Rabun, in the Blue Ridge; 34°46′N 83°24′W. Recreation area; mfg. (apparel).

Lakemoor, village (1990 pop. 1,322), McHenry and Lake cos., NE Ill., residential suburb 42 mi/68 km NW of downtown Chicago, 4 mi/6.4 km ESE of McHenry, at E end of Lily L.; 42°20′N 88°12′W. Volo Bog State Natural Area to N.

Lakemore, village (1990 pop. 2,684), Summit co., NE Ohio, 6 mi/10 km SE of downtown Akron; 41°01′N 81°25′E. Inc. 1920.

Lakeport, city (1990 pop. 4,390), ⊙ Lake co., NW Calif., 17 mi/27 km ESE of Ukiah, at W end of Clear L.; 39°02′N 122°55′W. Resort, farm trade center. Agr. (pears, grapes, oats, walnuts; cattle); mfg. (glass prods.). Mendocino Natl. Forest to N; Clear L. State Park to SE. Founded 1861, inc. 1888.

Lakeport 1 village, Belknap co., central N.H., industrial section of Laconia (city), 1 mi/1.6 km NE of city center, on L. Paugus, E of channel connecting Paugus and Opeche bays of L. Winnipesaukee. Mfg. (outerwear, commercial printing, metal doors). **2** village (1990 pop. 710), Gregg co., E Texas, residential suburb 7 mi/11.3 km SSE of downtown Longview, on Sabine R.; 32°23′N 94°42′W. Cattle; oil and natural gas. L. Cherokee reservoir to SE. Gregg Co. Airport to S.

Lakeport Dam, Laconia, Belknap co., SE N.H., on the Winnipesaukee R.; 44°32′N 71°28′W. Max. capacity 2,400,000 acre-ft; 14 ft/4 m high. Gravity dam built in 1851 for textile mills. Forms L. Winnipesaukee (recreation area).

Lakeridge, uninc. town, King co., W Wash., residential suburb Seattle, at S end of L. Washington.

Lakes District, suburban area (1990 pop. 60,300), Pierce co., W Wash., residential suburb 7 mi/11.3 km SW of Tacoma, near Puget Sound, drained by Chambers and Clover creeks. General name for area of small lakes, including Steilacoom, Gravelly, and American lakes, and including communities of Lakewood Center, Clover Park, Lakeview, Lake City, and Interlaken. Three fish hatcheries on creeks. Fort Lewis Military Reservation to S; McChord Air Force Base to E.

Lakeshire, town (1990 pop. 1,467), St. Louis co., E Mo., residential suburb 10 mi/16 km SSW of downtown St. Louis; 38°32′N 90°20′W.

Lakeshore 1 uninc. village, Fresno co., central Calif., 45 mi/72 km NE of Fresno, in Sierra Nevada, Sierra Natl. Forest, at E end of Huntington L. reservoir (Big Creek). Resort area; China Peak Ski Area; McKinley Grove Big Trees to SE. **2** uninc. village, Hancock, co., SE Miss., 7 mi/11.3 km SW of Bay St. Louis, near Mississippi Sound, Gulf of Mexico. Mfg. (boats and barges, boat docks).

Lakeside 1 uninc. city (1990 pop. 39,412), San Diego co., S Calif., residential suburb 17 mi/27 km NE of downtown San Diego, on San Diego R.; 32°51′N 116°55′W. Agr. (fruit, avocados; dairying; poultry; flowers, ornamental plants); mfg. (bldg. materials, fabricated metal prods.). Part of Cleveland Natl. Forest (E); Capitan Grande Indian Reservation (E); Barona Ranch Indian Reservation (NE); El Capitan Reservoir (E); San Vicente Reservoir (N). S terminus of San Diego Aqueduct. **2** city (☐ 17 sq mi/44 sq km; 1990 pop. 29,137), Leon co., NW Fla., 3 mi/4.8 km S of Tallahassee; 30°07′N 81°46′W. **3** uninc. city, Henrico co., E central Va., residential suburb 5 mi/8 km NW of downtown Richmond; 37°37′N 77°28′W. J. Sargeant Reynolds Community Col. (Parham Campus) is here.

Lakeside 1 town (1990 pop. 5,360), Jefferson co., N central Colo. residential suburb 5 mi/8 km NW of downtown Denver, near Clear Creek, bounded by Denver (and Denver co.) on N and E, Wheat Ridge on W, Mountain View on S. Elev. 5,360 ft/1,634 m. **2** resort town (1990 pop. 522), Buena Vista co., NW Iowa, just SE of Storm L.; 42°37′N 95°10′W. Inc. 1933. **3** town (1990 pop. 1,437), Coos co., SW Oregon, 12 mi/19 km N of North Bend, 3 mi/4.8 km E of Pacific Ocean, at joining of North Tenmile and South Tenmile lakes; 43°34′N 124°10′W. Lumber. Tourism. Eel L. and William M. Tugman State Park (N); Elliott State Forest (E); Oregon Dunes Natl. Recreation Area (W). **4** town (1990 pop. 292), Tarrant co., N Texas, residential suburb 10 mi/16 km NW of downtown Fort Worth, near L. Worth (E) and W Fork Trinity R.; 28°06′N 97°51′W. Fort Worth Nature Center and Refuge to N.

Lakeside 1 village, Litchfield co., Conn., 10 mi/16 km SW of Torrington, resort town on S side of Bantam L. Postal section of Morris. **2** village, Berrien co., extreme SW Mich., 14 mi/23 km NE of Michigan City, Ind., on L. Michigan; 41°50′N 86°40′W. Resort area. Warren Dunes State Part to NE. **3** village (1990 pop. 600), Flathead co., NW Mont., 13 mi/21 km SSE of Kalispell, on W shore of Flathead L., near N end of lake. Residential and recreational community. Flathead Natl. Forest to W. **4** resort village, Ottawa co., N Ohio, on Marblehead Peninsula in L. Erie, 7 mi/11 km NNW of Sandusky. **5** village, Chelan co., central Wash., 2 mi/3.2 km W of Chelan, and on L. Chelan.

Lakeside, Ariz.: see PINETOP-LAKESIDE.

Lakeside City, town (1990 pop. 865), Archer co., N Texas, residential suburb 6 mi/9.7 km SSW of downtown Wichita Falls, on S shore of L. Wichita (Holiday Creek); 33°49′N 98°32′W. Cattle; oil and natural gas.

Lakeside Park, town (1990 pop. 3,062), Kenton co., N Ky., residential suburb 6 mi/9.7 km SW of Cincinnati, Ohio, and 4 mi/6.4 km SW of Covington, Ky.; 39°01′N 84°34′W. Thomas More Col. to S. Inc. 1930.

Laketon, village (1990 pop. 500), Wabash co., N central

Ind., 12 mi/19 km N of Wabash, on Eel R. Corn, soybeans; cattle. Mfg. (asphalt, fuel oil, petroleum prods., gasoline). Laid out 1836.

Laketown, village (1990 pop. 261), Rich co., N Utah, at S end of Bear L., 28 mi/45 km ENE of Logan; 41°49'N 111°19'W. Rendezvous Beach State Park is NW; Circo Beach State Park to NNE (E shore); Wasatch Natl. Forest (W).

Lakeview 1 uninc. town (1990 pop.1,448), Riverside co., S Calif., 17 mi/27 km SE of Riverside, on San Jacinto R.; 33°50'N 117°07'W. Colorado R. Aqueduct passes to S. Mfg. (pharmaceuticals). **2** town, Montcalm co., central Mich., 38 mi/61 km NNE of Grand Rapids, on W end of small Tamarack L. (resort); 43°26'N 85°16'W. Agr. area (livestock; potatoes, grain, fruit, beans, apples, dairy prods.); mfg. (brass fittings). Winterskȍl Ski Area to SW. **3** town (1990 pop. 2,526), ⊙ Lake co., S Oregon, 70 mi/113 km E of Klamath Falls, N of Goose L.; 42°11'N 120°20'W. Elev. 4,798 ft/1,462 m; RR terminus. Sawmills, woodworking plants. Ranching; tourism. Meat processing. Wheat, oats, barley; sheep, cattle. Booth State Wayside to W; Chandler State Wayside and L. Abert to N; Drews Reservoir to W; parts of Fremont Natl. Forest to W and E; Goose L. State Recreation Area to S; Warner Valley (geyser basin) to E. Founded 1876, inc. 1884.

Lakeview 1 village (1990 pop. 1,108), Calhoun co., S Mich., just SSW of Battle Creek; 43°27'N 85°16'W. Part of city of Battle Creek. **2** residential village (1990 pop. 5,476), Nassau co., SE N.Y., on W L.I., just SW of Hempstead; 40°41'N 73°39'W. State park nearby. **3** resort village (1990 pop. 1,056), Logan co., W central Ohio, 12 mi/19 km NW of Bellefontaine, on Indian L.; 40°29'N 83°55'W. **4** village (1990 pop. 202), Hall co., NW Texas, 32 mi/51 km NW of Childress; 34°40'N 100°42'W. Peanuts; cattle. **5** village, McLennan co., E central Texas, 6 mi/9.7 km N of Waco.

Lakeville, city (1990 pop. 24,854), Dakota co., SE Minn., suburb 18 mi/29 km S of Minneapolis, and 22 mi/35 km SW of St. Paul; 44°40'N 93°14'W. Agr. area (grain, soybeans; livestock, poultry; dairying); mfg. (patterns and prototypes, machinery, paper prods., bldg. materials, plastic prods., furniture; millwork, food and beverage processing, printing and publishing). Airlake Park Airport to S; Crystal L. on N boundary, Marion L. in W center.

Lakeville 1 resort town in Salisbury town, Litchfield co., NW Conn., on L. Wononskopomuc. Hotchkiss preparatory school (1892) here. Ethan Allen made Revolutionary War munitions here. **2** town (1990 pop. 655), St. Joseph co., N Ind., 11 mi/18 km S of South Bend; 41°32'N 86°16'W. Mfg. (transportation equip.); agr. Potato Creek State Park nearby (W). **3** agr. town (1990 pop. 7,785), Plymouth co., SE Mass., on Assawompsett Pond, and 15 mi/24 km N of New Bedford; 41°50'N 70°58'W. Mfg. (paper prods.). Nearby ponds include Long, Great Quittacas, and Snipatuit. Hq. of Ocean Spray Cranberries, Inc. Settled 1717, inc. 1853.

Lakeville 1 village, Ashtabula co., NE Ohio, surrounding city of Conneaut. Inc. 1944. **2** village, Holmes co., central Ohio, near Mohican R., 27 mi/43 km ESE of Mansfield.

Lakeville, plantation (1990 pop. 45), Penobscot co., E central Maine, 50 mi/80 km NNE of Bangor, in wilderness area; 45°18'N 68°06'W. Hunting, fishing.

Lakeway, Village of, town (1990 pop. 4,044), Travis co., S Texas, residential suburb 15 mi/24 km WNW of downtown Austin. Agr. area (cotton, grain, pecans; cattle; dairying); recreation. L. Travis (Colorado R.) to N.

Lakewood 1 city (1990 pop. 73,557), Los Angeles co., S Calif., a suburb 15 mi/24 km SSE of Los Angeles, and 5 mi/8 km NE of Long Beach; 33°51'N 118°07'W. Bounded on E by San Gabriel R. Extensive aerospace, high-technology, and electronic industries in area; light mfg. Archtypical Amer. suburb; 1st of 17,500 houses built on assembly line principles bet. 1950 and 1952. Long Beach Airport (Daugherty Field) to SW. Site of Lakewood Center Mall, one of the largest shopping centers in U.S. Inc. 1954. **2** city (1990 pop. 126,095), Jefferson co., N central Colo., a growing suburb 7 mi/11.3 km SW of downtown Denver; 39°42'N 105°06'W. Elev. 5,440 ft/1,658 m. Drained by Bear Creek in S. The city has become a major suburban business center with the development of high-technology industries and corporate offices, including the huge Denver Federal Center. Mfg. (medical equip., laboratory equip., fabricated metal prods., consumer goods, soda ash; printing and publishing). Belmar Mus. here; Jefferson co. stadium at center of city. Bear Creek Reservoir in SW; Front Range of Rocky Mts. to W. County fairgrounds to W; Red Rock Natural Amphitheater to SW. Inc. 1969. **3** city (1990 pop. 59,718), Cuyahoga co., NE Ohio, a suburb of Cleveland, on L. Erie; 41°29'N 81°48'W. Many varied industries. City was settled as East Rockport and renamed in 1889. Inc. 1911. **4** uninc. city (1990 pop. 58,412), Pierce co., W Wash., suburb 6 mi/9.7 km SW of downtown Tacoma, near Puget Sound, in Lakes District; 47°10'N 122°32'W. Service and residential area for McChord Air Force Base and Fort Lewis Military Reservation, both to S. Steilacoom and Gravelly lakes are in city. Site of Lakewood Mall, one of the largest shopping centers in U.S.

Lakewood, town (1990 pop. 26,095), Ocean co., E central N.J., 9 mi/14.5 km N of Toms River, on the Metedeconk R. A resort in a scenic region near the Atlantic coast and center for Hassidic schools. It has plants making a variety of prods. Lakewood was the site of early ironworks and of the Rockefeller estate, which has become a state arboretum. Georgian Court Col. is here. Settled 1800, inc. 1892.

Lakewood 1 village (1990 pop. 1,609), McHenry co., NE Ill., residential satellite community of Chicago, W of village of Crystal Lake (town), near Crystal L., 8 mi/12.9 km SE of Woodstock; 42°13'N 88°22'W. In agr. area (dairying; corn). **2** uninc. village, Eddy co., SE N.Mex., on W shore of L. McMillan reservoir (Pecos R.), and 17 mi/27 km NNW of Carlsbad. In irrigated region; grain, cotton, pecans. Brantley L. State Park to SE. **3** resort village (□ 1 sq mi/2.6 sq km; 1990 pop. 3,564), Chautauqua co., extreme W N.Y., on Chautauqua L., 5 mi/8 km W of Jamestown; 42°06'N 79°19'W. Truck and bus engines. Settled 1809, inc. 1893.

Lakewood, Maine: see SKOWHEGAN.

Lakewood Bluff, Wis.: see MAPLE BLUFF.

Lakewood Park, town (□ 6 sq mi/15.5 sq km; 1990 pop. 7,211), St. Lucie co., Fla., 6 mi/9.7 km S of Vero Beach; 27°32'N 80°23'W.

Lakin (LAIK-uhn), town (1990 pop. 2,060), ⊙ Kearny co., SW Kansas, on Arkansas R., and 21 mi/34 km W of Garden City; 37°56'N 101°15'W. Wheat, cattle. L. McKinney, irrigation reservoir to NE.

Lakota 1 town (1990 pop. 281), Kossuth co., N Iowa, 22 mi/35 km NNE of Algona; 43°22'N 94°05'W. **2** town (1990 pop. 898), ⊙ Nelson co., NE central N.Dak., 24 mi/39 km ESE of Devils L.; 48°02'N 98°20'W. Livestock; wheat. RR junction; Stump L. to S.

Lamadrid (lah-mah-DREED), town (1990 pop. 1,971), Coahuila, N Mexico, 26 mi/42 km WNW of Monclova, off Mexico Highway 130, on RR; 27°05'N 101°49'W. Elev 2,362 ft/720 m. Cereals; cattle.

Lamar 1 (luh-MAHR), county (□ 605 sq mi/1,567 sq km; 1990 pop. 15,715), W Ala.; ⊙ Vernon. Level region bordering on Miss., drained by Buttahatchee R. Corn, timber; crude-oil and natural-gas production. Formed 1867. **2** county (□ 181 sq mi/469 sq km; 1990 pop. 13,038), W central Ga.; ⊙ Barnesville; 33°04'N 84°08'W. Piedmont agr. cotton, corn, soybeans, wheat; cattle, hogs, poultry; lumber and wood prods. Formed 1920. **3** county (□ 500 sq mi/1,295 sq km; 1990 pop. 30,424), SE Miss.; ⊙ Purvis; 31°12'N 89°30'W. Drained by Wolf R., and by Black and Red creeks, source of Wolf R. in SW. Agr. (cotton, corn, pecans; poultry, cattle); pine timber; oil and natural gas. Outskirts (W) of Hattiesburg in NE. Formed 1904. **4** county (□ 932 sq mi/2,414 sq km; 1990 pop. 43,949), NE Texas; ⊙ Paris; 33°40'N 95°34'W. Bounded N by Red R. (here the Okla. state line), S by North Fork of Sulphur R. Diversified agr. cotton, hay, peanuts; cattle; timber; mfg. at Paris. Pat Mayse L. in N; L. Crook reservoir near center. Formed 1840.

Lamar (luh-MAHR), city (1990 pop. 4,168), ⊙ Barton co., SW Mo., on branch of Spring R., and 32 mi/51 km NNE of Joplin; 37°29'N 94°16'W. Agr. (wheat, corn, hay, sorghum; cattle); mfg. (furniture, metal prods.). Founded c.1856. Harry S. Truman b. here 1884. Truman State Historic Site.

Lamar 1 (luh-MAHR), town (1990 pop. 768), Johnson co., NW Ark., 14 mi/23 km NW of Russellville, near Arkansas R., and L. Dardanelle; 35°26'N 93°23'W. Mfg. (wooden truss parts). **2** town (1990 pop. 8,343), ⊙ Prowers co., SE Colo., on Arkansas R., and 50 mi/80 km ENE of La Junta; 38°04'N 102°37'W. Elev. 3,622 ft/1,104 m. Junction of RR spurs to Wiley and Hartman. Food-processing center for grain and cattle region; mfg. (transit buses, forage tubs, clay prods., alfalfa prods.). Lamar Community Col., Madonna of the Trail Monument, Big Timbers Mus. here. Cluster of reservoirs to N; Thurston, King, Nee Shah, Nee Nashe, Nee So Pah, and Nee Grande (the Nee reservoirs). Inc. 1886. **3** uninc. town (1990 pop. 1,200), Clinton co., N central Pa., 9 mi/14.5 km SW of Lock Haven, on Fishing Creek; 41°00'N 77°31'W. Agr. (livestock; dairying). Laman Natl. Fish Hatchery to S. Bald Eagle State Park to NW. **4** town (1990 pop. 1,125), Darlington co., NE central S.C., 17 mi/27 km W of Florence; 34°10'N 80°04'W. Mfg. (tables, metal fabrication, apparel, machinery); agr. (poultry, livestock; dairying; grain, soybeans, tobacco).

Lamar 1 (luh-MAHR), village (1990 pop. 80), Spencer co., SW Ind., 3 mi/4.8 km S of Santa Claus. Bituminous-coal mining and processing. **2** village, Benton co., N Miss., 12 mi/19 km NNE of Holly Springs. In agr. area. **3** village (1990 pop. 31), Chase co., S Nebr., 17 mi/27 km W of Imperial, near Colo. state line; 40°34'N 101°58'W. **4** village (1990 pop. 97), Hughes co., central Okla., 16 mi/26 km E of Holdenville, near Canadian R.; 35°06'N 96°07'W. In agr. area; mfg. (consumer goods).

Lamar Heights, village (1990 pop. 176), Barton co., SW Mo., suburb 1 mi/1.6 km W of Lamar; 37°29'N 94°17'W. Residential and commercial area.

Lamb, county (□ 1,017 sq mi/2,634 sq km; 1990 pop. 15,072), NW Texas; ⊙ Littlefield; 34°04'N 102°20'W. On the Llano Estacado; elev. c.3,500 ft/1,070 m–3,900 ft/1,190 m. Drained by intermittent Blackwater Draw (center) and Running Water Draw (NE). Rich agr. and livestock region (cattle, sheep) with irrigated areas; leads in Texas production of grain sorghum; also grows cotton, corn, vegetables; hay; soybeans. Oil, natural-gas wells; potash deposits; stone. Formed 1876.

Lambert, town (1990 pop. 1,131), Quitman co., NW Miss., 15 mi/24 km E of Clarksdale; 34°12'N 90°16'W. Agr. (cotton, rice, sorghum, soybeans); mfg. (apparel). O'Keefe Wildlife Management Area to E.

Lambert 1 village (1990 pop. 160), Richland co., NE Mont., on Fox Creek, tributary of Yellowstone R., and 22 mi/35 km W of Sidney. Wheat, barley, hay; cattle. Fox L. Wildlife Management Area to W. Originally called Fox Lake. **2** village (1990 pop. 11), Alfalfa co., N Okla., 15 mi/24 km ESE of Alva; 36°40'N 98°25'W. In grain-growing area.

Lamberton, town (1990 pop. 972), Redwood co., SW Minn., near Cottonwood R., 23 mi/37 km SSW of Redwood Falls; 44°13'N 95°15'W. Grain, soybeans; livestock; dairying.

Lambertville, city (1990 pop. 3,927), Hunterdon co., W N.J., 14 mi/23 km NW of Trenton, and on Delaware R. (bridged here) opposite New Hope, Pa.; 40°22'N 74°56'W. Mfg. (industrial ceremics, clothing, luggage); stone quarries; agr. (livestock, poultry; vegetables). Founded 1732; inc. 1849.

Lambityeco (lahm-beet-YE-ko), a historic site, in central Oaxaca, Mexico, 19 mi/30 km S of Oaxaca de Juárez, off Highway 190. This Zapotec site is still being excavated and has not yet been restored.

Lambs Grove, village (1990 pop. 212), Jasper co., central Iowa, suburb 2 mi/3.2 km W of Newton; 41°42'N 93°04'W. Corn, oats; cattle, hogs, sheep.

Lambton (LAM-tuhn), county (□ 1,124 sq mi/ 2,911 sq km; 1991 pop. 128,943), S Ont., Canada, on L. Huron, and on St. Clair and Thames rivers, on Mich. border; ⊙ Sarnia; 42°50′N 82°05′W.

Lambton, village (1991 pop. 1,485), S Que., Canada, near L. St. Francis, 20 mi/32 km NNW of Megantic. Lumbering, dairying. Dam across S end of L. St. Francis nearby.

Lambton, Cape, S extremity of Banks Isl., SW Franklin dist., N.W.T., Canada, on Amundsen Gulf; 71°04′N 123°09′W.

Lame Deer, town (1990 pop. 1,918), Rosebud co., SE Mont., on Lame Deer Creek, and 48 mi/77 km ESE of Hardin; 45°37′N 106°37′W. Agr. (cattle, sheep, horses; wheat, barley, oats); mfg. (lumber prods., apparel). Hq. of Northern Cheyenne Indian Reservation, Dull Knife Memorial Col.

Lamentin 1 (lah-mawng-TANG), town, NE Basse-Terre, Guadeloupe, 6 mi/9.7 km WNW of Pointe-á-Pitre. In sugar growing region; mfg. of alcohol (Grosse-Montaque Distillery). **2** town, W Martinique, at head of Fort-de-France Bay, 3 mi/4.8 km E of Fort-de-France. Trade center on fertile plain (bananas, cacao); rum distilling; limekiln; industrial center.

Lamentin, Plain of (lah-mawng-TANG), W Martinique, along Fort-de-France Bay, only extensive level land on the isl. Sugar-growing area. Site of Lamentin Internatl. Airport.

Lamesa (luh-MEE-suh), city (1990 pop. 10,809), ⊙ Dawson co., NW Texas, in the Llano Estacado; 32°43′N 101°57′W. Elev. 2,975 ft/907 m. Processing and shipping center for an irrigated area where cattle and hogs are raised; cotton, sorghum, wheat. Agribusiness center. Mfg. (electric motors, sheet metal fabricating, cottonseed oil and cotton prods., apparel). The city has several oil- and natural-gas wells. Inc. 1917.

Lamine River (luh-MEEN), c.70 mi/113 km long, central Mo.; rises in several branches in Morgan and Pettis cos.; flows N to the Missouri 6 mi/9.7 km W of Boonville.

Lamoille (lah-MOIL), county (□ 463 sq mi/1,199 sq km; 1990 pop. 19,735), N central Vt., with Green Mts. in W; ⊙ Hyde Park; 44°36′N 72°39′W. Includes Mt. Mansfield (winter sports), highest peak of Green Mts.; resorts. Drained by Lamoille R. Dairying; mfg. (machinery, wood prods., textiles); talc, asbestos, lumber; maple sugar. Organized 1835.

Lamoille, uninc. town, Elko co., NE Nev., lies in the W foothills of the Ruby Mts. One of the older communities in N Nev.; a stopping place along the California Trail in the 1840s (nearby Camp Halleck provided a military presence and security). Originally est. as a community of small land-holding ranchers and grain farmers. Lamoille has become increasingly gentrified since the 1980s; ranches sold to movie moguls, lawyers, doctors, and other well-to-do. Heli-skiing in the Ruby Mts.; wildlife in Ruby and Franklin marshes; cultural amenities in Elko. Voted "the best small place to live in America" in 1990. Elko airport (12 mi/19 km distant).

Lamoille River (lah-MOIL), c.70 mi/113 km long, NW Vt.; rises near Hardwick; flows generally W, through the range, past Morrisville (dam forms L. Lamoille here), to L. Champlain 10 mi/16 km N of Burlington. Receives North Branch (c.20 mi/32 km long) near Cambridge.

Lamoine (luh-MOIN), fishing and resort town (1990 pop. 1,311), Hancock co., S Maine, on Frenchman Bay just N of Mt. Desert Isl., and 8 mi/12.9 km SE of Ellsworth; 44°29′N 68°18′W.

Lamoka Lake, Schuyler co., W central N.Y., in Finger Lakes region, 10 mi/16 km W of Watkins Glen; 1.5 mi/ 2.4 km long; 42°24′N 77°05′W. Connected by stream to Waneta L. (N).

Lamoni (lah-MO-nei), town (1990 pop. 2,319), Decatur co., S Iowa, near Mo. state line 14 mi/23 km SW of Leon; 40°37′N 93°56′W. Mfg. (concrete blocks, dairy prods.). Has Graceland Jr. Col. Plotted 1879, inc. 1885.

Lamont (luh-MAHNT), town (1991 pop. 1,574), central Alta., Canada, 30 mi/48 km ENE of Edmonton; 53°45′N 112°47′W. Grain elevators, lumbering. Gateway to Elk Isl. Natl. Park (S).

Lamont, uninc. city (1990 pop. 11,517), Kern co., S central Calif., a residential suburb 9 mi/14.5 km SE of Bakersfield; 35°16′N 118°55′W. Agr. (cotton, potatoes, vegetables, tomatoes, sugar beets, beans, melons, fruit, nuts; dairying; cattle). Sequoia Natl. Forest to NE.

Lamont, town (1990 pop. 471), Buchanan co., E Iowa, near Maquoketa R., 15 mi/24 km NE of Independence; 42°36′N 91°38′W. Sand and gravel pits nearby.

Lamont 1 village (1990 pop. 454), Grant co., N Okla., 26 mi/42 km NE of Enid, near Salt Fork Arkansas R.; 36°41′N 97°33′W. In agr. area. **2** village (1990 pop. 91), Whitman co., SE Wash., 40 mi/64 km SW of Spokane; 47°12′N 117°54′W. In agr. region; wheat, barley; cattle.

Lamorandière (lah-mo-rahd-YER), village, W Que., Canada, 22 mi/35 km ENE of Amos; gold mining.

Lampasas, county (□ 714 sq mi/1,849 sq km; 1990 pop. 13,521), central Texas; ⊙ Lampasas; 31°11′N 98°14′W. Bounded W by Colorado R.; drained by Lampasas R. Wool, mohair shipped; agr. (grain sorghum, corn, watermelons, peanuts; cattle). Glass-sand mining; sand and gravel; stone. Mineral springs (health resort) at Lampasas. Formed 1856.

Lampasas, town (1990 pop. 6,382), ⊙ Lampasas co., central Texas, on a tributary of Lampasas R., and c.60 mi/97 km NNW of Austin; 31°03′N 98°10′W. Elev. 1,025 ft/312 m. Cattle ranching; agr. (peanuts, corn, watermelons); mfg. (livestock feed, food processing, rubber prods., cut stone). Originally named Burleson. Settled 1854; inc. 1874.

Lampasas River, c.110 mi/177 km long, central Texas; rises in Hamilton co.; flows SE and E through Stillhouse Hollow L. reservoir 8 mi/12.9 km SE of Killeen, to join Leon R. c.9 mi/14.5 km S of Temple, to form Little R.

Lampazos de Naranjo (lahm-PAH-sos dai nah-RAHN-ho), city (1990 pop. 4,222) and township, ⊙ Lampazos de Naranjo municipio, Nuevo León, N Mexico, on RR, and 70 mi/113 km SW of Nuevo Laredo on Mexico Highway 1; 27°01′N 100°30′W. Elev. 1,115 ft/340 m. Agr. center (cotton, wheat, livestock); iron ore. Old colonial town; former Span. mission.

Lampman, town (1991 pop. 647), SE Sask., Canada, 20 mi/32 km NE of Estevan; 49°23′N 102°45′W. RR junction; grain elevators.

Lamprey River (LAM-prai), c.40 mi/64 km long, SE N.H.; rises in Pawtuckaway Pond in Nottingham; flows S, then generally E past Raymond, Epping, and Lee, to Great Bay, tidal inlet of Atlantic Ocean at Newmarket.

Lamy (LAI-mee), village, Santa Fe co., N central N.Mex., in foothills of Sangre de Cristo Mts., 16 mi/26 km S of Santa Fe. Elev. c.6,482 ft/1,976 m. RR junction, spur N to Santa Fe; cattle, sheep. Santa Fe Natl. Forest to E; Glorieta Mesa to E.

Lanagan (LA-nuh-guhn), town (1990 pop. 501), McDonald co., extreme SW Mo., on branch of Elk R., 5 mi/8 km W of Pineville; 36°36′N 94°27′W. Printing.

Lanai (LAH-NAH-ee), island (□ 141 sq mi/365 sq km), Maui co., central Hawaii, W of Maui isl. across the Auau Channel, separated from Molokai to N by Kalohi Channel; from Kahoolawe to SE by Kealaikahiki Channel. Mt. Lanaihale (3,370 ft/1,027 m), in E, is the isl.'s highest point. Administered as a dist. of Maui co. For many years the isl. was used for sugarcane raising and cattle grazing. In 1922 it was purchased by Dole pineapple company and developed as a pineapple-growing center. Lanai City (1990 pop. 2,400) is near center of isl.; and Kaumalapau port is on W coast; village of Manele on S coast. In 1961, 98% of the isl. became the property of the Castle and Cook company, with plans to limit tourism and to designate a large majority of Lanai for the development of forests, meadows, and some agr. Palawai Basin in S center; Garden of the Gods rock formation in NW.

Lanai City (LAH-NAH-ee), town (1990 pop. 2,400), central Lanai, Maui co., Hawaii, 70 mi/113 km SE of Honolulu; 20°49′N 156°55′W. Mfg. (food preparations). Lanai Airport to SW; Palawai Basin to S; Garden of the Gods to NW (by trail); junction of Kaumalapau Highway and Manele Road; Lanaihale (3,370 ft/1,027 m), highest point on Lanai, to SE; Hulopoe Beach Park to S. Founded 1922 by Dole pineapple company.

Lanark (LAH-nuhrk), county (□ 1,138 sq mi/2,947 sq km; 1991 pop. 54,803), SE Ont., Canada, on Ottawa R., and on Rideau L.; ⊙ Perth; 45°00′N 76°15′W.

Lanark, village (1991 pop. 890), SE Ont., Canada, on Clyde R., and 10 mi/16 km NW of Perth. Knitting and lumber mills; dairying.

Lanark, city (1990 pop. 1,382), Carroll co., NW Ill., near Rock Creek, 8 mi/12.9 km E of Mount Carroll; 42°06′N 89°49′W. Trade and shipping center in rich agr. area (grain; livestock); mfg. of food prods. Inc. 1867.

Lancaster 1 (LANG-KA-stuhr), county (□ 846 sq mi/ 2,191 sq km; 1990 pop. 213,641), SE Nebr.; ⊙ Lincoln and of the state; 40°46′N 96°41′W. Commercial and agr. region in part urbanized; a part of the Loess-Drift Hills of SE Nebr. Drainage is NE to the Platte through Salt Creek, and SE to the Nemaha. Diversified agr., with corn, wheat, sorghum, soybeans, cattle hogs, dairying. The 7 state recreational areas are Stagecoach L. and Wagon Train in SE; Bluestem L. and Olive Creek L. in SW; Conestoga L. and Pawnee L. in W; and Branched Oak L. in NW. Formed 1859. **2** (LANG-ki-stuhr), county (□ 983 sq mi/2,546 sq km; 1990 pop. 422,822), SE Pa.; ⊙ Lancaster. Bounded S by Md. state line, W and SW by Susquehanna R. (dams form Conowingo Reservoir, L. Aldre and L. Clarke), SE by Octoraro Creek and its East Branch, NW by Conewago Creek. Rich agr. area, gently rolling landscape (corn, wheat, oats, barley, hay, alfalfa, soybeans, potatoes, apples; sheep, hogs, cattle, chickens and eggs; dairying). Mfg. at Lancaster, Lititz, Deaver, Ephrata, Leola, New Holland. Major center for tourism. First settled 1709 by Swiss and French, later by Germans, Welsh, English, and Scotch-Irish. Conestoga wagon and Kentucky rifle were early prods. Co. has several covered bridges. Muddy Run Reservoir in SW corner. Formed 1729. **3** county (□ 555 sq mi/1,437 sq km; 1990 pop. 54,516), N S.C.; ⊙ Lancaster; 34°41′N 80°42′W. Bounded W by Catawba R., N by N.C. Mfg. (mica, clay, sand, shale, gold, silver); agr. (corn, wheat, oats, hay, soybeans; turkeys, cattle; timber) Formed 1785. **4** county (□ 231 sq mi/598 sq km; 1990 pop. 10,896), E Va.; ⊙ Lancaster; 37°42′N 76°24′W. On Northern Neck peninsula; bounded W and S by Rappahannock R. estuary, SE by Chesapeake Bay (estuary enters bay at SE tip of co.); shores indented by many inlets. Agr. (esp. tomatoes, vegetables, barley, wheat, corn, soybeans; poultry, cattle); timber (pine); fish, oysters, crabs. Resort area. Formed 1652.

Lancaster 1 (LAN-KA-stuhr), city (1990 pop. 97,291), Los Angeles co., S Calif., suburb 42 mi/68 km NNE of downtown Los Angeles, in Antelope Valley, and in the Mojave Desert; 34°42′N 118°11′W. It developed as a trade center for an irrigated farming area (vegetables, fruit, nuts; cotton), and has since become an important site for electronic, aerospace, aircraft, and defense industries. Mfg. (business forms, metal stampings); printing and publishing. Local borax mining and Edwards Air Force Base to NE, in Mojave Desert, a major military installation, add to Lancaster's economy. The city is the seat of Antelope Valley Col. (2-year), Antelope Valley Indian Mus. with prehistoric artifacts. Calif. Poppy Preserve to W; Saddleback Butte State Park to E. Laid out 1894. **2** (LANG-ki-stuhr), city (1990 pop. 785), ⊙ Schuyler co., N Mo., near Chariton R., 23 mi/ 37 km N of Kirksville; 40°31′N 92°31′W. Corn, soybeans; sheep, cattle, hogs. Inc. 1856. **3** (LAN-KA-stuhr), city (1990 pop. 34,507), ⊙ Fairfield co., S central Ohio, on the Hocking R.; 39°43′N 82°35′W. In a livestock and dairying area; founded 1800 by Ebenezer Zane, inc. as a village 1831. Mfg. (glassware, shoes, heating equip., and automotive parts). The birthplace of the brothers Gen. William T. Sherman and Senator John Sherman has been preserved. In the area are many covered bridges and a Native Amer. mound in the form of a cross. The city contains a campus of Ohio Univ. **4** (LANG-ki-stuhr), city (1990 pop. 55,551), ⊙ Lancaster co., SE Pa., 33 mi/53 km ESE of Harrisburg, on the Conestoga R., in the heart of the Pa. Dutch country;

40°02′N 76°17′W. It is the commercial center for a productive agr. co. with a huge farmer's market. Agr. area (livestock, poultry; grain, potatoes, soybeans, alfalfa, apples; dairying); mfg. (electrical, concrete, and aluminum prods., security prods., automotive parts, medical equip., food prods., advertising specialties; commercial printing). Lancaster is the seat of Franklin and Marshall Col. and a theological seminary, and it is noted for its large Amish and Mennonite communities. The area was settled by Ger. Mennonites c.1709 and was a starting point for W-bound pioneers. The famous Conestoga wagon was developed here. The borough of Lancaster was laid out in 1730 and was one of the first inland cities in the country. A munitions center during the Revolution, it was briefly (1777) a meeting place of the Continental Congress and served as capital of the state for more than 10 years before 1812. Robert Fulton was born nearby. Lancaster Airport to N. Tourist center. Points of interest include Wheatland, the home of President James Buchanan to W (built in 1828; a natl. historic site since 1962), and the Fulton Opera House (1854), a historic monument; also Heritage Center Mus., North Mus. of Natural History and Science, Pa. Victorian Wine Cellars to W; Pa. Dutch Visitors Bureau to E, Pa. Farm Mus. to NE; Du. Wonderland Amish Homestead, Mennonite Information Center, to E; several covered bridges in area. Inc. as a city 1818. **5** (LANG-KA-stuhr), city (1990 pop. 22,117), Dallas co., in NE Texas, suburb 11 mi/18 km S of downtown Dallas; 32°36′N 96°46′W. Elev. 512 ft/156 m. Tenmile Creek drains S sect. It is a processing and shipping center for a fruit, vegetable, and cotton region; agr to S (dairying; cattle; peanuts, cotton, vegetables). Mfg. (chemicals, transportation equip., bricks, brass valves, fabricated metal prods., packaging). Lancaster has grown significantly as part of the expanding Dallas–Fort Worth metropolitan area. Lancaster Municipal Airport to SE. Seat of Cedar Valley Col. (2-year). Town destroyed by 1994 tornado. Settled 1846, inc. 1886.

Lancaster 1 (LAN-ki-stuhr), town (1990 pop. 3,421), ⊙ Garrard co., central Ky., 31 mi/50 km S of Lexington, in Bluegrass region; 37°37′N 84°34′W. Agr. (burley tobacco, corn, wheat, hay; horses, cattle, hogs): mfg. (wheels, apparel, machinery, crushed stone and lime, lumber, fiberglass boats). Cottage industry (hooked rugs) in vicinity. Carry Nation Birthplace; Historic Garrard County Jail. Herrington L. reservoir (Dix R.) to NW. **2** (LANG-KA-stuhr), town (1990 pop. 6,661), Worcester co., N central Mass., on Nashua R., and 15 mi/24 km NNE of Worcester, N of Wachusett Reservoir; 42°29′N 71°41′W. Luther Burbank b. here. Has fine Bulfinch church (1817). Includes South Lancaster village (1990 pop. 1,772). State prison. Settled 1643, inc. 1653. **3** town (1990 pop. 3,522), ⊙ Coos co., NW N.H., 19 mi/31 km W of Berlin; 44°28′N 71°32′W. Bounded W by Connecticut R. (Vt. state line), drained by Israel R. (flows into Connecticut R.). Mfg. (lumber, inductors, food processing, polyethylene bags; printing and publishing); agr. (vegetables, nursery crops; poultry, livestock; dairying). Part of White Mt. Natl. Forest in E; Weeks State Park in S; 2 covered bridges. Includes village of Grange, in center. Inc. 1764. **4** (LANG-ki-stuhr), town (1990 pop. 8,914), ⊙ Lancaster co., N S.C., 23 mi/4.8 km SE of Rock Hill, near the Wateree; 34°43′N 80°46′W. Mfg. (metal fabrication, apparel, textiles, fabricated metal prods., batteries, asphalt; printing and publishing); agr. (poultry, livestock; grains, soybeans). Branch campus of Univ. of S.C. here. Andrew Jackson State Park to N. Courthouse and jail date from 1823. Bordered by several mill villages. **5** (LAN-KA-stuhr), town (1990 pop. 4,192), ⊙ Grant co., extreme SW Wis., 23 mi/37 km N of Dubuque, Iowa; 42°51′N 90°42′W. In livestock and dairying area. Dairy prods.; mfg. (canned foods, beverages, veterinary remedies, feed, timber; ships, transportation equip., flexible packaging). Agr. research station. Settled before 1840, inc. 1878.

Lancaster (LANG-kuh-stuhr), village (1991 pop. 739), SE Ont., Canada, on the St. Lawrence, and 15 mi/24 km NE of Cornwall. Dairying; mixed farming.

Lancaster 1 (LANG-KA-stuhr), village (1990 pop. 299), Atchison co., NE Kansas, 10 mi/16 km W of Atchison, near Corn Belt; 39°34′N 95°17′W. **2** (LAN-KA-stuhr), village (1990 pop. 342), Kittson co., NW Minn., 8 mi/12.9 km NE of Hallock, near Man. (Canada) border, on North Branch Two Rivers; 48°51′N 96°47′W. Wheat, potatoes, sugar beets, alfalfa, sunflowers; sheep; mfg. (agr. equip.). Skull Lake Wildlife Area to NE; port of entry of U.S.-Can. border, 9 mi/14.5 km N. **3** village (□ 2 sq mi/5.2 sq km; 1990 pop. 11,940), Erie co., W N.Y.; 42°53′N 78°40′W. Its industries include lumber mills, dairy farms, and stone quarries. Inc. 1849. **4** (LANG-ki-stuhr), uninc. village, ⊙ Lancaster co., E Va., 24 mi/39 km NNE of Gloucester; Chesapeake Bay to E. Mfg. (shellfish and seafood processing); agr. (tomatoes, vegetables, grain, soybeans; cattle); timber; fish, oysters, crabs from nearby coastal towns.

Lancaster Mills (LANG-ki-stuhr), uninc. village (1990 pop. 2,373), Lancaster co., N S.C., residential suburb 3 mi/4.8 km WNW of Lancaster; near Catawba R.; 34°42′N 80°47′W.

Lancaster Sound, arm of Baffin Bay, c.200 mi/320 km long and 40 mi/60 km wide, Baffin region, N.W.T., Canada. It extends W bet. Devon and Baffin isls. and is part of the shortest water route across N Canada to the Beaufort Sea. William Baffin, the Eng. explorer, visited here in 1616.

Lance Amour, Canada: see ANSE AMOUR, L'.

Lance au Loup, Canada: see ANSE AU LOUP, L'.

Lance Creek, village, Niobrara co., on Lance Creek, E Wyo., 21 mi/34 km NNW of Lusk. In oil field.

Land Between the Lakes, recreation area, Stewart co. in NW Tenn. and Tipton co. in SW Ky., bordered E by Barkley Reservoir (Cumberland R.), W by Kentucky Reservoir (Tenn. R.); 36°45′N 82°02′W. Covers 170,000 acres/68,799 ha; managed by TVA for fishing, hunting, hiking, camping. Living history farm (The Homeplace, 1850) is here.

Land o' Lakes, town (□ 12 sq mi/31 sq km; 1990 pop. 7,892), Pasco co., W central Fla., 18 mi/29 km N of Tampa; 28°13′N 82°27′W. Industries include lumber and light mfg.

Land o' Lakes, village, Vilas co., N Wis., on Wis.-Mich. state line, 37 mi/60 km NNE of Rhinelander. Mfg. (fishing tackle, lumber); resort center in wooded lake region. Gateway Ski Area to S; Ottawa Natl. Forest beyond state boundary.

Landa, village (1990 pop. 38), Bottineau co., N N.Dak., 22 mi/35 km W of Bottineau; 48°53′N 100°54′W. J. Clark Salyer Natl. Wildlife Refuge to W. Near Souris R. (Mouse R.).

Landa de Matamoros (LAHN-dah dai mah-tah-MO-ros), town (1990 pop. 784), NE Querétaro, Mexico, 7 mi/12 km E of Jalpan de Serra on Mexico Highway 120; 21°13′N 99°20′W. Elev. 3,363 ft/1,025 m. Very steep, rugged terrain crossing the Sierra Gorda. Hot climate. Agr. (coffee, sugarcane, corn); forestry; mining (magnesium, silver, and lead on a small scale).

Landaff (LAN-daf), town (1990 pop. 350), Grafton co., NW N.H., 11 mi/18 km SW of Littleton; 44°08′N 71°52′W. Drained by Ammonoosuc R. in NW corner, by Wild Ammonoosuc R. in S. In mt. recreational area. Timber. Part of White Mt. Natl. Forest in S.

Lander (LAN-duhr), county (□ 5,519 sq mi/14,294 sq km; 1990 pop. 6,266), N central Nev.; ⊙ Battle Mountain; 39°57′N 117°01′W. Drained by Humboldt and Reese rivers. Gold, silver, lead, copper deposits; cattle and sheep ranches. Formed 1863. Parts of Toiyabe Natl Forest in S cover N-S running Shoshone,Toiyabe, and Toquima mt. ranges. Geographic center of Nev. in SE corner.

Lander, town (1990 pop. 7,023), ⊙ Fremont co., W central Wyo., on Popo Agie R., just E of Wind R. Range, and 120 mi/193 km W of Casper; 42°49′N 108°43′W. Elev. c.5,357 ft/1,633 m. Resort and trade center for Popo Agie Valley; hq. for Washakie Natl. Forest. Agr. (cattle, sheep; sugar beets); mfg. (fabrics, concrete, metal art castings, underground mining equip, lumber; log homes; printing and publishing). Oil wells, gold and coal mines in vicinity. Agr. experiment station of state univ., large Wind R. Indian Reservation to N. Fremont County Pioneer Mus., Shoshone Natl. Forest, and Sinks Canyon State Park to SW. To SE is site of 1st oil well drilled in Wyo. (1884). Settled in 1870s around military post, inc. 1890.

Landero y Coss (lahn-DE-ro ee KOS), town (1990 pop. 1,375), Veracruz, E Mexico, 15 mi/24 km NE of Xalapa Enríquez. Fruit, corn. In Totanac Indian area. Also known as San Juan.

Landfill, village (1990 pop. 683), Washington co., E Minn., residential suburb 6 mi/9.7 km E of downtown St. Paul bet. Tanners L. (NW) and Battle Creek L. (SW).

Landgrove, town (1990 pop. 134), Bennington co., S central Vt., in Green Mts., 19 mi/31 km W of Springfield; 43°15′N 72°50′W.

Landing, resort village, Morris co., N N.J., at S end of L. Hopatcong, 12 mi/19 km NW of Morristown. In suburbanizing area. Boating; state park nearby.

Landingville, borough (1990 pop. 192), Schuylkill co., E central Pa., 7 mi/11.3 km SE of Pottsville, on Schuylkill R. Agr. (dairying); mfg. (contract sewing).

Landis, town (1990 pop. 2,333), Rowan co., central N.C., suburb 4 mi/6.4 km N of Kannapolis; 35°32′N 80°36′W. Agr. area (tobacco, grain, soybeans; poultry, livestock; dairying). Mfg. (meat processing, brake linings, textiles).

Landisburg, borough (1990 pop. 178), Perry co., S central Pa., 24 mi/39 km WNW of Harrisburg, near Sherman Creek. Agr. (dairying).

Landisville, uninc. town (1990 pop. 3,309), Lancaster co., SE Pa., 7 mi/11.3 km NW of Lancaster near Chickies Creek; 40°05′N 76°24′W. Mfg. (concrete, rare earth magnets, fabricated metal prods.; millwork); agr. (dairying; livestock, poultry and eggs; grain, potatoes, soybeans). Covered bridges in area. Salunga is 1 mi/1.6 km to NW.

Landisville, village, Atlantic co., S N.J., 12 mi/19 km WNW of Mays Landing. Clothing; poultry; vegetables.

Lando, uninc. town, Chester co., N S.C., 10 mi/16 km S of Rock Hill. Mfg. (blankets); agr. (livestock; dairying; grain, sorghum).

Landon, uninc. village (1990 pop. 1,117), Harrison co., SE Miss., suburb 5 mi/8 km N of Gulfport, on Bernard Bayou, at intersection of Interstate Highway 10 and U.S. Highway 49; 30°30′N 89°07′W.

Landover, town (1990 pop. 2,074), Prince Georges co., central Md., suburb 7 mi/11.3 km NE of Washington, D.C. Inc. after 1940, it has outstripped the adjacent Landover Hills in pop. and is a major food distribution point. Capital Center Sports Arena built in 1973 for Washington Bullets basketball and Caps hockey teams; Jack Kent Cooke Stadium opened in 1997 for the Washington Redskins football team.

Landover Hills, Md.: see LANDOVER.

Landrail Point, village, S Bahamas, on NW Crooked Isl., 8 mi/12.9 km NW of Colonel Hill; 22°50′N 74°20′W.

Landrienne (lah-dree-EN), village (1991 pop. 1,044), W Que., Canada, 8 mi/13 km E of Amos; 48°33′N 77°57′W. Gold mining.

Landrum (LAND-ruhm), town (1990 pop. 2,347), Spartanburg co., NW S.C., 22 mi/35 km NW of Spartanburg, at N.C. state line; 35°10′N 82°11′W. Mfg. (textile, fabricated metal prods., electronics. paper prods.; machining); agr. (dairying; livestock; grain, soybeans, sorghum, peaches, apples).

Lands Lokk, island, NE Franklin dist., N.W.T., Canada, in the Arctic Ocean, at N end of Nansen Sound, off NW Ellesmere Isl.; 20 mi. long, 8 mi. wide; 81°45′N 91°45′W.

Landusky (lan-DUHS-kee), village, Phillips co., N central Mont., in Lewis and Clark Natl. Forest, 48 mi/77 km SW of Malta. Gold; livestock. Little Rocky Mts. and Fort Belknap Indian Reservation to N.

Lane 1 county (□ 717 sq mi/1,857 sq km; 1990 pop. 2,375), W central Kansas; ⊙ Dighton; 38°28′N 100°28′W. Located in Smokey Hill region, rolling plain, with low hills in E and NE. Drained by Walnut Creek. Wheat, sorghum; cattle. Formed 1886. **2** county (□ 4,721 sq mi/12,227 sq km; 1990 pop. 282,912), W Oregon, ⊙ Eugene; 43°57′N 122°52′W. Mt. area in Coast and Cascade ranges, bounded on W by Pacific Ocean, crossed by

Willamette and Siuslaw rivers. Agr. (wheat, barley, oats, corn, brans, strawberries, blackberries, blueberries, grapes, apples, cherries, pears, plums, peaches; hogs, sheep, cattle); wineries, nurseries. Salmon fishing. Part of Willamette Natl. Forest in E; part of Umpqua Natl. Forest in SE; part of Siuslaw Natl. Forest in W; part of Oregon Dunes Natl. Recreation Area in extreme SW. Fern Ridge Reservoir in center. Co. has more than 12 state parks, notably Elijah Bristow and Armitage in center, Morton in NE, and Devils Elbow on coast. Formed 1851.

Lane 1 village (1990 pop. 247), Franklin co., E Kansas, on Pottawatomie Creek, and 16 mi/26 km SE of Ottawa; 38°26′N 95°04′W. Livestock; grain. **2** village (1990 pop. 523), Williamsburg co., E central S.C., 10 mi/16 km S of Kingstree; 33°31′N 79°52′W. Industry includes timber, livestock, grain, soybeans, cotton. **3** village (1990 pop. 71), Jerauld co., SE central S.Dak., 8 mi/12.9 km E of Wessington Springs, near Firesteel Creek; 44°04′N 98°25′W.

Lane Island, Knox co., S Maine, in Carvers Harbor; bridged to Vinalhaven isl.; ½ mi/⅕ km long.

Lanesboro 1 town (1990 pop. 182), Carroll co., W central Iowa, near Raccoon R., 12 mi/19 km NE of Carroll; 42°10′N 94°41′W. **2** or **Lanesborough**, agr. town (1990 pop. 3,032), Berkshire co., NW Mass., 5 mi/8 km N of Pittsfield, near Pontoosuc L. Resort; 42°32′N 73°14′W. Settled c.1753; inc. 1765. Includes state forest and villages of Berkshire and Balance Rock. **3** town (1990 pop. 858), Fillmore co., SE Minn., 32 mi/51 km SE of Rochester, on Duschee Creek, S of its confluence with Root R.; 43°43′N 91°58′W. Grain, soybeans; livestock, poultry; dairying; mfg. (corrugated dunnage, gopher traps). Richard J. Dorer Memorial Hardwood State Forest to N and E.

Lanesboro, borough (1990 pop. 659), Susquehanna co., NE Pa., 1 mi/1.6 km NE of Susquehanna Depot, near N.Y. state line. Agr. (dairying); mfg. (electronic coils).

Lanesville, town (1990 pop. 512), Harrison co., S Ind., 8 mi/12.9 km E of Corydon; 38°14′N 85°59′W. In agr. area. Laid out 1817.

Lanesville, resort village (1990 pop. 350), Greene co., SE N.Y., in the Catskills, 20 mi/32 km NW of Kingston; 42°16′N 74°16′W.

Lanesville, Mass.: see GLOUCESTER.

Lanett, city (1990 pop. 8,985), Chambers co., E Ala., on Chattahoochee R., 13 mi/21 km E of Lafayette, and 20 mi/32 km NE of Opelika. Adjoins West Point, Ga. Mfg. and processing of cotton fabrics. Fort Tyler, site of one of the last Civil War battles E of the Mississippi R. (April 1865), nearby. Inc. 1893.

Lanexa, uninc. village, New Kent co., E Va., 14 mi/23 km NW of Williamsburg, near Chickahominy R.; 37°25′N 76°54′W. Mfg. (catfish processing, apparel); agr. (grain, soybeans; poultry; cattle); catfish.

Lanezi Lake, E B.C., Canada, in Cariboo Mts., 65 mi/105 km E of Quesnel, S of Issac L.; 12 mi/19 km long, 1 mi/2 km wide. Drained W by Cariboo R. through Sandy L. (5 mi/8 km long) into Quesnel R.

Lang, village (1991 pop. 206), S Sask., Canada, 40 mi/64 km SSE of Regina; 49°55′N 104°22′W. Wheat.

Langdon 1 town (1990 pop. 580), Sullivan co., SW N.H., 13 mi/21 km S of Claremont, near Vt. state line; 43°10′N 72°22′W. Drained by Cold R. Agr. (nursery crops, hay; cattle, poultry). Two covered bridges in S. **2** town (1990 pop. 2,241), ⊙ Cavalier co., NE N.Dak., 85 mi/137 km NW of Grand Forks; 48°45′N 98°22′W. Durum wheat, barley, grain-distribution center, dairy prods., livestock; mfg. (farm equip., concrete, lawn and garden sprayers). Seat of state agr. experiment station. Inc. 1888.

Langdon, village (1990 pop. 62), Reno co., S central Kansas, 26 mi/42 km SW of Hutchinson; 37°51′N 98°19′W. In wheat region.

Langeloth (LAN-guh-lawth), uninc. town (1990 pop. 1,112), Smith township, Washington co., SW Pa., 16 mi/26 km NW of Washington; 40°21′N 80°24′W. Agr. (corn, hay; livestock, dairying). Mfg. (sporting goods); coal. Hillman State Park to N; Cross Creek Co. Park to S.

Langenburg (LANG-uhn-buhrg), town (1991 pop. 1,156), SE Sask., Canada, 40 mi/64 km SE of Yorkton, near Man. (Canada) border; 50°50′N 101°42′W. Mixed farming.

Langevin (lahzh-VE) or **Saint Justine** (seht zhuhs-TEEN), village, SE Que., Canada, 50 mi/80 km SE of Quebec. Dairying; pigs.

Langford, village, SW B.C., Canada, on SE Vancouver Isl., 6 mi/10 km W of Victoria; 48°27′N 123°30′W. Logging; mixed farming, fruit growing, vegetables, dairying. Formerly Langford Station.

Langford, village (1990 pop. 298), Marshall co., NE S.Dak., 14 mi/23 km S of Britton; 45°36′N 97°49′W. Fort Sisseton State Park to E.

Langham (LANG-uhm), town (1991 pop. 1,185), central Sask., Canada, near North Saskatchewan R., 20 mi/32 km NW of Saskatoon; 52°22′N 106°58′W. Grain elevators; dairying; ranching.

Langhorne, borough (1990 pop. 1,361), Bucks co., SE Pa., 19 mi/31 km NE of Philadelphia, and 9 mi/14.5 km WSW of Trenton, N.J., near Neshaminu Creek. Agr. to N (livestock; dairying); mfg. (machinery, medical instruments, sand blasting equip., valves, steel processing, metal fabrication, power transmission gears, plastic prods., printing, folding cartons). Buehl Field airport to NE. Sesame Place, theme park based upon *Sesame Street* television show, to E. Laid out 1783, inc. 1874.

Langhorne Manor, borough (1990 pop. 807), Bucks co., SE Pa., residential suburb, 18 mi/29 km NE of downtown Philadelphia and 1 mi/1.6 km S of Langhorne.

Langlade (LANG-laid), county (□ 887 mi/1,427 km; 1990 pop. 19,505), NE Wis.; ⊙ Antigo; 45°15′N 89°04′W. Lumbering is chief industry; agr. (barley, oats, wheat, corn, beans, potatoes; poultry). Drained by Wolf and Eau Claire rivers. Numerous lakes, especially N and far E; part of Nicolet Natl. Forest in extreme E; Langlade Fish Hatchery in E. Formed 1879.

Langlade, village, W central Que., Canada, 60 mi/97 km ESE of Senneterre. Garnet mining.

Langley, city (1991 pop. 19,765), SW B.C., Canada, in lower Fraser R. valley, 20 mi/32 km SE of Vancouver; 49°06′N 122°39′W. In dairying, fruit- and hops-growing region. Formerly called Langley Prairie.

Langley 1 uninc. town, Fairfax co., NE Va., residential suburb 7 mi/11.3 km NW of Washington, D.C., on Potomac R.; 38°56′N 77°09′W. Federal Highway Administration Research Station and Central Intelligence Agency (CIA) hq. are here. Little Falls Dam to E. **2** town (1990 pop. 845), Island co., NW Wash., on Whidbey Isl. on Saratoga Passage, and 10 mi/16 km WNW of Everett; 48°02′N 122°25′W. Resort; trade center for agr. area (livestock; berries; dairy prods.).

Langley 1 uninc. village (1990 pop. 500), Floyd co., E Ky., 9 mi/14.5 km S of Prestonburg, on Right Fork R. Bituminous coal, natural gas. Mfg. (natural gas processing). **2** village (1990 pop. 526), Mayes co., NE Okla., 13 mi/21 km SSE of Vinita; 36°27′N 95°02′W. Mfg. (signs). Pensacola Dam (Neosho R.) is E; forms L. of the Cherokees. Inc. 1939. **3** uninc. village, Aiken co., SW S.C., 7 mi/11.3 km WSW of Aiken. Mfg. (sealants); kaolin clay processing.

Langley Air Force Base, U.S. military installation, Hampton city, SE Va., 4 mi/6.4 km N of downtown Hampton; on Back R. estuary, arm of Chesapeake Bay. Covers 3,195 acres/1,293 ha. Named for aviation pioneer Samuel P. Langley. Oldest continuously active air force base in U.S.; hq. of Tactical Air Command; air-defense missile units. NASA Langley Research Center. Est.1916.

Langley, Mount (14,027 ft/4,275 m), on Inyo/Tulare co. line, E Calif., in the Sierra Nevada, c.5 mi/8 km SSE of Mt. Whitney and on E boundary of Sequoia Natl. Park. Formerly called Mt. Corcoran.

Langley Park, uninc. town (1990 pop. 17,474), Prince Georges co., W central Md., a suburb of Washington, D.C.; 38°59′N 76°59′W. The town has grown with the development of the greater Washington, D.C. metropolitan area. Light industries and businesses.

Langston, town (1990 pop. 1,471), Logan co., central Okla., 10 mi/16 km ENE of Guthrie, near Cimarron R. Seat of Langston Univ.

Langton Bay, Canada: see FRANKLIN BAY.

Langtry (LANG-tree), uninc. village (1990 pop. 30), Val Verde co., SW Texas, on the Rio Grande (Mex. border), near mouth of the Pecos and c.50 mi/80 km NW of Del Rio. Elev. 1,315 ft/401 m. Nearby, at old town of Langtry, Judge Roy Bean, "the law west of the Pecos," meted out justice in his frontier saloon. Amistad Reservoir and Amistad Natl. Recreation Area downstream (SE); Seminole Canyon State Park to E.

L'Anguille River (lan-GWEEL), c.110 mi/177 km long, E Ark.; rises in Craighead co., S of Jonesboro; flows S and SE, past Forrest City and Marianna, to St. Francis R. in Lee co.

Lanham (LA-nuhm), village (1990 pop. 16,792), Prince Georges co., central Md., ENE of Washington, D.C.; 38°58′N 76°50′W. Next to Washington Bible Col. is the private estate of Azalea Acres, where the public can view the flowers in season. Pop. figure includes Seabrook.

Lanier (luh-NIR), county (□ 200 sq mi/518 sq km; 1990 pop. 5,531), S Ga.; ⊙ Lakeland; 31°02′N 83°04′W. Coastal plain area intersected by Alapaha R. Agr. (corn, tobacco, peanuts, soybeans, cotton, fruit; cattle, hogs); forestry prods. Formed 1919.

Lanier (lah-nee-ER), swamps, Isla de la Juventud, off S coast of Cuba, extending c.25 mi/40 km E-W across central part of the isl.; 21°34′N 82°45′W. Formerly called Liguanea.

Lanier, Lake, in Dawson, Fulton, Gwinnett, and Hall cos., Ga., NE of Atlanta. Built in the 1950s for flood control, electrical power generation, and to assist downriver shipping, the lake has become the leading recreational facility in the state and the source of the fresh water supply for most residents of metropolitan Atlanta.

Lanigan, town (1991 pop. 1,397), S central Sask., Canada, 70 mi/113 km ESE of Saskatoon; 51°51′N 105°02′W. Grain elevators, lumbering.

Lanikai (LAH-nee-KEI), village, E Oahu, Honolulu co., Hawaii, on NE coast, 14 mi/23 km N of Honolulu, bet. Alala Point and Wailea. Mokulua Isls. offshore are state seabird sanctuaries.

Lankershim, Calif.: see NORTH HOLLYWOOD.

Lankin, village (1990 pop. 152), Walsh co., NE N.Dak., 25 mi/40 km WSW of Grafton, near N branch of Forest R.; 48°18′N 97°55′W.

Lannon, town (1990 pop. 924), Waukesha co., SE Wis., suburb 14 mi/23 km NW of Milwaukee; 43°08′N 88°09′W. In dairy and farm area. Mfg. (fabricated metal prods., packaging).

L'Annonciation (lah-no-see-ah-see-O), village (1991 pop. 2,163), SW Que., Canada, in the Laurentians, 40 mi/64 km NW of Ste. Agathe des Monts; 46°24′N 74°52′W. Dairying.

Lanoraie (lah-no-RAI), village (1991 pop. 1,793), S Que., Canada, on the St. Lawrence R., 35 mi/56 km NNE of Montreal; 45°58′N 73°13′W. Dairying; resort.

Lansdale, borough (1990 pop. 16,362), Montgomery co., SE Pa., suburb 20 mi/32 km NNW of Philadelphia; 40°14′N 75°16′W. It is a farm processing and industrial center. Mfg. (food prods.; bldg. materials, apparel, plumbing equip., commercial printing, machinery). Agr. (grain, apples; livestock; dairying). Evansburg State Park to W. The Jenkins House here dates from 1702. Inc. 1872.

Lansdowne, village, SE Ont., Canada, 27 mi/43 km ENE of Kingston; 60°16′N 134°17′W. Dairying, mixed farming.

Lansdowne, uninc. town (1990 pop. 15,509), Baltimore co., NE Md., suburb of Baltimore; 39°14′N 76°39′W. Settled by an Irishman named McGrath who named the area after the Marquis of Lansdowne, the postmaster of England in 1782. Iron was mined here in the 18th cent. and the Lansdowne Christian Church has a small Civil War mus.

Lansdowne, borough (1990 pop. 11,712), Delaware co., SE Pa., a residential suburb 6 mi/9.7 km WSW of Philadelphia, on Darby Creek; 39°56′N 75°16′W. Mfg. (paper prods., printing). Inc. 1893.

L'Anse (LANZ), town (1990 pop. 2,151), ⊙ Baraga co.,

NW Upper Peninsula, Mich., 27 mi/43 km SSE of Houghton, at head of Keweenaw Bay; 46°45′N 88°27′W. In farm and lumber area. Fisheries; mfg. (acoustical ceiling panels, lumber). Keweenaw Bay Indian Reservation is E; L'Anse Indian Reservation to NE and NW (both sides of bay); Ottawa Natl. Forest to W; 6-story-high copper statue on the lake bluff of Father Frederick Baraga, the Snowshoe Priest, honoring his good works in area. Baraga State Park to W. Inc. 1873.

Lanse (LANS), uninc. village, Cooper township, Clearfield co., central Pa., 6 mi/9.7 km NE of Philipsburg; 40°58′N 78°07′W. Surface bituminous coal.

L'Anse Amour, Canada: see ANSE AMOUR, L'.

L'Anse aux Epines (LANS uh-PEEN) or **Lance aux Epines** (lans-o-PEEN), peninsula, Grenada, West Indies; 11°59′N 61°45′W. Beach hotel and resort area on S coast.

L'Anse aux Meadows National Historic Park, N N.F., Canada, at northernmost tip of isl., 12 mi/19 km N of St. Anthony. Covers 20,000 acres/8,094 ha. Site of Viking settlement on Sacred Bay, Strait of Belle Isle; est. c. A.D. 1000. Declared federal historic park, 1970; World Heritage Area, 1988. Reconstructed stone and sod-roofed village. Wooden huts protect excavations.

Lansford, village (1990 pop. 249), Bottineau co., N N.Dak., 28 mi/45 km N of Minot; 48°37′N 101°22′W. Dairy prods.; wheat; livestock. RR junction.

Lansford (LANS-fuhrd), borough (1990 pop. 4,583), Carbon co., E Pa., 8 mi/12.9 km WSW of Jim Thorpe. Agr. (hay, potatoes, dairying); mfg. (apparel). Founded 1846, inc. 1877.

Lansing, city (1990 pop. 127,321), ⊙ Mich. and Ingham, Clinton, and Eaton cos., S Mich., 75 mi/121 km NW of Detroit, on the Grand R. at its confluence with the Red Cedar R.; 42°42′N 84°32′W. Lansing is a trade and processing center for its surrounding agr. area. Mfg. (paper prods., machinery, medical equip., fabricated metal and plastic prods., bldg. materials, printing). RR junction. The city grew after it was made the state capital (1847), and industrial development came with the RRs (1870s) and the automobile industry (1897). The state capitol houses a mus., Fenner Arboretum; the state office bldg. contains the state lib. and the state historical office. Lansing Community Col. and the Mich. School for the Blind are here. Amer. author Ray Baker was b. here. The adjacent suburb of East Lansing is the seat of Mich. State Univ. Sleepy Hollow State Park to NE; Capital City Airport to N. Inc. 1859.

Lansing 1 town (1990 pop. 1,007), Allamakee co., extreme NE Iowa, at foot of bluffs on Mississippi R. (bridged here), 14 mi/23 km ENE of Waukon; 43°21′N 91°13′W. Limestone quarries, lead and zinc deposits nearby. Large group of Indian effigy mounds and a state fish hatchery are in vicinity. Laid out 1851, inc. 1867. **2** town (1990 pop. 7,120), Leavenworth co., NE Kansas, suburb 4 mi/6.4 km S of Leavenworth and 16 mi/26 km NW of Kansas City, near Missouri R.; 39°15′N 94°53′W. In general agr. region. Kansas State Prison is here. St. Mary Col. in N.

Lansing 1 village (1990 pop. 28,086), Cook co., NE Ill., S suburb of Chicago, near the Ind. state line; 41°34′N 87°32′W. Among the industries are meat packing, food processing, and mfg. of metal prods. Inc. 1893. **2** village, Mower co., SE Minn., on Cedar R., 6 mi/9.7 km N of Austin; 43°44′N 92°58′W. Corn, soybeans; livestock; dairying; mfg. (feeds). **3** village (1990 pop. 171), Ashe co., NW N.C., 24 mi/39 km NNE of Boone, on North Fork of New R.; 36°30′N 81°30′W. Mfg. (machinery). **4** village, Belmont co., E Ohio, 5 mi/8 km NNW of Bellaire, and on small Wheeling Creek, in coal-mining area, near W.Va. state line. Mfg.

Lansing, Lake, Mich.: see HASLETT.

Lantana (lan-TAN-nuh), town (□ 2 sq mi/5.2 sq km; 1990 pop. 8,392), Palm Beach co., SE Fla., 9 mi/14.5 km S of West Palm Beach, on L. Worth lagoon; 26°34′N 80°03′W. Large Finn.-Amer. community. Hq. of *The National Enquirer.*

Laona (lai-O-nuh), village, Forest co., NE Wis., 36 mi/58 km ESE of Rhinelander, in Nicolet Natl. Forest, in lake region. Lumbering, logging; tourism; fishing, hatchery. Logging mus.; Potawatomi Indian Reservation to SE.

Laotto, village (1990 pop. 361), Noble co., NE Ind., 15 mi/24 km N of Ft. Wayne. Mfg. (metal prods.). Corn, wheat; cattle. Laid out 1871.

Lapaz or **La Paz**, town (1990 pop. 562), Marshall co., N Ind., 8 mi/12.9 km N of Plymouth. In agr. area.

Lapeer (luh-PIR), county (□ 663 sq mi/1,717 sq km; 1990 pop. 74,768), E Mich.; 43°05′N 83°13′W; ⊙ Lapeer. Drained by Flint (Holloway Reservoir on W boundary) and Belle rivers and by short Mill Creek. Agr. (cattle, hogs, sheep, poultry; dairying; apples, corn, wheat, oats, soybeans, barley, potatoes, carrots, sugar beets, beans, celery, onions). Mfg. at Lapeer (motor vehicle parts, fabricated metal prods., machining, plumbing equip., plastic prods.). Numerous small lakes, especially in W. Organized 1833.

Lapeer (luh-PIR), city (1990 pop. 7,759), ⊙ Lapeer co., E Mich., 20 mi/32 km E of Flint, on South Branch of Flint R.; 43°02′N 83°19′W. In dairying and grain-growing area; mfg. (metal prods., transportation equip., plastics prods., furniture). Has state home and school for mentally ill. Airport to E. Metamora-Hadley State Recreation Area to S. Settled 1831, inc. as city 1869.

Lapeer Heights (luh-PIR), village, Genesee co., SE central Mich., suburb of Flint, 3 mi/4.8 km E; 43°00′N 83°35′W. Now part of city of Burton.

Lapel, town (1990 pop. 1,742), Madison co., E central Ind., 8 mi/12.9 km WSW of Anderson; 40°04′N 85°51′W. In livestock and grain area; glass prods. Laid out 1876.

Laporte 1 village, Larimer co., N Colo., E of Front Range, 4 mi/6.4 km NW of Fort Collins, on Cache La Poudre R. Elev. 5,061 ft/1,543 m. Supply point.; mfg. (cement). Lory State Park and Horestooth Reservoir to SW. **2** village (1990 pop. 101), Hubbard co., N central Minn., 19 mi/31 km SSE of Bemidji; 47°12′N 94°45′W. Mfg. (stained glass). Leech L. reservoir and Leech L. Indian Reservation to E, Paul Bunyan State Forest to SW; several small natural lakes in area, including Garfield L. to NE.

Laporte (LA-port), borough (1990 pop. 328), ⊙ Sullivan co., NE Pa., 32 mi/51 km ENE of Williamsport, on L. Mokoma reservoir. Agr. (hay, dairying); timber. Worlds End State Park to NW; Wyoming State Forest to W.

Laprairie (lah-PRAI-ree), county (□ 170 sq mi/440 sq km), S Que., Canada, on the St. Lawrence R., just S of Montreal; ⊙ Laprairie; 45°20′N 73°35′W.

Laprairie, town, ⊙ Laprairie co., S Que., Canada, on the St. Lawrence R., near E end of the Lachine Rapids, opposite Montreal; 45°25′N 73°29′W. Food processing, mfg. (metalworking machinery, electrical components, baked goods). Suburb of Montreal. Settled 1673, it was site of fort built by Frontenac; attacked (1691) by New Englanders under Peter Schuyler. The 1st RR in Canada was built (1836) bet. here and St. Jean.

Lapwai, town (1990 pop. 932), Nez Perce co., W Idaho, 10 mi/16 km E of Lewiston, in W part of Nez Perce Indian Reservation; 46°24′N 116°48′W. Trade center; logging; cattle; alfalfa, wheat, barley; potatoes, vegetables; mfg. (agr. lime, machinery, logs) and agency hq. for Coeur d'Alene and Nez Perce Indian reservations in Idaho, and for Kalispel Indian Reservation in Wash. Spalding Mission (1836) to N, now Spalding Area Unit of Nez Perce Natl. Historical Park.

Laramie (LA-ruh-mee), county (□ 2,687 sq mi/6,959 sq km; 1990 pop. 73,142), SE Wyo.; ⊙ Cheyenne; 41°19′N 104°41′W. Agr. area bordering on Colo. (S) and Nebr. (E); watered by Chugwater, Horse, North Bear, Little Bear, and Lodgepole creeks. Agr. (wheat, sugar beets, hay, alfalfa, corn, beans, oats; cattle, sheep); dairying; timber. Foothills of Laramie Mts. in W; Curt Gowdy State Park in SW. Formed 1867.

Laramie (LA-ruh-mee), city (1990 pop. 26,687), ⊙ Albany co., SE Wyo., on the Laramie R., 40 mi/64 km WNW of Cheyenne, 20 mi/32 km N of Colo. state line; 41°18′N 105°34′W. Elev. 7,165 ft/2,184 m. It is a commercial, RR, and industrial center for a livestock and timber region. Laramie has RR yards, sawmills, a cement factory, and meat storage facilities. Mfg. also includes beverages; cabinetry; printing and publishing; and computer software. Tourism is an important economic activity; the city is surrounded by mt. ranges and many nearby ski, hunting, and fishing areas. The city is the seat of the Univ. of Wyoming. Fairgrounds to S; airport to W. Laramie was settled in 1868 with the arrival of the RR and grew with the development of the surrounding ranch country and local mining enterprises. Historic Territorial Prison at Wyo. Territorial State Park, in W part of city. It is hq. for the Medicine Bow Natl. Forest. Nearby is the site of Fort Sanders, est. in 1866 to protect the Overland Trail and workers on the Union Pacific RR. Laramie Mts. to E; part of Medicine Bow Natl. Forest to E, includes Vedauwoo Recreation Area to SE, rock formations; Curt Gowdy State Park also to SE. Hutton Lake Natl. Wildlife Refuge to SW. Inc. 1874.

Laramie Basin, Wyo.: see LARAMIE PLAINS.

Laramie, Fort, Wyo.: see FORT LARAMIE.

Laramie Mountains, range of the Rocky Mts., N extension of Front Range in Colo., c.130 mi/209 km long and c.20 mi/32 km wide; mainly in SE Wyo., from N of Fort Collins, Colo., to Casper and North Platte R. (N); Laramie Plains are to W. Highest point is Laramie Peak (10,274 ft/3,132 m), on boundary bet. Converse co. and Albany co., Wyo. N part of range in Medicine Bow Natl. Forest.

Laramie Peak (LA-ruh-mee) (10,272 ft/3,131 m), highest point in Laramie Mts., Albany and Converse cos., SE Wyo., 65 mi/105 km N of Laramie, in Medicine Bow Natl. Forest.

Laramie Plains (LA-ruh-mee) or **Laramie Basin** (7,000 ft/2,134 m–8,000 ft/2,438 m), Albany and Carbon cos., SE Wyo.; high basin drained by Medicine Bow and Laramie rivers; bounded E and NE by Laramie Mts., W by Medicine Bow Mts.; cattle-grazing area. City of Laramie is on E edge of plains.

Laramie River, 216 mi/348 km long, in N Colo. and SE Wyo.; rises in Front Range, W Larimer co, N Colo., near Continental Divide; flows N and NE, past Laramie, Wyo., through the Laramie Plains and Wheatland Reservoir, through Laramie Mts. and Grayrocks Reservoir, to North Platte R. opposite Fort Laramie. Supplies water to Cache la Poudre R. in N Colo. through Laramie-Poudre, or Greeley-Poudre, Tunnel (c.2 mi/3.2 km long; finished 1911), unit in irrigation project.

Larch River, 270 mi/435 km long, N Que., Canada; issues from Lower Seal Lakes, just N of Clearwater L.; flows NE to confluence with Kaniapiskau R., 50 mi/80 km SW of Fort Chimo, here forming Koksoak R., which flows NE to Ungava Bay. Numerous rapids.

Larchmont, upper-income suburban residential village (□ 1 sq mi/2.6 sq km; 1990 pop. 6,181), part of town of Mamaroneck, Westchester co., SE N.Y., on harbor on L.I. Sound, bet. New Rochelle (SW) and Mamaroneck; 40°55′N 73°45′W. A few small light industries. Yachting center (annual regattas). Joyce Kilmer lived here. Developed c.1845, inc. 1891.

Larchwood, town (1990 pop. 739), Lyon co., extreme NW Iowa, near Minn. state line, 13 mi/21 km W of Rock Rapids; 43°27′N 96°26′W. State park and site of large Indian village are nearby.

Larder Lake, town (1991 pop. 1,030), E Ont., Canada, on Larder L., 45 mi/72 km N of Haileybury; 48°07′N 79°41′W. Gold mining. Inc. 1938.

L'Ardoise (lahrd-WAHZ), fishing village, E N.S., Canada, on S coast of Cape Breton Isl. 30 mi/48 km E of Port Hawkesbury. In mid-18th cent. it was important center of Acadian fishing and slate quarrying region, with active fur trade.

Laredo 1 (luh-RAI-do), city (1990 pop. 205), Grundy co., N Mo., 10 mi/16 km ESE of Trenton; 40°01′N 93°27′W. Corn, wheat; cattle. **2** city (1990 pop. 122,899), ⊙ Webb co., S Texas, 130 mi/209 km WSW of Corpus Christi, on the Rio Grande; 27°31′N 99°29′W. It is a port of entry on the U.S.-Mexico border, with a thriving export-import trade and a tourist industry. During the 1980s and early 1990s, Laredo became one of the fastest growing U.S. cities. It is a wholesale and retail center for a large area on both sides of the Rio Grande. Important to its economy are cattle ranching, irrigated farming (vegetables; cotton; sorghum), oil production, and mining and smelting. A wide variety of prods. are manufactured, such as clothing, military supplies, candles, fabricated steel prods., and leather goods. Laredo has close economic ties with its large sister city in Mex., Nuevo Laredo ("New Laredo," 1990 pop. 350,000; founded 1775), with which it is linked by 2 internatl. bridges. Laredo, a blend of Span., Mex., and Amer. frontier influences, grew as a post on the road to San Antonio and other Texas cities. After the Texas Revolution its ownership remained in doubt until the S boundary of Texas was established by the Mex.-Amer. War; during that period the city was the capital of the "Republic of the Rio Grande" (the capitol bldg., erected in 1755, still stands). Laredo's growth was aided by the arrival of the RR (1880s), the development of irrigated farming, the discovery of oil and natural gas, and the opening (1936) of a highway to Mexico city. Laredo Internatl. Airport to E. The former army post Fort McIntosh was founded in 1849 and intermittently rebuilt and used until 1946. Texas A and M Internatl. Univ. and Laredo Jr. Col. are on grounds of fort. An extension center of the Texas Arts and Industries Univ. is also there. Casa Blanca L. and L. Casa Blanca State Park to E. Founded 1755, inc. 1852.

Laredo (luh-RAI-do), village, Hill co., N Mont., near Big Sandy Creek, 12 mi/19 km SW of Havre, at N edge of Rocky Boy's Indian Reservation. Grain, livestock region. Fort Assiniboine to NE, Beaver Creek Park and Reservoir to E.

Lares (LAH-res), town (1990 pop. 29,015), W P.R., W of Guajataca R., 15 mi/24 km SW of Arecibo. Elev. 1,125 ft/343 m. Agr. (coffee, oranges, plantains, bananas); varied light mfg. Copper deposits in area.

Largo, city (□ 14 sq mi/36 sq km; 1990 pop. 65,674), Pinellas co., W central Fla., on the Pinellas peninsula and the Gulf coast, 15 mi/24 km W of Tampa; 27°54′N 82°46′W. It is a packing, canning, and shipping center in a citrus fruit–growing and fishing area. Its beaches and many recreational facilities make it a popular resort spot. Settled 1853, inc. 1905.

Largo, Cayo (LAHR-go, KEI-yo), narrow islet, largest key at E part of Los Canarreos Archipelago, within Isla de la Juventud Special Municipality, off S coast of Cuba, on Jardines Bank, 65 mi/105 km WSW of Cienfuegos; 21°41′N 81°30′W. Islet is 15 mi/24 km long NE-SW; its 6 hotels and 13,000-ft/3,962-m airplane runway cater to tourists. Also has 3 small fishing villages.

Larimer, county (□ 2,633 sq mi/6,819 sq km; 1990 pop. 186,136), N Colo.; ⊙ Fort Collins; 40°38′N 105°27′W. Irrigated agr. area, bordering on Wyo. (N); drained by Cache la Poudre and Laramie rivers. Continental Divide forms co. boundary in SW. Limestone, timber; cattle, sheep; fruit, vegetables, wheat, hay, beans, barley, corn, sugar beets. Mfg. at Fort Collins and Loveland. Feature of irrigation system is Laramie-Poudre (or Greeley-Poudre) Tunnel, connecting Laramie and Cache la Poudre rivers; used to irrigate 125,000 acres/50,588 ha in Larimer and Weld cos. Includes part of Rocky Mt. Natl. Park in SW and of Front Range in W; part of Roosevelt Natl. Forest in W ½ of co.; Picnic Rock, Lory, and Boyd Lake state parks in E; small part of Colorado State Forest on W boundary. Formed 1861.

Larimer (LER-i-muhr), uninc. town (1990 pop. 800), North Huntingdon township, Westmoreland co., SW Pa., residential suburb 15 mi/24 km SE of Pittsburgh; 40°20′N 79°43′W.

Larimore, town (1990 pop. 1,464), Grand Forks co., E N.Dak., 28 mi/45 km W of Grand Forks; 47°54′N 97°37′W. Dairy; livestock; grain, potatoes. RR junction on Turtle R. Turtle R. State Park to NE. Inc. 1883.

Larkspur, city (1990 pop. 11,070), Marin co., W Calif., prestigious residential suburb 12 mi/19 km NNW of San Francisco, 2 mi/3.2 km S of San Rafael, and 2 mi/3.2 km W of San Francisco Bay, near Mt. Tamalpais; 37°57′N 122°32′W. The region's scenic beauty and excellent beaches attract many visitors. Nearby Larkspur Canyon has a redwood grove. Sharpe General Depot to NE; Mt. Tamalpais State Park and Muir Woods Natl. Monument to W. Inc. 1908.

Larkspur, village (1990 pop. 232), Douglas co., central Colo., 33 mi/53 km S of Denver, 27 mi/43 km N of Colorado Springs, on Plum Creek, at E edge of Front Range; 39°10′N 104°54′W. Elev. 6,680 ft/2,036 m. Cattle; fruit, nuts, wheat; timber; mfg. of wood prods. Pike Natl. Forest to W.

Larksville, borough (1990 pop. 4,700), Luzerne co., NE central Pa., residential suburb 2 mi/3.2 km WNW of Wilkes-Barre, on Susquehanna R. Light mfg. Larksville Mt. to NW. Inc. 1909.

Larned (LAHR-ned), town (1990 pop. 4,490), ⊙ Pawnee co., SW central Kansas, on Arkansas R., at mouth of Pawnee R., 22 mi/35 km SW of Great Bend; 38°10′N 99°05′W. RR junction. Trade center for agr. area (wheat, alfalfa, sugar beets); dairying. Mfg. (meat packing). Fort Larned Natl. Historical Site 3 mi/4.8 km to W. Laid out 1873, inc. 1886.

Larose (luh-ROZ), uninc. town (1990 pop. 5,772), Lafourche parish, SE La., 30 mi/48 km SW of New Orleans, on Bayou Lafourche, at intersection of Intracoastal Waterway; 29°34′N 90°22′W. Mfg. (boats, oil-field equip., concrete). Pointe au Chien State Wildlife Area to SW.

Larrabee, town (1990 pop. 175), Cherokee co., NW Iowa, 8 mi/12.9 km N of Cherokee; 42°51′N 95°32′W.

Larrainzar (lah-rah-een-SAHR), town (1990 pop. 1,636), Chiapas, S Mexico, in Sierra de Hueytepec, 12 mi/19 km NW of San Cristóbal de las Casas; 16°53′N 92°44′W. Wheat, fruit. A Tzotzic Mayan community. Also known as San Andrés Larrainzar.

Larsen Bay, S Alaska, S arm of Uyak Bay, inlet of Shelikof Strait, W Kodiak Isl., 60 mi/97 km WSW of Kodiak, 20 mi/32 km long; 57°32′N 154°03′W. Salmon canning. Larsen Bay village is on shore.

Larson, village (1990 pop. 26), Burke co., NW N.Dak., 29 mi/47 km WNW of Bowbells; 48°53′N 102°52′W.

Larto, Lake (LAHR-to), oxbow lake, Catahoula parish, E central La., formed by a cutoff of Ouachita R., 30 mi/48 km E of Alexandria; 31°22′N 91°55′W. Lake is c.10 mi/16 km long. Fishing. Catahoula L. Diversion Canal runs E-W to N of L. Larto. Saline State Wildlife Area adjacent to W.

Larue (luh-ROO), county (□ 263 sq mi/681 sq km; 1990 pop. 11,679), central Ky.; ⊙ Hodgenville; 37°32′N 85°42′W. Bounded E and NE by Rolling Fork; drained by Nolin R. Rolling agr. area (burley tobacco, corn, hay, alfalfa, soybeans, wheat; hogs, cattle, poultry; dairying); limestone quarries, timber. Includes Abraham Lincoln Birthplace Natl. Historic Site, at center of co., near Hodgenville, Lincoln boyhood home in NE, near White City. Formed 1843.

Larwill, town (1990 pop. 219), Whitley co., NE Ind., 7 mi/11.3 km WNW of Columbia City; 41°11′N 85°37′W. In agr. area. Laid out 1854.

Las Animas, county (□ 4,775 sq mi/12,367 sq km; 1990 pop. 13,765), SE Colo.; ⊙ Trinidad; 37°19′N 104°02′W. Largest co. in Colo.; bordering on N.Mex.; drained by Purgatoire and Apishapa rivers. Coal-mining and cattle-grazing area; cattle, horses; wheat, hay, sorghum. Part of Sangre de Cristo Mts. and San Isabel Natl. Forest in W; Trinidad State Park in W center; parts of Comanche Natl. Grassland in E and NE. Pinon Canyon Military Reserve in N. Formed 1866.

Las Animas, town (1990 pop. 2,481), ⊙ Bent co., SE Colo., on Arkansas R., W of mouth of Purgatoine R., 75 mi/121 km E of Pueblo; 38°04′N 103°13′W. Elev. 3,901 ft/1,189 m. Trade center in irrigated vegetables, wheat, barley, corn, sorghum, cattle region. Kit Carson Mus. (in cabin where the scout died) and U.S. veterans' hosp. RR junction to E; John Martin Reservoir to E; Adobe Creek Reservoir (Blue L.) to N; Horse Creek Reservoir to NW; Bent's Old Fort to W. Oldest active courthouse in Colo. (1888). City founded 1869, moved to present site 1873 to be on RR; inc. 1886.

Las Choapas (lahs cho-AH-pahs), city (1990 pop. 43,868), SE Veracruz, Mexico, 7 mi/11 km SE of the port of Coatzacoalcoson, located in a plains region on the banks of the Tonalá R., which forms the border between the states of Veracruz and Tabasco; 17°56′N 94°05′W. There is a RR line to Campeche, and roads connect with those that go from Coatzacoalcos to Salina Cruz and Villahermosa. There are many roads built by Petroleos Mexicanos. Hot climate. Petroleum center.

Las Cotorras, Trinidad and Tobago: see FIVE ISLANDS.

Las Cruces (lahs KROO-suhs) [Span. = the crosses], city (1990 pop. 62,126), ⊙ Dona Ana co., SW N.Mex., 42 mi/68 km NNW of El Paso, 225 mi/362 km S of Albuquerque, on the Rio Grande; 32°20′N 106°45′W. Elev. 3,896 ft/1,188 m. In a farm area irrigated by the Elephant Butte system. The 2d-largest city in N.Mex. and one of the country's fastest growing metropolitan areas in 1990s. Its economy is based chiefly on agr. and the nearby White Sands Missile Range, testing grounds for the 1st atomic bomb and a major military and NASA testing site. Cattle, sheep; dairying; vegetables, melons, corn, cotton, pecans, triticale. Mfg. (food processing, winery, beverages, printing and publishing, aircraft parts, concrete, consumer goods, wood prods., dairy prods.). The city has a textile industry and canning and processing plants for various prods., such as sugar beets, pecans, and cotton. The name refers to a massacre (1830) of some 40 travelers by Apaches on this site. N.Mex. State Univ. is to the SE. Donã Ana Branch Community Col. is here. Nearby are the historic village of La Mesilla to SW, Fort Fillmore (1851) ruins to S, the village of Tortugas to S. Aguirre Springs Natl. Recreation Area to E, in Organ Mts.; Leasburg Dam State Park and Fort Selden (1865) State Monument to NW; Las Cruces Airport to W; White Sands Missile Range to NE. Founded 1848, inc. 1907.

Las Cuevas, Mexico: see MATAMOROS, town.

Las Esperanzas (lahs es-pai-RAHN-sahs), mining settlement (1990 pop. 3,870), Múzquiz municipio, Coahuila, N Mexico, in Sabinas coal dist., on RR, 12 mi/19 km SE of Múzquiz.

Las Guaranas (lahs GWAH-rah-nahs), town (1993 pop. 9,623), 8 mi/13 km SE of San Francisco de Macorís, Duarte prov., central Dominican Republic; 19°12′N 70°13′W.

Las Lomas, uninc. town (1990 pop. 2,127), Monterey co., W Calif., residential suburb 3 mi/4.8 km SSE of Watsonville, 4 mi/6.4 km E of Pacific Ocean; 36°52′N 121°44′W.

Las Margaritas (lahs mahr-gahr-REE-tahs), city (1990 pop. 8,637), ⊙ Las Margaritas municipio, Chiapas, S Mexico, in Sierra Madre, 11 mi/18 km ENE of Comitán de Domíngeiz. Elev. 4,970 ft/1,515 m. Sugarcane, cereals, fruit; stock. Tojolabal-speaking Maya Indians occupy rural areas of the municipio.

Las Marías (lahs mah-REE-yahs), town (1990 pop. 9,306), W P.R., 10 mi/16 km ENE of Mayagüez. Coffee center. Agr. (coffee, oranges, grapefruit); light mfg.

Las Matas (lahs MAH-tas) or **Las Matas de Farfán**, town (1993 pop. 18,064), San Juan prov., W Dominican Republic, in irrigated San Juan Valley, on highway, 20 mi/32 km W of San Juan. Agr. (coffee, bananas, vegetables, cereals).

Las Matas de Santa Cruz (lahs MAH-tas dai SAHN-tah croos), town (1993 pop. 7,502), 19 mi/30 km SE of Monte Cristi, Monte Cristi prov., NW Dominican Republic; 19°40′N 71°30′W. In banana-producing region.

Las Minas (lahs MEE-nahs), town (1990 pop. 305), Veracruz, E Mexico, 19 mi/31 km NW of Xalapa Enríquez on Bobos R. Elev. 5,755 ft/1,754 m. Hydroelectric plant. In Totomac Indian area.

Las Piedras (lahs pee-AI-drahs), town (1990 pop. 27,896), E P.R., 3 mi/4.8 km NW of Humacao. Industrial center. Native artisanry (wood, thread, and clay prods., hammocks).

Las Rosas (lah RO-sahs), town (1990 pop. 12,193), ⊙ Las Rosas municipio, Chiapas, S Mexico, at SW foot of Sierra de Hueytepec, 29 mi/47 km SE of San Cristóbal de las Casas. Agr. center (cereals, sugarcane, coffee, fruit; livestock; timber). Called Pinola until 1934.

Las Tres Vírgenes, Volcán (lahs trais VIR-he-nes), volcanic massif in Baja California Sur, NW Mexico, near coast of Gulf of California, 25 mi/40 km NW of Santa Rosalía in El Vizcaíno Biosphere Reserve. Rises to 6,547 ft/1,996 m. Last erupted 1746.

Las Tunas (lahs TOO-nuhz), province (□ 2,662 sq mi/ 6,376 sq km), E Cuba; ⊙ Las Tunas. Created from former Camagüey and Oriente provs. in 1976. Bordered N by Atlantic Ocean, S by Gulf of Guacanayabo and Granma prov., E by Holguín prov., and W by Camagüey prov. Important centers are Las Tunas, Puerto Padre, Amancio, and Jobabo. The prov. produces c.9% of the nation's total amount of sugar each year; and processing at 3 mills (Peru, Argelia Libre, and Antonio Guiteras) is just over ½ of provincial total.

Las Tunas (lahs TOO-nuhz), town (1994 est. pop. 120,000), ⊙ Las Tunas prov., E Cuba, on Central Highway and RR, 100 mi/161 km NW of Santiago de Cuba; 20°56′N 76°56′W. Linked by RR with Manatí (25 mi/ 40 km N) on N coast. Trading and agr. center (sugarcane, bananas, oranges, cattle, beeswax, honey). Airfield, with 7,200 ft/2,195 m runway. Steel structures and glass are manufactured there. Scene of fighting in revolutionary war of 1950s.

Las Vegas, Cuba: see VEGAS.

Las Vegas 1 city (□ 83 sq mi/215 sq km; 1990 pop. 258,295), ⊙ Clark co., SE Nev.; 36°12′N 115°13′W. Elev. 2,025 ft/617 m. Only the N ½ of physical city (much of it commercial) is inc. The area generally S of Sahara Ave., including the Las Vegas Boulevard gambling and entertainment dist. (the Strip) is uninc., and its pop. is counted as part of the uninc. cities of Paradise and Winchester. It is the largest city in Nev. and one of the fastest growing cities in the country, which is largely caused by an influx of retirees and the growth of industries that support the retirement community. The city's pop. increased by more than 56% bet. 1980 and 1990. It is considered *the* gambling capital of the world; gambling was legalized in 1931. Revenue from hotels, gambling, entertainment, and other tourist-oriented industries forms the backbone of Las Vegas's economy. Its nightclubs, casinos, and championship boxing matches are world famous, and entertainment enterprises have led to an increasing array of music, sports, and gambling centers up and down the Strip, a.k.a "Glitter Gulch." The city is also the commercial hub of a ranching and mining area. Mfg. (paper prods., printing and publishing, apparel, chemicals, signs, machinery, gaming equip. and devices, electronics, dairy prods., fabricated metal prods., lumber, bldg. materials, hardware, beverages, jewelry, cut stone and stone prods., furniture, consumer goods). In the 19th cent., Las Vegas was a watering place for travelers to S Calif. In 1855–1857 the Mormons maintained a fort there, and in 1864, Fort Baker was built by the U.S. Army. In 1867, Las Vegas was detached from the Ariz. Territory and joined to Nev. Its main growth began with the completion of a RR in 1905. The Univ. of Nev. is in uninc. S part of city. Large Nellis Air Force Bombing and Gunnery Range to the NE of the city; Hoover Dam is 25 mi/ 40 km SE, forms large L. Mead (L. Mead Natl. Reservoir Area). Old Las Vegas Mormon Fort State Park at Las Vegas Boulevard and Washington Ave. Floyd Lamb State Park to NW. Mt. Charleston, in Toiyabe Natl. Forest to W. Desert View Natural Area to NW. Indian Springs Air Force Base to NW. Valley of Fire State Park to NE. Pabco Gypsum Mines 14 mi/ 23 km to NE. McCarran Internatl. Airport in S uninc. part of city. Convention Center in uninc. S part of city. Nev. State Mus.; Las Vegas Natural History Mus. Inc. 1911. **2** city (1990 pop. 14,753), ⊙ San Miguel co., N central N.Mex., on Gallinas R., in Sangre de Cristo Mts., 64 mi/103 km ESE of Santa Fe, in irrigated region; 35°36′N 105°13′W. Elev. 6,435 ft/1,961 m. Las Vegas is a mt. and health resort, as well as shipping center for livestock, lumber, wool, and hides in grain (alfalfa, peas) and livestock (cattle, sheep) area. N.Mex. Highlands Univ. is here. Hot springs 6 mi/9.7 km N; ruins of Fort Union (1851–1891), dude ranches, and parts of Santa Fe Natl. Forest to W and S; Las Vegas Natl. Wildlife Refuge to SE, at McAllister L.; Storrie L. State Park to N; Villanueva State Park to SSW. Founded 1609.

Las Vigas de Ramírez, town, ⊙ Las Vigas de Ramírez municipio, Veracruz, E Mexico, in Sierra Madre Oriental, on RR, 13 mi/21 km NW of Xalapa Enríquez on Mexico Highway 140. Elev. 4,265 ft/1,300 m. Agr. center (cereals, coffee, fruit).

Lasalle (luh-SAL) or **Ville Lasalle,** city (1991 pop. 73,804), S Que., Canada, SW of Montreal on the St. Lawrence R. at the head of the Lachine Rapids. Suburb of Montreal.

Lascahobas (lah-skah-O-bahs), town (1982 pop. 3,805), Centre dept., S central Haiti, on Artibonite Plain, 32 mi/51 km NE of Port-au-Prince; 18°50′N 71°56′W. Tobacco, sisal, sugarcane, coffee.

Lashburn, town (1991 pop. 748), W Sask., Canada, 20 mi/ 32 km SE of Lloydminster, near Alta. border; 53°07′N 109°37′W. Wheat.

Lasker, village (1990 pop. 139), Northampton co., NE N.C., 21 mi/34 km ESE of Roanoke Rapids; 36°21′N 77°18′W. Tobacco, peanuts, cotton, grain; livestock. Mfg. (feeds).

Lasqueti Island (las-KE-tee) (□ 26 sq mi/67 sq km), SW B.C., Canada, in Strait of Georgia just S of Texada Isl., 50 mi/80 km WNW of Vancouver; 10 mi/16 km long, 3 mi/5 km wide. Copper and gold mining in N central area. Village of Lasqueti is on W shore.

Lassen, county (□ 4,558 sq mi/11,805 sq km; 1990 pop. 27,598), NE Calif.; ⊙ Susanville; 40°39′N 120°35′W. On high volcanic plateau (more than 4,000 ft/1,219 m) extending E from Cascade Range; the Sierra Nevada is along SW and S borders, bounded by Nev. on E. The co.'s highest elev. (more than 8,000 ft/2,438 m) is at Warner Mts (NE), Drained by Pit and Susan rivers. Densely forested (pine, fir, cedar); logging and lumber milling are chief industries. Timber; stock grazing (cattle); farms (some irrigation) chiefly in Honey L. valley produce potatoes, rice, wheat, barley, oats, garlic, strawberries. Fishing, hunting, camping, winter sports attract vacationers. Includes part of Lassen Volcanic Natl. Park in SW. Much of co. is in natl. forests: Modoc (N), Plumas (S), and Lassen (W). Eagle and Honey lakes are here. Sierra Army Depot in SE, SE of Honey L. Region resisted with arms (1863) Calif.'s jurisdiction until Lassen co. was formed in 1864.

Lassen Peak or **Mount Lassen** (10,457 ft/3,187 m), SE Shasta co., N Calif., at S end of Cascade Range, N of the Sierra Nevada, c.50 mi/80 km E of Redding. In W part of Lassen Volcanic Natl. Park. Until Mt. St. Helens erupted in 1980, Lassen was considered to be the only active volcano in the continental U.S. The last major eruption here occurred in 1914, and the volcano was intermittently active until 1921. Discovered (probably 1821) by Luis Argüello, later named for Peter Lassen, pioneer and guide. The peak was a prominent landmark in the mid-1800s for westward travelers to Calif. Lassen Peak Ski Area to S.

Lassen Volcanic National Park (□ 166 sq mi/ 430 sq km), Shasta and Lassen cos., also extends into Plumas and Tehama cos., N Calif., at the S end of the Cascade Range. The park contains volcanic peaks, lava flows, vents, and hot springs. Lassen Peak (10,457 ft/ 3,187 m), in W part of park, is an active volcano. Est. 1916.

L'Assomption (lah-sop-SYO), county (□ 247 sq mi/ 640 sq km; 1991 pop. 91,537), S Que., Canada, on the St. Lawrence, N of Montreal; ⊙ L'Assomption; 45°45′N 73°30′W.

L'Assomption, town (1991 pop. 5,706), ⊙ L'Assomption co., S Que., Canada, on L'Assomption R., and 22 mi/ 35 km NNE of Montreal; 45°49′N 73°26′W. Lumbering, woodworking, light mfg.; market in tobacco growing, dairying region. Site of Agr. Canada Experimental Farm.

L'Assomption River, 100 mi/161 km long, S Que., Canada; rises in the Laurentians in Mont Tremblant Park; flows past to Joliette, thence S, past L'Assomption, to the St. Lawrence at N end of Montreal Isl.

Last Mountain (2,275 ft/693 m), S central Sask., Canada, 50 mi/80 km NNW of Regina. Nearby is Last Mt. L.

Last Mountain Lake (□ 89 sq mi/231 sq km), S central Sask., Canada, 22 mi/35 km NW of Regina, 58 mi/93 km long, 3 mi/5 km wide. Drains S into Qu'Appelle R.

Lastrup (LAS-truhp), village (1990 pop. 112), Morrison co., central Minn., 17 mi/27 km ENE of Little Falls on Little Mink Creek; 46°02′N 94°03′W. Dairying; mfg. (feeds).

Latah (LAI-tah), county (□ 1,076 sq mi/2,787 sq km; 1990 pop. 30,617), in Palouse region, N Idaho; ⊙ Moscow; 46°49′N 116°43′W. Situated bet. Coeur d'Alene (N) and Nez Perce (S) Indian reservations. Long, rolling hills, drained by Palouse and Potlatch rivers. Borders on Wash. (W). Lumber; sheep, cattle; alfalfa; wheat, oats, barley; peas, lentils. Includes part of St. Joe Natl. Forest in N. Formed 1888.

Latah (LAI-tah), village (1990 pop. 175), Spokane co., E Wash., 28 mi/45 km SE of Spokane, on Hangman Creek; 47°17′N 117°09′W. Grain, peas; sheep, hogs.

Latchford, town (1991 pop. 345), E Ont., Canada, on Montreal R., 12 mi/19 km SW of Haileybury; 47°20′N 73°54′W. In mining region (silver, cobalt, nickel, bismuth, arsenic); lumbering. World's shortest covered bridge (18 ft/5 m).

Laterrière or **La Terrière** (both: lah-te-ree-ER), town (1991 pop. 4,690), S central Que., Canada, 9 mi/14 km SSW of Chicoutimi. Lumbering; dairying.

Latex, village (1990 pop. 289), Houston co., E Texas, 5 mi/8 km N of Crockett. Agr. area; oil and natural gas. Mfg. (chemicals, plastics).

Latham (LAI-thum), city (1990 pop. 160), Butler co., SE Kansas, 23 mi/37 km SE of El Dorado; 37°32′N 96°38′W. In cattle region. Butler State Fishing L. to NW.

Latham 1 (LAI-thuhm), village (1990 pop. 482), Logan co., central Ill., 13 mi/21 km NW of Decatur; 39°58′N 89°09′W. In agr. area. **2** (LAI-thuhm), uninc. community, Moniteau co., central Mo., 8 mi/12.9 km SW of California.

Lathrop 1 (LAI-thruhp), city (1990 pop. 6,841), San Joaquin co., central Calif., 9 mi/14.5 km S of Stockton, near San Joaquin R.; 37°49′N 121°17′W. RR junction. Fruit, pumpkins, nuts, vegetables, grain, sugar beets; nursery prods.; dairying; cattle; mfg. (concrete, glass, and rubber prods., bldg. components, pesticides, feeds, prefabricated bldgs.). Caswell Memorial State Park to S. **2** city (1990 pop. 1,794), Clinton co., NW Mo., 30 mi/ 48 km SE of St. Joseph; 39°32′N 94°19′W. Corn, soybeans; cattle; historic mule market (shipped 170,000 mules during Boer War in South Afr. and 90,000 to Europe during WWI). Mfg. (candy). Platted 1867.

Lathrup Village (LA-thrup), village (1990 pop. 4,329), Oakland co., SE Mich., residential suburb 15 mi/24 km NW of Detroit; 42°29′N 83°13′W. Completely surrounded by city of Southfield. Light mfg.

Latimer, county (□ 729 sq mi/1,888 sq km; 1990 pop. 10,333), SE Okla.; ⊙ Wilburton; 34°52′N 95°14′W. Drained by small Fourche Maline Creek; in Ouachita Mts. Cattle; lumbering, coal mining (though activity has declined); mfg. (apparel, electric motors); oil and natural-gas wells; some agr. Includes Robbers Cave State Park in NW. Sardis L. reservoir on S boundary; Sansbois Mts. (extension of Ouachitas) on N boundary. Formed 1907.

Latimer 1 town, Franklin co., N central Iowa, 8 mi/ 12.9 km W of Hampton. In livestock and grain area. **2** uninc. town (1990 pop. 3,222), Jackson co., SE Miss., 9 mi/14.5 km NNE of Biloxi, near Tchoutacabouffa R., at SE edge of De Soto Natl. Forest; 30°30′N 88°51′W. Timber.

Latimer, village (1990 pop. 20), Morris co., E central Kansas, 20 mi/32 km W of Council Grove; 38°44′N 96°50′W. Grazing, farming.

Latir Peak (luh-TIR) (12,708 ft/3,873 m), Sangre de Cristo Mts., NE Taos co., N N.Mex., near Colo. state line, 9 mi/14.5 km NE of Questa on N boundary of Carson Natl. Forest. Latir Lakes to NE.

Laton, uninc. town (1990 pop. 1,415), Fresno co., central Calif., 7 mi/11.3 km NNW of Hanford, on Kings R.; 36°26′N 119°42′W. Citrus, nuts, cotton, grain; cattle; dairying.

Latouche Island (lah-TOOSH), S Alaska, in Gulf of Alaska, at entrance of Prince William Sound, off E coast of Kenai Peninsula, 50 mi/80 km E of Seward;

60°00′N 147°55′W. Rises to c.2,000 ft/610 m; 12 mi/19 km long, 2 mi/3.2 km–4 mi/6.4 km wide. Named by George Vancouver in 1794. Latouche village, NW.

Latrobe, borough (1990 pop. 9,265), Westmoreland co., SW Pa., 33 mi/53 km ESE of Pittsburgh, on Loyalhanna Creek, in the foothills of the Allegheny Mts.; 40°18′N 79°22′W. Mfg. (foam rubber, asphalt, lumber, printing and publishing, bldg. materials, steel, plastic prods., beer). Agr. (corn, hay; livestock; dairying). St. Vincent Col. to SW. County Airport to SW. Keystone State Park to N. Inc. 1854.

Latta (LAT-ah), town (1990 pop. 1,565), Dillon co., NE S.C., 21 mi/34 km NE of Florence; 34°20′N 79°25′W. Mfg. includes plastics, apparel, ordnance. Trading and shipping center for cotton, grain, soybeans, livestock.

Lattimore, village (1990 pop. 183), Cleveland co., S N.C., 6 mi/9.7 km W of Shelby; 35°19′N 81°39′W. Cotton, grain; livestock.

Lattingtown, residential village (☐ 3 sq mi/7.8 sq km; 1990 pop. 1,859), Nassau co., SE N.Y., on N shore of W L.I., just NE of Glen Cove; 40°53′N 73°35′W.

Latty, village (1990 pop. 205), Paulding co., NW Ohio, 17 mi/27 km SW of Defiance; 41°05′N 84°35′W. In agr. area.

Lauderdale 1 (LAW-duhr-dail), county (☐ 718 sq mi/1,860 sq km; 1990 pop. 79,661), extreme NW Ala.; ⊙ Florence, 34°54′N 87°38′W. Borders Miss. and Tenn., drained in S by Pickwick Landing Reservoir, Wilson L., and Wheeler L. Wilson and Wheeler dams provide hydroelectric power for industries at Florence. Cattle, poultry; corn, cotton, hay, and soybeans. Formed 1918. **2** county (☐ 715 sq mi/1,852 sq km; 1990 pop. 75,555), E Miss., bordering E on Ala.; ⊙ Meridian; 32°30′N 88°40′W. Drained by Chunky, Okatibbee, and Bucatunna creeks. Agr. (cotton, corn, sweet potatoes; cattle, hogs); timber. Meridian Naval Air Station in N; Sam Dale Memorial State Historical Site in N; Okatibbee L. reservoir in NW; L. Tom Bailey State L. in E. Formed 1833. **3** county (☐ 487 sq mi/1,261 sq km; 1990 pop. 23,491), W Tenn.; ⊙ Ripley; 35°46′N 89°38′W. Bounded W by the Mississippi, N by Forked Deer R., S by Hatchie R. Timber and agr. area (cotton, corn, soybeans, wheat, sorghum, fruit; livestock). Formed 1835.

Lauderdale, town (1990 pop. 2,700), Ramsey co., E Minn., residential suburb 5 mi/8 km WNW of St. Paul, and 3 mi/4.8 km ENE of Minneapolis; 44°59′N 93°12′W.

Lauderdale Lakes (LAW-duhr-dail), city (☐ 3 sq mi/7.8 sq km; 1990 pop. 27,341), Broward co., SE Fla., 3 mi/4.8 km NW of Fort Lauderdale; 26°10′N 80°12′W. Mfg. includes furniture, commercial glass.

Lauderdale-by-the-Sea (LAW-duhr-dail), town (☐ 1 sq mi/2.6 sq km; 1990 pop. 2,990), Broward co., SE Fla., 7 mi/11.3 km N of Fort Lauderdale on the Atlantic Ocean; 26°11′N 80°05′W.

Lauderhill (LAW-duhr-hil), city (☐ 7 sq mi/18.1 sq km; 1990 pop. 49,708), Broward co., SE Fla., 5 mi/8 km NW of Fort Lauderdale; 26°10′N 80°13′W. Mfg. includes plastic prods., furniture, commercial printing, shelving, motor vehicle parts.

Laughery Creek, c.50 mi/80 km long, in SE Ind.; rises in N Ripley co.; flows S past Versailles, to Friendship, where it turns ENE to flow along the boundary bet. Dearborn and Ohio cos. to join the Ohio R. SE of Aurora.

Laughlin (LAHF-lin), uninc. town (1990 pop. 4,791), Clark co., SE Nev., 72 mi/116 km SSE of Las Vegas, 20 mi/32 km N of Needles (Calif.), on Colorado R. (bridged), below (S of) Davis Dam (forms L. Mohave), opposite Bullhead City, Ariz.; 35°08′N 114°37′W. Elev. 535 ft/163 m. The southernmost town in Nev., Laughlin began with a couple of casinos and a fishing dock in mid-1980s; by 1996, it was 3rd in gambling revenue in Nev. with many hotels. Located at extreme S end of L. Mead Natl. Recreation Area; Fort Mohave Indian Reservation to S; Grapevine Canyon to N. Laughlin/Bullhead City Airport to E in Ariz. Lowest point in Nev. (469 ft/143 m) 10 mi/16 km to SSW, on Colorado R., at S tip of state.

Launay (lo-NAI), village (1991 pop. 272), W Que., Canada, 20 mi/32 km WNW of Amos. Gold mining.

Laupahoehoe (LOU-pah-HOI-HOI), village (1990 pop. 508), NE Hawaii isl., Hawaii co., Hawaii, 21 mi/34 km NNW of Hilo, on Hamakua coast; 19°58′N 155°14′W. On leaf-shaped point is a memorial to victims of the 1946 tidal wave; lighthouse. Hilo Forest Reserve to S; Manowaialee Forest Reserve to SW.

Laura, village (1990 pop. 483), Miami co., W Ohio, 15 mi/24 km SW of Piqua, in agr. area; 39°59′N 84°24′W.

Laurel, county (☐ 443 sq mi/1,147 sq km; 1990 pop. 43,438), SE Ky.; ⊙ London; 37°06′N 84°07′W. Bounded W by Rockcastle R., NE in part by South Fork of Rockcastle R., S by Laurel R. (forms Laurel R. L. reservoir); drained by several creeks. Mt. agr. area, in Cumberland foothills (cattle, hogs, poultry; dairying; burley tobacco, corn, hay, alfalfa); coal mines, timber. Includes Levi Jackson Wilderness Road State Park in center and part of Daniel Boone Natl. Forest in W ½. Formed 1825.

Laurel 1 city (1990 pop. 19,438), Prince Georges co., central Md., about halfway bet. Wash., D.C., and Baltimore; 39°06′N 76°52′W. Originally a small industrial center known as Laurel Factory, now primarily residential, Laurel has light mfg. and a growing number of businesses. The Wash., D.C. Children's Center and the famous Laurel racetrack (opened in 1911) are here. Montpelier, one of Maryland's famous mansions, completed about 1783 and now owned by the state, is one of several in the area. Fort George G. Meade is also here. Patented in the late 1600s, inc. 1870. **2** city (1990 pop. 18,827), ⊙ Jones co., SE Miss., on Tallahala Creek; 31°41′N 89°08′W. Agr. (cotton, corn; cattle, poultry; dairying); timber; mfg. (automotive parts, wood prods., apparel, chemicals, furniture, machinery, concrete, electrical equip., fabricated metal prods., food processing); oil and natural gas. The city was founded as the site of a sawmill in 1882. Oil was discovered in the vicinity in 1944. Southeastern Baptist Col. is in Laurel. L. Bogue Homa State L. to E; De Soto Natl. Forest to SE; Hesler-Noble Municipal Airport in SW. Inc. 1892. **3** uninc. city, Henrico co., E central Va., residential suburb 8 mi/12.9 km NNW of Richmond; 37°37′N 77°30′W. V.E. Randolph Mus. and Meadow Farm Mus. are here. Henrico County Govt. Center in S.

Laurel 1 town (1990 pop. 3,226), Sussex co., SW Del., 15 mi/24 km N of Salisbury, Md., on Broad Creek; 38°32′N 75°34′W. Shipping center for fruit, vegetables. Mfg. (wood prods.). Robert L. Graham Wildlife Area to W. Mason-Dixon Marker (1768), in SW corner of Del., 8 mi/12.9 km to SW. Numerous ponds in the area make Laurel a popular boating, fishing, and recreation center. Laid out 1802, inc. 1883. **2** town (☐ 5 sq mi/13 sq km; 1990 pop. 8,245), Sarasota co., W central Fla., 15 mi/24 km S of Sarasota; 27°08′N 82°27′W. **3** town (1990 pop. 544), Franklin co., SE Ind., 13 mi/21 km NW of Brookville; 39°30′N 85°11′W. In agr. area. On West Fork of Whitewater R. Laid out 1836. **4** town (1990 pop. 271), Marshall co., central Iowa, 12 mi/19 km S of Marshalltown; 41°52′N 92°55′W. In agr. area. **5** town (1990 pop. 5,686), Yellowstone co., S Mont., on Yellowstone R., near mouth of Clarks Fork, 16 mi/26 km SW of Billings; 45°40′N 108°46′W. Oil refinery; shipping point for copper, zinc, lumber, grain, hay, livestock, wool. Dairying; sugar beets, honey. Mfg. (petroleum prods., meat processing). Herbsfest. Laurel Municipal Airport and Canyon Creek Battlefield–Nez Perce Natl. Historical Park to N; large Crow Indian Reservation to SE. Inc. 1908. Formerly called Carlton. **6** town (1990 pop. 981), Cedar co., NE Nebr., 17 mi/27 km SSE of Hartington, on Logan Creek; 42°25′N 97°05′W. Livestock; grain, alfalfa mill.

Laurel Bay, uninc. town (1990 pop. 4,972), Beaufort co., S S.C., 6 mi/9.7 km W of Beaufort, on broad R. U.S. Marine Base to E; 32°27′N 80°47′W. Industry in fish and oysters. Agr. interests in vegetables.

Laurel Fork, river, c.50 mi/80 km long, E W.Va.; rises in E Randolph co.; flows NNE, receives Gandy Creek from S and Glady Creek from SW, turns WNW, joins Shavers Fork at Parsons to form Cheat R.

Laurel Hill, ridge (2,400 ft/732 m–2,900 ft/884 m) in the Allegheny Mts., in SW Pa., on Fayette/Somerset co. line, runs 55 mi/89 km NE from S Fayette co. to just W of Nanty Glo; 40°13′N 79°06′W–39°49′N 79°26′W. Youghiogheny R. cuts through just below Confluence, Conemaugh R. cuts through W of Johnstown. Much of ridge in Forbes State Forest. Bituminous coal, limestone, sandstone, clay, shale.

Laurel Hill, W.Va.: see LAUREL RIDGE.

Laurel Hollow, village (☐ 3 sq mi/7.8 sq km; 1990 pop. 1,748), Nassau co., SE N.Y., on N shore of L.I., 3 mi/4.8 km W of Huntington; 40°51′N 73°28′W. In summer-resort area. JFK Internatl. Airport to the SW. Until 1935, called Laurelton.

Laurel Mountain, borough (1990 pop. 195), Somerset co., SW Pa., 15 mi/24 km SE of Latrobe on Laurel Hill Ridge; 40°12′N 79°10′W. Ski resort to W. Several state parks and forests in area.

Laurel Park, town (1990 pop. 1,322), Henderson co., W N.C., residential suburb 2 mi/3.2 km W of Hendersonville; 35°18′N 82°30′W.

Laurel Ridge or **Laurel Hill** (c.3,300 ft/1,006 m), N W.Va., in the Allegheny Mts. Extends SSW from Cheat R. W of Rowlesburg to Tygart R. W of Elkins; 32 mi/51 km long. Rich Mt. is its S continuation. Scene (July 8, 1861) of Civil War engagement (Battle of Laurel Hill) E of Belington, in which Confederate troops were forced to retreat.

Laurel River, 38 mi/61 km long, SE Ky.; rises in the Cumberlands in E Laurel co.; flows generally SW past Corbin and through Laurel R. L. reservoir, to Cumberland R. 11 mi/18 km W of Corbin.

Laurel River Lake, reservoir, on the border bet. Laurel and Whitley cos. SE Ky., on Laurel R., in Daniel Boone Natl. Forest, 18 mi/29 km SW of London; c.13 mi/21 km long; 36°57′N 84°17′W. Max. capacity 435,600 acre-ft. Formed by Laurel R. Dam (282 ft/86 m high), built by the Army Corps of Engineers for flood control and power generation.

Laurel Run, borough (1990 pop. 708), Luzerne co., NE central Pa., residential suburb 2 mi/3.2 km SE of Wilkes-Barre. Wilkes-Barre Mt. in SE.

Laurel Springs (law-RUHL), borough (1990 pop. 2,341), Camden co., SW N.J., 10 mi/16 km SE of Camden; 39°49′N 75°00′W. Largely residential. Inc. 1913.

Laureldale, borough (1990 pop. 3,726), Berks co., SE central Pa., suburb 3 mi/4.8 km N of Reading. Mfg. (fabricated steel prods., textiles, commercial printing, batteries). Settled 1902, inc. 1930.

Laureles, Mexico: see BENITO JUÁREZ, Michoacán state.

Laurelton, residential section of SE borough of Queens, N.Y. city, SE N.Y., NE of JFK Internatl. Airport, 2.5 mi/4 km W of Valley Stream. Predominantly Afr.-Amer. pop., many from the Caribbean.

Laurelton, N.Y.: see LAUREL HOLLOW.

Laurelville, village (1990 pop. 605), Hocking co., S central Ohio, 16 mi/26 km NE of Chillicothe; 39°28′N 82°44′W. In agr. area; grain prods., lumber.

Laurens 1 (LOR-uhns), county (☐ 818 sq mi/2,119 sq km; 1990 pop. 39,988), central Ga.; ⊙ Dublin; 32°28′N 82°56′W. Coastal plain agr. (tobacco, wheat, cotton, corn, peanuts; cattle, hogs) and timber area intersected by Oconee R. Formed 1807. **2** (LOR-enz), county (☐ 722 sq mi/1,870 sq km; 1990 pop. 58,092), NW central S.C.; ⊙ Laurens; 34°28′N 82°00′W. Bounded SW by Saluda R., NE by Enoree R.; part of L. Greenwood is in S. Includes part of Sumter Natl. Forest. Mfg. includes granite, sand, vermiculite, textiles. Agr. includes chickens, hogs, cattle; eggs; dairying; corn, wheat, rye, soybeans, sorghum, hay. Formed 1785.

Laurens (LOR-enz), city (1990 pop. 9,694), ⊙ Laurens co., NW S.C.; 34°30′N 82°01′W. Mfg. includes printing and publishing, ceramics, motor vehicle parts, glass and fiberglass prods., machining, textiles, paper prods. Agr. includes livestock; dairying, grain, soybeans, sorghum. Inc. 1875.

Laurens, town (1990 pop. 1,550), Pocahontas co., N central Iowa, 11 mi/18 km NW of Pocahontas; 42°51′N 94°50′W. Inc. 1890.

Laurens, village (1990 pop. 293), Otsego co., central N.Y., 4 mi/6.4 km N of Oneonta; 42°31′N 75°05′W. In dairying area. Nearby is Gilbert L. State Park.

Laurentian Mountains (lo-REN-shuhn) or **Laurentides**, S Que., Canada, N of the St. Lawrence and Ottawa rivers, rising to 3,150 ft/960 m in Mt. Tremblant. The Gatineau, L'Assomption, Lièvre, Montmorency, and St. Maurice rivers rise in lakes in this region, which is a popular year-round recreational area, esp. for Montreal and Ottawa. Mt. Tremblant Provincial Park is here.

Laurentian Plateau, Canada: see CANADIAN SHIELD.

Laurentides (LO-ruhn-teidz), town (1991 pop. 2,336), SW Que., Canada, 25 mi/40 km NNW of Montreal; 45°51′N 73°46′W. Woodworking; vegetable growing; dairying; tobacco growing and processing. Sir Wilfrid Laurier b. here. Town was called St. Lin until it was inc. 1883.

Laurentides, Canada: see LAURENTIAN MOUNTAINS.

Laurentides Park, provincial park (□ 4,000 sq mi/ 10,360 sq km), S central Que., Canada, on the Laurentian Plateau, N of Quebec, and S of L. St. John; 80 mi/ 129 km long, 60 mi/97 km wide. Rises to 3,800 ft/1,158 m (S). Public recreation ground and game reserve, park contains c.1,600 lakes and vast network of streams. Chicoutimi R. rises in center of park. Est. 1895.

Laurier (lor-ee-AI), uninc. village (1990 pop. 30), Ferry co., NE Wash., port of entry at B.C. (Canada) border, opposite Cascade (B.C.), 11 mi/18 km ESE of Grand Forks (B.C.), 32 mi/51 km NE of Republic. Christian L. (B.C.) to NE, part of Colville Natl. Forest to E and W.

Laurierville (LO-ree-ai-ivil), village (1991 pop. 885), S Que., Canada, 22 mi/35 km NW of Thetford Mines. Dairying.

Laurin (lah-RAI), village (1990 pop. 40), Madison co., SW Mont., on Ruby R., 48 mi/77 km SSE of Butte. In livestock region. Parts of Beaverhead Natl. Forest to NE and SE. Robbers Roost to NW. Formerly called Cicero.

Laurinburg (LAW-ruhn-buhrg), city (1990 pop. 11,643), ⊙ Scotland co., S N.C., 37 mi/60 km SW of Fayetteville, near S.C. state line; 34°46′N 79°28′W. RR junction. Mfg. (pharmaceuticals, metal fabricating, bldg. materials, cobalt powder, wooden prods., textiles, feeds, glass prods.). Agr. area (cotton, tobacco, grain, soybeans, chickens, hogs). St. Andrews Presbyterian Col., Indian Mus. of the Carolinas, Native Amer. Lib. Inc. 1877.

Laurium (LAW-ree-uhm), town (1990 pop. 2,268), Houghton co., NW Upper Peninsula, Mich., 11 mi/ 18 km NE of Houghton; 47°14′N 88°26′W. Former copper-mining region. Inc. 1889.

Laurys Station, uninc. town (1990 pop. 950), Lehigh co., E Pa., 9 mi/14.5 km NNW of Allentown, on Lehigh R.; 40°43′N 76°31′W. Mfg. (wood prods.). Agr. includes dairying, livestock; grain; timber.

Laussedat, Mount (los-DAH) (10,035 ft/3,059 m), SE B.C., Canada, near Alta. border, in Rocky Mts., in Hamber Park, 65 mi/105 km WNW of Banff; 51°35′N 116°58′W.

Lava Beds National Monument (□ 73 sq mi/ 189 sq km), Siskiyou and Modoc cos., N Calif., 12 mi/ 19 km S of Oregon state line. Bounded by Tule L. Natl. Wildlife Refuge on N, by Modoc Natl. Forest W, S, and E, Klamath Natl. Forest to SW. Examples of rugged volcanic landscape. Used as a fortress by Native Americans during Modoc Indian War of 1872–1873. Canby's Massacre Site in N; Ice Caves in SW. Authorized 1925.

Lava Hot Springs, village (1990 pop. 420), Bannock co., SE Idaho, 25 mi/40 km SE of Pocatello, on Portneuf R.; 42°37′N 112°01′W. Elev. 5,072 ft/1,546 m. Part of Caribou Natl. Forest to NW; Portneuf Reservoir partially in SE corner of Fort Hall Indian Reservation to N.

Lavaca, county (□ 970 sq mi/2,512 sq km; 1990 pop. 18,690), S Texas; ⊙ Hallettsville; 29°22′N 96°56′W. In coastal plains region; drained by Lavaca and Navidad rivers. Cattle; agr. (corn, milo, rice, hay). Some oil and natural gas fields. Formed 1846.

Lavaca (luh-VAK-uh), town (1990 pop. 1,253), Sebastian co., W Ark., 13 mi/21 km ESE of Fort Smith, near Arkansas R.; 35°19′N 94°10′W. Light mfg. Fort Chaffee Military Reservation to S.

Lavaca River, 100 mi/161 km long, S Texas; rises in N Lavaca co., N of Moulton; flows generally SSE to Lavaca Bay, the NW arm of Matagorda Bay. Receives Navidad R. 11 mi/18 km above mouth.

Laval (lah-VAHL), former county, S Que., Canada. Now it is Île Jésus co., which is coextensive with Île Jésus (isl.).

Laval, city (1991 pop. 314,398), coextensive with Île Jésus (□ 94 sq mi/243 sq km), S Que., Canada, bet. the Rivière des Mille Îles and the Rivière des Prairies, just NW of Montreal; 45°36′N 73°44′W. The 2nd-largest city in Que., Laval was created in 1965, when 14 small communities on the isl. were amalgamated. It is a largely residential suburb of Montreal, with summer tourism facilities. The isl. was known as Montmagny Isl. until 1699, when it was granted to the Jesuits of Que. and began to be settled.

Lavallette (lah-vuh-LET), resort borough (1990 pop. 2,299), Ocean co., E N.J., on peninsula bet. Barnegat Bay and the Atlantic, 7 mi/11.3 km ENE of Toms River; 39°58′N 74°04′W.

Lavaltrie (lah-vahl-TREE), village (1991 pop. 4,365), SW Que., Canada, on the St. Lawrence R., 9 mi/14 km SW of Sorel; 45°53′N 73°17′W. Dairying. Just E, in the St. Lawrence, is islet of Lavaltrie.

Laveen, uninc. town (1990 pop. 800), Maricopa co., central Ariz., residential suburb 7 mi/11.3 km SW of Phoenix, S of Salt R. Mfg. (cotton milling, ironworks). Phoenix South Mt. Park to SE. Gila R. Indian Reservation to SW, including St. Johns Mus.

L'Avenir (lahv-NIR), village (1991 pop. 1,164), 3 Que., Canada, near St. Francis R., 12 mi/19 km SE of Drummondville. Dairying; cattle, pigs.

Laverlochère (lah-ver-lo-SHER), village (1991 pop. 854), W Que., Canada, 16 mi/26 km W of Haileybury; 47°25′N 79°17′W. Gold mining.

Laverne, town (1990 pop. 1,269), Harper co., NW Okla., 33 mi/53 km NW of Woodward, near North Canadian (Beaver) R.; 36°42′N 99°54′W. In agr. area (wheat; cattle); mfg. (meat processing).

Lavina (luh-VEE-nuh), village (1990 pop. 151), Golden Valley co., S central Mont., on Musselshell R. opposite mouth of Big Coulee Creek, 40 mi/64 km NW of Billings; 46°18′N 108°57′W. Wheat; sheep, cattle, sheepdogs.

Lavon, village (1990 pop. 303), Collin co., N Texas, 27 mi/ 43 km ENE of Dallas, on urban fringe of Dallas–Fort Worth area; 33°01′N 96°26′W. Agr. area. L. Lavon reservoir (East Fork of Trinity R.) to NW; L. Ray Hubbard reservoir to SW.

Lavon Lake, reservoir (□ 33 sq mi/85 sq km), Collin co., NE Texas, on East Fork of Trinity R., 25 mi/40 km NE of Dallas; 33°02′N 96°29′W. Max. capacity 921,100 acreft. Formed by Lavon Dam (81 ft/25 m high), built (1974) by Army Corps of Engineers for water supply; also used for flood control and recreation.

Lavonia (luh-VO-nee-uh), town (1990 pop. 1,840), Franklin co., NE Ga., near S.C. state line, 16 mi/26 km SE of Toccoa; 34°26′N 83°07′W. Mfg. includes apparel, textiles, feeds, train parts, industrial machinery.

Lavoy (luh-VOI), village (1991 pop. 100), central Alta., Canada, 9 mi/14 km ESE of Vegreville; 53°28′N 111°52′W. Grain, dairying.

Lawai (LAH-WAH-ee), town (1990 pop. 1,787), Kauai isl., Kauai co., Hawaii, 2 mi/3.2 km inland from S coast, on Lawai Stream, 9 mi/14.5 km WSW of Lihue, on Kaumualii Highway; 21°55′N 159°30′W. Sugarcane, fruit. Aepoalua Reservoir and several smaller reservoirs to SE. Natl. Tropical Botanical Garden to S. Lihue-Koloa Forest Reserve to N.

Lawler, town (1990 pop. 517), Chickasaw co., NE Iowa, 8 mi/12.9 km E of New Hampton; 43°04′N 92°09′W. In corn, hog, dairy, fertilizer and concrete area.

Lawn, village (1990 pop. 358), Taylor co., W central Texas, 21 mi/34 km S of Abilene; 32°08′N 99°45′W. In cotton, cattle area.

Lawndale, city (1990 pop. 27,331), Los Angeles co., S Calif., residential suburb 12 mi/19 km SW of Los Angeles and 3 mi/4.8 km NE of Pacific Ocean, in the Centinela Valley; 33°54′N 118°21′W. The pop. of Lawndale grew rapidly in the 1950s, but has been stable since early 1960s. Inc. 1959.

Lawndale, village (1990 pop. 573), Cleveland co., S N.C., 8 mi/12.9 km N of Shelby; 35°24′N 81°33′W. Cotton, grain; livestock. Mfg. (rugs, fabric dyeing and finishing, furniture, motor vehicle parts).

Lawnside, borough (1990 pop. 2,841), Camden co., SW N.J., 7 mi/11.3 km SE of Camden; 39°52′N 75°01′W. Site bought by abolitionists for free blacks (1840), and 1st called Free Haven. Pop. is overwhelmingly Afr.-Amer. Inc. 1926.

Lawnton, uninc. town (1990 pop. 3,221), Dauphin co., S Pa., residential suburb near Spring Creek; 40°16′N 76°47′W.

Lawrence 1 county (□ 718 sq mi/1,860 sq km; 1990 pop. 31,513), NW Ala.; ⊙ Moulton; 34°32′N 87°20′W. Drained in N by Wheeler Reservoir (in Tennessee R.). Part of William B. Bankhead Natl. Forest is in S. Cotton, corn, soybeans; poultry, cattle; deposits of coal, limestone, and asphalt. Formed 1818. **2** county (□ 592 sq mi/1,533 sq km; 1990 pop. 17,457), NE Ark.; ⊙ Walnut Ridge; 36°02′N 91°07′W. Bounded E by Cache R. and on N in part by Spring R.; drained by Black R., and Strawberry rivers. Agr. (cattle, hogs; rice, wheat, soybeans, sorghum). L. Charles State Park near center; Shirey Bay–Rainey Brake Wildlife Management Area in SW. Formed 1815. **3** county (□ 373 sq mi/966 sq km; 1990 pop. 15,972), SE Ill., bounded E by Wabash R.; ⊙ Lawrenceville; 38°42′N 87°43′W. Drained by Embarras R. Agr. area, with oil and natural-gas wells; livestock; soybeans, corn, wheat. Oil refineries also other mfg. at Lawrenceville. Includes Red Hills State Park and Lincoln Trail State Memorial. Formed 1821. **4** county (□ 452 sq mi/1,171 sq km; 1990 pop. 42,836), S Ind.; ⊙ Bedford; 38°50′N 86°29′W. Drained by Salt Creek and East Fork of White R. Large limestone quarries; agr. (fruit, corn, soybeans); mfg. at Bedford, Mitchell. Site of Purdue Univ. Moses Fell Annex Farm W of Bedford. Avoca State Fishing Area in NW, Williams Dam State Fishing Area in W, Spring Mill State Park in SE. Hoosier Natl. Forest in NE and SW. Karst topography (sinkholes) in S. Formed 1818. **5** county (□ 420 sq mi/ 1,088 sq km; 1990 pop. 13,998), NE Ky.; ⊙ Louisa; 38°04′N 82°46′W. Bounded E by Big Sandy and Tug Fork Big Sandy rivers (both form W.Va. state line here); drained by Levisa Fork, Big Sandy R., and Blaine Creek (forms Yatesville L. reservoir in center of co.). Mt. agr. area (corn, burley tobacco, hay, alfalfa; cattle); oil and gas wells, coal mines, fireclay, and sand pits; timber. Formed 1821. **6** county (□ 435 sq mi/1,127 sq km; 1990 pop. 12,458), S central Miss.; ⊙ Monticello; 31°33′N 90°06′W. Drained by Pearl R. Agr. (cotton, corn; poultry, cattle, hogs); timber. L. Mary Crawford State L. in W. Formed 1874. **7** county (□ 619 sq mi/1,603 sq km; 1990 pop. 30,236), SW Mo.; ⊙ Mt. Vernon; 37°07′N 93°50′W. In the Ozarks, drained by Spring R. Wheat, hay, oats, barley, corn, apples, peaches, vegetables; turkeys, cattle; dairying. Mfg. at Aurora, Mt. Vernon, Pierce City, and Marionville (dairy and grain prods.); limestone. Formed 1845. **8** county (□ 456 sq mi/ 1,181 sq km; 1990 pop. 61,834), S Ohio; ⊙ Ironton; 38°35′N 82°33′W. Bounded S by Ohio R., here forming boundary with Ky. and W.Va.; drained by small Symmes Creek. In the Unglaciated Plain physiographic region. Agr. (dairy prods.; livestock; grain, fruit, tobacco, hay); mfg. (chemicals, steel, and iron) at Ironton; limestone quarrying. Formed 1816. **9** county (□ 362 sq mi/ 938 sq km; 1990 pop. 96,246), W Pa.; ⊙ New Castle; 40°59′N 80°19′W. Bounded W by Ohio state line; drained by Shenango, Mahoning, and Beaver rivers, and Neshannock Creek. Agr. (corn, oats, wheat, hay, alfalfa, apples; sheep, hogs, cattle, dairying); sand and gravel, limestone, coal. Mfg. at New Castle. Iron center in mid-19th cent. McConnells Mill State Park in E. Formed 1849. **10** county (□ 800 sq mi/2,072 sq km; 1990 pop. 20,655), W S.Dak., on Wyo. state line; ⊙ Deadwood, 44°21′N 103°47′W. Drained by Spearfish R. and Whitewood and Elk creeks. Farming (in N), forest and mining region in Black Hills. Gold, silver, quartz, timber; cattle, dairying; grain; honey; tourism. Development of co. parallels growth of Homestake Mining Company and legalized gaming at Deadwood. S ⅔ of co. in Black Hills Natl. Forest, except for pocket around Lead and Deadwood that is set aside for mining interests; Terry Peak is near Lead. Roughneck Falls in W; Terry Peak and Deer Mt. Ski Areas in SW. Formed 1875. **11** county (□ 634; 1990 pop. 35,303), S Tenn.; ⊙ Lawrenceburg; 35°13′N 87°23′W. Bounded S by Ala.; drained by upper Buffalo R. and Shoal Creek. Upland agr. region; peanuts, fruit, cotton, corn, livestock, dairy prods.; timber; phosphate mining. Formed 1817.

Lawrence 1 city (1990 pop. 26,763), Marion co., central Ind., residential suburb 7 mi/11.3 km NE of Indianapolis, on Fall Creek; 39°52′N 85°59′W. Light mfg. Fort Benjamin Harrison is here. **2** city (1990 pop. 65,608), ⊙ Douglas co., a metropolitan statistical area in NE Kansas, on the Kansas R., 32 mi/51 km WSW of Kansas City, 23 mi/37 km ESE of Topeka; 38°57′N 95°15′W. RR junction. Although agr. trade and light mfg. are economically important (esp. as the hq. of the greeting card company Hallmark), the city's major employer is the Univ. of Kansas, which has hundreds of administrative offices, laboratories, and research facilities. Mfg. (printing, medical equip., construction machinery, feeds, fertilizers, chemicals, communications equip., textiles, asphalt, paper prods., concrete, pharmaceuticals, plastics prods.). Lawrence was founded in 1854 by the New England Emigrant Aid Company. The political center of the Free Staters, it was actually, though not legally, capital for a short time after 1857. Lawrence was an important stop on the Underground Railroad and the base for many Abolitionist organizations. In 1856 a proslavery raid on the town instigated the retaliatory Pottawatamie killings by John Brown. In 1863 the town was again sacked and burned by William Quantrill. The Plymouth Congregational Church here was the 1st church built (1854) by settlers in Kansas. Clinton L. reservoir and Clinton State Park to W. The Haskell Indian Community Col. (1884), a large school for Native Americans, is here. Natural History Mus., Spencer Art Mus. here. Lawrence Municipal Airport to NE. Inc. 1858. **3** city (□ 7 sq mi/18.1 sq km; 1990 pop. 70,207), ⊙ Essex co., NE Mass., on the Merrimack R.; 42°42′N 71°10′W. It is a port of entry. Textiles, clothing, electrical equip., athletic shoes, and rubber and paper prods. are manufactured. High-technology industries in the area also contribute to Lawrence's economy. Boston capitalists laid out an industrial town here in 1845 and built a granite dam on the Merrimack R. They also built mills and workers' dwellings, which were soon crowded with laborers, mainly from Europe, and Lawrence became one of the world's greatest centers for woolen textiles. By 1911 it was known as the "cloth-making capital of the world" (it was the hq. for American Woolen Company, among others). Several disastrous events have occurred here—the collapse and burning of the Pemberton Mill in 1860, when over 500 trapped workers were killed or injured; the tornado of 1890; and the protracted labor strike by members of the Internatl. Workers of the World in 1912. Leonard Bernstein was b. here. Has a community col. Heritage State Park. Settled 1655, set off from Andover and Methuen 1847, inc. as a city 1853.

Lawrence, uninc. town (1990 pop. 800), Peters township, Washington co., SW Pa., suburb 11 mi/18 km SSW of Pittsburgh, 12 mi/19 km NE of Washington, on Chartiers Creek; 40°18′N 80°07′W. Mfg. (machinery, data communications equip., commercial printing). Also known as Lawrence Hills.

Lawrence 1 village (1990 pop. 915), Van Buren co., SW Mich., 8 mi/12.9 km W of Paw Paw, on Paw Paw R., in fertile area; 42°13′N 86°02′W. Agr. (vegetables, fruit; hogs, poultry); mfg. (food processing, walk-in coolers and freezers, canned and frozen fruits and vegetables, electroplating, molded plastic prods.). **2** village (1990 pop. 323), Nuckolls co., S Nebr., 12 mi/19 km NW of Nelson; 40°17′N 98°15′W. Dairying; grain; livestock. **3** affluent residential village (□ 4 sq mi/10.4 sq km; 1990 pop. 6,513), Nassau co., SE N.Y., one of "5 Towns of Long Island," on S shore of W L.I., 9 mi/14.5 km SE of Jamaica; 40°36′N 73°42′W. A few light industries (machine parts, canvas). In resort area. Inc. 1897.

Lawrence, township (1990 pop. 25,787), Mercer co., central N.J., 6 mi/9.7 km N of Trenton; 40°17′N 74°43′W. Inc. 1798.

Lawrence, Cape, NE Ellesmere Isl., NE Franklin dist., N.W.T., Canada, on Kennedy Channel; 80°21′N 69°15′W.

Lawrence Hills, Pa.: see LAWRENCE.

Lawrence Park, township (1990 pop. 4,310), Erie co., NW Pa., residential suburb 3 mi/4.8 km ENE of Erie, on L. Erie; 42°08′N 80°01′W.

Lawrenceburg 1 city (1990 pop. 4,375), ⊙ Dearborn co., SE Ind., on Ohio R., 50 mi/80 km S of Richmond; 39°06′N 84°52′W. In agr. area; mfg. (whiskey, feed, machinery, lumber). Port of entry. Prehistoric fortifications found near here. Laid out 1802. Inundated by flood in 1937. **2** city (1990 pop. 10,412), ⊙ Lawrence co., S Tenn., on Shoal Creek (source of hydroelectric power), 32 mi/51 km SSW of Columbia; 35°14′N 87°20′W. In timber, livestock-raising, dairying, cotton-growing area; lumber milling; clothing, motor vehicle parts, bicycles, lawnmowers. Founded c.1815. David Crockett State Park is just W.

Lawrenceburg, town (1990 pop. 5,911), ⊙ Anderson co., central Ky., 22 mi/35 km W of Lexington; 38°01′N 84°53′W. Trade center in Bluegrass agr. region (dairying; poultry, horses; burley tobacco, corn, hay); mfg. (paper prods., motor vehicle parts, communications equip., distilled whiskey, crushed limestone, computer equip.). Buckley Hills Wildlife Sanctuary to N; Beaver L. reservoir 10 mi/16 km to SW. Settled 1776; inc. 1820.

Lawrencetown, village, W N.S., Canada, on Annapolis R., 20 mi/32 km NE of Annapolis Royal. Apple packing, barrel mfg.; fishing, hunting center.

Lawrenceville, village (1991 pop. 612), SW Que., Canada, 19 mi/31 km E of Granby. Dairying, lumbering, woodworking.

Lawrenceville 1 city (1990 pop. 16,848), ⊙ Gwinnett co., N central Ga., 26 mi/42 km ENE of Atlanta; 33°57′N 83°59′W. Suburb of Atlanta. Diversified economy with business and industrial parks. Mfg. of displays, industrial machinery, consumer goods, paper prods., printing and publishing, foods, plastics. New municipal govt. center opened in mid-1990s. Inc. 1821. **2** city (1990 pop. 4,897), ⊙ Lawrence co., SE Ill., on Embarras R. near the Wabash, 8 mi/12.9 km WNW of Vincennes (Ind.); 38°43′N 87°41′W. In oil, natural gas, and agr. area. Oil refineries; mfg. (metal industries, electronic components). Livestock; soybeans, corn, wheat. Oil was discovered here in 1906. Founded 1821, inc. 1835.

Lawrenceville, town (1990 pop. 1,486), ⊙ Brunswick co., S Va., on Great Creek, near Meherrin R., 40 mi/64 km SW of Petersburg; 36°45′N 77°50′W. Mfg. (clothing, motors, wood prods., furniture, textiles, plastic and metal prods., lumber); in agr. area (tobacco, grain, cotton, peanuts; livestock; dairying). St. Paul's Col.; Southside Va. Community Col. (Christiana campus) to NW at Cochran. Founded 1814; inc. 1874.

Lawrenceville 1 village (1990 pop. 6,446), Mercer co., W N.J., 5 mi/8 km NNE of Trenton; 40°17′N 74°43′W. Turbine mfg. Lawrenceville School for Boys (1810) and Rider Univ. are located here. Largely residential. Settled 1692. **2** village (1990 pop. 304), Clark co., W central Ohio, 5 mi/8 km NNW of Springfield; 39°59′N 83°52′W.

Lawrenceville, borough (1990 pop. 481), Tioga co., N Pa., 13 mi/21 km N of Mansfield, 17 mi/27 km WSW of Elmira, at N.Y. state line, on Tioga R. Agr. (dairying).

Lawson, city (1990 pop. 1,876), Ray and Clay cos., NW Mo., 16 mi/26 km NW of Richmond; 39°26′N 94°12′W. Corn, soybeans; hogs, cattle.

Lawson Army Airfield, airport for Fort Benning located on the Fort Benning Military Reservation, Ga. Built on site of Cusseta Town, which was the capital of the Lower Creek Nation before its removal. Floodplain of Chattahoochee R.

Lawson Heights, uninc. town (1990 pop. 2,464), Westmoreland co., SW Pa., residential suburb 2 mi/3.2 km SSW of Latrobe; 40°17′N 79°23′W. Agr. includes dairying. St. Vincent Col. to W.

Lawsonia (law-SO-nee-uh), village (1990 pop. 1,326), Somerset co., SE Md., on the Eastern Shore near Tangier Sound, 31 mi/50 km SSW of Salisbury; 37°58′N 75°50′W. Nearby is Pocomoke Sound Wildlife Management Area.

Lawton, city (1990 pop. 80,561), ⊙ Comanche co., SW Okla., 72 mi/116 km SW of Oklahoma City; drained by Cache Creek; 34°36′N 98°25′W. Elev. 1,117 ft/340 m. It is a commercial and trade center for the surrounding cotton, wheat, and cattle area and for Fort Sill, a military reservation to N. The fort is the largest local civilian employer; 25 mi/40 km long (E-W), and c.5 mi/8 km wide, it is practically a twin city to Lawton. Mfg. (machining, bakery prods., meat, rubber prods., apparel, fabricated steel, publishing and printing, concrete). Cameron Univ. is in the city. Comanche Tribal Hq.; Mus. of the Great Plains; Fort Sill Mus. at Fort Sill; co. fairgrounds. Nearby is a large limestone quarry and the Wichita Mts. Wildlife Refuge to NW. Inc. 1901.

Lawton 1 town (1990 pop. 482), Woodbury co., W Iowa, 11 mi/18 km E of Sioux City; 42°28′N 96°10′W. In agr. area, with mfg. of construction equip. and nylon rope. **2** town (1990 pop. 1,685), Van Buren co., SW Mich., 16 mi/26 km SW of Kalamazoo; 42°10′N 85°50′W. In area of vineyards and small lakes (to S). Mfg. (vegetables and fruit canning, food processing, juices and jellies, tools, foundry prods.).

Lawton, village (1990 pop. 63), Ramsey co., NE N.Dak., 27 mi/43 km NE of Devils L.; 48°17′N 98°22′W.

Lawtonka, Lake, reservoir, Comanche co., SW Okla., on branch of Cache Creek, at edge of Wichita Mts., 12 mi/19 km NW of Lawton; 5 mi/8 km long; 34°44′N 98°30′W. Formed by dam built for water supply. Fort Sill Military Reservation just S.

Lay Lake, on border of Chilton and Coosa cos., central Ala., in Coosa R., 41 mi/66 km NNW of Montgomery; c.4.8 mi/77 km long; 32°57′N 86°31′W. Extends NNE into Talladega and Shelby cos. to Logan Martin Dam. Formed by Lay Dam (104 ft/32 m high, 1,603 ft/489 m long), a privately built power dam completed 1914; crossed by road.

Laymantown, uninc. town, Botetourt co., W central Va., 9 mi/14.5 km NE of Roanoke; 37°22′N 79°51′W. George Washington Natl. Forest, Appalachian Trail to N.

Layou, town (1989 est. pop. 6,381), W St. Vincent, West Indies, on Mt. Wynn Bay, 4 mi/6.4 km NW of Kingstown; 13°12′N 61°16′W. Cotton, arrowroot; fishing.

Layou River (luh-YOO), c.10 mi/16 km long, W central Dominica, B.W.I., flows W, through Layou Plateau, to the coast.

Laysan (lai-SAHN), island, N Pacific, part of Honolulu co., Hawaii, c.890 mi/1,432 km NW of Honolulu, c.160 mi/257 km N of Tropic of Cancer, 25°46′N 171°44′W. Coral with hypersaline lagoon; known for its large bird pop. (rookery for albatross, frigate birds, gulls). Annexed 1857 by Hawaiian kingdom; now U.S. possession. Part of Hawaiian Isls. Natl. Wildlife Refuge.

Layton, city (1990 pop. 41,784), Davis co., N Utah, suburb 9 mi/14.5 km S of Ogden and 21 mi/34 km N of Salt Lake City, near Great Salt L.; 41°04′N 111°57′W. Elev. 4,400 ft/1,341 m. In an irrigated farm area served by the Weber basin project. Drained by Holmes and Hobbs creeks. Fruits and vegetables; dairying; cattle, sheep; mfg. (bakery goods, dairy prods., computer software). Causeway leads to Antelope Isl. State Park, in Great Salt L., to W. During the 1970s and 1980s the city profited from the prosperous commercial and financial activities of nearby Salt Lake City. Housing developments, business offices, and light mfg. plants were constructed in Layton to accommodate its increased growth and industry. Hill Air Force Base, with 17,000 workers, is Utah's largest employer. Wasatch Range and Natl. Forest to E; Hill Air Force Base to N. Layton Heritage Mus.

Laytonsville, town (1990 pop. 248), Montgomery co., central Md., 23 mi/37 km NNW of Washington, D.C.; 39°13′N 77°08′W. The 1st house here was believed to have been built by John Layton. For one year, 1848, it was called Cracklintown in honor of a nearby tavern where cracklin' bread was made.

Laytonville, uninc. town (1990 pop. 1,133), Mendocino co., NW Calif., 38 mi/61 km NNW of Ukiah, in Coast Ranges; 39°40′N 123°30′W. Laytonville Indian Reservation to W; Roud Valley Ind. Reservation to NE. Fruit; cattle; nursery stock; timber.

Lázaro Cárdenas, Mexico: see SANCTÓRUM.

Le Cap, Haiti: see CAP-HAÏTIEN.

Le Center, town (1990 pop. 2,006), ⊙ Le Sueur co., S Minn., 20 mi/32 km NE of Mankato, near Le Sueur Creek; 44°23′N 93°43′W. Elev. 1,066 ft/325 m. Agr. area (corn, oats, peas, alfalfa; livestock; dairying); mfg. (bldg. materials, fiberglass prods., plastics, machinery). Co. fairgrounds. Settled 1864, inc. 1876. Known as Le Sueur Center until 1931.

Le Claire, town (1990 pop. 2,734), Scott co., E Iowa, on outer Mississippi R., suburb 12 mi/19 km ENE of Davenport; 41°36′N 90°21′W. Mfg. (metal, wood and limestone prods.). Lock and Dam No. 14 is immediately downstream; Buffalo Bill Mus. here. Spring flooding occurred in 1993.

Le Conte, Mount (luh-KAWNT) (6,593 ft/2,010 m), in Great Smoky Mts., Sevier co., E Tenn., 6 mi/10 km SE of Gatlinburg. Tourist lodge, campsite here.

Le Droit Park, small, historic residential section in NW Washington, D.C., SE of Howard Univ.; 38°55′N 77°01′W. Many fine homes were built, beginning in 1873. By 1900, the area had become one of Washington's 1st "suburban" developments open to Afr.-Amer. residents.

Le Flore (luh FLOR), county (□ 1,608 sq mi/4,165 sq km; 1990 pop. 43,270), SE Okla.; ⊙ Poteau; 34°53′N 94°42′W. Bounded N by Arkansas R., E by Ark. state line; drained by Poteau and Kiamichi rivers; in Ouachita Mts. Agr. (corn, fruit, vegetables, hay, soybeans, potatoes; cattle, poultry); oil and natural gas wells; timber. Part of Ouachita Natl. Forest is in co., mostly in S half. Kiamichi Mts. (extension of Ouachitas) in S; Spiro Mounds in N. Heavener-Runestone State Park in E; L. Wister State Park at center; Talimena State Park in W. Robert S. Kerr Lock and Dam on Arkansas R. in NW corner. Formed 1907.

Le Flore, village (1990 pop. 119), Le Flore co., E Okla., 20 mi/32 km WSW of Poteau, near Fourche Maline Creek; 34°53′N 94°58′W. Agr. and timber area. Ouachita Natl. Forest to SE.

Le Grand 1 uninc. town (1990 pop. 1,205), Merced co., central Calif., 12 mi/19 km ESE of Merced; 37°13′N 120°16′W. Cattle, poultry; dairying; alfalfa, grain, sugar beets, tomatoes, melons, almonds. **2** town (1990 pop. 854), Marshall co., central Iowa, near Iowa R., 7 mi/11.3 km ESE of Marshalltown; 42°00′N 92°46′W. Concrete, asphalt. Limestone quarries nearby.

Le Mars, city (1990 pop. 8,454), ⊙ Plymouth co., NW Iowa, on Floyd R., 23 mi/37 km NNE of Sioux City; 42°47′N 96°10′W. RR junction; agr.-trade and mfg. center; dairy prods., apparel, detergents, printing, rendering plant, meat processing; grain mill (cereals, feed), creameries; cement work. Sand and gravel pits nearby. Westmar Col. (est. 1890) and historical mus. are here. Founded in late 1870s; inc. 1881.

Le Raysville (LUH RAIS-vil), borough (1990 pop. 336), Bradford co., NE Pa., 14 mi/23 km ENE of Towanda. Agr. (dairying).

Le Roy, city (1990 pop. 2,777), McLean co., central Ill., 14 mi/23 km SE of Bloomington; 40°20′N 88°45′W. Trade and processing center in rich agr. area; food processing. Near Moraine View State Park. Inc. 1857.

Le Roy 1 town (1990 pop. 34), Decatur co., S Iowa, 13 mi/21 km NE of Leon; 40°52′N 93°35′W. In livestock area. **2** town (1990 pop. 904), Mower co., SE Minn., on Upper Iowa R., near Iowa state line, 26 mi/42 km ESE of Austin; 43°30′N 92°30′W. Corn, oats, soybeans, alfalfa, peas; cattle, sheep, hogs, poultry; dairying; mfg. (feeds, fertilizers, electrical equip., furniture). Limestone deposits nearby. L. Louise State Park to NE.

Le Roy 1 village (1990 pop. 568), Coffey co., E Kansas, on Neosho R., 9 mi/14.5 km SE of Burlington; 38°05′N 95°37′W. In grain area. Mfg. (fabricated metal prods., meat, eggs). **2** village (1990 pop. 251), Osceola co., central Mich., 14 mi/23 km S of Cadillac; 44°02′N 85°27′W. In stock-raising area. Mfg. (hardwood lumber, machining); lake resorts. **3** village (□ 2 sq mi/5.2 sq km; 1990 pop. 4,974), Genesee co., W N.Y., 10 mi/16 km E of Batavia; 42°58′N 77°59′W. Mfg. of porcelain and polymer insulators, motor vehicle parts, dairy prods., office supplies, machinery; canning. In rich agr. area (poultry; fruit). In 1897, Pearl Bixby Wait, a local carpenter, perfected the formula for Jello gelatin dessert, then sold it for $450. Until 1964, General Foods had a plant that produced Jello in the village. Jello Mus. is housed in Le Roy Historical Society Bldg. Settled 1793, inc. 1834.

Le Sueur (luh SOOR), county (□ 473 sq mi/1,225 sq km; 1990 pop. 23,239), S Minn.; ⊙ Le Center; 44°22′N 93°43′W. Bordered W by Minnesota R. Agr. area (soybeans, alfalfa, peas; sheep, hogs, cattle, poultry; dairying); silica, sand, marble, limestone. Part of Sakatah L. State Park in SE corner; numerous small lakes in co., especially in S and E. Formed 1853.

Le Sueur (luh SOOR), town (1990 pop. 3,714), Le Sueur co., S Minn., 20 mi/32 km N of Mankato, on Minnesota R. at mouth of Le Sueur Creek; 44°27′N 93°54′W. Grain, soybeans, peas; livestock; dairying; mfg. (whey and dairy prods., baked goods, frozen food and beverages, greeting cards, injection molding, printing and publishing). Municipal Airport to S. Home of W.W. Mayo, founder of Mayo Clinic in Rochester (built 1859). Settled 1852.

Le Sueur Center, Minn.: see LE CENTER.

Le Sueur River (luh SOOR), 80 mi/129 km long, S Minn.; rises in N Freeborn co., c.9 mi/14.5 km NNW of Albert Lea; 43°46′N 93°28′W. Flows N and W, in very serpentine course, passes NE of New Richland and SW of Waseca, past St. Clair, receives Big Cobb and Maple rivers S of Mankato, enters Blue Earth R. 4 mi/6.4 km SW of Mankato and 3 mi/4.8 km S of its confluence with Minnesota R.

Lea (LEE), county (□ 4,394 sq mi/11,380 sq km; 1990 pop. 55,765), extreme SE N.Mex., in Llano Estacado; ⊙ Lovington; 32°47′N 103°25′W. Cattle, sheep; dairying; chiles, corn, sorghum, hay, alfalfa, melons, peas, spinach, pecans, peanuts, cotton, wheat, oats, barley, millet, rye. Bounded S and E by Texas (Central-Mountain time zone boundary on both sides; N.Mex. in Mountain time zone). Petroleum, natural-gas fields. Harry McAdams State Park in E corner, at Hobbs. Formed 1917.

Leachville, town (1990 pop. 1,743), Mississippi co., NE Ark., 20 mi/32 km W of Blytheville, near Mo. state line; 35°55′N 90°15′W. In cotton, rice, and soybean area. Mfg. (consumer goods, printing).

Leacock (LEE-kahk), uninc. town (1990 pop. 3,685), Lancaster co., SE Pa., residential suburb 5 mi/8 km NE of Lancaster; 40°05′N 76°12′W.

Lead, town (1990 pop. 3,632), Lawrence co., W S.Dak., 30 mi/48 km NW of Rapid City, in the Black Hills. It is the site of the famous Homestake Mine to E, which has been in operation since 1877. Tourism, gold and silver mining; surface tours; RR terminus. Deer Mt. and Terry Peak ski areas to W. Laid out 1876 after the discovery of gold here, inc. 1890.

Lead Hill, village (1990 pop. 283), Boone co., N Ark., 17 mi/27 km NE of Harrison, in the Ozarks, near Mo. state line; at base of peninsula of Bull Shoals L. reservoir (White R.) to N; 36°24′N 92°54′W.

Leadbetter Island (LED-be-tuhr), Knox co., S Maine, in Penobscot Bay just W of Vinalhaven Isl.; 1 mi/1.6 km long, ½ mi/⅘ km wide.

Leader (LEE-duhr), town (1991 pop. 999), SW Sask., Canada, 45 mi/72 km SSW of Kindersley; 50°53′N 109°33′W. RR junction; grain elevators, flour mills.

Leadore, village (1990 pop. 74), Lemhi co., E Idaho, on Lemhi R., 45 mi/72 km SSE of Salmon, on Lemhi R.; 44°41′N 113°22′W. Sheep, cattle; alfalfa; oats. Salmon Natl. Forest to NE and SW.

Leadville, town (1990 pop. 2,629), ⊙ Lake co., central Colo., near the headwaters of the Arkansas R., in the Rocky Mts.; 39°15′N 106°17′W. Elev. c.10,152 ft/3,094 m. Some mining and smelting are still carried on (at nearby Climax to NE huge deposits of molybdenum are mined), and farming, ranching, and the tourist trade have kept this famous city from becoming another ghost town. Rich placer gold deposits were discovered c.1860 in California Gulch. Oro City, the principal camp, flourished for about 2 years. The camps were virtually deserted until 1877, when the discovery of carbonates of lead with a high silver content again transformed Oro City into a boomtown. By 1880, 2 years after its incorporation, Leadville had become one of the greatest silver camps in the world. In 1893, with the repeal of the Sherman Silver Act, silver mining collapsed; but in the late 1890s, with the discovery of gold nearby, Leadville again revived. The spectacular history of Leadville is epitomized in the life of Horace Tabor. Points of interest include the restored Tabor home; the Matchless Mine, now a mus.; and the Healy House–Dexter Cabin Mus. Turquoise L. reservoir to W, parts of San Isabel Natl. Forest to N, W, and S. Pike Natl. Forest to E (beyond co. line), Leadville Natl. Fish Hatchery to W. Inc. 1878.

Leadwood (LED-wud), village (1990 pop. 1,247), St. Francois co., E Mo., in St. Francois Mts., 3 mi/4.8 km W of Park Hills; 37°51′N 90°35′W. Former mining town, primarily residential; sand and gravel.

Leaf Rapids, town (1986 pop. 1,950), Man., Canada, 1.9 mi/3.1 km S of Churchill R., 606 mi/975 km NW of Winnipeg. Copper-mine community; inc. 1974.

Leaf River, village (1990 pop. 546), Ogle co., N Ill., on Leaf R. and 6 mi/9.7 km NW of Oregon; 42°07′N 89°24′W. In rich agr. area.

Leaf River, 300 mi/483 km long, N Que., Canada; issues from L. Minto; flows NE, through tidal Leaf L. (30 mi/48 km long, 15 mi/24 km wide), to Ungava Bay 65 mi/105 km NNW of Fort Chimo.

Leaf River 1 c.25 mi/40 km long, N Ill.; rises S of Freeport; flows generally SE to Rock R. N of Oregon; 42°08′N 89°41′W. **2** 50 mi/80 km long, in W and W central Minn.; rises in E central Otter Tail co., in Ground L., SE of Otter Tail L.; 46°24′N 95°25′W. Flows E, through West and East Leaf lakes, past Bluffton and to N of Wadena, to Crow Wing R. 10 mi/16 km NNW of Staples. **3** c.180 mi/290 km long, in S central and SE Miss.; rises in Scott co.; flows S past Taylorsville and Hattiesburg, then SE past Beaumont and McLain, joining Chickasawhay R. to form Pascagoula R. in N George co.

League City, city (1990 pop. 30,159), Galveston co., SE Texas, suburb 13 mi/21 km NW of Texas City and 21 mi/34 km SE of Houston; 29°29′N 95°06′W. Near Galveston Bay, bounded by Clear L. (NE) and Clear Creek (N). The aeronautics industry is of prime importance to the area; the Lyndon B. Johnson Space Center is to N. Diversified light mfg. Inc. 1961.

Leake (LEEK), county (□ 585 sq mi/1,515 sq km; 1990 pop. 18,436), central Miss.; ⊙ Carthage; 32°45′N 89°31′W. Drained by Pearl and Yockanookany rivers and Lobutcha Creek. Includes 2 small Native Amer. reservations in center and SE (Choctaw). Agr. (cotton, corn; poultry, cattle; dairying); timber. Natchez Trace (Natl.) Parkway passes through NW. Formed 1833.

Leakesville (LEEKS-vil), town (1990 pop. 1,129), ⊙ Greene co.; 31°08′N 88°33′W, SE Miss., 45 mi/72 km ESE of Hattiesburg and on Chickasawhay R. Agr. (cotton, corn; cattle, poultry); timber; mfg. (lumber, wood processing). Parts of De Soto Natl. Forest to NW and SW.

Leakey, village (1990 pop. 399), ⊙ Real co., SW Texas, 36 mi/58 km N of Uvalde and on Frio R.; 29°43′N 99°45′W. Elev. 1,609 ft/490 m. In ranching area (goats, sheep, cattle). The scenic Frio Canyon is here. Cedar timber; mfg. (cedar wood oil, perfume). Lost Maples State Park to E.

Leaksville, town, Rockingham co., N N.C., 11 mi/18 km NNW of Reidsville, on Dan R. Merged with Spray (1 mi/1.6 km to NE) in the late 1960s to form city of Eden.

Leal, village (1990 pop. 35), Barnes co., E central N.Dak., 20 mi/32 km NW of Valley City; 47°06′N 98°18′W.

Lealman (LEEL-muhn), city (☐ 5 sq mi/13 sq km; 1990 pop. 21,748), W central Fla., Pinellas co., 3 mi/4.8 km N of St. Petersburg; 27°49′N 82°41′W.

Leamington (LEE-ming-tuhn), town (1991 pop. 14,182), S Ont., Canada, on L. Erie; 42°03′N 82°35′W. In a market-gardening area, it has large food-processing plants. Gateway to Point Pelée Natl. Park.

Leamington, village (1990 pop. 253), Millard co., W central Utah, 20 mi/32 km NE of Delta, on Sevier R.; 39°31′N 112°17′W. Irrigated agr. area. White Sand Dunes and Little Sahara Recreation Area to NW; Fishlake Natl. Forest to SE. Fool Creek reservoir to SW.

Leander, town (1990 pop. 3,398), Williamson co., central Texas, 22 mi/35 km NNW of Austin; 30°33′N 97°51′W. In agr. area (cotton, corn, wheat; cattle); limestone quarries; mfg. (concrete, plumbing equip., power supplies).

Learned (LUHR-ned), village (1990 pop. 111), Hinds co., W Miss., 22 mi/35 km WSW of Jackson; 32°12′N 90°32′W. Agr. and timber area. Natchez Trace (Natl.) Parkway passes to NW.

Leary, town (1990 pop. 701), Calhoun co., SW Ga., 20 mi/32 km WSW of Albany; 31°29′N 84°31′W.

Leary, village (1990 pop. 395), Bowie co., NE Texas, 8 mi/12.9 km W of Texarkana; 33°28′N 94°12′W. Agr. area. Oil and natural gas.

Leasburg, town (1990 pop. 289), Crawford co., E central Mo., in the Ozarks, near Meramec R., 9 mi/14.5 km N of Steelville; 38°05′N 91°17′W. Elev. 1,024 ft/312 m. Onondaga Cave State Park to SE.

Leask (leesk), village (1991 pop. 442), central Sask., Canada, 40 mi/64 km WSW of Prince Albert. Farming, dairying.

Leatherman Peak, Idaho: see LOST RIVER RANGE.

Leaton, Fort, Texas: see PRESIDIO, co. and town.

Leavenworth (LEV-uhn-wuhrth), county (☐ 468 sq mi/1,212 sq km; 1990 pop. 64,371), NE Kansas; ⊙ Leavenworth; 39°12′N 95°02′W. Gently rolling to hilly area, bounded E by Missouri R. and Mo., S by Kansas R. Wheat, sorghum, soybeans, hay, vegetables, apples; cattle, hogs, poultry; dairying; paper prods., industrial machinery. Oil. Formed 1855.

Leavenworth (LEV-uhn-wuhrth), city (1990 pop. 38,495), ⊙ Leavenworth co., NE Kansas, on the Missouri R. Satellite community of Kansas City, Kansas; 39°19′N 94°55′W. RR junction. It is the commercial center of a farm and livestock region, with flour mills and plants that make automobile batteries, machinery, furniture, and metal prods. Nearby Fort Leavenworth, with its various institutions (including U.S. Army Command and General Staff College and the federal penitentiary, which is located on the grounds although operated by the Justice Dept.), is central to the city's economy. St. Mary Col. is nearby. Leavenworth is the oldest city in Kansas and was the 1st city in the state to be incorporated. It was settled (1854) near the fort by proslavery Missourians, but later became a Union supporter during the Civil War. It also flourished as a supply point on westward travel routes. The state's 1st newspaper was printed here in 1854. Flooding occurred in the area in 1993. Inc. 1855.

Leavenworth 1 town (1990 pop. 320), Crawford co., S Ind., near Ohio R., 11 mi/18 km SSE of English; 38°12′N 86°21′W. In agr. area. Mfg. (crushed stone). Moved (1937–1938) to higher ground from flood-ravaged former site on Ohio R. Harrison-Crawford State Forest and Wyandotte Cave nearby to E. **2** town (1990 pop. 1,692), Chelan co., central Wash., 20 mi/32 km NW of Wenatchee and on Wenatchee R., near mouth of Icicle Creek; 47°35′N 120°40′W. Apples, pears; timber; mfg. (fishing lures). Camping, fishing; winter sports; Leavenworth Ski Area to N. Stevens Pass (4,061 ft/1,238 m), U.S. Highway 2, and Cascade RR Tunnel (8 mi/12.9 km long) through crest of Cascade Range 20 mi/32 km to NW. Surrounded, except NE, by Wenatchee Natl. Forest, including Alpine Lakes Wilderness Area to W. L. Wenatchee reservoir and State Park to N. Inc. 1906.

Leavenworth, Fort, Kansas: see FORT LEAVENWORTH.

Leavitt Peak (11,569 ft/3,526 m), Thuolumne/Mono co line, E Calif., in the Sierra Nevada, 32 mi/51 km NW of Mono L.

Leavittsburg (LE-vits-buhrg), village, Trumbull co., NE Ohio, 3 mi/5 km W of Warren and on Mahoning R.

Leawood (LEE-wud), city (1990 pop. 19,693), Johnson co., NE Kansas, suburb 8 mi/12.9 km S of Kansas City; 38°54′N 94°37′W. It is an agr.-trading and -processing point that has undergone major suburban development as an outgrowth of Kansas City. Business offices and light mfg. are located here. Mfg. (meat prods.). State Line Airport in S. Borders Mo. on E. Inc. 1948.

Lebanon, county (☐ 362 sq mi/938 sq km; 1990 pop. 113,744), SE central Pa.; ⊙ Lebanon. Drained by Swatara Creek. Agr. (corn, wheat, oats, barley, hay, alfalfa, soybeans; sheep, hogs, cattle, chickens, eggs, dairying) area; limestone. Mfg. at Lebanon, Myerstown, and Palmyra. Stiegel glassware made here in 18th cent. Indiantown Gap Military Reservation in NW, 10 mi/16 km NW of Lebanon, est. 1935. Appalachian Trail passes through N part of co., on stony and Blue Mt. ridges; Swatara State Park in N; Lebanon Valley in S; part of Middle Creek Waterfowl Management Area in SE. Settled c.1710 by Germans; formed 1813.

Lebanon 1 (LE-buh-nuhn), city (1990 pop. 3,688), St. Clair co., SW Ill., suburb of St. Louis, near Silver Creek, 12 mi/19 km NE of Belleville; 38°36′N 89°48′W. In agr. area (wheat, soybeans; hogs, poultry; dairy prods.). Seat of McKendree Col. Main Street has 19th cent. bldgs. with shops, taverns, restaurants; an old inn (1830) is here. Scott Air Base to SW. Settled in early 19th cent.; inc. 1857. **2** city (1990 pop. 12,059), ⊙ Boone co., central Ind., 25 mi/40 km NW of Indianapolis; 40°03′N 86°28′W. In dairying and farming area; mfg. (machinery, electrical equip., animal feed, plastics, paper prods., asphalt, frozen foods). Laid out 1832. **3** city (1990 pop. 9,983), ⊙ Laclede co., S central Mo., in the Ozarks, 47 mi/76 km NE of Springfield; 37°40′N 92°39′W. Shipping center for grain and dairy prods.; major service center on I-44. Mfg. (wood prods., machinery, fabricated metal prods., electrical equip., apparel, electric motors, food-processing plants). Bennett Spring State Park to W (Dallas co.). Founded c. 1849. **4** city (1990 pop. 12,183), Grafton co., W N.H., 43 mi/69 km NW of Concord; 43°38′N 72°15′W. Bounded W by Connecticut R. (Vt. state line), drained by Mascoma R. Includes village of West Lebanon. Mfg. (machinery, software, structural steel prods., printing and publishing, consumer goods); soapstone quarrying; agr. (nursery crops, apples, vegetables; cattle, poultry; dairying). RR junction at West Lebanon. Part of Moose Mts. in NE. Founded 1761. **5** city (1990 pop. 10,453), ⊙ Warren co., SW Ohio, 28 mi/45 km NE of Cincinnati and on small Turtle Creek; 39°25′N 84°13′W. Nearby is Fort Anc. State Memorial Park. Laid out 1802. **6** city (1990 pop. 10,950), Linn co., W Oregon, on South Santiam R., 12 mi/19 km SE of Albany; 44°31′N 122°54′W. RR junction. Fruits, grains; dairy prods. Lumber milling. Fish hatchery to NE. Foster Reservoir, with fish hatchery and Green Peter Reservoir, to SE. Site of Lebanon Strawberry Festival. Inc. 1878. **7** city (1990 pop. 24,800), ⊙ Lebanon co., SE Pa., 28 mi/45 km E of Harrisburg, on Quittapahilla Creek, in Pa. Dutch farm country; 40°20′N 76°24′W. RR junction. Mfg. (consumer goods, fabricated metal prods., lumber, commercial printing, apparel, machinery, tools, machinery, textiles, fertilizers, wood prods., food, plastic prods.). It has steel and steel-fabricating industries, although the industry declined significantly in the 1970s and 1980s. Agr. (grain, soybeans, apples; livestock; dairying). Lebanon was a flourishing town before 1790, and early 18th-cent. Ger. religious groups are still represented here. Lebanon Valley Airport to E. The city has a historical mus., Lebanon Historical Society, Stoy Mus., and horse shows. Also in the area are the Cornwall Furnace (operated 1742–1883) and the Union Canal tunnel, a civil engineering landmark. Swatara State Park and Appalachian Trail to N; Fort Indiantown Military Reservation and Memorial L. State Park to NW. Founded 1753, inc. as a city 1868. **8** city (1990 pop. 15,208), ⊙ Wilson co., N central Tenn., 28 mi/45 km E of Nashville; 36°12′N 86°18′W. In timber, tobacco, livestock area; mfg. of luggage, consumer goods, footwear, textiles, concrete, metal, plastic, wood, and marble prods. Seat of Cumberland Univ. and a community col. Sam Houston practiced law here. Fine antebellum homes nearby include the Hermitage. Cedars of Lebanon state park and forest are in the extensive cedar glades. Founded c.1802.

Lebanon 1 (LE-buh-nuhn), town (1990 pop. 6,041), New London co., E central Conn., 11 mi/18 km NW of Norwich; 41°37′N 72°14′W. Egg production and farming. Revolutionary War Office (1727), Gov. Trumbull house (1740; now historical mus.), other 18th-cent. houses here. Inc. 1700. **2** town (1990 pop. 5,695), ⊙ Marion co., central Ky., 28 mi/45 km WSW of Danville, in outer Bluegrass region; 37°34′N 85°15′W. Agr. (burley tobacco, grain; dairying); mfg. (textiles, wood prods., fabricated metal prods., metal fabrication, bldg. materials, paper prods., printing and publishing). Springfield-Lebanon Airport to N. Lebanon Natl. Cemetery is here; St. Mary's Col. to W at St. Mary. Est. 1815. **3** town (1990 pop. 4,263), York co., SW Maine, near Salmon Falls R., 9 mi/14.5 km SW of Alfred; 43°23′N 70°54′W. Settled 1738, inc. 1767. **4** town (1990 pop. 3,386), ⊙ Russell co., SW Va., 22 mi/35 km NNE of Bristol, on Little Cedar Creek; 36°53′N 82°04′W. Mfg. (bldg. materials, apparel, motor vehicle parts); agr. (corn, soybeans; livestock; dairying); timber.

Lebanon 1 (LE-buh-nuhn), village (1990 pop. 364), Smith co., N Kansas, 12 mi/19 km ENE of Smith Center; 39°48′N 98°33′W. Corn; livestock. Geographic center (39°50′N 98°35′W) of the continental U.S. is 2 mi/3.2 km NW of here. **2** village (1990 pop. 75), Red Willow co., S Nebr., 20 mi/32 km SE of McCook, on Beaver Creek, near Kansas state line; 40°02′N 100°16′W. **3** village (1990 pop. 115), Potter co., N central S.Dak., 10 mi/16 km ENE of Gettysburg; 45°04′N 99°46′W.

Lebanon (LE-buh-nuhn), borough (1990 pop. 1,036), Hunterdon co., W N.J., 9 mi/14.5 km N of Flemington; 40°38′N 74°50′W. Agr. area; machinery mfg.

Lebanon Junction (LE-buh-nuhn), town (1990 pop. 1,741), Bullitt co., central Ky., near Rolling Fork, 11 mi/18 km S of Shepherdsville; 37°49′N 85°43′W. In agr. area (burley tobacco, grain; livestock; dairying); mfg. (machinery, printing and publishing). Fort Knox Military Reservation to NW.

Lebanon Valley, Pa.: see LEBANON, co.

Lebec, uninc. village, Kern co., S central Calif., in Tehachapi Mts., 37 mi/60 km S of Bakersfield. Oil refining. Cattle; dairying; grain. Los Padres Natl. Forest to SW; Site of Fort Tejon State Historical Park; Tejon Pass to S.

Lebo (LEE-bo), village (1990 pop. 835), Coffey co., E Kansas, 16 mi/26 km NNW of Burlington; 38°24′N 95°51′W. In livestock and grain region.

Lebret (luh-BRET), village (1991 pop. 201), SE Sask., Canada, on the Fishing Lakes, 16 mi/26 km N of Indian Head. Mixed farming, fishing.

Lecanto (luh-KAN-to), town (☐ 6 sq mi/15.5 sq km; 1990 pop. 1,243), Citrus co., W central Fla., 10 mi/16 km W of Inverness; 28°51′N 82°29′W. Mfg. includes bldg. materials, furniture.

Leche Lagoon (LAI-chai), Camagüey prov., E Cuba, 3 mi/4.8 km N of Morón, and bounded N by Turiguanó Isl. ; 22°12′N 78°37′W. Lagoon is 7 mi/11.3 km long, up to 5 mi/8 km wide. Linked by tidal marshes with the sea (inlets of Old Bahama Channel). Its milky color is due to lime sulphates.

Lechuguilla Island (le-choo-GEE-yah) (☐ 13 sq mi/34 sq km), narrow barrier isl. in SE Gulf of California, off coast of Sinaloa, NW Mexico, at mouth of Río Fuerte, 9 mi/14 km W of Topolobampo; 12 mi/19 km long, 1 mi/1.6 km–2 mi/3.2 km wide.

Leclercville (luh-KLERK-vil), village (1991 pop. 315), S Que., Canada, on the St. Lawrence R., 30 mi/48 km NE of Trois Rivières; 46°34′N 72°00′W. Lumbering; dairying.

Lecompte (luh-KAHMP), town (1990 pop. 1,592), Rapides parish, central La., 15 mi/24 km S of Alexandria; 31°05′N 92°24′W. In agr. area (cotton, sugarcane; cattle, horses); timber; mfg. (feeds, charcoal). Alexander State Forest to W. Settled c.1855.

Lecompton (luh-KAHMP-tuhn), village (1990 pop. 619), Douglas co., NE Kansas, on the Kansas R., 10 mi/16 km NW of Lawrence; 39°02′N 95°23′W. The pro-slavery Lecompton Constitution was formulated here Sept. 1857, and it was rejected by Kansas voters in 1858. Clinton L. reservoir and Clinton State Park to S.

Leduc (luh-DOOK), town (1991 pop. 13,970), central Alta., Canada, S of Edmonton; 53°16′N 113°32′W. It is the center of the Leduc oil field (discovered 1947), which is now mostly depleted. The town is an oil storage and pumping station and also serves as an agr. distribution center.

Ledyard 1 town (1990 pop. 14,913), New London co., SE Conn.; 41°26′N 72°01′W. It is a farm center. The site of Fort Decatur is marked here. The Foxwoods casino complex, opened in 1991 by the Mashantucket Pequots on their reservation overlooking the Thames R., had grown into the largest casino in the world (measured by gaming area) by 1996. The complex (located on the former site of nuclear reactor components) includes gaming rooms, hotels, and historical reference rooms that cover the history of the Mashantucket Pequots. A tribal mus. was under construction in early 1996. Settled c.1653, inc. 1836. **2** town (1990 pop. 164), Kossuth co., N Iowa, near Minn. state line, 25 mi/40 km N of Algona; 43°25′N 94°09′W.

Lee 1 county (□ 615 sq mi/1,593 sq km; 1990 pop. 87,146), E Ala.; ⊙ Opelika. Piedmont area leveling off to flat farm lands below Fall Line; bounded on E by Chattahoochee R. and Ga. Cotton, corn; textiles. Granite, dolomite, manganese. Formed 1866. **2** county (□ 619 sq mi/1,603 sq km; 1990 pop. 13,053), E Ark.; ⊙ Marianna; 34°46′N 90°46′W. Bounded E by the Mississippi; drained by St. Francis and L'Anguille rivers and Rig Creek. Agr. (wheat, cotton, rice, soybeans; hogs); timber. Industries at Marianna. Part of St. Francis Natl. Forest in SE; La. Purchase State Historical Monument at SW corner. Formed 1873. **3** county (□ 1,212 sq mi/3,139 sq km; 1990 pop. 335,113), SW Fla., on Gulf of Mexico (W); ⊙ Fort Myers; 26°34′N 81°55′W. Lowland area, swampy in SE, drained by Caloosahatchee R. Bordered by a chain of barrier isls. (Lacosta, Captiva, San ibel, and Estero isls.) sheltering several lagoons (Pine Isl. Sound, San Carlos Bay, Estero Bay) and Pine Isl. Agr. (gladioli growing; citrus fruit, vegetables), cattle raising, fishing, and major tourist industry. Formed 1887. Major growth around Fort Myers since 1970s has made this one of nation's fastest growing cos. **4** county (□ 362 sq mi/938 sq km; 1990 pop. 16,250) SW central Ga.; ⊙ Leesburg; 31°47′N 84°08′W. Bounded E by Flint R.; drained by Kinchafoonee R. and Muckalee Creek. Coastal plain agr. (peanuts, soybeans, cotton, wheat, corn; cattle, hogs) and timber area. Formed 1826. **5** county (□ 729 sq mi/1,888 sq km; 1990 pop. 34,392), N Ill.; ⊙ Dixon; 41°44′N 89°17′W. Agr. (corn, soybeans; cattle, poultry; dairying). Mfg. (food prods., cement prods., metal prods., industrial machinery). Sand, gravel pits. Drained by Rock, Green, and Kyte rivers, and Bureau Creek. Formed 1839. **6** county (□ 538 sq mi/1,393 sq km; 1990 pop. 38,687), extreme SE Iowa; ⊙ Fort Madison and Keokuk; 40°38′N 91°28′W. Bounded NE by Skunk R., E by Mississippi R. (forms Ill. state line here), and S by Des Moines R. (forms Mo. state line here). Prairie agr. area (hogs, cattle, poultry, sheep; corn, oats, soybeans); limestone quarries, coal deposits. Mfg. at Fort Madison and Keokuk. Lock and Dam No. 19 at Keokuk. Part of Shimek State Forest in W. Formed 1836. **7** county (□ 211 sq mi/546 sq km; 1990 pop. 7,422), E central Ky.; ⊙ Beattyville; 37°35′N 83°43′W. In the Cumberland Mts.; drained by Kentucky R. and its North, Middle, and South forks. Mt. agr. area, (livestock; burley tobacco, hay); coal oil; hardwood timber; limestone. Includes part of Daniel Boone Natl. Forest in W ½ of co. Formed 1870. **8** county (□ 453 sq mi/1,173 sq km; 1990 pop. 65,581), NE Miss.; ⊙ Tupelo; 34°17′N 88°40′W. Drained by Chiwapa and Oldtown creeks. Agr. (cotton, corn, soybeans, wheat, honey; poultry, cattle; dairying); timber. Brices Cross Roads Natl. Battlefield Site in N (W of Baldwin); Tupelo Natl. Battlefield Site in W part of Tupelo; Tombigbee State Park in E; L. Lamar Bruce State L. in W; Natchez Trace (Natl.) Parkway passes SW-NE through co. Formed 1866. **9** county (□ 259 sq mi/671 sq km; 1990 pop. 41,374), central N.C.; ⊙ Sanford; 35°28′N 79°10′W. In forested Piedmont region in N and sandhill area in S; bounded NE by Cape Fear R. and NW by Deep R. Agr. area (esp. tobacco; cotton, corn, wheat, oats, soybeans, hay; chickens), timber. Mfg. at Sanford. Sand, stone quarrying. Formed 1907. **10** county (□ 411 sq mi/1,064 sq km; 1990 pop. 18,437), NE central S.C.; ⊙ Bishopville; 34°09′N 80°15′W. Drained by Lynches and Black rivers. Mfg. of clay and sand. Agr. area (cotton, peanuts, corn, oats, soybeans, hay; hogs, cattle); timber. State Penitentiary and Lee State Park (□ 2,839 acres/1,149 ha) is on Lynches R. in E. Formed 1902. **11** county (□ 634 sq mi/1,642 sq km; 1990 pop. 12,854), S central Texas; ⊙ Giddings; 30°18′N 96°57′W. Bounded NE by E Yegua Creek, SE in part by Yegua Creek, head of Somerville L. reservoir in E corner, confluence of the 2 creeks. Diversified agr., hogs, cattle; peanuts, corn, sorghum. Oil and gas, clay, Fuller's earth. Formed 1874. **12** county (□ 437 sq mi/1,132 sq km; 1990 pop. 24,496), extreme SW Va., in wedge formed by Ky. (NW) and Tenn. (S) state lines; ⊙ Jonesville; 36°42′N 83°07′W. Westernmost co. in Va.; mt. and valley region, with Cumberland Mts. along Ky. state line, Cumberland Gap pass at SW tip, part of Cumberland Gap Natl. Historical Park in SW (extends into Ky., Tenn.), part of Powell Mt. in E; includes parts of Jefferson Natl. Forest in NE, including Cave Springs Recreational Area. Drained by Powell R. Agr. (tobacco, corn, hay, alfalfa; cattle); timber; extensive bituminous-coal mining, limestone quarrying. Limestone caves. Formed 1792.

Lee 1 town (1990 pop. 832), Penobscot co., E central Maine, 45 mi/72 km NNE of Bangor; 45°22′N 68°17′W. In hunting, fishing area. **2** town (1990 pop. 5,849), Berkshire co., W Mass., in the Berkshires, on Housatonic R., 9 mi/14.5 km S of Pittsfield; 42°18′N 73°14′W. Includes Lee village. Resort; paper and lumber mills; marble quarries. October Mt. State Forest nearby. Villages of East Lee, South Lee, and Jacobs Pillow (resort and site of summer dance festival). Settled 1760, set off from Great Barrington and Washington in 1777. **3** town (1990 pop. 3,729), Strafford co., SE N.H., 9 mi/14.5 km SW of Dover; 43°07′N 71°00′W. Drained by Lemprey, North, and Oyster rivers. Mfg. (machinery); agr. (nursery crops, corn, apples; cattle; dairying).

Lee, village (1990 pop. 319), in Lee and De Kalb cos., N Ill., 18 mi/29 km SW of Sycamore; 41°47′N 88°56′W. In rich agr. area.

Lee City, village, Wolfe co., E central Ky., in the Cumberlands, 50 mi/80 km ESE of Winchester. Agr. (tobacco, corn; cattle).

Lee, Fort, Va.: see PETERSBURG.

Lee Lake, Washington co., W Miss., and Chicot co., Ark., E of Mississippi R., 8 mi/12.9 km S of Greenville. Oxbow lake is c.8 mi/12.9 km long. The sect. inside of this former bend in Mississippi R. remained part of Ark. when river channel shifted W.

Lee Park, uninc. town (1990 pop. 3,800), Luzerne co., NE central Pa., residential suburb 3 mi/4.8 km WSW of Wilkes-Barre on Solomon Creek; 41°13′N 75°54′W.

Lee State Park, S.C.: see LEE.

Lee Vining, uninc. village, Mono co., E Calif., 52 mi/84 km NNW of Bishop, in the Sierra Nevada, near W shore of Mono L. In mining and recreational region. Cattle. Canyon of Lee Vining Creek (W) has hydroelectric plant. E gateway to Yosemite Natl. Park (boundary 7 mi/11.3 km to W) via Tioga Pass (9,941 ft/3,030 m). Inyo Natl. Forest to W, Toiyabe Natl. Forest to NW; Saddleburg L. to W.

Leech Lake (□ 251 sq mi/650 sq km), Cass co. (W end extends into Hubbard co.), N central Minn., 25 mi/40 km SE of Bemidji, largely in Leech L. Indian Reservation; 47°10′N 94°25′W. The 2d-largest lake in Minn., after Red L. Fed by Kabekuna and Steamboat rivers at W end, by Boy R. at E end; drains from NE end through Leech R. (c.30 mi/48 km long; dammed just W of Federal Dam village) into Mississippi R. Lake is 20 mi/32 km long, max. width 15 mi/24 km; elev. 1,296 ft/395 m. Max. capacity c.1,000,000 acre-ft. Bear Isl. (3.5 mi/5.6 km long, 1 mi/1.6 km wide) is in SE. Fishing, bathing, and boating resorts. Town of Walker is on SW shore, on Walker Bay. Lake is surrounded by Chippewa Natl. Forest and used as reservoir. Shoreline indented by large bays, Boy and Headquarters bays in E, Socker Bay in N, Steamboat and Walker bays in W.

Leechburg, borough (1990 pop. 2,504), Armstrong co., W central Pa., 24 mi/39 km NE of Pittsburgh, on Kiskiminetas R. Agr. (corn, hay; dairying); mfg. (fabricated steel, medical equip., metal fabrication); bituminous coal. Crooked Creek L. reservoir and park to NE. Laid out 1828, inc. 1850.

Leedey (LEE-dee), village (1990 pop. 468), Dewey co., W Okla., 39 mi/63 km S of Woodward; 35°52′N 99°20′W. In agr. area; mfg. (furniture).

Leeds, city (1990 pop. 9,946), on Jefferson–St. Clair co. line, N central Ala., 10 mi/16 km E of Birmingham. In coal, iron, and limestone area; lumber and steel and wire prods., plastics, furniture. Founded 1881.

Leeds, town (1990 pop. 1,669), Androscoggin co., SW Maine, on the Androscoggin, 15 mi/24 km NNE of Auburn; 44°17′N 70°07′W. Vegetables; food processing.

Leeds 1 resort village (1990 pop. 750), Green co., SE N.Y., on Catskill Creek 3 mi/4.8 km NW of Catskill; 42°15′N 73°53′W. Has 18th-cent. stone bridge, one of the oldest stone structures in the state. **2** village (1990 pop. 542), Benson co., N central N.Dak., 30 mi/48 km WNW of Devils L.; 48°17′N 99°26′W. Hurricane L. to NNW, L. Ibsen to SE. **3** village (1990 pop. 254), Washington co., SW Utah, 15 mi/24 km NE of St. George; 37°14′N 113°21′W. Fruit; cattle. Dixie Natl. Forest, incl. Pine Valley Mt. Wilderness Area, to NW; Quail Creek reservoir and State Park to SW. Mining boom 1870s and 1880s. Pop. has grown in 1980s and 1990s with influx of retired citizens.

Leeds, Mass.: see NORTHAMPTON.

Leeds and Grenville United Counties (□ 1,309 sq mi/3,390 sq km; 1991 pop. 90,235), SE Ont., Canada, on the St. Lawrence, and on N.Y. border; ⊙ Brockville; 44°50′N 75°40′W. Leeds co. (□ 900 sq mi/2,331 sq km), chief town, Brockville. Grenville co. (□ 463 sq mi/1,199 sq km), chief town, Prescott.

Leedstown, uninc. village, Westmoreland co., E Va., 30 mi/48 km SE of Fredericksburg, on Rappahannock R. Agr. (grain, soybeans; cattle). Here, in 1766, were drawn up the Leedstown Resolutions, embodying points later included in Declaration of Independence.

Leelanau (lee-LA-nou), county (□ 2,533 sq mi/6,560 sq km; 1990 pop. 16,527), NW Mich.; ⊙ Leland. A peninsula (Leelanau Peninsula) bounded W by L. Michigan and E by Grand Traverse Bay and its W arm; 45°07′N 86°01′W. Area known for cherry growing; also apples, plums, strawberries, grapes, corn, wheat; cattle, hogs, poultry. Fisheries; resorts. It is a former lumber region. Lighthouse and Leelanau State Park at tip of peninsula (N). Sleeping Bear Dunes on L. Michigan shore, including N and S Manitou Isls. Timber Line Ski Area in S, Sugar Loaf Mt. Ski Area in center. Organized 1863.

Leelanau, Lake (lee-LA-nou), Leelanau co., NW Mich., on Leelanau Peninsula, just E of Leland; c.4.5 mi/7.2 km long; 44°54′N 85°43′W. Resort. Connected to Lower Leelanau L. (c.9 mi/14.5 km long; just S) by short stream.

Leelanau Peninsula, Mich.: see LEELANAU, co.

Leeper, Mount (9,603 ft/2,927 m), S Alaska, in Chugach Mts., 20 mi/32 km NE of Cape Yakataga; 60°17′N 142°05′W.

Lees, village, Cumberland co., S N.J., on Maurice R., 10 mi/16 km SSE of Millville. Farming area. State prison is nearby.

Lee's Summit, city (1990 pop. 46,418), Jackson and Cass co., W Mo., large residential and industrial suburb 16 mi/26 km SSE of Kansas City. Trucking center. Mfg. (communications equip., appliances, pharmaceuticals, plastic containers, tool and die, metal prods.).

Richards-Gebaur Airport nearby. James A. Reed Memorial Wildlife Area to SE; L. Jacomo Park to E; Longview Community Col. Inc. 1868.

Leesburg (LEEZ-buhrg), city (1990 pop. 16,202) ⊙ Loudoun co., N Va., 32 mi/51 km WNW of Washington, D.C., near the Potomac R.; 39°06′N 77°33′W. Mfg. (bldg. materials, printing and publishing, concrete blocks, wine); agr. (grain, apples, soybeans); dairying. Trade center in region known for livestock breeding (horses, cattle). Limestone quarrying. Site of Civil War engagement of Ball's Bluff (Oct. 1861) to NE, on Potomac R.; a Confederate victory. Balls Bluff Natl. Cemetery. Oatlands, home of George Carter; Oak Hill, home of James Monroe, to S. Dulles Internatl. Airport 10 mi/16 km to SE. Settled 1749; inc. 1758.

Leesburg 1 town (□ 12 sq mi/31 sq km; 1990 pop. 14,903), Lake co., central Fla., in a hill and lake region, 30 mi/48 km SE of Ocala; 28°48′N 81°52′W. Processing and shipping center in a citrus fruit–growing and farming area. Cattle raising and the mfg. of such items as crates, athletic equip., and mobile homes are also important. Inc. 1875. **2** town (1990 pop. 1,452), ⊙ Lee co., SW central Ga., 10 mi/16 km N of Albany, near Kinchafoonee R.; 31°44′N 84°10′W. Mfg. includes apparel, crushed stone, machine parts. **3** town (1990 pop. 584), Kosciusko co., N Ind., 6 mi/9.7 km N of Warsaw; 41°20′N 85°51′W. In agr. area. Laid out 1835.

Leesburg, village (1990 pop. 1,063), Highland co., SW Ohio, 10 mi/16 km NNE of Hillsboro, in livestock-raising and farming area; 39°20′N 83°33′W.

Leesport, borough (1990 pop. 1,270), Berks co., SE central Pa., suburb 7 mi/11.3 km NNW of Reading on Schuylkill R.; 40°26′N 75°58′W. Mfg. includes crushed stone, concrete, apple cider, copper alloy, furniture, fertilizer, and medical equip. Agr. includes dairying, livestock; grain, apples, soybeans. Reservoirs nearby.

Leesville, city (1994 pop. 8,587), ⊙ Vernon parish, W La., 50 mi/80 km WSW of Alexandria; 31°08′N 93°16′W. Mfg. (apparel, bottled water, lumber, printing and publishing); agr. (livestock; corn, sweet potatoes). Fort Polk Military Reserve and Kisatchie Natl. Forest are SE; Peason Ridge State Wildlife Area to N; Anacoco L. and Anacoco Prairie State Game and Fish Preserve to W; Boise-Vernon State Wildlife Area to SW. W La. Frontier Festival. Inc. 1899.

Leesville, village (1990 pop. 156), Carroll co., E Ohio, 24 mi/39 km SSE of Canton; 40°27′N 81°12′W. Flood-control dam nearby impounds Leesville Reservoir (capacity 37,400 acre-ft) in a small tributary of Tuscarawas R.

Leesville 1 Conn.: see EAST HADDAM. **2** S.C.: see BATESBURG.

Leesville Lake, reservoir, on Pittsylvania and Campbell co. border, SW central Va., on Roanoke (Staunton) R., extends SW into Bedford co., 25 mi/40 km SSW of Lynchburg; 37°05′N 79°23′W. Max. capacity 94,960 acre-ft; c.20 mi/32 km long. Formed by Leesville Dam (83 ft/25 m high), built (1963) for power generation.

Leeton, town (1990 pop. 632), Johnson co., W central Mo., 12 mi/19 km S of Warrensburg; 38°34′N 93°42′W.

Leetonia (lee-TO-nee-yuh), village, St. Louis co., NE Minn., in Mesabi Iron Range 2 mi/3.2 km W of Hibbing; 47°25′N 92°59′W. RR spur terminus. Iron mines nearby. **2** village (1990 pop. 2,070), Columbiana co., E Ohio, 15 mi/24 km S of Youngstown; 40°52′N 80°46′W. Laid out 1866.

Leetsdale, borough (1990 pop. 1,387), Allegheny co., W Pa., suburb 15 mi/24 km NW of Pittsburgh, on Ohio R., bet. mouths of Big Sewickley (NW) and Little Sewickley (SE) creeks. Agr to NE (corn, hay; livestock; dairying); mfg. (fabricated metal prods., office supplies, plastic prods.). Settled 1796, inc. 1904.

Leeville, uninc. village, Lafourche parish, extreme SE La., 39 mi/63 km SE of Houma, on navigable Bayou Lafourche, in marshy region bet. Caminada and Timbalier bays, c.50 mi/80 km S of New Orleans; 29°14′N 90°12′W. Center of oil field; shrimp processing. Wisner State Wildlife Area to E.

Leeward Islands, N group of the Lesser Antilles in the West Indies, extending SE from P.R. to the Windward Isls. The principal isls. are the Virgin Isls. of the U.S.; the Fr. isl. and overseas dept. of Guadeloupe and its dependencies; the Du. isls. of St. Eustatius and Saba; the jointly owned (Du. and Fr.) St. Martin; the isls. of the independent states of St. Kitts and Nevis and Antigua; and the isls. of the Br. dependent territories of Anguilla, Montserrat, and the Br. V.I. Largely volcanic in origin, the Leeward Isls. have lush, subtropical vegetation, rich soil, and abundant rainfall. The warm, delightful climate is tempered by the surrounding water so that there is little variation in temp. Most of the isls. have become popular tourist destinations. Prods. for the most part are agr. — fruits, vegetables, sugar, cotton, coffee, and tobacco. Columbus 1st sighted the Leeward Isls. in 1493, but settlement began only after the British arrived in the 17th cent. Sir Thomas Warner, sent to St. Kitts in 1623, was made governor general of the yet uncolonized neighboring isls. (Nevis, Antigua, Montserrat, and Barbuda), and in the same year the Frenchman Pierre Bélain d'Esnambuc also established a colony on St. Kitts. By 1632, when the English had settled the neighboring isls., the sharp, 3-way colonial conflict of England, France, and Spain had begun. The Spanish were forced from the struggle, but for nearly 2 cents. the isls. were pawns in the Anglo-Fr. worldwide wars. They changed hands with each fresh attack by Br. or Fr. forces and were reshuffled in ownership whenever a new treaty was signed. Their final disposition did not come until the end of the Napoleonic Wars in 1815.

Leflore (luh-FLOR), county (□ 606 sq mi/1,570 sq km; 1990 pop. 37,341), W central Miss.; ⊙ Greenwood; 33°32′N 90°17′W. Tallahatchie and Yalobusha rivers join in E center to form Yazoo R. Agr. (cotton, rice, sorghum, wheat, soybeans; cattle); catfish. Greenwood is market, processing center. Matthews Brake Natl. Wildlife Refuge in S; Florewood R. Plantation State Park in center. Formed 1871.

Lefors, village (1990 pop. 656), Gray co., extreme N Texas, in the Panhandle, 65 mi/105 km ENE of Amarillo and on North Fork of Red R.; 35°26′N 100°47′W. In oil, gas, and cattle area; wheat, sorghum, corn, forage crops; mfg. (gas processing). McClellan Creek Natl. Grassland to S.

Lefroy, Mount (luh-FROI) (11,230 ft/3,423 m), on Alta.-B.C. border, Canada, in Rocky Mts., on W edge of Banff Natl. Park, 35 mi/56 km WNW of Banff; 51°22′N 116°16′W.

Legal (luh-GAL), village (1991 pop. 973), central Alta., Canada, near Manawan L. (4 mi/6 km long), 28 mi/45 km N of Edmonton; 53°57′N 113°38′W. Grain elevators, mixed farming. Fr.-Can. settlement, founded 1898.

Legget, uninc. village (1990 pop. 375), Polk co., E Texas, 30 mi/48 km S of Lufkin. Timber. Oil and natural gas. Mfg. (liquid-propane processing). Alabama and Coushatta Indian Reservation to SE.

Leggett, village (1990 pop. 108), Edgecombe co., E central N.C., 14 mi/23 km ENE of Rocky Mount, near Tar R.; 35°59′N 77°34′W. Grain, tobacco, cotton, peanuts; livestock.

Lehi (LEE-hei), town (1990 pop. 8,475), Utah co., N central Utah, 25 mi/40 km S of Salt Lake City, 14 mi/23 km NW of Provo, on Dry Creek, near Jordan R. Wasatch Range and Uinta Natl. Forest to E; 40°23′N 111°50′W. Elev. 4,562 ft/1,390 m. Trading point for agr. area; alfalfa, flour mill; dairying; mfg. (cheese, explosives, clay prods.). Calcite and clay mining; limestone quarrying. Saratoga Resort to SW on lake. Surrounding region is irrigated by water from Utah L. (just S) and Provo R. Formerly called Lehi City. Settled by Mormons 1850; inc. 1852.

Lehigh (LEE-hei), county (□ 348 sq mi/901 sq km; 1990 pop. 291,130), E Pa.; ⊙ Allentown. Bounded in NE and drained by Lehigh R., and Jordan and Little Lehigh creeks. Rolling industrial and farm area with Blue Mt. ridge running length of NW boundary. Agr. (corn, wheat, oats, barley, hay, alfalfa, soybeans, potatoes, apples; chicken, sheep, hogs, cattle; dairying); limestone,

slate; sand and gravel. Mfg. at Allentown, Emmaus, and Bethlehem. Trexler Lehigh Co. Game Preserve in N center; 5 covered bridges in center, on Jordan Creek. The co. is urbanized in SE around twin cities of Allentown and Bethlehem. Formed 1812.

Lehigh, town (1990 pop. 536), Webster co., central Iowa, on Des Moines R., 12 mi/19 km SSE of Fort Dodge; 42°21′N 94°02′W. Brick and tile plant. Clay, sand, gravel pits nearby. Dolliver Memorial State Park in NW; Brushy Creek State Park in NE.

Lehigh 1 (LEE-hei), village (1990 pop. 180), Marion co., central Kansas, 16 mi/26 km W of Marion; 38°22′N 97°17′W. In grain, livestock, and oil-producing region. **2** village, Stark co., W N.Dak., 5 mi/8 km E of Dickinson, and on Heart R.; 46°52′N 102°41′W. Lignite briquettes are made here. **3** village (1990 pop. 303), Coal co., S central Okla., 5 mi/8 km S of Coalgate, near Muddy Boggy Creek; 34°28′N 96°13′W. In agr. area.

Lehigh (LEE-hei), river, 103 mi/166 km long, on Lackawanna-Wayne co. line, NE Pa.; rises in group of small ponds; flows SW through Francis Walter Reservoir, turns S at White Haven, flows past Jim Thorpe, Lehighton, and Allentown, then E past Bethlehem to Delaware R. at Easton; 41°16′N 75°24′W. Area around Allentown, Bethlehem, and Easton once noted for its anthracite-coal mining and steel mills.

Lehigh Acres (LEE-hei), town (□ 8 sq mi/20.7 sq km; 1990 pop. 13,611), Lee co., SW Fla., 13 mi/21 km E of Fort Myers; 26°36′N 81°37′W. Planned community surrounded by wilderness. Mfg. includes bldg. materials, printing and publishing.

Lehighton (LEE-hei-tuhn), borough (1990 pop. 5,914), Carbon co., E Pa., 20 mi/32 km NW of Allentown, on Lehigh R. Agr. (corn, hay, potatoes; dairying; timber); mfg. (machinery, fabricated metal prods., lumber, insulation, apparel). Jake Arner Memorial Airport to W. Mauch Chunk L. reservoir to W; Beltzville State Park to E. Settled 1746, inc. 1866.

Lehman Caves National Monument (LEE-muhn) (□ 1 sq mi/2.6 sq km), White Pine co., E Nev., 35 mi/56 km ESE of Ely. Monument (est. 1922) was included with Great Basin Natl. Park when the park was est. in 1985.

Lehr (LER), village (1990 pop. 191), Logan and McIntosh cos., S N.Dak., 17 mi/27 km N of Ashley; 46°16′N 99°20′W. Green L. and Doyle Memorial State Park to SW.

Lehua (lai-HOO-ah), small island ½ mi/%₁₀ km off N tip of Niihau, Kauai co., Hawaii. Highest point rises to 702 ft/214 m. Light beacon. Kaulakahi Channel to E.

Leicester 1 (LES-tuhr), residential town (1990 pop. 10,191), Worcester co., central Mass., just W of Worcester; 42°14′N 71°55′W. Has a jr. col. Includes villages of Leicester Center, Cherry Valley, and Rochdale. Settled 1713, inc. 1722. **2** town (1990 pop. 871), Addison co., W Vt., near L. Dunmore, in Green Mts., 11 mi/18 km S of Middlebury; 43°52′N 73°05′W.

Leicester (LES-tuhr), village (1990 pop. 405), Livingston co., W central N.Y., 32 mi/51 km SSW of Rochester; 42°46′N 77°54′W.

Leidy, Mount (LEI-dee) (10,317 ft/3,145 m), peak in Rocky Mts.,Teton co., NW Wyo., 25 mi/40 km NE of Jackson. Rises above E side of Jackson Hole.

Leigh (LEE), village (1990 pop. 447), Colfax co., E Nebr., 20 mi/32 km NNW of Schuyler; 41°42′N 97°14′W. Livestock; grain. Mfg. (fertilizer, feed).

Leighton 1 (LAI-tuhn), town (1990 pop. 988), Colbert co., NW Ala., 10 mi/16 km E of Tuscumbia. **2** town (1990 pop. 142), Mahaska co., S central Iowa, 8 mi/ 12.9 km WNW of Oskaloosa; 41°20′N 92°47′W. Meat processing.

Leipsic 1 (LIP-sik), village (1990 pop. 236), Kent co., central Del., 6 mi/9.7 km N of Dover, and on Leipsic R., 5 mi/8 km W of its mouth on Delaware Bay; 39°14′N 75°31′W. Named for Leipzig, Germany. An early fur-trading center and port. Oystering remains an important industry. **2** village (1990 pop. 2,203), Putnam co., NW Ohio, 18 mi/29 km WNW of Findlay; 41°05′N 83°59′W. In grain-growing area; food and dairy prods., clay and cement prods.

Leisenring (LEI-suhn-ring), uninc. town (1990 pop. 800), Franklin township, Fayette co., SW Pa., 2 mi/3.2 km WSW of Connellsville; 39°59′N 79°38′W.

Leisure Village–Pine Lake Park, uninc. area (1990 pop. 10,139), retirement community, Ocean co., E central N.J., 4 mi/6.4 km E of Lakehurst.

Leitches Creek (LEE-chiz), village, NE N.S., Canada, NE Cape Breton Isl., on Sydney Harbour, 6 mi/10 km WNW of Sydney.

Leitchfield (LICH-feeld), town (1990 pop. 4,965), ⊙ Grayson co., W central Ky., 36 mi/58 km NNE of Bowling Green; 37°28′N 86°17′W. In agr. (dairying; livestock; burley tobacco, corn, hay; timber), stone-quarrying area; mfg. (lumber, machinery, cheese, apparel, furniture, crushed limestone). Grayson County Airport to S. Jack Thomas House (c.1810). Nolin R. L. reservoir to SE; Rough R. L. reservoir and Rough R. Dam State Resort Park to NW.

Leiters Ford, village (1990 est. pop. 300), Fulton co., N Ind., 10 mi/16 km WNW of Rochester. In agr. area. Mfg. (lighting fixtures).

Leitersburg (LEET-erz-berg), village, Washington co., W Md., 6 mi/9.7 km NE of Hagerstown. A grain mill has operated here since 1792. Nearby is a Mennonite church, in use since 1835. Small plastic works here.

Leith, uninc. town (1990 pop. 950), South Union township, Fayette co., SW Pa., suburb 1 mi/1.6 km S of Uniontown; 39°53′N 79°43′W.

Leith (LEETH), village (1990 pop. 43), Grant co., S N.Dak., 52 mi/84 km SW of Bismarck; 46°21′N 101°38′W.

Lejunior (lah-JOON-yuhr), village (1990 pop. 597), Harlan co., SE Ky., 11 mi/18 km ENE of Harlan, on Clover Fork of Cumberland R. Bituminous coal. Timber. Formerly called Highsplint.

Leland 1 town (1990 pop. 311), Winnebago co., N Iowa, on Lime Creek, 4 mi/6.4 km N of Forest City; 43°19′N 93°38′W. **2** (LEE-luhnd), town (1990 pop. 6,366), Washington co., W Miss., 10 mi/16 km E of Greenville, on Deer Creek; 33°23′N 90°54′W. RR junction. Agr. (cotton, grain, soybeans; cattle); timber; mfg. (machinery, furniture, light mfg.). "Birthplace of the Frog," boyhood home of Jim Henson, creator of the Muppets. Stoneville Natl. Wildlife Refuge to N. Settled 1847, laid out 1884. **3** (LEE-luhnd), town (1990 pop. 1,801), Brunswick co., SE N.C., 6 mi/9.7 km WNW of Wilmington, near Cape Fear R.; 34°14′N 78°00′W. RR junction. Agr. area (tobacco, grain, soybeans, sweet potatoes; livestock). Mfg. (textiles, metal fabricating, bldg. materials).

Leland 1 village (1990 pop. 862), La Salle co., N Ill., 18 mi/29 km N of Ottawa; 41°36′N 88°47′W. In agr. area. **2** (LEE-luhnd), village, ⊙ Leelanau co., NW Mich., 19 mi/31 km NNW of Traverse City, bet. L. Leelanau (E) and L. Michigan; 45°01′N 85°45′W. In dairy, livestock-raising, and fruit area; lumber; printing; winery; resort. Sleeping Bear Dunes Natl. Lakeshore to SW; ferries to N and S Manitou Isls., part of natl. lakeshore.

Leland Grove, village (1990 pop. 1,679), Sangamon co., central Ill., residential suburb 2 mi/3.2 km SW of Springfield, nearly surrounded by city of Springfield; 39°46′N 89°40′W.

Leland, Mount (LEE-luhnd) (7,810 ft/2,380 m), on Alaska–B.C. (Canada) border, in St. Elias Mts., 40 mi/64 km W of Skagway; 59°22′N 136°29′W.

Lemberg, town (1991 pop. 395), SE Sask., Canada, 24 mi/39 km NE of Indian Head; 50°44′N 103°12′W. Grain-shipping center; grain elevators; dairying; livestock raising.

Lemhi, county (□ 4,569 sq mi/11,834 sq km; 1990 pop. 6,899), E Idaho; ⊙ Salmon; 44°58′N 113°57′W. Mt. and valley area drained by Salmon R. and tributaries and bounded on E by Bitterroot Range and Mont. (Continental Divide). Sheep, cattle; alfalfa, oats; mining (lead, silver, copper); manganese and uranium deposits; tourism, recreation, white water rafting on Salmon R. In Bitterroot Mt. Region; Salmon R. and Yellowjacket mts. are in NW, Lemhi Range in E. Parts of Salmon Natl. Forest throughout co., especially E; small part of Targhee Natl. Forest in SE; part of Frank Church R. of No Return Wilderness Area. Formed 1869.

Lemhi Range, range, E Idaho, running NW-SE bet. Salmon city and Snake R. Plain, mainly in Lemhi co., in Salmon Natl. Forest. Flatiron Mt. (11,019 ft/3,359 m) is highest point.

Lemhi River, 70 mi/113 km long, E Idaho, near Mont. state line; formed by confluence of several forks in E Lemhi co.; flows NNW, bet. Bitterroot and Lemhi ranges; to Salmon R. at Salmon. River is entirely within Lemhi co.

Lemington, town (1990 pop. 102), Essex co., NE Vt., on the Connecticut R., 20 mi/32 km N of Guildhall; 44°52′N 71°36′W. In hunting, fishing region. Monadnock Mt. is here.

Lemmon, town (1990 pop. 1,614), Perkins co., NW S.Dak., 140 mi/225 km NW of Pierre, on N.Dak. state line; 45°56′N 102°09′W. Trading point for large grain and livestock region in N.Dak. and S.Dak.; wheat, alfalfa; mfg. (jewelry). Grand R. Natl. Grassland to S and W; Petrified Wood Park to S; Standing Rock Indian Reservation to E. Llewellyn Johns Memorial and Shadehill State Recreational Area to S.

Lemmon, Mount, highest peak (9,157 ft/2,791 m) in Santa Catalina Mts., SE Ariz., 17 mi/27 km NNE of Tucson. On N side is the site of Biosphere 2, in which researchers lived in an enclosed self-contained environment. Mt. Lemmon Ski Valley. Sometimes called Lemmon Mt.

Lemon Fair River, c.20 mi/32 km long, W Vt., rises near Sudbury; flows N to Otter Creek near Weybridge.

Lemon Grove, city (1990 pop. 23,984), San Diego co., S Calif. residential suburb 7 mi/11.3 km E of San Diego; 32°44′N 117°02′W. It is agr., with some small industries (mfg. of wire prods., motor vehicle parts, and bricks, printing). Lemon Grove has benefited from the growth of nearby San Diego.

Lemon, Lake, reservoir, Monroe and Brown cos., S central Ind., on Beanblossom Creek, 10 mi/16 km NE of Huntington; 3 mi/4.8 km long; 39°16′N 86°24′W. Formed by L. Lemon Dam.

Lemon Reservoir (□ 1 sq mi/2.6 sq km), La Plata co., SW Colo., on Florida R., in San Juan Natl. Forest, in the Rocky Mts., 12 mi/19 km NE of Durango; 37°23′N 107°40′W. Max. capacity 487,660 acre-ft. Formed by Lemon Dam (284 ft/87 m high), built (1963) by the Bureau of Reclamation for irrigation; also used for flood control, recreation, and power generation. Transfer State Park on N end of Reservoir.

Lemont (lah-MONT), village (1990 pop. 7,348), Cook co., NE Ill., SW of Chicago, on Des Plaines R., Sanitary and Ship Canal (Illinois and Michigan Canal Natl. Heritage Corridor), 10 mi/16 km NNE of Joliet; 41°40′N 87°59′W. Oil refining; mfg. of aluminum prods.; limestone quarries. Ships petroleum, stone. Argonne Natl. Laboratory (for atomic research) and Argonne Forest Preserve (recreational area) are nearby. Inc. 1873.

Lemonweir River, c.60 mi/97 km long, W Wis.; rises in Jackson co.; flows SE, past New Lisbon and Mauston, to Wisconsin R. 11 mi/18 km E of Mauston.

Lemoore, city (1990 pop. 13,622), Kings co., S central Calif., in San Joaquin Valley, 30 mi/48 km S of Fresno; 36°18′N 119°48′W. Dairying; poultry; cantaloupes, plums, peaches, nectarines, olives, pistachios, almonds, cotton, barley; mfg. (textiles, printing and publishing). Lemoore Naval Air Station to W. Tulare L. irrigation reservoir to S. Inc. 1900.

Lemoyne (LUH-moin), borough (1990 pop. 3,959), Cumberland co., S central Pa., suburb 2 mi/3.2 km SW of Harrisburg, on Susquehanna R. (bridged). RR junction. Mfg. (meat processing, signs). Northernmost point of Confederate advance, 1863. Camp Hill State Correctional Institution to SW.

Lempster, town (1990 pop. 947), Sullivan co., SW N.H., 9 mi/14.5 km S of Newport; 43°13′N 72°10′W. Mfg. (lumber, metal fabrication); timber; agr. (nursery crops, hay; cattle, poultry). Part of Honey Brook State Forest in SW. Long Pond in SE.

Lena 1 (LEE-nah), village (1990 pop. 2,605), Stephenson co., N Ill., near Wis. state line, 11 mi/18 km NW of Freeport; 42°22′N 89°49′W. In agr. area; processes dairy prods. Inc. 1869. **2** (LEE-nuh), village (1990 pop. 175), Leake co., central Miss., 10 mi/16 km SSW of Carthage; 32°35′N 89°35′W. Agr. (cotton, corn; cattle); mfg. (apparel). Bienville Natl. Forest to S. **3** village (1990 pop. 590), Oconto co., NE Wis., 30 mi/48 km N of Green Bay; 44°57′N 88°02′W. Dairying region; vegetables; wood prods. Near Copper Culture State Park.

Lena Beach (LEE-nuh), fishing village, SE Alaska, on Lynn Canal, 15 mi/24 km NW of Juneau, and on Glacier Highway; 58°24′N 134°45′W.

Lenapah (LE-nuh-pah), village (1990 pop. 253), Nowata co., NE Okla., 10 mi/16 km N of Nowata; 36°51′N 95°37′W. In livestock area; crushed rock.

Lenape Heights (LE-nah-pee), uninc. town (1990 pop. 1,355), Armstrong co., W central Pa., residential suburb 1 mi/1.6 km SE of Ford City; 40°45′N 79°31′W.

Lenawee (LE-nuh-wee), county (□ 761 sq mi/1,971 sq km; 1990 pop. 91,476), SE Mich.; 41°53′N 84°04′W; ⊙ Adrian. Bounded S by Ohio state line; drained by R. Raisin and its branches, and by Tiffin R. Agr. (soybeans, wheat, oats, sugar beets, corn, beans; cattle, hogs, sheep, dairy prods.); mfg. at Adrian, Hudson, Morenci, and Tecumseh; hatcheries; sand and gravel; chrysanthemum raising; lake resorts. Walter J. Hayes State Park in N on Wamplers L.; L. Hudson State Recreation Area in W; Devils L. in NW. Organized 1826.

Lenexa (luh-NEK-suh), city (1990 pop. 34,034), Johnson co., E Kansas, suburb 12 mi/19 km SW of Kansas City; 38°57′N 94°17′W. Mfg. (apparel, machinery, electronic equip., plastics, medical equip., printing, bakery prods., ink, consumer goods, beverages, paper prods.).

L'Enfant Jésus, Canada; see VALLÉE JONCTION.

Lengby (LENG-bee), village (1990 pop. 112), Polk co., 32 mi/51 km W of Bemidji, on N shore of Spring L., near Poplar R.; 47°30′N 95°37′W. White Earth Indian Reservation to S. Dairying; grain.

Lengua de Pájaro, Cuba: see NICARO.

Lengua de Vaca Pass (LEN-gwah de VAH-kah), on Michoacán-Mexico state border, central Mexico, on Mexico Highway 41 from Toluca de Lerdo to Zitácuaro, 45 mi/72 km W of Toluca. Elev. 9,348 ft/2,849 m.

Lenhartsville (LEN-uhrts-vil), uninc. town (1990 pop. 195), Berks co., E central Pa., 16 mi/26 km N of Reading, on Maiden Creek. Agr. (grain; livestock; dairying); light mfg. Pa. Dutch Folk Culture Center is here.

Lennox, uninc. city (1990 pop. 22,757), Los Angeles co., S Calif., residential suburb 9 mi/14.5 km SW of Los Angeles, bet. Inglewood (N) and Hawthorne (S); 33°57′N 118°22′W. Los Angeles Internatl. Airport to W, Hawthorne Municipal Airport to S. Hollywood Park racetrack to NE.

Lennox, town (1990 pop. 1,767), Lincoln co., SE S.Dak., 15 mi/24 km SW of Sioux Falls; 43°21′N 96°54′W. Livestock center; grain, animal feed; meat prods. Mfg. (food processing, smoked fish). Co. fair takes place here. Settled 1879, inc. 1906.

Lennox and Addington, county (□ 1,170 sq mi/3,030 sq km; 1991 pop. 37,243), SE Ont., Canada, on L. Ontario; ⊙ Napanee; 44°40′N 77°10′W.

Lennoxville, town (1991 pop. 4,046), S Que., Canada, at the confluence of the St. Francis and Massawippi rivers, SE of Sherbrooke; 45°22′N 71°52′W. Chiefly a residential town. Seat of Bishop's Univ. (1843).

Lenoir (luh-NOR), county (□ 402 sq mi/1,041 sq km; 1990 pop. 57,274), E central N.C.; ⊙ Kinston; 35°14′N 77°38′W. Bounded NE by Contentnea Creek. On coastal plain; drained by Neuse R. source of Treat R. in S. Agr., esp. tobacco; also corn, cotton, wheat, soybeans, hay, sweet potatoes; chickens, turkey, hogs. Mfg. at Kinston. Formed 1791.

Lenoir, city (1990 pop. 14,192), ⊙ Caldwell co., W central N.C.; 35°54′N 81°31′W. Mfg (medical equip., pharmaceuticals, machinery, apparel, wood, synthetic, and plastic prods., furniture, printing and publishing). Seat of Caldwell Community Col. and Technical Inst. Tuttle Educational State Forest to SW; Pisgah Natl. Forest to W; L. Rhodhiss reservoir (Catawba R.) to S. Inc. 1851.

Lenoir City (luh-NOOR), city (1990 pop. 6,147), Loudon

co., E Tenn., on Tennessee R., 23 mi/37 km SW of Knoxville; 35°48′N 84°16′W. In timber and agr. area; mfg. of textiles, furniture, locks, processed meats; lumbering. Fort Loudon Dam and Reservoir (water power) nearby. Founded 1890.

Lenora (luh-NOR-uh), village (1990 pop. 329), Norton co., NW Kansas, on North Fork of Solomon R., 16 mi/26 km SSW of Norton; 39°36′N 100°00′W. RR terminus. Wheat, corn; cattle.

Lenore Lake, central Sask., Canada, 17 mi/27 km NNE of Humboldt; 17 mi/27 km long, 3 mi/5 km–7 mi/11 km wide.

Lenox 1 (LEN-uhks), town (1990 pop. 783), Cook co., S Ga., 12 mi/19 km SSE of Tifton; 31°16′N 83°28′W. **2** town (1990 pop. 1,303), Taylor co., SW Iowa, 16 mi/26 km NNW of Bedford; 40°52′N 94°33′W. Shipping point in livestock, grain area. Inc. 1875. **3** resort town (1990 pop. 5,069), including Lenox village, Berkshire co., W Mass., in the Berkshires, 7 mi/11.3 km S of Pittsfield; 42°22′N 73°17′W. Paper mill. Scene of annual Tanglewood Music Festival (begun 1934) at "Tanglewood," a former estate, mainly in adjoining Stockbridge town. At Edith Wharton's estate, the Mount, there is an annual performance of Shakespeare's plays. Hawthorne's cottage, burned in 1890, was rebuilt and dedicated as shrine in 1948. Lenox is noted for its many estates. Settled c.1750, set off from Richmond 1767. Includes state forest and villages of New Lenox and Lenox Dale.

Lenwood, uninc. town (1990 pop. 3,190), San Bernardino co., S Calif., 5 mi/8 km WSW of Barstow, in Mojave Desert, on Mojave R.; 34°54′N 117°06′W. Cattle.

Lenzburg, village (1990 pop. 510), St. Clair co., SW Ill., 18 mi/29 km SSW of Belleville; 38°17′N 89°49′W. In bituminous-coal and agr. area.

Leo, town (1990 pop. 1,200), Allen co., NE Ind., 10 mi/16 km NE of Ft. Wayne. Corn, soybeans; cattle. Mfg. (furniture). Laid out 1849.

Léogâne (lai-o-GAHN), town (1982 pop. 5,782), Ouest dept., S Haiti, port on NE coast of Jacmel Peninsula, 18 mi/29 km W of Port-au-Prince; 18°31′N 72°38′W. Tobacco, coffee and sugar growing. Has grotto.

Leola (lee-O-lah), uninc. town (1990 pop. 750), Lancaster co., SE Pa., industrial suburb 6 mi/9.7 km NE of Lancaster; 40°05′N 76°11′W. Light mfg.

Leola 1 (lee-O-luh), village (1990 pop. 476), Grant co., central Ark., 33 mi/53 km W of Pine Bluff; 34°10′N 92°35′W. Mfg. (food processing; lumber; bldg. materials). Jenkins Ferry Battleground State Historical Monument to NE. **2** village (1990 pop. 521) ⊙ McPherson co., N S.Dak., 28 mi/45 km NW of Aberdeen; 45°43′N 98°56′W. Shipping point for grain and hogs; duck hunting in vicinity.

Leominster (LE-min-stuhr), city (1990 pop. 38,145), Worcester co., N central Mass.; 42°31′N 71°46′W. Mfg. (plastics, metal fabrication, locks, processed foods, and chemicals). Birthplace of John Chapman (Johnny Appleseed). Leominster State Forest here. Set off from Lancaster 1740, inc. as a city 1915.

León (lai-ON), city (1990 pop. 758,270) and township, ⊙ León municipio, Guanajuato state, central Mexico; 21°07′N 101°01′W. It is located in a fertile river valley 6,184 ft/1,885 m high, but with a mild, temperate climate. Site of a famous flood, which in 1888 almost washed the city away. León, on the main RR line bet. El Paso, Texas, and Mexico city, and on Mexico Highways 37 and 45, is a commercial, agr., and mining center and one of Mexico's leading leather working and shoemaking cities. The local mines yield gold, copper, silver, lead, and tin. León was officially founded in 1577. Formerly called León de los Aldama.

Leon 1 (LEE-on), county (□ 701 sq mi/1,816 sq km; 1990 pop. 192,493), NW Fla., on Ga. state line (N), bounded W by Ochlockonee R. and L. Talquin; ⊙ Tallahassee; 30°27′N 84°16′W. Rolling terrain in N, coastal plain in S; includes many lakes and part of Apalachicola Natl. Forest. Agr. (corn, peanuts, cotton, vegetables; cattle, hogs, poultry; dairy prods.), and forestry (lumber). Industry at Tallahassee, which is also the state capital. Formed 1824. **2** county (□ 1,080 sq mi/2,797 sq km; 1990 pop. 12,665), E central Texas; ⊙ Centerville; 31°18′N 96°00′W. Bounded W by Navasota R., E by Trinity R. Agr., (cattle, hogs; grain, vegetables, watermelons, hay); timber; oil and natural-gas wells; lignite; iron ore. Hunting; fishing. Formed 1846.

Leon, city (1990 pop. 2,047), ⊙ Decatur co., S Iowa, c.60 mi/97 km S of Des Moines; 40°44′N 93°45′W. Mfg. (dairy prods., concrete blocks, wood, bldg. materials, apparel). Nine Eagles State Park to S. Settled 1840, inc. 1867.

Leon 1 (LEE-ahn), village (1990 pop. 707), Butler co., SE Kansas, 10 mi/16 km SE of El Dorado; 37°41′N 96°46′W. In cattle and grain area. Oil wells nearby. **2** village (1990 pop. 350), Cattaraugus co., W N.Y., 17 mi/27 km NE of Jamestown; 42°17′N 79°00′W. Dairy prods. **3** village (1990 pop. 101), Love co., S Okla., near Red R., 26 mi/42 km SW of Ardmore; 33°52′N 97°25′W. In diversified farm area. **4** (LEE-ahn), village (1990 pop. 145), Mason co., W W.Va., on Kanawha R., 12 mi/19 km SE of Point Pleasant; 38°45′N 81°57′W.

Leon River, c.145 mi/233 km long, central Texas; rises in Eastland co. W of Eastland; flows generally SE, through L. Leon (Eastland co.) and Proctor L. (Comanche co.), past Gatesville. It continues through large Belton L. reservoir, on E side of Fort Hood Military Reservation, past city of Temple, joining Lampasas R. to form Little R. c.9 mi/14.5 km S of Temple.

Leon Valley, town (1990 pop. 9,581), Bexar co., S central Texas, residential suburb 8 mi/12.9 km WNW of San Antonio, near Leon Creek; 29°30′N 98°36′W.

Leona (lee-O-nuh), village (1990 pop. 39), Doniphan co., NE Kansas, 12 mi/19 km W of Troy; 39°47′N 95°19′W. Agr. (chiefly apples). Brown State Fishing L. to NW.

Leona River, c.75 mi/121 km long, S central Texas; rises N of Uvalde, flows generally SE through livestock-ranching area, to the Frio R. 10 mi/16 km S of Pearsall.

Leonard 1 town (1990 pop. 90), Shelby co., NE Mo., 10 mi/16 km NW of Shelbyville; 39°53′N 92°10′W. Corn, soybeans; cattle, hogs. **2** town (1990 pop. 1,744), Fannin co., NE Texas, 9 mi/14.5 km S of Bonham; 33°22′N 96°16′W. Market in cotton, sorghum, soybeans, cattle. Agribusiness; mfg. (office supplies, crushed stone). Settled c.1880.

Leonard 1 village (1990 pop. 357), Oakland co., SE Mich., 18 mi/29 km. NE of Pontiac; 42°52′N 83°08′W. Mfg. (motor vehicle parts). **2** village (1990 pop. 26), Clearwater co., NW Minn., 21 mi/34 km NW of Bemidji, bet. Four Legged L. (S) and Stenlund L. (N); 47°38′N 95°16′W. Dairying.

Leonard Wood, Fort, Mo.: see FORT LEONARD WOOD.

Leonardo (lee-uh-NAR-do), village (1990 pop. 3,788), Monmouth co., E N.J., near Sandy Hook Bay, 15 mi/24 km NE of Freehold; 40°25′N 74°03′W. Largely residential.

Leonardo Bravo, Mexico: see CHICHIHUALCO.

Leonardtown, town (1990 pop. 1,475), ⊙ St. Marys co., S Md., c.45 mi/72 km SSE of Washington, D.C., and on navigable estuary entering the Potomac; 38°18′N 76°38′W. Laid out as Shepherd's Old Fields in 1708, the name was changed in honor of Benedict Leonard Calvert, the 4th Lord Baltimore, in 1728. Has been the co. capital since 1710. Raided by the British in the War of 1812, its business today revolves around tobacco, seafood, and summer visitors. The many historic bldgs. in the town include St. Francis Xavier Church (built 1767 on site of church erected c.1654), the oldest Catholic church in Md.; and Tudor Hall, built in the early 18th cent., once owned by ancestors of Francis Scott Key and now the co. public lib. The cannon outside the Old Jail (c.1895), now St. Mary's County Historical Society, is reputed to have come from the Ark, a ship that transported the original settlers to Md. in 1634.

Leonardville, village (1990 pop. 374), Riley co., NE Kansas, 20 mi/32 km NW of Manhattan; 39°21′N 96°51′W. Trading point in livestock and grain region.

Leonia (lee-O-nee-uh), residential borough (1990 pop. 8,365), Bergen co., NE N.J., 3 mi/4.8 km ESE of Hackensack, near W approach to George Washington Bridge; 40°51′N 73°59′W. Inc. 1894.

Leonidas (lee-YAW-nuh-duhs), village (1990 pop. 70), St. Louis co., NE Minn., in Mesabi Iron Range, 4 mi/6.4 km SSW of Virginia, 1 mi/1.6 km W of Eveleth; 47°28′N 92°34′W. Iron mines nearby.

Leonore, village (1990 pop. 134), La Salle co., N Ill., 12 mi/19 km SW of Ottawa; 41°11′N 88°58′W. In agr. area.

Leonville (lee-AHN-vil), town (1990 pop. 825), St. Landry parish, S central La., 16 mi/26 km NNE of Lafayette, and on Bayou Teche; 30°28′N 91°59′W. In agr. area (rice, vegetables, peaches, sweet potatoes, sugarcane, cotton; cattle; dairying); timber.

Leopold Island, E Franklin dist., N.W.T., Canada, in Davis Strait, off Cape Mercy, SE Baffin Isl., near entrance of Cumberland Sound; 64°59′N 63°18′W. Isl. is 7 mi/11 km long. Steep cliffs rise to c.2,000 ft/610 m.

Leoti (lee-O-tee), town (1990 pop. 1,738), ⊙ Wichita co., W Kansas, c.45 mi/72 km NW of Garden City, N of White Women Creek; 38°28′N 101°21′W. Elev. 3,297 ft/1,005 m. Shipping point for grain and cattle area.

Leoville (LEE-o-vil), village (1991 pop. 370), W central Sask., Canada, 70 mi/113 km NE of North Battleford; 53°38′N 107°33′W. Mixed farming; dairying.

Lepanto (luh-PAN-to), town (1990 pop. 2,033), Poinsett co., NE Ark., 26 mi/42 km SE of Jonesboro, on left-hand chute of Little R.; 35°36′N 90°19′W. In agr. area; mfg. (apparel). Inc. 1909.

L'Épiphanie (lai-pee-fah-NEE), village (1991 pop. 3,469), S Que., Canada, 4 mi/6 km NW of L'Assomption; 45°51′N 73°29′W. Woodworking; dairying.

Lepreau, Point (luh-PRO), promontory on the Bay of Fundy, S N.B., Canada, 24 mi/39 km SW of St. John; 45°03′N 66°28′W. Lighthouse; fishing ports; blueberries. N.B.'s only nuclear power plant is here.

Lerdo, Mexico: see CIUDAD LERDO.

Lerdo de Tejada (LER-do de te-HE-dah), city (1990 pop. 18,964) and township, Veracruz, SE Mexico, at edge of Papaloapan R. flood plain, and 24 mi/38 km NW of San Andres Tuxtla on Mexico Highway 180. Agr. center (sugarcane, fruit, cattle); sugar processing center.

Lerma (LER-man), river, c.350 mi/563 km long; rising in Mexico state, central Mexico; flowing NW and W through Guanajuato state to L. Chapala, crossing the part of the central plateau known as the Anáhuac. The river draining the lake to N, and flowing NW through Jalisco state to the Pacific Ocean is generally called the Río Grande de Santiago (c.200 mi/320 km long) but it is considered a continuation of the Lerma. The river system is extensively used for irrigation and hydroelectric power.

Lerma de Villada (ler-mah dai vee-YA-dah), city (1990 pop. 9,358) and township, Mexico state, central Mexico, on upper Lerma R., and 28 mi/45 km WSW of Mexico city, 8 mi/12.9 km E of Toluca de Lerdo; ⊙ Lerma Municipio; 19°17′N 99°28′W. Elev. 8,458 ft/2,578 m. On RR and on Mexico City-Toluca Espressway (Mexico Highway 15). Cereals, livestock.

Lerna, village (1990 pop. 301), Coles co., E central Ill., 8 mi/12.9 km SW of Charleston; 39°25′N 88°17′W. In rich agr. area.

Leroy (luh-ROI), town (1991 pop. 456), S central Sask., Canada, 22 mi/35 km SE of Humboldt; mixed farming, dairying.

Leroy, village (1990 pop. 292), McLennan co., E central Texas, 14 mi/23 km NNE of Waco; 31°43′N 97°01′W. Cattle; dairying; grain. Feeds.

Les Cayes (lai-KAI), **Cayes**, or **Aux Cayes**, town (1990 est. pop. 37,550), SW Haiti, on the Caribbean Sea; ⊙ Sud dept.; 18°12′N 73°45′W. Haiti's chief S port and fishing port, it handles exports, mainly molasses and coffee. Tobacco, cotton; cattle; sugarcane growing and processing; cigar mfg.

Les Cheneaux Islands (LE shuh-NO), Mich., group of about 35 small wooded isls. in L. Huron, just S of SE Upper Peninsula, and NE of the Straits of Mackinac; 45°58′N 84°20′W. Locally called "The Snows." Resort area; annual regatta. Largest of group is Marquette Isl., c.5 mi/8 km long.

Les Coteaux (lai ko-TO), village, W Tobago, Rep. of Trinidad and Tobago, 3 mi/5 km N of Scarborough at crossroads in Courland Valley. Agr. (cacao and coconut growing).

Leshara (le-SHAHR-uh), village (1990 pop. 118), Saunders co., E Nebr., 7 mi/11.3 km SE of Fremont, and on Platte R.; 41°19′N 96°25′W.

Leslie, county (□ 404 sq mi/1,046 sq km; 1990 pop. 13,642), SE Ky.; in Cumberland Mts., in Daniel Boone Natl. Forest; ⊙ Hyden; 37°05′N 83°22′W. Drained by Middle Fork Kentucky R. (forms Buckhorn L. reservoir, on N boundary) and Cutshin Creek. Mt. agr. area, (livestock; burley tobacco); timber; bituminous-coal mines. Formed 1878.

Leslie 1 town (1990 pop. 1,872), Ingham co., S central Mich., 14 mi/23 km N of Jackson; 42°27′N 84°25′W. In agr. area (livestock; dairy; grain, apples, corn, soybeans); light mfg. Settled 1836, inc. 1869. **2** town (1990 pop. 134), Franklin co., E central Mo., in Ozark region, 15 mi/24 km SW of Washington; 38°25′N 91°13′W. Hay, cattle.

Leslie 1 (LES-lee), village (1990 pop. 446), Searcy co., N Ark., c.50 mi/80 km N of Conway, and near Middle Fork of Little Red R.; 35°49′N 92°33′W. **2** village (1990 pop. 445), Sumter co., SW central Ga., 12 mi/19 km SE of Americus; 31°57′N 84°05′W.

Lesser Antilles, Caribbean: see WEST INDIES.

Lesser Slave Lake, central Alta., Canada, NW of Edmonton; 60 mi/97 km long and 3 mi/5 km–10 mi/16 km wide. It drains E into the Athabasca R. by the Lesser Slave R. Commercial fishing; lumbering and farming on shores.

Lester, town (1990 pop. 257), Lyon co., NW Iowa, 8 mi/12.9 km W of Rock Rapids; 43°26′N 96°19′W. Livestock, grain.

Lester, village (1990 pop. 420), Raleigh co., S W.Va., 7 mi/11.3 km WSW of Beckley; 37°44′N 81°17′W. Semibituminous-coal area. Light mfg.

Lester B. Pearson International Airport, S central Ont., Canada; covers 4,428 acres/1,792 ha. Official name of Toronto Internatl. Airport, 12 mi/19 km W of downtown Toronto at Malton, in N part of city of Mississauga, just NW of MacDonald-Cartier Freeway. Canada's largest and busiest airport with 3 terminals. Built in 1938 and greatly expanded in the 1960s through 1980s. Surrounded by light mfg. and office parks, hotels, commercial areas.

Lester Prairie, town (1990 pop. 1,180), McLeod co., S central Minn., 40 mi/64 km WSW of Minneapolis, on South Fork Crow R. W of mouth of Otter Creek; 44°52′N 94°02′W. Mfg. (feeds, plastic prods., construction materials).

Lesterville, village, (1990 pop. 168) Yankton co., SE S.Dak., 15 mi/24 km NW of Yankton; 43°02′N 97°35′W.

Lestock, village (1991 pop. 313), SE central Sask., Canada, 65 mi/105 km NNE of Regina. Wheat; dairying.

L'Estrie or **Cantons de l'est**, S Que., Canada, collective name of townships S of the St. Lawrence, centered on Sherbrooke, 1st surveyed after 1791, when Eng. land laws briefly replaced Fr. system of seigneurial tenure. Name was used to distinguish region from the Western Townships, N of the St. Lawrence and on the Bay of Quinte, Ont., surveyed 1783–1784; latter designation is no longer used.

L'Étang du Nord, Canada: see ÉTANG DU NORD.

Letcher (LECH-uhr), county (□ 339 sq mi/878 sq km; 1990 pop. 27,000), SE Ky.; ⊙ Whitesburg; 37°07′N 82°50′W. In the Cumberland Mts. Bounded E and SE by Va.; drained by North Fork Kentucky R. and Poor Fork of Cumberland R. and Rockhouse Creek. Important bituminous-coal-mining area; clay, sand, and gravel pits, stone quarries, timber; some agr. (livestock; burley tobacco). Includes part of Pine Mt. and part of Jefferson Natl. Forest, both on SE boundary; Kingdom Come State Park on SW boundary. Lilley Cornett Woods preserve in SW; Pine Mt. Wildlife Management Area and Bad Branch State Nature Preserve in S. Formed 1842.

Letcher, village (1990 pop. 164), Sanborn co., SE central S.Dak., 15 mi/24 km NNW of Mitchell; 43°53′N 98°08′W. Trade center for diversified farming region; (corn, hogs, poultry). Twin Lakes State Lakeside Use Area to NW.

Letchworth State Park, N.Y.: see GENESEE RIVER.

Letellier (luh-tehl-YAI, luh-TEHL-yah), village, SE Man., Canada, on Marais R., and 11 mi/18 km NW of Emerson. Grain, livestock.

Lethbridge (LEHTH-brij), city (1991 pop. 60,974), S Alta., Canada, on the Oldman R.; 49°42′N 112°50′W. Formerly a coal-mining center, Lethbridge is now a commercial and service center for an irrigated farming and ranching dist. Diverse mfg. includes food, fabricated metal prods., and electronic equip. Federal agr. and veterinary research stations. The Univ. of Lethbridge (1967).

Letona (lee-TO-nuh), village (1990 pop. 218), White co., central Ark., 9 mi/14.5 km NW of Searcy; 35°21′N 91°49′W.

Letts, town (1990 pop. 390), Louisa co., SE Iowa, 12 mi/19 km WSW of Muscatine; 41°19′N 91°13′W. Livestock, grain.

Leupp, uninc. town (1990 pop. 857), Coconino co., N central Ariz., 39 mi/63 km E of Flagstaff, in SW part of Navajo Indian Reservation, on Little Colorado R. Sheep, cattle. Crafts.

Levack, town, SE central Ont., Canada, 21 mi/34 km WNW of Sudbury; 46°38′N 81°23′W. Nickel and copper mining.

Levan (LUH-van), village (1990 pop. 416), Juab co., central Utah, 10 mi/16 km SSW of Nephi; 39°33′N 111°51′W. Elev. 5,314 ft/1,620 m. Wheat, barley, alfalfa; cattle. Chicken Creek reservoir to SW; Sevier Bridge Reservoir and Painted Rock State Park to S. San Pitch Mts. and part of Uinta Natl. Forest to E.

Levant (lev-ANT), agr. town (1990 pop. 1,627), Penobscot co., S Maine, 8 mi/12.9 km NW of Bangor; 44°53′N 68°59′W.

Levasy (LE-vuh-see), town (1990 pop. 279), Jackson co., W Mo., 25 mi/40 km E of downtown Kansas City, on Mo. R.; 39°07′N 94°07′W. Soybeans, wheat, corn; cattle. Fort Osage National Historic Landmark to N.

Level Park, village, Calhoun co., S Mich., suburb 7 mi/11.3 km NW of Battle Creek, on Kalamazoo R.; 42°21′N 85°16′W.

Level Plains, town (1990 pop. 1,473), Dale co., SE Ala., 4 mi/6.4 km W of Daleville; 31°18′N 85°46′W.

Levelland, city (1990 pop. 13,986), NW Texas, 30 mi/48 km W of Lubbock on the Llano Estacado; ⊙ Hockley co.; 33°34′N 102°21′W. Elev. 3,523 ft/1,074 m. The economy is based chiefly on oil and natural gas, agr. (cotton; cattle), and mfg. (food, transportation equip.). South Plains Col. (2-year) is in Levelland. Inc. 1926.

Levelock (LE-ve-lawk), village (1990 pop. 105), SW Alaska, 50 mi/80 km E of Dillingham; 59°06′N 156°53′W.

Leverett (LEV-ret), town (1990 pop. 1,785), Franklin co., N central Mass., 10 mi/16 km SSE of Greenfield; 42°28′N 72°29′W.

Levering, village, Emmet co., NW Mich., 11 mi/18 km SSW of Mackinaw City, in lake region; 45°38′N 84°47′W. Ships farm produce. L. Paradise to NE.

Lévis (lai-VEE), county (□ 272 sq mi/704 sq km), S Que., Canada, on the St. Lawrence, just S of Que.; ⊙ Lévis; 46°40′N 71°10′W.

Levisa Bay (lai-VEE-suh), small inlet, of the Atlantic Ocean, in Holguín prov., E Cuba, on N coast, 7 mi/11.3 km E of Mayarí; 8 mi/12.9 km long, 4 mi/6.4 km wide. Connects with sea through narrows; 20°43′N 75°31′W. Boca Carenerito Nicaro is on S shore.

Levisa Fork (luh-VAL-zuh), river, 164 mi/264 km long, SW Va. and E Ky.; rises in E Buchanan co., Va.; flows NW past Grundy, into Pike co., Ky., through Fishtrap L. reservoir, past Pikeville and Prestonsburg, and N past Paintsville, joins Tug Fork at Louisa to form Big Sandy R. Partially navigable; has locks, dams. Receives Russell Fork R. from SE 3 mi/4.8 km W of Fishtrap L.

Levis-Lauzon, city (1991 pop. 39,452), S central Que., Canada, suburb 1 mi/2 km SSE of Quebec City, on SE shore of St. Lawrence R. Connected to Que. by ferry. Shipbuilding, mfg. (industrial machinery, plastic prods.); general farming.

Levittown 1 uninc. city (1990 pop. 55,362), Bristol township, Bucks co., E Pa., suburb 20 mi/32 km NE of downtown Philadelphia, and 6 mi/9.7 km SW of Trenton,

N.J., near Delaware R.; 40°08′N 74°50′W. Mfg. (fabricated metal prods., electronic equip., printing and publishing, plastic prods.). It was the 2d housing development built (1951–1955) by Levitt and Sons, Inc., who repeated the low-cost residence plan of their Levittown, N.Y., development. The very name itself, Levittown, has come to symbolize the U.S. post-World War II suburban phenomenon, which first gave middle-class families the option of inexpensive, single-unit housing outside the urban sector. Pennsbury Manor State Park to E; Historic Fallsington to NE. Van Sliver L. (backwater lake) to E. **2** uninc. residential city (□ 6 sq mi/15.5 sq km; 1990 pop. 53,286), Nassau co., SE N.Y., on L.I.; 40°43′N 73°30′W. It was originally developed by Levitt and Sons, Inc. a as mass-produced area of private, low-cost housing, and became the prototype for many postwar housing developments throughout the country. Founded 1947.

Levy (LE-vee), county (□ 1,412 sq mi/3,657 sq km; 1990 pop. 25,923), N central Fla., bounded by Gulf of Mexico (S, W) and by Suwannee (W) and Withlacoochee (S) rivers; ⊙ Bronson; 29°16′N 82°47′W. Flatwoods area, with many small lakes and some swamps. Livestock raising (hogs, cattle), farming (corn, vegetables, peanuts), lumbering, fishing, and some quarrying (limestone, dolomite). Formed 1845.

Lewarae (LOO-uh-rai), uninc. village, Richmond co., S N.C., 4 mi/6.4 km W of Rockingham.

Lewellen, village (1990 pop. 307), Garden co., W Nebr., 10 mi/16 km ESE of Oshkosh, and on North Platte R.; 41°19′N 102°08′W. Livestock, grain, sunflower seeds Ash Hollow State Historical Park to SE.

Lewes (LOO-is), resort town (1990 pop. 2,295), Sussex co., SE Del., 15 mi/24 km NE of Georgetown, just W of Cape Henlopen, on Lewes and Rehoboth Canal; shore of Delaware Bay 2 mi/3.2 km to NE; 38°46′N 75°09′W. RR and car (U.S. Highway 9) ferry to Cape May, NJ. Deep-sea fishing; sand and gravel pits. Port of entry. Former Fort Miles Military Reservation to E, is now Cape Henlopen State Park. Prime Hook Natl. Wildlife Reserve to NW. Settled by Dutch in 1631 as 1st white settlement along the Delaware R. Many historic homes and buildings still stand. Historic and maritime exhibits are at Zwaanendael Mus. Inc. 1857.

Lewes and Rehoboth Canal, SE Del., waterway connecting Delaware Bay and N end of Rehoboth Bay; c.15 mi/24 km long; 38°45′N 75°06′W. Starts in N at Broadkill Creek, extends SE parallel to Delaware Bay, past Lewes and Cape Henlopen (to NE) turns S parallel to Atlantic coast, to N end of Rehoboth Bay. For small craft. N entrance 2 mi/3.2 km NW of Lewes; S entrance to ocean via Indian R. Bay and Passage.

Lewes River (LOO-is), 338 mi/544 km long, in S Yukon, Canada, on the upper course of Yukon R.; issues from Tagish L. on B.C. border, flows N, through Marsh L., past Whitehorse (head of navigation), through L. Laberge, and NW past Carmacks, to confluence with Pelly R. at Fort Selkirk, forming Yukon R. proper. Receives Teslin R.

Lewis 1 county (□ 479 sq mi/1,241 sq km; 1990 pop. 3,516), W Idaho; ⊙ Nezperce; 46°14′N 116°26′W. Agr. area bounded on E by Clearwater R., on, in part, by Salmon R. (extreme S), and by Lawyer's Creek. Cattle; alfalfa; barley, wheat; beans; lumber. Includes part of Nez Perce Indian Reservation, covers all but S end of co. Winchester L. State Park on W boundary. Formed 1911. **2** county (□ 495 sq mi/1,282 sq km; 1990 pop. 13,029), NE Ky.; ⊙ Vanceburg; 38°32′N 83°29′W. Bounded N by Ohio R. (Ohio state line) SW by North Fork Licking R.; drained by Grassy Fork and Kinniconick creeks. Rolling agr. area (burley tobacco, hay, alfalfa, soybeans, wheat, corn; cattle, poultry; dairying); some mfg. at Vanceburg. Formed 1806. **3** county (□ 505 sq mi/1,308 sq km; 1990 pop. 10,233), NE Mo.; ⊙ Monticello; 40°06′N 91°43′W. Bounded E by Mississippi R., drained by Wyaconda R. and North and Middle Fabius rivers. Corn, wheat, soy beans; hogs, cattle; lumber; mfg. at La Grange. Formed 1832. **4** co. (□ 1,289 sq mi/3,339 sq km; 1990 pop. 26,796), N central N.Y.; ⊙ Lowville; 43°47′N 75°27′W. Rises to foothills of the Adirondacks in E;

drained by Black and Moose rivers (water power). Mfg. of paper, wood prods., food; lumbering; major dairying area. Named for Morgan Lewis, N.Y. governor at time of co.'s creation. Historically part of romantic scheme to settle refugees from Fr. Revolution. L. Bonaparte named for Napoleon's brother Joseph, once King of Spain, who owned large tract of land here. Bldg. of Black R. canal from Utica to Carthage begun in 1836; it encompasses large part of Tug Hill Plateau, a winter recreational region and major source of pulpwood for paper and lumber mills. Canal ceased operation in 1922. E half of co. in Adirondack foothills, separated from the Tug Hill by the broad Black R. valley. Formed 1805. **5** county (□ 285; 1990 pop. 9,247), central Tenn.; ⊙ Hohenwald; 35°31′N 87°30′W. Drained by Buffalo R. and small Swan Creek. Lumbering, dairying, livestock raising, some agr. (corn, hay, cotton). Contains Meriwether Lewis Natl. Monument. Formed 1843. **6** county (□ 2,436 sq mi/6,309 sq km; 1990 pop. 59,358), SW Wash.; ⊙ Chehalis; 46°35′N 122°24′W. Drained by Cowlitz and Chehalis rivers. Peas, alfalfa, hay, oats, vegetables; dairying; poultry; quicksilver; food processing. Riffa L. (Mossyrock Dam) and Mayfield L. (Mayfield Dam) in S center; part of Mt. Saint Helens Natl. Volcanic Monument in SE. Includes parts of Mt. Baker–Snoqualmie (NE) and Gifford Pinchot (E) natl. forests and S part of Mt. Rainier Natl. Park (NE); includes Tatoosh Wilderness Area and parts of Goat Rocks and William O. Douglas Wilderness areas, in E; Lewis and Clark and Ike Kinswa state parks in S center; Rainbow Falls State Park in W. Formed 1845. **7** county (□ 389 sq mi/1,008 sq km; 1990 pop. 17,223), central W.Va.; ⊙ Weston; 39°00′N 80°30′W. On Allegheny Plateau; drained by the West Fork R. (a headstream of the Monongahela R.). Agr. (corn, potatoes, alfalfa, hay); cattle, sheep. Mfg. at Weston. Natural-gas and oil wells. Timber. Stonewall Jackson L. reservoir (State Park and Wildlife Management Area) in S; part of Stonecoal L. reservoir (Wildlife Management Area) in SE; Jackson's Mill historic site and state 4-H camp in N. Formed 1816.

Lewis, town (1990 pop. 433), Cass co., SW Iowa, on East Nishnabotna R., and 8 mi/12.9 km SSW of Atlantic, near Cold Springs State Park; 41°18′N 95°04′W. In rich agr. region; limestone quarry.

Lewis 1 village (1990 pop. 451), Edwards co., S central Kansas, 9 mi/14.5 km E of Kinsley; 37°56′N 99°15′W. In grain area. Light mfg. **2** lumbering village (1990 pop. 450), Essex co., NE N.Y., in the Adirondacks, 30 mi/48 km SSW of Plattsburgh; 44°17′N 73°34′W.

Lewis and Clark, county (□ 3,497 sq mi/9,057 sq km; 1990 pop. 47,495), W central Mont.; ⊙ Helena; 47°07′N 112°23′W. Mt. region crossed by Continental Divide that passes through W ½ of co.; drained by Missouri, Dearborn, and Blackfoot rivers. N boundary formed by North Fork Sun and Sun rivers (forms Gibson Reservoir; NW). Wheat, barley, oats, hay, cattle, sheep. Sand and gravel, gold. Missouri R. forms 3 reservoirs: Holter L. in E, Hauser L. (and Black Sandy State Park) in SE, and part of large Canyon Ferry L. (and state park) in SE corner. Gates of the Mts. (Missouri R. Canyon) in E. Part of Lewis and Clark Natl. Forest in NW, all 3 forests include parts of Bob Marshall and Scapegoat wilderness areas, in NW. Lincoln State Forest and Great Divide Ski Area in SW; sections of Helena Natl. Forest in SE and W; Willow Creek Wildlife Management Area and Reservoir in N. Initially formed 1865; present boundaries est. 1941. First called Edgerton Co., then Lewis and Clarke Co. (1870); the "e" was later dropped.

Lewis and Clark Affiliated Area, Mo., Neb., S.Dak., N.Dak., Mont., Idaho, Oregon, historic trail (4,500 mi/7,242 km long), commemorates the Lewis and Clark expedition. Authorized 1978.

Lewis and Clark Caverns State Park, , SE Jefferson co., SW Mont., recreational area in canyon of Jefferson R., 34 mi/55 km ESE of Butte. Includes large limestone cave consisting of underground passages and chambers fretted with stalactites and stalagmites. Formerly known as Morrison Cave and Lewis and Clark Caverns Natl. Monument. Covers 2,735 acres/1,107 ha.

Lewis and Clark Lake, reservoir (□ 50 sq mi/130 sq km), on Nebr. (Knox co.) and extreme SE S.Dak. (Yankton co.) border, on Missouri R., 7 mi/11 km E of Yankton; 42°51′N 97°29′W. Max. capacity 540,000 acre-ft. Formed by Gavins Point Dam (74 ft/23 m high), built (1958) by Army Corps of Engineers for flood control; also used for power generation, irrigation, navigation, and recreation.

Lewis Cass, Mount (6,864 ft/2,092 m), on Alaska-B.C. border, in Coast Range, 50 mi/80 km E of Wrangell; 56° 24′N 131°05′W.

Lewis, Fort, Wash.: see TACOMA.

Lewis Hills, sect. of the Long Range rising to 2,672 ft/814 m, W Newfoundland Isl., S of the Bay of Isls. Highest point on the isl.

Lewis Range, E Front Range of Rocky Mts. in NW Mont., extends c.160 mi/257 km SSE from near Waterton L. on U.S.-Canada border, through Glacier Natl. Park, to Blackfoot R. NW of Helena. Forms part of Continental Divide, follows length of range. Within park is highest portion of range, including some of the most spectacular summits of the Rockies; chief peaks are Mt. Cleveland (10,466 ft/3,185 m, highest in range and park), Mt. Stimson (10,142 ft/3,091 m), Kintla Peak (10,110 ft/3,079 m), Mt. Jackson (10,052 ft/3,064 m), Mt. Siyeh (10,014 ft/3,052 m), Going-to-the-Sun Mt. (9,642 ft/2,939 m). Within park, range is crossed by Marias and Logan passes.

Lewis River 1 c.30 mi/48 km long, in NW Wyo.; rises in geyser region of S central Yellowstone Natl. Park; flows S through Shoshone L. and Lewis L., to Snake R. near S boundary of park. **2** c.95 mi/153 km long, W of Mt. Adams, in NE Skamania co., SW Wash.; rising in the Cascade Range, and flowing SW to S of Mt. Saint Helens through to the Columbia R. c.15 mi/24 km N of Vancouver, Wash. Swift Reservoir, Yale L. reservoir, and L. Mervin reservoir furnish hydroelectric power and form a string of lakes along the river's middle course.

Lewis River, Idaho: see SNAKE RIVER.

Lewis Run, borough (1990 pop. 578), McKean co., N Pa., 5 mi/8 km S of Bradford, on East Branch Tunungant Creek. Agr. (grain; livestock; dairying); light mfg. Bradford Regional Airport 4 mi/6.4 km to S. Allegheny Natl. Forest to W.

Lewis Smith Lake, on border of Cullman and Walker cos., N central Ala., on Sipsey Fork R., 34 mi/55 km NW of Birmingham; 33°57′N 87°05′W. Sprawling reservoir has 3 major arms; NW arm extends c.35 mi/56 km into William B. Bankhead Natl. Forest. Max. capacity of 2,203,000 acre-ft. Formed by Lewis Smith Dam (265 ft/81 m high), built (1961) by the Alabama Power Co. for hydroelectric power generation and flood control. Major recreation area.

Lewisberry, borough (1990 pop. 314), York co., S Pa., 9 mi/14.5 km S of Harrisburg. Agr. (grain; livestock; dairying); light mfg. Gifford Pinchot State Park to S.

Lewisburg, city (1990 pop. 9,879), central Tenn., 15 mi/24 km SE of Columbia; ⊙ Marshall co.; 35°27′N 86°48′W. Trade, shipping, processing center for prosperous livestock-raising, dairying, grain-growing, and hardwood-timber region; mfg. of food, electronic equip., lumber. Inc. 1837.

Lewisburg 1 town (1990 pop. 772), Logan co., S Ky., near Mud R., 10 mi/16 km NNW of Russellville; 36°59′N 86°57′W. In agr. and timber area; mfg. (lumber, apparel). L. Malone reservoir and State Park to NW. **2** town (1990 pop. 3,598), SE W.Va., near Greenbrier R., 25 mi/40 km ENE of Hinton; ⊙ Greenbrier co.; 37°48′N 80°25′W. Elev. c.2,300 ft/701 m. Resort area. Grain, apples; tobacco; livestock; dairying. Limestone quarrying. Mfg. (construction equip., transportation equip., food, printing and publishing). Greenbrier Valley Airport to NE. Greenbrier Military School. Old stone church (1796), and site of Fort Savannah (later Fort Union). Carnegie Hall (1902). Lost World Caverns to N; W.Va. State Fairgrounds to S; Greenbrier State Forest to SE; S terminus of Greenbrier R. State Trail to E. Inc. 1782.

Lewisburg, village (1990 pop. 1,584), Preble co., W Ohio, 21 mi/34 km WNW of Dayton, and on small Twin Creek; 39°51′N 84°32′W. Trade center for farm and orchard area; nurseries.

Lewisburg, borough (1990 pop. 5,785), central Pa., 20 mi/32 km SSE of Williamsport, on West Branch of Susquehanna R.; ⊙ Union co. Agr. area (grain, soybeans; poultry, livestock, dairying); mfg. (food prods., fabricated metal prods., lumber, wood prods., printing and publishing); gypsum. Bucknell Univ. here. Lewisburg Federal Penitentiary to N. Tiadaghton State Forest to NW; Shamokin Mt. ridge to S. Laid out 1785, inc. 1813.

Lewisport, town (1990 pop. 1,778), Hancock co., NW Ky., 17 mi/27 km NE of Owensboro, on the Ohio R.; 37°55′N 86°54′W. In agr. area (burley and dark tobacco, grain; livestock). Squire Pate House (1822) and Emmick Plantation House (1850) to E.

Lewiston 1 city (1990 pop. 28,082), NW Idaho, at the Wash. state line, and on Snake R. at mouth of Clearwater R., opposite Clarkston, Wash., 185 mi/298 km NNW of Boise, and 85 mi/137 km SSE of Spokane; ⊙ Nez Perce co.; 46°23′N 117°00′W. It is the commercial and industrial center of a timber, grain, and livestock region (cattle; wheat, barley; alfalfa; vegetables, potatoes) that also has lime, clay, and silica deposits. The city has food processing plants, a large pulp and paper mill, a small arm ammunitions factory, and lumber factories. Lewis and Clark camped there in 1805. At nearby Lapwai, Henry H. Spalding estab. (1836) a mission and operated the first printing press in the Pacific Northwest. Lewiston grew as a supply and shipping center after gold was discovered on the Clearwater R. It was the first capital (1863–1864) of Idaho Territory and had the first newspaper, the *Golden Age* (1862), in Idaho. Lewiston-Nez Perce Airport on S part of city. Lewis-Clark State Col. is in the city, Nez Perce County Historical Mus. Lowest point in Idaho 710 ft/216 m, 2 mi/3.2 km N, where Snake R. turns W into Wash. Umatilla Natl. Forest to SW (Wash.), Nez Perce Indian Reservation to E; Hells Gate State Park to S. Founded 1861. **2** industrial city (1990 pop. 39,757), Androscoggin co., SW Maine, on the E band of the Androscoggin R. opposite Auburn; 44°05′N 70°10′W. A 50 ft/15 m waterfall supplied power for early textile mills; diversified industry. Bates Col. (1855) and the Memorial Armoury (1927), with its large auditoriums, are in Lewiston. Nearby is a bird sanctuary. Inc. 1795.

Lewiston 1 uninc. town (1990 pop. 1,187), Trinity co., NW Calif., 7 mi/11.3 km ESE of Weaverville, on Trinity R. (forms Lewiston L. reservoir to N and the larger Clair Engle L. reservoir, Trinity Dam, 7 mi/11.3 km NNE, both lakes in Trinity Unit of Whiskeytown-Shasta-Trinity Natl. Recreation Area); 40°42′N 122°48′W. Shasta-Trinity Natl. Forest to NE and NW. Timber, hay, cattle, sheep, lambs. **2** town (1990 pop. 1,298), Winona co., SE Minn., 13 mi/21 km WSW of Winona; 43°58′N 91°52′W. Grain; livestock; poultry; dairying; mfg. (feeds, fertilizers, electronics, printing and publishing). Richard J. Dorer Hardwood State Forest to S, N, and E. Whitewater Wildlife Area to NW. **3** town (1990 pop. 1,532), Cache co., N Utah, at Idaho state line, 17 mi/27 km N of Logan, near Bear R., in Cache Valley; 41°57′N 111°52′W. Elev. 4,506 ft/1,373 m. Dairying and irrigated agr. area; wheat, barley, alfalfa, sugar beets, vegetables; dairying (56 dairy farms within city limits); mfg. (plastic prods.). Settled 1870 by Mormons; inc. 1904.

Lewiston 1 village, Montmorency co., N Mich., c.45 mi/72 km SW of Alpena near Twin Lakes (each c.2 mi/3.2 km long); 44°53′N 84°18′W. In resort and agr. region. Light mfg. **2** village (1990 pop. 64), Pawnee co., SE Nebr., 15 mi/24 km NW of Pawnee City; 40°14′N 96°24′W. **3** village (□ 1 sq mi/2.6 sq km; 1990 pop. 3,048) and port of entry, Niagara co., W N.Y., on Niagara R. (bridged here to Queenston, Ont.), just N of Niagara Falls, 20 mi/32 km NNW of Buffalo; 43°10′N

79°02'W. Mfg. (chemicals, construction materials). Massive 2.4-million kw hydroelectric pumped storage project S and E of village. As with Lewis co., named after Gov. Morgan Lewis. Artpark, a 200-acre/81-ha theater and arts complex here. Settled c.1796, inc. 1822.

Lewiston Lake, reservoir (□ 1 sq mi/2.6 sq km), Trinity co., N central Calif., on Trinity R., at S end of Clair Engle L. in Whiskeytown Shasta-Trinity Natl. Recreational Area within Trinity Natl. Forest, 23 mi/37 km WNW of Redding; 40°44'N 122°48'W. Max. capacity 14,660 acre-ft. Formed by Lewiston Dam (91 ft/28 m high), built (1963) by the Bureau of Reclamation for irrigation.

Lewiston-Woodville, town (1990 pop. 788), Bertie co., NE N.C., 15 mi/24 km NW of Windsor; 36°06'N 77°10'W. Agr. area (cotton, tobacco, grain, peanuts; poultry, livestock). Light mfg. State Research Station nearby.

Lewistown, city (1990 pop. 2,572), central Ill., 36 mi/58 km WSW of Peoria; ⊙ Fulton co.; 40°23'N 90°09'W. In agr. and bituminous-coal-mining area; corn, wheat, livestock. City was the home of Edgar Lee Masters. The territory, its people, and legends are reflected in his *Spoon R. Anthology*. Lincoln and Douglas delivered speeches here. Dickson Mounds Mus. is nearby. Settled 1821, inc. 1857.

Lewistown 1 town (1990 pop. 453), Lewis co., NE Mo., near Middle Fabius R., 6 mi/9.7 km W of Monticello; 40°04'N 91°48'W. Agr. **2** town (1990 pop. 6,051), central Mont., on Big Spring Creek, and 90 mi/145 km ESE of Great Falls; ⊙ Fergus co.; 47°04'N 109°26'W. Trade center for agr. and mining region; coal, gypsum, kaolin clay (whiteware clay) gold mines; cattle, sheep, hogs, wheat, barley, oats, dairying; some mfg. Judith Mts. to NE; Big Snowy Mts. in part of Lewis and Clark Natl. Forest to S; Big Springs Trout Hatchery to SE. Laid out as Reed's Fort 1882, inc. as Lewistown 1899.

Lewistown, village, Frederick co., N Md., 9 mi/14.5 km N of Frederick. The town was laid out by Daniel Fundenburg in 1815. A fish hatchery here, constructed by the WPA in the 1930s on Fishing Creek, was recently consolidated with the one on Beaver Creek near South Mt. because of a dwindling water supply.

Lewistown, borough (1990 pop. 9,341), central Pa., 42 mi/68 km NW of Harrisburg, on the Juniata R.; ⊙ Mifflin co.; 40°36'N 77°34'W. Mfg. (paper prods., electronic equip., machinery, printing and publishing, construction materials, fabricated metal prods., apparel, wood prods., plastic prods.). In a lush farm and dairy area (grain, soybeans; livestock, poultry, dairying). Many Amish live and farm in the surrounding area. Lewiston Airport to SW. McCoy House (late 1700s). Blue Mt. ridge to SE, Jacks Mt. ridge to NW; Reeds Gap State Park to NE; Tuscarora State Forest to S. Inc. 1795.

Lewistown Junction, uninc. village, Granville township, Mifflin co., central Pa., 1 mi/1.6 km SW of Lewiston, on Junction R.; 40°35'N 77°34'W.

Lewisville, city (1990 pop. 46,521), Denton co., N Texas, suburb 22 mi/35 km NNW of Dallas–Fort Worth; 33°02'N 96°58'W. Elev. 490 ft/149 m. Rapidly growing urban margin of Dallas in farm area (cattle; wheat; peanuts; cotton). Mfg. (fabricated metal prods., machinery, furniture, concrete, chemicals). Lewisville L. reservoir and L. Lewisville State Park to N; 5 mi/8 km-long dam (on Elm Fork Trinity R.) on N edge of city.

Lewisville 1 town (1990 pop. 1,424), SW Ark., 27 mi/43 km E of Texarkana, near Red R.; ⊙ Lafayette co.; 33°21'N 93°34'W. RR junction. In diversified agr. area; mfg. (furniture, feeds), oil and gas field. L. Erling reservoir to S. **2** town (1990 pop. 437), Henry co., E Ind., near Flatrock R., 9 mi/14.5 km S of New Castle; 39°49'N 85°21'W. In agr. area. Laid out 1829. **3** uninc. town (1990 pop. 3,206), Forsyth co., N central N.C., residential suburb 10 mi/16 km W of Winston-Salem, near Yadkin R.; 36°05'N 80°24'W. In agr. area (tobacco, grain, cattle).

Lewisville 1 village (1990 pop. 471), Jefferson co., SE Idaho, 5 mi/8 km WNW of Rigby, inside bend of Snake R.; 43°42'N 112°01'W. Elev. 4,790 ft/1,460 m. RR terminus of RR spur from Ucon. Grain; sugar beets, potatoes; alfalfa; cattle, sheep; dairying; mfg. (food). **2** village (1990 pop. 255), Watonwan co., S Minn., 11 mi/18 km ESE of St. James; 43°55'N 94°26'W. Grain, soybeans; livestock. **3** village (1990 pop. 261), Monroe co., central Ohio, 15 mi/24 km S of Barnesville, in agr. area; 39°46'N 81°13'W.

Lewisville Lake, reservoir (15 mi/24 km long), at Lewisville, Denton co., N Texas, on Elm Fork of the Trinity R., 23 mi/37 km NW of Dallas; 38°04'N 96°59'W. Max. capacity 2,329,900 acre-ft. Has 8 mi/12.9 km NE arm. Formed by Lewisville Dam (118 ft/36 m high), built (1954) by the Army Corps of Engineers for water supply and flood control. Residential community of L. Dallas on W shore. Lake Lewisville State Park on E shore.

Lexington, county (□ 759 sq mi/1,966 sq km; 1990 pop. 167,611), central S.C.; ⊙ Lexington; 33°53'N 81°16'W. Bounded NE by Congaree R., SW by North Fork of the Edisto; drained by Saluda R. (dammed to form L. Murray) in N. In Sand Hill belt. Sand, clay, shale, grantie kaolin; some agr. (chickens, hogs; dairying; vegetables, corn, wheat, rye, oats, soybeans, hay, peaches). Residential and mfg. suburbs of Columbia in E. Formed 1785.

Lexington 1 city (1990 pop. 1,809), McLean co., central Ill., 15 mi/24 km NE of Bloomington; 40°38'N 88°46'W. Trade and shipping center in rich agr. area; corn, wheat, soybeans, livestock, dairy prods. Settled 1828, inc. 1867. **2** city (1990 pop. 225,366), central Ky., in the heart of the Bluegrass region; ⊙ Fayette co.; 38°02'N 84°27'W. Elev. 983 ft/300 m. The outstanding center in the U.S. for the raising of thoroughbred horses (several hundred horse farms in 35 mi/56 km radius), it is also an important market for burley tobacco, cattle, hogs, and bluegrass seed as well as a RR shipping point for E Kentucky's oil, coal, farm produce, and quarry prods. Lexington has RR junction and center, mfg. (fixtures, printing and publishing, fabricated metal prods., consumer goods, food, machinery, transportation equip., electronic equip.). The city was named in 1775 by a group of hunters who were encamped on the site when they heard the news of the battle of Lexington. Lexington Airport (Blue Grass Field) in W; Civic Center (Rupp Arena); Bluegrass Army Depot (chemical weapons). The city is the seat of the Univ. of Ky., Transylvania Univ. Places of interest include "Ashland," the home of Henry Clay (designed by Latrobe in 1806 and rebuilt with the original materials in the 1850s); "Hopemont," the home of John Hunt Morgan (1814); the Thomas Hart house (1794); the home of Mary Todd Lincoln; and the lib., which has a file of the *Kentucky Gazette*, founded by John Bradford in 1787. Hq. of American Thoroughbred Breeding Center. Aviation Mus. of Ky.; Whitney Mus.; Boone Station State Historic Site in SE; Waveland State Historic Site in S; Ky. Horse Park (State Park) in N, includes Internatl. Mus. of the Horse; Red Mile Harness Track (1875), Keeneland Racetrack in W. Lexington cemetery contains the graves of Clay, Morgan, J. C. Breckinridge, and the author James Lane Allen. A number of hosps. and a federal narcotics facility are located in the city. Lexington Natl. Cemetery in N. Inc. 1832. **3** city (1990 pop. 4,860), W central Mo., on Missouri R. and 35 mi/56 km E of Kansas City; ⊙ Lafayette co.; 39°10'N 93°52'W. Corn, sorghum, soybeans, wheat; cattle, hogs; mfg. (apparel, wood prods.); former coal mines, limestone, rock quarries. Wentworth Military Col. (jr.) here. Civil War battle, September 18-20, 1861. Historic court house (1847-1849). Numerous historic bldgs. Laid out 1822, inc. 1845. **4** city (1990 pop. 16,581), central N.C., 22 mi/35 km S of Winston-Salem; ⊙ Davidson co.; 35°48'N 80°15'W. High Rock L. reservoir (Yadkin R.) to SW. Mfg. (paper prods., food, machinery; printing and publishing, lumber, furniture, textiles). Davidson County Community Col. Boone's Cave State Park to W. Inc. 1827. **5** city (1990 pop. 5,810), W Tenn., 24 mi/39 km E of Jackson; ⊙ Henderson co.; 35°39'N 88°24'W. In cotton, corn, hardwood area; mfg. of electronic equip., apparel, wood prods. Natchez Trace Forest State Park is nearby. **6** independent city (□ 11 sq mi/28 sq km; 1990 pop. 6,959), NW Va., in Shenandoah Valley; ⊙ surrounding Rockbridge co.; 37°46'N 79°26'W. Mfg. (printing and publishing, fixtures); agr. in lush farm area (dairying; livestock, horses; grain, soybeans, apples, peaches). Bombarded and partially burned by Gen. David Hunter in 1864. Va. Military Institute (V.M.I.); Washington and Lee Univ. (including burial site of Robert E. Lee and George C. Marshall Mus.). Stonewall Jackson also buried in city; Stonewall Jackson Home. Natural Bridge to S., Va. Horse Center to N. Laid out 1777, inc. 1841.

Lexington 1 town (1990 pop. 28,974), Middlesex co., E Mass., a residential suburb 7 mi/11.3 km NW of Boston; 42°27'N 71°14'W. Mfg. (printing and publishing, computer software). Corporate hq. for major defense company. On April 19, 1775, the 1st battle of the Revolution was fought here. The site is marked by a monument on the triangular green, around which are several 17th-cent. bldgs. that include Buckman Tavern (1710), where the minutemen assembled. Other attractions are Monroe Tavern (1695), Br. hq. during the battle; and the Hancock-Clarke House (1698), where John Hancock and Samuel Adams were awakened by Paul Revere's alarm. The 1st state normal school in the country, now Farmington State Col., was est. here in 1839. The theologian and reformer Theodore Parker was born in Lexington. Mus. of Our Natl. Heritage. Minutemen Natl. Park. Settled c.1640, inc. 1713. **2** town (1990 pop. 2,279), Anoka co., E Minn., 11 mi/18 km NNE of downtown Minneapolis; 45°08'N 93°10'W. Light mfg. Small natural lakes to E. **3** town (1990 pop. 2,227), central Miss., 29 mi/47 km SSE of Greenwood; ⊙ Holmes co.; 33°07'N 90°02'W. Agr. (cotton, corn, soybeans, sorghum; cattle); timber; mfg. (textiles, apparel); sand and gravel. Booker-Thomas Mus.; Hillside Natl. Wildlife Refuge to W. Inc. 1836. **4** town (1990 pop. 6,601), S central Nebr., 35 mi/56 km W of Kearney and on Platte R.; ⊙ Dawson co.; 40°46'N 99°44'W. Flour; grain, livestock, dairy and poultry prods. Mfg. (food, machinery). Johnson Reservoir and Johnson L. State Recreation Area to S. Laid out as Plum Creek (on the Oregon Trail) 1872, changed to Lexington 1889. **5** town (1990 pop. 1,776), Cleveland co., central Okla., 33 mi/53 km SSE of Oklahoma City, on Canadian R., opposite Purcell; 35°01'N 97°20'W. Trading point in agr. area (wheat, oats, livestock; dairying); light mfg. Settled 1889. **6** town (1990 pop. 3,289), central S.C., 12 mi/19 km W of Columbia, near L. Murray; ⊙ Lexington co.; 33°59'N 81°13'W. Mfg. includes food, plastics, electronic equip., printing and publishing, apparel; agr. area includes chickens, eggs, hogs, dairying, vegetables, apples, and peaches. **7** town (1990 pop. 953), Lee co., S central Texas, c.40 mi/64 km ENE of Austin; 30°24'N 97°00'W. Elev. 456 ft/139 m. In agr. area (cotton, cattle, corn); mfg. (fixtures). Estab. 1850s. **8** uninc. town (1990 pop. 800), Cowlitz co., SW Wash., residential suburb 3 mi/4.8 km N of Kelso, on Cowlitz R., opposite mouth of Ostrander Creek. Mud flows from 1980 eruption of Mt. St. Helens, which surged down Toutle-Cowlitz river system, reached as far as Lexington. Dairying, vegetables.

Lexington 1 village (1990 pop. 230), NE Ga., 17 mi/27 km ESE of Athens; ⊙ Oglethorpe co.; 33°52'N 83°07'W. **2** village (1990 est. pop. 300), Scott co., S Ind., 7 mi/11.3 km ESE of Scottsburg. In agr. area. Lumber, crushed stone, agr. lime. Founded c.1811. **3** village (1990 pop. 779), Sanilac co., E Mich., 21 mi/34 km NNW of Port Huron, on L. Huron; 43°16'N 82°31'W. Fisheries; lumber; tourism, resorts; light mfg. **4** resort village (1990 pop. 500), Greene co., SE N.Y., in the Catskills, on Schoharie Creek, 24 mi/39 km NW of Saugerties; 42°12'N 74°21'W. **5** village (1990 pop. 4,124), Richland co., N central Ohio, 6 mi/10 km SW of Mansfield and on Clear Fork of Mohican R.; 40°40'N 82°35'W. **6** village (1990 pop. 286), Morrow co., N Oregon, 9 mi/14.5 km NW of Heppner, on Willow Creek; 45°27'N

119°41′W. Agr. (wheat, alfalfa, potatoes, onions; sheep, cattle).

Lexington Hills, uninc. town (1990 pop. 2,064), Santa Clara co., W Calif., residential suburb 11 mi/18 km SSW of downtown San Jose; 37°10′N 121°58′W. Surrounds Lexington Reservoir (Los Gatos Creek) in Santa Cruz Mts.; Sierra Azul to E.

Lexington Park, village (1990 pop. 9,943), St. Marys co., S Md., 10 mi/16 km E of Leonardtown; 38°16′N 76°27′W. Patuxent Naval Air Test Center is nearby. On the grounds of the center, Mattapany, built early in the 18th cent., is the official residence of the commanding officer. First established as a mission by Jesuits, it was reclaimed by Lord Baltimore in 1641 to prevent the priests from establishing independent communities. It was called Jarboesville, for an early postmaster, until 1950.

Leyden (LEI-den), agr. town (1990 pop. 662), Franklin co., NW Mass., on Green R., and 8 mi/12.9 km N of Greenfield; 42°42′N 72°38′W.

Liard (LEE-ahrd), river, 755 mi/1,215 km long, SE Yukon Territory, Canada; rising in the Pelly Mts. and flowing SE into N B.C., passes through the main range of the Rocky Mts., thence NE through densely wooded country to the Mackenzie R. at Fort Simpson, Fort Smith Region, N.W.T. It is navigable to Fort Liard, an old Hudson's Bay Co. post, c.165 mi/270 km from its mouth. The South Nahanni and Fort Nelson rivers are its chief tributaries. Part of its course is followed by the Alaska Highway.

Libby, town (1990 pop. 2,532), NW Mont., 56 mi/90 km WNW of Kalispell, and on Kootenai R., at mouth of Libby Creek, just NE of Cabinet Mts.; ⊙ Lincoln co.; 48°23′N 115°34′W. Visitors center; trade center for timber area; agr. (hay, some livestock). Gold, silver, lead, zinc, vermiculite mines nearby. Area surrounded by Kootenai Natl. Forest; Cabinet Mts. Wilderness Area to SW; Kootenai Falls on Kootenai R. to W; Turner Mt. Ski Area to N. Libby Dam on Kootenai R., 10 mi/16 km to E (upstream), forms L. Koocanusa, which extends 85 mi/137 km, including 40 mi/64 km into Canada (B.C.). Founded as mining village in 1860s, inc. 1910. Heritage Mus.; Montana City Old Town; Logger Days (second week of July), Nordicfest (mid-Sept.).

Libbyville, Alaska: see NAKNEK.

Liberal 1 city (1990 pop. 16,573), SW Kansas; ⊙ Seward co.; 37°02′N 100°56′W. Elev. 2,836 ft/864 m. RR junction. It is the trade center for a grazing and farm area. Mfg. (food, helium). Sand and gravel; oil and natural gas are extracted. The traditional Internatl. Pancake Race bet. the housewives of Liberal and Olney, England, is held annually on Shrove Tuesday. Seward Co. Community Col. is in Liberal. County Mus. here. Founded 1888, inc. 1945. **2** city (1990 pop. 684), Barton co., SW Mo., 15 mi/24 km NE of Pittsburg, Kansas; 37°33′N 94°31′W. Corn, wheat, sorghum; cattle. Prairie State Park to SW.

Liberta, village (1991 pop. 1,473), S Antigua, Antigua and Barbuda Republic, West Indies, 6 mi/9.7 km SSE of St. John's. Sugarcane, sea-island cotton. Founded after emancipation of slaves (1834).

Libertad, La, Mexico: see LA LIBERTAD.

Libertador, village, Dominican Republic: see PEPILLO SALCEDO.

Libertador, prov., Dominican Republic: see DAJABÓN.

Liberty 1 county (☐ 843 sq mi/2,183 sq km; 1990 pop. 5,569), NW Fla., bounded by Ochlockonee (E) and Apalachicola (W) rivers; ⊙ Bristol; 30°13′N 84°53′W. Lumber; agr. (livestock, corn, peanuts). S half of co. included in Apalachicola Natl. Forest. Formed 1855. **2** county (☐ 602 sq mi/1,559 sq km; 1990 pop. 52,745), SE Ga.; ⊙ Hinesville; 31°48′N 81°28′W. Bounded SE by the Atlantic, NE by Canoochee R. Includes St. Catherines Isl. Coastal plain agr. (corn, sugarcane, rice, tobacco; cattle, hogs, poultry); lumber, logging and wood prods.; fishing area. Fort Stewart military reservation in NW part of co. Formed 1777. **3** county (☐ 1,447 sq mi/3,748 sq km; 1990 pop. 2,295), N Mont.; ⊙ Chester; 48°33′N 111°02′W. Agr. area bordering on Canada (Alta.) in N; drained in S by Marias R., source of Sage Creek in NE. Wheat, barley, oats, hogs. Light mfg. Tiber Dam forms L. Elwell reservoir in W. Formed 1920. **4** county (☐ 1,176 sq mi/3,046 sq km; 1990 pop. 52,726), SE Texas; ⊙ Liberty; 30°08′N 94°48′W. S part is on Gulf of Mexico coastal plain; N is rolling, wooded. Bounded SW by Cedar Bayou; drained by Trinity R. (shallow-draft navigation to Liberty) and San Jacinto R. (NW). Agr. (rice, soybeans, sorghum, corn); livestock (esp. cattle). Timber (chiefly pine), lumber milling; oil and natural-gas wells, oil refining; sulphur production; sand and gravel. parts of Big Thicket Natl. Preserve in NE. Formed 1836.

Liberty, city (1990 pop. 20,459), satellite city 13 mi/21 km NW of downtown Kansas City; W central Mo.; ⊙ Clay co.; 39°14′N 94°25′W. Shipping point and regional service center; grain elevators. Corn, wheat, soybeans; hogs, cattle; mfg. (printing and publishing, fabricated metal prods., food). William Jewell Col. is here. Laid out 1822.

Liberty 1 town (1990 pop. 2,051), E Ind., 13 mi/21 km S of Richmond; ⊙ Union co.; 39°38′N 84°56′W. In agr. area (livestock; dairying; grain). Laid out 1822. **2** town (1990 pop. 1,937), central Ky., on Green R., and 22 mi/35 km SSW of Danville; ⊙ Casey co.; 37°19′N 84°55′W. Agr. (burley tobacco, corn; livestock, poultry; dairying); timber, limestone; mfg. (apparel, furniture, lumber). Settled 1791. One of 5 places so named in Ky. **3** resort town (1990 pop. 790), Waldo co., S Maine, 14 mi/23 km WSW of Belfast; 44°21′N 69°20′W. Wood prods., fabricated metal prods. Includes part of L. St. George State Park. **4** town (1990 pop. 2,047), Randolph co., central N.C., 18 mi/29 km SE of Greensboro near source of Rocky R.; 35°51′N 79°34′W. Agr. area (tobacco, soybeans, grain; dairying; poultry, livestock). Mfg. (feeds, construction materials, fixtures, textiles, apparel). **5** town (1990 pop. 3,228), Pickens co., NW S.C., 17 mi/27 km WSW of Greenville; 34°47′N 82°42′W. Mfg. includes transportation equip., food, apparel; agr. includes dairying, poultry, hogs, corn. **6** town (1990 pop. 391), De Kalb co., central Tenn., 8 mi/13 km NW of Smithville; 36°00′N 85°58′W. **7** town (1990 pop. 7,773), SE Texas, on Trinity R. at head of shallow-draft navigation, and 40 mi/64 km NE of Houston; ⊙ Liberty co.; 30°03′N 94°47′W. Elev. 30 ft/9 m. Trade center in agr. (rice, sorghum, soybeans, corn, cattle), timber, oil and natural-gas producing area. Mfg. (chemicals, machinery). Founded c.1830.

Liberty 1 village (1990 pop. 140), Montgomery co., SE Kansas, on Verdigris R., and 9 mi/14.5 km N of Coffeyville; 37°09′N 95°35′W. Livestock raising. Oil and gas fields nearby. Montgomery State Fishing L. to W. **2** village (1990 pop. 624), SW Miss., 42 mi/68 km SE of Natchez, bet. East and West forks Amite R.; ⊙ Amite co.; 31°09′N 90°47′W. Agr. (cotton, corn; cattle; dairying); catfish; some mfg. **3** village (1990 pop. 74), Gage co., SE Nebr., 18 mi/29 km SE of Beatrice, and on branch of Big Blue R., near Kansas state line; 40°05′N 96°28′W. Light mfg. **4** vacation and summer-resort village (☐ 2 sq mi/5.2 sq km; 1990 pop. 4,128), Sullivan co., SE N.Y., in the Catskills, 30 mi/48 km NW of Middletown; 41°47′N 74°45′W. Neversink and Roundout reservoirs, both part of N.Y. city's water supply, nearby. Settled 1793, inc. 1870. **5** village (1990 pop. 155), Tulsa co., NE Okla., 18 mi/29 km SSE of downtown Tulsa; 35°51′N 95°58′W. Agr. area located in margin of urban growth.

Liberty 1 borough (1990 pop. 2,744), Allegheny co., SW Pa., residential suburb 11 mi/18 km SE of downtown Pittsburgh, and 2 mi/3.2 km SSW of McKeensport, near Youghiogheny R. Inc. c.1912. **2** borough (1990 pop. 199), Tioga co., N Pa., 23 mi/37 km N of Williamsport. Agr. (dairying; livestock; grain); light mfg. Tioga State Forest to N, Tidaghton State Forest to SE.

Liberty Center, village (1990 pop. 1,084), Henry co., NW Ohio, 7 mi/11 km ENE of Napoleon, near Maumee R.; 41°26′N 84°00′W.

Liberty Hill, uninc. village (1990 pop. 300), Williamson co., central Texas, 29 mi/47 km NNW of Austin, on S Fork San Gabriel R. Light mfg. L. Georgetown reservoir to NE.

Liberty Island, N.Y.: see STATUE OF LIBERTY NATIONAL MONUMENT.

Liberty Lake, uninc. town, Spokane co., E Wash., industrial suburb 15 mi/24 km E of Spokane, 12 mi/19 km WSW of Coeur d'Alene, Idaho, 2 mi/3.2 km W of Idaho state line, on Liberty L. reservoir; 47°39′N 117°05′W. Mfg. (plastic prods., electronic equip., computers, machinery, printing and publishing).

Libertytown, village, Frederick co., N Md., 10 mi/16 km ENE of Frederick. Highway junction in agr. area.

Libertyville, town (1990 pop. 264), Jefferson co., SE Iowa, 6 mi/9.7 km SW of Fairfield, in bituminous-coal-mining and livestock area; 40°57′N 92°02′W.

Libertyville, village (1990 pop. 19,174), Lake co., NE Ill., in a lake area; 42°16′N 87°58′W. Remnant agr.: mfg. (paper prods., electronic equip.). A naval training station is nearby. Inc. 1882.

Library, uninc. town (1990 pop. 3,600), South Park township, Allegheny co., W Pa., residential suburb 10 mi/16 km SSW of downtown Pittsburgh; 40°17′N 80°00′W. Some mfg. South Regional Park to N.

Library of Congress, U.S. govt. institution, Independence Ave. and 1st St., SE Washington, D.C. A complex of 3 bldgs. containing the world's largest collection of books, maps, manuscripts, media items, etc. The Jefferson Bldg. (1897) contains the impressive Main Reading Room. The Adams Bldg. (1939) and Madison Bldg. (1980) have added much-needed shelf space for the more than 1 million items added to the collection each year.

Libres (LEE-bres), town (1990 pop. 9,284), ⊙ Libres municipio, Puebla state, central Mexico, 45 mi/72 km NE of Puebla on RR, on Mexico Highway 129; 19°27′N 97°41′W. Elev. 7,808 ft/2,380 m. Cereals, maguey; livestock. Formerly called San Juan de los Llanos.

Lick Observatory, astronomical observatory, on Mt. Hamilton, Santa Clara co., Calif., 15 mi/24 km E of San Jose, in Diablo range of Coast Ranges. The 1st mountaintop observatory in the world, it was founded through gifts made by James Lick in 1874–1875 and came under the direction of the Univ. of Calif. in 1888. The original telescope at the observatory is a 36 in/91 cm refracting telescope, 2d largest in the world after the 40 in/102 cm refractor at Yerkes. The principal research instrument is now a 120 in/305 cm reflecting telescope that went into operation in 1959. Other equip. includes 36 in/91 cm and 22 in/56 cm reflectors, a 12 in/30 cm refractor, and a 20 in/51 cm twin astrographic telescope.

Licking, county (☐ 686 sq mi/1,777 sq km; 1990 pop. 128,300), central Ohio; ⊙ Newark; 40°05′N 82°30′W. Drained by Licking R. and Raccoon Creek. Includes part of Buckeye L. (recreation). In the Glaciated Plain physiographic region. Agr. area (hogs; dairy prods.; corn); mfg. (tires; stone, clay, and glass prods.; commercial printing; motor vehicle parts); sand and gravel pits. Formed 1808.

Licking, town (1990 pop. 1,328), Texas co., S central Mo., in the Ozarks, 14 mi/23 km N of Houston; 37°30′N 91°51′W. Elev. 1,259 ft/384 m. Grain; cattle; lumbering; mfg. (apparel). Has center for a recreational area. Montauk State Park to E.

Licking River 1 E and N Ky., c.320 mi/515 km long; rises in SE Magoffin co., E Ky.; flows NW past Salyersville and West Liberty, through Cave Run L. reservoir, receives North Fork from E, then South Fork from S at Falmouth, enters Ohio R. at Covington and Newport, opposite Cincinnati, Ohio. The Licking was an important means of travel for Native Americans and pioneers and later a busy trade route. In 1780, at the river's mouth, George Rogers Clark's frontiersmen gathered for their march up the Little Miami; the battle of Blue Licks (1782) occurred in the Licking valley. **2** In central Ohio, formed by North and South forks and Raccoon Creek at Newark, flows c.40 mi/64 km E and SE to the Muskingum at Zanesville; 39°56′N 82°00′W. North Fork rises in Knox co., flows c.35 mi/56 km E and S. South Fork rises in Licking co., flows SE and NE for c.30 mi/48 km. Raccoon Creek (c.25 mi//40 km long), entirely within Licking co., flows SE to junction with the other headstreams.

Lida, Lake (LEI-duh), (□ 10 sq mi/26 sq km), Otter Tail co., W Minn., 19 mi/31 km NNE of Fergus Falls, separated by narrow land bridges from Crystal L. (N) and L. Lizzie (NW), throughout which it drains to Pelican R.; 4 mi/6.4 km long, 2.5 mi/4 km wide. Causeway separates South Arm (2 mi/3.2 km long) from remainder of lake; 46°34′N 95°58′W. Elev. 1,313 ft/400 m. Resorts. Maplewood State Park at S end.

Lidderdale, town (1990 pop. 202), Carroll co., W central Iowa, 6 mi/9.7 km NE of Carroll; 42°07′N 94°46′W. Feed milling.

Lidgerwood, town (1990 pop. 799), Richland co., SE N.Dak., 29 mi/47 km SW of Wahpeton; 46°04′N 97°09′W. Dairy prods.; poultry; grain. (Sisseton) Wahpeton Indian Reservation to S. L. Tewaukon and Tewaukon Natl. Wildlife Refuge to SW. Inc. 1901.

Lido Isle, residential island in Newport Bay, Calif.

Liebenthal (LEE-buhn-thahl), village (1990 pop. 112), Rush co., W central Kansas, 8 mi/12.9 km N of La Crosse; 38°38′N 99°19′W. In wheat and cattle area.

Lièvre, (lee-AI-vruh), river, c.200 mi/320 km long, S Que., Canada; rising in Kempt L.; flowing generally SW into the Ottawa R. near Buckingham. Parts of it are navigable. There are 5 hydroelectric plants along its course; 2 of the most important are at Masson and High Falls.

Lièvres, Île aux, Canada: see HARE ISLAND.

Liggett (LIG-et), uninc. village (1990 pop. 75), Harlan co., SE Ky., in the Cumberland Mts., 8 mi/12.9 km SSW of Harlan. Bituminous coal.

Light Oak, uninc. town (1990 pop. 1,339), Cleveland co., S N.C., residential suburb 4 mi/6.4 km ESE of Shelby; 35°16′N 81°28′W.

Lighthouse Point, town (□ 2 sq mi/5.2 sq km; 1990 pop. 10,378), Broward co., SE Fla., 3 mi/4.8 km S of Deerfield Beach; 26°16′N 80°05′W. Mfg. includes flow pumps.

Lignite (LIG-neit), village, Burke co., NW N.Dak., 15 mi/24 km WNW of Bowbells, near lignite-mining center; 48°52′N 102°33′W. RR junction to W.

Lignite, locality, S central Alaska, NE of Mt. McKinley Natl. Park, 5 mi/8 km N of Healy. On Alaska RR; subbituminous-coal deposits.

Ligon (LIG-uhn), village (1990 pop. 350), Floyd co., E Ky., in Cumberland foothills, 14 mi/23 km SW of Pikeville. Bituminous coal.

Ligonier (lig-uh-NEER), city (1990 pop. 3,443), Noble co., NE Ind., on Elkhart R., and 9 mi/14.5 km NW of Albion; 41°28′N 85°35′W. Trade center in dairying and poultry-raising area; mfg. (bldg. materials, gaskets, hydraulic equip., marshmallows, plastic prods., flour and feed milling, motor vehicle parts, molded prods., sample books). Laid out 1835.

Ligonier (LI-guh-nir), borough (1990 pop. 1,638), Westmoreland co., SW Pa., on Loyalhanna Creek, 17 mi/27 km ESE of Greensburg. Agr. (corn, hay; dairying); mfg. (wood prods.); bituminous coal; timber. Fort Ligonier built c.1758. Linn Run State Park and Forbes Satte Forest to S, Laurel Ridge State Park to SE and E; Chestnut Ridge to NW. Laid out 1817; inc. 1834.

Liguanea, Cuba: see LANIER.

Liguanea Plain, fertile lowland in SE Jamaica, includes all Kingston area and lower St. Andrew; 17°58′N–18°01′N 76°45′W–76°52′W. Vere Plain continues it W.

Lihue (LEE-HOO-ai), town (1990 pop. 5,536), ⊙ Kauai co., SE Kauai, Hawaii, near Nawiliwili Harbor, 110 mi/177 km WNW of Honolulu; 21°58′N 159°20′W. Junction of Kaumualii Highway, to S coast, and Kuhio Highway, to N coast. Mfg. (coatings, printing and publishing, lumber, soaps, sugarcane processing, construction machinery). Lihue Plantation to W. Kauai Community Col. to W at Puhi. Grove Farm Homestead Mus. Kauai Mus. Kilohana Crater (1,133 ft/345 m) to NW; Lihue-Koloa Forest Reserve to NW; Haleia Natl. Wildlife Refuge to NW; Wailua River State Park (including Wailua Falls) to N; Ahukini State Recreational Park to NE.

Lila Lake, Hamilton co., NE central N.Y., on branch of Beaver R., in the Adirondack Mts., in Adirondack Park,

30 mi/48 km SW of Saranac Lake town; c.2.5 mi/4 km long, max. 1.5 mi/2.4 km wide; 44°00′N 74°45′W.

Lilbourn (LIL-buhrn), city (1990 pop. 1,378), New Madrid co., extreme SE Mo., near Mississippi R., 5 mi/8 km W of New Madrid; 36°35′N 89°36′W. Cotton, rice, wheat, soybeans; lumber mills. Inc. as city 1910.

Lilburn, suburb (1990 pop. 9,301) of Atlanta, Gwinnett co., Ga., 5 mi/8 km E of Doraville; 33°53′N 84°08′W. Bedroom community for Atlanta region as well as an emerging business hub. Mfg. (glass, concrete, printing plates, steel fabricating, signs).

Liliesville (LEILZ-vil), village (1990 pop. 468), Anson co., S N.C., 2 mi/3.2 km E of Wadesboro; 34°58′N 79°59′W. In agr. (cotton, grain; poultry, livestock) and timber area. Mfg. (sand and gravel processing, fabric goods, lumber). Blewitt Falls L. reservoir to E.

Lillington (LIL-ing-tuhn), town (1990 pop. 2,048), ⊙ Harnett co., central N.C., 28 mi/45 km SSW of Raleigh, on Cape Fear R.; 35°23′N 78°49′W. Agr. area (grain, tobacco, cotton, sweet potatoes; poultry, livestock); mfg. (vanity tops and bathtubs, mobile homes, neon signs, gun holsters, workshirts, electronic counter measurers). Raven Rock State Park to NW.

Lillinonah, Lake, reservoir (□ 2 sq mi/5.2 sq km), Fairfield co., SW Conn., on Housatonic R., 12 mi/20 km E of Danbury; 41°23′N 73°10′W. Max. capacity 37,200 acre-ft. Formed by Stevenson Dam (83 ft/25 m high), built (1919) for power generation. Paugussett State Forest (W) and state parks here.

Lillooet (LI-loo-eht), village (1991 pop. 1,782), S B.C., Canada, on Fraser R., near Seton L., 70 mi/113 km W of Kamloops; 50°41′N 121°56′W. In gold-mining and mixed farming region; hydroelectric power.

Lillooet Lake, SW B.C., Canada, expansion of Lillooet R., in Coast Mts., 40 mi/64 km SW of Lillooet; 21 mi/34 km long, 1 mi/2 km–2 mi/3 km wide.

Lillooet River, 130 mi/209 km long, SW B.C., Canada; rises in Coast Mts. at foot of Mt. Dalgleish, W of Lillooet; flows SE, through Lillooet L., to NW end of Harrison L., which drains into Fraser R.

Lilly (1990 pop. 138), Dooly co., central Ga., 6 mi/9.7 km WNW of Vienna; 32°09′N 83°53′W.

Lilly, borough (1990 pop. 1,162), Cambria co., W central Pa., 21 mi/34 km ENE of Johnstown, on Little Conemaugh R. Agr. (corn, hay; dairying); mfg. (dresses); bituminous coal.

Lilly Grove, uninc. town (1990 pop. 950), Mercer co., S W.Va., 2 mi/3.2 km NW of Princeton.

Lily, uninc. town (1990 pop. 800), Laurel co., SE Ky., 5 mi/8 km N of Corbin, in Cumberland foothills, on Laurel R. Bituminous coal; mfg. (machining, mining lights). London-Corbin Airport to N. Levi Jackson Wilderness Road State Park to NE.

Lily, village (1990 pop. 26), Day co., NE S.Dak., 13 mi/21 km SW of Webster; 45°10′N 97°40′W. Waubay L. and Natl. Wildlife Refuge to SE; Pickerel L. State Rec. Area to E.

Lily Bay, bay, Piscataquis co., central Maine, on Moosehead L., and 31 mi/50 km NW of Dover-Foxcroft. Lily Bay State Park.

Lily Dale, resort village (1990 pop. 500), Chautauqua co., extreme W N.Y., 9 mi/14.5 km S of Dunkirk, on Cassadaga Lakes; 42°21′N 79°20′W. In agr. area. This small, gated community has been a center of spiritualism since organization of Lily Dale Assembly (1879), attracting thousands of summer tourists. Technically part of Poufret township.

Lily Lake, village (1990 pop. 542), Kane co., NE Ill., 10 mi/16 km WNW of Geneva; 41°56′N 88°28′W.

Lilydale, village (1990 pop. 506), Dakota co., SE Minn., residential suburb 3 mi/4.8 km SW of downtown St. Paul, 8 mi/12.9 km SE of downtown Minneapolis, on Mississippi R. (bridged), immediately below (E of) mouth of Minnesota R.; 44°54′N 93°07′W.

Lilypons (LIL-ee-ponz), village, Frederick co., central Md., 10 mi/16 km S of Frederick. Named after the opera singer. Tropical fish ponds here are described as the largest commercial operation of this kind in the country.

Lima (LEI-muh), city (1990 pop. 45,549), ⊙ Allen co.,

NW Ohio; 40°45′N 84°07′W. Located in a fertile farm area, it is a processing and marketing center for grain, dairy, and meat prods. Auto engines, school buses, electric signs and motors, cranes and power shovels, petroleum prods. (refinery), steel castings, machine tools, plastics, chemicals, engines, and fertilizers are produced in the city. Lima, formerly a large oil producer (1885–1910), houses a symphony orchestra and a branch of Ohio State Univ. Settled 1831; inc. 1842.

Lima 1 (LEI-muh), village (1990 pop. 120), Adams co., W Ill., 16 mi/26 km N of Quincy; 40°10′N 91°22′W. In agr. area. **2** village (1990 pop. 265), Beaverhead co., extreme SW Mont., 40 mi/64 km S of Dillon, near Idaho state line, and on Red Rock R. at mouth of Junction Creek; 44°38′N 112°35′W. Sheep, cattle; hay, potatoes. Continental Divide to S. Parts of Beaverhead Natl. Forest to S, W, and NE. Lima Reservoir used for irrigation and recreation to E on Red Rock R. Originally called Allerdice, then Spring Hill. **3** village (□ 1 sq mi/2.6 sq km; 1990 pop. 2,165), Livingston co., W central N.Y., 18 mi/29 km S of Rochester; 42°54′N 77°36′W. Makes concrete; agr. (wheat, vegetables, and fruits). **4** village (1990 pop. 133), Seminole co., central Okla., 6 mi/9.7 km WNW of Wewoka; 35°10′N 96°35′W. In agr. area. **5** (LEE-muh), uninc. village, Greenville co., NW S.C., in the Blue Ridge, on North Saluda R. and 17 mi/27 km N of Greenville.

Lima Reservoir (LEI-muh), SW Mont., in Beaverhead co., just S of Snowcrest Range, near Idaho state line, formed by Lima Dam in Red Rock R.; 8 mi/12.9 km long, 1 mi/1.6 km wide. Irrigates livestock region. Town of Lima 12 mi/19 km W. Red Rock Lakes Natl. Wildlife Refuge, important nesting site of trumpeter swan, upstream (E) from lake.

Limaville (LEI-muh-vil), village (1990 pop. 152), Stark co., E central Ohio, 17 mi/27 km NE of Canton; 40°59′N 81°08′W.

Limbé (lang-BAI), town (1982 pop. 10,476), Nord dept., N Haiti, 12 mi/19 km WSW of Cap-Haïtien; 19°42′N 72°24′W. Agr. (cacao, coffee, cotton, oranges, limes, sugarcane); copper deposits nearby. Old colonial town. Also called Le Limbé.

Lime Creek, 78 mi/126 km long, S Minn. and N Iowa; rises in Bear L., Freeborn co., Minn., 7 mi/11.3 km SW of Albert Lea, 43°31′N 93°29′W; flows SSW into Winnebago co., N Iowa to Ford city, then ESE, through Mason City, to Shell Rock R. 2 mi/3.2 km S of Rockford. From Forest City to its mouth the stream is called Winnebago R.

Lime Hall, town, St. Ann parish, N Jamaica, 2 mi/3.2 km S of St. Ann's Bay; 18°24′N 77°11′W. In agr. region (citrus fruits, corn, pimentos, coffee; cattle).

Lime Kiln, village, Frederick co., N Md., near Monocacy R., 4 mi/6.4 km S of Frederick. Always associated with limestone operations, it was once called Slabtown because many houses and walls were made of limestone slabs. The B&O RR still carries out lime-based portland cement.

Lime Lake, Cattaraugus co., W N.Y., resort lake (c.1 mi/1.6 km long), 25 mi/40 km N of Olean; 42°26′N 78°29′W. Lime L. village on N shore; Machias just SW.

Lime Ridge, uninc. town (1990 pop. 1,051), Columbia co., E central Pa., residential suburb 5 mi/8 km W of Berwick on Susquehanna R.; 41°01′N 76°21′W.

Lime Ridge, village (1990 pop. 152), Sauk co., S central Wis., 21 mi/34 km W of Baraboo; 43°28′N 90°09′W. In dairy and livestock region.

Lime Rock, Conn.: see SALISBURY.

Lime Springs, town (1990 pop. 438), Howard co., NE Iowa, near Upper Iowa R., 10 mi/16 km NW of Cresco; 43°27′N 92°16′W. Feed milling. Limestone quarries, sand and gravel pits nearby.

Limedale, village, Putnam co., W central Ind., 2 mi/3.2 km SSW of Greencastle. Limestone quarries. Laid out 1864.

Limerick (LIM-uhr-ik), town (1990 pop. 1,688), York co., SW Maine, 15 mi/24 km NNW of Alfred; 43°41′N 70°47′W. Yarn mills. Settled c.1775; inc. 1787.

Limerick, village (1991 pop. 155), S Sask., Canada, 13 mi/21 km W of Assiniboia; 49°39′N 106°16′W. Wheat.

Limerick 1 and 2 Nuclear Power Plants, Pa.: see MONTGOMERY CO.

Limerock, R.I.: see LINCOLN.

Limestone 1 county (☐ 607 sq mi/1,572 sq km; 1990 pop. 54,135), N Ala.; ⊙ Athens. Bounded N by Tenn., drained by Wheeler L. (on Tennessee R.) and Elk R. Cotton, timber, corn, soybeans. First Ala. co. invaded in Civil War, 1862. Nuclear power plants: Browns Ferry 1 (initial criticality, August 17, 1973), Browns Ferry 2 (initial criticality, July 20,1974), and Browns Ferry 3 (initial criticality, August 8, 1976) are 10 mi/16 km NW of Decatur. Use cooling water from the Tennessee R., and each has a max. dependable capacity of 1,065 MWe. Formed 1818. **2** county (☐ 933 sq mi/2,416 sq km; 1990 pop. 20,946), E central Texas; ⊙ Groesbeck; 31°32′N 96°34′W. Drained by Navasota R. Agr. (cotton, corn, peaches, hay, vegetables, pecans, nursery crops); dairying; livestock (cattle, horses, hogs, sheep, goats). Oil, natural gas; clay, stone, lignite, sand and gravel. Mfg. at Groesbeck, Mexia. Includes Fort Parker State Park and Old Fort Parker State Historic Site, near L. Mexia, in N center; Confederate Reunion Grounds State Historic Site in N; part of L. Limestone in SE. Formed 1846.

Limestone, town (1990 pop. 9,922), Aroostook co., NE Maine, 17 mi/27 km NNE of Presque Isle, at N.B. border; 46°54′N 67°51′W. In potato and pea country. Port of entry; terminus of Bangor and Aroostook RR. Loring Air Force Base (closed) here. Settled 1849; inc. 1869.

Limestone, village (☐ 1 sq mi/2.6 sq km; 1990 pop. 459), Cattaraugus co., W N.Y., on Allegheny R., 10 mi/16 km WSW of Olean; 42°01′N 78°37′W. Located near the N edge of the "Pennsylvania field," which extends through SW N.Y. state as well as into W Pa., W. Va., and Ohio. The field was the 1st major oil-producing region in the U.S. When the 1st well was successfully drilled near Titusville, Pa., in 1859, Allegany, Cattaraugus, and Chautaugua cos. all shared in the prosperity. Small amounts of oil and natural gas are still extracted.

Limestone, Lake, reservoir (☐ 21 sq mi/54 sq km), Robertson co., E central Texas, on Navasota R., 50 mi/80 km ESE of Waco; 31°20′N 96°19′W. Max. capacity 557,878 acre-ft. Formed by Sterling C. Robertson Dam (65 ft/16 m high), built (1978) for water supply; also used for irrigation and recreation.

Limington (LI-ming-ton), town (1990 pop. 2,796), York co., SW Maine, on Saco R., and 18 mi/29 km N of Alfred; 43°43′N 70°42′W. Wood prods.

Limon, town (1990 pop. 1,831), Lincoln co., E central Colo., on Big Sandy Creek, 80 mi/129 km SE of Denver, and 65 mi/105 km NE of Colo. Springs; 39°16′N 103°41′W. Agr. trade region: wheat, sunflowers; cattle; mfg. (concrete). Founded 1888; inc. 1909.

Limón, El, Mexico: see EL LIMÓN.

Limonade (lee-mo-NAHD), town (1982 pop. 2,590), Nord dept., N Haiti, near the Atlantic, 8 mi/12.9 km SE of Cap-Haïtien; 19°40′N 72°07′W. Agr. (coffee, tobacco, sugarcane, bananas, citrus fruits); essential oils distillery; copper deposits nearby.

Limonar (lee-mo-NAHR), town, Matanzas prov., W Cuba, on Central Highway, on RR, and 12 mi/19 km ESE of Matanzas; 22°46′N 81°25′W. In sugar-growing region. Also apiculture; cattle raising. Nearby are refineries and centrals of Horacio (NE) and Fructoso Rodríguez (S).

Linares (lee-NAH-res), city (1990 pop. 44,436) and township, Nuevo León, N Mexico, at foot of Sierra Madre Oriental, at junction Mexico Highways 60 and 85, RR, on Inter-Amer. Highway, and 75 mi/121 km SE of Monterrey; 24°51′N 99°34′W. Elev. 2,244 ft/684 m. Trading center in rich farming (sugarcane, oranges, cotton, cereals) and grazing dist. Old colonial churches.

Lincoln, town (1986 pop. 14,391), S Ont., Canada, on Niagara Peninsula, immediately W of St. Catharines. Fruits; nurseries; wineries. Light industries. Suburban.

Lincoln, plantation (1990 pop. 38), Oxford co., W Maine, on Magalloway R., and c.35 mi/56 km NW of Rumford; 44°57′N 71°00′W.

Lincoln, county (☐ 332 sq mi/834 sq km), S Ont., Canada, on L. Ontario, and on Niagara R., on N.Y. border; ⊙ St. Catharines; 43°05′N 79°34′W. Lincoln and Welland cos. form regional municipality of Niagara.

Lincoln 1 county (☐ 572 sq mi/1,481 sq km; 1990 pop. 13,690), SE Ark.; ⊙ Star City; 33°58′N 91°44′W. Bounded NE by Arkansas R.; drained by Bayou Bartholomew. Agr. (cotton, soybeans, wheat, rice; cattle, hogs, poultry). Joe Harden Lock and Dam in N; Cane Creek State Park at center. Formed 1871. **2** county (☐ 2,586 sq mi/6,698 sq km; 1990 pop. 4,529), E central Colo.; ⊙ Hugo; 39°03′N 103°27′W. Agr. area, drained by Big Sandy, Horse, Rush, and Hell creeks. Wheat, sunflowers; cattle. Source of S and N Forks Arikaree R. and S Fork Republican R in N. Formed 1889. **3** county (☐ 257 sq mi/666 sq km; 1990 pop. 7,442), NE Ga.; ⊙ Lincolnton; 33°47′N 82°27′W. Bounded E by S.C. state line, formed here by Savannah R., and S by Little R. Piedmont agr. (cotton, corn, hay, agr., fruits); cattle, hogs, poultry; mfg. (apparel, textiles); sawmilling. Formed 1796. **4** county (☐ 1,205 sq mi/3,121 sq km; 1990 pop. 3,308), S Idaho; ⊙ Shoshone; 42°59′N 114°08′W. In Snake R. plain; watered by Big Wood and Little Wood rivers. Irrigated region in SW, around Shoshone, produces cattle; alfalfa, oats, barley, corn, sugar beets, potatoes, dry beans. Shoshone Ice Caves in NW. Formed 1895. **5** county (☐ 719 sq mi/1,862 sq km; 1990 pop. 3,653), central Kansas; ⊙ Lincoln; 39°03′N 98°12′W. Smoky Hills region, drained by Saline R. and Salt Creek. Wilson L. and Dam on W border, with Wilson State Park on S shore (in Russell co.). Cattle, sheep; wheat, sorghum, alfalfa, hay. Formed 1870. **6** county (☐ 336 sq mi/870 sq km; 1990 pop. 20,045), central Ky.; ⊙ Stanford; 37°27′N 84°40′W. Drained by Dix and Green rivers and Fishing and Buck creeks (source of latter 3 streams). Rolling upland agr. area, partly in outer Bluegrass region (burley tobacco, hay, alfalfa, soybeans, wheat, corn; hogs, cattle, poultry; dairying; timber). Isaac Shelby State Historic Site in NW; William Whitley House State Historic Site in E. Formed 1780 from Kentucky co., Va., one of 3 original cos. of Kentucky dist. of Va. **7** coastal county (☐ 699 sq mi/1,810 sq km; 1990 pop. 30,357), S Maine; ⊙ Wiscasset; 44°03′N 69°32′W. Fishing and resort area, with some agr. in N part; boatbuilding, shipping, and canning of seafood. Resorts dot its rugged coast and isls. Sheepscot and Eastern rivers, Damariscotta and Medomak inlets. Formed 1760. Maine Yankee Nuclear Power Plant, initial criticality October 23, 1972, is 10 mi/16 km N of Bath, uses cooling water from the Back R., and has a max. dependable capacity of 860 MWe; was temporarily closed for repair in 1995. **8** county (☐ 548 sq mi/1,419 sq km; 1990 pop. 6,890), SW Minn.; ⊙ Ivanhoe; 44°25′N 96°16′W. Bounded by S.Dak. on W. Agr. area (oats, wheat, soybeans, hay, alfalfa; sheep, hogs, cattle, poultry; dairying). Includes part of Coteau des Prairies; several lakes scattered through co., including L. Benton in S and L. Hendricks on W boundary. Formed 1873. **9** county (☐ 588 sq mi/1,523 sq km; 1990 pop. 30,278), SW Miss.; ⊙ Brookhaven; 31°32′N 90°27′W. Drained by Bogue Chitto and East Fork Amite rivers. Agr. (cotton, corn; cattle, poultry; dairying); timber. Part of Homochitto Natl. Forest in NW. Formed 1870. **10** county (☐ 629 sq mi/1,629 sq km; 1990 pop. 28,892), E Mo.; ⊙ Troy; 39°04′N 90°58′W. Bounded E by Mississippi R., drained by the Cuivre. Soybeans, corn, apples; cattle, hogs; limestone; mfg. at Troy. Cuivre R. State Park NE of Troy. Formed 1818. **11** county (☐ 3,675 sq mi/9,518 sq km; 1990 pop. 17,481), extreme NW Mont.; ⊙ Libby; 48°32′N 115°25′W. Mt. region bordering on Canada (B.C.; N) and Idaho (W); drained by Kootenai R. (L. Koocanusa formed by Libby Dam, E center). W state line forms Mountain/Pacific time zone boundary. Lowest point in Mont. (c.1,800 ft/549 m) at point where Kootenai R. flows W into Idaho. Kootenai Natl. Forest covers most of co., including part of Cabinet Mts. Wilderness Area in S, parts of Kaniken Natl. Forest along W boundary, part of Stillwater State Forest in E, Turner Mts. Ski Area in NW center. Thompson Lakes source of Thompson R., in SE corner, source of Stillwater R. in E. Kootenai Natl. Forest and Yaak R., Cabinet Mts. in SW, Purcell Mts. in NW, Whitefish Range in NE, Salish Mts. in E. Hay; lumber; some cattle, sheep; lead, silver, gold. Formed 1909. **12** county (☐ 2,575 sq mi/6,669 sq km; 1990 pop. 32,508), SW central Nebr.; ⊙ North Platte; 41°03′N 100°46′W. The South Platte and North Platte rivers join here to form the Platte. Grazing and agr. area: cattle, hogs; dairying; corn, wheat, alfalfa, wild hay, sunflower seeds. Central/Mountain time zone boundary follows W boundary. Ft. McPherson Natl. Cemetery in E, S of Maxwell; L. Maloney State Recreation Area at center, S of North Platte; Sutherland State Recreation Area in W. Old Oregon Trail follows S side of Platte/South Platte River. Formed 1860. **13** county (☐ 10,637 sq mi/27,550 sq km; 1990 pop. 3,775), SE Nev.; ⊙ Pioche; 37°40′N 114°40′W. Seventh largest U.S. co. in land area. Mt. region bordering on Ariz. and Utah, both on E; E boundary is also Pacific/Mountain time zone boundary; watered by Meadow Valley Wash. Part of Desert Natl. Wildlife Range in SW, also part of Nellis Air Force Bombing and Gunnery Range in SW. Pahranagat Natl. Wildlife Refuge in SW center. Beaver Dam, Kershaw-Ryan, Spring Valley, and Cathedral Gorge state parks in E; Echo Canyon State Recreational Area in E. White R. Petroglyphs Archaeological Site, Leviathan Cave Natural Area, and small part of Humboldt Natl. Forest in W. Mining (perlite, sand and gravel), ranching. Part of Egan Range is in N. Formed 1866. **14** county (☐ 4,831 sq mi/12,512 sq km; 1990 pop. 12,219), S central N.Mex.; ⊙ Carrizozo; 33°44′N 105°27′W. Parts of Lincoln Natl. Forest in center and N; ranges of Sacramento Mts. extend N-S. Lincoln State Monument and Smokey Bear Historical State Park in S center; Valley of Fires Natl. Recreation Area, in the Malpais volcanic flow area, in W; Ski Apache ski area in S; part of Cibola Natl. Forest in N. Sheep, cattle; hay, alfalfa, some wheat, oats; watered by Rio Hondo. Formed 1869. **15** county (☐ 307 sq mi/795 sq km; 1990 pop. 50,319), W central N.C.; ⊙ Lincolnton; 35°28′N 81°13′W. In Piedmont region; bounded E by Catawba R. (Cowans Ford Dam forms L. Norman reservoir in upper reach of Mountains Isl. L. reservoir below [S] dam). Drained by South Fork Catawba R. Agr. (cotton, corn, wheat, hay, oats, barley, soybeans; poultry, cattle; dairying); mfg. at Lincolnton; stone quarrying. Formed 1779. **16** county (☐ 965 sq mi/2,499 sq km; 1990 pop. 29,216), central Okla.; ⊙ Chandler; 35°42′N 96°52′W. Intersected by the Deep Fork of the Canadian R. (touches SW corner). Diversified agr. (cotton, sorghum, castor beans, vegetables, pecans); dairying; livestock and poultry raising; beekeeping; mfg. (dairy prods., apparel, electronic components) at Chandler. Oil (at Chandler and Stroud) and natural-gas wells. Formed 1890. **17** county (☐ 1,193 sq mi/3,090 sq km; 1990 pop. 38,889), W Oregon; ⊙ Toledo; 44°38′N 123°54′W. Bounded W by Pacific Ocean, drained by Alsea, Siletz, and Yaquina rivers. Small portion of co. in S transferred (1949) to Benton co. (E). Home of Oregon's leading fishing company (salmon, tuna, halibut, crabs, shrimp, clams). Paper prods.; timber; dairy prods.; poultry, sheep, cattle. Coast Range to E. Part of Siuslaw Natl. Forest in N and S; Ellmaker State Park in E. More than 20 state parks and waysides on or near coast, notably Devils Lake State Park in NW, Yaquina Bay State Park in W, and Beachside State Park in SW. Formed 1893. **18** county (☐ 578 sq mi/1,497 sq km; 1990 pop. 15,427), SE S.Dak.; ⊙ Canton; 43°18′N 96°46′W. Rolling prairie region bounded E by Big Sioux R. (Iowa state line). Corn, soybeans; cattle, hogs. Urbanized in N central part with Sioux Falls and other area towns. Drained in W by E Fork Vermillion R. Newton Hills State Park in E, S of Canton. Formed 1862. **19** county (☐ 581 sq mi/1,505 sq; km; 1990 pop. 28,157), S Tenn.; ⊙ Fayetteville; 35°08′N 86°36′W. Bounded S by Ala.; crossed by Elk R. Rich agr. area (timber; livestock; corn, grain, fruits, sweet potatoes, tomatoes; dairy prods.). Some industry at Fayetteville. Formed 1809. **20** county (☐ 2,339 sq mi/6,058 sq km; 1990 pop. 8,864), E Wash.; ⊙ Davenport;

47°34′N 118°25′W. Bounded on N by Columbia and Spokane rivers; Grand Coulee Dam (just beyond NW corner of co.) forms Franklin D. Roosevelt L., which also creates Spokane R. Arm in NE; Little Falls and Long Lake dams on Spokane R. in NE; Coulee Dam Natl. Recreation Area surrounds lake and area. Potatoes, wheat, alfalfa, hay, barley, oats, rye. Formed 1883. **21** county (☐ 439 sq mi/1,137 sq km; 1990 pop. 21,382), W W.Va.; ⊙ Hamlin; 38°10′N 82°04′W. On Allegheny Plateau; drained by Guyandotte, Mud, and Coal rivers. Agr. (corn, potatoes, alfalfa, hay, nursery crops, tobacco); cattle; honey. Oil and natural-gas wells; bituminous coal. Big Ugly Wildlife Management Area in S; Hilbert Wildlife Management Area in NE. Formed 1867. **22** county (☐ 906 sq mi/2,347 sq km; 1990 pop. 26,993), N central Wis.; ⊙ Merrill; 45°19′N 89°45′W. Wooded lake region in N is resort area; dairying and farming (barley) in S part. Paper milling and mfg. at Merrill and Tomahawk. Drained by Wisconsin R. Contains Council Grounds State Park in S. Camp and Ten and Harrison Hills ski areas in NE. Formed 1874. **23** county (☐ 4,089 sq mi/10,591 sq km; 1990 pop. 12,625), W Wyo.; ⊙ Kemmerer; 42°15′N 110°42′W. Grain (barley, hay, alfalfa); livestock (sheep, cattle); dairying area bordering Utah and Idaho; drained by Green, Snake, Greys, and Salt rivers; Green R. forms Fontenelle Reservoir in E. Coal, oil, and phosphate found here. Salt R. Range and Bridger-Teton Natl. Forest in N part, Grand Canyon of the Snake R. in far N. Pine Creek Ski Area in W; Fossil Butte Natl. Monument in SW. Formed 1911.

Lincoln (LING-kuhn), parish (☐ 469 sq mi/1,215 sq km; 1990 pop. 41,745), N La.; ⊙ Ruston; 32°32′N 92°39′W. Drained by Middle Fork of Bayou D'Arbonne. Agr. (peaches, blueberries, home gardens, hay; cattle, poultry); logging; mfg. (lumber, wood prods., glass containers, metal prods., lighting fixtures); oil and natural gas. Small part of Jackson Bienville State Wildlife Area on S boundary. Named after President Abraham Lincoln. Formed 1873.

Lincoln 1 city (1990 pop. 2,941), Talladega co., E central Ala., 18 mi/29 km W of Anniston, and 13 mi/21 km N of Talladega, near Coosa R.; 33°36′N 86°08′W. **2** city (1990 pop. 7,248), Placer co., central Calif., 25 mi/40 km NNE of Sacramento, in Sacramento Valley; 38°54′N 121°19′W. Ships fruits, grain, vegetables; mfg. (plastics and clay prods., sawmilling, cabinets). Inc. 1890. **3** city (1990 pop. 15,418), ⊙ Logan co., central Ill.; 40°08′N 89°22′W. The city was plotted and promoted (1853) with the aid of Abraham Lincoln and named for him when he was still an unknown country lawyer. Lincoln practiced law there from 1847 to 1859, and bldgs. and places associated with him have been preserved or reconstructed, including Postville Courthouse Historic Site. Lincoln Col., Lincoln Christian Col., and Lincoln and Logan Correctional Centers are here. Edward A. Madigan State Park, formerly Railsplitter State Park, to S. It is a shipping and industrial center. In agr. area (corn, soybeans; cattle, hogs); mfg. (glass containers, electrical controls, corrugated containers, cleaning prods., and shampoos). Inc. 1865. **4** city (1990 pop. 191,972), ⊙ Nebr. and Lancaster co., SE Nebr.; 40°49′N 96°41′W. Major RR junction and center. It is the trade and industrial center for a large grain and livestock area. Mfg. (printing and publishing, processed and prepared foods, beverages, construction materials, electronics, motorcycles, sports equip., valves and cylinders, asphalt, automotive parts). Cattle are slaughtered and processed. Many insurance companies have their home offices here. It is the seat of the Univ. of Nebr. (2 campuses), Union Col., Nebr. Wesleyan Univ., and Southeast Community Col. (Lincoln campus). Lied Center for Performing Arts, which attracts musicians and other performers from around the world, is located on Univ. of Nebr. campus. It has a planetarium, Sheldon Art Gall., State Historical Society Mus. and State Mus., Germans from Russia Mus. (Natl.), sculpture garden, and several parks. Several state recreation areas to S and W. State fairgrounds, veterans hospital, state penitentiary S of city, municipal airport. The state capitol, designed by B. G. Goodhue, with sculptures by Lee Lawrie, was completed in 1934. William Jennings Bryan lived in Lincoln from 1887 to 1916; his home is preserved. Founded in 1864 as Lancaster, the city was chosen as the site of the capital in 1867 and renamed. Inc. 1869.

Lincoln 1 town (1990 pop. 1,460), Washington co., NW Ark., 17 mi/27 km WSW of Fayetteville, in the Ozarks, near Okla. state line; 35°57′N 94°25′W. Poultry; mfg. (egg processing, compost turners, poultry houses, printing). **2** town (1990 pop. 173), Tama co., central Iowa, 20 mi/32 km NNW of Toledo; 42°15′N 92°41′W. In agr. area. **3** or **Lincoln Center**, town, ⊙ Lincoln co., N central Kansas, on Saline R. and 32 mi/51 km WNW of Salina. RR junction. Shipping center for grain and cattle area. Mfg. (acrylics, crushed stone). Founded 1871; inc. 1879. **4** town (1990 pop. 5,587), including Lincoln village, Penobscot co., central Maine, on the Penobscot and c.45 mi/72 km N of Bangor, on Mattanawcook Pond; 45°21′N 68°27′W. Trade center, with wood prods., pulp and paper mill. Settled c.1825; inc. 1829. **5** residential town (1990 pop. 7,666), Middlesex co., E Mass., 14 mi/23 km WNW of Boston; 42°26′N 71°19′W. Agr., in suburbanizing area. Gropius, the Ger. architectural founder of the Bauhaus School, lived here. Cambridge Reservoir to the E. Site of Decordova Mus. and park. Drumlin Farm hq. of Mass. Audobon Society. Settled c.1650; inc. 1754. **6** town (1990 pop. 874), Benton co., central Mo., 9 mi/14.5 km N of Warsaw; 38°23′N 93°19′W. Corn, wheat; cattle. **7** town (1990 pop. 1,229), Grafton co., N central N.H., 18 mi/29 km SSE of Littleton; 44°05′N 71°34′W. Drained by Pemigewasset R. and its East Branch. RR terminus. Agr. (cattle; dairying; timber); mfg. (electrical connections, printing and publishing). Parts of White Mt. Natl. Forest in E and W; Hancock and Big Rock state campgrounds in E; Kancamagus Pass (2,860 ft/872 m) on Kancamagus Highway on E boundary; Loon Mt. Ski Area in SE; Appalachian Trail crosses in NE. Inc. 1764. **8** town (1990 pop. 1,132), Burleigh co., S central N.Dak., suburb 4 mi/6.4 km SE of Bismarck, on Apple Creek, near Bismarck Municipal Airport; 46°46′N 100°42′W. Residential. **9** town (☐ 18 sq mi/47 sq km; 1990 pop. 18,045), Providence co., NE R.I. Set off from Smithfield, named for Abraham Lincoln; 41°55′N 71°27′W. Includes villages of Manville, Saylesville, Limerock, and part of Lonsdale. Once a textile town, its mfg. includes wire, tubing, metal parts, and thread. Corporate hq. for Cross Pens. Limestone has been quarried here since colonial times. Many pre-Revolutionary houses, a state park, and Lincoln Downs (racetrack) are in the town. Inc. 1871. **10** town (1990 pop. 974), Addison co., W central Vt., on New Haven R. and 11 mi/18 km NE of Middlebury, in Green Mts.; wood prods.; 44°05′N 72°58′W. Settled 1795 by Quakers.

Lincoln 1 uninc. village (1990 pop. 300), Bonneville co., SE Idaho, residential suburb 4 mi/6.4 km E of Idaho Falls. Agr. area. **2** village (1990 pop. 337), Alcona co., NE Mich., 7 mi/11.3 km WNW of Harrisville, near L. Huron; 44°41′N 83°24′W. Mfg. (cutting tools). Small lakes (resorts) nearby. Mt. Maria Ski Area and Hubbard L. to NW. **3** village (1990 pop. 530), Lewis and Clark co., W central Mont., 35 mi/56 km NW of Helena, bet. Blackfoot R. and Keep Cool Creek, at center of Lincoln State Forest, which is surrounded by Helena Natl. Forest. One of the country's largest open-pit gold and silver mines. Lead, copper, molybdenum are also mined. Cattle, hay, timber; sport fishing. Mfg. (wood fuel pellets, beef snacks). Continental Divide to E. Scapegoat Wilderness Area to N. Setting for novel *A River Runs Through It* by Norman Maclean. **4** village, Lincoln co., central N.Mex., on Rio Bonito, just S of Capitan Mts., 31 mi/50 km SSE of Carrizozo; elev. c.5,715 ft/1,742 m. Agr.; livestock. Center of Lincoln co. cattle war, 1877–1878. State mus., formerly co. courthouse, in Lincoln State Monument, contains historical and archaeological collection. Billy the Kid imprisoned here 1881. Parts of Lincoln Natl. Forest to N and SW. El Capitan Mt. (10,083 ft/3,073 m), in Capitan Mts., to NE. **5** uninc. village, Ephrata township, Lancaster co., SE Pa., suburb 2 mi/3.2 km NW of Ephrata; 40°11′N 76°12′W. In rich agr. area.

Lincoln, borough (1990 pop. 1,187), Allegheny co., W Pa., 12 mi/19 km SSW of Pittsburgh and 4 mi/6.4 km SSW of McKeesport on Monongahela R.; 40°17′N 79°50′W. Agr. includes dairying; livestock; corn, hay.

Lincoln Boyhood National Memorial, Spencer co., SW Ind. near Lincoln City and Lincoln State Park. Site of the farm where Abraham Lincoln was raised and the burial place of his mother, Mary Hanks Lincoln. Authorized 1962.

Lincoln Center for the Performing Arts, arts center, on Upper W Side of Manhattan, SE N.Y., occupying a triangular area NW of Columbus Circle and bounded by Broadway on NE, by Columbus Ave. on E, by Amsterdam Ave. on W, by W. 66th St. on N, and by 62nd St. on S. Perhaps the foremost performing arts center of its kind in the world, it is the realization of the 1930s dream of Charles Spafford, 1 of the "Dukes of New York," a group of anonymous, powerful people serving on boards of most of the city's major institutions. John D. Rockefeller III was chairman of the Exploratory Committee that ultimately led to the Center's construction, and he was instrumental in raising its $185 million cost from corporations, foundations, foreign countries, state and federal funds, and private contributions. The site of the project was an area W of Central Park known as Lincoln Sq., which had become 1 of the city's most congested slums by the late 1940s. Completed in 1965, the complex has 6 main bldgs.: Philharmonic Hall, N.Y. State Theater, Metropolitan House, Lib. and Mus. of the Performing Arts, Vivian Beaumont Theater, and Julliard Bldg. Tenants include the Metropolitan Opera, N.Y. Philharmonic, N.Y. City Ballet, N.Y. City Opera, Chamber Music Society of Lincoln Center, School of American Ballet, Julliard School of Music, N.Y. Public Lib. at Lincoln Center, Lincoln Center Theater, and Film Society of Lincoln Center. Damrosch Park, with its grove of trees, a public plaza, a fountain, and sculptures, is also part of the Center.

Lincoln City, town (1990 pop. 5,892), Lincoln co., W Oregon, 46 mi/74 km W of Salem, on Pacific Ocean, N of Siletz Bay and mouth of Siletz R.; 44°58′N 124°00′W. Fish, timber, tourism. Mfg. (textile prods.). Part of Siuslaw Natl. Forest to E; Devils L. State Park to E and S; several state waysides along coast.

Lincoln City, village, Spencer co., SW Ind., 34 mi/55 km ENE of Evansville. Laid out 1872 on site of farm of Thomas Lincoln (Abraham Lincoln's father). Lincoln State Park (just S). Nearby Lincoln Boyhood Natl. Memorial has grave of Nancy Hanks Lincoln and site of Lincoln cabin built in 1816.

Lincoln Heights, uninc. town (1990 pop. 1,250), Westmoreland co., SW Pa., residential suburb 2 mi/3.2 km S of Jeannette; 40°18′N 79°37′W. Agr. includes dairying; corn, hay.

Lincoln Heights, village (1990 pop. 4,805), Hamilton co., extreme SW Ohio, suburb 10 mi/16 km N of downtown Cincinnati; 39°14′N 84°27′W. Inc. 1946.

Lincoln Highway, in U.S., road extending for more than 3,300 mi/5,311 km from N.Y. city to San Francisco; built 1913–1927.

Lincoln Homestead, Natl. Historic Site, central Ill., located in Springfield. Authorized 1971. Only private home owned by Abraham Lincoln; he was living there when he was elected president.

Lincoln Homestead State Park, Ky.: see SPRINGFIELD.

Lincoln Log Cabin State Historic Site, E central Ill., 8 mi/12.9 km S of Charleston, on site of last Lincoln family homestead in Ill.; contains reconstruction of Lincoln cabin built in 1837; 39°22′N 88°12′W. Covers 86 acres/35 ha.

Lincoln Memorial, monument, 164 acres/66 ha, in Potomac Park, Washington, D.C. Authorized 1911; built 1914–1917. The bldg., designed by Henry Bacon and styled after a Gr. temple, has 36 Doric columns representing the states of the Union at the time of Lincoln's death. Inside the bldg. is a heroic statue of Lincoln by Daniel Chester French and 2 murals by Jules Guerin.

Lincoln, Mount (14,286 ft/4,354 m), in Park Range, NW Park co., central Colo., 12 mi/19 km NE of Leadville in Pike Natl. Forest. Highest peak in range. Continental Divide passes to N, source of South Platte R. 5 mi/8 km SW of Summit.

Lincoln, Mount, N.H.: see FRANCONIA MOUNTAINS.

Lincoln Mountain, W central Vt., in Green Mts., 15 mi/24 km NE of Middlebury; one of its summits, Mt. Ellen (4,135 ft/1,260 m), is 3d highest in range. Sugarbush Valley and Mad River Glen ski areas are nearby.

Lincoln Park, city (□ 5 mi/8 km; 1990 pop. 41,832), Wayne co., SE Mich., a suburb 7 mi/11.3 km SW of downtown Detroit; 42°14′N 83°10′W. Borders N Branch Ecorse R. on N and E, drained by S Branch Ecorse in S., ½ mi/8/10 km W of Detroit R. Light mfg. It is a residential community in an area marked by a significant decline in industry. Inc. 1921.

Lincoln Park 1 uninc. town (1990 pop. 3,728), Fremont co., S central Colo., suburb 2 mi/3.2 km SE of Cañon City, near Arkansas R.; 38°25′N 105°12′W. In coal-mining area. Glass, machinery. **2** uninc. town (1990 pop. 1,800), Berks co., SE central Pa., residential suburb 3 mi/4.8 km WSW of Reading; 40°18′N 75°59′W.

Lincoln Park 1 village (1990 pop. 1,755), Upson co., W central Ga., just S of Thomaston; 32°52′N 84°19′W. **2** village (□ 1 sq mi/2.6 sq km; 1990 pop. 2,457), Ulster co., SE N.Y.; 41°57′N 74°00′W.

Lincoln Park, borough (1990 pop. 10,978), Morris co., N N.J., 7 mi/11.3 km W of Paterson; 40°55′N 74°17′W. Vegetable farming; mfg. of fixtures, chemicals, machinery. Inc. 1922.

Lincoln Tunnel, 3-tube vehicular tunnel under Hudson R. bet. midtown Manhattan borough of N.Y. city and Weehawken, N.J.; 40°44′N 74°01′W. The tunnel is 8,215 ft/2,504 m long (portal to portal), nearly 100 ft/30 m below surface of the river. Opened 1937.

Lincoln University, uninc. village, Chester co., SE Pa., 3 mi/4.8 km ENE of Oxford; 39°48′N 75°55′W. Seat of Lincoln Univ. Founded 1854 as one of 1st U.S. univ. for Afr.-Americans.

Lincoln Village, uninc. town (1990 pop. 4,236), San Joaquin co., central Calif., residential suburb 4 mi/6.4 km NNW of downtown Stockton; 38°00′N 121°20′W.

Lincolnia, uninc. city, Fairfax co., NE Va., residential suburb 5 mi/8 km W of Alexandria, 9 mi/14.5 km SW of Washington, D.C.; 38°49′N 77°09′W.

Lincolnia Heights, uninc. town, Fairfax co., NE Va., residential suburb 5 mi/8 km WNW of Alexandria, 8 mi/12.9 km SW of Washington, D.C.; 38°49′N 77°08′W. L. Barcroft reservoir to N.

Lincoln's New Salem Historic Site, restored historic village (a state historical site), Sangamon co., central Ill., on Sangamon R., and 16 mi/26 km NW of Springfield; 39°58′N 89°50′W. Here was home of Abraham Lincoln, 1831–1837; bldgs, which were standing in Lincoln's day (including the Rutledge Tavern, Danton Offut's store, and the Lincoln-Berry store) have been restored. A small mus. houses pioneer relics. Settled 1828; decline and abandonment came after 1839. Official title is Lincoln's New Salem Historic Site.

Lincolnshire, village (1990 pop. 4,931), Lake co., NE Ill., suburb 30 mi/48 km NNW of downtown Chicago, 6 mi/9.7 km W of Highland Park; 42°12′N 87°55′W. Drained by Des Plaines R. Mfg. (construction and mining equip., educational aids, toxic-gas–monitoring equip., storage tanks).

Lincolnton, city (1990 pop. 6,955), ⊙ Lincoln co., W central N.C., 28 mi/45 km NW of Charlotte, on South Fork Catawba R.; 35°28′N 81°15′W. RR junction. Agr. area (cotton, grain, chickens, hogs, cattle; dairying). Mfg. (textiles, apparel, pharmaceuticals, furniture, machinery, printing and publishing, food). Inc. 1785.

Lincolnton, town (1990 pop. 1,476), ⊙ Lincoln co., NE Ga., 34 mi/55 km NW of Augusta, near Savannah R.; 33°47′N 82°29′W. Mfg. (lumber, apparel, yarns, wood prods. food processing).

Lincolnville, resort town (1990 pop. 1,809), Waldo co., S Maine, on Penobscot Bay, and 10 mi/16 km S of Belfast; 44°17′N 69°04′W.

Lincolnville 1 village (1990 pop. 197), Marion co., E central Kansas, 10 mi/16 km NNE of Marion; 38°29′N 96°57′W. In grain and livestock region. **2** village (1990 pop. 716), Charleston co., SE S.C., 20 mi/32 km NW of Charleston, and 1 mi/1.6 km E of Summerville; 33°00′N 80°09′W. Agr. (poultry, hogs; corn, cotton).

Lincolnwood, village (1990 pop. 11,365), Cook co., NE Ill., residential suburb 9 mi/14.5 km NW of downtown Chicago; 42°00′N 87°43′W. Bounded by Skokie on N, by Chicago all other sides. Mfg. (machinery, bags, food prods., audio visual equip., computer equip., lighting systems). Until 1935 called Tessville.

Lind, village (1990 pop. 472), Adams co., SE Wash., 15 mi/24 km SW of Ritzville, on Lind Coulee; 46°58′N 118°37′W. In Columbia Basin agr. region (wheat; cattle, poultry).

Lind Island, Canada: see JENNY LIND ISLAND.

Linda, uninc. city (1990 pop. 13,033), Yuba co., N central Calif., residential suburb 3 mi/4.8 km ESE of Marysville, near Yuba R.; 39°07′N 121°33′W. Beals Air Force Base to E. Seat of Yuba Col. Agr. (grain, walnuts, peaches, prunes, olives; dairying, cattle).

Linda Vista, suburban section of San Diego, San Diego co., S Calif., 5 mi/8 km N of downtown San Diego; San Diego R. to S. Miramar Naval Air Station to NE; Tecolote Canyon Natural Park to NW; Mission Bay to W. Residential area.

Lindale, town (1990 pop. 2,428), Smith co., E Texas, 13 mi/21 km NNW of Tyler, near Sabine R.; 32°30′N 95°24′W. Canning, shipping center. Agr. (fruit, vegetables, horticultural crops, rose bushes). Mfg. (food prods., printing and publishing).

Lindale, village (1990 pop. 4,187), Floyd co., NW Ga., 4 mi/6.4 km S of Rome; 34°11′N 85°10′W. Textile mfg.

Linden, city (1990 pop. 36,701), Union co., NE N.J.; 40°37′N 74°14′W. During the 1st half of the 20th cent., Linden changed from an agr. dist. to a city of diverse mfg. (chemicals, petroleum prods., plastics, advertising signs, transportation equip.). The city, named for the linden trees in the vicinity, was part of Elizabeth until 1861. Inc. 1925.

Linden 1 town (1990 pop. 2,548), ⊙ Marengo co., W Ala., 15 mi/24 km S of Demopolis; 32°17′N 87°47′W. Corn area. Mfg. (apparel); lumber milling. Founded 1823. **2** uninc. town (1990 pop. 1,339), San Joaquin co., central Calif., 12 mi/19 km ENE of Stockton, near Mormon Slough; Calaveras R. to N; 38°01′N 121°06′W. Agr. (dairying, cattle; fruit, nuts, vegetables, sugar beets, beans, nursery prods., grain). Mfg. (farm machinery, printing and publishing). **3** town (1990 pop. 718), Montgomery co., W Ind., 17 mi/27 km S of Lafayette; 40°11′N 86°54′W. In agr. area. **4** town (1990 pop. 201), Dallas co., central Iowa, 9 mi/14.5 km N of Crawfordsville; 41°38′N 94°16′W. In agr. area, Mfg. (feed). **5** town (1990 pop. 2,415), Genesee co., SE central Mich., 14 mi/23 km SSW of Flint; 42°49′N 83°46′W. In lake and farm area. Food processing. Summer resort. Several lakes to E and SW. **6** town (1990 pop. 1,099), ⊙ Perry co., W central Tenn., on Buffalo R., and 46 mi/74 km W of Columbia; 35°37′N 87°50′W. Trade center for lumbering and agr. area. Mfg. (rubber, auto parts). **7** town (1990 pop. 2,375), ⊙ Cass co., NE Texas, 33 mi/53 km N of Marshall; 33°00′N 94°21′W. Elev. 410 ft/125 m. Agr. (vegetables, fruits; chickens); timber. Mfg. (oil and gas equip.). Founded c.1850.

Linden 1 village (1990 pop. 180), Cumberland co., S central N.C., 15 mi/24 km NNE of Fayetteville on Little R. (mouth in Cape Fear R. 3 mi/4.8 km to E); 35°15′N 78°45′W. **2** uninc. village, Warren co., N Va., 7 mi/11.3 km E of Front Royal, at Manassas Gap. Mfg. (sparkling cider, wine). **3** village (1990 pop. 429), Iowa co., SW Wis., 8 mi/12.9 km SW of Dodgeville; 42°55′N 90°16′W. Cheese; in dairying and hog-raising area.

Lindenhurst 1 village (1990 pop. 8,038), Lake co., NE Ill., residential suburb, 35 mi/56 km NW of downtown Chicago, 10 mi/16 km WNW of Waukegon, on Hastings Creek; 42°25′N 88°01′W. Small lakes in area; recreation. **2** village (□ 3 sq mi/7.8 sq km; 1990 pop. 26,879), Suffolk co., SE N.Y., on S L.I.; 40°41′N 73°22′W. Primarily residential. Mfg. (paper, chemicals, electronic equip.). Inc. 1923.

Lindenwold, borough (1990 pop. 18,734), Camden co., SW N.J., 9 mi/14.5 km SE of Camden; 39°49′N 74°59′W. Mfg. (plastics, nails, machinery, food). Terminus for a light RR line from Philadelphia. Settled 1742, inc. 1929.

Lindon, town (1990 pop. 3,818), Utah co., N central Utah, suburb 7 mi/11.3 km NNW of Provo, and 43 mi/69 km SSE of Salt Lake City; 40°20′N 111°43′W. Elev. 4,700 ft/1,433 m. Agr. (berries, vegetables, alfalfa; dairying; cattle, sheep). Mfg. (metal galvanizing, wood trusses). Served by Provo R. irrigation project. Geneva Steel Plant nearby. Mt. Timpanagos (11,750 ft/3,581 m) to NE. Uinta Natl. Forest to E; Utah L. to SW. Originally called Stringtown.

Lindsay, town (1991 pop. 16,696), SE Ont., Canada, on the Scugog R., 53 mi/85 km NE of Toronto; 44°21′N 78°44′W. Industrial town, with woolen, flour, and lumber mills, in an agr. and scenic lake dist.

Lindsay, city (1990 pop. 8,338), Tulare co., S central Calif., 12 mi/19 km SE of Visalia, in Sierra Nevada foothills; 36°13′N 119°05′W. Packs and ships oranges, olives, grapes, pistachios, almonds, walnuts. Cattle; poultry. Mfg. (citrus pulp, food and beverage machinery, plastic prods.). Inc. 1910.

Lindsay (LIN-zee), town (1990 pop. 2,947), Garvin co., S central Okla., 23 mi/37 km WNW of Pauls Valley, and 23 mi/37 km SE of Chickasha, and on Washita R.; 34°50′N 97°36′W. In agr. area. Mfg. (machinery, fishing lures). Historic Murray-Lindsay Mansion.

Lindsay 1 village (1990 pop. 321), Platte co., E central Nebr., 23 mi/37 km NW of Columbus, and on branch of Platte R.; 41°42′N 97°41′W. Agr. (grain, livestock). Mfg. (irrigation systems). **2** village (1990 pop. 610), Cooke co., N Texas, 3 mi/4.8 km W of Gainesville, near Elm Fork Trinity R.; 33°38′N 97°13′W. Agr. area (cattle, sheep, goats; grain).

Lindsborg (LINZ-buhrg), town (1990 pop. 3,076), McPherson co., central Kansas, on Smoky Hill R., and 13 mi/21 km N of McPherson; 38°34′N 97°40′W. RR junction. Trade center for wheat and livestock area; flour. Mfg. (signs, metal prods.). Seat of Bethany Col. (Lutheran; founded 1881). Founded 1868, inc. 1879.

Lindsey (LIN-zee), village (1990 pop. 529), Sandusky co., N Ohio, 7 mi/11 km NW of Fremont; 41°25′N 83°13′W. In agr. area. Mfg. (meat prods.).

Lindstrom, town (1990 pop. 2,461), Chisago co., E Minn., 33 mi/53 km NNE of St. Paul; 45°23′N 92°50′W. Agr. area (grain; cattle, poultry, dairying). Mfg. (food prods., plastic prods., consumer goods, printing and publishing). Bet. 4 lakes: North Lindstrom (NW), South Lindstrom (SW), South Center (SE), North Center (NE). St. Croix Wild River State Park to NE; Carlos Avery Wildlife Area to W. Early Swed. settlement.

Linekin Neck (LIN-uh-kin), peninsula, Lincoln co., S Maine, E of Boothbay Harbor, terminating in Ocean Point. Resort villages.

Linesville, borough (1990 pop. 1,166), Crawford co., NW Pa., 14 mi/23 km W of Meadville, on Lineville Creek, at its entrance on NE shore of Pymatuning Reservoir (causeway). Agr. area (dairying, livestock; potatoes, corn). Mfg. (aluminum processing, fiberglass boxes and units, machinery, lumber). Pymatuning Airport to NW. Inc. 1862.

Lineville 1 town (1990 pop. 2,394), Clay co., E Ala., just NE of Ashland. Mfg. (apparel; food prods., plastic prods.); lumber. **2** town (1990 pop. 289), Wayne co., S Iowa, at Mo. state line, 15 mi/24 km SW of Corydon; 40°35′N 93°31′W. Livestock; grain.

Linfield, uninc. village, Limerick township, Montgomery co., SE Pa., 5 mi/8 km SE of Pottstown, on Schuylkill R.; 40°12′N 75°34′W.

Lingle, village (1990 pop. 473), Goshen co., SE Wyo., on North Platte R., and 9 mi/14.5 km NW of Torrington; 42°08′N 104°20′W. Elev. 4,165 ft/1,269 m. Shipping point for sugar beets, beans, and cattle; in irrigated region.

Linglestown, uninc. town (1990 pop. 5,862), Dauphin

co., S Pa., residential suburb 7 mi/11.3 km NE of Harrisburg; 40°20′N 76°47′W. Blue Ridge Mts. to N.

Linière (leen-YER) or **Saint Côme** (san KOM), village (1991 pop. 1,143), S Que., Canada, on affluent of Chaudière R., 40 mi/64 km NNE of Megantic; 46°03′N 70°31′W. Lumbering; dairying.

Link River, small stream 2 mi/3.2 km long, Klamath co., S Oregon, at city of Klamath Falls; connects Upper Klamath L. with L. Ewauna, which is drained by Klamath R. Site of small dam.

Linn 1 county (□ 724 sq mi/1,875 sq km; 1990 pop. 168,767), E Iowa; ⊙ Cedar Rapids; 42°04′N 91°35′W. Prairie agr. area (hogs, cattle, poultry; corn, oats) drained by Cedar and Wapsipinicon rivers and Buffalo Creek. Many limestone quarries, sand and gravel pits. Mfg. at Cedar Rapids and Marion. Duane Arnold nuclear power plant, initial criticality March 23, 1974, is 8 mi/12.9 km NW of Cedar Rapids, uses cooling water from the Cedar Rapids R., and has a max. dependable capacity of 515 MW. Palisades Kepler State Park in SE; Pleasant Creek State Park in NW. Flooding occurred along rivers in 1993. Formed 1837. **2** county (□ 606 sq mi/1,570 sq km; 1990 pop. 8,254), E Kansas; ⊙ Mound City; 38°12′N 94°50′W. Prairie region, bordering E on Mo.; drained (NE) by Marais des Cygnes R. Agr. (cattle, hogs; wheat, sorghum, soybeans; hay). Formed 1855. **3** county (□ 624 sq mi/1,616 sq km; 1990 pop. 13,885), N central Mo.; ⊙ Linneus; 39°52′N 93°06′W. Agr. (corn, wheat, hay, soybeans; sheep, cattle, hogs). Coal; mfg. at Brookfield and Marceline. Pershing State Park SW of Laclede; Fountain Grove Conservation Area in SW corner. Gen. Pershing b. here 1860. Formed 1837. **4** county (□ 2,309 sq mi/5,980 sq km; 1990 pop. 91,227), W Oregon; ⊙ Albany; 44°29′N 122°31′W. Level farm land rising E to Cascade Range, bounded W by Willamette R. Most of N boundary formed by North Santiam R., forms Detroit L. Reservoir in NE. Mfg. (paper prods., food processing, metal industries); logging. Agr. (corn, beans, wheat, oats, barley; poultry, hogs, sheep, cattle); dairy prods.; nurseries, wineries. Part of Willamette Natl. Forest in E, including part of Mt. Washington Wilderness Area in SE and part of Mt. Jefferson Wilderness Area in NE. Summit of Mt. Jefferson (10,495 ft/3,199 m) marks NE corner of co. Foster and Green Peter Reservoirs, Cascadia State Park in E. Formed 1847.

Linn, city (1990 pop. 1,148), ⊙ Osage co., central Mo., 19 mi/31 km ESE of Jefferson City; 38°28′N 91°50′W. Agr. (corn, wheat, vegetables; cattle, dairying; poultry). Mfg. (transportation equip., plastic prods.); clay pits. Linn State Technical Col.

Linn 1 village (1990 pop. 472), Washington co., N Kansas, 10 mi/16 km S of Washington; 39°40′N 97°05′W. Shipping point in grain and livestock region; dairying; poultry and produce packing. **2** uninc. village (1990 pop. 450), Hidalgo co., S Texas, 26 mi/42 km NNE of McAllen, N of Rio Grande Valley. Cattle; cotton. Oil and natural gas.

Linn Creek, town (1990 pop. 232), Camden co., central Mo., in the Ozarks, on L. of the Ozarks, just N of Camdenton; 38°02′N 92°42′W. Mfg. (model RR accessories). Tourism; resorts. Original town of Linn Creek was submerged by the L. of the Ozarks in 1931.

Linn Grove, town (1990 pop. 194), Buena Vista co., NW Iowa, on Little Sioux R., and 18 mi/29 km N of Storm L.; 42°53′N 95°14′W. Mfg. (hydraulic cylinder components). Sand and gravel pits nearby. Wanata State Park to NW.

Linndale, village (1990 pop. 159), Cuyahoga co., N Ohio, a SW suburb of Cleveland; 41°26′N 81°46′W.

Linneus (LIN-nee-uhs), city (1990 pop. 364), ⊙ Linn co., N central Mo., 8 mi/12.9 km NW of Brookfield; 39°52′N 93°11′W. Corn, wheat, soybeans; sheep, cattle, hogs.

Linneus (LIN-ee-uhs), town (1990 pop. 810), Aroostook co., E Maine, 8 mi/12.9 km SW of Houlton; 46°02′N 67°58′W. In agr., hunting, fishing area.

Linntown, uninc. town (1990 pop. 1,640), East Buffalo township, Union co., central Pa., residential suburb 1 mi/1.6 km SW of Lewisburg; 40°57′N 76°54′W.

Lino Lakes (LEI-no), town (1990 pop. 8,807), Anoka co., E Minn., residential suburb 14 mi/23 km NNE of downtown Minneapolis, and 14 mi/23 km N of downtown St. Paul; 45°09′N 93°04′W. Chain of small natural lakes through center of community along Rice Creek; lakes also in SE corner. Mfg. (plastic prods., machining, bldg. materials, corrosion inhibiting prods., electrical prods.). Minn. Correctional Facility to W.

Linstead, town (1991 pop. 14,144), St. Catherine parish, central Jamaica, on RR, and 12 mi/19 km NNW of Spanish Town; 18°09′N 77°01′W. Annatto, tropical fruit, coffee; livestock.

Linthicum (LIN-thi-cum), suburban village (1990 pop. 7,547), Anne Arundel co., central Md., 7 mi/11.3 km SSW of downtown Baltimore; 39°13′N 76°40′W. Abner Linthicum bought the land here in 1801, and he and his descendants farmed it until 1908, when the estate was broken up. Baltimore-Washington Internatl. Airport is nearby.

Linton, city (1990 pop. 5,814), Greene co., SW Ind., 12 mi/19 km W of Bloomfield; 39°02′N 87°10′W. In agr. area. Mfg. (machinery, coal industry equip., furniture); bituminous-coal mines. Settled 1816. Laid out 1850; inc. as town in 1886, as city in 1900.

Linton, town (1990 pop. 1,410), ⊙ Emmons co., S N.Dak., 46 mi/74 km SSE of Bismarck, and on Beaver Creek, 15 mi/24 km E of Missouri R. (L. Oahe Reservoir); 46°16′N 100°13′W. Farming center (grain; livestock; dairying). Plotted 1883.

Linville, uninc. village, Avery co., NW N.C., 24 mi/39 km NNW of Morganton, and on Linville R. at edge of Pisgah Natl. Forest (N and E). Mfg. (gravel processing). Nearby are Linville Dam and Linville Falls (S) and Linville Caverns (12 mi/19 km SSW), with stalactite and stalagmite formations. Blue Ridge Parkway passes to SE.

Linville River, c.30 mi/48 km long, NW N.C.; rises in the Blue Ridge Mts. in central Avery co.; flows S, past Linville, Catawba R. in L. James reservoir, forms NW arm extending 4 mi/6.4 km from dam. Linville Falls, 2 cascades, and Linville Caverns, S of Linville. On upper course is Linville Dam (160 ft/49 m high, 1,326 ft/404 m long; for hydroelectric power; completed 1919).

Linwood 1 city (1990 pop. 409), Leavenworth co., NE Kansas, on Kansas R., 11 mi/18 km ENE of Lawrence; 39°00′N 95°01′W. General agr. **2** city (1990 pop. 6,866), Atlantic co., SE N.J., 7 mi/11.3 km W of Atlantic City; 39°20′N 74°34′W. Mfg. (lightweight boats, lumber prods.). Inc. as borough 1889, as city 1931.

Linwood 1 town (1990 pop. 342), Walker co., NW Ga., just NW of La Fayette; 34°43′N 85°17′W. **2** uninc. town (1990 pop. 3,425), Delaware co., SE Pa., residental suburb 15 mi/24 km SW of downtown Philadelphia, and 2 mi/3.2 km WSW of Chester, near Delaware state line; Delaware R. 1 mi/1.6 km to SE; 39°49′N 75°25′W. Mfg. (sheet-metal fabrication).

Linwood, village, S Ont., Canada, 15 mi/24 km NW of Kitchener. Dairying, mixed farming.

Linwood, village (1990 pop. 91), Butler co., E Nebr., 15 mi/24 km NE of David City, near Platte R.; 41°24′N 96°55′W.

Linwood, Mass.: see NORTHBRIDGE.

Linzee, Cape, westernmost point of Cape Breton Isl., NE N.S., Canada, on Gulf of St. Lawrence, 3 mi/5 km NNW of Port Hood; 46°03′N 61°32′W.

Lionel Town, town (1991 pop. 4,669), Clarendon parish, S central Jamaica, 9 mi/15 km S of May Pen; 17°48′N 77°14′W. Market town in sugarcane growing area. Sugar factory.

Lions Head, village (1991 pop. 491), S Ont., Canada, on Saugeen Peninsula, on Georgian Bay, 33 mi/53 km NNW of Owen Sound; 44°59′N 81°15′W. Dairying, mixed farming.

Lionville (LAI-uhn-vil), uninc. town (1990 pop. 6,468), Chester co., SE Pa., 9 mi/14.5 km SW of Phoenixville; 40°03′N 75°39′W. Mfg. (sump pumps, electronic equipment). Agr. (dairying, livestock, poultry; grain, apples). Marsh Creek State Park to W. Thomas Newcomer Lib. and Mus. to E.

Lipanos, Bolsón de los (lee-PAH-nos, bol-SON dai los), arid depression in N outliers of Sierra Madre Oriental of Coahuila, N Mexico, on Chihuahua border, NE of Bolsón de Mapimí. Elev. c.3,000 ft/914 m.

Lipon, village (1990 pop. 354), Hood co., N central Texas, 43 mi/69 km WSW of Fort Worth. Agr. area (cattle; peanuts, pecans).

Lipscomb, county (□ 932 sq mi/2,414 sq km; 1990 pop. 3,143), extreme N Texas; ⊙ Lipscomb; 36°16′N 100°16′W. Elev. 2,500 ft/762 m–2,800 ft/853 m. In NE corner of the Panhandle. In W, high plains broken by deep valley of Wolf Creek, also drained by Kiowa Creek in NW; in E, rolling hills. Grain (wheat, grain sorghum, milo, alfalfa); cattle. Oil and gas. Hunting for quail, wild turkey, deer. Formed 1876. Acquired part of Ellis co., Okla., in resurvey of 100th meridian (1930).

Lipscomb (LIPS-kuhm), city (1990 pop. 2,892), Jefferson co., N central Ala., a suburb 8 mi/12.9 km SW of Birmingham. Settled c.1890, inc. 1910.

Lipscomb, uninc. village (1990 pop. 45), ⊙ Lipscomb co., extreme N Texas, on edge of high plains of the Panhandle, c.55 mi/89 km WSW of Woodward, Okla., and on Wolf Creek. Elev. 2,430 ft/741 m. In farm, livestock area.

Lipton, village (1991 pop. 352), SE central Sask., Canada, 45 mi/72 km NE of Regina; 50°54′N 103°51′W. Grain elevators, lumbering, mixed farming.

Lisbon 1 (LIZ-bin), town (1990 pop. 3,790), New London co., SE Conn., on Quinebaug R., and 7 mi/11 km NE of Norwich; 41°36′N 72°00′W. Garbage incinerator plant, capable of burning 500 tons/551 metric tons of trash per day to generate electricity. Also an agr. center. Inc. 1786. **2** town (1990 pop. 1,452), Linn co., E Iowa, near Cedar R., 15 mi/24 km ESE of Cedar Rapids; 41°55′N 91°23′W. Mfg. (feed; chiropractic equip.). Limestone quarries nearby. **3** (LIZ-buhn), town (1990 pop. 9,457), Androscoggin co., SW Maine, on the Androscoggin, and 7 mi/11.3 km SE of Lewiston; 44°01′N 70°05′W. Light mfg. at Lisbon Falls (1990 pop. 4,674) and Lisbon Center villages. In Bowdoin until inc. 1799. **4** town (1990 pop. 1,664), Grafton co., NW N.H., 10 mi/16 km SSW of Littleton; 44°14′N 71°52′W. Drained by Ammonoosuc R. Mfg. (women's shoes, wire prods., furniture, maple prods.); timber. Agr. (vegetables, nursery crops, sugar maples; poultry, cattle; dairying). Iron, gold, other minerals formerly mined. Settled 1753, was named Concord until 1824. **5** town (1990 pop. 2,177), ⊙ Ransom co., SE N. Dak., 52 mi/84 km SW of Fargo, and on Sheyenne R.; 46°26′N 97°40′W. Agr., dairy prods. Site of state soldiers' home. Settled 1878, inc. 1883. Fort Ransom State Park and Historic Site to NW. Fish hatchery and sunflower prods.

Lisbon 1 village (1990 pop. 216), Kendall co., NE Ill., 20 mi/32 km SSW of Aurora; 41°28′N 88°28′W. In rich agr. area. **2** (LIZ-buhn), village (1990 pop. 160), Claiborne parish, N. La., 43 mi/69 km WNW of Monroe; 32°48′N 92°52′W. L. Claiborne State Park to SW. In agr. area; oil and natural gas; gasoline and diesel fuel processing. Two small units of Kisatchie Natl. Forest to NE and NW. **3** village, on Kent/Ottawa co. line, SW Mich., 14 mi/23 km NNW of Grand Rapids. In farm area. **4** village (1990 pop. 3,037), ⊙ Columbiana co., E Ohio, 22 mi/35 km SSW of Youngstown; 40°46′N 80°46′W. In coal, clay, and limestone area. Founded as New Lisbon in 1802.

Lisbon Falls, Maine: see LISBON.

Lisburne, Cape (LIZ-buhrn), NW Alaska, on Chukchi Sea, 40 mi/64 km NNE of Point Hope; 68°53′N 166°04′W. Here are large rookeries. Coal deposits nearby.

Liscomb, town (1990 pop. 258), Marshall co., central Iowa, near Iowa R., 11 mi/18 km NNW of Marshalltown; 42°11′N 93°00′W. Feed milling.

Lisianski Inlet (li-see-YAN-skee), SE Alaska, long narrow fjord on NW coast of Chichagof Isl.; 25 mi/40 km long, opening into Cross Sound at 57°06′N 136°28′W.

Lisianski Island, N Pacific, part of Honolulu co., Hawaii, c.1,080 mi/1,738 km NW of Honolulu, 170 mi/274 km N of Tropic of Cancer; 26°04′N 173°58′W. Level; coral and coral sand. Annexed 1857 by Hawaiian kingdom. Part of Hawaiian Isls. Natl. Wildlife Refuge. Sometimes written Lisyanski.

Cross references are shown in SMALL CAPITALS. The pronunciation key is on page xv. The dates of population figures are on page xii.

Lisle 1 village (1990 pop. 19,512), Du Page co., NE Ill., residential suburb 23 mi/37 km W of downtown Chicago; 41°47′N 88°05′W. East Du Page R. runs through village. Remnant agr. (oats, corn). Diverse mfg. Illinois Benedictine Col. here. Morton Arboretum to NE. **2** village (1990 pop. 361), Broome co., S N.Y., on Tioughnioga R., 18 mi/29 km NNW of Binghamton; 42°21′N 76°00′W. In dairying area.

L'Islet (lee-LAI), county (□ 773 sq mi/2,002 sq km), S Que., Canada, on the St. Lawrence and on Maine border; ⊙ St. Jean Port Joli; 47°00′N 70°00′W.

L'Islet or **Bon Secours** (bo suh-KOOR), town (1991 pop. 937), SE Que., Canada, on the St. Lawrence, and 14 mi/23 km NE of Montmagny. Lumbering, woodworking, dairying, metal casting.

Lisman (LIS-muhn), town (1990 pop. 481), Choctaw co., SW Ala., near Miss. state line, 7 mi/11.3 km NW of Butler; 32°10′N 88°17′W. Lumber.

Lismore (LIZ-mor), village (1990 pop. 248), Nobles co., SW Minn., 21 mi/34 km NW of Worthington; 43°45′N 95°57′W. Grain, soybeans; livestock; dairying.

Listowel (lis-TO-uhl), town (1991 pop. 5,404), S Ont., Canada, on Middle Maitland R., and 24 mi/39 km N of Stratford; 43°44′N 80°58′W. Dairying. Textile milling, furniture mfg.

Lisyanski Island, Hawaii: see LISIANSKI ISLAND.

Litchfield, county (□ 944 sq mi/2,445 sq km; 1990 pop. 174,092), NW Conn., on Mass. and N.Y. state lines; ⊙ Winsted and Litchfield; 41°47′N 73°15′W. Diversified mfg. in Torrington, Thomaston, and Winsted (metal prods., electrical equip., consumer goods, machinery, glass and plastic prods., textiles, apparel, machinery, furniture). Agr. (dairy prods., vegetables, fruit; tobacco; poultry). Many resorts on lakes and in Litchfield Hills; Mt. Frissell (2,380 ft/725 m), highest point in Conn., is near Salisbury. Includes part of L. Candlewood, and Waramaug, Wononskopomuc, Highland, and Bantam lakes, several state parks and forests; winter sports center at Mohawk Mt. State Park. Drained by Housatonic, Naugatuck, Shepaug, Farmington, Pomperaug, and Still rivers. Constituted 1751.

Litchfield, city (1990 pop. 6,883), Montgomery co., SW central Ill., 9 mi/14.5 km W of Hillsboro; 39°10′N 89°39′W. Trade center for bituminous coal–mining and agr. area (corn, wheat, soybeans; livestock). Mfg. (metal prods., dairy prods.). Oil was 1st commercially produced in Ill. here in 1880s. Inc. 1859.

Litchfield 1 town (1990 pop. 8,365), a ⊙ Litchfield co., W Conn., just SW of Torrington; 41°44′N 73°11′W. Includes boroughs of Litchfield and Bantam (1990 pop. 757). Agr. (poultry; fruit; dairy prods.). Resorts on Bantam L. (S); has state parks. First U.S. school exclusively for law students here, 1784–1833. Ethan Allen, Henry Ward Beecher, Harriet Beecher Stowe b. here. Inc. 1719. **2** (LICH-feeld), town (1990 pop. 2,650), Kennebec co., S Maine, 10 mi/16 km SW of Augusta; 44°09′N 69°56′W. In farming, resort region. **3** town (1990 pop. 1,317), Hillsdale co., S Mich., 10 mi/16 km NW of Hillsdale, and on St. Joseph R.; 42°02′N 84°45′W. Agr. (poultry; farming; dairy). Mfg. (apparel, transportation equip., metal prods.). **4** town (1990 pop. 6,041), ⊙ Meeker co., S central Minn., 63 mi/101 km W of Minneapolis; 45°07′N 94°31′W. Elev. 1,134 ft/346 m. Trading point in agr. area (grain, soybeans, peas, beans; livestock, poultry; dairying). Mfg. (mfg. equip., leather prods., food, wood prods., machinery, apparel, textiles, transportation equip.). L. Ripley to S, several small lakes in area. Settled 1856, plotted 1869, inc. 1872. **5** town (1990 pop. 5,516), Hillsborough co., S N.H., 10 mi/16 km S of Manchester, and 5 mi/8 km N of Nashua; 42°50′N 71°27′W. Bounded W by Merrimack R. Agr. (fruit, vegetables, nursery prods.; livestock, poultry; dairying).

Litchfield, village (1990 pop. 314), Sherman co., central Nebr., 12 mi/19 km SW of Loup City, and on Mud Creek; 41°09′N 99°09′W. Grain; livestock.

Litchfield Hills, NW Conn., S extension of the Berkshires running E of Housatonic R., in NW Litchfield co.

Litchfield Park, town (1990 pop. 3,303), Maricopa co., S central Ariz., near Agua Fria R., suburbs 19 mi/31 km W of downtown Phoenix; 33°30′N 112°21′W. Irrigated agr. area, especially to SW (fruit, vegetables, grain; cattle, sheep). Luke Air Force Base to N.

Litchville, village (1990 pop. 205), Barnes co., SE N.Dak., 21 mi/34 km SSW of Valley City; 46°39′N 98°11′W. Cattle, poultry; dairy prods.

Lithia Springs (LITH-ee-uh), suburb (1990 pop. 11,403), Douglas co., Ga., 8 mi/12.9 km NE of Douglasville, and 16 mi/26 km W of Atlanta; 33°47′N 84°40′W. Bedroom community for Atlanta and a growing commercial center. Mfg. (plastic prods., printing, glass prods., consumer goods, crushed stone, concrete).

Lithonia (lith-O-nee-uh), town (1990 pop. 2,448), DeKalb co., NW central Ga., 16 mi/26 km ESE of Atlanta; 33°43′N 84°07′W. Emerging suburban residential and commercial area in metropolitan Atlanta. Mfg. (plastics, crushed stone, concrete, processed foods, computer equip., metal prods., transportation equip.); granite processing.

Lithopolis (lith-AH-puh-lis), village (1990 pop. 563), Fairfield co., central Ohio, 15 mi/24 km SE of Columbus; 39°48′N 82°49′W.

Lititz (LI-tits), borough (1990 pop. 8,280), Lancaster co., SE Pa., 8 mi/12.9 km N of Lancaster; 40°08′N 78°18′W. Agr. (grain, soybeans, apples; eggs; livestock; dairying). Mfg. (footwear, machinery, commercial printing, consumer goods, millwork, food processing, crushed stone, transportation equip., pharmaceuticals, furniture). Lancaster Airport to S. Speedwell Forge L. reservoir to N. Settled c.1740 by Moravians, laid out 1757, inc. 1759.

Little Abaco Island, Abaco dist., N Bahama Isls., just NW of Great Abaco Isl., NE of Grand Bahama Isl., 125 mi/201 km N of Nassau; 26°53′N 77°43′W.

Little America, village, Sweetwater co., SW Wyo., 20 mi/32 km W of Green River town, near Blacks Fork R., on N side of Interstate Highway 80. Home base of chain of Little America truck stops located across Wyo., other W states.

Little Arkansas River (ahr-KAN-zez), 90 mi/145 km long, S central Kansas; rises in N Rice co. N of Lyons; flows SE past Butler and Halsted to Arkansas R. at Wichita.

Little Auglaize River (o-GLAIZ), c.45 mi/72 km long, W Ohio; rises W of Lima; flows generally N to the Auglaize just N of Melrose; 41°06′N 84°24′W.

Little Bahama Bank, shoal, NW Bahama Isls., N of Grand Bahama Isl., 60 mi/97 km E of West Palm Beach (across Straits of Florida); c.150 mi/241 km long NW-SE, c.50 mi/80 km wide. Surrounded by many cays and isls.

Little Barren River, c.45 mi/72 km long, S central Ky.; rises in SE Metcalfe co., SE of Edmonton; flows N past Edmonton, enters Green R. 9 mi/14.5 km W of Greensburg. Barren R. is to SW.

Little Bay, SE N.J., small inlet just S of Great Bay; protected from the Atlantic by isls.; traversed by Intracoastal Waterway channel.

Little Bay De Noc (duh NAHK), a N arm of Green Bay indenting SW shore of Delta co., Upper Peninsula, Mich.; c.16 mi/26 km long N-S, 1 mi/1.6 km–4 mi/6.4 km wide; 45°46′N 87°00′W. Escanaba is on W shore. Peninsula separates it from Big Bay De Noc (E).

Little Bay Island (□ 2 sq mi/5.2 sq km; 1991 pop. 261), E N.F., Canada, in Notre Dame Bay, 25 mi/40 km SW of Cape St. John; 49°39′N 55°50′W. Fishing.

Little Bear Creek Reservoir, Franklin co., NW Ala., on Little Bear Creek, 30 mi/48 km SW of Florence; 34°26′N 87°58′W. Formed by Little Bear Creek Dam (69 ft/21 m high), built (1974) by the TVA for flood control and recreation.

Little Bear Peak (14,037 ft/4,278 m), in Rocky Mts., Alamosa Costilla co., S Colo., 10 mi/16 km NNW of Fort Garland, and 1 mi/1.6 km SW of Blanca Peak.

Little Bear River, 50 mi/80 km long, N Utah; rises in Wasatch Range NNE of Ogden; flows generally N, through Hyrum Reservoir past Hyrum and Wellsville, to Bear R. 8 mi/12.9 km NW of Logan. Hyrum Dam (98 ft/30 m high, 540 ft/165 m long; completed 1935), just SW of Hyrum, is used for irrigation. Hyrum Reservoir State Park in Cache co. is a state recreation area.

Little Beaver River, c.7 mi/11 km long, E Ohio and W Pa.; formed by Middle, West, and North forks in SE Columbiana co., Ohio; flows SE to the Ohio just across Pa. state line. Main headstream (Middle Fork, c.35 mi/56 km long) rises in Mahoning co., flows SE.

Little Belt Mountains, range of Rocky Mts. in central Mont., rise SE of Great Falls, extend c.68 mi/109 km SE to Musselshell R. Lie within Lewis and Clark Natl. Forest. Judith River Wildlife Management Area on E side, has sapphire mine; Showdown Ski Area at center of range. Highest point, Big Baldy Mt. (9,175 ft/2,797 m). Silver, lead, gold, zinc, sapphires, coal mined.

Little Bighorn, river, c.90 mi/145 km long, N Wyo. and S Mont.; rising in the Bighorn Mts. in NW Sheridan co., N Wyo., and flowing N past Crow Agency to join the Bighorn R. at Hardin in S Mont. On June 25–26, 1876, Sioux and Cheyenne warriors defeated the forces of Col. George Custer in the Little Bighorn valley. Little Bighorn Battlefield Natl. Monument occupies the site of the battle at Crow Agency.

Little Bighorn Battlefield, national monument (765 acres/310 ha), Big Horn co., SE Mont., 14 mi/23 km SE of Hardin, 2 mi/3.2 km SE of Crow Agency. Authorized 1879. Site of the battle between the Seventh Cavalry, in NE part Crow Indian Reservation, commanded by George Armstrong Custer, and the Sioux and Northern Cheyenne. Battle of Little Bighorn June 25–26, 1876. Formerly Custer Battlefield Natl. Monument, the name was changed in 1993. Includes Custer Natl. Cemetery, within Monument park.

Little Blue River, 450 mi/724 km long, in S Nebr. and N Kansas; rises in Kearney co.; flows ESE, past Hebron and Fairbury, Nebr., then SSE to Big Blue R. at Blue Rapids, Kansas.

Little Boars Head, N.H.: see GREAT BOARS HEAD.

Little Bonaire (bawn-ER), Du. *Klein Bonaire*, islet, just off W coast of Bonaire isl., Neth. Antilles, 40 mi/64 km E of Willemstad; 2 mi/3.2 km long, 1.5 mi/2.4 km wide; 12°10′N 68°19′W.

Little Brewster Island, Mass.: see BREWSTER ISLANDS.

Little Calumet River, Ill. and Ind.: see CALUMET RIVER.

Little Canada, town (1990 pop. 8,971), Ramsey co., E Minn., suburb 5 mi/8 km N of downtown St. Paul, and 9 mi/14.5 km ENE of downtown Minneapolis; 45°01′N 93°04′W. RR junction. Mfg. (plastic prods., store fixtures, printing, medical supplies). Numerous small lakes in area; Gervais L. in E.

Little Captain Island, SW Conn., 2 small isls. joined by reefs, in L.I. Sound, 2 mi/3.2 km offshore, S of Greenwich. Public recreation center here.

Little Cayman, island (□ 9.2 sq mi/23.8 sq km; 1989 pop. 33) of Cayman Isls., Br. crown colony, West Indies, separated by narrow channel from Cayman Brac (E), and 60 mi/97 km ENE of Grand Cayman; c.9 mi/14.5 km long, 1 mi/1.6 km wide; 19°40′N 80°05′W. Tourism at small lodges, scuba diving, sport fishing.

Little Cedar River 1 c.40 mi/64 km long, in SW Upper Peninsula, Mich.; rises NW of Hermansville in Menominee co.; flows S, past Hermansville and Daggett, to Menominee R. 8 mi/12.9 km S of Stephenson; 45°45′N 87°39′W. **2** 60 mi/97 km long, in Minn. and Iowa; rises in Mower co., SE Minn., c.25 mi/40 km SSW of Rochester; flows S, into N Iowa, past Stacyville, to Cedar R. at Nashua; 43°38′N 92°45′W.

Little Chazy River (shai-ZEE), c.20 mi/32 km long, NE N.Y.; rises in E central Clinton co.; flows E and NE, past Chazy, to L. Champlain 6 mi/9.7 km S of Rouses Point.

Little Chebeague Island (shuh-BEEG), SW Maine, in Casco Bay off Portland; c.¾ mi/1.2 km long.

Little Chenier, ridge, Cameron parish, SW La.; 29°50′N 92°59′W. One of the Cheniers (oak tree–covered ridges) paralleling the Gulf coast of SW Louisiana. There are numerous Native Amer. sites.

Little Choptank River, c.15 mi/24 km long, E Md.; tidal arm of Chesapeake Bay, penetrating the Eastern Shore in Dorchester co., just N of Taylors Isl.

Little Chuckwalla Mountains, Calif.: see CHUCKWALLA MOUNTAINS.

Little Chute, city (1990 pop. 9,207), Outagamie co., E Wis., opposite Kimberly, on Fox R., and a suburb 5 mi/ 8 km ENE of Appleton; 44°17′N 88°18′W. Mfg. (printing, bldg. materials, prepared food, cheese, concrete). A dam is here. Settled 1850, inc. 1899.

Little City, village, Marshall co., S Okla., 9 mi/14.5 km E of Madill. In agr. area. L. Texoma to E and S.

Little Colinet Island, Canada: see GREAT COLINET ISLAND.

Little Colorado River, 315 mi/507 km long, largely in Ariz.; rises in SE Apache co., E Ariz.; flows generally NW through Ariz., past St. Johns, Holbrook, and Winslow, along Painted Desert, to Colorado R. in the Grand Canyon, in Grand Canyon Natl. Park, 70 mi/113 km N of Flagstaff. Stream is dammed, forms Lyman L. (State Park), for irrigation 10 mi/16 km S of St. Johns.

Little Compton, town (1990 pop. 3,339), Newport co., SE R.I., bet. Sakonnet R. and Mass. state line, and bounded S by the Atlantic; 41°31′N 71°10′W. Agr., fishing, resort area. Includes villages of Adamsville, Little Compton, and Sakonnet. John and Priscilla Alden's daughter Elizabeth lived and is buried here; Benjamin Church also lived here. R.I. Red fowl originated in the town. Inc. as a Plymouth Colony town in 1682, passed to R.I. 1747.

Little Creek, village (1990 pop. 167), Kent co., E Del., 4 mi/6.4 km E of Dover, on Little Creek; 39°10′N 75°27′W. Oysters. Little Creek Wildlife Area to SE.

Little Curaçao (kyoo-ruh-SOU), Du., *Klein Curaçao*, islet in Neth. Antilles, 20 mi/32 km ESE of Willemstad, Curaçao; 12°00′N 68°40′W. Lighthouse.

Little Current, town (1991 pop. 1,511), S Ont., Canada, on N Manitoulin isl., on North Channel of L. Huron; 45°58′N 81°56′W. A port and a popular yachting resort; RR connections with the mainland.

Little Cypress Bayou, c.50 mi/80 km long, NE Texas; rises E of Winnsboro in SW Camp co., near source of Big Cypress Creek in several streams N of Gilmer; flows generally SE, then NE into Cypress Bayou at W end of Caddo L. c.6 mi/9.7 km E of Jefferson.

Little Diomede Island (DEI-yo-meed), Diomede Isls., NW Alaska, in Bering Strait, 20 mi/32 km WNW of Cape Prince of Wales (Seward Peninsula), 27 mi/43 km SE of Cape Dezhnev (Siberia), and 4.5 mi/7.2 km E of Rus. isl. of Ratmanov (Big Diomede); 2 mi/3.2 km long, 1 mi/1.6 km wide; 65°45′N 168°57′W. Rises to 1,200 ft/ 366 m. On W coast is Inuit settlement of Diomede village (1990 pop. 178); school. Inuit inhabitants noted for skill as seamen. Just W is internatl. boundary bet. U.S. and Rus. Far East. Discovered by Bering, 1728. Also known as Kruzenshtern (Krusenstern) and Ignaluk (IG-nuh-luhk).

Little Dragoon Mountains, Ariz.: see DRAGOON MOUNTAINS.

Little Eau Pleine River (oh PLAIN), c.35 mi/56 km long, central Wis.; rises NW of Marshfield near Clark/Marathon co. line; flows generally SE through Rice L. to Wisconsin R. (DuBay Reservoir) 12 mi/19 km NNW of Stevens Point.

Little Edisto Island, S.C.: see EDISTO ISLAND.

Little Egg Harbor, township (1990 pop. 13,333), Ocean co., E central N.J., on Little Egg Harbor, 15 mi/24 km NE of Atlantic City; 39°36′N 74°20′W. Inc. 1798.

Little Egg Harbor, SE N.J.; inlet of the Atlantic E of Tuckerton; sheltered from ocean by S end of Long Beach isl.; c.6 mi/9.7 km long, 4 mi/6.4 km wide. Link in Intracoastal Waterway, entering from Manahawkin Bay (N) and continuing into Great Bay (S). Beach Haven Inlet, S of Beach Haven, and Little Egg Inlet are entrances from the Atlantic.

Little Elm, town (1990 pop. 1,255), Denton co., N Texas; residential suburb 25 mi/40 km NNW of downtown Dallas, on Lewisville L. reservoir (bridged); 33°09′N 96°55′W. Agr. and recreation area. Mfg. (printing press blankets). Lake Lewisville State Park to S.

Little Exuma Island, central Bahama Isls., southernmost (apart from small Hog Cay) of the Exuma isls., and adjoining Great Exuma Isl., 150 mi/241 km SE of

Nassau; 13 mi/21 km long, c.1 mi/1.6 km wide; 23°27′N 75°37′W. It is crossed by the Tropic of Cancer. Main settlement is Williams Town.

Little Falls 1 city (1990 pop. 7,232), ⊙ Morrison co., central Minn., on Mississippi R., and 30 mi/48 km NNW of St. Cloud, on both sides of Mississippi R. (4 bridges); 45°58′N 94°21′W. Elev. 1,118 ft/341 m. Resort and trade center for agr. area (grain, sunflowers, potatoes; livestock; dairying). Mfg. (metal prods., hardwood prods., beverages, paper, concrete, transportation equip., plastic prods., printing and publishing). Granite quarry nearby. Grew with establishment of mills that used falls in river as source of water power. Little Falls–Morrison County Airport to SE. Point of interest is Charles Lindbergh State Park to SW, surrounding aviator's childhood home. Camp Ripley Military Reservation to N. Settled 1855, inc. as village 1879, as city 1889. **2** city (□ 3 sq mi/7.8 sq km; 1990 pop. 5,829), Herkimer co., central N.Y., 18 mi/29 km ESE of Utica; 43°02′N 74°51′W. At falls of Mohawk R. (water power) and on N.Y. State Barge Canal (locks here). Mfg. (paper, fiberglass prods. and fabrication, printed packaging materials, consumer goods, apparel). Home of Gen. Nicholas Herkimer, hero of Battle of Oriskany. Settled c.1725; inc. as city 1895.

Little Falls, township (1990 pop. 11,294), Passaic co., NE N.J., on Passaic R., and 3 mi/4.8 km SW of Paterson; 40°52′N 74°13′W. Large laundry plant; mfg. (metal prods., athletic goods, concrete prods.). Includes Singac village. Settled 1711.

Little Ferry, borough (1990 pop. 9,909), Bergen co., NE N.J., on Hackensack R., and 4 mi/6.4 km ESE of Paterson; 40°51′N 74°02′W. Mfg. (machinery, bldg. materials, metal prods.). Settled 1636, inc. 1894.

Little Fogo Island (FO-go), group of 10 islets at entrance of Notre Dame Bay, E N.F., Canada, 5 mi/8 km N of Fogo. Northernmost isl. has lighthouse (49°49′N 54°07′W).

Little Fork River, 150 mi/241 km long, N Minn.; rises in Swampy area of St. Louis co., 9 mi/14.5 km E of Cook and S of Vermilion L.; flows 1st W past Cook, then NW through Koochiching State Forest, past Littlefork (Little Fork) village, to Rainy R. on Can. (Ont.) border, 10 mi/ 16 km SW of Internatl. Falls; 47°49′N 92°27′W. Mouth of Big Fork R., on Rainy R., 6 mi/9.7 km to W.

Little Goose Creek, c.30 mi/48 km long, N Wyo.; rises in Bighorn Mts. near Cloud Peak in NW Johnson co.; flows N to Goose Creek at Sheridan.

Little Goose Lock and Dam, Wash.: see BRYAN, LAKE.

Little Grand Lake, W N.F., Canada, 23 mi/37 km S of Corner Brook; 10 mi/16 km long, 1 mi/2 km wide. Drains into Grand L.

Little Gull Island, N.Y.: see GULL ISLANDS.

Little Gunpowder Falls, stream, c.25 mi/40 km long, N Md.; flows SE, forming part of Baltimore-Harford co. line, to Gunpowder R. (estuary), c.15 mi/24 km ENE of Baltimore.

Little Humboldt River, c.60 mi/97 km long, N Nev.; intermittent stream formed in E Humboldt co. by joining of North and South Forks in Chimney Dam Reservoir 70 mi/113 km NE of Winnemucca; flows W and SW to Humboldt R. 4 mi/6.4 km NE of Winnemucca. North Fork, c.45 mi/72 km long, rises in NE Humboldt co.; South Fork, c.40 mi/64 km long, rises in W Elko co., flows NNW, through SW.

Little Inagua Island, S Bahama Isls., just NE of Great Inagua Isl., SW of Caicos Isls., 360 mi/579 km SE of Nassau; roughly 10 mi/16 km long, up to 10 mi/16 km wide; 21°30′N 73°00′W. Practically uninhabited. Little Inagua Land and Sea Park.

Little Italy, S central borough of Manhattan, N.Y. city, SE N.Y., bounded approximately by Canal St. on S, East Houston St. on N, the Bowery on E, and Cleveland Pl. and Lafayette St. on W; 40°43′N 73°59′W. The dist.'s ethnic flavor was est. 1890–1924 with the arrival of a flood of Ital. immigrants. In 1932, 98% of the pop. was Ital., but now the dist. is becoming more ethnically mixed due to the encroachment of Chinatown from the S.

Little Juniata River, Pa.: see JUNIATA RIVER.

Little Kanawha River (kuh-NAW-uh), c.160 mi/257 km long, central and NW W.Va.; rises in S Upshur co.; flows generally W through Burnsville L. reservoir (Wildlife Management Area), past Burnsville, Glenville, and Grantsville, then NW to Ohio R. at Parkersburg; receives Hughes R. from E, 12 mi/19 km SE of Parkersburg.

Little Kentucky River, c.35 mi/56 km long, N Ky.; rises in SW Henry co., flows generally N, enters Ohio R. 2 mi/3.2 km W of Carrollton, and 1 mi/1.6 km W of mouth of Kentucky R.

Little Lake, in extreme SE La., inlet of Gulf of Mexico, c.25 mi/40 km SSW of New Orleans, c.10 mi/16 km long. Joined directly to Barataria Bay (SE) and L. Salvador and the Intracoastal Waterway (N). Indirect connection to Barataria Bay through Bayou St. Denis (ESE).

Little Lake, N.Y.: see WANETA LAKE.

Little London, town (1991 pop. 1,848), Westmoreland parish, SW Jamaica, in coastal lowland, 5 mi/8 km WNW of Savanna-la-Mar; 18°18′N 78°12′W. Sugar, rice, breadfruit; livestock.

Little Lost River, c.60 mi/97 km long, E Idaho; rises in Lemhi Range, Custer/Lemhi co. line; flows SSE, terminating in a depression ENE of Arco in E part of Butte co., in tract of Idaho Engineering Laboratory. Same termination area as Big Lost R.

Little Machipongo Inlet, Va.: see HOG ISLAND; PARRAMORE ISLAND.

Little Madawaska River (mad-uh-WAHS-kuh), c.35 mi/56 km long, NE Maine; rises in NE Aroostook co.; flows NE and SE to the Aroostook near Caribou.

Little Malad River, c.45 mi/72 km long, SE Idaho; formed by confluence of 2 forks in Oneida co.; flows S, through Daniels Reservoir, joining Deep Creek and Devil Creek near Malad City to form Malad R.

Little Manistee River (MAN-is-TEE), c.50 mi/80 km long, W Mich.; rises near Luther in Lake co.; flows NW to Manistee L. and Manistee R., near L. Michigan, at Manistee; 44°00′N 85°36′W.

Little Martinique, St. Vincent and the Grenadines: see PETITE MARTINIQUE.

Little Meadows, borough (1990 pop. 326), Susquehanna co., NE Pa., 17 mi/27 km NW of Montrose, at N.Y. state line, on Appalachin Creek; 41°59′N 76°07′W. Agr. (corn, hay; dairying).

Little Missouri, river, c.560 mi/901 km long, Wyo., Mont., and S.Dak.; rising in W Crook co., NE Wyo., and flowing NE through SE corner of Mont., NW corner of S.Dak., where it flows through Little Missouri Natl. Grassland and N and S units of Theodore Roosevelt Natl. Park, and past Elkhorn Ranch Site into Garrison Reservoir on the Missouri R. 13 mi/21 km N of Kildere, where it forms Little Missouri Bay (Little Missouri Bay State Park on S shore), an arm of the reservoir c.30 mi/48 km long. Joins Missouri R. channel c.25 mi/40 km NE of Kildere.

Little Missouri River, c.145 mi/233 km long, SW Ark.; rising in the Ouachita Mts., SE Polk co., and flowing generally SE to join the Ouachita R. N of Camden. North of Murfreesboro is Narrows Dam (1950), which impounds L. Greeson.

Little Moose Mountain (3,630 ft/1,106 m), Hamilton co., NE central N.Y., in Adirondack Mts., 15 mi/24 km NW of Speculator; 43°40′N 74°35′W. Little Moose L. (c. 1 mi/1.6 km long) just NE.

Little Mountain, village (1990 pop. 235), Newberry co., NW central S.C., 24 mi/39 km WNW of Columbia; 34°12′N 81°24′W. Mfg. (marine transmissions). Agr. (livestock, poultry; grain); timber.

Little Muddy River, c.60 mi/97 km long, S Ill.; rises in SE Washington co.; flows generally S, into Big Muddy R. W of Hurst; 38°21′N 89°12′W.

Little Muskegon River (mus-KEE-guhn), c.35 mi/ 56 km long, central Mich.; rises in small lakes in Mecosta co.; flows SW, past Morley, to Muskegon R. 7 mi/ 11.3 km E of Newaygo; 43°34′N 85°16′W.

Little Muskingum River (muhs-KING-guhm, muhs-KING-uhm), c.65 mi/105 km long, SE Ohio; rises in Monroe co.; flows generally SW, through Washington co., to Ohio R. 3 mi/5 km SE of Marietta; 39°22′N 81°24′W.

Little Narragansett Bay, on R.I.-Conn. state line, inlet of the Atlantic estuary of Pawcatuck R. Sheltered by curving peninsula, site of WATCH HILL resort village. Yatching, fishing, harbor.

Little Neck, residential section of NE Queens borough of N.Y. city, SE N.Y., on Little Neck Bay; 40°46′N 72°45′W.

Little Neck Bay, inlet of L.I. Sound indenting N shore of W L.I., Nassau co.; SE N.Y., bet. Queens borough (W) and Great Neck peninsula (E); c.1.5 mi/2.4 km wide at entrance, 2.5 mi/4 km long; 40°48′N 72°46′W.

Little Nemaha River (nee-MAH-hah), c.75 mi/121 km long, SE Nebr.; rises near Lincoln, Lancaster co.; flows SE, past Syracuse and Auburn, to Missouri R. near Nemaha. Channel straightened in parts.

Little Niangua River (nei-ANG-gwuh), c.40 mi/64 km long, central Mo.; rises in the Ozarks in Dallas co.; flows NE to Niangua arm of L. of the Ozarks in Camden co.

Little Ocmulgee River (OK-muhl-gee), c.70 mi/113 km long, S central Ga.; rises in S Twiggs co.; flows SE, past McRae, to Ocmulgee R. just SE of Lumber City; 32°07′N 82°54′W.

Little Osage River (O-saij), 68 mi/109 km long, in W Mo. and E Kansas; rises near Moran, Kansas; flows E, joining Marais des Cygnes R. to form Osage R. SE of Rich Hill, Mo.

Little Ossipee Pond (AHS-uh-pee), SW Maine, center of Waterboro resort area; 2.5 mi/4 km long; drains N into Little Ossipee R. (17 mi/27 km long), which enters the Saco at Limington.

Little Patuxent River (puh-TUX-ent), c.35 mi/56 km long, central Md.; rises in N Howard co.; flows SE, past Fort George G. Meade, to the Patuxent 4 mi/6.4 km ESE of Bowie.

Little Peconic Bay, SE N.Y., bet. N and S peninsulas of E L.I., E of Great Peconic Bay; c.6 mi/9.7 km long, 4.5 mi/7.2 km wide; 41°00′N 72°24′W.

Little Pee Dee River, c.90 mi/145 km long, E S.C.; rises in E Marlboro co. near N.C. state line; flows SE past Dillon to Great Pee Dee R., 18 mi/29 km W of Myrtle Beach.

Little Pigeon Creek, c.27 mi/43 km long, SW Ind.; rises in E Warrick co.; flows SW along most of the boundary bet. Warrick and Spencer cos. to join the Ohio R. c.5 mi/8 km SE (upstream) of Newburgh.

Little Platte River, c.170 mi/274 km long, SW Iowa and NW Mo.; rises near Creston, Iowa; flows generally S to Missouri R., below Leavenworth, Kansas. Sometimes called Platte R.

Little Point, village, Morgan co., central Ind., 14 mi/23 km NW of Martinsville. In agr. area. Founded 1829.

Little Popo Agie River, Wyo.: see POPO AGIE RIVER.

Little Powder River, c.100 mi/161 km long, in Wyo. and Mont.; rises in NE Campbell co., NE Wyo., 25 mi/40 km NNE of Gillette at joining of Cottonwood and Rawhide creeks; flows N to Powder R. 5 mi/8 km NE of Broadus, Powder River co., SE Mont.

Little Red River, 105 mi/169 km long, NW Ark.; rising in the Boston Mts., and flowing SE to the White R. Archeys Fork (30 mi/48 km long) joins south Fork at Clinton (40 mi/64 km long); both rise in W Van Buren co. Middle Fork (60 mi/97 km long) rises in S Searcy co., and joins South Fork at Edgemont, Cleburne co., in Greers Ferry L. Main river continues another 75 mi/121 km to White R., part Searcy. Greers Ferry Dam and reservoir (completed 1964) provide flood control and hydroelectric power.

Little Rich Mountain (3,320 ft/1,012 m), in the Blue Ridge, Greenville co., NW S.C., c.25 mi/40 km NNW of Greenville, near N.C. state line.

Little River, county (□ 564 sq mi/1,461 sq km; 1990 pop. 13,966), extreme SW Ark.; ⊙ Ashdown; 33°42′N 94°14′W. Bounded W by Texas, S by Red R., N and E by Little R. Agr. (wheat, soybeans; cattle, hogs). Mfg. (wood prods.); lumber milling. Timber; sand, gravel, limestone. Millwood L. (Little R.) and State Park in E. Formed 1867.

Little River, town (1990 pop. 3,470), Horry co., E S.C., 25 mi/40 km E of Conway, and on tidal Little R. near N.C. state line; 33°52′N 78°37′W. Mfg. (pulpwood). Agr. (timber; livestock; watermelons, vegetables, grain).

Little River, village (1990 pop. 496), Rice co., central Kansas, on Little Arkansas R., and 11 mi/18 km ENE of Lyons; 38°23′N 98°00′W. In wheat area. Oil wells nearby.

Little River 1 c.30 mi/48 km long, in NE Ala.; formed by confluence of 2 headstreams in Lookout Mt., NE Ala.; flows SW to Weiss L., 5 mi/8 km NNE of Centre. **2** c.25 mi/40 km long, in E Conn.; rises near Hampton; flows S to Shetucket R., 5 mi/8 km NNE of Norwich. **3** c.75 mi/121 km long, E Ga.; rises near Maxeys; meanders E to Savannah R., 20 mi/32 km NW of Augusta; 33°37′N 82°52′W. **4** c.70 mi/113 km long, in SW Ky.; formed in Christian co. S of Hopkinsville by junction of its North and South forks (North Fork rises in Hopkinsville, flows S c.10 mi/16 km; South Fork rises in E Christian co., flows WSW c.20 mi/32 km.); flows SW, then WNW, past Cadiz, to Cumberland R. 8 mi/12.9 km W of Cadiz, receives Muddy Fork (rises in NW Christian co., flows WSW c.30 mi/48 km.) 3 mi/4.8 km W of Cadiz; river below Cadiz forms E arm of L. Barkley reservoir. **5** c.90 mi/145 km long, in central La.; formed N of Georgetown by junction of Dugdemona R. and Castor Creek; flows SE to Catahoula L., and ENE to Ouachita R. (Black R.) at Jonesville; 31°37′N 91°48′W. Little R. State Wildlife Area on W bank. **6** c.70 mi/113 km long, SE Mo.; formerly the outflow of swamps and wetlands of SE Missouri in New Madrid, Pemiscot, and Dunklin cos., into which the Castor and Whitewater rivers emptied. Now completely channelized to the Ark. state line and referred to as the Little River drainage channels. Remnants of the original channel remain. Continues in Ark. as Little River and joins the St. Francis R. at Marked Tree, Ark. Swamps and wetlands were affected by New Madrid earthquakes 1811–1812. **7** 90 mi/145 km long, central Okla.; rises SE of Oklahoma City; flows generally SE, through city of Norman and part of Macomb, to Canadian R., in Hughes co., c.5 mi/8 km S of Holdenville. Dammed in Cleveland co., forming L. Thunderbird. Little R. State Park on L. Thunderbird, at Norman. **8** c.220 mi/354 km long, Okla. and Ark.; rises S of Pine Valley in Ouachita Mts. (Kiamichi Mts.) in SW Le Flore co., Okla.; flows SW, then SE, past Wright City, into Ark., through Millwood L. reservoir, where it receives Saline R. from N; joins Red R. just W of Fulton, Ark. Mountain Fork, c.40 mi/64 km long, rises in W Ark., enters McCurtain co., Okla., through Broken Bow L. reservoir, entering main stream 10 mi/16 km SE of Broken Bow. Pine Creek L. formed in McCurtain co. Millwood Reservoir (for flood control) is c.10 mi/16 km NW of Fulton. Little R. crosses into Ark. at elev. 287 ft/87 m, the lowest in Okla. **9** c.50 mi/80 km long, in E Tenn.; rises in Great Smoky Mts. Natl. Park, on Clingmans Dome, near N.C. state line; flows NW past Elkmont, Townsend, and Walland, to Fort Loudoun Reservoir (Tennessee R.) 8 mi/13 km S of Knoxville; 35°52′N 83°59′W. **10** c.75 mi/121 km long, in central Texas; formed by Leon and Lampasas rivers 9 mi/14.5 km S of Temple; flows generally SE and E past Cameron, to Brazos R., c.5 mi/8 km W of Hearne. **11** c.30 mi/48 km long, N Va.; rises in NE Fauquier co.; flows NE to Goose Creek (a tributary of Potomac R.), in Loudoun co., 3 mi/4.8 km SE of Leesburg. **12** c.50 mi/80 km long, SW Va.; rises in NE Floyd co.; flows S and WNW, to New R., 3 mi/4.8 km S of Radford. **13** c.40 mi/64 km long, central Va.; rises in E Louisa co.; flows SE to North Anna R., 5 mi/8 km NNW of Hanover.

Little River, Ga.: see WITHLACOOCHEE RIVER.

Little River Dam, S.C.: see KEOWEE, LAKE.

Little River–Academy, town (1990 pop. 1,390), Bell co., central Texas, suburb 7 mi/11.3 km S of Temple, NE of point where Leon and Lampasas rivers form Little R.; 30°59′N 97°20′W. Agr. area. Mfg. (feeds, fertilizers).

Little Rocher (LI-tuhl rahsh), village, SE N.B., Canada, on Chignecto Bay, 18 mi/29 km SW of Hopewell Cape. Gypsum quarrying.

Little Rock, city (1990 pop. 175,795), ⊙ of state and of Pulaski co., central Ark., on the Arkansas R.; 34°43′N 92°20′W. Drained by Fourche Creek. Murray Lock and Dam to NW; L. Maumelle reservoir and Pinnacles State Park to NW. It is a river port and the administrative, commercial, transportation, and cultural center of the state. Diversified mfg. and consumer goods. The city's industries process agr. prods. fish, beef, poultry, and bauxite and timber. Its mfg. industries are closely related with those of North Little Rock across the river. The settlement was a well-known river crossing when Arkansas Territory was est. in 1819. It became territorial capital in 1821 and state capital when Ark. entered the Union in 1836. In the Civil War the battle of Little Rock (1863) was fought there. The city became a center of world attention in 1957, when Federal troops were sent there to enforce a 1954 U.S. Supreme Court ruling against segregation in the public schools. Little Rock is the seat of Philander Smith Col., Ark. Baptist Col., the Univ. of Ark. at Little Rock, and several other branches of the Univ., including the law and medical schools. Of interest are the beautiful old statehouse (which served as capitol from 1836 to 1910) and several mus.; the present capitol bldg. was built in 1911. The city also contains several state institutions. Little Rock Air Force Base is to NE in Jacksonville. Ark. School for Blind and Deaf here. Camp Robinson Natl. Guard Training Area to N; Metropolitan Vocational Technical Educational Center. Livestock Showgrounds and Barton Coliseum; Adams Field Municipal Airport and Little Rock Post Industrial Park (on Arkansas R.) in E end. Inc. 1831.

Little Rock, town (1990 pop. 493), Lyon co., NW Iowa, on Little Rock R., and 15 mi/24 km E of Rock Rapids; 43°26′N 95°52′W. In livestock and grain area.

Little Rock River, 40 mi/64 km long, SW Minn. and NW Iowa; rises in central Nobles co., SW Minn., c.10 mi/16 km W of Washington, flows SW into NW Iowa, past Little Rock village, to Rock R. 4 mi/6.4 km NE of Rock Valley; 43°36′N 95°40′W.

Little Sac River (SAK), c.45 mi/72 km long, SW central Mo.; rises in the Ozarks N of Springfield; flows NW to Sac R. in Cedar co., as part of Stockton L.

Little Saint Lawrence, village, SE N.F., Canada, on SW side of Placentia Bay, on Burin Peninsula, 22 mi/35 km ESE of Grand Bank; 46°55′N 55°21′W. Hydroelectric station supplies power for nearby fluorspar mines. Tsunami from Grand Banks earthquake (Nov. 1929) destroyed villages along S end of Burin Peninsula, killing 29 people; largest earthquake toll in Can. history.

Little Salkehatchie River, S.C.: see COMBAHEE RIVER.

Little Salmon River, 40 mi/64 km long, W Idaho; rises in mt. region S of New Meadows, E Adams co.; flows N, through deep canyon, to Salmon R. at Riggins, in SW Idaho co.

Little San Bernardino Mountains (c.4,000 ft/1,219 m–5,500 ft/1,676 m), mainly Riverside co., S Calif., extends NW into San Bernardino co., SE continuation of San Bernardino Mts., extend c.40 mi/64 km NW-SE along E side of Coachella Valley. Partly (E slope) within SW part of Joshua Tree Natl. Monument. Colorado R. aqueduct passes along SW base of range.

Little San Salvador, islet, central Bahama Isls., just W of N Cat Isl., 95 mi/153 km ESE of Nassau; a narrow, bifurcated bar, c.6 mi/9.7 km long W-E; 24°35′N 75°55′W. San Salvador or Watling Isl., where Columbus made his 1st landfall, is 95 mi/153 km ESE, on the other side of Cat Isl.

Little Sandy River, c.90 mi/145 km long, NE Ky.; rises in SW Elliott co.; flows generally NNE, past Sandy Hook, through Grayson L. reservoir, and past Grayson, to Ohio R. at Greenup.

Little Satilla River (suh-TIL-uh), c.30 mi/48 km long, in SE Ga.; rises in E Brantley co.; flows ESE forming the co. border bet. Glynn and Camden cos., emptying into Saint Andrews Sound bet. the sea islands of Jekyll and Cumberland; 31°07′N 81°40′W.

Little Scioto River (sei-O-tuh), c.40 mi/64 km long, S Ohio; rises in Jackson co.; flows S through Scioto co. to the Ohio 6 mi/10 km E of Portsmouth; 38°45′N 82°53′W.

Little Sebago Lake (suh-BAI-go), SW Maine, in central

Cumberland co., E of Sebago L.; 6 mi/9.7 km long, ½ mi/⅕ km–1 mi/1.6 km wide. Drains SSW into Presumpscot R.

Little Silver, borough (1990 pop. 5,721), Monmouth co., E N.J., just SE of Red Bank, and 13 mi/21 km NE of Freehold; 40°19′N 74°01′W. Fort Monmouth nearby. Inc. 1923.

Little Sioux, town (1990 pop. 205), Harrison co., W Iowa, on Little Sioux R. near its mouth on Missouri R., and 17 mi/27 km NW of Logan; 41°48′N 96°01′W.

Little Smoky River, 185 mi/298 km long, Alta., Canada; rises in Rocky Mts. N of Jasper Natl. Park; flows E and N to Smoky R. 60 mi/97 km NE of Grande Prairie.

Little Snake River, c.150 mi/241 km long, in NW Colo. and S Wyo.; rises in N tip of Park Range, N Routt co., near Continental Divide, Routt Natl. Forest Colo.; flows W, along Wyo./Colo. state line, meanders into Carbon co., Wyo.; past Dixon and Baggs, Wyo., then SW into Colo., to Yampa R. c.45 mi/72 km W of Craig, E of Dinosaur Natl. Monument.

Little Sodus Bay, inlet of L. Ontario, Cayuga co., W central N.Y., 12 mi/19 km E of Sodus Bay; c.2 mi/3.2 km long, ½ mi/⁸⁄₁₀ km–0.75 mi/1.21 km wide; 43°20′N 76°43′W. Fair Haven (resort); Fair Haven Beach State Park.

Little Sound, Bermuda: see PORT ROYAL BAY.

Little Squam Lake, N.H.: see SQUAM LAKE.

Little Switzerland, uninc. village, McDowell co., W N.C., 12 mi/19 km NNW of Marion, in the Blue Ridge Mts., in Pisgah Natl. Forest. Blue Ridge Parkway passes to NW. Resort area. Gems, Emerald Village, N.C. Mining Mus.

Little Tallahatchie River, Miss.: see TALLAHATCHIE RIVER.

Little Tallapoosa River (tal-uh-POO-suh), c.90 mi/145 km long, in W Ga. and E Ala.; rises in N Carroll co.; flows SW, past Carrollton, into Ala. to Tallapoosa R., 6 mi/9.7 km W of Wedowee; 33°46′N 84°57′W.

Little Tancook Island, islet in Mahone Bay, S N.S., Canada, 8 mi/13 km SE of Chester; 44°28′N 64°08′W.

Little Tennessee River, c.135 mi/217 km long, Ga., N.C., and Tenn.; rising in the Blue Ridge, NE Ga., and flowing generally NW across SW N.C. and through E Tenn. to the Tennessee R. opposite Lenoir City; 34°55′N 83°26′W. On the river in N.C., near the Tenn. state line, is Fontana Dam (480 ft/146 m high; 2,365 ft/721 m long; completed 1945), impounding Fontana L. It is part of the TVA and is the highest dam E of the Rocky Mts. The dam provides flood control, river regulation, and hydroelectricity. Cheoah Dam in N.C., and Calderwood and Chilhowee dams in Tenn., are also part of the TVA.

Little Tobago Island (to-BAI-go), islet off NE Tobago, 18 mi/29 km NE of Scarborough; 11°13′N 60°30′W. Noted as reserve for birds of paradise, introduced from Du. New Guinea in 1909. The isl. (c.500 acres/202 ha) was presented to govt. of Trinidad and Tobago in 1929. Sometimes called Bird of Paradise Isl.

Little Traverse Bay, NW Mich., inlet of L. Michigan, c.15 mi/24 km NE of Grand Traverse Bay; c.10 mi/16 km long, 5 mi/8 km wide; 45°24′N 85°00′W. Bay View, Petoskey, Harbor Springs, and resort villages are on its shores.

Little Truckee River, c.30 mi/48 km long, E Calif.; rises in Weber L. in the Sierra Nevada; flows E and S past Sierraville, and through Boca Reservoir to Truckee R. 6 mi/9.7 km NE of Truckee, near Nev. state line. Boca Dam (1,629 ft/497 m long, 116 ft/35 m high; completed 1939 by Bureau of Reclamation) is on lower course near mouth. Forms small reservoir (capacity 40,900 acre-ft.) and is chief unit in Truckee storage project. Water from reservoir is released into Truckee R. and used for irrigation of 30,000 acres/12,141 ha in Washoe and Storey cos., W Nev., and to supplement Carson and Truckee rivers in supplying Newlands irrigation project in vicinity of Fallon, W Nev.

Little Tupper Lake, N.Y.: see TUPPER LAKE.

Little Unadilla Lake, N.Y.: see MILLERS MILLS.

Little Valley, village (□ 1 sq mi/2.6 sq km; 1990 pop. 1,188), ⊙ Cattaraugus co., W N.Y., 7 mi/11.3 km NNW

of Salamanca; 42°15′N 78°47′W. Mfg. (feed; printing, lumber milling). Agr. (grain, hay, fruit; livestock, poultry). Inc. 1876.

Little Vermilion River, c.55 mi/89 km long, in E Ill. and W Ind.; rises in SE Champaign co., Ill.; flows generally E to the Wabash just E of Newport, Ind.; 39°58′N 88°02′W.

Little Wabash River 1 (WAH-bash), c.30 mi/48 km long, in NE Ind.; rises in W Allen co. at Fort Wayne; flows SW, past Huntington, to the Wabash c.2 mi/3.2 km W of Huntington. **2** c.200 mi/322 km long, E central and SE Ill.; rises near Mattoo; flows S and SE to the Wabash near New Haven; 39°28′N 88°27′W. Dam impounds L. Mattoon near Mattoon.

Little Washita River (WAHSH-uh-tah), c.30 mi/48 km long, S Okla.; rises in SE Caddo co.; flows SE and then NE, through Grady co., to Washita R. just SE of Chickasha.

Little Watts Island, Va.: see WATTS ISLAND.

Little White River, c.135 mi/217 km long, S S.Dak.; rises in SE Shannon co.; flows E past Martin, then NNE past Rosebud and village of White River to White R. near town of White R. 12 mi/19 km SSE of Murdo; 43°11′N 102°09′W. Formerly South Fork of White R.

Little Wichita River, c.50 mi/80 km long, N Texas; rises in Archer co.; flows generally NE to Red R. 14 mi/23 km ENE of Henrietta. Dam impounds L. Kickapoo (capacity 105,000 acre-ft.), 26 mi/42 km SW of Wichita Falls. L. Arrowhead 13 mi/21 km SE of Wichita Falls.

Little Wood River, 90 mi/145 km long, S central Idaho; rises in Pioneer Mts., N Blaine co., flows S, through Little Wood R. reservoir, and past Richfield, then W, past Shoshone, to Big Wood R. just W of Gooding.

Little York, town (1990 pop. 155), Washington co., S Ind., 13 mi/21 km NE of Salem; 38°42′N 85°54′W. Agr. area. Laid out 1831.

Little York, village (1990 pop. 349), Warren co., NW Ill., 20 mi/32 km W of Galesburg; 41°00′N 90°45′W. In agr. area. On Cedar Creek.

Littlefield, town (1990 pop. 6,489), ⊙ Lamb co., NW Texas, on the Llano Estacado, 35 mi/56 km NW of Lubbock; 33°55′N 102°19′W. Elev. 3,556 ft/1,084 m. Trade, shipping, processing center for agr. and livestock (grain sorghum, cotton). Mfg. (fibers, turbine pumps). Lakes nearby (hunting, fishing). Settled 1912, inc. 1925; became co. seat 1946.

Littlefield, uninc. village, Mohave co., NW Ariz., 23 mi/37 km WSW of St. George, Utah, and 9 mi/14.5 km ENE of Mequite, Nev., on Virgin R., at mouth of Beaver Dam Wash. Elev. 1,858 ft/566 m. Cattle. Virgin Mts. to S; Paiute Wilderness Area, in Black Rock Mts., to SE; Beaver Dam Mts. Wilderness Area to E. Service center on Interstate Highway 15 the only viable community in this isolated NW corner of Ariz.

Littlefork, town (1990 pop. 838), Kochiching co., N Minn., on Little Fork R. 6 mi/9.7 km SW of International Falls; 48°23′N 93°33′W. Agr. (cattle; alfalfa). Mfg. (lumber, fishing lures); timber. Nett Lake Indian Reservation to SE; Koochiching State Forest to SW; Smokey Bear State Forest to NW. Often spelled Little Fork.

Littlejohn Island, resort isl., SW Maine, in Casco Bay off Yarmouth; 1 mi/1.6 km long. Bridge connects with Cousins Isl.

Littleport, town (1990 pop. 88), Clayton co., NE Iowa, on Volga R., and 7 mi/11.3 km S of Elkader; 42°45′N 91°22′W. In corn, hog, dairy region.

Littlerock, uninc. town (1990 pop. 1,320), Los Angeles co., S Calif., 14 mi/23 km SE of Lancaster; 34°32′N 117°59′W. Californian Aqueduct passes to S. San Gabriel Mts. to S. Pears, grain; dairying; poultry, cattle.

Littlestown, borough (1990 pop. 2,974), Adams co., S Pa., 10 mi/16 km SE of Gettysburg, near Md. state line; 39°44′N 77°05′W. Agr. area (grain, soybeans; poultry, livestock; dairying). Mfg. (furniture, consumer goods, machinery, metal prods., food prods.). Long Arm Reservoir to E. Laid out 1765, inc. 1864.

Littleton, city (1990 pop. 33,685), ⊙ Arapahoe co., N central Colo., suburb 7 mi/11.3 km S of downtown Denver, on South Platte R.; 39°35′N 105°00′W. Located in

an irrigated farm area rapidly being displaced by urbanization. Mfg. (construction materials, electronic games, medical supplies, metal prods., consumer goods, furniture). Arapahoe Community Col., Littleton Historical Mus., Arapaho County Fairgrounds, and a thoroughbred racing track, Continental Racetrack, are here. Chatfield L. and State Park to SW. Plotted 1812, inc. 1890.

Littleton 1 town (1990 pop. 956), Aroostook co., E Maine, 8 mi/12.9 km N of Houlton; 46°13′N 67°50′W. In potato-growing area. Inc. 1856. **2** rural town (1990 pop. 7,051), Middlesex co., NE central Mass., 13 mi/21 km SW of Lowell; 42°32′N 71°29′W. Agr. (poultry; dairying; apples). Mfg. (consumer goods, medical supplies, computer equip.). Skiing at Nashoba Valley. Includes village of Littleton Common. Settled on site of "praying Indian" village of Nashoba, est. c.1656; inc. 1715. **3** town (1990 pop. 5,827), Grafton co., NW N.H.; bounded NW by Connecticut R. (Vt. state line); 44°19′N 71°48′W. Drained by Ammonoosuc R. Agr. (cattle, poultry; dairying; vegetables; nursery crops, sugar maples; timber). Mfg. (electrical equip., food prods., machinery, lumber, pharmaceuticals, printing and publishing, metal prods.). Moore Dam on Connecticut R. forms Moore Reservoir in N. Settled 1769, inc. 1784.

Littleton 1 village (1990 pop. 181), Schuyler co., W Ill., 8 mi/12.9 km NNW of Rushville; 40°13′N 90°37′W. In agr. area. **2** village (1990 pop. 691), Warren and Halifax cos., N N.C., 15 mi/24 km W of Roanoke Rapids; 36°25′N 77°54′W. Agr. (tobacco; peanuts, grain, sweet potatoes; livestock). Mfg. (wood prods., apparel). L. Gastona reservoir (Roanoke R.) to N. Founded before 1775. **3** village (1990 pop. 198), Wetzel co., N W.Va., 19 mi/31 km ENE of New Martinsville, on Fish Creek; 39°42′N 80°30′W. SW corner of Pa. (W end of Mason-Dixon Line) 2 mi/3.2 km to NNE.

Littleville Lake, reservoir, on Hampden/Hampshire co. border, W Mass., on Middle Branch Westfield R., 12 mi/19 km WSW of Northampton; 4 mi/6.4 km long; 42°15′N 72°50′W. Max. capacity 40,500 acre-ft. Formed by Littleville Dam (earth construction; 159 ft/48 m high), built (1965) by the Army Corps of Engineers for flood control, water supply, and recreation.

Lituya Bay (li-TOO-yuh), SE Alaska, inlet of Gulf of Alaska, 100 mi/161 km SE of Yakutat, SSW of Mt. Fairweather; 9 mi/14.5 km long, 2 mi/3.2 km wide; 58°38′N 137°34′W. At head of bay, mts. rise to 11,924 ft/3,634 m. Discovered 1786 by Count de la Pérouse, who named it Port des Français. Famous for extraordinary high tides.

Litz Manor, village, Sullivan co., NE Tenn., suburb SE of Kingsport.

Live Oak, county (□ 1,078 sq mi/2,792 sq km; 1990 pop. 9,556), S Texas, ⊙ George West; 28°21′N 98°07′W. Drained by Frio, Atascosa, and Nueces rivers. Cattle ranching, hogs, agr. (grain sorghum, corn, cotton; hay). Oil, natural gas wells; sand and gravel. Tips State Recreation Park in center; part of Choke Canyon L. reservoir (Frio R) and State Park on W boundary; part of L. Corpus Christi (Nueces R.) in SE corner. Formed 1856.

Live Oak 1 city (1990 pop. 4,320), Sutter co., N central Calif., in Sacramento Valley, near Feather R., 10 mi/16 km N of Yuba City; 39°16′N 121°40′W. Trade and shipping center for agr. area (vegetables, melons, walnuts, prunes, peaches, pears); millwork. Sutter Butte to SW. Inc. 1947. **2** city (□ 6 sq mi/15.5 sq km; 1990 pop. 6,332), ⊙ Suwannee co., N central Fla., c.80 mi/129 km E of Tallahassee; 30°17′N 82°59′W. RR junction; chief bright-leaf tobacco market of the state; lumber milling; mfg. (naval stores, apparel). Fla. Memorial Col. is here. **3** city (1990 pop. 10,023), Bexar co., S central Texas, suburb 14 mi/23 km NE of downtown San Antonio; 29°33′N 98°20′W. Agr. area; oil and natural gas. Mfg. (dog and fish food).

Live Oak, uninc. town (1990 pop. 15,212), Santa Cruz co., W Calif., residential suburb 1 mi/1.6 km NE of Santa Cruz, 2 mi. N of Monterey Bay, Pacific Ocean; 36°59′N

121°59′W. New Brighton State Beach to S. Apples, berries, plums, nursery stock.

Live Oak Manor, uninc. town, (1990 pop. 2,150), Jefferson parish, SE La., residential suburb 7 mi/11 km W of downtown New Orleans, on the Mississippi R. Elev. 9 ft/3 m.

Livengood (LEI-ven-gud), village, central Alaska, 50 mi/80 km NNW of Fairbanks, at N end of Elliott Highway from Fairbanks. Placer gold mining; outfitting center for prospectors. Airfield. Near Alaska Pipeline and Dalton Highway.

Livermore, city (1990 pop. 56,741), Alameda co., W central Calif., suburb 28 mi/45 km ESE of downtown Oakland, in Livermore Valley; 37°42′N 121°46′W. Agr. (grapes, oats; nursery prods., roses; cattle); wineries. Mfg. (construction materials, household items, metal and plastic prods., communications equip.). Lawrence Radiation Laboratory of the Univ. of Calif. conducts nuclear research. Los Positas Col. (2-year). Livermore Municipal Airport to SW. Del Valle State Recreation Area to E. Hetch Hetchy Aqueduct passes E-W to S. Inc. 1876.

Livermore 1 town (1990 pop. 436), Humboldt co., N central Iowa, near East Des Moines R., 10 mi/16 km N of Dakota City; 42°52′N 94°10′W. Feed milling. **2** town (1990 pop. 1,534), McLean co., W Ky., 18 mi/29 km S of Owensboro, on Green R., mouth of Rough R. to SE; 37°29′N 87°07′W. In agr. area (tobacco, grain; livestock). Mfg. (metal fabrication, plastic prods., furniture). **3** town (1990 pop. 1,950), Androscoggin co., SW Maine, 20 mi/32 km N of Auburn; 44°24′N 70°12′W. Farming. Includes villages of Livermore and North Livermore. Inc. 1795. **4** town, Grafton co., N central N.H., 20 mi/32 km NNE of Plymouth, in White Mt. Natl. Forest; 44°01′N 71°27′W. Drained by Sawyer R. Crossed by Kancamagus Highway. Timber.

Livermore Falls, town (1990 pop. 3,455), Androscoggin co., SW Maine, 25 mi/40 km N of Lewiston, and on the Androscoggin R.; 44°25′N 70°09′W. Paper mills; shoes. Called East Livermore until 1930. Settled 1786, inc. 1843.

Livermore, Mount (8,381 ft/2,555 m), extreme W Texas, 24 mi/39 km NNW of Marfa; highest peak in Davis Mts. and 2d highest in state. Sometimes called Baldy Peak or Old Baldy.

Liverpool, town (1991 pop. 3,113), ⊙ Queens co., SW N.S., Canada, at head of Liverpool Bay (5 mi/8 km long) of the Atlantic, at mouth of Mersey R., 70 mi/113 km SW of Halifax; 44°02′N 64°43′W. Fishing center. Shipbuilding; paper-, pulp-, sawmilling.

Liverpool 1 village (1990 pop. 2,624), Onondaga co., central N.Y., on Onondaga L., just N of Syracuse; 43°06′N 76°12′W. Mfg. (computers, computer equip., machinery, corrugated containers, electrical equip., rubber prods.). Agr. (dairy prods.; poultry). Part of town of Salina. Inc. 1830. **2** village (1990 pop. 396), Brazoria co., SE Texas, residential suburb 32 mi/51 km S of downtown Houston, and 22 mi/35 km WSW of Texas City, on Chocolate Bayou; 29°18′N 95°16′W. Agr. area. Oil and natural gas.

Liverpool, borough (1990 pop. 934), Perry co., central Pa., 22 mi/35 km NNW of Harrisburg, on Susquehanna R. (ferry to Millersburg 2 mi/3.2 km to S); 40°34′N 76°59′W. Agr. area (corn, hay; dairying). Mfg. (modular homes, molded rubber prods.). Buffalo Mt. ridge to SW, end of Mahantango Mt. ridge to E.

Liverpool, Cape, N Bylot Isl., E Franklin dist., N.W.T., Canada, on Baffin Bay, at E end of Lancaster Sound; 73°45′N 77°45′W.

Livingston 1 county (□ 1,045 sq mi/2,707 sq km; 1990 pop. 39,301), E central Ill; ⊙ Pontiac; 40°53′N 88°33′W. Agr. (corn, wheat, soybeans; livestock; dairy prods.). Limestone, clay. Diversified mfg. Drained by Vermilion R. Site of max. security Pontiac Correctional Center. Formed 1837. **2** county (□ 342 sq mi/886 sq km; 1990 pop. 9,062), W Ky.; ⊙ Smithland; 37°12′N 88°20′W. Bounded W and N by Ohio R. (Ill. state line), S by Tennessee R. (joins Ohio R. at SW tip of co.); crossed by Cumberland R. (forms part of E boundary in SE). Kentucky Dam and part of Kentucky L. reservoir are on S boundary (Tennessee R.), Barkley Dam and part of L. Barkley reservoir on SE boundary. Gently rolling agr. area (tobacco; corn, wheat, soybeans; hay, alfalfa; hogs, cattle, poultry; dairying); catfish. Limestone quarries. Tourism. Formed 1798. **3** county (□ 585 sq mi/1,515 sq km; 1990 pop. 115,645), SE Mich.; ⊙ Howell; 42°36′N 83°54′W. Drained by Red Cedar, Huron, and Shiawassee rivers. Agr. (cattle, hogs, sheep, poultry; corn, wheat, oats, soybeans, apples; dairy prods.). Mfg. at Howell. Summer resorts; numerous small lakes in SE ¼ and extreme NE. Pinckney State Recreation Area on S boundary, Island L. State Recreation Area, Brighton State Recreation Area, and Mt. Brighton Ski Area, all in SE. Organized 1836. **4** county (□ 533 sq mi/1,380 sq km; 1990 pop. 14,592), N central Mo.; ⊙ Chillicothe; 39°46′N 93°32′W. Drained by Grand R. Agr. (corn, wheat, soybeans; cattle). Mfg. at Chillicothe. Fountain Grove Conservation Area in SE. Severe flooding on Grand R. in 1993. Formed 1837. **5** county (□ 640 sq mi/1,658 sq km; 1990 pop. 62,372), W central N.Y.; ⊙ Geneseo; 42°43′N 77°46′W. In Finger Lakes region; bisected S-N by broad Genesee R. valley; drained also by Canaseraga and Honeoye creeks. Conesus and Hemlock lakes in co. Some mfg. at Avon, Geneseo, Dansville, Caledonia. Rich agr. area (dairying; grain, vegetables, hay; poultry). Salt mines; gypsum and limestone quarries. Horse farms. James and William Wadsworth of Conn., most prominent early settlers, purchased 55 sq mi/142 sq km of land here and encouraged liberal settlement in the early 19th cent. Named for Robert Livingston, Continental Congress delegate and drafter of Declaration of Independence. Well-known Genesee Valley Hunt founded 1876; nation's 2d oldest. Includes N part of Letchworth State Park. Formed 1821.

Livingston, parish (□ 665 sq mi/1,722 sq km; 1990 pop. 70,526), SE La.; ⊙ Livingston; 32°30′N 90°45′W. Bounded W by Amite R. and S by Petite Amite and Blind rivers, partly E by Natalbany R., SE by L. Maurepas; drained by Tickfaw R. Agr. (home gardens, nursery crops, cucumbers, peppers; cattle, horses, poultry, exotic fowl, hogs; dairying); alligators; logging. Hunting, fishing. Named after Edward Livingston, who formulated La.'s code of law. Located in the "Fla. parishes" of La., part of former Br. colony of W Florida. Formed 1832.

Livingston, city (1990 pop. 7,317), Merced co., central Calif., in San Joaquin Valley, near Merced R., 14 mi/23 km NW of Merced; 37°23′N 120°43′W. Agr. (dairying; poultry; grain, vegetables, fruit, almonds; cotton, alfalfa). Mfg. (farm machinery); poultry processing, dehydrated fruits and vegetables.

Livingston 1 town (1990 pop. 3,530), ⊙ Sumter co., W Ala., 22 mi/35 km W of Demopolis, bet. Tombigbee R. and Miss. state line. Mfg. (paper prods. apparel). Livingston Univ. here. Founded c.1833. **2** town (1990 pop. 999), ⊙ Livingston parish, SE La., 25 mi/40 km E of Baton Rouge; 30°30′N 90°45′W. In lumbering area. Mfg. (wood prods., apparel); oil deposits. Founded 1918. **3** town (1990 pop. 6,701), ⊙ Park co., S Mont., 24 mi/39 km E of Bozeman, on Yellowstone R., N of Yellowstone Natl. Park, and just NW of Absaroka Range; 45°40′N 110°34′W. RR; tourism; trade center for mining and agr. area. Coal, arsenic, silver, gold mines; marble, granite. Agr. (dairying; cattle; vegetables, barley, oats, alfalfa). Mfg. (pottery, fishing flies, printing and publishing, wood prods.). Parts of Gallatin Natl. Forest to SE, SW, NW, and NE; Absaroka-Beartooth Wilderness Area to SE; Paradise Valley of Yellowstone R. to SW, scenic area leading to Yellowstone Natl. Park (U.S. Highway 89). Calamity Jane lived here. Livingston Professional Cowboys Assoc. Rodeo (July 4 weekend). Park County Mus., Depot Center, Sleeping Giant Wildlife Mus. to S. Originally called Clark City. Founded 1882, inc. 1889. **4** town (1990 pop. 3,809), ⊙ Overton co., N Tenn., 18 mi/29 km NNE of Cookeville; 36°23′N 85°19′W. In coal, timber, agr. (poultry, corn, hay) area. Mfg. (lumber; wood prods., furniture, apparel). Standing Stone State Park and Dale Hollow Reservoir are nearby. **5** town (1990 pop. 5,019), ⊙ Polk co., E Texas, 45 mi/72 km S of Lufkin; 30°42′N 94°56′W. Elev. 194 ft/59 m. Trade, shipping center in oil, timber. Mfg. (lumber, machinery, printing); wood processing. Alabama-Coushatta Indian Reservation is c.15 mi/24 km E. Oil discovered 1940s. Part of Big Thicket Natl. Preserve to SE; L. Livingston reservoir and State Park to SW.

Livingston 1 village (1990 pop. 928), Madison co., SW Ill., 14 mi/23 km NE of Edwardsville; 38°58′N 89°45′W. In agr. area. Inc. 1905. **2** village (1990 pop. 241), Rockcastle co., central Ky., on Rockcastle R., and 27 mi/43 km NE of Somerset, in Daniel Boone Natl. Forest; 37°17′N 84°13′W. Coal mining, agr. Hunting and fishing in vicinity. Great Saltpetre Cave to NE; Camp Wildcat Battle Monument to S. **3** village (1990 pop. 171), Orangeburg co., W central S.C., 15 mi/24 km WNW of Orangeburg; 33°32′N 81°07′W. **4** village (1990 pop. 576), Grant and Iowa cos., SW Wis., 11 mi/18 km N of Platteville; 42°53′N 90°25′W. In dairy and diversified-farming area.

Livingston, township (1990 pop. 26,609), Essex co., NE N.J., near Passaic R., 8 mi/12.9 km NW of Newark; 40°47′N 74°19′W. Beverages. Largely residential.

Livingston, Fort, La.: see GRAND TERRE ISLAND.

Livingston, Lake, reservoir, on San Jacinto/Polk co. border, E Texas, on Trinity R., 6 mi/9.7 km SSW of Livingston, extends NW into Trinity and Walker cos.; c.45 mi/72 km long; 30°38′N 95°10′W. Max. capacity 2,040,000 acre-ft. Formed by Livingston Dam (89 ft/27 m high), built (1968) by the city of Houston for water supply.

Livingston Manor, village (□ 3 sq mi/7.8 sq km; 1990 pop. 1,482), Sullivan co., SE N.Y., in Catskill Mts., on small Willowemoc Creek, 8 mi/12.9 km NW of Liberty; 41°53′N 74°49′W. Mfg. (corrugated pipe); lumber milling. State brown trout hatchery 7 mi/11.3 km NE. Summer and winter (skiing) resort; heart of Delaware-Sullivan cos. trout and fly-fishing region.

Livingstone, Fort, post of North West Mounted Police, W Man., Canada, near town of Swan R. From 1875 to 1877, was capital of N.W.T. and hq. of Mounted Police.

Livonia (li-VON-yah), city (1990 pop. 100,850), Wayne co., SE Mich., a suburb of Detroit; 42°23′N 83°22′W. Drained in S by Middle R. Rouge (parkway), in NE by Upper R. Rouge. Mfg. (transportation equip., plastic and steel prods., textiles); food processing. The city is the seat of Madonna Univ. and Schoolcraft Junior Col. The Wolverine Harness Raceway is here. Nankin Mills Nature Center on S boundary with Westland. Founded 1835, inc. 1950.

Livonia 1 (li-VON-yuh), town (1990 pop. 136), Washington co., S Ind., 10 mi/16 km WSW of Salem; 38°34′N 86°17′W. Agr. area. Laid out 1819. **2** town (1994 pop. 1,144), Pointe Coupee parish, SE central La., 22 mi/35 km WNW of Baton Rouge, on Bayou Maringouin; 30°34′N 91°33′W. RR junction. Agr. area (cotton, rice, sugarcane, vegetables; cattle); timber; crawfish. Mfg. (concrete, lumber). Atchafalaya Natl. Wildlife Refuge to SW. **3** town (1990 pop. 126), Putnam co., N Mo., on Chariton R., and 15 mi/24 km E of Unionville; 40°29′N 92°42′W.

Livonia, village (1990 pop. 1,434), Livingston co., W central N.Y., near Conesus L., 23 mi/37 km S of Rochester; 42°49′N 77°40′W. In agr. area. Summer residences and recreation.

Lizella (luh-ZEL-uh), town (1990 pop. 600), Bibb co., Ga., 11 mi/18 km SW of Macon; 32°48′N 83°49′W. Pottery.

Lizton, town (1990 pop. 410), Hendricks co., central Ind., 8 mi/12.9 km N of Danville; 39°53′N 86°32′W. In agr. area. Mfg. (lawn mowers).

Lizzie, Lake (□ 8 sq mi/20.7 sq km), Otter Tail co., W Minn., 22 mi/35 km N of Fergus Falls; 4 mi/6.4 km long, 3 mi/4.8 km wide; 46°37′N 96°00′W. Flows W through short stream to Prairie L. L. Lida to SE drains into L. Lizzie; Crystal L. to E; Pelican L. to N flows through short stream to L. Lizzie. Resorts.

Llanerch, Pa.: see HAVERFORD.

Llano (LAN-o), county (□ 966 sq mi/2,502 sq km; 1990 pop. 11,631), central Texas; ⊙ Llano; 30°42′N 98°40′W.

Elev. 650 ft/198 m–1,800 ft/549 m. Hilly area on E Edwards Plateau, bounded E by Colorado R. (forms L. Buchanan, Inks L., and L. Lyndon B. Johnson); drained by Llano R. and tributaries. Ranching (cattle, sheep, goats, hogs) and agr. (peanuts, pecans, peaches, grapes, grain; hay). Granite, stone, vermiculite quarrying. Scenery, hunting, fishing attract tourists. Formed 1856.

Llano (LAN-o), town (1990 pop. 2,962), ⊙ Llano co., central Texas, on Edwards Plateau, c.65 mi/105 km NW of Austin, and on Llano R. RR terminus in ranching (cattle and sheep) and agr. (grain, peanuts, peaches, grapes) area. Granite quarrying and cutting; light mfg. Tourism (hunting, fishing). L. Buchanan is c.12 mi/ 19 km E; Enchanted Rock State Natural Area to SW (Gillespie co.). Founded 1855; inc. 1901.

Llano Estacado (YAH-no es-tah-KAH-do), level, semiarid, plateaulike region of the S Great Plains (□ c.40,000 sq mi/103,600 sq km), E N.Mex. and W Texas, bet. the Pecos R. and the Caprock escarpment. Most irrigation is drawn from subsurface water tables, leading to concern over groundwater depletion. The High Plains (c.4,000 ft/1,220 m) of the Texas Panhandle, centered around Amarillo, are usually distinguished from the somewhat lower South Plains (c.2,500 ft/760 m), centered around Lubbock. Both are wind-swept grasslands. Formerly used for cattle ranching, the plains are dotted with dry-land and irrigated farms as well as oil and natural-gas fields. Also called the Staked Plain.

Llano River (LAN-o), c.105 mi/169 km long, in central Texas; formed at town of Junction, Kimble co., by N Llano and S Llano rivers, both rising on Edwards Plateau; flows generally E to the Colorado R. 50 mi/80 km NW of Austin. N Llano rises in Sutton co., flows c.60 mi/97 km E to Junction. S Llano rises NW Edwards co., flows c.80 mi/129 km E and NE to Junction.

Llanos, Los, Dominican Republic: see LOS LLANOS.

Llanura de Guacanayabo (yuh-NOOR-uh dai gwah-kahn-nah-YAH-bo), flood plain, Granma prov., Cuba, straddling the isl.'s longest river. Part of 3,463 sq mi/ 8,969 sq km watershed in E Cuba. Rich agr. lands. Also known as Llanura del Coato.

Llera, Mexico: see LLERA DE CANALES.

Llera de Canales (YE-rah dau kah-NAH-les), town (1990 pop. 3,915), ⊙ Llera township, Tamaulipas, NE Mexico, in E outliers of Sierra Madre Oriental, 30 mi/ 48 km SSE of Ciudad Victoria; 23°19′N 99°01′W. In agr. area.

Llewellyn (loo-WEL-lin), uninc. town (1990 pop. 800), Branch township, Schuylkill co., E central Pa., 4 mi/ 6.4 km W of Pottsville, on West Creek; 40°40′N 76°16′W. In anthracite-coal region.

Lloyd George, Mount, (10,000 ft/3,048 m), N central B.C., Canada, in Rocky Mts.; 57°51′N 124°57′W.

Lloyd Harbor, affluent village (□ 10 sq mi/26 sq km; 1990 pop. 3,343), Suffolk co., SE N.Y., on L.I. N shore, on Lloyd Neck near Lloyd Harbor (arm of L.I. Sound), 2 mi/3.2 km NW of Huntington; 40°55′N 73°27′W.

Lloyd Harbor, arm of L.I. Sound indenting E shore of Lloyds Neck in N L.I., SE N.Y.; extends c.2.5 mi/4 km W from its mouth on Huntington Bay N of Huntington; ¼ mi/ km–1 mi/1.6 km wide; 40°55′N 73°26′W.

Lloyd Neck, peninsula on L.I. N shore, SE N.Y., bet. Oyster Bay (W) and Huntington Bay (E) c.5 mi/8 km long, 1.5 mi/2.4 km–3.5 mi/5.6 km wide; 40°56′N 73°28′W. E shore deeply indented by Lloyd Harbor. Lloyd Point at tip. Caumsett State Park; Target Rock Natl. Wildlife Refuge.

Lloyd Point, N.Y.: see LLOYD NECK.

Lloyd Shoals Reservoir, Ga.: see JACKSON LAKE.

Lloydell (LOI-del), uninc. village (1990 est. pop. 300), Adams township, Cambria co., W central Pa., 12 mi/ 19 km E of Johnstown, on South Fork of Little Conemaugh R.; 40°18′N 78°41′W. Beaverdam Run Reservoir to E.

Lloydminster (LOID-min-stuhr), city (1991 pop. in Alta. 10,042; in Sask. 7,241), on the Alta.-Sask. border, Canada. The city is chartered by both provs. Farming and ranching; oil, natural gas, coal, and salt deposits.

Lloyds Lake, SW N.F., Canada, on Lloyds R., and 45 mi/ 72 km SSE of Corner Brook; 12 mi/19 km long, 1 mi/

2 km wide; 48°25′N 57°35′W. On S shore are Annieopsquotch Mts.

Lloyds River, SW N.F., Canada, upper course of Exploits R., flows 60 mi/97 km ENE, through King George IV L., Lloyds L., and Red Indian L., where it becomes Exploits R. proper.

Lluidas Vale (loo-EI-dus), town (1994 pop. 2,161), St. Catherine parish, central Jamaica, 15 mi/24 km NW of Spanish Town; 18°07′N 77°09′W. Sugar-growing center in lush green valley. In 1600s, rebel slaves formed one of the 1st free black settlements in the New World here.

Loa, village (1990 pop. 444), ⊙ Wayne co., S central Utah, 35 mi/56 km SE of Richfield, and on Fremont R.; 38°23′N 111°38′W. Elev. 7,020 ft/2,140 m. Alfalfa, barley; dairying; cattle; mfg. (cheese). Fish L. reservoir to NW; Fishlake Natl. Forest to E and N. Loa Fish Hatchery to NE; Bicknell Bottoms Fish Hatchery to SE. Named for Mauna Loa Volcano by Mormon missionary to Hawaii. Settled 1870's.

Loami (loe-AM-ih), village (1990 pop. 802), Sangamon co., central Ill., 13 mi/21 km SW of Springfield; 39°40′N 89°50′W. In agr. area.

Lobos Cay, Bahama Isls.: see CAY LOBOS.

Lobos Island (□ 5.5 sq mi/14.2 sq km), in Gulf of California, off coast of Sonora, NW Mexico, 45 mi/72 km SSE of Guaymas; low and sandy, 11 mi/19 km long, c.1 mi/1.6 km wide; 27°28′N 97°13′W. Lighthouse on W coast, at Point Lobos (27°22′N 110°38′W). Separated from mainland by Estero de Lobos.

Lobos, Point 1 promontory, San Francisco co., W Calif., on S side of entrance to Golden Gate Strait, entrance to San Francisco Bay, 3 mi/4.8 km WSW of Golden Gate Bridge, 6 mi/9.7 km W of San Francisco. Within Golden Gate Natl. Recreation Area. **2** promontory on S shore of Carmel Bay, Monterey co., W Calif., 6 mi/ 9.7 km SW of Monterey, S of Monterey Bay. Point Lobos State Reserve.

Lobster House, mountain (1,916 ft/584 m), W central N.F., Canada, 14 mi/23 km NNW of Buchans.

Lobster Lake, Piscataquis co., W central Maine, 27 mi/ 43 km N of Greenville, just E of Moosehead L.; irregularly shaped; 4 mi/6.4 km long, 2 mi/3.2 km wide. In recreational area.

Lobutcha Creek (lo-BOO-chuh), c.50 mi/80 km long, in central Miss., rises in NW Winston co., flows SW to Pearl R. 3 mi/4.8 km E of Carthage.

Loch Lomond, uninc. town, Prince William co., NE Va., residential suburb 2 mi/3.2 km N of Manassas, near Bull Run creek; 38°46′N 77°28′W. Manassas Natl. Battlefield Park to NW.

Loch Lynn, town, Garret co., W Md., in the Alleghenies, just SE of Oakland.

Loch Lynn Heights, town (1990 pop. 461), Garrett co., W Md., 2 mi/3.2 km E of Oakland; 39°23′N 79°22′W. It originated as a rival resort to Mountain Lake Park. Now mainly residential. Inc. 1896.

Loch Raven Reservoir (LOK RAI-ven), Baltimore co., N Md., on Gunpowder Falls R., in Loch Raven Park, 10 mi/16 km NNE of Baltimore; 21 mi/16 km long; 39°25′N 76°32′W. Formed by Loch Raven Dam (75 ft/ 23 m high, 650 ft/198 m long), built (1922) for Baltimore water supply.

Loch Sheldrake, resort village (1990 pop. 1,050), Sullivan co., SE N.Y., on small Loch Sheldrake, 5 mi/8 km SE of Liberty; 41°46′N 74°39′W.

Lochbuie, town (1990 pop. 1,168), Weld co., N central Colo., 25 mi/40 km NW of Denver; 40°00′N 104°43′W. Elev. 4,980 ft/1,518 m. Cattle; grain, sugar beets, beans, fruit. Denver Internatl. Airport to S. Barr Lake State Park to SW; Horse Creek Reservoir to E.

Lochmoor, Mich.: see GROSSE POINTE WOODS.

Lochsa River (lock-sah), c.65 mi/105 km long, in N Idaho; rises in NE Idaho co. in Bitterroot Range, near Lolo Pass; flows WSW past Lochsa Historic Ranger Station, joining Selway R. at Lowell to form Middle Fork Clearwater R. Nez Perce Natl. Forest to E.

Lock and Dam Number 13, Ark., see JAMES W. TRIMBLE LOCK AND DAM.

Lock and Dam Number 5, Jefferson co., central Ark.,

on Arkansas R., 23 mi/ km SSE of Little Rock; 34°25′N 92°06′W. Dam (54 ft/16 m high) built (1968) by Army Corps of Engineers for flood control, recreation, and as a fish and wildlife pond. Also known as Pool Number 5.

Lock Haven, city (1990 pop. 9,230), ⊙ Clinton co., N central Pa., 28 mi/45 km WSW of Williamsport, on West Branch Susquehanna R., 2 mi/3.2 km W of mouth of Bald Eagle Creek; 41°08′N 77°27′W. Mfg. (prefabricated housing, concrete, paper, printing, aircraft). Agr. (grain; livestock; dairying). Seat of Lock Haven State Col. Piper Memorial Airport to E. Bald Eagle State Park to SW; Seroul State Forest to NW, Bald Eagle State Forest to SE, Tiadaghton State Forest and Ravensburg State Park to E. Settled 1769, inc. as a city 1870.

Lock Springs, town (1990 pop. 57), Daviess co., NW Mo., near Grand R., 10 mi/16 km SE of Gallatin; 39°51′N 93°46′W. Damaged by flooding in 1993.

Lockbourne (LAHK-burn), village (1990 pop. 173), Franklin co., central Ohio, 10 mi/16 km S of Columbus; 39°48′N 82°58′W.

Locke, village (1990 pop. 550), Cayuga co., W central N.Y., in Finger Lakes region, 20 mi/32 km SSE of Auburn; 42°39′N 76°25′W. President Millard Fillmore b. here.

Locke Mills, Maine: see GREENWOOD.

Locke, Mount, Texas: see DAVIS MOUNTAINS.

Lockeford, uninc. town (1990 pop. 2,722), San Joaquin co., central Calif., 17 mi/27 km NE of Stockton, on Calaveras R.; 38°09′N 121°10′W. Nuts, fruits, grapes, pumpkins, vegetables, grain, nursery prods., sugar beets; dairying; cattle. Mfg. (prefabricated metal bldgs., wood fiber prods.). Mokelumne Aqueduct passes to SE; Calamanche Reservoir is to NE.

Lockeport (LAHK-port), town (1991 pop. 798), SW N.S., Canada, on Lockeport Harbour (14 mi/23 km long) of the Atlantic, 50 mi/80 km ESE of Yarmouth. Fishing.

Lockesburg, town (1990 pop. 608), Sevier co., SW Ark., 10 mi/16 km ESE of De Queen; 33°58′N 94°10′W. Mfg. (industrial control systems).

Lockhart 1 town (1990 pop. 9,205), ⊙ Caldwell co., S central Texas, 27 mi/43 km S of Austin; 29°52′N 97°40′W. Agr. area (cotton, sorghum, corn; turkeys; eggs); mfg. (sausage processing, laboratory equip., apparel, printing). Oil fields nearby. Lockhart State Park to SE is on site of battle of Plum Creek (1840), Texan defeat of Comanche Indians after they swept through the area's settlements. Founded 1848, inc. 1870. **2** town (1990 pop. 484), Covington co., S Ala., 22 mi/35 km SSE of Andalusia, near Fla. state line. **3** town (□ 4 sq mi/ 10.4 sq km; 1990 pop. 11,636), Orange co., central Fla., 5 mi/8 km NW of Orlando; 28°37′N 81°26′W. Light mfg.

Lockhart, village (1990 pop. 58), Union co., N W S.C., on Broad R., and 18 mi/29 km ESE of Spartanburg; 34°47′N 81°27′W. Textiles. Sumter Natl. Forest to S.

Lockington, village (1990 pop. 214), Shelby co., W Ohio, on Great Miami R., and 4 mi/6 km N of Piqua; 40°12′N 84°14′W. Lockington dam is just S.

Lockland, village (1990 pop. 4,357), Hamilton co., extreme SW Ohio, 10 mi/16 km NNE of Cincinnati; 39°13′N 84°27′W. Plotted 1828, inc. 1865.

Lockney, town (1990 pop. 2,207), Floyd co., NW Texas, on the Llano Estadaco, c.45 mi/72 km NE of Lubbock, near White R.; 34°07′N 101°26′W. Cattle; wheat, sorghum, cotton, soybeans, pumpkins, sunflowers. Beef processing, farm equipment. Settled 1894, inc. 1907.

Lockport 1 city (1990 pop. 9,401), Will co., NE Ill., 5 mi/ 8 km N of Joliet, at locks connecting Sanitary and Ship Canal with Des Plaines R.; 41°35′N 88°02′W. In agr. (corn, soybeans; dairying) area; mfg. (aluminum powders and pigments, plastic pipe, auto parts, farm equipment). Historic locks of old Illinois and Michigan Canal and Visitor Center. Lewis Univ. campus; airport on border with Romeoville. Stateville state prison across river. Laid out 1837, inc. 1853. **2** industrial city (□ 8 sq mi/20.7 sq km; 1990 pop. 24,426), ⊙ Niagara co., W N.Y., on N.Y. State Barge Canal; 43°10′N 78°42′W. Mfg. includes automotive radiators, metal and paper prods., chemicals, plastics. In a rich fruit and dairy region. Built around a series of locks on the old Erie Canal. Settled 1821, inc. 1865.

Lockport, town (1990 pop. 2,503), Lafourche parish, SE La., 34 mi/55 km SW of New Orleans, and on Bayou Lafourche; 29°39′N 90°33′W. Offshore oil exploration and outfitting center; mfg. (drilling platforms, paper, phenolic resin, shipbuilding). Also called Longville.

Lockport, village (1990 pop. 84), Henry co., N Ky., 18 mi/29 km NNW of Frankfort, on Kentucky R. Zinc and lead deposits in area. Tobacco; concrete and asphalt mixers.

Lockridge, town (1990 pop. 270), Jefferson co., SE Iowa, 11 mi/18 km E of Fairfield; 40°59′N 91°45′W.

Lockwood, city (1990 pop. 1,041), Dade co., SW Mo., 38 mi/61 km NE of Joplin; 37°23′N 93°57′W. Corn, sorghum, wheat, cattle; light mfg.; limestone quarries.

Lockwood, Cape, W Ellesmere Isl., NE Franklin dist., N.W.T., Canada, on Greely Fjord; 80°29′N 82°55′W.

Loco, village (1990 pop. 160), Stephens co., S Okla., 20 mi/32 km SE of Duncan; 34°19′N 97°40′W. Agr. area in oil region.

Locust, town (1990 pop. 1,940), Stanly co., S central N.C., 15 mi/24 km SSW of Albemarle and 23 mi/37 km E of Charlotte; 35°15′N 80°25′W. Cotton, grain, soybeans; livestock; dairying; light mfg. Read Gold Mine State Historical Site to N, first gold mine in U.S. (1799).

Locust Creek, c.85 mi/137 km long, in S Iowa and N Mo., rises 10 mi/16 km SE of Corydon in Wayne co. (Iowa); flows S, into Mo., to Grand R. 2 mi/3.2 km W of Sumner.

Locust Fork, stream, c.110 mi/177 km long; rises near Boaz, NE Ala.; flows SW to Mulberry Fork c.20 mi/32 km W of Birmingham, forming Black Warrior R.

Locust Gap, uninc. village, Mt. Carmel township, Northumberland co., E central Pa., 14 mi/23 km NW of Pottsville; 40°46′N 76°26′W.

Locust Grove 1 town (1990 pop. 1,681), Henry co., N central Ga., 11 mi/18 km NE of Griffin; 33°21′N 84°07′W. Exurban RR community S of Atlanta. Light mfg. **2** town (1990 pop. 1,326), Mayes co., NE Okla., 12 mi/19 km SE of Pryor; 36°12′N 95°10′W. In livestock-raising and agr. area; mfg. (chemical plant equip., boilers). L. Hudson (Markham Ferry Dam) to N, Fort Gibson L. to SW, both on Neosho R.

Locust Valley, village (□ 1 sq mi/2.6 sq km; 1990 pop. 3,963), Nassau co., SE N.Y., near N shore of W L.I., 3 mi/4.8 km E of Glen Cove; 40°52′N 73°35′W. Affluent residential area. Some light mfg.

Loda (LOW-dah), village (1990 pop. 390), Iroquois co., E Ill., 4 mi/6.4 km NNE of Paxton; 40°31′N 88°04′W. Corn, soybeans; cattle, hogs; egg and poultry processing; fertilizer.

Lodge, village (1990 pop. 147), Colleton co., S central S.C., 30 mi/48 km S of Orangeburg; 33°04′N 80°57′W. Timber; livestock; grain; watermelons.

Lodge Grass, village (1990 pop. 90), Big Horn co., S Mont., on Little Bighorn R. at mouth of Lodge Grass Creek, and 30 mi/48 km SSE of Hardin, in E part of Crow Indian Reservation; 45°18′N 107°22′W. Cattle. Lodge Grass Storage Reservoir to SW; Rosebud Battlefield State Park to E; Bighorn Canyon Natl. Recreation Area to W, including Old Fort C. F. Smith and Yellowtail Dam.

Lodgepole, village (1990 pop. 368), Cheyenne co., W Nebr., 20 mi/32 km E of Sidney, and on Lodgepole Creek; 41°08′N 102°38′W. Dairying; livestock; grain.

Lodgepole Creek, 212 mi/341 km long, in Wyo., Nebr., and Colo.; rises at elev. of 8,000 ft/2,438 m in Laramie Mts., SE Albany co., SE Wyo., c.10 mi/16 km E of Laramie; flows E past Pine Bluffs, Wyo., and Kimball, Sidney, and Chappell, W Nebr., then SE to join South Platte R. 5 mi/8 km WSW of Julesburg, NE Colo.

Lodi 1 city (1990 pop. 51,874), San Joaquin co., central Calif., 8 mi/12.9 km NNE of Stockton, and 30 mi/48 km S of Sacramento, on the Mokelumne R.; 38°07′N 121°17′W. In a rich farm area (nursery prods.; sugar beets, fruit, nuts, grapes, pumpkins, vegetables, grain; dairying; cattle). Diversified mfg; food processing, wineries. San Joaquin County Historical Mus. to S. Founded in 1869 and settled by wheat farmers from the Dakotas, mostly of Ger. descent. Inc. 1906. **2** (LO-dei), city (1990 pop. 2,093), Columbia co., S central Wis., on small Spring Creek, and 18 mi/29 km NNW of Madison; 43°19′N 89°31′W. In diversified farming area. Food processing, machinery and equip. mfg. Inc. as village in 1872, as city in 1941.

Lodi, village (1990 pop. 3,042), Medina co., N Ohio, 27 mi/43 km WSW of Akron, and on East Branch Black R.; 41°02′N 82°01′W.

Lodi (LO-dei), industrial borough (1990 pop. 22,355), Bergen co., NE N.J.; 40°52′N 74°04′W. Chemical, plastic, and ink mfg. Inc. 1894.

Logan 1 county (□ 731 sq mi/1,893 sq km; 1990 pop. 20,557), W Ark.; ⊙ Booneville and Paris; 35°13′N 93°42′W. Bounded N by Arkansas R.; drained by Petit Jean R. Soybeans; chickens, cattle, hogs; timber. Coal mining, sawmilling, cotton ginning. Hunting, fishing. Part of Ozark Natl. Forest in SE; part of Ouachita Natl. Forest in SW; part of Blue Mt. reservoir (Petit Jean R.) in S. Magazine Mt. is in co. Formed 1873 as Sarber co., renamed 1874. **2** county (□ 1,844 sq mi/4,776 sq km; 1990 pop. 17,567), NE Colo.; ⊙ Sterling; 40°43′N 103°06′W. Irrigated agr. area, bordering on N Nebr., drained by South Platte R. Sugar beets, beans, wheat, hay, sunflowers, corn; cattle. Sterling Reservoir and North Sterling State Park in W center; Julesburg Reservoir in NE on E boundary. Formed 1887. **3** county (□ 619 sq mi/1,603 sq km; 1990 pop. 30,798), central Ill.; ⊙ Lincoln; 40°07′N 89°21′W. Agr. (corn, wheat, soybeans; cattle, hogs). Some mfg. Drained by Salt and Kickapoo creeks and small Sugar Creek. Edward R. Madigan (formerly Railsplitter) State Park is S of Lincoln. Formed 1839. **4** county (□ 1,073 sq mi/2,779 sq km; 1990 pop. 3,081), W Kansas; ⊙ Oakley (in far NE corner); 38°55′N 101°09′W. Farming and grazing area, drained by Smoky Hill R. Wheat, sorghum, cattle. Logan State Fishing L. at center. In Central time zone: Mountain/Central time zone boundary follows W co. border. Formed 1887. **5** county (□ 557 sq mi/1,443 sq km; 1990 pop. 24,416), S Ky.; ⊙ Russellville; 36°51′N 86°52′W. Bounded S by Tenn.; drained by Mud, Red, and Gasper rivers and Whippoorwill, Wolf Lick, and Elk Lick creeks. Rolling agr. area (dark and burley tobacco, corn, wheat, barley, soybeans, alfalfa, hay; cattle, hogs, poultry; dairying; timber). Bituminous-coal and asphalt mines, limestone quarries. Some mfg. at Russellville. Part of L. Malone reservoir in NW corner, L. Herndon reservoir in center. Formed 1792. **6** county (□ 571 sq mi/1,479 sq km; 1990 pop. 878), central Nebr.; ⊙ Stapleton; 41°33′N 100°28′W. Located in Sand Hills region. Drained by South Loup R. Grazing area; cattle, hogs, corn. Formed 1885. **7** county (□ 1,000 sq mi/2,590 sq km; 1990 pop. 2,847), S N.Dak.; ⊙ Napoleon; 46°27′N 99°28′W. Agr. area watered by Beaver Creek. Cattle; sunflowers, wheat, barley; dairy prods. Rush L. in NW. Alkali L. on N boundary. Beaver L. State Park near center. Formed 1873. **8** county (□ 461 sq mi/1,194 sq km; 1990 pop. 42,310), W central Ohio; ⊙ Bellefontaine; 40°22′N 83°46′W. Drained by Great Miami and Mad rivers and small Mill and Rush creeks. Includes Indian L. State Park (resort) and Campbell Hill (1,550 ft/472 m), state's highest point. In Till Plains physiographic region. Agr. area (livestock, dairy prods., grain); mfg. at Bellefontaine. Formed 1817. **9** county (□ 748 sq mi/1,937 sq km; 1990 pop. 29,011), central Okla.; ⊙ Guthrie; 35°54′N 97°27′W. Intersected by Cimarron R. (forms part of NE boundary) and by small Ephraim and Cottonwood creeks. Diversified agr. (wheat, fruit); cattle and poultry; dairying. Mfg. at Guthrie. Formed 1890. **10** county (□ 456 sq mi/1,181 sq km; 1990 pop. 43,032), SW W.Va.; ⊙ Logan; 37°49′N 81°56′W. On Allegheny Plateau; drained by Guyandotte R. Bituminous-coal-mining region; natural-gas fields. Mfg. at Logan. Some agr. (tobacco). Chief Logan State Park in N center. Formed 1824.

Logan 1 city (1990 pop. 6,725), ⊙ Hocking co., S central Ohio, 34 mi/55 km SW of Zanesville, and on Hocking R.; 39°32′N 82°24′W. In rich agr. area. Mfg. (rubber and plastic prods.). Oil and gas wells. Founded 1816, inc. 1839. **2** city (1990 pop. 32,762), ⊙ Cache co., N Utah, on the Logan R.; 41°44′N 111°50′W. It is the center of an irrigated dairy and farm area, with huge cheese plants, other food-processing facilities, and diverse light mfg. A Latter-Day Saints tabernacle, Logan Temple, and Utah State Univ. are located there. Utah Festival Opera. Wasatch Natl. Forest to E. Logan Peak is visible from the city. Mt. Naomi Wilderness Area to NE. Founded by Mormons and inc. 1859.

Logan 1 town (1990 pop. 1,401), ⊙ Harrison co., W Iowa, on Boyer R., and 26 mi/42 km N of Council Bluffs; 41°38′N 95°47′W. RR junction. Mfg. (textbook printing; limestone prods.; conveyors). Settled as Boyer Falls; renamed Logan 1864; inc. 1876. **2** town (1990 pop. 633), Phillips co., N Kansas, on North Fork Solomon R., and 15 mi/24 km WSW of Phillipsburg; 39°39′N 99°34′W. In corn, wheat, cattle area. Mfg. (bakery prods.). Hansen Memorial Mus. **3** township (1990 pop. 5,147), Gloucester co., S N.J., 15 mi/24 km W of Woodbury; 39°47′N 75°21′W. Inc. 1877. **4** town (1990 pop. 870), Quay co., E N.Mex., on Canadian R., near Texas border, and 24 mi/39 km NE of Tucumcari; 35°21′N 103°26′W. Cattle- and sheep-ranching region; cotton, grain. Ute L. reservoir and State Park nearby. **5** town (1990 pop. 2,206), ⊙ Logan co., SW W.Va., on Guyandotte R., 38 mi/61 km SW of Charleston; 37°51′N 81°59′W. Coal mining; gas wells. Some agr. (tobacco). Trade center. Mfg. (mining equip., hydraulic cylinders, concrete, printing and publishing). South West Va. Community Col. Chief Logan State Park to NW.

Logan, village (1990 pop. 100), Gallatin co., SW Mont., on Gallatin R., 5 mi/8 km SE of Missouri R. headwaters, and 25 mi/40 km NW of Bozeman. In grain and livestock region. Madison Buffalo Jump State Park to S; Missouri Headwaters State Park to NW. Originally called Cannon House.

Logan, Ill.: see HANAFORD.

Logan Creek, 85 mi/137 km long, in E Nebr.; rises in Cedar co.; flows SSE and S past Wakefield, Pender, and Lyons, to Elkhorn R. at Winslow.

Logan Glacier, in St. Elias Mts. glacier system, S Alaska, 3 mi/4.8 km wide, extends 65 mi/105 km WNW from Mt. Logan, near 60°50′N 141°00′W. Flows into Chitina R.

Logan Martin Lake, reservoir, on the border of St. Clair and Talladega cos., NE central Ala., on the Coosa R., 27 mi/43 km ESE of Birmingham; c.40 mi/64 km long; 33°24′N 86°20′W. Extends NNE to H. Neely Henry Dam. Max. capacity 642,000 acre-ft. Formed by Logan Martin Dam (75 ft/23 m high), built in 1964 by the Alabama Power Co. for power generation and flood control.

Logan, Mount 1 (19,850 ft/6,050 m), extreme SW Yukon Territory, Canada, just E of Alaska; highest mt. in Canada and 2nd highest in N. Amer. It caps an immense tableland and is the center of the greatest glacial expanse in N. Amer. The first ascent was made in 1925. **2** (3,700 ft/1,128 m), E Que., Canada, on NW Gaspé Peninsula, in Shickshock Mts., 40 mi/64 km E of Matane.

Logan Pass (6,646 ft/2,026 m), in Lewis Range, NW Mont., near center of Glacier Natl. Park, on Continental Divide and Glacier/Flathead co. line; crossed by Going-to-the-Sun Highway. Nearby points of interest are Logan Pass Visitor Center, Logan Pass Boardwalk Wildlife Viewing Area, Hidden L. to SW, and Hanging Gardens (with colorful displays of wildflowers).

Logan Peak (9,710 ft/2,960 m), Cache co., N Utah, 5 mi/8 km E of Logan, in Wasatch Natl. Forest.

Logansport, city (1990 pop. 16,812), ⊙ Cass co., N central Ind., at the confluence of Wabash and Eel rivers; 40°45′N 86°22′W. In a fertile farm area. Diversified mfg. (pork prods., power equip., lumber, electronic controls, fibercoating, stampings, cement and masonry powders, motor vehicle parts, animal feeds). Grissom Air Base is nearby. Laid out 1828. Inc. 1838.

Logansport, town (1994 pop. 1,670), De Soto parish, NW La., 40 mi/64 km SSW of Shreveport, and on Sabine R. (here forming Toledo Bend Reservoir and Texas state line; bridged to Joaquin, Texas); 31°58′N 93°57′W.

Cotton, cattle, timber; dairying; mfg. of plaster molds, lumber, plywood. Gas field nearby. Founded in 1830s.

Loganton (LO-guhn-tuhn), borough (1990 pop. 443), Clinton co., central Pa., 10 mi/16 km SE of Lock Haven. Agr. (grain; livestock, dairying); light mfg. Ravensburg State Park to NE, part of Bald Eagle State Forest to N and S.

Loganville, town (1990 pop. 3,180), Walton and Gwinnett cos., N central Ga., 29 mi/47 km ENE of Atlanta; 33°50′N 83°54′W. Exurban community on fringe of Atlanta region. Light mfg.

Loganville, village (1990 pop. 228), Sauk co., S central Wis., on small Narrows Creek, and 15 mi/24 km W of Baraboo; 43°26′N 90°02′W. In dairy and livestock region. Natural Bridge State Park to SE.

Loganville (LO-guhn-vil), borough (1990 pop. 954), York co., S Pa., 8 mi/12.9 km. SSE of York. Agr. (grain, apples; livestock, dairying); mfg. (electrical connectors).

Loggieville, village (1991 pop. 762), NE N.B., Canada, on Miramichi R. estuary, and 5 mi/8 km NE of Chatham. Lumber port.

Lohman, town (1990 pop. 154), Cole co., central Mo., 11 mi/18 km W of Jefferson City. In agr. area (grain, soybeans; hogs; cattle).

Lohrville, town (1990 pop. 453), Calhoun co., central Iowa, 10 mi/16 km SSE of Rockwell City; 42°16′N 94°32′W. Metal prods.; feed; fertilizer.

Lohrville (LOR-vil), village (1990 pop. 368), Waushara co., central Wis., 29 mi/47 km W of Oshkosh; 44°02′N 09°07′W. In dairy and farm area.

Loíza (lo-EE-zah), town (1990 pop. 29,307), NE P.R., E of Loíza R., 15 mi/24 km ESE of San Juan. Industrial and commercial area; light mfg.; tourism. Has one of highest percentages of Afr. descendants (Yoruban slaves) of all isl. towns; the center of Afr.-Hispanic culture. Known for traditional masks. San Patricio Church (begun 1645), one of the oldest on isl., still active. Settled 1511 at site of a pre-Columbian village. Frequently attacked during 16th cent. by Carib Indians. Formerly Loíza Aldea. Piñones Forest Reserve is W.

Loíza Aldea, P.R.: see LOÍZA.

Loíza River (lo-EE-zah) or **Río Grande de Loíza**, c.40 mi/64 km long, in E P.R.; rises in the Sierra de Cayey S of San Lorenzo; flows N and NE through fertile Caguas valley, past San Lorenzo, Caguas, Trujillo Alto, and Carolina, to the Atlantic at Loíza. Used for irrigation.

Loki, Mount (LO-kee) (9,090 ft/2,771 m), SE B.C., Canada, in Selkirk Mts., 35 mi/56 km NE of Nelson; 49°51′N 116°45′W.

Loks Land, island, E Franklin dist., N.W.T., Canada, in Davis Strait, off SE Baffin Isl., at entrance of Frobisher Bay; 20 mi/32 km long, 15 mi/24 km wide; 62°27′N 64°35′W.

Lola Mount, (9,143 ft/2,787 m), Nevada co., E Calif., peak of the Sierra Nevada N of Donner Pass and W of Independence L., 30 mi/48 km W of Reno, Nev. Tahoe Natl. Forest.

Lolita, uninc. village (1990 pop. 300), Jackson co., S Texas, 25 mi/40 km E of Victoria, near confluence of Lavaca and Navidad rivers. Agr. area (rice, cotton, cattle). Mfg. (plastic bags). L. Texana reservoir to N.

Lolo, town (1990 pop. 2,746), Missoula co., W Mont., 10 mi/16 km SSW of Missoula, on Bitterroot R.; 46°46′N 114°07′W. Cattle, horses; hay. Lolo Natl. Forest to E and W; Sapphire Mts. to E, Bitterroot Range to W. Selway-Bitterroot Wilderness Area to SW; Lolo Hot Springs and Lolo Pass to W.

Lolo Pass (5,235 ft/1,596 m), between Idaho and Mont., in Bitterroot Range, Idaho co. (Idaho) and Missoula co. (Mont.), 32 mi/51 km WSW of Missoula. Lolo Pass Visitors Center on Idaho side.

Lolotla (lo-LOT-lah), town (1990 pop. 658), Hidalgo, central Mexico, 50 mi/80 km N of Pachuca de Soto, on Mexico Highway 105; 20°49′N 98°36′W. Elev. 5,577 ft/1,700 m. Cereals, beans; fruit; livestock.

Loma 1 (LOM-uh), village, Mesa co., W Colo., near Colorado R. and Utah state line, 15 mi/24 km NW of Grand

Junction. Elev. 4,511 ft/1,375 m. In irrigated agr. and livestock region. Oil and gas. Highline State Recreation Area to N. **2** village (1990 pop. 27), Cavalier co., NE N.Dak., 12 mi/19 km SSW of Langdon; 48°38′N 98°31′W.

Loma Bonita (LO-mah bo-NEE-tah), city (1990 pop. 30,720) and township, Oaxaca, S Mexico, on RR, on Mexico Highway 145, in Papaloapan lowlands, 16 mi/26 km E of Tuxtepec; 18°00′N 95°58′W. Pineapplegrowing center, developed in 1930s, most important central producer for state; exports to U.S. and Canada. Cattle raising.

Loma de Cabrera (LO-mah dai kah-BRAI-rah), town (1993 pop. 6,180), Dajabón prov., NW Dominican Republic, on Massacre R., near Haiti border, and 6 mi/9.7 km SSE of Dajabón; 19°25′N 71°35′W. Agr. center (coffee, rice; goats; hides; beeswax, honey). Formerly La Loma.

Loma de Tierra (LO-muh dai tee-ER-uh), town, La Habana prov., W Cuba, on Central Highway, and 10 mi/16 km SE of Havana; 23°02′N 82°15′W. In sugar-growing and dairying region.

Loma Linda, city (1990 pop. 17,400), San Bernardino co., S Calif., suburb 5 mi/8 km SSE of San Bernardino and 56 mi/90 km E of Los Angeles; 34°02′N 117°15′W. Drained by Santa Ana Wash. Citrus and vegetable region being rapidly displaced by urban development. Loma Linda Univ. Hosp. Tri-City Airport in NW. Norton Air Force Base to NE. San Timoteo Canyon to SE.

Loma, Point, San Diego co., S Calif., S tip of high rugged peninsula sheltering San Diego Bay from the Pacific, opposite North Island (peninsula) and Coronado, W of San Diego. Old lighthouse (1855) on crest near tip is included in Cabrillo Natl. Monument (est. 1913, includes former U.S. Fort Rosecrans Military Reservation), set aside in memory of Juan Rodríquez Cabrillo, who discovered the bay (1542). Point Loma residential dist. of San Diego is on peninsula. Point Loma Nazarene Col. and U.S. Internatl. Univ.

Loma Rica, uninc. town (1990 pop. 1,852), Yuba co., N central Calif., 15 mi/24 km NE of Marysville, in W foothills of Sierra Nevada; 39°19′N 121°24′W. Grain, nuts, fruit; cattle; dairying; timber.

Loma Tina, Dominican Republic: see TINA, MONTE.

Lomas de Chapultepec (LO-mahs dai chah-POOL-te-pek), neighborhood, Federal dist., Mexico. An exclusive residential area of Miguel Hidalgo Delegación, Mexico city.

Lomax, uninc. town (1990 pop. 3,554), Howard co., W central Texas, 12 mi/19 km SW of Big Spring, near Beals Creek. Oil and natural gas. Cattle; cotton, vegetables, sesame.

Lomax (LOW-max), village (1990 pop. 473), Henderson co., W Ill., on the Mississippi R., and 9 mi/14.5 km S of Burlington, Iowa; 40°40′N 91°04′W. Grain; livestock.

Lombard, village (1990 pop. 39,408), Du Page co., NE Ill., a residential suburb of Chicago; 41°52′N 88°00′W. Mfg. (plastics). The village is known for its lilacs. Inc. 1869.

Lombardía (lom-bahr-DEE-ah), town (1990 pop. 10,203), ⊙ municipality of Gabriel Zamora, central Michoacán, Mexico, on N bank of Cupatitzio R., on RR, on road, and 23 mi/37 km N of Uruapan; 19°09′N 102°02′W. Semidry climate. Corn, beans, rice, avocado, oranges, lemons; livestock. Formerly Gabriel Zamora.

Lometa, village (1990 pop. 625), Lampasas co., central Texas, near the Colorado R., c.50 mi/80 km SE of Brownwood; 31°13′N 98°23′W. RR junction in agr. (cattle; peanuts, watermelons) area; mfg. (farm gates and equip.). Colorado Bend State Park to SW.

Lomira (lo-MEI-ruh), town (1990 pop. 1,542), Dodge co., E Wis., 13 mi/21 km S of Fond du Lac; 43°35′N 88°26′W. In dairying region. Light mfg.

Lomita, city (1990 pop. 19,382), Los Angeles co., S Calif., residential suburb 18 mi/29 km SSW of Los Angeles, S of Torrance, W of San Pedro sect. of Los Angeles; 33°48′N 118°19′W. Torrance Municipal Airport to W. South Coast Botanical Gardens to SW.

Lomond (LO-muhnd), village (1991 pop. 167), S Alta., Canada, 50 mi/80 km N of Lethbridge. Wheat, flax; cattle.

Lomond, Loch, lake, S N.B., Canada, 10 mi/16 km NE of St. John; 4 mi/6 km long, 1 mi/2 km wide.

Lompoc, city (1990 pop. 37,649), Santa Barbara co., S Calif., 44 mi/71 km WNW of Santa Barbara, on Santa Ynez R., and 8 mi/12.9 km E of Pacific Ocean; 34°40′N 120°28′W. RR terminus. In oil and agr. (fruit, avocados, grain; cattle) area. It has a huge flower-seed industry and 2 large silica earth mines. Petroleum processing; light mfg.; food processing. Lompoc Mus. and Lompoc Valley Historical Mus. La Purisima Mission (1791) State Historical Park to NE. Vandenberg Air Force Base, a large missile testing base with a launch site for military satellites, is to the NW. Point Arguello to SW. Inc. 1888.

Lonaconing (lon-ah-KON-ing), mining town (1990 pop. 1,122), Allegany co., W Md., in the Alleghenies, and 14 mi/23 km WSW of Cumberland; 39°34′N 78°59′W. In bituminous-coal area. An old iron furnace said to have been built in 1837 and the first in the nation to use coke is on the Register of Historic Places. The name is either derived from several Indian words with different meanings or from an Indian scout called Nemacolin, but the inhabitants refer to it as "Coney." Big Savage Mt. and Savage R. State Forest are just W. Settled 1835.

London, city (1991 pop. 303,165), SE Ont., Canada, on the Thames R., and 100 mi/161 km SW of Toronto. In one of Canada's richest agr. dists., it is an industrial, commercial, service, and financial center. Mfg. includes electrical prods., locomotive and motor vehicle parts. The Univ. of Western Ont. (1878) and the affiliated Ursuline and Huron colls. are here. The site was chosen in 1792 by Government Simcoe to be capital of Upper Canada, but York was made capital instead. Its streets and bridges are named for those of London in England. Settled 1826.

London, city (1990 pop. 7,807), ⊙ Madison co., central Ohio, 24 mi/39 km WSW of Columbus; 39°53′N 83°26′W. In livestock and grain area; fish hatchery. State Correctional Inst. Founded 1811, inc. 1831.

London 1 town (1990 pop. 825), Pope co., N central Ark., 8 mi/12.9 km WNW of Russellville, and on L. Dardanelle (Arkansas R.); 35°19′N 93°14′W. **2** uninc. town (1990 pop. 1,638), Tulare co., S central Calif., 13 mi/21 km NW of Visalia; 36°29′N 119°27′W. Citrus, peaches, plums, olives, nuts, nursery prods.; cattle, hogs, poultry. **3** town (1990 pop. 5,757), ⊙ Laurel co., SE Ky., in Cumberland foothills, 29 mi/47 km E of Somerset; 37°07′N 84°04′W. Trade center for agr. (poultry; dairy; tobacco, corn, wheat), coal, and timber area. Light mfg. Seat of Sue Bennet Col. (1897). Colonel Harlan Sanders' original chicken restaurant 10 mi/16 km to S at Corbin. Annual World Chicken Festival (Sept.). Camp Wildcat Battle Monument to NW. Levi Jackson Wilderness Road State Park to SE; Daniel Boone Natl. Forest to W and E; Holly Bay Recreation Area on Laurel River L. reservoir to SW; Wood Creek L. reservoir to NW.

London, uninc. village (1990 pop. 750), Kanawha co., W central W.Va., on Kanawha R., c.17 mi/27 km SE of Charleston.

London Mills, village (1990 pop. 485), Fulton co., W central Ill., on Spoon R. (bridged here), 16 mi/26 km NW of Canton, and 24 mi/39 km NNW of Lewiston; 40°42′N 90°16′W. In agr. (corn, wheat, sorghum; cattle) and bituminous-coal-mining area. Feed milling.

Londonderry 1 (LUHN-duhn-de-ree), town (1990 pop. 19,781), Rockingham co., SE N.H., 10 mi/16 km SSE of Manchester, and 7 mi/11.3 km NE of Nashua; 42°52′N 71°23′W. Drained by Beaver Brook. Diversified mfg. Agr. (vegetables, beans, apples; cattle; dairying). Former NW section now in Derry. Settled by Scots Irish 1719, chartered 1722. **2** town (1990 pop. 1,506), Windham co., S central Vt., on West R., and 20 mi/32 km NNW of Newfane; 43°12′N 72°47′W. Lumber; wood prods. Partly in Green Mt. Natl. Forest.

Lone Cone, peak (12,613 ft/3,844 m), in San Juan Mts., San Miguel and Dolores cos., SW Colo., 23 mi/37 km W of Telluride, in Uncompahre Natl. Forest.

Lone Elm, village (1990 pop. 32), Anderson co., E Kansas,

13 mi/21 km S of Garnett; 38°04′N 95°14′W. Livestock; grain; dairying.

Lone Grove, town (1990 pop. 4,114), Carter co., S Okla., suburb 8 mi/12.9 km W of Ardmore; 34°11′N 97°16′W. Agr. and oil production area. Mfg. (glass and fiberglass prods.).

Lone Oak, town (1990 pop. 161), Meriwether co., W Ga., 14 mi/23 km NE of La Grange; 33°10′N 84°49′W.

Lone Oak 1 village (1990 pop. 465), McCracken co., W Ky., 5 mi/8 km SW of Paducah; 37°02′N 88°40′W. Tobacco, sorghum, grain; livestock. **2** village (1990 pop. 521), Hunt co., NE Texas, near Sabine R., 14 mi/23 km SE of Greenville; 33°00′N 95°56′W. In agr. area. L. Tawakoni reservoir to S.

Lone Pine, uninc. town (1990 pop. 1,818), Inyo co., E Calif., in Owens Valley, 65 mi/105 km ENE of Visalia, on Owens R.; 36°34′N 118°05′W. Lead and silver mining; cattle. Los Angeles Aqueduct passes to W. Mt. Whitney, highest point in U.S. outside of Alaska, 10 mi/16 km W; Death Valley Natl. Monument (E); Sequoia Natl. Park to W; part of Inyo Natl. Forest to W; L. Owens (dry) to SE. Lone Pine Indian Reservation to S.

Lone Rock, town (1990 pop. 185), Kossuth co., N Iowa, 11 mi/18 km NNW of Algona; 43°13′N 94°19′W.

Lone Rock, village (1990 pop. 641), Richland co., SW Wis., on Wisconsin R., on RR, and 14 mi/23 km SE of Richland Center; 43°10′N 90°12′W. In timber and agr. area. Lumber; cheese; feeds; hunting.

Lone Star, town (1990 pop. 1,615), Morris co., NE Texas, 30 mi/48 km N of Longview; 32°56′N 94°42′W. In agr. area (poultry; peanuts, watermelons). Mfg. (construction materials; coal tar and slag processing). Ellison Creek Reservoir to W; L. O' the Pines (Big Cypress Creek) to S.

Lone Star, village, Calhoun co., central S.C., 18 mi/29 km ENE of Orangeburg. In agr. area (cotton, soybeans). L. Marion to E.

Lone Tree, town (1990 pop. 979), Johnson co., E Iowa, 13 mi/21 km SSE of Iowa City; 41°29′N 91°25′W. Feed milling.

Lone Wolf, village (1990 pop. 576), Kiowa co., SW Okla., 8 mi/12.9 km WSW of Hobart; 34°59′N 99°15′W. In cotton, grain, livestock area. Altus L. reservoir to SW.

Lonerock, village (1990 pop. 11), Gilliam co., N Oregon, 24 mi/39 km SW of Heppner, on Lone Rock Creek; 45°05′N 119°52′W. Part of Umatilla Natl. Forest to S.

Long, county (□ 404 sq mi/1,046 sq km; 1990 pop. 6,202), SE Ga.; ⊙ Ludowici; 31°46′N 81°45′W. Bounded SW by Altamaha R. Coastal plain agr. (corn, soybeans, tobacco); livestock (hogs, cattle), and forestry area. Formed 1920.

Long, village, W Alaska, 24 mi/39 km S of Ruby. Placer gold mining. Airfield.

Long Barn, uninc. village, Tuolumne co., central Calif., in the Sierra Nevada, 15 mi/24 km NE of Sonora. Resort area. In Stanislaus Natl. Forest.

Long Beach 1 city (1990 pop. 429,433), Los Angeles co., S Calif., suburb 18 mi S of Los Angeles, on San Pedro Bay; 33°48′N 118°10′W. Drained in W by Los Angeles R., in E by San Gabriel R. Having an excellent harbor, it serves as Los Angeles's port and a year-round resort noted for its long, wide beaches and active marina. The city has a large oil industry; oil (discovered in 1921) is found both underground and offshore. Mfg. includes aircraft, automobile parts, electronic equip., audio/visual equip., oil well services, and home furnishings. The city grew rapidly as a result of the high-technology and aerospace industries in the area, and its pop. increased significantly 1940–1960 and continued to increase 1960 to 1990. It has the largest Cambodian community in U.S. Points of interest include an adobe ranch house (1844) that has become a mus.; four man-made oil islands in the harbor; and the ocean liner *Queen Mary*, which was purchased in 1967 and converted into a museum, hotel, and tourist center. California State Univ., Long Beach and Long Beach City Col. Long Beach Marina at Alamitos Bay in SE corner. Long Beach Airport (Daugherty Field) in N. Long Beach Naval Shipyard in W, on Terminal Island, scheduled on Pentagon list of 1995 for closing. Ferries to Santa Catalina Isl. Inc. 1888. **2** city (1990 pop. 15,804), Harrison co., SE Miss., 4 mi/6.4 km WSW of Gulfport, on Mississippi Sound; 30°21′N 89°10′W. Mfg. (restaurant chinaware, industrial prototypes, vacuum cleaners, banking machines). Seat of Gulf Park Col. Gulfport Naval Center in NE; Univ. of Southern Miss. (Gulfport campus). Beach resort area. **3** suburban city and beach community (□ 3 sq mi/7.8 sq km; 1990 pop. 33,510), Nassau co., SE N.Y., on barrier isl. off S shore of W L.I. (RR, highway connections), 8 mi/12.9 km SE of Jamaica; 40°35′N 73°40′W. Mfg. (clothing, machinery, umbrellas). RR terminus. Former resort. Popular beach. Inc. 1922.

Long Beach 1 town (1990 pop. 2,044), La Porte co., NW Ind., on L. Michigan, 11 mi/18 km NW of La Porte; 41°45′N 86°51′W. **2** township (1990 pop. 3,407), Ocean co., SE N.J.; 39°38′N 74°12′W. Resort and summer art colony communities on coastal Long Beach Isl. Inc. 1899. **3** town (1990 pop. 3,816), Brunswick co., SE N.C., 26 mi/42 km SSW of Wilmington, on Oak Isl., on Atlantic Ocean (S); 33°55′N 78°09′W. Beach resort area. Intracoastal Waterway canal passes to N. Lockwood Folly Inlet to W, mouth of Cape Fear R. estuary to E. **4** town (1990 pop. 1,236), Pacific co., SW Wash., on coast, 5 mi/8 km N of mouth of the Columbia R., and 15 mi/24 km NW of Astoria, Oregon; 46°22′N 124°03′W. Mfg. (printing and publishing); beach resorts. Willapa Bay and Natl. Wildlife Refuge to NE.

Long Beach, village (1990 pop. 204), Pope co., W Minn., 2 mi/3.2 km W of Glenwood, on N shore of L. Minnewaska; 45°38′N 95°25′W. Pelican L. to W.

Long Beach, narrow island (c.19 mi/31 km long), E N.J., sheltering Little Egg Harbor, Manahawkin Bay, and S end of Barnegat Bay from the Atlantic. Barnegat City is at Barnegat Light at N end, Beach Haven and Beach Haven Inlet are at S end. Other resorts: Harvey Cedars, Surf City, Ship Bottom (bridge to mainland here).

Long Branch, residential city (1990 pop. 28,658), Monmouth co., E central N.J., on the Atlantic coast; 40°17′N 73°59′W. Mfg. (apparel, cabinetmaking, electronic prods.). Presidents Grant, Hayes, Garfield, and Arthur summered here, and President Wilson's summer house (now part of Monmouth Col.) was at West Long Branch. President Garfield died in Long Branch in 1881. Historical mus., art center. Monmouth Park Racetrack is nearby. Settled 1740, inc. 1904.

Long Branch, borough (1990 pop. 482), Washington co., SW Pa., 3 mi/4.8 km S of Charleroi, near Monongahela R. Corn, hay; dairying.

Long Cay, islet (10 mi/16 km long NE-SW, c.1 mi/1.6 km wide; 1980 pop. 35) and district (□ 8 sq mi/20.7 sq km), S Bahama Isls., just W of Crooked Isl., 250 mi/402 km SE of Nassau. Main settlement, Albert Town (center); 22°37′N 74°20′W. Also known as Fortune Isl.

Long Creek 1 village (1990 pop. 1,250), Macon co., central Ill., suburb 7 mi/11.3 km ESE of Decatur; 39°47′N 88°50′W. Corn, soybeans. Spitler Woods State Natural Area to S. **2** village (1990 pop. 249), Grant co., NE central Oregon, 70 mi/113 km SSW of Pendleton; 44°42′N 119°05′W. Elev. 3,754 ft/1,144 m. Grain; livestock. Malheur Natl. Forest in SE; Umatilla Natl. Forest to NE.

Long Grove, town (1990 pop. 605), Scott co., E Iowa, 11 mi/18 km N of Davenport; 41°41′N 90°34′W. In agr. area.

Long Grove, village (1990 pop. 4,740), Lake co., NE Ill., suburb 29 mi/47 km NW of Chicago, 10 mi/16 km W of Highland Park; 42°12′N 88°00′W.

Long Island, plantation, Hancock co., S Maine, on Long Isl. (c.2 mi/3.2 km diameter), which is site of Frenchboro village (1990 pop. 44), and on smaller Placentia, Black, Great Duck (lighthouse), and Little Duck (bird sanctuary) isls.; c.8 mi/12.9 km S of Mt. Desert Isl., near entrance to Blue Hill Bay.

Long Island 1 village (1990 pop. 170), Phillips co., N Kansas, on Prairie Dog Creek, near Nebr. state line, and 17 mi/27 km NW of Phillipsburg; 39°57′N 99°31′W. Corn; livestock. **2** village, Sullivan co., NE Tenn., suburb just S of Kingsport.

Long Island, the Bahamas: see BAHAMAS.

Long Island 1 (□ 13 sq mi/34 sq km), SE N.F., Canada, in Placentia Bay, 65 mi/105 km W of St. John's; 15 mi/24 km long, 2 mi/3 km wide; 47°35′N 54°05′W. On SE coast is fishing settlement of Harbour Buffet. **2** E N.F., Canada, in Notre Dame Bay, 25 mi/40 km SSW of Cape St. John; 6 mi/10 km long, up to 4 mi/6 km wide; 49°35′N 55°40′W. **3** in the Atlantic, W N.S., Canada, at entrance to Bay of Fundy, forming SW shore of St. Mary Bay, 30 mi/48 km SW of Digby; 12 mi/19 km long, 2 mi/3 km wide. At its extremities are Boar Head (N) and Dartmouth Point (S).

Long Island, Canada: see GAULTOIS ISLAND.

Long Island 1 SE Alaska, in Cordova Bay, N arm of Dixon Entrance, 55 mi/89 km SW of Ketchikan; 15 mi/24 km long, 2 mi/3.2 km–6 mi/9.7 km wide; 54°51′N 132°42′W. Fishing at Howkan village (W) and in Elbow Bay region (NE). Sometimes called Howkan Isl. **2** (□ 1,723 sq mi/4,463 sq km; 1990 pop. 6,861,454), 118 mi/190 km long, and 12 mi/19 km–20 mi/32 km wide, SE N.Y.; 4th-largest isl. of the U.S. and the largest outside Alaska and Hawaii. Separated from Staten Isl. by The Narrows, from Manhattan and the Bronx by the East R., and from Conn. by the L.I. Sound; on the S is the Atlantic Ocean. Comprises 4 cos.—Kings, Queens, Nassau, and Suffolk; Kings (Brooklyn) and Queens are boroughs of N.Y. city. E L.I. has 2 flukelike peninsulas separated by Great and Little Peconic Bays. The N fluke, terminating in Orient Point, follows part of the Harbor Hill moraine, a hilly ridge that extends W along N L.I. to The Narrows and was deposited by melting ice during the last stage of the Pleistocene epoch. The S fluke, terminating in Montauk Point, follows the Ronkonkoma moraine, a somewhat older morainal ridge that extends W to join the Harbor Hill moraine at L. Success. Low, wooded hills, capped by glacial deposits, lie N of the moraines and contrast with a broad, low-lying outwash plain to S; the highest point on the isl. is c.400 ft/122 m above sea level. Long beaches, backed by dunes and shallow lagoons, fringe the S shore; the N shore has low cliffs, deeply indented by bays. With no large streams, water supply is limited and is obtained from groundwater. Large recharge basins catch surplus rainwater to replenish underground supplies, and strict conservation measures have been imposed to prevent further contamination of groundwater from sewage disposal and detergents and from encroachment by seawater. Both the Dutch and the English established farming, whaling, and fishing settlements on L.I., but it remained sparsely settled until RR, bridges, and highways provided easy access to N.Y. city. The L.I. Expressway is particularly high-trafficked. Fashionable summer estates started being built on the N Shore—known as "The Gold Coast"—in early 20th cent. Industrial and residential growth, largely concentrated in Nassau co. and the boroughs, occurred rapidly after World War II. During the same period, central L.I. communities and those along both shores experienced major residential growth. Despite the decline in farming in E L.I., the region still retains a rural character, quite in contrast with isl. to the W. Sand and gravel are quarried from the isl.'s glacial deposits. Sport and commercial fishing is important on the S and E coasts. The S shore is a popular recreational area and includes Fire Isl. Natl. Seashore, Robert Moses, and Jones Beach state parks, Coney Isl., and parts of Gateway Natl. Recreation Area. The L.I. Pine Barrens in Suffolk co., with pitch pine and scrub oak, overlie the aquifers. The Barrens have been set aside as a preserve where development is either precluded or highly regulated. Also here is an affluent residential and beach community called the Hamptons. LaGuardia and JFK Internatl. airports are on W L.I.; MacArthur Airport is in Holbrook, in central L.I. Brookhaven Natl. Laboratory is in the E. State Univs. of N.Y. at Stonybrook and Westbury, L.I. Univ., Hofstra Col., N.Y. Inst. of Technology, Adelphi Univ., branches of City Univ. of N.Y., and Suffolk Community Col. **3** (c.1 mi/1.6 km long), E Mass., in Quincy bay section of Boston Harbor, SE of downtown Boston. Connected to mainland by bridge (3 mi/4.8 km long) opened 1951, it is site of city hosp. and a lighthouse. Largest isl. in Boston Harbor. Linked to Moon Isl. by bridge and from Moon via causeway to Squantum on mainland. Restricted to use by the city of Boston. **4** resort, fishing, and farming island (c.1.4 sq mi/3.6 sq km) off Portland, Maine, in Casco Bay.

Long Island City, area of N.Y. city, in SW Queens co., SE N.Y., on L.I.; 40°45′N 73°55′W. An industrial and residential dist., it has a waterfront on the East R., and is connected with Manhattan by the Queensborough Bridge. Mfg. (food prods., machinery, furniture, pianos, footwear); service industries; film and television studios.

Long Island Expressway (L.I.E.), SE N.Y., one of 3 major E-W highways connecting Manhattan to the boroughs of Brooklyn and Queens, and Nassau and Suffolk cos.; Interstate Route 495 (I-495) from Manhattan via the Queens Midtown Tunnel to Calverton, 5 mi/8 km W of Riverhead in E Long Isl. By mid-1950s N.Y. state recognized need for thoroughfare through central Long Isl. for commercial vehicles and trucks. Of monumental size for the era, the project completed the 1st sect. (from East River to Rock Shelter Rd.) in 1958, and by 1962 the 6-lane highway stretched through Nassau co. to the Suffolk co. line. Its construction spurred industrial development throughout the area, particularly around Roosevelt Field, Jericho, Farmingdale, and Hicksville. The system is barely able to handle the congestion of rush-hour traffic; it has been nicknamed "the world's longest parking lot."

Long Island Sound, arm of the Atlantic Ocean, c.90 mi/145 km long, and 3 mi/4.8 km–20 mi/32 km wide, separating L.I., N.Y., from the SE N.Y. mainland and Conn.; 41°00′N 73°15′W. On the W the East R. joins it with N.Y. Bay. The sound is fed from the N by the Housatonic, Connecticut, and Thames rivers. It is a popular leisure-boating center. New Haven, New London, and Bridgeport, Conn., are the largest port cities; many residential communities line the sound.

Long Key, narrow barrier island (c.6 mi/9.7 km long) and resort area, Pinellas co., W central Fla., in Gulf of Mexico, near mouth of Tampa Bay, 7 mi/11.3 km WSW of St. Petersburg; connected by causeway with nearby mainland.

Long Lake, town (1990 pop. 1,984), Hennepin co., E Minn., suburb 15 mi/24 km W of Minneapolis on S shore of Long L., surrounded by Orono; 44°59′N 93°34′W. Light mfg. Morris T. Baker Park Reserve to NW; L. Minnetonka to S.

Long Lake 1 uninc. village (1990 pop. 2,888), Lake co., NE Ill., suburb 38 mi/61 km NW of Chicago, 15 mi/24 km W of Waukegan, on S side of Long L.; 42°22′N 88°07′W. In agr. area. **2** resort village (1990 pop. 500), Hamilton co., NE central N.Y., in the Adirondacks, on E shore of Long L. (14 mi/23 km long, c.1 mi/1.6 km wide), c.75 mi/121 km NE of Utica; 43°57′N 74°25′W. L. receives and discharges Raquette R. **3** village (1990 pop. 64), McPherson co., N S.Dak., 18 mi/29 km NW of Leola, at E end of Long L.; 45°51′N 99°12′W.

Long Lake 1 (□ 3 sq mi/8 sq km), N central N.B., Canada, 40 mi/64 km E of Grand Falls; 6 mi/10 km long, 1 mi/2 km wide. **2** (□ 75 sq mi/194 sq km), central Ont., Canada, 150 mi/241 km NE of Port Arthur; 45 mi/72 km long, 2 mi/3 km wide. Drains S into L. Superior. At N end is Longlac.

Long Lake 1 Sierra co., NE Calif., in the Sierra Nevada, at base of Mt. Elwell, 9 mi/14.5 km NE of Downieville, and near Gold L. Campgrounds; fishing. Tahoe Natl. Forest. **2** Aroostook co., N Maine, lake in course of the Allagash R., in recreational area 68 mi/109 km W of Presque Isle; 4 mi/6.4 km long. **3** Aroostook co., N Maine, S of Can. border, 10 mi/16 km W of Van Buren, and c.25 mi/40 km NNW of Presque Isle; 11 mi/18 km long; easternmost of FISH RIVER LAKES. **4** Cumberland co., SW Maine, center of resort area; 13.5 mi/23 km long, ½ mi/⅘ km–1 mi/1.6 km wide. Discharges S through Songo R. into Sebago L. **5** Alpena and Presque Isle cos., NE Mich., 9 mi/11.3 km N of Alpena, near L. Huron; c.8 mi/12.9 km long, 1 mi/1.6 km wide; 45°12′N 83°29′W. Resort. **6** Grand Traverse co., NW Mich.,

c.6 mi/9.7 km SW of Traverse City, in forested resort area; c.4 mi/6.4 km long, 1 mi/1.6 km wide; 44°42′N 85°44′W. **7** Hubbard co., W Minn., 4 mi/6.4 km E of Park Rapids; 6 mi/9.7 km long, ½ mi/⅘ km wide; 46°54′N 94°59′W. Drains S past small dam through small stream into Fish Hook R., which flows short distance (½ mi/⅘ km) S to Shell R. Resort area. Village of Hubbard at S end. **8** Burleigh and Kidder cos., S central N.Dak., 30 mi/48 km ESE of Bismarck; 20 mi/32 km long, 2 mi/3.2 km wide; 46°41′N 100°17′W. Used as migratory waterfowl refuge. Slade Natl. Wildlife Refuge to NE.

Long Lake 1 reservoir, Washburn co., NW Wis., on N branch of Red Cedar R., 11 mi/18 km SE of Spooner; c.13 mi/21 km long, with 4 mi/6.4 km NE arm at S end; 45°40′N 91°41′W. Narrow, fishhook-shaped. Lumber; resort area, fishing (pike and walleye). **2** reservoir, Lincoln co., NE Wash., on Spokane R., 23 mi/37 km NW of Spokane; 47°50′N 117°52′W. Max. capacity 105,080 acre-ft. Formed by Long Lake Dam (213 ft/65 m high), built (1915) for power generation; also used for recreation. Spokane Indian Reservation just W.

Long Lake Dam, Wash.: see SPOKANE RIVER.

Long Pine, village (1990 pop. 396), Brown co., N Nebr., 8 mi/12.9 km E of Ainsworth; 42°31′N 99°42′W. Resort. Livestock; vegetables; lumber. Long Pine State Recreation Area and dam nearby.

Long Point, peninsula, S Ont., Canada, extends 20 mi/32 km E into L. Erie, ESE of Port Rowan; 1 mi/2 km–4 mi/6 km wide.

Long Point, village (1990 pop. 208), Livingston co., N central Ill., 16 mi/26 km WNW of Pontiac; 41°00′N 88°53′W. In agr. area.

Long Point, SE Mass., sandspit on N tip of Cape Cod; curves SE to shelter Provincetown harbor. Has lighthouse at 42°02′N 70°12′W.

Long Pond, village, Somerset co., W Maine, on Long Pond (8 mi/12.9 km long, 1 mi/1.6 km wide), and 27 mi/43 km NW of Greenville. In lumbering, hunting, fishing area.

Long Pond, reservoir, Plymouth and Bristol cos., SE Mass., on short stream draining N to Assawompsett Pond, 9 mi/14.5 km SE of Taunton; c.3.5 mi/5.6 km long; 41°48′N 70°56′W. Heaven Heights village on W shore.

Long Pond, N.Y.: see WILLSBORO.

Long Prairie, town (1990 pop. 2,786), ⊙ Todd co., central Minn., on Long Prairie R., 25 mi/40 km W of Little Falls; 45°58′N 94°51′W. Elev. 1,295 ft/395 m. Trading point in agr. area (grain, potatoes, beans; livestock, poultry; dairying); mfg. (animal protein prods., food processing, dump trailers, printing and publishing). Winnebago Indian Agency here 1848–1855. Plotted 1867, inc. 1883.

Long Prairie River, 120 mi/193 km long; rises in chain of lakes, E Douglas co., W Minn. (L. Carlos is source of main stream; 45°58′N 95°19′W); flows generally E in very serpentine course, passes L. Osakis on N (manmade channel connects river with lake), past Long Prairie, then N past Brownesville, and NE to Crow Wing R. 2 mi/3.2 km SE of Motley.

Long Range, c.300 mi/480 km long, W N.F., Canada, rising to 2,672 ft/814 m in the Lewis Hills. It forms the Great Northern Peninsula of NW N.F. Part of the Appalachian system, the range consists of parallel ridges that rise steeply from the coast and slope gently E. A depression, of which Grand L. and St. George's Bay are part, divides Long Range into 2 sects. Timber. Gros Morne Natl. Park is here.

Long Sault Island (SOO), St. Lawrence co., N.Y., in the St. Lawrence R. (Long Sault rapids here), at Ont. border, 3 mi/4.8 km W of Massena; c.4.5 mi/7.2 km long, ¼ mi/ km–1 mi/1.6 km wide; 44°58′N 74°55′W.

Long Sault Rapids (SOO), in the St. Lawrence R., SE Ont., Canada, 12 mi/19 km WSW of Cornwall; 9 mi/14 km long. Bypassed by Cornwall Canal (11 mi/18 km long).

Long Tom River, 50 mi/80 km long, in Lane co., W Oregon; rises 10 mi/16 km W of Beneta, on E slopes of Coast Range; flows E past Veneta and into Fern Ridge

Reservoir, then N past Munroe to Willamette R. 12 mi/19 km S of Corvallis.

Long View, town (1990 pop. 2,995), Catawba co., W central N.C., residential suburb 2 mi/3.2 km W of Hickory. Hickory Regional Airport to NW.

Longboat Key, town (1990 pop. 5,937), Sarasota and Manatee cos., W central Fla., 12 mi/19 km NW of Sarasota; 27°23′N 82°38′W. Mfg. (printing and publishing).

Longboat Key, narrow barrier island (□ 17 sq mi/44 sq km; 1990 pop. 5,937), sheltering Sarasota Bay, in Gulf of Mexico, W central Fla.; c.10 mi/16 km long; 27°23′N 82°38′W. Exclusive resort located here.

Longdale, village (1990 pop. 281), Blaine co., W central Okla., 21 mi/34 km NNW of Watonga; 36°07′N 98°32′W. In agr. area (grain; livestock). Oil and natural-gas deposits. Canton L. to SW (North Canadian R.).

Longfellow Historic Site, Cambridge, E Mass., home of Henry Wadsworth Longfellow (1837–1882); also George Washington's hq. during the siege of Boston (1775–1776). Authorized 1972.

Longfellow-Evangeline Memorial State Commemorative Area, St. Martin parish, S central La., along Bayou Teche, just N of St. Martinville; area of 157 acres/64 ha; 30°08′N 91°49′W. Est. 1934 to commemorate supposed real-life heroine of Longfellow's poem *Evangeline* and commemorates Fr. history of S La. Depicts plantation life in 1800s.

Longford, village (1990 pop. 68), Clay co., N central Kansas, 17 mi/27 km SW of Clay Center; 39°10′N 97°19′W. Grain; livestock.

Longhorn Caverns State Park, limestone cave, Burnet co., central Texas, 8 mi/12.9 km SW of Burnet; area of 639 acres/259 ha. On the N edge of the Edwards Plateau, the cave lies beneath a triangular ridge rising above the valley of the Colorado R.; 2 mi/3.2 km long. Nature trails on surface. Home of prehistoric cave dwellers. Gunpowder manufactured here for Confederate Army. Mus.

Longhurst, uninc. village, Person co., N N.C., 2 mi/3.2 km NNE of Roxboro. Tobacco, grain; livestock.

Longlac (LONG-lak), town (1991 pop. 2,073), central Ont., Canada, on Long L., 150 mi/241 km NE of Port Arthur. Elev. 1,035 ft/315 m. Gold mining.

Longmeadow, town (1990 pop. 15,467), Hampden co., SW Mass., a residential suburb adjoining Springfield, on the Connecticut R.; 42°03′N 72°34′W. Settled 1644; set off and inc. 1783; Bay Path Col. is here.

Longmont, city (1990 pop. 51,555), Boulder co., N Colo. 28 mi/45 km NNW of Denver, on St. Vrain Creek; 40°10′N 105°06′W. Elev. 4,979 ft/1,518 m. RR junction. Growing trade and processing center for a rich farm area of the St. Vrain Valley, irrigated by the Colorado–Big Thompson project. Mfg. (vitamins, primary metal prods., consumer prods., mfg. equip., publishing and printing, building materials). Dickens Opera House; Pioneer Mus. here. Roosevelt Natl. Forest and Rocky Mt. Natl. Park to W; Barbour Ponds State Park to E. Inc. 1885.

Longport, borough (1990 pop. 1,224), Atlantic co., SE N.J., on the Atlantic coast, 5 mi/8 km SW of Atlantic City; 39°18′N 74°31′W.

Longs Peak (14,255 ft/4,345 m), Larimer and Boulder cos., N Colo., in the Front Range of the Rocky Mts., just E of Continental Divide, in SE Rocky Mt. Natl. Park. On E side of its snow-capped peak is a 2,000 ft/610 m drop to Chasm L. Peak named for explorer Stephen H. Long.

Longstreet, village (1990 pop. 189), De Soto parish, NW La., 31 mi/50 km SSW of Shreveport; 32°06′N 93°57′W. In agr. area.

Longton, village (1990 pop. 389), Elk co., SE Kansas, on Elk R., and 12 mi/19 km SE of Howard; 37°22′N 96°04′W. Shipping and trading point in grain and cattle area.

Longtown, town (1990 pop. 107), Perry co., E Mo., 6 mi/9.7 km SE of Perryville; 37°40′N 89°46′W.

Longueuil, city (1991 pop. 129,874), S Que., Canada, on the St. Lawrence R. opposite Montreal. Residential and industrial suburb of Montreal. It annexed Montreal

South in 1961, and it merged with the city of Jacques-Cartier in 1969.

Longview 1 city (1990 pop. 70,311), ⊙ Gregg co., extends E into Harris co., E Texas, 22 mi/35 km W of Marshall, and 34 mi/55 km NE of Tyler, near Sabine R.; 32°31′N 94°45′W. Elev. 339 ft/103 m. A growing mfg., business, and distributing center for the rich E Texas oil field. Highly industrialized city located in major oil-producing area. Cattle, race horses; timber. Mfg. (RR cars, oil field equipment, travel trailers, natural gas processing, printing, machinery). Also a livestock center. City boomed with the discovery of the oil field in 1930. It is the seat of LeTourneau Univ. Gregg co. airport to SE. Annual horse and cattle shows are held in Longview. L. Cherokee reservoir to SE; Lone Star Speedway. Settled early 1800s; inc. 1872. **2** city (1990 pop. 31,499), Cowlitz co., SW Wash., a port of entry on the Columbia R., at mouth of Cowlitz R.; 46°09′N 122°57′W. It is a RR junction and transportation center, with the Lewis and Clark Bridge (highway) across the Columbia to Oregon. Its mfg. includes plastic, paper, and wood prods.; aluminum; steel foundry; logging. The city was founded in 1922 as a lumber town on the site of the historic settlement Monticello, which had been swept away by a flood in 1867. Twin city with Kelso, adjoins Longview to NE. The Lower Columbia Col. (2-year) is here; art mus. L. Sacajewa at center of city; Seaquest State Park, on Silver R. reservoir to NE. Inc. 1924.

Longview 1 village, Champaign co., E Ill., 18 mi/29 km SSE of Champaign; 39°53′N 88°03′W. In agr. area. **2** village, Oktibbeha co., E Miss., 7 mi/11.3 km WSW of Starkville. Noxubee Natl. Wildlife Refuge to S.

Longville, village (1990 pop. 224), Cass co., N central Minn., 42 mi/68 km N of Brainerd, at NE end of Woman L., S of boundary of Leech Lake Indian Reservation, and at S edge of Chippewa Natl. Forest; 46°59′N 94°13′W. Dairying; livestock; oats; timber. Leech L. to NW; numerous small lakes in area.

Longwood, suburb (□ 5 sq mi/13 sq km; 1990 pop. 13,316) of Orlando, Seminole co., central Fla., 11 mi/18 km N of Orlando; 28°41′N 81°20′W. Has experienced major growth since 1975.

Longwood Park, uninc. village, Richmond co., S N.C., 3 mi/4.8 km N of Hamlet.

Lonoke (LO-nok), county (□ 802 sq mi/2,077 sq km; 1990 pop. 39,268), central Ark.; ⊙ Lonoke; 34°45′N 91°52′W. Bounded N by Cypress Bayou; drained by Wabbaseka, Meto, and Two Prairie (forms part of E boundary) bayous. Agr. (rice, cotton, wheat, strawberries, soybeans; livestock). Mfg. of wood prods.; rice milling. Toltec Mounds State Park (on Mound L.) in SW; Arkansas R. to W. Formed 1873.

Lonoke (LO-nok), city (1990 pop. 4,022), ⊙ Lonoke co., central Ark., 21 mi/34 km E of Little Rock, near Bayou Meto; 34°47′N 91°54′W. Trade center and shipping point for area producing rice, cotton, pecans, strawberries. Mfg. (wooden cabinets, apparel, ordnance, safety gates).

Lonsdale, town (1990 pop. 1,252), Rice co., S Minn., 35 mi/56 km SW of St. Paul; 44°28′N 93°25′W. Grain; livestock; dairying; mfg. (die-cutting and laminating, light mfg.). Small lakes in area.

Lonsdale 1 (LAHNZ-dail), village (1990 pop. 127), Garland co., central Ark., 14 mi/23 km E of Hot Springs; 34°32′N 92°48′W. **2** industrial village in Cumberland and Lincoln towns, Providence co., NE R.I., on Blackstone R. (bridged here), and 6 mi/9.7 km N of Providence. Former textile center.

Loogootee (lo-GO-dee), city (1990 pop. 2,884), Martin co., SW Indiana, near East Fork of White R., 7 mi/11.3 km W of Shoals; 38°41′N 86°55′W. In agr. area (wheat, corn, hay; livestock); lumber milling; mfg. (animal feed, textiles). Bituminous-coal mines to W.

Lookeba (LOOK-uh-bah), village (1990 pop. 141), Caddo co., W central Okla., 25 mi/40 km WSW of El Reno, on Sugar Creek; 35°21′N 98°22′W. In agr. area. Red Rock Canyon State Park to N.

Looking Glass River, c.65 mi/105 km long, S central Mich.; rises in NW Livingston co.; flows N and W, past De Witt, to Grand R. at Portland; 42°46′N 84°08′W.

Lookout, village (1990 pop. 600), Pike co., E Ky., in the Cumberland Mts., 11 mi/18 km S of Pikesville. Bituminous coal.

Lookout, Cape, N Ont., Canada, on Hudson Bay, 65 mi/105 km W of entrance of James Bay; 55°18′N 83°55′W.

Lookout, Cape 1 Tillamook co., NW Oregon, coastal promontory c.10 mi/16 km SW of Tillamook. Site of Cape Lookout State Park. **2** promontory, Carteret co., E N.C., at SW end of Hatteras Isl., in Outer Banks (sand barrier isls. on Atlantic Ocean coast). Morehead City 14 mi/23 km SE of Cape Lookout Natl. Seashore. Cape Lookout Lighthouse (1859); ferry to Harkers Isl., near mainland.

Lookout Heights, Ky.: see FORT WRIGHT.

Lookout Mountain, residential town (1990 pop. 1,901), Hamilton co., SE Tenn., along N ridge of Lookout Mt. at Ga. state line, suburb 3 mi/5 km SW of Chattanooga; reached by road and cable RR from Chattanooga; 34°59′N 85°21′W. Elev. 2,126 ft/648 m. Has limestone caves, interesting rock formations, Adolph S. Ochs Observatory and Mus. (dedicated 1940). Ruby Falls, an underground waterfall, and Rock City Gardens, were made famous by barn-roof advertising. Civil War "Battle above the Clouds" fought here. Part of surrounding area is in Chickamauga and Chattanooga Natl. Military Park.

Lookout Mountain, suburb (1990 pop. 1,636), Walker co., Ga. a suburb of Chattanooga, Tenn., 3 mi/4.8 km S across Tenn.-Ga. state line from Lookout Mountain, Tenn.; 34°58′N 85°22′W. Named for the mt., this village has become a tourist destination due to the beautiful vistas from the mt. The world's 1st miniature golf course was built in Lookout Mountain in the 1920s. Mfg. of display boards, lamps.

Lookout Mountain, narrow ridge (c.2,000 ft/610 m) of the Cumberland Plateau in Tenn., Ga., and Ala., parallel to Sand Mt.; from Moccasin Bend of Tennessee R. near Chattanooga, Tenn., extends c.75 mi. SSW, across NW corner of Ga., to Gadsden, Ala.; summit, 35°00′N 85°20′W. Cable RR and road ascend NE end (elev. 2,392 ft/729 m); a popular tourist area with a magnificient view, interesting limestone caverns, notable Rock City Gardens, and Adolph S. Ochs Observatory and Mus. This portion of ridge contains residential town of Lookout Mountain, was site (1863) of Civil War Battle of Lookout Mountain ("Battle above the Clouds"), and is partly included in Chickamauga and Chattanooga Natl. Military Park.

Lookout Mountain 1 peak (6,505 ft/1,983 m) in the Sierra Ancha, Gila co., central Ariz., c.60 mi/97 km NE of Phoenix. **2** peak (7,375 ft/2,248 m) in Front Range, Jefferson co., N central Colo., 2 mi/3.2 km SW of Golden. Reached by Lariat Loop road from N, by Lookout Mt. road from S. On summit is grave of William F. Cody (Buffalo Bill). **3** peak (9,128 ft/2,782 m) in W N.Mex., in Zuñi Mts., 34 mi/55 km SE of Gallup, NE of Continental Divide, in Cibola Natl. Forest.

Lookout, Point, low headland, St. Marys co., S Md., at N side of mouth of the Potomac on Chesapeake Bay; lighthouse (built 1830). Visitors can picnic, swim, and fish in 700 acres/283 ha Point Lookout State Park, where a notorious prison housed 20,000 Confederate soldiers during the Civil War, of whom 3,384 died. One survivor was Sidney Lanier, the poet.

Lookout Point Lake, reservoir (□ 7 sq mi/18.1 sq km), Lane co., W central Oregon, on Middle Fork Willamette R., on western edge of Willamette Natl. Forest, 19 mi/31 km SE of Eugene; 43°55′N 122°45′W. Max. capacity 477,700 acre-ft. Formed by Lookout Point Dam (276 ft/84 m high), built (1953) by Army Corps of Engineers and U.S. Department of Agr. Forest Service for flood control.

Lookout Shoals Lake, reservoir, on Iredell-Catawba co. border and in Alexander co., W central N.C., on Catawba R., 15 mi/24 km E of Hickory, and 3 mi/4.8 km N of Catawba; c.10 mi/16 km long; 35°44′N 81°04′W. Max. capacity 366,840 acre-ft. Formed by Oxford Dam (97 ft/30 m high), built by Duke Power Co. for power generation. Lake Norman reservoir below dam.

Loomis, city (1990 pop. 5,705), Placer co., central Calif., in Sacramento Valley, 23 mi/37 km NE of Sacramento; 38°49′N 121°11′W. Ships plums, kiwi fruit, vegetables, walnuts; sheep, cattle; mfg. (lumber, sheet metal work, screw machine prods.). Folsom L. State Recreation Area (American R.) to SE.

Loomis, village (1990 pop. 376), Phelps co., S Nebr., 6 mi/9.7 km WNW of Holdrege; 40°28′N 99°30′W. Mfg. (clothing).

Loon Lake, resort village (1990 pop. 100), Franklin co., NE N.Y., on Loon L. (c.2 mi/3.2 km long), 31 mi/50 km WSW of Plattsburgh; 44°33′N 74°04′W.

Loon Lake 1 Piscataquis co., NW Maine, 47 mi/76 km N of Greenville, in wilderness recreational area; 4.5 mi/7.2 km long. **2** El Dorado co., central Calif., on Gerle Creek, 21 mi/34 km WNW of S. Lake Tahoe, in Eldorado Natl. Forest; 4 mi/6.4 km long; 39°00′N 120°20′W. Elev. 6,378 ft/1,944 m. Extends NE; max. capacity of 76,500 acre-ft. Formed by Loon Lake Dam (100 ft/30 m high), built (1963) for Sacramento water supply and debris control.

Loosahatchie River (loo-suh-HA-chee), c.65 mi/105 km long, SW Tenn.; rises SW of Hardeman; flows W past Somerville, to Mississippi R. near Memphis; 35°12′N 90°03′W. Upper course canalized.

Lopatcong, township (1990 pop. 5,052), Warren co., NW N.J., 3 mi/4.8 km E of Phillipsburg; 40°42′N 75°09′W. Inc. 1851.

López (LO-pes), town (1990 pop. 2,246), Chihuahua, N Mexico, on Florido R., and 40 mi/64 km E of Hidalgo del Parral. Elev. 3,707 ft/1,130 m. Corn, wheat, cotton, tobacco; livestock. Also known as Villa López.

Lopez 1 uninc. village, Colley township, Sullivan co., NE Pa., 34 mi/55 km W of Scranton, on Loyalsock Creek; 41°27′N 76°20′W. **2** uninc. village (1990 pop. 600), San Juan co., NW Wash., on W side of Lopez Isl., San Juan Isls., 5 mi/8 km E of Friday Harbor, on San Juan Channel. Fishing. Tourism. Lopez Isl. Airport to S. Terminus of ferries from Anacortes and Friday Harbor, landing 4 mi/6.4 km NNE at Upright Head. Spencer Spit State Park to NE.

Lopez Island (12 mi/19 km long; 5 mi/8 km wide), San Juan co., NW Wash., in E part of San Juan Isls. Bounded E by Lopez Sound, N by Upright Channel, W by San Juan Channel, S by Strait of Juan de Fuca. Village of Lopez in NW; Spencer Spit State Park in NE. Ferry landing at N end. Dairying; cattle; hay. Fishing. Tourism.

Lopez Point, Monterey co., W Calif., coastal promontory c.40 mi/64 km SSE of Monterey.

Lorado (lor-AID-o), uninc. village (1990 pop. 500), Logan co., SW W.Va., 15 mi/24 km ESE of Logan. Coal-mining region.

Lorain (lo-RAIN), county (□ 495 sq mi/1,282 sq km; 1990 pop. 271,126), N Ohio; ⊙ Elyria; 41°20′N 82°09′W. Bounded N by L. Erie; drained by Black and Vermilion rivers. Agr. area (grain, fruit; poultry, livestock; dairy prods.); mfg. at Lorain, Elyria, Wellington. Commercial fishing; sandstone quarries; lake resorts. Formed 1824.

Lorain (lo-RAIN), city (1990 pop. 71,245), Lorain co., N Ohio, on L. Erie at the mouth of the Black R.; 41°26′N 82°11′W. Once an important ore-shipping point, Lorain has shipyards, steel works, automobile-assembly plants, and commercial fisheries. Port activities, once integral to the city's economy, have declined in bulk and importance over the years. Power equip., automotive and bldg. materials, navigation equip., and toys are among the manufactures. Lorain also has numerous boating facilities. Inc. 1834.

Loraine 1 village (1990 pop. 331), Adams co., W Ill., 18 mi/29 km NNE of Quincy; 40°08′N 91°13′W. In agr. area. **2** village (1990 pop. 15), Renville co., N N.Dak., 8 mi/12.9 km N of Mohall; 48°52′N 101°34′W. **3** village (1990 pop. 731), Mitchell co., W Texas, 8 mi/12.9 km E of Colorado City; 32°24′N 100°42′W. Oil and gas. Cattle, sheep; grains, cotton, alfalfa. Inc. 1907.

Lorain (LUH-rain), borough (1990 pop. 824), Cambria co., SW central Pa., residential suburb 2 mi/3.2 km SE of Johnstown; 40°17′N 78° 54′W.

Loramie Creek (LO-ruh-mee), c.40 mi/64 km long, W Ohio; rises in Shelby co., flows SW, from N Shelby co., to L. Loramie or Loramie Reservoir (c.7 mi/11 km long) just SE of Minster, then SE to Great Miami R. just N of Piqua; 40°11′N 84°14′W.

Loramie, Lake, Ohio: see LORAMIE CREEK.

Lorane (LUH-rain), uninc. town (1990 pop. 2,580), Berks co., SE central Pa., residential suburb 5 mi/8 km SE of Reading on Schuylkill R.; 40°17′N 75°50′W. Agr. includes dairying, livestock, poultry; apples, plums, grain. Daniel Boone Homestead State Historical Site to E.

Lordsburg, town (1990 pop. 2,951), ⊙ Hidalgo co., SW N.Mex., 44 mi/71 km SW of Silver City, near Ariz. state line; 32°20′N 108°42′W. Elev. 4,258 ft/1,298 m. RR junction. Trade center, resort. Cattle; vegetables, cotton, chiles, jalapeños, wheat, oats, barley, alfalfa, Christmas trees. Copper, silver, gold, and lead mines in vicinity. Southwest N.Mex. fair and livestock show take place here. Part of Gila Natl. Forest, in Burro Mts., to NE; Shakespeare Ghost Town to S; Stein's Ghost Town to SW.

Lore City, village (1990 pop. 384), Guernsey co., E Ohio, 7 mi/11 km ESE of Cambridge; 39°59′N 81°27′W.

Loreauville (luh-RO-vil), village (1990 pop. 860), Iberia parish, S La., 6 mi/10 km NE of New Iberia, and on Bayou Teche; 30°04′N 91°45′W. In agr. area (sugar, rice; cattle); catfish, crawfish; mfg. (aluminum boats, harvesting equip.).

Lorena, town (1990 pop. 1,158), McLennan co., E central Texas, 10 mi/16 km SSW of Waco; 31°22′N 97°12′W. Agr. area (cattle; dairying; cotton, grain). Light mfg.

Lorenzo, town (1990 pop. 1,208), Crosby co., NW Texas, on the Llano Estacado, 20 mi/32 km ENE of Lubbock; 33°40′N 101°31′W. Wheat; cotton; cattle; oil and gas; mfg. (textile yarns).

Loreto (lo-RE-to), town (1990 pop. 15,022), Zacatecas, N central Mexico, on RR, and 50 mi/80 km SE of Zacatecas; 22°18′N 102°00′W. Grain; livestock.

Loreto (lo-RE-to), village, La Paz municipio, Baja California Sur, NW Mexico, port on Gulf of California, on highway, and 145 mi/233 km N of La Paz; 26°00′N 111°20′W. Sugarcane, dates, figs. Formerly a Jesuit mission, founded 1697. The oldest of the Californian missions; site of planned tourist resort development begun in the early 1990s.

Loretteville (lo-REHT-vil), town (1991 pop. 14,219), S central Que., Canada, on short Nelson R., and 8 mi/13 km NW of Quebec. Mfg. of gloves, skis, canoes. Huron settlement began here 1697; village was known as Indian Lorette or Jeune Lorette. Nearby is Ancienne Lorette.

Loretto, city (1990 pop. 1,515), Lawrence co., S Tenn., 13 mi/21 km SSW of Lawrenceburg; 35°05′N 87°26′W. Fruit.

Loretto (luh-RET-o), town (1990 pop. 820), Marion co., central Ky., 27 mi/43 km E of Elizabethtown; 37°38′N 85°24′W. Mfg. (whiskey). Hq. of Sisters of Loretto; Holy Cross Church (1820s).

Loretto, village (1990 pop. 404), Hennepin co., E Minn., suburb 18 mi/29 km W of downtown Minneapolis, surrounded by Medina; 45°03′N 93°38′W. Mfg. (wedding cakes, metal stampings).

Loretto (luh-RE-to), borough (1990 pop. 1,072), Cambria co., SW central Pa., 5 mi/8 km ENE of Ebensburg; 40°30′N 78°38′W. Agr. area (corn, hay, potatoes; dairying); mfg. (dairy prods.). St. Francis Col. here.

L'Orignal (lo-reen-YAHL), village (1991 pop. 2,164), ⊙ Prescott and Russell cos., SE Ont., Canada, on Ottawa R., and 50 mi/80 km ENE of Ottawa. Lumbering center, dairying; resort.

Lorimor, town (1990 pop. 377), Union co., S Iowa, 17 mi/27 km ENE of Creston; 41°07′N 94°03′W. Metal prods.

Loring, fishing village, SE Alaska, on W side of Revillagigedo Isl., 20 mi/32 km N of Ketchikan.

Loris (LOR-is), town (1990 pop. 2,067), Horry co., E S.C., 17 mi/27 km NNE of Conway, near N.C. state line; 34°03′N 78°53′W. Diversified mfg. Agr. includes watermelons, tobacco, grain, strawberries; livestock.

Lorman, uninc. village (1990 pop. 500), Jefferson co., SW Miss., 26 mi/42 km NE of Natchez. Cotton, rice, corn; cattle; catfish. Old Country Store, in continuous operation since 1890s. Natchez Trace Parkway passes to W; Canemount (c.1855), and Rosewood (c.1857) plantations to NW. Alcorn State Univ. 4 mi/6.4 km NW.

Lorrain (lo-RAIN), village, E Ont., Canada, on Montreal R., and 5 mi/8 km WSW of Cobalt. Silver and cobalt mining.

Lorrain (law-RANG), town, NE Martinique, on the Atlantic, and 15 mi/24 km N of Fort-de-France. Rum distilling. Sometimes called Le Lorrain.

Lorraine (lo-RAIN), village (1990 pop. 147), Ellsworth co., central Kansas, 11 mi/18 km SSW of Ellsworth; 38°34′N 98°19′W. RR junction. Wheat; cattle.

Lorrainville (lo-RAIN-vil), village (1991 pop. 1,061), W Que., Canada, 16 mi/26 km ESE of Haileybury. Dairying, cattle raising; gold-mining region.

Lorton, uninc. city, Fairfax co., NE Va., suburb 15 mi/24 km SE of Wash., D.C.; 38°42′N 77°14′W. Mfg. (metal finishing, printing and publishing, lumber, concrete). Site of Dist. of Columbia Correctional Facility. Gunston Cove of Potomac R., Fort Belvoir Military Reservation to E, Mason Neck State Park and Natl. Wildlife Refuge, Pohick Bay Regional Park to SE, Occoquan Regional Park to W, Gunston Hall historic site to SE.

Lorton, village (1990 pop. 61), Otoe co., SE Nebr., 10 mi/16 km WSW of Nebraska City, and on branch of Little Nemaha R.; 40°36′N 96°01′W.

Los Alamitos, city (1990 pop. 11,676), Orange co., NE of Long Beach, S Calif., suburb 18 mi/29 km SSE of downtown Los Angeles, and 7 mi/11.3 km E of Long Beach, on San Gabriel R.; 33°48′N 118°04′W. Diversified mfg. Los Alamitos Racetrack to N; Los Alamitos Naval Air Station in SE; U.S. Naval Weapons Center to S, at Seal Beach; Alamitos Bay, Pacific Ocean, and Long Beach Marina, 5 mi SW. Inc. 1960.

Los Alamos (LOS AH-lah-mos), county (□ 109 sq mi/282 sq km; 1990 pop. 18,115), N N.Mex.; ⊙ Los Alamos; 35°52′N 106°18′W. Smallest co. in N.Mex. Includes uninc. community of Los Alamos and part of White Rock. All govt. is at co. level. High plateau area largely within Valle Grande Mts. Atomic research at Los Alamos. Formed 1949 from parts of Sandoval and Santa Fe cos. Part of Jemez Mt. in W; small part of Santa Fe Natl. Forest along N and W boundaries; Pajarito Ski Area in W; bounded by Bandelier Natl. Monument on S; part of Bandelier Natl. Monument in SE; bounded by Rio Grande in SE.

Los Alamos, uninc. city (1990 pop. 11,455), ⊙ Los Alamos co., N central N.Mex., 23 mi/37 km NW of Santa Fe; 35°53′N 106°16′W. Elev. 7,410 ft/2,259 m. It is on a long mesa extending E from Jemez Mt. The U.S. govt. chose the site in 1942 for atomic research, and the first atomic bombs were produced and tested here. In 1947 the Atomic Energy Commission took over the town. In 1962 govt. control ended; the co. was incorporated in 1969, and all govt. is at the co. level. Light, high-technology mfg. and incipient tourism. Has the only fully operational plutonium plant in country. Nuclear weapons design ended in 1988, and bombs now being dismantled. Bradbury Science Mus. The Los Alamos Scientific Laboratory, operated by the Univ. of California, is a natl. historic landmark. Santa Clara Indian Reservation to N; Bandelier Natl. Monument to S; Santa Fe Natl. Forest to N and SW; Pajarito Ski Area to W.

Los Alamos, uninc. village, Santa Barbara co., SW Calif., 16 mi/26 km SSE of Santa Maria. Oil field nearby.

Los Aldamas (los ahl-DAH-mahs), town (1990 pop. 11,991), Nuevo León, N Mexico, in lowland, on San Juan R. near Marte R. Gómez dam, and 75 mi/121 km ENE of Monterrey; 26°02′N 99°12′W. Cotton, corn, sugarcane.

Los Altos, city (1990 pop. 26,303), Santa Clara co., W Calif., residential suburb 9 mi/14.5 km WNW of downtown San Jose, and 30 mi/48 km SSE of downtown San Francisco; 37°22′N 122°06′W. Drained by Adobe Creek. Diversified light mfg. Junior col. is in nearby Los Altos Hills. Moffett Field Naval Air Station to NE. Hetch Hetchy Aqueduct runs E-W to N. Portola and Castle Rock state parks and Santa Cruz Mts. to SW. Inc. 1952.

Los Altos Hills, city (1990 pop. 7,514), Santa Clara co., W Calif., residential suburb 14 mi/23 km W of downtown San Jose, and 30 mi/48 km SSE of downtown San Francisco, SW of Los Altos, in NE foothills of Santa Cruz Mts.; 37°22′N 122°08′W. Stanford Univ. to N. Portola and Castle Rock state parks to S. Seat of Foothills Col. (2-yr.).

Los Angeles, county (□ 4,060 sq mi/10,515 sq km; 1990 pop. 8,863,164), S Calif.; ⊙ LOS ANGELES; 34°11′N 118°16′W. The fertile Los Angeles basin, a plain reaching to the Pacific on W, is almost surrounded by mts. covering c.½ of co.'s surface; in the basin and in tributary San Fernando Valley are the scores of cities of the metropolitan area, many of them virtually part of Los Angeles, and all including large suburban and semirural areas. By mid-1990s even areas at the edge of the desert, N of San Gabriel, had experienced rapid development. Many cities near the city of Los Angeles have now declined economically. Largest (in pop.) are LONG BEACH, PASADENA, GLENDALE, BURBANK, SANTA MONICA, ALHAMBRA, TORRANCE, and SOUTH GATE. San Gabriel Mts. (NE wall of basin) have peaks over 10,000 ft/3,048 m; coastal ranges (including Santa Monica Mts., Santa Susana Mts.) are lower. Antelope Valley (part of Mojave Desert; irrigated agr.) is in N. Off coast, which is indented by San Pedro Bay (Los Angeles Harbor here) and Santa Monica Bay, are Channel Islands, including Santa Catalina (also called Catalina), noted resort, and San Clemente Isl. Intermittent Los Angeles and San Gabriel rivers (both are large calverts) and their tributaries have flood-control works. California Aqueduct crosses N part of co. NW-SE, Los Angeles Aqueduct crosses co. N-S. Co.'s mediterranean climate and its resorts have long attracted winter residents and year-round tourists. Has some of nation's most valuable farmland (irrigation required; c.½ of farms under 10 acres/4 ha), but much of it has been replaced by urbanization. Important industries (motion pictures, at HOLLYWOOD, CULVER CITY, Burbank; oil refining, automobile assembling; mfg. of aircraft, tires and tubes, steel, foundry prods., clothing, furniture, food prods., computer equip. and software), rich oil and natural-gas fields. Chief farm prods. are dairy prods.; cattle, poultry; honey, strawberries, peaches, onions, barley; ornamentals and bedding plants. Part of Edwards Air Force Base on N boundary in NE; part of Santa Monica Mts. Natl. Recreation Area in W; parts of Angeles Natl. Forest in center (San Gabriel Mts.) and NW; Saddleback Butte State Park in NE; part of Mojave Desert in NE; part of Antelope Valley in NW; numerous state beaches on coast. Formed 1850.

Los Angeles, city (1990 pop. 3,485,398), ⊙ Los Angeles co., S Calif., bounding Pacific Ocean in 3 places, at Pacific Palisades c.15 mi/24 km W of downtown, at Venice 12 mi/19 km SW of downtown, and at San Pedro (Long Beach area) 20 mi/32 km S of downtown; 34°07′N 118°25′W. Drained by Los Angeles R., a large concrete flood control channel that can swell into a raging torrent during Pacific storms. A port of entry on the Pacific coast, with a fine harbor at San Pedro Bay, it is the 2d largest U.S. city in pop. and 7th largest in area. Two low mt. ranges, the Santa Monica and Verdugo, cut across the center of the city. Los Angeles's warm climate is tempered by cool ocean currents that flow S along the coast from the N Pacific. Los Angeles is a shipping, industrial, communication, financial, fashion, and distribution center for the W U.S. and much of the the Pacific Rim. It is also the motion-picture, television, radio, and recording capital of the U.S., if not the world, with numerous studios. Once an agr. distribution center, Los Angeles is the country's largest center of the clothing and textile industries. It is also a leading producer of aircraft, computers, paper, toys, glass, furniture, wire prods., prods. used in the biomedical industry, electrical and electronic machinery, pharmaceuticals, petrochemicals, and fabricated metal. Tourism, multimedia and cybernet entertainment software technology, printing and publishing, food processing, and oil refining are also major industries. Growth in many of these areas has offset a decline in financial, real estate, and insurance sectors that has occurred in the mid-1990s, as well as the relocation of several large corporate hq. Oil and natural gas fields in part of city and environs. Los Angeles Harbor and Long Beach Harbor, together, are Los Angeles's port, part in City of Long Beach and part in Los Angeles (the 2 cities adjoin each other). Los Angeles has one of the busiest ports in the U.S.; roughly half of its commerce is foreign. There is a smaller boat harbor in Marina del Rey, Venice area. It is the principal financial center for the West Coast and the E Pacific Basin. The vast Los Angeles metropolitan area covers 5 cos. (Los Angeles, Orange, Riverside, San Bernardino, and Ventura) and encompasses 34,000 sq mi/88,060 sq km with over 14.5 million people. Los Angeles metro area has practically merged with San Diego's metro area to S. The Los Angeles metropolitan area is connected by a freeway system that is increasingly unable to accommodate the area's traffic. The enormous number of motor vehicles, combined with the city's valley location, creates dangerously high levels of smog. A light-RR system (Southern Calif. Rapid Transit; opened in 1990) and bus service alleviate only a small percentage of freeway congestion. A new subway RR line, scheduled for completion in the early 21st cent., linking existing light-RR lines from the downtown area to Long Beach in the S and El Segundo/L.A. Internatl. Airport in the N, will provide some relief; however, there are concerns about earthquakes affecting the line. The subway links will be extended N to Hollywood and Pasadena. Maintaining an adequate water supply has long been a problem; the metropolitan area obtains its water from the Sierra Nevada (via Los Angeles Aqueduct), the Colorado R. (via Colorado R. Aqueduct) to E, and from N Calif. (via California Aqueduct) through California's Central Valley to the N. As Los Angeles rapidly expanded throughout the 20th cent., it absorbed numerous communities and enclosed independent municipalities. Among the communities now part of Los Angeles are Century City, Brentwood, Hollywood, San Pedro, Sylmar, Watts, Westwood, Bel-Air, and Boyle Heights, and several large suburbs in the San Fernando Valley, such as Northridge, Sherman Oaks, and Van Nuys. Two moderate earthquakes (1971 and 1994), each claiming more than 60 lives, were epicentered in the San Fernando Valley. Independent municipalities surrounded by Los Angeles include SANTA MONICA (1990 pop. 86,905), BEVERLY HILLS (1990 pop. 31,971), and SAN FERNANDO (1990 pop. 22,580). Inc. cities in the broader metropolitan region with populations of 80,000 or more include ALHAMBRA, ANAHEIM, BURBANK, DOWNEY, EL MONTE, FULLERTON, GARDEN GROVE, GLENDALE, HUNTINGTON BEACH, IRVINE, INGLEWOOD, LAKEWOOD, LONG BEACH, MORENO VALLEY, NORWALK, OCEANSIDE, ONTARIO, ORANGE, OXNARD, PASADENA, POMONA, RANCHO CUCAMONGA, RIVERSIDE, SAN BERNARDINO, SANTA ANA, SANTA CLARITA, SANTA MONICA, SIMI VALLEY, THOUSAND OAKS, , and TORRANCE, in addition to Los Angeles itself. The site of the city was visited by the Sp. explorer Gaspar de Portola in 1769, and in 1781 El Pueblo de Nuestra Señora de los Angeles de Porciuncula (The Town of Our Lady the Queen of the Angels of Porciuncula) was founded. The city served several times as the capital of the Sp. colonial province of ALTA CALIFORNIA and was a cattle-ranching center. In 1846, Los Angeles was captured from the Mexicans by U.S. forces. The arrival of the RR (Southern Pacific in 1876; Santa Fe in 1885) and the discovery of oil in the early 1890s stimulated expansion, as did the development of the motion-picture industry in the early 20th cent. During World War II, Los Angeles boomed as a center for the production of war supplies and munitions and thousands of African-Americans migrated to Los Angeles to fill factory jobs. After the war, massive suburban growth made the city enormously prosperous, but also created or exacerbated a variety of urban problems. In 1965, the African-American community of WATTS was the site of 6 days of rioting that left 34 people dead and caused over $200 million in property damage. In the 1970s and 1980s Los Angeles experienced dramatic growth through immigration. Today, Los Angeles is one of the most racially and ethnically diverse cities in the U.S. In 1990 the Hispanic pop. of metropolitan Los Angeles was almost 5 million (almost 40% of the pop.) and the area's Asian pop. was over 1.3 million. In addition to an already well established Jap.-Amer. community, recent immigration has come from China, South Korea, Vietnam, Cambodia, the Philippines, and other nations. Chinatown N of downtown, Little Tokyo SE of downtown. In the 1980s, violent gang warfare over the illegal drug (especially crack) trade became a serious problem for law enforcement officials. In April 1992, 4 white Los Angeles police officers were found not guilty of police brutality after they had been videotaped beating Rodney King, a black motorist they were pursuing. The acquittal touched off riots in S-central Los Angeles and a number of other areas that resulted in 58 deaths, thousands of arrests, and approximately $1 billion in property damage. In Los Angeles are botanical gardens; the Los Angeles Co. Mus. of Art; the Mus. of Contemporary Art; history, movie, industrial, and science museums; and many parks, including Griffith Park, one of the largest urban parks in the world, with a zoo and a planetarium. The La Brea Tar Pits, near Beverly Hills, are famous for Ice Age fossils. The Los Angeles Philharmonic is internationally famous as is the city's opera company. In 1987, Los Angeles gained its 2d Natl. Football League team (the other being the Rams) when the Oakland Raiders moved to the city, but as of early 1996, the Rams had moved to St. Louis and the Raiders back to Oakland, leaving Los Angeles without a Natl. Football League franchise. In baseball, the Natl. League's Los Angeles Dodgers and the Amer. League's California Angels (who play in Anaheim) represent the area. The city also has 2 Natl. Basketball Association teams (the Lakers and the Clippers) and a Natl. Hockey League team (the Kings). The motion-picture and television industries, the proximity of many resorts and theme parks (Six Flags Magic Mt. and Six Flags Hurricane Harbor), the fine beaches, and a climate that encourages year-round outdoor recreation attract millions of tourists annually to Los Angeles. Other attractions in the region include the Santa Anita and Hollywood Park racetracks, Knott's Berry Farm, and Disneyland (at Anaheim). Among the city's many educational institutions are the Univ. of Southern Calif.; the Univ. of Calif., Los Angeles; Calif. State Univ., Los Angeles in NE, and Calif. State Univ., Northridge, in NW; Occidental Col.; Loyola Marymount Univ.; Mt. St. Marys Col.; Fashion Inst. of Design and Merchandising (2-year), and numerous other 2-year cols. Will Rogers State Historical Park and State Beach in W; Topanga State Park and State Beach in W; Los Encinos State Historical Park in W; El Pueblo de Los Angeles State Historical Park in downtown, across the street from Union Station; Venice City and Dockweiler state beaches in W; Royal Palms State Beach in S; Santa Monica Mts. Natl. Recreation Area in W, extends W into Ventura co.; Angeles Natl. Forest, in San Gabriel Mts., to N; Busch Gardens in San Fernando Valley. Inc. 1850.

Los Angeles Aqueduct, Calif.; see OWENS RIVER.

Los Angeles Harbor, Los Angeles co., S Calif., man-made port of Los Angeles city, on San Pedro Bay, 20 mi/32 km S of city's center, at San Pedro and Wilmington. Adjoins Long Beach Harbor to E; both share same breakwater system shelter and both function as Los Angeles's port. Consists of 2 major parts: outer harbor (U.S. Navy's chief Pacific coast anchorage) in San Pedro Bay, sheltered by breakwater (in 2 sections; 4.5 mi/7.2 km long), extending E from Point Fermin; inner harbor, consisting of channels and turning basins dredged in former mudflats and of Terminal Isl. (largely artificial) lying bet. inner and outer harbors. Cerritos Channel connects Inner Harbor with Long Beach Harbor (E) at U.S. Naval Shipyard (Los Angeles/Long Beach), forms Terminal Isl. Port generally ranks high in U.S., and 1st on Pacific coast, in volume of cargo, most of which is outgoing (foreign and coastwise); 12th largest in U.S., Long Beach 10th largest, together 4th largest in U.S. Ships coal, oil and petroleum prods., manufactured goods, citrus and other fruit, canned fish, vegetables, cotton, borax, potash, soda ash, cement; receives iron, steel, lumber, bananas, copra, jute, hemp, fertilizers, rubber, sugar, spices, coffee, tea, newsprint, wool. Harbor dist. (Wilmington, San Pedro, Harbor City) is served by 120 mi/193 km RR, connecting with 3 transcontinental lines; container port transfers cargo directly from trains and trucks to container ships. Port has c.25 mi/40 km of dock frontage, oil terminals and refineries, shipyards, dry docks, a foreign trade zone (free port) opened in 1949, a naval operating base and other naval and coast guard installations, a fishing port (at Terminal Isl.; has large canneries, by-products plants at W end), which generally leads Calif. in catches (tuna, mackerel, sardines); also passenger terminals (at Wilmington); and automobile-assembling and other industrial plants. Harbor's modern development began in 1899, when breakwater was begun in exposed anchorage that had been in use as port since 1850s, and which had been connected (1869) by RR to Los Angeles; Los Angeles annexed San Pedro and Wilmington in 1909, and formed a harbor dist. to coordinate development; dredging of inner harbor was done 1912–1914. Opening in 1914 of Panama Canal, and the accelerating agr. and commercial growth of S. Calif., as well as development of area's great oil fields, stimulated trade of port and led to subsequent improvements.

Los Angeles River, channeled intermittent stream, c.50 mi/80 km long, Los Angeles co., S Calif.; rises c.25 mi/40 km NW of downtown Los Angeles, in Santa Susana Mts., enters Los Angeles city, drains San Fernando Valley, flows E along N base of Santa Monica Mts., through Sepulveda Flood Control Dam, where it receives Los Angeles Aqueduct from N, then S, past E end of range and through downtown Los Angeles, S through its S industrial dist. and SE suburbs, to San Pedro Bay at Long Beach. Torrential rainy-season flows are controlled by masonry embankments and huge catchment basins on upper river and tributaries (Pacoima R., Tujunga Creek, short Rio Hondo). Dry concrete culverts become raging torrents during storms.

Los Arabos (los ah-RAH-boz), town, Matanzas prov., W Cuba, on Central Highway and 60 mi/97 km ESE of Matanzas; 22°44′N 80°44′W. RR junction in agr. region (sugarcane, bananas). The refinery and central of México is NE.

Los Banos, city (1990 pop. 14,519), Merced co., central Calif., in San Joaquin Valley, 22 mi SW of Merced; 37°04′N 120°51′W. Dairying; poultry; irrigated farming (beans, tomatoes, sweet potatoes, almonds, rice, wheat, corn, cotton); mfg. (electrical machinery; printing and publishing). Fremont Ford State Recreation Area to N, San Luis State Recreation Area to W; San Luis and Merced natl. wildlife refuges to NE. Delta Mendota Canal and California Aqueduct to SW.

Los Cabos, Mexico: see SAN JOSÉ DEL CABOS.

Los Cerrillos (LOS se-REE-os), village (1990 pop. 500), Santa Fe co., N central N.Mex., on Gallisteo Creek, and 27 mi/43 km SSW of Santa Fe. Elev. 5,888 ft/1,795 m. Cattle, sheep; corn, grain, alfalfa. Several Pueblo Indian villages in vicinity. Santo Domingo Indian Reservation to W.

Los Chaves (LOS CHAH-ves), uninc. village (1990 pop. 3,872), Valencia co., central N.Mex., 27 mi/43 km S of Albuquerque, on Rio Grande; 34°43′N 106°45′W. Agr. area (dairying; cattle, sheep; grain, alfalfa, grapes). Senator William M. Chaves State Park located here.

Los Duranes (LOS du-RAHN-es), village, Bernalillo co., central N.Mex., on Rio Grande, part of city of Albuquerque, near Old Albuquerque (Old Town).

Los Fresnos, town (1990 pop. 2,473), Cameron co., extreme S Texas, 12 mi/19 km N of Brownsville; 26°04′N 97°28′W. Rich irrigated farming area (cotton, vegetables, sugarcane) of lower Rio Grande valley; mfg. (bldg. materials, meat rendering). Palo Alto Battlefield Natl.

Historic Site to S; Laguna Atacosca Natl. Wildlife Refuge to NE. Inc. after 1940.

Los Gatos, city (1990 pop. 27,357), Santa Clara co., W Calif., suburb 9 mi/14.5 km SSW of San Jose, at S edge of Bay Area urbanized area; 37°14′N 121°58′W. Drained by Los Gatos Creek. It is an affluent residential community. Agr. to S (cherries, vegetables, nursery prods.; poultry; dairying); mfg. (electronic components, computer peripherals). Los Gatos, Span. for "the cats," got its name from the wildcats that abounded in the Santa Clara valley at the time the city was founded. Santa Cruz Mts. to SW; Forest of Nisene Marks State Park to S; Big Basin Redwoods State Park to W; Lexington Reservoir to S. Inc. 1887.

Los Herreras (los he-RE-rahs), town (1990 pop. 2,351), Nuevo León, N Mexico, on RR, on Pesquería R., and 60 mi/97 km ENE of Monterrey. Elev. 656 ft/200 m. Cotton, sugarcane, cereals, fruit.

Los Llanos (los YAH-nos), officially Villa de San José de Los Llanos, town (1993 pop. 3,622), San Pedro de Macorís prov., SE Dominican Republic, 28 mi/45 km ENE of Santo Domingo; 18°38′N 69°30′W. Sugar; cattle. Sugar mill to SE.

Los Lunas (LOS LOON-uhs), town (1990 pop. 6,013), ⊙ Valencia co., central N.Mex., on Rio Grande, and 32 mi/ 51 km S of Albuquerque; 34°48′N 106°44′W. Elev. 4,852 ft/1,479 m. Trade center, dairying and livestock-shipping point (cattle, sheep) in irrigated grain- and vegetable-farming (corn, alfalfa) area. Mfg. (trailers). Univ. of N.Mex., Valencia campus (2 year). Isleta Pueblo Indian village to N in Isleta Indian Reservation; Manzano Mts. to E in part of Cibola Natl. Forest to E; Senator Willie M. Chavez State Park to S.

Los Mármoles (los MAR-mo-les), national park (□ 75 sq mi/194 sq km), in NW Hidalgo, Mexico, on Mexico Highway 85 N of Zimapán. Has natural springs and a large canyon (San Vicente). The forest terrain includes oak, pine, fir, and walnut trees. The park is underdeveloped and has no visitor facilities. Named for large marble outcrops.

Los Mochis (los MO-chees), city (1990 pop. 162,659) and township, ⊙ Ahome Municipio, Sinaloa state, W Mexico, on RR, and on Mexico Highway 15, 140 mi/226 km SW of Ciudad Obregon; 25°48′N 109°00′E. It is the commercial and processing center of the rich agr. area (Río Fuerte Irrigation dist.) irrigated by the Fuerte R. Prods. include grains, sugarcane, and tomatoes, as well as cattle and pigs. Los Mochis is additionally a tourist center.

Los Molinos, uninc. town (1990 pop. 1,709), Tehama co., N Calif., 12 mi/19 km SSE of Red Bluff, on Sacramento R., at mouth of Mill R.; 40°02′N 122°06′W. Woodson Bridge State Recreation Area to S. Part of Lassen Natl. Forest to E; Tehama State Game Refuge to E. Olives, walnuts, prunes; dairying; poultry.

Los Nietos, uninc. town, Los Angeles co., S Calif., suburb 10 mi/16 km SE of downtown Los Angeles, near Whittier, on San Gabriel R. Oil wells. Pio Pico State Historical Park to NE.

Los Olivos, uninc. village, Santa Barbara co., SW Calif., 26 mi/42 km NW of Santa Barbara. Fruit, grapes; grain; cattle. Winery. Los Padres Natl. Forest and Sierra Madre to NE.

Los Osos, uninc. city (1990 pop. 10,200), San Luis Obispo co., SW Calif., 10 mi/16 km WNW of San Luis Obispo, 1 mi/1.6 km SE of Baywood Park, 2 mi/3.2 km E of Pacific Ocean. Statistically reported as Baywood–Los Osos (1990 pop. 14,733). Flowers, nursery stock, strawberries, apples, avocados, vegetables, grain; cattle. Morro Bay State Park and Atascadero State Beach to NW; Montana de Oro State Park to S.

Los Palacios (los pah-LAH-see-oz), town, Pinar del Río prov., W Cuba, on Los Palacios R., on RR, and 30 mi/ 48 km ENE of Pinar del Río; 22°36′N 83°15′W. In agr. region (sugarcane, tobacco, pineapples; cattle). Mfg. of cigars.

Los Pinos (los PEE-noz), town, La Habana prov., W Cuba, on RR, W of Havana, and midway between Havana and Matanzas. In dairying region.

Los Pinos River, c.75 mi/121 km long, in SW Colo. and

NW N.Mex.; rises at Continental Divide, in San Juan Mts. in S central Hinsdale co., SW Colo., source within 2 mi/3.2 km of Rio Grande, across Divide; flows SSW through Valecito Reservoir, past Bayfield and Ignacio (Colo.), to San Juan R. (Navajo Reservoir) in San Juan co., N.Mex. Sometimes called Pine R. Vallecito Dam (162 ft/49 m high, 4,010 ft/1,222 m long; completed 1941) is 10 mi/16 km N of Bayfield; creates Vallecito Reservoir (capacity 129,700 ft/39,533 m), used to irrigate 33,100 acres/13,396 ha. Lower 8 mi/12.9 km forms N arm of Navajo Reservoir.

Los Ramones (los rah-MO-nes), town (1990 pop. 1,479), Nuevo León, N Mexico, on RR, on Pesquería R., and 40 mi/64 km E of Monterrey. Cotton, sugarcane, grain.

Los Ranchos de Albuquerque (LOS RAHN-chos de Al-buh-kuhr-kee), town (1990 pop. 3,955), Bernalillo co., N central N.Mex., residential suburb 4 mi/6.4 km N of downtown Albuquerque, on Rio Grande; 35°10′N 106°39′W.

Los Reyes 1 (los RE-yes), residential town, part of Coyoacán delegación, Federal dist., central Mexico, 6 mi/ 9.7 km S of Mexico city. **2** town (1990 pop. 637), Veracruz, E Mexico, in Sierra Madre Oriental, 17 mi/ 27 km SSW of Córdoba. Elev. 4,134 ft/1,260 m. Fruit.

Los Reyes Acaquilpan (los RE-yes ah-kah-KEEL-pahn), city (1990 pop. 134,544), ⊙ La Paz municipio, Mexico state, central Mexico, 12 mi/19 km SE of Mexico city. RR junction. Part of the Area Metropolitana de la Ciudad de México. Formerly an agr. community, now rapidly urbanizing. Also known as Los Reyes la Paz.

Los Reyes de Juárez (los RE-yes dai HWAH-res), town (1990 pop. 12,127), Puebla, central Mexico, on RR, and 28 mi/45 km ESE of Puebla. Agr. center (cereals, maguey, fruit).

Los Reyes de Salgado (los RE-yes dai sahl-GAH-do), town (1990 pop. 32,474), Michoacán, central Mexico, in Mex. Volcanic Axis, 30 mi/48 km SSW of Zamora de Hidalgo on Mexico Highway 40; 19°35′N 102°29′W. Agr. center (corn, sugarcane, tobacco, fruit; livestock).

Los Reyes la Paz, Mexico: see LOS REYES ACAQUILPAN.

Los Serranos, uninc. town (1990 pop. 7,099), San Bernardino co., S Calif., residential suburb 32 mi/51 km ESE of downtown Los Angeles, and 7 mi/11.3 km SW of Ontario; 33°58′N 117°42′W. Prado Flood Control Basin (Santa Ana R.) to SE. Chino Hills State Park to S.

Los Tuxtlas, Mexico: see SAN ANDRÉS TUXTLA.

Losantville, town (1990 pop. 253), Randolph co., E Ind., 14 mi/23 km SW of Winchester; 40°01′N 85°11′W. Agr. area. Also called Bronson.

Lost Cabin, village, Fremont co., central Wyo., on Badwater Creek on branch of Bighorn R., and 75 mi/121 km WNW of Casper.

Lost Creek, uninc. town (1990 pop. 800), Schuylkill co., E central Pa., 2 mi/3.2 km NW of Frackville, on Shenandoah Creek; 40°48′N 76°14′W. In anthracite- coal region.

Lost Creek, village (1990 pop. 413), Harrison co., N W.Va., 8 mi/12.9 km S of Clarksburg; 39°09′N 80°20′W. Corn; cattle, poultry. Mfg. (meat processing, limestone processing). Watters Smith Memorial State Park to W.

Lost Hills, uninc. town (1990 pop. 1,212), Kern co., S central Calif., 42 mi/68 km NW of Bakersfield, on California Aqueduct; 35°37′N 119°42′W. Agr. cotton, grain, sugar beets, fruits, nuts; cattle; dairying. Kern Natl. Wildlife Refuge to N; Temblor Range to SW.

Lost Mine Peak, Texas: see CHISOS MOUNTAINS.

Lost Nation, town (1990 pop. 467), Clinton co., E Iowa, 34 mi/55 km WNW of Clinton; 41°58′N 90°49′W. Feed milling; fertilizers.

Lost River, village (1990 pop. 29), Custer co., central Idaho, 13 mi/21 km WNW of Arco; 43°43′N 113°32′W. Challis Natl. Forest to W.

Lost River 1 c.70 mi/113 km long, in Calif. and Oregon; begins at joining of North and South forks, 30 mi/ 48 km NW of Alturas, Modoc Natl. Forest, N Modoc co.; flows W 5 mi/8 km to Clear L. reservoir, then NW (inflow and outflow are both in NE corner of reservoir), into Oregon, W past Bonanza, to 5 mi/8 km SE of Klamath Falls, then SSE, re-entering Calif. and into

Tule L. (Natl. Wildlife Refuge), 4 mi/6.4 km S of Oregon state line, and N of Lava Beds Natl. Monument. Dam at reservoir and system of small diversion dams and canals along middle course are units in Klamath irrigation project, supplying water to agr. area in Siskiyou co., Calif., and Klamath co., Oregon. **2** c.75 mi/121 km long, S Ind.; rises in W Wash. co.; flows W (partly in subterranean channel), past West Baden Springs, to East Fork of White R. in S Martin co.

Lost River 1 N.H.: see KINSMAN NOTCH. **2** W.Va.: see CACAPON RIVER.

Lost River Range, in Custer and Butte cos., E Idaho, bet. Big Lost and Little Lost rivers, in part of Challis Natl. Forest. Chief peaks are Borah Peak (12,662 ft/ 3,859 m; highest point in state), Dorion Peak (12,016 ft/ 3,662 m), Leatherman Peak (12,228 ft/3,727 m), Invisible Mt. (11,330 ft/3,453 m), Dickey Peak (11,141 ft/3,396 m).

Lost Springs 1 village (1990 pop. 106), Marion co., central Kansas, 16 mi/26 km N of Marion; 38°34′N 96°57′W. In grain-, livestock-, and oil-producing area. **2** village (1990 pop. 4), Converse co., E Wyo., 23 mi/ 37 km E of Douglas; 42°46′N 104°55′W. Elev. 4,996 ft/ 1,523 m. Coal mines and oil field nearby. Formerly Lost Spring.

Lostant, village (1990 pop. 510), La Salle co., N Ill., 13 mi/ 21 km SW of Ottawa; 41°08′N 89°03′W. In agr. area.

Lostine (LAHS-teen), village (1990 pop. 231), Wallowa co., NE Oregon, 9 mi/14.5 km NW of Enterprise, on Lostine R.; 45°29′N 117°25′W. Grain; livestock. Wallowa R. 2 mi/3.2 km to E. Part of Wallowa-Whitman Natl. Forest to SW, including Eagle Cap Wilderness Area.

Lotbiniére (lot-been-YER), county (□ 726 sq mi/ 1,880 sq km; 1991 pop. 26,633), S Que., Canada, on the St. Lawrence; ⊙ Ste. Croix.

Lotbiniére, village (1991 pop. 975), S Que., Canada, on the St. Lawrence, and 35 mi/56 km WSW of Quebec. Lumbering, dairying.

Lothair 1 (LO-thur), village (1990 pop. 600), Perry co., SE Ky., 2 mi/3.2 km SE of Hazard, in Cumberland foothills, near North Fork of Kentucky R. Bituminous coal. **2** (LAHT-HER), village, (1990 pop. 30), Liberty co., N Mont., 12 mi/19 km W of Chester. Wheat, barley, oats, rye, hay; cattle, hogs, sheep; gas and oil. L. Elwell reservoir (formed by Tiber Dam on Marias R.) to S.

Lott, town (1990 pop. 775), Falls co., E central Texas, near Brazos R., 25 mi/40 km S of Waco; 31°12′N 97°01′W. In cotton, corn, cattle area; light mfg.

Lottsburg, uninc. village, Northumberland co., E Va., 58 mi/93 km SE of Fredericksburg, near Coan R., arm of Potomac R. estuary; 37°57′N 76°31′W. Mfg. (canned seafoods); agr. (tomatoes, grain; poultry; cattle); fish, crabs, oysters.

Lotus Island, St. Lawrence co., N N.Y., in the St. Lawrence R., at Ont. border, 2.5 mi/4 km NE of Alexandria Bay; c.1 mi/1.6 km in diameter; 44°23′N 75°54′W.

Louann (loo-AN), village (1990 pop. 158), Ouachita co., S Ark., 15 mi/24 km NW of El Dorado; 33°23′N 92°47′W.

Loudon (LOU-duhn), county (□ 240 sq mi/622 sq km; 1990 pop. 31,255), E Tenn.; ⊙ Loudon; 35°44′N 84°19′W. In Great Appalachian Valley; crossed by Tennessee and Little Tennessee rivers; bounded NW by Clinch R. Includes part of Fort Loudoun L. (reservoir). Agr. (corn, tobacco, hay, fruit), livestock raising, dairying, wineries; barite mines; large timber tracts (pine, oak). Mfg. at Loudon and Lenoir City. Formed 1870.

Loudon 1 town (1990 pop. 4,114), Merrimack co., S central N.H., 7 mi/11.3 km NE of Concord; 43°19′N 71°26′W. Drained by Soucook R. and Bee Hole Brook. Agr. (poultry; cattle); corn, vegetables, nursery crops; dairying); light mfg. Site of New Hampshire Internatl. Speedway. **2** town (1990 pop. 4,026), ⊙ Loudon co., E Tenn., on Tennessee R., and 28 mi/45 km SW of Knoxville; 35°45′N 84°20′W. Trade, shipping center for timber and farm area; makes tissue, chairs, wine, corn syrup. Nearby is site of Fort Loudon (built 1756), which fell to the Cherokee in 1760 after a long siege. Fort

Loudoun Dam and Reservoir are NE. Settled 1828; inc. 1927.

Loudon, Mount (10,550 ft/3,216 m), SW Alta., Canada, near B.C. border, in Rocky Mts., near Banff Natl. Park, 65 mi/105 km NW of Banff.

Loudonville, village (1990 pop. 2,915), Ashland co., N central Ohio, 17 mi/27 km ESE of Mansfield, and on Black Fork of Mohican R.; 40°38′N 82°14′W. Mfg. foodstuffs, oils. Mohican State Forest and Pleasant Hill Dam are nearby. Laid out 1814.

Loudonville, residential suburb (□ 5 sq mi/13 sq km; 1990 pop. 10,822) of Albany, Albany co., E N.Y., 3 mi/4.8 km N of downtown; 42°42′N 73°46′W. Seat of St. Bernardine of Siena Col.

Loudoun, county (□ 521 sq mi/1,349 sq km; 1990 pop. 86,129), N Va.; ⊙ Leesburg; 39°05′N 77°38′W. In rolling Piedmont region, rising to the Blue Ridge in W; bounded NW by W.Va. state line, N and NE by Potomac R. (Md. state line); drained by Little R. and short Goose Creek. Agr. and country-estate area (known for horse and cattle breeding, fox hunting; also wheat, corn, barley, hay, soybeans, alfalfa, tobacco, apples; cattle, sheep, poultry; dairying); timber; limestone. Part of Harpers Ferry Natl. Historical Park in W. Part of Dulles Internatl. Airport in SE. Appalachian Trail parallels W co. boundary. Formed 1757.

Louds Island, S Maine, in Muscongus Bay, just E of Bristol; 3 mi/4.8 km long, c.½ mi/⅘ km wide. Sometimes called Muscongus Isl.

Louellen (loo-EL-en), village, Harlan co., SE Ky., on Clover Fork of Cumberland R., and 13 mi/21 km ENE of Harlan. Bituminous coal.

Lougheed (lah-HEED, LAH-heed), village (1991 pop. 231), E Alta., Canada, 30 mi/48 km WSW of Wainwright. Grain elevators, stockyards.

Lougheed Island, largest (□ 504 sq mi/1,305 sq km) of the Findlay Isls., NW Franklin dist., N.W.T., Canada, in the Arctic Ocean, N of Bathurst Isl., and separated from Borden Isls. (W) by Prince Gustav Adolph Sea and from Ellef Ringnes Isl. (NE) by Maclean Strait; 77°30′N 105°W. Isl. is 50 mi/80 km long, 12 mi/19 km–15 mi/24 km wide.

Loughman (LOU-muhn), town (□ 3 sq mi/7.8 sq km; 1990 pop. 1,214), Polk co., central Fla., 4 mi/6.4 km SW of Kissimmee; 28°14′N 81°34′W.

Louin (LOO-in), village (1990 pop. 289), Jasper co., E central Miss., 38 mi/61 km WSW of Meridian; 32°04′N 89°15′W. Agr. (cotton, corn; cattle, poultry; dairying); timber. Bienville Natl. Forest to N.

Louis Napoleon, Cape, E Ellesmere Isl., NE Franklin dist., N.W.T., Canada, on Kane Basin, at end of Darling Peninsula (20 mi/32 km long); 79°38′N 72°17′W. Shoreline was explored by Shackleton, 1935.

Louisa 1 county (□ 417 sq mi/1,080 sq km; 1990 pop. 11,592), SE Iowa, on Ill. state line (to E; here formed by Mississippi R.); ⊙ Wapello; 41°13′N 91°15′W. Prairie agr. area (cattle, hogs, poultry; corn, oats, wheat, soybeans) drained by Iowa R. Fertile E sect. (bet. the Iowa and the Mississippi) is artificially drained (pumping stations, ditches). Gypsum and limestone quarries. Lock and Dam No. 17 above Toolesburg. Mark Twain State Wildlife Refuge in E; Toolesburg Indian Mounds in SE near Miss. R. Widespread flooding in 1993. Formed 1836. **2** county (□ 510 sq mi/1,321 sq km; 1990 pop. 20,325), central Va.; ⊙ Louisa; 37°59′N 77°57′W. Bounded N and NE by North Anna R.; drained by South Anna R. Agr. (tobacco, barley, wheat, corn, soybeans, hay; cattle); some timber. North Anna 1 and North Anna 2 nuclear power plants are in NE on L. Anna reservoir in town of Mineral. Formed 1742.

Louisa 1 town (1990 pop. 1,990), ⊙ Lawrence co., NE Ky., 26 mi/42 km S of Ashland, on Big Sandy R. (here formed by junction of Levisa and Tug forks); 38°06′N 82°35′W. Trade and shipping center for mt. agr. area (livestock; corn, alfalfa, tobacco); mfg. (apparel, beverages); also coal mines and fireclay and sand pits. Birthplace of U.S. Supreme Court Justice Fred Vinson. Yatesville L. reservoir, on Blaine Creek, to W. Settled 1789; est. 1822. **2** town (1990 pop. 1,088), ⊙ Louisa co., central Va., 26 mi/42 km E of Charlottesville; 38°01′N 78°00′W. Mfg. (plastic prods., printing and publishing, tobacco processing, paper prods., lumber, clothing); in agr. area (tobacco, grain, soybeans; cattle, poultry; dairying); timber. Green Springs Natl. Historic Landmark Dist.

Louisa (luh-WEE-suh), uninc. village, St. Mary parish, S La., 33 mi/53 km SSE of Lafayette, near W Cote Blanche Bay, Gulf of Mexico, on Cote Blanche Isl. salt dome. Shallow-draft port; mfg. (boat parts, shrimp processing). Cypremort Point State Park to SW.

Louisburg (LOO-is-buhrg), town (1991 pop. 1,261), E Cape Breton Isl., N.S., Canada. The town, an ice-free port, is near the site of the great fortress of Louisbourg, built (1720–1740) by France as its Gibraltar in Amer. Plans were drawn by the great Fr. engineer Vauban, but the work was poorly done, and the garrison was inadequately supplied and at odds with the civilian pop. Fr. privateers, using the harbor as a base, preyed on New England fishermen working the Grand Banks, until 1745, when a small force of New Englanders under William Pepperrell, supported by a fleet of merchantmen commanded by Sir Peter Warren, attacked Louisbourg and forced its surrender. In 1748 it was returned to France by the Treaty of Aix-la-Chapelle in exchange for Madras, India, but it fell (1758) to a Brit. land and sea attack led by Gen. Jeffrey Amherst and Admiral Boscawen, which reduced it to ruins. The site is a natl. historic park, and reconstruction of a portion of the fortified town is completed.

Louisburg 1 town (1990 pop. 1,964), Miami co., E Kansas, near Mo. state line, 10 mi/16 km ENE of Paola; 38°37′N 94°40′W. Shipping point for livestock. Gas transmission and distribution. **2** town (1990 pop. 3,037), ⊙ Franklin co., N central N.C., on Tar R., 28 mi/45 km NE of Raleigh; 36°06′N 78°17′W. RR spur terminus. Trade center for agr. area (tobacco, cotton). Mfg. (food processing, apparel, steel frames, office furniture, wooden prods., lumber). Seat of Louisburg Col. Laurel Mills (1769) to NE. Settled 1758.

Louisburg (LOO-wis-buhrg), village (1990 pop. 42), Lac qui Parle co., SW Minn., near Minnesota R., 11 mi/18 km N of Madison; 45°10′N 96°10′W. Grain; dairying; livestock. Marsh L. (Minnesota R.) to NE, in Lac qui Parle Wildlife Area.

Louise (loo-EEZ), village (1990 pop. 343), Humphreys co., W Miss., 15 mi/24 km SSW of Belzoni; 32°58′N 90°35′W. In agr. area (cotton, grain; cattle). Delta Natl. Forest to SW.

Louise Island (□ 105 sq mi/272 sq km), W B.C., Canada, one of the Queen Charlotte Isls., in Hecate Strait, E of N Moresby Isl.; 15 mi/24 km long, 2 mi/3 km wide. Rises to 3,550 ft/1,082 m.

Louise, Lake, SW Alta., Canada, in the Rocky Mts., in Banff Natl. Park. Lake is 2 mi/3 km long, elev. 5,680 ft/1,731 m. Noted for its scenic beauty, esp. its sunrises, it is surrounded by high peaks, glaciers, and snow fields, which are reflected in its waters. The lake was explored in 1882 and later was named for Princess Louise. It has become a popular year-round tourist and mt.-climbing center. The lake drains to the E into the Bow R.

Louiseville (loo-EEZ-vil), town (1991 pop. 8,000), ⊙ Maskinonge co., S Que., Canada, on R. du Loup, near its mouth on the St. Lawrence, 20 mi/32 km WSW of Trois Rivières. Milling, lumbering, food processing; mfg.

Louisiana (luh-wee-zee-AN-uh), state (□ 51,843 sq mi/134,275 sq km; 1995 est. pop. 4,342,334), S central U.S., admitted to the Union in 1812 as the 18th state; ⊙ BATON ROUGE; 31°04′N 92°00′W. Baton Rouge is the state's 2d-largest city; the largest city is NEW ORLEANS, whose seaport is the busiest in the nation. Other major cities are SHREVEPORT, LAKE CHARLES, KENNER, and LAFAYETTE. La. is bounded on the N by Ark., on the E by Miss. (the state line is formed by the Mississippi R. in the N, by the Pearl R. in the extreme SE), on the S by the Gulf of Mexico, and on the W by Texas (the Sabine R. marks most of the boundary). A low country on the Gulf coastal plain and the Mississippi alluvial plain, La. rises gradually into low hills in NW; highest point is Driskill Mt. (535 ft/163 m) in Bienville parish near Ark. The rainy coast country contains marshes and fertile delta lands; inland are rolling pine hills and prairies. The Mississippi R. dominates the many waterways, but there are other rivers (e.g., the Red R., the Ouachita, the Atchafalaya, and the Calcasieu). The "Pelican State," especially the coast, is threaded by many slow-moving bayous (e.g., the Teche, the Macon, and the Lafourche), all former channels of the Mississippi R. and other rivers that continue to provide outlets during floods. The marshy coast is indented by bays and salt-water lakes, the largest being L. PONTCHARTRAIN, N of New Orleans. There are numerous backwater lakes throughout the delta and coastal areas, and oxbow and horseshoe lakes abound along river margins. Manmade canals criss-cross the state, constructed for shipping and floodwater diversion. The state's canal system is dominated by the Gulf branch of the Intracoastal Waterway, which provides a sheltered barge canal from Fla. to Texas. Major La. shipping outlets include the Mississippi R. Gulf Outlet SE of New Orleans, Houma Navigation Canal, and Port Allen–Morgan City Alternate Route. The system allows for direct ship-to-barge transfer of goods. The climate (subtropical in the S and temperate in the N), together with the rich alluvial soil, makes the state one of the nation's leading producers of sweet potatoes, rice, and sugarcane. Other major agr. commodities are soybeans, cotton; cattle; and dairy prods. Strawberries, vegetables, corn, hay, pecans, and watermelons are also produced in great quantity. Home gardens and nursery crops are major agr. income sources. Fishing is a major industry; shrimp, menhaden, crawfish, crabs, and oysters are principal catches, as well as catfish on inland waters. La. is a leading fur-trapping state (nutria is the primary source of fur); its marshes (7,409 sq mi/19,189 sq km of the state's area is underwater) supply most of the country's muskrat furs. Pelts are also obtained from mink, coypus, opossums, otter, and raccoon. The raising of ratite birds (emus, ostriches) for their meat has become a widespread activity. Alligators are farmed throughout the marshy S part of the state for their meat and hides. The state has great mineral wealth. It leads the nation in the production of salt and sulfur, and it ranks 2d in the production of crude petroleum (of which many deposits are offshore), natural gas, and natural-gas liquids. Timber is plentiful; forests cover almost 50% of the land area. There is 1 natl. forest. The state rapidly industrialized in the 1960s and 1970s. It has giant oil refineries, petrochemical plants, metal foundries, and sawmills and paper mills. Other industries produce foods, transportation equip., and electronic equip. Cajun and Creole foods, music, and traditions have become popular throughout the U.S. during the 1980s and 1990s, resulting in increased tourism to the state. New Orleans, with its exciting nightlife and Old World charm, is the major attraction. It is esp. noted for its picturesque Fr. Quarter, which has many celebrated restaurants, and for the colorful Mardi Gras—perhaps the most famous festival in the U.S.—held annually, on the day leading up to Ash Wednesday, since 1838. Another yearly attraction is the Sugar Bowl football game, staged in the Superdome on New Year's Day. Elsewhere a variety of recreational facilities makes the state an excellent vacationland; some of its lakes (e.g., Pontchartrain) have been highly developed as resort areas, and there is superb hunting and fishing throughout much of the region. La. is rich in tradition and legend, and 3 different groups have contributed to its unique heritage: the Creoles, descendants of the original Fr. colonists; the Cajuns (term derived from Acadian), whose Fr. ancestors were expelled from the Acadia region of N.S., Canada, by the British in the 18th cent.; and the Amer. cotton planters. Along the rivers, bayous, and cypress swamps overhung with Span. moss, some of the old mansions remain, recalling the elegance and splendor of Southern antebellum days. Plantation tours from Baton Rouge, Natchitoches, and many other cities are very popular, while the Cajun country in the Mississippi delta land also attracts visitors—most particularly the Longfellow Evangeline State Commemorative Area, at St. Martinville; and Jean Lafitte Natl. Historic Park, with 4 units in and around New Orleans and Lafayette. La. has a long and colorful history. The region was possibly visited by Cabeza de Vaca and his fellow survivors of a Span. expedition of 1528, and it was certainly seen by some of De Soto's men (1541–1542). In 1682, La Salle reached the mouth of the Mississippi and claimed for France all of the land drained by that river and its tributaries, naming it Louisiana after Louis XIV. Europeans did not permanently settle here until 1699, when Pierre le Moyne, sieur d'Iberville, founded a settlement near Biloxi. This settlement became the seat of govt. for La., an enormous territory embracing the entire Mississippi drainage basin. In 1702, Iberville's brother, the sieur de Bienville, was appointed governor and moved the territorial govt. to Fort Louis on the Mobile R. This colony was later moved (1710) to the present site of Mobile (Ala.), and Mobile became capital of La. Fr. missionaries and fur traders explored some of the vast territory, and Natchitoches (the oldest settlement within the present boundaries of the state of La.) grew from a Fr. military and trading post est. (c.1714) to protect the Red R. area from the Spanish. To increase the value of the colony, France granted (1712) a monopoly of commercial privileges, which in 1717 passed to a company organized by John Law. The promise of riches under Law's Mississippi Scheme brought many settlers to La., and a large number of them remained even after his scheme had collapsed. New Orleans was founded in 1718, and in 1723 became the capital. Large numbers of blacks were brought in as slaves, and the *Code Noir*, adopted in 1724, provided for the rigid control of their lives and the protection of the whites. After the French lost the last conflict of the Fr. and Indian Wars (1754–1763), they secretly ceded (by the Treaty of Fontainebleau in 1762) the area W of the Mississippi and the "Isle of Orleans" to Spain to keep the entire La. territory from falling into the hands of the British. By the Treaty of Paris (1763), Great Britain gained control of all La. E of the Mississippi except the Isle of Orleans; these changes were announced in 1764. The Fr. colonists resisted the new Span. rule, but were subdued and finally Span. mercantilistic monopoly of trade was instituted. During the Span. years, agr. flourished with the cultivation of rice and sugarcane, and New Orleans grew as a major port and trading center. The Span. govt. welcomed thousands of Acadians to the area from Canada, and they settled what came to be known as the Cajun country. During the Amer. Revolution, New Orleans was a center for Span. aid to the colonies. After Spain declared war on Great Britain in 1779, Bernardo de Gálvez, governor of La., became an active ally of the revolutionists, capturing Baton Rouge and Natchez (1779), Mobile (1780), and Pensacola (1781). After the war La.'s control of the great inland trade route, the Mississippi, led to heated controversy with the Americans. In the secret Treaty of San Ildefonso (1800), Napoleon I forced the retrocession of the territory to France. Revelation of this treaty caused profound concern in the U.S. President Jefferson attempted to purchase the Isle of Orleans from France. To the surprise of the Amer. representatives in France, Napoleon decided to sell all of La. to the U.S. The U.S. took possession in 1803, and in 1804 the territory was divided into 2 parts. The S part, which was called the Territory of Orleans, was admitted to the Union in 1812 as the state of La. Settlement (1819) of the W Fla. Controversy gave La. the area bet. the Mississippi and Pearl rivers, which formerly had been part of Fla. After statehood Fr. and Span. influence remained, not only in the Creole and Cajun societies but also in the civil law (based on Fr. and Span. codes) and in the division of the state into parishes rather than cos. In the early years of the 19th cent. the diverse people of La. – the French, the Spanish, the Germans, and Isleños brought by Gálvez from the Canary Isls. – united behind Andrew Jackson to defeat (1815) the British at the Battle of New Orleans during the War of 1812. This victory brought Jackson to natl. prominence even though the war was officially over by the time the battle was fought. (The battle site is contained in Chalmette Natl. Historical Park.) With settlers pouring in from other Southern states, great sugar and cotton plantations developed rapidly in the fertile lowlands, and the less productive uplands also were settled. The state capital was moved several times, finally ending up at Baton Rouge in 1849. The advent of steam propulsion on the Mississippi (the 1st steamboat to navigate the river arrived in New Orleans in 1812) was a boon to the state's economy; by 1840, New Orleans was the nation's 2d-largest port. Plantation owners, with their large landholdings and many slaves (more than 50% of the pop.) dominated politics and largely controlled the state. On Jan. 26, 1861, La. seceded from the Union and 6 weeks later joined the Confederacy. The fall of New Orleans to David G. Farragut in 1862 prefaced the detested military occupation under Gen. B. F. Butler. Occupied La. was a proving ground for Lincoln's moderate restoration program, but after Lincoln's assassination radical Republicans seized control, and La. suffered greatly during Reconstruction. The Ku Klux Klan was particularly active from 1866 to 1871. In the election of 1872 the radical Republican candidate for governor lost but was installed with the help of Federal troops. Reconstruction in La. finally ended with the disputed presidential election of 1876, when La.'s electoral votes were "traded" to the Republicans (whose candidate was Rutherford B. Hayes) in exchange for the withdrawal of Federal troops from the state. Francis R. T. Nicholls, a Democrat, became governor, and white control of the state was reestablished. Economic recovery was slow. The disrupted plantation system was largely replaced by farm tenancy and sharecropping. The decline of steamboat traffic was offset somewhat by new RR bldg. and the opening of the Mississippi R. for oceangoing vessels from New Orleans to the sea (a feat accomplished by James B. Eads) with the construction of jetties at the mouth of the river. Mississippi floods constituted a serious problem, and levee building increased after the flood of 1882; it was only after the flood of 1927 (at the time called Amer.'s greatest peacetime disaster), however, that the Federal govt. undertook a vast control system. The water resources development program encompasses flood control, navigation, drainage, and irrigation. The pattern of La. economy was changed by the discovery of oil and natural gas in 1901, and industries began to grow on the basis of cheap fuel and cheap labor. Medical advances helped to curb the yellow-fever epidemics that had periodically disrupted the state. Industrial growth and the continuing woes of the tenant farmers did not alter control of the state by "Bourbon" Democrats, but in 1928 a virtual revolution occurred when Huey P. Long was elected governor. His almost dictatorial rule, detested by liberals across the nation, brought material progress at the cost of widespread official corruption. Long withstood all outside pressures, including the opposition of President Franklin D. Roosevelt's administration. Long resigned the governorship in 1931 to become a U.S. senator, but he retained control over the state. After his assassination in 1935, his political heirs made their peace with the New Deal, and Federal funds, withheld during Long's last years, were poured into the state. The Bonnet-Carre Spillway, built to divert Mississippi floodwaters into L. Pontchartrain and protect New Orleans and other downstream communities from flood damage, was completed in 1935. The state has a large Afr.-Amer. pop., and the issue of civil rights has long been a bitter one. The process of integration following the 1954 Supreme Court ruling against racial segregation in the public schools was difficult. In 1965, Hurricane Betsy struck La., killing 74 and causing property damage in excess of $1 billion. Hurricane Camille (1969) was much more destructive, ravaging La. and a number of other states and killing 256 people. In April 1973, the Mississippi R. rose to its highest level recorded in La. Its floodwaters, together with those from its tributaries and distributaries, covered more than 10% of the state and caused millions of dollars of damage to crops and property. In 1992, Hurricane Andrew, after bringing severe damage to S Fla., struck S central La., killing 11. La. enjoyed an oil boom in the early 1980s, but when oil prices collapsed in 1986, the state economy did as well. The state's unemployment rate rose to the highest in the nation, and it suffered the effects of massive out-migration. This has placed an ever-greater economic burden on the tourist industry and led to increased efforts to diversify the state economy. Environmental problems also plagued La. during the 1980s and early 1990s. It was discovered that natural erosion, oil exploitation, and river control projects have severely degraded La.'s freshwater marshlands and their wildlife and plant communities, especially the Mississippi delta land. The state has had 11 constitutions since it was admitted to the Union in 1812. Its present constitution (1975) replaced the constitution of 1921, which had been amended more than 500 times. The state's executive branch is headed by a governor elected for a 4-year term and allowed 1 reelection. La.'s bicameral legislature has a senate with 39 members and a house of representatives with 105 members, all elected for 4-year terms. The state elects 2 senators and 7 representatives to the U.S. Congress. Among the state's more prominent institutions of higher learning are Tulane Univ., Univ. of New Orleans, Dillard Univ., Southern Univ., Loyola Univ., and Newcomb Col., all at New Orleans; La. State Univ. and Agr. and Mechanical (A&M) Col., main campus at Baton Rouge; Southern Univ. and Agr. and Mechanical (A&M) Col. (the largest predominantly Afr.-Amer. institution in the country), main campus in Lafayette; Grambling State Univ., at Grambling; Manesse State Univ. in Lake Charles; and La. Tech Univ., at Ruston. La. has 64 parishes: ACADIA, ALLEN, ASCENSION, ASSUMPTION, AVOYELLES, BEAUREGARD, BIENVILLE, BOSSIER, CADDO, CALCASIEU, CALDWELL, CAMERON, CATAHOULA, CLAIBORNE, CONCORDIA, DE SOTO, EAST BATON ROUGE, EAST CARROLL, EAST FELICIANA, EVANGELINE, FRANKLIN, GRANT, IBERIA, IBERVILLE, JACKSON, JEFFERSON, JEFFERSON DAVIS, LAFAYETTE, LAFOURCHE, LA SALLE, LINCOLN, LIVINGSTON, MADISON, MOREHOUSE, NATCHITOCHES, ORLEANS, OUACHITA, PLAQUEMINES, POINTE COUPEE, RAPIDES, RED RIVER, RICHLAND, SABINE, SAINT BERNARD, SAINT CHARLES, SAINT HELENA, SAINT JAMES, SAINT JOHN THE BAPTIST, SAINT LANDRY, SAINT MARTIN, SAINT MARY, SAINT TAMMANY, TANGIPAHOA, TENSAS, TERREBONNE, UNION, VERMILION, VERNON, WASHINGTON, WEBSTER, WEST BATON ROUGE, WEST CARROLL, WEST FELICIANA, and WINN.

Louisiana (loo-WEE-zee-a-nuh), city (1990 pop. 3,967), Pike co., E Mo., on Mississippi R. (here spanned by Champ Clark Bridge), 25 mi/40 km SE of Hannibal; 39°26'N 91°03'W. Agr. (grain, soybeans, corn; hogs; nursery prods.); mfg. (apparel, chemicals, machinery, metal fabrication, tools). Ammonia plant has been converted for study and production of synthetic fuels. Laid out 1818.

Louisiana Point, extreme SW point of La., on Gulf coast at E side of Sabine Pass entrance, 14 mi/23 km SSE of Port Arthur (Texas). Sabine Pass lighthouse (29°43'N 93°51'W) is 2 mi/3.2 km N.

Louisville 1 (LOO-is-vil), city (1990 pop. 12,361), Boulder co., N central Colo., just E of Front Range, suburb 15 mi/24 km NNW of Denver; 39°58'N 105°08'W. Elev. 5,337 ft/1,627 m. Coal-mining point in grain, sugar-beet region. Mfg. (medical equip., communications equip., information storage systems). Inc. 1892. **2** city (1990 pop. 215), Pottawatomie co., NE Kansas, on small affluent of Kansas R., 14 mi/23 km ENE of Manhattan, 3 mi/4.8 km N of Wamego; 39°15'N 96°19'W. Livestock; grain. **3** (LOO-uh-vuhl), city (1990 pop. 269,063), ⊙ Jefferson co., N Ky., on the Ohio R., at the Falls of the Ohio, opposite Jeffersonville and New Albany (Ind.); 38°13'N 85°44'W. Commonly referred to as Falls City and "gateway to the South." It is the largest city in Ky., a major river port, and one of the important industrial, financial, marketing, and shipping centers for the South and Midwest. A diverse mfg. base, including motor vehicles, consumer goods, naval ordnance, and whiskey; other mfg. (wood and paper prods., tobacco prods., food processing, computers and software, chemical processing, aluminum processing, concrete, printing and publishing). Louisville Slugger baseball bat factory and baseball mus. moved here from Jeffersonville, Ind., in 1996. Since the 1970s many industries have relocated to the city's suburbs, following the trend of many U.S. cities. Naval Surface Warfare Center scheduled to close. A settlement grew around a fort built by George Rogers Clark (1778) a base of operations against the British and the Native Americans. The city was chartered by the Va. legislature in 1780 (when Ky. was part of Va.) and named for Louis XVI of France. Louisville developed at the falls, as a portaging place (a canal was built in 1830; the McAlpine Locks currently allow modern barge traffic to pass the falls). After the arrival of the RRs in the mid-19th cent., its role as a shipping center became even more important. During the Civil War it was a center of pro-Union activity in the state and a military and supply base for Federal forces. Louisville Internatl. Airport (Standiford Field) in S part of city, Bowman Field airport is E of downtown. The Univ. of Louisville (est. 1798), Bellarmine Col., Spalding Univ., Jefferson Community Col. (Univ. of Ky.), and Presbyterian and Southern Baptist Theological Seminaries are here. Commonwealth Convention Center. Churchill Downs, a noted horse racetrack and scene of the Kentucky Derby (held annually in May since 1875), is S of downtown; also includes Kentucky Derby Mus. The city has many parks and is the site of the Ky. Fair and Exhibition Grounds. Among the many points of interest are the Amer. Printing House for the Blind; the J. B. Speed Art Mus.; Howard Steamboat Mus. (in Jeffersonville, Ind.), Sons of Amer. Revolution Mus., Col. Harland Sanders Mus. at Kentucky Fried Chicken hq.; Farmington historic home built 1810; the Filson Club, with a historical lib. and mus.; Louisville Zoo; Bernheim Arboretum and Research Forest; Whitehall Mansion (1855); the Jefferson County Courthouse (1850); and old Cave Hill Cemetery (E of downtown), where George Rogers Clark is buried. Nearby is "Locust Grove," built 1790, the last home of Clark; and the Zachary Taylor Natl. Cemetery, in the E suburbs, where President Taylor and his wife are buried. The Fort Knox gold bullion depository is 20 mi/32 km SSW (downstream on Ohio R.) is in the area. E.P. "Tom" Sawyer State Park to E. Inc. 1780. **4** (LOO-is-vil), city (1990 pop. 8,087), Stark co., E central Ohio, 6 mi/10 km ENE of Canton; 40°50′N 81°16′W.

Louisville 1 (LOO-ee-vil), town (1990 pop. 728), Barbour co., SE Ala., 10 mi/16 km SW of Clayton. Lumber; pecans. **2** (LOO-is-vil), town (1990 pop. 2,429), ⊙ Jefferson co., E Ga., on Ogeechee R., c.40 mi/64 km SW of Augusta; 33°00′N 82°24′W. Mfg. of textiles, clothing, electrical transformers. Has old slave market (built before 1800) referred to locally as Mauat House in the center of Broad Street, Several late-18th-cent. houses. Laid out 1786 as the prospective capital of Ga. State bldgs. completed 1795; seat of govt. until 1804, when Milledgeville became capital. The Ga. legislature held its 1st session here in 1776. Town sq. **3** (LOO-is-vuhl), town (1990 pop. 7,169), ⊙ Winston co.; 33°07′N 89°02′W, E central Miss., 45 mi/72 km SW of Columbus. In agr. area (cotton, corn; dairying); timber; mfg. (apparel, furniture, bricks, lumber, consumer goods, motor vehicle parts, construction equip.). Legion State Park to N; Noxubee Natl. Wildlife Refuge to NE; part of Tombigbee Natl. Forest to N: Nanih Waiya Historical Site, anc. Choctaw burial mounds, to SE. Inc. 1836. **4** town (1990 pop. 998), Cass co., E Nebr., 20 mi/32 km SW of Omaha, and on Platte R; 41°00′N 96°09′W. RR junction. Grain; mfg. (Portland cement). Louisville Lakes State Recreation Area nearby.

Louisville (LOU-is-vil), village (1990 pop. 1,098), ⊙ Clay co., S central Ill., 22 mi/35 km W of Olney; 38°46′N 88°30′W. In agr., oil, and natural gas area; corn, wheat, fruit; poultry. On Little Wabash R.

Loup (LOOP), county (□ 571 sq mi/1,479 sq km; 1990 pop. 683), central Nebr.; ⊙ Taylor; 41°55′N 99°27′W. Sand Hills grazing region drained by Calamus and North Loup rivers. Cattle, hogs; corn. Formed 1883.

Loup City (LOOP), town (1990 pop. 1,104), ⊙ Sherman co., central Nebr., 40 mi/64 km NW of Grand Isl. and on Middle Loup R.; 41°16′N 98°58′W. Grain. Bowman L. State Recreation Area to SW; Sherman Reservoir and State Recreation Area to NE. Settled 1873.

Loup River (LOOP), 68 mi/109 km long, E central Nebr.; formed by North and Middle Loup rivers in Howard co., near St. Paul; flows E, past Fullerton and Genoa, to Platte R. at Columbus. Its tributaries flow SE: North Loup, 212 mi/341 km long, rises in Cherry co.; flows past Ord to join the Middle Loup, which also rises in Cherry co. and flows 221 mi/356 km, past part of Nebr. Natl. Forest and Loup City. South Loup, 152 mi/245 km long, rises in Logan co.; flows past Ravenna to join Middle Loup E of Boelus. Calamus R. joins the North Loup, Dismal R. the Middle Loup, and Cedar R. the main stream. Diversion dam SW of Genoa is unit in Loup R. power project, directing water through a canal to generators at Monroe and Columbus.

Lourdes (LOOR-daiz), town, Villa Clara prov., N central Cuba; 22°51′N 80°27′W. Small agr. community in sugarcane region, on RR. Located 6 mi/10 km W of Quntín Banderas sugar mill and 7 mi/12 km W of José R. Riquelme sugar mill.

Louvicourt (loo-vee-KOOR), village, W Que., Canada, 11 mi/18 km ENE of Val d'Or. Gold and copper mining.

Louviers, uninc. village, Douglas co., central Colo., on Plum Creek, near South Platte R., 15 mi/24 km S of Denver, near E edge of Front Range. Elev. 5,680 ft/1,731 m. Mfg. (prefabricated bldgs.). Roxborough State Park and Pike Natl. Forest to W.

Love, county (□ 531 sq mi/1,375 sq km; 1990 pop. 8,157), S Okla.; ⊙ Marietta; 33°57′N 97°15′W. Bounded S by Red R., here forming Texas state line. Includes part of L. Murray (with state park) in NE and hq. of L. Texoma in SE (Red R.). Agr. area (grain, corn, asparagus and other vegetables, watermelons, hay, peanuts; cattle, sheep, hogs, horses); mfg. at Marietta. Formed 1907.

Love, village (1991 pop. 94), E central Sask., Canada, 10 mi/16 km NW of Nipawin. Wheat; dairying.

Love Canal, section of Niagara Falls, N.Y., and a former chemical disposal site. The empty canal was used 1942–1953 by Hooker Chemicals and Plastics Corp. to dump 22,000 tons/19,954 metric tons–25,000 tons/22,675 metric tons of toxic waste; the waste was sealed in metal drums in a manner that has since been declared illegal. The canal was then filled in and the land sold for $1 to the expanding city of Niagara Falls by the chemical company. Housing and an elementary school were built on the site. By the late 1970s several hazardous chemicals had leaked through their drums and risen to the surface. Investigations confirmed the existence of toxins in the soil and determined that they were responsible for the area's unusually high rates of birth defects, miscarriages, cancer, illness, and chromosome damage. Families were evacuated by N.Y. state from the area in 1978 and in 1980, the Love Canal was proclaimed by President Jimmy Carter to be a Federal Disaster Area. At the same time, reacting to the resulting natl. outrage over hidden industrial pollution and triggered by the Love Canal situation, Congress created the Federal Superfund. In early 1980s, the govt. bought and razed 238 houses located next to the dump; 550 houses, farther away, were bought, and ⅔ of them were declared in 1986 to be habitable. In March 1995 N.Y. state closed its public information office, declaring the Love Canal neghborhood to be safe. Since then, the 234 homes in the Emergency Declaration Area Habitable Zone put back on the market have been sold and the neighborhood renamed Black Creek. The original corporation's successor in Dec. 1995 settled with the federal govt., agreeing to pay $102 million to the Federal Superfund and an additional $27 million to the Federal Emergency Management Agency, which handled the early evacuation crisis. N.Y. state settled their suit with the same company for $98 million in June 1994. Total estimated cost of the cleanup was $129 million, and more than $20 million in damages was paid by the chemical company and the city of Niagara Falls to a group of former residents.

Love Point, Md.: see KENT ISLAND.

Love Valley, village (1990 pop. 67), Iredell co., W central N.C., 17 mi/27 km NNW of Statesville; 35°59′N 80°59′W. Tobacco, grain; livestock; timber.

Lovejoy, town (1990 pop. 754), Clayton co., N central Ga., 21 mi/34 km S of Atlanta; 33°26′N 84°19′W. Exurb of Atlanta. Mfg. includes motor vehicle parts, meat prods., food-processing equip.

Lovejoy, Ill.: see BROOKLYN.

Lovelady, village (1990 pop. 587), Houston co., E Texas, 13 mi/21 km S of Crockett; 31°07′N 95°27′W. In agr. area; timber; mfg. (oil and gas processing, plastic processing).

Loveland 1 city (1990 pop. 37,352), Larimer co., N Colo., 10 mi/16 km S of Fort Collins on Big Thompson R.; 40°25′N 105°04′W. Elev. 4,982 ft/1,519 m. Loveland lies in a fertile farm area, irrigated by the Colorado–Big Thompson project, where sugar beets and wheat are grown, also fruit and vegetables, beans, barley; cattle, sheep. The city is also a growing industrial hub, mfg. (bldg. materials, metal prods., electrical equip., computer equip., chemicals, printing and publishing, concrete, medical equip.). Gateway to Rocky Mt. State Park 25 mi/40 km to W; Roosevelt Natl. Forest to W; Boyd L. State Park to NE; Carter L. to SW. Inc. 1881. **2** city (1990 pop. 9,990), on Clermont-Hamilton-Warren co. line, SW Ohio, 18 mi/29 km NE of Cincinnati, on Little Miami R., on edge of suburban development; 39°16′N 84°13′W. Settled 1825, inc. 1876.

Loveland, village (1990 pop. 13), Tillman co., SW Okla., 15 mi/24 km ESE of Frederick; 34°17′N 98°46′W. In agr. area (cotton, grain, peanuts).

Loveland, Lake, Calif.: see SWEETWATER RIVER.

Loveland Pass (11,992 ft/3,655 m), N central Colo., crosses Continental Divide, in Front Range, c.55 mi/89 km W of Denver. U.S. Highway 6 passes through it. Eisenhower Memorial Tunnel to NW, carries Interstate 70 across Divide. Winter sports area. Grays Peak is just E.

Lovell 1 (LUHV-uhl), town (1990 pop. 888), Oxford co., W Maine, on Kezar L., 20 mi/32 km WSW of South Paris; 44°11′N 70°53′W. In resort area; wood prods. **2** town (1990 pop. 2,131), Big Horn co., N Wyo., on Shoshone R., near Mont. state line, 70 mi/113 km W of Sheridan, 65 mi/105 km S of Billings (Mont.); 44°50′N 108°23′W. Elev. 3,814 ft/1,163 m. Supply and processing point in irrigated sugar-beet and grain region; agr. (beet sugar, sugar-beet pellets and pulp, beans); cattle, sheep; mfg. (concrete; gypsum prods., steel fabricating). Oil wells in vicinity. Big Horn L. reservoir (Big Horn R.) and Big Horn Canyon Natl. Recreation Area to E; Big Horn Mts. and Big Horn Natl. Forest also to E. Pryor Mt. Wild Horse Range to NE; Medicine Wheel Natl. Historic Site to E. Laid out 1900 by Mormons.

Lovell, village, Logan co., central Okla., 17 mi/27 km NW of Guthrie. In agr. area.

Lovell's Island (LUH-vuhlz), island, E Mass., in Quincy Bay sect. of Boston Harbor, 6 mi/9.7 km SE of Boston. Part of Boston Harbor Isls. State Park. Former site of Fort Standish, abandoned after World War II.

Lovelock (LUHV-LAHK), town (1990 pop. 2,069), ⊙ Pershing co., W central Nev., on Humboldt R., bet. Trinity (W) and Humboldt (E) ranges, and c.83 mi/134 km NE of Reno; 40°10′N 118°28′W. Elev. 3,977 ft/1,212 m. Trade center for Humboldt irrigation project (barley; cattle, sheep; dairying). Gold, silver, copper, lead, and diatomite are mined in vicinity. Humboldt Sink in Humboldt Wildlife Management Area to SW. Rye Patch Reservoir and State Recreation Area to N, on Humboldt R. Mus. Settled 1860, inc. 1917.

Lovely (LUHV-lee), uninc. town (1990 pop. 900), Martin co., E Ky., 13 mi/21 km NW of Williamson, W Va., on Tug Fork R. (W.Va state line) at mouth of Wolf Creek, in Cumberland Mts. Bituminous coal. Mfg. (coal processing).

Lovenia, Mount, peak (13,219 ft/4,029 m) of Uinta Mts., N Duchesne co., NE Utah, 38 mi/61 km N of Duchesne, in High Uintas Wilderness Area, Ashley Natl. Forest.

Loves Park, city (1990 pop. 15,462), Winnebago co., N Ill., on the Rock R.; 42°20′N 89°00′W. It is chiefly residential. Next to Rock Cut State Park. Inc. 1947.

Lovett (LUHV-et), town, Laurens co., central Ga., 11 mi/ 18 km NE of Dublin; 32°38′N 82°46′W.

Lovettsville, town (1990 pop. 749), Loudoun co., N Va., 8 mi/12.9 km NNE of Leesburg, near Potomac R. (Md. state line), 2 mi/3.2 km S of Brunswick (Md.) across the river; 39°16′N 77°38′W. Light mfg.; agr. (dairying; livestock; grain, apples, soybeans). Harpers Ferry Natl. Historical Park to W.

Lovewell Mountain (LUH-vuhl), peak (2,496 ft/761 m), SW N.H., on Sullivan-Merrimack co. line, near Washington.

Lovewell Pond, Oxford co., W Maine, near Fryeburg; 2 mi/3.2 km long. Monument marks site of victory over Indians, 1725.

Lovewell Reservoir (□ 12 sq mi/31 sq km), Jewell co., N central Kansas, on White Rock Creek, 64 mi/103 km NNW of Salina; 39°53′N 98°02′W. Max. capacity 186,290 acre-ft. Formed by Lovewell Dam (93 ft/28 m high), built (1957) by the Bureau of Reclamation for flood control; also used for irrigation and recreation. Lovewell State Park on N shore.

Lovilia, town (1990 pop. 551), Monroe co., S Iowa, near Cedar Creek, 9 mi/14.5 km NW of Albia; 41°08′N 92°54′W. In bituminous-coal-mining and livestock area; mfg. (feed, concrete blocks).

Loving, county (□ 676 sq mi/1,751 sq km; 1990 pop. 107), W Texas; ⊙ Mentone; 31°50′N 103°34′W. High rolling prairies; bordered N by N.Mex. state line, SW by Pecos R. Elev. c.2,500 ft/762 m–3,400 ft/1,036 m. Some cattle ranching. Oil and natural gas. Red Bluff L. (Pecos R.), used for irrigation and recreation on co. line in NW. Smallest co. (in terms of pop.) in Texas. Formed 1887.

Loving, town (1990 pop. 1,243), Eddy co., SE N.Mex., near Pecos R., 13 mi/21 km SSE of Carlsbad; 32°17′N 104°05′W. In irrigated cotton and alfalfa region; potash and salt mining. Carlsbad Caverns Natl. Park to WSW. Junction of RR spur to potash mines to NE.

Lovingston, uninc. village, ⊙ Nelson co., central Va., 29 mi/47 km NE of Lynchburg. Mfg. (clothing); agr. (primarily apples; also corn, alfalfa; cattle).

Lovington, town (1990 pop. 9,322), ⊙ Lea co., SE N.Mex., on Llano Estacado, near Texas state line, 20 mi/ 32 km NW of Hobbs; 32°57′N 103°20′W. RR terminus. Trade center in livestock, grain, vegetables, melons; dairying and poultry raising, cotton. Mfg. (food, engines). Potash mines and oil wells in vicinity. Rodeo and co. fair take place here in August. Founded 1908.

Lovington, village (1990 pop. 1,143), Moultrie co., central Ill., 17 mi/27 km ESE of Decatur; 39°42′N 88°37′W. Corn, wheat, soybeans; livestock; dairy products. Inc. 1873.

Low and Burbanks Grant, land grant, Coos co., N central N.H., 13 mi/21 km SW of Berlin. Wilderness area in White Mt. Natl. Forest in Presidential Range of White Mts.

Low, Cape, S extremity of Southampton Isl., E Keewatin dist., N.W.T., Canada, on Hudson Bay; 63°07′N 85°18′W.

Low Moor, town (1990 pop. 280), Clinton co., E Iowa, 9 mi/14.5 km WSW of Clinton; 41°47′N 90°20′W. In agr. area.

Low Moor, uninc. village, Alleghany co., NW Va., 5 mi/ 8 km E of Covington, on Jackson R., in George Washington Natl. Forest; 37°47′N 79°59′W. Light mfg.; agr. (grain, apples; cattle); timber.

Low Point, cape, NE N.S., Canada, on NE Cape Breton Isl., 9 mi/14 km N of Sydney; 46°16′N 60°07′W. Lighthouse.

Lowden, town (1990 pop. 726), Cedar co., E Iowa, 12 mi/ 19 km NE of Tipton; 41°51′N 90°55′W. Limestone quarries nearby.

Lowden, uninc. village (1990 pop. 50), Walla Walla co., SE Wash., 11 mi/18 km W of Walla Walla, on Walla Walla R. Grain, vegetables, grapes; livestock. Wineries.

Lowe, Mount (5,603 ft/1,708 m), Los Angeles co., S Calif., in San Gabriel Mts., N of Pasadena and just NW of Mt. Wilson. Astronomical observatory (built 1894).

Formerly had incline RR to summit. In Angeles Natl. Forest. Bear Canyon to N.

Lowell (LO-uhl), city (□ 14 sq mi/36 sq km; 1990 pop. 103,439), ⊙ Middlesex co., NE Mass., at the confluence of the Merrimack and Concord rivers; 42°38′N 71°19′W. High-technology computer industries have developed here; other mfg. includes electronic, electrical, and telecommunications equip., textiles, rubber prods., chemicals, machine parts, foodstuffs, shoes, paper, and plastics. The city grew after textile mills were built at Pawtucket Falls, and it became one of the major textile centers of the country. It has rebounded somewhat after the collapse of the computer mfg. industry in 1992. Lowell State Col. and Lowell Technological Inst. and a branch of Univ. of Mass. are here. Now home of 2d-largest Cambodian pop. in U.S. The city has several fine parks, and James Whistler's birthplace is preserved. Oldest American boat shop (1793) still in operation is here. Charles Dickens visited Lowell in 1842 and described it in *American Notes*. Site of Lowell Natl. Historical Park, commemorating Amer. Industrial Revolution; Heritage State Park. Settled 1653, set off from Chelmsford 1826, inc. as a city 1836.

Lowell 1 town (1990 pop. 1,224), Benton co., extreme NW Ark., suburb 5 mi/8 km from Rogers (W) and Springdale (S), in the Ozarks; 36°16′N 94°08′W. Mfg. (sheet metal). **2** town (1990 pop. 6,430), Lake co., NW Ind., 10 mi/16 km SSW of Crown Point; 41°17′N 87°25′W. Consumer goods, automotive parts, furniture. Settled 1849, laid out 1853. **3** town (1990 pop. 267), Penobscot co., central Maine, 30 mi/48 km NNE of Bangor; 45°13′N 68°30′W. In hunting, fishing area. **4** town (1990 pop. 3,983), Kent co., SW Mich., 17 mi/27 km E of Grand Rapids, on Grand R. at mouth of Flat R.; 42°55′N 85°20′W. RR junction. In agr. area (apples, cherries); mfg. (motor vehicle parts, wire prods., chemical sprayers). Resort. Settled 1821, inc. 1859. **5** town (1990 pop. 2,704), Gaston co., S N.C., suburb 4 mi/ 6.4 km E of Gastonia near South Fork of Catawba R.; 35°16′N 81°05′W. Mfg. (metal fabrication; dye, textiles). **6** town (1990 pop. 785), Lane co., W Oregon, 17 mi/ 27 km SE of Eugene, on Middle Fork of Willamette R., below Lookout Point Dam; 43°55′N 122°46′W. Timber; dairying; poultry. Fall Creek reservoir to N. Elijah Bristow State Park to W; Willamette Natl. Forest to E; Umpqua Natl. Forest to SE. **7** town (1990 pop. 594), Orleans co., N Vt., on Missisquoi R., 16 mi/26 km SW of Newport; 44°47′N 72°27′W. Asbestos mining.

Lowell 1 village, Cochise co., SE Ariz., in Mule Mts., near Mex. border, 3 mi/4.8 km SE of Bisbee. Elev. 5,250 ft/ 1,600 m. Copper mining. **2** village (1990 pop. 617), Washington, SE Ohio, 8 mi/13 km NNW of Marietta, and on Muskingum R., in agr. area; 39°31′N 81°30′W. **3** village, Snohomish co., NW Wash., suburb 3 mi/4.8 km S of Everett, on Snohomish R. **4** village (1990 pop. 300), Dodge co., S central Wis., 8 mi/12.9 km S of Beaver Dam; 43°20′N 88°49′W. In dairying region. Cheese.

Lowell Historical Park (LO-uhl), NE Mass., authorized 1978. Restored site of 1st integrated textile mill. Natl. Historic Site maintained by Natl. Park Service.

Lowell, Lake, reservoir, Canyon co., SW Idaho, bet. Snake (SW) and Boise (N) rivers, in Deer Flat Natl. Wildlife Refuge, 5 mi/8 km W of Nampa; 43°34′N 116°45′W. Max. capacity c.177,000 acre-ft; 9 mi/14.5 km long, 2 mi/3.2 km wide. Formed by 3 earth-fill dams; fed by irrigation canal extending W from diversion dam on Boise R. 7 mi/11.3 km SE of Boise. Supplies water for Arrow Rock division of Boise irrigation project. Also known as Deer Flat Reservoir.

Lowell Observatory, astronomical observatory located in Flagstaff, Coconino co., N central Ariz., on Mars Hill, near Thorpe park, W of downtown. It was founded in 1894 by Percival Lowell, the Amer. amateur astronomer who popularized the idea that Mars might support intelligent life. Its original telescope, still in operation, is a 24-in/61-cm refractor. A 42-in/107-cm reflector was added, and in 1929 the 13-in/33-cm A. Lawrence Lowell photographic camera began operation. Also at the observatory's original Mars Hill site

and at its nearby Anderson Mesa station are 72-in/183-cm, 31-in/79-cm, 24-in/61-cm, and 21-in/53-cm reflecting telescopes. Many discoveries of fundamental importance were made at the observatory, especially by V. M. Slipher, its director from 1916 to 1954. By 1917 he had determined through spectroscopic analysis the radial velocities of most spiral nebulae then known. His discovery that nearly all these nebulae, now known as galaxies, were apparently moving away from the earth led to Hubble's work and the discovery of the expanding universe. Beginning in 1905 the observatory made a concerted search for a trans-Neptunian planet; this led to the discovery of Pluto by Clyde Tombaugh in 1930. Principal research programs involve the discovery and determination of orbits for new asteroids, a search for nearby stars, and the measurement of light and motion of close double stars, nebulae, and other galactic objects.

Lowellville, village (1990 pop. 1,349), Mahoning co., E Ohio, 8 mi/13 km SE of Youngstown, on Mahoning R., near Pa. state line; 41°02′N 80°32′W. Settled c.1800, inc. 1836.

Lower, township (1990 pop. 20,820), Cape May co., S N.J., 2 mi/3.2 km N of Cape May; 38°58′N 74°54′W. Inc. 1798.

Lower Allen, uninc. town (1990 pop. 6,329), Cumberland co., S Pa., residential suburb 5 mi/8 km SW of Harrisburg; 40°13′N 76°54′W. Camp Hill State Correctional Center to E.

Lower Ammonoosuc River, N.H.: see AMMONOOSUC RIVER.

Lower Arrow Lake, Canada: see ARROW LAKES.

Lower Burrell, city (1990 pop. 12,251), Westmoreland co., SW Pa., suburb 18 mi/29 km NE of Pittsburgh, on Allegheny R., Little Pucketta Creek to S; 40°34′N 79°42′W. Mfg. (steel fabrication, machinery, fabricated metal prods.). Agr. (grain, soybeans, apples; livestock; dairying). City's steel-based economy declined in the 1970s and 1980s. Inc. 1959.

Lower California: see BAJA CALIFORNIA.

Lower Canada: see QUEBEC, prov.

Lower Chateaugay Lake, N.Y.: see UPPER CHATEAUGAY LAKE.

Lower Crystal Springs, reservoir (□ 2 sq mi/5.2 sq km), San Mateo co., central Calif., on San Mateo Creek, in San Andreas Rift Zone and San Francisco State Fish and Game Refuge, 6 mi/9.7 km WSW of San Mateo; 37°32′N 122°22′W. Max. capacity 71,570 acre-ft. Formed by Lower Crystal Springs Dam (140 ft/43 m), built (1888) for water supply; owned by City and County of San Francisco.

Lower East Side, section of SE Manhattan, N.Y. city, SE N.Y., bounded on E by East R., S by Fulton and Franklin Sts., W by Pearl St. and Broadway, and N by 14th St.; 40°43′N 73°59′W. Prototypical immigrant neighborhood of N.Y. city, 1st populated by Irish immigrants in the 1840s. Its distinctive character, however, was established by the flood (beginning in the 1880s) of E Eur. Jews, Russians, Ukrainians, Slovaks, Romanians, Hungarians, Poles, Greeks, and Italians. In 1920 the Jewish enclave alone numbered 400,000, fostering some 500 synagogues and religious schools. By the late 19th cent., it was such a rundown slum that it defied even the efforts of noted reformer Jacob A. Riis to improve it. In 1936, in an attempt to replace the squalid tenements here, the city's housing authority constructed its 1st houses at 3rd St. and 1st Ave. Following World War II, it became the 1st integrated neighborhood in the city, with an influx of Afr. Americans and Puerto Ricans. Now it is heavily Chin., esp. in the S part; other ethnic groups living here include E and S Asians, Dominicans, and Latin and Central Americans. Home of such artists and entertainers as Al Jolson, George and Ira Gershwin, Irving Berlin, and the Marx Brothers.

Lower Fox River, Wis.: see FOX RIVER.

Lower Granite Lake, reservoir, on Garfield-Whitman co. border, SE Wash., on Snake R., extends SE into Asotin and Nez Perce cos., 13 mi/21 km SW of Pullman;

46°38′N 117°11′W. Max. capacity 483,800 acre-ft; 58 mi/ 93 km long. Clearwater R. enters from E at Lewiston, forming 15-mi/24-km E arm. Formed by Lower Granite Lock and Dam (105 ft/32 m high), built (1975) by the Army Corps of Engineers for power generation and navigation.

Lower Kalskag, village (1990 pop. 291), SW Alaska, near Kalskag, on Kuskokwim R.; 61°31′N 160°20′W.

Lower Klamath Lake, intermittent lake in NE corner of Siskiyou co., N Calif., near Oregon state line, c.20 mi/ 32 km S of Klamath Falls, Oregon. Variable in size and depth. Serves as catch basin for surplus irrigation water, which is pumped (NW) into Klamath R. through Klamath Strait (7 mi/11.3 km long; largely in Oregon) and used to generate power at Copco No. 1 Dam on Klamath R. in Calif. U.S. bird refuge (□ c.82,000 acres/ 33,185 ha) occupies N half of Lower Klamath L. and extends N into Klamath co., Oregon.

Lower Lake, uninc. town (1990 pop. 1,217), Lake co., NW Calif., at S end of Clear L., 30 mi/48 km NNE of Santa Clara, on Cache Creek; 38°55′N 122°37′W. Farm center (walnuts, pears, grapes, oats; cattle). Mineral springs (resorts) nearby. Clear L. State Park to NW.

Lower Leelanau Lake, Mich.: see LEELANAU, LAKE.

Lower Merion, township and upper-income residential suburb (1990 pop. 58,003) of Philadelphia, Montgomery co., SE Pa. 8 mi/12.9 km WNW of downtown; 39°59′N 75°16′W. Includes Ardmore (chief center of township); Bala-Cynwyd, part of Bryn Mawr, seat of Bryn Mawr Col. (in W); Gladwyne; Merion (or Merion Station); Penn Wynne; West Manayunk; Wynnewood; and part of Rosemont, seat of Rosemont Col. (in W). Bounded NW by Schuylkill R., also in part of NW and SE by Philadelphia. Eastern Baptist Theological Seminary and St. Charles Borromeo Seminary in S. Appleford-Parsons Bank Arboretum and Henry Foundation Botanical Research Center in N.

Lower Michigan, region (□ 40,494 sq mi/104,879 sq km; 1990 pop. 8,981,382), S Mich. The region lies S of Straits of Mackinac, which separate it from the Upper Peninsula (U.P.), or Upper Mich.; connected to the Upper Peninsula by Mackinac Bridge. Also referred to as the lower peninsula, it is bounded W by L. Michigan, N by the Straits, E by L. Huron, St. Clair R., L. St. Clair, Detroit R., and L. Erie, S by Ohio and Ind. Comprises 67 of state's 83 cos. Unlike the Upper Peninsula, it is highly industrialized, esp. S ½, and it is noted for its agr. prods., esp. its fruits and vegetables. It is characterized by low moraines, sand dunes, marshes, and lakes, all remnants of past glaciation.

Lower Paia (PAH-EE-ah), village, N Maui, Maui co., Hawaii, 8 mi/12.9 km ENE of Wailuku, on coast. Paia Sugar Mill at Paia to SE. Mantokui Buddhist Mission to NE; H.P. Baldwin Beach Park to SW.

Lower Red Lake, Minn.: see RED LAKE.

Lower Red Rock Lake, Mont.: see RED ROCK LAKES.

Lower Rice Lake, Clearwater co., NW central Minn., 27 mi/43 km WSW of Upper Rice L., fed from S and drained NW by Wild Rice R.; also fed from NE by Mosquito R.; 47°21′N 95°28′W. Marshy area in White Earth Indian Reservation.

Lower Saint Croix National Scenic Riverway (KROI) (□ 15 sq mi/39 sq km), Washington and Chisago cos., E Minn. and Pierce, St. Croix, and Polk cos., NW Wis. Scenic lower course (52 mi/84 km) of the St. Croix R.; lower 27 mi/43 km federally owned. Part of the Wild and Scenic Rivers System. Hq. at St. Croix Falls, Wis. Authorized 1972.

Lower Saint Mary Lake, Mont.: see GLACIER NATIONAL PARK.

Lower Saint Regis Lake, N.Y.: see SAINT REGIS RIVER.

Lower Salem (SAI-luhm), village (1990 pop. 103), Washington co., SE Ohio, 10 mi/16 km NNE of Marietta; 39°34′N 81°23′W.

Lower Saranac Lake, N.Y.: see SARANAC LAKES.

Lower Savage Islands, group of 3 small isls., SE Franklin dist., N.W.T., Canada, off SE Baffin Isl., in Gabriel Strait (arm of Hudson Strait); 61°48′N 65°24′W.

Lower Tallassee Dam, Ala.: see THURLOW DAM.

Lower Vacherie (VASH-ree), uninc. town (1990 pop.

3,462), St. James parish, La., 9 mi/14.5 km SE of Convent; 29°56′N 90°40′W. Oak Alley plantation 5 mi/8 km N; gas field nearby.

Lower Yosemite Falls, Calif.: see YOSEMITE NATIONAL PARK.

Lowesville (LOZ-vil), uninc. town (1990 pop. 1,092), Lincoln co., W central N.C., residential community 16 mi/26 km NNW of Charlotte, near Catawba R.; 35°25′N 81°00′W. (Mountain Isl. L. reservoir SE; Cowans Ford Dam to NE forms L. Norman reservoir). Cotton, grain, sweet potatoes; livestock; dairying.

Lowndes 1 (LOUNDS), county (□ 725 sq mi/ 1,878 sq km; 1990 pop. 12,658), S central Ala.; ⊙ Hayneville. In the Black Belt; bounded N by Alabama R.; drained by its tributaries. Cotton, corn, soybeans; dairying; poultry; lumber milling. Formed 1830. **2** (LOUNDZ), county (□ 511 sq mi/1,323 sq km; 1990 pop. 75,981), S Ga.; ⊙ Valdosta; 30°50′N 83°16′W. Bounded S by Fla. state line; drained by Withlacoochee R. Coastal plain agr. (tobacco, cotton, soybeans, peanuts, corn); cattle, hogs; forestry (lumber and byprods.). Formed 1825. **3** county (□ 516 sq mi/ 1,336 sq km; 1990 pop. 59,308), E Miss.; ⊙ Columbus; 33°28′N 88°26′W. Bordered E by Ala. state line; drained by Tombigbee R. (forms Columbus L. reservoir on NW boundary) and Luxapalila Creek. Agr. (cotton, corn, hay, soybeans, wheat; cattle); timber. L. Lowndes State Park in E; Buttahatchie R. forms part of N boundary. Formed 1830.

Lowndesville (LOUNZ-vil), village (1990 pop. 162), Abbeville co., NW S.C., 19 mi/31 km S of Anderson; 34°12′N 82°39′W. Agr. area.

Lowry 1 (LOU-ree), village (1990 pop. 233), Pope co., W Minn., 7 mi/11.3 km NW of Glenwood; 45°42′N 95°31′W. Livestock; grain; dairying; mfg. (printing and publishing). L. Reno to NE. **2** village (1990 pop. 15), Walworth co., N central S.Dak., 13 mi/21 km S of Selby, on Swan Creek; 45°19′N 99°58′W.

Lowry Air Force Base, Colo.: see DENVER.

Lowry City (LOU-ree), city (1990 pop. 723), St. Clair co., W Mo., near Truman L. (Osage R.), 7 mi/11.3 km N of Osceola; 38°08′N 93°43′W. Corn, hay; cattle.

Lowry Crossing, town (1990 pop. 865), Collin co., N Texas, residential suburb 28 mi/45 km NE of Dallas, and 5 mi/8 km E of McKinney, on East Fork of Trinity R., just N of L. Lavon reservoir; 33°10′N 96°32′W. Agr. area on urban fringe.

Lowrys (LOU-reez), village (1990 pop. 200), Chester co., N S.C., 15 mi/24 km SW of Rock Hill; 34°47′N 81°14′W. Agr. in area includes livestock; grain; dairying.

Lowther Island, central Franklin dist., N.W.T., Canada, in Barrow Strait, bet. Bathurst Isl. and Prince of Wales Isl.; 74°35′N 97°35′W. Isl. is 17 mi/27 km long, 2 mi/ 3 km–6 mi/10 km wide.

Lowville (LOU-vil), village (□ 1 sq mi/2.6 sq km; 1990 pop. 3,632), ⊙ Lewis co., N central N.Y., on Black R., 25 mi/40 km SE of Watertown; 43°47′N 75°29′W. Trade center in dairying area; mfg. of dairy prods., sporting goods; timber. Settled 1798, inc. 1854.

Loxley, town (1990 pop. 1,161), Baldwin co., SW Ala., 19 mi/31 km ESE of Mobile; 30°37′N 87°45′W. Cotton ginning; meat processing and rendering; furniture mfg.; metal fabrication; wood prods.

Loyal, town (1990 pop. 1,244), Clark co., central Wis., 17 mi/27 km WNW of Marshfield; 44°44′N 90°30′W. In dairying region. Cheese; agr. machinery. Inc. as city in 1948.

Loyal, village (1990 pop. 76), Kingfisher co., central Okla., 13 mi/21 km NW of Kingfisher; 35°58′N 98°07′W. In agr. area; mfg. (steel items). Inc. 1930.

Loyalhanna (LOI-uhl-HA-nah), uninc. town (1990 pop. 1,700), Westmoreland co., SW Pa., suburb 1 mi/1.6 km ENE of Latrobe; 40°19′N 79°21′W. Mfg. (metal and plastic fabrication, electrical equip.).

Loyalhanna Creek (LOI-uhl-HA-nah), c.50 mi/80 km long, SW Pa.; rises in S Westmoreland co., flows 1st NE, then NNW past Ligonier and Latrobe, joins Conemaugh R. at Saltsburg to form Kiskiminetas R.; 40°07′N 79°20′W. Loyalhanna L., flood-control reservoir, 4.5 mi/7.2 km above mouth.

Loyall (LOI-uhl), town (1990 pop.1,100), Harlan co., SE Ky., 2 mi/3.2 km W of Harlan, in the Cumberland Mts., on Cumberland R.; 36°51′N 83°20′W. Bituminous coal; timber; mfg. (concrete, signs). Kentenia State Forest to NE; part of Daniel Boone Natl. Forest to N. Inc. 1928.

Loyalsock Creek, c.60 mi/97 km long, N central Pa.; rises in E Sullivan co. at Wyoming co. line; 41°28′N 76°14′W. Flows WSW past Mildred, through Wyoming and Tiadaghton state forests, to West Branch of Susquehanna R. at Montoursville, 3 mi/ 4.8 km E of Williamsport.

Loyalton, city (1990 pop. 931), Sierra co., NE Calif., in Sierra Valley of the Sierra Nevada, 23 mi/37 km NW of Reno (Nev.); 39°41′N 120°14′W. Dairying; alfalfa, hay, field crops; cattle.

Loyalton, village, Edmunds co., N central S.Dak., 16 mi/ 26 km SW of Ipswich; 45°17′N 99°16′W.

Loyola, uninc. town (1990 pop. 3,076), Santa Clara co.; W Calif., residential suburb 12 mi/19 km W of San Jose, and 4 mi/6.4 km SSW of Mountain View; 37°21′N 122°06′W. Castle Rock State Park to S; Portola State Park to SW. Santa Cruz Mts. to SW.

Luana, town (1990 pop. 190), Clayton co., NE Iowa, 15 mi/24 km N of Elkader; 43°03′N 91°27′W. In corn, livestock, dairying (cheese, cream, whey prods.) region.

Luana Point, cape, St. Elizabeth parish, SW Jamaica, 4 mi/6.4 km W of Black River; 18°03′N 77°55′W.

Lubbock, county (□ 900 sq mi/2,331 sq km; 1990 pop. 222,636), NW Texas; ⊙ Lubbock; 33°36′N 101°49′W. Elev. 3,000 ft/914 m–3,500 ft/1,067 m. Drained by intermittent N Fork Double Mt. Fork of Brazos R. (forms Buffalo Springs L. in SE), Yellow House Draw and Blackwater Draw. Major RR junction and center; one of state's leading agr. cos.(cotton, sorghum, wheat, hay, vegetables, sunflowers, soybeans; beef cattle, sheep, hogs, poultry; eggs). Oil and gas; stone, sand, and gravel. Lubbock L. Landmark State Park at center of co., in Lubbock city. Hunting, fishing. Formed 1876.

Lubbock, city (1990 pop. 186,206), ⊙ Lubbock co., NW Texas, c.260 mi/418 km WNW of Fort Worth; 33°34′N 101°52′W. Elev. 3,241 ft/988 m. In the LLANO ESTACADO region of the Great Plains, on N Fork Double Mt. Fork of the Brazos R., at confluence of Yellow House Draw and Blackwater Draw. Lubbock was settled in 1879 by Quakers. It is the trade center for the cotton- and grain-growing region of Texas and E N.Mex. Mfg. (cottonseed oil, earth-moving equip., wineries, food processing, dairy prods., pumps, and irrigation equip.). Lubbock Internatl. Airport in N. In Mackenzie Park a prairie-dog town has been preserved. Lubbock L. Landmark State Park is N part of city. Site is an important geological formation; Buffalo Springs L. reservoir to SE. Texas Tech Univ. and Lubbock Christian Univ. are in the city. Reese Air Force Base where jet pilots are trained, is at W end of city. Buddy Holly Statue and Walk of Fame honors Texas music legends. Inc. 1909.

Lubec (loo-BEK), town (1990 pop. 1,853), Washington co., E Maine, on the coast, 25 mi/40 km ENE of Machias; 44°49′N 67°01′W. Resort, fishing (sardine canning). West Quoddy Head, SE of Lubec village (1990 pop. 1,536), is easternmost point of U.S. On Treat's Isl., in Cobscook Bay, is North Lubec village. Settled c.1780, inc. 1811.

Lubeck (loo-BEK), uninc. town (1990 pop. 1,579), Wood co., NW W.Va., 5 mi/8 km SW of Parkersburg; 39°14′N 81°32′W. Agr. (grain, tobacco); livestock; poultry. Blennerhassett Isl. Historic State Park, on Blennerhassett Isl. in Ohio R., to N.

Lublin, village (1990 pop. 129), Taylor co., central Wis., 41 mi/66 km NE of Eau Claire; 45°04′N 90°43′W. In lumbering and dairying region. On the S edge of Chequamegon Natl. Forest to NE.

Lucama (LOOK-uh-mah), town (1990 pop. 933), Wilson co., E central N.C., 7 mi/11.3 km SW of Wilson; 35°38′N 78°00′W. Tobacco, cotton, peanuts, sweet potatoes, grain, poultry, livestock. Mfg. (sportswear, pallets).

Lucan (LOO-kuhn), village (1991 pop. 1,847), S Ont., Canada, 16 mi/26 km NW of London; 43°11′N 81°24′W. Lumbering, fruit growing.

Lucan (loo-KAN), village (1990 pop. 235), Redwood co., SW Minn., 17 mi/27 km SW of Redwood Falls, near Sleepy Eye Creek; 44°24′N 95°24′W. Corn, oats, soybeans; livestock; dairying; mfg. (chassis liners, millwork).

Lucania, Mount, 17,147 ft/5,226 m high, in the St. Elias Mts., SW Yukon Territory, Canada, near the Alaska border; Canada's 3rd-tallest peak.

Lucas 1 county (□ 434 sq mi/1,124 sq km; 1990 pop. 9,070), S Iowa; ⊙ Chariton; 41°01′N 93°27′W. Prairie agr. area (hogs, cattle, poultry, corn, hay) drained by Chariton R. and Whitebreast Creek. Bituminous-coal deposits mined in E. Has state parks. Formed 1846. **2** county (□ 343 sq mi/888 sq km; 1990 pop. 462,361), NW Ohio; 41°39′N 83°40′W. Bounded N by Mich. state line, SE by Maumee R., and NE by W end of L. Erie. Chief agr. prods. are corn, vegetables, wheat; agr. bedding plants. Mfg. (paper prods., glass, motor vehicles and associated prods.). Includes Fallen Timbers State Park and site of old Fort Meigs. Formed 1835.

Lucas 1 town (1990 pop. 224), Lucas co., S Iowa, on Whitebreast Creek, and 7 mi/11.3 km W of Chariton; 41°01′N 93°27′W. In livestock and grain area. John L. Lewis b. here in 1880. **2** town (1990 pop. 2,205), Collin co., N Texas, residential suburb 25 mi/40 km NE of Dallas, and 10 mi/16 km ENE of Plano, near W shore of L. Lavon reservoir, in rapidly growing urban fringe; 33°06′N 96°34′W. Recreation.

Lucas 1 (LOO-kuhs), village (1990 pop. 452), Russell co., central Kansas, 18 mi/29 km NE of Russell; 39°03′N 98°32′W. Livestock, grain. Mfg. (farm machinery, feeds). Concrete sculpture of the Garden of Eden is here. Wilson L. Reservoir and dam; Wilson State Park to S. **2** village (1990 pop. 730), Richland co., N central Ohio, 6 mi/10 km SE of Mansfield; 40°42′N 82°25′W.

Lucasville, uninc. village (1990 pop. 1,575), Scioto co., S Ohio, 9 mi/14 km N of Portsmouth; 38°52′N 82°59′W. Location of a federal maximum security prison.

Lucaya (loo-KIE-yuh), locality, just E of Freeport, on Grand Bahama Isl., N Bahamas; 26°32′N 78°40′W. A resort and residential community with marinas, golf courses, and a Mus. of Underwater Exploration.

Luce (LOOS), county (□ 1,911 sq mi/4,949 sq km; 1990 pop. 5,763), NE Upper Peninsula, Mich.; ⊙ Newberry; 46°45′N 85°35′W. Bounded N by L. Superior; drained by Tahquamenon R. and small Two Hearted R. Forest and farm area (forage, potatoes, hay, oats; cattle, livestock); lumbering; recreation. Some mfg. at Newberry. Includes part of Manistique L. and North Manistique L. Part of Tahquamenon Falls State Park in NE; Muskallonge L. State Park in N; Big Village Ski Area in S. Formed and organized 1887.

Lucea, town (1991 pop. 5,419), ⊙ Hanover parish, NW Jamaica, minor port 17 mi/27 km W of Montego Bay, 95 mi/153 km WNW of Kingston; 18°27′N 78°10′W. Has fine, almost landlocked, harbor. Exports bananas and yams. Has old churches. Phosphate deposits nearby.

Lucedale (LOOS-dail), town (1990 pop. 2,592), ⊙ George co.; 30°55′N 88°35′W, SE Miss., 36 mi/58 km WNW of Mobile, Ala., and 38 mi/61 km N of Pascagoula, Miss. In agr. (cotton, corn, vegetables) and timber area; mfg. (storage tanks, jewelry, concrete, wood prods., knitting kits). Pascagoula River Wildlife Management Area to SW; Palestine Gardens to N, 20-acre/8-ha scale model of the Holy Land.

Lucerne 1 (loo-SUHRN), uninc. town (1990 pop. 2,011), Lake co.; NW Calif., 21 mi/34 km ESE of Ukiah, on N shore of Clear L. Mendocino Natl. Forest to N; 39°05′N 122°49′W. Walnuts, pears, oats, cattle. Tourism. **2** town (1990 pop. 51), Putnam co., N Mo., 16 mi/26 km W of Unionville; 40°27′N 93°17′W.

Lucerne, village, Cass co., N central Ind., 8 mi/12.9 km NNW of Logansport. In agr. area (corn, soybeans, hogs); mfg. (food grinding, fertilizer blending).

Lucerne Lake, San Bernardino co., S Calif., intermittently dry bed, in Mojave Desert, 17 mi/27 km E of Victorville; c.6 mi/9.7 km long. Town of Lucerne Valley to S.

Lucerne Mines (LOO-suhrn) or **Lucerne**, uninc. town (1990 pop. 1,074), Center township, Indiana co., W central Pa., 4 mi/6.4 km S of Indiana, on Yellow Creek, just NE of its mouth on Two Lick Creek; 40°32′N 79°09′W. Agr. (corn, hay, dairying); mfg. (voltage suppressors, hydraulic equip.).

Lucerne Valley, uninc. town (1990 pop. 1,300), San Bernardino co., S Calif., 30 mi/48 km NE of San Bernardino, at N edge of San Bernardino Mts., and SW edge of Mojave Desert. Cattle, fruit, alfalfa, grain. Mfg. (cement, industrial chemicals). Limestone quarrying. San Bernardino Natl. Forest to S.

Lucerne-in-Maine, Maine: see DEDHAM.

Luceville (LOOS-vil), village (1991 pop. 1,399), SE Que., Canada, near the St. Lawrence, 11 mi/18 km NE of Rimouski; 48°31′N 68°20′W. Dairying, pig raising.

Lucien (LOO-see-en), village, Noble co., N Okla., 9 mi/14.5 km W of Perry.

Luck, town (1990 pop. 1,022), Polk co., NW Wis., 37 mi/60 km WNW of Rice L., in wooded lake area; 45°34′N 92°28′W. Mfg. (food prods., wood moldings and picture frames; wire screen cloth, lumber, furniture).

Luckenbach (LOO-ken-bahk), uninc. village (1990 pop. 25), Gillespie co., S central Texas, 55 mi/89 km NNW of San Antonio; elev 1,561 ft/476 m. Cattle-ranching area; tourism. German hamlet est. 1850; purchased in 1970s by Texas humorist Hondo Crouch.

Luckey, village (1990 pop. 848), Wood co., NW Ohio, 10 mi/16 km ENE of Bowling Green; 41°27′N 83°29′W. Limestone quarries.

Lucknow (LUHK-no), village (1991 pop. 1,129), S Ont., Canada, 18 mi/29 km NE of Goderich, 43°57′N 81°31′W. Mfg.; dairying.

Lucky, town (1990 pop. 342), Bienville parish, La., 16 mi/26 km W of Jonesboro; 32°15′N 93°00′W.

Lucky Hill, village (1991 pop. 750), St. Mary parish, N Jamaica, just S of Gayle, and 8 mi/12.9 km SW of Port Maria; 18°18′N 77°01′W. A community project. Principal crops are bananas, citrus fruit, corn, peas, cacao.

Lucky Lake, village (1991 pop. 341), SW Sask., Canada, near Lucky L. (4 mi/6 km long, 3 mi/5 km wide), 55 mi/89 km NE of Swift Current; 50°59′N 107°08′W. Magnesium-sulphate production; grain elevators, lumbering.

Lucky Peak Reservoir, SW Idaho, on Boise R., 10 mi/16 km SE of Boise; c.10 mi/16 km long; 43°30′N 116°04′W. Max. capacity 307,000 acre-ft. Formed by Lucky Peak Dam (230 ft/70 m high), built (1955) by the Army Corps of Engineers for flood control.

Lucky Shot, hamlet, Lucky Shot Landing, S Alaska, 40 mi/64 km NNE of Anchorage. Airstrip.

Lucrecia Cape (loo-KRAI-see-uh), on Atlantic coast of E Cuba, Holguín prov., 45 mi/72 km ENE of Holguín; 21°05′N 75°37′W.

Ludden (LUHD-uhn), village (1990 pop. 41), Dickey co., SE N.Dak., 9 mi/14.5 km S of Oakes, near James R.; 46°00′N 98°07′W.

Ludington, town (1990 pop. 8,507), ⊙ Mason co., W Mich., on L. Michigan at mouth of Pere Marquette R.; 43°57′N 86°26′W. Port for Great Lakes shipping; RR terminus. Mfg. (furniture, industrial chemicals, industrial machinery, styrofoam, wire prods., RR maintenance equip., aluminum fabrication). Agr. (apples, cherries, peaches, vegetables). Mason Co. Airport to E. Historical mus. Resort; fishing in many nearby streams and lakes. Has monument on site of 1st burial place (1675) of Father Marquette. Car ferry to Manitowoc, Wis., carries U.S. Highway 10 across L. Mich. (4 hour crossing). Ludington State Park, with its dunes, to N, bet. Hankin L. and L. Mich. Manistee Natl. Forest to N. Inc. as city 1873.

Ludlam Bay (LUHD-luhm), SE N.J., inlet of the Atlantic (c.2.5 mi/4 km long) NW of Sea Isle City; entered from ocean by Corsons Inlet (NE); crossed by Intracoastal Waterway. Bet. bay and ocean is Ludlam Beach, barrier isl. (c.7 mi/11.3 km long) bet. Corsons Inlet (N) and Townsends Inlet (S); site of Sea Isle City (bridge to mainland here).

Ludlow 1 (LUHD-lo), town (1990 pop. 4,736), Kenton co., N Ky., residential suburb 2 mi/3.2 km WSW of Cincinnati, Ohio, 1 mi/1.6 km W of Covington, Ky., on the Ohio R. (RR bridge); 39°05′N 84°32′W. Diverse light mfg. Settled c.1790; inc. as village 1864, as city 1925. **2** agr. town (1990 pop. 430), Aroostook co., E Maine, 10 mi/16 km W of Houlton; 46°09′N 67°58′W. **3** town (1990 pop. 18,820), Hampden co., SW Mass., on the Chicopee R.; 42°11′N 72°28′W. Residential suburb of Springfield and Chicopee. Manufactures include industrial molds, plastic prods., twines. Ludlow State Park is within the town. Settled c.1750, set off from Springfield 1774, inc. 1775. **4** town (1990 pop. 147), Livingston co., N central Mo. on Shoal Creek, 12 mi/19 km SW of Chillicothe; 39°38′N 93°42′W. **5** uninc. town (1990 pop. 850), McKean co., N Pa., 12 mi/19 km SE of Warren, on Twomile Run, in Allegheny Natl. Forest; 41°43′N 78°56′W. Timber; mfg. (lumber). **6** town (1990 pop. 2,302), including Ludlow village, Windsor co., S central Vt., on Black R., and 20 mi/32 km SSW of Woodstock, in Green Mts.; mfg. (woolens, wood prods.); winter sports; 43°23′N 72°42′W. Okemo State Forest Park and Okemo Ski Area are nearby. Calvin Coolidge attended Black R. Acad. here.

Ludlow, village (1990 pop. 323), Champaign co., E Ill., 19 mi/31 km NNE of Champaign; 40°23′N 88°07′W. In agr. area.

Ludlow Falls, village (1990 pop. 300), Miami co., W Ohio, 12 mi/19 km SSW of Piqua; 39°59′N 84°20′W.

Ludowici (loo-duh-WEE-see), town (1990 pop. 1,291), ⊙ Long co., SE Ga., c.45 mi/72 km SW of Savannah, near the Altamaha R.; 31°43′N 81°45′W.

Lueders, village (1990 pop. 365), Jones co., W central Texas, 25 mi/40 km N of Abilene, and on Clear Fork of the Brazos; 32°47′N 99°37′W. In cotton, cattle area; limestone deposits; oil refinery.

Luella, village (1990 pop. 559), Grayson co., N Texas, 5 mi/8 km SE of Sherman; 33°34′N 96°32′W. Cattle, wheat, peanuts. Oil and natural gas.

Lufkin, city (1990 pop. 30,206), ⊙ Angelina co., E Texas, 115 mi/185 km NNE of Houston; 31°19′N 94°43′W. Elev. 328 ft/100 m. Forest industries with many sawmills; the first plant to make newsprint from native pine. RR junction; mfg. (pumping units, iron castings, trailer parts, carbonated beverages, electronics for missiles, industrial chrome plating); agr. (cattle, poultry; hay). Fuller's earth is found in the region. Angelina Col. (2-year), and a state school for the mentally retarded are in Lufkin. Angelina Natl. Forest to E, David Crockett Natl. Forest to W, and Sam Rayburn L. Inc. 1890.

Lugareño (loo-gahr-AIN-yo), sugar-mill village of Sierra de Cubitas, Camagüey prov., E Cuba, on RR, and 28 mi/45 km ENE of Camagüey; 21°34′N 77°28′W.

Lugoff (LOOG-ahf), uninc. town (1990 pop. 3,211), Kershaw co., N central S.C., 5 mi/8 km W of Camden, near Wateree R.; 34°13′N 80°40′W. Mfg. includes tools, chassis, synthetic fibers, contract embroidery, laundry bags, machining, industrial gases, women's sportswear; vessels and tanks; silica sand processing. Agr. (poultry, cattle, grain, and cotton). Wateree Dam and reservoir to NW; L. Wateree State Park in SW shore.

Luis Moya (LOO-ees MO-yah), town (1990 pop. 5,366), Zacatecas, N central Mexico, 30 mi/48 km SE of Zacatecas, on Mexico Highway 45; 22°28′N 102°17′W. Maguey, grain, beans, livestock. Formerly San Francisco de los Adame.

Lukachukai (loo-kuh-choo-kei), uninc. village, Apache co., NE Ariz., 117 mi/188 km NNE of Holbrook, Ariz., and 36 mi/58 km SW of Shiprock, N.Mex., on Lukachukai Creek, in Navajo Indian Reservation. Elev. 6,450 ft/1,966 m. Cattle, sheep; crafts. Chuska Mts. to NE. Canyon de Chelly Natl. Monument to S.

Luke, town (1990 pop. 184), Allegany co., W Md., on North Branch of the Potomac at mouth of Savage R., and 20 mi/32 km SW of Cumberland; 39°29′N 79°04′W. The town is named for the Luke family, which began a paper mill here in 1888 that is now one of the largest in the world. The mill turns out 1,000 tons/1,102 metric tons of high quality paper using 60 million gals/227.1 million liters of water from the Potomac every day, 24-hours a day.

Lukeville, uninc. village, Pima co., SW Ariz., 34 mi/55 km S of Ajo, on Mex. border, opposite Sonoita, Sonora, in

S part of Organ Pipe Cactus Natl. Monument. Elev. 1,814 ft/553 m. Gulf of Calif. (Puerto Penasco) 45 mi/72 km to SW.

Lula (LOO-luh), town (1990 pop. 1,018), Hall co., NE Ga., 10 mi/16 km NE of Gainesville, near source of Oconee R.; 34°23′N 83°40′W. Industry includes poultry processing equip. and light mfg.

Lula (LOO-luh), village (1990 pop. 224), Coahoma co., NW Miss., 18 mi/29 km NNE of Clarksdale; 34°27′N 90°28′W. Timber. Many antebellum homes in the vicinity. Moon L., natural oxbow lake near Mississippi R. and source of Sunflower R. (c.4 mi/6.4 km long; resort) is to W.

Luling 1 (LOO-ling), uninc. town (1990 pop. 2,803), St. Charles parish, SE La., on W bank (levee) of the Mississippi R., and 16 mi/26 km W of New Orleans; 29°55′N 90°22′W. Elev. 9 ft/3 m. Sugarcane, vegetables (esp. okra); catfish, alligators, crabs; mfg. (safety valves, chemicals). Highway bridge to Destrehan. **2** town (1990 pop. 4,661), Caldwell co., S central Texas, on San Marcos R., and c.40 mi/64 km S of Austin; 29°40′N 97°39′W. Elev. 418 ft/127 m. Oil field supply and shipping center; mfg. (oil field storage tanks, concrete, rubber prods., machining). Palmetto State Park to SE. Founded 1874; long a cow town, it boomed after oil discovery, 1922.

Lumber Bridge, village (1990 pop. 109), Robeson co., S N.C., 16 mi/26 km SW of Fayetteville near Big Swamp R.; 34°53′N 79°04′W. Grain, tobacco, poultry, livestock. Mfg. (storm windows and doors, poultry processing).

Lumber City, town (1990 pop. 1,429), Telfair co., S central Ga., 22 mi/35 km WNW of Baxley, near junction of Ocmulgee and Little Ocmulgee rivers; 31°56′N 82°41′W. Shipping point for hardwood and pine lumber. Mfg. (steel tire cords, animal feeds). Inc. 1889.

Lumber City, borough (1990 pop. 83), Clearfield co., W central Pa., 4 mi/6.4 km SW of Curwensville, on West Branch Susquehanna R.; 40°55′N 78°34′W. Agr. (corn, hay, dairying). Curwensville L. reservoir to NE.

Lumber River, c.125 mi/201 km long, in N.C. and S.C.; rises as Drowning Creek on Montgomery-Moore co. line E of Biscoe in central N.C.; flows SE, past Lumberton, approximate point of name change at Lumber R., receives Big Swamp R. from N as it turns to SSW into S.C., to Little Pee Dee R. 3 mi/4.8 km SSW of Nichols; c.50 mi/80 km as Lumber R.; c.65 mi/105 km as Drowning Creek.

Lumberport, town (1990 pop. 1,014), Harrison co., N W.Va., on West Fork R. (headstream of Monongahela R.), 6 mi/9.7 km NNW of Clarksburg; 39°22′N 80°20′W. Coal; oil. Agr. (corn); cattle; poultry; dairying. Inc. 1901.

Lumberton, city (1990 pop. 18,733), ⊙ Robeson co., SE N.C., 32 mi/51 km S of Fayetteville, on the Lumber R.; 34°37′N 79°00′W. (Drowning Creek changes name to Lumber R. about here). RR junction. Agr. area (tobacco, grain, soybeans, cattle, dairying, hogs); timber. Mfg. (transformers, textiles; sheet metal fabricating, children's clothing, athletic shoes; loudspeakers; textile dyeing and finishing; concrete, polypropylene; folding cartons, corrugated boxes). Seat of Pembroke State Univ. to W at Pembroke. Robeson Co. Planetarium. Lumber R. State Park to SE. Founded 1787, inc. 1852.

Lumberton 1 town (1990 pop. 2,121), Lamar co., SE Miss., on Red R., 24 mi/39 km SSW of Hattiesburg, on Red R. and Red Creek; 31°00′N 89°27′W. In agr. (cotton, corn, pecans; cattle, poultry) and pine-timber area. Mfg. (electrical transformers, concrete, feeds, apparel, petroleum refining); oil and natural gas. Large pecan nursery. De Soto Natl. Forest to E. Settled in 1880s. **2** township (1990 pop. 6,705), Burlington co., S N.J., 2 mi/3.2 km S of Mount Holly; 39°57′N 74°47′W. Boat mfg., printing. Inc. 1860. **3** town (1990 pop. 6,640), Hardin co., SE Texas, 13 mi/21 km NNW of Beaumont; 30°15′N 94°12′W. RR junction. Timber; oil and natural gas; cattle. Mfg. (heat exchangers and pressure valves, refractory anchors, industrial flanges). Main unit of Big Thicket Natl. Preserve is to E and S. Village Creek State Park is here.

Lumby, village (1991 pop. 1,265), S B.C., Canada, 14 mi/23 km E of Vernon; 50°15′N 118°58′W. Fruit, vegetables.

Lumière, Cape (loom-YER), in Northumberland Strait, E N.B., Canada, 40 mi/64 km N of Moncton; 46°40′N 64°43′W.

Lummi Island (LUHM-mee), Whatcom co., NW Wash., 8 mi/12.9 km SW of Bellingham; 9 mi/14.5 km long; ½ mi/⁹⁄₁₀ km–1 mi/1.6 km wide. Rosario Strait to S, Strait of Georgia to NW, Bellingham Bay to E. Hale Passage to NE separates isl. from mainland. Village of Lummi on narrow part of isl. in NW. Ferry from Lummi Peninsula, to N. Fish; oysters, crabs. Highest point, Lummi Peak, 1,509 ft/460 m. San Juan Isls. to W.

Lumpkin, county (□ 285 sq mi/738 sq km; 1990 pop. 14,573), N Ga., ⊙ Dahlonega; 34°34′N 84°00′W. In Blue Ridge area, drained by Chestatee and Etowah rivers. Agr. (corn, hay, potatoes); poultry, cattle, hogs; timber. Chattahoochee Natl. Forest occupies N ½ of co. Formed 1832.

Lumpkin, town (1990 pop. 1,250), ⊙ Stewart co., SW Ga., 30 mi/48 km SSE of Columbus; 32°03′N 84°48′W. Mfg. of dyes and paints. Inc. 1831.

Lumsden (LUHMZ-duhn), town (1991 pop. 1,477), S Sask., Canada, on Qu'Appelle R., and 17 mi/27 km NW of Regina; grain elevators, livestock.

Luna (LOO-nuh), county (□ 2,965 sq mi/7,679 sq km; 1990 pop. 18,110), SW N.Mex.; ⊙ Deming; 32°10′N 107°45′W. Livestock and grain (cattle, some sheep; melons, grapes, fruit, nuts, jalapeños, chiles, onions, green beans, cabbage, some lettuce; pecans, cotton, corn, sorghum, hay, alfalfa, wheat, oats, barley) area bordering on Mexico (Chihuahua state) in S. Fla. Mts. in SE, part of Mimbre Mts., including Cooke's Peak, in N. Formed 1901.

Lund (LUHNT), uninc. village (1990 pop. 330), White Pine co., E Nev., 27 mi/43 km SSW of Ely, on White R. Cattle, sheep. Egan Range to E; parts of Humboldt Natl. Forest to W and N; Wayne E. Kirch Wildlife Management Area to S.

Lundale, uninc. village (1990 pop. 500), Logan co., SW W.Va., 12 mi/19 km ESE of Logan.

Lundy's Lane, locality in S Ont., Canada, just W of Niagara Falls, scene of a stubborn engagement of the War of 1812, fought July 25, 1814. The Amer. forces commanded by Gen. Winfield Scott and led by Gen. Jacob J. Brown, pushing into Canada, encountered Br. troops posted along Lundy's Lane. After prolonged fighting, the Americans fell back to Fort Erie, their former position.

Lunenburg (LOO-nuhn-buhrg), county (□ 1,169 sq mi/3,028 sq km; 1991 pop. 47,634), SW N.S., Canada, on the Atlantic; ⊙ Lunenburg; 44°22′N 64°19′W.

Lunenburg, town (1991 pop. 2,781), SW N.S., Canada, on Lunenburg Bay, SW of Halifax. Large fishing fleet and a fisheries mus. The dist. was chiefly settled c.1750 by Germans from Hanover.

Lunenburg, county (□ 432 sq mi/1,119 sq km; 1990 pop. 11,419), S Va.; ⊙ Lunenburg; 36°57′N 78°14′W. Rolling agr. region; bounded S by Meherrin R., N by Nottoway R. Mfg. at Kenbridge; lumber milling; agr. (tobacco; also hay, wheat, barley, soybeans; cattle); timber (pine, oak). Formed 1746.

Lunenburg 1 (LOO-nen-buhrg), agr. town (1990 pop. 9,117), Worcester co., N Mass., 22 mi/35 km N of Worcester; 42°35′N 71°43′W. Settled 1721, inc. 1728. Large community of Finnish origin. Amusement park. **2** (LOON-uhn-buhrg), town (1990 pop. 1,176), Essex co., NE Vt., on Connecticut R., and 16 mi/26 km E of St. Johnsbury, in agr. region; 44°28′N 71°42′W. Includes village of Gilman. Chartered 1763.

Lunenburg, uninc. village, ⊙ Lunenburg co., S Va., 25 mi/40 km SSE of Farmville, 3 mi/4.8 km SW of Victoria. Agr. (cattle; tobacco, grain, soybeans).

Lunging Island, N.H.: see ISLES OF SHOALS.

Luperón (loo-pe-RON), town (1993 pop. 3,014), Puerto Plata prov., N Dominican Republic, on small inlet of the Atlantic, and 17 mi/27 km WNW of Puerto Plata; 19°50′N 71°03′W. In agr. region (coffee, cacao, tobacco, corn). Until 1927, called Blanco. The ruins of ISABELA are 9 mi/14.5 km W.

Lupton City, village, Hamilton co., SE Tenn., N suburb of Chattanooga, N of the Tennessee.

Luquillo (loo-KEE-yo), town (1990 pop. 18,100), NE P.R., on the Atlantic, 27 mi/43 km ESE of San Juan. Industrial, commercial, and tourism area. Luquillo Beach bathing resort (one of isl.'s most beautiful beaches), towered over by Sierra de Luquillo.

Luquillo, Sierra de (loo-KEE-yo, see-YER-rah dai), mountain range in NE P.R., 20 mi/32 km SE of San Juan. The Caribbean Natl. Forest is located here; extends c.15 mi/24 km SW-NE, rising to c.3,494 ft/1,065 m. Its highest and best-known peak is El Yunque. Largely forested; timber is used for charcoal. Resort area. El Portal del Yunque, a visitor center, with ecological exhibits on the tropical forest.

Luray 1 town (1990 pop. 70), Clark co., extreme NE Mo., near North Wyaconda R., 9 mi/14.5 km WNW of Kahoka; 40°27′N 91°52′W. **2** town (1990 pop. 4,587), ⊙ Page co., N Va., 27 mi/43 km NE of Harrisonburg, on Hawksbill Creek, in Shenandoah Valley; 38°39′N 78°27′W. Mfg. (automotive door panels, canoes, printing and publishing; clothing, leather finishing); in agr. area (apples, peaches, grain; poultry, livestock; dairying). Hq. of Shenandoah Natl. Park. George Washington Natl. Forest is N and W. The Luray Caverns to W discovered in 1878, noted for their large stalagmite and stalactite formations, and water pools. Inc. 1812.

Luray 1 (lor-AI), village (1990 pop. 261), Russell co., central Kansas, 16 mi/26 km NNE of Russell; 39°07′N 98°41′W. Livestock, grain. **2** (luh-RAI), village (1990 pop. 102), Hampton co., SW S.C., 15 mi/24 km SSE of Allendale; 32°48′N 81°14′W. Cotton, soybeans, watermelons; livestock.

Lure, Lake, N.C.: see LAKE LURE TOWN.

Luretha, Ky.: see FERGUSON.

Lusby (LUZ-bee), village, Calvert co., S Md., near Chesapeake Bay, 12 mi/19 km SE of Prince Frederick. Nearby is "Charlesgift," formerly called Preston-at-Patuxent (built 1650), one of oldest Md. houses. Nearby is the Calvert Cliffs Nuclear Power Station, and the nearby beach area famous for marine fossils.

Luscar (LUH-skuhr), village, W Alta., Canada, in Rocky Mts. at foot of Luscar Mt. (8,534 ft/2,601 m), near E side of Jasper Natl. Park, 30 mi/48 km ENE of Jasper; 53°04′N 117°24′W. Coal mining; cattle.

Luseland (LOOS-land), town (1991 pop. 658), W Sask., Canada, 65 mi/105 km SW of North Battleford; 52°05′N 109°26′W. Wheat.

Lushton, village (1990 pop. 28), York co., SE Nebr., 12 mi/19 km SW of York, and on West Fork of Big Blue R; 40°43′N 97°43′W.

Lusk (LUHSK), town (1990 pop. 1,504), ⊙ Niobrara co., E Wyo., on Niobrara R. (intermittent), and 100 mi/161 km E of Casper; 42°45′N 104°27′W. Elev. 5,015 ft/1,529 m. Trading point in dry-farming, cattle, and sheep region; wheat, oats. Lance Creek oil field to NW. Silver and radium once mined here. Town refers to itself as seat of least populated co. in least populated state (in numbers, Wyo. is 50th); oil boom of 1918 briefly swelled pop. to 10,000. Inc. 1898.

Lutcher (luhch-uhr), town (1990 pop. 3,907), St. James parish, SE central La., on E bank (levee) of the Mississippi R. (toll ferry here), and 36 mi/58 km W of New Orleans; 30°04′N 90°43′W. In agr. area (okra, sugarcane, cattle); crawfish; chemicals. Mfg. (concrete). Founded c.1890. Chemical plants in area.

Lutesville, former town, Bollinger co., SE Mo., 17 mi/27 km SW of Jackson; annexed by Marble Hill in 1986.

Luther 1 town (1990 pop. 154), Boone co., central Iowa, 8 mi/12.9 km SSE of Boone; 41°58′N 93°49′W. In agr. area. **2** town (1990 pop. 1,560), Oklahoma co., central Okla., a residential suburb 22 mi/35 km NE of downtown Oklahoma City, near the Deep Fork of Canadian R.; 35°39′N 97°10′W.

Luther, village (1990 pop. 343), Lake co., W central Mich., 20 mi/32 km SW of Cadillac; 44°02′N 85°40′W. In farm area. Part of Manistee Natl. Forest to NE.

Luthersville (LOO-thurs-vil), town (1990 pop. 741), Meriwether co., W Ga., 19 mi/31 km NE of La Grange; 33°13′N 84°44′W. Lumber.

Lutherville, suburban village (1990 pop. with Timonium 16,442), Baltimore co., N Md., bet. Loch Raven Reservoir and L. Roland, and 9 mi/14.5 km N of downtown Baltimore; 39°26′N 76°37′W. Named for Martin Luther by its founder, John C. Morris, it is the seat of former Md. Col. for Women (seminary chartered 1853). The Fire Mus. of Md. is located here. Timonium Fairgrounds here, one of the 3 ½-mi/⅕-km race tracks in Md., is the site every year of the 10-day state fair held by the Baltimore State Fair and Agr. Society of Baltimore Co.

Lutsen (LOOT-suhn), uninc. village, Cook co., NE Minn., 15 mi/24 km WSW of Grand Marai; 47°38′N 90°40′W. Resort community on L. Superior, in Superior Natl. Forest. Mfg. of draperies and upholstery. Cascade River State Park to NE; Ray Berglund State Wayside to SW. Lutsen Ski Area to N. Lutsen Mts. Resort to SW.

Luttrell (LUH-truhl), town (1990 pop. 812), Union co., NE Tenn., 17 mi/27 km NNE of Knoxville; 36°13′N 83°45′W.

Lutz, town (□ 14 sq mi/36 sq km; 1990 pop. 10,552), Hillsborough co., W central Fla., 10 mi/16 km N of Tampa; 28°08′N 82°27′W. Mfg. (neon signs, metal roofing; printing and publishing; hydraulic units).

Luverne (LUH-vuhrn), city (1990 pop. 4,382), ☉ Rock co., extreme SW Minn., 27 mi/43 km ENE of Sioux Falls, S.Dak., and 24 mi/39 km SSE of Pipestone, on Rock R.; 43°38′N 96°12′W. Elev. 1,454 ft/443 m. Trading point in agr. area (grain, milk, soybeans; livestock, poultry; dairying). Mfg. (water tanks, truck mounts, and farm equip., printing); granite quarries. Blue Mounds State Park to N. Settled 1867, plotted 1870, inc. as village 1877, as city 1904.

Luverne (town (1990 pop. 2,555), ☉ Crenshaw co., S Ala., on Patsaliga Creek, and 45 mi/72 km S of Montgomery; 31°42′N 86°15′W. Processing and shipping point in corn, peanut, and poultry area; clothing; soft drink bottling; lumber. Inc. 1891. **2** town, on Humboldt-Kossuth co. line, N central Iowa, 15 mi/24 km NNE of Dakota City. Livestock, grain.

Luverne (loo-VUHRN), village (1990 pop. 41), Steele co., E N. Dak., 23 mi/37 km NE of Valley City, near Sheyenne R.; 47°15′N 97°55′W. L. Ashtabula Reservoir to W.

Luxemburg 1 town, Dubuque co., E Iowa, 21 mi/34 km WNW of Dubuque. State park nearby. **2** town (1990 pop. 1,151), Kewaunee co., E Wis., on Door Peninsula, 15 mi/24 km E of Green Bay; 44°32′N 87°42′W. Dairying; mfg. (wood cabinets, cheese, plastic bottles). RR junction to W. Speedway here.

Luxora (luhks-OR-uh), town (1990 pop. 1,338), Mississippi co., NE Ark., 10 mi/16 km S of Blytheville, near the Mississippi; 35°45′N 89°55′W. In cotton-growing and rice area. Mfg. (asphalt, metal stampings). Founded 1882.

Luz, La, Mexico: see LA LUZ.

Luzerne (LOO-suhrn), county (□ 907 sq mi/2,349 sq km; 1990 pop. 328,149), E central Pa.; ☉ Wilkes-Barre. Bounded SE by Lehigh R.; drained by Susquehanna R. (forms part of NE boundary); Nescopeck Mt. ridge crosses E-W in center, Wyoming Valley in NE center. Agr. (corn, wheat, oats, hay, alfalfa, vegetables, potatoes, apples; hogs, cattle; dairying); some anthracite coal; sandstone. Mfg. at Wilkes-Barre, Mountain Top, Hazleton, West Hazleton, and Kingston. First permanent settlements (1753) by people from Conn. Part of Ricketts Glen State Park in NW, Frances Slocum State Park in NE; part of Lackawanna State Forest in N center. Nuclear power plants: Susquehanna 1 (initial criticality Sept. 10, 1982; max. dependable capacity of 1040 MWe) and Susquehanna 2 (initial criticality May 8, 1984; max. dependable capacity of 1044 MWe) are 7 mi/11.3 km NE of Berwick; both use cooling water from the Susquehanna R. Formed 1786.

Luzerne, town (1990 pop. 110), Benton co., E central Iowa, 19 mi/31 km SSW of Vinton; 41°54′N 92°10′W. In agr. area.

Luzerne, borough (1990 pop. 3,206), Luzerne co., NE central Pa., suburb 3 mi/4.8 km N of Wilkes-Barre, on Huntsville Creek; 41°17′N 75°54′W. Mfg. (sheet-metal components, wood prods.); some anthracite coal in area. Frances Slocum State Park to N. Inc. 1882.

Luzerne, N.Y.: see LAKE LUZERNE.

Lycoming (lei-KO-ming), county (□ 1,243 sq mi/3,219 sq km; 1990 pop. 118,710), N central Pa.; ☉ Williamsport. Hilly agr. and forested region; drained by West Branch of Susquehanna R. and by Lycoming (forms part of N boundary), Loyalsock, and Pine creeks; 41°21′ 77°03′. Agr. (corn, wheat, oats, barley, hay, alfalfa, soybeans, potatoes, apples; sheep, hogs, cattle; dairying). Mfg. at Williamsport, Montgomery, Montoursville, and Muncy. Largest co. in land area in Pa. Part of Allenwood Federal Prison Camp in SE. Little Pine and Upper Pine Bottom state parks in W, Susquehanna State Park in S center, at Williamsport; parts of Tiadaghton State Forest throughout co., especially in N and S. Formed 1795.

Lydia (LID-ee-uh), uninc. town (1990 pop. 1,136), Iberia parish, La., 6 mi/9.7 km SE of New Iberia; 31°55′N 91°48′W.

Lydia, village, Darlington co., central S.C., 10 mi/16 km SW of Hartsville. Agr. includes soybeans, wheat, cotton, corn.

Lydia Mills, textile village, Laurens co., NW S.C., adjacent to Clinton.

Lydick, village, St. Joseph co., N Ind., 7 mi/11.3 km WNW of South Bend.

Lyell, Mount (11,495 ft/3,504 m), on Alta.-B.C. border, Canada, in Rocky Mts., on W edge of Banff Natl. Park, 75 mi/121 km SE of Jasper; 51°57′N 117°06′W.

Lyell, Mount, NE Madera co., E Calif., peak (13,114 ft/3,997 m) of the Sierra Nevada, in Yosemite Natl. Park, near its E boundary, and c.20 mi/32 km SW of Mono L. Has small glacier.

Lyerly (LEI-uhr-lee), village (1990 pop. 493), Chattooga co., NW Ga., 17 mi/27 km NW of Rome, and on Chattooga R.; 34°24′N 85°24′W. Mfg. of work gloves and carpets.

Lyford, town (1990 pop. 1,674), Willacy co., extreme S Texas, 15 mi/24 km NNW of Harlingen; 26°24′N 97°47′W. In irrigated farm area (sugarcane, vegetables, cotton; cattle); oil and gas.

Lykens (LEI-kens), borough (1990 pop. 1,986), Dauphin co., E central Pa., 22 mi/35 km NNE of Harrisburg, on Wiconisco Creek. Mfg. (heat exchangers, work clothes). Part of Weiser State Forest to E and SW. Settled c.1740; laid out 1848; inc. 1872.

Lyle, uninc. town (1990 pop. 850), Klickitat co., S Wash., 8 mi/12.9 km NW of The Dallas, Oregon, on Columbia R. (Bonneville reservoir), at mouth of Klickitat R. RR junction. Wheat, alfalfa; cattle.

Lyle, village (1990 pop. 504), Mower co., SE Minn., on Iowa state line, near Cedar R., and 11 mi/18 km S of Austin; 43°30′N 92°56′W. RR junction. Alfalfa, soybeans, grain; dairying; poultry; mfg. (feeds, grain processing).

Lyman, county (□ 1,707 sq mi/4,364 sq km; 1990 pop. 3,638), S central S.Dak.; ☉ Kennebec; 43°53′N 99°50′W. Agr. and cattle-raising region bounded S by White R., E by Missouri R.; Lower Brule Indian Reservation is in N. Corn, wheat; cattle, hogs, poultry; dairy prods. Part of Fort Pierre Natl. Grassland in NW. Formed 1890.

Lyman 1 (LEI-muhn), uninc. town (1990 pop. 1,117), Harrison co., SE Miss., 8 mi/12.9 km N of Gulfport. Timber; corn, cotton, pecans, citrus. De Soto Natl. Forest to NE. **2** town (1990 pop. 388), Grafton co., NW N.H., 8 mi/12.9 km WSW of Littleton; 44°16′N 71°56′W. Agr. (cattle, poultry; vegetables; dairying; nursery crops, sugar maples); mfg. (briefcases and portfolios); recreational area. Gardner Mt. (2,330 ft/710 m) on NW boundary. **3** town (1990 pop. 2,271), Spartanburg co., NW S.C., near Tyger R., 11 mi/18 km W of Spartanburg; 34°57′N 82°07′W. Mfg. includes gears, copper film negatives, apparel fabrics. Agr. includes dairying; livestock, poultry; grain, soybeans, peaches, apples. **4** town (1990 pop. 1,896), Uinta co., SW Wyo., 35 mi/56 km E of Evanston near Blacks Fork R.; 41°19′N 110°17′W. Elev 6,695 ft/2,041 m.

Lyman 1 (LEI-men), village (1990 pop. 452), Scotts Bluff co., W Nebr., 20 mi/32 km WNW of Scottsbluff, near North Platte R., and at Wyo. state line; 41°55′N 104°02′W. livestock; beet sugar, grain, potatoes. Mfg. (screw machine prods.). **2** (LEI-muhn), village (1990 pop. 198), Wayne co., S central Utah, 2 mi/3.2 km E of Loa; 38°23′N 111°35′W. Elev. c.7,200 ft/2,195 m Cattle; alfalfa, barley. Fishlake Natl. Forest to E; Loa State Fish Hatchery to N. **3** village (1990 pop. 275), Skagit co., NW Wash., 15 mi/24 km NE of Mt. Vernon, and on Skagit R.; 48°31′N 122°04′W. Lumber; vegetables, berries; poultry; dairying. Mt. Baker–Snoqualmie Natl. Forest to NE and SE, Mt. Baker (10,775 ft/3,284 m) to NE.

Lyme 1 town (1990 pop. 1,949), New London co., SE Conn., on the Connecticut R., and 12 mi/19 km WNW of New London; 41°23′N 72°20′W. Agr.; dairying; resorts. Includes Hadlyme village and Hamburg (surrounds Hamburg Cove, finger offshoot of the Connecticut R.; with yacht harbor at mouth of Eight Mile R.; 3 state parks. Formerly included towns of East Lyme and Old Lyme. Motor vehicle sales and repairs. **2** town (1990 pop. 1,496), Grafton co., W N.H., 12 mi/19 km NNE of Lebanon; 43°47′N 72°07′W. Bounded on W by the Connecticut R. (Vt. state line). Agr. (cattle, poultry; vegetables; dairying; nursery crops; timber); mfg. (software). Dartmouth Skiway Ski Area in E; Appalachian Trail crosses town in E.

Lynbrook, village (□ 1 sq mi/2.6 sq km; 1990 pop. 19,208), Nassau co., SE N.Y.; 40°39′N 73°40′W. It is a suburb of N.Y. on S shore of L.I. Sheet-metal and furniture mfg. Old Church dates from 1800. The area was settled in 1785 and was called Bloomfield. The name *Lynbrook* (formed by reversing the syllables in *Brooklyn*) was adopted in 1895. Inc. 1911.

Lynch (LINCH), town (1990 pop. 1,166), Harlan co., SE Ky., 5 mi/8 km E of Cumberland, in the Cumberland Mts. near Va. state line; 36°57′N 82°54′W. Bituminous coal; coal processing. Black Mt. (4,139 ft/1,262 m), highest peak in Ky., is to S. Portal 31 Mine Tour. Jefferson Natl. Forest to E. Founded 1917.

Lynch, village (1990 pop. 296), Boyd co., N Nebr., 20 mi/32 km ESE of Butte, and on Ponca Creek; 42°49′N 98°28′W. Livestock; grain. Excavation of prehistoric settlements was begun nearby in 1936.

Lynchburg, independent city (□ 50 sq mi/130 sq km; 1990 pop. 66,049), central Va., 100 mi/161 km WSW of Richmond, on James R.; separate from adjoining Amherst, Bedford, and Campbell cos.; 37°23′N 79°11′W. RR junction; trade center and tobacco market in the foothills of the Blue Ridge Mts.; mfg. (machining, shelving, heating equip., sheet metal fabrication, conveyor systems, nuclear power prods., crushed limestone, lumber, power transformers, printing and publishing, iron pipe, communications equip., automatic teller machines, pharmaceuticals, bakery prods., metal plating, electronic capacitors, corrugated containers, furniture, prepared foods, gravure ink, cosmetics, dairy prods, metal cylinders, motor vehicle parts, footwear, tools, lumber, and wood prods.). Confederate supply base in the Civil War; Union attack repulsed (1864). Randolph-Macon Woman's Col., Lynchburg Col., Liberty Univ., Va. Theological Seminary and Col., Lynchburg Baptist Col., Central Va. Community Col., Maier Mus. of Art; Pest House Medical Mus. Notable historic houses include Poplar Forest to SW, built by Thomas Jefferson. Lynchburg Regional Airport to S. Settled 1757; inc. as a city 1852.

Lynchburg 1 uninc. town (1990 pop. 2,071), De Soto co., NW Miss., residential suburb 14 mi/23 km SSW of downtown Memphis, Tenn., and 3 mi/4.8 km E of Walls; 34°58′N 90°05′W. **2** town (1990 pop. 4,721), ☉ Moore co., S Tenn., 11 mi/18 km SW of Tullahoma; 35°17′N 86°22′W. In timber and agr. area; major bourbon whiskey producer. Community col.

Lynchburg 1 village (1990 pop. 1,212), Highland co., SW Ohio, 14 mi/23 km S of Wilmington, and on East Fork of Little Miami R.; 39°14′N 83°47′W. **2** village (1990 pop. 475), Lee co., NE central S.C., 18 mi/29 km NE of Sumter, near Lynches R., and 20 mi/32 km SW of Florence; 34°03′N 80°04′W. Fabric finishing, draperies, house furnishings.

Lynches River (LIN-chez), c.140 mi/225 km long long, S. N.C. and NE S.C., in south Union co.; rises just over state line in N.C.; flows SE Johnsonville, S.C. Enters Great Pee Dee R. 4 mi/6.4 km ENE of Johnsonville. Lee State Park is along river near Bishopville.

Lynd (LIND), village (1990 pop. 287), Lyon co., SW Minn., 5 mi/8 km SW of Marshall, on Redwood R.; 44°23′N 95°54′W. Agr. (dairying; poultry, livestock; grain, soybeans). Camden State Park to SW.

Lyndeborough (LIND-buh-ro), town (1990 pop. 1,294), Hillsboro co., S N.H., 15 mi/24 km WSW of Manchester; 42°53′N 71°46′W. Drained by Purgatory Brook. Agr. (livestock, poultry; fruits, vegetables; dairying; timber). Wapack Natl. Wildlife Refuge in W.

Lynden, town (1990 pop. 5,709), Whatcom co., NW Wash., 15 mi/24 km N of Bellingham, and on Nooksack R.; 48°57′N 122°28′W. Dairying; poultry; berries; tulips. Port of entry 3 mi/4.8 km S of Can. (B.C.) border; Aldergrove, B.C., 7 mi/11.3 km N. Mfg. (iron furniture, farm machinery, structural wood prods., millwork, printing and publishing, fertilizer). Pioneer Mus. Settled c.1860; inc. 1891.

Lynden (LIN-den), village, S Ont., Canada, 16 mi/26 km W of Hamilton. Dairying; fruits.

Lyndhurst (LIND-hurst), village, SE Ont., Canada, on Gananoque R., and 30 mi/48 km NE of Kingston. Dairying; mixed farming.

Lyndhurst, city (1990 pop. 15,982), Cuyahoga co., NE Ohio; 41°31′N 81°29′W. It is a residential suburb of Cleveland. Inc. 1917.

Lyndhurst (LIND-huhrst), township (1990 pop. 18,262), Bergen co., NE N.J., near Passaic R., 5 mi/8 km NNW of Jersey City; 40°47′N 74°06′W. Mfg. (machinery, metal prods., clothing, paints, asphalt). Inc. 1852.

Lyndon 1 (LIN-duhn), town (1990 pop. 964), ⊙ Osage co., E Kansas, 30 mi/48 km S of Topeka; 38°36′N 95°41′W. Elev. 1,030 ft/314 m. Trade center in livestock and grain region; paper prods., metal prods. Melvin L. and State Park to SW; Pomona L. and State Park to NE. **2** town (1990 pop. 8,037), Jefferson co., N Ky., residential suburb, 9 mi/14.5 km E of downtown Louisville; 38°15′N 85°35′W. Herr House here (built 1789) is one of earliest brick houses in Ky. **3** town (1990 pop. 5,371), Caledonia co., NE Vt., on Passumpsic R., and 7 mi/ 11.3 km N of St. Johnsbury; 44°32′N 72°00′W. Includes villages of Lyndon Center, seat of teachers col., and Lyndonville. Settled 1788.

Lyndon, village (1990 pop. 615), Whiteside co., NW Ill., on Rock R., and 7 mi/11.3 km SSE of Morrison; 41°43′N 89°55′W. In agr. area.

Lyndon B. Johnson National Historic Site (□ 2.45 sq mi/6.35 sq km), SE Texas. Sites of the birthplace, boyhood home, and ranch (and grandparents' ranch) of President Lyndon B. Johnson; covers 1,571 acres/ 636 ha. Authorized 1969; redesignated 1980.

Lyndon Baines Johnson Memorial Grove on the Potomac, memorial, Washington D.C. Grove (17 acres/ 7 ha) of 500 white pines overlooking Potomac R.; vista of the Capitol. Authorized 1973.

Lyndon Station, village (1990 pop. 474), Juneau co., S central Wis., near the Dells of the Wisconsin, 10 mi/ 16 km SE of Mauston; 43°42′N 89°53′W. Lumber; mfg. (wood prods.).

Lyndonville 1 (LIN-duhn-vil), village (□ 1 sq mi/ 2.6 sq km; 1990 pop. 953), Orleans co., W N.Y., 35 mi/ 56 km NE of Buffalo, near L. Ontario; 43°19′N 78°23′W. Mfg. (electronic equipment, apple juice, cider, and vinegar); agr. (fruits, grain). Inc. 1903. **2** village (1990 pop. 1,255), in Lyndon, Caledonia co., NE Vt.; 44°31′N 72°00′W. Veterinary medicines, dairy prods., maple sugar.

Lyndora (lin-DOR-ah), uninc. town (1990 est. pop. 3,000), Butler township, Butler co., W Pa., residential suburb 2 mi/3.2 km SW of Butler, on Connoquinessing Creek; 40°51′N 79°55′W. Mfg. (industrial chemicals).

Lynhurst, village, Marion co., central Ind., a W suburb 4 mi/6.4 km W of downtown Indianapolis, just S of the Indianapolis Speedway. Became part of Indianapolis 1970.

Lynn, county (□ 893 sq mi/2,313 sq km; 1990 pop. 6,758),

NW Texas; ⊙ Tahoka; 33°10′N 101°49′W. On the Llano Estacado; elev. c.3,000 ft/914 m. Irrigated agr. area, with large crops of grain sorghum, cotton, wheat; livestock (beef cattle, hogs, sheep). Oil and gas; stone. Includes Tahoka L., in NE corner, and other intermittently dry lakes. Formed 1876.

Lynn, city (1990 pop. 81,245), Essex co., E Mass., on Massachusetts Bay; 42°28′N 70°58′W. Lynn is an old industrial center. The 1st ironworks (1643) and the 1st fire engine (1654) in the country were built here. Formerly the shoe industry was important, but jet engines, marine turbines, dairy prods., plastics, and electrical instruments have become the major prods. The home of Mary Baker Eddy, the founder of Christian Science, is in Lynn. Lynn Beach and Lynn Woods Reservation are here. Inc. as a town 1631; as a city 1850.

Lynn, town (1990 pop. 1,183), Randolph co., E Ind., 9 mi/ 14.5 km SSE of Winchester; 40°03′N 84°56′W. Corn, oats, soybeans; poultry, livestock; mfg. (burial caskets, foundry filters). Five mi/8 km SE is state's highest point (1,257 ft/383 m) near Bethel, in Wayne co.

Lynn Canal, natural inlet; SE Alaska, c.90 mi/145 km long, 7 mi/11.3 km–12 mi/19 km wide. It connects in the S with Chatham Strait and Stephens Passage and thrusts N bet. mts. to break finally into the inlets of the Chilkoot and Chilkat rivers. Navigable to its head, Lynn Canal connects Skagway with Juneau and is an important shipping lane. During the Alaska gold rush (1896) it was a major route to the gold fields.

Lynn Garden, village, Sullivan co., NE Tenn., suburb just N of Kingsport; 36°35′N 82°34′W.

Lynn Haven, town (1990 pop. 9,298), Bay co., NW Fla., 5 mi/8 km N of Panama City; 30°14′N 85°39′W. Mfg. includes automotive disc brakes, feeders, table lamps, vinyl windows.

Lynn Lake, town (1991 pop. 834), NW Man., Canada, 200 mi/322 km N of The Pas; 56°51′N 101°03′W. Nickel- and copper-mining center; mfg. of ammonium sulphate fertilizer. Succeeded (early 1950s) exhausted copper property of Sherridon, 120 mi/193 km S, from which RR was extended to Lynn L.

Lynndyl, village (1990 pop. 120), Millard co., W Utah, on Sevier R., 17 mi/27 km NE of Delta; 39°30′N 112°23′W. Irrigated agr. area: alfalfa, barley, wheat, sugar beets; dairying; cattle. Little Sahara Rec. Area to N; Fool Creek reservoir to S. Fishlake Natl. Forest to SE. RR junction.

Lynnfield, town (1990 pop. 11,274), Essex co., NE Mass. Primarily residential, Lynnfield is a suburb 8 mi/ 12.9 km N of Boston; 42°32′N 71°02′W. Inc. 1814.

Lynnhaven, urbanized area, part of Virginia Beach city, SE Va., 15 mi/24 km E of Norfolk, on 2-branched Lynnhaven Bay, an arm (c.5 mi/8 km long) of Chesapeake Bay, which it joins via narrow Lynnhaven Inlet (bridged). Oysters.

Lynnview, town (1990 pop. 1,017), Jefferson co., N Ky., residential suburb 5 mi/8 km SSE of downtown Louisville; 38°10′N 85°42′W. Louisville International Airport (Standiford Field) to W.

Lynnville 1 town (1990 pop. 640), Warrick co., SW Ind., 10 mi/16 km N of Boonville; 38°12′N 87°19′W. In agr. and bituminous-coal area. **2** town (1990 pop. 393), Jasper co., central Iowa, on North Skunk R., and 15 mi/ 24 km SE of Newton; 41°34′N 92°47′W. Livestock; grain. Lynnville Mill upstream. **3** town (1990 pop. 344), Giles co., S Tenn., 12 mi/19 km N of Pulaski; 35°22′N 87°00′W. In agr., livestock area.

Lynnville, village (1990 pop. 125), Morgan co., W central Ill., 7 mi/11.3 km WSW of Jacksonville; 39°41′N 90°20′W. In agr. area.

Lynnwood, city (1990 pop. 28,695), Snohomish co., W central Wash., a suburb 15 mi/24 km N of downtown Seattle, and 12 mi/19 km SSW of Everett, near Puget Sound (2 mi/3.2 km NW of city center); 47°50′N 122°18′W. Mfg. (aerospace parts, communications equip., electrical equip. and electronic components, metal stampings, precious metal jewelry, scales and balances, textile bags). The city has rapidly developed in the 1980s and early 1990s along with the Seattle area. Edmonds Community Col. is located here. Inc. 1959.

Lynnwood, uninc. town (1990 pop. 1,400), Fayette co., SW Pa., 3 mi/4.8 km SE of Monessen; 40°07′N 79°50′W. Agr. includes dairying.

Lynwood, city (1990 pop. 61,945), Los Angeles co., S Calif., a suburb 10 mi/16 km S of downtown Los Angeles; 33°55′N 118°12′W. Although primarily residential, Lynwood has printing presses and varied light mfg., such as truck equip., furniture, metal prods., die casting, and gears. Los Angeles R. to E. Founded 1896; inc. 1921.

Lynwood, village (1990 pop. 6,535), Cook co., NE Ill., suburb 25 mi/40 km SSE of downtown Chicago, borders Ind. on E; 41°31′N 87°32′W. Mfg.: screw machine prods., light mfg. Lansing Municipal Airport to N.

Lynxville, village (1990 pop. 153), Crawford co., SW Wis., on the Mississippi (Iowa state line), and 14 mi/23 km NNE of Prairie du Chien, in livestock and dairy region; 43°15′N 91°02′W. A U.S. fish hatchery is here. Lock and Dam No. 9 to S.

Lyon 1 (LEI-uhn), county (□ 587; 1990 pop. 11,952), extreme NW Iowa; ⊙ Rock Rapids; 43°22′N 96°12′W. Prairie agr. area (sheep, hogs, cattle, poultry; corn, oats), drained by Rock and Little Rock rivers, and bounded N by Minn. and S.Dak. (5 mi/8 km of N boundary borders S.Dak.) and W by Big Sioux R. (forms S.Dak. state line here). Formed 1851. **2** county (□ 855 sq mi/2,214 sq km; 1990 pop. 34,732), E central Kansas; ⊙ Emporia; 38°27′N 96°09′W. Located in Flint Hills region, level to hilly area, drained by Neosho and Cottonwood rivers. Poultry, cattle, hogs; corn, wheat, sorghum, hay. Lyon State Fishing L. in NE. Formed 1860. **3** county (□ 256 sq mi/663 sq km; 1990 pop. 6,624), W Ky.; ⊙ Eddyville; 37°01′N 88°04′W. Bounded SW by Tennessee R. (Kentucky L. reservoir), NW by Cumberland R. Includes part of Kentucky Woodlands Wildlife Refuge; part of Land Between the Lakes Recreation Area in S; Barkley Dam, on Cumberland R. on W co. boundary, forms L. Barkley reservoir, which crosses co.; Mineral Mound State Park, on L. Barkley, in E center. Gently rolling agr. area (burley and dark tobacco, corn, wheat, soybeans, hay, alfalfa; hogs, cattle; catfish); limestone quarries, hardwood timber. Formed 1854. **4** county (□ 721 sq mi/1,867 sq km; 1990 pop. 24,789), SW Minn.; ⊙ Marshall; 44°24′N 95°50′W. Drained by Yellow Medicine, Cottonwood, and Redwood rivers. Agr. area (corn, oats, wheat, hay, alfalfa, soybeans; hogs, sheep, cattle, poultry; dairying; honey). Camden State Park in SW corner; small lakes in SW and NE corner. Formed 1868. **5** county (□ 2,016 sq mi/ 5,221 sq km; 1990 pop. 20,001), W Nev.; ⊙ Yerington; 39°00′N 119°11′W. East and West Walker rivers form the Walker R. above Yerington at center of co. Drained by Carson R. in N; forms Lahontan Reservoir, Lahontan State Recreational Area; reservoir supplies water for irrigation. Part of Toiyabe Natl. Forest is in S, in Sierra Nevada. Mason Valley Wildlife Management Area in N center. Part of Walker R. Indian Reservation in NE. Fort Churchill State Historical Park in N. Fernley Wildlife Mangement Area in N. Artesia L. Wildlife Management Area in W. Borders Calif. on SW. Cattle, sheep, poultry; dairying; hay, vegetables; cement, sand and gravel, gypsum; copper, gold, silver, diatomite. Formed 1861.

Lyon, village (1990 pop. 446), Coahoma co., NW Miss., 2 mi/3.2 km NE of Clarksdale, on Sunflower R.; 34°13′N 90°32′W. In agr. area (cotton, corn, soybeans, rice; cattle); mfg. (cotton processing).

Lyon, Fort, Colo.: see LAS ANIMAS.

Lyon Mountain, village, Clinton co., extreme NE N.Y., in the Adirondacks, 22 mi/35 km W of Plattsburgh. Lyon Mt. (elev. 3,810 ft/1,161 m) is just SE; 44°43′N 73°55′W.

Lyon Station, Pa.: see LYONS.

Lyons 1 (LEI-uhnz), town (1990 pop. 1,227), Boulder co., N Colo., at junction of N and S St. Vrain creeks, just E of Front Range, 15 mi/24 km N of Boulder; 40°13′N 105°16′W. Elev. c.5,374 ft/1,638 m. Mining, building stone, and lumbering point. Rocky Mt. Natl. Park to W; Roosevelt Natl. Forest to W. **2** town (1990 pop. 4,502), ⊙ Toombs co., E central Ga., 5 mi/8 km ESE of Vidalia; 32°12′N 82°19′W. In agr. and timber area. Mfg.

Area in square miles is shown by the symbol □   capital city or county seat by ⊙

includes storage tanks, clothing, textiles, concrete prods., veneers. Inc. 1897. **3** town (1990 pop. 753), Greene co., SW Ind., 9 mi/14.5 km WSW of Bloomfield; 38°59′N 87°05′W. In agr. and bituminous-coal area. **4** town (1990 pop. 3,688), ⊙ Rice co., central Kansas, 25 mi/40 km NW of Hutchinson; 38°21′N 98°12′W. RR junction. Salt mining and processing. Oil and natural-gas fields. County Mus. here. Quivira Relics archaeological site to W. Laid out 1876 on Santa Fe Trail; inc. 1880. **5** town (1990 pop. 1,144), Burt co., NE Nebr., 17 mi/27 km NW of Tekamah, and on Logan Creek, near Missouri R.; 41°56′N 96°28′W. Grain; livestock; mfg. (metal fabrication, alfalfa prods.). Inc. 1869. **6** town (1990 pop. 938), Linn co., W Oregon, 20 mi/32 km SE of Salem, on North Santiam R.; 44°46′N 122°36′W. Timber; fruits, vegetables. Mfg. (veneer). North Santiam State Park and Willamette Natl. Forest to E.

Lyons 1 village (1990 pop. 9,828), Cook co., NE Ill., a residential suburb of Chicago, on the Des Plaines R.; 41°48′N 87°49′W. Lyons was settled at the edge of an early travel route, the portage bet. the Chicago and the Des Plaines rivers. Inc. 1888. **2** village (1990 pop. 824), Ionia co., S central Mich., 6 mi/9.7 km E of Ionia, and on Grand R.; 42°58′N 84°57′W. In farm area; furniture mfg. **3** village (1990 pop. 4,280), ⊙ Wayne co., W N.Y., on the New York State Barge Canal and Clyde R., and 32 mi/51 km ESE of Rochester; 43°05′N 77°00′W. Mfg. (canned foods, chemicals, condiments, clothing, furniture, silk, brandy); in fruit-growing region. Summer resort. Settled 1800; inc. 1831. **4** village (1990 pop. 579), Fulton co., NW Ohio, 27 mi/43 km W of Toledo, near Mich. state line; 41°42′N 84°04′W. **5** village, Minnehaha co., SE S.Dak., 13 mi/21 km NW of Sioux Falls. Clear L. to SW; 43°43′N 96°52′W. Agr. area (corn, soybeans; cattle, hogs). Mfg. (fire trucks, printing). **6** village, Walworth Co., SE Wis., 6 mi/9.7 km SW of Burlington. Vegetables; livestock. Mfg. (thermofoam clamshells, light aircraft components).

Lyons (LEI-uhns) or **Lyon Station**, borough (1990 pop. 499), Berks co., E central Pa., 12 mi/19 km NE of Reading; 40°28′N 75°45′W. Agr. (grain; livestock; poultry; dairying); mfg. (electrical equip.).

Lyons Falls, village (☐ 1 sq mi/2.6 sq km; 1990 pop. 698), Lewis co., N central N.Y., on Black R. (falls here) at junction with Moose R., and 14 mi/23 km SSE of Lowville; 43°37′N 75°21′W. Paper milling. Co-generation of electric power (hydro and burning of wood residue) here and at Lyonsdale, 2 mi/3.2 km E. on Moose R. Paper milling also at Lyonsdale. At N terminus of 35 mi/56 km Black R. Canal, begun in 1838, completed in 1858, ceased operation in 1922. Never successfully competed with RR. Completely abandoned in 1926 when its final function as a feeder of water to the New York State Barge Canal was assumed by Delta L. (NE of Rome) and Hinckley Reservoir, N of Utica.

Lysander, planned residential village (☐ 5 sq mi/13 sq km; 1990 pop. 16,346) in township of Lysander, Onondaga co., central N.Y., 12 mi/19 km NW of Syracuse, 1 mi/1.6 km E of Baldwinsville; 43°10′N 76°22′W. Locally recognized name, although no central business dist. exists. Created as 1 of many residential, commercial, and industrial projects by N.Y. state's Urban Development Corp. that were meant to accommodate pop. growth in the area. Housing was to be provided for people of all income levels (planned capacity 18,000 residents), and 795 acres/322 ha were set aside for industrial uses. Despite fears of local residents of increased taxes, the loss of rural character, stifling of industrial competition, and the possibility of slums developing due to subsidized low-income housing, the community has been very successful.

Lyster (LI-stuhr), village (1991 pop. 1,740), S Que., Canada, on Bécancour R., and 35 mi/56 km SW of Que.; 46°22′N 71°37′W. Lumbering; dairying: livestock.

Lytle, town (1990 pop. 2,255), Atascosa co., SW Texas, 23 mi/37 km SW of San Antonio, near source of Atascosa R.; 29°13′N 98°47′W. Agr. area (cotton, corn, peanuts, vegetables); mfg. (feeds).

Lytle Creek, uninc. village (1990 pop. 700), San Bernardino co., S Calif., 14 mi/23 km NW of San Bernardino, on Lytle Creek, in San Bernardino Mts. and San Bernardino Natl Forest. San Gabriel Mts. to W. Tourism. Mfg. (transportation equip.).

Lytle, Lake, W central Texas, impounded by dam in small Lytle Creek (a S tributary of Clear Fork of Brazos R.), in city of Abilene; 1 mi/1.6 km long.

Lytton, village (1991 pop. 335), S B.C., Canada, on Fraser R. at mouth of Thompson R., and 65 mi/105 km SW of Kamloops; 50°14′N 121°34′W. Fruit and vegetable growing; gold mining; lumbering. Commercial apple growing in B.C. began in this area.

Lytton, town (1990 pop. 320), on Calhoun-Sac co. line, central Iowa, 7 mi/11.3 km E of Sac City; 42°25′N 94°51′W. In agr. area.

M

Maalaea Bay (MAH-ah-LEI-ah), arm of Pacific Ocean, on S coast of isthmus, Maui, Maui co., Hawaii, 6 mi/9.7 km S of Wailuku.

Mabank, town (1990 pop. 1,739), Kaufman co., NE Texas, c.50 mi/80 km SE of Dallas; 32°22′N 96°05′W. In agr. (cattle; cotton, sorghum, wheat), timber area; mfg. (turbines; diversified light mfg.); oil wells. Purtis Creek State Park to E; Cedar Creek Reservoir to SW.

Mabel, village (1990 pop. 745), Fillmore co., SE Minn., near Iowa state line, 19 mi/31 km SE of Preston, on Riceford Creek; 43°31′N 91°46′W. Grain, soybeans; livestock, poultry; dairying. Richard J. Dorer Memorial Hardwood State Forest to N.

Mabel Lake, S B.C., W Canada, 27 mi/43 km SW of Revelstoke; 22 mi/35 km long, 1 mi/2 km–2 mi/3 km wide. Drained W by Shuswap R. into Shuswap L.

Maben (MAI-buhn), town (1990 pop. 752), Oktibbeha and Webster cos., E Miss., 17 mi/27 km WNW of Starkville; 33°32′N 89°04′W. Agr. (cotton, corn, soybeans; cattle); mfg. (wood prods., apparel; meat processing). Natchez Trace (Natl.) Parkway passes to NW.

Mableton, growing suburb (1990 pop. 25,725), Cobb co., Ga., 5 mi/8 km NW of Atlanta; 33°30′N 84°35′W. Mfg. of lumber, aerospace parts, signs, coil coatings, plastic prods., wood prods., forestry equip., vegetable oil, machining.

Mabou (MA-boo), village, NE N.S., E Canada, W Cape Breton Isl., on Mabou R., near its mouth, on the Gulf of St. Lawrence, 12 mi/19 km SSW of Inverness; 46°04′N 61°22′W.

Mabou River, 15 mi/24 km long, NE N.S., E Canada, on W Cape Breton Isl.; rises in the Craignish Hills 4 mi/6 km SE of Mabou; flows WNW, past Mabou, to Gulf of St. Lawrence 5 mi/8 km W of Mabou.

Mabscott, town (1990 pop. 1,543), Raleigh co., S W.Va., suburb, 3 mi/4.8 km SW of Beckley; 37°46′N 81°12′W. Semibituminous-coal region. Mfg. (concrete). Inc. 1906.

Mabton, town (1990 pop. 1,482), Yakima co., S Wash., near Yakima R., and 35 mi/56 km SE of Yakima; 46°13′N 120°00′W. At E edge of Yakima Indian Reservation. Feeds. Horse Heaven Hills to S.

Macamic (mah-kah-MEEK), village, W Que., E Canada, on Macamic L., 35 mi/56 km N of Rouyn; 48°46′N 79°00′W. Lumbering; dairying; mining region. Also spelled Makamik.

MacArthur, uninc. town (1990 pop. 1,595), Raleigh co., S W.Va., suburb, 2 mi/3.2 km SSW of Beckley; 37°45′N 81°12′W. Coal region. Mfg. (bldg. materials, wood prods.).

MacArthur, Fort, Calif.: see SAN PEDRO.

Macclenny (muh-KLEN-nee), town (□ 3 sq mi/7.8 sq km; 1990 pop. 3,966), ⊙ Baker co., NE Fla., 28 mi/45 km W of Jacksonville; 30°16′N 82°07′W. In lumbering and farming area.

Maccles Lake (□ 12 sq mi/31 sq km), E N.F., E Canada, 30 mi/48 km SE of Gander; 8 mi/13 km long, 5 mi/8 km wide.

Macclesfield (MAK-uhlz-feeld), village (1990 pop. 493), Edgecombe co., E central N.C., 13 mi/21 km E of Wilson; 35°45′N 77°40′W. Tobacco, cotton, peanuts, grain; poultry, livestock.

MacDonald Pass (6,320 ft/1,926 m), on Continental Divide, on border bet. Powell and Lewis and Clark cos., W central Mont., 14 mi/23 km W of Helena. Named for Alexander MacDonald, who built and maintained 1st road (1870–1875) through pass; now U.S. Highway 12.

MacDonald-Cartier Freeway (Highway 401), S Ont., central Canada, 600 mi/966 km divided expressway from Windsor to Montreal (Que.). Commonly referred to as "The 401," it is considered Canada's "Main Street" and is central to Ontario's 400-series freeway system.

Built during the late 1960s and early 1970s, it links London, Kitchener/Waterloo, Toronto, Kingston, and Cornwall. Follows N shore of L. Ontario and St. Lawrence R. It enters Que. 40 mi/64 km SW of Montreal, where it becomes Highway 20 and connects with Montreal's Boulevard Metropolitain. One sect. in suburban Toronto has 16 lanes.

Macdougall, Lake (□ 265 sq mi/686 sq km), NW Keewatin dist., N.W.T., N Canada, NE of L. Garry; 66°00′N 99°00′W; 37 mi/60 km long, 1 mi/2 km–10 mi/16 km wide. Drained SE by Back R.

MacDowell Colony, N.H.: see PETERBORO.

Macedon, village (□ 1 sq mi/2.6 sq km; 1990 pop. 1,400), Wayne co., W N.Y., on the Barge Canal, and 12 mi/19 km SE of Rochester; 43°04′N 77°17′W. Mfg. of food flavorings, bases, and syrups.

Macedonia, city (1990 pop. 7,509), Summit co., NE Ohio, 14 mi/23 km N of Akron, just off U.S. Interstate 480, in a primarily urban area that stretches from S Cleveland to Akron; 41°19′N 81°29′W.

Macedonia, town (1990 pop. 262), Pottawattamie co., SW Iowa, on West Nishnabotna R., and 24 mi/39 km ESE of Council Bluffs; 41°11′N 95°25′W. In agr. region.

Macedonia, village (1990 pop. 58), Hamilton co., S Ill., 8 mi/12.9 km WSW of McLeansboro; 38°02′N 88°42′W. In agr. area.

Maces Bay, fishing village, SW N.B., E Canada, on Maces (or Mace) Bay (inlet of the Bay of Fundy), 24 mi./39 km SW of St. John.

MacGregor, village (1991 pop. 852), S Man., central Canada, 22 mi/35 km W of Portage la Prairie; 49°58′N 98°46′W. Grain elevators.

Machesney Park (ma-CHEZ-nee), city (1990 pop. 19,033), Winnebago co., N central Ill., suburb, 6 mi/9.7 km NNE of downtown Rockford, on Rock R.; 42°21′N 89°02′W. Diversified light mfg. Rock Cut State Park to E.

Machias (muh-CHEI-uhs), town (1990 pop. 2,569), including Machias village, ⊙ Washington co., E Maine, 65 mi/105 km ESE of Bangor, near mouth of the Machias R.; 44°40′N 67°27′W. Lumbering center. Site of Univ. of Maine campus. Eng. trading post here (1633) destroyed shortly thereafter by the French. Burnham Tavern (1770), historical mus., has mementos of early naval battle of Machiasport. Settled 1763, inc. 1784.

Machias, village (1990 pop. 900), Cattaraugus co., W N.Y., 25 mi/40 km N of Olean; 42°23′N 78°31′W. Resort, with small Lime L. nearby. Dairy and maple-sugar prods.; poultry. Lumber, wood prods.

Machias Bay (muh-CHEI-uhs), Washington co., E Maine, at mouths of Machias and East Machias rivers, just SE of Machias; 7 mi/11.3 km long, 4 mi/6.4 km wide.

Machias Lakes (muh-CHEI-uhs), Washington co., E Maine, 5 lakes (First to Fifth Machias lakes) in upper course of Machias R.; 1 mi/1.6 km–5 mi/8 km long.

Machias River 1 (muh-CHEI-uhs), c.65 mi/105 km long, in E Maine; rises in W Washington co., forms Machias Lakes in its upper course; flows c.40 mi/64 km S and SE to Machias Bay at Machiasport. **2** c.35 mi/56 km long, in N Maine; rises in Big Machias L. in Aroostook co.; flows SE and E to the Aroostook R. near Ashland.

Machias Seal Islands (muh-CHEI-uhs), group of islets, Washington co., off Maine and N.B. coasts, 24 mi/39 km SE of Machias, Maine. Can.-operated lighthouse (44°39′N 67°06′W) on Machias Seal, the southernmost isl.

Machiasport (muh-CHEI-uhs-port), town (1990 pop. 1,166), Washington co., E Maine, at head of Machias Bay, E of Machias; 44°37′N 67°24′W. Earthworks of Revolutionary War fort taken (1814) by British in state park. Offshore, in June 1775, a Br. ship was captured in what became known as "1st naval battle of the Revolution." Set off from Machias 1862.

Machinery City, Ga.: see FAIR OAKS.

MacIntyre, Mount (5,112 ft/1,558 m), Essex co., NE N.Y., 10 mi/16 km S of Lake Placid village; 44°08′N 74°01′W. Highest peak of MacIntyre Mts., a short range of the

Adirondack Mts. The peak faces Wallface Mt. (W) across scenic Indian Pass.

Mack, village, Mesa co., W Colo., near Utah state line (to W) and Colorado R., 20 mi/32 km NW of Grand Junction. Elev. 4,523 ft/1,379 m. In cattle and agr. region producing wheat, potatoes, beans, oats, barley. Nearby are deposits of coal and petroleum. Highline State Park to NE.

Mackay (ma-kee), village (1990 pop. 574), Custer co., S central Idaho, 25 mi/40 km NW of Arco, on Big Lost R.; 43°55′N 113°37′W. Elev. 5,897 ft/1,797 m. RR terminus. Gold, silver, zinc; agr. Mackay Reservoir to NW; Borah Peak (12,662 ft/3,859 m; highest point in Idaho) to NNW, in Lost R. Range; parts of Challis Natl. Forest to NE and SW.

Mackenzie, district, provisional administrative division (□ 527,490 sq mi/1,366,199 sq km) of N.W.T., N Canada, comprising W mainland part of territory, bounded S by Sask., Alta., and B.C., W by the Yukon, N by several arms of the Arctic Ocean (Beaufort Sea, Amundsen Gulf, Coronation Gulf, Dease Strait, and Queen Maud Gulf), and E by Keewatin Dist.; 65°00′N 115°00′W. In W are Mackenzie Mts., N range of the Rocky Mts., here rising to 9,049 ft/2,758 m on Mt. Sir James McBrien. E of this range extends the Mackenzie R. valley, widest part of which lies bet. Great Bear and Great Slave lakes. E of lakes is plateau, c.350 mi/563 km wide (E-W), followed by plain E of line bet. Dubawnt L. and Bathurst Inlet. Dist. is drained by Mackenzie R. and its tributaries (Hay, Slave, Liard, Arctic Red, and Great Bear rivers), and by Coppermine, Anderson, and Thelon rivers. N coastline is irregular and indented by several large bays. Gold mining is centered on Yellowknife, largest town of the N.W.T., site of discovery of important deposits in 1934. Uranium and pitchblende are mined on E shore of Great Bear L.; operations centered on Port Radium. Oil is found near Norman Wells; during World War II, terminal of *Canol* project pipeline. Copper, found near Coppermine, is not exploited because of transportation difficulties. Norman Wells is the chief oil-producing town. In the early 1970s large natural-gas fields were discovered in the Mackenzie delta region. A plan to construct the Mackenzie Valley Pipeline from the Arctic Ocean to Alta., which would have been the greatest construction project ever undertaken, was shelved in 1977 after a federal royal commission concluded that, though feasible, the project involved serious legal, political, and environmental problems. Tungsten-copper mined at Tungsten, on Yukon border. Lead-zinc mining at Pine Point, 1962–1987. Fur trapping and crafts are major occupations of Native (Inuit and other pop.). Chief towns are Fort Smith, Inuvik, and Hay River; other important trading posts are Aklavik, Fort Norman, Fort Simpson, Fort Providence, Fort Reliance, Hay River, Coppermine, Fort Liard, and Arctic Red River. There are extensive game preserves, including the Reindeer Grazing Reserve and Mackenzie Mts., Yellowknife, and Slave River preserves. Thelon Game Sanctuary has largest herd of musk ox on N.Amer. mainland. Transportation in dist. is by river and lake ships during summer navigation season (June-Oct.), winter road system during freeze-up. Nearly all localities served by scheduled air service; private planes are principal means of transportation. Created 1895, present borders defined 1918. NE part, from Keewatin dist. border NW to Clinton Point to be included in Territory of Nunavut (1999).

Mackenzie, river, c.1,120 mi/1,802 km long, N.W.T., N Canada; issues from Great Slave L., Fort Smith Region; flows generally NW to the Arctic Ocean through a great delta. Bet. Great Slave L. and L. Athabasca it is known as the Slave R. At L. Athabasca, the Finlay-Peace river system and the Athabasca R. join the Mackenzie. The Finlay-Peace-Mackenzie system (c.2,600 mi/4,180 km long) is the 2d-longest continuous stream in N. Amer. The Liard R. is the largest tributary flowing directly into the Mackenzie. The river is navigable from the Arctic Ocean to Great Slave L. bet. June and Oct. Bet. Great Slave L. and L. Athabasca there are rapids (14 mi/23 km) that must be portaged; above the rapids are over 400 mi/644 km of navigable waters. The Liard R. affords transportation bet. Fort Nelson (B.C.), and the Arctic; the Athabasca-Mackenzie system is followed by a major shipping route bet. Edmonton (Alta.), and the Arctic. Numerous lakes in the Mackenzie basin act as reservoirs and natural flood controls. The basin, flanked by the Rocky Mts. and the Can. Shield, is the N portion of the Great Plains of N. Amer.; Arctic air masses follow the valley S into the interior of the continent. Much of the Mackenzie valley is heavily forested and, where climate permits, its deep soil is well suited to agr. Numerous trading posts were established along the Mackenzie in the early part of the 19th cent. and fur trapping is still an important activity here; the chief trading posts are Fort Simpson, Fort Providence, and Aklavik. The region was the domain of fur traders until the 1930s when vast oil fields and other mineral resources were discovered. Peter Pond was possibly the 1st European to enter (1777) the Mackenzie drainage area, but Sir Alexander Mackenzie, the 19th-cent. Can. explorer, was the 1st to descend (1789) the river to the Arctic Ocean.

Mackenzie, town (1990 pop. 148), St. Louis co., E Mo., residential suburb of St. Louis, 8 mi/12.9 km SW of downtown.

Mackenzie Bay, NW Mackenzie dist., N.W.T., N Canada, inlet of Beaufort Sea of the Arctic Ocean, at mouth of Mackenzie R. delta; 100 mi/161 km long, 120 mi/193 km wide at mouth; 68°40′–69°45′N 134°30′–139°00′W. On E side of bay are Richards, Ellice, and several smaller isls.; on W side is Herschel Isl.

Mackenzie Highway, NW Alta. and SW N.W.T., W Canada; begins in S at Grimshaw (Alta.), 14 mi/23 km W of Peace River; continues N through Manning, High Level, Meander R. to Enterprise (N.W.T.), S of Great Slave L., where it turns WNW and continues to Fort Simpson and Wrigley. A winter road extension beyond Wrigley goes to Fort Norman, Norman Wells, and Fort Good Hope. Major river crossings include bridge over Hay R. at Meander R. ferry crossing of Liard R. E of Fort Simpson, ferry crossing of Mackenzie R. 40 mi/64 km NW of Fort Simpson. The highway and its branches to Yellowknife, Hay R. Fort Smith, and Fort Resolution are collectively referred to as the Mackenzie Route. The system is used to transfer goods and services N and raw materials, mainly from mining, S. Total distance, Grimshaw to Wrigley, 720 mi/1,159 km. Original highway and branches constructed during World War II; sect. to Fort Simpson, 1970s; to Wrigley, 1994.

Mackenzie Mountains, N range of Rocky Mts. in E Yukon and SW Mackenzie dist., N.W.T., NW Canada; extends c.500 mi/805 km SE-NW bet. B.C. border to Peel R. valley, forming S part of Yukon-N.W.T. border. Highest peak, Mt. Sir James McBrien (9,049 ft/2,758 m); other peaks higher than 8,000 ft/2,438 m are Mt. Hunt, Keele Peak, Dome Peak, Mt. Sidney Dobson, and Mt. Ida. In S part of range is Mackenzie Mts. Preserve, game reserve (□ 69 sq mi/179 sq km–440 sq mi/1,140 sq km) est. 1938.

Mackinac (MA-ki-naw), historic region of the Old Northwest (former NORTHWEST TERRITORY), a shortening of Michilimackinac. The name, in the past, was variously applied to different areas: to Mackinac Isl., to Mich., to the whole fur-trading region supplied from the isl., to the N mainland shore (St. Ignace, Mich., has been sometimes called Anc. Michilimackinac), and to the S mainland shore, where Mackinaw City (Mich.) is located and where a fort called Old Mackinac once stood. The Straits of Mackinac, a passage bet. the Upper and Lower peninsulas of Mich., connecting L. Michigan and L. Huron, served for many years as an important Native Amer. gathering place. In 1634 the Fr. explorer Jean Nicolet was the 1st European to pass through the straits. The Fr. Jesuit Claude Allouez, in 1665, was the 1st missionary to come here; he was followed by Father Jacques Marquette, who established a mission at St. Ignace in 1671. A fort was later built here, and it became the hq. of Fr. trade operations in New France and an important military post in the Old Northwest; its importance declined when Detroit was founded in 1701. The region passed into Br. hands in 1761 during the last conflict of the Fr. and Indian Wars. In 1763 members of the Br. garrison at Old Mackinac were attacked and killed by the Ottawa during Pontiac's Rebellion. During the Amer. Revolution, the fort and town at Old Mackinac, threatened by the exploits of the Amer. general George Rogers Clark, were moved to Mackinac Isl. The isl. and the straits were awarded to the U.S. in 1783 by the Treaty of Paris, but they remained in Br. hands until 1794. One of the 1st events of the War of 1812 was the Br. capture of Mackinac; it was returned to U.S. control by the Treaty of Ghent in 1814. After the war, Mackinac Isl. became the center of operations of John Jacob Astor's Amer. Fur Company, which thrived until the 1830s, when fur trading declined. After the 1840s the straits area changed from an important crossroads to an out-of-the-way shipping point, and the U.S. army post on the isl. was abandoned in 1894. Mackinac Isl. became a Mich. state park and, along with Bois Blanc Isl., a popular summer resort. Iron-ore mining revitalized the area in the early 20th cent., but the mineral was soon depleted. The Mackinac Straits Bridge (3,800 ft/1,158 m long; opened 1957) spans the straits and links St. Ignace with Mackinaw City. The connection has stimulated the economy of the Upper Peninsula as a result of the added transportation route for tourists, vacationers and sports enthusiasts. The straits are an important link in the Great Lakes-St. Lawrence waterway.

Mackinac (MA-ki-naw), county (□ 2,099 sq mi/5,436 sq km; 1990 pop. 10,674), SE Upper Peninsula, N Mich.; ⊙ St. Ignace; 46°00′N 85°00′W. Bounded S by lakes Michigan and Huron and by their connection, the Straits of Mackinac; drained by Carp and small Pine rivers. Part of historic MACKINAC region; includes Mackinac and Bois Blanc isls. Forest, resort, and agr. area (forage crops, oats; cattle; dairy prods.). Several lakes (part of Manistique; and South Manistique, Brevoort, Milakokia, Millecoquins) are in co. Hiawatha Natl. Forest in E center; Straits State Park; Mackinac Isl. State Park in SE. Formed 1818.

Mackinac Island (MA-ki-naw), village (1990 pop. 469), Mackinac co., SE Upper Peninsula, N Mich., 5 mi/8 km E of St. Ignace, on S end of Mackinac Isl. (c.3 mi/4.8 km long, 2 mi/3.2 km wide; a state park since 1895), in the Straits of Mackinac; 45°51′N 84°37′W. Summer resort, connected by passenger ferry with Mackinaw City and St. Ignace. No motorized vehicles on isl. Has airport; only accessible by air in winter. Village maintains original 1890s bldgs.; transportation by bicycle, horseback, and carriage. The Astor House (built c.1817 by Amer. Fur Company), and restored Fort Mackinac (est. 1780), with 14 restored bldgs., are reminders of isl.'s military, strategic role in history of MACKINAC region. Grand Hotel has the longest porch in world. Also called Mackinac.

Mackinac, Straits of (MA-ki-naw), N Mich., channel in heart of historic MACKINAC region separating Upper and Lower peninsulas and forming important waterway bet. lakes Huron (E) and Michigan (W); c.4 mi/6.4 km wide. To E and SE of St. Ignace (on N shore) are Mackinac, Round, and Bois Blanc isls. in L. Huron. St. Helena Isl., to W, near N shore of L. Michigan. South Channel of straits lies bet. Bois Blanc Isl. and the Lower Peninsula; 45°49′N 84°45′W. Spanned by the Mackinac Straits Bridge (3,800 ft./1,158 m long; opened 1957).

Mackinaw (MA-ki-naw), village (1990 pop. 1,331), Tazewell co., central Ill., on Mackinaw R. (bridged here), and 16 mi/26 km E of Pekin; 40°32′N 89°21′W. In agr. area; sand, gravel pits.

Mackinaw City (MA-ki-naw), village (1990 pop. 875), Sheboygan and Emmet cos., N Mich., 15 mi/24 km NW of Cheboyan, on the S shore of the Straits of Mackinac; 45°46′N 84°45′W. Mfg. (candy). The region was well traveled by traders, missionaries, and explorers during the 17th and 18th cent. Fr. troops, sent to garrison Fort Michilimackinac in 1715, remained for several years until the fort was occupied by Br. forces. Fort Michilimackinac W of town near base of bridge in Michilimackinac State Park. Mackinaw City was formerly linked with the Upper Peninsula only by car ferry. The completion of the Mackinac Straits Bridge (1957) now links the village with St. Ignace, on Upper Peninsula, to N. Passenger ferry to Mackinac Isl. to NE (summer). Old Mill Creek State Historical Park to SE; Wilderness State Park to W. Settled 1681, inc. 1882.

Mackinaw River, c.130 mi/209 km long, central Ill.; rises in W Ford co.; flows W, SW, and N, to Illinois R. below Pekin; 40°35′N 88°21′W.

Macklin, town (1991 pop. 1,105), W Sask., W Canada, on Alta. border, 75 mi/121 km WSW of North Battleford; 52°20′N 109°57′W. RR junction, with grain elevators, stockyard; dairying.

Macks Creek, town (1990 pop. 272), Camden co., central Mo., in Ozarks, near L. of the Ozarks, c.14 mi/23 km WSW of Camdenton; 37°58′N 92°58′W. Tunnel Dam hydroelectric power station on Niangua R. to E. Timber; cattle. Recreational area.

Macksburg, town (1990 pop. 110), Madison co., S central Iowa, 12 mi/19 km SW of Winterset; 41°12′N 94°11′W. In agr. area.

Macksburg, village (1990 pop. 218), Washington co., SE Ohio, 14 mi/23 km N of Marietta; 39°38′N 81°27′W.

Macksville, village (1990 pop. 488), Stafford co., S central Kansas, 11 mi/18 km WSW of St. John; 37°57′N 98°58′W. In wheat and livestock region. Antique Car Mus.

Mackworth Island, SW Maine, in Casco Bay just NE of Portland, near Falmouth, to which a bridge leads, and just NE of Portland; c.½ mi/⅘ km in diameter

Maclean Strait, N.W.T.: see PRINCE GUSTAV ADOLPH SEA.

Macmillan, river, c.200 mi/320 km long, E Yukon Territory, NW Canada; rises in 2 main forks in the Selwyn Mts.; flows generally W to the Pelly R. Important route to the goldfields, c.1890–1900.

MacNutt, village (1991 pop. 103), SE Sask., W Canada, on Man. border, 40 mi/64 km ESE of Yorkton. Mixed farming.

Macomb (muh-KOM), county (□ 569 sq mi/1,474 sq km; 1990 pop. 717,400), SE Mich., in Detroit metropolitan area, just N of Detroit; 42°40′N 82°54′W; ⊙ Mt. Clemens. Bounded SE by L. St. Clair and Anchor Bay; drained by Clinton R. and its affluents. Farm area (corn, wheat, oats, soybeans, apples, peaches; dairy prods.). Mfg. (fabricated metal prods., paper prods., transportation equip., machinery). Highly urbanized in S; mainly residential and commercial in W; industrial and office parks. Major suburban cities include Warren, Sterling Heights, St. Clair Shores. Selfridge Air Natl. Guard Base in L. St. Clair in E. Dodge Brothers State Park No. 8 at Sterling Heights; Rochester-Utica State Recreation Area in SW. Formed and organized 1818.

Macomb, city (1990 pop. 19,952), ⊙ McDonough co., W Ill., c.59 mi/95 km WSW of Peoria; 40°28′N 90°40′W. A trade and mfg. center in a rich farm, clay, and coal region, the city is known for its artistic clay prods. Other mfg. includes insulated containers and roller bearings. Seat of Western Ill. Univ. State park nearby. Inc. as a city 1841.

Macomb, Fort (muh-KOM), old U.S. fortification, Orleans parish, within city of New Orleans, SE La., on W bank of Chef Menteur Pass bet. lakes Pontchartrain and Borgne, c.20 mi/32 km ENE of downtown New Orleans; 30°03′N 89°48′W. Built c.1828. Partly restored; in State Commemorative area (16 acres/6.5 ha).

Macon 1 (MAI-kuhn), county (□ 613 sq mi/1,588 sq km; 1990 pop. 24,928), E Ala.; ⊙ Tuskegee, 32°24′N 85°49′W. In the Black Belt; drained by Tallapoosa R. and its branches. Cotton, corn, soybeans, peanuts, sweet potatoes; cattle; dairying. Contains Tuskegee Natl. Forest. Formed 1832. **2** county (□ 406 sq mi/1,052 sq km; 1990 pop. 13,114), central Ga.; ⊙ Oglethorpe; 32°21′N 84°02′W. Drained by Flint R. Coastal plain agr. area (cotton, corn, soybeans, wheat, peanuts); timber. Formed 1837. **3** county (□ 585 sq mi/1,515 sq km; 1990 pop. 117,206), central Ill.; ⊙ Decatur; 39°52′N 88°58′W. Agr. (corn, soybeans; livestock). Diversified mfg. Decatur is industrial and commercial center. Bituminous-coal mining. Drained by Sangamon R., dammed to form L. Decatur (recreation area). Includes Spitler Woods Natural Area and Lincoln Trail Homestead State Park. Formed 1829. **4** county (□ 814 sq mi/2,108 sq km; 1990 pop. 15,345), N central Mo.; ☉ Macon; 39°50′N 92°33′W. Drained by Chariton and Salt rivers. Agr. (corn, wheat, soybeans, hay); cattle, sheep, hogs; mfg. at Macon. Former coal-mining area. Long Branch L. and State Park to NW, Thomas Hill Reservoir in SW. Formed 1828. **5** county (□ 519 sq mi/1,344 sq km; 1990 pop. 23,499), W N.C., on Ga. (S) state line; ☉ Franklin; 35°08′N 83°25′W. SE corner near common corner at Ga., S.C., and N.C. Part of Blue Ridge Mts. in SE; crossed N-S by Nantahala Mts.; drained by Nantahala R. (forms Nantahala L. reservoir in W) and the Little Tennessee R. Included in Nantahala Natl. Forest. Agr. area (vegetables, apples, corn, hay, tobacco; cattle; dairying); timber, mica mining; resort area. L. Sequayah reservoir in SE. Appalachian Trail passes N-S through W part of co. Formed 1828. **6** county (□ 304 sq mi/787 sq km; 1990 pop. 15,906), N Tenn., on Ky. (N) state line; ☉ Lafayette; 36°32′N 86°01′W. Drained by affluents of Barren and Cumberland rivers. Timber; agr. (corn, tobacco); livestock raising. Formed 1842.

Macon 1 city (1990 pop. 106,612), ☉ Bibb co., central Ga., at the head of navigation on the Ocmulgee R.; 32°50′N 83°40′W. It is the industrial, processing, and shipping center for an extensive agr. area. Many antebellum mansions remain (the city was spared from Sherman's March during the Civil War). Known for its cherry blossom festival in spring. Mfg. includes processing of agr. prods. (cotton, peanuts, soybeans; poultry; dairy prods.), chemicals, wood prods., fabricated metal prods., bldg. materials, waste systems, transportation equip., shipping materials; printing and publishing. Est. 1806 on the E side of the Ocmulgee and renamed Newtown in 1821. A 2d Macon (for Nathaniel Macon) was laid out on the W side in 1823; Newtown was annexed in 1829. Seat of Wesleyan Col., Mercer Univ., a state school for the blind, and Macon Col. (2-year). Also in Macon are the birthplace of Sidney Lanier, a restored grand-opera house (1884), Fort Hawkins (1806; partially restored), a mus. of arts and sciences, and a planetarium. Nearby are Robins Air Force Base and the Ocmulgee Natl. Monument. Home of Georgia Music Hall of Fame. Inc. 1823. **2** city (1990 pop. 1,282), Macon co., central Ill., 8 mi/12.9 km S of Decatur; 39°42′N 89°00′W. In agr. (corn, soybeans, oats) and bituminous-coal area. **3** city (1990 pop. 5,571), ☉ Macon co., N central Mo., 25 mi/40 km S of Kirksville; 39°44′N 92°28′W. Ships agr. prods. (corn, wheat, soybeans) and livestock (cattle, hogs); former coal mines; mfg. (frozen foods, appliances). Long Branch L. and State Park on NW side of city. Inc. 1859.

Macon, town (1990 pop. 2,256), ☉ Noxubee co., E Miss., 28 mi/45 km SSW of Columbus, and on Noxubee R.; 33°06′N 88°33′W. Agr. (cotton, corn, wheat, soybeans; cattle; dairying); timber; mfg. (lumber, bricks, apparel, vinyl prods., feeds, transportation equip.). Co. Historical Society Mus. Inc. 1836.

Macon, village (1990 pop. 154), Warren co., N N.C., 4 mi/6.4 km NE of Warrenton; 36°26′N 78°04′W. Tobacco, grain; livestock.

Macon, Bayou (MAI-kuhn, BAH-yoo), c.175 mi/282 km long; rising in Desha co., SE Ark., S of Dumas; flows S into NE La. to the Tensas R. 18 mi/29 km SSE of Winnsboro (La.). Extremely serpentine esp. in N; closely parallels Mississippi R. (to E) for most of its length. It was used as a rendezvous by the bandits Frank and Jesse James.

Macouba (mah-koo-BAH), town, N Martinique, 18 mi/29 km NNW of Fort-de-France. Cacao growing; rum distilling.

Macoupin (ma-KOO-pin), county (□ 867 sq mi/2,246 sq km; 1990 pop. 47,679), SW central Ill.; ☉ Carlinville; 39°15′N 89°55′W. Agr. (corn, wheat, soybeans, sorghum; cattle, hogs, poultry; dairy prods.). Bituminous-coal mining; clay pits. Some mfg. (transportation

equip., food prods., wood prods.). Drained by Macoupin, Cahokia, and small Otter creeks. Formed 1829.

Macoupin Creek, c.100 mi/161 km long, SW Ill.; rises in NW Montgomery co.; flows SW and W to Illinois R. SE of Hardin; 39°24′N 89°34′W.

Macungie (mah-KUHNG-gee), borough (1990 pop. 2,597), Lehigh co., E Pa., 7 mi/11.3 km SSW of Allentown, near Swabia Creek; 40°31′N 75°32′W. Agr. area (apples, grain, potatoes, soybeans; livestock, poultry; dairying); mfg. (consumer goods, apparel, fabricated metal prods., wood prods.).

Macuspana (mah-koos-PAH-nah), city (1990 pop. 22,244) and township, Tabasco, SE Mexico, on Puxcatan R. (affluent of Grijalva R.), 27 mi/43 km SE of Villahermosa, 2 mi/3km NE of Mexico Highway 186; 18°46′N 92°36′W. Tropical agr.; petroleum production.

Macwahoc (muhk-WAH-hahk), plantation (1990 pop. 114), Aroostook co., E Maine, 40 mi/64 km SSW of Houlton; 45°38′N 68°14′W. Hunting, fishing.

Macy, town (1990 pop. 218), Miami co., N central Ind., 15 mi/24 km NNW of Peru; 40°58′N 86°08′W. In agr. area. Laid out 1860.

Macy, village (1990 pop. 836), Thurston co., Nebr., 50 mi/80 km N of Omaha, on Omaha Reservation. Tribal agency here. Annual Omaha tribal powwow held here in late Aug.

Mad River 1 c.95 mi/153 km long, N Calif.; rises in SE Trinity co. c.45 mi/72 km SW of Redding; flows NW to the Pacific Ocean 10 mi/16 km N of Eureka and NW of Arcata. **2** c.15 mi/24 km long, Grafton co., central N.H.; rises in White Mts. E of Woodstock; flows SW to Pemigewasset R. near Campton. **3** c.60 mi/97 km long, W Ohio; rises in Logan co.; flows S and SW, past Springfield, to Great Miami R. at Dayton; 39°45′N 84°11′W. **4** c.25 mi/40 km long, in W central Vt.; rises S of Warren, in Green Mts.; flows NE to Winooski R. W of Montpelier. Winter-sports area (skiing at Mad R. Glen) near Waitsfield.

Mad River Glen, ski area, Washington co., central Vt., in Fayston, and 10 mi/16 km WSW of Montpelier.

Madame Island or **Isle Madame** (eel mah-DAHM), in the Atlantic, E N.S., E Canada, just S of Cape Breton Isl., 8 mi/13 km N of Canso, near entrance of the Strait of Canso; 12 mi/19 km long, 9 mi/14 km wide. On S coast is Arichat.

Madawaska (ma-duh-WAH-skuh), county (□ 1,262 sq mi/3,269 sq km; 1991 pop. 36,554), NW N.B., E Canada, on U.S. (Maine) and Quebec borders; ☉ Edmundston.

Madawaska (mad-uh-WAHS-kuh), town (1990 pop. 4,803), Aroostook co., N Maine, on St. John R., opposite Edmundston (N.B.), and 15 mi/24 km NE of Fort Kent; 47°17′N 68°15′W. Port of entry; paper mills. Includes Madawaska village and Saint David, agr. village. Settled 1785 by Acadians, inc. 1869.

Madawaska River 1 250 mi/402 km long, SE Ont.; central Canada; rises in Algonquin Provincial Park; flows E, through several lakes, to Chats L. of Ottawa R. at Arnprior. **2** 30 mi/48 km long, SE Quebec and NW N.B., E Canada; issues from SE end of L. Temiscouata; flows SE to St. John R. at Edmundston (N.B.).

Madbury (1990 pop. 1,404), Strafford co., SE N.H., 3 mi/4.8 km SW of Dover; 43°10′N 70°56′W. Drained by Bellamy R. (forms Bellamy Reservoir in W). Agr. (cattle; vegetables, nursery crops; dairying); mfg. (wood prods.; commercial printing).

Maddock (MA-dahk), village (1990 pop. 559), Benson co., central N.Dak., 33 mi/53 km WSW of Devils L.; 47°57′N 99°31′W. Dairy prods.; grain; livestock, poultry. Mfg. (machinery).

Madeira (muh-DEE-ruh), city (1990 pop. 9,141), Hamilton co., extreme SW Ohio, a NE suburb of Cincinati; 39°11′N 84°22′W.

Madeira Beach (muh-DIR-ruh), town (□ 3 sq mi/7.8 sq km; 1990 pop. 4,225), Pinellas co., W central Fla., 10 mi/16 km WNW of St. Petersburg, on the Gulf of Mexico; 27°48′N 82°47′W.

Madeleine, îles-de-la-, Que.: see MAGDALEN ISLANDS.

Madelia (muh-DEE-lyuh), town (1990 pop. 2,237), Watonwan co., S Minn., 23 mi/37 km WSW of Mankato,

on Watonwan R.; 44°02′N 94°25′W. Agr. area (grain, soybeans; livestock, poultry); mfg. (poultry prods., bldg. materials, foods; printing and publishing). Feji L. to NE. Settled 1855, plotted 1857, inc. 1873.

Madeline Island, Wis.: see APOSTLE ISLANDS.

Madera (mah-DAI-rah), city (1990 pop. 13,774) and township, ☉ Madera municipio, Chihuahua, N Mexico, in Sierra Madre Occidental, on RR, and 125 mi/201 km WNW of Chihuahua; 29°17′N 107°52′W. Elev. 6,821 ft/2,079 m. Agr. (corn, beans, potatoes, fruits); woods.

Madera, county (□ 2,138 sq mi/5,537 sq km; 1990 pop. 88,090), central Calif.; ☉ Madera; 37°13′N 119°46′W. From level San Joaquin Valley in W, co. stretches NE to crest of the Sierra Nevada; Mt. Ritter rises to 13,156 ft/4,010 m. San Joaquin R., forms most of SW, S, and SE border, Chowchilla forms part of NW border. Watered by Fresno R. and Madera Canal (a unit of Central Valley project). Includes part of Yosemite Natl. Park (N), part of Sierra Natl. Forest (N and NE), and Devil Postpile Natl. Monument (NE). Rich irrigated valley lands produce cotton, oats, corn, wheat, barley, beans; pistachios, almonds, apples, figs, oranges, raisins, vegetables, honey; dairying; cattle, turkeys, poultry. Lumbering (chiefly pine); mining of pumice, gold, copper, sand and gravel; granite quarries. Mfg. at Madera and Chowchilla. Pacific Coast Trail crosses co. near NE border; part of Millerton L. State Recreation Area in SE; Mammoth Pool Reservoir (NE). Formed 1893.

Madera, city (1990 pop. 29,281), ☉ Madera co., central Calif., 20 mi/32 km NW of Fresno, on Fresno R., in the San Joaquin valley; 36°58′N 120°05′W. Winery. Cattle, poultry; dairying; nuts, fruit, grain, grapes, honey. Mfg. (machinery, consumer goods, plastic prods., ornamental metal work). Granite quarry. To the NE is Yosemite Natl. Park; Sierra Natl. Forest to NE; Millerton L. reservoir and State Recreation Area to E; Adobe Hill (566 ft/173 m) to NE. Inc. 1907.

Madera (mah-DUHR-ah), uninc. town (1990 pop. 900), Bigler township, Clearfield co., central Pa., 22 mi/35 km N of Altoona, on Clearfield Creek; 40°49′N 78°26′W. Agr. (dairying); mfg. of clothing. Surface bituminous coal.

Madera Acres, uninc. town (1990 pop. 5,245), Madera co., central Calif., residential suburb, 2 mi/3.2 km NNE of Madera, on Fresno R.; 37°01′N 120°04′W.

Madera Canal, Madera co., S central Calif. An irrigation unit (completed 1945) of Central Valley project; conducts San Joaquin R. water (by gravity) 37 mi/60 km NW from Friant Dam (Millerton L. reservoir), to supply Madera co. farmlands.

Madero, Mexico: see VILLA MADERO.

Madero, Ciudad, Mexico: see CIUDAD MADERO.

Madill (muh-DIL), town (1990 pop. 3,069), ☉ Marshall co., S Okla., 21 mi/34 km ESE of Ardmore, near L. Texoma; 34°05′N 96°46′W. Mfg. (peanut processing; transportation equip., apparel, fabricated metal prods.). L. Texoma State Park to SE; Tishomingo Natl. Wildlife Refuge to NE. A recreation center for nearby L. Texoma. Settled c.1900, inc. 1905.

Madison 1 county (□ 812 sq mi/2,103 sq km 1990 pop. 238,912), N Ala., on Tenn. (N) state line; ☉ Huntsville, 34°44′N 86°34′W. Drained in SW by Wheeler L. (in Tennessee R.), crossed (N-S) by Flint R. Cotton, corn, wheat, soybeans; mules, cattle, poultry; hay. Textiles. Formed 1808. **2** county (□ 837 sq mi/2,168 sq km; 1990 pop. 11,618), NW Ark., in the Ozark region; ☉ Huntsville; 36°00′N 93°42′W. Drained by White and Kings rivers and small War Eagle Creek. Agr. (cattle, hogs, chicken, turkeys); timber. Madison Co. Wildlife Management Area and Withrow State Park in N; part of Hobbs Wildlife Management Area in NW corner; part of Ozark Natl. Forest in S. Formed 1836. **3** county (□ 715 sq mi/1,852 sq km; 1990 pop. 16,569), N central Fla., on Ga. state line (N); ☉ Madison, 30°26′N 83°28′W. Flatwoods area with swamps and many small lakes; bounded by Aucilla (W), Withlacoochee (NE), and Suwannee (SE) rivers. Agr. (corn, peanuts, cotton, tobacco; hogs, poultry) and some forestry (lumber, naval stores). Formed 1827. **4** county (□ 286 sq mi/741 sq km; 1990 pop. 21,050), NE Ga.; ⊙ Danielsville, 34°08′N 83°13′W. Drained by Broad R. Mfg. includes apparel, textiles, wood prods.; printing and publishing. Piedmont agr. area (cotton, wheat, soybeans, sweet potatoes, hay); cattle, poultry, hogs. Formed 1811. **5** county (□ 473 sq mi/1,225 sq km; 1990 pop. 23,674), E Idaho; ⊙ Rexburg; 43°48′N 111°40′W. Irrigated agr. region in Snake R. Plain. Teton R. joins Henrys Fork R. in N which joins Snake R. in SW. Potatoes, sugar beets; wheat, barley, alfalfa; sheep, cattle; dairying. Part of Targhee Natl. Forest in SE; Kelly Canyon Ski Area in SE. Formed 1913. **6** county (□ 740 sq mi/1,917 sq km; 1990 pop. 249,238), SW Ill., bounded W by Mississippi R.; ⊙ Edwardsville; 38°50′N 89°54′W. Part of St. Louis metropolitan area. Agr. (wheat, soybeans, sorghum; cattle, poultry; dairy prods.) in E. Oil. Mfg. at major cities of Edwardsville, Granite City, Alton, Collinsville, and adjacent communities. Drained by Cahokia and Silver creeks. Campus of Southern Ill. Univ. at Edwardsville. Horseshoe L. State Park in SW (large oxbow lake). Formed 1812. **7** county (□ 452 sq mi/1,171 sq km; 1990 pop. 130,669), E central Ind.; ⊙ Anderson; 40°10′N 85°43′W. Drained by West Fork of White R. and by small Pipe, Kilbuck, Fall, Duck, and Lick creeks. Rich agr. area (hogs, cattle; corn, tomatoes, soybeans, vegetables; poultry). Diversified mfg.: includes processing of farm and dairy prods. Limestone quarrying. Ind. Reformatory in S at Pendleton. Mounds State Park E of Anderson. Formed 1823. **8** county (□ 562 sq mi/1,456 sq km; 1990 pop. 12,405), S central Iowa; ⊙ Winterset, 41°20′N 94°01′W. Prairie agr. area (hogs, cattle; corn, soybeans) drained by North and Middle rivers. Bituminous coal deposits, clay, limestone quarries. Pammel State Park SW of Winterset; Badger Creek State Park in NE. Formed 1846. **9** county (□ 443 sq mi/1,147 sq km; 1990 pop. 57,508), central Ky.; ⊙ Richmond, 37°44′N 84°18′W. Bounded NW, N, and NE by Kentucky R., W in part by Paint Lick creek; drained by Silver, Muddy, and Red Lick creeks. Rolling agr. area, in Bluegrass region (burley tobacco, corn, hay, alfalfa; poultry, cattle, horses; dairying); bituminous coal mines; clay pits. Mfg. at Berea and Richmond. Small parts of Daniel Boone Natl. Forest in SE; White Hall State Historic Site in NW; Lexington-Bluegrass Army Depot (chemical weapons) in center. Formed 1785. **10** county (□ 742 sq mi/1,922 sq km; 1990 pop. 53,794), central Miss.; ⊙ Canton; 32°37′N 90°01′W. Bounded by Pearl (SE) and Big Black (NW) rivers. Agr. (cotton, corn, hay, vegetables, potatoes; poultry, cattle; dairying); timber. Mfg. at Canton, Madison, and Ridgeland. S part of co. is urbanized, including part of city of Jackson and its environs. Miss. Petrified Forest in SW; Natchez Trace (Natl.) Parkway passes through SE, on Pearl R.; Cypress Swamp natural area to NE. Formed 1828. **11** county (□ 496 sq mi/1,285 sq km; 1990 pop. 11,127), SE Mo.; ⊙ Fredericktown; 37°29′N 90°21′W. Partly in St. Francois Mts., drained by St. Francis and Castor rivers. Farming (wheat, corn, hay; livestock) and mining (tungsten, manganese, lead, zinc, iron, cobalt, copper, antimony, nickel, granite); mfg. at Fredericktown. Part of Mark Twain Natl. Forest extends across co. E-W. St. Francis R. is popular rafting, canoeing, kayaking stream. Mining began in 1720s. Formed 1818. **12** county (□ 3,602 sq mi/9,329 sq km; 1990 pop. 5,989), SW Mont., ⊙ Virginia City; 45°18′N 111°55′W. Agr. and mining region, drained by Madison, Ruby, Beaverhead, and Jefferson rivers. SE corner borders on Idaho, forms Continental Divide. Several small mt. lakes in S and center; Beaverhead Rock State Park on border; Ennis L. reservoir in E; part of Earthquake L., formed (1959) by earthquakes in SE corner. Cattle, sheep, horses; hay, wheat, barley, potatoes. Talc mining, marble, gold, silver, lead, lignite. Parts of Beaverhead Natl. Forest in S, SE, and center; parts of Deerlodge Natl. Forest in N and NW; part of Gallatin Natl. Forest in E, forest includes parts of Lee Metcalf Wilderness Area; Tobacco Root Mts. in N; Gravelly Mts. in S; part of Madison Range in E and Ruby Range in W. Formed 1865. **13** county (□ 575 sq mi/1,489 sq km; 1990 pop. 32,655), NE central Nebr.; ⊙ Madison; 41°55′N 97°36′W. Agr. area drained by Elkhorn R. Cattle, hogs; dairying; poultry prods.; corn, soybeans. Mfg. at Norfolk. Formed 1867. **14** county (□ 661 sq mi/1,712 sq km; 1990 69,120), central N.Y.; ⊙ Wampsville; 42°56′N 75°39′W. Named for James Madison, who was Secretary of State in 1806, when co. was formed. Almost entire co. was part of the Twenty Town tract purchased by Gov. George Clinton from Oneidas in 1788. Colgate Univ. founded (1817) at Hamilton as the Baptist Education Society. The "Perfectionists" sect, led by John H. Noyes, established the communistic Oneida Community, which turned capitalistic by producing Oneida silverware and sharing stock in Oneida Community, Ltd. Lorenzo, an estate at S end of Cazenovia L., is a State Historic Site; has a Federal-period house. Drained by Chenango and Unadilla rivers and several creeks. Includes Cazenovia L., and many small lakes and several reservoirs; resorts. Dairying; field crops (esp. onions, cabbage); grain; poultry. Mfg. concentrated at Oneida and Canastota. **15** county (□ 451; 1990 pop. 16,953), W N.C.; ⊙ Marshall; 35°51′N 82°42′W. Appalachian Mt. region, bounded N by Tenn. state line; Bald Mts. along N border; drained by French Broad R. Agr. area (tobacco, corn, hay, potatoes), cattle; timber; resort area. Some mfg. at Marshall. Part of Pisgah Natl. Forest. Formed 1851. **16** county (□ 464 sq mi/1,202 sq km; 1990 pop. 37,068), central Ohio; ⊙ London, 39°52′N 83°26′W. Drained by Deer, Paint, and Darby creeks. Agr. area (livestock; corn, wheat, soybeans, fruit); some mfg. at London and Mount Sterling (metal prods., transportation equip.). Formed 1810. **17** county (□ 561 sq mi/1,453 sq km; 1990 pop. 77,982), W Tenn.; ⊙ Jackson; 35°37′N 88°51′W. Drained by Middle and South forks of Forked Deer R. Agr. area (vegetables, soybeans, strawberries, cotton; livestock); sand pits; diversified mfg. at Jackson. Extensive Native Amer. mounds at Pinson Mounds State Park, SE of Jackson. Formed 1821. **18** county (□ 472 sq mi/1,222 sq km; 1990 pop. 10,931), E central Texas; ⊙ Madisonville; 30°58′N 95°55′W. Bounded W by Navasota R., E by Trinity R., SE by Bedias Creek. Livestock (cattle, hogs, horses); forage crops; timber. Formed 1853. **19** county (□ 321 sq mi/831 sq km; 1990 pop. 11,949), N Va.; ⊙ Madison, 38°24′N 78°16′W. In N Piedmont region; rises in NW to Blue Ridge; bounded SW and S by Rapidan R.; drained by short Robinson R. Agr. (barley, wheat, corn, alfalfa, soybeans, hay, apples, peaches; cattle, sheep, hogs; dairying); timber. Trout fishing. Includes part of Shenandoah Natl. Park in NW. Blue Ridge (Natl.) Parkway follows NW border. Formed 1792.

Madison, parish (□ 662 sq mi/1,715 sq km; 1990 pop. 12,463), NE La.; ⊙ Tallulah; 32°25′N, 91°11′W. Bounded W by Bayou Macon, E by Mississippi R. (Miss. state line); intersected by Tensas R. Fertile delta lowland agr. area (cotton, corn, sorghum, rice, soybeans, wheat; cattle, hogs; home gardens), crawfish. Fishing and waterfowl hunting on oxbow lakes formed by the Mississippi. Possesses many Native Amer. mounds. Named after President Madison. Formed 1838. Part of Big L. State Wildlife Area in SW, part of Tensas River Natl. Wildlife Refuge in S.

Madison 1 city (1990 pop. 14,904), Madison co., N Ala., 9 mi/14.5 km WSW of Huntsville. Mfg. (machine tools, machinery, fiber optics, paper prods.). **2** city (1990 pop. 4,629), Madison and St. Clair cos., SW Ill., suburb of St. Louis, on the Mississippi R., and 5 mi/8 km N of East St. Louis, within St. Louis metropolitan area; 38°40′N 90°09′W. Mfg. (fabricated metal prods., wood prods.; aluminum and magnesium extrusion and production). Grew with establishment of steel industry in early 1890s. Gateway Natl. Raceway to S. Part of Granite City Ordnance Plant near river. Inc. 1891. **3** city (1990 pop. 12,006), ⊙ Jefferson co., SE Ind., on the Ohio R.; 38°46′N 85°24′W. Port of entry and a tobacco-marketing center. Mfg. (transportation equip., tool and die, shoes, fabricated metal prods., machinery, chemicals). Has fine examples of Georgian, Federal, Classical Revival, Gothic, Italianate, and Victorian architecture. An annual regatta is held on the Ohio R. Hanover Col. and Clifty Falls State Park are to W; branch of Ind. Vocational and Technical Col., Jefferson Proving Grounds to N. Settled 1805, inc. 1838. **4** city (1990 pop. 518), Monroe co., NE central Mo., 12 mi/19 km ENE of Moberly; 39°28′N 92°12′W. Corn, wheat, soybeans; cattle, saddle horses. **5** city (1990 pop. 191,262), ⊙ Wis. and Dane co., S central Wis., city center and state capitol on an isthmus bet. lakes Monona (SE) and Mendota (NW), in the Four Lakes group; 43°04′N 89°23′W. Metropoitan area; trading and mfg. center in a fertile agr. region. Mfg. (printing and publishing; dairy prods., chemicals, foods and beverages, machinery, lumber, packaging, paper goods, medical and medical research supplies, wood prods., fabricated metal prods., chemicals and chemical supplies, consumer goods). Seat of the Univ. of Wis., Edgewood Col., and Madison Area Technical Col. Many parks that dot the wooded lake shores make it an attractive residential city. Among its points of interest are the elaborate capitol, which houses the legislative lib. organized by Charles McCarthy; a Unitarian church designed by Frank Lloyd Wright; Univ. of Wis. Arboretum; and Vilas Park, which contains a zoo. Madison Art Center, a U.S. Forest-Prods. Laboratory (on Univ. of Wis. campus), Mendota Mental Health Inst., and Central Wis. Center are also here. Gov. Nelson State Park to NW, on opposite side of L. Mendota. Dane co. Regional Airport (Truax Field) in NE. Founded in 1836, and chosen (through the efforts of James Duane Doty) territorial capital before it was settled; inc. 1856.

Madison 1 town (1990 pop. 1,263), St. Francis co., E Ark., 4 mi/6.4 km E of Forrest City, and on St. Francis R.; 35°01′N 90°43′W. In agr. area; mfg. (chemicals). **2** resort town (1990 pop. 15,485), New Haven co., S Conn., on Hammonasset R. and L.I. Sound, and 17 mi/27 km E of New Haven; 41°20′N 72°37′W. Mostly residential with summer family resort at Hammonasset Beach State Park. Many fine 17th- and 18-cent. houses; once a shipbuilding, shipping center. Includes Madison and East R. (on small East R.) villages and Hammonasset Beach State Park, at Hammonasset Point. Set off from Guilford 1826. **3** town (□ 2 sq mi/5.2 sq km; 1990 pop. 3,345), ⊙ Madison co., N central Fla., near Ga. state line, c.50 mi/80 km E of Tallahassee; 30°28′N 83°25′W. Trade center for farming region. **4** town (1990 pop. 3,483), ⊙ Morgan co., N central Ga., 26 mi/42 km SSW of Athens; 33°35′N 83°29′W. Agr. trade center; mfg. (clothes, furniture, lumber, consumer goods, plastics, plywood, rope). Has antebellum houses restored by residents attracted here from Atlanta and elsewhere since the 1970s. Inc. 1809. **5** town (1990 pop. 845), Greenwood co., SE Kansas, on Verdigris R., and 18 mi/29 km S of Emporia; 38°07′N 96°08′W. Mfg. point in oil-producing and agr. region; produces gasoline. Oil wells nearby. Laid out 1879, inc. 1885. **6** town (1990 pop. 4,725), including Madison village, Somerset co., central Maine, on the Kennebec R., near Skowhegan; 44°49′N 69°47′W. Its water power developed paper and textile mills. Lakewood resort is E of village. Inc. 1804. **7** town (1990 pop. 1,951), ⊙ Lac qui Parle co., SW Minn., near S.Dak. state line, 23 mi/37 km WNW of Montevideo; 45°00′N 96°11′W. Elev. 1,091 ft/333 m. RR terminus. Agr. trade center (grain, soybeans; livestock, poultry; dairying); mfg. (fertilizers, bakery prods., fabricated metal prods., feeds). Lac qui Parle Wildlife Area, surrounds Lac qui Parle and Marsh lakes; Minnesota R. to NE. Settled c.1875, plotted 1884, inc. as city 1902. **8** town (1990 pop. 7,471), Madison co., central Miss., suburb 13 mi/21 km NNE of downtown Jackson, on Ross Barnett Reservoir (Pearl R.); 32°27′N 90°06′W. Agr. to N and W (cotton, corn, vegetables; poultry; dairying); mfg. (liquid carbon dioxide, wood prods., fabricated metal prods.). Bruce Campbell Field airport is here. Natchez Trace (Natl.) Parkway passes through SE, along reservoir. **9** town (1990 pop. 2,135), ⊙ Madison co., NE central Nebr., 14 mi/23 km S of Norfolk, and on branch of Elkhorn R; 41°49′N 97°27′W. Grain; dairy and poultry prod.; watermelons. Mfg. (wood prods;, hog slaughtering). Inc. 1873. **10** town (1990 pop. 1,704), Carroll co., E N.H., 29 mi/47 km NE of Laconia;

43°53′N 71°09′W. Drained by Silver R. and Forrest Brook. Agr. (livestock, poultry; vegetables; dairying; timber); mfg. (machine parts, asphalt). Resort area. Silver L. in SW (includes village of Silver Lake; mfg. wooden prods., safety equip.); Madison Boulder State Reservation in NW; King Pine Ski Area in E. **11** town (1990 pop. 2,371), Rockingham co., N N.C., on Dan R., and 27 mi/43 km NE of Winston-Salem, and 2 mi/3.2 km S of Mayodan; 36°23′N 79°58′W. Tobacco, grain, soybeans; poultry, livestock; dairying. Mfg. (leather prods., embroidery, bldg. materials, textiles; commercial printing). Belews L. reservoir to SW. Laid out 1818. **12** town (1990 pop. 6,257), ⊙ Lake co., SE S.Dak., 38 mi/61 km NW of Sioux Falls; 44°00′N 97°06′W. Trade center for agr. region; resort. RR terminus. Dairy prods.; livestock, poultry; grain; flour. Mfg. (machinery, wood prods.; egg processing). Seat of Dakota State Univ., 1st in S.Dak. (1881). Hosp. and airport. L. Madison and L. Herman State Park to SW. Plotted 1873. **13** town (1990 pop. 307), ⊙ Madison co., N Va., near E foot of Blue Ridge, 26 mi/42 km NNE of Charlottesville, near Robinson R.; 38°22′N 78°15′W. Mfg. (wood prods., lumber, clothing); agr. (grain, apples, soybeans; livestock; dairying); timber. **14** town (1990 pop. 3,051), ⊙ Boone co., W central W.Va., on Little Coal R. (left tributary of Big Coal R.), 23 mi/37 km SSW of Charleston; 38°03′N 81°47′W. RR junction. Bituminous-coal region. Timber. Mfg. (lumber, coal processing). Agr. (tobacco, honey). Inc. 1906.

Madison 1 fishing village, Dorchester co., E Md., 9 mi/14.5 km WSW of Cambridge. Agr. area; vegetable cannery. Originally called Little Tobacco Stick when laid out in 1760, it was renamed in honor of James Madison, the 4th President. In local lore, it was the home of a legendary white mule which refused every effort to harness him, was driven into the swamps by a posse, and returned drunk to harrass the town until he sobered up and became a parson. In 1814, men from here captured Capt. Phipps and the 18-member crew of a Br. tender from HMS *Dauntless*, which had gone around on James Point. **2** village (1990 pop. 316), Madison co., central N.Y., 20 mi/32 km SW of Utica; 42°53′N 75°30′W. In dairying area. **3** village (1990 pop. 2,477), Lake co., NE Ohio, 15 mi/24 km WSW of Ashtabula, near L. Erie; 41°46′N 81°03′W. Makes fabricated metal prods., wood prods., wine, mats; nurseries. Resort. **4** residential village, Davidson co., N central Tenn., suburb, 7 mi/11 km NE of Nashville, on Cumberland R.; 36°16′N 86°42′W. Mfg. transportation equip.

Madison 1 borough (1990 pop. 15,850), Morris co., NE N.J.; 40°45′N 74°25′W. Residential area. Corporate hq. Seat of Drew Univ. and part of Fairleigh Dickinson Univ. Originally called Bottle Hill, it was renamed in 1834. Sayre House (1745) in Madison was Gen. Anthony Wayne's hq. Noted for its roses. Settled 1685, inc. 1889. **2** borough (1990 pop. 539), Westmoreland co., SW Pa., 8 mi/12.9 km SW of Greensburg; 40°15′N 79°40′W. Agr. (grain; livestock; dairying); mfg. (fabricated metal prods.).

Madison, river, 183 mi/295 km long, in Wyo. and Mont.; rises in Yellowstone Natl. Park in Park co., NW Wyo.; flows W then N through SW Mont. to join the Jefferson and Gallatin rivers at the Three Forks of the Missouri at Three Forks, Mont. Impounded by Hebgen Dam (Hebgen L.), Gallatin co. (Mont.), in its upper course and by Madison Dam (Ennis L.) Madison co. (Mont.), a power facility, at midcourse. The river is used for irrigation. Earthquake or Quake, L., just downstream from Hebgen Dam was formed by an earthquake in 1959.

Madison Avenue, celebrated street of Manhattan, borough of N.Y. city., SE N.Y. Runs from Madison Sq. (23d St.) to the Madison Bridge (to the Bronx) over the Harlem R. (138th St.). In the 1940s and 1950s, some of the major U.S. advertising agencies had hq. in its Midtown sect., and the name of the avenue became synonymous with the advertising industry. Now lined by expensive shops bet. 42nd and 96th Sts.

Madison Heights 1 city (1990 pop. 32,196), Oakland co., SE Mich., a suburb, 12 mi/19 km NNW of downtown Detroit; 42°30′N 83°05′W. Mfg. (tool design and prototypes, encoder prods., displays, machinery, fabricated metal prods., apparel). Inc. 1955. **2** uninc. city, Amherst co., central Va., suburb, 1 mi/1.6 km NE of Lynchburg, on James R.; 37°26′N 79°05′W. Mfg. (machinery, paper prods., lumber, furniture; machining); in agr. area (corn, apples, peaches; cattle); timber.

Madison Lake, village (1990 pop. 643), Blue Earth co., S Minn., 9 mi/14.5 km ENE of Mankato; 44°12′N 93°48′W. Grain; livestock; light mfg. Madison L. to SE, Eagle L. to W, numerous small natural lakes in area.

Madison, Lake, lake, Lake co., E S.Dak., SE of Madison; 4 mi/6.4 km long, 1.5 mi/2.4 km wide; 43°57′N 97°01′W. Popular resort.

Madison, Mount, N.H.: see PRESIDENTIAL RANGE.

Madison Range, in Rocky Mts. of SW Mont., Gallatin and Madison cos., rises SW of Bozeman, extends c.44 mi/71 km S, bet. Gallatin and Madison rivers, to Hebgen L. Partly within Gallatin and Beaverhead Natl. Forests, includes units of Lee Metcalf Wilderness Area. Highest points are Hilgard Peak (11,316 ft/3,449 m), Koch Peak (11,286 ft/3,440 m). Lone Mt. (11,166 ft/3,403 m).

Madison Square Garden, sports and entertainment complex, mid-Manhattan, N.Y. city, SE N.Y., bounded E by 7th Ave., W by 8th Ave., N by 33d St., and S by 31st St. The 820,000 sq ft/76,178 sq m of space includes the 20,000-seat Arena, the 5,600-seat Theater, and the 36,000-sq-ft/3,344-sq-m Exposition Rotunda, as well as an office tower and shops. Located directly above the Pennsylvania Station (L.I. RR, N.J. Transit, and Amtrak). Completed in 1967, the present complex is the 4th to bear this name; the 1st was an 1879 conversion of Barnum's Madison Sq. Hippodrome, formerly the Grand Central Depot. Each successive incarnation of the "Garden" has moved farther uptown. Home stadium of the NHL N. Y. Rangers and NBA N.Y. Knicks.

Madisonville, city (1990 pop. 16,200), ⊙ Hopkins co., W Ky., 36 mi/58 km SW of Owensboro; 37°20′N 87°30′W. Major RR junction. Agr. (tobacco, grain, soybeans; livestock); mfg. (coal processing; machinery, bldg. materials, dairy prods., ordnance, soft drinks); coal is mined here, both surface and subsurface. Madisonville Municipal Airport to E. Hopkins Co. Historical Society Lib. and Mus. Seat of Madisonville Community Col. (Univ. of Ky.). L. Pee Wee reservoir to W; White City Wildlife Management Area to E. Inc. 1807.

Madisonville 1 town (1994 pop. 796), St. Tammany parish, SE La., 8 mi/13 km SW of Covington, and on Tchefuncte R., 2 mi/3 km N of its entrance to L. Pontchartrain; 30°24′N 90°10′W. Barge building, mfg. (treated wood). Hosts Wooden Boat Festival. Fairview-Riverside State Park is here. **2** town (1990 pop. 3,033), ⊙ Monroe co., SE Tenn., 14 mi/23 km NE of Athens; 35°31′N 84°22′W. Agr.; lumbering; some mfg. (clothing, wood prods.). Seat of Hiwassee Col. **3** town (1990 pop. 3,569), ⊙ Madison co., E central Texas, c.85 mi/137 km NNW of Houston; 30°56′N 95°54′W. Shipping, trade center in agr. area (cattle, horses, hogs); timber; mfg. (mushroom processing; feeds, transportation equip.).

Madoc (MAI-dahk), village (1991 pop. 1,397), SE Ont., central Canada, on Deer Creek, and 24 mi/39 km N of Belleville; 44°31′N 77°29′W. Milling, dairying, mixed farming. Resort area.

Madras (MAD-ruhs), town (1990 pop. 3,443), ⊙ Jefferson co., N central Oregon, 40 mi/64 km N of Bend; 44°37′N 121°07′W. Elev. 2,242 ft/683 m. Mfg. (millwork; wood prods., bldg. materials, fertilizer). Grain, potatoes; sheep, cattle. L. Chinook (Round Butte Dam) to SW and L. Simtustus (Pelton Dam) to W, both on Deschutes R. Cove Palisades State Park surrounds L. Chinook. Warm Springs Indian Reservation to W; Deschutes Natl. Forest to SW; Crooked R. Natl. Grassland to S.

Madre, Laguna, Texas and Mexico: see LAGUNA MADRE.

Madrid (MAD-rid), city (1990 pop. 2,395), Boone co., central Iowa, near Des Moines R., 14 mi/23 km SSE of Boone; 41°52′N 93°49′W. In agr. and mfg. area. Plotted 1852, inc. 1883.

Madrid 1 town, Houston co., SE Ala., 14 mi/23 km S of Dothan, near Fla. state line. **2** town (1990 pop. 178), Franklin co., W central Maine, on branch of Sandy R., and 21 mi/34 km NW of Farmington; 44°53′N 70°25′W. Settled c.1807, inc. 1836.

Madrid 1 village (1990 pop. 288), Perkins co., SW central Nebr., 10 mi/16 km E of Grant; 40°51′N 101°32′W. Grain, beans, sunflower seeds. **2** uninc. village, Santa Fe co., N central N.Mex., 30 mi/48 km SSW of Santa Fe. Elev. 6,020 ft/1,835 m. Cattle, sheep; corn, grain, alfalfa. Several Pueblo villages, ruins of Paako Pueblo nearby. **3** village (1990 pop. 700), St. Lawrence co., N N.Y., on Grass R., and 17 mi/27 km ENE of Ogdensburg; 44°46′N 75°07′W.

Madruga (mah-DROO-guh), town, La Habana prov., W Cuba, on Central Highway, on RR, and 34 mi/55 km ESE of Havana; 22°53′N 81°52′W. Spa and agr. center (sugarcane, tobacco, coffee). The Boris Luís Santa Coloma sugar central is just SW.

Maeser, village (1990 pop. 2,598), Uintah co., NE Utah, 10 mi/16 km NW of Vernal, in S foothills of Uinta Mts. (in Ashley Natl. Forest); 40°28′N 109°34′W. Oil and natural gas. Uintah and Ouray Indian Reservation to W.

Maestra, Sierra, Cuba: see SIERRA MAESTRA.

Maffo (MAH-fo), town, Santiago de Cuba prov., E Cuba, at N slopes of the Sierra Maestra, 32 mi/51 km WNW of Santiago de Cuba; 21°18′N 76°15′W. Fruit and sugar region.

Magadalena Mixtepec (mahg-dah-LAI-nah MEESH-te-pek), town (1990 pop. 481), in central Oaxaca, Mexico, 16 mi/25 km SW of Oaxaca de Juárez; 16°54′N 96°54′W. Zapotec community. Farming (corn, beans). No access by road.

Magaguadavic River (ma-guh-DAI-vik), 80 mi/129 km long, SW N.B., E Canada; rises WSW of Fredericton; flows S, through L. Magaguadavic (□ 11 sq mi/28 sq km), past St. George (hydroelectric station), to Passamaquoddy Bay 5 mi/8 km W of St. George.

Magalloway (muh-GAL-uh-wai), plantation (1990 pop. 45), Oxford co., W Maine, c.30 mi/48 km NW of Rumford, near Rangeley Lakes; 44°51′N 70°58′W.

Magalloway Mountain (muh-GA-luh-wai), peak (3,360 ft/1,024 m), Coos co., N.H., in wilderness area, 20 mi/32 km NE of Colebrook, 4 mi/6.4 km W of Maine state line. First Connecticut L. to NW. Source of Dead Diamond R.

Magalloway River (muh-GAL-uh-wai), c.15 mi/24 km long, NW Maine and NE N.H.; rises in N Oxford co. (Maine); flows S, through Parmachenee L., to Aziscohos L. (formed by dam), thence generally SW into N.H. where, with outlet of Umbagog L., it forms Androscoggin R.

Magazine, town (1990 pop. 799), Logan co., W Ark., 37 mi/60 km ESE of Fort Smith, 7 mi/11.3 km E of Boonville; 35°08′N 93°48′W. In rich farmland of Petit Jean valley. Mfg. (apparel). Ozark Natl. Forest to E. Magazine Mt. is nearby.

Magazine Mountain, W central Ark., the highest peak (2,753 ft/839 m) in state, c.45 mi/72 km SE of Fort Smith, in Ouachita Mts., Ozark Natl. Forest, and 10 mi/16 km SSE of Paris.

Magdalen Islands (MAG-duh-luhn) or **Îles-de-la-Madeleine** (EEL–duh–lah–mahd-LEN), group of 9 main isls. and numerous islets, Que., E Canada, in the Gulf of St. Lawrence N of P.E.I. Discovered (1534) by Jacques Cartier. The main isls. are Alright, Amherst, Brion, Coffin, East, Entry, Grindstone, Grosse, and Wolf. Fishing and sealing are the chief occupations of the islanders, most of whom are of Fr. descent.

Magdalena 1 (MAHG-dah-LAI-nah), town (1990 pop. 11,021), Jalisco, W Mexico, on L. Magdalena, on RR, and 45 mi/72 km WNW of Guadalajara, on Mexico Highway 15. Elev. 4,610 ft/1,405 m. Agr. center (grain, maguey, sugarcane, cotton, vegetables, fruit; livestock). **2** town (1990 pop. 219), Veracruz, E Mexico, in Sierra Madre Oriental, 7 mi/11.3 km SSE of Orizaba. Coffee.

Magdalena (MAG-duh-le-nuh), town (1990 pop. 861), Socorro co., W central N.Mex., just NW of Magdalena Mts., 27 mi/43 km WNW of Socorro; 34°06′N

107°13′W. Elev. 6,573 ft/2,003 m. Trade and shipping point in livestock area (cattle, sheep); alfalfa, chilies. Lead, zinc deposits nearby. Natl. Radio Observatory and Very Large Array (V.L.A.) radiotelescope facillity to W, at NE end of Plains of San Agustin on 3-pronged track system. Parts of Cibola Natl. Forest NW, SE and SW; South Baldy Peak (10,283 ft/3,134 m) 9 mi/14.5 km SSE; Gallinas Mts. to NW; Alamo Band Navajo Tribe Reservation to NW. Founded 1884.

Magdalena Apasco (mahg-dah-LAI-nah ah-PAHS-ko), town (1990 pop. 2,040), in central Oaxaca, Mexico, 19 mi/30 km NW of Oaxaca de Juárez, on RR, and on Mexico Highway 190; 17°14′N 96°48′W. Elev. 5,446 ft/1,660 m. In Etla arm of Oaxaca Valley irrigated by the Atoyac R. Temperate climate. Agr. (corn, beans, fruit), woods; cattle raising. Also known as Magdalena Apasco Etla and Magdalena Apazco.

Magdalena Bay (MAHG-dah-LAI-nah), inlet of Pacific Ocean, SW coast of Baja California, NW Mexico, SSW of Ciudad Constitución, sheltered by several isls., including Santa Margarita (S); 17 mi/27 km long NW-SE, 12 mi/19 km wide. Well known as good harbor and fishing ground.

Magdalena Contreras, La, Mexico: see LA MAGDALENA CONTRERAS.

Magdalena de Kino (MAHG-dah-LAI-nah dai KEE-no), city (1990 pop. 17,181), ⊙ Magdalena municipio, Sonora, NW Mexico, on Magdalena R., and 110 mi/177 km N of Hermosillo, 50 mi/80 km S of Nogales, on RR, and on Mexico Highway 15; 30°37′N 111°03′W. Elev. 2,464 ft/751 m. Agr. center (wheat, fruit, chickpeas, vegetables, cotton) in rich silver- and copper-mining area. Yearly Native Amer. festivals (Oct.) in honor of St. Francis Xavier draw many pilgrims. Nearby Gold Placers were known to Aztecs.

Magdalena Jaltepec (mahg-dah-LAI-nah HAHL-tai-pek), town (1990 pop. 639), in W Oaxaca, Mexico, 28 mi/45 km NW of Oaxaca de Juárez, 8 mi/12 km S off Mexico Highway 190, on unpaved road; 17°18′N 97°12′W. Elev. 2,625 ft/800 m. Temperate humid climate. Agr. (corn, beans, wheat, fruits), woods; cattle. Pottery.

Magdalena Jicotlán, Mexico: see SANTA MAGDALENA JICOTLÁN.

Magdalena, La, Mexico: see LA MAGDALENA TLATLAUQUITEPEC.

Magdalena Mountains (MAG-duh-le-nuh), W central N.Mex., in Socorro co., W of Socorro and the Rio Grande, largely within part of Cibola Natl. Forest. Prominent peaks include North Baldy (9,858 ft/3,005 m) and South Baldy (10,783 ft/3,287 m; highest point). Zinc is mined.

Magdalena Ocotlán (mahg-dah-LAI-nah o-kot-LAHN), town (1990 pop. 924), in S central Oaxaca, Mexico, 4 mi/6 km SSW of Ocotlán de Morelos, in the Valle Grande Arm of the Oaxaca Valley, just W of Mexico Highway 175; 16°43′N 96°42′W. Elev. 5,085 ft/1,550 m. The total pop. of the municipality live here in its capital city. Temperate climate. Agr. (cereals and fruits); woods and mezcal.

Magdalena Peñasco (mahg-dah-LAI-nah pen-YAHS-ko), town (1990 pop. 437), in W Oaxaca, Mexico, 56 mi/90 km W of Oaxaca de Juárez, 9 mi/14 km E of Tlaxiaco, on unpaved road; 17°14′N 97°34′W. Elev. 6,201 ft/1,890 m. In the Mixteca Alta. Temperate climate. Agr. (corn, beans, wheat, fruits), woods, mezcal; cattle. Woven textiles.

Magdalena River, c.200 mi/322 km long, Sonora, NW Mexico; rises SE of Nogales near U.S. border; flows SW and W, past Imuris, Magdalena de Kino, Santa Ana, and Caborca, to Gulf of California 22 mi/35 km NW of Cape Tepoca. Receives Altar R., whose name sometimes designates its lower course; lower course also called Asunción R., the sect. above its mouth Concepción R. Used for irrigation in an otherwise arid region; chickpeas, fruit, cereals, vegetables are produced. Intermittent stream.

Magdalena Teitipac (mahg-dah-LAI-nah tai-EE-tee-PAHK), town (1990 pop. 2,986), in S central Oaxaca, Mexico, 16 mi/25 km SE of Oaxaca de Juárez, 6 mi/-

10 km SW of Tlacolula; 16°55′N 96°36′W. Elev. 5,440 ft/1,658 m. In Tlacolula arm of Oaxaca Valley. Temperate climate. Agr.; woven textiles; mezcal processing.

Magdalena Tequisistlán (mahg-dah-LAI-nah tai-kwee-seest-LAHN), town (1990 pop. 4,093), in SE Oaxaca, Mexico, 31 mi/50 km NW of the port of Salina Cruz, on Mexico Highway 190; 16°22′N 95°15′W. Agr. (corn, coffee, sugarcane, fruits), woods. Textiles from local artisans.

Magdalena Tlacotepec (mahg-dah-LAI-nah tlah-KO-tai-pek), town (1990 pop. 1,152), in SE Oaxaca, Mexico, 8 mi/13.5 km SW of Ciudad Ixtepec; 16°30′N 95°12′W. Hot climate.

Magdalena Yodocono de Porfirio Díaz (mahg-dah-LAI-nah yo-do-KO-no dai por-FEE-ree-o DEE-ahs), town (1990 pop. 822), NW Oaxaca, Mexico, 7 mi/12 km SW of Asunción Nochixtlán; 17°23′N 97°22′W. Elev. 6,332 ft/1,930. Resources are livestock and poultry breeding. Formerly Yodocono de Porfirio Diaz.

Magdalena Zahuatlán (mahg-dah-LAI-nah zah-waht-LAHN), town (1990 pop. 409), in NW Oaxaca, Mexico, 43 mi/70 km NW of Oaxaca de Juárez, and 4.3 mi/7 km S of Nochixtlán. Elev. 7,087 ft/2,160 m. A Mixtec community. Agr.

Magee (muh-GEE), town (1990 pop. 3,607), Simpson co., S central Miss., 38 mi/61 km SE of Jackson, near Okatoma Creek; 31°52′N 89°43′W. RR junction to SE. Agr. (cotton, corn; poultry; cattle); timber; mfg. (apparel, wood prods., bldg. materials; millwork). State sanitorium to NW. Simpson Co. Legion L. (state lake) to NW.

Magens Bay (MAI-ginz), bay of N St. Thomas Isl., U.S. V.I., c.1.5 mi/2.4 km N of Charlotte Amalie. Fine beach and public park; popular tourist site.

Maggie L. Walker, natl. historic site, downtown Richmond, E central Va., at 110 1/2 East Lehigh St. Home of Afr.-Amer. ex-slave's daughter who became bank president, early leader in the women's movement. Covers area of 1.3 acres/0.5 ha. Authorized 1978.

Maggie Valley, village (1990 pop. 183), Haywood co., W N.C., 6 mi/9.7 km WNW of Waynesville; 35°31′N 83°05′W. Great Smoky Mts. Natl. Park to N; parts of Pisgah Natl. Forest to S and NE; Blue Ridge Parkway passes to SW. Corn, tobacco, potatoes; livestock; dairying.

Maggotty, town (1991 pop. 1,359), St. Elizabeth parish, W Jamaica, on Black R., on Jamaica RR, and 23 mi/37 km SE of Montego Bay; 18°09′N 77°46′W. In agr. region (corn, spices; livestock). Known for nearby Maggotty Falls.

Magic Dam, Idaho: see BIG WOOD RIVER.

Maglia, uninc. town (1990 pop. 8,987), Butte co., N central Calif., 11 mi/21 km ENE of Chico, near Butte R. Plumas Natl. Forest to E. E. L. Oroville reservoir to SE. Cattle; fruit, nuts, grain; timber.

Magna, village (1990 pop. 17,829), Salt Lake co., N Utah, suburb 10 mi/16 km W of downtown Salt Lake City; 40°42′N 112°05′W. Elev. 4,261 ft/1,299 m. RR junction. Copper, silver, gold, lead processed. Diversified farming (grain, fruit, sugar beets) in vicinity; mfg. (solid propulsion prods., chemicals). Great Salt L. (S shore) State Park to W. Large Kennecott Tailings Pond is here.

Magness (MAG-nes), village (1990 pop. 158), Independence co., NE central Ark., 10 mi/16 km ESE of Batesville, near White R.; 35°42′N 91°28′W.

Magnet, village (1990 pop. 69), Cedar co., NE Nebr., 15 mi/24 km SW of Hartington; 42°27′N 97°28′W.

Magnetawan (mag-NE-tuh-wahn), village (1991 pop. 267), SE central Ont., central Canada, on Magnetawan R., and 30 mi/48 km NE of Parry Sound; 45°40′N 79°38′W. Lumbering.

Magnetawan River, 100 mi/161 km long, SE central Ont., central Canada; rises in NW part of Algonquin Provincial Park; flows SW and W, past Magnetawan, to Georgian Bay of L. Huron, through the Bying Inlet, 40 mi/64 km NW of Parry Sound.

Magnetic Peak (10,008 ft/3,050 m), SE Maui isl, Maui co., Hawaii, at SW rim of Haleakala Crater, on boundary of Haleakala Natl. Park. Maui's 2d-highest point; ½

mi/⁹⁄₁₀ km SE of Puu Ulaula (Red Hill), Maui's highest point.

Magnetic Springs, village (1990 pop. 373), Union co., central Ohio, 17 mi/27 km SSW of Marion; 40°21′N 83°16′W.

Magnolia, city (1990 pop. 11,151), ⊙ Columbia co., SW Ark.; 33°16′N 93°14′W. Mfg. (fabricated metal prods., apparel, chemicals, lumber, bldg. materials). Its oil industry has been important since 1938. Seat of Southern Ark. Univ. Inc. 1855.

Magnolia 1 town (1990 pop. 204), Harrison co., W Iowa, 6 mi/9.7 km NW of Logan; 41°41′N 95°52′W. In agr. area. **2** town (1990 pop. 2,245), ⊙ Pike co., SW Miss., 7 mi/11.3 km S of McComb, near Tangipahoa R.; 31°08′N 90°27′W. Agr. (cotton, corn; cattle; dairying); timber; mfg. (bldg. materials, apparel, wood prods., chemicals, lab equip.). Percy Quin State Park to NW. **3** town (1990 pop. 747), Duplin co., SE N.C., 34 mi/55 km S of Goldsboro; 34°53′N 78°03′W. In agr. area (tobacco, grain, cotton, sweet potatoes; poultry, livestock). **4** town (1990 pop. 940), Montgomery co., SE Texas, 40 mi/64 km NW of Houston; 30°12′N 95°45′W. Agr. area (cattle, horses, ostriches; nursery prods.). Timber. Oil and natural gas. Mfg. (machinery, oil field linings).

Magnolia 1 village (1990 pop. 211), Kent co., E Del., 6 mi/9.7 km SSE of Dover; 39°04′N 75°28′W. In agr. region; grain, vegetables, fruit; poultry, livestock; dairying. Harvey Conservation Area to E. **2** village (1990 pop. 261), Putnam co., N central Ill., 12 mi/19 km SE of Hennepin; 41°06′N 89°12′W. In agr. area. **3** village (1990 pop. 155), Rock co., extreme SW Minn., 7 mi/11.3 km E of Luverne, near Iowa state line; 43°38′N 96°04′W. Grain; livestock; dairying; mfg. (feeds, protein blending). **4** village (1990 pop. 937), on border bet. Stark and Carroll cos., E Ohio, 11 mi/18 km SSE of Canton; 40°39′N 81°17′W.

Magnolia, residential borough (1990 pop. 4,861), Camden co., SW N.J., 8 mi/12.9 km SE of Camden; 39°51′N 75°02′W. Inc. 1915.

Magnolia, Mass.: see GLOUCESTER.

Magnolia Beach, village, Calhoun co., S Texas, on Lavaca Bay, and 7 mi/11.3 km SE of Port Lavaca.

Magoffin (muh-GAHF-uhn), county (□ 309 sq mi/800 sq km; 1990 pop. 13,077), E Ky., in the Cumberland Mts.; ⊙ Salyersville; 37°42′N 83°03′W. Drained by Licking R. and by several creeks. Agr. area (burley tobacco, corn, hay; cattle). Bituminous-coal mines, oil wells; timber. Formed 1860.

Magog, city (1991 pop. 14,034), S Que., E Quebec, on L. Memphremagog, SW of Sherbrooke; 45°16′N 72°09′W. Founded by Loyalist emigrants from the U.S. after 1776, Resort and trade center, with textile mills, food processing, and dairying.

Magothy River (MAG-ah-thee), irregular arm of Chesapeake Bay, c.12 mi/19 km long, central Md.; penetrates Anne Arundel co. just N of Sandy Point.

Magrath (muh-GRATH), town (1991 pop. 1,743), S Alta., W Canada, 19 mi/31 km S of Lethbridge; 49°25′N 112°53′W. Coal mining; oil and gas; wheat, flax, sugar beets; cattle. Mormon settlement, founded 1899.

Magruder Mountain, Nev.: see SILVER PEAK RANGE.

Maguarichi, mining settlement (1990 pop. 339) and township, Chihuahua, N Mexico, in Sierra Madre Occidental, on RR, 23 mi/37 km WNW of Creel, and 130 mi/209 km SW of Chihuahua, in Sierra Tarahumara. Silver and gold mining. Formerly Maguarichic.

Maguarichic, Mexico: see MAGUARICHI.

Maguse Lake (□ 540 sq mi/1,399 sq km), SE Keewatin dist., N.W.T., N Canada, near Hudson Bay; 45 mi/72 km long, 1 mi/2 km–7 mi/11 km wide; 61°30′N 95°W. Drained E into Hudson Bay by Maguse R. (35 mi/56 km long); at mouth of river is trading post.

Mahaffey (ma-HA-fee), borough (1990 pop. 341), Clearfield co., central Pa., 22 mi/35 km WSW of Clearfield, on West Branch of Susquehanna R., at mouth of Chest Creek; 40°52′N 78°43′W. Agr. (grain; cattle; dairying); lumber.

Mahanoy City (mah-HA-noi), borough (1990 pop. 5,209), Schuylkill co., E central Pa., 10 mi/16 km NNE of Pottsville, on Mahanoy Creek; 40°48′N 76°08′W. Agr. (corn, hay; poultry); dairying. Anthracite coal. In area are Locust L. (S) and Tuscarora (E) state parks. Settled 1859, inc. 1863.

Mahanoy Creek (mah-HA-noi), c.60 mi/97 km long, E central Pa.; rises in NE Schuylkill co.; flows W, past Mahony City, Fruckville, and Ashland, through anthracite coal-mining area, to Susquehanna R. 9 mi/14.5 km S of Sunbury; 40°49′N 76°05′W.

Mahantango Creek (mai-uhn-TANG-go), c.35 mi/56 km long, E central Pa.; rises in W Schuylkill co.; flows WSW to Susquehanna R. 5 mi/8 km N of Millersburg; 40°43′N 76°27′W. Forms border bet. Northumberland and Dauphin cos.

Mahaska, county (□ 573 sq mi/1,484 sq km; 1990 pop. 21,522), S central Iowa; ⊙ Oskaloosa; 41°19′N 92°38′W. Rolling prairie agr. area (hogs, cattle, sheep, poultry; corn, oats, hay) drained by Des Moines, Skunk, and North Skunk rivers. Bituminous-coal deposits mined in SW; limestone quarries. Includes L. Keomah State Park in E. River flooding in 1993. Formed 1843.

Mahaska (muh-HAS-kuh), village (1990 pop. 98), Washington co., N Kansas, near Nebr. state line, 20 mi/32 km NW of Washington; 39°59′N 97°20′W. In grain and livestock area.

Mahnomen (muh-NO-men), county (□ 583 sq mi/1,510 sq km; 1990 pop. 5,044), NW Minn.; ⊙ Mahnomen; 47°19′N 95°48′W. Drained by Wild Rice and White Earth rivers. Agr. area (wheat, hay, alfalfa, oats, barley, sunflowers, wild rice). Nearly entire co. is within White Earth Indian Reservation which extends into Clearwater (E) and Baker (S) cos.; small sect. of White Earth State Forest in E and SE. Formed 1906.

Mahnomen, town (1990 pop. 1,154), ⊙ Mahnomen co., NW Minn., 48 mi/77 km WSW of Bemidji, on Wild Rice R., at mouth of White Earth R., in White Earth Indian Reservation; 47°18′N 95°58′W. Elev. 1,212 ft/369 m. Trading point for agr. area (livestock; wild rice, grain, sunflowers, alfalfa); mfg. (bldg. materials, chemicals, apparel). White Earth State Forest to E.

Mahomet (mah-HOM-it), village (1990 pop. 3,103), Champaign co., E central Ill., on Sangamon R., and 9 mi/14.5 km WNW of Champaign; 40°11′N 88°24′W. In agr. area.

Mahone Bay (muh-HON), town (1991 pop. 1,096), S N.S., E Canada, on W shore of Mahone Bay, 40 mi/64 km WSW of Halifax; 44°26′N 64°22′W. Shipbuilding, lumbering.

Mahone Bay, inlet of the Atlantic Ocean, off S N.S., E Canada, 30 mi/48 km WSW of Halifax; 12 mi/19 km long, 9 mi/14 km wide at entrance. On bay are towns of Chester and Mahone Bay. There are numerous isls., including Oak Isl., reputed site of Captain Kidd's hidden treasure. Great Tancook Isl. (3 mi/5 km long) is the largest.

Mahoning (muh-HO-ning), county (□ 419 sq mi/1,085 sq km; 1990 pop. 264,806), E Ohio, on Pa. (E) state line; ⊙ YOUNGSTOWN; 41°02′N 80°46′W. Intersected by Mahoning and Little Beaver rivers. Agr. (livestock, poultry; grains; dairy prods.). Mfg. industrial machinery. Coal mining; limestone quarries. Includes Milton Reservoir and part of Berlin Reservoir. Formed 1846.

Mahoning (muh-HON-ing), river, c.90 mi/145 km long, Ohio and Pa.; rises in NE Ohio, E of Canton; 40°57′N 80°22′W; flows NW to Alliance, then NE past Warren, where it turns SE to flow past Youngstown into NW Pa. and joins the Shenango R. to form the Beaver R. The river drains a fertile valley. Berlin Dam (completed 1943), on the upper Mahoning, provides flood control and water supply.

Mahoning Creek (ma-HO-ning), c.60 mi/97 km long, W central Pa.; rises in W Clearfield co.; flows generally W, past Punxsutawney, through Mahoning Creek L. (flood-control reservoir), to Allegheny R., just N of Templeton, 9 mi/14.5 km N of Kittanning; 41°02′N 78°42′W. Flood-control dam is c.22 mi/35 km above mouth. Another Mahoning Creek in E Pa.; rises in E Schuylkill co.; flows E c.15 mi/24 km to Lehigh R. at Lehighton.

Mahopac (mah-HO-pak), residential village (□ 6 sq mi/15.5 sq km; 1990 pop. 7,755), Putnam co., SE N.Y., on E shore of L. Mahopac (c.1.5 mi/2.4 km in diameter), 12 mi/19 km NE of Peekskill; 41°22′N 73°44′W.

Mahtomedi (mah-duh-MEE-dei), town (1990 pop. 5,569), Washington co., E Minn., 9 mi/14.5 km NNE of downtown St. Paul, on E and SE shore of White Bear L.; 45°03′N 92°57′W. Agr. area (corn, oats, soybeans, alfalfa; cattle, sheep); light mfg. Northport Airport to NE, Lakewood Communtiy Col. to W, in White Bear Lake city; Northeast Metropolitan Technical Col. is here. Numerous small natural lakes in area. Inc. 1931.

Mahwah (MAH-wah), village (1990 pop. 17,905), Bergen co., extreme N N.J., near Ramapo R. and N.Y. state line, 12 mi/19 km N of Paterson; 41°04′N 74°11′W. Mfg of transportation equip. and electronics; former auto plant. Largely residential. Seat of Ramapo Col. of N.J. Center for the 3,000 Ramapough mt. people, who also live in nearby Ringwood (N.J.) and Hillbury (N.Y.); subjects of an ongoing dispute regarding their status as a Native Amer. tribe or as descendants of late-16th-cent. Afr. and Du. farmers.

Maida (MAI-duh), village, Cavalier co., NE N.Dak., port of entry at Can. (Man.) border, 15 mi/24 km N of Langdon; 48°59′N 98°21′W.

Maiden, town (1990 pop. 2,470), Catawaba co., W central N.C., 6 mi/9.7 km S of Newton. Agr. area (grain, soybeans, hay; chickens, cattle, hogs; dairying). Mfg. (textiles, security alarms, apparel, wood prods., furniture, conveyor components).

Maiden Rock, village (1990 pop. 146), Pierce co., W Wis., on L. Pepin (Mississippi R.), 11 mi/18 km E of Red Wing (Minn.), surrounded by bluffs; 44°34′N 92°18′W. Mfg. (concrete prods.). Silicate-rock mine is nearby.

Maidens, uninc. village, Goochland co., central Va., 1 mi/1.6 km S of Goochland, 24 mi/39 km WNW of Richmond, on James R.

Maidstone, town (1991 pop. 985), W Sask., W Canada, 50 mi/80 km WNW of North Battleford; 53°05′N 109°18′W. Grain elevators.

Maidstone, town (1990 pop. 131), Essex co., NE Vt., on the Connecticut R., just above Guildhall. Maidstone L. (c.3 mi/4.8 km long; fishing), with state park, is W.

Maidsville, uninc. village, Monongalia co., N W.Va., 4 mi/6.4 km N of Morgantown, on Monongahela R. Agr. (grain, strawberries); livestock, poultry. Bituminous coal. Mfg. (coal processing).

Maili (MAH-EE-lee), town (1990 pop. 6,059), Oahu isl., Honolulu co., Hawaii, 20 mi/32 km WNW, on W coast, near mouth of Maililii Stream; 21°25′N 158°10′W. Poultry, cattle. Lualualei Naval Reservation to E. Waianae Mts. to E; Maili Point to S.

Maimon (mei-MON), town (1993 pop. 9,337), 10 mi/16 km SE of Bonao, Monseñor Nouel prov., central Dominican Republic; 18°54′N 70°18′W. Nickel-mining center.

Main à Dieu (man uh DOO), village, NE N.S., E Canada, E Cape Breton Isl., on the Atlantic Ocean, 19 mi/31 km SE of Sydney; 46°00′N 59°51′W. Fishing.

Main Topsail, mountain (1,822 ft/555 m), W central N.F., E Canada, 30 mi/48 km E of NE end of Grand L.; 49°08′N 56°33′W.

Maine, state (□ 35,387 sq mi/91,683 sq km; 1995 est. pop. 1,241,382), in the extreme NE corner of the U.S.; ⊙ AUGUSTA 45°50′N 69°17′W. Largest of the New England states. Admitted as the 23d state of the Union in 1820. The Can. provs. of Que. and N.B. border Maine from the NW around to the SE coast, with the St. John and the St. Croix rivers forming part of the internatl. border with N.B. To the S is the Atlantic Ocean (the Bay of Fundy lies off to the E). N.H. (to the W) is the only state bordering Maine. Geologic action laid down a bedrock of sandstone, shale, and limestone. Much of the soft rock eroded into tableland valleys, while the more resistant rock remained, forming the generally mountainous W, the mts. of Mt. Desert Isl. in the E, and isolated peaks including Katahdin (5,268 ft/1,606 m), the highest point in the state. Receding glaciers deposited long drift ridges across the countryside and dammed the valleys to form more than 2,200 lakes (Moosehead L. is the largest) and to establish new, rugged watercourses for more than 5,000 streams and rivers. The major rivers are the St. John, the Penobscot, the Kennebec, the Androscoggin, and the Saco. The sea has encroached on the low coastal valleys, leaving a jigsawed, fjorded, coastline of 2,500 mi/3,219 km and numerous irregular and rocky isls. offshore. E of the Kennebec the coast of Maine is rugged, but W of the river the shoreline has sandy beaches and marshy lowlands. More than 80% of Maine is forested with great stands of white pine (Maine is known as the "Pine Tree State"), hemlock, spruce, fir, and hardwoods. In the shelter of lakes and woods, particularly in the N cos., wildlife has found refuge. Moose, deer, black bear, and smaller game are still found; fish and fowl are plentiful. Much of Maine's natural and industrial resources remain undeveloped. Many varieties of granite, including some superior ornamental types, have been used for construction throughout the nation. Sand and gravel, zinc, and peat are found in addition to stone. The pop. of Maine is centered on the cleared land along the coast and major rivers. Due to a variety of economic factors—generally poor soil and a short growing season, geographical remoteness from production centers, an inadequate distribution system, lack of coal and steel, and a reluctance to adopt modern methods of production and merchandising—Maine had a very low pop. increase 1860–1970 after which it experienced unprecedented growth. The economic revival experienced in port and factory towns during World War II did not continue after the war. In 1949–1950 the textile industry, after enjoying a brief expansion, suffered severely from competitive markets, and many of the old mills and plants were closed. Sharp decline in the shoe- and food-processing industries followed with 1980s. However, in the 1980s, Maine successfully transformed a major portion of its economy into trade, service, and finance industries, the greatest growth occurring in and near Portland and, in addition, the picturesque coastal and isl. resorts of Maine hold a strong appeal for visitors and tourists and, combined with abundant wildlife to attract sportsmen, make the tourist trade a most important feature of Maine's economy. Many of Maine's traditional economic activities have experienced difficult times. Fishing, one of the state's earliest industries, has declined considerably (with the exception of lobsters, still caught in abundance). Lumbering—the 1st sawmill in America was built in 1623 on the Piscataqua R.—dominated industry and the export trade from the days when the straight white pines provided masts for the Br. navy. However, since the virgin timber has been largely cut off, the timber trade has declined. Maine is still a leading producer of paper and paper prods., which remain the most valuable of all manufactures in the state. The proximity of harbors and forests early encouraged extensive shipbuilding, which reached its peak in the 19th cent. After the decline of shipbuilding and timber trading, commercial activity slackened. Portland, the largest port, operates far below its capacity. However, Portland, Bangor, and Rockland (with Lewiston, the state's largest cities) are still important cities and during the summer months serve a vast resort region. Portland has also attracted commercial development for the banking, insurance, and real estate industries. Mfg. is the largest economic sector, accounting for ⅓ of all production. Limited amounts of leather goods (esp. shoes), and food prods. are still produced in addition to transportation equip., paper, and wood prods. Printing, publishing and electronic components are also important. Agr. has been developed despite adverse soil and climatic conditions. Since the opening of the prairie and grasslands of the W, Maine has tended to concentrate on dairying, poultry raising, and market gardening to serve local and New England markets. The state is a leading producer of brown eggs. The growing of potatoes, particularly in Aroostook co., was stimulated by the completion of the Aroostook RR in 1894 and in recent years maintained by introduction of freezing process. Blueberries, hay, apples, and oats are the other chief crops. The earliest human habitation in what is now Maine extends back to prehistoric times, as evidenced by the burial mounds of the Red Paint people found in the S central part of the state. The Native Americans who came later left enormous shell heaps, variously estimated to be 1,000–5,000 years old. At the time of settlement by Europeans the Abnaki were scattered along the coast and in some inland areas. The coast of Maine may have been visited by the Norsemen and was included in the grant that James I of England awarded to the Plymouth Co., and colonists set out under George Popham in 1607. This settlement, Fort St. George, on the present site of Phippsburg, at the mouth of the Kennebec (then called the Sagadahoc) R., did not prosper, and the colonists returned to England in 1608. The French came to the area in 1613 and established a new colony and a Jesuit mission on Mt. Desert Isl.; however, the English under Sir Samuel Argall expelled them. In 1620 the Council for New England (successor to the Plymouth Co.) granted Ferdinando Gorges and Captain John Mason the territory bet. the Kennebec and Merrimack rivers extending 60 mi/ 97 km inland. At this time, the region became known as Maine. Neglected after Gorges' death in 1647, Maine settlers came under the jurisdiction of the Mass. Bay Colony in 1652. King Philip's War (1675–1676) was the 1st of many struggles bet. the British on 1 side and the French and Native Americans on the other. In 1691 Mass. received a new charter that confirmed its hold on Maine, and with Sir William Phips, a Maine native, as governor and the territorial question settled, local govt. and institutions in the Mass. tradition really took root here. Maine soon had prosperous fishing, lumbering, and shipbuilding industries. Dissatisfaction with Br. rule was 1st expressed openly after Parliament passed the Stamp Act in 1765. During the Amer. Revolution, Falmouth was devastated by a Br. fleet (1775). Benedict Arnold, in 1775, led his grueling, unsuccessful expedition against Que. N through here. During the war supplies were cut off and conflict with Native Americans was frequent, but with Amer. independence won, economic development was rapid in what was then called the Dist. of Maine. However, the Embargo Act of 1807 and the War of 1812 interrupted the thriving commerce and turned the dist. to industrial development. Agitation for statehood, which had been growing since the Revolution, now became widespread. Dissatisfaction with Mass. was aroused by the inadequate military protection provided during the War of 1812; by the land policy, which encouraged absentee ownership; and by the political differences bet. conservative Mass. and democratic Maine. The imminent admission of Mo. into the Union as a slave state hastened the separation of Maine from Mass., and equality of power bet. North and South was preserved by admitting Maine as a free state in 1820, as part of the Missouri Compromise. With Portland as its capital (moved to Augusta in 1832) the new state entered a prosperous period. During the 1st ½ of the 19th cent. Maine enjoyed its greatest pop. increase until the 1970s. A highly profitable timber trade was carried on with the West Indies, Europe, and Asia, and towns such as BATH became America's leaders in shipbuilding. The long-standing Northeast Boundary Dispute almost precipitated border warfare bet. Maine and N.B. in the so-called Aroostook War of 1839; the controversy was settled by the Webster-Ashburton Treaty with Great Britain in 1842. Political life was vigorous, particularly in the 1850s, when the reluctance of the Democrats, who had been dominant since 1820, to take a firm antislavery stand swept the new Republican party into power. Hannibal Hamlin was a leading Republican politician and was Vice President during Abraham Lincoln's 1st administration. Antislavery sentiment was strong, and Maine made sizable contributions of men and money to the Union in the Civil War. Gens. Oliver O. Howard and Joshua L. Chamberlain were from Maine. For decades regulation of the liquor traffic was the chief political issue in Maine, and the state was the 1st to adopt (1851)

a prohibition law. It was incorporated into the constitution in 1884 and was not repealed until 1934. State politics entered a hectic stage in 1878 when the newly organized Greenback party combined with the Democrats to carry the election, ending more than 20 years of Republican rule. The following year the coalition was accused of manipulating election returns, a charge sustained by the state supreme court, which seated a rival legislature elected by the Republicans. In 1880 the fusionists were again successful, but from that time until the 1950s the state was generally Republican, providing that party with such natl. leaders as James G. Blaine, Thomas B. Reed, and Margaret Chase Smith, who in 1948 became the 1st female Republican U.S. senator. Former U.S. Secretary of State Edmund S. Muskie was elected governor in 1954. In 1964 and 1968 (when Muskie, then a U.S. senator, ran unsuccessfully for Vice President) the state voted Democratic in the presidential election for the 1st time since 1912. In 1969 personal and corporate income taxes were added to the sales tax within the state. Maine's pop. grew 13.2% during the 1970s and 9.2% during the 1980s, its largest increases since the 1840s. Maine has a long tradition of concern for environmental issues. In the 1970s the state prohibited the use of rivers to transport logs in order to protect the salmon, and dams which produce hydroelectric energy may be removed for the same reason. The need for energy, however, led Maine voters to narrowly defeat a 1988 anti-nuclear-power referendum. Maine is governed under the 1820 constitution as amended. There is a 2-house legislature of 35 senators and 151 representatives, all elected for 2-year terms; the governor is elected for a 4-year term and may succeed himself once. Maine elects 2 Representatives and 2 Senators to the U.S. Congress and has 4 electoral votes. Localities are classified as cities, towns, townships, and "plantations," a minor civil div. for remote and sparsely populated places. Places of interest in Maine include Acadia Natl. Park on Mt. Desert Isl.; Baxter State Park, which includes the beginning of the APPALACHIAN TRAIL at Mt. Katahdin in the N Maine wilderness; and the Old York Gaol (1653), one of the oldest public bldgs. in New England. Among the state's leading educational institutions are Bowdoin Col., at Brunswick; Colby Col., at Waterville; Bates Col., at Lewiston; and the Univ. of Maine, at Orono. Maine has 16 cos.: ANDROS-COGGIN, AROOSTOOK, CUMBERLAND, FRANKLIN, HAN-COCK, KENNEBEC, KNOX, LINCOLN, OXFORD, PENOB-SCOT, PISCATAQUIS, SAGADAHOC, SOMERSET, WALDO, WASHINGTON, and YORK.

Maine, Gulf of, part of the Atlantic Ocean, bet. SE Maine and SW N.S., at the entrance of the Bay of Fundy. The area is noted for its scenery and fishing.

Maine Turnpike, part of Maine highway and interstate (also designated I-95) system extending NE from near Portsmouth (N.H.) to Augusta. Toll road.

Maine Yankee Nuclear Power Plant, Maine: see LINCOLN.

Mainero, Mexico: see VILLA MAINERO.

Maineville, village (1990 pop. 359), Warren co., SW Ohio, 20 mi/32 km NE of Cincinnati; 39°19′N 84°13′W. In agr. area.

Maisí (mei-SEE), scenic beach resort in Guantánamo prov., at E end of Cuba, at foot of Meseta with same name; 20°15′N 74°09′W.

Maisí, Cape (mei-SEE) or **Maisí Point**, easternmost headland of Cuba, Guantánamo prov., on Windward Passage, 110 mi/177 km E of Santiago de Cuba, 50 mi/ 80 km WNW of Cape St. Nicolas (Haiti); 20°15′N 74°08′W. Has lighthouse. Old spelling, Maysí.

Maisonette Point (mai-zuhn-EHT), cape on Chaleur Bay, NE N.B., E Canada, 35 mi/56 km NE of Bathurst; 47°50′N 65°00′W. Lighthouse.

Maïssade (mah-ee-SAHD), town (1982 pop. 3,493), Centre dept., central Haiti, 40 mi/64 km S of Cap-Haïtien; 19°10′N 72°08′W. Agr. (fruit, sugarcane, coffee, cotton); cattle; beekeeping. Lignite deposits nearby.

Maitland, village, central N.S., E Canada, on Chignecto Bay, at mouth of Shubenacadie R., 12 mi/19 km WSW

of Truro; 45°19′N 63°31′W. Dairying, mixed farming; former shipbuilding center.

Maitland (MAIT-luhnd), city (1990 pop. 338), Holt co., NW Mo., on Nodaway R., and 33 mi/53 km NNW of St. Joseph; 40°12′N 95°04′W. Corn; cattle, hogs.

Maitland (MAIT-luhnd), town (□ 4 sq mi/10.4 sq km; 1990 pop. 9,110), Orange co., central Fla., 5 mi/8 km N of Orlando; 28°37′N 81°22′W. Heart of major office complex along I-4. One of largest suburban business centers in SE U.S.

Maitland, uninc. village (1990 pop. 200), McDowell co., S W.Va., 2 mi/3.2 km ESE of Welch.

Maíz, Mexico: see CIUDAD DEL MAÍZ.

Maize (MAIZ), town (1990 pop. 1,520), Sedgwick co., S Kansas, suburb, 10 mi/16 km NW of Wichita; 37°46′N 97°27′W. In wheat region.

Majagua (mah-HAH-gwuh), town, Ciego de Ávila prov., E Cuba, on RR, and 15 mi/24 km WNW of Ciego de Ávila; 21°55′N 79°00′W. Sugarcane, fruit; cattle. Orlando González sugar mill is 6 mi/9.7 km S.

Majestic, uninc. village (1990 pop. 600), Pike co., E Ky., in the Cumberland Mts. near Tug Fork, 13 mi/21 km SE of Williamson. Bituminous coal. States of W.Va., Va., and Ky. converge 7 mi/11.3 km to E (easternmost point in Ky.).

Majestic Mountain (10,125 ft/3,086 m), W Alta., W Canada, near B.C. border, in Rocky Mts., in Jasper Natl. Park, 11 mi/18 km SE of Jasper; 52°53′N 118°13′W.

Major, county (□ 957 sq mi/2,479 sq km; 1990 pop. 8,055), NW Okla.; ⊙ Fairview; 36°18′N 98°32′W. Drained by Cimarron R. (forms W part of N border) and Eagle Chief Creek. North Canadian R. drains SW corner. Agr. (wheat, oats, soybeans, corn; cattle). Oil and natural-gas deposits. Formed 1907.

Makaha (MAH-KAH-hah), town (1990 pop. 7,990), Oahu isl., Honolulu co., Hawaii, 23 mi/37 km WNW of Honolulu, on W coast, near mouth of Makaha Stream. Cattle; fish. Kaneaki Heiau (Temple) to NE. Makaha and Keeau beach parks to NW. Keeau Point State Park to NW. Waianae Mts. and Waianae Kai Forest Reserve to NE.

Makaha Valley (MAH-KAH-hah), town (1990 pop. 1,012), Oahu isl., Honolulu co., Hawaii, 23 mi/37 km WNW of Honolulu, 1 mi/1.6 km NE of Makaha and W coast; 21°28′N 158°11′W. Site of Kaneaki Heiau (Temple). Waianae Mts. to NE.

Makahuena Point (MAH-kah-HOO-EI-nah), SE coast, Kauai isl., Kauai co., Hawaii, 8 mi/12.9 km SW of Lihue, SE of Poipu; 21°52′N 159°26′W.

Makakilo City (MAH-kah-KEE-lo), city (1990 pop. 9,828), Oahu isl., Honolulu co., Hawaii, 15 mi/24 km WNW of Honolulu, 3 mi/4.8 km inland from W coast, and 4 mi/6.4 km from S coast, at S end of Waianae Mts.; 21°21′N 158°05′W. Dairying; poultry. Barbers Point Naval Air Station to S; Kahe Point Beach Park to W.

Makamik, Que.: see MACAMIC.

Makanalua Peninsula, Hawaii: see KALAUPAPA.

Makanda (mah-KAHN-dah), village (1990 pop. 404), Jackson co., SW Ill., 12 mi/19 km SSE of Murphysboro; 37°37′N 89°14′W. In agr. region. Giant City State Park nearby.

Makapala (MAH-kah-PAH-lah), village, N Hawaii, Hawaii co., Hawaii, on Kohala Peninsula, 52 mi/84 km NW of Hilo. Kohala Forest Reserve to SE; Keokea Beach Park to E, near Akoakoa Point.

Makapuu Point (MAH-kah-POO-oo), SE Oahu isl., Honolulu co., Hawaii, 12 mi/19 km E of Honolulu; 21°18′N 157°39′W. Easternmost point on Oahu. Site of lighthouse built 1909. Manana (Rabbit) Isl. to N.

Makawao (MAH-kah-WOU), town (1990 pop. 5,405), NE Maui, Maui co., Hawaii, in interior, 6 mi/9.7 km S of N coast; 20°51′N 156°19′W. Holds annual 4th of July Rodeo. Univ. of Hawaii Agr. Station to SE. Olinda Prison Camp to SE. Koolau Forest Reserve to E; pine forest region to NE; eucalyptus forests to S; Makawao Forest Reserve to SE.

Makena Bay (MAH-KAI-nah), village, SW Maui, Hawaii. Molokini isl. 3.5 mi/5.6 km WSW, in Alalakeiki Channel. Makena Golf Course overlooks bay.

Cross references are shown in SMALL CAPITALS. The pronunciation key is on page xv. The dates of population figures are on page xii.

Makkovik (muh-KOO-vik), village (1991 pop. 370), E Lab., E Canada, on Makkovik Bay of the Atlantic Ocean; 55°05′N 59°06′W. Fishing port.

Makkovik, Cape, on the Atlantic Ocean, E Lab., E Canada; 55°15′N 59°04′W.

Makoti (mah-KO-tee), village (1990 pop. 145), Ward co., NW central N.Dak., 31 mi/50 km SW of Minot; 47°57′N 101°47′W. Fort Berthold Indian Reservation just W.

Makushin (MA-koo-shin), native fishing village, N Unalaska Isl., Aleutian Isls., SW Alaska.

Makushin Volcano (6,680 ft/2,036 m), NE Unalaska Isl., Aleutian Isls., SW Alaska, 15 mi/24 km W of Dutch Harbor; 53°53′N 166°55′W. Flat-topped, snow-covered, active volcano.

Malabar (MA-luh-bahr), town (□ 13 sq mi/34 sq km; 1990 pop. 1,977), Brevard co., E central Fla., 4 mi/6.4 km S of Melbourne; 27°59′N 80°34′W. Mfg. includes machinery; commercial graphics.

Malad City, town (1990 pop. 1,946), ⊙ Oneida co., SE Idaho, on Deep Creek, near Little Mallad R., near Utah state line, and 18 mi/29 km WNW of Preston; 42°11′N 112°15′W. Elev. 4,700 ft/1,433 m. RR terminus; shipping point for agr. area (sugar beets, wheat, barley, potatoes); dairying; cattle; mfg. (pumice aggregate, glue flour). Caribou Natl. Forest to E, Curlew Natl. Grassland to W; Devil Creek Reservoir to NE; Malad Summit (pass; 5,976 ft/1,821 m) to N. Settled by Mormons 1864.

Malad River, c.50 mi/80 km long, in SE Idaho and N Utah; formed by confluence of Little Malad R. with Deep and Devil creeks in Oneida co., Idaho; flows S, into Box Elder co., Utah, entering Bear R. NW of Brigham City.

Malaga 1 (MA-luh-guh), village, Gloucester co., S N.J., on Maurice R., and 5 mi/8 km NNW of Vineland. In fruit and vegetable area. **2** uninc. village, Chelan co., central Wash., 7 mi/11.3 km ESE of Wenatchee, on the Columbia R. (Rock Island L. reservoir). Apples, pears; cattle, sheep. Mfg. (primary aluminum production). Rock Island Dam to SE.

Malaga Lake, W N.S., E Canada, 13 mi/21 km W of Bridgewater; 8 mi/13 km long, 3 mi/5 km wide. Fed and drained by Medway R.

Malagash (MA-luh-gash), village, N N.S., E Canada, at head of Tatamagouche Bay, 40 mi/64 km WNW of New Glasgow; 45°46′N 63°23′W. Salt-production center; fish, lobster, scallops, potatoes.

Malakoff, town (1990 pop. 2,038), Henderson co., E Texas, 27 mi/43 km ENE of Corsicana; 32°10′N 96°00′W. Agr. (vegetables, nursery crops; cattle, horses); clay; oil and gas; lignite mines; mfg. (powdered aluminum, transportation equip., bldg. materials). Cedar Creek Reservoir to NW. Inc. after 1940.

Malartic (mah-lahr-TEEK), town (1991 pop. 4,326), W Que., E Quebec, 40 mi/64 km ESE of Rouyn; 48°08′N 78°07′W. Mining center (gold, copper, molybdenum, zinc, lead). Inc. 1939.

Malaspina (ma-luh-SPEE-nuh), glacier (□ c.1,500 sq mi/3,890 sq km), SE Alaska, bet. Yakutat and Icy bays and flowing into the Gulf of Alaska. Named for an Ital. navigator who explored this region for Spain in 1791. Largest piedmont glacier in N. Amer.

Malbaie, La (MAL-bai, lah) or **Murray Bay**, village, E Que., E Canada, on the St. Lawrence R., at mouth of Malbaie R., and 80 mi/129 km NE of Quebec. Lumbering, dairying; resort.

Malbaie River (MAL-bai) or **Murray River**, S Que., E Canada, 100 mi/161 km long; rises in E part of Laurentides Natl. Park, flows in an arc NE and then SSE to the St. Lawrence R. at La Malbaie.

Malcolm, town (1990 pop. 447), Poweshiek co., central Iowa, 9 mi/14.5 km N of Montezuma; 41°42′N 92°33′W. In agr. area; feeds.

Malcolm, village (1990 pop. 181), Lancaster co., SE Nebr., 10 mi/16 km NW of Lincoln; 40°54′N 96°52′W. In area are Branched Oak L. (N) and Pawnee L. (S) state recreation areas.

Malcolm Island (□ 32 sq mi/83 sq km), SW B.C., SW Canada, in Queen Charlotte Strait just off N Vancouver Isl., 3 mi/5 km N of Alert Bay; 15 mi/24 km long, 2 mi/

3 km–4 mi/6 km wide. Lumbering; farming; salmon fishing. Sointula is trade center.

Malden 1 (MAWL-duhn), city (1990 pop. 53,884), Middlesex co., E Mass., a residential, commercial, and industrial suburb of Boston, in the Mystic R. valley; 42°26′N 71°04′W. Bordered N by the cliffs of Middlesex Fells. Mfg. includes electronic parts, fabricated metal prods., paint, clothing, and footwear. A number of old historic churches are here. Michael Wigglesworth was minister here for many years. Adoniram Judson and Saul Cohen b. here. Pine Barks shared with Melrose. Settled 1640, inc. 1881. **2** city (1990 pop. 5,123), Dunklin co., extreme SE Mo., in Mississippi alluvial plain, 29 mi/47 km SE of Poplar Bluff; 36°34′N 89°58′W. Soybeans, rice, cotton; mfg. (transportation equip., fabricated metal prods., milling tools); ships cotton, livestock. Plotted 1877.

Malden, uninc. town, Kanawha co., W central W.Va., suburb, 5 mi/8 km ESE of Charleston, on Kanawha R. Agr. (corn, tobacco); cattle, poultry. Mfg. (quilts).

Malden, village (1990 pop. 189), Whitman co., SE Wash., 25 mi/40 km N of Colfax, on Pine Creek; 47°14′N 117°28′W. Agr. region in Palouse Country.

Malheur (muh-LOOR), county (□ 9,930 sq mi/25,719 sq km; 1990 pop. 26,038), SE Oregon; ⊙ Vale; 43°12′N 117°37′W. Drained by Malheur and Owyhee rivers, which flow to Snake R. Borders on Nev. (S) and Idaho (E). Twelfth-largest co. in U.S. Agr. (sugar beets, corn, onions, potatoes, wheat, oats, barley; hogs, sheep, cattle); dairy prods. OWYHEE DAM, 20 mi/32 km SW of Nyssa, creates Owyhee Reservoir in E. Warm Springs Reservoir on W border. Small part of Malheur Natl. Forest on NW border; Ontario State Park in NE; L. Owyhee Reservoir and State Park and Succor Creek State Recreation Area in E. Duck Pond L., intermittent, in SW. Lava beds in S center. Formed 1887.

Malheur (muh-LOOR), river, c. 165 mi/266 km long, SE Grant co., Oregon; rises at confluence of Big and Lake creeks, in Malheur Natl. Forest, in the Strawberry Range, E Oregon; flows S then SE through Warm Springs Reservoir, receives the South Fork, then flows generally NE past Juntura, where it receives the North Fork, past Vale to the Snake R., N of Ontario. Flood-control projects; Vale project uses the Malheur for irrigation.

Malheur Lake (muh-LOOR), semidry lake, Harney co., SE Oregon, 20 mi/32 km SE of Burns; c.15 mi/24 km long and up to 5 mi/8 km wide. Harney Basin in NW part of Great Basin. Fed by Silvies (from NW) and Donner und Blitzen (from S) rivers. Connected by channel to Harney L. in SW. Lakes have no outlet. Separate units of Malheur Natl. Wildlife Refuge surround Malheur and Harney lakes and Donner und Blitzen R.

Malibu, uninc. city (1990 est. pop. 10,000), S Calif., suburb, 26 mi/42 km W of Los Angeles and 11 mi/18 km W of Santa Monica, on Pacific Ocean coast (faces S) at Malibu Point, at mouth of Malibu Creek. Mfg. (electronics research; printing and publishing). Popular beach resort. Its relatively secluded area has made Malibu attractive to many of the entertainment and business personalities. Elaborate residences line a beach escarpment extending N from shore of Santa Monica Bay. Of interest is the J. Paul Getty Mus., 7 mi/11.3 km E at Topanga. Seat of Pepperdine Univ. In area are Malibu Lagoon (E) and Leo Carillo (W) state beaches; Malibu Creek State Park to N.

Malibu Lake, reservoir, Los Angeles co., S Calif., on Malibu Creek, at center of residential development 6 mi/9.7 km NNW of Malibu, in Santa Monica Mts. Natl. Recreation Area; 1.5 mi/2.4 km long; 34°05′N 118°42′W. Formed by small dam.

Malibu Riviera, Calif.: see POINT DUME.

Malignant Cove, village, E N.S., E Canada, on Northumberland Strait, 12 mi/19 km NNW of Antigonish; 45°48′N 62°02′W. Resort.

Maligne Lake (muh-LEEN), W Alta., W Canada, in Rocky Mts., in Jasper Natl. Park, at foot of Mt. Unwin, 21 mi/34 km SE of Jasper; 20 mi/32 km long, 1 mi/2 km

wide. Elev. 5,490 ft/1,673 m. Recognized for its scenic beauty. Drains NW into Athabaska R.

Maligne Mountains, W Alta., W Canada, range of peaks in Rocky Mts., in Jasper Natl. Park, extends 20 mi/32 km SE from Jasper; rises to 9,157 ft/2,791 m. Overlooks upper Athabaska R. valley.

Malin (muh-LIN), village (1990 pop. 725), Klamath co., S Oregon, 1 mi/1.6 km N of Calif. state line, 25 mi/40 km SE of Klamath Falls. Agr. (barley, wheat, potatoes; cattle); dairy prods. Nearby, in Calif. are Tule L. (SW) and Clear L. (SE) natl. wildlife refuges.

Malinalco (mah-lee-NAHL-ko), town (1990 pop. 5,385), Mexico state, central Mexico, 25 mi/40 km SSE of Toluca de Lerdo; 18°57′N 99°30′W. Sugarcane, cereals, fruit; livestock. Site of important archaeological site, famous pre-Aztec murals.

Malinaltepec (mah-lee-NAHL-te-pek), town (1990 pop. 1,465), Guerrero, SW Mexico, in Sierra Madre del Sur, 35 km SSW of Tlapa de Comonfort; 17°03′N 98°40′W. An isolated community in the Sierra Madre del Sur. No access by road. Cereals, sugarcane, fruit; livestock.

Malinche (mah-LEEN-chai), dormant volcano (14,636 ft/4,461 m), central Mexico, on Puebla-Tlaxcala border, 16 mi/26 km NE of Puebla. Has several extinct craters; snowcapped during winter. Aztec name is Matlalcueyatl. Also written Malintzi or Malinzi.

Malinta (muh-LIN-tuh), village (1990 pop. 294), Henry co., NW Ohio, 7 mi/11 km SE of Napoleon; 41°19′N 84°02′W. Clay, concrete, and plaster prods.

Malintzi, Mexico: see MALINCHE.

Malinzi, Mexico: see MALINCHE.

Mallaig (MA-laig), village, E Alta., W Canada, 65 mi/105 km NNW of Vermilion. Mixed farming, lumbering.

Mallard, town (1990 pop. 360), Palo Alto co., NW Iowa, 12 mi/19 km S of Emmetsburg; 42°56′N 94°40′W. Livestock; grain.

Mallory, uninc town (1990 pop. 1,126), Logan co., SW W.Va., near Guyandotte R., 11 mi/18 km SSE of Logan; 37°43′N 81°49′W. Coal mining. Mfg. (rebuilt mining equip.). R. D. Bailey L. (reservoir) and Wildlife Management Area to SE.

Malmo, village (1990 pop. 114), Saunders co., E Nebr., 6 mi/9.7 km NW of Wahoo, and on branch of Platte R.; 41°16′N 96°43′W.

Malmstrom Air Force Base, U.S. military installation (□ 6 sq mi/15.5 sq km), W central Mont., 4 mi/6.4 km E of Great Falls, Cascade co. Est. 1942 during World War II as the take-off point for Soviet-bound lend-lease material; after the war it was a training base for crews in the Berlin Airlift. The Strategic Air Command (SAC) assumed command in 1954; SAC's 1st Minuteman missile wing was est. here in 1961. The missile complex adjoining the base is one of the largest in the world. Scheduled for closing in late 1990s.

Malone 1 village (□ 2 sq mi/5.2 sq km; 1990 pop. 6,777), ⊙ Franklin co., N N.Y., on Salmon R., near Canada (Que.) border, and 30 mi/48 km ESE of Massena; 44°51′N 74°17′W. Port of entry. Mfg. of aluminum and bronze powder, footwear, bldg. materials, paper, clothing, cheese, lumber, furniture, machinery; RR shops. In agr. (dairy prods.; potatoes; grain). Summer resort. Was gathering point for the Fenians, who raided Canada in 1866. Seat of North Country Community Col. Settled c.1800, inc. 1833. **2** village (1990 pop. 306), Hill co., central Texas, 15 mi/24 km SE of Hillsboro; 31°55′N 96°53′W. In farm area. Mfg. (meat prods.). Navarro Mills L. reservoir to E.

Maloy, town (1990 pop. 36), Ringgold co., S Iowa, on Little Platte R., and 10 mi/16 km WSW of Mount Ayr; 40°40′N 94°24′W.

Malpais, Mexico: see SAN NICOLÁS DE BUENOS AIRES.

Malpais, The (MAL-pei) [Span.=bad lands], name given to lava fields in central and W N.Mex. One area is in Lincoln and Otero cos., central N.Mex., c.45 mi/72 km N of Alamogordo and SW of Carrizozo, in N part of Tularosa Valley, E of Sierra Oscura, W of Sierra Blanca, and with Valley of Fires Natl. Recreation Area in N. The other area is in Cibola co., W N.Mex., c.70 mi/113 km WSW of Albuquerque, S of Grants.

Much of area covered by El Malpais Natl. Monument. La Ventana Natural Arch in E; Bandera Volcano and Ice Cave to W.

Malpeque Bay (MOL-pek), inlet (12 mi/19 km long, 10 mi/16 km wide at entrance) of the Gulf of St. Lawrence, NW P.E.I., E Canada, 4 mi/6 km N of Summerside. Entrance of bay is protected by several islets. Oyster beds.

Malta, city (1990 pop. 2,340), ⊙ Phillips co., N Mont., on Milk R., near L. Bowdoin, and 58 mi/93 km WNW of Glasgow; 48°21′N 107°52′W. Trading point in irrigated agr. area; cattle; wheat, barley, hay. Natural-gas wells to NE. L. Bowdoin and Bowdoin Natl. Wildlife Refuge (known for its waterfowl) to E. Phillips Co. Mus. here. Inc. 1909.

Malta 1 village (1990 pop. 171), Cassia co., S Idaho, 25 mi/40 km SE of Burley, on Raft R.; 42°19′N 113°22′W. Irrigated agr. area. Cattle; dairying; grain, alfalfa. **2** village (1990 pop. 865), De Kalb co., N Ill., 10 mi/16 km WSW of Sycamore; 41°55′N 88°51′W. In rich agr. area. Kishwaukee Community Col. nearby. **3** (MOL-tuh), village (1990 pop. 802), Morgan co., SE Ohio, on Muskingum R., opposite McConnelsville; 39°39′N 81°52′W.

Malta Bend, town (1990 pop. 289), Saline co., central Mo., near Missouri R., 10 mi/16 km NW of Marshall; 39°11′N 93°21′W. Grain; livestock. Grand Pass Conservation Area (wetlands) to N.

Maltrata (mahl-TRAH-tah), town (1990 pop. 8,732), Veracruz, E Mexico, in valley at S foot of Pico de Orizaba, on RR, and 12 mi/19 km WSW of Orizaba. Coffee-growing center.

Malvern (MAL-vuhrn), city (1990 pop. 9,256), ⊙ Hot Spring co., central Ark., 17 mi/27 km SE of Hot Springs, near Ouachita R.; 34°22′N 92°49′W. In diversified agr. area. Mfg. (apparel, bldg. materials, chemicals, lumber, fiberboard, electrical goods, wood prods.); sawmilling. L. Catherine (Ouachita R.) and L. Catherine State Park are to NW. Inc. as city 1876.

Malvern, town (1991 pop. 3,262), St. Elizabeth parish, SW Jamaica, resort, 9 mi/14.5 km SE of Black River town; 17°58′N 77°43′W. In agr. region (corn, tropical fruit and spices; livestock).

Malvern 1 town (1990 pop. 570), Geneva co., SE Ala., 21 mi/34 km NE of Geneva. **2** town (1990 pop. 1,210), Mills co., SW Iowa, on Silver Creek, and 9 mi/14.5 km ESE of Glenwood; 41°00′N 95°35′W. In hay, grain, livestock area; feed milling. Founded 1869 with coming of RR; inc. 1870.

Malvern, village (1990 pop. 1,112), Carroll co., E Ohio, 13 mi/21 km ESE of Canton, and on small Sandy Creek; 40°41′N 81°11′W. In dairying area; makes clay prods.

Malvern (MAL-vuhrn), borough (1990 pop. 2,944), Chester co., SE Pa., suburb, 19 mi/31 km WNW of downtown Philadelphia; 40°01′N 75°30′W. Some agr. (vegetables; livestock; dairying; nursery stock); mfg. (biotechncal prods., electronic equip., chemicals, consumer goods, plastic prods., restaurant equip., transportation equip., computers, machinery; publishing). Settled 1866, inc. 1889.

Malverne, residential village (☐ 1 sq mi/2.6 sq km; 1990 pop. 9,054), in Hempstead town, Nassau co., SE N.Y., on L.I.; 40°40′N 73°40′W. Settled in the early 1800s, inc. 1921.

Mama (MAH-mah), town (1990 pop. 2,430), Yucatán, SE Mexico, 15 mi/24 km NE of Ticul; 20°29′N 89°22′W. Henequen, sugarcane, fruit.

Mamaroneck (mah-MA-ruh-nek), residential village and town (1990 pop. 17,325), Westchester co., SE N.Y., a suburb of N.Y. city, on L.I. Sound; 40°55′N 73°43′W. Initially a farming community, Mamaroneck is a boating center with an excellent marina. There is some light mfg. in addition to office and corporate activity. Mixed middle- and upper-class pop. Town includes Larchmont village. Settled 1661, inc. 1895.

Mamawi Lake, NE Alta., W Canada, 8 mi/13 km SW of Fort Chipewyan, in Wood Buffalo Natl. Park, bet. L. Claire and L. Athabasca; 16 mi/26 km long, 10 mi/16 km wide; 58°35′N 111°30′W.

Mamey, El, Mexico: see MINATITLÁN.

Mameyes (mah-MAI-yes), village, NE P.R., 23 mi/37 km ESE of San Juan. Cultivates the mamey tree, which yields preserves and candy.

Mammoth, town (1990 pop. 1,845), Pinal co., SE Ariz., on San Pedro R., and 39 mi/63 km NNE of Tucson; 32°43′N 110°38′W. Elev. 2,348 ft/716 m. Cattle, sheep. Molybdenum deposits. Busy mining (gold, silver) camp in 1880s. Galiuro Mts. to NE; parts of Coronado Natl. Forest to E and SW; Aravaipa Canyons Wilderness area and Holy Joe Peak (6,145 ft/1,873 m) to NE.

Mammoth Cave, cavern near San Andreas, Calaveras co., central Calif. Has many chambers and a subterranean lake.

Mammoth Cave National Park (☐ 82 sq mi/212 sq km), Edmonson, Hart, and Barren cos., S central Ky., in Pennyroyal region. Site of Mammoth Cave, one of the largest known caves in the world, located in hilly, forested region drained by Green and Nolin rivers. Composed of a series of subterranean chambers and narrow passages formed by the dissolution of limestone, the cave has 5 separate levels. The cave has at least 330 mi/531 km of explored passageways with a large variety of limestone formations (stalactites, stalagmites, and columns), and subterranean lakes and rivers. Echo R., c.360 ft/110 m below the surface, flows through the cave's lowest level and drains into the Green R. Also Hanson's Lost R., joins Mammoth Cave with the extensive Flint Ridge cave system; this long-sought link was discovered in 1972. The temp. (54°F/12°C) and relative humidity (87%) remain constant during the year throughout the cave. The cave contains the mummified body of a man believed to date from the pre-Columbian period. Eyeless fish, bats, and insects are also found. Mammoth Cave was a long-time Native Amer. habitation before it was explored by Ky. pioneers in 1799. During the War of 1812, saltpetre was mined in the cave for gunpowder. Numerous other caves in and around park. Variety of surface wildlife and flora. Authorized 1926.

Mammoth Hot Springs, Wyo.: see YELLOWSTONE NATIONAL PARK.

Mammoth Lakes, city (1990 pop. 4,785) Mono co., E Calif., resort settlement and region of many small lakes, in the Sierra Nevadas, 35 mi/56 km NW of Bishop; 37°38′N 119°00′W. Elev. c.8,900 ft/2,713 m. Fishing, boating, camping, hiking, horseback riding, winter sports. Devil Postpile Natl. Monument is 5 mi/8 km W. Scene of small-scale gold rush, 1879–1880. Surrounded by Inyo Natl. Forest to W, Sierra Natl. Forest to W, beyond Sierra Crest; world-class Mammoth Mt. Ski Area to W; L. Crowley reservoir to E.

Mammoth Mountain Ski Area, Calif.: see MAMMOTH LAKES.

Mammoth Onyx Cave, Ky.: see MUNFORDVILLE.

Mammoth Pool Reservoir, S central Calif., on border of Fresno and Madera cos., on San Joaquin R., 47 mi/76 km NNE of Fresno, in Sierra Natl. Forest; 9 mi/14.5 km long; 37°18′N 119°18′W. Elev. 3,330 ft/1,015 m. Extends NE; max. capacity 123,000 acre-ft. Formed by Mammoth Pool Dam (375 ft/114 m high), built by the Southern Calif. Edison Company for power generation and water supply

Mammoth Spring (MAM-uth), town (1990 pop. 1,097), Fulton co., N Ark., c.65 mi/105 km NW of Jonesboro, at Mo. state line; 36°29′N 91°32′W. In agr. area. Has natl. fish hatchery. Named for spring (N end of town), one of largest in U.S. Mammoth Spring State Park, which feeds Spring R.; site of resort, power plant. Mfg. (catfish processing; walking canes).

Mamou (MAH-moo), town (1990 pop. 3,483), Evangeline parish, S central La., 8 mi/13 km ESE of Ville Platte; 30°38′N 92°25′W. In cotton- and rice-producing area; light mfg. Oil field nearby.

Mamulique Pass (mah-moo-LEE-ke) (2,280 ft/695 m), in N outliers of Sierra Madre Oriental, Nuevo León, N Mexico, on Inter-Amer. Highway (85) and 40 mi/64 km NNW of Monterrey.

Man, town (1990 pop. 914), Logan co., SW W.Va., 10 mi/16 km SW of Logan; 37°44′N 81°52′W. RR junction to E. Bituminous-coal area. Mfg. (mining machine parts).

R. D. Bailey L. reservoir and Wildlife Management Area to SE. Inc. 1918.

Man of War Bay, deep inlet of NW Tobago, Trinidad and Tobago, 14 mi/23 km NE of Scarborough; c.2 mi/3.2 km long, 2 mi/3.2 km wide; 11°19′N 60°34′W. On it is Charlotteville. High cliffs. Sometimes spelled Man-of-War Bay.

Manacas (mah-NAH-kahs), town, Villa Clara prov., central Cuba, on Central Highway, on RR, and 27 mi/43 km NW of Santa Clara; 22°42′N 80°21′W. Sugarcane, tobacco, fruit; cattle. George Washington sugar mill 2 mi/3.2 km SE.

Managua (mah-NAH-gwuh), town, La Habana prov., W Cuba, at N foot of Managua hills, part of Alturas de Bejucal, 15 mi/24 km SSE of Havana; 22°57′N 82°18′W. Sugarcane; livestock.

Manahawkin (ma-nuh-HUH-kin), village (1990 pop. 1,594), Ocean co., E N.J., near Atlantic coast, 18 mi/29 km S of Toms River village; 39°42′N 74°15′W. Manahawkin Bay is E; link in N.J. sect. of Intracoastal Waterway, which enters from Barnegat Bay (N) and continues S into Little Egg Harbor. Bay is crossed SE of Manahawkin by highway bridge to Long Beach isl., barrier bet. bay and the Atlantic.

Manakin-Sabot, uninc. village, Goochland co., central Va., 14 mi/23 km WNW of Richmond, near James R. Mfg. (stone processing, millwork); agr. (grain, tobacco, soybeans; cattle); limestone.

Manalapan (ma-nuh-LA-puhn), township (1990 pop. 26,716), Monmouth co., NE N.J., 5 mi/8 km E of Hightstown; 40°16′N 74°20′W. Inc. 1848. Former farm community, now rapidly growing suburb.

Manasquan (MA-nuhs-kwahn), resort borough (1990 pop. 5,369), Monmouth co., E N.J., on coast, at N mouth of Manasquan R., and 15 mi/24 km SE of Freehold; 40°06′N 74°02′W. Fishing; wood millwork. Inc. 1887.

Manasquan River (MA-nuhs-kwahn), c.30 mi/48 km long, E N.J.; rises S of Freehold; flows generally SE to the Atlantic Ocean at Manasquan. Manasquan Inlet, at mouth of river, is N entrance of Intracoastal Waterway, which continues S, through the Point Pleasant Canal, to head of Barnegat Bay.

Manassa, town (1990 pop. 988), Conejos co., S Colo., near Conejos R., just E of San Juan Mts., and 20 mi/32 km S of Alamosa; 37°10′N 105°56′W. Elev. 7,683 ft/2,342 m. Mfg. (jewelry). Trading point in San Luis Valley. Jack Dempsey b. here; mus.

Manassas 1 (muh-NA-suhs), city (1990 pop. 123), Tattnall co., E central Ga., 7 mi/11.3 km W of Claxton; 32°10′N 82°01′W. **2** independent city (☐ 10 sq mi/26 sq km; 1990 pop. 27,957), ⊙ surrounding Prince William co., NE Va., separate from surrounding Prince William co.; 38°45′N 77°29′W. Mfg. (bldg. materials, medical equip., food, machinery, electronic equip.; printing and publishing, steel fabrication, bindery services). Agr. area to W and NW (grain, soybeans; livestock; dairying). Manassas has become a growing residential town with retail shopping centers and added housing; its development has been spurred by the expansion of Washington, D.C., suburbs, further into N Va. Key Civil War RR junction; battles of BULL RUN fought nearby; sites are locally marked. Northern Va. Community Col. (Manassas Campus) to N. George Mason Univ. Prince William Campus to W. Manassas Mus. Manassas Natl. Battlefield Park to NW. Manassas Regional Airport (Davis Field) to SW. Inc. 1873, rechartered 1938.

Manassas (muh-NA-suhs), Natl. Battlefield Park (☐ 8 sq mi/20.7 sq km), Prince William and Fairfax cos., N Va., 5 mi/8 km NNW of Manassas; 38°49′N 77°31′W. Site of Civil War First (July 21, 1861) and Second (Aug. 28–Aug. 30, 1862) battles of Manassas. Authorized 1940.

Manassas Gap (c.950 ft/290 m), N Va., on border bet. Warren and Fauquier cos., lowest pass in Blue Ridge Mts., 8 mi/12.9 km E of Front Royal. RR and Interstate highway Route 66 pass through. Linden village, just W, in Warren co., was formerly called Manassas Gap. Appalachian Trail crosses gap N-S.

Manassas Park, independent city (1990 pop. 6734), N

Va., residential suburb, 2 mi/3.2 km NE of Manassas, near Bull Run creek, separate from surrounding Prince William co. and adjoining city of Manassas; 38°46′N 77°27′W. Manassas Natl. Battlefield Park to NW.

Manatee (MAN-uh-tee), county (□ 892 sq mi/2,310 sq km; 1990 pop. 211,707), W central Fla., on Gulf of Mexico and Tampa Bay; ⊙ Bradenton; 27°28′N 82°21′W. Level and rolling terrain, drained by Manatee and Myakka rivers; has scattered lakes, part of Sarasota Bay, and small offshore isls., including Anna Maria Key. Farming and citrus fruit-growing area, with dairying, poultry raising, some fishing, and lumbering. Formed 1855.

Manatee (MAN-uh-tee), town, Manatee co., W central Fla., fishing port on Manatee R. near its mouth on Tampa Bay, and 3 mi/4.8 km E of Bradenton; 27°29′N 82°39′W. Ships citrus fruit and vegetables.

Manatee Bay, small Caribbean inlet, St. Catherine parish, S Jamaica, at foot of low Hellshire Hills, 14 mi/23 km SW of Kingston; 17°50′N 77°00′W.

Manatee River (MAN-uh-tee), c.50 mi/80 km long, W central Fla.; rises in small lake in E Manatee co.; flows SW and W to Tampa Bay near Bradenton. Lower course dredged.

Manatí (mah-nah-TEE), town (1990 pop. 38,692), N P.R., 24 mi/39 km W of San Juan. Pineapples; livestock; dairying (milk); mfg. (chemical, plastic, and pharmaceutical prods.). Tourism at Mar Chiquita Beach, just N. Referred to as the "Athens of Puerto Rico." In the Karst region.

Manatí (mah-nuh-TEE), sugar-mill village, Las Tunas prov., E Cuba, near Puerto Manatí Bay (6 mi/9.7 km long, 3 mi/4.8 km wide) of the Atlantic Ocean, on RR, and 25 mi/40 km N of Las Tunas city; 21°19′N 76°55′W.

Manatí River (mah-nah-TEE) or **Río Grande de Manatí**, c.40 mi/64 km long, central and N P.R.; rises in Cordillera Central just N of Barranquitas; flows NW, past Ciales, to the Atlantic Ocean 4 mi/6.4 km NW of Manatí.

Manawa, town (1990 pop. 1,169), Waupaca co., central Wis., on Little Wolf R. (tributary of Wolf R.), and 32 mi/51 km E of Stevens Point; 44°27′N 88°55′W. In dairying and farming area. Mfg. (marine accessories, mill prods., transportation equip.).

Mancelona (man-se-LO-nuh), village (1990 pop. 1,370), Antrim co., NW Mich., 29 mi/47 km NE of Traverse City, adjoining Antrim; 44°53′N 85°03′W. In dairy and agr. area (livestock; cherries, apples; dairy); mfg. (transportation equip., metal stampings, storage tanks, wood prods.). Schuss Mt. and Shanty Creek ski areas to NW. Inc. 1889.

Manchac, Bayou (MAN-shak, BEI-yoo), partly navigable waterway once connected with the Mississippi R., c.19 mi/31 km long, SE La.; begins S of Baton Rouge; flows E, entering Amite R. 9 mi/14 km S of Denham Springs; 30°20′N 90°53′W. Also known as Bayou Iberville.

Manchac, Pass (MAN-shak), navigable waterway (shallow-draft vessels), c.6 mi/10 km long, SE La., connecting L. Pontchartrain (E) and L. Maurepas (W), c.27 mi/43 km NW of New Orleans; 30°17′N, 90°18′W. Manchac State Wildlife Area on S side of channel.

Manchaug, Mass.: see SUTTON.

Manchester, parish (1991 pop. 156,723), Middlesex co., W central and S Jamaica; ⊙ Mandeville; 18°15′N–17°51′N 77°38′W–77°21′W. Bordered E by Clarendon, N by Trelawny, and W by St. Elizabeth parishes. This predominantly mountainous region of no rivers and scarce water supply has a salubrious climate of 55°F/13°C–88°F/31°C. Its leading settlements, such as Mandeville, Christiana, and Williamsfield, are popular resorts. Tropical prods. (grapefruit, oranges, annatto, ginger, pimento) are grown widely. Traversed by Jamaica RR.

Manchester 1 city (1990 pop. 5,137), ⊙ Delaware co., E Iowa, on Maquoketa R., and 38 mi/61 km W of Dubuque; 42°29′N 91°27′W. Agr. trade and processing center (dairy prods.); mfg. (paper goods., fabricated metal prods., electronic prods., chemicals, machinery). A U.S. fish hatchery to SE. Settled 1850, inc. 1886. **2** city (1990 pop. 99,567), Hillsborough co., S N.H., on both sides of the Merrimack R.; 42°58′N 71°26′W. Also drained by Piscataquog R. and Cohas Brook. Largest city in N.H. Mfg. (computer equip. and accessories, electronic prods. and equip., machinery, lobster holding systems, foods and beverages, clothing, hats, concrete products, industrial brushes, fabricated metal prods., plastics, bldg. materials, medical supplies, paper prods., chemicals, sterilization systems, tool and die, machinery). The Amoskeag Falls on the Merrimack provided power for the 1st textile mills. In 1838 textile interests founded the city and established a huge textile-mfg. company. Until the depression of the 1930s and the moving of much of the textile industry to the South, Manchester was heavily dependent on this industry. Seat of St. Anselm Col. and the Currier Gall. of Art. Also Univ. of N.H. at Manchester, Notre Dame Col., N.H. Technical Col. (2 year), Inst. of Arts and Sciences, Hesser Col., N.H. Col. (to N). John Stark lived and is buried here. Municipal Airport to S. Massabesic L. is on E border. McIntyre Ski Area to NE. Settled 1722, inc. as a city 1846. **3** city (1990 pop. 7,709), ⊙ Coffee co., central Tenn., near Duck R., 12 mi/19 km NE of Tullahoma; 35°29′N 86°05′W. Shipping center in timber and farm area; clothing, metal parts, caskets. Settled 1836; inc. 1905. Old Stone Fort State Park is nearby.

Manchester 1 town (1990 pop. 51,618), Hartford co., central Conn.; 41°46′N 72°31′W. Prerevolutionary sawmills and paper mills. Was also known for its production of grandfather clocks and cheney silks. Mfg. today includes transportation equip., tools, and dairy and paper prods. A major retail shopping area has developed along the Interstate 84 corridor here. Seat of Manchester Community-Technical Col. Settled c.1672, inc. 1823. **2** town (1990 pop. 4,104), Meriwether and Talbot cos., W Ga., 33 mi/53 km NE of Columbus, on N face of Pine Mt. (S extremity of the Appalachian Mts.); 32°51′N 84°37′W. In agr. and livestock area. Mfg. includes bldg. materials, chemicals, consumer goods; various light mfg. Franklin D. Roosevelt State Park, warm springs, and Callaway Gardens nearby. Settled 1905; inc. 1909. **3** town (1990 pop. 1,634), ⊙ Clay co., SE Ky., 18 mi/29 km E of London, on Goose Creek, in Cumberland foothills, in Daniel Boone Natl. Forest; 37°08′N 83°46′W. In coal-mining, timber, and agr. (corn, tobacco, hay; livestock) area; mfg. (lumber, tool and die, consumer goods, bldg. materials; coal processing; window treatments). Has airport. Seat of Eastern Ky. Univ.–Manchester Campus and Oneida Baptist Inst. Beech Creek Wildlife Management Area to E. Est.1798; inc. 1932. **4** town (1990 pop. 2,099), Kennebec co., S Maine, just W of Hallowell and Augusta, and on L. Cobbosseecontee; 44°19′N 69°51′W. **5** town (1990 pop. 2,810), Carroll co., N Md., 29 mi/47 km NW of Baltimore; 39°40′N 76°53′W. Clothing and meat factories. Near site of Native Susquehannock town, whose members were massacred in battles with Seneca tribes and Colonel John Washington in 1675. Subsequent raids on Eur. settlers contributed to Bacon's Rebellion. Laid out in 18th cent. by Capt. Richard Richards, and named after his home city of Manchester (England). **6** suburban town (1990 pop. 5,286), Essex co., NE Mass., on Mass. Bay, and 8 mi/12.9 km NE of Salem; 42°34′N 70°46′W. Includes village of West Manchester. Former upper-class resort. Known for Singing Beach. Offshore is Norman's Woe Rock. Settled 1626, inc. 1645. **7** town (1990 pop. 1,753), Washtenaw co., SE Mich., 18 mi/29 km SW of Ann Arbor; 42°08′N 84°02′W. In diversified agr. area; feed milling. Mfg. (machinery, fabricated metal prods., transportation equip.). Inc. 1867. **8** town (1990 pop. 6,447), St. Louis co., E Mo., residential suburb, 17 mi/27 km W of downtown St. Louis, and 2 mi/3.2 km E of Ballwin, near Meramec R. Castlewood State Park to SW. Mfg. (fabricated metal prods., tool and die; printing). **9** township (1990 pop. 35,976), Ocean co., E central N.J., 2 mi/3.2 km SW of Lakehurst; 39°57′N 74°22′W. Inc. 1865. **10** resort town (1990 pop. 3,622), including Manchester village, ⊙ Bennington co. (along with Bennington); 43°09′N 73°04′W. SW Vt., on Batten Kill, and 20 mi/32 km N of Bennington, bet. the Taconic (W) and Green mts.; also includes Manchester Center and Manchester Depot villages. Seat of Burr and Burton Seminary (1829). Major retail center (factory outlet shops); mfg. (consumer goods; printing); lumber, marble. Summer, winter resort; skiing at nearby Bromley Mt. (also known as Big Bromley), ski touring at Hildere. Southern Vt. Art Center; Mt. Equinox is just W. Vt. Council of Safety met here 1777. Settled c.1764, laid out 1784. **11** uninc. town (1990 pop. 900), Kitsap co., W Wash., 10 mi/16 km WSW of downtown Seattle, on Kitsap Peninsula, on Puget Sound. Fishing. Manchester State Park and U.S. Naval Station to N; Blake Isl. State Park to SE.

Manchester 1 uninc. village, Mendocino co., NW Calif., near the Pacific Ocean coast, 25 mi/40 km WSW of Ukiah. Farming (cattle; apples, pears, grapes); dairying; fish, urchins. Manchester State Beach at Point Arena, to SW. **2** village (1990 pop. 347), Scott co., W central Ill., 9 mi/14.5 km SE of Winchester; 39°32′N 90°19′W. In agr. area. **3** village (1990 pop. 80), Dickinson co., N central Kansas, 13 mi/21 km NNW of Abilene; 39°05′N 97°19′W. Wheat; cattle. **4** village (1990 pop. 69), Freeborn co., S Minn., 7 mi/11.3 km NW of Albert Lea; 43°43′N 93°27′W. Dairying; mfg. (fabricated metal prods.). **5** village (□ 1 sq mi/2.6 sq km; 1990 pop. 1,598), Ontario co., W central N.Y., on Canandaigua Outlet (the stream draining Canandaigua L.), and 23 mi/37 km SE of Rochester; 42°58′N 77°13′W. Truck freight transfer point; mfg. (packaging, fabricated metal prods., plastic parts and gears); agr. (field and vegetable crops). Inc. 1892. **6** village (1990 pop. 2,223), Adams co., S Ohio, on the Ohio R., and 35 mi/56 km W of Portsmouth; 38°42′N 83°36′W. Mfg. (textiles, machinery). One of Ohio's earliest towns, founded 1791. **7** village (1990 pop. 106), Grant co., N Okla., 40 mi/64 km N of Enid, near Kansas state line; 36°59′N 98°02′W. In agr. area (grain; livestock); mfg. (machinery).

Manchester, borough (1990 pop. 1,830), York co., S Pa., 6 mi/9.7 km N of York; 40°03′N 76°43′W. Agr. (dairying; livestock, poultry; grain, soybeans, apples); mfg. (plastic prods., foods, fabricated metal prods., transportation equip., electronic prods.; machining). Laid out c.1815, inc. c.1869.

Manchioneal, town (1991 pop. 2,185), Portland parish, NE Jamaica, on Jamaica Channel, 14 mi/23 km SE of Port Antonio; 18°03′N 76°17′W. Bananas, coconuts.

Mancos, town (1990 pop. 842), Montezuma co., SW Colo., in La Plata Mts., NE Montezuma co., on Mancos R., near mouth of Chicken Creek, 23 mi/37 km W of Durango; 37°21′N 108°17′W. Elev. 7,030 ft/2,143 m. Cattle, sheep-shipping and outfitting point. Wheat, oats, barley, beans. Mfg. (wood fiber). Coal and silver mines in vicinity. Mesa Verde Natl. Park to SW; Ute Mt. Indian Reservation to SW; Mancos State Park and L. to N; San Juan Natl. Forest to NE.

Mancos River, c.60 mi/97 km long, in Colo. and N.Mex.; formed in La Plata Mts., NE Montezuma co., SW Colo., past E tip of Mesa Verde Natl. Park, by confluence of West Mancos (20 mi/32 km long) and East Mancos (15 mi/24 km long) rivers, 2 mi/3.2 km ENE of Mancos; Middle Mancos R. (c.10 mi/16 km long) joins East Mancos 3 mi/4.8 km ENE of Mancos. All 3 rise in NE Montezuma co. Mancos R. flows intermittently SW and WSW, through part of Ute Mt. Indian Reservation, to San Juan R. just across state line in extreme NW N.Mex., in Navajo Indian Reservation, 20 mi/32 km NW of Shiprock (N.Mex.). Jackson Gulch Reservoir (181 ft/55 m high, 1,900 ft/579 m long; completed 1948), on diversion canal W of West Mancos R.; canal continues into Chicken Creek, branch of West Mancos, 4 mi/6.4 km N of Mancos.

Mandan, city (1990 pop. 15,177), ⊙ Morton co., S N.Dak., on the Missouri R., at the mouth of Heart R., opposite Bismarck; 46°49′N 100°53′W. A RR division point, it is the distributing center for a grain, livestock, and dairy region; mfg. (printing and publishing; bldg. materials, wood prods.). Has a large cattle market and food-processing plants. Industry includes iron, fabricated metal prods., tile. Lewis and Clark wintered here (1804–1805) in the Mandan Native Amer. villages. A state industrial school is in the city, and a U.S. agr. experiment station is nearby. Fort Lincoln State Park to S. In Central time zone; Mountain/Central time zone border (Missouri R.) skirts around Mandan and NE corner of Morton co. Inc. 1883.

Manderson, village (1990 pop. 83), Big Horn co., N Wyo., on Big Horn R., just W of Big Horn Mts., and 8 mi/12.9 km SSE of Basin; 44°16′N 107°57′W. Elev. 3,890 ft/1,186 m. Agr. (sugar beets, beans, alfalfa; cattle, sheep); mfg. (utility poles). Medicine Lodge State Archaeological Site to E, with prehistoric glyphs (petroglypyhs, pictographs).

Mandeville (MAN-di-vil), city (1994 pop. 9,362), St. Tammany parish, SE La., on L. Pontchartrain, 23 mi/37 km N of New Orleans; 30°22′N 90°05′W. Mfg. (wood prods., electronic equip., cultured marble, caskets, meat prods., signs). N end of 30-mi/48-km Pontchartrain Causeway from New Orleans is 1 mi/2 km W. Fontainbleau State Park and St. Tammany State Refuge to SE. Hosts Mandeville Seafood Festival. Founded c.1830, inc. 1840.

Mandeville, town (1991 pop. 39,945), ⊙ Manchester parish, central Jamaica; 18°02′N 77°30′W. Elev. c.2,000 ft/610 m. An inland resort town known for its cool climate and quiet, "Eng.-village" character.

Manele (MAH-NAI-lai), village, Lanai isl., Maui co., Hawaii, on Manele Bay, S coast, 6 mi/9.7 km S of Lanai City (connected by road). Tourism. Hulopoe Beach Park to W.

Manganese (MAIN-guh-neez), village, Crow Wing co., central Minn., 15 mi/24 km NE of Brainerd, and 4 mi/6.4 km NW of Crosby, surrounded by Crow Wing State Forest; 40°31′N 94°00′W. In lake and forest area. Iron mines nearby in Cuyuna Iron Range. Cole L. to W.

Mangham (MANG-guhm), town (1990 pop. 598), Richland parish, NE La., 24 mi/39 km SE of Monroe, on Big Creek; 32°19′N 91°47′W. Cotton; mfg. (apparel).

Manglar Zapoton Ecological Reserve (mahn-glahr zah-po-TON), nature reserve, in S Chiapas, Mexico, 5 mi/8 km W of Huixtla, on the Pacific coast.

Mangles Islands (MAHN-glaiz) [=mangrove], group of keys off SW Cuba in Gulf of Batabanó, 8 mi/12.9 km N of Isla de la Juventud, forming NW isls. of Los Canarreos archipelago; 22°04′N 82°53′W.

Mango, town (□ 4 sq mi/10.4 sq km; 1990 pop. 8,700), Hillsborough co., W central Fla., 8 mi/12.9 km E of Tampa; 27°59′N 82°18′W.

Mangrove Bay, inlet of Somerset Isl., Bermuda.

Mangrove Cay, settlement, W Bahama Isls., on E Andros Isl., 60 mi/97 km SSW of Nassau.

Manguito (mahn-GEE-to), town, Matanzas prov., W Cuba, on RR, and 35 mi/56 km SE of Cárdenas; 22°41′N 80°55′W. In agr. region (sugarcane, fruit; poultry, cattle). Nearby sugar mills include Seis de Agosto (NE), Jesús Rabí (SE), and Reynold García (SW).

Mangum (MANG-guhm), town (1990 pop. 3,344), ⊙ Greer co., SW Okla., near Salt Fork of Red R., and 20 mi/32 km NNW of Altus; 34°52′N 99°30′W. Elev. 1,608 ft/490 m. Trade center for irrigated agr. area (peanuts; sheep); mfg. (bricks). Seat of Mangum Jr. Col. Quartz Mt. State Park and Lodge (recreation) on Altus L. to E; Old Greer Co. Mus. Laid out 1883, inc. 1900.

Manhasset (man-HA-suht), affluent residential village (□ 2 sq mi/5.2 sq km; 1990 pop. 7,718), Nassau co., SE N.Y., on N shore of W L.I., near head of Manhasset Bay, 4 mi/6.4 km NNW of Mineola; 40°47′N 73°41′W. In estates area. Some light mfg. (electrical and electronic goods, consumer goods, textiles). Retailing center for area nicknamed "Miracle Mile."

Manhasset Bay, inlet of L.I. Sound indenting N shore of W L.I., SE N.Y., just E of Great Neck; c.3.5 mi/5.6 km long; 40°50′N 73°44′W. Is 1 mi/1.6 km wide at entrance, which lies bet. Barker Point on Manhasset Neck (E) and Hewlett Point (W). Yachting. On or near its shores are Port Washington, Plandome, Manhasset, Great Neck.

Manhasset Neck, peninsula on N shore of W L.I., SE N.Y., bet. Manhasset Bay (W) and Hempstead Harbor (E); c.5 mi/8 km long, 1.5 mi/2.4 km–3 mi/4.8 km wide; 40°50′N 73°41′W. At its blunt tip are (SW to NE) Barker Point, Sands Point (lighthouse), Prospect Point. Residential area.

Manhattan (man-HAT-uhn), city (1990 pop. 37,712), ⊙ Riley co., NE Kansas, at the confluence of the Big Blue and Kansas rivers; 39°11′N 96°35′W. Trade and processing center of a farm area. RR junction. Mfg. (printing and publishing, food industry and meat processing, research; bldg. materials, apparel). Much of the economy is dependent upon Kansas State Univ. and nearby Fort Riley. Author Damon Runyon b. here. Pottawatonic State Fishing L. No. 2 to NE; Tuttle Creek Dam and Reservoir and State Park to N. Inc. 1857.

Manhattan (man-HAT-tuhn), town (1990 pop. 1,034), Gallatin co., SW Mont., on Gallatin R., and 20 mi/32 km NW of Bozeman; 45°52′N 111°20′W. Mfg. (wood prods.); dairying; cattle, sheep, hogs; wheat, barley, oats, potatoes. Madison Buffalo Jump State Park to SW. Formerly called Moreland and Hamilton.

Manhattan, village (1990 pop. 2,059), Will co., NE Ill., 8 mi/12.9 km SSE of Joliet; 41°25′N 87°59′W. In agr. area.

Manhattan, borough (□ 33 sq mi/85 sq km; 1990 pop. 1,487,536), N.Y. city, SE N.Y., coextensive with N.Y. co.; 40°46′N 73°58′W. Composed chiefly of Manhattan Isl., and is bounded W by the Hudson R., S by N.Y. Bay, E by the East R., NE and N by the Harlem R. and Spuyten Duyvil Creek. Many bridges, tunnels, and ferries link it to the other boroughs and to N.J. A large number of Manhattan's workers commute to the borough every day. Manhattan is the cultural and commercial heart of the city, and its dramatic skyline symbolizes N.Y. city around the world. It began as a Du. colonial town built at the S tip of the isl. called New Amsterdam and served as capital of the colony of New Netherland during the Du. period. In 1664 the English captured New Netherland and renamed it N.Y. The city line 1st extended beyond Manhattan Isl. when some Westchester co. towns were annexed in 1874. In the consolidation of 1898, Manhattan became 1 of the city's 5 boroughs. For its history, cultural, educational, and religious institutions, and other points of interest, see NEW YORK, city.

Manhattan, locality, Nye co., central Nev., 65 mi/105 km S of Austin, in Toquima Range. Former gold-mining town. Great gold producer (1906–1915), still actively mined. Surrounded, except W, by Toiyabe Natl. Forest.

Manhattan Beach, city (1990 pop. 32,063), Los Angeles co., S Calif., suburb, 13 mi/21 km SW of downtown Los Angeles, on Santa Monica Bay, Pacific Ocean; 33°54′N 118°25′W. Residential and beach community with an oil refinery and factories in adjacent communities that produce transportation equip., electrical equip., computers, and pottery. Manhattan State Beach is here. Inc. 1912.

Manhattan Beach, village (1990 pop. 61), Crow Wing co., central Minn., 26 mi/42 km N of Brainerd, at N end of (Lower) Whitefish L.; 46°43′N 94°08′W. Crow Wing State Forest to S.

Manhattan Beach, N.Y.: see CONEY ISLAND.

Manheim (MAN-heim), borough (1990 pop. 5,011), Lancaster co., SE Pa., 10 mi/16 km NW of Lancaster, on Chickies Creek; 40°09′N 76°24′W. Agr. area (dairying; livestock, poultry; grain, potatoes, soybeans, apples); mfg. (foods and beverages, machinery, tool and die, consumer goods, apparel, plastic prods.; commercial printing); stone quarries. Mt. Hope Estate and Winery to N; covered bridges in area. Settled 1716, laid out c.1760 by H. W. Stiegel, who probably produced the 1st flint glass in Amer. here. Inc. 1848.

Maní (mah-NEE), town (1990 pop. 3,418), Yucatán, SE Mexico, 12 mi/19 km E of Ticul; 20°23′N 89°24′W. Henequen, sugarcane, fruit. Maya ruins nearby.

Manicaragua (mah-nee-kahr-RAH-gwuh), town (1994 est. pop. 28,000), Villa Clara prov., central Cuba, on upper Arimao R., and 17 mi/27 km S of Santa Clara; 80°07′N 79°58′W. Tobacco-growing and -processing center. Copper deposits to ESE.

Manicouagan River (man-i-KWAHG-uhn), 310 mi/499 km long, Que., E Canada; rises in E central Que.; flows S to the St. Lawrence R. near Baie Comeau. The river is an important source of hydroelectricity. Also spelled Manikuagan R.

Manikuagan River, Que.: see MANICOUAGAN RIVER.

Manila (muh-NIL-uh), town (1990 pop. 2,635), Mississippi co., NE Ark., 15 mi/24 km WSW of Blytheville, near Right Hand Chute; 35°52′N 90°09′W. Big L. Natl. Wildlife Reservoir to E; Big L. Wildlife Management Area beyond it. Inc. 1901.

Manila, village (1990 pop. 207), ⊙ Daggett co., NE Utah, 35 mi/56 km NNW of Vernal, near Wyo. state line and Uinta Mts.; 40°59′N 109°43′W. Elev. 6,375 ft/1,943 m. Sheep; timber; tourism. Uinta Mts. and Ashley Natl. Forest to S. Flaming Gorge reservoir and Natl. Recreation Area to E. Sheep Rock Canyon to SW. Surveyed in 1898 during capture of Manila (Philippines) by U.S.

Manilla, town (1990 pop. 898), Crawford co., W Iowa, on branch of West Nishnabotna R., and 10 mi/16 km SSE of Denison; 41°53′N 95°14′W. Wood prods.; seeds; fertilizers. Inc, 1887.

Manion Creek, village, N central B.C., W Canada, 150 mi/241 km NW of Prince George, 20 mi/32 km SW of Williston L., on Manson Creek, on dirt logging road from Fort St. James. Lodge; no other services.

Manistee (MAN-is-TEE), county (□ 1,280 sq mi/3,315 sq km; 1990 pop. 21,265), NW Mich.; 44°17′N 86°18′W; ⊙ MANISTEE. Bounded W by L. Michigan; drained by Manistee and Little Manistee rivers and small Bear Creek. Fruit growing (apples, cherries, peaches, berries); also cattle, hogs, poultry; potatoes, forage crops; mfg. (paper prods., chemicals, mineral prods.) at Manistee; salt mines; fisheries; resorts. Includes part of Manistee Natl. Forest to S and SE; Orchard Beach State Park in SW. Portage, Bear, and Manistee lakes are in W. Bear L. in NW; Tippy Dam Pond in SE. Organized 1855.

Manistee (MAN-is-TEE), city (1990 pop. 6,734), ⊙ Manistee co., NW Mich., c.45 mi/72 km SW of Traverse City, port on L. Michigan, at mouth of Manistee R. (here draining Manistee L., just E); 44°14′N 86°19′W. Resort, shipping, and industrial center; salt mining and processing, mfg. (salt, salt prods., bulk bags, chemicals, paper, furniture, wood prods., boats, textiles); fisheries. Agr. prods. (fruit, potatoes; cattle, hogs, poultry). Annual forest festival held here. Co. Mus. Manistee-Blacker Airport NE of town. Orchard Beach State Park to N; Manistee Natl. Forest to E. Inc. as city 1869.

Manistee Lake, Mich.: see MANISTEE RIVER.

Manistee River (MAN-is-TEE), c.170 mi/274 km long, NW Mich.; rises in lakes near border bet. Otsego and Antrim cos.; flows generally SW, past Mesick through Hodenpyl Dam and Tippy Dam ponds, and Manistee Natl. Forest, to L. Michigan at Manistee. Widens into Manistee L. (c.5 mi/8 km long, 1 mi/1.6 km wide) before entering L. Michigan; 44°56′N 84°52′W.

Manistique (MAN-is-TEEK), town (1990 pop. 3,456), ⊙ Schoolcraft co., S Upper Peninsula, N Mich., c.40 mi/64 km ENE of Escanaba, at mouth of Manistique R., on L. Michigan; 45°57′N 86°15′W. Mfg. (wood prods., paper, bldg. materials). Resort, industrial, and shipping center; lumber and paper milling, processing of hardwood prods. Limestone quarrying nearby. Indian L., with Indian L. (E and W units) and Palm Book state parks, is just NW. Senny Natl. Wildlife Refuge to NE; Hiawatha Natl. Forest to W, including Thunder Bowl Ski Area in NW. Inc. as village 1885, as city 1901.

Manistique Lake (MAN-is-TEEK), SE Upper Peninsula, N Mich., on border bet. Luce (N) and Mackinac (S) cos., 13 mi/21 km SW of Newberry; c.7 mi/11.3 km long, 3 mi/4.8 km wide. Drained by Manistique R.; joined by streams to South Manistique L. (c.4.5 mi/7.2 km long, 2 mi/3.2 km wide), just S, and to North Manistique L. (c.2 mi/3.2 km long, 1.5 mi/2.4 km wide), just NE. Village of Curtis at SE end, Helmer on NE end; 46°14′N 85°47′W.

Manistique River (MAN-is-TEEK), c.35 mi/56 km long, S Upper Peninsula, N Mich.; rises in Manistique L.; flows SW to L. Michigan just below Manistique; 46°14′N 85°51′W. Receives many small tributaries from N and NW.

Manito (MAN-i-to), village (1990 pop. 1,711), Mason co., central Ill., 20 mi/32 km SSW of Peoria, near Sand Ridge State Forest; 40°25′N 89°46′W. Corn, wheat, watermelons, vegetables.

Manito Lake (MA-ni-too) (□ 67 sq mi/174 sq km), W Sask., W Canada, near Alta. border, 55 mi/89 km W of North Battleford; 12 mi/19 km long, 7 mi/11 km wide.

Manitoba (man-i-TO-buh), province (□ 250,934 sq mi/650,930 sq km, including 39,215 sq mi/101,580 sq km of water surface; 1991 pop. 1,091,942), W central Canada; ⊙ WINNIPEG, largest city, accounting for more than ½ of the prov.'s pop. in its metropolitan area; 55°00′N 97°00′W. Other important cities are BRANDON, THOMPSON, PORTAGE LA PRAIRIE, and SELKIRK. Easternmost of the Prairie Provs., Man. is bounded N by Keewatin region of the N.W.T. (with a NE shoreline on Hudson Bay), E by Ont., S by U.S. (Minn. and N.Dak.), and W by Sask. Because of its central location it is a major natl. transportation center. The S and central part of Man. was once covered by L. Agassiz (see AGASSIZ, LAKE). As its waters receded into Hudson Bay, it left behind numerous lakes (Winnipeg, Manitoba, and Winnipegosis) and rivers (Nelson, Churchill, and Hayes), which flow NE into the bay. In some places rock formations were swept bare, and in others they were covered with rich deposits of black loam. Miles of almost uninhabited treeless tundra surround the port of Churchill. Extending S from Churchill and E from L. Winnipeg, the topography is that of the Can. Shield; limited areas have been cleared for general farming and dairying, and the mineral and timber resources have been partly developed. The S part of Man. is dominated by lakes, with the Winnipeg paralleled in the W by Winnipegosis and Manitoba. To the W and N of the Red R. valley, the land rises in an escarpment extending into the plateaus of the Pembina, Turtle, Riding, Duck, and Porcupine mts. Much of this heavily forested area has been set off as reserves, and the Riding Mt. area is a natl. park. To the S, where most of the pop. is concentrated, are fields of wheat, barley, oats, rye, and flax. The well-settled Souris plains in the SW are esp. famous for their wheat fields. Canada's wheat industry originated here, and Man.'s bread wheat has set the standards for the world. Grain is shipped in quantity from Churchill (the only port in the Prairie Provs.) during the 3 ice-free months of the year. Although agr. has been continually extended—esp. in mixed farming, dairying, and poultry and livestock raising—mfg. has nevertheless displaced it as the leading industry in the prov. Foods, minerals, clothing, electrical items, chemicals, furniture, leather, fabricated metals, and transportation equip. are major prods. Continuing developments in mining, pulp and paper mfg., and extensive hydroelectric production promise to preserve Man.'s industrial growth. In the SW, near Brandon, are large oil reserves, and the municipal dists. of Flin Flon and The Pas, on the Saskatchewan R., are gateways to the rich mineral deposits (chiefly nickel, copper, and zinc) and timberlands of the central W. Man. ranks 2d only to Ont. in the production of nickel; the mines at Thompson provide most of Man.'s nickel. Beluga whales are still caught by native fishermen at Churchill, and fur farming in the N places Man. 3d of all the provs. in the production of fur. The modern history of Man. began along Hudson Bay. The search for the elusive NW Passage to the Pacific Ocean drew such explorers as Henry Hudson, Thomas Button, Pierre Radisson, and Médard Chouart des Groseilliers, some of whom returned to England laden with beaver furs. To exploit this fur wealth, King Charles II granted (1670) the Hudson's Bay Company propriety over all the lands draining into Hudson Bay. This vast area included the present-day prov. of Man., then occupied by the Assiniboin, the Ojibwa, and the Cree peoples. The company established a trading post at Port Nelson and soon extended its operations S to the strategic Red R. valley. In 1717, Fort Prince of Wales was built at the mouth of the Churchill R. (rebuilt in stone 1732–1771, it is now in Fort Prince of Wales Natl. Historic Park). Man. was explored and posts were established by the French as well as by the British; their rival claims were resolved when England's conquest of Canada in the Fr. and Indian Wars was confirmed by the Treaty of Paris in 1763. Scotsmen took over much of the Fr. fur trade, organized the North West Company, and challenged the monopoly of the Hudson's Bay Company. A crisis came when the earl of Selkirk established the Red R. Settlement at present-day Assiniboine in North West Company territory. The resulting violence deterred colonization until the merger of the 2 companies in 1821. From then until 1870, when the Hudson's Bay Company sold its vast domain to the newly created confederation of Canada, that company was in sole control, and settlement of the area increased. Prearrangements for the transfer of the land to the new dominion govt. led to conflict bet. govt. representatives and Métis (people of mixed Eur. and Native Amer. ancestry), who had long enjoyed almost total autonomy under the Hudson's Bay Company's rule. Fearing political persecution and the loss of their land, they staged (1869) the Red R. Rebellion under the leadership of Louis Riel. The rebellion was nominally successful and the Métis were granted land and cultural rights, but after Man. was organized as a prov. in 1870, most of the Métis were harassed into moving further W. Agr. settlement in Man. proceeded slowly, but when the RRs came (1870 and 1881), they provided access to and from the grain markets on the Great Lakes, and, during the 1880s, the pop. doubled. Man.'s area was enlarged in 1881, and in 1912 it was given its present extension to Hudson Bay. The depression of 1913 and the opening of the Panama Canal in 1914 ended this period of prosperity, during which Winnipeg had served as a great transportation center. With the completion of the Hudson Bay RR to Churchill in 1929, the prov. was in a position to use the shorter sea route E. During the last part of the 19th cent. and the 1st part of the 20th, the Can. govt. advertised for immigrants to settle the prairies, and huge numbers of Russians, Poles, Estonians, Scandinavians, and Hungarians came from Europe. Man. remains Canada's most ethnically diverse prov. The largest single immigrant group was the Ukrainians, who now constitute more than 11% of the pop. and are an important part of Man. culture. A natl. Ukr. festival is held each year, and there is a Ukr. culture mus. in Winnipeg. The prov. provided a multilingual school system from 1897 to 1916, but abolished it when the number of ethnic groups requesting such facilities grew too large. Further immigration came with World War I when Amer. pacifist sects (e.g., the Mennonites and Hutterites), seeking to avoid military service, set up colonies of their own here. Man. still has problems amalgamating its many ethnic groups; they include the Métis, who have settlements (such as St. Boniface) in the prov. Man. sends 6 senators (appointed) and 14 representatives (elected) to the natl. Parliament. The Univ. of Man. and the Univ. of Winnipeg are at Winnipeg.

Manitoba, Lake (□ 1,817 sq mi/4,706 sq km), SW Man., central Canada; one of the largest lakes of N. Amer. A remnant of glacial L. Agassiz, it is fed by L. Winnipegosis and drains into L. Winnipeg. Its shores are marshy. Commercial fisheries.

Manitou (MA-ni-too), village (1991 pop. 811), S Man., central Canada, in Pembina Mts., 50 mi/80 km S of Portage la Prairie; 49°14′N 98°32′W. Elev. 1,590 ft/485 m. Grain elevators; dairying, mixed farming.

Manitou (MAN-uh-too), village (1990 pop. 244), Tillman co., SW Okla., 9 mi/14.5 km NNE of Frederick; 34°30′N 98°58′W. In cotton and grain area. L. Frederick reservoir to E.

Manitou Beach, village (1991 pop. 138), S Sask., W Canada, on Little Manitou L., 4 mi/6 km N of Watrous. Resort.

Manitou Beach (MAN-i-too), town, Lenawee co., SE Mich., on Devils L., and 15 mi/24 km WNW of Adrian; 41°58′N 85°18′W.

Manitou Falls, Big, Wis.: see BLACK RIVER.

Manitou Island (MAN-i-too), Keweenaw co., off Upper Peninsula, N Mich., in L. Superior, 3 mi/4.8 km E of Keweenaw Point; c.3 mi/4.8 km long, 1 mi/1.6 km wide; 47°25′N 87°37′W. Manitou Isls. are in L. Michigan.

Manitou Islands (MAN-i-too), NW Mich., two islands in L. Michigan, c.14 mi/23 km W of Leelanau Peninsula; southernmost isls. of BEAVER ISLANDS archipelago. North Manitou Isl. is 8 mi/12.9 km long, 4 mi/6.4 km wide; South Manitou Isl. is c.4 mi/6.4 km long, 3 mi/4.8 km wide. Passenger ferry from Leland connects both isls. to each other and to mainland. Resorts; sand dunes, small lakes. Part of Sleeping Bear Dunes Natl. Lakeshore. MANITOU ISLAND is NW, in L. Superior.

Manitou Lake (□ 60 sq mi/155 sq km), W Ont., central Canada, 50 mi/80 km E of Whitefish Bay (L. of the Woods); 27 mi/43 km long, 5 mi/8 km wide. Divided into Upper Manitou and Lower Manitou lakes by narrow strait. Drains S into Rainy L.

Manitou, Lake, Ind.: see ROCHESTER.

Manitou Springs, town (1990 pop. 4,535), El Paso co., central Colo., on Fountain Creek, at foot of Pikes Peak, and 5 mi/8 km W of Colorado Springs; 38°51′N 104°54′W. Elev. 6,412 ft/1,954 m. Tourist and health resort with mineral springs and sanitarium. Light mfg. Cliff Dwellings Mus. and Historic Miramont Castle are here. Road and cog RR to summit of Pikes Peak (W). Nearby are Pike Natl. Forest (N, W, and S), Cave of the Winds (N), and Garden of the Gods (N). Founded 1872, inc. 1888.

Manitoulin (ma-ni-TOO-lin), district (□ 1,588 sq mi/4,113 sq km; 1991 pop. 11,192), S central Ont., central Canada; ⊙ Gore Bay; 45°45′N 82°30′W. Comprises Manitoulin Isl., in L. Huron, and surrounding isls.

Manitoulin Islands (man-uh-TOO-lin), archipelago consisting of 3 large isls. and several smaller ones, in N L. Huron, NW of Georgian Bay, Ont., central Canada. The isls., in a noted fishing region, are popular resorts. The permanent pop. is mainly Native Amer. Dairying, lumbering, mixed farming, and tourism are the major activities. Manitoulin, c.80 mi/130 km long and from 2 mi/3 km–30 mi/48 km wide, is the world's largest lake isl. It encloses over 100 lakes and has a much-indented, rugged coast. Cockburn and Drummond isls. are also rocky and forested. Drummond Isl. belongs to Mich., and the others of the group to Ont.

Manitouwadge, township (1986 pop. 3,522), NW Ontario, central Canada, 247 mi/397 km NE of Thunder Bay; 49°08′N 85°48′W. Mining copper, lead, silver, and zinc. Ont. govt.-designed model town.

Manitowaning, village, S central Ont., central Canada, on NE Manitoulin Isl., on Manitowaning Bay, 18 mi/29 km SSE of Little Current; 45°44′N 81°48′W. Lumbering, dairying, mixed farming.

Manitowash Waters, village, Vilas Co., N Wis., 27 mi/43 km SE of Ironwood (Mich.), in Northern Highland State Forest. Numerous lakes in area. Turtle Flambeau Flowage reservoir to W. Mfg. (archery and craft feathers).

Manitowik Lake (ma-ni-TOU-ik), central Ont., central Canada, 100 mi/161 km N of Sault Ste. Marie; 12 mi/19 km long, 2 mi/3 km wide; 48°10′N 84°24′W. Drained S into L. Superior by Michipicoten R.

Manitowish River, c.45 mi/72 km long, N Wis.; rises in lake region in Vilas co.; flows W and SW through wooded lake area to Flambeau R., immediately E (upstream) of Turtle-Flambeau Reservoir. Fishing, white-water canoeing.

Manitowoc, county (□ 1,493 sq mi/3,867 sq km; 1990 pop. 80,421) E Wis.; ⊙ Manitowoc; 44°08′N 87°32′W. Agr. (barley, oats, wheat, corn, soybeans, peas, brans, alfalfa, hay; poultry, cattle; dairying); marble and stone. Mfg. at Manitowoc, Two Rivers, and Kiel. Bounded E by L. Michigan; drained by Manitowoc R. Point Beach State Forest in NE, in L. Michigan; Hidden Valley Ski Area in N. Nuclear power plants, Point Beach 1 (initial criticality November 2, 1970) and Point Beach 2 (initial criticality May 30, 1972), are 13 mi/21 km NNW of Manitowoc; use cooling water from L. Michigan, and each has a max. dependable capacity of 485 MWe. Formed 1836.

Manitowoc, city (1990 pop. 32,520), ⊙ Manitowoc co., E Wis., 75 mi/121 km NNE of Milwaukee, a port of entry on L. Michigan at the mouth of the Manitowoc R.; 44°06′N 87°40′W. Mfg. (electric equip., malt, foods, toys, printing, fabricated metal prods., consumer goods, textiles, transportation equip., furniture, plastics prods., lubrication equip., machinery, bakery prods., yachts, bldg. materials). RR junction and a ship and RR transfer point. Its shipbuilding industry dates from 1847; submarines were made here in World War II. The North West Company established a trading post on the site in 1795. Manitowoc and its twin city, Two Rivers (6 mi/9.7 km NE), were founded in 1836. Silver L. Col., Univ. of Wis.-Manitowoc campus, and a maritime mus. and submarine memorial are located here. Point Beach State Forest to NE; L. Michigan car ferry to Ludington (Mich.) carries U.S. Highway 10 (last of 8 ferry crossings of L. Mich.). Inc. 1870.

Manitowoc River, c.40 mi/64 km long, E Wis.; formed by several branches rising in W Calumet co. near L. Winnebago; flows generally E to L. Michigan at Manitowoc.

Maniwaki (ma-ni-WO-kee), town (1991 pop. 4,605), ⊙ Gatineau co., SW Que., E Canada, on Gatineau R., at mouth of Desert R., and 70 mi/113 km NNW of Ottawa; 46°22′N 75°58′W. Lumbering, pulp milling, dairying.

Mankato (man-KAY-do), city (1990 pop. 31,477), ⊙ Blue Earth co., extends NW into Nicollet co., S Minn., 63 mi/101 km SSE of Minneapolis, on Minnesota R., E of mouth of Blue Earth R; 44°10′N 93°59′W. Elev. 793 ft/242 m. Trade and processing center for a farm region (grain, alfalfa; livestock; dairying [esp. to N and E]). Mfg. (soybean processing, dairy prods., oilseed processing, printing and publishing, flour, feeds, bldg. materials, computer equip., machinery, paper prods., fabricated metal prods., consumer goods, lumber, electronic equip., plastic prods.). Mankato stone has been quarried here for more than 100 years. Mankato Municipal Airport. Seat of Mankato State Univ. and Bethany Col. Sibley Park in Mankato was the site of Camp Lincoln, where more than 300 Sioux were held and 38 of them hanged, after their revolt in 1862. Minneopa State Park, with waterfalls to W; Mt. Kato Ski Area to S; numerous small natural lakes to NE. Inc. 1865.

Mankato (man-KAI-to), town (1990 pop. 1,037), ⊙ Jewell co., N Kansas, 33 mi/53 km NW of Concordia; 39°47′N 98°12′W. RR junction. Trading center for grain and livestock area. Lovewell Reservoir and State Park to NE; Jewall State Fishing L. to SW. Founded 1872, inc. 1880.

Mankota (man-KO-tuh), village (1991 pop. 381), SW Sask., W Canada, 50 mi/80 km WSW of Assiniboia; 49°25′N 107°04′W. Wheat. In coal-mining region.

Manlio Fabio Altamirano (mahn-lee-o FAH-dee-o ahl-tah-mee-RAh-no), town (1990 pop. 4,236), ⊙ Manlio Rabio Altamirando municipio, Veracruz, E Mexico, 14 mi/23 km SW of Veracruz; 19°06′N 96°20′W. Corn, fruit. Sometimes called, after its RR station, Purga or La Purga.

Manlius 1 village (1990 pop. 365), Bureau co., N Ill., 12 mi/19 km WNW of Princeton; 41°27′N 89°40′W. In agr. area. **2** residential commuter village (☐ 1 sq mi/2.6 sq km; 1990 pop. 4,764), Onondaga co., central N.Y., 9 mi/14.5 km ESE of Syracuse; 43°00′N 75°58′W. Mfg. (electronic equip., fabricated metal prods., machinery, plastic prods.). Settled 1789 inc. 1842.

Manly, town (1990 pop. 1,349), Worth co., N Iowa, 11 mi/18 km N of Northwood; 43°17′N 93°12′W. Soybean prods. Inc. 1898.

Manly, uninc. village, Moore co., central N.C., 1 mi/1.6 km NE of Southern Pines. Fort Bragg Military Reserve to SE.

Mannford, town (1990 pop. 1,826), Creek co., central Okla., 22 mi/35 km W of Tulsa, near Cimarron R.; 36°07′N 96°19′W. In agr., oil-producing area; mfg. (fabricated metal prods.). Keystone L. reservoir and Keystone State Park to NE.

Manning, town (1991 pop. 1,139), NW Alta., W Canada, 48 mi/77 km NNW of Peace River, on Mackenzie Highway, and RR line to Hay River (N.W.T.), on S bank of Notikewin R. Est. 1947 as service center for transportation, mining, and agr. region. Outfitting for sports fishing, hunting.

Manning 1 town (1990 pop. 1,484), Carroll co., W central Iowa, on West Nishnabotna R. (hydroelectric plant), and 15 mi/24 km SSW of Carroll; 41°54′N 95°03′W. Mfg. (feed, fertilizer). Inc. 1880. **2** town (1990 pop. 4,428), ⊙ Clarendon co., E central S.C., 17 mi/27 km SSE of Sumter, near Pocotaligo R.; 33°41′N 80°13′W. Mfg. includes clothing, wood prods., lumber, fabricated metal prods., textiles, bldg. materials. Agr. includes dairying; tobacco, cotton, sweet potatoes, soybeans, grain.

Manning, village (1990 pop. 49), ⊙ Dunn co., W central N.Dak., 25 mi/40 km N of Dickinson, and on Knife R; 47°13′N 102°46′W. L. Ilo Natl. Wildlife Refuge to NNE.

Mannington, town (1990 pop. 2,184), Marion co., N W.Va., 12 mi/19 km WNW of Fairmont; 39°31′N 80°20′W. RR terminus and processing center in oil, natural-gas, and bituminous-coal region. Mfg. (machining; lumber). Agr. (corn, apples); livestock, poultry. Inc. 1871.

Mannington, village (1990 pop. 225), Christian co., SW Ky., 18 mi/29 km N of Hopkinsville. Bituminous coal; agr. (tobacco, soybeans, grain; livestock; dairying).

Manns Choice, borough (1990 pop. 249), Bedford co., S Pa., 5 mi/8 km WSW of Bedford, on Raystown Branch of Juniata R.; 40°00′N 78°35′W. Agr. (corn, oats, hay; livestock; dairying); mfg. (lumber). Shawnee L. reservoir and Shawnee State Park to NW.

Manns Harbor, village, Dare co., NE N.C., on Croatan Sound (bridged) opposite Roanoke Isl. Fishing.

Mannsville 1 village (1990 pop. 444), Jefferson co., N N.Y., 20 mi/32 km SSW of Watertown; 43°43′N 76°04′W. **2** village (1990 pop. 396), Johnston co., S Okla., 15 mi/24 km E of Ardmore, near Washita R.; 34°11′N 96°52′W. In farm area.

Mannville, village (1991 pop. 774), E Alta., W Canada, near Vermilion R., 14 mi/23 km W of Vermilion; 53°20′N 111°10′W. Dairying; grain growing.

Manoa, Pa.: see HAVERFORD.

Manoir Lake, N.W.T.: see MAUNOIR, LAC.

Manokin River (mah-NOK-in), c.25 mi/40 km long, SE Md.; rises in NE Somerset co.; flows SW, past Princess Anne (head of navigation), to Tangier Sound just S of Deal Isl. Its mouth is 5 mi/8 km wide.

Manokotak, village (1990 pop. 385), SW Alaska, on small Igushik R., and 22 mi/35 kmWSW of Dillingham; 58°59′N 159°03′W.

Manomet, Mass.: see PLYMOUTH.

Manor (MA-nor), village (1990 pop. 326), SE Sask., W Canada, at foot of Moose Mt., 40 mi/64 km SSW of Moosomin; 49°36′N 102°05′W. Mixed farming.

Manor 1 (MA-nor), town (1990 pop. 300), Ware co., Ga., 15 mi/24 km SW of Waycross. Mfg. of wood prods. **2** (MAI nor), town (1990 pop. 1,041), Travis co., S central Texas, 12 mi/19 km ENE of Austin; 30°21′N 97°33′W. In cotton, grain area. Mfg. (electronic prods., computer equip.).

Manor (MA-nor), borough (1990 pop. 2,627), Westmoreland co., SW Pa., suburb, 18 mi/29 km SE of Pittsburgh, and 2 mi/3.2 km W of Jeannette, on Brush Creek; 40°21′N 79°40′W. Mfg. (wood prods., fabricated metal prods.). Laid out 1873, inc. 1890.

Manor Ridge, uninc. town (1990 pop. c.1,000), Lancaster co., SE Pa., residential suburb, 4 mi/6.4 km W of Lancaster; 40°02′N 76°21′W. Garden Spot Airport to W.

Manorhaven, village (1990 pop. 5,672), Nassau co., SE N.Y., on N shore of W L.I., just NE of Port Washington; 40°50′N 73°42′W. In water recreation-oriented area. Inc. 1930.

Manorville, borough (1990 pop. 418), Armstrong co., W central Pa., 2 mi/3.2 km S of Kittanning, and 1 mi/1.6 km NNE of Ford City, on Allegheny R.; 40°47′N 79°31′W. Agr. (corn, hay; dairying).

Manotick, village, SE Ont., central Canada, on Rideau R. and Rideau Canal, and 14 mi/23 km S of Ottawa; 45°15′N 75°37′W. Commuter suburb, on S edge of city of Nepean. Dairying; mixed farming.

Mansel Island (☐ 1,317 sq mi/3,411 sq km), E Keewatin dist., N.W.T., N Canada, in Hudson Bay, off N Ungava Peninsula; 62 mi/100 km long, 4 mi/6 km–30 mi/48 km wide. Created reindeer reserve in 1920. On N coast is trading post (62°25′N 79°36′W).

Mansfield 1 (MANS-feeld), city (1994 pop. 5,040), ⊙ De Soto parish, NW La., 33 mi/53 km S of Shreveport; 32°02′N 93°42′W. Trading and shipping center for fertile agr. area; oil and natural-gas wells; timber. Lumber milling; mfg. (fabricated metal prods., transportation equip.). Clear and Smithport lakes to NE. Mansfield State Commemorative Area, to SE, marks the site of the Civil War battle of Sabine Crossroads (April 8, 1864), a Confederate victory. Inc. 1847. **2** industrial city (1990 pop. 50,627), ⊙ Richland co., N central Ohio; 40°46′N 82°31′W. In a hilly region surrounded by fertile farmlands. Mfg., commercial, and insurance center. Major mfg. (steel, automotive body assembly). Among its many other diverse prods. are tires, electrical appliances, sports vehicles, and brass goods. A branch of Ohio State Univ. is here. The home of Louis Bromfield is used as an ecological center and experimental farm. Also of interest are South Park, with a reconstructed blockhouse of the War of 1812, and Kingwood Center and Gardens, with landscaped floral displays and a pre-Civil War Fr.-provincial mansion. Inc. 1828. **3** city (1990 pop. 15,607), Tarrant and Johnson cos., N Texas, suburb 16 mi/26 km SE of Fort Worth; 32°34′N 97°07′W. In agr. area to S (cotton, corn; dairying), agr. is being edged out by rapid urban growth. Mfg. (machinery, bldg. materials, transportation equip., electronic equip., modular bldgs., chemicals). L. Joe Pool reservoir and Cedar Hill State Park to W.

Mansfield 1 town (1990 pop. 1,018), on border bet. Sebastian and Scott cos., W Ark., 24 mi/39 km SSE of Fort Smith; 35°03′N 94°15′W. In farm area; lumber. Ouachita Natl. Forest to S. **2** town (1990 pop. 21,103), Tolland co., NE Conn.; 41°47′N 72°13′W. Agr. and mfg. town, The Univ. of Conn. is in Storrs, which is included within Mansfield. The town also includes Mansfield Hollow, the site of a large flood-control project. Mansfield Training School for Mentally Retarded, which was the oldest such institution in the state, closed in 1993. Settled c.1692, inc. 1702. **3** town (1990 pop. 16,568), including Mansfield village, Bristol co., SW Mass., 15 mi/24 km NE of Providence (R.I.); 42°01′N 71°13′W. Machine parts, metal prods., chocolate, medical and scientific instruments and equip., chemicals and inks. Settled 1659, set off from Norton 1770. Great Woods Outdoor Performing Arts Center is here.

Mansfield 1 village (1990 pop. 341), Newton co., N central Ga., 9 mi/14.5 km SE of Covington; 33°31′N 83°44′W. Mfg. (textiles, machinery). **2** village (1990 pop. 929), Piatt co., central Ill., 14 mi/23 km NNE of Monticello; 40°12′N 88°30′W. In grain-growing area. **3** village, Parke co., W Ind., 9 mi/14.5 km SE of Rockville, and on Big Raccoon Creek. Agr. area (corn, soybeans; hogs, cattle). Covered bridges in area. Seasonal tourist site, esp. in autumn. **4** village (1990 pop. 311), Douglas co., central Wash., 15 mi/24 km NE of Wenatchee; 47°49′N 119°38′W. RR terminus. In Columbia basin agr. region (wheat, barley, alfalfa; cattle, sheep).

Mansfield, borough (1990 pop. 3,538), Tioga co., N Pa., 24 mi/39 km SW of Elmira, N.Y., on Tioga R.; 41°48′N 77°04′W. Agr. area (grain, soybeans; livestock; dairying); mfg. (wood prods.); natural gas. Seat of Mansfield Univ. of Pa. Hills Creek State Park to W; Hammond and Tioga reservoirs (joined by channel, to NW). Laid out 1824, inc. 1857.

Mansfield, township (1990 pop. 7,154), Warren co., NW N.J., 3 mi/4.8 km SW of Hackettstown; 40°48′N 74°54′W. Inc. 1798.

Mansfield Dam, Texas: see TRAVIS, LAKE.

Mansfield Hollow Dam, Conn.: see NATCHAUG RIVER.

Mansfield Hollow Lake, reservoir (☐ 1 sq mi/2.6 sq km), Tolland and Windham cos., N central Conn., on Nachaug R., 3 mi/5 km NNE of Willimantic; 41°46′N 72°11′W. Max. capacity 79,000 acre-ft. Formed by Mansfield Hollow Dam (78 ft/24 m high), built

(1952) by Army Corps of Engineers for flood control. Mansfield Hollow State Park at N end of reservoir.

Mansfield, Mount, peak (4,393 ft/1,339 m), N central Vt., highest peak in the Green Mts. and in Vt. Most of the mt. is in Mt. Mansfield State Forest. At the foot of the mt. is a deep gorge called Smugglers Notch. With major ski area, Mt. Mansfield is a winter-sports center offering some of the finest skiing in New England.

Manson, town (1990 pop. 1,844), Calhoun co., central Iowa, 10 mi/16 km NE of Rockwell City; 42°31'N 94°32'W. Twin Lakes State Park nearby. Founded 1872, inc. 1877.

Mansonville, village, S Que., E Canada, on Missisquoi R., near U.S. (Vt.) border, 35 mi/56 km SW of Sherbrooke. Dairying.

Mansura (man-SOO-ruh), town (1990 pop. 1,601), Avoyelles parish, E central La., 29 mi/47 km SE of Alexandria; 31°04'N 92°03'W. In sugarcane and cotton area; timber; mfg. (custom millwork, valves). Spring Bayou State Wildlife Area to NE, Grand Cote Natl. Wildlife Refuge to NW.

Mantachie (man-TACH-ee), village (1990 pop. 651), Itawamba co., NE Miss., 5 mi/8 km NW of Fulton; 34°19'N 88°29'W. Agr. (cotton, corn, soybeans; cattle, poultry); mfg. (furniture).

Mantador (MANT-uh-dor), village (1990 pop. 77), Richland co., extreme SE N.Dak.,19 mi/31 km WSW of Wahpeton, and on Wild Rice R.; 46°10'N 96°58'W.

Mante, Ciudad, Mexico: see CIUDAD MANTE.

Manteca, city (1990 pop. 40,773), San Joaquin co., central Calif., 10 mi/16 km SSE of Stockton; 37°48'N 121°13'W. RR junction. Diverse agr. (grapes, sugar beets, fruit, nuts, beans, vegetables, pumpkins; nursery prods.); mfg. (frozen fruits and vegetables, cut stone, electrical machinery; sugar processing. Casweel Memorial State Park to S; Sharpe General depot to NW. Founded 1870, inc. 1918.

Mantee (man-TEE), village (1990 pop. 134), Webster co., central Miss., 22 mi/35 km NW of Starkville; 33°43'N 89°03'W. Agr. and timber; mfg. (wood prods.). Natchez Trace (Natl.) Parkway passes to E.

Manteno (man-TEE-no), village (1990 pop. 3,488), Kankakee co., NE Ill., 9 mi/14.5 km N of Kankakee; 41°15'N 87°50'W. In agr. area. Inc. 1878.

Manteo (man-TEE-o), town (1990 pop. 991), ⊙ Dare co., NE N.C., near N end of Roanoke Isl., 40 mi/64 km SE of Elizabeth City, on Roanoke Sound; 35°53'N 75°40'W. Fort Raleigh Natl. Historic Site to NW. Atlantic Ocean 5 mi/8 km to E. Bridges to mainland (across Crouton Sound to W, and to Outer Banks, to E Roanoke Sound). Mfg. (wood prods.; printing and publishing). N.C. State Aquarium is here. Elizabeth II State Historical Site, replica of original masted ship which brought Eng. colonists to Amer., moored here.

Manter (MAN-tuhr), village (1990 pop. 186), Stanton co., SW Kansas, 7 mi/11.3 km SW of Johnson, near Colo. state line; 37°31'N 101°52'W. Grain.

Manti (MAN-tei), town (1990 pop. 2,268), ⊙ Sanpete co., central Utah, near San Pitch R., in irrigated Sanpete Valley, 70 mi/113 km S of Provo; 39°16'N 111°38'W. Elev. c.5,530 ft/1,686 m. Processing point in cattle, sheep, hogs, poultry, and dairying area; mfg. (apparel). Oolite quarries nearby. Mormon temple (built 1877–1888) here. Founded by Mormons 1849. Wasatch Plateau is just E, in Manti Natl. Forest. Gunnison Reservoir to SW. Palisade State Park to S. Settled 1849, inc. 1851.

Mantoloking (man-tuh-LO-king), resort borough (1990 pop. 334), Ocean co., E N.J., on peninsula bet. Barnegat Bay (bridged here) and the Atlantic Ocean, 10 mi/16 km NE of Toms R.; 40°02'N 74°02'W.

Manton, town (1990 pop. 1,161), Wexford co., NW Mich., 11 mi/18 km N of Cadillac; 44°24'N 85°24'W. Livestock; fruit, potatoes, beans. Mfg. (machinery, bldg. materials, lumber prods.). Settled 1871 as lumber town; inc. as village 1877, as city 1924.

Mantorville, town (1990 pop. 874), ⊙ Dodge co., SE Minn., 15 mi/24 km WNW of Rochester, and 2 mi/3.2 km N of Kasson, on South Branch Middle Zumbro R.; 44°04'N 92°45'W. Elev. 836 ft/255 m. Grain, soybeans, peas; livestock; poultry; dairying.

Mantua (mahn-TOO-uh), town, Pinar del Río prov., W Cuba, on small Mantua R., and 40 mi/64 km WSW of Pinar del Río; 22°18'N 84°18'W. Tobacco, fruit; cattle; lumbering.

Mantua, uninc. town, Fairfax co., N Va., residential suburb 12 mi/19 km WSW of Washington, D.C., 3 mi/4.8 km E of Fairfax; 38°51'N 77°15'W. Northern Va. Community Col. (Annandale Campus) to SE.

Mantua 1 (MAN-choo-ah), village (1990 pop. 10,074), Gloucester co., SW N.J., on Mantua Creek, and 10 mi/16 km S of Camden, in suburbanizing area; 39°45'N 75°10'W. **2** (MAN-tuh-wai), village (1990 pop. 1,178), Portage co., NE Ohio, 20 mi/32 km NE of Akron, and on Cuyahoga R.; 41°17'N 81°13'W. In dairy, poultry, and vegetable area **3** (MAN-oo-ai), village (1990 pop. 665), Box Elder co., N Utah, 5 mi/8 km NE of Brigham City, on Mantua Reservoir; 41°30'N 111°55'W. Agr. Elev. 5,175 ft/1,577 m. In Wasatch Range and Natl. Forest.

Mantua Creek (MAN-chuh), c.16 mi/26 km long, Gloucester co., SW N.J., rises N of Glassboro; flows generally NW, past Wenonah and Paulsboro, to Delaware R. opposite S Philadelphia. Navigable for c.9 mi/14.5 km above mouth.

Mantua River (mahn-TOO-uh), 41 mi/66 km long, Pinar del Río prov., W Cuba; rises in the Sierra de los Organos; flows SW, past Mantua, to the Ensenada de Guadiana, Gulf of Mexico.

Manuel Benavides (mahn-WEL bai-nah-VEE-des), town (1990 pop. 1,051), Chihuahua, N Mexico, near Rio Grande, 43 mi/69 km ESE of Ojenaga; 29°06'N 103°54'W. On unpaved road. Lead mining; cattle raising. Also San Carlos.

Manuel Doblado, Mexico: see CIUDAD MANUEL DOBLADO.

Manuel M. Diéguez, town (1990 pop. 662), Jalisco, central Mexico, on central plateau, 55 mi/89 km SE of Sayula; 19°34'N 102°55'W. Grain, beans, fruit; livestock. Also Santa María del Oro.

Manvel, town (1990 pop. 3,733), Brazoria co., SE Texas, suburb 18 mi/29 km S of downtown Houston, on Mustang Bayou; 29°28'N 95°21'W. Urban growth area in agr. region. Oil and natural gas. Mfg. (plastic prods., electronic equip.).

Manvel (MAN-vuhl), village (1990 pop. 333), Grand Forks co., E N.Dak., 13 mi/21 km NNW of Grand Forks, and on Turtle R.; 48°04'N 97°10'W.

Manville 1 village in Lincoln town, Providence co., NE R.I., on Blackstone R., and 11 mi/18 km N of Providence. **2** village (1990 pop. 97), Niobrara co., E Wyo., 10 mi/16 km W of Lusk; 42°46'N 104°37'W. Elev. c.5,245 ft/1,599 m. Trading point in ranching and wheat region.

Manville, borough (1990 pop. 10,567), Somerset co., central N.J.; 40°32'N 74°35'W. Laid out 1906, inc. 1929.

Many (ME-nee), town (1990 pop. 3,112), ⊙ Sabine parish, W La., c.70 mi/113 km S of Shreveport; 31°34'N 93°28'W. Commercial center for lumber, oil and natural gas, and agr. area (cattle, poultry, exotic fowl; dairying); timber. Mfg. (transportation equip., poultry feed, consumer goods; publishing and printing). Settled in early 19th cent. Recreation. Fort Jesup and Los Adaes state commemorative areas to NE. Rebel State Commemorative Areas to N. Sabine State Wildlife Area to W.

Many Farms, uninc. town (1990 pop. 1,294), Apache co., NE Ariz., 107 mi/172 km NNE of Holbrook, near Chinle Creek. Cattle, sheep; hay. Crafts.

Manzanar, historic site, Inyo co., E Calif., W of Owens R., in Owens Valley, bet. Lone Pine and Independence. Site during World War II of a relocation camp for interned Pacific Coast residents of Jap. descent.

Manzanilla (MAHN-zah-nil-ah), village, E Trinidad, Trinidad and Tobago, 33 mi/53 km ESE of Port of Spain, near Manzanilla Bay; 10°37'N 61°08'W. Manzanilla Beach, lined by coconut palms, is a popular tourist site. Manzanilla Point is 3 mi/4.8 km E.

Manzanilla, La, Mexico: see LA MANZANILLA DE LA PAZ.

Manzanillo (mahn-zah-NEE-yo), city, (1994 est. pop. 98,000), Granma prov., SE Cuba, a port on the Guacanayabo Gulf of the Caribbean Sea; 20°21'N 77°08'W.

A leading city on Cuba's S coast, Manzanillo is a commercial center and the exportation point for the agr. produce (sugarcane, rice, tobacco) of the Cauto plain. Founded in 1784; long a smuggling center involving Br. merchants from Jamaica. An attack by Great Britain in 1792 destroyed numerous Span. ships in the harbor and led to the fortification of the city.

Manzanillo (mahn-sah-NEE-yo), city (1990 pop. 67,697) and township, Colima state, SW Mexico. One of Mexico's chief Pacific ports, Manzanillo has a fine harbor and modern RR and highway connections with Mexico City. It handles many imports and ships out minerals, fruit, and lumber. Excellent beaches, a tropical climate, and resources for hunting and fishing have made Manzanillo a popular internatl. resort.

Manzanillo Bay (mahn-zahn-NEE-yo), Fr. *Baie de Mancenille*, inlet of Atlantic Ocean on N coast of Hispaniola, at border bet. Haiti and Dominican Republic; 19°45'N 71°45'E. Sheltered by Manzanillo Point (N). Port of Pepillo Salcedo is on S shore, at mouth of Massacre (Dajabón) R.

Manzanillo Keys (mahn-zah-NEE-yo), tiny coral reefs in the Gulf of Guacanayabo, Granma prov., SE Cuba, just outside Manzanillo, the harbor of which they protect; 20°23'N 77°11'W. Covered by mangroves. On Perla Key (W) is a lighthouse.

Manzanita (man-zuh-NEET-uh), town (1990 pop. 513), Tillamook co., NW Oregon, on the Pacific Ocean, 32 mi/51 km SSW of Astoria; 45°43'N 123°55'W. Dairy prods. Timber. Tourism. Oswald West State Park to NW; Tillamook State Forest to E.

Manzano Mountains (mahn-ZAHN-o), central N.Mex., E of Rio Grande; extends c.40 mi/64 km N from Mountainair; largely within parts of Cibola Natl. Forest and part of Isleta Indian Reservation. Prominent points are Mosca (9,509 ft/2,898 m), Manzano (10,098 ft/3,078 m) peaks.

Manzanola, village (1990 pop. 437), Otero co., SE central Colo., on Arkansas R., near mouth of Apishapa R., and 40 mi/64 km ESE of Pueblo; 38°06'N 103°52'W. Elev. 4,252 ft/1,296 m. Trading point in region producing cantelopes, melons, vegetables, sugar beets, wheat, beans, corn; cattle. L. Meredith Reservoir to NE.

Mao, town (1993 pop. 42,547), Santiago prov., NW Dominican Republic, in fertile Cibao region, 25 mi/40 km WNW of Santiago. Rice-growing and -milling center. Lumbering and gold washing in vicinity. Also called Valverde.

Mapastepec (mah-PAHS-te-pek), town (1990 pop. 12,572), ⊙ Mapastepec municipio, Chiapas, S Mexico, in Pacific lowland, on RR, and 55 mi/89 km NW of Tapachula, on Mexico Highway 200; 15°25'N 92°54'W. Elev. 105 ft/32 m. Cacao, tobacco, sugarcane, fruit; livestock.

Mapimí (mah-pee-MEE), town (1990 pop. 4,229), ⊙ Mapimí municipio, Durango, N Mexico, at S edge of Bolsón de Mapimí, 29 mi/46 km NW of Gómez Palacio, on Mexico Highway 30; 25°51'N 103°50'W. Elev. 4,485 ft/1,367 m. Silver, gold, lead mining.

Mapimí, Bolsón de (mah-pee-MEE, bo-SON dai), arid depression in plateau of N Mexico, in states of Chihuahua. Coahuila, and Durango, N of Mapimí (Durango). Desert region. Potentially fertile; has been irrigated in S, where cotton, wheat, alfalfa are grown. Average elev. c.4,485 ft/1,367 m.

Maple, village, in city of Vaughan, S Ont., central Canada, 15 mi/24 km N of Toronto; 43°51'N 79°31'W. Suburban community. Dairying; vegetable gardening. Mfg. (concrete prods., electronic goods, plastics, structural wood). Site of Canada's Wonderland amusement park.

Maple Bluff, village (1990 pop. 1,352), Dane co., S Wis., at E end of L. Mendota, a suburb, 2 mi/3.2 km N of downtown Madison; 43°06'N 89°22'W. Executive Mansion is here. Inc. 1930 as Lakewood Bluff; renamed 1931.

Maple Creek, town (1991 pop. 2,334), SW Sask., W Canada, on Maple Creek, and 55 mi/89 km ESE of Medicine Hat, at foot of the Cypress Hills; 49°55'N 109°28'W. Grain elevators; dairying; lumbering; livestock raising.

Maple Glen, uninc. town (1990 pop. 5,881), Montgomery

co., SE Pa., residential suburb, 12 mi/19 km N of downtown Philadelphia; 40°10′N 75°10′W. Willow Grove Naval Air Station to NE.

Maple Grove, city (1990 pop. 38,735), Hennepin co., E Minn., suburb, 12 mi/19 km NW of downtown Minneapolis; 45°06′N 93°27′W. Mfg. (machining, gun drilling, sheet metal fabricating; ink, furniture, concrete prods., machinery, aerospace material, bldg. materials, foam prods., wood prods., burglar alarms, tool and die prods., transportation equip., medical equip.). Several small lakes in vicinity. Elm Creek Park Reserve on N border.

Maple Heights, city (1990 pop. 27,089), Cuyahoga co., NE Ohio; 41°24′N 81°34′W. Chiefly a residential suburb of Cleveland, major shopping centers and miscellaneous mfg. Inc. 1932.

Maple Hill, city (1990 pop. 406), Wabaunsee co., NE Kansas, on Mill Creek, near its confluence with Kansas R., 14 mi/23 km ENE of Alma; 39°05′N 96°01′W. In cattle, poultry, and grain area.

Maple Lake, town (1990 pop. 1,394), Wright co., S central Minn., 7 mi/11.3 km WNW of Buffalo; 45°13′N 94°00′W. Grain, soybeans; livestock, poultry; dairying. Mfg. (metal fabrication; frozen foods, consumer goods, feeds and fertilizers, boats). Several small natural lakes in area, including Maple (E) and Mink (N) lakes; L. Marion State Park to N.

Maple Park, village (1990 pop. 641), Kane co., NE Ill., 15 mi/24 km W of Geneva; 41°54′N 88°35′W. In agr. area (dairy prods.; livestock).

Maple Plain, town (1990 pop. 2,005), Hennepin co., E Minn., suburb 18 mi/29 km W of downtown Minneapolis; 45°00′N 93°39′W. Bounded on N, W, and S by Independence, on E by Medina. Dairying in area; mfg. (concrete prods., industrial patterns, wood prods., machinery, molding; machining). Morris T. Baker Park Reserve to E; L. Independence to NE; L. Minnetonka to SE.

Maple Rapids, village (1990 pop. 680), Clinton co., S central Mich., 9 mi/14.5 km NW of St. Johns, and on Maple R.; 43°06′N 84°41′W. In farm area.

Maple Ridge, city (1991 pop. 48,422), SW B.C., SW Canada, suburb 27 mi/43 km ESE of downtown Vancouver, on N bank of Fraser R.; 49°13′N 122°36′W. Includes locality of Haney. River port. Logging, sawmilling, shipbuilding; dairying; fruit.

Maple River 1 90 mi/145 km long, W Iowa; rises in Buena Vista co., flows S, past Ida Grove, and SW to Little Sioux R. 7 mi/11.3 km ESE of Onawa. **2** c.65 mi/105 km long, S central Mich.; rises S of Corunna in Shiawassee co.; flows NW, past Ovid and Elsie, then W and SW, past Maple Rapids, to Grand R. at Muir; 42°56′N 84°03′W. **3** S Minn.; rises in Penny L., on border bet. Fairbault and Freeborn cos.; flows W past Wells, then NW, receives waters from Minnesota L. from 2 outflows, then N 5 mi/8 km W of Mapleton, past Good Thunder, to Le Sueur R. 5 mi/8 km S of Mankato; 43°47′N 93°38′W. **4** 100 mi/161 km long, E N.Dak.; rises in Steele co.; flows S largely through Cass co. to Enderlin, then NE to Sheyenne R., 10 mi/16 km NW of Fargo, near its confluence with Red R. of the North; 47°27′N 97°50′W.

Maple Shade, village (1990 pop. 19,211), Burlington co., SW N.J., 5 mi/8 km E of Camden; 39°57′N 75°00′W. Mfg. (clothing, paper prods.). Largely residential.

Maple Springs, resort village (1990 pop. 400), Chautauqua co., extreme W N.Y., on Chautauqua L., 11 mi/18 km NW of Jamestown; 42°12′N 79°25′W.

Maple Valley, uninc. town (1990 pop. 1,211), King co., W Wash., suburb 20 mi/32 km SE of downtown Seattle, on Cedar R.; 47°24′N 122°02′W. RR junction. Mfg. (wood prods.). L. Youngs reservoir to W.

Maplecrest, resort village (1990 pop. 150), Greene co., SE N.Y., in the Catskill Mts., 17 mi/27 km WNW of Catskill; 42°16′N 74°11′W.

Maplesville, town (1990 pop. 725), Chilton co., central Ala., on Mulberry R., 15 mi/24 km WSW of Clanton. Paper, lumber and veneer.

Mapleton 1 town (1990 pop. 1,294), Monona co., W Iowa, on Maple R., and 40 mi/64 km SE of Sioux City;

42°10′N 95°47′W. Concrete. Inc. 1878. **2** town (1990 pop. 1,853), Aroostook co., NE Maine, just W of Presque Isle; 46°42′N 68°07′W. Potato-producing area. Inc. 1880. **3** town (1990 pop. 1,526), Blue Earth co., S Minn., 17 mi/27 km S of Mankato, near Maple R.; 43°55′N 93°57′W. Grain; livestock; light mfg. Laid out and inc. 1878. **4** town (1990 pop. 3,572), Utah co., N central Utah, suburb, 8 mi/12.9 km SE of Provo, on Hobble Creek; 40°07′N 111°34′W. Elev. 4,537 ft/1,383 m. Fruit, vegetables; dairying; cattle, sheep. Spanish Fork Peak to SE; Utah L. to NW. Unita Natl. Forest and Wasatch Range to E. Originally named Union Beach, name changed in 1901.

Mapleton 1 village (1990 pop. 96), Bourbon co., SE Kansas, 15 mi/24 km NW of Fort Scott; 38°01′N 94°52′W. Dairying, general agr. **2** uninc. village, Hertford co., NE N.C., 37 mi/60 km E of Roanoke Rapids, near Meherrin R. Tobacco, cotton, peanuts; grain; chickens, livestock. **3** village (1990 pop. 682), Cass co., E N.Dak., 12 mi/19 km W of Fargo, and on Maple R.; 46°53′N 97°02′W.

Mapleton Depot, borough (1990 pop. 529), Huntingdon co., S central Pa., 3 mi/4.8 km W of Mt. Union, on Juniata R.; 40°23′N 77°56′W. Agr. (alfalfa; livestock, poultry); mfg. (feeds, glass sand). Parts of Rothrock State Forest to S, NE, and W. Also known as Mapleton.

Mapleview, village (1990 pop. 206), Mower co., SE Minn., 2 mi/3.2 km N of Austin, on Cedar R.; 43°41′N 92°58′W. Grain; dairying.

Maplewood 1 city (1990 pop. 30,954), Ramsey co., SE Minn., residential suburb, 5 mi/8 km NE of downtown St. Paul, immediately SW of city of St. Paul, with S extension adjoining entire E border of St. Paul; 44°59′N 93°01′W. Mfg. (dairy prods., signs). Mississippi R. to SW; numerous small lakes in area. Inc. 1957. **2** city (1990 pop. 9,962), St. Louis co., E Mo., a suburb, 7 mi/11.3 km SW of downtown St. Louis; 38°36′N 90°19′W. Mfg. (fabricated metal prods., tools, transportation equip., machinery). Settled 1825, inc. 1908.

Maplewood, uninc. village, Calcasieu parish, SW La., 6 mi/10 km W of L. Charles, and 4 mi/6 km E of Sulphur; 30°12′N 93°18′W. RR junction; oil and natural gas.

Maplewood, township (1990 pop. 21,756), Essex co., NE N.J., just W of Newark; 40°43′N 74°16′W. Primarily residential area. Maps.

Maplewood, N.H.: see BETHLEHEM.

Maplewood Heights, uninc. town (1990 pop. 3,300), King co., W Wash., residential suburb, 12 mi/19 km SE of downtown Seattle, 4 mi/6.4 km E of Renton, on Cedar R. L. Youngs reservoir to N.

Mappsville, uninc. village, Accomack co., E Va., 10 mi/16 km NNE of Accomac, in Eastern Shore area, W of Atlantic Ocean, and E of Chesapeake Bay; 37°50′N 75°34′W. Mfg. (clam processing; bronze sculptures); agr. (dairying; livestock; vegetables); fish, oysters, clams.

Maquapit Lake (MA-kwuh-pit) (□ 7 sq mi/18 sq km), S N.B., E Canada, 20 mi/32 km E of Fredericton, and 2 mi/3 km W of Grand L.; 5 mi/8 km long, 2 mi/3 km wide.

Maqueripe Bay (MAH-kah-reep), swimming beach, NW Trinidad, Trinidad and Tobago, 8 mi/12.9 km NW of Port of Spain; 10°44′N 61°37′W.

Maquoit Bay (muh-KOIT), SW Maine, indentation of Casco Bay, just SW of Brunswick, and E of Freeport; 4 mi/6.4 km long.

Maquoketa (ma-KO-kid-uh), city (1990 pop. 6,111), ☉ Jackson co., E Iowa, on Maquoketa R., near mouth of North Fork Maquoketa R., and 32 mi/51 km S of Dubuque; 42°04′N 90°40′W. Mfg. (consumer goods, machinery, fabricated metal prods., feeds, concrete prods., textiles, transportation equip.; printing). Maquoketa Caves State Park to W. Flooding occurred in 1993. Inc. 1853.

Maquoketa River, E Iowa, c.130 mi/209 km long; rises in SE Fayette co.; flows SE, past Manchester, Monticello, and Maquoketa, to Mississippi R. 7 mi/11.3 km SE of Bellevue. Receives North Fork (c.75 mi/121 km long) near Maquoketa.

Maquon, village (1990 pop. 331), Knox co., W central Ill., on Spoon R., and 15 mi/24 km SE of Galesburg; 40°47′N 90°09′W. In agr. area.

Mar Muerto (mahr moo-ER-to), lagoon of Gulf of Tehuantepec, on coast of Oaxaca and Chiapas, S Mexico de Zaragoza, 60 mi/97 km ESE of Juchitán; 45 mi/72 km long, 2 mi/3.2 km–7 mi/11.3 km wide; 16°15′N 94°15′W. Connected to Mar Muerto Inferior by marshes and channels.

Mar Muerto Inferior (mahr moo-ER-to een-fai-REE-or), lagoon in Oaxaca, S Mexico, on Isthmus of Tehuantepec, 18 mi/29 km SE of Juchitán de Zaragoza Bay; connected through narrow channels with Mar Muerto Superior and Gulf of Tehuantepec.

Mar Muerto Superior (mahr moo-ER-to soo-pai-REE-or), inlet of Gulf of Tehuantepec, in Oaxaca, S Mexico, S of Juchitán de Zaragoza; 18 mi/29 km long, 5 mi/8 km–12 mi/19 km wide. Connected by narrow channel with Mar Muerto Inferior.

Mar Vista, SW residential sect. of Los Angeles city, Los Angeles co., S Calif., 10 mi/16 km W of downtown Los Angeles, 1 mi/1.6 km W of Culver City.

Mara Vista, Mass.: see FALMOUTH.

Marabella (MAH-rah-bel-ah), village, W Trinidad, Trinidad and Tobago, on the Gulf of Paria, on RR, and 2 mi/3.2 km N of San Fernando. Coconuts; manjak deposits. Thermal springs nearby.

Maracas (MAH-rah-kas), village, NW Trinidad, Trinidad and Tobago, at S foot of Tucuche Mt., 7 mi/11.3 km E of Port of Spain. The Maracas Falls are 2 mi/3.2 km N. Public beach, destination for day visitors; Maracas Bay village resort scheduled for development.

Maracas Bay, inlet of N Trinidad, Trinidad and Tobago, towered over by the forest-clad Tucuche Mt., 16 mi/26 km NE of Port of Spain; 10°45′N 61°26′W. Resort.

Marais des Cygnes (muhr-ee dah SEEN), river, c.140 mi/225 km long, Kansas and Mo.; rises in S Wabaunsee co. c.25 mi/40 km SW of Topeka, E central Kansas; flows SE through Melvern L. Reservoir, past Ottawa and Osawatonie, then into W Mo. to join the Little Osage R. 6 mi/9.7 km W of Scheli City to form the Osage R. Subject to heavy flooding, the river has many flood control projects.

Maramec (MAR-uh-mek), village (1990 pop. 110), Pawnee co., N Okla., 9 mi/14.5 km SE of Pawnee; 36°14′N 96°40′W. In agr. area.

Marana, town (1990 pop. 2,187), Pima co., S Ariz., near Santa Cruz R., 21 mi/34 km NW of Tucson; 32°24′N 111°10′W. Elev. 2,055 ft/626 m. Trade center in cotton-growing area; cattle; mfg. (machinery parts). Tortolita Mts. to NE; Tucson Mt. unit of Saguaro Natl. Monument to S.

Maranacook, Lake (muh-RAN-uh-kuk), lake, Kennebec co., S Maine, just N of Winthrop; 5.5 mi/8.9 km long.

Marathon, county (□ 1,576 sq mi/4,082 sq km; 1990 pop. 115,400), central Wis.; ☉ Wausau; 44°53′N 89°45′W. Primarily a dairying area, co. is a major producer of cheese; lumbering; agr. (oats, barley, corn, potatoes, alfalfa, hay, ginseng, cranberries; cattle, sheep, hogs, poultry); diversified mfg. at Wausau. Drained by Wisconsin R. and its tributaries (Eau Claire, Big and Little Eau Pleine), Big Rib, and Placer rivers and Big Eau Pleine and Du Bay reservoirs (both in S). Rib Mt. State Park, SW of Wausau, at center, including Rib Mt. (1,940 ft/591 m), winter sports center. N fringe of city of Marshfield in SW. Formed 1850.

Marathon (MA-ruh-thahn), town (1991 pop. 5,064), central Ont., central Canada, on L. Superior, 130 mi/209 km E of Thunder Bay; 49°46′N 86°26′W. Gold mining; paper mill. Secondary airport. Formerly Peninsula.

Marathon 1 town (□ 6 sq mi/15.5 sq km; 1990 pop. 8,857), ☉ Monroe co., located in middle Fla. Keys, half-way bet. Key West and Key Largo; 24°42′N 81°04′W. Center of a major resort area. **2** town (1990 pop. 320), Buena Vista co., NW Iowa, near source of Raccoon R., 18 mi/29 km NE of Storm Lake; 42°51′N 94°58′W. In livestock and grain area. **3** town (1990 pop. 1,606), Marathon co., central Wis., on Big Rib R., and 10 mi/

16 km W of Wausau; 44°55′N 89°50′W. In dairying and lumbering area. Mfg. (dairy prods., lumber, beverages, bldg. materials, wood prods., feeds and fertilizers).

Marathon 1 village (1990 pop. 1,107), Cortland co., central N.Y., on Tioughnioga R., and 25 mi/40 km NNW of Binghamton; 42°26′N 76°02′W. Mfg. (boats, transportation equip.); agr. (dairy prods.; poultry; field corn and hay). **2** uninc. village (1990 pop. 800), Brewster co., extreme W Texas, 28 mi/45 km SE of Alpine. Elev. 4,043 ft/1,232 m. In ranch region (sheep, cattle, goats); mfg. (machinery). Hq. for Big Bend Natl. Park (c.35 mi/56 km S).

Maraval (MAH-rah-val), N residential suburb of Port of Spain, N Trinidad, Trinidad and Tobago.

Maravatío de Ocampo (mah-rah-vah-TEE-o dai o-KAHM-po), city (1990 pop. 22,133) and township, ⊙ Maravatío municipio, Michoacán, central Mexico, on central plateau, 45 mi/72 km ENE of Morelia; 19°53′N 100°26′W. Elev. 6,824 ft/2,080 m. RR junction; processing and agr. center (cereals, fruit, vegetables; livestock); flour milling, tanning, lumbering; mfg. (shoes, textiles).

Marbial (bahr-BYAHL), Ouest dept., S Haiti, rural region just N of Jacmel; 18°20′N 72°28′W. Coffee and fruit growing.

Marble 1 village (1990 pop. 64), Gunnison co., W central Colo., on Crystal R., in foothills of Elk Mts., and 40 mi/64 km NNW of Gunnison; 39°04′N 107°11′W. Elev. 7,950 ft/2,423 m. Quarries produce high-grade marble. Paonia State Park to SW, surrounded by Gunnison Natl. Forest; White River Natl. Forest to N. **2** village (1990 pop. 618), Itasca co., N central Minn., 14 mi/23 km ENE of Grand Rapids, in Mesabi Iron Range; 47°19′N 93°17′W. Open-pit iron mines in area. Swan L. 5 mi/8 km E. **3** uninc. village, Cherokee co., extreme W N.C., 8 mi/12.9 km NE of Murphy in Nantahala Natl. Forest. Timber; marble quarrying. Mfg. (textiles, apparel, wood chips).

Marble Canyon, Coconino co., N Ariz., extends c.60 mi/97 km S along Colorado R. from mouth of Paria R., near Utah state line, to mouth of Little Colorado R., at E end of Grand Canyon Natl. Park. Also known as Marble Gorge. Sometimes defined as upper part of Grand Canyon. Est. as 1969 as Marble Canyon Natl. Monument; added to Grand Canyon Natl. Park 1975 (in NE extension of park).

Marble City, village (1990 pop. 232), Sequoyah co., E Okla., 8 mi/12.9 km N of Salisaw; 35°34′N 94°49′W. In agr. area; mfg. (limestone processing). Crystal Caves and Sallisaw State Park (to S) are nearby.

Marble Cliff, village (1990 pop. 633), Franklin co., central Ohio, just W of Columbus, on Scioto R.; 39°59′N 83°04′W. Limestone quarry gave its name; generally suburban.

Marble Falls, town (1990 pop. 4,007), Burnet co., central Texas, on Colorado R. (bridged), and 39 mi/63 km NW of Austin; 30°34′N 98°16′W. Elev. 764 ft/233 m. RR terminus. Agr. (cattle, sheep; pecans, fruit); cedar timber; granite quarries. Mfg. (crushed stone, oil field tanks, electronic components). L. Marble Falls (Colorado R.) impounds here, L. Lyndon B. Johnson dammed to W; Longhorn Caverns State Park to NW. Settled 1887, inc. 1908.

Marble Hill, town (1990 pop. 1,447), ⊙ Bollinger co., SE Mo., 24 mi/39 km W of Cape Girardeau; 37°17′N 89°58′W. Corn, wheat; livestock; timber; mfg. (headwear). Annexed adjacent Lutesville in 1986.

Marble Hill, a residential district of Manhattan borough of N.Y. city, SE N.Y., across Harlem R. from N end of Manhattan Isl. and surrounded W, N, and E by the Bronx. Was originally part of Manhattan Isl. until Harlem R. was redirected S of it in 1895, cutting it off; in 1913, it was physically joined to the Bronx by landfill. Pop. largely Lat.-Amer. and Afr.-Amer.

Marble Rock, town (1990 pop. 361), Floyd co., N Iowa, on Shell Rock R., and 11 mi/18 km WSW of Charles City; 42°57′N 92°52′W. In livestock area; limestone quarries.

Marblehead (MAHR-buhl-hed), suburban town (1990 pop. 19,971), Essex co., NE Mass., on the Atlantic coast;

42°29′N 70°51′W. A fishing village for many years, Marblehead became a resort in the 19th cent.; it is a picturesque town esp. famous for yachting and antiques. Has many 18th-cent. bldgs., including politician Elbridge Gerry's birthplace. Abbot Hall contains Archibald Willard's painting *Spirit of '76.* In Burial Hill cemetery are the graves of hundreds of Amer. Revolutionary soldiers and a monument to the 65 Marblehead residents who died in a gale in 1846. The Revolutionary War Fort Sewall is in a seaside park. Includes village of Clifton. Site of Marblehead Regatta held every July. Inc. 1649.

Marblehead, village (1990 pop. 745), Ottawa co., N Ohio, 6 mi/10 km N of Sandusky, at tip of Marblehead Peninsula, which extends c.15 mi/24 km E into L. Erie and shelters Sandusky Bay on N; 41°32′N 82°43′W. Resort, fishing center; has lighthouse. Limestone quarries; fruit orchards.

Marbleton, village (1990 pop. 634), Sublette co., W Wyo., near Green R., 25 mi/40 km SW of Pinedale, and 1 mi/1.6 km N of Big Piney; 42°33′N 110°05′W. Elev. 6,850 ft/2,088 m.

Marbury, village (1990 pop. 1,244), Charles co., S Md., near Mattawoman Creek, 24 mi/39 km SSW of Washington; 38°34′N 77°10′W. Nearby is Smallwood State Park and Indian Head Naval Ordnance Station.

Marcelin (MAHRS-lin), village (1991 pop. 193), central Sask., W Canada, 45 mi/72 km WSW of Prince Albert; 52°56′N 106°47′W. Mixed farming, dairying.

Marceline (mahr-suh-LEEN), city (1990 pop. 2,645), Linn and Chariton cos., N central Mo., 8 mi/12.9 km SE of Brookfield; 39°43′N 92°57′W. Shipping center in grain, livestock (esp. dairy), cattle, hogs; mfg. (printing, publishing, steel fabrication). Coal area but no longer mined. Plotted 1887. Boyhood home of Walt Disney.

Marcellina, Mount, peak (11,349 ft/3,459 m) in Rocky Mts., Gunnison co., W Colo., 14 mi/23 km WNW of Crested Butte, in the Raggeds Wilderness.

Marcellus (mahr-SEL-uhs), town (1990 pop. 1,193), Cass co., SW Mich., 22 mi/35 km SSW of Kalamazoo; 42°01′N 85°48′W. In farm and lake resort area. Mfg. (logging, machining). Fish and Saddlebag lakes to NW. Inc. 1879.

Marcellus, village (1990 pop. 1,840), Onondaga co., central N.Y., 10 mi/16 km WSW of Syracuse; 42°58′N 76°20′W. Mfg. (paper, feed); agr. (dairy prods.). Inc. 1846.

March Air Force Base, Calif.: see RIVERSIDE.

Marchand (mahr-SHAH), village (1991 pop. 1,229), S Que., E Canada, on St. Maurice R., and 10 mi/16 km NW of Trois Rivières; 49°26′N 96°23′W. Mining.

Marco Island, town (1990 pop. 9,493), Collier co., SW Fla., 15 mi/24 km SSE of Naples. Center of resort complex that covers Marco Isl.

Marconi, Mount (mahr-KO-nee) (10,190 ft/3,106 m), SE B.C., W Canada, near Alta. border, in Rocky Mts., 60 mi/97 km N of Fernie; 50°23′N 115°07′W.

Marcus, town (1990 pop. 1,171), Cherokee co., NW Iowa, 14 mi/23 km WNW of Cherokee; 42°49′N 95°48′W. Feed. Inc. 1892.

Marcus, village (1990 pop. 135), Stevens co., NE Wash., 11 mi/18 km NW of Colville, and on Columbia R. (Franklin D. Roosevelt L. reservoir), opposite mouth of Kettle R.; 48°40′N 118°04′W. Terminus of RR spur from Kettle Falls. Agr. (wheat, alfalfa, barley; hogs). Coulee Dam Natl. Recreation Area on both shores of reservoir; part of Colville Natl. Forest to W. City moved (1941) from site c.1.5 mi/2.4 km S, now covered by reservoir.

Marcus Baker, Mount (13,176 ft/4,016 m), S Alaska, in Chugach Mts., 55 mi/89 km WNW of Valdez; 61°26′N 147°46′W.

Marcus Hook, borough (1990 pop. 2,546), Delaware co., SE Pa., 15 mi/24 km SW of downtown Philadelphia, and 2 mi/3.2 km SW of Chester, on Delaware R. (N.J. state line), at Del. state line (SW); 39°48′N 75°25′W. Mfg. (petroleum refining; vinyl prods., chemicals, lumber, chemicals). Early 18th-cent. pirate rendezvous. Settled c.1640 by Swedes, laid out c.1701, inc. 1893.

Marcy, Mount (5,344 ft/1,629 m), Essex co., NE N.Y., in

the Adirondack Mts., c.12 mi/19 km SSE of Lake Placid village; 44°07′N 73°56′W. Highest peak in the state. L. Tear of the Clouds, on its S slope, is the source of the main headstream (Feldspar Creek–Opalescent R.) of the Hudson R. Was 1st ascended in 1837.

Mardela Springs (mahr-DE-lah), town (1990 pop. 360), Wicomico co., E Md., 11 mi/18 km NW of Salisbury; 38°28′N 75°46′W. Originally called Barren Springs, the name was changed to the combination of the names of Md. and Del. in 1906. A natural spring (now polluted) was reputed to have health-giving qualities.

Mare Island, Calif.: see VALLEJO.

Marea del Portillo (mah-RAI-yo dail por-TEE-yo), small town, Granma prov., SE Cuba, near mouth of Silantros R., on Caribbean coast; 19°55′N 77°11′W.

Marengo (muh-REN-go), county (□ 982 sq mi/2,543 sq km; 1990 pop. 23,084), W Ala., in the Black Belt; ⊙ Linden. Bounded W by Tombigbee R. Corn, hay; cattle; lumber milling; textiles. Demopolis is in N. Formed 1818.

Marengo 1 (mo-REN-go), city (1990 pop. 4,768), McHenry co., N Ill., on Kishwaukee R., and 11 mi/18 km SW of Woodstock; 42°15′N 88°35′W. In dairy and farm area; makes fabricated metal prods. Settled 1835; inc. as town in 1857, as city in 1893. **2** city (1990 pop. 2,270), ⊙ Iowa co., E central Iowa, on Iowa R., and 24 mi/39 km WSW of Cedar Rapids; 41°47′N 92°04′W. Mfg. (bldg. materials; printing). Amana Colonies to E. Inc. 1859.

Marengo, town (1990 pop. 856), Crawford co., S Ind., on a tributary of Blue R., and 7 mi/11.3 km ENE of English; 38°22′N 86°20′W. In agr. area; limestone quarries; timber. Marengo Cave here is a tourist attraction.

Marengo (muh-RENG-go), village (1990 pop. 393), Morrow co., central Ohio, 22 mi/35 km SE of Marion; 40°24′N 82°49′W.

Marenisco (mahr-en-IS-ko), village, Gogebic co., W Upper Peninsula, NW Mich., 24 mi/39 km ESE of Ironwood, on Presque Isle R., in Ottawa Natl. Forest; 46°22′N 89°41′W. In lumbering, and agr. area. Mfg. (wood prods.). L. Gogebic State Park on W shore of large L. Gogebic, 8 mi/12.9 km NE.

Marfa, town (1990 pop. 2,424), ⊙ Presidio co., extreme W Texas, c.175 mi/282 km SE of El Paso, just S of Davis Mts. Elev. 4,688 ft/1,429 m. Market, shipping center for ranching (cattle, horses), silver-mining region; mfg. (solar pump jacks, feeds); tourist trade. Old Fort D. A. Russell here was founded 1833. Hunting nearby. Marfa Mystery Lights, unexplained phenomenon 1st reported in 1883. Founded 1881, inc. 1887.

Marfrance (MAHR-frans), uninc. town (1990 pop. 100), Greenbrier co., SE W.Va., 23 mi/37 km NNW of Lewisburg.

Margaree (mahr-guh-REE), village, NE N.S., E Canada, on Cape Breton Isl., on Margaree R., 22 mi/35 km NW of Inverness; 46°23′N 61°04′W. Salmon-fishing center. At mouth of Margaree R., on the Gulf of St. Lawrence, 4 mi/6 km NW, is fishing port of Margaree Harbour.

Margaree River, 10 mi/16 km long, NE N.S., E Canada, on NE Cape Breton Isl.; rises in 2 branches: Southwest Margaree R. issues from L. Ainslie, 8 mi/13 km ESE of Inverness; flows 15 mi/24 km N; Northeast Margaree R. rises 20 mi/32 km SW of Ingonish; flows 40 mi/64 km S and E; the branches unite 4 mi/6 km S of Margaree, forming Margaree R., which flows NNW to the Gulf of St. Lawrence at Margaree Harbour.

Margaret, village (1990 pop. 616), St. Clair co., N central Ala., 12 mi/19 km SW of Ashville. Coal mines.

Margaretsville, uninc. village, Northampton co., NE N.C., 18 mi/29 km ENE of Roanoke Rapids, at Va. state line, near Meherrin R. Tobacco, grain; livestock.

Margaretville, summer-resort village (1990 pop. 639), Delaware co., S N.Y., in the Catskill Mts., on East Branch of Delaware R., and 37 mi/60 km NW of Kingston; 42°08′N 74°39′W.

Margarita Island, Mexico: see SANTA MARGARITA ISLAND.

Margaritas, Las, Mexico: see LAS MARGARITAS.

Margate, city (□ 8 sq mi/20.7 sq km; 1990 pop. 42,985),

Broward co., SE Fla., 5 mi/8 km W of Pompano Beach; 26°15′N 80°12′W. Mfg. includes commercial printing and light mfg.

Margate City (MAHR-gait), resort and residential city (1990 pop. 8,431), Atlantic co., SE N.J., on the Atlantic Ocean, c.4 mi/6.4 km S of Atlantic City; 39°19′N 74°30′W. Known for its pleasant beaches and for its large, old homes, intermixed with expensive, renovated modern residences. Inc. 1897.

Margrethe, Lake (mahr-GRETH), Crawford co., N central Mich., 4 mi/6.4 km SW of Grayling; c.3 mi/4.8 km long, 1 mi/1.6 km wide; 44°39′N 84°47′W. Drained from W by a headstream of Manistee R. Located within Camp Grayling Natl. Guard Reservation.

Maria, village (1991 pop. 2,491), E Que., E Canada, S Gaspé Peninsula, on Cascapedia Bay of Chaleur Bay, 20 mi/32 km ENE of Dalhousie. Fishing port; lumbering. Resort.

María Cleófas Island, Mexico: see TRES MARÍAS, LAS.

Maria Islands, two small islands, off SSE St. Lucia, Caribbean Sea; 13°43′N 60°55′W. Nature preserve inhabited by rare species of snakes, lizards, birds.

María Madre Island, Mexico: see TRES MARÍAS, LAS.

María Magdalena Island, Mexico: see TRES MARÍAS, LAS.

María Trinidad Sánchez, province (□ 508 sq mi/1310 sq km; 1993 pop. 122,165), NE Dominican Republic, on the Atlantic Coast; ⊙ Nagua; 19°30′N 70°00′W. Agr. (bananas) in S part.

Marianao (mah-ree-uh-NOU), county and city, (1982 est. pop. 130,000), Ciudad de la Habana prov., W Cuba, a commercial and residential suburb of Havana in W metropolitan area; 23°05′N 82°25′W. Marianao encloses the N. Amer.-built military base of Columbia, now called Ciudad Libertad. Chemicals, beer, and textiles are produced here. Has a fine beach. Founded in 1719 by Dominican and Augustinian monks, the city was destroyed by fire in 1726. Rebuilt in 1765 as Quemados de Marianao and grew with the sugar boom in the 19th cent.

Marianna 1 town (1990 pop. 5,910), ⊙ Lee co., E Ark., c 50 mi/80 km SW of Memphis (Tenn.), and on L'Anguille R.; 34°46′N 90°46′W. Agr. (cotton, rice, soybeans); mfg (transportation equip., fabricated metal prods.). The small St. Francis Natl. Forest is to SE. Inc. 1877. **2** town (□ 6 sq mi/15.5 sq km; 1990 pop. 6,292), ⊙ Jackson co., NW Fla., on Chipola R., and c.60 mi/97 km WNW of Tallahassee; 30°46′N 85°14′W. RR junction. Lumber milling; mfg. of consumer goods and millwork articles, barrels, feed. Limestone quarrying.

Marianna (MER-ee-A-nah), borough (1990 pop. 616), Washington co., SW Pa., 13 mi/21 km SE of Washington on Tenmile Creek; 40°00′N 80°06′W. Agr. (corn, hay; dairying). Inc. 1901.

Mariano Arista, Nancamilpa de, Mexico: see NANACAMILPA.

Mariano Escobedo (mah-ree-AH-no es-ko-BAI-do), town (1990 pop. 2,157), Veracruz, E Mexico, in Sierra Madre Oriental, 5 mi/8 km N of Orizaba. Coffee, fruit.

Marias (muh-REI-uhs), river, c.210 mi/338 km long, N Mont.; formed by joining of Cut Bank Creek and Two Medicine R. on border bet. Glacier and Pondersa cos.; flows E, passes 8 mi/12.9 km S of Shelby and through L. Elwell (Tiber Reservoir), then SE and receives Teton R. just before entering Missouri R. at Loma. Used for irrigation. Tiber Dam (completed 1956), is part of the Missouri R. Basin Project.

Marías, Las, P.R.: see LAS MARÍAS.

Marias Pass (muh-REI-uhs) (5,280 ft/1,609 m), in Lewis Range of Continental Divide, on border bet. Glacier and Flathead cos., NW Mont., at Summit, on SE border of Glacier Natl. Park, and 50 mi/80 km SW of Cut Bank. Nearby are Lewis and Clark (NE) and Flathead (SW) natl. forests. Discovered 1889 by John F. Stevens, the pass is now crossed by U.S. Highway 2 and Burlington Northern RR.

Mariaville (muh-REI-uh-vil), town (1990 pop. 270), Hancock co., S Maine, 12 mi/19 km N of Ellsworth; 44°45′N 68°23′W. In recreational area.

Maricao (mah-ree-KOU), town (1990 pop. 6,206), W P.R., in W outliers of the Cordillera Central, 11 mi/18 km E of Mayagüez. Elev. 1,416 ft/432 m. Coffee-trading and producing center; citrus fruits, plantains; resort. Pharmaceuticals factory. Fish hatchery nearby. Adjoining S is extensive reforestation project. Maricao Forest Reserve nearby (S).

Maricopa, county (□ 9,224 sq mi/23,890 sq km; 1990 pop. 2,122,101), central and S central Ariz.; ⊙ Phoenix, the state capital; 33°20′N 112°29′W. McDowell Mts., part of Mazatzal Mts., and part of Tonto Natl. Forest are in NE. Irrigated agr. region extends along banks of Salt, Gila, Santa Cruz, Verde, and Agua Fria (which forms L. Pleasant reservoir and part of N border) rivers. Long-staple cotton, citrus, vegetables, hay, alfalfa, wheat, barley; cattle, sheep, hogs; tourism. Mfg. at Phoenix, Glendale, Tempe, Scottsdale, Mesa, Chandler, other suburban cities. Sixteenth-largest co. in U.S. Highly urbanized in NE around Phoenix; large retired pop.; Phoenix area has attracted large numbers of businesses and residents to its warm climate. Hummingbird Springs, Big Horn Mts., and parts of Eagletail Mts. and Harquahala Mts. wilderness areas in NW; part of Tohono O'odham (Papago) Indian Reservation in S; Gila Bend Indian Reservation in SW; Salt R. and Fort McDowell Reservations in NE. Luke Air Force Base W of Phoenix; part of large Barry M. Goldwater (formerly Luke) Air Force Range in SW. Gila R. Indian Reservation to S. Nuclear power plants, Palo Verde 1 (initial criticality May 25, 1985), Palo Verde 2 (initial criticality April 18, 1986), and Palo Verde 3 (initial criticality Oct. 25, 1987), are 36 mi/58 km W of Phoenix; use cooling water from a sewage treatment facility, and each has a max. dependable capacity of 1221 MWe. Formed 1871.

Maricopa, city (1990 pop. 1,193), Kern co., S central Calif., 30 mi/48 km SW of Bakersfield, in S part of San Joaquin Valley; 35°04′N 119°24′W. Oil wells. Cattle; dairying; fruit, grain. Los Padres Natl. Forest to S; Buena Vista L., irrigation reservoir to NE.

Maricopa Mountains, Maricopa co., SW central Ariz., E of Gila R. and Gila Bend; rise to c.3,000 ft/914 m. Javelina Mt. in S, 3,571 ft/1,088 m.

Marie-Galante: see GUADELOUPE.

Mariel (mah-ree-AIL), town, La Habana prov., W Cuba, on sheltered bay, 27 mi/43 km WSW of Havana; 23°00′N 82°46′W. In agr. region (sugarcane, tobacco; cattle). Mfg. of cement and cigars. Shark fishing. Nearby are Cuba's principal asphalt reserves and a geothermal power plant. There are also limestone and guano deposits; sulphurous springs. In the outskirts is the Cuban Naval Acad. Site of 1980 Mariel boat lift, when over 100,000 Cubans left for Fla. through its port. The Central San Ramón is 3 mi/4.8 km SW.

Mariemont (muh-REE-mahnt), village (1990 pop. 3,118), Hamilton co., extreme SW Ohio, an E suburb of Cincinnati; 39°08′N 84°22′W. Bakery prods., electrical apparatus, beverages. Laid out 1922, inc. 1941.

Marienville (MER-ee-ahn-vil), uninc. town (1990 pop. 1,400), Forest co., NW Pa., 28 mi/45 km NE of Clarion; 41°28′N 79°07′W. Allegheny Natl. Forest immediately to N; Clear Creek State Forest to S.

Maries (MER-reez), county (□ 526 sq mi/1,362 sq km; 1990 pop. 7,976), central Mo., in the Ozark Mts.; ⊙ Vienna; 38°10′N 91°55′W. Drained by Gasconade R. Agr. (wheat, corn) and livestock (cattle) region; timber, charcoal. Rolla Airport and weather station at Vichy in SE. Formed 1855.

Marietta 1 (mar-ee-ET-uh), city (1990 pop. 44,129), ⊙ Cobb co., NW Ga.; 33°57′N 84°32′W. A growing and important suburb of Atlanta, its industry is largely involved in the production of aircraft. Other mfg. includes bldg. materials, plastics, food and beverages, consumer goods, textiles, chemicals, hardware and security equip.; poultry processing, marble and granite production, printing and publishing. Near Kennesaw Mt., Marietta was the scene of a Union defeat in the Civil War; Kennesaw Mt. Natl. Battlefield Park marks the site. Many Civil War dead are buried in the city's large natl. cemetery. Kennesaw House played a role in the Civil War. The Zion Baptist Church, built in 1888, is an important Afr.-Amer. institution. Seat of Kennesaw and Southern Polytechnic univs. Dobbins Air Force Base is nearby. Inc. 1834. **2** city (1990 pop. 15,026), ⊙ Washington co., SE Ohio, at the confluence of the Muskingum and Ohio rivers; 39°25′N 81°26′W. Trading center for an agr. and dairying area. Mfg. includes machinery, plastics, chemicals, ventilators, and paint. The 1st planned, permanent settlement in Ohio and the Northwest Territory. Founded in 1788 by the Ohio Company of Associates, among local Mound Builders' earthworks, Marietta grew as a shipbuilding and shipping center for a farm area. First houses were in stockaded enclosure called Campus Martius. Seat of Marietta Col. Points of interest include the Ohio R. Mus. (est. 1972); Mound Cemetery, where numerous Revolutionary officers are buried; and the Campus Martius Memorial State Mus. Inc. 1801.

Marietta (mar-ee-ET-uh), town (1990 pop. 2,306), ⊙ Love co., S Okla., 16 mi/26 km S of Ardmore; 33°55′N 97°07′W. Elev. 843 ft/257 m. In diversified agr. area (peanuts; sheep, hogs); mfg. (machinery, apparel, foods); gas and oil. L. Murray State Park and Lodge is 10 mi/16 km N; headwaters of L. Texoma on Red R. to E. Founded c.1887.

Marietta 1 (mar-ee-ET-uh), village (1990 pop. 142), Fulton co., W central Ill., 15 mi/24 km NW of Lewiston; 40°30′N 90°23′W. In agr. and bituminous-coal area. **2** village (1990 pop. 211), Lac qui Parle co., SW Minn., near S.Dak. state line, 11 mi/18 km W of Madison; 45°00′N 96°25′W. Grain; livestock; dairying. **3** village (1990 pop. 287), Prentiss co., NE Miss., 20 mi/32 km NE of Tupelo, near East Fork Tombigbee R.; 34°30′N 88°28′W. John Bell Williams Wildlife Management Area to SE. Natchez Trace Parkway passes to SE. Mfg. (furniture, apparel). **4** village (1990 pop. 206), Robeson co., SE N.C., 18 mi/29 km SSW of Lumberton, near S.C. state line; 34°22′N 79°07′W. Grain, sunflowers, tobacco; livestock. Mfg. (air filters). Lumber R. State Park to NE. **5** (mar-ee-ET-uh), uninc. village, Greenville co., NW S.C., and 13 mi/21 km NNW of Greenville, on N Saluda R. Mfg. includes fabric finishing, synthetic textiles, wood prods. Agr. includes, timber; livestock, poultry; grain.

Marietta (mer-ee-E-tah), borough (1990 pop. 2,778), Lancaster co., SE Pa., 13 mi/21 km W of Marietta, on Susquehanna R.; 40°03′N 76°32′W. Agr. (grain, soybeans, potatoes; livestock, poultry; dairying); mfg. (bldg. materials, fabricated metal prods., pharmaceuticals). Elizabethtown-Marietta Airport to N. Marietta Ordnance Depot to W. Settled 1718, inc. 1812.

Marieville (MAH-ree-vil), town (1991 pop. 5,164), ⊙ Rouville co., S Que., E Canada, near Richelieu R., 20 mi/32 km ESE of Montreal; 45°26′N 73°10′W. Mfg., woodworking; dairying.

Marigot (MA-ree guht), village (1991 pop. 2,919), NE Dominica, B.W.I., 18 mi/29 km NNE of Roseau; 15°32′N 61°18′W. Coconuts, limes. At the Carib Reserve, 4 mi/6.4 km S, live a few survivors of aboriginal inhabitants. Nearby (W) is Melville Hall Airport.

Marigot (mah-ree-GO), agr. town (1982 pop. 1,332), Sud-Est dept., S Haiti, on the Caribbean Sea, 18 mi/29 km E of Jacmel; 18°14′N 72°19′W. Coffee; fruit. Fishing port.

Marigot (mah-ree-GO), village, St. Martin isl., Fr. West Indies, on W coast of isl., 160 mi/257 km NW of Basse-Terre (Guadeloupe); 18°04′N 63°05′W. Principal settlement of the Fr. sect. of the isl., with a good harbor. Produces some sugarcane, tropical fruit, cotton, and cattle for local use.

Marigot Bay (mahr-ee-GO), W coast of St. Lucia, 4 mi/6.4 km S of Castries; 13°58′N 61°01′W. One of the most beautiful and protected yachting anchorages in Caribbean Sea. Hotel and yacht chartering facilities. Also known as Hurricane Hole.

Mariguana, Bahama Isls.: see BAHAMAS

Marin, county (□ 520 sq mi/1,347 sq km; 1990 pop. 230,096), W Calif.; ⊙ San Rafael; 38°02′N 122°45′W. Many residential suburbs of San Francisco, linked by Golden Gate Bridge to San Francisco (S) and by Richmond–San Rafael Bridge to Contra Costa co. (E).

Wooded, hilly Marin Peninsula reaches S to the Golden Gate, and bet. San Pablo and San Francisco bays (E) and Pacific Ocean (W); Pacific coast is indented by Bodega, Tomales, Drakes, and Bolinas bays. Petaluma R. forms NE border. Dairying; poultry and livestock raising (cattle, sheep), farming (oats, nuts, fruit); fishing (oysters, clams, mussels); nurseries. Stone, sand, gravel, clay quarrying; mercury. Hamilton Air Force Base in E. Mt. Tamalpais State Park and Muir Woods Natl. Monument are in S, W of Mill Valley. Includes Angel Isl. State Park, largest in San Francisco Bay; Point Reyes Natl. Seashore is in SW; part of Golden Gate Natl. Recreation Area is in S, on Golden Gate strait. State prison at San Quentin. Formed 1850.

Marin (mah-RANG), town, SE Martinique, minor port on bay, 16 mi/26 km SE of Fort-de-France; 14°28′N 60°52′W. Trading and processing (alcohol), in agr. region (cacao). Sometimes called Le Marin.

Marín, town, Nuevo León, N Mexico, 22 mi/35 km NE of Monterrey; 25°55′N 100°00′W. Cereals, cactus fibers; livestock.

Marina, city (1990 pop. 26,436), Monterey co., W Calif., on Pacific Ocean, 8 mi/12.9 km W of Salinas, on Monterey Bay; 36°41′N 121°48′W. Agr. (artichokes, vegetables, fruit); dairying; cattle. Mfg. (printing and publishing). Fort Ord Military reservation to S.

Marina del Rey (mah-REE-nah del RAI), uninc. town (1990 pop. 7,431), Los Angeles co., S Calif., residential suburb 11 mi/18 km WSW of downtown Los Angeles (borders it on all sides except NE), 3 mi/4.8 km SE of Santa Monica, near Pacific Ocean, SW of Culver City; 33°59′N 118°27′W. Mfg. (electronic equip., machinery); service industry. Marina del Rey boat harbor extends inland here from coast. Hughes Airport is here; Los Angeles Internatl. Airport to S.

Marina Hemingway, recreational marine facility, at W edge of Havana, Ciudad de la Habana prov., W Cuba; 23°05′N 82°31′W. An important sports-fishing and leisure-boating facility. Hosts annual spring fishing. Small craft can moor here for 72 hours without immigration visa or tourist card.

Marine, village (1990 pop. 972), Madison co., SW Ill., 10 mi/16 km E of Edwardsville; 38°47′N 89°46′W. In agr. area (wheat; dairy prods.; poultry, cattle).

Marine, Minn.: see MARINE ON SAINT CROIX.

Marine City, town and port (1990 pop. 4,556), St. Clair co., E Mich., 18 mi/29 km S of Port Huron, and on St. Clair R. at mouth of Belle R.; 42°42′N 82°30′W. Mfg. (transportation equip.; machining); grain elevator. Salt mines. Ferry to Sombra (Ont.). Inc. as village 1865; named Marine City 1867; inc. as city 1887.

Marine on Saint Croix (KROI), village (1990 pop. 602), Washington co., E Minn., 23 mi/37 km NE of downtown St. Paul, and 10 mi/16 km N of Stillwater, on St. Croix R.; 45°22′N 92°45′W. One of 1st Eur. settlements in Minn. William O'Brian State Park to N; Lower St. Croix Natl. Scenic Riverway on St. Croix R.; numerous small lakes in area, esp. Big Marine L. to NW. Also known as Marine.

Mariners' Harbor, neighborhood, in borough of Staten Island, N Staten Isl. on W side of Willowbrook Expressway, N.Y. city, SE N.Y. state; 40°38′N 74°09′W. Formerly a major industrial, warehousing, and transshipment center on S end of Newark Bay–Kill Van Kull. In 1972, the 1st Mitchell-Lama project, known as North Shore Plaza, was planned for Staten Isl. in an attempt to revive the economically depressed North Shore communities. Formerly a prosperous community whose economy was based on oyster fishing; little evidence now remains of the fine Classic Revival homes of Captain's Row. Mfg. (chemicals, metal prods.). Goethals and Bayonne bridges to N.J. are nearby.

Marinette, county (□ 1,550 sq mi/4,015 sq km; 1990 pop. 40,548), NE Wis., ⊙ Marinette; 45°20′N 88°00′W. Lumbering; wheat, corn, beans. Mfg. at Marinette. Lake resorts. Bounded E by Menominee R. (Mich. state line and border bet. Central and Eastern time zones), SE by Green Bay. Wooded region, drained by Peshtigo R. Thunder R. State Fish Hatchery and Winterset Ski Area in W; Mt. LeBett Ski Area in SW; Nicolet Natl. Forest immediately beyond W border. Formed 1879.

Marinette, city (1990 pop. 11,843), ⊙ Marinette co., NE Wis., 43 mi/69 km NNE of Green Bay city, on Green Bay of L. Michigan, at the mouth of the Menominee R.; 45°05′N 87°37′W. Mfg. (consumer goods, transportation equip., wood prods., paper prods., tanks and vessels, chemicals). RR junction. A port of entry, it is the center of a tri-city area embracing Peshtigo and Menominee (Mich.). Fur trading began here c.1795 and gave way to lumbering, which flourished until the 1930s. The city was named for a Menominee Native Amer. queen, who established a trading post on the river and built the 1st frame house here. Inc. 1887.

Maringouin (MER-in-gwin), town (1990 pop. 1,149), Iberville parish, SE central La., 19 mi/31 km W of Baton Rouge, on Bayou Maringouin; 30°30′N 91°31′W. Mfg. (lumber). Atchafalaya Natl. Wildlife Refuge to W.

Marinuka, Lake, Wis.: see GALESVILLE.

Marinwood, uninc. town (1990 pop. 5,982), Marin co., W Calif., residential suburb 17 mi/27 km NNW of downtown San Francisco, 2 mi/3.2 km W of San Pablo Bay, on Miller Creek. Lucas valley to W. Hamilton Air Force Base to NE. Big Rock Ridge to N. Statistically reported as Lucas Valley–Marinwood.

Marion 1 (MAR-ee-uhn), county (□ 743 sq mi/1,924 sq km; 1990 pop. 29,830), NW Ala.; ⊙ Hamilton; 34°08′N 87°52′W. Agr. area bordering on Miss. (W), drained by Buttahatchee R., crossed (N-S) by fall line. Corn, soybeans, wheat; poultry. Coal mines; lumber; textiles. Formed 1818. **2** county (□ 640 sq mi/1,658 sq km; 1990 pop. 12,001), N Ark., in the Ozark region; ⊙ Yellville; 36°15′N 92°40′W. Bounded N by Mo. state line; intersected by White R. (site of Bull Shoals Dam in NE), drained by Buffalo R. and small Crooked Creek. Agr. (cattle, hogs, turkeys). Some mfg. at Yellville. Lead, zinc mines; timber. Bull Shoals State Park at dam, large Bull Shoals L. dominates N ¼ of co.; part of Buffalo Natl. R. in SE. Formed 1835. **3** county (□ 1,663 sq mi/4,307 sq km; 1990 pop. 194,833), N central Fla.; ⊙ Ocala; 29°12′N 82°03′W. Flatwoods area with scattered lakes, including Lakes Weir and Kerr; drained by Oklawaha R. Ocala Natl. Forest occupies E part. Agr. (citrus fruit, vegetables, corn, peanuts); livestock raising (cattle, hogs); forestry (lumber, naval stores); and quarrying (limestone, phosphate). Formed 1844. **4** county (□ 368 sq mi/953 sq km; 1990 pop. 5,590), W Ga.; ⊙ Buena Vista; 32°21′N 84°32′W. Drained by Kinchafoone R. Coastal plain agr. (soybeans, wheat, corn, peanuts); cattle, poultry, hogs; timber. Formed 1827. **5** county (□ 575 sq mi/1,489 sq km; 1990 pop. 41,561), S central Ill.; ⊙ Salem; 38°39′N 88°56′W. Largest town is Centralia in SW corner. Oil-producing, and gas area. Agr. (wheat, soybeans, corn, sorghum; cattle, poultry; dairying). Some mfg. (metal prods., plastics prods., machinery, transportation equip., electronic equip., food prods., clothing). Drained by Skillet Fork, Crooked Creek, and East Fork of Kaskaskia R. Formed 1823. Stephen A. Forbes State Park in NE. **6** county (□ 403 sq mi/1,044 sq km; 1990 pop. 797,159), central Ind.; ⊙ INDIANAPOLIS; 39°47′N 86°08′W. Transportation (RR, highway), commercial, market, political, and mfg. center at Indianapolis. Drained by West Fork of White R. and small Eagle, Fall, and Buck creeks. Largely urbanized; some farming (corn, vegetables, soybeans); livestock raising (cattle, hogs); dairying. Eagle Creek (NW) and Geist (NE) reservoirs. Indianapolis Internatl. Airport in W. Fort Benjamin Harrison at Lawrence in NE. On Jan. 1, 1970, Indianapolis consolidated with co. (except for municipalities of Lawrence, Speedway, Southport, and Beech Grove). Indianapolis 500 Speedway (auto race track) at Speedway in W. Formed 1822. **7** county (□ 570 sq mi/1,476 sq km; 1990 pop. 30,001), S central Iowa; ⊙ Knoxville, 41°19′N 93°05′W. Rolling prairie agr. area (hogs, cattle, poultry, sheep; corn) drained by Skunk and Des Moines rivers and by Whitebreast Creek. Many bituminous-coal mines, some limestone quarries. Sunset Ski Area in NE, W of Pella; large Red Rock Reservoir (Des Moines R.) NE of Knoxville where there is a Corps of Engineers recreational area and Elk Rock State Park on N shore. Widespread flooding along rivers in 1993. Formed 1845. **8** county (□ 953 sq mi/2,468 sq km; 1990 pop. 12,888), E central Kansas; ⊙ Marion; 38°24′N 97°09′W. Gently rolling to hilly area, drained by Cottonwood R. Wheat, sorghum, apples; livestock (cattle), poultry. Industrial machinery; food processing; marble and granite. Formed 1860. **9** county (□ 346 sq mi/896 sq km; 1990 pop. 16,499), central Ky.; ⊙ Lebanon, 37°33′N 85°16′W. Drained by Rolling Fork and Beech rivers. Rolling upland agr. area, partly in SW part of Bluegrass region (burley tobacco, corn, hay, alfalfa, soybeans, wheat; hogs, cattle, poultry; dairying); timber; stone quarries. Some mfg. at Lebanon. Formed 1834. **10** county (□ 548 sq mi/1,419 sq km; 1990 pop. 25,544), S Miss.; ⊙ Columbia; 31°13′N 89°49′W. Partly bounded S by La. state line. Drained by Pearl R. Agr. (cotton, corn; cattle; dairying); timber. L. Bill Waller and L. Columbia, state lakes in E. Formed 1811. **11** county (□ 440 sq mi/1,140 sq km; 1990 pop. 27,682), NE Mo.; ⊙ Palmyra; 39°49′N 91°36′W. Bounded E by Mississippi R., drained by North and South Fabius rivers. Corn, wheat, soybeans; dairying; hogs, cattle. Mfg. at Hannibal and Palmyra; limestone. Formed 1826. **12** county (□ 405 sq mi/1,049 sq km; 1990 pop. 64,274), central Ohio; ⊙ Marion, 40°35′N 83°10′W. Intersected by Scioto R.; also drained by Olentangy and Little Scioto rivers and small Tymochtee Creek. Agr. (livestock; dairy prods.; grain); mfg. at Marion (glass and primary metal industries); limestone quarries, sand and gravel pits. Formed 1823. **13** county (□ 1,195 sq mi/3,095 sq km; 1990 pop. 228,483), NW Oregon; ⊙ Salem; 44°54′N 122°34′W. Bounded S by North Santiam R., forms Detroit L. Reservoir in SE (Detroit L. State Park). Bounded N, in part, by Butte Creek. Mfg. (food processing; electronic components, wood prods.). Agr. (fruit, peas, onions, potatoes, mint, wheat, barley; poultry); wineries. Ankeny Natl. Wildlife Refuge in SW; Champoeg and Willamette Mission state parks in NW; Silver Falls State Park in center; North Santiam State Park in S; part of Mt. Hood and Willamette natl. forests in E, including parts of Mt. Jefferson and Bull of the Woods Wilderness Area. Cascade Range in E. Formed 1843. **14** county (□ 494 sq mi/1,279 sq km; 1990 pop. 33,899), E S.C.; ⊙ Marion, 34°05′N 79°26′W. Bounded Great Pee Dee (W) and Little Pee Dee (E) rivers, which join at SE tip of co. Mfg. of sand and clay. Agr. area (tobacco, corn, oats, sorghum, hay; hogs, cattle). Formed 1798. **15** county (□ 507 sq mi/1,313 sq km; 1990 pop. 24,860), SE Tenn.; ⊙ Jasper; 35°08′N 85°37′W. Partly in the Cumberlands; bounded S by Ala. and Ga.; drained by Tennessee and Sequatchie rivers and small Little Sequatchie R. Includes Hales Bar Reservoir. Coal, iron-ore deposits; dairying; livestock raising; some agr. (corn, hay, soybeans, cotton), esp. in the Sequatchie valley. Formed 1817. **16** county (□ 420 sq mi/1,088 sq km; 1990 pop. 9,984), E Texas; ⊙ Jefferson; 32°48′N 94°21′W. Bounded E by La. state line, S in part by Big Cypress Creek and Little Cypress Bayou; drained by Big Cypress Creek, includes part of Caddo L. (hunting, fishing). Timber, oil, natural-gas wells; gravel; lignite. Agr. (peaches, pecans, vegetables, blueberries; horticulture; hay); cattle, horses, hogs, ratites (ostriches, emus, rheas). Most of L. O' the Pines reservoir in W. Formed 1860. **17** county (□ 312 sq mi/808 sq km; 1990 pop.57,249), N W.Va.; ⊙ Fairmont; 39°30′N 80°14′W. On Allegheny Plateau; Tygart and West Fork rivers join at Fairmont in SE to form Monongahela R. Coal mining declined rapidly in the 1990s; gas and oil fields. Aluminum and iron industries. Mfg. at Fairmont. Agr. (corn, alfalfa, hay, apples); cattle, poultry, sheep. Pricketts Fort State Park in NE; part of Valley Falls State Park in SE. Formed 1842

Marion 1 (MAR-ee-uhn), city (1990 pop. 4,211), ⊙ Perry co., W central Ala., 23 mi/37 km NW of Selma, near Cahaba R. Lumber; clothing, cheese; poultry; catfish processing. Seat of Judson Col. and Marion Military Inst. Settled 1817. Talladega Natl. Forest is E and N. U.S. fish hatchery nearby. **2** city (1990 pop. 14,545), ⊙ Williamson co., S Ill.; 37°43′N 88°56′W. Commercial and retail center of a farm and coal area and has a large soft drink-bottling plant. A maximum-security Federal prison is 8 mi/12.8 km S, known as "the new Alcatraz." Robert Ingersoll and John A. Logan lived here. Inc. 1841. **3** city (1990 pop. 32,618), ⊙ Grant co., E central Ind., on the Mississinewa R.; 40°33'N 85°40'W. Trade, processing, and industrial center in a farm area. Mfg. (transportation equip., glassware, paper prods., electronic equip., corn prods., dry ice, fabricated metal prods., machinery, wood prods.; printing). Developed with the discovery of gas and oil in the late 1880s. Seat of Indiana Wesleyan Univ. (formerly Marion Col.); Taylor Univ. is in nearby Upland. Settled 1826, inc. 1889. **4** city (1990 pop. 20,403), Linn co., E central Iowa, adjoining Cedar Rapids; 42°01'N 91°35'W. A chiefly residential city, home construction and concrete mfg. are its main industries. Mfg. also includes furniture, machinery, feeds and fertilizers, plastic prods., electrical prods. Flour and dairy prods. are also processed here. Airfield to E; Squaw Creek Regional Park to S. Inc. 1865. **5** city (1990 pop. 34,075), ⊙ Marion co., central Ohio; 40°35'N 83°07'W. A RR, industrial, and agr. center noted for production of major machinery, consumer goods. Limestone quarries in the area. Home of President Warren G. Harding; his house is preserved as a mus., and his burial place is marked by a circular marble monument. A branch of Ohio State Univ. is here. Appliance mfg. Inc. 1830.

Marion 1 (MAR-ee-uhn), town (1990 pop. 4,391), ⊙ Crittenden co., E Ark., 12 mi/19 km WNW of Memphis (Tenn.); 35°12'N 90°12'W. In cotton-and rice-growing area. Mfg. (bldg. materials, wood prods.). **2** town (1990 pop. 1,906), ⊙ Marion co., E central Kansas, on Cottonwood R., and 45 mi/72 km NNE of Wichita; 38°21'N 97°01'W. RR junction. Shipping center for grain and livestock area; food processing. Co. fair takes place here annually in Oct. Damaged by flood of July 1951. Marion L. Reservoir to NW. Co. mus. Settled 1860, laid out 1866, inc. 1875. **3** town (1990 pop. 3,320), ⊙ Crittenden co., W Ky., 34 mi/55 km ENE of Paducah, on Crooked Creek; 37°19'N 88°04'W. In oak-timber and agr. (corn, burley tobacco, oats, wheat; dairying) area. Mfg. (industrial ceramics, plastic prods., bldg. materials, electrical equip.); limestone quarrying and crushing, lumber milling. Co. mus., Clement Mineral Mus. Free ferry crosses Ohio R. to Cave-In-Rock (Ill.), 10 mi/16 km to NNW. Amish community to N, est. 1977. Inc. 1844. **4** town (1990 pop. 4,496), Plymouth co., SE Mass., on W shore of Buzzards Bay, and 10 mi/16 km NE of New Bedford; 41°42'N 70°45'W. Resort. Formerly shipbuilding. Settled 1679, set off from Rochester 1852. **5** uninc. town (1990 pop. 1,359), Lauderdale co., E Miss., residential suburb 5 mi/8 km NE of Meridian; 32°25'N 88°39'W. Cotton, corn; cattle, hogs; light mfg. **6** town (1990 pop. 4,765), ⊙ McDowell co., W N.C., 31 mi/50 km ENE of Asheville, in the Blue Ridge Mts., near Catawba R., forms lake; 35°40'N 82°00'W. James reservoir to NE; L. James State Park to NE. RR junction. Agr. (corn, soybeans; poultry; dairying); mfg. (medical supplies, lumber and paper prods., electronics equip., machinery, transportation equip., tools, apparel, textiles, furniture; food processing); timber; stone quarrying. Linville Caverns are N; Pisgah Natl. Forest and L. Tahoma reservoir to NW. **7** uninc. town (1990 pop. c.1,000), Franklin co., S Pa., 5 mi/8 km SSW of Chambersburg; 40°38'N 77°16'W. Light mfg. Agr. includes dairying; livestock, poultry; grain, potatoes, apples. **8** town (1990 pop. 7,658), ⊙ Marion co., E S.C., 20 mi/32 km E of Florence; 34°10'N 79°24'W. Trade center in agr. area (livestock; grain, tobacco, cotton, sorghum.). Mfg. (transportation equip., textiles, apparel, millwork, ceramic tile, foods). **9** town (1990 pop. 831), Turner co., SE S.Dak., 7 mi/11.3 km WNW of Parker; 43°25'N 97°15'W. Hosp. and clinic for persons suffering with bone disorders are here. Mfg. (feeds, machinery). **10** town (1990 pop. 984), Guadalupe co., S central Texas, 24 mi/39 km NE of San Antonio, and on Guadalupe R.; 29°34'N 98°08'W. In agr. area (peanuts, cotton; poultry). Mfg. (machinery). **11** town (1990 pop. 6,630), ⊙ Smyth co., SW Va., 38 mi/61 km NE of Bristol, near South Fork of Holston R., bet. Walker Mt. (N) and Iron Mts. (S); 36°50'N 81°30'W. Mfg. (machining, printing and publishing; beverages, wood prods., furniture, transportation equip., consumer goods, apparel). Agr. area (tobacco, grain; livestock; dairying); limestone quarrying. Hungry Mother State Park to N; Mt. Rogers, highest point in Va. (5,729 ft/1,746 m) 12 mi/19 km to S, within Mt. Rogers Natl. Recreation Area (part of Jefferson Natl. Forest). Inc. 1832. **12** town (1990 pop. 1,242), Waupaca and Shawano cos., E central Wis., on small Pigeon R., and c.40 mi/64 km WNW of Green Bay; 44°40'N 88°53'W. In timber, dairy, and grain area. Dairy prods.; mfg. (wood prods., foods, chemicals, transportation equip.). Settled 1878; inc. as village in 1898, as city in 1939.

Marion 1 (MER-ee-uhn), village (1990 pop. 775), Union parish, N La., 29 mi/47 km NNW of Monroe; 32°54'N 92°14'W. In agr. area (cotton); lumbering; sawmill; pulpwood. Upper Ouachita Natl. Wildlife Refuge to E, Union State Wildlife Area to W. **2** village (1990 pop. 807), Osceola co., central Mich., 16 mi/26 km SE of Cadillac; 44°06'N 85°09'W. In farm area. Mfg. (light mfg.). **3** village (1990 pop. 1,100), Wayne co., W N.Y., 20 mi/32 km E of Rochester; 43°09'N 77°12'W. In fruit-growing region. **4** village (1990 pop. 169), La Moure co., SE central N.Dak., 18 mi/29 km N of La Moure; 46°36'N 98°19'W. RR terminus.

Marion Center, borough (1990 pop. 476), Indiana co., W central Pa., 11 mi/18 km NNE of Indiana; 40°46'N 79°02'W. Agr. area (grain, soybeans; dairying; livestock); light mfg.; subsurface bituminous coal.

Marion Heights, borough (1990 pop. 837), Northumberland co., E central Pa., 1 mi/1.6 km N of Kulpmont; 40°47'N 76°28'W. Agr. (corn, hay; poultry); anthracite coal.

Marion, Lake, reservoir (□ 156 sq mi/404 sq km), on border bet. Berkeley (N) and Clarendon and Calhoun (S) cos., E central S.C., on Santee R., 25 mi/40 km NNW of Charleston; 33°28'N 80°09'W. Largest lake in S.C. Max. capacity 1,230,000 acre-ft. Connected to L. Moultrie on SE. Formed by Santee Dam (50 ft/15 m high), built (1942) for power generation; owned by S.C. Public Service Authority. Santee Natl. Wildlife Refuge on N shore, Santee State Park on W shore.

Marion, Mount (9,750 ft/2,972 m), SE B.C., W Canada, in Selkirk Mts., 55 mi/89 km N of Nelson; 50°17'N 117°13'W.

Marion Station, village, Somerset co., SE Md., on the Eastern Shore, near Big Annemessex R., 25 mi/40 km SSW of Salisbury. Named for a daughter of the developer, John C. Horsey, it was the self-proclaimed strawberry capital of the world until the 1920s when growing centers shifted to the West Coast.

Marionville, city (1990 pop. 1,920), Lawrence co., SW Mo., in the Ozark Mts., 24 mi/39 km SW of Springfield; 37°00'N 93°38'W. Apples, berries, peaches, vegetables; cattle; dairying. Mfg. (wood prods., apparel, magnetic coils). Laid out 1854.

Mariposa, county (□ 1,451 sq mi/3,758 sq km; 1990 pop. 14,302), central Calif.; ⊙ Mariposa; 37°35'N 119°55'W. On W slope of the Sierra Nevada, at S end of Mother Lode gold country; has peaks over 10,000 ft/3,050 m in NE. Part of Yosemite Natl. Park in NE. Also includes parts of Sierra and Stanislaus natl. forests NW-SE through center. Drained by Merced R. (forms McClure Reservoir) in W, Chowchilla R. forms part of S border. Includes Merced and Mariposa groves of the big trees *Sequoia gigantea.* Region famed for scenery and recreational resources (resorts; hunting, lake and stream fishing, camping, hiking, winter sports). A leading gold-mining co. (quartz mines) of Calif. Timber (pine, fir, spruce). Livetock raising (some cattle, sheep, hogs, poultry); little farming. Sand and gravel pits; silver mining. Mariposa, Hornitos, Coulterville, and ruins of old gold camps are reminders of gold rush. Badger Pass Ski Area in Yosemite Natl. Park. Formed 1850.

Mariposa, uninc. town (1990 pop. 1,152), ⊙ Mariposa co., central Calif., 32 mi/51 km NE of Merced; 37°30'N 119°58'W. Cattle; mfg. (electronic components). Gateway to Yosemite Natl. Park and Sierra Natl Forest (NE). Airport nearby. An old gold rush town; its courthouse (1854) is said to be oldest in state. Stanislaus Natl. Forest to N; L. McClure reservoir to W.

Mariposa Grove, Calif.: see YOSEMITE NATIONAL PARK.

Mariposa Monarca Ecological Reserve (mah-ree-PO-sah mo-NAHR-kah), a biological reserve in E Michoacán, Mexico, 3.7 mi/6 km S of the village of Angangueo, near El Rosario. Ths is the winter grounds for a migrant species of monarch butterfly (*Danaus plexipus*). Some 100 million butterflies make a c.5,000-mi/8,000-km trip from Canada and the U.S. to stay 3 months in this area. Logging and pollution threaten survival of these insects.

Mariscala de Juárez (mah-rees-KAH-lah dai HWAH-rez), town (1990 pop. 1,659), in far NW Oaxaca, Mexico, 25 mi/40 km W of Huajuapam de Peón. Elev. 3,675 ft/1,120 m. Mountainous terrain on the Mixteco R. Temperate to hot climate. Agr. (corn, beans, sugarcane, chilies), straw textiles. Cattle. Connected by unpaved road to Huajuapam de León.

Marissa, village (1990 pop. 2,375), St. Clair co., SW Ill., 24 mi/39 km SE of Belleville; 38°15'N 89°45'W. Stone and wood prods.; bituminous-coal mines; agr. (corn, wheat; dairy prods.; poultry, livestock). Inc. 1882.

Maritime Provinces, E Canada, term applied to NOVA SCOTIA, NEW BRUNSWICK, and PRINCE EDWARD ISLAND, which before the formation of the Can. confederation (1867) were politically distinct from Canada proper.

Mark, village (1990 pop. 391), Putnam co., N central Ill., 5 mi/8 km SSW of Spring Valley; 41°15'N 89°15'W. In agr. area (corn, wheat, barley; cattle); mushroom processing.

Mark Twain Lake, reservoir (□ 13 sq mi/34 sq km), Ralls co., NE Mo., on Salt R., 48 mi/77 km NE of Columbia; 39°32'N 91°38'W. Max. capacity 1,861,889 acre-ft. Formed by Clarence Cannon Dam, built (1984) by Army Corps of Engineers for flood control; also used for power generation and recreation. Mark Twain State Park and Mark Twain State Historical Site near center of reservoir.

Markagunt Plateau, Kane co., SW Utah, high tableland (rising to 11,307 ft/3,446 m in Brian Head peak) in Iron, Garfield, and Kane cos., E of Cedar City. Bounded E by Paunsaugunt Plateau, S by Pink Cliffs. Covered by a unit of Dixie Natl. Forest; includes Cedar Breaks Natl. Monument in SW.

Markdale, village (1991 pop. 1,370), S Ont., central Canada, on Rocky Saugeen R., and 22 mi/35 km SE of Owen Sound; 44°19'N 80°39'W. Dairying; woodworking, lumbering; mfg. (frozen foods, footwear); in mixed farming area.

Marked Tree, town (1990 pop. 3,100), Poinsett co., NE Ark., on St. Francis R., at mouth of Little R., and 26 mi/42 km SE of Jonesboro; 35°31'N 90°25'W. In agr. area (cotton, corn). Mfg. (industrial storage tanks, furniture, machinery, leather prods.). St. Francis Sunken Lands Wildlife Management Area to N. Settled c.1870.

Markesan (MAHRK-i-san), town (1990 pop. 1,496), Green Lake co., central Wis., on Grand R., and 28 mi/45 km WSW of Fond du Lac; 43°42'N 88°59'W. In farming, dairying, and livestock-raising region. Mfg. (canned vegetables, fabricated metal prods.). RR terminus.

Markham, city (1990 pop. 13,136), Cook co., NE Ill., suburb 19 mi/31 km SSW of downtown Chicago; 41°36'N 87°41'W. Mfg. (bldg. materials, industrial brushes, wood prods.). Native prairie preserved at Indian Boundaries Prairies. Inc. 1925.

Markham, town (1991 pop. 153,811), S Ont., central Canada, on Rouge R., and 15 mi/24 km NNE of Toronto; 43°52'N 79°16'W. Suburban community. High technology industries; mfg. (chemicals, medical supplies, transportation equip., machinery, ordnance, computers, motor vehicles, frozen foods, paper goods, furniture, apparel, flour), book publishing, printing.

Markham (MAHRK-uhm), village, Creek co., central Okla., 10 mi/16 km NE of Cushing.

Markland, village, SE N.F., E Canada, in central part of

Avalon Peninsula, 40 mi/64 km WSW of St. John's. Scene of agr. resettlement scheme, begun 1934, for unemployed.

Markle, town (1990 pop. 1,208), in Huntington and Wells cos., NE central Ind., on the Wabash R., and 9 mi/14.5 km SE of Huntington; 40°50′N 85°20′W. Mfg. (machinery, fabricated metal prods.).

Markleeville, uninc. village (1990 pop. 500), ⊙ Alpine co., E Calif., 18 mi/29 km SSE of South Lake Tahoe, on East Fork Carson R., in the Sierras, 32 mi/51 km S of Carson City (Nev.). Mineral springs (Grover Hot Springs State Park) to NW. Hunting, fishing in region. Kirkwood Ski Area to W; Toiyabe Natl. Forest to W, S, and E; Pacific Crest Trail to W.

Marklesburg (MAHR-kuhls-buhrg), borough (1990 pop. 165), Huntingdon co., S central Pa., 11 mi/18 km SW of Huntingdon; 40°22′N 78°10′W. Agr. (corn, hay; dairying). Post office is James Creek.

Markleville, town (1990 pop. 412), Madison co., E central Ind., 9 mi/14.5 km SE of Anderson; 39°59′N 85°37′W. Agr. area. Mfg. (bldg. materials, wood prods.). Laid out 1852.

Markleysburg (MAHR-klees-buhrg), borough (1990 pop. 320), Fayette co., SW Pa., 18 mi/29 km SE of Uniontown, 1 mi/1.6 km N of Md. state line, and 2 mi/3.2 km NE of corner of W.Va. state line; 39°44′N 79°27′W. Agr. (dairying); mfg. (concrete). In area are Youghiogheny R. L. (E) and L. Courage (W) reservoirs.

Marks, town (1990 pop. 1,758), ⊙ Quitman co., NW Miss., 18 mi/29 km ENE of Clarksdale, and on Coldwater R.; 34°15′N 90°16′W. Trade center in rich agr. area (soybeans, cotton, corn); mfg. (apparel, electrical equip.; soybean processing). O'Keefe Wildlife Management Area to SE. Inc. 1906.

Marksville, city (1990 pop. 5,526), ⊙ Avoyelles parish, E central La., 24 mi/39 km SE of Alexandria, near Red R.; 31°08′N 92°04′W. In agr. area (cotton, corn, sugarcane, soybeans, sweet potatoes); food processing, mfg. (apparel, foods); logging. Fort De Russey, site of Civil War fighting, nearby. Marksville State Commemorative Area (covers 43 acres/17 ha), with Native Amer. mounds dating to 140 B.C., is here. Spring Bayou State Wildlife Area to E, with L. Ophelia (NE) and Grand Cote (W) natl. wildlife refuges in area. Near giant casino on land owned by Tunica, Native Biloxi tribe in Avoyelles parish. Settled in late 18th cent. by Acadians.

Marland (MAHR-land), village (1990 pop. 280), Noble co., N Okla., 10 mi/16 km SSW of Ponca City; 36°33′N 97°09′W. In oil- and natural-gas-producing area.

Marlboro, county (☐ 485 sq mi/1,256 sq km; 1990 pop. 29,361), NE S.C., on N.C. (N and NE) state line; ⊙ Bennettsville; 34°36′N 79°40′W. Bounded SW by Great Pee Dee R. Mfg. of sand, gravel, clay. Mainly agr., including hogs; corn, rye, oats, tobacco, soybeans, hay, cotton, vegetables; some timber. Mfg. at Bennettsville. Formed 1785.

Marlboro (MAHRL-buh-ro), town (1990 pop. 924), Windham co., SE Vt., 8 mi/12.9 km W of Brattleboro; 42°53′N 72°44′W. Lumber. Seat of Marlboro Col. Annual summer music festival.

Marlboro, village (1990 pop. 2,200), Ulster co., SE N.Y., on W bank of the Hudson R., and 7 mi/11.3 km N of Newburgh; 41°36′N 73°58′W. Mfg. (bldg. materials, dairy and canned foods, beverages); agr. (vegetables, grapes, tree fruit). Also spelled Marlborough.

Marlboro (MAWRL-buh-ruh), township (1990 pop. 27,974), Monmouth co., E N.J., 4 mi/6.4 km N of Freehold; 40°20′N 74°15′W. In suburbanizing agr. area. Marlboro State Hosp. nearby.

Marlborough, city (1990 pop. 31,813), Middlesex co., E Mass.; 42°21′N 71°33′W. Shoe-mfg. center for many years; mfg. also includes plastic and paper prods., consumer goods, machinery, computer equip., processed foods, and chemicals. Growing site of suburban office activity. Skiing at Jericho Hill. Almost destroyed (1676) in King Philip's War. Settled on the site of a Native Amer. village 1657, inc. as a city 1890.

Marlborough 1 (MAHRL-buh-ro), town (1990 pop. 5,535), Hartford co., central Conn., 15 mi/24 km SE of Hartford; 41°38′N 72°27′W. In rural area that mainly is a residential community. Has 18th-cent. tavern. **2** town (1990 pop. 1,949), St. Louis co., E Mo., 10 mi/16 km SW of downtown St. Louis; 38°34′N 90°20′W. Residential and commercial suburb of St. Louis. Watson Road (old Route 66) runs length of town; known for its old motels, restaurants, and drive-in theatres. **3** town (1990 pop. 1,927), Cheshire co., SW N.H., 4 mi/6.4 km ESE of Keene; 42°53′N 72°10′W. Drained by Minnewawa Brook. Agr. (cattle, poultry; vegetables, nursery crops; dairying); mfg. (plastics, consumer goods, other light mfg.). Inc. 1776.

Marlette (mahr-LET), town (1990 pop. 1,924), Sanilac co., E Mich., 21 mi/34 km N of Imlay; 43°19′N 83°04′W. In farm area (grain, sugar beets, apples; livestock; dairy prods.). Mfg. (bldg. materials, hose clamps, transportation equip.); grain elevator. Inc. 1881.

Marlin, town (1990 pop. 6,386), ⊙ Falls co., E central Texas, near Brazos R., 23 mi/37 km SE of Waco; 31°18′N 96°53′W. Elev. 383 ft/117 m. Health resort (mineral springs); trade center for agr. area (cotton, corn; cattle). Hot artesian wells discovered 1890s. Est. 1830s.

Marlinton (MAHR-lin-tuhn), town (1990 pop. 1,148), ⊙ Pocahontas co., E W.Va., on Greenbrier R., 50 mi/80 km S of Elkins, within W edge of Monongahela Natl. Forest; 38°13′N 80°5′W. Mfg. (lumber, wood prods.). Agr. (grain, apples); livestock, poultry; timber. Summer resort in hunting area. Greenbrier R. State Trail passes through town; Watoga State Park to S; Seneca State Forest to NE; Edray State Fish Hatchery to N. Settled 1747 as Marlin's Bottom, 1st settlement W of Allegheny Mts.

Marlow 1 (MAHR-lo), town (1990 pop. 650), Cheshire co., SW N.H., 13 mi/21 km NNE of Keene; 43°07′N 72°12′W. Drained by Ashuelot R. Agr. (cattle, sheep, poultry; vegetables, apples; dairying; nursery crops). Mfg. (electronic equip.). **2** town (1990 pop. 4,416), Stephens co., S Okla., 10 mi/16 km N of Duncan; 34°38′N 97°57′W. In agr. area (corn, watermelons, peanuts; cattle; mfg. (medical supplies, meat prods.). Settled 1892.

Marlton, village (1990 pop. 10,228), Burlington co., W N.J., 11 mi/18 km E of Camden; 39°53′N 74°55′W. Has Baptist church (1805). Largely residential.

Mar-Mac (MAHR–mak), uninc. town (1990 pop. 3,282), Wayne co., E central N.C., residential suburb 6 mi/9.7 km SSW of downtown Goldsboro, near Neuse R.; 35°19′N 78°03′W.

Marmaduke (MAHR-muh-dook), town (1990 pop. 1,164), Greene co., NE Ark., 10 mi/16 km NE of Paragould, near St. Francis R.; 36°11′N 90°23′W. In agr. area. Mfg. (plastic prods.).

Marmarth (MAHR-muhth), village (1990 pop. 144), Slope co., SW N.Dak., 26 mi/42 km WNW of Bowman, near Mont. state line, on Little Missouri R., in Little Missouri Natl. Grassland; 46°17′N 103°55′W. Ships livestock; wheat, hay. Fort Dilts Historic Site to E.

Marmaton River (MAHR-muh-tuhn), 73 mi/117 km long, including longest fork, SE Kansas and Mo.; rises in E Allen co. (Kansas), NE of Moran; flows S then E, past Fort Scott, to Little Osage R. 7 mi/11.3 km SSE of Rich Hill (Mo.).

Marmelade (mahr-muh-LAHD), town (1982 pop. 1,419), Artibonite dept., N Haiti, in Massif du Nord, 20 mi/32 km SSW of Cap-Haïtien; 19°31′N 72°21′W. Fruits; coffee growing.

Marmet (mahr-MET), town (1990 pop. 1,879), Kanawha co., W central W.Va., on Kanawha R., 9 mi/14.5 km SSE of Charleston; 38°15′N 81°34′W. Coal-mining region. Agr. (corn, tobacco); cattle, poultry. Mfg. (chemicals). Kanawha State Forest to W. Inc. 1921.

Marmion Lake (MAHR-mee-uhn), W Ont., central Canada, 30 mi/48 km W of Lac des Milles Lacs, 110 mi/177 km WNW of Thunder Bay; 14 mi/23 km long, 6 mi/10 km wide; 48°54′N 91°30′W. Elev. 1,363 ft/415 m. Drained S by Seine R.

Marmora (MAHR-muh-ruh), village (1991 pop. 1,538), SE Ont., central Canada, 27 mi/43 km NW of Belleville; 44°29′N 77°41′W. In mining area (gold, iron, marble); stellite refining, lumber milling.

Marmot Peak (11,735 ft/3,577 m), in Rocky Mts., Chaffee and Park cos., central Colo., 7 mi/11.3 km N of Buena Vista.

Marne, town (1990 pop. 149), Cass co., SW Iowa, 6 mi/9.7 km NW of Atlantic; 41°27′N 95°06′W.

Maroa (mah-RO-ah), city (1990 pop. 1,602), Macon co., central Ill., 12 mi/19 km N of Decatur; 40°02′N 88°57′W. In agr. area (corn, soybeans).

Maroon Peak (14,156 ft/4,315 m), in Elk Mts., Pitkin and Gunnison cos., W central Colo., 12 mi/19 km SW of Aspen. One of 3 peaks, collectively called the Maroon Bells, SW of Maroon L., among the most photographed areas of Colo. In Maroon Bells Snowman Wilderness Area.

Maroon Town, town (1991 pop. 2,669), St. James parish, NW Jamaica, in the Cockpit Country, 14 mi/23 km SE of Montego Bay; 18°21′N 77°49′W. Here the Maroon leader Cudjoe signed a peace treaty with the British in 1739 and was given 1,500 acres/607 ha, which they named "Trelawny Town." Later rebellious maroons made their last stand (1795). Formerly Trelawny Town.

Marquand (MAHR-kwahnd), town (1990 pop. 278), Madison co., SE Mo., in the St. Francois Mts., on Castor R., and 11 mi/18 km SE of Fredericktown; 37°25′N 90°10′W. Cattle; timber. Surrounded by Mark Twain Natl. Forest.

Marqués, Villa de, Mexico: see LA CAÑADA.

Marquette 1 (mahr-KET), county (☐ 3,426 sq mi/8,873 sq km; 1990 pop. 70,887), NW Upper Peninsula, NW Mich., on L. Superior (N); 46°39′N 87°35′W; ⊙ Marquette. Bordered S and SW by Menominee, Dickinson and Iron City cos. and Central time zone (co. in Eastern time zone). Drained by Dead and Michigamme rivers, and by several branches of Escanaba R. Includes the Marquette Iron Range and Huron Mts. Some mining; lumbering; food processing. Mfg. at Marquette. Cattle; forage, potatoes. Resorts (fishing, hunting, camping). A natl. experimental forest, fish hatchery and several lakes are in co. Small sub-unit of Ottawa Natl. Forest on E border; Van Ripen State Park in W; Huron Mts. Wilderness in NW; Moose Range Cliffs Ridge Ski Area in NE. Nearby K.I. Soyer Air Force Base was closed in 1995 and there is an ongoing attempt to redevelop its facilities into commercial and industrial services. Organized 1851. **2** county (☐ 464 sq mi/1,202 sq km; 1990 pop. 12,321), S central Wis.; ⊙ Montello; 43°49′N 89°23′W. Agr. (corn, soybeans; hogs, sheep); mfg. (processing of dairy prods.); granite quarries. Drained by Fox R. and its tributaries; includes Buffalo L. at center of co.; several small lakes in N. Westfield State Fish Hatchery in W. Formed 1836.

Marquette (mahr-KET), city (1990 pop. 21,977), ⊙ Marquette co., N Mich., Upper Peninsula, 140 mi/225 km W of Sault Sainte Marie, on L. Superior; 46°32′N 87°24′W. Once an iron ore shipping port, it is now a shipping center for a lumber, cattle, and resort region. RR spur terminus (ship/RR transfer). Mfg. includes chemicals, wood prods., and mining machinery, dairy and bakery prods.; publishing. Ore Docks handle 7 million tons/6.4 million metric tons of iron ore annually. Seat of Northern Mich. Univ. (has Olympic Training Center). Marquette Co. Airport to W. A branch of the state prison is also here. Maritime Mus. Cliffs Ridge Ski Area to S. Settled 1849, inc. as a city 1871.

Marquette, town (1990 pop. 479), Clayton co., NE Iowa, on Mississippi R. (bridged here), opposite Prairie du Chien (Wis.), and 13 mi/21 km NE of Elkader; 43°02′N 91°10′W. Asphalt plant equip.; storage silos. Upper Mississippi Natl. Wildlife Refuge; Effigy Mounds Natl. Monument 3 mi/4.8 km N; Yellow R. State Forest 10 mi/16 km N.

Marquette 1 (mahr-KET), village (1990 pop. 593), McPherson co., central Kansas, on Smoky Hill R., and 23 mi/37 km SSW of Salina; 38°33′N 97°49′W. Grain milling. **2** village (1990 pop. 211), Hamilton co., SE central Nebr., 9 mi/14.5 km N of Aurora, near Platte R.; 41°00′N 98°00′W. Mfg. (foods).

Marquette Heights, city (1990 pop. 3,077), Tazewell co., central Ill., residential suburb 5 mi/8 km S of downtown Peoria, and S of Creve Coeur, near Illinois R.; 40°37′N 89°35′W.

Marquette Iron Range (mahr-KET), NW Upper Peninsula, NW Mich., low range in Marquette co., lying generally W of Marquette. Once a rich iron-mining region with mining center at Ishpeming and Negaunee. Natl. Mine still active with 7,000,000 tons/ 7,714,000 metric tons shipped out of Marquette annually. Also known as Marquette Range. Mich. Iron Industry Mus. here.

Marquette Island, Mich.: see LES CHENEAUX ISLANDS.

Marquette Range, Mich.: see MARQUETTE IRON RANGE.

Marquez, village (1990 pop. 270), Leon co., E central Texas, 40 mi/64 km N of Bryan, near Navasota R. (forms L. Limestone to NW); 31°14′N 96°15′W. RR junction to SW. Agr. area.

Marrero (MER-ER-o), uninc. city (1990 pop. 36,671), Jefferson parish, SE La., on the Mississippi R., suburb opposite New Orleans, 3 mi/5 km SSW of downtown; 29°54′N 90°07′W. Mfg. (machinery, bldg. materials). Bayou Segnette State Park to SW.

Marrowbone, uninc. village (1990 pop. 300), Cumberland co., S Ky., 7 mi/11.3 km WNW of Burkesville, on Marrowbone Creek. Burley tobacco, corn; cattle; diarying. Mfg. (apparel).

Mars, borough (1990 pop. 1,713), Butler co., W Pa., 16 mi/ 26 km N of Pittsburgh, on Breakneck Creek; 40°42′N 80°00′W. Agr. (corn, hay, apples; livestock; dairying). Mfg. (consumer goods, fabricated metal prods., bldg. materials, machinery; steel fabrication). Inc. 1882.

Mars Hill 1 agr. town (1990 pop. 1,760), Aroostook co., E Maine, 27 mi/43 km N of Houlton, and on Presque Isle R., near Can. (N.B.) border; 46°33′N 67°50′W. Ships potatoes. Takes name from Mars Hill (1,550 ft/ 472 m), 2 mi/3.2 km E. Includes Mars Hill village. **2** town (1990 pop. 1,611), Madison co., W N.C., 16 mi/ 26 km N of Asheville; 35°49′N 82°32′W. In agr. area (tobacco, corn; cattle). Mfg. (electrical prods., apparel). Seat of Mars Hill Col. (4-year). Parts of Pisgah Natl. Forest to N and E.

Marseilles (mahr-SAILZ), city (1990 pop. 4,811), La Salle co., N Ill., on Illinois R. (water power), and 8 mi/ 12.9 km E of Ottawa; 41°19′N 88°41′W. Mfg. (bldg. materials, food prods., chemicals). Marseilles Canal carries Illinois Waterway shipping around rapids in Illinois R. here. Illini State Park and Marseilles Natl. Guard Training Area are nearby. Inc. 1861.

Marseilles, village (1990 pop. 130), Wyandot co., N central Ohio, 12 mi/19 km ENE of Kenton; 40°42′N 83°23′W.

Marsh Harbour, town, N Bahama Isls., on E central shore of Great Abaco Isl., 5 mi/8 km W of Hope Town; 26°33′N 77°04′W. Lumbering; fishing.

Marsh Island, low marshy island, Iberia parish, S La., 25 mi/40 km S of New Iberia, bet. Gulf of Mexico (S) and Vermilion, West Cote Blanche, and East Cote Blanche bays (NW, N, and E); 21 mi/34 km long, 2 mi/ 3 km–10 mi/16 km wide; 29°33′N 91°50′W. Southwest Pass separates isl. and mainland on W. Several small lakes, including Ferme, Oyster (S), and Sand (E). Entire isl. comprises Russell Sage Natl. Wildlife Refuge.

Marsh Lake, reservoir, Minnesota R., Lac qui Parle, Swift and Big Stone cos., W Minn., 13 mi/21 km ESE of Ortonville; 7.5 mi/12.1 km long, 2 mi/3.2 km wide. Elev. 938 ft/286 m. Created by dam at SE end. In Lac qui Parle Wildlife Area. Nearby are Lac qui Parle (SE) and Big Stone (NW) reservoirs.

Marsh Peak (12,240 ft/3,731 m), Uinta Mts., NW Uintah co., Utah, in Ashley Natl. Forest, 22 mi/35 km NNW of Vernal. Highest point in E part of range.

Marshall 1 county (□ 623 sq mi/1,614 sq km; 1990 pop. 70,832), NE Ala.; ⊙ Guntersville, 34°23′N 86°20′W. Bounded N by Paint Rock R. Agr. area (poultry, cattle; corn, soybeans, hay); textiles. Wheeler and Guntersville reservoirs are on Tennessee R. Formed 1836. **2** county (□ 398 sq mi/1,031 sq km; 1990 pop. 12,846), N central Ill.; ⊙ Lacon; 41°02′N 89°22′W. Agr. (corn, wheat, soybeans, fruit; livestock). Some mfg. (food prods., books, chemicals, clothing). Drained by Illinois R. and small Sandy Creek. Formed 1839. Includes Goose and Billsbach lakes. Southernmost co. to span Illinois R. **3** county (□ 449 sq mi/1,163 sq km; 1990 pop. 42,182), N Ind.; ⊙ Plymouth; 41°20′N 86°16′W. Agr. area (grain, soybeans, oats, vegetables, fruit; dairy prods.; cattle, poultry, hogs), esp. noted for vegetable and mint growing; processing of spearmint and peppermint oil. Several lakes, glacial in origin, concentrated in SW part of co., some with resorts; largest is L. Maxinkuckie near Culver. Drained by Yellow and Tippecanoe rivers. Formed 1835. **4** county (□ 573 sq mi/1,484 sq km; 1990 pop. 38,276), central Iowa; ⊙ Marshalltown, 42°02′N 93°00′W. Prairie agr. area (cattle, hogs, poultry; corn, oats) drained by Iowa and North Skunk rivers. Bituminous-coal deposits (W), limestone quarries (E). Mfg. at Marshalltown. Formed 1846. **5** county (□ 904 sq mi/2,341 sq km; 1990 pop. 11,705), NE Kansas, on Nebr. (N) state line; ⊙ Marysville; 39°48′N 96°33′W. Gently rolling to hilly area; drained by Big Blue, Black Vermillion, and Little Blue rivers. Wheat, sorghum, strawberries, soybeans; hogs, cattle. Transportation equip.; gypsum prods. N extremity of Tuttle Creek Reservoir in S. Formed 1855. **6** county (□ 340 sq mi/ 881 sq km; 1990 pop. 27,205), W Ky.; ⊙ Benton; 36°52′N 88°21′W. Bounded N and E by Tennessee R., forms Kentucky L. reservoir on E (Kentucky Dam); drained by East and West forks of Clarks R. Agr. area (corn, dark and burley tobacco, alfalfa, hay, soybeans, wheat, corn; hogs, cattle); timber; clay pits. Mfg. at Benton and Calvert City. Includes Kentucky Dam State Resort Park in NE. Formed 1842. **7** county (□ 1,812 sq mi/ 4,693 sq km; 1990 pop. 10,993), NW Minn., on Red R. (W; N.Dak. state line); ⊙ Warren; 48°21′N 96°22′W. Drained by Snake, Thief, Tamarac, and Middle rivers. Agr. area (wheat, oats, flax, hay, alfalfa, sugar beets, beans, sunflowers, potatoes; poultry, cattle, sheep); timber. Thief L. Wildlife Area in NE; Agassiz Natl. Wildlife Refuge, surrounds Mud L., in E center; Old Mill State Park in center. Formed 1879. **8** county (□ 709 sq mi/1,836 sq km; 1990 pop. 30,361), N Miss., on Tenn. (N) state line, and on Tallahatchie R. (S); ⊙ Holly Springs; 34°46′N 89°30′W. Drained by Coldwater R. Hilly agr. area (cotton, corn, hay, soybeans, wheat; cattle; dairying); clay prods.; processing of farm prods. Includes part of Holly Springs Natl. Forest in SE; Wall Doxey State Park in S center. Formed 1836. **9** county (□ 426 sq mi/1,103 sq km; 1990 pop. 10,829), S Okla.; ⊙ Madill; 34°01′N 96°46′W. Bounded E and S by L. Texoma, formed by Denison Dam in Red R., and E by Washita Arm of L. Texoma. Cattle-raising, recreation, and agr. area (corn, pecans, barley); tourism. Includes L. Texoma State Park in SE; part of Tishomingo Natl. Wildlife Refuge in NE. Formed 1907. **10** county (□ 885 sq mi/2,292 sq km; 1990 pop. 4,844), NE S.Dak., on N.Dak. (N) state line; ⊙ Britton; 45°46′N 97°36′W. Rich farming and cattle-raising region, with numerous lakes. Corn, wheat, flax, hay; dairy produce; poultry. Fort Sisseton, historic military outpost, and part of L. Traverse (Sisseton Wahpeton) Indian Reservation in E. Sica Hollow (?is)& Roy L. State Parks and Clear L. State Lakeside Use Area in E. Formed 1885. **11** county (□ 377; 1990 pop. 21,539), central Tenn.; ⊙ Lewisburg; 35°28′N 86°46′W. Drained by Duck R. and its tributaries. Agr. (livestock; dairy prods.; fruit, hay, grain, tobacco); timber; some mfg. Formed 1836. **12** county (□ 312 sq mi/808 sq km; 1990 pop. 37,356), N W.Va., southernmost co. of N Panhandle, on Ohio R. (W; Ohio state line) and on Pa. (E) state line; ⊙ Moundsville; 39°52′N 80°40′W. Drained by small Wheeling, Fish, and Grave creeks. Industrial area; mfg. at Moundsville, Cameron, and Benwood is based on region's coal, natural gas, oil, glass-sand, clay, and timber. Some agr. (honey, corn, potatoes, alfalfa, hay, nursery crops); cattle, hogs, sheep, poultry. Grave Creek Mound State Park in W; Burches Run Wildlife Management Area in NE. Formed 1835.

Marshall 1 city (1990 pop. 3,555), ⊙ Clark co., E Ill., 16 mi/26 km WSW of Terre Haute (Ind.); 39°23′N 87°41′W. In agr. area; oil wells. Inc. 1853. On historic Natl. Road. **2** city (1990 pop. 12,023), ⊙ Lyon co., SW Minn., 87 mi/140 km WNW of Mankato, on Redwood R.; 44°27′N 95°47′W. Elev. 1,174 ft/358 m. Trade and shipping center for agr. area (grain; livestock, poultry; dairying); mfg. (honey and beeswax, bldg. materials, lumber, corn prods., feed supplements, electronic prods., foods and beverages; printing and publishing, custom welding). Municipal Airport to W. Camden State Park to SW. Settled 1871, plotted 1872, inc. 1901. **3** city (1990 pop. 12,711), ⊙ Saline co., N central Mo.; 39°06′N 93°12′W. RR junction. Grain-, egg-, and meat-processing center of a large farm area (corn, wheat, oats, soybeans; hogs, poultry). Mfg. (frozen foods, animal fats, gloves, egg prods., bldg. materials). Seat of Missouri Valley Col. Nearby are Van Meter (NW) and Arrow Rock (SW) state parks. Inc. 1839. **4** city (1990 pop. 23,682), ⊙ Harrison co., E Texas, 23 mi/37 km E of Longview, and 35 mi/56 km W of Shreveport (La.). Elev. 375 ft/114 m. In a pine-covered hill and lake area. Oak-shaded streets and mansions recall the plantation past of the city, which has since declined economically. RR junction. Mfg. (stoneware pottery, ceramic tiles, consumer goods, wood prods., chemicals). Seat of East Texas Baptist Col., Texas State Technical Col. and Wiley Univ. L. O' the Pines reservoir to NW, Caddo L. reservoir and State Park to NE; Ginocchio Natl. Historic Dist., 3-block area, Starr Mansion State Historic Site. Inc. 1844.

Marshall 1 town (1990 pop. 1,318), ⊙ Searcy co., N Ark., 34 mi/55 km SE of Harrison, in the Ozark Mts.; 35°54′N 92°38′W. Mfg. (lumber, apparel). Buffalo Natl. River to N. **2** town (1990 pop. 379), Parke co., W Ind., 6 mi/ 9.7 km NNE of Rockville; 39°51′N 87°11′W. Agr. area; mfg. (plastic prods.). Tourist area around Turkey Run State Park to N; canoeing on Sugar Creek. Covered bridges in area. Laid out 1878. **3** town (1990 pop. 6,891), ⊙ Calhoun co., S Mich., 12 mi/19 km SE of Battle Creek, and on Kalamazoo R.; 42°15′N 57°84′W. In farm area (livestock, poultry; grain). Mfg. (plastic prods., transportation equip., foods, fabricated metal prods., chemicals); vehicle-component testing lab. Historical homes. Settled 1831; inc. as village 1836, as city 1859. **4** town (1990 pop. 809), ⊙ Madison co., W N.C., 15 mi/ 24 km NNW of Asheville, on French Broad R.; 35°47′N 82°40′W In agr. area (corn, burley tobacco; cattle). Mfg. (fabricated metal prods., electrical prods., apparel). Pisgah Natl. Forest to NW. Settled 1816; inc. 1952. **5** town (1990 pop. 2.329), Dane co., S Wis., on small Waterloo Creek, and 17 mi/27 km ENE of Madison; 43°10′N 89°03′W. Farm area. Dairy prods.; feed mill; mfg. (construction; pet foods).

Marshall 1 village (1990 pop. 273), W Alaska, on Yukon R., and 75 mi/121 km N of Bethel; 61°52′N 162°03′W. Placer gold mining. Scene of gold rush, 1913. Also called Fortuna Ledge. **2** or **New Marshall**, village (1990 pop. 288), Logan co., central Okla., 22 mi/35 km NW of Guthrie; 36°09′N 97°37′W. In agr. area. **3** uninc. village, Fauquier co., N Va., 10 mi/16 km N of Warrenton. Mfg. (clothing); in agr. area (grain, soybeans, apples; livestock). Nearby is "Oak Hill" (1773), home of John Marshall.

Marshall Hall, excursion resort, Charles co., S Md., on the Potomac R., c.16 mi/26 km below Washington, D.C. An amusement park is located on an estate granted to William Marshall in 1690. The Marshall Hall House, containing period furniture, dates from the Colonial era when George Washington was a frequent visitor. Cruise ships from Washington, D.C. stop here daily most of the year and at Mt. Vernon on the other side of the river. A jousting (Md. state sport) tournament is held here every Aug., as knights on horseback try to spear suspended rings.

Marshall Island, Maine: see SWANS ISLAND.

Marshall Pass, Colo.: see SAWATCH MOUNTAINS.

Marshallton 1 uninc. town (1990 pop. 1,765), New Castle co., N Del., residential suburb 5 mi/8 km W of Wilmington, on White Clay Creek; 39°44′N 75°38′W. Del. Park Horse Race Track to SW. **2** uninc. town (1990 pop. 1,482), Northumberland co., E central Pa., residential suburb 1 mi/1.6 km E of Shamokin, near Shamokin Creek; 40°47′N 76°31′W.

Marshalltown, city (1990 pop. 25,178), ⊙ Marshall co., central Iowa, on the Iowa R.; 42°02′N 92°54′W. RR junction. RR and trade center of a rich grain and livestock area as well as a busy mfg. city. Mfg. (plastic prods., rubber prods., paints, machinery, fabricated metal prods., seeds, shipping containers, furnaces, canned goods; pork processing). The Iowa Veterans' Home and Marshalltown Community Col. are here; Union Grove State Park is to the NE. Inc. 1863.

Marshallville 1 town (1990 pop. 1,457), Macon co., W central Ga., 7 mi/11.3 km SSW of Fort Valley; 32°27'N 83°56'W. In a peach-growing area. **2** town (1990 pop. 1,457), Macon co., Ga., 13 mi/21 km W of Perry; 32°28'N 83°56'W.

Marshallville, village (1990 pop. 758), Wayne co., N central Ohio, 13 mi/21 km NE of Wooster; 40°54'N 81°44'W. In agr. area; meat prods.

Marshes Siding, uninc. town (1990 pop. 800), McCreary co., S Ky., 2 mi/3.2 km N of Whitley City. Timber; tobacco; cattle. Area surrounded by Daniel Boone Natl. Forest. Big South Fork Natl. R. and Recreation Area to SW.

Marshfield 1 city (1990 pop. 4,374), ⊙ Webster co., S central Mo., in the Ozark Mts., 22 mi/35 km ENE of Springfield; 37°20'N 92°54'W. Cattle; dairying; hay, wheat, fruit. Mfg. (apparel, machinery, caskets). Settled c.1830. **2** city (1990 pop. 19,291), Wood and Marathon cos., central Wis.; 44°39'N 90°10'W. In a dairy area. Mfg. (food and beverages, machinery, furniture, fabricated metal prods., apparel, hydraulic cylinders, bldg. materials). Has agr. research station. Inc. 1883.

Marshfield 1 town (1990 pop. 21,531), Plymouth co., SE Mass., on the Atlantic coast, 9 mi. NNW of Plymouth; 42°07'N 70°43'W. Sand and gravel are chief prods., also electronic prods. Resort. Has several colonial bldgs. Daniel Webster lived and is buried here. Includes villages of Brant Park, Green Harbor, Humarock, Marshfield Hills, Ocean Bluff, Sea View. Settled 1632, inc. 1640. **2** town (1990 pop. 1,331), including Marshfield village, Washington co., central Vt., on Winooski R., 15 mi/24 km NE of Montpelier; 44°18'N 72°22'W. Includes part of Plainfield village.

Marshfield or **Base Station**, Coos co., N central N.H., valley station at W end of 3-mi/4.8-km-long Mt. Washington cog RR, 15 mi/24 km SSW of Berlin; completed 1869 (1st of its kind in the world).

Marshfield oregon: see COOS BAY.

Marshfield Hills, Mass.: see MARSHFIELD.

Marshville, town (1990 pop. 2,020), Union co., S N.C., 10 mi/16 km E of Monroe; 34°59'N 80°22'W. Timber; cotton, grain; poultry, livestock; dairying. Mfg. (wood prods., textiles; turkey processing).

Marshyhope Creek, c.40 mi/64 km long, W central Del. and E Md.; rises in swamps in SW central Kent co. (Del.), 10 mi/16 km SW of Dover; flows generally SSW, into Md, past Federalsburg (head of navigation), and through Dorchester co., turns to SE to the Nanticoke R. 2 mi/3.2 km below SW of Sharpstown. Formerly called Northwest Fork of Nanticoke R.

Marsing, town (1990 pop. 798), Owyhee co., SW Idaho, on Snake R., and 30 mi/48 km W of Boise, near Deer Flat Reservoir; 43°33'N 116°49'W. RR terminus and trading point in agr. area (potatoes, grain; livestock). Served by Owyhee project. L. Lowell reservoir, surrounded by Deer Flat Natl. Wildlife Refuge, to E; Jump Creek Canyon to SW, Squaw Creek Canyon to S.

Marsland, village (1990 pop. 10), Dawes co., NW Nebr., 30 mi/48 km SSW of Chadron, and on Niobrara R.; 42°26'N 103°17'W. Box Butte Reservoir State Recreation Area to E.

Marston, city (1990 pop. 691), New Madrid co., in the bootheel of extreme SE Mo., near Mississippi R., 7 mi/11.3 km SW of New Madrid; 36°31'N 89°36'W. Soybeans, rice, cotton; rice milling.

Marstons Mills, Mass.: see BARNSTABLE.

Mart, town (1990 pop. 2,004), McLennan co., E central Texas, 17 mi/27 km E of Waco; 31°32'N 96°49'W. Cotton, corn; dairying; cattle, hogs. Tradinghouse Creek Reservoir to W. Settled 1875, inc. 1903.

Martell, uninc. village, Amador co., central Calif., 2 mi/3.2 km NW of Jackson, near Jackson Creek, in 1849 Calif. Gold Rush region. Logging; walnuts, grapes, grain; cattle.

Martelle, town (1990 pop. 290), Jones co., E Iowa, 16 mi/26 km E of Cedar Rapids; 42°01'N 91°21'W. Soybean prods.

Martensdale, town (1990 pop. 491), Warren co., S central Iowa, 6 mi/9.7 km W of Indianola; 41°22'N 93°44'W.

Martha, village (1990 pop. 217), Jackson co., SW Okla., 7 mi/11.3 km NNW of Altus, near the Salt Fork of Red R.; 34°43'N 99°23'W. In cotton and grain area.

Martha Brae River, c 20 mi/32 km long, Trelawny parish, N Jamaica; rises in N Cockpit Country; flows E and N to the Caribbean Sea at Falmouth, for which it supplies water; 18°28'N 77°38'W. The village of Martha Brae is 2 mi/3.2 km S of Falmouth.

Martha's Vineyard, island (□ c.100 sq mi/260 sq km; 1990 est. pop. 8,850), Dukes co., SE Mass., separated from the Elizabeth Isls. and Cape Cod by Vineyard and Nantucket sounds. As a result of glaciation, the isl. has morainal hills composed of boulders and clay deposits in the N, and low, sandy plains in the S. The English were the 1st Europeans to settle here (1642); they engaged in farming, brickmaking, salt production, and fishing. Martha's Vineyard became an important commercial center, with whaling and fishing as the main occupations, in the 18th and early 19th cents. In the late 1800s the isl., with its harbors, beaches, and scenic attractions, developed into a summer resort. Ferry service from Woods Hole, Falmouth, and Hyannis; Dukes Co. Airport. Divided into the towns of Chilmark, Edgartown (to which Chappaquiddick Isl. is connected), Gay Head, Oak Bluffs, Tisbury, and West Tisbury. Much of the isl.'s interior is set aside as a state forest. Edgartown is the largest harbor and site of annual Edgartown Regatta. Gay Head glacial clay cliffs are most famous physical feature. Summer homes of many famous people include the late Jacqueline Kennedy Onassis. State beach and park.

Marthasville, town (1990 pop. 674), Warren co., E central Mo., near Missouri R., 6 mi/9.7 km NW of Washington; 38°37'N 91°02'W. Grain; livestock. Electronic prods., paper prods. Original Daniel and Rebecca Boone graves 2 mi/3.2 km to E. Area of Ger. settlement beginning 1830s.

Marthaville (MAHR-thuh-vil), uninc. town (1990 pop. 932), Natchitoches parish, NW central La., 18 mi/29 km W of Natchitoches; 31°44'N 93°23'W. In agr. area; cotton gins, sawmills. In area are Rebel (NW) and Los Adaes (E) state commemorative areas.

Martí 1 (mahr-TEE), town, Camagüey prov., E Cuba, on Central Highway, and 33 mi/53 km ESE of Camagüey; 21°10'N 77°27'W. RR junction in sugarcane region. **2** town, Matanzas prov., W Cuba, on RR, and 17 mi/27 km ESE of Cárdenas; 22°56'N 80°55'W. In agr. region (sugarcane, oranges, sisal). Asphalt deposits and mineral springs in vicinity. Nearby is the sugar mill of Esteban Hernández (WNW). Formerly called Lacret.

Martin 1 county (□ 752 sq mi/1,948 sq km; 1990 pop. 100,900), E central Fla., bet. L. Okeechobee (W) and the Atlantic Ocean (E), and partly sheltered E by Jupiter Isl. (barrier beach); ⊙ Stuart; 27°04'N 80°24'W. Lowland area, with swamps and many small lakes in W; crossed by St. Lucie Canal. Produce and citrus-fruit region, with some cattle raising and fishing. Formed 1925. **2** county (□ 340 sq mi/881 sq km; 1990 pop. 10,369), SW Ind.; ⊙ Shoals; 38°43'N 86°48'W. Drained by Lost R. and East Fork of White R. Agr. (corn, hay; cattle, hogs); gypsum, limestone; timber. Mfg. at Loogootee, Shoals. Hoosier Natl. Forest in SE quarter; Hindostan Falls State Fishing Area in SW. Martin State Forest in E. Crane Naval Weapons Support Center (including Greenwood L. reservoir) in N ¼ of co. Formed 1820. **3** county (□ 230 sq mi/596 sq km; 1990 pop. 12,526), E Ky., in the Cumberland Mts.; ⊙ Inez; 37°47'N 82°31'W. Bounded E by Tug Fork of Big Sandy R. (W.Va. state line); drained by several creeks. Mt. agr. area (livestock; tobacco); bituminous-coal mines. Formed 1870. **4** county (□ 729 sq mi/1,888 sq km; 1990 pop. 22,914), S Minn., on Iowa (S) state line; ⊙ Fairmont; 43°40'N 94°33'W. Watered by numerous lakes, most in 4 distinct groupings, including Middle Chain of Lakes and East Chain of Lakes, also in S center (including Okamanpedan L. on Iowa state line), and chain of lakes in NW. Agr. area (corn, oats, soybeans, alfalfa; hogs, sheep, cattle). Formed 1857. **5** county (□ 462 sq mi/1,197 sq km; 1990 pop. 25,078), E N.C.; ⊙ Williamston; 35°50'N 77°05'W. Coastal plain; bounded N by Roanoke R. Agr. area (corn, wheat, oats, soybeans, cotton, peanuts, tobacco; chickens, hogs); timber (pine, gum). Fishing, tobacco, and peanut processing. Fort Branch Battlefield State Historical Site in NW. Formed 1774. **6** county (□ 915 sq mi/2,370 sq km; 1990 pop. 4,956), W Texas; ⊙ Stanton; 32°17'N 101°57'W. On S Llano Estacado, with E-facing Caprock escarpment in NW; elev. 2,600 ft/790 m–3,000 ft/915 m. Cattle-ranching area; also hogs, sheep, goats; some agr. (grains, sorghum). Some oil and gas production. Formed 1876.

Martin, city (1990 pop. 8,600), Weakley co., NW Tenn., 13 mi/21 km ESE of Union City; 36°21'N 88°51'W. Trade center for timber and agr. area. Makes consumer goods, wood prods., apparel. Univ. of Tenn. branch campus here. Founded 1873.

Martin, town (1990 pop. 1,151), ⊙ Bennett co., S S.Dak., 90 mi/145 km SE of Rapid City; 43°10'N 101°43'W. Trading point for farm and livestock region; wheat, flax; honey; feeds. Lacreek L. and Natl. Wildlife Refuge to E. Pine Ridge Indian Reservation to N&W; Rosebud Indian Reservation to E (both in neighboring cos.). Founded 1912, inc. 1926.

Martin 1 village (1990 pop. 243), Stephens co., NE Ga., 9 mi/14.5 km SE of Toccoa, near S.C. state line; 34°29'N 83°11'W. **2** village (1990 pop. 694), Floyd co., E Ky., in Cumberland foothills, 15 mi/24 km WNW of Pikeville, on Beaver Creek; 37°34'N 82°45'W. In bituminous-coal area; mfg. (machinery, electrical prods.). One of 2 places so named in Ky. **3** village (1990 pop. 545), Red River parish, NW La., 36 mi/58 km SW of Shreveport, near Black L. Bayou; 32°06'N 93°13'W. In agr. area (cotton, soybeans, vegetables; cattle); timber. **4** village (1990 pop. 462), Allegan co., SW Mich., 11 mi/18 km E of Allegan; 42°32'N 85°38'W. Mfg. (plastic prods.). **5** village (1990 pop. 117), Sheridan co., central N.Dak., 10 mi/16 km NW of Harvey; 47°49'N 100°06'W.

Martin Bay, N Lab., E Canada, arm of Labrador Sea, 255 mi/410 km NNW of Nain. Site of unmanned Nazi weather station located on SE lobe of Hutton Peninsula. On Oct. 22, 1943, crew of U-Boat 537 landed and set up station. It remained operational for 2 weeks before signal was jammed.

Martin Bluff, uninc. town (1990 pop. 1,928), Jackson co., SE Miss., residential suburb 10 mi/16 km NNW of Pascagoula, on Pascagoula R.; 30°27'N 88°38'W. Cotton, corn, fruit. Miss. Sandhill Crane Natl. Wildlife Refuge to SW; Ward Bayou Wildlife Management Area to N.

Martin City, village (1990 pop. 400), Flathead co., NW Mont., 18 mi/29 km NE of Kalispell, and 1 mi/1.6 km E of Hungry Horse. Tourism. Timber. Area surrounded by Flathead Natl. Forest; Flathead Range to E, Swan Range to SW, Glacier Natl. Park to NE; Hungry Horse Reservation to SE.

Martin, Lake (□ c.62 sq mi/161 sq km), Tallapoosa co., E Ala., on Tallapoosa R., 30 mi/48 km NE of Montgomery; average width 5 mi/8 km; 32°40'N 85°54'W. Large and irregular-shaped. Formed by Martin Dam (168 ft/51 m high, 2,000 ft/610 m long; completed 1927), used for hydroelectric power and river control. Wind Creek State Park on W shore.

Martin Luther King Jr. Historic Site, Atlanta, N Ga.; 33°45'N 84°22'W. The site is run by the Natl. Park Service and is located on Auburn Ave. in downtown Atlanta. Dr. King was born, reared, and buried here. The MLK center contains Dr. King's gravesite, his church (the Ebenezer Baptist Church), Dr. King's boyhood home, Freedom Hall, the Martin Luther King, Jr. Center for Nonviolent Social Change, and a visitors center. Authorized 1980.

Martin Point, NE Alaska, near Canada (Yukon) border,

cape on Beaufort Sea, 10 mi/16 km E of Barter Isl.; 70°08′N 143°12′W.

Martin River, 25 mi/40 km long, S Alaska; rises in Martin R. Glacier at 60°29′N 144°19′W; flows SW to Gulf of Alaska E of Cordova.

Martin Siding, village, S Ont., central Canada, in Muskoka lakes region, 35 mi/56 km E of Parry Sound. Diatomite mining.

Martin Van Buren National Historic Site, home of the 8th U.S. president, Columbia co., SE N.Y., 9 mi/14.5 km NE of Hudson, and 2 mi/3.2 km S of Kinderhook, on Kinderhook Creek; 42°22′N 73°42′W. Legend has it that Van Buren 1st used the abbreviation O.K. ("Old Kinderhook") to indicate approval of paperwork. Authorized 1974.

Martindale, town (1990 pop. 904), Caldwell co., S central Texas, 6 mi/9.7 km ESE of San Marcos, on San Marcos R.; 29°50′N 97°50′W. Oil and natural gas. Agr. area (turkeys; eggs; cotton, sorghum, corn).

Martinez, city (1990 pop. 31,808), ⊙ Contra Costa co., W Calif., suburb 12 mi/19 km NNE of downtown Oakland, on Carquinez Strait (Benicia-Martinez Bridge) bet. San Pablo and Suisun bays; 38°00′N 122°07′W. RR junction. In a farm area. Its major industry is petroleum refining; also machinery, consumer goods, construction materials, steel. Seat of John F. Kennedy Univ. Home of the naturalist John Muir; John Muir Natl. Historic Site in S. Part of the Central Valley project is nearby. Inc. 1884.

Martinez (mahr-teen-EZ), suburb (1990 pop. 33,731), on border bet. Columbia and Richmond cos., Ga., 33°30′N 82°04′W. Fast-growing suburb of Augusta. Commercial center. Mfg. (bldg. materials, textiles); granite and marble processing, steel fabricating.

Martínez de la Torre (mahr-TEE-nes dai lah TO-rai), city (1990 pop. 37,092) and township, Veracruz, E Mexico, in Gulf lowland, 33 mi/53 km SE of Papantla de Olarte; 20°05′N 97°02′W. Corn, sugarcane, coffee.

Martinique (mahr-tee-NEEK), overseas department and administrative region (☐ 425 sq mi/1,101 sq km; 1990 est. pop. 349,000), of France, in the Windward Isls., West Indies, coextensive with the isl. of Martinique; ⊙ FORT-DE-FRANCE 14°40′N 61°00′W. Of volcanic origin, the isl. is rugged and mountainous and reaches its greatest ht. in Pelée volcano. Most agr. exists in the hot valleys and along the coastal strips; about 80% of this area is devoted to sugarcane, which was introduced from Brazil in 1654 and which provides Martinique's major export, rum. The isl.'s industries consist mainly of sugar and rum production, pineapple canning, and petroleum refining. Tourism constitutes a major sector of the economy. Visited by Columbus, probably in 1502, the isl. was ignored by the Spanish; colonization began in 1635, when the French, who had promised the native Caribs the W ½ of the isl., established a settlement. The French proceeded to eliminate the Caribs and later imported Afr. slaves as sugar plantation workers. In the 18th cent. Martinique's sugar exports made it one of France's most valuable colonies; although slavery was abolished in 1848, sugar continued to hold a dominant position in the economy. A target of dispute during the Anglo-Fr. worldwide colonial struggles, Martinique was finally confirmed as a Fr. possession after the Napoleonic wars. Martinique supported the Vichy regime after France's collapse in World War II, but in 1943 a U.S. naval blockade forced the isl. to transfer its allegiance to the Free French. It became a dept. of France in 1946 and an administrative region in 1974. Although the isl. has recovered from the extensive damage caused by a hurricane in 1980, France has continued its attempts to improve the economic life of Martinique, which is plagued by overpopulation and a lack of development.

Martinique Passage, channel in the Windward Isls., West Indies, bet. Dominica (N) and Martinique (S); c.25 mi/40 km wide.

Martins Creek, uninc. town (1990 pop. 1,200), Lower Mt. Bethel township, Northampton co., E Pa., 6 mi/9.7 km N of Easton, on Martins Creek (1 mi/1.6 km N of its mouth on Delaware R.); 40°47′N 75°11′W. Agr. (corn, hay, potatoes, soybeans, apples; livestock; dairying). Mfg. (flour, textiles). Franklin Hill Winery to N.

Martins Ferry, city (1990 pop. 7,990), Belmont co., E Ohio, on the Ohio R., opposite Wheeling (W.Va.); 40°06′N 80°43′W. Formerly an industrial coal-mining and steel-mfg. city. The novelist William Dean Howells was b. here. In Walnut Grove Cemetery are the graves of Elizabeth (Betty) and Ebenezer Zanec. Settled 1780, inc. as a city 1885.

Martins Location, land grant, Coos co., N central N.H., 9 mi/14.5 km S of Berlin, in White Mt. Natl. Forest. Drained by Peabody R.

Martinsburg, city (1990 pop. 14,073), ⊙ Berkeley co., NE W.Va., in the E Panhandle; 39°27′N 77°58′W. RR center in agr. region (apples, peaches). Mfg. (bldg. materials, glassware, textiles, fiberglass, fabricated metal prods., ceramics, wood prods., modular homes, transportation equip., ordnance; printing and publishing). Limestone is quarried nearby. During the Civil War, the city's strategic location on the RR made it a frequent military objective. Belle Boyd, the Confederate spy, lived here and was imprisoned in the old courthouse. Sleepy Creek Wildlife Management Area to W. Settled 1732, inc. as a city 1859.

Martinsburg 1 town (1990 pop. 157), Keokuk co., SE Iowa, 11 mi/18 km S of Sigourney; 41°10′N 92°15′W. Livestock; grain. **2** town (1990 pop. 337), Audrain co., NE central Mo., 13 mi/21 km ESE of Mexico; 39°06′N 91°39′W. Grain; livestock; lumber.

Martinsburg 1 village (1990 pop. 90), Dixon co., NE Nebr., 7 mi/11.3 km WSW of Ponca, 42°30′N 96°49′W. **2** village (1990 pop. 213), Knox co., central Ohio, 11 mi/18 km SE of Mount Vernon; 40°16′N 82°21′W.

Martinsburg, borough (1990 pop. 2,119), Blair co., S central Pa., 13 mi/21 km SSE of Altoona; 40°18′N 78°19′W. RR terminus. Agr. (dairying; livestock; corn, hay, apples). Mfg. (leather prods., food prods.). Altoona Blair Co. Airport to S. Settled c.1793, laid out 1815, inc. 1832.

Martinsdale, village (1990 pop. 70), Meagher co., central Mont., on South Fork 3 mi/4.8 km SW of confluence with North Fork (forming Musselshell R.), and 30 mi/48 km ESE of White Sulphur Springs. Sheep, cattle, poultry; hay. Mfg (pottery). Martinsdale Reservoir to E; parts of Lewis and Clark Natl. Forest to N, S, and NW.

Martinsville 1 city (1990 pop. 1,161), Clark co., E Ill., 12 mi/19 km WSW of Marshall; 39°20′N 87°52′W. Agr. (corn, apples); oil wells; foundry, oil-storage and -pumping station. Plotted 1833, inc. 1875. On historic Natl. Road. **2** city (1990 pop. 11,677), ⊙ Morgan co., central Ind., on West Fork of White R., and 28 mi/45 km SSW of Indianapolis; 39°25′N 86°25′W. In grain-growing area. Mfg. (electronic prods., wood prods., furniture); timber; sand and gravel. Artesian springs. Settled 1822. **3** independent city (☐ 11 sq mi/28 sq km; 1990 pop. 16,162), ⊙ surrounding Henry co., S Va., separate from surrounding Henry co., in Blue Ridge foothills near N.C. state line, 27 mi/43 km WNW of Danville, on Smith R.; 36°40′N 79°51′W. RR junction. Mfg. (furniture, prefabricated homes, textiles, clothing, bldg. materials, wood prods., machinery, plastic prods., chemicals, wood prods., consumer goods, transportation equip.; tobacco processing). Patrick Henry Community Col. to N. Va. Mus. of Natural History. Philpott Reservoir and Fairy Stone State Park to NW; Martinsville Speedway to S. Founded 1793, inc. as a city 1928.

Martinsville 1 village (1990 pop. 476), Clinton co., SW Ohio, 33 mi/53 km ENE of Cincinnati; 39°19′N 83°49′W. **2** uninc. rural community, Harrison co., NW Mo., 8 mi/12.9 km NW of Bethany.

Martinton, village (1990 pop. 299), Iroquois co., E Ill., 10 mi/16 km N of Watseka; 40°55′N 87°43′W. In agr. area (corn, soybeans, sorghum; cattle, hogs).

Mártir de Cuilapan, Mexico: see APANGO.

Mártires de Tacubaya (MAHR-tee-res dai tah-koo-BAH-yah), town (1990 pop. 1,659), in far NW Oaxaca, Mexico, on the border of the state of Guerrero, on unpaved road 11 mi/18 km ENE of Cuajinicuilapa (Guerrero). Hot climate. Agr. (corn, coffee, sugarcane, beans, fruits), woods.

Martre, Lac la (MAHR-truh, lahk lah), lake (☐ 840 sq mi/2,176 sq km), S central Mackenzie dist., N.W.T., N Canada, 100 mi/161 km WNW of Yellowknife; 50 mi/80 km long, 12 mi/19 km–28 mi/45 km wide; 63°20′N 118°W. Drains SE into Great Slave L.

Martwick, uninc. village, Muhlenberg co., W Ky., 5 mi/8 km NE of Central City. In bituminous-coal-mining and agr. area.

Marvel, village, Bibb co., central Ala., c.17 mi/27 km NE of Centreville.

Marvell, town (1990 pop. 1,545), Phillips co., E Ark., 18 mi/29 km W of Helena; 34°33′N 90°54′W. In agr. area.

Marvin, village (1990 pop. 38), Grant co., NE S.Dak., 14 mi/23 km W of Milbank; 45°15′N 96°54′W. L. Traverse (Sisseton Wahpeton) Indian Reservation to W.

Marvin, Lake, Hemphill co., extreme N Texas, impounded by dam in a small N tributary of Canadian R., 11 mi/18 km E of town of Canadian; c.1 mi/1.6 km long. Fishing, hunting in area.

Marvine, Mount, highest peak (11,610 ft/3,539 m) in Fish L. Mts., S Sevier co., S central Utah, 25 mi/40 km ESE of Richfield.

Marwayne, village (1991 pop. 484), E Alta., W Canada, near Sask. border, near Vermilion R., 24 mi/39 km NE of Vermilion; 53°31′N 110°20′W. Dairying; grain; livestock.

Mary Alice, village, Harlan co., SE Ky., 3 mi/4.8 km S of Harlan, in the Cumberland Mts. Bituminous coal.

Mary Esther, town (☐ 1 sq mi/2.6 sq km; 1990 pop. 4,139), Okaloosa co., NW Fla., on the Gulf of Mexico, 32 mi/51 km E of Pensacola; 30°24′N 86°39′W.

Mary Island, SE Alaska, in Gravina Isls., in Revillagigedo Channel, 25 mi/40 km SE of Ketchikan; 4 mi/6.4 km long, 2 mi/3.2 km wide; 55°05′N 131°12′W.

Mary Island, N.Y.: see WELLESLEY ISLAND.

Mary, Lake, S Douglas co., W Minn., 5 mi/8 km SW of Alexandria; 4 mi/6.4 km long, 1.5 mi/2.4 km wide; 45°49′N 95°28′W. Fishing resorts. Andrew L. to E.

Mary McLeod Bethune Council House Historic Site, Wash., D.C. Home and political hq. of the educator and activist. The carriage house contains the Bethune Archives. Authorized 1982.

Marydel, town (1990 pop. 143), Caroline co., E Md., on Del. state line, 12 mi/19 km WSW of Dover (Del.); 39°07′N 75°45′W. Named for its position on the state line. Scene of a duel (Jan. 3, 1877) bet. James Gordon Bennett, owner of The N.Y. *Herald*, and Frederick May, a well-known explorer, over May's broken engagement to Bennett's sister. Both men missed, and, subsequently, Bennett exiled himself to Paris.

Maryfield, agr. village (1991 pop. 408), SE Sask., W Canada, on Man. border, 22 mi/35 km SSE of Moosomin; 49°50′N 101°32′W. RR junction.

Maryknoll, locality (1990 pop. 600), Westchester co., SE N.Y., near Ossining. Catholic Foreign Mission Society of Amer. trains missionaries (the Maryknoll Fathers) here. Seat of Maryknoll School of Theology, a graduate-level institution with distinctive degree programs in Justice and Peace, and in Mission Ministry.

Maryland, state (☐ 12,406 sq mi/32,132 sq km; 1995 est. pop. 5,042,438), E U.S., in the Middle Atlantic region, 1 of the original 13 Colonies; ⊙ ANNAPOLIS 38°59′N 76°34′W. BALTIMORE, with a large percentage of the state's pop., is the dominant metropolis. A seaboard state, E Md. is divided by Chesapeake Bay, which runs almost to the N border, separating the Eastern Shore from the main part of the state. Bounded N by Pa. (see MASON-DIXON LINE) and E by Del. and the Atlantic Ocean. For the most part, the erratic course of the Potomac R. separates the main part of Md. from Va. (to the S) and the long, narrow W handle from W.Va. (to the S and W). The Potomac R. lies entirely within Md., as the state line with Va. on the S shore. The D.C. cuts a rectangular indentation into the state just below the falls of the Potomac. The main part of the state is divided by the fall line, which runs bet. the upper end of Chesapeake Bay and Wash., D.C.; to the N and W is the rolling Piedmont, rising to the Blue Ridge and to the Pa. hills. The heavily indented shores of Chesapeake

Bay fringe the land with bays and estuaries, which helped in the development of a farm economy relying on water transport. In the mild winters and hot summers of the coastal plains typically Southern trees, such as the loblolly pine and the magnolia, flourish, while the cooler uplands have woods of black and white oak and beech. Md. has nearly 3 million acres/1.2 million ha of forest land. Chesapeake Bay dominates the E sect. of the state. Although the fishing industry is declining, the catch of fish and shellfish from Chesapeake Bay yields an annual income in the millions of dollars, and the state's annual catch of crabs is the largest in the nation. The coastal marshes abound in wild fowl. In the W part of Md. are the mineral resources of bldg. stone and coal, which have declined significantly. The iron mines, active in the 19th cent., have declined along with other mining activity. Important industries include mfg. of primary metals, food prods., missiles, transportation equip., clothing, and electrical machinery. Shipping (Baltimore is a major port), tourism (esp. along Chesapeake Bay), and printing and publishing are also big industries. Services are the largest sector of the economy, ahead of finance, insurance, and real estate, all of which have surpassed govt. work and mfg. Although mfg. well exceeds agr. as a source of income, Md.'s, farms yield corn, hay, tobacco, soybeans, and other crops. Income from livestock, esp. cattle and chickens, and livestock prods., is almost twice that from crops; dairy and poultry farms thrive, and Md. is famous for breeding horses. Giovanni da Verrazano, an Ital. navigator in the service of France, probably visited (1524) the Chesapeake region, which was certainly later explored (1574) by Pedro Menéndez Marqués, governor of Span. Fla. In 1603 the region was visited by an Englishman, Bartholomew Gilbert, and it was charted (1608) by Capt. John Smith. In 1632, Charles I granted a charter to George Calvert, the 1st Baron Baltimore, yielding him feudal rights to the region bet. lat. 40°00'N and the Potomac R. Disagreement over the boundaries of the grant led to a long series of border disputes with Va. The territory was named "Maryland" in honor of Henrietta Maria, queen consort of Charles I. Before the great seal was affixed to the charter, George Calvert died, but his son Cecilius Calvert, the 2d Baron Baltimore, undertook development of the colony as a haven for his persecuted fellow Catholics and also as a source of income. In 1634 the ships *Ark* and *Dove* brought settlers (both Catholic and Protestant) to the Western Shore, and a settlement called St. Mary's was set up. The Algonquian-speaking Native Americans withdrew gradually and for the most part peacefully from the area during the colonial period, sparing Md. the conflicts other colonies experienced. Religious conflict, however, was strong in ensuing years as the Puritans, growing more numerous in the colony and supported by Puritans in England, set out to destroy the religious freedom guaranteed with the founding of the colony. The next cent. saw the emergence of commercially oriented Baltimore, which by 1800 had a pop. of over 30,000 and a flourishing coastal trade. Tobacco became the basis of the economy by 1730. In 1767 the demarcation of the Mason-Dixon Line ended a long-standing border dispute with Pa. Economic and religious grievances led Md. to support the growing colonial agitation against England. At the time of the Amer. Revolution most Marylanders were stalwart patriots and vigorous opponents of the Br. colonial policy. In 1776, Md. adopted a declaration of rights and a state constitution and sent soldiers and supplies to aid the war for independence. At Annapolis Congress ratified the Treaty of Paris ending the Revolutionary War in 1783. In 1791 Md. and Va. contributed land and money for the new natl. capital. Industry, already growing in conjunction with renewed commerce, was furthered by the skills of Ger. immigrants. The War of 1812 was marked by the Br. attack of 1814 on Baltimore and the defense of Fort McHenry, immortalized in Francis Scott Key's "The Star-Spangled Banner." After the war the state entered a period of great commercial and industrial expansion. This was accelerated by the building of the Natl. Road, which tapped the rich resources of the West; the opening of the Chesapeake and Delaware Canal (1829); and the opening (1830) of the Baltimore and Ohio RR, the 1st RR in the U.S. open for public traffic. Southern ways and sympathies persisted, however, among the plantation owners, and as the rift bet. North and South widened, Md. was torn by conflicting interests and the intense internal struggle of the true border state. In 1860 there were 87,000 slaves in Md., but industrialists and businessmen had special interests in adhering to the Union; and despite the urgings of Southern sympathizers, the state remained in the Union. At the beginning of the Civil War, President Lincoln suspended habeas corpus and sent troops to Md. who imprisoned large numbers of secessionists. Nevertheless, Marylanders fought on both sides, and families were often split. Gen. Lee's Army of Northern Va. invaded Md. in 1862 and was repulsed by Union forces at Antietam. In 1863, Lee again invaded the North and marched across Md. on the way to and from Gettysburg. Throughout the war, Md. was the scene of many minor battles and skirmishes. With the end of the Civil War, industry was quickly revived and became a dominant force, economically and politically. New RR lines traversed the state, making it more than ever a crossing point bet. North and South. Labor troubles hit Md. with the Panic of 1873, and 4 years later RR wage disputes resulted in large-scale rioting in Cumberland and Baltimore. During the 20th cent., however, Md. became a leader in labor and other reform legislation. The great influx of pop. into the state during World War I was repeated and accelerated in World War II — war workers poured into Baltimore, where vital shipbuilding and aircraft plants were in operation, and military and other govt. employees moved into the area around Wash., D.C. Since World War II, public-works legislation, particularly that concerning roads and other traffic arteries, has brought major changes. The opening of the Chesapeake Bay Bridge in 1952 spurred significant industrial expansion on the Eastern Shore; a parallel bridge was opened in 1973. The Patapsco R. tunnel under Baltimore harbor was completed in 1957, and the Francis Scott Key Bridge (1977), crosses the Patapsco. Other projects include the Baltimore-Wash. Internatl. Airport, formerly called Friendship Internatl. Airport (1950), S of Baltimore, and the Baltimore-Wash. Parkway (1954). Md. experienced tremendous suburban growth in the 1980s, esp. the metropolitan Wash., D.C. area. This growth occured in spite of a decline in govt. jobs, as service sector employment rose dramatically. Suburban Baltimore grew as well while the city proper lost 6.4% of its pop. during the 1980s. Baltimore undertook major revitalization projects in the 1980s and the early 1990s, including the construction of Orioles Park at Camden Yards, the new home of the Baltimore Orioles baseball team. In 1968, Md. Gov. Spiro T. Agnew was elected Vice President. Md. is governed under a constitution adopted in 1867. The general assembly consists of 47 senators and 141 delegates, all elected for 4-year terms. The governor, also elected for a 4-year term, may succeed himself once. The state elects 2 U.S. Senators and 8 Representatives. It has 10 electoral votes. Md. has become increasingly popular as a vacation area — Ocean City is a popular seashore resort, and both sides of Chesapeake Bay are lined with beaches and small fishing towns. The Chesapeake Bay Bridge has brought the culture of the Eastern Shore, formerly quite distinctive, into a more homogenous unity with that of the rest of the state; the area, however, is still noted for its unique rural beauty and architecture, strongly reminiscent of the Eng. countryside left behind by early settlers. Annapolis, with its well-preserved Colonial architecture and 18th-cent. waterfront, is the site of the U.S. Naval Acad. Tourists are also attracted to the Antietam Natl. Battlefield Site and the natl. cemetery at Sharpsburg; the Fort McHenry Natl. Monument, near Baltimore's inner harbor; and the historic towns of Frederick and St. Marys City. Racing enthusiasts attend the annual Preakness and Pimlico Cup horse races at Baltimore. There are several military establishments, including Fort George G. Meade and Andrews Air Force Base. The Natl. Inst. of Health in Bethesda is a civilian govt. establishment. A Natl. Agr. Research Center (□ 19 sq mi/49 sq km) is located at Beltsville. Md.'s medical, educational, and cultural institutions greatly benefited from philanthropic gifts in the late 19th cent. from Johns Hopkins, George Peabody, and Enoch Pratt. Institutions of higher learning in the state include Johns Hopkins Univ., at Baltimore; St. John's Col., at Annapolis; Towson State Univ. at Towson; and the Univ. of Md., at Col. Park and Baltimore. Md. has 23 cos.: ALLEGANY, ANNE ARUNDEL, BALTIMORE, CALVERT, CAROLINE, CARROLL, CECIL, CHARLES, DORCHESTER, FREDERICK, GARRETT, HARFORD, HOWARD, KENT, MONTGOMERY, PRINCE GEORGES, QUEEN ANNES, SAINT MARYS, SOMERSET, TALBOT, WASHINGTON, WICOMICO, WORCESTER.

Maryland Heights, town, St. Louis co., E central Md., on Missouri R., W of St. Louis and NE of Chesterfield; 38°43'N 90°28'W. Mfg. (machinery, rubber prods., electronic equip., bldg. materials, fertilizers, plastic prods.; printing, metal processing).

Maryland Park, village, Prince Georges co., central Md., E suburb of Wash., D.C.

Marylhurst, locality, Clackamas co., NW Oregon, on Willamette R., bet. West Linn and Lake Oswego. Seat of Marylhurst Col.

Mary's Harbour, settlement (1991 pop. 470), SE Lab., E Canada, on inlet of the Atlantic Ocean, 10 mi/16 km WNW of Battle Harbour; 52°19'N 55°51'W. Fishing port and seaplane anchorage.

Marys Igloo, Alaska: see IGLOO.

Marys River (ME-reez), c.45 mi/72 km long, NE Nev.; rises in N Elko co. in Humboldt Natl Forest; flows S to Humboldt R. 16 mi/26 km W of Wells. Also written Mary's R.

Marystown, town (1986 pop. 6,660), N.F., E Canada, on E side of Burin Peninsula; 47°10'N 55°10'W. Fine natural harbor; shipbuilding, fish processing.

Marysvale, village (1990 pop. 364), Piute co., SW central Utah, on Sevier R., and 23 mi/37 km SSW of Richfield; 38°26'N 112°15'W. Elev. 5,866 ft/1,788 m. Trading point for mining and agr. area (alfalfa, corn, potatoes; dairying; sheep, cattle). Gold, silver, potash, and alunite mines nearby. RR terminus. Tushar Mts. are just W. Marysvale Peak (10,943 ft/3,335 m) is 7 mi/11.3 km ENE, in Sevier Plateau. Parts of Fishlake Natl. Forest to E and West Piute Reservoir and State Park to S. Mt. Belknap (12,137 ft/3,699 m) to W. Settled 1860s.

Marysville, town, S N.B., E Canada, on Nashwaak R., suburb 3 mi/5 km NE of Fredericton; 45°59'N 66°35'W. Lumber milling.

Marysville (MAI-reez-vil), village, SE B.C., W Canada, on St. Mary R., and 4 mi/6 km SE of Kimberley; 49°38'N 115°57'W. Timber; tourism.

Marysville 1 city (1990 pop. 12,324), ⊙ Yuba co., N central Calif., opposite (E of) Yuba City, on Feather R., at mouth of Yuba R., in Sacramento Valley, and 35 mi/56 km N of Sacramento; 39°09'N 121°35'W. RR junction, trade, and shipping center for fruit-growing region (peaches, prunes, kiwi fruit); walnuts, almonds, wheat, corn, rice. Mfg. (meat processing; beverages, valves and fittings). Gold dredging on Yuba R. Hydraulic mining raised Yuba R. bed above town, necessitating large levees (begun 1875). City was supply point in gold rush, when it was head of Feather R. navigation. Seat of Yuba Col. (2-year); Beale Air Force Base to E. Founded 1849, inc. 1851. **2** city (1990 pop. 9,656), ⊙ Union co., central Ohio, 27 mi/43 km NW of Columbus; 40°14'N 83°22'W. Ohio State Reformatory for Women is here. Motor-vehicle-assembly plant. Settled 1816. **3** city (1990 pop. 10,328), Snohomish co., NW Wash., 5 mi/8 km N of Everett, and on Possession Sound (arm of Puget Sound), at mouth of Snohomish R.; 48°04'N 122°09'W. Timber; strawberries, vegetables; poultry, cattle; dairying; logging. Mfg. (steel foundry, sawmill; machinery parts, log homes, abrasive prods., fabricated metal prods.; printing and publishing, leather tanning). RR junction to N. Tulalip Indian Reservation to W (has casino); Wenberg State Park to NW. Inc. 1890.

Marysville 1 town (1990 pop. 65), Marion co., S central Iowa, near Cedar Creek, 13 mi/21 km SSE of Knoxville; 41°10′N 92°57′W. In agr. area. **2** town (1990 pop. 3,359), ⊙ Marshall co., NE Kansas, on Big Blue R., and 70 mi/113 km NW of Topeka; 39°51′N 96°38′W. RR div. point in grain and livestock region; dairying, poultry packing. Mfg. (honey, meats, machinery, paper prods.). Pony Express Station. Former ferry crossing (1849) on Oregon Trail. Inc. 1861. **3** town (1990 pop. 8,515), St. Clair co., E Mich., 5 mi/8 km SSW of Port Huron, and on St. Clair R.; 42°54′N 82°28′W. Mfg. (machinery, plastic prods., fabricated metal prods., transportation equip., plastics and resins, rubber prods.); salt mining. St. Clair Co. Internatl. Airport to W. Inc. as village 1921, as city 1924.

Marysville 1 uninc. village (1990 pop. 200), Fremont co., E Idaho, 15 mi/24 km NE of St. Anthony, and 2 mi/3.2 km E of Ashton, bet. Falls and Henry's Fork rivers. Elev. 5,245 ft/1,599 m. Targhee Natl. Forest to NE. **2** village (1990 pop. 70), Lewis and Clark co., W central Mont., 15 mi/24 km NW of Helena. Helena Natl. Forest to SW; Great Divide Ski Area to W, just NE of Continental Divide. Nearby Drumlummon mine, once immensely rich in gold and silver.

Marysville, borough (1990 pop. 2,425), Perry co., S central Pa., 6 mi/9.7 km NW of Harrisburg, on Susquehanna R. (Rockville Bridge, RR), at mouth of Fishing Creek; 40°20′N 76°55′W. Agr. area (corn, hay; poultry; dairying); mfg. (food prods.). Appalachian Trail passes to W and N. Laid out 1861, inc. 1866.

Marysville Buttes, Calif.: see SUTTER BUTTES.

Marytown, uninc. village (1990 pop. 135), McDowell co., S W.Va., on Tug Fork R., 6 mi/9.7 km NW of Welch.

Maryville 1 city (1990 pop. 10,663), ⊙ Nodaway co., NW Mo., near One Hundred and Two R., and 40 mi/64 km N of St. Joseph; 40°20′N 94°52′W. Agr. service center. Corn, wheat; hogs. Mfg. (milk prods., electrical goods, transportation equip., fabricated metal prods., bldg. materials; machining). Seat of Northwest Mo. State Univ. Benedictine convent nearby. Settled c.1845. **2** (MER-ee-vil), city (1990 pop. 19,208), ⊙ Blount co., E Tenn., 15 mi/24 km S of Knoxville; 35°45′N 83°59′W. With its twin city, ALCOA, Maryville is an important center for the production of aluminum and aluminum prods. Lumber, automotive parts, and ski boats are also produced. Corn and tobacco are grown. Limestone and marble quarries nearby. Seat of Maryville Col. The Great Smoky Mts. Natl. Park and the Tuckaleechee Caverns are in the area. Settled around Fort Craig (built 1785), inc. as a town 1830, as a city 1927.

Maryville, village (1990 pop. 2,576), Madison co., SW Ill., suburb of St. Louis, 12 mi/19 km ENE of East St. Louis; 38°43′N 89°57′W. Agr. (corn, wheat; cattle); mfg. marble prods.

Masardis (muh-SAHR-dis), town (1990 pop. 305), Aroostook co., NE Maine, on the Aroostook R., and 21 mi/34 km SW of Presque Isle; 46°31′N 68°21′W.

Mascareen Peninsula (mas-kuh-REEN), SW N.B., E Canada, on E side of Passamaquoddy Bay, opposite St. Andrews; 8 mi/13 km long, 5 mi/8 km wide; 45°03′N 65°49′W. Cod, scallops, lobster; aquaculture industry (salmon farms). Includes villages of Latete, Letang, Back Bay. Ferry to Deer Isl.

Mascoma Lake (mas-KO-muh), Grafton co., W N.H., resort lake 5 mi/8 km E of Lebanon; 4.5 mi/7.2 km long. Mascoma R. (c.30 mi/48 km long) rises in S central Grafton co. c.16 mi/26 km NE of Lebanon, flows S then W through Mascoma L. and Lebanon to Connecticut R. at W. Lebanon. Shaker village and Shrine of Our Lady of LaSalette on SW shore.

Mascot, village, Knox co., E Tenn., 13 mi/21 km ENE of Knoxville; 36°04′N 83°45′W. Zinc mines.

Mascota (mas-KO-tah), town (1990 pop. 7,396) and township, Jalisco, W Mexico, 48 mi/77 km W of Ameca; 20°34′N 104°49′W. Agr. center (grain, sugarcane, cotton, tobacco, fruit, rice).

Mascotte (muh-SKAHT-tee), town (1990 pop. 1,761), Lake co., central Fla., 16 mi/26 km S of Leesburg; 28°34′N 81°53′W. In citrus-fruit region.

Mascouche (mas-KOOSH), town (1991 pop. 25,828), S Que., Canada, 18 mi/29 km N of Montreal. Agr.

Mascoutah (mass-COO-tah), city (1990 pop. 5,511), St. Clair co., SW Ill., satellite community of St. Louis, 20 mi/32 km ESE of East St. Louis; 38°30′N 89°48′W. Bituminous coal mines; agr. (wheat, soybeans, corn, apples, poultry, hogs; dairy prods.). Inc. 1839.

Mashapaug, Conn.: see UNION.

Mashpee (MASH-pee), resort town (1990 pop. 7,884), Barnstable co., SE Mass., on W Cape Cod, 10 mi/16 km WSW of Barnstable; 41°37′N 70°29′W. Includes villages of Seconsett, New Seabury, and Popponesset. Two state parks in vicinity. Site of Native Amer. church and praying ground and lands of Wampanoag tribe. South Cape Beach State Park, Popponesset Beach.

Maskell, village (1990 pop. 54), Dixon co., NE Nebr., 16 mi/26 km NW of Ponca, near Missouri R.; 42°41′N 96°58′W.

Maskinonge, Fr. *Maskinongé* (mah-skee-noh-ZHAI), county (□ 2,378 sq mi/6,159 sq km), S Que., E Canada, extending NW from the St. Lawrence R.; ⊙ Louisville; 46°23′N 73°05′W.

Maskinonge, Fr. *Maskinongé*, village (1991 pop. 1,022), S Que., E Canada, on Maskinonge R. near its mouth on the St. Lawrence R., and 24 mi/39 km WSW of Trois Rivières; 46°13′N 73°01′W. Dairying; pig raising.

Maskinonge River, Fr. *Maskinongé*, 35 mi/56 km long, S Que., E Canada; issues from L. Maskinonge (4 mi/6 km long), 25 mi/40 km NNW of Sorel; flows SE and then S, past Maskinonge, to the St. Lawrence R. 10 mi/16 km NNE of Sorel. Above its mouth it has a falls of over 300 ft/91 m.

Mason 1 county (□ 563 sq mi/1,458 sq km; 1990 pop. 16,269), central Ill.; ⊙ Havana; 40°14′N 89°54′W. Bounded W by Illinois R. and S by Sangamon R. and Salt Creek. Slough lakes along the Illinois. Includes Chautauqua Natl. Wildlife Refuge and Sand Ridge State Forest. Agr. (corn, wheat, soybeans, vegetables; melons). Diversified mfg.; river, RR shipping. Formed 1841. Much agr. benefits from outer-pivot irrigation. **2** county (□ 246 sq mi/637 sq km; 1990 pop. 16,666), NE Ky., on Ohio R. (N; Ohio state line); ⊙ Maysville; 38°36′N 83°49′W. Drained by North Fork of Licking R. Gently rolling upland agr. area (burley tobacco, corn, wheat, soybeans, hay, alfalfa; cattle, poultry; dairying), in N part of Bluegrass region; limestone. Mfg. at Maysville. Formed 1788. **3** county (□ 1,241 sq mi/3,214 sq km; 1990 pop. 25,537), W Mich., on L. Michigan (W); 44°01′N 86°30′W; ⊙ Ludington. Drained by Pere Marquette Big Sable and Little Manistee rivers and short Lincoln R. Agr. (cattle; apples, cherries, peaches, green beans; dairy prods.). Mfg. at Ludington. Fisheries. Resorts. Ludington State Park, with its large sand dunes, is in W bet. L. Mich. and large Hamlin L.; Manistee Natl. Forest in E and N margins of co. Organized 1855. **4** county (□ 932 sq mi/2,414 sq km; 1990 pop. 3,423), central Texas; ⊙ Mason; 30°43′N 99°13′W. On Edwards Plateau; elev. c.1,200 ft/366 m–2,300 ft/701 m. Drained by San Saba R., Llano R. and its tributaries. Ranching (beef cattle, sheep, goats); wool, mohair marketed; agr. (peanuts, watermelons; hay). Topaz found in area. Hunting, fishing, scenery attract visitors. Formed 1858. **5** county (□ 1,051 sq mi/2,722 sq km; 1990 pop. 38,341), W Wash.; ⊙ Shelton; 47°21′N 123°11′W. Mt. area indented in NE by Hood Canal. Timber; fish, clams, oysters; hay; dairying; poultry. Part of Olympic Natl. Forest in NW (includes Wonder Mts. and Mt. Skokomish wilderness areas), Squaxin Isl. (E) and Skokomish (N) Indian reservations; L. Cushman reservoir in N. Formed 1854. **6** county (□ 445 sq mi/1,153 sq km; 1990 pop. 25,178), W W.Va., on Ohio R. (N and W; Ohio state line); ⊙ Point Pleasant; 38°46′N 82°01′W. Drained by Kanawha R., which joins Ohio in NW. Bituminous-coal mines; some natural-gas wells. Agr. (honey, corn, wheat, oats, tobacco, potatoes, alfalfa, hay, vegetables, nursery crops); cattle, hogs, sheep; dairying. Mfg. at Point Pleasant and New Haven. Chief Cornstalk (S center) and Clifton F. McClintic (NW) wildlife management areas. Formed 1804.

Mason, city (1990 pop. 11,452), Warren co., SW Ohio, 21 mi/34 km NE of Cincinnati; 39°22′N 84°18′W.

Mason 1 town (1990 pop. 387), Effingham co., SE central Ill., 12 mi/19 km SSW of Effingham; 38°57′N 88°37′W. Agr. (cattle, hogs; wheat, soybeans, sorghum). **2** town (1990 pop. 6,768), ⊙ Ingham co., S central Mich., 12 mi/19 km SSE of Lansing; 42°34′N 84°26′W. In farm area (dairying; livestock; beans, cabbage, vegetables, apples). Mfg. (printing; fabricated metal prods., consumer goods). **3** town (1990 pop. 1,212), Hillsborough co., S N.H., on Mass. (S) state line, 14 mi/23 km W of Nashua; 42°45′N 71°45′W. Drained by Spaulding Brook. Agr. (livestock, poultry; fruit, vegetables, corn; dairying; nursery crops, sugar maples); mfg. (maple syrup). **4** town (1990 pop. 337), Tipton co., W Tenn., 34 mi/55 km NE of Memphis; 35°25′N 89°32′W. In cotton-growing area. **5** town (1990 pop. 2,041), ⊙ Mason co., central Texas, on Edwards Plateau, 85 mi/137 km SE of San Angelo, and on Comanche Creek in Llano R. valley; 30°45′N 99°13′W. Elev. 1,550 ft/472 m. Shipping center for cattle, sheep, goats; peanuts, watermelons; wool, mohair. Mfg. (beverages). Resort (hunting, fishing nearby). Site of historic Fort Mason, foundations of 23 bldgs. Settled by Germans before Civil War. Inc. after 1940. **6** town (1990 pop. 1,053), Mason co., W W.Va., near the Ohio R. (bridged), 14 mi/23 km NNE of Point Pleasant, and 2 mi/3.2 km SE of (opposite) Pomeroy (Ohio); 39°01′N 82°01′W. Agr. (grain); livestock; dairying. Coal-mining area. Clifton F. McClintic Wildlife Management Area to S.

Mason, village (1990 pop. 102), Bayfield co., N Wis., 13 mi/21 km SW of Ashland; 46°26′N 91°03′W. Lumber. Chequamegon Natl. Forest to N, W and S.

Mason City 1 city (1990 pop. 2,323), Mason co., central Ill., 28 mi/45 km N of Springfield; 40°12′N 89°42′W. In agr. (corn, wheat, soybeans) and clay area; mfg. (edible oils). Inc. 1869. **2** city (1990 pop. 29,040), ⊙ Cerro Gordo co., N central Iowa; 43°08′N 93°12′W. Major RR junction and trade and industrial center of a large agr. area. The major industries are food processing, meatpacking, and the mfg. of cement and fertilizers. Also mfg. of soybean prods., foods, feeds, electrical goods, fabricated metal prods., paper prods., bldg. materials, machinery; printing, meat processing). Seat of North Iowa Area Community Col. (1918; oldest in the state). A large band festival is held here annually. McIntosh Woods and Clear L. state parks to W. Inc. 1874.

Mason City, village (1990 pop. 160), Custer co., central Nebr., 20 mi/32 km SE of Broken Bow, and on Mud Creek; 41°13′N 99°17′W. Grain; cattle.

Mason Dam oregon: see PHILLIPS RESERVOIR.

Mason Hall, village, central Tobago, Trinidad and Tobago, 3 mi/4.8 km NW of Scarborough. Cacao growing.

Masonboro, uninc. town (1990 pop. 7,010), New Hanover co., SE N.C., residential suburb 6 mi/9.7 km ESE of downtown Wilmington, on Intracoastal Waterway, at Hewletts Creek estuary; 34°10′N 77°52′W. Masonboro Inlet to Atlantic Ocean 2 mi/3.2 km to E.

Mason-Dixon Line, state line bet. Md. and both Pa. and Del., surveyed by the Eng. astronomers Charles Mason and Jeremiah Dixon bet. 1763 and 1767. The ambiguous description of the borders in the Md. and Pa. charters led to a protracted disagreement bet. the proprietors of the 2 colonies; the dispute was submitted to the Eng. court of chancery in 1735. A compromise bet. the Penn and Calvert families in 1760 resulted in the appointment of Mason and Dixon. By 1767 the surveyors had run their line 244 mi/393 km W from the Del. border, every 5th milestone bearing the Penn and Calvert arms. The survey was completed to the W limit of Md. in 1773; in 1779 the line was extended to mark the S border of Pa. with Va. (the present-day W.Va. state line). Before the Civil War the term "Mason-Dixon Line" popularly designated the boundary dividing the slave from the free states, and it is still used to distinguish the South from the North. Also known as Mason and Dixon's Line.

Masontown, town (1990 pop. 737), Preston co., N W.Va., 10 mi/16 km SE of Morgantown. Agr. (grain); livestock, poultry. Coal-mining area. Mfg. (coal processing; bldg. materials). Upper Decker Creek Wildlife Management Area to SW; Coopers Rock State Forest to N.

Masontown (MAI-suhn-toun), borough (1990 pop. 3,759), Fayette co., SW Pa., 11 mi/18 km WSW of Uniontown, near Monongahela R.; 39°51′N 79°54′W. Agr. area (corn, hay; dairying); mfg. (apparel, crushed stone, machinery); bituminous coal, natural gas, lumber. Friendship Hill Natl. Historic Site to S. Inc. 1876.

Masonville, town (1990 pop. 129), Delaware co., E Iowa, 7 mi/11.3 km W of Manchester; 42°28′N 91°35′W. Fertilizers. Limestone quarries nearby.

Maspeth (MAS-puhth), a residential and industrial section of W Queens borough of N.Y. city, SE N.Y., at head of Newtown Creek; 40°43′N 73°55′W. Several cemeteries here. Mainly working-class residents.

Mass, village, Ontonagon co., NW Upper Peninsula, NW Mich., 13 mi/21 km SE of Ontonagon; 46°45′N 89°05′W. Also known as Mass City. Ottawa Natl. Forest to S; Adventure Mt. Ski Area to N.

Massabesic Lake (ma-suh-BEE-sik), Hillsborough and Rockingham cos., SE N.H., 4 mi/6.4 km E of downtown Manchester; 4 mi/6.4 km long; 3 mi/4.8 km wide; 42°59′N 71°21′W. Irregularly shaped. Drained from SW end by Cohas Brook (c.5 mi/8 km long) to Merrimack R.

Massac (MAH-SAK), county (□ 242 sq mi/627 sq km; 1990 pop. 14,752), extreme S Ill., on Ohio R. (S; Ky. state line), across from Paducah (Ky.); ⊙ Metropolis; 37°13′N 88°42′W. Bordered NW by Cache R. Agr. area (wheat, sorghum, corn, soybeans; cattle), with some mfg. (clothing, chemicals, cerment). Includes part of Shawnee Natl. Forest along NE border; and Fort Massac State Park and Mermet L. Conservation Area. Lock and Dam No. 52 near Brookport. Formed 1843. One of 17 Ill. cos. to retain Southern-style commission form of govt.

Massac, Fort, Ill.: see METROPOLIS.

Massachusetts (MAS-suh-CHOO-suhts), officially the Commonwealth of Massachusetts, state (□ 10,554 sq mi/27,335 sq km; 1995 est. pop. 6,073,550), NE U.S., in New England, on Atlantic Ocean (E and SE), 1 of the 13 Colonies; ⊙ BOSTON 42°10′N 71°11′W. Bordered NE by Vt., NW by N.H., S by R.I. (which also borders SE Mass. on the W) and Conn., and W by N.Y. The E part, including the CAPE COD peninsula and the isls. lying off it to the S—the ELIZABETH ISLANDS, MARTHA'S VINEYARD, and NANTUCKET—is a low coastal plain. In this area short, swift rivers such as the Merrimack have long supplied industry with power, and an indented coastline provides many good natural harbors, with Boston a major port. In the interior rise uplands separated by the rich Connecticut R. valley, and farther W lies the Berkshire valley, surrounded by the Berkshire Hills, part of the Taconic Mts. The W streams feed both the Hudson and the Housatonic rivers. The state has a mean elev. of c.500 ft/150 m, and Mt. Greylock in the Berkshires is the highest point (3,491 ft/1,064 m). The climate is variable with 4 seasons-cool winter, warm summer, and spectacular autumn foliage season. Traditionally an industrial state, and, with its predominantly urban pop., one of the most densely settled in the nation. It has diverse mfg., chiefly electrical and electronic equip., computers, industrial equip., plastic prods., shoes and leather goods, clothing and textiles, paper and paper prods., machinery, tools, and metal and rubber prods. Shipping, printing, and publishing are important, and the jewelry industry dates from before the Amer. Revolution. Leading agr. prods. include cranberries, apples, vegetables, greenhouse and nursery items, and milk and other dairy goods; poultry is also raised. The fishing fleets of Gloucester and New Bedford still bring in a large and varied catch, and the coastal waters abound in shellfish. Lime, clay, sand, gravel, and stone are the chief mineral resources. High-technology research and development, finance, insurance, and trade industries have become the mainstays of the Mass. economy. Service sector industries, of which education and tourism are primary, made up over ⅓ of the state's gross state prod. (GSP) in 1986. Important cities include Boston (the largest), WORCESTER, SPRINGFIELD, LOWELL, NEW BEDFORD, CAMBRIDGE, BROCKTON, FALL RIVER, and QUINCY. The coast of what is now Mass. was probably skirted by Norsemen in the 11th cent., and Europeans of various nationalities (but mostly Eng.) sailed offshore in the late 16th and early 17th cents. Settlement began when the Pilgrims arrived on the Mayflower and landed 1st at Provincetown (1620) then to a point which they named PLYMOUTH (for their port of embarkation in England). The Plymouth Colony took firm hold and eventually prospered. Other Englishmen soon established fishing and trading posts nearby, such as Naumkeag (SALEM), which in 1628 became the nucleus of a Puritan colony led by John Endecott of the New England Company (later, the Mass. Bay Company) and chartered by the private Council for New England. In 1630, John Winthrop led the 1st large Puritan migration from England (900 settlers on 11 ships). Boston supplanted Salem as capital of the colony, and Winthrop replaced Endecott as governor. After some initial adjustments to allow greater popular participation and the representation of outlying settlements in the General Court (consisting of a governor, deputy governor, assistants, and deputies), the "Bay Colony" continued to be governed as a private company for the next 50 years. It was also a thoroughgoing Puritan theocracy, in which clergymen such as John Cotton enjoyed great political influence. The status of freeman was restricted (until 1664) to church members, and the state was regarded as an agency of God's will on earth. Due to a steady stream of newcomers from England, the South Shore (i.e., area S of Boston), the North Shore, and the interior were soon dotted with firmly rooted communities. The early Puritans were primarily agr. people, although a merchant class soon formed. Most of the inhabitants lived in villages, beyond which lay their privately owned fields. The typical village was composed of houses (also individually owned) grouped around the common—a plot of land held in common by the community. The dominant structure on the common was the meetinghouse, where the pastor, the most important figure in the community, held long Sabbath services. In the meetinghouse of the chief village of a town (in New England a town corresponds to what is usually called a township elsewhere in the U.S.) was also held the town meeting, traditionally regarded as a foundation of Amer. democracy. In practice the town meeting served less to advance democracy than to enforce unanimity and conformity, and participation was as a rule restricted to male property holders and church members. Because they valued the ability of everyone to study scripture and always insisted on a learned ministry, the Puritans also zealously promoted the development of educational facilities. The Boston Lat. School was founded in 1635, 1 year before Harvard Univ. was established, and in 1647 a law was passed requiring elementary schools in towns of 50 families. These were not free schools, but they were open to all and are considered the beginning of popular education in the U.S. Native Amer. resentment of the Puritan presence resulted in the Pequot War of 1637, after which the 4 Puritan colonies (Mass. Bay, Plymouth, Conn., and New Haven) formed the New England Confederation, the 1st voluntary union of Amer. colonies. In 1675–1676, the confederation broke the power of the Native Americans of S New England in King Philip's War. In the course of the Fr. and Indian Wars, however, frontier settlements such as DEERFIELD were devastated. The withdrawal of the charter of the Mass. Bay Colony (1684) occurred because the colony had consistently violated the terms of the charter and repeatedly evaded or ignored royal orders by operating an illegal mint, establishing religious rather than property qualifications for suffrage, and discriminating against Anglicans. In 1691, a new charter united Mass. Bay, Plymouth, and Maine into the 1 royal colony of Mass. This charter abolished church membership as a test for voting, although Congregationalism remained the established religion. Widespread anxiety over loss of the original charter contributed to the witchcraft panic that reached its climax in Salem in the summer of 1692. Nineteen persons were hanged and 1 crushed to death for refusing to confess to the practice of witchcraft. The Salem trials ended abruptly when colonial authorities, led by Cotton Mather, became alarmed at their excesses. By the mid-18th cent. the Mass. colony had come a long way from its humble agr. beginnings. Fish and lumber were exported along with farm prods. in a lively trade carried by ships built here and manned by local seamen. That the menace of Fr. Canada was removed by 1763 was due in no small measure to the unstinting efforts of the mother country, but the increasing Br. tendency to regulate colonial affairs, esp. trade, without colonial advice, was most unwelcome. Because of the colony's extensive shipping interests, e.g., the traffic in molasses, rum, and slaves (the "triangular trade"), it sorely felt these restrictions. In 1761, James Otis opposed a Mass. superior court's issue of the writs of assistance (general search warrants to aid customs officers in enforcing collection of duties on imported sugar), arguing that this act violated the natural rights of Englishmen and was therefore void. He thus helped set the stage for the political controversy which, coupled with economic grievances, culminated in the Amer. Revolution. The Stamp Act (1765) and the Townshend Acts (1767) preceded the Boston Massacre (1770), and the Tea Act (1773) brought on the Boston Tea Party. The rebellious colonials were punished for this with the Intolerable Acts (1774), which troops under Gen. Thomas Gage were sent to enforce. Through Committees of Correspondence, Mass. and the other colonies had been sharing their grievances, and in 1774 they called the First Continental Congress at Philadelphia for united action. The mounting tension in Mass. exploded in April 1775, when Gen. Gage decided to make a show of force. Warned by Paul Revere and William Dawes, the Mass. militia engaged the Br. force at Lexington and Concord. Patriot militia from other colonies hurried to Mass., where, after the battle of BUNKER HILL (June 17, 1775), George Washington took command of the patriot forces. The British remained in Boston until March 17, 1776, when Gen. William Howe evacuated the town. In 1780 a new constitution, drafted by a constitutional convention under the leadership of John Adams, was ratified by direct vote of the citizenry. Victorious in the Revolution, the colonies faced depressing economic conditions. Nowhere were those conditions worse than in W Mass., where discontented Berkshire farmers erupted in Shays' Rebellion in 1786. The uprising was promptly quelled, but it frightened conservatives into support of a new natl. constitution that would displace the weak govt. under the Articles of Confederation; this constitution was ratified by Mass. in 1788 (the 6th state to do so). Independence had closed the old trade routes within the Br. Empire, but newer ones were soon opened up, and trade with China became esp. lucrative. Boston and lesser ports boomed, and the prosperous times were reflected politically in the commonwealth's unwavering adherence to the Federalist party, the party of the dominant commercial class. Eur. wars at the beginning of the 19th cent. further stimulated the carrying trade until it led to interference with Amer. shipping. To avoid war Congress resorted to Jefferson's Embargo Act of 1807, a severe blow to the economy of Mass. and the rest of the nation. War with Great Britain came anyway in 1812, and it was violently unpopular in New England. There was talk of secession at the abortive Hartford Convention of New England Federalists. As it transpired, however, the embargo and the War of 1812 had an unexpectedly favorable effect on the economy of Mass. With Eng. manufactured goods shut out, the U.S. had to begin mfg. on its own, and the infant industries that sprang up after 1807 tended to concentrate in New England, and esp. in Mass. These industries, financed by money made in shipping and shielded from foreign competition by protective tariffs after 1816, grew rapidly, transforming the character of the commonwealth and its people. Labor was plentiful and often ruthlessly exploited. The power loom, perfected by Francis Cabot Lowell, as well as Eng. techniques for textile mfg. (based on plans smuggled out of England) made Mass. an early center of the Amer. textile industry. The water power of the Merrimack R. became the basis for the Lowell's cotton textile industry in the 1820s. Agr., on the other hand, went into a sharp decline because Mass. could not compete with the new agr. states of the West, a region more readily accessible after the opening of the ERIE CANAL (1825). Farms were abandoned by the score; some farmers turned to work in the new factories, others moved to the West. In 1820, Maine was separated from Mass. and admitted to the Union as a separate state under the terms of the Missouri Compromise. In the same year the Mass. constitution was considerably liberalized by the adoption of amendments that abolished all property qualifications for voting, provided for the incorporation of cities, and removed religious tests for officeholders. (Mass. is the only 1 of the original 13 states that is still governed under its original constitution, the one of 1780, although this was extensively amended by the constitutional convention of 1917–1919.) In the 1830s and 1840s the state became the center of religious and social reform movements, such as Unitarianism and transcendentalism. Of the transcendentalists, Ralph Waldo Emerson and Henry Thoreau were quick to perceive and decry the evils of industrialization, while Bronson Alcott, Margaret Fuller, Nathaniel Hawthorne, and Emerson had some association with Brook Farm, an outgrowth of Utopian ideals. Horace Mann set about establishing an enduring system of public education in the 1830s. The 1st normal school in U.S. was est. 1839 and is now Farmington State Col. During this period Mass. gave to the nation the architect Charles Bulfinch; such writers and poets as Richard Henry Dana, Emily Dickinson, Oliver Wendell Holmes, Henry Wadsworth Longfellow, James Russell Lowell, and John Greenleaf Whittier; the historians George Bancroft, John Lothrop Motley, Francis Parkman, and William Hickling Prescott; and the scientist Louis Agassiz. In the 1830s reformers began to devote energy to the antislavery crusade. This was regarded with great displeasure by the mill tycoons, who feared that an offended South would cut off their cotton supply. The Whig party split on the slavery issue, and Mass. turned to the new Republican party and voted for John C. Frémont in 1856 and Abraham Lincoln in 1860. Mass. was the 1st state to answer Lincoln's call for troops after the firing on Fort Sumter. Mass. soldiers were the 1st to die for the Union cause when the Sixth Mass. Regiment was fired on by a secessionist mob in Baltimore. In the course of the war over 130,000 men from the state served in the Union forces, including an Afr.-Amer. regiment. After the war Mass., with other Northern states, experienced rapid industrial expansion. Mass. capital financed many of the nation's new RRs, esp. in the West. Although people continued to leave the state for the West, labor remained cheap and plentiful as Eur. immigrants streamed into the state. The Irish, oppressed by both famine and the British, began arriving in droves even before the Civil War (beginning in the 1840s), and they continued to land in Boston for years to come. After them came Fr. Canadians, arriving later in the 19th cent., and followed in the early 20th cent. by Portuguese, Italians, Poles and other Slavs, Russian Jews, and Scandinavians. Also from the Br. Isles came Englishmen, Scots, and Welshmen. Of all the immigrant groups, Eng.-speaking and non-Eng.-speaking, the Irish came to be the most influential, esp. in politics. Their R.C. religion and their Democratic political faith definitely set them apart from the old native Yankee stock. Practically all of the immigrants went to work in the factories. The halcyon days of shipping were over. The carrying trade had bounded back triumphantly after the War of 1812, but the supplanting of sail by steam, the growth of RRs, and the destruction caused by Confederate cruisers in the Civil War helped reduce shipping to its present negligible state—a far cry from the colorful era of the clipper ships, which

were perfected by Donald McKay of Boston. Whaling, once the glory of New Bedford and Nantucket, faded quickly with the introduction of petroleum. The rise of industrialism was accompanied by a growth of cities, although the small mill town, where the factory hands lived in company houses and traded in the company store, remained important. Labor unions struggled for recognition in a long, weary battle marked by strikes, sometimes violent, as was the Lawrence textile strike of 1912. World War I, which caused a vast increase in industrial production, improved the lot of workingmen, but not of Boston policemen, who staged and lost their famous strike in 1919. For his part in breaking the strike, Gov. Calvin Coolidge won natl. fame and went on to become Vice President and then President, the 3d Mass. citizen (after John and John Quincy Adams) to hold the highest office in the land. The Sacco-Vanzetti Case, following the police strike, attracted internatl. attention, as liberals raged over the seeming lack of regard for the spirit of the law in a state that had given the nation such an eminent jurist as Oliver Wendell Holmes (1841–1935). Labor unions finally came into their own in the 1930s under the New Deal. Industry spurted forward again during World War II, and in the postwar era the state has continued to develop. The decline of the textile industry has been offset by the growth of the electronics industry, attracted by the skilled labor in the Boston area. This growth in the computer and electronics industries helped Mass. to gain economic prosperity throughout much of the 1980s and was a significant factor in the major pop. growth of suburban Boston. In 1989, the state economy was devastated by the effects of a nationwide recession and the burden of a huge state budget. Unemployment rose and the state's real estate market collapsed after years of growth. On the political scene, Mass. was home of the nation's 35th President, John F. Kennedy. The governor of Mass. is elected for a 4-year term. The legislature (the General Court) has a senate of 40 members and a house of representatives with 160 members, all of whom serve 2-year terms. Mass. sends 10 Representatives and 2 Senators to the U.S. Congress, and has 12 electoral votes. As a recreation and vacation area, Mass. has great stretches of seashore in the E and many lakes and streams in the wooded Berkshire Hills in the W. There are numerous state parks, forests, and beaches, and Cape Cod is the site of a natl. seashore. Provincetown, on Cape Cod, and Rockport, on Cape Ann, are artist colonies; Marblehead is a noted yachting center. The state is also famed for its historic points of interest, among them being those at Sturbridge, Salem, Concord (Minute Man Historical Park), and Lexington; and at 6 historic sites— Adams, Salem Maritime, Longfellow, John Fitzgerald Kennedy, Saugus Iron Works, and Dorchester Heights. Cultural attractions include the noted Tanglewood music festival and the many educational facilities of the state. In the field of higher learning Mass. continues strong. Besides Harvard Univ. and the Mass. Inst. of Technology, at Cambridge, educational institutions include Radcliffe Col., also at Cambridge; Amherst Col., at Amherst; the Univ. of Mass., at Amherst and Boston; Boston Col., at Newton; Boston Univ., Simmons Col., and Northeastern Univ., at Boston; Brandeis Univ., at Waltham; Clark Univ., Col. of the Holy Cross, and Worcester Polytechnic Inst., at Worcester; Lowell Univ., at Lowell; Mount Holyoke Col., at South Hadley; Smith Col., at Northampton; Tufts Univ., at Medford; Wellesley Col., at Wellesley; Wheaton Col., at Norton; Williams Col., at Williamstown; and several state cols. The state is also renowned for its excellent private secondary schools, such as Phillips Acad. Mass. has 14 cos.: BARNSTABLE, BERKSHIRE, BRISTOL, DUKES, ESSEX, FRANKLIN, HAMPDEN, HAMPSHIRE, MIDDLESEX, NANTUCKET, NORFOLK, PLYMOUTH, SUFFOLK, WORCESTER.

Massacre River, c.35 mi/56 km long, along Dominican Republic–Haiti border; flows N, past Dajabón (Dominican Republic) and Ouanaminthe (Haiti), to the Atlantic Ocean at Pepillo Salcedo (Dominican Republic); 19°42′N 71°45′W.

Massanutten, uninc. town, Rockingham co., NW Va., 9 mi/14.5 km ESE of Harrisonburg; 38°24′N 78°44′W. Tourism. Part of George Washington Natl. Forest to N. Massanutten Resort is here.

Massanutten Mountain, N Va., ridge in center of N Shenandoah Valley, parallels Allegheny Mts. (W) and Blue Ridge (E); extends from point E of Harrisonburg c.45 mi/72 km NNE to point W of Front Royal in sect. of George Washington Natl. Forest; rises to c.3,000 ft/914 m. North and South forks of Shenandoah R. meet at N end. Massanutten Resort and Caverns, at S end, Luray Caverns at E side. Observation tower near N end, E of Woodstock. Masanutten Visitors' Center in center of ridge.

Massapequa (ma-suh-PEE-kwuh), uninc. city (☐ 4 sq mi/10.4 sq km; 1990 pop. 22,018), Nassau co., SE N.Y., on S shore of L.I.; 40°40′N 73°28′W. Chiefly residential.

Massapequa Park (ma-suh-PEE-kwuh), residential village (☐ 2 sq mi/5.2 sq km; 1990 pop. 18,044), Nassau co., SE N.Y., on L.I.; 40°40′N 73°27′W. Bethpage State Park is 5 mi/8 km to N. Bordered by the Massapequa Preserve greenbelt to W. Inc. 1931.

Massawippi, Lake (ma-suh-WI-pee), S Que., E Canada, 10 mi/16 km SSW of Sherbrooke; 8 mi/13 km long, 2 mi/3 km wide. Noted for scenic beauty. Drains N to St. Francis R.

Massena, city (☐ 4 sq mi/10.4 sq km; 1990 pop. 11,719), St. Lawrence co., extreme N N.Y., on the St. Lawrence R.; 44°55′N 74°53′W. Aluminum and aluminum prods. are the chief mfg. Two locks and 2 dams of the St. Lawrence Seaway are nearby. In a summer resort area and has a state park. An internatl. bridge connects the city with Cornwall (Ont.). Settled 1792, inc. 1886.

Massena, town (1990 pop. 372), Cass co., SW Iowa, on West Nodaway R., and 16 mi/26 km SE of Atlantic; 41°15′N 94°46′W. In agr. area.

Masset, village (1991 pop. 1,476), W B.C., W Canada, on N Graham Isl., on an inlet of Dixon Entrance, 80 mi/129 km WSW of Prince Rupert across Hecate Strait; 54°02′N 132°09′W. W terminus of Yellowhead Highway (Rte. 16). Trade center, inhabited largely by Native Haida. Salmon fishing, once a mainstay of the economy, is now declining, with a ban on commercial chinook fishing in effect and fishermen selling their licenses back to the govt. in a plan to reduce fishing activity. Tourist center. Haida Village native cultural center, totem poles. Scheduled seaplane service.

Masset Inlet, W B.C., W Canada, central Graham Isl., 20 mi/32 km S of Massett, connected with Dixon Entrance by Masset Sound (25 mi/40 km long); 20 mi/32 km long, 2 mi/3 km–8 mi/13 km wide; 53°42′N 132°20′W. In lumbering and fishing area. Port Clements is on E shore; Massett village is at mouth of Masset Sound.

Massey, town (1991 pop. 1,186), SE central Ont., central Canada, on Spanish R., and 55 mi/89 km WSW of Sudbury; 46°12′N 82°05′W. Nickel, copper, and gold mining; lumbering.

Massey, village, Kent co., E Md., 19 mi/31 km NW of Dover, Del.

Massillon (MAS-i-lahn), city (1990 pop. 31,007), Stark co., NE Ohio, on the Tuscarawas R.; 40°47′N 81°31′W. Industrial city; mfg. includes fabricated metal prods., transportation equip., medical supplies, food prods., plastics. Jacob S. Coxey, the social reformer, lived here and was mayor in the early 1930s. State mental hosp. and prison facility are nearby. Inc. 1853.

Massive, Mount, peak (14,421 ft/4,396 m), in W Lake co., W central Colo., in the Sawatch Mts.; at Continental Divide, 4 mi/6.4 km NNW of Mt. Elbert; in San Isabel Natl. Forest. It is the 2d-highest peak in the U.S. Rocky Mts.

Masson (MA-so), village (1991 pop. 5,753), SW Que., E Canada, on Lièvre R., just above its mouth on Ottawa R., and 16 mi/26 km ENE of Ottawa; 45°33′N 75°25′W. Lumbering; dairying; livestock raising.

Mastic (MAS-tik), residential village (☐ 4 sq mi/10.4 sq km; 1990 pop. 13,778), Suffolk co., SE N.Y., on an inlet of Moriches Bay, on S shore of L.I., 2 mi/3.2 km W of Center Moriches; 40°47′N 72°50′W.

Mastic Beach (MAS-tik), village (□ 5 sq mi/13 sq km; 1990 pop. 10,293), Suffolk co., SE N.Y., 10 mi/16 km E of Patchogue; 40°45′N 72°50′W.

Masury (MA-zhuh-ree), village, Trumbull co., NE Ohio, 11 mi/18 km NE of Youngstown, at Pa. state line.

Mata (MAH-tuh), town, Villa Clara prov., central Cuba, on RR, and 15 mi/24 km N of Santa Clara; 22°40′N 79°56′W. Sugar growing. Sugar mills Braulio Coroneaux (1.9 mi/3 km S) and El Vaquerito (1.9 mi/3 km NW).

Mata Palacio (MAH-tah pah-LAH-see-o), town, Hato Mayor prov., E Dominican Republic, 15 mi/24 km N of San Pedro de Macorís. In agr. region (sugarcane, cacao, coffee, rice, fruit; cattle).

Matachi (mah-TAH-chee), town (1990 pop. 2,230), Chihuahua, N Mexico, on headstream of Yaqui R., in Sierra Madre Occidental, on RR, and 105 mi/169 km W of Chihuahua. Corn, wheat, beans, fruit; cattle. Formerly Matachic.

Matachic, Mexico: see MATACHI.

Matador, town (1990 pop. 790), ⊙ Motley co., NW Texas, just below Caprock escarpment of Llano Estacado, 45 mi/72 km SW of Childress, near huge Matador Ranch; 34°01′N 100°49′W. Elev. 2,347 ft/715 m. In cattle-ranching region, also producing cotton, wheat, peanuts; oil and gas. Matador State Wildlife Management Area to E (Cottle co.).

Matagami, village, W central Que., E Canada, 110 mi/177 km NNE of Val d'Or, on S side of L. Matagami; 49°45′N 77°38′W. Mining center; road connection from S. Scheduled air service.

Matagorda (ma-tuh-GOR-duh), county (□ 1,612 sq mi/4,175 sq km; 1990 pop. 36,928), S Texas; ⊙ Bay City; 28°46′N 96°00′W. On Matagorda and East Matagorda bays, sheltered from Gulf of Mexico by Matagorda Peninsula, a sand barrier paralleling coast, and traversed by Gulf Intracoastal Waterway (also parallels coast 1 mi/1.6 km inland); drained by Colorado R. E border formed in part by Linville Bayou and Caney L. Creek. RR terminus. A leading Texas cattle co.; also agr. (esp. rice; also cotton, grain). Oil, natural gas, salt. Tourism; beaches, fishing attract visitors. Formed 1836. Nuclear power plants include South Texas 1 (initial criticality March 8, 1988) and South Texas 2 (initial criticality March 12, 1989), both 12 mi/19 km SSW of Bay City; they use cooling water from the Colorado R., and each has a max. dependable capacity of 1251 MW. Big Boggy Natl. Wildlife Refuge in SE; Matagorda Peninsula State Park in S.

Matagorda (ma-tuh-GOR-duh), uninc. village (1990 pop. 605), Matagorda co., S Texas, on Intracoastal Waterway, at E end of Matagorda Bay and on SW East Matagorda Bay, at mouth of Colorado R., and 20 mi/32 km S of Bay City. Fisheries; seafood, shell market. Matagorda Peninsula State Park 7 mi/11.3 km to NE on Gulf Coast; Big Boggy Natl. Wildlife Refuge to NE. Christ Church here was built 1839. Settled 1825; served as port for Austin's colony.

Matagorda Bay (ma-tuh-GOR-duh), inlet of the Gulf of Mexico, SE Texas, separated from Gulf by a long sand spit, Matagorda Peninsula; 30 mi/48 km long and 3 mi/4.8 km–12 mi/19 km wide. Receives the Colorado R. at E end, is separated from peninsula with mainland, and is crossed by the Intracoastal Waterway. Matagorda Isl. is a sandbar farther S extending beyond tip of Matagorda Peninsula into entrance of San Antonio Bay. Lavaca Bay in NW arm of Matagorda Bay, East Matagorda Bay, inlet of Gulf of Mexico, extends 20 mi/32 km NE, from neck of land separating it from Matagorda Bay (SW); separated from gulf by E extension of Matagorda Peninsula. At E end of Matagorda Bay is the site of the village of Matagorda, which was settled in 1825 and served as a port for Stephen F. Austin's colony. Matagorda is known principally for fishing and oyster gathering. The area is often struck by hurricanes. Big Boggy Natl. Wildlife Refuge on N shore. Intracoastal Waterway is 1 mi/1.6 km inland from mainland shore.

Matagorda Island (ma-tuh-GOR-duh), Calhoun co., S Texas, low sandy barrier isl. bet. San Antonio and Espiritu Santo bays (NW; bet. isl. and mainland), and the Gulf of Mexico (SE); 36 mi/58 km long, 1 mi/1.6 km–4 mi/6.4 km wide. Separated by channel from St. Joseph Isl. (SW) and by Cavallo Pass from tip of Matagorda Peninsula (NE), both continuations on the sand barrier that rings much of the Texas Gulf Coast. At E end, Matagorda Isl. State Park and Wildlife Area; former air force base used for bombing practice, now restored to natural status.

Matagorda Peninsula (ma-tuh-GOR-duh), Matagorda co., S Texas, sand barrier paralleling Texas Gulf Coast; c.50 mi/80 km. Connected to mainland by 7 mi/11.3 km neck of land, 25 mi/40 km S of Bay City. Extends NE c.20 mi/32 km, separating East Matagorda Bay from Gulf of Mexico, and c.30 mi/48 km SW, separating Matagorda Bay from gulf. The SW extension is breached in 3 places, the work of numerous hurricanes and tropical storms. SW tip separated from Mustang Isl. by Pass Cavallo. NE tip separated from mainland by small entrance to East Matagorda Bay. Matagorda Peninsula State Park at base of peninsula, S of village of Matagorda.

Mataguá (mah-tah-GWUH), small town, Villa Clara prov., central Cuba, on RR line, and secondary highway, 11 mi/18 km S of Santa Clara; 22°14′N 80°00′W. Between small ranges of Sierra del Escambray (NE) and Sierra de Potrerillo (SW).

Matahambre, Cuba: see MINAS DE MATAHAMBRE.

Matamoras (me-tuh-MO-ruhs), village (1990 pop. 1,965), Washington co., SE Ohio, on the Ohio R. (W.Va. state line), and 21 mi/34 km ENE of Marietta; 39°31′N 81°04′W. In agr. area.

Matamoras (MA-tah-MOR-uhs), borough (1990 pop. 1,934), Pike co., NE Pa., 1 mi/1.6 km SW of Port Jervis (N.Y.), on Delaware R. (bridged NE to N.Y., SE to N.J.); 41°22′N 74°42′W. Agr. (dairying; cattle); mfg. (medical supplies; commercial printing). Easternmost point in Pa. Part of Del. State Forest to W; High Point State Park (N.J.) to S.

Matamoros (mah-tah-MO-ros), city (1990 pop. 39,091) and township, Coahuila, N Mexico, in Laguna dist., 12 mi/19 km E of Torreón; 25°33′N 103°15′W. RR junction. Agr. center (cotton, corn, wheat, wine, vegetables).

Matamoros (mah-tah-MUH-ros), town (1990 pop. 2,417), Chihuahua, N Mexico, 13 mi/21 km SSE of Hidalgo del Parral, on Mexico Highway 45; 26°48′N 105°35′W. Silver and lead mining. Also Villa Matamoros. Formerly Las Cuevas or San Isidro de las Cuevas.

Matamoros 1 Mexico: see IZÚCAR DE MATAMOROS.
2 Mexico: see HEROICA MATAMOROS.

Matane (muh-TAN), county (□ 1,631 sq mi/4,224 sq km), E Que., E Canada, on N shore of Gaspé Peninsula, on the St. Lawrence R.; ⊙ Matane; 48°45′N 67°05′W.

Matane (muh-TAN), town (1991 pop. 12,756), SE Que., E Canada, on the St. Lawrence R. at the mouth of the Matane R., at the beginning of the Gaspé Peninsula; 48°51′N 67°32′W. Fishing (shrimp), lumbering, and pulpwood-shipping center; mfg. (concrete, prepared meats, fresh and frozen fish); summer resort.

Matanilla Reef, northernmost part of the Bahama Isls., B.W.I., 50 mi/80 km NNE of West End (Grand Bahama Isl.); 27°25′N 78°42′W.

Matanuska (ma-duh-NOO-skuh), village, S Alaska, 30 mi/48 km NE of Anchorage.

Matanuska River (ma-duh-NOO-skuh), 75 mi/121 km long, S Alaska; rises in Chugach Mts., near 61°47′N 147°40′W; flows SW past Moose Creek, Palmer, and Matanuska, to Knik Arm 30 mi/48 km NE of Anchorage. Lower course flows through Matanuska Valley agr. region. Source includes Matanuska glacier. Paralleled by Glenn Highway.

Matanuska Valley (ma-duh-NOO-skuh), region (□ c.1,000 sq mi/2,590 sq km) of S Alaska, on lower Matanuska R., NE of Anchorage, extends c.40 mi/64 km ENE from head of Knik Arm, bet. Talkeetna (NNW) and Chugach (SSE) mts.; c.9,000 acres/3,642 ha are

under cultivation, producing oats, barley, fodder grasses, vegetables, potatoes, berries, hogs; dairy prods. Growing suburban region for Anchorage. Region served by Glenn Highway. Market center is Palmer. Climate is temperate, with adequate rainfall. Univ. of Alaska has Matsu Community Col. Transportation Mus., Palmer Fair, Tourism. Valley became site of Federal experiment in rural resettlement (May 1935), when 208 families from Middle Western drought areas were est. here with aid of Federal loans. Matanuska Valley Farmers' Cooperating Assn. was est. (1937) at Palmer. Control of project transferred (Sept. 1938) to Dept. of the Interior.

Matanuska-Sustina, borough (□ 24,694 sq mi/63,958 sq km; 1990 pop. 39,683), S Alaska. Main town is Palmer. Bounded on S in part by Cook Inlet. Part of Alaska Range to NW and Talkeetna Mts. are in SE center. Part of Denali Natl. Park and Preserve to NW, small part of L. Clark Natl. Park and Preserve in SW corner. Matanuska Valley, Alaska's main agr. area, in the S. Agr. (vegetables, potatoes, rutabagas, hay); dairying. Fishing.

Matanzas (mah-TAHN-zuhs), province (1990 pop. 601,500;□ 30,225 sq mi/78,253 sq km), W central Cuba; ⊙ Matanzas. Well endowed with natural resources. The N coast is lined with ports and bays and contains one of the world's finest beaches, at Varadero ("Playa Azul"). In the N ½ of the prov. are plains of deep red-clay soil with good drainage; in the S are low-lying wetlands. The S coast includes Cienaga de Zapata (a swamp with over 500,000 tons/454,000 metric tons of dry peat) and Cochinos Bay, the site of the Bay of Pigs invasion (1961). Sugarcane (with 21 mills) and henequen are the major crops; subsistence agr. is also practiced, and there is some cattle raising. The prov. produced 30% of Cuba's citrus crop in 1994. Has the Fr.-designed Antonio Guiteras thermoelectric generating station, which can generate 330 MW, the 5th-most powerful in Cuba. Tourist industry; many mineral springs. Important cities include Cárdenas, Colón, Jovellanos, and Jagüey Grande.

Matanzas (mah-TAHN-zuhs), city (1994 est. pop. 115,000), ⊙ Matanzas prov., W central Cuba; 23°04′N 81°33′W. A port with a large, deep harbor, it exports sugar (16% of Cuba's total 1994 sugar exports, 2d only to Cienfuegos), fruits, and sisal. Industries in the city include sugar refineries and textile mills. Petrochemical and petroleum-storage and -distribution facilities on port. The port has capacity to handle 6 ships simultaneously on 3,630-ft/1,106-m-long piers. On the highway bet. Havana and Varadero Beach; popular stopover for vacationers, who explore the picturesque Yumurí R. valley and the caves of Bellamar, famous for their calcite crystal formations. Founded in 1693, it was once a pirate haven but by the early 19th cent. had become Cuba's 2d city, mainly because of the growth of the sugar industry. As the industry moved E, the city's importance declined. Matanzas remains an important cultural center for the area.

Matanzas (mah-TAHN-zahs), officially San José de Matanzas, town, Samaná prov., N Dominican Republic, on Escocesa Bay, 15 mi/24 km NW of Sánchez. In agr. region (rice, cacao, corn, coconuts, coffee, fruit). Damaged by 1946 earthquake and tidal waves.

Matanzas River (muh-TAN-zuhs), narrow lagoon, c.17 mi/27 km long, St. Johns co., NE Fla.; sheltered from the Atlantic Ocean by Anastasia Isl.; extends from St. Augustine (N end; ocean outlet) to Matanzas Inlet, which connects its S end with the ocean. Followed by Intracoastal Waterway.

Matapa, Mexico: see VILLA PESQUEIRA.

Matapeake, Md.: see KENT ISLAND.

Matapedia (ma-tuh-PEE-dee-uh), Fr. *Matapédia* (mah-tah-PAI-dee-ah), county (□ 1,751 sq mi/4,535 sq km), E Que., E Canada, in central part of Gaspé Peninsula; ⊙ Amqui; 48°25′N 67°25′W.

Matapedia, Fr. *Matapédia*, village (1991 pop. 786), E Que., E Canada, SE Gaspé Peninsula, on Restigouche R., at mouth of Matapedia R., 12 mi/19 km WSW of

Campbellton; 47°58′N 66°56′W. RR junction. Lumbering, dairying.

Matapedia, Lake (ma-tuh-PEE-dee-uh), E Que., E Canada, at the base of the Gaspé Peninsula, and S of Matane; 14 mi/23 km long and 2 mi/3 km wide. Drained S by the Matapedia R., famous for salmon fishing. Well-known tourist center.

Matapedia River, Fr. *Matapédia River*, 50 mi/80 km long, E Que., E Canada, at base of Gaspé Peninsula; issues from L. Matapedia; flows SE, past Amqui and Causapscal, to Restigouche R. at Matapedia. Noted salmon stream.

Matas, Las, Dominican Republic: see LAS MATAS.

Matawan (MA-tuh-WAHN), borough (1990 pop. 9,270), Monmouth co., E N.J., 11 mi/18 km N of Freehold, in suburban region; 40°24′N 74°14′W. Mfg. (metal goods, rubber and plastic goods, concrete prods.). Has 18th-cent. bldgs. Called New Aberdeen before 1715, inc. 1895.

Matehuala (mah-te-WAH-law), city (1990 pop. 54,713) and township, ⊙ Matehuala municipio, San Luis Potosí, N central Mexico, on interior plateau, 105 mi/169 km NNE of San Luis Potosí, on Mexico Highway 57; 23°38′N 100°38′W. Elev. 5,299 ft/1,615 m. RR terminus. Gold and silver mining; tanning; maguey processing (textile fibers, liquor). Airfield.

Matelot (MA-tai-lot), village, N Trinidad, Trinidad and Tobago, 18 mi/29 km ENE of Port of Spain. Swimming, fishing.

Matewan (MAIT-wahn), village (1990 pop. 619), Mingo co., SW W.Va., on Tug Fork R., at Ky. state line, 7 mi/11.3 km SE of Williamson; 37°37′N 82°10′W. Bituminous-coal region. Mfg. (coal processing). One site of Hatfield-McCoy feud. Scene of bloody confrontation (May 1920) bet. mine owners and miners. Inc. 1895.

Matfield Green, village (1990 pop. 33), Chase co., E central Kansas, on S fork of Cottonwood R., and 14 mi/23 km S of Cottonwood Falls; 38°09′N 96°33′W. Livestock; grain.

Mather, uninc. town (1990 pop. 1,300), Greene co., SW Pa., 7 mi/11.3 km ENE of Waynesburg, near South Fork Tenmile Creek; 39°56′N 80°04′W. Agr. (dairying; corn).

Mather (MA-duhr), village, S Man., central Canada, 60 mi/97 km SE of Brandon. Grain; livestock.

Mather Air Force Base, Calif.: see SACRAMENTO.

Mather, Mount (12,123 ft/3,695 m), S central Alaska, in Alaska Range, in Mt. McKinley Natl. Park, 140 mi/225 km N of Anchorage; 63°11′N 150°26′W.

Matherville, village (1990 pop. 708), Mercer co., NW Ill., on Edwards R., and 9 mi/14.5 km ENE of Aledo; 41°15′N 90°36′W. In agr. area.

Matheson Point, E extremity of King William Isl., S Franklin dist., N.W.T., N Canada, on Rae Strait; 68°49′N 95°10′W.

Mathews, county (□ 251 sq mi/650 sq km; 1990 pop. 8,348), E Va.; ⊙ Mathews; 37°25′N 76°16′W. In Tidewater region; bounded E by Chesapeake Bay, N by Piankatank R. estuary and S by Mobjack Bay. Agr. (corn, soybeans, vegetables, melons, bulbs; poultry); fish, crabs, oysters. Seasonal homes in area; waterfowl hunting. Formed 1791.

Mathews, uninc. town (1990 pop. 3,009), Lafourche parish, on Bayou Lafourche, 4 mi/6.4 km SE of Raceland; 29°41′N 90°33′W. Fishing; sugarcane.

Mathews, uninc. village, ⊙ Mathews co., E Va., near Chesapeake Bay, 28 mi/45 km ESE of West Point. Mfg. (wood prods.); agr. (vegetables, corn, soybeans; poultry; bulb growing).

Mathews Dam, Calif.: see MATHEWS, LAKE.

Mathews, Lake, Riverside co., S Calif., reservoir at W end of Colorado R. Aqueduct (enters E end of lake through 8-mi/12.9-km-long Valverde Tunnel), 9 mi/14.5 km S of Riverside; c.5 mi/8 km long. Impounded by Mathews Dam (210 ft/64 m high, 2,170 ft/661 m long; completed 1938). From lake, gravity carries water to cities of Los Angeles metropolitan dist. Santa Ana Mts. to SW. Formerly Cajalco (kah-HAL-ko) Reservoir.

Mathis, town (1990 pop. 5,423), San Patricio co., S Texas, 34 mi/55 km NW of Corpus Christi, near Nueces R; 28°05′N 97°49′W. RR, trade, shipping point in agr. and

oil-producing area; mfg. (fertilizers). Just W is L. Corpus Christi; L. Corpus Christi and Lipantitlan state parks to SW. Inc. 1937.

Mathiston (MATH-is-tuhn), town (1990 pop. 818), Webster and Choctaw cos., central Miss., 18 mi/29 km WNW of Starkville, near Big Black R.; 33°32′N 89°07′W. Mfg. (lumber, apparel, machinery). Seat of Wood Jr. Col. Natchez Trace (Natl.) Parkway passes to NW.

Matías Romero, city (1990 pop. 19,692) and township, ⊙ Matías Romero municipio, Oaxaca, S Mexico, in foothills of Sierra Madre del Sur, on RR, and 22 mi/35 km NNE of Ixtepec; 16°52′N 95°21′W. Elev. 659 ft/201 m. RR center. Processing, lumbering, and agr. center (cereals, sugarcane, fruit; livestock). Mfg. materials and bldg. equip.

Matinecock, residential village (□ 2 sq mi/5.2 sq km; 1990 pop. 872), Nassau co., SE N.Y., on NW L.I., just E of Glen Cove; 40°51′N 73°34′W. In water-oriented recreational area. Oyster Bay Natl. Wildlife Refuge 3.5 mi/5.6 km to E.

Matinicock Point, small peninsula extending N into L.I. Sound, SE N.Y., just N of Glen Cove, and marking E side of entrance to Hempstead Harbor; 40°54′N 73°38′W.

Matinicus Isle (muh-TIN-ik-uhs), plantation (1990 pop. 67), Knox co., S Maine, in the Atlantic Ocean, c.20 mi/32 km SE of Rockland; 43°53′N 68°54′W. Includes Matinicus (□ c.1 sq mi/2.6 sq km), Ragged (with Criehaven village), Seal, and Wooden Ball isls., and Matinicus Rock (lighthouse).

Matlalcueyatl, Mexico: see MALINCHE.

Matlock, town (1990 pop. 92), Sioux co., NW Iowa, 17 mi/27 km NNE of Orange City; 43°14′N 95°55′W. Livestock; grain.

Matoaka (muh-TO-kuh), town (1990 pop. 366), Mercer co., S W.Va., 9 mi/14.5 km WNW of Princeton; 37°25′N 81°14′W. Coal-mining and lumbering area.

Matouba (mah-too-BAH), thermal springs, S Basse-Terre isl., Guadeloupe, near Saint-Claude, 2 mi/3.2 km NNE of Basse-Terre.

Matsqui (MAT-skwee), village, SW B.C., W Canada, near Fraser R., 16 mi/26 km WSW of Chilliwack. Lumbering; fruit, hops, tobacco.

Mattabesset River (MA-te-BAI-sit), c.12 mi/19 km long, central Conn.; rises SE of New Britain; flows generally SE to the Connecticut R. just above Middletown.

Mattagami (muh-TA-guh-mee), river, 275 mi/443 km long; rises in the lake dist., E Ont., central Canada, SW of Timmins; flows N to join the Missinaibi R., with which it forms the Moose R.

Mattagami Lake (muh-TA-guh-mee) (□ 88 sq mi/228 sq km), W Que., E Canada, 120 mi/193 km N of Val d'Or; 26 mi/42 km long, 10 mi/16 km wide. Elev. 765 ft/233 m. Drained NW by Nottaway R.

Mattamuskeet, Lake (ma-tuh-muh-SKEET), E N.C., in central Hyde co., N and NW of Pamlico Sound; c.15 mi/24 km long E-W, 6 mi/9.7 km wide. State Highway 94 causeway crosses center of lake. Entirely within L. Mattanuskeet Natl. Wildlife Refuge. Intracoastal Waterway (Alligator-Pungo Canal) passes to N.

Mattapan, Mass.: see BOSTON.

Mattapoisett (ma-duh-POI-set), town (1990 pop. 5,850), Plymouth co., SE Mass., on W shore of Buzzards Bay, 6 mi/9.7 km E of New Bedford; 41°40′N 70°49′W. Resort; mfg. (boats, apparel); good harbor. Formerly had shipbuilding and whaling. Includes villages of Antasawamock Neck and East Mattapoisett. Settled 1750, inc. 1857.

Mattaponi River (ma-tah-po-NEI), 120 mi/193 km long, E Va.; formed in NW Caroline co. by joining of Matta and Poni rivers; flows SE, past Bowling Green, joins Pamunkey R. at West Point to form York R. estuary, arm of Chesapeake Bay. Navigable for c.40 mi/64 km above mouth; chief cargoes are wood prods.

Mattawa (MAH-tuh-wo), town (1991 pop. 2,454), E Ont., central Canada, on Ottawa R. at mouth of Mattawa R., and 36 mi/58 km E of North Bay; 46°19′N 78°42′W. Lumbering, plywood mfg., mica mining.

Mattawa (MAT-uh-wah), town (1990 pop. 941), Grant

co., E central Wash., 29 mi/47 km ENE of Yakima, near Columbia R. (Priest Rapids L. reservoir); 46°45′N 119°54′W. Irrigated agr. area (vegetables, fruit, sugar beets). Priest Rapids (to S) and Wanapum (to N) dams. U.S. Military Reservation–U.S. Dept. of Energy Hanford Site to E and SE.

Mattawa River, 45 mi/72 km long, central Ont., central Canada; issues from Trout L. (8 mi/13 km long), 3 mi/5 km E of North Bay; flows E to Ottawa R. at Mattawa.

Mattawamkeag (mat-uh-WAHM-keg), town (1990 pop. 830), Penobscot co., E central Maine, on the Penobscot R., at mouth of the Mattawamkeag R., and c.50 mi/80 km NNE of Bangor; 45°32′N 68°18′W. Mfg. wood prods. Hunting, fishing.

Mattawamkeag Lake, Aroostook co., E central Maine, 18 mi/29 km SW of Houlton; 7 mi/11.3 km long. In lumbering, recreational area. A source of Mattawamkeag R.

Mattawamkeag River, c.70 mi/113 km long, E central Maine; rises in 2 branches in S Aroostook co.; flows generally S and SW to the Penobscot R. at Mattawamkeag.

Mattawin River (MA-tuh-win), 100 mi/161 km long, S Que., E Canada; rises near Mont Tremblant; flows E, through L. Toro, to St. Maurice R. 25 mi/40 km NNW of Grand'Mere. Several falls.

Mattawoman Creek (ma-tah-WO-muhn), c.35 mi/56 km long, S Md.; rises just SE of Brandywine; flows generally W through swampland, forming part of border bet. Charles and Prince Georges cos., to the Potomac R. c.4 mi/6.4 km below Indian Head.

Matteawan, N.Y.: see BEACON.

Matteseunk Lake (MA-tuh-suhnk), Aroostook co., E Maine, 17 mi/27 km ESE of Millinocket; 3 mi/4.8 km long.

Matteson (MAT-ih-sun), village (1990 pop. 11,378), Cook co., NE Ill., S commuter suburb of Chicago; 41°30′N 87°44′W. Lincoln Mall is here.

Matthew Town, minor port in S Bahama Isls., on W tip of Great Inagua Isl., 350 mi/563 km SE of Nassau, 55 mi/89 km NNE of Cape Maisí (E Cuba); 20°57′N 73°40′W. Salt (company hq. for Bahamas).

Matthews, city (1990 pop. 13,651), Mecklenburg co., S N.C., a suburb 10 mi/16 km SE of Charlotte; 35°07′N 80°42′W. Agr. to E and S (grain; livestock; dairying). Mfg. (machinery, plastics, paper prods., lab equip., bldg. materials, safety valves, textiles, consumer goods; metal fabricating).

Matthews 1 town, Jefferson co., E Ga., 25 mi/40 km SW of Augusta; 33°12′N 82°18′W. **2** town (1990 pop. 571), Grant co., E central Ind., 14 mi/23 km SSE of Marion. In agr. area; electrical equip. **3** town (1990 pop. 614), New Madrid co., extreme SE Mo., 12 mi/19 km NNW of New Madrid; 36°45′N 89°34′W. Soybeans, cotton, corn.

Matthews Peak (9,512 ft/2,899 m), Apache co., NE Ariz., in Chuska Mts., near N.Mex. state line, c.55 mi/89 km SW of Farmington (N.Mex.).

Mattituck (MA-ti-tuk), resort village (□ 10 sq mi/26 sq km; 1990 pop. 3,902), Suffolk co., SE N.Y., on NE L.I., on inlet of L.I. Sound, 8 mi/12.9 km NE of Riverhead; 41°00′N 72°32′W. Mfg. of zinc prods. for marine industry, machinery. Popular for summer recreational activities.

Mattole River, c.50 mi/80 km long, NW Calif.; rises in NW Mendocino co., 3 mi/4.8 km inland from Pacific Ocean, 10 mi/16 km NW of Leggett; flows NW to the Pacific c.35 mi/56 km SW of Eureka, N of Punta Gorda cape. King Mt. Range separates river from ocean.

Mattoon (mat-TOON), city (1990 pop. 18,441), Coles co., E central Ill., 11 mi/18 km W of Charleston; 39°28′N 88°22′W. Processing, RR, and industrial center for a farming region. Agr. (corn, soybeans, sorghum). Mfg. (paper prods., electrical equip., machinery, consumer goods, fire-prevention equip., signs, bldg. materials; vegetable processing). Nearby are many oil wells, a fish hatchery, and L. Mattoon (6 mi/9.7 km SW). The farm and grave of Abraham Lincoln's father and stepmother are SE of the city. Lake Land Col. 5 mi/8 km S. Inc. 1859.

Mattoon (mah-TOON), village (1990 pop. 431), Shawano co., E central Wis., 29 mi/47 km ENE of Wausau; 45°00′N 89°02′W. Lumbering; mfg. (wood and wood-related prods.). Menominee Indian Reservation (all of Menominee co.) to E.

Matty Island, S Franklin dist., N.W.T., N Canada, in James Ross Strait, bet. Boothia Peninsula (NE) and King William Isl. (SW); 20 mi/32 km long, 15 mi/24 km wide; 69°30′N 95°30′W.

Matunuck (ma-TOO-nuhck), summer resort village, in South Kingstown, Washington co., R.I., on coast of Block Isl. Sound. Fishing; many public beaches.

Mauckport, town (1990 pop. 95), Harrison co., S Ind., on Ohio R., and 13 mi/21 km S of Corydon; 38°01′N 86°12′W. In agr. area; hardwood veneer.

Maud 1 town (1990 pop. 1,204), Pottawatomie and Seminole cos., central Okla., 16 mi/26 km SE of Shawnee, near Wolf Creek; 35°07′N 96°46′W. In agr. area (oats, wheat; livestock); oil wells. Inc. 1929. **2** town (1990 pop. 1,049), Bowie co., NE Texas, 18 mi/29 km WSW of Texarkana, near Sulphur R. (Wright Patman L. to S); 33°19′N 94°20′W. Dairying; blueberries, vegetables; timber. Mfg. (electronics).

Maugansville (MO-gans-vil), village, Washington co., W Md., 4 mi/6.4 km NNW of Hagerstown. Named for Jonathan and Abraham Maughan in the 1880s, its development is recent. Washington Co. Regional Airport nearby.

Maui (MOU-ee), county (☐ 2,398 sq mi/6,211 sq km; 1990 pop. 100,374), Hawaii, includes KAHOOLAWE, LANAI, MAUI, MOLOKAI isls.; ⊙ Wailuku, on Maui; 20°52′N 156°37′W. Locally administered by 13 dists., 1 on Maui, 2 on Molokai, and 1 on Lanai. Largest city is Kahului. KALAWAO CO., on Molokai, is officially a dist. of Maui co. and is part of Kaulapapa Natl. Historical Park; Kahoolawe owned by U.S. military.

Maui (MOU-ee), island (☐ 728 sq mi/1,886 sq km; 1990 est. pop. 82,500), Maui co., Hawaii, 2d-largest isl. in the state of Hawaii, separated from the isl. of Hawaii to SE by the Alenuihaha Channel, from Molokai (NW) by the Pailolo Channel, from Lanai (NW) by Auau Channel, from Kahoolawe (SW) by Alakeiki Channel. Locally administered by 10 dists. Maui is made up of 2 mt. masses, the Haleakala in SE, in main sect. of isl., and West Maui Mts. in NW; on West Maui Peninsula, connected by isthmus 7 mi/11.3 km wide. The highest point on the isl. is Puu Ulaula (Red Hill) on SW rim of Haleakala crater (10,023 ft/3,055 m) in HALEAKALA NATIONAL PARK. In West Maui, Puu Kukui rises to 5,788 ft/ 1,764 m. The isl.'s chief industries are tourism and the cultivation of sugarcane (esp. W), cattle, pineapples, and timber (pine, eucalyptus). The principal ports are Kahului (largest city on isl. and in co.) and Lahaina. Wailuku (1990 pop. 10,688) is the 2d-largest town and the capital of Maui co. (1990 pop. 100,374), which includes the isls. of Maui, Lanai, Kahoolawe, and Molokai. Wailuku/Kahului and Lahaina have become major tourist centers. Launiupoko (W) and Waianapanapa Cave (E) state parks; Poli Poli Springs State Recreational Area in S; Kaumahina and Puaa Kaa state waysides in NE; West Maui (NW), Koolau and Makawao (NE), Hana (E), and Kula, Kahikinui, and Kipahulu (S) forest reserves.

Mauldin (MAWL-duhn), city (1990 pop. 11,587), Greenville co., NW S.C., suburb 6 mi/9.7 km SSE of Greenville, near Reedy R.; 34°47′N 82°17′W. Mfg. includes machinery, textile and textile prods., plastic prods., computer equip., food prods. Agr. includes grain, tomatoes, soybeans, sorghum, peaches; livestock, poultry.

Maumee (mo-MEE), residential city (1990 pop. 15,561), Lucas co., NW Ohio, on the Maumee R.; 41°34′N 83°39′W. Site of Fort Miami, a Br. post surrendered to the Americans during the War of 1812. Nearby is Fallen Timbers, the historical monument commemorating the battle fought in 1794. The Maumee R. courses N and NE through Toledo, where it enters L. Erie through Maumee Bay and is navigable. Automotive stamping plant. Inc. 1838.

Maumee River, c.130 mi/209 km long, in Ind. and Ohio; formed at Fort Wayne (Ind.) by junction of St. Joseph and St. Mary's rivers; flows NE, past Defiance and Toledo (Ohio), to Maumee Bay, an arm of L. Erie just NE of Toledo. For several miles above its mouth, the Maumee serves as harbor of Toledo. Receives Auglaize R. at Defiance.

Maumelle, Lake (maw-MEL), Pulaski co., central Ark., on Big Maumelle R., 15 mi/24 km WNW of Little Rock, and 2 mi/3.2 km W of the Arkansas R.; c.12 mi/19 km; 34°50′N 92°30′W. Max. capacity 220,000 acre-ft. Formed by L. Maumelle Dam (62 ft/19 m high), built (1957) by the City of Little Rock for its water supply.

Mauna Kea (MOU-nah KAI-ah), dormant volcano (13,796 ft/4,205 m), in the N central part of the isl. of Hawaii, Hawaii co., Hawaii, 25 mi/40 km WNW of Hilo. Highest point in Hawaii and Hawaiian Isl. chain; highest seamount in the world, rising c.32,000 ft/ 9,754 m from the Pacific Ocean floor; a 2d peak, Puu Makanaka (11,633 ft/3,546 m), is 3 mi/4.8 km to NE. It has many cinder cones on its flanks and a great crater at the summit. Its fertile lower slopes are used for agr., esp. the growing of coffee beans. The upper slopes are snow-covered in winter. Onizuka Astronomy Center S of summit. Observatory complex at summit. Pohakuloa Military Training Area to SW. Surrounded by Mauna Kea Forest Reserve; Mauna Kea Ice Age Natural Area Reserve on S slopes; Mauna Kea State Recreational Area to SW; large Parker Ranch to NW.

Mauna Kea Observatory, astronomical observatory at Mauna Kea peak, Hawaii co., Hawaii, c.25 mi/40 km WNW of Hilo; at elev. of over 13,796 ft/4,205 m. Observatory complex immediately N of peak. Operated by the Inst. for Astronomy of the Univ. of Hawaii. Instruments include the Canada-France-Hawaii 142-in/ 361-cm telescope, the U.K. Infrared 150-in/381-cm telescope, the 120-in/305-cm Infrared Telescope Facility, an 88-in/224-cm reflecting telescope, and twin 24-in/61-cm reflectors as well as 2 telescopes used for observations in the submillimeter portion of the electromagnetic spectrum. The W. M. Keck 33-ft/10-m telescope, with its array of 36 segmented mirrors, began observations in 1991. A computer adjusts each small mirror many times per second so that a single image is formed of the object under study. New twin telescopes (Keck I 1993 and Keck III 1996) are the world's largest, with 4 times the power of the 200-in/508-cm telescope at Mt. Palomar. Onizuka Astronomy Center to S of peak.

Mauna Loa (MOU-nah LO-ah), volcano (13,677 ft/ 4,169 m), S central Hawaii isl., Hawaii co., Hawaii, 35 mi/56 km WSW of Hilo, in W part of Hawaii Volcanoes Natl. Park. Mokuaweoweo, Mauna Loa's crater, lies at N end of the Southwest Rift Zone, which extends to S end of isl. Mauna Loa has erupted 4 times (1942, 1949, 1975, and 1984) since its period of greatest activity in 1881. Mauna Loa (atmospheric) Observatory 5 mi/ 8 km to N. Kau (SE), Mauna Loa (N), Kapapala (SE) forest reserves.

Maunabo (mou-NAH-bo), town (1990 pop. 12,347), SE P.R., near coast, N of Maunabo R., and 14 mi/23 km E of Guayama. Agr. (plantains; livestock). Tourism at its beaches. Its port (beach/resort) is 1.5 mi/2.4 km SSE.

Maunaloa (MOU-nah-LO-ah), village (1990 pop. 405), W Molokai, Maui co., Hawaii, inland c.5 mi/8 km from both N and W coasts, 3 mi/4.8 km from S coast, and 13 mi/21 km WNW of Kaunakakai; 21°08′N 157°12′W. Terminus of Manualoa Highway (State Highway 460). Molokai Ranch Wildlife Park to NW.

Maunalua Bay (MOU-nah-LOO-ah), SE Oahu isl., Honolulu co., Hawaii, bet. Diamond Head (W) and Koko Head (E), in city of Honolulu, 6 mi/9.7 km ESE of downtown.

Maunawili (MOU-nah-WEE-lee), town (1990 pop. 4,847), SE Oahu isl., Honolulu co., Hawaii, 8 mi/ 12.9 km ENE of Honolulu, and 2 mi/3.2 km SW of Kailua and E coast, at intersection of Kalanianaole and Pali highways. Waimanalo Forest Reserve to SW.

Maunie (maw-NEE), village (1990 pop. 119), White co., SE Ill., on Wabash R., and 8 mi/12.9 km ESE of Carmi; 38°02′N 88°02′W. In agr. area (corn, wheat, soybeans); oil and natural gas.

Maunoir, Lac (mon-WAHR, lahk), lake, NW Mackenzie dist., N.W.T., N Canada, NW of Great Bear L.; 30 mi/ 48 km long, 1 mi/2 km–15 mi/24 km wide; 67°30′N 125°W. Drains NE into Anderson R. Sometimes called Manoir L.

Maupin (MAW-pin), village (1990 pop. 456), Wasco co., N Oregon, 30 mi/48 km S of The Dalles, on Deschutes R., at mouth of Bakeoven Creek; 45°10′N 121°04′W. Timber. Wheat, fruit; sheep, cattle. Fish hatchery to N. Warm Springs Indian Reservation to SW. Mt. Hood Natl. Forest to W.

Maurepas, Lake (MAHR-i-paw), SE La., c.28 mi/45 km NW of New Orleans; c.13 mi/21 km long; 30°15′N, 90°29′W. Receives navigable Tickfaw R. from N, Amite and Petite Amite rivers from W; connected to L. Pontchartrain (E) by the Pass Manchac waterway.

Maurice, town (1990 pop. 243), Sioux co., NW Iowa, 6 mi/9.7 km W of Orange City; 42°58′N 96°10′W. In livestock and grain area.

Maurice (MAHR-ees), village (1990 pop. 432), Vermilion parish, S La., 12 mi/19 km NNW of Abbeville, and 8 mi/ 13 km SW of Lafayette, on Indian Bayou; 30°07′N 92°07′W. Rice; cattle. Gas field nearby.

Maurice River (maw-REES), township (☐ over 94 sq mi/243 sq km; 1990 pop. 6,648), Cumberland co., S N.J., 6 mi/9.7 km SW of Millville; 39°17′N 74°56′W. Sparsely populated. Inc. 1798.

Maurice River (maw-REES), c.50 mi/80 km long, S N.J.; rises near Glassboro; flows S, past Millville (dam here forms 3-mi/4.8-km-long Union L.), to Maurice R. Cove on Delaware Bay, 2 mi/3.2 km S of Port Norris. Navigable to Millville; oystering, fishing docks at mouth.

Mauricetown (maw-REES-toun), village, Cumberland co., S N.J., on Maurice R., and 8 mi/12.9 km SSE of Millville. Oystering.

Mauriceville, uninc. town (1990 pop. 2,046), Orange co., SE Texas, 12 mi/19 km NW of Orange; 30°13′N 93°52′W. RR junction. Agr. (cattle; rice; horticulture). Timber. Oil and natural gas. Mfg. (machinery).

Maury (MOR-ree), county (☐ 614 sq mi/1,590 sq km; 1990 pop. 54,812), central Tenn.; ⊙ Columbia; 35°37′N 87°05′W. Drained by Duck R. Livestock raising (esp. cattle and mules); dairying; agr. (corn, hay, tobacco, wheat, sorghum, pecans). Phosphate rock deposits. Graphite plant and other mfg. at Columbia, some mfg. at Mt. Pleasant. Formed 1807.

Maury (MOR-ee), uninc. village, Greene co., E central N.C., 15 mi/24 km N of Kinston. In agr. area (tobacco, grain, cotton; poultry; livestock). Mfg. (clothing, wood prods., fabricated metal prods.).

Maury City, town (1990 pop. 782), Crockett co., W Tenn., 26 mi/42 km NW of Jackson; 35°49′N 89°14′W. In diversified farm area.

Maury River, c.90 mi/145 km long, NW Va.; rises in SW Augusta co., 10 mi/16 km W of Staunton; flows SSW, receiving Calfpasture R. from NW near Goshen, turns SE, continuing past Lexington and Buena Vista, then S to James R. at Glasgow. Sect. below Goshen formerly called North R.

Mauston (MAWS-tun), town (1990 pop. 3,439), ⊙ Juneau co., central Wis., on Lemonweir R., and 55 mi/ 89 km E of La Crosse; 43°47′N 90°04′W. In agr. area. Agr. (grain, hay, potatoes); mfg. (fabricated metal prods., machine tools, machinery, pork and dairy prods., beverages, furniture, cigars). Castle Rock Dam and L. to NE. Settled c.1840, inc. 1883.

Maverick, county (☐ 1,291 sq mi/3,344 sq km; 1990 pop. 36,378), SW Texas, on Rio Grande (SW; Mex. border); ⊙ Eagle Pass; 28°45′N 100°19′W. Bridged at Eagle Pass. Rich agr. area (part of Winter Garden region), irrigated by the Rio Grande; grain sorghum, oats, wheat; pecans, vegetables; uplands are ranching region (cattle); oil and gas; sand and gravel. Formed 1856.

Mavis Bank, village (1991 pop. 1,756), St. Andrew parish, SE Jamaica, in interior mts., 11 mi/18 km NE of Hope Botanical Gardens; 18°01′N 76°40′W. Elev. c.2,000 ft/ 610 m. Coffee dist. Noted scenery.

Max, village (1990 pop. 301), McLean co., central N.Dak., 29 mi/47 km S of Minot; 47°49′N 101°17′W. RR junction. L. Sakakawea to S.

Max Meadows, uninc. village, Wythe co., SW Va., 7 mi/11.3 km E of Wytheville. Mfg. (machining); in rich agr. area (grain, apples, soybeans; livestock; dairying).

Max Patch Mountains, N.C. and Tenn.: see BALD MOUNTAINS.

Maxbass, village (1990 pop. 123), Bottineau co., N N.Dak., 33 mi/53 km WSW of Bottineau; 48°43′N 101°08′W.

Maxcanú (mahsh-kahn-DO), town (1990 pop. 10,082), Yucatan, SE Mexico, on RR, and 36 mi/58 km SW of Mérida, at a highway junction (Mexico Highways 180 and 184); 20°35′N 90°00′W. Henequen-growing center. Oxkintoc ruins (NE) and Calcehtoc grotto (E) nearby.

Maxeys (MAKS-eez), town (1990 pop. 180), Oglethorpe co., NE Ga., 19 mi/31 km SE of Athens; 33°45′N 83°10′W.

Maxfield, town (1990 pop. 86), Penobscot co., S central Maine, 35 mi/56 km N of Bangor; 45°17′N 68°45′W. Lumbering.

Máximo Gómez (MAHKS-ee-mo GO-maiz), town, Matanzas prov., W Cuba, 14 mi/23 km SE of Cárdenas; 22°53′N 81°03′W. RR junction in agr. region (sugarcane, fruit, sisal; cattle).

Máximo River (MAHKS-ee-mo), c.35 mi/56 km long, Camagüey prov., E Cuba; rises at S foot of the Sierra de Cubitas; flows ENE to N coast 15 mi/24 km NW of Nuevitas.

Maxinkuckee, Lake, SW Marshall co., N Ind., at Culver; c.3 mi/4.8 km long. Ind.'s 2d-largest natural lake. Glacially formed. Average depth is 88 ft/27 m. Resort area.

Maxton, town (1990 pop. 2,373), Robeson co., S N.C., 6 mi/9.7 km ESE of Laurinburg, near Drowning Creek (becomes Lumber R. downstream from here, to E); 34°44′N 79°20′W. RR terminus. Agr. (grain, tobacco, soybeans, cotton; chickens, cattle, hogs). Mfg. (foods, furniture, wood prods.; textiles, apparel, paper).

Maxville, village (1991 pop. 840), SE Ont., central Canada, 19 mi/31 km N of Cornwall; 45°17′N 74°51′W. Dairying, mixed farming.

Maxwell, town (1990 pop. 788), Story co., central Iowa, 10 mi/16 km S of Nevada; 41°53′N 93°24′W. Bldg. materials.

Maxwell 1 uninc. village, Colusa co., N central Calif., 10 mi/16 km NW of Colusa, on Stone Corral Creek. Rice, wheat, sugar beets, walnuts, almonds; cattle; rice milling. Colusa R. to E. Nearby are Sacramento (N), Delevan (NE), and Colusa (SE) natl. wildlife refuges; Colusa–Sacramento R. State Recreation Area to E. **2** village, Hancock co., central Ind., 4 mi/6.4 km N of Greenfield. In agr. area; mfg. (concrete prods.). **3** village (1990 pop. 285), Lincoln co., central Nebr., 13 mi/21 km ESE of North Platte city, near Platte R.; 41°04′N 100°31′W. Fort McPherson Natl. Cemetery and State Wayside Area to S. **4** village (1990 pop. 247), Colfax co., NE N.Mex., on Canadian R., N of mouth of Vermejo R., near Sangre de Cristo Mts., and 26 mi/42 km S of Raton; 36°32′N 104°32′W. Elev. 5,909 ft/1,801 m. Shipping point in irrigated region; sheep, cattle. Maxwell Natl. Wildlife Refuge is here; Dorsey Mansion State Monument to E; Stubblefield L. reservoir to NW. **5** uninc. village (1990 pop. 185), Caldwell co., S central Texas, 8 mi/12.9 km E of San Marcos. Poultry; eggs; cotton, sorghum. Oil and natural gas. Mfg. (fabricated metal prods.).

Maxwell Air Force Base, Alabama: see MONTGOMERY.

May 1 village (1990 pop. 42), Harper co., NW Okla., 22 mi/35 km WNW of Woodward, and on North Canadian (Beaver) R.; 36°37′N 99°45′W. In grain and livestock area. **2** uninc. village (1990 pop. 285), Brown co., central Texas, 19 mi/31 km N of Brownwood. In rich farm area.

May, Cape, N.J.: see CAPE MAY.

May Pen, town (1991 pop. 45,903), ⊙ Clarendon parish, S Jamaica, on Minho R., on Jamaica RR, 30 mi/48 km W of Kingston; 17°58′N 77°14′W. RR junction, road and marketing center; citrus-processing plant, canneries, rope factory.

Maya, La, Cuba: see LA MAYA.

Mayaguana: see BAHAMAS.

Mayaguana Passage, Atlantic channel, S Bahama Isls., bet. Mayaguana isl. (E) and cays off E Acklins Isl. (W); c.25 mi/40 km wide.

Mayagüez (mah-yah-GWAIZ), city (1990 pop. 100,371), W P.R., facing Mona Passage. Port of entry and shipping and mfg. center. Tuna-processing plants, breweries. Other mfg. (food processing; candy, chemical prods., machinery, electronics, scientific instruments). Recent expansion of pharmaceutical industries and offshore assembly plants. Tourism. Long known for its embroidery. Communications and cultural center with a growing pop. Has campus of Univ. of P.R., a U.S. govt. agr. research station, and 2 television stations. Mayagüez Zoo here. Internatl. airport. Founded c.1760.

Mayajigua (mei-yuh-HEE-gwuh), town, Sancti Spíritus prov., central Cuba, on RR, and 33 mi/53 km SE of Caibarién; 22°15′N 78°59′W. Resort with mineral springs.

Mayapán (mah-yah-PAHN), town (1990 pop. 1,929), Yucatán, SE Mexico, 24 mi/39 km SSE of Mérida; 20°28′N 89°11′W. In henequen-growing area. Was capital of a post-classic Maya state; ruins are extensive but not reconstructed.

Mayarí (mah-yuh-REE), town, Holguín prov., E Cuba, on small Mayarí R., near Nipe Bay (Atlantic Ocean), and 40 mi/64 km ESE of Holguín; 23°40′N 75°44′W. Lumbering and agr. center (sugarcane, tobacco, fruit), in important quarry and mining region (laterites; chromium and iron refined at Felton, 8 mi/12.9 km NE). The sugar central Guatemala is 7 mi/11.3 km NNE.

Mayarí Arriba (mah-yuh-REE ah-REE-buh), town, Santiago de Cuba prov., SE Cuba, in mts., 31 mi/50 km NNE of Santiago de Cuba; 20°25′N 75°32′W. Food processing.

Mayarí River (mah-yuh-REE), 66 mi/107 km long, Holguín prov., E Cuba; rises SE of Mayarí; flows N, past Mayarí, to Nipe Bay. Drains 475 sq mi/1,231 sq km. Navigable for small boats below Mayarí. Fourth longest river on N coast.

Mayaro (MA-yah-ro), county (□ 145.69 sq mi/377.34 sq km; Nariva-Mayaro 1990 pop. 36,250), SE Trinidad, Trinidad and Tobago, on the Atlantic Ocean; 10°10′N 61°05′W. Forms (together with St. David, St. Andrew, and Nariva) the administrative dist. of Eastern Cos.

Mayaro (MA-yah-ro), village, E Trinidad, Trinidad and Tobago, on N Mayaro Bay, 30 mi/48 km E of San Fernando. In coconut-growing region. Fine beaches along the coast.

Mayaro Bay (MA-yah-ro), along SE coast of Trinidad, Trinidad and Tobago, ribbon of fine sand beaches, c.12 mi/19 km long (N-S); 10°15′N 60°58′W. Lined by coconut palms.

Maybee, town (1990 pop. 500), Monroe co., extreme SE Mich., 9 mi/14.5 km NW of Monroe; 42°00′N 83°31′W. In farm area. Limestone.

Maybeury (MAI-be-ree), uninc. village (1990 pop. 700), McDowell co., S W.Va., 13 mi/21 km ESE of Welch.

Maybrook, village (□ 1 sq mi/2.6 sq km; 1990 pop. 2,802), Orange co., SE N.Y., 10 mi/16 km WSW of Newburgh; 41°29′N 74°12′W. Mfg. of textiles and apparel. Inc. 1925.

Mayer (MAI-yuhr), village (1990 pop. 471), Carver co., S central Minn., on South Fork Crow R., and 32 mi/51 km W of Minneapolis; 44°52′N 93°53′W. Dairying; poultry; grain, soybeans, alfalfa.

Mayersville (MEI-uhrs-vil), village (1990 pop. 329), ⊙ Issaquena co., W Miss., on the Mississippi R., and 34 mi/55 km S of Greenville; 32°53′N 91°02′W. Agr. (cotton, grain; cattle). Indian Bayou Waterfall Area to E; Anderson-Tully and Shipland wildlife management areas to S.

Mayerthorpe (MAI-uhr-thorp), village (1991 pop. 1,692), central Alta., W Canada, 70 mi/113 km WNW of Edmonton. Lumbering, mixed farming.

Mayes (MAIZ), county (□ 683 sq mi/1,769 sq km; 1990 pop. 33,366), NE Okla.; ⊙ Pryor; 36°17′N 95°14′W. Intersected by Neosho R. (impounded near center by Pensacola Dam), forming L. of the Cherokees; Fort Gibson L. reservoir downstream (S). Cherokee Plains

in W. Cattle; recreation; agr. (corn, soybeans, sorghum, wheat, oats; dairying). Mfg. (food prods., apparel, chemicals, machinery; metal industry). Salina and Snowdale state parks, near center; Spavinaw, Cherokee, and Little Blue–Disney state parks in NE. Formed 1907.

Mayesville, village (1990 pop. 694), Sumter co., E central S.C., 8 mi/12.9 km ENE of Sumter, near Black R.; 33°59′N 80°12′W. Mfg. of wood prods.; agr. includes livestock; grain, tobacco, cotton, peanuts.

Mayetta (mai-ET-uh), village (1990 pop. 267), Jackson co., NE Kansas, 8 mi/12.9 km S of Holton; 39°20′N 95°43′W. Trading point in livestock and grain area. Potawatomi Indian Reservation is W.

Mayfield, town (1990 pop. 9,935), ⊙ Graves co., W Ky., 23 mi/37 km S of Paducah; 36°44′N 88°39′W. RR terminus. In an area of farms and clay deposits, it is an agr. trade center with a tobacco market. Mfg. (tobacco processing; transportation equip., apparel, RR ties, industrial packaging, plastics prods.). Mayfield–Graves Co. Airport to E. Woolridge Monument, in Maplewood Cemetery, 18 statues designed by Harry C. Woolridge from 1840. Western Ky. Mus. Kaler Brothers (to NE) and Obion Creek (to W) wildlife management areas. Founded 1823.

Mayfield 1 village (1990 pop. 110), Summer co., S Kansas, 8 mi/12.9 km W of Wellington; 37°15′N 97°32′W. In wheat area. **2** village (□ 1 sq mi/2.6 sq km; 1990 pop. 817), in Mayfield town (1990 pop. 5,738), Fulton co., E central N.Y., on Sacandaga Reservoir, 6 mi/9.7 km NE of Gloversville; 43°06′N 74°16′W. **3** village (1990 pop. 3,462), Cuyahoga co., N Ohio, 13 mi/21 km E of downtown Cleveland, and on Chagrin R., just S of Mayfield Heights; 41°33′N 81°26′W. Insurance is major employer. **4** village (1990 pop. 438), Sanpete co., central Utah, on Twelve Mile Creek, 10 mi/16 km SSW of Manti; 39°07′N 111°42′W. Alfalfa, barley; dairying; cattle, sheep, poultry. Elev. 5,500 ft/1,676 m. Manti–La Sal Natl. Forest to E. Settled 1876.

Mayfield, borough (1990 pop. 1,890), Lackawanna co., NE Pa., 11 mi/18 km NE of Scranton; 41°32′N 75°31′W. Agr. (dairying; cattle; corn); mfg. (fabricated metal prods., plastics prods.). Former anthracite-coal center. Archbald Pothole State Park to SW; Merli Sarnoski Park to N. Founded c.1840.

Mayfield Creek, c.70 mi/113 km long, SW Ky.; rises in W Calloway co.; flows generally NNW, past Mayfield, then W to the Mississippi R. 1 mi/1.6 km S of Wickliffe. Receives West Fork Mayfield Creek (c.25 mi/40 km long; rises SW of Mayfield, 6 mi/9.7 km ESE of Wickliffe).

Mayfield Heights, city (1990 pop. 19,847), Cuyahoga co., NE Ohio, a suburb of Cleveland; 41°31′N 81°27′W. It is primarily residential. Inc. 1925.

Mayflower, town (1990 pop. 1,415), Faulkner co., central Ark., 18 mi/29 km NNW of Little Rock, near Arkansas R.; 34°58′N 92°25′W. Mfg. (plastic and wood prods.). L. Conway reservoir to NE; Camp Robinson Wildlife Management Area to E; Camp Robinson Natl. Guard Training Area to SE.

Mayflower Village, uninc. town (1990 pop. 4,978), Los Angeles co., S Calif., residential suburb 12 mi/19 km ENE of downtown Los Angeles, 2 mi/3.2 km SE of Arcadia; 34°07′N 118°01′W. El Monte Airport to SW.

Mayhill, uninc. village (1990 pop. 300), Otero co., S N.Mex., in E foothills of Sacramento Mts., 30 mi/48 km E of Alamogordo, in Lincoln Natl. Forest. Elev. 6,580 ft/2,006 m. Timber; sheep; fruit. Cloudcraft Ski Area to W; Mescalero Apache Indian Reservation to N.

Maynard 1 town (1990 pop. 513), Fayette co., NE Iowa, 14 mi/23 km SSW of West Union; 42°46′N 91°52′W. Dairying; limestone quarry. **2** town (1990 pop. 10,325), Middlesex co., NE central Mass., on Assabet R., and 21 mi/34 km WNW of Boston; 42°26′N 71°28′W. Computer company hq. Site of former wool textile mill. Settled 1638, inc. 1871.

Maynard 1 village (1990 pop. 354), Randolph co., NE Ark., 12 mi/19 km NNE of Pocahontas, near Mo. state line; 36°25′N 90°54′W. Lumber. **2** village (1990 pop. 419), Chippewa co., SW Minn., 13 mi/21 km E of Montevideo, on Hawk Creek; 44°53′N 95°28′W.

Grain, soybeans, sugar beets; hogs, sheep; mfg. (plastic prods.).

Maynardville, city (1990 pop. 1,298), ⊙ Union co., NE Tenn., 20 mi/32 km NNE of Knoxville; 36°15′N 83°48′W. In fertile farm area. Mfg. (apparel).

Mayne Island (□ 9 sq mi/23 sq km), SW B.C., W Canada, Gulf Isls., in Strait of Georgia just off Vancouver Isl., bet. Galiano (NW) and Saturna (SE) isls., 30 mi/ 48 km S of Vancouver; 6 mi/10 km long, 1 mi/2 km– 3 mi/5 km wide; 48°50′N 123°18′W. Lumbering, farming. Village is at NW end.

Mayo, village (1991 pop. 243), central Yukon, NW Canada, on Stewart R., and 110 mi/177 km ESE of Dawson; 63°36′N 135°53′W. Silver- and lead-mining center, furtrapping region. Govt. services. Formerly called Mayo Landing.

Mayo (MAI-o), uninc. town (1990 pop. 1,569), Spartanburg co., NW S.C., near Pacolet R., 10 mi/16 km NNE of Spartanburg; 35°04′N 81°50′W. Agr. includes dairying; livestock; grain, peaches, apples.

Mayo, village (1990 pop. 917), ⊙ Lafayette co., N central Fla., c.60 mi/97 km WNW of Gainesville; 30°03′N 83°10′W. Lumbering; limestone quarrying.

Mayo River (MAH-yo), c.220 mi/354 km long, NW Mexico; rises in Chihuahua NE of Ocampo; flows SW into Sonora, past Navojoa, and Etchojoa, to a lagoon inlet of Gulf of California, 5 mi/8 km SW of Huatabampo. Used for irrigation (Mocuzari Dam); along lower course; agr. (beans, corn, rice).

Mayo River, c. 15 mi/24 km long, Va. and N.C.; formed on state line by joining of North and South Mayo rivers 13 mi/21 km SW of Martinsville (Va.); flows S into N.C. past Mayodan to Dan R. just E of Madison. North Mayo R. rises in E Patrick co., flows SE c. 20 mi/32 km; South Mayo R. rises in SE Patrick co., flows c. 15 mi/ 24 km ESE.

Mayodan (MAI-o-dan), town (1990 pop. 2,471), Rockingham co., N N.C., 29 mi/47 km NE of Winston-Salem, and 2 mi/3.2 km N of Madison, near Dan R.; 36°24′N 79°58′W. Tobacco, grain, soybeans; poultry, livestock; dairying. Mfg. (textiles, apparel). Belews L. reservoir to NE. Settled 1894; inc. 1897.

Maypearl, town (1990 pop. 781), Ellis co., N central Texas, 11 mi/18 km SW of Waxahachie; 32°19′N 97°00′W. In agr. (cotton; corn, wheat; dairying; cattle, horses) area; oil and gas.

Mayport, town, Duval co., extreme NE Fla., 14 mi/ 23 km E of Jacksonville, on St. Johns R. near its mouth on the Atlantic Ocean. Fishing. Major service center for adjacent Mayport U.S. Naval Station.

Mayrán, Laguna de (mah-ee-RAHN, lah-GOO-nah dai), depression in Laguna dist. of Coahuila, N Mexico, 45 mi/72 km E of Torreón; 25 mi/40 km long, c.15 mi/ 24 km wide. Contains water only during rainy period, when Nazas R. flows to it. Construction of dams has left the laguna dry, covered with clay. Desert climate. Also known as Desierto de Mayran.

Mayreau (MEI-ro) islet (□ 1.5 sq mi/3.9 sq km; 1994 est. pop. 200), St. Vincent and the Grenadines, West Indies, bet. Canouan and Union isls., 35 mi/56 km S of St. Vincent; 12°39′N 61°23′W. Sometimes called Mayaro or Mayero.

Mays Landing, resort village (1990 pop. 2,090), ⊙ Atlantic co., S N.J., on Great Egg Harbor R., and 16 mi/ 26 km WNW of Atlantic City; 39°27′N 74°43′W. Poultry; vegetables. Seat of Atlantic Community Col. Settled c.1710.

Mays Lick, uninc. village (1990 pop. 430), Mason co., NE Ky., 9 mi/14.5 km SSW of Maysville. Burley tobacco, grain; livestock; dairying. Mfg. (feeds, fertilizer).

Maysí, Cape, Cuba: see MAISÍ, CAPE.

Maysville, city (1990 pop. 1,176), ⊙ De Kalb co., NW Mo., 26 mi/42 km ENE of St. Joseph; 39°53′N 94°21′W. Corn, wheat, soybeans; cattle; light mfg. Settled 1845.

Maysville 1 town (1990 pop. 170), Scott co., E Iowa, 10 mi/16 km NW of Davenport; 41°38′N 90°43′W. In agr. area. **2** town (1990 pop. 7,169), ⊙ Mason co., NE Ky., 50 mi/80 km SE of Cincinnati (Ohio), on the Ohio R. (bridged here to Aberdeen, Ohio), in N part of Bluegrass region; 38°37′N 83°46′W. Elev. 514 ft/157 m. RR junction; trade and industrial center, with air, RR, and river connections. Mfg. (machinery, fabricated metal prods., textiles, apparel, transportation equip., bldg. materials; lime processing, paper converting). Agr. (burley tobacco, soybeans, grain; livestock, poultry; dairying). Daniel Boone and his wife operated a tavern here (c.1786–1789). Ulysses S. Grant attended a local school. Singer Rosemary Clooney's Childhood Home. Site of Kenton's station, a stockaded trading post, is nearby. Fleming–Mason Co. Airport to S. Maysville Community Col. (Univ. of Ky.). Mason Co. Mus., Opera House (1851). Valley Pike Covered Bridge to W. Settled c.1782 by Simon Kenton and others as Limestone; est. 1787 by Va. legislature; inc. 1833. **3** town (1990 pop. 892), Jones co., E N.C., 18 mi/29 km SW of New Bern, on White Oak R.; 34°53′N 77°13′W. Agr. (grain, beans, tobacco, peanuts, cotton; livestock). Mfg. (crushed stone, apparel). Croatan Natl. Forest to E; Hoffman Forest to W. **4** town (1990 pop. 1,203), Garvin co., S central Okla., 12 mi/19 km WNW of Pauls Valley; 34°49′N 97°24′W. In agr. area; mfg. (fabricated metal prods., paper prods.); oil and gas.

Maysville, village (1990 pop. 728), Banks and Jackson cos., NE Ga., 14 mi/23 km E of Gainesville; 34°15′N 83°34′W. Textile mfg.

Maytown, uninc. town (1990 pop. 1,720), Lancaster co., SE Pa., near Susquehanna R., 15 mi/24 km W of Lancaster; 40°04′N 76°34′W. In agr. area (grain, soybeans; livestock, poultry; dairying). Elizabethtown-Marietta Airport to N, Marietta Ordnance Depot to S.

Mayview, town (1990 pop. 279), Lafayette co., W central Mo., 9 mi/14.5 km S of Lexington; 39°02′N 93°49′W. Corn, soybeans; cattle.

Mayville 1 town (1990 pop. 2,092), Traill co., E N.Dak., 49 mi/79 km NNW of Fargo, and on Goose R. Terminus of 1 of 2 RR spurs; joins Portland spur 4 mi/ 6.4 km NNW. Trade center; grain; livestock. Mfg. (printing; concrete, alfafa pellets). Seat of Mayville State Univ. Settled 1881, inc. 1883. **2** town (1990 pop. 4,474), Dodge co., S central Wis., on Rock R., and 15 mi/24 km ENE of Beaver Dam; 43°30′N 88°32′W. In farming, dairying, and resort area. Mfg. (metal prods., dairy prods., canned foods, cheese, maple syrup, cable and hose reels, work platforms, tool and die, furniture, fabricated metal prods., paper goods; sheet metal fabricating, printing). RR spur terminus. Horicon Natl. Wildlife Refuge to NW; Horicon Marsh Wildlife Area to SW. Settled c.1844, inc. 1885.

Mayville 1 village (1990 pop. 1,010), Tuscola co., E Mich., suburb 3 mi/4.8 km ESE of Saginaw; 43°20′N 83°20′W. In agr. area; mfg. (calcium chloride; machining). **2** resort village (□ 1 sq mi/2.6 sq km; 1990 pop. 1,636), ⊙ Chautauqua co., extreme W N.Y., at NW end of Chautauqua L., 17 mi/27 km NW of Jamestown; 42°15′N 79°30′W. Mfg. of furniture and lights. Inc. 1830.

Maywood, city (1990 pop. 27,850), Los Angeles co., S Calif., a suburb 5 mi/8 km SE of downtown Los Angeles; 34°00′N 118°11′W. Although chiefly residential, it has plants that make a variety of prods., such as chemicals, signs, foods, flat glass; industry base has declined. Inc. 1924.

Maywood 1 village (1990 pop. 27,139), Cook co., NE Ill., a suburb of Chicago, on the Des Plaines R.; 41°52′N 87°50′W. Agr. marketing and processing point and mfg. center. Nearby are the Loyola Univ. Medical Center and a VA hosp. Inc. 1881. **2** village (1990 pop. 313), Frontier co., S Nebr., 35 mi/56 km SSE of North Platte; 40°39′N 100°37′W. Grain; livestock, poultry. **3** suburban village (1990 pop. 3,400), Albany co., E N.Y., 8 mi/12.9 km NW of downtown Albany; 42°45′N 73°52′W.

Maywood, borough (1990 pop. 9,473), Bergen co., NE N.J., a residential suburb bet. Hackensack and Paterson; 40°53′N 74°03′W. Chemicals. Inc. 1894

Maywood Park, town (1990 pop. 781), Multnomah co., NW Oregon, residential suburb 4 mi/6.4 km ENE of downtown Portland, near Columbia R.; 45°32′N 122°33′W.

Maza (MAIZ-uh), village (1990 pop. 12), Towner, Benson, and Ramsey cos., N N.Dak., 8 mi/12.9 km S of Cando; 48°23′N 99°12′W. Wheat and livestock area. L. Alice Natl. Wildlife Refuge to SE (formerly Lac Aux Mortes); L. Alice and Chain L. to SE; L. Irvine to S.

Mazama, Mount oregon: see CRATER LAKE NATIONAL PARK.

Mazamitla (mah-sah-MEET-lah), town (1990 pop. 5,470), Jalisco, central Mexico, 37 mi/60 km E of Sayula, on Mexico Highway 110; 19°55′N 103°02′W. Grain, beans; livestock.

Mazapa de Madero (mah-SAH-pah dai mah-DAI-ro), town (1990 pop. 1,179), Chiapas, S Mexico, near Guatemala border, on Mexico Highway 190, 4 mi/6.4 km E of Motozintinde Mendoza; 15°23′N 92°11′W. Sugarcane. Also Mazapa.

Mazapil (mah-SAH-peel), city (1990 pop. 500) and township, ⊙ Mazapil municipio, Zacatecas, N central Mexico, on interior plateau, near Coahuila state border, 65 mi/105 km SW of Saltillo; 24°40′N 101°35′W. Elev. 7,677 ft/2,340 m. Mining center (gold, silver, lead, zinc, mercury).

Mazapiltepec de Juárez (mah-sah-PEEL-tai-pek dai HWAH-res), town (1990 pop. 1,287), Puebla, central Mexico, 35 mi/56 km ENE of Puebla. Elev. 7,940 ft/ 2,420 m. Cereals, maguey, fruit; livestock.

Mazatán 1 (mah-sah-TAHN), town (1990 pop. 4,220), Chiapas, S Mexico, in Pacific lowland, 13 mi/21 km WSW of Tapachula. Coffee, sugarcane, cacao, mangoes; livestock. **2** town (1990 pop. 1,600), Sonora, NW Mexico, 55 mi/89 km E of Hermosillo; 29°00′N 110°10′W. Grain, beans; cattle.

Mazateca, Sierra, Mexico: see OAXACA, SIERRA MADRE DE.

Mazatecochco (mah-sah-te-KOCH-ko), town (1990 pop. 6,320), ⊙ Mazatecochco de José María Morelos, Tlaxcala, central Mexico, at W foot of Malinche volcano, 10 mi/16 km N of Puebla; 19°11′N 98°10′W. Grain; livestock. Also known as José María Morelos.

Mazatecochco de José María Morelos, Mexico: see MAZATECOCHCO.

Mazatepec (mah-SAH-tai-pek), city (1990 pop. 3,592) and township, Morelos, central Mexico, 16 mi/26 km SW of Cuernavaca. Sugarcane, rice, fruit, vegetables.

Mazatlán (mah-saht-LAHN), city (1990 pop. 262,705) and township, Sinaloa state, W Mexico, on the Pacific coast; 23°11′N 106°25′W. One of the largest commercial and industrial centers of W Mexico, Mazatlán is one of Mexico's major Pacific seaports. It is on a RR bet. the U.S. and Mexico city, and its location makes it the country's primary ferry link to Baja California. Although the climate is hot, Mazatlán is a popular resort with a beautiful setting. Span. colonial trade with the Philippines stimulated the development of the port. Buena internatl. airport to N.

Mazatlan de Flores, Mexico: see MAZATLÁN VILLA DE FLORES.

Mazatlán Villa de Flores (mah-zaht-LAHN VEE-yah dai FLO-res), town (1990 pop. 522), in N central Oaxaca, Mexico, in S part of Sierra Mazateca, on the Chiquito R. (a tributary of the Santo Domingo R.), on unpaved road to Huautla, and 12 mi/19 km SE of Teotitlán de Flores Magón; 18°02′N 96°54′W. Elev. 3,937 ft/ 1,200 m. In Teotitlán judicial dist. Temperate climate. Mazatec-speaking area. Agr. (corn, sugarcane, mangoes). Formerly known as San Cristóbal Mazatlán.

Mazatzal Mountains, Maricopa, Gila and Yavapai cos., central Ariz., NE of Phoenix, extend c.50 mi/80 km N-S, E of along Verde R. from East Verde to Salt rivers, in Tonto Natl. Forest. Mazatzal Peak (7,903 ft/2,409 m) is highest in the range; Four Peaks (7,645 ft/2,330 m) and Mt. Ord (7,128 ft/2,173 m) are other high points.

Mazeppa (muh-ZE-puh), village (1990 pop. 722), Wabasha co., SE Minn., 18 mi/29 km NNW of Rochester, on North Fork Zumbro R.; 44°16′N 92°32′W. Grain; livestock, poultry; dairying; mfg. (fabricated metal prods., hog troughs). Richard J. Dorer Memorial Hardwood State Forest to E.

Mazomanie (maiz-o-MAIN-ee), town (1990 pop. 1,377), Dane co., S Wis., on tributary of Wisconsin R., and 22 mi/35 km WNW of Madison; 43°10′N 89°47′W. Lumber; shipping point and trade center for agr. area. RR junction. Timberline Ski Area to W.

Mazon (MAH-ZON), village (1990 pop. 764), Grundy co., NE Ill., 8 mi/12.9 km S of Morris; 41°14′N 88°25′W. In agr. area. Near the Mazon R., a classic source of fossils from a middle Pennsylvanian formation.

McGuire 1 and 2 Nuclear Power Plants, N.C.: see NORMAN, LAKE.

McAdam, village (1991 pop. 1,600), SW N.B., Canada, 40 mi/64 km SW of Fredericton, 5 mi/8 km ENE of Vanceboro (Maine); 45°35′N 67°20′W. RR junction; lumbering; hunting; tourist center.

McAdenville (mik-AD-uhn-vil), town (1990 pop. 830), Gaston co., S N.C., suburb 15 mi/24 km W of Charlotte, 7 mi/11.3 km E of Gastonia, on South Fork of Catawba R.; 35°15′N 81°04′W. Mfg. (textiles).

McAdoo (mahk-A-doo), borough (1990 pop. 2,459), Schuylkill co., E central Pa., 5 mi/8 km S of Hazleton; 40°53′N 75°59′W. Agr. (corn, hay; poultry; dairying); mfg. (cigars, bldg. materials, motor vehicles); anthracite coal. Tuscarora State Park to S. Founded 1880, inc. 1896.

McAlester (muh-KAL-uh-stuhr), city (1990 pop. 16,370), ⊙ Pittsburg co., SE Okla., 55 mi/89 km SSW of Muskogee, 26 mi/42 km SSW of Eufaula; 34°55′N 95°45′W. Elev. 740 ft/226 m. RR junction. A former coal-mining and farming community, McAlester has become a regional distribution center with a busy stockyard. Agr.; mfg. (apparel, motor vehicles, chemicals, ammunition, animal feeds, concrete), printing and publishing, food processing. McAlester Army Munitions Plant to SW, at Savanna. McAlester Municipal Airport to S. Inc. 1899.

McAlisterville (muh-KA-luhs-tuhr-vil), uninc. town (1990 pop. 750), Juniata co., central Pa., 8 mi/12.9 km ENE of Mifflintown on Little Lost Creek, 40°38′N 77°16′W. Mfg. of lumber, wooden prods., RR ties; agr. includes dairying; livestock; grain; timber.

McAllen, city (1990 pop. 84,021), Hidalgo co., extreme S Texas, 50 mi/80 km WNW of Brownsville, on the Rio Grande; 26°13′N 98°14′W. It is a RR junction, a port of entry, and a packing and processing center for the citrus fruit, vegetables and other produce, and flowers grown in the lower Rio Grande valley. The growing city has oil refineries and mfg. (medical supplies, apparel, marble prods., printing, steel fabrication). It is also a winter resort. Its nickname, "the City of Palms," came from the fact that 40 palm varieties flourish here. McAllen, connected by bridge with Reynosa, Mexico (8 mi/12.9 km SSW), saw a 50% increase in pop. from 1970 to 1990. Miller Internatl. Airport in S part of city. Bentsen–Rio Grande Valley State Park is to W; Santa Ana Natl. Wildlife Refuge to SE. Inc. 1911.

McAlpin, locality, Raleigh co., S W.Va., 8 mi/12.9 km SW of Beckley.

McAndrews (muh-KAND-rooz), uninc. village (1990 pop. 500), Pike co., E Ky., in the Cumberland Mts., 7 mi/11.3 km S of Williamson (W.Va.). Bituminous coal.

McArthur, village (1990 pop. 1,541), ⊙ Vinton co., S Ohio, 27 mi/43 km ESE of Chillicothe; 39°14′N 82°28′W. In livestock area; chemicals, lumber, clay prods. Plotted 1815, inc. 1851.

McArthur Falls, waterfalls in SE Man., Canada, on Winnipeg R., at N end of Lac du Bonnet, 65 mi/105 km NE of Winnipeg. Hydroelectric power center.

McArthur, Mount 1 peak (9,892 ft/3,015 m), SE B.C., Canada, near Alta. border, in Rocky Mts., in Yoho Natl. Park, 50 mi/80 km NW of Banff; 51°32′N 116°36′W. 2 peak (14,400 ft/4,389 m), SW Yukon, Canada, near Alaska border, in St. Elias Mts., 180 mi/290 km W of Whitehorse; 60°36′N 140°12′W.

McArthur–Burney Falls State Park, Calif.: see BURNEY.

McBain, village (1990 pop. 692), Missaukee co., N central Mich., 10 mi/16 km SE of Cadillac; 44°11′N 85°12′W. Mfg. (sawmill; feeds).

McBaine, town (1990 pop. 29), Boone co., central Mo., on Missouri R., 7 mi/11.3 km SW of Columbia. Virtually destroyed by 1993 flood.

McBee, town (1990 pop. 715), Chesterfield co. NE S.C., 38 mi/61 km NW of Florence; 34°28′N 80°15′W. Mfg.

includes printing equip., wire, apparel, water heaters, steel prods. Agr. includes peaches, watermelons; livestock.

McBride, village (1991 pop. 580), E B.C., Canada, on Fraser R., 120 mi/193 km ESE of Prince George; 53°18′N 120°10′W. Lumbering.

McBride, village (1990 pop. 236), Montcalm co., central Mich., 4 mi/6.4 km NNE of Stanton; 43°21′N 85°02′W. In agr. area.

McCall, town (1990 pop. 2,005), Valley co., W Idaho, on North Fork of Payette R., at S end of Payette L., 27 mi/43 km N of Cascade in recreation area; 44°55′N 116°07′W. Elev. 5,025 ft/1,532 m. Lumber milling, concrete mfg. Hq. Idaho Natl. Forest. Nearby deposits of thorium; summer and winter tourism. Upper Payette L. to N, Cascade Reservoir to S; Ponderosa State Park to E; parts of Payette Natl. Forest to E and W; Brundage Mt. Ski Area to N; Payette L. Ski Resort to W.

McCallsburg, town (1990 pop. 292), Story co., central Iowa, 11 mi/18 km NNE of Nev.; 42°10′N 93°23′W. Livestock; grain.

McCamey, town (1990 pop. 2,493), Upton co., W Texas, 60 mi/97 km S of Midland, near Pecos R.; 31°07′N 102°13′W. Elev. 2,441 ft/744 m. Distributing center for oil and gas and cattle- and sheep-ranching region. Agr. (cotton, pecans). Oil refinery; mfg. (petroleum production). Founded 1925 after oil discovery; inc. 1926.

McCammon, village (1990 pop. 722), Bannock co., SE Idaho, 20 mi/32 km SE of Pocatello, on Portneuf R.; 42°39′N 112°11′W. Elev. 4,751 ft/1,448 m. RR junction. Wheat, barley, alfalfa, hay, sheep, cattle, grain milling, mfg. (grain-milling equip.). Parts of Caribou Natl. Forest to NE, NW, and SW.

McCandless, township (1990 pop. 28,781), Allegheny co., W Pa., residential suburb 10 mi/16 km N of Pittsburgh; 40°34′N 80°01′W. Includes the communities of Highland and Fox Ridge.

McCarthy, village, S Alaska, 120 mi/193 km NE of Cordova, at foot of Wrangell Mts., 3 mi/4.8 km S of Kennicott. Airstrip. Formerly terminus of Copper R. and Northwestern RR, closed down 1938. Sometimes called Shushanna Junction.

McCaskill (muh-KAS-kil), village (1990 pop. 75), Hempstead co., SW Ark., 18 mi/29 km N of Hope; 33°55′N 93°38′W.

McCauley Island (☐ 108 sq mi/280 sq km), W B.C., Canada, in Hecate Strait W of Pitt Isl.; 53°40′N 130°15′W. Isl. is 18 mi/29 km long, 2 mi/3 km–12 mi/19 km wide.

McCausland, town (1990 pop. 308), Scott co., E Iowa, near Wapsipinicon R., 15 mi/24 km NNE of Davenport; 41°44′N 90°27′W.

McCaysville (muh-KAIZ-vil), town (1990 pop. 1,065), Fannin co., N Ga., 35 mi/56 km ENE of Dalton, near Tenn.-N.C. state line, in copper-mining region; 34°59′N 84°22′W. Once made barren from sulfuric acid by-prods. from smelting. Vegetation is now rebounding. Nearby Burra Mine site and Ducktown Basin Mus. are located across the state line in Tenn.

McChord Air Force Base, Wash.: see TACOMA.

McClain (muh-KLAIN), county (☐ 580 sq mi/1,502 sq km; 1990 pop. 22,795), central Okla.; ⊙ Purcell; 35°00′N 97°26′W. Bounded NE by Canadian R. and drained by small creeks; Washita R. beyond S boundary. Agr. (cotton, alfalfa, hay, soybeans, vegetables; cattle; dairying). Natural-gas wells. NW corner is partially urbanized, opposite Oklahoma City and Norman. Formed 1907.

McCleary, town (1990 pop. 1,235), Grays Harbor co., W Wash., 17 mi/27 km W of Olympia, on Wildcat Creek; 47°04′N 123°16′W. Mfg. (lumber, bldg. materials). Historic McCleary Hotel.

McClellan Air Force Base, Calif.: see SACRAMENTO.

McClellan Creek, c.40 mi/64 km long, extreme N Texas; rises in Carson co.; flows E and NE to North Fork of Red R. 10 mi/16 km N of McLean. In upper course, dam impounds L. McClellan, in McClellan Creek Natl. Grassland. Recreational area (fishing, bathing, camping) here.

McClellan, Fort, Ala.: see ANNISTON.

McClelland, town (1990 pop. 139), Pottawattamie co., SW Iowa, 10 mi/16 km ENE of Council Bluffs; 41°19′N 95°40′W.

McClellanville (muh-KLE-len-vil), village (1990 pop. 333), Charleston co., SE S.C., on the coast, on Intracoastal Waterway, and 23 mi/37 km SSW of Georgetown; 33°05′N 79°28′W. Fishing industry. Mfg. includes seafood processing. Nearby are Harrietta House and Gardens.

McClintock Channel, arm of the Arctic Ocean, S Franklin dist., N.W.T., Canada, bet. Victoria Isl. and Prince of Wales Isl.; 72°00′N 103°00′W. Opens N on Viscount Melville Sound; 170 mi/274 km long, 65 mi/105 km–130 mi/209 km wide.

McCloud, uninc. town (1990 pop. 1,555), Siskiyou co., N Calif., near McCloud R., 17 mi/27 km SE of Weed, at S base of Mt. Shasta; 41°15′N 122°08′W. Cattle, sheep, lambs; potatoes, onions. Pacific Crest Trail passes to S; parts of Shasta Natl. Forest to N and S.

McCloud River, c.50 mi/80 km long, N Calif.; rises in S Siskiyou co., at Shasta co. line; flows 1st N, then SW, passes SE of McCloud to join Sacramento R. and its branch, the Pit R., at Shasta L. reservoir; forms long arm of the lake, 19 mi/31 km S of Dunsmuir.

McClure, village (1990 pop. 781), Henry co., NW Ohio, 10 mi/16 km E of Napoleon, near Maumee R.; 41°22′N 83°57′W.

McClure (muh-KLUHR), borough (1990 pop. 1,070), Snyder co., central Pa., 15 mi/24 km NE of Lewistown; 40°42′N 77°18′W. In agr. area (corn, hay; livestock; dairying); mfg. (apparel, steel prods., lumber, concrete prods.). Snyder-Middleswarth State Park to NE; parts of Bald Eagle State Forest to E and N; Blue Mt. ridge to SE.

McClure, Cape, N extremity of Banks Isl., W Franklin dist., Baffin region, N.W.T., Canada, on McClure Strait; 74°28′N 120°41′W.

McClure Strait, arm of Beaufort Sea of the Arctic Ocean, W Franklin dist., Baffin region, N.W.T., Canada, extending W from Viscount Melville Sound, bet. Melville and Eglinton isls. (N) and Banks Isl. (S); 75°00′N 118°00′W. Channel is 170 mi/274 km long, 60 mi/97 km wide. In 1954, U.S. icebreakers cut through the strait for the 1st time, opening the last obstacle to the shortest water route across the Can. arctic region.

McClusky (muh-KLUHS-kee), village (1990 pop. 492), ⊙ Sheridan co., central N.Dak., 50 mi/80 km NNE of Bismarck, on McClusky Irrigation Canal; 47°28′N 100°26′W.

McColl (muh-KAHL), town (1990 pop. 2,685), Marlboro co., NE S.C., 8 mi/12.9 km ENE of Bennettsville, at N.C. state line; 34°40′N 79°32′W. Mfg. includes apparel; agr. includes cotton, grains, soybeans, vegetables; hogs.

McCollum Lake, village (1990 pop. 1,033), McHenry co., NE Ill., residential suburb 2 mi/3.2 km N of McHenry.

McComas (mik-O-muhs), uninc. town (1990 pop. 800), Mercer co., S W.Va., 7 mi/11.3 km W of Princeton. Coal region.

McComb (muh-KOM), city (1990 pop. 11,591), Pike co., SW Miss., 72 mi/116 km S of Jackson; 31°14′N 90°28′W. It is the trade and RR center of an agr. area (cotton, corn, soybeans; cattle); timber; mfg. (wire prods., printing and publishing, textile prods., concrete, lumber; poultry processing. Percy Quin State Park to SW. Inc. 1872.

McComb, village (1990 pop. 1,544), Hancock co., NW Ohio, 9 mi/14 km WNW of Findlay; 41°06′N 83°47′W. Corn, wheat, oats; glass prods.

McComb Mountain (4,425 ft/1,349 m), Essex co., NE N.Y., in the High Peak sect. of the Adirondacks, 9 mi/14.5 km SE of Mt. Marcy, c.20 mi/32 km SE of Lake Placid village; 44°03′N 73°47′W.

McConaughy, Lake, Nebr.: see C. W. MCCONAUGHY, LAKE.

McCone, county (☐ 2,682 sq mi/6,946 sq km; 1990 pop. 2,276), NE Mont.; ⊙ Circle; 47°39′N 105°48′W. Agr. region bounded N by Missouri R.; drained by Redwater R. Wheat, barley, hay; sheep, cattle; oil. In W is part of

Dry Arm (Big Dry Creek) of Fort Peck Reservoir. Reservoir is surrounded by Charles M. Russell Natl. Wildlife Refuge. Formed 1919.

McConnells, village (1990 pop. 157), York co., N S.C., 12 mi/19 km WSW of Rock Hill; 34°52′N 81°13′W. Agr. includes cotton, grain; livestock. Formerly called McConnellsville.

McConnellsburg (muh-KAH-nuhls-buhrg), borough (1990 pop. 1,106), ☉ Fulton co., S Pa., 22 mi/35 km W of Chambersburg; 39°55′N 78°00′W. Agr. area (corn, hay; livestock; dairying); mfg. (construction equip., machinery parts, toys, food processors); mt. resort. James Buchanan's Birthplace State Historical Park to SE. Cowans Gap State Park to NE; Meadow Grounds L. reservoir to SW; Tuscarora Mt. ridge and part of Buchanan State Forest to E. Settled c.1730, laid out 1786, inc. 1814.

McConnellsville, S.C.: see MCCONNELLS.

McConnelsville, village (1990 pop. 1,804), ☉ Morgan co., E central Ohio, on Muskingum R., 20 mi/32 km SSE of Zanesville; 39°39′N 81°51′W. Gas and oil wells. Plotted 1817.

McCook, county (□ 577 sq mi/1,494 sq km; 1990 pop. 5,688), SE S.Dak.; ☉ Salem; 43°40′N 97°21′W. Agr. area drained by East and West forks of Vermillion R. Corn, soybeans; cattle, hogs. L. Vermillion State Recreational Area in E. Formed 1873.

McCook, town (1990 pop. 8,112), ☉ Red Willow co., S Nebr., 65 mi/105 km S of North Platte and on Republican R., near Kansas state line; 40°12′N 100°37′W. Trade center, RR div. point in rich grain-raising region; livestock. Mfg. (fertilizers, rubber prods., concrete, printing, bakery prods.). Mus. of the High Plains here. Red Willow Reservoir (Hugh Butler L.) and State Recreation Area to N (both in Frontier co.). Founded as Fairview 1881; named McCook 1882; inc. 1883.

McCook, village (1990 pop. 235), Cook co., NE Ill., industrial suburb 12 mi/19 km WSW of Chicago; 41°47′N 87°50′W. Large locomotive div. plant here; mfg. (consumer goods, boxes, oils, aluminum prods., chemicals, crushed stone).

McCool (muh-KOOL), village (1990 pop. 169), Attala co., central Miss., 17 mi/27 km NE of Kosciusko; 33°12′N 89°20′W. Agr. (cotton, grain, soybeans; cattle).

McCool Junction, village (1990 pop. 372), York co., SE Nebr., 9 mi/14.5 km S of York, and on West Fork of Big Blue R.; 40°44′N 97°35′W.

McCordsville, town (1990 pop. 684), Hancock co., central Ind., 15 mi/24 km NE of Indianapolis; 39°55′N 85°56′W. Mfg. (machinery, fabricated metal prods.). Corn, soybeans. Geist Reservoir to NW. Laid out 1865.

McCormick, county (□ 393 sq mi/1,018 sq km; 1990 pop. 8,860), W S.C.; ☉ McCormick; 33°53′N 82°17′W. Bounded SW by Savannah R.; includes part of Sumter Natl. Forest. Agr. area, includes chickens, cattle; hay; timber; textile milling. Several state parks in area. Formed 1916.

McCormick, town (□ 3 sq mi/7.8 sq km; 1990 pop. 1,659), ☉ McCormick co., W S.C., 21 mi/34 km SSW of Greenwood; 33°54′N 82°17′W. Mfg. of lumber, apparel, textiles. Large retirement community here. Sumter Natl. Forest nearby.

McCoy, Camp, Wis.: see SPARTA.

McCracken (muh-KRAK-uhn), county (□ 268 sq mi/694 sq km; 1990 pop. 62,879), W Ky.; ☉ Paducah; 37°03′N 88°43′W. Bounded N by Ohio R. (Ill. state line), NE by the Tennessee R. (enters Ohio R.); drained by Clarks R. and its East and West forks and by Mayfield Creek. Gently rolling agr. area (dark and burley tobacco, corn, sorghum, hay, soybeans, wheat; hogs, cattle, poultry; dairying). Clay, sand and gravel, coals; timber. Mfg. at Paducah. Barkley Regional Airport in W. West Ky. Wildlife Management Area in NW; Lock and Dam No. 52 in NE, on Ohio R. at Paducah. Formed 1824.

McCracken (muh-KRAK-uhn), village (1990 pop. 231), Rush co., W central Kansas, 13 mi/21 km WNW of La Crosse; 38°34′N 99°34′W. Wheat; cattle.

McCreary (muh-KRIR-ee), county (□ 430 sq mi/1,114 sq km; 1990 pop. 15,603), S Ky.; ☉ Whitley City.

In the Cumberland Mts. Bounded S by Tenn., N and NE by Cumberland R., W in part by Little South Fork river; drained by South Fork of the Cumberland R.; 36°44′N 84°28′W. Bituminous-coal-mining and timber region; oil wells, some farms (burley tobacco, hay; cattle). Some lumber milling. Daniel Boone Natl. Forest covers nearly all of co. Includes a natural bridge, caves, and parts of Cumberland Falls State Park in NE; part of Big South Fork Natl. R. and Recreation Area in S, extends into Tenn. Formed 1912.

McCrory (muh-KROR-ee), town (1990 pop. 1,971), Woodruff co., E central Ark., 28 mi/45 km NW of Forrest City, and on Cache R.; 35°15′N 91°12′W. Agr. (rice, soybeans). Mfg. (paper prods., plastics, fertilizer, feeds). Settled 1886.

McCulloch, county (□ 1,073 sq mi/2,779 sq km; 1990 pop. 8,778), central Texas; ☉ Brady; 31°11′N 99°20′W. Geographical center of state, on N Edwards Plateau, with Brady Mts. (c.2,000 ft/610 m) crossing E-W; bounded N by Colorado R. and drained by San Saba R. and Brady Creek (forms Brady reservoir in W center). Diversified agr. and livestock raising; oats, peanuts, cotton, wheat; hay; cattle, sheep, and goats (wool, mohair). Oil and gas; sand and gravel. Formed 1856.

McCune (muh-KYOON), village (1990 pop. 462), Crawford co., extreme SE Kansas, 18 mi/29 km WSW of Pittsburg; 37°21′N 95°01′W. In diversified agr. area. Coal mines nearby.

McCurtain, county (□ 1,901 sq mi/4,924 sq km; 1990 pop. 33,433), extreme SE Okla.; ☉ Idabel; 34°06′N 094°46′W. Bounded E by Ark. state line, S by Red R., here forming Texas state line; drained by Little R. and Mountain Fork; part of Ouachita Mts. in N. Lumbering; agr. (corn, alfalfa, hay, soybeans; cattle, poultry); tourism, recreation. Pine Creek L. reservoir in W; part of Ouachita Natl. Forest in SE (separate unit beyond N boundary). Broken Bow L. reservoir in NE center; Beavers Bend and Hochatown state parks at S end of lake at dam. McCurtain Co. Wilderness Area on N end of lake. Formed 1907.

McCurtain, village (1990 pop. 465), Haskell co., E Okla., 20 mi/32 km WNW of Poteau; 35°08′N 94°58′W. In agr. area. Sansbois Mts. to SW.

McDade, uninc. village (1990 pop. 345), Bastrop co., S central Texas, 30 mi/48 km E of Austin.

McDermitt (muh-DUHR-mit), uninc. village (1990 pop. 373), Humboldt co., N Nev., 68 mi/109 km N of Winnemucca, on Oregon state line; 41°58′N 117°35′W. Cattle, sheep. On U.S. Highway 95, one of most remote gateways to Nev., small gambling resort developed to attract travelers entering and leaving state. Main sect. of Fort McDermitt Indian Reservation to E; Santa Rosa Range, in sect. of Humboldt Natl. Forest, to SE. Trout Creek Mts. (Oregon) to NW.

McDonald, county (□ 540 sq mi/1,399 sq km; 1990 pop. 16,938), extreme SW Mo., in Ozarks, borders Okla. on W, Ark. on S; ☉ Pineville; 36°37′N 94°20′W. Drained by Elk R. Fruit (berries, grapes, tomatoes), vegetables, grain; dairying; turkeys, chickens, broilers. Mfg. (food); lumber; tourism; major broiler (chicken) producer. Huckleberry Ridge State Forest at center; Bluff Dwellers Cave S of Noel. Formed 1849.

McDonald 1 village (1990 pop. 184), Rawlins co., NW Kansas, 16 mi/26 km W of Atwood; 39°47′N 101°22′W. In grain region. **2** village (1990 pop. 88), Robeson co., SE N.C., 10 mi/16 km WSW of Lumberton; 34°32′N 79°10′W. Grain, tobacco; livestock. **3** village (1990 pop. 3,526), Trumbull co., NE Ohio, just NW of Youngstown, and on Mahoning R.; 41°10′N 80°43′W.

McDonald, borough (1990 pop. 2,252), Washington and Allegheny cos., SW Pa., suburb 14 mi/23 km WSW of Pittsburgh, on Robinson Run; 40°22′N 80°13′W. Agr. (corn, apples; dairying); diversified light mfg.; bituminous coal, oil (gas and oil field to SE).

McDonald, Lake, Mont.: see GLACIER NATIONAL PARK.

McDonald Observatory, astronomical observatory, on Mt. Locke (6,791 ft/2,070 m), near Fort Davis, Texas. Founded in 1932, sponsored by the Univ. of Texas in cooperation with the Univ. of Chicago at the bequest of amateur astronomer William J. McDonald. Its

equip. includes 107-in/272-cm, 82-in/208-cm, 32-in/81-cm, and 30-in/76-cm reflecting telescopes. The 107-in/272-cm reflecting telescope, which began operation in 1968 as the 3d-largest telescope in the world, was built under contract with NASA; it is housed in a large dome.

McDonald Peak, Mont.: see MISSION RANGE.

McDonough (muh-DUHN-uh), county (□ 590 sq mi/1,528 sq km; 1990 pop. 35,244), W Ill.; ☉ Macomb; 40°27′N 90°40′W. Agr. (livestock; corn, sorghum, soybeans, hay; dairy). Bituminous-coal mining; clay pits. Macomb is trade and mfg. center, with diversified prods. Drained by La Moine R. and branches. Includes Western Ill. Univ. and Argyle L. State Park. Formed 1826.

McDonough (muh-DUHN-uh), town (1990 pop. 2,929), ☉ Henry co., N central Ga., 24 mi/39 km SSE of Atlanta; 33°27′N 84°08′W. Romanesque Revival courthouse in center square Emerging Atlanta suburb. Mfg. includes apparel, machinery parts, plastics, cleaners, animal feeds, computer equip.; pulpwood processing. Inc. 1823.

McDowell 1 county (□ 446 sq mi/1,155 sq km; 1990 pop. 35,681), W central N.C.; ☉ Marion; 35°40′N 82°02′W. In the Blue Ridge Mts.; drained by Catawba R. (forms L. James reservoir in NE); N part in Pisgah Natl. Forest. Farming (corn, apples, soybeans, hay; chickens, cattle), timber. Stone quarrying. Resort area; mfg. at Marion. Blue Ridge Parkway follows NW boundary. Formed 1842. **2** county (□ 535 sq mi/1,386 sq km; 1990 pop. 35,233), S W.Va.; ☉ Welch; 37°22′N 81°39′W. On Allegheny Plateau; bounded W, S, and SE by Va.; drained by Tug Fork and Dry Fork rivers (headstreams of the Big Sandy R.). Extensive semi-bituminous-coal mining (Pocahontas coalfield); some natural gas. Timber. Some agr. (apples). Panther State Forest to W; Berwind L. Wildlife Management Area in S; Anawalt Wildlife Management Area in E. Formed 1858.

McDowell 1 uninc. village (1990 pop. 500), Floyd co., E Ky., in the Cumberland Mts., 12 mi/19 km W of Pikeville, on Beaver Creek. Bituminous coal. **2** uninc. village, Highland co., NW Va., in the Alleghany Mts., 8 mi/12.9 km SE of Monterey, on Bullpasture R. Mfg. (lumber); agr. (alfalfa); timber.

McDowell Mountains, Maricopa co., central Ariz.; rise to 4,035 ft/1,230 m in McDowell Peak, c.20 mi/32 km NE of Phoenix. McDowell Mts. Park in S; Verde R. to E.

McDuffie (muh-DUHF-ee), county (□ 266 sq mi/689 sq km; 1990 pop. 20,119), E Ga.; ☉ Thomson; 33°29′N 82°29′W. Bounded N by Little R. Intersected by the fall line. Agr. (cotton, vegetables, fruit); cattle; timber. Formed 1870.

McEwen (muh-YOO-uhn), city (1990 pop. 1,442), Humphreys co., central Tenn., 45 mi/72 km W of Nashville; 36°07′N 87°38′W. In timber region.

McEwensville (muh-YOO-uhns-vil), borough (1990 pop. 273), Northumberland co., E central Pa., 14 mi/23 km N of Sunbury; 41°04′N 76°49′W. Agr. (corn, hay; poultry; dairying).

McFadden, village, Carbon co., SE Wyo., near Rock Creek, near foothills of Medicine Bow Mts., and 36 mi/58 km NW of Laramie. Elev. c.7,200 ft/2,195 m. Oil wells.

McFall, city (1990 pop. 142), Gentry co., NW Mo., near Grand R., 40 mi/64 km NE of St. Joseph; 40°06′N 94°13′W. Corn, soybeans; hogs, cattle.

McFarlan (mik-FAHR-luhn), village (1990 pop. 98), Anson co., S N.C., 12 mi/19 km SSE of Wadesboro, near Great Pee Dee R., near S.C. state line; 34°48′N 79°58′W. Cotton, grain; livestock.

McFarland, city (1990 pop. 7,005), Kern co., S central Calif., 22 mi/35 km NNW of Bakersfield, near Friant-Kern Canal (irrigation); 35°41′N 119°14′W. RR junction to S. Cotton, fruit, nuts, vegetables, grain; dairying; cattle.

McFarland, town (1990 pop. 5,232), Dane co., S Wis., suburb 7 mi/11.3 km SE of Madison, near Yahara R., on E end of L. Waubesa; 43°01′N 89°17′W. In dairy and lake-resort region. Mfg. (telecomunications equip., metal fabricating, paper prods.).

McFarland, village (1990 pop. 224), Wabaunsee co., NE central Kansas, 19 mi/31 km ESE of Manhattan and 3 mi/4.8 km NE of Alma; 39°02′N 96°14′W. RR junction. In cattle and grain region.

McGehee (muh-GEE), town (1990 pop. 4,997), Desha co., SE Ark., 25 mi/40 km NW of Greenville (Miss.); 33°37′N 91°23′W. RR junction. In livestock-raising and agr. area. Mfg. (apparel, paper). Inc. 1906.

McGill (muh-GIL), town (1990 pop. 1,258), White Pine co., E Nev., bet. Schell Creek Range (E), and Egan Range (W), 12 mi/19 km NNE of Ely, near Duck Creek; 39°23′N 114°46′W. Elev. 6,210 ft/1,893 m. Cattle, sheep; gold, silver. Terminus of RR spur from Ely. Pony Express station site 25 mi/40 km to N. Goshute Indian Reservation (Utah-Nev.) 45 mi/72 km to NE. Part of Humboldt Natl Forest to E. North Schell Park (elev. 11,883 ft/3,622 m) to E.

McGillivray Falls (muh-GI-liv-ree), ghost town, SW B.C., Canada, in Coast Mts., on Anderson L., 23 mi/37 km WSW of Lillooet; 50°37′N 122°26′W. Former gold-mining area.

McGovern, uninc. town (1990 pop. 2,504), Washington co., SW Pa., residential suburb 2 mi/3.2 km SSW of Canonsburg, on Chartiers Creek; 40°14′N 80°13′W. Agr. includes dairying; apples.

McGrann, uninc. village, Manor township, Armstrong co., W Pa., on Allegheny R., residential suburb 1 mi/1.6 km NNE of Ford City; 40°46′N 79°31′W.

McGrath 1 village (1990 pop. 528), SW central Alaska, on upper Kuskokwim R. (head of navigation), 220 mi/354 km NW of Anchorage; 62°58′N 155°35′W. Has airfield. Est. 1905. **2** village (1990 pop. 62), Aitkin co., E Minn., on Snake R., 30 mi/48 km SE of Aitkin; 46°14′N 93°16′W. Solano State Forest to NE; Mille Lacs L. to W.

McGraw, village (1990 pop. 1,074), Cortland co., central N.Y., 4 mi/6.4 km E of Cortland; 42°35′N 76°05′W. Mfg. of jewelry, silverware, apparel. Inc. 1869.

McGregor 1 town (1990 pop. 797), Clayton co., NE Iowa, on Mississippi R. almost opposite mouth of Wisconsin R., 3 mi/4.8 km SW of Prairie du Chien (Wis.), in hilly "Little Switzerland" region; 43°01′N 91°10′W. Mfg. (dairy prods.; consumer goods, beverages). Upper Mississippi Natl. Wildlife Refuge; Effigy Mounds Natl. Monument 5 mi/8 km N; McGregor Heights and Pikes Peak State Parks to S. Settled 1836, inc. 1857. **2** town (1990 pop. 4,683), McLennan co., E central Texas, 18 mi/29 km SW of Waco, near branch of Bosque R.; 31°26′N 97°22′W. Mfg. (motors, furniture and bedding, office supplies, air conditioning equip.). Mother Neff State Park is SW, on Belton L. reservoir. An ordnance plant was nearby in World War II. Est. 1882.

McGregor, village (1990 pop. 376), Aitkin co., E central Minn., 20 mi/32 km ENE of Aitkin; 46°36′N 93°18′W. Mfg. (motor vehicle parts, wood prods., machinery). Sandy L. Fur Post (1794) to N; Savanna State Forest to NE; Savanna Portage State Park to NE; Rice L. Natl. Wildlife Refuge to S; East L. Indian Reservation to S; Sandy L. Indian Reservation to NE; Big Sandy L. reservoir to N. Numerous small natural lakes in area.

McGregor, Lake, S Alta., Canada, 60 mi/97 km SE of Calgary. Drains N into Bow R.; 23 mi/37 km long, 1 mi/2 km–3 mi/5 km wide. Irrigation dams at N and S extremities.

McGrew, village (1990 pop. 99), Scotts Bluff co., W Nebr., 15 mi/24 km SE of Scottsbluff, and on North Platte R.; 41°45′N 103°25′W.

McGuffey, village (1990 pop. 550), Hardin co., W central Ohio, 9 mi/14 km WNW of Kenton; 40°42′N 83°47′W.

McGuire, Mount (10,082 ft/3,073 m), Lemhi co., E Idaho, in Yellowjacket Mts., 32 mi/51 km W of Salmon, in Frank Church R. of No Return Wilderness Area. S of confluence of Salmon and Middle Fork Salmon rivers.

McHenry 1 county (□ 611 sq mi/1,582 sq km; 1990 pop. 183,241), NE Ill., on Wis. state line (N); ⊙ Woodstock; 42°19′N 88°27′W. Urban growth has extended into co. from Chicago. Larger communities are Woodstock, McHenry, Crystal Lake, and Algonquin. Dairying area; also livestock; corn, hay. Several lakes; fishing. Drained by Fox and Kishwaukee rivers. Formed 1836. **2** county (□ 1,879 sq mi/4,867 sq km; 1990 pop. 6,528), N central N.Dak.; ⊙ Towner; 48°13′N 100°38′W. Agr. area with extensive lignite deposits; drained by Souris R (Mouse R.), Wintering R. and Spring Coulee Creek. Cattle, poultry; dairy prods.; wheat, rye, barley, hay. Formed 1873. North L. and Buffalo Lodge L. at center; George L., Smoky L., and other small lakes in E; part of J. Clark Salyer Natl. Wildlife Refuge in N.

McHenry, city (1990 pop. 16,177), McHenry co., NE Ill., on Fox R. (bridged here), satellite community of Chicago, 22 mi/35 km W of Waukegan; 42°20′N 88°17′W. Trade and processing center in dairying, remnant agr.; mfg. (plastics, rubber prods., fabricated metal prods., packaging, electrical motors); fishing. Settled 1836; inc. as village in 1855, as city in 1923.

McHenry 1 (muh-KEN-ree), village (1990 pop. 414), Ohio co., W Ky., 3 mi/4.8 km WSW of Beaver Dam; 37°22′N 86°55′W. Bituminous coal; agr. (tobacco, grain; livestock; timber); mfg. (copper prods., furniture). **2** village (1990 pop. 85), Foster co., E central N.Dak., 27 mi/43 km ENE of Carrington; 47°34′N 98°35′W.

McHenry, summer resort, Garrett co., W Md., in the Alleghenies on Deep Creek L., 32 mi/51 km WSW of Cumberland. Named for James McHenry, Washington's secretary of war for whom Fort McHenry was also named. McHenry purchased land here about 1805. State game refuge near. Garrett Community Col. and Garrett County Fairgrounds.

McHenry, Fort, Md.: see FORT MCHENRY.

McIntire, town (1990 pop. 147), Mitchell co., N Iowa, near Minn. state line, on Wapsipinicon R., 15 mi/24 km NE of Osage; 43°26′N 92°35′W. Limestone quarries, sand pits nearby.

McIntosh 1 county (□ 575 sq mi/1,489 sq km; 1990 pop. 8,634), SE Ga.; ⊙ Darien; 31°29′N 81°22′W. Bounded SE by the Atlantic Ocean, SW by Altamaha R.; includes Sapelo Isl. Agr., fishing, and sawmilling area; seafood canning at Darien. Formed 1793. **2** county (□ 991 sq mi/2,567 sq km; 1990 pop. 4,021), S N.Dak., borders S.Dak. on S; ⊙ Ashley; 46°07′N 99°26′W. Rich prairie land watered by South Branch of Beaver Creek. Farm machinery; dairy prods., wheat, rye; cattle. Doyle Memorial State Park, on Green L. is to the N; L. Hoskins is to the S. Formed 1883. **3** county (□ 715 sq mi/1,852 sq km; 1990 pop. 16,779), E Okla.; ⊙ Eufaula; 35°22′N 95°40′W. Bounded S by Canadian R. (forming Eufaula L. here; Eufaula Dam in SE corner); intersected by North Canadian and Deer Fork of Canadian rivers (forming arms of Eufaula L.). Agr. (soybeans, peanuts; cattle; dairying). Some mfg.; timber; tourism. Fountainhead State Park at center on L. Eufaula. Formed 1907.

McIntosh 1 village (1990 pop. 665), Polk co., NW Minn., on Poplar R., 35 mi/56 km ESE of Crookston; 47°38′N 95°53′W. Grain, sunflowers; livestock; dairying. **2** village (1990 pop. 302), ⊙ Corson co., N S.Dak., 55 mi/89 km NW of Mobridge; 45°55′N 101°20′W. Livestock; grain.

McIntosh, Fort, Texas: see LAREDO.

McIntyre, village (1990 pop. 552), Wilkinson co., central Ga., 26 mi/42 km E of Macon; 32°51′N 83°11′W. Mfg. includes wood prods.; kaolin clay processing.

McIntyre Mountain (1,030 ft/314 m), SW Cape Breton Isl., E N.S., Canada, 12 mi/19 km N of Port Hawkesbury. Highest in Craignish Hills.

McKay Creek (muh-KAI), 20 mi/32 km long, NE Oregon; rises at the line bet. Umatilla and Union cos.; flows W and N through McKay Reservoir to Umatilla R., just W of Pendleton. McKay Dam (180 ft/55 m high, 2,700 ft/823 m long; completed 1927) is 5 mi/8 km S of Pendleton. Used for irrigation.

McKay Lake, central Ont., Canada, 28 mi/45 km E of Geraldton, 10 mi/16 km E of Long L. Lake is 12 mi/19 km long, 3 mi/5 km wide; elev. 1,052 ft/321 m. Drains S into L. Superior through Pie R.

McKay, Mount (1,581 ft/482 m), W Ont., Canada, overlooking entrance of Thunder Bay, 3 mi/5 km S of Thunder Bay.

McKean, county (□ 984 sq mi/2,549 sq km; 1990 pop. 47,131), N Pa.; ⊙ Smethport; 41°47′N 78°34′W. Plateau area. Bounded N by N.Y. state line; drained by Allegheny R. Largest producer of Pa. lubricating oils. Agr. (corn, oats, hay, alfalfa; hogs, cattle; dairying); petroleum, natural gas. Mfg. at Bradford. Kinzua Bridge State Park in S center; small part of Susquehannock State Forest in SE; part of Allegheny Natl. Forest in W ½, including Kinzua Bay and Sugar Bay, arms of Allegheny Reservoir. Formed 1804.

McKean, borough (1990 pop. 418), Erie co., NW Pa., 9 mi/14.5 km SSW of Erie, on Elk Creek; 42°00′N 80°08′W. Agr. (dairying); mfg. (wood prods.). Formerly called Middleboro.

McKee (muh-KEE), town (1990 pop. 870), ⊙ Jackson co., E Ky., in the Cumberland Mts., 40 mi/64 km SSE of Winchester, in Cumberland Natl. Forest, surrounded by Daniel Boone Natl. Forest; 37°25′N 83°59′W. Agr. (corn, hay, tobacco; cattle; dairying); coal mines, timber; mfg. (consumer goods; limestone processing).

McKees Rocks, borough (1990 pop. 7,691), Allegheny co., SW Pa., industrial suburb 4 mi/6.4 km WNW of Pittsburgh, on the Ohio R. (bridged); 40°28′N 80°03′W. Mfg. (fabricated steel prods., lubricants, food prods., furniture, metal fabrication). The regional coal and steel industries formerly based here have collapsed, thus leading to unemployment and industrial decline. Pittsburgh State Correctional Inst. is here. Settled c.1764, inc. 1892.

McKeesport, city (1990 pop. 26,016), Allegheny co., SW Pa., suburb 10 mi/16 km SE of Pittsburgh, on Monongahela R., at mouth of Youghiogheny R.; 40°20′N 79°50′W. A steel and industrial city, McKeesport has undergone rapid decline and increased unemployment since the collapse of the U.S. steel industry in the 1980s. Present-day mfg. includes electrical equip., solvents, metal fabrication, coal tar prods., meat processing, tools). Pa. State Univ.–McKeesport Campus is here. Settled 1755, inc. as a city 1890.

McKenney, town (1990 pop. 386), Dinwiddie co., SE central Va., 23 mi/37 km SW of Petersburg; 36°59′N 77°43′W. Mfg. (consumer goods; tobacco processing); in agr. area (tobacco, peanuts, grain, soybeans; livestock). Fort Pickett Military Reservation to W.

McKenzie, county (□ 2,735 sq mi/7,084 sq km; 1990 pop. 6,383), W N.Dak., borders Mont. on W, borders Missouri R. (L. Sakakawea) on N; ⊙ Watford City; 47°43′N 103°23′W. Agr. area watered by Yellowstone R. in W, Little Missouri R. in SE; rich in lignite, oil, and natural gas. Wheat, sugar beets; cattle. Irrigation projects in NW along Missouri R. Little Missouri Natl. Grassland in S and E; N unit of Theodore Roosevelt Natl. Park in S; part of Fort Berthold Indian Reservation, including Four Bears State Recreational Area in E. The boundary bet. Mountain and Central time zones follows the Mont. state line for short distance S then crosses S part of co.; N ¾ of co. is in Central time zone, S ¼ in Mountain. Formed 1883; eliminated 1891 due to lack of settlement and reorganized in 1905.

McKenzie, city (1990 pop. 5,168), in Carroll, Weakley, and Henry cos., NW Tenn., 10 mi/16 km N of Huntingdon; 36°08′N 88°32′W. In cotton, corn, timber area; clay, sand, and gravel pits. Mfg. (furniture, lawn and garden equip., apparel). Inc. 1868.

McKenzie, town (1990 pop. 464), Butler co., S Ala., 20 mi/32 km S of Greenville.

McKenzie River (muh-KEN-zee), 86 mi/138 km long, W Oregon; formed in Cascade Range in NE Lane co., near the Three Sisters peaks; flows W to Willamette R. N of Eugene. South Fork, c. 30 mi/48 km long, rises in W Lane co., flows NNW through Cougar Reservoir, joins main stream c.25 mi/40 km W of source.

McKinley, county (□ 5,456 sq mi/14,131 sq km; 1990 pop. 60,686), NW N.Mex.; ⊙ Gallup; 35°34′N 108°15′W. Livestock-grazing area, watered by Rio Puerco and Zuñi R.; borders on Ariz. (W); Continental Divide crosses co. from NE corner to S center, at angle. Uranium, molybdenum, copper; hay, alfalfa, timber; cattle, sheep; wool, Native Amer. artifacts, pottery. Coal mines near Gallup. Includes parts of Zuñi Mts. (S), parts of Cibola Natl. Forest (S and SE), and parts of Navajo (NW), Zuni (SW), and Ramah (SW) Indian reservations. Bluewater L. State Park S of boundary; Red Rock State Park in W center. Formed 1899.

McKinley, village (1990 pop. 116), St. Louis co., NE Minn., 7 mi/11.3 km E of Virginia, in Mesabi Iron Range; 47°30′N 92°24′W. Iron mines in area.

McKinley, Mount, peak (20,320 ft/6,194 m), S central Alaska, in the Alaska Range. Highest point in N. Amer. Permanent snowfields cover more than ½ the mt. and feed numerous glaciers. Known locally as *Denali* [= the great one], Mt. McKinley was 1st scaled successfully by the Amer. explorer Hudson Stuck in 1913. It is included in Denali Natl. Park and Preserve.

McKinley Park, village, central Alaska, on Alaska RR and Parks Highway, 100 mi/161 km SW of Fairbanks. Tourist gateway to Mt. McKinley Natl. Park; numerous hotels.

McKinleyville, uninc. city (1990 pop. 10,749), Humboldt co., NW Calif., 10 mi/16 km N of Eureka, near Pacific Ocean and mouth of Mud R.; 40°57′N 124°07′W. Trinidad State Beach and Patrick's Point State Park to N. Cattle, sheep; dairying; timber. Redwood Natl. Park to N.

McKinney, city (1990 pop. 21,283), ⊙ Collin co., N Texas, suburb 30 mi/48 km NNE of Dallas, on East Fork of Trinity R.; 33°12′N 96°39′W. It is a shipping point for cotton, cattle, and grains (wheat, sorghum) and has grown as industrial center, mfg. (electronic equip., leather prods., marble items, consumer goods, food, copper wire). Located on the blackland prairie, it was one of the principal cotton cities before the Civil War. The restored 1836 home of Collin McKinney, for whom the city was named, is here. Collin Co. Community Col. A wildlife sanctuary and a mus. of natural science are just outside the city. Inc. 1849.

McKinney, uninc. village (1990 pop. 475), Lincoln co., central Ky., 7 mi/11.3 km SSE of Stanford. Historic RR depot. Tobacco, grain; livestock. Mfg. (concrete prods.).

McKinney, Lake, Kearny co., SW Kansas, on Mattox Draw (intermittent sidestream N of Arkansas R.), 18 mi/29 km W of Garden City; 5 mi/8 km long, 1 mi/ 1.6 km wide; 37°57′N 101°16′W. Used for irrigation.

McKittrick, town (1990 pop. 66), Montgomery co., E central Mo., on Missouri R., across river from Hermann (bridge); 38°44′N 91°26′W. Feed mill. Flooded in 1993.

McKittrick, uninc. village, Kern co., S central Calif., at E base of Temblor Range, 35 mi/56 km W of Bakersfield. Oil and natural-gas field. Cattle; grain, cotton.

McLain, village (1990 pop. 536), Greene co., SE Miss., 31 mi/50 km SE of Hattiesburg, on Leaf R.; 31°06′N 88°49′W. Cotton, corn; cattle, poultry; timber. Mfg. (furniture). De Soto Natl. Forest to W and S.

McLaughlin (muh-LAWF-lin), town (1990 pop. 780), Corson co., N S.Dak., 27 mi/43 km NW of Mobridge, near Oak Creek, in Standing Rock Indian Reservation; 45°48′N 100°48′W. Trading point for ranching and farming area.

McLean 1 (muh-KLAIN), county (□ 1,186 sq mi/ 3,072 sq km; 1990 pop. 129,180), central Ill.; ⊙ Bloomington; 40°29′N 88°50′W. Drained by Sangamon and Mackinaw rivers and by Kickapoo, Salt, and small Money and Sugar creeks. Includes L. Bloomington (with residences, resort), Evergreen L., and Moraine View State Park. Agr. (corn, wheat, soybeans; livestock; dairy prods.). Gravel and sand pits. Mfg., includes motor vehicle plant at Normal. Includes Ill. State Univ., Ill. Wesleyan Univ., Heartland Col., and a branch of Lincoln Col. Formed 1830. **2** county (□ 256 sq mi/ 663 sq km; 1990 pop. 9,628), W Ky.; ⊙ Calhoun; 37°31′N 87°15′W. Bounded W by Green and Pond rivers; drained by Green R. and Cypress Creek. Agr. area (soybeans, corn, wheat, dark and burley tobacco, tomatoes, hay, alfalfa; hogs, cattle; timber); bituminous-coal mines. Some mfg. at Livermore and Calhoun. Formed 1854. **3** county (□ 2,065 sq mi/5,348 sq km; 1990 pop. 10,457), central N.Dak.; ⊙ Washburn; 47°36′N

101°19′W. Agr. area in W and S by Missouri R. Lignite mines; cattle; dairy prods.; wheat, barley, rye, flax. Audubon Natl. Wildlife Refuge on L. Audubon, E part of L. Sakakawea, at co. center; several small lakes in NE ¼; Fort Stevenson State Park on N shore of L. Sakakawea; Fort Mandan Historic Site in S; McClusky Canal crosses E part; part of Fort Berthold Indian Reservation in W part. The boundary bet. Mountain and Central time zones follows river upstream as far as Little Missouri R., including L. Sakakawea above Garrison Dam. Formed 1883.

McLean, uninc. city (1990 pop. 38,168), Fairfax co., N Va., suburb 8 mi/12.9 km WNW of Washington, D.C., near Potomac R.; 38°56′N 77°10′W. Mfg. (foods, satellite components, printing and publishing, computer and telecommunications equip.). Hq. of the CIA, Federal Highway Administration Research Station to NE in Langley. George Washington Memorial Parkway (Natl. Park unit) to E, follows Potomac R., includes Turkey Run Park. Tyson's Corner Center, one of the largest shopping centers in the U.S., is here.

McLean, town (1990 pop. 849), Gray co., extreme N Texas, in the Panhandle, 75 mi/121 km E of Amarillo; 35°13′N 100°35′W. Elev. 2,812 ft/857 m. In cattle, wheat, cotton region; gas and oil wells. L. McClellan and McClellan Creek Natl. Grassland to W. Settled 1901, inc. 1909.

McLean 1 (mik-LAIN), village (1990 pop. 797), McLean co., central Ill., 14 mi/23 km SW of Bloomington; 40°19′N 89°10′W. In rich agr. area. **2** village (1990 pop. 49), Pierce co., NE Nebr., 13 mi/21 km N of Pierce; 42°23′N 97°28′W.

McLean Canyon, Canada: see CHURCHILL FALLS.

McLeansboro (muh-KLAINZ-bur-oh), city (1990 pop. 2,677), ⊙ Hamilton co., SE Ill., 25 mi/40 km SE of Mount Vernon; 38°05′N 88°31′W. In agr. area; corn, wheat; livestock. Inc. 1840.

McLeansville (muh-KLEENZ-vil), uninc. town (1990 pop. 1,154), Guilford co., N central N.C., residential suburb 10 mi/16 km ENE of Greensboro; 36°06′N 79°39′W. In agr. area (tobacco, grain, soybeans; poultry, cattle; dairying).

McLellan Reservoir, Arapahoe and Douglas cos., N central Colo., on Dad Clark Gulch (sidestream of South Platte R.), 11 mi/18 km S of Denver; 39°35′N 104°54′W. Max. storage capacity of 8,952 acre-ft; 1 mi/ 1.6 km long. Formed by McLellan Dam (111 ft/34 m high), built (1969) by the City of Englewood for water supply.

McLemoresville (mak-luh-MORZ-vil), town (1990 pop. 280), Carroll co., NW Tenn., 8 mi/13 km W of Huntington; 35°59′N 88°34′W.

McLennan, town (1991 pop. 1,020), W Alta., Canada, on Kimiwan L. (7 mi/11 km long, 4 mi/6 km wide), 40 mi/ 64 km SSE of Peace R., 40 mi/64 km NW of Lesser Slave L.; 55°42′N 116°54′W. Lumbering; wheat; mixed farming.

McLennan, county (□ 1,060 sq mi/2,745 sq km; 1990 pop. 189,123), E central Texas; ⊙ Waco; 31°33′N 97°12′W. Commercial, distribution, mfg. center for wide region. Drained by Brazos R. and Bosque R. and its North and Middle branches, and Aquilla and Tradinghouse creeks; includes L. Waco. Rich agr. area (oats, wheat, hay, cotton, corn, grain sorghum, pecans); extensive dairying; beef cattle, hogs. Limestone, clay, stone, sand and gravel; oil and gas. Fishing. Tradinghouse Creek Reservoir in E; L. Waco (Bosque R.) in center. Formed 1850.

McLeod (muh-KLOUD), county (□ 505 sq mi/ 1,308 sq km; 1990 pop. 32,030), S central Minn.; ⊙ Glencoe; 44°49′N 94°16′W. Watered by South Fork of Crow R. and Buffalo Creek. Agr. area (corn, oats, wheat, hay, alfalfa, soybeans, peas; hogs, cattle, poultry; dairying). Many small lakes in co. Formed 1856.

McLeod, Fort, trading post, E central B.C., Canada, on McLeod L. (14 mi/23 km long), 75 mi/121 km N of Prince George. Est. 1805 by Simon Fraser for the North West Company; taken over 1821 by Hudson's Bay Company.

McLoud, town (1990 pop. 2,493), Pottawatomie co., central Okla., 12 mi/19 km NW of Shawnee, 21 mi/34 km E of Oklahoma City, on North Canadian R.; 35°24′N 97°05′W. In rich agr. area (corn, wheat, peanuts; dairy prods.).

McLoughlin House National Historic Site (muh-GLAHK-luhn), in McLoughlin Park, Oregon City, NW Oregon; an affiliated area of the Natl. Park Service. Home of fur trader Dr. John McLoughlin, the "Father of Oregon." Authorized 1941.

McLoughlin, Mount (muh-GLAHK-luhn) (9,495 ft/ 2,894 m), E Jackson co., near Klamath co. line, SW Oregon, in Cascade Range, W of Upper Klamath L., c.30 mi/48 km NE of Klamath Falls.

McLouth (muh-KLOUTH), village (1990 pop. 719), Jefferson co., NE Kansas, 6 mi/9.7 km E of Oskaloosa; 39°12′N 95°12′W. In livestock-raising, dairying, and general farming region. Leavenworth State Fishing L. to SE.

McMechen (mik-MEK-uhn), town (1990 pop. 2,130), Marshall co., N W.Va., in N Panhandle, on the Ohio R., 8 mi/12.9 km S of Wheeling; 39°59′N 80°43′W. Industrial area; mfg. (concrete, machining). Inc. 1895.

McMicken Heights, village, King co., W Wash., residential suburb 13 mi/21 km SSE of Seattle. Seattle-Tacoma Internatl. Airport (Sea-Tac) to W.

McMillan, village, Luce co., NE Upper Peninsula, Mich., 9 mi/14.5 km W of Newberry; 46°20′N 85°41′W. In lumbering and agr. area.

McMillan, Lake, N.Mex.: see PECOS, river.

McMinn, county (□ 435; 1990 pop. 42,383), SE Tenn.; ⊙ Athens; 35°25′N 84°37′W. In Great Appalachian Valley; Cherokee Natl. Forest lies along SE border; bounded SW by Hiwassee R. Agr. (corn, wheat, fruit, tobacco, hay); livestock raising; dairying. Limestone, barite. Timber (pine, hardwood). Mfg. at Athens. Formed 1819.

McMinnville 1 (muhk-MIN-vil), city (1990 pop. 17,894), ⊙ Yamhill co., NW Oregon, 33 mi/53 km SW of Portland, at confluence of North and South Yamhill rivers (from Yamhill R.); 45°12′N 123°11′W. RR junction to NE. Trade and processing center in fertile Willamette Valley. Mfg. (foods, textiles, bldg. materials, printing and publishing, rubber prods., concrete, steel milling, medical equip.). Agr. (apples, cherries, plums, peaches, pears, grapes, nuts, berries, wheat, barley, oats; poultry); dairy prods.; wineries. Linfield Col. Siuslaw Natl. Forest to W; Erratic Rock Wayside State Park to SW. Inc. 1876. **2** city (1990 pop. 11,194), ⊙ Warren co., central Tenn., on branch of Caney Fork, 38 mi/61 km SE of Murfreesboro; 35°41′N 85°46′W. In timber and farm area; mfg. of wood prods., wood-working machinery, motors; tree nurseries. Marble and granite quarries nearby. Great Falls Dam is NE, Center Hill Reservoir N. Settled 1800; inc. 1808.

McMullen, county (□ 1,142 sq mi/2,958 sq km; 1990 pop. 817), S Texas; ⊙ Tilden; 28°21′N 98°34′W. Drained by Frio and Nueces rivers. Cattle ranching; agr. (grain sorghum, corn). Oil, natural-gas wells; sulphur. Part of Choke Canyon L. reservoir (Frio R.) in NE, Choke Canyon State Park on S shore, on co. line. Formed 1858.

McMurray, uninc. town (1990 pop. 4,082), Washington co., SW Pa., industrial suburb 12 mi/19 km SSW of Pittsburgh on urban fringe; 40°16′N 80°05′W. Mfg. includes printing and publishing, medical equip., aerospace components, TV and microwave transmitters, wooden prods.

McMurray, Canada: see FORT MCMURRAY.

McNab, village (1990 pop. 95), Hempstead co., SW Ark., 14 mi/23 km W of Hope, near Little R.; 33°39′N 93°49′W. Grassy L. (backwater lake) to NW.

McNabb, village (1990 pop. 310), Putnam co., N central Ill., 12 mi/19 km SSW of Peru; 41°10′N 89°12′W. Corn, soybeans.

McNair, uninc. village, Harris co., S Texas, suburb 20 mi/ 32 km E of Houston, on Goose Creek. Area is gradually being annexed by Baytown, to S. Highlands Reservoir to N.

McNairy (muhk-NAI-ree), county (□ 569 sq mi/ 1,474 sq km; 1990 pop. 22,422), SW Tenn.; ⊙ Selmer;

35°11′N 88°34′W. Bounded S by Miss.; drained by tributaries of South Fork of Forked Deer, Hatchie, and Tennessee rivers. Cotton, corn, hay, soybeans, vegetables; livestock raising; timber. Mfg. at Adamsville, Selmer. Formed 1823.

McNary 1 (mik-NER-ee), village, Apache co., E Ariz., near White R., in NE part of Fort Apache Indian Reservation, 40 mi/64 km SW of St. Johns. Elev. 7,505 ft/ 2,288 m. Lumber milling; wood prods. Natl. forests nearby. White Mts. to E. Apache-Sitgreaves Natl. Forest to N; source of White R. to SE; fish hatchery is here. **2** village (1990 pop. 248), Rapides parish, central La., 23 mi/37 km SSW of Alexandria; 30°60′N 92°35′W. In agr. area. Cocodrie L. to E. Kisatchie Natl. Forest to NW. **3** village (1990 est. pop. 250), Hudspeth co., extreme W Texas, 50 mi/80 km SE of El Paso, near the Rio Grande (Mex. border). In irrigated farm area (cotton, vegetables, alfalfa; cattle, hogs). Ruins of old Fort Quitman are SE.

McNary Lock and Dam oregon: see WALLULA, LAKE.

McNeil, village (1990 pop. 686), Columbia co., SW Ark., 6 mi/9.7 km NNE of Magnolia; 33°21′N 93°12′W. RR junction. In agr. area; mfg. (aluminum for aircraft industry). Logoly State Park is here.

McNeil Island, Pierce co., W Wash., in Puget Sound WSW of Tacoma and just W of Steilacoom; c.3 mi/ 4.8 km long. Site of McNeil Isl. Federal Penitentiary. Ferry from Steilacoom via Anderson Isl. to S end. Carr Inlet (N), Pitt Passage and Kitsap Peninsula (NW), Balch Passage and Anderson Isl. (S).

McNeill, uninc. village (1990 pop. 600), Pearl River co., SE Miss., 10 mi/16 km NNE of Picayune. Agr. area (cotton, corn, berries; cattle; dairying). Mfg. (apparel).

McNutt Island, in the Atlantic, at entrance to Shelburne Harbour, SW N.S., Canada, 7 mi/11 km S of Shelburne; 43°38′N 65°47′W. Isl. is 4 mi/6 km long, 2 mi/3 km wide.

McPhee, former village, Montezuma co., SW Colo., on Dolores R., 11 mi/18 km NNE of Cortez. Elev. c.7,000 ft/2,134 m. Mesa Verde Natl. Park nearby. Now called McPhee Reservoir.

McPhee, reservoir (□ 8 sq mi/20.7 sq km), Montezuma co., extreme SW Colo., on Dolores R., 10 mi/16 km N of Cortez; 37°34′N 108°35′W. Max. capacity 399,200 acre-ft. Formed by McPhee Dam (295 ft/90 m high), built (1984) by the Bureau of Reclamation for irrigation; also used for water supply, power generation, recreation, and as a fish and wildlife pond. Escalante Ruins Historical Site and Anasazi Heritage near dam.

McPherson 1 (muhk-FUHR-suhn), county (□ 901 sq mi/2,334 sq km; 1990 pop. 27,268), central Kansas; ⊙ McPherson; 38°23′N 97°39′W. Rolling plain, drained (NW) by Smoky Hill R. Wheat, soybeans, alfalfa, hay; poultry, cattle, hogs, sheep; chemicals, petroleum refining, plastics prods., mineral wool. Oil and gas fields. Formed 1870. **2** county (□ 860 sq mi/ 2,227 sq km; 1990 pop. 546), W central Nebr., in Sand Hills region; ⊙ Tryon; 41°34′N 101°03′W. Grazing area; cattle, hogs; corn. Boundary bet. Central and Mountain time zones follows N and W boundaries of co., and W part of S boundary. Brown L. and White Water L. in NW, Diamond Bar L. in SW, all of them small natural lakes. Formed 1887. **3** (mik-FIR-suhn), county (□ 1,151 sq mi/2,981 sq km; 1990 pop. 3,228), N S.Dak., on N.Dak. state line; ⊙ Leola; 45°46′N 99°13′W. Agr. (wheat, flax) and cattle-raising region. Drained by Spring Creek in NW and Foot Creek in SE. Formed 1873.

McPherson (muhk-FUHR-suhn), city (1990 pop. 12,422), ⊙ McPherson co., central Kansas, in a farm area on the old Santa Fe Trail; 38°22′N 97°39′W. Mfg. (plastics prods., RR equip., motor vehicles, petroleum refining, animal feeds, plating, pharmaceuticals). The city is named for Gen. James B. McPherson, the highest ranking Union general to die in the Civil War. McPherson Col. here. Inc. 1874.

McQueen, Mont.: see MEADERVILLE.

McQueeney, town (1990 pop. 2,063), Guadalupe co., S central Texas, 5 mi/8 km WNW of Seguin, on L.

McQueeney reservoir (c.1.5 mi/2.4 km long) to N, on Guadalupe R.; 29°36′N 98°02′W. Agr. diverse area (cattle; cotton, peanuts); greyhound breeding; mfg. (bldg. materials, pottery); clay; recreational area.

McRae, town (1990 pop. 3,007), ⊙ Telfair co., S central Ga., 32 mi/51 km S of Dublin, adjacent to Helena (W), and on Little Ocmulgee R.; 32°04′N 82°54′W. Mfg. includes lumber, beverages, clothing; pecan processing, seed packaging. Little Ocmulgee State Park nearby. Est. by Scottish settlers in mid-19th cent. Inc. 1874.

McRae, village (1990 pop. 669), White co., central Ark., 37 mi/60 km NE of Little Rock; 35°06′N 91°49′W. In agr. area.

McSherrystown, borough (1990 pop. 2,769), Adams co., S Pa., suburb 2 mi/3.2 km W of Hanover, near South Branch of Conewago Creek; 39°47′N 77°01′W. Agr. (grain, soybeans, potatoes, apples; livestock; dairying); mfg. (electronic equip., cigars). Hanover Airport to S. Conewago Chapel (1787) to NW. Long Arm Reservoir to SE. Inc. 1882.

McVeigh (muhk-VAI), uninc. village (1990 pop. 400), Pike co., E Ky., in the Cumberland Mts., 9 mi/14.5 km. S of Williamson (W.Va.). In bituminous-coal-mining area.

McVeytown, borough (1990 pop. 408), Mifflin co., central Pa., 12 mi/19 km SW of Lewistown, on Juniata R.; 40°30′N 77°44′W. Agr. (dairying; livestock; corn, alfalfa); mfg. (feeds). Tuscarora State Forest to SE; Rothrock State Forest to NW.

McVille (mak-VIL), village (1990 pop. 559), Nelson co., E central N.Dak., 22 mi/35 km N of Cooperstown, near Sheyenne R.; 47°46′N 98°10′W.

McWatters, village (1991 pop. 1743), W Que., Canada, 6 mi/10 km ESE of Rouyn; 48°13′N 78°55′W. Gold mining.

Mead, uninc. town (1990 pop. 2,150), Spokane co., E Wash., suburb 8 mi/12.9 km NNE of Spokane, on Deadmans Creek. Agr. area (vegetables, wheat; dairying; cattle, sheep, hogs). Mfg. (food; iron foundry; aluminum production). Mead Airport to N.

Mead 1 village (1990 pop. 456), Weld co., N Colo., 8 mi/ 12.9 km NE of Longmont; 40°13′N 104°59′W. Elev. 5,140 ft/1,567 m. Mfg. (chemicals, machinery). Barbour Ponds State Park to S. **2** village (1990 pop. 513), Saunders co., E Nebr., 7 mi/11.3 km E of Wahoo, near Platte R.; 41°13′N 96°29′W. U.S. and Univ. of Nebr. agr. experiment station. Packaging.

Mead, Lake (□ 247 sq mi/640 sq km), reservoir, on the Nev.-Ariz. border, on Colorado R., c.25 mi/40 km SE of Las Vegas; 36°01′N 114°46′W. Shoreline is 550 mi/ 885 km long; reservoir is 115 mi/185 km long, 1 mi/ 1.6 km–8 mi/12.9 km wide; max. depth 589 ft/180 m. Formed by Hoover Dam. Surrounded by L. Mead Natl. Recreation Area, which also extends S, below dam, to take in L. Mohave (Devil Dam). Has 30-mi/48-km-long N arm formed by Virgin R. Grand Canyon Natl. Park at headwaters of lake in Ariz. Valley of Fire State Park (Nev.) on Virgin R. arm.

Meade 1 county (□ 979 sq mi/2,536 sq km; 1990 pop. 4,247), SW Kansas; ⊙ Meade; 37°14′N 100°21′W. Rolling prairie region, in High Plains region, bordered S by Okla.; drained by Crooked Creek. Wheat, corn, sorghum; cattle; volcanic ash deposits. Meade State Park in SW center. Formed 1885. **2** county (□ 324 sq mi/ 839 sq km; 1990 pop. 24,170), N Ky.; ⊙ Brandenburg; 37°58′N 86°13′W. Bounded N and NW by Ohio R. (Ind. state line); drained in E by Otter Creek. Rolling agr. area (burley tobacco, hay, alfalfa, soybeans, wheat; hogs, cattle; timber); limestone quarries. Otter Creek Park in E; part of Fort Knox Military Reservation and Gold Depository in E. Formed 1823. **3** county (□ 3,482 sq mi/9,018 sq km; 1990 pop. 21,878), W central S.Dak.; ⊙ Sturgis; 44°34′N 102°42′W. Ranching and agr. area rich in mineral resources. Drained by Belle Fourche R. and Elk, Sulphur, Beaver Dam, and Cherry creeks; and bounded E by Cheyenne R. Gold, manganese, lignite, bentonite, fuller's earth; marble; corn, soybeans, hay, sugar beets; cattle, hogs, sheep; dairying. Bear Butte State Park in W; small part of Black Hills

Natl. Forest in SW. Ellsworth Air Force Base on S boundary. Formed 1889.

Meade, town (1990 pop. 1,526), ⊙ Meade co., SW Kansas, on Crooked Creek, 35 mi/56 km SSW of Dodge City; 37°17′N 100°20′W. Shipping point for cattle and grain area. Dalton Gang Hideout and Mus. here. Meade State Park to SW. Inc. 1885.

Meade, Fort George G., Md.: see FORT GEORGE G. MEADE.

Meade River, c.250 mi/402 km long, N Alaska, S of Point Barrow; rises near 69°15′N 158°30′W; flows N to Arctic Ocean at 70°50′N 155°46′W. Atkasuk, 60 mi/ 97 km SSW of Barrow. Inuit village.

Meaderville (MEE-duhr-vil), NE suburb of Butte, Silver Bow co., SW Mont. Copper mines with precipitating plant that recovered pure copper from water pumped out of mines; closed 1983. Originally called Gunderson.

Meadow 1 village (1990 pop. 547), Terry co., NW Texas, on the Llano Estacado, 25 mi/40 km SW of Lubbock; 33°20′N 102°12′W. In agr. area; oil and gas. **2** village (1990 pop. 250), Millard co., W Utah, 8 mi/12.9 km SW of Fillmore; 38°53′N 112°24′W. Elev. 5,000 ft/1,524 m. Wheat, barley, alfalfa; cattle. Fishlake Natl. Forest to E; Kanosh Indian Reservation to SE. Clear L. Waterfowl Management Area to NW. Black Rock Desert to W.

Meadow Bridge, village (1990 pop. 325), Fayette co., S central W.Va., 20 mi/32 km SE of Fayetteville; 37°51′N 80°51′W. Coal-mining and agr. region. New R. Gorge Natl. R. to W.

Meadow Grove,, village (1990 pop. 332), Madison co., NE central Nebr., 15 mi/24 km W of Norfolk, on Elkhorn R.; 42°01′N 97°44′W. Grain; livestock. Millstone State Wayside Area to E.

Meadow Lake, town (1991 pop. 4,318), W Sask., Canada, on Meadow L. (6 mi/10 km long, 3 mi/5 km wide), 100 mi/161 km N of North Battleford; 54°08′N 108°26′W. Grain elevators; woodworking; lumbering; fur trapping; fishing.

Meadow Lands, uninc. town (1990 pop. 980), Canton township, Washington co., SW Pa., suburb 3 mi/4.8 km NE of Washington and 3 mi/4.8 km SW of Canonsburg, on Chartiers Creek; 40°13′N 80°13′W. Agr. area (corn, hay; dairying); mfg. (fabricated metal prods., polyurethane and rubber prods., electrical equip., motor vehicle parts); coal. Also spelled Meadowlands.

Meadow Mountain, ridge (c.3,000 ft/914 m) of the Alleghenies, NW Md.; extends NE c.20 mi/32 km from Deep Creek L. to state line just SE of Salisbury, Pa. On it is part of Savage R. State Forest.

Meadow River, 53 mi/85 km long, S central W.Va.; rising on Keeney Knob in N Summers co.; flows generally NW, through Meadow R. Wildlife Management Area, to Gauley R. 14 mi/23 km E of Gauley Bridge; lower 5 mi/8 km in Gauley R. Natl. Recreation Area.

Meadow Valley Wash, c.110 mi/177 km long, SE Nev.; rises in mt. region of E Lincoln co.; flows S, past Panaca and Caliente, to Muddy R. N of L. Mead.

Meadow Vista, uninc. town (1990 pop. 3,067), Placer co., E Calif., 8 mi/12.9 km NNE of Auburn; 39°00′N 121°02′W. Fruit, nuts, grain; cattle, sheep.

Meadowbrook, uninc. village (1990 pop. 1,082), Madison co., SW Ill., residential suburb 21 mi/34 km NNE of St. Louis (Mo.), 2 mi/3.2 km E of Behalto, near Indian Creek; 38°53′N 90°00′W.

Meadowlands, village (1990 pop. 92), St. Louis co., NE Minn., on Whiteface R., 35 mi/56 km NW of Duluth; 47°04′N 92°43′W. Dairying; poultry; oats, alfalfa; mfg. (furniture); Whiteface R. State Forest to E.

Meadowood, uninc. town (1990 pop. 3,011), Butler co., NW Pa., residential suburb 1 mi/1.6 km SSE of Butler; 40°50′N 79°53′W.

Meadows, town (1990 pop. 4,606), Fort Bend co., SE Texas, residential suburb 15 mi/24 km WSW of Houston, near Keegans Bayou; 29°38′N 95°35′W.

Meadows of Dan, uninc. village, Patrick co., SW Va., 30 mi/48 km W of Martinsville, near source of Dan R. Mfg. (furniture, food, lumber, clothing); agr. (apples, grain; cattle; dairying); timber. Pinnacles of Dan mt. (2,655 ft/809 m) to SW, Lovers Leap mt. (3,300 ft/ 1,006 m) to E. Blue Ridge Parkway passes to W.

Meadowview, uninc. town, Washington co., SW Va., 7 mi/11.3 km NE of Abingdon. Mfg. (machining); agr. (dairying; livestock; corn, alfalfa). Walker Mt. ridge to W. Emory 2 mi/3.2 km to NE.

Meadville 1 (MEED-vil), city (1990 pop. 360), Linn co., N central Mo., near Grand R., 12 mi/19 km W of Brookfield; 39°47′N 93°17′W. Corn, wheat, soybeans; cattle. **2** city (1990 pop. 14,318), ⊙ Crawford co., NW Pa., 33 mi/53 km S of Erie, on French Creek, at mouth of Cussewago Creek; 41°38′N 80°09′W. Mfg. (metal fabrication, furniture, plastic prods., pet food, electrical components, food prods., concrete, printing and publishing, glass). Agr. area (corn, hay, potatoes; dairying). Oil deposits are located near the city. Seat of Allegheny Col. Port Meadville Airport to W. Woodcock L. reservoir to NE, Tamarack L. reservoir to SE, Conneaut L. (natural) to W. Settled 1788, inc. 1866.

Meadville (MEED-vil), village (1990 pop. 453), ⊙ Franklin co., SW Miss., 30 mi/48 km ESE of Natchez; 31°28′N 90°53′W. Timber area surrounded by Homochitto Natl. Forest.

Meaford (MEE-fuhrd), town (1991 pop. 4,520), S Ont., Canada, on Nottawasaga Bay, inlet of Georgian Bay, 18 mi/29 km E of Owen Sound; 44°36′N 80°35′W. Port; fruit processing; woodworking; shipbuilding; dairying; apple-growing, trout-fishing region.

Meagher (MAI-guhr), county (□ 2,394 sq mi/6,200 sq km; 1990 pop. 1,819), central Mont.; ⊙ White Sulphur Springs; 46°35′N 110°52′W. Mt. region drained by Smith R. (source in S center), also Sixteenmile Creek (source in SE); and South Fork and North Fork (sources in E), form Musselshell R. just E of E boundary. Barley, wheat, hay; cattle, sheep, hogs. Smith R. State Park in NW; part of Little Belt Mts. in NE; part of Big Belt Mts. in W; part of Lewis and Clark Natl. Forest in NE, center, and SE; part of Helena Natl. Forest in W; small part of Gallatin Natl. Forest in SW corner. Formed 1867. Present boundaries est. 1911.

Meaghers Grant (MEE-guhrz), village, S N.S., Canada, on Musquodoboit R., 26 mi/42 km NE of Halifax; 44°55′N 63°14′W. Lumbering; in gold-mining region. Settled 1692.

Mealy Mountains, range, SE Lab., Canada; extending c.120 mi/193 km SW-NE along S shore of L. Melville; rises to 4,300 ft/1,311 m. There are several peaks over 3,000 ft/914 m high; numerous small lakes.

Meander Creek Reservoir (□ 3 sq mi/7.8 sq km), Trumbull co., NE Ohio, on Meander Creek, 5 mi/8 km WNW of Youngstown; 41°09′N 80°48′W. Max. capacity 62,000 acre-ft. Formed by Mineral Ridge Dam (60 ft/18 m high), built (1932) for water supply.

Meander River, village, NW Alta., Canada, on Mackenzie Highway, 175 mi/282 km N of Peace River, on SE side of Hay R., on RR to town of Hay River, N.W.T. Transportation service center to and from N.W.T. Timber, furs.

Meansville (MEENZ-vil), town (1990 pop. 250), Pike co., W central Ga., 16 mi/26 km S of Griffin; 33°03′N 84°19′W.

Meares, Cape (MIR), promontory (700 ft/213 m) with lighthouse, Tillamook co., NW Oregon, 5 mi/8 km NW of Tillamook. Site of Cape Meares State Park.

Meares Island (□ 27 sq mi/70 sq km), SW B.C., Canada, in Clayoquot Sound off W Vancouver Isl., 45 mi/72 km W of Port Alberni; 49°10′N 125°50′W. Isl. is 10 mi/16 km long, 2 mi/3 km–7 mi/11 km wide. Kakawis village (W); lumbering.

Meauwataka (myoo-WAH-tah-kuh), village, Wexford co., NW Mich., 10 mi/16 km NW of Cadillac, near small Meauwataka L.; 44°21′N 85°32′W. In Manistee Natl. Forest.

Mebane (MEB-in), town (1990 pop. 4,754), Alamance and Orange cos., N central N.C., 9 mi/14.5 km E of Burlington; 36°05′N 79°16′W. Tobacco, grain, soybeans; cattle, chickens; dairying. Mfg. (consumer goods, furniture, textiles, apparel, heating and automotive components, lumber, tools; plastic, metal, and rubber prods.). Founded 1854.

Mecatina, Cape (me-kuh-TEE-nuh), on the Gulf of St. Lawrence, E Que., Canada; 50°44′N 59°W. Air base; lighthouse.

Mecatlán (me-kaht-LAHN), town (1990 pop. 3,679), Veracruz, E Mexico, in Sierra Madre Oriental foothills, 28 mi/45 km SW of Papantla de Olarte. Corn, coffee, tobacco, sugarcane. In Totomac Indian area.

Mecayapan, town (1990 pop. 3,535), Veracruz, SE Mexico, 29 mi/47 km W of Coatzacoalcos. Tobacco, fruit.

Mecca 1 uninc. town (1990 pop. 1,966), Riverside co., S Calif., 12 mi/19 km SE of Indio, 32 mi/51 km SE of Palm Springs, in Coachella Valley, 4 mi/6.4 km NW of the N end of Salton Sea; 33°35′N 116°04′W. Dates, citrus. Painted Canyon, a spectacular many-colored gorge, in Orocopia Mts. is East Salton Sea State Recreation Area to SE; Joshua Tree Natl. Monument to NE; Coachella Canal to E; Torrez Martinez Indian Reservation to S and SW. Town is below sea level. **2** town (1990 pop. 331), Parke co., W Ind., 17 mi/27 km NNE of Terre Haute, on Raccoon Creek, near Wabash R.; 39°44′N 87°20′W. Covered bridges in area. Hogs, cattle; wheat, corn. Laid out 1890.

Mecham, Cape (MEE-chuhm), S extremity of Prince Patrick Isl., W Franklin dist., N.W.T., Canada, on Beaufort Sea of the Arctic Ocean, at entrance of McClure Strait; 75°44′N 121°23′W.

Mechanic Falls (muh-KAN-ik), town (1990 pop. 2,919), Androscoggin co., SW Maine, on the Little Androscoggin, and 8 mi/12.9 km W of Auburn; 44°06′N 70°24′W. Set off from Minot and Poland 1893.

Mechanicsburg 1 village (1990 pop. 538), Sangamon co., central Ill., 13 mi/21 km E of Springfield; 39°48′N 89°24′W. In agr. area. **2** village (1990 pop. 1,803), Champaign co., W central Ohio, 18 mi/29 km ENE of Springfield; 40°04′N 83°33′W. In agr. area; drugs, tools, farm equip.

Mechanicsburg (me-KA-niks-buhrg), borough (1990 pop. 9,452), Cumberland co., S central Pa., suburb 8 mi/12.9 km WSW of Harrisburg; 40°12′N 77°00′W. In agr. area (grain, soybeans, apples; livestock; dairying); mfg. (printing and publishing, machine parts, plastic prods., microwave equip., motor vehicle parts, concrete, fabricated steel, food prods.). Camp Hill State Correctional Inst. to E; Navy Ships Control Center to NE. Williams Grove amusement park to S. Appalachian Trail passes to W. Settled c.1790, inc. 1828.

Mechanicsville, uninc. city (1990 pop. 22,027), Hanover co., E central Va., suburb 5 mi/8 km NE of Richmond, on Chickahominy R.; 37°37′N 77°21′W. Mfg. (sporting equip., machinery, dry ice, printing and publishing); agr. area (dairying; cattle, poultry; grain, soybeans, peanuts, tobacco). Site of inconclusive Civil War battle of Mechanicsville (or Battle of Beaver Dam Creek), one of Seven Days Battles (June 26, 1862) nearby.

Mechanicsville 1 town (1990 pop. 1,012), Cedar co., E Iowa, 11 mi/18 km NW of Tipton; 41°53′N 91°15′W. Feed mfg.; corn, soybeans; pigs. **2** uninc. town (1990 pop. 2,803), Mahoning township, Montour co., central Pa., residential suburb 1 mi/1.6 km NE of Danville; 40°58′N 76°35′W.

Mechanicsville, borough (1990 pop. 540), Schuylkill co., E central Pa., residential suburb 1 mi/1.6 km ENE of Pottsville, on Schuylkill R.; 40°41′N 76°10′W.

Mechanicsville, Conn.: see THOMPSON.

Mechanicville, city (1990 pop. 5,249), Saratoga co., E N.Y., on the canalized Hudson, and 18 mi/29 km N of Albany; 42°53′N 73°41′W. Mfg. of metal goods; RR shops; in dairying area. Settled before 1700; inc. as village in 1859, as city in 1915.

Mechant, Lake (mi-SHANT), Terrebonne parish, SE La., 24 mi/39 km SW of Houma, in marshy coastal region; 29°18′N 90°57′W. Lake is c.5 mi/8 km long, 3 mi/5 km wide; waterways connect it with Caillou L. and Gulf of Mexico (both S).

Mecklenburg 1 (MEK-luhn-buhrg), county (□ 549 sq mi/1,422 sq km; 1990 pop. 511,433), S N.C.; ⊙ Charlotte; 35°15′N 80°49′W. In Piedmont region; bounded SW by S.C. state line, W by Catawba R. (forms L. Wylie reservoir, on S.C. state line, and Mountain Isl. and L. Norman reservoirs). Agr. area (cattle; dairying; corn, oats, barley, hay); timber (pine, oak). Mfg. at Charlotte,

Matthews, Davidson, Pineville, and Huntersville. Most of co. is highly urbanized, esp. in S and center, centered on Charlotte, largest city in N.C. James K. Polk Memorial State Historical Site at Pineville in S. Formed 1762. **2** county (□ 679 sq mi/1,759 sq km; 1990 pop. 29,241), S Va.; ⊙ Boydton; 36°40′N 78°22′W. Bounded S by N.C. state line, N by Meherrin R.; drained by Roanoke (Staunton) R., joined by Dan R. on W boundary. Mfg. at Clarksville, Chase City, South Hill; agr. (tobacco, wheat, barley, corn, soybeans, cotton, hay, alfalfa, peanuts; cattle, hogs, poultry; dairying); some timber. Buffalo Springs resort area. Kerr Reservoir (Buggs Isl. L.), L. Gaston reservoir, both on Roanoke R., in S. Occoneechee State Park in SW; Staunton R. State Park on W boundary, both on Kerr Reservoir. Formed 1765.

Meckling, village, Clay co., SE S.Dak., 8 mi/12.9 km NW of Vermillion; 42°50′N 97°04′W. In farming region.

Mecosta (me-KOS-tuh), county (□ 571 sq mi/1,479 sq km; 1990 pop. 37,308), central Mich.; 43°38′N 85°19′W; ⊙ Big Rapids. Drained by Muskegon, Little Muskegon, Chippewa, and Pine rivers. Agr. (cattle, hogs, sheep; potatoes, apples, corn; dairy prods.). Mfg. at Big Rapids. Resorts. Fish hatchery. Manistee Natl. Forest is in SW. Organized 1859.

Mecosta (me-KOS-tuh), village (1990 pop. 393), Mecosta co., central Mich., 14 mi/23 km ESE of Big Rapids; 43°37′N 85°13′W. In lake-resort and farm area.

Medaryville, town (1990 pop. 689), Pulaski co., NW Ind., on a tributary of Big Monon Creek, 15 mi/24 km W of Winamac; 41°05′N 86°53′W. Agr.; apparel. Medaryville Correctional Unit nearby.

Meddybemps (MED-ee-bemps), town (1990 pop. 133), Washington co., E Maine, 14 mi/23 km SW of Calais; 45°02′N 67°21′W. On Meddybemps L. (6 mi/9.7 km long); resort area.

Medellín, Mexico: see MEDELLÍN DE BRAVO.

Medellín de Bravo (mai-de-YEEN), town (1990 pop. 1,140), Veracruz, E Mexico, in Gulf lowland, on RR, 11 mi/18 km S of Veracruz; 19°04′N 96°09′W. Popular weekend resort. Site of anc. Indian town with prehistoric Xicalango (Xicalanco) ruins in forest nearby. Cortés, who founded the new town, naming it after his native town in Estremadura, Spain, resided here briefly (1526).

Medfield, residential town (1990 pop. 10,531), Norfolk co., E Mass., on Charles R., 18 mi/29 km SW of Boston; 42°11′N 71°19′W. Mfg. (laboratory equip., scientific instruments). Includes Medfield village. Settled and inc. 1650.

Medford 1 city (1990 pop. 57,407), Middlesex co., E Mass., residential and industrial suburb of Boston, on the Mystic R.; 42°25′N 71°07′W. Wax, paper, clothing, and furniture are among its prods. A shipping and shipbuilding center from the 17th to the 19th cents., Medford was also known for its rum. It is the seat of Tufts Univ. Several 18th-cent. bldgs. stand in the city. Includes village of West Medway. Settled 1630, inc. as a city 1892. **2** city (1990 pop. 46,951), ⊙ Jackson co., SW Oregon, 115 mi/185 km S of Eugene, on Bear Creek; 42°20′N 122°50′W. Elev. 1,382 ft/421 m. Junction of logging RR to White City. Growing trade, shipping, and medical center in an agr. area. Mfg. (food processing; lumber, furniture, veneer, electrical equip.; boatbuilding). Tourism. Bet. 1836 and 1856, the area was the scene of a number of bloody conflicts bet. white settlers and Native Americans of Rogue R. descent. Gold was discovered nearby in 1851. The gold-mining town of Jacksonville has been restored. Medford is the hq. for Crater L. Natl. Park, 50 mi/80 km to NE. Tou Velle State Park to N; parts of Rogue R. Natl. Forest to S and E. Pear blossom festival. Inc. 1884.

Medford 1 town (1990 pop. 1,172), ⊙ Grant co., N Okla., 24 mi/39 km W of Blackwell; 36°47′N 97°44′W. Elev. 1,094 ft/333 m. RR junction. In agr. area (wheat, alfalfa, oats, cotton; cattle); mfg. (concrete). **2** town (1990 pop. 4,283), ⊙ Taylor co., N central Wis., on Black R., 37 mi/60 km NW of Wausau; 45°08′N 90°20′W. Lumbering, livestock-raising, and dairying area. Dairy prods.; mfg. (food processing; crushed concrete, bldg. materials). S unit of Chequamegon Natl. Forest to NW. Nearby is a Mennonite colony. Inc. 1889.

Medford 1 village (1990 pop. 733), Steele co., SE Minn., on Straight R., 8 mi/12.9 km S of Fairbault; 44°10′N 93°14′W. Dairying; poultry; grain, soybeans, beans; mfg. (concrete blocks, exercise equip.). Inc. 1936. **2** village (□ 10 sq mi/26 sq km; 1990 pop. 21,274), Suffolk co., SE N.Y., on central L.I., 4 mi/6.4 km N of Patchogue; 40°49′N 72°58′W. Mfg. (machinery, cement prods., bldg. materials); in farming area.

Medford, township (1990 pop. 20,526), Burlington co., W central N.J., c.15 mi/24 km E of Camden, near Rancocas R.; 39°51′N 74°49′W. Friends' meetinghouse here built 1814.

Medford Lakes, borough (1990 pop. 4,462), Burlington co., W central N.J., 9 mi/14.5 km S of Mount Holly; 39°51′N 74°48′W. Small lakes here.

Medfra, village, S central Alaska, on upper Kuskokwim R., 30 mi/48 km ENE of McGrath; 63°06′N 154°43′W.

Media, village (1990 pop. 146), Henderson co., W Ill., 13 mi/21 km SE of Oquawka; 40°46′N 90°49′W. In agr. area.

Media, borough (1990 pop. 5,957), ⊙ Delaware co., SE Pa., residential suburb 12 mi/19 km W of Philadelphia, on Ridley Creek; 39°55′N 75°23′W. Mfg. (printing and publishing, diversified light mfg.). Tyler Arboretum to W. Ridley Creek State Park to NW; Springton Reservoir to N. Seat of Penn State Univ.–Delaware Co. Campus. Settled 1682, laid out c.1848, inc. 1850.

Media Luna (MAI-dee-uh LOO-nuh), site of sugar mill Juan Manuel Márquez, Granma prov., SE Cuba, with nearby small port on Gulf of Guacanayabo; 20°09′N 77°27′W.

Media Luna, Mexico: see OXCHUC.

Media Luna, Cayo (MAH-dee-uh LOO-nuh, KEI-yo), islet in the Gulf of Guacanayabo, E Cuba, 55 mi/89 km S of Camagüey; 20°34′N 77°53′W. Fishing.

Mediapolis, town (1990 pop. 1,637), Des Moines co., SE Iowa, 14 mi/23 km N of Burlington; 41°00′N 91°09′W.

Medical Lake, town (1990 pop. 3,664), Spokane co., E Wash., 15 mi/24 km SW of Spokane, and on Medical L.; 47°34′N 117°42′W. Light mfg. Several lakes in area, largest in Silver L., to E. Four Lakes Battle Monument to SE. Fairchild Air Force Base to N. Inc. 1889.

Medicine Bow, village (1990 pop. 389), Carbon co., S Wyo., on Medicine Bow R., 15 mi/24 km N of N end of Medicine Bow Mts., 50 mi/80 km NW of Laramie; 41°53′N 106°12′W. Elev. c.6,563 ft/2,000 m. Supply point in oil and livestock area. Petrified forest in vicinity. Shirley Mts. to NW. Como Bluff, dinosaur fossil site, to E.

Medicine Bow Mountains, outlying E range of the Rocky Mts., SE Wyo. and N Colo. It extends from village of Elk Mountain, Wyo., WNW of Laramie, S c.80 mi/129 km to Cameron Pass, Colo. Peaks include Medicine Bow Peak (12,013 ft/3,662 m) and Elk Mt. (11,156 ft/3,400 m). Wyo. part is in Medicine Bow Natl. Forest (natl. forest includes part of Laramie Mts.), Colo. part is in Colo. State Forest.

Medicine Bow River, 195 mi/314 km long, S Wyo.; rises in N Medicine Bow Mts. in SE Carbon co.; flows N past village of Medicine Bow, then W, joining North Platte R. at Seminoe Reservoir.

Medicine Creek 1 c.100 mi/161 km long, S Iowa and N Mo.; rises in S Iowa; flows S to Grand R. 10 mi/16 km SE of Chillicothe. **2** SW central Nebr.; rises in Lincoln co.; flows to SE, joining Republican R. at Cambridge. Medicine Creek Reservoir (Harry D. Strunk L.) has state recreation area.

Medicine Hat, city (1991 pop. 43,625), SE Alta., Canada, on the South Saskatchewan R.; 50°02′N 110°41′W. Center of a farming and ranching area. Natural-gas deposits. Light industries; glassblowing; rubber plants.

Medicine Lake 1 village (1990 pop. 385), Hennepin co., E Minn., residential suburb 7 mi/11.3 km W of Minneapolis, on small peninsula on S shore of Medicine L. (2 mi/3.2 km long, 1 mi/1.6 km wide), W of outflow of Bassett Creek; 45°00′N 93°25′W. Village is surrounded by city of Plymouth. **2** village (1990 pop. 357), Sheridan co., NE Mont., on Medicine L., near Big

Muddy Creek, 20 mi/32 km S of Plentywood; 48°30′N 104°30′W. Hogs, sheep; wheat, barley, oats, sugar beets; hay. Fort Peck Indian Reservation to W, Medicine L. Natl. Wildlife Refuge to SE, Homestead L. unit of refuge to SW. Holds state's high-temp. record (117°F/47°C). Winter temp. commonly falls below −40°F/−40°C.

Medicine Lake, reservoir, Sheridan co., NE Mont., on Lake Creek, in Medicine L. Natl. Wildlife Refuge, 20 mi/32 km S of Plentywood; 9 mi/14.5 km long, 4 mi/6.4 km wide; 48°28′N 104°24′W. Drains W into Big Muddy Creek.

Medicine Lodge, town (1990 pop. 2,453), ⊙ Barber co., S Kansas, on Medicine Lodge R., 70 mi/113 km WSW of Wichita; 37°17′N 98°34′W. Trade and refining point in wheat and livestock area; mfg. Oil and gas wells, gypsum mines in vicinity. Quinquennial pageant (since 1927) commemorates signing of treaty (1867) nearby with Plains tribe. Carry Nation started antisaloon crusade here in 1899. Medicine Lodge Stockade and Mus. here. Barber State Fishing L. to N. Founded 1873, inc. 1879.

Medicine Lodge River, 101 mi/163 km long, in Kansas and Okla.; rises in Kiowa co. in S Kansas; flows SE past Medicine Lodge (Kansas), into Alfalfa co. in Okla., to Salt Fork of Arkansas R.

Medicine Park, village (1990 pop. 285), Comanche co., SW Okla., 11 mi/18 km NNW of Lawton, and N of Fort Sill Military Reservation. Located at S end of L. Lawtonka, W end of dam. Wichita Mts. Natl. Wildlife Refuge to NW. Recreation area.

Medina 1 (muh-DEI-nuh), county (□ 424 sq mi/1,098 sq km; 1990 pop. 19,231), N Ohio; ⊙ Medina; 41°06′N 81°53′W. Drained by Rocky and Black rivers and small Chippewa Creek. Includes Chippewa L. (resort). In the Till Plains and Glaciated Plain physiographic regions. Agr. area (poultry, sheep; corn, vegetables); mfg. (food prods., rubber and plastic prods., fabricated metal prods., machinery). Formed 1818. **2** (MAH-dee-nah), county (□ 1,334 sq mi/3,455 sq km; 1990 pop. 27,312), SW Texas; ⊙ Hondo; 29°21′N 99°06′W. Crossed E-W by Balcones Escarpment, separating Edwards Plateau (in N) from plains of S. Drained by Medina R., source of Atascosa R. in SE. Ranching (cattle, sheep, goats); wool, mohair marketed; agr. (corn, grain sorghum, peanuts; cotton); irrigated vegetable farming. Some oil, natural gas; clay mining; sand and gravel. Part of Medina L. (forms part of N boundary), used for irrigation and recreation, is in NE; Frio R., SW corner. Landmark Inn State Historic Site in E at Castroville. Formed 1848.

Medina (muh-DEI-nuh), city (1990 pop. 19,231), ⊙ Medina co., N Ohio; 41°08′N 81°52′W. Paints, roofing, industrial prods.; aluminum and lumber processing, light industry. Town center was restored in early 20th cent. Laid out 1818, inc. as a city 1950.

Medina 1 (muh-DEI-nuh), town (1990 pop. 3,096), Hennepin co., E Minn., residential suburb 15 mi/24 km WNW of Minneapolis; 45°01′N 93°35′W. Includes community of Hamel in NE. Mfg. at Hamel (motor vehicle parts, paper prods., fabricated metal prods., machining, bldg. equip.). Several small lakes esp. in W; L. Minnetonka to S; L. Independence on W boundary. Morris T. Baker Park Reserve in SW. **2** town (1990 pop. 658), Gibson co., NW Tenn., 12 mi/19 km N of Jackson; 35°48′N 88°46′W. In timber and farm area. **3** uninc. town (1990 pop. 2,981), King co., W Wash., residential suburb 4 mi/6.4 km E of Seattle, 2 mi/3.2 km W of Bellevue, on E shore of L. Washington; 47°37′N 122°14′W. Evergreen Point Bridge to Seattle to NW.

Medina 1 (muh-DEI-nuh), industrial village (□ 3 sq mi/7.8 sq km; 1990 pop. 6,686), Orleans co., W N.Y., on the Barge Canal and Oak Orchard Creek, 30 mi/48 km NE of Buffalo; 43°13′N 78°23′W. Mfg. of sheet metal, clothing, paper prods., consumer goods, metal fabrication, machinery, medical equip.) Agr. (fruit); sandstone quarries. Inc. 1832. **2** village (1990 pop. 387), Stutsman co., central N.Dak., 29 mi/47 km W of Jamestown; 46°53′N 99°17′W. Chase L. Natl. Wildlife Refuge to NW. **3** (mah-DEE-nah), uninc. village (1990

pop. 515), Bandera co., SW Texas, on Medina R., c.50 mi/80 km NW of San Antonio; 29°48′N 99°15′W. In livestock-ranching area (cattle, sheep, goats); guest ranches; mfg. (leather prods.). Hill Country State Park to SE, Lost Maples State Park to SW.

Medina Dam, Texas: see MEDINA RIVER.

Medina Lake, Texas: see MEDINA RIVER.

Medina River (MAH-dee-nah), c.100 mi/161 km long, S central Texas; rises on Edwards Plateau NW of Medina; flows generally SE to San Antonio R. 14 mi/23 km S of San Antonio. Medina Dam (180 ft/55 m high, 1,580 ft/482 m long), built in 1913, 26 mi/42 km WNW of San Antonio, impounds Medina L. (capacity 327,000 acre-ft), 1st large Texas irrigation reservoir. Fishing, recreation.

Medomak, Maine: see BREMEN.

Medomak River (muh-DAHM-uhk), c.15 mi/24 km long, S Maine; rises in Knox co.; flows S, widening below Waldeboro, to Muscongus Bay.

Medon (MEE-duhn), town (1990 pop. 137), Madison co., W Tenn.,11 mi/18 km S of Jackson; 35°27′N 88°52′W.

Medora, town (1990 pop. 805), Jackson co., S Ind., 8 mi/12.9 km SW of Brownstown; 38°49′N 86°10′W. In agr. area.

Medora 1 village (1990 pop. 420), Macoupin co., SW Ill., 16 mi/26 km SW of Carlinville; 39°10′N 90°08′W. In agr. and bituminous-coal area. **2** village (1990 pop. 101), ⊙ Billings co., W N.Dak., on Little Missouri R., 36 mi/58 km W of Dickinson; 46°54′N 103°31′W. Cattle raising; grain. Nearby is site of Chimney Butte Ranch, where Theodore Roosevelt engaged in livestock raising; it is at entrance to S Unit of Theodore Roosevelt Natl. Park; in Little Missouri Natl. Grassland; Sullys Creek State Primitive Park to S; Camel Hump Reservoir to W; Chateau de Mores Historic Site to SW.

Medstead, village (1991 pop. 172), W Sask., Canada, 40 mi/64 km NNE of North Battleford; 53°18′N 108°05′W. Wheat; mixed farming.

Medulla (muh-DULL-uh), town (□ 5 sq mi/13 sq km; 1990 pop. 3,977), Polk co., W central Fla., 7 mi/11.3 km S of Lakeland; 27°57′N 81°59′W.

Meduncook River (muh-DUHN-kuk), inlet of Muscongus Bay, 5.5 mi/8.9 km long, Knox co., S Maine, bet. Friendship and Cushing.

Meduxnekeag River (muh-DUHKS-nuh-keg), 35 mi/56 km long, in Maine and N.B., Canada; North and South branches rise in SE Aroostook co., Maine; flow c.20 mi/32 km to junction 8 mi/12.9 km NE of Houlton (on South Branch), in N.B., then c.15 mi/24 km SE to St. John R. at Woodstock, N.B.

Medway 1 town (1990 pop. 1,922), Penobscot co., E central Maine, on the Penobscot, c.60 mi/97 km NNE of Bangor; 45°37′N 68°30′W. In lumbering area. **2** town (1990 pop. 9,931), Norfolk co., E Mass., on Charles R., 22 mi/35 km N of Providence (R.I.); 42°09′N 71°26′W. Treadmills, tools, plastics. Settled 1657, set off from Medfield 1713. Includes West Medway and Medway villages.

Medway River, c.75 mi/121 km long, W N.S., Canada; rises ESE of Annapolis Royal; flows SE, through Malaga and Ponbook lakes, to the Atlantic 8 mi/13 km NE of Liverpool.

Meeker, county (□ 645 sq mi/1,671 sq km; 1990 pop. 20,846), S central Minn.; ⊙ Litchfield; 45°07′N 94°31′W. Drained by North and South forks of Crow R. Agr. area (corn, oats, barley, wheat, hay, alfalfa, soybeans, beans, peas; sheep, hogs, cattle, poultry; dairying). Numerous small lakes in co.; Washington L. in SE, L. Koronis in N boundary in NW. Formed 1856.

Meeker 1 town (1990 pop. 2,098), ⊙ Rio Blanco co., NW Colo., on White R., and 75 mi/121 km NNE of Grand Junction; 40°02′N 107°53′W. Elev. 6,249 ft/1,905 m. Resort and trading point in grain and livestock area; sheep, cattle; hay. Mining. Nearby is Meeker Monument, at scene of "Meeker Massacre" (1879), in which Utes killed a small group of whites including Nathan Meeker, Indian agent and co-founder of Greeley. White R. Natl. Forest to E and SE; L. Avery reservoir to E; Piceans State Wildlife Area to W. Inc. 1885. **2** town (1990 pop. 1,003), Lincoln co., central Okla., 10 mi/

16 km N of Shawnee; 35°29'N 96°53'W. Trading point for agr. area; N terminus of RR spur from Shawnee. Mfg. (machinery, consumer goods).

Meelpaeg Lake (MEEL-puh-eg) (□ 37 sq mi/96 sq km), central N.F., Canada, 40 mi/64 km SSE of Buchans; 15 mi/24 km long, 5 mi/8 km wide. Contains numerous islets. Drained by Grey R.; connected SE with L. Ebbegunbaeg by 4-mi/6 km-long stream.

Meeteetse (muh-TEET-see), village (1990 pop. 368), Park co., NW Wyo., on Greybull R., in SE foothills of Absaroka Range, and 27 mi/43 km SSE of Cody; 44°09'N 108°52'W. Elev. 5,797 ft/1,767 m. In sheep-raising region. Barley, sugar beets.

Megantic (muh-GAN-tik) or **Mégantic** (mai-gah-TEEK), county (□ 780 sq mi/2,020 sq km), S Que., Canada, on L. St. Francis; ⊙ Inverness; 46°15'N 71°30'W.

Megantic, Mégantic, or **Lac Mégantic**, town, ⊙ Frontenac co., SE Que., Canada, on Chaudière R., at N end of L. Megantic, 50 mi/80 km ENE of Sherbrooke, near Maine border. RR center; pulp milling, lumbering, dairying; resort.

Megantic, Lake, S Que., Canada; extends S from Megantic, 50 mi/80 km E of Sherbrooke. Elev. 1,294 ft/394 m. Drained by Chaudière R. into the St. Lawrence; 9 mi/14 km long, 2 mi/3 km wide. Also spelled L. Mégantic.

Megantic Mountain (3,625 ft/1,105 m), S Que., Canada, 16 mi/26 km SW of Megantic, near N.H. border. Also spelled Mégantic Mt.

Megargel, village (1990 pop. 244), Archer co., N Texas, 40 mi/64 km SW of Wichita Falls; 33°27'N 98°55'W. In farm, ranch area.

Meggett (MEG-git), town (1990 pop. 787), Charleston co., SE S.C., 18 mi/29 km WSW of Charleston; 32°42'N 80°15'W. On Wadmalaw Isl. Mfg. includes vegetable prods.

Megunticook Lake (me-GUHN-tuh-kuk), reservoir, Knox and Waldo cos., S Maine, source of Megunticook R., 3 mi/4.8 km NW of Camden, in recreational area; 44°15'N 69°05'W. Reservoir is 3 mi/4.8 km long, 1.5 mi/2.4 km wide; river (c.4 mi/6.4 km long) flows SE to Atlantic Ocean at Camden.

Megunticook, Mount, Maine: see CAMDEN HILLS.

Meherrin River, 126 mi/203 km long, in Va. and N.C.; formed by headstreams joining on the border of Lunenburg and Mecklenburg cos., S Va.; flows ESE to N of South Hill, past Emporia, and SE into N.C., past Murfreesboro (head of navigation), to Chowan R. 8 mi/12.9 km E of Murfreesboro.

Mehoopany, uninc. village, Wyoming co., NE Pa., 6 mi/9.7 km W of Tunkhannock; 41°33'N 76°03'W. Mfg. includes paper prods. Agr. includes dairying; timber.

Meighen Island (MEE-uhn) (□ 360 sq mi/932 sq km), Sverdrup Isls., N Franklin dist., N.W.T., Canada, in the Arctic Ocean, separated from Ellef Ringnes and Amund Ringnes isls. (S) by Peary Channel and from Axel Heiberg Isl. (E) by Sverdrup Channel; 80°00'N 99°00'W. Isl. is 30 mi/48 km long, 8 mi/12.9 km–15 mi/24 km wide; central plateau rises to over 1,000 ft/305 m. Named 1921 by Stefansson after Arthur Meighen, Can. prime minister.

Meigs 1 (MEGZ), county (□ 434 sq mi/1,124 sq km; 1990 pop. 22,987), SE Ohio; ⊙ Pomeroy, 39°06'N 82°01'W. Bounded SE by Ohio R., here forming W.Va. line; drained by small Shade R. and Leading Creek. In the Unglaciated Plain physiographic region. Agr. (poultry; grain); mfg. (electronic equip.); coal mines, limestone quarries. Formed 1819. **2** county (□ 213 sq mi/552 sq km; 1990 pop. 8,033), SE Tenn.; ⊙ Decatur; 35°31'N 84°49'W. In Great Appalachian Valley; bounded NW by the Tennessee; drained by Hiwassee R. Includes parts of Chickamauga and Watts Bar reservoirs. Livestock raising, tobacco; lumbering; sawmills and planing mills. Formed 1836.

Meigs (MEGZ), town (1990 pop. 1,120), Thomas and Mitchell cos., S Ga., 17 mi/27 km NNW of Thomasville; 31°04'N 84°05'W. Mfg. includes textiles, apparel, consumer goods.

Meigs, Fort, Ohio: see FORT MEIGS.

Meiners Oaks, uninc. town (1990 pop. 3,329), Ventura co., S Calif., 12 mi/19 km N of Ventura, near Ventura R., in Ojai Valley; 34°27'N 119°16'W. Strawberries, citrus, vegetables; flowers; nursery stock. Los Padres Natl. Forest to N; L. Casitas Reservoir to SW; Pine Mt. (7,510 ft/2,289 m) to NE.

Meire Grove, village (1990 pop. 124), Stearns co., central Minn., 35 mi/56 km WNW of St. Cloud; 45°37'N 94°52'W. Grain; livestock; dairying.

Mekoryok, village (1990 pop. 177), SW Alaska, on N shore of Nunivak Isl.; 60°24'N 166°11'W.

Melba, village (1990 pop. 252), Canyon co., SW Idaho, 25 mi/40 km SW of Boise, near Snake R.; 43°22'N 116°32'W. Center of irrigated area (cattle, sheep; seed growing); mfg. (feeds, birdseed; meat processing). Deer Flat Natl. Wildlife Refuge at L. Lowell, to NW.

Melbeta (mel-BAI-tuh), village (1990 pop. 116), Scotts Bluff co., W Nebr., 10 mi/16 km ESE of Scottsbluff, and on North Platte R; 41°46'N 103°31'W.

Melbourne, village (1991 pop. 513), S Que., Canada, on St. Francis R., opposite Richmond. Dairying.

Melbourne (MEL-buhrn), city (1990 pop. 59,646), Brevard co., E central Fla., on Indian R. (a lagoon). Tourist and aerospace center near the Atlantic Ocean. The leading industries are fruit processing and shipping, electronic equip. and boat mfg. Since the development of nearby Cape Canaveral, the aerospace industry has bolstered Melbourne's economy and pop. Fla. Inst. of Technology is in the city, and Patrick Air Force Base is nearby. Inc. 1888.

Melbourne 1 town (1990 pop. 1,562), ⊙ Izard co., N Ark., 23 mi/37 km NW of Batesville; 36°03'N 91°54'W. Stock raising, agr.; mfg. (aircraft parts, hardwood flooring, apparel). Ozark Natl. Forest to W. **2** town (1990 pop. 669), Marshall co., central Iowa, 12 mi/19 km SW of Marshalltown; 41°56'N 93°05'W.

Melbourne (MEL-buhrn), village (1990 pop. 660), Campbell co., N Ky., 8 mi/12.9 km SE of Cincinnati, Ohio, on the Ohio R.; 39°01'N 84°22'W. Tobacco, alfalfa, soybeans, corn; cattle. Mfg. (bldg. materials).

Melbourne Beach (MEL-buhrn), town (□ 1 sq mi/2.6 sq km; 1990 pop. 3,021), Brevard co., E central Fla., 3 mi/4.8 km E of Melbourne; 28°04'N 80°33'W. Light mfg.

Melbourne Island, S Franklin dist., N.W.T., Canada, in Queen Maud Gulf, just E of base of Kent Peninsula, opposite SE Victoria Isl.; 68°30'N 104°15'W. Isl is 18 mi/29 km long, 10 mi/16 km wide. On N coast is Eskimo winter camp.

Melcher, town (1990 pop. 1,302), Marion co., S central Iowa, near Whitebreast Creek, 9 mi/14.5 km SW of Knoxville; 33 mi/53 km SE of Des Moines; 41°13'N 93°14'W. Merged in mid-1980s with Dallas (1 mi/1.6 km N). Mfg. of wood prods.; coal mining.

Melchor Ocampo 1 (mel-CHOR o-KAHM-po) or **Ocampo**, town (1990 pop. 23,089), Mexico state, central Mexico, 20 mi/32 km N of Mexico city, and in the Zona Metropolitana de la Ciudad de México; 18°00'N 102°13'W. Cereals; livestock. **2** town (1990 pop. 1,641), Nuevo León, N Mexico, 55 mi/89 km ENE of Monterrey. Corn, cactus fibers. Formerly called Charco Redondo. **3** town (1990 pop. 493), ⊙ Melchor Campo municipio, Zacatecas, N central Mexico, on Coahuila border, 55 mi/89 km SW of Saltillo Elev. 7,415 ft/2,260 m. RR terminus; mining center (copper, lead, gold, silver). Formerly called San Pedro Ocampo.

Melena del Sur (mai-LAI-nuh del soor), town, La Habana prov., W Cuba, on RR, 26 mi/42 km S of Havana; 22°47'N 82°12'W. Sugar-growing center, with the Gregorio Arlee Mañalich sugar mill 1.5 mi/2.4 km N. Limekiln.

Melfa, town, Accomack co., E Va., 6 mi/9.7 km SSW of Accomac, in Eastern Shore area, bet. Atlantic Ocean (E) and Chesapeake Bay (W); 37°38'N 75°44'W. Mfg. (waste disposal systems, bronze sculptures); agr. (vegetables, grain; livestock. Co. Airport to W; Accomack Vineyards to S. Eastern Shore Community Col.

Melfort (MEL-fuhrt), city (1991 pop. 5,628), central Sask., Canada, on Melfort Creek, 55 mi/89 km ESE of Prince Albert; 52°52'N 104°36'W. Livestock-shipping

and oil-distributing center; flour and lumber milling, dairying; cold storage plant.

Melissa, village (1990 pop. 557), Collin co., N Texas, 37 mi/60 km NNE of Dallas, near East Fork of Trinity R.; 33°16'N 96°34'W. Agr. area just beyond fringe of Dallas–Fort Worth urban area. Cotton, wheat, sorghum; cattle. Mfg. (concrete, steel fabricating).

Melita (muh-LI-tuh), town (1991 pop. 1,134), SW Man., Canada, on Souris R., 60 mi/97 km SW of Brandon; 49°16'N 100°59'W. Dairying; mixed farming; livestock raising.

Mella (MAI-yuh), village, Santiago de Cuba prov., E Cuba, at S foot of Sierra de Nipe, 28 mi/45 km N of Santiago de Cuba; 20°22'N 75°55'W. Sugar mills. Formerly called Miranda.

Mellen, town (1990 pop. 935), Ashland co., N Wis., on branch of Bad R., 20 mi/32 km SSE of Ashland, in wooded lake region, near Gogebic Range; 46°19'N 90°39'W. Commercial center for dairying area; woodworking; mfg. (lumber, plywood, pulpwood). RR junction. Copper Falls State Park is to N; Chequamegon Natl. Forest to W and S; small lakes to SE. Settled 1886, inc. 1907.

Mellette, county (□ 1,309 sq mi/3,390 sq km; 1990 pop. 2,137), S S.Dak.; ⊙ White R.; 43°34'N 100°45'W. Farming and cattle-raising region bounded N by White R. Wheat; cattle. Drained by Little White R. and Oak and Black Pipe creeks. In Mountain time zone; the boundary bet. Mountain and Central time zones follows E co. boundary to E part of N boundary to U.S. Highway 83. Formed 1909.

Mellette (MEL-let), village (1990 pop. 184), Spink co., NE central S.Dak., 20 mi/32 km N of Redfield; 45°08'N 98°30'W.

Mellott, town (1990 pop. 222), Fountain co., W Ind., 13 mi/21 km E of Covington; 40°10'N 87°09'W. Agr.

Melocheville (muh-losh-VEEL), village (1991 pop. 2,292), SW Que., Canada, on L. St. Louis, near NE end of Beauharnois Canal, 25 mi/40 km SW of Montreal; 45°19'N 73°56'W. Quartz mining; dairying; resort. Formerly called Lac Saint Louis.

Melozitna River, 180 mi/290 km long, central Alaska; rises NW of Tanana, near 66°01'N 152°45'W; flows SW to Yukon R. opposite Ruby.

Melrose, city (1990 pop. 28,150), Middlesex co., E Mass., suburb of Boston; 42°27'N 71°04'W. It is chiefly residential. The opera star Geraldine Farrar was b. here. Settled c.1629, set off from Malden and inc. 1850.

Melrose 1 town (1990 pop. 150), Monroe co., S Iowa, on Cedar Creek, 14 mi/23 km WSW of Albia; 40°58'N 93°02'W. In bituminous-coal–mining and livestock area. **2** town (1990 pop. 2,561), Stearns co., central Minn., on Sauk R., 32 mi/51 km WNW of St. Cloud; 45°40'N 94°48'W. Trade and shipping point (grain; livestock; dairying; mfg. (cheese, feeds, machine parts, furniture; food processing). Little and Big Birch lakes to N; Birch L. State Forest to N. Settled 1857, inc. as city 1898.

Melrose 1 village, Silver Bow co., SW Mont., on Big Hole R. at mouth of Camp Creek, 28 mi/45 km SSW of Butte. Trout-fishing center. Cattle, sheep. **2** village (1990 pop. 662), Curry co., E N.Mex., 20 mi/32 km W of Clovis; 34°25'N 103°37'W. Cattle, sheep; alfalfa, pumpkins, vegetables; grain (esp. wheat); dairying. **3** village (1990 pop. 307), Paulding co., NW Ohio, 13 mi/21 km SSW of Defiance, near Auglaize R.; 41°05'N 84°25'W. **4** village (1990 pop. 551), Jackson co., W central Wis., 24 mi/39 km NNE of La Crosse, 44°07'N 91°00'W. Creamery; feeds.

Melrose Park 1 village (1990 pop. 20,859), Cook co., NE Ill., industrial suburb W of Chicago; 41°53'N 87°51'W. It has large RR yards and shops, steel mills, TV mfg., and factories that make a wide variety of prods. Inc. 1893. **2** village (□ 4 sq mi/10.4 sq km; 1990 pop. 2,091), Cayuga co., W central N.Y.; 42°53'N 76°31'W. **3** uninc. village, Cheltenham township, Montgomery co., SE Pa., suburb 8 mi/12.9 km N of Philadelphia (at the city limits); 40°03'N 75°07'W. Light mfg.

Melstone (MELS-tuhn), village (1990 pop. 166), Musselshell co., central Mont., on Musselshell R., 66 mi/-

106 km NNE of Billings; 46°36′N 107°52′W. Sheep, cattle; wheat, hay. Oil fields in area.

Melvern, city (1990 pop. 423), Osage co., E Kansas, on Marais des Cygnes R., 3 mi/4.8 km downstream (E) of Melvin Dam, 8 mi/12.9 km SSE of Lyndon; 38°30′N 95°38′W. Livestock; grain.

Melvern Lake, Osage co., E Kansas, on Marais des Cygnes R., 24 mi/39 km WSW of Ottawa; 38°30′N 95°42′W. Max. capacity 363,000 acre-ft; 13 mi/21 km long. Formed by Melvern Dam (93 ft/28 m high) built (1972) for flood control. Eisenhower State Park on N shore.

Melville (MEL-vuhl), city (1991 pop. 4,905), SE Sask., Canada, 25 mi/40 km SW of Yorkton; 50°56′N 102°48′W. Grain elevators; flour mills; dairying.

Melville, town (1990 pop. 1,562), St. Landry parish, S central La., 23 mi/37 km ENE of Opelousas and on Atchafalaya R. (toll ferry); 30°42′N 91°45′W. In agr. area (cattle, vegetables, cotton, sugarcane, rice), catfish, crawfish; mfg. of food prods., wood prods. Heavily damaged by floods in 1927. Famous for Melville crevaise (levee break). Settled c.1875, inc. 1911.

Melville, village (1990 pop. 20), Sweet Grass co., S Mont., 19 mi/31 km N of Big Timber on Sweet Grass Creek. Cattle, sheep, and horses and other rodeo stock. Dude ranches. Crazy Mts. to W; Upper and Lower Glaston lakes to SE.

Melville Island (□ c.16,400 sq mi/42,500 sq km), W Baffin region, N.W.T., Canada, N of Victoria Isl.; largest of the Parry Isls.; 75°30′N 112°00′W. Generally hilly (rising to c.1,500 ft/460 m), it has several ice-covered areas in the interior. There are musk oxen on the isl. Sir William Parry, the Br. explorer, visited Melville Isl. in 1819, and its S coast was explored (1851) by Sir Francis McClintock.

Melville, Lake (□ 1,133 sq mi/2,934 sq km), SE Lab., Canada; extending c.120 mi/190 km inland from Hamilton Inlet, an arm of the Atlantic Ocean; 53°45′N 59°30′W. The saltwater lake receives the Churchill R. in Goose Bay, its SW arm, and the Naskaupi R. Towns of Goose Bay and Happy Valley at SW end.

Melville Peninsula (□ 24,156 sq mi/62,564 sq km), Baffin region, Franklin dist., N.W.T., Canada, bet. the Gulf of Bothnia and Foxe Basin, and separated from Baffin Island to the N by the Fury and Hecla Strait; it is joined to the mainland by the Rae Isthmus. Peninsula is c.250 mi/400 km long and 70 mi/113 km–135 mi/217 km wide. Numerous streams radiate from the peninsula's central hilly sect., which rises to 1,850 ft/564 m. Hall L. (□ c.200 sq mi/520 sq km) lies near the NE coast, and in the S portion of the peninsula are many connected lakes. The tundra-covered region is virtually uninhabited and is of little importance economically. Weather station at Mackar Inlet on W coast; trading post at Repulse Bay and Hall Beach on the S coast; air station near Hall Beach.

Melville Sound, Canada: see VISCOUNT MELVILLE SOUND.

Melvin, town (1990 pop. 250), Osceola co., NW Iowa, 11 mi/18 km SE of Sibley; 43°17′N 95°36′W. In livestock and grain area.

Melvin 1 village (1990 pop. 466), Ford co., E central Ill., 12 mi/19 km NNW of Paxton; 40°34′N 88°15′W. Agr. (grain; livestock); feed milling. **2** village (1990 pop. 148), Sanilac co., E Mich., 15 mi/24 km NE of Imlay City; 43°10′N 82°51′W. In farm area. **3** village (1990 pop. 184), McCulloch co., central Texas, on Brady Creek, 15 mi/24 km WNW of Brady; 31°11′N 99°34′W. In cotton, cattle region.

Melvin Village, N.H.: see TUFTONBORO.

Melvina (mee-VEI-nuh), village (1990 pop. 115), Monroe co., W Wis., 23 mi/37 km E of La Crosse; 43°47′N 90°46′W.

Melvindale, city (1990 pop. 11,216), Wayne co., SE Mich., SW residential suburb 6 mi/9.7 km SW of Detroit; 42°16′N 83°10′W. Borders Detroit on E, R. Rouge on N, North Branch of George R. on S. Mfg. (animal oils, meat processing, fabricated metal prods., paper prods., metal plating). Settled 1870, inc. as city 1932.

Memphis 1 city (1990 pop. 2,094) ⊙ Scotland co., NE Mo., on North Fabius R., 28 mi/45 km NE of Kirksville; 40°27′N 92°10′W. Livestock (sheep, cattle, hogs); soybeans and grain (corn); mfg. (clothing, beverages). Settled 1838. **2** city (1990 pop. 610,337), ⊙ Shelby co., extreme SW Tenn., on the Fourth, or Lower, Chickasaw Bluff above the Mississippi R., at the mouth of the Wolf R., 235 mi/378 km S of St. Louis (Mo.); 35°08′N 90°04′W. A river port with excellent anchorages on the Wolf, Memphis is the largest city in the state, a port of entry, a RR and air distribution center, and a leading hardwood lumber, cotton, and livestock market. Its wide variety of mfg. includes textiles, consumer goods, paints, and automotive parts. A number of corporations have their natl. hq. in the city, and its internatl. airport handles the largest amount of domestic freight of any airport in the U.S. With the rise of gambling casinos in nearby Miss., casino management has become a major industry here. De Soto possibly crossed the Mississippi near the site of Memphis, and La Salle's Fort Prudhomme may have been built here. The area was strategically important during the time of the Br., Fr., and Span. rivalries in the 18th cent. A U.S. fort was erected in 1797. The city was est. 1819 by Andrew Jackson, Marcus Winchester, and John Overton. In the Civil War it fell, on June 6, 1862, to a Union force led by the elder Charles Henry Davis. Severe yellow-fever epidemics occurred in the 1870s, and thousands died. So many people fled the city that its charter had to be surrendered (1879); it was not restored until 1891. Memphis was a key site during the nation's civil rights struggles in the 1960s; the Lorraine Motel, where Rev. Dr. Martin Luther King was shot in 1968, is now a natl. civil rights mus. The city is the seat of the Univ. of Memphis, the Univ. of Tenn. Medical Units, Rhodes Col., Christian Brothers Col., Lemoyne-Owen Col., the Memphis Acad. of Arts, Southern Col. of Optometry and Shelby State Community Col. It has a mus. of natural history, a planetarium, an opera company, a ballet company, a symphony orchestra, an art gallery, a notable park system, botanical gardens, a nature center, a zoo, an aquarium, a coliseum, a professional theater, a speedway, and a coliseum shaped like an Egyptian pyramid (tribute to the city's Egyptian heritage). It is the seat of a large medical center, St. Jude Children's Research Hosp., and a state mental hosp. The Mid-South Fairgrounds and Libertyland Amusement Park are here, as is a modern convention hall. An annual week-long cotton carnival is held, and the Liberty Bowl post-season col. football game is played here each year. A number of Victorian homes in the city have been restored. Graceland, former home of Elvis Presley, is one of the nation's largest tourist attractions. Beale St., another popular site, was made famous by W. C. Handy, the blues composer. A number of military installations are in and near the city, including Memphis Naval Air Station at Millington. A trans-Mississippi bridge connects Memphis with Ark. Inc. 1826.

Memphis 1 town (□ 3 sq mi/7.8 sq km; 1990 pop. 6,760), Manatee co., W central Fla., 2 mi/3.2 km N of Bradenton.; 27°32′N 82°33′W **2** town (1990 pop. 325), Macomb and St. Clair cos., SE Mich., 18 mi/29 km SW of Port Huron and on Belle R.; 42°53′N 82°46′W. Mfg. (electronic equip., tools, machining). **3** town (1990 pop. 2,465), ⊙ Hall co., NW Texas, 28 mi/45 km NW of Childress; 34°43′N 100°32′W. Elev. 2,067 ft/630 m. Trade, processing center for agr. area (cotton; peanuts; cattle); mfg. (fabricated metal prods., peanut processing). Founded 1889, inc. 1906.

Memphis 1 village, Clark co., SE Ind., 5 mi/8 km NW of Charlestown. Agr. area; mfg. (beef and pork processing). **2** village (1990 pop. 70), De Soto co., NW Miss., residential suburb 13 mi/21 km SSW of Memphis (Tenn.); 34°55′N 90°08′W. **3** village (1990 pop. 117), Saunders co., E Nebr., 12 mi/19 km SE of Wahoo near Platte R; 41°05′N 96°25′W. Farm trade center in fertile valley. Nearby are recreation grounds and artificial lake. Memphis L. State Recreation Area to W.

Memphremagog, Lake (mehm-fruh-MAI-gahg), in S Que., Canada, and N Vt., Mainly in Que. Newport, Vt., and Magog, Que., are trade centers and resorts here. Lake is c.30 mi/48 km long, with a max. width of 4 mi/6 km. Drains through Magog R. and L. Magog into St. Francis R., Que.

Memramcook (MEM-ruhm-kahk), village, SE N.B., Canada, on Memramcook R., and 13 mi/21 km ESE of Moncton; 46°00′N 64°33′W. Lumbering; potatoes, grain. Nearby is St. Joseph, site of Acadian cultural center.

Memramcook River, 25 mi/40 km long, SE N.B., Canada; rises E of Moncton; flows ESE and S to Shepody Bay at Dorchester.

Mena (MEEN-uh), town (1990 pop. 5,475), ⊙ Polk co., W Ark., in Ouachita Mts., c.55 mi/89 km S of Fort Smith; 34°34′N 94°14′W. In farming area. Mfg. (wood prods., food processing, apparel, printing, automobile parts). Ouachita Natl. Forest surrounds the town and vicinity except to SW; Queen Wilhelmina State Park to NW; L. Wilhelmina reservoir to W. Founded 1896.

Menahga (me-NAH-guh), town (1990 pop. 1,076), Wadena co., W central Minn., 22 mi/35 km N of Wadena, on Blueberry R.; 46°45′N 95°05′W. Sheep, cattle, poultry; oats, barley, rye, beans; dairying; mfg. (animal feeds, consumer goods, hardwood lumber, concrete blocks, wood prods., rubber prods.). Hutersville State Forest to E; Smoky Hills State Forest to NW; several small natural lakes to E and NE.

Menan, village (1990 pop. 601), Jefferson co., SE Idaho, 5 mi/8 km NW of Rigby, inside bend of Snake R.; 43°43′N 112°00′W. Elev. 4,798 ft/1,462 m. Irrigated agr. area (dairying, cattle, sheep; sugar beets, potatoes, fruit; wheat); mfg. (log homes).

Menands (muh-NANZ), suburban village (□ 3 sq mi/7.8 sq km; 1990 pop. 4,333), Albany co., E N.Y., on the Hudson R., just N of Albany; 42°41′N 73°43′W. Regional wholesale produce center. Inc. 1924.

Menard 1 (muh-NAHRD), county (□ 315 sq mi/816 sq km; 1990 pop. 11,164), central Ill.; ⊙ Petersburg; 40°01′N 89°47′W. Agr. (corn, wheat, soybeans). Some mfg. Drained by Sangamon R. and Salt Creek (both partly forming N boundary of co.). Includes New Salem Historic Site, a reconstruction of the town in which Lincoln lived during 1831–1837. One of 17 Ill. cos. to retain the Southern-style commission form of co. govt. Formed 1839. **2** county (□ 902 sq mi/2,336 sq km; 1990 pop. 2,252), W central Texas; ⊙ Menard; 30°53′N 99°49′W. Elev. 1,800 ft/549 m–2,450 ft/747 m. On Edwards Plateau; drained by San Saba R. Ranching (sheep, goats, cattle); wool, mohair marketed; some irrigated agr. (grains, pecans). Oil and natural gas. Scenery, hunting, fishing attract tourists. Formed 1858.

Menard, town (1990 pop. 1,606), ⊙ Menard co., W central Texas, on Edwards Plateau, c.55 mi/89 km SE of San Angelo; 30°55′N 99°46′W. Elev. 1,960 ft/597 m. Market for wool, mohair; ranching region (cattle, sheep, goats); irrigated agr. (pecans, grain); oil and gas; mfg. (feeds; meat processing); resort. Ruins of Span. mission and a presidio (restored), both est. 1757, are nearby.

Menasha (men-ASH-uh), city (1990 pop. 14,711), Winnebago and Calumet cos., E Wis., suburb 5 mi/8 km S of Appleton, on the Fox R.; forms a continuous community with twin city of Neenah; 44°12′N 88°26′W. Mfg. (wires, printing and publishing, asphalt, paper prods., inks, machinery); dairy farms; summer resort. RR junction. Menasha's large papermaking industry, which is served by water power, dates from the late 19th cent. The region at the lake outlet was visited by Jean Nicolet (c.1634; the site is marked) and other Fr. explorers and was described by Jonathan Carver in his *Travels* (1778). Univ. of Wis.–Fox Valley Center. Settled 1840s, inc. 1874.

Mendenhall (MEN-duhn-hawl), town (1990 pop. 2,463), ⊙ Simpson co., S central Miss., 29 mi/47 km SE of Jackson, near Strong R.; 31°57′N 89°52′W. Agr. (corn, cotton; cattle, poultry); timber; mfg. (steel fabrication, lumber, equip. parts). Simpson Co. Legion L. (state lake) to SE.

Mendenhall Glacier, SE Alaska, 25 mi/40 km NW of Juneau; 58°26′N 134°33′W. Glacier (17 mi/27 km long,

3 mi/4.8 km wide) is accessible by highway from Juneau.

Méndez (MEN-des), town (1990 pop. 797), Tamaulipas, NE Mexico, 85 mi/137 km SW of Matamoros; 25°05′N 98°32′W. Cereals, sugarcane; livestock. Also Villa de Méndez.

Mendham (MEN-duhm), residential borough (1990 pop. 4,890), Morris co., N central N.J., 6 mi/9.7 km WSW of Morristown; 40°46′N 74°35′W. Has pre-Revolutionary tavern. Settled before 1750, inc. 1906.

Mendocino, county (☐ 3,509 sq mi/9,088 sq km; 1990 pop. 80,345), NW Calif., on the coast; ☉ Ukiah; 39°26′N 123°26′W. Mt. and valley region, traversed by several of the Coast Ranges; in E are summits over 6,000 ft/1,829 m. Bounded W by Pacific Ocean. Drained by Eel, Russian, Big, Noyo, and Navarro rivers. Extensive timber, sawmilling; wineries, breweries. Cattle; farms in valleys produce fruit (apples, pears), grapes, hops, beans; dairying. Ocean fisheries (urchins, fish). Hot springs (resorts); trout and steelhead fishing, deer hunting. Part of Mendocino Natl. Forest (NE). Round Valley Indian Reservation is in N. Large stands of redwood near coast; inland are pine, fir, and oak. Mackerricher, Russian Gulch, and Van Damme state parks in W, Manchester State Beach in SW, all on Pacific Ocean; Hendy Woods State Park in S. Formed 1850.

Mendocino, uninc. village, Mendocino co., NW Calif., at mouth of Big R., 31 mi/50 km WNW of Ukiah. Redwood, pine timber; fish, urchins; tourism. Jackson State Forest to NE; Russian Gulch State Park to N, Van Damme State Park to S; Point Cabrillo to N.

Mendocino, Cape, promontory, Humboldt co., NW Calif., 27 mi/43 km S of Eureka, on Pacific Ocean; 40°26′N 124°24′W. Westernmost point of Calif. Rainbow Ridge to E.

Mendon 1 (MEN-duhn), town (1990 pop. 4,010), Worcester co., S Mass., 17 mi/27 km SE of Worcester; 42°05′N 71°33′W. Agr. Settled 1660, inc. 1667. **2** town (1990 pop. 207), Chariton co., N central Mo., 13 mi/21 km S of Brookfield; 39°35′N 93°07′W. Corn, wheat, soybeans. Dairying; livestock raising. Swan L. Natl. Wildlife Refuge on N side. **3** town (1990 pop. 1,049), Rutland co., W central Vt., just NE of Rutland, partly in Green Mt. Natl. Forest; 43°37′N 72°52′W.

Mendon 1 village (1990 pop. 854), Adams co., W Ill., 11 mi/18 km NNE of Quincy; 40°05′N 91°16′W. In agr. area (corn, sorghum, soybeans; cattle). **2** village (1990 pop. 920), St. Joseph co., SW Mich., 21 mi/34 km SSE of Kalamazoo, on St. Joseph R.; 42°00′N 85°27′W. Rich farm area. Mfg. (plastic prods.). **3** village (1990 pop. 717), Mercer co., W Ohio, 9 mi/14 km N of Celina, and on St. Marys R.; 40°40′N 84°31′W. In agr. area; cannery. **4** village (1990 pop. 684), Cache co., N Utah, 8 mi/12.9 km W of Logan, near Little Bear R.; 41°42′N 111°58′W. Elev. 4,520 ft/1,378 m. Wheat; dairying; cattle. Part of Wasatch Natl. Forest, including Wellsville Wilderness Area, to W. Settled 1857.

Mendota 1 city (1990 pop. 6,821), Fresno co., central Calif., in San Joaquin Valley, 33 mi/53 km W of Fresno; 36°46′N 120°23′W. Melons, cotton, sugar beets, figs, vegetables, almonds, grain; cattle; mfg. (beet sugar). Near here is terminus of Delta-Mendota Canal; Calif. aqueduct to SW. Inc. 1942. **2** city (1990 pop. 7,018), La Salle co., N Ill., 19 mi/31 km NW of Ottawa; 41°32′N 89°07′W. Processing and shipping center in agr. area; mfg. (food processing, woodworking machinery, tools, concrete prods.); corn, wheat, soybeans; livestock. Inc. 1859.

Mendota 1 (men-DO-duh), village (1990 pop. 164), Dakota co., SE Minn., suburb 5 mi/8 km SW of St. Paul and 7 mi/11.3 km SE of Minneapolis, at confluence of Minnesota (W) and Mississippi (N) rivers; 44°53′N 93°09′W. Mfg. (consumer goods). The 1st permanent white settlement in Minn. Served as meeting place for traders and trappers before 1819 and known as St. Peter's. Settled 1834, name changed 1837. Homes of Henry Hastings Sibley (Sibley House Mus.), 1st governor of Minn., and of Jean Baptiste Fairbault, early trader and fur trapper, are here. Reconstructed in 1930s, bldgs.

date back, respectively, to 1835 and 1837. Mendota Bridge (4,119 ft/1,255 m long, completed 1926) crosses Minnesota R. here. Minneapolis–St. Paul Internatl. Airport to W. Fort Snelling State Park to W and SW. **2** uninc. village, Washington co., SW Va., on North Fork of Holston R., 12 mi/19 km W of Abingdon. Agr. (dairying; livestock; corn, alfalfa).

Mendota Heights (men-DO-duh), town (1990 pop. 9,451), Dakota co., SE Minn., residential suburb 5 mi/8 km SSW of St. Paul and 8 mi/12.9 km SE of Minneapolis, near confluence of Mississippi (NW) and Minnesota (W) rivers (both bridged here); 44°52′N 93°08′W. RR junction; mfg. (rubber prods., concrete, printing, medical equip., food, pharmaceuticals, machinery). Small lakes in area; Rogers L. in S. Part of Fort Snelling State Park in W.

Mendota, Lake (men-DO-tuh), largest of the Four Lakes, Dane co., S Wis.; c.6 mi/9.7 km long, c.4 mi/6.4 km wide. A resort lake stocked with fish, it is fed by Yahara R. from N and drained by it to SE to L. Monona. Downtown Madison is on SE shore, city also bounds it on NE and SW; city of Middleton on W end. Univ. of Wis. on S shore; Gov. Nelson State Park on NW shore.

Mendoza, Mexico: see CIUDAD MENDOZA.

Menemsha, Mass.: see CHILMARK.

Meneses (mai-NAI-saiz), town, Sancti Spíritus prov., central Cuba, in low Sierra de Meneses, 23 mi/37 km SE of Caibarién; 22°15′N 79°16′W. Sugarcane, tobacco; cattle.

Menfro, uninc. community, Perry co., E Mo., near Mississippi R., 9 mi/14.5 km ENE of Perryville.

Menifee (MEN-uh-fee), county (☐ 206 sq mi/534 sq km; 1990 pop. 5,092), E central Ky.; ☉ Frenchburg; 37°57′N 83°35′W. Bounded NE by Licking R. (Cave Run L. reservoir), S by Red R.; drained by several creeks. Rolling agr. area (burley tobacco, hay; cattle); oil and gas wells, timber; some sawmills. Most of co. (except E and W ends) in Daniel Boone Natl. Forest. Part of Red R. Geological Area, including Red R. Gorge, in S. Formed 1869.

Menlo, town (1990 pop. 356), Guthrie co., W central Iowa, near source of North R., 12 mi/19 km SSE of Guthrie Center; 41°31′N 94°24′W. In livestock and grain area.

Menlo 1 (MEN-lo), village (1990 pop. 538), Chattooga co., NW Ga., 24 mi/39 km NW of Rome, near Ala. line and Lookout Mt.; 34°29′N 85°29′W. Mfg. of jewelry, apparel, lumber. **2** village (1990 pop. 50), Thomas co., NW Kansas, near source of South Fork of Solomon R., 16 mi/26 km E of Colby; 39°21′N 100°43′W. In agr. and cattle region.

Menlo Park, city (1990 pop. 28,040), San Mateo co., W Calif., residential suburb 25 mi/40 km SSE of San Francisco, 4 mi/6.4 km SSW of San Francisco Bay; 37°29′N 122°08′W. Bounded by San Francisquito Creek in SE. Mfg. (electronic and communications equip., liquor, pharmaceuticals, medical equip., wire and plastic prods., aerospace parts, computer equip.). Menlo Col. and Stanford Univ. are located 1 mi/1.6 km SE at Stanford. Santa Cruz Mts. to SW; Hetch Hetchy Aqueduct passes to N; Stanford Linear Accelerator to S. Inc. 1874.

Menlo Park, uninc. residential community, Middlesex co., central N.J. It is the site of Edison Memorial Tower and state park, where Thomas Edison kept his laboratories (1876–1887). The laboratories have since been transferred to the Edison Inst. of Technology in Greenfield Village Mus. at Dearborn, Mich. Menlo Park developed into a suburban community after World War II.

Menno, town (1990 pop. 768), Hutchinson co., SE S.Dak., 27 mi/43 km NNW of Yankton; 43°14′N 97°34′W. Cooperative creamery and grain elevator.

Meno (MEEN-o), village (1990 pop. 155), Major co., NW Okla., 17 mi/27 km W of Enid; 36°23′N 98°10′W. Wheat, corn; cattle; oil and natural gas.

Menominee 1 (me-NAH-me-nee), county (☐ 1,337 sq mi/3,463 sq km; 1990 pop. 24,920), SW Upper Peninsula, N Mich.; ☉ Menominee; 45°31′N 87°31′W. Bounded SE by Green Bay and SW by Wis.; drained by

Menominee, Big Cedar, and Little Cedar rivers. Agr. (cattle, poultry; forage, corn, oats; dairy prods.). Mfg. at Menominee. Fishing, lumbering. Resorts. Mich. Pottawatomi Indian Reservation in NE. J. W. Wills State Park in E on Green Bay. One of 4 Mich. cos. in Central time zone; border bet. Central and Eastern time zones follows N and E borders. Organized 1863. **2** county (☐ 365 sq mi/945 sq km; 1990 pop. 3,890), E central Wis., ☉ Keshena; 45°01′N 88°42′W. Formerly part of Shawano co. (to S). Drained by Wolf and Red rivers. Several small lakes, esp. in SE corner. Barley, oats, alfalfa; cattle, hogs, sheep; dairying. Lumber.

Menominee (me-NAH-me-nee), city (1990 pop. 9,398), ☉ Menominee co., N Mich., W Upper Peninsula, on Green Bay of L. Michigan at the mouth of the Menominee R.; 45°07′N 87°37′W. A distribution center for upper Mich. and N Wis. Mfg. (fabricated metal prods., machinery, consumer goods, paper prods., lumber and wood prods.). Co. Airport to NW. Of interest is the "mystery ship," raised (1969) from the bottom of Green Bay, where it sank in 1864. A bridge connects Menominee with Marinette (Wis.). Inc. 1883.

Menominee, village (1990 pop. 187), Jo Daviess co., extreme NW Ill., on short Little Menominee R. (bridged here), and 8 mi/12.9 km NW of Galena; 42°28′N 90°32′W.

Menominee Iron Range (me-NAH-me-nee), mainly in Iron co., SW Upper Peninsula, N Mich., along Mich.-Wis. state line NW of Iron Mountain (Mich.). Timber; tourism (sport fishing, hunting). Iron Mt. Mine still active. Also called Menominee Range.

Menominee River (me-NAH-me-nee), 118 mi/190 km long, N Mich.; formed by the union of the Brule and the Michigamme rivers above Iron Mountain, W Upper Peninsula; flows SE into Green Bay at Menominee; 45°57′N 88°11′W. It passes through a once plentiful iron-ore region and forms part of the Wis.-Mich. state line for its entire length. Numerous small dams. Piers Gorge, near Norway (Mich.) named for piers built to slow river's flow.

Menominee River, Wis.: see MENOMONEE RIVER.

Menomonee Falls, city (1990 pop. 26,840), Waukesha co., SE Wis., on the Menominee and Fox rivers, a suburb 17 mi/27 km NW of Milwaukee, and 8 mi/12.9 km NE of Waukesha; 43°08′N 88°07′W. Mfg. (publishing and printing; wire, fabricated metal prods., paper prods., concrete prods., plumbing fixtures, furniture, fiberglass prods., machine tools, machinery, oil lamps and lamp oils, marble prods., accoustical materials, medical supplies and equip.; steel and aluminum foundry). Founded 1843; settled originally by Ger. immigrants. Inc. 1892.

Menomonee River, c.25 mi/40 km long, SE Wis.; rises at Germantown in SE Washington co.; flows SE through Menomonee Falls and Wauwatosa to Milwaukee R. at its mouth on L. Michigan at Milwaukee. Sometimes spelled Menominee. Menomonee Parkway follows mid-course.

Menomonie, city (1990 pop. 13,547), ☉ Dunn co., W Wis., 20 mi/32 km WNW of Eau Claire, on the Red Cedar R. (forms L. Menomonie); 44°53′N 91°54′W. Once a lumber town, it is a trade center in an area of poultry and dairy farms. Mfg. (fabricated metal prods., foods, machinery). N terminus of Red Cedar State Trail; Hoffman Hills State Recreation Area to NE. The Univ. of Wis.-Stout campus is here. The ornate civic center bldg. was erected (1890s) by a lumber baron. Plotted 1859, inc. 1882.

Mentasta Lake, village (1990 pop. 96), E Alaska, 40 mi/64 km SW of Tanacross, in Mentasta Pass, on Tok Cutoff; 62°51′N 143°45′W. Sometimes called Mentasta.

Mentasta Mountains, E Alaska, SE extension of Alaska Range, bet. Tanana R. (NE) and Wrangell Mts. (SW); extend 50 mi/80 km NW from upper Nabesna R. Rise to 8,300 ft/2,530 m (62°35′N 142°50′W). Continued SE by Nutzotin Mts.

Mentone 1 (MEN-tuhn), resort town (1990 pop. 474), De Kalb co., NE Ala., on Lookout Mt., 12 mi/19 km NE of Fort Payne, near Ga. state line. **2** uninc. town (1990 pop. 5,675), San Bernardino co., S Calif., suburb 9 mi/

14.5 km SE of San Bernardino, and 63 mi/101 km E of downtown Los Angeles, just E of Redlands. Poultry; dairying; citrus fruit, vegetables; nursery prods. Agr. is being displaced by urban development. Mfg. (machinery, wood prods.). Redlands Municipal Airport to NW. San Bernardino Mts., in San Bernardino Natl. Forest, to N. **3** town (1990 pop. 912), Kosciusko co., N Ind., 11 mi/18 km SW of Warsaw; 41°10′N 86°02′W. In agr. area; eggs, chickens; lumber. Mfg. (livestock feed mixing, poultry processing; mechanical springs, powder coating).

Mentone, uninc. village (1990 pop. 50), ⊙ Loving co., W Texas, 19 mi/31 km NNW of Pecos, and on Pecos R. Elev. 2,683 ft/818 m. Oil and gas; some cattle. One of the smallest co. seats in U.S., only locality within co.

Mentor, city (1990 pop. 47,358), Lake co., NE Ohio, on L. Erie; 41°42′N 81°20′W. Mfg. of machinery. James Garfield was living here when elected President; his home, "Lawnfield," is preserved. Seat of Lakeland Community Col. Founded 1799, inc. 1855.

Mentor, village (1990 pop. 94), Polk co., NW Minn., 23 mi/37 km ESE of Crookston; 47°42′N 96°08′W. Grain; dairying. Maple L. to S.

Mentor-on-the-Lake, city (1990 pop. 8,271), Lake co., NE Ohio, on L. Erie, just NW of Mentor, and 21 mi/34 km NE of Cleveland; 41°43′N 81°22′W.

Meoqui (me-O-kee), city (1990 pop. 16,428) and township, Chihuahua, N Mexico, on affluent of Conchos R., and 45 mi/72 km SE of Chihuahua, on Mexico Highway 45; 28°18′N 105°30′W. Cotton center; cereals, beans, fruit; cattle.

Meota (mee-O-tuh), village (1991 pop. 268), W Sask., W Canada, on Jackfish L. (10 mi/16 km long, 6 mi/10 km wide), 20 mi/32 km NNW of North Battleford. Resort.

Mequon (ME-kawn), city (1990 pop. 18,885), Ozaukee co., SE Wis., a suburb 10 mi/16 km N of downtown Milwaukee, on L. Michigan and the Milwaukee R.; 43°14′N 87°59′W. Mfg. (transportation equip., wire forms, fabricated metal prods., levels and carpentry tools, machinery, consumer goods, bldg. materials, glass prods.). R.C. training center, a Lutheran seminary, and an automotive mus. are here. Est. 1846, inc. 1957.

Mer Rouge (MER ROOZH), village (1994 pop. 751), Morehouse parish, NE La., 8 mi/13 km E of Bastrop; 32°47′N 91°48′W. In agr. area (cotton, rice, sweet potatoes, vegetables; cattle); timber. Handy Brake Natl. Wildlife Refuge to N.

Meramec River (mer-uh-MAK), 207 mi/333 km long, E Mo.; rises in the Ozark Mts. E of Salem; meanders N, NE, and SE to the Mississippi R. 20 mi/32 km below St. Louis. Fishing, boating, recreation. Receives the Bourbeuse and the Big rivers. Numerous caves and springs along it, as well as several state parks.

Merasheen Island (mee-ruh-SHEEN), (☐ 46 sq mi/ 119 sq km), SE N.F., E Canada, in Placentia Bay, 70 mi/ 113 km W of St. John's; 21 mi/34 km long, 5 mi/8 km wide; 47°30′N 54°15′W. At S end is fishing settlement of Merasheen.

Meraux (muh-RO), uninc. city (1990 pop. 8,849), St. Bernard parish, extreme SE La., suburb 8 mi/13 km E of downtown New Orleans, on the Mississippi R., bet. Chalmette and Violet; 29°56′N 89°55′W. Mfg. (gasoline, kerosene). Holds La. Shrimp Festival.

Mercado, Cerro de, Mexico: see VICTORIA DE DURANGO.

Merced, county (☐ 1,929 sq mi/4,996 sq km; 1990 pop. 178,403), central Calif.; ⊙ Merced; 37°11′N 120°43′W. Extends across San Joaquin Valley from Diablo Range (W and SW) to foothills of the Sierra Nevada (E and NE). Fertile agr. area, irrigated by Merced, San Joaquin, and Chowchilla rivers. Grapes, alfalfa, grain, sweet potatoes, tomatoes, corn, cantaloupes, wheat, barley, oats, rice, beans, sugar beets; dairying; cattle, turkeys and poultry raising. Sand and gravel. Farm prods. processing (fruit drying and canning, meat and poultry packing), lumber milling, cement mfg. Crossed in SW (SE to NW) by Delta Mendota Canal and Calif. Aqueduct. San Luis and Merced natl. wildlife refuges in center; George Hatfield State Park and Fremont Ford State Recreation Area in NW; San Luis Reservoir and State

Recreation Area in W; Ortigalita Peak (3,305 ft/1,007 m) in S corner (Diablo Range) Formed 1855.

Merced, city (1990 pop. 56,216), ⊙ Merced co., central Calif., 50 mi/80 km NW of Fresno; 37°18′N 120°29′W. Growing city and a center for tourism and farm trade in cotton, fruit, and dairying; poultry; grain, alfalfa, almonds, sugar beets. Concentration of Hmong immigrants. Mfg. (prefabricated wood bldgs., fabricated metal prods., machinery, transportation equip., paper prods.). Seat of Merced Col. (2-year). Merced and San Luis natl. wildlife refuges to SW; Castle Air Force Base to NW, Yosemite Natl. Park c.50 mi/80 km NE. Inc. 1889.

Merced Falls, village, Merced co., central Calif., on Merced R., near Sierra Nevada foothills, and 17 mi/ 27 km NE of Merced. Cattle; alfalfa, grain, fruit, nuts. Large tailings left by gold-dredging operations. L. McClure formed by New Exchequer Dam, to NE.

Merced River, c.45 mi/72 km long, central Calif.; rises in Edna L. in the Sierra Nevada SW Yosemite Natl. Park, extreme NE Madera co.; flows N briefly, then W through small Merced L. and dramatic Yosemite Valley, at center of park, then SW; receives South Fork from E 10 mi/16 km W of park boundary, continues WSW through L. McClure, formed by New Exchequer Dam, past Livingston, to San Joaquin R., c.25 mi/40 km WNW of Merced. South Fork Merced rises 1 mi/1.6 km S of source of main stream, flows SW then W through S part of Yosemite Natl. Park, then NW to Merced R.

Mercedes, city (1990 pop. 12,694), Hidalgo co., extreme S Texas, 12 mi/19 km WSW of Harlingen, in the lower Rio Grande valley, 70 mi/113 km N of Rio Grande (Mex. border); 26°08′N 97°55′W. Mfg. (footwear, wood prods., cheese, clay prods., sheet metal, machine-shop prods.), meatpacking. Irrigated citrus, vegetable region. Pipeline (1,840 mi/2,961 km long) to N.Y. area from oil field here. Founded 1907, inc. 1909.

Mercer 1 county (☐ 568 sq mi/1,471 sq km; 1990 pop. 17,290), NW Ill.; ⊙ Aledo; 41°12′N 90°44′W. Bounded W by Mississippi R.; drained by Edwards R. and Pope Creek. Agr. (cattle, hogs; corn, soybeans, hay; dairy prods.). Some mfg. Formed 1825. **2** county (☐ 253 sq mi/655 sq km; 1990 pop. 19,148), central Ky.; ⊙ Harrodsburg; 37°47′N 84°52′W. Bounded NE by Kentucky R., SE by Dix R.; forms Herrington L. by Dix Dam; drained by Salt and Chaplin rivers. Rolling agr. area in Bluegrass region (burley tobacco, soybeans, wheat, corn, hay, alfalfa; hogs, cattle, poultry; dairying); calcite mines, limestone quarries. Mfg. at Harrodsburg. Includes Old Fort Harrod (E center) and High Bridge state parks. Formed 1785. **3** county (☐ 456 sq mi/ 1,181 sq km; 1990 pop. 3,723), N Mo.; ⊙ Princeton; 40°25′N 93°34′W. Drained by Weldon and Thompson rivers. Soybeans, corn; hogs (corporate hog farms), cattle. Mfg. at Princeton. L. Paho W of Princeton. Formed 1845. **4** county (☐ 228 sq mi/591 sq km; 1990 pop. 325,824), W N.J., bounded W by the Delaware R.; ⊙ TRENTON; 40°16′N 74°42′W. Varied mfg. (wire and wire rope, pottery, electrical equip., rubber prods., machinery, hardware). Agr. (poultry, livestock; vegetables, grains; dairy prods.; fruit). Crossed by Delaware and Raritan Canal; drained by Millstone R. and Crosswicks Creek. Formed 1837. **5** county (☐ 1,041 sq mi/ 2,696 sq km; 1990 pop. 9,808), central N.Dak.; ⊙ Stanton; 47°17′N 101°49′W. Agr. area drained by Knife R.; bounded N and E by Missouri R. Lignite mines. Wheat; cattle. Organized 1884. Garrison Dam forms L. Sakakawea on N; Sakakawea State Park at Garrison Dam in NE; Knife R. Indian Village Historic Site is in E; part of Fort Berthold Indian Reservation in NW. Border bet. Mountain and Central time zones follows Missouri R.; co. is in Mountain time zone. **6** county (☐ 454 sq mi/ 1,176 sq km; 1990 pop. 39,443), W Ohio, on Ind. (W) state line; ⊙ Celina, 40°33′N 84°38′W. Drained by Wabash and St. Marys rivers; part of Grand L. is in E. Includes Fort Recovery State Park. In the Till Plains physiographic region. Agr. area (poultry, sheep; corn, soybeans). Mfg. (meat prods., machinery; printing and publishing). Limestone quarries; timber. Formed 1824. **7** county (☐ 682 sq mi/1,766 sq km; 1990 pop. 121,003),

NW Pa., on Ohio (W) state line; ⊙ Mercer; 41°18′N 80°15′W. Drained by Shenango R. and Neshannock and Wolf creeks. Agr. (corn, wheat, oats, barley, hay, alfalfa, potatoes; hogs; cattle; dairying). Bituminous coal, sandstone, limestone. Mfg. at Sharon, Farrell, Greenville, Mercer, and Grove City. L. Wilhelm reservoir in NE; large Shenango R. L. reservoir, on Shenango R. and its tributary, Pymatuning Creek in W. Settled by veterans of Revolution. Formed 1800. **8** county (☐ 421 sq mi/1,090 sq km; 1990 pop. 64,980), S W.Va., on Allegheny Plateau, and on Va. (S) border; ⊙ Princeton; 37°24′N 81°06′W. Drained by Bluestone R. Bluefield, semibituminous-coal-mining center in Pocahontas coalfield, is partly in Va. Coal, limestone deposits. Timber. Mfg. at Bluefield and Princeton. Agr. (corn, oats, tobacco, potatoes, alfalfa, hay, nursery crops); cattle, sheep. Includes Camp Creek State Forest in N, and Pinnacle Rock State Park in SW. Formed 1837.

Mercer 1 (MUHR-suhr), town (1990 pop. 593), Somerset co., central Maine, on Sandy R., and 12 mi/19 km SW of Skowhegan; 44°40′N 69°54′W. Farming, lumbering. **2** town (1990 pop. 297), Mercer co., N Mo., near Weldon R., 9 mi/14.5 km N of Princeton; 40°30′N 93°31′W.

Mercer 1 village (1990 pop. 104), McLean co., central N.Dak., 48 mi/77 km NE of Bismark; 47°29′N 100°42′W. Several small lakes to NW. **2** village, Iron co., N Wis., 20 mi/32 km SSE of Hurley. In wooded lake region; fishing. Mfg. (forest prods.). Nearby is a fish hatchery. Large Turtle–Flambeau flowage reservoir to SW; Lac du Flambeau Indian Reservation and Northern Highland State Forest to SE.

Mercer, borough (1990 pop. 2,444), ⊙ Mercer co., W Pa., 22 mi/35 km ENE of Youngstown (Ohio), near Otter Creek; 41°13′N 80°14′W. Agr. (potatoes, corn, hay; livestock; dairying). Mfg. (fabricated metal prods., transportation equip., food prods., machinery); bituminous coal. Shenango R. L. reservoir to NW; L. Latonka reservoir (residential development) to NE. Settled 1795, laid out 1803, inc. 1814.

Mercer Island, city (1990 pop. 20,816), King co., W Wash., residential suburb 4 mi/6.4 km ESE of downtown Seattle, including all of Mercer Isl., in S end of L. Washington; 47°34′N 122°14′W. Mercer Isl. (Morrow) Bridge connects N end of isl. to both shores of lake. Mfg. (machinery, wood prods., furniture, fabricated metal prods.).

Mercer Island, Wash.: see WASHINGTON LAKE.

Mercersburg, borough (1990 pop. 1,640), Franklin co., S Pa., 15 mi/24 km SW of Chambersburg; 39°49′N 77°54′W. Agr. area (grain, potatoes, apples; poultry, livestock; dairying). Mfg. (lumber, machinery, medical equip., apparel). Buchanan's Birthplace Historic State Park to NW; Buchanan State Forest to NW; Cove Mt. ridge to W. Settled c.1729, laid out 1780, inc. 1831.

Merchantville, residential borough (1990 pop. 4,095), Camden co., SW N.J., just E of Camden; 39°57′N 75°02′W. Settled 1852, inc. 1874.

Mercoal, village, W Alta., W Canada, in Rocky Mts., near E side of Jasper Natl. Park, on McLeod R., and 40 mi/64 km SW of Edson; 53°10′N 117°06′W. Coal mining; timber.

Mercur, town, Tooele co., NW Utah, 20 mi/32 km WSW of Lehi, in Oquirrh Mts. Elev. 6,700 ft/2,042 m. Deposits of gold and silver. Barnick Mercur Gold Mine Historical Site.

Mercury, uninc. village (1990 pop. 166), McCulloch co., near geographical center of Texas, 22 mi/35 km NE of Brady.

Mercy, Cape, SE Baffin Isl., E Franklin dist., N.W.T., N Canada, on Davis Strait, on N side of entrance of Cumberland Sound; 64°56′N 63°39′W.

Mere Point (MIR), SW Maine, peninsula extending 4 mi/6.4 km into Casco Bay, near Brunswick. Site of summer colony.

Meredith, town (1990 pop. 4,837), Belknap co., central N.H., 8 mi/12.9 km N of Laconia; 43°38′N 71°30′W. Bounded NE by L. Winnipesaukee, which dominates E part of town, SE by Winnisquam L. Agr. (cattle, poultry; dairying; nursery crops; timber); mfg. (consumer goods., electronic goods; machining). Resort, water sports. Site of Annalee Doll Mus. Waukewan L. on NW border, Wickwas L. in S. Inc. 1768.

Meredith, Lake, reservoir (□ 10 sq mi/26 sq km), Crowley co., SE Colo., on Bob Creek, 14 mi/23 km NNW of La Junta; 38°10′N 103°44′W. Max. capacity 41,412 acreft. Fed by Colorado Canal. Formed by L. Meredith Dam (30 ft/9 m high), built (1900) for irrigation; also used for recreation and as a fish and wildlife pond.

Meredith Lake, reservoir (□ 48 sq mi/124 sq km), Potter, Moore, and Hutchinson cos., NW Texas, on Canadian R., in L. Meredith Natl. Recreation Area, 37 mi/60 km NNE of Amarillo; c.30 mi/48 km long; 35°43′N 101°34′W. Max. capacity 2,434,220 acre-ft. Formed by Sanford Dam (228 ft/69 m high), built (1965) by the Bureau of Reclamation for water supply; also used for flood control and recreation. Alibates Flint Quarries Natl. Monument on SE shore.

Meredosia (mer-i-DO-shah), village (1990 pop. 1,134), Morgan co., W central Ill., on Illinois R., and Meredosia L. (c.5 mi/8 km long; a slough lake of Illinois R.), 18 mi/29 km WNW of Jacksonville; 39°49′N 90°33′W. In agr. area (corn, wheat, soybeans, sorghum; cattle, hogs; dairying); mfg. (chemicals).

Mérida (ME-ree-dah), city (1990 pop. 523,422) and township, ⊙ Yucatán state, SE Mexico; 20°59′N 89°39′W. It is the chief commercial, communications, and cultural center of the Yucatán peninsula. Founded (1542) by Francisco de Montejo (the younger), on the site of a ruined Mayan city, Mérida has many fine examples of Span. colonial architecture, notably the 16thcent. cathedral. Rooftop windmills, characteristic of this region, are used to pump water from underground wells and streams. Commercial, administrative, agr., and tourist center. Once dependent upon the large crops of henequen from the surrounding region. Tourists visiting nearby Mayan ruins, notably Chichén Itzá and Uxmal, contribute work to the local economy. Internatl. airport to SW.

Meriden (ME-ri-duhn), city (1990 pop. 59,479), New Haven co., S central Conn.; 41°32′N 72°47′W. Known for its silver industry. Silverware and pewter were made here in the 18th cent. by Samuel Yale and later by the Rogers Brothers and a forerunner of the Internatl. Silver Company. Industry now diversified. Settled 1661, inc. as a town 1806, as a city 1867, town and city consolidated 1922.

Meriden 1 (ME-ri-duhn), town (1990 pop. 193), Cherokee co., NW Iowa, 5 mi/8 km WNW of Cherokee; 42°47′N 95°37′W. In agr. area. **2** town (1990 pop. 622), Jefferson co., NE Kansas, on branch of Delaware R., and 13 mi/21 km W of Oskaloosa; 39°11′N 95°34′W. Grain growing; dairying and general agr.

Meriden, N.H.: see PLAINFIELD.

Meridian 1 (muh-RID-ee-uhn), city (1990 pop. 9,596), Ada co., SW Idaho, suburb 10 mi/16 km W of downtown Boise; 43°37′N 116°24′W. In agr. area (fruit, grain; cattle, sheep, poultry). Mfg. (machinery, bldg. materials, millwork). Served by Boise irrigation project. Founded 1891, inc. 1902. **2** city (1990 pop. 41,036), ⊙ Lauderdale co., E Miss., 85 mi/137 km E of Jackson, near Ala. state line; 32°22′N 88°42′W. Drained in W by Okatibbee Creek, forms Okatibbee L. reservoir to NW. RR junction. Important RR and highway point and the trade, shipping, and industrial center for a farm and timber area. Agr. (cotton, corn; livestock); mfg. (bldg. materials, wire, food and beverages, transportation equip., industrial scales, furniture, apparel, paper prods., electronic equip., fabricated metal prods., and wood prods.; printing and publishing). In the Civil War, Meridian was the temporary capital of Miss. (1863); it was destroyed by General Sherman in Feb. 1864. Two junior cols. and a state mental hosp. are here. Key Field airport in SW; Meridian Naval Air Station to NE; Temple Theatre (1923); "Merrehope," Gr. Revival cottage (1858); Mus. of Art; Jimmie Rodgers Mus., "Father of Country Music"; Grand Opera House (c.1890); Highland Park Carousel (1890s); Sam Dale State Historical Site to N; L. Tom Bailey (state lake) to E. Settled 1831, inc. 1860.

Meridian 1 uninc. town (1990 pop. 3,473), Butler co., W Pa., residential suburb 5 mi/8 km WSW of Butler; 40°51′N 79°57′W. Agr. area (corn, hay, apples; livestock; dairying). **2** town (1990 pop. 1,390), ⊙ Bosque co., central Texas, on Bosque R., and c.40 mi/64 km NW of Waco; 31°55′N 97°39′W. Elev. 791 ft/241 m. In diversified livestock (cattle) and agr. (corn, wheat, pecans, peaches) area; mfg. of tile. Meridian State Park to SW; L. Whitney reservoir to E. Settled 1854, inc. 1886.

Meridian 1 uninc. village, Sutter co., N central Calif., on Sacramento R., and 16 mi/26 km W of Yuba City. Agr. (grain, vegetables, fruit, nuts, sugar beets); waterfowl hunting. Sutter Buttes to NE. **2** village (1990 pop. 351), Cayuga co., W central N.Y., 17 mi/27 km N of Auburn; 43°09′N 76°32′W. In agr. area. **3** village (1990 pop. 45), Logan co., central Okla., 10 mi/16 km ESE of Guthrie; 35°50′N 97°15′W. In agr. area.

Meridian Dam oregon: see MIDDLE FORK.

Meridian Hills, town (1990 pop. 1,728), Marion co., central Ind., suburb 7 mi/11.3 km N of downtown Indianapolis, near White R.; 39°53′N 86°10′W. Former municipality, merged with Indianapolis 1970.

Meridian Township, suburb, Ingham co., S central Mich., 6 mi/9.7 km E of Lansing, on Red Cedar R.; 42°41′N 84°21′W. Includes former suburbs of Haslett and Okemos. L. Lansing in NE corner of city.

Meridianville, village (1990 pop. 2,852), Madison co., N Ala., 11 mi/18 km N of Huntsville; 34°52′N 86°34′W. Electronics mfg.

Merigold, village (1990 pop. 572), Bolivar co., NW Miss., 6 mi/9.7 km N of Cleveland; 33°50′N 90°43′W. Agr. (cotton, corn, soybeans; cattle).

Merigomish (me-ri-guh-MISH), village, E N.S., E Canada, on Northumberland Strait, 12 mi/19 km ENE of New Glasgow; 45°37′N 62°25′W. Fishing.

Merigomish Island, NE N.S., E Canada, in Northumberland Strait, sheltering small Merigomish Bay, 12 mi/19 km E of Pictou; 5 mi/8 km long, 2 mi/3 km wide; 45°40′N 62°25′W.

Merino, village (1990 pop. 238), Logan co., NE Colo., on South Platte R., and 14 mi/23 km SW of Sterling; 40°28′N 103°20′W. Elev. 4,035 ft/1,230 m. Shipping point in irrigated sugar-beet region. Mfg. (machinery). Prewitt Reservoir to S, Summit Springs Battlefield to SE.

Merino Village, Mass.: see DUDLEY.

Merion (MER-ee-ahn) or **Merion Station**, uninc. town, in Lower Merion township, Montgomery co., SE Pa., residential suburb 5 mi/8 km WNW of downtown Philadelphia; 39°59′N 75°15′W. Mfg. (commercial printing). St. Charles Borromeo Seminary and Eastern Baptist Theological Seminary to W. Barnes Mus. here.

Merion Station, Pa.: see MERION.

Meriwether (MER-ee-weth-uhr), county (□ 505 sq mi/1,308 sq km; 1990 pop. 22,411), W Ga.; ⊙ Greenville; 33°02′N 84°41′W. Bounded E by Flint R. Mfg. includes apparel, textiles, wood prods.; printing and publishing; lumber. Piedmont peach-growing area; also produces pecans, melons, peppers; cattle, hogs. Formed 1827.

Merkel, town (1990 pop. 2,469), Taylor co., W central Texas, 16 mi/26 km W of Abilene; 32°28′N 100°00′W. In agr. (cotton, wheat), cattle-ranching area. Mfg. (apparel). Settled c.1875, inc. 1906.

Merlin, uninc. town (1990 pop. 500), Joseph co., SW Oregon, 6 mi/9.7 km NW of Grants Pass, on Jumpoff Joe Creek. Timber; livestock, poultry; dairying; pears, apples, plums; grain. Mfg. (lumber, veneer, wood stoves). Siskiyou Natl. Forest to W.

Mermentau (MUHR-muhn-to), village (1990 pop. 760), Acadia parish, S La., 13 mi/21 km W of Crowley, and shallow-draft port on navigable Mermentau R.; 30°11′N 92°35′W. In rice-growing area; commercial fishing (crawfish, alligators), mfg. (milled rice). Oil and natural-gas field nearby.

Mermentau River (MUHR-muhn-to), c.71 mi/114 km long, S La.; formed just above Mermentau by junction of Nezpique and des Cannes bayous; flows SW to Gulf of Mexico, S of Oak Grove, 48 mi/77 km E of Sabine Pass; 29°43′N 93°06′W. Navigable. Widens to form L. Arthur (c.7 mi/11 km long) at Lake Arthur town, Grand

L. (c.10 mi/16 km long, 2 mi/3 km–10 mi/16 km wide) in central Cameron parish, and small Upper Mud and Lower Mud lakes in marshy coastal area above mouth. Intersected by Intracoastal Waterway through N part of Grand L., which in turn is joined by navigation canals to White L. (SE) and thence to Freshwater Bayou Canal.

Merna, village (1990 pop. 377), Custer co., central Nebr., 9 mi/14.5 km NW of Broken Bow; 41°28′N 99°45′W. Grain; livestock. Victoria Springs State Recreation Area to N.

Merom, town (1990 pop. 257), Sullivan co., SW Ind., on the Wabash R., bet. Wabash R. (W) and Turtle Creek Reservoir (E), 8 mi/12.9 km WSW of Sullivan; 39°04′N 87°34′W. Oil and natural-gas wells nearby. Grain; melon-growing area. Spectacular view of the Wabash R. (W edge of town) at Meron Bluff. Laid out 1817.

Merriam (MER-ee-uhm), city (1990 pop. 11,821), Johnson co., E Kansas, suburb 7 mi/11.3 km SW of Kansas City; 39°01′N 94°41′W. Mfg. (lumber, concrete, clothing, electrical and electronic goods).

Merrick, county (□ 494 sq mi/1,279 sq km; 1990 pop. 8,042), E central Nebr.; ⊙ Central City; 41°10′N 98°01′W. Irrigated agr. region bounded S by Platte R., N border approaches Loup R. Mfg. at Central City. Leading well irrigation co. Mfg. of mobile homes, chemicals and fertilizer. Cattle, hogs; dairying; corn. Mormon Trail State Wayside Area in E, near Clarks. Hord L. State Recreation Area in S central co., at Central City. Formed 1858.

Merrick, uninc. city (□ 5 sq mi/13 sq km; 1990 pop. 23,042), Nassau co., SE N.Y., on L.I.; 40°38′N 73°32′W. Although chiefly residential, it has some light mfg.

Merrickville, village (1991 pop. 989), SE Ont., central Canada, on Rideau R. and Rideau Canal, and 35 mi/56 km SSW of Ottawa; 44°55′N 75°50′W. Light mfg.; resort area.

Merricourt, village (1990 pop. 9), Dickey co., SE N.Dak., 18 mi/29 km NW of Ellendale; 46°12′N 98°45′W. Whitestone Battlefield Historic Site to SW.

Merrifield, uninc. town, Fairfax co., NE Va., residential suburb 10 mi/16 km W of Washington, D.C., 4 mi/6.4 km ENE of Fairfax; 38°52′N 77°14′W. Mfg. (commercial printing). Natl. Memorial Park Cemetery to E.

Merrifield, uninc. village, Crow Wing co., central Minn., 7 mi/11.3 km N of Brainerd, at E end of North Long L.; 46°27′N 94°10′W. Mfg. (fabricated metal prods., consumer goods, electronic prods.); agr. (cattle; dairying; oats); timber. Numerous small lakes in area. Crow Wing State Forest to NE.

Merrill, city (1990 pop. 9,860), ⊙ Lincoln co., N central Wis., at confluence of Wisconsin and small Prairie rivers, 16 mi/26 km N of Wausau; 45°10′N 89°42′W. In dairying and farming area; mfg. (paper and paper goods, apparel, wood prods., wire prods., fabricated metal prods., consumer goods, shoes, furniture, textiles, beverages). Nearby are the Grandfather Falls of the Wisconsin and Council Grounds State Park to NW. Settled c.1847, Merrill grew as lumbering town; inc. 1883.

Merrill 1 town (1990 pop. 729), Plymouth co., NW Iowa, on Floyd R., near confluence of West Branch Floyd R., and 6 mi/9.7 km SW of Le Mars; 42°43′N 96°15′W. Livestock, and grain area. Sand, gravel pits nearby. **2** town (1990 pop. 837), Klamath co., S Oregon, 15 mi/24 km SE of Klamath Falls, on Lost R.; 42°01′N 121°35′W. Elev. 4,064 ft/1,239 m. Barley, wheat, potatoes; sheep, cattle; dairy prods. Lava Beds Natl. Monument and Tule L. Natl. Wildlife Refuge to S, in Calif. Lower Klamath Natl. Wildlife Refuge (Calif. and Oregon) to SW.

Merrill 1 village (1990 pop.755), Saginaw co., E central Mich., 19 mi/31 km W of Saginaw; 43°24′N 84°20′W. In agr. area. Mfg. (machinery, tool and machine parts). **2** resort village (1990 pop. 450), Clinton co., extreme NE N.Y., on Upper Chateaugay L., 25 mi/40 km WNW of Plattsburgh; 44°46′N 73°57′W.

Merrill, township (1990 pop. 296), Aroostook co., E Maine, 20 mi/32 km WNW of Houlton; 46°09′N 68°13′W. In lumbering area.

Merrill Peak, Ariz.: see PINALENO MOUNTAINS.

Merrillan (MER-i-lan), village (1990 pop. 553), Jackson co., W central Wis., 40 mi/64 km SE of Eau Claire; 44°27'N 90°50'W. RR junction. In dairying region. Black R. State Forest to SE; Bruce Mound Ski Area to E.

Merrillville 1 town, Thomas co., S Ga., 10 mi/16 km NE of Thomasville; 30°56'N 83°52'W. **2** town (1990 pop. 27,257), Lake co., NW Ind., suburb 12 mi/19 km S of Gary; 41°28'N 87°20'W. Drained by Deep R. in SE and Turkey Creek in NW. Mfg. (chemicals, aluminum and plastic prods., transportation equip., foods). Agr. to S and E (dairying; vegetables). Settled 1847, inc. 1970.

Merrimac 1 (ME-ri-mak), rural town (1990 pop. 5,166), including Merrimac port village, Essex co., NE Mass., on Merrimack R., near N.H. state line, and 13 mi/21 km NE of Lawrence; 42°51'N 71°01'W. Settled 1638, set off from Amesbury 1876. **2** uninc. town, Montgomery co., SW Va., residential suburb 4 mi/6.4 km N of Christiansburg, 3 mi/4.8 km S of Blacksburg; 37°11'N 80°25'W.

Merrimac (ME-ri-mak), village (1990 pop. 392), Sauk co., S central Wis., on Wisconsin R. at W end of L. Wisconsin, and 24 mi/39 km NNW of Madison; 43°22'N 89°37'W. Mfg. (printing and publishing). RR junction to W. Agr. research station to SW. Ferry (free). Devil's L. State Park to NW; Devil's Head Ski Area to N. Post office name formerly Merrimack.

Merrimack (ME-ri-mak), county (□ 956 sq mi/2,476 sq km; 1990 pop. 120,005), S central N.H.; ⊙ Concord; 43°17'N 40°71'W. Mfg. at Concord, Franklin, Hooksett, and Suncook; agr. (nursery crops, vegetables, corn, apples, sugar maples, hay; cattle, poultry; dairying). Granite quarrying, mica mining, sand and gravel. Resorts on lakes. Hilly region, drained by Merrimack, Contoocook, Suncook, Soucook, Blackwater, and Lane rivers. Winslow and Rollins state parks in center. Wadleigh and part of Mt. Sunapee state parks in W; part of Low State Forest in SW; part of Bear Brook State Park in SE; Sunapee L. on W border; N.H. State Forest Nursery in center. Formed 1823.

Merrimack (ME-ri-mak), town (1990 pop. 22,156), Hillsborough co., S N.H., 8 mi/12.9 km S of Manchester, and 7 mi/11.3 km N of Nashua; 42°51'N 71°31'W. Bounded E by Merrimack R.; drained by Souhegan R. and Baboosic and Naticook brooks. Mfg. (machinery, beverages, chemicals, fiberglass, electronic prods., computers and computer prods., consumer goods, plastic prods., wood prods.); agr. (fruit, vegetables, corn, nursery prods.; poultry, livestock; dairying). Town includes village of Thorntons Ferry in S. Covered bridge in NW. Busch Clydesdale Hamlet in S. Naticook Pond in SW. Inc. 1746.

Merrimack, Wis.: see MERRIMAC.

Merrimack River (ME-ri-mak), c.110 mi/177 km long, SE N.H. and NE Mass.; formed at Franklin, S central N.H., by the junction of the Pemigewasset (rises in the White Mts.) and Winnipesaukee (flows SW out of L. Winnipesaukee and Winnisquam L.) rivers; flows S past Concord, Manchester, Merrimack, and Nashua (all in N.H.), and into NE Mass., past Dracut, Lowell, Haverhill, and Lawrence, then turns ENE to the Atlantic Ocean at Newburyport, widens into 3-mi/4.8-km-wide bay before entering ocean through narrow channel. With its numerous tributaries, the river drains most of S N.H. and NE Mass. The river was a source of power for textile mills from c.1820 to 1930 with several large dams; this traditional industrial base has since moved to the Carolinas and other states. Receives Contoocook R. from SW above Concord, Nashua R. from SW at Nashua, Concord R. from S at Lowell, and Shawsheen R. from S at Lawrence.

Merriman, village (1990 pop. 151), Cherry co., N Nebr., 60 mi/97 km W of Valentine, and on branch of Niobrara R., near S.Dak. state line; 42°55'N 101°42'W.

Merriman Dam, N.Y.: see RONDOUT CREEK.

Merrionette Park, village (1990 pop. 2,065), Cook co., NE Ill., SW suburb of Chicago; 41°40'N 87°42'W. Inc. 1947.

Merritt, city (1991 pop. 6,253), S B.C., W Canada, on Nicola R. at mouth of Coldwater R., and 45 mi/72 km SSW of Kamloops; 50°07'N 120°47'W. Elev. 2,030 ft/619 m. Lumbering and plywood; fox farming; cattle raising. Craigmont copper mine closed 1980s. Economy boosted by 1986 opening of new Coquihalla Tollway.

Merritt, reservoir (□ 5 sq mi/13 sq km), Cherry co., N central Nebr., on Snake R., 24 mi/39 km SW of Valentine; 42°38'N 100°52'W. Max. capacity 86,134 acre-ft. Extends E-W. Formed by Merritt Dam (115 ft/35 m high), built (1964) by the Bureau of Reclamation for irrigation; also used for recreation. Samuel R. McKelvie Natl. Forest to N. Merritt Reservoir State Recreational Area on N shore.

Merritt Island, city (1990 pop. 32,886), Brevard co., E central Fla., 2 mi/3.2 km E of Cocoa; 28°18'N 80°39'W. Mfg. includes fabricated metal prods., machining, fiberglass prods.

Merritt Island (□ 47 sq mi/122 sq km; 1990 pop. 32,886), E central Fla., separated from the mainland by Indian R. (a lagoon) and from the Canaveral peninsula (E) by Banana R. (a lagoon); c.40 mi/64 km long and c.6 mi/9.7 km wide; 28°18'N 80°39'W. It produces citrus fruits and is noted for its birds and other wildlife. The Merritt Isl. Wildlife Refuge and the John F. Kennedy Space Center, a division of NASA, are here. Tourism is a major isl. industry.

Merritt Parkway, landscaped limited-access road, in Conn., part of state's express highway system; extends from N.Y. state line E of White Plains, where it joins N.Y. parkway system. Generally parallel to shore as far as New Haven, then to NE, through Hartford, by Wilbur Cross Parkway, where it merges with Interstate 84. First limited-access highway in U.S.

Merritton (ME-ri-tuhn), town, S Ont., central Canada, on Welland Ship Canal, SE suburb of St. Catharines. Steel, paper, and pulp milling.

Merry Oaks, uninc. village, Chatham co., central N.C., 22 mi/35 km SW of Raleigh. Brick mfg. Recreation area. Jordan L. reservoir to N, Harris L. reservoir to E.

Merrymeeting Bay, Sagadahoc co., SW Maine, tidal bay 5 mi/8 km NE of Brunswick. Formed by junction of Androscoggin and Kennebec rivers below Bowdoinham, it extends 16 mi/26 km further S to the Atlantic Ocean. The surrounding marshes are noted for duck hunting.

Merrymeeting Lake (ME-ree-mee-ting), Strafford co., E central N.H., in New Durham, 27 mi/43 km NE of Concord; 3 mi/4.8 km long. Drains through Merrymeeting R. (c.10 mi/16 km long), which turns NW at New Durham Village, flows past Alton to S end of L. Winnipesaukee to W. Powder Mill Fish Hatchery located below lake's outlet.

Merrymount, Mass.: see QUINCY.

Merryville (MER-ee-vil), town (1990 pop. 1,235), Beauregard parish, W La., 17 mi/27 km WSW of De Ridder, near Sabine R. (Texas state line); 30°45'N 93°32'W. In agr. area (soybeans, squash, blueberries, watermelons; cattle; dairying); wool market; logging. Oil field nearby. Boise-Vernon State Wildlife Area to N.

Mershon (MUHR-shuhn), town (1990 pop. 200), Pierce co., Ga., 12 mi/19 km N of Blackshear; 31°28'N 82°15'W. Mfg. of hydraulic equip.

Mertens, village (1990 pop. 104), Hill co., N central Texas, 14 mi/23 km E of Hillsboro; 32°03'N 96°53'W. In farm area (cattle; cotton).

Merton, town (1990 pop. 1,199), Waukesha co., SE Wis., on Bark R., and 20 mi/32 km NW of Milwaukee; 43°08'N 88°18'W. In dairying region. Mfg. (cleaning prods.). Lakes nearby.

Mertzon, town (1990 pop. 778), ⊙ Irion co., W Texas, 25 mi/40 km SW of San Angelo, and on a tributary of Concho R.; 31°15'N 100°49'W. Elev. 2,250 ft/686 m. Retail, shipping point for sheep-ranching region; wool warehouses; mfg. (natural gas processing, meat prods.).

Merwin, town (1990 pop. 75), Bates co., W Mo., 17 mi/27 km NW of Butler; 38°23'N 94°35'W.

Merwin, Lake, reservoir (□ 6 sq mi/15.5 sq km), Clark and Cowlitz cos., SW Wash., on Lewis R., 23 mi/37 km SE of Longview; 46°00'N 122°29'W. Max. capacity 422,000 acre-ft. Formed by Merwin Dam (313 ft/95 m high), built for power generation; also used for recreation and as a fish and wildlife pond.

Mesa, county (□ 3,341 sq mi/8,653 sq km; 1990 pop. 93,145), W Colo., on Utah (W) border; ⊙ Grand Junction; 39°01'N 108°28'W. N part is extensively irrigated farming area. Drained by Colorado and Gunnison rivers. Fruit (peaches, grapes), beans, wheat, hay, oats, barley, corn, potatoes; cattle, sheep. Marble quarrying. Oil and natural gas. Includes Colo. Natl. Monument and Grand Valley and large part of Grand Mesa Natl. Forest in E; part of White R. Natl. Forest in NE; part of Uncompahgre Natl. Forest in S; small part of Manti La Sal Natl. Forest in SW corner; Highline State Park in NW; Colorado R. and Isl. Acres state parks in N; Vega State Park in NE. Part of Grand Mesa Lakes on SE border. Numerous reservoirs (c.100) on either side of border bet. Mesa and Delta cos. Powderhorn Ski Area in NE. Formed 1883.

Mesa, city (1990 pop. 288,091), Maricopa co., S central Ariz., suburb 12 mi/19 km ESE of downtown Phoenix, on Salt R. (intermittent), in the irrigated Salt R. valley; 33°25'N 111°44'W. Mfg. includes electronic prods., fabricated metals, aircraft, and machine tools. One of the fastest-growing U.S. cities, marked by a pop. increase of 89% bet. 1980 and 1990. Tourism is important, and the citrus and farm prods. of the area are packed and processed here. The Mormons who founded the city in 1878 used old Native Amer. irrigation canals for farming in the Salt R. valley. A Mormon temple, Mesa community col., training camp of Chicago Cubs baseball team, and the chief agr. experimental farm of the Univ. of Ariz. are here. Usery Mt. Park in E; Mesa Municipal Airport (Falcon Field) in NE; Williams Air Force Base in SE; Ariz. Boys Ranch to SE. Inc. 1883

Mesa (MAI-suh), village (1990 pop. 252), Franklin co., SE Wash., 24 mi/39 km N of Pasco; 46°34'N 119°00'W. Agr. area (wheat, alfalfa, vegetables; sheep, hogs). Mesa L. reservoir to W.

Mesa Verde National Park (□ 81 sq mi/210 sq km), Montezuma co., 10 mi/16 km SE of Cortez, SW Colo. It includes the most notable and best-preserved cliff dwellings and relics in the U.S., covering 4 archaeological periods. There are museums and a lib. The mesa rises 1,800 ft/549 m–2,000 ft/610 m above the surrounding land. It is cut by many canyons where anc. Native Americans built pit and cliff dwellings A.D. 500–A.D. 1300. Bounded by Ute Mt. Indian Reservation on S and W. Authorized 1906.

Mesaba (muh-SAH-buh), locality, St. Louis co., NE Minn., near E end of Mesabi Iron Range, 19 mi/31 km ENE of Virginia, and 5 mi/8 km ENE of Aurora; 47°34'N 92°07'W. Site of extensive open-pit iron mining operations of Erie Mining Company. RR delivers ore to Taconite Harbor, on L. Superior, 57 mi/92 km to E. Iron reserves and mining activity have declined in late 1900s.

Mesabi Iron Range (muh-SAH-bee), range of low hills, in iron-mining dist., St. Louis and Itasca cos., NE Minn. The ores were found in a belt c.110 mi/177 km long and 1 mi/1.6 km–3 mi/4.8 km wide, bet. Babbitt and Grand Rapids, occurring in horizontal layers (up to 500 ft/152 m thick) near the surface and mined by the open pit method (Mesaba open-pit mine, 5 mi/8 km ENE of Aurora). Reserves of high-grade hematite iron are now exhausted, and lower-grade taconite deposits are being worked. The taconite contains mostly chert and magnetite (an iron-bearing mineral) and must undergo a costly and complex beneficiation process before being shipped in the form of pellets containing c.60% iron. Mining centers include communities of Babbitt, Aurora, Biwabik, Gilbert, Virginia, Mountain Iron, Buhl, Chisholm, Hibbing, Marble, and Coleraine. Most of the ore found is shipped by company RRs to Duluth, Taconite Harbor, Silver Bay, and Two Harbors. The Mesabi iron ore deposits were 1st discovered in 1887 by Leonidas Merritt and his brothers, who organized the Mountain Iron Company in 1890 to mine the ore; John D. Rockefeller gained control of the company in the Panic of 1893. Productivity

Cross references are shown in SMALL CAPITALS. The pronunciation key is on page xv. The dates of population figures are on page xii.

has declined due to dwindling reserves and environmental restrictions. Vermilion Iron Range parallels Mesabi Range, c.10 mi/16 km to N.

Mescala, Río, Mexico: see BALSAS, RÍO.

Mescalero (mes-kuh-LER-o), town (1990 pop. 1,159), Otero co., S N.Mex., in Sacramento Mts., 29 mi/47 km NNE of Alamogordo, in Mescalero Apache Indian Reservation; 33°08′N 105°47′W. Elev. 6,600 ft/2,012 m. Timber; sheep, cattle. Mfg. (ponderosa pine lumber). Reservation hq. here; reservation has ski resort and gambling. In 1996, proposed as temporary nuclear-waste-storage site. Parts of Lincoln Natl. Forest to N and S; L. Mescalero reservoir to NE; Sierra Blanca (11,977 ft/3,651 m) to NNW.

Meservey, town (1990 pop. 292), Cerro Gordo co., N Iowa, 22 mi/35 km SW of Mason City; 42°55′N 93°28′W.

Meshoppen, borough (1990 pop. 439), Wyoming co., NE Pa., 25 mi/40 km NW of Scranton, on Susquehanna R., at Meshoppen Creek; 41°36′N 76°02′W. Agr. (corn, hay; dairying); light mfg.; quarrying.

Mesic (ME-sik), village (1990 pop. 310), Pamlico co., E N.C., 26 mi/42 km ENE of New Bern, near Bay R. estuary; 35°12′N 76°39′W. Cotton, peanuts, grain; hogs.

Mesick (ME-sik), village (1990 pop. 406), Wexford co., NW Mich., 19 mi/31 km NW of Cadillac, and on Manistee R., at end of Hodenpyl Dam Pond; 44°23′N 85°43′W. Mfg. (tool and die; machining). Manistee Natl. Forest to S. Annual mushroom festival.

Mesilla Park (ME-SEE-uh), uninc. town, Doña Ana co., S N.Mex., suburb 2 mi/3.2 km SSE of downtown Las Cruces, near Rio Grande. Mfg. (ceramic tile, tortillas, jewelry).

Mesones Hidalgo (mai-SO-nes hee-DAHL-go), town (1990 pop. 901), in far W Oaxaca, Mexico, 87 mi/140 km W of Oaxaca de Juárez. On the border of the state of Guerrero. Mt. valley with temperate climate. Agr. (corn, beans, coffee, fruits), woods, mezcal; cattle. Fabric. Formerly Hidalgo, also San José Mesones.

Mesquite (MES-keet), city (1990 pop. 101,484), Dallas co., N Texas, a suburb, 10 mi/16 km E of downtown Dallas, adjoining city of Dallas; 32°46′N 96°35′W. Elev. 491 ft/150 m. Bounded in SE by East Fork Trinity R. Mfg. industrial power supplies, also bldg. materials, medical equip., bank supplies, machinery, paper prods. Hq. of several major Texas corporations, such as the Texas Power and Light Company and Lonestar Gas Company Agr. to E and SE (dairying; cotton, peanuts). It has been one of the fastest-growing U.S. cities, marked by a pop. increase of more than 51% bet. 1980 and 1990; it is now surrounded on all but SE by other municipalities. Eastfield Col. (2-year) is in NW of city, and an annual rodeo is held here every Oct. L. Ray Hubbard reservoir to NE; Devil's Bowl Speedway is here; Phil L. Anderson Airport in E. Inc. 1887.

Mesquite 1 (mes-KEET), town (1990 pop. 1,871), Clark co., SE Nev., 70 mi/113 km NE of Las Vegas, on Ariz. state line, on Virgin R.; 36°47′N 114°06′W. One of several towns developed on Nev. state line to offer gambling opportunities to travelers. Desert Valley Mus. Virgin Mts. to SE; Virgin Mt. to S; Virgin R. State Recreation Area to SW. **2** (muh-SKEET), uninc. town (1990 pop. 500), Dona Ana co., S N.Mex., 12 mi/19 km SSE of Las Cruces, on Rio Grande. Cattle, sheep; dairying; chilies, jalapenos, vegetables, grain, alfalfa, nuts. Mfg. (dairy prods., fertilizer).

Messalonskee Lake (mes-uh-LAHN-skee), reservoir (□ 6 sq mi/15.5 sq km), Kennebec co., central Maine, on Messalonskee Stream, c.7 mi/11 km W of Waterville; 10 mi/16 km long, c.1 mi/1.6 km wide; 44°32′N 69°44′W. Max. capacity 118,300 acre-ft. Formed by Snow Pond Dam (13 ft/4 m high), built (1992) for power generation. One of Belgrade Lakes.

Meta (MEE-tuh), town (1990 pop. 249), Osage co., central Mo., near Osage R., 20 mi/32 km SSW of Linn.; 38°18′N 92°10′W. Pet food; charcoal prods.

Meta Incognita or **Kingait,** peninsula, SE Baffin Isl., SE Franklin dist., N.W.T., Canada, extending SE into the Atlantic, bet. Frobisher Bay (NE) and Hudson Strait (SW); 61°52′N 65°55′W–63°30′N 70°W. Mountainous

surface rises to c.2,500 ft/762 m in center; 170 mi/274 km long, 30 mi/48 km–80 mi/129 km wide. On NE coast, near mouth of Frobisher Bay, are Grinnell Ice Cap (c.3,000 ft/914 m high) and Southeast Ice Cap (c.2,800 ft/853 m high), both extending tongues to Frobisher Bay.

Meta Pond (MEE-tuh), lake, SE N.F., Canada; 8 mi/13 km long, 2 mi/3 km wide; 48°03′N 54°53′W.

Metabetchouan (mee-tuh-behch-WAHN) or **Saint Jérôme** (seh zhai-ROM), town (1991 pop. 3,379), S central Que., Canada, on SE shore of L. St. John, 13 mi/21 km SE of St. Joseph d'Alma; 48°26′N 71°52′W. Dairying; lumbering; pig raising. Also spelled Métabetchouan.

Metabetchouan River or **Métabetchouan River,** 50 mi/80 km long, S central Que., Canada; rises in N part of Laurentides Provincial Park; flows N to L. St. John at Desbiens.

Metairie (MET-uh-ree), uninc. city (1990 pop. 149,428), Jefferson parish, SE La., NW suburb, 7 mi/11 km WNW of New Orleans, on S shore of L. Pontchartrain; 30°00′N 90°11′W. Mfg. (cultured marble, fabricated metal prods., motor vehicle parts, concrete blocks, dairy prods.), printing and publishing. Mississippi R. to S. Named for the metairies, or little farms, that developed from the original plantations.

Metaline (met-ah-LEEN), village (1990 pop. 198), Pend Oreille co., NE Wash., on Pend Oreille R., 31 mi/50 km NE of Colville, 10 mi/16 km S of Canada (B.C.) border; 48°51′N 117°23′W. Lead, zinc, copper; timber. Box Canyon Dam to S, Boundary Dam to N. Crawford State Park to N, on Can. boundary; parts of Colville Natl. Forest to E and W.

Metaline Falls (met-ah-LEEN), village (1990 pop. 210), Pend Oreille co., NE Wash., port of entry near B.C. line, 33 mi/53 km NE of Colville, near Pend Oreille R. 9 mi/14.5 km S of Canada (B.C.) border, port of entry (Nelway, B.C.); 48°52′N 117°22′W. RR terminus. Timber; lead, zinc, copper. Sullivan L. reservoir to SE; parts of Colville Natl. Forest to E and W, including Salmo-Priest Wilderness Area, to NE. Box Canyon Dam to S, Boundary Dam to N.

Metamora 1 (met-a-MORE-ah), village (1990 pop. 2,520), Woodford co., central Ill., 12 mi/19 km ENE of Peoria; 40°47′N 89°21′W. In agr. area; canned foods. Former capital of Woodford co. Old courthouse is now state memorial to Lincoln, who often argued cases here. Inc. 1845. **2** village, Franklin co., SE Ind., on the West Fork of Whitewater R., and 7 mi/11.3 km WNW of Brookville. Located on the old Whitewater Canal, a sect. of which still goes through the village and is a tourist attraction. Laid out 1838. **3** (ME-ta-MOR-uh), village (1990 pop. 447), Lapeer co., E Mich., 7 mi/11.3 km S of Lapeer; 42°56′N 83°17′W. In farm area. Mfg. (plastic molding, machining). Metamura-Hadley State Recreation Area to W. **4** (me-tuh-MO-ruh), village (1990 pop. 543), Fulton co., NW Ohio, 19 mi/31 km W of Toledo, at Mich. line; 41°43′N 83°54′W. Agr. (tomatoes, corn); poultry hatcheries.

Metapa de Domínguez (me-TAH-pah dai do-MEEN-ges), town (1990 pop. 2,026), ⊙ Metapa municipio, Chiapas, S Mexico, near Guatemala border, 6 mi/9.7 km SE of Tapachula; 14°50′N 92°11′W. Coffee, sugarcane; bee keeping.

Metasville (MET-uhs-vil), town, Wilkes co., NE Ga., 8 mi/12.9 km ENE of Washington; 33°46′N 82°36′W.

Metcalf (MET-kaf), town, Thomas co., S Ga., 9 mi/14.5 km S of Thomasville, near Fla. state line; 30°42′N 83°59′W.

Metcalf, village (1990 pop. 227), Edgar co., E Ill., 14 mi/23 km NNW of Paris; 39°47′N 87°48′W. In agr. area.

Metcalfe (MET-kaf), county (□ 290 sq mi/751 sq km; 1990 pop. 8,963), S Ky.; ⊙ Edmonton; 36°59′N 85°37′W. Drained by Little Barren R. and Beaver and Marrowbone creeks. Rolling agr. area (corn, wheat, burley tobacco, soybeans, hay, alfalfa; cattle, poultry; dairying; timber). Formed 1860.

Metcalfe (MET-kaf), town (1990 pop. 1,092), Washington co., W Miss., residential suburb, 4 mi/6.4 km NE

of Greenville; 33°27′N 91°00′W. Greenville Municipal Airport here. Stoneville Natl. Wildlife Refuge to E.

Metedeconk River (muh-TEE-duh-KUHNGK), E N.J.; rises SW of Freehold in North Branch (c.20 mi/32 km long) and South Branch (c.15 mi/24 km long), which flow SE to junction c.6 mi/9.7 km above mouth on Barnegat Bay; navigable below the junction.

Meteghan (meh-TAI-guhn), village, W N.S., Canada, on the Atlantic, at entrance of St. Mary Bay, 25 mi/40 km N of Yarmouth; 44°11′N 66°09′W. Fishing; wood-working.

Meteor Crater, large crater, SE Coconino co., N central Ariz., 35 mi/56 km ESE of Flagstaff. Created by meteorites; 4,150 ft/1,265 m in diameter, 570 ft/174 m deep, with rim rising 120 ft/37 m–160 ft/49 m above surrounding plain, about 1 mi/1.6 km wide. Fragments of iron, containing some nickel, have been found. NASA used the crater as training ground for Apollo astronauts before their missions to the moon. Mus. of Astrogeology is at site. Sometimes called Diablo Crater.

Metepec 1 (ME-te-pek), town (1990 pop. 1,320), Hidalgo, central Mexico, 27 mi/43 km ENE of Pachuca de Soto. Corn, maguey; livestock; mfg. of metal pipes. **2** town (1990 pop. 116,203), Mexico state, central Mexico, on RR, 5 mi/8 km SE of Toluca de Lerdo, on Mexico Highway 55. Known for pottery and colorful market. Agr. center (grain, fruit; livestock); dairying.

Methow River (MET-hou), c.80 mi/129 km long, Okanogan co., N Wash.; rises in Cascade Range N of L. Chelan; flows N then generally SE through irrigated agr. valley (apples), past Winthrop and Twisp, to Columbia R. (L. Pateros reservoir) at Pateros.

Methuen (me-THOO-uhn), town (1990 pop. 39,990), Essex co., NE Mass., suburb of Boston; 42°44′N 71°11′W. Methuen is industrial, and among its prods. are food items, computer and microwave components, medical supplies, and textiles. The Tenney Estate was converted into St. Basil's Seminary and Presentation of Mary Acad. Settled c.1642, set off from Haverhill 1725.

Methy Lake (MEE-thee), NW Sask., Canada, 20 mi/32 km NW of Peter Pond L.; 21 mi/34 km long, 5 mi/8 km wide; 56°25′N 109°30′W. Elev. 1,460 ft/445 m. Main headstream of Churchill R. rises here.

Metinic Island (muh-TIN-ik), I., Knox co., S Maine, 6 mi/9.7 km SE of Tenants Harbor; 2 mi/3.2 km long, ¼ mi/⅖ km wide.

Metis Beach (MEH-tis) or **Métis sur Mer** (mai-TEE suhr MER), village (1991 pop. 239), E Que., Canada, on the St. Lawrence, 25 mi/40 km WSW of Matane; 48°40′N 67°59′W. Resort.

Metlakahtla, Alaska, see: METLAKATLA.

Metlakatla (MET-luh-KAT-luh), village, SE Alaska, on W shore of Annette Isl., 17 mi/27 km S of Ketchikan. A model cooperative village of the Tsimshian Indians. Fishing, logging; cooperative cannery and sawmill. Est. 1887 by Rev. William Duncan, missionary, and Indians emigrating from Fort Simpson, B.C. Also spelled Metlakahtla.

Metlatónoc (met-lahn-TO-nok), town (1990 pop. 1,886), Guerrero, SW Mexico, in isolated zone of Sierra Madre del Sur, near Oaxaca border, 25 mi/40 km SE of Tlapa de Comonfort; 17°11′N 98°20′W. No paved roads. Cereals, fruit; stock.

Metlatoyuca (me-tlah-YOO-kah), town (1990 pop. 3,735), ⊙ Francisco Z. Mena municipio, Puebla, central Mexico, in foothills of Sierra Madre Oriental, 33 mi/53 km SW of Túxpam de Rodríguez Cano; 20°44′N 97°51′W. Sugarcane, coffee, tobacco, fruit. Pre-Columbian ruins nearby.

Metolius (met-O-lee-uhs), village (1990 pop. 450), Jefferson co., N central Oregon, 5 mi/8 km SW of Madras; 44°35′N 121°10′W. Grain, livestock; frozen potatoes. Crooked R. Natl. Grassland to SE. Warm Springs Indian Reservation to NW. Cove Palisades State Park, on L. Chinook Reservoir, to SW.

Metolius River (met-O-lee-uhs), c. 60 mi/97 km long, SW Jefferson co., N central Oregon; rises in Cascade Range in Deschutes Natl. Forest; flows N, then SE, forming S boundary of Warm Springs Indian Reservation and long W arm of L. Chinook Reservoir. Metolius Bench, level plateau area, to N.

Metompkin Inlet, Va.: see METOMPKIN ISLAND.

Metompkin Island, Accomack co., E Va., 5 mi/8 km E of Accomac, separated from mainland by narrow channel (Wire Passage; to W); c.6 mi/9.7 km long. Metompkin Inlet, Cedar Isl. to S; Gargathy Inlet, Assawoman Isl. to N.

Metropolis (meh-TROP-o-lis), port city (1990 pop. 6,734), ⊙ Massac co., extreme S Ill., on Ohio R., and 28 mi/45 km ENE of Cairo; 37°08′N 88°42′W. In agr. and lumbering area; mfg. (clothing); shipping center for corn, wheat, livestock. Fort Massac State Park (1,470 acres/595 ha), on site of Fr. fort (1757); Kincaid Indian Mounds nearby. Inc. 1859. Annual celebration honoring Superman.

Mettawa, village (1990 pop. 348), Lake co., NE Ill., residential suburb, 29 mi/47 km NNW of downtown Chicago, 5 mi/8 km W of Lake Forest, on Des Plaines R.; 42°14′N 87°55′W.

Mettawee River (ME-tuh-wee), c.50 mi/80 km long, in Vt. and N.Y.; rises in Taconic Mts. near Dorset, Vt.; flows NW, past Pawlet, Vt., and Granville, N.Y., to L. Champlain near Whitehall, N.Y.

Metter, town (1990 pop. 3,707), ⊙ Candler co., E central Ga., 17 mi/27 km W of Statesboro, near Canoochee R.; 32°24′N 82°04′W. Welcome center on I-16. William Bartram-inspired Charles C. Harrold Nature Preserve nearby operated by nature conservancy features sand hill formations. Mfg. includes clothing, boats, metal fabrication, commercial printing; tobacco market; lumber; pecan and peanut processing.

Metuchen (muh-TUH-chuhn), borough (1990 pop. 12,804), Middlesex co., NE N.J.; 40°32′N 74°21′W. Chiefly residential; light mfg. includes fabricated metal prods., packaging equip., consumer goods, machinery, and electric appliances. In June 1777, a brief but bloody skirmish occurred here bet. Br. troops under Gen. William Howe and a small Amer. force led by William Alexander. Settled before 1700, inc. 1900.

Metz, town (1990 pop. 91), Vernon co., W Mo., on Little Osage R., and 12 mi/19 km NNW of Nevada; 38°00′N 94°26′W. Sorghum, hay; cattle.

Metzquititlán (metz-kee-tee-TLAHN), town (1990 pop. 1,183), ⊙ San Agustín Metzquititlán municipio, Hidalgo, central Mexico, 30 mi/48 km NNE of Pachuca de Soto on Mexico Highway 105; 20°32′N 98°39′W. Corn beans, maguey, fruit; livestock.

Metztitlán (metz-tee-TLAHN), town, Hidalgo, central Mexico, on central plateau, near L. Metztitlán, 33 mi/53 km N of Pachuca de Soto; 20°36′N 98°45′W. Elev. 4,413 ft/1,345 m. Agr. center (corn, beans, oranges, melons, tomatoes; livestock).

Mexcala River, Mexico: see BALSAS, RÍO.

Mexcaltitán (meks-kahl-teet-LAHN), village, W central Nayarit, Mexico, 21 mi/34 km NW of Tepic. Some people believe this tiny fishing village was a stop-off for the Mexico (Aztec) people during their seach for a homeland. It can be reached by a paved road or by dugout canoe. This canoe trip is through a mangrove forest. Some of the houses are built on platforms because the isl. floods during the rainy season. The economy is based on shrimp in the lagoon.

Mexia, town (1990 pop. 6,933), Limestone co., E central Texas, 39 mi/63 km ENE of Waco; 31°40′N 96°28′W. Elev. 534 ft/163 m. Commercial, processing center for agr. (cotton, grain; cattle), oil-producing area; mfg. of clay prods. Old Fort Parker State Historic Site and Fort Parker State Park to SW; Confederate Reunion Grounds State Historic Site to N; L. Mexia to W. Settled 1873; oil discovery (1920) led to boom.

Mexicali (meks-ee-KAHL-ee), city (1990 pop. 438,377) and township, ⊙ Mexicali municipio and of Baja California state, NW Mexico, across the border from Calexico, Calif.; 32°39′N 115°30′E. Once noted chiefly as the center of a cotton- and cereal-raising area, it has experienced extensive construction of foreign-owned mfg. plants called *maquiladoras.* A large and rapidly growing labor force and lower employment and production costs in Mexico have stimulated the development of *maquiladoras* in the border areas. Also center of irrigated agr., lower Colorado R.

Mexicaltzingo (meks-hee-kahlt-seen-go), town (1990 pop. 6,438), ⊙ Mexicalcingo municipio, Mexico state, central Mexico, on RR, and 8 mi/12.9 km SE of Toluca de Lerdo, on Mexico Highway 55; 19°21′N 99°07′W. Cereals; livestock; dairying.

Mexico (MEKS-i-ko), Span. *México* or *Méjico,* (both: ME-hee-ko), officially called the United States of Mexico, Span. *Estados Unidos Mexicanos,* republic (□ 753,665 sq mi/1,951,992 sq km; 1990 pop. 81,249,645), S N. Amer., bordering on the U.S. in the N, on the Gulf of Mexico and the Caribbean Sea in the E, on Belize and Guatemala in the SE, and on the Pacific Ocean in the S and W. Mexico is divided into 31 states and the Federal Dist., which includes MEXICO city. The states are AGUASCALIENTES, BAJA CALIFORNIA, BAJA CALIFORNIA SUR, CAMPECHE, CHIAPAS, CHIHUAHUA, COAHUILA, COLIMA, DURANGO, GUANAJUATO, GUERRERO, HIDALGO, JALISCO, MEXICO, MICHOACÁN, MORELOS, NAYARIT, NUEVO LEÓN, OAXACA, PUEBLA, QUERÉTARO, QUINTANA ROO, SAN LUIS POTOSÍ, SINALOA, SONORA, TABASCO, TAMAULIPAS, TLAXCALA, VERACRUZ, YUCATÁN, and ZACATECAS. Most of Mexico is highland or mountainous; only about 20% of the land is arable. Lowland areas include most of the Yucatán peninsula and the Isthmus of Tehuantepec in the SE, and low-lying strips of land along the Gulf of Mexico, the Pacific Ocean, and the Gulf of California (known in Mexico as *Mar de Cortés*) separating the Baja, or Lower, California peninsula from the rest of the country. The Mex. Plateau (c.700 mi/1,130 km long and c.4,000 ft/1,219 m–8,000 ft/2,438 m high) makes up the heart of Mexico. It is fringed by 2 mt. ranges, the Sierra Madre Oriental (E) and the Sierra Madre Occidental (W). Some of the country's major cities are located within drainage basins contained within the plateau. The LAGUNA DISTRICT, for example, was the scene of a major irrigation development and land colonization project (1936). In the N the plateau is mostly arid; some of the area has been irrigated and is used principally for raising livestock. The broad, shallow lakes of the ANÁHUAC region, famous for its rich cultural heritage, lie S of the deserts. S. of the Anáhuac, which includes the Valley of Mexico, is the Transverse Volcanic Axis, a chain of volcanoes, including CITLALTEPÉTL or Orizaba (elev. 18,700 ft/5,700 m; the highest point in Mexico); POPOCATÉPETL; and IZTACCIHUATL. Further S are jumbled masses of mts. and the Sierra Madre del Sur. Mexico contains a few large rivers including the Río Bravo del Norte (Rio Grande), which forms the boundary with Texas, and its tributaries; and the Río Grijalva, Río Papaloapan, and Río Úsumacinta, which flow into the Gulf of Mexico. The climate of the country varies with elev.: *tierra caliente* (up to c.3,000 ft/1,220 m), *tierra templada* (c.3,000 ft/914 m–c.6,000ft/1,829 m), and *tierra fría* (above c.6,000 ft/1,829 m). Most of the citizens are of mixed Span. and Native Amer. descent; Span. is the country's official language. Since 1920 the pop. of Mexico has had a very high rate of growth; from 1940 to 1990 the pop. grew from 19.6 million to 81.1 million. However, declining fertility rates indicate a slow down in the pop. growth. The vast majority of people are R.C., with Protestant minorities. The Mex. govt. plays a major role in planning the economy and owns and operates some basic industries (including the petroleum industry) and means of transport. About 40% of the country's workers are engaged in farming, which is slowly becoming modernized. Because rainfall is inadequate outside the coastal regions, agr. depends largely on extensive irrigation. Mexico produces a wide variety of agr. prods. (basic grains, sugarcane, citrus fruits, cotton, coffee, and tomatoes); maguey is widely grown and is processed into the alcoholic beverages pulque and mescal. Livestock raising and fishing are also significant sources of economic activity. Mexico is among the world's leading producers of many minerals, including silver, fluorite, zinc, and mercury, and its petroleum reserves are one of its most valuable assets. In the late 1970s and early 1980s petroleum constituted about ¾ of Mexico's exports. That figure fell drastically in the mid-1980s. While diversification of industry has helped to keep Mexico's trade economy from becoming dependent once more on a single export, the petroleum industry has also recovered substantially. The country's principal industrial centers include Mexico city, GUADALAJARA, MONTERREY, CIUDAD JUÁREZ, TIJUANA, DURANGO, LEÓN, QUERÉTARO, and PUEBLA. There is also a petrochemical center at Coatzacoalcos-Minatitlán and an iron-steel complex at Lázaro Cárdenas on the Isthmus of Tehuan tepec. Leading mfg. includes iron and steel, motor vehicles, cement, refined petroleum and petrochemicals, processed food, electronic prods., and textiles. Mexico is also known for its handicrafts, esp. pottery, woven goods, and silverwork. Tourism is now Mexico's 2d-greatest source of income. Favorite tourist centers include ACAPULCO, CANCÚN, COZUMEL, PUERTO VALLARTA, MAZATLÁN, CABO SAN LUCAS, and TIJUANA, as well as Mexico city itself and some of the highland centers like Guadalajara and Puebla. The country's chief ports are Veracruz, Tampico, COATZACOALCOS, Mazatlán, and ENSENADA. The leading imports (machinery, motor vehicles, electronic equip., chemicals, consumer goods, and grain); main exports (petroleum, cotton, sugar, coffee, tomatoes, shrimp, sulfur, and zinc). Until recently, the annual value of Mexico's imports was considerably higher than the value of its exports. Since the early 1980s, however, there has been considerable foreign investment in *maquiladoras,* which take advantage of a large, low-cost labor force to produce finished goods for export to the U.S. The *maquiladoras* have increased Mexico's export production considerably, as well as contributing to the diversification of the industrial sector. The principal trade partners are the U.S., the EU, and Japan. Mexico is a member of the UN, the OAS, the Latin Amer. Integration Assn., and the Latin Amer. Economic System. The country has numerous univs., notably in Mexico city, Saltillo, Guadalajara, Monterrey, and Puebla. A number of great civilizations flourished in Mexico; earliest of these were the Olmec civilization, reaching its high point bet. 800 and 400 B.C. The Maya civilization flourished bet. about A.D. 300 and 900, followed by the Toltec (900–1200) and the Aztec (1200–1519). Other notable civilizations of pre-Columbian Mexico are the Mixtec and the Zapotec. The 1st Europeans to visit Mexico were Francisco Fernández de Córdoba in 1517 and Juan de Grijalva in 1518. The conquest of Mexico was begun from Cuba in 1519 by Hernán Cortés, who conquered the Aztec capital, TENOCHTITLÁN, in 1521. The territory was constituted the viceroyalty of New Spain in 1535. The Spanish had difficulty establishing control, as is evidenced by such events as the Mixtón War (1541), but at last they managed to establish their power over the indigenous pop. The society slowly developed 3 different status groupings—Spaniards, Native Americans, and mestizos (mixed Span. and Native Amer.). The growth of an underprivileged mestizo class and the antagonism bet. those born in Spain (*gachupines*) and those born in America (*criollos,* or creoles) created internal stress and conflict. During this period, the Spanish continued to conquer new territory. Most of present-day Mexico and the former Span. holdings in the present-day U.S. were occupied early. NE Mexico and Texas began to be occupied by Europeans in large numbers in the middle and late 18th cent. Around this time, discontent with Span. rule began to grow, sparking a revolution in the early 19th cent. A priest named Miguel Hidalgo y Costilla began the rebellion by issuing the *Grito de Dolores* [Span. = cry of Dolores] on Sept. 16, 1810, a revolutionary tract calling for racial equality and the redistribution of land. Armies made up mostly of mestizos and Native Americans fought against the Span. army. Although successful at first, the rebels were ultimately overmatched; by 1815, their armies had either been defeated in battle or driven into the wilds. A few years later another more peaceful rebellion was fostered by the royalist general Augustín de Iturbide among others. The resulting Plan of Iguala (Feb. 1821) called for an independent monarchy, equality for Spaniards and creoles, and the maintenance of the privileged position of the church. Spain accepted

Mex. independence that Sept., and an empire was est. in 1822 with Iturbide at its head. In 1823, the republican leaders drove out Iturbide and est. Mexico as a republic. Political unrest and frequent turnover of govts. continued for the next several years. In 1836, Texas, calling itself a republic, withdrew from Mexico leading to the Mex.-Amer. War (1846–1848). By the terms of the Treaty of Guadalupe Hidalgo, the U.S. took over all Mex. lands N of the Rio Grande. After the war, the Mex. govt. remained unstable, and in 1855 it was again overthrown by a group of reform-minded men led by Benito Juárez. They drafted a liberal constitution (1857) that secularized church property and reduced the privileges of the army. Conservative opposition began the War of Reform (1858–1861); however, the liberals emerged victorious, and Juárez became president. At the invitation of the conservatives, Napoleon III of France intervened in 1864, unseating Juárez and setting up an empire. But the empire quickly collapsed (1867), and Juárez again assumed control of Mexico. Porfirio Díaz led a successful armed revolt in 1876 and, except for the period from 1880 to 1884, firmly held the reins of power as president until 1911. It was a period of considerable economic growth, but social inequality increased. Despite some liberal opposition, repressive and dictorial regime continued into 1914 when a successful revolution broke out under the leadership of Venustiano Carranza, Francisco "Pancho" Villa, and Emiliano Zapata. With the influence of U.S. military intervention, Carranza became president (1914). Civil war broke out again later that year, but by the end of 1915 Carranza had reestablished control. A constitution ratified in 1917 est. Mexico as a federal republic with a president and a bicameral legislature. In 1920 Carranza was deposed by General Álvaro Obregón, his former military chief, who was subsequently elected president. The Obregón administration (1920–1924) redistributed lands and undertook educational reforms. His successor, Plutarco Elías Calles, continued the agrarian and educational programs, but he became embroiled in serious disagreements with the U.S. over rights to petroleum and with the church over the separation of church and state. Despite his loss of the 1928 presidency, Calles remained a powerful political influence. He organized the Natl. Revolutionary Party (1929; renamed the Institutional Revolutionary Party—PRI—in 1946), the chief political party in Mexico to this day. Lázaro Cárdenas (1934) instituted reforms to improve the lot of the underprivileged. He redistributed land and supported the Mex. labor movement. Under his political term, RRs were nationalized; foreign holdings, particularly in petroleum fields, were expropriated with compensation; educational opportunities were increased and illiteracy reduced; medical facilities were extended; transport and communications were improved; and plans were drawn up for land reclamation and for hydroelectric and industrial projects. Relations with the U.S. improved in the 1940s. In World War II, Mexico declared war (1942) on the Axis powers; it made substantial contributions to the Allied cause and also received considerable U.S. economic aid. Since the end of World War II, Mexico has embarked upon an ambitious program of economic development (esp. of its industrial plants) and implemented many of Cárdenas plans. Most of the benefits of this economic progress, however, have accrued to the middle and upper classes, and the relative welfare of poorer people has remained the same or deteriorated. The improvements made in Mexico's RR network and the opening of the INTER-AMERICAN HIGHWAY aided the tourist trade and thus increased the commercial value of one of the country's greatest assets: the beauty of its land. Mexico remained on friendly terms with the U.S., ratifying treaties that settled long-standing border disputes in the El Paso, Texas, region (1964, 1967) and called (1965) for the U.S. to maintain the freshwater content of the Colorado R., whose waters are used for irrigation in Mexico. Mexico maintained diplomatic relations with post-Castro Cuba, but it supported the U.S. during the Cuban missile crisis (1962). In the 1970s Mexico continued to expand its economy, borrowing significantly on the strength of its petroleum reserves, but when oil prices fell sharply in the early 1980s the country's ability to meet its internatl. debt obligations was severely strained. In addition, pop. increases and inflation contributed to food shortages and unemployment. Private and foreign investment dropped sharply, and the pop. began to migrate from rural areas into the cities and into the U.S. The govt. responded with economic austerity policies, a renegotiation of Mexico's internatl. debt, and a loosening of direct foreign investment regulations. The economic crisis, the austerity measures, and the added blow of a major earthquake in the city of Mexico in 1985 all contributed to a popular discontent with the PRI. Salinas has continued economic reform, encouraging foreign investment, privatizing many natl. industries, investigating corruption in public offices, and working toward increased trade with the U.S. A continued problem in Mexico's relations with the U.S., however, has been the flow of illegal immigrants and drugs across the border. By 1990, debt relief, diversification and privatization of the economy, and foreign investment began to show positive effects, and Mexico's economic growth rate returned to historic levels. In 1992 Mexico, the U.S., and Canada negotiated the North American Free Trade Agreement (NAFTA), which was designed to erase many trade barriers among the 3 govts. and create a trading bloc of 370 million people; it was inaugurated in Jan. 1994. Also in Jan. 1994, a guerilla uprising by the Zapatista Natl. Liberation Army (EZLN) began in the SE state of Chiapas; the often-violent conflict continues, and another rebel group, the Popular Revolutionary Army (EPR), has begun to agitate against the govt. as well. In the presidential election of 1994, the PRI candidate, Luis Donaldo Colosio Murrieta, was assassinated in Tijuana; his successor, Ernesto Zedillo Ponce de León, was subsequently elected. In early 1995, soon after Zedillo took office, Mexico suffered a major economic crisis, with devaluation of the peso and near-catastrophic financial instability. An austerity plan and U.S. aid relieved the situation and saved the peso from complete collapse.

Mexico (MEKS-i-ko), Span. *México* or *Méjico* (both: ME-hee-ko), state (□ 8,286 sq mi/21,461 sq km; 1990 pop. 9,815,795), S central Mexico; ⊙ TOLUCA DE LERDO; 18°22′N 98°35′W. The N sect. of the state, containing most of the Valley of Mexico (part of the Anáhuac plateau), has broad, shallow lakes and is broken by low mts. There are steeper mts. and valleys in the E, and the S and W areas are dominated by the rugged volcanic belt extending across the center of the country. On the state's SE border are the Popocatépetl and Iztaccíhuatl volcanoes. The principal river is the Lerma. Except on the S, the state encircles the Federal Dist., with the nation's capital, Mexico city, and most of the E part lies within the Mexico City Metropolitan Zone. Suburbs of Mexico city which lie within Mexico State include Ciudad Nezahualcóyotl, a huge (more than 2 million) working-class neighborhood that developed as a squatter settlement in former bed of L. Texcoco, and the major industrial centers of Naucalpan, Tlalnepantla, Ecatepec, Tultitlán, and Cuautitlán. The state is highly industrialized; a leading producer of automobiles, paper, chemicals, textiles, other light manufactures, iron, and steel. Mining (gold, silver, lead, zinc), and agr. (maguey, beans, and cereals) are other economic activities. Mexico is one of the country's most densely populated states.

Mexico (MEKS-i-ko), Span. *Ciudad de México* or *Méjico* (both: ME-hee-ko), city (1990 pop. 15,047,685), central Mexico, ⊙ and largest city of Mexico, near the S end of the plateau of Anáhuac; 19°26′N 99°07′W. Elev. c.7,349 ft/2,240 m; the horizons of the city are almost obscured by mt. barriers, and the peaks of Popocatépetl and Iztaccíhuatl are not far off. The climate is cool and dry. Much of the surrounding valley is a lake basin with no outlet, and in the past during the rainy seasons, floods of runoff swelled the lakes. From the time when the Aztec capital of Tenochtitlán stood on an isl. in L. Texcoco—now the heart of the metropolis—measures have been taken to protect the city and provide for expansion by draining Texcoco and the other lakes, Chalco and Xochimilco. In 1607–1608 an 8-mi-13-km-long drainage canal and tunnel were built to drain floodwaters from the basin N to the Tula R. In 1900 a central canal was completed that reached to the headwaters of the Pánuco R. The Caracol [Span. = snail], a 12-mi/19-km spiral system fed by longitudinal canals begun in 1936, acts as an evaporating basin, from which valuable minerals are taken. Drainage and artesian wells have lowered the water table so that the alluvial soil, formerly saturated by subsoil water, can no longer sustain the heavier bldgs. of the city, which are sinking c.4 in/10.2 cm–12 in/30 cm a year. Some of Mexico's finest bldgs. have been damaged, among them the old cathedral (begun in 1553 near the site of an Aztec temple) and the Palace of Fine Arts. Modern office bldgs. have been shored up with pilings. In addition to the soft subsoil, the city is located in a region of high seismic activity; earthquakes in 1957 and 1985 caused substantial damage. Nevertheless, many monuments of Span. colonial architecture remain. The cathedral and the Natl. Palace are on the great central square, or Plaza de la Constitución, where the streets of the old town crisscross in a rough gridiron. From the Plaza the great avenues span out to the far sections of the capital. Many colonial churches are to be found. The Paseo de la Reforma cuts across the city to CHAPULTEPEC. Public bldgs. of the 19th cent. have a ponderous grandeur that shows Fr. influence, but the newly built edifices are starkly modern. Some old bldgs. as well as the newer (e.g., the Palace of Fine Arts, the Natl. Palace, and the Natl. Preparatory School) have murals by the modern artists Diego Rivera, José Clemente Orozco, and David Alfaro Siqueiros. The Natl. Univ. of Mexico, founded in the 16th cent., is housed in University City (opened 1952), built on El Pedregal, a lava outcrop in the outskirts, with famous mosaics designed by Juan O'Gorman. The city was the metropolis of Mexico even before New Spain was created. It is built on the ruins of the Aztec city of TENOCHTITLAN, which was begun in c.1325 and razed by Hernán Cortés in 1521. During the colonial period Mexico city served as the capital of New Spain and was for a time the cultural and social center of Spain's Amer. empire. It was taken in 1847 by Winfield Scott's Amer. army, after an inland march from Veracruz in the Mex.-Amer. War. The Fr. army captured Mexico city in 1863, and Emperor Maximilian, crowned in 1864, did much to beautify it before it was recaptured by Mexicans under Benito Juárez. In the years of revolution after 1910, it was a magnet for divergent insurrectionary forces. Perhaps the most spectacular incidents were the occupations (1914–1915) by Pancho Villa and Emiliano Zapata. Today Mexico City forms the core of the Federal Dist. and is the commercial, industrial, financial, political, and cultural center of the nation. Among its diverse and important manufactures are chemicals, petroleum, food products, textiles, motor vehicles, machinery, pharmaceuticals, and consumer goods. Pop. has increased rapidly in a city that had already spread out in many residential sections called *colonias*. Overcrowding has become a major problem and traffic concentrations, combined with the atmospheric conditions of the city's surrounding valley, have resulted in heavy air pollution. The Metro, Mexico city's subway system, helps to reduce traffic congestion and pollution. The 1st of the 9 lines was opened in 1969. Ixtapalapa and Delegations A. Madero are the largest suburbs of the Federal Dist.; Coyoacán is the oldest, with a palace built by Cortés. Among noted religious and recreational centers are Guadalupe Hidalgo and Xochimilco. Azcapotzalco is the transport and industrial hub of the city. Its rich local color and extraordinary cultural attractions, make it a focal point for tourists, especially from the U.S. The Olympics were held in Mexico City in 1968. Benito Juárez Internatl. Airport to E.

Mexico, city (1990 pop. 11,290), ⊙ Audrain co., central Mo., 28 mi/45 km NW of Columbia; inc. 1857; 39°10′N 91°52′W. Regional farm service area. Livestock markets.

Saddle horses. Refractory clay deposits. Wheat, corn, soybeans; hogs, cattle; mfg. (soybean processing, prefabricated homes, cloth bags, fire-clay and aluminum brick and insulation, trailers, plastic prods., ceramic tile and bricks, copper wire, carpet tack). A saddle-horse mus., Mo. Military Acad., and a Missouri Veterans' Home are also in the city. John D. Moore b. here.

Mexico, residential town (1990 pop. 3,344), including Mexico village, W Maine, on Androscoggin R., opposite industrial Rumford; 44°35′N 70°30′W. Inc. 1818.

Mexico 1 village (1990 pop. 1,003), Miami co., N central Ind., 5 mi/8 km NW of Peru, on Eel R; 40°49′N 86°07′W. Soybeans, corn; cattle; dairying. Laid out 1834. **2** village (□ 2 sq mi/5.2 sq km; 1990 pop. 1,555) in Mexico town (1990 pop. 5,050), Oswego co., central N.Y., 13 mi/21 km E of Owego; 43°27′N 76°14′W. Rich agr. area (berries, sweet and field corn); mfg. of canned specialities, diabetic foods, flour, wood prods., burial vaults. Inc. 1851.

Mexico Beach, village (□ 1 sq mi/2.6 sq km; 1990 pop. 992), Bay co., NW Fla., 21 mi/34 km SE of Panama City; 29°56′N 85°24′W.

Mexico, Gulf of, arm of the Atlantic Ocean (□ c.700,000 sq mi/1,813,000 sq km), SE N. Amer. The Gulf stretches more than 1,100 mi/1,770 km from W to E and c.800 mi/1,287 km from N to S. It is bordered by the Gulf coast of the U.S. from Fla. to Texas, and the E coast of Mexico from Tamaulipas to Yucatán. Near the entrance of the Gulf is the isl. of Cuba. On the N side of Cuba the Gulf is connected with the Atlantic Ocean by the Straits of Florida (from which the Gulf Stream ocean current originates); on the S side of Cuba it is connected with the Caribbean Sea by the Yucatán Channel. The Bay of Campeche (Bahía de Campeche), Mexico, and Apalachee Bay, Florida, are the Gulf's largest arms. Sigsbee Deep (12,714 ft/3,875 m), the deepest part of the Gulf, lies off the Mex. coast. The shoreline is generally low, sandy, and marshy, with many lagoons. Chief of the many rivers entering the Gulf are the Mississippi, Alabama, Brazos, and Rio Grande. The U.S. Intracoastal Waterway follows the Gulf's coastline from S Fla. to the Rio Grande. Oil deposits from the continental shelf are tapped by offshore wells, esp. along the coast of Texas and La. Most of the U.S. shrimp catch comes from the Gulf Coast; menhaden is another important catch. The chief ports along the Gulf of Mexico are at Tampa and Pensacola, Fla.; Mobile, Ala.; New Orleans; Galveston and Corpus Christi, Texas; Tampico and Veracruz, Mexico.

Mexico, Valley of, oval basin of interior drainage in Federal Dist. and Mexico state, central Mexico; part of the large central plateau S of Pánuco R. system; 50 mi/80 km by 40 mi/64 km. Once occupied by a system of connected shallow lakes (Chaldo, Texcoco, Xaltocan, Xochimiyco Andzumpango). The basin has been drained by a complex of canals and tunnels to control flodding and facilitate Mexico city urban expansion. Average elev. c.7,500 ft/2,286 m; temperate to subtropical climate. Site of Mexico city, it is one of Mexico's most densely populated areas, with important agr. and industrial activities.

Mexquitic de Carmona (mash-KEE-teek dai kahr-MO-nah), town (1990 pop. 632), San Luis Potosí, N central Mexico, 12 mi/19 km NW of San Luis Potosí, on Mexico Highway 49; 22°16′N 101°07′W. Corn, beans, maguey. Sometimes spelled Mezquitic.

Mexticacán (mesh-tee-kah-KAHN), town (1990 pop. 3,152), Jalisco, central Mexico, 13 mi/21 km SW of Teocaltiche; 21°13′N 102°43′W. Grain, vegetables; livestock.

Meyers Chuck, Alaska: see MYERS CHUCK.

Meyers Lake, village (1990 pop. 493), suburb of Canton, Stark co., E central Ohio, on small Meyers L. (former site of amusement park at streetcar line terminus); 40°49′N 81°25′W.

Meyersdale, borough (1990 pop. 2,518), Somerset co., SW Pa., 14 mi/23 km SSE of Somerset, on Casselman R., at mouth of Flaugherty Creek; 39°48′N 79°01′W. RR junction. Mfg. (wooden prods., fire tankers, apparel); surface coal. Agr. (corn, oats, hay, soybeans, potatoes; livestock; dairying). Laid out 1844, inc. 1871.

Meyronne (MAI-ruhn), village (1991 pop. 56), SW Sask., Canada, on Pinto Creek and 40 mi/64 km W of Assiniboia; 49°40′N 106°51′W. Mixed farming; livestock.

Mezcala River, Mexico: see BALSAS, RÍO.

Mezquital, Mexico: see SAN FRANCISCO DEL MEZQUITAL.

Mezquital del Oro (mes-KEE-tahl del O-ro), town (1990 pop. 1,203), ⊙ Mezquital del Oro municipio, Zacatecas, N central Mexico, 35 mi/56 km S of Tlaltenango de Sánchez Román, an isolated community in the Sierra Madre Occidental. Elev. 3,839 ft/1,170 m. Grain, fruit, vegetables; livestock.

Mezquital River, c.250 mi/402 km long, in W Mexico; rises in Sierra Madre Occidental 45 mi/72 km ENE of Durango; flows S, past Nombre de Dios and Mezquital, into Nayarit, then W, past Tuxpan, to coastal lagoons which drain into the Pacific. Sometimes called Tuxpan R. Its lower course is also called San Pedro R.

Mezquital River, Mexico: see SAN PEDRO RIVER.

Mezquitic (mes-KEE-tik), town (1990 pop. 2,019), Jalisco, W Mexico, on headstream of Bolaños R., near Zacatecas border, and 38 mi/61 km NW of Colotlán. An isolated community in the S Sierra Madre Occidental. Cereals, beans, chili, alfalfa; livestock.

Mezquitic, Mexico: see MEXQUITIC DE CARMONA.

Miacatlán (mee-an-kat-LAHN), town (1990 pop. 6,451), Morelos, central Mexico, 12 mi/19 km SW of Cuernavaca; 18°46′N 99°22′W. Sugar, rice, coffee, wheat, fruit; livestock.

Miahuatlán (mee-ah-waht-LAHN), town (1990 pop. 2,387), Veracruz, E Mexico, in Sierra Madre Oriental, 13 mi/21 km NNE of Xalapa Enríquez. Corn, sugarcane, coffee, tobacco. Also called San José Miahuatlán.

Miahuatlán 1 Mexico: see SAN JOSÉ MIAHUATLÁN. **2** Mexico: see SANTIAGO MIAHUATLÁN.

Miahuatlán de Porfirio Díaz (mee-ah-wat-LAHN dai por-FEE-ree-o DEE-yahs), city (1990 pop. 12,102), in central Oaxaca, Mexico; 16°20′N 96°35′W. Elev. 5,272 ft/1,607 m. On the bank of the Miahuatlán R., 61.1 mi/98.4 km S of Oaxaca de Juárez, on Mexico Hwy. 175. Hot climate. Major production of castor-oil plant along with corn and beans. Significant cattle-raising and livestock industry. Forestry with pine and oak trees, coffee, aguardiente (liquor). The major commercial center for coffee production in the whole region. Coffee is exported through Puerto Angel or Oaxaca de Juárez. Formerly known as Miahuatlán San Andrés.

Miami (mei-A-mee), village, S Man., Canada, 40 mi/64 km S of Portage la Prairie, in Pembina Mts.; 49°22′N 98°15′W. Lumbering; grain elevators; clay and bentonite quarrying.

Miami 1 (mei-AM-ee), county (□ 377 sq mi/976 sq km; 1990 pop. 36,897), N central Ind.; ⊙ Peru; 40°46′N 86°03′W. Intersected by Wabash, Mississinewa, and Eel rivers, and by Deer Creek. Agr. (grain, fruit; livestock, poultry; dairy prods.). Mfg. at Peru. Grissom Air Base in SW. Mississinewa Reservoir and Miami State Recreation Area in SE. Formed 1832. **2** county (□ 590 sq mi/1,528 sq km; 1990 pop. 23,466), E Kansas; ⊙ Paola; 38°33′N 94°49′W. Rolling plain region, bordering E on Mo.; drained by Marais des Cygnes R. and Pottawatomie Creek. Agr. (corn, oats, soybeans, sorghum; hogs, cattle); metal prods., navigation equip. Hillsdale L. Reservoir in NW. Formed 1861. **3** county (□ 407 sq mi/1,054 sq km; 1990 pop. 93,182), W Ohio; ⊙ Troy; 40°03′N 84°14′W. Intersected by Great Miami and Stillwater rivers. In the Till Plains physiographic region. Agr. area (livestock; corn, tobacco, wheat); mfg. (furniture, fixtures, rubber and plastic prods., newspaper, steel pipe and tubes, aluminum die-castings, ordnances), mainly at Piqua, Troy, Tipp City; sand and gravel pits, stone quarries; nurseries. Formed 1807.

Miami 1 city (□ 54 sq mi/140 sq km; 1990 pop. 358,548), ⊙ Dade co., SE Fla., on Biscayne Bay, at the mouth of the Miami R.; 25°46′N 80°12′W. The 2d-largest city in the state, a port of entry, and the transportation and business hub of SE Fla., it is also a popular and famous resort of the E U.S. Tourism remains a major industry, closely followed by mfg. and commerce. Miami has an internatl. airport with more direct connections to Lat. and S. Amer. than any other U.S. city and is the principal port for cruise ships to the Caribbean. The city is also the processing and shipping hub of a large agr. region and an aircraft service center. Mfg. includes clothing, transportation equip., machinery, plastics, and electronics. Other industries are printing and publishing, fishing, and shellfishing. The 1st settlement was made here in the 1870s near the site of Fort Dallas, built in 1836 during the Seminole War. In 1895, Henry M. Flagler took charge of the area; he made Miami a RR terminus in 1896, built a major hotel, dredged the harbor, began to develop a recreational center, and promoted tourism. The city received its greatest impetus during the Fla. land boom of the mid-1920s. Since 1959 the large influx of Cubans to the city has created "Little Havana," an ethnic community of Miami; by the late 1990s about 50% of the city's pop. was Hispanic, heavily of Cuban descent. Since 1980 Miami's position in SE Fla. has eroded as a result of massive suburban growth, spurred by the increase of high-technology industries in the Miami area. Metrorail, the elevated transit system that opened in 1984, has been unsuccessful. Miami is the seat of a number of institutions of higher education, such as Barry Col., St. Thomas Univ. (formerly Biscayne Col.), Fla. Memorial Col., Fla. Internatl. Univ., and Miami-Dade Community Col., the largest 2-year col. in the country. The Univ. of Miami is in nearby Coral Gables. A number of state parks, gardens, and major tourist attractions such as the Seaquarium are in the area. The region of Greater Miami encompasses all of metropolitan Dade co., including Miami, Miami Beach, Coral Gables, Hialeah, and many smaller communities. **2** city (1990 pop. 142), Saline co., central Mo., on Missouri R., and 14 mi/23 km N of Marshall; 39°19′N 93°13′W. Wheat, corn; cattle. Highway bridge. **3** city (1990 pop. 13,142), ⊙ Ottawa co., 70 mi/113 km NE of Tulsa, and 20 mi/32 km WSW of Joplin, Mo., extreme NE Okla., in the foothills of the Ozarks; 36°53′N 94°52′W. Elev. 801 ft/244 m. On the headwaters of Grand L., which provides both electric power and recreation. It is a trade, shipping, and marketing center for a tristate livestock and dairy region where lead and zinc are mined. Mfg. (apparel, fabricated metal prods., electronic materials, leather prods., motor coaches, fiberglass boats; vegetable processing, publishing and printing). Northeast Oklahoma A&M Col. here. Twin Bridges State Park to SE; Spring River State Park to NE.

Miami, town (1990 pop. 2,018), Gila co., E central Ariz., 68 mi/109 km E of Phoenix, and 5 mi/8 km W of Globe; 33°23′N 110°52′W. Mines (copper, gold, silver, lead, molybdenum, perlite) nearby. Mfg. machine parts; cattle, hay. Pinal Mts. to S; Tonto Natl. Forest to S, W, and N; San Carlos Indian Reservation to E. Founded 1908.

Miami, village (1990 pop. 675), ⊙ Roberts co., extreme N Texas, in high plains of the Panhandle, 23 mi/37 km NE of Pampa; 35°41′N 100°38′W. Elev. 2,744 ft/836 m. Cattle, hogs; wheat, milo, corn; gas and oil.

Miami Beach, city (□ 18 sq mi/47 sq km; 1990 pop. 92,639), Dade co., SE Fla., on an isl. bet. Biscayne Bay and the Atlantic Ocean; 25°48′N 80°08′W. It is connected to Miami by four causeways. Miami Beach is a popular year-round resort, famous for its hotel strip, Art Deco dist., and recreational facilities. The city's chief source of income derives from tourism. The glamorous hotel and vacation industry, however, declined in the 1970s and 1980s; a spurt in less-expensive development led to the influx of a younger pop., and the larger and wealthier retired community primarily moved to other developing Fla. (resort) cities. Efforts in the late 1980s and early 1990s have been made for the architectural revival of the Art Deco bldgs. in the S part of the city known as South Beach, a rebuilt beach that had lost much of its sand to erosion. The large Convention Hall complex in Miami Beach has hosted several natl. political conventions, including the Democratic and Republican conventions in 1972. Inc. 1915.

Miami Lakes, planned town (□ 4 sq mi/10.4 sq km; 1990 pop. 12,750), Dade co., SE Fla., 10 mi/16 km NW of

Miami; 25°54′N 80°18′W. Mfg. includes apparel, medical equip., and plastic prods.

Miami Shores, town (□ 3 sq mi/7.8 sq km; 1990 pop.10,084), Dade co., SE Fla., a suburb 7 mi/11.3 km N of Miami, from which it was separated in 1932; 25°52′N 80°10′W. Barry Univ. is here.

Miami Springs, town (□ 2 sq mi/5.2 sq km; 1990 pop. 13,268), Dade co., SE Fla., a residential suburb, 5 mi/ 8 km NW of Miami; 25°49′N 80°17′W. Miami Internatl. Airport is just S of the city. Inc. 1926.

Miamisburg (mei-AM-eez-buhrg), city (1990 pop. 17,834), Montgomery co., SW Ohio, on the Miami R.; 39°38′N 84°16′W. Metal and paper prods. are the leading manufactures. Atomic Energy Commission operates Mound Laboratory (tritium research). A large Native Amer. mound is nearby. Laid out 1818; inc. 1932.

Miamisburg Mound, Montgomery co., W Ohio, just SSW of Miamisburg; largest prehistoric conical mound in Ohio; 39°37′N 84°16′W. Height (68 ft/21 m); c.2 acres/1 ha in extent. Picnic grounds here.

Mianus River, c.25 mi/40 km long, N.Y. and Conn.; rises NE of Armonk, N.Y.; flows NE then S, through Conn., to L.I. Sound at Cos Cob Harbor in Greenwich town.

Mica Mountain, Pima co., SE Ariz., highest peak (8,666 ft/2,641 m.) in Rincon Mts., c.25 mi/40 km E of Tucson, in Saguaro Natl. Monument.

Micanopy (mik-uh-NO-pee), village (□ 1 sq mi/ 2.6 sq km; 1990 pop. 612), Alachua co., N central Fla., 10 mi/16 km S of Gainsville; 29°30′N 82°16′W. Citrus fruit; artist and writer's colony.

Micaville (MEIK-uh-vil), uninc. village, Yancey co., W N.C., 8 mi/12.9 km W of Spruce Pine, near South Toe R. Mica and feldspar mining; stone quarrying. Mfg. (bldg. stone, fabricated metal prods., apparel). Parts of Pisgah Natl. Forest to N and SW.

Micco (MIK-o), town (□ 9 sq mi/23.3 sq km; 1990 pop. 8,757), Brevard co., E central Fla., 15 mi/24 km SSE of Melbourne; 27°52′N 80°31′W.

Miccosukee, Lake (mi-kuh-SOO-kee), Jefferson co., NW Fla., 20 mi/32 km ENE of Tallahassee. Triangular shaped; c.7 mi/11.3 km long, 1 mi/1.6 km–5 mi/8 km wide.

Michael J. Kirwan Lake, reservoir (□ 4 sq mi/ 10.4 sq km), Portage co., NE Ohio, on W. Branch of Mahoning R., 23 mi/37 km ENE of Akron; 41°10′N 81°05′W. Max. capacity of 124,000 acre-ft. Formed by Michael J. Kirwan Dam (77 ft/23 m high), built (1966) by Army Corps of Engineers for flood control; also used for recreation and water supply. West Branch State Park on SE shore.

Michel (MI-chuhl), village, SE B.C., Canada, near Alta. border, in Rocky Mts., on Elk R., and 18 mi/29 km NE of Fernie; 49°43′N 114°49′W. Elev. 3,861 ft/1,177 m. Open-pit coal mining; cattle; timber.

Michelson, Mount, (8,855 ft/2,699 m), NE Alaska, in Romanzof Mts., NE Brooks Range; 69°19′N 144°15′W.

Miches (MEE-ches), town (1993 pop. 7,679), Seibo prov., E Dominican Republic, on the coast, at entrance of Samaná Bay, 17 mi/27 km N of Seibo; 18°55′N 69°00′W. Agr. prods. (cacao, coffee, coconuts, rice, corn, fruit). Until 1936, Jovero or El Jovero.

Michiana (mish-ee-AN-uh), village (1990 pop. 164), Berrien co., extreme SW Mich., at Ind. line, suburb 3 mi/ 4.8 km NE of Michigan City, Ind.; 41°45′N 86°48′W.

Michiana Shores, town (1990 pop. 378), La Porte co., NW Ind., on L. Michigan, 11 mi/18 km NNW of La Porte, adjacent to Mich. state boundary; 41°46′N 86°49′W. Tourist area.

Michigamme, Lake (mish-i-GAM-ee), Marquette and Baraga cos., NW Upper Peninsula, Mich., c.26 mi/ 42 km W of Ishpeming; c.6 mi/9.7 km long, 1.5 mi/ 2.4 km wide; 46°30′N 88°06′W. Resort. Michigamme village is on NW shore. Source of Michigamme R.; Michigamme Reservoir is further downstream on Michigamme R., in Iron co.; 10 mi/16 km long and 2.5 mi/ 4 km wide, formed by Way Dam. Van Ripen State Park at E end.

Michigamme River (mish-i-GAM-ee), c.60 mi/97 km long, SW Upper Peninsula, Mich.; rises in L. Michigamme; flows SSW through Michigamme Reservoir (Way Dam) and Peavy Pond reservoir, both in Iron co., joining Brule R. in SE Iron co. to form Menominee R. Has 2 dams in lower course; 46°29′N 88°04′W.

Michigan, state (□ 96,810 sq mi/250,738 sq km; 1995 est. pop. 9,549,353), N U.S., in the Great Lakes region, admitted to the Union 1837 as the 26th state; ⊙ LANSING. DETROIT is the largest city. Other major cities are GRAND RAPIDS, WARREN, FLINT, and ANN ARBOR. The Lower Peninsula, shaped like a mitten, thrusts N from Ind. and Ohio. On the E it is separated from Ont. (Canada) by L. Erie and L. Huron, and by the Detroit R. and the St. Clair R., which together link the 2 Great Lakes; on the W it is separated from Wis. by L. Michigan. Across L. Michigan, NE of Wis., the Upper Peninsula stretches E, separating L. Michigan from L. Superior, and itself separated from Ont. only by the narrow St. Marys R.; 44°43′N 85°32′W. The Upper Peninsula is separated from the Lower Peninsula by the Straits of Mackinac; a bridge connecting the 2 peninsulas was opened in 1957 and has spurred the development of the Upper Peninsula. The E portion of the Upper Peninsula has swampy flats and limestone hills on the L. Michigan shore, while sandstone ridges rise abruptly from the rough waters on L. Superior; in the W the land rises to forested mts., rich in copper and iron. The whole of the Upper Peninsula is N woods country, with what has been described as "ten months of winter and two months of poor sledding." The abundance of furred animals and the trees early attracted fur traders and lumbermen. The animals were trapped out, forests were aggressively logged; copper and iron ore mining declined. Hunting (deer, bears, small game; fish). Modern reforestation efforts have aided in second growth. The Lower Peninsula has different topography, flora, and fauna. Its forests were also cut over in the lumber boom of the late 19th cent., when busy sawmills made Mich. the temporary leader in lumber production. The soil of these cut-over lands, unlike the productive earth in other areas of the Lower Peninsula, proved generally unsuitable for agr., and reforestation has been undertaken. Mineral mining (gypsum, sandstone, limestone, salt, cement, sand, and gravel). Warm climate, due to the surrounding lakes, allow for a long growing season. However, they also contribute to the heavy snowfall, esp. on the windward (E) side of L. Michigan, and on Keweenaw Peninsula on L. Supreme. Agr. is important ot the state's economy, esp. in the S cos. and Michigan's noted fruit belt lining the shore of L. Michigan. Crops account for almost ½ of farm income; corn is the chief crop, followed by hay, soybeans, and apples; noted for its cherries. Livestock raising and dairying are also important. Mfg. accounts for 30% of the state's economic production, more than twice as much as any other sector. The manufacture of transportation equip. is by far the state's chief industry, and Detroit, Dearborn, Flint, Pontiac, and Lansing are historically centers for motor vehicle mfg. Mich. is most readily identified with the automobile industry, and its mass-production methods were the core of the early 20th-cent. industrial revolution. Other industries produce nonelectrical machinery, fabricated metal prods., primary metals, chemicals, and food prods. Industrial centers include Saginaw, Bay City, Muskegon, and Jackson. The chemical industry in Midland is one of the nation's largest; Kalamazoo is an important paper-mfg. and pharmaceuticals center; Grand Rapids is noted for its furniture, and Battle Creek for its breakfast cereals. Mich.'s lack of mfg. diversity makes it particularly susceptible to the fluctuations of the natl. economy. The state has attempted in recent years to stabilize its economy by attracting high-technology industry and developing the service sector. Although mining contributes less to income in the state than either agr. or mfg., Mich. in 1989 was the nation's 4th leading state in nonfuel mineral production. The chief minerals produced are iron ore, cement, sand, and gravel. Mich. is a leading producer of peat, bromine, calcium-magnesium

chloride, gypsum, and magnesium compounds. Upper Peninsula is generally pre-Cambrian, an extension of the Canadian Shield. Many minerals such as copper and iron ore have been mined, but the industry has diminished. Economies of depleted mining areas have been partially sustained by tourism and to lesser extent by forestry and fishing. Michigan's abundant natural beauty makes it a popular destination for tourists. Much of lower Michigan (Lower Peninsula) is composed of series of moraines (formed during glaciation) and dune ridges (formed since glaciation) causing the formation of numerous lakes, the irregular flow of rivers, and marshland. Large sand dunes on L. Michigan E shore, (Berrien, Mason, Leelanau and other cos.), sand blocks out flowing rivers, forming small lakes behind dunes. The Ojibwa, the Ottawa, the Potawatomi, and other Algonquin-speaking Native Amer. groups were living in Mich. when the Fr. explorer Étienne Brulé landed at the narrows of Sault Ste. Marie in 1618, probably the first Eur. man to have reached present Mich. Later, Fr. explorers, traders, and missionaries came, including Jean Nicolet, who was searching for the NW Passage; Jacques Marquette, who founded a mission in the Mackinac region; and the empire builder, Robert Cavelier, sieur de La Salle, who came on the *Griffon*, the first ship to sail the Great Lakes. Fr. posts were scattered along the lakes and the rivers, and Mackinac Isl. (in the Straits of Mackinac) became a center of the fur trade. Fort Pontchartrain, later Detroit, was founded in 1701 by Antoine de la Mothe Cadillac. The vast region was weakly held by France until lost to Great Britain in the last conflict (1754–1763) of the Fr. and Indian Wars. The Native Americans of Mich., who had lived in peace with the French, resented the coming of the British, who were the allies of the much-hated Iroquois tribes. Under Pontiac they revolted against the Br. occupation. The rebellion, which began in 1763, was short-lived, ending in 1766, and the Native Americans subsequently supported the British during the Amer. Revolution. Native Amer. resistance to U.S. control was effectively ended at the Battle of Fallen Timbers in 1794 with the victory of Gen. Anthony Wayne. Despite provisions of the Treaty of Paris which ended the Amer. Revolution (1783), the British held stubbornly to Detroit and Mackinac until 1796. After passage of the NW Ordinance in 1787, Mich. became part of the NORTHWEST TERRITORY. However, even after the NW Territory was broken up and Detroit was made (1805) capital of Mich. Territory, Br. agents still maintained great influence over the Native Americans, who fought on the Br. side in the War of 1812. In that war Mackinac and Detroit fell almost immediately to the British as a result of the ineffective control of U.S. Gen. William Hull and his troops. Mich. remained in Br. hands through most of the war until Gen. William Henry Harrison in the battle of Thames and Oliver Hazard Perry in the battle of L. Erie restored U.S. control. After peace came, pioneers moved into Mich. The policy of pushing Native Americans W and opening the lands for settlement was largely due to the efforts of Gen. Lewis Cass, who was governor of Mich. Territory (1813–1831) and later a U.S. senator. Steamboat navigation on the Great Lakes and sale of public lands in Detroit both began in 1818, and the Erie Canal was opened in 1825. Farmers came to the Mich. fields, and the first sawmills were built along the rivers. The move toward statehood was slowed by the desire of Ohio and Ind. to absorb parts of present S Mich. and by the opposition of S states to the admission of another free state. The Mich. electorate organized a govt. without U.S. sanction and in 1836 operated as a state, although outside the Union. To resolve the boundary dispute Congress proposed that the Toledo strip be ceded to Ohio and Ind. with compensation to Mich. of land in the Upper Peninsula. Though the Mich. electorate rejected the offer, a group of Democratic leaders accepted it, and by their acceptance Mich. became a state in 1837. (The admission of Ark. as a slaveholding state offset that of Mich. as a free state.) Detroit served as the capital until 1847, when it was replaced by Lansing. After statehood, Mich. promptly adopted a program of internal improvement through the building of RRs, roads, and canals, including the Soo Locks Ship Canal at Sault Ste. Marie. At the same time lumbering was expanding, and the pop. grew as Ger., Irish, and Du. immigrants arrived. In 1854 the Republican party was organized at Jackson (Mich.). During the Civil War, Mich. fought on the side of the Union, contributing 90,000 troops to the cause. After the war the state remained firmly Republican until 1882. Then Mich. farmers, moved by the same financial difficulties and outrage at high transportation and storage rates that aroused other Western farmers, supported movements advocating agrarian interests, such as the Granger movement and the Greenback party. The farmers joined with the growing numbers of workers in the mines and lumber camps to elect a Greenback-Democratic governor in 1882 and succeeded in getting legislation passed for agrarian improvement and public welfare. Reforms influenced by the labor movement were the creation of a state board of labor (1883), a law enforcing a 10-hr day (1885), and a moderate child-labor law (1887). The lumbering business, with its yield of wealth to the timber barons, declined to virtually nothing. Some of the loggers joined the ranks of industrial workers, which were further swelled by many Pol. and Nor. immigrants. With the invention of the automobile and the construction of automotive plants, industry in Mich. was radically altered. Henry Ford established the Ford Motor Co. in 1903 and introduced conveyor-belt assembly lines in 1918. General Motors and the Chrysler Corp. were established shortly after Ford. Along with the development of mass-production methods came the growth of the labor movement. In the 1930s, when the automobile industry was well established in the state, labor unions struggled for recognition. The conflict bet. labor and the automotive industry, which continued into the 1940s, included sit-down strikes and was sometimes violent. Walter Reuther, a pioneer of the labor movement, was elected president of the United Auto Workers (UAW) in 1946. During World War II, Mich. produced large numbers of tanks, airplanes, and other war materiel. Industrial production again expanded after the Korean War broke out in 1950. In the early 1960s, however, economic growth lagged and unemployment became a problem in the state. The St. Lawrence Seaway opened in 1959 and increased export trade by bringing many ocean-going vessels to the port of Detroit. Detroit was shaken by severe race riots in 1967 that left 43 persons dead and many injured, in addition to $200 million in damage. In the wake of the rioting, programs were undertaken to improve housing facilities and job opportunities in the city, but these failed as the city suffered massive outmigration. While Detroit deteriorated, the suburbs experienced dramatic growth, spreading throughout SE Mich. Resistance to busing was a major political issue in the state in the early 1970s. The state's dependence on the auto industry was exhibited during the recession of the early 1980s, when car sales slumped, many factories closed, and Michigan's unemployment rose. The federal govt. helped bail out the Chrysler Corp. in 1979, authorizing $1.5 billion in loan guarantees. After a brief period of recovery through limited diversification of the state economy, Mich. was again esp. hard hit by natl. recession and continuing foreign competition in the early 1990s, as General Motors layed off 35,000 employees (a large percentage in Mich.) in 1991. The N Mich. wilds, numerous inland lakes, and some 3,000 mi/4,828 km of shoreline, combined with a pleasantly cool summer climate, have long attracted vacationers. In the winter Michigan's snow-covered hills bring skiers from all over the Midwest. Places of interest in the state include Greenfield Village, a re-creation of a 19th-cent. U.S. village, and the Henry Ford Mus., both at Dearborn; Pictured Rocks and Sleeping Bear Dunes natl. lake shores; and Isle Royale Natl. Park. Major isls. include, Isle Royale (L. Superior), Beaver N and S, Manitou N and S, Fox Isls. (N L. Michigan), Bois Blanc, Drummond, Mackinac (L. Huron), Sugar and Neebish (St. Marys R.). The state normally ranks among the top 10 states annually in tourism expenditures. Michigan's constitution, adopted in 1963, provides for an elected governor as the state's chief executive. The governor serves for a term of 4 years and may succeed himself in the office. The state legislature is made up of a senate and house of representatives. The senate has 38 members elected for terms of 4 years and the house of representatives has 110 members elected for 2-year terms. Mich. sends 16 representatives and 2 senators to the U.S. Congress and has 18 electoral votes in presidential elections. John Engler, a Republican, was elected governor in 1990. Educational institutions include the Univ. of Mich., at Ann Arbor; Mich. State Univ., at East Lansing; the Univ. of Detroit Mercy and Wayne State Univ., at Detroit; Western Mich. Univ. and Kalamazoo Col., at Kalamazoo; Eastern Mich. Univ., at Ypsilanti; Northern Mich. Univ., at Marquette; and many other private and state cols. Many of the small-lakes dists. outside Detroit (Oakland co.) and other parts of S Mich., and S part of L. Michigan shore, once resorts, have given over to permanent and seasonal residences. Mich. has 83 cos.: ALCONA, ALGER, ALLEGAN, ALPENA, ANTRIM, ARENAC, BARAGA, BARRY, BAY, BENZIE, BERRIEN, BRANCH, CALHOUN, CASS, CHARLEVOIX, CHEBOYGAN, CHIPPEWA, CLARE, CLINTON, CRAWFORD, DELTA, DICKINSON, EATON, EMMET, GENESEE, GLADWIN, GOGEBIC, GRAND TRAVERSE, GRATIOT, HILLSDALE, HOUGHTON, HURON, INGHAM, IONIA, IOSCO, IRON, ISABELLA, JACKSON, KALAMAZOO, KALKASKA, KENT, KEWEENAW, LAKE, LAPEER, LEELANAU, LENAWEE, LIVINGSTON, LUCE, MACKINAC, MACOMB, MANISTEE, MARQUETTE, MASON, MECOSTA, MENOMINEE, MIDLAND, MISSAUKEE, MONROE, MONTCALM, MONTMORENCY, MUSKEGON, NEWAYGO, OAKLAND, OCEANA, OGEMAW, ONTONAGON, OSCEOLA, OSCODA, OTSEGO, OTTAWA, PRESQUE ISLE, ROSCOMMON, SAGINAW, SAINT CLAIR, SAINT JOSEPH, SANILAC, SCHOOLCRAFT, SHIAWASSEE, TUSCOLA, VAN BUREN, WASHTENAW, WAYNE, WEXFORD.

Michigan, village (1990 pop. 413), Nelson co., E central N.Dak.,10 mi/16 km E of Lakota; 48°01′N 98°07′W. Livestock, poultry; dairy prods.; wheat. Also called Michigan City.

Michigan Center, village (1990 pop. 4,863) Jackson co., S Mich., 4 mi/6.4 km SE of Jackson, on small Michigan Center L.; 42°13′N 84°19′W.

Michigan City, city (1990 pop. 33,822), La Porte co., NW Ind., on L. Michigan; 41°43′N 86°53′W. An area with sand-dune beaches and a state park, Michigan City has industries that produce goods such as machinery, consumer articles, alumina powder, kitchen equip., concrete anchoring systems, wire prods., transportation equip., magnetic steel laminates, chemicals, apparel, and cast-iron boilers. Indiana State Prison is located here, as is the Lakeside Correctional Center. Laid out 1832. Inc. 1836.

Michigan, Lake (□ 22,178 sq mi/57,441 sq km), bordered by Mich., Ind., Ill., and Wis.; 3d-largest of the Great Lakes and the only one entirely within the U.S.; 307 mi/494 km long and 30 mi/48 km–120 mi/193 km wide. Its surface is 581 ft/177 m above sea level, and the lake is 923 ft/281 m deep. The Straits of Mackinac, its only natural outlet, connects the lake with L. Huron to the northeast; the Illinois Waterway links L. Michigan with the Mississippi R. and the Gulf of Mexico. Many isls. are found in the N part of the lake; the N shorelines are indented, with Green Bay and Grand Traverse Bay the largest bays. The S part of L. Michigan has a regular shoreline, necessitating the bldg. of artificial harbors such as the Calumet Harbor, NE Ill. The Muskegon, Grand, Kalamazoo, Fox, and Menominee are the chief rivers flowing into L. Michigan; the lake's current tends to clog the mouths of the rivers with sand. The Chicago R. formerly flowed into the lake, but its course was reversed in 1900. Sand dunes border the E and S shores of the lake; Indiana Dunes Natl. Lakeshore is here. The forested N region of L. Michigan is generally sparsely populated. The S portion, located near the heart of the Midwest, is industrially important; the Gary-Chicago-Milwaukee urbanized area extends along the SW shore. Michigan City, Gary, Chicago, Racine, Milwaukee, and Escanaba are the major lakeside cities. Such urban and industrial concentration has led to growing pollution problems associated with the lake's waters. Prevailing westerly winds tempered by the lake give the E shore a moderate climate, making it a rich fruit belt and popular resort area. L. Michigan was discovered in 1634 by the Fr. explorer Jean Nicolet and was later explored by the Fr. traders Marquette and Joliet. Fr. missionary and trade centers thrived there by the late 1600s. As part of the bitterly contested Northwest territory, the area passed to England in 1763 and later to the U.S. in 1796. The area was isolated until the 1830s, when improvements in transportation brought settlers there. Ore, coal, and limestone are the main items moved on the lake. The Saint Lawrence Seaway has opened L. Michigan to internatl. trade. The S part of the lake does not freeze over in the winter, but storms and ice halt interlake movement from Dec. to April.

Michigantown, town (1990 pop. 472), Clinton co., central Ind., 8 mi/12.9 km ENE of Frankfort; 40°20′N 86°23′W. Agr. area. Laid out 1830.

Michikamau Lake (mi-chi-KAH-mo), SW Lab., Canada, near Quebec border; 65 mi/105 km long, 30 mi/48 km wide, 53°50′N 63°22′W–51°30′N 64°48′W. Elev. 1,650 ft/503 m. It is largest body of water in region of numerous small lakes; drained by Hamilton R.

Michilimackinac, Mich.: see MACKINAC, region.

Michipicoten Harbour (mi-chi-pi-KO-tuhn), village, central Ont., Canada, on Michipicoten Bay of L. Superior, at mouth of Michipicoten R., 110 mi/177 km NNW of Sault Ste. Marie. Iron and pulp shipping port; gold, iron mining.

Michipicoten Island, central Ont., Canada, in NE part of L. Superior, at entrance of Michipicoten Bay, 110 mi/177 km NW of Sault Ste. Marie; 17 mi/27 km long, 3 mi/5 km–6 mi/10 km wide. Rises to 1,598 ft/487 m (W).

Michipicoten River, 70 mi/113 km long, central Ont., Canada; issues from L. Wabatongushi, 120 mi/193 km N of Sault Ste. Marie; flows generally SW, through Dog and Manitowick lakes, to Michipicoten Bay of L. Superior, 3 mi/5 km SE of Michipicoten Harbour.

Michoacán (mee-cho-an-KAHN) or **Michoacán de Ocampo**, state (□ 23,202 sq mi/60,093 sq km; 1990 pop. 3,548,199), S Mexico; ⊙ MORELIA; 17°55′N 100°44′W. Dominated by the Transverse Volcanic Axis of central Mexico, Michoacán extends from the Pacific Ocean northeastward into the central plateau. The Lerma R. and L. Chapala form part of its N boundary with the state of Jalisco; the Río Balsas constitutes the S border with Guerrero. The climate and soil variations caused by topography and differences in elev. make Michoacán a diverse agr. state, producing both temperate and tropical cereals, fruits, and vegetables. Michoacán's forests yield fine cabinet woods and dyewoods. Mining is a leading industry; gold and silver are most important, but iron, coal, and zinc are also major minerals. Industrial development is modest, centering around iron and steel production at Lázaro Cárdienas. Michoacán ships its prods. from the cities of Morelia, Uruapan, and Lázaro Cárdenas. Federally sponsored irrigation and hydroelectric power projects, esp. the Infiernillo Dam on Río Balsas, have aimed at developing Michoacán's Pacific coastal region. L. Pátzcuaro (where UNESCO and the OAS have a training center for Latin Amer. rural teachers) and the Parícutin volcano attract many tourists. Most of the state's inhabitants are native Tarascans. Michoacán played a leading role in Mexico's revolution against Spain and in subsequent struggles.

Micoud (mee-KOO), village (1991 pop. 3,251), SE St. Lucia, minor port 14 mi/23 km SE of Castries; 13°49′N 60°56′W. Agr. (bananas, other tropical fruit); fishing.

Micro, village (1990 pop. 417), Johnston co., central N.C.,

10 mi/16 km NE of Smithfield; 35°33′N 78°12′W. Tobacco, cotton, peanuts, grain; livestock, poultry.

Midale, town (1991 pop. 497), SE Sask., Canada, 27 mi/43 km SE of Weyburn; 49°24′N 103°24′W. Mixed farming.

Mid-Canada Line, Canada: see DEW LINE.

Middle, township (1990 pop. 14,771), Cape May co., S N.J., 20 mi/32 km N of Cape May; 39°05′N 74°50′W. Inc. 1798.

Middle Bass Island, Ohio: see BASS ISLANDS.

Middle Brewster Island, Mass.: see BREWSTER ISLANDS.

Middle Caicos or **Grand Caicos**, island (□ 48 sq mi/124 sq km; 1990 pop. 272), Turks and Caicos Isls., crown colony of Great Britain, West Indies, just W of East Caicos; 25 mi/40 km long, 12 mi/19 km wide; 21°50′N 71°45′W. Largest and least developed isl. of the archipelago. Conch Bar caves, with underground salt lakes, are open to visitors. Small airfield.

Middle Chain of Lakes, 19 small natural lakes and several lesser bodies of water running N-S in nearly straight line c.20 mi/32 km long, mainly in Martin co., S Minn., extends into Emmet co., N Iowa. Located in relatively lake-free agr. prairie. From Iowa L. on S, on Iowa-Minn. state line, the lakes drain N through South Silver, North Silver, Wilmert, Mud, Aires, Amber, Hall, Budd, Sisseton, and George lakes (latter 4 in Fairmont city), connected by Center Creek; Buffalo, Canright and Kiester lakes drain S to Elm Creek; Charlotte, High, and Martin lakes drain N to Elm Creek; Murphy L. drains S into Elm Creek; Perch L. drains N, source of Perch Creek. Lake chain follows course of retreating Pleistocene glacier. East Chain of Lakes, 5 mi/8 km to E, c.15 mi/24 km long N-S, includes Goose and Burt Lakes, Kossuth co. (Iowa), Sway L. (on Iowa-Minn. border), East Chain L. (2 mi/3.2 km long), Sager, Rose, Little Hall and Imogene lakes (Martin co., Minn.).

Middle Creek, Ky.: see PRESTONSBURG.

Middle Fabius River, Mo.: see FABIUS RIVER.

Middle Fork or **Middle Fork of Wilamette River**, river, c.115 mi/185 km long, W Oregon; formed by confluence of several small branches in Cascade Range near Emigrant Pass (5,000 ft/1,524 m); flows NW through Hills Creek Reservoir, past Oakridge, through Lookout Point Reservoir; joins Coast Fork 3 mi/4.8 km SE of Eugene to form Willamette R. About 20 mi/32 km SE of Eugene is Lookout Point Dam (250 ft/76 m high, 3,106 ft/947 m long; begun 1947), a unit of Willamette R. flood-control plan; also called Meridian Dam.

Middle Granville, village (1990 pop. 600), Washington co., E N.Y., near Vt. line, 20 mi/32 km ENE of Glens Falls; 43°26′N 73°17′W. In slate-quarrying area.

Middle Grove, uninc. community, Monroe co., NE central Mo., 15 mi/24 km SW of Paris.

Middle Haddam, Conn.: see EAST HAMPTON.

Middle Island, S Ont., Canada, tiny isl. in L. Erie just S of Pelee Isl., near Ohio boundary; southernmost point of Canada (41°41′N).

Middle Island, village, W St. Kitts, West Indies, 7 mi/11.3 km NW of Basseterre. Has St. Thomas Church and tomb of Sir Thomas Warner, founder of the Br. colony, who d. in 1648.

Middle Island Creek, c.85 mi/137 km long, NW W.Va.; rises in SE Doddridge co., 15 mi/24 km SW of Clarksburg; flows NW past West Union and Middlebourne, and SSW to Ohio R., 1 mi/1.6 km NW of St. Marys.

Middle Loup River, Nebr.: see LOUP RIVER.

Middle Nodaway River, Iowa: see NODAWAY RIVER.

Middle Pease River, Texas: see PEASE RIVER.

Middle Point, village (1990 pop. 639), Van Wert co., W Ohio, 7 mi/11 km E of Van Wert, and on Little Auglaize R., in agr. area; 40°51′N 84°26′W.

Middle Raccoon River, Iowa: see RACCOON RIVER.

Middle River, uninc. town (1990 pop. 24,616), Baltimore co., N Md.; 39°20′N 76°26′W. An industrial and growing residential suburb of Baltimore. Martin Airport, named for John Martin, founder of the Martin-Marieta Company. The river for which the town is named is an inlet bet. the Gunpowder and Back R. estuaries.

Middle River, village (1990 pop. 285), Marshall co., NW Minn., on Middle R., and 22 mi/35 km N of Thief R.; 48°26′N 96°09′W. Falls. Wheat, sugar beets, potatoes, beans, sunflowers; mfg. (flour milling, transportation equip.). Thief L. Wildlife Area to NE; large Mud L., and Agassiz Natl. Wildlife Refuge to SE.

Middle River 1 105 mi/169 km long, S central Iowa; rises in SW Guthrie co.; flows SE and ENE to Des Moines R. 13 mi/21 km SE of Des Moines. **2** 70 mi/113 km long, Minn.; rises in marshy area of E central Marshall co., NW Minn., just E of village at Middle R.; 48°24′N 96°00′W; flows W past Newfolden and Argyle, to Snake R. 12 mi/19 km N of Alvarado and 6 mi/9.7 km SE of its confluence with Red R. **3** c.60 mi/97 km long, NW Va.; rises in S Augusta co.; flows NE (W and N of Staunton) to North R., 2 mi/3.2 km SW of Port Republic.

Middle Saranac Lake, N.Y.: see SARANAC LAKES.

Middle Teton, Wyo.: see GRAND TETON NATIONAL PARK.

Middle Valley, town (1990 pop. 3,150), Hamilton co., SE Tenn., 12 mi/19 km NNE of Chattanooga.

Middle Village, a residential sect. of Queens borough of N.Y. city, SE N.Y.; 40°43′N 73°54′W. Mfg. (metal and plate fabrication, airplane parts, furniture, apparel).

Middle West Side, N.Y.: see CLINTON.

Middle Yuba River, Calif.: see YUBA RIVER.

Middleboro, town (1990 pop. 17,867), Plymouth co., SE Mass.; 41°53′N 70°53′W. Cranberry-processing is a major industry in the town; other mfg. (fire apparatus, chemicals, and shoes). The town was destroyed by Native Americans in King Philip's War but later rebuilt. Of interest are a Native Amer. site believed to date from 2500 B.C.; restored Revolutionary industries, such as a slitting mill and an iron foundry. The Tom Thumb historical mus. The name is also spelled Middleborough. Inc. 1669.

Middleboro, Pa.: see MCKEAN.

Middlebourne (MID-uhl-buhrn), town (1990 pop. 922), ⊙ Tyler co., NW W.Va., 37 mi/60 km NE of Parkersburg, on Middle Isl. Creek. Agr. (corn); cattle; dairying. Gas, oil region. Mfg. (secondary aluminum processing, wooden mouldings). Jug and Conaway Run Wildlife Management Area to E; Lewis Wetzel Wildlife Management Area to E.

Middleburg, town (1990 pop. 549), Loudoun co., N Va., 17 mi/27 km N of Warrenton, near Little R.; 38°58′N 77°44′W. Mfg. (lumber, wine, leather goods; printing and publishing); agr. (dairying; livestock; grain, apples, grapes, soybeans). Center of country-estate area known for fox hunting, horse breeding.

Middleburg 1 village (□ 1 sq mi/2.6 sq km; 1990 pop. 1,436), Schoharie co., E central N.Y., on Schoharie Creek, and 30 mi/48 km WSW of Albany; 42°36′N 74°19′W. Trade center for dairying and farming area. Settled 1712, inc. 1881. **2** village (1990 pop. 131), Vance co., N N.C., 6 mi/9.7 km NE of Henderson; 36°23′N 78°19′W. Grain, tobacco, soybeans; chickens, livestock. Mfg. (lumber). Large S arm of Kerr reservoir to NW.

Middleburg, borough (1990 pop. 1,422), ⊙ Snyder co., central Pa., 15 mi/24 km WSW of Sunbury, on Middle Creek; 40°47′N 77°02′W. Agr. area (corn, hay, apples; dairying); mfg. (concrete prods., cutting tools, sportswear, food prods.). Parts of Bald Eagle State Forest to S and NW. Settled c.1760, laid out 1800, inc. 1856.

Middleburg Heights, city (1990 pop. 14,702), Cuyahoga co., N Ohio, a SW suburb of Cleveland; 41°22′N 81°49′W.

Middlebury 1 town (1990 pop. 6,145), New Haven co., SW Conn., just W of Waterbury; 41°31′N 73°07′W. In summer resort area; mfg. (watches, clocks). Corporate hqs. Quassapaug Pond just W. Settled in early 18th cent., inc. 1807. **2** town (1990 pop. 2,004), Elkhart co., N Ind., on small Little Elkhart R., and 9 mi/14.5 km NE of Goshen; 41°40′N 85°43′W. In agr. area; livestock. Mfg. (plastics., recreational vehicles, modular and prefabricated homes, furniture, wood prods., transportation equip., window blinds, wire harnesses, store display fixtures, and agr. machinery; food processing). Laid out 1835. **3** town (1990 pop. 8,034), including Middlebury village, ⊙ Addison co., W Vt., on Otter Creek, and 32 mi/51 km S of Burlington; 44°00′N 73°07′W. Agr. (poultry; dairy prods., fruit); mfg. (wood prods., electronic equip.). Resort area; winter sports at Middlebury Col. Snow Bowl. Seat of Middlebury Col., and art mus. (1829). Partly in Green Mt. Natl. Forest. Chartered 1761; 1st settled 1773; permanently settled 1783.

Middlefield 1 industrial town (1990 pop. 3,925), Middlesex co., S Conn., bet. Middletown and Meriden; 41°31′N 72°42′W. Mfg. (ordnances, transportation equip., tools, cement prods., thermometers, fabricated metals, fixtures, consumer goods); agr. (apples, peaches). Includes Rockfall village. State park here. Dinosaur tracks found here now in Peabody Mus. of Yale Univ. Settled c.1700, set off from Middletown 1866. **2** town (1990 pop. 392), Hampshire co., W Mass., 14 mi/23 km ESE of Pittsfield; 42°21′N 73°01′W.

Middlefield, village (1990 pop. 1,898), Geauga co., NE Ohio, 30 mi/48 km E of Cleveland; 41°27′N 81°04′W. In agr. area; rubber, plastic and metal prods., lumber, food prods.

Middleport 1 village (1990 pop. 1,876), Niagara co., W N.Y., on the Barge Canal, and 30 mi/48 km NNE of Buffalo; 43°12′N 78°28′W. Mfg. (water- and ground-water-metering equip., agr. chemicals, machinery). Grew after completion of Erie Canal (1825). Settled 1812, inc. 1859. **2** village (1990 pop. 2,725), Meigs co., SE Ohio, on Ohio R., and 18 mi/29 km NNE of Gallipolis; 38°59′N 82°03′W. Coal mines, gas and oil wells. RR shops; mfg. of food prods., cement blocks.

Middleport, borough (1990 pop. 520), Schuylkill co., E central Pa., 8 mi/12.9 km ENE of Pottsville, on Schuylkill R.; 40°43′N 76°05′W. Anthracite coal. Locust State Park and part of Weiser State Forest to N.

Middlesboro, city (1990 pop. 11,328), Bell co., S Ky., c.105 mi/169 km SE of Lexington, on Yellow R., in the Cumberland Mts., 2 mi/3.2 km W of the point where Ky., Tenn., and Va. meet; 36°36′N 83°43′W. Elev. 1,138 ft/347 m. It is a coal-mining center, with the mfg. (plastic pipe, elastic webbing, apparel; printing and publishing, meat processing, leather tanning, coal processing). Said to be the only U.S. city built within a meteor crater. Airport to NW. Southeast Community Col.—Middlesboro Campus. Coal House and Mus. Cumberland Gap Tunnel Project (completed 1996). Cumberland Gap Natl. Historical Park to E; Ky. Ridge State Forest to NW; Pine Mt. State Resort Park to N. Est. 1889.

Middlesex, county (□ 1,420 sq mi/3,678 sq km; 1991 pop. 372,274), S Ont., Canada, on Thames R.; ⊙ London; 43°00′N 81°30′W.

Middlesex, county (1991 pop. 991,929), central Jamaica, bet. Cornwall (W) and Surrey cos. (E); 17°42′N 77°33′W–18°28′N 76°54′W. Consists of St. Catherine, St. Mary, Clarendon, St. Ann, and Manchester parishes. Set up 1758; no longer has administrative functions.

Middlesex 1 county (□ 439 sq mi/1,137 sq km; 1990 pop. 143,196), S Conn., on L.I. Sound, bisected by Connecticut R.; ⊙ Middletown; 41°25′N 72°31′W. Agr. (tobacco, potatoes, produce, fruit; dairy prods., poultry); mfg. (tools, hardware, electrical equip., boats, textiles, metal prods., consumer goods, piano parts, paper and fiber prods., clothing, transportation equip., agr. machinery, chemicals, asbestos, cigars); fishing; sandstone and feldspar quarries. Resorts on shore. Includes Pocotopaug L., several state parks and forests. Drained by Connecticut (E boundary) Hammonasset (W boundary), Salmon, and Mattabesset rivers. Constituted 1785. Former site of Haddam Neck nuclear power plant, built in the mid-1960s on the banks of the Connecticut R., closed in 1996 for safety reasons. Site heavily contaminated. **2** county (□ 847 sq mi/2,194 sq km; 1990 pop. 1,398,468), NE Mass., bordering N on N.H.; ⊙ Cambridge and Lowell; 42°29′N 71°23′W. Intersected by Merrimack and Nashua rivers, and drained by Charles, Concord, Sudbury, and Assabet rivers, which furnish water power. Industrial towns include Lowell, Cambridge, Somerville, Framingham, Everett, Malden, Waltham. Produces shoes, textiles, machinery and other metal prods., electronic and computer components, watches, food and wood prods., rubber goods, and agr. produce. Formed 1643. **3** county (□ 322 sq mi/834 sq km; 1990 pop. 671,780), E N.J., bounded E by

Raritan Bay and Arthur Kill; ⊙ New Brunswick; 40°26′N 74°24′W. Industrial, agr., rapidly suburbanizing residential area, with extensive clay deposits and allied industries. Oil refineries, ore smelters and refineries; shipyards, drydocks on Raritan Bay. Diversified mfg. (chemicals, plastics, and machinery prods.); agr. (produce, soybeans, fruit; poultry). Drained by Raritan R. (navigable) and Millstone and South rivers. Formed 1675. **4** county (□ 210 sq mi/544 sq km; 1990 pop. 8,653), E Va.; ⊙ Saluda; 37°36′N 76°30′W. In Tidewater region; bounded N by Rappahannock R., S by short Dragon Run and Piankatank R., E by Chesapeake Bay. Agr. (hay, barley, wheat, soybeans, tobacco, corn, melons; cattle, hogs, poultry); timber (pine, oak); fish, oysters. Resort area. Formed 1673.

Middlesex 1 town (1990 pop. 730), Nash co., NE central N.C., 25 mi/40 km E of Raleigh; 35°47′N 78°12′W. Tobacco, cotton, peanuts, grain; poultry, livestock. Mfg. (aerospace hose lines, transportation equip., apparel, roof and floor trusses). **2** town (1990 pop. 1,514), Washington co., central Vt., on Winooski R., just NW of Montpelier; 44°18′N 72°38′W.

Middlesex, resort village (1990 pop. 400), Yates co., W central N.Y., near Canandaigua L., 19 mi/31 km SW of Geneva; 42°43′N 77°17′W. In grape-growing region.

Middlesex, borough (1990 pop. 13,055), Middlesex co., N central N.J. Diversified mfg. includes adhesives, plastics, and chemicals. Inc. 1913.

Middleton, city (1990 pop. 13,289), Dane co., S Wis., on W end of L. Mendota, suburb, 7 mi/11.3 km W of Madison; 43°06′N 89°30′W. In farming and dairying area; mfg. (brewery, furniture, textiles, transportation equip., medical instruments, household furnishings; food and beverage processing, genetic engineering). Morey Airport to NW. Governor Dodge State Park to NE. Inc. 1905.

Middleton, town (1991 pop. 1,819), W N.S., Canada, on Annapolis R., and 25 mi/40 km ENE of Annapolis Royal; 44°57′N 65°40′W. Furniture mfg., lumbering; agr. market in fruitgrowing area.

Middleton 1 town, Elbert co., NE Ga., 6 mi/9.7 km ESE of Elberton, near Savannah R.; 32°05′N 82°46′W. **2** town (1990 pop. 1,851), Canyon co., SW Idaho, 5 mi/8 km NE of Caldwell, and on Boise R.; 43°43′N 116°37′W. In fruit and grain area. **3** town (1990 pop. 4,921), Essex co., NE Mass., on Ipswich R., and 8 mi/12.9 km NW of Salem; 42°36′N 71°01′W. Resort; mfg. (chemicals). State forest nearby. Settled 1659, organized 1728. **4** town (1990 pop. 1,183), Strafford co., SE N.H., 12 mi/19 km NNW of Rochester; 43°28′N 71°04′W. Mfg. (lumber); timber; agr. (produce, vegetables; cattle; dairying). Sunrise L. in S. **5** town (1990 pop. 536), Hardeman co., SW Tenn., 40 mi/64 km S of Jackson; 35°03′N 88°53′W. Cotton, corn; livestock.

Middleton Island, S Alaska, in Gulf of Alaska, 80 mi/129 km SSW of Cordova; 5 mi/8 km long; 59°26′N 146°20′W.

Middletown 1 industrial city (1990 pop. 42,762), Middlesex co., central Conn., on the W bank of the Connecticut R.; 41°32′N 72°39′W. Mfg. (transportation equip., marine hardware, rubber footwear, apparel, computer industry, and textiles). Shipping brought early prosperity to Middletown, and during colonial days it was the state's leading shipping, commercial, and cultural center. Settled 1650; inc. 1784; town and city consolidated 1923. It is the seat of Wesleyan Univ. and Middlesex Com. Technical Col. Also in the city are a state mental hosp., a state correctional school, and a state park. A bridge (1938) spans the Connecticut R. to Portland. **2** industrial city (□ 4 sq mi/10.4 sq km; 1990 pop. 24,160), Orange co., SE N.Y., on the Wallkill R.; 41°27′N 74°25′W. At the intersection of E-W Route I-84, which gives access to and from New England, the mid-Hudson valley and the N.Y. State Thruway, and NYS Route 17 (Southern Tier Expressway), which funnels travel bet. N.Y. city and the Catskills–Upstate N.Y. region. Middletown serves as the major regional hub for the region S and E of the Catskills which is also an easy distance away for N.Y. city residents. Summer homes on the numerous natural lakes and ponds and in the mts. and the large number and variety of recreational facilities and activities draw many downstate New Yorkers for extended visits. These people heavily influence the character of the city and its hinterland. Dairying and farming on the extensive mucklands S of the city are still viable industries. Diverse mfg. includes furniture, clothing, electronic, medical instruments, footwear, tools, perfumes, flavors and extracts, pig lead and alloys, and machinery. Seat of Orange Co. Community Col. Rockland Psychiatric Center and Middletown Residential Center (state youth correctional facility) are here. Settled 1756, inc. as a city 1888. **3** industrial city (1990 pop. 46,022), Butler co., SW Ohio, on the Great Miami R.; 39°30′N 84°22′W. In a farm area; mfg. (steel, aircraft parts, and paper prods.). Major mfg. employment sector: steel. Miami Univ. has a branch in the city. Inc. 1866.

Middletown 1 town (1990 pop. 3,834), New Castle co., W Del., 25 mi/40 km SSW of Wilmington, near Silver L., and 3 mi/4.8 km E of Md. state line; 39°27′N 75°42′W. Marketing and shipping center in agr. area; mfg. (asbestos prods., plastics prods.). Nearby is pre-Revolutionary St. Anne's Episcopal Church. Inc. 1861. **2** town (1990 pop. 2,333), Henry co., E central Ind., on small Fall Creek, and 13 mi/21 km NNW of New Castle; 40°04′N 85°32′W. Livestock; grain, tomatoes. Mfg. (bedding materials). Laid out 1829. **3** town (1990 pop. 386), Des Moines co., SE Iowa, 8 mi/12.9 km W of Burlington; 40°49′N 91°15′W. In agr. area. **4** town (1990 pop. 5,016), Jefferson co., N Ky., residential, 15 mi/24 km E of downtown Louisville; 38°14′N 85°31′W. Mfg. (sheet-metal fabricating). **5** town (1990 pop. 1,834), Frederick co., W Md., in Middletown Valley, and 8 mi/12.9 km WNW of Frederick; 39°26′N 77°32′W. Trade center in agr. area (grain; dairy prods.); mfg. (shoes). Martenbox Church, Revolutionary War cemetary. **6** town (1990 pop. 217), Montgomery co., E central Mo., near West Fork of Cuivre R., 11 mi/18 km NNE of Montgomery City; 39°07′N 91°24′W. Agr. **7** township (1990 pop. 68,183), Monmouth co., E N.J., 4 mi/6.4 km NW of Red Bank; 40°23′N 74°04′W. Mfg. includes telecommunications hardware and software. Marlpit Hall (c.1684) now a mus. Adjoins Gateway Natl. Recreation Center; 1st Baptist church in N.J. (1668) built here. Settled 1665. **8** uninc. town (1990 pop. 6,866), Northampton co., E Pa., residential suburb, 2 mi/3.2 km ENE of Bethlehem on Lehigh R.; 40°38′N 75°19′W. **9** residential and resort town (1990 pop. 19,500), Newport co., SE R.I., on Rhode Island (Aquidneck) and Narragansett Bay; set off from Newport; 41°31′N 71°17′W. Nursery farms. Inc. 1743. Its name is derived from its location bet. Newport and Portsmouth. During the Amer. Revolution, Middletown was pillaged (1776) by the British. **10** town (1990 pop. 1,061), Frederick co., N Va., in Shenandoah Valley, 12 mi/19 km SSW of Winchester; 39°01′N 78°16′W. Agr. (apples, grain; livestock; dairying). Site of Union victory in Civil War on Cedar Creek, small N tributary of North Fork of Shenandoah R. (Oct. 19, 1864). Belle Grove (1794) Natl. Historic Landmark. Lord Fairfax Community Col.

Middletown 1 uninc. village, Lake co., NW Calif., 22 mi/35 km NNE of Santa Rosa, in a valley of the Coast Ranges, near Putah Creek. Agr. (grapes, pears, walnuts, oats; cattle); winery. Mineral springs (resorts) nearby. **2** village (1990 pop. 436), Logan co., central Ill., 20 mi/32 km N of Springfield; 40°06′N 89°35′W. Agr. (corn, soybeans; cattle, hogs).

Middletown, borough (1990 pop. 9,254), Dauphin co., S Pa., 8 mi/12.9 km SE of Harrisburg, on Susquehanna R., at mouth of Swatara Creek; 40°12′N 76°43′W. Agr. (grain, soybeans, apples; poultry, livestock; dairying); mfg. (electronic connectors, power supplies; diesel engines). Penn State Harrisburg, Capital Col. is here. Harrisburg Internatl. Airport on Susquehanna R. to W. Olmsted Air Force Base. Thee Mile Isl. Nuclear Power Plant 3 mi/4.8 km to S. Laid out 1755; inc. 1828.

Middletown Springs, town (1990 pop. 686), Rutland co., W Vt., on Poultney R., and 11 mi/18 km SW of Rutland; 43°28′N 73°07′W.

Middletown Valley, Frederick co., NW Md., fertile agr. valley, drained by Catoctin Creek; extends N from the Potomac bet. prongs (Catoctin Mt. on E, South Mt. on W) of the Blue Ridge; c.15 mi/24 km long, 6 mi/9.7 km wide. It includes Middletown, Brunswick, Myerstown, Berkittville, and Petersville.

Middleville, town (1990 pop. 1,966), Barry co., SW Mich., 20 mi/32 km SE of Grand Rapids, and on Thornapple R.; 42°42′N 85°28′W. In farm area. Mfg. (clothing, machinery, transportation equip., metal fabrication). Middleville Ski Area to N; Yankee Springs State Recreational Area to SW.

Middleville, village (1990 pop. 624), Herkimer co., central N.Y., on W. Canada Creek, and 13 mi/21 km ENE of Utica; 43°08′N 74°58′W. In dairying area.

Midfield, suburb (1990 pop. 5,559), Jefferson co., N central Ala., just W of Birmingham; 33°27′N 87°55′W. Mfg. of chain-link fencing and glazed blocks.

Midland, town (1991 pop. 13,865), S Ont., Canada, on Georgian Bay, NW of Toronto; 44°45′N 79°54′W. Midland is a port; mfg. (grain elevators, textiles, cameras, optical goods). The Martyrs' Shrine, commemorating the deaths of 5 Jesuit priests who were among the 8 N. Amer. martyrs canonized in 1930, and other remembrances of the early colonial period are nearby.

Midland 1 county (□ 527 sq mi/1,365 sq km; 1990 pop. 75,651), E central Mich.; 43°38′N 84°23′W; ⊙ MIDLAND. Drained by Tittabawassee (Sanford L. reservoir in N), Pine, and Chippewa rivers. Agr. (cattle, hogs; corn, wheat, oats, soybean, beans, sugar beets). Oil wells, salt deposits, coal mines. Midland city is a chemical and metallurgical center. Organized 1855. **2** county (□ 902 sq mi/2,336 sq km; 1990 pop. 106,611), W Texas; ⊙ Midland; 31°53′N 102°01′W. On S Llano Estacado. Elev. c.2,500 ft/762 m–3,000 ft/914 m. Drained by tributaries of Colorado R. Important oil fields (development begun 1950–1951); ranching (cattle, horses), irrigated agr. (cotton; alfalfa, pecans). Mfg. at Midland city, hq. for many oil companies. Formed 1885.

Midland 1 city (1990 pop. 38,053), ⊙ Midland co., central Mich., 17 mi/27 km W of Bay City, in the Saginaw valley, at the confluence of the Tittabawassee and Chippewa rivers; 43°37′N 84°13′W. Elev. 629 ft/192 m. Midland owes its development after 1890 to the Dow Chemical Co.; corporate hq. here. Mfg. includes silicone prods., chemicals, magnesium, and plastics; other mfg. (exhibits, metal cutting machinery; printing). Oil, coal, and salt are found in the area. Chippewa Nature Center; Dow Gardens, original gardens at home of Dr. Herbert H. Dow, founder of Dow Chemical Corporation, and Dow Gardens Library and Center for Arts are in Midland; Saginaw Valley State Univ. at University Center, 12 mi/19 km E. Inc. 1887. **2** city (1990 pop. 89,443), ⊙ Midland co., W Texas, 18 mi/29 km NE of Odessa, and 110 mi/177 km S of Lubbock, on the S edge of the Llano Estacado; 32°01′N 102°05′W. Elev. 2,779 ft/847 m. Midland has prospered partly because of its cattle ranches, but the city's reputation for spectacular wealth and its great spurt in pop. after 1940 resulted from the drilling of oil. Midland sits in the heart of the Permian Basin "oil patch" and has thus attracted numerous oil-company offices to the city. Prefabricated metal bldgs., oil field equip., transportation equip., paving materials, gas processing. The busy city continued to increase in terms of pop. from 1970 into the 1980s but growth slowed by the early 1990s, although travelers remain attracted to Midland. Midland Col. (2-year), a symphony orchestra, a planetarium, Permian Basin Petroleum Mus., and Hall of Fame are in the city. Inc. 1906.

Midland 1 town (1990 pop. 574), Allegany co., W Md., in the Alleghenies, 11 mi/18 km WSW of Cumberland; 39°35′N 78°57′W. Once called Koontz for an early settler, it has always been a mining town. The Thrasher Mus. displays horse-drawn carriages and wagons in a former school bldg. **2** uninc. town (1990 pop. 760), Cabarrus co., S central N.C., 20 mi/32 km E of Charlotte, on Rocky R. Cotton, grain, soybeans; poultry; livestock; dairying. Mfg. (apparel, feeds, machining, wood prods.). **3** uninc. town (1990 pop. 5,687), Pierce co., W Wash., residential suburb, 5 mi/8 km S of downtown Tacoma; 47°10′N 122°25′W. Pacific Lutheran Univ. in SW. McChord Air Force Base and Fort Lewis Military Reservation to SW.

Midland 1 village (1990 pop. 220), Sebastian co., W Ark., 20 mi/32 km S of Fort Smith, near Okla. line; 35°05′N 94°20′W. Mfg. (blasting agents). Sugarloaf L. to W. **2** uninc. village, Riverside co., S Calif., 20 mi/32 km NNW of Blythe, in N Palo Verde Valley. Gypsum quarrying, processing. Big Maria Mts. to NE, Palen Mts. to W **3** village (1990 pop. 319), Clinton co., SW Ohio, 35 mi/56 km ENE of Cincinnati; 39°18′N 83°55′W. **4** uninc. village, Chartiers township, Washington co., SW Pa., residential suburb, 2 mi/3.2 km W of Canonsburg; 40°15′N 80°13′W. **5** village (1990 pop. 233), Haakon co., central S.Dak., 25 mi/40 km NE of Kadoka, and on Bad R.; 44°04′N 101°09′W. Livestock; grain. **6** uninc. village, Fauquier co., N Va., 8 mi/12.9 km SSE of Warrenton; 38°35′N 77°43′W. Mfg. (food processing, machining, machinery, concrete prods.); agr. (grain, apples, soybeans; livestock).

Midland, borough (1990 pop. 3,321), Beaver co., W Pa., 28 mi/45 km NW of Pittsburgh, on Ohio R.; 40°38′N 80°27′W. Agr. (dairying); mfg. (metal recovery, stainless steel finishing, machinery, steel foundry). Nuclear Power Plant at Shipping port 2 mi/3.2 km to E. Settled c.1820.

Midland City, town (1990 pop. 1,819), Dale co., SE Ala., 8 mi/12.9 km NW of Dothan. Mfg. structural steel.

Midland Park, borough (1990 pop. 7,047), Bergen co., NE N.J., 5 mi/8 km N of Paterson; 40°59′N 74°08′W. Mfg. (textiles, towels). Inc. 1894. Largely residential.

Midlothian, town (1990 pop. 5,141), Ellis co., N Texas, 25 mi/40 km SSW of Dallas; 32°29′N 97°00′W. RR junction in rich cotton, grain, cattle area; mfg. (industrial gases, structural steel, portland cement); limestone. Cedar Hill State Park and L. Joe Pool reservoir to NW. Settled 1880; inc. 1898.

Midlothian 1 (mid-LO-thi-an), village (1990 pop. 14,372), Cook co., NE Ill., suburb, 16 mi/26 km SW of downtown Chicago; 41°37′N 87°43′W. Mfg. (sportswear, cleaning compounds, water treatment chemicals). Inc. 1927. **2** uninc. village, Chesterfield co., E central Va., suburb, 11 mi/18 km WSW of Richmond; 37°30′N 77°38′W. Mfg. (crushed granite, machinery, lumber, concrete, commercial printing, business forms); agr. (tobacco, grain; livestock). Granite quarrying. Pocahontas State Forest and Park to SE, Swift Creek Reservoir to S. John Tyler Community Col. (Midlothian Campus).

Midvale, city (1990 pop. 11,886), Salt L. co., N Utah, suburb 10 mi/16 km S of Salt L. City, and on Jordan R.; 40°36′N 111°54′W. In mining area (lead, zinc, copper, gold, silver); has large smelter. Alfalfa, sugar beets; dairying; cattle, sheep; mfg. (men's outerwear, computer platforms and software, medical devices, circuit boards, soap, catheters; food processing). RR junction. Elev. 4,390 ft/1,338 m. Settled 1859, known as Brigham Junction and East Jordan, named Midvale and inc. 1909.

Midvale 1 village (1990 pop. 110), Washington co., W Idaho, 18 mi/29 km NNE of Weiser, and on Weiser R.; 44°28′N 116°44′W. Center of agr. area. Crane Creek Reservoir to SE, Mann Creek Reservoir to SW; Payette Natl. Forest to NW. **2** village in Wanaque borough, Passaic co., NE N.J., on Wanaque Reservoir, and 11 mi/18 km NW of Paterson. Largely residential. **3** village (1990 pop. 575), Tuscarawas co., E Ohio, 5 mi/8 km SE of New Philadelphia, and at junction of Tuscarawas R. and Stillwater Creek; 40°26′N 81°22′W.

Midvale, Pa.: see PLAINS.

Midville, village (1990 pop. 620), Burke co., E Ga., 23 mi/37 km SSW of Waynesboro, and on Ogeechee R; 32°49′N 82°14′W. Steel fabrication and light industry.

Midway 1 town (1990 pop. 455), Bullock co., SE Ala., 12 mi/19 km SE of Union Springs. **2** town (1990 pop. 863), Liberty co., SE Ga., 27 mi/43 km SW of Savannah; 31°48′N 81°26′W. Mfg. of trailer panels, paper prods., and textiles. **3** town (1990 pop. 1,290), Woodford co., central Ky., near Elkhorn Creek, 12 mi/19 km WNW of Lexington, in Bluegrass region; 38°08′N 84°40′W. Agr. (burley tobacco, grain; cattle, horses); mfg. (corn meal, flour). Midway Col. Weisenberger Mill (1862), on Elkhorn Creek to N. Estab. 1833. **4** uninc. town (1990 pop. 1,506), LaSalle parish, La., 2 mi/3.2 km W of Jena; 31°43′N 92°09′W. In agr. area (cotton, soybeans; cattle); timber. **5** uninc. town (1990 pop. 2,254), Conewago township, Adams co., S Pa., residential suburb, 1 mi/1.6 km NW of Hanover; 39°47′N 77°00′W. **6** town (1990 pop. 1,554), Wasatch co., N central Utah, 5 mi/8 km W of Heber City, and on Provo R.; 40°30′N 111°28′W. Dairying; limestone. Wasatch Mt. State Park to W; Uinta Natl. Forest to W. Deer Creek reservoir and Midway Fish Hatchery to S. Elev. 5,567 ft/1,697 m. Settled in 1866 by Swiss.

Midway, village (1991 pop. 611), S B.C., Canada, on Wash. border, on Kettle R., at mouth of Boundary Creek, and 14 mi/23 km W of Grand Forks; 49°02′N 118°45′W. Elev. 2,000 ft/610 m. Fruit, vegetables; tourism, Mt. Baldy ski resort.

Midway 1 village (1990 pop. 289), Madison co., central Ohio, 10 mi/16 km S of London; 39°44′N 83°29′W. Also called Sedalia. **2** village (1990 pop. 274), Madison co., E central Texas, 26 mi/42 km SW of Crockett; 31°01′N 95°45′W. Livestock area (cattle, horses, hogs); oil and gas.

Midway, borough (1990 pop. 1,043), Washington co., SW Pa., 15 mi/24 km WSW of Pittsburgh, on Robinson Run; 40°22′N 80°17′W. Agr. (corn, hay; dairying); coal, natural gas. Hillman State Park to NW; Cherry Valley Reservoir to SW.

Midway City, uninc. village, Orange co., S Calif., suburb, 26 mi/42 km SSE of downtown Los Angeles, and 10 mi/16 km E of Long Beach. Pacific Ocean coast 4 mi/6.4 km SW.

Midway Park, uninc. village, Onslow co., E N.C., residential suburb 5 mi/8 km SE of downtown Jacksonville, on N boundary of Camp Lejeune Marine base.

Midway Village, Va.: see STEELES TAVERN.

Midwest, region of the United States centered on the W Great Lakes and the upper-middle Mississippi valley. It is a somewhat imprecise term that has been applied to the N sect. of the land bet. the Appalachians and the Rocky Mts. More often it is restricted to the Old NW Territory and the neighboring states to the S border of Missouri, E of the Great Plains. Also called Middle West, it thus includes Ohio, Ind., Ill., Mich., Wis., Minn., Iowa, Mo., Kansas, and Nebr. The area has some of the richest farmland in the world and is known for its corn and cattle. The extended area also includes great wheat fields, particularly W of the Missouri R. The heavily industrialized parts of the Midwest known as the Rustbelt declined in the 1970s and 1980s but started on the road to recovery in the 1990s, as industries modernized on the basis of high technology; financial and other services increased in importance. The chief cities are Chicago, Detroit, St. Louis, Milwaukee, and Minneapolis-St. Paul.

Midwest, village (1990 pop. 495), Natrona co., central Wyo., on Salt Creek, and 40 mi/64 km N Casper; 43°24′N 106°16′W. Elev. 4,820 ft/1,469 m. Oil wells. Teapot Dome to SSE.

Midwest City, city (1990 pop. 52,267), Oklahoma co., central Okla., a suburb, 9 mi/14.5 km E of downtown Oklahoma City; 35°27′N 97°22′W. Mfg. (sporting goods, transportation equip., sheet-metal prods., apparel, silica sand, crushed granite prods.; publishing and printing). Rose State Col. (2-year). The developer and builder W. P. Atkinson planned the city as a model for an area of spacious parks and curved streets. Founded 1942 with the activation of adjoining Tinker Air Force Base (to S), a logistics center.

Mier (MEE-er), city (1990 pop. 6,190) and township, Tamaulipas, N Mexico, near Rio Grande, S of Falcon Dam, and 90 mi/145 km NE of Monterrey on Mex. Highway 2; 26°28′N 99°10′W. Agr. center (cotton, sugarcane, corn; livestock).

Mier y Noriega (mee-er ee no-ree-AI-gah), town (1990 pop. 1,096), Nuevo León, N Mexico, in Sierra Madre Oriental, 37 mi/60 km ESE of Matehuala (Zacatecas); 23°25′N 100°07′W. Elev. 5,515 ft/1,681 m. Grain; livestock; lumbering.

Miesville (MEES-vil), village (1990 pop. 135), Dakota co., SE Minn., 9 mi/14.5 km S of Hastings, in Richard J. Dorer Memorial Hardwood State Forest; 44°36′N 48°92′W. Agr. (grain; livestock; dairying). Mississippi R. to NE.

Mifflin, county (□ 413 sq mi/1,070 sq km; 1990 pop. 46,197), central Pa.; ⊙ Lewistown; 40°36′N 77°37′W. Stone Mt. ridge in NW boundary, Long Mt. ridge on N boundary, Blue Mt. ridge on SE boundary; bisected NE-SW by Jacks Mt. ridge (2 mi/3.2 km wide) in center of co.; drained by Juniata R. (forms part of SW boundary); also by Kishacoquilla Creek. Agr. region, (corn, wheat, oats, hay, alfalfa; sheep, hogs, cattle, poultry and eggs, dairying); limestone, sand. Mfg. at Lewistown. Reeds Gap State Park in NE center; part of Rothrock State Forest in NW, part of Tuscarora State Forest is S, part of Bald Eagle State Forest in NE. Formed 1789.

Mifflin, village (1990 pop. 162), Ashland co., N central Ohio, 8 mi/13 km E of Mansfield; 40°46′N 82°22′W. Nearby on Black Fork of Mohican R. is Charles Mill Reservoir (capacity 88,000 acre-ft.), built for flood control.

Mifflin, borough (1990 pop. 660), Juniata co., central Pa., 9 mi/14.5 km ESE of Lewistown, on Juniata R. opposite (W of) Mifflintown; 40°34′N 77°24′W. Agr. (corn, hay, apples; livestock, poultry; dairying); timber; light mfg. Part of Tuscarora State Forest and Blue Mt. ridge to NW.

Mifflinburg, borough (1990 pop. 3,480), Union co., central Pa., 9 mi/14.5 km WSW of Lewisburg, near Buffalo Creek; 40°55′N 77°02′W. Agr. (poultry; dairying); timber; mfg. (yarn, apparel, mobile and modular homes, furniture). Bald Eagle State Forest to SW and NW. Laid out 1792; inc. 1827.

Mifflintown, borough (1990 pop. 866), ⊙ Juniata co., central Pa., 10 mi/16 km ESE of Lewistown, on Juniata R., opposite (E) of Mifflin; 40°34′N 77°24′W. Agr. (corn, hay, apples; poultry, livestock; dairying); mfg. (wooden prods., picnic tables, food processing, apparel; printing and publishing); limestone and shale quarries. Mifflintown Airport to N. Part of Tuscarora State Forest and Blue Mt. ridge to NW. Laid out 1791, inc. 1833.

Mifflinville, uninc. town (1990 pop. 1,329), Columbia co., E central Pa., 3 mi/4.8 km SW of Berwick on Susquehanna R.; 41°01′N 76°17′W. Mfg. (food prods., sprinkler systems, swimming pools); agr. (dairying; livestock, poultry; corn, hay, potatoes, apples.

Mignon (MIN-yon), village (1990 pop. 1,548), Talladega co., E central Ala., 20 mi/32 km SW of Talladega.

Miguel Alemán, Mexico: seeCIUDAD MIGUEL ALEMÁN.

Miguel Auza (mee-GEL AH-oo-sah), town (1990 pop. 11,899), ⊙ Miguel Auza municipio, Zacatecas, N central Mexico, on interior plateau, near Durango border, 3 mi/5 km W of Juan Aldama; 24°20′N 103°30′W. Elev. 6,683 ft/2,037 m. Silver mining; livestock raising. Also known as San Miguel de Mezquital.

Miguel Hidalgo (mee-GEL hee-DAHL-go), delegación, (1990 pop. 406,868), in the W part of Distrito Federal, Mexico, 10 mi/16 km NW of Tlalpan. Created in 1970. Part of the Mexico city metropolitan area.

Miguel Hidalgo y Costilla, Mexico: see ACUAMANALA.

Milaca (muh-LAH-kuh), town (1990 pop. 2,182), ⊙ Mille Lacs co., E Minn., 28 mi/45 kmENE of St. Cloud, on Rum R; 45°45′N 93°39′W. Elev. 1,084 ft/330 m. Trading point in agr. area (grain; livestock, poultry; dairying); mfg. (concrete, coin and currency wrappers, medical instruments; printing and publishing). Part of Rum R. State Forest to NE. Settled 1888; inc. 1897.

Milakokia Lake (mi-luh-KO-kee-uh), Mackinac co., SE Upper Peninsula, N Mich., 22 mi/35 km NE of Manistique, and 6 mi/9.7 km N of L. Michigan; c.3 mi/4.8 km long, 1.5 mi/2.4 km wide; 46°04′N 85°48′W.

Milam (MEI-lem), county (□ 1,021 sq mi/2,644 sq km; 1990 pop. 22,946), central Texas; ⊙ Cameron; 30°47′N 96°58′W. Bounded NE by Brazos R., drained by Little R. and San Gabriel R., and E Yegua Creek. Diversified agr. (esp. cotton; also corn, grain sorghum, wheat);

livestock (cattle, poultry, hogs, some sheep). Large lignite deposits. Oil wells; large aluminum plant at Rockdale. Formed 1836.

Milan 1 (MEI-luhn), city (1990 pop. 1,767), ⊙ Sullivan co., N Mo., 28 mi/45 km W of Kirksville; 40°12'N 93°07'W. Corn, soybeans; sheep, cattle, hogs. Corporate hog farming; poultry processing. Laid out 1845. **2** city (1990 pop. 7,512), Gibson co., NW Tenn., 11 mi/18 km ESE of Trenton; 35°55'N 88°46'W. In fruit, vegetable, cotton-growing region; mfg. (apparel, food cartons, rubber goods; cotton gins). U.S. arsenal and wildlife management area here.

Milan 1 (MEI-luhn), town (1990 pop. 1,056), Telfair and Dodge cos., S central Ga., 13 mi/21 km SSE of Eastman; 32°01'N 83°04'W. **2** town (1990 pop. 1,529), Ripley co., SE Ind., 7 mi/11.3 km NE of Versailles; 39°08'N 85°08'W. In agr. area. Laid out 1854. **3** town (1990 pop. 980), Washtenaw and Monroe cos., SE Mich., 14 mi/23 km SSE of Ann Arbor, and on small Saline R.; 42°04'N 83°40'W. RR junction. In farm area (beans, sugar beets). Mfg. (auto bumpers, plastic components, coated seals, surface measuring equip., wood floors and trusses, nonclay refractories, corrugated containers, lumber). Inc. 1885. **4** town (1990 pop. 1,295), Coos co., N N.H., 7 mi/11.3 km N of Berlin; 44°33'N 71°13'W. Drained by Androscoggin and Upper Ammonoosuc rivers. Mfg. (lumber); timber; agr. (poultry, livestock; dairying). Includes village of West Milan in NW. Part of White Mt. Natl. Forest in SW; Milan Hill State Forest in NW. **5** (mee-LAHN), town (1990 pop. 1,911), Cibola co., W N.Mex., suburb 2 mi/3.2 km NW of Grants, on Rio San Jose; 35°11'N 107°53'W. Cattle, sheep, alfalfa, triticale. Mfg. (machine tool accessories, bottled water, wood molding). Part of Cibola Natl. Forest to E and W. El Malpais Natl. Monument to S.

Milan 1 (MEI-luhn), village (1990 pop. 5,831), Rock Island co., NW Ill., on Rock R. (bridged), suburb, 4 mi/6.4 km S of downtown Rock Isl.-Moline; 41°26'N 90°33'W. In agr. (corn, soybeans; cattle, hogs; dairying); bituminous-coal-mining area. Mfg. (forklift components, printing, packaging and assembly, lighting fixtures). Inc. 1865. Quad Cities Airport to E. **2** (mil-AHN), village (1990 pop. 109), Sumner co., S Kansas, 15 mi/24 km W of Wellington, near Chikaskia R.; 37°15'N 97°40'W. Wheat. **3** (MEI-luhn), village (1990 pop. 353), Chippewa co., SW Minn., 14 mi/23 km NW of Montevideo, near Lac qui Parle L. (reservoir on Minnesota R.); 45°06'N 95°54'W. Grain, soybeans, sugar beets; mfg. (dolls). Las qui Parle Wildlife Area to SW and S, on river; Lac qui Parle State Park to S. **4** village (1990 pop. 1,464), Erie co., N Ohio, 12 mi/19 km SSE of Sandusky, and on Huron R.; 41°17'N 82°36'W. Beer. Thomas A. Edison was b. here. Settled 1804 by Moravian missionaries.

Milano, village (1990 pop. 408), Milam co., central Texas, 29 mi/47 km W of Bryan; 30°42'N 96°51'W. RR junction in cattle, cotton, corn area.

Milbank, town (1990 pop. 3,879), ⊙ Grant co., NE S.Dak., 30 mi/48 km NE of Watertown, near Minn. state line; 45°13'N 96°37'W. Granite quarries furnish material for gravestones and monuments; mfg. (orthopedic braces, cheese, printing and publishing). Inkapa-Du-Ta Ski Area to NE.

Milbridge, town (1990 pop. 1,305), Washington co., E Maine, 25 mi/40 km WSW of Machias, at mouth of the Narraguagus, and on Pleasant Bay; 44°28'N 67°51'W. Light mfg.; fishing, lumbering area. Inc. 1848. Sometimes spelled Millbridge.

Milburn, village (1990 pop. 264), Johnston co., S Okla., on Blue R., and 8 mi/12.9 km E of Tishomingo; 34°14'N 96°32'W. Tishomingo Natl. Wildlife Refuge and L. Texoma (Washita R.) to SW.

Milden, village (1991 pop. 228), SW central Sask., Canada, 21 mi/34 km E of Rosetown; 51°29'N 107°31'W. Wheat.

Mildmay, village (1991 pop. 1,095), S Ont., Canada, 7 mi/11 km SSE of Walkerton; 44°02'N 81°07'W. Dairying; lumbering.

Mildred, village (1990 pop. 46), Allen co., SE Kansas, 14 mi/23 km NE of Iola; 38°01'N 95°10'W. Livestock, grain; dairying.

Miles 1 town (1990 pop. 409), Jackson co., E Iowa, 18 mi/29 km E of Maquoketa; 42°02'N 90°19'W. Livestock, grain. **2** town (1990 pop. 793), Runnels co., W central Texas, 17 mi/27 km NE of San Angelo, near Concho R; 31°36'N 100°10'W. Elev. 1,800 ft/549 m. In cattle, sheep, grain, cotton area. Old Opera House (1904).

Miles City, town (1990 pop. 8,461), ⊙ Custer co., SE Mont., on Yellowstone R., at mouth of Tongue R., and 140 mi/225 km ENE of Billings; 46°25'N 105°51'W. In irrigated area. Trade center, shipping point for wool, livestock. RR shops; gas wells. Agr. (wheat, oats, corn, alfalfa, sugar beets; horses and rodeo stock, cattle, sheep, hogs); mfg. (leather goods, flour, feeds, concrete prods., printing, explosives, pond liners). Pirogue Isl. State Park in Yellowstone R. to NE. Fort Keogh, 3 mi/4.8 km to SW, (served from 1877–1908) has been rebuilt and, with former military reservation, is now the Fort Keogh Agr. Experiment Station, livestock research, includes large tract of range. Rodeo and fair; Custer County Art Center, Range Riders Mus. Inc. 1887. Originally called Milestown.

Miles, Fort, Del.: see HENLOPEN, CAPE.

Miles Glacier, in Chugach Mts., S Alaska, N of Martin R. Glacier; 60°40'N 144°45'W. Flows into Copper R. ENE of Cordova.

Miles River, E Md., irregular estuary entering Eastern Bay (arm of Chesapeake Bay) in Talbot co.; c.20 mi/32 km long. Originally called St. Michael's R., the saintly reference was deleted and the name was abbreviated.

Milesburg (MAI-uhls-buhrg), borough (1990 pop. 1,144), Centre co., central Pa., 2 mi/3.2 km N of Bellefonte, on Bald Eagle Creek; 40°56'N 77°47'W. Agr. (corn, hay; livestock; dairying); mfg. (electronic equip., plastic prods.). Bald Eagle State Park, including Howard State Nursery, to NE.

Milestone, town (1991 pop. 593), S Sask., Canada, 32 mi/51 km S of Regina, in the rich prairie region. Grain elevators, lumbering.

Milford 1 residential city (1990 pop. 49,938), New Haven co., SW Conn., on L.I. Sound; 41°13'N 73°03'W. Oysters and clams are gathered there for commercial use, and the city also has light mfg., such as the production of writing pens and electrical prods. Major retail shopping area adjacent to Interstate 95 and along U.S. Route 1. Milford Acad. is here. Settled 1639, inc. as a city 1959. **2** city (1990 pop. 5,660), on Clermont-Hamilton co. line, SW Ohio, 14 mi/23 km E of downtown Cincinnati, and on Little Miami R.; 39°10'N 84°17'W. Makes burial vaults, hosp. supplies, wood prods., consumer goods.

Milford 1 town (1990 pop. 6,040), Kent and Sussex cos., E Del., 18 mi/29 km SSE of Dover, and at head of navigation on Mispillion R., which divides city into North and South Milford; 38°54'N 75°25'W. Trade and shipping center in vegetable and fruit-farming area; mfg. (fabricated plate work, draperies, industrial machinery, wooden pallets, plastics materials). Has several 18th-cent. bldgs. Milford Neck Wildlife Area to NE. Inc. 1867. **2** town (1990 pop. 1,388), Decatur co., SE central Ind., 7 mi/11.3 km W of Greensburg; 41°25'N 85°51'W. Laid out 1835. **3** town (1990 pop. 126), Kosciusko co., N Ind., 12 mi/19 km N of Warsaw; 39°21'N 85°37'W. Poultry area. Mfg. (motor vehicles, grain bins, livestock feeding and watering equip., poultry processing, feed mixing, mobile restrooms). Laid out 1836. **4** town (1990 pop. 2,170), Dickinson co., NW Iowa, 6 mi/9.7 km S of Spirit L., near Okoboji lakes and Little Sioux R.; 43°19'N 95°09'W. Agr. trade center and summer resort; wood prods. Founded 1869, inc. 1892. **5** town (1990 pop. 2,884), Penobscot co., S central Maine, on the Penobscot, 11 mi/18 km NNE of Bangor; 44°59'N 68°34'W. Light mfg.; hunting, fishing. **6** industrial town (1990 pop. 25,355), Worcester co., S Mass., on the Charles R.; 42°10'N 71°31'W. Infarm area; pink granite has been quarried there since the mid-1800s. Mfg. (glass containers, electronics, metal fabrication, precision and analytical instruments). Settled 1662 and set off from Mendon; inc. 1780. **7** town (1990 pop. 5,511), Oakland co., SE Mich., 16 mi/26 km WSW of Pontiac, and on Huron R.; 42°35'N 83°35'W. Mfg. (transportation equip., machinery). General Motors proving ground is nearby. Highland State Recreational Area to N; Proud L. State Recreational Area to SE; Island L. State Recreational Area and Kennington Metropark to SW; numerous lakes in area. Inc. 1869. **8** town (1990 pop. 886), Seward co., SE Nebr., 10 mi/16 km S of Seward, and on Big Blue R. Grain. Community Col. **9** town (1990 pop. 11,795), Hillsborough co., S N.H., 10 mi/16 km WNW of Nashua; 42°49'N 71°40'W. Drained by Souhegan R. Mfg. (diamond tools, crystal materials, corrugated packaging, medical equip., printing and publishing, electronics, plastics prods.; metal fabrication, commercial printing); agr. (nursery crops, fruit, vegetables, corn; poultry, livestock; dairying); granite quarries. Milford State Fish Hatchery in NW. Set off 1794. **10** town (1990 pop. 1,107), Beaver co., SW Utah, on Beaver R., and 21 mi/34 km WNW of Beaver; 38°23'N 113°00'W. RR and trade center for dairying and irrigated agr. area (alfalfa, peas, potatoes, barley). Ships cattle. Lead, silver, and gold deposits, copper mines nearby. Town was once dependent on mining. Elev. 4,957 ft/1,511 m. Squaw Springs to W. Settled 1870, inc. 1903.

Milford 1 village (1990 pop. 1,512), Iroquois co., E Ill., 11 mi/18 km S of Watseka, on Sugar Creek; 40°37'N 87°42'W. Trade and shipping center in agr. area (corn, soybeans, sorghum; cattle, hogs; dairy prods.). Mfg. (food processing, electrical motors). Settled c.1830; plotted 1836; inc. 1874. **2** village (1990 pop. 384), Geary co., NE central Kansas, on Republican R., and 11 mi/18 km NNW of Junction City; 39°10'N 96°54'W. Livestock; grain. On W shore of Milford L. Reservoir and W of Fort Riley Military Reserve. **3** village (1990 pop. 462), Otsego co., central N.Y., on the Susquehanna R., and 11 mi/18 km NNE of Oneonta; 42°35'N 74°57'W. In dairying area. Brewery. **4** village (1990 pop. 711), Ellis co., N central Texas, c.45 mi/72 km SSW of Dallas, and 13 mi/21 km NE of Hillsboro; 32°07'N 96°57'W. In cotton, grain, cattle, dairying area. **5** uninc. village, Caroline co., E Va., 20 mi/32 km SSE of Fredericksburg, on Mattaponi R. Mfg. (stone prods., concrete, lumber, ladders); in agr. area (grain, potatoes; cattle); timber.

Milford 1 borough (1990 pop. 1,273), Hunterdon co., W N.J., on Delaware R., and 13 mi/21 km WNW of Flemington; 40°34'N 75°05'W. Paper mill; agr. (poultry; produce, grain; dairy prods.). **2** borough (1990 pop. 1,064), ⊙ Pike co., NE Pa., 7 mi/11.3 km SW of Port Jervis, N.Y., on Delaware R., at mouth of Sawkill Creek; 41°19'N 74°47'W. Agr. (dairying; cattle); mfg. (electronics, apparel, diversified light mfg.); resort area. Delaware Water Gap Natl. Recreation Area to S; part of Del. State Forest to NW. Settled 1733.

Milford Center, village (1990 pop. 651), Union co., central Ohio, 5 mi/8 km SSW of Marysville, and on Darby Creek; 40°10'N 83°26'W. In agr. area.

Mililani Town (MEE-lee-LAH-nee), city (1990 pop. 29,359), central Oahu isl., Honolulu co., Hawaii, 12 mi/19 km NW of Honolulu, 2 mi/3.2 km S of Wahiawa, on Waikele Stream, and on Kamehameha Highway; 21°26'N 158°01'W. Wheeler Air Force Base and Schofield Barracks Military Reservation to N.

Milk, river, 729 mi/1,173 km long, Mont. and Alta. (Canada); rising in the Rocky Mts., formed by joining of South and Middle Forks 21 mi/34 km N of Browning, Glacier co., NW Mont. South Fork (c.30 mi/48 km long) and Middle Fork (c.20 mi/32 km long) rise in the Blackfeet Indian Reservation just E of Glacier Natl. Park; then the river flows ENE into Alta., where it receives North Fork of the Milk R., then curves E past town of Milk River and Writing-on-Stone Provincial Park, SE into Montana again, through Fresno Reservoir, past Havre, then forms N boundary of Fort Belknap Indian Reservation. From there, it then flows past Malta and Glasgow to the Missouri R., 10 mi/16 km downstream, (NE) of Fort Peck Dam, in SW corner of Fort Peck Indian Reservation. The Milk R. reclamation project (est. 1911) irrigates c.134,000 acres/54,230 ha.

Cross references are shown in SMALL CAPITALS. The pronunciation key is on page xv. The dates of population figures are on page xii.

The largest of several dams is the Fresno Dam (completed 1939). Malta, Chinook, Glasgow, and Harlem (Mont.) are in the project area.

Milk River, town (1991 pop. 926), S Alta., Canada, near Mont. border, on Milk R., and 50 mi/80 km SW of Lethbridge; 49°08'N 112°05'W. Coal mining; mixed farming; ranching; cattle; flax, wheat, sugar beets.

Milk River, c.20 mi/32 km long, Clarendon parish, S Jamaica; rises N of Porus; flows S, past village of Milk River (spa), to the Caribbean; 17°55'N 77°20'W. Abounds in fish. Navigable for 2 mi/3.2 km upstream. Spa waters known as curative.

Mill Basin, SE section of Brooklyn borough of N.Y. city, SE N.Y., bounded on E, S, and W by Mill Creek Basin (an inlet of Jamaica Bay), and on N by Ave. U. Land sold to Dutch by Native Americans in 1664. Until early 20th cent. economy was largely based on abundant shellfish from its tidal marshlands, estuaries, and Jamaica Bay. In 1906, industrial development of the marshlands, channel dredging, and construction of wharves began. The area's seedy industrial character began to become more residential after World War II. Now this is one of Brooklyn's most exclusive sects., with large homes, circular streets, and private boat docks. The pop. is largely of Ital. and Irish heritage. In 1971 Harbor Village, a 904-family co-op development was proposed to be built on a 40-acre/16-ha rubble-strewn wasteland adjacent to the neighborhood. But area residents were afraid that middle-income families would avoid the project because rents would be too high and that N.Y. city would in turn provide rent subsidies that would encourage occupancy by low-income families. The City Board of Estimates rescinded its approval, and the project was cancelled.

Mill City, town (1990 pop. 1,555), Linn and Marion cos., W Oregon, on North Santiam R., 30 mi/48 km ESE of Salem; 44°45'N 122°28'W. Lumber. Grain, fruit; dairy prods. North Santiam State Park to W; Willamette Natl. Forest to E. Inc. 1947.

Mill Creek, uninc. town (1990 pop. 7,172), Snohomish co., NW Wash., residential suburb 18 mi/29 km NNE of Seattle, and 10 mi/16 km S of Everett; 47°52'N 122°13'W. Agr. area (dairying; poultry; berries, vegetables) in rapidly growing urban fringe.

Mill Creek 1 village (1990 pop. 87), Union co., S Ill., 8 mi/12.9 km S of Jonesboro; 37°20'N 89°15'W. **2** village (1990 pop. 336), Johnston co., S Okla., 10 mi/16 km SE of Sulphur; 34°23'N 96°49'W. Sand quarrying. **3** village (1990 pop. 685), Randolph co., E central W.Va., on Tygart R., 15 mi/24 km SSW of Elkins; 38°43'N 79°58'W. Mfg. (lumber). Monongahela Natl. Forest to E, includes Valley Bend Wetland to N.

Mill Creek, borough (1990 pop. 392), Huntingdon co., central Pa., 5 mi/8 km SE of Huntingdon, on Juniata R., at mouth of Mill Creek; 40°26'N 77°55'W. Agr. (corn, hay, alfalfa; livestock); mfg. (wood prods., stoves); glass sand. Swigart Mus., vintage autos. Part of Rothrock State Forest to E.

Mill Creek 1 c.50 mi/80 km long, N Calif.; rises in Lassen Volcanic Natl. Park in SE Shasta co.; flows SW into Tehama co., through Shasta Natl. Forest to Sacramento R. near Tehama; in orchard region, 10 mi/16 km SSE of Red bluff. **2** c.50 mi/80 km long, W central Ind.; rises in W Hendricks co.; flows SW and NW to Eel R. in SW Putnam co.

Mill Grove, uninc. community, Mercer co., N Mo., on Weldon R., 7 mi/11.3 km S of Princeton.

Mill Hall, borough (1990 pop. 1,702), Clinton co., N central Pa., 2 mi/3.2 km SW of Lock Haven, near Bald Eagle Creek; 41°06'N 77°29'W. Drained by Fishing Creek. Agr. (grain; livestock; dairying); mfg. (consumer goods, cosmetics, lumber, food prods.). Laid out 1806, inc. 1850.

Mill Island, SE Franklin dist., N.W.T., Canada, in Hudson Strait, at S end of Foxe Channel; 20 mi/32 km long, 14 mi/23 km wide; 63°59'N 78°W. Isl.

Mill Neck, residential village (□ 2 sq mi/5.2 sq km; 1990 pop. 977), Nassau co., SE N.Y., on N shore of L.I., on an inlet of Oyster Bay Harbor, 2 mi/3.2 km NW of Oyster Bay village; 40°52'N 73°33'W.

Mill River 1 c.17 mi/27 km, SW Conn.; rises W of Monroe; flows S to L.I. Sound, forming harbor at Fairfield. Dam on river forms Easton Reservoir 4 mi/6.4 km NW of Trumbull. **2** c.25 mi/40 km, W central Mass.; rises in ponds in N Hampshire co.; flows SE to the Connecticut at Northampton.

Mill River, Mass.: see NEW MARLBORO.

Mill Shoals, village (1990 pop. 247), White co., SE Ill., near Skillet Fork, 15 mi/24 km NW of Carmi; 38°15'N 88°20'W. In agr. area.

Mill Springs, village, Wayne co., SE Ky., 9 mi/14.5 km NNE of Monticello, on the Cumberland R. (forms L. Cumberland reservoir). Mill Springs Park, site of the opening battle of the Ky.-Tenn. campaign of the Civil War and the 1st important Union victory in the West (Jan. 19, 1862), is here. Includes 1840 grist mill.

Mill Valley, city (1990 pop. 13,038), Marin co., W Calif., 11 mi/18 km NNW of San Francisco; 37°55'N 122°33'W. Residential suburb, set in heavily timbered hills and valleys; redwood trees predominate. Mfg. (printing and publishing, light mfg.). Golden Gate Baptist Theological Seminary is here. Mt. Tamalpais (2,572 ft/784 m) to NW; Mt. Tamalpais Game Refuge in Richardson Bay, to SE; Mt. Tamalapis State Park and Muri Woods Natl. Monument to W; part of Golden Gate Natl. Recreation Area to SW; Golden Gate Bridge to S. Inc. 1900.

Mill Village, borough (1990 pop. 429), Erie co., NW Pa., 17 mi/27 km SSE of Erie, on French Creek; 41°52'N 79°58'W. Agr. (corn, hay, potatoes; dairying); mfg. (plant food).

Milladore (MIL-uh-dor), village (1990 pop. 314), Wood co., central Wis., 14 mi/23 km N of Wisconsin Rapids; 44°36'N 89°50'W. In dairy belt.

Millard, county (□ 6,828 sq mi/17,685 sq km; 1990 pop. 11,333), W Utah; ⊙ Fillmore; 39°02'N 113°05'W. Agr. area bordering on Nev. (W) and watered by Sevier R., which flows into intermittent Sevier L. at center of co. Irrigated lands around Delta produce alfalfa, wheat, sugar beets, barley. Dairying; beryllium ore, mining, limestone, precious metals. Fort Deseret State Historical Park in NE corner. Kanosh Indian Reservation in SE. Desert Range Experimental Station in SW. Fishlake Natl. Forest and Pavant Mts. in E, semiarid region in W. Co. formed 1852.

Millard, suburb of Omaha, Douglas co., E Nebr., 8 mi/12.9 km WSW of downtown. Part of city of Omaha.

Millbank, village, S Ont., Canada, on tributary of Nith R., 18 mi/29 km WNW of Kitchener. Dairying; mixed farming.

Millboro, uninc. village, Bath co., NW Va., in Allegheny Mts., 15 mi/24 km NNW of Lexington, in George Washington Natl. Forest. Mfg. (handicrafts, apparel); in agr. area (cattle); timber. Resort area.

Millboro Springs, uninc. village, Bath co., NW Va., 17 mi/27 km NNW of Lexington, on Cowpasture R., in George Washington Natl. Forest. Agr. (catte); timber. Resort area.

Millbourne, borough (1990 pop. 831), Delaware co., SE Pa., residential suburb, 4 mi/6.4 km W of Philadelphia, on Cobbs Creek; 39°57'N 75°15'W.

Millbrae, city (1990 pop. 20,412), San Mateo co., W Calif., residential suburb, 12 mi/19 km S of San Francisco, on San Francisco Bay; 37°36'N 122°24'W. Mfg. (chemicals, light mfg.). San Francisco Internatl. Airport adjoins the city to NE. Montana Mt. and San Francisco State Fish and Game Refuge, including San Andreas L. Resevoir to SW (on San Andreas Fault). Inc. 1948.

Millbridge, Maine: see MILBRIDGE.

Millbrook, city (1990 pop. 6,050), Elmore co., E. central Ala., 8 mi/12.9 km N of Montgomery; 32°29'N 86°22'W. Mfg. of aircraft engine parts and apparel.

Millbrook, village (1991 pop. 1,259), S Ont., Canada, 15 mi/24 km SW of Peterborough; 44°09'N 78°27'W. Lumbering; dairying; mixed farming.

Millbrook, residential and resort village (□ 1 sq mi/2.6 sq km; 1990 pop. 1,339), Dutchess co., SE N.Y., 12 mi/19 km NE of Poughkeepsie; 41°46'N 73°41'W. In dairying and limited stock-raising area. Seat of Inst. of Ecosystem Studies–N.Y. Botanical Gardens; Millbrook Preparatory School. Many estates and 2d homes for New Yorkers. Noted for polo playing. Inc. 1896.

Millbrook, Mass.: see DUXBURY.

Millburn, residential township (1990 pop. 18,630), Essex co., NE N.J., on Rahway and Passaic rivers, 7 mi/11.3 km W of Newark; 40°44'N 74°19'W. Includes Short Hills, site of shopping mall. The Paper Mill Playhouse, the oldest continually running nonprofit playhouse, is here. Settled c.1725, inc. 1857.

Millbury, town (□ 16 sq mi/41 sq km; 1990 pop. 12,228), Worcester co., S Mass., on Blackstone R., 6 mi/9.7 km SSE of Worcester; 42°11'N 71°47'W. Woolens, textile supplies, wire, tools, castings, and veterinary pharmaceuticals. Includes village of W. Millbury. In 1870, town had the world's largest felt mill. Settled 1716, inc. 1813.

Millbury, village (1990 pop. 1,081), Wood co., NW Ohio, 9 mi/14 km SE of Toledo; 41°34'N 83°25'W.

Millcreek, township (1990 pop. 46,820), Erie co., NW Pa., residential suburb, 4 mi/6.4 km SW of Erie; 42°04'N 80°09'W. Includes the communities of Glenruadh, Westminster, Lakewood, Eaglehurst, Charter Oaks, Highland Park, Chestnut Hill, Kearsarge, and Bell Valley. Erie Internatl. Airport in NW.

Milldale, Conn.: see SOUTHINGTON.

Mille Îles River or **Milles Îles River** (both: meel EEL), S Que., Canada, branch of Ottawa R., flowing from L. of the Two Mountains NE along shore of Jesus Isl. to the St. Lawrence. Also spelled Mille Isles.

Mille Lacs (MIL laks), county (□ 681 sq mi/1,764 sq km; 1990 pop. 18,670), E central Minn.; ⊙ Milaca; 45°55'N 93°37'W. Drained by Rum R. Resort area; agr. (alfalfa, hay, corn, oats, barley, rye; hogs, cattle, poultry; dairying); timber; peat; sand and gravel. Part of Mille Lacs Wildlife Area here. S ½ of Mille Lacs L. in N; parts of Mille Lacs Indian Reservation in NW and NE corners; Father Hennipen State Park in NE; Mille Lacs Kathio State Park in NW, both on shore of Mille Lacs L.; parts of Rum R. State Forest in NW and E center. Formed 1857.

Mille Lacs, Lac des (MIL laks, laks dai), lake (□ 102 sq mi/264 sq km), NW Ont., Canada, 60 mi/97 km WNW of Port Arthur. Elev. 1,496 ft/456 m; 18 mi/29 km long, 12 mi/19 km wide. Drains SW into Rainy L.

Mille Lacs Lake (□ 207 sq mi/536 sq km), Aitkin, Mille Lacs, and Crow Wing cos., NE central Minn., 90 mi/145 km NNW of Minneapolis; 46°16'N 93°48'W. Elev. 1,251 ft/381 m. Minn.'s 3d-largest lake, after Red and Leech lakes. Drains S through the Rum R. Marshy area; lake fed by small side streams; numerous small lakes to W and N. Sieur Duluth, a Fr. explorer, visited (1679) the Ojibwas who lived on the shore. In 1680, Louis Hennepin, a Fr. friar and explorer of N. Amer., and his companions were held captive near the lake by the Ojibwas for several weeks. The region is a center for tourists and sportsmen. Part of Mille Lacs Indian Reservation is on the SW shore. Wealthwood State Forest on N shore; Father Hennepin State Park on SE shore; Mille Lacs Kathio State Park on SW shore.

Mille Roches (meel ROSH), village, SE Ont., Canada, on Cornwall Canal, and 5 mi/8 km W of Cornwall. Dairying, mixed farming.

Millecoquins Lake (mil-i-KAH-kinz), Mackinac co., SE Upper Peninsula, Mich., c.40 mi/64 km ENE of Manistique; 46°09'N 85°30'W. Lake is c.2.5 mi/4 km long, 1.5 mi/2.4 km wide; drained by Furlong Creek. Resort.

Milledgeville, city (1990 pop. 17,727), ⊙ Baldwin co., central Ga., on the Oconee R., in a fertile agr. area; 33°05'N 83°14'W. Laid out in 1803 as the site of the state capital, which was there from 1807 to 1868. Mfg. includes clothing, carpets, aircraft parts, printing and publishing, lumber. Many antebellum homes survive in the Federal Gr. Revival and Classical Revival styles. The old state capitol (1807) is now part of Georgia Military Col., a prep school. The city is also the site of Ga. Col. and State Univ., a unit of the Univ. System of Ga.; the univ. president maintains an office in the former governor's mansion. Central State Hosp., founded in 1837 as a mental instutution, is now used as a state prison. Inc. 1836.

Area in square miles is shown by the symbol □ capital city or county seat by ⊙

Milledgeville 1 village (1990 pop. 1,076), Carroll co., NW Ill., 14 mi/23 km NNW of Sterling, on Elkhorn Creek; 41°57′N 89°46′W. Dairying; corn; mfg. (fabricated aluminum). **2** village (1990 pop. 120), Fayette co., S central Ohio, 9 mi/14 km WNW of Washington Court House; 39°35′N 83°35′W.

Millen (MIL-uhn), town (1990 pop. 3,808), ⊙ Jenkins co., E Ga., on Ogeechee R., c.45 mi/72 km S of Augusta; 32°49′N 81°56′W. Big buckhead church established in 1787 located nearby. Mfg. includes motor vehicles, clothing, fertilizer. Magnolia Spring State Park nearby. Settled early 1830s; inc. 1881.

Miller 1 county (□ 637 sq mi/1,650 sq km; 1990 pop. 38,467), extreme SW Ark.; ⊙ Texarkana; 33°18′N 93°52′W. Bounded W by Texas, S by La., E and N by Red R.; drained by Sulphur R. Agr. (wheat, soybeans; cattle, hogs, chickens). Timber; oil and gas. Mfg. at Texarkana. Sulphur R. Wildlife Management Area in S. Formed 1874. **2** county (□ 284 sq mi/736 sq km; 1990 pop. 6,280), SW Ga.; ⊙ Colquitt; 31°10′N 84°44′W. Coastal plain agr. (corn, peanuts, sugarcane, cotton, oats); cattle, hogs. Area drained by Spring Creek. Formed 1856. **3** county (□ 603 sq mi/1,562 sq km; 1990 pop. 20,700), central Mo.; ⊙ Tuscumbia; 38°13′N 92°25′W. In Ozark region; drained by Osage R. Resort, recreational, and commercial development at Osage Beach and L. Ozark. Corn, wheat; cattle, poultry; timber; hydroelectricity; mfg. at Eldon, Iberia, and St. Elizabeth. Bagnell Dam on Osage R. forms L. of the Ozarks. Major recreation area about equidistant bet. St. Louis and Kansas City. L. of the Ozarks State Park in SW (largest state park in Mo.). Formed 1837.

Miller 1 town (1990 pop. 753), Lawrence co., SW Mo., 7 mi/11.3 km N of Mt. Vernon; 37°13′N 93°50′W. Agr., flour mills. Corn, hay. Cattle; dairying. **2** town (1990 pop. 1,678), ⊙ Hand co., central S.Dak., 70 mi/113 km ENE of Pierre and on Turtle Creek; 44°31′N 98°59′W. In agr. region. L. Louise State Rec. Area to NW. Settled 1882, inc. as city 1910.

Miller, village (1990 pop. 130), Buffalo co., S central Nebr., 23 mi/37 km NW of Kearney, and on Wood R.; 40°55′N 99°23′W.

Miller City, village (1990 pop. 173), Putnam co., NW Ohio, 7 mi/11 km NW of Ottawa; 41°06′N 84°08′W.

Miller Creek, uninc. town (1990 pop. 1,787), Wilkes co., NW N.C., 6 mi/9.7 km NW of Wilkesboro; 36°11′N 81°14′W. Rendezvous Mt. State Educational Forest to W; W. Kerr Scott reservoir (Yadkin R.) to S. Timber; tobacco, grain, soybeans; poultry, cattle; dairying. Mfg. (lumber).

Miller Field, tract of open parkland on E side of Staten Isl. borough of N.Y., SE N.Y., 2.5 mi/4 km NE of Great Kills Harbor; 40°35′N 74°05′W. Area is 203 acres/82 ha. Part of the 6-mi/9.7-km Gateway Natl. Recreation Area fronting on Lower N.Y. Bay and the Atlantic.

Miller, Mount (11,000 ft/3,353 m), S Alaska, in Robinson Mts. 30 mi/48 km NNE of Cape Yakataga; 60°28′N 142°14′W.

Miller Peak (9,466 ft/2,885 m), Cochise co., SE Ariz., highest in Huachuca Mts., near Mex. border, 11 mi/18 km S of Fort Huachuca.

Millers Creek Reservoir (□ 5 sq mi/13 sq km), Throckmorton and Baylor cos., N central Texas, on Millers Creek, 55 mi/88 km SW of Wichita Falls; 33°25′N 99°22′W. Max. capacity 131,000 acre-ft. Formed by Millers Creek Dam (75 ft/23 m high), built (1974) for water supply.

Millers Falls, village (1990 pop. 1,084) in Erving and Montague towns, Franklin co., NW Mass., on Millers R., and 5 mi/8 km E of Greenfield; 42°35′N 72°29′W. Tool mfg.

Millers Ferry Dam, Ala.: see WILLIAM "BILL" DANNELLY RESERVOIR, .

Millers Mills, resort village (1990 pop. 85), Herkimer co., central N.Y., 15 mi/24 km SSE of Utica, on Little Unadilla R.; 42°55′N 75°05′W. In winter, cutting of slabs of lake ice is a tradition and popular attraction here.

Millers River, c.60 mi/97 km long, N Mass.; rises in N Worcester co.; flows SW and W to the Connecticut R. c.5 mi/8 km E of Greenfield.

Millers Tavern, uninc. village, Essex co., E Va., 37 mi/60 km NE of Richmond. Mfg. (lumber, motor vehicle parts); agr. (grain, soybeans; cattle); timber.

Millersburg 1 town (1990 pop. 854), Elkhart co., N Ind., 9 mi/14.5 km SE of Goshen; 41°32′N 85°42′W. Mfg. (motor vehicles). Laid out 1855. **2** town (1990 pop. 188), Iowa co., E central Iowa, 15 mi/24 km S of Marengo; 41°34′N 92°09′W. In agr. area. **3** town (1990 pop. 937), Bourbon co., N central Ky., 8 mi/12.9 km NE of Paris, on Hinkston Creek, in Bluegrass region; 38°17′N 84°09′W. Mfg. (machinery). Colville Covered Bridge to NW.

Millersburg 1 village (1990 pop. 250), Presque Isle co., NE Mich., 13 mi/21 km SW of Rogers City, and on short Ocqueoc R.; 45°19′N 84°03′W. In farm area. Lumber. **2** village (1990 pop. 3,051), ⊙ Holmes co., central Ohio, 32 mi/51 km SW of Canton, on Killbuck Creek; 40°33′N 81°55′W. In agr. area; dairy prods., rubber prods., furniture. Coal mines. Settled 1816. **3** village (1990 pop. 715), Linn co., W Oregon, suburb, 2 mi/3.2 km NE of Albany, on Willamette R.; 44°40′N 123°04′W. Albany Municipal Airport to SE.

Millersburg, borough (1990 pop. 2,729), Dauphin co., central Pa., 20 mi/32 km NNW of Harrisburg, on Susquehanna R. (ferry), at mouth of Wiconisco Creek; 40°32′N 76°57′W. Agr. (grain, soybeans; livestock; dairying); mfg. (plastic prods., tools, contract embroidery, textiles, consumer goods). Berry Mt. ridge to S, Mahantango Mt. ridge to W. Settled c.1790, laid out 1807, inc. 1850.

Millersport, village (1990 pop. 1,010), Fairfield co., central Ohio, 24 mi/39 km E of Columbus, near Buckeye L. (resort), in agr. area; 39°54′N 82°32′W.

Millerstown, borough (1990 pop. 646), Perry co., central Pa., 25 mi/40 km NW of Harrisburg, on Juniata R.; 40°32′N 77°09′W. Agr. (corn, hay; dairying); mfg. (lumber, wood prods., food prods.). Tuscarora Mt. to NW.

Millersville, city (1990 pop. 2,575), Sumner co., N central Tenn., 15 mi/24 km NNE of Nashville; 36°22′N 86°42′W. Inc. 1981.

Millersville, borough (1990 pop. 8,099), Lancaster co., SE Pa., 4 mi/6.4 km SW of Lancaster, near Conestoga R.; 40°00′N 76°20′W. Agr. (grain, soybeans, apples; livestock; dairying); light mfg. Seat of Millersville Univ. of Pa. Inc. 1932.

Millerton, town (1990 pop. 44), Wayne co., S Iowa, 6 mi/9.7 km N of Corydon; 40°51′N 93°18′W. Livestock; grain.

Millerton 1 village (1990 pop. 884), Dutchess co., SE N.Y., near Conn. border, 28 mi/45 km NE of Poughkeepsie; 41°57′N 73°30′W. In dairying area. Working-class pop. **2** village (1990 pop. 234), McCurtain co., SE Okla., 12 mi/19 km WNW of Idabel; 33°58′N 95°01′W. In agr. area.

Millerton Lake, reservoir, central Calif., on San Joaquin R. (border of Fresno and Madera cos.), 17 mi/27 km NNE of Fresno; 37°00′N 119°41′W. Elev. 561 ft/171 m; 15 mi/24 km long. Extends NE. Formed by Friant Dam (3,430 ft/1,045 m long, 320 ft/98 m high; completed 1944), key irrigation and flood-control unit of Central Valley project. Madera and Friant-Kern canals extend from dam to irrigate the valley farms. Dam destroyed fish-spawning run. Millerton L. State Recreation Area surrounds reservoir.

Millerville, village (1990 pop. 104), Douglas co., W Minn., 16 mi/26 km NW of Alexandria, near Chippewa R., in region of small natural lakes; 46°04′N 95°32′W. Grain; livestock; dairying. Inspiration Peak State Park is to N. Aaron and Moses lakes to W.

Milles Îles River, Canada: see MILLE ÎLES RIVER.

Millet (MI-lit), town (1991 pop. 1,782), central Alta., Canada, 30 mi/48 km S of Edmonton; 53°05′N 113°28′W. Coal mining; oil and gas; barley, wheat; cattle.

Millfield, village, Athens co., SE Ohio, 8 mi/13 km N of Athens, in coal region. Mine disaster here (1930) killed 82 men.

Millhaven, village, SE Ont., Canada, 12 mi/19 km WSW of Kingston, on North Channel, L. Ontario; 44°12′N 76°45′W. Ferry to Amherst Isl. Mixed farming; dairying; apples.

Millheim, borough (1990 pop. 847), Centre co., central Pa., 16 mi/26 km E of Bellefonte, on Elk Creek, in Penns Valley; 40°53′N 77°28′W. Agr. (corn, wheat, hay, vegetables; livestock, dairying; timber); mfg. (electronic equip.). Poe Valley State Park to S; Penn's Cave to W; part of Bald Eagle State Forest to SE.

Millhousen, town (1990 pop. 151), Decatur co., SE central Ind., 9 mi/14.5 km S of Greensburg; 39°13′N 85°26′W. In agr. area. Near Muscatatuck R. Settled 1838, plotted 1858.

Milligan, village (1990 pop. 328), Fillmore co., SE Nebr., 10 mi/16 km E of Geneva, and on branch of Big Blue R.; 40°30′N 97°23′W. Grain; feeds and alfalfa pellets.

Milligan College, town, Carter co., NE Tenn., 4 mi/6 km ESE of Johnson City. Milligan Col. (1881) here.

Milliken, town (1990 pop. 1,605), Weld co., N Colo., on Big Thompson R., at mouth of Little Thompson R., 10 mi/16 km SW of Greeley; 40°19′N 104°50′W. Elev. 4,760 ft/1,451m. Sugar beets, beans, wheat, barley, oats, vegetables, fruits; cattle. Mfg.

Millington, city (1990 pop. 17,866), Shelby co., SW Tenn., 14 mi/23 km N of Memphis; 35°20′N 89°52′W. In a livestock and cotton region. The U.S. Naval Air Station provides a major source of employment. Inc. 1903.

Millington 1 town (1990 pop. 409), Kent and Queen Annes cos., E Md., 18 mi/29 km WNW of Dover (Del.); 39°16′N 75°50′W. Was 1st called Head of Chester for its location at the head of navigation on Chester R.; the name was changed in 1827 because of the numerous mills in the area. The Higman Mill, whose foundations are believed to date back to the 1760s, ground corn with water wheel and millstone until the early 1950s. Millington Wildlife Refuge is nearby. **2** town (1990 pop. 1,114), Tuscola co., E Mich., 19 mi/31 km NNE of Flint; 43°16′N 83°31′W. In agr. area (potatoes, beans, wheat, corn, soybeans, sugar beets; poultry, hogs); mfg. (fiberglass prods., steel fabrication). Murphy L. to E.

Millington, village, Morris co., N central N.J., on Passaic R., 8 mi/12.9 km SSW of Morristown. Suburbanizing area.

Millington, Conn.: see EAST HADDAM.

Millinocket (mil-uh-NAHK-et), town (1990 pop. 6,956), Penobscot co., central Maine, on West Branch of Penobscot R.; 45°38′N 68°42′W. Developed around paper mills built here 1899–1900. Wood prods. are still important here. Millinocket L. (c.6 mi/9.7 km wide) and Mt. Katahdin are NW. Inc. 1901.

Millinocket Lake (mil-uh-NAHK-et), lake, Piscataquis co., N central Maine, 43 mi/69 km NNW of Millinocket; 46°13′N 68°50′W. Lake is 3 mi/4.8 km long, recreation (winter sports).

Millinocket Lake (mil-uh-NAHK-et), reservoir, Penobscot and Piscataquis cos., N central Maine, on Sandy Stream, small branch of Penobscot R., 5 mi/8 km NNW of Millinocket; 45°43′N 68°43′W. Formed by dam; 6 mi/9.7 km long, 4 mi/6.4 km wide. Mt. Katahdin, in Baxter State Park, to NW.

Millis, town (1990 pop. 7,613), Norfolk co., E Mass., on Charles R., 20 mi/32 km SW of Boston; 42°10′N 71°22′W. Settled 1657, inc. 1885.

Millport, town (1990 pop. 1,203), Lamar co., W Ala., 14 mi/23 km S of Vernon.

Millport, village (1990 pop. 342), Chemung co., S N.Y., 12 mi/19 km N of Elmira; 42°16′N 76°50′W. In agr. area.

Millry, town (1990 pop. 781), Washington co., SW Ala., 11 mi/18 km N of Chatom. Lumber; clothing.

Mills 1 county (□ 439 sq mi/1,137 sq km; 1990 pop. 13,202), SW Iowa, on Nebr. state line (W; formed here by Missouri R.); ⊙ Glenwood; 41°01′N 95°37′W. Prairie agr. area (corn, cattle, poultry; corn, oats) drained by West Nishnabotna R. and by Keg and Silver creeks. Bituminous-coal deposits. Widespread river flooding in 1993. Formed 1851. **2** county (□ 749 sq mi/1,940 sq km; 1990 pop. 4,531), central Texas; ⊙ Goldthwaite; 31°30′N 98°35′W. Bounded SW by Colorado R.; drained by Pecan Bayou and other tributaries. Ranching area: sheep, goats, beef and dairy cattle; grains, pecans. Formed 1887.

Mills, town (1990 pop. 1,574), Natrona co., central Wyo., on North Platte R., suburb, 2 mi/3.2 km W of Casper; 42°51′N 106°22′W. Mfg. (motor vehicles; fabricated metal). Fort Casper and fairgrounds here. Site of Mormon Ferry built (1847) by Brigham Young.

Mills, uninc. village, Harding co., NE N.Mex., 26 mi/42 km NW of Mosquero, in section of Kiowa Natl. Grasslands. Canadian R. Canyon to W; Chicosa L. State Park to SE.

Millsap, village (1990 pop. 485), Parker co., N central Texas, 38 mi/61 km W of Fort Worth; 32°45′N 98°00′W. Agr. area (cattle, horses; peanuts, pecans). Stone, clay. Mfg. (crushed rock and asphalt, brick). L. Mineral Wells State Park to N.

Millsboro, town (1990 pop. 1,643), Sussex co., SE Del., 8 mi/12.9 km SSE of Georgetown, and on Indian R.; 38°35′N 75°17′W. Agr. area (grain, vegetables, fruit; poultry, cattle, hogs; dairying); mfg. (sawmill, biological prods.). Cypress Swamp to S. Founded 1792. In early 19th cent., over 15 grist mills and sawmills were in the area.

Millsfield, town, Coos co., N N.H., 23 mi/37 km NNW of Berlin. Drained by Clear Stream. Timber; livestock; dairying.

Millstadt (MIL-staht), village (1990 pop. 2,566), St. Clair co., SW Ill., 11 mi/18 km SSE of East St. Louis; 38°27′N 90°05′W. Flour milling, mfg. (food processing systems); bituminous-coal mines; agr. (wheat, apples; dairy prods.; hogs, poultry). Inc. 1878.

Millstone 1 village, New London co., SE Conn. Site of the Millstone Nuclear Power Station, completed in 1969, which serves Waterford as well as the larger New England area. **2** village (1990 pop. 400), Letcher co., SE Ky., 3 mi/4.8 km E of Whitesburg, in the Cumberland Mts., on North Fork of Kentucky R. Bituminous coal. Jefferson Natl. Forest to SE.

Millstone, borough (1990 pop. 450), Somerset co., central N.J., on Millstone R., and 4 mi/6.4 km S of Somerville; 40°30′N 74°35′W.

Millstone 1, 2, and 3 Nuclear Power Plants, Conn.: see NEW LONDON, CO.

Millstone River, c.40 mi/64 km long, central N.J.; rises SW of Freehold; flows NW and N, past Hightstown, Princeton (dam here forms L. Carnegie), and Millstone, to Raritan R below Somerville.

Milltown, town, SW N.B., Canada, on St. Croix R. (internatl. bridge), opposite Milltown and Calais, Maine, and 60 mi/97 km W of St. John; 45°10′N 67°18′W. Lumbering.

Milltown 1 town (1990 pop. 917), Crawford and Harrison cos., S Ind., on Blue R., and 25 mi/40 km WNW of New Albany; 38°20′N 86°16′W. Limestone quarrying and processing; poultry hatcheries. Laid out 1839. **2** town (1990 pop. 786), Polk co., NW Wis., 39 mi/63 km NNE of Hudson; 45°31′N 92°30′W. Dairying area; vegetable canning. Light mfg.

Milltown (MIL-toun), village (1990 pop. 320), Missoula co., W Mont., 6 mi/9.7 km E of Missoula, on Clark Fork R., at mouth of Blackfoot R. Small Milltown Dam at confluence. Largest lumber mill in Mont. Cattle, horses; hay. Lolo Natl. Forest to N and S. Originally called Riverside, then Finntown.

Milltown, borough (1990 pop. 6,968), Middlesex co. E N.J., 3 mi/4.8 km S of New Brunswick; 40°27′N 74°25′W. Mfg. (health-care prods., typewriter and computer ribbons, paper prods.); sand, gravel, clay pits; agr. (poultry; fruit; dairy prods.). Settled before 1800, inc. 1889.

Milltown, Maine: see CALAIS.

Millvale, borough (1990 pop. 4,341), Allegheny co., SW Pa., residential suburb, 3 mi/4.8 km NNE of downtown Pittsburgh; 40°28′N 79°58′W. Settled c.1844, inc. 1868.

Millville, city (1990 pop. 25,992), Cumberland co., S N.J., on the Maurice R., in a poultry, fruit, and vegetable-farm area; 39°23′N 75°02′W. Settled 1756, inc. 1866. The principal industries produce glass, tools, canned seafood, and machinery; aircraft engines are repaired in Millville.

Millville 1 residential town (1990 pop. 2,236), Worcester co., S Mass., on Blackstone R., and 20 mi/32 km SE of Worcester, at R.I. state line; 42°02′N 71°35′W. Settled 1662, set off from Blackstone 1916. **2** town (1990 pop. 1,202), Cache co., N Utah, 3 mi/4.8 km S of Logan; 41°40′N 111°49′W. Fruit, vegetables, wheat, barley; dairying; cattle. Part of Wasatch Natl. Forest to E. Elev. 4,542 ft/1,384 m. Est. 1859.

Millville 1 village (1990 pop. 206), Sussex co., SE Del., 18 mi/29 km SE of Georgetown; 38°32′N 75°06′W. Vegetables, fruit; poultry, cattle, hogs. Holts Landing State Park to N, on Indian River Bay. **2** village, Henry co., E Ind., 6 mi/9.7 km E of New Castle. Agr. area. Wilbur Wright Birthplace State Memorial nearby to N. Laid out 1854. **3** village (1990 pop. 163), Wabasha co., SE Minn., on Zumbro R., 18 mi/29 km NNE of Rochester, in Richard J. Dorer Memorial Hardwood State Forest; 44°15′N 92°17′W. Dairying. **4** village (1990 pop. 755), Butler co., extreme SW Ohio, 5 mi/8 km W of Hamilton; 39°23′N 84°39′W.

Millville, borough (1990 pop. 969), Columbia co., E central Pa., 10 mi/16 km NNW of Bloomsburg, on Little Fishing Creek; 41°07′N 76°31′W. Agr. (grain, soybeans, apples; livestock, poultry, dairying); mfg. (crates, washing equip., paper filing prods.). Covered bridges in area.

Millwood 1 uninc. town (1990 pop. 1,070), Sumter co., central S.C., residential suburb, 2 mi/3.2 km S of Sumter, on Pocotaligo R; 33°54′N 80°23′W. **2** town (1990 pop. 1,559), suburb, 7 mi/11.3 km E of downtown Spokane, Spokane co., E Wash; 47°42′N 117°17′W. RR center. Foits Field Municipal Airport to W.

Millwood Lake, reservoir (☐ 45 sq mi/117 sq km), on Little River–Hempstead co. border, Little River Co., SW Ark., on Little R., 7 mi/11.3 km ENE of Ashdown; 33°42′N 93°58′W. Max. capacity 1,854,930 acre-ft. Fed by Saline R. Formed by Little River Dam (88 ft/27 m high), built (1966) by Army Corps of Engineers for water storage, recreation, and as a fish and wildlife pond. Millwood State Park on S shore.

Milner, village (1990 pop. 321), Lamar co., W central Ga., 10 mi/16 km SSE of Griffin; 33°07′N 84°12′W. Mfg. of lumber and pork rinds.

Milner Pass (10,758 ft/3,279 m), Grand and Larimar cos., N central Colo., across Continental Divide, on Trail Ridge Road, 15 mi/24 km WNW of Estes Park. In Rocky Mt. Natl. Park.

Milnor (MIL-nuhr), village (1990 pop. 651), Sargent co., SE N.Dak.,17 mi/27 km SE of Lisbon; 46°15′N 97°27′W.

Milo 1 (MEI-lo), town (1990 pop. 864), Warren co., S central Iowa, 8 mi/12.9 km SE of Indianola; 41°17′N 93°26′W. In agr. area. **2** town (1990 pop. 2,600), Piscataquis co., central Maine, at confluence of the Piscataquis and the Sebec, 12 mi/19 km ENE of Dover-Foxcroft; 45°15′N 68°58′W. Trade center, with mfg. (lumber prods.). Center for Schoodic, Seboois, and Sebec lakes region. Settled 1803, inc. 1823. **3** town (1990 pop. 76), Vernon co., W Mo., 7 mi/11.3 km SSE of Nevada; 37°45′N 94°18′W.

Milo (MEI-lo), village (1991 pop. 104), S Alta., Canada, near N end of L. McGregor, 60 mi/97 km N of Lethbridge; 50°34′N 112°53′W. Wheat, flax, cattle.

Milot (mee-LO), village (1982 pop. 3,762), Nord dept., N Haiti, in foothills of the Massif du Nord, 9 mi/14.5 km S of Cap-Haïtien; 19°37′N 72°13′W. In agr. region (sugarcane, cacao, citrus fruit, tobacco; cattle). Base for visitors to nearby Sans Souci palace and Citadelle La Ferrière, both built by Henri Christophe, king of Northern Haiti (1811–1820).

Milpa Alta (MEEL-pah AHL-tah), town (1990 pop. 63,654) and delegación, Federal Dist., central Mexico, 18 mi/29 km SSE of Mexico city; 19°11′N 99°01′W. Part of the Mexico city metropolitan area. Agr. center (cereals, fruit, vegetables; stock).

Milpitas, city (1990 pop. 50,686), Santa Clara co., W Calif., a growing suburb, 7 mi/11.3 km N of downtown San Jose; 37°26′N 121°54′W. Agr. area to W (vegetables, strawberries, cherries, mushrooms, grain); dairying; poultry; nursery prods. High-tech mfg; other industries include food distributing, paint production, and an automobile assembly plant. Branch of Hetch Hetchy Aqueduct runs through city; Coyote Creek drains city on W. Inc. 1954.

Milroy 1 village (1990 pop. 900), Rush co., E central Ind., 7 mi/11.3 km S of Rushville. Mfg. (paper prods., canned tomatoes). Hogs; corn, wheat. Laid out 1830. **2** village (1990 pop. 297), Redwood co., SW Minn., 23 mi/37 km WSW of Redwood Falls; 44°25′N 95°32′W. Grain, soybeans; livestock; dairying; mfg. (feeds). **3** uninc. village (1990 pop. 1,456), Mifflin co., central Pa., 9 mi/14.5 km N of Lewistown, on Laurel Creek; 40°42′N 77°35′W. Agr. (corn, hay; poultry, livestock, dairying); mfg. (crushed limestone, lumber, cabinets, audio speakers, pharmaceuticals). Laurel Creek Reservoir to NW; Reeds Gap State Park to E; Rothrock State Forest to W.

Milstead, village, Rockdale co., N central Ga., just N of Conyers; 33°41′N 83°59′W.

Milton, village, SW N.S., Canada, on Mersey R. and 3 mi/5 km NW of Liverpool. Lumbering center.

Milton, industrial suburb (1991 pop. 32,075) of Toronto, Ont., Canada; 43°31′N 79°53′W. Part of Halton Regional Municipality. Mfg. (trucks, cranes, vehicle parts, screws and bolts); warehousing, mixed farming; copper foundry.

Milton 1 town (1990 pop. 1,417), Sussex co., SE Del., 10 mi/16 km W of Lewes, and on Broadkill R.; 38°46′N 75°18′W. In farm area; vegetables, fruit; poultry, livestock; dairying; mfg. (canned fruits and vegetables, sausages). Lake Cannon Mus. is here; Prime Hook Natl. Wildlife Refuge to NE. The town is well known for Victorian architecture **2** town (☐ 4 sq mi/10.4 sq km; 1990 pop. 7,216), ⊙ Santa Rosa co., NW Fla., on Blackwater R., and 18 mi/29 km NE of Pensacola; 30°37′N 87°02′W. Lumber milling. Founded c.1825. **3** town (1990 pop. 634), Wayne co., E Ind., on Whitewater R., and 14 mi/23 km W of Richmond; 39°47′N 85°10′W. **4** town (1990 pop. 506), Van Buren co., SE Iowa, near Mo. state line, 10 mi/16 km WSW of Keosauqua; 40°40′N 92°09′W. In livestock and grain area. **5** town (1990 pop. 25,725), Norfolk co., E Mass., a residential suburb, just S of Boston, on the Neponset R.; 42°14′N 71°05′W. Granite quarries are nearby. Milton is the seat of Curry Col. and several preparatory schools, including Milton Academy (1798). Meteorological observatory is on Blue Hill (tallest coastal feature in Mass.). Includes village of East Milton. Blue Hill Ski Area; Blue Hill Reservation Park. Settled 1636, set off from Dorchester and inc. 1662. **6** town (1990 pop. 3,691), Strafford co., SE N.H., on Salmon Falls R., 7 mi/11.3 km N of Rochester (separated from Rochester in 1802); 43°27′N 71°00′W. Bounded E by Salmon Falls R. (Maine state boundary), which flows through Milton and Northeast ponds in E center. Agr. (nursery crops, corn, apples; cattle; dairying). N.H. Farm Mus. Includes village of Milton Mills (in N). **7** town (1990 pop. 8,404), including Milton village, Chittenden co., NW Vt., on Lamoille R. and L. Champlain, and 12 mi/19 km N of Burlington; 44°38′N 73°09′W. Dairy prods. Sandbar Refuge Management Area is here. Settled 1782, organized 1788. **8** town (1990 pop. 4,995), Pierce co., W central Wash., suburb, 6 mi/9.7 km E of Tacoma; 47°15′N 122°19′W. Mfg. (engines, pleating and stitching); logging. Evergreen Airport to N. **9** town (1990 pop. 2,242), Cabell co., W W.Va., on Mud R., 16 mi/26 km E of Huntington; 38°25′N 08°82′W. Agr. (corn, tobacco); cattle; poultry. Coal, gas, and oil region. Known as "Glass Town" for its glass mfg. (hand-blown glassware, stained glass); also plastic dies, machining, back supports. Mountaineer Opry House. Mill Creek Wildlife Management Area to N. Inc. 1876. **10** town (1990 pop. 4,434), Rock co., S Wis., near L. Koshkonong (resort), 8 mi/12.9 km NE of Janesville; 42°46′N 88°57′W. In farming and dairying area; mfg. RR junction. Milton House State Historical Site. Inc. 1904.

Milton 1 village, Pike co., W Ill., near Illinois R., 9 mi/14.5 km ESE of Pittsfield; 39°33′N 90°39′W. In agr. area. **2** village (1990 pop. 563), Trimble co., N Ky., on the Ohio R. (bridge to Madison, Ind.), and 40 mi/64 km NNE of Louisville; 38°42′N 85°22′W. Agr. (tobacco, grain, soybeans; cattle; dairying); mfg. (sand and gravel processing). **3** village (☐ 1 sq mi/2.6 sq km; 1990 pop. 1,140), Ulster co., SE N.Y., on W bank of the Hudson R., and 4 mi/6.4 km S of Poughkeepsie; 43°01′N

73°50′W. Agr. (tree fruit, grapes). Pop. includes Heritage Hills and Heritage Knolls. **4** village (1990 pop. 185), Caswell co., N N.C., 15 mi/24 km NW of Roxboro, and 13 mi/21 km ESE of Danville, on Dan R., at Va. state line; 36°32′N 79°12′W. Tobacco, grain; poultry. Hyco reservoir (Hyco R.) to SE. **5** village (1990 pop. 133), Cavalier co., NE N.Dak., 18 mi/29 km SE of Langdon; 48°37′N 98°02′W.

Milton, borough (1990 pop. 6,746), Northumberland co., E central Pa., 11 mi/18 km NNW of Sunbury, on West Branch of Susquehanna R.; 41°00′N 50°76′W. Agr. (corn, hay; livestock, poultry; dairying); diversified mfg.; limestone. Milton Airport to S. Tiadaghton State Forest to W, Bald Eagle State Forest to NW; Milton State Park, on isl. in river, to W. Laid out 1792, inc. 1817.

Milton Center, village (1990 pop. 200), Wood co., NW Ohio, 10 mi/16 km WSW of Bowling Green, in agr. area; 41°18′N 83°49′W.

Milton Junction, village, Rock co., S Wis., bet. L. Koshkonong and Janesville, 1 mi/1.6 km W of Milton. Inc. 1949.

Milton, Lake, reservoir (□ 3 sq mi/7.8 sq km), Mahoning co., NE Ohio, on Mahoning R., 10 mi/16 km NW of Alliance; 41°08′N 80°59′W. Max. capacity 46,605 acre-ft. Formed by Lake Milton Dam (30 ft/9 m high), built (1916) for recreation; also used for water supply. Lake Milton State Park on W shore.

Milton Lake, Ohio: see MAHONING RIVER.

Milton Mills, N.H.: see MILTON.

Miltona (mil-TO-nuh), village (1990 pop. 181), Douglas co., W Minn., E of L. Miltona, 12 mi/19 km NNE of Alexandria; 46°02′N 95°17′W. Grain; poultry; dairying; mfg. (concrete, golf course repair tools). L. Carlos State Park to S; Irene L. to NW.

Miltona, Lake (mil-TO-nuh) (□ 8 sq mi/20.7 sq km), Douglas co., W Minn., 10 mi/16 km N of Alexandria; 5.5 mi/8.9 km long, 2 mi/3.2 km wide; 46°02′N 95°21′W. Elev. 1,365 ft/416 m. Miltona village is E. Drains S into L. Ida. Resorts.

Milton-Freewater, town (1990 pop. 5,533), Umatilla co., NE Oregon, 10 mi/16 km S of Walla Walla, Wash., on Walla Walla R., 23 mi/37 km NE of Pendleton. Mfg. (canned vegetables, frozen fruit). Wheat. Timber. Site of Frazier Farmstead Mus. Umatilla Natl. Forest, including Umatilla Wilderness Area, to SE and E. Inc. 1886.

Miltonsburg, village (1990 pop. 56), Monroe co., Ohio, 6 mi/10 km NNW of Woodsfield, in agr. area; 39°50′N 81°10′W. Limestone quarry.

Miltonvale, village (1990 pop. 484), Cloud co., N central Kansas, 19 mi/31 km SE of Concordia; 39°21′N 97°27′W. In wheat region.

Milverton, village (1991 pop. 1,664), S Ont., Canada, 15 mi/24 km NNE of Stratford; 43°34′N 80°55′W. Light mfg., mixed farming, dairying; flour, apples; cattle; wood prods.

Milwaukee, county (□ 1,189 sq mi/3,080 sq km; 1990 pop. 959,275), SE Wis.; ⊙ Milwaukee; 42°58′N 87°40′W. All of co. is incorporated. The city of Milwaukee comprises 96 sq mi/249 sq km of the co., mainly in center and NW; remainder is comprised of Wauwatosa, West Allis, Franklin, Oak Creek, and 14 other cities and villages. Bounded E by L. Michigan; drained by Milwaukee, Menomonee, and Root rivers. Highly industrialized area, centered at Milwaukee. Small areas of remnant agr., mainly in far S (wheat, soybeans). Formed 1834.

Milwaukee, city (1990 pop. 628,088), ⊙ Milwaukee co., SE Wis., at the point where the Milwaukee, Menomonee, and Kinnickinnic rivers enter L. Michigan; 43°03′N 87°58′W. Borders L. Michigan on E; city is hemmed in on all sides by neighboring municipalities, preventing annexation (other than by merges). A metropolitan area, it is the largest city in the state, and it is a port of entry, shipping heavy cargo from the entire Midwest to other lake ports and world ports via the St. Lawrence Seaway. It is a producer of heavy machinery and electrical equip. and a principal manufacturer of diesel and gasoline engines, tractors, and beer; Milwaukee once dominated the country's beer-brewing industry. Various light and heavy mfg. In 1673, Father

Jacques Marquette visited the site, which was then a Native Amer. gathering and trading center. In 1795 the North West Company established a fur-trading post. Solomon Juneau, a fur trader, arrived in 1818, and in 1838 several settlements merged to form Milwaukee village. It grew as a shipping center and became famous for its numerous industries, notably brewing and meat packing. German refugees arrived in large numbers after 1848, stimulating the city's political, economic, and social growth. The Knights of Saint Crispin foreshadowed the city's growing labor movement after the Civil War. Victor L. Berger, the Socialist leader, exerted a dominant influence there, and Daniel W. Hoan made Milwaukee known for efficient administration. Among the city's educational institutions are Marquette Univ., the Univ. of Wis. (Milwaukee), Alverno Col., Cardinal Stritch Col. (in Fox Point), Wisconsin Lutheran Col. (in Wauwatosa), Milwaukee Inst. of Art and Design, the Wisconsin Conservatory of Music, the Milwaukee School of Engineering, and the Milwaukee Area Technical Col. Local attractions include the breweries, with their guided tours; a public library and mus.; an art center; a church built by Frank Lloyd Wright; a performing arts center; and the water tower. Havenswood Environmental Awareness Center. Among the numerous parks are Washington Park; Mitchell Park, with enclosed botanical gardens; Juneau Park; Estabrook Park, containing one of the city's oldest houses. Milwaukee has professional basketball and baseball teams, and the Green Bay Packers football team play several games a year here. Economically, the city was hit hard in the 1979–1982 recession years; more than 60,000 jobs were lost in the industrial sector. Prosperity reoccurred in the late 1980s as mfg. jobs became more prevalent, aided principally by the economic efforts of major Milwaukee companies in areas such as the internatl. export of tools and machinery. Inc. 1846

Milwaukee, uninc. village, Northampton co., NE N.C., 24 mi/39 km E of Roanoke Rapids. Peanuts, cotton, tobacco; livestock.

Milwaukee Deep, trench, ocean depth at 28,232 ft/8,605 m, in the Puerto Rico Trench, 19°35′N 66°30′W. Deepest point in the Atlantic Ocean.

Milwaukee River, c.75 mi/121 km long, SE Wis.; rises in lake region of Fond du Lac co.; flows S, past West Bend, turns E, then generally S, past Grafton, reaching L. Michigan at Milwaukee.

Milwaukie, city (1990 pop. 18,692), Clackamas and Multnomah cos., NW Oregon, suburb, 5 mi/8 km SSE of downtown Portland on the Willamette R., at mouths of Johnson and Kellogg Creeks; 45°26′N 122°37′W. RR junction. Mfg. (apparel, furniture prods., fabricated metal). The city is a distribution center for farms and orchards of the Willamette Valley and has numerous warehouse facilities. Fruit trees brought here by covered wagon from Iowa (1848) inaugurated the state's important cherry-growing industry. Inc. 1903.

Mimbres (MIM-bruhs), uninc. village (1990 pop. 300), Grant co., SW N.Mex., 18 mi/29 km ENE of Silver City, on Mimbres R. Elev. 5,977 ft/1,822 m. Resort with hot mineral springs. Gila Natl. Forest to W, N, and E; Black Range, Black Peak, on Coninental Divide, to NW; Mimbres Mts. to E.

Mimbres Mountains (MIM-bruhs), SW N.Mex., extending N from Cooks Range to Black Range, on Grant and Sierra co. line; extending S into Luna co. Chief peaks: Pine Flat Mt. (7,875 ft/2,400 m), Thompson Cone (7,932 ft/2,418 m), Seven Brothers Mt. (8,690 ft/2,649 m). Cooke's Peak (8,408 ft/2,563 m) in S. Range is largely within Gila Natl. Forest.

Mimms, Fort, Ala.: see FORT MIMMS.

Mimosa Park (mi-MO-suh), uninc. town (1990 pop. 4,516), St. Charles parish, 5 mi/8 km SE of Hahnville; 29°54′N 90°21′W.

Mims (MIMZ), town (□ 25 sq mi/65 sq km; 1990 pop. 9,412), Brevard co., E central Fla., 6 mi/9.7 km N of Titusville; 28°40′N 80°50′W. Mfg. includes liquified gases, heat-sealing prods., fruit packing, structural steel fabrication, chemically treated fittings.

Mina (MEE-nah), town (1990 pop. 2,822), Nuevo León,

N Mexico, in foothills of Sierra Madre Oriental, near Salinas R., 27 mi/43 km NW of Monterrey, on Mexico Highway 53; 26°00′N 100°33′W. Cereals, cactus fibers, livestock.

Mina (MEE-nuh), uninc. village (1990 pop. 400), Mineral co., W Nev., 34 mi/55 km SE of Hawthorne. Elev. 4,540 ft/1,384 m. Cattle. Excelsior Mts. to W; Pilot Peak (9,184 ft/2,799 m), in Monte Cristo Range, to E. Southern Pacific Spring to NE; Rhodes Salt Marsh to S.

Minarets, The, Madera-Mono co. line, E Calif. Jagged summits (c.12,000 ft/3,658 m) in the Sierra Nevada, in scenic region SE of Yosemite Natl. Park.

Minas (MEE-nahs), town (pop. 15,000), Camagüey prov., E Cuba, on RR, and 20 mi/32 km ENE of Camagüey; 21°29′N 77°37′W. Asphalt, iron, and copper mining.

Minas Basin (MEI-nuhs), central N.S., Canada, central part of deep inlet of the Bay of Fundy, with which it is connected (W) by Minas Channel; 24 mi/39 km long, up to 25 mi/40 km wide. Continued E by Cobequid Bay. Narrows bet. Cape Sharp and Cape Split separate it from Minas Channel. On N coast is Parrsboro. Receives Cornwallis, Avon, and several smaller rivers.

Minas Channel, inlet, N central N.S., connects the Bay of Fundy (W) with the Minas Basin (E); 24 mi/39 km long, 10 mi/16 km–14 mi/23 km wide. Its mouth is bet. Cape Chignecto and Cape Sharp. N shore is indented by Advocate Bay (4 mi/6 km long, 8 mi/13 km wide) and Greville Bay (5 mi/8 km long, 16 mi/26 km wide). On S side, Cape Split extends 6 mi/10 km into the channel. On N shore is Port Greville. High tides of Bay of Fundy extend into Minas Channel.

Minas de Matahambre (MEE-nahs dai mah tah-AHM-brai), town, Pinar del Río prov., W Cuba, 20 mi/32 km NW of Pinar del Río; 22°41′N 83°56′W. Copper-mining center. Also called Matahambre.

Minatare (MI-nuh-tahr-ai), village (1990 pop. 807), Scotts Bluff co., W Nebr., 8 mi/12.9 km ESE of Scottsbluff, and on North Platte R; 41°48′N 103°30′W. Beet sugar, dairy and poultry produce, grain. Nearby is L. Minatare, artificial lake created (1915) for irrigation. State Recreation Area to N (part of North Platte Natl. Wildlife Refuge). Mfg. (sickle sharpeners).

Minatitlán (mee-nah-tee-TLAHN), city (1990 pop. 142,060) and township, Veracruz, SE Mexico, port on navigable Coatzacoalcos R. (20 mi/32 km from mouth), on Isthmus of Tehuantepec, 135 mi/217 km SE of Veracruz; 17°59′N 94°32′W. RR terminus; along with Coatzacoalcos, the center of Mexico's oil and petrochemical industry (pipeline to Salina Cruz); lumber mills. Agr. prods.: coffee, rice, corn, sugarcane, fruit; livestock.

Minatitlán (mee-nah-tee-TLAHN), town (1990 pop. 3,843), Colima, W Mexico, 24 mi/39 km WNW of Colima; 17°59′N 94°32′W. Rice, corn, beans, sugarcane, cotton, coffee, fruit; livestock; iron mining. Also known as El Mamey.

Minburn, town (1990 pop. 346), Dallas co., central Iowa, 10 mi/16 km N of Adel; 41°45′N 94°01′W. In agr. area.

Minburn, village (1991 pop. 105), E Alta., Canada, 22 mi/35 km W of Vermilion. Mixed farming, wheat, flax; cattle.

Minchumina, Lake, Alaska: see LAKE MINCHUMINA.

Minco (MINK-o), town (1990 pop. 1,411), Grady co., central Okla., 18 mi/29 km N of Chickasha; 35°19′N 97°57′W. In agr. area (cotton, corn, wheat, peanuts; livestock); honey, lye soap.

Minden (MIN-DIN), city (1990 pop. 13,661), ⊙ Webster parish, NW La., 23 mi/37 km ENE of Shreveport; 32°37′N 93°17′W. RR junction. Shipping center of an area rich in timber, oil, and natural gas. In agr. area (cotton, sweet potatoes, vegetables, watermelons; cattle; dairying); diversified mfg. Oil and gas field nearby. German colony. Established as a socialist-utopian commune in 1835. Kisatchie Natl. Forest to N. Inc. 1850.

Minden 1 (MIN-duhn), town (1990 pop. 498), Pottawattamie co., SW Iowa, on Keg Creek, and 20 mi/32 km NE of Council Bluffs; 41°28′N 95°32′W. **2** town (1990 pop. 2,749), ⊙ Kearney co., S Nebr., 14 mi/23 km SSE of Kearney, and on branch of Little Blue R; 40°30′N 98°57′W. RR junction. Grain; livestock; dairy and poultry produce. Mfg. (fiberglass parts, plastic aircraft components). Harold Warp's Pioneer Village here. Ft. Kearney State Historical Park to NW. City founded 1876. **3** uninc. town (1990 pop. 1,441), ⊙ Douglas co., W Nev., on East Carson R., and 15 mi/24 km S of Carson City; 38°57′N 119°46′W. Alfalfa, potatoes, grain; cattle; poultry; mfg. (lightning protection equip.); tourism. Toiyabe Natl. Forest to W and SE. Jacks Valley Wildlife Management Area to N. Douglas co. Airport to N. Est. 1905 as RR town. **4** uninc. town (1990 pop. 980), Fayette co., S central W.Va., near New R., 2 mi/3.2 km NE of Oak Hill. Coal-mining region.

Minden (MIN-duhn), village, ⊙ Haliburton co., S Ont., Canada, bet. Minden L. (N) and Gullfoot L. (S), 40 mi/64 km N of Lindsay; 44°56′N 78°44′W. Dairying, mixed farming.

Minden City, village (1990 pop. 233), Sanilac co., E Mich., 17 mi/27 km NNE of Sandusky, near source of Black R.; 43°40′N 82°46′W. In farm area. Light mfg. Also called Minden.

Minden Lake, S Ont., Canada, 3 mi/5 km N of Minden, 50 mi/80 km NNW of Peterborough; 3 mi/5 km long, 1 mi/2 km wide. Drains S through Gull R. into Balsam L. and Trent Canal.

Mindenmines (MIN-din-meinz), city (1990 pop. 346), Barton co., SW Mo., 8 mi/12.9 km NE of Pittsburg, Kansas; 37°28′N 94°35′W. In a former strip coal-mining area; oil field. Wheat, corn, sorghum; cattle. Prairie State Park to N.

Mine Centre, village, W Ont., Canada, on Little Turtle L. (7 mi/11 km long, 5 mi/8 km wide), 40 mi/64 km ENE of Fort Frances; 48°46′N 92°37′W. Gold, iron mining.

Mine Hill, township (1990 pop. 3,333), Morris co., N central N.J., 8 mi/12.9 km NW of Morristown; 40°52′N 74°35′W. Ships crushed stone, sand. Iron mine here opened 1858, reopened 1939, since closed.

Mine La Motte, (MEIN luh MAHT), uninc. community, historic lead-mining village, Madison co., SE Mo., in St. François Mts. 5 mi/8 km N of Fredericktown. First lead mine in present-day Mo. was opened here in c.1720 by Antoine de la Motte Cadillac.

Mineola, town (1990 pop. 4,321), Wood co., NE Texas, near Sabine R., 24 mi/39 km NNW of Tyler; 32°40′N 95°29′W. Elev. 414 ft/126 m. RR junction; in agr. and mfg. (sleeping bags, feeds, food processing, wooden cabinets) area; timber. Settled 1872, inc. 1873.

Mineola, suburb (□ 1 sq mi/2.6 sq km; 1990 pop. 18,994) of N.Y. city, ⊙ Nassau co., SE N.Y., on L.I., 18 mi/29 km E of midtown Manhattan; 40°45′N 73°38′W. Chiefly residential, it is a commercial center, with some light industry. Inc. 1906.

Miner, county (□ 572 sq mi/1,481 sq km; 1990 pop. 3,272), E central S.Dak.; ⊙ Howard; 44°01′N 97°36′W. Agr. area watered by W Fork Vermillion R. and Rock and Redstone creeks. Corn, wheat, soybeans; dairy produce; cattle, hogs, poultry. Lake Carthage State Lakeside Use Area in N. Formed 1873.

Miner (MEI-nuhr), town (1990 pop. 1,218), Scott co., SE Mo., suburb, 2 mi/3.2 km E of Sikeston; 36°53′N 89°31′W. Residential. Highway service center.

Mineral 1 county (□ 877 sq mi/2,271 sq km; 1990 pop. 558), SW Colo.; ⊙ Creede; 37°41′N 106°55′W. Continental Divide forms part of N boundary, winds SSW through Hinsdale co., turns SSE in San Juan co., crossing back through Hinsdale co. and across S part of Mineral co. Mining and livestock-grazing region, drained by headwaters of Rio Grande. Silver, lead. Includes ranges of Rocky Mts. Most of N ¾ of co. in Rio Grande Natl. Forest; most of S part, S of divide, in San Juan Natl. Forest. Wheeler Natl. Monument is in NE. Formed 1893. **2** county (□ 1,223 sq mi/3,168 sq km; 1990 pop. 3,315), W Mont.; ⊙ Superior; 47°09′N 114°59′W. Forested region bordering on Idaho; drained by the Clark Fork and St. Regis rivers. Some sheep, cattle; hay; forest industries; mining. Lolo Natl. Forest covers all of co., except margins of Clark Fork. Bitter root Range in W. Formed 1914. **3** county (□ 3,813 sq mi/-

9,876 sq km; 1990 pop. 6,475), W Nev.; ⊙ Hawthorne; 38°32′N 118°25′W. Mt. region bordering on Calif. Gold, silver; sand and gravel; cattle; recreation. Formed 1911. Walker L. (Walker L. State Recreational Area on W shore) and Wassuk Range in W. U.S. naval ammunition depot at Hawthorne, in W center; part of Walker R. Indian Reservation in NW. Excelsior Mts. in S. Gillis Range in N center. Part of Toiyabe and Inyo Natl. Forests in SW. Formerly entirely within Esmeralda co. **4** county (□ 329 sq mi/852 sq km; 1990 pop. 26,697), W.Va., in Eastern Panhandle; ⊙ Keyser; 39°25′N 78°56′W. Bounded N and NW by North Branch of the Potomac R. (forms Md. state line; Jennings Randolph L. reservoir in W); drained by Patterson Creek; traversed by Knobly and Patterson Creek Mt. ridges (on W boundary) and others. Coal mines; timber. Agr. (corn, wheat, oats, barley, rye, tobacco, alfalfa, hay); cattle, hogs, sheep, poultry. Mfg. at Keyser, esp. glass. Nancy Hanks Memorial in S. Parts of Springfield Wildlife Management Area in E. Formed 1866.

Mineral, town (1990 pop. 471), Louisa co., central Va., 30 mi/48 km E of Charlottesville; 38°00′N 77°54′W. Mfg. (clothing, wooden pallets, lumber); agr. (tobacco, grain, soybeans; cattle).

Mineral 1 uninc. village, Tehama co., N Calif., 35 mi/56 km ENE of Red Bluff, near Mill Creek. Hq. for Lassen Volcanic Natl. Park (to NE). **2** village (1990 pop. 250), Bureau co., N Ill., 20 mi/32 km W of Princeton; 41°22′N 89°50′W. In agr. area.

Mineral Bluff, village (1990 pop. 153), Fannin co., N Ga., 4 mi/6.4 km NE of Blue Ridge; 34°55′N 84°17′W.

Mineral City, village (1990 pop. 725), Tuscarawas co., E Ohio, 9 mi/14 km NE of New Philadelphia, in coal mining area; 40°36′N 81°22′W.

Mineral de Angangueo (mee-NAI-ral de ahn-gahn-GWAI-o), town (1990 pop. 4,579), ⊙ Angangueo municipio, Michoacán, central Mexico, on central plateau, 45 mi/72 km NW of Toluca de Lerdo, on RR; 19°39′N 100°25′W. Elev. 8,622 ft/2,628 m. In the past, one of richest mining centers (silver, lead, copper, zinc).

Mineral de la Reforma, Mexico: see PACHUQUILLA.

Mineral del Chico (mee-NE-rahl del CHEE-ko) or **El Chico**, town (1990 pop. 528), Hidalgo, central Mexico, 6 mi/9.7 km N of Pachuca de Soto; 20°12′N 98°43′W. Elev. 7,713 ft/2,351 m. located within El Chico Natl. Park. Former mining center. Resort in majestic mt. setting nearby.

Mineral del Monte (mee-ne-rahl del MON-te), city (1990 pop. 10,666) and township, ⊙ municipio Mineral del Monte, Hidalgo, central Mexico, on central plateau, 4 mi/6.4 km E of Pachuca de Soto; 20°08′N 98°40′W. Elev. 8,789 ft/2,679 m. Important silver- and gold-mining center worked by Welsh miners in 1800s, active; foundries; mfg. of explosives. Sometimes Real del Monte.

Mineral Hills, village (1990 pop. 200), Iron co., SW Upper Peninsula, Mich., 2 mi/3.2 km NNW of Iron River city; 46°06′N 88°38′W.

Mineral Hot Springs, village, Saguache co., S central Colo., on San Luis Creek, in S foothills of Sawatch Mts., and 13 mi/21 km ENE of Saguache. Elev. 7,747 ft/2,361 m. Sheep, cattle, feed. Resort. Ouray Peak is 19 mi/31 km NW. Parts of Rio Grande Natl. Forest to NW and NE.

Mineral Mountains, in Beaver co., SW Utah, extend 25 mi/40 km N from Minersville. Max. elev. 7,583 ft/2,311 m.

Mineral Point 1 town (1990 pop. 384), Washington co., E central Mo., in the Ozarks, 3 mi/4.8 km E of Potosi; 37°57′N 90°43′W. Former lead-mining dist.; mfg. (valves). Missouri State Correctional Center to NW. **2** town (1990 pop. 2,428), Iowa co., S Wis., 7 mi/11.3 km SSW of Dodgeville; 42°51′N 90°10′W. In dairy and livestock area; dairy prods. light mfg. Winery. Inc. 1857. Has restored Cornish miners' houses dating from lead-mining activity of mid-19th cent.

Mineral Ridge, unincorporated village (1990 pop. 3,928), Trumbull co., NE Ohio, 7 mi/11 km SE of Warren; 41°08′N 80°46′W. Steel prods., canned foods.

Mineral Springs, town (1990 pop. 1,004), Howard co.,

SW Ark., 6 mi/9.7 km SW of Nashville; 33°52′N 93°55′W. Mfg. (floor and roof trusses). Millwood L. reservoir to SW.

Mineral Springs, uninc. village, Union co., S N.C., 7 mi/11.3 km SW of Monroe. Cotton; livestock; poultry. Mfg. (yarn, fertilizer).

Mineral Wells, city (1990 pop. 14,870), Palo Pinto and Parker cos., N Texas, 45 mi/72 km W of Fort Worth; 32°49′N 98°04′W. Elev. 925 ft/282 m. Mfg. (aluminum prods., bottled mineral water, clothing, building materials, gas processing, pharmaceuticals). The mineral water (Waters of Crazy Well were discovered 1885) made this hill city a popular health resort in the late 19th and early 20th cent., and oil activity in the area also spurred the city's growth. Cattle, horses; peanuts, wheat; cedar timber. To the E is L. Mineral Wells State Park, a reservoir in the Trinity R. system. Inc. 1882.

Mineral Wells or **Mineralwells**, uninc. town (1990 pop. 1,698), Wood co., NW W.Va., 5 mi/8 km S of Parkersburg, near Little Kanawha R.; 39°10′N 81°30′W. Agr. (grain, tobacco); livestock; poultry. Mfg. (trailer and truck bodies, sand and gravel processing). W.Va. Motor Speedway is here. W.Va. Interstate Fair held in July.

Minersville, village (1990 pop. 608), Beaver co., SW Utah, on Beaver R., and 17 mi/27 km WSW of Beaver, just SW of Mineral Mts.; 38°12′N 112°55′W. Irrigated agr. area (alfalfa, corn, fruit, potatoes. barley); cattle. Town was once dependent on mining. Elev. 5,625 ft/1,715 m. Minersville Reservoir and State Park to E. Settled 1858; 1st mine in Utah.

Minersville, borough (1990 pop. 4,877), Schuylkill co., E central Pa., 3 mi/4.8 km NNW of Pottsville; 40°41′N 76°15′W. Agr. (poultry, dairying); mfg. (concrete, apparel); anthracite coal. Schuylkill Co. Airport 5 mi/8 km to W. Settled c.1793, inc. 1831.

Minerva 1 resort village (1990 pop. 300), Essex co., NE N.Y., in the Adirondacks, 37 mi/60 km NNW of Glens Falls; 43°51′N 74°02′W. Hunting nearby. **2** village (1990 pop. 4,318), on Stark-Carroll co. state line, E Ohio, 15 mi/24 km ESE of Canton, in agr. area; 40°43′N 81°06′W. Brick, tile. Founded 1835.

Minerva Park, village (1990 pop. 1,463), Franklin co., central Ohio, suburb N of Columbus; 40°04′N 82°57′W.

Minetto, village (□ 3 sq mi/7.8 sq km; 1990 pop. 1,252) in Minetto town (1990 pop. 1,822), Oswego co., N central N.Y., on Oswego R., just S of Oswego; 43°23′N 76°28′W.

Mineville, village (1990 pop. 950), Essex co., NE N.Y., near L. Champlain, 18 mi/29 km NNW of Ticonderoga; 44°05′N 73°31′W. Named after iron mining once conducted in area.

Mingan (MING-guhn), village, E Que., Canada, on Jacques Cartier Strait of Gulf of St. Lawrence, and 100 mi/161 km E of Sept-Îles, 400 mi/644 km NE of Quebec; 50°18′N 64°02′W. Radio station, airfield. Coastal highway extended from Sept-Îles to Havre–St.-Pierre (via Mingan) in late 1960s; ferry continues beyond to S end of Lab.

Mingan Archipelago National Park Reserve (□ 58 sq mi/150 sq km), c. 40 islands in Jacques Cartier Passage at mouth of St. Lawrence R., E Que., Canada, near Havre-St-Pierre, 93 mi/150 km E of Sept-Iles. Est. 1985; natl. park status pending settlement of Aboriginal land claims. Flowerpot isls. of limestone, eroded at base by tides. Atlantic puffins, other seabirds; wildflowers. Camping, hiking.

Mingan Islands (MING-guhn), group of 15 small isls. and many islets, E Que., Canada, in the St. Lawrence R., N of Anticosti isl. They were visited (1535) by Jacques Cartier, the Fr. explorer. In 1836 the isls. were acquired by the Hudson Bay Company.

Mingan Passage, E Que., Canada, channel (30 mi/48 km wide) of the St. Lawrence, bet. Mingan, on Que. mainland, and Anticosti Isl. Near N coast are Mingan Isls.

Mingo (MING-o), county (□ 423 sq mi/1,096 sq km; 1990 pop. 33,739), SW W.Va.; ⊙ Williamson; 37°43′N 82°8′W. Bounded SW by Tug Fork R. (Ky. state line). Extensive bituminous-coal fields; natural gas and oil wells; timber. Some agr. Laurel Creek Wildlife Management Area in N; part of R.D. Bailey L. (reservoir) Wildlife Management Area in SE. Formed 1895.

Mingo, town (1990 pop. 252), Jasper co., central Iowa, 14 mi/23 km WNW of Newton; 41°46′N 93°16′W. Livestock, grain.

Mingo Junction, village (1990 pop. 4,297), Jefferson co., E Ohio, 4 mi/6 km S of Steubenville, and on Ohio R.; 40°19′N 80°37′W. Truck and fruit farming. Settled 1809, inc. 1882. Coal mines nearby.

Mingus, village (1990 pop. 215), Palo Pinto co., N central Texas, c.65 mi/105 km WSW of Fort Worth; 32°32′N 98°25′W. In agr. area (cattle; peanuts, wheat); oil and gas.

Mingus Mountain, peak (7,743 ft/2,360 m) in Black Hills, central Ariz., 25 mi/40 km ENE of Prescott, and 3 mi/4.8 km S of Jerome. Copper was mined nearby. In Prescott Natl. Forest.

Minho River, c.40 mi/64 km long, W central and S Jamaica; rises just E of Spaldings; flows SE and S through a fertile valley, past Frankfield, Chapleton, May Pen, and Alley, to the coast; 18°05′N 77°14′W. Not navigable. Also known as Rio Minho.

Minidoka, county (□ 763 sq mi/1,976 sq km; 1990 pop. 19,361), S Idaho; ⊙ Rupert. Bounded by Snake R. on S and SE. Irrigated farmlands receive water from L. Walcott, formed by Minidoka Dam (SE boundary of co.) on Snake R. Potatoes, sugar beets, dry beans, alfalfa; sheep, cattle; dairying; oats, barley, wheat. Part of Minidoka Natl. Wildlife Refuge in SE corner, at dam; part of Lava Crater in N; Snake River Plain. Formed 1913.

Minidoka, village (1990 pop. 67), Minidoka co., S Idaho, 15 mi/24 km NE of Rupert; 42°45′N 113°29′W. Elev. 4,286 ft/1,306 m. RR center in irrigated agr. area. Minidoka Dam (L. Walcott Reservoir; Snake R.) is 6 mi/9.7 km S. Minidoka Natl. Wildlife Refuge to SE on reservoir.

Minidoka Dam, Idaho: see WALCOTT, LAKE.

Minier (mei-NEER), village (1990 pop. 1,155), Tazewell co., central Ill., 17 mi/27 km W of Bloomington; 40°25′N 89°18′W. In agr. area.

Miniota (mi-nee-O-tuh), village (1991 pop. 1,048), SW Man., Canada, on Assiniboine R., and 50 mi/80 km WNW of Brandon; 50°08′N 101°02′W. Dairying; grain, stock.

Mink Creek, uninc. village (1990 pop. 50), Franklin co., SE Idaho, 11 mi/18 km NE of Preston, near Bear R. Poultry, dairy. Cache Natl. Forest to E.

Minneapolis, city (1990 pop. 368,383), ⊙ Hennepin co., E Minn., at the head of navigation on the Mississippi R., at St. Anthony Falls; 44°57′N 93°16′W. Lock and Dam No. 1 at falls; river flows through center of city. The largest city in the state and a port of entry, it is a major industrial and RR hub. Served by Twin Cities internatl. airport in nearby Richfield. With adjacent St. Paul to E, the 2 are known as the Twin Cities; similar in size, Minneapolis is the dominant twin, downtown St. Paul is 8 mi/12.9 km ESE of downtown Minneapolis. It is the processing, distributing, and trade center for a vast grain and cattle area. Minneapolis is also a banking and financial center with a significant high-technology industry that primarily developed in the 1980s. Diversified mfg., both heavy and light. Although the central city's pop. has declined since the 1970s, the outlying suburbs have grown significantly, including Bloomington (S), Plymouth, and Minnetonka (W). The falls were visited by Louis Hennepin in 1683; Fort Snelling was est. in 1819; and a sawmill was built at the falls in 1821. The village of St. Anthony was settled c.1839 on the E side of the river near the falls. Minneapolis originated on the W side of the river c.1847 and included much of the reservation of Fort Snelling. It annexed St. Anthony in 1872. The city became the country's foremost lumber center, and after the plains were planted with wheat and the RR were built, flour milling developed, with the 50 ft/15 m falls supplying power. The city was laid out with wide streets and has 22 lakes and 153 parks. In Minnehaha Park, in SE, is the Stevens House (1849), the 1st frame house in Minneapolis, and Minnehaha Falls, on Minnehaha Creek. Fort Snelling State Park and Natl. Cemetery, also to SE, several art galleries and mus. (including the Amer. Swedish Inst.), the Guthrie Theater, and the Minneapolis Grain Exchange. The Minn. Symphony was founded here in 1903. The city is the seat of the Univ. of Minn., Augsburg Col., Minneapolis Community Col., and Natl. Education Center-Brown Inst. Campus. Hennepin Co. Historical Society Mus., Minneapolis Inst. of Arts, Minneapolis Col. of Art and Design, all 3 at Morrison Park in S. In the early 1960s, the main shopping avenue was converted into a 10-block mall lined with trees and flowers; a skyway system of sidewalks was provided for pedestrians; and a 51-story skyscraper and other noteworthy bldgs. were erected. State Theatre; Orchestra Hall; Convention Center; Bell Mus. of Natural History; Weissman Art Mus., and Mariucci Area at Univ. of Minn.; Minn. Zoo at suburban Apple valley, 15 mi/24 km to S; Como Park Zoo in St. Paul to E; Dunwoody Industrial Inst. Hubert Humphrey Metrodome (1982), stadium in downtown, replaced Metropolitan Stadium in Bloomington, to S, old stadium site is now Mall of America, 3d-largest shoping center in world, a major tourist destination. Inc. 1856.

Minneapolis (min-ee-AP-uh-lis), town (1990 pop. 1,983), ⊙ Ottawa co., N central Kansas, on Solomon R. and 20 mi/32 km NNW of Salina; 39°07′N 97°42′W. RR junction. Trade and shipping center for livestock, grain, and poultry region; grain storage. Mfg. (motor homes). Ottawa State Fishing L. to E, large, smooth sandstone formations. Laid out 1866, inc. 1871.

Minnedosa (mi-ni-DO-suh), town (1991 pop. 2,526), SW Man., Canada, on Minnedosa R., and 30 mi/48 km N of Brandon; 50°15′N 99°50′W. Lumbering, mixed farming; resort.

Minnedosa River, SW Man., Canada; rises in Riding Mt. Natl. Park; flows c.150 mi/241 km in a winding course generally S, past Minnedosa, to Assiniboine R., 8 mi/13 km W of Brandon.

Minnehaha, [=laughing water], county (□ 813 sq mi/2,106 sq km; 1990 pop. 123,809), E S.Dak., on Minn. line; ⊙ Sioux Falls; 43°40′N 96°47′W. Highly productive agr. area drained by Big Sioux R. and Pinestone Creek. Mfg. at Sioux Falls. Corn, soybeans, hay; cattle, hogs, sheep; dairy produce; honey. Urbanized in S central part, Sioux Falls and adjacent towns. Formed 1862.

Minnehaha Falls (min-nee-HAH-huh), Hennepin co., SE Minn., 53 ft/16 m high, in Minnehaha Creek, which flows from L. Minnetonka (23 sq mi/60 sq km) SE to the Mississippi R. (at its outflow to Mississippi R. is Lock and Dam No. 1 just N of confluence); 44°54′N 93°12′W. The surrounding area, including the gorge cut by the receding falls, is in Minnehaha Park, SE corner of city of Minneapolis. Most of the year only a thin trickle of water passes over the falls. The name *Minnehaha* (meaning "laughing water") is immortalized in Longfellow's *The Song of Hiawatha.*

Minneiska (mi-nee-IS-kuh), village (1990 pop. 127), Wabasha co., SE Minn., on Mississippi R., and 15 mi/24 km NW of Winona; 44°11′N 91°52′W. Grain; livestock, poultry; dairying. Lock and Dam No. 5 to SE; Whitewater Wildlife Area to SW.

Minneola (mi-nee-O-luh), town (□ 1 sq mi/2.6 sq km; 1990 pop. 1,515), Lake co., central Fla., 23 mi/37 km W of Orlando, on small lake; 28°34′N 81°45′W. Ships citrus fruit.

Minneola (min-ee-O-luh), village (1990 pop. 705), Clark co., SW Kansas, 22 mi/35 km NW of Ashland; 37°26′N 100°00′W. Shipping point in wheat and livestock region. Oil and gas exploration and refining.

Minneota (mi-nee-YO-duh), town (1990 pop. 1,417), Lyon co., SW Minn., on South Branch of Yellow Medicine R., 12 mi/19 km NW of Marshall; 44°33′N 95°58′W. Grain; livestock, poultry; dairying; mfg. (fertilizers, transformers, trusses and rafters). Settled 1868, inc. 1881.

Minnesota, state (□ 86,943 sq mi/225,182 sq km; 1995 est. pop. 4,609,548), N central U.S., in the Great Lakes region, admitted as the 32d state of the Union in 1858; ⊙ SAINT PAUL; 46°29′N 94°04′W. St Paul and its twin city MINNEAPOLIS are 2d-largest and largest cities, respectively. BLOOMINGTON (suburb of Minneapolis) and DULUTH (in NE, on L. Superior) are other major cities. Except for Alaska, Minn. is the northernmost of all the states (reaching lat. 49°24′N). Minn. is bounded on the N by Canada (Man. to NW, Ont. to N and NE), on the E by L. Superior (forms boundary with Mich. and part of Wis.) and Wis. (the St. Croix and Mississippi rivers form most of border), on the S by Iowa, and on the W by S.Dak. and N.Dak. The climate is humid continental. Winter locks the land in snow, and spring is brief; summers are warm. Prehistoric glaciers left marshes, boulder-strewn hills, numerous lakes, and rich, gray drift soil stretching from the N pine wilderness to the broad S prairies. State referred to as "Land of 10,000 Lakes." In the E part of the state are mts. from which iron ore is decreasingly extracted. The Vermilion and Cuyuna ranges (discovered in 1884 and 1911) are virtually depleted, and the once rich MESABI iron range (1890) has seen major decline because of the depletion and environmental restrictions; all 3 mining districts are in N and NE. As richer ores diminished, new methods were developed to use lower-grade ores such as taconite. In spite of the decline, Minn. led the nation in iron ore production in 1988. Granite (from St. Cloud) and sand and gravel production are also among the largest in the country. S of the iron country, famous for its former boom towns, lie rolling hills. In the S and the W are prairies, the fertile farming country of Minn. Wheat, once paramount in the fields, has yielded its preeminence to corn, soybeans, and livestock. The state is a leader in the production of creamery butter, dry milk, cheese, and sweet corn. In the early 1950s mfg. displaced agr. as the major source of income in Minn. Major industries in the state include the mfg. of processed foods, electronic equip., machinery, paper prods., chemicals, and stone, clay, and glass prods. Minn. also pioneered the development of computers and other high-technology mfg. Printing and publishing are also important. Reforestation and the use of smaller trees for pulpwood have helped to keep timber as one of Minnesota's assets, even though the "big woods" of the early 19th cent. have been to a large extent recklessly felled. The state is roughly 30% forestland and has Chippewa Natl. Forest in N center; Superior Natl. Forest in NE, including Boundary Waters Canoe Area; Voyageur Natl. Park on Rainy L., on Can. border. Numerous state forests, especially in N; Richard J. Dorer Memorial Hardwood State Forest in SE. The days of logging in Minn., immortalized in the stories of the legendary Paul Bunyan and his prized possession, Babe the Blue Ox, were brief, but they helped build a number of large fortunes, such as that of Frederick Weyerhaeuser. Mountainous in NE along North Shore (Arrow Country, referring to triangular shape of NE corner); lowest point is L. Superior (602 ft/183 m), shared by the cos. of St. Louis, Lake, and Cook. Highest point is Eagle Mt. (2,301 ft/701 m), Cook co., only 13 mi/21 km from L. Superior. Another great resource of Minn. is its water, which has been extensively developed near industrial centers. The state has more than 10,000 lakes, many of which create chains of lakes; numerous streams and rivers. The rivers feed 3 major river systems: the Red R. and its tributaries in the W run N to Hudson Bay; the streams that run E into L. Superior are part of the St. Lawrence R. System (Atlantic Ocean); and the Mississippi flows S from its humble beginning in L. Itasca, gathering volume from the waters of the Minnesota and St. Croix rivers and others before leaving the state. Other rivers include Big Sioux R. and Missouri R., both part of Mississippi R. system. Locks and other improvements enable barge traffic to pass around the Falls of St. Anthony to reach upstream beyond Minneapolis. Duluth, at the western tip of L. Superior, has the largest inland harbor in the U.S.; W head of navigation of Great Lakes–St. Lawrence Seaway System. With the completion of the SAINT LAWRENCE SEAWAY (1959) and a marine terminal, the city became a key port for overseas trade. In 1991 it handled almost 41 million tons/45 million metric tons of cargo. Archaeological evidence indicates that Minn. was inhabited long before the time of the Mound Builders. A skeleton ("Minnesota Man"), found in 1931 near Pelican Falls, is believed to date from the Pleistocene epoch, c.20,000 years ago. Much important archaeological information concerning the early inhabitants of N. Amer. has been found in Minn. There are some experts who argue on the basis of the Kensington Rune Stone and other evidence that the 1st Europeans to reach Minn. were the Norsemen; that Fr. fur traders came in the mid-17th cent. is undeniably true. Other traders, explorers, and missionaries of New France also penetrated the country. Among these were Radisson and Groseilliers, Verendrye, the Sieur Duluth, and Father Hennepin and Michel Aco, who discovered the Falls of St. Anthony (the site of Minneapolis). At the time the French arrived, the dominant groups of Native Americans were the Ojibwa in the E and the Sioux in the W. Both were friendly to the French and contributed to the fur-trading empire of New France. Minn. remained excellent country for fur trade throughout the Br. regime that followed the Fr. and Indian Wars and continued so after the War of 1812, when the Amer. Fur Company became dominant and the company's men helped to develop the area. The E part of Minn. had been included in the NORTHWEST TERRITORY and was governed under the Ordinance of 1787; the W part was joined to the U.S. by the Louisiana Purchase. Further exploration was pursued by Jonathan Carver (1766–1767), Zebulon M. Pike (1805–1806), Henry Schoolcraft (1820, 1829), and Stephen H. Long (1823). Only after the War of 1812, however, did settlement begin in earnest. In 1820, Fort St. Anthony (later Fort Snelling) was founded as a guardian of the frontier. A gristmill established there in 1823 initiated the industrial development of Minneapolis. Treaties (1837, 1845, 1851, and 1855) with the Ojibwa and the Sioux, by which the U.S. govt. took over Native Amer. lands, and the opening of a land office at St. Croix Falls in 1848 initiated a period of real expansion. In 1849 Minn. became a territory. The Missouri and White Earth rivers were the W boundary. A land boom grew as towns were plotted, RRs chartered, and roads built. Attention was turned to education, and the Univ. of Minn. was started in 1851. The school, with its many associated campuses, exerts a great influence on the cultural life of the state. The building (1851–1853) of the Soo Ship Canal at Sault Ste. Marie, Mich., opened an E water route for lake shipping. The Panic of 1857 hit Minn. particularly hard because of land speculation, but difficult times did not prevent the achievement of statehood in 1858, with St. Paul as the capital and Sibley as the state's 1st governor. The pop. had swelled from 6,000 in 1850 to more than 150,000 in 1857; by 1870 there were nearly 440,000 inhabitants. Chiefly a land of small farmers (mainly of Br., Ger., and Irish extraction), Minn. supported the Union in the Civil War and supplied much wheat to the Northern armies. During the war years and afterward, the Sioux reacted to broken promises, fraudulent dealings, and the encroachment of settlers on their lands with violent resistance. A Sioux force under Little Crow was defeated by H. H. Sibley, virtually ending Native Amer. resistance. Meanwhile, settlement boomed, aided by the Homestead Act of 1862. Later in the cent. came immigrants from Scandinavia—Swedes, Norwegians, and Finns. Lumbering, which had begun in 1839 with a sawmill on the St. Croix, became paramount, and logging camps were established. Fortunes were made quickly in the 1870s and 1880s as the RR pushed W. A boom in wheat made the Minn. flour mills famous across the world and brought wealth to flour producers such as John S. Pillsbury. Farmers, however, suffered from such natural disasters as the blizzard of 1873 and insect plagues from 1874 to 1876. To these were added the miseries that accompanied the downward trend of the natl. economy, and Minn. became a center of farmers' discontent, expressed in the Granger movement. The opening of the iron mines gave new impetus to Minnesota's economy but also created discontent among the laborers. They joined forces with the farmers in the 1890s in the Populist party, one of several 3d-party movements that challenged the Republican party's traditional leadership in Minn. Ignatius Donnelly was one of the Populists' most powerful figures. Renewed agrarian discontent led to the founding of the Nonpartisan League in 1915. Farmers and laborers joined forces again in 1920 in the Farmer-Labor party, which was dominant in the 1930s. The Republicans returned to power in 1939 with the election of Harold Stassen as governor. In 1944 the Farmer-Labor party and the Democrats merged. The most successful leader of the new party, the Democratic Farmer Labor party (DFL), has been Hubert H. Humphrey, who was elected to the U.S. Senate 4 times and was Vice President from 1965 to 1969. Orville Freeman, DFL governor from 1955 to 1961, was Secretary of Agr. from 1961 to 1969. Walter F. Mondale, a Humphrey protégé, was a U.S. senator from 1964 to 1977. He was elected Vice President as Jimmy Carter's running mate in 1976 and ran for President in 1984, losing to incumbent Ronald Reagan. Since the 1950s the DFL and the Republicans have vied sharply in contests for state offices. In the 1970s the Republican party changed its name to the Independent Republican party. With the exception of 1952, 1956, and 1972, Minn. has voted Democratic in every presidential election since 1932. The state is governed under the 1858 constitution. The legislature has 67 senators elected for 4-year terms and 134 representatives elected for 2-year terms. The governor is elected for a 4-year term and may succeed himself. Arne Carlson, an Independent Republican, was elected governor in 1990. Minn. sends 2 senators and 8 representatives to Congress; it has 10 electoral votes. The state has been notable for experimentation in novel features of local govt. and has also been a leader in the use of cooperatives. This phenomenon is perhaps explained by the cooperative heritage present among its many people of Scandinavian descent. Credit unions, cooperative creameries, grain elevators, and purchasing associations were supported by legislation in 1919 that protected the institutions and instructed the state department of agr. to encourage them. There are several thousand cooperative associations. in Minn. serving diversified needs. A nuclear power plant built by the Atomic Energy Commission is located at Elk River, on Mississippi R. NW of Minneapolis. Since the mid-19th cent. the state has become progressively more urban. In 1970 the urban pop. was ⅔ of the total. Since 1970 dramatic suburban growth has taken place, especially in the Minneapolis–St. Paul metropolitan area. Minneapolis–St. Paul Internatl. Airport has become an important hub for the region. Nearby is the massive Mall of America (1992), in suburban Bloomington, the nation's 3d-largest shopping center. Many people come to Minn. for treatment at the famous Mayo Clinic in Rochester (also hq. of IBM), and surgeons at the Univ. of Minn. have won recognition for their development of new heart-surgery techniques. The beauty of Minnesota's lakes and dense green forests has long attracted vacationers, and the abundant fish in the state's many rivers, lakes, and streams provide excellent fishing. Also of interest to tourists are the Grand Portage (in NE) and Pipestone (SW) natl. monuments, Itasca State Park, in NW (site of the headwaters of the Mississippi R.), the Minn. Mus. of Mining (near Chisholm), in N, and the world's largest open-pit iron mine at HIBBING. The Minn. Symphony Orchestra is nationally known, and a theater in Minneapolis houses the professional company of Tyrone Guthrie. Many Minnesotans are of Scandinavian descent; one local tradition is *lutefisk*, cod cured in lye, served during the holiday season at church dinners, attracting thousands of people. Minn. has contributed important literary figures to the nation, including Sinclair Lewis, F. Scott Fitzgerald, and O.E. Rølvaag. The economist Thorstein Veblen and Charles A. Lindbergh were also born in the state. Minn. has 87 COS.: AITKIN, ANOKA, BECKER, BELTRAMI, BENTON, BIG STONE, BLUE EARTH, BROWN, CARLTON, CARVER, CASS, CHIPPEWA, CHISAGO, CLAY, CLEARWATER, COOK, COTTONWOOD, CROW WING, DAKOTA, DODGE, DOUGLAS, FARIBAULT, FILLMORE, FREEBORN, GOODHUE, GRANT, HENNEPIN, HOUSTON, HUBBARD, ISANTI, ITASCA, JACKSON, KANABEC, KANDIYOHI, KITTSON, KOOCHICHING, LAC QUI PARLE, LAKE, LAKE OF THE WOODS, LE SUEUR, LINCOLN, LYON, MCLEOD, MAHNOMEN, MARSHALL, MARTIN, MEEKER, MILLE LACS, MORRISON, MOWER, MURRAY, NICOLLET, NOBLES, NORMAN, OLMSTED, OTTER TRAIL, PENNINGTON, PINE, PIPESTONE, POLK, POPE, RAMSEY, RED LAKE, REDWOOD, RENVILLE, RICE, ROCK, ROSEAU, SAINT LOUIS, SCOTT, SHERBURNE, SIBLEY, STEARNS, STEELE, STEVENS, SWIFT, TODD, TRAVERSE, WABASHA, WADENA, WASECA, WASHINGTON, WATONWAN, WILKIN, WINONA, WRIGHT, YELLOW MEDICINE.

Minnesota City, village (1990 pop. 258), Winona co., SE Minn., 7 mi/11.3 km NW of Winona, near Mississippi R, (Lock and Dam No. 5 to NW, Lock and Dam No. 5A to SE); 44°05′N 91°45′W. RR junction. Grain; livestock, poultry; dairying; light mfg. John A. Latsch State Park to NW; Richard J. Dorer Memorial Hardwood State Forest to SW.

Minnesota Lake, village (1990 pop. 681), Faribault co., S Minn., 27 mi/43 km NW of Albert Lea, on E shore of Minnesota L. (3 mi/4.8 km long, 2 mi/3.2 km wide); 43°50′N 93°49′W. Lake has 2 outflows (S and W) to Maple R.; small dams at both. Corn, oats, peas, soybeans; livestock, poultry.

Minnesota River, 332 mi/534 km long, S Minn.; rising in Big Stone L. (lake forms part of Minn.-S.Dak. state line; fed from NW by Little Minnesota R.), exits lake through small dam at Ortonville, Minn., and Big Stone City, S.Dak., immediately entering Minn.; flows SE through Marsh L. and Lac Qui Parle L. reservoirs, past Montevideo, Granite Falls, and New Ulm, turns N at Mankato and passes St. Peter, and Le Sueur, then flows NE past Belle Plaine, Shakopee, and Bloomington; enters Mississippi R. 6 mi/9.7 km SW of downtown St. Paul and 6 mi/9.7 km SSE of downtown Minneapolis, in Fort Snelling State Park; 45°18′N 96°27′W. Minneapolis–St. Paul Internatl. Airport is W of mouth. Minnesota R. enters Mississippi R. at its head of commercial navigation and is itself navigable only by small craft. Minnesota Valley State Trail and Natl. Wildlife Refuge follow lower course of river. Earlier called the St. Peter or St. Pierre, it was an important route of explorers and fur traders. The river follows the valley of the prehistoric R. Warren, the outlet of prehistoric L. Agassiz.

Minnesott Beach (MIN-uh-saht), village (1990 pop. 266), Pamlico co., E N.C., 10 mi/16 km NE of Havelock, on Neuse R. estuary (ferry); 34°58′N 76°49′W. Croatan Natl. Forest to S; Cherry Point Marine Corps Air Station to SW.

Minnetonka (mi-ne-TAWN-kuh), city (1990 pop. 48,370), Hennepin co., SE Minn., a suburb, 9 mi/14.5 km WSW of downtown Minneapolis, E of L. Minnetonka (Gray's Bay on W boundary, receives Minnehaha Creek); 44°55′N 93°27′W. Diversified mfg. Its pop. has increased significantly since 1970 due to the influx of former central-city Minneapolis residents to the outlying suburbs. Glen Lake Sanitorium in S. Inc. 1956.

Minnetonka Beach (mi-ne-TAWN-kuh), village (1990 pop. 573), Hennepin co., E Minn., residential suburb, 16 mi/26 km W of downtown Minneapolis, on small peninsula in L. Minnetonka bet. Crystal Bay (N) and Lafayette Bay (S); 44°56′N 93°35′W.

Minnetonka, Lake (mi-ne-TAWN-kuh) (□ 23 sq mi/60 sq km), E Minn., largely in Hennepin co., extends S into Carver co., 12 mi/19 km W of downtown Minneapolis; 10 mi/16 km long, max. width 2.5 mi/4 km; 44°56′N 93°36′W. Has deeply indented shoreline (97 mi/156 km long), including peninsulas and land bridges, some manmade, and several small isls. Residential on all but SW shore, complex shoreline provides max. access to residents. Drains through Minnehaha Creek (E) into Mississippi R. Lake is divided into Upper (W) and Lower (E) lakes by isthmus crossed by narrow channels; lake is further divided into arms and bays, some of them lakes in their own right, especially in NW. Lake is on W urban fringe of Minneapolis–St. Paul (Twin Cities); municipalities on lake include Orono and Wayzata (N), Minnetonka (E),

Shorewood and Victoria (S), Mound and Minnetrista (W), Spring Park and Tonka Bay (center). Lake is celebrated in songs by Thurlow Lieurance ("By the Waters of Minnetonka") and Charles W. Cadman ("From the Land of the Sky-Blue Water"). Recreation area.

Minnetrista (mi-ne-TRIS-tuh), town (1990 pop. 3,439), Hennepin co., E Minn., residential suburb, 19 mi/31 km WSW of downtown Minneapolis, bounded on SE by Upper L. and NE by Jennings Bay, both on L. Minnetonka; 44°56′N 93°42′W. Oak L. in N. Carver Park Reserve to SE.

Minnewanka, Lake (mi-ni-WAHNG-kuh) SW Alta., Canada, near B.C. border, in Rocky Mts., in Banff Natl. Park, 6 mi/10 km NE of Banff, at foot of Mts. Aylmer and Girouard; 12 mi/19 km long, 1 mi/1.6 km wide. Elev. 4,769 ft/1,454 m.

Minnewaska, Lake (mi-nee-WAW-skuh) (□ 19 sq mi/ 49 sq km), Pope co., W Minn.; 7.5 mi/12.1 km long, 2 mi/3.2 km wide; 45°36′N 95°27′W. Elev. 1,138 ft/347 m. Town of Glenwood at NE end; town of Starbuck at SW end; resorts. Drains SW through Outlet Creek to L. Emily, 6 mi/9.7 km SW. Fed by short stream from W through Pelican L., enters at NE end.

Minnewaska, Lake, N.Y.: see LAKE MINNEWASKA.

Minnewaukan (min-uh-WAW-kuhn), village (1990 pop. 401), ⊙ Benson co., central N.Dak., 18 mi/29 km WSW of the city of Devils L., near W end of Devils L.; 48°04′N 99°15′W. Grain area; RR junction. Devils L. Sioux Indian Reservation to SE.

Minnewawa, Lake, Aitkin co., NE central Minn., just SE of Sandy L., 22 mi/35 km NE of Aitkin in Savanna State Forest; 5 mi/8 km long, max. width 2 mi/3.2 km irregular shoreline; 46°42′N 93°16′W. Resorts. Sheshabee village on SE shore. Drains S and W to Sandy R. through Minnewawa Creek. Separated from Big Sandy L. to NW by ½ mi/⅓ km neck of land.

Minoa (min-O-ah), residential village (□ 1 sq mi/ 2.6 sq km; 1990 pop. 3,745), Onondaga co., central N.Y., 8 mi/12.9 km E of Syracuse; 43°04′N 76°00′W. In dairying area.

Minocqua (min-AHK-waw), resort village, Oneida co., N Wis., 21 mi/34 km NW of Rhinelander, in lake region. Lumbering. Light mfg. N terminus of Bear Skin State Trail. Amer. Legion State Forest to E.

Minong (MEI-nahng), village (1990 pop. 521), Washburn co., NW Wis., 43 mi/69 km SSE of Superior, in wooded region with numerous lakes; 46°06′N 91°49′W. Mfg. (meat snacks, mailing machines).

Minonk (mi-NUNK), city (1990 pop. 1,982), Woodford co., central Ill., 18 mi/29 km NE of Eureka; 40°53′N 89°02′W. Mfg. (paper prods.). Agr. (dairy prods.; livestock; grain). Inc. 1867.

Minooka (mi-NOO-kah), village (1990 pop. 2,561), Grundy co., NE Ill., 11 mi/18 km WSW of Joliet; 41°27′N 88°15′W. In agr. area.

Minooka (mi-NOO-kah), suburb, Lackawanna co., NE Pa., residential section, 3 mi/4.8 km SW of downtown Scranton, on Lackawanna R.; 41°22′N 75°41′W. Part of city of Scranton.

Minor, suburb (1990 pop. 3,133), Jefferson co., N central Ala., just W of Birmingham; 33°31′N 86°57′W.

Minor Lane Heights, town (1990 pop. 1,675), Jefferson co., N Ky., residential suburb, 8 mi/12.9 km S of downtown Louisville; 38°07′N 85°43′W.

Minot (MEI-naht), city (1990 pop. 34,544), seat of Ward co., NW N.Dak., on the Souris R.; 48°13′N 101°17′W. Inc. 1887. It is a commercial and transportation center for an extensive agr. area. RR junction. There are lignite mines and oil basins in the region. Industries include building materials, petroleum compounds, farm machinery; dairy and meat prods. Minot State Univ. (1913) and a state agr. experiment station are there. Minot Air Force Base is 10 mi/16 km N.; Upper Souris Natl. Wildlife Refuge to NW.

Minot (MEI-naht), town (1990 pop. 1,664), Androscoggin co., SW Maine, on the Little Androscoggin just W of Auburn; 44°08′N 70°19′W. Light mfg.

Minot, Mass.: see SCITUATE.

Minots Ledge (MEI-nuhts), E Mass., reef in Massachusetts Bay, c.2.5 mi/4 km off Cohasset; 42°16′N 70°46′W.

The 1st lighthouse here (built 1850) destroyed by gale in 1851; present 114–ft/35–m structure built 1860.

Minster, village (1990 pop. 2,650), Auglaize co., W Ohio, 10 mi/16 km S of St. Marys, near L. Loramie; 40°23′N 84°22′W. Inc. 1833.

Mint Hill, city (1990 pop. 11,567), Mecklenburg co., S N.C., residential suburb, 10 mi/16 km ESE of downtown Charlotte; 35°10′N 80°30′W. Agr. area to E.

Minter, town, Laurens co., central Ga., 10 mi/16 km ESE of Dublin; 32°29′N 82°45′W.

Minto 1 village (1991 pop. 665), SW Man., Canada, 30 mi/48 km S of Brandon. Grain, stock. **2** village (1991 pop. 3,096), central N.B., Canada, near NW shore of Grand L., 60 mi/97 km N of St. John; 46°05′N 66°05′W. Coal mining center. Coal was 1st shipped to New England from here in 1643.

Minto 1 village (1990 pop. 218), central Alaska, in Minto Flats, 40 mi/64 km W of Fairbanks, on Elliot Highway; 65°01′N 149°31′W. Gold mining. **2** village (1990 pop. 560), Walsh co., NE N.Dak.9 mi/14.5 km S of Grafton, and on Forest R. ; 48°17′N 97°22′W. Mfg. (farm equip.). L. Ardoch to SE.

Minto Inlet, W Victoria Isl., SW Franklin Dist., N.W.T., Canada, arm of Amundsen Gulf, at S end of Prince of Wales Strait; 75 mi/121 km long, 8 mi/13 km–25 mi/ 40 km wide; 71°15′N 117°W.

Minto, Lake (□ 485 sq mi/1,256 sq km), N Que., Canada; 60 mi/97 km long, 15 mi/24 km wide; 57°25′N 74°30′W. Drained by Leaf R.

Minto Mine, town, SW B.C., Canada, in Coast Mts., on Bridge R., and 40 mi/64 km WNW of Lillooet; 50°54′N 122°46′W. Site has been flooded by Carpenter Lake Reservoir (1970s). Cattle, timber in area.

Minturn, town (1990 pop. 1,066), Eagle co., W central Colo., on Eagle R., just W of Gore Range, and 25 mi/ 40 km NNW of Leadville; 39°34′N 106°25′W. Elev. 7,817 ft/2,383 m. Mfg. (printing and publishing). Surrounded by White River Natl. Forest. To NE is Vail ski resort.

Minturn (MIN-tuhrn), village (1990 pop. 124), Lawrence co., NE Ark., 20 mi/32 km WNW of Jonesboro; 35°58′N 91°01′W.

Minute Man Historical Park (□ 1 sq mi/2.6 sq km), Lexington and Concord E Mass., 10 mi/16 km ENE of Boston. Authorized 1959. Scene of fighting on the opening day of the Revolutionary War; includes North Bridge, Minute Man statue, Battle Road, and the home of Nathaniel Hawthorne.

Mio (MEE-o), village (1990 pop. 1,886), ⊙ Oscoda co., NE central Mich., c.45 mi/72 km SW of Alpena, and on Au Sable R.; 44°39′N 84°08′W. Mfg. (pipe bending, thermocouple alloys); resort. Surrounded by Huron Natl. Forest on W, S, and E. Mio Mt. Ski Area to S.

Miquihuana (mee-kee-WAH-nah), town (1990 pop. 1,327), Tamaulipas, NE Mexico, in Sierra Madre Oriental, 45 mi/72 km WSW of Ciudad Victoria; 23°35′N 99°46′W. Cereals, livestock.

Miquon (ME-kwahn), uninc. village, Montgomery co., SE Pa., suburb, 9 mi/14.5 km NW of Philadelphia, on Schuylkill R.; 40°03′N 76°15′W. Mfg. of fine paper.

Mira Bay (MEI-ruh), inlet of the Atlantic, NE N.S., Canada, on NE coast of Cape Breton Isl., 12 mi/19 km SE of Sydney. Leads inland into Mira R.

Mira Loma, uninc. city (1990 pop. 15,786), Riverside co., S Calif., 10 mi/16 km W of Riverside; 33°59′N 117°31′W. Vineyards; mfg. (printing and publishing, fabricated metal prods., transportation equip.).

Mira Por Vos, [Span. = look out for yourself], islets and reefs, S central Bahama Isls., 15 mi/24 km W of S tip of Acklins Isl., 270 mi/435 km SE of Nassau; 22°10′N 74°32′W. Low, dangerous rocks.

Mira River (MEI-ruh), tidal inlet in E part of Cape Breton Isl., NE N.S., Canada, extending 30 mi/48 km W and S from Mira Bay; 1 mi/2 km–2 mi/3 km wide.

Mira Vista, uninc. town (1990 pop. 7,744), Ventura co., S Calif., 10 mi/16 km N of Ventura, on Ventura R. (forms L. Casitas reservoir to SW). Citrus, avocados, vegetables, flowers, nursery prods. Los Padres Natl. Forest to N; Emma Wood State Beach, on Pacific Ocean, to S.

Mirabel International Airport, S central Que., Canada, 25 mi/40 km NW of downtown Montreal, SW of Laurentian Autoroute. Montreal's second intl. airport.

Miragoâne (mee-rah-GWAHN), town (1982 pop. 4,327), Grande-Anse dept., SW Haiti, minor port on N Jacmel Peninsula, 50 mi/80 km W of Port-au-Prince; 18°27′N 73°06′W. Port ships coffee, fruit; logwood. Tobacco growing; sisal processing. Fishing port. Bauxite deposits in vicinity.

Miramar (MI-ruh-mahr), city (□ 31 sq mi/80 sq km; 1990 pop. 40,663), Broward co., SE Fla.; 25°58′N 80°19′W. Located 15 mi/24 km NW of Miami, it is a residential community in the rapidly growing I-75 corridor. Inc 1955.

Miramar (mee-rah-MAHR), resort, Tamaulipas, NE Mexico, on Gulf at mouth of Pánuco R., 6 mi/9.7 km NE of Tampico.

Miramar Beach (MI-ruh-mahr), town (□ 4 sq mi/ 10.4 sq km; 1990 pop. 1,644), Walton co., NW Fla., 8 mi/ 12.9 km ESE of Destin on Gulf of Mexico; 30°22′N 86°21′W.

Miramichi (mi-ruh-muh-SHEE), river system in N central N.B., Canada, consisting of several streams rising in N central highlands of prov. and flowing E to estuarial sect., which begins at Newcastle and extends 15 mi/24 km ENE, past Chatham, to Miramichi Bay, inlet (20 mi/32 km long, 15 mi/24 km wide at mouth) of the Gulf of St. Lawrence. Main river of Miramichi system, the Southwest Miramichi, is 135 mi/217 km long. Miramichi Bay, visited by Cartier in 1534, contains several small isls.; on shore are Acadian fishing settlements. Noted for salmon fishing. Ongoing struggle to keep salmon pop. stable; pressure from increased tourism and sport fishing. Logging, lumber mills.

Mirando City, uninc. village (1990 pop. 559), Webb co., S Texas, 30 mi/48 km E of Laredo. In oil field; some mfg. Cattle.

Mirebalais (meer-bah-LAI), town (1982 pop. 6,096), Centre dept., S central Haiti, on Artibonite R., and 25 mi/40 km NE of Port-au-Prince; 18°50′N 72°06′W. Agr. (coffee, limes, sugarcane, sisal, cotton, rice); sugar processing.

Mirror Lake, village, Carroll co., E N.H., in town of Tuftonboro, 11 mi/18 km NE of Laconia, and 5 mi/8 km SW of town center, bet. Mirror L. (E) and N end of Winter Harbor of L. Winnipesaukee. Resort area. Libby Mus. to SE.

Mirror Lake, small alpine lake, SW Alta., Canada, near B.C. border, in Rocky Mts., in Banff Natl. Park, 4 mi/ 6 km WSW of L. Louise. Drains E into Bow R.

Mirror Lake 1 N.J.: see BROWNS MILLS. **2** N.Y.: see LAKE PLACID. **3** Wis.: see DELL CREEK.

Mirror Landing, Alta., Canada: see SMITH.

Misantla (mee-SAHNT-lah), city (1990 pop. 19,203) and township, Veracruz, E Mexico, in Sierra Madre Oriental foothills, 29 mi/47 km N of Xalapa Enríquez; 19°56′N 96°51′W. Agr. center (corn, sugarcane, coffee, tobacco). Anc. ruins nearby.

Miscou Island (MI-skoo), in Gulf of St. Lawrence, NE N.B., Canada, at entrance to Chaleur Bay just N of Shippagan Isl.; 9 mi/14 km long, 5 mi/8 km wide; 47°55′N 64°30′W. Lobster, clams, oysters, cod fisheries; peat. Lighthouse in operation since 1856. Beach areas.

Miscouche (mis-KOOSH), village (1991 pop. 672), W P.E.I., Canada, 5 mi/8 km WNW of Summerside; 46°26′N 63°52′W. Mixed farming, dairying; potatoes.

Misery Island, Mass.: see GREAT MISERY ISLAND.

Misery, Mount (3,711 ft/1,131 m), NW St. Kitts, Leeward Isls., 7 mi/11.3 km NW of Basseterre.

Misery Point, N extremity of Belle Isle, N N.F., Canada, 40 mi/64 km NE of Cape Norman; 52°01′N 55°17′W. Lighthouse.

Mishawaka, city (1990 pop. 42,608), St. Joseph co., N Ind., on both banks of the St. Joseph R., and adjacent to South Bend. A growing industrial city, Mishawaka's industries are closely associated with those of South Bend. Mfg of military vehicles, aerospace parts, chemicals, plastics, transportation equip., fabricated metal prods.). Natl. Steel Co. hq. The city is the seat of Bethel Col. Settled c.1830, laid out 1833, inc. 1899.

Mishicot (MISH-i-kaht), town (1990 pop. 1,296), Manitowoc Co., E Wis., 8 mi/12.9 km NW of Two Rivers; 44°13′N 87°38′W. Point Beach State Forest to SE. Dairying. Cherries, cranberries, grain. Light mfg.

Mishongnovi, Hopi Indian pueblo, NE Ariz., in Hopi Indian Reservation c.55 mi/89 km N of Winslow. Elev. 6,230 ft/1,899 m. The Snake Dance is held here biennially.

Misión, Mexico: see LA MISIÓN.

Mispillion River (mis-PIL-yun), 15 mi/24 km long, E Del.; rises in streams W of Milford; flows E and NE past Milford (head of navigation) to Delaware Bay, 16 mi/26 km NW of Cape Henlopen.

Misquah Hills (MIS-kwah), Cook co., extreme NE Minn., bet. Can. border (N) and L. Superior (SE), in the Arrowhead region; 47°59′N 90°33′W. Small group of monadnock-type hills, rising to 2,230 ft/680 m. Eagle Mt. is highest point in Minn.

Misquamicut (mis-KWAW-mi-kut), summer resort village in Westerly town, Washington co., SW R.I., on Block Isl. Sound, and 4 mi/6.4 km S of Westerly village. Renamed from Pleasant View 1928.

Missaukee (mi-SAW-kee), county (□ 573 sq mi/1,484 sq km; 1990 pop. 12,147), N central Mich.; ⊙ Lake City; 44°20′N 85°05′W. Drained by Muskegon R. and its affluents. Cattle, hogs; corn, oats, forage, dairy prods. Mfg. at Lake City. Resorts. Cluster of about 7 small lakes W of Lake City, in W, largest is L. Missaukee. A state forest is in co. Organized 1871.

Missaukee, Lake, Mich.: see LAKE CITY.

Missinaibi (mi-si-NAI-bee), river, c.265 mi/430 km long, central Ont., Canada; rising in Missinaibi L.; flowing N and NE to the Mattagami R., SW of Moosonee, to form the Moose R.

Missinipi River, Canada: see CHURCHILL river.

Mission, rural village, SW B.C., Canada, on Fraser R., residential satellite community, 35 mi/56 km E of Vancouver; 49°08′N 122°18′W. Elev. 100 ft/30 m. Fruit and vegetable canning, fruit-jam making, lumbering, dairying, fishing. Established c.1860 as mission station. Seminary of Christ the King is here.

Mission 1 city (1990 pop. 9,504), Johnson co., E Kansas, a suburb, 4 mi/6.4 km SSW of downtown Kansas City, Kansas; 39°01′N 94°39′W. Mfg. (printing and publishing, consumer goods, plastic prods.). Area referred to as Shawnee Mission. Inc. after 1950. **2** city (1990 pop. 28,653), Hidalgo co., extreme S Texas, suburb, 5 mi/8 km W of McAllen, near Rio Grande (Mex. border); 26°12′N 98°19′W. Elev. 134 ft/41 m. It is a processing and canning center for citrus fruits (especially grapefruit) and vegetables grown in the irrigated lower Rio Grande valley, Anzalduas Dam (irrigation) to S. Mfg. (consumer goods, concrete). Oil wells are also in Mission, which has been marked by a pop. growth since 1970. The city was founded on property that had belonged to the Oblate Fathers; their chapel still stands on the Rio Grande. Bentsen–Rio Grande State Park to SW. Inc. 1910.

Mission, town (1990 pop. 730), Todd co., S S.Dak., 75 mi/121 km S of Pierre, and 33 mi/53 km NNW of Valentine, Nebr. on Antelope Creek; 43°18′N 100°39′W. Trading point near center of Rosebud Indian Reservation (comprises all of co.); cattle feed, livestock.

Mission Bay, San Diego co., S Calif., shallow lagoon, at mouth of San Diego R., 6 mi/9.7 km NW of downtown San Diego, within San Diego city limits; c.3 mi/4.8 km wide and long. Isls. and small peninsula to S, bet. bay and San Diego city are in Mission Bay Park (city park); Sea World on S shore of bay.

Mission Beach, suburban section of San Diego city, San Diego co., S Calif., 7 mi/11.3 km NW of downtown San Diego, on narrow strip of land bet. Pacific Ocean (W) and Mission Bay; mouth of bay and San Diego R. to S. Mission Bay Park to E; Sea World theme park to SE. Beach resort.

Mission Beach, Calif.: see SAN DIEGO, city.

Mission Hill, village (1990 pop. 180), Yankton co., SE S.Dak., 7 mi/11.3 km ENE of Yankton; 42°55′N 97°16′W. In farming region.

Mission Hills, city (1990 pop. 3,446), Johnson co., E Kansas, a suburb, 5 mi/8 km S of Kansas City, Kansas; 39°00′N 94°37′W. Borders Mo. on E.

Mission Hills, suburban section of Los Angeles city, Los Angeles co., S Calif., 18 mi/29 km NW of downtown Los Angeles, and 2 mi/3.2 km SW of San Fernando, in San Fernando Valley; 34°42′N 120°27′W. Area suffered heavy damage in Jan. 17, 1994, Northridge Earthquake; Northridge area to W. Van Nuys Airport and Busch Gardens theme park to S. San Fernando Mission to N.

Mission Range, in Rocky Mts. of NW Mont., Lake and Missoula cos., rises bet. Flathead L. and Swan R., extends c.45 mi/72 km S toward Missoula. Numerous small lakes throughout center and S part of range; mt. divide forms E boundary of Flathead Indian Reservation. Mission Mts. Wilderness Area and Mission Mts. Tribal Wilderness Area at center of range. Highest point, McDonald Peak (9,820 ft/2,993 m).

Mission River, c.25 mi/40 km long, in Refugio co., S Texas; coastal stream formed by Blanco (c.50 mi/80 km) and Medio (c.65 mi/105 km) creeks; both rise in Karnes co., to NW, NW of Refugio; flow SE past Refugio, through oil fields, to Copano Bay.

Mission San Jose, uninc. village, Alameda co., W Calif. suburb, 14 mi/23 km N of San Jose, 3 mi/4.8 km SE of Fremont. Site of San Jose Mission (mission San Jose de Guadalupe), built 1797.

Mission Viejo, uninc. city (1990 pop. 78,820), Orange co., S Calif., residential suburb, 43 mi/69 km SE of downtown Los Angeles, and 8 mi/12.9 km ENE of Laguna Beach and Pacific Ocean; 33°37′N 117°39′W. Irrigated agr. (citrus, nursery prods., flowers; dairying; poultry). Mfg. (printing and publishing, pharmaceuticals, diverse light mfg.). Historic Mission Viejo to SE; Mission San Juan Capistrano to S, site of annual return of swallows March 19. Santa Ana Mts. and Cleveland Natl. Forest to NE. Seat of Saddleback Col. (2-year).

Mission Woods, village (1990 pop. 182), Johnson co., E Kansas, a suburb, 4 mi/6.4 km S of downtown Kansas City, Kansas; 39°01′N 94°36′W. Borders Mo. on E. Flour milling.

Missionary Ridge (c.1,000 ft/305 m), in Tenn. and Ga., in Great Appalachian Valley, E of Chattanooga; 34°59′N 85°16′W. A Civil War battleground (1863) where Union forces won a costly victory; partly included in Chickamauga and Chattanooga Natl. Military Park.

Missiquoi River (MIS-i-koi), c.100 mi/161 km long, in N Vt. and S Que.; rises near Lowell, Vt.; flows N, past Troy, into Que., thence W and SW, reentering Vt. near Richford, thence generally W, through Green Mts., to L. Champlain N of Swanton.

Missisquoi (mi-SI-skwoi), county (□ 375 sq mi/971 sq km), S Que., Canada, on Vt. border; ⊙ Bedford; 45°10′N 73°00′W.

Mississagi River (mi-si-SAH-gee), flows in a wide arc 170 mi/274 km W, S, and SE, in central Ont., Canada; issues from Mississagi L. (6 mi/10 km long) at 47°9′N 82°32′W; flows through several small lakes, to L. Huron 3 mi/5 km W of Blind R. Several rapids: Aubrey Falls (108 ft/33 m high), 50 mi/80 km NNW of Blind R.; Grand Falls (150 ft/46 m), 30 mi/48 km NW of Blind R.; and L. Falls (55 ft/17 m), 20 mi/32 km WNW of Blind R.

Mississauga (mis-si-SAW-guh), city (1991 pop. 463,388), S Ont., Canada, 12 mi/20 km W of Toronto, on L. Ontario; 43°09′N 79°30′W. A residential suburb of Toronto and a growing transportation and industrial center, it is one of Canada's fastest-growing cities. Mfg. includes aircraft, motor vehicles, engines, chemicals, petroleum, steel and rubber prods., cement, appliances, and printing and publishing. It has a port and is the site of Lester B. Pearson Internatl. Airport. Originally an agr. and then residential area, it had a pop. of 15,000 in 1945.

Mississinewa Lake, reservoir (c.12 mi/19 km long), Miami and Wabash cos., N central Ind., on Mississinewa R., 5 mi/8 km SE of Peru; 40°42′N 85°56′W. Max. capacity of 368,400 acre-ft. Formed by Mississinewa Dam (122 ft/37 m high), built (1967) by the Army Corps of Engineers for flood control. State recreation areas along W shore.

Mississinewa River (MI-si-SI-nuh-wah), c.100 mi/161 km long, in Ohio and Ind.; rises in Darke co., W Ohio; flows W into Ind., then generally NW, past Marion, to the Wabash at Peru; 40°45′N 86°01′W.

Mississippi, state (□ 48,434 sq mi/125,444 sq km; 1995 est. pop. 2,697,243), S U.S., admitted as the 20th state of the Union in 1817; 32°45′N 89°31′W. JACKSON, the ⊙ and largest city is in SW center. Other important cities are BILOXI, GREENVILLE, HATTIESBURG, and MERIDIAN; also part of suburban Memphis, Tenn., extends into De Soto co. in NW. Bounded W by Mississippi R. (Ark. and part of La. state lines, actual state boundary follows river channel that existed when boundary was established; present-day channel has left stranded numerous oxbow, or horseshoe, lakes on both sides of river and with them pieces of opposite states); bounded S by La.; bounded E by Ala. (including NE corner of Tennessee R., which forms Pickwick L. reservoir); bounded N by Tenn; S extension of Miss. in SE bounded by Gulf of Mexico (Mississippi Sound) and W by La. (Pearl R.). The generally hilly land reaches its highest point at Woodall Mt. (806 ft/246 m), in Tishomingo co., in the NE corner. The most distinctive region in the state's varied topography is the Delta, a flat alluvial plain bet. The Mississippi and the Yazoo rivers; Yazoo follows former channel of Mississippi. A wide belt of longleaf yellow pine (the piny woods) covers most of S Miss. to within a few mi/km of the coastal-plain grasslands. Important there are lumbering and allied industries. Most of the state's rivers belong to either the Mississippi or the Alabama river system, with the Pontoctoc Ridge the divide and include the Pearl, Pascagoula, Tallahatchie, and Yalobusha rivers. The climate of Miss. is subtropical along Gulf Coast to temperate in the northern part; the average annual rainfall is more than 50 in/127 cm. Traditionally one of the more rural and economically depressed U.S. states. Since the 1960s, mfg. has taken over as the leading industrial sector; many companies from industrial NE states have relocated here to take advantage of cheaper labor. In 1990, though declining, Miss. ranked 3d (after Texas and Calif.) in the nation in the production of cotton. Soil erosion, resulting from overcultivation of the crop, and the destruction caused by the boll weevil have led to the increased adoption of scientific farming techniques and to agr. diversification. The most important crops are soybeans, rice, and hay. There has been a great rise in cattle, poultry, and hog raising and, especially, dairying. The state's most important and valuable mineral resources, petroleum and natural gas, have been developed only since the 1930s; especially important is the Tinsley Oil Field S of Yazoo City, in W center. Sand and gravel and clays are also produced. Industry has grown rapidly since oil development began and has been helped by the TVA and the state's program to balance agr. with industry. Under this program many communities have subsidized and attracted new industries; industrial prods., including wood prods., foods, and chemicals, have exceeded in value those of agr. in recent years. The state has become a major producer of furniture, especially upholstered furniture, and also of apparel. On the Gulf coast there is a profitable fishing and seafood-processing industry, including shrimp and crabs. Catfish farming is a major industry in the Delta region in W. Mississippi ranks among the country's highest gambling revenue states. Despite modernization efforts, however, the state's per capita income is the lowest in the nation. The Tennessee-Tombigbee Waterway in NE, extended from Tennessee R. in N, SSE along Tombigbee R. into Ala., allows alternate route to Mississippi R. for barge traffic to Gulf. Natl. forests include 2 sections of Holly Springs Natl. Forest in N, 2 sections of Tombigbee Natl. Forest in NE center, Bienville Natl. Forest in E center, 2 sections of De Soto Natl. Forest in SE, Delta Natl. Forest in W, and Homochitto Natl. Forest in SW. Also there are several natl. wildlife refuges, especially Miss. Sandhill Crane Natl. Widlife Refuge in SE; Panther Swamp Natl. Wildlife Refuge in W, and Noxubee Natl. Wildlife Refuge in NE center. The Choctaw Indian Reservation is in Neshoba co., and several smaller reservations are in the E center. Hernando De Soto's expedition undoubtedly passed (1540–1542) through the region, then inhabited by the Choctaw, Chickasaw, and Natchez, but the first permanent Eur. settlement was not made until 1699, when Pierre le Moyne, sieur d'Iberville, established a Fr. colony on Biloxi Bay. Settlement accelerated in 1718, when the colony came under the French Mississippi Co., headed by the speculator John Law. The region was part of La. until 1763, when, by the Treaty of Paris England received practically all the Fr. territory E of the Mississippi R. and also E Fla. and W Fla., which had belonged to Spain. Eng. colonists, many of them retired soldiers, had made the Natchez dist. a thriving agr. community, producing tobacco and indigo, by the time Bernardo de Gálvez captured it for Spain in 1779. By the Treaty of Paris of 1783 at the end of the Amer. Revolution, the U.S., with Eng. approval, claimed as its S boundary in the W lat. 31°N (most of the present-day state of Miss. was included in the area). Spain denied this claim, and the long, involved W Fla. Controversy ensued. In the Pinckney Treaty (1795), Spain accepted lat. 31°N as the N boundary of its territory but did not evacuate Natchez until the arrival of U.S. troops in 1798. Congress immediately created the Mississippi Territory, with Natchez as the capital and William C. C. Claiborne as the governor. After Georgia's cession (1802) of its Western lands to the U.S. and the Louisiana Purchase (1803), a land boom swept Miss. The high price of cotton and the cheap, fertile land brought settlers thronging in, most of them via the NATCHEZ TRACE, from the Southern Piedmont region and even from New England. A few attained great wealth, but most simply managed a living. In 1817, Miss. became a state, with substantially its present-day boundaries; the E sect. of Miss. was organized as Ala. The aristocratic planter element of the Natchez region initially dominated Mississippi's govt., as the state's first constitution (1817) showed. With the spread of Jacksonian democracy, however, the small farmer came into his own, and the new constitution adopted in 1832 was quite liberal for its time. Land hunger increased as more new settlers arrived, lured by the continuing cotton boom. By a series of treaties (1820, 1830, 1832), the Native Americans in the state were pushed westward across the Mississippi. Mississippians were among the leading Southern expansionists seeking new land for cotton and slavery. After 1840 slaves in the state outnumbered Whites. On Jan. 9, 1861, Miss. became the 2d state to secede from the Union. State pride was highly gratified by the choice of Jefferson Davis as president of the Confederacy. Civil War fighting did not reach Miss. until April 1862, when Union forces were victorious at CORINTH and Iuka. Grant's brilliant Vicksburg campaign ended large-scale fighting in the state, but further destruction was caused by Gen. W. T. Sherman in his march from Vicksburg to Meridian. Moreover, cavalry of both the North and the South, particularly the Confederate forces of Gen. N. B. Forrest, continued active. After the war, Miss. abolished slavery but refused to ratify the Thirteenth and Fourteenth Amendments, and in March 1867, under the Congressional plan of Reconstruction, it was organized with Ark. into a military dist. commanded by Gen. E.O.C. Ord. After much agitation, a Republican-sponsored constitution guaranteeing basic rights to blacks was adopted in 1869. Miss. was readmitted to the Union early in 1870 after ratifying the Fourteenth and Fifteenth Amendments and meeting other Congressional requirements. While Republicans were in power, the state govt. was composed of new immigrants from the North, blacks, and cooperative white Southerners. A. K. Davis became the state's first black lieutenant governor in 1874. The establishment of free public schools was a noteworthy aspect of Republican rule. As former Confederates were permitted to return to politics and blacks were increasingly intimidated, the Democrats regained strength. The Republicans were defeated in the bitter election of 1875. Lucius Q. C. Lamar figured largely in the Democratic triumph and was the state's most prominent natl. figure for many years. In Reconstruction days the Republicans could win only with solid black support. After Reconstruction, blacks were virtually disenfranchised. White supremacy was bolstered by the Constitution of 1890, later used as a model by other Southern states; under its terms a prospective voter could be required to read and interpret any of the constitution's provisions. Because at the turn of the century most Miss. blacks could not read (neither could many whites, but the test was rarely applied to them) and because the county registrar could disqualify a prospective voter if that person disagreed with the interpretation of the constitution, blacks were legally disenfranchised. On the ruins of the shattered plantation economy rose the sharecropping system, and the merchant and the banker replaced the planter in having the largest financial interest in farming. Too often the system made the sharecroppers, white as well as black, little more than economic slaves. The landowners, however, maintained their hold on politics until 1904, when the small farmers, still the dominant voting group, elected James K. Vardaman governor. Nevertheless this agrarian revolt did not alter a deep-seated obscurantism that was reflected in the Jim Crow laws (1904) and in the ban on the teaching of evolution in the public schools (1926). Another reflection of the social structure of the state was prohibition, put into effect in 1908 and not repealed until 1959. Since the disastrous flood of 1927 the Federal govt. has taken over flood-control work—constructing levees, floodwalls, floodways, and reservoirs; stabilizing riverbanks; and improving channels. Navigation, too, has not been neglected; the Intracoastal Waterway provides a protected channel along the entire Miss. coastline and links the state's ports with all others along the Gulf coast and with all inland waterway systems emptying into the Gulf of Mexico. The TENNESSEE-TOMBIGBEE WATERWAY, opened in 1985, connects the Tennessee R. in NE Miss. with the Tombigbee R. in W Ala. The state has made attempts to wipe out illiteracy, but it still has the highest illiteracy rate in the country. Miss. is still plagued by racial problems, which have changed the state's alignment in natl. politics. In 1948, Miss. abandoned the Democratic party because of the natl. Democratic party's stand on civil rights, and the state supported J. Strom Thurmond, the States' Rights party candidate, for President. The 1954 Supreme Court ruling against racial segregation in public schools occasioned massive resistance. Citizens Councils, composed of White men and dedicated to maintaining segregation, began to spring up throughout the state. In the 1960 presidential election Mississippians again rebelled against the Democratic natl. platform by giving victory at the polls to unpledged electors, who cast their electoral col. votes not for John F. Kennedy but for Harry F. Byrd, the conservative senator from Va. In 1964 the conservative Republican Barry Goldwater carried the state; in 1968 Gov. George Wallace of Ala., who had become famous for opposing integration, won the state. In 1961 mass arrests and violence were touched off when "freedom riders," actively seeking to spur integration, made Miss. a major target. However, there was not even token integration of public schools in Miss. until 1962, when the state govt. under the leadership of Gov. Ross R. Barnett tried unsuccessfully to block the admission of James H. Meredith, a black, to the Univ. of Miss. at Oxford. In the conflict the Federal and state govts. clashed, and the U.S. Dept. of Justice took legal action against state officials, including Barnett; 2 persons were killed in riots, and Federal troops had to restore order. Racial antagonisms resulted in many more acts of violence. Churches and black homes were bombed. Medgar Evers, an official of the Natl. Assn. for the Advancement of Colored People, was killed in 1963; 3 civil rights workers (2 White, 1 Black) were murdered the next year. After the Federal Voting Rights Act of 1965, many blacks succeeded in registering and voting. In 1967, for the first time since 1890, a Black was elected to the legislature, and blacks are now as well represented in Miss. politics as any state, with a large degree of cross-racial voting. However, in 1992 the U.S. Supreme Court ordered the state col. system to end its tradition of segregation. Mississippi's economic problems continued in the 1980s as the state was unable to shift emphasis from mfg. to the service sector and was unable to avoid the natl. trend of industrial decline. Miss. is governed under the 1890 constitution. The bicameral legislature consists of 52 senators and 122 representatives, all elected for 4-year terms. The governor is also elected for a 4-year term. The state has 2 U.S. senators, 5 representatives, and 7 electoral votes. In August 1969, Miss. and La. were devastated by Camille, one of the cent.'s worst hurricanes. In April 1973, the Mississippi R. rose to record levels in the state. The floodwaters from the river and its tributaries covered about 9% of the state, including parts of Vicksburg and Natchez, causing millions of dollars of damage to property. U.S. govt. installations include Meridian Naval Air Station in E, Keesler Air Force Base and Gulfport Naval Center in SE, and NASA's Stennis Space Center, on Pearl R., in SE. Among the institutions of higher learning are the Univ. of Miss. at Oxford, Miss. State Univ., near Starkville, the Univ. of Southern Miss., at Hattiesburg, Jackson State Univ., at Jackson, and Miss. Univ. for Women, at Columbus. Historical sites in the state include Old Spanish Fort, the oldest house on the Mississippi R., near Pascagoula, and Vicksburg Natl. Military Park, Brices Cross Roads Natl. Battlefield Site, and Tupelo Natl. Battlefield Site. Miss., in the path of waterfowl migrations down the Mississippi valley, is noted for its duck and quail hunting. Along the Gulf Coast, a favorite fishing area, are several resort cities and part of Gulf Isls. Natl. Seashore. Long, narrow sandy isls. lie generally 10 mi/16 km offshore in Gulf of Mexico, including Ship, Cat, Horn, and Petit Bois isls., and Dog Keys; all except Ship Isl. are in Gulf Islands Natl. Seashore (Miss. and Fla). Intracoastal Waterway runs parallel to coast in Mississippi Sound. In Natchez and Biloxi are many fine antebellum mansions. Natchez Trace Parkway (unit of Natl. Park system) traverses state from NE corner to Natchez in SW and follows old Native American road and former colonial trade route. Miss. has 82 cos.: ADAMS, ALCORN, AMITE, ATTALA, BENTON, BOLIVAR, CALHOUN, CARROLL, CHICKASAW, CHOCKTAW, CLAIBORNE, CLARKE, CLAY, COAHOMA, COPIAH, COVINGTON, DE SOTO, FORREST, FRANKLIN, GEORGE, GREENE, GRENADA, HANCOCK, HARRISON, HINDS, HOLMES, HUMPHREYS, ISSAQUENA, ITAWAMBA, JACKSON, JASPER, JEFFERSON, JEFFERSON DAVIS, JONES, KEMPER, LAFAYETTE, LAMAR, LAUDERDALE, LAWRENCE, LEAKE, LEE, LEFLORE, LINCOLN, LOWNDES, MADISON, MARION, MARSHALL, MONROE, MONTGOMERY, NESHOBA, NEWTON, NOXUBEE, OKTIBBEHA, PANOLA, PEARL RIVER, PERRY, PIKE, PONTOTOC, PRENTISS, QUITMAN, RANKIN, SCOTT, SHARKEY, SIMPSON, SMITH, STONE, SUNFLOWER, TALLAHATCHIE, TATE, TIPPAH, TISHOMINGO, TUNICA, UNION, WALTHALL, WARREN, WASHINGTON, WAYNE, WEBSTER, WILKINSON, WINSTON, YALOBUSHA, YAZOO.

Mississippi 1 county (□ 919 sq mi/2,380 sq km; 1990 pop. 57,525), NE Ark.; ⊙ Blytheville and Osceola; 35°45′N 90°02′W. Bounded N by Mo. line, E by Mississippi R.; drained by East Hand and West Hand Chutes of Little R. Agr. (cattle, hogs; cotton, soybeans, sorghum, wheat, rice); timber. Industries at Blytheville and Osceola. Hampson Mus. State Park at Wilson in E; Big Lake Natl. Wildlife Refuge and Wildlife Management Area in N. Formed 1833. **2** county (□ 411 sq mi/1,064 sq km; 1990 pop. 14,442), extreme SE Mo.; on Mississippi R. (levees), with drainage channels; ⊙ Charleston; 36°49′N 89°17′W. Agr. region (corn, cotton, soybeans, wheat, potatoes, popcorn, melons; livestock); cotton processing; lumber; mfg. at Charleston and E. Prairie. Big Oak Tree State Park in S; Towasahgy Archaeological Site at Dorena. Formed 1845.

Mississippi Palisades State Park, Ill.: see SAVANNA.

Mississippi River, c.100 mi/160 km long, S Ont., Canada; rising E of the Kawartha Lakes; flowing NE through Mississippi L., then N to the Ottawa R. near Arnprior.

Mississippi River, principal river of the U.S. c.2,350 mi/3,780 km long, exceeded in length only by the Missouri R., chief of its numerous tributaries. The combined Missouri-Mississippi system (from the Missouri's headwaters in the Rocky Mts. to the mouth of the Mississippi R.) is c.3,740 mi/6,020 km long and ranks as the world's 3d-longest river system after the Nile and the Amazon. With its tributaries, the Mississippi drains c.1,231,000 sq mi/3,188,290 sq km of the central United States, including all or part of 31 states and c.13,000 sq mi/33,670 sq km of Alberta and Saskatchewan in Canada. The Mississippi R. rises in small streams that feed L. Itasca (alt. 1,463 ft/446 m) in N Minnesota; flows generally S to enter the Gulf of Mexico through a huge delta in SE Louisiana. A major economic waterway, the river is navigable from the sediment-free channel maintained through South Pass in the delta to the Falls of St. Anthony in Minneapolis, with canals circumventing the rapids near Rock Island, Ill., and Keokuk, Iowa. For the low-water months of July, August, and September, there is a 45-ft/13.7-m channel navigable by oceangoing vessels from Head of the Passes to Baton Rouge, La., and a 9-ft/2.7-m channel from Baton Rouge deep enough for barges and towboats to Minneapolis. The Mississippi connects with the Intracoastal Waterway in the S and with the Great Lakes-St. Lawrence Seaway system in the N by way of the Illinois Waterway. Along the river's upper course shipping is interrupted by ice from Dec. to March; thick, hazardous fogs frequently settle on the cold waters of the unfrozen sections during warm spells from Dec. to May. In its upper course the river is controlled by numerous dams and falls (c.700 ft/210 m) in the 513-mi/826-km stretch from L. Itasca to Minneapolis and then falls (c.490 ft/150 m) in 856 mi/1,378 km from Minneapolis to Cairo, Ill. The Mississippi R. receives the Missouri R. 17 mi/27 km N of St. Louis and expands to a width of c.3,500 ft/1,070 m; it swells to c.4,500 ft/1,370 m at Cairo, where it receives the Ohio R. The lower Mississippi meanders in great loops across a broad alluvial plain (25 mi/40 km–125 mi/201 km wide) that stretches from Cape Girardeau, Mo., to the delta region S of Natchez, Miss. The plain is marked with oxbow lakes and marshes that are remnants of the river's former channels. Natural levees, built up from sediment carried and deposited in times of flood, border the river for much of its length; sediment has also been deposited on the river bed, so that in places the surface of the Mississippi is above that of the surrounding plain, as evidenced by the St. Francis, Black, Yazoo, and Tensas river basins. Breaks in the levees frequently flood the fertile bottomlands of these and other low-lying areas of the plain. After receiving the Arkansas and Red rivers, the Mississippi enters a birdsfoot-type delta, which was built outward by sediment carried by the main stream since A.D. c.1500. It then discharges into the Gulf of Mexico through a number of distributaries, the most important being the Atchafalaya R. and Bayou Lafourche. The main stream continues SE through the Delta to enter the Gulf through several mouths, including Southeast Pass, South Pass, and Pass à Loutre. Indications that the Mississippi R. might abandon this course and divert through the Atchafalaya R. have led to the construction of a dam by the U.S. Army Corps of Engineers, known as the Old River Control Structure, to prevent such an occurrence. Regarding the Delta, environmentalists and those in the seafood industry are concerned with the fact that it loses 25 sq mi/65 sq km–45 sq mi/117 sq km of marsh a year. The loss has been attributed to subsidence and a decrease in sediment largely due to dams, artificial channeling, and land conservation measures. Pollution and the cutting of new waterways for petroleum exploration and drilling have also taken their toll on the Delta. Louisiana has enacted environmental protection laws that are expected to slow, but not halt, the loss of the Delta marshes. Sluggish bayous and freshwater lakes dot the Delta region. The flow of the river is greatest in the spring, when heavy rainfall and melting snow on the tributaries (especially the Missouri and the Ohio) cause the main stream to rise and frequently overflow its banks and levees, inundating vast areas of the plain. Since the disastrous flood of 1927 the U.S. Congress has authorized the construction of dams on the upper Mississippi and its tributaries to regulate the flow; the building of c.1,600 mi/2,580 km of levees below Cape Girardeau to contain the swollen river; and the establishment of floodways to divert water at critical points, such as the Cairo–New Madrid, Atchafalaya, and Morganza floodways and the Bonnet Carre Spillway at New Orleans, which diverts water into L. Pontchartrain. Cutoffs have eliminated the dangerous winding channels, and an improved main channel has increased the river's flood-carrying capacity. Nonetheless, serious, record-breaking floods again occurred in the rainy spring of 1973, when the river crested at St. Louis at 43.3 ft/13.2 m, remained at flood stage for 77 days, and drove about 50,000 persons from their homes and again in 1993. In 1988 a severe drought brought water levels down to their lowest point in recorded history and halted most river traffic. The Span. explorer Hernando De Soto is credited with the Eur. discovery of the Mississippi R. in 1541. The French explorers Jacques Marquette and Louis Joliet reached it through the Wisconsin R. in 1673, and in 1682, La Salle traveled down the river to the Gulf of Mexico and claimed the entire territory for France. The French founded New Orleans in 1718 and effectively extended control over the upper river basin with settlements at Cahokia, Kaskaskia, Prairie du Chien, and St. Louis. France ceded the river to Spain in 1763 but regained it in 1800; the United States acquired the Mississippi R. as part of the Louisiana Purchase in 1803. A major artery for Native Americans and the fur-trading Fr., the river became in the 19th cent. the principal outlet for the newly settled areas of mid-America; exports were floated downstream with the current, and imports were poled or dragged upstream on rafts and keelboats. The 1st steamboat plied the river in 1811, and successors became increasingly luxurious as river trade increased in profitability and importance. Traffic from the north ceased after the outbreak of the Civil War. During the Civil War the Mississippi was an invasion route for Union armies and the scene of many important battles. Especially decisive were the capture of New Orleans (1862) by Adm. David Farragut, the Union naval commander, and the victory of Union forces under General Grant at Vicksburg in 1863. River traffic resumed after the end of the war; it is colorfully described in Mark Twain's *Life on the Mississippi* (1883). However, much of the trade was lost to the RR in the mid-1800s. With modern improvements in the river channels, traffic has increased, especially since the mid-1950s, with principal freight items being petroleum products, chemicals, sand, gravel, and limestone. Cotton and rice are important crops in the lower Mississippi valley; sugarcane is raised in the Delta. The Mississippi is abundant in freshwater fish; shrimp are taken from the briny Delta waters. The Delta also yields sulfur, oil, and gas. A 220-acre/89-ha model of the Mississippi R. basin is located at Clinton, Miss., which has been used by the U.S. Corps of Engineers to simulate various conditions in the basin.

Mississippi River Gulf Outlet, canal, Orleans and St. Bernard parishes, SE La., SE extension of Gulf Intracoastal Waterway; 29°50′N 89°39′W. Begins in N 8 mi/13 km ENE of downtown New Orleans, flows SE c.30 mi/48 km into shallow Breton Sound. Roughly parallels SW end of L. Borgne, coming within 1 mi/2 km of its shore. Provides direct access between offshore oil and natural-gas fields and processing facilities in New Orleans and Baton Rouge. It also reserves the Mississippi R. natural channel for deepwater shipping from Port of New Orleans.

Mississippi Sound, arm of the Gulf of Mexico, extending from L. Borgne in La. on the W to Mobile Bay in Ala., on the E; c.100 mi/161 km long and 7 mi/11 km–15 mi/24 km wide; 30°18′N, 88°55′W. It is part of the Intracoastal Waterway and is separated from the Gulf by a series of narrow isls. and sandbars. Main isls. are Cat, Ship, Horn, Petit Bois (Miss.), and Dauphin (Ala.). Gulfport, Biloxi, and Pascagoula, Miss., are on the Mississippi Sound. Ship, Horn, and Petit Bois, along with a small mainland unit, comprise Gulf Isls. Natl. Seashore.

Mississippi State, village, Oktibbeha co., E Miss., suburb 1 mi/1.6 km SE of Starkville. Seat of Miss. State Univ. Formerly called State College.

Misson Hills, uninc. town (1990 pop. 3,112), Santa Barbara co., SW Calif., 3 mi/4.8 km NNE of Lompoc, near Santa Ynez R., in Puritma Hills. Fruit, avocados, grain, cattle. La Purisma Mission State Historic Park to SE.

Missoula (muh-SUL-uh), county (□ 2,618 sq mi/6,781 sq km; 1990 pop. 78,687), W Mont., borders Idaho in SW; ⊙ Missoula; 47°02′N 113°56′W. Irrigated agr. region (wheat, barley, hay; cattle; dairying; poultry); timber; mining. Drained by the Clark Fork, Bitterroot, Swan, Clearwater, and Blackfoot rivers. Frenchtown Pond and Council Group state parks in W; Placid L. and Salmon L. state parks in NE; part of Flathead Natl. Forest in far N; part of Mission Mts. Wilderness and Flathead Indian Reservation in N; small part of Bitterroot Natl. Forest and Selway-Bitterroot Wilderness Area on S boundary; parts of Lolo Natl. Forest throughout co., especially W and N. Formed 1865.

Missoula (muh-SUL-uh), city (1990 pop. 42,918), W Mont., 89 mi/143 km W of Helena, on the Clark Fork river, 5 mi/8 km E of mouth of Bitterroot R.; ⊙ Missoula co.; 46°52′N 114°01′W. Elev. 3,210 ft/978 m. Third-largest city in Mont. In the midst of well-watered valleys, large forests, and dairy and cattle area. Missoula is a commercial center with a busy lumber and paper industry; mfg. (printing and publishing, food, chemicals, construction materials, furniture, lumber, fabricated metal prods.). The "Salish Council" of 1855 opened the area to white settlement. Hell Gate town was founded nearby in 1860 and moved to the Missoula site 6 years later. The coming of the RR (1883, 1908) stimulated Missoula's growth. In the city are the Missoula campus of the Univ. of Montana; Historical Mus. at Fort Missoula to SW, Missoula Mus. of the Arts; and a regional hq. of the U.S. Forest Service. Smokejumper Visitor Center located at Missoula Co. Internatl. Airport NW of city. Rocky Mt. Elk Foundation Visitor Center. Montana Snowbowl Ski Area to N; parts of Lolo Nalt. Forest to N, W, and SE. Inc. 1889.

Missouri, state (1995 est. pop. 5,323,523), 69,709 sq mi/180,546 sq km, central U.S., admitted as the 24th state of the Union in 1821; 38°13′N 92°25′W. The ⊙ is JEFFERSON CITY, and the largest cities are KANSAS CITY, SAINT LOUIS, SPRINGFIELD, and INDEPENDENCE. Mo. is bounded on the N by Iowa; on the W by Nebr., Kansas, and Okla.; on the S by Ark.; and on the E, where the Mississippi R. forms the border, by Ill., Ky., and Tenn. The state lies N of lat. 36°30′N except for a small area (called the "bootheel") in the extreme SE that protrudes into Ark. The center of pop. of the U.S., for both 1980 and 1990, was located in the N Ozarks of Mo.'s 2 great rivers, the Mississippi and the Missouri, have had a great influence on the development of Mo. Mo. is a diverse state, topographically, culturally, and economically, often considered a microcosm of the nation, possessing characteristics of the U.S.'s 4 quadrants. The Mississippi R. tied the region to the South, particularly to New Orleans. The Missouri crosses the state from W to E and enters the Mississippi near St. Louis. The portion of the Missouri Valley bet. St. Louis and Kansas City was the greatest avenue of pioneer advance westward across the continent. The region N of the Missouri R. is largely prairie land, where, not unlike the Iowa plains to the N, corn and livestock are raised. Most of the region S of the Missouri is covered by foothills and by the dissected plateau of the Ozark highlands, a unique region of hill scenery originally populated by a relatively isolated, self-reliant people. The rough, heavily forested eastern sect. of the Ozarks extends into the less hilly farming region in the W and encompasses the irregular, twisting L. of the Ozarks to the NW. In SW Mo. is a long, narrow area of flat land, the Osage Plains, which are part of the Great Plains, where livestock and forage crops are raised. In the SE, S of Cape Girardeau are the cotton, rice, and soybean fields of the Mississippi flood plain, an area that was once swampy but was converted to agriculture after the establishment of a drainage system in the early part of the 20th cent. The state's rivers have periodically flooded. Record flood levels were attained at many places in floods of 1993. Mo.'s share of the flood of 1993 was first brought about by heavy rains in Iowa and Minn. in spring, which swelled the Mississippi and Missouri rivers downstream in Mo., then exacerbated by locally heavy rains, which also caused flash flooding in smaller streams. Ironically SE Mo. was being affected by the severe drought that gripped the SE U.S. that same year. Missouri has extensive bituminous coal deposits in the W and N central sections. Fire, or refractory, clays occur in central and NE Mo., and barite in E central Mo. The Ozarks is a great metalliferous region, including lead, zinc, silver, manganese, copper, and iron. Much of the state is underlain by limestone and dolomite. Lead, cement, and stone are the chief minerals produced in the mid 1990s. Mo. is, by far, the leading state in the production of lead. Mo.'s economy, however, rests chiefly on industry. The manufacture of aerospace and transportation (cars, vans, trucks, RR) vehicles and equip. is the major industry in the state; food and chemicals are next in commercial importance, followed by printing and publishing. Machinery, fabricated metal prods., and electrical equip. are also produced. St. Louis is an important center for the mfg. of planes, cars, metals, and chemicals. In Kansas City, long a leading market and agr. business center for livestock and wheat, the mfg. of vending machines and of cars and trucks are leading industries. Mo. remains important agriculturally, and farming contributes substantially to the state's income. The most valuable farm prods. are cattle, hogs, soybeans, corn, and dairy items. Mo. ranked 6th in the production of hogs in 1990 and 7th in the production of cattle. After soybeans, the chief crops are corn, hay, and wheat. Mo. is 2nd in the nation in number of farms and also has important wine producing areas, especially along Missouri R. bet. St. Louis and Jefferson City. The development of resorts and recreation facilities in the Ozarks has encouraged tourism and retirement communities and added to the state's income. Services and wholesale and retail trade closely follow mfg. in economic importance. Mo.'s recorded history begins in the latter ½ of the 17th cent. when the Fr. explorers Jacques Marquette and Louis Joliet descended the Mississippi R., followed by Robert Cavelier, sieur de La Salle, who claimed the whole area drained by the Mississippi R. for France and called the territory Louisiana. When the Fr. explorers came the area was inhabited by Native Americans of the Osage and the Mo. groups and by the end of the 17th cent., Fr. trade with the Native Americans flourished. In the early 18th cent. the Fr. worked the area's lead mines and made numerous trips through Mo. in search of furs. Trade down the Mississippi prompted the settlement of Ste. Geneviève before 1750 and the founding of St. Louis in 1764 by Pierre Laclede and René Auguste Chouteau, who were both in the fur-trading business. Although not involved in the last conflict (1754–1763) of the Fr. and Indian Wars, Mo. was affected by the Fr. defeat when in 1762, France secretly ceded the territory W of the Mississippi to Spain. In 1800 the Louisiana Territory (including the Mo. area) was retroceded to France, but in 1803 it passed to the U.S. as part of the Louisiana Purchase. Fr. influence remained dominant, even though by this time Americans had filtered into the territory. At the time of the Lewis and Clark expedition (1803–1806), St. Louis was already known as the gateway to the Far West. The U.S. Territory of Mo. was set up in 1812, and settlement proceeded rapidly after the War of 1812. The coming of the steamboat increased traffic and trade on the Mississippi. Planters from Kentucky and Virginia brought slaves into the territory in which the Fr. had been using Black slaves since the 1720s. The question of admitting the Mo. Territory as a state became a burning natl. issue because it involved the question of extending slavery into the territories west of the Mississippi R. The dispute was resolved by the Missouri Compromise, which admitted (1821) Mo. to the Union as a slave state but excluded slavery from other lands of the Louisiana Purchase N of lat. 36°30′. Slaveholding interests became politically powerful in the new state. In 1822, W. H. Ashley (who later made a fortune in fur trading) led an expedition of the adventurous trappers, who became known as mt. men, up the Missouri R. to explore the West for furs. From Mo. traders established a thriving commerce over the SANTA FE TRAIL with the inhabitants of N.Mex., and pioneers followed the OREGON TRAIL to settle the NW. Franklin, Westport, Independence, and St. Joseph became famous as the points of origin of these expeditions. Settlement of Mo. itself quickened, spreading in the 1820s over the river valleys into central Mo. and by the 1830s into W Mo. The final boundaries of the state were formed after Native Americans gave up their claim to the Platte country in 1836; this strip of land in the NW corner of Mo. was added to the state. Mormon immigrants came to settle Mo. in the 1830s, but their opposition to slavery, their friendliness with Native Americans, and their growing numbers made them unwelcome, and they were driven by force from the state in 1839. Ger. immigrants, however, were cordially received during the 1840s and 1850s, settling principally in the counties in the St. Louis area. In 1854 the problem of slavery was made acute with the passage of the Kansas-Nebraska Act, leaving the question of slavery in the Kansas and Nebr. territories to the settlers themselves. The proslavery forces in Mo. became very active in trying to win Kansas for the slave cause and contributed to the violence and disorder that tore the territory apart in the years just prior to the Civil War. Nevertheless Mo. also had leaders opposed to slavery, including one of its senators, Thomas Hart Benton. During the Civil War most Missourians remained loyal to the Federal govt. A state convention, which met in March 1861, voted against secession, and in 1862, the convention set up a provisional govt. because the pro-Southern governor had set up a separate state gov't in SW Mo. Guerrilla activities persisted during this period, and the lawlessness bred by civil warfare persisted in Mo. after the war in the activities of outlaws such as Jesse James. A new Mo. rose out of the war. The semi-Southern atmosphere, along with the river life and steamboating, began to decline, but the flavor of the period was preserved in the works of one of Missouri's most celebrated sons, Mark Twain (Samuel L. Clemens). The coming of the RR brought the eventual decay of many of Mo.'s river towns and tied the state more closely to the East and North. Urbanization and industrialization progressed, and the Louisiana Purchase Exposition, held at St. Louis in 1904, dramatically revealed Missouri's economic growth. St. Louis was the nation's 4th-largest city. Although during World War I general prosperity prevailed in the state, the Depression years of the 1930s sent farm values crashing down, and many banks, especially in rural areas, failed. Prosperity returned during World War II, when both St. Louis and Kansas City served as vital midcontinental transportation centers. After the war Missouri's industrialization increased enormously. During this period, Mo. became the 2d-largest (behind Mich.) producer of automobiles in the nation. Although most industry remains centered around the major urban centers of Kansas City and St. Louis, the smaller cities and towns have had success in attracting light and heavy industry. The central cities of the two metropolitan areas have experienced dramatic outmigration, often to nearby suburbs. The pop. of St. Louis declined 53% from 1950 to 1990. In 1945, Mo. adopted a new state constitution that remains in effect. As independent city, St. Louis is prohibited by Mo. Constitution to annex into adjacent St. Louis co., thereby unable to balance its inner city decline with suburban growth. The governor of the state is elected for a term of 4 years. The general assembly, or legislature, has a senate with 34 members elected for 4 years and a house of representatives with 163 members elected for 2 years. The state also elects 9 representatives and 2 senators to the U.S. Congress and has 11 electoral votes in presidential elections. Since the brief period of radical Republican rule from 1864 to 1870, Mo. has been permanently wedded to neither major party. While tending toward the Republicans in the days of Theodore Roosevelt, it turned solidly Democratic for Franklin D. Roosevelt and helped to elect Missourian Harry S. Truman to the presidency in 1948. Political machines in the large cities have attracted natl. attention, notably the machine of Thomas J. Pendergast (1872–1945) in Kansas City. Mo. has contributed to the U.S. such outstanding statesmen as Champ Clark, James Reed, and W. Stuart Symington. Thomas Hart Benton, a descendant of the Mo. senator of the same name, was one of the country's important artists. Places of cultural and historic interest in Mo. include the Jefferson Natl. Expansion Memorial, a natl. historic site, in St. Louis; George Washington Carver Natl. Monument, in Diamond; Wilson's Creek Natl. Battlefield, near Springfield; the William Rockhill Nelson Gall. of Art, in Kansas City; the Harry S. Truman Memorial Lib., in Independence; the Mus. of the Amer. Indian, in St. Joseph. and the State Capitol in Jefferson City. Mo.'s schools were desegregated following the Supreme Court decision in 1954. Insts. of higher learning include the Univ. of Mo., with four campuses, including the main one at Columbia; Saint Louis Univ., Washington Univ., and Webster Col., at St. Louis; Rockhurst Col., at Kansas City; and Westminster Col., at Fulton. Mo. has 1 independent city and 114 cos.: ADAIR, ANDREW, ATCHISON, AUDRAIN, BARRY, BARTON, BATES, BENTON, BOLLINGER, BOONE, BUCHANAN, BUTLER, CALDWELL, CALLAWAY, CAMDEN, CAPE GIRARDEAU, CARROLL, CARTER, CASS, CEDAR, CHARITON, CHRISTIAN, CLARK, CLAY, CLINTON, COLE, COOPER, CRAWFORD, DADE, DALLAS, DAVIESS, DE KALB, DENT, DOUGLAS, DUNKLIN, FRANKLIN, GASCONADE, GENTRY, GREENE, GRUNDY, HARRISON, HENRY, HICKORY, HOLT, HOWARD, HOWELL, IRON, JACKSON, JASPER, JEFFERSON, JOHNSON, KNOX, LACLEDE, LAFAYETTE, LAWRENCE, LEWIS, LINCOLN, LINN, LIVINGSTON, MCDONALD, MACON, MADISON, MARIES, MARION, MERCER, MILLER, MISSISSIPPI, MONITEAU, MONROE, MONTGOMERY, MORGAN, NEW MADRID, NEWTON, NODAWAY, OREGON, OSAGE, OZARK, PEMISCOT, PERRY, PETTIS, PHELPS, PIKE, PLATTE, POLK, PULASKI, PUTNAM, RALLS, RANDOLPH, RAY, REYNOLDS, RIPLEY, SAINT CHARLES, SAINT CLAIR, SAINT FRANCOIS, SAINT LOUIS, SAINT LOUIS (INDEPENDENT CITY), SAINTE GENEVIEVE, SALINE, SCHUYLER, SCOTLAND, SCOTT, SHANNON, SHELBY, STODDARD, STONE, SULLIVAN, TANEY, TEXAS, VERNON, WARREN, WASHINGTON, WAYNE, WEBSTER, WORTH, WRIGHT.

Missouri, river, c.2,565 mi/4,130 km long (including its Jefferson-Beaverhead-Red Rock headstream), the longest river of the U.S. and the principal tributary of the Mississippi R. The length of the combined Missouri-Mississippi system from the headwaters of the Missouri to the mouth of the Mississippi is c.3,740 mi/6,020 km, making it the world's 3d-longest river after the Nile and the Amazon. The Missouri R. drains an area of c.580,000 sq mi/1,502,200 sq km, including 2,550 sq mi/6,600 sq km in Canada. The principal headwaters of the Missouri are the Jefferson, Madison, and Gallatin rivers, which rise high in the Rocky Mts., SW Mont., and join to form the Missouri near Three Forks, Mont. The Missouri's upper course flows N through scenic mt. terrain including Gate of the Mts., a deep gorge. At Great Falls, Mont., the river enters a 10-mi/16-km stretch of cataracts that prevented navigation to the upper river and effectively established Fort Benton, Mont., as the head of navigation for 19th-cent. riverboats. Below Fort Benton, the Missouri follows a meandering course E and then SE across the Great Plains of W-central U.S., crossing Mont., N.Dak., and S.Dak.

and forming part of the boundaries of Nebr., Kansas, and Iowa before crossing Mo. and entering the Mississippi R. 17 mi/27 km N of St. Louis. Nicknamed "Big Muddy" for its heavy load of silt, the brown waters of the Missouri do not readily mix with the gray waters of the Mississippi until c.100 mi/160 km downstream. The Yellowstone, Platte, Kansas, and Osage rivers are the Missouri's chief tributaries. Above Sioux City, Iowa, the Missouri's fluctuating flow is regulated by 7 major dams (Gavins Point, Fort Randall, Big Bend, Oahe, Garrison, Fort Peck, and Canyon Ferry) and more than 80 other dams on tributary streams. These dams, with their reservoirs, are part of the coordinated, basinwide Missouri River basin project (authorized by the U.S. Congress in 1944), which provides for flood control, navigation, hydroelectric power, irrigation water, and recreational facilities. The dams serve to impound for later use the spring rains and snow melt that swell the volume of the river in March and April and also the 2d flood stage that frequently occurs in June as the snow melts in the more remote mt. regions. Because the dams have no locks, Sioux City is the head of navigation for the 9-ft/2.7-m channel maintained over the 760-mi/ 1,223-km stretch downstream to the Mississippi. Tugboats pushing strings of barges move freight along this route. From Dec. to March, navigation is interrupted by ice and low water levels (resulting from upstream freezing); summer water levels, which frequently fall so low as to cause riverboats to go aground, are now maintained at safe levels by the release of water from Gavins Point Dam. Silt, fertilizers, and pesticides, which are contained in the runoff from agr. lands, and urban areas pollute the river at selected times of the year. The Missouri R. was an important artery of commerce for Native Amer. villages of the Plains culture long before the Fr. explorers Jacques Marquette and Louis Joliet passed the mouth of the river in 1683 and the Canadian explorer Vérendrye visited the upper reaches of the river in 1738. David Thompson, a Can. fur trader, explored part of the river in 1797. Meriwether Lewis and William Clark followed the Missouri on their journey (1803–1806) to the Pacific Ocean and described it at length. The 1st steamboat ascended the river in 1819 and hundreds more later navigated the uncertain waters to Fort Benton. Mormons bound for Utah and pioneers bound for Oregon and Calif. followed the Missouri valley and that of the Platte overland to the West. R. traffic declined with the loss of freight to the RR after the Civil War, but it has been revitalized in the 20th cent., in the sect. below Sioux City, through the navigational improvements and flood control efforts of the Missouri R. basin project. The Missouri R. is the water supply for several million persons. Occasional high floods cause considerable damage. The Great Flood of 1993 on the river below Omaha, which set record crests and record discharges, and another flood in 1995, have prompted reevaluation of river management, goals, and strategies.

Missouri City 1 city (1990 pop. 348), Clay co., W Mo., on Missouri R., and 20 mi/32 km NE of Kansas City; 39°14′N 94°17′W. Concrete and crushed limestone. **2** city (1990 pop. 36,176), Fort Bend and Harris cos., SE Texas, suburb, 14 mi/23 km SW of downtown Houston; 29°34′N 95°32′W. Near Brazos R. Drained by Oyster Creek. Agr. area (rice, cotton, nursery crops, vegetables). Oil and natural gas. Some mfg. Blue Ridge State Prison Farm to E.

Missouri Mountain (14,067 ft/4,288 m), Chaffee co., central Colo., in Collegiate Range of Rocky Mts., in San Isabel Natl. Forest, E of Continental Divide, 15 mi/ 24 km WNW of Buena Vista.

Missouri Valley, city (1990 pop. 2,888), Harrison co., W Iowa, near Boyer R., 7 mi/11.3 km SW of Logan; 41°33′N 95°54′W. Mfg. (feed, beverages, concrete blocks). Settled 1854, inc. 1871.

Missouri Wild and Scenic River and Riverway, park, S.Dak. to Neb., authorized 1978. Free-flowing portion of Missouri River with isls., bars, and chutes; 59 mi/ 95 km long, from Gavins Point Dam, near Yankton, S.Dak., downstream to Ponca, Nebr. Authorized 1978. Limited recreational facilities.

Mist Mountain (10,303 ft/3,140 m), SW Alta., Canada, near B.C. border, in Misty Range of Rocky Mts., 50 mi/ 80 km SW of Calgary; 50°33′N 114°55′W.

Mistassibi River (mis-tuh-SI-bee), 200 mi/322 km long, central Que., Canada; rises E of L. Mistassini; flows S to Mistassini R. at Dolbeau, near L. St. John.

Mistassini (mis-tuh-SEE-nee), village, S central Que., on Mistassibi R., near its mouth on Mistassini R., 3 mi/ 5 km NE of Dolbeau; 48°54′N 72°12′W. Agr. (dairying; pigs); blueberry processing.

Mistassini, Lake (☐ c.840 sq mi/2,180 sq km), S Que., Canada, NW of L. St. John. In sparsely settled country, it drains W to James Bay by way of the Rupert R. (380 mi/612 km long).

Mistassini River, 200 mi/322 km long, central Que.; rises E of L. Mistassini; flows S, past Dolbeau, where it receives Mistassibi R., to St. John. On upper course are numerous rapids.

Mita Point (MEE-tah), cape on the Pacific, at NE entrance of Banderas Bay, W Mexico, 65 mi/105 km SW of Tepic; 20°46′N 105°33′W. Lighthouse.

Mitchel Air Force Base, former U.S. installation at Mitchel Field, Nassau co., SE N.Y., just E of Garden City; 40°43′N 73°36′W. Air Defense Command hq. here until 1951. Used to be the largest military airfield on the East Coast.

Mitchell, town (1991 pop. 3,382), S Ont., Canada, on Thames R., and 12 mi/19 km NW of Stratford; 43°28′N 81°11′W. Food processing.

Mitchell 1 county (☐ 514 sq mi/1,331 sq km; 1990 pop. 20,275), SW Ga.; ⊙ Camilla; 31°13′N 84°11′W. Bounded NW by Flint R. Coastal plain agr. (corn, pecans, soybeans, peanuts; cotton, tobacco; cattle, hogs, poultry); in sawmilling area. Mfg. at Camilla and Pelham. Formed 1857. **2** county (☐ 469 sq mi/1,215 sq km; 1990 pop. 10,928), N Iowa, on Minn. line; ⊙ Osage; 43°21′N 92°47′W. Prairie agr. region (dairying; cattle, hogs; corn, hay) drained by Wapsipinicon, Cedar, and Little Cedar rivers. Has many limestone quarries, sand, clay and gravel pits. Pioneer State Park in SE. General flooding in 1993. Formed 1851. **3** county (☐ 718 sq mi/ 1,860 sq km; 1990 pop. 7,203), N Kansas; ⊙ Beloit; 39°23′N 98°12′W. Smoky Hills region, drained by Solomon R. Agr. (cattle, sheep, hogs; wheat, soybeans). Mfg. (farm machinery). Waconda L. Reservoir and Glen Elder State Park (at dam) in W. Formed 1870. **4** county (☐ 222 sq mi/575 sq km; 1990 pop. 14,433), W N.C.; ⊙ Bakersville; 36°00′N 82°09′W. Bounded N by Tenn. state line, W by Nolichucky R., SW by Toe R.; Unaka Mts. in N, the Blue Ridge Mts. in S. Largely in Pisgah Natl. Forest in N ½ and SE corner. Agr. area (tobacco, corn, apples; hay; cattle). Mining (mica, feldspar, quartz, kaolin). Resort area. Appalachian Trail follows state line in N. Blue Ridge Parkway follows SE co. line. Formed 1861. **5** county (☐ 915 sq mi/2,370 sq km; 1990 pop. 8,016), W Texas; ⊙ Colorado City; 32°17′N 100°55′W. Elev. 1,900 ft/579 m–2,600 ft/792 m. Rolling prairies, drained by Colorado R. and Beals Creek. Ranching (cattle, sheep), agr. region (cotton, grains). Oil and natural gas wells. Chamion Creek Reservoir and L. Colorado City (State Park) at center of co. Formed 1876.

Mitchell 1 city (1990 pop. 4,669), Lawrence co., S Ind., 9 mi/14.5 km S of Bedford; 38°44′N 86°29′W. Agr. (fruit, grain). Mfg. (cement, transportation equip., machinery, crushed stone, lime); limestone quarrying. Spring Mill State Park (recreation), with restored pioneer village, is nearby to E. Karst topography. Settled 1813, laid out 1853. **2** city (1990 pop. 13,798), seat of Davison co., SE S.Dak; 43°43′N 98°01′W. Mitchell is a trade, distribution, and shipping center for a dairy and livestock area. Mfg. (printing, trailers, transportation equip., machinery, computer equip.); food processing. L. Mitchell to N; RR junction. Dakota Wesleyan Univ.; Mitchell Area Vocational Tech. Institute; Corn Palace, opera house and music hall. Friends of the Middle Border Mus.; Oscar Howe Art Center. Inc. 1881.

Mitchell 1 town (1990 pop. 170), Mitchell co., N Iowa, 4 mi/6.4 km NW of Osage; 43°19′N 92°52′W. Livestock; grain. **2** town (1990 pop. 1,743), Scotts Bluff co., W Nebr., 8 mi/12.9 km NW of Scottsbluff, and on North Platte R; 41°56′N 103°48′W. In irrigated agr. region; beet sugar, honey, dairy prods., potatoes.

Mitchell 1 village (1990 pop. 181), Glascock co., E Ga., c.45 mi/72 km WSW of Augusta, near Ogeechee R; 33°13′N 82°42′W. Lumber. **2** village (1990 pop. 163), Wheeler co., N central Oregon, 30 mi/48 km S of Fossil on Bridge Creek; 44°34′N 120°09′W. Ochoco Natl. Forest and Bridge Creek Wilderness Area to S. John Day Fossil Beds Natl. Monument (Painted Hills Unit) to NW.

Mitchell Heights, village (1990 pop. 265), Logan co., SW W.Va., 5 mi/8 km N of Logan, on Guyandotte R. Residential. Chief Logan State Park to W.

Mitchell, Lake, Wexford co., NW Mich., 3 mi/4.8 km W of Cadillac; c.3 mi/4.8 km long, 3 mi/4.8 km wide; 44°15′N 85°29′W. In resort area. Joined to L. Cadillac (E) by short stream.

Mitchell Lake, E B.C., Canada, in Cariboo Mts., 75 mi/ 121 km E of Quesnel; 10 mi/16 km long, 2 mi/3 km wide; 52°53′N 120°36′W. Elev. 3,170 ft/966 m. Drains SW into Quesnel L.

Mitchell, Lake, reservoir, Davison co., SE central S.Dak., on Firesteel Creek, 2 mi/3.2 km N of Mitchell; 3 mi/ 4.8 km long, 1 mi/1.6 km wide; 43°39′N 98°00′W. Formed by dam. Recreational area.

Mitchell Lake (☐ 9 sq mi/23.3 sq km), on border of Chilton and Coosa cos., central Ala., in Coosa R., 30 mi/48 km NNW of Montgomery; c.14 mi/23 km long; 32°48′N 86°26′W. Extends NNW to Lay Dam; has 4-mi/6.4-km E arm. Formed by privately built (1923) Mitchell Dam (106 ft/32 m high, 1,264 ft/385 m long).

Mitchell, Mount, peak (6,684 ft/2,037 m), Yancey co., W N.C., in the Black Mts. of the Appalachian system. Highest mt. in N. Amer. E of Rocky Mts. In Mt. Mitchell State Park, surrounded by Pisgah Natl. Forest. Road access to summit from SW; restaurant and observation tower. Blue Ridge Parkway passes to S and SE.

Mitchell Peak (7,951 ft/2,423 m), Greenlee co., E Ariz., in Blue Range, 10 mi/16 km N of Morenci. Apache-Sitgreaves Natl. Forest.

Mitchellville 1 town (1990 pop. 1,670), Polk co., central Iowa, near Skunk R., 14 mi/23 km ENE of Des Moines; 41°39′N 93°21′W. In agr. and coal-mining area. Seat of Iowa Correctional Inst. for Women. **2** town (1990 pop. 193), Summer co., N Tenn., near Ky. line, 22 mi/35 km NE of Springfield; 36°38′N 86°32′W.

Mitkof Island, SE Alaska, in Alexander Archipelago, bet. Kupreanof Isl. (W) and mainland (E), 10 mi/16 km NW of Wrangell; 24 mi/39 km long, 7 mi/11.3 km–17 mi/ 27 km wide; 56°40′N 132°47′W. Rises to 3,960 ft/1,207 m (SE). Petersburg town, N.

Mitla (MEE-tlah) [Nahuatl = abode of the dead], archaeological site, religious center of the Zapotec at San Pablo Villa de Mitla, near Oaxaca, SW Mexico; 16°56′N 96°19′W. Probably built in the 13th cent., the bldgs., unlike the pyramidal structures of most Middle Amer. architecture, are low, horizontal masses enclosing the plazas. Mitla is thought to represent the highest expression of Zapotec architectural talent, although some decorative elements have been attributed to the Mixtec, who conquered Mitla as well as Monte Albán.

Mitontic (mee-to-TEEK), town (1990 pop. 666), Chiapas, S Mexico, in Sierra de Hueytepec, 10 mi/16 km NNE of San Cristóbal de las Casas. Elev. 6,135 ft/ 1,870 m. Agr. (wheat, fruit). A Tzotzil Maya community. Also known as San Miguel.

Mi-Wuk village (me–wook), uninc. town (1990 pop. 1,175), Toulumne co., central Calif., 12 mi/19 km NE of Sonora, in Sierra Nevada; 38°04′N 120°11′W. Timber, cattle, hay. Area surrounded by Stanislaus Natl. Forest.

Mixcoac (meesh-ko-AHK), SW sect. of Mexico city, central Mexico, and part of Benito Juárez Delegacion. Mfg. suburb (cement plant, processing industries); nursery gardens. Alvaro Obregón adjoins (S).

Mixistlán de la Reforma (meesh-ko-AHK de lah re-FOR-mah), town (1990 pop. 594), in E central Oaxaca, Mexico, 48 km ENE of Tlacolula de Matamords. Elev.

5,906 ft/1,800 m. Mountainous region with temperate climate. Agr. (cereals and fruits), and woods. A Mixe-speaking town. Formerly known as Santa María Mixistlán.

Mixquiahuala (meesh-kee-ah-WAH-lah), town (1990 pop.19,536), ⊙ Mixquiahuala de Juárez municipio, Hidalgo, central Mexico, on Tula R., and 32 mi/51 km WNW of Pachuca de Soto, on RR; 20°11′N 99°10′W. Elev. 6,549 ft/1,996 m. Grain, beans, potatoes, fruit; livestock.

Mixquic (meesh-KEEK), town, Federal Dist., Tláhuac delegación, central Mexico, 18 mi/29 km SE of Mexico city, and part of the Mexico city metropolitan area. Cereals, fruit, vegetables; livestock.

Mixtla, Mexico: see SAN FRANCISCO MIXTLA.

Mixtla de Altamirano (MEESH-tlah dai ahl-mee-RAH-no), town (1990 pop. 83), Veracruz, E Mexico, in Sierra Zongolica, 21 mi/34 km SSW of Córdoba. An isolated town in mountainous area. Coffee, sugarcane, fruit.

Mixtlán (meesh-TLAHN), town (1990 pop. 1,657), Jalisco, W Mexico, 23 mi/37 km WSW of Ameca. Isolated town in Sierra Verde. Corn, chickpeas, beans, sugarcane.

Mize (MEIZ), village (1990 pop. 312), Smith co., S central Miss., 27 mi/43 km WNW of Laurel, on Oakahay Creek; 31°52′N 89°32′W. Agr. (corn, cotton; poultry, cattle); mfg. (electrical components, lumber, polishing machinery)

Mizpah 1 (MIZ-puh), village (1990 pop. 100), Koochiching co., N Minn., 60 mi/97 km SW of International Falls; 47°55′N 94°13′W. In forest area. Timber, alfalfa; cattle; mfg. (valve lifters). Pine Island State Forest to N and E. **2** village, Atlantic co., S N.J., 5 mi/8 km NW of Mays Landing. In agr. area. Founded by Jewish immigrants in the late 19th cent.

Mizzen Topsail, mountain (1,761 ft/537 m), W central N.F., Canada, 25 mi/40 km E of NE end of Grand L.; 49°5′N 56°37′W.

Moa (MO-uh), deep-water port city (1994 pop. 44,000), on NE coast of Holguín prov., E Cuba; 20°40′N 74°56′W. Ships nickel and sugar; nickel smelter and quarries. Airport (runway 6,000 ft/1,829 m).

Moa, Cayo Grande de, Cuba: see GRANDE DE MOA, CAYO.

Moa, Cuchillas de (MO-uh, koo-CHEE-yahz dai), small range, Holguín prov., NE Cuba, NW of Baracoa, extends c.20 mi/32 km NW along Atlantic coast; rises to 1,175 m at Pico de Toldo. Yields timber; has iron deposits. Has 300 ft/91 m cascade on small Moa R.

Moab (MO-ab), town (1990 pop. 3,971), ⊙ Grand co., E Utah, on Colorado R. (crossed here by bridge), and 100 mi/161 km SE of Price; 38°34′N 109°32′W. Elev. 4,025 ft/1,227 m. Tourist point; trade center for cattle, sheep; irrigated agr. area. Oil and natural-gas processing; salt, potassium mining. Vanadium and uranium mines nearby. La Sal Mts. are E, in sect. of La Sal Natl. Forest (hq. at Moab); Arches Natl. Park is N. Canyonlands Natl. Park and Dead Horse Point State Park to SW. Settled 1855; grew as ranching point after 1876.

Moapa (MO-puh) or **Moapa Valley**, uninc. village (1990 pop. 3,444), Clark co., SE Nev., 44 mi/71 km NE of Las Vegas; 36°34′N 114°28′W. Small farming community at entrance to Moapa Indian Reservation, to SW. Junction of RR spur to Overton. Cattle; poultry; vegetables; mfg. (concrete). Valley of Fire State Park and Lake Mead Natl. Recreation Area to SE. Warm Springs Resort, desert tourist oasis, is here.

Mobeetie, village (1990 pop. 154), Wheeler co., extreme N Texas, in the Panhandle, 30 mi/48 km E of Pampa; 35°31′N 100°26′W. In farming and cattle region; oil. Nearby is Old Mobeetie, site of old Fort Elliot. Historic jail is now a mus.

Moberly, city (1990 pop. 12,839), Randolph co., N central Mo.; 39°25′N 92°26′W. Mfg. (instant ice packs, automobile components, gym equip.). Limestone quarries. Former coal-mining region. Former important RR center. Moberly Area Junior Col. State Correctional Center (penitentiary) to S. Inc. 1868.

Mobile (MO-beel), county (□ 1,644 sq mi/4,258 sq km; 1990 pop. 378,643), extreme SW Ala.; ⊙ Mobile.

Coastal plain, bounded S by Mississippi Sound, E by Mobile Bay and Mobile R., W by Miss. Corn, soybeans, pecans, berries, subtropical fruits; seafood; paper mills; crude- oil and natural-gas production. City of Mobile (mfg. center) is Ala.'s only seaport. Formed 1812.

Mobile (MO-beel), city (1990 pop. 196,278), ⊙ Mobile co., SW Ala., at the head of Mobile Bay, at the mouth of the Mobile R. It is one of the country's major ports, the only seaport in Ala., and the 2d-largest city in the state. Oil refineries; paper, textiles, aluminum, and chemicals; iron smelting. After the Tennessee-Tombigbee waterway was completed in 1984, connecting N Miss.'s Tennessee R. with the Tombigbee R. in W Ala. and providing access to the Gulf of Mexico, Mobile enjoyed a boom in business growth and redevelopment. Mobile was the capital of Fr. Louisiana (1710–1719). The Br. held it (1763–1780), before Bernardo de Gálvez took it for Spain. Mobile was seized by the U.S. in 1813. During the Civil War, ships from Mobile evaded the Federal blockade until Admiral Farragut's victory at Mobile Bay (1864); Gen. E. R. S. Canby captured the city in April, 1865. Mobile has many beautiful antebellum homes and magnificent gardens. Also noteworthy are a R.C. cathedral, the city hall (1858), and Marine Hosp. (1842). Of historical interest are forts Morgan and Gaines at the entrance to Mobile Bay. Mobile is the seat of Spring Hill Col., Univ. of Mobile, the Univ. of South Ala., and Bishop State Community Col. Brookley, a coast guard station, and a coast guard aviation training center are here. The USS *Alabama* Battleship Memorial Park, USS *Drum* submarine, and numerous aircraft are here. The colorful annual Mardi Gras was begun in the early 1700s; the Azalea Trail Festival dates from 1929. The Bankhead Tunnel lies under the Mobile R. Inc. 1814.

Mobile Bay (MO-beel), arm of the Gulf of Mexico, SW Ala., extending c.35 mi/56 km from the Gulf to the mouth of the Mobile R.; 8 mi/12.9 km–18 mi/29 km wide. A ship channel connects Mobile Bay with the Gulf. The Intracoastal Waterway passes through the S part of the bay. Mobile is on the NW shore. Admiral David Farragut, a Civil War naval hero, won the celebrated battle of Mobile Bay on Aug. 5, 1864.

Mobjack Bay, arm of Chesapeake Bay, Gloucester and Mathews cos., E Va., 25 mi/40 km N of Newport News; c.5 mi/8 km wide at SE entrance, up to 10 mi/16 km long. Has several inlets.

Mobridge, town (1990 pop. 3,768), Walworth co., N S.Dak., on Missouri R., and 80 mi/129 km N of Pierre; 45°32′N 100°26′W. Trade and distribution point for agr. region; lignite coal; cement blocks, concrete; beverages; livestock, dairy produce. Lutheran academy is here. Sports fishing center. Mountain-Central time zone boundary runs through center of river. Large Standing Rock Indian Reservation to W (including Sitting Bull's Grave and Sacajawea Monument across river); large Cheyenne River Indian Reservation to SW. Founded 1906, inc. 1908.

Moca (MO-kah), city (1993 pop. 45,217), ⊙ Espaillat prov., N Dominican Republic, on S slope of Cordillera Septentrional, on highway, and 13 mi/21 km ESE of Santiago; 19°25′N 70°30′W. Coffee-growing center; also cacao and tobacco. Founded 1780.

Moca (MO-kah), town (1990 pop. 32,926), NW P.R., 3 mi/4.8 km SE of Aguadilla. Livestock; light mfg; rope hammock-making artisan shops. Famous for mundillo (lace-making).

Mocambo, Mexico: see BOCA DEL RÍO.

Mocanaqua (MO-kah-NAH-kwah), uninc. town (1990 pop. 1,100), Conyngham township, Luzerne co., E central Pa., 15 mi/24 km SW of Wilkes-Barre, on Susquehanna R., at mouth of Turtle Creek; 41°08′N 76°08′W. Light mfg.

Moccasin 1 (MAH-kuh-suhn), uninc. village, Mohave co., NW Ariz., 18 mi/29 km SW of Kanab, Utah, hq. of Kaibab Indian Reservation. Pipe Spring Natl. Monument is to S, within reservation. **2** village (1990 pop. 80), Judith Basin co., central Mont., 22 mi/35 km WSW of Lewistown. RR junction. Wheat, barley, hay; livestock. Agr. research center to W. Ackley Lake State Park to S.

Mochis, Mexico: see LOS MOCHIS.

Mochitlán (mo-chee-TLAHN), town (1990 pop. 3,887), Guerrero, SW Mexico, in Sierra Madre del Sur, 9 mi/14.5 km ESE of Chilpancingo de Dravo. Cereals, sugarcane, fruit, forest prods. (resin, vanilla).

Mock Horn Island, marshy isl., Northampton co., E Va., off Atlantic Ocean coast, 6 mi/9.7 km E of Cape Charles town; 8 mi/12.9 km long, 2 mi/3.2 km wide. Separated from Delmarva (Eastern Shore) peninsula by Mockhorn (NW) and Magothy (SW) bays; separated from Wreck and Ship Shoal isls. to E by South Bay. Mockhorn Isl. Wildlife Management Area covers isl.

Mockingbird Valley, town (1990 pop. 177), Jefferson co., N Ky., residential suburb, 4 mi/6.4 km NE of Louisville, and near Ohio R.; 38°16′N 85°40′W.

Mocksville, town (1990 pop. 3,399), ⊙ Davie co., central N.C., 22 mi/35 km SW of Winston-Salem; 35°53′N 80°33′W. Tobacco, soybeans, grain; chickens, livestock; dairying. Light mfg. Joppa Cemetery, burial site of Squire and Sarah Boone, parents of pioneer Daniel Boone. Settled before 1750.

Moclips (MO-klips), uninc. town (1990 pop. 770), Grays Harbor co., W Wash., 23 mi/37 km NW of Hoquiam, on Pacific, at mouth of Moclips R. RR junction. Logging. Copalis Natl. Wildlife Refuge, including coastal rocks, offshore. Quinault Indian Reservation to N.

Mocochá (mo-ko-CHAH), town (1990 pop. 1,582), Yucatán, SE Mexico, 13 mi/21 km NE of Mérida, on Mexico Highway 281. Henequen.

Mocorito (mo-ko-REE to), city (1990 pop. 6,458) and township, Sinaloa, NW Mexico, on small Evora R., and 55 mi/89 km NW of Culiacán (Rosales); 25°30′N 107°53′W. Agr. center (corn, sugarcane, tomatoes, chickpeas, fruit).

Moctezuma (mok-te-SOO-mah), city (1990 pop. 2,949) and township, San Luis Potosí, N central Mexico, on interior plateau, 43 mi/69 km N of San Luis Potosí; 22°46′N 101°06′W. Grain, beans, cotton, maguey. Thermal springs nearby.

Moctezuma (mok-te-SOO-mah), town (1990 pop. 3,529), Sonora, NW Mexico, on Moctezuma R., and 90 mi/145 km NE of Hermosillo; 29°50′N 109°40′W. Copper-mining, wheat-growing center.

Moctezuma River 1 (mok-te-SOO-mah), c.175 mi/282 km long, in N central and NE Mexico; rises in Sierra Madre Oriental SW of San Juan del Rio; flows NE along Querétaro-Hidalgo border, past Tamazunchale and Tanquián in fertile La Huasteca plains (San Luis Potosí), to join Santa María (or Tamuin) R. in forming Pánuco R. on Veracruz border, 50 mi/80 km SW of Tampico. Used for irrigation. **2** c.110 mi/177 km long, in Sonora, NW Mexico; rises in W outliers of Sierra Madre Occidental; flows S past Cumpas and Moctezuma to Yaqui R. at Plutarco Elias Calles Reservoir; 21°59′N 98°34′W.

Modale, town (1990 pop. 289), Harrison co., W Iowa, near mouth of Soldier R. on Missouri R., 11 mi/18 km W of Logan; 41°37′N 96°00′W. In agr. area.

Modena (mo-DEE-nuh), borough (1990 pop. 563), Chester co., SE Pa., 1 mi/1.6 km S of Coatesville, on West Branch of Brandywine Creek; 39°57′N 75°47′W. Agr. (grain, apples; livestock; dairying); mfg. (metal bins, paper). Formerly Paperville.

Modena (mo-DEE-nuh), uninc. rural community, Mercer co., N Mo., bet. Thompson and Weldon rivers, 8 mi/12.9 km SW of Princeton.

Modesto, city (1990 pop. 164,730), seat of Stanislaus co., central Calif., 50 mi/80 km ENE of San Jose on the Tuolumne R. (S) and Modesto Main Canal (N), near the N part of the San Joaquin valley; 37°40′N 121°00′W. Elev. 27 ft/8 m. The center of a farming and fruit-growing area, it has food processing, tomato canning, wineries, fruit orchards, and diversified mfg.; also much agr. (dairying; cattle, poultry; nuts, vegetables, beans, pumpkins, melons, rice); and fishing (codfish). RR junction. Riverbank Army Ammunition Plant 7 mi/11.3 km to NE, on Stanislaus R.; Hetch Hetchy Aqueduct to N. It is one of the fastest-growing U.S. cities, marked by a pop. increase of 54% bet. 1980 and 1990. Modesto 2-yr col. is here. Inc. 1884.

Modesto, village (1990 pop. 240), Macoupin co., SW central Ill., 16 mi/26 km NNW of Carlinville; 39°28′N 89°58′W. In agr. (cattle, hogs; corn, wheat, sorghum, soybeans) and bituminous-coal area. Otter L. 5 mi/8 km SE.

Modesto Reservoir, Calif.: see TUOLUMNE RIVER.

Modoc, county (□ 3,944 sq mi/10,215 sq km; 1990 pop. 9,678), NE Calif.; ⊙ Alturas; 41°36′N 120°43′W. Bounded N by Oregon, E by Nev. On high, semiarid volcanic plateau (lowest elev. in co. is 4,000 ft/1,219 m), with extensive lava beds; rises to Eagle Peak (9,892 ft/3,015 m) in Warner Mts. (E). Cattle, sheep; timber; potatoes, onions, horseradish, wheat, barley, oats, sugar beets; pumice, sand and gravel. Drained by Pit R. Includes Clear L. Reservoir (for irrigation) and Clear Lake Natl. Wildlife Refuge in NW; part of Goose L. on N boundary, extends into Oregon; Surprise Valley (in E), which contains intermittently dry upper, middle, and lower Alkali lakes; Cow Head L. (dry) in NE; Fort Bidwell Indian Reservation in NE; part of Klamath irrigation project (N); Modoc Natl. Forest covers large part of co., esp. in center and NW, and Warner Mts. in E; small part of Shasta Natl. Forest in SW corner; Big Sage Reservoir in center; part of Tule L. Natl. Wildlife Refuge and part of Lava Reeds Natl. Monument on W boundary; parts of XL Ranch Indian Reservation in E center and at S end of Goose L. Good waterfowl and deer hunting, fishing. Formed 1874.

Modoc 1 (MO-dahk), town, Emanuel co., E central Ga., 5 mi/8 km N of Swainsboro; 32°39′N 82°18′W. **2** town (1990 pop. 218), Randolph co., E Ind., 11 mi/18 km SW of Winchester; 40°02′N 85°08′W.

Moenkopi, uninc. town (1990 pop. 924), Coconino co., N central Ariz., 64 mi/103 km NNE of Flagstaff, and 2 mi/3.2 km S of Tuba City, in W part of Navajo Indian Reservation, on Moenkopi Wash and Moenkopi Plateau. Crafts. Dinosaur tracks site to W.

Moffat, county (□ 4,751 sq mi/12,305 sq km; 1990 pop. 11,357), extreme NW Colo.; ⊙ Craig; 40°36′N 108°12′W. Livestock-grazing area; borders on Utah (W) and Wyo. (N); drained by Yampa, Little Snake, and Green rivers. Elkhead Reservoir on E boundary; Elkhead Creek forms part of E county line. Cattle; wheat, oats, barley. Part of Dinosaur Natl. Monument in W (extends into Utah); parts of Routt Natl. Forest (in NE); parts of White River Natl. Forest (SE); Browns Park Natl. Wildlife Reserve in NW. Formed 1911.

Moffat, village (1990 pop. 99), Saguache co., S Colo., on San Luis Creek Saguache Creek to W, and 14 mi/23 km ESE of Saguache; 38°00′N 105°54′W. Elev. 7,561 ft/2,305 m. Shipping point in livestock region. Crestone Peak, 18 mi/29 km E; Great Sand Dunes Natl. Monument to SE; Sangre De Cristo Mts. to E; parts of Rio Grande Natl. Forest to NE, NW, and W.

Moffat Tunnel, RR tunnel, N central Colo., on the Continental Divide, NW of Denver; 24 ft/7 m high, 18 ft/5 m wide, and 6.2 mi/10 km long. One of the country's longest RR tunnels, it was built bet. 1922 and 1927. At an elev. of 9,094 ft/2,772 m, it passes through James Peak. An adjacent bore carries water to Denver. Extends from Winter Park, Grand co., on W, to East Portal, Gilpinco, on E, S of Rollins Pass.

Moffet Inlet, Anglican mission station, N Baffin Isl., SE Franklin Dist., N.W.T., Canada, on E side of Admiralty Inlet, 65 mi SSE of Arctic Bay trading post; 77°11′N 84°28′W.

Moffett, village (1990 pop. 219), Sequoyah co., E Okla., on Arkansas R. (bridged), suburb, 3 mi/4.8 km WNW of Fort Smith, Ark; 35°23′N 94°27′W. Residential, commercial, and agr. area.

Moffett Air Force Base, Calif.: see SUNNYVALE.

Mogadore (MAH-guh-dor), village (1990 pop. 4,008), Summit co., NE Ohio, just E of Akron; 41°03′N 81°24′W. Tools, clay prods., composites, plastic prods.

Mogollon (muh-guh-YON), uninc. village (1990 pop. 35), Catron co., SW N.Mex., near San Francisco R., W of Mogollon Mts., 52 mi/84 km NNW of Silver City. Elev. 6,620 ft/2,018 m. Silver mines in vicinity. Snow L. to E; the Catwalk to SW.

Mogollon Mountains (muh-guh-YON), Gila and Grant cos., SW N.Mex., just E of San Francisco R., in Gila Natl. Forest, near Ariz. state line. Prominent points: Granite Peak (8,731 ft/2,661 m), Mogollon Baldy (10,778 ft/3,285 m), Whitewater Baldy (10,892 ft/3,320 m). Silver mining.

Mogollon Plateau (muh-guh-YON) or **Mogollon Mesa**, tableland, E central Ariz., part of the Colorado Plateau. Elev. from 7,000 ft/2,134 m to 8,000 ft/2,438 m. It is covered by pine forests, parts of which are included in Coconino, Tonto, and Apache-Sitgreaves natl. forests. Its S edge is a rugged S-facing escarpment called the Mogollon Rim, which forms Coconino-Gila co. line in NW, and N boundary of Fort Apache Indian Reservation in E. The plateau is not directly connected with the Mogollon Mts. in W N.Mex.

Mohall (MO-hawl), town (1990 pop. 931), ⊙ Renville co., N N.Dak., 38 mi/61 km N of Minot.; 48°46′N 101°30′W.

Mohave, county (□ 13,470 sq mi/34,887 sq km; 1990 pop. 93,497), NW Ariz.; ⊙ Kingman, 35°42′N 113°45′W. Mining (lead, silver, zinc, gold, copper); agr. (cattle; alfala, wheat, barley, sorghum, lettuce, honeydews). Hualpai, Mohave, and Black mts. in SW. Drained by Big Sandy R. in SE. Parts of Grand Canyon Natl. Park in N center and NE; parts of L. Mead Natl. Recreation Area in NW and N center. Colorado R. bounds co. in large part on W., foms lakes Havasu, Mohave, and Mead and state boundary of Nev. (part) and Calif.; entire W state line forms Pacific-Mountain time zone boundary (Ariz is in Mountain); Colorado R. crosses co. in N and forms part of E boundary; bounded by Utah on N, with Kaibab Creek forming NE boundary; Bill Williams and Santa Maria rivers form S boundary. Part of large Hualapai Indian Reservation in NE center, small sections of reservation NE and SW of Kingman; part of Kaibab Indian Reservation in far NE; part of Fort Mojave Indian Reservation in SW corner, on Colorado R., next to Calif. and Nev. Mt. Nuff, Warm Springs, and Wabayuma Peak wilderness areas in SW corner, 2 sects. of Havasu Natl. Wildlife Refuge in SW; Paints and Beaver Dam wilderness areas in NW corner; Hualapai Mt. Park in center, SE of Kingman; L. Havasu State Park in SW. Hoover Dam forms L. Mead on Nev. border. Fifth-largest co. in U.S. in land area. Formed 1864.

Mohave, Lake, Ariz.: see DAVIS DAM.

Mohave Mountains, Mohave co., W Ariz., E side of Colorado R., just N of Lake Havasu City, Ariz., and E of Needles, Calif. Rise to 5,102 ft/1,555 m (Grossman Peak) in Ariz., to 3,688 ft/1,124 m in Calif.

Mohawk 1 village, Keweenaw co., NW Upper Peninsula, Mich., 17 mi/27 km NE of Houghton; 47°18′N 88°21′W. RR terminus. Mfg. (cedar furniture); acorn nuts. **2** village (1990 pop. 2,986), Herkimer co., central N.Y., on Mohawk R. and the Barge Canal, and 13 mi/21 km SE of Utica; 43°00′N 75°00′W. Mfg. (measuring tapes, fishing reels; metal fabrication). Settled 1826, inc. 1844. **3** village, Coshocton co., central Ohio, 12 mi/19 km WNW of Coshocton.

Mohawk Dam; Mohawk Reservoir, Ohio: see WALHONDING RIVER.

Mohawk, Lake, reservoir, Sparta, Sussex co., NW N.J., on Wallkill R., 7 mi/11.3 km ESE of Newton; c.2.5 mi/4 km long; 41°01′N 74°38′W. Recreational area.

Mohawk River 1 (MO-hawk), 10 mi/16 km long, Coos co., N N.H.; rises in Mud Pond, 3 mi/4.8 km N of Dixville Notch; flows SW and W to the Connecticut R. at Colebrook. **2** largest tributary of the Hudson R., c.140 mi/225 km long, central and E N.Y.; rises in Oneida co.; flows S and SE, past Rome, Utica, Amsterdam, and Schenectady, to the Hudson R. at Cohoes (falls here). Drains 3,412 mi/5,491 km. From Rome to its mouth, river is either paralleled by or part of N.Y. State Barge Canal joining Great Lakes and E coast ports via Hudson R. The beautiful and fertile Mohawk valley, as the E-W passage bet. the Adirondacks (N) and the Allegheny Plateau, or Upland (S), was scene of many battles in the Fr. and Indian War and in the Amer. Revolution and was an important route for westbound pioneers; the old Erie Canal followed the river in much the same manner as the Barge Canal.

Mohawk Trail (MO-hawk), motor highway extending c.30 mi/50 km across N Mass. from Greenfield to North Adams. Follows a trail blazed originally by the Mohawks. Traversing the scenic Hoosac Mts. and Berkshire Hills, the route is popular with tourists. A number of state forests are along the route.

Mohawk Trail, old road in central N.Y. state following the Mohawk R. in part; c.100 mi/160 km long. It was the major route through the Appalachians by which thousands of settlers emigrated from the E seaboard to the Midwest. It traverses territory once occupied by the Iroquois Confederacy. In the Colonial period it was a series of turnpikes that began at Schenectady and extended to Rome, with lesser trails stretching W. The Erie Canal rendered the road less important, and when the RRs were built, its value was further diminished.

Mohawk Valley, Calif.; see BLAIRSDEN.

Mohegan, village, Burrillville town, R.I.; 41°59′N 71°37′W.

Mohegan (mo-hee-GIN), community, New London co., Conn. Attained Native American reservation status in 1995. Casino gambling complex under development in early 1996.

Mohegan Lake, village (1990 pop. 3,600), Westchester co., SE N.Y., on L. Mohegan (c.1 mi/1.6 km long), 5 mi/8 km NE of Peekskill; 41°19′N 73°52′W.

Mohican, Cape (mo-HEE-kin), W Alaska, W extremity of Nunivak Isl., on Bering Sea; 60°12′N 167°24′W.

Mohican River, c.40 mi/64 km long, central Ohio; formed by junction of forks in region E of Mansfield; flows S, joining Kokosing R. to form Walhonding R. 16 mi/26 km NW of Coshocton; 40°21′N 82°09′W. Among its headstreams and tributaries (some with flood-control works) are Black, Lake, Clear, and Jerome forks.

Mohicanville Dam, Ashland co., N central Ohio, on Lake Fork Mohican R., 13 mi/21 km WSW of Wooster; 40°43′N 82°08′W. Reservoir is dry except during flood periods; max. potential capacity 102,000 acre-ft.; extends NNE into Wayne co.

Mohinora, Cerro (mo-ee-NO-rah), peak (10,663 ft/3,250 m) in Sierra Madre Occidental, Chihuahua, N Mexico, 80 mi/129 km NNE of Culiacán Rosales; near 00°26′N 107°04′W. Sometimes known as Muinora.

Mohinora River, Mexico: see SINALOA RIVER.

Mohnton (MON-tuhn), borough (1990 pop. 2,484), Berks co., SE central Pa., suburb, 5 mi/8 km SW of Reading; 40°17′N 75°59′W. Mfg. (apparel, communications systems, food prods., commercial printing, machinery). Maple Grove Raceway (drag racing). Founded 1850, inc. 1907.

Mohonk, Lake (MO-hawnk), small lake in scenic resort area of the Shawangunk range, Ulster co., SE N.Y., 4 mi/6.4 km WNW of New Paltz; 41°46′N 74°09′W. Mohonk L. village is here. Mohonk Mountain House, a private resort on the 12-sq-mi/31-sq-km public Mohonk Preserve, is a major vacation destination.

Moiese (mo-EEZ), village (1990 pop. 5), Lake co., W Mont., 40 mi/64 km NW of Missoula, on Mission Creek in Flathead Indian Reservation. Hq. for Natl. Bison Range to S.

Moira River (MOI-ruh), SE Ont., Canada; rises W of Sharbot L.; flows 60 mi/97 km SW to the Bay Quinte at Belleville. Course is rapid; supplies water power.

Moisie (mwah-ZEE), town (1991 pop. 776), E Que., Canada, on the St. Lawrence, near mouth of Moisie R., 10 mi/16 km E of Sept Îles; 50°11′N 66°06′W. Hudson's Bay Company trading post.

Moisie (mwah-ZEE), river, 210 mi/338 km long; rises in E Que., Canada, near the Lab. border; flows S to the St. Lawrence; 50°11′N 66°05′W. The Hudson's Bay Company has an important trading post at the village of Moisie near the river's mouth.

Mojada, Sierra, low NW spur of Sierra Madre Oriental, on Coahuila-Chihuahua border, N Mexico, W of Esmeralda; c.30 mi/48 km long NW-SE; average elev. c.5,000 ft/1,524 m. Rich in minerals (silver, gold, lead, copper, zinc).

Mojave (mo-hah-vai), uninc. village (1990 pop. 3,763), Kern co., S central Calif., in Mojave Desert, c.47 mi/

76 km ESE of Bakersfield; 35°03′N 118°11′W. Supply point for mines (tungsten, silver, borax, gold); cattle and wheat ranches. Mfg. (cement, aircraft parts). RR junction. Los Angeles Aqueduct and Pacific Crest Natl. Scenic Trail pass to W; Edwards Air Force Base and Rogers L. (dry) to SE; Red Rock Canyon State Recreation Area to N.

Mojave Dam, Calif., see SILVERWOOD LAKE.

Mojave Desert or **Mohave** (both: mo-hah-vai) (□ c.15,000 sq mi/38,850 sq km), region of low, barren mts. and flat valleys, 2,000 ft/610 m to 5,000 ft/1,525 m high, S Calif.; part of the Great Basin of the U.S. (all rivers leading into basin have no outlet to sea). Bordered on the N and W by the Sierra Nevada and the Tehachapi; on SW by San Gabriel, and San Bernardino mts.; it merges with the Colorado Desert in SE; N part includes Death Valley (282 ft/86 m below sea level) lowest point in W Hemisphere. Beneath it lies the Fenner Basin, a large aquifer 3,506 ft/1,069 m below the surface. Once a part of an anc. interior sea, the desert was formed by volcanic action (lava surfaces with cinder cones are present) and by material deposited by the Colorado R. The temp. is uniformly warm to very hot, with cold nights throughout the year, with a wide variation from day to night. Strong, dry winds blow in the afternoon and evening. Located in the rain shadow of the Coast Ranges, the Mojave receives an average annual rainfall of 5 in/12.7 cm., mostly in winter. Juniper and Joshua trees are found on the higher, outer mt. slopes; desert-type vegetation, and numerous intermittent lakes and streams are present in the valleys. The Mojave R. enters from SW and is the largest stream. Minerals found in the desert include borax and other salines; gold, silver, and iron. The desert is crossed by 2 RR lines and 2 highways. Military installations were est. in the Mojave during World War II; modern istallations include China Lake Naval Weapons Center, Fort Irwin Military Reservation, and Twentynine Palms Marine Corps Base. A solar-power plant has been built using molten salt to store energy from sunlight. Ward Valley, 20 mi/32 km from Colorado R. and Ariz. border, contains a 1,000-acre/400-ha tract that is scheduled to become a low-level nuclear waste dump. Death Valley Natl. Monument is in N, and Joshua Tree Natl. Monument is in S.

Mojave River or **Mohave** (mo-hah-vai) c.100 mi/161 km long; rises in the San Bernardino Mts., San Bernardino co., S Calif. at L. Arrowhead Reservoir, (as Deep Creek for first c.20 mi/32 km); flows N past Victorville, then NE past Barstow to disappear in the Mojave Desert, SW of Soda L. (dry). Due to the porous soil and rapid evaporation, it is intermittent for much of its course except during the short wet season.

Mokane (mo-KAIN), town (1990 pop. 186), Callaway co., central Mo., on Missouri R., and 12 mi/19 km S of Fulton; 38°40′N 91°52′W. Grain, livestock.

Mokapu Point (MO-KAH-poo), E Oahu Isl., Honolulu co., Hawaii, 11 mi/18 km NE of Honolulu; 21°27′N 157°43′W. NE corner of Mokapu Peninsula; Kaneohe Marine Corps Air Station occupies most of peninsula, which is bounded by Kaneohe Bay (W), by Kailua Bay (SSE). Moku Manu Isl. 1 mi/1.6 km NNE of point.

Mokelumne Hill, uninc. village, Calaveras co., central Calif., near Mokelumne R., and c.40 mi/64 km NE of Stockton, in 1849 Calif. gold rush region. Cattle; walnuts olives, honey. During gold rush, it was co. seat for a time and an important freighting point for the mines. Pardee Reservoir to W.

Mokelumne Peak, (9,332 ft/2,844 m), Amador co., E Calif., in the Sierra Nevada, 27 mi/43 km S of L. Tahoe. In El Dorado Natl. Forest.

Mokelumne River, 80 mi/129 km long, E central Calif.; rises in the Sierra Nevada in S central Alpine co., formed by joining of North and South Forks 9 mi/14.5 km E of Jackson. North Fork rises in Sierra Nevada, 30 mi/48 km S of South L. Tahoe, in central Alpine co., E Calif.; flows c.60 mi/97 km WSW through Salt Springs Reservoir, to South Fork. South Fork rises in Sierra Nevada 40 mi/64 km E of Jackson, in E Calaveras co.; flows c.30 mi/48 km SW then W. The combined Mokelumne R. flows SW, past Mokelumne Hill through Pardee and Camanche reservations and past Lodi, then NW and SW to San Joaquin R. 20 mi/32 km NW of Stockton (San Joaquin R. forms shipping channel to Suison Bay at this point). Near Mokelumne Hill, Pardee Dam (358 ft/109 m high, 1,337 ft/408 m long; completed 1929) impounds Pardee Reservoir, which supplies water to cities on E shore of San Francisco Bay. On a headstream (N. Fork), on Calaveras/Amador co. line, is Salt Springs Dam (328 ft/100 m high, 1,260 ft/384 m long; completed 1931; for power). Mokelumne Aqueduct diverts water from Camanche Reservoir to Stockton and N Bay area.

Mokena (mo-KEE-nah), village (1990 pop. 6,128), Will co., NE Ill., 10 mi/16 km E of Joliet; 41°31′N 87°52′W. In agr. area (corn, soybeans; dairying). Mfg. (water pollution control equip.; galvanized ducts and fittings; food processing equip., plastic injection molds).

Mokuaweoweo (MO-koo-AH-WAI-o-WAI-o), crater and caldera of Mauna Loa volcano, S central Hawaii isl., Hawaii co., Hawaii, at W end of Hawaii Volcanoes Natl. Park. 2nd-largest active crater (□ 3.7 sq mi/9.6 sq km, length 3.7 mi/6 km, width 1.7 mi/2.7 km) in world; Kilauea, also on Hawaii isl., is larger. Lava flow of 1880–1881 was 50 mi/80 km long.

Mokuleia (MO-koo-LAI-ee-ah), town (1990 pop. 1,776), NW Oahu isl., Honolulu co., Hawaii, 26 mi/42 km NW of Honolulu, on N coast at mouth of Makaleha Stream; 21°34′N 158°10′W. Kukui nuts; cattle; fish. Dillingham Air Force Base (inactive) to W, Kaena Military Reservation lies farther W at Kaena Point. Mokuleia Beach Park to W; Waianae Mts. to S.

Molalla (mo-LAL-uh), town (1990 pop. 3,651), Clackamas co., NW Oregon, 14 mi/23 km S of Oregon City, near Molalla R.; 45°08′N 122°34′W. RR terminus. Timber. Berries, apples, potatoes; poultry, hogs, sheep, cattle; nurseries. Table Rock Wilderness Area to SE; Mt. Hood Natl. Forest to E.

Molango (mo-LAHN-go), town (1990 pop. 3,062), ⊙ Molango de Escamilla municipio, Hidalgo, central Mexico, 45 mi/72 km N of Pachuca de soto, on Mexico Highway 105; 20°48′N 98°44′W. Corn, wheat, beans, fruit; livestock.

Molcaxac (mol-KAH-hak), town (1990 pop. 1,456), Puebla, central Mexico, near Atoyac R., 29 mi/47 km SE of Puebla. Grain, maguey.

Molena (mo-LEE-nuh), village (1990 pop. 439), Pike co., W central Ga., 13 mi/21 km NW of Thomaston, near Flint R; 33°01′N 84°30′W. Fabric dyeing.

Môle-Saint-Nicolas (mol–sang–nee-ko-LAH), coastal town (1982 pop. 1,960), Nord-Ouest dept., NW Haiti, port on inlet of Windward Passage, 115 mi/185 km NW of Port-au-Prince, near NW extremity of Hispaniola isl. (site of Columbus's landing on Dec. 6, 1492); 19°48′N 73°23′W. Banana growing; beekeeping. Fishing port.

Moline (mo-LEEN), city (1990 pop. 43,202), Rock Island co., NW Ill., on the Mississippi R. (N), Rock R. (S); 41°29′N 90°29′W. In a coal area. It is a transportation and industrial center. Mfg. (dairy prods., concrete, metal fabricating, printing and publishing; elevators and elevator door openers; industrial equip.; nonferrous die castings, presses and punches, small airplanes, ice cream). Has been a major producer of farm machinery since the industrialist John Deere moved there in 1847. A military arsenal is nearby. Moline, with Bettenforf, Iowa; Rock Island, Ill.; and Davenport, Iowa, is part of an economic unit called the Quad Cities. Site of Black Hawk Col. Quad Cities Campus. Inc. 1855.

Moline, village (1990 pop. 473), Elk co., SE Kansas, 7 mi/11.3 km S of Howard; 37°21′N 96°17′W. Shipping point in cattle and grain region; dairying. Crushed stone.

Moline Acres, town (1990 pop. 2,710), St. Louis co., E Mo.; residential suburb, 11 mi/18 km N of downtown St. Louis; 38°45′N 90°14′W.

Molino (mo-LEE-no), town (□ 6 sq mi/15.5 sq km; 1990 pop. 1,207), Escambia co., extreme NW Fla., 22 mi/35 km NNW of Pensacola; 30°43′N 87°19′W. Agr.-produce shipping point, with brickworks and clay pits.

Molino de las Flores National Park (mo-LEE-no dai lahs FLOR-es), a national park, in Texcoco de Mora, in E México, Mexico. Park is partly restored 17th-cent. hacienda and nearby pre-Hispanic ruins, the baths of King Netzahualcóyotl.

Molino del Rey (mo-LEE-no del rai), group of massive stone bldgs., SW section of Mexico city, Mexico, just W of CHAPULTEPEC. Scene (Sept. 8, 1847) of battle in Mexican War in which U.S. forces were victorious.

Molino, El, Mexico: see VISTA HERMOSA DE NEGRETE.

Moller, Port (MO-luhr), bay (20 mi/32 km long, 10 mi/16 km wide at mouth), SW Alaska, on Alaska Peninsula, on Bristol Bay; 56°N 160°26′W. Port Moller village is on N shore.

Moloacán (mo-lo-ah-KAHN), town (1990 pop. 1,853), Veracruz. SE Mexico, on Isthmus of Tehuantepec, 13 mi/21 km E of Minatitlán. Fruit. Petroleum production.

Moloch, Mount (MO-lahk), (10,195 ft/3,107 m), SE B.C., Canada, in Selkirk Mts., near Glacier Natl. Park, 16 mi/26 km NNW of Revelstoke; 51°20′N 117°56′W.

Molokai (MO-lo-KAH-ee), island (1990 pop. 6,587), 261 sq mi/676 sq km, Maui co., Hawaii, bet. Oahu (W, separated by Kaiwi Channe)l, Lanai (S, separated by Kalohi Channel), and Maui (separated by Pailolo Channel). Molokai is generally mountainous, with Mt. Kamakou (4,970 ft/1,515 m) the highest peak in E end. On the N coast is the Kalaupapa peninula, separated by a rocky mt. wall from the rest of the isl. and accessible only over a 2,000 ft/610 m pass, on which the Kalaupapa leper colony existed (1886–1969) and is now included in Kalaupapa Historical Park; much of E part of isl. is in Molokai Forest Reserve. Molokai has many cattle ranches. Most pineapple plantations have reverted to hayfields and other crops. The chief town and port is Kaunakakai, on central S shore, from which the isl.'s prods. are shipped to Honolulu for export. Palauu State Park in N center, just SW of Kalaupapa; Molokai Ranch Wildlife Park at W end.

Molokini (MO-lo-KEE-nee), island, Maui co., Hawaii, bet. Maui and Kahoolawe isls., in Alalakeiki Channel. Barren, rocky; lighthouse.

Molson, village (1990 pop. 30), Okanogan co., N Wash., 1 mi/1.6 km S of Canada (B.C.) border, 11 mi/18 km ENE of Oroville. Old Mission, Molson Mus. and Ghost Town.

Molson Lake (MOL-suhn), central Man., Canada, 50 mi/80 km NE of L. Winnipeg; 27 mi/43 km long, 12 mi/19 km wide. Drains N into Hayes R.

Molunkus Lake (mo-LUHNK-uhs), c.35 mi/56 km long, Aroostook co., E central Maine, 20 mi/32 km E of Millinocket; 3 mi/4.8 km long. Drains into Molunkus Stream, which rises to NW, flows SE to Mattawamkeag R.

Momauguin, Conn.: see EAST HAVEN.

Momax (mo-MAKS), town (1990 pop. 1,621), Zacatecas, N central Mexico, 12 mi/19 km NNW of Tlaltenango de Sánchez Román, on Tlalt enengo R. Grain, chickpeas, tobacco, alfalfa; livestock.

Mombin-Crochu (mong-BANG–kro-SHYOO), town (1982 est. pop. 11,000), Nord-Est dept., Haiti, 29 mi/47 km SE of Cap-Haïtien; 18°18′N 73°13′W. Coffee, citrus fruit growing.

Momence (mo-MENS), city (1990 pop. 2,968), Kankakee co., NE Ill., on Kankakee R. (bridged here) and 10 mi/16 km E of Kankakee; 41°09′N 87°39′W. RR junction. In agr. area (corn, soybeans; dairying); mfg. (food prods.). Plotted 1844, inc. 1874.

Mona, village and institution (1991 pop. 3,426), St Andrew parish, SE Jamaica, 7 mi/11.3 km from Kingston, an amalgam of Mona Heights, Univ. Heights, the Col. Commons and Mona Reservoir lands; 18°00′N 76°44′W. Bounded SW by Long Mt. and Beverley Hills, N by Hope Botanical Gardens and the Col. of Arts, Science and Technology and separated from the Hope R. by Papine Village. Home of Univ. of the W. Indies and Univ. Col. Hospital. The univ. was est. in 1948 as the 1st degree-granting institution in the West Indies and today has campuses in Port-of-Spain, Trinidad, and Cave Hill, Barbados. In 1962 the college received its charter to be an independent univ. Mona Heights, W of the univ., is a private housing development.

Cross references are shown in SMALL CAPITALS. The pronunciation key is on page xv. The dates of population figures are on page xii.

Mona, village (1990 pop. 584), Juab co., central Utah, 8 mi/12.9 km N of Nephi, on Current Creek, at S end of Mona Reservoir; 39°49′N 111°51′W. Alfalfa, barley, wheat; cattle. Mona Reservoir (5 mi/8 km long, 1 mi/1.6 km wide) is just N, formed by dam on small tributary of Utah L. Mt. Nebo (11,928 ft/3,636 m) is E, in Wasatch Range. In Mt. Nebo Wilderness Area of Uinta Natl. Forest. Elev. 4,025 ft/1,227 m. Settled 1851.

Mona, P.R.: see MONA ISLAND.

Mona Island (MO-nah), Span. *Isla de Mona* (□ c.20 sq mi/52 sq km), part of the Commonwealth of P.R., c.50 mi/80 km W of Mayaguez. Uninhabited isl. It was discovered by Columbus in 1493, and in 1508 Ponce de León stopped here. In 1511 the isl. was ceded to Columbus's younger brother Bartolomé, but it soon became a haven for pirates and corsairs. Here is a nature reserve (bird sanctuary), turtle nesting sites, high cliff walls (up to 200 ft/61 m), and caves. Lighthouse on N side. Administered by the Department of Natural and Environmental Resources of the Commonwealth of P.R.

Mona Passage (MO-nah), strait, bet. P.R. and the Dominican Republic; c.80 mi/129 km wide. Connecting the N Atlantic Ocean with the Caribbean Sea, it is a favored shipping lane.

Monaca (MAH-nah-kah), borough (1990 pop. 6,739), Beaver co., W Pa., on Ohio R., opposite mouth of Beaver R., 22 mi/35 km NW of Pittsburgh, and 1 mi/1.6 km SE of Beaver; 40°40′N 80°16′W. RR junction. Agr. (corn, hay; livestock, dairying); mfg. (metal fabrication and prods., glassware, printing). Community Col. of Beaver Co. here; Penn State Univ. Beaver Campus to W. Settled 1813, inc. 1839.

Monadnock Mountain 1 (muh-NAD-nawk), peak (3,165 ft/965 m), Cheshire co., SW N.H., 9 mi/14.5 km SE of Keene, in Monadnock State Park. It is a popular hiking and cross-country skiing area. Geomorphic term *monadnock* referring to a hill or mt. isolated from larger highland mass by erosion is derived from this mt. which is a classical example of an erosional remnant above the base level of a peneplane surface. **2** (muhn-AD-nawk), isolated peak (3,140 ft/957 m), NE Vt., near the Connecticut, in Lemington town, opposite Colebrook, N.H.

Monahans (1990 pop. 8,101), ⊙ Ward co., extreme W Texas, in the Pecos valley, 35 mi/56 km WSW of Odessa; 31°38′N 103°03′W. Elev. 2,613 ft/796 m. Trade, shipping, processing center for oil fields; cattle ranches nearby; mfg. (gas processing, light mfg.). Est. 1881; inc. 1928.

Monango (mo-NANG-o), village (1990 pop. 53), Dickey co., SE N.Dak., 12 mi/19 km NNW of Ellendale; 46°10′N 98°35′W. Whitestone Battlefield Historic Site to W.

Monarch, village, Chaffee co., central Colo., on branch of Arkansas R., in Sawatch Mts., 16 mi/26 km W of Salida. Elev. c.10,000 ft/3,048 m. Limestone quarries. Monarch Ski Resort here. In San Isabel Natl. Forest; Continental Divide to W. Gunnison Natl. Forest beyond Divide. Monarch Pass to SW, Mt. Shavano 7 mi/11.3 km NNE.

Monarch, S.C.: see MONARCH MILLS.

Monarch Mills, village (1990 pop. 2,214), Union co., N S.C., suburb, 2 mi/3.2 km E of Union; 34°43′N 81°34′W. Agr. area of poultry, livestock, dairying, grain, peaches, apples. Sumter Natl. Forest to S.

Monarch Mountain (11,714 ft/3,570 m), W B.C., Canada, in Coast Mts., 200 mi/322 km NW of Vancouver; 51°56′N 125° 56′W.

Monarch Pass (11,312 ft/3,448 m), central Colo., in Sawatch Mts., bet. Chaffee and Gunnison cos. Crossed by U.S. Highway 50. View from highest point on pass includes 12 peaks exceeding 14,000 ft/4,267 m to N. Gunnison Natl. Forest (S); San Isabel Natl. Forest (N).

Monarch, The, mountain (9,528 ft/2,904 m), SE B.C., Canada, near Alta. border, in Rocky Mts., on SE edge of Kootenay Natl. Park, 16 mi/26 km SW of Banff.

Monashee Mountains (muh-NA-shee), range of Rocky Mts., SE B.C., Canada, W of Selkirk Mts., extending c.200 mi/322 km N from Wash. state line bet. Columbia

R. and Arrow Lakes (E) and upper North Thompson R., Shuswap L., and Okanagan L. (W). Peaks include Hallam Peak (10,560 ft/3,219 m) and Cranberry Mt. (9,470 ft/2,886 m). Bet. Revelstoke and Shuswap L., the range is crossed by Can. Pacific RR. In S part is important mining (gold, silver, copper, lead, zinc) region.

Monaville (MO-nuh-vil), uninc. village (1990 pop. 500), Logan co., SW W.Va., 2 mi/3.2 km S of Logan.

Monción (mon-see-ON), town (1993 pop. 4,560), Monte Cristi prov., NW Dominican Republic, in N outliers of the Cordillera Central, 32 mi/51 km W of Santiago; 19°28′N 71°10′W. Agr. region (tobacco, coffee, cacao; beeswax; hides). Sometimes Benito Monción; formerly Guaraguanó.

Moncks Corner, town (1990 pop. 5,607), ⊙ Berkeley co., SE S.C. 28 mi/45 km N of Charleston, and on Cooper R; 33°12′N 80°00′W. Pinopolis Dam and Hydroelectric plant of Santee-Cooper power and navigation development nearby. Mfg. includes plastic tubing, timing belts, noise control equip., cargo shipping liners. Agr. includes cotton, tobacco, corn, soybeans; hogs, cattle, poultry.

Monclova, city (1990 pop. 177,792) and township, ⊙ Monclova municipio, Coahuila state, Mexico; 26°54′N 101°25′W. Elev. 1,923 ft/586 m. Situated within outlier ranges of the Sierra Madre Oriental on Mexico Highways 30, 53, and 57, it is a regional commercial and industrial center. Monclova's chief industry is the production of iron and steel. It is the 3d-largest city in Coahuila state.

Moncton (MUHNGK-tuhn), city (1991 pop. 57,010), SE N.B., Canada, on the Petitcodiac R.; 46°06′N 64°47′W. It is an air and RR transportation center. Service and distribution center for region and prov. Textiles as well as wood, metal, and meat prods. are mfg., and wood and meat are processed; pulp mill; mfg. (plastic prods., mattresses and bedsprings). It was called The Bend until 1833, when it was renamed in honor of the Br. general Robert Monckton. Magnetic Hill, an optical illusion, and the Tidal Bore, a high tide occurring twice daily, are features of the city. The Université de Moncton (1963) is here.

Moncure (MAHN-kyor), uninc. village, Chatham co., central N.C., 28 mi/45 km SW of Raleigh, and 1 mi/1.6 km W of Haywood, near confluence of Haw and Deep rivers, which form Cape Fear R. Timber. Mfg. (industrial yarns, industrial resins, fiberboard, crushed stone).

Mondamin, town (1990 pop. 403), Harrison co., W Iowa, near Soldier R., 14 mi/23 km NW of Logan; 41°42′N 96°01′W.

Mondovi (mahn-DO-vee), town (1990 pop. 2,491), Buffalo co., W Wis., on Buffalo R. (hydroelectric plant), and 19 mi/31 km SSW of Eau Claire; 44°34′N 91°40′W. Dairy prods., poultry hatcheries; mfg. (lumber, cabinets). W terminus of Buffalo R. State Trail. Settled 1855, inc. 1889.

Moneague, village (1991 pop. 2,880), St. Ann parish, central Jamaica, resort at N foot of Mt. Diablo, 30 mi/48 km NW of Kingston; 18°17′N 77°06′W.

Monee (mo-KNEE), village (1990 pop. 1,044), Will co., NE Ill., 19 mi/31 km ESE of Joliet; 41°25′N 87°45′W. In agr. area.

Monessen (mo-NE-suhn), city (1990 pop. 9,901), Westmoreland co., SW Pa., 20 mi/32 km S of Pittsburgh, on the Monongahela R. (bridged); 40°08′N 79°52′W. Mfg. (wire prods., printing and publishing, fencing). Monessen's steel mill was closed as a result of the industry's decline. Founded 1898, inc. 1921.

Moneta, town (1990 pop. 29), O'Brien co., NW Iowa, 13 mi/21 km WE of Primghar; 43°07′N 95°23′W. In agr. area.

Moneta 1 uninc. village, Bedford co., SW central Va., 18 mi/29 km ESE of Roanoke; 37°10′N 79°37′W. Mfg. (lumber, concrete, meat processing, printing and publishing); agr. (dairying; livestock; grain, tobacco). Smith Mt. L. reservoir and State Park to S. **2** village, Fremont co., central Wyo., on Poison Creek, on branch of Big Horn R., and 75 mi/121 km WNW of Casper.

Elev. 5,428 ft/1,654 m. Castle Gardens, area of picturesque sandstone formations, and Gas Hills Uranium Mining Dist. to S.

Monett (mo-NET), city (1990 pop. 6,529), Barry and Lawrence cos., SW Mo., in the Ozarks, 35 mi/56 km ESE of Joplin; 36°55′N 93°55′W. Cattle and dairying. Ships fruit; light mfg. Surveyed 1887.

Monetta (muh-NET-ah), village (1990 pop. 285), Aiken and Saluda cos., SW S.C., 21 mi/34 km NNE of Aiken; 33°51′N 81°36′W. Mfg. includes fiberglass truck bodies. Agr. includes livestock, poultry; grain, cotton, peanuts.

Monette (mo-NET), town (1990 pop. 1,115), Craighead co., NE Ark., 21 mi/34 km S of Jonesboro; 35°53′N 90°20′W. In agr. area; mfg. (plastic molding, shoes). St. Francis Sunken Lands Wildlife Management Area to W. Inc. 1900.

Monhegan (mahn-HEE-guhn), island (□ 2.5 sq mi/6.5 sq km), Lincoln co., c.10 mi/16 km off the coast of S Maine. It is a summer resort favored by artists for its scenery. In the War of 1812 the USS *Enterprise* defeated the HMS *Boxer* SE of the isl. Settled c.1622.

Monida (muh-NEI-duh), village, Beaverhead co., extreme SW Mont., 50 mi/80 km SSE of Dillon, at SE extremity of Bitterroot Range, on Idaho state line, just N of Monida Pass (6,870 ft/2,094 m), crosses the Continental Divide into Idaho. Targhee Natl. Forest (Idaho) to S; Beaverhead Natl. Forest to SW; Lima Reservoir to N (Red Rock R.); Red Rock Lakes Natl. Wildlife Refuge to E; important nesting site of Trumpeter swan, Sandhill crane, Barrow's Goldeneye, and Great Blue heron.

Moniteau (mah-ni-TAW), county (□ 418 sq mi/1,083 sq km; 1990 pop. 12,298), central Mo.; ⊙ California; 38°37′N 92°34′W. Bounded NE by Missouri R. Agr. (wheat, corn, soybeans), cattle, poultry, limestone; mfg. at California and Tipton. Formed 1845.

Monitor Range, central Nev., largely in Nye co., extends N into Lander co., E of Toquema Range. Lies in Toiyabe Natl. Forest. Antelope Peak (10,220 ft/3,115 m) and Summit Mt. (10,461 ft/3,189 m) are in N.

Monjas (MON-hahs), town (1990 pop. 12,102), in S central Oaxaca, Mexico, 50 mi/80 km S of Oaxaca de Juárez, on Mexico Highway 175. Elev. 4,921 ft/1,500 m. A mountainous region with a temperate climate. Agr. on the Atoyac River.

Monkey Point, W Trinidad, Trinidad and Tobago, on the Gulf of Paria, just W of village of California, 18 mi/29 km S of Port of Spain; 10°25′N 61°30′W.

Monkeys Eyebrow, uninc. village, Ballard co., W Ky., 20 mi/32 km WNW of Paducah, near Ohio R. Lock and Dam No. 53 to W, on Ohio R. Ballard Co. Wildlife Management Area to SW.

Monkton, town (1990 pop. 1,482), Addison co., W Vt., 17 mi/27 km S of Burlington; 44°13′N 73°07′W. Dairying.

Monmouth (MUHN-muhth), county (□ 665 sq mi/1,722 sq km; 1990 pop. 553,124), E N.J., bounded E by the Atlantic, N by Raritan and Sandy Hook bays; ⊙ Freehold; 40°17′N 74°09′W. Many coastal resorts, including Asbury Park, Manasquan, and Long Branch. Agr. area inland produces large potato, vegetable, and fruit crops; poultry prods.; some mfg. (rugs, textiles, clothing, clay prods., food prods., chemicals, other goods). Drained by Metedeconk, Manasquan, and Shark rivers; Navesink R. and Shrewsbury R. estuaries, Navesink Highlands, and Sandy Hook are in NE. Formed 1675. Largely residential and seasonal resort communities along the coast.

Monmouth, city (1990 pop. 9,489), ⊙ Warren co., W Ill.; 40°54′N 90°38′W. Located in a farm area, it is a trade center with a packing plant. Mfg. (pottery, farm tools, feed). Monmouth Col. is in the city. Wyatt Earp was b. here. Inc. 1852.

Monmouth 1 (MAHN-muhth), town (1990 pop. 169), Jackson co., E Iowa, 11 mi/18 km W of Maquoketa; 42°04′N 90°52′W. Livestock, grain. **2** town (1990 pop. 3,353), Kennebec co., S Maine, 15 mi/24 km SW of Augusta, near L. Cobbosseecontee; 44°14′N 70°00′W. Orchard center, with Univ. of Maine agr. experiment station. Seat of Monmouth Acad. Settled 1775, inc. 1792. **3** town (1990 pop. 6,288), Polk co., NW Oregon, 11 mi/

18 km SW of Salem near Willamette R.; 44°51′N 123°13′W. Agr. (fruit, hops, corn, brans; poultry, hogs, sheep, cattle); dairy prods.; wineries. Site of Paul Jensen Arctic Mus. and Western Oregon State Col. Baskett Slough Natl. Wildlife Refuge to N; Helmick State Park to S; McDonald State Forest to S. Plotted in 1855.

Monmouth Beach (MUHN-muhth), resort borough (1990 pop. 3,303), Monmouth co., E N.J., bet. the coast and Shrewsbury R. inlet, 2 mi/3.2 km N of Long Branch, and 16 mi/26 km ENE of Freehold; 40°20′N 73°59′W.

Monmouth, Fort, N.J.: see RED BANK.

Monmouth, Mount (10,470 ft/3,191 m), SW B.C., Canada, in Coast Mts., 120 mi/193 km NNW of Vancouver; 51°N 123°45′W.

Mono, county (□ 3,046 sq mi/7,889 sq km; 1990 pop. 9,956), E Calif.; ⊙ Bridgeport; 37°55′N 118°52′W. Rugged Sierra Nevada country; crest of range (with peaks over 13,000 ft/3,962 m) forms W and is crossed by scenic Tioga Pass (E entrance to Yosemite Natl. Park). Bounded E by Nev. state line; drained by Owens, East Walker, and West Walker rivers; hydroelectric plants. Sweetwater Mts. in NE, White Mts. in SE. Much of co. is in Toiyabe (N) and Inyo (S and SE) Natl. Forests. Bodie State Historical Park in center. Recreational region (hiking, camping, hunting, fishing, winter sports); includes saline Mono L., in center; Mammoth Lakes and June L. in SW; Mammoth Mt. Ski Area; many other small lakes (fishing), part of John Muir Trail on W boundary and scenic wilderness preserves. Stock raising (cattle, sheep), mining (pumice, gold, lead, silver, andalusite). Timber stands (chiefly pine) remain largely intact. Formed 1861.

Mono Craters, Mono co., E Calif., group of about 20 geologically recent volcanic cones (max. elev c.9,000 ft/2,743 m), just S of Mono L.

Mono Lake (□ 87 sq mi/225 sq km), Mono co., E Calif., saline lake c.50 mi/80 km NW of Bishop, just E of Sierra Nevada crest. Elev. c.6,407 ft/1,953 m. It has no outlet, and its waters, which contain many natural impurities, support brine shrimp. Supports varied migratory birdlife, principally California gull pop. Has 2 small volcanic isls; larger is Paoha Isl. Fed mainly by small mt. streams of Sierra Nevada.

Mono Pass (c.10,650 ft/3,246 m), Tuolumne-Mono co. line, E Calif., in the Sierra Nevada, c.10 mi/16 km SW of Mono L. Foot trail passes through. On E boundary of Yosemite Natl. Park.

Mono Vista, uninc. town (1990 pop. 2,599), Tuolumne co., E central Calif., 6 mi/9.7 km ENE of Sonora, in W foothills of Sierra Nevada; 38°01′N 120°16′W. Timber. Stanislaus Natl. Forest to E; Tuolumne Indian Rancheria (Indian reservation) to SE.

Monocacy (mah-no-kah-see), river, c.60 mi/97 km long; formed at Pa.-Md. state line 8 mi/12.9 km S of Gettysburg by joining of Marsh and Rock Creeks (39°43′N 77°13′W); flows S across Md., passes E of Frederick, to join the Potomac R. 13 mi/21 km S of Frederick. On its banks, just E of Frederick, the Civil War battle of Monocacy was fought on July 9, 1864. Although the Union forces under Gen. Lew Wallace were defeated, they delayed the Confederate forces under Gen. J. A. Early long enough to give Gen. Ulysses Grant time to dispatch troops to defend Washington and drive Early back into Va.

Monocacy National Battlefield (□ c.2 sq mi/5.2 sq km), Frederick co., W Md., 3 mi/4.8 km SSE of Frederick. Authorized 1976. On July 7, 1864, Gen. Lew Wallace, who later wrote *Ben Hur*, took a position at the RR junction on the Moncacy R. with 2,650 Union soldiers facing 17,500 Confederate troops under Gen. Jubal Early. On July 8, Wallace was reinforced by an an additional 3,500 making the odds 3, rather than 7, to 1. When the 2 forces clashed the next day, the Union forces were decisively defeated, but the Confederates lost their best opportunity to seize the capital. Both sides lost more than 1,300 men each.

Monolith, village, Kern co., S central Calif., in Tehachapi Mts., just E of Tehachapi.

Monomonac, Lake (muh-NAW-muh-nak), on N.H.-Mass. state line, N of Rindge, N.H., 17 mi/27 km NW of Fitchburg, Mass.; 2.5 mi/4 km long. Drains SW to Millers R.

Monomoy Island, Mass.: see CHATHAM.

Monon, town (1990 pop. 1,585), White co., NW central Ind., on small Little Monon Creek, and 10 mi/16 km NW of Monticello; 40°52′N 86°53′W. RR junction. Agr. area (corn, oats, soybeans); diversified mfg.; stone quarrying. Laid out 1853, inc. 1879.

Monona, county (□ 698 sq mi/1,808 sq km; 1990 pop. 10,034), W Iowa, on Nebr. state line (W; formed here by Missouri R.); ⊙ Onawa; 42°02′N 95°57′W. Prairie agr. area (corn; hogs, cattle, poultry) drained by Little Sioux, Maple, and Soldier rivers; Blue L., Oxbow L. of Missouri R. in W. Bituminous-coal deposits (E, S), sand and gravel pits. Lewis and Clark State Park on N end of Blue L., near Mo. R. in W; Preparation Canyon State Park in S. Formed 1851; lost territory in 1943 to Burt co., Nebr.

Monona (muh-NO-nuh), city (1990 pop. 8,637), Dane co., S Wis., on S shore of L. Monona, a suburb, 2 mi/3.2 km SE of downtown Madison; 43°02′N 89°19′W. In dairy region; mfg. (wood prods.). Yahara R. flows through city connecting L. Monona with L. Waubesa in S. Inc. 1938.

Monona, town (1990 pop. 1,520), Clayton co., NE Iowa, 14 mi/23 km N of Elkader; 43°02′N 91°23′W. In grain, dairy, and timber area; mfg. (farm equip., electrical wiring harnesses). Airfield here. Inc. 1897.

Monona Lake (muh-NO-nuh), one of the Four Lakes, Dane co., S Wis.; downtown Madison is on NW shore (bet. L. Monona and L. Mendota); roughly triangular, c.4 mi/6.4 km long, c.3 mi/4.8 km wide. City of Menona is on S shore. City of Madison borders on all other sides. Yahara R. drains into it from L. Mendota, to NW, and out of it to L. Waubesa, to SE.

Monongah (muh-NAHN-guh), town (1990 pop. 1,018), Marion co., N W.Va., on the West Fork R., 5 mi/8 km WSW of Fairmont; 39°27′N 80°13′W. Bituminous-coal-mining region. Agr. (corn, apples); livestock; poultry. In 1907, a mine disaster here killed 361 men. Founded c.1768.

Monongahela (mah-nahn-gah-HEE-lah), city (1990 pop. 4,928), Washington co., SW Pa., 17 mi/27 km S of Pittsburgh, on Monongahela R., at mouth of Pigeon Creek; 40°12′N 79°55′W. Agr. (grain, soybeans; livestock; dairying); mfg. (business forms, sheet metal fabrication, concrete, specialty chemicals, scrap metal processing, sledge hammers); bituminous coal, gas. A center of Whisky Rebellion, 1794. Settled 1770, inc. as borough 1833, as city 1873.

Monongahela (mah-nahn-gah-HEE-lah), river, 128 mi/206 km long, N W.Va; formed at Fairmont by the joining of the West Fork and Tygart rivers; flows NE past Morgantown and Star City and enters Pa.; receives Cheat R. from SE and turns N, flows past Friendship Hill Natl. Historic Site, past Fredericktown, California, Monessen, Monongahela, and Clairton; receives Youghiogheny R. from SE at McKeesport, turns NW at Duquesne, joins Allegheny R. (enters from NE) in downtown Pittsburg to form Ohio R. The channelized river is navigable for most of its length. Iron, steel, and coal are the chief prods. moved on the river. The Monongahela R. was the first river in the U.S. to be improved for navigation.

Monongalia (muh-nahn-GAIL-yuh), county (□ 366 sq mi/948 sq km ; 1990 pop. 75,509), N W.Va.; ⊙ Morgantown; 39°37′N 80°2′W. On Allegheny Plateau; bounded N by Pa.; drained by Monongahela and Cheat rivers. Coal mining; gas and oil fields; limestone quarries, sand pits. Mfg. (lumber, glass, metal prods., chemicals) at Morgantown. Agr. (honey, corn, oats, alfalfa, hay, strawberries, nursery crops); cattle; poultry; sheep. Part of Chestnut Ridge Park and part of Coopers Rock State Forest in NE. Formed 1776.

Monos Island (MO-nos) (□ 1.52 sq mi/3.94 sq km), off NW Trinidad, Trinidad and Tobago, in the Dragon's Mouth, 11 mi/18 km W of Port of Spain; 10°41′N 61°41′W. Elev. 942 ft/287 m. Bathing and fishing resort. Its central sect. was leased to U.S. in 1941. Now part of Forest Reserve.

Monowi (MI-no-wee), village, Boyd co., N Nebr., 27 mi/43 km ESE of Butte, and on Ponca Creek, near Missouri R; 42°49′N 98°19′W.

Monroe 1 (muhn-RO), county (□ 1,034 sq mi/2,678 sq km; 1990 pop. 23,968), SW Ala.; ⊙ Monroeville. Coastal plain, bounded SW by Alabama R., S by the Little R. Cotton, peanuts, corn, soybeans; timber; crude-oil and natural-gas production. Formed 1815. **2** county (□ 621 sq mi/1,608 sq km; 1990 pop. 11,333), E central Ark.; ⊙ Clarendon; 34°40′N 91°12′W. Drained by White (forms SW boundary) and Cache rivers. Agr. (cotton, rice, wheat, soybeans; hogs); timber. Mfg. at Brinkley and Clarendon. Commercial fishing. Louisiana Purchase State Historical Monument on E boundary; part of large White R. Natl. Wildlife Refuge at S end; Dagmar Wildlife Management Area in N. Formed 1829. **3** county (□ 3,737 sq mi/9,679 sq km; 1990 pop. 78,024), SW Fla. and Fla. Keys, at tip of peninsula; ⊙ Marathon; 25°07′N 81°09′W. Consists of sparsely populated Everglades area on the Fla. peninsula (including Cape Sable, Whitewater Bay, and part of Everglades Natl. Park) and all of the Fla. Keys, enclosing Fla. Bay. Has large Seminole Indian Reservation in N. Fishing, dairying, and poultry raising; citrus-fruit growing (esp. limes) on Fla. Keys. Major tourist industry (Keys). Formed 1824. **4** county (□ 398 sq mi/1,031 sq km; 1990 pop. 17,113), central Ga.; ⊙ Forsyth; 33°01′N 83°55′W. Bounded E by Ocmulgee R. Piedmont agr. (corn, wheat, vegetables, pecans, fruit); cattle, poultry; in timber area. Textile mfg. at Forsyth. Formed 1821. **5** county (□ 397 sq mi/1,028 sq km; 1990 pop. 22,422), SW Ill.; ⊙ Waterloo; 38°16′N 90°10′W. Bounded W by Mississippi R., E by Kaskaskia R. In N, is part of St. Louis metropolitan area. Agr. (wheat, hay, barley, sorghum; poultry; dairy prods.); limestone quarries; caves. Formed 1816. Dominant town is Columbia in N. A large portion of W part of co. damaged by floods, 1993. Valmeyer relocated itself to bluff site as result. One of 17 Ill. counties to retain southern-style commission form of county government. **6** county (□ 411 sq mi/1,064 sq km; 1990 pop. 108,978), S central Ind.; ⊙ Bloomington; 39°10′N 86°31′W. Drained by White R., Salt Creek, and small Beanblossom and Clear creeks. Agr. (corn; cattle; dairying); limestone quarrying; clay, timber. Mfg. at Bloomington. Hoosier Natl. Forest in SE corner (including Hardin Ridge Recreation Area and Monroe Reservoir); Paynetown and Fairfax State Recreation Areas (both on Monroe Reservoir) in S. Part of Morgan-Monroe State Forest in NE. Karst topography in S. Formed 1818. **7** county (□ 434 sq mi/1,124 sq km; 1990 pop. 8,114), S Iowa; ⊙ Albia; 41°01′N 92°52′W. Prairie agr. (hogs, cattle, poultry, sheep; corn, oats, hay) and coal-mining area. Unit of Stephens State Forest in NW. Formed 1843. **8** county (□ 332 sq mi/860 sq km; 1990 pop. 11,401), S Ky.; ⊙ Tompkinsville; 36°42′N 85°43′W. Bounded S by Tenn.; drained by Cumberland and Barren rivers and Skaggs creek. Hilly agr. area (corn, wheat, hay, alfalfa, burley tobacco, soybeans; cattle, poultry; dairying; timber); limestone quarries. Includes Old Mulkey Meeting House State Historic Site, SW of Tompkinsville, in S center of co. Formed 1820. **9** county (□ 680 sq mi/1,761 sq km; 1990 pop. 133,600), SE corner of Mich.; 41°55′N 83°30′W; ⊙ Monroe. Bounded S by Ohio state line, E by L. Erie, NE by Huron R.; drained by R. Raisin. Cattle, hogs, sheep, poultry, dairying; agr. (corn, wheat, soybeans, sugar beets, apples); nurseries. Mfg. at Monroe and Dundee. Limestone quarrying. Formed 1817. Fermi 2 nuclear- power plant, initial criticality June 21, 1985; is 25 mi/40 km NE of Toledo, Ohio, uses cooling water from Lake Erie, and has a max. dependable capacity of 1060 MWe. **10** county (□ 772 sq mi/1,999 sq km; 1990 pop. 36,582), E Miss.; ⊙ Aberdeen; 33°53′N 88°29′W. Bordered E by Ala. state line. Drained by Buttahatchie R. and East Fork of the Tombigbee R., which forms Aberdeen L. reservoir in center. Tennessee-Tombigbee Waterway runs parallel to the river. Agr. (cotton, corn, soybeans, wheat; cattle; dairying); timber. Formed 1821.

11 county (□ 669 sq mi/1,733 sq km; 1990 pop. 9,104), NE central Mo.; ⊙ Paris; 39°30′N 92°00′W. Drained by Salt R. Agr. (corn, soybeans, wheat); cattle, sheep and saddle horses; lumber; mfg. at Monroe City. Union Covered Bridge SW of Paris. Mark Twain L. in E; Mark Twain State Park and Birthplace at Florida. Formed 1831. **12** county (□ 1,364 sq mi/3,533 sq km; 1990 pop. 713,968), W N.Y.; ⊙ Rochester; 43°17′N 77°41′W. Bounded N by L. Ontario (resorts); crossed by the Barge Canal; drained by Genesee R. and Honeoye and other creeks. Extensive mfg., esp. in Rochester, East Rochester, Fairport, and Webster. Dairy prods., horticultural and vegetables, grain. Named for James Monroe, who was U.S. President at time co. was created. George Eastman brought fame to area with invention of instant photography in 1878. With the coming of the Erie Canal in 1823, Rochester became known as the Flour City for its milling of the W N.Y. wheat region (nation's leading wheat-growing region in the mid-1800s). The growth of Rochester as a science and mfg. center never overshadowed the agr. wealth of the co. Even today, despite suburbanization, the agr. landscape is still dynamic. Monroe co. is one of the top 14 cos. and/or independent cities in U.S. in terms of value added. Formed 1821. **13** county (□ 455 sq mi/1,178 sq km; 1990 pop. 15,497), E Ohio; ⊙ Woodsfield, 39°44′N 81°04′W. Bounded SE by Ohio R., here forming W.Va. state line; also drained by small Sunfish Creek and by Little Muskingum R. In the Unglaciated Plain physiographic region. Agr. (cattle; dairy prods.; corn); mfg. (primarily metal industries, aluminum sheet, plate, and foil); coal mines, limestone quarries. Formed 1815. **14** county (□ 616 sq mi/1,595 sq km; 1990 pop. 95,709), E Pa.; ⊙ Stroudsburg; 41°03′N 75°20′W. Bounded E by Delaware R. (N.J. state line). Pocono Mts. plateau is in W; series of long high ridges in S, separated by narrow valleys. Agr. (corn, wheat, oats, hay, alfalfa; cattle; dairying); resort area. Mfg. at Stroudsburg and East Stroudsburg. Parts of Delaware Water Gap Natl. Recreation Area in SE and NE; Delaware Natl. Scenic River on E boundary; part of Delaware State Forest in NE; Gouldsboro and Tobyhanna state parks in N; Big Pocono State Park in center; Appalachian Trail follows S boundary on Kittatinny and Blue mt. ridges. The 1st settlers (1725) worked copper mines. Formed 1836. **15** county (□ 665 sq mi/1,722 sq km; 1990 pop. 30,541), SE Tenn.; ⊙ Madisonville; 35°27′N 84°15′W. Bounded SE and E by N.C., NE by Little Tennessee R.; drained by its tributaries; Unicoi Mts. lie along S border. Includes Tellico Wildlife Management Area and part of Cherokee Natl. Forest. Lumbering, livestock raising, dairying, agr. (fruit, tobacco, hay, corn), dairying. Barite mines. Some gold was mined here in the 19th cent. Formed 1819. **16** county (□ 474 sq mi/1,228 sq km; 1990 pop. 12,406), SE W.Va.; ⊙ Union; 37°33′N 80°32′W. Bounded SE and SW by Va.; drained by Indian and Potts creeks. Mountainous region, with Peters Mt. along Va. state line and summits of the Allegheny Mts. (including Bickett Knob) to W. Agr. (corn, oats, barley, rye, alfalfa, hay); cattle; dairying; hogs; poultry; sheep. Limestone and iron-ore deposits; some natural gas. Mfg. (aircraft parts). Moncove State Park and Wildlife Management Area in NE; part of Jefferson Natl. Forest in SE; Appalachian Trail follows part of Va. and W.Va. state line in S. Formed 1799. **17** county (□ 908 sq mi/2,352 sq km; 1990 pop. 36,633), W central Wis.; ⊙ Sparta; 43°57′N 90°37′W. Dairying and farming area (tobacco, cranberries, corn, soybeans, alfalfa, hay; cattle); timber. Processing of dairy prods., lumber. Drained by Lemonweir, Black (bounds NW corner), La Crosse, and Kickapoo rivers. Part of Central Wis. Conservation Area in NE corner. Fort McCoy Military Reserve in N corner. Mill Bluff State Park on E boundary. Formed 1854.

Monroe 1 (muhn-RO), city (1994 pop. 57,049), ⊙ Ouachita parish, SE La., 75 mi/121 km NNE of Alexandria, on the Ouachita R.; 32°31′N 92°05′W. The center of the great Monroe Natural Gas Field (discovered 1916). Mfg. (apparel, food and beverages, construction materials), printing and publishing. The 1st settlers founded (c.1785) Fort Miró. The community was renamed in 1819 after the *James Monroe*, the 1st steamship to come up the Ouachita. Northeast La. Univ. is in the city. Of interest are Masur Mus. of Art, Louisiana. Purchase Garden and Zoo, and antebellum houses in area. Site of the Louisiana Folklife Festival. Russell Sage State Wildlife Area to E, D'Arbonne Natl. Wildlife Refuge to NW, Cheniere Brake State Fish Preserve and lake to SW. Founded c.1785, inc. as a city 1900. **2** city (1990 pop. 22,902), ⊙ Monroe co., SE Mich., 19 mi/31 km NE of Toledo, Ohio, and 38 mi/61 km SW of Detroit, on L. Erie; 41°54′N 83°23′W. Paper prods., heating equip., plastic tubing, flour, and auto parts are made. The city has large nurseries and is the shipping point for a farm region. Monroe was the scene of the R. Raisin massacre during the War of 1812 and the center of the "Toledo War." George A. Custer lived here, and the local mus. has a large collection of Custer memorabilia. A community col. is in the city, General Custer Historic Site, and Sterling State Park to NE. Settled 1778, inc. 1837. **3** city (1990 pop. 16,385), ⊙ Union co., S N.C., 24 mi/39 km SE of Charlotte, in the Piedmont region; 34°59′N 80°32′W. RR junction. Has diverse agr. (cotton, soybeans, grain, sorghum; poultry, livestock; dairying); mfg. (metal fabricating and casting, textiles and apparel, plastic and stone prods., pharmaceuticals, printing and publishing, industrial machinery, lighting fixtures, aviation and electronic equip.; food processing). Wingate Col. (4-yr) to E at Wingate. Source of Lynches R. to S. Settled 1751; inc. 1844. **4** city (1990 pop. 10,241), ⊙ Green co., S Wis., 35 mi/56 km SSW of Madison; 42°36′N 89°38′W. Dairying region. One of state's leading cheese-producing centers; mfg. (food and beverages, electronic equip., wood prods.). Inhabitants mostly of Swiss descent; annual cheese fair is held. Brownstone-Cadiz State Recreation Area (former Cadiz Springs State Park) to W. Inc. as village c.1859, as city in 1882.

Monroe 1 (muhn-RO), town (1990 pop. 16,896), Fairfield co., SW Conn., on the Housatonic, and 10 mi/16 km N of Bridgeport; 41°20′N 73°13′W. Chiefly residential; some light industry. Settled c.1775, inc. 1823. **2** town (1990 pop. 9,759), ⊙ Walton co., N central Ga., 37 mi/60 km E of Atlanta; 33°47′N 83°43′W. Mfg. of apparel, printing and publishing, steel molds, plastics, roofing materials; machining. Has some fine old houses in classic-revival style. Birthplace of 8 former governors. The Georgia Trust for Historic Preservation maintains the 1887 McDaniel-Tichenor house. Inc. 1821. **3** town (1990 pop. 788), Adams co., E Ind., 6 mi/9.7 km S of Decatur; 40°44′N 84°56′W. Mfg. (truck trailers). There is also a Monroe in Tippecanoe co., 13 mi/21 km SE of Lafayette. **4** town (1990 pop. 1,739), Jasper co., central Iowa, 13 mi/21 km SSW of Newton; 41°31′N 93°05′W. In agr. area. Mfg. (seeds, plastic containers, feeds). Laid out 1851. **5** town (1990 pop. 802), Waldo co., S Maine, 11 mi/18 km N of Belfast; 44°36′N 69°02′W. **6** rural town (1990 pop. 115), Franklin co., NW Mass., on Deerfield R. (power dam) and 9 mi/14.5 km E of North Adams; 42°43′N 72°59′W. Includes Monroe Bridge village. Former paper mill town. Several state forests in vicinity. **7** town (1990 pop. 746), Grafton co., NW N.H., 13 mi/21 km WSW of Littleton; 44°17′N 72°00′W. Bounded W and NW by Connecticut R. (Vt. state line). Mfg. (egg and poultry processing); agr. (nursery crops, vegetables; cattle, poultry; dairying). Commerford Dam, hydroelectric plant. Gardner Mt. (2,330 ft/710 m) in NE corner. **8** town, Overton co., N Tenn., 5 mi/8 km NE of Livingston. **9** town (1990 pop. 1,472), Sevier co., SW central Utah, in Sevier R. valley, 10 mi/16 km S of Richfield; 38°37′N 112°07′W. Alfalfa, barley; dairying; cattle. Hot springs nearby. Units of Fishlake Natl. Forest to E and NW. Elev. 5,395 ft/1,644 m. Sevier Plateau is E. Settled 1863. **10** town (1990 pop. 4,278), Snohomish co., NW Wash., suburb, 15 mi/24 km SE of Everett, and 24 mi/39 km NE of downtown Seattle, on Skykomish R., in W foothills of Cascade Range; 47°52′N 121°59′W. RR junction. Vegetables, berries; dairying; poultry; salmon. Granite quarrying; mfg. (aircraft parts, business forms, salmon processing, wood furniture, boat building, feeds and fertilizer); food processing. Mt. Baker-Snoqualmie Natl. Forest to E; L. Roesiger to N. Evergreen State Fair.

Monroe 1 village (1990 pop. 309), Platte co., E central Nebr., 12 mi/19 km W of Columbus, and on Loup R; 41°28′N 97°35′W. **2** summer residential and recreational village (□ 3 sq mi/7.8 sq km; 1990 pop. 6,672), Orange co., SE N.Y., 15 mi/24 km SW of Newburgh; 41°19′N 74°11′W. Mfg. of steel prods. Small lakes nearby. Inc. 1894. **3** village (1990 pop. 4,490), Butler co., extreme SW Ohio, 11 mi/18 km ENE of Hamilton; 39°26′N 84°20′W. **4** village (1990 pop. 448), Benton co., W Oregon, 20 mi/32 km NNW of Eugene; 44°19′N 123°17′W. Farm trade center. Berries, grapes; wineries. Timber. Washburne Wayside State Park to SE; William L. Finley Natl. Wildlife Refuge to N. **5** village (1990 pop. 151), Turner co., SE S.Dak., 7 mi/11.3 km NNW of Parker; 43°29′N 97°13′W. **6** uninc. village, Amherst co., central Va., 6 mi/9.7 km NNE of Lynchburg. Mfg. (wood-burning stoves, lumber, steel fabrication); agr. (corn, apples; cattle); timber.

Monroe, township (1990 pop. 22,255), Middlesex co., central N.J., 12 mi/19 km S of New Brunswick; 40°19′N 74°25′W. Inc. 1838.

Monroe, Pa.: see MONROETON.

Monroe Bridge, Mass.: see MONROE.

Monroe City (muhn-RO), city (1990 pop. 2,701), Monroe and Marion cos., NE central Mo., near Salt R., 20 mi/32 km W of Hannibal; 39°38′N 91°43′W. RR junction. Poultry-shipping center; corn, soybeans; hogs; mfg. (aluminum and magnesium die castings); lumber. Mark Twain b. in nearby Florida; Mark Twain L. to S. Inc. 1869.

Monroe City, town (1990 pop. 538), Knox co., SW Ind., 10 mi/16 km SE of Vincennes; 38°37′N 87°21′W. In agr. and bituminous-coal area.

Monroe, Lake, a shallow widening of St. Johns R., central Fla., on Seminole-Volusia co. line; c.5 mi/8 km long, 3 mi/4.8 km wide. Sanford is on S shore.

Monroe Lake, reservoir, Monroe and Brown cos., S central Ind., on Salt Creek (formed here by North and South forks), 12 mi/19 km N of Bloomington; 15 mi/24 km long; 39°00′N 86°31′W. Has 2 arms. Formed by Monroe Dam, built by Army Corps of Engineers for water supply. On shores are state recreation areas and Whitewater State Park (NE).

Monroe, Mount, N.H.: see PRESIDENTIAL RANGE.

Monroe Peak (11,227 ft/3,422 m), in Sevier Plateau, S Sevier co., SW central Utah, 7 mi/11.3 km SSE of Monroe. In Fishlake Natl. Forest.

Monroeton (MUHN-ro-tuhn), borough (1990 pop. 540), Bradford co., NE Pa., 4 mi/6.4 km SSW of Towanda, on Towanda Creek; 41°42′N 76°28′W. Mfg. includes dowels, commercial printing, feeds. Agr. includes dairying; livestock; corn, hay. Towanda Airport to SE. Formerly called Monroe.

Monroeville 1 (muhn-RO-vil), town (1990 pop. 6,993), ⊙ Monroe co., SW Ala., 75 mi/121 km NE of Mobile. Trade center in agr. area (cotton, corn); clothing mfg., lumber, paper, concrete. Factory outlet mall located here. Tourism. Ala. Southern Community Col. here. Setting for Harper Lee's novel *To Kill a Mockingbird.* Settled c.1815. **2** town (1990 pop. 1,232), Allen co., NE Ind., 14 mi/23 km ESE of Fort Wayne, near Ohio line; 40°59′N 84°52′W. In agr. area (corn, soybeans). Mfg. (fertilizer blending). Settled 1841, inc. 1865.

Monroeville, village (1990 pop. 1,381), Huron co., N Ohio, 14 mi/23 km S of Sandusky and on West Branch of Huron R.; 41°14′N 82°42′W.

Monroeville (MUHN-ro-vil), borough (1990 pop. 29,169), Allegheny co., SW Pa., suburb, 12 mi/19 km E of downtown Pittsburgh; 40°25′N 79°45′W. Bounded by Turtle Creek on S. Primarily residential, spurred by the suburban growth in 1980s and 1990s from the Pittsburgh area. Monroeville has chemical and nuclear research centers. Community Col. of Allegheny Co.–Boyce Campus. Pittsburgh Monroeville Airport in N. Koppers Research Center in NE. Boyce Regional Park and Ski Area to N. Settled 1810, inc. 1952.

Monrovia, city (1990 pop. 35,761), Los Angeles co., S Calif., suburb, 16 mi/26 km NE of downtown Los Angeles, in the foothills of the San Gabriel Mts.; 34°10'N 118°00'W. Diversified Mfg. Bounded N and NE by Angeles Natl. Forest, including San Gabriel Wilderness to N., Ma Wilson Observatory to NW; San Gabriel and Morris reservoirs to NE, on San Gabriel R. Inc. 1886.

Monrovia, town (1990 pop. 600), Morgan co., central Ind., 5 mi/8 km SW of Mooresville. Hogs; soybeans, corn, apples. Laid out 1834.

Monsanto, Ill.: see SAUGET.

Monseñor Nouel (mon-sen-YOR no-WEL), province (☐ 388 sq mi/1,004 sq km; 1993 pop. 144,327), central Dominican Republic, located on N flank of Cordillera Central; ⊙ BONAO; 18°55'N 70°25'W. Agr. (sugarcane, sugarcane refining, coffee, cacoa, fruit). Formerly part of La Vega prov.

Monsey, residential suburb (☐ 2 sq mi/5.2 sq km; 1990 pop. 13,986) of Suffern, Rockland co., SE N.Y., 5 mi/8 km E of city center; 41°07'N 74°04'W.

Monson 1 (MAHN-suhn), town (1990 pop. 744), Piscataquis co., central Maine, on small Hebron Pond, and 15 mi/24 km NW of Dover-Foxcroft; 45°17'N 69°30'W. Known for its slate quarries. **2** town (1990 pop. 7,776), including Monson village, Hampden co., S Mass., 13 mi/21 km E of Springfield; 42°05'N 72°19'W. Woollens granite; dairying; poultry, vegetables. Settled 1715, inc. 1760.

Mont Alto (MAHNT AL-to), borough (1990 pop. 1,395), Franklin co., S Pa., 6 mi/9.7 km N of Waynesboro, on West Branch Antietam Creek; 39°50'N 77°32'W. Agr. area (grain, apples; poultry, livestock; dairying). Mont Alto Arboretum. Mont Alto State Park to E; Appalachian Trail passes to E.

Mont Belvieu, town (1990 pop. 1,323), Chambers co., SE Texas, suburb, 28 mi/45 km E of Houston, on Cedar Bayou, 6 mi/9.7 km inland from Trinity Bay; 29°51'N 94°52'W. Urban growth area. In oil-producing and agr. area (rice, soybeans; cattle); natural-gas and gas-liquids processing.

Mont Clare (MAHNT KLER), uninc. town (1990 pop. 1,800), Upper Providence township, Montgomery co., SE Pa., on Schuylkill R., residential suburb, opposite (1 mi/1.6 km N of) Phoenixville; 40°08'N 75°30'W.

Mont Laurier (mon LO-ree-ai), town (1991 pop. 7,862), SW Que., Canada, on the Lièvre R., N of Ottawa; 46°33'N 75°30'W. Located in the Laurentian Mts., it is a winter resort in a lumbering and potato-growing region and has a hydroelectric-power station.

Mont Réal, Canada: see MOUNT ROYAL.

Mont Tremblant (mo trah-BLAH), village (1991 pop. 707), SW Que., Canada, in the Laurentians, at foot of Mt. Tremblant, on small L. Mercier, 20 mi/32 km NW of Ste. Agathe des Monts; 46°12'N 74°38'W. Dairying; skiing center. Resort.

Montagne Tremblante Park (moh-TAH-nyuh trah-BLAHT), provincial park in the Laurentians, S Que., Canada, c.70 mi/113 km NW of Montreal. Mt. Tremblant (Trembling Mt.) rises to 3,150 ft/960 m. Resort area, notably for skiing.

Montague (MAHN-tuh-goo), town (1991 pop. 1,901), E. P.E.I., Canada, on short Montague R., near its mouth on Cardigan Bay, 24 mi/39 km ESE of Charlottetown; 46°10'N 62°39'W. Agr. market in dairying, cattle-raising, potato-growing region.

Montague, county (☐ 938 sq mi/2,429 sq km; 1990 pop. 17,274), N Texas; ⊙ Montague; 33°40'N 97°43'W. Bounded N by Red R. (here the Okla. state line); source of Elm Fork Trinity R., and Clear, Denton, and Big Sandy creeks. Diversified agr. (peanuts, cotton, corn, grains, fruit, truck); large poultry, dairy industries; cattle ranching. Oil, natural gas fields; timber. Mfg., processing at Bowie, Nocona. L. Nocona reservoir in N (on tributary of Red), L. Carter reservoir in SW (Big Sandy Creek). Formed 1857.

Montague, city (1990 pop. 1,415), Siskiyou co., N Calif., at W base of Cascade Range, 6 mi/9.7 km E of Yreka, and on Shasta R.; 41°44'N 122°32'W. Dairying; cattle, sheep, lambs; grain. L. Shastina reservoir to SE; part of Klamuth Natl. Forest to NW.

Montague 1 town (1990 pop. 8,316), Franklin co., NW Mass., on Connecticut R. just SE of Greenfield; 42°33'N 72°31'W. Machinery, dies, fishing tackle. Large hydroelectric plant. Villages include Montague City, Turners Falls (1990 pop. 4,731) (site of 1st dam across the Connecticut), Millers Falls, and Lake Pleasant. Settled 1715, set off from Sunderland 1754. **2** (MON-tawg), town (1990 pop. 2,276), Muskegon co., SW Mich., 14 mi/23 km NNW of Muskegon, at head of White L., near L. Michigan, opposite Whitehall; 43°24'N 86°21'W. Shipping point for agr. (fruits and vegetables; poultry) and dairying area; mfg. (food prods.); mfg. (horticultural labels, pharmaceuticals, cast aluminum prods., machining). Resort; winter ice fishing. Duck L. State Park to S. Inc. as village 1883, as city 1935.

Montague, uninc. village (1990 pop. 500), ⊙ Montague co., N Texas, 47 mi/76 km ESE of Wichita Falls. Elev. 1,075 ft/328 m. In agr. area (dairying; cattle; watermelons, cantaloupes; peanuts; wheat); oil and gas; stone.

Montague Island 1 S Alaska, on W side of entrance of Prince William Sound, 60 mi/97 km E of Seward; 50 mi/80 km long, 5 mi/8 km–12 mi/19 km wide; 60°05'N 147°23'W. **2** (☐ 18 sq mi/47 sq km), Lower California, NW Mexico, at mouth of Colorado R., at head of Gulf of California, 75 mi/121 km SE of Mexicali; 6 mi/9.7 km long, 3 mi/4.8 km wide. Flat, alluvial, uninhabited.

Montague Strait, S Alaska, entrance from Gulf of Alaska (S) to Prince William Sound (N), bet. Montague Isl. (E) and Latouche Isl. (W); 60°08'N 147°38'W.

Montana, state (☐ 147,046 sq mi/380,849 sq km; 1995 est. pop. 870,281), NW U.S., in the Rocky Mt. region; ⊙ HELENA; 47°15'N 109°13'W. Admitted as the 41st state of the Union in 1889; 4th-largest state in U.S. Helena, BILLINGS, and GREAT FALLS are the largest cities; other places of importance include MISSOULA and BUTTE. The state lies on the N border of the contiguous U.S., S of the Can. provinces of B.C., Alta., and Sask. It is bounded by N.Dak. and S.Dak. on the E, by Wyo. and Idaho on the S, and by Idaho on the W. Mont. is thinly populated and has many remote areas. Life in the state's W mt. area differs greatly from that on its E plains. In the E ½ of the state are broad rolling plains, punctuated by buttes and outlier ranges of Rocky Mts., drained by the Missouri R., which originates in SW Mont., and by its tributaries, the Milk, the Marias, the Sun, and esp. the Yellowstone. Much of Montana's W boundary is marked by the crest of the lofty Bitterroot Range, part of the Rocky Mts., which dominate the W sect. of the state and along which, in SW Mont., runs the CONTINENTAL DIVIDE (forms Idaho and Mont. boundary in S and SW, continues N through W Mont. to Glacier Natl. Park). Montana's very name is derived from the Span. word *montaña*, meaning mt. country. High granite peaks, green forests, blue lakes, and such natural wonders as those of Glacier Natl. Park in NW and part of Yellowstone Natl. Park in SW have helped make tourism the state's 2d-ranking industry. The mts., moreover, offer more than massive beauty, for in and around the mountainous W region are the large mineral deposits for which Mont. is famous—copper, silver, gold, platinum, zinc, lead, and manganese. The E part of the state is noted for its petroleum and natural gas, and there are also vast coal deposits. In addition, Mont. mines vermiculite, chromite, cadmium, talc, molybdenum, and tungsten. Mfg. includes forest prods. (timber is important in W ½ of state), processed food, refined petroleum, and coal prods. In E Mont. the high grass of the Great Plains once nourished herds of buffalo and later sustained the cattle and sheep of huge ranches; much of the high grass is gone, but the cattle and sheep remain, grazing mainly on short grass. Despite the dangers of drought and the severe years that drove many farmers out of the state—turning farming communities into ghost towns—agriculture, both rain-fed and irrigated, provides an important share of Montana's income. Agr., coal, and petroleum contribute to growth of Billings, Mont.'s fastest-growing city. Cattle are the most valuable farm item; sheep, horses, and hogs are regionally important. The principal crops raised are wheat, hay, barley, potatoes, and sugar beets. Important for hydroelectric development and for irrigation, Mont.'s rivers were once avenues of travel for the Native Americans known to have inhabited the region at the time Europeans first explored it. Ethnic groups included the Blackfeet, the Sioux, the Shoshoni, the Atsina (Gros Ventre), the Kootenai, the Cheyenne, the Salish, Crow, the Pend D'Oreille, Assiniboine, the Ojibway, the Cree, and others. Major Indian Reservations: Blackfeet Indian Reservation and Flathead Indian Reservation in NW, Rocky Boy's Indian Reservation and Fort Belknap Indian Reservation in N center, Fort Peck Indian Reservation in NE, Crow and Northern Cheyenne Indian reservations in S. Early explorers of the country also traveled along the rivers. Exploration of the region began in earnest after most of Mont. had passed to the U.S. under the Louisiana Purchase (1803). The Lewis and Clark expedition traveled W across Mont. in 1805, and François Antoine Larocque, along with his North West Company of Canada, explored the Yellowstone R. after 1805. The 1st trading post in Mont. was established at the mouth of the Bighorn in 1807 by a trading expedition under Manuel Lisa that came up the Missouri from St. Louis. For some years both Can. and Amer. fur traders continued to open the territory. David Thompson of the North West Company built several trading posts in NW Mont. bet. 1807 and 1812, and beaver in the mt. streams and lakes attracted adventurous trappers, the so-called "mountain men." The Amer. Fur Company, with its posts on the Missouri and the Yellowstone, dominated the later years of the region's fur trade, which diminished in the 1840s. The U.S. claim to NW Mont., the area bet. the Rockies and the N Idaho border, was legalized in the Oregon Treaty of 1846 with the British. Mont. was then still a wilderness of forest and grass, with a few trading posts and some missions. Montana's 1st period of growth was the rapid, boisterous, and unstable expansion brought on by a gold rush. The discovery of gold, made initially in 1852, brought many people to mushrooming mining camps such as those at Bannack (1862) and Virginia City (1864). Crude shanty towns were built, complete with saloons and dance halls—ephemeral settlements as colorful as the earlier gold-rush camps in Calif. and perhaps even more lawless. Previously part of, successively, the territories of Oregon, Wash., Nebr., Dakota, and Idaho, Mont. itself became a territory in 1864. The territory was still a rough frontier, however, and the 1st governor, Sidney Edgerton, was driven out of the region, and later Thomas Francis Meagher, appointed temporary governor, died mysteriously. After the Civil War, the grasslands attracted ranchers. Although cattle had been introduced into Mont. by missionaries, traders, and the Métis before the gold rushes, large-scale ranching dates from the acquisition of cattle by Richard Grant in the Beaverhead Basin in 1850. Yet it was not until after wars with the Sioux that ranching was safe. The Sioux did not tamely submit to having their lands taken from them; in 1876 at the battle of the Little Bighorn, they defeated Gen. George A. Custer and his force in one of the greatest of Native Amer. victories. The Sioux were eventually subdued, and the gallant attempt of Chief Joseph of the Nez Percé to lead his people into Canada to escape pursuing U.S. troops had its pitiful end in the Bears Paws Mts. in Mont. Great ranches spread out across the plains, and cow towns that were to grow into cities, such as Billings, sprang up as the RRs were built in the West (c.1880–c.1910). Achievement of statehood in 1889 and the building of the RR put an end to the era of the open range. Mining continued to dominate Mont.: the discovery of silver at Butte (1875) had been followed (c.1880) by discovery of copper at that same "richest hill on earth." Mont.'s fate was subsequently linked to copper, and the Anaconda Copper Mining Company came to play a major role in Mont. life. The titans of the mines, Marcus Daly and William A. Clark, fought bitterly not only for ownership of the mineral deposits but for political control, and their rivalry was physically fought out by the miners. Fritz Augustus Heinze also entered the scramble for copper claims, challenging the claims of the Amalgamated Copper Company. Amalgamated ruled triumphant, however, exercising control over state affairs. Struggles bet. the company and the workingmen led to strikes, disorder, and bloodshed, but they also resulted in the enactment of some early measures for social security. This was an important achievement, for over the years the livelihood of the residents of the mining towns has been dependent on the market price of copper. Despite fluctuating metals prices, the mines have contributed a large amount to the state's wealth. After the coming of the RRs, farmers came by the trainload to develop the lands of E Mont. They planted their fields in the 2d decade of the 20th cent.; the initial yield of wheat was great, but it did not last long. The calamitous drought of 1919 and the consequent dust storms seared the fields, and in the 1920s the farms began to disappear as rapidly as they had been established. When the great natl. depression began in 1929, Mont. was already accustomed to depression. In subsequent years vigorous measures were taken to aid agr. in the state, and by the late 1940s, Federal dam and irrigation projects — on the Missouri, the Yellowstone, the Marias, the Sun, and elsewhere — opened many acres to cultivation. Some of the vast grazing lands were brought under planned use, and the development of hydroelectric power continued. Major multipurpose dams in Mont. producing power include Fort Peck Dam (Missouri R., NE central Mont.), Hungry Horse Dam (South Fork Flathead R., NW), and Canyon Ferry (Missouri R., W center). Large Fort Peck L. reservoir surrounded by Charles M. Russell Natl. Wildlife Refuge. Flathead L., in NW, is Mont.'s largest natural lake. There are also many reclamation projects. The demand for copper in World War II and the E Mont. oil boom of the early 1950s stimulated Montana's economy. The state, however, still faces problems regarding high transportation costs, lack of manpower, and the necessary regulation of resources. There has been a beneficial if slow trend toward a more diversified economy, with mfg. growing in importance in relation to farming and mining. The latter sector of the economy has declined in importance, while tourism has been growing. Development of vast recreational facilities along the Gallatin R. stirred protests from conservationists in the early 1970s. In the 1970s the exploitation of coal increased dramatically. The Anaconda Mining Company closed its largest copper smelter in the 1970s and closed down operations in Butte altogether in 1983, primarily the results of strict environmental regulations. Much of Mont. is still largely undeveloped and unpopulated. Places of interest, besides Glacier Natl. Park, include Little Bighorn (formerly Custer) Battlefield Natl. Monument, Big Hole Natl. Battlefield, Grant-Kohrs Ranch Natl. Historic Site, and part of Fort Union Trading Post Natl. Historic Site, on N.Dak. state line. Also the Natl. Bison Range, near Ravalli, where herds of bison may still be seen. Strips of Yellowstone Natl. Park, including the N and W entrances, are also in Mont. Bighorn Canyon Natl. Recreation Area on Wyo. boundary in S. Upper Missouri (N center) and Flathead (NW) natl. wild and scenic rivers. Natl. forests: Kootenai, Kaniksu, Lolo, and Flathead in NW; Beaverhead, Bitterroot, and Deerlodge in SW; Helena and Lewis and Clark in W center; Custer Natl. Forest in SE. The many kinds of fish found in the rushing mt. streams and innumerable lakes bring fishing enthusiasts to the state, and the abundant wildlife — wapiti, elk, deer, antelope, moose, bear, and waterfowl — attract hunters. The state's outstanding recreational areas also include facilities for skiing, hiking, boating, and swimming. In 1973, Mont. implemented a new constitution, which replaced the one adopted in 1889. The governor of the state is elected for a term of 4 years and may be reelected. The Legislative Assembly is made up of a senate with 50 members and a house of representatives with 100 members. State senators are elected for terms of 4 years and representatives for terms of 2 years. Mont. is represented in the U.S. Congress by 1 representative and 2 senators, and the state has 3 electoral votes in presidential campaigns. The state's major institutions of higher learning are included in the Univ. of Mont. and Mont. State Univ. systems. Mont. has 56 cos.: BEAVERHEAD, BIG HORN, BLAINE, BROADWATER, CARBON, CARTER, CASCADE, CHOUTEAU, CUSTER, DANIELS, DAWSON, DEER LODGE, FALLON, FERGUS, FLATHEAD, GALLATIN, GARFIELD, GLACIER, GOLDEN VALLEY, GRANITE, HILL, JEFFERSON, JUDITH BASIN, LAKE, LEWIS AND CLARK, LIBERTY, LINCOLN, MCCONE, MADISON, MEAGHER, MINERAL, MISSOULA, MUSSELSHELL, PARK, PETROLEUM, PHILLIPS, PONDERA, POWDER RIVER, POWELL, PRAIRIE, RAVALLI, RICHLAND, ROOSEVELT, ROSEBUD, SANDERS, SHERIDAN, SILVER BOW, STILLWATER, SWEET GRASS, TETON, TOOLE, TREASURE, VALLEY, WHEATLAND, WIBAUX, YELLOWSTONE.

Montara, uninc. town (1990 pop. 2,552), San Mateo co., W Calif., on the Pacific, suburb 17 mi/27 km SSW of downtown San Francisco, and 1 mi/1.6 km N of Moss Beach; 37°33′N 122°30′W. Artichokes, brussel sprouts, flowers, grains. Nearby Montara Point has lighthouse and radio compass station. Montara Mt. (extension of Santa Cruz Mts.) and San Francisco State Fish and Game to E; Montara State Beach is here; Grey Whale Cove State Beach to N.

Montauban (moh-to-BAH), village, S central Que., Canada, on Batiscan R., and 27 mi/43 km NE of Grand'-Mère. Dairying; cattle, pig, poultry raising.

Montauban les Mines (lai MEEN), village, S central Que., Canada, 23 mi/37 km NE of Grand'-Mère. Mining.

Montauk, resort village (□ 19 sq mi/49 sq km; 1990 pop. 3,001), Suffolk co., SE N.Y., on E L.I. near tip of its S peninsula, 14 mi/23 km ENE of East Hampton; 41°02′N 71°57′W. E terminus of S Shore line of Long Isl. RR. Commercial- and sport-fishing center. Mfg. (electronic components, high-temperature alloys). Prize fishing area, with over 30 world records for marlin, shark, and tuna. Just E is L. Montauk (c.2 mi/3.2 km long), sheltered inlet of L.I. Sound; yacht harbor. Montauk Point State Park is 5 mi/8 km E; Hither Hills State Park (camping) is 4 mi/6.4 km WSW. Name derived from Montauk word for "hilly land." Founded on land bought from Montauks in 1686 by settlers from nearby East Hampton to raise cattle. Site of oldest cattle ranch in U.S.

Montauk Point, E extremity of the S peninsula of L.I., the "South Fork," SE N.Y.; 41°04′N 71°52′W. Approximately 115 mi/185 km E of Manhattan, it is the easternmost point of land of the state. In 1792 President George Washington signed order for construction of the Montauk Point Lighthouse. Built by John McComb Jr., a famous early Amer. naval architect, on spot where Royal Navy had kept signal bonfires for its ships during Amer. Revolution. Lighthouse completed in 1796 at cost of $22,300. The area is included in Montauk Point State Park.

Montcalm (mahnt-KAHM), county (□ 3,894 sq mi/ 10,085 sq km), SW Que., Canada, N of the St. Lawrence, on Gatineau R.; ☉ Ste. Julienne; 47°28′N 76°00′W.

Montcalm, county (□ 721 sq mi/1,867 sq km; 1990 pop. 53,059), central Mich.; ☉ Stanton; 43°18′N 85°09′W. Drained by Flat and Pine rivers, Fish Creek, and short Tamarack R. Agr. (potatoes, apples, corn, wheat, beans; cattle, hogs, sheep; dairy prods.). Mfg. at Greenville; lake resorts. Has state game area. Wintersköl Ski Area in NW; small part of Manistee Natl. Forest in NW corner. Organized 1850.

Montcalm (mahnt-KAHM), uninc. town (1990 pop. 1,023), Mercer co., S W.Va., 6 mi/9.7 km N of Bluefield, near Bluestone R.; 37°21′N 81°15′W. RR junction. Agr. (grain, tobacco); livestock; bituminous coal. Pinnacle Rock State Park to SW.

Montclair 1 city (1990 pop. 28,434), San Bernardino co., SE Calif., suburb 32 mi/51 km E of downtown Los Angeles, and 3 mi/4.8 km W of Ontario; 34°04′N 117°42′W. Light mfg. Citrus-fruit–growing area replaced in 1990s by urbanization. San Gabriel Mts. and San Bernardino Natl. Forest to N; Angeles Natl. Forest to NW; Cable Airport to N; Mt. Baldy Ski Area to N. Inc. 1956. **2** uninc. city, Prince William co., NE Va., residential suburb 25 mi/40 km SSW of Washington, D.C., near Potomac R. Prince William Forest Park (natl. park unit) to W, Leesylvania State Park to E; 38°36′N 77°20′W.

Montclair, town (1990 pop. 37,729), Essex co., NE N.J., a suburb of Newark and N.Y. city, 6 mi/9.7 km NNW of Newark, on a slope of the Watchung Mts. Although chiefly residential, it has plants that make chemicals, paint, and metalware. The art mus. contains several paintings by George Inness, who lived here. Montclair State Univ. is in Upper Montclair (notable for its many large mansions). Settled c.1666 as part of Newark, set off from Newark 1812, set off from Bloomfield and inc. 1868.

Monte Albán (MOH-te ahl-BAHN), anc. city, c.7 mi/ 11.3 km from Oaxaca, SW Mexico; ☉ Zapotec. Monte Albán was built on an artificially leveled, rocky promontory above the Valley of Oaxaca. Located around an enormous plaza about 1,000 ft/305 m long and 650 ft/ 198 m wide are long, low bldgs. set off by sunken courts and stairways. The tombs, particularly Tomb 7, have yielded great archaeological treasure — jewelry of gold, copper, jade, rock crystal, obsidian, and turquoise mosaic, and bone and wood carving showing elaborate religious symbolism. Excavation was begun (1931) by the Mex. archaeologist Alfonso Caso. The Zapotec apparently had an advanced culture here c.200 B.C. and already were using the bar and dot system of numerals used by the Maya. The final epoch (c.1300–1521), terminated by the Span. Conquest, covers the ascendancy of the Mixtec, when the Zapotec were driven from Monte Albán and Mitla. Tomb 7 belongs to the final period. Cultural links with the Olmec and the Toltec have been found.

Monte Alto, uninc. town (1990 pop. 1,769), Hidalgo co., S Texas, 23 mi/37 km NE of McAllen. Located in irrigated Rio Grande Valley agr. area (citrus, vegetables, cotton). Mfg. (frozen foods).

Monte Cristi (MON-te KREE-stee) or **Montecristi**, province (□ 1,150 sq mi/2,979 sq km; 1993 pop. 94,427), NW Dominican Republic, on the coast, bordering W on Haiti; ☉ Monte Cristi; 19°40′N 71°25′W. Watered by the Yaque del Norte, the irrigated valley of which here forms W sect. of fertile Cibao region; adjoined by Cordillera Septentrional (N) and Cordillera Central (S). Lumbering; livestock raising; agr. (rice, bananas, cocoa, corn; beeswax, honey; dairy prods.; hides; hardwood). Main center is Monte Cristi city, with nearby harbor. Port of Pepillo Salcedo, built 1945, ships bananas. Prov. was set up 1879; in 1938 Dajabón prov. was separated from it.

Monte Cristi (MON-te KREE-stee), officially San Fernando de Montecristi, city (1993 pop. 11,520), ☉ Monte Cristi prov., NW Dominican Republic, near coast and near mouth of the Yaque del Norte, 65 mi/105 km WNW of Santiago, 150 mi/241 km NW of Santo Domingo; 19°51′N 71°40′W. Trading and agr. center (rice, cotton, coffee, bananas; goats) in irrigated W sect. of the fertile Cibao region. Exports hides and skins through its fine harbor (1 mi/1.6 km away). Founded 1533 by Span. peasants on a site explored and named by Columbus in 1493. Leveled 1606 by the Spanish because of illegal trade with pirates; rebuilt c. 1750. Also spelled Montecristi. Sometimes called San Fernando de Monte Cristi.

Monte Escobedo (MON-te es-ko-BE-do), town (1990 pop. 3,502), Zacatecas, N central Mexico, 45 mi/72 km SW of Jérez de García Salinas; 22°20′N 103°30′W. Grain, alfalfa, sugarcane, livestock.

Monte Negro, Mexico: see SANTIAGO JOCOTEPEC.

Monte Plata (MON-te PLAH-tah), province (□ 841 sq mi/2,179 sq km; 1993 pop. 162,630), S central Dominican Republic; ☉ MONTE PLATA; 18°50′N 69°50′W. Includes S flank of Cordillera Central and coastal plain. Agr. (rice, cacao, coffee, bananas). Formerly part of San Cristóbal prov., also called Trujillo.

Monte Plata (MON-te PLAH-tah), town (1993 pop. 162,630), ⊙ Monte Plata prov., S Dominican Republic, at S foot of Cordillera Central, 23 mi/37 km NNE of Santo Domingo; 18°45′N 69°51′W. Agr. (rice, cacao, coffee).

Monte Rio, uninc. town (1990 pop. 1,058), Sonoma co., W Calif., on Russian R., and 15 mi/24 km W of Santa Rosa; 38°28′N 123°01′W. Grapes, apples, grain; dairying; sheep. Armstrong Redwoods State Park and Austin Creek State Recreation Area to N.

Monte Sereno, city (1990 pop. 3,287), Santa Clara co., W Calif., residential suburb 7 mi/11.3 km SW of downtown San Jose; 37°14′N 122°00′W. Santa Cruz Mts. to SW; Los Gatos Creek to E.

Monte Vista, town (1990 pop. 4,324), Rio Grande co., S Colo., on Rio Grande, just E of San Juan Mts., in San Luis Valley, and 17 mi/27 km NW of Alamosa; 37°34′N 106°08′W. Elev. 7,663 ft/2,336 m. Shipping point in potato area; mfg. (starches, light mfg.). Hq. of Rio Grande Natl. Forest to W. Dude ranches, gold and silver mines in vicinity. Nearby are state soldiers' and sailors' home, Rio Grande Natl. Forest, and Picture Rocks, with pictographs. Monte Vista Natl. Wildlife Refuge. Junction of RR spur to center to SE. Inc. 1886.

Monteagle (mawnt-EE-guhl), town (1990 pop. 1,138), Grundy and Marion cos., S central Tenn., 32 mi/51 km NW of Chattanooga, on Monteagle Mt. in the Cumberlands; 35°15′N 85°50′W. Elev. c.1,900 ft/579 m. Summer resort; vineyards.

Montebello (mahn-ti-BEHL-o), village (1991 pop. 1,022), SW Que., Canada, on the Ottawa R. NE of Ottawa; 45°39′N 74°56′W. Summer resort in a lumbering and farming area.

Montebello, city (1990 pop. 59,564), Los Angeles co., S Calif., a residential and industrial suburb 7 mi/11.3 km ESE of Los Angeles; 34°01′N 118°07′W. Diversified mfg. A wide variety of prods. are mfg. in Montebello, developed significantly during the 1970s along with the S California area. The city is also known for its oil wells. Bounded on E by branch of Los Angeles R., bounded W by Los Angeles. Inc. 1920.

Montebello, village (□ 4 sq mi/10.4 sq km; 1990 pop. 2,950), Rockland co., SE N.Y., 1 mi/1.6 km NNE of Suffern, 9 mi/14.5 km NW of Nyack; 41°07′N 74°07′W.

Montecito, uninc. town, Santa Barbara co., SW Calif., residential suburb near Pacific Ocean, 3 mi/4.8 km E of Santa Barbara.

Montego Bay, city (1991 pop. 82,002), ⊙ St. James parish, NW Jamaica; 18°28′N 77°55′W. One of the most popular tourist resorts in the Caribbean with highly developed tourism facilities, Montego Bay is also a port and commercial center. Active trade in sugar, bananas, coffee, rum. Various light mfg. industries. Internatl. airport.

Montegut (MAHN-ti-guht), town (1990 pop. 1,784), Terrebonne parish, La., 13 mi/21 km SE of Houma; 29°28′N 90°33′W. Fishing (shrimp, crabs, finfish).

Montello, town (1990 pop. 1,329), ⊙ Marquette co., central Wis., at E end of Buffalo L., at confluence of Fox R. and small Montello R. (E end of Montrello L.), 45 mi/72 km W of Fond du Lac; 43°47′N 89°19′W. Resort; livestock, grain; granite quarries; mfg. (lumber mill, wood prods.). Settled 1849, inc. 1938.

Montemorelos (mon-te-mo RE-los), city (1990 pop. 35,508) and township, Nuevo León, N Mexico, in E foothills of Sierra Madre Oriental, on RR, and 45 mi/72 km SE of Monterrey on Inter-Amer. Highway (Mexico Highway 85); 25°12′N 99°50′W. Agr. center (oranges, sugarcane, pecans, cactus fibers, livestock). Known for yearly fiesta in July.

Monterey, county (□ 3,322 sq mi/8,604 sq km; 1990 pop. 355,660), W Calif., on the Pacific and Monterey Bay; ⊙ Salinas; 36°14′N 121°19′W. Bounded N by Pajaro R. valley; Salinas R. valley in its center is flanked E by Gabilan and Diablo ranges, W by Santa Lucia Range (rising here to 5,862 ft/1,787 m at Junipero Serra Peak). Monterey Peninsula (site of historic towns of Monterey and Carmel) in NW is famed scenic resort region. Co. includes Big Sur (redwoods); scenic Big Sur coastal drive (state highway 1) S from Monterey; Monterey State Beach, Asilomar State Beach and Point Lobos State Reserve in NW; Fremont Peak and Moss Landing state parks in N; Andrew Molera Pfeiffer Big Sur and Julia Pfeiffer Burns state parks in SW; old Soledad (center), Carmel, and San Antonio de Padua (SW) missions; U.S. Fort Ord Military Reservation (NW) and Hunter Liggett Military Reservation (S); part of Los Padres Natl. Forest (SW); part of Pinnacles Natl. Monument on NE boundary. Agr. (grain, tomatoes, asparagus, peppers, olives, celery, spinach, mushrooms, artichokes, carrots, broccoli, lettuce, strawberries, grapes); wineries; cattle; dairying; asbestos mining at King City; sand and gravel. Formed 1850.

Monterey, city (1990 pop. 31,954), Monterey co., W Calif., 12 mi/19 km W of Salinas, a port on Monterey Bay, at base of Monterey Pennisula to W; 36°36′N 121°53′W. Mfg. (printing and publishing, calculating machines, computers, electrical aparatus, paperboard boxes). It is a popular resort, the home of many artists and writers, and one of the oldest cities in Calif. The bay was visited by Juan Cabrillo in 1542 and entered and named by Sebastián Vizcaíno in 1602. In 1770 an expedition under Gaspar de Portolá arrived and established a presidio. Junípero Serra remained to found a Franciscan mission. Monterey was the capital of Alta California during many of the years bet. 1775 and 1846. In 1846 the city was taken by a U.S. naval force under Commodore John D. Sloat, and in 1849 the state constitutional convention met there. An early whaling and fishing center, Monterey's 20th-cent. economy is based on tourism (Fisherman's Wharf, restaurants, shops, seafood markets) and the revenues and employment derived from nearby military installations, such as Fort Ord to E. Calif.'s 1st theater (1844) and 1st brick bldg. (1847) still stand, and it was in Monterey that Calif.'s 1st newspaper was established in 1846. Numerous mus. are in the city, as is the Presidio of Monterey (1770) and the Monterey Bay Aquarium. Monterey Peninsula Col. (2-year), the Monterey Inst. of Internatl. Studies, and the U.S. Postgraduate School are there. Calif. State Univ. at Monterey (1995), Carmel Bay to SW; Monterey Pennisula Airport to SE; Monterey State Beach is here. Founded 1770; inc. 1850.

Monterey 1 town (1990 pop. 230), Pulaski co., NW Ind., on Tippecanoe R., and 9 mi/14.5 km NE of Winamac; 41°10′N 86°29′W. In agr. area. Tippecanoe River State Park to W. Laid out 1849. **2** town (1990 pop. 805), Berkshire co., SW Mass., in the Berkshires, 19 mi/31 km S of Pittsfield; 42°11′N 73°14′W. Beartown State Forest. **3** (MON-tuh-rai), town (1990 pop. 2,559), Putnam co., central Tenn., 14 mi/23 km E of Cookeville; 36°09′N 85°16′W. In timber, coal, and farm area; processes meat for fast food industry. Small Monterey L. (resort) is nearby. **4** town (1990 pop. 222), ⊙ Highland co., NW Va., in Allegheny Mts., 32 mi/51 km NW of Staunton; 38°24′N 79°34′W. Mfg. (printing and publishing, fish processing); agr. (alfalfa); timber; freshwater fish.

Monterey (mahn-tuh-RAI), village (1990 pop. 164), Owen co., N Ky., on Kentucky R., and 16 mi/26 km N of Frankfort; 38°25′N 84°52′W. Agr. (tobacco, corn; dairying); recreation (fishing, camping). Larkspur Press, small book printer using handset type.

Monterey, Minn.: see TRIMONT.

Monterey Bay, W Calif., Monterey and Santa Cruz cos., crescent shaped inlet of the Pacific formed by break in Coast Ranges, c.65 mi/105 km S of San Francisco; 26 mi/42 km long. Santa Cruz Mts. (with Santa Cruz at their base) rise steeply to NE, Santa Lucia Range (behind Monterey, on Monterey Peninsula) to S. Pajaro R. enters from E; fertile Salinas R. valley extends SE from bay. Fisheries; beaches. Sighted (1542) by Cabrillo; entered (1602) and named by Vizcaíno.

Monterey Park, city (1990 pop. 60,738), Los Angeles co., S Calif., a residential suburb 6 mi/9.7 km E of Los Angeles; 34°03′N 118°08′W. Wholesale, retail center, and financial service center. There is some light industry. Light mfg. East Los Angeles Col. (2-year) is located here. Calif. State Univ.–Los Angeles to W, in Los Angeles. Has the 1st suburban Chinatown, and 1st city in continental U.S. with Asian majority. Inc. 1916.

Monterey Peninsula, W Calif., rugged, almost square peninsula jutting 4 mi/6.4 km NW into the Pacific bet. Monterey Bay (N) and Carmel Bay (S). Communities of Monterey, Pacific Grove, Del Monte Forest, Del Ray Oaks, Pebble Beach, Carmel, Asilomar, other resorts. Seventeen-Mile Drive is a scenic toll road around shore. Point Piños (lighthouse), is N tip; Cypress Point its W extremity; Pescadero Point in S. Pebble Beach, site of world golf classics, and other popular golf courses; Asilomar and Monterey state beaches in N.

Monterrey (mon-te-RAI), city (1990 pop. 1,068,996) and township, ⊙ Nuevo León state, NE Mexico, c.150 mi/241 km S of Laredo (Texas), at the mouth of a valley surrounded by mts. on 3 sides; 25°40′N 100°20′W. The 3d-largest city of Mexico, Monterrey is the RR and highway hub of NE Mexico. It is also Mexico's 2d-most important industrial center. The site of the nation's largest iron and steel foundries and a major producer of cement. Monterrey's modern industrial complex also includes a wide range of light mfg. (including glass and beverages). The city has experienced further growth with the construction of maquiladoras, foreign-owned plants that use low-wage labor for goods exported to the U.S. Natural gas, coal and petroleum from the neighboring states of Coahuila and Tamaulipas are also major sources of industrial activity. Its moderate, dry climate, cool mountains, and hot springs make the Monterrey area a popular resort. Monterrey is the home of the Univ. of Nuevo León and Monterrey Technical Inst., one of Mexico's most prestigious institutions of higher education. The city was founded in 1579.

Montesano (mahn-tuh-SAI-no), town (1990 pop. 3,064), ⊙ Grays Harbor co., W Wash., 10 mi/16 km E of Aberdeen, and on Chehalis R., near mouth of Wyandotte R.; 47°01′N 123°59′W. RR junction. Peas, hay; lumber, dairy prods.; mfg. (lumber, pumps). L. Sylvia State Park 1 mi/1.6 km to N. Inc. 1883.

Montevallo 1 (mahn-tuh-VAH-lo), town (1990 pop. 4,239), Shelby co., central Ala., 17 mi/27 km WSW of Columbiana; 33°06′N 86°51′W. Cotton area; lumber milling and wood prods. Univ. of Montevallo here. Talladega Natl. Forest is S. Settled c.1815, inc. 1848. **2** (mahn-tee-VAL-o), uninc. town, Vernon co., W Mo., 16 mi/26 km SE of Nevada. Cattle, hay, sorghum, corn. Destroyed during the Civil War. Rebuilt 1 mi/1.6 km from original site.

Montevideo (MAWN-te-vi-dee-yo), town (1990 pop. 5,499), ⊙ Chippewa co., SW Minn., 35 mi/56 km SW of Willmar on Minnesota R. at mouth of Chippewa R.; 44°57′N 95°43′W. Elev. 955 ft/291 m. Agr. trade center; grain, soybeans, sugar beets; livestock; dairying; mfg. (tarpaulins, fertilizers, computer sub-assemblies, mobile systems, miniature aircraft motors). To W is Camp Release State Memorial with granite monument commemorating release (1862) of 269 white captives of Sioux Indians. Lac qui Parle Wildlife Area and Lac qui Parle State Park, both of Minnesota R., to NW. Plotted 1870, inc. as village 1879, as town 1908.

Montezuma, county (□ 2,040 sq mi/5,284 sq km; 1990 pop. 18,672), SW Colo.; ⊙ Cortez; 37°20′N 108°35′W. Bordering on N.Mex. (S) and Utah (W); SW corner of co. forms Four Corners Area (Utah, Ariz., N.Mex., Colo. meet), bounded E by La Plata Mts.; drained by Dolores R. San Juan R. crosses SW corner, Dolores R. forms McPhee Reservoir in N. Sheep, wheat, hay, beans, oats, barley, cattle, peaches; aspen timber. Mesa Verde Natl. Park in SE; Yucca House Natl. Monument at center; part of Ute Mt. Indian Reservation in S; part of San Juan Natl. Forest in NE; Mancos State Park in E; unit of Havenwood Natl. Monument in W (other parts in Utah). Formed 1889.

Montezuma 1 (mahn-tuh-ZOO-muh), town (1990 pop. 4,506), Macon co., central Ga., c.45 mi/72 km SW of Macon, and on Flint R. opposite Oglethorpe; 32°18′N 84°02′W. Mfg. includes plastic pipe, motor vehicle seats, clothing, frozen fruits and vegetables. Mennonite farm community to the E. Inc. 1854. **2** town (1990 pop. 1,134), Parke co., W Ind., on Wabash R., and 7 mi/11.3 km NW of Rockville; 39°47′N 87°22′W. In agr. and bituminous-coal area; mfg. (lumber); fisheries; gravel and clay pits; mineral springs. Settled c.1821, plotted 1849, inc. 1851. **3** town (1990 pop. 1,651), ⊙ Poweshiek co., central Iowa, 21 mi/34 km NNE of Oskaloosa, near source of South Fork of English R.; 41°34′N 92°31′W. Mfg. (wood prods., chemicals, epoxy prods., polishing compounds, automotive parts, balsa wood and model airplane kits, printing, tankage). Fun Valley Ski Area to W. Inc. 1868.

Montezuma 1 (mahn-tuh-ZOO-muh), village (1990 pop. 60), Summit co., central Colo., on branch of Blue R., in Front Range, and 5 mi/8 km SW of Grays Peak, 12 mi/19 km NE of Breckenridge; 39°34′N 105°52′W. Elev. c.10,280 ft/3,133 m. Continental Divide 1 mi/1.6 km to E. Skiing. Arapaho Basin Ski Area to N. In Arapaho Natl. Forest; Pike Natl. Forest E of Divide. **2** village (1990 pop. 838), Gray co., SW Kansas, 14 mi/23 km SSW of Cimarron; 37°36′N 100°26′W. Wheat-shipping point. **3** village (1990 pop. 199), Mercer co., W Ohio, 4 mi/6 km SSE of Celina, and on Grand L.; 40°29′N 84°32′W.

Montezuma (mahn-tuh-ZOO-muh), a RR community, San Miguel co., N.Mex., 6 mi/9.7 km N of Las Vegas. Site of an historic 75-room hotel built to receive guests from the Santa Fe RR. In 1982 Armand Hammer bought the bldg. and donated it to the United World Col. as the site for one of its campuses.

Montezuma Castle National Monument, Yavapai co., on Wet Beaver Creek, central Ariz. Consists of 858 acres/347 ha. Montezuma Castle, built by a farming culture, c.1250, is a 5-story, 20-room apartment house perched high in the cavity of a cliff. It was named by early settlers who believed it had been built by the Sinagua. The monument has 2 sects.; main sect. 2 mi/3.2 km NNE of Camp Verde has cliff dwellings, Montezuma Well, which has a continuous spring, 1,500,000 gals/5,677,950 liters per day, is 9 mi/14.5 km NE of Camp Verde. Both units are bounded by Presott Natl. Forest. Authorized 1906.

Montfort, village (1990 pop. 676), Grant co., SW Wis., 16 mi/26 km N of Platteville; 42°58′N 90°25′W. In agr. area (dairying; poultry; grain farms); cheese.

Montgomery 1 county (□ 800 sq mi/2,072 sq km; 1990 pop. 209,085), E central Ala; ⊙ Montgomery; 32°14′N 86°14′W. In the Black Belt. Bounded NW by Alabama R., N by Tallapoosa R. Cotton, livestock, grain. Mfg. at Montgomery. Formed 1816. **2** county (□ 800 sq mi; 1990 pop. 7,841), W Ark.; ⊙ Mount Ida; 34°32′N 93°39′W. Drained by Ouachita, Caddo, and Little Missouri rivers; in Ouachita Mts. region. Agr. (cattle, hogs, chickens); dairy prods.; cotton ginning, sawmilling, food processing, stone quarrying. All of co. except a narrow margin in SE is within Ouachita Natl. Forest, (8 forest campgrounds), W ½ of large L. Ouachita reservoir in E; Little Missouri Falls in SW. Formed 1842, organized 1844. **3** county (□ 247 sq mi/640 sq km; 1990 pop. 7,163), E central Ga.; ⊙ Mount Vernon; 32°10′N 82°32′W. Bounded W by Oconee R., S by Altamaha R. Mfg. (apparel, textiles, beer and distilled beverages); agr. (cotton, corn, tobacco, peanuts); cattle, hogs; in timber area. Formed 1793. **4** county (□ 709 sq mi/1,836 sq km; 1990 pop. 30,728), S central Ill.; ⊙ Hillsboro; 39°14′N 89°29′W. Agr. (corn, wheat, sorghum, soybeans, cattle; dairy prods.). Some mfg. (food prods., paper boxes, glass jars, metal prods., industrial machinery, transportation equip.). Drained by Shoal and Macoupin creeks. Has several recreational reservoirs, including L. Lou Yaeger, L. Glenn Shoals, Coffeen L. Largest town is Litchfield. in W. Formed 1821. **5** county (□ 505 sq mi/1,308 sq km; 1990 pop. 34,436), W central Ind.; ⊙ Crawfordsville; 40°02′N 86°53′W. Drained by Sugar and Raccoon creeks. Agr. (soybeans, corn, wheat, cattle, hogs, sheep, poultry; dairy prods.). Clay pits; timber. Commerce and mfg. at Crawfordsville. Shades State Park in SW; canoeing on Sugar Creek. Formed 1822. **6** county (□ 424 sq mi/1,098 sq km; 1990 pop. 12,076), SW Iowa; ⊙ Red Oak, 41°02′N 95°10′W. Prairie agr. area (hogs, cattle; corn, wheat, oats) drained by East Nishnabotna, West Nodaway, and Tarkio rivers and by Walnut Creek; bituminous-coal deposits. Formed 1851. **7** county (□ 651 sq mi/1,686 sq km; 1990 pop. 38,816), SE Kansas; ⊙ Independence; 37°12′N 95°44′W. Level to hilly region, bordering S on Okla.; drained by Verdigris and Elk rivers. Livestock; grain; dairying; wheat, sorghum, soybeans, hay, strawberries; petroleum refining, plastics prods., industrial machinery. Numerous oil and gas fields. Formed 1869. **8** county (□ 198 sq mi/513 sq km; 1990 pop. 19,561), E central Ky.; ⊙ Mt. Sterling; 38°03′N 83°55′W. Drained by Hinkston and Slate creeks. Rolling upland agr. area, mainly in NE part of Bluegrass region (burley tobacco, corn, soybeans, hay, alfalfa; cattle, poultry; dairying). Mfg. at Mt. Sterling. Formed 1796. **9** county (□ 506 sq mi/1,311 sq km; 1990 pop. 757,027), central Md.; ⊙ Rockville; 39°08′N 77°12′W. Bounded NE by Patuxent R., S by Dist. of Columbia, W and SW by Potomac R. (forms Va. state line here); drained by Rock Creek. Rolling piedmont area containing many residential suburbs (including Chevy Chase, Bethesda, Takoma Park) of Washington. Agr. hinterland produces dairy prods., truck, apples, wheat, hay, cattle, poultry; some mfg. (esp. scientific instruments, wood prods.). Formed in 1776 and named for Gen. Richard Montgomery, killed leading the Amer. attack on Quebec in 1775, the county ceded 60 sq mi/155 sq km to the Federal government in 1790 to form the Dist. of Columbia. One of the most affluent communities in the country, the co. operates 168 parks with a total area of 19,000 acres/7,689 ha. Govt. installations, esp. the Dept. of Health and Human Services and the Food and Drug Administration in Rockville, Bethesda, and Silver springs employ thousands. The Takoma Park Campus of Montgomery Col. was founded in 1945 as the 1st junior col. in the nation. Includes some of Natl. Capital Parks (W), among them Great Falls Park. Josiah Henson, the inspiration for Harriet Beecher Stowe's *Uncle Tom's Cabin*, grew up as a slave in Montgomery co. His mother had been sold to a Montgomery co. planter and his father to a Southern plantation owner. Henson fled to Canada in 1830, and wrote a book, *Truth Stranger than Fiction*, describing his life. An oak log cabin restored near Md. 355 and Old Georgetown Road may have been the home in which Henson, who became a Methodist preacher and Abolitionist speaker, grew up. His descendant, Matthew Henson, accompanied Admiral Robert E. Peary to the North Pole in 1902. **10** county (□ 407 sq mi/1,054 sq km; 1990 pop. 12,388), central Miss.; ⊙ Winona; 33°30′N 89°36′W. Drained by Big Black R. Agr. (cotton, corn, soybeans; cattle); timber. Mfg. at Winona. Formed 1871. **11** county (□ 533 sq mi/1,380 sq km; 1990 pop. 11,355), E central Mo.; ⊙ Montgomery City; 38°58′N 91°29′W. On Missouri R. and drained by the Loutre. Agr. (corn, wheat, soybeans), cattle, sheep, hogs; mfg. at Montgomery City and Jonesburg; limestone, fire-clay pits. Graham Cave State Park in W. Flooding in 1993 destroyed Rhineland and McKittrick in S. Formed 1818. **12** county (□ 410 sq mi/1,062 sq km; 1990 pop. 51,981), E central N.Y.; ⊙ Fonda; 42°53′N 74°25′W. Lies in fertile Mohawk R. valley; traversed by the N.Y. State Barge Canal; also drained by Schoharie Creek. Dairying region, with mfg. centers: Amsterdam (carpets), Canajoharie, Fort Plain, and St. Johnsville. Formed 1772. **13** county (□ 501 sq mi/1,298 sq km; 1990 pop. 23,346), central N.C.; ⊙ Troy; 35°19′N 79°54′W. Bounded W by Yadkin R. (joined by Rocky R., from W, to form Pee Dee R. in SW corner) which forms Badin and Tillery reservoirs; Uwharrie and Little rivers. Bounded SE by Drowning Creek. In forested Piedmont region; agr. area (wheat, soybeans, hay, sweet potatoes, peaches, cotton, tobacco, corn; chicken, cattle, hogs). Some mfg. at Troy and Biscop. Part of Uwharrie Natl. Forest covers most of co., in S center, W, and N. Town Creek Indian Mound State Historical Site in S (16th-cent. reconstruction). Formed 1778. **14** county (□ 465 sq mi/1,204 sq km; 1990 pop. 573,809), W Ohio; ⊙ Dayton; 39°45′N 84°18′W. Intersected by Great Miami, Stillwater, and Mad rivers, and by small Bear, Wolf, and Twin creeks. Miamisburg Mound, and Englewood Dam are here. In the Till Plains physiographic region. Agr. area (hogs, corn, soybeans, tobacco); extensive mfg., especially at Dayton. Sand and gravel pits: cement plants. Formed 1803. **15** county (□ 487 sq mi/1,261 sq km; 1990 pop. 678,111), SE Pa.; ⊙ Norristown; 40°12′N 75°22′W. Bounded SE by Philadelphia; drained by Schuylkill R. (forms part of SW boundary, in W) and Perkiomen Creek (forms Green Lane Reservoir in N) and Pennypack Creek. Co. is highly urbanized in SE and center rural in NW. Agr. (corn, wheat, barley, hay, alfalfa, soybeans; hogs, cattle, dairying); sand and gravel, limestone. Mfg. at Lansdale, Norristown, Hatfield, Telford, Conshohocken, and Collegeville. Part of Valley Forge Natl. Historical Park in SW; Evansburg State Park in center, Fort Washington State Park in S center. Nuclear power plants: Limerick 1 (initial criticality Dec. 22, 1984) and Limerick 2 (initial criticality Aug. 12, 1989) are 21 mi/34 km NW of Philadelphia. Use cooling water from the Schuylkill R., and each has a max. dependable capacity of 1055 MWe. First settled by Swedes and Welsh; later by Germans. Formed 1784. **16** county (□ 543; 1990 pop. 100,498), N Tenn.; ⊙ Clarksville; 36°30′N 87°23′W. Bounded N by Ky.; drained by Cumberland and Red rivers. Agr. (esp. strawberries and dark tobacco), livestock raising. Diversified mfg. at Clarksville. Iron ore and limestone deposits. Has part of Fort Campbell Army base. Formed 1796. **17** county (□ 1,076 sq mi/2,787 sq km; 1990 pop. 182,201), SE Texas; ⊙ Conroe; 30°18′N 95°30′W. Drained by West Fork (forms L. Conroe in NW) of San Jacinto R. and Peach Creek (forms NE boundary). Bounded S by Spring Creek. Oil, natural gas production and processing; sand and gravel are important industries. Also cattle, horses, ratites (ostriches, emus, rheas); fruit, some corn, cotton; nursery and greenhouse prods. Hunting, fishing. Fringe of Houston urbanized area and extension of Houston city limits are in S and SE edge of co. Includes parts of Sam Houston Natl. Forest in NW and NE. Formed 1837. **18** county (□ 389 sq mi/1,008 sq km; 1990 pop. 73,913), SW Va.; ⊙ Christiansburg, 37°10′N 80°23′W. Independent city of Radford, in W, separate from co. Mainly in Great Appalachian Valley, traversed by ridges; Allegheny Mts. are NW, Blue Ridge in SE; bounded W by New R., SW and S by Little R., Roanoke R., and Craig Creek. Mfg. at Christiansburg, Blacksburg; agr. (corn, alfalfa, hay, apples; cattle, sheep; dairying); some bituminous-coal mining; stone quarrying. Includes part of Jefferson Natl. Forest. in NW. Appalachian Trail passes through N corner. Formed 1776.

Montgomery 1 city (1990 pop. 187,106), ⊙ Ala. and Montgomery co., E central Ala. Near the head of navigation on the Alabama R. just below the confluence of the Coosa and Tallapoosa rivers, and in the rich Black Belt. It is an important market center for lumber and agr. goods, esp. livestock and dairy prods. Mfg. includes commercial fertilizer, furniture, air conditioning and heating units, automotive wiring, food items, and paper. Montgomery became the capital of Ala. in 1847 and boomed as a river port and cotton market. The city has been called the "Cradle of the Confederacy." In the capitol bldg. (erected 1857) the convention met (Feb. 1861) that formed the Confederate States of America. Jefferson Davis was inaugurated president on the capitol steps, and the city served as the Confederate capital until the seat was moved to Richmond in May 1861. The city was occupied by Federal troops in the spring of 1865. During the civil rights movement in the 1950s and 1960s, Montgomery was marked by Afr.-Amer. demonstrations, led by Martin Luther King, Jr., who was a minister in Montgomery in the mid-1950s. In Dec. 1955, Afr.-Americans organized a nonviolent boycott of the segregated public bus system; by the following year a desegregation edict regarding public transportation was issued. Racial unrest ensued here in the 1960s. The city is the seat of Ala. State Univ., Auburn Univ. at Montgomery, Huntingdon Col., Troy State Univ., Faulkner Univ., 2 technical schools, and Southern Christian Univ. Maxwell Air Force Base, home of Air Univ., the center of professional military education for the U.S. Air Force, adjoins the city on the NW. In addition to the historic state capitol, points of interest in Montgomery include the "1st White House of the Confederacy" (built c.1825), preserved as a Confederate mus.; a planetarium; a mus. of fine arts; the state archives and history mus.; a zoo; the Ala. Shakespeare festival and many antebellum homes and bldgs. Inc. 1819. **2** city (1990 pop. 9,753), Hamilton co., extreme SW Ohio, a NE suburb of Cincinnati; 39°14′N 84°20′W.

Montgomery 1 town (1990 pop. 645), Grant parish, central La., 36 mi/58 km NW of Alexandria, and on Red R.; 31°40′N 92°54′W. In agr. area (cotton, vegetables, soybeans, cattle); lumber; mfg. (septic tanks). Kisatchie Natl. Forest to N. **2** town (1990 pop. 759), Hampden co., SW Mass., 14 mi/23 km NW of Springfield; 42°13′N 72°49′W. **3** town (1990 pop. 2,399), Le Sueur co., S Minn., 40 mi/64 km SSW of Minneapolis; 44°26′N 93°34′W. Agr. trade center (grain, peas, soybeans; livestock, poultry; dairying); mfg. (canned peas and corn, fireplaces, printing and publishing, hardware). Numerous small lakes in area. Platted 1877, inc. 1902. **4** town (1990 pop. 823), Franklin co., NW Vt., on small Trout R., and 23 mi/37 km E of St. Albans, 44°51′N 72°36′W. Agr., dairying. Chartered 1789, settled 1793. **5** town (1990 pop. 2,449), Kanawha and Fayette cos., W central W.Va., on Kanawha R. (bridged), 22 mi/35 km SE of Charleston; 38°10′N 81°19′W. Bituminous-coal mines; gas and oil wells. Mfg. (coal processing, concrete). Agr. (grain); livestock. W.Va. Univ. Inst. of Technology. Inc. 1890.

Montgomery 1 village (1990 pop. 4,267), Kane co., NE Ill., on Fox R., just SW of Aurora, residential satellite community c.35 mi/56 km WSW of Chicago; 41°43′N 88°20′W. In agr. area (dairy prods.; corn, soybeans); mfg. **2** village (1990 pop. 351), Daviess co., SW Ind., 6 mi/9.7 km E of Washington; 38°40′N 87°03′W. Glendale State Fish and Wildlife Area to S. Mfg. (post buildings, wood trusses). Turkeys, cattle; grain. Bituminous-coal area, surface mines. Laid out 1865. **3** village (1990 pop. 388), Hillsdale co., S Mich., 13 mi/21 km SW of Hillsdale, near Ind. state line (NE corner of Ind.), Ohio state line 5 mi/8 km SE; 41°46′N 84°48′W. In farm area; egg processing; mfg. (auto parts). **4** village (□ 1 sq mi/ 2.6 sq km; 1990 pop. 2,696), Orange co., SE N.Y., on small Wallkill R., and 11 mi/18 km W of Newburgh; 41°31′N 74°14′W. Light mfg. **5** village (1990 pop. 356), Montgomery co., SE Texas, 15 mi/24 km WNW of Conroe; 30°23′N 95°42′W. Timber and agr. area. Light mfg. L. Conroe reservoir to NE. Sam Houston Natl. Forest to N.

Montgomery, borough (1990 pop. 1,631), Lycoming co., N central Pa., 10 mi/16 km ESE of Williamsport, on West Branch of Susquehanna R. (bridged); 41°10′N 76°52′W. Agr. area (grain, potatoes, soybeans; livestock, dairying); mfg. (paper processing equip., lumber, truck bodies, commercial printing, wooden furniture, aluminum and vinyl blinds, apparel, plastic prods.). Allenwood Federal Prison Camp to SW; Muncy State Correctional Inst. to NE. Tiadaghton State Forest to N. Settled 1778, inc. 1887.

Montgomery, township (1990 pop. 9,612), Somerset co., N N.J., 10 mi/16 km N of Princeton; 40°25′N 74°40′W. Inc. 1798.

Montgomery City, city (1990 pop. 2,281), ⊙ Montgomery co., E central Mo., 25 mi/40 km ENE of Fulton; 38°58′N 91°30′W. Corn, wheat, soybeans; cattle; mfg. (commercial printing, toll booths, feeds, apparel). Laid out 1853.

Montgomery Pass (mahnt-GUHM-ree) (7,132 ft/ 2,174 m), SW Nev., in N White Mts., N of Boundary Peak, 60 mi/97 km W of Tonopah, 8 mi/12.9 km NE of Calif. state line. U.S. Highway 6 passage. In Inyo Natl. Forest.

Montgomery Peak, Calif.: see WHITE MOUNTAINS.

Montgomeryville, uninc. town (1990 pop. 9,114), Montgomery co., SE Pa., suburb 20 mi/32 km N of Philadelphia; 40°15′N 75°14′W. Mfg. includes fabricated metal prods., infrared detectors, cement paste, commercial printing, caulking compounds, plastic prods., clothing, fencing, microwave components.

Monticello 1 city (1990 pop. 4,549), ⊙ Piatt co., central Ill., on Sangamon R. (bridged here) and 24 mi/39 km ENE of Decatur; 40°01′N 88°24′W. In rich agr. area; mfg. (drugs, food prods.); corn, soybeans, wheat, livestock, dairy prods. Inc. 1841. **2** city (1990 pop. 5,237), ⊙ White co., NW central Ind., on Tippecanoe R., bet. Shafer and Freeman lakes, and 21 mi/34 km W of Logansport; 40°45′N 86°46′W. In agr. area (corn, oats, soybeans; hogs); Light mfg. Resort area. Settled 1831, laid out 1834, inc. 1853. **3** city (1990 pop. 3,522), Jones co., E Iowa, on Maquoketa R., and 10 mi/16 km NE of Anamosa; 42°14′N 91°11′W. Mfg. (farm equip., feed, concrete prods.). Limestone quarries nearby. Settled 1836, inc. 1867.

Monticello 1 (mahn-tuh-SEL-o), town (1990 pop. 8,116), ⊙ Drew co., SE Ark., c.45 mi/72 km SSE of Pine Bluff; 33°37′N 91°47′W. Industrial center for agr. area; lumber milling, mfg. (printing, tables, elastomeric liquid containers, recreational boats, polyester and nylon textile yarns, trash bags, lumber). Univ of Ark. at Monticello campus SW of town. **2** town (□ 3 sq mi/ 7.8 sq km; 1990 pop. 2,573), ⊙ Jefferson co., N central Fla., 27 mi/43 km ENE of Tallahassee, near Ga. state line and L. Miccosukee; 30°32′N 83°52′W. Farm trade center, plywood mfg. Settled in early 19th cent. **3** town (1990 pop. 2,289), ⊙ Jasper co., central Ga., 32 mi/ 51 km N of Macon, 33°19′N 83°41′W. Mfg. of lumber, industrial axles, plywood; feldspar mining and processing. Inc. 1810. Oconee Natl. Forest in area. **4** town (1990 pop. 5,357), ⊙ Wayne co., S Ky., in Cumberland foothills, 23 mi/37 km SW of Somerset; 36°50′N 84°50′W. In area of agr. (corn, burley tobacco, wheat; livestock; timber). Mfg. (poultry processing, steel pipes, sleepwear, shirts and blouses, houseboats, kitchen cabinets, blue jeans). Wayne County Airport to NW. Camp Earl Wallace Conservation Education Center to SW. Large L. Cumberland reservoir (Cumberland R.) to NW. Settled before 1800. **5** town (1990 pop. 872), Aroostook co., E Maine, on Meduxnekeag R., and 13 mi/21 km N of Houlton; 46°19′N 67°50′W. Potatoes shipped. Settled 1830, inc. 1846. **6** (mawn-ti-SE-lo), town (1990 pop. 4,941), Wright co., E Minn., on Mississippi R., and 35 mi/56 km NW of Minneapolis; 45°17′N 93°47′W. Grain, soybeans; livestock; dairying; mfg. (molded prods., hand tools, cabinets, fabricated structural metals). Several small lakes in area. L. Maria State Park to W; Sherburn Natl. Wildlife Refuge and Sand Dunes State Forest to NE. Nuclear Power Plant. Inc. 1856. **7** (mahnt-uh-SEL-o), town (1990 pop. 1,755), ⊙ Lawrence co., S central Miss., 20 mi/32 km E of Brookhaven, and on Pearl R.; 31°33′N 90°06′W. In agr. (cotton, corn; cattle, hogs, poultry) and timber area; mfg. (linerboard, sportswear, industrial screens, lumber). RR junction to N. L. Mary Crawford State L. to W; Armstrong-Lee House (1856); Fox House (1848). Founded 1798. **8** (mahn-tee-SEL-o), town (1990 pop. 106), ⊙ Lewis co., NE Mo., on North Fabius R., near the Mississippi, and 20 mi/32 km NW of Quincy, Ill.; 40°07′N 91°42′W. Corn, soybeans; cattle, hogs. **9** town (1990 pop. 1,806), ⊙ San Juan co., SE Utah, 50 mi/ 80 km SSE of Moab; 37°52′N 109°20′W. Flour-milling point in wheat and cattle area; mining of uranium and vanadium ores. Abajo Mts. are just W, in sect. of La Sal Natl. Forest. Elev. 7,066 ft/2,154 m. Canyonlands Natl. Park and Newspaper Rock State Park to NW. Settled 1888. **10** town (1990 pop. 1,140), Green co., S Wis., 10 mi/16 km N of Monroe; 42°45′N 89°35′W. In agr. area; mfg. cooperative (feed, cheese, wire garment hangers). On Sugar R. State Trail.

Monticello, resort village (□ 3 sq mi/7.8 sq km; 1990 pop. 6,597), ⊙ Sullivan co., SE N.Y., 20 mi/32 km NW of Middletown; 41°38′N 74°41′W. In timber, dairying, and declining recreational lake area; mfg. (furniture, steel fabrication, construction materials); sand and gravel. Inc. 1830.

Monticello, [Ital. = little mountain], estate, Albemarle co., central Va., 4 mi/6.4 km SE of Charlottesville, on Rivanna R.; home of Thomas Jefferson for 56 years. Covers of 640 acres/259 ha. The mansion, which he designed, was begun in 1770 on property inherited from his father. The bldg. materials — stone, brick, lumber, and nails — were prepared on the estate, and most of the construction work was carried out by Jefferson's artisan slaves. By 1772, when Jefferson took his bride there to live, part of the house was ready for occupancy; for many years afterward, he added to the bldg. The house is one of the earliest examples of the Amer. classic revival style. Not long after Jefferson's death, his daughter, unable to maintain the property, sold it, retaining only the family burial plot in which Jefferson is interred. Monticello was later bought by Uriah P. Levy, a naval officer, who bequeathed it to "the people of the United States," but his heirs successfully contested the will. By 1879, Jefferson P. Levy was in full ownership, but he sold Monticello in 1923 to the Thomas Jefferson Memorial Foundation. Dedicated as a natl. shrine in 1926, and extensively renovated during the next 30 years, the estate was opened to the public in 1954.

Monticello Nuclear Power Plant, Minn.: see WRIGHT, CO.

Mont-Joli (moh zho–LEE), town (1991 pop. 6,265), E Que., Canada, near the St. Lawrence, 18 mi/29 km NE of Rimouski; 48°35′N 68°11′W. On RR spur to Matane; RR junction, highway junction. RR workshops, metal foundries, lumber mill; hydroelectric station. Dairying, pig-raising region. Airfield.

Montmagny (moh-mahn-YEE), county (□ 630 sq mi/ 1,632 sq km; 1991 pop. 23,667), SE Que., Canada, on the St. Lawrence R. and Maine border; ⊙ Montmagny; 46°50′N 70°20′W.

Montmagny, town (1991 pop. 11,861), SE Que., Canada, on the St. Lawrence R.; 46°58′N 70°33′W. Mfg. includes textiles, furniture, and household appliances.

Montmartre, village (1991 pop. 471), SE Sask., near small Chapleau Lakes, 23 mi/37 km SE of Indian Head; 50°13′N 103°27′W. Mixed farming.

Montmorenci 1 village (1990 pop. 300), Tippecanoe co., W central Ind., 7 mi/11.3 km NW of Lafayette. Mfg. Corn, soybeans, cattle, hogs. Laid out 1838. **2** (mahnt-muh-REN-see), uninc. village, Aiken co., SW S.C., 5 mi/8 km ESE of Aiken. Agr. includes livestock; grain, cotton, peanuts, poultry.

Montmorency, county (□ 562 sq mi/1,456 sq km; 1990 pop. 8,936), N Mich.; 45°01′N 84°07′W; ⊙ Atlanta. Drained by Thunder Bay, Rainy, and Black rivers. Dairying, corn; cattle; industrial machinery; also a recreation area, with state forest, game refuge, small lakes. Clear L. State Park in N, Sheridan Valley Ski Area in SW; large Fletcher Pond on E boundary. Organized 1881.

Montmorency (mahnt-muh-REHN-see), town, S Que., Canada, at the confluence of the St. Lawrence and Montmorency rivers; now part of the municipality of Beauport; 46°53′N 71°09′W. It is a suburb of Quebec city and the site of the scenic Montmorency Falls.

Montmorency, river, c.60 mi/100 km long, Canada; rising in the Laurentian Mts., S Que.; flowing generally S to the St. Lawrence R.; 46°53′N 71°09′W. Near its mouth are Montmorency Falls (275 ft/84 m high), providing hydroelectric power.

Montmorency No. 1 and **Montmorency No. 2** (moh-mo-rah-SEE), county (□ 2,198 sq mi/5,693 sq km), S Que., Canada, on the St. Lawrence. Montmorency No. 1 (47°30′N 71°15′W) consists of mainland, from St. Lawrence NW into Laurentides Prov. Park. Montmorency No. 2 (46°55′N 70°58′W) consists of Île d'Orléans in St. Lawrence; ⊙ Sainte Famille.

Mont-Organisé (mong–or-gah-nee-ZAI), agr. town (1982 pop. 1,513), Nord-Est dept., NE Haiti, near Dominican Republic border, 17 mi/27 km SSE of Fort Liberté; 19°24′N 71°47′W. Coffee growing and processing; citrus fruit; gold deposits.

Montour (mahn-TOOR), county (□ 132 sq mi/ 342 sq km; 1990 pop. 17,735), central Pa.; ⊙ Danville; 41°01′N 76°39′W. Drained by Susquehanna R. (forms part of S boundary) and Chillisquaque Creek. Agr.

(corn, wheat, oats, barley, hay, alfalfa, soybeans; sheep, hogs, cattle, poultry; dairying); limestone. Mfg. at Danville. Smallest co. in land area in Pa. L. Chillisquaque reservoir in Montour Preserve in N. Formed 1850.

Montour, town (1990 pop. 312), Tama co., central Iowa, on Iowa R. and 7 mi/11.3 km E of Toledo; 41°58′N 92°43′W. Limestone quarries nearby.

Montour Falls, village (☐ 3 sq mi/7.8 sq km; 1990 pop. 1,845), Schuyler co., W central N.Y., in Finger Lakes region, just SE of Watkins Glen, and on small Catherine Creek; 42°21′N 76°50′W. Summer resort. Chequaga (or Shequaga) Falls (156 ft/48 m) here attract tourists, esp. when snowmelt in the spring enhances the awesome spectacle.

Montoursville (mahn-TOORS-vil), borough (1990 pop. 4,983), Lycoming co., N central Pa., suburb 4 mi/ 6.4 km E of Williamsport, on West Branch of Susquehanna R., at mouth of Loyalsock Creek; 41°15′N 76°55′W. Mfg. (paper, fabricated metal prods., concrete, printing, furniture). Williamsport-Lycoming Co. Airport in S. Parts of Tiadaghton State Forest to N and S. Settled 1807, laid out 1820, inc. 1850.

Montpelier, city (1990 pop. 1,880), Blackford co., E Ind., on Salamonie R., and 8 mi/12.9 km NE of Hartford City. In agr. area (livestock; dairy prods.; soybeans; corn, grain); mfg. (grip nuts, corrugated containers, glass prods., gloves); old natural gas and oil wells; stone quarries. Settled 1836, laid out 1837, inc. 1937.

Montpelier, town, St. James parish, NW Jamaica, on Jamaica RR, and 8 mi/12.9 km S of Montego Bay; 18°23′N 77°56′W. In fertile agr. region, growing principally bananas.

Montpelier (mahnt-PEEL-yuhr), city (1990 pop. 8,247), ☉ Washington co. and Vt. (since 1805), central Vt., at the junction of the Winooski and North Branch rivers; 44°16′N 72°34′W. The economy is dominated by state govt. and insurance industries. It is also a trading center in a lumber, granite, and winter-resort area. Granite is processed here; mfg. includes printing, plastics, textiles, and sawmill machinery. Montpelier shares an airport with Barre to SE. Vermont Col. of Norwich Univ., a community col., the state historical society, and a state school for children with special needs are here. Of interest are the state capitol and an art gallery for wood sculpture. Surrounded by mts., the city has an excellent view of Mt. Mansfield, the highest point in the state. Admiral George Dewey b. here. Airport. Inc. 1855.

Montpelier, town (1990 pop. 2,656), Bear Lake co., extreme SE Idaho, near Bear R., 70 mi/113 km SE of Pocatello; 42°19′N 111°18′W. Elev. c.5,943 ft/1,811 m. RR div. point, trade and shipping center for agr. and grazing area; dairying; mfg. (dairy feeds, light mfg.). Phosphate deposits nearby. Founded 1864 by Mormons. Early names: Clover Creek, Belmont. Renamed (1865) by Brigham Young in honor of Vt. capital. Has Mormon tabernacle. Caribou Natl. Forest to NE, Cache Natl. Forest to W.

Montpelier 1 (mahnt-PEEL-yuhr), village (1990 pop. 247), St. Helena parish, SE La., 33 mi/53 km ENE of Baton Rouge, on Tickfaw R.; 30°41′N 90°39′W. Agr. and timber area. Mfg. (feeds, dog food, sausage). **2** village (1990 pop. 82), Stutsman co., SE central N.Dak., 16 mi/ 26 km SSE of Jamestown, and on James R.; 46°42′N 98°35′W. **3** village (1990 pop. 4,299), Williams co., extreme NW Ohio, on St. Joseph R., and 8 mi/13 km NNW of Bryan; 41°35′N 84°36′W. Wood fixtures, metal stampings, truck bodies. Settled 1855, inc. 1875. **4** uninc. village, Hanover co., E Va., 25 mi/40 km NNW of Richmond. Agr. (dairying; livestock; grain).

Montreal (mahn-tree-OL), city (1991 pop. 1,017,666), S Que., Canada, on Montreal isl., surrounded by St. Lawrence R. and Rivière des Prairies; 45°31′N 73°34′W. Montreal is the 2d-largest metropolitan area in Canada, after Toronto, and is a cultural, tourist, commercial, financial, and industrial center. It is the 2d-largest Fr.-speaking city in the world, though most of its inhabitants also speak Eng. Montreal lies at the foot of Mt. Royal—the source of its name—and has an excellent harbor on the St. Lawrence Seaway, which connects the city to the great industrial centers of the Great Lakes.

Canada's most important port, Montreal is a transshipment point for oil, grain, sugar, machinery, and manufactured goods. It is also an important RR hub, and it has 2 internatl. airports, Dorval and Mirabel. Montreal's underground RR system, the Métro, was inaugurated in 1966. Mfg. includes steel, electronic equip., refined petroleum, transportation materials and equip., raw textiles, clothing, food and beverages, printed materials, and tobacco. Once Canada's preeminent city, Montreal has been eclipsed by Toronto as the country's economic center. Tensions over Que.'s insistence on enforcing its francophone culture have caused an outmigration of Eng.-speaking people to Ontario and to the growing W provs. Despite these changes, Montreal remains one of N. Amer.'s great cosmopolitan cities, and had a burst of prosperity in the 1980s due to its growth as a financial service center. A stockaded Native-Amer. village, Hochelaga, was found on the site (1535) by Cartier, and the isl. was visited in 1603 by Champlain, but it was not settled by the French until 1642, when a band of priests, nuns, and settlers under Paul de Chomedey, Sieur de Maisonneuve, founded the Ville Marie de Montréal. The settlement grew to become an important center of the fur trade and the starting point for the W expeditions of Jolliet, Marquette, La Salle, Vérendrye, and Duluth. It was fortified in 1725 and remained in Fr. possession until 1760, when Vaudreuil de Cavagnal surrendered it to Brit. forces under Amherst. Americans under Richard Montgomery occupied it briefly (1775–1776) during the Amer. Revolution. The city's growth was aided by the opening in 1825 of the Lachine Canal, making possible water communications with the Great Lakes. From 1844 to 1849, Montreal was the capital of United Canada. The Can. Pacific RR established its hq. here in the 1880s. The area of Old Montreal has undergone extensive restoration and few buildings from the Fr. period are extant. Among the city's notable buildings are the Gothic Church of Notre Dame (c.1820), St. Sulpice Seminary (1685), the Château de Ramezay (1705), and the Place Ville Marie (1962). Montreal is the seat of McGill Univ., the Univ. of Montreal, the Univ. of Que. at Montreal, and Concordia Univ. Expo '67, the intl. exposition of 1967, was held in the city. Montreal hosted the 1976 Summer Olympics, which created a great financial burden. Its professional hockey team, the Montreal Canadiens, has won 23 Stanley Cups, making it one of the athletic world's most enduring dynasties. In late 1960s, Montreal experienced a high-rise building boom; a system of underground promenades of shops and restaurants was created, linking office bldgs. (Place Ville Marie and Place Bonaventure), the Queen Elizabeth Hotel, train station, subway, arts center, and other facilities.

Montreal (mahn-tree-AWL), town (1990 pop. 838), Iron co., N Wis., in Gogebic Range, 2 mi/3.2 km W of Hurley, on Gile Flowage near Gile Falls; 46°25′N 90°14′W. Iron mining; forestry. Inc. 1924.

Montreal Island 1 S Franklin dist., N.W.T., Canada, in Chantrey Inlet, on E side of Adelaide Peninsula; 13 mi/ 21 km long, 2 mi/3 km–4 mi/6 km wide; 67°52′N 96°20′W. **2** (☐ 201 sq mi/521 sq km), S Que., Canada, bounded by L. St. Louis (S), the St. Lawrence (E), and R. des Prairies (NW), branch of Ottawa R.; 30 mi/ 48 km long, up to 10 mi/16 km wide. Isl. is coextensive with Montreal Isl. co., including former cos. of Hochelaga and Jacques Cartier. Great part of isl. is occupied by Montreal city and its suburbs.

Montreal Lake, (☐ 162 sq mi/420 sq km), central Sask., Canada, 60 mi/97 km N of Prince Albert; 32 mi/51 km long, 7 mi/11 km wide. Drains N into Churchill R. through Lac la Ronge.

Montreal River, 90 mi/145 km long, central Ont., Canada; flows S and WSW to L. Superior 50 mi/80 km NNW of Sault Ste. Marie. Montreal Falls (150 ft/46 m) is 10 mi/16 km above its mouth; hydroelectric power.

Montreal River, c.40 mi/64 km long, in Wis. and Mich.; rises in Iron co., N Wis., in small Pine L.; flows N and NW, past Ironwood, Mich., and Hurley, Wis., to L. Superior; forms part of Mich.-Wis. state line for most of its length.

Montreal-Nord, city (1991 pop. 85,516), S central Que., Canada, residential suburb 6 mi/10 km NW of downtown Montreal, on Montreal isl., on SE bank of Prairies R.; 45°36′N 73°37′W. Bounded on S by city of Montreal, on E by St.-Leonard.

Montreal-Ouest, city (1991 pop. 5,180), S central Que., Canada, residential suburb 5 mi/8 km SSW of downtown Montreal, on Montreal isl.; 45°27′N 73°39′W. Canal Lachine on SE.

Montreat (MAHN-treet), village (1990 pop. 693), Buncombe co., W N.C., 14 mi/23 km E of Asheville, in the Blue Ridge Mts.; 35°38′N 82°17′W. Cattle, poultry, corn, tobacco. Montreat-Anderson Col. (2-yr). Pisgah Natl. Forest to NE.

Montrose, village (1986 pop. 1,183), 3.1 mi/5 km SE of Trail, B.C., Canada. Residential settlement near smelter town.

Montrose, county (☐ 2,242 sq mi/5,807 sq km; 1990 pop. 24,423), W Colo., ☉ Montrose; 38°24′N 108°16′W. Agr. region bordering Utah; drained by Dolores, San Miguel, and Uncompahgre rivers. Fruit, beans, hay, livestock. Mining of uranium, radium, coal, silver, copper. Includes parts of Uncompahgre, Gunnison, and La Sal natl. forests and, in NE, Black Canyon of the Gunnison Natl. Monument. Crystal Reservoir and part of Morrow Point Reservoir Natl. Recreation Area (part of Curecanti Natl. Recreation Area) in E; part of Gunnison Natl. Forest in far E; part of Uncompahgre Natl. Forest in center, part of Manti La Sal Natl. Forest on W boundary (with Utah). Uncompahgre Plateau bisects co. NW-SE; regular highway connections via neighboring counties. Formed 1883.

Montrose (mahn-TROZ), city (1990 pop. 440), Henry co., W central Mo., 14 mi/23 km SW of Clinton; 38°15′N 93°58′W. Corn, wheat, soybeans; cattle; mfg. (lead castings, fishing lures). Montrose Conservation Area to N. Strip coal mining. Coal-fired electric power generating plant (Kansas City).

Montrose 1 uninc. town, Los Angeles co., S Calif., in foothills of San Gabriel Mts., suburb 11 mi/18 km N of downtown Los Angeles, N of Glendale. Mfg. (electronic coils, plastics prods.). **2** town (1990 pop. 8,854), ☉ Montrose co., W Colo., on Uncompahgre R., and 55 mi/89 km SE of Grand Junction; 38°28′N 107°52′W. Elev. 5,794 ft/1,766 m. RR terminus spur from Delta. Trade center in irrigated fruit, potato, sugarbeet region; meat and dairy prods., flour; mfg. (signs, lumber, hydroelectric testing equip., boxed chocolates). Carnotite deposits nearby are source of radium and uranium. Black Canyon of the Gunnison Natl. Monument to NE. Nearby Gunnison Tunnel conducts water from Gunnison R. to Uncompahgre valley. Ute Indian Mus. to S, Curranti Natl. Recreation Area to E. Founded and inc. 1882. **3** town (1990 pop. 957), Lee co., extreme SE Iowa, on Mississippi R. and 10 mi/16 km SE of Fort Madison, in livestock area; 40°31′N 91°25′W. One of the 1st permanent white settlements in Iowa was made here in 1799, when Louis Tesson, a Fr. Canadian, established a trading post. Town was laid out in 1837. **4** (mahn-TROS), town (1990 pop. 1,811), Genesee co., SE central Mich., suburb 15 mi/24 km NW of Flint; 43°10′N 83°53′W. In farm area; lumber. **5** (MAWN-troz), town (1990 pop. 1,008), Wright co., S central Minn., 8 mi/ 12.9 km S of Buffalo; 45°04′N 93°54′W. Poultry; dairying; mfg. (speaker systems, color dispensers). Small natural lakes in area. **6** uninc. town, Henrico co., E central Va., residential suburb 4 mi/6.4 km ESE of downtown Richmond; 37°31′N 77°22′W. Richmond National Cemetery to W, Richmond Internatl. Airport to E.

Montrose 1 (MAHN-troz), village (1990 pop. 528), Ashley co., SE Ark., 12 mi/19 km W of Lake Village; 33°17′N 91°30′W. Mfg. (barbecue sauce). **2** (mahn-TROZ), village (1990 pop. 117), Laurens co., central Ga., 15 mi/ 24 km W of Dublin; 32°34′N 83°09′W. **3** village (1990 pop. 306), Effingham co., SE central Ill., 8 mi/12.9 km ENE of Effingham; 39°10′N 88°22′W. In agr. area. **4** (mahnt-ROZ), village (1990 pop. 106), Jasper co., E central Miss., 35 mi/56 km WSW of Meridian, in Bienville Natl. Forest; 32°07′N 89°14′W. Agr. and timber area. **5** village (1990 pop. 420), McCook co., SE S.Dak., 10 mi/16 km E of Salem; 43°42′N 97°10′W. Lake Vermillion State Rec. Area to S. **6** (MAHN-troz), uninc. village (1990 pop. 140), Randolph co., E W.Va., 11 mi/18 km N of Elkins; 39°04′N 79°48′W. Monongahela Natl. Forest to E.

Montrose (MAHN-tros), borough (1990 pop. 1,982), ⊙ Susquehanna co., NE Pa., 31 mi/50 km NNW of Scranton; 41°49′N 75°52′W. Agr. (corn, hay; livestock; dairying); mfg. (wooden prods., cabinet parts, machinery, printing and publishing, cement reinforcing materials, textile prods.); mt. resort area with numerous small lakes. Salt Springs State Park to N. Settled 1799, inc. 1824.

Montrose-Ghent, uninc. village (1990 pop. 4,906), Summit co., NE Ohio, just NW of Akron; 41°10′N 81°38′W. Large-scale retailing.

Montross, town (1990 pop. 359), ⊙ Westmoreland co., E Va., 38 mi/61 km ESE of Fredericksburg; 38°05′N 76°49′W. Mfg. (printing and publishing, seafood processing, computer cable assemblies, lumber); agr. (grain, soybeans; cattle). George Washington Birthplace Natl. Monument to NW; "Stratford Hall," birthplace of Robert E. Lee, Westmoreland State Park to N.

Mont-Royal or **Mount Royal**, city (1991 pop. 18,212), S central Que., Canada, suburb 3 mi/5 km W of downtown Montreal, on Montreal isl.; 45°31′N 73°39′W. Bounded N and S by Montreal, E by Outremont, W by St.-Laurent.

Monts, Pointe des (MOII, pwcht dai), cape on the Gulf of St. Lawrence, E Que., Canada, on N side of mouth of the St. Lawrence, opposite Gaspé Peninsula, 36 mi/58 km ENE of Baie Comeau; 49°20′N 67°22′W; lighthouse.

Montserrat (mawn-suh-RAHT), island and Br. dependency in Lesser Antilles (□ 38 sq mi/98 sq km; 1994 est. pop. 13,000), West Indies, one of the Leeward Isls.; ⊙ Plymouth. It is a rugged, scenic isl. of volcanic origin. Plymouth is only outlet for the cotton and other agr. prods. of the isl. Tourism has become the economic mainstay, accounting for 25% of the isl.'s GNP. Mainly known for producing calypso music records (there's a recording studio on the isl.). Highest point is Chance's Peak in the Soufrière Hills (elev. 3,002 ft/915 m). Columbus sighted the isl. in 1493 and named it Santa María de Montserrat after a monastery near Barcelona. Was 1st settled in 1632 by Irish Catholics from St. Kitts, possibly seeking religious freedom. It developed a prosperous sugar industry, which suffered from the abolition of slavery in 1834 and was replaced by raising limes. After changing hands several times bet. France and Britain, it was ceded to Great Britain in 1783. The isl. was a member of the former Leeward Isls. colony and of the Federation of the West Indies. In 1966, Montserrat rejected self-government. The isl. suffered extensive damage from a hurricane in 1989 and again when the Soufrière Hills volcano erupted in July 1997 after 400 years of dormancy. The eruption buried the S ½ of the isl. under lava and ash, and most of the pop. had to be evacuated.

Montserrat Hills (mon-sai-RAHT), low range in W central Trinidad, Trinidad and Tobago, 20 mi/32 km SE of Port of Spain. Rises to 918 ft/280 m.

Montvale, borough (1990 pop. 6,946), Bergen co., NE N.J., 10 mi/16 km N of Hackensack; 41°02′N 74°02′W. Makes clothing and paperboard. Inc. 1894. In suburban area.

Montverde (mahn-tuh-VER-dee), village (□ 1 sq mi/2.6 sq km; 1990 pop. 890), Lake co., central Fla., near L. Apopka, 19 mi/31 km W of Orlando; 28°36′N 81°40′W. Grapes.

Montville, town (1990 pop. 16,673), New London co., SE Conn., 7 mi/11.3 km NNW of New London; 41°27′N 72°09′W. Paper prods., sheet metal, computer boards, tachometers, aluminum doors and windows, and boxes are made. High security state prison; former nuclear submarine building site. Nearby are the Tantaquidgeon Native-Amer. Mus. and a state park. Founded 1670, inc. 1786.

Montville, township (1990 pop. 15,600), Morris co., N

N.J., 10 mi/16 km W of Paterson; 40°54′N 74°21′W. Mfg. (drugs, crushed stone). Largely residential.

Montville, Mass.: see SANDISFIELD.

Monument, town (1990 pop. 1,020), El Paso co., central Colo., on Monument Creek, in SE foothills of Front Range, 15 mi/24 km N of Colorado Springs, and 45 mi/72 km S of Denver; 39°04′N 104°51′W. Elev. 6,961 ft/2,122 m. Mfg. (cable prods., light mfg.). Pike Natl. Forest to W. U.S. Air Force Acad. to S. Natl. Carvers Mus. to S.

Monument 1 uninc. village (1990 pop. 300), Lea co., SE N.Mex., 13 mi/21 km WSW of Hobbs. Diversified irrigated agr. area on Llano Estacado. Cattle, sheep, cotton, grain, alfalfa, dairying. Mfg. (oil and natural gas production). **2** village (1990 pop. 162), Grant co., NE central Oregon, 27 mi/43 km NW of Canyon City, on North Fork of John Day R.; 44°49′N 119°25′W. Part of Umatilla Natl. Forest to N.

Monument Beach, Mass.: see BOURNE.

Monument Creek, 34 mi/55 km long, central Colo.; rises in Front Range in NW El Paso co.; flows generally S, past Palmer L. and Monument towns, through E side of U.S. Air Force Acad., to Fountain Creek at Colorado Springs.

Monument Mountain (1,710 ft/521 m), peak of the Berkshires, SW Mass., in Monument Mt. State Reservation (□ 260 acres/105 ha), 4 mi/6.4 km N of Great Barrington.

Mooar (MOO-are), village, Lee co., extreme SE Iowa, 15 mi/24 km SW of Madison. Explosives plant.

Moodus (MOO-duhs), village (1990 pop. 1,170), East Haddam town, Middlesex co., S Conn., near the Connecticut R.; 41°30′N 72°27′W. "Moodus noises," subterranean rumblings about which Indians had legends, believed to be caused by minor earthquakes beneath hill here. Summer camps and resorts. Former poultry raising.

Moody, county (□ 521 sq mi/1,349 sq km; 1990 pop. 6,507), E S.Dak., on Minn. state line; ⊙ Flandreau; 44°01′N 96°40′W. Rich farming and livestock-raising region drained by Big Sioux R. and Pipestone Creek. Corn, soybeans; hogs, cattle, sheep; dairying. Flandreau Indian Reservation N of Flandreau. Formed 1873.

Moody 1 town (1990 pop. 4,921), St. Clair co., N central Ala., c.15 mi/24 km E of Birmingham; 33°35′N 86°29′W. **2** town (1990 pop. 1,329), McLennan co., E central Texas, 21 mi/34 km SSW of Waco; 31°18′N 97°21′W. Elev. 783 ft/239 m. In farm area (cattle; grains; dairying); mfg. (pecan and honey processing). Mother Neff State Park on Belton L. reservoir to W. Inc. 1901.

Moody Air Force Base, U.S. military base, Lowndes co., S Ga., N of Valdosta. Established at the beginning of World War II. Largest employer in co.

Mooers, village (1990 pop. 467), Clinton co., extreme NE N.Y., on Great Chazy R., and 20 mi/32 km NNW of Plattsburgh; 44°58′N 73°35′W. Port of entry, at Que. border 3.3 mi/5.3 km NNW.

Moomaw, Lake (□ 4 sq mi/10.4 sq km), Alleghany and Bath cos., W Va., on Jackson River, in Monongahela Natl. Forest, 10 mi/16 km N of Covington; 37°58′N 79°57′W. Max. capacity 421,500 acre-ft. Formed by Gathright Dam (also known as Moomaw Dam; 257 ft/78 m high), built (1978) by Army Corps of Engineers for flood control; also used for recreation.

Moon, Pa.: see CARNOT-MOON.

Moon Island, in Boston Harbor, E Mass., 5 mi/8 km S of Boston, E of Quincy. Connects to Quincy by causeway. Former site of sewage treatment plant. Later Boston Police Dept. outdoor firearms range and bomb disposal, also Boston Fire Dept. training facility. Connected to Long Isl. by Long Isl. Bridge. Restricted use by the city of Boston.

Moon Lake, Miss.: see LULA.

Moon Lake Dam, Utah: see LAKE FORK.

Moon Run, uninc. town (1990 pop. 800), Robinsoe township, Allegheny co., W Pa., suburb 5 mi/8 km W of downtown Pittsburgh; 40°27′N 80°06′W. In bituminous-coal and agr. area.

Moonachie (moo-NAH-KEE), borough (1990 pop.

2,817), Bergen co., NE N.J., 3 mi/4.8 km S of Hackensack; 40°50′N 74°03′W. Inc. 1910. Largely residential. Hq. for milk distribution; soy; plastics.

Moonridge, uninc. town (1990 pop. 2,700), San Bernardino co., S Calif., ENE of San Bernardino, on S shore of Big Bear L. Recreation area. Tourism. Area surrounded by San Bernardino Natl. Forest.

Moorcroft, town (1990 pop. 768), Crook co., NE Wyo., on Belle Fourche R., and 30 mi/48 km WSW of Sundance; 44°15′N 104°57′W. Elev. c.4,206 ft/1,282 m. Trade and shipping center in livestock, timber region; oil refinery. Oil wells nearby. Keyhole Reservoir (Belle Fourche R.) and Keyhole State Park to NE.

Moore 1 county (□ 706 sq mi/1,829 sq km; 1990 pop. 59,013), central N.C.; ⊙ Carthage; 35°18′N 79°28′W. Forested sand hills in Piedmont region; drained by Deep R., bounded SE by Little R., SW by Drowning Creek. Agr. area (tobacco, peaches, corn, wheat, oats, barley, soybeans, hay, cattle, hogs); timber; sawmilling, textile mfg. Bounded in SE by Fort Bragg Military Reserve. House in the Horseshoe State Historical Site in NE. Weymouth Wood State Park (Sandhills Nature Preserve) in SE. Formed 1784. **2** county (□ 122 sq mi/316 sq km; pop. 130), S Tenn.; ⊙ Lynchburg; 35°17′N 86°22′W. Bounded SE by Elk R. Livestock, corn, tobacco, timber. Formed 1871. **3** county (□ 909 sq mi/2,354 sq km; 1990 pop. 17,865), extreme N Texas; ⊙ Dumas; 35°50′N 101°53′W. Elev. 3,000 ft/914 m–4,000 ft/1,219 m. In high plains of the Panhandle; drained in SE by Canadian R. One of richest areas in the huge Panhandle natural gas and oil field; helium production; wheat, corn, sorghum, pinto beans farming, cattle ranching. Part of L. Meredith reservoir (Canadian R.) and L. Meredith Natl. Recreation Area in SE corner. Formed 1876.

Moore, city (1990 pop. 40,318), Cleveland co., central Okla., suburb 9 mi/14.5 km S of downtown Oklahoma City; 35°19′N 97°28′W. Mfg. (lightning and surge protection equip., packaging for food condiments, bumpers and grill guards, printing). Inc. 1887.

Moore 1 village (1990 pop. 190), Butte co., SE central Idaho, 7 mi/11.3 km NNW of Arco, on Big Lost R.; 43°44′N 113°22′W. Parts of Challis Natl. Forest to E and W. **2** village (1990 pop. 211), Fergus co., central Mont., 13 mi/21 km WSW of Lewistown; 46°58′N 109°42′W. Livestock; wheat, barley, hay. Ackley Lake State Park to W. Part of Lewis and Clark Natl. Forest to SE. **3** uninc. village, Spartanburg co., NW S.C., 8 mi/12.9 km SSW of Spartanburg, near Tyger R. Mfg. includes silicon wafers, contract embroidery, recycled cotton waste. **4** uninc. village (1990 pop. 230), Frio co., SW Texas, c.40 mi/64 km SW of San Antonio. Winter vegetables, melons, corn, peanuts; hogs, cattle; natural gas wells.

Moore Haven, town (□ 1 sq mi/2.6 sq km; 1990 pop. 1,432), ⊙ Glades co., S central Fla., c.50 mi/80 km ENE of Fort Myers, on W shore of L. Okeechobee near entrance (lock here) to Caloosahatchee R.; 26°49′N 81°05′W. Small-scale farming, fishing.

Moore Reservoir, NW N.H. and NE Vt., on Connecticut R., 4 mi/6.4 km WNW of Littleton, N.H.; c.10 mi/16 km long; 44°20′N 71°51′W. Max. capacity 115,000 acre-ft. Formed by Moore Dam (178 ft/54 m), built (1956) by the Connecticut R. Power Company for power generation.

Moore Town, town (1991 pop. 1,054), Portland parish, E Jamaica, on the Rio Grande, 7 mi/11.3 km. SSE of Port Antonio; 18°04′N 76°25′W. Site of anc. Maroon settlement.

Moorefield, village, S Ont., Canada, on Conestoga R., and 25 mi/40 km NNW of Kitchener. Dairying, mixed farming.

Moorefield, town (1990 pop. 2,148), ⊙ Hardy co., NE W.Va., 27 mi/43 km S of Keyser, in Eastern Panhandle, on South Branch of the Potomac R., at mouth of South Fork, South Branch Potomac R. In hunting, fishing area. Agr. (grain, soybeans); livestock; poultry. Mfg. (kitchen cabinets and counter tops, limestone processing, marble prods., poultry processing, poultry feed). Lost R. State Park to SE. Settled 1777.

Cross references are shown in SMALL CAPITALS. The pronunciation key is on page xv. The dates of population figures are on page xii.

Moorefield, village (1990 pop. 52), Frontier co., S Nebr., 5 mi/8 km NE of Curtis; 40°41′N 100°24′W.

Mooreland 1 town (1990 pop. 465), Henry co., E Ind., 8 mi/12.9 km NE of New Castle; 40°00′N 85°15′W. In agr. area. **2** town (1990 pop. 1,157), Woodward co., NW Okla., 10 mi/16 km E of Woodward; 36°26′N 99°12′W. In grain, oil and natural gas area; also alfalfa, livestock; mfg. (farm supplies, feeds). Boiling Springs State Park to W.

Moores Creek National Battlefield, Pender co., SE N.C., 20 mi/32 km NW of Wilmington, near Black R. Park consists of 87 acres/35 ha. The patriot victory over the Loyalists at Moores Creek Bridge on Feb. 27, 1776, prevented the intended Br. invasion of N.C. and spurred revolutionary sentiment in the South; the battle is often called the Lexington and Concord of the South. Est. 1926.

Moores Hill, town (1990 pop. 649), Dearborn co., SE Ind., 12 mi/19 km W of Lawrenceburg; 39°07′N 85°05′W. In agr. area. Laid out 1838.

Moore's Mill, NE suburb (1990 pop. 3,362), of Huntsville, Madison co., N Ala.; 34°51′N 86°31′W.

Moores Mills, lumbering village, SW N.B., Canada, 7 mi/11 km N of St. Stephen; 45°17′N 67°16′W.

Mooresboro, village (1990 pop. 294), Cleveland co., SW N.C., 8 mi/12.9 km W of Shelby; 35°17′N 81°42′W. Cotton, grain; livestock. Mfg. (rugs, seat covers).

Moorestown (MAWRZ-toun), township (1990 pop. 16,500), Burlington co., SW N.J., an industrial suburb of the Camden, N.J.–Philadelphia area, 9 mi/14.5 km E of Camden; 39°58′N 74°56′W. Electronic equip., metal prods., and chemicals are the principal mfg. Of interest are several 18th-cent. houses. Settled 1682 by Quakers, inc. 1922.

Mooresville 1 town (1990 pop. 54), Limestone co., N Ala., 5 mi/8 km E of Decatur, across Tennessee R. **2** town (1990 pop. 5,541), Morgan co., central Ind., on Whitelick Creek, and 16 mi/26 km SW of downtown Indianapolis; 39°37′N 86°22′W. Agr. area (grain, fruit; dairy prods.); varied mfg. Laid out 1824. **3** town (1990 pop. 100), Livingston co., N central Mo., near Grand R., 9 mi/14.5 km WSW of Chillicothe; 39°45′N 93°43′W. **4** town (1990 pop. 9,317), Iredell co., W central N.C., 14 mi/23 km SSE of Statesville, near Lake Norman; 35°34′N 80°48′W. Ironworks. Varied mfg. L. Norman reservoir (Catawba R.) to W; Duke Power State Park, on L. Norman, named for Duke Power Company, which built lake to NW. Bahari Racing to W. Founded 1868.

Mooreton (MOR-tuhn), village (1990 pop. 193), Richland co., SE N.Dak., 13 mi/21 km W of Wahpeton, on Antelope Creek; 46°16′N 96°52′W.

Moorhead (MOOR-hed), city (1990 pop. 32,295), ⊙ Clay co., NW Minn., on the Red R.; 46°51′N 96°45′W. Elev. 910 ft/277 m. A sister city of Fargo, N.Dak., 1 mi/1.6 km E of Fargo. RR junction. It is a shipping and processing center for an agr. area; cattle, poultry, sheep, hogs; dairying. Mfg. (sugar and molasses, barley malt, soft drinks, printing and publishing, dairy bottles, fiberglass tanks). Seat of Moorhead State Univ. and Concordia Col. The Plains Art Mus.; Archie's West Ltd. Art Gal.; Rourke Art Gal. are here. Buffalo R. State Park to E. Inc. 1881.

Moorhead 1 town (1990 pop. 259), Monona co., W Iowa, on Soldier R., and 14 mi/23 km SE of Onawa; 41°55′N 95°50′W. In livestock and grain area. State park nearby. **2** town (1990 pop. 2,417), Sunflower co., W Miss., 20 mi/32 km W of Greenwood; 33°27′N 90°30′W. In rich soybean and cotton-growing area; also corn, rice; catfish; mfg. (canned vegetables, catfish feed). Miss. Delta Community Col. Inc. 1899.

Mooringsport (MOR-eeng-sport), town (1990 pop. 873), Caddo parish, extreme NW La., on S shore of Caddo L., 17 mi/27 km NW of Shreveport; 32°41′N 93°58′W. In oil-producing and agr. area; timber, clay; mfg. (bricks). Soda Lake State Wildlife Area to SE.

Moorland, town (1990 pop. 209), Webster co., central Iowa, 7 mi/11.3 km SW of Fort Dodge; 42°26′N 94°17′W. In agr. area.

Moorland, village (1990 pop. 467), Jefferson co., N Ky.,

residential suburb 10 mi/16 km E of downtown Louisville; 38°16′N 85°34′W.

Moorpark, city (1990 pop. 25,494), Ventura co., S Calif., 18 mi/29 km ENE of Oxnard, and 42 mi/68 km NW of Los Angeles; 34°17′N 118°53′W. Heavy and high-technology mfg.; citrus orchards, vegetables, strawberries; flowers, nursery prods.; oil fields nearby. Moorpark Col. (2 year). Santa Susana Mt. to N.

Moose, village, Teton co., NW Wyo., near Snake R., and 12 mi/19 km N of Jackson. Service center located at center of Grand Teton Natl. Park. Teton Range to W.

Moose, river, c.50 mi/80 km long, Canada; formed in central Ont., by the Mattagami and Missinaibi rivers; flows NE to its confluence with the Abitibi R. and into SW James Bay near Moosonee.

Moose Creek, village, SE Ont., Canada, 20 mi/32 km NW of Cornwall. Dairying, mixed farming.

Moose Creek, village, S Alaska, in Matanuska Valley, on Matanuska R., and 40 mi/64 km NE of Anchorage. Fishing; tourism.

Moose Factory, trading post, NE Ont., Canada, near the mouth of the Moose R. on James Bay. A fort was built here by Charles Bayly, gov. of the Hudson's Bay Company, in the early 1670s. In the struggle bet. the English and French in Canada, the fort changed hands several times and shortly after 1696 was destroyed. In 1730 the company built a post close to the ruins of the original fort. This post has been in continuous operation since.

Moose Island, Washington co., E Maine, at mouth of Indian R., just NW of Jonesport; 2 mi/3.2 km long, .75 mi/1.2 km wide.

Moose Jaw, city (1991 pop. 33,593), S central Sask., Canada; 50°24′N 105°33′W. RR and distribution center. Oil refineries; meat-packing and dairy-processing plants, flour; lumber, woolen mills; stockyards. Canada's largest jet-training base.

Moose Lake 1 E B.C., Canada, near Alta. border, in Rocky Mts., in Mt. Robson Provincial Park, 30 mi/48 km W of Jasper; 8 mi/13 km long, 2 mi/3 km wide. Elev. 3,386 ft/1,032 m. Drained NW by Fraser R. **2** (□ 525 sq mi/1,360 sq km), W Man., Canada, 32 mi/51 km E of The Pas; 43 mi/69 km long, 30 mi/48 km wide. Drained S into L. Winnipeg by Saskatchewan R., through Cedar L.

Moose Lake, town (1990 pop. 1,206), Carlton co., E Minn., 38 mi/61 km SW of Duluth; 46°27′N 92°46′W. Oats, alfalfa; timber; poultry; dairying; mfg. (feeds, fishing tackles). Moose L. State Park to SE; Sand and Island lakes to S. Founded as lumber town before 1875, rebuilt after destruction by forest fire, 1918.

Moose Mountain, range, SE Sask., Canada; extends 30 mi/48 km E-W near Man. border; rises to 2,725 ft/831 m, 50 mi/80 km NNE of Estevan. Here is Moose Mtn. Provincial Park (□ 152 sq mi/394 sq km), a region of woods, lakes, resorts.

Moose Pass, village, S Alaska, on E Kenai Peninsula, 25 mi/40 km N of Steward. On Seward Highway.

Moose Pond, reservoir, at Denmark, Oxford and Cumberland cos., SW Maine, on small stream; c.8 mi/12.9 km long; 44°02′N 70°47′W. Drains S into the Saco R.

Moose River, township (1990 pop. 233), Somerset co., W Maine, just N of Jackman in wilderness area; 45°42′N 70°13′W. Lumbering, recreation.

Moose River 1 62 mi/100 km long, in W Maine; rises in N Franklin co.; flows generally E to Moosehead L., near Rockwood. **2** c.30 mi/48 km long, in N central N.Y.; rises in the W Adirondacks in North, Middle, and South branches, which join near Fulton Chain of Lakes (drained by Middle Branch); flows SW and W to Black R. at Lyons Falls. **3** c.30 mi/48 km long, NE Vt.; rises near East Haven; flows S and W, past Concord, to the Passumpsic at St. Johnsbury.

Moosehead Lake, reservoir (□ 120 sq mi/311 sq km), on Piscataquis and Somerset co. border, W central Maine, on Kennebec R., 2 mi/3.2 km S of Rockwood; c.30 mi/48 km long, max. 10 mi/16 km wide; 49°34′N 69°42′W. Elev. 1,029 ft/314 m. Max. capacity

714,980 acre-ft. Extensions include Lily and Spencer bays (E) and North Bay (N). Moose R. enters from W 2 mi/3.2 km WNW of Rockwood. Formed by Western Outlet Dam (gravity dam; 7 ft/2.1 m high), built (1960) by Kennebec Logging Company for logging activities. New outlet at Moosehead, 6 mi/9.7 km S of Rockwood. Has an irregular shoreline and numerous isls., including Sugar (SE), Deer (S), and Famr (NW) isls. Lily Bay State Park on SE shore. Mt. Kineo (1,789 ft/545 m high) is located on a peninsula that extends into the lake.

Mooseheart, Ill.: see BATAVIA.

Mooselookmeguntic Lake (moos-luk-mi-GUHN-tik), reservoir (□ 25 sq mi/65 sq km), Oxford co., W Maine, on Rapid R., adjacent to Richardson L., 26 mi/42 km NNW of Rumford; 44°53′N 70°52′W. Max. capacity 192,039 acre-ft. Formed by Upper Dam.

Moosic (MOO-sik), borough (1990 pop. 5,339), Lackawanna co., NE Pa., suburb 5 mi/8 km SW of Scranton, on Lackawanna R.; 41°21′N 75°42′W. Mfg. (explosives, cardboard cartons, contract sewing, food prods., textile printing). Wilkes-Barre Scanton Internatl. Airport to S. Lackawanna Co. Stadium to E. Montage Ski Area and Waterslide to E; Moosic Mts. to SE.

Moosilauke, Mount (MOO-si-lawk), peak (4,810 ft/1,466 m), Grafton co., W N.H., White Mts., 7 mi/11.3 km W of North Woodstock, S of Kinsman Notch, in White Mt. Natl. Forest.

Moosomin (MOO-so-min), town (1991 pop. 2,436), SE Sask., Canada, near Man. border, 80 mi/129 km WNW of Brandon; 50°09′N 101°40′W. Grain elevators; dairying; livestock raising.

Moosonee (MOO-suh-nee), village, NE Ont., Canada, on the Moose R. near James Bay; 51°16′N 80°39′W. It is the N terminus of the Ont. Northland RR and the prov.'s only saltwater port. Popular tourist center. Meteorological station.

Moosup (MOO-suhp), industrial village (1990 pop. 3,289), Plainfield town, Windham co., E Conn., on small Moosup R. (water power), and 16 mi/26 km NE of Norwich; 41°43′N 71°52′W. Textiles, thread, metal and wood prods., oil burners.

Moosup River (MOOS-up), c.25 mi/40 km long, R.I. and Conn.; rises in W R.I.; flows S and W, past Sterling and Moosup, Conn. (water power), to Quinebaug R. near Wauregan village.

Mora (MOR-uh), county (□ 1,933 sq mi/5,006 sq km; 1990 pop. 4,264), NE N.Mex.; ⊙ Mora; 36°01′N 104°56′W. Livestock and agr. region, watered by Mora R.; bounded E by Canadian R. Fruit, hay, alfalfa, wheat, nuts; cattle, some sheep. Part of Sangre de Cristo Mts. in (Crest forms most of W boundary) W; part of Santa Fe Natl. Forest in SW. Charette Lakes in N; part of Kiowa Natl. Grasslands in E; Morphy L. State Park in SW; Coyote Creek State Park in NW; Fort Union Natl. Monument in S center. Formed 1860.

Mora (MOR-uh), town (1990 pop. 2,905), ⊙ Kanabec co., E Minn., c.60 mi/97 km N of Minneapolis on Snake R., N of mouth of Ann R.; 45°52′N 93°17′W. Elev. 1,010 ft/308 m. Trading point in oats, barley, potatoes; livestock, poultry; dairying; mfg. (yachts, plastic molding, printing and publishing, tool and die, dairy machinery). Mus. of Izaak Walton League is here. Ann L. Wildlife Area to NW; Knife L. to N; Fish L. to S. Plotted 1881.

Mora (MOR-uh), uninc. village, ⊙ Mora co., N N.Mex., on Mora R., in Sangre de Cristo Mts., and 29 mi/47 km N of Las Vegas. Elev. 7,179 ft/2,188 m. In irrigated fruit region; farming; cattle, some sheep; grain, alfalfa, fruits, nuts; resort. Santa Fe Natl. Forest to W; Carson Natl. Forest to NW; dude ranch nearby. Morphy L. State Park to SW; Coyote Creek State Park to N; Fort Union Natl. Monument to E.

Mora River (MOR-uh), 75 mi/121 km long, N N.Mex.; rises 7 mi/11.3 km NW of Mora in Sangre de Cristo Mts.; flows SE, past Mora and Watrous, and E to Canadian R., 45 mi/72 km ENE of Las Vegas, N.Mex. Receives Sapello Creek from W below Mora.

Morada, uninc. town (1990 pop. 3,570), San Joaquin co., central Calif., 4 mi/6.4 km NE of Stockton, and 5 mi/

8 km S of Lodi, on Mosher Creek; 38°02′N 121°14′W. Fruit, nuts, olives, grain, vegetables; dairying; cattle. San Joaquin Co. Historic Mus. to N.

Moraga, city (1990 pop. 15,852), Contra Costa co., W Calif., residential suburb 7 mi/11.3 km E of downtown Oakland, in Berkeley Hills E of Oakland; 37°51′N 122°07′W. Light mfg. St. Mary's Col. is to NE. Berkley Hills to W; Upper San Leandro Reservoir to S; Redwood Regional Park to SW; Las Trampas Regional Park to E.

Moraine, city (1990 pop. 5,989), Montgomery co., SW Ohio, just S of Dayton on U.S. Interstate 75; 39°42′N 84°13′W. Mfg. (truck components, power-train systems).

Moraine Lake, SW Alta., Canada. Small glacial lake formed by moraine nestled in Rocky Mts., Banff Natl. Park, near B.C. border, 7 mi/11 km S of L. Louise. Flows E into Bow R. About ½ mi/⅘ km in diameter. Popular tourist attraction.

Moran 1 (mor-AN), village (1990 pop. 551), Allen co., SE Kansas, 13 mi/21 km E of Iola; 37°55′N 95°10′W. Livestock; grain; dairying. Mfg. (hand tools, limestone). **2** village (1990 pop. 285), Shackelford co., N Texas, 33 mi/53 km E of Abilene; 32°32′N 99°10′W. In wheat, cattle, oil area.

Moran Junction (mor-AN), village, Teton co., NW Wyo. in Grand Teton Natl. Park, on Snake R., at mouth of Blackrock Creek, and 28 mi/45 km NNE of Jackson. Elev. 6,742 ft/2,055 m. Service center at E entrance to park. Jackson L. Dam, unit in Minidoka reclamation project, to W, raises level of natural lake.Teton Range to W; Jackson Hole Biological Research Station also to W. Bridger-Teton Natl. Forest to NE and SE.

Morant Bay, town (1991 pop. 9,602), ⊙ St. Thomas parish, SE Jamaica, port with open roadstead, at mouth of small Morant R., 25 mi/40 km ESE of Kingston (linked by highway); 17°53′N 76°25′W. Ships cacao, coffee, pimento, ginger, coconuts, copra, honey, rum. Sea resort. Scene of 1865 rebellion.

Morant Cays, group of 3 Caribbean islets, dependency of Jamaica, at S entrance of Jamaica Channel, 45 mi/72 km SE of Morant Bay (SE Jamaica). Northeast Cay is at 17°25′N 75°58′W, Southwest Cay at 17°23′N 75°58′W. The uninhabited isls. are of little economic importance, though sea-bird eggs and guano are collected. They were occupied by the British in 1862 and annexed to Jamaica in 1882. Sometimes called, together with Pedro Cays (120 mi/193 km WSW), Guano Isls.

Morant Point, cape at E extremity of Jamaica, on Jamaica Channel, and 40 mi/64 km E of Kingston; 17°55′N 76°10′W. Lighthouse. Another headland, South East Point, is c 1 mi/1.6 km S.

Morattico (mour-A-ti-ko), uninc. village, Lancaster co., E Va., 17 mi/27 km SE of Tappahannock, on Rappahannock R. estuary, at mouth of Lancaster Creek; 37°47′N 76°37′W. Mfg. (crab-meat processing); fish, oysters, crabs.

Moravia, town (1990 pop. 679), Appanoose co., S Iowa, 11 mi/18 km NNE of Centerville; 40°53′N 92°49′W. Mfg. of cement blocks. Limestone quarry nearby.

Moravia, village (1 sq mi/2.6 sq km; 1990 pop. 1,559), Cayuga co., W central N.Y., near S end of Owasco L., 26 mi/42 km WSW of Syracuse; 42°42′N 76°25′W. Agr. (cabbage, field corn, hay; dairying; and beef cattle). Fillmore Glen State Park and the birthplace of President Millard Fillmore are nearby. Inc. 1837.

Moravian Falls (mor-AIV-ee-uhn), uninc. town (1990 pop. 1,736), Wilkes co., NW N.C., 5 mi/8 km S of North Wilkesboro; 36°06′N 81°10′W. Tobacco, grain, soybeans; poultry; dairying; honey. Mfg. (beehives). Wilkesboro reservoir is W.

Morden, town (1991 pop. 5,273), S Man., Canada, SW of Winnipeg. In an agr. region. Mfg. includes farm machinery and food- and fiber-processing plants. Govt. experimental farm in the town.

Moreau River (MOR-o), NW S.Dak.; north and south forks rise in SE Harding co., and converge in Perkins co.; flows E through Cheyenne R. Indian Reservation to Missouri R. S of Mobridge; 45°08′N 102°49′W.

Moreauville (MOR-o-vil), village (1990 pop. 919), Avoyelles parish, E central La., 33 mi/53 km SE of Alexandria; 31°02′N 91°59′W. In cotton-growing area; mfg. (fabricated structural metal).

Morehead, town (1990 pop. 8,357), ⊙ Rowan co., NE Ky., 58 mi/93 km ENE of Lexington, surrounded by Daniel Boone Natl. Forest; 38°11′N 83°23′W. In timber, clay, burley tobacco, corn, and cattle area; mfg. (apparel, lumber, wood prods.; metal prod.; furniture, printing and publishing). Seat of Morehead State Univ., including Ky. Folk center. Cave Run L. reservoir to S, including Minor Clark State Fish Hatchery.

Morehead City, town (1990 pop. 6,046), Carteret co., E N.C., 32 mi/51 km SSE of New Bern, on W side of mouth of Beaufort Harbor (bridged to Beaufort 3 mi/4.8 km E; receives Newport R. from NW) and N shore of Bogue Sound (bridged to Bogue Isl.), and just W of Beaufort; 34°43′N 76°43′W. Ocean port (with shipping terminal built 1935–1937; resort, fishing center; mfg. (seafood processing, diversified light mfg.). Carteret Community Col. Fort Macon State Park to SE, on Bogue Isl., one of 2 N.C. state parks (other in Wilmington). Croatan Natl. Forest to NW. Cape Lookout 14 mi/23 km to SE. Founded 1857; inc. 1860.

Morehouse, parish (□ 804 sq mi/2,082 sq km; 1990 pop. 31,938), NE La.; ⊙ Bastrop; 32°46′N, 91°55′W. Bounded E by Boeuf R., W by Ouachita R., N by Ark. state line; intersected by Bayou Bartholomew and Bayou Bonne Idee; lies mostly in Mississippi R. delta land. Agr. (cotton, corn, wheat, sorghum, home gardens, rice, soybeans, sweet potatoes, vegetables, cattle, horses), catfish. Logging, some mfg., including processing of agr. prods., timber, paper prods., apparel. Includes Chemin-a-Haut State Park in N (recreation), Georgia Pacific State Wildlife Area in NW, small part of Upper Ouachita Natl. Wildlife Refuge in NW corner, Handy Brake Natl. Wildlife Refuge in N center, Coulee State Game Refuge in S, and part of Russell Sage State Wildlife Refuge in far S. Abraham Morehouse was one of its early settlers. Formed 1844.

Morehouse, city (1990 pop. 1,068), New Madrid co., extreme SE Mo., on Little R., and 6 mi/9.7 km WSW of Sikeston; 36°51′N 89°41′W. Cotton, rice, soybeans; woodworking plant. Settled 1880.

Moreland, town (1990 pop. 366), Coweta co., W Ga., 6 mi/9.7 km S of Newman; 33°17′N 84°46′W.

Moreland, uninc. village (1990 pop. 300), Bingham co., SE Idaho, 4 mi/6.4 km W of Blackfoot. Irrigated agr. area near Snake R. Sheep, cattle, wheat, oats, barley, potatoes, sugar beets. Junction of RR spur to Blackfoot.

Morelia (mo-RAI-lee-ah), city (1990 pop. 489,756) and township, ⊙ Michoacán state, W Mexico; 19°40′N 101°11′W. It is the commercial and processing center of an irrigated agr. and cattle-raising area. Founded as Valladolid in 1541 by Antonio de Mendoza, Morelia is built on a rocky hill and is surrounded by a fertile valley at the W edge of the central plateau. High peaks border the valley on 3 sides. The climate is warm and healthful. The city is supplied with water by an aqueduct dating from the colonial period. The most imposing Span. structure is the cathedral, begun in 1640; colonial architecture, some modern bldgs., and shaded plazas give the city a pleasant atmosphere. The Colegio de San Nicolás, founded (1540) in Pátzcuaro and transferred in 1580 to Morelia, is the oldest institution of higher learning in Mexico. Morelia was the birthplace of Agustín de Iturbide and of the patriot José María Morelos y Pavón, for whom it was renamed in 1828.

Morell (mo-REHL), village (1991 pop. 349), NE P.E.I., Canada, on St. Peters Bay, 23 mi/37 km ENE of Charlottetown; 46°25′N 62°42′W. Lobster, fisheries.

Morelos (mo-RAI-los), state (□ 1,917 sq mi/4,965 sq km; 1990 pop. 1,195,059), S Mexico, ⊙ CUERNAVACA. Morelos is separated from the Federal Dist. and from Mexico state by the Transverse Volcanic Axis crossing central Ciudad Mexico. Morelos itself is mountainous, with many broad, semiarid valleys in the S. The climate is cold in the mts. and hot in the valleys. Chiefly agr., the state grows sugarcane, rice, cereals, tropical fruits,

and vegetables. Industry is progressing; automobile mfg. is significant, and mining is being developed. The principal towns are Cuernavaca and CUAUTLA, which is famous for its defense (1812) by José María Morelos y Pavón in the war against Spain. The state, created in 1869, was named in his honor. It is one of Mexico's most densely populated states.

Morelos 1 (mo-RAI-los), town (1990 pop. 414), Chihuahua, N Mexico, in valley of Sierra Madre Occidental, 120 mi/193 km W of Hidalgo del Parral. Extremely isolated, no road access. Corn; cattle; timber. Sometimes Real Morelos. **2** town (1990 pop. 5,534), Coahuila, N Mexico, on RR and 27 mi/43 km SW of Piedras Negras (Texas border); 28°28′N 100°52′W. Cattle raising; wheat, bran, istle fibers, candelilla wax. **3** town (1990 pop. 4,733), Zacatecas, N central Mexico, 8 mi/12.9 km N of Zacatecas, at junction of Mexico Highways 45, 49, and 54; 22°51′N 102°32′W. Elev. 7,621 ft/2,323 m. Active silver mining; agr. (cereals, maguey; livestock).

Morelos 1 Mexico: see MORELOS CAÑADA. **2** Mexico: see VILLA MORELOS.

Morelos Cañada, town (1990 pop. 3,158), ⊙ Cañada Morelos municipio, Puebla, central Mexico, on RR, and 18 mi/29 km S of Serdán; 18°44′N 97°25′W. Elev. 7,667 ft/2,337 m. Wheat, corn, vegetables. Sometimes Morelos.

Morelos, Ciudad, Mexico: see CUAUTLA.

Morelos, Villa, Mexico: see VILLA MORELOS.

Morena Dam, Calif.: see COTTONWOOD CREEK.

Morenci 1 uninc. town, Greenlee co., SE Ariz., at S tip of Blue Range, 110 mi/177 km NE of Tucson. Elev. 4,710 ft/1,436 m. Cattle; grain, alfalfa. Built on steep hillside. Rich copper mines here, discovered 1872. San Carlos Indian Reservation to NW; Gila Box Riparian Natl. Conservation Area to S; Apache-Sitgreaves Natl. Forest to N. **2** (muhr-EN-see), town (1990 pop. 2,342), Lenawee co., SE Mich., on Tiffin R., and 15 mi/24 km SW of Adrian, near Ohio state line; 41°43′N 84°13′W. In diversified farm area (corn, grain, apples, sugar beets; livestock; dairy). Mfg. (broaching tools, metal fabrication). Inc. as city 1934.

Moreno Valley, city (□ 49 sq mi/127 sq km; 1990 pop. 118,779), Riverside co., S Calif., suburb 12 mi/19 km ESE of Riverside, in Moreno Valley; 33°56′N 117°13′W. Mfg. (office chairs, printing and publishing). As of 1990, Moreno Valley was California's fastest growing city, with a pop. increase of more than 300% bet. 1980 and 1990, includes former wine area of Morena, Sunnymead and Edgemont. Among its developing industries are high-technology electronics, steel and other metals, home construction and improvement enterprises, engineering, and retailing. March Air Force Base in SW, the oldest base in the W United States, is hq. for the Strategic Air Command's 15th Air Force; it employs a large proportion of the city's workers. Moreno Valley is the seat branch of Chapman Univ., and a growing number of cultural institutions. L. Perris Reservoir and State Recreation Area to S; Riverside Auto Race Track in W; Colorado R. Aqueduct runs E-W to S. Inc. 1984.

Moresby Island (□ 1,060 sq mi/2,745 sq km), W B.C., Canada, Queen Charlotte Isls., in the Pacific, separated from mainland by Hecate Strait, and just S of Graham Isl., from which it is separated by Skidegate Inlet; 85 mi/137 km long, 4 mi/6 km–34 mi/55 km wide. Queen Charlotte Mts. here rise to 3,810 ft/1,161 m. Lumbering, fishing; cattle. Chief villages are Sandspit and Aliford Bay, both on NE coast. Inhabitants are mostly Haida Indians.

Moretown, town (1990 pop. 1,415), Washington co., central Vt., on Mad R., 11 mi/18 km W of Montpelier; 44°15′N 72°43′W.

Morey, Lake, in town of Fairlee, Orange co., E Vt., 26 mi/42 km SE of Barre, and 1 mi/1.6 km W of Connecticut R.; c.2 mi/3.2 km long; 43°55′N 72°10′W. Resort.

Morgan 1 county (□ 599 sq mi/1,551 sq km; 1990 pop. 100,043), N Ala.; ⊙ Decatur, 34°27′N 86°51′W. Agr. area drained in N by Wheeler L. (in Tennessee R.). Cotton, corn, soybeans; poultry, livestock; textiles. Deposits of coal, sandstone, fuller's earth, asphalt. Formed 1818. **2** county (□ 1,293 sq mi/3,349 sq km; 1990 pop. 21,939), NE Colo.; ⊙ Fort Morgan; 40°16′N 103°49′W. Irrigated agr. region, drained by South Platte R. Cattle, wheat, hay, sunflowers, brans, barley, corn, sugar beets. Empire Reservoir on W boundary; Jackson Reservoir and Jackson State Park in NW; Bijou Reservoir in W. Formed 1889. **3** county (□ 355 sq mi/919 sq km; 1990 pop. 12,883), N central Ga.; ⊙ Madison; 33°35′N 83°29′W. Bounded NE by Apalachee R., drained by Little R. Piedmont. agr. (cotton, corn, wheat, peaches; cattle, hogs, poultry); in lumbering area. Formed 1807. **4** county (□ 572 sq mi/1,481 sq km; 1990 pop. 36,397), W central Ill.; ⊙ Jacksonville; 39°43′N 90°13′W. Bounded W by Illinois R.; drained by Apple, Sandy, Mauvaise Terre, and Indian creeks. Agr. (corn, wheat, sorghum, soybeans, cattle, hogs; dairying). Food processing; mfg. of bookbinding, paper prods., chemicals; coal. Includes part of L. Meredosia. Formed 1823. One of 17 Ill. cos. to retain Southern-style commission form of co. govt. Includes Illinois Col. and MacMurray Col. **5** county (□ 409 sq mi/1,059 sq km; 1990 pop. 55,920), central Ind.; ⊙ Martinsville; 39°29′N 86°27′W. Agr. area (hogs, wheat, corn, fruit; poultry). Mfg. at Martinsville and Mooresville. Clay deposits; timber; artesian springs. Part of Morgan-Monroe State Forest on S boundary; Cikana State Fish Hatchery E of Martinsville. Drained by West Fork of White R., Whitelick Creek, and small Indian Creek. Formed 1821. **6** county (□ 383 sq mi/992 sq km; 1990 pop. 11,648), E Ky.; ⊙ West Liberty; 37°55′N 83°16′W. Drained by Licking R. (upper reach of Cave Run L. reservoir in NW) and several creeks. Hilly agr. area in Cumberland foothills (corn, burley tobacco, sorghum, hay, alfalfa; cattle); bituminous-coal mines. Includes part of Daniel Boone Natl. Forest in NW; part of Paintsville L. reservoir in SE. Formed 1822. **7** county (□ 596 sq mi/1,544 sq km; 1990 pop. 15,574), central Mo.; ⊙ Versailles; 38°25′N 92°52′W. In the Ozarks, on L. of the Ozarks; drained N by Lamine R.; drained by Osage R. Commercial, recreational, and residential development along lake at Laurie, and Gravois Mills. Wheat, corn; cattle, poultry; mfg. at Versailles; former barite mines; timber; tourist region in S. Large Amish community N of Versailles. Formed 1833. **8** county (□ 418 sq mi/1,083 sq km; 1990 pop. 14,194), E central Ohio; ⊙ McConnelsville; 39°37′N 81°50′W. Intersected by Muskingum R. and small Meigs and Wolf creeks. Agr. area (livestock; dairy prods.; corn, wheat, cabbages); mfg. at McConnelsville; limestone quarries, coal mines. Formed 1818. **9** county (□ 539 sq mi/1,396 sq km; 1990 pop. 17,300), NE central Tenn.; ⊙ Wartburg; 36°08′N 84°39′W. On Cumberland Plateau. Lumbering, agr. (corn, hay, tobacco, vegetables), livestock raising, dairying; coal, oil, and gas deposits. Formed 1817. Part of Obed Natl. Wild and Scenic R. system is here. **10** county (□ 610 sq mi/1,580 sq km; 1990 pop. 5,528), N Utah; ⊙ Morgan; 41°06′N 111°38′W. Irrigated agr. area watered by Weber R. Alfalfa, barley, sugar beets, vegetables; dairying; cattle. Wasatch Range throughout. Wasatch Natl. Forest in NE, N, and W. East Canyon Reservoir and State Park in S. Lost Creek Reservoir and State Park in NE. Formed 1862. **11** county (□ 223 sq mi/578 sq km; 1990 pop. 12,128), NE W.Va., in East Panhandle; ⊙ Berkeley Springs; 39°33′N 78°15′W. Bounded N and W by Potomac R. (Md. state line), S, in part, by Va.; drained by Cacapon R. Agr. (honey, corn, wheat, oats, barley, alfalfa, hay, apples); cattle; poultry. Mfg. (furniture). Glass-sand pits; timber. Cacapon State Park is here, includes Cacapon Mt.; Berkeley Springs State Park in N; part of Sleepy Creek Wildlife Management Area in E. Formed 1820.

Morgan, city (1990 pop. 252), ⊙ Calhoun co., SW Ga., 23 mi/37 km W of Albany, and on Ichawaynochaway Creek; 31°32′N 84°36′W. Declining agr. service center symbolized by abandoned cotton gin.

Morgan 1 town (1990 pop. 965), Redwood co., SW Minn., 24 mi/39 km WNW of New Ulm; 44°25′N 94°55′W. Grain, soybeans, sugar beets, alfalfa; livestock, poultry; dairying; mfg. (electrical components, feeds, fertilizer). Lower Sioux Indian Reservation to NW, on Minnesota R. **2** uninc. town (1990 pop. 800), South Fayette township, Allegheny co., W Pa., suburb 10 mi/16 km SW of downtown Pittsburgh, on Millers Run creek; 40°21′N 80°08′W. Mfg. (novelty items). **3** or **Morgan City**, town (1990 pop. 2,023), ⊙ Morgan co., N Utah, on Weber R. at mouth of East Canyon Creek, in Wasatch Range, and 22 mi/35 km NNE of Salt L. City; 41°02′N 111°40′W. Trade center for agr. region; sugar beets, alfalfa, vegetables, barley; dairying; mfg. (cement, luggage, small arms). Elev. 5,068 ft/1,545 m. Lost Creek Reservoir and State Park to NE; East Canyon Reservoir and State Park to S. Wasatch Natl. Forest to N, W, and S. Settled 1852 by Mormons. Surrounding area served by irrigation works on Weber R. **4** town (1990 pop. 497), Orleans co., N Vt., on Seymour L. and 9 mi/14.5 km E of Newport; 44°53′N 71°58′W. Resorts.

Morgan 1 village, Phillips co., N Mont., port of entry at Canada (Sask.) border, c.44 mi/71 km N of Malta. Mixed livestock and cash-crop farming. **2** village (1990 pop. 451), Bosque co., central Texas, 7 mi/11.3 km N of Meridian; 32°01′N 97°36′W. In farm area. L. Whitney reservoir to E. **3** uninc. rural community, Laclede co., S central Mo., in the Ozarks, near Osage Fork of Gasconade R., 12 mi/19 km S of Lebanon.

Morgan Acres, uninc. town (1990 pop. 1,500), Spokane co., E Wash., suburb 5 mi/8 km NE of downtown Spokane. RR center.

Morgan City, city (1990 pop. 14,531), St. Mary parish, S La., 48 mi/77 km S of Baton Rouge; 29°41′N 91°12′W. Elev. 8 ft/3 m. Fishing port on the Atchafalaya R. (connected to the Intracoastal Waterway). Hq. for offshore petroleum drilling; oil and gas wells. Shipyards; large shrimp and crawfish fleet, an oyster industry, and alligator farms. Mfg. (barges, propeller shafts, crew boats, yachts), printing and publishing. Holds La. Shrimp and Petroleum Festival. L. Palourde to NE. Inc. 1860.

Morgan City, village (1990 pop. 139), Leflore co., W central Miss., 14 mi/23 km SW of Greenwood, near Yazoo R.; 33°22′N 90°20′W. Cotton, grain; cattle.

Morgan, Fort, historic site, Baldwin co., SW Ala., 21 mi/34 km W of Gulf Shores at the entrance to Mobile Bay. Crucial to Confederate defense of Mobile, Fort Morgan surrendered to the North in Aug. 1864 after the Battle of Mobile Bay.

Morgan Hill, city (1990 pop. 23,928), Santa Clara co., W Calif., 20 mi/32 km SE of San Jose, in Santa Clara Valley; 37°08′N 121°39′W. Varied mfg; mushrooms (abundant mines), fruit, vegetables, grapes, cherries; diversified agr.; cattle, poultry; dairying, eggs; nursery prods.; timber. Anderson Reservoir to NE, Coyote Reservoir to SE (both on Coyote Creek); Henry W. Coe State Park to NE; Santa Cruz Mts. to SW. Inc. 1906.

Morgan, Mount (13,748 ft/4,190 m), Inyo co., E Calif., in the Sierra Nevada, 19 mi/31 km W of Bishop, in Inyo Natl. Forest.

Morganfield, town (1990 pop. 3,776), ⊙ Union co., W Ky., 21 mi/34 km WSW of Henderson; 37°40′N 87°54′W. RR terminus. Bituminous-coal-mining and agr. (corn, wheat, hay, alfalfa; livestock) area; mfg. (wire prods., automobile parts and accessories, paper cones, meat processing, coal processing). Morganfield Airport to E. U.S. Camp Breckinridge to E (inactive) was active in World War II. Higgins-Henry Wildlife Management Area to SE.

Morgans Point, village (1990 pop. 341), Harris co., S Texas, on Galveston Bay, and 20 mi/32 km ESE of downtown Houston, on W side of mouth of San Jacinto R.–Houston Ship Channel.

Morgan's Point Resort, town (1990 pop. 1,766), Bell co., central Texas, residential and recreational suburb 7 mi/11.3 km WNW of Temple, on E shore of L. Belton reservoir; 31°09′N 97°27′W.

Morganton, city (1990 pop. 15,085), ⊙ Burke co., W N.C., 63 mi/101 km NW of Charlotte, on the Catawba R. at upper reach of L. Rhodhiss reservoir; L. James reservoir upstream (to W), in the foothills of the Blue Ridge Mts.; 35°44′N 81°42′W. Mfg. (textiles, apparel, chemicals, furniture, foam rubber, auto and tool parts, metal and fiberglass fabricating, electronics, printing and publishing). South Mt. State Park to S; Tuttle Educational State Forest to NE. Founded 1784, inc. 1885.

Morganton, village (1990 pop. 295), Fannin co., N Ga., 4 mi/6.4 km E of Blue Ridge, and on Blue Ridge L.; 34°52′N 84°14′W. Mfg. of lumber and clothing.

Morgantown, city (1990 pop. 25,879), ⊙ Monongalia co., N W.Va., near the Pa. state line, on the Monongahela R.; 39°38′N 79°57′W. Shipping point for coal and limestone region. Mfg. (glass, chemicals, printing and publishing, office furniture, mining equip., organic phosphate, crushed limestone, lumber, pharmaceuticals, airport equip., machining). Agr. (strawberries, grain); livestock; poultry. Morgantown Airport to E. W.Va. Univ. (2 main campuses). Kennedy Youth Center, Natl. Training Center for Boys, to S. Chestnut Ridge Park and Coopers Rock State Forest to NE. Fort Morgan built here (1772), and the 1st settlers arrived the same year. Iron, discovered in 1789, was the principal industry until the Civil War. Inc. 1785.

Morgantown 1 town (1990 pop. 978), Morgan co., central Ind., near small Indian Creek, 8 mi/12.9 km SE of Martinsville; 39°22′N 86°16′W. In agr. area. Laid out 1831. **2** town (1990 pop. 2,284), ⊙ Butler co., W central Ky., on Green R., and 20 mi/32 km NW of Bowling Green; 37°13′N 86°42′W. Agr. (dark and burley tobacco, grain; livestock; catfish); coal mining; mfg. (apparel, rubber prods., lumber, plastic molding, leather prods.). Read's Ferry crosses Green R. to NW. Est. 1813. **3** uninc. town (1990 pop. 900), Berks co., SE central Pa., 12 mi/19 km S of Reading; 40°09′N 76°53′W. Mfg. includes smelting, testing instruments, truck and van bodies, electronic assemblies, gantry cranes, crushed stone, log home kits; limestone. Agr. includes dairying; livestock; grain, soybeans, potatoes.

Morganville, village (1990 pop. 181), Clay co., N Kansas, on Republican R., and 8 mi/12.9 km NNW of Clay Center; 39°28′N 97°12′W. Grain; livestock. Mfg. (farm machinery).

Morganza (mor-GAN-zuh), village (1990 pop. 759), Pointe Coupee parish, SE central La., on the Mississippi R., 32 mi/51 km NW of Baton Rouge; 30°45′N 91°35′W. Agr. (cotton, rice, vegetables, sugarcane, cattle), crawfish. Morganza Spillway (Floodway) 25 mi/40 km NW of Baton Rouge, diverts Mississippi R. floodwaters into Atchafalaya Basin.

Moriah (MO-rei-ah), village, central Tobago, Trinidad and Tobago., 4.5 mi/7.2 km N of Scarborough. Cacao.

Moriah, village (1990 pop. 400), Essex co., NE N.Y., near L. Champlain, 14 mi/23 km NNW of Ticonderoga; 44°02′N 73°31′W. In former iron-mining area.

Moriah, Mount 1 Nev.: see SNAKE RANGE. **2** N.H.: see CARTER-MORIAH RANGE.

Moriarty (mor-ee-AHR-i-tee), town (1990 pop. 1,399), Torrance co., central N.Mex., 37 mi/60 km E of Albuquerque; 35°00′N 106°02′W. Elev. 6,217 ft/1,895 m. Cattle, corn, pumpkins, grain, alfalfa; mfg. (metal stampings). Manzano Mts. to SW; Sandia Mts. to NW; El Cuervo Butte (6,947 ft/2,117 m) to NE.

Morice Lake (□ 40 sq mi/104 sq km), W central B.C., Canada, in Coast Mts., 50 mi/80 km SSW of Smithers, near Tweedsmuir Park; 27 mi/43 km long, 1 mi/2 km–5 mi/8 km wide. Drains N into Bulkley R.

Moriches, village (1990 pop. 1,500), Suffolk co., SE N.Y., on SE L.I., on Moriches Bay, 9 mi/14.5 km E of Patchogue, in resort; 40°48′N 72°49′W. Agr. (potatoes, sweet corn, cauliflower) and poultry.

Morinville, town (1991 pop. 6,104), central Alta., Canada, 18 mi/29 km NNW of Edmonton; 53°48′N 113°39′W. RR junction; mixed farming, dairying.

Moris (MO-rees), town (1990 pop. 758), ⊙ Moris municipio, Chihuahua, N Mexico, 165 mi/266 km ESE of Hermosillo; 28°08′N 108°35′W. Elev. 2,507 ft/764 m. Silver, gold, lead mining.

Morland, village (1990 pop. 234), Graham co., NW Kansas, on South Fork of Solomon R., and 13 mi/21 km W of Hill City; 39°21′N 100°04′W. Trade and shipping center for grain region.

Morley 1 town (1990 pop. 85), Jones co., E Iowa, 12 mi/19 km S of Anamosa; 42°00′N 91°15′W. Livestock, grain.

2 town (1990 pop. 683), Scott co., SE Mo., in Mississippi alluvial plain, 6 mi/9.7 km SSW of Benton; 37°02′N 89°36′W. Mfg.: motor vehicle parts.

Morley, village (1990 pop. 528), Mecosta co., central Mich., 15 mi/24 km S of Big Rapids, and on Little Muskegon R.; 43°29′N 85°27′W. Machining. Newaygo State Park, on Hardy Dam Pond and Manistee Natl. Forest to W.

Mormon Flat Dam, Ariz., see CANYON LAKE.

Mormon Lake (☐ 12 sq mi/31 sq km), Coconino co., central Ariz., 20 mi/32 km SE of Flagstaff; 4 mi/6.4 km long, 3 mi/4.8 km wide. Summer resorts. Mt. Mormon (8,440 ft/2,573 m) is near W shore.

Mormon Pioneer Affiliated Area, historic trail running through Ill., Mo., Kansas, Colo., Utah. Follows the route of Brigham Young; authorized 1978.

Morne Diablotin, Dominica: see DIABLOTIN, MORNE.

Morne Fortune (morn for-too-NAY), hill, St. Lucia, 1 mi/1.6 km E of Castries; 14°00′N 61°00′W. Spectacular views overlooking Castries harbor. Site of governor general's mansion. Ruins of fortifications.

Morne Garu, central mountain range, St. Vincent, St. Vincent and the Grenadines, West Indies; 13°17′N 61°10′W. Soufrière (4,049 ft/1,234 m) is an active volcano and major mt. on N side of this range.

Morne-à-l'Eau (mawr-nah–LO), town, W Grande-Terre, Guadeloupe, on the Grand Cul de Sac, 7 mi/11.3 km N of Pointe-à-Pitre. Rum distilling, sugar milling.

Morne-Rouge (mawrn–ROOZH), town, N Martinique, at S foot of Mont Pelée, 12 mi/19 km NNW of Fort-de-France; 15°53′N 61°17′W. In sugar-growing region; rum distilling. Destroyed (1902) by eruption of Pelée.

Morning Sun, town (1990 pop. 841), Louisa co., SE Iowa, 7 mi/11.3 km SSW of Wapello, and 25 mi/40 km SSW of Muscatine; 41°05′N 15°91′W. Rendering works; limestone quarries nearby.

Morningdale, Mass.: see BOYLSTON.

Morningside, town (1990 pop. 930), Prince Georges co., central Md., suburb SE of Washington, D.C.; 38°50′N 76°53′W. Formed in 1949, many residents work in nearby Andrews Air Force Base or govt. agencies such as the U.S. Census in Suitland.

Morningside Heights, section of the W side of Manhattan borough of N.Y. city, SE N.Y., lying bet. Riverside Park along the Hudson (W) and Morningside Park (E), N of 110th St.; 40°49′N 73°57′W. Manhattanville sect. adjoins on N. Site of Columbia Univ., Teachers Col., Columbia Univ., Cathedral of St. John the Divine, Riverside Church, Union Theological Seminary, Jewish Theological Seminary of Amer.

Moro (MOR-o), plantation (1990 pop. 38), Aroostook co., E Maine, on Rockabema L., and 25 mi/40 km W of Houlton; 46°10′N 68°22′W. In hunting, fishing area.

Moro 1 (MOR-o), village (1990 pop. 287), Lee co., E Ark., 19 mi/31 km SW of Forrest City; 34°47′N 90°59′W. **2** (MOR-o), village (1990 pop. 292), ⊙ Sherman co., N Oregon, 23 mi/37 km ESE of The Dalles; 45°29′N 120°43′W. Elev. 1,807 ft/551 m. Wheat, barley, oats; poultry, cattle. Deschutes River State Recreation Area to W.

Moro Bayou (MOR-o), c.65 mi/105 km long, S Ark.; rises in Dallas co. NW of Fordyce; flows S past Fordyce to Ouachita R. at Moro Bay State Park, 19 mi/31 km NE of El Dorado.

Morocco, town (1990 pop. 1,044), Newton co., NW Ind., near Ill. state line, 12 mi/19 km N of Kentland; 40°57′N 87°27′W. In agr. area; corn, soybeans, cattle. Mfg. (insert moldings). Settled 1833, laid out 1851, inc. 1890.

Moroleón (mo-ro-le-ON), city (1990 pop. 41,136) and township, ⊙ Moroleón municipio, Guanajuato, central Mexico, on central plateau, 38 mi/64 km N of Mexico Highway 430; 20°07′N 101°11′W. Elev. 5,814 ft/1,772 m. Agr. center (grain, sugarcane, fruit; livestock); mfg. (shoes, scarves, shawls).

Morón (mor-ON), city (1994 pop. 53,000), Ciego de Ávila prov., E Cuba, near N coast (Leche Lagoon), 65 mi/105 km NW of Camagüey; 22°09′N 78°39′W. RR junction, trading and processing center in rich agr. region (sugarcane, tobacco, cacao, coffee, fruit; cattle). Lumbering; mfg. of meat prods. Airfield. Has several sugar mills in outskirts, including Patria o Muerte (SE), Máximo Gómez (SW), and Enrique Varona (NW). Town core possesses housing stock built by Amer. sugar interests in early decades of 20th cent.

Moron (mo-RONG), town (1982 pop. 1,310), Grande-Anse dept., SW Haiti, on W Jacmel Peninsula, 12 mi/19 km SW of Jérémie; 18°34′N 74°15′W. Cacao, coffee.

Morongo Valley, uninc. town (1990 pop. 1,544), San Bernardino co., S Calif., 40 mi/64 km ESE of San Bernardino, and NNW of Palm Springs, in E part of San Bernardino Mts.; 34°04′N 116°36′W. San Bernardino Natl. Forest to NW; Morongo Indian Reservation; Joshua Tree Natl. Monuments to E. Pacific Coast Natl. Scenic Trail to W. Desert resort area. Cattle.

Moroni (muh-RO-nei), town (1990 pop. 1,115), Sanpete co., central Utah, 17 mi/27 km SE of Nephi, near San Pitch R.; 39°31′N 111°34′W. Elev. c.5,600 ft/1,707 m. Poultry, cattle, sheep; barley, wheat, alfalfa. Mfg. (turkey feed, turkey processing). Uinta Natl. Forest to W. Terminus of RR spur from Ephraim.

Morovis (mo-RO-vis), town (1990 pop. 25,288), N central P.R., 21 mi/34 km WSW of San Juan. Industrial and commercial area. Agr. (some coffee, plantains); dairying (milk production); mfg. (clothing, plastic prods.).

Morral (MAH-ruhl), village (1990 pop. 373), Marion co., central Ohio, 8 mi/13 km NW of Marion; 40°41′N 83°13′W. Metal prods., food prods.

Morrice (MOR-is), village (1990 pop. 630), Shiawassee co., S central Mich., 21 mi/34 km NE of Lansing, and 2 mi/3.2 km E of Perry; 42°50′N 84°10′W. In agr. area.

Morrill, county (☐ 1,429 sq mi/3,701 sq km; 1990 pop. 5,423), W Nebr.; ⊙ Bridgeport, located in Platte R. valley. Irrigated farm area drained by North Platte R. and its branches. Sugar beets, beans, cattle, hogs, corn, wheat. Several small natural lakes in NE corner, including McCarthy, Wildhorse, Rush, Storm, and Goose lakes. Chimney Rock Natl. Historical Site in W; Bridgeport State Recreation Area at center. Formed 1909.

Morrill 1 (MAHR-uhl), town (1990 pop. 644), Waldo co., S Maine, just W of Belfast; 44°25′N 69°10′W. In agr., recreational area. **2** town (1990 pop. 974), Scotts Bluff co., W Nebr., 15 mi/24 km WNW of Scottsbluff, and on North Platte R.; 41°57′N 103°55′W. Dairy prods.; livestock; grain, sugar beets, potatoes. Mfg. (feeds, dry beans and peas, rubber decoys).

Morrill (mor-EL), village (1990 pop. 299), Brown co., NE Kansas, 10 mi/16 km NW of Hiawatha, near Nebr. state line; 39°55′N 95°41′W. In grain and livestock region (corn belt).

Morrilton (MOR-uhl-tuhn), town (1990 pop. 6,551), ⊙ Conway co., central Ark., 40 mi/64 km NW of Little Rock, and on Arkansas R. (here bridged; Arthur V. Ormond Lock and Dam to SW); 35°09′N 92°44′W. Stock raising, sawmilling, dairying, mfg. (light machinery, food prods., textiles). Petit Jean State Park to W; Brewer L. reservoir to NE, on Petit Jean Mt. Founded in 1870s.

Morrin, village (1991 pop. 235), S Alta., Canada, 14 mi/23 km N of Drumheller; 51°40′N 112°46′W. Wheat.

Morris, town (1991 pop. 1,616), S Man., Canada, on Red R., at mouth of small Morris R., and 40 mi/64 km SSW of Winnipeg; 49°21′N 97°22′W. Grain elevators; livestock raising, dairying; oil distributing point.

Morris 1 county (☐ 702 sq mi/1,818 sq km; 1990 pop. 6,198), E central Kansas; ⊙ Council Grove; 38°41′N 96°38′W. Located in Flint Hills region, watered by Neosho R. Hogs, cattle; wheat, barley, hay, soybeans; industrial machinery. Council Grove L. reservoir in E. Formed 1859. **2** county (☐ 481 sq mi/1,246 sq km; 1990 pop. 421,353), N N.J., bounded SE and E by Passaic R.; ⊙ Morristown; 40°52′N 74°32′W. Hilly estate and resort area, with many lakes and mt. ridges. Dairying, agr. (fruit, nursury prods.; poultry), nurseries; mfg. (electrical, electronic, and radar equip., pharmeceutical hq., metal prods., machinery, explosives, chemicals, rubber goods, clothing, wood prods.); telecommunications, research and development. Drained by Pequannock, Rockaway, Whippany, and Musconetcong rivers, and branches of Raritan R.; includes Morristown Natl. Historical Park and part of L. Hopatcong. E largely suburbanized. In W half still agr. but that is quickly becoming suburbanized. Formed 1739. **3** county (☐ 258 sq mi/668 sq km; 1990 pop. 13,200), NE Texas; ⊙ Daingerfield; 33°07′N 94°43′W. Bounded N by Sulphur R., S by Big Cypress Creek and Ellison Creek (Ellison Creek Reservoir in S). Diversified agr., peanuts, watermelons; cattle, poultry. Iron-ore deposits. Timber (mainly pine). Daingerfield State Park in S. Formed 1875.

Morris, city (1990 pop. 10,270), ⊙ Grundy co., NE Ill., on Illinois R., and 21 mi/34 km SW of Joliet; 41°22′N 88°25′W. Shipping and industrial center in agr., clay area; mfg. (paper prods., chemicals, plastics prods.). Plotted 1842, inc. 1853. Nearby is Gebhard Woods State Park (30 acres/12 ha) along old Illinois and Michigan Canal Parkway.

Morris 1 resort town (1990 pop. 2,039), Litchfield co., W Conn., on Bantam L., the state's largest natural lake, and 10 mi/16 km SW of Torrington; 41°41′N 73°12′W. Includes Lakeside village resort, part of state park, game sanctuary, agr. and light industry. **2** town (1990 pop. 5,613), ⊙ Stevens co., W Minn., near Pomme de Terre R., and 50 mi/80 km NW of Willmar; 45°35′N 95°54′W. Elev. 1,136 ft/346 m. RR junction. Wheat, corn, oats, barley, soybeans, alfalfa, sunflowers; hogs, cattle, sheep; mfg. (truck trailers, bulk ethanol, printing and publishing, belt conveyors). Plotted 1869, inc. as village 1878, as city 1903. **3** town (1990 pop. 1,216), Okmulgee co., E central Okla., 6 mi/9.7 km E of Okmulgee; 35°36′N 95°51′W. In oil-producing and coal-mining area, mfg. (lead fishing weights).

Morris, township (1990 pop. 19,952), Morris co., N N.J.; 40°47′N 74°29′W. Includes the capital of co., Morristown. Inc. 1798. Pharmeceuticals.

Morris, village (1990 pop. 642), Otsego co., central N.Y., 13 mi/21 km NW of Oneonta; 42°32′N 75°15′W. In dairying area; mfg. of veterinary medicines. Gilbert L. State Park is c.5 mi/8 km NE. Otsego co. fairground here.

Morris Canal, N.J., abandoned canal (c.100 mi/161 km long) joining Delaware R. at Phillipsburg and Newark Bay at Newark. Chartered 1824 as outlet for Pa. coal regions; opened 1831; extended to Jersey City, 1836; declined after peak traffic in 1860s; finally abandoned 1923. Bed at Newark utilized for subway (1935).

Morris Dam, Calif.: see SAN GABRIEL RIVER.

Morris Island, Charleston co., S S.C., one of the Sea Isls. at S side of entrance to Charleston Harbor; c.3.5 mi/5.6 km long. Charleston lighthouse on S tip. James Isl. to W, Folly Isl. to S, Atlantic Ocean to E.

Morris Plains, residential borough (1990 pop. 5,219), Morris co., N N.J., just N of Morristown; 40°50′N 74°28′W. Pharmaceuticals, tea, electrical equip., and office equip. are produced here. State mental hosp. (1871) nearby. Inc. 1926.

Morris Run, uninc. village, Hamilton township, Tioga co., N Pa., 2 mi/3.2 km E of Blossburg, on Morris Run creek; 41°40′N 77°01′W. Mfg. (wooden prods.).

Morrisania, residential section of S Bronx borough of N.Y. city, SE N.Y.; 40°50′N 73°54′W. Depressed area, mostly Afr.-American and Hispanic.

Morrisburg, village (1991 pop. 2,429), SE Ont., Canada, on the St. Lawrence R.; 44°54′N 75°11′W. Mfg. includes concrete prods., brooms and brushes, surgical and dental supplies. Just E of the village is the Upper Canada Village, a model of a typical 19th-cent. community.

Morrisdale, uninc. village (1990 pop. 600), Clearfield co., central Pa., 12 mi/19 km SE of Clearfield; 40°56′N 78°13′W. Surface bituminous coal.

Morrison, county (☐ 1,153 sq mi/2,986 sq km; 1990 pop. 29,604), central Minn.; ⊙ Little Falls; 46°00′N 94°16′W. Agr. area drained by Mississippi R. Bounded in NW by Crow Wing R. (Mississippi R. forms parts of N and S co. boundary). Alfalfa, hay, potatoes, corn, oats, barley, rye, sunflowers, beans; timber; sheep, hogs, cattle, poultry; dairying; deposits of marl and peat. Numerous small lakes in NW, including L. Alexander. Camp Ripley Military Reservation in NW. Charles A. Lindbergh State Park in W center. County formed 1855.

Morrison, city (1990 pop. 4,363), ⊙ Whiteside co., NW Ill., on Rock Creek (bridged here), and 12 mi/19 km E of Clinton (Iowa); 41°48′N 89°58′W. In farming and dairying area; mfg. (dairy prods.). Rockwood State Park nearby. Founded 1855, inc. 1867.

Morrison 1 town (1990 pop. 113), Grundy co., central Iowa, 5 mi/8 km E of Grundy Center; 42°20′N 92°40′W. In agr. area. **2** town (1990 pop. 160), Gasconade co., E central Mo., on Missouri R., 7 mi/11.3 km W of Hermann; 38°40′N 91°37′W. Corn, soybeans, cattle. Damged by flood of 1993. **3** town (1990 pop. 570), Warren co., central Tenn., 10 mi/16 km SW of McMinnville; 35°36′N 85°55′W.

Morrison 1 village (1990 pop. 465), Jefferson co., N central Colo., on Bear Creek, suburb 10 mi/16 km SW of Denver; 39°38′N 105°10′W. Elev. c.5,800 ft/1,768 m. Light mfg. Resort; entrance to Denver mt. park system. Red Rocks Natural Amphitheater, used for concerts, to NW. Front Range of Rocky Mts. to W; Bear Creek L. reservoir to E. Formerly Mt. Morrison. **2** village (1990 pop. 640), Noble co., N Okla., 12 mi/19 km NNE of Stillwater, on Black Bear Creek; 36°17′N 97°00′W. In agr. area (grain, livestock).

Morrison City, village, Sullivan co., NE Tenn., 4 mi/6 km N of Kingsport, near Tenn.-Va. state line; 36°35′N 82°35′W.

Morrisonville 1 village (1990 pop. 1,113), Christian co., central Ill., 14 mi/23 km SW of Taylorville; 39°25′N 89°27′W. Agr. (grain; livestock); soybean prods. Inc. 1872. **2** village (□ 2 sq mi/5.2 sq km; 1990 pop. 1,742), Clinton co., extreme NE N.Y., on Saranac R., and 5 mi/ 8 km W of Plattsburgh; 44°41′N 73°32′W.

Morristown, city (1990 pop. 21,385), ⊙ Hamblen co., NE Tenn., 40 mi/64 km ENE of Knoxville; 36°12′N 83°18′W. An important tobacco, poultry, timber, and dairy center; mfg. of furniture, wood prods., hosiery, jet and auto parts; 2 community cols. (Walters State and Knoxville Col. at Morristown). Cherokee Reservoir (Holston R.) is N; state fish hatchery nearby. Settled 1783, inc. 1855.

Morristown 1 town (1990 pop. 980), Shelby co., central Ind., on Big Blue R., and 11 mi/18 km NNE of Shelbyville; 39°40′N 85°42′W. In agr. area; mfg. (motor vehicle leaf springs, seals, steering components, hamburger buns, plastic moldings, windows and doors). Laid out 1828. **2** town (1990 pop. 784), Rice co., S Minn., 10 mi/16 km WSW of Faribault, on Cannon R.; 44°13′N 93°26′W. Grain, soybeans; livestock; dairying. Small lakes in area. Sakatah L. State Park to W, Cannon L. to NE, both on Cannon R. **3** town (1990 pop. 16,189), ⊙ Morris co., N N.J., on the Whippany R.; 40°47′N 74°28′W. Although chiefly residential, it has electronics, health and beauty aids, autoparts, chemicals, milk cartons, and hose mfg. plants; telecommunication research and development center. Morristown also has become a burgeoning center of corporate activity. It was a principal area of Revolutionary maneuvers, particularly in the winters of 1777 and 1779–1780, when the Continental army encamped here. Benedict Arnold was court-martialed in the town. S. F. B. Morse and Alfred Vail perfected (c.1837) the telegraph here. Of interest are the Schuyler-Hamilton House (1760), where Alexander Hamilton courted (1779–1780) Elizabeth Schuyler (it has become hq. for the Daughters of the American Revolution); and the courthouse (1826). Other notable residents of Morristown were the cartoonist Thomas Nast, the writer Bret Harte, and the humorist Frank R. Stockton. Morristown Natl. Historical Park includes the Ford Mansion, which was Washington's hq. in 1779–1780; a historical mus. at the rear of the Ford Mansion; and the reconstructed sites of encampment of the Continental army at Fort Nonsense and at Jockey Hollow. The engine of the *Savannah*, the 1st steamship to cross the Atlantic Ocean, was made near Morristown. Settled c.1710, inc. 1865. **4** town (1990 pop. 4,733), Lamoille co., N central Vt., on Lamoille R., and just S of Hyde Park, in agr. region; 44°32′N 72°38′W. Includes Morrisville village. Chartered 1781.

Morristown 1 village (□ 1 sq mi/2.6 sq km; 1990 pop. 490), St. Lawrence co., N N.Y., on the St. Lawrence, opposite Brockville, Ont. (ferry), and 12 mi/19 km SW of Ogdensburg; 44°34′N 75°39′W. Fishing center; port

of entry. **2** village (1990 pop. 296), Belmont co., E Ohio, 8 mi/13 km W of St. Clairsville, in coal-mining area; 40°04′N 81°04′W. **3** village (1990 pop. 64), Corson co., N S.Dak., 18 mi/29 km W of McIntosh, and on N.Dak. state line; 45°56′N 101°43′W. Supply point for ranching region; in Standing Rock Indian Reservation.

Morristown National Historical Park (□ 2 sq mi/ 5.2 sq km), N N.J. Authorized 1933. Site of military encampments during the Revolution; George Washington's headquarters, 1779–1780.

Morrisville 1 town (1990 pop. 293), Polk co., central Mo., near Little Sac R., 8 mi/12.9 km S of Bolivar; 37°28′N 93°25′W. **2** town (1990 pop. 1,499), Wake co., central N.C., suburb 9 mi/14.5 km W of downtown Raleigh, and 11 mi/18 km SSE of downtown Durham; 35°49′N 78°49′W. Mfg. (concrete and glass blocks, pharmaceuticals, trade show exhibits, machine parts, carbide cutting tools, laminated wood prods.). Research Triangle Park to NW, Raleigh-Durham Intl. Airport to NE. L. Crabtree reservoir to NE. **3** uninc. town (1990 pop. 1,365), Greene co., SW Pa., residential suburb 1 mi/ 1.6 km E of Waynesburg; 39°53′N 80°10′W. Agr. includes dairying, hay. Greene co. Airport to E.

Morrisville 1 village (□ 1 sq mi/2.6 sq km; 1990 pop. 2,732), Madison co., central N.Y., 28 mi/45 km ESE of Syracuse, in dairying area; 42°53′N 75°38′W. The SUNY Col. of Agr. and Technology at Morrisville is here. **2** village (1990 pop. 1,984) in Morristown town, Lamoille co., N central Vt.; 44°33′N 72°35′W. Lumber, dairy prods. Winter sports.

Morrisville, borough (1990 pop. 9,765), Bucks co., SE Pa., suburb 1 mi/1.6 km SW of downtown Trenton, N.J., and 27 mi/43 km NE of downtown Philadelphia, on the Delaware R.; 40°12′N 74°46′W. Mfg. (water pumps, clutches, coatings, concrete prods., rubber prods., coated coils, foam fabrication, wire screens, printing and publishing, gases and chemicals). Steel fabricating to S at Fairless Hills. George Washington had his hq. here Dec. 8–14, 1776. Pennsbury Manor State Park, with reconstructed Pennsbury, which was William Penn's home, to S. Settled c.1624 by the Du. West India Company, inc. 1804.

Morro Bay, city (1990 pop. 9,664), San Luis Obispo co., SW Calif., 12 mi/19 km NW of San Luis Obispo, on Morro Bay (an inlet of Estero Bay, Pacific Ocean); 35°22′N 120°52′W. A 4 mi/6.4 km long spit separates Morro Bay from the ocean, opening on the N. Guarded by Morro Rock (576 ft/176 m). Mfg. (medical equip.); cattle; grain, flowers, nursery stock apples, avocados, vegetables, strawberries. Section of Los Padres Natl. Forest to NE; Montana de Oro State Park and Atascadero State Beach to S. Morro Bay State Park is here.

Morro Castle 1 fort, at the entrances to Havana harbor, Ciudad de La Habana prov., W Cuba; 23°09′N 82°19′W. Erected by the Span. under the direction of architect-engineer Batista Antonelli in 1589 to protect the city from buccaneers and was also used as a prison. It was captured by the British in 1762. **2** fort, at entrance to Santiago de Cuba harbor, Santiago de Cuba prov., SE Cuba; 21°33′N 75°17′W. Built shortly after the Morro Castle of Havana. It was taken by the Amer. forces in the Span.-Amer. War (1898).

Morro Castle (MOR-ro) or **Castillo del Morro**, fort at harbor of San Juan, P.R.

Morro Point (MO-ro), headland on coast of Campeche, SE Mexico, on W Yucatán Peninsula, 15 mi/24 km SW of Campeche; 19°41′N 90°42′W. Occasionally Morros Point.

Morrow 1 county (□ 404 sq mi/1,046 sq km; 1990 pop. 27,749), central Ohio; ⊙ Mount Gilead; 40°32′N 82°47′W. Drained by Kokosing R. and small Whetstone and Big Walnut creeks. In the Till Plains physiographic region. Agr. area (hogs, cattle; corn); mfg. mainly at Mount Gilead and Cardington (machinery, paper prods., electric lighting). Formed 1848. **2** (MAHR-o), county (□ 2,048 sq mi/5,304 sq km; 1990 pop. 7,625), N Oregon; ⊙ Heppner; 45°25′N 119°34′W. Bounded N by Columbia R. (forms Wash. state line). Drained by Willow Creek. Agr. (alfalfa, grapes, corn, wheat, oats,

barley, onions, potatoes; sheep, cattle). Umatilla Ordnance Depot on NE boundary. Part of Umatilla Natl. Forest in SE; parts of Umatilla Natl. Wildlife Refuge in N. Formed 1885.

Morrow (MAHR-o), town (1990 pop. 5,168), Clayton co., NW central Ga., 12 mi/19 km S of Atlanta; 33°35′N 84°20′W. Emerging suburb of Atlanta. The Atlanta Beach Recreation Complex gained fame as the site of beach volleyball competition during the 1996 summer Olymic Games. Reynolds Memorial Nature Preserve and mus. here. Mfg. of cleaning chemicals, plastics, hydraulic cylinders; steel fabrication.

Morrow, village (1990 pop. 1,206), Warren co., SW Ohio, 7 mi/11 km SE of Lebanon, and on Little Miami R.; 39°20′N 84°07′W.

Morrow Point Reservoir, Montrose and Garrison cos., W Colo., on Gunnison R., in Curecanti Natl. Recreation Area, 18 mi/29 km S of Montrose; 11 mi/18 km long; 38°27′N 107°33′W. Extends E to Blue Mesa Dam. Max. capacity of 121,500 acre-ft. Formed by Morrow Point Dam (400 ft/122 m high), built (1968) by the Bureau of Reclamation for power generation and flood control.

Morrowville, village (1990 pop. 173), Washington co., N Kansas, 7 mi/11.3 km WNW of Washington; 39°50′N 97°10′W. Grain; livestock. Washington State Fishing L. to N.

Morse, town (1991 pop. 313), S Sask., Canada, 35 mi/ 56 km ENE of Swift Current. Grain elevators, lumbering.

Morse, town (1990 pop. 782), Acadia parish, S La., 10 mi/ 16 km SW of Crowley; 30°07′N 92°30′W. In agr. (rice) area; mfg. (mops).

Morse Bluff, village (1990 pop. 128), Saunders co., E Nebr., 15 mi/24 km WSW of Fremont, and on Platte R; 41°25′N 96°46′W.

Morse Reservoir, water supply reservoir, Hamilton co., central Ind., 22 mi/35 km NNE of downtown Indianapolis. Located on Cicero Creek and built by the Indianapolis Water Co.

Mortimer, town, Caldwell co., W central N.C., 14 mi/ 23 km WNW of Lenoir.

Mortlach (mort-LAKH), town (1991 pop. 296), S Sask., Canada, 23 mi/37 km W of Moose Jaw; 50°27′N 106°04′W. Wheat.

Morton 1 county (□ 729 sq mi/1,888 sq km; 1990 pop. 3,480), extreme SW Kansas; ⊙ Elkhart; 37°12′N 101°48′W. Rolling plain, bordered W by Colo. and S by Okla.; drained by Cimarron R. Wheat and grain sorghums; cattle, livestock. Gas field in E. Includes Cimarron Natl. Grassland at center of co. (Mountain/Central time zone boundary). Formed 1886. **2** county (□ 1,920 sq mi/4,973 sq km; 990 pop. 23,700), central N.Dak.; ⊙ Mandan; 46°43′N 101°16′W. Agr. area drained by Big Muddy Creek and Heart R.; bounded by Missouri R. (L. Oahe Reservoir S of Mandan) on E (forms the border bet. the Mountain and Central time zones, except for NE corner of co., including Mandan, which is in Central). Mfg. food prods., petroleum refining; diversified farming, cattle; hogs; dairying; wheat, barley, hay. Fort Lincoln State Park in E; Fort Rice Historic Site in SE; Sweet Briar Reservoir in N. Formed 1873.

Morton 1 town (1990 pop. 3,212), Scott co., central Miss., 32 mi/51 km E of Jackson, in Bienville Natl. Forest; 32°21′N 89°39′W. Mfg. (paper mill equip., wooden pallets and boxes, poultry processing). Roosevelt State Park to SW. **2** town (1990 pop. 2,597), ⊙ Cochran co., NW Texas, on the Llano Estacado, c.55 mi/89 km W of Lubbock; 33°43′N 102°45′W. Elev. 3,758 ft/1,145 m. Shipping, storage, trade center for agr. and cattle-ranching area (cotton, wheat, sorghum); mfg. (meat packing); oil and gas. Muleshoe Natl. Wildlife Refuge to N. Inc. 1934. **3** town (1990 pop. 1,130), Lewis co., SW Wash., 34 mi/55 km E of Chehalis; 46°34′N 122°17′W. Agr.; dairying; mfg. (lumber, wood prods.). Mt. Saint Helens Natl. Volcanic Monument to SE; parts of Gifford Pinchot Natl. Forest to N, NE, and SE. Riffe L. reservoir (Mossyrock Dam) to S.

Morton 1 village (1990 pop. 13,799), Tazewell co., central

Ill.; 40°36′N 89°28′W. In a grain-farming and livestock area. Mfg. (food processing, tractor parts, washing machines, pottery). Inc. 1877. **2** village (1990 pop. 448), Renville co., SW Minn., on Minnesota R., and 7 mi/ 11.3 km E of Redwood; 44°32′N 94°58′W. Grain, soybeans, peas, sugar beets; livestock, poultry; dairying; mfg. (rubber prods.). Lower Sioux Indian Reservation to S; Birch Coulee Battlefield Historic Site, set aside in commemoration of battle bet. Sioux Indians and U.S. Cavalry in 1862.

Morton, borough (1990 pop. 2,651), Delaware co., SE Pa., suburb 9 mi/14.5 km WSW of downtown Philadelphia; 39°54′N 75°19′W. Mfg. (RR, wheels and axles, plastics prods.). Inc. 1898.

Morton Grove, village (1990 pop. 22,408), Cook co., N of Chicago, NE Ill.; 42°02′N 87°47′W. It has research laboratories and mfg. plants (pumps, electrical equip., cosmetics). On North Branch of Chicago R. Inc. 1895.

Mortons Gap, town (1990 pop. 987), Hopkins co., W Ky., 7 mi/11.3 km S of Madisonville; 37°14′N 87°28′W. RR junction. In coal-mining, agr. (burley tobacco, grain; livestock; timber) area; mfg. (barrel staves). White City Wildlife Management Area to NE.

Moruga (mo-ROO-ga), village, S Trinidad, Trinidad and Tobago, 18 mi/29 km SE of San Fernando; 10°08′N 61°19′W. In cacao- and coconut-growing region; beach.

Morvant (MOR-vah), village, NW Trinidad, Trinidad and Tobago, 1.5 mi/2.4 km E of Port of Spain. In coconut and citrus fruit region; sawmilling. Has new housing development and residential suburbs.

Morven 1 village (1990 pop. 536), Brooks co., S Ga., 16 mi/26 km WNW of Valdosta; 30°56′N 83°30′W. **2** village (1990 pop. 590), Anson co., S N.C., 8 mi/ 12.9 km SSE of Wadesboro; 34°51′N 80°00′W. Cotton, grain, tobacco; livestock. Mfg. (home furnishings).

Morzhovoi (mor-SHO-vee), village, SW Alaska, on SW Alaska Peninsula, on narrow strait bet. the Pacific and Bering Sea, opposite Unimak Isl.; 54°55′N 163°18′W. Native pop. works in fishing industry during summer.

Mosby, town (1990 pop. 194), Clay co., W Mo., 8 mi/ 12.9 km NNE of Liberty; 39°19′N 94°17′W.

Mosca, hamlet, Alamosa co., S Colo., 12 mi/19 km N of Alamosa. Elev. 7,550 ft/2,301 m. In agr. region of the San Luis valley. Great Sand Dunes Natl. Monument and San Luis Lakes State Park are E.

Mosca Pass (9,713 ft/2,961 m), S Colo., in Sangre de Cristo Mts., bet. Huerfano and Alamosa cos. Crossed by trail, co. road reaches Mosca Pass radio tower from E.

Mosca Peak, N.Mex.: see MANZANO RANGE.

Moscow, city (1990 pop. 18,519), ⊙ Latah co., NW Idaho, 23 mi/37 km N of Lewiston, at the Wash. state line, and 10 mi/16 km E of Pullman, Wash., near South Fork of Palouse R.; 46°44′N 117°00′W. Elev. 2,564 ft/782 m. It is a trade center for a lumber and farm area where wheat, peas, lentils, and dairy items are produced. Mfg. (semiconductors, printing and publishing, erosion control blankets, concrete, wooden cabinets). Originally part of the Nez Perce Reservation, it was first settled by whites in 1871. The Univ. of Idaho is there, as well as a historical museum and a U.S. govt. forest sciences laboratory. Nez Perce Indian Reservation to SE. Inc. 1887.

Moscow 1 (MAW-skou), town (1990 pop. 608), Somerset co., W central Maine, on the Kennebec and 22 mi/ 35 km NNW of Skowhegan; 45°07′N 69°52′W. **2** town (1990 pop. 384), Fayette co., SW Tenn., on Wolf R., and 34 mi/55 km E of Memphis; 35°04′N 89°24′W.

Moscow 1 village, Rush co., E central Ind., on Flatrock R., and 10 mi/16 km SW of Rushville. Agr. area. Settled 1822, laid out 1832. **2** (MAHS-kou), village (1990 pop. 252), Stevens co., SW Kansas, 12 mi/19 km NE of Hugoton; 37°19′N 101°12′W. In agr. area. **3** village (1990 pop. 279), Clermont co., SW Ohio, 15 mi/24 km S of Batavia, and on Ohio R. (here forming Ky. state line); 35°52′N 84°13′W. Grant Memorial Bridge is nearby.

Moscow (MAHS-kou), borough (1990 pop. 1,527), Lackawanna co., NE Pa., 9 mi/14.5 km SE of Scranton, on Roaring Brook, forms Elmhurst Reservoir to N; 41°20′N 75°31′W. Agr. area (corn, hay; cattle; dairying);

timber; mfg. (lumber, metal fabrication). Lackawanna State Forest to SW; Moosic Mts. to NW. Settled 1830.

Moscow Mills (mahs-ko-MILZ), town (1990 pop. 924), Lincoln co., E Mo., on Cuivre R., and 4 mi/6.4 km SE of Troy; 38°57′N 90°55′W. Agr. Residential growth from St. Louis metropolitan area.

Moselle (mo-ZEL), uninc. rural community, Franklin co., E central Mo., on Meramec R., and 8 mi/12.9 km SE of Union.

Moses Lake, city (1990 pop. 11,235), Grant co., central Wash., on E shore of Moses L., 68 mi/109 km NE of Yakima; 47°08′N 119°17′W. A distributing and shipping point for the Columbia basin project, its chief prods. are sugar beets, potatoes, and milk. Heavy mfg. Grant County Airport to N; Municipal Airport to E. Columbia Natl. Wildlife Refuge to S; Moses Lake State Park to W. Central part of city is on peninsula bet. Parker Horn and Pelican Horn, horn-shaped arms of lake. Large Potholes Reservoir to S. Adam East Mus.; Big Bend Community Col. here. Settled 1897, inc. 1938.

Moses Lake, reservoir, Grant co., E Wash., on Crab Creek, 2 mi/3 km SW of Moses Lake; 47°05′N 119°20′W. Max. capacity 50,000 acre-ft. Formed by Moses L. South Dam (20 ft/6 m high), built (1962) by the Bureau of Reclamation for irrigation. Moses L. State Park on S bank.

Moses Point, locality, W Alaska, on SE Seward Peninsula, on Norton Sound, at mouth of Norton Bay, 100 mi/161 km E of Nome; 64°45′N 161°46′W. Air field. In the Elim Indian Reservation.

Moshassuck River (mo-SHASS-uck), c.10 mi/16 km long, N R.I.; rises in Lincoln; flows generally SSE, past Saylesville and Central Falls, through Providence, joining Woonasquatucket R. just before entering Providence R.

Mosier (MO-zhuhr), village (1990 pop. 244), Wasco co., N Oregon, 12 mi/19 km NW of The Dalles, and on Columbia R. (Bonneville Reservoir) at mouth of Mosier Creek; 45°40′N 121°23′W. Agr. (apples, cherries, grapes). Koberg Beach Wayside State Park to W; Memaloose and Mayer State Parks to E; Mt. Hood Natl. Forest to S.

Mosinee, town (1990 pop. 3,820), Marathon co., central Wis., on Mosinee Flowage of Wisconsin R., and 12 mi/ 19 km SSW of Wausau, at head of Du Bay Reservoir; 44°47′N 89°40′W. In lumbering and dairying area; paper and sawmilling, cheese making. Mfg. (trailer components, papers, nylon slings). Big Eau Pleine Reservoir to SW. Inc. 1931. Central Wisconsin Regional Airport to SE.

Mosquero (mos-KER-o), village (1990 pop. 164), Harding–San Miguel co. line, ⊙ Harding co., NE N.Mex., 45 mi/72 km NNW of Tucumcari; 35°46′N 103°57′W. Cattle, alfalfa, wheat, oats, barley, millet. Chicosa L. State Park and section of Kiowa Natl. Grasslands to NW.

Mosquito (mos-KEE-to), village on NW Vieques Isl., E P.R., 5 mi/8 km WSW of Isabel Segunda. Fishing.

Mosquito Creek 1 c.60 mi/97 km long, SW Iowa; rises in Shelby co.; flows SW, to Missouri R. 5 mi/8 km S of Council Bluffs. **2** c.30 mi/48 km long, in NE Ohio; rises in Ashtabula co.; flows S, past Cortland, to Mahoning R. at Niles; 41°10′N 80°45′W. About 9 mi/14 km above mouth, a flood control dam (5,650 ft/1,722 m long, 47 ft/14 m high) impounds Mosquito Creek Reservoir (capacity 104,100 acre-ft.).

Mosquito Creek Lake, reservoir (□ 12 sq mi/31 sq km), Trumbull co., NE Ohio, on Mosquito Creek, 7 mi/ 11 km NE of Warren; 41°24′N 80°46′W. Max. capacity 180,000 acre-ft. Formed by Mosquito Creek Dam (43 ft/13 m high), built (1944) by Army Corps of Engineers for flood control; also used for recreation and water supply.

Mosquito Lagoon, in Volusia and Brevard cos., E central Fla., separated from the Atlantic by narrow barrier beach; c.17 mi/27 km long, 2 mi/3.2 km wide. Contains many small isls. Followed by Intracoastal Waterway.

Mosquito Pass (13,186 ft/4,019 m), Park-Lake cos., central Colo., in Park Range, just N of Mount Sherman. County road passes through it.

Moss Beach, uninc. town, (1990 pop. 3,002), San Mateo co., W Calif., residential suburb c.18 mi/29 km SSW of downtown San Francisco; 37°31′N 122°31′W. Fishing; ornamentals, flowers, artichokes, brussels sprouts, grain; marine gardens offshore. Half Moon Bay Airport to SE. Montana Mt. (extension of Santa Cruz Mts.) and San Francisco State Fish and Game Refuge to NE.

Moss Landing, uninc. village, Monterey co., W Calif., on Monterey Bay, now mouth of Pajaro R., 15 mi/ 24 km N of Monterey. Fishing docks; artichokes, vegetables, fruit; dairying; cattle; oil loading pipeline; power plant.

Moss Point, city (1990 pop. 17,837), Jackson co., extreme SE Miss., 4 mi/6.4 km N of Pascagoula, on E channel of Pascagoula R. at mouth of Escatawba R.; 30°25′N 88°31′W. Mfg. (rubber and latex, gears and pumps, shipbuilding, metal fabrication, fish oil). Regional airport to N; Escatawba R. forms Robertson and Beardsley lakes in W part of city; Grand Bay Natl. Wildlife Refuge to SE; Miss. Sandhill Crane Natl. Wildlife Refuge to W.

Moss Town, town, central Bahama Isls., on central Great Exuma Isl., 5 mi/8 km WNW of George-Town; 23°30′N 75°51′W. Livestock raising (sheep, goats, hogs).

Mossbank, town (1991 pop. 400), S Sask., Canada, near Johnstone L., 35 mi/56 km SW of Moose Jaw; 49°56′N 105°58′W. Coal mines, grain elevators.

Mossyrock, village (1990 pop. 452), Lewis co., SW Wash., on Cowlitz R., and 25 mi/40 km SE of Chehalis; 46°32′N 122°29′W. Dairying; timber. Parts of Gifford Pinchot Natl. Forest to N and SE; Ike Kinswa State Park, on Mayfield L. reservoir, to NW. Mossyrock Dam, forms Riffe L., to E.

Mossyrock Dam, Wash.: see RIFLE LAKE.

Moswansicut River (mos-WAN-si-cut), N central R.I., short stream entering N arm of Scituate Reservoir. Formerly joined Ponaganset R. to form North Branch of Pawtuxet R. in area now flooded by reservoir.

Motembo, Minas de (mo-TAIM-bo, MEE-nuhz dai), village, Matanzas prov., W Cuba, 26 mi/42 km ESE of Cárdenas; 22°50′N 80°41′W. Petroleum wells.

Mother Lode, belt of gold-bearing quartz veins, Mariposa, Calaveras, Amados, El Dorado, and Placer cos., central Calif., along the W foothills of the Sierra Nevada. The term is sometimes limited to a strip c.70 mi/ 113 km long and from 1 mi/1.6 km to 6.5 mi/10.5 km wide, running NW from Mariposa. Popularly it is used to mean the gold-bearing area E of the Sacramento and San Joaquin rivers and W of the Sierra Nevada. The discovery of alluvial gold at Sutter's Mill on the South Fork of the Amer. R. in 1848 led to the gold rush centered on this territory in 1849. Those traveling here to seek gold were nicknamed "The Fortyniners" and constructed the lawless boom towns of Angel's Camp, Volcano Eruption, and Sonora. Mark Twain and Bret Harte helped make the Mother Lode famous. Highway 49, named for the 1st year of the Gold Rush, runs through most of the historic towns. The area around Sonora and Tuolumne cos. is now middle-income suburbs.

Motley, county (□ 989 sq mi/2,562 sq km; 1990 pop. 1,532), NW Texas; ⊙ Matador; 34°04′N 100°47′W. In broken plains just below Caprock escarpment of Llano Estacado; drained by North, South, and Middle Pease rivers. Chiefly cattle-ranching region, producing also cotton, peanuts, grain sorghum. Oil, gas fields; sand and gravel; timber. Formed 1876.

Motley (MAWT-lee), village (1990 pop. 441), Morrison co., central Minn., 22 mi/35 km W of Brainerd on Crow Wing R., at mouth of Long Prairie R.; 46°20′N 94°38′W. Mfg. (feeds, smoked fish, imitation seafood). Small lakes in area; Shamineau L. to SE.

Motozintla de Mendoza (mo-to-SEEN-tlah dai men-DO-sah), town (1990 pop. 11,316), ⊙ Motozintla municipio, Chiapas, S Mexico, in Sierra Madre, near Guatemala border, 33 mi/53 km N of Tapachula on Mexico Highway 190; 15°21′N 92°14′W. Sugarcane, coffee, fruit.

Mott, town (1990 pop. 1,019), ⊙ Hettinger co., SW N.Dak., 42 mi/68 km SE of Dickinson, and on Cannonball R.; 46°22′N 12°19′W. Flour, dairy prods., wheat. Inc. 1928.

Mott Haven, industrial section of SW Bronx borough of N.Y. city, SE N.Y., along Harlem R. (bridges to Manhattan); 40°50′N 73°56′W. Mfg. of machinery, metal prods.; RR yards. Site of Yankee Stadium and Bronx County Bldg. Lower-income pop., mainly Afr.-Amer. and Puerto Rican, with a growing number of middle-class Afr. Americans moving into rehabilitated areas.

Motte, Lac La (MOT, lahk lah), lake (8 mi/13 km long, 6 mi/10 km wide), W Que., Canada, 16 mi/26 km NW of Val d'Or, in gold-mining region. Drained N by Harricanaw R.

Motul de Carrillo Puerto (mo-TOOL dai kah-REE-yo poo-ER-to), town (1990 pop. 17,410), ⊙ Motul municipio, Yucatán, SE Mexico, on RR, and 23 mi/37 km ENE of Mérida; 21°09′N 89°19′W. Henequen, corn, tropical fruit, livestock. Archaeological remains nearby.

Mouchoir Bank, shoal with reefs, in the West Indies, 60 mi/97 km N of Hispaniola, separated from Turk Isls. (W) by Mouchoir Passage (c.60 mi/97 km long), Silver Bank is 25 mi/40 km E, beyond Silver Bank Passage.

Mould Bay, U.S.-Can. Arctic weather station, SE Prince Patrick Isl., W Franklin dist., N.W.T.; 76°05′N 119°45′W.

Moule (MOOL), town, E Grande-Terre, Guadeloupe, minor port 14 mi/23 km ENE of Pointe-à-Pitre. Trading (rum, fruit, lumber); distilling; fishing. Archaeological mus. and hotels. Sometimes Le Moule.

Moule à Chique, Cape (MOOL ah SHEEK), headland on S St. Lucia, 20 mi/32 km S of Castries; 13°43′N 60°57′W. Forms a narrow neck of land running into the sea for 3 mi/4.8 km. Lighthouse.

Moulton 1 (MUL-tuhn), town (1990 pop. 3,248), ⊙ Lawrence co., NW Ala., 20 mi/32 km WSW of Decatur. Clothing mfg., lumber milling, limestone quarrying. **2** town (1990 pop. 613), Appanoose co., S Iowa, near Mo. state line and source of North Fabius R., 11 mi/18 km ESE of Centerville; 40°41′N 92°40′W. Settled 1867. **3** town (1990 pop. 923), Lavaca co., S Texas, 20 mi/32 km N of Yoakum, near source of Lavaca R.; 29°34′N 97°09′W. In cattle area; some oil and gas; mfg. (oil field equip.).

Moultonborough (MOL-tuhn-buh-ro), town (1990 pop. 2,956), Carroll co., E central N.H., 15 mi/24 km NNE of Laconia; 43°43′N 71°22′W. Bounded SW in part by L. Winnipesaukee, SE by Moultonborough Bay, in NW corner by Squam L. Mfg. (machine parts, book publishing); agr. (nursery crops, apples, vegetables; cattle, poultry; dairying). Castle in the Clouds in E; Red Hill (2,029 ft/618 m) in NW; L. Kanasatka in W; Snow Peak (2,975 ft/907 m) part of Ossipee Mts. in E; Ossipee Mt. Ski Area in E center. Includes Long Isl. (in S), bridged to mainland; L. Winnipesaukee largest isl.

Moultrie (MOL-tree), county (□ 344 sq mi/891 sq km; 1990 pop. 13,930), central Ill.; ⊙ Sullivan, 39°38′N 88°37′W. Agr. (corn, wheat, soybeans; livestock). Mfg. (candy, wood prods., farm machinery). Drained by Kaskaskia R. L. Shelbyville in S. Formed 1843.

Moultrie (MOL-tree), city (1990 pop. 14,865), ⊙ Colquitt co., SW Ga., on the Ochlockonee R.; 31°10′N 83°46′W. Mfg. includes furniture, printing and publishing, fertilizer, lighting fixtures, cotton processing, concrete, animal feeds, aircraft, meat processing, paper prods., agr. equip., steel and aluminum prods. The town grew as a lumbering and naval stores center, but the timber has since been depleted. Now center of commercial produce production. Airport. The Colquitt County Farmer's Market is here. Inc. 1890.

Moultrie, Fort, S.C.: see FORT MOULTRIE.

Moultrie, Lake, reservoir (□ 94 sq mi/243 sq km), Berkeley co., SE S.C., on West Branch Cooper R., 25 mi/40 km N of Charleston; 33°16′N 79°58′W. Max. capacity of 1,110,000 acre-ft. Connected to L. Marion at NW. Formed by Pinopolis Dam (75 ft/23 m high), built (1942) for power generation; owned by S.C. Public Service Authority. Francis Marion Natl. Forest to E; Old Santee Canal State Park just S.

Moultrie, Lake, S.C.: see SANTEE RIVER.

Moultrieville, S.C.: see SULLIVANS ISLAND.

Mound, town (1990 pop. 9,634), Hennepin co., E Minn.,

residential suburb 20 mi/32 km W of downtown Minneapolis, bounded by extension of L. Minnetonka: Upper L. and Cooks Bay in S, West Arm and Jennings Bay in NE; Langdon L. in W; 44°55′N 93°39′W. Diverse light mfg.) Dutch L. on N boundary. Settled 1854, inc. 1912.

Mound, village (1990 pop. 16), Madison parish, NE La., near the Mississippi, 8 mi/13 km W of Vicksburg, Miss.; 32°20′N 91°01′W. Derives name for an Indian mound at the site. Agr.

Mound Bayou, town (1990 pop. 2,222), Bolivar co., NW Miss., 25 mi/40 km SSW of Clarksdale; 33°52′N 90°43′W. In rich agr. area (cotton, corn, rice, soybeans; cattle).

Mound City 1 city (1990 pop. 765), ⊙ Pulaski co., extreme S Ill., on Ohio R., and 5 mi/8 km N of Cairo; 37°05′N 89°09′W. Mfg. of mineral prods.; agr. (grains, vegetables; livestock). Important Union naval base in Civil War. Natl. cemetery is nearby. City severely damaged in 1937 flood. Inc. 1857. **2** city (1990 pop. 1,273), Holt co., NW Mo., 32 mi/51 km NW of St. Joseph; 40°08′N 95°13′W. Fruit, grain; hogs, cattle. Big Lake State Park and Squaw Creek Natl. Wildlife Refuge to SW. Laid out 1857.

Mound City, town (1990 pop. 789), ⊙ Linn co., E Kansas, 22 mi/35 km NNW of Fort Scott; 38°08′N 94°49′W. In livestock and fruit region. Annual co. fair is held here. Big Hill L. Reservoir to N.

Mound City, village (1990 pop. 89), ⊙ Campbell co., N S.Dak., 20 mi/32 km ENE of Mobridge; 45°43′N 100°04′W.

Mound City Group Monument, S Ohio. Authorized 1923, Prehistoric mounds of Hopewell Native Americans.

Mound Station, village (1990 pop. 147), Brown co., W Ill., 6 mi/9.7 km W of Mount Sterling; 40°00′N 90°52′W. In agr. area. Also called Timewell.

Mound Valley, village (1990 pop. 405), Labette co., SE Kansas, 11 mi/18 km SW of Parsons; 37°12′N 95°24′W. In grain and diversified-farming area. Big Hill L. reservoir to N.

Moundhouse, locality, Carson City, independent city (formerly Ormsby co.), W Nev., 5 mi/8 km NE of Carson City proper, on Carson R. Agr. area (dairying; poultry; vegetables, hay); mfg. (truck bodies, fishing rods, aerospace fasteners, printed circuit boards).

Moundridge, town (1990 pop. 1,531), McPherson co., central Kansas, 14 mi/23 km SSE of McPherson; 38°12′N 97°31′W. Flour, feed. Mfg. (steel-processing equip., lawn and garden equip., fertilizers, farm machinery, meat packaging). Oil and gas wells nearby.

Mounds, city (1990 pop. 1,407), Pulaski co., extreme S Ill., 3 mi/4.8 km NNW of Mound City; 37°06′N 89°12′W. In agr. area (corn). Inc. 1904.

Mounds, town (1990 pop. 980), Creek co., central Okla., 20 mi/32 km SW of Tulsa; 35°52′N 96°03′W. In oil-producing and agr. area.

Mounds View, city (1990 pop. 12,541), Ramsey co., E Minn., suburb 9 mi/14.5 km NNE of downtown Minneapolis and 12 mi/19 km NW of downtown St. Paul, E of Mississippi R., drained by Rice Creek; 45°06′N 93°12′W. Mfg. (tools, skates, gaskets, data communications equip., business checks). Spring L. on W boundary.

Moundsville, city (1990 pop. 10,753), seat of Marshall co., N W.Va., 120 mi/193 km NNE of Charleston, in the Northern Panhandle, on the Ohio R. (bridged); 39°55′N 80°44′W. Coal was once the chief industry, and some is still mined. Mfg. (asphalt, roofing materials, petroleum calcined coke, hygiene prods.). Agr. (corn, potatoes); livestock; poultry. Moundsville State Penitentiary. Palace of Gold, temple of New Vrindaban Spiritual Community. Grave Creek Mound State Park (Native Amer. burial site) to S. Burches Run Wildlife Management Area to NE. Settled 1771, inc. 1865.

Moundville 1 town (1990 pop. 1,348), Hale co., W Ala., on Black Warrior R., and 20 mi/32 km N of Greensboro; 33°00′N 37°87′W. Trade and shipping point in cotton, corn, and vegetable area; cotton ginning, lumber milling; feed. Nearby state monument includes

group of large Native Amer. mounds and mus. (dedicated 1939). **2** town (1990 pop. 140), Vernon co., W Mo., 7 mi/11.3 km SW of Nevada; 37°46′N 94°27′W.

Mount Airy, village (1990 pop. 543), Habersham co., NE Ga., 11 mi/18 km WSW of Toccoa; 34°31′N 83°30′W.

Mount, town, Carroll and Frederick cos., N Md., 30 mi/48 km W of Baltimore. In agr. area.

Mount Aetna, town (1990 pop. 3,608), Washington co., W Md., 39°37′N 77°40′W. A recently discovered iron furnace apparently lit up the hillside village; it most likely provided the inspiration for the name when it was founded in 1761. The largest limestone caverns in Md. are also here. The numerous formations have been given names such as the Great Wall of China and Jefferson Davis, because of fancied resemblances. They were discovered by Boy Scouts in 1928, but closed to the public in 1932.

Mount Airy 1 town (1990 pop. 3,730), Carroll and Frederick cos., central Md., 6 mi/9.7 km SW of Westminster; 39°22′N 77°10′W. Situated on Parr's Ridge with a water tower visible for miles around, Mount Airy was settled by Henry Bussard in 1814, and annexed neighboring Ridgeville in 1966. A series of inclined planes had to be built by the Baltimore and Ohio RR to allow its early engines to negotiate Parr's Ridge. A tunnel was built through the ridge in 1890. The once well-known Mary Garrett Childrens' Hosp. located here has been converted into apartments. Mostly in Carroll co., the town splits into Frederick co. **2** town (1990 pop. 7,156), Surry co., NW N.C., 34 mi/55 km NW of Winston-Salem, in Blue Ridge foothills, near Va. state line; 36°30′N 80°36′W. RR terminus. Granite quarrying. Mfg. (stone, granite, and plastic prods.; apparel, lumber, store displays, utility bldgs.; furniture, bucket trucks). Pilot Mt. State Park to SE. Inc. 1885.

Mount Albert, village, S Ont., Canada, 32 mi/51 km N of Toronto; 44°08′N 79°19′W. Now part of city of East Gwillimbury. Dairying, mixed farming.

Mount Allen, uninc. town (1990 pop. 2,110), Cumberland co., S Pa., residential suburb 7 mi/11.3 km SW of Harrisburg; 40°10′N 76°58′W.

Mount Angel, town (1990 pop. 2,778), Marion co., NW Oregon, 13 mi/21 km NE of Salem near Pudding R., in Willamette R. Valley; 45°04′N 122°47′W. Trade center for fruit, grain, and dairy prods. Mfg. (bakery prods., soft drinks, vitamins). Agr. (vegetables, mint, berries, tulips, iris; poultry, cattle). Mt. Angel Seminary (Roman Catholic) to SE. Inc. 1905.

Mount Arlington, borough (1990 pop. 3,630), Morris co., N N.J., on L. Hopatcong, and 12 mi/19 km NW of Morristown; 40°55′N 74°38′W.

Mount Auburn 1 town (1990 pop. 138), Shelby co., E Ind., 11 mi/18 km SSW of Shelbyville; 39°49′N 85°11′W. In agr. area. Laid out 1837. **2** town (1990 pop. 134), Benton co., E central Iowa, near Cedar R., 9 mi/14.5 km NNW of Vinton; 42°15′N 92°05′W. In agr. area.

Mount Auburn, village (1990 pop. 544), Christian co., central Ill., near Sangamon R., 21 mi/34 km E of Springfield; 39°46′N 89°15′W. Grain; livestock.

Mount Auburn, Mass.: see CAMBRIDGE.

Mount Ayr 1 town (1990 pop. 151), Newton co., NW Ind., 15 mi/24 km NNE of Kentland; 40°57′N 87°18′W. In agr. area. **2** town (1990 pop. 1,796), ⊙ Ringgold co., S Iowa, 24 mi/39 km SSE of Creston; 40°42′N 94°14′W. In livestock and grain area. Mfg. (stadium bleachers, automotive wire harnesses, motor-home leveling systems). Airfield here; fish hatchery to N. Founded c.1855, inc. 1875.

Mount Beacon, N.Y.: see BEACON.

Mount Blanchard (BLAN-chuhrd), village (1990 pop. 491), Hancock co., NW Ohio, 10 mi/16 km SSE of Findlay, and on Blanchard R.; 40°54′N 83°33′W.

Mount Braddock, uninc. village, Menallen township, Fayette co., SW Pa., 6 mi/9.7 km NE of Uniontown; 39°56′N 79°38′W. Connellsville Airport to NW.

Mount Brydges, village, S Ont., Canada, 15 mi/24 km WSW of London; 42°54′N 81°29′W. Dairying, farming.

Mount Calm, village (1990 pop. 303), Hill co., central Texas, 20 mi/32 km NE of Waco, near source of Navasota R.; 31°45′N 96°52′W. In cotton area; dairying; horses.

Mount Calvary, village (1990 pop. 558). Fond du Lac co., E Wis., near Sheboygan R., 10 mi/16 km ENE of Fond du Lac, in dairying region; 43°49′N 88°15′W. Kettle Moraine State Forest to SE; Sheboygon Marsh Co. Park to NE.

Mount Carbon, borough (1990 pop. 132), Schuylkill co., E central Pa., residential suburb, 1 mi/1.6 km SE of Pottsville, on Schuylkill R.; 40°40′N 76°11′W.

Mount Carmel, city (1990 pop. 8,287), ⊙ Wabash co., SE Ill., on the Wabash (bridged here), and 24 mi/39 km SSW of Vincennes, Ind.; 38°25′N 87°46′W. Center of rich agr. area (corn, wheat, soybeans); mfg. of electronic equip., metal prods.; RR shops. Oil obtained nearby. Musselshell industry flourished here after 1900. Indian mounds nearby have yielded artifacts. Inc. 1825. Wabash Valley Col. is nearby.

Mount Carmel 1 town (1990 pop. 108), Franklin co., SE Ind., 7 mi/11.3 km ESE of Brookville; 39°25′N 84°53′W. In agr. area. **2** (KAHR-mel), town (1990 pop. 4,082), Hawkins co., NE Tenn., 6 mi/10 km W of Kingsport, on Holston R., near Holston army ammunition plant; 36°33′N 82°39′W. Inc. 1961.

Mount Carmel 1 uninc. village (1990 pop. 4,462), Clermont co., extreme SW Ohio, a far E suburb of Cincinnati; 39°05′N 84°17′W. **2** (KAHR-muhl), village (1990 pop. 117), McCormick co., W S.C., 14 mi/23 km NW of McCormick, and on W edge of Sumter Natl. Forest; 34°00′N 82°30′W. **3** uninc. village, Kane co., SW Utah, on East Fork Virgin R., and 15 mi/24 km NNW of Kanab. Agr., cattle. Elev. 5,314 ft/1,620 m. Coral Pink Sand Dunes State Park to S. Zion Natl. Park to W; Dixie Natl. Forest to N. Highway extends 25 mi/40 km W to Zion Canyon, in Zion Natl. Park. Mt. Carmel Junction 2 mi/3.2 km SW.

Mount Carmel, borough (1990 pop. 7,196), Northumberland co., E central Pa., 20 mi/32 km ESE of Sunbury, near North Branch Shamokin Creek (source to NE); 40°47′N 76°24′W. Agr. area (grain, apples; poultry, livestock, dairying); mfg. (aluminum doors and windows, corrugated boxes, plastic prods.); anthracite coal. Laid out 1835, inc. 1864.

Mount Carmel, Conn.: see HAMDEN.

Mount Carmel Junction, uninc. village (1990 pop. 133), Kane co., S Utah, 14 mi/23 km NNW of Kanab, on East Fork Virgin R. Elev. 5,191 ft/1,582 m. Cattle. East gateway to Zion Natl. Park. Coral Pink Cliffs State Park to S.

Mount Carroll, city (1990 pop. 1,726), ⊙ Carroll co., NW Ill., 22 mi/35 km SW of Freeport; 42°06′N 89°58′W. In rich agr. area (dairy prods., grain; livestock, poultry). Founded 1843, inc. 1867.

Mount Chase, plantation (1990 pop. 254), Penobscot co., N central Maine, 31 mi/50 km NNE of Millinocket; 46°04′N 68°30′W. In hunting, fishing area.

Mount Clare, uninc. town (1990 pop. 850), Harrison co., N W.Va., 5 mi/8 km S of Clarksburg. Agr. (corn); cattle; poultry.

Mount Clemens, city (1990 pop. 18,405), ⊙ Macomb co., suburb 22 mi/35 km NE of downtown Detroit, SE Mich., on the Clinton R.; 42°36′N 82°52′W. The city is known for its mineral waters. It has a large floral industry and mfg. of tool and die, enamels, powder coatings, tool holders and publishing. Natl. Guard Base to E. Settled c.1798, inc. as a city 1879.

Mount Cobb, uninc. town (1990 pop. 2,043), Lackawanna co., NE Pa., 9 mi/14.5 km E of Scranton; 41°25′N 75°30′W. Agr. includes dairying, livestock; corn, hay. Several reservoirs in area.

Mount Cory, village (1990 pop. 245), Hancock co., NW Ohio, 11 mi/18 km SW of Findlay; 40°56′N 83°49′W. In agr. area.

Mount Crawford, village (1990 pop. 228), Rockingham co., NW Va., in Shenandoah Valley, 6 mi/9.7 km SSW of Harrisonburg, on North R.; 38°21′N 78°56′W. Mfg. (fertilizer, poultry packaging, dairy prods.); agr. (poultry, livestock; dairying; grain, apples, peaches). Blue Ridge Community Col. is 6 mi/9.7 km to S.

Mount Croghan (KRO-guhn), village (1990 pop. 131), Chesterfield co., N S.C., 20 mi/32 km WNW of Cheraw, near N.C. state line; 34°46′N 80°13′W. Mfg. includes textile parts, knit goods; agr. includes livestock, poultry, grain, peaches.

Mount Desert (DEZ-zert), township (1990 pop. 1,899), Hancock co., S Maine, on Mt. Desert Isl.; 44°19′N 68°19′W. Includes villages of Seal Harbor, Northeast Harbor, and Asticou. Settled 1762; formerly called Somesville; inc. 1789.

Mount Desert Island (□ c.100 sq mi/259 sq km), largest isl. off the coast of Maine, separated from the mainland by Frenchman Bay, Mt. Desert Narrows, and Western Bay. The isl.'s rugged topography is a result of glacial action. It is almost equally divided into E and W halves by Somes Sound, a fjord. A chain of rounded granite peaks dominates the isl., culminating in Cadillac Mt. (1,530 ft/467 m high). The peaks were named *Monts Deserts*, meaning "wilderness mts.," by the Fr. explorer Samuel de Champlain, who landed on the isl. in 1604. The 1st Fr. Jesuit mission and colony in Amer. was est. here in 1613; the 1st permanent Eng. settlement began in 1762. The isl. developed as a fishing and lumbering center, and by the end of the 19th cent. it had become a famous resort area. A forest fire in 1947 damaged much of the E ½ of the isl. Bar Harbor, Mt. Desert, Tremont, and Southwest Harbor are the main towns. The major part of the isl. is in Acadia Natl. Park.

Mount Dora (DAW-ruh), town (□ 5 sq mi/13 sq km; 1990 pop. 7,196), Lake co., central Fla., 23 mi/37 km NW of Orlando, on L. Dora; 28°48′N 81°38′W. Yachting resort; citrus-fruit shipping center with packing houses, cannery, box and fertilizer factories. Settled 1874, inc. 1912.

Mount Dora (DO-ruh), village, Union co., NE N.Mex., 18 mi/29 km WNW of Clayton, near Cieneguilla del Burro or Seneca Creek. Elev. 5,686 ft/1,733 m. Livestock; alfalfa, and grain.

Mount Eaton, village (1990 pop. 236), Wayne co., N central Ohio, 14 mi/23 km ESE of Wooster; 40°42′N 81°42′W. In agr. area.

Mount Eden, uninc. village, Alameda co., W Calif., suburb 15 mi/24 km SSE of downtown Oakland and E of San Francisco Bay, at E end of San Mateo Bridge (toll).

Mount Enterprise, village (1990 pop. 501), Rusk co., E Texas, 16 mi/26 km SSE of Henderson. In pine timber; cattle; vegetable-growing area.

Mount Ephraim (EE-free-uhm), residential borough (1990 pop. 4,517), Camden co., SW N.J., 5 mi/8 km S of Camden; 39°52′N 75°05′W. Settled before 1800, inc. 1926.

Mount Erie, village (1990 pop. 137), Wayne co., SE Ill., 12 mi/19 km NE of Fairfield; 38°30′N 88°13′W. In agr. area.

Mount Etna, town (1990 pop. 111), Huntington co., NE central Ind., on Salamonie R., and 10 mi/16 km SSW of Huntington; 40°44′N 85°34′W. In agr. area.

Mount Forest, town (1991 pop. 4,266), S Ont., Canada, on branch of Saugeen R., and 40 mi/64 km NNW of Kitchener; 43°58′N 80°44′W. Light mfg.; dairying, woodworking.

Mount Gay, uninc. town (1990 pop. 1200), Logan co., SW W.Va., suburb 2 mi/3.2 km W of Logan. Mfg. (electrical boxes, machining). Agr. (tobacco). Chief Logan State Park to N. Also called Gay.

Mount Gerdine (guhr-DEEN), mountain (11,258 ft/3,834 m), S Alaska, in Tordrillo Mts., 90 mi/145 km WNW of Anchorage; 61°35′N 152°29′W. Named for topographic engineer in late 19th cent.

Mount Gilead (GIL-ee-uhd), town (1990 pop. 1,336), Montgomery co., S central N.C., 14 mi/23 km SE of Albemarle; 35°13′N 80°00′W. Agr. area (cotton, tobacco, grain; livestock); mfg. (barcode equip., boots, wood chips, socks and hosiery). L. Tillery reservoir to W, on Yadkin R. Town Creek Indian Mound State Historical Site to SE.

Mount Gilead, village (1990 pop. 2,846), ⊙ Morrow co., central Ohio, 16 mi/26 km ESE of Marion; 40°33′N 82°50′W. Mfg.(hydraulic presses, electrical apparatus, chemicals); seed growing. Site of annual gourd festival. Founded c.1824; renamed Mount Gilead in 1832.

Mount Gretna, borough (1990 pop. 303), Lebanon co., SE central Pa., 6 mi/9.7 km SSW of Lebanon, suburb of Mount Gretna Heights ½ mi/⅘ km to E; 40°15′N 76°28′W. Agr. (grain; poultry, livestock, dairying). Conewago L. reservoir, on Conewago Creek, in town.

Mount Hamilton Range, Calif.: see DIABLO RANGE.

Mount Healthy, city (1990 pop. 7,580), Hamilton co., extreme SW Ohio, a N suburb of Cincinnati; 39°14′N 84°32′W. Makes tools, brick. Founded 1817.

Mount Hermon, resort village, Santa Cruz co., W Calif., in Santa Cruz Mts., 5 mi/8 km N of Santa Cruz. Redwood groves and a Narrow Gauge RR nearby.

Mount Hermon, Mass.: see NORTHFIELD.

Mount Holly, city (1990 pop. 7,710), Gaston co., S N.C., suburb 12 mi/19 km WNW of Charlotte, and 10 mi/16 km ENE of Gastonia, on Catawba R. (L. Wylie reservoir) dam here forms Mountain Isl. L.; 35°18′N 81°01′W. RR junction. Agr. area (cotton, tobacco, grain; livestock, poultry, dairying). Light Mfg. Hydroelectric plant nearby. Inc. 1879.

Mount Holly 1 township (1990 pop. 10,639), ⊙ Burlington co., W N.J., on Rancocas Creek, and 18 mi/29 km E of Camden; 40°00′N 74°47′W. Mfg. (computers, auto weather stripping, packaging materials); trade center for agr. region. Settled by Friends c.1680; occupied by British in Revolution. Friends' meetinghouse (1775), courthouse (1796), John Woolman memorial bldg. (1771), and other 18th-cent. bldgs. survive. **2** town (1990 pop. 1,093), Rutland co., S central Vt., 13 mi/21 km SE of Rutland; 43°26′N 72°48′W. Partly in Green Mtn. Natl. Forest.

Mount Holly, uninc. village, Berkeley co., SE S.C., suburb 16 mi/26 km NNW of Charleston. Mfg. includes primary aluminum production, aluminum foil, scrap metal. Charleston Naval Base to SE; Cypress Gardens to E.

Mount Holly Springs, borough (1990 pop. 1,925), Cumberland co., S Pa., 6 mi/9.7 km S of Carlisle, near Yellow Breeches Creek; 40°06′N 77°10′W. Mfg. (filter paper, oscillators and quartz crystals, capacitor paper, candy). Kings Gap Environmental Training Center to W. Appalachian Trail passes to S; Pine Grove State Park Furnace to SW. Laid out 1815.

Mount Hope 1 town (1990 pop. 805), Sedgwick co., S central Kansas, 22 mi/35 km NW of Wichita; 37°52′N 97°39′W. In wheat, livestock, and poultry area. Oil wells nearby. **2** town (1990 pop. 1,573), Fayette co., S central W.Va., 8 mi/12.9 km N of Beckley; 37°53′N 81°10′W. RR junction. Bituminous-coal fields. Mfg. (lumber, rebuilt mining machinery, urethane castings). Agr. (grain); cattle. New R. Gorge Natl. R. to E; Plum Orchard Wildlife Management Area to NW. Inc. 1897.

Mount Hope 1 village, Morris co., N central N.J., 9 mi/14.5 km NNW of Morrisville, in lake and hill region. Once an important iron-mining area. **2** village (1990 pop. 173), Grant co., extreme SW Wis., 16 mi/26 km ESE of Prairie du Chien; 42°58′N 90°51′W. Livestock and dairy region. Eagle Valley Nature Preserve to E.

Mount Hope Bay, R.I. and Mass., NE arm of Narragansett Bay, just W of Fall R., Mass.; c.6 mi/9.7 km long, 3 mi/4.8 km wide. Opens S into Sakonnet R., SW into Narragansett Bay at N end of Rhode Isl., where it is crossed by Mt. Hope Bridge (1929), one of largest in New England.

Mount Hopkins Observatory, N Santa Cruz co., S Ariz., astronomical observatory located 35 mi/56 km S of Tucson, W of Mt. Wrightson, in section of Coronado Natl. Forest, at an elev. of 8,500 ft/2,591 m. It is operated jointly by the Smithsonian Astrophysical Observatory and the Univ. of Arizona. The principal instrument is the multiple-mirror telescope (MMT), scheduled for conversion to a 6-m single mirror telescope. The MMT consists of 6 identical 72–in/183–cm reflecting telescopes mounted in a hexagonal array on a common mounting and feeding their images to a single focus. A 30–in/76–cm reflector in the center of the mounting serves as a guide telescope. The combined light-gathering power of the MMT is equal to that of a conventional 176–in/447–cm reflector. It is designed for observations in both the optical and the infrared part of the spectrum. Also at Mt. Hopkins are a 60–in/152–cm and a 394–in/10–m dish with 248 small

Cross references are shown in SMALL CAPITALS. The pronunciation key is on page xv. The dates of population figures are on page xii.

mirrors used for gamma-ray astronomy observations. Gamma rays come from particular objects such as supernovae remnants and black holes.

Mount Horeb (HO-reb), town (1990 pop. 4,182), Dane co., S Wis., 19 mi/31 km WSW of Madison; 43°00′N 89°43′W. In dairying and farming area; processes dairy prods., feed; mfg. (plastic injection molding). On Military Ridge State Trail. Settled 1860 by Norwegians and Swiss; inc. 1899.

Mount Ida, town (1990 pop. 775), ⊙ Montgomery co., W Ark., 32 mi/51 km W of Hot Springs, in Ouachita Natl. Forest; 34°32′N 93°37′W. Mfg. (machining, ladies' shoes). Large L. Ouachita Natl. Forest to NW.

Mount Irvine Bay, SW Tobago, Trinidad and Tobago; popular bathing resort, 7 mi/11.3 km W of Scarborough. Also known as Little Courland Bay.

Mount Jackson, town (1990 pop. 1,583), Shenandoah co., NW Va., 24 mi/39 km NNE of Harrisonburg, on North Fork of Shenandoah R.; 38°45′N 78°38′W. Mfg. (fruit processing, concrete prods., furniture, apparel, fertilizer); agr. (apples, grain, soybeans; poultry, livestock; dairying). Shenandoah Caverns to SW are a tourist attraction.

Mount Jewett, borough (1990 pop. 1,029), McKean co., N Pa., 16 mi/26 km S of Bradford, near Kinzua Creek; 41°43′N 78°38′W. RR junction. Agr. (hay; livestock, dairying); timber; mfg. (particleboard, electronic components). Bradford Regional Airport to N. Kinzua Bridge State Park (bridge originally built of iron 1882, rebuilt 1900 of steel; 301 ft/92 m high, 2,110 ft/643 m long; on abandoned RR line); Allegheny Natl. Forest to W. Settled c.1838, inc. 1893.

Mount Joy, borough (1990 pop. 6,398), Lancaster co., SE Pa., 12 mi/19 km NW of Lancaster, on Little Chikies Creek; 40°06′N 76°30′W. Agr. (grain, potatoes, soybeans; livestock, poultry and eggs, dairying); mfg. (telecommunications components, commercial printing, apparel, printing and publishing, machinery, flour, aluminum castings, food prods.). Covered bridges in area. Settled 1768, laid out 1812, inc. 1851.

Mount Juliet, city (1990 pop. 5,389), Wilson co., central Tenn., 15 mi/24 km E of Nashville; 36°12′N 86°31′W. In farming area near Old Hickory Reservoir (Cumberland R.). Inc. 1972.

Mount Kisco, residential village in Mount Kisco town (☐ 3 sq mi/7.8 sq km; 1990 pop. 9,108), Westchester co., SE N.Y., 13 mi/21 km N of White Plains; 41°12′N 73°43′W. Some light industry (electronics). Affluent community. Inc. 1874.

Mount Laurel, township (1990 pop. 30,270), Burlington co., W central N.J., 8 mi/12.9 km S of Willingboro; 39°57′N 74°54′W. Site of housing dispute resolved by N.J. Supreme Court in 1975 and clarified in Mount Laurel II (1985), which validated low-and moderate-income housing. Residential.

Mount Lebanon, town (1990 pop. 102), Bienville parish, La., 9 mi/14.5 km SW of Arcadia; 32°30′N 93°03′W. In timber area, oil and gas nearby.

Mount Lebanon, township (1990 pop. 33,262), Allegheny co., SW Pa., residential suburb 5 mi/8 km SSW of downtown Pittsburgh; 40°22′N 80°02′W.

Mount Lehman (LEE-muhn), village, SW B.C., Canada, 4 mi/6 km WSW of Mission across Fraser R. Dairying; livestock, vegetables, fruit.

Mount Leonard, town (1990 pop. 96), Saline co., central Mo., near Missouri R., 10 mi/16 km W of Marshall; 39°07′N 93°23′W.

Mount Marion, village (1990 pop. 130), Ulster co., SE N.Y., near Esopus Creek and the Hudson 3 mi/4.8 km SSW of Saugerties, in resort and agr. area; 42°02′N 74°00′W.

Mount McKinley National Park, Alaska: see DENALI NATIONAL PARK AND PRESERVE.

Mount Moriah (mo-REI-yuh), town (1990 pop. 104), Harrison co., NW Mo., 13 mi/21 km NE of Bethany; 40°19′N 93°47′W.

Mount Morris, city (1990 pop. 3,292), Genesee co., SE central Mich., suburb 7 mi/11.3 km N of Flint; 43°07′N 83°42′W. In farm area (grain, potatoes; dairy prods.);

mfg. (packaging, machining). Settled 1842; inc. as village 1867, as city 1930.

Mount Morris, uninc. town (1990 pop. 900), Greene co., SW Pa., 13 mi/21 km SSE of Waynesburg, and 8 mi/12.9 km NNW of Morgantown, W.Va., near W.Va. state line, on Dunkard Creek; 39°43′N 80°04′W. Mfg. (lumber); subsurface coal mining; agr. (hay; livestock, dairying).

Mount Morris 1 village (1990 pop. 2,919), Ogle co., N Ill., 6 mi/9.7 km WNW of Oregon; 42°02′N 89°25′W. In rich agr. area; large printing plant. Settled 1838, inc. 1857. **2** village (☐ 2 sq mi/5.2 sq km; 1990 pop. 3,102), Livingston co., W central N.Y., on Genesee R., and 34 mi/55 km SSW of Rochester; 42°43′N 77°52′W. N entrance to Letchworth State Park is here. Mt. Morris Dam (550 ft/168 m long, 216 ft/66 m high; for flood control) is on the Genesee here.

Mount Morrison, Colo.: see MORRISON.

Mount Natazhat (NAH-zuhr-raht), mountain, S Alaska, in St. Elias Mts., 150 mi/241 km NNW of Yakutat; 61°31′N 141°09′W.

Mount Olive, city (1990 pop. 2,126), Macoupin co., SW central Ill., 18 mi/29 km SSE of Carlinville; 39°04′N 89°43′W. In agr. and bituminous-coal-mining area. Inc. 1917. Has graves of "Mother" Jones and "General" Alexander Bradley, pioneers in miners' union movement.

Mount Olive 1 town (1990 pop. 914), Covington co., S central Miss., 36 mi/58 km NNW of Hattiesburg, on Okatoma Creek; 31°45′N 89°39′W. RR junction to N. Agr. (cotton, corn; poultry, cattle); mfg. (sportswear). L. Ross Barnett State Lake to NE. **2** town (1990 pop. 4,582), Wayne and Duplin cos., E central N.C., 13 mi/21 km SSW of Goldsboro; 35°12′N 78°04′W. Agr. area (poultry, livestock; grain, tobacco, peppers, cotton, cucumbers). Mfg. (furniture, food processing, electrical equip., printing and publishing, plastic prods.). Founded 1839–1840.

Mount Olive, township (1990 pop. 21,282), Morris co., N N.J., 10 mi/16 km W of Morristown; 40°52′N 74°44′W. Inc. 1871.

Mount Oliver, borough (1990 pop. 4,160), Allegheny co., SW Pa., residential suburb 2 mi/3.2 km S of downtown Pittsburgh near Monongahela R.; 40°24′N 79°59′W. Bounded on all sides by city of Pittsburgh. Inc. 1892.

Mount Olivet (AHL-uh-vet), village (1990 pop. 384), ⊙ Robertson co., N Ky., 17 mi/27 km WSW of Maysville; 38°31′N 84°02′W. In Bluegrass agr. region (dairying; poultry, cattle; corn, burley tobacco); mfg. (hand-made soap). Johnson Creek Covered Bridge to S; Blue Licks Battlefield State Park to S.

Mount Orab (O-ruhb), village (1990 pop. 1,929), Brown co., SW Ohio, 11 mi/18 km N of Georgetown, in tobacco and grain area; 39°01′N 83°55′W.

Mount Pearl, city (1991 pop. 23,689), SE N.F., Canada, suburb 4 mi/6 km SW of St. John's, on both sides of Waterford R. Mfg. (kitchen cabinets, wood prods.); mixed farming, potatoes, dairying.

Mount Penn, borough (1990 pop. 2,883), Berks co., SE central Pa., residential suburb 1 mi/1.6 km SE of Reading near Schuylkill R.; 40°19′N 75°53′W. Mt. Penn, with observation tower and the Pagoda, to NW. Laid out 1884, inc. 1902.

Mount Pleasant 1 city (1990 pop. 8,027), ⊙ Henry co., SE Iowa, 25 mi/40 km WNW of Burlington; 40°57′N 91°32′W. Mfg. (consumer goods, food processing, printing, fabricated metal prods., construction material). Limestone quarries nearby. Has Iowa Wesleyan Col.; Mount Pleasant Correctional Center; and Midwest Old Settlers and Threshers Heritage Mus. Oakland Mills State Park to SW; Grode State Park to SE. Founded 1839, inc. 1842. **2** city (1990 pop. 23,285), ⊙ Isabella co., central Mich., on the Chippewa R.; 43°36′N 84°46′W. The city grew after oil was found nearby in 1928. Oil wells and refineries are there. Mfg. (motor assemblies, machinery, foil stamping). Municipal airport to E. Mount Pleasant is the seat of Central Mich. Univ. Isabella Indian Reservation surrounds and includes city. Settled before 1860, inc. as a city 1889. **3** city (1990 pop. 30,108), Charleston co., SE S.C., residential suburb 4 mi/6.4 km E of downtown Charleston, across

Charleston Harbor (here bridged); 32°49′N 79°51′W. Port facilities, boat repairs. Mfg. includes marine equip., plastic prods., signs, and seafood processing. Upper middle-class suburb and one of the state's fastest-growing areas. A 300-year-old tradition of weaving baskets from local marsh grass and sweet grass by the local Afr.-Amer. community is continued today. **4** city (1990 pop. 4,278), Maury co., central Tenn., 11 mi/18 km SW of Columbia; 35°32′N 87°12′W. In phosphate-mining, lumbering, agr. area; makes fertilizer, chemicals, clothing; aluminum processing. Meriwether Lewis Natl. Monument is 14 mi/23 km W. **5** city (1990 pop. 12,291), ⊙ Titus co., NE Texas, c.50 mi/80 km SE of Paris; 33°10′N 94°58′W. Elev. 416 ft/127 m. Trade, RR junction, shipping center for agr. (poultry; dairying; cattle; watermelons, corn), oil, timber region; mfg. (food processing, trailers, concrete, insulated wire, doors, printing). Northwest Texas Community Col. is at nearby Chappell Hill, (serves Camp, Morris and Titus cos.). Formerly a lumbering center; settled before mid-19th cent., inc. 1900.

Mount Pleasant 1 town (1990 pop. 1,027), Cabarrus co., S central N.C., 8 mi/12.9 km E of Concord; 35°23′N 80°26′W. Agr. area (grain, soybeans, poultry, livestock, dairying). Mfg. (hosiery, marble bathtubs and vanities, lumber, yarn). **2** town (1990 pop. 2,092), Sanpete co., central Utah, 22 mi/35 km NNE of Manti, near San Pitch R., in irrigated Sanpete Valley; 39°32′N 111°27′W. Shipping point for cattle, sheep, hogs, poultry and agr. area (alfalfa, wheat, barley, oats; dairying); mfg. (flour, cheese). Elev. c.5,924 ft/1,806 m. Wasatch Range in Manti–La Sal Natl. Forest is E. Old Pioneer Mus. Settled 1852 by Mormons, inc. 1868.

Mount Pleasant 1 uninc. village, New Castle co., W Del., 17 mi/27 km SSW of Wilmington; 39°31′N 75°43′W. Recreational waterfowl hunting. **2** village (1990 pop. 498), Jefferson co., E Ohio, 17 mi/27 km SSW of Steubenville; 40°10′N 80°48′W.

Mount Pleasant, borough (1990 pop. 4,787), Westmoreland co., SW Pa., 30 mi/48 km SE of Pittsburgh; 40°08′N 79°32′W. Bituminous coal; mfg. (food processing, technical equip., fabricated metal prods., consumer goods); timber. Agr. area (corn, hay, apples, dairying). Chestnut Ridge to SE; Bridgeport Reservoir (Jacobs Creek) to SE; Mt. Pleasant–Scottsdale Airport to S. Laid out c.1897, inc. 1828.

Mount Pleasant, residential sect. in NW Washington, D.C., E of Rock Creek and N of Irving St.; 38°56′N 77°02′W. Early suburb of Washington, largely developed in the 1870s. Formerly the site of a Civil War hosp. The community today has a large Hispanic and 1st-generation immigrant pop.

Mount Plymouth, town (☐ 1 sq mi/2.6 sq km; 1990 pop. 1,752), Lake co., central Fla., 20 mi/32 km NW of Orlando; 28°48′N 81°31′W.

Mount Pocono, borough (1990 pop. 1,795), Monroe co., E Pa., 12 mi/19 km NW of Stroudsburg in Pocono Mts.; 41°07′N 75°21′W. Elev. 1,658 ft/505 m. Tourism, large resort community. Light mfg. Numerous residential developments to N and W. Pocono Mts. Municipal Airport to N; Pennsylvania Du. Farm to E; Pocono Internatl. Raceway to SW; Pocono Manor Ski Area to S; Mt. Airy Ski Area to SE; Tobyhanna State Park to NW; Tobyhanna Depot to NW.

Mount Prospect, village (1990 pop. 53,170), Cook co., NE Ill.; 42°04′N 87°56′W. Inc. 1917. It is a large and growing residential suburb NW of Chicago.

Mount Pulaski (poo-LAS-kei), city (1990 pop. 1,610), Logan co., central Ill., 25 mi/40 km NE of Springfield; 40°00′N 89°16′W. In agr. area. Was ⊙ Logan co., 1847–1853; inc. 1893. The old courthouse (1847) was made a state monument in 1936.

Mount Rainier, city (1990 pop. 7,954), Prince Georges co., central Md., suburb NE of Wash., D.C.; 38°56′N 76°58′W. Land in the area once belonged to Army officers from Seattle, hence the name. Est. 1902.

Mount Rainier National Park (rai-NIR) (☐ 368 sq mi/953 sq km), Pierce and Lewis cos., W central Wash., in the Cascade Range. The area is dominated by Mt. Rainier (14,411 ft/4,392 m), a dormant, glaciated volcanic peak. The mt. is snow-crowned and has 26 glaciers; its heavily forested lower slopes and alpine meadows are popular with hikers. Bounded W, N, and E by Snoqualmie Natl. Forest, S by Gifford Pinchot Natl. Forest. Numerous waterfalls; road access in E and S, NW corner. Est. 1899.

Mount Repose, uninc. village (1990 pop. 3,093), Clermont co., extreme SW Ohio, a NE suburb of Cincinnati, c.16 mi/26 km from downtown; 39°11′N 84°13′W. Adjacent to Mulberry.

Mount Revelstoke National Park (□ 100 sq mi/259 sq km), SE B.C., Canada, in the Selkirk Mts., just E of the Columbia R. valley. Est. 1914. Situated on a high plateau, rising to c.7,000 ft/2,134 m at Mt. Revelstoke, the park has several small lakes and glaciers. A popular resort area, noted especially for winter sports.

Mount Robson Provincial Park (RAHB-suhn) (□ 803 sq mi/2,080 sq km), E B.C., Canada, in the Rocky Mts. W of Jasper, Alta.; 52°58′N 118°50′W. Est. 1913. High peaks, glaciers, lakes, waterfalls, and headwaters of Fraser R. Mt. Robson (12,972 ft/3,954 m), in the park, is the highest peak in the Can. Rocky Mts.

Mount Royal or **Mont Réal** (mo-rai-AHL) (900 ft/274 m), S Que., Canada, in N part of Montreal city. On its upper slopes is Mount Royal Park (□ 463 acres/187 ha); on S slope is McGill Univ., on N slope Montreal Univ. Residential dist.

Mount Rushmore National Memorial (□ 2 sq mi/5.2 sq km), Pennington and Custer cos., SW S.Dak., in the Black Hills at Keystone, 17 mi/27 km SW of Rapid City, N of Custer State Park. Carved on the face of the mt. and visible for 60 mi/100 km, are the enormous busts of four U.S. Presidents—Washington, Jefferson, Lincoln, and Theodore Roosevelt. The sculpture, nearly completed when the sculptor, Gutzon Borglum, died (1941), was finished later that year by his son Lincoln. It took 14 years to complete the figures. Visitors' Center. Est. 1925, dedicated 1927.

Mount Saint George, village, E Tobago, Trinidad and Tobago, 4 mi/6.4 km ENE of Scarborough, opens onto Hillsborough Bay. Coconuts. Formerly called Georgetown, former capital of Tobago.

Mount Saint Helens National Volcanic Monument (172 sq mi/445 sq km); in Skamania, Cowlitz, and Lewis cos., SW Wash., 55 mi/89 km NNE of Portland, Oregon, and 120 mi/193 km S of Seattle, Wash. Est. 1982 to protect the area around Mt. Saint Helens volcano and to commemorate the event of May 18, 1980, when Mt. Saint Helens erupted, one of the most significant geologic events of recorded N. Amer. history. Spirit L. in NE; Ape Cave in S.

Mount Savage, village, Allegany co., W Md., in the Alleghenies near Pa. state line, 7 mi/11.3 km WNW of Cumberland. Bituminous-coal and clay mining; firebrick plant, RR shops. A blast furnace was built here in 1839 by Eng. entrepreneurs, after coal and iron ore both were found nearby, making the village an early industrial center. They sold out to Amer. investors in the Mount Savage Iron Co., which made the first iron rails in Amer. The iron works failed when the ore proved inferior, but a firebrick plant, headed by President Franklin Delano Roosevelt's father, James, in the 1880s, is still operating. Big Savage Mt. is just nearby.

Mount Shasta, city (1990 pop. 3,460), Siskiyou co., N Calif., tourist center at SW foot of Mt. Shasta; 41°19′N 122°19′W. Cattle, sheep, lambs; grain, potatoes, onions; mfg. (printing and publishing); timber, fish hatchery nearby. RR junction. Settled in 1850s, inc. 1905. Known as Sisson until 1925. Castle Crags State Park to S; near Sacramento R., its source is c.10 mi/16 km to SW; parts of Shasta Natl. Forest to NE and SW. Sisson Mus.

Mount Snow, ski area and year-round resort, Windham co., S Vt., in Dover town, and 15 mi/24 km ENE of Bennington.

Mount Sterling, city (1990 pop. 1,922), ⊙ Brown co., W Ill., 33 mi/53 km E of Quincy; 39°58′N 90°45′W. In agr. area (corn, soybeans, cattle, hogs). Settled 1830, inc. 1837. Western Ill. Correctional Inst. near here.

Mount Sterling 1 town (1990 pop. 53), Van Buren co., SE Iowa, near Mo. state line, on Fox R., and 7 mi/11.3 km S of Keosauqua; 40°37′N 91°56′W. Livestock, grain. **2** town (1990 pop. 5,362), ⊙ Montgomery co., E central Ky., 31 mi/50 km E of Lexington; 38°03′N 83°57′W. Elev. 940 ft/287 m. Trade center in NE part of Bluegrass region. Agr. (dairying; livestock, poultry; burley tobacco, corn, wheat) area; varied mfg. Mt. Sterling-Montgomery County Airport to W. Gaitskill Mounds, burial mounds of Adena Indians (c.800 B.C.–700 A.D.) to N. Ascension Church (1878). Platted 1793. Captured and sacked (1863) by Confederate Gen. John Hunt Morgan in Civil War.

Mount Sterling 1 village (1990 pop. 1,647), Madison co., central Ohio, 15 mi/24 km SE of London, and on Deer Creek, in agr. area; 39°43′N 83°16′W. Founded 1828. **2** village (1990 pop. 217), Crawford co., SW Wis., 21 mi/34 km NNE of Prairie du Chien; 43°18′N 90°55′W. Hog-raising and dairying area. Goat cheese and milk. Quarry here.

Mount Stewart, village (1991 pop. 315), N P.E.I., Canada, on Hillsborough R., and 16 mi/26 km NE of Charlottetown; 46°22′N 62°52′W. Mixed farming, dairying; potatoes.

Mount Summit, town (1990 pop. 238), Henry co., E Ind., 6 mi/9.7 km N of New Castle; 40°00′N 85°23′W. In agr. area. Mfg. (food processing). Laid out 1854.

Mount Tabor, town (1990 pop. 214), Rutland co., S central Vt., in hunting, fishing area of Green Mtn. Natl. Forest, 16 mi/26 km S of Rutland; 43°21′N 72°55′W. Former charcoal center.

Mount Tom, Mass.: see EASTHAMPTON.

Mount Tremper, resort village (1990 pop. 650), Ulster co., SE N.Y., in the Catskills, on Esopus Creek, and 16 mi/26 km WNW of Kingston; 42°03′N 74°17′W.

Mount Union, town (1990 pop. 140), Henry co., SE Iowa, 10 mi/16 km NE of Mount Pleasant; 41°03′N 91°23′W. In livestock area.

Mount Union, borough (1990 pop. 2,878), Huntingdon co., S central Pa., 29 mi/47 km ESE of Altoona, on Juniata R.; 40°22′N 77°52′W. Mfg. (screw machine prods., clothing, fiberglass, storage tanks); timber; agr. (alfalfa, grain; poultry, dairying). Mt. Union Airport to S; Tuscarora State Forest to E; part of Rothrock State Forest to N and NW. Laid out 1849, inc. 1867.

Mount Utsayantha, N.Y.: see STAMFORD.

Mount Van Hoevenberg, N.Y.: see MOUNT VAN HOEVENBERG STATE RECREATION AREA, .

Mount Van Hoevenberg State Recreation Area, Essex co., N N.Y., 5.5 mi/8.9 km SE of L. Placid, on NE slopes and to NE of Mt. Van Hoevenberg (elev. 2,940 ft/896 m); 44°13′N 73°56′W. Major winter sports recreation destination. The 1st bobsled run in N. Amer. was built here for the 1932 Winter Olympics. Site of the bobsled, luge, cross-country, and biathlon events of the 1980 Winter Olympic Games held at L. Placid.

Mount Vernon 1 city (1990 pop. 16,988), ⊙ Jefferson co., SE Ill.; 38°19′N 88°54′W. Settled 1819, inc. 1837. It is a trade, RR, and industrial center in a farm and coal region. Mfg. (tools, tires, transformers, coal-mining equip., neon signs, rebuilt locomotives); diversified agr. State game farm nearby. Rend L. Col. 10 mi/16 km S. **2** city (1990 pop. 7,217), ⊙ Posey co., extreme SW Ind., 18 mi/29 km W of Evansville, and on Ohio R. near influx of the Wabash; 37°56′N 87°54′W. Trade center for agr. area; oil refining; mfg. of petroleum and coal prods., flour grinding, asphalt roofing shingles, plastics, gases, feed mixing. Ohio R. port. Settled 1816, inc. 1865. **3** city (1990 pop. 3,726), ⊙ Lawrence co., SW Mo., near Spring R., 30 mi/48 km W of Springfield; 37°06′N 93°49′W. Wheat, corn, produce; dairying; cattle; mfg. (woodburning stoves, apparel, aluminum cans, motor vehicle equip.). Missouri Rehabilitation Center and Missouri Veterans' Home. Laid out 1845. **4** city (1990 pop. 67,153), Westchester co., SE N.Y., bet. the Bronx and Hutchinson rivers and adjacent to the Bronx; 40°55′N 73°50′W. Settled 1664, inc. 1892. Although primarily a residential suburb of N.Y. city, its mfg. includes pharmaceuticals and electronic components. John Peter Zenger was arrested there for libel in 1733. The city itself was not founded until 1851, when a cooperative group, the Industrial Home Assn., bought the land and built a planned community. St. Paul's Church (c.1761), a natl. historic site, is here. The city, which has a large Afr.-Amer. pop., has been the scene of a great deal of controversy over school and housing integration in the 1970s, 1980s, and 1990s. **5** city (1990 pop. 14,550), ⊙ Knox co., central Ohio, on the Kokosing R.; 40°23′N 82°28′W. Laid out 1805, inc. as a city 1880. Livestock and dairy farms; mfg. (diesel engines, steel, turbines, and glass). Mount Vernon has a junior col. **6** uninc. city (1990 pop. 27,485), Fiarfax co., NE Va., residential suburb 7mi/11 km S of Alexandria and 14 mi/23 km SSW of Washington, D.C., on Potomac R. Mt. Vernon historical site is here, as well as the Woodlawn Plantation and George Washington Grist Mill Historic State Park to the W. Tourism. **7** city (1990 pop. 17,647), ⊙ Skagit co., NW Wash., 25 mi/40 km SSE of Bellingham and on Skagit R., near Skagit Bay of Puget Sound (to SW); 48°25′N 122°19′W. Berries, vegetables, tulips; dairying; poultry; mfg. (fabricated metal prods., fresh and frozen seafoods, farm machinery, service industry machinery, signs, printing and publishing, poultry processing); stone quarrying. Swinomish Indian Reservation to W; Bay View State Park to NW. Skagit Valley Community Col. is here. Settled c.1877.

Mount Vernon 1 town (1990 pop. 1,914), ⊙ Montgomery co., E central Ga., 9 mi/14.5 km W of Vidalia, near Oconee R.; 32°11′N 82°35′W. Mfg. includes apparel, textiles, lumber. **2** town (1990 pop. 3,657), Linn co., E Iowa, 13 mi/21 km ESE of Cedar Rapids; 41°55′N 91°25′W. Mfg. (feed). Cornell Col. (Methodist, 1853) is here. State park nearby. Inc. 1869. **3** town (1990 pop. 2,654), ⊙ Rockcastle co., central Ky., 32 mi/51 km SE of Danville, on old Wilderness Road; 37°21′N 84°20′W. RR junction to E. In coal-mining, agr. (corn, burley tobacco; livestock; dairying) area; coal mines; mfg. (crushed limestone, plastic packaging materials, uniform pants). Daniel Boone Natl. Forest to E (including Great Saltpeter Caves). Hunting in vicinity. Renfro Valley Entertainment Center to N; L. Linville reservoir to N. Settled 1810; inc. 1818. **4** town (1990 pop. 1,362), Kennebec co., S Maine, 17 mi/27 km NW of Augusta; 44°28′N 69°57′W. In lake dist.; agr., resorts, lumbering. **5** town (1990 pop. 1,812), Hillsborough co., S N.H., 13 mi/21 km SW of Manchester; 42°53′N 71°40′W. Drained by Beaver Brook and Ceasans Brook. Mfg. (canvas goods); agr. (fruit, vegetables; poultry, livestock; dairying). **6** town (1990 pop. 2,219), ⊙ Franklin co., NE Texas, 70 mi/113 km WSW of Texarkana, and near White Oak Creek; 33°10′N 95°13′W. Elev. 476 ft/145 m. In agr., oil, timber area; varied mfg. (furniture, wiring). Lakes Bob Sandlin, Cypress Springs and Monticello to SE, L. Bob Sandlin State Park to SE. Inc. 1910.

Mount Vernon 1 village (1990 pop. 902), Mobile co., SW Ala., near Mobile R., 27 mi/43 km N of Mobile. Lumber, flooring. **2** village (1990 pop. 538), Grant co., NE central Oregon, on John Day R., at mouth of Beech Creek, 6 mi/9.7 km W of John Day; 44°25′N 119°06′W. Elev. 2,871 ft/875 m. Trading point for agr. and livestock. Strawberry Mts. to SE. Clyde Holliday State Park to E; parts of Malheur Natl. Forest to N and S. **3** village (1990 pop. 368), Davison co., SE central S.Dak., 10 mi/16 km W of Mitchell; 43°42′N 98°15′W.

Mount Vernon, historic site, Fairfax co., NE Va., overlooking Potomac R., 7 mi/11.3 km S of Alexandria, 14 mi/23 km SSW of downtown Wash., D.C.; home of George Washington from 1747 until his death in 1799. The land was patented in 1674, and the house was built in 1743 by Lawrence Washington, George Washington's half brother. Mount Vernon was named for Admiral Edward Vernon, Lawrence's commander in the Brit. navy. George Washington inherited it in 1754 and made additions that were not completed until after the Revolution. The mansion is a wooden structure of Georgian design, 2½ stories high, with a broad, columned portico; wide lawns, fine gardens, and subsidiary bldgs. surround it. The mansion has been restored, after Washington's detailed notes, with much of the original furniture, family relics, and duplicate pieces of the period. Purchased in 1860 by the Mount Vernon Ladies'

Association (organized 1856), its permanent custodian. Tombs (built 1831–1837) of George and Martha Washington and other family members.

Mount Victory, village (1990 pop. 551), Hardin co., W central Ohio, 9 mi/14 km SSE of Kenton, in agr. area; 40°32'N 83°31'W.

Mount Vsevidof, snow-covered volcano, SW Alaska, on W Umnak Isl., Aleutian Isls., 15 mi/24 km NNE of Nikolski; 60°40'N 143°00'W.

Mount Washington 1 town (1990 pop. 5,226), Bullitt co., NW Ky., 15 mi/24 km SE of Louisville; 38°02'N 85°32'W. Agr. area (burley tobacco, grain, livestock, poultry, dairying). Mfg. (concrete, materials handling equip., executive coaches). **2** resort town (1990 pop. 135), Berkshire co., SW Mass., in the Berkshires, near N.Y. state line, 25 mi/40 km SSW of Pittsfield; 42°06'N 73°28'W. Includes Union Church village and Mt. Everett. Bash Bish Falls State Park nearby; state forest.

Mount Washington, Md.: see BALTIMORE.

Mount Wilson Observatory, Los Angeles co., S Calif. at Mt. Wilson, San Gabriel Mts., 16 mi/26 km NE of downtown Los Angeles and 7 mi/11.3 km NE of Pasadena in Angeles Natl. Forest. Mt. Wilson Observatory was founded in 1904 by George E. Hale. Its equip. includes 100 in/254 cm and 60 in/152 cm reflecting telescopes and 2 solar tower telescopes 150 ft/46 m and 60 ft/18 m in length. Principal research programs that have been conducted at the observatory include studies of the structure and dimensions of the universe and the physical nature, chemical composition, and evolution of celestial bodies. An ongoing program on the 60 in/152 cm telescope is a long-term study of singly ionized calcium lines to monitor sunspot cycles on nearby solar-type stars. Formerly part of the Hale Observatories jointly administered by the California Inst. of Technology and the Carnegie Inst., in 1985 the Carnegie Inst. closed the 100 in/254 cm telescope, and a few years later transferred the observatory's management to the newly formed Mount Wilson Inst.

Mount Wolf, borough (1990 pop. 1,365), York co., S Pa., 7 mi/11.3 km NNE of York, 2 mi/3.2 km to SW of Susquehanna R.; 40°03'N 76°42'W. Mfg. (food prods., corrugated containers, steel wire and fiberglass mesh prods.); agr. (grain, soybeans, apples; poultry, livestock, dairying).

Mount Zion, city (1990 pop. 511), Carroll co., W Ga., 7 mi/11.3 km NW of Carrollton, near Ala. state line; 33°38'N 85°11'W.

Mount Zion, village (1990 pop. 4,522), Macon co., central Ill., 6 mi/9.7 km SE of Decatur; 39°46'N 88°52'W. In agr. area. Spitler Woods State Natural Area nearby.

Mountain, village (1990 pop. 134), Pembina co., NE N.Dak., 13 mi/21 km SW of Cavalier; 48°40'N 97°51'W. Icelandic State Park to NE.

Mountain Brook, suburb (1990 pop. 19,810), Jefferson co., N central Ala. A residential suburb E of Birmingham. Inc. 1942.

Mountain City 1 town (1990 pop. 784), Rabun co., extreme NE Ga., 3 mi/4.8 km N of Clayton, in the Blue Ridge; 34°55'N 83°23'W. Mfg. of apparel and wood prods. Black Rock Mt. Park has the highest elev. among nearby state parks. **2** town (1990 pop. 2,169), extreme NE Tenn., 33 mi/53 km ENE of Johnson City, bet. Stone Mts. (E) and Iron Mts. (W); ⊙ Johnson co.; 36°28'N 81°48'W. Farm-trade center (strawberries, tobacco) in summer-resort region; lumbering; mfg. of apparel, wood prods.

Mountain City, uninc. village (1990 pop. 100), Elko co., NE Nev., on East Fork Owyhee R., and 70 mi/113 km N of Elko in Humboldt Natl. Forest, beyond SE corner of Duck Valley Indian Reservation. Elev. c.5,620 ft/1,713 m. Trading point. Rio Tinto (just SW) is former company-owned, copper-mining town, 10 mi/16 km S of Idaho state line.

Mountain Creek Lake, Dallas co., N Texas, reservoir impounded 10 mi/16 km WSW of Dallas by dam in small Mountain Creek (also forms L. Joe Pool to S), a S tributary of West Fork of Trinity R. Dallas Naval Air Station on N shore; Dallas Baptist Univ. on SE shore.

Mountain Dale, resort village (1990 pop. 200), Sullivan co., SE N.Y., in the Catskills, 8 mi/12.9 km ENE of Monticello; 41°42'N 74°33'W.

Mountain Fork, Okla. and Ark.: see LITTLE RIVER.

Mountain Grove, city (1990 pop. 4,182), Wright co., S central Mo., in the Ozarks, 55 mi/89 km E of Springfield; 37°07'N 92°15'W. Agr., livestock, timber area; trade center; mfg. (metal stamping, feeds and fertilizers, exercise equip., caps); lumber; limestone quarries. State fruit experiment station nearby. Settled 1851, inc. 1882.

Mountain Home 1 town (1990 pop. 9,027), ⊙ Baxter co., N Ark., c.40 mi/64 km ENE of Harrison, in the Ozarks, bet. White R. (Bull Shoals Dam and Reservoir) to W and the North Fork (Norfork Reservoir) to E; 36°20'N 92°22'W. Mfg. (printing, motor vehicle equip., rubber, health care prods., consumer goods). Bull Shoals State Park to W. Tourism and recreation, growing retirement pop. **2** town (1990 pop. 7,913), ⊙ Elmore co., SW Idaho, near Snake R., 40 mi/64 km SE of Boise; elev. 3,145 ft/959 m; 43°08'N 115°42'W. Wool-shipping point in irrigated agr. area (sheep, cattle, fruit, potatoes, sugar beets; hay); mfg. (potato skins). Mountain Home U.S. Air Force Base to SW. Plans for further land reclamation in vicinity have been made. Zinc, silver, gold mines to N. Boise Natl. Forest to N; Long Tom Reservoir to N; Bruneau Dunes State Park to S, at Bruneau. Inc. 1896. **3** uninc. town (1990 pop. 1,898), Henderson co., SW N.C., 16 mi/26 km S of Asheville, and 4 mi/6.4 km N of Hendersonville; 35°22'N 82°30'W. Pisgah Natl. Forest to W. Agr. area (dairying, cattle, hay, corn, potatoes). Mfg. (metal, paper, and ceramic prods.).

Mountain Iron, town (1990 pop. 3,362), St. Louis co., NE Minn., in Mesabi Iron Range 4 mi/6.4 km W of Virginia; 47°31'N 92°37'W. Mfg. (crushers and shovels, taconite, pallets, steel fabrication). Superior Natl. Forest to N. Grew with development of iron deposits. West Two Rivers Reservoir to S. Settled 1890, inc. 1892.

Mountain Island Lake, N.C.: see CATAWBA RIVER.

Mountain Lake, town (1990 pop. 1,906), Cottonwood co., SW Minn., 10 mi/16 km ENE of Windom, near Watonwan R., forms Mountain L. to NW; 43°56'N 94°55'W. Grain, soybeans; livestock; mfg. (slurry pumps, oak furniture, light mfg.). Laid out 1872, settled by Mennonites.

Mountain Lake, in chain of lakes on Can.-U.S. border, in Cook co., NE Minn., and Thunder Bay dist., W Ont., 25 mi/40 km NNE of Grand Marais, Minn.; 7 mi/11.3 km long, 1 mi/1.6 km wide; 48°06'N 90°13'W. Minn. part in Boundary Waters Canoe Area of Superior Natl. Forest. Fed From Watap L. by small stream from W; drains E through small stream to Moose L. and Pigeon R.; all on U.S.-Can. border.

Mountain Lake, reservoir, Greenville co., NW S.C., in the Blue Ridge Mts., on South Saluda R., and 19 mi/31 km N of Greenville. Resort area.

Mountain Lake Park, town (1990 pop. 1,938), Garrett co., W Md., in the Alleghenies just SE of Oakland; 39°24'N 79°23'W. Vegetable cannery. Founded in 1881, the village was originally an extensive complex of hotels, sporting facilities, and a tabernacle called the "Mountain Chautaugua." Thousands gathered here to listen to William Jennings Bryan, perennial Presidential candidate famed for his "Cross of Gold" speech; Samuel Gompers, president of the Amer. Federation of Labor; and President William Howard Taft—when magicians, jugglers, and bell ringers were not performing.

Mountain Lakes, residential borough (1990 pop. 3,847), Morris co., N N.J., 6 mi/9.7 km NNE of Morristown; 40°53'N 74°26'W. Has several artificial lakes. Settled 1915 as real estate development, inc. 1924.

Mountain Meadow, located in Dixie Natl. Forest, small valley in extreme SW Utah, N central Washington co., near headwaters of Santa Clara R. where in 1857 a party of some 140 emigrants bound for Calif. were massacred by Indians led by fanatical Mormons settlers after a 3-day battle; the incident exacerbated tensions bet. Mormons and non-Mormons.

Mountain Mesa, uninc. town (1990 pop. 1,153), Kern co., S central Calif., residential community 4 mi/6.4 km ENE of Lake Isabella town, on S shore of L. Isabella reservoir (Kern R.), in Sierra Nevada; 35°38'N 118°25'W. Cattle, hay, timber. Area surrounded by parts of Sequoia Natl. Forest.

Mountain Park, village, W Alta., Canada, in Rocky Mts., near Jasper Natl. Park, 35 mi/56 km E of Jasper; 52°56'N 117°17'W. Elev. 5,815 ft/1,772 m. Coal mining; timber; tourism. Near source of McLeod R.

Mountain Park, city (1990 pop. 544), Fulton co., NW central Ga., 12 mi/19 km NE of Marietta; 34°05'N 84°25'W.

Mountain Park, village (1990 pop. 473), Kiowa co., SW Okla., 25 mi/40 km SSE of Hobart; 34°42'N 98°57'W. In agr. area. Great Plains State Park nearby, on Tom Steed L. reservoir, to N.

Mountain Pine, town (1990 pop. 866), Garland co., central Ark., 8 mi/12.9 km NW of Hot Springs, and on Ouachita R., at E end of Blakely Mt. Dam; 34°34'N 93°10'W. Mfg. (lumber, wooden furniture). Tourism and recreation. Large L. Ouachita reservoir to NW; L. Ouachita State Park to N; Ouachita Natl. Forest to W.

Mountain Point, village, SE Alaska, on S shore of Revillagigedo Isl., SE of Ketchikan; 55°18'N 131°32'W.

Mountain Rest, village, Oconee co., NW S.C., in the Blue Ridge, 9 mi/14.5 km NW of Walhalla; near Ga. state line in Sumter Natl. Forest. Oconee State Park to E., fish hatchery to N.

Mountain Top, uninc. town (1990 pop. 750), Fairview township, Luzerne co., NE Pa., industrial suburb, 5 mi/8 km S of Wilkes-Barre; 41°10'N 75°52'W. Elev. 1,680 ft/512 m. Diversified mfg. Crystal L. reservoir to E. Founded 1788.

Mountain View, village, S Alta., Canada, near Mont. border, 50 mi/80 km SW of Lethbridge. Gateway to Waterton Lakes Natl. Park; cattle, sheep.

Mountain View, city (1990 pop. 67,460), Santa Clara co., W Calif., suburb 8 mi/12.9 km WNW of downtown San Jose, and 31 mi/50 km SSE of San Francisco, on San Francisco Bay; 37°24'N 122°05'W. Located in an area that grew rapidly in 1960s–1970s, Mountain View is a major part of the Silicon Valley industrial complex. Varied high-technology mfg. It also has research organizations, and diverse mfg. industries. Fruits and vegetables are shipped from the city. Saint Patrick's Col. is there. Moffet Naval Air Station adjoins the city to NE. Drained by Stevens Creek; Stevens Creek Reservoir to S; Santa Clara Mts. to SW; branch of Hetch Hetchy Aqueduct runs through city. Inc. 1902.

Mountain View 1 town (1990 pop. 2,439), ⊙ Stone co., N Ark., 27 mi/43 km WNW of Batesville, in the Ozarks; 35°52'N 92°06'W. Agr.; varied mfg. Part of Ozark Natl. Forest to N; Blanchard Springs Caverns and Recreation Area to NW; Ozark Folk Center State Historical Park is here. **2** town (1990 pop. 3,075), SE Hawaii isl., Hawaii co., Hawaii, 12 mi/19 km S of Hilo inland, 12 mi/19 km from NE coast, 15 mi/24 km from SE coast, on Volcano Road (Hawaii Belt Road); 19°31'N 155°09'W. Hawaii Volcanoes Natl. Park 12 mi/19 km SW, active craters and lava flows to sea 12 mi/19 km S. Waiakea Forest Reserve to N; Puna Forest Reserve and Wao Kele O Puna Natural Area Reserve to SE. **3** town (1990 pop. 2,036), Howell co., S Mo., in the Ozarks, near Eleven Point R., 20 mi/32 km NNE of West Plains; 36°59'N 91°42'W. Grain, livestock, lumber prods. **4** uninc. town (1990 pop. 3,697), Catawba co., W central N.C., 5 mi/8 km SSW of Hickory, bet. Henrys Fork and Jacobs Fork rivers; 35°40'N 81°22'W. Agr. area (grain, soybeans, poultry, livestock, dairying). **5** town (1990 pop. 1,086), Kiowa co., SW Okla., 20 mi/32 km ENE of Hobart, and on Washita R., N of Wichita Mts.; 35°06'N 98°45'W. In wheat, livestock, cotton area. **6** town (1990 pop. 1,189), Uinta co., SW Wyo., 5 mi/8 km SSW of Lyman, on Williams Creek; 41°16'N 110°20'W. Elev. 6,795 ft/2,071 m. Cattle, sheep; alfalfa, hay; timber. Wasatch Natl. Forest to S.

Mountain View 1 village (1990 pop. 550), Jefferson co., N central Colo., residential suburb 5 mi/8 km NW of downtown Denver; 39°46'N 105°03'W. Elev. 5,385 ft/1,641 m. Bounded E by Denver, N by Lakeside, W and S by Wheat Ridge. **2** residential village, Passaic co., NE N.J., on Pompton R., and 5 mi/8 km W of Paterson.

Mountain View Acres, uninc. town (1990 pop. 2,469), San Bernardino co., S Calif., residential suburb 4 mi/ 6.4 km SW of Victorville, and 5 mi/8 km NNW of Hesperia; 34°30'N 117°21'W. Agr. (citrus, pears, apples, nursery prods., grain); dairying; cattle. Roy Rogers/ Dale Evans Mus. to NE; George Air Force Base to N. Irrigated agr. area at SW edge of Mojave Desert.

Mountain Village, village, W Alaska, on Yukon R., and 110 mi/177 km NW of Bethel; 62°5'N 163°43'W.

Mountainair, town (1990 pop. 926), Torrance co., central N.Mex., 65 mi/105 km NW of Socorro, bet. Manzano Range (NW) and Chupadero Mesa (S); 34°31'N 106°14'W. Elev. 6,499 ft/1,981 m. Agr. shipping point for cattle, corn, beans, pumpkins, grains, alfalfa. Mfg. (hydro pressure filters, traffic control devices). Abo Pueblo Ruins to W, Quarai Pueblo Ruins to NW, Gran Quivira Pueblo Ruins (Socorro co.) to SE; all 3 are units comprising Salinas Pueblo Missions Natl. Monument. Manzano Peak (10,098 ft/3,078 m) to W; Manzano Mt. State Park to NW; parts of Cibola Natl. Forest to W and E.

Mountainburg, village (1990 pop. 488), Crawford co., NW Ark., 21 mi/34 km NE of Fort Smith on Frog Bayou, at S edge of the Ozarks; 35°37'N 94°10'W. Mfg. (printed circuit boards). Tourism and resort area. Lake Fort Smith State Park and Ozark Natl. Forest to NE.

Mountainhome, uninc. town (1990 pop. 1,042), Monroe co., E Pa., 13 mi/21 km NNW of Stroudsburg in Pocono Mts.; 41°10'N 75°15'W. Mfg. includes food prods. and fabricated metal prods. Tourism important to the economy. Delaware State Forest to E. Ski area here.

Mountainside, residential borough (1990 pop. 6,657), Union co., NE N.J., 11 mi/18 km SW of Newark; 40°40'N 74°21'W. Park and bird sanctuary here. Inc. 1895.

Mountainville 1 village, Hunterdon co., W N.J., 13 mi/ 21 km N of Flemington, in agr. area. **2** village (1990 pop. 600), Orange co., SE N.Y., 12 mi/19 km SSW of Newburgh, in Hudson highlands; 41°24'N 74°05'W. Site of Storm King Art Center.

Mountlake Terrace, city (1990 pop. 19,320), Snohomish and King cos., NW Wash., a residential suburb 13 mi/ 21 km N of downtown Seattle; 47°48'N 122°19'W. Mfg. (refrigeration systems, printing and publishing, switchgear, netting, communications equip.). Puget Sound to W, N end of L. Washington to SE. Ballinger L. (in Snohomish co.) is in city. Inc. 1954.

Mountrail, county (□ 1,819 sq mi/4,711 sq km; 1990 pop. 7,021), NW central N.Dak.; ⊙ Stanley; 48°12'N 102°22'W. Rich agr. area borders Missouri R. (L. Sakakawea) on SW, Van Hook Arm of L. Sakakawea on S and drained by White Earth and Little Knife rivers and Shell Creek. Lignite mines; cattle, dairy produce, wheat, rye. Formed 1909. Powers, Cottonwood, White and Lower Lostwood lakes in N, Shell L. in E; part of Fort Berthold Indian Reservation in S; Shell Lake Natl. Wildlife Refuge in SE.

Mountville, town, Troup co., W Ga., 8 mi/12.9 km E of La Grange, in agr. area; 33°02'N 84°52'W.

Mountville, uninc. village, Laurens co., NW S.C., 9 mi/ 14.5 km SSE of Laurens.

Mountville, borough (1990 pop. 1,977), Lancaster co., SE Pa., 6 mi/9.7 km W of Lancaster; 40°02'N 76°25'W. Mfg. (tool and die, plastic prods.); agr. (grain, apples, soybeans; poultry, livestock, dairying). Laid out 1814.

Mousam Lake (MOOS-uhm), SW Maine, W York co.; c.6.5 mi/10.5 km long. Drains SE into Mousam R.

Mousam River (MOOS-uhm), 23 mi/37 km long, SW Maine; rises in Mousam L. (5 mi/8 km long), W York co.; flows SE to the Atlantic 4 mi/6.4 km below Kennebunk, where it furnishes water power.

Moville, town (1990 pop. 1,306), Woodbury co., W Iowa, on West Fork Little Sioux R., and 17 mi/27 km E of Sioux City; 42°29'N 93°04'W. In agr. area.

Moweaqua (mo-WEE-kwah), village (1990 pop. 1,785), Shelby co., central Ill., 14 mi/23 km S of Decatur; 39°37'N 89°01'W. Agr. (corn, wheat, soybeans; dairy prods.; livestock). Inc. 1877.

Mower (MOU-wuhr), county (□ 711 sq mi/1,841 sq km; 1990 pop. 37,385), SE Minn.; ⊙ Austin; 43°40'N

92°45'W. Agr. area bordering Iowa on S, drained by Cedar R. and headwaters of Root and Little Cedar rivers. Hay, soybeans, corn, oats, peas, alfalfa; sheep, hogs, cattle, poultry; dairying; meat processing at Austin; limestone. Lake Louise State Park in SE corner. Formed 1855.

Mowrystown (MOU-reez-TOUN), village (1990 pop. 460), Highland co., SW Ohio, 13 mi/21 km SSW of Hillsboro; 39°02'N 83°45'W.

Moxee (MAHK-see), town (1990 pop. 814), Yakima co., S Wash., 8 mi/12.9 km SE of Yakima, near Roza Canal; 46°34'N 120°24'W. RR terminus. Fruits, vegetables, hops; dairying; mfg. (fertilizers, millwork, furniture, mattresses). Yakima Ridge to N; Yakima Indian Reservation to SW. U.S. Military Reservation Yakima Training Center and Firing Range to NE.

Moxie Mountain (MAKS-ee) (2,925 ft/892 m), Somerset co., W central Maine, 30 mi/48 km NNW of Skowhegan.

Moxie Pond (MAKS-ee), reservoir, Somerset co., W central Maine, on branch of Kennebec R., 40 mi/64 km N of Skowhegan; 7 mi/11.3 km long; 45°20'N 69°51'W. Formed by dam S of Lake Moxie village. Recreation area.

Moyahua, Mexico: see MOYAHUA DE ESTRADA.

Moyahua de Estrada (mo-YAH-wah dai es-TRAH-dah), town (1990 pop. 2,358), Zacatecas, N central Mexico, on Juchipila R., and 35 mi/56 km SSE of Tlaltenango de Sánchez Román on Mexico Highway 54; 21°18'N 103°09'W. Grain, sugarcane, fruit, vegetables; livestock.

Moyie (MOI-ee), village, SE B.C., Canada, in Purcell Mts., at S end of Moyie L. (8 mi/13 km long), on Moyie R., 16 mi/26 km S of Cranbrook; 49°17'N 115°50'W. Timber; tourism.

Moyie Springs, village (1990 pop. 415), Boundary co., N Idaho, 8 mi/12.9 km E of Bonners Ferry, on Moyie R., near its confluence with Koutanai R., near Mont. state line; 48°43'N 116°11'W. Timber; mfg. (heating logs, lumber). Moyie Falls to NE; Kaniksu Natl. Forest to N and S.

Muchalat Inlet (moo-CHA-lit), SW B.C., Canada, in W Vancouver Isl., W arm (24 mi/39 km long) of Nootka Sound, 50 mi/80 km W of Courtenay.

Muckalee Creek (MUHK-uh-lee), c.65 mi/105 km long, SW central Ga.; rises SE of Buena Vista; flows SSE, past Americus, to Kinchafoonee R. just N of Albany; 32°18'N 84°31'W.

Mucurapo (myoo-ko-RAH-po), NW suburb of Port of Spain, W Trinidad, Trinidad and Tobago.

Mud Creek 1 77 mi/124 km long, central Nebr.; rises in Custer co. near Broken Bow; flows SE to South Loup R. near Ravenna. **2** c.65 mi/105 km long, S Okla.; rises SE of Duncan in Stephens co.; flows SE, through Jefferson co., to Red R. in Love co., 23 mi/37 km SW of Ardmore.

Mud Lake, village (1990 pop. 179), Jefferson co., E Idaho, 32 mi/51 km NW of Idaho Falls; 43°51'N 112°29'W. Wheat, alfalfa, sheep, cattle. Mfg. at Terreton, 2 mi/ 3.2 km E (feeds, conveyor chain), Mud L. reservoir to NE; Camas Natl. Wildlife Refuge to NE; large tract of Idaho Natl. Engineering Laboratory to W.

Mud Lake 1 NW Nev., intermittent body of water in Washoe co., NNE of Pyramid L., S of Gerlach; c.20 mi/ 32 km long, 6 mi/9.7 km wide. Sometimes known as Mud Flat. Pah-Rum Peak to SW. **2** in Jefferson co., N N.Y., 6 mi/9.7 km SE of Alexandria Bay; c.2.5 mi/4 km long, ½ mi/¹⁄₁₀ km wide; 44°17'N 75°49'W. Resort; fishing. **3** Traverse co., W Minn. and Roberts co., NE S.Dak., on Bois de Sioux R., 1 mi/1.6 km NE of outflow of L. Traverse reservoir, also on Minn.-S.Dak. state line; 5 mi/8 km long, 2 mi/3.2 km wide at S end. Marshy area. **4** NW Minn., E central Marshall co., 17 mi/27 km NE of Thief River Falls, in Agassiz Natl. Wildlife Refuge; 6 mi/9.7 km wide, 11 mi/18 km long. Irregular shape. Fed by Mud R. from E, drains into Thief R., which passes immediately to W. Marshy area; waterfowl.

Mud Mountain Dam, Wash.: see WHITE RIVER.

Mud River 1 c.70 mi/113 km long, S Ky.; rises in Logan

co. E of Russellville; flows generally N to Green R. at Rochester. **2** 72 mi/116 km long, W W.Va.; rises in W Boone co. W of Madison; flows NNW and W past Milton to Guyandotte R. at Barboursville, near Ohio R.

Muddy Boggy Creek, c.110 mi/177 km long, SE Okla.; rises E of Ada; flows SE, past Atoka, to junction with Clear Boggy River in Choctaw co., c.18 mi/29 km WNW of Hugo.

Muddy River 1 c.70 mi/113 km long, S central Utah; rises at Sanpete-Sevier co. line, in Wasatch Plateau; flows SE past Emery, joining Fremont R. in Wayne co., N of Henry Mts., to form Dirty Devil R. Its main tributary, Muddy Creek, rises in SE Sevier co., flows c.35 mi/ 56 km SSE, joining Muddy R. 8 mi/12.9 km SSE of Emery. **2** c.60 mi/97 km long, SE Nev.; rises in Sheep Range; flows SE to N arm (Virgin R.) of L. Mead just SE of Overton. Sometimes called Muddy Creek. Meadow Valley Wash is tributary.

Muenster, town (1990 pop. 1,387), Cooke co., N Texas, 14 mi/23 km W of Gainesville, Elm Fork Trinity R.; 33°38'N 97°22'W. Elev. 970 ft/296 m. Mfg. (cheese and dairy prods., meat packing).

Muerto, Mar, Mexico: see MAR MUERTO.

Muertos, P.R.: see CAJA DE MUERTOS ISLAND.

Múgica, Mexico: see NUEVA ITALIA DE RUIZ.

Mugu, Point, Ventura co., S Calif., low foreland just SE of Port Hueneme, and 7 mi/11.3 km SSE of Oxnard. Point Mugu Naval Air Station. Point Mugu State Park is here.

Muhlenberg (MYOO-luhn-buhrg), county (□ 479 sq mi/1,241 sq km; 1990 pop. 31,318), W Ky.; ⊙ Greenville; 37°12'N 87°09'W. Bounded NE by Green R., E by Mud R., W by Pond R.; drained by Pond, Cypress, and Rocky creeks. Important bituminous-coal-mining area; agr. (soybeans, burley and dark tobacco, wheat, hay, alfalfa, corn; hogs, cattle; timber); limestone. Mfg. at Greenville and Central City. L. Malone reservoir (Rocky Creek) and State Park on S boundary. Formed 1798.

Muir (MEER), uninc. town (1990 pop. 900), Schuylkill co., E central Pa., 2 mi/3.2 km E of Tower City; 40°35'N 76°31'W. Agr. includes dairying, livestock, poultry; corn, hay. Former anthracite-coal region.

Muir (MYOOR), village (1990 pop. 667), Ionia co., S central Mich., 7 mi/11.3 km E of Ionia; and on Grand R. at mouth of Maple R.; 43°00'N 84°56'W. In farm area.

Muir Glacier, Alaska: see GLACIER BAY NATIONAL PARK AND PRESERVE.

Muir, Mount (14,015 ft/4,272 m), E central Calif., in the Sierra Nevada, just S of Mt. Whitney, and on Inyo/ Tulare co. line, on E boundary of Sequoia Natl. Park.

Muir Woods, Natl. Monument, Marin co., W Calif., 12 mi/19 km NW of downtown San Francisco. Authorized 1908. Covers 554 acres/224 ha. Grove of virgin redwood trees on Pacific side of Peninsula. Bounded N, W, and S by Mt. Tamalpais State Park; Pacific Ocean 2 mi/3.2 km to SW. Named for natural conservationist, co-founder of the Sierra Club.

Muirkirk (MYOOR-kuhrk), village, Prince Georges co., central Md., 18 mi/29 km NE of Washington, D.C. William and Elias Ellicott built an iron furnace in 1847 that was the precursor of the present Mineral Pigments Corp. Muirkirk iron, used in cannons, gun carriages and RR wheels, was noted for its tensile strength. In 1924, the works were converted to the production of dry pigments from ores. The nearby Ammendale Normal Inst. (R.C.), est. in 1880, is the provincial house and novitiate of the Christian Brothers for the Diocese of Baltimore.

Mujeres Island, Mexico: see ISLA MUJERES.

Mukilteo (muh-kuhl-TEE-o), town (1990 pop. 7,007), Snohomish co., W Wash., on Possession Sound passage between Puget Sound (S) and Possession Sound, extension of Puget (N), suburb 5 mi/8 km SW of Everett, and 23 mi/37 km N of downtown Seattle; 47°56'N 122°19'W. Ferry to Clinton, on Whidbey Isl. (W). Varied mfg. Mukilteo State Park is here.

Mukwonago (muhk-WAHN-uh-go), town (1990 pop. 4,457), Waukesha co., SE Wis., on small Phantom L.,

24 mi/39 km SW of Milwaukee; 42°52′N 88°19′W. In dairying, livestock-raising, and farming region; mfg. (bottled water, pump components). Rail junction. Kettle Moraine State Forest (S unit) to W.

Mulberry 1 town (1990 pop. 1,448), Crawford co., NW Ark., 22 mi/35 km ENE of Fort Smith, and on Mulberry R.; 35°30′N 94°04′W. N of its confluence with Arkansas R. Mfg. (farm gates and corral panels); trade center for agr. area. Ozark Natl. Forest to N. **2** town (□ 3 sq mi/7.8 sq km; 1990 pop. 2,988), Polk co., central Fla., 10 mi/16 km S of Lakeland; 27°53′N 81°58′W. Processes phosphate from nearby mines; also mfg. of fertilizer, steel. **3** town (1990 pop. 1,262), Clinton co., central Ind., 10 mi/16 km NW of Frankfort; 40°21′N 86°40′W. In agr. area (corn, soybeans, hogs). Laid out 1858. **4** uninc. town (1990 pop. 2,339), Wilkes co., NW N.C., 6 mi/9.7 km N of Wilkesboro; 36°13′N 81°10′W. Agr. area (tobacco, grain, soybeans, poultry, hogs; dairying); timber. **5** uninc. town (1990 pop. 1,097), Sumter co., central S.C., residential suburb 3 mi/4.8 km E of Sumter; 33°57′N 80°19′W.

Mulberry 1 village (1990 pop. 555), Crawford co., SE Kansas, at Mo. state line, 11 mi/18 km NNE of Pittsburg; 37°33′N 94°37′W. In livestock, poultry, and grain area. Coal mines nearby. **2** uninc. village (1990 pop. 2,856), Clermont co., extreme SW Ohio, a NE suburb of Cincinnati, c.15 mi/24 km from downtown; 39°11′N 84°14′W. Adjacent to Mt. Repose and just off U.S. I-275.

Mulberry Fork, river, c.100 mi/161 km long, in N Ala.; rises in NE Cullman co.; flows SW, past Cordova, to join Locust Fork c.20 mi/32 km W of Birmingham, forming Black Warrior R.

Mulberry Gap (3,100 ft/945 m), on Wilkes and Alleghany co. line, NW N.C., pass through the Blue Ridge, 15 mi/24 km N of Wilkesboro.

Mulberry Grove, village (1990 pop. 660), Bond co., S central Ill., 8 mi/12.9 km ENE of Greenville; 38°55′N 89°16′W. In agr. area (corn, wheat; livestock; dairy prods.); ships sand.

Mulberry River 1 c.35 mi/56 km long, in central Ala.; rises in Chilton co., W of Clanton; flows S to Alabama R. 9 mi/14.5 km E of Selma. **2** c.70 mi/113 km long, in NW Ark.; rises NE in Johnson co., in the Ozarks; flows SW to Arkansas R. just S of Mulberry. Most of upper course is in Ozark Natl. Forest. Famous for canoeing.

Mulchatna River, Alaska: see NUSHAGAK RIVER.

Muldoon, uninc. village (1990 pop. 98), Fayette co., S central Texas, near Colorado R., 14 mi/23 km SE of Smithville. Agr. area.

Muldraugh (MUHL-duhr), town (1990 pop. 1,376), Mead co., N Ky., 37 mi/60 km SSW of Louisville, near Ohio R., within Fort Knox Military Reserve, U.S. Gold Bullion Depository to S. Otter Creek Park to W; 37°56′N 85°59′W.

Muldrow (MUHL-dro), town (1990 pop. 2,889), Sequoyah co., E Okla., 5 mi/8 km ESE of Salislaw; 35°23′N 94°35′W. In agr. area; mfg. (furniture).

Mule Mountains, Cochise co., SE Ariz., W of Bisbee, near Mex. border; rise to 7,500 ft/2,286 m in Mt. Ballard. Copper, gold, and silver are mined near Bisbee and Warren, in S part of range.

Mulegé (moo-le-HE), village, Baja California Sur, NW Mexico, near Gulf of California, 35 mi/56 km S of Santa Rosalía on Mexico Highway 1; 26°54′N 112°00′W. Manganese-mining and agr. center (sugarcane, coconuts, dates, figs, grapes). Mission Santa Rosade Mulegé (1705–1828) is nearby.

Mulegé, Mexico: see SANTA ROSALÍA.

Muleshoe, town (1990 pop. 4,571), ⊙ Bailey co., NW Texas, on the Llano Estacado, c.65 mi/105 km NW of Lubbock, on Blackwater Draw Creek; 34°13′N 102°43′W. In cattle-ranching and irrigated agr. region; agribusiness; dairying; cotton, wheat, corn, sorghum; vegetables, potatoes; food processing (corn flour, seed packaging, tortillas, potato packaging). Muleshoe Natl. Wildlife Refuge to S; Coyote L. to SW. Settled 1913, inc. 1926.

Mulga, town (1990 pop. 261), Jefferson co., N central Ala., just W of Birmingham.

Mulgrave (MUHL-graiv), town (1991 pop. 935), E N.S., Canada, on W shore of Strait of Canso, 30 mi/48 km E of Antigonish; 45°37′N 61°24′W. Fishing; port.

Mulhall (MUHL-hawl), village (1990 pop. 199), Logan co., central Okla., 13 mi/21 km N of Guthrie; 36°03′N 97°24′W. In farming area.

Mullan, town (1990 pop. 821), Shoshone co., N Idaho, 6 mi/9.7 km E of Wallace in Coeur d'Alene Mts., near Mont. state line; 47°28′N 115°48′W. Elev. 3,277 ft/999 m. Terminus of RR spur from Wallace. Lead, silver, zinc mines. Founded 1884 at time of lead-silver strike. Lookout Pass (4,725 ft/1,440 m) on state line and Lookout Pass Ski Area (Mont.) to E. Inc. 1904.

Mullen, village (1990 pop. 554), ⊙ Hooker co., central Nebr., 60 mi/97 km NNW of North Platte, near Middle Loup R.; 42°02′N 101°02′W. In heart of Sand Hills region. Beef cattle, livestock.

Mullens, town (1990 pop. 2,006), Wyoming co., S W.Va., on Guyandotte R., 23 mi/37 km NNW of Bluefield; 37°34′N 81°23′W. Bituminous- and semibituminous-coal region. Agr. (corn, potatoes); cattle. Timber. Twin Falls State Park to NW.

Mullet Bay, Sint Maarten, Neth. Antilles, beach area on SW shore, 6 mi/9.7 km E of Philipsburg. Location of large resort and casino complex, near Princess Juliana airport.

Mullett Lake, Cheboygan co., N Mich., 5 mi/8 km S of Cheboygan; c.11 mi/18 km long, 3 mi/4.8 km wide; 45°33′N 84°31′W. Mullett L., resort village, is on NW shore. Village of Aloha and Aloha State Park on E shore. Villages of Mullet L. and Topinabee on W shore. Source of Cheboygan R.

Mullica (MUH-li-kuh), township (1990 pop. 5,896), Atlantic co., S N.J., along Mullica R., SW of Batsto; 39°36′N 74°40′W. Inc. 1838.

Mullica Hill (MUH-li-kuh), village (1990 pop. 1,117), Gloucester co., SW N.J., on Raccoon Creek, and 15 mi/24 km SSW of Camden, in rich fruit and produce region; 39°44′N 75°13′W. Residential development starting in area.

Mullica River (MUH-li-kuh), c.55 mi/89 km long, SE N.J.; rises near Berlin; flows generally SE, forming part of Burlington-Atlantic co. line, to Great Bay SW of Tuckerton. Receives Batsto, Wading, and Bass rivers. Navigable for c.23 mi/37 km above mouth.

Mulliken, village (1990 pop. 590), Eaton co., S central Mich., 17 mi/27 km W of Lansing; 42°45′N 84°54′W. In farm area; mfg. (metal fabrication).

Mullin, village (1990 pop. 194), Mills co., central Texas, 21 mi/34 km SE of Brownwood; 31°33′N 98°39′W. In grain, livestock area.

Mullins, town (1990 pop. 5,910), Marion co., E S.C., 28 mi/45 km E of Florence, near Little Pee Dee R.; 34°12′N 79°15′W. Mfg. includes clothing, meat processing, military food rations, light bulbs, lumber. Important tobacco market; grain, sorghum, cotton, timber. Little Pee Dee State Park to N.

Mullinville, village (1990 pop. 289), Kiowa co., S Kansas, 10 mi/16 km W of Greensburg; 37°35′N 99°28′W. Grain, livestock.

Multnomah (muhlt-NO-muh), county (□ 465 sq mi/1,204 sq km; 1990 pop. 583,887), NW Oregon; ⊙ Portland; 45°32′N 122°24′W. Bounded N by Columbia R., forms Wash. state line. Drained by Willamette R. Mfg. and shipping center at Portland. Urbanized in W; agr. areas in center and extreme NW. Agr. (wheat, oats, barley, potatoes, corn, berries, apples, cherries, pears, plums, peaches, hops); nurseries, wineries. Part of Mt. Hood Natl. Forest, including Columbia Wilderness Area. In E. Co. has 12 state parks, all E of Portland, along the Columbia R., most notably Bridal Veil Falls, Benson and John B. Yeon State Parks.

Multnomah Falls (muhlt-NO-muh), waterfall (c. 850 ft/259 m high, including upper and lower falls), NW Oregon, in Multnomah Creek, rising on Larch Mt. (4,100 ft/1,250 m) and plunging into Columbia R. gorge 9 mi/14.5 km WSW of Bonneville, near Benson State Park. Site of historic Multnomah Falls Lodge.

Mulvane (muhl-VAIN), town (1990 pop. 4,674), on Sedgwick-Sumner co. line, S Kansas, on Arkansas R.,

and 16 mi/26 km SSE of Wichita; 37°28′N 97°14′W. RR junction. In diversified-farming area. Sand and gravel plant here. Laid out 1879, inc. 1883.

Mumford, village (1990 pop. 800), Monroe, co., W N.Y., 17 mi/27 km SSW of Rochester, in agr. area; 42°59′N 77°52′W.

Mummery, Mount (10,918 ft/3,328 m), SE B.C., Canada, near Alta. border, in Rocky Mts., in Hamber Provincial Park, 65 mi/105 km NW of Banff; 51°40′N 116°51′W.

Mummy Mountain, Colo.: see MUMMY RANGE.

Mummy Range, spur of Front Range in NE corner of Rocky Mt. Natl. Park, Larimer co., N Colo. Prominent peaks include Mt. Dunraven (12,571 ft/3,832 m), Mt. Chiquita (c.13,069 ft/3,983 m), Mt. Chapin (12,454 ft/3,796 m), Mummy Mt. (13,425 ft/4,092 m), Mt. Fairchild (13,502 ft/4,115 m), Ypsilon Mt. (13,514 ft/4,119 m), Hague's Peak (13,562 ft/4,134 m). Rowe Glacier is in NE tip of range.

Mumtrak (MUHM-trak), village, SW Alaska, near N shore of Goodnews Bay, 13 mi/21 km NE of Platinum; 59°08′N 161°31′W. In mining area.

Muna (MOO-nah), town (1990 pop. 9,418), Yucatán, S Mexico, on RR, and 35 mi/56 km SSW of Mérida; 20°29′N 89°41′W. Agr. center (henequen, sugarcane, corn, fruit, timber).

Muncie, city (1990 pop. 71,035), ⊙ Delaware co., E Ind., on the White R.; 40°12′N 85°23′W. It is a trade, processing, and mfg. center. The city is in a fertile agr. area with dairying, soybean, fruit, corn, oats, and vegetables. Mfg. (machinery, electronic equip., plastics, glass, motor vehicle equip., metal fabrication, consumer goods). Area 1st settled by peoples of Native Amer. Delaware culture; town was named for one of their tribes. In 1818 the land passed by treaty to the U.S. govt. Industrialization came after the discovery (1886) of natural gas in the co. Muncie is the seat of Ball State Univ. Settled 1818, laid out 1827, inc. 1854.

Muncie, village (1990 pop. 182), Vermillion co., E Ill., 10 mi/16 km W of Danville; 40°07′N 87°50′W. In agr. and bituminous-coal area.

Muncy (MUHN-see), borough (1990 pop. 2,702), Lycoming co., N central Pa., 12 mi/19 km E of Williamsport, on West Branch of Susquehanna R. (bridged), at mouth of Muncy Creek; 41°12′N 76°47′W. Mfg. (grain-processing equip., aluminum and plastic prods., printing, food prods., modular wood bldgs., conveyor systems, pneumatic conveyors). Agr. area (potatoes, soybeans, grain; livestock; dairying). Tiadaghton State Forest to W; Muncy State Correctional Inst. to W. Laid out 1797, inc. 1826.

Muncy Creek (MUHN-see), c.40 mi/64 km long, E central Pa.; rises in SE Sullivan co.; flows SW past Hughesville to West Branch of Susquehanna R. 1 mi/1.6 km NW of Muncy; 41°12′N 76°48′W.

Mundare, town (1991 pop. 596), central Alta., Canada, 14 mi/23 km NW of Vegreville; 53°36′N 112°20′W. Mixed farming, dairying.

Munday, town (1990 pop. 1,600), Knox co., N Texas, 72 mi/116 km WSW of Wichita Falls; 33°27′N 99°37′W. In cattle-ranching and irrigated agr. area (cotton, sorghum, wheat; vegetables); mfg. (portable bldgs.). Inc. 1906.

Munday, Mount (11,000 ft/3,353 m), W B.C., Canada, in Coast Mts., 170 mi/274 km NW of Vancouver, just SE of Mt. Waddington; 51°21′N 125°14′W.

Mundelein, village (1990 pop. 21,215), Lake co., NW of Chicago, NE Ill.; 42°16′N 88°00′W. Founded 1835 as Mechanics Grove, inc. 1909. The name was changed in 1926 to honor George Cardinal Mundelein. Its light mfg. produces a variety of household goods. St. Mary of the L. Seminary is in Mundelein.

Munden, village (1990 pop. 143), Republic co., N Kansas, 8 mi/12.9 km NE of Belleville; 39°54′N 97°32′W. In corn and wheat region.

Munford, town (1990 pop. 2,326), Tipton co., W Tenn., 11 mi/18 km SSW of Covington; 35°27′N 89°49′W. In cotton-growing area.

Munford, village, Talladega co., E Ala., 11 mi/18 km NE of Talladega. Cheaha Mt. (2,407 ft/734 m), the highest point in Ala., is 10 mi/16 km E. Civil War battle here (1865).

Munfordville, town (1990 pop. 1,556), ☉ Hart co., central Ky., 35 mi/56 km ENE of Bowling Green, on Green R., in limestone cave region; 37°16′N 85°54′W. Agr. (poultry; dairying; burley tobacco, corn; timber); mfg. (lumber, mattress pads). Indian relics found in vicinity. Mammoth Onyx Cave, containing onyx formations is to S. In Civil War, Confederate Gen. Braxton Bragg captured Union fort and garrison here in Sept. 1863. Hart Co. Historical Mus. Mammoth Cave Natl. Park to SW. Est. 1801.

Munhall, borough (1990 pop. 13,158), Allegheny co., SW Pa., residential suburb 6 mi/9.7 km ESE of downtown Pittsburgh, on the Monongahela R. (bridged); 40°23′N 79°54′W. The once-large steel and iron works here have declined significantly along with the natl. steel industry. Part of large U.S. Steel complex is here. Mfg. (office furniture, insulation tape). Munhall was a site of the Homestead Strike in 1892. Sandcastle water theme park is here. Inc. 1901.

Munich (MYOO-nik), village (1990 pop. 310), Cavalier co., N N.Dak., 23 mi/37 km SW of Langdon; 48°40′N 98°49′W. RR junction.

Municipality of Murrysville, city (1990 pop. 17,240), Westmoreland co., SW Pa., suburb 15 mi/24 km E of Pittsburgh; 40°26′N 79°39′W. Mfg. includes aluminum dies, construction equip., metal stampings, gas detectors, patient ventilation prods., vinyl windows, roof and floor trusses. Agr. includes dairying. Usually just called Murrysville.

Munising (MUHN-is-ing), town (1990 pop. 2,783), ☉ Alger co., N Upper Peninsula, Mich. 36 mi/58 km ESE of Marquette on small Munising Bay of L. Superior, and facing Grand Isl. Resort; 46°25′N 86°38′W. Lumbering and agr. in area. Mfg. (paper and wood prods., including log homes); fisheries. Hq. for Pictured Rocks Natl. Lakeshore (to NE); Hiawatha Natl. Forest to W, S, and E; Wagner Falls State Park to S. Inc. as village 1897, as town 1916.

Munn Bay, Canada: see CORAL HARBOUR.

Munn, Cape, N extremity of Southampton Isl., E Keewatin dist., N.W.T., Canada, on Roes Welcome Sound; 65°55′N 85°28′W.

Munnsville, village (1990 pop. 438), Madison co., central N.Y., on Oneida Creek, and 19 mi/31 km SW of Utica; 42°58′N 75°35′W. Quarry.

Muñoz (moon-YOS), town (1990 pop. 1,373), ☉ Munoz de Domingo Arenas Municipio, N Tlaxcala, Mexico, 7 mi/11 km NW of Apizaco. Relatively flat region in the Pie Grande Valley with water from the Zahuapan R. Temperate climate. Agr. (corn, beans, potatoes, pulque, fruits, medicinal plants). Pop. is mostly indigenous.

Muñoz de Domingo Arenas, Mexico: see MUÑOZ.

Munroe Falls, city (1990 pop. 5,359), Summit co., NE Ohio, 6 mi/10 km NE of Akron, and on Cuyahoga R. Paper prods.

Munsey Park, residential village (1990 pop. 2,692), Nassau co., SE N.Y., on NW L.I., bet. Manhasset (W) and Roslyn on North Shore; 40°47′N 73°40′W.

Munson, agr. village (1991 pop. 159), S central Alta., Canada, near Red Deer R., 7 mi/11 km N of Drumheller; 51°34′N 112°45′W.

Munson Corners, village (1990 pop. 2,432), Cortland co., central N.Y., 1 mi/1.6 km SW of Cortland; 42°35′N 76°12′W.

Munster, town (1990 pop. 19,949), Lake co., NW Ind., 13 mi/21 km NW of Crown Point on the Ill. state line; 41°33′N 87°30′W. Light mfg. (soft drinks, printing, aluminum alloys). It is a primarily residential suburb in the industrialized Hammond–East Chicago area. Settled 1855.

Munsungan Lake (muhn-SUHN-guhn), Piscataquis co., N central Maine, 50 mi/80 km NNW of Millinocket; 7.5 mi/12.1 km long, 2 mi/3.2 km wide; 46°22′N 68°55′W. Drained ESE by Munsungan Stream into Aroostook R. Wilderness recreational area. Chase L. immediately upstream (to NW).

Munuscong Lake (mi-NE-skahng), in S central Ont.,

Canada, and E Upper Peninsula, Mich., a widening of St. Marys R., 23 mi/37 km SSE of Sault Ste. Marie and W of St. Joseph Isl.; c.15 mi/24 km long, 5 mi/8 km wide. Mich.-Ont. line passes through lake. Receives Munuscong R. (c.15 mi/24 km long) from SW.

Murchinson, village (1990 pop. 510), Henderson co., E Texas, 26 mi/42 km WSW of Tyler; 32°16′N 95°45′W. Oil and natural gas. Agr. area. Mfg. (gas processing). L. Athens reservoir to S.

Murchison, Cape, NE Ellesmere Isl., NE Franklin dist., N.W.T., Canada, on Hall Basin, at S end of Robeson Channel, near N entrance of Lady Franklin Bay; 81°42′N 64°05′W.

Murchison Mount (10,659 ft/3,249 m), SW Alta., Canada, near B.C. border, in Rocky Mts., in Banff Natl. Park, 70 mi/113 km NW of Banff; 51°55′N 116°38′W.

Murchison Promontory, N extremity of Boothia Peninsula, S Franklin dist., N.W.T., Canada, on Bellot Strait; 71°58′N 94°28′W. Rises steeply to c.2,500 ft/762 m.

Murderkill River, 19 mi/31 km long, central Del.; rises in W Kent co.; flows E through Killen's Pond (state park) and NE, past Frederica (head of navigation), to Delaware Bay at Bowers (Bowers Beach).

Murdo, town (1990 pop. 679), ☉ Jones co., S central S.Dak., 40 mi/64 km SSW of Pierre; 43°53′N 100°42′W. Mountain/Central time zone boundary to E.

Murdock 1 village (1990 pop. 282), Swift co., SW Minn., 19 mi/31 km WNW of Willmar; 45°13′N 95°23′W. Alfalfa, beans, sugar beets; grain; livestock, poultry; dairying. **2** village (1990 pop. 267), Cass co., SE Nebr., 23 mi/37 km ENE of Lincoln, near Platte R.; 40°55′N 96°16′W.

Murfreesboro (MUHR freez-BUHR-o), city (1990 pop. 44,922), ☉ Rutherford co., central Tenn., on Stones R.; 35°50′N 86°25′W. The city is the processing center of a dairy, livestock, and farm area. Mfg. includes appliance motors, packaged foods, boats, outdoor furniture. Murfreesboro, capital of Tenn. from 1819 to 1826, was the site of the Civil War battle of Murfreesboro (or Stones R.) Dec. 31, 1862–Jan. 2, 1863. Stones River Battlefield commemorates the battle, and Civil War dead are buried in Stones River Natl. Cemetery. Oakland Mansion is another historic attraction. Middle Tennessee State Univ. is here. Inc. 1817.

Murfreesboro 1 (MUHR-freez-BUHR-o), town (1990 pop. 1,542), ☉ Pike co., SW Ark., c.45 mi/72 km SW of Hot Springs, near Little Missouri R.; 34°03′N 93°41′W. Narrows Dam to N; forms L. Greerson. In agr. area; mercury mines. Crater of Diamonds State Park is on the site of only diamond reserve in U.S. (N). **2** town (1990 pop. 2,580), Hertford co., NE N.C., on Meherrin R., and 31 mi/50 km E of Roanoke Rapids; 36°26′N 77°05′W. Tobacco, peanuts, soybeans, corn, cotton, chickens, hogs. Mfg. (socks, clothing, baskets and crates, steel fabricating).

Murillo (moo-RI-lo), village, W Ont., Canada, 12 mi/19 km W of Thunder Bay. Dairying; grain.

Murphy 1 town (1990 pop. 1,575), ☉ Cherokee co., extreme W N.C., on Hiwassee R., and 90 mi/145 km WSW of Asheville, in Nantahala Natl. Forest, near Ga. state line; 35°05′N 84°01′W. RR terminus. Mfg. (motors, wooden cabinets and pallets, clothing, jeans, thread, veneers). Timber; tobacco, corn, apples, soybeans, cattle, chickens. Hiwassee and Apalachia reservoirs are near. Founded c.1830. **2** town (1990 pop. 1,547), Collin co., N Texas, residential suburb 17 mi/27 km NE of downtown Dallas, in urban growth area; 33°00′N 96°36′W.

Murphy, uninc. village (1990 pop. 75), ☉ Owyhee co., SW Idaho, 25 mi/40 km S of Nampa. One of the smallest co. seats in U.S.; county mus. here.

Murphy Islands, group of 6 small islands, St. Lawrence co., N N.Y., in the St. Lawrence R., 11 mi/18 km SW of Massena; 44°53′N 75°09′W.

Murphys, uninc. town (1990 pop. 1,517), Calaveras co., central Calif., 45 mi/72 km ENE of Stockton, on Angels Creek; 38°09′N 120°28′W. Walnuts, olives, grapes, oats, cattle; timber. Mfg. (printing and publishing). El Dorado Natl. Forest and Calaveras Big Trees State Park to NE.

Murphysboro, city (1990 pop. 9,176), ☉ Jackson co., S Ill., on the Big Muddy R., 7 mi/11.3 km WNW of Carbondale; 37°46′N 89°20′W. It is a trade and distributing center for a fertile farm area. Shoes, feed, and fertilizer are made there. A memorial to John A. Logan is in the city. Nearby are a state park and a natl. forest. Inc. 1867.

Murray 1 (MUHR-ee), county (□ 347 sq mi/899 sq km; 1990 pop. 26,147), NW Ga.; ☉ Chatsworth; 34°47′N 84°45′W. Bounded N by Tenn. state line, W by Conasauga R. Mfg. of textiles; agr. area for corn, hay, soybeans, fruit; cattle, hogs, poultry; sawmilling; talc mining. Part of Chattahoochee Natl. Forest (E). Formed 1832. **2** county (□ 719 sq mi/1,862 sq km; 1990 pop. 9,660), SW Minn.; ☉ Slayton; 44°01′N 95°45′W. Agr. area drained by Des Moines R., which forms L. Shetek (state park) in N. Corn, oats, alfalfa, soybeans; hogs, sheep, cattle, poultry; dairying. Several small lakes in co. Formed 1857. **3** county (□ 423 sq mi/1,098 sq km; 1990 pop. 12,042), S Okla.; ☉ Sulphur; 34°29′N 97°04′W. Intersected by Washita R. (forms border on N and S). Includes part of Arbuckle Mts. (to W, including Turner and Price falls), and Chickasaw Natl. Recreation Area and Arbuckle Reservoir in E. Livestock raising, agr. (corn, wheat, poultry, fruit), dairying; mfg. (oil and gas field machinery). Mining (limestone, sand). Recreation. Sulphur is resort, with mineral springs. Formed 1907.

Murray 1 (MUHR-ee), city (1990 pop. 14,439), ☉ Calloway co., W Ky., 35 mi/56 km SSE of Paducah on East Fork Clarke R.; 36°36′N 88°19′W. Elev. 515 ft/157 m. Varied light Mfg., agr. (dark and burley tobacco, grain; livestock, poultry; dairying), and tourism are important; recreation and retirement area. Murray State Univ., including Wrather-West Mus. (history of W Ky.) is here. Kenlake State Resort Park to NE, Kentucky L. reservoir (Kenlake; Tenn. R.) to E. Est. 1822; inc. 1844. **2** city (1990 pop. 31,282), Salt L. co., N central Utah, suburb 7 mi/11.3 km S of downtown Salt Lake City on Jordan R., at mouths of Big Cottonwood and Little Cottonwood creeks; 40°38′N 111°53′W. Elev. 4,300 ft/1,311 m. Retail center; dairying; cattle, sheep; mfg. (fish food, cabinets). Wasatch Range and Natl. Forest to E, including Mt. Olympus Wildlife Area. The county fairgrounds are in Murray. Settled 1890s, inc. 1903.

Murray, town (1990 pop. 731), Clarke co., S Iowa, 9 mi/14.5 km W of Osceola; 41°02′N 93°57′W. In livestock and grain area; mfg. of automotive wiring harnesses.

Murray (MUHR-ee), village (1990 pop. 418), Cass co., SE Nebr., 7 mi/11.3 km S of Plattsmouth, near Missouri R.; 40°55′N 95°55′W.

Murray Bay, Canada: see LA MALBAIE.

Murray Canal, SE Ont., Canada, connects Bay of Quinte with L. Ontario, cutting across narrow isthmus that connects peninsula of Prince Edward co. with mainland. Completed 1889.

Murray City, village (1990 pop. 499), Hocking co., S central Ohio, 13 mi/21 km E of Logan, in coal-mining area.

Murray Harbour, village (1991 pop. 390), SE P.E.I., Canada, on Murray Harbour of the Gulf of St. Lawrence, at mouth of Murray R., 33 mi/53 km ESE of Charlottetown. Lobster, oyster, fisheries.

Murray Hill, town, Union co., N.J., 10 mi/16 km from Elizabeth. Major center for Lucent Technologies, Inc.

Murray Hill, business and residential dist. of S central Manhattan borough of N.Y. city, SE N.Y., on the East Side S of 42d St.; 40°44′N 73°58′W.

Murray Isle, one of the Thousand Isls., Jefferson co., N N.Y., in the St. Lawrence, bet. Wellesley and Grindstone isls., 7 mi/11.3 km SW of Alexandria Bay; 44°17′N 76°03′W. Isl. is 1.1 mi/1.8 km long, elongated NE-SW; highest elev. c.345 ft/105 m. Popular for summer-resort homes. Post office in Clayton.

Murray, Lake 1 reservoir and resort lake, Love and Carter cos., S Okla., on small tributary of Red R., 8 mi/12.9 km SSE of Ardmore; c.15 mi/24 km long; 34°01′N 97°01′W. L. Murray State Park on W shore. **2** reservoir, Lexington, Saluda, Newberry cos., central S.C., on Saluda R., 12 mi/19 km WNW of Columbia; 30 mi/48 km long; 34°02′N 81°12′W. Formed by Saluda Dam (formerly Dreher Shoals Dam), built for power generation. Dreher Isl. State Park along W part of lake.

Murray Lock and Dam, Pulaski co., central Ark. Dam is 68 ft/21 m high and is on the Arkansas R. It was built by the Army Corps of Engineers in 1969 for navigational purposes. The reservoir it creates has a max. capacity of 108,500 acre-ft.

Murray River, village (1991 pop. 485), SE P.E.I., Canada, on small Murray R., and 30 mi/48 km ESE of Charlottetown. Mixed farming, dairying; potatoes.

Murray River, Canada: see MALBAIE RIVER.

Murrayville, village (1990 pop. 673), Morgan co., W central Ill., 10 mi/16 km S of Jacksonville; 39°34′N 90°15′W. In agr. area (corn, wheat, soybeans, cattle, hogs).

Murrels Inlet (MUH-ruhls), uninc. town (1990 pop. 3,334) Georgetown co., E S.C., 18 mi/29 km NE of Georgetown; 33°32′N 79°02′W. Fishing, boatbuilding. Brookgreen Gardens to W. Mfg. includes fish processing, printing, concrete.

Murrieta, uninc. village (□ 2 sq mi/5.2 sq km; 1990 pop. 1,628), Riverside co., S Calif., 30 mi/48 km S of Riverside on Murrieta Creek; 33°34′N 117°13′W. Resort, with thermal springs. Mfg. (optical instruments, screw machine parts, biological prods., medical instruments, signs). This part of SW Riverside co. has grown rapidly from 1980 to mid-1990s and is projected to continue to grow in 21st cent. Murrieta and Temecula hot springs to E; Santa Ana Mts. to SW; parts of Cleveland Natl. Forest to W and SE.

Murrieta Springs, uninc. town (1990 pop. 1,938), Riverside co., S Calif., 2 mi/3.2 km E of Riverside, 2 mi/3.2 km E of Murrieta; 33°34′N 117°09′W. Murrieta and Temecula hot springs are here. Established resort area now at fringe bet. Los Angeles and San Diego.

Murrysville, Pa.: see MUNICIPALITY OF MURRYSVILLE.

Murtaugh, village (1990 pop. 134), Twin Falls co., S Idaho, 15 mi/24 km ESE of Twin Falls, on Snake R.; 42°29′N 114°10′W. Elev. 4,082 ft/1,244 m. Agr. (potatoes); mfg. (potato starch). Commercial fish hatcheries. Milner Dam to E; Murtaugh L. to S. Inc. 1937.

Murtle Lake, E B.C., Canada, in Cariboo Mts., in Wells Gray Provincial Park, 100 mi/161 km NNE of Kamloops; 17 mi/27 km long, 1 mi/2 km–6 mi/10 km wide. Elev. 3,650 ft/1,113 m. Drains W into North Thompson R.

Muscatatuck National Wildlife Refuge (□ c.12 sq mi/31 sq km), in E Jackson co. and W Jennings co., SE Ind. Diversified habitat of farmland, timber, lakes, marshes, and ponds. Ducks, geese, wild turkeys, deer. Only natl. wildlife refuge in Ind.

Muscatatuck River, 45 mi/72 km long, S Ind.; formed in W Jefferson co. by junction of Big Graham Creek and Big Chicken Run; flows SW and W to East Fork of White R. 3 mi/4.8 km S of Medora.

Muscatine, county (□ 449 sq mi/1,163 sq km; 1990 pop. 39,907), SE Iowa, bounded SE by Mississippi R. (forms Ill. state line here); ⊙ Muscatine; 41°29′N 91°06′W. Prairie agr. area (sheep, hogs, cattle, poultry; corn, soybeans) drained by Cedar R. Limestone; sand and gravel pits; bituminous-coal deposits. Mfg. and Lock and Dam No. 16 at Muscatine. Wildcat Den State Park in SE. Formed 1836.

Muscatine, city (1990 pop. 22,881), ⊙ Muscatine co., SE Iowa, on the Mississippi R.; 41°25′N 91°04′W. An early center of river traffic and lumbering, Muscatine is the shipping and processing center of a rich agr. area. Grains; diversified light mfg. Muscatine Community Col., an airfield, and Lock and Dam No. 16 are there; Wildcat Den State Park to E. Serious flooding occurred along Mississippi R. in 1993. Inc. 1851.

Muscle Shoals, town (1990 pop. 9,611), Colbert co., NW Ala., on the Tennessee R. S of Florence. Center of experimental development of phosphate and nitrate fertilizers and animal foods. Various prods. are made in the chemical works here; mfg. (truck trailers, nuts, screws, and bolts). Inc. 1923.

Muscoda (muhs-KO-duh), town (1990 pop. 1,287), Grant co., SW Wis., on Wisconsin R., and 35 mi/56 km WNW of Prairie du Chien; 43°11′N 90°25′W. In livestock and dairy region; mfg. (lumber, cheese, whey protein).

Muscogee (muhs-KO-gee), county (□ 221 sq mi/-572 sq km; 1990 pop. 179,278), W Ga.; ⊙ Columbus; 32°31′N 84°52′W. Bounded W by Ala. state line; drained by Chattahoochee R. Intersected by the fall line. Mfg. at Columbus; dairying, cattle, vegetable farming. Fort Benning is S. Formed 1826.

Musconetcong (MUHS-kuh-NET-kuhng), river, c.44 mi/71 km long, NW N.J.; rises NE of L. Hopatcong, in SE Sussex co.; flows generally SW forming part of the Sussex-Morris and Warren-Morris and Warren-Hunterdon co. lines, joining the Delaware R. at Riegezsuille.

Musconetcong, Lake (MUHS-kuh-NET-kuhng), reservoir, Sussex and Morris cos., NW N.J., on Musconetcong R., 12 mi/19 km NW of Morristown; 40°54′N 74°41′W. Formed SW of L. Hopatcong.

Musconetcong Mountain (MUHS-kuh-NET-kuhng) (c.800 ft/244 m–900 ft/274 m), ridge of Appalachians; extends NE from Delaware R. near Riegelsville, paralleling on SE the fertile valley of Musconetcong R., which drains L. Musconetcong and L. Hopatcong in SE Sussex co. The river flows c.45 mi/72 km SW to the Delaware at Riegelsville.

Muscongus Bay (muhs-KAHNG-uhs), S Maine, bet. Pemaquid Point and Port Clyde; c.15 mi/24 km across, 8 mi/12.9 km long.

Muscongus Island, Maine: see LOUDS ISLAND.

Muscotah (muhs-KO-tuh), village (1990 pop. 194), Atchison co., NE Kansas, on Delaware R., and 21 mi/34 km W of Atchison; 39°32′N 95°31′W. Diversified farming.

Muscoy, uninc. town (1990 pop. 7,541), San Bernardino co., S Calif., residential suburb 54 mi/87 km ENE of downtown Los Angeles, and 4 mi/6.4 km NW of San Bernardino, near Lytle Creek, in S foothills of San Bernardino Mts. (San Bernardino Natl. Forest); 34°09′N 117°21′W. Glen Helen Regional Park to NW. Calif. State Univ. (San Bernardino) to NW.

Muse, uninc. town (1990 pop. 1,250), Washington co., SW Pa., 14 mi/23 km SW of Pittsburgh, and 2 mi/3.2 km N of Canonsburg; 40°17′N 80°12′W. Mfg. (printing).

Music Mountain, peak (6,761 ft/2,061 m), Mohave co., NW Ariz.; rises from tableland (elev. c.6,000 ft/1,829 m) at S end of Grand Wash Cliffs, 30 mi/48 km NE of Kingman. In Music Mts., small range at SW edge of Hualapai Indian Reservation.

Muskeget Channel (muh-SKEE-get), SE Mass., separates Nantucket and its adjacent isls. from Martha's Vineyard, opening N on Nantucket Sound; c.7 mi/11.3 km wide. Muskeget Isl. (c.1.5 mi/2.4 km long) is just off NW tip of Tuckernuck Isl.

Muskego (muhs-KEE-go) or **Muskego Center**, city (1990 pop. 16,813), Waukesha co., SE Wis., a suburb 14 mi/23 km SW of downtown Milwaukee, on Big Muskego, Little Muskego, and Denmoor lakes in city; 42°53′N 88°07′W. Varied light mfg.

Muskegon (mus-KEE-guhn), county (□ 1,459 sq mi/3,779 sq km; 1990 pop. 158,983), SW Mich.; 43°17′N 86°27′W; ⊙ Muskegon. Bounded W by L. Michigan; drained by Muskegon and White rivers, and by small Crockery Creek. Agr. (cattle, hogs; apples, cherries, vegetables, corn, wheat, oats, grain; dairy prods.). Mfg. at Muskegon. Fisheries. Resorts. Muskegon County Airport at Morton Shores, S of Muskegon. P.F. Hoffmaster, Muskegon, and Duck L. state parks, in W, on or near L. Michigan; part of Manistee Natl. Forest is in N. Formed and organized 1859.

Muskegon (mus-KEE-guhn), city (1990 pop. 40,283), ⊙ Muskegon co., W Mich., 33 mi/53 km WNW of Grand Rapids, on L. Michigan; 43°13′N 86°15′W. Elev. 620 ft/189 m. A port of entry, the city is a car-ferry terminus and a ship/RR transfer point for a farm, fruit, and industrial region. Mfg. (motor vehicle equip. and parts, foundry prods., chemicals, paper prods., sporting goods equip., ink pigments, gasoline pumps, and heavy machinery). A fur-trading post was est. here c.1810. The first sawmill was built in 1837, and the lumber industry thrived until 1890, when the city was swept by fire. Muskegon Community Col. is here. Manistee Natl. Forest to NE; P.F. Hoffmaster State Park to S at Norton

Shores, Muskegon State Park to W, both on L. Michigan. Inc. as a city 1869.

Muskegon Heights (mus-KEE-guhn), city (1990 pop. 13,176), Muskegon co., W Mich., a suburb 2 mi/3.2 km S of Muskegon; 43°12′N 86°14′W. Light mfg. (foundry items, restaurant furniture, tanks and hoppers, lubricants). Mona L. on S border. Inc. 1903.

Muskegon River (mus-KEE-guhn), 227 mi/365 km long, N central Mich.; rising in Houghton L.; flowing SW past Evart and Big Rapids, through Rogers, Hardy and Croton Dam ponds, then past Newaygo to L. Michigan at Muskegon; 44°23′N 84°47′W. At its mouth the river widens into Muskegon L., forming a harbor c.2.5 mi/4 km wide and c.5.5 mi/8.9 km long.

Muskingum (mus-KING-guhm), county (□ 667 sq mi/1,728 sq km; 1990 pop. 82,068), central Ohio; ⊙ ZANESVILLE; 39°57′N 81°57′W. Intersected by Muskingum and Licking rivers and small Salt and Jonathan creeks. In the Unglaciated Plains physiographic region. Agr. (hogs, cattle; dairy prods.; corn, fruit); mfg. mainly at Zanesville, Roseville (lumber and wood prods., stone, clay, and glass prods., pottery prods., engines and other electrical equip.). Coal mines, limestone quarries; sand, gravel, and clay pits. Formed 1804. There are a number of state parks at the various dams on the Muskingum R.

Muskingum (muhs-KING-guhm), river, 111 mi/179 km long, formed in NE Ohio, at Coshocton, by the union of the Walhonding and Tuscarawas rivers and flowing S through Zanesville, then SE to the Ohio R. at Marietta; 39°24′N 81°27′W. The Muskingum R. system has extensive flood control projects. The canalized lower river is navigable. The upper river was a link bet. the Ohio and the Erie Canal.

Muskogee (muh-SKO-gee), county (□ 839 sq mi/2,173 sq km; 1990 pop. 68,078), E Okla.; ⊙ Muskogee; 35°36′N 95°22′W. Bounded N in part by Arkansas R., S by Canadian R. Agr. (corn, hay, soybeans; cattle; dairying). Varied mfg. esp. food prods. Mfg. at Muskogee. Oil and natural-gas fields. Fort Gibson Natl. Cemetery and Stockade in NE; Fort Gruber Natl. Guard Training Facility in E. Greenleaf State Park in E; part of Sequoyah Natl. Wildlife Refuge in far SE. Formed 1907.

Muskogee (muh-SKO-gee), city (1990 pop. 37,708), ⊙ Muskogee co., 38 mi/61 km SE of Tulsa, E Okla., on Arkansas R., opposite confluences of Verdigris and Neosho (Grand) rivers, near the junction of the Arkansas, Verdigris, and Grand rivers; 35°45′N 95°20′W. It is an important transportation, trade, and industrial center in the agr. Arkansas valley, with a modern port (port of Muskogee, NE part of city; opened 1971) on the McClellan–Kerr Arkansas R. Navigation System. Mfg. (machinery, rubber prods., food prods., consumer goods). Bacone Col. (2-year) here. Fairgrounds. Chouteau Dam (on Verdigris R.) to N; Sequoyah and Bay state parks on Ft. Gibson reservoir to NE. Fort Gruber Natl. Guard Training Facility to SE. Hatbox Airport in W. Five Civilized Tribes Mus. and Fort Gibson (1824, restored) to E, with its natl. cemetery. Inc. 1898.

Muskoka (muh-SKO-kuh), district (□ 1,585 sq mi/4,105 sq km; 1991 pop. 48,005), S Ont., Canada, on Georgian Bay of L. Huron; ⊙ Bracebridge; 45°00′N 79°20′W.

Muskoka, Lake, S Ont., Canada, 30 mi/48 km SE of Parry Sound; 15 mi/24 km long, 5 mi/8 km wide. Drained W by Muskoka R. into Georgian Bay. It is one of the Muskoka lakes (which also include Rosseau L., L. Joseph, and L. of Bays) in a popular resort region of forests, ponds, and rivers, drained by Muskoka R. into Georgian Bay (W).

Muskoka River, 120 mi/193 km long, S Ont., Canada; rises in Algonquin Provincial Park in 2 branches that unite at Bracebridge (waterfalls near by); flows W through L. Muskoka to Georgian Bay 25 mi/40 km S of Parry Sound. Drains Muskoka lake region.

Muskwa (MUH-skwuh), village, NE B.C., Canada, on Muskwa R. at mouth of Prophet R., on Alaska Highway, and 5 mi/8 km W of Fort Nelson; lumbering.

Muskwa River, 160 mi/257 km long, NE B.C., Canada;

rises in Stikine Mts. near 57°45′N 124°50′W; flows generally NE to confluence with Sikanni Chief R. at Fort Nelson, forming Fort Nelson R.

Musquacook Lakes (muhs-KWAH-kuk), Piscataquis and Aroostook cos., N Maine, 13-mi/21-km chain of 5 lakes (First to Fifth Musquacook lakes), c.58 mi/93 km W of Presque Isle; drain N, through Musquacook Stream, into Allagash R.

Musquodoboit Harbour (muh-sko-DO-bit), village, S N.S., Canada, at head of an inlet of the Atlantic, at mouth of Musquodoboit R., 25 mi/40 km ENE of Halifax. Lumbering, salmon and trout fishing.

Musquodoboit River, 60 mi/97 km long, central N.S., Canada; rises in Cobequid Mts. NW of Sheet Harbour; flows SW and S to the Atlantic, 22 mi/35 km E of Halifax.

Musselshell (MUH-suhl-SHEL), county (□ 1,870 sq mi/4,843 sq km; 1990 pop. 4,106), central Mont.; ⊙ Roundup; 46°29′N 108°24′W. Agr. region drained by Musselshell R. Wheat, oats, hay, some corn, dairying, cattle, sheep, hogs. Oil, gas, and coal. Formed 1911.

Musselshell (MUH-suhl-SHEL), village (1990 pop. 125), Musselshell co., central Mont., 58 mi/93 km NNE of Billings. on Musselshell R., at mouth of Hawk Creek. Grain, livestock. Bull Mts. to the S.

Musselshell River (MUH-suhl-SHEL), 292 mi/470 km long, central Mont.; rises in several branches in the Crazy, Castle, and Little Belt mts., formed by joining of North and South Forks in W Wheatland co., just E of Meagher co. line; flows E past Harlowton, NE past Roundup, and N to Fort Peck L. Not navigable.

Mustang, city (1990 pop. 434), Canadian co., central Okla., suburb 13 mi/21 km WSW of downtown Oklahoma City, near Canadian R. Mfg. (electronics).

Mustang Creek, N. Mex. and Texas: see RITA BLANCA CREEK.

Mustang Island, Nueces co., S Texas, barrier isl., across entrance to Corpus Christi Bay, 17 mi/27 km E of Corpus Christi; 25 mi/40 km long, 1 mi/1.6 km–4 mi/6.4 km wide. Port Aransas is on Aransas Pass, shipping channel to Corpus Christi dug through N end of isl., at NE end; narrow channel that separated is. from Padre Isl. (S) is now filled. Causeway from Corpus Christi connects Padre and Mustang isls. with mainland; ferry to Harbor Isl. from N end connects with causeway to town of Aransas Pass. Mustang Isl. State Park straddles S part.

Mustang Mountain, SW Nev., in N White Mts., near Calif. state line, 60 mi/97 km WNW of Goldfield. Elev. 10,316 ft/3,144 m.

Mustinka River (muhs-TEEN-kuh), 80 mi/129 km long, W Minn.; rises S of Fergus Falls, SW Otter Tail co.; flows S through Lightning L., and to W of Elbow Lake town, then W past Norcross, receiving West Branch Mustinka (c.30 mi/48 km long) from S, then SW past Wheaton to NE end of Traverse L., in Bois de Sioux R., on S.Dak. state line, 8 mi/12.9 km SW of Wheaton; 46°12′N 96°06′W.

Mustique (mus-TEEK), island (□ 5 mi/8 km; 1994 est. pop. 800), St. Vincent and the Grenadines, West Indies, SE of Bequia, 18 mi/29 km S of St. Vincent; 12°53′N 61°11′W. Privately managed tourist isl. under govt. control. Sea-island cotton, coconut and citrus trees. Britannia Bay is small port and center.

Muttontown, affluent residential village (□ 6 sq mi/-

15.5 sq km; 1990 pop. 3,024), Nassau co., SE N.Y., on NW Long Isl., just SE of Glen Cove; 40°49′N 73°32′W.

Mutual 1 village (1990 pop. 126), Champaign co., W central Ohio, 6 mi/10 km ESE of Urbana. **2** village (1990 pop. 68), Woodward co., NW Okla., 19 mi/31 km SE of Woodward; 36°13′N 99°10′W. In livestock, grain, and oil and natural-gas area.

Muxupip (moo-shoo-PEEP), town (1990 pop. 2,092), Yucatán, SE Mexico, 20 mi/32 km E of Mérida; 21°02′N 82°20′W. Henequen, corn.

Muzon, Cape, SE Alaska, S tip of Dall Isl., Alexander Archipelago, in Dixon Entrance, 60 mi/97 km SW of Ketchikan; 54°40′N 132°41′W.

Múzquiz (MOOS-kees), city (1990 pop. 29,819) and township, Coahuila, N Mexico, 25 mi/40 km W of Sabinas, on Mexico Highway 53; 27°52′N 101°30′W. Elev. 1,654 ft/504 m. RR terminus. Mexico's major coal-mining center; also silver, gold, lead, zinc. Agr. center (grain; cattle). Formerly Ciudad Melchor Múzquiz.

Myakka River (mei-AK-kuh), c.50 mi/80 km long, W central Fla.; rises in E Manatee co.; flows SW, through swamps of Sarasota co., then SE, into Charlotte Harbor c.7 mi/11.3 km W of Punta Gorda. Last 10 mi/16 km an estuary.

Myers Chuck, village, SE Alaska, on W side of Cleveland Peninsula, on Clarence Strait 37 mi/60 km NW of Ketchikan. Trading center; fishing. Also spelled Meyers Chuck.

Myerstown (MAI-uhrs-toun), borough (1990 pop. 3,236), Lebanon co., SE Pa., between Myerstown NE of Lebanon, on Tulpehocken Creek; 40°22′N 76°18′W. Varied heavy mfg. Agr. (grain, soybeans, apples; poultry, livestock, dairying). Lebanon Valley Airport to W. Laid out 1768, inc. c.1910.

Myersville, town, St. Elizabeth parish, SW Jamaica, 26 mi/42 km W of May Pen; 17°58′N 77°38′W. Corn, spices; livestock.

Myersville, town (1990 pop. 464), Frederick co., W Md., on Catoctin Creek, bet. Catoctin and South Mts., and 11 mi/18 km N of Frederick; 39°31′N 77°34′W. Founded by James Stottlemeyer in 1742, it has escaped development despite being bet. Routes 40 and 70.

Mylo (MEI-lo), village (1990 pop. 20), Rolette co., N N.Dak., 16 mi/26 km S of Rolla; 48°38′N 99°37′W. Group of small lakes to SW.

Myrnam (MUHR-nuhm), village (1991 pop. 342), E Alta., Canada, near North Saskatchewan R., 26 mi/42 km NW of Vermilion; 53°40′N 111°14′W. Mixed farming, grain, livestock. Fort De L'Isle Historical Site nearby.

Myrtle 1 (MUHR-tuhl), village (1990 pop. 72), Freeborn co., S Minn., near Iowa state line, 12 mi/19 km SE of Albert Lea; 43°33′N 93°09′W. Dairying. **2** village (1990 pop. 358), Union co., N Miss., 8 mi/12.9 km NW of New Albany; 34°33′N 89°07′W. Agr. (cotton, corn; cattle; dairying); timber; mfg. (upholstered furniture). Holly Springs Natl. Forest to W and N.

Myrtle Beach, city (1990 pop. 24,848), Horry co., E S.C., on the coast, 14 mi/23 km SE of Conway; 33°42′N 78°53′W. Year-round beach resort; largest seashore resort in state. Socastee yacht basin, on Intracoastal Waterway, is nearby. Myrtle Beach Air Force Base. Mfg. includes ceramic capacitors, concrete, wire harnesses, industrial component parts, printing and publishing, signs, bricks. Inc. 1938.

Myrtle Beach, uninc. town (1990 pop. 4,275), New Hanover co., SE N.C., residential suburb 7 mi/11.3 km SSE

of Wilmington, near Intracoastal Waterway 1 mi/1.6 km to E, Atlantic Ocean 2 mi/3.2 km to E.; 34°07′N 77°52′W.

Myrtle Creek (MUHR-tuhl), town (1990 pop. 3,063), Douglas co., SW Oregon, 13 mi/21 km S of Roseburg, on South Umpqua R., at mouth of Myrtle Creek; 43°01′N 123°16′W. Timber.

Myrtle Grove, suburb (□ 6 sq mi/15.5 sq km; 1990 pop. 17,402) of Pensacola, Escambia co., extreme NW Fla., 6 mi/9.7 km W of city center; 30°25′N 87°17′W.

Myrtle Point (MUHR-tuhl), town (1990 pop. 2,712), Coos co., SW Oregon, South Fork of Coquille R. (forms main stream) at confluence of North Fork, 23 mi/37 km S of Coos Bay; 43°03′N 124°07′W. Pacific Ocean 15 mi/24 km to W. Trade center for dairy prods. and livestock. Timber. Fish hatchery to NE. Maria C. Jackson State Park to NE; Hoffman Memorial Wayside and Coquille and Myrtle Grove State Parks to S; Siskiyou Natl. Forest to S. Settled 1858, inc. 1903.

Myrtletowne, uninc. town (1990 pop. 4,413), Humboldt co., NW Calif., residential suburb 4 mi/6.4 km E of Eureka, near Humboldt Bay; 40°48′N 124°08′W. Dairying, cattle, sheep, lambs; timber.

Mystic, city (1990 pop. 545), Appanoose co., S Iowa, 4 mi/6.4 km NW of Centerville; 40°46′N 92°56′W. Inc. 1899.

Mystic, town (1990 pop.), Irwin co., S central Ga., 9 mi/14.5 km SW of Fitzgerald; 31°37′N 83°20′W.

Mystic, village (1990 pop. 2,618), at the mouth of the Mystic R., SE Conn.; 41°21′N 71°57′W. Mystic is a postal section of both Groton and Stonington, since the village of Mystic is split bet. the 2 towns. It is a major tourist area, known for the Mystic Marinelife Aquarium, from which Robert Ballard and the Inst. for Undersea Exploration operate. Mystic Seaport Mus. chronicles the village's historical importance in colonial Conn.'s fishing and whaling industries and offers river and sound cruises aboard historic ships. Olde Misticke retail center on outskirts of village. Tourist traffic on the narrow main street in village center often comes to a patient standstill in the summertime as the drawbridge over the Mystic R. opens and closes, allowing sailboats to go in and out of the Mystic harbor. Major sidewalk art festival annually in Aug.

Mystic (MIS-tik), river, c.7 mi/11 km long; rising in Mystic Lakes, E Mass.; and flowing SE, past Medford, into Boston Harbor at Charlestown. Medford was one of the important early settlements on its banks. Former inner sect. of Boston Harbor and spanned by Mystic R. Bridge bet. Boston and Chelsea.

Mystic Lakes (MIS-tik), reservoir consisting of 2 lakes, on Medford-Arlington city border, and in Winchester town, Middlesex co., E Mass., on Mystic R., 6 mi/9.7 km NNW of downtown Boston; c.2 mi/3.2 km long; 42°26′N 71°08′W. Includes Upper Mystic and Lower Mystic ponds. Residential area.

Mystic River, c.10 mi/16 km long; rising in SE Conn.; flowing S past Old Mystic to L.I. Sound, where it divides the village of Mystic into 2 municipal dists., one in town of Groton (W), another in Stonington (E).

Myton, village (1990 pop. 468), Duchesne co. NE Utah, 18 mi/29 km E of Duchesne, and on Duchesne R.; 40°11′N 110°03′W. Wheat, barley, alfalfa; cattle, sheep; uintaite deposits, oil and natural gas. Elev. 5,084 ft/1,550 m. At S edge of Uintah and Ouray Indian Reservation. Originally an Indian trading post. Est. 1905.

N

Naalehu (NAH-AH-LAI-hoo), town (1990 pop. 1,027), S Hawaii isl., Hawaii co., Hawaii, 1 mi/1.6 km from coast, 53 mi//85 km SSW of Hilo; 19°04'N 155°34'W. Whittington (to E) and Punaluu Black Sand (to NE), beach parks; Kau Forest Reserve to NW.

Nabesna (nah-BES-nuh), village, E Alaska, near Can. (Yukon) border, on Nabesna R., and 70 mi/113 km S of Tanacross, on N slope of Wrangell Mts. Airfield. Another Nabesna is c.50 mi/80 km downstream on Nabesna R. opposite Northway.

Nabesna Glacier (nah-BES-nuh), E Alaska, extends N from Wrangell Mts., 20 mi/32 km long, 3 mi/4.8 km wide; near 62°5'N 142°55'W.

Nabesna River (nah-BES-nuh), 70 mi/113 km long, E Alaska; rises in Nabesna Glacier, in the Wrangell Mts., near 62°14'N 142°55'W; flows NNE, past Nabesna, to Tanana R. at 63°02'N 141°53'W.

Nabesna Village (nah-BES-nuh), Native Amer. village, E Alaska, near Can. (Yukon) border, on Nabesna R., and 50 mi/80 km SE of Tanacross, near Alaska Highway.

Nacajuca (nah-kah-HOO-kah), city (1990 pop. 7,469) and township, Tabasco, SE Mexico, on arm of Grijalva R., and 13 mi/21 km NNW of Villahermosa; 18°12'N 93°01'W. In an important oil-producing region. Corn, rice, beans, tobacco, fruit; livestock.

Naches (NA-cheez), village (1990 pop. 569), Yakima co., S Wash., 12 mi/19 km NW of Yakima, and on Naches R.; 46°44'N 120°42'W. RR terminus. Fruit; dairying; mfg. (wood prods., lumber); logging. Snoqualmie Natl. Forest to W.

Naches Pass (NA-cheez) (4,923 ft/1,501 m), on border bet. Pierce and Yakima cos., central Wash., gateway through Cascade Range used by pioneers, c.50 mi/80 km E of Tacoma, NE of Mt. Rainier Natl. Park.

Naches River (NA-cheez), c.75 mi/121 km long, central Wash.; rises in Cascade Range near Naches Pass as Little Naches R.; flows c.20 mi/32 km SE, joins American R. (from SW) to form Naches R., 20 mi/32 km SW of Cle Elum, flows another 55 mi/89 km SE past Naches to Yakima R. bet. Yakima and Selah.

Nachvak Fiord (NACH-vak), inlet of the Atlantic Ocean, NE Lab., E Canada, at foot of Cirque Mt.; 30 mi/48 km long, 3 mi/5 km wide; 59°3'N 63°40'W.

Nacimiento Mountains (nah-see-MYEN-to), range in Sandoval and Rio Arriba cos., NW N.Mex., just E of Rio Puerco; extend c.30 mi/48 km S from Cuba. Prominent points include Pajarito Peak (9,040 ft/2,755 m), San Miguel Mt. (9,473 ft/2,887 m), Nacimiento Peak (9,801 ft/2,987 m). Range is partly in Santa Fe Natl. Forest.

Nacimiento Reservoir (□ 8 sq mi/20.7 sq km), San Luis Obispo co., SW Calif., on Nacimiento R., in Santa Lucia Range, 12 mi/19 km NW of Paso Robles; 35°44'N 120°53'W. Max. capacity 470,000 acre-ft. Formed by Nacimiento Dam (215 ft/66 m high), built (1957) for power generation; also used for irrigation, water supply, recreation, and flood control. Hunter Liggett Military Reservation nearby.

Nacmine (NAK-mein), village, S Alta., W Canada, on Red Deer R., and 4 mi/6 km W of Drumheller. Coal mining. Cattle; wheat.

Naco (NAH-ko), town (1990 pop. 4,035), Sonora, NW Mexico, in NW spurs of Sierra Madre Occidental, on U.S. border adjoining Naco (Ariz.), on RR, and 60 mi/97 km E of Nogales; 31°20'N 109°53'W. In rich copper belt; cattle.

Naco (nah-ko), uninc. village, Cochise co., SE Ariz., on Mex. border, opposite and adjacent to Naco (Sonora, Mexico), 24 mi/39 km W of Douglas. Elev. 4,680 ft/1,426 m. Agr. (cattle sheep). U.S. customs and Mex. consulate are here. Mule Mts. are N.

Nacogdoches (NAH-kah-do-ches), county (□

981 sq mi/2,541 sq km; 1990 pop. 54,753), E Texas; ⊙ Nacogdoches; 31°36'N 94°36'W. Rolling, wooded area; chief industries are timber; dairying, poultry raising; vegetables. Bounded W and S by Angelina R., E by Attoyac Bayou. Oil found here 1866; natural gas; clay, some mfg. Part of Angelina Natl. Forest in SE; L. Nocogdoches in W. Formed 1836.

Nacogdoches (NAH-kah-do-ches), city (1990 pop. 30,872), ⊙ Nacogdoches co., E Texas, 60 mi/97 km S of Longview; 31°36'N 94°39'W. In a pine and hardwood forest area. Highly industrialized city including lumbering, livestock and poultry raising and processing, mfg. (feed, wood prods., motor homes, electronic prods., furniture). Tourism is also important; to the SE is the large Sam Rayburn Reservoir and Angelina Natl. Forest; L. Nacogodoches is to W. Area explored by La Salle (1687), and a Span. mission was founded here in 1716. The state's 1st oil wells were drilled nearby in 1859. Seat of Stephen F. Austin State Univ., Span. presidio built in 1779 on campus.

Nácori Chico (NAH-ko-ree CHEE-ko), town (1990 pop. 1,149), Sonora, NW Mexico, on affluent of Yaqui R., in W outliers of Sierra Madre Occidental, and 135 mi/217 km ENE of Hermosillo; 29°38'N 108°49'W. Elev. 3,550 ft/1,082 m. Livestock raising and wheat growing.

Nacozari de García (nah-ko-SAH-ree dai gahr-SEE-ah), town (1990 pop. 1,040), ⊙ Nacozari de García muncipio, Sonora, NW Mexico, in broad valley of W outliers of Sierra Madre Occidental, on RR, and 70 mi/113 km S of Douglas (Ariz.); 30°22'N 109°41'W. Elev. 3,412 ft/1,040 m. Cattle-raising and copper-mining center; silver, gold, lead, zinc mines.

Nadadores (nah-dah-DO-RES), town (1990 pop. 4,116), Coahuila, N Mexico, 15 mi/24 km NW of Monclova, on RR, on Mexico Highway 30; 27°02'N 101°38'W. Cereals, wine; livestock.

Naden Harbour (NAI-duhn), inlet of Virago Sound, Dixon Entrance, in N Graham Isl., W B.C., W Canada, 17 mi/27 km W of Massett; 8 mi/13 km long, 1 mi/2 km– 3 mi/5 km wide; 54°00'N 132°35'W. Salmon fishing.

Nagai Island (nuh-GEI), Shumagin Isls., SW Alaska, off SW Alaska Peninsula; 32 mi/51 km long, 1 mi/1.6 km– 11 mi/18 km wide; 55°6'N 160°W.

Nags Head, town (1990 pop. 1,838), Dare co., E N.C., 4 mi/6.4 km NNE of Manteo, barrier beach on Outer Banks, sand barrier bet. Atlantic Ocean (E) and Roanoke Sound (W), SE of Albermarle Sound; 35°56'N 75°37'W. Bridge to mainland is 4 mi/6.4 km to S. Swimming, game hunting; commercial fishing. Beach resort area. Mfg. (crab meat processing; consumer goods). Jockey's Ridge State Park to N, largest sand dunes on E coast. Nags Head Woods, a natl. natural landmark (□ 2 sq mi/5.2 sq km) of forest, dunes and wetlands.

Nagua (NAH-gwah), town (1993 pop. 25,969), on Escocesa Bay, N Dominican Republic, ⊙ María Trinidad Sánchez prov.; 19°23'N 69°50'W. Fishing port and tourist center in a rice- and cocoa-growing area. Formerly called Julia Molina or Villa Julia Molina.

Naguabo (nah-GWAH-bo), town (1990 pop. 22,620), E P.R., near the coast, 6 mi/9.7 km ENE of Humacao. Mfg. (electronics, apparel, fabricated metal prods.); dairying (milk prods.); livestock, hogs, poultry. Fishing. Tourism at nearby beaches. Its port, Playa de Naguabo, is 2 mi/3.2 km SE.

Nahanni National Park (nuh-HAN-ee) (□ c.1,840 sq mi/4,770 sq km), Fort Smith region, N.W.T., N Canada, W of Fort Simpson, just E of the Yukon border. Extends along the lower portion of the South Nahanni R. The river's spectacular course passes through 3 deep canyons and over Virginia Falls (c.300 ft/90 m high) and numerous rapids. A wilderness area, the park has hot springs and caves and a variety of plant and animal life. Est. 1972.

Nahant (nuh-HAHNT), resort and residential town (1990 pop. 3,828), Essex co., E Mass., on rocky peninsula jutting S of Lynn into Mass. Bay; 42°25'N 70°55'W. Site of Nahant Beach. East point site of former coastal artillery World War II. Present town park and research station for Northeastern Univ. Settled 1630, inc. 1853.

Nahma (NAH-muh), village, Delta co., S Upper Peninsula, N Mich., 20 mi/32 km ENE of Escanaba, on Big Bay De Noc; 45°50'N 86°39'W. In Hiawatha Natl. Forest. Lumber milling. Native Amer. settlement nearby.

Nahmakanta Lake (nah-muh-KAN-tuh), Piscataquis co., central Maine, 20 mi/32 km WNW of Millinocket; 4 mi/6.4 km long. In lumbering, recreational area. Joined by stream to Pemadumcook L.

Nahuatzén (nah-hwat-SEN), town (1990 pop. 7,025), Michoacán, central Mexico, 17 mi/27 km NNE of Uruapan; 19°42'N 101°50'W. Sugarcane, fruit, tobacco, corn; livestock.

Nahunta (nah-HUHN-tuh), city (1990 pop. 1,049), ⊙ Brantley co., SE Ga., 22 mi/35 km E of Waycross; 31°13'N 81°59'W. Light mfg. and vegetable processing.

Naica (nah-EE-kah), mining settlement, Chihuahua, N Mexico, in E outliers of Sierra Madre Occidental, 70 mi/113 km SE of Chihuahua; 27°51'N 105°30'W.

Naicam (NAI-kuhm), town (1991 pop. 826), central Sask., W Canada, 30 mi/48 km ENE of Humboldt; 52°25'N 104°30'W. Grain elevators.

Nain (NAIN), town (1991 pop. 1,069), NE Lab., E Canada, on inlet of the Atlantic Ocean; 56°33'N 61°41'W. Fishing port.

Nain, town (1991 pop. 2,373), St. Elizabeth parish, SW Jamaica, 8 mi/13 km SW of Mandeville; 17°58'N 77°36'W. Road junction town. Airfield.

Najasa (nah-HAH-suh), town, Camagüey prov., E central Cuba, at crossroads of secondary highways, 23 mi/37 km SSE of Camagüey city, at foot of hills with same name; 21°10'N 77°45'W.

Najasa River (nah-HAH-suh), 64 mi/104 km long, Camagüey prov., E Cuba; rises SE of Camagüey; flows SW and S to the Caribbean Sea, 4 mi/6.4 km E of Santa Cruz del Sur. Sometimes called San Juan de Najasa R. Small Sierra Najasa lies along its upper (left) course. Drains 346 sq mi/895 sq km.

Nakina (nuh-KEE-nuh), town (1991 pop. 635), N central Ont., central Canada, near Upper Twin L. (10 mi/16 km long), 150 mi/241 km NE of Thunder Bay. Elev. 1,052 ft/321 m. Gold mining.

Naknek, village (1990 pop. 575), S Alaska, near head of Alaska Peninsula, on Kvichak Bay of Bristol Bay at mouth of Naknek R.; 58°40'N 157°01'W. Fishing and fish processing. Formerly known as Libbyville, Pawik, Suwarof, or Suworof.

Naknek Lake, S Alaska, near base of Alaska Peninsula; 40 mi/64 km long, 3 mi/4.8 km–8 mi/12.9 km wide; 58°40'N 156°12'W. Game-trout fishing. E part is in Katmai Natl. Monument. Drains W into Kvichak Bay of Bristol Bay by Naknek R. (35 mi/56 km long).

Nakusp (nuh-KUHSP), village (1991 pop. 1,374), SE B.C., W Canada, on Upper Arrow L. (Columbia R.), and 55 mi/89 km SSE of Revelstoke; 50°15'N 117°48'W. Fruit; mixed farming. Tourism; Nakusp Hot Springs.

Namakagon River, Wis.: see NAMEKAGON RIVER.

Namakan Lake (NA-muh-kuhn), St. Louis co., NE Minn. and Rainy Lake dist., W Ont., in chain of lakes on border bet. U.S. and Canada, 35 mi/56 km ESE of International Falls; 12 mi/19 km long, 3 mi/4.8 km wide; 48°30'N 92°38'W. Drains NW into Rainy L., through Short Kettle Falls R., Kettle Falls Dam enlarges both lakes, is continuous with Kabetogama L. (reservoir), to W. Fed from E by Namakan R., which flows across part of Ont. from Lac La Croix (also on border); also receives Pipestone, Seine, and Turtle rivers from Ont. U.S. portion in Voyageurs Natl. Park.

Nambe (NAHM-BAI), pueblo (□ 29 sq mi/75 sq km; 1990 pop. 1,246), Santa Fe co., N central N.Mex., 15 mi/24 km N of Santa Fe, in Nambe Pueblo land grant bet. Sangre de Cristo Mts. and the Rio Grande. Elev. 6,082 ft/1,854 m. Chief activity is agr. (grain, chilies, fruit).; metal alloy pottery. Inhabitants are Mexicans and Native Amer. Pueblo; languages spoken are Span., Eng., and Tewa.

Namekagon River (NAM-e-KAH-gun), c.95 mi/153 km long, NW Wis.; rises E of Namekagon L., in SE Bayfield co.; flows SW, past Hayward, then NW, to St. Croix R., 45 mi/72 km S of Superior. Entire length of river below Namekagon L. is S branch of St. Croix Natl. Scenic

Riverways. Trout fishing. Formerly spelled Namakagon.

Namiquipa (nah-mee-KEE-pah), town (1990 pop. 1,801), ⊙ Namiquipa municipio, Chihuahua, N Mexico, in Sierra Madre Occidental, on Santa María R., and 90 mi/145 km WNW of Chihuahua; 29°15′N 107°25′W. Elev. 5,997 ft/1,828 m. Corn, beans, fruit; cattle.

Nampa, city (1990 pop. 28,365), Canyon co., SW Idaho, in the fertile Treasure Valley; 43°35′N 116°34′W. Elev. 2,484 ft/757 m. RR junction and the commercial, processing, and shipping center for an irrigated agr., orchard, and dairy region. Has food-processing plants and a large sugar factory. Consumer goods, furniture, fabricated metal prods., and wood prods. are also manufactured. Seat of Northwest Nazaréne Col. Canyon Co. Historic Mus. Deer Flat Wildlife Refuge at L. Lowell, to SW. Inc. 1890.

Nanacamilpa (nah-nah-kah-MEEL-pah) or **San José Nanacamilpa** (sahn ho-ZAI nah-nah-kah-MEEL-pah), town (1990 pop. 9,768), ⊙ Nanacamilpa de Mariano Arista municipio, Tlaxcala, central Mexico, 22 mi/ 35 km NW of Tlaxcala; 19°29′N 98°33′W. Maguey, cereals; livestock.

Nanacamilpa de Mariano Arista, Mexico: see NANACAMILPA.

Nanaimo (nuh-NEI-mo), city (1991 pop. 60,129), SW B.C., W Canada, on Vancouver Isl.; 49°09′N 123°55′W. A port, the base of a commercial fishing fleet, and the trade center for a farm and lumbering region. It is the site of a federal fisheries and oceanographic research station. A tourist center, Nanaimo hosts an annual Bathtub Race across the straits to Vancouver.

Nanakuli (NAH-NAH-KOO-lee), city (1990 pop. 9,575), Oahu, Honolulu co., Hawaii, on W coast, 19 mi/31 km WNW of Honolulu; 21°23′N 158°09′W. Lualualei U.S. Naval Reservation to N. Waianae Range to E; Maili Point to NW; Nanaikapono Beach Co. Park to N; Kalanianaoli Beach Co. Park is here.

Nancamilpa (nahn-kah-MEEL-pah), town (1990 pop. 12,837), ⊙ Nancamilpa municipio, Tlaxcala, Mexico, 22 mi/35 km WNW of Tlaxcala, 5 mi/8 km off Mexico Highway 136, on paved road, near Zoquiapan Natl. Park; 19°29′N 98°33′W. Elev. 8,858 ft/2,700 m. Agr., small farming (corn, beans, agave). Also called Mariano Arista.

Nance, county (□ 448 sq mi/1,160 sq km; 1990 pop. 4,275), E central Nebr.; ⊙ Fullerton; 41°23′N 97°59′W. Agr. region drained by Loup and Cedar rivers. Cattle, hogs; dairying; corn, soybeans, sorghum. Formed 1879.

Nanchital de Lázaro Cárdenas del Río (nahn-shee-TAHL dai LAH-zah-ro KAHR-dai-nahs del REE-o), city (1990 pop. 25,593), SE Veracruz, Mexico, 2.5 mi/ 4 km S of the port of Coatzacoalcos, on the banks of the Coatzacoalcos R., 4.3 mi/7 km S of Mexico Highway 180, and near RR. Hot climate. Important because of rich petroleum deposits.

Nanga Parbat, Mount (10,780 ft/3,286 m), on border bet. W Alta. and E B.C., W Canada, in Rocky Mts., at W edge of Banff Natl. Park, 2 mi/3 km SE of Mt. Freshfield in the Freshfield Icefield, and 65 mi/105 km NW of Banff; 51°43′N 116°52′W.

Nanoose Bay (na-NOOS), village, SW B.C., W Canada, on SE Vancouver Isl., on Strait of Georgia, 13 mi/21 km WNW of Nanaimo; 49°15′N 124°11′W. Lumber-shipping port.

Nansemond River, c.25 mi/40 km, SE Va.; rises in W Suffolk city; flows N, through Suffolk to James R. estuary, in Hampton Roads harbor; lower 10 mi/16 km widens into tidal river.

Nansen Sound or **Fridtjof Nansen Sound**, NE Franklin dist., N.W.T., N Canada, arm of the Arctic Ocean, bet. Axel Heiberg (W) and NW Ellesmere (E) isls.; 90 mi/ 145 km long, 10 mi/16 km–35 mi/56 km wide; 81°00′N 90°00′W. Connects Eureka Sound and Greely Fjord (SE) with Arctic Ocean (NW). In N entrance are Lands Lokk and Fjeldhdmen isls.

Nantachie, Lake (nuh-TACH-ee), reservoir, Grant parish, central La., 8 mi/13 km NW of Colfax; c.2 mi/3 km long; 31°37′N; 92°48′W. Drains S through tributary of Red R.

Nantahala Mountains (nan-tuh-HAI-luh), mostly in far SW N.C. , extends into NE Ga., transverse range of the Appalachians bet. Great Smoky Mts. (N) and the Blue Ridge (S); from confluence of Nantahala and Little Tennessee rivers in N.C. extend c.50 mi/80 km S to Tallulah Falls (Ga.). Highest points are Wine Spring Bald mt. (c.5,500 ft/1,676 m), 13 mi/21 km SW of Franklin (N.C.), and Wayah Bald mt. (5,342 ft/1,628 m), 11 mi/ 18 km W of Franklin. In Nantahala (N.C.) and Chattahoochee (Ga.) natl. forests.

Nantahala River (nan-tuh-HAI-luh), 40 mi/64 km long, W N.C.; rises in Nantahala Mts. 65 mi/105 km SW of Asheville, in SW Macon co. at Ga. state line; flows NNW and N, through Nantahala L. reservoir to Little Tennessee R., in Fontana L. reservoir where it forms S arm, 8 mi/12.9 km W of Bryson City. Entirely within Nantahala Natl. Forest. In lower course, traverses scenic, 8-mi/12.9-km-long Nantahala Gorge, with steep sides up to 2,000 ft/610 m high. Nantahala Dam (250 ft/ 76 m high, 1,042 ft/318 m long; completed 1942), privately built power dam in middle course, is c.20 mi/ 32 km SW of Bryson City; forms Nantahala Reservoir (5 mi/8 km long, 1 mi/1.6 km wide), sometimes known as Aquone L.

Nantasket Beach, beach village, of Hull town, Plymouth co., E Mass., 3 mi/4.8 km NNE of Hingham, on narrow Nantasket Peninsula (5 mi/8 km long), which extends NW into Mass. Bay to Point Allerton, then bends W to end at Windmill Point. State public beach.

Nanticoke, city (1986 pop. 20,202), SE Ont., central Canada, on N shore of L. Erie, 36 mi/58 km SW of Hamilton; 42°48′N 80°04′W. Heavy industries including Steel Co. Canada complex, oil refinery, and coal-generated electric plant. Inc. 1974 by almagamation of 7 municipalities, including village of Nanticoke.

Nanticoke (NAN-ti-KOK), city (1990 pop. 12,267), Luzerne co., NE Pa., 7 mi/11.3 km WSW of Wilkes-Barre, on the Susquehanna R. (bridged); 41°12′N 76°00′W. Largely residential. Mfg. (plastic prods.). Formerly the heart of a major anthracite-coal-mining region, but production has declined. State Correctional Institution to W; part of Lackawanna State Forest to N. Founded 1793, inc. as a city 1926.

Nanticoke (NAN-TEE-kok), fishing village, Wicomico co., SE Md., on the Eastern Shore, 17 mi/29 km WSW of Salisbury, and on an estuary of Nanticoke R. Tomato cannery; ships, seafood. The name comes from a Native Amer. tribe known as "tide-water people."

Nanticoke River, c.50 mi/80 km long, S Del. and E Md.; rises in several small branches in S Sussex co. (Del.); flows SW, past Seaford (Del.; head of navigation and tides), Sharptown and Vienna (Md.), to N end of Tangier Sound near Nanticoke; marsh-bordered estuary is 3 mi/4.8 km wide at mouth. Fishing Bay Wildlife Management Area on W shore. Wicomico R. shares entrance to sound, enters from ENE. Main tributary is Marshyhope Creek, formerly called NW Fork of Nanticoke R.

Nanton, town (1991 pop. 1,589), S Alta., W Canada, 50 mi/80 km SSE of Calgary; 50°21′N 113°46′W. Flour and cereal foods milling; dairying; ranching; wheat; livestock. Mineral springs. Large source of bottled mineral water.

Nantucket (nan-TUH-ket), island (□ 303 sq mi/ 785 sq km), Nantucket co., SE Mass., c.25 mi/40 km S of Cape Cod (separated by Nantucket Sound) and across Muskeget Channel from Martha's Vineyard (W); c.14 mi/23 km long, 3 mi/4.8 km–6 mi/9.7 km wide; 41°15′N 70°08′W. Airport; ferry service from Woods Hole and Hyannis. Exhibiting evidence of glaciation (terminal moraine, outwash plain), Nantucket has sandy beaches and low, rolling hills composed of sand and gravel. It is sparsely vegetated; wild cranberries, beach plums, heather, and wild roses predominate. Nantucket and the small adjacent isls. constitute both Nantucket town (1990 pop. 6,012) and Nantucket co. Settled by Europeans in 1659, the isl. was part of N.Y. (1660–1692), when it was ceded to Mass. Major whaling port until the decline of the industry (c.1850); later developed into a well-known resort and artists' colony.

The village of Nantucket is the trade center of the isl. and is known for its many old houses and fishing port. Siasconset, or 'Sconset, is a summer resort on Atlantic coast (E). The isl. has a whaling mus. and an 18th-cent. windmill. The 1st U.S. lightship station (est. 1856) is located near Nantucket. Great Point forms the N tip of the isl. (lighthouse here). Sankaty Head and lighthouse in Siasconset on entrance.

Nantucket Sound, channel of the Atlantic Ocean, off SE Mass., bet. S shore of Cape Cod (N) and Nantucket Isl. and Martha's Vineyard (S); c.30 mi/48 km long, c.25 mi/40 km wide.

Nanty Glo (NAN-tee GLO), borough (1990 pop. 3,190), Cambria co., W central Pa., 10 mi/16 km NNE of Johnstown, on South Branch Blacklick Creek; 40°28′N 78°49′W. Bituminous coal. Light mfg. Ebensburg Airport to E. Founded 1888.

Nanuet (NA-noo-et), village (□ 5 sq mi/13 sq km; 1990 pop. 14,065), Rockland co., SE N.Y., 5 mi/8 km W of Nyack; 41°06′N 74°01′W. Mfg. of wood prods., fabricated metal prods., electrical prods., machinery. Internatl. Shrine of St. Anthony is here.

Nanvarnarluk, village, SW Alaska, on Bethel Bay, 60°00′N 162°00′W.

Naolinco, Mexico: see NAOLINCO DE VICTORIA.

Naolinco de Victoria (mah-o-LEEN-ko de veek-TO-ree-ah), city (1990 pop. 6,526) and township, ⊙ Naolinco municipio, Veracruz, E Mexico, in Sierra Madre Oriental, 9 mi/14.5 km NNE of Xalapa Enríquez; elev. 5,266 ft/1,605 m; 19°39′N 96°51′W. Agr. center (coffee, corn, sugarcane, fruit).

Naomi Wilderness Area, Mount, Utah: see RICHMOND, town.

Napa (NA-puh), county (□ 754 sq mi/1,953 sq km; 1990 pop. 110,765), W Calif.; ⊙ Napa; 38°30′N 122°19′W. Bounded S by San Pablo Bay, it is a mountainous area, in Coast Ranges. Napa Valley (wine growing) extends SE from base of Mt. St. Helena to near San Pablo Bay. S co. line comes within 0.5 mi/0.8 km of San Pablo Bay. Petrified redwood forest, hot springs (resorts) near Calistoga. Grapes, walnuts; nursery prods.; dairying; cattle. Wine making (since 1850s) is principal industry, together with neighboring Sonoma co. (to W); also fruit processing, some mfg. (at Napa). Mining and quarrying (mercury, pumice, sand and gravel). Formed 1850.

Napa (NA-puh), city (□ 17 sq mi/44 sq km, 1990 pop. 61,842), ⊙ Napa co., W Calif., 33 mi/53 km NNE of San Francisco, on the Napa R.; 38°18′N 122°18′W. Mfg. (wineries; medical equip., electronic equip., beverages, computer prods., apparel, plastic prods., wood prods.; printing and publishing). Grapes and other fruits (esp. citrus fruit) are grown in the adjacent Napa valley, which is famous for the wines that have been made here since the late 1870s. Numerous wineries in the region. Growing city, almost doubled in pop. bet. 1970 and 1990. Seat of Napa Valley Col. (2-year). Napa Co. Airport to S. Inc. 1872.

Napa River, c.50 mi/80 km long, Napa co., W Calif.; rises in NW Napa co. near Mt. St. Helena; flows S; through Napa Valley in the Coast Ranges, past St. Helena and Napa (head of navigation and of tidewater), to Mars Isl. Strait, narrow arm of San Pablo Bay. Wine-producing dist. Also has dairying; cattle; walnuts, nursery stock.

Napaimiut (nuh-PAI-mee-yoot), native village, W Alaska, on Kuskokwim R., and 60 mi/97 km SE of Holy Cross; 61°32′N 158°48′W. Airfield. Sometimes called Napai, Napamute, or Napamiute.

Napaiskak (nuh-PEI-yi-skak) or **Napakiak**, Inuit village (1990 pop. 318), W Alaska, near mouth of Kuskokwim R., 11 mi/18 km SW of Bethel.

Napakiak, Alaska: see NAPAISKAK.

Napamute, Alaska: see NAPAIMIUT.

Napanee (NA-puh-nee), town (1991 pop. 5,179), ⊙ Lennox and Addington co., SE Ont., central Canada, on Napanee R., near its mouth on the Bay of Quinte, and 23 mi/37 km W of Kingston; 44°15′N 76°57′W. Milling, food processing, brick and tile mfg.; dairying.

Napanoch (NA-puh-nawk), resort village (□ 1 sq mi/ 2.6 sq km; 1990 pop. 1,068), Ulster co., SE N.Y., on

Rondout Creek, just W of the Shawangunk range, and 2 mi/3.2 km NE of Ellenville; 41°45′N 74°22′W. Rondout Reservoir is 3 mi/4.8 km NW.

Napatree Point, R.I.: see WATCH HILL.

Napavine, town (1990 pop. 745), Lewis co., SW Wash., 8 mi/12.9 km S of Chehalis; 46°35′N 122°55′W. In agr., dairying area; poultry. Lewis and Clark State Park to SE.

Naper (NAIP-uhr), village (1990 pop. 130), Boyd co., N Nebr., 13 mi/21 km WNW of Butte, bet. S.Dak. state line and Keya Paha R.; 42°57′N 99°05′W.

Naperville, city (1990 pop. 85,351), Du Page and Will cos., NE Ill., on the Du Page R., suburb 30 mi/48 km W of downtown Chicago; 41°45′N 88°09′W. It has become a major office and corporate center, marked by an economy that has grown since the early 1980s. Mfg. (fabricated metal prods., electrical equip., food prods., paper prods., machinery, medical supplies, plastic prods.; printing). Remnant agr. (corn, oats, vegetables). The city's pop. has grown 4-fold bet. 1970 and 1990. Seat of North Central Col. Settled 1831–1832, inc. as a city 1890.

Napierville (NAI-pyuhr-vil), county (□ 149 sq mi/ 386 sq km), S Que., E Canada, bet. the St. Lawrence R. and the U.S. (N.Y.) border; ⊙ Napierville; 45°10′N 73°30′W.

Napierville, village (1991 pop. 2,909), ⊙ Napierville co., SW Que., E Canada, on Little Montreal R., and 24 mi/ 39 km SSE of Montreal; 45°11′N 73°24′W. Dairying; vegetables.

Napili Bay (NAH-PEE-lee), town (1990 pop. 2,300), Maui isl., Maui co., Hawaii, on NW coast of West Maui Peninsula, on Napili Bay, at mouth of Honokeana Stream. Pineapples.

Napinka (nuh-PING-kuh), village, SW Man., central Canada, on Souris R., and 55 mi/89 km SW of Brandon; 49°19′N 100°51′W. Grain elevators.

Naplate (na-PLAIT), village (1990 pop. 609), La Salle co., N Ill., just W of Ottawa, on Illinois R.; 41°19′N 88°52′W. Buffalo Rock State Park to W.

Naples, resort city (□ 13 sq mi/34 sq km; 1990 pop. 19,505), Collier co., SW Fla., on the Gulf of Mexico; 26°08′N 81°47′W. Borders the Big Cypress Swamp. Tourism (noted beach is popular year-round), fishing, and shrimp fisheries are the staples of the economy. Site of the Caribbean Gardens and Collier Seminole State Park. Rapidly growing metropolitan area. Inc. 1927.

Naples 1 town (1990 pop. 130), Scott co., W central Ill., on Illinois R., and 11 mi/18 km WNW of Winchester; 39°45′N 90°36′W. In agr. area. **2** resort town (1990 pop. 2,860), Cumberland co., SW Maine, on Sebago and Long lakes, 27 mi/43 km NW of Portland; 43°58′N 70°36′W. Includes part of Sebago L. State Park. **3** town (1990 pop. 1,508), Morris co., NE Texas, 40 mi/64 km WSW of Texarkana; 33°12′N 94°40′W. In agr. area (cattle; peanuts, watermelons); timber; mfg. (bldg. materials; peanut processing). Inc. 1909. **4** town (1990 pop. 1,334), Uintah co., NE Utah, 2 mi/3.2 km SE of Vernal, near Ashley Creek; 40°25′N 109°29′W. Residential community. Sheep, cattle; dairying; alfalfa, barley, wheat. Oil and natural gas.

Naples 1 village (1990 pop. 1,237), Ontario co., W central N.Y., in Finger Lakes region, near S end of Canandaigua L., 20 mi/32 km SSW of Canandaigua; 42°37′N 77°24′W. In grape-growing Naples valley; mfg. (wine, grape juice); timber. Inc. 1894. **2** village (1990 pop. 35), Clark co., E central S.Dak., 13 mi/21 km SE of Clark; 44°46′N 97°30′W. In farming region.

Naples Manor, town (1990 pop. 4,574), Collier co., SW Fla., 5 mi/8 km SE of Naples.

Naples Park, town (□ 2 sq mi/5.2 sq km; 1990 pop. 8,002), Collier co., SW Fla., 8 mi/12.9 km N of Naples; 26°15′N 81°49′W.

Napoleon, city (1990 pop. 8,884), ⊙ Henry co., NW Ohio, on Maumee R., and 14 mi/23 km ENE of Defiance. Market center for agr. area; machinery, preserved fruits and vegetables, transportation equip., consumer goods, metal prods., bldg. materials.

Napoleon 1 town (1990 pop. 238), Ripley co., SE Ind., 8 mi/12.9 km SW of Batesville; 39°13′N 85°20′W. In agr.

area. Mfg. (wood prods.). Laid out 1820. **2** town (1990 pop. 233), Lafayette co., W central Mo., on Missouri R., and 9 mi/14.5 km WSW of Lexington; 39°07′N 94°05′W. Soybeans, corn, wheat; cattle. **3** town (1990 pop. 930), ⊙ Logan co., S N.Dak., 54 mi/87 km ESE of Bismarck; 46°30′N 99°46′W. Livestock; grain; dairy prods. Beaver State Park to SE.

Napoleonville (nuh-PO-lee-uhn-vil), village (1990 pop. 802), ⊙ Assumption parish, SE La., 30 mi/48 km SSE of Baton Rouge, on Bayou Lafourche; 29°57′N 91°02′W. In agr. area (sugarcane; cattle); crawfish, crabs. Food processing, mfg. (raw sugar). Oil and gas field nearby. Has fine old church, antebellum houses. Founded c.1818, inc. 1878.

Naponee (nuh-PAWN-ee), village (1990 pop. 97), Franklin co., S Nebr., 10 mi/16 km W of Franklin, and on Republican R.; 40°04′N 99°08′W. Harlan Co. Dam and Reservoir and State Recreation Area to W (upstream).

Napoopoo (NAH-PO-o-PO-o), village (1990 pop. 350), Hawaii isl., Hawaii co., Hawaii, 55 mi/89 km WSW of Hilo, 2 mi/3.2 km SW of Captain Cook, on Kealakekua Bay, Kona (W) Coast. Coffee, fruit; fish. Napoopoo Beach Park and Mokuohai Battleground to SW; Kealakekua Bay State Underwater Park to N.

Nappanee, city (1990 pop. 5,510), Elkhart co., N Ind., 14 mi/23 km SW of Goshen; 41°27′N 85°59′W. In agr. area (mint, onions, grain; livestock); mfg. (furniture, fabricated metal prods.; electrical goods, transportation equip.; wood prods.; motor vehicles and motor homes, manufactured housing). Plotted 1874, inc. 1926.

Narada Falls (nuh-RA-duh), waterfall (168 ft/51 m), on Paradise Creek, in S Mt. Rainier Natl. Park, Lewis co., W central Wash.

Naramata (na-ruh-MA-tuh), village, S B.C., W Canada, on Okanagan L., 7 mi/11 km N of Penticton. Fruit, vegetables.

Naranja (nuh-RAN-juh), town (□ 1 sq mi/2.6 sq km; 1990 pop. 5,790), Dade co., SE Fla., 24 mi/39 km SW of Miami; 25°31′N 80°25′W. Adjacent to Homestead Air Force Base. Virtually destroyed by Hurricane Andrew in 1992.

Naranjal (nah-RAHN-hahl), town (1990 pop. 1,842), Veracruz, E Mexico, 6 mi/9.7 km S of Córdoba, on Blanco R. Elev. 2,799 ft/853 m. Coffee, fruit.

Naranjito (nah-rahn-HEE-to), town (1990 pop. 27,914), N central P.R., 14 mi/23 km SW of San Juan. Commercial and industrial center. Agr. (coffee, bananas, plantains; livestock). A hydroelectric plant with artificial lake is nearby on the La Plata R.

Naranjo, Bahía de (nah-RAHN-ho, bah-HEE-uh dai), small sheltered inlet, on NE coast of Cuba, in Holguín prov., 10 mi/16 km E of Gibara; c.2 mi/3.2 km long, 1 mi/1.6 km wide; 21°07′N 75°52′W.

Naranjos (nah-RAHN-hos), town (1990 pop. 19,389), ⊙ Amatlán Tuxpan, Veracruz, E Mexico, 33 mi/53 km NW of Túxpam de Rdoríguez Cano; 21°22′N 97°43′W. Corn, sugar, fruit. Petroleum wells.

Narberth (NAHR-buhrth), borough (1990 pop. 4,278), Montgomery co., SE Pa., residential suburb 6 mi/ 9.7 km WNW of downtown Philadelphia; 40°00′N 75°15′W. Light mfg. Settled 1860, inc. 1895.

Nardin (NAHR-din), village (1990 pop. 75), Kay co., N Okla., 22 mi/35 km WNW of Ponca City; 36°48′N 97°27′W. In agr. area.

Nares Abyssal Plain, flat area of ocean floor N of the P.R. Trench, 20°00′N 24°00′N, one of the deepest in the N Atlantic, with depths of 19,029 ft/5,800 m– 19,685 ft/6,000 m.

Nares, Cape, N Ellesmere Isl., NE Franklin dist., N.W.T., N Canada, on the Arctic Ocean; 83°06′N 71°45′W.

Nariva (nuh-REE-vuh), county (□ 206.3 sq mi/ 534.3 sq km), E Trinidad, Trinidad and Tobago, on the Atlantic Ocean; 10°22′N 61°10′W. Forms, together with St. David, St. Andrew, and Mayaro, the administrative dist. of the Eastern Cos.

Nariva Swamp (nuh-REE-vuh), E Trinidad, Trinidad and Tobago, c.35 mi/56 km SE of Port of Spain, a low area stretching from palm-lined Cocos Bay on E coast c.5 mi/8 km inland. Wetlands haven for migratory birds.

Narka, village (1990 pop. 113), Republic co., N central Kansas, 14 mi/23 km NE of Belleville, near Nebr. state line; 39°57′N 97°25′W. In grain region.

Narragansett (na-ruh-GAN-set), town (1990 pop. 14,985), Washington co., S R.I., along W shore entrance of Narragansett Bay, N of Point Judith, 27 mi/43 km S of Providence; 41°23′N 71°29′W. Suburban settlements, resorts; fishing; agr. Includes resort village Narragansett Pier (1990 pop. 3,721), fishing village of Galilee, and a state reservation with Scarborough Beach. Point Judith lighthouse dates from 1816. Settled in mid-17th cent., set off from South Kingstown 1888. A fire in 1900 and the 1938 hurricane did great damage. The town takes its name from a Native Amer. tribe that once lived in the territory. In 1675, Colonists engaged the Narragansetts and prevailed. Inc. 1901.

Narragansett Bay, arm of the Atlantic Ocean, deeply indenting the state of R.I.; 30 mi/48 km long, 3 mi/ 4.8 km–12 mi/19 km wide. Its many inlets provided harbors that were advantageous to Colonial trade and later to resort development. At the head of the bay is Providence; at the SE corner of the N bay portion is Newport. Conanicut and Prudence isls. are also in the bay, which is spanned by Newport Bridge (built 1969; 1,600 ft/488 m), which links Newport with Jamestown.

Narragansett Indian Reservation, Native Amer. land (1990 pop. 31), in Charlestown, Washington co., S R.I.; 41°25′N 71°40′W. The Narragansetts, an Algonquian tribe of Native Americans, sold their reservation lands c.1880 and only regained them over a cent. later. The tribe claimed an estimated 2,100 members in the 1990s. The reservation preserves ruins illustrative of Narragansett life, as well as small burial grounds and a Native church (1859) of hewn granite.

Narragansett Pier, R.I.: see NARRAGANSETT.

Narraguagus River (nar-uh-GWAI-guhs), c.30 mi/ 48 km long, SE Maine; rises in Hancock and Washington cos.; flows SE to Narraguagus Bay.

Narrows, town (1990 pop. 2,082), Giles co., SW Va., in Allegheny Mts., near W. Va. state line, 22 mi/35 km WNW of Blacksburg, on New R., at mouth of Wolf Creek; 37°19′N 80°48′W. In agr. area (alfalfa, apples; cattle, poultry); mfg. (cellulose prods., machinery, textiles); timber; coal mining. Civil War Confederate garrison. Inc. 1904.

Narrows Arm, NE arm of Seechelt Inlet, SW B.C., W Canada, 45 mi/72 km NW of Vancouver; 10 mi/16 km long, 1 mi/2 km wide. In lumbering area.

Narrows Dam, Ark.: see LITTLE MISSOURI RIVER.

Narrows, The, Caribbean strait, Leeward Isls., bet. St. Kitts (NW) and Nevis (SE); c.2 mi/3.2 km wide; at c.17°13′N 62°37′W.

Narrows, The, narrow passage in the U.S.V.I., bet. St. John (S) and Great Thatch and Tortola (N) isls., 12 mi/ 19 km ENE of Charlotte Amalie; c.1 mi/1.6 km wide.

Narrowsburg, resort village (1990 pop. 750), Sullivan co., SE N.Y., on Delaware R. (here forming Pa. state line), and 20 mi/32 km WSW of Monticello; 41°36′N 75°03′W.

Naschitti (nah-SHI-tee), settlement, San Juan co., N.Mex., 39 mi/63 km N of Gallup, on the Navajo Reservation. The site of one of the 1st trading posts on the E side of the Chuska Mts.

Naselle (nai-SEL), uninc. town (1990 pop. 1,000), Pacific co., SW Wash., 12 mi/19 km N of Astoria (Oregon), on Naselle R., at mouth of South Naselle R. Timber; dairying. Stone quarrying. Willapa Natl. Wildlife Refuge and Willapa Bay to NW; Columbia R. estuary 5 mi/8 km S.

Nash, county (□ 542 sq mi/1,404 sq km; 1990 pop. 76,677), NE central N.C.; ⊙ Nashville; 35°58′N 77°59′W. In coastal plain area; bounded NE by Fishing Creek; drained by Tar R. Agr. (wheat, oats, soybeans, hay, sweet potatoes, peanuts, tobacco, cotton, corn; chickens, cattle, hogs); pine timber. Mfg. at Rocky Mount, Spring Hope, and Nashville. Formed 1777.

Nash, town (1990 pop. 2,162), Bowie co., NE Texas, suburb 7 mi/11.3 km WNW of downtown Texarkana; 33°26′N 94°07′W. Agr. area (dairying; cattle, wheat; soybeans, rice). Oil and natural gas. Mfg. (wood prods., plastic prods., transportation equip., fabricated metal prods.).

Nash or **Nashville**, village (1990 pop. 281), Grant co., N Okla., 21 mi/34 km NNW of Enid, near Salt Fork of Arkansas R.; 36°40′N 98°02′W. In grain-growing and dairying area. Great Salt Plains State Park (Natl. Wildlife Refuge) and L. to NW.

Nash Harbor, village, W Alaska, on N shore of Ninivak Isl.; 60°15′N 166°44′W.

Nash Island, Washington co., E Maine, small lighthouse isl. just E of entrance to Pleasant Bay.

Nashoba (na-SHO-buh), former community, Shelby co., SW Tenn., on Wolf R. just E of Memphis. Founded 1827 by Frances Wright as a colony in which slaves were to be educated for freedom, Nashoba failed as a social experiment and by 1830 had been dissolved.

Nashotah (nuh-SHO-tuh), village (1990 pop. 567), Waukesha co., SE Wis., 24 mi/39 km W of Milwaukee, in farm and lake resort region; 43°05′N 88°24′W. Mfg. (plastic prods., cable assembly, wood prods.). Seat of Nashotah House, an Episcopal seminary.

Nashua (NA-shoo-wuh), city (1990 pop. 79,662), ⊙ Hillsborough co., S N.H., 15 mi/24 km S of Manchester, on Mass. (S) state line, and 35 mi/56 km NW of Boston (Mass.); 42°45′N 71°29′W. Bounded E by Merrimack R.; drained by Nashua R. and Salmon Brook. RR junction. Because of the availability of water power, Nashua developed (early 19th cent.) as a textile mill town; the closing of these mills after World War II, however, prompted the development of diverse mfg. Mfg. (machinery, rubber prods., wood prods., bldg. materials, computers and computer equip., fabricated metal prods., transportation equip., electrical and electronic goods, furniture, chemicals, shoes, paper prods., airshafts, plastic prods., defense systems; machining). The city has also grown as a satellite community of the Boston urbanized area and is popular for its tax-free shopping. Seat of Rivier Col., N.H. Technical Col., Daniel Webster Col. The Federal Aviation Agency has an Air Traffic Control Center here. Federal Fish Hatchery. Municipal Airport to W. Silver L. State Park to W, in Hollis. Settled c.1655, inc. as a city 1853.

Nashua, town (1990 pop. 1,476), Chickasaw co., NE Iowa, on Cedar R. at mouth of Little Cedar R., and 15 mi/24 km WSW of New Hampton; 42°57′N 32°92′W. Mfg. (machinery, metal and wood prods.).

Nashua 1 (NA-shoo-wuh), village (1990 pop. 63), Wilkin co., W Minn., 21 mi/34 km SE of Breckenridge; 46°02′N 96°17′W. Grain, sunflowers; dairying. **2** (NA-shwuh), village (1990 pop. 375), Valley co., NE Mont., 13 mi/21 km ESE of Glasgow, at the confluence of Porcupine Creek and Milk R.; 48°08′N 106°22′W. Fort Peck L. and Dam to S; large Fort Peck Indian Reservation to E. Sheep, cattle; irrigated agr. Growth stimulated by construction of dam.

Nashua River (NA-shoo-uh), c.30 mi/48 km long, Mass. and N.H.; formed in E Worcester co. (Mass.) by junction of its N and S branches near Lancaster; flows NNE to the Merrimack R. at Nashua (N.H.). Water power. N branch rises W of Fitchburg (Mass.), flows c.30 mi/48 km generally SE, past Fitchburg (water power), joining S branch c.5 mi/8 km below its issuance from Wachusett Reservoir.

Nashville 1 city (1990 pop. 3,202), ⊙ Washington co., SW Ill., 18 mi/29 km SW of Centralia; 38°21′N 89°22′W. Mfg. (machinery); agr. (corn, wheat, fruit, seed; livestock, poultry). Inc. 1853. **2** city (1990 pop. 510,784), ⊙ Tenn., coextensive with Davidson co., central Tenn., on the Cumberland R., 195 mi/314 km NE of Memphis; 36°10′N 86°46′W. In a fertile farm area, Nashville is a port of entry and an important commercial and industrial center. The city has RR shops and diverse mfg., including wood, glass, and rubber prods., shoes, aircraft parts, and steel. Noted for its music business; it is a major recording center, esp. for country music. It also has many publishing houses producing religious materials, school annuals, magazines, and telephone directories. Several large insurance and finance companies have their hq. here, and the country's largest healthcare conglomerate, Hospital Corp. of Amer., is based here. Founded (1779) by a group of pioneers under James Robertson. Fort Nashborough was built on the banks of the river, and the next year 60 families arrived to settle the area. As the N terminus of the Natchez Trace, the settlement developed early as a cotton center and river port and later as a RR hub. It became the permanent state capital in 1843. After the fall of Fort Donelson in Feb. 1862, Nashville was abandoned to Union troops under D. C. Buell and became an important Union base for the remainder of the Civil War. Sometimes called the "Athens of the South," Nashville has many buildings of Classical design, including a replica of the Parthenon, built in 1897. Among its many institutions of higher education are Vanderbilt Univ., Fisk Univ., Tenn. State Univ., the Univ. of Tenn. at Nashville, Meharry Medical Col., Amer. Baptist Col., David Lipscomb Col., Belmont Col., Free Will Baptist Bible Col., Aquinas Junior Col., and a state school for the blind. Nashville has many cultural amenities, including a symphony orchestra, ballet and opera companies, and several theater troupes, art galleries, and mus. Points of interest include the capitol (completed 1855) with the tomb of James K. Polk; the war memorial bldg.; the Country Music Hall of Fame and mus.; Opryland; Ryman auditorium (original home of the Grand Ole Opry); a replica of Fort Nashborough; and several old churches and antebellum homes, including Belle Meade mansion. Nearby is the Hermitage, home of Andrew Jackson. Inc. as a city 1806, merged with Davidson co. 1963.

Nashville 1 town (1990 pop. 4,639), ⊙ Howard co., SW Ark., 38 mi/61 km NNE of Texarkana; 33°56′N 93°50′W. RR junction. Shipping point for agr. area (poultry; grain); mfg. (consumer goods, bldg. materials, lumber, plastic prods., machinery, poultry prods., beverages). **2** town (1990 pop. 4,782), ⊙ Berrien co., S Ga., 26 mi/42 km N of Valdosta; 31°12′N 83°15′W. Tobacco market. Mfg. includes fiberglass prods., transportation equip., clothing, bldg. materials; food canning; lumber. Inc. 1892. **3** town (1990 pop. 873), ⊙ Brown co., S central Ind., on Salt Creek, and 40 mi/64 km S of Indianapolis; 39°12′N 86°14′W. Densely forested; hilly terrain. Timber. Beautiful scenery here attracts tourists esp. in autumn; town has an art gallery and several resident painters. Brown Co. State Park to S; Yellowood State Forest to W. Laid out 1836. **4** town (1990 pop. 3,617), ⊙ Nash co., NE central N.C., 10 mi/16 km W of Rocky Mount; 35°58′N 77°57′W. In agr. area (cotton, tobacco, peanuts, grain; poultry, livestock); timber. Mfg. (feeds, mobile homes, fabricated metal prods., apparel, lumber; printing and publishing).

Nashville 1 village (1990 pop. 118), Kingman co., S Kansas, 21 mi/34 km SW of Kingman; 37°26′N 98°25′W. In wheat area. **2** village (1990 pop. 1,654), Barry co., SW Mich., 10 mi/16 km ESE of Hastings, and on Thornapple R.; 42°36′N 85°05′W. In agr. area; mfg. tool and die. Plotted 1865, inc. 1869. **3** village (1990 pop. 181), Holmes co., central Ohio, 11 mi/18 km WNW of Millersburg.

Nashwaak River (NASH-wok), 70 mi/113 km long, central N.B., E Canada; issues from the small Nashwaak L., 30 mi/48 km NE of Woodstock; flows SE and S, past Marysville, to St. John R. opposite Fredericton.

Nashwaaksis (NASH-wok-sis), lumbering village, S central N.B., E Canada, on St. John R., at mouth of Nashwaak R., just NW of Fredericton.

Nashwauk (NASH-wawk), town (1990 pop. 1,026), Itasca co., NE Minn., 13 mi/21 km WSW of Hibbing, in Mesabi Iron Range; 47°22′N 93°10′W. Iron mining; timber; mfg. (pulpwood). Growth followed discovery of iron nearby in early 1900s. George Washington State Forest to N; Hill Annex Mine State Park to W. Swan L. to S.

Naskaupi River (nas-KO-pee), 180 mi/290 km long, Lab., E Canada; issues from small lake 30 mi/48 km E of Michikamau L. at 54°08′N 63°05′W; flows E and SE, through Grand L. (30 mi/48 km long, 2 mi/3 km wide), to W end of L. Melville, 20 mi/32 km NE of Goose Bay air base. On its upper course are waterfalls.

Naskeag Point (NAS-keg), Hancock co., S Maine, 3-mi/4.8-km peninsula in Blue Hill Bay, S of Brooklin. Br. raid repulsed here, 1778. Naskeag village is in Brooklin town.

Nason, city (1990 pop. 235), Jefferson co., S Ill., 10 mi/16 km SSW of Mount Vernon; 38°10′N 88°58′W. In agr. area (wheat, sorghum; cattle). Rend L. nearby.

Nasonville, village, in Burrillville, Providence co., N central R.I., ¼ mi/⅖ km W of Slatersville Reservoir. Little Flower Home here.

Nass River (NAS), 236 mi/380 km long, Canada; rises in the Coast Mts., W B.C.; flows SW to Portland Inlet of the Pacific Ocean. Navigable for 25 mi/40 km. Valuable salmon fisheries.

Nassau 1 (NA-saw), county (□ 725 sq mi/1,878 sq km; 1990 pop. 43,941), extreme NE Fla., on Atlantic Ocean (E) and Ga. (N) state line (formed here by St. Marys R.); ⊙ Fernandina Beach; 30°36′N 81°46′W. Lowland area, with Amelia barrier isl. (E). Agr. (poultry; dairy prods.; corn), forestry (naval stores, lumber; paper), and fishing. Formed 1824. **2** county (□ 285 sq mi/738 sq km; 1990 pop. 1,287,348), SE N.Y., on W L.I., bet. L.I. Sound (N) and the Atlantic Ocean (S) and immediately E of N.Y. city (Queens borough); ⊙ Mineola; 40°43′N 73°35′W. Bordered E by Suffolk co. Part of N.Y. city metropolitan area; chiefly residential, with many suburban shopping centers including Roosevelt Field shopping complex NW of Levittown. Deeply indented N shore has country-estate communities; yachting, fishing. The S shore has resorts; its bays, with many marshy isls., are sheltered from the Atlantic by fine barrier beaches (swimming, surf fishing) which are linked to L.I. by causeways; Jones Beach State Park is here. Co. is traversed by several highways and is served by several lines of L.I. RR. Includes several state parks (notably Bethpage, Jones Beach), several racetracks (notably Belmont Park, in W). Pollution, dredging, and overfishing have combined to severely limit the once-major shellfish industry. Urbanization and residential tracts and industry have likewise excluded commercial agr., with the exception of nurseries and greenhouse horticultural crops, sod farms, and some aminal husbandry. Diversified mfg. Named for William of Nassau, Prince of Orange. First co. to adopt charter form of govt. Originally the E part of Queens co.; created Jan. 1, 1899, after the W part of Queens co. became part of N.Y. city.

Nassau, city (1990 pop. 172,196), ⊙ the BAHAMAS, port on New Providence isl.; 25°05′N 77°21′W. Has a large and beautiful harbor; the commercial and social center of the country. Its warm, healthful climate and colorful atmosphere have made it a popular resort. Casino gambling at the 2 main resort areas in nearby Paradise Isl. and Cable Beach. Nassau Internatl. Airport is located here. Formerly called Charles Towne, the isl. was renamed Nassau in 1695. In the 18th cent. it was a rendezvous for pirates, among them Blackbeard. Three forts, Nassau (1697), Charlotte (1787–1794), and Fincastle (1793), were built to ward off the numerous Span. invasions. Amer. revolutionists in 1776 captured and held it a short time.

Nassau 1 (NA-saw), village (1990 pop. 83), Lac qui Parle co., SW Minn., on S.Dak. state line, 13 mi/21 km WNW of Madison, near Yellow Bank R.; 45°04′N 96°26′W. Grain; mfg. (feeds, fertilizers). **2** village (1990 pop. 1,254), Rensselaer co., E N.Y., 15 mi/24 km SSE of Troy; 42°30′N 73°36′W. Mfg. (textiles, apparel, food and beverages, plastic and wood household furniture). Co. fairgrounds are here.

Nassau Bay, town (1990 pop. 4,320), Harris co., SE Texas, residential suburb 22 mi/35 km SE of downtown Houston, in area referred to as Clear Lake City, on Clear Creek (S) and Clear L. (E); 29°33′N 95°05′W. NASA Johnson Space Center immediately N.

Nassau, Fort:, N.Y. and N.J.: see FORT NASSAU.

Nassau River, c.40 mi/64 km long, extreme NE Fla.; rises in central Nassau co.; meanders E to Nassau Sound, a small inlet of the Atlantic Ocean bet. Amelia (N) and Talbot (S) isls.; lower course an estuary.

Nassawadox, town, Northampton co., E Va., 17 mi/27 km NNE of Cape Charles town, in Eastern Shore area, bet. Atlantic Ocean (E) and Chesapeake Bay (W);

37°28′N 75°51′W. Mfg. (seafood processing); agr. (vegetables, grain; poultry, livestock); fish, oysters, crabs.

Nasworthy, Lake, Texas: see CONCHO RIVER.

Natal (nuh-TAL), village, SE B.C., W Canada, near Alta. border, in Rocky Mts., on Elk R., and 19 mi/31 km NE of Fernie; 49°44′N 114°50′W. Elev. 3,782 ft/1,153 m. Open-pit coal mining; dairying; cattle; timber.

Natalbany (nuh-TAHL-buh-nee), uninc. town (1990 pop. 1,289), Tangipahoa parish, 4 mi/6.4 km NW of Hammond; 30°32′N 90°29′W. In agr. (cattle) and timber area. On Danville's map of 1732.

Natalbany River (nuh-TAHL-buh-nee), c.45 mi/72 km long, SE La.; rises in E St. Helena parish near Miss. state line; flows S to L. Maurepas, receives Tickfaw R. 2 mi/3 km above its mouth; 30°21′N, 90°29′W. Catfish, crawfish.

Natalia, town (1990 pop. 1,216), Medina co., SW Texas, 25 mi/40 km SW of San Antonio; 29°11′N 98°51′W. In irrigated farm area (vegetables, peanuts; grain; cotton); mfg. (textiles).

Natashkwan (nat-ash-KWAHN), river, 241 mi/388 km long, E Canada; rises in S Lab.; flows S across E Que. to the Gulf of St. Lawrence; 50°06′N 61°49′W. Noted for trout and salmon fishing. Iron-bearing sands found along its banks are mined. Also spelled Natashquan.

Natazhat, Mount (13,435 ft/4,095 m), S Alaska, in St. Elias Mts., 150 mi/241 km NNW of Yakutat; 61°31′N 141°09′W.

Natchaug River (NAT-chahg), c.25 mi/40 km long, NE Conn.; rises near Mass. state line; flows SW, joining Willimantic R. to form Shetucket R. at Willimantic. Mansfield Hollow Dam (for flood control) is just above Willimantic.

Natchez (NA-chez), city (1990 pop. 19,460), ⊙ Adams co., SW Miss., 85 mi/137 km SW of Jackson, on the Mississippi R. (bridged), opposite Vidalia (La.); 31°33′N 91°23′W. RR terminus. It is the trade, shipping, and processing center for a cotton, livestock, and timber area. Agr. (soybeans, corn, cotton); timber; mfg. (printing and publishing, steel fabrication, pulpwood and lumber processing; transportation equip., machinery; bldg. materials). One of the oldest towns on the Mississippi R., Natchez was founded in 1716 when Fort Rosalie was established; in 1729 the Native Amer. Natchez attacked and killed the garrison members. The area passed to England (1763), to Spain (1779), and to the U.S. (1798). Capital of the Mississippi Territory, 1798–1802. The city became a great river port and the cultural center of the planter aristocracy before the Civil War. Served as state capital 1817–1821. In the Civil War it was taken by Federal forces in 1863. The city has preserved its antebellum charm, and of over 500 historic homes, about 20 are available for touring and are visited during the annual festival period in March and April. Natchez Natl. Historical Park; St. Catherine Creek Natl. Wildlife Refuge to SW; Homochitto Natl. Forest to SE; SW terminus of Natchez Trace Parkway; Natchez Natl. Cemetery to N; Natchez Mus. of Afr.-Amer. History and Culture; Mostly Afr. Market, with arts and crafts; Grand Village of the Natchez (1682–1729); Emerald Mound (c.1300 A.D.) and Natchez State Park to NE; Old South Winery. Settled 1716, inc. 1803.

Natchez (NA-chez), village (1990 pop. 434), Natchitoches parish, NW central La., 8 mi/13 km SSE of Natchitoches; 31°40′N 93°03′W. Kisatchie Natl. Forest and Red Dirt Natl. Wildlife Refuge to S. Timber. In agr. area. Catfish, crawfish.

Natchez National Historical Park, Adams co., SW Miss. One of the best preserved concentrations of antebellum bldgs. in the U.S. Interprets history of Natchez area. Includes Melrose Mansion and WIlliam Johnson House. Covers 80 acres/32 ha. Authorized 1988.

Natchez Trace, historic road, in Tenn., Ala., Miss., from Nashville (Tenn.) to Natchez (Miss.), of great commercial and military importance from the 1780s to the 1830s. Grew from a series of Native Amer. trails (following trails originally traced by migrating buffalos up to 8,000 years ago) later used in the 18th cent. by Fr., Eng., and Span. traders, trappers, and missionaries.

Traveled originally mainly N from Natchez to Nashville; goods were later floated S to New Orleans by flatboat on Cumberland, Ohio, and Mississippi rivers, and boatmen then used the Trace to trek back N. Its general use was replaced with development of steamboats, which could ply the rivers in both directions. Its heyday was in the late 1700s and early 1800s. It was made a post road in 1800 and was improved by the army. Andrew Jackson marched over the Trace to New Orleans in the War of 1812. With the coming of steamboat transportation in the 1830s, however, it passed into decline. The Natchez Trace Parkway and the Natchez Trace Natl. Scenic Trail memorialize and generally follow the old Natchez Trace. Meriwether Lewis and Ackia Battleground natl. monuments were disestablished and inc. 1961 into Natchez Trace Parkway.

Natchez Trace National Scenic Trail (NACH-ez) 445 mi/716 km long, Ala. and Tenn. Trail extends from Nashville (Tenn.), via Tupelo and Jackson, to Natchez (all in Miss.). Parallels Natchez Trace Parkway, unit (□ 17 sq mi/44 sq km), of Natl. Park System. Trail is undeveloped. Authorized 1983.

Natchez Trace Parkway, scenic 2-lane drive in central Tenn., follows the route of the old Natchez Trace, trade route bet. Nashville (Tenn.) and Natchez (Miss.). Administered by the Natl. Park Service, the route passes numerous Native Amer. mounds, historical sites, state parks, and campgrounds. From Nashville it goes SSW, passes W of Columbia (Tenn.), and Florence (Ala.), and into Miss., past Tupelo, Kosciusko, and Jackson, to Natchez on Mississippi R. Total length is 445 mi/716 km, of which 400 mi/644 km are completed. Construction began in 1937 as a Depression-era relief project, yet incomplete segments still remain near Natchez and Jackson. The parkway has been designed for leisurely recreational driving rather than high speeds.

Natchitoches (NA-ki-tish), parish (□ 1,297 sq mi/3,359 sq km; 1990 pop. 36,689), NW central La.; ⊙ Natchitoches; 31°46′N, 93°06′W. Bounded on E by Saline and Red rivers, on N in part by Black L. Bayou and Bayou Pierre. Intersected by Red R. and Cane River L.; includes Saline and Black lakes (N), both part of NW La. State Wildlife Area. Agr. (cotton, corn, sorghum, hay, rice, soybeans; cattle, poultry), catfish, crawfish, alligators; timber. Some mfg., including processing of timber, paper prods., and farm prods. Oil and natural gas deposits. Formed 1807. The parish courthouse has been restored. Red Dirt Natl. Wildlife Refuge in S, part of Peason Ridge State Wildlife Area in far S, Rebel and Los Adaes State Commemorative Areas in W, Fort St. Jean Baptiste State Commemorative Area at center, part of Kisatchie Natl. Forest in far NE and S, including Kisatchie Hills Wilderness in S.

Natchitoches (NA-ki-tish), city (1990 pop. 16,609), ⊙ Natchitoches parish, NW La., 42 mi/68 km NW of Alexandria; 31°46′N 93°06′W. Industry centered on the production, processing, and shipping of farm prods., including cotton, lumber, poultry, and cattle; also catfish, crawfish, alligators. Mfg. (concrete prods., poultry prods., lumber, cottonseed oil), printing and publishing. The 1st permanent settlement in the Louisiana Purchase Territory, Natchitoches was founded c.1714 as a Fr. military and trading post. It served as the dividing line bet. Fr. and Span. territory. The city was an important port on the Red R. until the river changed its course in the early 1800s, leaving the 33-mi/53-km meandering riverbed known as Cane R. L. Occupied by the Union army during the Civil War. The lasting old homes and plantations attract tourists. Northwestern State Univ. of La. is here. Sibley L. reservoir to W, Natl. Fish Hatchery to S, Fort St. Jean Baptiste State Commemorative Area to S (reproduction of 1730s Fr. fort). Inc. 1819.

Nathorst, Cape, S extremity of Ellef Ringnes Isl., N Franklin dist., N.W.T., N Canada; 77°44′N 100°05′W.

Natick (NAI-dik), town (1990 pop. 30,510), Middlesex co., E Mass., residential and industrial suburb of Boston, on L. Cochituate; 42°17′N 71°21′W. Founded as a village by John Eliot in 1651, inc. 1781. Major retailing center. Mfg. includes electronic components, computer

software, medical equip., clocks, machine parts; food processing. Site of U.S. army research facility. Includes village of South Natick (includes historic dist. and park on Charles R.). Site of Cochituate State Park and Broadmoor Wildlife Sanctuary.

National City, city (□ 9 sq mi/23.3 sq km; 1990 pop. 54,249), San Diego co., S Calif., suburb 6 mi/9.7 km SE of downtown San Diego, on E side of San Diego Bay; 32°40′N 117°06′W. Mfg. (fabrication of structural metal, printing and publishing, shipbuilding, recycling machinery; plastics prods., transportation equip., electrical and electronic prods., signs, furniture, clothing). Primarily residential, marked by a steady growth in pop. bet. 1970 and 1990. Serves as the hq. of the Pacific Reserve Fleet. Sweetwater R. to S. Inc. 1887.

National City 1 or **National Stockyards**, village (1990 pop. 57), St. Clair co., SW Ill., adjoining East St. Louis (N), industrial suburb of St. Louis, near Mississippi R.; 38°38′N 90°09′W. Once large stockyards; periodic fires have destroyed most of facilities. Mfg. (scrap metal, meat waste prods.). Gateway Internatl. Raceway nearby. **2** village, Iosco co., NE Mich., 11 mi/18 km WSW of Tawas City; 44°14′N 83°43′W. Gypsum quarrying and processing.

National Forest System, federally owned reserves (□ c.343,000 sq mi/888,600 sq km), administered by the Forest Service of the U.S. Dept. of Agr. The system is made up of 154 natl. forests and 19 natl. grasslands in 41 states and P.R. The majority of reserves are found in the Western states, with Alaska, Idaho, and Calif. having the most extensive holdings. In the East, large natl. forests are in the Green, White, Allegheny, and Blue Ridge mts. The natl. grasslands are found on the Great Plains. By law the reserves must be used for timber production, watershed land, wildlife preservation, livestock grazing, mining, and recreation. In 1891, Congress authorized the president to set aside forest reserves; Yellowstone Park Timber Reserve (now Shoshone Natl. Forest) in Wyo. was the 1st (1891) to be established. The forest reserves were administered by the General Land Office of the Dept. of the Interior until 1905, when they were transferred to the Forest Service by President Teddy Roosevelt. They were designated natl. forests in 1907.

National Mall, landscaped park, Washington, D.C., part of the city's L'Enfant Plan. Extends from the U.S. Capitol (E) to the Washington Monument (W), bet. Constitution and Independence aves. The mall is the location of most Smithsonian Inst. bldgs. Authorized 1933.

National Park, residential borough (1990 pop. 3,413), Gloucester co., SW N.J., on Delaware R., and 7 mi/11.3 km SW of Camden; 39°52′N 75°11′W. Monument here commemorates Revolutionary battle of Red Bank (1777), named for former locality here. Inc. 1902.

National Road, U.S. highway, built in the early 19th cent. At the time of its construction, the Natl. Road was the most ambitious road-building project ever undertaken in the U.S. It finally extended from Cumberland (Md.) to St. Louis and was the great highway of Western migration. Agitation for a road to the West began c.1800. Congress approved the route and appointed a committee to plan details in 1806. Contracts were given in 1811, but the War of 1812 intervened, and construction did not begin until 1815. The 1st sect. (called the Cumberland Road) was built of crushed stone. Opened in 1818, it ran from Cumberland to Wheeling (W.Va.), following in part the Native Amer. trail known as Nemacolin's Path. Largely through the efforts of Henry Clay it was continued (1825–1833) W through Ohio, using part of the road built by Ebenezer Zane. By this time the older part of the road was badly in need of repair. Control of the road was therefore turned over to the states through which it passed, where tolls for maintenance were collected. It was carried on to Vandalia (Ill.), and finally to St. Louis. The old route became part of U.S. Highway 40. At points on the road copies of a statue called the *Madonna of the Trail* have been erected to honor the pioneer women who went West over the Natl. Road.

National Stockyards, Ill.: see NATIONAL CITY.

Natividad (nah-tee-vee-DAHD), town (1990 pop. 1,373), in W central Oaxaca, Mexico, 31 mi/50 km NE of Oaxaca de Juárez. Elev. 6,234 ft/1,900 m.

Natividad Island (nah-tee-vee-DAHD), islet (□ 3.3 sq mi/8.5 sq km) off Pacific coast of Baja California Sur, NW Mexico, at SW edge of Sebastián Vizcaíno Bay; 3.75 mi/6.03 km long, ½ mi/⅘ km–1.5 mi/2.4 km wide; 27°50′N 115°11′W. Elev. 492 ft/150 m. Barren; rocky.

Natívitas, Mexico: see SANTA MARÍA NATÍVITAS.

Natoma (nuh-TO-muh), village (1990 pop. 392), Osborne co., N central Kansas, on small affluent of Saline R., and 23 mi/37 km NNW of Russell; 39°11′N 99°01′W. Grain; livestock.

Natrona (nuh-TRO-nuh), county (□ 5,375 sq mi/13,921 sq km; 1990 pop. 61,226), central Wyo.; ⊙ Casper; 42°58′N 106°47′W. Livestock and mining region; watered by North Platte and Sweetwater rivers, and headstreams of Powder R., Alcova Reservoir and part of Pathfinder Reservoir in S. Agr. (hay, alfalfa; cattle, sheep); oil, coal. N end of Laramie Mts. in SE corner; Hogaden Ski Area in SE. S end of Bighorn Mts. in NW corner. Edness Kimball Wilkins State Park in E. Part of Pathfinder Natl. Wildlife Refuge in S. Formed 1888.

Natrona (nah-TRO-nah), village, Harrison township, Allegheny co., W central Pa., suburb 19 mi/31 km NE of downtown Pittsburgh, on Allegheny R.; 40°36′N 79°43′W. Mfg. (fabricated metal prods., chemicals). Saltworks founded here 1853.

Natrona Heights (nah-TRO-nah), uninc. city (1990 pop. 11,700), Allegheny co., W central Pa., residential suburb 19 mi/31 km NE of Pittsburgh; 40°37′N 79°43′W. Mfg. includes commercial printing; tool and die, plastic prods., bldg. materials. Dairying; livestock, poultry; grain to N.

Natural Bridge 1 village (1990 pop. 600), Jefferson co., N N.Y., 8 mi/12.9 km NE of Carthage; 44°04′N 75°30′W. Indian R. has cut through limestone here to form a bridge and caverns that are a popular tourist attraction. **2** uninc. village, Rockbridge co., NW Va., in Shenandoah Valley, 12 mi/19 km SSW of Lexington. Mfg. (industrial prototypes); agr. (dairying; livestock; grain, apples). Nearby, over gorge of Cedar Creek, is famous Natural Bridge, a limestone arch 215 ft/66 m high with a span of 90 ft/27 m, once owned by Thomas Jefferson, who built a visitors' cabin and kept a guest book. A public highway now crosses the bridge. Founded 1774.

Natural Bridge State Resort Park (□ 3 sq mi/7.8 sq km), Powell and Wolfe cos., E central Ky., 10 mi/16 km ESE of Stanton, just SE of Slade, surrounded by Daniel Boone Natl. Forest. Wooded, hilly area, with lodge and recreational facilities, nature preserve; chief attraction is Ky. Natural Bridge, a span of Paleozoic limestone; largest natural bridge in Ky.; arch has c.90-ft/27-m clearance, is c.75 ft/23 m wide. The cliffs and overhangs are home to Virginia big-eared Bat.

Natural Bridges National Monument (□ 12 sq mi/31 sq km), central San Juan co., SE Utah. Located in an area of colored cliffs and box canyons, the monument contains 3 huge natural sandstone bridges: Owachomo (also called Rock Mound), 106 ft/32 m high with a span of 180 ft/55 m; Kachina, 210 ft/64 m high with a span of 206 ft/63 m; and Sipapu, 220 ft/67 m high with a span of 268 ft/82 m. Native Amer. Anasazi ruins under 1 bridge. Drained by White Canyon. Est. 1908.

Natural Tunnel, Scott co., SW Va., natural passageway on SE side of Powell Mt., 10 mi/16 km WNW of Gate City, in Natural Tunnel State Park (603 acres/244 ha); 75 ft/23 m–100 ft/30 m high, c.900 ft/274 m long. Small stream and RR pass through it.

Naturita, village (1990 pop. 434), Montrose co., SW Colo., at mouth of Naturita Creek, on San Miguel R., and 40 mi/64 km SW of Montrose; 38°13′N 108°34′W. Elev. 5,431 ft/1,655 m. Uranium and vanadium mined here; also coal. Cattle, sheep; wheat, beans, corn. Uncompahgre Natl. Forest to NE.

Naubinway (NAW-bin-wai), village, Mackinac co., SE Upper Peninsula, N Mich., 39 mi/63 km NW of St. Ignace, on L. Michigan; 46°05′N 85°26′W. Resort.

Naucalpan de Juárez (nah-oo-KAHL-pahn dai HWAH-res), city (1990 pop. 772,483) and township, ⊙ Naucalpan municipio, Mexico state, S central Mexico; 19°29′N 99°14′W. It is an industrial extension of Mexico city.

Naugatuck, industrial borough (1990 pop. 30,625), New Haven co., SW Conn., on both sides of the Naugatuck R.; 41°29′N 73°02′W. In 1843, Charles Goodyear established a rubber plant here, which became famous for its Goodyear tires. Other mfg. includes machinery, chemicals, and electrical and metal (esp. brass, and copper) prods., candy, and medical supplies. Settled 1704, inc. 1844.

Naugatuck (NAW-guh-tuhk), uninc. village, Mingo co., SW W.Va., 10 mi/16 km NNW of Williamson, on Tug Fork R. Mfg. (coal processing). Bituminous-coal mining. Laurel Creek Wildlife Management Area.

Naugatuck, river, 65 mi/105 km long, Conn.; rises in NW Conn.; flows S, past Waterbury, to the Housatonic R. at Derby. It furnishes water power for the remaining industrial plants along its shores. Thomaston Dam (completed 1960), built for flood control, forms 1 reservoir on the river. Has a number of dams.

Nauhcampatépetl, Mexico: see COFRE DE REROTE NATIONAL PARK.

Naupan (nah-OO-pahn), town (1990 pop. 1,203), Puebla, central Mexico, in Sierra Madre Oriental, 5 mi/8 km NW of Huauchinango; 20°14′N 98°07′W. No all-weather roads. Corn, coffee, sugar.

Nauset Harbor (NAW-set), SE Mass., sheltered inlet of the Atlantic Ocean, on E coast of Cape Cod, bet. Eastham and Orleans. Lighthouse and coast guard station. Part of Cape Cod Natl. Seashore.

Naushon Island, Mass.: see ELIZABETH ISLANDS.

Nautla (nah-OO-tlah), town (1990 pop. 2,616), Veracruz, E Mexico, at mouth of small Nautla R., in Gulf lowland, 40 mi/64 km SE of Papantla de Olarte, on Mexico Highway 180; 20°15′N 96°45′W. Minor port; tobacco growing.

Nauvoo (nah-VOO), city (1990 pop. 1,108), Hancock co., W Ill., on heights overlooking the Mississippi R., 9 mi/14.5 km N of Keokuk (Iowa); 40°32′N 91°22′W. In agr. area (fruit, corn, soybeans); mfg. (wine, cheese). Tourism is major industry. Settled as Commerce shortly after 1830; occupied and renamed by Mormons under Joseph Smith in 1839. Pop. reached c.20,000 under the Mormons and was briefly the largest Ill. city; after Smith and his brother were killed (1844) by a mob in nearby Carthage, the group left Ill. for Utah (1846). The Icarians, a colony of Fr. communists under Étienne Cabet, occupied the city, 1849–1856. Smith's house, part of an old hotel, and other old bldgs. are still standing. Church interests protect historic town site on flats below bluff and its square street pattern. Town damaged in 1993 floods. Nauvoo State Park nearby. Inc. 1841.

Nauvoo (NAW-voo), town (1990 pop. 240), Walker co., NW Ala., 16 mi/26 km NW of Jasper. Lumber.

Nauzontla (nah-oo-SON-tlah), town (1990 pop. 1,617), Puebla, central Mexico, 18 mi/29 km NW of Teziutlán; 19°58′N 97°35′W. Corn, fruit, vegetables, coffee.

Nava (nah-wah), town (1990 pop. 13,192), Coahuila, N Mexico, on RR, and 25 mi/40 km SW of Piedras Negras, on Mexico Highway 57; 28°28′N 100°45′E. Wheat, corn; cattle; thistle fibers, candelilla wax.

Navajo, county (□ 9,960 sq mi/25,796 sq km; 1990 pop. 77,658), E Ariz., on Utah (N) state line; ⊙ Holbrook; 35°23′N 110°19′W. Nation's 11th-largest co. Agr. (sheep, cattle, hogs; alfalfa, hay, corn); Native Amer. handicraft; tourist trade. Mt. area crossed in S by Little Colorado R. Black Mesa in far N, parts of Painted Desert in N center; part of Petrified Forest Natl. Park on E border, and parts of Navajo and Hopi Indian reservations cover N ½ of co.; parts of Mogollon Rim escarpment crosses co. in S, forms border of Apache-Sitgreaves Natl. Forest (N) and Fort Apache Indian Reservation (S); bounded by Black R. in extreme SE. Navajo Natl. Monument is in N, near Utah state line. Homolovi Ruins State Park in W center; Monument Valley, with dramatic buttes, scene in many movie westerns, in NE. Formed 1895.

Navajo (NAH-vuh-ho), uninc. town (1990 pop. 1,985), McKinley co., NW N.Mex., 26 mi/42 km NNW of Gallup, at Ariz. state line, in Navajo Indian Reservation; 35°53′N 109°01′W. Cattle, sheep. Timber. Mfg. (lumber). Reservation has 4 coal mines and 2 electric power plants. In the late 1970s to the mid-1980s some coal was converted to gas, but process then discontinued. Red and Asaayi lakes to NE. Canyon de Chelly Natl. Monument (Ariz.) to NW. Chuska Peak (8,795 ft/2,681 m), in Chuska Mts., to E.

Navajo Lake (NAH-vuh-ho), NW Kane co., SW Utah, in Markagunt Plateau and Dixie Natl. Forest, 20 mi/32 km SE of Cedar City; 3 mi/4.8 km long, ½ mi/⅘ km wide. Elev. 9,035 ft/2,754 m. Fishing, camping. Sometimes called Duck L. Cedar Breaks Natl. Monument 5 mi/8 km NW.

Navajo Lake (NAH-vuh-ho), reservoir, NW N.Mex. and SW Colo., on San Juan R., 22 mi/35 km ENE of Bloomfield (N.Mex.); c.25 mi/40 km long; 36°48′N 107°36′W. Max, capacity 1,986,000 acre-ft. Los Pinos R. forms 8-mi/12.9-km N arm at dam. Receives Piedra R. in Colo. Formed by Navajo Dam (402 ft/123 m high, 3,648 ft/1,112 m long), a major unit of the Colorado R. storage project built (1958–1963) by the U.S. Bureau of Reclamation for irrigation and flood control. Navajo L. State Park (N.Mex.) and Navajo Reservoir State Recreation Area (Colo.) are here.

Navajo Mountain (NAH-vuh-ho) (10,388 ft/3,166 m), Laccolith formation, S Utah, near Ariz. state line 11 mi/18 km S of junction of San Juan and Colorado rivers, 5 mi/8 km SE of Rainbow Bridge Natl. Monument, 38 mi/61 km ENE of Page (Ariz.). On Navajo Indian Reservation.

Navajo National Monument, Navajo and Coconino cos., NE Ariz. Ruins of large elaborate cliff dwellings. Betatakin Ruin Unit and hq. 16 mi/26 km WSW of Kayenta; Keet Seel Ruin Unit 14 mi/23 km WNW of Kayenta, both units in Navajo co. Additional acreage in Coconino co. Covers 360 acres/146 ha. Proclaimed 1909.

Navarre (nuh-VAHR), town, Santa Rosa co., NW Fla., 23 mi/37 km E of Pensacola. Mfg. includes consumer goods, neon signs, bldg. materials.

Navarre, village (1990 pop. 1,635), Stark co., E central Ohio, 9 mi/14 km SW of Canton, and on Tuscarawas R. Agr. trade center; makes foods, fabricated metal prods. Fort Laurens State Park is nearby.

Navarro (NAH-vahr-o), county (□ 1,086 sq mi/2,813 sq km; 1990 pop. 39,926), E central Texas; ⊙ Corsicana; 32°02′N 96°28′W. Mainly rich blackland prairies; bounded NE by Trinity R; drained by Richland, Chambers and Waxahachie creeks. Diversified agr. (cotton, corn, grains, vegetables; sorghum, wheat; herbs); livestock (beef and dairy cattle, hogs, horses, emus). Oil, natural gas wells. Mfg., processing of farm prods. and petroleum at Corsicana. Navarro Mills L. reservoir in W (Richland Creek); large part of Richland Chambers Reservoir in S. Formed 1846.

Navarro Mills Lake (NAH-vahr-o), reservoir, Navarro and Hill cos., E central Texas, on Richland Creek, 18 mi/29 km SW of Corsicana; c.12 mi/19 km long; 31°57′N 96°42′W. Max. capacity 335,800 acre-ft. Formed by Navarro Mills Dam (77 ft/23 m high), built (1963) by the Army Corps of Engineers for water supply and flood control.

Navarro River, c.40 mi/64 km long, NW Calif.; rises in SE Mendocino co.; flows NW, through Hendy Woods State Park, to the Pacific Ocean 18 mi/29 km S of Fort Bragg.

Navasota, town (1990 pop. 6,296), Grimes co., E central Texas, on Navasota R. (near its confluence with the Brazos R.), and c.60 mi/97 km NW of Houston; 30°23′N 96°05′W. Cattle; timber; agribusiness (fruit); dairying; mfg. (machinery, fabricated metal prods., honey). Statue of La Salle commemorates tradition that he was killed nearby. Active in Texas Revolution; laid out 1858.

Navasota River, c.130 mi/209 km long, E central Texas; rises in Limestone co.; flows SE, through L. Mexia and

L. Limestone reservoirs then S to the Brazos R. 5 mi/8 km SW of Navasota.

Navassa (nah-VAH-suh), village (1990 pop. 445), Brunswick co., SE N.C., 5 mi/8 km NW of Wilmington, on Cape Fear R. (RR bridge); 34°15′N 78°00′W. RR junction. Mfg. (wood prods.).

Navassa Island (nuh-VA-suh), Fr. *La Navase*, U.S.-owned Caribbean islet (□ c.1 sq mi/2.6 sq km), bet. Haiti and Jamaica, 35 mi/56 km W of Cape Irois (Haiti); 18°25′N 75°02′W. Formerly yielded guano. Lighthouse.

Navesink (NA-vuh-sink), village, Monmouth co., E N.J., on Navesink R., and 16 mi/26 km NE of Freehold. Largely residential.

Navesink Highlands (NA-vuh-sink), Monmouth co., E N.J., coastal ridge (c.276 ft/84 m) bet. Sandy Hook Bay (N) and Navesink R. estuary (S). One of highest points on U.S. Atlantic coast; site of the Twin Towers, one of most powerful U.S. lighthouses (40°24′N 73°59′W). Often called Atlantic Highlands, Highlands of Navesink.

Navesink River (NA-vuh-sink), estuary, c.8 mi/12.9 km. long, Monmouth co., E N.J.; extending ENE from Red Bank (head of navigation) to junction with Shrewsbury R. estuary at entrance to passage to Sandy Hook Bay near Highlands. Navesink Highlands are N, on mainland.

Navidad River, c.100 mi/161 km long, S Texas; rises in headstreams in Fayette co.; flows generally SSE and parallel to Lavaca R., joining it 11 mi/18 km above its mouth of Lavaca Bay. Forms L. Texana 13 mi/21 km above mouth.

Navina (na-VEI-nuh), village, Logan co., central Okla., 9 mi/14.5 km WSW of Guthrie. In agr. area.

Navojoa (nah-VO-ho-ah), city (1990 pop. 82,618) and township, Sonora, NW Mexico, on lower Mayo R., in coastal plain, on Gulf of California, and 100 mi/161 km SE of Guaymas; 27°04′N 109°28′E. RR junction; agr. center (wheat, corn, chickpeas, fruit; cattle); flour milling; native handicrafts, textiles.

Navolato (nah-vo-LAH-to), city (1990 pop. 938) and township, Sinaloa, NW Mexico, on Culiacán R., and 20 mi/32 km WSW of Culiacán Rosales, on RR; 24°45′N 107°41′W. Agr. center (sugarcane, chickpeas, corn, vegetables, fruit); lumbering.

Navy Board Inlet, N Baffin Isl., SE Franklin dist., N.W.T., N Canada, arm of Lancaster Sound, bet. Borden Peninsula of Baffin Isl. (W) and Bylot Isl. (E); 70 mi/113 km long, 6 mi/10 km–18 mi/29 km wide; 73°N 80°50′W.

Navy Island, in the Niagara R., just above Niagara Falls, S Ont., central Canada. Famous as the scene of the last stand made by William Lyon Mackenzie and some of his fellow rebels in the Upper Canada Rebellion of 1837.

Navy Yard City, uninc. town (1990 pop. 2,905), Kitsap co., W Wash., 3 mi/4.8 km SW of Bremerton, on Sinclair Inlet arm of Puget Sound; 47°33′N 122°40′W.

Nawiliwili Harbor (NAH-WEE-lee-WEE-lee), SE Kauai, Kauai co., Hawaii, principal deep water port of isl., 1 mi/1.6 km SE of Lihue; ½ mi/⅘ km wide. Inner extension of Nawiliwili Bay, separated by jetty; receives Huleia Stream from NW. Port of Nawiliwili, on N side, harbors cruise ships, cargo ships.

Nayarit, state (□ 10,664 sq mi/27,620 sq km; 1990 pop. 824,643), W Mexico, on the Pacific Ocean; ⊙ TEPIC 20°37′N 23°00′N. Mostly wild and rugged, Nayarit is broken by W spurs of the Sierra Madre Occidental. In the NE are broad, tropical plains watered by the Santiago R., a continuation of the Lerma R. Nayarit has 2 large volcanoes, Ceboruco (7,480 ft/2,280 m) and Sangangüey (7,546 ft/2,300 m). The volcanic soil, heavy rains, and elev. variations permit cultivation of a variety of prods. of tropical and temperate agr. — grain, sugarcane, cotton, coffee, and tobacco. Cattle raising is also important. Forest wealth, little exploited in the past, is rapidly being developed. Mining is a significant part of the state's economy; gold has been mined in Amatlán de Cañas municipio and in Santa Maria del Oro muncipio. Silver has been extracted in Compostela and La Yesca (moderate); large deposits of lead, copper, silver, and gold in the state. The coastal swamps are noted bird refuges. The Nayarit region was known to the Spanish early in the 16th cent., and one of its towns, Compostela (near Tepic), was the 1st capital of Nueva Galicia. Spain did not finally conquer the area until the early 17th cent. Shortly afterward, Nayarit became a dependency of Guadalajara and, upon Mex. independence, part of Jalisco. Continued turbulence led to Nayarit's separation as a territory in 1884; it became a state in 1917. The name Nayarit is given to pre-Columbian clay figurines that are found in the vicinity.

Naylor, city (1990 pop. 642), Ripley co., S Mo., 13 mi/21 km E of Doniphan; 36°34′N 90°36′W. Fruit; timber; cattle; mfg. (apparel).

Naylor, village (1990 pop. 111), Lowndes co., S Ga., 13 mi/21 km ENE of Valdosta, near Alapaha R.; 30°55′N 83°05′W. Mfg. of furniture.

Nazan, Alaska: see ATKA.

Nazareno Etla (nah-zah-RAI-no ET-lah), town (1990 pop. 3,207), in central Oaxaca, Mexico, 7 mi/12 km NW of Oaxaca de Juárez, off Mexico Highway 190; 17°10′N 96°49′W. Elev. 5,194 ft/1,583 m. Agr. irrigated by the Atoyac R.

Nazareth 1 (NAZ-uh-reth), uninc. village (1990 pop. 400), Nelson co., Ky., 3 mi/4.8 km N of Bardstown. Tobacco, grain; livestock; dairying. **2** village (1990 pop. 293), Castro co., NW Texas, 50 mi/80 km SSW of Amarillo; 34°32′N 102°05′W. Agr. area (cattle, sheep; wheat, cotton).

Nazareth (NA-zah-reth), borough (1990 pop. 5,713), Northampton co., E Pa., 6 mi/9.7 km NW of Easton, on Shoeneck Creek; 40°44′N 75°18′W. Mfg. (beef processing, limestone processing; bldg. materials, textiles, consumer goods, paper prods., plastic prods.). Agr. (apples, soybeans, grain; livestock; dairying). Settled c.1740, inc. 1863.

Nazas (NAH-sahs), city (1990 pop. 3,325) and township, Durango, N Mexico, on Nazas R., and 55 mi/89 km SW of Torreón; 25°15′N 104°06′W. Agr. center (corn, wheat, cotton, sugar, vegetables, fruit).

Nazas (NAH-sahs), river, c.180 mi/290 km long, N Mexico; rises in the Sierra Madre Occidental, Durango state; flows generally E to disappear through evaporation near Torreón. During the wet season it usually inundates a vast desert basin and sometimes reaches Laguna de Mayran. With its control dams, it provides water for irrigating the Laguna dist. Also called Sextín R. Dammed for irrigation at Lazaro Cardenas Dam and at Francisco Zarco.

Neah Bay (NEE-uh), uninc. town (1990 pop. 916), Clallam, co., NW Wash., on Neah Bay of Strait of Juan de Fuca, and 60 mi/97 km NW of Port Angeles, in (and hq. of) Makah Indian Reservation (1990 pop. 1,214); 48°22′N 124°37′W. Fishing. Makah Cultural Center; Cape Flattery 4 mi/6.4 km W. N end of Olympic Natl. Park; coastal sect. to S. State's 1st Eur. settlement made here by Spaniards in 1791.

Nealtican, Mexico: see SAN BUENAVENTURA NEALTICAN.

Near Islands, Alaska: see ALEUTIAN ISLANDS.

Nebo (NEE-bo), town (1990 pop. 227), Hopkins co., W Ky., 9 mi/14.5 km WNW of Madisonville; 37°22′N 87°38′W. In coal-mining and agr. (tobacco, grain; livestock) area.

Nebo 1 (NEE-bo), village (1990 pop. 402), Pike co., W Ill., 12 mi/19 km S of Pittsfield; 39°26′N 90°47′W. Grain, fruit; livestock. **2** uninc. village, McDowell co., W central N.C., 5 mi/8 km ENE of Marion, L. James reservoir (Catawba R.) to N. Mfg. (wood prods.). L. James State Park to NE.

Nebo, Mount (NEE-bo), central Utah, on border bet. Utah and Juab cos., 27 mi/43 km S of Provo, in Mt. Nebo Wilderness Area of Uinta Natl. Forest. Elev. 11,877 ft/3,620 m. Mt. Nebo is the southernmost extent of the middle Rocky Mts. in the Wasatch Range.

Nebraska, state (□ 77,358 sq mi/200,357 sq km; 1995 est. pop. 1,637,112), central U.S., in the Great Plains region, admitted as the 37th state of the union in 1867; ⊙ LINCOLN 41°23′N 99°43′W. The state is roughly rectangular, except in the NE and the E where the border is formed by the irregular course of the Missouri R. and in the SW where the state of Colo. cuts out a rectangular corner. Elsewhere Nebr. is bounded W by Wyo., N by S.Dak., E by Iowa and Mo., and S by Kansas. The land rises more or less gradually from 840 ft/256 m in the E to 5,426 ft/1,654 m in the W. The Platte R., too shallow and braided for navigation, is formed in W Nebr. by the junction of the North Platte and the South Platte rivers, and flows across the state from W to E to join the Missouri S of Omaha. The river valleys have long provided routes westward, and today several of the transcontinental RRs, pioneered by the Union Pacific in the mid-1860s, and highways follow the valleys. From the Missouri westward over about ½ the state stretch undulating farm lands, where the fertile silt is underlaid by deep loess soil both E and S of the Sand Hills, which occupy much of the NW interior. Nebr.'s pop. is concentrated there, many being farmers who produce grains for the market or for feeding hogs and dairy cattle. Both along the Platte and along the margins of the Sand Hills, irrigation, mainly from wells, permits intensive farming, commonly with ranching and/or wheat farming, which are dependent on rainfall. Beef, both from farming and ranching, is the chief agr. prod. of the state. The underground water resources are the greatest to be found in the Great Plains. In this region also are Nebr.'s 2 major cities — Omaha, the largest and an important meat- and grain-distribution and -processing center, and Lincoln, state govt. and important insurance center — as well as many of the state's larger towns. To the W and NW the Sand Hills of Nebr. dominate the landscape, their wind-eroded contours now more or less stabilized by grass coverage suitable only for cattle grazing, the low sand hills provide protection from the severe prairie winters. The climate of Nebr. is continental; a low of −40°F/−40°C in the winter is not unusual, and during the short intense summers temperatures may easily reach 110°F/43°C. Rainfall is almost twice as heavy in the E as in the W. In the far W, sandstone bedrock foundations have led to such spectacular formations as Chimney Rock and Scotts Bluff. Mineral deposits of oil (discovered in Cheyenne co. in 1949–1950), sand and gravel, and stone contribute to the state's economy, but agr. remains the dominant occupational pursuit. To promote agr. the Univ. of Nebr. maintains experimental agr. stations throughout the state. A program of soil conservation has been developed to avert a repeat of the 1930s Dust Bowl effect of overgrazing and overplowing of the fragile prairie soils. Forest plantations have been established in parts of the Sand Hills, including Nebr. and Samuel R. McKelvie natl. forests. Nebr.'s chief agr. prods. are cattle, corn, hogs, soybeans, and wheat. Nebr. ranked 2d among the states in cattle production in 1990. Nebr.'s largest industry is food processing, which derives much of its raw materials from the state's farm prods. The state has diversified its industries since World War II, and the mfg. of electrical machinery, primary metals, and transportation equip., is also important. The Native Americans of the plains — notably the Pawnee — were devoted to hunting the bison, which roamed in great number across the prairie, as well as the pronghorn and lesser animals. The Span. explorer Francisco Vásquez de Coronado and his men were the 1st Europeans to visit the region. They probably came through Nebr. in 1541. The French also came and in the 18th cent. engaged in fur trading, but development began only after the area passed from France to the U.S. in the Louisiana Purchase of 1803. The Lewis and Clark expedition (1804) and the explorations of Zebulon M. Pike (1806) increased knowledge of the country, but the activities of the fur traders were more immediately valuable in terms of settlement. Manuel Lisa, a fur trader, probably established the 1st trading post in the Nebr. area in 1813. Bellevue, the 1st permanent settlement in Nebr., developed originally as a trading post. Steamboating on the Missouri R., initiated in 1819, brought much business to the river ports of Omaha and Brownville. The natural highway formed by the Platte valley was used extensively by pioneers going W over the Oregon Trail and also the Calif. and Mormon trails. Nebr. settlers made money supplying the wagon trains with fresh mounts and pack animals as well as food. Nebr. became a territory after passage of the Kansas-Nebr. Act in 1854. The territory, which initially extended from lat. 40°00′N to the Can. border, was firmly Northern and Republican in sympathy during the Civil War. In 1863 the territory was reduced to its present-day size by the creation of the territories of Dakota and Colo. Congress passed an enabling act for statehood in 1864, but the original provision in the state constitution limiting the franchise to whites delayed statehood until 1867. In that year the Union Pacific RR was built across the state, and the land boom, already vigorous, became a rush. Farmers settled on free land obtained under the Homestead Act of 1862, and E Nebr. took on a settled look. The pop. rose from 28,841 in 1860 to 122,993 in 1870. The Pawnee were defeated in 1859, and by 1880 war with the Sioux and other Native Amer. resistance was over. With the coming of the RRs, cow towns, such as Ogallala and Schuyler, were built up as shipping points on overland cattle trails. Buffalo Bill's Wild West Shows were opened in Nebr. in 1882. Farmers had long since been staking out homestead claims across the Sand Hills to the high plains, but ranches also prospered in the state. The ranchers, trying to preserve the open range, ruthlessly opposed the encroachment of the farmers, but the persistent farmers won. Many conservationists believe that much land was plowed under that should have been left with grass cover to prevent erosion in later dust storms. Nature was seldom kind to the people of Nebr. Ranching was esp. hard hit by the ruinous cold of the winter of 1880–1881, and farmers were plagued by insect hordes from 1856 to 1875, by prairie fires, and by the recurrent droughts of the 1890s. Many farmers joined the Granger movement in the lean 1870s and the Farmers' Alliances of the 1880s. In the 1890s many beleaguered farmers, faced with ruin and angry at the monopolistic practices of the RRs and the financiers, formed marketing and stock cooperatives and voiced their discontent by joining the Populist party. The 1st natl. convention of the Populist party was held at Omaha in 1892, and Nebr.'s most famous son, William Jennings Bryan, headed the Populist and Democratic tickets in the presidential election of 1896. Populists held the governorship of the state from 1895 to 1901. Improved conditions in the early 1900s caused Populism to decline in the state, and the return of prosperous days was marked by progressive legislation, the building of highways, and conservation measures. The flush of prosperity, largely caused by the demand for foodstuffs during World War I, was almost feverish. Overexpansion of credits and overconfidence made the depression of the 1920s and 1930s all the more disastrous. Many farmers were left destitute, and many were able to survive only because of the moratorium on farm debts in 1932. They received Federal aid in the desperate years of drought in the 1930s. Better weather and the huge food demands of World War II renewed prosperity here. Since the war, efforts have continued to make the best use of the water supply, notably in such Federal plans as the Missouri R. basin project, a vast dam and water-diversion scheme, but the big increase in irrigation from wells has been far more important for Nebr. Nebr. has attempted to diversify its economic base in order to reduce its dependence on meat processing and agr., industries, which have destabilized the state economy for decades. These efforts have been generally successful in existing cities. Nebr.'s present constitution was adopted in 1875. It was amended in 1982 to ensure that rangeland and farmland could only be sold to individuals and family-farm corporations. The executive branch is headed by a governor elected for a 4-year term. By constitutional amendment in 1934 the legislature was made unicameral, with 49 members elected on a nonpartisan basis for terms of 4 years. The state elects 3 representatives and 2 senators to the U.S. Congress and has 5 electoral votes in presidential elections. Among Nebr.'s noted citizens have been the pioneer and historian Julius Sterling Morton, who originated Arbor Day for tree planting, and author Willa Cather, who depicted pioneer Nebr. in her novels *My Antonia*and *O Pioneers!* Points of interest include Father Flanagan's Boys Town, near Omaha; the Fort Niobrara Natl. Wildlife Refuge, near Valentine; the Oglala Natl. Grassland in NW corner; and the Homestead Natl. Monument, near Beatrice. The pioneers' migration W over the Oregon Trail is commemorated by the Scotts Bluff Natl. Monument and the Chimney Rock Natl. Historic Site. Agate Fossil Beds Natl. Monument in far W protects major Miocene mammal fossil site. The prairie, esp. Sand Hills, abounds in beaver and native and migratory bird species. Hundreds of fresh and alkali lakes in the state attract sportsmen and campers. The state's leading institution of higher education is the Univ. of Nebr., mainly at Lincoln. The Strategic Air Command (SAC) at Offutt Air Force Base is S of Omaha. Nebr. has 93 COS.: ADAMS, ANTELOPE, ARTHUR, BANNER, BLAINE, BOONE, BOX BUTTE, BOYD, BROWN, BUFFALO, BURT, BUTLER, CASS, CEDAR, CHASE, CHERRY, CHEYENNE, CLAY, COLFAX, CUMING, CUSTER, DAKOTA, DAWES, DAWSON, DEUEL, DIXON, DODGE, DOUGLAS, DUNDY, FILLMORE, FRANKLIN, FRONTIER, FURNAS, GAGE, GARDEN, GARFIELD, GOSPER, GRANT, GREELEY, HALL, HAMILTON, HARLAN, HAYES, HITCHCOCK, HOLT, HOOKER, HOWARD, JEFFERSON, JOHNSON, KEARNEY, KEITH, KEYA PAHA, KIMBALL, KNOX, LANCASTER, LINCOLN, LOGAN, LOUP, MCPHERSON, MADISON, MERRICK, MORRILL, NANCE, NEMAHA, NUCKOLLS, OTOE, PAWNEE, PERKINS, PHELPS, PIERCE, PLATTE, POLK, RED WILLOW, RICHARDSON, ROCK, SALINE, SARPY, SAUNDERS, SCOTTS BLUFF, SEWARD, SHERIDAN, SHERMAN, SIOUX, STANTON, THAYER, THOMAS, THURSTON, VALLEY, WASHINGTON, WAYNE, WEBSTER, WHEELER, YORK.

Nebraska City, town (1990 pop. 6,547), ⊙ Otoe co., SE Nebr., 40 mi/64 km S of Omaha, and on Missouri R. at Iowa state line; 40°40′N 95°51′W. Elev. 1,029 ft/314 m. RR junction. Commercial, processing center for cattle-raising, agr. region; dairy prods.; livestock; grain, apples. Mfg. (die casting, beef processing; machinery, apparel). State school for blind. Arbor Lodge State Historical Park (has over 100 species of trees honoring J. Sterling Morton, founder of Arbor Day, on W edge of town), Arbor Day Lied Conference Center designed to serve conservation groups. City is referred to as Apple Capital (by Nebraskans). Riverview Marina State Recreation Area to N. Inc. 1855. Grew as river port; has barge dock.

Necaxa, Mexico: see NUEVO NECAXA.

Necaxa River (ne-KA-shah), c.125 mi/201 km long, in Puebla and Veracruz, Mexico; rises NW of Zacatlán; flows NE, past Huauchinango, to the Gulf of Mexico at Tecolutla; 20°16′N 97°27′W. Used extensively for irrigation and hydroelectric power. Its lower course in Veracruz is called Tecolutla. The large Necaxa Falls are NW of Huauchinango, near Veracruz state border.

Necedah (ne-SEE-duh), village (1990 pop. 743), Juneau co., central Wis., on Yellow R., and 28 mi/45 km SSW of Wisconsin Rapids; 44°01′N 90°04′W. RR junction. Wood prods., dairy prods.; mfg. (machinery, wood prods., fabricated metal prods.). Necedah Natl. Wildlife Refuge to NW; Central Wis. Conservation Area to W; Petenwell Dam and L. to NE; Buckhorn State Park to SE, on Castle Rock L. reservoir.

Necessity, Fort, Pa.: see FORT NECESSITY.

Nechako (ni-CHAK-o), river, 287 mi/462 km long, B.C., W Canada; rises in Tetachuck and Ootsa lakes, central B.C.; flows NE, then E to the Fraser R. at Prince George. Kenney Dam (325 ft/99 m high; completed 1952) and Kemano Dam (320 ft/98 m high; completed 1954) are among the highest dams in Canada.

Neche (NECH-ee), village (1990 pop. 434), Pembina co., NE N.Dak., near Can. (Man.) border, port of entry 14 mi/23 km NNE of Cavalier, and on Pembina R.; 48°58′N 97°32′W.

Neches River (NAI-chiz), 416 mi/669 km long, E Texas; rises in Van Zandt co.; flows generally SE, past Beaumont, to head of Sabine L. Has deepwater channel (an arm of Sabine-Neches Waterway) from Beaumont (port) to Sabine L., NE of Port Arthur. Plans were developed in 1947 for Rockland Dam and reservoir (for flood control, power, navigation) in N Tyler co. L. Palestine reservoir 15 mi/24 km SW of Tyler; B.A. Steinhagen L. reservoir 50 mi/80 km N of Beaumont (flows through Big Thicket Natl. Preserve bet. lakes and Beaumont).

Neck City, city (1990 pop. 132), Jasper co., SW Mo., on Spring R., and 12 mi/19 km N of Joplin; 37°15′N 94°26′W.

Necker Island, in N Pacific, Honolulu co., Hawaii, c.430 mi/692 km NW of Honolulu, 8 mi/12.9 km N of Tropic of Cancer; 23°34′N 164°42′W. Under jurisdiction of city and co. of Honolulu. Once had small Hawaiian settlement. Highest elev. 277 ft/84 m. Part of Hawaiian Isls. Natl. Wildlife Refuge. From here, Necker Ocean Ridge branches to SW from the Hawaiian Ridge.

Neddick, Cape (NED-ik), promontory, SW Maine, with offshore lighthouse, 3 mi/4.8 km NNE of York Harbor.

Nederland, city (1990 pop. 16,192), Jefferson co., SE Texas, suburb 6 mi/9.7 km NW of downtown Port Arthur, near Neches R.; 29°58′N 94°00′W. Primarily a residential suburb bet. Beaumont and Port Arthur, it has 2 oil companies and a chemical industry. Rice is a major cash crop; soybeans; cattle. Mfg. (electric prods., barges, chemicals and chemical processing). Founded by Du. settlers as a rice-farming community in 1897. Jefferson Co. Airport to SW. Inc. 1940.

Nederland, town (1990 pop. 1,099), Boulder co., N central Colo., on headstream of Boulder Creek, on W end of Barler Reservoir, in Front Range, and 30 mi/48 km WNW of Denver; 39°57′N 105°30′W. Elev. 8,236 ft/2,510 m. Resort; tungsten mines. L. Eldora dam serves hydroelectric plant. Univ. of Colo. Observatory. Area surrounded by Roosevelt Natl. Forest.

Nedrow, village (1990 pop. 2,700), Onondaga co., central N.Y., just S of Syracuse; 42°59′N 76°08′W. Quarrying. Onondaga Indian Reservation is nearby.

Neebish Island (NEE-bish), E Upper Peninsula, N Mich., in St. Marys R., (U.S.-Can. border), just W of St. Joseph Isl. (Ont.), and 15 mi/24 km SSE of Sault Ste. Marie; c.8 mi/12.9 km long, 4 mi/6.4 km wide; 46°17′N 84°09′W. Resort; some agr. Car ferry from Barbeau, on mainland.

Needham (NEE-duhm), town (1990 pop. 27,557), Norfolk co., E Mass., suburb of Boston; 42°17′N 71°14′W. Although largely residential, paper prods., electronic equip. and software, and other items are manufactured here. Founded 1680, set off from Dedham and inc. 1711.

Needham's Point, headland, protecting S end of Carlisle Bay, roadstead off Bridgetown, S coast of Barbados. Now site of large hotel. Has fort and lighthouse.

Needle Mountain, Wyo.: see ABSAROKA RANGE.

Needles, city (□ 30 sq mi/78 sq km; 1990 pop. 5,191), San Bernardino co., SE Calif., 150 mi/241 km ENE of San Bernardino, and 38 mi/61 km SW of Kingman (Ariz.), on Colorado R., on upper reach of L. Havasu Reservoir (Ariz. state line); 34°49′N 114°37′W. Mfg. (bldg. materials). Trade center for mines, irrigated farms, and Fort Mojave Indian Reservation (Ariz., Nev., Calif.) to N. Fishing; waterfowl hunting in river marshes. Temps. here are extremely high (often over 100°F/38°C), with wide daily range and low humidity. Davis Dam (L. Mead Natl. Recreation Area) 22 mi/35 km to N; L. Havasu Natl. Wildlife Refuge (Ariz.) to SE; Chemehuevi Indian Reservation to SE; Sacramento Mts. to SW. Founded 1883, inc. 1913.

Needville, town (1990 pop. 2,199), Fort Bend co., SE Texas, 11 mi/18 km S of Rosenberg; 29°23′N 95°50′W. RR junction; agr. area (cattle; rice; cotton; soybeans, vegetables; nurseries); oil and gas; mfg. (meat processing). Brazos Bend State Park to E.

Neely Henry Lake, Ala., see H. NEELY HENRY LAKE.

Neelyville, town (1990 pop. 381), Butler co., SE Mo., near Black R., 15 mi/24 km SSW of Poplar Bluff; 36°33′N 90°30′W. Cotton, rice.

Neenah, [Native Amer. = water], city (1990 pop. 23,219), Winnebago co., E Wis., a suburb 7 mi/11.3 km SSW of Appleton, on L. Winnebago at the mouth of the Fox R.; 44°10′N 88°28′W. RR junction. Located in a dairy-farming region, Neenah is known, with its twin city Menasha, as a center for the mfg. of paper and paper prods. Mfg. (rubber prods., dairy prods., chemicals, clothing, wood prods., paper prods.; printing and publishing; foundries). Neenah's industrial development began c.1850 when nearby flour mills were opened. In 1865 its paper industry was established. Of interest is a replica of the home of James Duane Doty, who was the 2d governor of Wis. Territory. Hydroelectric power is generated for Neenah and Menasha by falls of the Fox R. Bergstrom Art Centre. Settled c.1835 on the site of a Winnebago village, inc. as a city 1873.

Neepawa (NEE-puh-wah), town (1991 pop. 3,258), SW Man., central Canada, on Whitemud R., and 35 mi/ 56 km NE of Brandon; 50°14′N 99°27′W. Woodworking, marble processing; grain; livestock.

Neeses (NEES-is), village (1990 pop. 410), Orangeburg co., W central S.C., 15 mi/24 km W of Orangeburg; 33°32′N 81°07′W. Agr. includes, livestock; grain, cotton, tobacco, pecans, peaches.

Neffs, uninc. village (1990 pop. 1,213), Belmont co., E Ohio, 6 mi/10 km ESE of St. Clairsville. In coal-mining area.

Neffsville (NEFS-vil), uninc. town (1990 pop. 980), Lancaster co., SE Pa., residential suburb 4 mi/6.4 km N of Lancaster; 40°06′N 76°18′W. Lancaster Airport to N; Pa. Farm Mus. to E.

Negaunee (nuh-GAW-nee), town (1990 pop. 4,741), Marquette co., NW Upper Peninsula, N Mich., 10 mi/ 16 km SW of Marquette, in Marquette Iron Range; 46°30′N 87°35′W. RR junction for mining spurs and RR spur to Marquette. Iron mining; wood prods.; cattle farming. Resort. Iron was discovered here in 1844. Mich. Iron Industry Mus. Settled 1846; inc. as village 1862, as city 1873.

Negril, township and resort (1991 pop. 4,184), Westmoreland parish, W Jamaica, just N of South Negril Point; 18°19′N 78°20′W. Extends from Half Moon Bay in Hanover through Long Bay S to Negril Light House (18°15′N 78°20′W). The area encloses 7 mi/11.3 km of white sand beach protected by coral reefs. Once a quiet fishing village, Negril is now a regional tourist mecca due to its laid-back atmosphere. Prime attractions include water sports and snorkling. Minor port ships logwood.

Negro Mountain, NW Md. and SW Pa., a ridge of the Alleghenies, rising to 3,213 ft/979 m in Mt. Davis, highest point on the Natl. Road; extends c.35 mi/56 km NNE from Deep Creek L. just SE of McHenry (Md.), to a point just S of Somerset (Pa.). Sect. of Savage R. State Forest is on the slopes in Md. During the Fr. and Indian War, an Afr.-American known as Nemisis, under the command of Colonel Thomas Cresap died in a skirmish with Native Americans here; hence the name.

Nehalem (nuh-HAI-luhm), village (1990 pop. 232), Tillamook co., NW Oregon, 38 mi/61 km S of Astoria, on Nehalem R., near mouth of North Fork; 45°43′N 123°53′W. Dairy prods.; cattle. Wineries. Fish hatcheries to E and NE. Oswald West State Park to NW.

Nehalem River, NW Oregon; rises in NW Wash. co.; flows NE past Vernonia, curves W and SW, then flows through Clatsop and Tillamook State Forest. Receives North Fork before entering Nehalem Bay, Pacific Ocean, near Nehalem. North Fork rises in S central Clatsop co., flows S and SW c. 25 mi/40 km.

Nehawka, village (1990 pop. 260), Cass co., SE Nebr., 11 mi/18 km NW of Nebraska City, and on Weeping Water Creek, near Missouri R.; 40°49′N 95°59′W. Traces of prehistoric man discovered near here.

Neiba (ne-EE-bah), city (1993 pop. 16,287), ⊙ Bahoruco prov., SW Dominican Republic, near E shore of L. Enriquillo, 100 mi/161 km W of Santo Domingo; 18°28′N 71°23′W. Produces sugarcane and fine construction wood. Provincial capital since 1943. Rock-salt and gypsum deposits nearby. Also spelled Neyba.

Neiba Bay (ne-EE-bah), small inlet of the Caribbean Sea, SW Dominican Republic; c.6 mi/9.7 km long, 6 mi/9.7 km wide; 18°15′N 71°02′W. Into it falls the Yaque del Sur. Barahona city on SW coast.

Neiba, Sierra de (ne-EE-bah, see-ER-rah dai), range in W Dominican Republic, S of the Cordillera Central,

bet. San Juan Valley (N) and L. Enriquillo (S), extending c.60 mi/97 km E from Haiti border to the Yaque del Sur; rises to 5,545 ft/1,690 m; 18°40′N 71°30′W.

Neihart, village (1990 pop. 53), Cascade co., central Mont., 51 mi/82 km SE of Great Falls, on Belt Creek, in Little Belt Mts., in Lewis and Clark Natl. Forest; 46°56′N 110°45′W. Elev. c.5,700 ft/1,737 m. Trading point. Silver, lead, sapphire mines. Showdown Ski Area to S.

Neilsville, town (1990 pop. 2,680), ⊙ Clark co., central Wis., on Black R., and 47 mi/76 km ESE of Eau Claire, in hilly region; 44°33′N 90°35′W. Commercial center for dairying, livestock-raising, and farming area; cheese, butter; mfg. (fabricated metal prods., machinery, beverages, canned vegetables). Has hydroelectric plant. St. Mary's Mission School is here. Bruce Mound Ski Area to SW. Settled c.1844, inc. 1882.

Nejapa de Madero (nai-HAH-pah dai mah-DAI-ro), town (1990 pop. 1,932), in SE Oaxaca, Mexico, 81 mi/ 130 km SE of Oaxaca de Juárez; 16°37′N 95°59′W. Elev. 3,281 ft/1,000 m. A mountainous region with flat areas irrigated by the Grande R. Hot climate. Mostly Zapotec pop. Agr. (cereals and fruits), fine woods, lumber, mezcal; cattle and poultry raising.

Nekoma (nuh-KO-muh), village (1990 pop. 63), Cavalier co., NE N.Dak., 13 mi/21 km S of Langdon; 48°34′N 98°22′W.

Nekoosa, town (1990 pop. 2,557), Wood co., central Wis., on Wisconsin R., and suburb 7 mi/11.3 km SSW of Wisconsin Rapids; 44°18′N 89°54′W. In dairy area; paper prods. State nursery across river to NE; large Petenwell Reservoir to S on Wisconsin R. Settled 1892, inc. 1926.

Nelagoney (nel-uh-GO-nee), village, Osage co., N Okla., 6 mi/9.7 km ESE of Pawhuska.

Nelchina Glacier, 22 mi/35 km long, S Alaska; rises in Chugach Mts. near 61°30′N 146°50′W; flows NW, drains into Tazlina L.

Neligh (NEE-lei), town (1990 pop. 1,742), ⊙ Antelope co., NE central Nebr., 30 mi/48 km WNW of Norfolk, and on Elkhorn R.; 42°07′N 98°01′W. Grain; mfg. (flags, wood prods.). Neligh Mills, restored water-powered mill. Inc. 1873.

Nellie, village (1990 pop. 130), Coshocton co., central Ohio, 12 mi/19 km WNW of Coshocton, and on Walhonding R. Mohawk Dam is nearby.

Nellie Juan, Port, bay, S Alaska, on E side of Kenai Peninsula 50 mi/80 km NE of Seward; 30 mi/48 km long, 3 mi/4.8 km wide; opens into Prince Williams Sound at 60°32′N 148°17′W. Fishing, fish processing.

Nellieburg, uninc. town (1990 pop. 1,208), Lauderdale co., E Miss., residential suburb 3 mi/4.8 km WNW of downtown Meridian; 32°23′N 88°46′W.

Nellis Air Force Base, Nev.: see LAS VEGAS.

Nelliston, village (□ 1 sq mi/2.6 sq km; 1990 pop. 569), Montgomery co., E central N.Y., on Mohawk R. (bridged), opposite Fort Plain, and 22 mi/35 km W of Amsterdam; 42°55′N 74°36′W.

Nelson 1 county (□ 424 sq mi/1,098 sq km; 1990 pop. 29,710), central Ky.; ⊙ Bardstown; 37°47′N 85°28′W. Bounded SW by Rolling Fork R., E by Beech Fork. Rolling agr. area, in Bluegrass region (burley tobacco, soybeans, wheat, corn, hay, alfalfa; hogs, cattle, poultry; dairying; hardwood timber). Mfg. at Bardstown. Co. is known for its whiskey distillery at Bardstown and Borton. Part of Taylorsville L. reservoir in NE corner; My Old Ky. Home State Park in center; part of Bernheim Forest preserve in NW. Formed 1784. **2** county (□ 995 sq mi/2,577 sq km; 1990 pop. 4,410), E central N.Dak., in Pothole region; ⊙ Lakota; 47°55′N 98°11′W. Agr. area watered by Sheyenne and Goose rivers; Stump L. in W. Dairy prods.; cattle; poultry; wheat, oats, sunflowers. Formed 1883. Small part of Devils L. Sioux Indian Reservation in W; Johnson L. Natl. Wildlife Refuge on SW corner. **3** county (□ 474 sq mi/1,228 sq km; 1990 pop. 12,778), central Va.; ⊙ Lovingston; 37°47′N 78°52′W. In rolling Piedmont region, with Blue Ridge in W and NW; bounded SE by James R.; drained by Rockfish R. Agr. (apples, hay, alfalfa, corn; cattle); mining (titanium ores, apatite), stone quarrying. Blue Ridge Parkway follows NW border, Appalachian Trail

crosses co. in NW, part of George Washington Natl. Forest in NW. Formed 1807.

Nelson, city (1991 pop. 8,760), SE B.C., W Canada, on the Kootenay R.; 49°29′N 117°17′W. Transportation and administrative center for a lumbering and farming region.

Nelson, city (1990 pop. 181), Saline co., central Mo., on Blackwater R., near the Missouri R., and 12 mi/19 km SE of Marshall; 38°59′N 93°01′W. Corn, wheat; cattle.

Nelson, town (1990 pop. 535), Cheshire co., SW N.H., 8 mi/12.9 km NE of Keene; 43°00′N 72°07′W. Agr. (cattle, poultry; vegetables; dairying; nursery crops). Spoonwood Pond and part of Nubanusit L. in E.

Nelson 1 village (1990 pop. 486), Pickens and Cherokee cos., N Ga., 32 mi/51 km W of Gainesville; 34°23′N 84°22′W. Marble fabrication. **2** village (1990 pop. 200), Lee co., N Ill., on Rock R., and 6 mi/9.7 km WSW of Dixon; 41°47′N 89°35′W. In rich agr. area. **3** village, Muhlenberg co., W Ky., 3 mi/4.8 km N of Central City. In bituminous-coal-mining and agr. area. **4** village (1990 pop. 177), Douglas co., W Minn., 5 mi/8 km E of Alexandria, in lake region; 45°53′N 95°16′W. Poultry, livestock; grain; dairying; mfg. (wood prods., dairy prods.). Smith (to S) and Victoria (to W) lakes nearby. **5** village (1990 pop. 627), ⊙ Nuckolls co., S Nebr., 30 mi/48 km SE of Hastings, and on branch of Little Blue R.; 40°12′N 98°04′W. Grain. **6** village (1990 pop. 388), Buffalo co., W Wis., near the Mississippi R. (bridged nearby), at mouth of Chippewa R., 30 mi/ 48 km NNW of Winona (Minn.), opposite Wabasha (Minn.); 44°25′N 92°00′W. Coulee region. Mfg. (RR ties, dairy prods.). Upper Mississippi R. Wildlife and Fish Refuge on river.

Nelson, river, c.400 mi/640 km long, Man., central Canada; issues from the NE end of L. Winnipeg, central Man.; flows NE to Hudson Bay at Port Nelson. With the Bow–South Saskatchewan–Saskatchewan river system, which enters NW L. Winnipeg, the Nelson is part of a 1,600-mi/2,575-km continuous stream from W Alta. to Hudson Bay. There are hydroelectric plants at Kettle Rapids, Long Spruce, and Kelsey. Nickel-mining and -refining operations at Thompson use electricity generated by the river. The Nelson's mouth was explored (1612) by Sir Thomas Button. The river was long followed by fur traders; from 1682 to 1957 the Hudson's Bay Co. maintained a trading post at York Factory on Hudson Bay.

Nelson Forks, Hudson's Bay Co. trading post, NE B.C., W Canada, near Yukon border, on Liard R., at mouth of Fort Nelson R., and 70 mi/113 km NW of Fort Nelson; 59°30′N 124°00′W.

Nelson Island, W Alaska, separated from mainland (E) by narrow channel, from Nunivak Isl. (SW) by Etolin Strait; 42 mi/68 km long, 20 mi/32 km–35 mi/56 km wide; 60°37′N 164°22′W. Tanunak village in W.

Nelson Peak (10,772 ft/3,283 m), SE B.C., W Canada, in Selkirk Mts., 60 mi/97 km SW of Banff; 50°28′N 116°21′W.

Nelson Reservoir, NE Mont., in Phillips co., 15 mi/ 24 km NE of Malta; 10 mi/16 km long, 2 mi/3.2 km max. width. Formed by dam on small branch of Milk R.

Nelsonville, city (1990 pop. 4,563), Athens co., SE Ohio, 12 mi/19 km NW of Athens, and on Hocking R. In coal- and clay-producing, dairying, and farming area; makes footwear, bricks, tile, machinery.

Nelsonville 1 village (□ 1 sq mi/2.6 sq km; 1990 pop. 585), Putnam co., SE N.Y., 9 mi/14.5 km N of Peekskill; 41°25′N 73°57′W. In dairying area. **2** village (1990 pop. 171), Portage co., central Wis., 12 mi/19 km E of Stevens Point; 44°29′N 89°18′W. Dairying area.

Nemacolin (NEE-ma-KO-lin), uninc. town (1990 pop. 1,097), Greene co., SW Pa., 14 mi/23 km E of Waynesburg, on Monongahela R.; 39°52′N 79°55′W. Hay; livestock; dairying.

Nemacolin's Path, Native Amer. trail bet. the Potomac and the Monongahela rivers, going from the site of Cumberland (Md.), to the mouth of Redstone Creek, where Brownsville (Pa.) is situated. It was blazed and cleared in 1749 or 1750 by Nemacolin, a Delaware chief, and Thomas Cresap, a Md. frontiersman. The path was of military importance as the route of George Washington's 1st Western expedition and of Gen. Edward Braddock's expedition in the last of the Fr. and Indian Wars. It was known as Braddock's Road until the Cumberland Road or NATIONAL ROAD was built on the same route.

Nemadji River (ne-MA-jee), c.20 mi/32 km long, Douglas co., NW Wis.; formed by joining of North Fork Nemadji and South Fork Nemadji rivers, 15 mi/24 km SSW of Superior (Wis.), at Minn. state line; flows NE to L. Superior, on Allouez Bay, 4 mi/6.4 km SE of Superior at Allouez. North Fork Nemadji R., Minn. and Wis., rises in S Carlton co., NE Minn., c.15 mi/24 km SSW of Carlton; 46°24′N 92°30′W; flows generally NE c.25 mi/40 km to join South Fork Nemadji R. in Douglas co., Wis, at Minn. state line. South Fork Nemadji R. Minn. and Wis., formed by joining of several small creeks in S Carlton co., NE Minn. c.13 mi/21 km S of Carlton; flows c.15 mi/24 km to North Fork to form Nemadji R.

Nemaha 1 (NEE-muh-hah), county (□ 719 sq mi/ 1,862 sq km; 1990 pop. 10,446), NE Kansas; ⊙ Seneca; 39°46′N 96°01′W. Gently sloping terrain, bordered N by Nebr.$ained by South Fork Nemaha R. Cattle, hogs, poultry; corn, oats, soybeans, wheat. Food prods., machinery, rubber prods. Nemaha State Fishing L. in center. Formed 1855. **2** (NEE-muh-huh), county (□ 411 sq mi/1,064 sq km, 1990 pop. 7,980), SE Nebr.; ⊙ Auburn; 40°23′N 95°50′W. Farming area bounded E by Missouri R. (Mo. state line); drained by Little Nemaha R. Soybeans, wheat, corn, sorghum; cattle, hogs; dairying and dairy and poultry prods. Cooper Station nuclear power plant (initial criticality February 21, 1974) is 23 mi/37 km S of Nebraska City; uses cooling water from the Missouri R., and has a max. dependable capacity of 778 MWE. Brownville State Recreation Area in E. Formed 1854.

Nemaha, town (1990 pop. 112), Sac co., W Iowa, near Raccoon R., 8 mi/12.9 km NNW of Sac City; 42°31′N 95°05′W.

Nemaha (NEE-muh-huh), village (1990 pop. 188), Nemaha co., SE Nebr., 10 mi/16 km ESE of Auburn, and on Missouri R; 40°20′N 95°40′W. Missouri R. flooded in 1993. Brownville State Recreation Area to N.

Nemiscau, village, W central Que., E Canada, 85 mi/ 137 km ESE of Waskaganish (Rupert House) and James Bay, on NW side of L. Nemiscau; 51°19′N 76°54′W. Located on SW margin of James Bay Hydro Project. Timber.

Nenana, village (1990 pop. 393), central Alaska, on Tanana R. (700-ft/213-m RR bridge) at mouth of Nenana R., and 45 mi/72 km WSW of Fairbanks; 64°32′N 149°05′W. Distributing and transshipment center from RR to Yukon R. tug boats and barges. RR mus. Scene of annual Nenana ice sweepstakes. Est. 1916 as base for construction of Alaska RR; at S end of bridge President Warren Harding opened RR, July 1923.

Nenana River, 150 mi/241 km long, central Alaska, S tributary of Tanana R.; rises in central Alaska Range, near 63°19′N 147°46′W; flows NNW to Tanana R. at Nenana. River rafting. Paralleled by Parks Highway and Alaska RR for c.100 mi/161 km.

Nenzel (NEN-zil), village (1990 pop. 8), Cherry co., N Nebr., 28 mi/45 km W of Valentine, near S.Dak. state line, and Niobrara R.; 42°55′N 101°05′W. Samuel B. McKelvie Natl. Forest to S.

Neodesha (nee-O-duh-shai), town (1990 pop. 2,837), Wilson co., SE Kansas, on Verdigris R., near mouth of Fall R., and 13 mi/21 km N of Independence; 37°25′N 95°40′W. Refining center in agr. (grain; livestock) and oil area. Mfg. (chemicals, boats, transportation equip., hand tools, machinery, plastics prods., wood prods.). Norman Oil Well to NE, replica of oil well W of Miss. Mus. Site of Neodesha Reservoir (for flood control on the Verdigris) is near. Inc. 1871.

Neoga (nee-O-gah), city (1990 pop. 1,678), Cumberland co., SE central Ill., 12 mi/19 km WNW of Toledo; 39°19′N 88°27′W. Corn, soybeans. Inc. 1869.

Neola, town (1990 pop. 894), Pottawattamie co., SW

Iowa, on Mosquito Creek, and 18 mi/29 km NE of Council Bluffs; 41°27′N 95°37′W. In corn, wheat, livestock area.

Neon, Ky.: see FLEMING-NEON.

Neopit (NEE-o-pit), village (1990 pop. 615), Menominee co., NE Wis., 18 mi/29 km NNW of Shawano, on mill pond, in Menominee Indian Reservation; 44°58′N 88°49′W. Sawmilling on mill pond. Lumber.

Neosho (nee-O-sho), county (□ 578 sq mi/1,497 sq km; 1990 pop. 17,035), SE Kansas; ⊙ Erie; 37°33′N 95°17′W. Sloping to gently rolling area, drained by Neosho R. Sorghum, wheat, soybeans, hay; hogs, cattle, poultry; dairying. Textiles, plastic prods., transportation equip. Oil, gas, coal. Neosho Waterfowl Refuge and Neosho State Fishing L. in SE. Formed 1864.

Neosho (nee-O-sho), city (1990 pop. 9,254), ⊙ Newton co., SW Mo., in the Ozark Mts., 16 mi/26 km SSE of Joplin; 36°50′N 94°22′W. RR junction. Apples, berries, vegetables; dairy prods.; cattle, poultry. Mfg. (foods, furniture, apparel; poultry processing, jet engine overhauling). Tourism. Crowder Col. to S. Pro-Confederate Mo. state convention passed an ineffective ordinance of secession here, 1862. Thomas Hart Benton (painter and muralist) b. here, 1889. Natl. fish hatchery. Inc. 1855.

Neosho (nee-O-sho), village (1990 pop. 658), Dodge co., S central Wis., on small Rubicon R., and 19 mi/31 km SE of Beaver Dam; 43°18′N 88°31′W. Dairying region.

Neosho (nee-O-sho), river, c.460 mi/740 km long, Kansas and Okla.; rises in Morris co., E central Kansas; flows SE through Council Grove L. Reservoir, past Council Grove and Emporia, through John Redmond Reservoir, then past Iola, Chanute, and Independence (all in Kansas), and Miami (Okla.) into NE Okla. (where it is generally known as the Grand R.) then S to join the Arkansas R. near Muskogee. Pensacola Dam (which impounds the huge L. of the Cherokees) and Fort Gibson dam and reservoir are in NE Okla.; there are several flood control units on the river in Kansas.

Neosho Falls (nee-O-sho), village (1990 pop. 157), Woodson co., SE Kansas, on Neosho R., and 12 mi/ 19 km NE of Yates Center; 38°00′N 95°33′W. Livestock; grain. Small oil fields nearby.

Neosho Rapids (nee-O-sho), village (1990 pop. 235), Lyon co., E central Kansas, on Neosho R., and 10 mi/ 16 km ESE of Emporia; 38°22′N 95°59′W. Cattle; grain.

Nepaug Reservoir, Conn.: see FARMINGTON RIVER.

Nepean, city (1991 pop. 107,627), SE Ont., central Canada, suburb 6 mi/10 km SSW of downtown Ottawa, part of Ottawa-Carleton Regional Municipality (1991 pop. 678,147). Borders Ottawa R. on NW, Rideau R. on SE. Seat of Algonquin Col. Rural area (mixed farming; dairying).

Nephi (NEE-fei), city (1990 pop. 3,515), ⊙ Juab co., central Utah, 38 mi/61 km SSW of Provo, in mt. region; 39°42′N 111°49′W. Elev. 5,133 ft/1,565 m. Cattle- and grain-shipping (wheat, barley, alfalfa) center; mfg. (rubber prods.). Parts of Uinta Natl. Forest to NE and SE, including Mt. Nebo Wilderness Area to NE. Fountain Green Fish Hatchery to E. Settled 1851 by Mormons.

Neponset (ni-PON-set), village, Bureau co., N Ill., 18 mi/ 29 km WSW of Princeton; 41°17′N 89°47′W. In agr. area.

Neponset River (ne-PAWN-set), c.25 mi/40 km long, E Mass.; rises in SW Norfolk co.; flows NE, past Milton (head of navigation), to SW side of Boston Harbor, bet. Boston and Quincy.

Neponsit, section of S Queens borough of N.Y. city, SE N.Y., on Rockaway Peninsula; 40°34′N 73°52′W. Residential; beachfront community.

Neptune, township (1990 pop. 28,148), Monmouth co., E N.J., on the Atlantic coast, and W and S of Asbury Park; 40°12′N 74°02′W. Mfg. (apparel, electrical equip., fabricated metal prods.); ironworks. Includes Ocean Grove (resort). Inc. 1879.

Neptune Beach, resort town (□ 6 sq mi/15.5 sq km; 1990 pop. 6,816), Duval co., extreme NE Fla., 15 mi/24 km E of Jacksonville, on the Atlantic Ocean; 30°18′N 81°23′W. Inc. 1931.

Neptune City, resort borough (1990 pop. 4,997), Monmouth co., E N.J., near the Atlantic coast, 2 mi/3.2 km SW of Asbury Park; 40°12′N 74°01′W. Inc. 1881.

Nequasset, Maine: see WOOLWICH.

Nerstrand (NUHR-strand), village (1990 pop. 210), Rice co., SE Minn., 11 mi/18 km ENE of Faribault; 44°20′N 93°03′W. Dairying; poultry; grain, soybeans; light mfg. Nerstrand Woods State Park to W. Holds annual "Ring Bologna Days."

Nesbit 1 (NEZ-bit), uninc. village, De Soto co., NW Miss., 18 mi/29 km S of Memphis (Tenn.), and 4 mi/ 6.4 km N of Hernando. Agr. area (cotton, corn; cattle). Mfg. (fabricated metal prods., wire racks, wood prods.). Site of Jerry Lee Lewis Ranch, home of the rock-'n'-roll star; has piano-shaped swimming pool. **2** village (1990 pop. 327), Harrison co., NE Texas, residential suburb 5 mi/8 km NW of downtown Marshall; 32°35′N 94°27′W. Located in cattle and timber area.

Nesconset, uninc. village, census-designated place (□ 3 sq mi/7.8 sq km; 1990 pop. 10,712), Suffolk co., SE N.Y., 3.5 mi/5.6 km SE of Smithtown; 40°51′N 73°09′W. Mfg. (transportation equip., electronic prods., plastic prods.).

Nescopeck (NES-ko-pek), borough (1990 pop. 1,651), Luzerne co., E central Pa., 23 mi/37 km SW of Wilkes-Barre, on Susquehanna R. (bridged; opposite Berwick to NW), at mouth of Nescopeck Creek; 41°02′N 76°12′W. Mfg. (transporation equip., ordnance, burial vaults). Agr. area (apples, potatoes, corn; livestock; dairying). Settled 1786, inc. 1896.

Nescopeck Creek (NES-ko-pek), c.45 mi/72 km long, E central Pa.; rises in E central Luzerne co., c.7 mi/ 11.3 km S of Wilkes-Barre; flows WSW, passes N of Freeland, turns NW to Susquehanna R. at Nescopeck, opposite Berwick; 41°05′N 75°50′W.

Neshaminy Creek (nuh-SHA-mi-nee), c.50 mi/80 km long, SE Pa.; rises in SW Bucks co. at joining of West and North branches; flows generally SE past Chalfant and Parkland to Delaware R. at Croydon; 40°16′N 75°12′W. West Branch (c.10 mi/16 km long) rises in NE Montgomery co., flows E; North Branch (c.15 mi/24 km long) rises in N Bucks co., flows SW through L. Galean reservoir.

Neshkoro (nesh-KAW-ruh), village (1990 pop. 384), Marquette co., central Wis., on small White R., and mill pond, 33 mi/53 km W of Oshkosh; 43°58′N 89°12′W. In livestock and dairy area. Hydroelectric plant.

Neshoba (nuh-SHO-buh), county (□ 571 sq mi/ 1,479 sq km; 1990 pop. 24,800), E central Miss.; ⊙ Philadelphia; 32°45′N 89°07′W. Drained by Pearl R. Includes Choctaw Indian Reservation in W; also small reservation SE of Philadelphia. Agr. (cotton, corn; poultry, cattle; dairying); timber. Mfg. at Philadelphia. Part of Nanih Waiya Memorial State Historical Site in NE; Neshoba Co. Legion L. (state lake) in SE; source of Chunky Creek in E. Formed 1833.

Nesowadnehunk Lake (ne-SOU-uh-duh-huhnk), Piscataquis co., central Maine, 32 mi/51 km NW of Millinocket, near W border of Baxter State Park; 3 mi/ 4.8 km long, 1 mi/1.6 km wide. Source of Nesowadnehunk Stream, which flows S to West Branch of Penobscot R. Formerly known as Sourdnahunk L.

Nespelem (nes-PEE-luhm), village (1990 pop. 187), Okanogan co., N Wash., in S end of Colville Indian Reservation, 30 mi/48 km SE of Okanogan, on Nespelem R. Indian Agency hq. for Colville and Spokane reservations; 48°10′N 118°58′W. Columbia R. 4 mi/6.4 km SE. Chief Joseph Memorial. Owhi L. reservoir to NE.

Nesquehoning (NUHS-kwa-HO-ning), borough (□ 22 sq mi/57 sq km; 1990 pop. 3,364), E Pa., 4 mi/6.4 km W of Jim Thorpe, on Nesquehoning Creek, extends from Lehigh R. to Schuylkill co. border; 40°51′N 75°49′W. Former anthracite-coal region. Mfg. (chemicals, vinyl prods., displays, apparel, transportation equip., fabricated metal prods.). Agr. area (potatoes, corn, hay; livestock; dairying). Mauch Chunk L. reservoir to S.

Ness (NES), county (□ 1,075 sq mi/2,784 sq km; 1990 pop. 4,033), W central Kansas; ⊙ Ness City; 38°28′N 99°55′W. Smoky Hills region to N, drained by Walnut

Creek and its North and South forks, which converge at center of co., and by Pawnee R. (S). Wheat, sorghum; cattle. Oil and gas extraction. Formed 1880.

Ness City (NES), town (1990 pop. 1,724), ⊙ Ness co., W central Kansas, on N Fork of Walnut Creek, and c.60 mi/97 km W of Great Bend; 38°27′N 99°54′W. Elev. 2,220 ft/677 m. In agr. area (wheat; cattle). Founded 1878, inc. 1886.

Nesselrode, Mount (8,105 ft/2,470 m), in Coast Range, on border bet. U.S. (SE Alaska) and Canada (B.C.), 50 mi/80 km N of Juneau (Alaska); 58°58′N 134°19′W.

Nesterville, town, central Ont., central Canada, on L. Huron, 3 mi/5 km NW of Thessalon. Dairying; mixed farming; lumbering. Also spelled Nestorville.

Nestorville, Ont.: see NESTERVILLE.

Netawaka (net-uh-WAH-kuh), village (1990 pop. 167), Jackson co., NE Kansas, 9 mi/14.5 km N of Holton; 39°36′N 95°43′W. Cattle; grain.

Netcong (NET-kuhng), borough (1990 pop. 3,311), Morris co., N N.J., near L. Musconetcong, and 13 mi/21 km NW of Morristown; 40°53′N 74°42′W. In resort area. Mfg. (machinery, consumer goods); agr. (poultry; fruit, vegetables). State park nearby. Inc. 1894; grew as residence for iron miners and ironworkers.

Nether Providence (NE-thur), township (1990 pop. 13,229), Delaware co., SE Pa., residential suburb 12 mi/19 km SW of Philadelphia; 39°53′N 75°22′W.

Nett Lake (□ 11 sq mi/28 sq km), in Koochiching and St. Louis cos., N Minn., in Nett L. Indian Reservation, 35 mi/56 km SSE of Internatl. Falls; 6 mi/9.7 km long, 4 mi/6.4 km wide; 48°07′N 93°07′W. Drains WNW through Nett Lake R. to Little Fork R. Nett Lake village is small Native Amer. community, on E shore of lake, at Big Point. Big Isl. in S.

Nettilling Lake (NE-chi-ling), freshwater lake (□ 1,956 sq mi/5,066 sq km), S Baffin Isl., N.W.T., N Canada. One of the largest lakes entirely within Canada. Located in an arctic lowland region and fed by Amadjuak L. and by numerous streams that drain the tundra. It empties through the Koukdjuak R. W into Foxe Basin. Frozen most of the year.

Nettleton 1 town, Craighead co., NE Ark., 2 mi/3.2 km ESE of Jonesboro; part of city of Jonesboro. Ships farm produce. Founded 1881. **2** town (1990 pop. 2,462), Lee and Monroe cos., E Miss., 13 mi/21 km SSE of Tupelo, near Chipawa R.; 34°05′N 88°37′W. Agr. (corn, cotton, wheat, soybeans; cattle; dairying), Mfg. (furniture, apparel, valves).

Netzahualcóyotl, Mexico: see CIUDAD NETZAHUAL-CÓYOTL.

Neudorf (NOO-dorf), village (1991 pop. 373), SE Sask., Canada, 17 mi/27 km SW of Melville; 50°43′N 103°00′W. Mixed farming; livestock.

Neuse Forest (NOOS), uninc. town (1990 pop. 1,110), Craven co., E N.C., 10 mi/16 km SSE of New Bern, on Neuse R., at N edge of Croatan Natl. Forest; 34°57′N 76°57′W. Cherry Point Marine Corps Air Station to SE.

Neuse River, c.275 mi/443 km long, E N.C.; formed 8 mi/12.9 km NE of Durham by junction of small Flat (c.25 mi/40 km long), Eno, and Little rivers; flows generally SE through Falls L. reservoir, passes to E of Raleigh, flows past Smithfield, Goldsboro, Kinston, and New Bern where it widens into an estuary (c.5 mi/8 km wide) extending c.40 mi/64 km SE and NE to Pamlico Sound.

Neustadt (NOO-stat), village (1991 pop. 551), S Ont., Canada, on South Saugeen R., and 35 mi/56 km S of Owen Sound. Dairying, mixed farming.

Neuville, village (1991 pop. 1,006), S Que., Canada, on the St. Lawrence, and 20 mi/32 km WSW of Quebec; 46°42′N 71°35′W. Dairying; fruit, vegetables.

Nevada, state (□ 110,566 sq mi/286,366 sq km; 1995 est. pop. 1,530,108), W U.S., admitted as the 36th state of the Union in 1864; ⊙ CARSON CITY; 39°59′N 117°01′W. Elev. 5,500 ft/1,676 m. LAS VEGAS is the largest city, and RENO is the 2d largest. Nev. is bounded on the W and SW by Calif., on the N by Oregon and Idaho, on the E by Utah, and on the SE by Ariz. (with the Colorado R. marking most of the border). Most of the state lies within the Basin and Range region, or "Great Basin"

or "Intermountain West." The rivers in the SE belong to the Colorado R. system, while those of the extreme N drain into the Columbia system (Snake). Like the Humboldt, Truckee, and Carson rivers, most Nev. rivers flow into brackish and intermittent lakes or dry sinks — which have no outlet to the oceans, where water loss due to evaporation, absorption, and human use is greater than inflow and precipitation — except where they have been diverted for irrigation and reclamation. About 500,000 acres/202,350 ha of land are being reclaimed by the Humboldt project, the Newlands project, and the Truckee R. storage project. The alkali sinks and great arid stretches clothed with sagebrush, tule (bulrushes), and creosote bush typify Nev.'s valley landscapes. There are more than 200 ranges in Nev. Its mt. chains generally run N and S, further segmenting the state. In its angled corner on its W boundary with Calif., are part of the Sierra Nevada range, practically the only exception to the state's dry basin and range landscape. The driest state in the nation, the days and nights are generally clear, and the temp. varies with the season as well as the elev. In the N and W the winters are extremely cold, while in parts of the S the summers approach ovenlike heat. Many of the high plateau areas are utilized for grazing; cattle and sheep raising are important industries in the state. Because of the prevailing dryness and the steep slopes, agr. is not highly developed, but is devoted mainly to growing forage crops, such as alfalfa and hay; however, potatoes, vegetables, cantaloupe, and barley are grown in irrigated valleys in W and far S; dairying and poultry are also important. Much of the state's foodstuffs are imported. The pop. has been sparse since the Paiute and other Native Amer. tribes eked out a living from the land and the animals. The fortune of Nev. has been not in its land but in the almost incredible wealth below the surface of the land. Mining drew people to Nev., swelling some mining districts to 20,000 and more. Nev. is the leading producer of gold, silver, diatomite, and mercury in the U.S. Copper mining, once a major industry, is now virtually nonexistent. Sand and gravel are also mined. Petroleum was discovered in 1954, and commercial exploitation began in the 1970s. There is also some mfg. (gaming machines and prods., aerospace equipment, military supplies, lawn and garden irrigation devices, seismic monitoring equip.). Nev.'s economy is now overwhelmingly based on tourism, especially the gambling (legalized in 1931), resort entertainment, and convention industries centered in Las Vegas and, to a lesser extent, Reno and Lake Tahoe. Gambling taxes are a primary source of state revenue; gambling and associated services account for half the state's employment. In addition to major gambling destinations like Las Vegas and Reno, several border towns have developed during 1970s and 1980s, some from nothing, to provide services to travelers entering and leaving the state: Laughlin, Mesquite, West Wendover, McDermitt, Jackpot, and Stateline. Liberal divorce laws made Reno "the divorce capital of the world" for many years, until other states liberalized their laws. The state has become a distribution center for the W U.S., including Calif. In the 1770s several Span. explorers came near the area of present-day Nev. but it wasn't until half a cent. later that fur traders venturing beyond the Rocky Mts. publicized the region. Jedediah S. Smith came across S Nev. on his way to Calif. in 1827. The following year Peter Skene Ogden, a Hudson's Bay Company man trading out of the Oregon country, entered NE Nev. Joseph Walker in 1833–1834 went along the Humboldt and crossed the Sierra Nevada to Calif. With Kit Carson, John C. Frémont had explored much of the state bet. 1843 and 1845, and his reports gave the Federal govt. its 1st comprehensive information on the area, which the U.S. acquired from Mexico in the Mex.-Amer. War. Later many wagon trains crossed Nev. on the way to Calif., especially during and after the gold rush of 1849. Travelers going to Calif. over the Old Span. Trail also crossed S Nev., and Las Vegas became a station on the route. Reports from these sources possibly aided Brigham Young when he was shepherding

the Mormons W to build a new home in Utah. When in 1850 the Federal govt. set up the Utah Territory, almost all of Nev. was included except the S tip, which was then part of N.Mex. Non-Mormons had been averse to settling in Mormon-dominated territory, but after gold was found in 1859 non-Mormons did come into the area. A rush from Calif. began and multiplied manyfold as news of the Comstock Lode silver strike spread. Most of the newcomers preferred to consider themselves as still being within Calif., and a political question was added to the general upheaval. Meanwhile, miners came helter-skelter, raising camps that grew overnight into such booming and raucous places as Virginia City. Partly to impose order on the lawless, wide-open mining towns, Congress made Nev. into a territory in 1861 as migrant prospectors and settlers poured in. The territory was then enlarged by increasing its E boundary by 1 degree of long. in 1862. It was rushed into statehood in 1864, with Carson City as its capital. President Lincoln (in order to get more votes to pass the 13th Amendment) had signed the proclamation even though the territory did not actually meet the pop. requirement for statehood. In 1866, Nev. acquired its present-day boundaries when the S tip was added and more E land was gained from Utah. Communications with the East, which had been briefly maintained by the pony express, were firmly established by the completion of the transcontinental RR in 1869. The state continued to be dependent on its precious ores, and its fate was affected by new strikes such as the "big bonanza" (1873), which enriched the silver kings, J. W. Mackay and J. G. Fair, and the discovery (1900) of silver deposits at Tonopah, of copper at Ely, and of gold at Goldfield (1902). In the 20th cent. the Federal govt. has played an active role in Nev., and in 1990 owned over 85% of the state's land. The Newlands Irrigation Project (1907) was the nation's first irrigation project built by the Federal govt. The HOOVER DAM was completed in 1936. The U.S. Atomic Energy Commission (now the Nuclear Regulatory Commission) began nuclear tests in Nev. at Frenchman Flat and Yucca Flat in the 1950s. In 1987, the U.S. Dept. of Energy named Yucca Mt. as a prospective site for the storage of high-level nuclear waste. The state bitterly opposed the decision and has continued to fight it. Nevada's pop. was the fastest growing in the nation during the 1980s and increased 650% from 1950 to 1990. A large influx of retired citizens has swelled pops. of existing cities and has led to creation of new communities, such as Pahrump and Gardnerville Ranches, and increased demand for water to the desert environment. Nevada's constitution was adopted in 1864. The legislature is composed of 20 senators elected for 4-year terms and 42 assemblymen elected for 2-year terms. The governor is elected for a 4-year term. The state elects 2 U.S. senators and 2 representatives; it has 4 electoral votes. Besides Reno and Las Vegas, there are many points of interest. Hoover Dam impounds L. Mead, one of the largest artificial lakes in the world. L. Mead Recreational Area has facilities for fishing, swimming, and boating. Other attractions include L. Tahoe, on the Nev.-Calif. state line, part of Death Valley Natl. Monument (mostly in Calif.), Great Basin Natl. Park (includes the former Lehman Caves Natl. Monument), and restored mining ghost towns like Virginia City. The state's leading institution of higher education is the Univ. of Nev., at Reno and at Las Vegas. State has widely scattered units of 2 natl. forests; Toiyabe, in center, W and S, and Humboldt in N and E; part of Inyo Natl. Forest is on SW boundary. Indian reservations: Pyramid L. and Walker R. in W, Summit Lake in NW, part of Duck Valley on N boundary (W Idaho), South Fork in NE, part of Goshute on E boundary (Utah), Moap R. Indian Reservation in SE. Nev. has 16 cos.: CHURCHILL, CLARK, DOUGLAS, ELKO, ESMERALDA, EUREKA, HUMBOLDT, LANDER, LINCOLN, LYON, MINERAL, NYE, PERSHING, STOREY, WASHOE, and WHITE PINE; and 1 independent city, CARSON CITY, (ORMSBY CO. until 1969).

Nevada 1 (nuh-VAI-duh), county (□ 620 sq mi; 1990 pop. 10,101), SW Ark.; ⊙ Prescott; 33°40′N 93°17′W.

Bounded N by Little Missouri R. and drained by Bayou Dorcheat and Terre Rouge and Caney creeks; White Oak L. State Park and Poison Springs Wildlife Management Area on E boundary. Agr. (chicken); lumber milling, oil and gas. Formed 1871. **2** county (□ 958 sq mi/2,481 sq km; 1990 pop. 78,510), E Calif.; ⊙ Nevada City; 39°18′N 120°46′W. Narrow strip extending E across foothills to crest of Sierra Nevada, here crossed by Donner Pass, bounded by Nev. state on E. Highest point is Mt. Lola (9,160 ft/2,792 m). Rugged, wooded mt. country, with many beautiful lakes (e.g., Donner L.). Popular recreational region (winter sports in Donner Pass area; camping, hiking, hunting, fishing). Most of E ⅔ in Tahoe Natl. Forest. Bear R. forms part of S boundary in SW; Middle Yuba and Yuba rivers form NW boundary. At N end of Mother Lode, it has been a leading Calif. co. in gold production (peak years were 1850s–1950s; also mining of silver, quarrying of sand and gravel. Agr. (apples, nursery stock; cattle; timber). Drained by South Yuba R. Middle and South forks converge at Englebright Reservoir in NW corner to form Yuba R. Part of Beale Air Force Base in SW; Malakoff Diggins State Historic Park in NE; Empire Mine State Historic Park in W center. Grass Valley is largest city. Formed 1851.

Nevada 1 (nuh-VAI-duh), city (1990 pop. 6,009), ⊙ Story co., central Iowa, 30 mi/48 km NNE of Des Moines; 42°01′N 93°27′W. RR junction; livestock shipping. Mfg. (food processing, agr. equip., printing, consumer goods). Airfield here. Founded c.1853, inc. 1869. **2** city (1990 pop. 8,597), ⊙ Vernon co., SW Missouri near Marmaton R., 52 mi/84 km N of Joplin; 37°50′N 94°20′W. RR junction; ships grain, livestock. Mfg. (furniture, china plumbing fixtures, apparel, leather prods.); asphalt and coal mines, oil wells. Cottey Col. State Southwest Mo. Mental Health Center. Evacuated and burned by Union forces in 1863, during Civil War. Osage (Indian) Village State Historic Site and Camp Clark nearby. Founded 1855.

Nevada 1 (nuh-VA-duh), village (1990 pop. 849), Wyandot co., N central Ohio, 8 mi/13 km E of Upper Sandusky. Mfg. (food prods., bldg. materials). **2** village (1990 pop. 456), Collin co., N Texas, 30 mi/48 km ENE of Dallas; 33°02′N 96°22′W. Agr. area just beyond urban fringe of Dallas–Fort Worth area (cotton, sorghum; cattle, horses).

Nevada City, city (□ 1 sq mi/2.6 sq km; 1990 pop. 2,855), ⊙ Nevada co., E central Calif., 55 mi/89 km NE of Sacramento, and 5 mi/8 km NE of Grass Valley on Deer Creek , on W slope of the Sierra Nevada; 39°16′N 121°01′W. Elev. c.2,500 ft/762 m. Mfg. (broadcasting equip., winery). Agr. (apples, grapes, nursery stock; cattle; timber). Center of rich placer–hydraulic-mining area after 1850; lode gold is still produced. Hq. of Tahoe Natl. Forest (Forest to E). Recreational region. Empire Mine State Historic Park to SW; Malakoff Diggins State Historic Park to NE. Laid out 1849, inc. 1851.

Nevada Falls, Calif.: See YOSEMITE NATIONAL PARK.

Nevada, Sierra: see SIERRA NEVADA.

Nevadaville, village, Gilpin co., N central Colo., in Front Range, 35 mi/56 km W of Denver. Elev. c.9,150 ft/2,789 m. Former gold-mining camp, now ghost town. Nearby is Glory Hole, huge mining pit still worked for ore.

Nevado de Toluca National Park (ne-VAH-do dai to-LOO-kah) (□ 199 sq mi/515 sq km), in SW Mexico state, Mexico, 14 mi/22 km SW of the city of Toluca de Lerdo. This park is named for the volcano Toluca, or Xinantécatl (14,954 ft/4,558 m). This volcano forms part of the Transverse Volcanic Axis SW of the city of Toluca. The park is served by a paved road branching S from Mexico Highway 130.

Never Summer Mountains, range of Rocky Mts. in N Colo.; extend c.20 mi/32 km N-S along Continental Divide; forms part of W boundary of Rocky Mt. Natl. Park, part of Jackson Co. line, and Continental Divide. Prominent peaks in park and range include Mt. Cumulus (12,724 ft/3,878 m), Mt. Nimbus (12,730 ft/3,880 m), Mt. Cirrus (12,797 ft/3,901 m), Howard Mt.

(12,810 ft/3,904 m), and Mt. Richthofen (12,940 ft/3,944 m). Range sometimes included within Medicine Bow Mts. of Wyo. and Colo. Includes the dramatic rock points of Nokhu Crags in N (S part of Colorado State Forest).

Neversink River, c.65 mi/105 km long, SE N.Y.; rises in the Catskills W of Ashokan Reservoir; flows SW and S, paralleling W base of the Shawangunk range in lower course, to the Delaware at Port Jervis. In upper course (called Neversink Creek) is earth-fill Neversink Dam (2,800 ft/853 m long, 200 ft/61 m high; begun 1941), impounding Neversink Reservoir. A 5-mi/8-km water tunnel extends to Rondout Reservoir, which connects with Delaware Aqueduct.

Neville (NE-vil), village (1990 pop. 226), Clermont co., SW Ohio, 18 mi/29 km S of Batavia, and on Ohio R. (here forming Ky. state line).

Neville, township (1990 pop. 1,273), Allegheny co., W Pa., suburb 7 mi/11.3 km NW of Pittsburgh; 40°30′N 80°08′W. Township is constituted entirely of Neville Isl. in Ohio R. Mfg. (fabricated metal prods., polyester resins, chemicals, portland cement). Emsworth Lock and Dam here.

Nevis (NEE-vis), village (1990 pop. 375), Hubbard co., central Minn., 11 mi/18 km ENE of Park Rapids, at E end of Elbow L.; 46°57′N 94°50′W. Agr. (oats, barley, rye, beans, alfalfa; sheep). Mfg. (wood prods.). Eighth Crow Wing L. to E.

Nevis (NEE-vis), island (□ 36 sq mi/93 sq km; 1997 est. pop. 10,000), Federation of St. Kitts–Nevis, West Indies; 17°09′N 62°35′W. The island is 2 of 2 isls. making up the federation. Located 2 mi/3.2 km SE of St. Kitts, linked by ferry boat service at Charlestown, the isl.'s commercial center. Dominated by volcanic, cone-shaped Nevis Peak (3,232 ft/985 m), surrounded by rainforests and woodlands. Columbus used the Span. word for snow, "nieves," to name this isl. with cloud-shrouded peak. Alexander Hamilton b. here. Extensive damage in 1989 Hurricane Hugo. Former sugarcane estates have been converted to hotels; Canadian-based Four Seasons complex (opened in 1991) is 1st full-service resort. Sea isl. cotton is chief crop; coconuts, green lemons, and spices also grown.

New Aberdeen, coal-mining suburb of Glace Bay, NE N.S., Canada, on Cape Breton Isl.

New Albany, city (1990 pop. 36,322), ⊙ Floyd co., S Ind., near the falls of the Ohio R. opposite Louisville, Ky., and at the foot of the Knobstone Escarpment, which lies to the W; 38°18′N 85°50′W. The city was a ship-building center in the 19th cent., and the riverboats *Robert E. Lee* and *Eclipse* were built there. Mfg. (wood prods., apparel, electronic equip., chemicals, food prods., paper prods., transportation equip., sheet metal, furniture). Bridges link New Albany with Louisville. William Vaughn Moody lived in the city. Seat of Ind. Univ. Southeast. Laid out 1813, inc. 1819.

New Albany (AWL-buh-nee), town (1990 pop. 6,775), ⊙ Union co., N Miss., 19 mi/31 km NW of Tupelo, on Tallahatchie R; 34°29′N 89°01′W. RR junction. Trade center for agr. area (cotton; corn, soybeans; cattle; dairying) and mfg. (machinery, marble tops, asphalt and foam prods., apparel, printing and publishing, furniture, concrete). Holly Springs Natl. Forest to W. Settled c.1840.

New Albany 1 village (1990 pop. 60), Wilson co., SE Kansas, on Fall R., and 7 mi/11.3 km WNW of Fredonia; 37°34′N 95°55′W. Livestock raising, farming. **2** village (1990 pop. 1,621), Franklin co., central Ohio, 13 mi/21 km NE of Columbus. In agr. area.

New Albany (NOO AHL-buh-nee), borough (1990 pop. 306), Bradford co., NE Pa., 12 mi/19 km S of Towanda, on South Branch of Towando Creek; 41°36′N 76°26′W. Mfg. (feeds and supplements, machining). Agr. (apples, corn, hay; dairying). Hatch Mt. to N.

New Albin, town (1990 pop. 534), Allamakee co., extreme NE Iowa, on Minn. state line, 18 mi/29 km NNE of Waukon, near Mississippi and Upper Iowa rivers; 43°30′N 91°17′W. Lumber. Limestone quarries and Indian Fish Farm mounds to S.

New Alexandria, uninc. town, Fairfax co., NE Va., residential suburb, 2 mi/3.2 km S of Alexandria, and 9 mi/14.5 km S of Washington, D.C., on Potomac R. Woodrow Wilson Memorial Bridge to NE

New Alexandria, village (1990 pop. 257), Jefferson co., E Ohio, 6 mi/10 km SW of Steubenville, in coal-mining area.

New Alexandria (NOO A-leks-AN-dree-ah), borough (1990 pop. 571), Westmoreland co., SW central Pa., 9 mi/14.5 km NE of Greensburg, on Loyalhanna Creek; 40°23′N 79°25′W. Mfg. (concrete, pool tables); coal, timber. Agr. (corn, hay; livestock, dairying). Keystone State Park to SE.

New Almaden, village, Santa Clara co., W Calif., 9 mi/14.5 km SSE of downtown San Jose, on Guadalupe Creek. Quicksilver mines (since 1845).

New Amsterdam, town (1990 pop. 30), Harrison co., S Ind., on Ohio R., near mouth of Indian Creek, and 11 mi/18 km SW of Corydon; 38°06′N 86°17′W. In agr. area. Laid out 1815.

New Amsterdam, Du. settlement at the mouth of the Hudson R. and on the S end of Manhattan isl.; est. 1624. It was capital of the colony of New Netherland from 1626 to 1664, when it was captured by the British and renamed N.Y. city.

New Ashford, agr. town (1990 pop. 192), Berkshire co., NW Mass., 11 mi/18 km N of Pittsfield; 42°37′N 73°14′W. Recreation; ski resort.

New Athens 1 (AI-thens), village (1990 pop. 2,010), St. Clair co., SW Ill., on Kaskaskia R., and 17 mi/27 km SSE of Belleville; 38°19′N 89°52′W. Mfg. (stoves, enamelware); bituminous coal mines. Agr. (corn, wheat, fruit; dairy prods., livestock). Inc. 1869. **2** (A-thinz), village (1990 pop. 370), Harrison co., E Ohio, 6 mi/10 km SE of Cadiz, in coal-mining area.

New Auburn 1 village (1990 pop. 363), Sibley co., S Minn., 8 mi/12.9 km N of Gaylord, on W shore of High Island L.; 44°40′N 94°13′W. Livestock; grain, soybeans; dairying. **2** village (1990 pop. 485), Chippewa co., W central Wis., 26 mi/42 km N of Eau Claire; 45°12′N 91°34′W. Dairying; livestock raising. State fishery.

New Augusta (aw-GUHS-tuh), village (1990 pop. 668), ⊙ Perry co., SE Miss., 17 mi/27 km ESE of Hattiesburg, on Leaf R.; 31°11′N 89°01′W. In N edge of De Soto Natl. Forest. Agr. (cotton, corn; poultry); timber. Mfg. (telephone poles, pulpwood processing). Camp Shelby Natl. Guard base, to W.

New Baden (BAY-den), village (1990 pop. 2,602), in Clinton and St. Clair cos., SW Ill., 15 mi/24 km E of Belleville; 38°32′N 89°42′W. In agr. (corn, wheat, poultry; dairy prods.) and bituminous-coal–mining area. Inc. 1867.

New Baltimore, city (1990 pop. 5,798), Macomb and St. Clair cos., E Mich., 10 mi/16 km NE of Mt. Clemens, on Anchor Bay of L. St. Clair; 42°40′N 82°44′W. Satellite community of Detroit. Resort. Agr. (apples; dairy, poultry). Mfg. (thermoplastic molding, fabricated metal prods.). Inc. as village 1867, as city 1931.

New Baltimore, village (1990 pop. 960), Greene co., SE N.Y., on W bank of the Hudson, and 15 mi/24 km. S of Albany; 42°25′N 73°51′W.

New Baltimore, borough (1990 pop. 162), Somerset co., S Pa., 16 mi/26 km E of Somerset, on Raystown Branch Juniata R.; 39°59′N 78°46′W. Corn, hay, oats; dairying.

New Bavaria (buh-VE-ree-uh), village (1990 pop. 92), Henry co., NW Ohio, 13 mi/21 km S of Napoleon.

New Beaver (NOO-BEE-vuhr), borough (1990 pop. 1,736), Lawrence co., W Pa., 8 mi/12.9 km SSW of New Castle; 40°52′N 80°21′W. Agr. (dairying; corn, hay).

New Bedford, city (1990 pop. 99,922), ⊙ Bristol co., SE Mass., at the mouth of the Acushnet R., on Buzzard's Bay; 41°40′N 70°57′W. Formerly one of the world's greatest whaling ports, it has become a leading port for the fishing and scalloping industries. During the Revolution the harbor was a haven for Amer. privateers, prompting the British to invade and burn the town in 1778. The whaling industry boomed after the Revolution, reaching a peak in the 1850s. The 1st cotton-textile mill in the city dates from 1846, but the textile industry declined in the 1920s. Mfg. (apparel, textiles, electrical and electronic equip., rubber prods., medical supplies, prepared food, metal prods.). The Seamen's Bethel, described by Herman Melville in *Moby Dick*; the Bourne Whaling Mus.; the Old Dartmouth Historical Society; Friends' Acad. (1810); and the Swain School of Design are in New Bedford. The Free Public Lib. holds a large collection of material on whaling. A sizable Port.-speaking pop. is in the city. Settled 1640, set off from Dartmouth 1787, inc. as a city 1847.

New Berlin (BUHR-lin), city (1990 pop. 33,592), Waukesha co., SE Wis., a suburb 10 mi/16 km WSW of downtown Milwaukee; 42°58′N 88°07′W. It is largely residential. Mfg. (rubber prods., computer equip., printing, wire forms, medical equip., electrical and electronic equip., plastic molding, transportation equip.). Founded 1840, inc. 1959.

New Berlin 1 (BER-lin), village (1990 pop. 797), Sangamon co., central Ill., 15 mi/24 km WSW of Springfield; 39°43′N 89°54′W. Bituminous-coal mining. Agr. (corn, wheat, soybeans). **2** (BUHR-lin), village (□ 1 sq mi/2.6 sq km; 1990 pop. 1,220), Chenango co., central N.Y., on Unadilla R., and 36 mi/58 km S of Utica; 42°37′N 75°20′W. In dairying and farming area. Agr. (feed, lumber, wood prods.). Inc. 1819.

New Berlin (BUHR-lin), borough (1990 pop. 892), Union co., central Pa., 11 mi/18 km SW of Lewisburg, on Penns Creek; 40°52′N 76°59′W. Mfg. (machinery, apparel). Agr. (grain, soybeans; poultry, livestock, dairying). Shamokin Mt. ridge to N; Bald Eagle State Forest to W.

New Bern, city (1990 pop. 17,363), ⊙ Craven co., E N.C., 40 mi/64 km SE of Greenville on Nuese R., at mouth of Treat R.; 35°07′N 77°04′W. RR junction. Mfg. (lumber, textiles, pharmaceuticals, asphalt, fabricated metal prods., food processing, transportation equip., apparel, plastic prods.). Settled in 1710 by Swiss and German colonists under Baron Christopher de Graffenried and John Lawson, New Bern was the 2d town in N.C. and an early colonial capital; in 1774 it was the seat of the first provincial convention. Notable among the old bldgs. is the beautiful Tryon Palace (1767–1770), which was the colonial capitol and governor's mansion; it was badly burned in 1798 and was not reconstructed until the 1950s. In the Civil War the city was captured (March 1862) by Union forces under Gen. S. E. Burnside. Hoffman Forest to SW, Croatan Natl. Forest to S, Cherry Point Marine Corps Air Station to SE. Tryon Palace Historical Site and Garden. Christ Episcopal Church (1752). Civil War Mus.; New Bern Acad. (opened 1764). First Presbyterian Church (opened 1822). Inc. 1723.

New Bethlehem (BETH-luh-hem), borough (1990 pop. 1,151), Clarion co., W central Pa., 16 mi/26 km NE of Kittanning, on Redbank Creek; 41°00′N 79°19′W. Mfg. (wooden prods., feeds, refractories); bituminous coal, former oil and gas center. Agr. area (grain, soybeans, potatoes; livestock; dairying). Settled 1785, laid out 1840, inc. 1853.

New Bloomfield, Pa.: see BLOOMFIELD.

New Bloomington, village (1990 pop. 282), Marion co., central Ohio, 10 mi/16 km W of Marion. In agr. area.

New Boston, city (1990 pop. 620), Mercer co., NW Ill., on the Mississippi (ferry here), and 14 mi/23 km W of Aledo; 41°10′N 91°00′W. In agr. area.

New Boston 1 town (1990 pop. 3,214), Hillsborough co., S N.H., 11 mi/18 km W of Manchester; 42°58′N 71°41′W. Drained by South Branch Piscataquog R. Joe English Hill (1,240 ft/378 m) in S. Agr. (livestock, poultry; vegetables; dairying; timber). Mfg. (prefabricated bldgs., robotics lighting systems, casting molds). **2** town (1990 pop. 5,057), Bowie co., NE Texas, 22 mi/35 km W of Texarkana; 33°27′N 94°25′W. Trade center in timber; agr. area (cattle; dairying; wheat, rice; vegetables). Oil and gas. Mfg. (lumber, printing, concrete, fabricated metal prods.). State prison. In area settled in 1820s; town inc. 1910.

New Boston 1 village, Wayne co., SE Mich., uninc, suburb 23 mi/37 km SW of downtown Detroit, and immediately S of Romulus, on Huron R.; 42°09′N 83°24′W. Mfg. (concrete, steel, plastic prods.). Detroit Metropolitan Wayne County Airport to NE. Lower

Huron Metropark along river. **2** village (1990 pop. 2,717), Scioto co., S Ohio, on the Ohio, just NE of Portsmouth. Mfg. (steel, metal prods.). Founded 1891. **3** (BAWS-tuhn), uninc. village, Mahanoy township, Schuylkill co., E central Pa., 1 mi/1.6 km SSW of Mahanoy City; 40°47′N 76°09′W. Anthracite-coal region.

New Boston, Mass.: see SANDISFIELD.

New Braintree (BRAIN-tree), town (1990 pop. 881), Worcester co., central Mass., 16 mi/26 km WNW of Worcester; 42°19′N 72°08′W. In agr. and dairying area. State police acad.

New Braunfels, city (1990 pop. 22,334), ⊙ Comal co., S central Texas, 30 mi/48 km NE of San Antonio, on the Guadalupe R.; 29°41′N 98°07′W. Elev. 620 ft/189 m. The economy is largely based on diversified mfg. (portland cement, consumer goods, crushed limestone, furniture, leather prods.) and food processing, and agr. (cattle, sheep, goats, hogs, exotic animals; corn, wheat, sorghum); winery; stone, lime, sand and gravel. New Braunfels was founded (1845) by Prince Carl von Solms-Braunfels and settled by thousands of Ger. immigrants. It still retains many Germanic features. Local attractions include a historical mus.; Landa Park, which contains Comal springs, river, and lake; Natural Bridge Caverns to W; L. McQueeney to SE. Inc. 1847.

New Bremen (BREE-muhn), village (1990 pop. 2,558), Auglaize co., W Ohio, 13 mi/21 km SW of Wapakoneta; 40°26′N 84°23′W. Agr. (dairy prods.). Mfg. (rubber goods, machinery). Inc. 1833.

New Brighton, city (1990 pop. 22,207), Ramsey co., SE Minn., a suburb 6 mi/9.7 km NE of Minneapolis, and 9 mi/14.5 km NW of St. Paul; 45°04′N 93°12′W. Drained by Rice Creek. RR junction. Mfg. (metal prods., machinery, leather, primary metals, printing and publishing, machining). A theological seminary is in New Brighton. Long L. in N. Inc. 1891.

New Brighton (BREI-tuhn), borough (1990 pop. 6,854), Beaver co., W Pa., 2 mi/3.2 km SSE of Beaver Falls, on Beaver R. (bridged); 40°44′N 80°18′W. Mfg. (chemicals, primary metals, fabricated metal prods., machinery, plastic prods.). Agr. (corn, hay; livestock; dairying). Merrick Art Gall. Lapic Winery to E. Blockhouse erected here 1789. Settled c.1801, inc. 1838.

New Brighton, section of Staten Isl. borough of N.Y. city, SE N.Y., on N Staten Isl., at junction of Kill Van Kull and Upper N.Y. Bay; 40°36′N 74°06′W. Residential, industrial. Sailors' Snug Harbor, a home for retired seamen, is nearby.

New Britain, industrial city (1990 pop. 75,491), Hartford co., central Conn.; 41°40′N 72°47′W. The tin shops and brassworks in the city were established in the 18th cent. New Britain became famous as the "Hardware City" because of its tool and household-hardware industry, which remains economically important. Central Conn. State Univ. is here. Of interest are the city hall (1884), a park designed by Frederick Law Olmsted in the center of the city, and a mus. of Amer. Art. Elihu Burritt b. here. Settled c.1686, inc. 1871.

New Britain (BRI-tuhn), borough (1990 pop. 2,174), Bucks co., SE Pa., residential suburb 3 mi/4.8 km WSW of Doylestown and 23 mi/37 km N of downtown Philadelphia; 40°17′N 75°10′W. Mfg. (concrete prods., rubber prods.). Agr. (grain, soybeans, apples; livestock, poultry, dairying). L. Galena reservoir to N; Peace Valley Winery to N. .

New Brockton, town (1990 pop. 1,184), Coffee co., SE Ala., 9 mi/14.5 km E of Elba; 31°22′N 85°55′W. Woodworking.

New Brookland, S.C.: see WEST COLUMBIA.

New Brunswick, province (□ 28,345 sq mi/73,414 sq km; 1991 pop. 723,900), E Canada; ⊙ FREDERICTON, 3d-largest city; 46°30′N 66°45′W. The largest city is SAINT JOHN and the 2d-largest is MONCTON. One of the Maritime Provinces, N.B. is bounded on the N by Chaleur Bay and Que. prov.; on the E by the Gulf of St. Lawrence, Northumberland Strait, and N.S.; on the S by the Bay of Fundy; and on the W by Maine. It is connected to the prov. of P.E.I. by a bridge (completed 1997) across Northumberland Strait at Cape Tormentine. Its irregular coastline provides excellent facilities

for fishing and shipping enterprises. Rivers cross the rolling countryside; they were the 1st means of transportation and are still important arteries of travel and commerce. The largest river, the St. John, crosses the prov. from NW to SE, and the Miramichi R. flows NE and drains the central lowlands. Most of the roads follow the river banks. Dairying thrives on fine pasturage, and the major crops are potatoes, hay, clover, oats, berries, and fruit. A careful conservation program maintains a supply of 2d-growth hardwoods and softwoods; forests cover about 90% of the total area, and lumbering is N.B.'s most important industry. Great quantities of pulpwood and paper are produced. Mfg. has greatly expanded since World War II; in addition to wood items and pulp and paper, prods. include food and beverages, ships, chemicals, refined oil, and shoes. Industry is generally run by hydroelectric power, and fuel resources include coal and much untapped water power, which is being developed. There is a nuclear reactor at Point Lepreau. Mining is an important industry, with zinc, silver, and lead the most important minerals. Other minerals include copper, bismuth, cadmium, gold, antimony, potash, oil, and natural gas. N.B.'s fisheries, even with periodic slumps in industry, are among the most valuable in Canada, with a variety of freshwater and saltwater fish (cod, salmon, herring, and sardines) as well as shellfish (lobsters, oysters, and clams). Trade flows in and out of the ports of St. John and Moncton, facilitated by RR connections throughout the prov., E to N.S. and W to Que. Tourism is one of N.B.'s most important industries. Its forests are still filled with bear, deer, and moose, and the rivers abound in trout and salmon, although overfishing and acid wastes from paper mills have reduced the salmon pop. Easy accessibility from the U.S. via I-95 has made Woodstock the gateway to the prov. Summer residences are concentrated around Passamaquoddy Bay. Natural attractions include the Grand Falls on the upper reaches of the St. John as well as the spectacular Fundy tides — the highest in the world, sometimes surging to over 50 ft/15 m. The tides in turn cause the Reversing Falls at St. John and the "Bore," a twice-daily tidal wave coming up the Petitcodiac R. They have also sculpted the famous Hopewell Rocks, another tourist attraction. N.B.'s 1st inhabitants were the Micmacs, a Native Amer. people whose settlements stretched along the coast from N.S. and P.E.I. to the S Gaspé Peninsula. The 1st European said to have sailed along the N.B. coast was a Port. navigator, Estevão Gomes (1525), although there is evidence of Basque fishermen at an earlier date. Jacques Cartier landed at Point Escuminac in 1534 and skirted the shores of Miramichi Bay. The 1st Eur. settlement was made in 1604 at the mouth of the St. Croix R. by Champlain and the sieur de Monts. During this period, while France and England made conflicting territorial claims, the present prov. of N.S. and the coast of N.B. were considered 1 region, called ACADIA by the French and N.S. by the British. Br. control of this region was confirmed by the Peace of Utrecht (1713–1714). Doubting the loyalty of the Acadians, the British expelled them in 1755, although many fled into the interior, which was still effectively controlled by the French. Others sought refuge in the 13 Amer. colonies or returned to France. (Today about 35% of the people of N.B. are Acadians.) Great Britain gained possession of the rest of N.B. when it gained all of Canada after the Fr. and Indian Wars. When the pop. of N.B. was increased by many thousands of Loyalists who fled New England after the Amer. Revolution, that area was organized (1784) into a separate colony. As trees were cut down for shipbuilding, the land was cleared for farming. By the middle of the 19th cent. lumbering and farming were extending into the interior, and St. John was a busy port and shipbuilding town. Dissatisfaction with the arbitrary rule of the provincial govt. resulted in the achievement of responsible (or cabinet) govt. in 1849. In 1867, under the Br. North Amer. Act, federation with the other provs. into the dominion of Canada was somewhat reluctantly accepted. N.B. sends 10 senators (appointed) and 10 representatives (elected) to the natl.

parliament. The prov.'s 4 univs. are Univ. of N.B., Université du Moncton, Mt. Allison Univ., and St. Thomas Univ.

New Brunswick, city (1990 pop. 41,711), ⊙ Middlesex co., central N.J., on the Raritan R.; 40°29′N 74°27′W. Originally developed as a commercial center (esp. for collecting and shipping grain), New Brunswick manufactures pharmaceuticals, electrical equip., transportation equip., and medical and surgical supplies. Hq. for large health-care prods. provider. The city is the seat of Rutgers Univ. and New Brunswick Theological Seminary. Washington, retreating from N.Y., stayed a week in New Brunswick in 1776. Joyce Kilmer b. here; his birthplace is an Amer. Legion post. Adjoining New Brunswick was Camp Kilmer, a major army base during World War II and the Korean War, and now the site for part of Rutgers Univ. campus. Settled 1681, inc. as a city 1784.

New Buffalo, town (1990 pop. 2,317), Berrien co., extreme SW Mich., 8 mi/12.9 km NE of Michigan City, Ind., on L. Michigan; 41°47′N 86°45′W. In orchard and farm area (fruits, vegetables). Mfg. (steel castings, plastic prods., air compressors); resorts. RR junction to NE. Settled 1835, inc. 1936.

New Buffalo (BUH-fah-lo), borough (1990 pop. 145), Perry co., central Pa., 14 mi/23 km NNW of Harrisburg, on Susquehanna R.; 40°27′N 76°58′W. Livestock, dairying.

New Bullards Bar Dam, Calif.: see YUBA RIVER.

New Burnside, village (1990 pop. 259), Johnson co., S Ill., 16 mi/26 km NE of Vienna; 37°34′N 88°46′W. Surrounded by Shawnee Natl. Forest.

New Butler, Wis.: see BUTLER.

New Cambria (KAIM-bree-yuh), town (1990 pop. 223), Macon co., N central Mo., near Chariton R., 15 mi/24 km W of Macon; 39°46′N 92°45′W. Agr.

New Cambria (KAIM-bree-uh), village (1990 pop. 152), Saline co., central Kansas, on Saline R. near its mouth on Smoky Hill R., and 6 mi/9.7 km ENE of Salina; 38°52′N 97°30′W. Wheat; livestock.

New Canaan, town (1990 pop. 17,864), Fairfield co., SW Conn.; 41°09′N 73°30′W. It is mainly a residential town, with specialty shops and small office bldgs. Silvermine Col. of Art is located in New Canaan. Settled c.1700, inc. 1801.

New Canada, plantation (1990 pop. 253), Aroostook co., NE Maine, on Fish R., and 42 mi/68 km NW of Presque Isle; 47°07′N 68°30′W. Hunting, fishing.

New Caney, uninc. town (1990 pop. 2,771), Montgomery co., SE Texas, 30 mi/48 km NNE of Houston. Agr. area on outer fringe of Houston urbanized area. Mfg. (machinery). L. Houston State Park to SE.

New Canton, town (1990 pop. 405), Pike co., W Ill., near the Mississippi, 16 mi/26 km W of Pittsfield; 39°38′N 91°05′W. In agr. area.

New Carlisle, city (1990 pop. 6,049), Clark co., W central Ohio, 12 mi/19 km W of Springfield, and on small Honey Creek; 39°57′N 84°01′W. In agr. area; food prods. Founded 1810.

New Carlisle, town (1990 pop. 1,446), St. Joseph co., N Ind., 14 mi/23 km W of South Bend; 41°42′N 86°31′W. In agr. area. Mfg. (animal by-products, construction materials, snow melting systems, steel prods., animal feed). Laid out 1835.

New Carlisle, village (1991 pop. 1,568), ⊙ Bonaventure co., E Que., Canada, on SE Gaspé Peninsula, on N side of entrance of Chaleur Bay, 50 mi/80 km E of Dalhousie; 48°00′N 65°20′W. Market center in lumbering, dairying region; resort.

New Carrollton, city (1990 pop. 12,002), Prince Georges co., central Md., 9 mi/14.5 km NE of Washington, D.C.; 38°58′N 76°53′W. A rapidly growing suburb of Washington, it was named Carrollton by the developer, Albert Turner after Charles Carroll of Carrollton. When a post office was opened in 1965, mail was misdirected to Carrollton, a small rural village in Carroll co., which had first claim on the name. The growing suburb became New Carrollton. A major light RR terminal for the D.C. subway system is located here. Inc. in 1953.

New Castle, county (□ 493 sq mi/1,277 sq km; 1990 pop.

441,946), N Del.; ⊙ WILMINGTON, state's largest city and main commercial and industrial center; 39°34′N 75°38′W. Bounded N by Pa. state line, W by Md. state line, S in part by Smyrna R., E by Delaware R. (New Jersey state line). Highest point in Del. (442 ft/135 m; unnamed) on Pa. state line 6 mi/9.7 km N of Wilmington. Agr. (dairy prods., poultry, livestock; corn, wheat); shipping at Wilmington. Crossed E-W at center by Chesapeake and Delaware Canal, part of Intracoastal Waterway; drained by Christina R., and Brandywine, Red Clay, and White Clay creeks. Highly urbanized in N, especially NE around Wilmington; continuation of Philadelphia metropolitan area, to NE. Smallest of Delaware's 3 cos. Silver Run and Augustine Wildlife Area in E; Canal Natl. Wildlife Refuge follows Chesapeake and Delaware Canal, at center; Brandywine Creek, Bellevue, and Fox Point state parks in NE; White Clay State Park in NW; Lums Pond State Park in W center, N of Canal; Fort Delaware and Fort Dupont state parks in E; 2 small sects. of Del., including Finn's Point, are on the New Jersey side of Delaware R. Univ. of Del. is at Newark. Formed 1672.

New Castle 1 city (1990 pop. 17,753), ⊙ Henry co., E Ind., 18 mi/29 km S of Muncie; 39°55′N 85°21′W. It is the trade center of an agr. and farm region. Mfg. (transportation equip., feed, steel prods., rubber prods.; food prods., construction materials, machinery, pharmaceuticals). The city has a number of prehistoric Native Amer. mounds. Wilbur Wright's birthplace is to the E. Laid out 1823, inc. 1839. **2** city (1990 pop. 28,334), ⊙ Lawrence co., W Pa., 40 mi/64 km NNW of Pittsburgh, at the junction of the Shenango R. and Neshannock Creek; 41°00′N 80°20′W. Shenango R. joins Mahoning R. 3 mi/4.8 km SW of city to form Beaver R. Fertile farm area (apples, soybeans, grain; livestock, dairying). Coal, limestone, and clay deposits found in the region contribute to the city's economy. Mfg. (fabricated metal prods., plastic prods., food prods., machinery, transportation equip., printing and publishing, consumer goods). The Hoyt Inst. of Fine Arts; County Historical Society; New Castle Municipal Airport to NW; McConnells Mill State Park to SE, including Hells Hollow Falls and McConnells Mill. Inc. 1825.

New Castle 1 town (1990 pop. 4,837), New Castle co., N Del., 5 mi/8 km S of Wilmington, on the Delaware R., opposite Pennsville, N.J.; 39°40′N 75°34′W. RR junction. mfg. (mineral prods., metal prods., beverages and food prods., signs, paper prods., gypsum prods., office machines); sawmill. Peter Stuyvesant built a Du. fort on the site, and the settlement was called Niew Amstel until it was renamed in 1664. The state of Del. was formed at a convention in New Castle on Sept. 21, 1776, and for a year the city served as state capital. The Immanuel Church (1710) is a historic landmark. Other colonial bldgs. are the Old Dutch House (dating from the late 1600s), the New Castle Court House (1732), and Amstel House Mus. Wilmington Col. (4-year) is here. Delaware Memorial Bridge (Delaware R.) 3 mi/4.8 km to NE. New Castle County Airport to NW. Fort Delaware State Park, on Pea Patch Isl., 5 mi/8 km to S. Colonial architecture and cobblestone streets make the town an important tourist destination. **2** town (1990 pop. 893), ⊙ Henry co., N Ky., 23 mi/37 km NW of Frankfort; 38°25′N 85°10′W. In Bluegrass agr. area. Drennon Springs, on Drennon Creek to E, site of annual storytelling festival (Oct.). Est. 1817. **3** town (1990 pop. 840), Rockingham co., SE N.H., on small isl. (□ .75 sq mi/1.9 sq km) in Portsmouth harbor; bridged to mainland, 12 mi/19 km SE of Dover; 43°03′N 70°43′W. Former summer resort now residential suburb of Portsmouth. Settlement here originally called Great Isl., was pre-Revolutionary governor's seat; here are ruins of Fort Constitution (then Castle William and Mary), seized by colonists in 1774. Chartered 1693. **4** town (1990 pop. 4,214), McClain co., central Okla., suburb 18 mi/29 km SSW of downtown Oklahoma City, on Canadian R. Agr. area; mfg. (consumer goods, computer equip.). **5** town (1990 pop. 152), ⊙ Craig co., SW Va., in Allegheny Mts., 17 mi/27 km NNW of Roanoke, on Craig Creek, in Jefferson Natl. Forest; 37°30′N

80°06′W. Mfg. (sand processing, apparel). Agr. (grain; cattle, sheep).

New Castle, village (1990 pop. 679), Garfield co., W Colo., on Colorado R., and 11 mi/18 km W of Glenwood Springs; 39°35′N 107°31′W. Elev. c.5,552 ft/1,692 m. In irrigated agr. region (cattle; oats, hay). Mfg. (wood roof trusses). Coal deposits. Part of White River Natl. Forest to N and S. Harvey Gap, Rifle Gap, and Rifle Falls state parks to NW.

New Castle Northwest (NOO KA-suhl NORTH-west), uninc. town (1990 pop. 1,515), Lawrence co., W Pa., residential suburb 2 mi/3.2 km NW of New Castle; 41°01′N 80°21′W.

New Centerville (NOO SEN-tuhr-vil), borough (1990 pop. 211), Somerset co., SW Pa., 8 mi/12.9 km SW of Somerset; 39°56′N 79°11′W. Agr. (corn, oats; livestock, dairying). Laurel Hill State Park to NW.

New Chicago, town (1990 pop. 2,066), Lake co., extreme NW Ind., SE of Gary, and N of Hobart; 41°34′N 87°16′W. In industrial area.

New City, suburb (□ 16 sq mi/41 sq km; 1990 pop. 33,673) of N.Y. city, ⊙ Rockland co., SE N.Y., 26 mi/42 km N of midtown Manhattan; 41°08′N 73°58′W. It is primarily residential.

New Cold Harbor, Va.: see COLD HARBOR.

New Columbia (NOO kuh-LUHM-bee-ah), uninc. village, Union co., E central Pa., 2 mi/3.2 km NNW of Milton, on West Branch of Susquehanna R. (bridged to N); 41°02′N 76°52′W. Mfg. (construction materials). Agr. (dairying). Parts of Bald Eagle and Tiadaghton state forests to NW; Allenwood Federal Prison Camp to NW.

New Columbus (ko-LUHM-buhs), uninc. village, Nesquehoning borough, Carbon co., E Pa., 1 mi/1.6 km NW of Nesquehoning town center; 40°52′N 75°50′W.

New Columbus (ko-LUHM-buhs), borough (1990 pop. 228), Luzerne co., NE central Pa., 22 mi/35 km WSW of Wilkes-Barre; 41°10′N 76°17′W. Drained by Pine Creek. Agr. (potatoes, corn, hay; livestock; dairying).

New Concord (KAHNG-kuhrd), village (1990 pop. 2,086), Muskingum co., central Ohio, 15 mi/24 km ENE of Zanesville; 39°59′N 81°44′W. In agr. area. Seat of Muskingum Col. William Rainey Harper b. here. Birthplace of John Glenn, 1st American to orbit earth (1962). Founded c.1827.

New Croton Dam and Aqueduct, SE N.Y., water supply system for N.Y. city and Westchester and Putnam cos.; 41°14′N 73°52′W. A complex, integrated system of 12 dams and reservoirs, watersheds, and above- and underground tunnels, it was constructed to supplement and eventually replace the Old Croton Dam and Aqueduct. The project began in 1885, and by 1890 additional water was being successfully delivered to the Central Park Reservoir. New Croton Dam, begun in 1892 at a site 4 mi/6.4 km downstream from Old Croton Dam, was finished in 1907. When the new system began operations, city consumption was able to rise from 102 million gal/386.1 million liters per day to 170 million gal/643.5 million liters. Today it supplies N.Y. city (esp. Manhattan's W Side and parts of the Bronx and Westchester co.) with 300 million gal/1,135,590,000 liters of water per day, although both quality and quantity are decreasing with the urbanization of the system's watersheds. But the system still does not adequately meet N.Y. city's water demands; the city's water supply is augmented with water from the Catskills and the Delaware R., and the city continues to look for supplementary water sources.

New Cumberland, town (1990 pop. 1,363), ⊙ Hancock co., N W.Va., in Northern Panhandle, 7 mi/11.3 km N of Weirton, on the Ohio R. (Ohio state line); 40°30′N 80°36′W. Light mfg. Agr. (grain, nursery crops); fruit farms in region. Tomlinson Run State Park to N; New Cumberland Lock and Dam (Ohio R.) are here. Plotted 1839.

New Cumberland (NOO KUHM-buhr-luhnd), borough (1990 pop. 7,665), Cumberland co., S central Pa., residential suburb 2 mi/3.2 km S of downtown Harrisburg, on Susquehanna R. (bridged to S end of Harrisburg), at mouth of Yellow Breeches Creek; 40°13′N

76°52′W. Mfg. (machinery, electronics assembly, diverse light mfg.). Defense Distribution Center (depot) and Central City Airport to SE. Camp Hill State Correctional Inst. to SW. Laid out c.1810, inc. 1831.

New Deal, village (1990 pop. 521), Lubbock co., NW Texas, 10 mi/16 km N of Lubbock, on Blackwater Draw creek; 33°43′N 101°50′W. Agr. area (cotton, wheat, sunflowers; cattle, sheep). Oil and natural gas.

New Denver, village (1991 pop. 571), SE B.C., Canada, on E side of Slocan Lake, 35 mi/56 km N of Nelson; 49°59′N 117°22′W. Highway junction. Tourism, ski resort.

New Dorp, section of Staten Isl. borough of N.Y. city, SE N.Y., on E central Staten Isl.; 40°34′N 74°06′W. Residential; some mfg.

New Dorp Beach, N.Y.: see SOUTH BEACH.

New Douglas, village (1990 pop. 387), Madison co., SW Ill., 20 mi/32 km NE of Edwardsville; 38°58′N 89°40′W. In agr. area (corn, wheat; dairy prods.; poultry, livestock).

New Dundee (duhn-DEE), village, S Ont., Canada, 8 mi/13 km SSW of Kitchener. Dairying, mixed farming.

New Durham, town (1990 pop. 1,974), Strafford co., E central N.H., 13 mi/21 km NW of Rochester; 43°28′N 71°08′W. Drained by Merrymeeting and Ela rivers. Agr. (cattle; dairying; nursery crops; timber). Mfg. (wire brushes). Merrymeeting L. and Powder Mill Fish Hatchery in NW.

New Eagle (EE-guhl), borough (1990 pop. 2,172), Washington co., SW Pa., 15 mi/24 km S of Pittsburgh, and 1 mi/1.6 km W of Monongahela, on Monongahela R.; 40°12′N 79°57′W. Mfg. (vermiculite and perlite, electronic prods.). Agr. (corn, hay; livestock; dairying). Inc. 1912.

New Echota Marker National Memorial (□ 0.92 acres/0.37 ha), near Calhoun, NW Ga.; site of the last capital of the Cherokee tribe in Ga. Native Amer. newspaper was printed here in syllabary devised by Sequoyah. Central site of Cherokee removal connected with the Trail of Tears, the march that led to the Cherokee's resettlement in Oklahoma. Est. 1930.

New Effington, village (1990 pop. 219), Roberts co., NE S.Dak., 25 mi/40 km NNE of Sisseton, in Lake Traverse (Sisseton Wahpeton) Indian Reservation; 45°51′N 96°55′W. Livestock; corn, wheat.

New Egypt, village (1990 pop. 2,327), Ocean co., central N.J., on Crosswicks Creek, and 17 mi/27 km SE of Trenton; 40°03′N 74°31′W. Agr., mfg. (apparel, canned cranberries).

New Ellenton, town (1990 pop. 2,515), Aiken co., W S.C., 10 mi/16 km S of Aiken; 33°25′N 81°41′W. Grew with the establishment of the Department of Energy's Savannah R. Nuclear Site (S). Agr. (livestock, poultry; grain, soybeans, cotton, peanuts, peaches).

New England, name applied to the region comprising 6 states of the NE U.S.— MAINE, NEW HAMPSHIRE, VERMONT, MASSACHUSETTS, RHODE ISLAND, and CONNECTICUT. The region is thought to have been so named by Capt. John Smith because of its resemblance to the Eng. coast (another source has it that Prince Charles, afterward Charles I, inserted the name on Smith's map of the country). Topographically it is partly delineated from the rest of the nation by the Appalachian Mts. on the W. From the Green Mts., the White Mts., and the Berkshire Hills, the land slopes gradually toward the Atlantic Ocean. Many short, swift rivers furnish water power. The Connecticut R. is the region's longest river. Because of the generally poor soil, agr. was never a major part of the region's economy. However, excellent harbors and nearby shallow banks teeming with fish made New England a fishing and commercial center. Shipbuilding was important until the end (mid-1800s) of the era of wooden ships. During the colonial period the region carried on a more extensive foreign commerce than the other Br. colonies and was therefore more affected by the passage of the Br. Navigation Acts. New England was the major center of the events leading up to the Amer. Revolution, particularly after 1765, and was the scene of the opening Revolutionary engagements. The return of peace necessitated a reorganization of commerce, with the result that connections were made with the Amer. NW and China. The War of 1812 had an adverse effect on the region's trade, and opposition to the war was so great that New England threatened secession. After the war the growth of mfg. (especially of cotton textiles) was rapid, and the region became highly industrialized. A large part of the great migration to the Old Northwest Territory originated here. Agr. dwindled with the growth of the West. Prior to the Civil War, this region furnished many social and humanitarian leaders and movements. New England has also long been a leading literary and educational center of the country. After World War II the character of New England industry changed. Traditional industries (e.g., shoe and textile) have been superseded by more modern industries such as electronics. Tourism, long a source of income for the region, remains important, especially the ski industry in winter. There is also stone quarrying, dairying, and potato farming. Boston has long been the chief urban center of New England; corporate activity, however, has sprung up in many of the smaller cities and suburbs. The area is abundant in educational institutions, having some of the foremost universities in the U.S.

New England, town (1990 pop. 663), Hettinger co., SW N.Dak., 24 mi/39 km S of Dickinson, and on Cannonball R.; 46°32′N 102°52′W.

New England Seamount Chain, chain of submarine volcanic mountains (6,562 ft/2,000 m–9,843 ft/3,000 m), SE of Georges Bank, bet. 36°N and 40°N, along the NE edge of the Bermuda Rise plateau in the NW Atlantic Basin, and extending to a distance of c.600 mi/966 km.

New Era, village (1990 pop. 520), Oceana co., W Mich., 9 mi/14.5 km S of Hart; 43°33′N 86°20′W. Fruit and vegetable canning.

New Fairfield, town (1990 pop. 12,911), Fairfield co., SW Conn., bet. N.Y. state line and L. Candlewood, 6 mi/9.7 km N of Danbury; 41°28′N 73°29′W. State park, state forest here; resorts. Mfg. (machine tools, electrical parts). Inc. 1740.

New Florence, town (1990 pop. 801), Montgomery co., E central Mo., 5 mi/8 km SSE of Montgomery City; 38°54′N 91°27′W. Agr. (corn, wheat, soybeans; hogs). Mfg. (barrel staves, wine, champagne); limestone quarries.

New Florence, borough (1990 pop. 854), Westmoreland co., SW central Pa., 10 mi/16 km WNW of Johnstown, on Conemaugh R. (bridged); 40°22′N 79°04′W. Agr. (soybeans, grain; livestock, dairying). Laurel Bridge State Park to SE.

New Fort Hamilton, village, W Alaska, on arm of Yukon R. delta, 80 mi/129 km SW of St. Michael. Sometimes called New Hamilton. Hamilton village 10 mi/16 km N.

New France: see CANADA.

New Franklin, city (1990 pop. 1,107), Howard co., central Mo., just N of Boonville across the Missouri; 39°01′N 92°44′W. Agr. (corn, apples, wheat, soybeans). Mfg. (concrete); lumber; limestone quarries. Laid out 1828 after the town of Franklin (est. 1816) was washed away by the Missouri R. The Santa Fe Trail began at Franklin–New Franklin in the 1820s. Boonslick State Park to NW.

New Freedom (FREE-duhm), borough (1990 pop. 2,920), York co., S Pa., 16 mi/26 km S of York on Md. state line; 39°44′N 76°42′W. RR junction. Mfg. (lumber, machinery, plastic molds). Agr. (apples, soybeans, grain; poultry, livestock, dairying); timber. Inc. 1879.

New Galilee, borough (1990 pop. 500), Beaver co., W Pa., 6 mi/9.7 km WSW of Ellwood City, on North Fork of Little Beaver Creek; 40°49′N 80°24′W. Mfg. (cement prods., candy); agr. (corn, hay, alfalfa; livestock; dairying).

New Germany, village, W N.S., Canada, on Lahave R., 15 mi/24 km N of Bridgewater.

New Germany 1 village, Garrett co., W Md., in the Alleghenies 18 mi/29 km W of Cumberland. Hq. for surrounding Savage R. State Forest. **2** village (1990 pop. 353), Carver co., S central Minn., 36 mi/58 km W of Minneapolis; 44°52′N 93°58′W. Grain, soybeans, alfalfa; livestock; dairying; light mfg.

New Germany State Park, within Savage R. State Forest, Garrett co., W Md., in the Alleghenies 18 mi/29 km W of Cumberland. One of 2 state parks in the forest (the other being Big Run). The stately virgin pines here, which the Natl. Road ran through, reminded some of cathedrals. Most pioneers, fearful of Indian attack, called them "Shades of Death."

New Glarus (GLAIR-us), town (1990 pop. 1,899), Green co., S Wis., on branch of Sugar R., 23 mi/37 km SW of Madison; 42°48′N 89°37′W. In dairying region. Mfg. (meat prods.); cheese center; makes Swiss embroidery. Annual Swiss festival held here; state trail. Swiss historical village. N terminus of Sugar R. State Trail. Founded by Swiss in 1845, inc. 1901.

New Glasgow, town (1991 pop. 4,134), N N.S., Canada, on East R.; 45°35′N 62°38′W. Industrial town in a coal region. Mfg. includes steel prods. and machinery; large pulp mill nearby.

New Gloucester (GLAHS-tuhr), rural town (1990 pop. 3,916), Cumberland co., SW Maine, 20 mi/32 km N of Portland; 43°57′N 70°17′W. In it is Sabbathday L. village, Shaker community settled 1793 near Sabbathday L., the last living Shaker community in the U.S. (mus., visitor center). Includes village of Upper Gloucester. Settled c.1743, inc. 1794.

New Goshen, village (1990 pop. 500), Vigo co., W Ind., 9 mi/14.5 km NNW of Terre Haute, bet. Wabash R. and Ill. Boundary. Corn, soybeans; cattle. Bituminous coal area, surface mines. Laid out 1853.

New Grand Chain, village (1990 pop. 273), Pulaski co., S Ill., 17 mi/27 km NW of Metropolis, near Ohio R.; 37°15′N 89°01′W. Grain, sorghum. Lock and Dam No. 53 to S. Shawnee Community Col. to NW.

New Hamburg (HAM-buhrg), village, S Ont., Canada, on Nith R., 12 mi/19 km WSW of Kitchener; 43°23′N 80°42′W. Suburb of Kichener. Within Regional Municipality of Waterloo (formerly Waterloo co.). Mfg. (furniture); mixed farming; dairying; tobacco, peanuts.

New Hamburg, uninc. community, Scott co., SE Mo., 3 mi/4.8 km NW of Benton. Agr.

New Hamilton, Alaska: see NEW FORT HAMILTON.

New Hampshire, state (□ 9,350 sq mi/24,219 sq km; 1995 est. pop. 1,148,253), NE U.S., in New England; 43°31′N 71°25′W; ⊙ CONCORD. One of the 13 original U.S. states and former Eng. colony. It is bounded on the N by Canada (Que. prov.), on the E by Maine and the Atlantic Ocean, on the S by Mass., and on the W by the Connecticut R. (Vt. state line). The largest city is MANCHESTER, followed by NASHUA; Concord is 3d. Other important cities are ROCHESTER, DOVER, KEENE, and PORTSMOUTH. The continental ice sheet once covered the entire state and, in receding, scraped the mts. and eroded the intervening upland areas, and rerouted the water courses into precipitous streams and beautiful lakes. Across the N central part of the state the residual White Mts. of the Appalachian chain form ranges abruptly broken by passes (locally referred to as notches) through their rocky walls. Bet. the Carter-Moriah Range and the Presidential Range in the E, the Ellis R. falls 80 ft/24 m on the side of Pinkham Notch. W of the Presidential Range (which includes Mt. Washington, highest peak in NE U.S. at 6,288 ft/1,917 m), the cascading courses of the Ammonoosuc and Saco rivers divide it from the Franconia Mts. at Crawford Notch. To the SW Franconia Notch contains the famous Old Man of the Mt. (rock profile resembling face), beneath which the Pemigewasset tumbles on its way to join the Merrimack. The northernmost gap, Dixville Notch, is surrounded by rocky pinnacles that look down upon a wild, fir-covered country abounding in lakes and streams. S of the mts. the lake and upland area is frequently interrupted by isolated peaks called "monadnocks," including Mt. Monadnock in SW. The weather changes rapidly, and occasional high winds and violent storms roar through the narrow valleys and sweep over the rocky summits, especially at Mt. Washington, which has clocked winds of 231 mph/372 km per hour.

Annual precipitation ranges from 30 in/76 cm to 70 in/180 cm, with snowfall mounting to 8 ft/2.4 m in the mt. regions. The S and coastal areas experience less snowfall than other parts, moderated by the ocean. Agr. is hampered by the mountainous topography and by extensive areas of unfertile and stony soil, but along the seacoast and along the valleys of the Merrimack and Connecticut R. there is good farmland. The upper Connecticut valley (known as "Coos country") is pleasantly pastoral. Agr. commodities include dairy prods., apples, eggs; greenhouse prods.; cattle, poultry. Agr. reached its peak in the 1880s and vast areas of farmland were abandoned in the cent. that followed. Today less than 5% of N.H.'s land is in farms and some of the best land is being taken for residential and industrial development. Since the late 1800s mfg. has been predominant. Based upon the percentage of pop. employed by industry, N.H. is one of the most industrialized states in the union. The textile mills and factories producing leather goods (such as shoes and boots), which once lined the state's fast-moving rivers, have moved to SE states and given way to high-technology firms, many of them migrating from the Boston area and its high tax rates. Moreover, many of the residents of S N.H. commute to the high-tech firms located in the Boston metropolitan area. Electrical and other machinery, as well as primary metals, fabricated metals, and plastics are also manufactured. Lumbering has been important since the 1st sawmill was built on the Salmon Falls R. in 1631. Most of the timber cut is for use in paper production, which is still important. The state's only port, Portsmouth, is situated on the estuary of the Piscataqua R. and serves as a commercial center in the state. Although N.H. has long been known as the Granite State, its large deposits of granite — used for bldg. as early as 1623 — are no longer extensively quarried, though some quarrying is still done around Concord. The use of steel and concrete in modern construction has greatly decreased the granite market. Today sand and gravel, stone, and clays are the state's leading minerals. Nevertheless, mineral production remains a minor factor in the N.H. economy. The year-round tourist trade is 2d only to industry in economic importance. Many visitors come to N.H. each year to enjoy the state's beaches, mts., and lakes. The largest lake, beautiful L. Winnipesaukee in the center of the state, is dotted with some 274 isls., while along the Atlantic shore 18 mi/29 km of curving beaches (many state-owned) attract vacationers. Of the rugged Isles of Shoals off the coast (partly in Maine), 3 belong to N.H. Landscape is dotted with covered bridges, especially in W and N. In the winter skiers flock N, and the state has responded to the increasing popularity of winter sports by greatly expanding its facilities. Ski resorts are distributed throughout state (except SE); hiking and backpacking are important during other seasons Some of N.H.'s industries include the mfg. of recreational equip. and hiking boots. The Appalachian Trail crosses state from Hanover on Vt. state boundary, continuing NE through White Mts. into Maine. Native crafts such as wood carving, weaving, and pottery making have been revived to attract the tourist market. N.H. has numerous state parks and forests, and the White Mts. Natl. Forest in N, which extends into Maine, has c.724,000 acres/293,000 ha in N.H. The state's scenic beauty and serenity have long inspired writers and artists. Hawthorne, Whittier, and Longfellow summered in N.H. Augustus Saint-Gaudens sculpted many of his finest works at the artist's colony at Cornish (Saint-Gaudens Natl. Historic Site on Connecticut R.) and the MacDowell Colony at Peterborough is a summer haven for musicians, artists, and writers; their ranks have included E. A. Robinson and Thornton Wilder. The state is most intimately connected with the works of Robert Frost; Frost himself once said that there was not one of his poems "but has something in it of New Hampshire." The region was 1st explored by Martin Pring (1603) and Samuel de Champlain (1605). In 1620 the Council for New England, formerly the Plymouth Company, received a royal grant of land bet. lat. 40°N and 48°N. One of the council's leaders, Sir Ferdinando Gorges, formed a partnership with Capt. John Mason and in 1622 obtained rights bet. the Merrimack and Kennebec rivers, then called the prov. of Maine. By a division Mason took (1629) the area bet. the Piscataqua and the Merrimack, naming it N.H. Portsmouth was founded by farmers and fishermen in 1630. Through claims based on a misinterpretation of its charter, Mass. annexed S N.H. bet. 1641 and 1643. Although N.H. was proclaimed a royal colony in 1679, Mass. continued to press land claims until the King-in-Council decided the E and S boundaries in 1741. Although they were technically independent of each other, the crown habitually appointed a single man to govern both colonies until 1741, when Benning Wentworth was made the 1st governor of N.H. alone. Wentworth was an expansionist and granted lands beyond the Connecticut R., close to the Hudson, thereby provoking a protracted controversy with N.Y. Although a royal order in 1764 est. the Connecticut R. as the W boundary of N.H., the dispute flared up again in the Amer. Revolution and was only settled when Vt. became a state. The Fr. and Indian Wars had prevented colonization of the inland areas, but after the wars a land rush began. Lumber camps were set up and sawmills were built along the streams. The Scots-Irish settlers had already initiated the textile industry by growing flax and weaving linen. By the time of the Revolution many of the inhabitants had tired of Br. rule and were eager for independence. In Dec. 1774, a band of patriots overpowered Fort William and Mary (later Fort Constitution) and secured the arms and ammunition for their cause. N.H. was the 1st colony to declare its independence from Great Britain and to establish its own govt. (Jan. 1776). N.H. became the 9th and last necessary state to ratify the new Constitution of the U.S. in 1788. N.H.'s N boundary was fixed in 1842 when the Webster-Ashburton Treaty set the internatl. line bet. Canada and the U.S. The Democrats remained in political control until their inability to take a united antislavery stand brought about their decline. When Franklin Pierce, the only U.S. president from N.H. (1853–1857), tried to smooth over the slavery quarrel and unite his party, antislavery sentiment was strong enough to alienate many of his supporters. During the Civil War, N.H. was a strong supporter of the Northern cause and contributed many troops to the Union forces. After the war its economy began to emerge as primarily industrial, and pop. growth was steady although never spectacular. The production of woolen and cotton goods and the mfg. of shoes led all other enterprises. The forests were rapidly and ruthlessly exploited, but in 1911 a bill was passed to protect big rivers by creating forest reserves at their headwaters, including the White Mt. Natl. Forest. Since that time numerous conservation measures have been enacted and large tracts of woodland have been placed under state and natl. ownership. The Great Depression of the 1930s severely dislocated the state's economy, especially in the 1-industry towns. The effort made then to broaden economic activities has been continually intensified. The recent establishment of important new industries such as electronics has successfully counterbalanced the departure to other states of older industries such as textiles. However, when Mass. fell into deep recession in the late 1980s and early 1990s, N.H was similarly affected. N.H.'s present constitution was adopted in 1784; it is the 2d-oldest in the country. N.H. is the only state in which amendments to the constitution must be proposed by convention; once every 7 years a popular vote determines the necessity for constitutional revision. The state's executive branch is headed by a governor and 5 powerful elected officers called councillors. The governor is elected for a 2-year term and is traditionally limited to 2 successive terms. Perhaps the most unusual feature of N.H. politics is the size of its bicameral legislature (General Court); it is one of the largest representative bodies in the Western world, with 24 senators and from 375 to 400 representatives, all elected for 2 years. The state elects 2 senators and 2 representatives to the U.S. Congress and has 4 electoral votes. The N.H. presidential primary is among the 1st to be held in election years and has often forecast natl. trends or influenced important political decisions. Republicans have dominated N.H. politics since the Civil War. Among the state's more prominent institutions of higher learning are Dartmouth Col., at Hanover, and the Univ. of N.H., at Durham. As in other New England states, N.H. cos. are subdivided into towns (townships) that are more important than cos. as secondary level of govt. Villages within towns have no govt. of their own. In Coos co., in far N, some mt. areas have land grants and land purchases instead of towns and have little or no pop. N.H. has 10 cos.: BELKNAP, CARROLL, CHESHIRE, COOS, GRAFTON, HILLSBOROUGH, MERRIMACK, ROCKINGHAM, STRAFFORD, , and SULLIVAN.

New Hampton 1 city (1990 pop. 3,660), ⊙ Chickasaw co., NE Iowa, 18 mi/29 km E of Charles City; 43°03′N 92°18′W. Mfg. (dairy prods., egg processing, food processing, feed, beverages, bldg. materials, motor vehicle parts). Inc. 1873. **2** city (1990 pop. 320), Harrison co., NW Mo., 8 mi/12.9 km W of Bethany; 40°16′N 94°12′W. Corn, wheat, soybeans; cattle.

New Hampton, town (1990 pop. 1,606), Belknap co., central N.H., 11 mi/18 km NW of Laconia; 43°37′N 71°37′W. Bounded W and SW by Pemigewasset R.; town center near river. Mfg. (machinery, commercial printing). Agr. (nursery crops; cattle, poultry; dairying). Seat of New Hampton School. New Hampton Fish Hatchery, state's oldest fish hatchery (1920). Winter sports. Pemigewasset L. in NE center. Winona L. and L. Waukewan in NE. Hersey Mt. (2,005 ft/611 m) on SE boundary.

New Hanover, county (□ 327 sq mi/847 sq km; 1990 pop. 120,284), SE N.C., ⊙ Wilmington; 34°10′N 77°51′W. Bounded E by Atlantic Ocean (Onslow Bay), W by Cape Fear R., N and NW by Northeast Cape Fear R. Forested tidewater area. Very little agr. Mfg. and shipping at Wilmington; beach resorts along coast. Stone quarrying. Intracoastal Waterway channel parallels coast S to Carolina Beach Inlet, continues S in Cape Fear R. estuary. Wrightsville Beach resort area in E. Pleasure Isl. in S, including Kure Beach and Carolina Beach resort areas, also Carolina Beach State Park, Ft. Fisher State Recreation Area and Historical Site. N.C. State Aquarium. Formed 1729.

New Harmony, town (1990 pop. 846), Posey co., SW Ind., on the Wabash R., 14 mi/23 km N of Mt. Vernon; 38°08′N 87°56′W. Agr. area (grain, melons, fruit; livestock). Founded 1814 by the Harmony Society under George Rapp. In 1825 the Harmonists sold their holdings to Robert Owen and moved to Economy, Pa., where their sect survived for another 78 years. Owen established a communistic colony in New Harmony that gained prominence as a cultural and scientific center and attracted many noted scientists, educators, and writers. Dissension arose, and in 1828 the community ceased to exist as a distinct enterprise, although the town remained an intellectual center. The nation's 1st kindergarten, 1st free public school, 1st free library, and 1st school with equal education for boys and girls were all established there. In New Harmony 25 old Rappite bldgs. remain. Harmony State Park nearby to SSW.

New Harmony, village (1990 pop. 101), Washington co., SW Utah, 18 mi/29 km SW of Cedar City, on Ash Creek; 37°28′N 113°18′W. Elev. 5,306 ft/1,617 m. Dixie Natl. Forest to W; Kolob Canyon sect. of Zion Natl. Park to E. Ash Creek reservoir to SE. Settled 1852.

New Hartford 1 resort town (1990 pop. 5,769), Litchfield co., NW Conn., on Farmington R., just SE of Winsted; 41°50′N 73°00′W. Agr.; mfg. of plumbing supplies, aircraft parts, electronics, blenders, springs, guitars, business forms, and plastics; skiing. Includes Pine Meadow village; state forest; part of Nepaug Reservoir. Flooded (1936) when nearby Greenwood Dam broke, and again in 1955. Sorner Dam and L. McDonough just E. Summer tubing down Farmington R. at nearby state park. Settled 1733, inc. 1738. **2** town (1990 pop. 683), Butler co., N central Iowa, 15 mi/24 km WNW of Waterloo; 42°34′N 92°37′W. Feeds.

New Hartford, village (1990 pop. 2,111), Oneida co., central N.Y., just SW of Utica; 43°04′N 75°17′W. Mfg. (paper prods., computer software, consumer goods). Settled c.1787, inc. 1870.

New Haven, county (□ 862 sq mi/2,233 sq km; 1990 pop. 804,219), S Conn., on L.I. Sound; ⊙ New Haven and Waterbury; 41°21′N 72°54′W. Mfg., agr., resort region, with industrial Waterbury, Wallingford, Naugatuck, New Haven, Ansonia, Derby, and Meriden, producing wide variety of goods, esp. metal prods., hardware, firearms, rubber goods, silverware, electrical equip. and appliances, bricks, textiles; oil refining; agr. (fruit, vegetables, dairy prods.; poultry); seed growing; fisheries; shore resorts. Drained by Housatonic (W boundary), Naugatuck, Quinnipiac, and Hammonasset (E boundary) rivers. Constituted 1666.

New Haven 1 city (1990 pop. 130,474), New Haven co., S Conn., port of entry where the Quinnipiac and other small rivers enter L.I. Sound; 41°18′N 72°55′W. Firearms and ammunition, clocks and watches, tools, rubber and paper prods., and textiles are among the mfg. The city is an educational center, being the seat of Yale Univ. and its allied institutions and of Albertus Magnus Col. and Southern Conn. State Univ. New Haven was founded in 1637–1638 by Puritans led by Theophilus Eaton and John Davenport. The city hosted the 1995 World Special Olympics, which attracted many internatl. heads of state. It was one of the 1st planned communities in Amer. and was the chief town of a colony that later included Milford, Guilford, Stamford, Branford, and Southold (on L.I.). Its govt. was theocratic; religion was a test for citizenship, and life was regulated by strict rules. In 1665 the colony was reluctantly united with Conn.; it was joint capital with Hartford from 1701 to 1875. In the late 18th and early 19th cents., New Haven was a thriving port. Mfg. grew, and New Haven firearms, hardware, coaches, and carriages became famous prods. New Haven was raided by a Br. and Tory force in the Amer. Revolution, and the port was blockaded during the War of 1812. The world's 1st commercial telephone exchange was est. there in 1879. The city centers upon a large public green, dating from 1680, on which stand 3 churches built bet. 1812 and 1816 — Center and United Churches (both Congregational) and Trinity Church (Episcopal). Many old bldgs. have been preserved, and there is a historic dist. Landmarks in the city are 2 traprock cliffs — West Rock, with the Judges' Cave, and East Rock. Since the 1950s, New Haven has received natl. attention for its pioneering urban renewal projects. The nation's 1st antipoverty program began there in 1962. Despite these improvements, the city suffered a serious racial riot in 1967. New Haven's mfg.-based economy has since declined, and by 1990 mfg. employed less than 20% of city's workforce. Noah Webster and Eli Whitney lived and are buried in the city. Inc. 1784. **2** city (1990 pop. 9,320), Allen co., NE Ind., on Maumee R., suburb 6 mi/9.7 km E of Fort Wayne; 41°04′N 85°02′W. Residential community. Mfg. (machinery, livestock feed, steel fabricating, consumer goods). Laid out 1839. **3** city (1990 pop. 1,757), Franklin co., E central Mo., on Missouri R., 12 mi/19 km W of Washington; 38°36′N 91°13′W. Corn, soybeans; dairying; cattle; mfg. (grain prods.,apparel, fabricated metal, sporting equip.). Laid out 1856. Settled by Ger. immigrants, 1840s.

New Haven 1 town (1990 pop. 796), Nelson co., central Ky., on Rolling Fork, 15 mi/24 km E of Elizabethtown; 37°39′N 85°35′W. Agr. (tobacco, grain; livestock; dairying); mfg. (furniture). Gethsemani Farms Trappist Monastery to E. Site of Knob Creek Farm, which was the Lincoln family home (1811–1816). Ky. RR Museum. **2** town (1990 pop. 2,331), Macomb co., SE Mich., 10 mi/16 km NNE of Mt. Clemens; 42°43′N 82°47′W. Satellite community of Detroit. In farm area; mfg. (motor vehicle parts, iron foundry). Inc. 1869. **3** town, Addison co., W Vt., on New Haven R., 9 mi/14.5 km N of Middlebury. Dairy prods. **4** town (1990 pop. 1,632), Mason co., W W.Va., near the Ohio R., 14 mi/23 km NE of Point Pleasant; 38°59′N 81°58′W. Agr. (grain, tobacco);

livestock; dairying. Coal-mining area. Mfg. (metal alloys, bricks, food). RR junction to S. Racine Lock and Dam (Ohio R.) to SE.

New Haven, village (1990 pop. 459), Gallatin co., SE Ill., on Little Wabash R. and 14 mi/23 km NNE of Shawneetown; 37°53′N 88°07′W. In agr. area.

New Haven River, c.25 mi/40 km long, W Vt.; rises in Green Mts. E of Middlebury; flows NW and SW to Otter Creek at Weybridge.

New Hebron (noo HEE-bruhn), village (1990 pop. 373), Lawrence co., S central Miss., 40 mi/64 km SSE of Jackson. Agr. (cotton, corn; livestock); mfg. (food, apparel).

New Hempstead, village (□ 2 sq mi/5.2 sq km; 1990 pop. 4,200), Rockland co., SE N.Y., 8 mi/12.9 km NW of Nyack; 41°08′N 74°02′W.

New Hogan Reservoir, Calaveras co., central Calif., impounded in Calaveras R. 9 mi/14.5 km W of San Andreas; c.8 mi/12.9 km long. North Fork of Calaveras R. enters upstream and from NE.

New Holland 1 village, Hall co., NE Ga., 3 mi/4.8 km NE of Gainesville; 34°18′N 83°48′W. Textile mfg. **2** village (1990 pop. 330), Logan co., central Ill., 13 mi/21 km WNW of Lincoln; 40°10′N 89°34′W. In agr. and bituminous coal area. **3** village (1990 pop. 841), Pickaway co., S central Ohio, 16 mi/26 km WSW of Circleville; 39°33′N 83°15′W. In livestock and general agr. area.

New Holland, borough (1990 pop. 4,484), Lancaster co., SE Pa., 12 mi/19 km ENE of Lancaster; 40°06′N 76°05′W. In Pa. Dutch region. Mfg. (feeds, wire and cable, farm equip., furniture, clothing, wood prods., concrete, lumber, printing and publishing, food prods.); agr. (grain, soybeans, apples; livestock; dairying). Settled 1728, inc. 1895.

New Holstein (HOL-steen), town (1990 pop. 3,342), Calumet co., E Wis., 23 mi/37 km NW of Sheboygan; 43°57′N 88°05′W. In dairying and grain-growing area. Mfg. (construction equip., machinery, animal feed, engines). Settled 1849, inc. 1926.

New Hope, city (1990 pop. 21,853), Hennepin co., E Minn., suburb 7 mi/11.3 km NW of Minneapolis; 45°02′N 93°23′W. Mfg. (lithography, electronic equip., printing). Several small lakes in area; Medicine L. to SW.

New Hope 1 uninc. town (1990 pop. 1,663), Lowndes co., E Miss., 6 mi/9.7 km ESE of Columbus, near Ala. state line; 33°27′N 88°19′W. Agr. (cotton, corn, soybeans; cattle). L. Lowndes State Park to S. **2** uninc. town (1990 pop. 5,694), Wake co., central N.C., residential suburb 5 mi/8 km NE of Raleigh, near Neuse R.; 35°48′N 78°33′W. **3** uninc. town (1990 pop. 4,491), Wayne co., E central N.C., residential suburb 8 mi/12.9 km ENE of Goldsboro. In agr. area. Seymour-Johnson Air Force Base to SW.

New Hope 1 village (1990 pop. 2,248), Madison co., N Ala., near Paint Rock R., 17 mi/27 km SE of Huntsville. **2** village (1990 pop. 523), Collin co., N Texas, residential suburb 32 mi/51 km NNE of Dallas; 4 mi/6.4 km ENE of McKinney, near East Fork of Trinity R.; 33°12′N 96°33′W. Agr. area in urban fringe.

New Hope, borough (1990 pop. 1,400), Bucks co., SE Pa., 14 mi/23 km NW of Trenton (N.J.), on Delaware R. (bridged), opposite Lambertville (N.J.); 40°21′N 57°74′W. Agr. area (grain, soybeans, apples, grapes; livestock; dairying); mfg. (concrete, furniture, optical instruments). Artist, literary, and theatrical colony. Tourist center, shops. Washington Crossing State Park to S, 1 of 2 places where George Washington crossed Delaware R. in 1776; Bucks Co. Winery to W; Buckingham Valley Winery to SW. Settled c.1712, inc. 1837.

New Houlka (HUHLK-uh), village (1990 pop. 558), Chickasaw co., NE central Miss., 24 mi/39 km SW of Tupelo, near source of Yalobusha R. Agr. (cotton, corn, soybeans; dairying; timber); mfg. (furniture). Part of Tombigbee Natl. Forest to E. Old Houlka 1 mi/1.6 km to E. Also called Houlka.

New Hudson, village, Oakland co., SE Mich., uninc. suburb 18 mi/29 km SW of Pontiac; 42°30′N 83°36′W. In farm area; mfg. (glass prods., motor vehicle parts, machinery). Oakland Southwest Airport is here. Island L. State Recreation Area to W.

New Hyde Park, village (1990 pop. 9,728), Nassau co., SE N.Y., on L.I.; 40°43′N 73°41′W. It is a residential community with some mfg. and a few farms. To the N is North New Hyde Park. Inc. 1927.

New Iberia (ei-BIR-ee-uh), city (1990 pop. 31,828), ⊙ Iberia parish, S La., 16 mi/26 km SSE of Lafayette, on Bayou Teche, which is connected to the Intracoastal Waterway by a canal; 30°01′N 91°49′W. RR junction. Printing and publishing, mfg. (oil and gas drilling equip., fabricated steel, food prods., hunting equip., ceramics, lumber, animal feeds); esp. known for pepper sauces. Acadian refugees from N.S., Canada, settled here beginning c.1765, and Fr. is still spoken by many of the inhabitants. Base for the pirate Jean Lafitte's slave trading. Numerous antebellum houses are in the area; among them are Justine (1822) and Shadows on the Teche (1834), a classic example of Gr. Revival architecture. A sugarcane festival is held in New Iberia every Sept. Has a gambling and red-light dist. Port of New Iberia, 5 mi/8 km SSW, shallow-draft facilities. Nearby are many wildlife refuges, sheltering a multitude of migratory birds. Longfellow Evangeline State Commemorative Area to N. Inc. 1836.

New Inlet, channel through the Outer Banks, Dare co., E N.C., connecting Pamlico Sound with the Atlantic c.30 mi/48 km N of Cape Hatteras. Channel closed by sand movements, linking Pea Isl. (N) with Hatteras Isl. (S).

New Ipswich, town (1990 pop. 4,014), Hillsborough co., S N.H., 20 mi/32 km W of Nashua; 42°44′N 71°52′W. Bounded S by Mass. state line; drained by Souhegan R. Mfg. (concrete prods., metal prods., textiles); agr. (fruit, vegetables, corn, nursery crops; poultry, cattle, hogs; dairying). State's 1st cotton mill built here (1803), 1st woolen mill (1801). Windblown Ski Touring Center in W; Annett State Forest to W in Rindge. Inc. 1762.

New Jersey, state (□ 8,722 sq mi/22,590 sq km; 1995 est. pop. 7,945,298), E U.S., one of the Mid-Atlantic states and 1 of the original 13 colonies; ⊙ TRENTON; 40°16′N 74°42′W. NEWARK is the largest city. Surrounded by water except along 50 mi/80 km of the N border with N.Y. state, N.J. is bounded on the E by the Hudson R., N.Y. Bay, and the Atlantic Ocean and on the S and W by Delaware Bay and the Delaware R. (which separate it from Del. and Pa.). The N ⅓ of N.J. lies within the Appalachian Highland region, where ridges running NE and SW shelter valleys containing pleasant streams and glacial lakes. Beyond the crest of wooded slopes are long-established farms given over to dairying and field crops. The Kittatinny Mts., with the state's highest elevations (up to 1,803 ft/550 m), stretch across the NW corner of N.J. from the N.Y. state line to the DELAWARE WATER GAP. SE of the Highlands lie the Triassic lowlands or piedmont plains, extending from the NE border to Trenton and encompassing every major city of the state except CAMDEN and ATLANTIC CITY. The monotony of the lowlands is broken by anc. trap-rock ridges that extend to the Palisades of the Hudson, and many commuter towns are located along the wooded slopes. E of Newark and HACKENSACK acres of tidal marshes have been converted to industrial, office, and commercial use. This area, called the Meadowlands, also contains a huge sports and entertainment complex. Drainage is provided by the state's major rivers, the Passaic, the Raritan, and the Hackensack. The busy lowlands give way in the SE to the coastal plains, which cover more than 50% the state. The coast itself is highly developed as a resort area. Offshore barrier isls. make large harbors impractical but provide 115 mi/185 km of sheltered waterways that have made possible a superior combination of bay and ocean facilities. Only 4 states are smaller in size than N.J., yet N.J. ranks 9th in the nation in pop., a fact indicative of its economic importance. It is a major industrial center, an important transportation terminus, and a long-established playground for summer vacationers. The state is noted for its output of chemicals and pharmaceuticals, machinery, and a host of other prods., including telecommunications research and development and electronic equip. Camden is an important port. Stone, zinc, and sand and gravel are the state's only native mineral resources of consequence. BAYONNE is the terminus of pipelines originating in Texas and Okla., and there are oil refineries at LINDEN, CARTERET, and Bayway. The area near PRINCETON has developed into a center for high-technology industry, and N.J. has been a leader in the research industry since Thomas Edison established a research facility at Menlo Park in 1876. The finance industry has also become important to the state's economy, attracting many corporations from N.Y. city. These developments have to a large extent reversed N.J.'s role as a suburban commuter area for N.Y. city and Philadelphia. A tremendous transportation system, concentrated in the industrial lowlands, moves prods. and a huge volume of interstate traffic through the state. Busy highways like the Garden State Parkway and the N.J. Turnpike are part of a network of toll roads and freeways. N.J. is linked to Del. and Pa. by many bridges across the Delaware R. Traffic to and from N.Y. is served by RR and subway tunnels and by the facilities of the Port Authority of N.Y. and N.J. — the double-decked George Washington Bridge, the Lincoln and Holland vehicular tunnels, and 3 bridges to Staten Isl. Airports are operated by many cities, and Newark airport (controlled by the Port Authority) ranks among the nation's busiest. Shipping in N.J. centers on the ports of the Newark Bay and N.Y. Bay areas, with relatively minor seagoing traffic on the Delaware as far N as Trenton. Because of this extensive transportation network, N.J.'s ocean beaches, inland lakes, forests, and low mt. areas are the basis for the state's traditional vacation industry. Tourism is N.J.'s 2d-largest industry, due largely to the emergence of Atlantic City as a major gambling center. In addition to being a center of industry, transportation, and tourism, N.J. is a leading state in agr. income per acre. The scrub pine area of the S inland region is used for cranberry and blueberry growing. N of the pine belt the soil is extremely fertile and supports a variety of crops, most notably potatoes, corn, hay, peaches, and vegetables (esp. tomatoes and asparagus). Dairy prods., eggs, and poultry are also important. Huge commercial and residential expansion, however, has taken over much of the state's farmland. The history of N.J. goes back to Du. and Swed. communities established prior to settlement by the English. Du. claims to the Hudson and Delaware valleys were based on the voyages of Henry Hudson, who sailed into Newark Bay in 1609. Under the auspices of the Du. West India Company. patroonships were offered for settlement, and small colonies were located on the present sites of Hoboken, Jersey City, and Gloucester City. Swedes and Finns of New Sweden, who predominated in the Delaware Valley after 1638, were annexed by the New Netherland colony in 1655. In 1664, New Netherland was seized for the English, but the Dutch disputed this claim. Proprietorship of lands bet. the Hudson (at lat. 41°N) and the northernmost point of the Delaware was granted to Lord John Berkeley and Sir George Carteret. The original grants to Berkeley and Carteret divided the region in 2 sects. The split was further defined in the Quintipartite Deed of 1676, which divided the prov. into East and West Jersey, East Jersey being held by Carteret. In 1681, William Penn and 11 other Quakers purchased East Jersey from Carteret's widow. In both Jerseys confusion resulting from the unwieldy number of proprietors together with widespread resentment against authority caused the proprietors to surrender voluntarily their governmental powers to the crown in 1702, although they retained their land rights. N.J.'s independence from N.Y. was recognized, but authority was vested in the governor of N.Y. until 1738, when Lewis Morris was appointed governor of N.J. alone. Under the royal governors the same problems persisted — land titles were in dispute and opposition to the proprietors culminated in riots in the 1740s. E Jersey was dominated by Calvinism, implanted by Scottish and New England settlers, while in W Jersey the Quakers soon developed a landed aristocracy with strong political and economic influence. Anti-Br. sentiment gradually spread from its stronghold in E Jersey throughout the colony and took shape in Committees of Correspondence. Although the Tory party was to prove strong enough to raise 6 Loyalist battalions, the patriot cause was generally accepted, and in June 1776, the provincial congress adopted a constitution and declared N.J. a state. Because of its strategic position, N.J. was of major concern in the Amer. Revolution. George Washington's memorable Christmas attack on the Hessians at Trenton in 1776, followed by his victory at Princeton, restored the confidence of the patriots. In June 1778, Washington fought another important battle in N.J., at Monmouth. Altogether, about 90 engagements were fought in the state, and Washington moved his army across it 4 times, wintering twice at MORRISTOWN. At the Federal Constitutional Convention in 1787, the delegates from N.J. sponsored the cause of the smaller states and carried the plan for equal representation in the Senate. N.J. was the 3d state to ratify (Dec. 1787) the U.S. Constitution. By this time N.J.'s pop. had grown from an estimated 15,000 in 1700 to approximately 184,000. Trenton became the state's capital in 1790. Agr. had been supplemented by considerable mining and processing of iron and copper and by the production of lumber, leather, and glass. During the next 50 years, a period of enormous economic expansion, the dominance of the landed aristocracy gave way to industrial growth and to a more democratic state govt. The important textile industry, powered by the falls of the Passaic, was initiated at Paterson. Potteries, shoe factories, and brickworks were built. Roads were improved, the Morris, Delaware, and Raritan canals were chartered, and the Camden and Amboy RR completed a line from N.Y. city to Philadelphia with monopoly privileges. Prior to the Civil War an era of reform resulted in the framing of a new state constitution (1844) in which property qualifications for suffrage were abolished, provisions were made for the popular election of the governor and the assemblymen, and a balance of power and responsibility was established among the executive, legislative, and judicial departments. In spite of some pro-Southern sentiment, N.J. recruited its quota of regiments in the Civil War and gave valuable financial aid to the Union. The war demands proved lucrative for commerce and industry, and the expanding labor market attracted large numbers of Eur. immigrants. By 1865 the pattern of the state's development was molded. Pop. and industry showed rapid and steady growth. Large economic interests grasped control of political power, giving rise to sporadic but unsustained popular movements for reform. The Camden and Amboy RR was transferred by lease to the Pa. RR in 1871, and its monopolistic power was lessened by legislation opening the state to all RR lines and by the assessment and taxation of RR properties. After the 1870s easy incorporation laws and low corporation tax rates attracted new trusts to incorporate through "dummy" offices in the state. There was much liberal sentiment against the power of "big business." A general reform movement sponsored by Woodrow Wilson when he was governor (1910–1912) resulted in such legislation as the direct primary, a corrupt practices act, and the "Seven Sisters" acts for the regulation of trusts (later repealed). The state voted predominantly Democratic from the Civil War until 1896. Since that time it has frequently voted Republican in natl. elections, and in state politics it has often divided power bet. Democratic governors and Republican legislatures. The powerful political machine of Frank Hague, centered in Jersey City, wielded great influence in the Democratic Party from 1913 to 1949, when it was defeated by insurgents within its ranks. In 1947 a new constitution was framed and accepted to replace the antiquated constitution of 1844. The liberal Bill of Rights was preserved and extended, governmental depts. were streamlined, the cumbersome court system was simplified, the executive power was strengthened, and labor's right to organize and bargain collectively was recognized. In 1966 another convention was called to rewrite those portions of the 1947 constitution invalidated by application of the U.S. Supreme Court's "1 man, 1 vote" rule to state legislatures. The convention drafted sweeping revisions, which were approved by the electorate in Nov. 1966. A 6-day race riot in Newark in July 1967 drew attention to the urgent need for social and political reform in many of the state's urban centers. Kenneth A. Gibson was elected as Newark's 1st Afr.-Amer. mayor in 1970. During the early 1970s the state govt. proposed plans for massive urban renewal and economic development projects, but the trend of movement away from central cities like Newark increased throughout the 1970s and 1980s and into the 1990s. During this period, N.J. lost thousands of mfg. jobs but replaced them through the dramatic development of the service and trade sectors of the economy. In 1976 the state legalized casino gambling and in 1978 the 1st casino opened in Atlantic City. The Meadowlands Sports Complex opened in 1976 and grew to include Giants Stadium (1977), home of professional football teams, and Continental Airlines Arena (1981), which hosts professional hockey, basketball, and special events. N.J. was hard hit by recession in the early 1990s as economic growth slowed and the state suffered the effects of overdevelopment. The N.J. legislature consists of a senate of 40 members, elected to serve 4-year terms, and an assembly of 80 members, elected for 2-year terms. The governor serves a 4-year term and may be reelected once. N.J. sends 13 representatives and 2 senators to the U.S. Congress and has 15 electoral votes. In the important area of water resources and rights, N.J. signed the Delaware R. Basin Compact in 1961 with 3 other states and the Federal govt. N.J.'s 2 best-known institutions of higher learning were est. in the 18th cent. — Princeton Univ., at Princeton, as the Col. of N.J. in 1746; and Rutgers Univ., mainly at New Brunswick, as Queen's Col. in 1766. Included among other N.J. educational institutions are Fairleigh Dickinson Univ., with 2 campuses; Seton Hall Univ., mainly at South Orange; Stevens Inst. of Technology, at Hoboken; and a number of state cols. The Inst. for Advanced Study, at Princeton, is one of the leading research centers of the country. Lucent Technologies in Murray Hill, Holmdel, and elsewhere remains the country's foremost research center and one of the world's most important scientific labs. N.J. has 21 cos.: ATLANTIC, BERGEN, BURLINGTON, CAMDEN, CAPE MAY, CUMBERLAND, ESSEX, GLOUCESTER, HUDSON, HUNTERDON, MERCER, MIDDLESEX, MONMOUTH, MORRIS, OCEAN, PASSAIC, SALEM, SOMERSET, SUSSEX, UNION, WARREN.,

New Jersey Turnpike, part of N.J. highway system extending NE from Deepwater on Delaware R. at Delaware Memorial Bridge to Ridgefield Park, with an extension to Fort Lee and the George Washington Bridge. Toll road.

New Kensington, city (1990 pop. 15,894), Westmoreland co., SW Pa., suburb 15 mi/24 km NE of Pittsburgh, on the Allegheny R. (bridged); 40°34′N 79°45′W. Coal-mining area. Mfg. (ceramics, machinery, concrete, plastic prods., crushed stone, chemical blending, rubber prods.). Pa. State Univ. (New Kensington campus). Laid out 1891 on the site of Fort Crawford (1778), inc. as a city 1933.

New Kent, county (□ 223 sq mi/578 sq km; 1990 pop. 10,445), E Va.; ⊙ New Kent; 37°30′N 77°00′W. Agr. (hay, barley, wheat, corn, soybeans, sweet and white potatoes; poultry); timber. In Tidewater region, bounded S by Chickahominy R., N by Pamunkey R., and NE by York R. estuary. Formed 1654.

New Kent, uninc. village, ⊙ New Kent co., E Va., 25 mi/40 km E of Richmond, near Pamunkey R. Agr. (potatoes, grain, soybeans; poultry). Co. seat since 1961.

New Kingston, resort village (1990 pop. 150), Delaware co., S N.Y., in the Catskills, c.40 mi/64 km NW of Kingston; 42°13′N 74°41′W.

New Knoxville, village (1990 pop. 838), Auglaize co., W Ohio, 8 mi/13 km SW of Wapakoneta; 40°29′N 84°19′W. Lumber, clay prods.

New Lebanon 1 village (1990 pop. 950), Columbia co.,

SE N.Y., near Mass. state line, 8 mi/12.9 km W of Pittsfield (Mass.); 42°28'N 73°26'W. Samuel Tilden was b. here. Site of R.C. Shrine of Our Lady of Lourdes. **2** village (1990 pop. 4,323), Montgomery co., W Ohio, 10 mi/16 km W of Dayton; 39°45'N 84°24'W. In agr. area.

New Lebanon (LE-bah-nahn), borough (1990 pop. 209), Mercer co., NW Pa., 16 mi/26 km SSE of Meadville; 41°25'N 80°04'W. Corn, hay; livestock; dairying. L. Wilhelm reservoir, in M. K. Goddard State Park, to SW.

New Leipzig, village (1990 pop. 326), Grant co., S N.Dak., 18 mi/29 km E of Mott, near Cannonball R.; 46°22'N 101°57'W.

New Lenox (LEN-iks), village (1990 pop. 9,627), Will co., NE Ill., 5 mi/8 km E of Joliet, residential satellite community of Chicago; 41°31'N 87°58'W. Agr. (corn, soybeans; dairying); mfg. (machinery, furniture). Inc. 1946.

New Lenox, Mass.: see LENOX.

New Lexington, city (1990 pop. 5,117), ⊙ Perry co., central Ohio, 19 mi/31 km SSW of Zanesville; 39°43'N 82°12'W. Trade center and distribution point for coal-, sand-, and oil-producing area; makes tile, machine tools. Laid out 1817.

New Liberty, town (1990 pop. 139), Scott co., E Iowa, 20 mi/32 km NW of Davenport; 41°43'N 90°52'W. In agr. area; mfg.

New Limerick (LIM-uhr-ik), town (1990 pop. 524), Aroostook co., E Maine, just W of Houlton; 46°07'N 67°58'W. Agr.

New Lisbon, town (1990 pop. 1,491), Juneau co., central Wis., on Lemonweir R., c.55 mi/89 km E of La Crosse; 43°52'N 90°09'W. RR junction. In dairying and farming region. Mfg. (furniture, machinery). Necedah Natl. Wildlife Refuge and Central Wis. Conservation Area to N. Inc. 1889.

New Liskeard (LI-skuhrd), town (1991 pop. 5,431), E Ont., Canada, at N end of L. Timiskaming, 5 mi/8 km NNW of Haileybury; 47°30'N 79°40'W. Mfg. (paper prods.), printing, pulp and lumber milling, food processing, dairying; resort. Market center for surrounding mining region.

New Llano (LAH-no), town (1990 pop. 2,660), Vernon parish, W La., 2 mi/3 km S of Leesville; 31°06'N 93°16'W. In agr. area (poultry, cattle; sweet potatoes, watermelons; dairying); timber. Llano Cooperative Colony, founded by a socialist utopian group, was est. here in 1917. Fort Polk Military Reservation to E, Anacoco Prairie State Game and Fish Preserve to W, Kisatchie Natl. Forest to SE. Also spelled Newllano.

New London, county (□ 771 sq mi/1,997 sq km; 1990 pop. 254,957), SE Conn., on L.I. Sound and R.I. state line, bounded W by the Connecticut; ⊙ New London and Norwich; 41°28'N 72°07'W. New London is a Coast Guard and submarine center; co. has diversified mfg. (textiles, metal prods., medical supplies, machinery, printing presses, paper prods., chemicals, clothing, consumer goods, silverware, boats, leather prods.); agr. (dairy prods.; poultry; fruit, vegetables). Resorts on coast. Drained by Yantie, Shetucket, Thames, Mystic, Quinebaug, Pawcatuck (E boundary), and Niantic rivers. Located 3.2 mi/5.1 km ENE of New London are 3 nuclear power plants: Millstone 1 (initial criticality Oct. 26, 1970; max. dependable capacity of 650 MWe), Millstone 2 (initial criticality Oct. 17, 1975; max. dependable capacity of 860 MWe), and Millstone 3 (initial criticality Jan. 23, 1986; max. dependable capacity of 1150 MWe); all use cooling water from L.I. Sound. Constituted 1666.

New London 1 city (1990 pop. 24,540), New London co., SE Conn., on the Thames R. near its mouth on L.I. Sound; 41°19'N 72°05'W. It is a deepwater port of entry, with mfg. (shipbuilding; textiles; high-technology research and engineering; bldg. materials; fishing, tourism; furniture, and paper prods.). New London survived a partial burning by the British under Benedict Arnold in 1781 and a Br. blockade during the War of 1812. The city reached the peak of its maritime prosperity in the 19th cent., when it flourished as a shipping, shipbuilding, and whaling port. The excellent harbor is used by the U.S. Navy as a principal submarine base, by yachters and students of the U.S. Coast Guard Acad. (located in the city), and by the Coast Guard Officers Training Command. Annual Yale-Harvard boat races are held on the Thames R. Conn. Col. and Mitchell Col. are here. The city has a whaling mus., an art mus., and many old bldgs., including the Hempsted House (1678) the old town mill (1650) and Old Fort Trumbull (1849). Laid out 1646 by John Winthrop, inc. 1784. **2** city (1990 pop. 988), ⊙ Ralls co., NE Mo., near Salt R., 8 mi/12.9 km S of Hannibal; 39°34'N 91°24'W. Soybeans, corn; hogs; mfg. (consumer goods); agr. trade center. Historic courthouse (1857–1858).

New London 1 town (1990 pop. 1,922), Henry co., SE Iowa, 8 mi/12.9 km ESE of Mt. Pleasant. In livestock and grain area. Founded as Dover; inc. 1860. **2** town (1990 pop. 971), Kandiyohi co., S central Minn., 14 mi/23 km NNE of Willmar, on Crow R.; 45°17'N 94°57'W. Mfg. (machinery, concrete). Fish hatchery here. Sibley State Park, on L. Andrew to W; Mt. Tom (1,375 ft/419 m) to W; Green L. to SE, Mud L. to N. **3** town (1990 pop. 3,180), Merrimack co., S central N.H., 27 mi/43 km NW of Concord, in hilly country; 43°25'N 71°59'W. Mfg. (printing and publishing); timber; agr. (nursery crops, vegetables; livestock; dairying). Seat of Colby-Sawyer Col. Resort and retirement area. Sunapee L. on SW boundary. Little Squam L. in W; Pleasant L. in E; Norsk Ski Touring Area in SE. **4** town (1990 pop. 926), Rusk co., E Texas, 21 mi/34 km ESE of Tyler; 32°16'N 94°55'W. Oil town in E Texas field; oil and gas; cattle, horses; dairying; vegetables, watermelons; timber. A school explosion here (March 18, 1937) took the lives of hundreds of pupils and teachers. **5** town (1990 pop. 6,658), on the border bet. Waupaca and Outagamie cos., E central Wis., at confluence of Wolf and Embarrass rivers, 27 mi/43 km NNW of Oshkosh; 44°23'N 88°44'W. RR junction. In agr. area (cabbage; poultry); mfg. (food, machinery, furniture, dairy prods., wood prods., brick); lumber milling. Has Carr Mus., with natural history and historical exhibits. Founded c.1853, inc. 1877.

New London 1 village (1990 pop. 414), Stanly co., S central N.C., 8 mi/12.9 km NW of Albemarle; 35°26'N 80°13'W. RR junction to S. Cotton, grain, soybeans; dairying; livestock; timber. Mfg. (lumber, furniture). Badin Limes to E, Tuckertown L. reservoir to NE, both on Yadkin R. **2** village (1990 pop. 2,642), Huron co., N Ohio, 15 mi/24 km SE of Norwalk; 41°04'N 82°24'W. Trade and shipping point; mfg. clay and cement prods. Settled 1816.

New Lothrop (LAH-thrup), village (1990 pop. 596), Shiawassee co., S central Mich., 16 mi/26 km NW of Flint; 43°07'N 83°58'W.

New Madison, village (1990 pop. 928), Darke co., W Ohio, 11 mi/18 km SSW of Greenville; 39°58'N 84°42'W. Canned foods; grain.

New Madrid, county (□ 679 sq mi/1,759 sq km; 1990 pop. 20,928), extreme SE Mo., the Mississippi R. on E; ⊙ New Madrid; 36°35'N 89°39'W. Crossed by Little R. and drainage channels. Land surface and drainage affected by the New Madrid earthquakes of 1811–1812. Cotton region; rice, soybeans, wheat, melons; mfg. (aluminum processing; telecommunications shelters). Settled c.1788 by Fr. Creoles and Americans. One of Mo.'s original 5 cos. Formed 1812.

New Madrid, city (1990 pop. 3,350), ⊙ New Madrid co., extreme SE Mo., on Mississippi R. and protected by high levees, and 35 mi/56 km SW of Cairo (Ill.); 36°35'N 89°32'W. Cotton, wood prods.; mfg. (aluminum processing; telecommunications shelters); river port. Laid out 1789 when under Span. rule. In Civil War, Federal troops captured city before taking (1862) nearby Isl. No. 10 in the Mississippi R.; isl., then Tenn. territory, has since vanished. The name has been given to the fault zone that runs SW to NE through several states. It and its branch faults have been the origin of numerous earthquakes, most notably the extremely high-energy quakes of 1811 and 1812. They reversed flow of Mississippi R., created Reelfort L. in Tenn., rang church bells in Boston, and were felt in Canada and Charleston (S.C.). Original townsite is in the Mississippi R. channel.

New Manchester, uninc. village, Hancock co., N W.Va., 9 mi N of Weirton, near Ohio R. Agr. (grain, nursery crops). Tomlinson Run State Park to N; Hillcrest Wildlife Management Area.

New Market 1 town (1990 pop. 614), Montgomery co., W central Ind., 6 mi/9.7 km S of Crawfordsville; 39°57'N 86°55'W. In agr. area; mfg. (grain mixing). **2** town (1990 pop. 454), Taylor co., SW Iowa, 10 mi/16 km WNW of Bedford; 40°43'N 94°54'W. In agr. area. **3** town (1990 pop. 328), Frederick co., Md., 8 mi/12.9 km ESE of Frederick; 39°23'N 77°16'W. Its many antiques shops are now popular with collectors. Laid out by Nicholas Hall in 1793. **4** town (1990 pop. 1,086), Jefferson co., E Tenn., 23 mi/37 km ENE of Knoxville; 36°06'N 83°33'W. In agr., zinc-mining area. **5** town (1990 pop. 1,435), Shenandoah co., NW Va., in Shenandoah Valley, 16 mi/26 km NE of Harrisonburg; 38°38'N 78°40'W. Mfg. (fabricated copper, apparel; bookbinding); agr. area. (apples, peaches, grain, soybeans; livestock; dairying). Site of Confederate Civil War victory (May 15, 1864). New Market Battlefield Park. Endless Caverns (S), Shenandoah Caverns (N).

New Market 1 village (1990 pop. 227), Scott co., S Minn., 28 mi/45 km S of Minneapolis; 44°34'N 93°20'W. Grain; livestock; dairying. Small lakes in area. **2** village, Middlesex co., NE N.J., 4 mi/6.4 km N of New Brunswick. Structural steel plant. Settled early in 18th cent.; site of a Revolutionary camp. Has house built (1814) by Duncan Phyfe. In suburban area. **3** uninc. rural community, Platte co., W Mo., 10 mi/16 km N of Platte City. Settled 1830.

New Marlboro or **New Marlborough**, town (1990 pop. 1,240), Berkshire co., SW Mass., in the Berkshires, 23 mi/37 km S of Pittsfield; 42°06'N 73°14'W. Dairy prods. Mill River village is seat of town; also includes Hartsville and Southfield villages.

New Martinsville, town (1990 pop.6,705), ⊙ Wetzel co., NW W.Va., on the Ohio R. (bridged), 30 mi/48 km SSW of Wheeling; 39°39'N 80°51'W. Agr. (corn, potatoes); cattle, poultry. Mfg. (glassware, chemicals, lumber, textiles). Oil and natural-gas wells; sandpits. Hannibal Lock and Dam to N, Lock and Dam No. 15 to S, both on Ohio R. Lewis Wetzel Wildlife Management Area to SE. Platted 1838.

New Meadows, village (1990 pop. 534), Adams co., W Idaho, 18 mi/29 km NNE of Council, on Little Salmon R.; 44°58'N 116°17'W. Uninc. village of Meadows 2 mi/3.2 km E. RR terminus in cattle-grazing area; mfg. (lumber); ski resort. Lost Valley Reservoir to W; Brundage Mt. Ski Area to NE, Payette Lakes Ski Area to E; parts of Payette Natl. Forest to W and E.

New Meadows River, SW Maine, inlet of Casco Bay extending from S tip of Sebascodegan Isl. c.12 mi/19 km inland, bet. Brunswick and Bath.

New Melones Lake, reservoir (□ 21 sq mi/54 sq km), on Calaveras-Tuolumne co. border, E central Calif., on Stanislaus R., on W edge of Stanislaus Natl. Forest in Mother Lode Country, 35 mi/56 km NE of Modesto; 37°57'N 120°31'W. Max. capacity 2,870,000 acre ft. Formed by New Melones Dam (625 ft/191 m), built (1979) by the Bureau of Reclamation for irrigation, flood control, recreation, and as a fish and wildlife pond.

New Mexico, state (□ 121,598 sq mi/314,939 sq km; 1995 est. pop. 1,685,401), SW U.S.; ⊙ SANTA FE; 34°38'N 105°50'W. The largest city is ALBUQUERQUE. Admitted to the Union in 1912 as the 47th state. The state is bounded on the N by Colo., on the E by Okla. and Texas, on the S by Texas and Mexico (Sonora and Chihuahua states), and on the W by Ariz. At its NW corner, Ariz., Utah, Colo., and N.Mex. meet at right angles—the only point in the U.S. common to 4 states (Four Corners). N.Mex. is roughly bisected by the Rio Grande and has an approximate mean elev. of 5,700 ft/1,737 m. The topography of the state is marked by broken mesas, wide deserts, heavily forested mt. wildernesses, and high, bare peaks. The mt. ranges, part of the Rocky Mts., rising to their greatest elev. (more than

13,000 ft/3,962 m) in the Sangre de Cristo Mts., are in broken groups, running N to S through central N.Mex. and flanking the Rio Grande. In the SW is the tumbled Gila Wilderness. Broad, semiarid plains, particularly prominent in S N.Mex., are covered with cactus, yucca, creosote bush, sagebrush, and desert grasses. Water is rare in these near-arid regions, where the scanty rainfall is subject to rapid evaporation. Because irrigation opportunities are few, most of the farmland is given over to grazing. There are many large ranches, and cattle and sheep graze year-round on the open range. The 2 notable rivers besides the Rio Grande—the Pecos and the San Juan—are used for some irrigation; the Carlsbad and Fort Sumner reclamation projects are on the Pecos, and the Tucumcari project is nearby. Other projects utilize the Colorado R. basin; however, the Rio Grande, harnessed by the Elephant Butte Dam, remains the major irrigation source for the area of most extensive farming (Doña Ana co.). In the regions that support dry farming, the major crops are hay and sorghum grains. Important are crops relating to the popular Mex. food industry, esp. chiles, jalapeños, and blue corn. Onions, potatoes, and dairy prods. are also very important, and several crops, such as piñon nuts, pinto beans, and chilies, are esp. characteristic of N.Mex. Much of the state's income is derived from its considerable mineral wealth. N.Mex. is a leading producer of uranium ore, manganese ore, potash, salt, perlite, copper ore, natural gas, beryllium, and tin concentrates. Petroleum and coal are also found in smaller quantities. Silver and turquoise have been used in making Indian jewelry since long before Eur. exploration. Navajo pottery, in NW and "Pueblo" pottery in N central. The Federal govt. is the largest employer in the state, accounting for over ¼ of N.Mex.'s jobs. A large percentage of govt. jobs in the state are related to the military. The climate of the state and the increasing pop. have aided N.Mex.'s effort to attract new industries; mfg., centered esp. around Albuquerque, includes food and mineral processing and the production of chemicals, electrical equip., and ordnance. High-technology mfg. has also become increasingly important, much of it in the defense industry. Pinewood is the chief commercial wood. Millions of acres of the state are under Federal control as natl. forests and monuments, and, together with the attractive climate and scenery, make tourism a chief source of income. Best known of the state's attractions are the Carlsbad Caverns Natl. Park in SE and the Aztec Ruins Natl. Monument in NW. Thousands of tourists annually visit the White Sands, Bandelier, Capulin Mt., El Morro, El Malpais, Fort Union, Gila Cliff Dwellings, and Salina Pueblo Missions (or Salinas) natl. monuments and the Chaco Culture Natl. Historical Park. Natl. forests include Carson and Santa Fe in N; Cibola, Gila, and part of Apache-Sitgreaves in W; Lincoln in S. Kiowa Natl. Grasslands in NE. In the S is part of large Fort Bliss Military Reserve (extends N from Texas) and Holoman Air Force Base. The state is a popular place for winter or year-round residence, particularly for retirees. Many writers and artists have made their homes in communities such as Taos and Santa Fe. In 1990, the Native Amer. pop. of N.Mex. was 134,355. The Apache, Navajo, and Ute live on Federal reservations within the state—the Navajo reservation, with over 16 million acres/6 million ha, is the largest in the country—and the Pueblo people live in pueblos scattered throughout the N part of the state. Indian reservations in the state include Mescalero Apache in S; Zuñi, Acoma, Laguna, Alamo Band–Navajo in W; parts of Navajo and Ute Mt. in NW; Jicarilla Apache in N; Isleta in center; several small Puelo Indian reservations and land grants in N. Over ⅓ of the pop. today is of Hispanic origin (some are recent immigrants from Mexico) and roughly the same percentage speak Span. fluently. The state has made a great effort to re-establish its Mex. roots. Use of the land and minerals goes back to the prehistoric time of the early Indian cultures in the Southwest that long preceded the flourishing sedentary civilization of the Pueblos that

the Spanish found along the Rio Grande and its tributaries. Word of the pueblos reached the Spanish through Cabeza de Vaca, who may have wandered across S N.Mex. bet. 1528 and 1536; they were identified by Fray Marcos de Niza as the fabulously rich 7 Cities of Cibola. A full-scale expedition (1540–1542) to find the cities was dispatched from New Spain, under the leadership of Francisco Vásquez de Coronado. The treatment of Native Americans by Coronado and his men led to the long-standing hostility bet. the Native Americans and the Spanish and slowed Span. conquest. The 1st regular colony at SAN JUAN was founded by Juan de Oñate in 1598. The Native Americans of ACOMA revolted against the Span. encroachment, and were severely suppressed. In 1609, Pedro de Peralta was made governor of the "Kingdom and Provs. of New Mexico," and a year later he founded his capital at Santa Fe. The little colony did not prosper greatly, although some of the missions flourished and haciendas were founded. The subjection of Native Americans to forced labor and attempts by missionaries to convert them resulted in violent revolt by the Apache in 1676 and the Pueblo in 1680. These revolts drove the Spanish entirely out of N.Mex. The Spanish did not return until the campaign of Diego de Vargas Zapata reestablished their control in 1692. In the 18th cent. the development of ranching and of some farming and mining was more thorough, laying the foundations for the Span. culture in N.Mex. to sites near present-day El Paso, Texas and Juarez, Mexico, that still persists. When Mexico achieved its independence from Spain in 1821, N.Mex. became a prov. of Mexico, and trade was opened with the U.S. By the following year the SANTA FE TRAIL was being traveled by the wagon trains of Amer. traders. In 1841, a group of Texans embarked on an expedition to assert Texan claims to part of N.Mex.; they were captured. The Mex.-Amer. War marked the coming of the Anglo-Amer. culture to N.Mex. Stephen W. Kearny entered (1846) Santa Fe without opposition, and 2 years later the Treaty of Guadalupe Hidalgo ceded N.Mex. to the U.S. The territory, which included Ariz. and other territories, was enlarged by the Gadsden Purchase (1853). A bid for statehood with an antislavery constitution was halted by the Compromise of 1850, which settled the Texas boundary question in N.Mex.'s favor and organized N.Mex. as a territory without restriction on slavery. In the Civil War, N.Mex. was initially occupied by Confederate troops from Texas, but was taken over by Union forces early in 1862. After the war and the withdrawal of the troops, the territory was plagued by conflict with the Apache and Navajo. The surrender of Apache chief Geronimo in 1886 ended conflict in N.Mex. and Ariz. (which was made a separate territory in 1863). However, there were local troubles even after that time. Already the ranchers had taken over much of the grasslands. The coming of the Santa Fe RR in 1879 encouraged the great cattle boom of the 1880s. There were typical cow towns, feuds among cattlemen as well as bet. cattlemen and the authorities (notably the Lincoln Co. War), and colorful characters such as Sheriff Pat Garrett and the outlaw Billy the Kid. The cattlemen were unable to keep out the sheepherders and were overwhelmed by the homesteaders and squatters, who fenced in and plowed under the "sea of grass." Land claims gave rise to bitter quarrels among the homesteaders, the ranchers, and the old Span. families, who made claims under the original grants. Despite overgrazing and reduction of lands, ranching survived and continues to be important together with the limited, but scientifically controlled irrigated and dry-land farming. Statehood was granted in 1912. Pancho Villa raided Columbus, N.Mex., in March 1916. In 1943 the U.S. govt. built LOS ALAMOS as a center for atomic research. The 1st atom bomb was exploded at the White Sands Proving Grounds in July 1945. The growth of military establishments and advanced research facilities, including Sandia Natl. Laboratory opened in 1956, has greatly contributed to the economic advance of N.Mex. in recent years. Since the 1970s, high-technology industries have become prominent in the state

economy. The scarcity of water, however, could slow N.Mex.'s impressive recent growth. The legislature has a senate of 42 members elected for 4-year terms and a house of representatives with 70 members elected for 2-year terms. The governor is elected for 4 years, and may be reelected. The state elects 2 U.S. senators and 3 representatives and has 5 electoral votes. N.Mex. has been generally Democratic in politics, although it joined the natl. trend toward conservatism in the 1980s. The most prominent educational institution in the state is the Univ. of N.Mex., at Albuquerque. The state has 33 cos.: BERNALILLO, CATRON, CHAVES, CIBOLA, COLFAX, CURRY, DE BACA, DOÑA ANA, EDDY, GRANT, GUADALUPE, HARDING, HIDALGO, LEA, LINCOLN, LOS ALAMOS, LUNA, MCKINLEY, MORA, OTERO, QUAY, RIO ARRIBA, ROOSEVELT, SANDOVAL, SAN JUAN, SAN MIGUEL, SANTA FE, SIERRA, SOCORRO, TAOS, TORRANCE, UNION, VALENCIA.,

New Miami (mei-A-mee), village (1990 pop. 2,555), Butler co., extreme SW Ohio, 4 mi/6 km NNE of Hamilton, and on Great Miami R.; 39°26′N 84°32′W.

New Middletown, town (1990 pop. 82), Harrison co., S Ind., 6 mi/9.7 km SE of Corydon; 38°10′N 86°03′W. In agr. area.

New Middletown, village (1990 pop. 1,912), Mahoning co., E Ohio, 10 mi/16 km SSE of Youngstown, near Pa. state line; 40°58′N 80°33′W.

New Milford, town (1990 pop. 23,629), Litchfield co., W Conn., on the Housatonic R.; 41°36′N 73°25′W. Situated in a dairy region; mfg. include paper prods. and electronic equip. The town hall is on the homesite of Roger Sherman, a drafter and signer of the Declaration of Independence. The Canterbury School is in New Milford. Inc. 1712.

New Millford, village (1990 pop. 463), Winnebago co., N central Ill., residential suburb 7 mi/11.3 km S of Rockford, on Kishwaukee R.; 42°10′N 89°04′W.

New Milford 1 borough (1990 pop. 15,990), Bergen co., NE N.J., on the Hackensack R., 2 mi/3.2 km NNE of Hackensack; 40°55′N 74°01′W. A suburb of N.Y. city, it is primarily residential. New Milford was settled in 1695 by Fr. Huguenots. One of the original homes still stands, and there is a Huguenot cemetery in the city. In 1776, George Washington's forces crossed the Hackensack R. here during their retreat from Fort Lee to Trenton. Washington used the New Bridge Inn (still standing). Inc. 1922. **2** borough (1990 pop. 953), Susquehanna co., NE Pa., 9 mi/14.5 km ENE of Montrose, on Salt Lick Creek; 41°52′N 75°43′W. Mfg. (plastic prods.). Agr. (corn, hay; dairying). Numerous small lakes in area; Salt Springs State Park to NW.

New Minden (MEN-din), village (1990 pop. 219), Washington co., SW Ill., 7 mi/11.3 km N of Nashville; 38°26′N 89°22′W. In agr. area (wheat, corn, soybeans; hogs, poultry); coal; oil.

New Munich (MYOO-nik), village (1990 pop. 314), Stearns co., central Minn., on Sauk R., 28 mi/45 km W of St. Cloud; 45°37′N 94°45′W. Grain; poultry; dairying; mfg. (concrete).

New Orleans (OR-lee-uhnz), city (1990 pop. 496,938), coextensive with Orleans parish, SE La., bet. the Mississippi R. (SW), L. Pontchartrain (N), and L. Borgne (SE), 107 mi/172 km by water from the river mouth; 30°04′N 89°56′W. City is c.32 mi/51 km long, reaching NE to the Rigolets Channel, only 4 mi/6 km W of Miss. state line. Chef Menteur Pass bisects city in E. Parts of the city/parish are undeveloped. It was built within a great bend of the Mississippi (and is therefore called the Crescent City) on subtropical lowlands, now protected from flooding by levees and by spillways located upstream, notably the Morganza and Bonnet Carre spillways. Level of Mississippi R. is higher than the city, but levees have been built for protection. The river is crossed here by the Algiers Bridge (completed 1991), the Huey P. Long Bridge (completed 1935), and the Greater New Orleans Bridge (completed 1958), which is one of the largest cantilever bridges in the country. There are also 3 toll ferries operating within the city. L. Pontchartrain is spanned by a 24-mi/39-km double causeway (opened 1957; longest bridge in world). The largest city in La. and one of the largest in the South, New Orleans is a major U.S. port of entry. It has long been one of the busiest and most efficient internatl. ports in the country, leading the nation in tonnage of goods conveyed. Coffee, sugar, and bananas are among its imports (the coffee and banana wharves are tourist attractions); exports include oil, petrochemicals, rice, cotton, and corn. Mfg. (wood prods., paper prods., consumer goods, fabricated metal prods., food and beverages, marble, granite, slate, medical equip., boats, concrete, communication systems, bldg. equip., apparel, aircraft parts, printing and publishing). Coastwise traffic is heavy (the city is at the junction of the Intracoastal Waterway and the Mississippi R.), and New Orleans is a major hub for RR, highway, air, river, and ocean transportation. New Orlean Internatl. Airport is 10 mi/16 km W, at Kenner. Its fine port accommodates ship and barge traffic, helping to make the New Orleans area one of the leading industrial transportation centers in the South. The region has extensive shipbuilding and repair yards as well as plants mfg. a wide variety of prods. A long corridor of oil and chemical plants lines the Mississippi R. between New Orleans and Baton Rouge. Although most of the larger industries have been developed recently, it was soon after the sieur de Bienville had the city plotted in 1718 it took prominence as a port, and in 1722 it became the capital of the Fr. colony. In the late 1700s thousands of Fr. settlers arrived from Acadia, N.S., after being expelled by British. The transfer of La. to Spain by the secret Treaty of Fontainebleau (1762) was confirmed by the Treaty of Paris (1763). New Orleans — deeply involved in the struggle for control of the Mississippi — was returned to Fr. hands only briefly before passing to the U.S. with the Louisiana Purchase (1803). Nevertheless, the tone of the city's life was dominated by Creole culture until late in the 19th cent., and the Fr. influence is still seen today. After Andrew Jackson's victory over the British at New Orleans (Jan. 8, 1815) had written a postscript to the War of 1812, the W movement in the U.S. carried the "Queen City of the Mississippi" to almost fabulous heights as a port and market for cotton and slaves. New Orleans then was stamped with its lasting reputation for glamour, extravagant living, elegance, and wickedness. Then, as now, Afr.-Americans were a large element in the pop., and they contributed to the exotic flavor of the city. Jazz had its origin in the late 19th cent. among the black musicians of New Orleans. The quadroon balls — sumptuous affairs attended by rich whites and their quadroon mistresses — disappeared with the Civil War, but Afr. folkways and stories of voodoo magic persist into the 20th cent. The golden era ended when in the Civil War the city fell (1862) to Admiral David G. Farragut and suffered under the occupation of Union troops led by Benjamin F. Butler. New Orleans recovered from Reconstruction and passed through the end of the river-steamboat era to emerge as a modern city. Its past, however, is perhaps a greater factor than the warm, damp climate in attracting visitors and artists and writers. The unusual life and history of the city have produced a literature, including the works of George W. Cable, Lafcadio Hearn, Grace Elizabeth King, Charles Gayarré, and Alcée Fortier. The picturesque Fr. Quarter (Vieux Carré) of the old city, N of broad Canal St., is a major tourist attraction. In the heart of the quarter is Jackson Square (the former Place d'Armes); fronting on the square are the Cabildo (1795), formerly the govt. bldg., it now houses part of the La. state mus.); St. Louis Cathedral (1794); and other 18th- and 19th-cent. structures. Known for its music and world-famous restaurants, specializing in seafood and spicy Cajun and Creole cooking, which uphold the New Orleans tradition of good living. The annual Mardi Gras on Shrove Tuesday is perhaps the best-known festival in the U.S. Also adding to the color of the city are the many parks, museums (including a voodoo mus. and the New Orleans Mus. of Art), and gardens. The metropolitan area has 2 racetracks. Jean Lafitte Natl. Historic Park includes a 33-block sect. of New

Orleans' Fr. Quarter, Chalmette Battlefield and Cemetery to E, and a large natural area in the swamps of Jefferson parish to S. The Superdome, home of the Natl. Football League's New Orleans Saints, is also the site of the annual Sugar Bowl football game. New Orleans is also an educational center, the seat of Dillard Univ., Loyola Univ., Tulane Univ., Univ. of New Orleans, Southern Univ. in New Orleans, La. State Univ. Medical Center, Delgado Community Col., Our Lady of Holy Cross Col., New Orleans Baptist Theological Seminary and several other theological seminaries. The 1st attempts to integrate New Orleans public schools aroused a great deal of controversy in 1960. Since then, blacks have come to comprise the large majority of students and teachers in the school system, as many whites have moved from the city to the suburbs. Many deaths and much property damage resulted from Hurricane Camille, which swept through the region in 1969. Since the 1960s, the pop. of the metropolitan area has risen at a rate slightly higher than that at which the pop. of the city has declined, reflecting the trend toward suburbanization that has left the inner city increasingly troubled by poverty and crime. Attempts have been made at urban revitalization; in the 1970s many new bldgs. were erected as the city benefited from high oil prices. In the 1980s, however, the economy suffered as oil prices fell and the state's energy industry floundered. In 1983 New Orleans hosted a world's fair, but the attention it attracted and its contribution to the local economy fell far below expectations. In response to rising crime rates, the police dept. has introduced many innovations and encouraged the formation of citizen patrols. The legalization of gambling in 1992 is expected to have a major impact and may transform the character of the Fr. Quarter. Points of interest include La. Nature and Science Center, an art mus., the Aquarium of the Americas with an IMAX theater, and the fairgrounds. Algiers U.S. Naval Station and U.S. Quarantine Station are here. L. St. Catherine is in NE, Bayou Savage State Wildlife Area is near center, Fort Pike State Commemorative Area is in NE, Fort Macomb State Commemorative Area is in SE, and Bayou Segnette State Park is to SW (Jefferson parish). Founded 1718 by the sieur de Bienville; inc. 1805.

New Oxford, borough (1990 pop. 1,617), Adams co., S Pa., 10 mi/16 km ENE of Gettysburg, on South Branch of Conewago Creek; 39°51′N 77°03′W. Mfg. (feeds, fabricated metal prods., paper prods., iron castings, food prods.). Agr. area (grain, soybeans, potatoes, apples; livestock; dairying); timber. Laid out 1792, inc. 1874.

New Palestine, town (1990 pop. 671), Hancock co., central Ind., on Sugar Creek, 8 mi/12.9 km SW of Greenfield; 39°43′N 85°53′W. Primarily a residential area of Indianapolis. In agr. area (grain). Laid out 1838.

New Paltz, town (1990 pop. 5,463), Ulster co., SE N.Y., on small Wallkill R., 13 mi/21 km SSW of Kingston; 41°45′N 74°05′W. In agr. area (dairying; poultry; fruit, vineyards, sweet corn, beans, and tomatoes). State Univ. of N.Y. Col. at New Paltz is here. Summer recreational area. Settled by Huguenots in 1677; inc. 1887.

New Paris 1 village (1990 pop. 1,007), Elkhart co., N Ind., 5 mi/8 km S of Goshen, near Elkhart R.; 41°30′N 85°50′W. RR Junction. Mfg. (motor vehicles, dairy prods., furniture, boats, wire prods., feed). Cattle, poultry; dairying. Laid out 1838. **2** village (1990 pop. 1,801), Preble co., W Ohio, on East Fork of Whitewater R., at Ind. state line, 12 mi/19 km NW of Eaton (Ind.); 39°51′N 84°48′W. Lumber.

New Paris, borough (1990 pop. 223), Bedford co., S Pa., 10 mi/16 km NW of Bedford, on Dunning Creek; 40°06′N 78°38′W. Agr. (grain; livestock; dairying). Several covered bridges to NE; Shawnee State Park to S.

New Pekin, town (1990 pop. 1,095), Washington co., S Ind., 8 mi/12.9 km SSE of Salem; 38°30′N 86°01′W. In agr. area.

New Perlican (PUHR-li-kuhn), town (1991 pop. 281), SE N.F., Canada, on E side of Trinity Bay, 13 mi/21 km NNW of Carbonear; 47°55′N 53°22′W. Fishing port; lumbering.

New Philadelphia, city (1990 pop. 15,698), ⊙ Tuscarawas co., E Ohio, on the Tuscarawas R., in a coal and clay area; 40°29′N 81°26′W. Foundry prods., machinery, and pottery are made. The Tuscarawas Regional Campus of Kent State Univ. is here. Nearby is the Schoenbrunn Village State Memorial, a reconstruction of the 1st settlement in Ohio. Outdoor epic theater of Moravian settlement and massacre of Christian Indians 1782 (3 mi/4.8 km). Founded 1804, inc. 1833.

New Philadelphia, borough (1990 pop. 1,283), Schuylkill co., E central Pa., 5 mi/8 km NE of Pottsville, on Schuylkill R., at mouth of Silver Creek; 40°43′N 76°07′W. Mfg. (textiles). Anthracite coal. Laid out c.1828, inc. 1868.

New Plymouth, town (1990 pop. 1,313), Payette co., SW Idaho, 10 mi/16 km SE of Payette and on Payette R., 5 mi/8 km upstream (SE) from its mouth (Snake R.); 43°58′N 116°49′W. Apples, peaches, plums, vegetables, sugar beets, grains; cattle, sheep; dairying.

New Plymouth, Bahamas: see GREEN TURTLE CAY.

New Point, town, Decatur co., SE central Ind., 9 mi/14.5 km E of Greensburg. In agr. area.

New Point Comfort, low promontory, Mathews co., E Va., bet. Chesapeake Bay (E) and Mobjack Bay (W), 8 mi/12.9 km SSE of Mathews; 37°18′N 76°16′W. Lighthouse. Villages of Bavon, New Point are nearby.

New Port, town, S Curaçao, Neth. Antilles, minor port 7 mi/11.3 km SE of Willemstad; 12°03′N 68°49′W. Ships phosphate, which is carried by cableway from Santa Barbara, 2.5 mi/4 km N. Sometimes spelled Newport.

New Port Richey, town (□ 4 sq mi/10.4 sq km; 1990 pop. 14,044), Pasco co., W central Fla., 25 mi/40 km NW of Tampa, near the Gulf of Mexico; 28°15′N 82°43′W. Citrus fruit; concrete prods. Major resort and retirement area; recreational fishing.

New Portland, town (1990 pop. 789), Somerset co., W central Maine, on the Carrabassett, 20 mi/32 km WNW of Skowhegan; 44°53′N 70°04′W. Wood prods.

New Prague (PRAIG), town (1990 pop. 3,569), Le Sueur and Scott cos., S Minn., 33 mi/53 km SSW of Minneapolis; 44°32′N 93°34′W. Grain; soybeans; livestock; dairying); mfg. (coffee, flours, food prods., fabricated steel, bldg. supplies, printing and publishing). Inc. as village 1877, as city 1891.

New Preston, Conn.: see WASHINGTON.

New Providence 1 town (1990 pop. 270), Clark co., SE Ind., 17 mi/27 km NW of Jeffersonville; 38°28′N 85°55′W. In agr. area. Clark State Forest nearby to ENE. **2** town (1990 pop. 240), Hardin co., central Iowa, 7 mi/11.3 km SW of Eldora; 42°16′N 93°10′W. In agr. area.

New Providence, village, Montgomery co., central Tenn., on the Cumberland just NW of Clarksville; 36°33′N 87°23′W. Old stone blockhouse (1788) here.

New Providence, borough (1990 pop. 11,439), Union co., NE N.J.; 40°42′N 74°24′W. It is largely residential but has some light industry. Roses and fruit are grown here commercially. Originally called Turkey Town, its name was changed to New Providence in 1778. Settled c.1720, set off and inc. 1899.

New Providence, island (□ 80 sq mi/207 sq mi; 1990 pop. 172,196), central Bahamas, 170 mi/275 km ESE of Miami, Fla.; 25°02′N 77°25′W. The most populous isl. in the Bahamas, with ⅔ of the nation's residents, it is the site of the capital, Nassau. Mostly flat, with low ridges and several shallow lakes, notably L. Killarney and L. Cunningham. The urban center of Nassau is on the NE coast, with suburban areas to the SE, S, and W. Nassau Internatl. Airport is near the W end of the isl. The isl. has become a major vacation resort, and the pine woodlands and swamps are giving way to golf courses, beach resorts, and residential developments. Some vegetables and tropical fruits are grown, and the rum industry is important. Settled in the late 17th cent., when the British built several forts. Fort Nassau was completed in 1697, and the city laid out in 1729. During the 18th cent., the Spanish and French made incursions into the area, although the isl. was eventually ceded by treaty to Great Britain. In the 1780s Amer. loyalists took refuge here. The British maintained an air base on the isl. during WWII.

New Quebec, Canada: see UNGAVA.

New Raymer, Colo.: see RAYMER.

New Richland, town (1990 pop. 1,237), Waseca co., S Minn., 12 mi/19 km S of Waseca; 43°53′N 93°29′W. Grain, soybeans; livestock; dairying; mfg. (feeds; grain processing).

New Richmond, town (1991 pop. 4,012), E Que., Canada, on S Gaspé Peninsula, on Chaleur Bay, at mouth of Little Cascapedia R., 26 mi/42 km ENE of Dalhousie; 48°10′N 65°50′W. Fishing port, in mining region.

New Richmond 1 town (1990 pop. 312), Montgomery co., W central Ind., 11 mi/18 km NNW of Crawfordsville; 40°11′N 86°59′W. In agr. area; mfg. (alfalfa). **2** town (1990 pop. 5,106), St. Croix co., W Wis., on small Willow R., 28 mi/45 km ENE of St. Paul (Minn.); 45°07′N 92°32′W. Mfg. (flour milling, food processing, machinery, wire prods., printing and publishing).

New Richmond, village (1990 pop. 2,408), Clermont co., SW Ohio, 19 mi/31 km SSW of Batavia, and on Ohio R.; 38°58′N 84°16′W. In agr. area; metal prods. Birthplace of Ulysses S. Grant is nearby. Founded 1816.

New Riegel (REE-guhl), village (1990 pop. 298), Seneca co., N Ohio, 8 mi/13 km WSW of Tiffin; 41°03′N 83°19′W.

New Ringgold (RING-old), borough (1990 pop. 315), Schuylkill co., E central Pa., 8 mi/12.9 km S of Tamaqua, on Little Schuylkill R.; 40°41′N 75°59′W. Mfg.; agr. (apples, grain; livestock; dairying). Appalachian Trail passes to SE, on Blue Mt. ridge.

New River, uninc. village, Pulaski co., SW Va., 2 mi/3.2 km NW of Radford, on New R.; 37°08′N 80°35′W. Coal mining nearby.

New River 1 c.320 mi/515 km long, N.C., Va., and W.Va.; rising in the Blue Ridge Mts., NW N.C., formed by joining of North and South forks on the line bet. Ashe and Alleghany cos.; flows NE into SW Va., through Clayton L. reservoir past Pulaski and Radford. Continues NW past Pearisburg, Va., and into W.Va. through Bluestone L. reservoir, past Hinton, and through New R. Gorge Natl. R. (natl. park unit), joins Gauley R. c.25 mi/40 km SE of Charleston to form Kanawha R., which flows NW to Ohio R., then joins with the Gauley R. to form the Kanawha R.; 34°42′N 77°26′W. It is used extensively to generate electricity. Bluestone Dam (completed 1952), near Hinton, W.Va., provides flood control and power, and its reservoir extends 36 mi/58 km upstream. The New R. Gorge Bridge, built (1977) across the New R. Gorge, is the largest steel-arch bridge in the U.S., with a 1,700-ft/518-m span on U.S. Highway 19 at Fayetteville. South Fork of New R. rises in S Watauga co., NW N.C., near Boone; flows NNE c.75 mi/121 km. North Fork of New R. rises on Watauga-Ashe co. line, NW N.C., near Tenn. state line; flows NE c.40 mi/64 km. **2** c.50 mi/80 km long, in SE N.C.; rises in NW Onslow co.; flows SSE past Jacksonville where it widens into estuary c.2 mi/3.2 km wide and meanders through Camp Lejeune Marine Base, to Onslow Bay, enters Atlantic Ocean via New R. Inlet. Intracoastal Waterway crosses entrance behind coastal sand barrier. **3** c.40 mi/64 km long, in S S.C.; rises in N Jasper co., near Ridgeland; flows S to the Atlantic Ocean S of Daufuskie Isl., N of mouth of Savannah R.; partly navigable.

New River Gorge National River (□ 97 sq mi/251 sq km), S central W.Va., in Fayette, Raleigh, and Summers cos., c.40 mi/64 km SE of Charleston, on New R., forms Bluestone L. bet. Charleston and Va. state line. The natl. river is a 52-mi/84-km-long sect. of one of oldest rivers in N. Amer. White-water stream flows through deep canyons; rafting. White-water rafting. Authorized 1978.

New Roads, city (1990 pop. 5,303), ⊙ Pointe Coupee parish, SE central La., 24 mi/39 km NW of Baton Rouge, and on False R. (a c.13-mi/21-km-long oxbow lake of the Mississippi R.); 30°42′N 91°27′W. In agr. area (pecans, corn, sugarcane, soybeans, rice); sawmilling; fishing (crawfish); light mfg. Oil and natural-gas fields. Toll ferry across Mississippi R. to St. Francisville, 5 mi/8 km NE. Primary recreational area for people from Baton Rouge. Annual Mardi Gras parade.

New Rochelle, city (□ 13 sq mi/34 sq km; 1990 pop.

67,265), Westchester co., SE N.Y., on L.I. Sound; 40°55′N 73°46′W. Although mainly a residential suburb of N.Y. city, it has some light industry. The house where Thomas Paine lived has been preserved. The city has also been the home of several artists, authors, and other celebrities, including Norman Rockwell and Lou Gehrig. Iona Col. and the Col. of New Rochelle are in the city. David's Isl., site of former Fort Slocomb, is here. Settled by Huguenots 1688, inc. as a village 1858, inc. as a city 1899.

New Rockford, town (1990 pop. 1,604), ⊙ Eddy co., E central N.Dak., 33 mi/53 km SW of Devils Lake and on James R.; 47°40′N 99°08′W. RR junction; dairy prods., wheat; livestock. Devils L. Sioux Indian Reservation to NE. Inc. 1912.

New Rome, village (1990 pop. 111), Franklin co., central Ohio, 7 mi/11 km W of Columbus; 39°57′N 83°08′W.

New Ross, town (1990 pop. 331), Montgomery co., W central Ind., near Raccoon Creek, 12 mi/19 km SE of Crawfordsville; 39°58′N 86°43′W. In agr. area (corn, soybeans; hogs).

New Salem 1 town (1990 pop. 802), Franklin co., central Mass., 14 mi/23 km ESE of Greenfield, near Quabbin Reservoir; 42°27′N 72°19′W. Fruit. **2** town (1990 pop. 909), Morton co., central N. Dak., 25 mi/40 km W of Mandan; 46°50′N 101°25′W. Dairy produce; livestock; printing, concrete. Sweet Briar Dam and Reservoir to NE.

New Salem 1 village (1990 pop. 147), Pike co., W Ill., 7 mi/11.3 km NNW of Pittsfield; 39°42′N 90°50′W. In agr. area (corn, wheat, soybeans; cattle, hogs). **2** uninc. village (1990 pop. 669), Menallen township, Fayette co., SW Pa., 6 mi/9.7 km WNW of Uniontown, on Dunlap Creek; 39°53′N 47°76′W. Mfg. (textiles); agr. (corn, hay; dairying).

New Salem (NOO SAI-luhm), borough, York co., S Pa., 5 mi/8 km SW of York, on Codorus Creek; 39°54′N 76°47′W. Agr. (apples, grain; livestock; dairying).

New Salisbury, village, Harrison co., S Ind., 6 mi/9.7 km N of Corydon. RR junction. Mfg. (furniture, lumber). Laid out 1830.

New Sarpy (SAHR-pee), uninc. town (1990 pop. 2,946), St. Charles parish, 2 mi/3.2 km E of Hahnville; 29°58′N 90°23′W. On E bank (levee) of Mississippi R. Name given to distinguish it from Sarpy (now called Norco).

New Sharon 1 town (1990 pop. 1,136), Mahaska co., S central Iowa, near Skunk R., 12 mi/19 km N of Oskaloosa; 41°28′N 92°39′W. Settled by Quakers. **2** town (1990 pop. 1,175), Franklin co., W central Maine, on Sandy R. and 7 mi/11.3 km ESE of Farmington; 44°38′N 70°00′W.

New Shoreham, R.I.: see BLOCK ISLAND.

New Smyrna Beach (SMUHR-nuh), town (□ 17 sq mi/44 sq km; 1990 pop. 16,543), Volusia co., E central Fla., 15 mi/24 km SSE of Daytona Beach, on Indian R. and on Ponce de Leon Inlet of Atlantic Ocean; 29°01′N 80°55′W. Resort and tourist area. Citrus-fruit packing; commercial fishing; seafood processing. Light mfg. Inc. 1903.

New Spain: see MEXICO, republic.

New Springville, section of Staten Isl. borough of N.Y. city, SE N.Y., on central Staten Isl., 6 mi/9.7 km SW of St. George; 40°35′N 74°09′W.

New Square, village (1990 pop. 2,605), Rockland co., SE N.Y., 2 mi/3.2 km N of Spring Valley, 7 mi/11.3 km NW of Nyack; 41°08′N 74°01′W. A community of Orthodox Hasidic Jews of the Skvirer sect lives here.

New Stanton, borough (1990 pop. 2,081), Westmoreland co., SW Pa., 7 mi/11.3 km SSW of Greersburg on Sewickley Creek; 40°13′N 79°36′W. Mfg. includes plastic prods., nuclear components, temp. controls, machine tools. Agr. includes dairying; livestock; corn. Natural gas in area.

New Straitsville, village (1990 pop. 865), Perry co., central Ohio, 8 mi/13 km SSW of New Lexington, in coal-mining area; 39°34′N 82°14′W. Founded 1870.

New Stuyahok (STOO-yah-hok), village (1990 pop. 391), SW Alaska, c. 50 mi/80 km NE of Dillingham; 59°28′N 157°15′W.

New Suffolk, resort village (1990 pop. 1,000), Suffolk co.,

SE N.Y., on N peninsula of E L.I., on Great Peconic Bay, 11 mi/18 km ENE of Riverhead; 41°00′N 72°29′W.

New Summerfield, village (1990 pop. 521), Cherokee co., E Texas, 29 mi/47 km SSE of Tyler; 31°59′N 95°05′W. Agr. and timber area. Mfg. (rubber prods.). L. Striker reservoir to E.

New Sweden, town (1990 pop. 715), Aroostook co., NE Maine, 20 mi/32 km NNW of Presque Isle; 46°58′N 68°07′W. Settled 1870 by Swed. immigrants.

New Sweden, Swed. colony (1638–1855), on the Delaware R.; included parts of what are now Pa., N.J., and Del. With the support of statesman Axel Oxenstierna (a Swede), Admiral Klas Fleming (a Finn), and Peter Minuit (a Dutchman), the New Sweden Company was organized in Sweden in 1633. The *Kalmar Nyckel* and the *Fogel Grip*, 2 ships commanded by Minuit, reached the Delaware R. in March 1638. Minuit immediately bought land from the Native Americans and founded Fort Christina, where Wilmington, Del., stands. In 1643, Tinicum Isl. (at Philadelphia) became the colony's capital. About ½ of the colonists were Finns. Peter Stuyvesant, with a Du. force larger than the pop. of New Sweden, took the little colony in 1655.

New Town, town (1990 pop. 1,388), Mountrail co., NW N. Dak., 25 mi/40 km SSW of Stanley, in Fort Berthold Indian Reservation; 47°58′N 102°29′W. Located near N end of Van Hook Arm, large bay of L. Sakakawea. RR terminus. Tribal community col., tribal casino. Four Bears State Recreation Area to W. Mfg. (printing, electronics).

New Trier (TREE-yuhr), village (1990 pop. 96), Dakota co., SE Minn., 10 mi/16 km S of Hastings; 44°36′N 92°55′W. Agr. area (grain; livestock; dairying). Richard J. Dorer Memorial Hardwood State Forest to E.

New Tulsa, village (1990 pop. 232), Wagoner co., NE Okla., residential suburb 16 mi/26 km ESE of Tulsa; 36°06′N 95°44′W.

New Ulm (UHLM), city (1990 pop. 13,132), ⊙ Brown co., S Minn., 25 mi/40 km WNW of Mankato, on the Minnesota R. at the mouth of Cottonwood R.; 44°18′N 94°27′W. Elev. 818 ft/249 m. New Ulm is a processing and trade center for agr. area (grain, soybeans, peas, sugar beets; livestock; dairying); mfg. (dairy prods., beer, electronics, metal fabrication, printing and publishing). It was settled in 1854 by Germans, who named it after Ulm, Germany. In 1862, C. E. Flandrau, then a justice of the Minn. supreme court, led the defense of the city during a Sioux uprising. Municipal Airport to W. Co. Fairgrounds here. Seat of Dr. Martin Luther King Col. Flandrau State Park at SW edge of city, on Cottonwood R. Inc. as a city 1876.

New Ulm, uninc. village (1990 pop. 650), Austin co., S Texas, 67 mi/108 km W of Houston, on San Bernard R. Oil and natural gas. Agr. area.

New Underwood, village (1990 pop. 553), Pennington co., SW central S.Dak., 20 mi/32 km E of Rapid City and on Box Elder Creek; 44°05′N 102°49′W. In farm region (grain; livestock).

New Vienna, town (1990 pop. 376), Dubuque co., E Iowa, 22 mi/35 km WNW of Dubuque; 42°32′N 91°06′W. In livestock area.

New Vienna, village (1990 pop. 932), Clinton co., SW Ohio, 14 mi/23 km ESE of Wilmington, and on East Fork of Little Miami R.; 39°19′N 83°42′W.

New Vineyard, town (1990 pop. 661), Franklin co., W central Maine, 9 mi/14.5 km NNE of Farmington; 44°48′N 70°07′W. Wood prods.

New Virginia, town (1990 pop. 433), Warren co., S central Iowa, 15 mi/24 km SSW of Indianola and 29 mi/47 km S of Des Moines; 41°10′N 93°43′W. In agr. area.

New Washington 1 village (1990 pop. 600), Clark co., S Ind., 10 mi/16 km NE of Charlestown. Cattle, poultry. **2** village (1990 pop. 1,057), Crawford co., N central Ohio, 12 mi/19 km NE of Bucyrus; 40°58′N 82°51′W. Fabricated metal prods., food prods.

New Washington, borough (1990 pop. 78), Clearfield co., W central Pa., 11 mi/18 km NNE of Barnesboro, on Chest Creek; 40°49′N 78°42′W. Corn; livestock; dairying.

New Washoe City (wuh-SHO), uninc. town (1990 pop.

2,875), Washoe co., W Nev., residential community 8 mi/12.9 km N of Carson City, near E shore of Washoe L.; 39°17′N 119°46′W. Washoe L. State Park to S; Mt. Davidson to E.

New Waterford, town (1991 pop. 7,695), on NE Cape Breton Isl., N.S., NE of Sydney; 46°15′N 60°05′W. Mine closures in the 1960s and 1970s caused steady outmigration from this traditional coal-mining center.

New Waterford, village (1990 pop. 1,278), Columbiana co., E Ohio, 9 mi/14 km ENE of Lisbon; 40°51′N 80°37′W. In agr. and coal area; furniture, pottery.

New Waverly, town (1990 pop. 936), San Jacinto co., E Texas, 14 mi/23 km S of Huntsville; 30°32′N 95°28′W. In timber and oil area; mfg. (lumber, oil field equip., tools). Settled in 1830s as plantation center. L. Conroe reservoir to SW; surrounded W, N, and E by Sam Houston Natl. Forest; Huntsville State Park to N.

New Westminster, city (1991 pop. 43,585), SW B.C., Canada, on the Fraser R., part of metropolitan Vancouver; 49°12′N 122°55′W. Founded in 1859 as Queensborough, it was the capital of B.C. until Victoria was made the capital after the union of B.C. and Vancouver Isl. in 1866. New Westminster is a year-round port, with an excellent harbor that is the base of the Fraser R. fishing fleet and a shipping point for grain, lumber, minerals, and canned goods. Among the city's industries are salmon, fruit, and vegetable canneries; distilleries and breweries; oil refineries; paper, lumber, and flour mills; and shipbuilding plants. Columbia and St. Louis cols. are in the city, as are Anglican and R.C. cathedrals.

New Weston, village (1990 pop. 148), Darke co., W Ohio, 16 mi/26 km N of Greenville; 40°21′N 84°39′W. In agr. area; ceramics.

New Whiteland, town (1990 pop. 4,097), Johnson co., central Ind., satellite community of Indianapolis, 15 mi/ 24 km S of downtown, and 4 mi/6.4 km NNW of Franklin; 39°34′N 86°06′W.

New Willard, uninc. village, Polk co., E Texas, 38 mi/ 61 km SSW of Lufkin. Lumbering.

New Wilmington (WIL-meeng-tuhn), borough (1990 pop. 2,706), Lawrence co., W Pa., 8 mi/12.9 km N of New Castle, near Little Neshannock Creek; 41°07′N 80°19′W. Mfg. (tools, cheese, printing and publishing). Agr. (apples, corn, hay; dairying). Westminister Col. Covered bridge to SE; Amish Town Farm to N. Inc. 1863.

New Windsor, town (1990 pop. 757), Carroll co., N Md., 19 mi/31 km ENE of Frederick, near Little Pipe R.; 39°32′N 77°06′W. Called Sulphur Springs when 1st settled in the early 19th cent., it was renamed in 1844 for Windsor in England. Site of the hq. of the Church World Service of the Natl. Council of the Church of Christ in the U.S.

New Windsor 1 village, Mercer co., NW Ill., 17 mi/27 km NNW of Galesburg; 41°12′N 90°26′W. Dairy prods., corn, soybeans. Corporate name is the Village of Windsor. **2** suburban village (1990 pop. 8,898), Orange co., SE N.Y., on W bank of the Hudson, just S of Newburgh; 41°28′N 74°07′W. Mfg. (textiles, furniture). Site of Stewart Internatl. Airport, an air force base opened to commercial aircraft in 1990 and now a regional airport. Industrial park located at the airport. Was home of George Clinton. De Witt Clinton was b. here.

New Woodville, village, Marshall co., S Okla., near L. Texoma, 2 mi/3.2 km N of Woodville and 11 mi/18 km, SSE of Madill.

New World Island (□ 62 sq mi/161 sq km), in Notre Dame Bay, E N.F., Canada; 20 mi/32 km long, 8 mi/ 13 km wide; 49°35′N 54°40′W. Fishing.

New Year's Point, Calif.: see AÑO NUEVO POINT.

New York, state (□ 54,475 sq mi/141,089 sq km; 1995 est. pop. 18,136,081), NE U.S., one of the Mid-Atlantic states and one of the original 13 colonies; ⊙ ALBANY; 42°54′N 75°40′W. N.Y. is known as the Empire State. NEW YORK is the largest city. The state is bounded on the N by the Can. provs. of Que. and Ont., with the St. Lawrence R. and L. Ontario marking the Ont. border. In the NW the Niagara R., with scenic NIAGARA FALLS, forms the border with Ont. bet. L. Ontario and L. Erie. L. Erie

itself and a minute portion of Pa. constitute the rest of the W border. Pa. and N.J. are to the S, except where the state extends into the Atlantic Ocean at N.Y. city and L.I. To the E, N.Y. borders on Conn., Mass., and Vt. L. Champlain's outlet, the Richlieu R., stretching past the Can. border, is part of the state line with Vt.; it is also the chief N feature of the Great Valley (including the Hudson R.) that dominates all E N.Y. The Hudson is noted for its beauty, as are L. Champlain and neighboring L. George, which have many resorts. W of the lakes are the Adirondack Mts., including the rugged High Peaks sect. of S Clinton, E Essex and N Warren cos., another major vacationland, with woods in the N and sports centers like L. Placid and Saranac L. Mt. Marcy (5,344 ft/1,629 m), the highest point in the state, is in the Adirondacks near L. Placid. The rest of NE N.Y. is hilly, sloping gradually to the valleys of the St. Lawrence and L. Ontario. The Mohawk R., which flows from Rome to the Hudson N of Albany, and Oneida lake are part of the NEW YORK STATE BARGE CANAL, a major route to the Great Lakes and the midwestern U.S. as well as the only complete natural route across the Appalachians Mts. Most of the S part of the state is on the Appalachian plateau, which rises in the SE just W of the Hudson Valley as the Catskill Mts., an area that attracts many vacationers from N.Y. city and its environs. N.Y. city, in turn, attracts multitudes of tourists from all over the world. The W extension of the state to Lakes Ontario and Erie contains many bodies of water, notably ONEIDA LAKE and the celebrated FINGER LAKES. The W region in rural areas has an abundance of farms (agr. is the state's single largest industry) as well as large, traditionally industrial cities such as BUFFALO on L. Erie, ROCHESTER on L. Ontario, SYRACUSE, and UTICA. The W sect. is drained SW by the Allegheny R., W by Cattaraugus Creek, N by the Genesee, and S by the Susquehanna and Delaware R. systems. The Delaware R. Basin Compact, signed in 1961 by N.Y., N.J., Pa., Del., and the Federal govt., regulates the utilization of water of the Delaware system. SCHENECTADY, Albany, and N.Y. city, once the major industrial cities of the lower Mohawk and the Hudson, continue their longtime mfg. decline, as have many cities in the NE U.S. Except in the mt. regions, the areas bet. cities are rich agriculturally. The Ontario L. plain, from the Niagara Frontier to near Oswego, is a major fruit- and vegetable-producing region. N.Y. ranks 2d only to Wash. state in the production of apples. The Finger Lakes region, one of N.Y.'s leading regions, has extensive vineyards and is famous for its wines. Other areas of the state produce diverse crops, esp. grains, vegetables, hay, and potatoes (grown in great quantity on E L.I.). N.Y.'s mineral resources include crushed stone, cement, salt, and zinc. The state has a complex system of RRs, air routes, and modern highways, notably the NEW YORK STATE THRUWAY. The rivers and the N.Y. State Barge Canal, an improvement of the old ERIE CANAL, still carries limited freight bet. Albany and Syracuse, and a comprehensive plan has been instituted for the historical and recreational development of the canal. Ocean shipping is handled by the port of N.Y. city and to a much lesser extent, by the upstate ports of Buffalo, Albany, OSWEGO, and OGDENSBURG. Hydroelectricity for N N.Y. is produced by the St. Lawrence power project and by the Niagara power project, which began producing in 1961. In spite of significant decline, N.Y. has retained some important mfg. industries, and, by virtue of N.Y. city, it has strengthened is position as a commercial and financial leader. Although the largest percentage of the state's jobs lie in the service sector, its mfg. is extremely diverse and includes apparel, food prods., machinery, chemicals, paper, electrical equip. (notably at Schenectady), computer equip., optical instruments and cameras (at Rochester), and transportation equip. Printing and publishing, mass communications, advertising, and entertainment are among N.Y. city's notable industries. Brookhaven Natl. Laboratory, an atomic energy testing and research center, is in central L.I. Many corporate hq. and research facilities have relocated to Westchester

co., N of N.Y. city. Fishing in Lakes Erie and Ontario is confined to sports fishing, while commercial fishing takes place in the waters around L.I. The state has c.29,336 sq mi/75,980 sq km of forest, and forestry is a major industry. It includes the harvesting and exporting of hardwoods, harvesting pulp for timber, and use for the mfg. of a variety of hardwood and forest prods., such as maple syrup, poles, pallets, and baseball and softball bats. Early in its history N.Y. state emerged as one of the cultural leaders of the nation. In the early 19th cent. local authors Washington Irving, William Cullen Bryant, and James Fenimore Cooper were among the country's foremost literary figures. The natural beauty of N.Y. inspired the noted Hudson R. School of Amer. landscape painters. With New England's decline as a literary hub, many writers came to N.Y. city from other parts of the nation, helping to make it a literary and publishing center and the cultural heart of the country. Outside of N.Y. city, the institutions of higher education in the state include Alfred Univ., Bard Col., Colgate Univ., Cornell Univ., Hamilton Col., Hobart Col., L.I. Univ., Rensselaer Polytechnic Inst., Sarah Lawrence Col., Skidmore Col., Syracuse Univ., U.S. Military Acad., Univ. of Rochester, Vassar Col., and Wells Col. The State Univ. of N.Y. has major campuses at Stony Brook, Albany, Binghamton, and Buffalo. In addition to the great forest preserves of the Adirondack and Catskill mts., N.Y. has many state parks, including JONES BEACH, and BUTTERMILK FALLS STATE PARK, and CHENANGO VALLEY STATE PARK. Part of FIRE ISLAND is a natl. seashore. The racetrack of Saratoga Springs and Saratoga Performing Arts Center makes it both a pleasure and health resort, and the THOUSAND ISLANDS are popular with summer vacationers. Among the several places of historic interest in the state under Federal administration are those at HYDE PARK, with the burial place of Eleanor and Franklin D. Roosevelt, and the VANDERBILT MANSION. Before Europeans began to arrive in the 16th cent., N.Y. was inhabited mainly by Algonquian- and Iroquoian-speaking Native Americans. The Algonquians, including the Mahican, Lenni Lenape, and Wappinger, lived chiefly in the Hudson valley and on L.I. The Iroquois, living in the central and W parts of the state, included the Cayuga, Mohawk, Oneida, Onondaga, and Seneca, who joined c.1570 to form the Iroquois Confederacy. Europeans 1st approached N.Y. from both the sea and from Canada. Giovanni da Verrazano, a Florentine in the service of France, visited (1524) the excellent harbor of N.Y. Bay but did little exploring. In 1609, Fr. explorer Samuel de Champlain traveled S on L. Champlain from Canada, and Henry Hudson, an Englishman in the service of the Dutch, sailed the Hudson nearly to Albany. The French, who had allied themselves with the Hurons of Ont., continued to push into N and W N.Y. from Canada, but met with resistance from the Iroquois Confederacy, which dominated W N.Y. The Dutch claimed the Hudson region early on, and the Du. West India Company (chartered in 1621, organized in 1623) planted (1624) their colony of NEW NETHERLAND, with its chief settlements at NEW AMSTERDAM on the lower tip of present-day Manhattan isl. (purchased in 1626 from the Canarsie for goods worth about $24) and at Fort Nassau, later called Fort Orange (present-day Albany). To speed up the slow pace of colonization the Dutch set up the patroon system in 1629, thus establishing the landholding aristocracy that became the hallmark of colonial N.Y. The last and most able of the Du. administrators was Peter Stuyvesant (in office 1647–1664). The English claimed the whole region on the basis of the explorations of John Cabot, and in 1664 an Eng. fleet sailed into the harbor of New Amsterdam. Stuyvesant surrendered without a struggle, and New Netherland then became the colonies of N.Y. and N.J. The popular governor Thomas Dongan (in office 1683–1688) put N.Y. on a firm basis and began to establish the alliance of the English with the Iroquois, which later played an important part in N.Y. history. The Fr. threat was continuous, and N.Y. was involved in a number of the Fr. and Indian Wars (1689–1763). Unrest from Native Americans caused much of W N.Y. to remain unsettled by colonists throughout the 18th cent. Slowly, however, the colony, with its busy shipping and fishing fleets, and its expanding farms, was beginning to establish its own separate identity from that of England. Colonial self-assertiveness grew after the warfare with the French ended; there was considerable objection to the restrictive commercial laws, and the Navigation Acts were flouted by smugglers. When the Stamp Act was passed, N.Y. was a leader of the opposition, and the Stamp Act Congress met (1765) in N.Y. city. The Stamp Act occasioned considerable complaint, and unrest grew. When trouble flared into the Amer. Revolution, New Yorkers were divided. About ⅓ of all the military engagements of the Amer. Revolution took place in N.Y. state. The 1st major military action in the state was the capture (May 1775) of Ticonderoga by Ethan Allen and his Green Mt. Boys and Benedict Arnold. In Aug. 1776, however, George Washington was unable to hold lower N.Y. against the British and lost battles at Harlem Heights and White Plains. The British successfully invaded N.Y. city; however, the state had declared independence, with KINGSTON as its capital. N.Y. was in 1777 the key to the overall Br. campaign plan, which was directed toward taking the entire state and thus separating New England from the S. This failed finally (Oct. 1777) in the battles near the present-day resort of SARATOGA SPRINGS. For the rest of the war there was more or less a stalemate in N.Y., with the British occupying N.Y. city and the patriots holding most of the rest of the state except for Westchester co. The E boundary of N.Y. was established after much conflict and violence when Vt. was admitted as a state in 1791. N.Y. city was capital of the new nation briefly and was also the state capital until 1797, when Albany succeeded it. From the 1780s increased commerce (somewhat slowed by the Embargo Act of 1807) and industry, esp. textile milling, marked the turn away from the old, primarily agr., order. In the War of 1812, N.Y. saw action in 1813–1814, with the Br. capture of Fort Niagara and particularly with the brilliant naval victory over the British on L. Champlain at Plattsburgh. The state continued its development, which was quickened and broadened by the building of the Erie Canal. The canal, completed in 1825, and RR lines constructed (from 1831) parallel to it made N.Y. the major E–W commercial route in the 19th cent. and helped to account for the growth and prosperity of the port of N.Y. Cities along the canal (Buffalo, Syracuse, Rome, Utica, and Schenectady) prospered, Albany grew, and N.Y. city became the financial capital of the nation. New constitutions broadened the suffrage in 1821 and again in 1846; slavery was abolished in 1827. Politics was largely controlled from the 1820s to the 1840s by the Albany Regency, which favored farmers, artisans, and small businessmen. N.Y. was a leader in numerous 19th-cent. reform groups, including antislavery and women's rights groups. Migrants from New England had been settling on the W frontier, and in the 1840s famine and revolution in Europe resulted in a great wave of Irish and Ger. immigrants, whose 1st stops in Amer. were usually ELLIS ISLAND and then N.Y. city. In 1850, Millard Fillmore became the 2d New Yorker to be President of the U.S.; the 1st was Martin Van Buren (1837–1841). The split of the Democrats over the slavery issue helped pave the way for N.Y.'s swing to the Republicans and Abraham Lincoln in the fateful election of 1860. During the Civil War, N.Y. state strongly favored the Union and contributed much to its cause. Industrial development was stimulated by the needs of the military, and RRs increased their capacity. N.Y. city's newspapers had considerable natl. influence, and after the war the publication of periodicals and books centered more and more in the city, whose libs. expanded. From 1867 to 1869, Cornelius Vanderbilt consolidated the N.Y. Central RR system. As economic growth accelerated, political corruption became rampant, particularly the Tweed Ring of N.Y. city, headed by William Marcy "Boss" Tweed. Chester A. Arthur (1881–1885) and Grover Cleveland (1885–1889, 1893–1897) were New Yorkers who served as Presidents of the U.S. in the late 19th cent. The inpouring after 1880 of immigrants from Ireland, Italy, and E Europe brought workers for the old industries, which were expanding, and for the new ones, including the electrical and chemical industries, which were being established. Working conditions worsened but were challenged by the growing labor movement in the state. Service as N.Y. city's police commissioner and then as reforming governor of N.Y. helped Theodore Roosevelt establish the natl. reputation that sent him to the vice presidency and then to the White House (1901–1909). In the early 20th cent., N.Y. politics seesawed from the Republicans to the Democrats and back again. Reform programs, emphasizing public works, conservation, reorganization of state finances, social welfare, and extensive labor laws, continued to gain ground, however. Franklin D. Roosevelt, former governor of N.Y., went to the White House in 1932, and then-Governor Herbert H. Lehman (1932–1942) followed the President's natl. New Deal program by instituting the Little New Deal in N.Y. state. At the same time Fiorello LaGuardia, Republican mayor of N.Y. city (1934–1945), enthusiastically supported Roosevelt's social and economic reforms. Thomas E. Dewey, elected governor in 1942, 1946, and 1950, had the immense task of coordinating state activities with natl. efforts in World War II, which strained N.Y.'s resources to the utmost. He also built upon the reforms of his predecessors. Nelson Rockefeller, elected governor in 1958, 1962, 1966, and 1970, increased the state's social welfare programs, greatly expanded the State Univ. (est. 1948), and was largely responsible for the construction of a large state office and cultural complex in Albany. N.Y.'s growth slowed considerably during the 1970s and 1980s as it lost its dominant position in mfg. However, N.Y. city remains the nation's most populous city (with twice the number of inhabitants as Los Angeles, which is 2d). N.Y. has 62 cos.: ALBANY, ALLEGANY, Bronx (coextensive with the BRONX borough of N.Y. city), BROOME, CATTARAUGUS, CAYUGA, CHAUTAUQUA, CHEMUNG, CHENANGO, CLINTON, COLUMBIA, CORTLAND, DELAWARE, DUTCHESS, ERIE, ESSEX, FRANKLIN, FULTON, GENESEE, GREENE, HAMILTON, HERKIMER, JEFFERSON, Kings (coextensive with the BROOKLYN borough of N.Y. city), LEWIS, LIVINGSTON, MADISON, MONROE, MONTGOMERY, NASSAU, NEW YORK, NIAGARA, ONEIDA, ONONDAGA, ONTARIO, ORANGE, ORLEANS, OSWEGO, OTSEGO, PUTNAM, QUEENS, RENSSELAER, RICHMOND, ROCKLAND, SAINT LAWRENCE, SARATOGA, SCHENECTADY, SCHOHARIE, SCHUYLER, SENECA, STEUBEN, SUFFOLK, SULLIVAN, TIOGA, TOMPKINS, ULSTER, WARREN, WASHINGTON, WAYNE, WESTCHESTER, WYOMING, and YATES.

New York, county (□ 33 sq mi/85 sq km; 1990 pop. 1,487,536), SE N.Y., coextensive with Manhattan borough of N.Y. city; 40°46′N 73°58′W.

New York, city (□ 309 sq mi/800 sq km; 1990 pop. 7,322,564), SE N.Y., largest city in the U.S. and one of the largest in the world, on N.Y. Bay at the mouth of the Hudson R.; 40°40′N 73°56′W. It comprises 5 boroughs, each coextensive with a co.: MANHATTAN (N.Y. co.), the heart of the city, an isl.; the BRONX (Bronx co.), on the mainland, NE of Manhattan and separated from it by the Harlem R.; QUEENS (Queens co.), on L.I., E of Manhattan across the East R.; BROOKLYN (Kings co.), also on L.I., on the East R. adjoining Queens and on N.Y. Bay; and STATEN ISLAND (Richmond co.), on Staten Isl., SW of Manhattan and separated from it by the Upper Bay. The metropolitan area (1990 est. pop. 18,087,251) encompasses parts of SE N.Y. state, NE N.J., and SW Conn. The port of N.Y. (which is now centered on the N.J. side of the Hudson R.), remains one of the leading ports in the world. The city is a vibrant center for commerce and business and one of the 3 "world cities" (along with London and Toyko) that control world finance. Mfg.—primarily of small but highly diverse types—accounts for a large but declining amount of employment. Clothing and other apparel, such as furs; chemicals; metal prods.; and processed foods are some of the principal mfg. N.Y. is also a major center of TV broadcasting, book publishing, advertising, and other facets of mass communications. The most celebrated newspapers are the N.Y. *Times* and the *Wall Street Journal.* N.Y. attracts many business and professional conventions. It was the site of 2 World's Fairs (1939–1940; 1964–1965), and in 1992 it hosted the Democratic Party's Natl. Convention. The city is served by 3 major airports: JFK (JOHN F. KENNEDY) INTERNATIONAL AIRPORT, and LAGUARDIA AIRPORT, both in Queens, and Newark Internatl. Airport, in N.J. RRs and interstate highways converge upon N.Y. from all points, giving access to outlying areas. With its vast cultural and educational resources, famous shops and restaurants, places of entertainment (including the theater dist. and many off-Broadway theaters), striking and diversified architecture (including the EMPIRE STATE BUILDING and the soaring towers of the WORLD TRADE CENTER), and parks and botanical gardens, N.Y. draws millions of tourists every year. Some of its streets and neighborhoods have become accepted symbols throughout the nation. WALL STREET means finance; BROADWAY, the theater; FIFTH AVENUE, fine shopping; and SOHO, art. N.Y. city is also famous for its ethnic diversity, manifesting itself in scores of communities representing virtually every nation on earth, each preserving its cultural identity. LITTLE ITALY, CHINATOWN, and the LOWER EAST SIDE (once a predominantly Jewish enclave, now a melange primarily consisting of E and S Asians, Dominicans, Central Americans, and Lat. Americans) date back to the mid-19th cent. Afr.-Americans from the South began to migrate to HARLEM after 1910, and in the 1940s large numbers of Puerto Ricans and other Hispanic-Americans began to settle in what is now known as Span. Harlem. The city's pop. has remained static, however, for over 50 years. In the 1980s, N.Y. city experienced a new wave of immigration largely from Lat. Amer. (esp. the Dominican Republic), Israel, E and S Asia, Jamaica, Haiti, Afr., and Russia. This new infusion, however, did little more than replace the 2d- and 3d-generation immigrants who were moving out of the city. The 1990 pop. of 7,322,564 is only slightly more than what it was in 1930. The city's many bridges include the GEORGE WASHINGTON BRIDGE, BROOKLYN BRIDGE, HENRY HUDSON BRIDGE, TRIBOROUGH BRIDGE, BRONX-WHITESTONE BRIDGE, THROGS NECK BRIDGE, and the VERRAZANO-NARROWS BRIDGE. The HOLLAND TUNNEL (the 1st vehicular tunnel under the Hudson) and the LINCOLN TUNNEL link Manhattan with N.J. The QUEENS-MIDTOWN TUNNEL and the BROOKLYN-BATTERY TUNNEL, both under the East R., connect Manhattan with W L.I. Isls. in the East R. include ROOSEVELT ISLAND (formerly Welfare Isl.), RIKERS ISLAND (site of a city penitentiary), and RANDALLS ISLAND (with Downing Stadium). In N.Y. Bay are Liberty Isl. (featuring the STATUE OF LIBERTY NATIONAL MONUMENT); GOVERNORS ISLAND; and ELLIS ISLAND. N.Y. city is the seat of the UNITED NATIONS HEADQUARTERS. LINCOLN CENTER FOR THE PERFORMING ARTS, is a complex of bldgs. housing the Metropolitan Opera Company, the N.Y. Philharmonic, the N.Y. City Ballet, the N.Y. City Opera, and the Juilliard School. Also in the city are Carnegie Hall and N.Y. City Center, featuring performances by musical and theatrical companies. Among the best known of the city's many museums and scientific collections are the Metropolitan Mus. of Art, the Mus. of Modern Art, the Solomon R. Guggenheim Mus. (designed by Frank Lloyd Wright), the Frick Collection (housed in the Frick mansion), the Whitney Mus. of Amer. Art, the Mus. of the City of N.Y., the Amer. Mus. of Natural History (with the Hayden Planetarium), the Pierpont Morgan Lib., the Mus. of Jewish Heritage (with a moving Holocaust memorial), the Mus. of the Amer. Indian, the mus. and lib. of the N.Y. Historical Society, and the Brooklyn Mus. The N.Y. Public Lib. is one of the largest in the U.S. Major educational institutions include the City Univ. of N.Y., Columbia Univ., Cooper Union, Fordham Univ., General Theological Seminary, Jewish Theological Seminary, New School for Social Research, N.Y. Univ., Pace Univ., Yeshiva Univ., Pratt Inst., and Union

Theological Seminary. A center for medical treatment and research, N.Y. has more than 130 hosps. and several medical schools. Noted hosps. include Bellevue Hosp., Mt. Sinai Hosp., Columbia-Presbyterian Medical Center, and N.Y. Hosp. Among N.Y.'s noted houses of worship are Trinity Church, St. Paul's Chapel (dedicated 1776), St. Patrick's Cathedral, the Cathedral of St. John the Divine, Riverside Church, and Temple Emanu-El. N.Y.'s parks and recreation centers include parts of GATEWAY NATIONAL RECREATION AREA CENTRAL PARK, The BATTERY, Washington Square Park, Riverside Park, and Fort Tryon Park (with the Cloisters) in Manhattan; the N.Y. Zoological Park (with the Bronx Zoo), the N.Y. Botanical Garden, and Van Cortlandt Park in the Bronx; and CONEY ISLAND (with boardwalks, beaches, and an aquarium) and PROSPECT PARK in Brooklyn. Sports events are held at MADISON SQUARE GARDEN in Manhattan, YANKEE STADIUM in the Bronx, and SHEA STADIUM in Queens. Among the many other places of interest are ROCKEFELLER CENTER; GREENWICH VILLAGE, with its cafés and restaurants; and TIMES SQUARE, with its lights and theaters. Of historic interest are Fraunces Tavern (built 1719), where Washington said farewell to his officers after the Amer. Revolution; Gracie Mansion (built late 18th cent.), now the official residence of the mayor; the Edgar Allen Poe Cottage; and Grant's Tomb. Although Giovanni da Verrazano was probably the 1st European to explore the region and Henry Hudson certainly visited the area, it was with Du. settlements on Manhattan and L.I. that the city truly began to emerge. In 1624 the colony of New Netherland was established, with the town of New Amsterdam on the lower tip of Manhattan as its capital. Peter Minuit of the chartered Du. West India Company supposedly bought the isl. from its Native Amer. inhabitants for about $24 worth of merchandise (the sale was completed in 1626). Under the Dutch, schools were opened and the Du. Reformed Church was established. The Native Amer. pop. was forced out of the area of Eur. settlement in a series of bloody battles. Charles II gave New Netherland to his brother James, Duke of York and Albany. In 1664 the duke sent a squadron of frigates to seize New Amsterdam, the seat of the colony's govt., headed by Director-Gen. Peter Stuyvesant. New Amsterdam was renamed N.Y. city, and it became capital of the new Br. prov. of N.Y. The Dutch returned to power briefly (1673–1674) before the reestablishment of Eng. rule. The autocratic rule of Br. governors was one of the causes of an insurrection that broke out in 1689. In 1741, an alleged plot by Afr.-Amer. slaves to burn N.Y. was ruthlessly suppressed. Throughout the 18th cent. N.Y. was an expanding commercial and cultural center. The city's 1st newspaper, the N.Y. *Gazette*, appeared in 1725, and its 1st institution of higher learning, Kings Col. (now Columbia Univ.), was founded in 1754. N.Y. was active in the colonial opposition to Br. measures after trouble in 1765 over the Stamp Act. As revolutionary sentiments increased, the N.Y. Sons of Liberty forced (1775) Gov. William Tryon and the Br. colonial govt. from the city. Although many New Yorkers were Loyalists, Continental forces commanded by George Washington tried to defend the city. After the patriot defeat in the Battle of L.I. and the succeeding actions at Harlem Heights and White Plains, Washington gave up N.Y., and the British occupied the city until the end of the war for independence. Under the Br. occupation 2 mysterious fires (1776 and 1778) destroyed a large part of the city. After the Revolution, N.Y. was briefly the 1st capital of the U.S. and was the state capital until 1797. New development was marked by such events as the founding (1784) of the Bank of N.Y. and the beginning of the stock exchange (c.1790). By 1790, N.Y. was the largest city in the U.S., with over 33,000 inhabitants; by 1800 the number had risen to 60,515. In 1811 plans were adopted for the laying out of most of Manhattan on a grid pattern. The opening of the Erie Canal (1825) made N.Y. city the seaboard gateway for the Great Lakes region, ushering in another era of commercial expansion. The N.Y. and Harlem RR was built in 1832. In 1835 a massive fire destroyed much of Lower Manhattan, but it brought about new bldg. laws and the construction of the OLD CROTON DAM AND AQUEDUCT water system. By 1840, N.Y. had become the leading port of the nation. A substantial wave of Irish and Ger. immigration after 1840 dramatically changed the character of urban life and politics in the city. The coming of the Civil War found New Yorkers unusually divided; many shared Mayor Fernando Wood's Southern sympathies, but under the leadership of Gov. Horatio Seymour most supported the Union. However, in the Draft Riots (1863), which broke out in protest against the Federal Conscription Act, the rioters—many of whom were Irish and other recent immigrants—directed most of their anger against Afr.-Americans. Extensive immigration had begun before the Civil War, and after 1865, with the acceleration of industrial development, another wave of immigration began, reaching its height in the late 19th and early 20th cents. As a result of this immigration, which was predominantly from E and S Europe, the city's pop. reached 3,437,000 by 1900 and 7 million by 1930. N.Y.'s many distinct neighborhoods, divided along ethnic and class lines, included such notorious slums as Five Points, CLINTON, also known as Hell's Kitchen, and the Lower East Side. They were often side-by-side with such exclusive neighborhoods as GRAMERCY PARK and BROOKLYN HEIGHTS. Until 1874, when portions of Westchester were annexed, the city's boundaries were those of present-day Manhattan. With the adoption of a new charter in 1898, N.Y. became a city of 5 boroughs—N.Y. city was split into the present Manhattan and Bronx boroughs, and the independent city of Brooklyn was annexed, as was the W portions of Queens co. and Staten Isl. The opening of the 1st subway line (1903) and other means of mass transportation spurred the growth of the outer boroughs, and this trend has continued into the 1990s. The Flatiron Bldg. (1902) foreshadowed the skyscrapers that today give Manhattan its famed skyline. In the 20th cent., N.Y. city has been served by such mayors as Seth Low, William J. Gaynor, James J. Walker (whose resignation was brought about by the Seabury investigation), Fiorello H. LaGuardia, Robert F. Wagner, Jr., John V. Lindsay, Edward I. Koch, David Dinkins (the city's 1st Afr.-Amer. mayor), and Rudolph Giuliani. The need for regional planning resulted in the nation's 1st zoning legislation of 1916 and the formation of such bodies as the Port of N.Y. Authority (1921; now the PORT AUTHORITY OF NEW YORK AND NEW JERSEY,), the Regional Plan Assn. (1929), the Municipal Housing Authority (1934), and the City Planning Commission (1938). In the period following World War II, N.Y. began to experience the urban problems that are common to most large U.S. cities. Urban renewal plans have done little to alleviate the growing poverty of large sects. of the city. These problems were highlighted in the near-bankruptcy of N.Y. city in 1975.

New York, uninc. village (1990 pop. 12), Henderson co., E Texas, 12 mi/19 km E of Athens. Noted for its cheesecakes, distributed throughout U.S. L. Athens to W; L. Palestine to E.

New York Bay, arm of the Atlantic Ocean at the mouth of the Hudson R., SE N.Y. and NE N.J., enclosed by the shores of NE N.J., E Staten Isl., S Manhattan, and W L.I. (Brooklyn) and opening on the SE to the Atlantic Ocean bet. Sandy Hook, N.J., and Rockaway Point, N.Y.; 40°40′N 74°02′W. It is a sheltered deep harbor able to accommodate the largest ships. The tidal range of the bay is very small and it is ice-free. N.Y. Bay is divided into Upper and Lower bays, which are connected by The Narrows, a strait (c.3 mi/4.8 km long; 1 mi/1.6 km wide) separating Staten Isl. from Brooklyn. The Verrazano-Narrows Bridge spans the strait bet. Fort Wadsworth and Fort Hamilton. Upper Bay, c.5.5 mi/8.9 km in diameter, is joined to Newark Bay (to the W) by Kill Van Kull and to L.I. Sound by the East R. Historically the bay has been one of the world's busiest harbors with port facilities on all shores, but now the N.J. waterfront is the most active. Ellis and Liberty isls. (both part of Statue of Liberty Natl. Monument) and Governors Isl. (site of Fort Jay) are in Upper Bay. Ferries cross the bay from Manhattan to Staten Isl. and N.J. The larger Lower Bay, which includes Raritan Bay on the W and Gravesend Bay on the NE is joined to Newark Bay by Arthur Kill. Jamaica Bay is an E extension of Lower Bay. Sections of Lower Bay's shoreline are part of Gateway Natl. Recreation Area. Ambrose Channel, federally maintained, crosses Sandy Hook bar at the bay's entrance and extends N to the piers of Upper Bay, where it is 2,000 ft/610 m wide.

New York Harbor, SE N.Y., port of entry for N.Y. city and the Greater N.Y. metropolitan area; at mouth of Hudson R. on N.Y. Bay, connects to L.I. Sound by the East R between the borough of Manhattan on the W and Queens and Brooklyn on the E. From the earliest colonial days, when fur trading put New Amsterdam on the map, to today's modern, massive container operations, the harbor has been vital to the regional and natl. economy. Simultaneous emergence of the jet age and containerized shipping of cargo, as well as changing trade patterns since the 1950s, have affected the harbor's maritime passenger and cargo movements; however, the modern port is still the 3d-largest container port in N. Amer., as well as one of the top 15 in the world. Harbor facilities and operations occur on both the N.Y. and N.J. sides. More than 400,000 motor vehicles now pass through the port each year, making it the leading U.S. port for auto importing and exporting. It is also a center for bulk and breakbulk cargoes. Planned, governed, and operated by the joint PORT AUTHORITY OF NEW YORK AND NEW JERSEY, the port serves not only the 17 million consumers within a defined 25-mi/40-km radius of the Statue of Liberty, but also N. Amer.'s largest marketplace of 80 million people, reaching into the Midwest, New England, and E Canada. The port dist. includes Upper and Lower N.Y. bays; Raritan, Gravesend, Flushing, Newark, and Jamaica bays; Hudson (North), East, Hackensack, Passaic, Raritan, and Harlem rivers, Newtown Creek, Arthur Kill, and Kill Van Kull. Cargo facilities within the N.Y. state confines of the harbor are the Green St. Lumber Exchange facilities (on the East R. in Queens); Pier 40 (on the Hudson R. side of Manhattan); the 40-acre/16-ha Red Hook Terminal (along the 40-ft/13-m deep Buttermilk Channel at the S end of the East R. in Brooklyn); the 2-mi/3.2-km S Brooklyn Marine Terminal; and the Howland Hook Marine Terminal (the W side of Staten Isl., bordering Arthur Kill). On the N.J. side of the harbor are 2 major port cargo facilities: the Auto Marine Terminal (on Upper N.Y. Bay) and the huge (□ 3 sq mi/7.8 sq km) Port Newark–Elizabeth Marine Terminal (on Newark Bay), the largest and most versatile terminal in the harbor. The harbor's leading general cargo exports include waste paper, plastic, motor vehicles and parts, lumber, and paper and paperboard. Major bulk exports are iron and steel, fuel oils, and corn. Leading imports include alcoholic beverages, organic chemicals, clothing, machinery, footwear, and motor vehicles and parts. Leading export markets for harbor goods are Europe and SE Asia. The N.Y. City Passenger Ship Terminal's 3 finger piers on Manhattan's W Side (bet. West 48th and West 52nd Sts.) are the only vestiges left of the scores of piers which once lined the Hudson to service the mainly trans-Atlantic passenger steamships. Today it primarily serves the seasonal cruise ship industry. From N.Y. city's earliest days, the history of the port has gone hand in hand with the history of the city. Its location directly on the Atlantic Ocean gave the city an early advantage over Philadelphia and Baltimore, and the 1825 opening of the Erie Canal made it the seaboard gateway for the vast Midwest. Fulton's steamship *Clemont* made its 1st voyage (1807) on the Hudson, and in 1838 the 1st vessels to cross the Atlantic entirely under steam power docked in the harbor. In both World Wars the harbor was one of the nation's most vital supply ports and ports of embarkation. In 1996 the Port Authority of N.Y. and N.J. agreed to undertake a large-scale dredging operation to deepen the harbor channels so larger vessels could be accommodated.

New York Mills, town (1990 pop. 940), Otter Tail co., W Minn., 14 mi/23 km WNW of Wadena; 46°31′N 95°22′W. Grain, sugar beets, sunflowers; poultry, livestock; dairying; mfg. (fabricated metal prods., furniture, printing and publishing). Rush L. to W.

New York Mills, village (□ 1 sq mi/2.6 sq km; 1990 pop. 3,534), Oneida co., central N.Y., 3 mi/4.8 km W of Utica; 43°06′N 75°17′W. Mfg. (machinery, textiles). Inc. 1922.

New York State Barge Canal, waterway system, 525 mi/ 845 km long, traversing N.Y. state and connecting the Great Lakes with the Hudson R. and L. Champlain. The canal, a modification and improvement of the old Erie canal, was authorized (1903) by public vote, begun in 1905, and completed in 1918. Its main sects. are the Erie Canal, extending from Troy to Tonawanda; the Champlain Canal, joining the Erie Canal at Waterford and extending N (via the Hudson as far as Fort Edward) to Whitehall on L. Champlain; the Oswego Canal, connecting the Erie Canal with Oswego on L. Ontario at Three Rivers, N of Syracuse; and the Cayuga and Seneca Canal, joining the Erie Canal with Cayuga and Seneca lakes at Montezuma. It is operated by the N.Y. State Thruway Authority's Canal Recreationway Commission, created by the state legislature in 1992. The Barge Canal (12 ft/4 m deep), with 57 electrically operated locks, can accommodate 2,000-ton/1,814-metric ton vessels. With the significant decline in the commercial shipping of commodities that occurred in the 1970s, N.Y. state has essentially abandoned the idea of modernizing the system and integrating it into the nation's extensive and commercially viable network of waterways. The state now envisions preserving the canal's history and environment, emphasizing leisuretime activities on and along the canal, and re-energizing adjacent communities through cooperative public-private projects under the canal corporation, a wholly owned subsidiary of the Canal Recreationway Commission. Numerous leisure craft use the canal. Additional uses provided by the canal system are as a supply of fresh water and a method of flood control and generating hydroelectric power.

New York State Thruway, toll expressway between N.Y. city and Ripley in W N.Y. (on the Pa. state line). Completed in 1960, in 1964 it was officially named the Gov. Thomas E. Dewey Thruway, after the state governor who sponsored legislation in 1950 for its construction. With a total length of 641 mi/1,032 km, it is the longest state expressway in the U.S. The main line originally stretched 426 mi/686 km between N.Y. city and Buffalo, the state's 2 largest cities. The main line and connections totalled 559 mi/900 km; the expressway grew another 11 mi/18 km in Apr. 1991 with the state's acquisition of the Cross Westchester Expressway (I-287), and another 71 mi/114 km in Oct. 1991 with the acquisition of I 84 from Port Jervis to the Conn. state line. Various sects. connect to New England states, Pa., N.J., the Midwest, and Canada. In Apr. 1987, a 540-ft/165-m span over Schoharie Creek collapsed, and 6 people were killed.

Newagen, Cape (noo-WAI-guhn), Lincoln co., SW Maine. Has summer colony at S tip of Southport town.

Newalla (noo-AHL-uh), village, Oklahoma co., central Okla., suburb 21 mi/34 km ESE of Oklahoma City. In oil-producing area; mfg. (plumbing equip.). Part of Oklahoma City.

Newark 1 (NOO-wuhrk), city (1990 pop. 37,861), Alameda co., W Calif., suburb 23 mi/37 km SSE of Oakland, 15 mi/24 km NNW of San Jose; 37°31′N 122°02′W. Mfg. (plastics prods., furniture, feeds, semiconductors, chemicals, machine parts, paper prods., food processing, gypsum prods., computers). Dumbarton Bridge crosses San Francisco Bay to Palo Alto (W); Hetch Hetchy Aqueduct passes through city in S and crosses San Francisco Bay S of Dunbarton Bridge; Sky Sailing Airport to SE; Coyote Hills Regional Park to NW; San Francisco Bay Natl. Wildlife Refuge visitors center to W. **2** (NOO-work), city (1990 pop. 25,098), New Castle co., NW Del., 11 mi/18 km WSW of Wilmington, on White Clay Creek; 39°41′N 75°45′W. Near Md. state line; Pa. state line to N. RR junction. The 3d-largest city

in the state, it is the seat of the Univ. of Del. Mfg. (metal prods., printing and publishing, electrical equip., machinery, consumer goods, food prods., transportation equip., plastics prods., construction materials, textiles). The only Revolutionary battle on Del. soil was fought (Sept. 1777) at nearby Cooch's Bridge. White Clay Creek State Park to N; Lums Pond State Park to S; Fair Hill Natural Resource Management Area and Covered Bridge to NW, in Md. Settled before 1700, inc. 1852. **3** city (1990 pop. 275,221), ⊙ Essex co., NE N.J., on the Passaic R. and Newark Bay, 8 mi/13 km W of N.Y. city. It is a port of entry and the largest city in the state. Newark is a transportation, industrial, commercial, and mfg. center. A major center for transshipment of RR, truck, and water freight; deepwater terminal (Port Newark), developed in World War I, and Newark Airport (opened 1929) are units of Port of N.Y. and Jersey City Authority. Its leather industry dates from the 17th cent., and its still-significant jewelry mfg. and insurance businesses began in the early 19th cent. Among the city's many other prods. are beer, cutlery, electronic equip., textiles, pharmaceuticals, fabricated metal items, paints. Newark Internatl. Airport is one of the nation's busiest, and the important seaport is operated by the Port Authority of N.Y. and N.J. The city was settled (1666) by Puritans from Conn. under the leadership of Robert Treat. It was the scene of Revolutionary skirmishes. Industrial growth began after the Amer. Revolution, aided by the development of transportation facilities. The Morris Canal was opened in 1832, and the RRs arrived in 1834 and 1835. A flourishing shipping business resulted, and Newark became the industrial center of the area. In the late 19th cent. its industry was further developed, esp. through the efforts of such men as Seth Boyden and J. W. Hyatt. Newark Port opened in 1915, and the city's shipbuilding played an important role in World War I. During the latter half of the 20th cent., Newark's economy and living standards have greatly declined. Many central city residents fled to the outlying suburbs, which have been marked by a boon in corporate development, shopping center growth, and housing construction. Poverty and unemployment have plagued Newark. In July 1967, the city was the scene of a major race riot, resulting in 26 deaths and more than 1,300 injuries before the Natl. Guard restored order. By the 1980s nearly 50% of the city's residents were black. Landmarks include Trinity Cathedral (1810, with the spire of a church built in 1743); the Sacred Heart Cathedral (begun 1898, completed 1953); the First Presbyterian Church (1791); the Newark Public Lib. (founded 1888); the Newark Mus. (1909); and the co. courthouse (1906), with Gutzon Borglum's statue of Lincoln in front. Other points of interest include Borglum's large group *Wars of Amer.* (1926) in Military Park (a Revolutionary War drilling ground and a Civil War tenting area) and many historic homes. Celluloid (1872) and photographic film (1887) 1st made here. Newark's educational institutions include Rutgers Univ. in Newark, the N.J. Inst. of Technology, Essex County Col., and a preparatory acad. founded in 1774. Aaron Burr and Stephen Crane b. here. Settled 1666, inc. as a city 1836, adopted commission govt. 1917. **4** city (1990 pop. 44,389), ⊙ Licking co., central Ohio, on the Licking R.; 40°04′N 82°25′W. In a livestock area. Farm trade and processing center, a transportation hub, and an industrial city. Mfg. includes glass, aluminum prods., automobile parts, and plastics. The city's Native Amer. mounds attract many visitors. The Newark Earthworks State Memorials include 3 locations within the city's limits: the Great Circle; the Octagon Mound, with smaller mounds inside the octagon; and the Wright Earthworks. Mus. of Native Amer. Art and Newark campus of the Ohio State Univ. are here. Inc. 1826.

Newark 1 (noo-AHRK), town (1990 pop. 1,159), Independence co., NE central Ark., 12 mi/19 km ESE of Batesville; 35°42′N 91°26′W. In agr. and timber area. Large electricity generator nearby. **2** (NOO-ahrk), town (1990 pop. 82), Knox co., NE Mo., on South Fabius R., and 16 mi/26 km SE of Edina; 39°59′N 91°58′W.

Limestone quarry. **3** town (1990 pop. 354), Caledonia co., NE Vt., 20 mi/32 km N of St. Johnsbury; 44°42′N 71°55′W.

Newark 1 village (1990 pop. 840), Kendall co., NE Ill., 10 mi/16 km SW of Yorkville; 41°32′N 88°34′W. In rich agr. area. **2** village, Worcester co., SE Md. 19 mi/31 km ESE of Salisbury. In farming and timber area; canneries. The RR station here is given the name Queponco to avoid confusion with other Newarks. **3** (NOO-wuhrk), village (□ 5 sq mi/13 sq km; 1990 pop. 9,849), Wayne co., W N.Y., on the Barge Canal, 29 mi/47 km ESE of Rochester; 43°02′N 77°05′W. In agr. area. Mfg. (metal prods., furniture). Inc. 1839. **4** village, Marshall co., NE S.Dak., 10 mi/16 km N of Britton, on N.Dak. state line; 45°55′N 97°47′W. In agr. area.

Newark, Canada: see NIAGARA-ON-THE-LAKE.

Newark Bay (NOO-uhrk), NE N.J., estuary at confluence of Passaic and Hackensack rivers, bet. shores of Newark and Elizabeth (W), Jersey City and Bayonne (E), and Staten Isl. (S); linked to Upper N.Y. Bay by Kill Van Kull, to Lower N.Y. Bay by Arthur Kill; 6 mi/ 9.7 km long, 1 mi/1.6 km wide. Port Newark is deepwater terminal on W shore, connected with dredged channel in bay.

Newark Valley, village (1990 pop. 1,082), Tioga co., S N.Y., on Owego Creek, 17 mi/27 km NW of Binghamton; 42°13′N 76°11′W. Wood prods.

Newaygo (ne-WAI-go), county (□ 861 sq mi/ 2,230 sq km; 1990 pop. 38,202), W Mich.; ⊙ White Cloud; 43°32′N 85°47′W. Drained by Muskegon, Pere Marquette, and White rivers and short Tamarack and Rogue rivers. Agr. (cattle, hogs, poultry; dairying; onions, carrots, asparagus, apples, cherries, peaches, grains). Some mfg. at Newaygo. Resorts. Manistee Natl. Forest, Newaygo State Park in E, White Cloud State Park at center; Manistee Natl. Forest covers NE ⅔ of co. except extreme NE corner, Hardy Dam is here. Organized 1851.

Newaygo (ne-WAI-go), town (1990 pop. 1,136), Newaygo co., W central Mich., 8 mi/12.9 km S of White Cloud, and on Muskegon R.; 43°25′N 85°47′W. In farm area (fruit, vegetables); dairy prods. Mfg. (machinery). Airport. Manistee Natl. Forest to NE. Settled 1836, inc. as village 1867.

Newberg, city (1990 pop. 13,086), Yamhill co., NW Oregon, 20 mi/32 km SW of Portland, on Willamette R.; 45°18′N 122°57′W. Agr. (wheat, barley, oats, fruit, nuts; poultry, cattle); dairy prods. Wineries nearby. Mfg. (chemicals, furniture, pulp, plastic prods., machinery, electronics assembly). George Fox Col. Bald Peak State Park to N; Champoag State Park to SE. Founded by Quakers; named, 1869, inc. 1893.

Newbern 1 town (1990 pop. 222), Hale co., W central Ala., 10 mi/16 km SE of Greenboro; 32°35′N 87°32′W. **2** town (1990 pop. 2,515), Dyer co., NW Tenn., 9 mi/ 14 km NE of Dyersburg, 36°07′N 89°16′W. In agr. and light mfg. area.

Newbern, uninc. village, Pulaski co., SW Va., 5 mi/8 km ENE of Pulaski, near New R., Claytor L. reservoir; 37°04′N 80°41′W. Mfg. (handmade carousel horses). Agr. (corn; cattle, sheep; dairying). Claytor L. State Park to E.

Newberry, county (□ 647 sq mi/1,676 sq km; 1990 pop. 33,172), NW central S.C.; ⊙ Newberry; 34°17′N 81°35′W. Bounded E by Broad R., S by Saluda R., N by Enoree R.; part of L. Murray in SE. Includes part of Sumter Natl. Forest. Mainly agr. (chickens, turkeys, hogs, cattle; eggs; corn, oats, soybeans, sorghum, hay); timber, granite. Mfg. at Newberry. Formed 1785.

Newberry 1 town (□ 2 sq mi/5.2 sq km; 1990 pop. 1,644), Alachua co., N central Fla., 17 mi/27 km W of Gainesville; 29°38′N 82°36′W. Small-scale farming; phosphate quarries nearby. **2** town (1990 pop. 207), Greene co., SW Ind., on West Fork of White R., and 9 mi/14.5 km SW of Bloomfield; 38°55′N 87°01′W. In agr. area (corn, wheat; turkeys). Mfg. (poultry prods.). Laid out 1822. **3** town (1990 pop. 1,873), ⊙ Luce co., NE Upper Peninsula, Mich., c.55 mi/89 km WSW of Sault Ste. Marie, near Tahquamenon R.; 46°21′N 85°30′W. Logging; trade point for farm area (cattle; forage crops, oats);

mfg. (strand board). Starting point for fishermen, scenic route to Tahquamenon Falls State Park, to NE. Big Valley Ski Area to S. Settled 1882, inc. 1886. **4** industrial town (1990 pop. 10,542), ⊙ Newberry co., NW central S.C., 45 mi/72 km WNW of Columbia; 34°16′N 81°36′W. Mfg. (textiles, wood prods., printing and publishing, paper prods., communication equip.); lumber, food processing; granite quarries. A fish hatchery is here. Seat of Newberry Col.

Newborn, village (1990 pop. 404), Newton co., N central Ga., 11 mi/18 km ESE of Covington; 33°31′N 83°42′W.

Newboro (NOO-buh-ruh), village (1991 pop. 282), SE Ont., Canada, on Newboro L. (8 mi/13 km long, 3 mi/5 km wide), 30 mi/48 km NNE of Kingston; 44°39′N 76°19′W. Dairying, mixed farming.

Newburg, city (1990 pop. 589), Phelps co., central Mo., in the Ozarks, on Little Piney R., 8 mi/12.9 km W of Rolla; 37°55′N 91°54′W. Artist colony. Surrounded by Mark Twain Natl. Forest. Settled 1823.

Newburg 1 village (1990 pop. 104), Bottineau co., N N.Dak. 23 mi/37 km WSW of Bottineau, near Souris R. (Mouse R.); 48°42′N 100°54′W. J. Clark Salyer Natl. Wildlife Refuge to E. **2** village (1990 pop. 378), Preston co., N W.Va., 10 mi/16 km ENE of Grafton; 39°23′N 79°50′W. Agr. and coal-mining area. **3** village (1990 pop. 875), Washington co., E Wis., 7 mi/11.3 km E of West Bend, on branch of Milwaukee R.; 43°25′N 88°02′W. Agr. (poultry; general farming). Mfg. (transportation equip., machinery).

Newburg 1 (NOO-buhrg), borough (1990 pop. 117), Clearfield co., central Pa., 22 mi/35 km SW of Clearfield, on Chest Creek; 40°50′N 41°78′W. Agr. (corn, hay; livestock; dairying). Post office name is La Jose. **2** borough (1990 pop. 312), Cumberland co., S Pa., 6 mi/9.7 km NNW of Shippensburg, near Conodoguinet Creek; 40°08′N 77°32′W. Mfg. (fruit juice, potpourri). Agr. (apples, grain; livestock; dairying).

Newburgh, city (□ 4 sq mi/10.4 sq km; 1990 pop. 26,454), Orange co., SE N.Y., on the W bank of the Hudson R., opposite Beacon; 41°30′N 74°01′W. The city has become an area wholesale and trucking center that ships fruit and dairy prods. Mfg. (transportation equip., machinery, scientific instruments, apparel, plastic goods, metal prods.). Growing Hispanic pop. Newburgh has many old houses, and the streets run sharply to the river. At Hasbrouck House (1750; now a mus.), Washington made his hq. from April 1782 to Aug. 1783. It was in Newburgh that the Continental Army was disbanded. Mt. St. Mary Col. is in the city. West Point is located a few miles to the S. Settled 1709 by Palatines; inc. 1800.

Newburgh 1 town (1990 pop. 2,880), Warrick co., SW Ind., on Ohio R., and 10 mi/16 km SW of Boonville; 37°57′N 87°24′W. Suburb of Evansville. Mfg. (aluminum ingots). Settled 1803, laid out 1818. **2** town (1990 pop. 1,317), Penobscot co., S Maine, 13 mi/21 km WSW of Bangor; 44°42′N 69°01′W. Includes Newburgh Center and Newburgh Village.

Newburgh (NOO-buhrg), village (1991 pop. 712), SE Ont., Canada, on Napanee R., and 7 mi/11 km NE of Napanee; 44°20′N 76°52′W. Paper milling.

Newburgh Heights (NOO-buhrg, NYOO-), village (1990 pop. 2,310), Cuyahoga co., N Ohio, a S suburb of Cleveland; 41°27′N 81°40′W. Ceramic plants.

Newbury 1 residential town (1990 pop. 5,623), Essex co., NE Mass., 15 mi/24 km ENE of Lawrence, just S of Newburyport; 42°46′N 70°53′W. Includes sects. of Byfield, South Byfield, and Plum Isl. Plum Isl. Airport. Site of Parker River Natl. Wildlife Refuge and Northeast Wildlife Management Area. Governor Dummer Acad. preparatory school in South Byfield. Plum Isl. State Park nearby. **2** town (1990 pop. 1,347), Merrimack co., S central N.H., 27 mi/43 km WNW of Concord; 43°18′N 72°01′W. Tourism. Timber; poultry; dairying. Sunapee L. on NW boundary with Mt. Sunapee State Park Beach at S end of lake. Mt. Sunapee Ski Area, in Mt. Sunapee State Park, in W. **3** town (1990 pop. 1,985), including Newbury village, Orange co., E Vt., on the Connecticut R., and 24 mi/39 km SE of Barre; 44°06′N 72°07′W. Site of Revolutionary fort and E terminus of military road built 1776. Includes industrial village of Wells River. Settled 1762 on site of Indian village.

Newbury, village (1991 pop. 419), S Ont., Canada, 28 mi/45 km NE of Chatham; 42°41′N 81°48′W. Fruit growing.

Newbury National Volcanic Monument, Deschutes co., 10 mi/16 km S of Bend, central Oregon, surrounded by Deschutes Natl. Forest. Includes Newbury Crater, 22 mi/35 km S of Bend, with E and W lakes in its caldera, also Lava Cast Forest, Lava R. Cave, and Lava Butte Geological Area.

Newbury Park, uninc. town, Ventura co., S Calif., independent suburb 4 mi/6.4 km W of Thousand Oaks, near Arroyo Conejo. Mfg. (metal prods., consumer goods, electrical and computer equip., communications equip., transportation equip., printing and publishing, machinery). Ranco Conejo Airport to N. Santa Monica Mts. Natl. Recreation Area to S.

Newburyport, city (1990 pop. 16,317), ⊙ Essex co., NE Mass., at the mouth of the Merrimack R. Its silverware industry dates from colonial times; textiles, scientific instruments, and electronic equip. are also made. Summer resort; antiques; fishing; whale watching. An early shipbuilding, whaling, and shipping center, it declined after Jefferson's embargo of 1808 and the War of 1812. Birthplace of U.S. Coast Guard and Plum Isl. Coast Guard Station. There are several historic and maritime museums here. Its notable old houses include the Coffin House (c.1651), the Swett-Isley House (c.1671), the Short House (c.1732), and Custom House Maritime Mus. William Lloyd Garrison and Francis Cabot Lowell were b. here. Natl. Wildlife Refuge nearby and state park. Settled 1635, set off from Newbury and inc. 1764.

Newcastle 1 town (1991 pop. 5,711), E central N.B., Canada, on the Miramichi R.; 47°00′N 65°34′W. In lumbering region. Sawmills and a large pulp mill. Newcastle was the birthplace of the Can. leader Peter Mitchell and was the boyhood home of Lord Beaverbrook. **2** town (1991 pop. 49,479), S Ont., Canada, on L. Ontario, 15 mi/24 km E of Oshawa; 43°55′N 78°35′W. Includes Bowmanville and large rural area. Dairying; mixed farming; apples.

Newcastle, town, St. Andrew parish, E Jamaica, in Blue Mts., 9 mi/14.5 km NE of Kingston; 18°04′N 76°43′W. Elev. c.3,700 ft/1,128 m. Mt. resort; military barracks.

Newcastle 1 town (1990 pop. 1,538), Lincoln co., S Maine, on Damariscotta R. inlet (bridged to Damariscotta), and 6 mi/9.7 km NE of Wiscasset; 44°02′N 69°34′W. **2** town (1990 pop. 3,003), ⊙ Weston co., NE Wyo., just SW of Black Hills, near S.Dak. state line, 50 mi/80 km WSW of Rapid City, S.Dak.; 43°51′N 104°12′W. Elev. 4,334 ft/1,321 m. Shipping point for cattle, lumber, oil prods., and bentonite. Mfg. (lumber, petroleum prods.). Pioneer relics at Anna Miller Mus. Scenic region of caves, canyons, lakes, and streams in nearby Black Hills. Thunder Basin Natl. Grassland to W. Founded 1889.

Newcastle 1 uninc. village, Placer co., central Calif., in Sacramento Valley, 3 mi/4.8 km SW of Auburn. Ships fruit, nuts; cattle, sheep. Mfg. (boatbuilding). Folsom L. State Recreation Area to SE. **2** village (1990 pop. 271), Dixon co., NE Nebr., 10 mi/16 km NW of Ponca, Iowa, near Missouri R; 42°38′N 96°52′W. In fertile agr. region (livestock, poultry prods.; grain). **3** village (1990 pop. 505), Young co., N Texas, near Brazos R., c.50 mi/80 km SSW of Wichita Falls; 33°11′N 98°44′W. Elev. 1,126 ft/343 m. Oil fields nearby. Agr. (livestock; cotton; wheat). Restored Fort Belknap (est. 1851) is just S. L. Graham reservoir to E. Formerly coal-mining center.

Newcomb, mining village (1990 pop. 300), Essex co., NE N.Y., in the Adirondacks, 38 mi/61 km WNW of Ticonderoga; 44°01′N 74°08′W. Ilmenite, magnetite.

Newcomerstown (NOO-kuh-muhrz-toun), village (1990 pop. 4,012), Tuscarawas co., E Ohio, 17 mi/27 km SSW of New Philadelphia, and on Tuscarawas R. Mfg. (tools, hardware, clay prods.). Settled 1815 on site of Delaware Indians' capital; inc. 1838.

Newdale, village (1990 pop. 377), Fremont co., E Idaho, 8 mi/12.9 km SE of St. Anthony; 43°54′N 111°36′W. Elev. 5,068 ft/1,545 m. Agr. (cattle, sheep; potatoes). Teton Dam Site 5 mi/8 km ENE; on June 5, 1976, the dam collapsed, sending billions of gallons of water into the Teton R. valley just W of Newdale, killing 11 people.

Newell 1 (NOO-uhl) town (1990 pop. 1,089), Buena Vista co., NW Iowa, 10 mi/16 km ESE of Storm L.; 42°36′N 95°00′W. Concrete prods., feed. **2** uninc. town (1990 pop. 900), Mecklenburg co., S N.C., residential suburb 6 mi/9.7 km NE of downtown Charlotte. Univ. of N.C., Charlotte, to N; Univ. Research Park to NW. Agr. to E (grain; livestock). **3** uninc. town (1990 pop. 1,724), Hancock co., N W.Va., in Northern Panhandle, 2 mi/3.2 km SW of East Liverpool, Ohio, across Ohio R. (bridged); 40°37′N 80°35′W. Mfg. (consumer goods, electrical equip., graphite, chemicals, bauxite), oil refining. Agr. (grain, nursery crops).

Newell, village (1990 pop. 675), Butte co., W S.Dak., 22 mi/35 km E of Belle Fourche; 44°43′N 103°25′W. In heart of irrigated area; diversified farming (sugar beets, grain, dairy prods., honey). Nearby is a substation of state experimental farm. Belle Fourche Reservoir (Orman Dam) to W.

Newell (NOO-uhl), borough (1990 pop. 518), Fayette co., SW Pa., 25 mi/40 km S of Pittsburgh, in sharp bend of Monongahela R.; 40°04′N 79°53′W. Mfg. (chemicals). Agr. (corn, hay; dairying).

Newellton (NOO-uhl-tuhn), town (1990 pop. 2,576), Tensas parish, NE La., 29 mi/47 km SW of Vicksburg, Miss., on NW end of L. St. Joseph; 32°04′N 91°14′W. In agr. area (cotton, rice, soybeans, peanuts, wheat; cattle). Tensas R. Natl. Wildlife Refuge to NW.

Newenham, Cape, SW Alaska, on Bering Sea, bet. Kuskokwim Bay (N) and Bristol Bay (S), 130 mi/209 km W of Dillingham; 58°39′N 162°02′W. Extremity of small peninsula formed by rugged mts.

Newfane, town (1990 pop. 1,555), including Newfane village, ⊙ Windham co., SE Vt., on West R., and 10 mi/16 km NW of Brattleboro; 42°58′N 72°42′W. Resort, winter and summer recreation.

Newfane, village (□ 4 sq mi/10.4 sq km; 1990 pop. 3,001), Niagara co., W N.Y., near L. Ontario, 25 mi/40 km NNE of Buffalo; 43°17′N 78°42′W. In fruit-growing area; nurseries.

Newfield, town (1990 pop. 1,042), York co., SW Maine, 14 mi/23 km NW of Alfred; 43°38′N 54°70′W. Severely damaged (1947) by forest fire.

Newfield, borough (1990 pop. 1,592), Gloucester co., S N.J., 10 mi/16 km N of Millville; 39°32′N 75°01′W. Mfg. (powdered metals, glass prods.).

Newfields, town (1990 pop. 888), Rockingham co., SE N.H., 10 mi/16 km WSW of Portsmouth; 43°02′N 70°58′W. Bounded E by Squamscott R; drained by Piscassic R. Agr. (cattle, poultry; vegetables; dairying; nursery crops). Mfg. (transportation equip., screen printing).

Newfolden (noo-FOL-duhn), village (1990 pop. 345), Marshall co., NW Minn., on Middle R., and 18 mi/29 km NNW of Thief R. Falls; 48°21′N 96°19′W. Agr. (potatoes, sugar beets, beans, wheat; cattle, sheep, poultry). Light mfg.

Newfound Gap, pass (5,048 ft/1,539 m), on Tenn.-N.C. state line, 8 mi/12.9 km SSE of Gatlinburg, Tenn. Crossed by highway bet. Gatlinburg and Cherokee, N.C., through Great Smoky Mts. Natl. Park.

Newfound Lake (NOO-found), Grafton co., central N.H., resort lake in hilly region 12 mi/19 km NNW of Franklin; 6 mi/9.7 km long, 2.5 mi/4 km wide. Drains S through Newfound R. (2.5 mi/4 km long), past Bristol (water power), to the Pemigewasset R.

Newfoundland and Labrador (NYOO-fuhn-luhnd, nyoo-fuhn-LAND), province, E Canada, consists of the isl. of N.F. and adjacent isls. (□ 43,359 sq mi/112,300 sq km; 1991 pop. 538,099) and the mainland area of Lab. and adjacent isls. (□ 112,826 sq mi/292,219 sq km; 1991 pop. 30,375), ⊙ SAINT JOHN'S; 52°00′N 56°00′W. N.F. isl. lies at the mouth of the Gulf of St. Lawrence and is bounded on the N, E, and S by the Atlantic Ocean and separated on the NW from Lab. by the Strait of Belle Isle. Lab., part of the LABRADOR-UNGAVA peninsula, forms the NE tip of the Can. mainland. It is bounded on the E by the Atlantic Ocean down to the Strait of Belle Isle and on the S and W by

Que. Cape Chidley, Lab.'s northernmost point, is on the Hudson Strait. N.F. has a rocky, irregular coast, indented with numerous inlets. The major portion of the isl. is a plateau, with many lakes and marshes, and with forests covering less than ½ the area. Throughout the prov. the inland wilderness has an abundance of waterfowl, fish, and fur-bearing animals, while caribou graze on the tundra of the N. The cod-fishing area of the Grand Banks is probably the best in the world. Lobster, flounder, redfish, herring, and salmon are caught throughout the coastal waters; cod fishing collapsed in mid-1990s due to overfishing and failure to rebound. The prov. has a generally cool and moist climate. In Lab., the cold Lab. current, bringing temperatures below freezing 8 months of the year, and the lack of transportation facilities have combined to retard economic development. However, Lab. is rich in mineral resources (iron, zinc, copper, asbestos, gold, oil, natural gas), timber, and water power. Exploitation of the tremendous iron reserves in the SW lake dist., begun in the 1950s, and the growth of the logging industry have brought new towns and roads. Also, what is believed to be the world's largest deposit of nickel was discovered in an 800-sq-mi/2,072-sq-km area surrounding Voisey's Bay; production is expected to begin in the year 2000. The area also has deposits of cobalt and copper. There is a giant hydroelectric project at Churchill Falls. A 65-year contract with Que. (1976) gives all but a fraction of revenue from project to Hydro Que. This and collapse of cod industry in mid-1990s has increased pressure on prov. to develop offshore oil and gas fields, of which there have been significant discoveries in recent years. These discoveries are expected to have a favorable economic impact on the prov.'s economy, although the negative impact upon coastal fishing is argued by environmentalists. Biggest concern is potential for spills and damage to oil rigs by icebergs, rough seas, and seismic activity. Mining is the main industry, and N.F. provides about ½ of Canada's iron ore. The processing of fish and the mfg. of wood prods. are also important. There are large pulp and paper mills at GRAND FALLS and CORNER BROOK, both on N.F. Agr. in the prov. is limited by the unfavorable soil and climate, and much of the food supply must be imported. The pop. is centered on the Avalon Peninsula, which is the prov.'s most important commercial and administrative region. Corner Brook is the 2d-largest city. Most of the inhabitants are of Eng. or Irish descent, but in Lab. there are small numbers of Inuit and Montagnais-Naskapi. The Beothuk, a Native Amer. tribe on the island of N.F., died out in the 19th cent., presumably of Eur. diseases. Vikings visited the area c.1000 and briefly established a settlement on N.F. at L'Anse aux Meadows, the sole confirmed Viking site in N. Amer. After the 2 voyages of John Cabot to the area at the end of the 15th cent., fishermen and explorers from several Eur. countries followed. In 1535–1536, Jacques Cartier sailed through the Cabot Strait and the Strait of Belle Isle. Sir Humphrey Gilbert claimed N.F. for England in 1583. The 1st settlers arrived in 1610. After it changed hands several times, the Treaty of Paris of 1763 definitively awarded N.F. and Lab. (where the French had established trading posts) to Great Britain. The Peace of Utrecht in 1713 granted France the fishing rights on the NW coast of N.F. and awarded St. Pierre and Miquelon to it. In 1783 the "French Shore" was redefined to include the entire W coast. In the early 19th cent. the Hudson's Bay Company developed the fur trade; this and the expanding fishing industry led to increased immigration from Europe, particularly from Ireland. Representative govt. was introduced in 1832 and parliamentary govt. in 1855. The port of Heart's Content became the W terminal of the transatlantic cable in 1866. In 1869 the voters of N.F. rejected union with Canada; in 1895, after a disastrous fire in St. John's and the failure of local banks, negotiations to join Canada resumed but were unsuccessful. In 1895 iron ore was discovered in the Grand Falls (now Churchill Falls) region of Lab. As part of the Anglo-Fr. Entente Cordiale of 1904, France abandoned the Fr. Shore. In 1927, the Br. Privy Council demarcated the W boundary, enlarged the Lab. land area, and confirmed N.F.'s title to it, but Que. continues to claim it. During the economic depression of the 1930s, Britain suspended N.F.'s self-govt. and assumed administrative and financial control. Actual authority was exercised by a joint commission of Newfoundlanders and British. During World War II, U.S. and Can. military bases were est. in Lab. and on N.F. After the war N.F. voted to join Canada, and in 1949 it became Canada's 10th prov. Joseph Smallwood, a Liberal who led the drive to join Canada, became premier and held office until 1972, when the Conservatives gained a majority under Frank Moores. Power has since moved back and forth. N.F. sends 6 senators and 7 representatives to the natl. parliament. Memorial Univ. of N.F. is in St. John's.

Newfoundland Canal, W central N.F., Canada, extends 10 mi/16 km WSW-ESE bet. NE end of Deer L. and NE end of Grand L.

Newfoundland Mountains, Box Elder co., NW Utah, in Great Salt L. Desert. Desert Peak (6,984 ft/2,129 m) is highest point. Small range c.15 mi/24 km N-S, Newfoundland Evaporation Basin to W; Hill Air Force Firing Range and Great Salt L. to E.

Newgulf, uninc. village (1990 pop. 963), Wharton co., S Texas, c.45 mi/72 km SW of Houston. In sulphur-mining area; oil wells. Agr. (rice; cotton).

Newhalen, village (1990 pop 160), Alaska, 225 mi/362 km SW of Anchorage, on N shore of Iliamna L., largest lake in Alaska (75 mi/121 km long, E-W; 20 mi/32 km wide); 59°43′N 154°52′W. Road connection to village of Iliamna and L. Clark, in L. Clark Natl. Park and Preserve. Fishing, hunting.

Newhall, town (1990 pop. 854), Benton co., E central Iowa, 15 mi/24 km W of Cedar Rapids; 41°59′N 91°58′W. Mfg. (feed, wood and metal prods.).

Newington, uninc. city, Fairfax co., NE Va. suburb 9 mi/14.5 km SW of Alexandria, 15 mi/24 km SW of Wash., D.C., on Accotink Creek; 38°44′N 77°12′W. Mfg. (concrete, fabricated metal prods., stains, commercial printing, satellites). Fort Belvoir Military Reservation to SE, Fort Belvoir Proving Ground to NW.

Newington 1 town (1990 pop. 29,208), Hartford co., central Conn., suburb of Hartford; 41°41′N 72°43′W. Chiefly residential. Industry includes milk processing and the mfg. of airplane parts, ball bearings, metal fabrication, tools, and plumbing supplies. Site of children's hosp. Settled 1670, inc. 1871. **2** town (1990 pop. 319), Screven co., E Ga., 16 mi/26 km SE of Sylvania, near S.C. state line; 32°35′N 81°31′W. **3** town (1990 pop. 990), Rockingham co., SE N.H., 5 mi/8 km NW of Portsmouth; 43°06′N 70°50′W. Bounded W by Great Bay, NW by Little Bay, NE by Piscataqua R. (Maine state line). Mfg. (lab equip., food processing, communications equip., swimming pools); agr. (nursery crops; cattle, poultry, seafood; dairying). Pease Internatl. Tradeport (including airport, formerly Pease Air Force Base), in E; shipping; oil and gas terminal.

Newkirk, town (1990 pop. 2,168), ⊙ Kay co., N Okla., 13 mi/21 km N of Ponca City; 36°52′N 97°03′W. Elev. 1,154 ft/352 m. Grain elevators; oil and gas wells; light mfg. Kaw L. is E. Settled c.1893.

Newland, village (1990 pop. 645), ⊙ Avery co., NW N.C., 27 mi/43 km NNW of Morganton, in the Blue Ridge Mts., at edge of Pisgah Natl. Forest; 36°05′N 81°55′W. North Toe R., near its source. Cattle; tobacco. Grandfather Mt. (5,964 ft/1,818 m) to E.

Newlands project, on the Carson and Truckee rivers, W Nev. Was the 1st irrigation project built by the U.S. Bureau of Reclamation (1903–1908), begun with Derby Dam. Nearby Lahontan Dam, completed in 1915, was built to produce electricity for the project.

Newlin, uninc. village (1990 pop. 31), Hall co., NW Texas, 17 mi/27 km NW of Childress and on Prairie Dog Town Fork of Red R. Cotton, peanuts; cattle.

Newman 1 city (□ 1 sq mi/2.6 sq km; 1990 pop. 4,151), Stanislaus co., central Calif., in San Joaquin Valley, 22 mi/35 km S of Modesto; 37°19′N 121°01′W. Dairying, farming (poultry; fruit, vegetables, grain, including rice); mfg. (cheese, fabricated metal prods., fruit). George J. Hatfield State Park to SE; Diablo Range to SW; San Joaquin R. to E (mouth of Merced R.). Laid out 1887, inc. 1908. **2** city (1990 pop. 960), Douglas co., E Ill., 17 mi/27 km E of Tuscola; 39°47′N 87°59′W. Ships grain. Founded 1857, inc. 1872.

Newman Grove, village (1990 pop. 787), Madison co., E central Nebr., 18 mi/29 km WSW of Madison, on Shell Creek of Platte R., in grassy Loess Hills; 41°45′N 97°46′W. Dairy prods.; grain.

Newmanstown, uninc. town (1990 pop. 1,410), Lebanon co., SE central Pa., 12 mi/19 km E of Lebanon, near Mill Creek; 40°21′N 76°12′W. Mfg. (furniture, apparel, steel fabrication); agr. (grain, soybeans; livestock; dairying). Middle Creek Waterfowl Management L. reservoir to S.

Newmarket, town (1991 pop. 45,474), S Ont., Canada, on Holland R., 27 mi/43 km N of Toronto; 44°03′N 79°28′W. Commuter suburb of Toronto. Mfg. (motor vehicle parts, hardware, furniture, rubber and plastic prods., electrical equip.; food processing.

Newmarket, town (1990 pop. 7,157), Rockingham co., SE N.H., 9 mi/14.5 km W of Portsmouth; 43°04′N 70°57′W. Bounded E by Great Bay, drained by Lamprey R. Mfg. (electrical prods., sheet metal fabrication); agr. (nursery crops; poultry, cattle; dairying). Set off from Exeter in 1727.

Newnan (NOO-nuhn), city (1990 pop. 12,497), ⊙ Coweta co., W Ga., 35 mi/56 km SW of Atlanta; 33°23′N 84°47′W. Emerging exurb of metropolitan Atlanta. Mfg. includes clothing, plastics, paper prods., consumer goods, textiles, crushed stone, electrical equip. Many old houses and gardens. Nearby planned community of Shenandoa established in the 1970s. Several important cultural institutions including the Male Acad. Mus. with Civil War artifacts and the Manget Bannon Alliance for the Arts gallery and theater. Inc. 1828.

Newnans Lake, Alachua co., N central Fla., 5 mi/8 km E of Gainesville; 4 mi/6.4 km long, 2 mi/3.2 km wide; 29°39′N 82°20′W.

Newport, county (□ 313 sq mi/811 sq km; 1990 pop. 87,194), SE R.I., on Mass. state line and the Atlantic, and including Conanicut, Prudence, and Rhode isls. (Aquidneck) in Narragansett Bay; ⊙ Newport; 41°31′N 71°16′W. Resort, agr. area, with mfg. (textiles, rubber and metal prods., electronic, computer and data-processing equip., jewelry; fisheries, boatbuilding, boat repair). Inc. 1703.

Newport 1 city (1990 pop. 18,871), ⊙ Campbell co., N Ky., suburb 1 mi/1.6 km SE of Cincinnati (Ohio), on the Ohio R. opposite Cincinnati at mouth of Licking R.; 39°05′N 84°29′W. Mfg. (wood prods., food prods., paper prods., bldg. equip., oil and gas, fabricated steel prods., printing, dairy prods.). Newport was a station on the Underground RR, and Ky's only antislavery newspaper was edited here in the 1850s. Riverboat Row Riverwalk. Laid out 1791, inc. as a city 1835. **2** city (1990 pop. 28,227), ⊙ Newport co., SE R.I., on Aquidneck Isl. (also called Rhode Isl.); 41°29′N 71°19′W. A port of entry, the city's economy revolves chiefly around tourism, educational institutions, and fishing. The mfg. of electrical equip. is also important. Founded in 1639, Newport was united (1640) with Portsmouth and then entered (1654) in a permanent federation with Providence and Warwick. Shipbuilding, dating from 1646, and foreign commerce brought pre-Revolutionary prosperity to Newport. In the Amer. Revolution the British occupied the town (1776–1779); many bldgs. were destroyed, most of the citizens moved away, and Newport never regained its former economic prestige. It was replaced in importance by Providence, with which it was joint state capital until 1900. In the 19th cent., Newport developed as a fashionable resort of the wealthy, and many palatial mansions were built. Outstanding tourist attractions are The Breakers, the former summer house of Cornelius Vanderbilt; Belcourt Castle; The Elms; Marble House; and Château-sur-Mer. Cliff Walk and Ocean Drive are known for their spectacular views of the ocean and the coastline. Of historic interest are the Wanton-Lyman-Hazard House

Cross references are shown in SMALL CAPITALS. The pronunciation key is on page 00. The dates of population figures are on pages 00–00.

(c.1675; scene of a Stamp Act riot in 1765); Trinity Church (1726); Touro Synagogue (1763), oldest in the country and since 1946 a natl. historic site; the Redwood Lib. and Athenaeum (1747); and the brick market house or city hall (1762). Also a natl. historic site. Fort Adams dates from 1776 and remained a coastal defense command post through World War II. Newport hosts yacht races, and it was the site of the Amer.'s Cup race until the early 1980s. Tennis was popularized here; the Natl. Tennis Hall of Fame is in the Newport casino. The Newport Jazz Festival was held until 1971, but other music and dance fests continue. The city is the seat of Salve Regina Col., the U.S. Naval War Col. (on a small isl. connected to the main isl. by a causeway), and other naval training schools. U.S. navy facilities that closed in the 1970s created significant unemployment. Pell Bridge (1969; commonly known as Newport Bridge) spans the E passage of Narragansett Bay, linking the city with Jamestown. Matthew Perry was born in Newport. Settled 1639, inc. 1784. **3** city (1990 pop. 7,123), ⊙ Cocke co., E Tenn., on Pigeon R., 40 mi/64 km E of Knoxville, at W foot of the Great Smokies; 35°58′N 83°11′W. Lumbering, wood extracts. John Sevier Fish and Game Preserve (□ 125,000 acres/50,588 ha), and Great Smoky Mts. Natl. Park are nearby. **4** city (1990 pop. 4,434), ⊙ Orleans co., N Vt., on L. Memphremagog, 50 mi/80 km NNE of Montpelier, near Que. (Canada) border; 44°56′N 72°12′W. Resort, trade center, port of entry; wood prods., clothing; lumber, dairy prods. Just W is Newport town, including Newport Center village (lumber). Settled 1793, chartered 1803, inc. 1917.

Newport 1 town (1990 pop. 7,459), ⊙ Jackson co., NE Ark., 37 mi/60 km WSW of Jonesboro and on White R.; 35°37′N 91°14′W. RR and commercial center for farm area (wheat; hogs; rice, pecans). Mfg. (machinery, lumber, RR equip., aluminum, motor vehicles, food). Jacksonport State Park to NW. Settled c.1873. **2** town (1990 pop. 1,240), New Castle co., N Del., and suburb 4 mi/6.4 km SW of Wilmington, on Christina R.; 39°42′N 75°36′W. Mfg. (plastics prods.). New Castle Co. Airport to S; Del. Park Horse Race Track to W. Founded in 1735. Birthplace of Oliver Evans, inventor of automatic flour-milling machinery (1785), which revolutionized grain processing. **3** town (1990 pop. 627), ⊙ Vermillion co., W Ind., 28 mi/45 km N of Terre Haute, on Little Vermilion R. near its mouth on Wabash R.; 39°53′N 87°25′W. Mfg. (ordnance, chemicals). Corn, wheat; cattle. **4** town (1990 pop. 3,036), including Newport village, Penobscot co., S central Maine, 25 mi/40 km W of Bangor and on Sebasticook L.; 44°51′N 69°13′W. Mfg. (textiles, wood prods.). Settled 1808, inc. 1814. . **5** town (1990 pop. 3,720), Washington co., SE Minn., on Mississippi R. (bridged), 7 mi/11.3 km SSE of St. Paul; 44°52′N 93°00′W. Mfg. (consumer goods, wood prods., steel). **6** town (1990 pop. 6,110), ⊙ Sullivan co., SW N.H., 8 mi/12.9 km E of Claremont; 43°22′N 72°12′W. Drained by Sugar R. and its South Branch, with Newport town center at confluence. Trade center, mfg. (printing and publishing, concrete prods.; sawmilling, machining; wood prods., ordnance, metal fabrication); timber; agr. (apples, nursery crops, hay, corn; poultry, cattle). Covered bridge in NW. Includes Guild, mill village. L. Sunapee to E. Inc. 1761. **7** town (1990 pop. 2,516), Carteret co., E N.C., 10 mi/16 km WNW of Morehead City, 7 mi/11.3 km SSE of Havelock, in Croatan Natl. Forest; 34°47′N 76°51′W. Mfg. (apparel). **8** town (1990 pop. 8,437), Lincoln co., W Oregon, at entrance of Yaquina Bay of the Pacific, estuary of Yaquina R., 40 mi/64 km W of Corvallis; 44°37′N 124°02′W. Mfg. (seafood processing, printing, publishing, boatbuilding). Timber-shipping point. Resort. Site of the Log Cabin Mus., Coast Aquarium. Part of Siuslaw Natl. Forest to SE; numerous state parks along coast to N and S; Yaquina Bay State Park and Lighthouse in town; South Beach State Park to S. Yaquina Head Lighthouse 3 mi/4.8 km to NW. Municipal airport to S. Settled c. 1855, inc. 1891. **9** town (1990 pop. 1,691), ⊙ Pend Oreille co., NE Wash., near Idaho state line opposite Old Town (Idaho), 40 mi/64 km NE of Spokane, on Pend Oreille R.; 48°11′N 117°03′W. RR junction. Potatoes, hay, alfalfa; dairying; mfg. (printing and publishing); timber. Kaniksu Natl. Forest to N; Pend Oreille State Park to SW. Co. Historical Society Mus. Albeni Falls Dam 2 mi/3.2 km E, in Idaho. Settled c.1885, inc. 1903.

Newport 1 village (1990 pop. 35), De Soto co., NW Miss., 17 mi/27 km SW of Memphis (Tenn.), near Mississippi R.; 34°53′N 90°13′W. Agr. area. **2** village (1990 pop. 136), Rock co., N Nebr., 10 mi/16 km E of Bassett; 42°36′N 99°19′W. Hay-shipping point. **3** village, Cumberland co., SW N.J., on short Nantuxent Creek, 9 mi/14.5 km SSE of Bridgeton. Sand pits. **4** village (1990 pop. 676), Herkimer co., central N.Y., 13 mi/21 km NE of Utica; 43°11′N 75°00′W.

Newport, borough (1990 pop. 1,568), Perry co., central Pa., 20 mi/32 km NW of Harrisburg, on Juniata R. at mouth of Little Buffalo Creek; 40°28′N 77°07′W. Mfg. (machinery, crushed stone, apparel, printing and publishing, flour); agr. (corn, hay; livestock; dairying); limestone. Little Buffalo State Park to SW. Settled 1789, laid out 1814, inc. 1840.

Newport Bay, at Newport Beach, Orange co., S Calif., dredged harbor (yachting, sport and commercial fishing) 10 mi/16 km S of Santa Ana. Balboa (resorts) on Balboa Isl. and Pennisula (part of Newport Beach City), street bridge to Balboa Isl., ferry to Balboa Peninsula; Corona del Mar and Corona del Mar State Beach are on SE shore; entrance to Pacific on E end of bay; Balboa Isl. in E; Lido Isl. in W.

Newport Beach, city (1990 pop. 66,643), Orange co., S Calif., suburb 33 mi/53 km SE of Los Angeles, 17 mi/27 km SE of Long Beach, on Newport Bay and the Pacific Ocean; 33°37′N 117°55′W. Upper Newport Bay divides city; Peters Canyon Wash enters from N. Mfg. (electrical equip., computers, medical equip., shipbuilding, adhesives, printing and publishing). It is a popular seaside resort and yachting center. John Wayne (Orange co.) Airport to N. Includes Balboa Isl. in bay and Peninsula bet. bay and ocean, residential and recreational sect.; Lido Isl. in W part of bay; Corona del Mar State Beach in S. Inc. 1906.

Newport Center, Vt.: see NEWPORT.

Newport Hills, uninc. town (1990 pop. 14,736), King co., W Wash., residential suburb 7 mi/11.3 km SE of Seattle, on SE shore of L. Washington; 47°33′N 122°10′W. Mercer Isl. is to W.

Newport News, independent city (□ 69 sq mi/179 sq km; 1990 pop. 170,045), SE Va., at mouth of James R., off Hampton Roads, 8 mi/12.9 km NW of Norfolk; 37°04′N 76°30′W. Bounded on E by independent city of Hampton. Port for transatlantic and intracoastal shipping; commodities handled include coal, oil, tobacco, grain, ores. One of the nation's major shipbuilding and repair centers, its shipbuilding industry began in 1886. The U.S.S. *Enterprise II*, the 1st nuclear-powered aircraft carrier, was constructed here. Mfg. (office equip., seafood processing, printing and publishing, plastic prods., apparel, dairy prods., shipbuilding, paper prods., bldg. materials, electronic equip.); oil refineries. Settled by Irish colonists c.1620 but did not grow appreciably until 1880, when it became E terminus of Chesapeake and Ohio RR. In 1862 battle bet. ironclad ships *Monitor* and *Merrimac* took place off Newport News. Mariners Mus., War Memorial Mus. of Va., Va. Living Mus. and Planetarium, and Victory Arch (1919, rebuilt 1962). Ft. Eustis Military Reservation, with Matthew Jones House (1660) on the fort's grounds in NW. Christopher Newport Univ. and Apprentice School of Newport News. Williamsburg–Newport News Internatl. Airport in E. Monitor-Merrimac Memorial Bridge connects S to Suffolk, James R. Bridge connects SW to Isle of Wight co., both bridges span James R. U.S. Naval Weapons Station to N. Inc. 1896.

Newry, town (1990 pop. 316), Oxford co., W Maine, on Bear R., 23 mi/37 km NNW of South Paris; 44°31′N 70°49′W. In recreational area.

Newry (NOO-ree), village, Oconee co., NW S.C., 5 mi/8 km NW of Clemson, on L. Keowee Reservoir at Little River Dam, on Keowee R.

Newry, borough (1990 pop. 288), Blair co., S central Pa., 8 mi/12.9 km S of Altoona, near Frankstown Branch of Juniata R.; 40°23′N 26°78′W. Mfg. (meat processing). Agr. (grain; livestock; dairying).

Newsoms, town (1990 pop. 337), Southampton co., SE Va., 12 mi/19 km WSW of Franklin; 36°37′N 77°07′W. Mfg. (lumber; meat processing); agr. (peanuts, cotton, grain, melons; livestock); timber.

Newton 1 county (□ 823 sq mi/2,132 sq km; 1990 pop. 7,666), NW Ark.; ⊙ Jasper; 35°55′N 93°13′W. Drained by Buffalo R. and its tributaries; situated in Ozark region. Agr. (cattle, hogs). Lead and zinc mining; lumber milling. Part of Ozark Natl. Forest is in S, small unit to N; W part of Buffalo Natl. R. crosses N part of co.; part of Gene Bush–Buffalo R. Wildlife Management Area in E. Formed 1842. **2** county (⊙ 279 sq mi/723 sq km; 1990 pop. 41,808), N central Ga.; ⊙ Covington; 33°33′N 83°50′W. Drained by Alcovy and Yellow rivers; includes part of Lloyd Shoals Reservoir. Textile mfg. Piedmont agr. area producing fruit; cattle and poultry. Formed 1821. **3** county (□ 403 sq mi/1,044 sq km; 1990 pop. 13,551), NW Ind.; ⊙ Kentland; 40°57′N 87°24′W. Bounded W by Ill. state line, N by Kankakee R.; also drained by Iroquois R. Native prairie grasses. Agr. area; corn, rye, oats, soybeans; cattle, hogs. Some mfg. at Kentland. Ships seeds, grain. Limestone quarrying. Part of LaSalle State Fish and Wildlife Area in NW corner; Willow Slough State Fish and Wildlife Area in W. Formed 1859 (the last co. organized in Ind.). **4** county (□ 579 sq mi/1,500 sq km; 1990 pop. 20,291), E central Miss.; ⊙ Decatur; 32°24′N 89°07′W. Drained by Chunky and Potterchitto creeks. Agr. (cotton, corn; poultry, cattle; dairying); timber. Part of Bienville Natl. Forest in SW corner. Formed 1836. **5** county (□ 629 sq mi/1,629 sq km; 1990 pop. 44,445), SW Mo.; ⊙ Neosho; 36°54′N 94°19′W. In the Ozarks; includes part of city of Joplin in NW. Vegetables, berries, hay, apples, corn, wheat; dairying; cattle, horses, poultry; oak timber. Mfg. at Neosho, Joplin, Granby and Seneca. George Washington Carver Natl. Monument in N. Crowder College at former Camp Crowder. Formed 1854. **6** county (□ 939 sq mi/2,432 sq km; 1990 pop. 13,569), E Texas; ⊙ Newton. Bounded E by Sabine R. (La. state line); drained by its tributaries. In pine-forest belt; lumbering is chief industry; peaches, vegetables; oil and natural gas. Toledo Bend Reservoir in NE corner. Formed 1846.

Newton 1 city (1990 pop. 3,154), ⊙ Jasper co., SE central Ill., on Embarras R., 22 mi/35 km SE of Effingham; 38°59′N 88°09′W. In agr. area; livestock; corn, wheat; dairy prods. Sam Parr State Park nearby. Settled 1828, inc. 1831. **2** city (1990 pop. 14,789), ⊙ Jasper co., central Iowa, 30 mi/48 km ENE of Des Moines; 41°42′N 93°02′W. Mfg. center (appliances, paper prods., steel fabrication, machinery, foundry prods.). Riverview Relenst Center (correctional facility) to S. Settled 1846, inc. 1857. **3** city (1990 pop. 16,700), ⊙ Harvey co., S central Kansas, 27 mi/43 km N of Wichita; 38°02′N 97°20′W. Elev. 1,420 ft/433 m. In an agr. area. It is a RR div. point with RR shops and has a large mobile home industry in addition to oil wells. Mfg. (machinery, flour milling, motor vehicle parts, plastic prods., glass, furniture, lumber, concrete). The Chisholm Trail passed through the site. In the early 1870s, Ger. Mennonites from Russia brought seed for what became the 1st hard winter wheat in Kansas. The city still has a large Mennonite pop., and a monument to their ancestors is here. Mus. here. Bethel Col. is in North Newton. Inc. 1872. **4** city (1990 pop. 82,585), Middlesex co., E Mass., suburb of Boston on the Charles R.; 42°20′N 71°13′W. Industries include publishing, chemicals, precision instruments, and computers. Newton is known as a regional education center. The city is the seat of Newton Col., Mount Alvernia Col., Andover Newton Theological School, Boston Col., Mt. Ida Col., Lovell Col., and Pine Manor Col. Horace Mann, Nathaniel Hawthorne, Mary Baker Eddy, and Samuel Francis Smith lived in Newton. It comprises 14 individual residential villages; including Auburndale, Eliot, Newton Centre, Newton Highlands, Newton Lower Falls, Newton Upper Falls,

Newtonville, Nonantum (or Silver Lake), Riverside, Waban, West Newton, Chestnut Hill, Oak Hill, Newton Corner. Settled before 1640, inc. as a city 1873. **5** city (1990 pop. 9,304), ⊙ Catawba co., W central N.C., 8 mi/12.9 km SE of Hickory 40 mi/64 km NNW of Charlotte; 35°40′N 81°13′W. RR junction. Mfg. (furniture, motor vehicle parts, textiles, apparel, printing, wood, paper, and metal prods.; flour, medical prods.). Co. Historical Mus. Hickory Motor Speedway to NW. Catawba Valley Community Col. to NW. Settled mid-18th cent.

Newton 1 town (1990 pop. 1,580), Dale co., SE Ala., on the Choctawhatchee, and 10 mi/16 km S of Ozark. In vegetable and pecan area. **2** town (1990 pop. 3,701), Newton co., E central Miss., 27 mi/43 km W of Meridian; 32°19′N 89°09′W. RR junction. Agr. (cotton, corn; poultry, cattle; dairying); hardwood timber; mfg. (fabricated metal prods., furniture, cheese, apparel, feeds). Bienville Natl. Forest to SW. **3** town (1990 pop. 3,473), Rockingham co., SE N.H., 7 mi/11.3 km N of Haverhill (Mass.), 9 mi/14.5 km SW of Exeter, N.H.; 42°52′N 71°02′W. Bounded SE by Mass. state line. Mfg. (consumer goods). Includes village of Newton Junction in W. **4** town (1990 pop. 7,521), ⊙ Sussex co., N N.J., 21 mi/34 km NW of Morristown; 41°02′N 74°45′W. Dairying center; mfg. (clothing, plastics, pharmaceuticals, metal fabrication); fur processing; poultry, fruit. Don Bosco Col. and Sussex Co. Community Col. here. Little Flower Monastery (Benedictine) nearby. Settled c.1760, inc. 1864. **5** town (1990 pop. 1,885), ⊙ Newton co., E Texas, near Sabine R., c.55 mi/89 km NNE of Beaumont; 30°51′N 93°45′W. In agr., timber region; lumber milling; mfg. (pulpwood, lumber, wood prods.).

Newton 1 village (1990 pop. 703), ⊙ Baker co., SW Ga., 22 mi/35 km SSW of Albany, on Flint R.; 31°19′N 84°20′W. Peanut processing. **2** village (1990 pop. 659), Cache co., N Utah, on Clarkston Creek near its confluence with Bear R., and 12 mi/19 km NW of Logan; 41°51′N 111°59′W. Irrigated agr. area; fruit, vegetables; dairying. Elev. 4,525 ft/1,379 m. Newton Dam is 3 mi/4.8 km N.

Newton Centre, Mass.: see NEWTON.

Newton Corner, Mass.: see NEWTON.

Newton Dam and Reservoir, Utah.: see CLARKSTON CREEK.

Newton Falls, city (1990 pop. 4,866), Trumbull co., NE Ohio, 8 mi/13 km SW of Warren and on Mahoning R.; 41°11′N 80°58′W. Mfg. of structural steel and tubing; also motor vehicles, machinery.

Newton Falls, village (1990 pop. 400), St. Lawrence co., N N.Y., near Cranberry L., on Oswegatchie R. (dam nearby) and 32 mi/51 km S of Potsdam; 44°13′N 75°00′W.

Newton Grove, village (1990 pop. 511), Sampson co., S central N.C., 22 mi/35 km SW of Goldsboro near Great Coharrie Creek; 35°15′N 78°21′W. Agr. area (grain, cotton, peanuts, tobacco, sweet potatoes; livestock). Mfg. (hog feeders; corn milling). Bentonville Battleground State Historical Site to N.

Newton Hamilton, borough (1990 pop. 287), Mifflin co., central Pa., 3 mi/4.8 km E of Mount Union, on Juniata R.; 40°23′N 77°50′W. Agr. (corn, hay; livestock; dairying). Tuscarora State Forest to E; Rothrock State Forest to NW.

Newton Highlands, Mass.: see NEWTON.

Newton Lake, reservoir, Jasper co., SE Ill., on Weather Creek (a tributary of the Big Muddy R.), 13 mi/21 km SW of Newton; 38°52′N 88°17′W. Sandy Creek (N) arm is 10 mi/16 km long, Laws Creek (NNE) arm 15 mi/24 km long. Max. capacity of 44,000 acre-ft. Formed by Newton Dam (52 ft/16 m high), built in 1974.

Newton Lower Falls, Mass.: see NEWTON.

Newton Upper Falls, Mass.: see NEWTON.

Newtonia, city (1990 pop. 204), Newton co., SW Mo., in the Ozarks, 10 mi/16 km E of Neosho; 36°52′N 94°10′W. Civil War battle, Sept. 30, 1862.

Newtonsville, village (1990 pop. 427), Clermont co., SW Ohio, 10 mi/16 km NNE of Batavia; 39°11′N 84°05′W.

Newtonville, Mass.: see NEWTON.

Newtown 1 town (1990 pop. 20,779), Fairfield co., SW Conn., on the Housatonic, 8 mi/12.9 km ENE of Danbury; 41°23′N 73°17′W. Dairy and fruit farms are in the area. Industry includes the mfg. of pressure gauges, plastics, paper prods., and fabricated metal prods. Maximum security state prison. Inc. 1711. **2** town (1990 pop. 243), Fountain co., W Ind., 7 mi/11.3 km SE of Attica. Agr. area. **3** town (1990 pop. 115), Sullivan co., N Mo., 16 mi/26 km NW of Milan; 40°22′N 93°19′W.

Newtown, village (1990 pop. 1,589), Hamilton co., extreme SW Ohio, suburb E of Cincinnati, across Little Miami R.; 39°07′N 84°21′W. Concrete prods., plastics, machinery. Laid out 1801.

Newtown, borough (1990 pop. 2,565), Bucks co., SE Pa., suburb 22 mi/35 km NNE of Philadelphia; 40°13′N 74°55′W. Diverse mfg.; agr. (grain, apples, soybeans; livestock; dairying). Tyler State Park to W; Bucks Co. Community Col. to W. Settled 1684, laid out 1733, inc. 1838.

Newtown, township (1990 pop. 11,366), Delaware co., SE Pa., residential suburb 11 mi/18 km W of Philadelphia; 39°59′N 75°24′W. Includes the communities of Florida Park, Newtown, and Newtown Square. State park to SW.

Newtown Battlefield State Park, N.Y.: see ELMIRA.

Newtown Creek, tidal arm of East R., within N.Y. city, SE N.Y.; c.4 mi/6.4 km long, partly separates Brooklyn and Queens boroughs. Carries shipping for industrial NW Queens.

Newtown Grant, uninc. town (1990 pop. 2,141), Bucks co., SE Pa., residential suburb 22 mi/35 km NNE of Philadelphia and 1 mi/1.6 km NW of Newtown; 40°15′N 74°57′W.

Newtown Square, uninc. village, Delaware co., SE Pa., suburb 11 mi/18 km W of Philadelphia; 39°59′N 75°24′W. Mfg. includes chemicals and plastics, pharmaceuticals, printing and publishing.

Newville, town (1990 pop. 531), Henry co., SE Ala., 12 mi/19 km SSW of Abbeville.

Newville, borough (1990 pop. 1,349), Cumberland co., S Pa., 11 mi/18 km WSW of Carlisle, on Big Spring Creek; 40°10′N 77°24′W. Mfg. (apparel, farm equip.). Agr. (grain, soybeans; livestock; dairying). Big Spring to S; Colonel Denning State Park to N. Laid out 1794, inc. 1817.

Nextlalpan de Felipe Sánchez Solís, town (1990 pop. 7,446), ⊙ Nextlalpan municipio, Mexico state, central Mexico, 22 mi/35 km N of Mexico city. Cereals; livestock.

Ney (nai), village (1990 pop. 331), Defiance co., NW Ohio, 10 mi/16 km NW of Defiance; 41°23′N 84°31′W. Grain and lumber mills.

Nez Perce, county (□ 856 sq mi/2,217 sq km; 1990 pop. 33,754), W Idaho; ⊙ Lewiston; 46°20′N 116°45′W. Livestock-raising and agr. area (cattle; potatoes, barley, wheat, alfalfa, vegetables) bounded W by Snake R. and Wash., far S by Salmon R.; drained by Clearwater R. Lumber milling at Lewiston. Lowest point in Idaho (710 ft/216 m) in NW, at point where Snake R. flows into Wash. state. Mts. are in S, part of Nez Perce Indian Reservation in E, covers about ½ co. Nez Perce Natl. Historical Park (spalding Area unit) in N; Soldier Meadow Reservoir in SE; Winchester L. State Park on SE boundary; Hells Gate in W, S of Lewiston. Formed 1861.

Nez Perce National Historical Park (□ 3 sq mi/7.8 sq km), Nez Perce, Idaho and Clearwater cos., NW Idaho. Comprises 24 sites that preserve and commemorate the history and culture of the Nez Perce. Includes Spalding Area site, Nez Perce co., which has a mus. and bldgs. from a Presbyterian Indian Agency (1861) and church (c.1885); also East Kamiah Site, E of Kamiah, and site S of Grangerville, both Idaho co., also some acreage in Clearwater co. Authorized 1965.

Nezahualcóyotl, Mexico: see CIUDAD NEZAHUALCÓYOTL.

Nezinscot River (ne-ZIN-skaht), c.11 mi/18 km long, W Maine; rises in 12-mi/19-km E and W branches in Oxford co., joining at Buckfield; flows E to the Androscoggin above Auburn.

Nezperce (NEZ-purse), village (1990 pop. 453), ⊙ Lewis co., W Idaho, 40 mi/64 km ESE of Lewiston, in Nez Perce Indian Reservation; 46°14′N 116°14′W. Wheat, alfalfa; cattle.

Nezpique, Bayou (nehz-PEEK, BEI-yoo), c.70 mi/113 km long, S La.; rises in Evangeline parish; flows S, joining Bayou des Cannes near Mermentau to form Mermentau R. Navigable by small shallow-draft boats for 23 mi/37 km of lower course.

Niagara, county (□ 1,139 sq mi/2,950 sq km; 1990 pop. 220,756), W N.Y.; ⊙ Lockport; 43°19′N 78°47′W. Bounded W by Niagara R. and L. Erie, N by L. Ontario; crossed by the Barge Canal; drained by Tonawanda Creek. Includes Niagara Falls resort area. Agr. (fruit; dairy prods.) and extensive mfg. area that produces chemicals, abrasives, electronic and electrical equip., and metal fabrication. Mining of wollastonite; oil refining. Contains Tuscarora and part of Tonawanda Indian reservations. Formed 1808.

Niagara, town (1990 pop. 1,999), Marinette co., NE Wis., at falls of Menominee R., 5 mi/8 km SSE of Iron Mountain (Mich.); 45°46′N 88°00′W. In potato-growing and dairy area. Mfg. (paper milling, iron and steel prods.). Inc. 1914.

Niagara, village (1990 pop. 73), Grand Forks co., E N.Dak., 40 mi/64 km WNW of Grand Forks; 48°00′N 97°52′W.

Niagara, river, 34 mi/55 km long, N.Y. and Ont.; issuing from L. Erie bet. Buffalo, N.Y., and Fort Erie, Ont. (Canada); flows N around Grand Isl. and over Niagara Falls to L. Ontario; the river forms part of the U.S.-Can. border. The upper sect. of the river is navigable for c.20 mi/32 km to a series of rapids above the falls; in its last 7 mi/11 km it is again navigable, from Lewiston, N.Y., to L. Ontario. The N.Y. State Barge Canal enters the river at Tonawanda, N.Y.; the Welland Canal, several miles W on the Ont. side, is a lake-freighter route around the falls. Hydroelectric power is generated by diverting water from the river above Niagara Falls to generating plants. Many bridges cross the Niagara R., notably Peace Bridge (1927); bridges linking Grand Isl. with both shores (1935); Rainbow Bridge (1941) below the falls; and American Rapids Bridge (1960), linking Goat Isl. with the mainland.

Niagara, Canada: see NIAGARA-ON-THE-LAKE.

Niagara Falls, city (1991 pop. 75,399), S Ont., Canada, on the Niagara R. opposite Niagara Falls (N.Y.); 43°06′N 79°03′W. Formerly called Clifton, it is a port of entry, an important industrial city, and the home of Can. factories for many well-known U.S. firms. Electric power supplied by the falls supports industries that make chemicals, abrasives, silverware, machinery, sporting equip., and paper prods. The falls are also an intl. tourist attraction. Bet. the city and the falls and along the gorge below the falls is Queen Victoria Park. Casino Niagara, a very large gambling casino operated by the provincial govt. of Ont., is 100 yd/91 m from the U.S. border.

Niagara Falls, city (□ 16 sq mi/41 sq km; 1990 pop. 61,840), Niagara co., W N.Y., at the great falls of the Niagara R.; 43°05′N 79°01′W. Tourism is one of its oldest industries, and many state parks are in the area, including N.Y. State Niagara Reservation. The city is also a port of entry; its mfg. includes abrasives, mechanical and electrochemical prods., and paper and aluminum goods. This was the site of one of the world's 1st hydroelectric power plants; it was replaced bet. 1963 and 1965 by a plant capable of producing 2,100 MW. Settled by Native Americans, the site was occupied by the French in the 1680s, captured by the British in 1759, and settled by Americans in 1805. Lost to the British during the War of 1812, it was regained by the U.S. after the Treaty of Ghent in Dec. 1814. Several bridges span the river to Canada. Niagara Univ. and a community col. are here, as well as a large casino opened by the provincial govt. of Ont. (Canada), 100 yd/91 m from the U.S. border. Inc. 1892.

Niagara Falls, in the Niagara R., W N.Y. and S Ont. (Canada); 43°05′N 29°04′W. One of the most famous spectacles in N. Amer., the falls are on the internatl.

border bet. the cities of Niagara Falls, N.Y., and Niagara Falls, Ont. Goat Isl. splits the cataract into the American Falls (167 ft/51 m high and 1,060 ft/323 m wide) and the Horseshoe, or Canadian, Falls (158 ft/48 m high and 2,600 ft/792 m wide). The falls were formed c.10,000 years ago as the retreating glaciers exposed the Niagara escarpment, thus permitting the waters of L. Erie to flow N to L. Ontario. The escarpment has been gradually eroded back toward L. Erie, a process that has formed the Niagara Gorge (c.7 mi/11.3 km long); the Whirlpool Rapids and the Whirlpool are here. Horseshoe Falls is eroding upstream at a faster rate than the American Falls because of the greater volume of water passing over it. A great rock slide occurred (1954) at the American Falls and formed a huge talus slope at its base. Water was diverted from the American Falls for several months in 1969 by the U.S. Corps of Engineers to study the bedrock and to remove some of the talus. Internatl. agreements control the diversion of water for hydroelectric power; weirs divert part of the flow above the Horseshoe Falls to supplement the flow in the shallower American Falls. Hydroelectric-power developments were authorized under the Niagara Diversion Treaty (1950), which stipulated a small flow to be reserved for the falls and the equal div. of the remaining flow bet. the U.S. and Canada. In the U.S. the project was undertaken by the Power Authority of the State of N.Y. Water is diverted from the river above the upper rapids into underground conduits (46 ft/14 m wide and 66 ft/20 m high). It is then conveyed overland, dropping 314 ft/96 m to a point below the lower rapids where, as it returns to the river, the water passes through turbines that power 13 generators of the Robert Moses Niagara Power Plant (1,950-MW capacity; opened 1961). Associated with the N.Y. hydroelectric-power project is the construction in the area of new roads, bridges, and parks. In Canada it was undertaken by the Hydro-Electric Power Commission of Ont. Water is diverted from the river above the falls and is fed into the Sir Adam Beck Generating Stations (1,775 MW; opened 1954) by way of a series of tunnels and canals. The govts. of the U.S. and Canada also control the appearance of the surrounding area, much of which has been included in parks since 1885. That the falls represented a major physical obstacle to the Great Lakes' full access to regional and ocean commerce via the St. Lawrence R. was recognized as early as 1829, when a canal-river bypass was constructed bet. Lakes Erie and Ontario. In 1839 the Can. govt. assumed ownership of the canal, enlarging it in 1845 and again in 1887. In 1932, the present Well and Ship Canal, part of the St. Lawrence Seaway system, was opened. In 1973 $110 million was allocated to straighten and enlarge 8 mi/12.9 km of this 27-mi/43-km-long canal, located 14 mi/23 km W of Niagara Falls. The earliest written description of the falls is that of Louis Hennepin (in *Nouvelle Découverte,* 1697), who was with the expedition of Fr. explorer Robert Cavalier, sieur de La Salle, in 1678. In the 19th cent., daredevils attempted to brave the falls in barrels, boats, and rubber balls. The great Blondin performed (1859) on a tightrope over the falls, which continue to be a major center of internatl. tourism. Historical and natural history material relating to the region is in the Niagara Falls Mus. in the city of Niagara Falls, N.Y.

Niagara, Fort, N.Y.: see FORT NIAGARA.

Niagara-on-the-Lake or **Niagara**, city (1991 pop. 12,945), S Ont., Canada, on L. Ontario at the mouth of the Niagara R.; 43°15′N 79°04′W. It was settled (1784) by Amer. Loyalists and in 1792 Lt. Gov. Simcoe made the town the capital of Upper Canada, renaming it Newark. The legislature met here until 1796. Fort George, built (1796–1799) to defend the settlement, was taken in 1813 by the U.S. but Canada took it back in the same year. The town, officially called Niagara-on-the-Lake to distinguish it from the Can. and U.S. cities of Niagara Falls, is an architectural and historical treasure, with many well-preserved 19th-cent. bldgs. It is the site of the Shaw Festival, an annual festival of plays.

Niangua (nei-ANG-gwuh), city (1990 pop. 459), Webster co., S central Mo., in the Ozarks, at headwaters of Niangua R., 29 mi/47 km ENE of Springfield; 37°23′N 92°49′W. Fruit; dairying; cattle.

Niangua River (nei-ANG-gwuh), c.90 mi/145 km long, central Mo.; rises in the Ozarks near Marshfield; flows N into the Niangua arm of L. of the Ozarks in Camden co. Bennett Spring State Park along the river in Dallas co. Canoeing, fishing.

Niantic (ni-ANT-ick), village (1990 pop. 647), Macon co., central Ill., 10 mi/16 km W of Decatur; 39°51′N 89°10′W. Grain; livestock; dairy prods.

Niantic, Conn.: see EAST LYME.

Nibley, town (1990 pop. 1,167), Cache co., N Utah, 4 mi/6.4 km S of Logan, on Blacksmith Creek; 41°40′N 111°50′W. Barley, wheat, vegetables; dairying; cattle. Part of Wasatch Natl. Forest to E.

Nicaragua, sugar-mill village, Holguín prov., E Cuba, on Banes Bay, 4 mi/6.4 km S of Banes; 20°55′N 75°58′W.

Nicaro (nee-KAHR-o), town, Holguín prov., E Cuba, on Levisa Bay (Atlantic Ocean), at base of small Lengua de Pájaro peninsula, 6 mi/9.7 km E of Mayarí; 20°43′N 75°32′W. Refining of nickel oxide, which is mined nearby (S) at foot of Sierra del Cristal. Refining operations were started in 1943.

Nicatous Lake (nik-uh-TOU-uhs), Hancock co., E central Maine, 36 mi/58 km NE of Bangor; 8.5 mi/13.7 km long. In hunting, fishing area.

Nice, uninc. town (1990 pop. 2,126), Lake co., NW Calif., 6 mi/9.7 km NE of Lakeport, at NW end of Clear L. (Redman Slough enters lake to W); 39°08′N 122°51′W. Cattle; grain, timber. Mendocino Natl. Forest to N and NE. Bloody Isl. Massacre Historic Marker to NW.

Niceville, town (□ 11 sq mi/28 sq km; 1990 pop. 10,507), Okaloosa co., NW Fla., c.45 mi/72 km ENE of Pensacola, on Choctawhatchee Bay; 30°31′N 86°28′W.

Nichicun Lake or **Nichikun Lake** (both: NI-chi-kuhn) (□ 150 sq mi/389 sq km), central Que., Canada, on St. Lawrence–Hudson Bay watershed, at foot of the Otish Mts.; 20 mi/32 km long, 12 mi/19 km wide; 53°5′N 71°W. Elev. 1,737 ft/529 m. Drained N by Fort George R. Just SE is Naokokan L. (18 mi/29 km long, 12 mi/19 km wide).

Nicholas 1 county (□ 196 sq mi/508 sq km; 1990 pop. 6,725), N Ky.; ⊙ Carlisle; 38°20′N 84°00′W. Bounded NE by Licking R. Gently rolling upland agr. area (burley tobacco, hay, alfalfa, corn; cattle, poultry; dairying), in Bluegrass region. Includes Blue Licks Battlefield State Park in N; Clay Wildlife Management Area in E. Formed 1799. **2** county (□ 649 sq mi/1,681 sq km; 1990 pop. 26,775), central W.Va.; ⊙ Summersville; 38°17′N 80°47′W. On Allegheny Plateau; bounded SW by Gauley and Meadow rivers; drained by Gauley, Cranberry, Cherry, and Birch rivers. Agr. (corn, potatoes, alfalfa, hay, apples); cattle, poultry. Bituminous-coal mining. Timber. Carnifex Ferry Battlefield State Park in center; part of Monongahela Natl. Forest in E; part of Gauley R. Natl. Recreation Area in SW; Summersville L. reservoir (Gauley R.) and Wildlife Management Area in center. Formed 1818.

Nicholas Channel or **Saint Nicholas Channel**, strait off NW coast of Cuba, 90 mi/145 km E of Havana, 80 mi/129 km SE of Key West (Fla.); 23°15′N 79°45′W. Extends c.100 mi/161 km E, bounded N by Cay Sal Bank (20 mi/32 km off Cuba). Continued E by Old Bahama Channel. Sometimes spelled Nicolas or Canal de San Nicolas.

Nicholasville, city (1990 pop. 13,603), ⊙ Jessamine co., central Ky., 13 mi/21 km SSW of Lexington, in Bluegrass region; 37°52′N 84°34′W. Agr. area (dairying; cattle, horses, hogs, poultry; burley tobacco, corn, wheat, soybeans); mfg. (shoes). Early gristmill (1782) nearby. Jim Beam Nature Preserve and Camp Nelson Natl. Cemetery to S. Settled 1798.

Nicholls, town (1990 pop. 1,003), Coffee co., S central Ga., 13 mi/21 km E of Douglas; 31°31′N 82°38′W. Mfg. (clothing and textiles).

Nicholls' Town, town, W Bahama Isls., on NE shore of Andros Isl., 40 mi/64 km W of Nassau; 25°8′N 77°59′W. Fishing. Submarine caverns nearby.

Nichols, town (1990 pop. 366), Muscatine co., SE Iowa, 13 mi/21 km WNW of Muscatine; 41°28′N 91°18′W. In agr. area.

Nichols 1 village (1990 pop. 366), Muscatine co., SE Iowa, 13 mi/21 km WSW of Muscatine. Corn, soybeans; cattle, hogs. **2** village (1990 pop. 573), Tioga co., S N.Y., near the Susquehanna, 25 mi/40 km WSW of Binghamton; 42°01′N 76°22′W. **3** village (1990 pop. 528), Marion co., E S.C., 35 mi/56 km E of Florence, on Lumber R. at its mouth on Little Pee Dee R.; 34°13′N 79°09′W. Mfg. includes furniture, fish processing, aquaculture; agr. prods. include sorghum, corn, cotton, tobacco; livestock; catfishing. **4** village (1990 pop. 254), Outagamie co., E Wis., 20 mi/32 km N of Appleton; 44°34′N 88°28′W. Dairying; poultry; grain. Mfg. (printing).

Nichols Hills or **Nichols Hill**, town (1990 pop. 4,020), Oklahoma co., central Okla., residential suburb 5 mi/8 km N of Oklahoma City; 35°32′N 97°32′W. Okla. Mus. of Art here. L. Hefner reservoir to NW. Inc. 1929.

Nicholson, town (1990 pop. 535), Jackson co., NE central Ga., 10 mi/16 km N of Athens; 34°07′N 83°26′W.

Nicholson, uninc. village, Pearl River co., SE Miss., 3 mi/4.8 km SSW of Picayune, on Pearl R. Mfg. (fireworks, concrete prods., chemicals). Stennis Space Center (NASA) to SE. Bogue Chitto Natl. Wildlife Refuge (La.) to W.

Nicholson (NI-kuhl-suhn), borough (1990 pop. 857), Wyoming co., NE Pa., 16 mi/26 km NNW of Scranton, on Tunkhannock Creek; 41°37′N 75°47′W. Mfg. (feeds); flagstone quarrying; agr. (corn, hay; dairying). Lackawanna State Park to SE; several small lakes to SE. Inc. 1875.

Nicholson, former trading post, N Mackenzie dist., N.W.T., Canada, at head of Liverpool Bay; on inlet (30 mi/48 km long, 5 mi/8 km–10 mi/16 km wide) of the Beaufort Sea, at mouth of Anderson R.; 69°45′N 128°52′W. Meteorological station. Formerly called Stanton.

Nickajack Lake, reservoir, Marion and Hamilton cos., SE Tenn., on the Tennessee R., 18 mi/29 km WSW of Chattanooga, 2 mi/3.2 km N of Ala. state line; 35°00′N 85°37′W. Max. capacity 252,400 acre-ft; c.50 mi/80 km long. Formed by Nickajack Dam (67 ft/20 m high), built (1967) by the TVA for navigation, flood control, and power generation. Prentice Cooper State Forest on N shore. Former Hales Bar Dam site at Haletown (Guild), 6 mi/9.7 km upstream.

Nickelsville, town, Scott co., SW Va., 16 mi/26 km NW of Bristol, near Copper Creek; 36°45′N 82°25′W. Agr. (dairying; livestock; tobacco, corn).

Nickerson, town (1990 pop. 1,137), Reno co., S central Kansas, on Arkansas R., 10 mi/16 km NW of Hutchinson; 38°08′N 98°05′W. In grain and livestock area. Inc. 1879.

Nickerson, village (1990 pop. 291), Dodge co., E Nebr., 6 mi/9.7 km N of Fremont, near Elkhorn R; 41°32′N 96°28′W. Productive terrace land.

Nicola River (NI-ko-luh), 100 mi/161 km long, S B.C., Canada; rises c.40 mi/64 km SSE of Kamloops; flows generally W, through Nicola L. (14 mi/23 km long), to Merritt, then NW to Thompson R. just ENE of Spences Bridge.

Nicolás Bravo (nee-ko-LAHS-BRAH-vo), town (1990 pop 538), Puebla, central Mexico, 10 mi/16 km N of Tehuacán. Corn, sugar, fruit; livestock. Also called San Felipe Maderas.

Nicolas Channel, Cuba: see NICHOLAS CHANNEL.

Nicolás Flores (nee-ko-LAHS FLO-res), town (1990 pop. 385), N central Hidalgo, Mexico, 8 mi/83 km N of Panchuca de Soto; 20°46′N 99°07′W. Agr. produces wheat and corn. No all-weather roads.

Nicolás Romero, Mexico: see VILLA NICOLÁS ROMERO.

Nicolás Ruiz (nee-ko-LAHS ROO-ees), town (1990 pop. 2,805), Chiapas, S Mexico, at SW foot of Sierra de Hueytepec, 23 mi/37 km SSE of San Cristóbal de las Casas; 16°24′N 92°32′W. Isolated Tzotzil Maya community. Fruit; livestock.

Nicolet (nee-ko-LAI), county (□ 626 sq mi/1,621 sq km), S Que., Canada, on the St. Lawrence; ⊙ Bécancour; 46°15′N 72°15′W.

Nicolet, town (1991 pop. 4,789), S Que., Canada, on Nicolet R., near its mouth on the St. Lawrence R., 9 mi/14 km SSW of Trois Rivières; 46°13′N 72°36′W. Textile knitting, mfg. of optical equip., hosiery, furniture; in dairying region. Seat of R.C. bishop; site of cathedral and seminary.

Nicolet, Lake, E Upper Peninsula, Mich., an expansion of St. Marys R., 4 mi/6.4 km SE of Sault Ste. Marie and W of Sugar Isl.; 46°25′N 84°14′W. Lake is c.13 mi/21 km long, 2 mi/3.2 km wide.

Nicolet River, 100 mi/161 km long, S Que., Canada; flows in a winding course generally NW, past Nicolet, to L. St. Peter.

Nicollet (NI-kuh-let), county (□ 466 sq mi/1,207 sq km; 1990 pop. 28,076), S Minn.; ⊙ St. Peter; 44°20′N 94°15′E. Triangular-shaped co., bounded SW and E by Minnesota R. Agr. area (corn, oats, alfalfa, hay, soybeans, peas; hogs, sheep, cattle, poultry; dairying). Swan and Middle lakes near center of co. Part of Fort Ridgely State Park in far NW corner. Formed 1853.

Nicollet (NI-kuh-let), town (1990 pop. 795), Nicollet co., S Minn., 11 mi/18 km NW of Mankato, on small stream which flows S out of Middle L. to Nicollet Creek; 44°16′N 94°11′W. Dairying; livestock; grain, soybeans, beans; mfg. (boating equip., wood prods.). Swan L. to NW, Minnesota R. to S.

Nicoma Park (nuh-KO-muh), town (1990 pop. 2,353), Oklahoma co., central Okla., residential suburb 10 mi/16 km E of Oklahoma City; 35°29′N 97°19′W. In oil-producing area.

Nielsville (NEELZ-vil), village (1990 pop. 100), Polk co., NW Minn., 19 mi/31 km SW of Crookston, near Red R.; 47°31′N 96°49′W. Grain.

Niesky, U.S. V.I.: see NISKY.

Nieves (nee-EH-ves), town (1990 pop. 5,430), ⊙ Francisco R. Murguía municipio, Zacatecas, N central Mexico, on interior plateau, 14 mi/23 km NE of Río Grande, 90 mi/145 km NNW of Zacatecas; 23°59′N 103°01′W. Elev. 6,617 ft/2,017 m. Silver mining still moderately active. Also known as Francisco Murguía.

Nieves Ixpantepec, Mexico: see IXPANTEPEC NIEVES.

Night Hawk Lake, E Ont., Canada, 15 mi/24 km E of Timmins; 13 mi/21 km long, 6 mi/10 km wide. Drains N into Abitibi R.

Nighthawk, village, Okanogan co., N Wash., port of entry at B.C. border, on Okanogan R., and 38 mi/61 km N of Okanogan.

Nightmute, village (1990 pop. 153), SW Alaska, on Nelson Isl., 70 mi/113 km W of Bethel; 60°27′N 164°48′W.

Nihoa (nee-HO-ah), uninhabited island, Honolulu co., Hawaii, 130 mi/209 km NW of Niihau, 270 mi/435 km NW of Honolulu, 20 mi/32 km S of Tropic of Cancer. Highest point 910 ft/277 m; covers 155 acres/63 ha. Under jurisdiction of city and co. of Honolulu. Once had small Hawaiian settlement. Most SE point of NW Hawaiian Isls. Part of Hawaiian Isls. Natl. Wildlife Refuge. Formerly Bird Isl.

Niihau (NEE-ee-HOU), island (□ 70 sq mi/181 sq km; 1990 pop. 230), Kauai co., Hawaii, N end 13 mi/21 km WSW of Mana Point; 18 mi/29 km long and 6 mi/9.7 km wide. It is mostly semiarid lowland, rising to 1,281 ft/390 m at Paniau Mt. on NE coast. Administered as a dist. of Kauai co. Villages of Puuwai and Nonopapa on W coast; Kii Landing, at NE tip, main transfer point to adjacent isls. Main industries are cattle raising, mfg. of shell leis. The isl. is inhabited mainly by pure-blooded Hawaiians who maintain their cultural heritage. Halulu and Halalii, intermittent natural lakes, in S center. Small Lehua Isl. off N end.

Nikolai, village (1990 pop. 109), S central Alaska, in upper reaches of Kuskokwim R., 35 mi/56 km E of McGrath; 63°00′N 154°23′W.

Nikolski, village (1990 pop. 35), SW Umnak Isl., Aleutian Isls., SW Alaska, 80 mi/129 km SW of Kashega; 52°55′N 168°47′W. Has church and school.

Niland, uninc. town (1990 pop. 1,183), Imperial co., S Calif., 18 mi/29 km N of Brawley, at N end of IMPERIAL VALLEY, 5 mi/8 km E of Salton Sea; 33°14′N 115°31′W. Citrus fruit, vegetables, tomatoes, dates, melons, sugar beets; cotton; cattle, sheep. Coachella Canal and Chocolate Mts. to NE.

Niles 1 city (1990 pop. 12,456), Berrien co., SW Mich., 10 mi/16 km N of South Bend, Ind.; 41°49′N 86°15′W. Part of urbanized area, on the St. Joseph R. In a farm and fruit area. Mfg. includes paper prods., transportation equip., fabricated metal prods., and machinery. It was the site of a Jesuit Mission (1690) and of Fort St. Joseph, built by the French (1697). The fort fell to the British (1761), to the Native Americans (Pontiac's Rebellion, 1763), and to the Spanish and Native Americans (1780, 1781). Permanent settlement began in 1827, and as a station on the stagecoach route bet. Detroit and Chicago, Niles grew as a commercial and industrial center. Airport to E. Ring Lardner was b. here. Over 1,000- acres/405-ha Botanic Garden here. Inc. 1829. **2** city (1990 pop. 21,128), Trumbull co., NE Ohio, on the Mahoning R., 4 mi/6.4 km SE of Warren; 41°11′N 80°45′W. Produces steel, bldg. materials, and lathes. There is a memorial to President William McKinley, who was b. here. Settled 1806, inc. as a city 1895.

Niles, uninc. town, Alameda co., W Calif., suburb 23 mi/37 km SE of Oakland and 2 mi/3.2 km E of Fremont, on Alameda Creek. RR junction. Niles Canyon (E) is recreational area.

Niles, village (1990 pop. 28,284), Cook co., NE Ill., a residential suburb just NW of Chicago, on the N branch of Chicago R.; 42°01′N 87°48′W. Settled 1832, inc. 1899. The village has a replica (½ size) of the leaning tower of Pisa. Niles Col. of Loyola Univ. is here.

Nilikluguk, village, SW Alaska, on Bethel Bay, 80 mi/129 km WSW of Bethel.

Niltepec, Mexico: see SANTIAGO NILTEPEC.

Nilwood, town (1990 pop. 238), Macoupin co., SW central Ill., 9 mi/14.5 km NNE of Carlinville; 39°23′N 89°48′W. In agr. and bituminous-coal area.

Nimbus, Mount, Colo.: see NEVER SUMMER MOUNTAINS.

Nimmons (NIM-uhnz), village (1990 pop. 96), Clay co., extreme NE Ark., 28 mi/45 km NE of Paragould, near St. Francis R.; 36°18′N 90°05′W.

Nimpkish River (NIMP-kish), 80 mi/129 km long, SW B.C., Canada, on Vancouver Isl.; rises near Victoria Peak; flows NW, through Nimpkish L. (□ 12 sq mi/31 sq km), to Johnstone Strait opposite Alert Bay.

Nimrod, village (1990 pop. 65), Wadena co., central Minn., on Crow Wing R., and 19 mi/31 km NE of Wadena; 46°38′N 94°52′E. Dairying. Lyons State Forest to S; Huntersville State Forest to N.

Nimrod Lake, reservoir (□ 6 sq mi/15.5 sq km), Yell co., W central Ark., on Fourche LaFave R., in Ouachita Natl. Forest, 35 mi/56 km NNE of Hot Springs; 34°57′N 93°00′W. Extends E-W. Max. capacity 336,000 acre-ft. Formed by Nimrod Dam (100 ft/30 m high), built (1942) by Army Corps of Engineers for power generation, recreation, and as a fish and wildlife pond.

Nine Mile Falls, uninc. village (1990 pop. 150), Spokane co., E Wash., suburb 9 mi/14.5 km NNW of downtown Spokane, on Spokane R., at Nine Mile Dam. Mfg. (furniture, wood prods.). Parts of Riverside State Park to SW and N.

Nine Mile Point Nuclear Plants, 2 nuclear power–generating stations, Oswego co., central N.Y., on S shore of L. Ontario, 7 mi/11 km NE of Oswego; 43°31′N 76°25′W. This is one of 3 nuclear power sites in N.Y. state. Nine Mile Point Unit 1 (opened in June 1969, 610-MW capacity) is owned by Niagara Mohawk Power Corp., while Unit 2 (opened in 1989 with a 1,080-MW capacity) is jointly owned by Niagara Mohawk and 4 other N.Y. state utilities. Lake water is used for cooling purposes.

Ninemile Peak, Nev.: see ANTELOPE RANGE.

Ninette (nin-EHT), village, SW Man., Canada, 15 mi/24 km N of Killarney, at NW end of Pelican L.; 49°24′N 99°38′W. Grain; livestock.

Ninety Six, town (1990 pop. 2,099), Greenwood co., W S.C., 7 mi/11.3 km E of Greenwood. Livestock, poultry; dairying; grain; knitted cloth, cotton fabrics, bricks. Saluda R. (E) forms into L. Greenwood reservoir (hydroelectric power); L. Greenwood state park here. Town settled around nearby trading post built c.1730; moved to present site with RR's arrival 1855.

Ninety Six Historic Site (□ 1 sq mi/2.6 sq km), NW S.C., located 2 mi/3.2 km S of Ninety Six town and 7 mi/11.3 km ESE of Greenwood; 34°10′N 82°01′W. A frontier trading post after 1769 and Revolutionary War stronghold. Authorized 1976.

Nineveh, village (1990 pop. 400), Broome co., S N.Y., 16 mi/26 km NE of Binghamton; 42°12′N 75°37′W.

Ninga (NING-guh), village, SW Man., Canada, 11 mi/18 km WNW of Killarney; 49°13′N 99°53′W. Grain; livestock.

Ninigret Pond, R.I.: see CHARLESTOWN.

Ninilchik, village (1990 pop. 10,523) on W coast of Kenai Peninsula, S Alaska, on Cook Inlet 75 mi/121 km W of Seward, on Kenai-Homer Highway; 60°15′N 152°25′W. Fishing, fish processing. Orthodox church. Ninilchik Recreation Area nearby. Founded c.1830 by employees of Rus. Amer. Company.

Ninnescah River (nin-ES-kuh), 49 mi/79 km long, S Kansas; formed by confluence of its North Fork (87 mi/140 km long; forms Cherry Reservoir N of Cherry) and South Fork (92 mi/148 km long) in Sedgwick co. 6 mi/9.7 km SE of Cheney; flows SE to Arkansas R. 19 mi/31 km NNW of Arkansas City.

Niobrara (nei-uh-BRAR-uh), county (□ 2,627 sq mi/6,804 sq km; 1990 pop. 2,499), E Wyo.; ⊙ Lusk; 43°02′N 104°28′W. Grain, livestock region, bordering on S.Dak. and Nebr.; watered by South Fork of Cheyenne R. and its branches. Agr. (wheat, oats, sheep); petroleum, natural gas. Small part of Thunder Basin Natl. Grassland near N boundary. Formed 1911.

Niobrara (nee-o-BRUH-ruh), village (1990 pop. 376), Knox co., NE Nebr., on Missouri R. (Lewis and Clark L.) at mouth of Niobrara R., at S.Dak. state line, and 20 mi/32 km NNW of Creighton; 42°45′N 98°01′W. Dairying; livestock; grain. Resort. Both Santee Indian agency and Ponca Indian agency here. Ponca tribal powwow in mid-Aug. Santee Indian Reservation to E. Niobrara State Park to W.

Niobrara (nei-uh-BRAR-uh), river, c.430 mi/692 km long; rises in the High Plains in S Niobrara co., E Wyo., flows E as an intermittent stream past Lusk, Wyo., into NW Nebr., through Agate Fossil Beds Natl. Monument, through Box Butte Reservoir (completed 1946), past Valentine and Butte, entering Missouri R. in Knox co., NE Nebr., 4 mi/6.4 km NNW of Niobrara.

Niota (nei-O-tuh), city (1990 pop. 745), McMinn co., SE Tenn., 45 mi/72 km SW of Knoxville; 35°30′N 84°32′W.

Niotaze (NEE-o-taiz), village (1990 pop. 99), Chautauqua co., SE Kansas, 5 mi/8 km NW of Caney, near Okla. state line; 37°04′N 96°00′W. In livestock and grain area. Oil fields nearby.

Nipawin (NI-puh-win), town (1991 pop. 4,419), E central Sask., Canada, on Saskatchewan R., and 75 mi/121 km E of Prince Albert; 53°22′N 104°01′W. Flour milling, dairying.

Nipe Bay (NEE-pai), sheltered Atlantic inlet, Holguín prov., NE Cuba, 50 mi/80 km N of Santiago de Cuba, and linked with sea by narrows; 14 mi/23 km long, 8 mi/12.9 km wide; 20°45′N 75°45′W. Receives Mayarí R. and small Nipe R. Preston is on E, Antilla on N shore.

Nipe, Sierra de (NEE-pai, see-ER-uh dai), range, Holguín and Santiago de Cuba provs., E Cuba, extending c.25 mi/40 km S from Nipe Bay towards Santiago de Cuba, forming divide bet. Nipe (W) and Mayarí (E) rivers. Rises to 3,264 ft/995 m at Loma de Mensura. Iron mined in N. Also called Los Pinales.

Nipigon (NI-pi-gahn), town (1991 pop. 2,338), W central Ont., Canada, on Nipigon Bay of L. Superior, at mouth of Nipigon R., 60 mi/97 km NE of Thunder Bay; 49°01′N 88°15′W. Lumbering.

Nipigon, Lake (NIP-i-gahn) (□ c.1,870 sq mi/4,840 sq km), central Ont., Canada. Has many islands. Its outlet, the Nipigon R. (40 mi/64 km long) flows S, past the logging town of Nipigon, into L. Superior.

Nipisiguit River (ni-PI-zi-gwit), c.100 mi/161 km long, N N.B., Canada; rises at foot of Mt. Carleton; flows E, turning NNE to Nipisiguit Bay, inlet of Chaleur Bay, at Bathurst. Grand Falls, 20 mi/32 km SSW of Bathurst, are 4 falls with total ht. of 140 ft/43 m.

Nipissing (NI-pi-sing), district (□ 7,560 sq mi/ 19,580 sq km; 1991 pop. 84,723), SE central Ont., Canada, on L. Nipissing; ⊙ North Bay; 46°15′N 79°00′W.

Nipissing, Lake (NIP-i-sing) (□ c.350 sq mi/910 sq km), S Ont., Canada, bet. the Ottawa R. and Georgian Bay. It extends W from the city of North Bay and is drained SW by the French R. c.50 mi/80 km to Georgian Bay.

Nipomo, uninc. town (1990 pop. 7,109), San Luis Obispo co., SW Calif. 5 mi/8 km NNW of Santa Maria, 10 mi/ 16 km E of Pacific Ocean; 35°02′N 120°29′W. Apples, strawberries, avocados, vegetables, grain, nursery prods.; cattle. Santa Maria R. to S; Twitchell Reservoir to E; Los Padres Natl. Forest, in Sierra Madre to E.

Nippersink Lake, Ill.: see CHAIN O' LAKES.

Nipple Mountain (12,199 ft/3,718 m), in Sangre de Cristo Mts., S central Colo. Boundaries of Fremont, Custer, and Saguache cos. converge at summit. San Isabel Natl. Forest to NE; Rio Grande Natl. Forest to SW.

Nipple Top, peak (4,620 ft/1,408 m) of the High Peaks sect. of the Adirondacks, in Essex co., NE N.Y., c.6 mi/ 9.7 km ESE of Mt. Marcy, and 16 mi/26 km SE of Lake Placid village; 44°05′N 73°50′W.

Niquero (nee-KER-o), town, Holguín prov., E Cuba, port on SE Guacanayabo Bay, 35 mi/56 km SW of Manzanillo; 20°30′N 75°46′W. In fertile region (sugarcane, fruit; livestock; timber). Airfield.

Nishnabotna River, c.100 mi/161 km long, in SW Iowa and NW Mo.; formed by East and West Nishnabotna rivers; rises in Carroll co., Iowa; both flow S and W, then join near Hamburg to form Nishnabotna R.; flows c.12 mi/19 km S to Missouri R. 2 mi/3.2 km W of Watson in extreme NW Mo. Used for hydroelectric power. Tributaries and main stream are canalized for flood control. Because of record rains, serious flooding occurred along the river in 1993.

Niskayuna, village and town (□ 1 sq mi/2.6 sq km; 1990 pop. 4,942), Schenectady co., E N.Y., on Mohawk R., and 5 mi/8 km E of Schenectady; 42°47′N 73°51′W.

Nisky (NES-kee), village, St. Thomas Isl., U.S. V.I., 1.5 mi/2.4 km W of Charlotte Amalie. Site of a Moravian mission (founded 1755), in picturesque setting. Sometimes spelled Niesky.

Nisland, village (1990 pop. 174), Butte co., W S.Dak., 15 mi/24 km E of Belle Fourche, and on Belle Fourche R.; 44°40′N 103°32′W. Butte co. fair takes place here.

Nisqually River (nuh-SKWAH-lee), 81 mi/130 km long, W central Wash.; fed by Nisqually Glacier on S slopes of Mt. Rainier, Mt. Rainier Natl. Park, SE Pierce co.; flows SW, then W through Alder L. reservoir, then NW past Yelm through part of Fort Lewis Military Reservation, and past Nisqually Indian Reservation to Puget Sound 10 mi/16 km ENE of Olympia. Alder Dam (completed 1944; 330 ft/101 m high, 1,600 ft/488 m long) and La Grande Dam (completed 1945; 215 ft/66 m high, 710 ft/216 m long) furnish power. Nisqually Natl. Wildlife Refuge on W side of mouth.

Nissequogue (NIS-uh-kwahg), residential village (□ 5 sq mi/13 sq km; 1990 pop. 1,620), Suffolk co., SE N.Y., on N shore of L.I., near mouth of Nissequogue R., 12 mi/19 km E of Huntington; 40°54′N 73°11′W. Residential and recreational area.

Nissequogue River (NIS-uh-kwahg), c.8 mi/12.9 km long, SE N.Y.; rises in small lake just S of Smithtown Branch on Long Isl.; flows SW and NE, past Smithtown, to Smithtown Bay 4 mi/6.4 km W of Stony Brook.

Nisswa (NIS-wah), town (1990 pop. 1,391), Crow Wing co., central Minn., 13 mi/21 km NNW of Brainerd; 46°30′N 94°17′W. Resort area. Dairying; poultry; oats, alfalfa; mfg. (boat lifts and docks, labels). Cullen L. to N, Gull L. reservoir to SW, Pelican L. to NE; Pillsbury State Forest to SW.

Nisutlin River S, 150 mi/241 km long, Yukon, Canada, headstream of Yukon R.; rises in SE part of Pelly Mts.; flows in wide arc W and S to Teslin L.

Nitchequon, village, E central Que., Canada, on NE shore of L. Nichicun, where La Grande R. exits and

flows N from lake; 53°12′N 70°55′W. Within James Bay Hydro Project. Populated by Cree Indians. Iron ore and timber reserves in area. Fishing, hunting.

Nith River, c.70 mi/113 km, SW Ont., Canada; rises SE of Listowel; flows SE, past New Hamburg, to Thames R. 9 mi/14 km SW of Galt. Receives Millbank R.

Nitinat Lake (□ 10 sq mi/26 sq km), SW B.C., Canada, on SW Vancouver Isl., 70 mi/113 km WNW of Victoria; 13 mi/21 km long, 1 mi/2 km wide.

Nitro (NEI-tro), town (1990 pop. 6,851), Putnam and Kanawha cos., W central W.Va., on Kanawha R. (bridged), suburb 11 mi/18 km WNW of Charleston; 38°25′N 81°49′W. Agr. (corn, tobacco); cattle; poultry. Coal-producing area. Mfg. (chemicals, glass, screens, protective castings; printing and publishing; IBM plant. A boomtown in World War I, govt. explosives plant here was later abandoned. Inc. 1932.

Nivelle, Mount (NI-vuhl), (10,620 ft/3,237 m), SE B.C., Canada, near Alta. border, in Rocky Mts., 50 mi/80 km SSE of Banff; 50°31′N 115°11′W.

Niwot, uninc. town (1990 pop. 2,666), Boulder co., N central Colo., suburb 8 mi/12.9 km NE of Boulder, and 5 mi/8 km SW of Longmont; 40°06′N 105°09′W. Elev. 5,090 ft/1,551 m. Mfg. of concrete, plastic parts; publishing; IBM plant.

Nixa (NIK-suh), town (1990 pop. 4,707), Christian co., SW Mo., in the Ozarks, near James R., 12 mi/19 km S of downtown Springfield; 37°02′N 93°17′W. Fruit; dairying; mfg. (plastic molding, deodorants, lamps, fixtures, aluminum and sand castings, furniture, pottery).

Nixon 1 uninc. town (1990 pop. 1,342), Butler co., W Pa., residential community 6 mi/9.7 km SSW of Butler; 40°46′N 79°55′W. Butler co. airport to W. **2** town (1990 pop. 1,995), Gonzales co., S central Texas, c.45 mi/72 km ESE of San Antonio; 29°16′N 97°45′W. Poultry-packing and -shipping center. Agr. (peanuts; corn, wheat; cattle, poultry).

Nixon, uninc. village (1990 pop. 400), Washoe co., W Nev., 33 mi/53 km NE of Reno, on Truckee R., 5 mi/ 8 km SE of its entrance to Pyramid L., in SE part of Pyramid L. Indian Reservation. Cattle, sheep. Pyramid L. State Park to NW; Anaho Isl. Natl. Wildlife Reserve to N.

Nizao (nee-ZOU), town (1993 pop. 5,594), Peravia prov., S Dominican Republic, on the coast, 26 mi/42 km SW of Santo Domingo; 18°15′N 70°13′W. Agr. (coffee, rice, bananas).

No Mans Land, SE Mass., isl. in the Atlantic, 6 mi/9.7 km S of Gay Head; c.2 mi/3.2 km long, ½ mi/⅘₀ km–1 mi/ 1.6 km wide. The isl. is a Natl. Wildlife Refuge. Formerly U.S. Navy bombing range.

Noatak, Inuit village (1990 pop. 333), NW Alaska, on Noatak R., and 50 mi/80 km NNW of Kotzebue; 67°34′N 163°00′W. Just W is Cape Krusenstern Natl. Monument.

Noatak Preserve (□ 10,272 sq mi/26,604 sq km), Alaska; authorized 1978. Mt.-ringed river basin.

Noatak River, c.400 mi/644 km long, NW Alaska; rises in Brooks Range, near 67°28′N 154°50′W; flows W to Kotzebue Sound opposite Kotzebue.

Noble 1 county (□ 417 sq mi/1,080 sq km; 1990 pop. 37,877), NE Ind.; ⊙ Albion; 41°24′N 85°25′W. Agr. area (hogs, cattle; poultry; fruit, corn, soybeans, produce; dairy). Mfg. (dairy- and farm-prods. processing) at Kendallville, Albion, Ligonier. Gravel pits. Drained by Elkhart R. Chain O' Lakes State Park in S central; part of Tri-County Fish and Wildlife Area in SW corner. Gene Stratton Porter State Memorial in N. About 20 small lakes, glacial in origin, scattered throughout co.; largest is Sylvan L. near Rome City in N. Formed 1836. **2** county (□ 404 sq mi/1,046 sq km; 1990 pop. 11,336), E Ohio; ⊙ Caldwell, 39°50′N 81°28′W. Drained by Wills Creek and small Duck and Seneca creeks. Includes Senecaville Reservoir. In the Unglaciated Plain physiographic region. Agr. (livestock; grain, tobacco; dairy prods.); mfg. (lumber and wood prods., motor vehicle parts and accessories, electrometallurgical products); coal mines, clay pits, limestone quarries. Formed 1851. **3** county (□ 742 sq mi/1,922 sq km; 1990 pop. 11,045),

N Okla.; ⊙ Perry; 36°23′N 97°14′W. Bounded NE by Arkansas R. in extreme NE. Drained by small Black Bear and Red Rock creeks. Agr. area (wheat, oats, barley; cattle). Mfg. (metal prods., construction machinery) at Perry. Oil and natural gas wells. Includes Tonkawa and Ponca Otoe Indian natl. hqs. and tribal lands. L. McMurtry is S; Sooner L. reservoir on E boundary. Formed 1893.

Noble, town (1990 pop. 4,710), Cleveland co., central Okla., suburb 6 mi/9.7 km SSE of Norman, and 22 mi/ 35 km SSE of downtown Oklahoma City, on Canadian R.; 35°08′N 97°22′W. In agr. area; mfg. (belt buckles, figurines).

Noble 1 village (1990 pop. 756), Richland co., SE Ill., 7 mi/11.3 km WSW of Olney; 38°42′N 88°13′W. In agr. area (corn, wheat, apples; livestock). **2** village (1990 pop. 225), Sabine parish, W La., 57 mi/92 km S of Shreveport; 31°42′N 93°41′W. Agr.; timber; recreation. Oil wells nearby. Large Toledo Bend reservoir (Sabine R.; Texas boundary) to W.

Noble, Dominican Republic: see VICENTE NOBLE.

Nobleboro, town (1990 pop. 1,455), Lincoln co., S Maine, on Damariscotta L., and 11 mi/18 km NE of Wiscasset; 44°06′N 69°28′W. Sometimes called Nobleborough.

Nobleford, village (1991 pop. 517), S Alta., Canada, 17 mi/ 27 km NW of Lethbridge; 49°53′N 113°03′W. Wheat; dairying.

Nobles, county (□ 722 sq mi/1,870 sq km; 1990 pop. 20,098), SW Minn.; ⊙ Worthington; 43°40′N 95°45′W. Bordered by Iowa on S and West Branch of Little Rock R. Agr. area (corn, oats, soybeans, alfalfa; hogs, sheep, cattle, poultry; dairying). Includes part of Coteau des Prairies; several small natural lakes of glacial origin in NE and SE, includes Ocheda and Okabena lakes (SE), West and East Graham lakes (NE). Formed 1857. Ocheda L. is in SE.

Noblestown, uninc. village (1990 pop. 350), North Fayette township, Allegheny co., W Pa., suburb 11 mi/18 km WSW of downtown Pittsburgh, on Robinson Run; 40°23′N 80°11′W. Gas and oil field. Pa. Motor Speedway is here.

Noblesville, city (1990 pop. 17,655), ⊙ Hamilton co., central Ind., on White R., and 20 mi/32 km NNE of Indianpolis; 40°04′N 86°02′W. Suburb of Indianpolis. RR junction. In livestock and grain area; mfg. (concrete and molded prods., ductile iron castings, plastics, medical prods., air springs, food prods., agr. products, consumer goods; printing and publishing); breeds horses. Morse Reservoir nearby to the NW. Laid out 1823; inc. as town in 1851, as city in 1887.

Nobska Point (NAWB-skuh), SW Cape Cod, Falmouth, Mass., low promotory just SE of Woods Hole; extends into Vineyard Sound. Lighthouse (41°31′N 70°39′W).

Nocatee (NAHK-uh-tee), village, De Soto co., central Fla., near Peace R., 4 mi/6.4 km S of Arcadia; 27°11′N 81°52′W. Large crate factory.

Noccalula Falls (nah-kuh-LOO-luh), in small Black Creek, just NW of Gadsden, Ala.; drop of c.100 ft/30 m over limestone ridge of Lookout Mt.; c.15 mi/24 km long.

Nochistlán, Mexico: see ASUNCIÓN NOCHIXTLÁN, Oaxaca.

Nochistlán, Mexico: see NOCHISTLÁN DE MEJÍA.

Nochistlán de Mejía (no-chees-TLAHN dai me-HEE-ah), city (1990 pop. 14,659) and township, Nochistlán de Mejía Zacatecas, N central Mexico, on interior plateau, 50 mi/80 km SW of Aguascalientes; 21°21′N 102°50′W. Elev. 6,332 ft/1,930 m. Agr. center (grain, sugarcane, beans, fruit; livestock).

Nockamixon, Lake, reservoir (□ 2 sq mi/5.2 sq km), Bucks co., E central Pa., on Tohickon Creek, in Nockamixon State Park, 16 mi/25 km SE of Bethlehem; 40°28′N 75°11′W. Max. capacity 71,000 acre-ft. Formed by Nockamixon Dam (102 ft/31 m high) built (1973) for recreation.

Nocona (NAH-ko-nah), town (1990 pop. 2,870), Montague co., N Texas, c.45 mi/72 km E of Wichita Falls; 33°46′N 97°43′W. Elev. 988 ft/301 m. In agr. ranching, oil-producing area; a leather goods mfg. center (belts, accessories, tack). L. Nocona to NE.

Nocupétaro de Morelos (no-koo-PE-tah ro dai moh-RE-los), town (1990 pop. 2,915), ⊙ Nocupétaro municipio, Michoacán, central Mexico, 45 mi/73 km S of Morelia; 18°50′N 101°02′W. Rice, sugarcane, fruit.

Nodaway (NAH-duh-wai), county (□ 877 sq mi/ 2,271 sq km; 1990 pop. 21,709), NW Mo.; ⊙ Maryville; 40°21′N 94°52′W. Drained by Nodaway R., Little Platte R., and One Hundred and Two R. Agr. region (corn, wheat, oats, soybeans; cattle, hogs); mfg. at Maryville. N.W. Mo. State Univ. at Maryville. Formed 1845.

Nodaway, town, Adams co., SW Iowa, on East Nodaway R., and 9 mi/14.5 km WSW of Corning.

Nodaway River, 188 mi/303 km long (including Middle Nodaway R.), in SW Iowa and NW Mo.; formed near Villisca in Montgomery co. (Iowa) by junction of Middle and West Nodaway rivers; flows to Missouri R. above St. Joseph; 40°56′N 94°54′W. Receives East Nodaway R. (c.60 mi/97 km long) near Shambaugh.

Noel (NO-wuhl), town (1990 pop. 1,169), McDonald co., extreme SW Mo., in the Ozarks, on Elk R., and 9 mi/ 14.5 km SSW of Anderson; 36°32′N 94°29′W. Sport fishing; berries, chickens, dairying; mfg. (poultry processing, wood prods.). Bluff Dwellers Cave to S. Plotted 1891.

Nogal Peak, N.Mex.: see SIERRA BLANCA.

Nogales (no-GAH-les), city (1990 pop. 20,447) and township, Veracruz, E Mexico, in valley of Sierra Madre Oriental, at S foot of Pico de Orizaba, on RR, and 4 mi/ 6.4 km WSW of Orizaba; 18°50′N 97°12′W. Textile-milling and agr. center (coffee, tobacco, sugarcane, fruit).

Nogales (NO-gah-les), city (1990 pop. 19,489), Santa Cruz co., S Ariz., 60 mi/97 km S of Tucson, on the Mex. (Sonoran) border opposite Nogales, Mexico; 31°21′N 110°55′W. Elev. 3,865 ft/1,178 m. RR terminus (transfer point to Mex. RR system).There are copper, silver, and lead mines. Skirmishes occurred in Nogales against Pancho Villa in 1916. Industrial development, primarily in the 1980s, in the Mex. city of Nogales has resulted in a growth of maquiladoras (mfg. plants operated by low-cost labor for the production of U.S. trading goods). Parts of Coronado Natl. Forest to E and W; Patagonia L. State Park to NE; Tubac Presidio State Historic Park and Tumacacori Natl. Monument to N.

Nogales, Mexico: see HEROICA NOGALES.

Nogamut (NO-guh-moot), Indian village, W Alaska, on Holitna R., and 75 mi/121 km SE of Aniak. Sometimes spelled Nugammute and Nogamiut.

NoHo, section of Lower Manhattan, N.Y. city, SE N.Y., bounded on S by East Houston St., on N by East 8th St., on E by the Bowery, and on W by Mercer where it abuts Greenwich Village; 40°43′N 73°59′W. Name is an emblematic acronym referring to the gentrification process that has occurred in the area "north of Houston St." (similar to the way the name SoHo stands for "south of Houston St."). Like SoHo, its more glamorous counterpart, NoHo is still zoned for light mfg., with joint living and working quarters for artists. In 1976, artists' request that the city re-zone the dist. in the same manner as SoHo—that is, as an historical, industrial mfg. area—was granted. Many of the former warehouses have been officially certified by N.Y.C. Dept. of Cultural Affairs as residences of artists. For young, less affluent artists, NoHo has developed as a cheaper alternative to SoHo, which is now characterized by skyrocketing rents and lack of space.

Nokomis, city (1990 pop. 2,534), Montgomery co., S central Ill., 16 mi/26 km NE of Hillsboro; 39°17′N 89°17′W. In agr. area; dairy prods. Inc. 1867.

Nokomis (no-KO-mis), town (1991 pop. 459), S central Sask., Canada, 22 mi/35 km SE of Watrous; 51°31′N 105°01′W. RR junction; grain elevators, lumbering.

Nokomis (nuh-KO-mis), town (□ 2 sq mi/5.2 sq km; 1990 pop. 3,448), Sarasota co., W central Fla., 17 mi/ 27 km SE of Sarasota; 27°07′N 82°26′W. Mfg. includes motor vehicles, printing and publishing, machining, aluminum fabricating.

Nolan, county (□ 914 sq mi/2,367 sq km; 1990 pop. 16,594), W Texas; ⊙ SWEETWATER. Drained by Sweetwater Creek and other tributaries of the Colorado and the Brazos rivers; 32°18′N 100°24′W. Elev. 2,000 ft/ 610 m–2,700 ft/823 m. Ranching, agr.; cattle, sheep, goats, hogs; cotton, sorghum, wheat, hay; oil and natural gas production; gypsum quarries, stone, sand and gravel, clay. Recreation areas at Sweetwater and Oak Creek lakes. Formed 1876.

Nolanville, town (1990 pop. 1,834), Bell co., central Texas, residential suburb 7 mi/11.3 km E of Killeen, and 14 mi/ 23 km WSW of Temple, on Nolan Creek; 31°04′N 97°36′W. Agr. area. Limestone. Large Fort Hood Military Reservation to N., Stillhouse Hollow L. reservoir to S.

Nolichucky (NAHL-uh-chuk-ee) river, c.150 mi/240 km long, W N.C.; rises in the Blue Ridge; flows NW and W to the French Broad R. W of Greeneville, Tenn. A power dam impounds Davy Crockett L. SW of Greeneville. The 1st settlement on the river was made in 1772.

Nolin Lake (NO-lin), reservoir (□ 9 sq mi/23.3 sq km), Edmonson co., central Ky., on Nolin R., 24 mi/39 km NNE of Bowling Green; 37°17′N 86°15′W. Max. capacity 609,400 acre-ft. Formed by Nolin L. Dam (146 ft/45 m high), built (1963) by Army Corps of Engineers for flood control; also used for recreation. Mammoth Cave Natl. Park just S. Also known as Nolin River L.

Nolin River (NO-lin), 105 mi/169 km long, central Ky.; rises in E Larue co., flows W past Hodgenville, and SSW through Nolin River L. reservoir and W end of Mammoth Cave Natl. Park, to Green R. 3 mi/4.8 km NE of Brownsville.

Nombre de Dios (NOM-brai dai DEE-os), city (1990 pop. 4,400) and township, Durango, N Mexico, on interior plateau, 30 mi/48 km ESE of Durango; 23°50′N 104°15′W. Grain, cotton, vegetables; livestock. Silver mines nearby. First Span. settlement in Durango. Also called La Villita.

Nome, city (1990 pop. 3,500), W Alaska, on the S side of Seward Peninsula, on Norton Sound; 64°30′N 165°24′W. Founded c.1898, when gold was discovered on the beach here. It is the commercial, govt., and supply center for NW Alaska, with an airport. Major economic mainstays are mining, tourism fishing, and govt. The city is also a center of Eskimo handicrafts. Nome was a gold rush town from 1899 to 1903; its pop. swelled to 30,000, but many died or left because of the hardships. Dredging, which replaced older methods of mining, ceased in 1962, renewed in 1980s. The city is the scene of an annual Midnight Sun Festival (late June), Iditarod Dog Sled Race (late Feb., from Anchorage) and the All-Alaska Championship Dog Race. Cape Nome lies to SE. Road system connects with Taylor (N), Keller (NW), and Ophir (NE).

Nome 1 (NOM), village (1990 pop. 67), Barnes co., SE N.Dak., 20 mi/32 km SE of Valley City; 46°40′N 97°49′W. RR junction to NE at Lucca. **2** village (1990 pop. 448), Jefferson co., SE Texas, 18 mi/29 km W of Beaumont; 30°01′N 94°25′W. Oil and natural gas. Cattle; rice, soybeans.

Nome, Cape, W Alaska, S Seward Peninsula, on N shore of Norton Sound, 12 mi/19 km ESE of Nome; 64°27′N 165°00′W.

Nominingue (no-meen-ENG), village, SW Que., Canada, on L. Nominingue (6 mi/10 km long, 3 mi/5 km wide), in the Laurentians, 45 mi/72 km NW of Ste. Agathe des Monts; 46°23′N 75°01′W. Dairying.

Nonacho Lake (□ 305 sq mi/790 sq km), SE Mackenzie dist., N.W.T., Canada, E of Great Slave L.; 61°42′N 109°40′W; 30 mi/48 km long, 1 mi/2 km–20 mi/32 km wide. Drained W into Great Slave L. by Taltson R.

Nonantum, Mass.: see NEWTON.

Nondalton, village (1990 pop. 178), S Alaska, at SW end of L. Clark, 190 mi/306 km WSW of Anchorage; 59°59′N 154°50′W. Fishing resort.

Nonesuch River, SW Maine, tidal stream; follows 12-mi/19-km semi-circular course, NE above Saco, then SE and S to the Atlantic at Scarboro.

Nonoava (no-no-AH-vah), town (1990 pop. 1,303), Chihuahua, N Mexico, on tributary of Conchos R., and 90 mi/145 km SW of Chihuahua; 27°30′N 106°41′W. Corn, cotton, beans; livestock; lumbering.

Nonquitt, Mass.: see DARTMOUTH.

Noodle, uninc. village (1990 pop. 40), Jones co., W central Texas, 20 mi/32 km WNW of Abilene. Agr. area (cotton, wheat; cattle).

Nooksack (NOOK-sak), village (1990 pop. 584), Whatcom co., NW Wash., 15 mi/24 km NE of Bellingham, and on Sumas R. (Nooksack R. is 2 mi/3.2 km W at Everson); 48°56′N 122°19′W. In agr. area; grain, vegetables, berries; dairying; cattle, poultry.

Nooksack River, c.25 mi/40 km long, NW Wash.; rises NE of Mt. Baker as North Fork (c.50 mi/80 km long); flows W and SW through Nooksack Falls (power plant), 1st joining Middle Fork, then South Fork; main stream flows NW, and SW again to Bellingham Bay on Lummi Indian Reservation, E Whatcom co.; receives South Fork (c.40 mi/64 km long) and Middle Fork (c.20 mi/32 km long). Has power plant at falls near source.

Noonan, village (1990 pop. 231), Divide co., NW N.Dak., port of entry 7 mi/11.3 km N of village of Crosby near Can. border; 48°53′N 103°00′W. Lignite mining; dairy prods., wheat, corn.

Noonen Reservoir, Arapahoe co., W Colo., on Deer Trail Creek, 53 mi/85 km E of Denver; 1 mi/1.6 km long; 39°43′N 103°58′W. Formed by Noonen Dam (42 ft/13 m high), built (1970) by private interests for flood control.

Noonmark, peak (elev. 3,552 ft/1,083 m) of the High Peaks sect. of the Adirondacks, in Essex co., NE N.Y., c.8 mi/ 12.9 km E of Mt. Marcy, and 16 mi/26 km SE of Lake Placid village; 44°08′N 73°47′W.

Noorvik (1990 pop. 531), NW Alaska, on Kobuk R., and 45 mi/72 km E of Kotzebue; 66°49′N 161°02′W. Within Noorvik Indian Reservation.

Nooseneck, R.I.: see WEST GREENWICH.

Nootka Island (NOOT-kuh) (□ 206 sq mi/534 sq km), SW B.C., Canada, in the Pacific, off W central coast of Vancouver Isl., 45 mi/72 km NW of Tofino; 21 mi/34 km long, 16 mi/26 km wide; center near 49°45′N 126°45′W. Fishing, lumbering. Nootka village on SE coast.

Nootka Sound, inlet of the Pacific Ocean and natural harbor on the W coast of Vancouver Isl., SW B.C., Canada, lying bet. the mainland and Nootka Isl. (□ 206 sq mi/534 sq km). The mouth of the sound was sighted (1774) by Juan Pérez, the Span. explorer. The sound itself was visited by Capt. James Cook (1778), who was the 1st European to land in that region. John Meares, the Br. explorer, established a trading post on Nootka Sound in 1788. Its seizure by Spaniards in 1789 became the subject of a controversy bet. Spain and England over claims in the region. The Nootka Convention (1790) resolved the dispute and opened the N Pacific coast to Br. settlement.

Nopala (no-PAH-lah), town (1990 pop. 913), ⊙ Nopala de Villagran municipio, Hidalgo, central Mexico, near RR, and 25 mi/40 km SE of San Juan del Río. Corn, beans, maguey; livestock.

Nopaltepec (no-PAHL-te-pek), town (1990 pop. 2,156), Mexico state, central Mexico, on RR, and 35 mi/56 km NE of Mexico city, in the Zona Metropolitana de la Ciudad de México; 19°41′N 98°25′W. Elev. 8,202 ft/ 2,500 m. Cereals, maguey.

Nopalucan de la Granja, town (1990 pop. 4,020), ⊙ Nopalucan municipio, Puebla, central Mexico, 28 mi/ 45 km NE of Puebla; 19°13′N 97°49′W. Cereals, beans, maguey.

Nora 1 village (1990 pop. 162), Jo Daviess co., NW Ill., 20 mi/32 km NW of Freeport; 42°27′N 89°56′W. In agr. area. Apple R. Canyon State Park is nearby. **2** village (1990 pop. 24), Nuckolls co., S Nebr., 10 mi/16 km NNE of Superior; 40°09′N 97°58′W. **3** uninc. village, Dickenson co., SW Va., in Cumberland Mts., 18 mi/29 km NE of Norton; 37°4′N 82°20′W. Agr. (cattle; tobacco); timber.

Nora Springs, town (1990 pop. 1,505), Floyd co., N Iowa, on Shell Rock R., and 17 mi/27 km WNW of Charles

City; 43°08′N 93°00′W. Concrete blocks. Limestone quarry, sand and gravel pits nearby. Inc. 1875.

Noranda, Canada: see ROUYN-NORANDA.

Norbertville, village (1991 pop. 270), S Que., Canada, 25 mi/40 km W of Thetford Mines. Dairying; cattle; wheat, potatoes.

Norbestos (nor-BE-stuhs), asbestos mining village, S Que., Canada, 5 mi/8 km NE of Asbestos.

Norborne (NAHR-buhrn), city (1990 pop. 856), Carroll co., NW central Mo., near Missouri R., 10 mi/16 km WSW of Carrollton; 39°17′N 93°40′W. Wheat, corn, soybeans; hogs, cattle. Laid out 1868.

Norcatur (nor-KAI-tuhr), village (1990 pop. 198), Decatur co., NW Kansas, 18 mi/29 km E of Oberlin; 39°49′N 100°11′W. Grain; cattle.

Norco, city (1990 pop. 23,302), Riverside co., SE Calif., suburb 35 mi/56 km ESE of downtown Los Angeles, 10 mi/16 km W of Riverside, on Santa Ana R.; 33°56′N 117°33′W. Diversified agr. being displaced by rapid urban development from Los Angeles. Mfg. (lubricating oils). Calif. Inst. for Women (prison) to W, Calif. Inst. for Men (prison) and Chino Aiport to NW, Corona Municipal Airport to SW. Chino Hills State Park to W; Prado Reservoir to SW. Inc. 1964.

Norco (NOOR-ko), uninc. town (1990 pop. 3,385), St. Charles parish, SE La., near E bank (levee) of the Mississippi R., c.20 mi/32 km W of New Orleans; 30°00′N 90°25′W. RR junction; oil refining; mfg. (gas and liquid oxygen, gasoline and other fuels, fabricated metals). Bonnet Carre Spillway to NW. L. Pontchartrain shore 4 mi/6 km NNE.

Norcross, town (1990 pop. 5,947), Gwinnett co., N central Ga., 15 mi/24 km NE of Atlanta; 33°56′N 84°13′W. Emerging center of high-tech innovation and production in this N Atlanta suburb. Many high-tech business and industrial parks house domestic and multinatl. firms. Mfg (chemicals, computer hardware, concrete blocks, ventilation equip., particleboard, consumer goods, telecommunications equip., apparel; sheet metal fabrication, printing and publishing).

Norcross, village (1990 pop. 86), Grant co., W Minn., on Mustinka R., and 14 mi/23 km SW of Elbow Lake town; 45°52′N 96°12′W. Dairying; grain.

Nord (NOR), department (1982 pop. 564,002), N Haiti, bounded on the W by Nord-Ouest and Artibonite depts., S by Artibonite and Centre depts., E by Nord-Est dept.; ⊙ Cap-Haïtien (Haiti's 2d-largest city); 19°36′N 72°18′W. Agr. (sugarcane, coffee, citrus fruits); copper deposits.

Nord, Massif du (NOR, mah-SEEF dyoo), range in N Haiti, bet. the Plaine du Nord (N) and Central Plain (S), continuing the Cordillera Central of the Dominican Republic; extends c.80 mi/129 km SE from Port-de-Paix; 19°30′N 72°15′W. Rises to 2,525 ft/770 m. The Plaine du Nord continues the Cibao region of the Dominican Republic; agr. (sugarcane, coffee, cacao, tobacco, bananas, citrus fruit, pineapples, sisal, fine wood); copper deposits.

Nordegg (NUHR-deg) or **Brazeau** (BRA-zo), town, SW Alta., Canada, in Rocky Mts., near North Saskatchewan R., 130 mi/209 km SW of Edmonton. Elev. 4,471 ft/1,363 m. Hydroelectricity; cattle; timber.

Norden, uninc. village, Nevada co., E Calif., in the Sierra Nevada, 35 mi/56 km SW of Reno (Nev.), on South Yuba R., at L. Van Norden. Elev. 6,880 ft/2,097 m. Donner Pass to E (Interstate Highway 80) and Norden Tunnel (RR; c.10,000 ft/3,048 m long).

Norden Tunnel, Calif.: see NORDEN.

Nord-Est (NOR-EST), department (1982 pop. 189,573), NE Haiti. Bounded on N by Atlantic Ocean, E by Dominican Republic, S by Centre dept., W by Nord dept.; ⊙ Fort Liberté; 19°32′N 71°42′W. Sugarcane, fruit, sisal growing; gold deposits.

Nordheim, village (1990 pop. 344), De Witt co., S Texas, 38 mi/61 km WNW of Victoria; 28°55′N 97°36′W. Cotton, corn; cattle, poultry, dairying; oil and gas.

Nordman, uninc. village (1990 pop. 50), Bonner co., N Idaho, 30 mi/48 km NW of Sandpoint, near Wash. state line, in Kaniksu Natl. Forest. Timber; tourism. N terminus of State Highway 57. Priest L. to E; Upper Priest L. Scenic Area to N.

Nord-Ouest (NOR-WEST), department (□ c.1,060 sq mi/2,745 sq km; 1982 pop. 293,531), NW Haiti; 19°45′N 73°05′W. To the N is the Atlantic Ocean, to the S the Gulf of Gonaïves and Artibonite dept., to the E Nord dept.; ⊙ Port-de-Paix. Coffee, rice, sisal, cocoa growing; beekeeping; has copper deposits.

Norfolk (NOR-fuhk), county (□ 634 sq mi/1,642 sq km), S Ont., Canada, on L. Erie; ⊙ Simcoe; 42°50′N 80°20′W.

Norfolk 1 county (□ 443 sq mi/1,147 sq km; 1990 pop. 616,087), E Mass.; ⊙ Dedham, S of Boston, with Quincy and Hingham bays on Boston Bay; bounded SW by R.I.; 42°10′N 71°11′W. Drained by Charles and Neponset rivers. NE area is thickly populated, with residential suburbs of Boston (e.g., Brookline, Milton). Mfg. (textiles, metal and wood prods., bldg. materials, machinery, paper prods.), printing and publishing; former granite quarrying in its industrial towns, notably Quincy. Agr. in SW. Formed 1793. State Prison. **2** former county, SE Va. is now the independent cities of PORTSMOUTH and CHESAPEAKE.

Norfolk 1 city (1990 pop. 21,476), Madison co., NE Nebr., on the Elkhorn R.; 42°01′N 97°25′W. Elev. 1,527 ft/465 m. RR terminus. A trade and RR center in a fertile farming region, it has a livestock market. Mfg. (animal feeds, food and beverages, electronics; printing and publishing, construction materials). Northeast Community Col., Nebr. Veteran's Home,. Karl Statan Memorial Airport. Inc. 1881. **2** independent city (□ 66 sq mi/171 sq km; 1990 pop. 261,229) SE Va., bounded N by Chespeake Bay, NW by Hampton Roads harbor, W by Elizabeth R. (Portsmouth opposite), S by Chesapeake city, E by Va. Beach city; 36°55′N 76°14′W. Lafayette R. estuary indents city from Elizabeth R. in center, South Branch Elizabeth R. in S. RR junction and terminus; port of entry; major commercial, industrial, shipping, and distribution center. Mfg. (lumber, steel and sheet metal fabrication, leather prods., agr. equip., motor vehicles, metal doors, textiles, shipbuilding, transportation equip., furniture; machining, meat processing, printing and publishing). With Portsmouth and Newport News, it forms the Port of Hampton Roads, one of world's best natural harbors. Waterfront (50 mi/80 km), extensive maritime trade; quantities of coal, grain, tobacco, seafood, farm prods. exported. Major military center; with Portsmouth the city forms an extensive naval complex. A rallying point for Tory forces at the start of the Amer. Revolution, Norfolk was attacked (1776) by Americans and in the ensuing battle caught fire and was nearly destroyed. Civil War Confederate naval base until the Union takeover (May 1862); battle bet. the *Monitor* and the *Merrimack* fought in Hampton Roads. St. Paul's Church (1738; only bldg. to survive the burning of 1776); Ft. Norfolk (1794); Gen. Douglas MacArthur Memorial, where the general is buried; Va. Zoological Park; Norfolk Botanical Gardens; Hermitage Foundation Mus.; many historic homes. Old Dominion Univ., Norfolk State Univ., Eastern Va. Medical School; Va. Wesleyan Col. on boundary with Virginia Beach. Chesapeake Bay Bridge-Tunnel and RR barge link Norfolk from Virginia Beach with Delmarva Peninsula (Cape Charles) and Hampton Roads Bridge-Tunnel with Hampton, Va. Norfolk Internatl. Terminal (shipping port) on Elizabeth R.; Norfolk Internatl. Airport in E, on Va. Beach boundary. Norfolk Naval Base in NW. Intracoastal Waterway passes through Elizabeth R. Founded 1682, inc. as a city 1845.

Norfolk 1 resort town (1990 pop. 2,060), Litchfield co., NW Conn., in Litchfield Hills, near Mass. line, 8 mi/12.9 km NW of Winsted; 41°58′N 73°12′W. Agr.; mfg. wooden and metal prods. Recreational area, with state parks; Annual Litchfield co. choral concerts began here, 1899. William Henry Welch b. here. Settled 1755, inc., 1758. **2** agr. town (1990 pop. 9,270), Norfolk co., E Mass., 22 mi/35 km SW of Boston; 42°07′N 71°20′W. State correctional institute here. Settled 1795, inc. 1870.

Norfolk, village (□ 1 sq mi/2.6 sq km; 1990 pop. 1,412), St. Lawrence co., N N.Y., on Raquette R., and 10 mi/16 km SSW of Massena; 44°47′N 74°59′W. Settled in 1809. Amish people moved into the area in the mid-1970s and opened a cheese mill, cheese factories, sawmills, and gristmills; they are all gone now, though. William P. Rogers, who grew up here, was appointed U.S. Attorney General in 1958.

Norfork, village (1990 pop. 394), Baxter co., N Ark., c.45 mi/72 km E of Harrison, at junction of White R. and the North Fork; 36°12′N 92°16′W. Norfork Dam is to NE on North Fork (White) R. backs up the North Fork R. in Norfolk L.

Norfork Lake, reservoir (□ 34 sq mi/88 sq km), mainly in extreme N central Ark. (Baxter co.) and Mo., on N. Fork of White R., 4 mi/6.4 km W of Mountain Home; 36°15′N 92°14′W. Max. capacity 1,983,000 acre ft. Extends N-S. Formed by Norfork Dam (216 ft/66 m high), built (1944) by Army Corps of Engineers for power generation, recreation, water supply and as a fish and wildlife pond.

Norge, uninc. village, James City co., SE Va., 7 mi/11.3 km NNW of Williamsburg; 37°22′N 76°46′W. Agr. (tobacco, grain, soybeans; cattle; dairying).

Noria de Ángeles (NO-ree-ah dai AHN-he-les), town (1990 pop. 1,606), Zacatecas, N central Mexico, 50 mi/80 km SE of Zacatecas; 22°26′N 101°54′W. Maguey, fruit; livestock; silver and copper deposits.

Noria de San Pantaleón (NO-ree-ah dai sahn pahn-tah-le-ON), mining settlement (1990 pop. 94), Sombrerete municipio, Zacatecas, N central Mexico, 10 mi/16 km ENE of Sombrerete; 23°40′N 103°46′W. Silver, gold, lead, copper deposits.

Norlina (nor-LEIN-uh), town (1990 pop. 996), Warren co., N N.C., 14 mi/23 km NE of Henderson; 36°27′N 78°12′W. Grain, soybeans, tobacco, chickens; livestock; dairying. Mfg. (textiles).

Normal 1 town, Madison co., N Ala., 3 mi/4.8 km N of Huntsville. Seat of Ala. Agr. and Mechanical Univ. **2** town (1990 pop. 40,023), McLean co., central Ill.; 40°31′N 89°00′W. It is the center of a productive farming area. Mfg. (motor vehicles). The town originally grew around Ill. State Univ. (1857; formerly called Illinois State Normal Univ., the first public Univ. in Ill.), which remains a major contributor to its economy. Inc. 1867.

Norman, county (□ 877 sq mi/2,271 sq km; 1990 pop. 7,975), NW Minn.; ⊙ Ada. Bounded W by Red R. of the North (N.Dak. state line) and drained by Wild Rice R.; 47°20′N 96°28′W. Agr. area (wheat, oats, barley, sugar beets, beans, sunflowers, soybeans, potatoes, alfalfa, hay). Formed 1881.

Norman, city (1990 pop. 80,071), ⊙ Cleveland co., central Okla., suburb 18 mi/29 km S of Oklahoma City, on Canadian R.; 35°13′N 97°20′W. Elev. 1,170 ft/357 m. It is the center of a livestock region. Oil wells; mfg. (machinery, communication equip., bakery prods., nutritional prods., consumer goods; food processing, publishing and printing). Norman is the seat of the Univ. of Okla. Max Westheimer Field airport here. L. Thunderbird reservoir and Little R. State Park in E part of city. The city has been marked by a pop. increase of more than 55% bet. 1970 and 1990. Inc. 1891.

Norman 1 village (1990 pop. 382), Montgomery co., W Ark., 35 mi/56 km W of Hot Springs, in Ouachita Natl. Forest; 34°27′N 93°40′W. Lumbering. **2** village (1990 pop. 48), Kearney co., S Nebr., 7 mi/11.3 km E of Minden; 40°28′N 98°47′W. **3** village (1990 pop. 105), Richmond co., S N.C., 16 mi/26 km NNE of Rockingham; 35°10′N 79°43′W. Tobacco, grain, cotton; livestock. RR terminus. Kerr Reservation to NW, L. Gaston reservoir to NE.

Norman, Cape, promontory at N extremity of N.F., Canada, on Strait of Belle Isle; 51°38′N 55°54′W. Lighthouse.

Norman Island, islet, Br. Virgin Isls., 3 mi/4.8 km E of St. John; 18°20′N 64°37′W. Has old pirates' caves.

Norman, Lake, reservoir, on Lincoln/Mecklenberg co. border and in Iredell and Catawba cos., SW N.C., on Catawba R., 18 mi/29 km NNW of Charlotte; c.25 mi/40 km long; 35°28′N 80°58′W. Max. capacity 1,092,429 acre-ft. Oxford Dam at N tip. Formed by Cowans Ford Dam (115 ft/35 m), built (1963) by the

Duke Power Co. for power generation. Duke Power State Park on NE shore. Site of Mc Guire 1 and 2 nuclear power plants.

Norman Park, city (1990 pop. 711), Colquitt co., S Ga., 9 mi/14.5 km NE of Moultrie; 31°16′N 83°41′W.

Norman Wells, village (1991 pop. 627), Inuvik Region, N.W.T., Canada, on the Mackenzie R., W of Great Bear L.; 65°17′N 126°51′W. River port and center of an oil region. In 1985 a pipeline to the Zama, Alta. oil field (S) was completed, continues on to Edmonton refineries. Radio, TV, scheduled air service. Originated as oil-producing town. Once the terminus of Canol Road (1942–1958) from Yukon (now Canol Heritage Trail); proposed extension of MacKenzie Highway (now a winter road).

Normandin (nor-ma-DA), town (1991 pop. 3,957), S central Que.,Canada, 26 mi/42 km NW of Roberval; 48°50′N 72°31′W. Lumbering; food processing.

Normandy 1 town (1990 pop. 4,480), St. Louis co., E Mo., residential suburb 8 mi/12.9 km NW of downtown St. Louis; 38°42′N 90°17′W. Served by Metrolink light RR; Univ. of Mo. campus in adjacent Bellerive. Inc. since 1940. **2** town (1990 pop. 118), Bedford co., central Tenn., on Duck R., and 13 mi/21 km SE of Shelbyville; 35°27′N 86°16′W. State fish hatchery, Normandy dam nearby.

Normandy Park, town (1990 pop. 6,709), King co., W Wash., residential suburb 10 mi/16 km S of downtown Seattle, on Puget Sound, 47°26′N 122°22′W. Three Tree Pt. to W. Seattle-Tacoma (SeaTac) Internatl. Airport to E.

Normangee, village (1990 pop. 689), Leon and Madison cos., E central Texas, 29 mi/47 km NE of Bryan; 31°01′N 96°07′W. Trade point in farm area (vegetables, watermelons; cattle, hogs). State park nearby.

Normans, Md.: see KENT ISLAND.

Normantown, town, Toombs co., E central Ga., 7 mi/11.3 km N of Vidalia; 32°18′N 82°22′W.

Normetal, village (1991 pop. 1,193), W Que., Canada, 55 mi/89 km NNW of Rouyn, near Ont. border; 49°00′N 79°22′W. Gold, copper, zinc mining.

Norphlet (NOR-flit), village (1990 pop. 706), Union co., S Ark., 7 mi/11.3 km N of El Dorado; 33°19′N 92°39′W.

Norquay (NOR-kwai), town (1991 pop. 524), E Sask., Canada, near Man. border, 23 mi/37 km NNW of Kamsack. Mixed farming.

Norridge, village (1990 pop. 14,459), Cook co., NE Ill., near W edge of Chicago; 41°58′N 87°49′W. Inc. since 1948.

Norridgewock (NOR-ij-wahk), town (1990 pop. 3,105), Somerset co., W central Maine, on the Kennebec, and 5 mi/8 km SW of Skowhegan; 44°43′N 69°48′W. Light mfg. (shoes). In 17th cent. Norridgewock Indians here were visited by Jesuit missionaries; monument commemorates chapel of Sébastien Rasles who, with the Indians, was killed by English in 1724. Inc. 1788.

Norris, city (1990 pop. 1,303), Anderson co., E Tenn., on Clinch R., and 16 mi/26 km NW of Knoxville; 36°12′N 84°04′W. Built originally as residential community for construction workers on nearby Norris Dam; hq. of forestry div. of TVA and regional hq. of U.S. Bureau of Mines. Nearby is Norris Park (resort) on Norris Reservoir, and the Mus. of Appalachia, a living history mus. Inc. 1949.

Norris, town (1990 pop. 884), Pickens co., NW S.C., c. 9 mi/14.5 km SSW of Pickens; 34°45′N 82°45′W. Mfg. of clothing; agr. includes dairying, poultry, hogs; corn.

Norris 1 village (1990 pop. 212), Fulton co., W central Ill., 18 mi/29 km NNE of Lewiston; 40°37′N 90°01′W. In agr. and bituminous-coal area. **2** village, Madison co., SW Mont., at the confluence of Burnt Creek and Hot Springs Creek, a branch of Madison R., and 32 mi/51 km WSW of Bozeman. Corundum of gem quality mined here, coal outcroppings; cattle. Norris Hot Springs. Tobacco Root Mts. to W; unit of Lee Metcalf Wilderness Area to SE. Units of Deerlodge and Beaverhead natl. forests to W, Gallatin Natl. Forest to SE.

Norris, reservoir (□ 23 sq mi/60 sq km), E Tenn., on Clinch R., 25 mi/40 km N of Knoxville; 36°13′N 84°05′W. Max. capacity 255,200 acre-ft. Has 2 main branches; W branch, on Yellow and Powell rivers extends NE from dam through Campbell, Union and Claiborne cos.; E branch on Clinch R extends E bet. Union and Claiborne (N) and Grainger (S) cos. Formed by Norris Dam (265 ft/81 m high), built (1936) by TVA for flood control; also used for power generation, navigation, and recreation. Chuck Swan Forest and Wildlife Management Area bet. W and E branches; Big Ridge Rustic Park situated directly S of reservoir.

Norris City, village (1990 pop. 1,341), White co., SE Ill., 13 mi/21 km SW of Carmi; 37°58′N 88°19′W. Trade center in agr. and bituminous-coal, oil field area; wheat, corn, soybeans; livestock. Inc. 1901.

Norristown, borough (1990 pop. 30,749), ⊙ Montgomery co., SE Pa., suburb 15 mi/24 km NW of downtown Philadelphia, on the Schuylkill R.; 40°07′N 75°20′W. Mfg. (textiles, medical equip., machinery, fabricated metal prods., petroleum prods., explosive devices, furniture, food prods., consumer goods, windows and doors; printing and publishing,). The borough is named for Isaac Norris (1671–1735), a Quaker merchant and a mayor of Philadelphia, who in 1704 bought a large tract of land here from his friend William Penn. Gen. Winfield Scott Hancock, a commander during the Civil War and Democratic candidate for president in 1880, was born in Norristown and is buried here. Norristown State Hosp. is here; Wings Field Airport to E; Elmwood Park Zoo; Fort Washington State Park to E; Evansburg State Park to N; Valley Forge Natl. Historical Park to W.

North, town (1990 pop. 809), Orangeburg co., W central S.C., 16 mi/26 km NW of Orangeburg; 33°37′N 81°05′W. Mfg. includes lumber, knife cases, screen doors, apparel. Agr. (timber; poultry, livestock; grain, cotton, peanuts, tobacco, pecans, peaches).

North Abington, Mass.: see ABINGTON.

North Adams, city (1990 pop. 16,797), Berkshire co., NW Mass., in the Berkshire Hills, on the Hoosic R. near the Vt. border; 42°42′N 73°07′W. The city is located in a summer resort and winter ski area. Mfg. include electronic and electrical components, paper prods., textiles, and machinery. Airport. North Adams State Col. was a normal school in 1894. New art mus. in city. Mt. Greylock State Reservation. Settled c.1737, set off from Adams and inc. 18/8.

North Adams, village (1990 pop. 512), Hillsdale co., S Mich., 6 mi/9.7 km NE of Hillsdale; 41°58′N 84°31′W. In agr. area; mfg. of screw machine prods., metal stampings.

North Amherst, Mass.: see AMHERST.

North Amity (AM-uh-tee), town, Aroostook co., E Maine, 15 mi/24 km S of Houlton, near N.B. border (Canada). Agr.; lumbering.

North Andover (nor-THAN-do-vuhr), town (1990 pop. 22,792), Essex co., NE Mass., on the Merrimack R.; 42°40′N 71°05′W. In a dairy and farm area. A former textile town, its mfg. includes telephone equip., chemicals, paper prods., valves, prepared foods, and plastics. It is the seat of Merrimack Col., Brooks Preparatory School, and a Boston Univ. theology center; textile mus. The scenic spring-fed L. Cochichewick is nearby. Boston Hill ski resort; Harold Parker State Forest. Settled c.1644, set off from Andover, and inc. 1855.

North Anna 1 and 2 Nuclear Power Plants, Va.: see LOUISA, CO.

North Anna Dam, Va.: see ANNA, LAKE.

North Anna River, c.70 mi/113 km long, central Va.; rises in Piedmont region in W Orange co. (38°09′N 78°05′W); flows SE, through L. Anna reservoir; joins South Anna R. c.20 mi/32 km N of Richmond to form Pamunkey R. .

North Apollo, borough (1990 pop. 1,391), Armstrong co., W central Pa., 1 mi/1.6 km N of Apollo, and 15 mi/24 km S of Kittanning, on Kiskiminetas R. opposite Vandergrift; 40°35′N 79°33′W. Mfg. (fabricated metal prods.); agr. (corn, hay; dairying). Inc. 1930.

North Arlington, borough (1990 pop. 13,790), Bergen co., NE N.J., 2 mi/3.2 km NNE of Newark; 40°47′N 74°07′W. A residential and industrial suburb of Newark, on the Passaic R. Settled 1700s, inc. 1896.

North Atlanta, town, De Kalb co., N central Ga., suburb of Atlanta; 33°51′N 84°20′W.

North Attleboro, industrial town (1990 pop. 25,038), Bristol co., SE Mass., near the R.I. line, 20 mi/32 km NNW of Fall River; 41°58′N 71°20′W. Jewelry (since 1807); other mfg. includes boxes, metal prods., eyewear; fish hatchery nearby. The Woodcock tavern dates from 1670. Settled 1669, set off from Attleboro and inc. 1887.

North Auburn, uninc. city (1990 pop. 10,301), Placer co., central Calif., residential suburb 2 mi/3.2 km N of Auburn, on North Fork American R., opposite mouth of Rubicon R.; 38°56′N 121°05′W. Cattle, sheep; apiary prods.; fruit, nuts.

North Augusta, city (1990 pop. 15,351), Aiken co., SW S.C., on the Savannah R. suburb of Augusta, Ga.; 33°31′N 81°57′W. Located in an agr. region, it is mostly residential. Mfg. includes reconditioned RR equip., bldg. materials, machinery, chemicals, furniture; printing and publishing. Agr (cotton, grain, peanuts, peaches, soybeans; livestock, poultry). Many local residents are employed at the Atomic Energy Commission's nearby Savannah R. Nuclear site and in Augusta, Ga. Settled c.1860, inc. 1906.

North Augusta, village, SE Ont., Canada, 12 mi/19 km W of Brockville. Dairying, mixed farming.

North Aurora (aw-ROR-ah), village (1990 pop. 5,940), Kane co., NE Ill., on Fox R. (bridged here), just N of Aurora; 41°47′N 88°19′W.

North Baldwin, hamlet of Baldwin township, Cumberland co., SW Maine, c.28 mi/45 km WNW of Portland; 43°50′N 70°41′W. Saddleback Hills nearby.

North Baldy, N.Mex.: see MAGDALENA MOUNTAINS.

North Baltimore, village (1990 pop. 3,139), Wood co., NW Ohio, 13 mi/21 km S of Bowling Green; 41°11′N 83°40′W. In diversified farming area (corn, wheat); leather goods, machine shop prods., rubber prods. Stone quarries nearby. Settled 1834.

North Barrington, village (1990 pop. 1,787), Lake co., NE Ill., residential suburb 27 mi/43 km NW of downtown Chicago, 2 mi/3.2 km N of Lake Zürich; 42°12′N 88°07′W. Mfg. greeting cards.

North Bass Island, Ohio; see BASS ISLANDS.

North Battleford, city (1991 pop. 14,350), W Sask., Canada, at the confluence of the North Saskatchewan and Battle rivers, opposite Battleford; 52°46′N 108°17′W. It is the service and distributing center for NW Sask., which has rich farming, lumbering, and fishing.

North Bay, city (1991 pop. 55,405), SE Ont., Canada, on L. Nipissing; 46°18′N 79°27′W. It is the transportation and commercial center of lumbering and mining dists. and a popular summer resort. Mining equip. is mfg. here. It is the site of a large air base.

North Bay, village (1990 pop. 246), Racine co., SE Wis., residential suburb 3 mi/4.8 km NNE of Racine, on L. Michigan; 42°45′N 87°46′W. Urban growth area.

North Beach, summer resort town (1990 pop. 1,173), Calvert co., S Md., on Chesapeake Bay, 19 mi/31 km S of Annapolis; 38°43′N 76°32′W. Declined in popularity since opening of Bay Bridge (Atlantic beaches). Fires have destroyed a boardwalk, 2 piers and hotels; hurricanes have eroded the beaches.

North Belle Vernon, borough (1990 pop. 2,112), Westmoreland co., SW Pa., 22 mi/35 km S of Pittsburgh, and 2 mi/3.2 km SE of Monessen, near Monongahela R.; 40°07′N 79°52′W. Agr. (corn, hay; dairying). Inc. 1876.

North Bellmore, uninc. town (1990 pop. 19,707), Nassau co., SE N.Y., on L.I.; 40°41′N 73°32′W. Chiefly residential.

North Bellport, village (1990 pop. 8,182), Suffolk co., SE N.Y., just E of Patchogue; 40°45′N 72°58′W. Pop. figure includes Hagerman.

North Belmont or **Belmont Junction**, village, Gaston co., S N.C., a suburb of Charlotte, 2 mi/3.2 km N of Belmont.

North Bend 1 town (1990 pop. 1,249), Dodge co., E Nebr., 15 mi/24 km W of Fremont, and on Platte R; 41°28′N 96°46′W. Livestock, poultry; grain; mfg. (fertilizer, pallets). **2** town (1990 pop. 9,614), Coos co., SW Oregon, on inside of large curve of Coos Bay estuary, c.70 mi/113 km SW of Eugene, adjoins city of Coos Bay on S side of bay; 43°24′N 124°14′W. Wood preserving; paper mills. Fisheries. Simpson Wayside State Park in NE part of town. North Bend Municipal Airport in NW part of town. Oregon Dunes Natl. Recreation Area to N. Settled 1853, inc. 1903. **3** uninc. town (1990 pop. 800), Chapman township, Clinton co., N central Pa., 3 mi/4.8 km ENE of Renovo, on West Branch of Susquehanna R.; 41°21′N 77°42′W. Area surrounded by Sproul State Forest. Hyner Run and Hyner View state parks to E. **4** town (1990 pop. 2,578), King co., W central Wash., suburb 25 mi/40 km ESE of Seattle, and on South Fork Snoqualmie R., 2 mi/3.2 km S of junction of South, Middle and North forks to form main stream; 47°30′N 121°48′W. Farm and dairy prods.; lumber. Chester Morse L., formed by Masonry Dam, to S; Mt. Si (4,167 ft/1,270 m) to E. Olallie State Park to SE; Mt. Baker–Snoqualmie Natl. Forest to S and E; Snoqualmie Pass (3,022 ft/921 m) and Ski Area to E.

North Bend, village (1990 pop. 541), Hamilton co., extreme SW Ohio, on the Ohio, and 11 mi/18 km W of Cincinnati; 39°08′N 84°45′W. Benjamin Harrison was b. here; William Henry Harrison Memorial State Park nearby. Founded 1789.

North Bennington, village (1990 pop. 1,520), of Bennington town, Bennington co., SW Vt., 4 mi/6.4 km N of Benington; 42°55′N 73°14′W. Wood prods., paper.

North Bergen, residential suburban township (1990 pop. 48,414), Hudson co., NE N.J., NE of Jersey City; 40°47′N 74°01′W. Mfg. (ink, electrical equip., radio parts, apparel, machinery, textiles, fiber optics, metal cans, foods, paper boxes). Inc. 1861.

North Berwick, town (1990 pop. 3,793), including North Berwick village, York co., SW Maine, on Great Works R., and 12 mi/19 km S of Alfred; 43°20′N 70°46′W. Mfg. (wood and metal prods., textiles). Settled c.1630, set off from Berwick 1831.

North Bessemer, uninc. village, Allegheny co., W Pa., 12 mi/19 km ENE of downtown Pittsburgh, now part of PENN HILLS borough; 40°29′N 79°47′W.

North Bimini, Bahama Isls.: see BIMINI ISLANDS.

North Bonneville, village (1990 pop. 411), Skamania co., SW Wash., 30 mi/48 km E of Vancouver, Wash. and on Columbia R., opposite Bonneville, Oregon, no bridge connection; 45°38′N 121°58′W. Downstream (1 mi/1.6 km W) from Bonneville Dam. Beacon Rock State Park to W; Gifford Pinchot Natl. Forest to N.

North Borden Island, Canada: see BORDEN ISLANDS.

North Bosque River, Texas: see BOSQUE RIVER.

North Braddock (BRA-duhk), borough (1990 pop. 7,036), Allegheny co., W Pa., residential suburb 8 mi/12.9 km ESE of downtown Pittsburgh, near the Monongahela R.; 40°23′N 79°50′W. Andrew Carnegie's 1st steel plant was built here in 1875. The borough was the site of Gen. Edward Braddock's defeat in the last conflict of the Fr. and Indian wars and of a mass meeting of farmers instituting the Whiskey Rebellion. Inc. 1897.

North Branch, town (1990 pop. 1,867), Chisago co., E Minn., 39 mi/63 km N of St. Paul, on North Branch Sunrise R., surrounded by municipality of Branch; 45°30′N 92°58′W. Grain; cattle, poultry; dairying; mfg. (metal stampings, feed ingredients, concrete, mops, tool and die, physical training devices; grain mill).

North Branch, village (1990 pop. 1,023), Lapeer co., E Mich., 14 mi/23 km NNE of Lapeer; 43°13′N 83°11′W. In area producing livestock; grain, apples, soybeans; dairying; mfg. (screw machine prods., rolled thread and nuts).

North Branford, town (1990 pop. 12,996), New Haven co., S Conn., on the Branford R.; 41°21′N 72°46′W. A large traprock quarry is here, as is some light industry. Settled c.1680, inc. 1831.

North Brentwood, town (1990 pop. 512), Prince Georges co., central Md., just NE of Washington, D.C.; 38°57′N 76°57′W. Originally called Highlands, the name was changed after the Civil War. Inc. in 1912, it is adjacent to Brentwood. Inc. in 1924.

North Bridgton, Maine: see BRIDGTON.

North Brookfield, town (1990 pop. 2,635), including North Brookfield village, Worcester co., central Mass., 14 mi/23 km W of Worcester; 42°16′N 72°05′W. Rubber

goods, beverages, poultry feed; dairying; poultry; fruit. Settled 1664, inc. 1812.

North Brother Island, SE N.Y., in East R., off S shore of Bronx borough of N.Y. city; 40°48′N 74°00′W. Covers 13 acres/5 ha.

North Brother Mountain (4,143 ft/1,263 m), Piscataquis co., N central Maine, 25 mi/40 km NW of Millinocket, in Katahdin State Game Preserve.

North Broughton Island, Canada: see BROUGHTON ISLAND.

North Brunswick, township (1990 pop. 31,287), Middlesex co., N N.J., 3 mi/4.8 km S of New Brunswick; 40°27′N 74°28′W. Inc. 1798.

North Buena Vista, town (1990 pop. 145), Clayton co., NE Iowa, on the Mississippi, and 26 mi/42 km ESE of Elkader; 42°40′N 90°57′W. In agr. and dairying region.

North Caicos, island (□ 54.1 sq mi/140.1 sq km; 1990 pop. 1,275), Turks and Caicos Isls., crown colony of Great Britain, West Indies, NW of Middle Caicos isl.; c.12 mi/19 km long; 21°50′N 72°W. Most populous of the group, with Kew and Bottle Creek villages. Tourism, swimming, scuba diving, sport fishing. Noted for its flamingos. Formerly site of many plantations, now in ruins.

North Caldwell, residential township (1990 pop. 6,706), Essex co., NE N.J., 6 mi/9.7 km SW of Paterson; 40°51′N 74°15′W. Inc. 1898.

North Canaan, town (1990 pop. 3,284), Litchfield co., NW Conn., in Taconic Mts., on Mass. state line, and 17 mi/27 km NW of Torrington; 42°01′N 73°17′W. Magnesium mining and reduction; agr.; limestone quarrying. Includes villages of CANAAN (S) and East Canaan.

North Canadian, river, 760 mi/1,223 km long, N.Mex., Texas, Okla.; rises in NW central Union co., E of Des Moines; flows E near N boundaries of Kiowa Natl. Grasslands (N.Mex.) and Rita Blanca Natl. Grassland (Okla.), through far W part of Okla. Panhandle, drops S briefly passing through extreme N Texas, continuing E in Okla., past Guymon and Beaver, leaving Panhandle and turning SE past Woodward (roughly paralleling Canadian R., for remainder of its course), through Canton L. reservoir, past Watonga, through El Reno and Oklahoma City, past Shawnee and passing S of Henryetta, joining Canadian R. in Eufala L. reservoir, forming large N arm of lake, also receiving Deep Fork Canadian R from NW, which form its own arm. Federal dams and reservoirs on the river and its tributary, Wolf Creek, are part of the Arkansas R. basin project for flood control and other purposes.

North Canton, city (1990 pop. 14,748), Stark co., NE Ohio, a suburb of Canton; 40°52′N 81°23′W. Vacuum cleaners and industrial die castings are among the city's manufactures. Diversified light mfg. Settled c.1815, inc. as a city 1961.

North Canton (KAN-tuhn), village, Cherokee co., NW Ga., near Canton and Allatoona Reservoir; 34°14′N 84°29′W.

North, Cape, NE extremity of Cape Breton Isl., NE N.S., Canada, on Cabot Strait, 60 mi/97 km NNW of Sydney; 47°2′N 60°25′W. Elev. 984 ft/300 m. Communications linkpoint, 1st undersea telegraph cable from N.F. (Canada) 1856.

North Caribou Lake, NW Ont., Canada, in NW Patricia dist.; 22 mi/35 km long, 14 mi/23 km wide; 52°49′N 90°46′W. Elev. 1,060 ft/323 m. Drains N into Severn R.

North Carolina, state (□ 53,821 sq mi/139,397 sq km; 1995 est. pop. 7,195,138), SE U.S., one of the original 13 U.S. states; ⊙ RALEIGH; 35°28′N 79°10′W. The largest city is CHARLOTTE; other major cities include GREENSBORO, WINSTON-SALEM, DURHAM, RALEIGH, and ASHEVILLE. The state is bounded on the N by Va., on the E by the Atlantic Ocean, on the S by S.C. and Ga., and on the W by Tenn. Serving as a buffer against the Atlantic is a long chain of sand barrier isls. and peninsulas referred to as the Outer Banks, with constantly shifting sand dunes, which open and close passages, or inlets, through the banks. Prominent capes (3) — Hatteras, Lookout, and Fear — point SE from the isl. chain and lie prone to the rigors of Atlantic storms. Bet. the Banks and the mainland are large lagoons — Albemarle Sound

and Pamlico Sound being the largest — that receive the Chowan, Roanoke, Tar, and Neuse rivers, each forming estuaries which protrude inland; the Cape Fear R. in SE and its estuary open directly into the ocean. WILMINGTON, N.C.'s chief port, lies at the head of Cape Fear R. estuary. Most of N.C.'s cities lie at least 100 mi/161 km inland from the coast. Intracoastal Waterway follows Atlantic coastline through channel less than 1 mi/1.6 km inland in S, and through canals in N linking the sounds and estuaries behind the Outer Banks. The mainland bordering the sounds is low, flat tidewater country, often swampy, including the (Great) Dismal Swamp in NE (Va.-N.C.), East Dismal Swamp in E, and Green Swamp in SE. In the upper coastal plain the land rises gradually from the tidewater level, reaching 500 ft/152 m at the fall line. There begins the Piedmont region, a rolling hill country with many swift streams such as the Broad, Catawba, and Pee Dee or Great Pee Dee rivers. Power from the Piedmont fall line contributed greatly to the development of textile mill industry in both Carolinas and the relocation of the industry from New England by 1960s. The hydroelectric power these rivers generate made this an important mfg. area. The Piedmont supports most of the state's pop. and has its largest cities. At the W edge of the Piedmont, the land rises abruptly in the Blue Ridge, and in the S, dips down to several basins, and rises again in the Great Smoky Mts. Asheville is the leading urban center of this mt. region, with Mt. Mitchell (6,684 ft/2,037 m) the highest peak E of the Mississippi R. The Fr. Broad R., the Watauga, and other rivers rising W of the Blue Ridge flow into the Mississippi system, almost all via the Tennessee R. Several reservoirs, including B. Everett Jordan L. (center; on Haw and New Hope rivers), Falls L. Reservoir (center; Neuse R.), L. Norman (W center; Catawba R.), part of John H. Keen Reservoir (N state line with Va.; on Roanoke R.). N.C., in the warm temperate zone, has a mild, generally uniform climate, and the rainfall is abundant and well distributed, although summer dry spells are common. The state leads the nation in the production of tobacco and is a major producer of textiles and furniture. While it grows 40% of all U.S. tobacco, it is also the country's 2d-largest producer of poultry and hogs. The continuing trend toward diversification has moved poultry and hogs ahead of tobacco in total value. Cattle; dairying; corn, soybeans, cotton, peanuts, and eggs are also important. Plentiful forests supply the thriving paper prods. and lumber industries. N.C. has long been a major textile manufacturer, producing cotton, knit, and synthetic goods. Other leading mfg. are electrical machinery, computers, and chemicals. The state also has mineral resources: it leads the nation in the production of feldspar, mica (primary source during World War II), and lithium materials and produces substantial quantities of olivine, crushed granite, talc, clays, and phosphate rock. There are valuable coastal fisheries, with shrimp, menhaden, and crabs the principal catches. N.C.'s congenial climate, its many miles of beaches, and its beautiful mts. attract large numbers of visitors and vacationers each year. Chief among the tourist attractions are the Cape Hatteras and Cape Lookout natl. seashores in E, part of the Blue Ridge Natl. Parkway in NW, and part of the Great Smoky Mts. Natl. Park in W. Wildlife abounds in the natl. forests, Nantahala and Pisgah (W), Uwharrie (center), Croatan (E); also Blade Lakes State Forest (SE). The Appalachian Trail (or Appalachian Natl. Scenic Trail) closely follows most of Tenn.-N.C. state boundary then crosses SW end of state to Ga. Main range of Appalachians on W boundary remains a formidable barrier to W states. Places of historic interest include Fort Raleigh Natl. Historic Site, on Roanoke Isl. and the Wright Brothers Natl. Memorial, at Kitty Hawk, both in E; Carl Sandburg Home Natl. Historic Site, at Flatrock, in SW; and Guilford Courthouse (N center) and Moores Creek (SE) natl. military parks. Among the largest military reservations in the nation are Fort Bragg, near Fayetteville in SE center, and Camp Lejeune Marine base, near Jacksonville, in SE, at mouth of the New R. N.C. has one Indian reservation, the Eastern Cherokee (also called Qualla Boundary) Indian Reservation in W, bordering on Great Smoky Mts. Natl. Park. The treacherous coast was explored by Verrazano in 1524, and possibly by some Span. navigators. In the 1580s, Sir Walter Raleigh attempted unsuccessfully to establish a colony on 1 of the isls. (see ROANOKE ISLAND). The first permanent settlements were made (c.1653) around Albemarle Sound by colonials from Va. Meanwhile, Charles I of England had granted (1629) the territory S of Va. bet. the 36th and 31st parallels (named Carolina in the king's honor) to Sir Robert Heath. Heath did not exploit his grant, and it was declared void in 1663. Charles II reassigned the territory to 8 court favorites, who became the "true and absolute Lords Proprietors" of Carolina. In 1664, Sir William Berkeley, governor of Va. and one of the proprietors, appointed a governor for the prov., which after 1691 was known as N.C. By 1700 there were only some 4,000 people, predominantly of Eng. stock, along Albemarle Sound. There, with the help of indentured servants and Afr. and Native Amer. slaves, they raised tobacco, corn, and livestock, mostly on small farms. The people were semi-isolated; only vessels of light draft could negotiate the narrow and shallow passages through the isl. barriers, and communication by land was almost impossible, except with Va., and even then swamps and forests made it difficult. There was some trade (primarily with Va., New England, and Bermuda), and in 1711, N.C. was made a separate colony. The destructive war with Native Americans of the Tuscarora tribe broke out that year. The Tuscarora were defeated, and in 1714 the remnants of the tribe moved N to join the Iroquois Confederacy. A long, bitter boundary dispute with Va. was partially settled in 1728 when a joint commission ran the state line 240 mi-386 km inland. The Br. govt. made N.C. a royal colony in 1729. Thereafter the region developed more rapidly. The Native Americans were gradually pushed back over the Appalachians as the Piedmont was increasingly occupied. Germans and Scotch-Irish followed the valleys down from Pa., and Highland Scots settled along the Cape Fear R. These varied racial and natl. elements, in addition to smaller groups of Swiss, French, and Welsh who had migrated to the region earlier in the cent., gradually amalgamated. In 1768, the back-country farmers, justifiably enraged by the excessive taxes imposed by a legislature dominated by the E aristocracy, organized the Regulator Movement in an attempt to effect reforms. The insurgents were suppressed at Alamance in 1771 by the provincial militia led by Gov. William Tryon, who executed 7 of the Regulators. After the outbreak of the Amer. Revolution, royal authority collapsed. A provisional govt. was set up, the disputed Mecklenburg Declaration of Independence was allegedly promulgated (May 1775), and the provincial congress instructed (April 12, 1776) the colony's delegates to the Continental Congress to support complete independence from Britain. Most Loyalists, including Highland Scots, fled N.C. after their defeat (Feb. 27, 1776) at the battle of Moores Creek Bridge near Wilmington. The British, however, did not give up hope of Tory assistance in the state until their failure in the Carolina Campaign (1780–1781). One explanation for the designation of North Carolinians as "Tar Heels" is said to have originated during that campaign when patriotic citizens poured tar into a stream across which Cornwallis's men retreated, and the British emerged with the substance sticking to their heels. Settlements had been established beyond the mts. before the Revolution and were increased after the war. In 1784, N.C. ceded its W lands to the U.S., spurring the transmontane people to organize a new, short-lived govt. (see FRANKLIN, STATE OF). Within the year N.C. repealed the act ceding the land; however, the cession was reenacted in 1789, and that territory became (1796) the state of Tenn. N.C. opposed a strong central govt. and did not ratify the Constitution until Nov. 1789, months after the new U.S. govt. had begun to function. Little social and economic progress was made under the state's undemocratic constitution (framed in 1776), which largely served the interests of the politically dominant, tidewater planter aristocracy, and N.C. appeared to be on the verge of revolution. In 1835, however, the W part of the state, now its most populous sect., finally succeeded in enacting a constitution that abolished the property and religious qualifications for voting and holding office (except for Jews) and provided for the popular election of governors. In the same year began the final forced removal of most of the Cherokee; but to check the steady, voluntary migration of whites, internal improvements, esp. the building of RRs and plank roads, were effected. The Public School Law (1839) inaugurated free education, and other important reforms were instituted. The period of progress continued until the Civil War. Few North Carolinians held slaves, and considerable antislavery sentiment existed until the 1830s, when the organized agitation of Northern abolitionists began, provoking a defensive reaction that North Carolinians shared with most Southerners. Yet it was a native of the state, Hinton Rowan Helper, who made the most notable Southern contribution to antislavery literature. Not until President Lincoln's call for troops after the firing on Fort Sumter did the state secede and join (May 1861) the Confederacy. The coast was ideal for blockade-running, and the last important Confederate port to fall (Jan. 1865) was Wilmington (see FORT FISHER). Gov. Zebulon B. Vance zealously defended the state's rights against what he considered encroachments by the Confederate govt. Although many small engagements were fought on N.C. soil, the state was not seriously invaded until almost the end of the war when Gen. William Sherman and his huge army moved N from Ga. After engagements at Averasboro and Bentonville in March, 1865, Confederate Gen. J. E. Johnston surrendered (April 26, 1865) to Sherman near Durham; next to Lee's capitulation at Appomattox, it was the largest (and almost the last) surrender of the war. In May, 1865, President Johnson applied his plan of Reconstruction to the state. The radical Republicans in Congress, however, adopted their own scheme in 1867, and the Carolinas, organized as the 2d military dist., were again occupied by Federal troops. The Reconstruction constitution of 1868 abolished slavery, removed all religious tests for holding office, and provided for the popular election of all state and co. officials. In 1871 the legislature, with conservatives again in control, impeached and convicted Gov. William H. Holden. The often maligned period of Reconstruction actually saw the beginning of the modern state, with a tremendous rise in industry in the Piedmont. Increased use of tobacco in the Civil War stimulated the growth of tobacco mfg., 1st centered at Durham, and the introduction of the cigarette-making machine in the early 1880s was an immense boon to the industry, creating tobacco barons such as James B. Duke and R. J. Reynolds. Agr., however, was in a critical condition. The old plantation system was replaced by farm tenancy, which long remained the dominant system of holding land. Much farm property was destroyed, credit was lacking, and transportation broke down. The nation-wide agrarian revolt reached N.C. in the Granger Movement (1875), the Farmers' Alliance (1887), and the Populist Party, which united with the Republicans to carry the state elections in 1894 and 1896. However, the Fusionists were blamed for the rise of black control in many tidewater towns and cos., and in the election of 1898, when the Red Shirts, like the Ku Klux Klan of Reconstruction days, were active, the Democrats regained control. The turn of the cent. marked the beginning of a new progressive era, typified by the successful airplane experiments of the Wright Brothers near Kitty Hawk. The crusade for public education for both races led by Gov. Charles B. Aycock, elected in 1900, achieved wide results, and new interest was created in developing the state's agr. and industrial resources. But one old pattern was strengthened when a suffrage amendment, the "grandfather clause" assuring white supremacy, was added (1900) to the state constitution. Since World War I the state govt. has increasingly followed a policy of consolidation and centralization, taking over the public school system and the supervision of co. finance and roads. A huge highway development program, begun by the cos. in 1921, was assumed by the state (1931) when the cos. could no longer meet the costs. Expenditures for higher education were greatly increased, and the 3 major state educational institutions were merged into a greater Univ. of N.C. N.C., more than many other Southern states, was able to make a peaceful adjustment to integration in the public schools following the Supreme Court's desegregation ruling in 1954. Industrialization burgeoned after World War II, and in the 1950s the value of manufactured goods surpassed that of agr. for the first time. In that period, and esp. in the administration of Gov. Luther H. Hodges, over $1 billion in new industry was established, making N.C. the leading industrial state of the South. This industrialization continued during the 1960s and early 1970s, increasing at a rate unmatched by any other Southern state. The Charlotte-Douglas and Raleigh-Durham airports were both transformed into major air traffic hubs during the 1980s, reflecting the tremendous growth (most of it suburban) in those metropolitan areas. Interstate Highway system criss-crosses state. In addition, N.C. has been able recently to shift from its traditional, low-skill industries to high-technology industries. With cooperation of Duke Univ., Univ. of N.C., and N.C. State Univ., Gov. Hodges was instrumental in establishing the Research Triangle Park, bet. Raleigh and Durham in late 1950s, which helped boost N.C.'s standing in technological research and development. N.C. experienced substantial pop. growth in the 1980s, becoming the 10th-largest state in the nation after the 1990 census. N.C.'s 1st constitution was adopted in 1776. Its present constitution dates from 1868 but was thoroughly revised in 1875–1876 as a result of Reconstruction experiences; it has been amended many times since. The state's executive branch is headed by a governor elected for a 4-year term. N.C.'s bicameral general assembly has a senate with 50 members and a house with 120 members, all elected for 2-year terms. The state elects 2 Senators and 12 Representatives to the U.S. Congress and has 14 electoral votes. James Martin, a Republican, was elected governor in 1984 and reelected in 1988. In 1992, Democrat James B. Hunt Jr. was elected governor. The state's other notable institutions of higher learning include E Carolina Univ., at Greenville; Appalachian State Univ., at Boone; and Wake Forest Univ., at Winston-Salem. N.C. has 100 cos.: ALAMANCE, ALEXANDER, ALLEGHANY, ANSON, ASHE, AVERY, BEAUFORT, BERTIE, BLADEN, BRUNSWICK, BUNCOMBE, BURKE, CABARRUS, CALDWELL, CAMDEN, CARTERET, CASWELL, CATAWBA, CHATHAM, CHEROKEE, CHOWAN, CLAY, CLEVELAND, COLUMBUS, CRAVEN, CUMBERLAND, CURRITUCK, DARE, DAVIDSON, DAVIE, DUPLIN, DURHAM, EDGECOMBE, FORSYTH, FRANKLIN, GASTON, GATES, GRAHAM, GRANVILLE, GREENE, GUILFORD, HALIFAX, HARNETT, HAYWOOD, HENDERSON, HERTFORD, HOKE, HYDE, IREDELL, JACKSON, JOHNSTON, JONES, LEE, LENOIR, LINCOLN, MCDOWELL, MACON, MADISON, MARTIN, MECKLENBURG, MITCHELL, MONTGOMERY, MOORE, NASH, NEW HANOVER, NORTHAMPTON, ONSLOW, ORANGE, PAMLICO, PASQUOTANK, PENDER, PERQUIMANS, PERSON, PITT, POLK, RANDOLPH, RICHMOND, ROBESON, ROCKINGHAM, ROWAN, RUTHERFORD, SAMPSON, SCOTLAND, STANLY, STOKES, SURRY, SWAIN, TRANSYLVANIA, TYRRELL, UNION, VANCE, WAKE, WARREN, WASHINGTON, WATAUGA, WAYNE, WILKES, WILSON, YADKIN, YANCEY.

North Carrollton, village (1990 pop. 578), Carroll co., central Miss., 15 mi/24 km E of Greenwood, and 1 mi/1.6 km N of Carrollton; 33°31'N 89°55'W. Agr. (cotton, corn; cattle); mfg. (furniture).

North Carver, Mass.: see CARVER.

North Cascades National Park, Skagit and Chelan cos., N Wash. Bounded by Mt. Baker–Snoqualmie Natl. Forest, E, W, and SW; by Wenatchee Natl. Forest, S; by Chelan Natl. Recreation Area in SE; N unit bounded by Canada (B.C.) to N. Covers 504,781 acres/204,285 ha. Area of great alpine scenery in the Cascade Range;

North and South units separated by Ross L. Natl. Recreation Area. Authorized 1968.

North Castle, township (1990 pop. 10,061), Westchester co., SE N.Y., abutting NW ½ of N.Y. state border with SW Conn, c.35 mi/56 km of N.Y. city; 41°10′N 73°43′W. Exclusive, suburban residential area (including the hamlets of Armonk, Banksville, East Patent, Middle Patent, North White Plains, Payne's Corners, and West Patent); site of IBM's internatl. hq. The hq. bldg. was designed in 1963 by the renowned architects Skidmore, Owings, and Merrill and features a glass atrium created by I. M. Pei. However, IBM plans to tear down this structure and replace it with several smaller ones that are more accommodating to high-tech needs. Westchester co. is planning to build a public golf course (194 acres/79 ha) in the adjacent township of New Castle; other future plans may include the construction of a huge golf-tennis-residential complex near Byram L. Reservoir. Town got its name from a barrier built by the Mohicans to protect themselves from attack.

North Catasauqua (KA-tah-SAW-kwah), borough (1990 pop. 2,867), Northampton and Lehigh cos., E Pa., residential suburb 4 mi/6.4 km N of downtown Allentown, on Lehigh R.; 40°39′N 75°28′W. Lehigh Valley Internatl. Airport to E. Inc. 1908.

North Channel, central Ont., Canada, N arm (120 mi/193 km long, 1 mi/2 km–20 mi/32 km wide) of L. Huron, bet. N shore of lake and Manitoulin Isls.; connects St. Marys R. (W) and Georgian Bay (E). Crossed by road and RR bridge to Manitoulin Isl. at Little Current.

North Charleroi (SHAHR-luh-roi), borough (1990 pop. 1,562), Washington co., SW Pa., suburb 1 mi/1.6 km NW of Charleroi, on Monongahela R. (bridged; Lock No. 4 to SE); 40°08′N 79°54′W. Agr. (grain; livestock; dairying). Inc. 1894.

North Charleston, city (1990 pop. 70,218), Charleston co., SE S.C., suburb 5 mi/8 km NNW of downtown Charleston, bet. Cooper and Ashley rivers; 32°54′N 80°02′W. RR junction. Mfg. includes military avionics, construction materials, consumer goods, fooda nd beverage processing, paper bags, ship conversion and repair, textiles, fabricated metal prods., machinery, steel drums, plastic prods., ferrochrome alloys, therapy units, electronics. Charleston Naval Base and U.S. Army Depot to SE, Charleston A.F.B. to NW; Charleston Internatl. Airport to W.

North Chatham, Mass.: see CHATHAM.

North Chelmsford, Mass.: see CHELMSFORD.

North Chicago, industrial city (1990 pop. 34,978), Lake co., NE Ill.; 42°19′N 87°51′W. Its economy is closely intertwined with the neighboring city of Waukegan, which has a harbor on L. Michigan. Pharmaceuticals, medical diagnostic testing equip., chemicals, steel, and automobile parts are among the many manufactures. A sit-down strike at a steel plant here in 1937 led to a U.S. Supreme Court decision (1939) ruling sit-down strikes illegal. Adjacent to the city is the Great Lakes Naval Training Center. Inc. 1895.

North Chili (CHEI-LEI), village (1990 pop. 2,300), Monroe co., W N.Y., 10 mi/16 km WSW of Rochester; 43°07′N 77°48′W. Seat of Roberts Wesleyan Col.

North City, village (1990 pop. 538), Franklin co., S Ill., 8 mi/12.9 km W of Benton; 37°59′N 89°03′W. In bituminous-coal and agr. area.

North Cohasset, Mass.: see COHASSET.

North College Hill, city (1990 pop. 11,002), Hamilton co., SW Ohio, a N suburb of Cincinnati; 39°13′N 84°33′W. Mostly residential. Clovernook Home for the Blind has a braille printing shop. Revolutionary War cemetery is in the city. Inc. as a city 1940.

North Collins, village (1990 pop. 1,335), Erie co., W N.Y., 22 mi/35 km S of Buffalo; 42°35′N 78°56′W. In fruit-growing region; mfg. (farm machinery, wire); natural-gas wells. Settled c.1810, inc. 1911.

North Conway, village (1990 pop. 2,032), Carroll co., E N.H., 28 mi/45 km S of Berlin, and 5 mi/8 km N of Conway village, in town of Conway, on Saco R.; 44°02′N 71°07′W. Year-round resort area; agr. (livestock; dairying; timber); mfg. (furniture, diversified light mfg.). White Mt. Natl. Forest to W and N; Mt. Cranmore Ski Area to NE; Echo L. State Park to W.

North Corbin, uninc. town (1990 pop. 1,601), Laurel co., SE Ky., in Cumberland foothills on Laurel R., 1 mi/1.6 km N of Corbin; 36°58′N 84°05′W. Laurel River L. reservoir to W.

North Country, region of N.Y. state that includes the Adirondacks, L. Champlain lowlands, and St. Lawrence. Key summer and winter tourist area; some farming in lowlands; also lumbering. Hydroelectric production. Plattsburgh, Massena, Ogdensburg, Lake Placid, and Watertown are main centers.

North Creek, resort village (1990 pop. 700), Warren co., E N.Y., in the High Peaks sect. of the Adirondacks, on the Hudson, and 32 mi/51 km NNW of Glens Falls; 43°42′N 74°00′W. Wood prods.; garnet mining. Just SW is Gore Mt. (elev. 3,595 ft/1,096 m), skiing center.

North Crows Nest, town (1990 pop. 57), Marion co., central Ind., on the White R., and 7 mi/11.3 km N of downtown Indianapolis. A suburb of and part of the city of Indianapolis.

North Dakota, state (□ 70,665 sq mi/183,022 sq km; 1995 est. pop. 641,367) N central U.S., admitted to the Union in 1889 simultaneously with S.Dak. (they are the 39th and 40th states). BISMARCK, on the E bank of the Missouri R., is the capital and FARGO is the largest city. N.Dak. is bounded on the N by the Can. provs. of Sask. and Man., on the E by the Red R. of the N and Bois des Sioux R. which separates it from Minn., on the S by S.Dak., and on the W by Mont. N.Dak. is drained by the Missouri, James, Sheyenne and Souris (also called Mouse) rivers. Situated in the geographical center of N. Amer., N.Dak. is subject to the extremes of a continental climate. Semiarid conditions prevail in the W ½ of the state, but in the E an average annual rainfall of 22 in/56 cm, much of it falling in the crop-growing months of spring and summer, enables the rich soil to yield abundantly. N.Dak. is one of the most rural states in the nation; the cities and towns supply the needs of neighboring farms, and industry is largely devoted to the processing of agr. prods. and agr. machinery. The E ½ of the state is in the central lowlands; agr. (flax, grain, sunflowers). E of the Man. Escarpment there is a wedge of land, c.40 mi/64 km wide at the Can. border and tapering to 10 mi/16 km in the S, that is the floor of the former glacial L. Agassiz. Treeless, except along the riversides, and relatively void of rocks, this flat land was transformed into the bonanza wheat fields of the 1870s and 1880s, with farms ranging in size from 3,000 acres/1,214 ha to 65,000 acres/26,306 ha. Today the average farm in the Red R. valley is about 1,009 acres/408 ha; (the state average is about 1,267 acres/513 ha), and its major crop, wheat, is varied with such crops as sugar beets, soybeans, pinto beans, canola, flax and seed potatoes. To the W of the valley a series of escarpments rises some 300 ft/91 m to meet the drift prairies, where rolling hills, scattered lakes, and occasional moraines form a pleasant and fertile countryside. The productivity of the soil makes N.Dak. a leader in spring wheat and durum wheat (ranking 2d in the nation), hay, barley, sugarbeets, oats, soybeans, and sunflowers. However, cattle and cattle prods. exceed all the crops except wheat in income earned. In the W part of the state a combination of unfavorable topography and scant rainfall precludes intensive cultivation except in the river valleys. An area some 50 mi/80 km E of the Missouri R. is a farm and grazing belt, divided from the drift prairies by the Missouri escarpment. W from the Missouri rolls an irregular plateau, covered with short prairie grasses and cut by deep coulees. Where wind and rain have eroded the hillsides there are unusual formations of sand and clay, glowing in yellows, reds, browns, and grays. Along the Little Missouri this sect. is called the Badlands, so named because the region (once described as "hell with the fires out") was difficult to traverse in early days. Here are the 3 units of the Theodore Roosevelt Natl. Park where from 1883 to 1886 the young Theodore Roosevelt spent part of each year ranching. Also in this area is the Little Missouri Natl. Grassland. On the plateau cattle graze, finding shelter in the many ravines, and large ranges are an economic necessity. In the NW area of the state oil was discovered in 1951, and petroleum is now the state's leading mineral prod., ahead of sand and gravel, lime, and salt. There are also natural gas fields. Underlying the W cos. are lignite coal reserves est. at 350 billion tons/386 billion metric tons, which are mixed in several areas. In close proximity to the lignite beds are fine deposits of clay of such varied types that they serve as both construction and pottery materials. Despite mineral production and some mfg., however, agr. continues to be the state's principal pursuit, and the processing of grain, meat, and dairy prods. is vital to such cities as Fargo, Grand Forks, Minot, and Bismarck. The Missouri and the Red R., once the major transportation routes, are more important now for their irrigation potential. Several dams have been built, notably Garrison Dam, and a number of Federal reclamation projects have been completed as part of the Missouri R. basin project. There has also been reforestation. With such attractions as the Badlands, the Internatl. Peace Garden on the Can. border, and recreational facilities provided by reservoirs (resulting from dam building in the 1950s), tourism has become N.Dak.'s 5th-ranking source of income, behind agr., Federal activities (2d), mineral production (3d), mfg. (4th). The first farmers in the region of whom there is definite knowledge were Native Americans of the Mandan tribe. Other agr. tribes were the Arikara and the Hidatsa. Seminomadic and nomadic tribes were the Cheyenne, Cree, Sioux, Assiniboine, Crow, and Ojibwa (Chippewa). With the Louisiana Purchase of 1803 the W ⅔ of N.Dak. became part of the U.S. The E ⅓ was acquired from Great Britain in 1818 when the internatl. line with Canada was fixed at the 49th parallel. Earlier the Lewis and Clark expedition had wintered (1804–1805) with the Mandan along the Missouri R. and the North West Company and the Hudson's Bay Company had established trading posts in the Red R. valley. These ventures introduced an industry that dominated the region for more than ½ a cent. Within that era the buffalo vanished from the plains and the beaver from the rivers. From its post at Fort Union (est. 1828), John Jacob Astor's Amer. Fur Company gradually gained monopolistic control for a time over the trade of the region. Supply and transport were greatly facilitated when a paddlewheel steamer, the *Yellowstone*, inaugurated steamboat travel on the turbulent upper Missouri in 1832. Additional transportation was provided by the supply caravans of Red R. carts, which went W across the Minn. prairies and returned to the Mississippi loaded with valuable pelts. In 1837, the introduction of smallpox by settlers decimated the Mandan and Hidatsa tribes. The first attempt at agr. colonization was made at Pembina in 1812, but the first permanent farming community was not established until 1851 when another group settled at Pembina. This was still the only farm settlement in the future state when Dakota Territory was organized in 1861 to include what eventually became present-day N.Dak., S.Dak., Mont., and Wyo. Several military posts had been established starting in 1857 to protect travelers and RR workers. Even when free land was opened in 1863 and the Northern Pacific RR was chartered in 1864 a preoccupation with the Civil War and the eruption of open warfare with the Native Americans prevented any appreciable settlement. Gen. Alfred H. Sully joined Gen. Henry H. Sibley of Minn. in campaigns against the Sioux in 1863–1866. A treaty was signed in 1868. In 1876, after gold was discovered on Native Amer. land in the Black Hills, the unwillingness of the whites to respect treaty agreements led to further war, and the force of George A. Custer was annihilated at the battle of the Little Bighorn in present-day Mont. Ultimately, however, the Sioux under Chief Sitting Bull fled to Canada, where they surrendered voluntarily; they were returned to reservations in the U.S. The first cattle ranch in N.Dak. was est. 1878. With the construction of RRs in the 1870s and

1880s, thousands of Eur. immigrants, principally Scandinavians and Germans (notably Germans from Russia) arrived. They worked the land on their own homesteads or on the large Eastern-financed bonanza wheat fields of the low central prairies. Borrowing the idea from Europe, they founded agr. cooperatives. Local politics was rapidly reduced to a struggle bet. the agrarian groups and the corporate interests. Alexander McKenzie of the Northern Pacific was for many years the most important figure in the state. Republicans held the elective offices. Agrarian groups formed the Farmers' Alliance and in 1892, 3 years after N.Dak. had achieved statehood, the Farmers' Alliance combined with the Democrats and Populists to elect Eli Shortridge, a Populist, as governor. Later, when the success of the La Follette Progressives in Wis. encouraged the growth of the Republican Progressive movement in N.Dak., a fusion with the Democrats elected "Honest John" Burke as governor for 3 terms (1906–1912). Much of the agrarian discontent was focused on marketing practices of the large grain interests. Although many small cooperative grain elevators were established, they did not prove effective, and the farmers pressed for state-owned grain elevators. When this movement failed in the legislature of 1915, the Nonpartisan League, directed in N.Dak. by Arthur C. Townley, was organized on a platform that included state ownership of terminal elevators and flour mills, state inspection of grain and grain dockage, relief of farm improvements from taxation, and rural credit banks operated at cost. Working primarily with the Republican Party because it was the majority party in N.Dak., the league captured the state legislature in 1919 and proceeded to enact virtually its entire platform. This included the establishment of an industrial commission to manage state-owned enterprises and the creation of the Bank of N.Dak. to handle public funds and provide low-cost rural credit. The right of recall was also enacted, by which voters could remove an elected official. The reforms were disappointing in operation. Dissension arose within the league, and the Independent Voters Assn. was organized to represent the conservative Republican position. The industrial commission was accused of maladministration, and the provision of recall was exercised 3 times, the 1st against Gov. L. J. Frazier in 1921. William Langer, who had been active with both the Nonpartisan League and the Independent Voters Assn., was elected governor in 1932 running as a Nonpartisan. Langer was convicted on a Federal charge of misconduct in office in 1934, although the conviction was later reversed. Langer again became governor in 1936, running as an individual candidate and not on the ticket of either party; subsequently he was elected to the U.S. Senate 4 times. In the 1950s and 1960s, a large number of military installations were built in N.Dak. The state's heavy dependence on wheat and petroleum has made it extremely vulnerable to the fluctuations of those markets. In 1991, N.Dak. sought alternative sources of revenue through the legalization of some Indian tribal casino gambling. In recent years N.Dak. has become more urbanized, but its overall pop. declined 2.1% in the 1980s. The state is governed under the 1889 constitution. The legislature consists of 53 senators elected to 4-year terms and 106 representatives elected to 2-year terms. The governor is elected for a 4-year term. N.Dak. elects 2 U.S. senators and 1 representative; it has 3 electoral votes. The state's institutions of higher education include the Univ. of N.Dak., at Grand Forks; N.Dak. State Univ., at Fargo; Jamestown Col., at Jamestown; and several other cols. N.Dak. has 53 cos.: ADAMS, BARNES, BENSON, BILLINGS, BOTTINEAU, BOWMAN, BURKE, BURLEIGH, CASS, CAVALIER, DICKEY, DIVIDE, DUNN, EDDY, EMMONS, FOSTER, GOLDEN VALLEY, GRAND FORKS, GRANT, GRIGGS, HETTINGER, KIDDER, LA MOURE, LOGAN, MCHENRY, MCINTOSH, MCKENZIE, MCLEAN, MERCER, MORTON, MOUNTRAIL, NELSON, OLIVER, PEMBINA, PIERCE, RAMSEY, RANSOM, RENVILLE, RICHLAND, ROLETTE, SARGENT, SHERIDAN, SIOUX, SLOPE, STARK, STEELE, STUTSMAN, TOWNER, TRAILL, WALSH, WARD, WELLS, WILLIAMS.,

North Dartmouth, Mass.: see DARTMOUTH.

North Dighton, Mass.: see DIGHTON.

North Dome, peak (elev. 3,593 ft/1,095 m) in Greene co., SE N.Y., in the Catskills, 20 mi/32 km WNW of Saugerties; 42°10′N 74°21′W.

North East, town (1990 pop. 1,913), Cecil co., NE Md., at head of navigation on Northeast R. (c.6 mi/9.7 km long), and 24 mi/39 km WSW of Wilmington, Del.; 39°36′N 75°56′W. Trade center for hay and grain area; sand, gravel pits; mfg. (fireworks, firebrick). Once nicknamed Herringtown because of the importance of commercial fishing. The Georgian bell tower of St. Anne's Protestant Episcopal Church (c.1742) was added in 1904 by Robert Brookings, founder of the Brookings Inst. in memory of his parents. The churchyard is older than the church and contains several Indian graves as well as those of colonists dating from the 1600s. Sandy Cove (summer resort) and Elk Neck (site of state forest, state park) are nearby.

North East, borough (1990 pop. 4,617), Erie co., NW Pa., 13 mi/21 km NE of Erie, on Sixteenmile Creek; L. Erie 1 mi/1.6 km to NW; 42°12′N 79°49′W. N.Y. state line 3 mi/4.8 km to E. Mfg. (frozen foods, powder coating, metal castings, electrical parts, wineries, juices and jams); agr. (cherries, tomatoes, apples, grapes, grain; livestock; dairying). Lake Shore RR Mus. here. Settled c.1800, inc. 1834.

North East Carry, resort village, Piscataquis co., W central Maine, on Moosehead L., and 28 mi/45 km N of Greenville. Hunting, fishing.

North East Point, St. Thomas parish, cape at NE extremity of Jamaica, on Jamaica Channel, 33 mi/53 km ENE of Kingston; 18°09′N 76°20′W.

North Eastham, Mass.: see EASTHAM.

North Easton, Mass.: see EASTON.

North Edwards, uninc. town (1990 pop. 1,259), Kern co., S central Calif., 44 mi/71 km W of Barstow, in Mojave Desert; 35°01′N 117°50′W. Edwards Air Force Base and Rogue L. (dry) to S. Service center for air base. Cattle; grain.

North Egremont, Mass.: see EGREMONT.

North El Monte, uninc. town (1990 pop. 3,387), Los Angeles co., S Calif., residential suburb 13 mi/21 km ENE of downtown Los Angeles, and 2 mi/3.2 km NE of El Monte; drained by San Gabriel R.; 34°06′N 118°01′W.

North Elba, township (□ 156 sq mi/404 sq km; 1990 pop. 7,870), Essex co., NE N.Y., in the Adirondacks, just SE of Lake Placid village; 44°15′N 74°00′W. Here are the farm, home (now a mus.), and grave of John Brown.

North English, town (1990 pop. 944), Iowa co., E central Iowa, 19 mi/31 km S of Marengo; 41°31′N 92°04′W.

North Enid (EEN-id), town (1990 pop. 874), Garfield co., N Okla., residential suburb 2 mi/3.2 km NNE of Enid; 36°27′N 97°51′W.

North Fabius River, Mo. and Iowa: see FABIUS RIVER.

North Fair Oaks, uninc. city (1990 pop. 13,912), San Mateo co., W Calif., residential suburb 24 mi/39 km SSE of downtown San Francisco, and 3 mi/4.8 km SW of San Francisco Bay; 37°28′N 122°12′W. Hetch Hetchy Aquaduct passes to NW.

North Fairfield, village (1990 pop. 504), Huron co., N Ohio, 10 mi/16 km S of Norwalk, and on East Branch of Huron R.; 41°06′N 82°37′W.

North Falmouth, Mass.: see FALMOUTH.

North Fond du Lac (fawn doo LAK), town (1990 pop. 4,292), Fond du Lac co., E Wis., on L. Winnebago, suburb 2 mi/3.2 km NW of Fond du Lac; 43°48′N 88°28′W. RR junction. In farm area. Light mfg.; RR shops. Inc. 1903.

North Fork or **North Fork Malheur River**, 55 mi/89 km long, E Oregon; rises in SW corner of Baker co.; flows S through Beulah Reservoir to Malheur R. at Juntura. Agency Valley Dam (55 mi/89 km high, 1,850 ft/564 m long; completed 1935),12 mi/19 km NNW of Juntura, forms Beulah Reservoir (2.5 mi/4 km long, 1.5 mi/2.4 km wide; capacity 59,900 acre-ft.). Unit in Vale Irrigation Project.

North Fork Blackfoot River, c.40 mi/64 km long, W Mont.; rises in NW Lewis and Clark co. at Continental

Divide; flows SSW to join Blackfoot R. 2 mi/3.2 km S of Ovando.

North Fork Musselshell River (MUH-suhl-SHEL), c.35 mi/56 km long, central Mont.; rises in Little Belt Mts., NE Meagher co.; flows S through Bair Reservoir, then SE, joins main Musselshell R. just W of Wheatland co. line.

North Fork of Red River, c.195 mi/314 km long, N Texas and SW Okla.; rises in the Llano Estacado W of Lefors, Gray co., N Texas; flows generally E to Sayre, Okla., then SSE through Altus L. reservoir and S to Red R. 10 mi/16 km WSW of Frederick, Okla. Elm Fork (c.90 mi/145 km long) rises in SW Wheeler co., Texas as an intermittent stream; flows ESE; enters from W, c.10 mi/16 km E of Mangum, Okla.

North Fork of Wichita River, Texas: see WICHITA RIVER.

North Fork Republican River, c.30 mi/48 km long, in Colo. and Nebr.; rises W of Wray, in Yuma co., NE Colo.; flows E, past Wray, Colo., into Dundy co., SW Nebr., receiving Arikaree R. from SW at Haigler, then joining South Fork Republican R. at Benkelman, forming Republican R.

North Fork River, c.100 mi/161 km long; rises in Douglas Co. in the Ozarks, S Mo.; flows S, into N Ark., to the White R. Near its mouth is Norfork Dam (completed 1944), which impounds Norfork L. and has a power plant. Popular canoeing, floating, and fishing stream above lake. Many springs feed it. Commonly called Norfork R. North Fork of the White R.

North Fork Virgin River, 40 mi/64 km long, SW Utah; rises in SE Iron co.; flows through Zion Canyon, the main focal point of Zion Natl. Park, joining East Fork Virgin R. at Springdale, just S of park, to form Virgin R.

North Fort Myers, city (□ 23 sq mi/60 sq km; 1990 pop. 30,027), Lee co., SW Fla., 3 mi/4.8 km NNW of Fort Myers; 26°42′N 81°53′W. Mfg. includes signs, concrete prods., shell prods., coil winding.

North Fox Island, Mich.: see FOX ISLANDS.

North Freedom, village (1990 pop. 591), Sauk co., S central Wis., on Baraboo R., and 6 mi/9.7 km W of Baraboo; 43°27′N 89°51′W. In dairy and livestock area. RR mus. Natural Bridge State Park to SW.

North Garden, uninc. village, Albermarle co., N central Va., 10 mi/16 km SW of Charlottesville; 37°56′N 78°38′W. Mfg. (lumber, concrete, apple brandy); agr. (dairying, livestock; grain, apples).

North Girard, Pa.: see LAKE CITY.

North Gower (gor), village, SE Ont., Canada, 18 mi/29 km S of Ottawa. Dairying, mixed farming.

North Grafton, Mass.: see GRAFTON.

North Grosvenor Dale, Conn.: see THOMPSON.

North Grove, village, Miami co., N central Ind., 12 mi/19 km SSE of Peru. In agr. area.

North Guilford, town, New Haven co., S Conn., 12 mi/19 km NE of New Haven, on Coginchaug R.

North Gulfport, uninc. town (1990 pop. 4,966), Harrison co., SE Miss., residential suburb 4 mi/6.4 km N of downtown Gulfport, on Bernard Bayou; 30°24′N 89°05′W.

North Haledon (HAIL-duhn), borough (1990 pop. 7,987), Passaic co., NE N.J., 3 mi/4.8 km N of Paterson; 40°57′N 74°11′W. Inc. 1901. Largely residential.

North Hampton, town (1990 pop. 3,637), Rockingham co., SE N.H., 7 mi/11.3 km SSW of Portsmouth, and 2 mi/3.2 km N of Hampton; 42°58′N 70°49′W. Bounded E by Atlantic Ocean. Agr. (poultry; dairying; nursery crops); mfg. (freight elevators, software, light mfg.). Fuller Gardens and Hampton Beach Casino in E. Set off from Hampton 1742.

North Hampton, village (1990 pop. 417), Clark co., W central Ohio, 8 mi/13 km NW of Springfield; 39°59′N 83°57′W.

North Hampton, uninc. suburb of Hampton, SE Va.

North Hanover, township (1990 pop. 9.994), Burlington co., S N.J., 8 mi/12.9 km N of Fort Dix; 40°04′N 74°35′W. Mfg. (transmitters, automotive parts, switches, wire, adhesive tape; printing). Inc. 1905.

North Hartsville, uninc. town (1990 pop. 2,906), Darlington co., NE S.C., 1 mi/1.6 km N of Hartsville; 34°23′N 80°04′W.

North Harwich, Mass.: see HARWICH.

North Hatley, village (1991 pop. 704), S Que., Canada, on L. Massawippi, 9 mi/14 km SSW of Sherbrooke; 45°25′N 71°54′W. Dairying; mixed farming. Resort.

North Haven 1 town (1990 pop. 22,249), New Haven co., S Conn., on the Quinnipiac R.; settled c.1650, set off from New Haven 1786; 41°22′N 72°51′W. Chiefly residential, it has some manufactures, such as aircraft parts, tools, chemicals, and machinery. Several 18th-cent. houses still stand in the town. **2** resort town (1990 pop. 332), Knox co., S Maine, on North Haven Isl. (8 mi/12.9 km long, ½ mi/⅘km–2 mi/3.2 km wide), in Penobscot Bay, and 12 mi/19 km ENE of Rockland; 44°09′N 68°53′W. Includes Pulpit Harbor village.

North Haven, resort village (□ 2 sq mi/5.2 sq km; 1990 pop. 713), Suffolk co., SE N.Y., on E L.I., just N of Sag Harbor, on peninsula just E of Noyack Bay; 41°01′N 72°19′W.

North Henderson, uninc. village, Vance co., N N.C., a suburb 1 mi/1.6 km N of Henderson.

North Hero, island and town (1990 pop. 502), ⊙ Grand Isle co., NW Vt., in L. Champlain, 10 mi/16 km W of St. Albans. Isl. (c.12 mi/19 km long) is bridged to Grand Isle (S) and Alburg (N); 44°50′N 73°16′W. Resorts; dairy farms. North Hero and Knight Point state parks are here.

North Hickory, uninc. town (1990 pop. 4,299), Catawaba co., W central N.C., residential suburb 3 mi/4.8 km NNE of Hickory L.; 35°46′N 81°19′W. Hickory reservoir (Catawba R.) to N and NW.

North High Shoals, town (1990 pop. 268), Oconee co., N central Ga.; 33°50′N 83°30′W.

North Highlands, uninc. city (1990 pop. 42,105), Sacramento co., N central Calif., a residential suburb 9 mi/14.5 km NE of downtown Sacramento, in the Sacramento valley; 38°40′N 121°23′W. Grew dramatically 1970s–1990s. Agr. (citrus, tomatoes, grain; nursery prods.; dairying; poultry); mfg. (draperies, concrete prods., lumber; printing and publishing). McClellan Air Force Base to SW.

North Hills, town (1990 pop. 849), Wood co., NW W.Va., residential suburb 4 mi/6.4 km NE of Parkersburg; 39°18′N 81°30′W.

North Hills, residential village (□ 2 sq mi/5.2 sq km; 1990 pop. 3,453), Nassau co., SE N.Y., on W L.I., c.2 mi/3.2 km N of Mineola; 40°46′N 40°73′W.

North Hollywood, suburban section, LOS ANGELES, Los Angeles co., S Calif., in San Fernando Valley, 12 mi/19 km W of downtown Los Angeles, just W of Burbank. Mfg. (wood containers, stationery, electronic capacitors, baked goods, musical instruments, metal prods.). Hollywood Burbank Airport to N; Universal Studios to S. Formerly called Lankershim.

North Hornell, village (1990 pop. 822), Steuben co., S N.Y., on Canisteo R., opposite Hornell; 42°21′N 77°39′W.

North Hudson, town (1990 pop. 3,101), St. Croix co., W Wis., on St. Croix R. (lower St Croix Natl. Scenic Riverway), 1 mi/1.6 km N of Hudson; 45°00′N 92°45′W. Dairying. Willow R. State Park to NE.

North Huntingdon, township (1990 pop. 28,158), Westmoreland co., SW Pa., suburb 14 mi/23 km SE of Pittsburgh; 40°23′N 79°44′W. Mfg. (machinery, tools, temperature controls); agr. (dairying; livestock; corn); however, agr. is losing ground to urban growth. Pop. centered in NW in Circleville, Sunset Valley; and NE in Westmoreland City. Shuster Cellars Winery to S.

North Hyde Park, Vt.: see HYDE PARK.

North Irwin (UHR-win), borough (1990 pop. 956), Westmoreland co., SW Pa., residential suburb 16 mi/26 km SE of Pittsburgh, and 1 mi/1.6 km NW of Irwin, on Brush Creek; 40°20′N 79°42′W. Inc. 1894.

North Island, S.C.: see WINYAH BAY.

North Island Naval Air Station, Calif.: see SAN DIEGO.

North Jay, Maine: see JAY.

North Johns or **Johns**, town (1990 pop. 177), Jefferson co., N central Ala., 20 mi/32 km SW of Birmingham.

North Judson, town (1990 pop. 1,582), Starke co., NW Ind., 10 mi/16 km SW of Knox; 41°13′N 86°47′W. Agr.

(grain; livestock); mfg. (dried foliage, meatpacking, furnaces and air conditioners). Laid out 1861.

North Kansas City, city (1990 pop. 4,130), Clay co., W Mo., on N bank of Missouri R., industrial suburb 3 mi/4.8 km N of downtown Kansas City; 39°08′N 94°33′W. Mfg. (foods, chemicals, metal prods., food processing, metal containers, fabricated structured steel, machinery, lighting fixtures, auto batteries, lamp bases, gypsum board; printing); Kansas City Downtown Airport on W side. Founded 1912.

North Kingstown, town (1990 pop. 23,801), Washington co., S central R.I., on Narragansett Bay; 41°34′N 71°27′W. Includes Quonset Point (former naval air station, now a state airport and industrial park) and the villages of Allentown, Davisville, Hamilton, Lafayette, Saunderstown, and Wickford. Mfg. (machine tools, primary metals, printing, chemicals, plastics, and textiles).The site of North Kingstown was settled in 1641 by Roger Williams, founder of Providence, R.I. It is a regional trade center and minor fishing port and attracts many tourists. Of interest are Smith's Castle (1678); Casey House (1725), which retains bullet holes made during skirmishes in the Revolutionary War; the birthplace (now a mus.) of Gilbert Stuart (1755–1828), the portrait painter. Narragansett Bay is used for recreational boating and fishing. Inc. 1674 as Kings Towne, divided into North Kingstown and South Kingstown 1723.

North Kingsville, village (1990 pop. 2,672), Ashtabula co., extreme NE Ohio, on L. Erie, 6 mi/10 km ENE of Ashtabula; 41°55′N 80°40′W. Wood prods.

North La Junta, uninc. village, Otero co., SE Colo., suburb just N of La Junta, bet. city and RR yards, on Arkansas R. Home of the Koshare Indian Dancers.

North Lake, town, Waukesha co., SE Wis., on small North L., 12 mi/19 km NW of Milwaukee. In farm and lake-resort region. Mfg. (lubricants).

North Lake, village, Marquette co., NW Upper Peninsula, Mich., 2 mi/3.2 km NW of Ishpeming; 46°29′N 87°43′W.

North Lake, Greene co., SE N.Y., in the Catskills, 2 mi/3.2 km E of Haines Falls; c.½ mi/⅘ km long; 42°12′N 74°02′W. State campsite.

North Laramie River (LAR-uh-mee), 69 mi/111 km, SE Wyo.; rises in Laramie Mts. in N Albany co.; flows 1st S then mainly E to Laramie R. 5 mi/8 km N of Wheatland.

North Las Vegas, city (□ 60 sq mi/155 sq km; 1990 pop. 47,707), Clark co., SE Nev., a suburb 3 mi/4.8 km N of Las Vegas; 36°16′N 115°08′W. Tourism and military expediture are the economic mainstays of this growing suburb. Mfg. (furniture, food prods., chemicals, sanitary food containers, septic tanks, fertilizers, gaming equip.). Community Col. of Southern Nev. The Garden of Cities there features trees and plants from cities throughout the U.S. Nellis Air Force Base to E and NE. Sunrise Mt. Natural Area to SE. Las Vegas Dunes Recreation Area to NE. Desert Natl. Wildlife Range to N. Part of Toiyabe Natl Forest, including Mt. Charleston, to W. Inc. 1946.

North Lauderdale, city (□ 3 sq mi/7.8 sq km; 1990 pop. 26,506), Broward co., SE Fla., 6 mi/9.7 km W of Pompano Beach; 26°12′N 80°13′W. Mfg. includes cabinets and commercial printing.

North Lewisburg, village (1990 pop. 1,160), Champaign co., W central Ohio, 13 mi/21 km NE of Urbana, near Darby Creek, 40°13′N 83°33′W. In agr. area.

North Liberty 1 town (1990 pop. 1,366), St. Joseph co., N Ind., 13 mi/21 km SW of South Bend; 41°32′N 86°26′W. Dairy prods., grain. Mfg. (aluminum extrusions). Potato Creek State Park is nearby to the E. Laid out 1836. **2** town (1990 pop. 2,926), Johnson co., E Iowa, 7 mi/11.3 km NNW of Iowa City; 41°44′N 91°36′W. State park nearby.

North Little Rock, city (1990 pop. 61,741), Pulaski co., central Ark., on the Arkansas R. (Murray Lock and Dam to W), opposite Little Rock; 34°47′N 92°15′W. RR center. North Little Rock lies in a cotton, rice, soybean, dairy-cattle, and produce area. Mfg. (consumer goods, food and food prods., fiberglass prods., printing, bldg.

materials, hospital garments, bakery prods., feed, furniture, fertilizers, electronic prods., chemicals). In the early 19th cent. the discovery of a small silver vein drew settlers to the area, which was then called Silver City. Most of the area later became part of Little Rock, but in 1903 local citizens pushed a bill through the Ark. legislature permitting a part of Little Rock to secede and join the small village of North Little Rock. Nearby is Camp Joseph T. Robinson Natl. Guard Training Area, to N of city. Settled c.1856, inc. as a city 1903.

North Logan, town (1990 pop. 3,768), Cache co., N Utah, suburb 2 mi/3.2 km N of Logan, W of Bear River range; 41°46′N 111°48′W. Elev. 4,700 ft/1,433 m. Mt. Nanomi Wilderness Area of Wasatch Natl. Forest to E. Settled 1878.

North Long Lake, Crow Wing co., central Minn., (□ 10 sq mi/26 sq km), 4 mi/6.4 km N of Brainerd; 6.5 mi/10.5 km long, 2 mi/3.2 km wide in middle. Drains NE to Edward L. Resorts. Distinct bays at E and W ends, connected to lake by narrow channels. Gull L. to W, Round L. to NW, Mississippi R. to SE.

North Loup (LOOP), village (1990 pop. 361), Valley co., central Nebr., 10 mi/16 km SE of Ord and on North Loup R; 41°29′N 46°98′W. Dairying, grain; mfg. (popcorn processing). Chalkmine State Wayside Area to SE (Greeley co.).

North Loup River, Nebr.: see LOUP RIVER.

North Lumberton, uninc. village, Robeson co., S N.C., a suburb 1 mi/1.6 km N of Lumberton.

North Madison, village, Jefferson co., SE Ind., just NW of Madison. In agr. area.

North Manchester, town (1990 pop. 6,383), Wabash co., NE central Ind., on Eel R., and 14 mi/23 km N of Wabash; 41°00′N 85°46′W. In agr. area (livestock; grain); mfg. (transportation equip., animal feed, mobile home axles, battery cables, agr. equip., appliances, iron castings). Seat of Manchester Col. Laid out 1837.

North Manistique Lake, Mich.: see MANISTIQUE LAKE.

North Manitou Island, Mich.: see MANITOU ISLANDS.

North Mankato (man-KAI-do), city (1990 pop. 10,164), Nicollet co., S Minn., suburb 1 mi/1.6 km NW of Mankato, on N side of Minnesota R.; 44°10′N 94°01′W. Agr. (grain, soybeans, peas; livestock, poultry; dairying); mfg. (awards, printers, electronics, trusses, food and beverage processing, lumber brake systems). North Mankato Vocational Technical School. Inc. 1922.

North Maroon Peak (14,014 ft/4,271 m), in Elk Mts., Pitkin co., near Gunnison co. boundary, W central Colo., 13 mi/21 km SW of Aspen, and 1 mi/1.6 km N of Maroon Peak.

North Merrick, uninc. village (1990 pop. 12,113), Nassau co., SE N.Y., on L.I.; 40°42′N 73°34′W. It is chiefly residential.

North Miami, city (□ 9 sq mi/23.3 sq km; 1990 pop. 49,998), Dade co., SE Fla., suburb 6 mi/9.7 km N of Miami, on Biscayne Bay; 25°53′N 80°10′W. It is mainly residential. Mfg. includes boats, wooden furniture, and aluminum prods.; substantial retail development since the 1980s. Inc. 1926.

North Miami, village (1990 pop. 450), Ottawa co., extreme NE Okla., suburb 3 mi/4.8 km N of Miami; 36°55′N 94°52′W. Mfg. (precast concrete structures).

North Miami Beach, city (□ 5 sq mi/13 sq km; 1990 pop. 35,359), Dade co., SE Fla., 10 mi/16 km N of Miami near the Atlantic coast; 25°55′N 80°10′W. Major office and retail area. Inc. 1931.

North Middletown, village (1990 pop. 602), Bourbon co., N central Ky., 9 mi/14.5 km ESE of Paris, in Bluegrass region; 38°08′N 84°06′W. Agr. (horses, cattle; burley tobacco, grain; dairying).

North Mountain (elev. c.2,000 ft/610 m–3,300 ft/1,006 m high), in Va. and W.Va., ridge of Allegheny Mts., extends c.50 mi/80 km SW-NE, partly along border bet. Hardy co., W.Va., and Shenandoah co., Va.; in George Washington Natl. Forest (both states). Shenandoah Valley to E. Also called Great North Mt.

North Mullins, uninc. village, Marion co., E S.C., 28 mi/45 km E of Florence.

North Muskegon (mus-KEE-guhn), town (1990 pop.

3,919), Muskegon co., SW Mich., on Muskegon L., suburb 1 mi/1.6 km N of Muskegon; 43°15′N 86°16′W. RR junction. Mfg. (agr. chemicals); fruit and vegetable farming. Muskegon State Park to W of L. Michigan; Manistee Natl. Forest to NE; Duck L. State Park to NW on L. Michigan. Inc. as village 1881, as city 1891.

North Myrtle Beach, town (1990 pop. 8,636), Horry co., E S.C., 15 mi/24 km NE of Myrtle Beach, on Atlantic Ocean, in Grand Strand Beach resort area; 33°49′N 78°40′W. Mfg. includes wire harnesses, food processing. Intracoastal Waterway to NW, bridged to N.

North Naples, town (□ 7 sq mi/18.1 sq km; 1990 pop. 13,422), Collier co., SW Fla., 4 mi/6.4 km N of Naples; 26°11′N 81°47′W.

North Negril Point, Hanover parish, cape at W end of Jamaica, 29 mi/47 km WSW of Montego Bay; 18°21′N 78°22′W. South Negril Point, westernmost cape of the isl., is 6 mi/9.7 km S.

North Newton, town (1990 pop. 1,262), Harvey co., S central Kansas, suburb 2 mi/3.2 km N of Newton; 38°04′N 97°20′W. Seat of Bethel Col.

North Oaks 1 uninc. town, Los Angeles co., S Calif., residential suburb 30 mi/48 km NNW of downtown Los Angeles, on Santa Clara R. San Gabriel Mts. to S; Bouquet Canyon to N. Dairying; cattle, poultry; bedding plants, peaches. Los Angeles Aqueduct passes N-S through area. **2** town (1990 pop, 3,386), Ramsey co., E Minn., residential suburb 9 mi/14.5 km N of downtown St. Paul, and 12 mi/19 km NE of downtown Minneapolis; 45°06′N 93°05′W. Numerous small lakes in area; Pleasant L. in center.

North Ogden, city (1990 pop. 11,668), Weber co., N Utah; residential suburb 5 mi/8 km N of Ogden; 41°18′N 111°57′W. Elev. 4,275 ft/1,303 m. Vegetables, cherries, apples, wheat, barley; dairying; cattle. Wasatch Range and Wasatch Natl. Forest to E. Settled 1851; inc. 1934.

North Olmsted (AHM-sted), city (1990 pop. 34,204), Cuyahoga co., NE Ohio, a suburb of Cleveland; 41°25′N 81°55′W. Mainly residential; chief industry, printed materials. First U.S. municipal bus line began operations in North Olmstead in 1931. Inc. as a city 1951.

North Oxford, Mass.: see OXFORD.

North Palisade, Calif.: see KINGS CANYON NATIONAL PARK.

North Palm Beach, town (□ 5 sq mi/13 sq km; 1990 pop. 11,343), Palm Beach co., SE Fla., 10 mi/16 km N of W. Palm Beach; 26°49′N 80°03′W.

North Patchogue, town (1990 pop. 7,373), Suffolk co., SE N.Y., 20 mi/32 km SW of Riverhead; 40°47′N 72°56′W. Residential area. Pop. figure includes Patchogue Highlands.

North Peak, Nev.: see BATTLE MOUNTAIN.

North Pease River, Texas: see PEASE RIVER.

North Pekin (PEE-kin), village (1990 pop. 1,556), Tazewell co., central Ill., suburb of Peoria, near Illinois R.; 40°36′N 89°37′W. In agr. area; mfg. (grinding wheels, machinery). Next to Pekin L. Conservation Area. Inc. 1948.

North Perry, village (1990 pop. 824), Lake co., NE Ohio, on L. Erie, 8 mi/13 km NE of Painesville; 41°48′N 81°07′W.

North Plainfield, residential borough (1990 pop. 18,820), Somerset co., NE N.J. Settled 1736, inc. 1885. A Revolutionary War cemetery is here.

North Plains, town (1990 pop. 972), Washington co., NW Oregon, 15 mi/24 km WNW of downtown Portland, on McKay Creek; 45°36′N 123°00′W. Dairying; poultry; berries, fruit, vegetables.

North Platte (PLAT), city (1990 pop. 22,605), ⊙ Lincoln co., W central Nebr., at the confluence of the North Platte and South Platte rivers, on point below the 2 rivers; 41°07′N 100°46′W. It is a processing and shipping point for grain and livestock. It has meatpacking plants and a large RR repair shop and clarification yard. Mfg. (concrete blocks, sheet metal fabrication, wooden doors, horse meat and zoo dists.; lawn ornaments, soft drinks, aprons; printing). Nearby are Scouts Rest Ranch (formerly a home of "Buffalo" Bill Cody, who lived in North Platte for 30 years) and Fort McPherson

Natl. Cemetery. A nightly rodeo is held in the city during summer at the Rodeo Arena at Buffalo Bills Scouts Resort Ranch NW of town, also has Mid-Plains Community Col. S of town. Maloney Reservoir (on Tri-Co. Supply Canal) and L. Maloney State Recreation Area to S, also has fish hatchery. Old Oregon Trail, once guarded by Ft. McPherson, follows S side Platte–South Platte rivers. Inc. 1873.

North Platte, river, c.680 mi/1,094 km long; rises in the Park Range, SW Jackson co., N Colo., at joining of Grizzly and Little Grizzly creeks, near Continental Divide, 23 mi/37 km SSW of Walden, Colo.; flows N into Wyo., past Saratoga, through Seminos, Pathfinder, and Alcova reservoirs, NE to Casper, then E, past N end of Laramir Mts., SE past Douglas and Torrington, Wyo., Scottsbluff, Bridgeport, and Oshkosh, Nebr., through L.C.W. McConaughy Reservoir (N of Ogallala), then joining South Platte at city of North Platte to form Platte R., lower 80 mi/129 km nearly parallels South Platte R. The North Platte project and the Kendrick project utilize the North Platte's water for power and irrigation. Kingsley Dam (170 ft/52 m high and 3.4 mi/5.5 km long; completed 1942) near Ogallala, Nebr., is one of many dams on the river, and there are also large reservoirs. The valley of the North Platte was a chief route used by W-bound pioneers. Fort Laramie Natl. Historic Site is on the river near the mouth of the Laramie R.

North Platte project (PLAT), unit of the U.S. Bureau of Reclamation, in the North Platte R. valley, W Nebr. and E Wyo. It supplies hydroelectric power to many towns and industries and provides irrigation for land extending along the valley from Guernsey, Wyo., to below Bridgeport, Nebr. Among the project's many dams and reservoirs are Guernsey Reservoir, formed by Guernsey Dam (completed 1927), and Pathfinder Reservoir, created by Pathfinder Dam (completed 1909). There are also several large dams on the branches of the North Platte. The power system of the project has been integrated with the Missouri R. basin project.

North Pleasureville, village, Henry co., N Ky., 18 mi/29 km NW of Frankfort, in Bluegrass agr. region.

North Plymouth, Mass.: see PLYMOUTH.

North Point, suburban village, Baltimore co., central Md., on North Point, extending into Chesapeake Bay at N side of Patapsco R. mouth (lighthouse), 12 mi/19 km SE of downtown Baltimore. Agr.; steel plant. Fort Howard Veterans Hosp. is here. Site of minor victory over British (Sept. 12, 1814).

North Point, NW extremity of P.E.I., Canada, on the Gulf of St. Lawrence, 7 mi/11 km NNE of Tignish; 47°04′N 63°59′W. Lighthouse.

North Port, town (□ 75 sq mi/194 sq km; 1990 pop. 11,973), Sarasota co., W central Fla., 12 mi/19 km E of Venice; 27°03′N 82°11′W. Contains Little Salt Springs archeological site.

North Portal, village (1991 pop. 164), SE Sask., Canada, frontier station on N.Dak. border, 23 mi/37 km ESE of Estevan; 49°00′N 102°33′W. Mixed farming.

North Powder, village (1990 pop. 448), Union co., NE Oregon, 22 mi/35 km SSE of La Grande, on Powder R., W of the confluence with Powder R.; 45°01′N 117°55′W. Elev. 3,256 ft/992 m. Agr. (wheat, potatoes, cherries, apples; sheep, cattle); timber. Parts of Wallowa-Whitman Natl. Forest to W and E.

North Prairie, town (1990 pop. 1,322), Waukesha co., SE Wis., 26 mi/42 km WSW of Milwaukee; 42°56′N 88°24′W. In dairying region. Dairy prods.; mfg. (wood pallets). Kettle Moraine State Forest (S unit) to W.

North Princeton, village, Mercer co., W N.J., near Princeton.

North Providence, town (1990 pop. 32,090), Providence co., NE R.I. Set off from Providence; 41°52′N 71°28′W. Once a large textile town, it is now mainly a residential suburb. A major portion of R.I. Col. is within the town's limits. Inc. 1765.

North Puyallup (pyoo-A-luhp), uninc. town (1990 pop. 2,886), Pierce co., W Wash., residential suburb 8 mi/12.9 km SE of downtown Tacoma, and 1 mi/1.6 km N of Puyallup, on Puyallup R.; 47°13′N 122°19′W.

North Randall, village (1990 pop. 977), Cuyahoga co., N Ohio, a SE suburb of Cleveland; 41°26′N 81°32′W. Site of Randall Park Mall, one of the largest shopping center in U.S. Extensive retailing; thoroughbred racing at Randall Park.

North Reading (RE-deeng), residential town (1990 pop. 12,002), Middlesex co., NE Mass., on the Ipswich R., 14 mi/23 km N of Boston; 42°35′N 71°05′W. Mfg. (athletic footwear). Settled 1651, set off from Reading and inc. 1853.

North Redwood, village (1990 pop. 203), Redwood co., SW Minn., 2 mi/3.2 km NE of Redwood Falls, on Redwood R. at its mouth on Minnesota R.; 44°33′N 95°05′W. Corn, oats, soybeans; dairying; livestock.

North Richland Hills, city (1990 pop. 45,895), Tarrant co., N Texas, residential suburb 9 mi/14.5 km NE of downtown Fort Worth; 32°51′N 97°13′W. Elev. 650 ft/198 m. Drained by Big Fossil (S) and Little Bear creeks (N). Mfg. (corrugated boxes, food prods., textiles). Its pop. more than doubled bet. 1970 and 1990 as a result of the economic development of the N Texas area. City is now surrounded by neighboring municipalities. Tarrant Co. Jr. Col. NE campus 1 mi/1.6 km E in Hurst. Inc. 1953.

North Ridgeville, city (1990 pop. 21,564), Lorain co., N Ohio, 18 mi/29 km WSW of downtown Cleveland; 41°23′N 82°01′W.

North River, 75 mi/121 km long, SW Que., Canada; flows S and SW, past Ste. Agathe des Monts, St. Jérôme, and Lachute, to W end of L. of the Two Mts.

North River 1 55 mi/89 km long, in W Ala.; formed by confluence of 2 headstreams E of Fayette; flows S through L. Tuscaloosa, to Black Warrior R. NE of Tuscaloosa. **2** c.70 mi/113 km long, in S central Iowa; rises near Menlo in Guthrie co.; flows E, to Des Moines R. 10 mi/16 km SE of Des Moines. **3** c.25 mi/40 km long, in E Mass.; rises in N Plymouth co.; flows NE, past Hanover, to Mass, Bay c.2 mi/3.2 km S of Scituate. Wildlife sanctuary. **4** c.70 mi/113 km, NE Mo.; rises in Knox co.; flows SE and E to the Mississippi below Quincy, Ill. **5** c.25 mi/40 km long, NW Va.; rises in Blue Ridge in NW Augusta co.; flows generally SE to SW of Harrisonburg, joins South R. near Port Republic to form South Fork of Shenandoah R.; 38°27′N 79°15′W. Receives Middle R. 2 mi/3.2 km W of its mouth.

North River, Va.: see MAURY RIVER.

North Riverside, village (1990 pop. 6,005), Cook co., NE Ill., residential suburb 11 mi/18 km W of downtown Chicago; 41°51′N 87°49′W. Inc. 1923. Mfg. trigger pumps. On Des Plains R.

North Robinson, village (1990 pop. 216), Crawford co., N central Ohio, 6 mi/10 km E of Bucyrus; 40°48′N 82°51′W.

North Royalton, city (1990 pop. 23,197), Cuyahoga co., NE Ohio, a growing suburb of Cleveland; 41°19′N 81°45′W. Dairy-processing and sawmilling center in the 19th cent., North Royalton has since developed a variety of light industries. Settled 1811, inc. as a village 1927, as a city 1960.

North Sacramento, city, Sacramento co., central Calif., suburb of Sacramento, across American R. Community Col. is here. Packed meat, brick, machinery. Part of Sacramento. Inc. 1924.

North Saint Paul, city (1990 pop. 12,376), Ramsey co., SE Minn., a suburb 6 mi/9.7 km NE of downtown St. Paul; 45°00′N 93°00′W. Mfg. (electronic equip., concrete prods., furniture, roofing materials, arrowheads [for archery], vending machines; millwork, printing and publishing). Silver L. in NE corner; White Bear L. to N. Inc. 1888.

North Salem, town (1990 pop. 499), Hendricks co., central Ind., 8 mi/12.9 km NW of Danville. In agr. area (corn, soybeans; hogs). Laid out 1835.

North Salem, village (1990 pop. 600), Rockingham co., SE N.H., suburb in town of Salem, 3 mi/4.8 km N of Salem center, at N end of Arlington Mill Reservoir. Mfg. (radar, outboard motor accessories). Amer.'s Stonehenge, Mystery Hill, prehistoric stone structures here; Robert Frost Farm to NE.

North Salem, township (1990 pop. 4,725), NE Westchester co., SE N.Y., 50 mi/80 km N of Manhattan; 41°20′N 73°35′W. Acknowledged as one of the most beautiful and underdeveloped areas in N.Y. city's metropolitan area, its tranquility is now being threatened by rapid growth. After decades of litigation, the zoning laws here have been changed, resulting in new homes and sub-divisions. Open fields and rugged hills surrounding Titicus Reservoir; horseback riding is popular, as is the raising of horses for hunting and jumping. DeLancey Town Hall, a restored 18th-cent. Georgian manor, is on the Natl. Register of Historic Places; mus., Jap. Stroll Garden are here. Along Titicus Road, there is a 60-ton/54–metric ton granite glacial erratic which has inspired a great deal of media attention and scientific speculation.

North Salt Lake, town (1990 pop. 6,474), Davis co., N central Utah, suburb 4 mi/6.4 km N of downtown Salt Lake City, at mouth of Jordan R. and Great Salt L.; 40°50′N 111°55′W. Elev. 4,300 ft/1,311 m. Gravel; mfg. (containers and luggage, medical equip., lighting fixtures; petroleum refining, meatpacking). Wasatch Range and Natl. Forest to E.

North Saskatchewan, Canada: see SASKATCHEWAN, river.

North Scituate, Mass.: see SCITUATE.

North Sewickley (SUH-wik-lee), uninc. village, Franklin township, Beaver co., W Pa., residential suburb 2 mi/3.2 km S of Ellwood City, on Connoquenessing Creek; 40°50′N 80°16′W.

North Sioux City, town (1990 pop. 2,019, Union co., SE S.Dak., suburb 6 mi/9.7 km WNW of downtown Sioux City, Iowa, on Big Sioux R.; 42°32′N 96°30′W. Agr. area (corn; cattle, hogs, poultry). Mfg. of computers, pet food, bakery goods, and hydraulic pumps.

North Skunk River, Iowa: see SKUNK RIVER.

North Slope, borough (□ 87,861 sq mi/227,560 sq km; 1990 pop. 5,979), N Alaska. Bounded on N by Arctic Ocean; E by Yukon Territory (Canada); includes most of the N Slope of the Brooks Range in S. Main town is Barrow. Part of the Gates of the Arctic Natl. Park and Preserve and the Noatak Natl. Preserve to S; part of the Arctic Natl. Wildlife Reservation to the East Alaska Pipeline crosses the borough N-S in center, terminating at Prudhoe Bay in NE. Fishing. Caribou hunting. Oil and natural gas extraction.

North Slope, Alaska: see ALASKA NORTH SLOPE.

North Smithfield, industrial town (1990 pop. 10,497), Providence co., N R.I., on Mass. line, on Branch R., and 13 mi/21 km NW of Providence; 41°59′N 71°33′W. Formerly an important textile center. Has several old inns. Includes villages of Forestdale and Slatersville (pop. center). Inc. 1871.

North Springfield 1 uninc. town (1990 pop. 5,451), Lane co., W Oregon, residential suburb 3 mi/4.8 km ENE of downtown Springfield, on McKenzie R.; 44°04′N 123°00′W.Va. **2** uninc. town, Fairfax co., Va., residential suburb 8 mi/12.9 km W of Alexandria, 11 mi/18 km SW of Washington, D.C.; 38°47′N 77°12′W. L. Accotink Park to SW.

North Star Lake, Itasca co., N central Minn., 22 mi/35 km N of Grand Rapids, in Chippewa Natl. Forest; 3 mi/4.8 km long, 1 mi/1.6 km wide; 47°33′N 93°39′W. Drained from N end by Potato Creek. Resort area. Sometimes called Potato L.

North Stonington, town (1990 pop. 4,884), New London co., SE Conn., on R.I. state line, 12 mi/19 km SE of Norwich; 41°28′N 71°52′W. Rural agr. town. State forest here. Inc. 1807.

North Stratford, N.H.: see STRATFORD.

North Swansea, Mass.: see SWANSEA.

North Sydney, town (1991 pop. 7,260), NE Cape Breton Isl., N.S., on Sydney Harbour; 46°12′N 60°15′W. It is the coal-shipping port for the nearby Sydney Mines and a winter base for the Cape Breton fisheries.

North Syracuse, suburb (□ 1 sq mi/2.6 sq km; 1990 pop. 7,363) of Syracuse, Onondaga co., central N.Y., 6 mi/9.7 km N of city center. Hancock Internatl. Airport; 43°07′N 76°07′W. Inc. 1925.

North Tarryall Peak, Colo.: see TARRYALL MOUNTAINS.

North Tazewell, former town, Tazewell co., SW Va., part of Tazewell co., with separate post office, in Allegheny Mts., 1 mi/1.6 km N of downtown Tazewell; 37°07′N 81°31′W. In agr. area; (hay, corn; cattle, sheep; dairying) mfg. (lumber, commercial printing); timber; coal-mining.

North Tisbury, Mass.: see WEST TISBURY.

North Tiverton, neighborhood, in Tiverton town, on Mount Hope Bay, Newport co., R.I., 17 mi/27 km SE of Providence.

North Tonawanda, industrial and commercial city (□ 10 sq mi/26 sq km; 1990 pop. 34,989), Niagara co., W N.Y., on the Niagara R. at the terminus of the Barge Canal; 43°02′N 78°52′W. It is a port of entry and has a variety of mfg., including furniture, chemicals, plastics, and castings. Settled c.1802, inc. as a city 1897.

North Troy, Vt.: see TROY.

North Truro, Mass.: see TRURO.

North Tunica (TOO-nik-uh), uninc. town (1990 pop. 1,314), Tunica co., NW Miss., residential suburb 2 mi/3.2 km N of Tunica; 34°42′N 90°22′W. Cotton, corn, rice, soybeans, sorghum; cattle; catfish.

North Turtle Lake, Otter Tail co., W Minn., 10 mi/16 km E of Fergus Falls; 5 mi/8 km long, 1 mi/1.6 km wide at E end; 46°18′N 95°48′W. Village of Underwood is near W end of lake. Smaller South Turtle L. (2 mi/3.2 km long, ½ mi/⅕ km wide) 1 mi/1.6 km to S.

North Twin Lake (□ 16 sq mi/41 sq km), central N.F., 25 mi/40 km WNW of Botwood; 8 mi/13 km long, 4 mi/6 km wide. Drains into Exploits R.

North Twin Lake, Vilas co., N Wis., 7 mi/11.3 km NE of Eagle R. city; c.5 mi/8 km long, 1.5 mi/2.4 km wide. Phelps is at E end. Connected to the smaller South Twin L. (2 mi/3.2 km wide, 2 mi/3.2 km long) at W end by narrow channel.

North Twin Lakes Reservoir (□ 28 sq mi/73 sq km), Penobscot co., N Maine, on West Branch Penobscot R., 16 mi/96 km N of Bangor; 45°38′N 68°47′W. Max. capacity 392,680 acre-ft. Formed by North Twin Dam (35 ft/11 m high), built (1934) for power generation; also used for flood control and recreation.

North Twin Mountain, N.H.: see FRANCONIA MOUNTAINS.

North Utica, village (1990 pop. 848), La Salle co., N central Ill., 4 mi/6.4 km E of La Salle, near Illinois R. On Ill. and Mich. State Trail; 41°20′N 89°00′W. Starved Rock and Mathiessen state parks to S.

North Valley Stream, uninc. town (□ 1 sq mi/2.6 sq km; 1990 pop. 14,574), Nassau co., SE N.Y., on L.I.; 40°40′N 73°42′W. It is chiefly residential.

North Vancouver, city (1991 pop. 38,436), SW B.C., on Burrard Inlet of the Strait of Georgia, opposite Vancouver, of which it is a suburb; 49°19′N 123°04′W. Shipbuilding, woodworking, and the shipping of grain, lumber, and ore are the chief industries.

North Vandergrift, uninc. town (1990 est. pop. 1,200), Armstrong co., W Pa., 25 mi/40 km NE of Pittsburgh, on Kiskiminetas R., opposite (1 mi/1.6 km NE of) East Vandergrift; 40°36′N 79°33′W. Agr. (grain; livestock; dairying). Listed as North Vandergrift–Pleasant View (1990 pop. 1,431) by Census Bureau; Pleasant View 1 mi/1.6 km to NW.

North Vernon, city (1990 pop. 5,311), Jennings co., SE Ind., 2 mi/3.2 km NW of Vernon; 39°01′N 85°38′W. Plastic injection moldings, wire harnesses, processed eggs, concrete, steel forgings, motor-vehicle fuel tubes, fixtures. Timber; limestone quarries. Selmier State Forest is nearby to the NE. Plotted 1854.

North Versailles (VER-sils), township (1990 pop. 12,302), Allegheny co., W Pa., residential suburb 12 mi/19 km ESE of Pittsburgh; 40°22′N 79°48′W. Mfg. of nylon and polyester bags, fabric printing, plastics molding.

North Vineland, village, Cumberland co., S N.J., 3 mi/4.8 km N of Vineland.

North Wales, borough (1990 pop. 3,802), Montgomery co., SE Pa., suburb 19 mi/31 km NNW of downtown Philadelphia; 40°12′N 75°16′W. Mfg. (paperboard boxes, power supplies, corrugated boxes, food-service

equip., pumps and valves, commercial printing, precision metal tubing, cutting blades, metal finishing, textile finishing); some agr. Settled 1850, laid out 1867, inc. 1869.

North Walpole, N.H.: see WALPOLE.

North Warren, uninc. town (1990 pop. 1,360), Warren co., NW Pa., residential suburb 2 mi/3.2 km N of Warren, on Conewango Creek; 41°52′N 79°09′W. Mfg. (wood prods.). Agr. area (corn, hay; dairying). Large Warren State Hosp. complex to N.

North Washington, town (1990 pop. 107), Chickasaw co., NE Iowa, 6 mi/9.7 km NW of New Hampton; 43°07′N 92°24′W.

North Webster, town (1990 pop. 881), Kosciusko co., N Ind., 10 mi/16 km NE of Warsaw; 41°20′N 85°42′W. In agr. area; mfg. (heaters). Recreation area. Tri-Co. State Fish and Wildlife Area is nearby to the NE.

North Weissport, uninc. town (1990 pop. 900), Carbon co., E Pa., residential suburb 1 mi/1.6 km N of Weissport, and 1 mi/1.6 km E of Lehighton, on Lehigh R.; 40°50′N 75°41′W.

North West Point, cape in Hanover parish, NW Jamaica, 19 mi/31 km W of Montego Bay; 18°28′N 78°14′W. Also known as Pedro Point.

North West River, town (1991 pop. 528), SE Lab., Canada, at W end of L. Melville, at mouth of Naskaupi R., 10 mi/16 km NE of Goose Bay; 53°32′N 60°09′W. Lumbering.

North Westchester, village, New London co., E central Conn., 16 mi/26 km WNW of Norwich, at confluence of Salmon and Pine rivers.

North Westminster, Vt.: see WESTMINSTER.

North Westport, Mass.: see WESTPORT.

North Weymouth, Mass.: see WEYMOUTH.

North Wilbraham, Mass.: see WILBRAHAM.

North Wildwood, resort city (1990 pop. 5,017), Cape May co., S N.J., on barrier isl. (bridged to mainland) off Cape May Peninsula, and 32 mi/51 km SW of Atlantic City; 39°00′N 74°47′W. Inc. 1917.

North Wilkesboro, town (1990 pop. 3,384), Wilkes co., NW N.C., 50 mi/80 km W of Winston-Salem, 1 mi/1.6 km N of Wilkesboro, across Yadkin R.; 36°10′N 81°08′W. Mfg. (glass mirrors, apparel, furniture, machinery, lumber, crushed stone, consumer goods; printing and publishing). Rendezvous Mt. Educational State Forest to NW; West Scott Kerr (Wilksboro) reservoir to W; Stone Mt. State Park to N. North Wilkesboro Speedway. Founded 1890; inc. 1891.

North Windham, village, Windham co., NE Conn., 4 mi/6.4 km NE of Willimantic.

North Woodstock, N.H.: see WOODSTOCK.

North Yarmouth (YAHR-muhth), town (1990 pop. 2,429), Cumberland co., SW Maine, on Royal R., and 15 mi/24 km NNE of Portland; 43°51′N 70°14′W. Inc. 1680, Yarmouth set off 1849.

North York, city (1991 pop. 562,564), borough of Metropolitan Toronto, S central Ont., Canada, 7 mi/11 km N of downtown Toronto. Humber R. on W boundary; E and W branches of Don R. in E part. MacDonald-Cartier Freeway (Highway 401) runs E-W. Major commercial and office complexes along Freeway and Yonge St. Ont. Science Centre, Black Creek Pioneer Village, Civic Gardens, North York Performing Arts Centre; Downsview Can. Air Force Base. York Univ. campus here. Inc. 1979.

North York, borough (1990 pop. 1,689), York co., S Pa., residential suburb 1 mi/1.6 km N of York; 39°58′N 76°43′W.

North Yukon National Park (□ 3,926 sq mi/10,168 sq mi), NW Yukon Territory, Canada. Bounded on W by Alaska, on NE by Beaufort Sea, on SE by Babbage R., S boundary follows divide to Alaska boundary. Excludes Herschel Isl. Traversed by Malcolm, Firth, and Trail rivers. British Mts. in S, Arctic Coastal Plain in N. Tundra; forested pockets in valleys. Snow geese, eagles, Arctic and red fox, Dall sheep, grizzly bears; caribou migration route and calving grounds. Est. 1984. Ranger station; no facilities. Backpacking, rafting, primitive camping.

North Zanesville, uninc. village (1990 pop. 2,121), Muskingum co., SE central Ohio, just N of Zanesville; 39°59′N 82°00′W.

North Zulch, uninc. village (1990 pop. 100), Madison co., E central Texas, 22 mi/35 km NE of Bryan, near Navasota R. In agr. area, mainly cattle, horses, hogs; oil and gas.

Northampton 1 (north-HAMP-tuhn),county (□ 550 sq mi/1,425 sq km; 1990 pop. 20,798), NE N.C.; ⊙ Jackson; 36°25′N 77°24′W. In Piedmont region, bounded N by Va. state line, SW by Roanoke R. (forms Roanoke Rapids and Gaston reservoirs in extreme W); drained by Meherrin R., forms part of NE boundary. Agr. area (peanuts, cotton, corn, tobacco, wheat, soybeans, sorghum, hay; poultry, hogs); timber. Formed 1741. **2** county (□ 377 sq mi/976 sq km; 1990 pop. 247,105), E Pa.; ⊙ Easton; 40°45′N 75°18′W. Industrial region; bounded E by Delaware R. (forms N.J. state boundary), NW by Lehigh R. (drained in S by Lehigh R.); Blue Mt. and Kittatinny Mt. (both ridges) along N boundary; Appalachian Trail follows N boundary. Mfg. at Bethlehem, Northampton, and Nazareth; slate quarrying. Agr. (corn, wheat, oats, barley, hay, alfalfa, soybeans, potatoes, apples; sheep, hogs, cattle, poultry; dairying). Small part of Delaware Water Gap Natl. Recreation Area in NE corner; Jacobsburg State Park in center. Settled 1st by English and Scotch-Irish, later by Germans. Formed 1752. **3** county (□ 795 sq mi/2,059 sq km; 1990 pop. 13,061), E Va.; ⊙ Eastville; 37°17′N 75°55′W. At S end of Eastern Shore (Delmarva) peninsula; Cape Charles at S tip, on N side of entrance to Chesapeake Bay; Chesapeake Bay Bridge-Tunnel (18 mi/29 km long) crosses mouth of bay. Many barrier and bay isls. lie off Atlantic coast. Fertile coastal plain. Mfg. (several canneries process seafood, farm produce); agr. (known for white and sweet potatoes; also strawberries, corn, barley, wheat, soybeans; poultry, hogs); pine timber; limestone; crabs, oysters. Cape Charles, resort town, is a port and a RR and ferry terminus. Kiptopeke State Park in S, Wreck Isl. State Natural Area in E, Fishermans Isl. National Wildlife Refuge in S. Intracoastal Waterway passes through bay to W. Formed 1663.

Northampton (nor-THAM-tuhn), city (1990 pop. 29,289), ⊙ Hampshire co., W Mass., on the Connecticut R.; 42°20′N 72°41′W. Includes village of Leeds. Brushes, wire, optical devices, and plastic prods. are made in Northampton. It is the seat of Smith Col. and has Clarke School for the Deaf. President Calvin Coolidge was a former mayor of Northampton; his papers and mementos are preserved in the Forbes Lib. Jonathan Edwards was pastor here, and Sylvester Graham lived and is buried in the city. Historic Deerfield is nearby. Dinosaur Footprint Park nearby. Inc. as a town 1656; as a city 1883.

Northampton (north-HAMP-tuhn), borough (1990 pop. 8,717), Northampton co., E Pa., suburb 5 mi/8 km N of Allentown, on Lehigh R.; 40°41′N 75°29′W. RR junction. Mfg. (machinery, metal castings, men's suits, flow meters, apparel), agr. (grain, apples, soybeans, potatoes; livestock; dairying). Allentown State Farm to E; Mary Immaculate Missionary Col. to N; Lehigh Valley Internat. Airport to SE. Settled c.1763; inc. 1901.

Northboro, town (1990 pop. 78), Page co., SW Iowa, near Mo. line, 16 mi/26 km SW of Clarinda; 40°36′N 95°17′W. In agr. region.

Northborough, town (1990 pop. 11,929), including Northborough village, Worcester co., E central Mass., 10 mi/16 km ENE of Worcester; 42°19′N 71°39′W. Mfg. (fiberoptics, electronics equip., rubber prods.). Settled c.1672; inc. 1766.

Northbridge, town (1990 pop. 13,371), Worcester co., S Mass., on the Blackstone R.; 42°08′N 71°39′W. It includes the villages of Whitinsville (1990 pop. 5,639) and Linwood. Mfg. (wood furniture, paper prods., stereo components); former textile-machinery mfg. Settled 1704; set off from Uxbridge and inc. 1772.

Northbrook, village (1990 pop. 32,308), Cook co., NE Ill., a suburb NW of Chicago; 42°07′N 87°49′W. It was inc. as Shermerville in 1901 and was reincorporated as Northbrook in 1923. Largely residential, it has some industry and research laboratories and is an insurance center. Once a farming community, Northbrook developed industry after the coming of a RR in 1871. Botanical gardens and a forest preserve are just E of the village. Settled 1836.

Northcrest, town (1990 pop. 1,725), McLennan co., E central Texas, residential suburb 7 mi/11.3 km NE of downtown Waco; 31°38′N 97°05′W. Agr. area (cattle; dairying; cotton). Seat of Texas State Tech. Col.; airport.

Northeast Cape Fear River, SE N.C.; rises SE Wayne co. at Duplin co. line; flows 130 mi/209 km S to Cape Fear R. at Wilmington; lower c.50 mi/80 km tidal.

Northeast Harbor, Maine: see MOUNT DESERT.

Northeast Providence Channel, Atlantic strait, Bahama Isls., NE of the Great Bahama Bank, bounded by New Providence Isl. and Eleuthera Isl. (S) and Great Abaco Isl. (N); c.110 mi/177 km long SWNNE. Leads through NW Providence Channel to Straits of Florida.

Northern Neck, E Va., Tidewater region peninsula bet. Potomac R. (N) and Rappahannock R. (S) estuaries, bounded E by Chesapeake Bay; extends c.65 mi/105 km SE from Port Royal and King George. Includes Westmoreland, Richmond, Northumberland, and Lancaster cos., and part of King George co. NE shore (except for inlets) forms Md.-Va. state line. Ferries from E end to Smith and Tangier isls.

Northern Panhandle, NW W.Va. (□ 584 sq mi/1,513 sq km), narrow arm of state, extending N bet. Pa. (E) and Ohio (W and N); Ohio R. forms N and W boundary; includes Marshall, Ohio, Brooke, and Hancock cos. Largely industrial, due to proximity to Pittsburgh steel dist. (to E) and to region's abundant natural resources (esp. coal, clay, natural gas, glass sand, salt). Weirton (steel) and Wheeling (diversified industries) are principal mfg. centers.

Northfield 1 city (1990 pop. 14,684), Rice co., SE Minn., 35 mi/56 km S of Minneapolis, on the Cannon R.; 44°27′N 93°10′W. RR junction and trade center for farming region (corn, oats, soybeans; livestock, poultry; dairying); mfg. (printed circuit boards, toys, feeds and seeds, cereals). On Sept. 7, 1876, Jesse and Frank James and their bandit gang attempted a bank robbery here, which failed and resulted in the deaths of 2 Northfield citizens. Each Sept., Northfield holds a festival that reenacts the robbery attempt. Carleton Col., St. Olaf Col., and the Laura Baker School for mentally challenged children are in the city. Historical Society Mus. Nestrand Woods State Park to SE. Inc. 1875. **2** city (1990 pop. 7,305), Atlantic co., SE N.J., 6 mi/9.7 km W of Atlantic City; 39°22′N 74°32′W. Inc. 1905.

Northfield 1 town (1990 pop. 898), Jefferson co., N Ky., residential suburb 6 mi/9.7 km ENE of downtown Louisville, near Ohio R.; 38°17′N 85°38′W. Zachary Taylor Natl. Cemetery to SW. **2** town (1990 pop. 99), Washington co., E Maine, 9 mi/14.5 km NW of Machias; 44°49′N 67°36′W. **3** town (1990 pop. 2,838), Franklin co., N Mass., on Connecticut R., and 10 mi/16 km NE of Greenfield, near N.H. state line; 42°41′N 72°27′W. A beautiful New England town. Dwight L. Moody b. here, founded Northfield Seminary (now Northfield School) for girls and Mt. Hermon School for boys. Hq. of Amer. Youth Hostels; 1st hostel opened here 1934. Town 1st settled 1672; permanently settled 1714; inc. 1723. Includes villages of East Northfield, South Vernon, and Mt. Hermon. **4** town (1990 pop. 4,263), Merrimack co., S central N.H., 4 mi/6.4 km S of Franklin; 43°24′N 71°34′W. Bounded W by Merrimack R., N by Winnipesaukee R. Agr. (livestock, poultry; vegetables, apples; dairying; nursery crops, timber); mfg. (boxes, batteries). Covered bridges in N. **5** town (1990 pop. 5,610), including Northfield village, Washington co., central Vt., 10 mi/16 km SW of Montpelier; 44°08′N 72°41′W. Maple sugar; granite. Winter sports. Seat of Norwich Univ. Chartered 1781; settled 1785; organized 1794.

Northfield 1 village (1990 pop. 4,635), Cook co., NE Ill., N suburb of Chicago, just W of Winnetka; 42°06′N 87°46′W. Food processing. **2** village (1990 pop. 3,624), Summit co., NE Ohio, 15 mi/24 km N of downtown Akron, near Cuyahoga R.; 41°20′N 81°31′W. Furnace Run Reservation (recreation) is nearby.

Northfork, village (1990 pop. 656), McDowell co., S W.Va., on Tug Fork R., 8 mi/12.9 km E of Welch; 37°25′N 81°25′W. Trade center for semibituminous-coal-mining region.

Northgate, village, SE Sask., Canada, frontier station on N.Dak. border, 35 mi/56 km ESE of Estevan.

Northgate 1 village, Burke co., NW N.Dak., port of entry at Can. border, 14 mi/23 km N of Bowbells; 48°59′N 102°15′W. Das Lacs Natl. Wildlife Refuge to E. **2** uninc. village (1990 pop. 7,864), Lucas co., NW Ohio, near Toledo; 39°15′N 84°35′W.

Northglenn, city (1990 pop. 27,195), Adams co., N central Colo., suburb 10 mi/16 km N of downtown Denver, near South Platte R.; 39°54′N 104°58′W. Elev. 5,460 ft/1,664 m. Mfg. of commercial greenhouses.

Northlake, city (1990 pop. 12,505), Cook co., NE Ill., a suburb of Chicago; 41°54′N 87°54′W. It has various manufactures. St. John Vianney R.C. Church, which is shaped like a fish, has the largest mosaic-tile mural in the Western Hemisphere. Inc. 1949.

Northlake, uninc. town (1990 pop. 3,162), Anderson co., NW S.C., residential suburb 4 mi/6.4 km NNW of Anderson, on NE arm of Hartwell L. reservoir; 34°34′N 82°40′W.

Northlakes, uninc. town (1990 pop. 1,219), Caldwell co., W central N.C., residential suburb 5 mi/8 km NW of Hickory, near Catawba R., forms Hickory L. reservoir to E and S; L. Rhodhiss reservoir to W; 35°46′N 81°22′W. Recreation area.

Northome (NORTH-hom), village (1990 pop. 283), Koochiching co., N Minn., c.40 mi/64 km NE of Bemidji; 47°52′N 94°16′W. Livestock; alfalfa; timber; mfg. (meat processing, printing); logging. Island L. and Chippewa Natl. Forest to SE; Pine Isl. State Forest to N and E.

Northport, city (1990 pop. 17,366), Tuscaloosa co., W central Ala., on Black Warrior R. opposite Tuscaloosa. Lumber; mfg. (apparel, fixtures).

Northport, resort town (1990 pop. 1,201), Waldo co., S Maine, on Penobscot Bay, and just S of Belfast; 44°21′N 68°59′W. Temple Heights Spiritualist camp of the Natl. Spiritual Assn. of Churches, founded 1882.

Northport 1 village (1990 pop. 605), Leelanau co., NW Mich., 25 mi/40 km N of Traverse City, on W shore of Grand Traverse Bay; 45°07′N 85°37′W. RR terminus. In cherry- and apple-producing area. Light mfg.; fisheries. Lighthouse; Leelanau State Park to NE. **2** residential village (□ 2 sq mi/5.2 sq km; 1990 pop. 7,572), Suffolk co., SE N.Y., on N shore of W L.I., on Northport Bay, 5 mi/8 km ENE of Huntington; 40°53′N 73°20′W. Sand, gravel pits. Settled c.1683, inc. 1894. **3** village (1990 pop. 308), Stevens co., NE Wash., 27 mi/43 km NNE of Colville, and 5 mi/8 km S of Can. border (B.C.) on Columbia R.; 48°55′N 117°47′W. Ports of entry to NW and NE. Mfg. (concrete). Parts of Colville Natl. Forest to E and W. Upper reach of Franklin D. Roosevelt L., formed by Grand Coulee Dam, 150 mi/241 km downstream.

Northport Bay, 3 mi/4.8 km long NNS, 2.5 mi/4 km wide, an arm of L.I. Sound indenting N shore of W L.I., SE N.Y., opens on E side of Huntington Bay, 2 mi/3.2 km NE of Huntington; 40°55′N 73°24′W. Northport is on its E shore.

Northridge, uninc. village, Montgomery co., SW Ohio, 3 mi/5 km N of Dayton. Former village absorbed into suburban development.

Northridge, suburban sect. of LOS ANGELES, Los Angeles co., S Calif., in San Fernando Valley, 20 mi/32 km NW of downtown Los Angeles. Mfg. (computer equip., electronic equip., pharmaceuticals, machinery). Seat of Calif. State Univ., Northridge. Northridge Fashion Center, one of the largest shopping centers in U.S., is here. Van Nuys Airport to SE. Santa Susana Mts. to N. Center of 1994 Northridge Earthquake.

Northrop, village (1990 pop. 276), Martin co., S Minn., 6 mi/9.7 km N of Fairmont; 43°44′N 94°26′W. Grain, soybeans; livestock. Middle Chain of Lakes to W, includes Martin, High, and Charlotte lakes.

Northumberland 1 (nor-THUHM-buhr-luhnd), county (□ 4,671 sq mi/12,098 sq km; 1991 pop. 52,983), N central N.B., Canada, on the Gulf of St. Lawrence; ⊙ Newcastle. **2** county (□ 734 sq mi/1,901 sq km; 1991 pop. 78,224), S Ont., Canada, on L. Ontario and on Rice L.; ⊙ Cobourg.

Northumberland 1 (north-UHM-buhr-luhnd), county (□ 477 sq mi/1,235 sq km; 1990 pop. 96,771), E central Pa.; ⊙ Sunbury; 40°51′N 42°76′W. Anthracite-coalmining region; drained by Susquehanna R. and its West Branch, joining at Northumberland; mountainous in S. Anthracite coal; mfg. at Sunbury, Northumberland, and Milton; limestone. Agr. (corn, wheat, oats, barley, alfalfa, vegetables, soybeans, potatoes, apples; poultry, sheep, hogs, cattle; dairying). Milton State Park in NW; part of Shikellamy State Park in NW. Formed 1772. **2** county (□ 285 sq mi/738 sq km; 1990 pop. 10,524), E Va.; ⊙ Heathsville; 37°51′N 76°22′W. On NE part of Northern Neck peninsula; bounded by Potomac R. estuary (NE) and Chesapeake Bay (E); coast has many bays and inlets; indented from E by Great Wicomico R. estuary. Reedville (fish-processing center) is a port. Mainly agr. (hay, barley, wheat, corn, soybeans, tomatoes; cattle, poultry); oysters, crabs, herring, fish. Shore resorts (fishing, bathing). Formed 1648.

Northumberland, town (1990 pop. 2,492), Coos co., NW N.H., 5 mi/8 km N of Lancaster; 44°34′N 71°31′W. Bounded W by Connecticut R. (Vt. state line); drained by Upper Ammonoosuc R. Includes village of Groveton (1990 pop. 1,255) in NE (covered bridge). Agr. (cattle, poultry; vegetables; dairying; nursery crops; timber); mfg. (pulp and paper). Cape Horn State Forest at center. Settled 1767, inc. 1779.

Northumberland (north-UHM-buhr-luhnd), borough (1990 pop. 3,860), Northumberland co., E central Pa., 2 mi/3.2 km N of Sunbury, on Susquehanna R., at mouth of West Branch Susquehanna R. (both rivers bridged); 40°53′N 76°47′W. Mfg. (transportation equip., food, wood prods.). Dr. Joseph Priestley lived here 1794–1804. Shikellamy State Park to SW and SE, partly on Packers Isl.; Sunbury Airport to E on Packers Isl. Laid out c.1775, inc. 1828.

Northumberland, Cape, SE Alaska, S extremity of Duke Isl., 35 mi/56 km SSE of Ketchikan; 54°52′N 131°21′W.

Northumberland Strait, c.200 mi/320 km long and from 9 mi/14 km to 30 mi/48 km wide, arm of the Gulf of St. Lawrence, separating P.E.I. from N.B. and N.S, Canada. A bridge across the strait (completed 1997) connects Cape Tormentine, N.B., to P.E.I.

Northvale, borough (1990 pop. 4,563), Bergen co., extreme NE N.J., 13 mi/21 km NE of Paterson, at N.Y. line; 41°00′N 73°57′W. Largely residential. Inc. 1916.

Northville, town (1990 pop. 3,367), Wayne and Oakland cos., SE Mich., suburb 23 mi/37 km NW of downtown Detroit, on upper reach of Middle R. Rouge; 42°26′N 83°29′W. Remnant farming; mfg. (glass prods., chemicals, computer equip., transportation equip., furniture). Mayberry State Park to W. Inc. 1867.

Northville 1 village (□ 1 sq mi/2.6 sq km; 1990 pop. 1,180), Fulton co., E central N.Y., on NW arm of Sacandaga Reservoir, 15 mi/24 km NE of Gloversville; 43°13′N 74°10′W. S terminus of 133-mi/214-km Northville–Lake Placid Trail. Inc. 1873. **2** village (1990 pop. 120), Suffolk co., SE N.Y., on NE L.I., 4 mi/6.4 km NE of Riverhead; 40°58′N 72°37′W. In summer-recreation area. **3** village (1990 pop. 105), Spink co., NE central S.Dak., 20 mi/32 km N of Redfield, and on Snake Creek; 45°08′N 98°34′W. Trading point for agr. area.

Northway, village (1990 pop. 113), E Alaska, near Yukon border, on Nabesna R., and 110 mi/177 km SW of Dawson; 62°57′N 141°57′W. Just off Alaska Highway.

Northwest Angle, Minn.: see LAKE OF THE WOODS.

Northwest Arctic, borough (□ 35,863 sq mi/ 92,885 sq km; 1990 pop. 6,113), NW Alaska, bounded on W by Chukchi Sea, indented by Kotzebue Sound and Hotham Inlet, drained by Kobuk R. Main town is Kotzebue. Part of Bering Land Bridge Natl. Preserve to SW; part of Noatak Natl. Preserve to N; part of Gates

of the Arctic Natl. Park and Preserve to E; Cape Krusenstern Natl. Monument to NW; Kobuk Valley Natl. Park in center; Selawik Natl. Wildlife Reserve to S. Arctic Circle crosses borough at its middle. Fishing. Caribou and seal hunting.

Northwest Fork of Nanticoke River, Del. and Md.: see MARSHYHOPE CREEK.

Northwest Gander River, central N.F., Canada, headstream of GANDER RIVER.

Northwest Harborcreek, uninc. town (1990 pop. 6,662), Erie co., NW Pa., residential suburb 6 mi/9.7 km ENE of downtown Erie, on Lake Erie at mouths of Sixmile and Sevenmile Creeks; 42°08′N 79°59′W.

Northwest Providence Channel, c.130 mi/209 km long, WNW-NESE, in Bahama Isls., just E of West Palm Beach, Fla., bet. Little Bahama Bank (N) and Great Bahama Bank (S), linking Straits of Fla. (W) with Northeast Providence Channel (E).

Northwest Territories, region (□ 1,304,903 sq mi/ 3,379,699 sq km; 1991 pop. 57,649), NW Canada. The N.W.T. lie W of Hudson Bay, N of lat. 60°N, and E of Yukon, and occupy more than 33% of Canada's area; 66°00′N 102°00′W. YELLOWKNIFE has been the territorial capital since 1967; before 1967 the govt. was conducted from Ottawa. The region is divided into 5 administrative dists.: Ft. Smith, near the Alta. border; Keewatin, W of Hudson Bay; Inuvik, E of Yukon; Kitikmeot, in the vicinity of Victoria Isl.; and Baffin, which includes Queen Elizabeth Isl. Geographically, the region is separated by the tree line, which runs roughly NW to SE, from the Mackenzie R. delta in the Arctic Ocean to the Churchill harbor area on Hudson Bay. The tundras extend over much of the N and E; there the Inuit and Native Americans derive their small incomes from hunting, trapping fur, and making arts and crafts, and obtain many necessities from fish, seals, reindeer, and caribou. Most of the development of the N.W.T. has taken place in the Fort Smith and Inuvik regions, areas well covered with softwoods and rich in minerals. In these regions are 2 of the largest lakes in the world, Great Slave and Great Bear. E from these lakes the geology of the region is that of the Can. Shield. Great Slave and Great Bear lakes are linked to the Arctic Ocean by one of the world's longest rivers, the Mackenzie, which runs 2,635 mi/4,241 km from its source in B.C. Agr. in the N.W.T. is virtually impossible except for limited cultivation S of the Mackenzie R. region. Govt. agr. experimental stations, however, are at Fort Simpson and Yellowknife. Trapping, the region's oldest industry, ranks 2d after mining. A thriving commercial fishing industry, based on whitefish and lake trout, is centered on the village of Hay River, on Great Slave L. Minerals are now the N.W.T.'s most valuable natural resource. Leading minerals are lead and zinc, both mined at Pine Point on Great Slave L. Oil is pumped and refined at Fort Norman and Norman Wells on the Mackenzie R.; gold is being produced in increasing quantities at Yellowknife and on the Snare R.; copper is extracted on the Coppermine R. and in Keewatin near Hudson Bay; and exceptionally high-grade iron ore has been discovered on Baffin Isl. The region also has tungsten, silver, cadmium, and nickel deposits. Important hydroelectric developments are on the Talston and Snake rivers. Transportation and communication in the N.W.T. are difficult. Long winters close the rivers to navigation for all but 2 months of the year, but allow the opening of winter roads for transport of goods. During World War II, oil pipeline from Norman Wells to Zama, Alta. was built. Despite the Great Slave RR and the Mackenzie highway system, which links Alta. to the Great Slave area, most commerce, supply, and travel continue to be airborne. An extensive N roads program, 1st announced in 1966, was expected to help open up the area when completed, and there are now extensive telecommunications services. The Liard Highway, opened in 1984, ties Ft. Simpson to the Alaska Highway. Original Native Amer. inhabitants were the hunting and fishing Inuit and Dene (de-NAI). About 1,000 Vikings from Greenland explored the E Arctic. Sir Martin Frobisher was the 1st in

a long line of explorers to seek a NORTHWEST PASSAGE, but it was Henry Hudson who discovered the gateway to the NW (Hudson Bay) in 1610. For several decades the Hudson's Bay Company sent out trader-explorers through the N sea lanes and coast, and in 1771 Samuel Hearne descended the Coppermine R. In 1789, Alexander Mackenzie, exploring for the North West Company, journeyed to the mouth of the Mackenzie R. Sir John Franklin made scientific expeditions to the Arctic NW in the early 19th cent., obtaining valuable geographical data. The area that is now the N.W.T. was part of the vast lands sold by the Hudson's Bay Company to the new Can. confederation in 1870. Some of those lands were added to the provs. of Que. and Ont. The prov. of Man. was carved from them in 1870, and Alta. and Sask. in 1905. The present boundaries of the N.W.T. were set in 1912. Since the patriation of the Can. constitution, several land claims by Native peoples have been making their way through the courts and the federal govt. In 1982 the N.W.T. voted to split the territory. The new territory of Nunavut, which will be controlled by the Inuit, is expected to come into force no later than Apr. 1, 1999. This action will split the N.W.T. along a zigzag line running from the Sask.-Man. border to the North Pole. The Inuit land claim currently under consideration would give them outright title to about 20% of the new territory, in addition to $1.4 billion over 14 years. Other Native groups making claims are the Dene, the Métis, and the Inuvialuit. Today the territory is administered by a commissioner and a 24-member council sitting in Yellowknife, backed up by the Royal Can. Mounted Police. The govt. operates a school system, and, with the aid of scattered missions throughout the vast region, provides extensive health and welfare services. The N.W.T. sends 1 senator and 2 representatives to the natl. parliament. With its valuable minerals and their strategic importance, enhanced by transpolar navigation, the region continues to present major challenges in every field of human endeavor. The N.W.T. are the site of the Nahanni and Baffin Islands natl. parks (both est. 1972).

Northwest Territory, first possession of the U.S., comprising the region known as the Old Northwest, S and W of the Great Lakes, NW of the Ohio R., and E of the Mississippi R., including the present states of Ohio, Ind., Ill., Mich., Wis., and part of Minn. Men from New France began to penetrate this rich fur country in the 17th cent.; in 1634, the Fr. explorer Jean Nicolet became the 1st to enter the region. He was followed by explorers and traders: Radisson and Groseilliers, Duluth, La Salle, Jolliet, Perrot, and Cadillac, as well as by missionaries such as Jogues, Dablon, and Marquette. The Great Lakes region was controlled by a few widely scattered Fr. posts, such as Kaskaskia, Vincennes, Prairie du Chien, and Green Bay; links were established bet. the Northwest settlements and those in Fr. Louisiana (St. Louis, New Orleans). The two chief posts of the Old Northwest were Detroit and Mackinac (Michilimackinac), but Fr. influence spread among the Native Amer. groups E to the Iroquois country. In the 18th cent. the NW was coveted not only by the Br. colonists in Canada, but also by those in the Amer. seaboard colonies, who organized the Ohio Company in 1747 for the purpose of extending the Va. settlements westward. At the same time, the French sought to strengthen their hold on the NW by building forts. The clash of Br. and Fr. interests culminated in the expedition led by George Washington that resulted in the loss of Fort Necessity and the outbreak of the last of the Fr. and Indian wars. The wars ended in 1763 with the Treaty of Paris, by which the British obtained Canada and the Old Northwest. Almost immediately after the British took over, Pontiac, an Ottawa chief, led an uprising against them. The Ottawa were somewhat appeased by the Br. Proclamation of 1763 that closed the region W of the Allegheny Mts. to white settlement in an attempt to protect the Native Amer. fur trade and lands; yet this action caused resentment among the Amer. frontiersmen and contributed to the Amer. Revolution. The mysterious machinations of Robert Rogers, an Amer. frontiersman, further endangered the Br. hold on the Old Northwest. During the Revolutionary War, an expedition led by the Amer. general George Rogers Clark penetrated deep into the region in 1778–1779, in one of the most daring and valuable exploits of the war. The Old Northwest, which became U.S. territory in 1783 by the Treaty of Paris ending the Revolution, soon became one of the most pressing problems before the U.S. Congress. The 4 so-called landed states — Va., Mass., N.Y., and Conn. — claimed portions of the Old Northwest, while states with no W land claims, esp. Md., argued that if the claims of the landed states were recognized, the wealth and population of the other states would be attracted to the W lands. The final solution was the cession of all the lands to the U.S. govt., which was thus greatly strengthened; N.Y. made its cession in 1780, Va. in 1784, Mass. in 1785, and Conn. in 1786. Two reserves were kept, the Va. Military Dist. and the Conn. Western Reserve in Ohio. The Ordinance of 1785 established the Township System for surveying, which used a rectangular grid system in order to divide the land. The Ordinance of 1787 set up the machinery for the organization of territories and the admission of states. Its terms prohibited slavery in the Northwest Territory, encouraged free public education, and guaranteed religious freedom and trial by jury. The Ohio Company of Associates, the most active force in early colonization, was followed by later companies that brought settlers into the territory. Br. traders, however, opposed Amer. expansion, and the Native Americans were also hostile to their encroachment. A series of campaigns against the Native Americans culminated in 1794, when Gen. Anthony Wayne won an Amer. victory at Fallen Timbers; his victory was solidified by the Greenville Treaty of 1795. Meanwhile, Jay's Treaty and subsequent negotiations smoothed out some of the Br.-Amer. difficulties. The Northwest posts were transferred to Americans in 1796, although Br. influence remained strong among the Native Americans. Settlers poured into the S part of the territory, and in 1799 a legislature was organized. In 1800 the W part was split off as Ind. Territory, and by 1802, the E portion was populated enough to seek admission as a state; it was admitted as Ohio in 1803. Other territories were then formed — Mich. in 1805, Ill. in 1809, and Wis. in 1836. The Br. traders, however, wanted the Northwest set aside as Native Amer. land. Unrest led Tecumseh and Shawnee Prophet to seek a permanent foothold for the Native Americans. Some W Americans, meanwhile, sought to extend the Northwest to Canada. The quarrel over the Northwest was a major cause of the War of 1812. The Treaty of Ghent, which ended the war, solved the problem of the Northwest. Despite opposition from Br. merchants in the region, Great Britain irrevocably gave the Northwest to the U.S.

Northwood 1 town (1990 pop. 1,940), N Iowa, near Minn. state line, on Shell Rock R.; and 20 mi/32 km N of Mason City; ⊙ Worth co.; 43°26′N 93°13′W. Mfg. (dairy prods., food, furniture, chemicals). Settled 1853, inc. 1875. **2** town (1990 pop. 3,124), Rockingham co., SE N.H., 11 mi/18 km SW of Rochester; 43°12′N 71°12′W. Agr. (cattle, poultry; vegetables; dairying; nursery crops, timber); mfg. (lumber, fabricated metal prods.). Source of Lamprey R. Northwood L. in W; Jenness Pond in NW. **3** town (1990 pop. 1,166), Grand Forks co., E N.Dak., 28 mi/45 km SW of Grand Forks; 47°44′N 97°34′W. Printing; dairy prods.; wheat, flax, potatoes. Settled 1879, inc. 1892.

Northwoods, town (1990 pop. 5,106), St. Louis co., E Mo., residential suburb 7 mi/11.3 km NW of downtown St. Louis; 38°42′N 90°16′W. Inc. 1939.

Norton, county (□ 881 sq mi/2,282 sq km; 1990 pop. 5,947), NW Kansas; ⊙ Norton; 39°46′N 99°54′W. Rolling plain region, bordering N on Nebr.; watered by Beaver, Prairie Dog creeks and North Fork Solomon R. Wheat, barley, oats, corn, sorghum; cattle, hogs; furniture. Prairie Dog State Park and Keith Sebelius L. Reservoir in W center. Formed 1872.

Norton 1 city (1990 pop. 3,017), NW Kansas, on Prairie Dog Creek, and c.70 mi/113 km NNW of Hays; ⊙ Norton co.; 39°50′N 99°53′W. Elev. 2,260 ft/689 m. Processing center for agr. region; dairying. Mfg. (fabricated metal prods.). Prairie Dog State Park and Keith Sebelius L. reservoir to SW. Inc. 1885. **2** independent city (□ 7 sq mi/18.1 sq km; 1990 pop. 4,247), SW Va., separate from surrounding Wise co., in Cumberland Mts., 33 mi/53 km NW of Bristol, on Guest R.; 36°55′N 82°37′W. Mfg. (apparel, explosives, printing and publishing, crushed stone); trade, processing and shipping center in bituminous-coal and agr. area; bituminous-coal mining. Settled 1787; inc. 1894.

Norton 1 town (1990 pop. 14,265), Bristol co., SE Mass., 11 mi/18 km SW of Brockton; 41°58′N 71°11′W. Light mfg. Wheaton Col., House in the Pines School here. Settled 1669, set off from Taunton 1711. **2** town (1990 pop. 169), Essex co., NE Vt., on Que. (Canada) border, port of entry; 44°58′N 71°48′W. Norton Pond (c.3 mi/4.8 km long; fishing) is S. Part of Averill village is in Norton town.

Norton Air Force Base, Calif.: see SAN BERNARDINO.

Norton Bay, W Alaska, NE arm of Norton Sound, on S side of base of Seward Peninsula; 30 mi/48 km long, 20 mi/32 km wide; 64°40′N 161°27′W. Receives Koyuk R.

Norton Reservoir (□ 10 sq mi/26 sq km), Norton co., NW Kansas, on Prairie Dog Creek, 70 mi/113 km NNW of Hays; 39°49′N 99°56′W. Max. capacity 193,023 acre-ft. Formed by Norton Dam (131 ft/40 m high), built (1964) by the Bureau of Reclamation for irrigation; also used for flood control and recreation. Also known as Keith Sebelius Reservoir.

Norton Shores, city (1990 pop. 21,755), Muskegon co., W Mich., on L. Michigan, residential suburb of Muskegon. 43°09′N 86°15′W. Airport is here. P. F. Hoffmaster State Park in SW part of city, on L. Michigan.

Norton Sound,, inlet of the Bering Sea, W Alaska, S of the Seward Peninsula; c.150 mi/240 km long and 125 mi/200 km across at its widest point. Norton Bay is its NE arm. Nome is on the N shore and the Yukon R. flows into the sound from the SE. It is navigable from May to Oct.

Nortonville, town (1990 pop. 1,209), Hopkins co., W Ky., 10 mi/16 km SSE of Madisonville; 37°11′N 87°27′W. RR junction. Coal mining; timber; agr. (burley tobacco, grain; hogs, cattle).

Nortonville, village (1990 pop. 643), Jefferson co., NE Kansas, 15 mi/24 km SW of Atchison; 39°25′N 95°19′W. Shipping point in grain, dairy, and poultry area.

Norvelt (NOR-velt), uninc. town (1990 pop. 1,000), Mt. Pleasant township, Westmoreland co., SW Pa., 7 mi/11.3 km SSE of Greensburg, near Sewickley Creek; 40°12′N 79°29′W. Mfg. (ceramics, apparel); agr. (corn, hay, dairying).

Norwalk 1 city (1990 pop. 94,279), Los Angeles co., S Calif., suburb 12 mi/19 km SE of downtown Los Angeles and 10 mi/16 km NE of Long Beach; 33°55′N 118°05′W. Bounded by San Gabriel R in W. Mfg. (fabricated metal prods., plastic prods., computer equip., furniture). With the arrival (1875) of the Southern Pacific RR, it became a center for the dairy and logging industries. Norwalk's main growth occurred after World War II, with rapid industrialization. Seat of Cerritos Col. (2-year). The city also holds an annual Space, Science, and Technology Show. Settled in the 1850s, inc. 1957. **2** city (1990 pop. 78,331), Fairfield co., SW Conn., at the mouth of the Norwalk R., on L.I. Sound; 41°05′N 73°25′W. An oyster center; mfg. of apparel, electronic and electrical equip., machinery, chemicals; aircraft research. Norwalk was burned by the Br. in the Amer. Revolution. It has a community col., Norwalk Com. Technical Col., and an amateur symphony orchestra. The city includes numerous small isls. in the harbor and the village of Silvermine, an artists' colony. The Maritime Center at Norwalk, an aquarium and marine-life education center, is here. Settled 1640, inc. 1913. **3** city (1990 pop. 14,731), N Ohio; ⊙ Huron co.; 41°14′N 82°37′W. Trade and processing center for a farm area, with factories that make furniture, rubber prods., fabricated metal prods., and machinery. City was settled (c.1817) by "Fire Sufferers" from Norwalk, Conn., whose homes had been burned by the Br. in the Amer. Revolution. Inc. 1881.

Norwalk, town (1990 pop. 5,726), Warren co., S central Iowa, near North R., 9 mi/14.5 km S of Des Moines, satellite community of Des Moines; 41°30′N 93°40′W. Agr. and bituminous-coal area; mfg. of food, concrete.

Norwalk, village (1990 pop. 564), Monroe co., W central Wis., on a branch of Kickapoo R., and 30 mi/48 km E of La Crosse; 43°49′N 90°37′W. In farm and dairy area. On La Crosse State Trail.

Norwalk River, c.30 mi/48 km long, SW Conn.; rises just E of Ridgefield; flows N, then S, past Georgetown and Wilton, to L.I. Sound at Norwalk.

Norway 1 town (1990 pop. 583), Benton co., E central Iowa, 14 mi/23 km WSW of Cedar Rapids; 41°53′N 91°55′W. In agr. area; light mfg. **2** town (1990 pop. 4,754), including Norway village, Oxford co., W Maine, 17 mi/27 km NW of Auburn, and on L. Pennesseewassee; 44°13′N 70°36′W. Mfg. (wood prods.), resort area. Settled 1786, inc. 1797. **3** town (1990 pop. 2,910), Dickinson co., SW Upper Peninsula, Mich., 8 mi/12.9 km ESE of Iron Mountain city; 45°47′N 87°54′W. In lumbering and farming region (potatoes; cattle). Mfg. (printing, transportation equip.). Norway Spring, artesian spring created in 1903 by 1,904 ft/580 m drill-hole made in search of iron deposits. Iron Mt. Iron Mine is here (tourist attraction). Vulcan U.S.A. Ski Area to E. Trout hatchery nearby. Settled c.1879, inc. 1891.

Norway, village (1990 pop. 401), Orangeburg co., W central S.C., 15 mi/24 km WSW of Orangeburg; 33°27′N 81°07′W. Agr includes poultry, livestock; grain, tobacco, peanuts, cotton, watermelons, peaches.

Norwegian Bay, N Franklin dist., N.W.T., Canada, arm (c.100 mi/161 km long, 90 mi/145 km wide) of the Arctic Ocean, off SW Ellesmere Isl.; 77°N 90°W.

Norwell (NOR-wel), town (1990 pop. 9,279), Plymouth co., E Mass., on North R., near coast, and 20 mi/32 km SE of Boston; 42°10′N 70°50′W. Light mfg. In suburbanizing area. Settled 1634, set off from Scituate 1888.

Norwich 1 industrial city (1990 pop. 37,391), SE Conn., on hilly ground, where the Yantic and Shetucket rivers form the Thames; ⊙ New London co.; 41°32′N 72°05′W. Chemicals, plastics, paper prods. The last great battle bet. the Mohegans and Narragansetts took place on this site in 1643, and the tribal chiefs are buried here. Norwich was a leading colonial industrial city; Thomas Danforth began making pewterware here in 1733. The many historic structures include the Leffingwell Inn (1675); the birthplace and home of Benedict Arnold; and the home of Samuel Huntington. Location of Three Rivers Community Col. and a state hosp. Settled 1659, inc. 1784, town and city consolidated 1952. **2** city (□ 2 sq mi/5.2 sq km; 1990 pop. 7,613), central N.Y., on Chenango R., and 35 mi/56 km NE of Binghamton; ⊙ Chenango co.; 42°31′N 75°31′W. Mfg. (pharmaceuticals, aerospace electrical systems, wood and metal prods., apparel), in dairying and farming area. Gail Borden b. here. Settled 1788. Inc. 1915.

Norwich (NOR-wich, NAH-rich), town (1991 pop. 10,146), S Ont., Canada, 12 mi/19 km SE of Woodstock; 42°59′N 80°36′W. Lumbering, food processing.

Norwich, town (1990 pop. 3,093), Windsor co., E Vt., on the Conn. R., opposite Hanover, N.H., and 12 mi/19 km NE of Woodstock; 43°44′N 72°19′W. In agr. area. Includes Pompanoosuc village. Settled before 1775.

Norwich 1 village (1990 pop. 455), Kingman co., S Kansas, 20 mi/32 km SE of Kingman; 37°27′N 97°50′W. RR junction. Wheat-shipping point. **2** village (1990 pop. 133), Muskingum co., central Ohio, 12 mi/19 km ENE of Zanesville; 39°59′N 81°48′W. In agr. area.

Norwood, city (1990 pop. 23,674), Hamilton co., SW Ohio, a suburb of Cincinnati; 39°09′N 84°27′W. Mfg. includes machinery, printing and publishing. Settled early 1800s, inc. 1888.

Norwood 1 (NOR-wud), town (1990 pop. 238), Warren co., E Ga., 12 mi/19 km W of Thomson; 33°28′N 82°43′W. **2** town (1990 pop. 28,700), Norfolk co., E

Mass.; 42°11′N 71°12′W. Chiefly residential; local industries include printing and publishing, plastics, apparel, computer software, electronic equip. Settled 1678, set off from Dedham and Walpole and inc. 1872. **3** town (1990 pop. 1,351), Carver co., S Minn., 34 mi/55 km WSW of Minneapolis; 44°46′N 93°55′W. RR junction. Agr. area (grain, soybeans, alfalfa; livestock, poultry; dairying); light mfg. **4** town (1990 pop. 449), Wright co., S central Mo., in the Ozarks, 9 mi/14.5 km W of Mountain Grove; 37°06′N 92°25′W. Dairy; cattle, poultry. **5** town (1990 pop. 1,617), Stanly co., S central N.C., 10 mi/16 km SSE of Albemarle L.; 35°13′N 80°07′W. Tillery reservoir to E on Yadkin R. RR junction. Agr. area (cotton, grain, soybeans; poultry, livestock; dairying); mfg. (textiles, apparel, fixtures, transportation equip.). Yadkin and Rocky rivers join 5 mi/8 km to SE to form Pee Dee (or Great Pee Dee) R. Settled c.1800; inc. 1882.

Norwood, village (1991 pop. 1,441), S Ont., Canada, on Ouse R., and 22 mi/35 km E of Peterborough; 44°23′N 77°59′W. Dairying, feed milling, woodworking.

Norwood 1 village (1990 pop. 429), San Miguel co., SW Colo., near San Miguel R., 30 mi/48 km NW of Telluride; 38°07′N 108°17′W. Elev. 7,014 ft/2,138 m. In diversified farming area; wheat, corn; cattle, sheep. San Miguel Mts. just S. Parts of Uncompahgre Natl. Forest to S and NE; Miramoric State Wildlife Area to S. **2** village (1990 pop. 495), Peoria co., central Ill., residential suburb 5 mi/8 km W of downtown Peoria; 40°42′N 89°42′W. Greater Peoria Airport to S. Wildlife Prairie Park to W. **3** village (1994 pop. 527), East Feliciana parish, SE central La., near Miss. state line to N, 35 mi/56 km N of Baton Rouge; 30°58′N 91°07′W. Light mfg. **4** village (□ 2 sq mi/5.2 sq km; 1990 pop. 1,841), St. Lawrence co., N N.Y., on Raquette R., and 13 mi/21 km SSW of Massena; 44°45′N 75°00′W. Originally an Adirondack–St. Lawrence Valley RR center and industrial village, but now it is purely a residential community. Inc. 1871.

Norwood 1 borough (1990 pop. 4,858), Bergen co., extreme NE N.J., 12 mi/19 km NE of Paterson, near N.Y. state line; 40°59′N 73°57′W. Largely residential. Inc. 1905. **2** borough (1990 pop. 6,162), Delaware co., SE Pa., residential suburb 9 mi/14.5 km SW of downtown Philadelphia, on Darby Creek; 39°53′N 75°17′W. Inc. 1893.

Norwood Court, town (1990 pop. 888), St. Louis co., E Mo., residential suburb 8 mi/12.9 km NW of downtown St. Louis, adjacent to Normandy; 38°43′N 90°17′W.

Norwoodville, uninc. village, Polk co., central Iowa, suburb 5 mi/8 km NW of downtown Des Moines, in residential area.

Norwottock, Mount, Mass.: see HOLYOKE RANGE.

Notasulga (nah-tuh-SUL-ga), town (1990 pop. 979), Lee and Macon cos., E Ala., 10 mi/16 km N of Tuskegee. Lumber.

Notre Dame, Ind.: see SOUTH BEND.

Notre Dame Bay, arm of the Atlantic Ocean, c.40 mi/60 km long and 50 mi/80 km wide, E N.F., Canada. The Exploit R. empties into it. The bay has an irregular shoreline and contains many isls.; Fogo Isl. is E of the bay. There are numerous fishing settlements along the coast; Botwood is the chief town and port.

Notre Dame de Portneuf, Canada: see PORTNEUF.

Notre Dame du Lac, town (1991 pop. 2,133), SE Que., Canada, on L. Temiscouata, 40 mi/64 km ESE of Rivière du Loup; ⊙ Temiscouata co.; 47°36′N 68°48′W. Dairying, lumbering.

Notre Dame Mountains (NO-tri DAIM), sect. of the Appalachian system, extending c.500 mi/805 km from the Green Mts. of Vt. into the Gaspé Peninsula, Canada. Worn low by erosion, the anc. mts. have an average elev. of c.2,000 ft/610 m.

Notre-Dame, village, E N.B., Canada, on Cocagne R., and 16 mi/26 km N of Moncton; 46°18′N 64°43′W. Mixed farming.

Notrees (NO-treez), uninc. village (1990 pop. 338), Ector co., W Texas, 23 mi/37 km WNW of Odessa. Agr. area (cattle, horses; pecans). Oil and natural gas.

Nottawa (NAH-tuh-wuh), village, S Ont., Canada, 3 mi/5 km S of Collingwood. Dairying, mixed farming.

Nottawasaga River (nah-tuh-wuh-SO-guh), 60 mi/97 km long, S Ont., Canada; rises NNE of Toronto, flows N of Nottawasaga Bay, S arm of Georgian Bay, 11 mi/18 km ENE of Collingwood.

Nottaway (NAHT-uh-WAI), river, c.140 mi/230 km long; issuing from Mattagami L., W Que., Canada; flows NW into S James Bay. The Waswanipi R. (c.195 mi/310 km long) is its chief headstream.

Nottely River (NAHT-lee), c.40 mi/64 km long, in N Ga. and W N.C.; rises in Blue Ridge Mts. 17 mi/27 km NE of Dahlonega; flows NW into Cherokee co., N.C., then NE to Hiwassee Reservoir (in Hiwassee R.) near Murphy; 34°45′N 83°50′W. Nottely Dam, in Ga., 9 mi/14.5 km NW of Blairsville, is major TVA dam (184 ft/56 m high, 2,300 ft/701 m long) completed 1942; used for flood control. Forms Nottely Reservoir (□ 6.7 sq mi/17.4 sq km; 20 mi/32 km long, 1 mi/1.6 km–3 mi/4.8 km wide; capacity 184,400 acre-ft.) in Union co., Ga.

Nottingham (NAW-deeng-ham), town (1990 pop. 2,939), Rockingham co., SE N.H., 14 mi/23 km SW of Dover; 43°07′N 71°07′W. Drained by Pawtuckaway R. (flows out of Pawtuckaway L. in S), North R., and Black Creek. Agr. (cattle, poultry; vegetables; dairying; timber); mfg. (plastic prods., lumber, fabricated metal prods.). Part of Pawtuckaway State Park in SW.

Nottingham (NAH-ting-ham), uninc. village, Chester co., SE Pa., 5 mi/8 km SW of Oxford near Md. state line; 39°45′N 76°00′W. Mfg. of food prods.; agr. includes dairying, livestock, poultry; grain, mushrooms. Nottingham Park to S.

Nottingham Island (□ 441 sq mi/1,142 sq km), SE Franklin dist., N.W.T., Canada, in Hudson Strait, bet. Ungava Peninsula (S) and Southampton Isl. (WNW); 38 mi/61 km long, 11 mi/18 km–22 mi/35 km wide; 63°20′N 78°00′W.

Nottoway (NAWT-uh-wai), county (□ 316 sq mi/818 sq km; 1990 pop. 14,993), central Va.; ⊙ Nottoway Court House; 37°08′N 78°02′W. Bounded S by Nottoway R.; source of Stony Creek in SE. Mfg. at Blackstone; agr. (mainly tobacco; also fruit, hay, barley, wheat, corn, soybeans; cattle, sheep, poultry; dairying); timber; granite quarrying. Part of Fort Pickett Military Reservation in SE. Formed 1788.

Nottoway Court House, uninc. village, central Va., 37 mi/60 km WSW of Petersburg, Lake Nottoway to NE; ⊙ Nottoway co. Agr. (tobacco, grain; livestock; dairying). Nottoway Correctional Center. Also called Nottoway.

Nottoway River, c.170 mi/274 km long, S Va.; rises in S Prince Edward co., c.7 mi ENE of Keysville flows generally SE past Courtland; joins Blackwater R. 9 mi/14.5 km S of Franklin, at N.C. state line to form Chowan R.; 37°06′N 78°19′W.

Notus, village (1990 pop. 380), Canyon co., SW Idaho, 8 mi/12.9 km NW of Caldwell, and on Boise R.; 43°44′N 116°48′W. In dairying and agr. area served by Boise irrigation project.

Nouveau Québec, Canada: see UNGAVA.

Nova Scotia (NO-vuh SKO-shuh) [Lat. = new Scotland], province (□ 21,425 sq mi/55,491 sq km; 1991 pop. 899,942), E Canada; ⊙ HALIFAX; 45°00′N 63°00′W. One of the Maritime Provs., it comprises a mainland peninsula and the adjacent Cape Breton Isl. In addition to Halifax, important cities are DARTMOUTH, SYDNEY, GLACE BAY, TRURO, and NEW GLASGOW. N.S. is bounded on the N by the Gulf of St. Lawrence, on the E and S by the Atlantic Ocean, and on the W by N.B., from which it is largely separated by the Bay of Fundy. The climate is moderate and the rainfall abundant. The E coast is rocky, with numerous bays and coves, and is dotted with many charming fishing villages. Off the beautiful S shore is Sable Isl., called the graveyard of the Atlantic; on the W coast huge Fundy tides wash the shores. There is considerable mining activity in N.S. Coal is mined principally in the Sydney–Glace Bay area of Cape Breton Isl. Gypsum, barite, and salt are also

mined. Fishing is more important than mining to N.S. Fleets operate on the continental shelf edging the coast and also move out to the Grand Banks. Cod fishing has been curtailed in recent years, but lobster, scallops, and haddock continue to be important. Inland, the forests yield spruce lumber, and the prov.'s industries produce much pulp and paper. In the NW there is dairying, the most important sector of N.S.'s agr. economy, and the region of Annapolis and Cornwallis supports valuable apple orchards. There are also important hay, grain, fruit, and vegetable crops. The bay lowlands, reclaimed by dikes in the 17th cent., are very productive. Mfg. is the largest production sector of N.S.'s economy. In addition to the iron and steel produced at Sydney, the prov.'s mfg. includes processed food (esp. fish), motor vehicles, tires, sugar, and construction materials. In addition to its all-year port facilities, Halifax is a RR terminus. The rivers of N.S. have a number of small hydroelectric stations that help support the economy. The charms of the rural and coastal countryside and an abundance of historical sites attract over 1 million tourists per year. Frequently visited historical spots include the Alexander Graham Bell Mus. at Baddeck, the Shrine of Evangeline at Grand Pré, and the town of Annapolis Royal, site of the 1st permanent Can. settlement (1610). Cape Breton Isl. (est. 1936) and Kejimkujik (est. 1968) natl. parks are in N.S. Sportsmen are attracted by abundant game and all types of fishing, and some of the best sailing on the continent. Two Algonquian tribes, the Abnaki and the Micmac, inhabited the area before Europeans arrived. John Cabot may have landed (1497) on the tip of Cape Breton Isl.; Eur. fishermen were already making regular stops during their yearly expeditions. An unsuccessful Fr. settlement was made in 1605 at Port Royal (now Annapolis Royal). In 1610 the French succeeded at the same site. For the next 150 years France and England contested bitterly for colonial rights to ACADIA, which included present-day N.S., N.B., and P.E.I. In 1621 Sir William Alexander obtained a patent from James I for the colonization of Acadia. Control alternated bet. France and England through several wars and treaties. Under the Peace of Utrecht (1713–1714), the N.S. peninsula was restored to England, although Cape Breton Isl. was retained by the French. Hostilities were renewed in 1744. During the Fr. and Indian War (1755–1763), a tragic incident was the expulsion of the Fr. Acadians — described by Longfellow in *Evangeline*. The Treaty of Paris (1763) gave all of Fr. N. Amer. to England. P.E.I., joined to N.S. in 1763, became separate in 1769. With the influx (c.1784) of United Empire Loyalists, additional settlement occurred. In 1784 N.B. and Cape Breton also became separate colonies; Cape Breton rejoined N.S. in 1820. During the early 19th cent. thousands of Scots and Irish emigrated to N.S. Under the leadership of Joseph Howe, N.S. became the 1st colony to achieve (1848) responsible (or cabinet) govt. It acceded to the Can. confederation as 1 of the 4 original members in 1867 after considerable difficulty over economic arrangements. In recent years N.S. has struggled to stabilize its economy. Federal govt. programs to develop secondary industries or to discover offshore oil or natural-gas deposits have been largely unsuccessful. The prov. sends 10 senators and 11 representatives to the natl. parliament. N.S. has pioneered in Can. history with the 1st newspaper (*Halifax Gazette*, 1752), the 1st printing press (1751), and the 1st univ. (King's Col., Windsor, 1788–1789). Additional educational institutions include Dalhousie Univ., St. Francis Xavier Univ., Saint Mary's, Mount Saint Vincent, Univ. Col. of Cape Breton, Sainte-Anne Univ., and the Technical Univ. of N.S.

Novar (NO-vahr), village, S Ont., Canada, 40 mi/64 km E of Parry Sound; 45°27′N 79°15′W. Diatomite mining.

Novato, city (1990 pop. 47,585), Marin co., W Calif., suburb 24 mi/39 km NNW of downtown San Francisco, on Novata Creek, 4 mi/6.4 km W of San Pablo Bay; 38°05′N 122°34′W. Dairying; poultry, lambs; fruit, nuts. Mfg. (cosmetics, fabricated metal prods., telephone apparatus, lumber, wiring devices). Its pop. has increased along with the economic development of N Calif. Hamilton Air Force Base to SE, a major West Coast installation, is situated in Novato, and the co. airport is just N of the city. City is surrounded by dairy farming. Annual celebration called Western Weekend is here. Petaluma Adobe State Historical Park to NE; Point Reyes Natl. Seashore, on Pacific Ocean, to SW. Inc. 1960.

Novelty, town (1990 pop. 143), Knox co., NE Mo., on North R., and 11 mi/18 km S of Edina; 40°00′N 92°12′W. Lumber.

Novi (NO-vee), city (1990 pop. 32,998), Oakland co., SE Mich., 24 mi/39 km WNW of downtown Detroit and 13 mi/21 km SW of Pontiac; 42°28′N 83°29′W. Drained in SE by Ingersoll Creek. Heavy mfg. Walled L. in N. Maybury State Park to SW (Wayne co.). Oakland Southwest Airport to NW. Borders Wayne co. on S.

Novice, village (1990 pop. 183), Coleman co., central Texas, 15 mi/24 km NW of Coleman; 31°59′N 99°37′W. Agr. area. L. Coleman reservoir to NE.

Novinger (NAH-vin-juhr), city (1990 pop. 542), Adair co., N Mo., on Chariton R., and 6 mi/9.7 km W of Kirksville; 40°13′N 92°42′W. Corn, soybeans; cattle, hogs, poultry. Settled 1830s; platted 1888. Former coal-mining town; pop. peaked c.1900 at c.5,000 inhabitants.

Nowata, county (☐ 580 sq mi/1,502 sq km; 1990 pop. 9,992), NE Okla.; ⊙ Nowata; 36°47′N 95°37′W. Bounded N by Kansas state line; drained by Verdigris R. Cattle; agr. (corn, wheat, oats, sorghum). Oil and natural-gas fields, limestone quarries; refineries. Mfg. at Nowata. Timber. Part of Oolagah L. in SE. Formed 1907.

Nowata (no-WAH-tuh), town (1990 pop. 3,896), ⊙ Nowata co., NE Okla., 20 mi/32 km E of Bartlesville; 36°42′N 95°38′W. Elev. 708 ft/216 m. In agr. and oil- and natural gas–producing area; mfg. (metal industries, lithographic printing; crushed limestone); timber. N end of Oologah L. reservoir (Verdigris R.) to SE. Has co. historical mus. Settled 1888, inc. 1895.

Nowitna River, 250 mi/402 km long, SW Alaska; rises N of upper Kuskokwim R., near 63°26′N 155°2′W; flows in a winding course generally N to Yukon R. at 64°56′N 154°20′W.

Noxapater (nahks-uh-PAI-tuhr), village (1990 pop. 441), Winston co., E central Miss., 9 mi/14.5 km S of Louisville; 32°59′N 89°03′W. Agr. (cotton, corn; poultry, cattle; dairying); mfg. (gloves, furniture, cabinets). Nanih Waiya Historical Site, Choctaw burial mounds, to SE.

Noxen, uninc. village, Noxen township, Wyoming co., NE Pa., 21 mi/34 km W of Scranton, on Bowman Creek; 41°25′N 76°03′W.

Noxon (NAHKS-uhn), village (1990 pop. 270), Sanders co., NW Mont., 37 mi/60 km NW of Thompson Falls, on the Clark Fork R., at upstream (SE) end of Cabinet Gorge Reservoir, near Idaho line. RR. Trapping; mining; logging; berries; hay; livestock. Noxon Rapids Dam (Noxon Reservoir), 3 mi/4.8 km SE on Clark Fork. Area surrounded by Kaniksu Natl. Forest; Cabinet Mts. Wilderness Area to E.

Noxon Reservoir (NAHKS-uhn), Sanders co., NW Mont., on Clark Fork river, 30 mi/48 km SSW of Libby, near Idaho state line; c.30 mi/48 km long; 47°57′N 115°57′W. Max. capacity 800,000 acre-ft. Formed by Noxon Rapids Dam (gravity and earth; 176 ft/54 m high), built (1960) by the Wash. Power Company for power generation, flood control, and irrigation.

Noxubee (NAHKS-uh-bee), county (☐ 700 sq mi/1,813 sq km; 1990 pop. 12,604), E Miss., bordering E on Ala.; ⊙ Macon; 33°06′N 88°34′W. Drained by Noxubee R. Agr. (cotton, corn, wheat, soybeans; cattle; dairying); timber. Part of Aliceville L. reservoir on NE, on W boundary; part of Noxubee Natl. Wildlife Refuge in NW corner. Formed 1833.

Noxubee River (NAHKS-uh-bee), c.140 mi/225 km long, in E Miss. and W Ala.; rises in SE Choctaw co., E central Miss.; flows first E through Tombigbee Natl. Forest (Choctaw Unit) and Noxubee Natl. Wildlife Refuge,

then SE, past Macon, into Sumter co., Ala.; enters Tombigbee R. near Gainesville.

Noyack Bay, inlet indenting N shore of S peninsula of L.I., SE N.Y., c.1 mi/1.6 km W of Sag Harbor; c.2 mi/3.2 km in diameter; 41°01′N 72°20′W. In summer-resort area; yachting; fishing.

Noyes (NOIZ), village, Kittson co., extreme NW Minn., port of entry on Can. (Man.) border, 20 mi/32 km NW of Hallock, 2 mi/3.2 km NNE of St. Vincent, and 1 mi/1.6 km E of Red R. (N.Dak. state line); 48°59′N 97°12′W.

Noyo, uninc. village, Mendocino co., NW Calif., on the Pacific Ocean, 35 mi/56 km NW of Ukiah, 2 mi/3.2 km S of Fort Bragg and mouth of Noyo R. Fruit; nursery stock, timber; fish, urchins.

Noyo River, c.30 mi/48 km long, NW Calif.; rises in central Mendocino co., 18 mi/29 km N of Ukiah, in Coast Ranges; flows W to the Pacific at Fort Bragg.

Nuangola (NOO-an-GO-lah), borough (1990 pop. 701), Luzerne co., NE central Pa., 7 mi/11.3 km SW of Wilkes-Barre, on Nuangola L. reservoir; 41°09′N 75°58′W.

Nuchek, Indian fishing village, S Alaska, on W coast of Hinchinbrook Isl., 35 mi/56 km WSW of Cordova. A 19th-cent. Rus. and Amer. trading post.

Nuckolls, county (☐ 576 sq mi/1,492 sq km; 1990 pop. 5,786), S Nebr.; ⊙ Nelson; 40°10′N 98°02′W. Agr. region bounded S by Kansas; drained by Republican and Little Blue rivers. Cattle; dairying; hogs, corn, wheat, sorghum. Historic Oregon Trail in NE. Formed 1871.

Nucla, village (1990 pop. 656), Montrose co., SW Colo., near San Miguel R., 39 mi/63 km WSW of Montrose; 38°16′N 108°32′W. Elev. 5,862 ft/1,787 m. In irrigated cattle, sheep, fruit, and vegetable area. Nearby deposits of carnotite yield vanadium and uranium. Coal. Uncompahgre Natl. Forest to NE.

Nueces (NOO-ai-sis), county (☐ 1,166 sq mi/3,020 sq km; 1990 pop. 291,145), S Texas; ⊙ CORPUS CHRISTI; 27°44′N 97°31′W. Deepwater port, industrial, commercial center. On Gulf plains; bounded E by Gulf of Mexico, N by Nueces R. and Nueces, and E by Corpus Christi Bay; Laguna Madre separates Mustang and Padre Isls. from mainland. A leading Texas oil and natural gas-producing co.; also lime, sand, and gravel; diversified irrigated agr. (cotton, grain sorghum, corn, wheat; some citrus); cattle. Resort beaches; fishing. Oil refining, diversified mfg. (esp. chemicals) centered in city of Corpus Christi, also processing of farm prods., seafood. Mustang Isl. State Park on Gulf Coast in E; part of Laguna Largo, inland lake, in SE; S fringe of King Ranch. Formed 1846.

Nueces Bay, Texas: see CORPUS CHRISTI BAY.

Nueces River (NOO-ai-sis), 315 mi/507 km long, Texas; rises on Edwards Plateau in Real co.; flows generally S past Crystal City then SE past Cotulla, NE to Three Rivers, then again SE to Nueces Bay, a NW arm of Corpus Christi Bay. Receives Frio R. at Three Rivers (Atascosa R. enters Frio 5 mi/8 km N). Dam 32 mi/51 km WNW of Corpus Christi impounds L. Corpus Christi. West Nueces R. rises in N Edwards co., flows S and SE c.85 mi/137 km to Nueces R., 10 mi/16 km NW of Uvalde.

Nueltin Lake (noo-EHL-tin) (☐ 336 sq mi/870 sq km), S Keewatin dist., N.W.T., and NW Man., Canada, W of Hudson Bay; 85 mi/137 km long, 3 mi/5 km–19 mi/31 km wide; 60°N 100°W. Drained NE by Thlewiaza R. into Hudson Bay.

Nuervo, uninc. town (1990 pop. 3,010), Riverside co., S Calif., 18 mi/29 km SE of Riverside, S of Colorado R. Aqueduct, on San Jacinto R.

Nuestra Senora de la Soledad, Mission, Calif.: see SOLEDAD.

Nueva Ciudad Guerrero, city (1990 pop. 4,182) and township, ⊙ Guerrero municipio, Tamaulipas, N Mexico, near Falcón Dam on Rio Grande (Texas border), and 50 mi/80 km SSE of Nuevo Laredo, on Mexico Highway 26°49′N 99°20′W. Agr. center (cotton, sugarcane, corn; cattle).

Nueva Galicia, Span. colonial administrative region, W Mexico, comprising roughly the present states of Jalisco and Nayarit with S Sinaloa. Conquered (1529–1531) by

Nuño de Guzmán and later governed by Francisco Vásquez de Coronado, the territory was the scene of the Mixtón War in 1541. In 1548 it was given its own audiencia at Guadalajara. Nominally subject to the viceroy of New Spain, it was essentially a separate administration controlled from Spain, and it came to be known after the creation (1563) of a presidential office of its own as the presidency of Nueva Galicia. Its independent character, however, declined as colonial-era authority was more and more centralized in Mexico city.

Nueva Gerona (NWAI-vah hai-RON-uh), principal town of Isla de la Juventud, SW Cuba, on small Las Casas R., and 90 mi/145 km SSW of Havana; 21°53′N 82°49′W. Resort, trading, and agr. center (citrus fruit, tobacco, potatoes, winter vegetables). Served by airline and linked through nearby landing (N) with Surgidero de Batabanó on main isl. A clean town of modern character with a customhouse and industrial art center. Fine beaches (fishing, bathing) and caves in picturesque surrounding region. Presidio Modelo penitentiary is 2 mi/3.2 km E. Marble, copper, iron, and gold deposits in vicinity.

Nueva Italia de Ruíz (NWAI-vah ee-TAH-lee-ah dai roo-EEZ), town (1990 pop. 27,008), ⊙ Múgica municipio, Michoacán, W Mexico, 35 mi/56 km SSW of Uruapan on Mexico Highway 37; 19°01′N 102°06′W. Cereals, rice, sugar, fruit.

Nueva Paz (NWAI-vah PAHZ), town, La Habana prov., W Cuba, 45 mi/72 km SE of Havana, on major highway; 22°46′N 81°45′W. Rice, sugarcane, vegetables, cattle. Rice mills. Manuel Isla sugar mill 4 mi/6.4 km NNE.

Nueva Rosita (NWAI-vah ro-SEE-tah), mining city (1990 pop. 36,284) and township, ⊙ San Juan de Sabinas municipio, Coahuila, N Mexico, in semiarid country, in Sabinas coal dist., 170 mi/274 km NW of Monterreyon Mexico Highway 53; 27°55′N 101°17′W. Elev. 1,411 ft/430 m. Connected by RR with Saltillo, Monterrey, Piedras Negras. Developed as prominent industrial city of N Mexico in 1930s. Coal mining; zinc smelter; mfg. (zinc sulfate and sulfuric acid). Sometimes called simply Rosita.

Nueva Villa de Padilla (NWAI-vah VEE-yah dai pah-DEE-yah), town (1990 pop. 5,164), ⊙ Padilla municipio, Tamaulipas, NE Mexico, 32 mi/51 km NE of Ciudad Victoria, on Mexico Highway 101; 24°00′N 98°47′W. Cereals, sugarcane, fruit; livestock.

Nueva Vizcaya, Mexico: see DURANGO.

Nuevas Grandes (NWAI-vahs GRAHN-dais), narrow inlet off N coast of Cuba, on Las Tunas–Camagüey prov. border, 20 mi/32 km ESE of Nuevitas; 8 mi/12.9 km long; 21°23′N 77°00′W. Receives small Cabreras R.

Nuevitas (nwai-VEE-tahs), city (1995 est. pop. 52,000), Camagüey prov., E Cuba, on the Guincho peninsula on the N coast; 21°33′N 75°17′W. Once the largest world port for sugar shipping, its salience declined in 1970s because of growth elsewhere. Nuevitas is sheltered by a huge harbor with an entrance through a twisted, rocky channel, has 2 auxiliary ports, and remains a major shipping point for Cuban sugar as well as other prods. from the surrounding agr. region. Ports handle about 6% of total sugar exports, serving 5 sugar mills from Camagüey and Ciego de Avila provs., and have cargo facilities for bulk grain handling. Thermoelectric plant, 10 de Octubre, has 442 MW capacity. Fertilizer and cement plants nearby. It is connected to Camagüey city by RR and a 2-lane highway. The large bay was sighted by Columbus in 1492. Founded in 1775, the city was moved to its present site in 1828.

Nuevo Casas Grandes (NWAI-vo KAH-sahs GRAHN-des), city (1990 pop. 44,087) and township, Chihuahua, N Mexico, on arid plateau, on Casas Grandes R. (irrigation), and 130 mi/209 km SW of Ciudad Juárez; 30°24′N 107°55′W. Elev. 4,833 ft/1,473 m. RR junction; agr. center (cotton, corn, beans, tobacco; cattle); tanning, flour milling, lumbering.

Cross references are shown in SMALL CAPITALS. The pronunciation key is on page xv. The dates of population figures are on page xii.

Nuevo Coahuayana, Mexico: see COAHUAYANA DE HI-
DALGO.

Nuevo Ideal (NWAI-vo ee-dai-AHL), city (1990 pop.
8,583), in central Durango, Mexico, 37 mi/60 km N of
Victoria de Durango; 24°53′N 105°02′W.

Nuevo Laredo (NWAI-vo lah-RAI-do), city (1990 pop.
218,413) and township, Nuevo Laredo municipio, Tamaulipas state, NE Mexico, across the Rio Grande from
Laredo, Texas; 27°30′N 99°31′W. Linked with the U.S.
by road and RR bridges, Nuevo Laredo is the N terminus of the natl. RR and the Inter-Amer. Highway, as
well as an important point of entry for U.S. tourists
driving to Mexico. It is also a center of internatl. trade
and the distribution point for an agr. (mainly cotton)
and livestock-raising area; commerce; tourism industry. Nuevo Laredo has been one of the many Mex. cities
affected by an influx of foreign capital, primarily due
to the establishment of foreign-owned industrial
plants, known as maquiladoras. Has developed into a
transportation–trans-shipment center since NAFTA
(1993). Founded in 1755, the city was part of Laredo
until the end of the Mex.-Amer. War in 1848. Nuevo
Laredo played a role in the Mex. revolution of 1910 and
was burned extensively in 1914.

Nuevo León (NWAI-vo lai-ON), state (□ 25,136 sq mi/
65,102 sq km; 1990 pop. 3,098,736), N Mexico; ☉ MON-
TERREY; 21°10′N 98°27′W. The S and W parts of the
state are traversed by the Sierra Madre Oriental, but
some of the extreme W portions lie within the vast,
semiarid basin lands of N Mexico, which are cultivable
under irrigation. Much of the N is arid, but to the E,
where the plains sweep down toward the lowlands of
Tamaulipas and are crossed by several large rivers, the
land is suitable for rain-fed agr. Grains and citrus fruits
are grown. Nuevo León has an extremely diversified
industrial structure which includes oil refining and extensive heavy and light mfg. The growth of maquiladoras, foreign-owned industrial plants that produce
goods for export to the U.S., has become important.
The area is also a leading natl. producer of iron, steel,
and chemicals. Road and RR connections within the
state are excellent, and Nuevo León enjoys one of the
highest living standards in Mexico. The area was explored and settled by the Spanish in the late 16th cent.
Nuevo León became a state in 1824.

Nuevo Morelos (NWAI-vo mo-RAI-los), town (1990
pop. 1,628), Tamaulipas, in E foothills of
Sierra Madre Oriental, 90 mi/145 km WNW of Tampico on Mexico Highway 80; 22°34′N 99°17′W. Agave,
fruit; livestock.

Nuevo Necaxa (NWAI-vo nai-KA-shah), town (1990
pop. 6,028), ☉ Juan Galindo municipio, Puebla, central
Mexico, in Sierra Madre Oriental, on Necaxa R., and
4 mi/6.4 km NE of Huauchinango. Sugarcane, coffee,
fruit. Hydroelectric plant, on Necaxa Falls (c.540 ft/
165 m high) nearby, supplies Mexico city. Sometimes
called Necaxa.

Nuevo Parangaricutiro, Mexico: see NUEVO SAN JUAN
PARANGARICUTIRO.

Nuevo, Río (NWAI-vo, REE-o) or **González River**,
c.75 mi/121 km long, Tabasco, SE Mexico, slough draining a portion of lower Grijalua, river marshes; formed
7 mi/11.3 km ENE of Cárdenas; flows E, N, and NW, to
Gulf of Campeche 6 mi/9.7 km ENE of Paraíso.

Nuevo San Juan Parangaricutiro (NWAI-vo sahn
hwahn pah-rahn-gah-ree-koo-TEE-ro), town (1990
pop. 9,765), ☉ Nuevo Parangaricutiro municipio, Michoacán, central Mexico, in Sierra de los Tarascos,
20 mi/32 km WNW of Uruapan; 19°24′N 102°08′W.
Elev. 7,415 ft/2,260 m. In agr. area. After eruption (1943)
of Parícutin volcano, 5 mi/8 km SSW, original town
was largely engulfed by lava flow, residents moved to
new site.

Nuevo Santo Tomás de los Plátanos (NWAI-vo
SAHN-to to-MAHS dai los PLAH-tah-nos), town
(1990 pop. 2,872), Mexico state, central Mexico, on Michoacán border, 40 mi/64 km WSW of Toluca de
Lerdo; 19°09′N 100°12′W. Sugarcane, fruit, corn.

Nuevo Soyaltepec (NWAI-vo so-YAHL-tai-pek), town
(1990 pop. 5,878), N Oaxaca, Mexico, 23 mi/37 km NW
of Tuxtepec, near Presidente Aleman Damand within
Temascal L. Natural Park. Elev. 1,640 ft/500 m. Hot
climate. Agr. (corn, beans, coffee, sugarcane, tropical
fruits); wood. Temascal hydroelectric plant (generating
capacity 154,080 kw) at Temascal Dam. Former town
name is Temascal. A Mazatec-speaking community.

Nuevo Urecho (noo-E-vo oo-RE-cho), town (1990 pop.
1,182), Michoacán, central Mexico, 22 mi/35 km SSE of
Uruapan. Fruit, cereals. Near RR, poor roads.

Nuevo Zoquiapam (NWAI-vo zo-kee-AH-pahm), town
(1990 pop. 1,400), central Oaxaca, Mexico, 16 mi/26 km
NE of Oaxaca de Juárez; 17°18′N 96°36′W. Mountainous terrain in the sierra of Ixtlán on a tributary of the
Río Grande. Temperate climate although there is a
slight variation from the E to the W. Farming (corn,
beans; livestock), Zapotec Indian community. Also
Santiago Zoquiápam.

Nugammute, Alaska: see NOGAMUT.

Nuka Bay, S Alaska, on SE coast of Kenai Peninsula,
opens into Gulf of Alaska; 20 mi/32 km long, 1 mi/
1.6 km–7 mi/11.3 km wide; 59°23′N 150°31′W.

Nuka Island, S Alaska, in Gulf of Alaska, off SE Kenai
Peninsula, 65 mi/105 km SW of Seward; 8 mi/12.9 km
long, 3 mi/4.8 km wide; 59°22′N 150°41′W. Entire isl.
used as fox farm.

Nulato (noo-LAH-do), Indian village (1990 pop. 359), on
W bank of Yukon R., W Alaska, 200 mi/322 km E of
Nome; 64°43′N 158°07′W. Airfield. Rus. blockhouse
built here 1838.

Nulhegan River (NUHL-i-gin), c.15 mi/24 km long, NE
Vt.; rises in Averil; flows E to the Connecticut at
Bloomfield.

Numa, town (1990 pop. 151), Appanoose co., S Iowa,
6 mi/9.7 km WSW of Centerville; 40°41′N 92°58′W.

Numarán (noo-mah-RAHN), town (1990 pop. 4,236),
Michoacán, central Mexico, on Lerma R., and 7 mi/
11.3 km SE of La Piedad de Cabadas; 20°15′N 101°56′W.
Cereals, fruit; livestock.

Nunachuak (noo-NAH-choo-wak), village, SW Alaska,
on Nushagak R., and 60 mi/97 km NE of Dillingham.

Nunapitchuk, village (1990 pop. 378), SW Alaska, 30 mi/
48 km SW of Bethel, near Kuskokwim R.; 60°30′N
162°25′W.

Nunavik, region, N Que., Canada, also includes N tip of
Lab. N of Ramah, and N.W.T. isls. of Killiniq and Ak-
patok (Ungava Bay), Salisbury and Nottingham (Hud-
son Strait), Mansel, Ottawa, Smith, and Gilmour
(Hudson Bay), North Twin and South Twin (James
Bay). The Que. portion includes land N of 56°30′N,
including land around Ungava Bay and all of Ungava
Peninsula; also Hudson Bay and James Bay shore lands
S to 53°N. Includes 14 coastal Inuit villages and the
Cree. Inuit village of Chisasibi, at mouth of La Grande
R. Name means "great land" in Inuit. Not a political
unit, the affairs and services of region are operated by
an Inuit corporation which draws much of its income
from agreements over the use of lands to SE of region
for the James Bay Hydroelectric Project. The corporation operates Air Inuit, which serves region and adjacent areas.

Nunavut, territory, NE Canada, created by a plebiscite
on May 4, 1992, the electorate of the N.W.T. approved
a boundary that would divide the territory along a zigzag line running from the Sask.-Man. border almost to
the North Pole. The estimated area (1992) was
772,260 sq mi/2,000,671 sq km. The new territory of
Nunavut, which will constitute the E portion of the
current N.W.T., will have a W boundary that runs N
to the Thelon R., W to just above the Great Bear L.,
and then N again to bisect Victoria and Melville isls.
The federal govt. anticipates that the new territorial
govt. will come into force no later than April 1, 1999.
The territory, Canada's 3d after the YUKON and the remaining N.W.T., will effectively be controlled by the
Inuit, who, with 17,500 people, make up the majority
of the area's pop. The region will include the isls. of
Ellesmere, Baffin, Devon, Prince of Wales, Southampton, and Coats, among others. The largest town in the
territory is IQALUIT (1991 pop. 3,552) on Baffin Isl. at
Frobisher Bay. Most of the richest and most well-de-
veloped parts of the current N.W.T., which lie along
the Mackenzie R., will not be included in Nunavut. The
new territory will have to rely on the development of
its mineral resources, in addition to hunting, fishing,
fur trapping, sealing, and the production of arts and
crafts, in order to establish its economic base. As a
result of their land claim with the federal govt., the
Inuit will hold outright title to about 20% of Nunavut,
including 13,896 sq mi/36,000 sq km of subsurface mineral rights. In the Inuit language, Nunavut means "our
land."

Nunda 1 (nun-DAI), village (1990 pop. 1,347), Livingston
co., W central N.Y., 23 mi/37 km NW of Hornell;
42°34′N 77°56′W. Mfg. (canned foods, dairy prods.,
machinery); agr. (poultry; grain). Letchworth State
Park along Genesee R. is NW. Inc. 1839. **2** village (1990
pop. 45), Lake co., E S.Dak., 12 mi/19 km NNE of Madison; 44°09′N 97°01′W.

Nunez (noo-NEZ), town (1990 pop. 135), Emanuel co.,
E central Ga., 7 mi/11.3 km S of Swainsboro; 32°29′N
82°21′W.

Nunivak, island (□ c.1,700 sq mi/4,400 sq km), off W
Alaska, in the Bering Sea. It is the 2d-largest isl. in the
Bering Sea. Fogbound most of the year, Nunivak is
covered with low vegetation and has a small Inuit pop.
engaged in hunting and fishing. Reindeer and musk
oxen have been introduced as part of a natl. wildlife
refuge here.

Nunn, village (1990 pop. 324), Weld co., N Colo., 20 mi/
32 km N of Greeley; near Lone Tree Creek; 40°42′N
104°46′W. Elev. 5,186 ft/1,581 m. Farm center in cattle-
grazing area, also wheat, corn, sugar beets, sunflowers.
Pawnee Natl. Grassland to E.

Nun's Island, S Que., Canada, in the St. Lawrence, opposite Montreal, near the Lachine Rapids; 2 mi/3 km
long, 1 mi/2 km wide.

Nushagak, village, SW Alaska, on Nushagak Bay, inlet
of Bristol Bay, 8 mi/12.9 km S of Dillingham. Fishing;
cannery.

Nushagak Bay, SW Alaska, on N shore of Bristol Bay;
50 mi/80 km long, 4 mi/6.4 km–20 mi/32 km wide;
58°37′N 158°31′W. Receives Nushagak R. Fishing and
canning region. Dillingham village, N.

Nushagak River, 280 mi/451 km long, SW Alaska; rises
in Alaska Range near 60°50′N 154°W; flows SW, past
Nunachuak and Ekwok, to Nushagak Bay, inlet of Bristol Bay, just E of Dillingham. Salmon stream. Upper
course called Mulchatna R.

Nutak, abandoned locality, N Lab., Canada, at SE end of
Okak Isl., off Labrador Sea coast. It and village of Okak,
at NW end of isl., were sites of Moravian missions, est.
1830s. Dec. 1918, supply ship *Harmony* brought influ-
enza to area, nearly wiping out Inuit pop.

Nutarawit Lake (noo-tuh-RO-wit) (□ 350 sq mi/
907 sq km), S central Keewatin dist., N.W.T., Canada,
just NW of Yathkyed L.; 62°55′N 98°50′W. Drains SE
into Kazan R. through Yathkyed L.

Nutley, town (1990 pop. 27,099), Essex co., NE N.J., a
residential suburb of Newark, 5 mi/8 km N of Newark,
on the Passaic R.; 40°49′N 74°09′W. Settled 1680, inc.
1902. Pharmaceuticals, dyestuffs, and machinery are
made. After the Civil War the town was a center for
writers and artists. Annie Oakley lived here.

Nutter Fort, town (1990 pop. 1,819), Harrison co., N
W.Va., 2 mi/3.2 km SE of Clarksburg; 39°15′N 80°19′W.
Light mfg. Agr. (corn); cattle; poultry. Settled 1770; inc.
1924.

Nutzotin Mountains (nood-ZO-tin), E Alaska and SW
Yukon, NW extension of St. Elias Mts., bet. Wrangell
Mts. (SW) and upper Tanana R. (NE); extend 75 mi/
121 km bet. upper Nabesna R. (NW) and upper White
R., Yukon (SE); 62°15′N 142°8′W. Rise to c.9,000 ft/
2,743 m; continued NW by Mentasta Mts.

Nuuanu Pali, sheer cliff and mountain pass (1,200 ft/
366 m), Koolau Range, SE Oahu isl., Honolulu co., Hawaii, 5 mi/8 km NE of Honolulu. One of 3 highway
routes bet. Honolulu and E Oahu. State highway 61
Freeway runs through pass and tunnel.

Nyac (NEI-yak), village, W Alaska, 70 mi/113 km ENE of
Bethel.

Nyack (NEI-yak), residential village (□ 1 sq mi/ 2.6 sq km; 1990 pop. 6,558), Rockland co., SE N.Y., on W bank of Tappan Zee (widening of the Hudson R.; bridge), opposite Tarrytown; 41°05′N 73°55′W. Mfg. of clothing, leather goods, optical goods. It was a 19th-cent. health resort, port, and boat-building center. Birthplace of artist Edward Hopper. Hook Mt. Park (□ c.650 acres/263 ha; a sect. of Palisades Interstate Park) is just N. Settled 1684, inc. 1833.

Nye, county (□ 18,159 sq mi/47,032 sq km; 1990 pop. 17,781), S and central Nev.; ⊙ Tonopah; 38°02′N 116°27′W. Mt. region bordering on Calif. on SW: 4 large sects. of Toiyabe Natl. Forest are in N, in Shoshone, Toiyabe, Toquima and Monitor ranges; small part of Toiyabe Natl. Forest in Spring Mts. in far E. Pahute Mesa, Amargosa Desert, and parts of Death Valley Natl. Monument (main part in Calif.) are in S. Mining (silver, gold, clay, magnesium, sand and gravel); cattle, sheep; ranching. Formed 1863. Berlin-Ichthyosaur State Park in NW. Nev. Test Site, and part of large Nellis Air Force Bombing and Gunnery Range in S center. Ash Meadows Wildlife Management Area in S. Natl. Wildhorse Management Area in SE center. Nev.'s only winery at Pahrump, a growing retirement community in extreme SE. Two parts of Humboldt Natl. Forest in NE, in White Pine and Grant ranges. RR Valley and Wayne E. Kirch Wildlife Management Areas in NE. Duckwater Indian Reservation in NE. Lunar Crater in NE center. Largest co. (land area) in Nev., 3d-largest co. in U.S. Drained by Amargosa R. (S), Reese R. (NW), White R. (NE).

Nyssa (NIS-uh), town (1990 pop. 2,629), Malheur co., E Oregon, on Snake R., 5 mi/8 km NNE of mouth of Owyhee R., 8 mi/12.9 km S of Ontario; 43°52′N 117°00′W. Elev. 2,178 ft/664 m. RR junction. Sugar-beet processing. The town is a market for irrigation projects on Owyhee and Boise rivers and for the Vale Irrigation Project. Site of an agr. mus. Owyhee Dam 20 mi/32 km to SW. L. Owyhee State Park to SW. Inc. 1903.

O

O. C. Fisher Lake, reservoir, Tom Green co., W central Texas, on North Concho R., 3 mi/4.8 km W of downtown San Angelo; 5 mi/8 km long; 31°30′N 100°28′W. Max. capacity 696,300 acre-ft. Formed by San Angelo Dam (122 ft/37 m high), built (1952) by the Army Corps of Engineers for water supply and flood control. City parks on S and SW shores.

O. H. Ivie Lake, reservoir (□ 30 sq mi/78 sq km), Coleman, Concho, and Runnels cos., central Texas, on Colorado R., 40 mi/64 km WSW of Brownwood; 31°30′N 99°40′W. Also fed by Concho R. Formed by Simon Freese Stacy Dam (148 ft/45 m high), built (1989) for water supply; also used for recreation.

Oacoma (O-uh-KO-muh), village (1990 pop. 367), Lyman co., S central S.Dak., 4 mi/6.4 km W of Chamberlain, across Missouri R.; 43°47′N 99°22′W. Manganese deposits nearby. Site of Fort Kiowa (1822) to N.

Oahe, Lake (O-AW-hee), reservoir, S.Dak. and N.Dak., on Missouri R., 6 mi/9.7 km N of Pierre (S.Dak.); c.250 mi/402 km long; 44°28′N 100°24′W. Has 3 arms (all in S.Dak.), formed by Cheyenne, Moreau, and Grand rivers. Formed by Oahe Dam (242 ft/74 m high), built (1948–1963) by the Army Corps of Engineers for power generation, flood control, irrigation, and recreation. Cheyenne R. (S.Dak.) and Standing Rock (N.Dak.) Indian reservations on W shore, as is Fort Rice Historic Site (N.Dak.); West Whitlock and Swan Creek state recreation areas (S.Dak.) on E shore.

Oahu (o-AH-hoo), island (□ 593 sq mi/1,536 sq km; 1990 pop. 836,231), 3d-largest and chief isl. of Hawaii, comprising (with offshore isls.) Honolulu co., separated from Kauai isl. (NW) by Kauai Pass, from Molokai isl. (E) by Kaiwi Channel. Oahu is composed of 2 parallel mt. ranges, Waianae (W) and Koolau (E), separated by a broad, rolling plain dissected by deep gorges. Mt. Kaala (4,046 ft/1,233 m) is the isl.'s highest peak. Oahu has no active volcanoes, but there are many extinct craters, among them Diamond Head, Koko Head, and Punchbowl. Pearl Harbor indents the isl.'s S coast. Honolulu, the state capital and the economic center of Hawaii, and capital of Honolulu co., is on the highly urbanized S coast of Oahu. Honolulu is the site of the Univ. of Hawaii (at Manoa), Chaminade Univ., Hawaii Pacific Univ., and Honolulu and Kapiolani community cols. The isl. is an important defense area that includes the hq. of the U.S. Marine Corps Pacific Command and the Pearl Harbor naval base and Hickam Air Force Base. Other military installations include Kaneohe Marine Corps Base (on Mokapu Peninsula), Barbers Point Naval Air Station (SW), Lualualei Naval Reservation (W), Schofield Barracks Military Reservation and Wheeler Army Air Field (center), Kaena Military Reservation (NW). There are many swimming beaches (including Waikiki at Honolulu). Large pineapple plantations persist in central rural areas of the isl., but sugarcane is no longer grown. Dairy farming, fruit, vegetables, and nursery crops and fishing are important activities, but services, tourism and military operations are the principal economic mainstay of Oahu. Honolulu is main mfg. center of Oahu and state; new industrial centers include Aiea, Waipahu, and Kapolei. Urban development has spread W, N and NE from Honolulu; 3 interstate highways extend in these directions. Numerous forest reserves protect mt. areas, including Waianae Kai Forest Reserve (W) and Kahuku, Ewa, Waiahole and Honolulu Watershed (E). Kahana Valley and Sacred Falls state parks and Malaekahana State Recreational Area in NE; Kuaiwa Heiau State Recreational Area in S; Kaena Point State Park in NW; Honolulu Stadium State Park and Diamond Head State Monument at Honolulu.

Oak, village (1990 pop. 68), Nuckolls co., S Nebr., 17 mi/27 km NNE of Superior, and on Little Blue R; 40°14′N 97°54′W.

Oak Bay, SE suburb (1991 pop. 17,815) of Victoria, SW B.C., W Canada, at SE extremity of Vancouver Isl., on Juan de Fuca Strait.

Oak Bluffs, town (1990 pop. 2,804), Dukes co., SE Mass., on NE Martha's Vineyard, 23 mi/37 km SE of New Bedford; 41°26′N 70°35′W. Resort. Passenger ferry connections with Woods Hole. Location of famous Methodist campground dating from 1870, Victorian Gingerbread cottages. Oldest operating carousel in U.S. Lighthouse at entrance. Oak Bluffs State Beach Park. Settled 1642, set off from Edgartown as Cottage City in 1880, renamed 1907.

Oak Brook, village (1990 pop. 9,178), Du Page co., NE Ill., suburb 16 mi/26 km W of Chicago; 41°50′N 87°57′W. High-rise office complexes; shopping dist. Mfg. (consumer goods, transportation equip., coated paper and film, detergents, machinery). Site of Oakbrook Shopping Center, one of the largest malls in the U.S.

Oak City 1 village (1990 pop. 389), Martin co., E N.C., 28 mi/45 km E of Rocky Mount; 35°57′N 77°17′W. Tobacco, cotton, peanuts, grain; chickens, hogs, cattle. Mfg. (apparel). **2** village (1990 pop. 587), Millard co., W central Utah, 12 mi/19 km E of Delta; 39°22′N 112°20′W. Elev. 5,105 ft/1,556 m. Alfalfa; dairying; cattle. Fishlake Natl. Forest to S and E; Fools Creek reservoir to N. Settled 1860, originally named Oak Creek.

Oak Creek, city (1990 pop. 19,513), Milwaukee co., SE Wis., a suburb 8 mi/12.9 km S of downtown Milwaukee, on L. Michigan; 42°52′N 87°54′W. Mfg. (machinery, electronic prods., plastic prods., computers, paper prods., chemicals, transportation equip., fabricated metal prods., concrete prods.; metal fabricating). Small farms dot the city's surrounding region. Inc. 1955.

Oak Creek, village (1990 pop. 673), Routt co., NW Colo., Oak co., in SW foothills of Park Range, and 15 mi/24 km SSW of Steamboat Springs; 40°16′N 106°57′W. Elev. 7,414 ft/2,260 m. Oil and gas. Cattle, sheep; wheat, hay, barley. Coal mines in vicinity. Parts of Routt Natl. Forest to E and SW; Stagecoach State Park to E. Inc. 1907.

Oak Forest, city (1990 pop. 26,203), Cook co., NE Ill., a residential suburb 20 mi/32 km SSW of downtown Chicago; 41°36′N 87°45′W. Residential development interspersed with remnant agr. (grain; livestock); mfg. (chemicals; commercial printing). Inc. 1947.

Oak Grove 1 city (1990 pop. 4,565), Jackson co., W Mo., 25 mi/40 km ESE of Kansas City; 39°00′N 94°07′W. Corn, wheat, sorghum; cattle. Satellite community of Kansas City. **2** uninc. city (1990 pop. 12,576), Clackamas co., NW Oregon, residential suburb 7 mi/11.3 km S of Portland, on Willamette R.; 45°24′N 122°38′W. Mfg. (machinery).

Oak Grove 1 town (1990 pop. 2,863), Christian co., SW Ky., 15 mi/24 km SSE of Hopkinsville, at Tenn. state line; 36°40′N 87°25′W. Agr. area (dark and burley tobacco, soybeans, grain; livestock; dairying). Limestone. Mfg. (concrete). Fort Campbell Military Reserve to W. **2** town (1990 pop. 2,126), ⊙ West Carroll parish, NE La., near Ark. state line, 50 mi/80 km NE of Monroe; 32°52′N 91°23′W. In agr. area (cotton, corn, vegetables; cattle); mfg. (canned vegetables, bldg. components). Inc. as village in 1908, as town in 1928. Bayou Macon State Wildlife Area to E. **3** uninc. town (1990 pop. 7,173), Lexington co., central S.C., residential suburb 6 mi/9.7 km SW of downtown Columbia. Columbia Municipal Airport to SE; 33°58′N 81°08′W. **4** town (1990 pop. 3,498), Washington co., NE Tenn., 8 mi/13 km NNE of Johnson City.

Oak Grove, village (1990 pop. 626), Rock Island co., NW Ill., 5 mi/8 km S of Rock Island; 41°24′N 90°34′W. Residential suburb in agr. area (corn, soybeans; livestock).

Oak Harbor, city (1990 pop. 17,176), Island co., NW Wash., on Whidbey Isl. and 30 mi/48 km NW of Everett. Dairying; wheat; poultry; mfg. (concrete prods., lab instruments). Whidbey Isl. Naval Air Station to N on Saratoga Passage, arm of Puget Sound. Joseph Whidbey (W) and Deception Pass (W) state parks nearby.

Oak Harbor, village (1990 pop. 2,637), Ottawa co., N Ohio, 11 mi/18 km W of Port Clinton, and on Portage R.; 41°31′N 83°08′W. Baskets, food prods., bldg. materials, barrels; ships fruit. Sometimes spelled Oakharbor.

Oak Hill, city (1990 pop. 4,301), Davidson co., central Tenn., residential suburb 6 mi/10 km S of Nashville; 36°04′N 86°47′W. Radnor L. State Natural Area is nearby. Inc. 1952.

Oak Hill 1 town (1990 pop. 28), Wilcox co., SW central Ala., 14 mi/23 km SE of Camden. **2** town (1990 pop. 6,812), Fayette co., S central W.Va., 6 mi/9.7 km S of Fayetteville; 37°58′N 81°09′W. RR junction. Bituminous-coal mines. Mfg. (bldg. materials, machinery). Agr. (grain, alfalfa); cattle. Timber. New R. Gorge Natl. R. to E; Plum Orchard Wildlife Management Area to SW. Settled 1820.

Oak Hill 1 village (1990 pop. 13), Clay co., N central Kansas, 14 mi/23 km SW of Clay Center; 39°15′N 97°20′W. In grain and livestock area. Also spelled Oakhill. **2** village (1990 pop. 400), Greene co., SE N.Y., in Catskill Mts., on Catskill Creek, and 20 mi/32 km NW of Catskill; 42°25′N 74°09′W. **3** village (1990 pop. 1,831), Jackson co., S Ohio, 12 mi/19 km SSE of Jackson. Forest area.

Oak Hill, Mass.: see NEWTON.

Oak Hills, uninc. town (1990 pop. 2,245), Butler co., W Pa., residential suburb 3 mi/4.8 km SSW of Butler; 40°49′N 79°54′W.

Oak Island, one of the Thousand Isls., St. Lawrence co., N N.Y., in the St. Lawrence R., near Can. (Ont.) border, just SW of Chippewa Bay; c.2 mi/3.2 km long, max. width c.1 mi/1.6 km; 44°26′N 75°48′W.

Oak Island, islet in Mahone Bay, S N.S., E Canada, 4 mi/6 km SW of Chester; 44°31′N 64°18′W. The treasure of Captain Kidd is reputedly hidden here; many unsuccessful attempts have been made to recover it.

Oak Lake, town (1991 pop. 350), SW Man., central Canada, near Assiniboine R., 30 mi/48 km W of Brandon; 49°46′N 100°38′W. Mixed farming; livestock; muskrat farms.

Oak Lawn, village (1990 pop. 56,182), Cook co., NE Ill., a suburb SE of Chicago; 41°43′N 87°45′W. It is chiefly residential with some light mfg. industries. Prods. include metalwork, wood prods., and school supplies. Inc. 1909.

Oak Orchard Creek, c.60 mi/97 km long, W N.Y.; rises in N central Genesee co.; flows N and W, then N and NE, crossing the Barge Canal at Medina, to L. Ontario 9 mi/14.5 km N of Albion.

Oak Park 1 city (1990 pop. 53,648), Cook co., NE Ill., a residential suburb adjacent to Chicago; 41°53′N 87°47′W. Some 25 houses in the village were designed by Frank Lloyd Wright, who lived here. Ernest Hemingway was b. here. Emmaus Bible School is here. Settled 1833, inc. 1901. **2** city (1990 pop. 30,462), Oakland co., SE Mich., a suburb 10 mi/16 km NW of downtown Detroit, and just N of Detroit city; 42°27′N 83°10′W. It is chiefly residential, but there is some industry. Mfg. (laser cutting, sheet metal forming; fabricated metal prods., foods, textiles). Marian Sandweiss b. here. Detroit Zoological Park to NE. Inc. 1927.

Oak Park 1 uninc. town (1990 pop. 2,412), Ventura co., SW Calif., residential suburb 6 mi/9.7 km ESE of Thousand Oaks, on Media Creek; 34°10′N 118°46′W. Simi Peak to N. **2** town (1990 pop. 269), Emanuel co., E central Ga., 16 mi/26 km S of Swainsboro; 32°22′N 82°19′W.

Oak Park Heights, town (1990 pop. 3,466), Washington co.,E Minn., suburb 16 mi/26 km ENE of downtown St. Paul, and 2 mi/3.2 km S of Stillwater, on L. St. Croix, natural lake on St. Croix R. (Wis. state line); 45°01′N 92°48′W. Light mfg.; agr. (cattle, sheep; corn, oats, alfalfa, soybeans). Minn. Correctional facilities are here and in adjacent Bayport (to S). Lower St. Croix Natl. Scenic Riverway on St. Croix R.

Oak Point, village, S Man., central Canada, on L. Manitoba, 55 mi/89 km NW of Winnipeg; 50°30′N 98°02′W. Fishing.

Oak Point, resort village, St. Lawrence co., N N.Y., on the St. Lawrence R., and 18 mi/29 km SW of Ogdensburg; 44°31′N 75°45′W.

Oak Ridge, city (1990 pop. 27,310), Anderson and Roane cos., E Tenn., on Black Oak Ridge and the Clinch R.,

17 mi/27 km WNW of Knoxville; 36°02'N 84°12'W. Many activities in the fields of atomic energy and nuclear physics are pursued; mfg. includes complex nuclear instruments, electronic prods., radioactive pharmaceuticals, and nuclear fuel. The site was chosen (1942) for what was then called the Clinton Engineer Works, and the city was built by the Federal govt. to house the workers who developed the uranium-235 and plutonium-239 for the atomic bomb. The existence and purpose of the community were kept secret from most of the country until the summer of 1945. The project was under the control of the Atomic Energy Commission, but the city has since (1955–1959) been turned over to its residents. The former Clinton Natl. Laboratory for nuclear research became (1948) the Oak Ridge Natl. Laboratory. The Oak Ridge Inst. of Nuclear Studies (1948), composed of many sponsoring educational institutions, and the Univ. of Tenn. Biomedical Science graduate school are also here. Tourist attractions include the Amer. Mus. of Atomic Energy; a nearby nuclear graphite reactor; the K-25 overlook, from which can be seen the Oak Ridge gaseous diffusion plant; and an arboretum. Founded by the U.S. govt. 1942, inc. as an independent city 1959.

Oak Ridge 1 town, St. Clair co., central Ala., 3 mi/4.8 km N of Pell City. **2** town (1990 pop. 202), Cape Girardeau co., SE Mo., bet. Mississippi and Whitewater rivers, 9 mi/14.5 km NNW of Jackson; 37°30'N 89°43'W. **3** uninc. town (1990 pop. 950), Guilford co., N central N.C., 12 mi/19 km NW of downtown Greensboro, near Haw R. Agr. area (tobacco, grain; poultry, livestock; dairying).

Oak Ridge, village (1990 pop. 174), Morehouse parish, NE La., 14 mi/23 km SSE of Bastrop; 32°37'N 91°46'W. An agr. area (cotton, rice, soybeans, vegetables; cattle). Coulee State Game Refuge to W.

Oak Ridge North, town (1990 pop. 2,454), Montgomery co., SE Texas, suburb 30 mi/48 km N of downtown Houston metropolitan area; 30°09'N 95°26'W. Agr. (cattle, ratites [ostriches, emus]; nursery and greenhouse crops).

Oak Ridge Reservoir (□ 1 sq mi/2.6 sq km), Morris co, N N.J., on Pequannock R., 14 mi/22 km NW of Parsippany; 41°02'N 74°31'W. Max. capacity 15,000 acre-ft. Formed by Oak Ridge Reservoir Dam (60 ft/18 m high), built (1892) for water supply.

Oak River, village, SW Man., central Canada, on Oak R., and 30 mi/48 km NW of Brandon. Grain; livestock.

Oak Vale, village, Lawrence co., S central Miss., 15 mi/24 km NNW of Columbia, near Pearl R. Also spelled Oakvale.

Oak View, uninc. town (1990 pop. 3,606), Ventura co., S Calif., 8 mi/12.9 km N of Ventura, on Ventura R.; 34°24'N 119°18'W. Avocados, citrus, vegetables; flowers, nursery prods. L. Casitas reservoir to W; Los Padres Natl. Forest to N; Emma Wood State Beach to S; San Buenaventura Mission to S.

Oakboro, village (1990 pop. 600), Stanly co., S central N.C., 11 mi/18 km SW of Albemarle, near Rocky R.; 35°13'N 80°19'W. Cotton, grain, soybeans; poultry, livestock; dairying. Mfg. (apparel and textiles, roller tubing, lumber, hats, machinery).

Oakbrook Terrace, city (1990 pop. 1,907), Du Page co., NE Ill., residential suburb 17 mi/27 km W of downtown Chicago, and NW of Oak Brook; 41°51'N 87°58'W.

Oakdale 1 city (1990 pop. 11,961), Stanislaus co., central Calif., in San Joaquin Valley, 25 mi/40 km ESE of Stockton, and on Stanislaus R.; 37°46'N 120°51'W. Dairying; irrigated farming (fruit, almonds, vegetables, grain, melons), horticulture; poultry. Mfg. (wood prods., machinery, chocolate; printing and publishing). Annual rodeo. Hetch Hetchy Aqueduct to SE, delivers water from Sierra Nevada range to San Francisco. Woodward and Farmington reservoirs to N. Inc. 1906. **2** city (1990 pop. 18,347), Washington co., E Minn., residential suburb 7 mi/11.3 km ENE of downtown St. Paul, in area of small natural lakes; 44°59'N 92°58'W. Mfg. (machinery, pressure vessels, plastic prods., polyethylene tubing). **3** city (1994 pop. 7,482), Allen parish, SW central La., 52 mi/84 km NE of L. Charles city, on Calcasieu R.; 30°49'N 92°40'W. In lumber and agr. area (soybeans, vegetables, peaches; cattle); mfg. (chemicals, plywood and wood prods., apparel). Laid out in 1886. West Bay State Wildlife Area to W.

Oakdale 1 uninc. town (1990 pop. 1,800), McCracken co., W Ky., residential suburb 3 mi/4.8 km SE of downtown Paducah, on Ohio R., at mouths of Tennessee and Clarks rivers. Includes villages of Woodlawn and Tyler, both names duplicated in other parts of Ky. **2** town (1990 pop. 268), Morgan co., NE central Tenn., 7 mi/11 km SE of Wartburg, in the Cumberlands; 35°59'N 84°33'W.

Oakdale 1 village, within Montville, New London co., SE Conn. **2** village (1990 pop. 362), Antelope co., NE central Nebr., 5 mi/8 km SE of Neligh, and on Elkhorn R; 42°04'N 97°58'W. Livestock; dairy prods.; grain. **3** residential village (□ 3 sq mi/7.8 sq km; 1990 pop. 7,875), Suffolk co., SE N.Y., on S shore of L.I., 2 mi/3.2 km NW of Sayville; 40°44'N 73°07'W. Seat of Dowling Col. Heckscher State Park is nearby.

Oakdale, borough (1990 pop. 1,752), Allegheny co., SW Pa., suburb 11 mi/18 km WSW of downtown Pittsburgh, on Robinson Run; 40°23'N 80°11'W. Diversified mfg.; oil. Settlers Cabin Park to NE. Inc. 1872.

Oakdale, Mass.: see WEST BOYLSTON.

Oakes, town (1990 pop. 1,775), Dickey co., SE N. Dak., 27 mi/43 km ENE of Ellendale, near James R.; 46°08'N 98°05'W. RR junction, agr. shipping center. Mfg. (machinery); dairy prods.; grain. Plotted 1886, inc. 1888.

Oakes Field, airport, just E of Nassau, New Providence Isl., N central Bahama Isls.

Oakesdale, village (1990 pop. 346), Whitman co., SE Wash., 18 mi/29 km NNE of Colfax, near Pine Creek, in the Palouse Hills; 47°08'N 117°15'W. Wheat, oats, peas, barley; mfg. (flour milling). Steptoe Butte State Park to S. Historic flour mill; historical mus.

Oakfield 1 town, Worth co., S central Ga., 20 mi/32 km NE of Albany, near Flint R.; 31°46'N 83°58'W. **2** agr. town (1990 pop. 846), Aroostook co., E Maine, 15 mi/24 km W of Houlton; 46°04'N 68°04'W. Inc. 1897. **3** town (1990 pop. 1,003), Fond du Lac co., E central Wis., 8 mi/12.9 km SSW of Fond du Lac; 43°40'N 88°32'W. RR spur terminus. In dairy and farm region. Mfg. (limestone prods.). Horicon Natl. Wildlife Refuge to SW.

Oakfield, village (1990 pop. 1,818), Genesee co., W N.Y., 7 mi/11.3 km NW of Batavia; 43°03'N 78°16'W. In wheat area. Food canning. Gypsum quarrying and processing. Iroquois Natl. Wildlife Refuge (□ 17 sq mi/44 sq km), featuring migratory waterfowl of E N. Amer., occupies much of Orchard Swamp, 5 mi/8 km NW of village center. Settled 1850, inc. 1858.

Oakford, village (1990 pop. 246), Menard co., central Ill., near Sangamon R., 10 mi/16 km NW of Petersburg; 40°06'N 89°58'W. In agr. area.

Oakham (O-kuhm), town (1990 pop. 1,503), Worcester co., central Mass., 13 mi/21 km WNW of Worcester; 42°21'N 72°03'W. Agr.

Oakhaven, village (1990 pop. 35), Hempstead co., SW Ark., 4 mi/6.4 km N of Hope; 33°43'N 93°37'W. Hope Wildlife Management Area to N.

Oakhurst, uninc. town (1990 pop. 2,602), Madera co., central Calif., 38 mi/61 km NNE of Fresno, on Fresno R., in W foothills of Sierra Nevada; 37°20'N 119°39'W. Cattle, poultry; dairying; nuts, fruit, grain. Mfg. (power valves; printing and publishing). Yosemite Natl. Forest to N and E.

Oakhurst 1 village (1990 pop. 4,130), Monmouth co., E N.J., near the Atlantic coast, 3 mi/4.8 km N of Asbury Park; 40°15'N 74°01'W. Residential. **2** village (1990 pop. 219), San Jacinto co., E Texas, 14 mi/23 km E of Huntsville, in N edge of Sam Houston Natl. Forest; 30°44'N 95°18'W. In timber, agr. area. L. Livingston reservoir to E.

Oakland, county (□ 908 sq mi/2,352 sq km; 1990 pop. 1,083,592), SE Mich.; 42°39'N 83°22'W; ⊙ Pontiac. Drained by Shiawassee, Huron, and Clinton rivers, and by the R. Rouge. Part of Detroit metropolitan area. Fruit growing (apples); agr. in N (vegetables, wheat, oats, corn; cattle, hogs, sheep, poultry; dairy prods.; nurseries). Mfg. at Pontiac, Ferndale, and Royal Oak. Highly urbanized in S ½ from neighboring city of Detroit. Many small lakes (resorts, esp. in W). Co. has 10 state parks and state recreational areas and 4 ski areas. Organized 1820.

Oakland 1 city (1990 pop. 372,242), ⊙ Alameda co., W Calif., 6 mi/9.7 km E of San Francisco, on the E side of San Francisco Bay; 37°46'N 122°13'W. Together with San Francisco and San Jose, the city comprises the 4th-largest metropolitan area in the U.S. A containerized shipping port and a major RR terminus, Oakland has shipyards, chemical plants, glassworks, food-processing establishments, and an iron foundry. Mfg. includes foods, cleaners, electronic goods, canvas prods., and fabricated metal prods. The SAN FRANCISCO–OAKLAND BAY BRIDGE was opened in 1936 and connects Oakland with other nearby cities. Oakland is the hq. and hub of the Bay Area Rapid Transit (BART), a 3-co. rapid transit system connected to San Francisco that began operation in 1972. Oakland Internatl. Airport, at Bay Farm Isl. (peninsula) in S. An extremely severe earthquake on Oct. 17, 1989, which struck during a World Series baseball game in the San Francisco Bay area, resulted in great damage to Oakland as well as to the San Francisco–Oakland Bay Bridge. About 1 mi/1.6 km of Interstate 880 highway, in Oakland collapsed. The earthquake's toll took 62 lives and injured thousands; major repair and reconstruction efforts immediately ensued. Other principal redevelopment since the 1970s has focused on Oakland's waterfront area. Of interest are the Oakland Mus., Chabot Observatory, the Morcom Rose Garden, and Jack London Square. The city has a symphony orchestra, notable parks, a state arboretum, a children's amusement park, and a zoo. Seat of Mills Col., Holy Names Col., Calif. Col. of Arts and Crafts, Laney Col., and Merritt Col.; Univ. of Calif. at Berkeley is to N. The large U.S. Naval Supply Depot and a Oakland Army Base are in W part of city, on bay; Alameda Naval Air Station to SW, in Alameda; Oak Knoll Naval Medical Center in SE. The Oakland–Alameda Co. Coliseum and Arena is the home of the city's major league professional baseball team (the Oakland Athletics). Anthony Chabot and Redwood regional parks to E; Upper San Leandro Reservoir to E, L. Chabot reservoir to SE, L. Merritt reservoir in city, E of downtown; Knowland State Park and Arboretum are in SE. Inc. 1852. **2** city (1990 pop. 996), Coles co., E Ill., near Embarras R., 14 mi/23 km NNE of Charleston; 39°39'N 88°01'W. In rich agr. area (corn, wheat, soybeans; livestock). Inc. 1855.

Oakland 1 town (1990 pop. 1,496), Pottawattamie co., SW Iowa, on West Nishnabotna R., and 25 mi/40 km E of Council Bluffs; 41°18'N 95°24'W. In livestock, grain, poultry area. Fabricated metal prods.; rendering works. Inc. 1882. **2** town (1990 pop. 5,595), including Oakland village, Kennebec co., S Maine, 16 mi/26 km N of Augusta, and on Messalonskee L.; 44°33'N 43°69'W. Wood prods. Set off from Waterville 1873. **3** town (1900 pop. 1,741), ⊙ Garrett co., extreme W Md., in the Alleghenies near W.Va. state line, c.40 mi/64 km WSW of Cumberland; 39°25'N 79°54'W. Trade center in resort and agr. area (dairy prods.; vegetables, grain); wood prods., maple sugar. Swallow Falls State Forest is just NW. William Armstrong, the 1st permanent settler, built a cabin in 1806 here at a ford where a packhorse trail crossed the Youghiogheny R. Resort hotels were built here in "Switzerland of Amer." after the Baltimore and Ohio RR came through in 1849. The RR station (c.1851) is a Natl. Historic Landmark. Buffalo Bill Cody came to the funeral in Crook's Crest of Gen. George Crook, who fought the Sioux and Apache after the Civil War, and retired here in 1890. Joseph E. Harwood, the former owner of Proudfoot's Drugstore, wrote a classic botany book, *Wildflowers of the Appalachians.* Deer Park Spring water, popular among late-19th-cent. presidents, is still available, although the famed Deer Park Hotel was razed in 1944. **4** town (1990 pop. 1,593), St. Louis co., E Mo., residential suburb 10 mi/16 km WSW of downtown St. Louis; 38°34'N 90°22'W. **5** town (1990 pop. 1,279), Burt co., E Nebr., 13 mi/21 km W of Tekamah, and on Logan Creek, near Missouri R; 41°50'N 96°28'W. Trade, shipping point for rich agr. area; livestock; grain. Printing. Settled 1863, inc. 1881. **6** town (1990 pop. 844), Douglas co., SW Oregon,15 mi/24 km N of Roseburg, on Calapooya Creek; 43°25′N 123°17′W. Wood prods.; dairy prods.; poultry, sheep, cattle. **7** uninc. town (1990 pop. 1,766), Union township, Lawrence co., W Pa., residential suburb 1 mi/1.6 km SW of New Castle; 40°59′N 80°22′W. **8** uninc. town (1990 pop. 1,298), Sumter co., central S.C., residential suburb 10 mi/16 km WNW of downtown Sumter, at NW edge of Shaw Air Force Base; 33°59′N 80°30′W. **9** town (1990 pop. 392), Fayette co., SW Tenn., 9 mi/14 km W of Somerville; 35°14′N 89°31′W.

Oakland 1 village (1990 pop. 202), Warren co., S Ky., 12 mi/19 km. ENE of Bowling Green; 37°02′N 86°15′W. In agr. area (tobacco, grain; livestock; dairying); mfg. (glass prods.). **2** village (1990 pop. 553), Yalobusha co., N central Miss., 20 mi/32 km NNW of Grenada; 34°02′N 89°54′W. Agr. (cotton, corn; cattle, poultry); timber; mfg. (lumber). Sect. of Holly Springs Natl. Forest to SE; Enid L. reservoir and George Payne Cossar State Park to NE. **3** village (1990 pop. 602), Marshall co., S Okla., 2 mi/3.2 km W of Madill, and 20 mi/32 km ESE of Ardmore; 34°06′N 96°47′W. In farm area. **4** village, in Burrillville, Providence co., R.I.

Oakland 1 residential borough (1990 pop. 11,997), Bergen co., NE N.J., near Ramapo R., 8 mi/12.9 km NW of Paterson; 41°01′N 74°14′W. Ramapo State Forest to W. **2** borough (1990 pop. 641), Susquehanna co., NE Pa., 37 mi/60 km N of Scranton, on Susquehanna R., opposite (N of) Susquehanna Depot; 41°57′N 75°36′W. Agr. (grain; livestock; dairying).

Oakland Acres, village (1990 pop. 152), Jasper co., central Iowa, 5 mi/8 km WSW of Grinnell; 41°43′N 92°49′W. Rock Creek State Park to N. Corn; cattle, hogs, sheep.

Oakland Beach, neighborhood, Warwick, Kent co., central R.I.

Oakland Beach, N.Y.: see SOUTH BEACH.

Oakland City, city (1990 pop. 2,810), Gibson co., SW Ind., 11 mi/18 km E of Princeton; 38°20′N 87°21′W. Grain farms. Bituminous coal, surface mines. Seat of Oakland City Col. Laid out 1856.

Oakland Park, city (□ 6 sq mi/15.5 sq km; 1990 pop. 26,326), Broward co., SE Fla., on Atlantic coast, 3 mi/4.8 km N of Fort Lauderdale; 26°10′N 80°09′W.

Oakley, uninc. city (1990 pop. 18,374), Contra Costa co., W Calif., suburb 34 mi/55 km NE of downtown Oakland, and 6 mi/9.7 km E of Antioch, near San Joaquin R.; 38°00′N 121°43′W. Fruit, vegetables (esp. asparagus); grain, nuts.

Oakley, town (1990 pop. 2,045), ⊙ Logan co., NW Kansas, 21 mi/34 km SSE of Colby; 39°07′N 100°50′W. RR junction. Trading point in grain, livestock region; dairying. Located in extreme NE corner of co., unusual for a co. seat. Fick Fossil Mus. Inc. 1887.

Oakley 1 village (1990 pop. 635), Cassia co., S Idaho, on Goose Creek, and 20 mi/32 km SSW of Burley; 42°14′N 113°53′W. Elev. 4,191 ft/1,277 m. RR terminus, in agr. area (potatoes, sugar beets, wheat; cattle, sheep); flour milling. Oakley Dam (145 ft/44 m high, 1,025 ft/312 m long) is on Goose Creek 4 mi/6.4 km SSW; forms Lower Goose Creek Reservoir (6 mi/9.7 km long, ½ mi/8/10 km wide), used for irrigation. Parts of Sawtooth Natl. Forest to E and W. City of Rocks Natl. Historic Landmark to SE; granite columns (c.600 ft/183 m high) were important landmark for pioneers. **2** village (1990 pop. 362), Saginaw co., E central Mich., 22 mi/35 km SW of Saginaw, near Shiawassee R.; 43°08′N 84°10′W. Lumber. **3** uninc. village, Pitt co., E N.C., 11 mi/18 km NNE of Greenville. **4** village (1990 pop. 522), Summit co., N Utah, 15 mi/24 km SSE of Coalville, and on Weber R.; 40°43′N 111°17′W. Elev. 6,517 ft/1,986 m. Rockport Reservoir and State Park to NW. Uinta Mts., in part of Wasatch Natl. Forest, to E. Originally named Oak Creek.

Oaklyn, residential borough (1990 pop. 4,430), Camden co., SW N.J., 4 mi/6.4 km SE of Camden; 39°53′N 75°04′W. Settled 1682 by Friends, laid out c.1890, inc. 1905.

Oakman 1 town (1990 pop. 846), Walker co., NW central Ala., 10 mi/16 km SW of Jasper. Coal mining. **2** town, Gordon co., NW Ga., 15 mi/24 km ENE of Calhoun; 34°33′N 84°42′W.

Oakmont, borough (1990 pop. 6,961), Allegheny co., SW Pa., suburb 10 mi/16 km NE of downtown Pittsburgh, on Allegheny R. (bridged); 40°31′N 79°50′W. Mfg. (wire, seals, plastic prods., fabricated metal prods., furniture, machinery, bldg. materials, electronic goods). Inc. 1889.

Oakmont, Pa.: see HAVERFORD.

Oakmulgee Creek (ok-MUL-gee), c.40 mi/64 km long, central Ala.; rises in SE Bibb co.; flows S to Cahaba R. 9 mi/14.5 km NW of Selma.

Oakridge, town (1990 pop. 3,063), Lane co., W Oregon, 38 mi/61 km SE of Eugene, on Middle Fork of Willamette R.; 43°45′N 122°28′W. Concrete, traffic counters. Timber. Fish hatchery to E. Willamette Pass to SE. Surrounded by Willamette Natl. Forest. Umpqua Natl. Forest to SW; Waldo L. Wilderness Area to E; Hills Creek Reservoir to SE. Inc. 1934.

Oaks, uninc. town (1990 pop. 850), Montgomery co., SE Pa., 20 mi/32 km WNW of Philadelphia, on Schuylkill R; 40°07′N 75°27′W. Diverse mfg. Agr. includes dairying; grain, apples.

Oaks, village (1990 pop. 431), Delaware co., NE Okla., 18 mi/29 km NNE of Tahlequah; 36°10′N 94°50′W. Agr. area. Rocky Ford State Park to S.

Oakton, uninc. city, Fairfax co., NE Va., 13 mi/21 km W of Washington, D.C., 2 mi/3.2 km N of Fairfax; 38°53′N 77°17′W. Dulles Internatl. Airport to W.

Oaktown, town (1990 pop. 655), Knox co., SW Ind., 14 mi/23 km NNE of Vincennes; 38°52′N 87°26′W. Fruit (esp. watermelons), wheat, corn. Oil wells. Laid out 1867.

Oakvale, village (1990 pop. 165), Mercer co., S W.Va., 8 mi/12.9 km ESE of Princeton, near Va. state line; 37°19′N 80°58′W. Coal-mining area. State fish hatchery.

Oakville, town (1991 pop. 114,670), Ont., central Canada, on L. Ontario, bet. Toronto and Hamilton; 43°26′N 79°40′W. A major component of the local economy is the Ford Motor Co. plant, one of the largest motor vehicle plants in Canada. Originally inhabited by the Mississauga, it became a shipbuilding center in the 19th cent. because of its good harbor.

Oakville, village, S Man., central Canada, 14 mi/23 km ESE of Portage la Priarie. Grain; livestock; dairying.

Oakville, town (1990 pop. 442), Louisa co., SE Iowa, on Iowa R., and 10 mi/16 km SE of Wapello; 41°06′N 91°02′W.

Oakville 1 uninc. village, Napa co., W Calif., in Napa R. valley, 15 mi/24 km E of Santa Rosa. Winery; grapes, walnuts; dairying; cattle; nursery prods. U.S. Dept. of Agr. experimental vineyard here. **2** village, sect. of Litchfield co., W Conn. **3** village (1990 pop. 493), Grays Harbor co., W Wash., 20 mi/32 km SW of Olympia, and on Chehalis R. Mfg. (wood prods., lumber). Chehalis Indian Reservation to SE; Black Hills to N.

Oakwood, city (1990 pop. 8,957), Montgomery co., W Ohio, just S of Dayton. Inc. as village in 1907; became city after 1930.

Oakwood 1 town (1990 pop. 1,464), Hall co., NE Ga., 5 mi/8 km SW of Gainseville; 34°14′N 83°53′W. Mfg. of animal feeds, paints, plastics, transportation equip.; commercial printing. **2** uninc. town (1990 pop. 2,541), Union township, Lawrence co., W Pa., residential suburb 1 mi/1.6 km W of New Castle, on Shenango R.; 41°00′N 80°22′W. New Castle Municipal Airport to NW.

Oakwood 1 uninc. village, Madison co., Ala. **2** village (1990 pop. 1,533), Vermillion co., E Ill., 7 mi/11.3 km W of Danville; 40°06′N 87°46′W. In agr. and bituminous-coal area. Kickapoo State Park is nearby. **3** village (1990 pop. 709), Paulding co., NW Ohio, on Auglaize R., and 11 mi/18 km ESE of Paulding. Agr. area. **4** village (1990 pop. 107), Dewey co., W Okla., 17 mi/27 km WNW of Watonga; 35°55′N 98°42′W. In agr. area (grain; cattle). **5** village (1990 pop. 527), Leon co., E central Texas, 17 mi/27 km SW of Palestine, near Trinity R.; 31°34′N 95°50′W. Lumbering center and agr. area. **6** uninc. village, Buchanan co., SW Va., 40 mi/64 km ENE of Norton; 37°12′N 82°00′W. Mfg. (concrete prods., machinery); agr. (tobacco, potatoes; cattle); bituminous coal.

Oakwood Hills, village (1990 pop. 1,498), McHenry co., NE Ill., residential suburb 4 mi/6.4 km ENE of Crystal Lake; 40°06′N 87°46′W.

Oatman, uninc. village, Mohave co., W Ariz., 20 mi/32 km SW of Kingman. Gold-mining town in W foothills of Black Mts. Mt. Nutt (NE) and Warm Springs (SE) wilderness areas nearby. Fort Mojave Indian Reservation to W.

Oaxaca (wah-HAH-kah), state (□ 36,375 sq mi/94,211 sq km; 1990 pop. 3,019,560), S Mexico, on the Pacific Ocean and its arm, the Gulf of Tehuantepec; ⊙ OAXACA DE JUÁREZ 16°45′N 94°10′W. The N part of the state is dominated by the Sierra de Oaxaca; there are deep, narrow valleys in the S and broad, open, semiarid valleys and plateaus in the N. Except on the W and the N the periphery of the state is tropical. The climate of the interior is generally temperate. Fertile valleys are farmed; agr. is the principal economic activity. Sugarcane, coffee (of which Oaxaca is a leading natl. producer), tobacco, cereals, and tropical and semitropical fruits are grown; livestock is raised. Oaxaca's reportedly extensive mineral deposits remain largely unexploited. The state's limited industrial activity centers around oil refining, beverage and paper mfg., and sugar and flour milling. Oaxaca is also known for its handicrafts, esp. handwoven textiles, pottery, and leather goods. Despite the existence of several highways, inadequate communications remain the chief barrier to the state's development. There are famous archaeological sites at Mitla and Monte Albán. Native Americans predominate here, as in few other states (notably Yucatán and Chiapas), with Mixtecs dominating in the Whighlands and Zapotecs elsewhere. Beach resorts are under development at Huatulco Bays and elsewhere on the S coast, which should augment the already important contribution of tourism to the state's economy. Porfirio Diás and Benito Juárez were b. here.

Oaxaca de Juárez (wah-HAH-kah dai HWAH-res), city (1990 pop. 212,818) and township, ⊙ Oaxaca state, S Mexico; 17°03′N 96°43′W. Commercial and tourist center situated in the Valley of Oaxaca. The church and monastery of Santo Domingo is a natl. monument and UN World Heritage Site. Noted for hand-wrought gold and silver filigree, pottery, and woven goods that rank among the finest in Mexico. The chief city of S Mexico, Oaxaca is linked with the federal capital by RR and the Inter-Amer. Highway (190). Subject to severe earthquakes. According to Aztec tradition, Oaxaca was founded as Huasyacac in 1486, during the brief ascendancy of the Aztecs over the Mixtecs and Zapotecs. Prominent in the Mex. revolution against Spain, the city also joined in the War of the Reform and in resistance to the Fr. intervention. Known as Antequera in colonial period.

Oaxaca, Sierra Madre de (wah-HAH-kah, see-ER-rah MAH-drai dai), mountain range, Oaxaca, Puebla, and Veracruz states, central Mexico; extending roughly 164 mi/200 km NW-SE and paralleling the Gulf of Mexico coast from Córdoba to the Isthmus of Tehuantepec; 18°30′N 97°00′W. A part of the Sierra Madre del Sur physiographic prov. Divided into several poorly demarcated ranges, including Sierra Zongolica (Puebla, Veracruz), Sierra Mazateca (Puebla, Oaxaca), and Sierra de Juárez (Oaxaca).

Oaxaca, Valley of (wah-HAH-kah), region, Oaxaca state, S Mexico, largest valley of Sierra Madre del Sur, surrounding the city of Oaxaca de Juárez. Broken into 3 arms: Etla, which extends N of Oaxaca de Juárez; Tlacolula, the E extension; and the Valle Grande, the S branch of the valley. Site of extensive Pre-Columbian settlement at Monte Albán, Mitla, and other sites; still, the heart of one of the country's most Indian regions, where those of non-Eur. descent predominate.

Oba (O-buh), village, central Ont., central Canada, on Oba L. (12 mi/19 km long, 2 mi/3 km wide), 100 mi/161 km SW of Kapuskasing; 49°04′N 84°06′W. Gold mining.

Obabika Lake (o-buh-BEE-kuh), SE central Ont., central Canada, 50 mi/80 km NE of Sudbury; 15 mi/24 km long, 2 mi/3 km wide. In gold-mining region. Drains E into L. Timagami.

Obalski Lake (o-BAHL-skee), W Que., E Canada, on Harricanaw R., 11 mi/18 km NE of Amos; 7 mi/11 km long, 2 mi/3 km wide. On shore are gold and copper deposits; airfield.

Obed Wild and Scenic River and Riverway (□ 7 sq mi/ 18 sq km), E central Tenn., on the Cumberland Plateau. Includes portions of Daddy's and Clear creeks and Emory and Obed rivers. Rugged scenery. Authorized 1976.

Oberlin, city (1990 pop. 8,191), Lorain co., N Ohio, 7 mi/ 11 km SW of Elyria; 41°17′N 82°13′W. In vegetable, dairy, and poultry area. Seat of Oberlin Col.

Oberlin 1 (O-buhr-lin), town (1990 pop. 2,197), ⊙ Decatur co., NW Kansas, on Sappa Creek, and 32 mi/ 51 km W of Norton; 39°49′N 100°31′W. RR terminus. Trading point in corn, barley, wheat, rye, cattle area; dairying. Mfg. (wood prods., foods). Site of last Native Amer. raid on Kansas soil 1878. Laid out 1878, inc. 1885. **2** town (1990 pop. 1,808), ⊙ Allen parish, SW central La., 38 mi/61 km NE of L. Charles city, near Calcasieu R.; 30°37′N 92°46′W. In agr. area (rice, soybeans, peaches; cattle; dairying); timber. West Bay State Wildlife Area to N.

Oberon (O-buhr-ahn), village (1990 pop. 103), Benson co., N central N.Dak., 21 mi/34 km SW of Devils Lake; 47°55′N 99°12′W. Junction of RR spur to Minnewaukan. Devils L. Sioux Indian Reservation just E; Fort Totten Historic Site to NE.

Obert, village (1990 pop. 39), Cedar co., NE Nebr., 12 mi/ 19 km ENE of Hartington, near Missouri R.; 42°41′N 97°01′W.

Obetz (O-bets), suburban village (1990 pop. 3,167), Franklin co., central Ohio, 5 mi/8 km SSE of Columbus; 39°52′N 82°57′W.

Obey River (O-bee), 58 mi/93 km long, N Tenn.; rises in E Putnam co.; flows NW and W to Cumberland R. at Celina; Dale Hollow Dam, 7 mi/11 km above mouth, impounds 51-mi/82-km-long Dale Hollow Reservoir; 36°33′N 85°30′W.

Obion (o-BEI-uhn), county (□ 550 sq mi/1,425 sq km; 1990 pop. 31,717), NW Tenn., on Ky. (N) state line; ⊙ Union City; 36°22′N 89°09′W. Bounded NW by Reelfoot L.; drained by Obion R. and its tributaries. Fertile farm region, producing chiefly soybeans, grain, cotton, wheat, sorghum; livestock; some mfg. at Union City. Formed 1823. Includes Gooch Wildlife Management Area and part of Reelfoot Natl. Wildlife Refuge.

Obion, town (1990 pop. 1,241), Obion co., NW Tenn., on Obion R., and 13 mi/21 km SSW of Union City; 36°16′N 89°12′W. In fertile farm area (apples, corn).

Obion Creek, c.50 mi/80 km long, SW Ky.; rises in S Graves co., c.15 mi/24 km S of Mayfield; flows NW through Obion Creek Wildlife Management Area, then SW to Mississippi R. 2 mi/3.2 km NE of Hickman.

Obion River, c.50 mi/80 km long, W Tenn.; formed in Obion co. by confluence of canalized North (c.45 mi/ 72 km long), South (c.55 mi/89 km long), and Rutherford (c.50 mi/80 km long) forks; flows SW past Obion, to Mississippi R. 13 mi/21 km NW of Ripley; 35°54′N 89°38′W. Receives Forked Deer R.

Oblatos, Barranca de, Mexico: see BARRANCA DE OBLATOS.

Oblong (OB-long), village (1990 pop. 1,616), Crawford co., SE Ill., 9 mi/14.5 km W of Robinson; 39°00′N 87°54′W. Oil, natural-gas wells. Agr. (livestock, poultry; corn, wheat, soybeans). Inc. 1883.

Obregón, Cañadas de, Mexico: see CAÑADAS DE OBREGÓN.

Obregón, Ciudad, Mexico: see CIUDAD OBREGÓN.

O'Brien, county (□ 575 sq mi/1,489 sq km; 1990 pop. 15,444), NW Iowa; ⊙ Primghar; 43°04′N 95°37′W. Prairie agr. area (hogs, cattle, sheep, poultry; corn, oats, barley) drained by Little Sioux and Floyd rivers. Mill Creek State Park in S. Field and stream flooding occurred in 1993. Formed 1851.

Observatory Inlet, W B.C., W Canada, long narrow arm of Portland Inlet (arm of Dixon Entrance), extending inland near and parallel to the S tip of the Alaska panhandle; 45 mi/72 km long, 1 mi/2 km–4 mi/6 km wide. Alice Arm extends E to Alice Arm village. On W side of Observatory Inlet is copper mining center of Anyox.

Obstruction Mountain (10,394 ft/3,168 m), SW Alta., W Canada, in Rocky Mts., near SE edge of Jasper Natl. Park, 60 mi/97 km SE of Jasper; 52°23′N 116°53′W.

Ocala (o-KA-lah), city (□ 28 sq mi/73 sq km; 1990 pop. 42,045), ⊙ Marion co., N central Fla.; 29°11′N 82°07′W. Trade and processing center for citrus fruit, vegetables, and other agr. goods. The surrounding region is known for its thoroughbred horses, cattle, lumber, and phosphates. Since 1970 the cattle-raising industry here has grown significantly. Tourism is also important to the city; fish and game abound in the many nearby lakes and streams and in the Ocala Natl. Forest. Inc. 1868.

Ocampo 1 (o-KAHM-po), city (1990 pop. 5,541) and township, Guanajuato, central Mexico, in Sierra Madre Occidental, 52 mi/84 km NW of Dolores Hidalgo, on Mexico Highway 51; 21°38′N 101°24′W. Beans, wheat, corn, mescal; livestock. **2** city (1990 pop. 4,746) and township, Tamaulipas, NE Mexico, in E foothills of Sierra Madre Oriental, 33 mi/54 km WNW of Ciudad Mante, on Mexico Highway 70; 22°50′N 99°20′W. Cereals, agave; livestock.

Ocampo 1 town (1990 pop. 2,570), Coahuila, N Mexico, on plateau E of Sierra Madre Oriental, 66 mi/107 km WNW of Monclova; 27°20′N 102°24′W. Elev. 3,773 ft/ 1,150 m. Silver, and lead mining. Also known as Villa Ocampo. **2** town (1990 pop. 2,295), Michoacán, central Mexico, on RR, and 10 mi/16.5 km N of Zitácuaro. Corn; livestock.

Ocampo (o-KAHM-po), mining settlement (1990 pop. 448), Chihuahua, N Mexico, in Sierra Madre Occidental, 92 mi/148 WSW of Cuantemoc on unpaved road; 28°12′N 108°24′W. Elev. 5,689 ft/1,734 m. Some silver, gold, lead, copper mining. Airfield.

Ocampo, Mexico: see VILLA OCAMPO.

Ocampo, San Pedro, Mexico: see MELCHOR OCAMPO.

Ocampo, Villa, Mexico: see VILLA OCAMPO.

Occidental, uninc. town (1990 pop. 1,300), Sonoma co., W Calif., 6 mi/9.7 km W of Sebastopol; 38°24′N 122°57′W. Apples, grapes, nursery prods.; dairying; poultry, cattle.

Occoquan (UH-kuh-kwahn), town (1990 pop. 361), Prince William co., NE Va., 20 mi/32 km SW of Wash. D.C., on Occoquan Creek, 3 mi/4.8 km NW of its mouth, on Potomac R.; 38°40′N 77°15′W. Occoquan Regional Park (Fairfax co.) to NW.

Occoquan River, c.20 mi/32 km long, NE Va.; formed 4 mi/6.4 km S of Manassas by joining of Broad Run and Cedar Run creeks; flows ENE through L. Jackson (L. Jackson Dam) and Occoquan reservoirs, receives Bull Run creek from NW, turns SE, flows past Occoquan to Occoquan Bay, arm of Potomac R., at Woodbridge. Occoquan Dam 5 mi/8 km above mouth, forming Occoquan Reservoirs.

Ocean, county (□ 915 sq mi/2,370 sq km; 1990 pop. 433,203), E N.J., on Barnegat Bay (E); ⊙ Toms River; 39°52′N 74°15′W. Long Beach isl. and Isl. Beach peninsula, bet. Barnegat Bay and the Atlantic Ocean, have many popular summer resorts and fisheries. Inland agr. area produces vegetables, fruit; poultry; dairy prods. Varied mfg. Part of co. is in pine barrens region (timber; cranberries, blueberries), here including Lebanon State Forest. Drained by Toms and Metedeconk rivers and Cedar Creek. Formed 1850. Oyster Creek Nuclear Power Plant, initial criticality May 3, 1969 (nation's 3d-oldest nuclear plant), in Forked River, 9 mi/14.5 km S of Toms River; uses cooling water from Barnegat Bay, and has a max. dependable capacity of 610 MWe; scheduled to be closed.

Ocean, township (1990 pop. 25,058), Monmouth co., E central NE N.J., 1 mi/1.6 km NW Asbury Park; 40°15′N 74°02′W. Inc. 1849.

Ocean Beach, suburban section of San Diego city, San Diego co., S Calif., 6 mi/9.7 km WNW of downtown San Diego, on Pacific Ocean. Mission Bay and mouth of San Diego R. to North Point Loma Naval Reservation and Cabrillo Natl. Monument to S. Point Loma Col. and Natl. Univ. are in area. San Diego Internatl. Airport to E. Residential and beach resort area.

Ocean Beach, N.Y.: see FIRE ISLAND.

Ocean Bluff, Mass.: see MARSHFIELD.

Ocean Cape, SE Alaska, on Gulf of Alaska, on E shore of entrance to Yakutat Bay; 59°32′N 139°52′W. Nearby are a Native fishing area and an air strip built in World War II.

Ocean City, city (1990 pop. 15,512), Cape May co., SE N.J., resort on the Atlantic coast, on an 8-mi/13-km-long isl. bet. the Atlantic Ocean and Great Egg Harbor Bay; linked to the mainland by a 2-mi/3.2-km causeway; 39°16′N 74°35′W. Its boardwalk, amusement rides, and proximity to other N.J. beaches make it a popular summer vacation spot. Inc. 1897.

Ocean City 1 town (□ 1 sq mi/2.6 sq km; 1990 pop. 5,422), Okaloosa co., NW Fla., directly N of Fort Walton Beach across Cinco Bayou; 30°26′N 86°36′W. **2** town (1990 pop. 5,146), Worchester co., SE Md., 28 mi/45 km E of Salisbury, and extends 10 mi/16 km along a barrier beach; 38°23′N 75°02′W. Largest ocean resort in the state. Originally patented in the 1870s as "The Ladies Resort to the Sea." Tourism is its economic mainstay and the pop. greatly increases during the summer. Storm tides here, particularly those of March 6–8, 1962, were the most devastating on the East Coast. A major center for deep-sea fishing. The Coast Guard Station here, est. on Aug. 4, 1790, is one of the oldest in the country. The First Md.-Del. Boundary Marker, at the foot of the Fenwick Isl. Lighthouse (no longer in operation), was erected in 1751. Inc. 1880.

Ocean Drive Beach, uninc. village, Horry co., E S.C., 20 mi/32 km NE of Myrtle Beach, on Atlantic Ocean, in Grand Strand Beach resort area.

Ocean Falls, town, W B.C., W Canada, on inlet of the Pacific Ocean, 300 mi/403 km NW of Vancouver; 52°22′N 127°41′W. Paper-milling and -shipping center; hydroelectric power.

Ocean Gate, borough (1990 pop. 2,078), Ocean co., E N.J., on Toms R., and 4 mi/6.4 km SE of Toms River; 39°55′N 74°08′W. In fishing and resort area.

Ocean Grove, part of Neptune Township (1990 pop. 4,818), Monmouth co., E N.J., on the Atlantic coast, just S of Asbury Park. Founded 1869 by Methodist camp meeting association as a tent city for summer camp meetings, with an auditorium (seating 7,000) designed according to biblical rules. Noted for its Victorian architecture. Blue laws kept cars off the roads, and clothes off the lines on Sundays. Roads in and out of here were roped off all day to keep the traffic out. The N.J. supreme court struck down the laws in 1979, thereby opening the streets to Sunday traffic.

Ocean Grove, Mass.: see SWANSEA.

Ocean Island, Hawaii: see KURE ATOLL.

Ocean Isle Beach, village (1990 pop. 523), Brunswick co., SE N.C., 40 mi/64 km SW of Wilmington, on Atlantic Ocean; 33°53′N 78°25′W. Tubbs Inlet to W; Intracoastal Waterway canal passes to N. Beach resort area.

Ocean Park, uninc. town (1990 pop. 1,409), Pacific co., SW Wash., 20 mi/32 km SW of Raymond, on North Beach Peninsula, on Pacific Ocean; 46°30′N 124°02′W. Beach resort; tourism. Mfg. (processed seafood). Willapa Bay 1 mi/1.6 km E. Leadbetter State Park, near entrance to Willapa Bay, to N. Parts of Willapa Natl. Wildlife Refuge to N and SE.

Ocean Pond, lake, E N.F., E Canada, 30 mi/48 km SW of Bonavista; 4 mi/6 km long, 2 mi/3 km wide; 48°19′N 53°39′W. Drains into Trinity Bay.

Ocean Ridge, town (□ 1 sq mi/2.6 sq km; 1990 pop. 1,570), Palm Beach co., SE Fla., 1 mi/1.6 km E of Boynton Beach, on the Atlantic Ocean; 26°31′N 80°03′W.

Ocean Shores, town (1990 pop. 2,301), Grays Harbor co., W Wash., 14 mi/23 km W of Aberdeen, on peninsula bet. Grays Harbor and Pacific Ocean; 46°58′N 124°09′W. Entrance to harbor and Point Brown to S. Ferry to Westport at S side of harbor. Ocean City State Park to N. Beach resort.

Ocean Springs, city (1990 pop. 14,658), Jackson co., extreme SE Miss., 3 mi/4.8 km ENE of Biloxi, at entrance to Biloxi Bay (bridged), on Gulf of Mexico; 30°24′N 88°47′W. Mfg. (electronics prods., plastics, optical goods, pottery, apparel, consumer goods, boats, wood prods.; printing and publishing, shrimp processing); fish, shrimp. Seat of marine research laboratory (1948). Walter Anderson Mus. of Art; The Doll House, doll mus.; Fort Maurepas (replica 1 mi/1.6 km from original 1699 site); Miss. Sandhill Crane Natl. Wildlife Refuge to NE; Gulf Isls. Natl. Seashore Visitors Center, on mainland, to E; De Soto Natl. Forest to N; Gulf Marine State Park is here; Deer Isl. to S. Town established on site of Old Biloxi, founded in 1699 by Iberville as 1st Eur. settlement in lower Mississippi valley.

Ocean View, village (1990 pop. 606), Sussex co., SE Del., 16 mi/26 km SSE of Lewes, on Assawoman Canal; 38°32′N 75°05′W. In poultry-raising region; fruit, vegetables; cattle, hogs; dairying. Atlantic Coast 2 mi/3.2 km to E; Indian R. Bay to N; Assawoman Wildlife Area to S. Gateway to Bethany Beach resort area.

Oceana (o-shee-AN-ah), county (□ 1,306 sq mi/3,383 sq km; 1990 pop. 22,454), W Mich., on L. Michigan (W); ⊙ Hart; 43°39′N 86°31′W. Drained by White R. and short Pentwater R. Fruit (apples, cherries, peaches) and vegetables; cattle, hogs, poultry; dairying. Some mfg. at Hart, Shelby, and Pentwater. Fisheries. Resort. Includes part of Manistee Natl. Forest in E and far N; several lakes, mainly in E and NW; Charles Mears (NW) and Silver L. (W) state parks, both on L. Michigan. Organized 1855.

Oceana (o-shee-AN-uh), town (1990 pop. 1,791), Wyoming co., S W.Va., on Clear Fork, 9 mi/14.5 km NW of Pineville; 37°41′N 81°37′W. Agr. (corn, potatoes); cattle. R. D. Bailey L. reservoir and Wildlife Management Area to SW.

Oceanlake, uninc. town, Lincoln co., W Oregon, on Pacific Ocean, 2 mi/3.2 km N of Lincoln City. Resort area. Roads End Beach State Wayside to N. Devils L. to SE.

Oceano, uninc. town (1990 pop. 6,169), San Luis Obispo co., SW Calif., on Pacific Ocean, 12 mi/19 km S of San Luis Obispo; 35°06′N 120°37′W. Flowers, nursery stock; vegetables, apples, strawberries, avocados, grain; cattle. Beach resort; tourism. Pismo State Beach is here.

Oceanport, borough (1990 pop. 6,146), Monmouth co., E N.J., on Shrewsbury R. estuary (head of navigation), and 3 mi/4.8 km NW of Long Branch; 40°19′N 74°01′W. Largely residential. Computer mfg. Fort Monmouth nearby. Inc. 1920.

Oceanside 1 city (1990 pop. 128,398), San Diego co., S Calif., suburb 36 mi/58 km NNW of downtown San Diego, on the Gulf of Santa Catalina; 33°14′N 117°19′W. RR junction. Commercial and trading center for an inland farm area and for Camp Pendleton Marine Corps Base to N. Mainly residential, the city produces rubber goods, electronic components, hardware, motors, and clothing; also has a large citrus, flower, and bulb industry. Deep-sea fishing and tourism, owing to its seaside location, are also important. Oceanside is one of the fastest-growing U.S. cities, marked by a pop. increase of over 67% bet. 1980 and 1990. Seat of Mira Costa Col. (2-year). Nearby is San Luis Rey Mission (founded 1798). Carlsbad (S) and San Onofre (NW) state beaches nearby. Inc. 1888. **2** uninc. residential city (□ 5 sq mi/13 sq km; 1990 pop. 32,423), Nassau co., SE N.Y., on the S shore of L.I.; 40°37′N 73°38′W.

Ocheda Lake (o-CHEE-duh), Nobles co., SW Minn., 3 mi/4.8 km S of Worthington; 7 mi/11.3 km long, 5 mi/8 km wide; 43°32′N 95°38′W. Fed from N by short stream from Okabena L. Drains S into Ocheyedan R. Lake is divided into 3 distinct sects., connected by narrow channels.

Ochelata (och-uh-LAIT-uh), village (1990 pop. 441), Washington co., NE Okla., 9 mi/14.5 km S of Bartlesville, near Caney R.; 36°36′N 95°58′W. In farm and ranch area.

Ocheyedan (o-CHEE-duhn), town (1990 pop. 539), Osceola co., NW Iowa, near Ocheyedan R., 11 mi/18 km E of Sibley; 43°25′N 95°32′W. Makes popcorn. Nearby is Ocheyedan Mound, highest point (1,675 ft/511 m) in Iowa.

Ocheyedan River, 58 mi/93 km long, Minn. and Iowa; rises in Nobles co., SW Minn., in Ochada L., 3 mi/4.8 km S of Worthington; flows S through L. Bella reservoir then SE into NW Iowa to Little Sioux R. at Spencer.

Ochiltree, county (□ 918 sq mi/2,378 sq km; 1990 pop. 9,128), extreme N Texas, on Okla. (N) state line; ⊙ Perryton; 36°16′N 100°48′W. On high plains of the Panhandle; elev. c.2,600 ft/792 m–3,100 ft/945 m. Drained by Wolf and Kiowa creeks, tributaries of the North Canadian R. A leading wheat-producing co. of U.S.; also cattle ranching; sheep, hogs, horses; cotton, wheat, sorghum; oil and gas, gypsum, sand and gravel, clay. Formed 1876.

Ochlocknee (ok-LAHK-nee), town (1990 pop. 588), Thomas co., S Ga., 10 mi/16 km NNW of Thomasville; 30°59′N 84°03′W. Also spelled Ochlochnee.

Ochlockonee River (ok-LAHK-uh-nee), c.150 mi/241 km long, in Ga. and Fla.; rises SW of Sylvester in SW Ga.; flows generally S, across NW Fla., into W end of Apalachee Bay of the Gulf of Mexico, 14 mi/23 km SSW of Crawfordville; 31°27′N 83°55′W. W of Tallahassee, a dam forms L. Talquin (c.14 mi/23 km long, 1 mi/1.6 km–4 mi/6.4 km wide).

Ocho Rios, town (1991 pop. 8,189), St. Ann parish, NE Jamaica, on the Caribbean Sea; 18°25′N 77°07′W. Major tourist center noted for its rivers and waterfalls, as well as a commercial port that exports mainly bauxite, logwood, and sugar.

Ochoco Creek (O-chuh-ko), c.40 mi/64 km long, Oregon; rises in mt. region of N Crook co., central Oregon; flows W to Crooked R. at Prineville. Ochoco Reservoir (4 mi/6.4 km long), 8 mi/12.9 km E of Prineville, is formed by small dam in upper course. Used for irrigation.

Ochre River, village (1991 pop. 991), W Man., central Canada, on Ochre R., near Dauphin L., 14 mi/23 km ESE of Dauphin; 51°03′N 99°47′W. Grain; mixed farming.

Ocilla (o-SIL-uh), town (1990 pop. 3,182), ⊙ Irwin co., S central Ga., 8 mi/12.9 km S of Fitzgerald; 31°36′N 83°15′W. Agr. trade center; mfg. includes chemicals, roasted nuts, clothing. Inc. 1897.

Ocmulgee (ok-MUHL-gee), river, c.255 mi/410 km long, central Ga.; formed SE of Atlanta, NW Ga., by the confluence of the Yellow, South, and Alcovy rivers; 33°19′N 83°50′W; flows SE past Macon to join the Oconee R. and form the Altamaha R. near Lumber City. Major river of middle Ga. The river passes the remains of prehistoric Native Amer. villages, preserved in Ocmulgee Natl. Monument in Macon near Fort Hawkins. Macon's cotton market flourished due to its location at the head of the river's navigation

Ocmulgee National Monument (ok-MUHL-gee) (□ 1 sq mi/1.6 sq km), central Ga., on Ocmulgee R., just E of Macon; 32°48′N 83°35′W. Mounds, pyramids, artifacts, and village remains of early Mississippian civilization; reconstructed earth lodge on 1 of 8 grass-covered mounds. Authorized 1934; est. 1936.

Ocoa Bay (o-KO-ah), inlet of the Caribbean, S Dominican Republic, 45 mi/72 km W of Santo Domingo; 18°22′N 70°39′W.

Ococingo, Mexico: see OCOSINGO.

Ocoee (o-KO-ee), town (□ 9 sq mi/23.3 sq km; 1990 pop. 12,778), Orange co., central Fla., 10 mi/16 km W of Orlando, near L. Apopka; 28°34′N 81°31′W. Ships citrus fruit and general produce.

Ocoee River (o-KO-ee), in N Ga. and SE Tenn., formed in Blue Ridge Mts. 9 mi/14 km SE of Blue Ridge city, Ga., by confluence of 2 headstreams; flows c.80 mi/129 km NW through Fannin co. (here called Toccoa R.), into Tenn., past Copper Hill, through Polk co., and N to Hiwassee R. 2 mi/3 km N of Benton; 90 mi/145 km long; 35°12′N 84°30′W. Drains forest area in both states. Drainage area is 639 sq mi/1,655 sq km. Dammed in upper course by BLUE RIDGE DAM, forming L. Toccoa. Three other dams are in Tenn. Ocoee No. 1 (135 ft/41 m high, 840 ft/256 m long; completed 1912) is in lower course, 6 mi/10 km S of Benton; forms L. Ocoee (7 mi/11 km long, .5 mi/.8 km wide; also known as Parksville Reservoir). Ocoee No. 2 (30 ft/9 m high, 450 ft/137 m long; completed 1913) is further upstream, 6 mi/10 km NW of Copperhill. Ocoee No. 3 (110 ft/34 m high, 612 ft/187 m long; completed 1943) is at Copperhill, just N of Ga. line. Major whitewater recreation area and scheduled site of the 1996 Summer Olympics kayaking events.

Oconee 1 (o-KO-nee), county (□ 186 sq mi/482 sq km; 1990 pop. 17,618), NE central Ga.; ⊙ Watkinsville; 33°50′N 83°26′W. Piedmont area drained by Apalachee and Oconee rivers. Mfg. includes furniture, fixtures, wholesale goods; agr. includes cotton, soybeans, fruit; cattle, poultry, hogs. Formed 1875. **2** county (□ 673 sq mi/1,743 sq km; 1990 pop. 57,494), extreme NW S.C.; ⊙ Walhalla; 34°45′N 83°04′W. Bounded NW by Chattooga R., SW by Tugaloo R., E by Keowee and Seneca rivers. Includes much of S.C. part of the Blue Ridge Mts.; summer-resort area, with part of Sumter Natl. Forest. Mfg. includes granite and sand. Agr. prods. include chickens, eggs, hogs, cattle, dairying, corn, wheat, soybeans, sorghum, hay, apples. Formed 1868. Nuclear power plants Oconee 1 (initial criticality April 19, 1973), Oconee 2 (initial criticality Nov. 11, 1973), and Oconee 3 (initial criticality Sept. 5, 1974) are 30 mi/48 km W of Greenville; they use cooling water from L. Keowee, and each has a max. dependable capacity of 846 MWe.

Oconee, village (1990 pop. 201), Shelby co., central Ill., 19 mi/31 km SW of Shelbyville; 39°17′N 89°06′W. In agr. area.

Oconee 1, 2, and 3 Nuclear Power Plants, S.C.: see OCONEE CO.

Oconee (o-KO-nee), river, 282 mi/454 km long; rising in the Appalachian Mts., N Ga.; flowing SE to the Ocmulgee R. to form the Altamaha R.; 34°23′N 83°39′W. Sinclair Dam (completed 1953) and Furman Shoals Dam (completed 1953) are on the Oconee.

Oconee, Lake (o-KO-nee), reservoir (□ 30 sq mi/78 sq km), Putnam, Morgan, and Greene cos., N central Ga., on Oconee R., 18 mi/29 km NNE of Milledgeville; 33°21′N 83°09′W. Max. capacity 370,000 acre-ft. Formed by Wallace Dam (117 ft/36m high) built (1980) for power generation. Oconee Natl. Forest at N end.

Oconee State Park, S.C.: see WALHALLA.

Oconomowoc (o-KAW-nuh-mo-wawk), city (1990 pop. 10,993), Waukesha co., SE Wis., on Oconomowoc R. (tributary of Rock R.), bet. small Fowler and La Belle lakes, and 13 mi/21 km ESE of Watertown; 43°06′N 88°30′W. Mfg. (dairying and baking prods., wheelchairs, labels, electronics, fabricated metal prods.; food processing); resort with mineral springs. Annual winter-sports carnival. Inc. 1875.

Oconto (o-KAWN-to), county (□ 1,149 sq mi/2,976 sq km; 1990 pop. 30,226), NE Wis.; ⊙ Oconto; 44°59′N 88°13′W. Primarily a dairying and lumbering area; agr. (barley, oats, wheat, brans, hay; cattle, hogs, poultry). Bounded E by Green Bay; drained by Oconto R. Menominee Indian Reservation W of co.; large sect. of Nicolet Natl. Forest in NW; Copper Culture Mound State Park in E. Formed 1851.

Oconto (o-KAWN-to), town (1990 pop. 4,474), ⊙ Oconto co., NE Wis., at mouth of Oconto R., on W shore of Green Bay, 28 mi/45 km NNE of Green Bay city; 44°53′N 87°52′W. RR junction. Commercial center for lumbering and dairying area. Mfg. (wood prods., textiles, beer, food processing, pleasure boats, machinery); fisheries. Father Allouez founded a mission here in 1669; the 1st Christian Science church was built here in 1886. Was important lumbering center. Copper Culture Mound State Park to SW. Inc. 1869.

Oconto, village (1990 pop. 147), Custer co., central Nebr., 20 mi/32 km SSW of Broken Bow, and on Wood R.; 41°08′N 99°45′W.

Oconto Falls (o-KAWN-to), town (1990 pop. 2,584), Oconto co., NE Wis., on Oconto R., and 26 mi/42 km NNW of Green Bay city; 44°52′N 88°09′W. RR terminus. Mfg. (paper milling, feeds and fertilizer, magnetic printing cylinders, paper prods.). Inc. 1919.

Oconto River (o-KAWN-to), 87 mi/140 km long, NE Wis.; rises in several small lakes in SE Forest co.; flows S and E, past Oconto Falls, to Green Bay at Oconto city.

Ocosingo (o-ko-SEEN-go), city (1990 pop. 12,826) and township, Chiapas, S Mexico, on N plateau of Sierra Madre, 36 mi/58 km NE of San Cristóbal de las Casas; 16°54′N 92°05′W. Corn, rice, mangoes, oranges. Anc. Maya ruins of great interest and artistic merit nearby. Sometimes spelled Ococingo. Pop. is largely Tzectal-speaking Maya Indian.

Ocotepec 1 (o-KO-te-pek), town (1990 pop. 2,792), Chiapas, S Mexico, in N spur of Sierra Madre, 30 mi/48 km N of Tuxtla Gutiérrez. Elev. 4,629 ft/1,411 m.

Cereals, sugarcane, fruit. No paved roads. A Zoque Indian town. **2** town (1990 pop. 1,414), Puebla, central Mexico, 7 mi/11 km ENE of Libres 1 mi/2 km E of Mexico Highway 129. Corn, maguey.

Ocotillo (o-ko-TEE-yo), uninc. town, Maricopa co., central Ariz., residential suburb 16 mi/26 km SE of downtown Phoenix. Gila R. Indian Reservation to W and S. Chandler Municipal Airport to NE.

Ocotlán (o-ko-TLAHN), city (1990 pop. 62,595) and township, Jalisco, central Mexico, on NE shore of L. Chapala, at outlet of Santiago (Lerma) R., and 45 mi/72 km SE of Guadalajara; 20°21′N 102°42′W. RR junction; processing and agr. center (grain, vegetables, fruit; livestock); milk canneries, rayon-yarn plants. Point of departure for L. Chapala resort dist.

Ocotlán de Morelos (o-ko-TLAHN dai mo-RE-los), city (1990 pop. 10,219) and township, Oaxaca, S Mexico, in Sierra Madre del Sur, on RR, and 19 mi/31 km S of Oaxaca de Juárez on Mexico Highway 175; 16°49′N 96°40′W. Agr. center (cereals, sugarcane, coffee, fruit; livestock; timber); silver and gold deposits.

Ocoyoacac (o-ko-yo-ah-KAHK), town (1990 pop. 17,631), Mexico state, central Mexico, 12 mi/19 km E of Toluca de Lerdo, off Mexico Highway 15; 19°16′N 99°26′W. Agr. center (cereals; livestock); dairying.

Ocoyucan, Mexico: see SANTA CLARA OCOYUCAN.

Ocozocoautla de Espinosa (o-ko-zo-ko-ah-OO-tlah), city (1990 pop. 20,563) and township, Chiapas, S Mexico, in Sierra Madre, 18 mi/29 km W of Tuxtla; 16°46′N 93°22′W. Agr. center (corn, beans, sugarcane, coffee, tobacco, fruit). A zoque Indian town.

Ocracoke (O-kruh-kok), uninc. village (1990 pop. 650), Hyde co., E N.C., 27 mi/43 km WSW of Cape Hatteras, on Pamlico Sound, near SW end of Ocracoke Isl. (c.12 mi/19 km long, 1 mi/1.6 km wide), in Outer Banks, sand barrier bet. the Atlantic Ocean and Pamlico Sound in Cape Hatteras Natl. Seashore. An important port before Civil War. Br. Cemetery, graves of 4 royal navy crewmen who d. here (1942). Ocracoke Inlet 3 mi/4.8 km to W. Ocracoke Lighthouse (1823), oldest operating lighthouse in N. C., at center of village. Toll ferries to Swan Quarter, on mainland (NW) and Cedar Isl. (SW, carries State Highway 12 traffic).

Ocracoke Inlet (O-kruh-kok), E N.C., passage connecting Pamlico Sound (NW) with the Atlantic Ocean (SE) bet. Ocracoke Isl. (Cape Hatteras Natl. Seashore) to NE and Portsmouth Isl. (Cape Lookout Natl. Seashore) to SW. Hyde-Carteret co. line passes through.

Octa (AHK-tuh), village (1990 pop. 78), Fayette co., S central Ohio, 10 mi/16 km WNW of Washington Court House; 39°37′N 83°36′W.

Octavia (awk-TAI-vee-uh), village (1990 pop. 132), Butler co., E Nebr., 7 mi/11.3 km NNE of David City, near Platte R; 41°21′N 97°03′W.

Octoraro Creek (AHK-to-RER-o), SE Pa. and NE Md.; formed by joining of West and East branches in Octoraro L. reservoir, 4 mi/6.4 km WNW of Oxford, Pa.; flows c.20 mi/32 km SE in Md. to Susquehanna R. at 8 mi/12.9 km NNW of Havre de Grace; 39°48′N 76°02′W. East Branch rises in NE Lancaster co., near Chester co. line, flows c.20 mi/32 km South West Branch rises in E Lancaster co., flows c.20 mi/32 km SSW and SE.

Ocuilan de Arteaga (o-KWEE-lahn dai ahr-te-AH-gah), town (1990 pop. 2,106), ⊙ Ocuilan municipio, Mexico state, central Mexico, 12 mi/20 km WSW of Cuernavaca; 18°58′N 99°25′W. Cereals, sugarcane, vegetables; livestock.

Ocuituco (o-kwee-TOO-ko), town (1990 pop. 3,730), Morelos, central Mexico, 12 mi/19 km NE of Cuautla; 18°52′N 98°46′W. Grain, sugar, fruit; livestock.

Odanah (o-DAN-uh), village (1990 pop. 190), Ashland co., extreme N Wis., 9 mi/14.5 km E of Ashland, on Bad R., in Bad R. Reservation (for Chippewa Indians), in barren, marshy area; 46°36′N 90°40′W. Wild rice. Near L. Superior.

Odebolt (O-duh-bolt), town (1990 pop. 1,158), Sac co., W Iowa, 15 mi/24 km SW of Sac Center; 42°18′N 95°15′W. Popcorn. Inc. 1877.

Odell (o-DEL), town, Coos co., N N.H., 20 mi/32 km NW of Berlin. Wilderness area in Nash Stream State Forest. Drained by Nash Stream. Timber.

Odell 1 (o-DEL), village (1990 pop. 1,030), Livingston co., NE central Ill., 10 mi/16 km NNE of Pontiac; 41°00′N 88°31′W. In agr. area; mfg. of clothing. **2** village (1990 pop. 291), Gage co., SE Nebr., 15 mi/24 km S of Beatrice, and on branch of Big Blue R., near Kansas state line; 40°02′N 96°47′W. Grain; livestock; dairy and poultry prods.; animal crates and cribs. **3** village (1990 pop. 131), Wilbarger co., N Texas, 15 mi/24 km NNW of Vernon, near Red R. (Okla. state line). In agr. area.

Odem, town (1990 pop. 2,366), San Patricio co., S Texas, 15 mi/24 km NW of Corpus Christi, near Nueces R.; 27°56′N 97°35′W. RR junction in farm area (cotton, sorghum; cattle). Oil and natural gas. W end of Nueces Bay to SE. Inc. as city 1929.

Oden 1 (O-duhn), village (1990 pop. 126), Montgomery co., W Ark., c.40 mi/64 km WNW of Hot Springs, on Ouachita R., in Ouachita Natl. Forest; 34°37′N 93°47′W. **2** village, Emmet co., NW Mich., on Crooked L., and 6 mi/9.7 km NE of Petoskey; 45°25′N 84°49′W. Has large state fish hatchery. Resort area.

Odenton (O-duhn-tuhn), village (1990 pop. 12,833), Anne Arundel co., central Md., 14 mi/23 km NW of Annapolis; 39°04′N 76°42′W. In vegetable-farming area; plastics, furniture and corrugated box plant. Named for Oden Bowie, who became governor of Md. in 1869. The town caters to Fort George G. Meade, just NW, and has fast-food restaurants lining the road.

Odenville, town (1990 pop. 796), St. Clair co., NE central Ala., c.9 mi/14.5 km NW of Pell City.

Oderin Island (o-DIR-in), SE N.F., E Canada, in Placentia Bay, 40 mi/64 km W of Argentia; 2 mi/3 km long; 47°18′N 54°49′W. Fishing.

Odessa 1 (o-DES-suh), village, SE Ont., central Canada, 12 mi/19 km WNW of Kingston; 44°17′N 76°43′W. Cheese making. **2** village (1991 pop. 239), S Sask., W Canada, 40 mi/64 km ESE of Regina. Wheat; dairying.

Odessa 1 city (1990 pop. 3,695), Lafayette co., W central Mo., 33 mi/53 km E of Kansas City; 39°00′N 93°57′W. Processes and ships farm prods. Corn, wheat, sorghum; cattle, hogs; mfg. (consumer goods). Plotted 1878. **2** city (1990 pop. 89,699), ⊙ Ector co., extends E into Midland co., W Texas, 18 mi/29 km SW of Midland, and 123 mi/198 km SSW of Lubbock; 31°52′N 102°20′W. Elev. 2,891 ft/881 m. Great oil deposits just to the S changed Odessa from a small ranch town into a large and growing oil center with refineries and plants that produce fuels, carbon black, chemicals, plastics, synthetic rubber, industrial gas, and machinery. The region is underlain by potash, salt, and limestone deposits. Schlemeyer Field airport to N, Midland Airport (to E) handles many commuters to and from Dallas and Houston. Co. Coliseum. Seat of Odessa Col. (2-year) and Univ. of Texas of the Permian Basin. Founded 1881, inc. 1927.

Odessa (o-DES-suh), town (1990 pop. 935), Lincoln co., E Wash., 32 mi/51 km SW of Davenport, on Crab Creek, at mouth of Duck Creek; 47°20′N 118°42′W. In Columbia basin agr. region; ships barley, oats, rye, potatoes, wheat, cattle. Coffeepot L. and Twin Lakes to NE; Pacific L. to N. Town settled by Germans and Russians.

Odessa 1 (o-DES-suh), village (1990 pop. 303), New Castle co., N central Del., 20 mi/32 km S of Wilmington; 39°27′N 75°39′W. In agr. region. Has 18th-cent. homes; Friends meetinghouse dates from 1783. Winterthur Mus. at Odessa. Silver Run Wildlife Area to NE. Named after Odessa, Ukraine (then Russia). Formerly called Cantwell's Bridge. A busy port for grain shipments until 1855, when the new RR bypassed the town, leaving it to serve as a small local trade center. **2** village (1990 pop. 155), Big Stone co., SW Minn., 7 mi/11.3 km ESE of Ortonville, on Minnesota R., near S.Dak. state line; 45°15′N 96°19′W. Grain. Lac qui Parle Wildlife Area to SE. **3** resort village (□ 7 sq mi/18.1 sq km; 1990 pop. 986), Schuyler co., W central N.Y., in Finger Lakes region, 15 mi/24 km WSW of Ithaca; 42°18′N 76°49′W.

Odessadale (o-DES-uh-dail), town, Meriwether co., W Ga., 12 mi/19 km ESE of La Grange; 33°00′N 84°48′W.

Odin 1 village (1990 pop. 1,150), Marion co., S central Ill., 5 mi/8 km W of Salem; 38°37′N 89°02′W. In agr. and oil-producing area. Inc. 1865. **2** village (1990 pop. 102), Watonwan co., S Minn., 10 mi/16 km SW of St. James, on South Fork of Watonwan R.; 43°52′N 94°44′W. Grain, soybeans; livestock; mfg. (agr. equip. parts, feeds). Small lakes in area.

Odin, Mount (9,751 ft/2,972 m), SE B.C., W Canada, in Monashee Mts., 30 mi/48 km S of Revelstoke; 50°33′N 118°08′W.

Odiorne's Point (O-dee-yuhr), SE N.H., small peninsula near mouth of the Piscataqua R., bet. Portsmouth and Rye. Odiorne State Park. Site of state's 1st Eur. settlement (1623).

Odon, town (1990 pop. 1,475), Daviess co., SW Ind., 15 mi/24 km NE of Washington; 38°50′N 86°59′W. In agr. area (corn, soybeans; dairying); mfg. (agr. and industrial supplies, concrete burial vaults, lumber). Laid out 1846.

O'Donnell, town (1990 pop. 1,102), Lynn and Dawson cos., NW Texas, on the Llano Estacado 45 mi/72 km S of Lubbock; 32°58′N 101°49′W. Elev. 3,110 ft/948 m. In irrigated agr. area (wheat, cotton; livestock); mfg. (farm tools). Settled 1908, inc. 1923.

Odum (O-duhm), village (1990 pop. 388), Wayne co., SE Ga., 10 mi/16 km NW of Jesup, on Little Satilla Creek; 31°40′N 82°02′W. Mfg. includes textile printing and meat processing.

Oella (O-el-lah), suburban village, Baltimore co., central Md., on Patapsco R., and 10 mi/16 km W of downtown Baltimore. The large cotton mill est. here in 1845 is said to have been named for the 1st woman in Amer. to spin cotton. Once exclusively a workers' town, it is becoming gentrified. Benjamin Banneker, "the free man of color" who helped lay out Washington, D.C. for Thomas Jefferson, was associated with the Mt. Gillboa Church. Patapsco Valley State Park is nearby and Baltimore and Ohio RR Mus.The stone mill is now a community center, gallery and crafts shop.

Oelrichs, village (1990 pop. 138), Fall R. co., SW S.Dak., 20 mi/32 km SE of Hot Springs, and on Horsehead Creek; 43°10′N 103°13′W. Buffalo Gap Natl. Grasslands to E, S (?is)& W.

Oelwein, city (1990 pop. 6,493), Fayette co., NE Iowa, 20 mi/32 km S of West Union; 42°40′N 91°54′W. RR center; poultry-packing plant; feed, beverages. Inc. 1888.

O'Fallon 1 city (1990 pop. 16,073), St. Clair co., SW Ill., suburb of St. Louis, 12 mi/19 km E of East St. Louis; 38°35′N 89°54′W. Bituminous coal in area; agr. area (corn, soybeans, wheat; hogs); flour mill, dairying. Scott Air Force Base is SE. City derives pop. and revenue from base personnel. Inc. 1865. **2** city (1990 pop. 18,698), St. Charles co., E Mo., residential and commercial suburb 25 mi/40 km WNW of St. Louis; 38°46′N 90°42′W. R.C. convent. Agr. remains mainly to N, along Mississippi R. (soybeans, corn, vegetables). Mfg. (paper prods., fabricated metal prods., transportation equip., consumer goods). Rapid urban growth since 1970s.

O'Fallon Creek (O-FAH-luhn), c.90 mi/145 km long, SE Mont.; rises in NW Carter co., flows N, past Ismay, to Yellowstone R. 7 mi/11.3 km ENE of Terry.

Offerle (AWF-uhr-lee), village (1990 pop. 228), Edwards co., S central Kansas, 8 mi/12.9 km WSW of Kinsley; 37°53′N 99°33′W. In wheat region.

Offutt Air Force Base, U.S. military installation (□ 3 sq mi/7.8 sq km; 1990 pop. 10,883), E Nebr., S of Omaha; 41°06′N 95°55′W. Est. 1896 as Fort Crook, an army base. Converted to an air base in the early 1900s and renamed in 1924, it is now the hq. of the Strategic Command. The Strategic Air Command (S.A.C) Mus. is on the base.

Ogallala (o-guh-LUH-luh), city (1990 pop. 5,095), ⊙ Keith co., SW central Nebr., 50 mi/80 km W of North Platte city, and on South Platte R.; 41°07′N 101°43′W. Mfg. (machinery, electronic prods., bldg. materials, textiles, foods, machine prods.; printing.). Livestock (cattle); wheat, corn, beans; dairy and poultry prods. Nearby, on North Platte R., are Kingsley Dam and Lake C. W. McConaughy (Kingsley Reservoir). Old Oregon Trail follows S side of river. L. McConanghy State Recreation Area to N and NW (7 units scattered along S sides of lake); L. Ogallala State Recreation Area to N, S of Kingsley Dam. Front St., reconstruction and reenactment of Old West town life. City laid out 1875, inc. 1930.

Ogallala Aquifer, region, Nebr.; the main source of irrigation water in Nebr. and the remainder of the High Plains, of which it is the chief component. The Ogallala, of Tertiary age, contains thick permeable materials, consisting largely of sand and gravel, and underlies the Nebr. Sand Hills, extending beyond, esp. at the S and E, where it merges with Quaternary sand and gravel. In places it is overlain by recent alluvium, as along the Platte R.

Ogden, city (1990 pop. 63,909), ⊙ Weber co., N Utah, at the confluence of the Ogden and Weber rivers; 41°13′N 111°58′W. Aerospace industries, Hill Air Force Base (Utah's largest employer, with 17,000 employees) and the Ogden Defense Depot to W are the major employers. The site of a trading post in the 1820s, the area was settled by Mormons in 1847. Seat of Weber State Univ. and a state industrial school; has a Mormon temple and tabernacle. Surrounded by mts., and major ski resorts in the area include Snow Basin to E (elev. 4,300 ft/1,311 m), Nordic Valley, and Powder Mt. Important RR center. Mfg. (paper mill; weapons design; transportation equip., machinery, fabricated metal prods., foods, bldg. materials, carbon fiber prods., chemicals, computer prods., electrical and electronic goods, consumer goods, apparel, motor vehicles, paper goods; printing and publishing, sugar beet refining). Wasatch Range and Natl. Forest to E. Mt. Ogden 5 mi/8 km to SE. Fort Buenaventura State Historical Park to W. Ogden Bay Waterfowl Management Area to W. Inc. 1851.

Ogden 1 town (1990 pop. 1,909), Boone co., central Iowa, 7 mi/11.3 km W of Boone; 42°02′N 94°01′W. In agr. area. Inc. 1878. **2** town (1990 pop. 1,494), Riley co., NE central Kansas, on Kansas R., and 9 mi/14.5 km SW of Manhattan; 39°06′N 96°42′W. Grazing; agr. At entrance to Fort Riley Military Reserve. **3** (AHG-duhn), uninc. town (1990 pop. 3,228), New Hanover co., SE N.C., residential suburb 7 mi/11.3 km ENE of Wilmington, near Middle Sound (Intracoastal Waterway); 34°16′N 77°47′W. Atlantic Ocean 4 mi/6.4 km to SE.

Ogden 1 village (1990 pop. 264), Little River co., extreme SW Ark., 11 mi/18 km N of Texarkana, and near Red R.; 33°34′N 94°02′W. **2** village (1990 pop. 671), Champaign co., E Ill., 14 mi/23 km E of Urbana; 40°07′N 87°57′W. In agr. area.

Ogden Dunes, town (1990 pop. 1,499), Porter co., NW Ind., on L. Michigan, 7 mi/11.3 km E of downtown Gary; 41°37′N 87°11′W. Residential suburb. Ind. Dunes State Park nearby to E.

Ogden Island, St. Lawrence co., N N.Y., in the St. Lawrence R. (rapids here), at Can. (Ont.) border, just N of Waddington; c.2.75 mi/4.43 km long, ½ mi/8⁄10 km–1.5 mi/2.4 km wide; 44°52′N 75°13′W. Connected to N.Y. shore by bridge.

Ogden, Mount 1 on border bet. U.S. (Alaska) and Canada (B.C.), in Coast Range, 40 mi/64 km ENE of Juneau (Alaska); 58°26′N 133°23′W. **2** (9,572 ft/2,918 m), N Utah, 5 mi/8 km SE of Ogden, in Wasatch Mts., Weber co., in Wasatch Natl. Forest. Snow Basin Ski Resort to NE.

Ogden River, 35 mi/56 km long, Utah; formed in the Wasatch Range Weber co., N Utah, at the convergence of its North, Middle,and South forks at Pineview Reservoir near Huntsville; flows SW through Wasatch Natl. Forest and city of Ogden to join the Weber R. just W of Ogden. The river has been used for irrigation for nearly a cent. The Ogden-Brigham Canal (c.20 mi/30 km long) carries water N to Brigham City. Pineview Dam, completed by the Bureau of Reclamation in 1937, is at the head of Ogden Canyon. The headwater region of the Ogden is a winter sports area. South Fork formed at Causey Reservoir in E Weber co. by 3 forks, flows W c.20 mi/32 km; Middle Fork rises in NE Weber co., flows SW c.15 mi/24 km; North Fork rises in N Weber co., flows SSE c.15 mi/24 km.

Ogdensburg, city (□ 8 sq mi/20.7 sq km; 1990 pop. 13,521), St. Lawrence co., N N.Y., on the St. Lawrence R. at the mouth of the Oswegatchie R., in a resort area, opposite Prescott (Ont.; connected by Ogdensburg Prescott Internatl. Bridge); 44°42′N 75°28′W. A variety of light industrial prods. are made here, including shade rollers and blinds. Settled by Fr. missionaries and trappers 1749; was strategically important in the War of 1812. Seat of Mater Dei, and Wadhams Hall Seminary and Col. and a mus. with works of Frederic Remington, who lived here. Rhoda Fox Graves was the 1st woman to serve the state's Assembly and Senate. Inc. as a city 1868.

Ogdensburg, village (1990 pop. 220), Waupaca co., central Wis., 7 mi/11.3 km N of Waupaca; 44°27′N 89°01′W. In farm area. Mfg. (fiberglass prods.).

Ogdensburg (AHG-duhnz-buhrg), borough (1990 pop. 2,722), Sussex co., NW N.J., on Wallkill R., and 8 mi/12.9 km ENE of Newton; 41°04′N 74°35′W. Inc. 1914.

Ogeechee River (o-GEE-chee), c.250 mi/402 km long, E Ga.; rises E of Greensboro; flows SE, past Louisville and Millen, to the Atlantic Ocean through Ossabaw Sound, 15 mi/24 km S of Savannah; 33°31′N 82°54′W. Rice plantations formerly located along lower reaches.

Ogema 1 (O-ge-muh), village (1990 pop. 164), Becker co., W Minn., 20 mi/32 km N of Detroit Lakes, in SW part of White Earth Indian Reservation, near Wild Rice R.; 47°06′N 95°55′W. Dairying; grain, wild rice. Numerous small lakes to E, including White Earth L. **2** village, Price co., N Wis., 28 mi/45 km W of Tomahawk. In forested area. Mfg. (wood prods., machinery). Timms Hill (1951.5 ft/594.8 m) highest point in Wis., 5 mi/8 km to E.

Ogemaw (AH-ge-maw), county (□ 574 sq mi/1,487 sq km; 1990 pop. 18,681), NE central Mich.; ⊙ West Branch; 44°19′N 84°07′W. Drained by Au Gres and Rifle rivers. Agr. (cattle, hogs; corn, wheat, oats, barley; dairy prods.). Part of Huron Natl. Forest in NE corner; state forest, game refuge, and many small lakes, esp. in E (resorts), are in co. Rifle R. State Park in NE. Organized 1875.

Ogilvie, village (1990 pop. 510), Kanabec co., E Minn., 7 mi/11.3 km WSW of Mora, on Groundhouse R.; 45°49′N 93°25′W. Grain, potatoes; livestock, poultry; dairying; mfg. Fish L. to E.

Ogilvie Range, E Yukon, NW Canada, at NW end of Mackenzie Mts., extending c.150 mi/241 km WNW from N.W.T. border.

Ogle (O-guhl), county (□ 763 sq mi/1,976 sq km; 1990 pop. 45,957), N Ill.; ⊙ Oregon; 42°02′N 89°19′W. Agr. (cattle, hogs; dairy prods.; corn, soybeans, hay). Food processing plants; mfg. (textile finishing, die-casting; paper prods.). Also other mfg. at Oregon and Rochelle. Drained by Rock, Leaf, and Kyte rivers, and by Kilbuck and Elkhorn creeks. Includes White Pines Forest, Lowden, and Castle Rock state parks and Lowder-Miller State Forest. John Deere home at Grand Detour (S). Nuclear power plants Byron 1 (initial criticality Feb. 2, 1985) and Byron 2 (initial criticality Jan. 9, 1987) are 17 mi/27 km SW of Rockford; use cooling water from the Rock R. and each has a max. dependable capacity of 1,105 MWe. Formed 1836.

Oglesby (O-guhlz-bee), city (1990 pop. 3,619), La Salle co., N Ill., on Illinois R., near mouth of Vermilion R., 3 mi/4.8 km SE of La Salle; 41°17′N 89°03′W. Mfg. (consumer goods., bldg. materials); agr. (dairying; corn, wheat, soybeans; cattle, hogs). Inc. 1902. Ill. Valley Community Col. 1 mi/1.6 km W.

Oglesby, village (1990 pop. 452), Coryell co., central Texas, near Leon R., 23 mi/37 km WSW of Waco; 31°25′N 97°30′W. In cattle, farm area; mfg. (machining). Beelton L. reservoir and Mother Neff State Park to S.

Oglethorpe (O-guhl-thorp), county (□ 442 sq mi/1,145 sq km; 1990 pop. 9,763), NE Ga.; ⊙ Lexington; 33°53′N 83°05′W. Piedmont agr. (wheat, fruit); cattle, hogs, poultry; in timber area. Formed 1793.

Oglethorpe (O-guhl-thorp), town (1990 pop. 1,302), ⊙ Macon co., W central Ga., c.45 mi/72 km SW of Macon, and on Flint R. opposite Montezuma; 32°17′N 84°04′W. Mfg. includes animal feeds, wood and paper prods. Inc. 1849.

Oglethorpe, Mount (O-guhl-thorp) (3,290 ft/1,003 m), Pickens co., N Ga., 6 mi/9.7 km NE of Jasper, at S end of the Blue Ridge, at SW terminus of Appalachian Trail; 34°29′N 84°19′W. A white marble shaft has been erected at its summit as a memorial to Gen. James E. Oglethorpe, founder of the Ga. colony. Called Grassy Mt. until 1929.

Ogoki (o-GO-kee), river, c.300 mi/480 km long, Ont., central Canada; rises in lakes W of L. Nipigon, W central Ont.; flows NE to the Albany R. A dam at Waboose Rapids forms a reservoir (45 mi/72 km long), which drains to the S into L. Nipigon; 51°38′N 85°57′W.

Ogualik Island, Canada: see COD ISLAND.

Ogunquit (o-GUHN-kwit), village (1990 pop. 974), in Wells town, York co., SW Maine, on the Atlantic coast, 17 mi/27 km SSE of Alfred; 43°15′N 70°36′W. Summer resort frequented esp. by artists; summer playhouse.

O'Hara (o-HER-ah), township (1990 pop. 9,096), Allegheny co., W Pa., residential suburb 6 mi/9.7 km NE of Pittsburgh; 40°30′N 79°54′W. Allegheny R. is township's S boundary.

Ohatchee (o-HAT-chee), town (1990 pop. 1,042), Calhoun co., E Ala., 12 mi/19 km NW of Anniston, bet. Ohatchee Creek and Neely Henry L. Mfg. (paint and children's clothes). Ohatchee is the incorporated name for Ohatchie. The Ohatchee Creek Ranch, which houses more than 50 different animal species, is located just E.

Ohaton (o-HA-tuhn), village, central Alta., Canada, 9 mi/14 km ESE of Camrose. Coal mining; oil and gas; wheat, oats, barley.

Ohio, state (□ 44,828 sq mi/116,105 sq km; 1995 est. pop. 11,150,506), N U.S., in the Great Lakes region of the Midwest, admitted as the 17th state of the Union in 1803; ⊙ COLUMBUS (the largest city). Other major cities are CLEVELAND, CINCINNATI, TOLEDO, and AKRON. The Ohio R., from which the state takes its name, separates it in the SE from W.Va. and in the S from Ky.; Ohio is bounded on the W by Ind., on the N by Mich. and L. Erie, and on the E (N of the Ohio R.) by Pa. From the dunes on L. Erie to the gorge-cut plateau along the Ohio R., the land is fairly flat, with some pleasant rolling country and in the SE rugged little hills leading to the mts. of W.Va. Before the coming of settlers to Ohio, it was covered with many square miles of virgin forest, but today only vestiges of the trees that helped to build the many cities remain. The state is highly industrialized. Yet it continues to draw from the earth: it leads the nation in the production of lime, is 2d in the production of clays, and ranks high in the production of salt. Also produced are sand and gravel, stone, and coal. The land supports rich farms, especially where the soil was improved ages ago by glacier-ground limestone. Although most of the state's income is derived from commerce and mfg., Ohio has extensive farms, and produces large amounts of corn, soybeans, hay, wheat, cattle, hogs, and dairy items. RRs and highways crisscross the state, bearing raw materials and manufactured goods. The L. Erie ports, Toledo and Cleveland, handle much iron and copper ore, coal, oil, and finished materials (including steel and automobile parts). In spite of massive decline in mfg. employment since the 1970s, the state still is a major mfg. center and the value added by mfg. is at an all-time high. Heavy industry is still significant but there is more employment in polymer industries now than in the steel industry at its peak. Leading prods. include polymers, transportation equip., primary and fabricated metals, and machinery. In prehistoric times Ohio was inhabited by the Mound Builders, many of whose mounds are preserved in state parks and in the Mound City Group Natl. Monument. Before the arrival of Europeans, E Ohio was the scene of warfare bet. the Iroquois and the Erie, resulting in the extermination of the Erie. In addition to the Iroquois, other Native Amer. tribes soon prominent in the region were the Miami, the Shawnee, and the Ottawa. La Salle began his explorations of the Ohio valley in 1669 and claimed the entire area for France. The Ohio R. became a magnet for fur traders and landseekers, and the British, moving in, hotly contested the Fr. claims. Rivalry for control of the forks of the Ohio R. (Pittsburgh, Pa.) led to the outbreak (1754) of the

OHIO 739

last of the Fr. and Indian Wars. The defeat of the French caused the transfer of the land to the British, but Br. possession was disturbed by Pontiac's Rebellion. The Br. govt. issued a proclamation in 1763 forbidding settlement W of the Appalachian Mts. Then in 1774, with the Quebec Act, the British placed the region bet. the Ohio R. and the Great Lakes within the boundaries of Canada. The colonists' resentment over these acts contributed to the discontent that led to the Amer. Revolution. In that war military operations were conducted in the Ohio country. Ohio was part of the vast area ceded to the U.S. by the Treaty of Paris (1783). Conflicting claims to land in that area made by Conn., Mass., and Va. were settled by relinquishment of almost all of the claims and the organization of the Old Northwest by the Ordinance of 1787. Ohio was the 1st region developed under the provisions of that ordinance, with the activities of the Ohio Company of Associates promoted by Rufus Putnam and Manasseh Cutler. Marietta, founded in 1788, was the first permanent Amer. settlement in the Old NW. In the years that followed, various land companies were formed, and settlers poured in from the E, down the Ohio on flatboats and barges, or across the mts. by wagon and pack horse—their numbers varying with conditions but steadily expanding the pop. The Native Americans, supported by the British, resisted Amer. settlement. A coalition of Indian tribes successfully opposed campaigns led by Josiah Harmar and Arthur St. Clair but were decisively defeated by Anthony Wayne in the battle of Fallen Timbers (1794). The British thereafter (1796) withdrew their outposts from the NW under the terms of Jay's Treaty, and the area was pacified. Ohio became a territory in 1799. General St. Clair, as the 1st governor, ruled in an arbitrary fashion that made Ohioans for many years afterward distrustful of all govt. In 1802 a state convention drafted a constitution, and in 1803 Ohio entered the Union, with Chillicothe as its capital. Columbus became the permanent capital in 1816. In the War of 1812 the Americans lost many of the 1st battles of the war in the Old Northwest, and their military frontier was pushed back to the Ohio R. The 2 Br. attacks on Ohio soil were successfully resisted: one against Fort Meigs at the mouth of the Maumee R. and another against Fort Stephenson on the Sandusky. The area was further secured with Oliver Hazard Perry's naval victory on L. Erie near Put-in-Bay, Ohio, and William Henry Harrison's victory in the battle of the Thames on Can. soil. After the war Ohio's growth was spurred by the building of the Erie Canal, other canals, and toll roads. The National Road facilitated settlement and was a vital commercial artery. Settlement of the Western Reserve by New Englanders (esp. those from Conn.) gives NE Ohio a decidedly New England cultural landscape. Before the opening of the Eric Canal (Buffalo to Albany). Ohio's society of small farms exported their produce down the Ohio and the Mississippi rivers to St. Louis and New Orleans. In 1837, Ohio won a territorial struggle with Mich. usually called the Toledo War. The Loan Law, adopted in the Panic of 1837, encouraged RR and industrial development. RRs gradually succeeded canals, preparing the way for the industrial expansion that followed the Civil War. In the war most Ohioans were sympathetic with the Union, and the state contributed many soldiers to the Union army. Native sons such as Joshua R. Giddings, Salmon P. Chase, and Edwin M. Stanton had long been prominent opponents of slavery. Nevertheless, the Peace Democrats, the Knights of the Golden Circle, and the Copperheads were very active; Clement L. Vallandigham, leader of the Copperheads, drew many votes in the gubernatorial election of 1863. Ohio was the scene of the northernmost penetration of Confederate forces in the war—the famous raid (1863) of John Hunt Morgan, which terrorized the people of the countryside until Morgan and most of his men were finally captured in the SE corner of the state. After the Civil War industrial development increased rapidly when the shipment of ore from the upper Great Lakes region was intensified and the development of the petroleum industry in NE Ohio shifted the center of economic activity from the banks of the Ohio R. to the shores of L. Erie, particularly around Cleveland. Immigrants began to swell the pop., and huge fortunes were made. Ohio became very important politically. The state contributed 7 Amer. presidents: Ulysses S. Grant, Rutherford B. Hayes, James A. Garfield, Benjamin Harrison, William McKinley, William Howard Taft, and Warren G. Harding. Big business and politics became entwined as in the relations of Marcus A. Hanna and William McKinley. City bosses such as Cincinnati's George B. Cox are consistent with this pattern. The state as a whole was for many years steadily Republican, despite the rise of organized labor in the late 19th cent. and considerable labor strife. In the 1890s the reforming mayor of Toledo, Samuel "Golden Rule" Jones, won natl. fame for his espousal of city ownership of municipal utilities. Floods in the many rivers flowing to the Ohio and in the Ohio R. itself have long been a problem; a devastating flood in 1913 led to the establishment of the Miami valley conservation project. Continuing long-term state and Federal projects have improved locks and dams along the entire length of the Ohio and its tributaries, for navigation as well as flood control purposes. The Muskingum Conservancy District maintains dams and lakes to control floodwaters on upstream tributaries, and for fishing and other recreational purposes. Both farms and industries in Ohio were hard hit by the Great Depression that began in 1929. In the 1930s the state was wracked by major strikes such as the sit-down strikes in Akron (1935–1936) and the so-called Little Steel strike (1937). World War II brought great prosperity to Ohio, but labor strife was later resumed in the steel strikes of 1949 and 1959. In 1970, 4 students were killed when natl. guardsmen fired on a group of Vietnam War protesters at Kent State Univ. Ohio's economy went into massive decline in the 1970s and 1980s as the automobile, steel, and coal industries virtually collapsed, causing unemployment to soar. Akron, once world famous as a major rubber center, stopped producing rubber prods. altogether by the mid-1980s. During this period, the state's N industrial centers were especially hard hit and lost much of their pop. Since then, Ohio has concentrated on diversifying its economy transforming its mfg. base by incorporating advanced mfg. techniques, through the attraction of Jap. automobile manufacturers and parts suppliers, the expansion of the service sector and the widespread expansion of polymer coatings and plastic prods. including composite materials. Ohio has become an important center for the health care industry with the opening of the Cleveland Clinic. Industrial research is also important, with Nela Park near Cleveland and Battelle Memorial Inst. in Columbus and 7 Edison Technology Centers: 2 for advanced mfg., 2 for materials, and 2 for biotechnologies being among the more no table research centers. There are still important polymer research laboratories in Akron and the Liquid Crystal Inst. in Kent. Ohio's cultural development has been marked by the fame achieved by the Cleveland Orchestra and by the unusually large number of institutions of higher learning located in the state. Among them are Antioch Univ. at Yellow Springs; Bowling Green State Univ., at Bowling Green; Case Western Reserve Univ. (formerly Western Reserve Univ. and Case Inst. of Technology), at Cleveland; Kent State Univ., at Kent; Kenyon Col., at Gambier; Miami Univ., at Oxford; Muskingum Col., at New Concord; Denison Univ. at Granville; Oberlin Col., at Oberlin; the Ohio State Univ., at Columbus; Ohio Univ., at Athens; Ohio Wesleyan Univ., at Delaware; Univ. of Cincinnati; Univ. of Toledo; and a large number of other state and private institutions. Ohio's present constitution was adopted in 1851. It has been amended many times, most notably in 1912 after a constitutional convention and the adoption of 33 changes, including many progressive labor provisions and such measures as initiative, referendum, and the direct primary. The state's executive branch is headed by a governor elected for a 4-year term, permitted 2 successive terms. Ohio's bicameral general assembly has a senate with 33 members, elected for 4-year terms (1/2 each 2 years) and a house with 99 members elected for 2-year terms. The state elects 2 Senators and 19 Representatives to the U.S. Congress and has 21 electoral votes in presidential elections. Ohio has 88 cos.: ADAMS, ALLEN, ASHLAND, ASHTABULA, ATHENS, AUGLAIZE, BELMONT, BROWN, BUTLER, CARROLL, CHAMPAIGN, CLARK, CLERMONT, CLINTON, COLUMBIANA, COSHOCTON, CRAWFORD, CUYAHOGA, DARKE, DEFIANCE, DELAWARE, ERIE, FAIRFIELD, FAYETTE, FRANKLIN, FULTON, GALLIA, GEAUGA, GREENE, GUERNSEY, HAMILTON, HANCOCK, HARDIN, HARRISON, HENRY, HIGHLAND, HOCKING, HOLMES, HURON, JACKSON, JEFFERSON, KNOX, LAKE, LAWRENCE, LICKING, LOGAN, LORAIN, LUCAS, MADISON, MAHONING, MARION, MEDINA, MEIGS, MERCER, MIAMI, MONROE, MONTGOMERY, MORGAN, MORROW, MUSKINGUM, NOBLE, OTTAWA, PAULDING, PERRY, PICKAWAY, PIKE, PORTAGE, PREBLE, PUTNAM, RICHLAND, ROSS, SANDUSKY, SCIOTO, SENECA, SHELBY, STARK, SUMMIT, TRUMBULL, TUSCARAWAS, UNION, VAN WERT, VINTON, WARREN, WASHINGTON, WAYNE, WILLIAMS, WOOD, or WYANDOT.

Ohio **1** county (□ 87 sq mi/225 sq km; 1990 pop. 5,315), SE Ind.; ⊙ Rising Sun; 38°57′N 84°58′W. Bounded E by Ky. state line, here formed by Ohio R.; drained by small Laughery Creek. Agr. area (hogs, cattle, tobacco); mfg. at Rising Sun. Smallest co. in Ind. (both pop. and area). Formed 1844. **2** county (□ 596 sq mi/1,544 sq km; 1990 pop. 21,105), W Ky.; ⊙ Hartford; 37°28′N 86°50′W. Bounded SW and SE (in part) by Green R.; drained by Rough R. and Caney and South Fork of Panther creeks. Rolling agr. area (burley and dark tobacco, hay, alfalfa, soybeans, wheat, corn; hogs, cattle); bituminous coal mines, limestone quarries; timber. Formed 1798. **3** county (□ 109 sq mi/282 sq km; 1990 pop. 50,871), N W.Va., in Northern Panhandle; ⊙ Wheeling; 40°6′N 80°37′W. Industrial and commercial center of the Panhandle. Bounded W by Ohio R. (Ohio state line), E by Pa.; drained by Wheeling Creek. Coal mines, natural-gas wells. Iron, steel, and metal-working industries and other mfg. at Wheeling. Agr. (corn, wheat, oats, barley, hay); cattle; dairying; hogs. Oglebay Park in W; Bear Rocks Lakes Wildlife Management Area in E; part of Castleman Run Wildlife Management Area in NE. Formed 1776.

Ohio **1** village, Gunnison co., W central Colo., just W of Sawatch Mts., 17 mi/27 km E of Gunnison, on Quartz Creek, at mouth of Gold Creek. Elev. 8,560 ft/2,609 m. Surrounded by Gunnison Natl. Forest. **2** village (1990 pop. 426), Bureau co., N Ill., 14 mi/23 km N of Princeton; 41°33′N 89°27′W. In agr. area; dairy prods.

Ohio, river, 981 mi/1,579 km long; formed by the confluence of the Allegheny and Monongahela rivers in SW Pa., in downtown Pittsburgh (40°26′N 80°00′W); 1st flows NW to Monaca, where it receives Beaver R. from N, then generally SW, forms Ohio-W.Va. state line and flows past Steubenville, Ohio, Wheeling and Huntington, W.Va., continuing WNW forming Ohio-Ky. state line, past Ashland, Ky., and Portsmouth and Cincinnati, Ohio, turns WSW, forms Ind.-Ky. and Ill.-Ky. state line, flowing past Louisville and Owensboro, Ky., Evansville, Ind., and Paducah, Ky., entering Mississippi R. at Cairo, Ill., opposite Mo. Receives Kentucky R. from S, 40 mi/64 km NE of Louisville; receives Wabash R. from N, 28 mi/45 km WSW of Evansville; receives Cumberland R. and Kentucky R. 12 mi/19 km ENE and 3 mi/4.8 km ESE of Paducah, respectively. The Ohio is navigable for its entire length; a series of locks and dams improves its navigability and controls flooding. The Ohio's course follows a portion of the S edge of the region covered by continental ice during the late Cenozoic era; glacial meltwater probably cut its original channel. The river is a major tributary of the Mississippi and supplies more water to it than does the Missouri R. The Ohio R. basin covers c.204,000 sq mi/528,360 sq km; the chief tributaries are the Tennessee, Cumberland, Wabash, and Kentucky. The Ohio is prone to spring flooding, and extensive flood-control and protection devices have been constructed along the river and its tributaries. These devices also improve the river's navigability; a 9-ft/2.7-m channel is maintained along its entire length. A system of modern locks and dams, constructed since 1955 to replace older structures, speeds the transit of barges and leisure craft. A canal (1st

Cross references are shown in SMALL CAPITALS. The pronunciation key is on page xv. The dates of population figures are on page xii.

opened in 1830) at Louisville bypasses the Falls of the Ohio, a 2.25-mi/3.62-km-long series of rapids having a 24 ft/7 m drop. Oil and steel account for most of the cargoes moved on the river. The principal river ports are Cincinnati, Louisville, and Pittsburgh. The Ohio R. basin is one of the most populated and industrialized regions of the U.S. Eight states (Ill., Ind., Ky., N.Y., Ohio, Pa., Va., and W.Va.) affected by the river's industrial pollution ratified (1948) the Ohio R. Valley Sanitation Compact. Some results of their cleanup efforts have become discernible, and the river now supports marinas and recreational facilities. The Fr. explorer La Salle reportedly reached the Ohio R. in 1669, but there was no significant interest in the valley until the French and the British began to struggle for control of the river in the 1750s. An early settlement was established at the forks of the Ohio (modern Pittsburgh) by the Ohio Co. of Virginia in 1749, but it was captured by the French in 1754, and the unfinished Fort Prince George was renamed Fort Duquesne; it was recaptured by the British and renamed Fort Pitt in 1758. At the end of the Fr. and Indian Wars, Britain gained control of the river by the treaty of 1763, but settlement of the area was prohibited. Britain ceded the region to the U.S. at the end of the Revolutionary War (1783), and it was opened to settlement by the Ordinance of 1787, which established the Northwest Territory. Until the opening of the Erie Canal in 1825, the Ohio R. was the main route to the newly opened West and the principal means of market transportation of the region's growing farm output. Traffic declined on the river after the RR was built in the mid-1800s, although it revived after World War II. The Ohio R. remains a vital link in the river transportation system of the Midwest. Most shipping is done with barges pushed by towboats.

Ohio and Erie Canal, former waterway of Ohio, 307 mi/494 km long, bet. L. Erie at Cleveland and the Ohio R. at Portsmouth; built 1825–1832. It utilized part of the courses of the Cuyahoga, Muskingum, and Scioto rivers and had 49 locks. It flourished as a means of transporting freight until the advent of the RR era in the 1850s. The canal was responsible for the growth of cities along its route, especially Cleveland, Akron, and Columbus.

Ohio Caverns, Ohio: see WEST LIBERTY.

Ohio City, village (1990 pop. 899), Van Wert co., W Ohio, 7 mi/11 km SSW of Van Wert; 40°46′N 84°37′W. Dairy prods., canned foods, grain prods.

Ohiopyle (o-HEI-yo-pai-uhl), borough (1990 pop. 81), Fayette co., SW Pa., 12 mi/19 km E of Uniontown, on the Youghiogheny R., at center of Ohiopyle State Park (□ 29 sq mi/75 sq km); 39°52′N 79°29′W. A recreation area including part of Potomac Natl. Scenic Trail. Tourism. Fallingwater, a home designed by Frank Lloyd Wright in 1936, is to N.

Ohioville (o-HEI-yo-vil), borough (1990 pop. 3,865), Beaver co., W Pa., 10 mi/16 km W of Beaver on Ohio state line; 40°40′N 80°28′W. Agr. includes dairying, corn, hay.

Ohiowa, village (1990 pop. 146), Fillmore co., SE Nebr., 10 mi/16 km SE of Geneva; 40°24′N 97°27′W.

Ohogamiut (o-HO-gah-mee-yoot), village, W Alaska, on lower Yukon R. and 55 mi/89 km N of Bethel; 61°35′N 161°56′W. Sometimes spelled Ohogamut. Also called Iguak.

Ohoopee (o-HOOP-ee), village, Toombs co., E central Ga.,10 mi/16 km E of Vidalia; 32°10′N 82°13′W.

Ohoopee River (o-HOOP-ee), c.100 mi/161 km long, E central Ga.; rises S of Sandersville; flows SE to Altamaha R. 13 mi/21 km S of Reidsville; 32°56′N 82°47′W. Receives Little Ohoopee R. (c.45 mi/72 km long).

Oies, Île aux (ZWAH, ee-lo) or **Island of Geese**, in the St. Lawrence, S Que., Canada, 40 mi/64 km ENE of Quebec; 6 mi/10 km long, 1 mi/2 km wide; 47°05′N 70°30′W. Just SW is Île aux Grues.

Oil Center, uninc. village (1990 pop. 236), Lea co., E N.Mex., 22 mi/35 km SSW of Hobbs. In oil and natural gas producing area of Llano Estacado. Cattle, sheep, cotton, grain.

Oil City, village, S Ont., Canada, 5 mi/8 km SSE of Petrolia. Oil production.

Oil City, city (1990 pop. 11,949), Venango co., NW Pa., 70 mi/113 km NNE of Pittsburgh, on the Allegheny R., at mouth of Oil Creek; 41°25′N 79°42′W. Mfg. (continuous casting equip., plastic prods., printing and publishing, aluminum castings, concrete production, motor oil, machinery, antioxidants, steel tubing). Agr. area (corn, hay; livestock, dairying). The city was founded after Edwin L. Drake struck (1859) oil nearby in Titusville. It is a refining and shipping center for the state's oil industry and a producer of oil-field equip. Clarion Col. (Venango campus) to SW; Oil Creek State Park to N. Inc. 1871.

Oil City, town (1990 pop. 1,282), Caddo parish, extreme NW La., 20 mi/32 km NW of Shreveport, near Caddo L. Enter of oil field discovered in 1906; 32°45′N 93°58′W. Caddo-Pine Isl. Oil and Historical Society mus. here. Caddo L. reservoir to SW.

Oil Creek 1 7 mi/11.3 km long, Teller co., central Colo.; rises W of Pikes Peak; flows SSW then NNW, joining Fourmile Creek at Mueller State Park. **2** c.45 mi/72 km long, NW Pa.; rises in headstreams in N Crawford co., in Canadohta L.; flows SE, past Titusville, and S, through Oil Creek State Park, through oil-producing region to Allegheny R. at Oil City; 41°48′N 79°50′W. On its banks near Titusville 1st successful oil well in U.S. was drilled in 1859.

Oil Springs, village (1991 pop. 690), S Ont., Canada, 7 mi/11 km SSE of Petrolia. Oil production.

Oil Trough, village (1990 pop. 208), Independence co., NE central Ark., 14 mi/23 km SE of Batesville and on White R.; 35°37′N 91°27′W. In agr. area.

Oildale, uninc. city (1990 pop. 26,553), Kern co., S central Calif., a residential suburb 1 mi/1.6 km N of Bakersfield, across Kern R.; 35°25′N 119°02′W. RR junction. Oil field center. Irrigated agr. area, cotton; dairying; cattle; grain, melons, pumpkins, fruit, nuts, grapes, sugar beets, beans, vegetables. Bakerfield Airport to N. Greenhouse Mts. and Sequoia Natl. Forest to NE.

Oilton (OIL-tuhn), town (1990 pop. 1,060), Creek co., central Okla., 34 mi/55 km W of Tulsa, and 10 mi/16 km NE of Cushing, on Cimarron R; 36°04′N 96°34′W. In petroleum and agr. area (grain, corn); mfg. (horse and stock trailers); oil and natural gas wells. Founded c.1915.

Oilton, uninc. village (1990 pop. 458), Webb co., S Texas, 31 mi/50 km E of Laredo. Oil and natural gas. Cattle.

Oilville, uninc. village, Goochland co., central Va., 22 mi/35 km WNW of Richmond; 37°42′N 77°47′W. Mfg. (tobacco processing, carrying cases, machining); agr. (grain, tobacco, soybeans; cattle).

Oistins (oi-STINZ), town, S Barbados, B.W.I., 5 mi/8 km ESE of Bridgetown. Fisheries, modern fish market. Sometimes Oistin's or Oistin's Town.

Ojai, city (1990 pop. 7,613), Ventura co., S Calif., 12 mi/19 km N of Ventura, near Ojai Creek; 34°27′N 119°15′W. In fertile Ojai Valley in Coast Ranges. RR terminus. Vegetables, citrus, avocados; flowers, nursery prods.; mfg. (cutting tools, printing and publishing). Seat of several private schools. Year-round resort. Los Padres Natl. Forest to N; Pine Mt. (7,510 ft/2,289 m) to N. Inc. 1921.

Ojibwa (o-JIB-wah), village, Sawyer co., N Wis., on Chippewa R., and 24 mi/39 km SE of Hayward. Lumbering, dairying. On Tuscobia State Trail. Relics of early logging days are exhibited here. Former Ojibwa State Roadside Park nearby (now a co. park).

Ojinaga (o-hee-NAH-gah), city (1990 pop. 18,177) and township, Chihuahua, N Mexico, on the Rio Grande, opposite Presidio (Texas), at mouth of Conchos R., on RR, terminus and Mexico Highway 16, 120 mi/193 km NE of Chihuahua; 29°35′N 104°26′W. Border trade; cotton and cattle center.

Ojo Caliente (O-ho kah-lee-EN-tai), uninc. village (1990 pop. 600), Rio Arriba and Taos cos., N N.Mex., on Rio Tusas, and 26 mi/42 km N of Española. Elev. 6,213 ft/1,894 m. Health resort with hot mineral springs. Mfg. (signs). Cattle, sheep, alfalfa; chiles. Pueblo ruins in area; Carson Natl. Forest surrounds village, except S.

Ojo Caliente, Chihuahua, Mexico: see CAMARGO.

Ojo del Toro (O-ho dail TOR-ro), peak (1,749 ft/533 m), Granma prov., E Cuba, near W end of the Sierra Maestra, 22 mi/35 km E of the Cape Cruz; 22°38′N 77°27′W.

Ojocaliente (o-ho-kah-lee-EN-tai), city (1990 pop. 14,412) and township, ⊙ Ojocaliente muncipio, Zacatecas, N central Mexico, on central plateau, 23 mi/37 km. SE of Zacatecas; 22°34′N 102°15′W. Elev. 6,936 ft/2,114 m. RR terminus. Gold, silver mining; sulphur plant.

Ojuelos de Jalisco (o-HWAI-los dai hah-LEES-ko), town (1990 pop. 7,265), Ojuelos de Jalisco muncipio, Jalisco, central Mexico, in Sierra Madre Occidental, near Zacatecas border, 45 mi/72 km SW of San Luis Potosí, at junction of Mexico Highways 51, 70, and 80; 21°52′N 101°40′W. A major highway hub; elev. 7,493 ft/2,284 m. Corn, beans, chilies; livestock.

Ojus (O-juhs), city (□ 3 sq mi/7.8 sq km; 1990 pop. 15,519), Dade co., SE Fla., 12 mi/19 km NNE of Miami; 25°57′N 80°09′W. Dairy prods.; limestone quarries.

Oka (O-kuh), village, S Que., Canada, on the N shore of the L. of the Two Mountains (a widening of the Ottawa R.) and SW of Montreal; 45°29′N 74°07′W. It is noted as the site of a Trappist monastery and farm (est. 1881), where Oka cheese is made. An agr. institute here is affiliated with the Univ. of Montreal. About 600 Native Americans live at Oka. In 1982, Oka Crisis was a native clash which resulted in death and lengthy stand-off with Que. govt.

Okabena (o-kuh-BEE-nuh), village (1990 pop. 223), Jackson co., SW Minn., 19 mi/31 km WNW of Jackson; 43°44′N 95°19′W. Grain; livestock. Heron L. to NE, South Heron L. to E.

Okabena Lake (o-kuh-BEE-nuh), Nobles co., SW Minn.; 2 mi/3.2 km long, 1 mi/1.6 km wide. Drains into Ocheda L., 3 mi/4.8 km S through Ocheyedan R. Worthington is at NE end and on N shore. Man-made channel links lake to Okabena Creek to N (no natural link).

Okak Islands (O-kak), group of 2 adjoining islands, NE Lab., Canada, at entrance of Okak Bay on the Atlantic; each isl. is 10 mi/16 km long, 10 mi/16 km wide; 57°21′–57°33′N and 61°36′–62°01′W. On NW isl. is fishing settlement of Nutak. Adjacent are several islets.

Okaloosa (o-kuh-LOOS-suh), county (□ 1,082 sq mi/2,802 sq km; 1990 pop. 143,776), NW Fla., bounded by Ala. state line (N) and Gulf of Mexico (S); ⊙ Crestview; 30°40′N 86°35′W. Rolling agr. area (corn, peanuts, cotton; hogs, cattle, poultry) drained by Blackwater, Yellow, and Shoal rivers. Also forestry (lumber, naval stores) and some fishing. Includes part of Choctawhatchee Natl. Forest and Choctawhatchee Bay. Formed 1915.

Okamanpeedan Lake (O-kuh-MAN-pee-dan), Martin co., S Minn., and Emmet co., NW Iowa, 10 mi/16 km SSW of Fairmont, Minn.; 7 mi/11.3 km long, 1 mi/1.6 km wide; 43°30′N 94°34′E. Fed and drained by East Fork Des Moines R. Okamanpeedan State Park is on S shore of lake, in Iowa. Also called Tuttle L.

Okanagan Lake (o-kuh-NAH-guhn), S B.C., Canada; 69 mi/111 km long and from 2 mi/3 km to 4 mi/6 km wide. It drains S through the Okanagan R. The lake is in a prosperous fruit-growing region.

Okanagan Landing, village, S B.C., Canada, on Okanagan L., 5 mi/8 km SW of Vernon; 50°14′N 119°22′W. Fruit, vegetables.

Okanagan River, U.S. and Canada: see OKANOGAN RIVER.

Okanogan (o-kuh-NAH-guhn), county (□ 5,281 sq mi/13,678 sq km; 1990 pop. 33,350), N Wash., bounded by Canada (B.C.) to N; ⊙ Okanogan; 48°33′N 119°45′W. Bounded S by Columbia R., forms L. Pateros (Wells Dam) SW, Rufus Woods L. (Chief Joseph Dam) S and SE; large Grand Coulee Dam in SE corner; drained by Okanogan and Methow rivers. Cascade Mts. in W. Timber; apples, barley, oats, alfalfa, wheat; cattle, sheep; gold, silver, copper; tourism and recreation, several ski resorts. Includes parts of Chelan and Colville natl. forests and Colville Indian Reservation. Pearrygin L. State Park in W; Osoyos L. State Park on N, lake extends N into B.C.; Conconally State Park in center; Alta L., Fort Okanogan, and Bridgeport state parks in S; nearly all of Okanogan Natl. Forest is in W, including Pasayten and part of L. Chelan-Sawtooth wilderness areas; several smaller sects. of Okanogan Natl. Forest in NE; part of large Colville Indian Reservation (roughly ½) in SE. Largest co. in land area in Wash. (ranks 55th in U.S.). Formed 1888.

Okanogan (o-kuh-NAH-guhn), town (1990 pop. 2,370), ⊙ Okanogan co., N Wash., 73 mi/117 km NNE of Wenatchee and on Okanogan R., at mouth of Salmon Creek; center of Okanogan irrigation project; 48°22′N 119°35′W. Settled 1886, c.20 mi/32 km from Fort Okanogan, which was 1st Amer. settlement in Wash.; inc. 1907. Silver, copper; timber, apples (in irrigated Okanogan R. valley), wheat; mfg. (concrete). Gateway to Chelan Natl. Forest (NW). Loup Loup Ski Area, at Loup Loup Pass, to W; Conconully State Park to NW. Co. Historical Mus. Okanogan Natl. Forest to W.

Okanogan River (o-kuh-NAH-guhn), 115 mi/185 km long, N Wash. and S B.C., Canada; issues from S end of Okanagan L. at Penticton, B.C.; flows S, through Skaha L., past Oliver, through Osoyoos L., in which it crosses B.C.-Wash. border, past Oroville, Omak and Okanogan, to Columbia R. 2 mi/3.2 km E of Brewster. Receives Similkameen R. from W at Oroville. Called Okanagan in Canada.

Okarche (o-KAHR-chee), town (1990 pop. 1,160), on Kingfisher-Canadian co. line, central Okla., 30 mi/48 km WNW of Oklahoma City; 35°43′N 97°58′W. In grain and livestock area; mfg. (fiber processing, concrete, commercial and industrial heating and air conditioning); oil and natural gas in region (declining).

Okatibbee Creek (o-kuh-TIB-ee), E Miss.; rises in W Kemper co.; flows through Okatibbee L. reservoir and past Meridian to W, joins Chunky Creek at Enterprise to form Chickasawhay R.

Okauchee (o-KAW-chee), village, Waukesha co., SE Wis., on Okauchee L. (c.3 mi/4.8 km long), 13 mi/21 km NW of Waukesha. Concrete.

Okawville, village (1990 pop. 1,274), Washington co., SW Ill., 12 mi/19 km WNW of Nashville; 38°25′N 89°32′W. Health resort, with mineral springs.

Okay, village (1990 pop. 528), Wagoner co., E Okla., suburb 8 mi/12.9 km SSE of Wagoner and 7 mi/11.3 km NNE of Muskogee, on Verdigris R. near its confluence with Arkansas R.; 35°51′N 95°18′W. In agr. area. Fort Gibson L. reservoir (Neosho R.) to NE, including Bay State Park.

O'Kean (o-KEEN), village (1990 pop. 250), Randolph co., NE Ark., 20 mi/32 km WNW of Paragould; 36°10′N 90°49′W.

Okeechobee (o-kee-CHO-bee), county (☐ 891 sq mi/2,308 sq km; 1990 pop. 29,627), central Fla., bounded W by Kissimmee R. and S by L. Okeechobee; ⊙ Okeechobee; 27°23′N 80°53′W. Cattle-raising area of grassy plains with many small lakes and some swamps; also poultry and vegetable farming. Formed 1917.

Okeechobee (o-kee-CHO-bee), town (☐ 4 sq mi/10.4 sq km; 1990 pop. 4,943), ⊙ Okeechobee co., central Fla., 35 mi/56 km SW of Fort Pierce, near N end of L. Okeechobee; 27°14′N 80°49′W. Shipping center for vegetables, poultry, fish, frog legs, and palm fronds.

Okeechobee, Lake (o-kee-CHO-bee) (☐ c.700 sq mi/1,813 sq km), S central Fla., N of the Everglades; 3d-largest freshwater lake and 4th-largest lake wholly within the U.S. It is c.35 mi/56 km long and up to 25 mi/40 km wide, with a max. depth of 15 ft/5 m. The Kissimmee R. is its chief source and the Caloosahatchee R. its main outlet. In reclaiming the Everglades and adjacent lands, many canals were built extending from the S part of the lake, itself a link in the Okeechobee Waterway. A levee, built after the disastrous hurricane of 1926, encircles the lake's shores and protects the region from flood waters. The levees and canals have impeded the flow of water from the lake into the Everglades, which now suffers from water shortages. The drained lands bordering the lake produce vegetables and sugarcane.

Okeechobee Waterway (o-kee-CHO-bee) or **Cross-Florida Waterway**, 155 mi/249 km long, across S central Fla., from Stuart on the Atlantic Ocean to Fort Myers on the Gulf of Mexico. Its main segments are the St. Lucie Canal, L. Okeechobee, L. Hicpochee, and Caloosahatchee R. The shallow (6 ft/1.8 m) waterway has 4 locks and is used by small commercial and leisure craft. It is also an outlet for the flood waters of L. Okeechobee.

Okeene (o-KEEN), town (1990 pop. 1,343), Blaine co., W central Okla., 31 mi/50 km SW of Enid, near Cimarron R.; 36°07′N 98°19′W. Wheat, oats; cattle; mfg. (wheat by-prods., gypsum, flour).

Okefenokee Swamp (o-kee-fuh-NO-kee) (☐ c.600 sq mi/1,554 sq km), SE Ga., extending into N Fla.; c.40 mi/64 km long and averaging 20 mi/32 km in width; 00°40′N 82°20′W. It is a saucer-shaped depression with low ridges and small isls. rising above the water and vegetation cover. Water depth averages 6 ft/2 m, but is as deep as 24 ft/8 m in places. It abounds in varied wildlife, and is drained by the Suwanee and St. Marys rivers. In Ga. the swamp makes up most of the Okefenokee Natl. Wildlife Refuge and Wilderness Area (est. 1937). Extensive timbering of cypress trees in the early 1990s. Many carniverous plants; wading birds, fish, and other waterfowl found here.

Okemah (o-KEE-muh), town (1990 pop. 3,085), ⊙ Okfuskee co., central Okla., 22 mi/35 km SW of Okmulgee; 35°25′N 96°17′W. Elev. 913 ft/278 m. In agr. area (grain, pecans, peanuts, corn). Mfg. (flex circuits, printing, aerospace parts, jeans). Was home of Woody Guthrie. Settled 1902.

Oketo (o-KEE-to), village (1990 pop. 116), Marshall co., NE Kansas, on Big Blue R., and 9 mi/14.5 km NNE of Marysville, near Nebr. state line; 39°57′N 96°35′W. Grain.

Okfuskee (ok-FUHS-kee), county (☐ 628 sq mi/1,627 sq km; 1990 pop. 11,551), central Okla.; ⊙ Okemah; 35°28′N 96°19′W. Intersected by North Canadian R. (forms co. boundary in SW) and Deep Fork of Canadian R. (in N). Agr. (melons, fruit, grain, pecans, peanuts); cattle; dairying; mfg. (machinery, apparel). Formed 1907.

Okikeska Lake (o-ki-KE-skuh), W Que., Canada, on Harricanaw R., 22 mi/35 km NW of Val d'Or; 7 mi/11 km long, 3 mi/5 km wide. In gold-mining region.

Oklahoma, state (☐ 69,902 sq mi/181,046 sq km; 1995 est. pop. 3,277,687), SW U.S.; ⊙ OKLAHOMA CITY. Admitted as the 46th state of the Union in 1907. The state is bounded on the N by Colo. and Kansas and on the E by Mo. and Ark.; the Red R. marks the S border with Texas; Texas also bounds the state on the W and on the S of the Okla. Panhandle, a 34–mi/55–km-wide strip of land that extends 166 mi/267 km W from the NW corner of the state, bordering N.Mex. on its W end. Oklahoma City and TULSA are important cities. Okla. is a land of climatic transition. The Ouachita Mts. of the SE average more than 50 in/120 cm of precipitation per year while Black Mesa averages less than 16 in/41 cm. Consequently, dense forests were the original cover for most of E Okla. while short grasslands dominated the W. The high, short-grass plains of W Okla. are part of the GREAT PLAINS and, like the rest of that area, are chilled by N winds in the winter and baked by intense heat in the summer. There are extensive grazing lands and wheat fields. The plains are broken here and there, notably by Black Mesa in the Panhandle and by the Wichita Mts. in the SW, but the general slope is downward to the E, and central and E Okla. is mostly prairie, rising in the NE to the Ozark and Boston Mts. and in the SE to the Ouachita Mts. Lesser ranges include the Arbuckle Mts. in S and Wichita Mts. in SW. The rivers that flow W-E across the state — the Arkansas, and its tributaries, the Cimarron and the Canadian (with the North Canadian) in the N; the Red R. with the Washita and other tributaries in the S — are much more prominent in the E. Formerly the major crop of Okla. was cotton, but now wheat is the leading cash crop; however, income from livestock (esp. cattle) exceeds that from crops. Other important crops are peanuts and sorghums. Also sheep, poultry, exotic fowl [emu, ostrich] gained popularity, in the 1980s, being raised for their meat. Many minerals are found in the state, including coal, but the resource that has given the state its wealth is oil. After the first well was drilled in 1888, the petroleum industry grew by fits and starts to enormous proportions, and Oklahoma City and Tulsa were among the great natural gas and petroleum centers of the world. Okla. remains a major — but declining — oil-producing state. Many of Okla.'s factories process raw materials found in the state and its chief industry includes non-electrical machinery and fabricated metal prods. Okla. has a rich Native Amer. heritage. The Native Amer. pop. is the largest in the nation; the 1990 census reported 252,420 Native Americans in Okla. (c.8% of total state pop.). Several Native Amer. cultures existed in the area before the first European visited here in 1541. Francisco Coronado almost certainly crossed Okla. in that year, and Hernando De Soto may have visited E Okla. Later Juan de Oñate passed through W Okla., and some other Span. explorers and traders and Fr. traders from La. visited the region, but there was no development of the area. Native Americans dominated the landscape, tribes of the Plains cultures — Osage, Kiowa, Comanche, and Apache — in the W, and the Wichita and other relatively sedentary tribes farther E. It is asserted that the first Eur. trading post was established at Salina by the Chouteau family of St. Louis before the territory was transferred to the U.S. by the Louisiana Purchase in 1803, but the land remained in control of the sparse and nomadic Native Amer. pop. For the most part only traders, official explorers (notably Stephen H. Long), and scientific and curious travelers (among them Washington Irving and George Catlin) came into the present-day state. In 1819 the Adams-Onís Treaty with Spain defined Okla. as the SW border of the U.S. After the War of 1812 the U.S. govt. invited the Cherokee of Ga. and Tenn. to move into the area, and a few had come to settle before intense white pressure for their lands, with the approval of President Andrew Jackson, forced the Cherokee and the others of the 5 Civilized Tribes (the Choctaw, the Chickasaw, the Creek, and the Seminole) to abandon their old homes E of the Mississippi and to take up residence in what was to become the INDIAN TERRITORY. Their tragic removal is known as the Trail of Tears. They settled on the hills and little prairies of the E sect. and built separate organized states and communities. The Cherokee particularly had a highly Europeanized culture, with a written language, invented by their great leader Sequoyah, and highly developed institutions. Some of the Cherokee were slaveholders and ran their agr. in the traditional Southern plantation pattern; others were small farmers. The 5 Civilized Tribes clashed briefly with the Plains Indians, particularly the Osage, but they were for a time free from white interference, and they were able to establish a civilization that strongly affected the whole history of the region. The troubles of the whites did not, however, long escape them, and the Civil War was a major disaster. Although no major battle of the war was fought in present-day Okla., there were innumerable skirmishes. Most Native Americans allied themselves with the Confederacy, but Unionist disaffection was widespread, and individual violence was so prevalent that many fled, leaving their farms to desolation. As a punishment for taking the Confederate side the 5 Civilized Tribes lost the W part of the Indian Territory, and the Federal govt. began assigning lands there to such landless Eastern tribes as the Delaware and the Shawnee, as well as to nomadic Plains tribes, who caused much trouble before they were subdued and settled on reservations. The territory was victimized by lawlessness and served as a hideout for white outlaws. After the establishment of a Federal court at Fort Smith, Isaac Parker became famous as the hanging judge. Immediately after the Civil War the long drives of cattle from Texas to the Kansas RR began to cross Okla., traveling over the cattle trails that became part of Western folklore. The best known is the CHISHOLM TRAIL. The cattle were fattened on the virgin ranges of Okla., and cattlemen began to look on the grasslands with speculative and covetous eyes. The first RR to cross Okla. was built bet. 1870 and 1872, and thereafter it was not possible to keep white settlers out. They came despite laws and treaties with the Native Americans, and by the 1880s there was a strong admixture of whites. Ranches were developed, too, nominally owned by Native Americans, but actually controlled by white cattlemen and their cowboys; the region took on a tinge of the Old West of the cattle frontier, a tinge that it has never wholly lost. In the 1880s, land-hungry frontier farmers, the boomers, agitated to obtain the "unassigned" lands in the central sect.—the lands not given to any Native Amer. tribe. The agitation succeeded, and a large strip was opened for settlement in 1889. On April 22, 1889, prospective settlers lined up on the territorial border, and at noon, at the sound of a pistol shot, were allowed to run into the state to compete for the best lands. Some settlers who illegally entered ahead of the set time were referred to as the Sooners, hence the state's nickname, the Sooner State. Later other strips of territory were opened, and settlers poured in from the Midwest and the South. The W sect. of what is now the state of Okla. became the Okla. Territory in 1890; it included the Panhandle, the narrow strip of territory that, taken from Texas by the Compromise of 1850, had become a no-man's-land where settlers came in undisturbed. In 1893 the Dawes Commission was appointed to implement a policy of dividing the tribal lands into individual holdings; the Native Americans resisted, but the policy was finally enforced in 1906. The wide lands of the Indian Territory were thus made available to whites. The Civilized Tribes made the best of a poor bargain, and the Indian Territory and Okla. Territory were united in 1907 to form the state of Okla., with a constitution that included provision for initiative and referendum. Already the oil boom had reached major proportions, and the young state was on the verge of great economic development. At the same time, cotton, wheat, and corn were major money crops, and cattle-land holdings, although shrinking, were still enormous. In World War I the great demand for farm prods. brought an agr. boom to the state, but in the 1920s the state fell upon hard times. Recurrent drought burned the wheat in the fields, and overplanting, overgrazing, and unscientific cropping aided the weather in making Okla. part of the DUST BOWL of the 1930s. Farm tenancy increased in the 1920s, and in both the E and W the farms tended more and more to be held by large interests and to be consolidated in large blocks. A great number of tenant farmers were compelled to leave their dust-stricken farms and went W as migrant laborers; the tragic plight of these Okies, many of whom took Route 66 (the Highway of the Okies) to Calif., is the theme of John Steinbeck's *The Grapes of Wrath*. A larger migration, however, took place within the state as rural residents moved to the cites. With the return of rains, however, and with increasing care in selecting crops and in conserving and utilizing water and soil resources, much of the Dust Bowl was again made into productive farm land. The demands for food in World War II and Federal price supports for agr. prods. after the war aided farm prosperity. Large state and Federal programs for conserving the water of rivers and for supplying irrigation have resulted in the construction of many large dams and reservoirs, such as the reservoir impounded by Kerr Dam on the Arkansas R., resulting in extension of barge navigation on the Arkansas R. Navigation System to the Tulsa area in 1971, improved agr. conditions and new recreation areas. (For more detailed information on irrigation projects, see separate articles on the rivers of Okla.) Okla. experienced a boom in its economy during the late 1970s when oil prices rose dramatically. In the mid-1980s, Okla.'s economy was hurt (as it had been in the 1930s) by dependence on a single industry as oil prices fell rapidly. Okla. has increased its industrial diversity and has moved, along with Texas, into the apparel industry (availability of cotton and low-cost labor). Also important is the state's aircraft and rocket industries. The bombing of the Murrah Federal Bldg. in Oklahoma City, on April 19, 1995, killed 166 people and interrupted the state's usual tranquillity. During the 1920s 2 governors, John C. Walton and Henry S. Johnston, were impeached. Prohibition, in effect since statehood, was repealed in 1959. The original 1907 constitution is still in effect. The Cheyenne and Arapacho tribes are currently suing the state govt., claiming that their tribal lands were illegally seized in 1883 and 1948, including a 12-sq-mi/31-sq-km piece of land (formerly the Army base of Fort Reno) with unmarked graves of their people and ritual dance grounds, as well as significant oil and gas reserves. They are asking for the land's return; as yet, the issue has not been resolved. Okla. has a legislature of 48 senators and 101 representatives, elected for 4- and 2-year terms, respectively. The governor is elected for a 4-year term. The state elects 2 U.S. senators and 6 representatives and has 8 electoral votes. The most important institutions of higher learning in the state are the Univ. of Okla., Okla. State Univ., and the Univ. of Tulsa. Okla. has 77 cos.: ADAIR, ALFALFA, ATOKA, BEAVER, BECKHAM, BLAINE, BRYAN, CADDO, CANADIAN, CARTER, CHEROKEE, CHOCTAW, CIMARRON, CLEVELAND, COAL, COMANCHE, COTTON, CRAIG, CREEK, CUSTER, DELAWARE, DEWEY, ELLIS, GARFIELD, GARVIN, GRADY, GRANT, GREER, HARMON, HARPER, HASKELL, HUGHES, JACKSON, JEFFERSON, JOHNSTON, KAY, KINGFISHER, KIOWA, LATIMER, LE FLORE, LINCOLN, LOGAN, LOVE, MCCLAIN, MCCURTAIN, MCINTOSH, MAJOR, MARSHALL, MAYES, MURRAY, MUSKOGEE, NOBLE, NOWATA, OKFUSKEE, OKLAHOMA, OKMULGEE, OSAGE, OTTAWA, PAWNEE, PAYNE, PITTSBURG, PONTOTOC, POTTAWATOMIE, PUSHMATAHA, ROGER MILLS, ROGERS, SEMINOLE, SEQUOYAH, STEPHENS, TEXAS, TILLMAN, TULSA, WAGONER, WASHINGTON, WASHITA, WOODS, WOODWARD.,

Oklahoma, county (□ 718 sq mi/1,860 sq km; 1990 pop. 599,611), central Okla.; ⊙ Oklahoma City, which extends into 3 adjacent cos.; 35°32′N 97°24′W. Other important cities include Edmond, Spencer, and Midwest City. Intersected by North Canadian R. and the Deep Fork of Canadian R. Dairying; cattle; wheat; agr. mostly in E and NW parts. Varied mfg. at Oklahoma City and Edmond. Oil and natural-gas fields; sand, granite; refineries. Most urbanized co. in state. Formed 1890.

Oklahoma, borough (1990 pop. 977), Westmoreland co., W central Pa., 24 mi/39 km ENE of Pittsburgh and 1 mi/1.6 km S of Vandergrift, on Kiskiminetas R.; 40°34′N 34°79′W.

Oklahoma City, city (1990 pop. 444,719), ⊙ state and of Oklahoma co., also Cleveland, Canadian, and Pottawatomie cos., central Okla., on the North Canadian R.; 35°28′N 97°30′W. The largest city in the state, it is an important livestock market, a wholesale, distributing, industrial, and financial center, and a farm trade and processing point. Oil is a major prod.; the city is situated in the middle of an oil field (opened 1928), with oil derricks even on the capitol grounds. Diversified light and heavy mfg. In SE part of city, Tinker Air Force Base, a logistics center with one of the world's largest air depots, has the largest employment at 1 site. Oklahoma City was quickly settled in a land rush after the area was opened to homesteaders on April 22, 1889. It became the state capital in 1910. One of the largest U.S. cities in terms of land area (604 sq mi/1,564 sq km), it extends into 3 cos. and has many parks. Of interest are the capitol, the state historical mus., the Natl. Cowboy Hall of Fame and Western Heritage Center, sports stadium, the state fairgrounds, the civic center bldgs. and monuments, a theater complex, a convention center, the state lib., the Okla. Health Sciences Center, and a zoo. Educational institutions include Oklahoma City Univ., Okla. Christian Univ. of Science and Arts, an Okla. State Univ. branch campus, the medical school of the Univ. of Okla., Southern Nazarene Univ. (in nearby Bethany), Oklahoma City Community Col., Okla. State Univ. (2-year branch), Univ. of Central Okla. in adjacent Edmond (N), Univ. of Okla. at Norman (S). The city also has a symphony orchestra. Reservoirs for recreation and water supply include L. Stanley Druper and Shawnee Reservoir (SE), Arcadia L. (N), L. Hefner and L. Overholder (W). Softball Hall of Fame; Firefighters Mus., Kirkpatrick Center Mus. Complex. Will Rogers World Airport in SW part of city; Wiley Post Airport in NW part. On April 19, 1995, Oklahoma City was the victim of the worst terrorist attack in U.S. history. A bomb explosion destroyed an entire side of the 9-storey Murrah Federal Bldg.; total death toll 166. Timothy McVeigh and Terry Nichols were convicted on Federal charges in association with the bombing. Inc. 1890.

Oklaunion, uninc. village (1990 pop. 138), Wilbarger co., N Texas, near Okla. state line, c.40 mi/64 km WNW of Wichita Falls. In agr. area.

Oklawaha River (ahk-lah-WAH-hah), c.140 mi/225 km long, central and N central Fla.; rises in extensive central Fla. lake system (with L. Apopka at its upper end); flows N, receiving outlets of Silver Springs and Orange L., then turns E, converging with St. Johns R. near Welaka. The upper course, extremely tortuous, is dredged to Leesburg.

Oklee, village (1990 pop. 441), Red Lake co., NW Minn., on Lost R., and 19 mi/31 km E of Red L.; 47°50′N 95°50′W. Falls. Grain, sugar beets, sunflowers, potatoes; cattle; mfg. (fertilizers, feeds).

Okmulgee (ok-MUHL-gee), county (□ 702 sq mi/1,818 sq km; 1990 pop. 36,490), E central Okla.; ⊙ Okmulgee; 35°38′N 95°58′W. Intersected by the Deep Fork; includes Okmulgee and Henryetta lakes (recreation). Agr. (peanuts, corn; cattle; dairy prods.). Mfg. (glass containers, metal stampings, chemicals) at Okmulgee and Henryetta. Oil and natural-gas fields; timber. Coal mining. State recreation area. L. Okmulgee reservoir and Okmulgee State Park in W. Formed 1907.

Okmulgee (ok-MUHL-gee), city (1990 pop. 13,441), ⊙ Okmulgee co., E central Okla., 31 mi/50 km S of Tulsa; 35°37′N 95°57′W. Elev. 670 ft/204 m. In an oil and farm area. An agr. processing center, it has oil and gas wells; mfg. (glass containers, marker boards, carbonated beverages, publishing and printing). It was founded on the site of the Creek capital (1868–1907) and boomed with the discovery of oil in 1907. An old Creek (Muscogee) Nation Council House (1878) is on the town square. Yucchi Tribal Hq. and Okla. State Univ. Technical Branch (2-year) here. L. Okmulgee and Okmulgee State Park to W; Eufaula L. reservoir to SE. Inc. 1900.

Okmulgee, Lake (ok-MUHL-gee), reservoir, Okmulgee co., E central Okla., in Okmulgee State Park, 6 mi/9.7 km WSW of Okmulgee; c.5 mi/8 km long; 35°36′N 96°03′W. Built for Okmulgee water supply.

Okoboji, town (1990 pop. 775), Dickinson co., NW Iowa, just S of Spirit Lake, bet. lakes East Okoboji (c.5 mi/8 km long) and West Okoboji (c.6 mi/9.7 km long); 43°23′N 95°08′W. Situated in popular resort area containing several state parks on West Okoboji L., and fish hatchery on Big Spirit L. to N.

Okolona (o-kuh-LO-nuh), uninc. city (1990 pop. 18,902), Jefferson co., N Ky., a residential suburb 10 mi/16 km SSE of downtown Louisville; 38°08′N 85°41′W. Agr. to SE; motor vehicle plant to NW.

Okolona (o-kuh-LO-nuh), town (1990 pop. 3,267), ⊙ Chickasaw co., NE central Miss., 18 mi/29 km S of Tupelo; 34°00′N 88°45′W. In agr., dairying, livestock, and timber area; mfg. (furniture, apparel, corrugated boxes). Seat of Okolona Col. Founded 1848; burned in Civil War. Has a Confederate cemetery. Nearby is a U.S. game preserve. Part of Tombigbee Natl. Forest to W; Natchez Trace (Natl.) Parkway passes to W.

Okolona (o-kuh-LO-nuh), village (1990 pop. 113), Clark co., S central Ark., 18 mi/29 km WSW of Arkadelphia; 34°00′N 93°20′W. In agr. area, near Antoine R.

Okotoks (O-kuh-tahks), town (1991 pop. 6,720), SW Alta., Canada, at foot of Rocky Mts., satellite community 23 mi/37 km S of Calgary; 50°44′N 113°59′W. Elev. 3,448 ft/1,051 m. Oil-shipping center for Turner Valley field; natural-gas and oil production, oil refining, pharmaceuticals mfg.; wheat, flax; cattle. Dormitory town for Calgary.

Oktaha, village (1990 pop. 266), Muskogee co., E Okla., 13 mi/21 km SSW of Muskogee; 35°34′N 95°28′W. In agr. area.

Oktibbeha (ok-TIB-uh-hah), county (□ 462 sq mi/1,197 sq km; 1990 pop. 38,375), E Miss.; ⊙ Starkville; 33°25′N 88°52′W. Drained by Noxubee and Oktibbeha rivers. Agr. (cotton, corn, hay, soybeans, honey; cattle; dairying); timber. Starr Forest Wildlife Management Area and part of Noxubee Natl. Wildlife Refuge in S; small part of Tombigbee Natl. Forest in SW. Formed 1833.

Ola (O-luh), town (1990 pop. 1,090), Yell co., W central Ark., 18 mi/29 km SSW of Russellville; 35°01′N 93°13′W. Mfg. (lumber). Petit Jean Wildlife Management Area to N; Ouachita Natl. Forest to W.

Area in square miles is shown by the symbol □ capital city or county seat by ⊙

Olaa, Hawaii: see KEAAU.

Olamon, Maine: see GREENBUSH.

Olancha Peak (12,123 ft/3,695 m), E Calif., in the Sierra Nevada, on Inyo-Tulare co. line, 24 mi/39 km S of Lone Pine. In Inyo Natl. Forest. Pacific Crest Trail passes peak.

Olanta (o-LANT-uh), village (1990 pop. 687), Florence co., E central S.C., 22 mi/35 km SSW of Florence; 33°56′N 79°55′W. Mfg. of yarn for motor vehicle industry. Agr. includes tobacco, grain, cotton; hogs, chickens.

Olar (O-luhr), village (1990 pop. 391), Bamberg co., W central S.C., 29 mi/47 km SW of Orangeburg; 33°10′N 81°11′W. Mfg. of hardwood veneers, fence posts.

Olathe (o-LAITH-uh), city (1990 pop. 63,352), ⊙ Johnson co., NE Kansas, suburb 19 mi/31 km SW of downtown Kansas City, Kansas; 38°53′N 94°48′W. In an area of livestock farms. Agr. to S and W. Mfg. Olathe has been growing at a fast rate; its pop. more than tripled bet. 1970 and 1990. The city's name is derived from the Shawnee word for *beautiful*. Kansas State School for the Deaf, Mid-Amer. Nazarene Col., and Johnson Community Vocational Technical School are located here. Inc. 1858.

Olathe, town (1990 pop. 1,263), Montrose co., W Colo., on Uncompahgre R. and 45 mi/72 km SE of Grand Junction; 38°36′N 107°58′W. Elev. 5,346 ft/1,629 m. Shipping point in cattle, sheep region; potatoes, onions, beans. Black Canyon of the Gunnison Natl. Monument to E; Switzer L. State Park to N.

Olcott, village (□ 5 sq mi/13 sq km, 1990 pop. 1,432), Niagara co., W N.Y., on L. Ontario, 30 mi/48 km NNE of Buffalo; 43°20′N 78°42′W. Mfg. (industrial chemicals).

Old Andreafsky (an-dree-YAF-skee), village, W Alaska, on Yukon R., and 100 mi/161 km NW of Bethel. Formerly important trading center (salmon fishing and packing) and port with dock installations now destroyed. Has Rus. Orthodox church. Trading post established by Russians, c.1853.

Old Appleton, town (1990 pop. 82), Cape Girardeau co., SE Mo., on Apple Creek, near Mississippi R.,13 mi/21 km SE of Perryville; 37°35′N 89°42′W. Settled 1808. Formerly Appleton. Old Appleton since 1917.

Old Bahama Channel, strait off N coast of Cuba and Camagüey Archipelago, S of Great Bahama Bank; c.100 mi/161 km long, 15 mi/24 km wide.

Old Baldy 1 Ariz.: see WRIGHTSON MOUNT. **2** Calif.: see SAN ANTONIO PEAK.

Old Bennington, Vt.: see BENNINGTON.

Old Bight, town, central Bahama Isls., on SW Cat Isl., 140 mi/225 km SE of Nassau; 24°22′N 75°22′W. Sisal, fruit.

Old Bridge, township (1990 pop. 56,475), Middlesex co., E N.J., on South R. and 7 mi/11.3 km SE of New Brunswick; 40°23′N 74°18′W. Concrete blocks. Largely residential.

Old Bridgeport, coal mining village, NE N.S., Canada, on NE coast of Cape Breton Isl., 9 mi/14 km NE of Sydney.

Old Brookville, village (□ 3 sq mi/7.8 sq km; 1990 pop. 1,823), Nassau co., SE N.Y., on W L.I., 4 mi/6.4 km SE of Glen Cove; 40°49′N 73°35′W.

Old Croton Dam and Aqueduct, Westchester and Putnam cos., SE N.Y., a 50-ft/15-m-high, granite-faced, timber-rock dam, and a 33-mi/53-km-long, brick-lined aqueduct that was the main source of N.Y. city's water supply 1842–1907. The 1st supply of public water to N.Y. city was a 21,000-gal/79,491-liter elevated tank, but it proved less than adequate. In 1832, Gov. DeWitt Clinton asked the state legislature for plans for new water sources. In 1834 the legislature approved the construction of a dam on Croton R., which would produce an est. yield of 20 million gals/75.7 million liters per day. The dam project started in 1837 and was completed in 1842. The aqueduct from Croton crossed over Harlem R. at High Bridge, then to Central Park reservoir, then to Bryant Park reservoir, an Egyptian-style enclosure with 50-ft/15-m-high, 25-ft/7.5-m-thick walls. That reservoir was used until 1890, and in 1897 it was razed to make way for the N.Y. Public Lib. at 42d St. and 5th Ave. Repairs to the system in 1881 strengthened it, increasing the yield to 95 million gals/359.6 million liters per day. The Old Croton System was used until 1907, when it was replaced by the New Croton Dam and Aqueduct. The Old Croton Aqueduct is listed on the Natl. Register of Historic Places. Today the aqueduct route is part of the 173-acre/70-ha Old Croton Trailways State Park; it stretches 20 miles/32 km from the dam along the public right-of-way following the Hudson R. to Van Cortlandt Park in the Bronx, a distance of 20 mi/32 km.

Old Crow, village (1991 pop. 256), N Yukon, on Porcupine R., at mouth of Old Crow R.; and 250 mi/402 km N of Dawson; 67°35′N 139°50′W. Trading post, Royal Can. Mounted Police station. Controversial archaeological finds of early occupation of Americas.

Old England, town, Manchester parish, S Jamaica, 6 mi/9.7 km SSE of Mandeville; 17°59′N 77°27′W. In agr. region (tropical spices and citrus; livestock).

Old Factory River, village, NW Que., Canada, on Old Factory Bay, on E side of James Bay; 52°36′N 78°43′W. Hudson's Bay Company trading post.

Old Faithful, Wyo.: see YELLOWSTONE NATIONAL PARK.

Old Field, village (□ 2 sq mi/5.2 sq km; 1990 pop. 765), Suffolk co., SE N.Y., on N shore of L.I., overlooking Smithtown Bay, and 5 mi/8 km NW of Port Jefferson; 40°57′N 73°07′W.

Old Field Point, promontory on N shore of W L.I., SE N.Y., at W side of entrance to Port Jefferson Harbor. Lighthouse (40°59′N 73°07′W).

Old Forge, resort village (1990 pop. 1,450), Herkimer co., N central N.Y., in the Adirondacks, on a lake of Fulton Chain of Lakes, c.45 mi/72 km NNE of Utica; 43°43′N 74°58′W. Popular winter-sports (snowmobiling) and summer-resort area; logging; hunting, fishing.

Old Forge, borough (1990 pop. 8,834), Lackawanna co., NE Pa., suburb 5 mi/8 km SW of Scranton, on Lackawanna R.; 41°22′N 75°44′W. Anthracite coal. Mfg. (food prods., winery, machinery, printing, apparel, consumer goods). Preate Winery is here. Settled 1798, inc. 1895.

Old Fort, town (1990 pop. 732), McDowell co., W central N.C., 21 mi/34 km E of Asheville on Catawba R., near its source; 35°37′N 82°10′W. Agr. area (corn, apples; chickens, cattle). Timber. Mfg. (motor vehicle parts, textiles, machine parts). Pisgah Natl. Forest to N.

Old Fort Harrod State Park, in Harrodsburg, Mercer co., central Ky. Covering an area of 32 acres/13 ha, it commemorates old fort pioneer settlement W of the Alleghenies, made here in 1774 by Capt. James Harrod. On site of old Fort Harrod, park includes reproduction of fort and pioneer cabins, George Rogers Clark memorial, cabin in which Nancy Hanks and Thomas Lincoln (Abraham Lincoln's parents) were married, pioneer cemetery, and a mus. Formerly called Pioneer Memorial State Park. Est. 1934.

Old Glory, uninc. village (1990 est. pop. 125), Stonewall co., NW central Texas, c.50 mi/80 km NNW of Abilene. Cattle; wheat, peanuts, hay.

Old Greenwich, Conn.: see GREENWICH.

Old Hamilton, Alaska: see HAMILTON.

Old Harbor, village (1990 pop. 284), Alaska, on SE Kodiak Isl., 60 mi/97 km SW of Kodiak; 57°15′N 153°22′W. Fishing, fish processing. Site of Three Saints Bay, Rus. settlement in Alaska, est. 1784.

Old Harbour, town (1991 pop. 17,778), St. Catherine parish, S Jamaica, in coastal lowland, on RR, 20 mi/32 km W of Kingston; 17°55′N 77°06′W. Sugarcane, tropical fruit, coffee. The minor port Old Harbour Bay (2 mi/3.2 km S), on bay of the same name, was once noted for shipbuilding.

Old Harbour Bay, town (1991 pop. 5,405), St. Catherine parish, S central Jamaica, 11 mi/18 km SW of Spanish Town; 17°54′N 77°06′W. Fishing center on S coast of Jamaica.

Old Harbour Bay, Caribbean inlet, St. Catherine parish, S Jamaica; bounded by Clarendon and St. Catherine parishes, c.20 mi/32 km SW of Kingston; 17°55′N 77°03′W. At its SW gate is Portland Ridge peninsula. The bay is dotted with many islets, such as Great Goat Isl. and Pigeon Isl., which, together with sects. of the shoreline, were leased to the U.S. for naval bases in 1940. The minor port of Old Harbour Bay is at its head. Sometimes called Portland Bight.

Old Hickory, village, Davidson co., N central Tenn., on Old Hickory Reservoir (Cumberland R.), 10 mi/16 km NNE of Nashville; 36°15′N 86°39′W. Formerly owned by E. I. du Pont de Nemours and Company, whose plant here was founded to make munitions during World War I. It now produces X-ray film and DMT, a component of dacron and polyester. Until 1923, called Jacksonville.

Old Hickory Lake, reservoir, on border of Davidson and Sumner cos. and in Wilson, Trousdale, and Smith cos., central Tenn., on Cumberland R., 12 mi/19 km NE of Nashville; 36°17′N 86°39′W. Serpentine; c.65 mi/105 km long. Cordell Hull Dam at E tip. Formed by Old Hickory Dam, built (1950s) by Army Corps of Engineers. Bledsoe Creek State Park on N shore.

Old Iliamna, Alaska: see ILIAMNA.

Old Kasaan National Monument, SE Alaska, on E Prince of Wales Isl., 30 mi/48 km WNW of Ketchikan. Area is 38 acres/15 ha. Includes historic ruins of abandoned Haida Indian village, with grave houses and totem poles. Est. 1916.

Old Lyme, residential and resort town (1990 pop. 6,535), New London co., SE Conn., on L.I. Sound, on the E side of the mouth of the Connecticut R.; 41°19′N 72°17′W. Its noteworthy old houses built by sea captains have attracted many artists. The Congregational Church (1817; burned in 1909, but carefully restored) has been portrayed by Childe Hassam. Chiefly a residential community that is home to art galleries, art museums, and the Lyme Art Acad. (Fine Arts). High Hopes Therapeutic Riding stables hosted equestrian events for 1995 World Special Olympics. Location of the initial discovery of Lyme disease. Seasonal tourism centered around the town's beaches, boating activities, and scenic beauty. Includes villages of South Lyme, Laysville, and Blackhall. Settled c.1655, inc. 1855.

Old Man's Pond, lake (8 mi/13 km long, 1 mi/2 km wide), W N.F., Canada, 10 mi/16 km NNE of Corner Brook.

Old Mill Creek, village (1990 pop. 73), Lake co., NE Ill., residential suburb 44 mi/71 km NNW of Chicago, 11 mi/18 km NW of Waukegan, near Wis. state line; 42°25′N 87°58′W. Drained by North Mill Creek.

Old Mission Peninsula, Mich.: see GRAND TRAVERSE BAY.

Old Mobeetie, Texas: see MOBEETIE.

Old Monroe, town (1990 pop. 242), Lincoln co., E Mo., on Cuivre R., near the Missouri, and 21 mi/21 km ESE of Troy; 38°55′N 90°45′W. Lumber; fertilizers and feed.

Old Mulkey Meeting House State Park, Ky.: see TOMPKINSVILLE.

Old Mystic, village, New London co., SE Conn., 8 mi/12.9 km ENE of New London, on Whitford R. Many old houses.

Old Ocean, uninc. town (1990 pop. 915), Brazoria co., SE Texas, 24 mi/39 km WNW of Freeport, near Linville Bayou. Oil and natural gas region. Agr. (rice, cotton, soybeans). Mfg. (petro-chemicals).

Old Orchard Beach, town (1990 pop. 7,789), York co., SW Maine, on the Atlantic coast; 43°31′N 70°23′W. For many years a popular summer resort, it has a beach and amusement facilities. A trading post was located nearby before 1630. Settled c.1631, inc. 1883.

Old Perlican (PUHR-li-kuhn), town (1991 pop. 745), SE N.F., Canada, on E side of Trinity Bay, 25 mi/40 km NNE of Carbonear; 48°05′N 53°01′W. Fishing. Just offshore is Perlican Isl.

Old Point Comfort, resort area, Hampton independent city, SE Va., on small peninsula (Old Point Comfort), on Chesapeake Bay, on N side of entrance to Hampton Roads harbor, 3 mi/4.8 km E of Hampton; 37°00′N 76°18′W. Bathing, fishing resort since 1830s. U.S. Fort Monroe (long known as Fortress Monroe), built 1819–1834 on site of 17th-cent. fortifications. Held by Union throughout Civil War; Jefferson Davis imprisoned here, 1865–1867. Long a coastal artillery post, it became (1946) hq. of U.S. Army field forces. Now Fort Monroe Military Reservation; historic Jefferson Davis Casemate. Hampton Roads Bridge-Tunnel 1 mi/1.6 km to SW.

Old Rampart, Indian village, NE Alaska, near Yukon (Canada) border, on Porcupine R., 110 mi/177 km ENE of Fort Yukon; 67°10′N 141°40′W. Est. 1869 as trading post of Hudson's Bay Company.

Old Ripley, village (1990 pop. 95), Bond co., SW central Ill., 8 mi/12.9 km W of Greenville; 38°53′N 89°34′W. In agr. area (corn, wheat; dairy prods.; livestock).

Old River, stream, 7 mi/11km long, S Concordia parish, La.; connects the Mississippi R. with the Red and Atchafalaya rivers; 31°04′N 91°30′W. The Old R. Control Structure, which prevents the Mississippi R. from being captured by the Atchafalaya R., is here.

Old River Control Structure, La.: see ATCHAFALAYA RIVER

Old River-Winfree, uninc. town (1990 pop. 1,233), Chambers co., SE Texas, residential suburb 30 mi/48 km ENE of Houston, on Old R., near Trinity R.; 29°52′N 94°49′W. Agr. area on urban fringe.

Old Road, village, W St. Kitts, West Indies, 5 mi/8 km WNW of Basseterre. Here landed (1623) Sir Thomas Warner with Br. settlers. Sometimes called Old Road Town.

Old San Juan (SAHN WAHN), neighborhood of San Juan, NE P.R., W portion of San Juan Islet, facing San Juan Bay and the Atlantic Ocean. A walled city within the city of San Juan, Old San Juan is characterized by its extraordinary Span. colonial architecture and its cobblestone streets. Important govt. offices are here, including La Fortaleza, where all governors of the isl. have lived since Juan Ponce de León. Administrative, commercial, banking, recreational, and tourist center of P.R.

Old Saratoga, village (1990 pop. 1,364), Saratoga co., E N.Y., on the Hudson, 11 mi/18 km E of Saratoga Springs; 43°06′N 73°34′W. Summer resort; light mfg. Scene of Burgoyne's surrender to Gates in Saratoga campaign of the Amer. Revolution. Saratoga Monument (155 ft/47 m high) is here. Revolutionary battles fought in vicinity are commemorated by Saratoga Natl. Historical Park 9 mi/14.5 km SE of Saratoga Springs. Settled in 17th cent. as Old Saratoga; inc. 1874. Name was changed to Schuylerville in 1831, but was changed back in 1997.

Old Saybrook, resort town (1990 pop. 9,552), Middlesex co., S Conn., on L.I. Sound, at mouth of the Connecticut R. (here bridged), 28 mi/45 km E of New Haven; 41°17′N 72°22′W. Agr.; fishing; tourism; mfg. (hardware, boats, food prods., electronics, printing, metal fabrication). Includes Fenwick (resort borough), Old Saybrook village, and Saybrook Point (summer colony). Collegiate School of Amer. here (early 18th cent.) was nucleus of Yale Univ. Settled 1635 as Saybrook colony, inc. 1854 as Old Saybrook. A town formerly named Saybrook (now Deep River) is N.

Old Shawneetown, village (1990 pop. 356), Gallatin co., S Ill., on Ohio R., 23 mi/37 km E of Harrisburg; 37°42′N 88°08′W. Highway bridge to Ky. Shawneetown State Historical Site is here. Shawnee Natl. Forest to SW. Gallatin Co. Courthouse and most residents moved to (new) Shawneetown in late 1930s after disastrous Ohio R. flood of 1937. One of state's oldest settlements; important area in the early 19th cent. The 1st state chartered bank opened here.

Old Spec Mountain (4,180 ft/1,274 m), Oxford co., W Maine, near N.H. state line, 20 mi/32 km W of Rumford.

Old Tappan, borough (1990 pop. 4,254), Bergen co., extreme NE N.J., 12 mi/19 km NE of Paterson, near Hackensack R. and N.Y. state line; 41°01′N 73°58′W. Largely residential.

Old Town, city (1990 pop. 8,317), Penobscot co., S central Maine, on the Penobscot, and 13 mi/21 km above Bangor; 44°57′N 68°44′W. Mfg. (canoes, pulp, paper; lumber mills). On small isl. N of Old Town village is a reservation for Penobscot Indians. Maine's 1st RR (1836) connected Old Town with Bangor. Includes villages of Stillwater and Great Works. Settled 1774, inc. 1840, city chartered 1891.

Old Westbury, residential village (□ 8 sq mi/20.7 sq km; 1990 pop. 3,897), Nassau co., SE N.Y., on W L.I., 3 mi/4.8 km NE of Mineola; 40°47′N 73°35′W. Old Westbury Gardens and manor of former Phipps estate rivals formal gardens of Europe. Seat of N.Y. Inst. of Technology's central campus; State Univ. of N.Y. Col. at Old Westbury. Inc. 1924.

Oldenburg, town (1990 pop. 715), Franklin co., SE Ind., 11 mi/18 km SW of Brookville; 39°20′N 85°12′W. In agr. area. Seat of Convent of the Immaculate Conception and Acad. (Oldenburg Franciscan Community of Sisters). Laid out 1837.

Oldham 1 (OLD-uhm), county (□ 196 sq mi/508 sq km; 1990 pop. 33,263), N Ky.; ⊙ La Grange; 38°23′N 85°26′W. Bounded W and NW by Ohio R. (Ind. state line); drained by Floyds Fork R. and Harrods Creek. Rolling upland agr. area (burley tobacco, corn, wheat, hay, alfalfa, soybeans; hogs, cattle, poultry; dairying); limestone, in N part of Bluegrass region. Urbanized in SW; extends from Louisville. Formed 1823. **2** county (□ 1,501 sq mi/3,888 sq km; 1990 pop. 2,278), extreme N Texas; ⊙ Vega, in high plains of Panhandle; 35°23′N 102°35′W. Elev. 3,200 ft/975 m–4,100 ft/1,250 m. Wheat, sorghum; cattle ranching; oil and gas, sand and gravel, stone. Drained by Canadian R. and Rita Blanca Creek. Formed 1876.

Oldham, village (1990 pop. 189), Kingsbury co., E S.Dak., 16 mi/26 km SE of De Smet; 44°13′N 97°18′W. In agr. area.

Oldhorn Mountain (10,125 ft/3,086 m), W Alta., Canada, near B.C. border, in Rocky Mts., in Jasper Natl. Park, 11 mi/18 km SW of Jasper; 52°46′N 118°13′W.

Oldman, river, c.250 mi/400 km long; rises in the Rocky Mts., SW Alta., Canada; flows generally E past Lethbridge to join the Bow R. W of Medicine Hat and form the South Saskatchewan R. The Belly R. is its chief tributary. The Oldman flows through a farming region; wheat and sugar beets are the main crops.

Oldmans Creek, c.25 mi/40 km long, SW N.J.; rises SW of Glassboro; flows generally NW, forming Gloucester-Salem co. line, to Delaware R. above Penns Grove. Navigable for c.11 mi/18 km above mouth.

Olds, town (1991 pop. 5,542), S Alta., Canada, N of Calgary, in a livestock-raising, dairy-producing, and wheat-farming region; 51°47′N 114°06′W. It has grain elevators and is the seat of a provincial agr. school.

Olds, town (1990 pop. 205), Henry co., SE Iowa, 12 mi/19 km N of Mount Pleasant; 41°07′N 91°32′W. In livestock area.

Oldsmar, town (□ 9 sq mi/23.3 sq km; 1990 pop. 8,361), Pinellas co., W central Fla., 10 mi/16 km ENE of Clearwater; 28°03′N 82°40′W.

Oldtown 1 village (1990 pop. 151), Bonner co., N Idaho, at Wash. state line adjacent to Newport (Wash.); 48°11′N 117°02′W. Mfg. (sawmill prods., lumber). **2** uninc. village (1990 pop. 570), Greenup co., NE Ky., 8 mi/12.9 km S of Greenup, on Little Sandy R. Tobacco, alfalfa, soybeans, corn; cattle. Oldtown Covered Bridge (1880) spans river. Greenbo State Resort Park to N. **3** village, Allegany co., W Md., on North Branch of the Potomac (bridged), 11 mi/18 km SE of Cumberland. It was originallly a ford called Skipton settled in 1741 by Col. Thomas Cresap on an old Indian trail known as "The Warriors' Path." The Six Nations of the Iroquois Confederacy of the N and the Cherokees, Catawbas, and Shawnees of the S raided each other over the path. Private toll bridge across Potomac to Green Springs (W.Va.); closed to motor vehicle traffic in 1995.

Olean (O-lee-AN), city (□ 6 sq mi/15.5 sq km; 1990 pop. 16,946), Cattaraugus co., W N.Y., on the Allegheny R. near the Pa. state line; 42°04′N 78°25′W. An important commercial center of the region. Once an oil-based economy emanating from nearby "Pennsylvania" oil fields, mfg. include turbines and compressors for the oil industry, electrical items, cutlery, and dairy prods. St. Bonaventure Univ. and Allegheny State Park are nearby. Major outfitting post for settlers moving W down the Allegheny and Ohio rivers in early 1800s. In 1972 a severe flood associated with Hurricane Agnes flooded large areas and damaged more than 2,900 homes. Settled 1804, inc. 1893.

Olean (O-lee-AN), town (1990 pop. 106), Miller co., central Mo., 5 mi/8 km N of Eldon; 38°24′N 92°31′W.

Olean Creek, N.Y.: see ISCHUA CREEK.

Olentangy River (O-luhn-TAN-jee), c.75 mi/121 km long, central Ohio; rises near Galion in Crawford co.; flows NW, then S, past Delaware and Worthington, to Scioto R. at Columbus; 39°57′N 83°01′W.

Oleum, oil-refining and -shipping point, Contra Costa co., W Calif., on San Pablo Bay, 9 mi/14.5 km NE of Richmond. Tanker docks.

Oley (O-lee), uninc. town (1990 pop. 900), Berks co., SE central Pa., 7 mi/11.3 km NE of Reading, on Little Manatawny Creek; 40°23′N 75°47′W. Light mfg.; agr. (grain; livestock; dairying).

Olin, town (1990 pop. 663), Jones co., E Iowa, 10 mi/16 km SE of Anamosa; 42°00′N 91°08′W.

Olinalá (o-LEE-nah-LAH), town (1990 pop. 4,821), Guerrero, SW Mexico, in Sierra Madre del Sur, 19 mi/30 km NNW of Tlapa de Comonfort on unpaved roads; 17°48′N 98°44′W. Cereals, sugarcane, coffee, fruit, forest prods. (resin, vanilla).

Olinda, uninc. village, Orange co., S Calif., 12 mi/19 km NNE of Santa Ana. Oil field here (since 1890s). Annexed by Brea.

Olintla (o-LEEN-tlah), town (1990 pop. 2,714), Puebla, central Mexico, 23 mi/37 km ESE of Huauchinango; 20°06′N 97°41′W. An isolated community in the S Sierra Oriental with Totonac Indian pop. Sugar, coffee, fruit. Also called San José Olintla.

Olive Branch, town (1990 pop. 3,567), De Soto co., extreme NW Miss., near Tenn. state line, suburb 15 mi/24 km SE of Memphis (Tenn.); 34°57′N 89°49′W. In agr. area (cotton, grain; cattle; dairying); mfg. (aluminum and metal prods., printing and publishing; textiles, machinery, furniture).

Olive Branch, uninc. village (1990 pop. 500), Alexander co., S Ill., 13 mi/21 km SE of Cape Girardeau (Mo.), near Mississippi R. Shawnee Natl. Forest to N; 37°10′N 89°21′W. Horseshoe L. State Conservation Area to S.

Olive Bridge Dam, N.Y.: see ASHOKAN DAM.

Olive Cove, fishing village, SE Alaska, on N shore of Etolin Isl., 20 mi/32 km S of Wrangell; 56°11′N 132°19′W.

Olive Hill, town (1990 pop. 1,809), Carter co., NE Ky., 12 mi/19 km W of Grayson, on Tygarts Creek; 38°17′N 83°10′W. In agr., clay, sand and gravel, and coal; mfg. (limestone processing, lumber, apparel, pumps, consumer goods). Northeastern Ky. Mus. to NE, near Carter Caves State Park. Carter Caves State Resort Park to NE; Cascade Caverns State Nature Preserve to NE; Grayson L. reservoir and State Park to SE; Tygarts State Forest to N; several caves and natural bridges in area.

Olive View, suburban section of Los Angeles, Los Angeles co., S Calif., in San Fernando Valley, just N of San Fernando co. In foothills of San Gabriel Mts. Veterans Administration Hosp. here. Pacoima Reservoir to NE; Angeles Natl. Forest to N and E.

Olivebridge, resort village (1990 pop. 400), Ulster co., SE N.Y., in the Catskills, near Ashokan Reservoir, 11 mi/18 km W of Kingston; 41°56′N 74°13′W. Also spelled Olive Bridge.

Olivebridge Dam, New York: see ASHOKAN DAM.

Olivehurst, uninc. town (1990 pop. 9,738), Yuba co., N central Calif., 3 mi/4.8 km SSE of Marysville; 39°05′N 121°33′W. Peaches, prunes, olives, walnuts, kiwi; dairying; cattle; mfg. concrete. Yuba Co. Airport is here. Beale Air Force Base to E.

Oliver, county (□ 720 sq mi/1,865 sq km; 1990 pop. 2,381), central N.Dak.; ⊙ Center; 47°06′N 101°20′W. Agr. area watered by Square Butte and Otter Creek; bounded E by Missouri R. (on border bet Mountain and Central time zones). Lignite mines; farming; cattle; wheat, barley, potatoes. Nelson L. SE of center; Cross Ranch State Park in E; Fort Clark Historic Site on N boundary. Formed 1885.

Oliver, town (1991 pop. 3,743), S B.C., Canada, near Wash. border, on Okanagan R., 22 mi/35 km S of Penticton; 49°11′N 119°33′W. In irrigated farming region; fruit and vegetable packing, canning.

Oliver (AH-li-vuhr), uninc. town (1990 pop. 3,271), North Union township, Fayette co., SW Pa., residential suburb 2 mi/3.2 km N of Uniontown; 39°55′N 79°43′W. RR junction.

Oliver 1 village (1990 pop. 242), Screven co., E Ga., 15 mi/24 km SSE of Sylvania; 32°31′N 81°32′W. Mfg. (wood processing). **2** village (1990 pop. 265), Douglas co., extreme NW Wis., 4 mi/6.4 km SW of Superior, on St. Louis R. (Minn. state line); 46°38′N 92°11′W. RR terminus. Grain growing. Mont Du Lac Ski Area to SW.

Oliver Springs, town (1990 pop. 3,433), Morgan, Roane, and Anderson cos., E Tenn., 23 mi/37 km WNW of Knoxville; 36°03′N 84°20′W. In coal-mining area.

Oliverea, resort village (1990 pop. 150), Ulster co., SE N.Y., in the Catskills, 26 mi/42 km WNW of Kingston; 42°04′N 74°28′W.

Olivet (ah-li-VET), town (1990 pop. 1,604), Eaton co., S central Mich., 16 mi/26 km NE of Battle Creek; 42°27′N 84°55′W. In farm area. Mfg. (fabricated metal prods.). Seat of Olivet Col.

Olivet 1 (ah-li-VET), village (1990 pop. 59), Osage co., E central Kansas, near Marais des Cygnes R., 9 mi/14.5 km S of Lyndon, on S side of Melvern L. Reservoir; 38°28′N 95°45′W. In livestock and grain area. **2** village (1990 pop. 74), ⊙ Hutchinson co., SE S.Dak., 30 mi/48 km NNW of Yankton; 43°14′N 97°40′W.

Olivette, town (1990 pop. 7,573), St. Louis co., E Mo., suburb 10 mi/16 km WNW of St. Louis; 38°40′N 90°22′W. Mfg. (paper prods., pharmaceuticals, cosmetics, glass prods. printing and publishing, bldg. materials, furniture); distillery (makes Southern Comfort). Inc. 1930.

Olivia, village (1990 pop. 2,623), ⊙ Renville co., SW Minn., 28 mi/45 km E of Granite Falls; elev. 1,086 ft/331 m; 44°46′N 95°00′W. Agr. area (grain, soybeans, beans, sugar beets; livestock, poultry; dairying); mfg. (agr. prods., canned food, food prods.). Plotted 1878, inc. 1881.

Olla (AH-luh), town (1990 pop. 1,410), La Salle parish, central La., c.45 mi/72 km NNE of Alexandria; 31°54′N 92°14′W. In agr. area (cotton, soybeans; cattle, hogs); mfg. (oil storage tanks, lumber).

Ollie, town (1990 pop. 207), Keokuk co., SE Iowa, 11 mi/18 km SE of Sigourney; 41°12′N 92°05′W. Limestone quarries nearby.

Olmito, uninc. village (1990 pop. 200), Cameron co., extreme S Texas, 8 mi/12.9 km N of Brownsville. In irrigated agr. area of lower Rio Grande valley; mfg. (radio equip., boats).

Olmitz (OL-mits), village (1990 pop. 130), Barton co., central Kansas, 14 mi/23 km NW of Great Bend; 38°31′N 98°56′W. In wheat region. Gas and oil fields nearby.

Olmos Dam, Texas: see OLMOS PARK.

Olmos Park, city (1990 pop. 2,161), Bexar co., S central Texas, residential suburb 3 mi/4.8 km N of San Antonio, near San Antonio R.; 29°28′N 98°29′W. Olmos Dam (flood control) built here across small Olmos Creek (tributary of San Antonio R.) after 1921 flood. Trinity Univ. in S. Inc. 1939.

Olmsted, county (☐ 654 sq mi/1,694 sq km; 1990 pop. 106,470), SE Minn.; ⊙ Rochester; 44°00′N 92°24′W. Drained by Root R. and South and Middle forks of Zumbro R. Agr. area (corn, oats, soybeans, peas, hay, alfalfa; sheep, hogs, cattle, poultry; dairying); mfg. at Rochester. Mayo Clinic at Rochester. Part of Whitewater Wildlife Area in NE corner; parts of Richard J. Dorer Memorial Hardwood State Forest in NW and S. Formed 1855.

Olmsted, village (1990 pop. 358), Pulaski co., extreme S Ill., 13 mi/21 km NNE of Cairo; 37°10′N 89°04′W. In agr. area. Near Lock and Dam 53 on Ohio R.

Olmsted Air Force Base, Pa.: see MIDDLETOWN.

Olmsted Falls, city (1990 pop. 6,741), Cuyahoga co., N Ohio, 14 mi/23 km SW of Cleveland and on Rocky R.; 41°22′N 81°54′W. Mfg. (tools).

Olmstedville, resort village (1990 pop. 400), Essex co., NE N.Y., in the Adirondacks, 35 mi/56 km NNW of Glens Falls; 43°46′N 73°56′W.

Olney (AWL-nee), city (1990 pop. 8,664), ⊙ Richland co., SE Ill., 30 mi/48 km W of Vincennes (Ind.); 38°43′N 88°05′W. Trade and shipping center in agr. (corn, wheat, apples; livestock); mfg. (dairy prods., vinegar). Olney Central Col. near here. Famous for white squirrels. Inc. 1841.

Olney, town (1990 pop. 3,519), Young co., N Texas, 40 mi/64 km S of Wichita Falls; 33°21′N 98°45′W. Elev. 1,184 ft/361 m. Commercial center for oil and gas; livestock (cattle, sheep, goats, hogs). Agr. area (wheat, cotton, pecans, nursery crops), oil refining; mfg. (aircraft components, bldg. materials, clothing, fabricated aluminum). Settled 1891, inc. 1909.

Olney, residential village (1990 pop. 23,019), Montgomery co., central Md., 17 mi/27 km N of Washington, D.C.; 39°09′N 77°05′W. Seat of co. hosp. It is said to have been named after a town in England which was the home of poet William Cowper. The summer theater here (popular with Washington residents) dates back to 1875.

Olney (AWL-nee), N residential section of Philadelphia, Pa.; 40°02′N 75°07′W.

Olney Springs, village (1990 pop. 340), Crowley co., SE central Colo., near Arkansas R., 10 mi/16 km WSW of Ordway; 38°10′N 103°56′W. Elev. 4,391 ft/1,338 m. In irrigated sugar-beet region.

Olpe (OL-pee), village (1990 pop. 431), Lyon co., E central Kansas, 10 mi/16 km S of Emporia; 38°15′N 96°10′W. Cattle; grain.

Olsburg, village (1990 pop. 192), Pottawatomie co., NE Kansas, 15 mi/24 km N of Manhattan, E of Tuttle Creek Reservoir; 39°25′N 96°37′W.

Olton, town (1990 pop. 2,116), Lamb co., NW Texas, on the Llano Estacado, 25 mi/40 km W of Plainview; 34°10′N 102°08′W. Cattle, sheep; cotton; oil and gas; mfg. (bldg. materials). Was the capital of Lamb co. until 1946.

Olustee (o LUHS-tee), village (1990 pop. 701), Jackson co., SW Okla., 8 mi/12.9 km SW of Altus, near Salt Fork of Red R.; 34°32′N 99°25′W. In cotton and grain area.

Oluta (o-LOO-tah), town (1990 pop. 9,659), Veracruz, SE Mexico, on Isthmus of Tehuantepec, 2 mi/3.2 km SE of Acayucan; 17°55′N 94°54′W. Rice, coffee, fruit; livestock. A Popoluca Indian town.

Olympia, city (1990 pop. 33,840), ⊙ of Wash. and of Thurston co., W Wash., 26 mi/42 km SW of Tacoma, a S extremity of Puget Sound, on Budd Inlet; 47°02′N 122°54′W. RR junction. A port of entry, it ships lumber prods. and agr. produce. Oyster fisheries are here; mfg. (printing and publishing, explosives, consumer goods, sports equip., plastic bottles, metal cans, plastic prods., paper prods., veneer, furniture, cheese, steel, aircraft engines, porcelain enamel); logging. State Capital Mus. Settled in 1846, it was made capital of the newly created Wash. Territory in 1853. Of interest are the state lib., the old capitol bldg. (1893), and the newer, imposing group of white sandstone capitol bldgs. Olympia Municipal Airport to S. Fort Lewis Military Reservation to E. Nisqually Natl. Wildlife Reservation to E; Nisqually Indian Reservation to NE. Millersylvania State Park to S; Tolmie State Park to NE. A local attraction is the annual salmon run from Budd Inlet into Capitol L. St. Martin's Col. (at Lacey, to E), South Puget Sound Community Col. and Evergreen State Col. are in Olympia. The Olympic Mts. can be seen to the N, and Mt. Rainier to the NE. Inc. 1859.

Olympia Fields, village (1990 pop. 4,248), Cook co., NE Ill., S suburb of Chicago, just W of Chicago Heights; 41°31′N 87°41′W. One of few upscale suburbs S of the city.

Olympian Village, village (1990 pop. 752), Jefferson co., E Mo., residential community 5 mi/8 km E of De Soto; 38°07′N 90°27′W.

Olympic Hot Springs, Clallam co., NW Wash., in Olympic Mts., Olympic Natl. Park, N of Mt. Olympus and 13 mi/21 km SW of Port Angeles, 4 mi/6.4 km W of L. Mills, on Boulder Creek, branch of Elwha R. Elev. c.2,000 ft/610 m. Former resort.

Olympic Mountains, range, highest part of the Coast Ranges, on the Olympic Peninsula, NW Wash. Mt. Olympus (7,965 ft/2,427 m) is the highest point in the mts. (has permanent snowcap), which are composed mainly of sedimentary rock. The W side of the mts. is in one of the areas of greatest precipitation in the U.S., with an annual rainfall of c.130 in/330 cm; the NE side, in the rain shadow, is in one of the driest areas on the West Coast. On the upper slopes are about 60 small glaciers fed by heavy winter snows. The greater part of the Olympic Mts. is included in Olympic Natl. Park (☐ 922,654 acres/373,398 ha); est. 1938. Rugged mts., alpine meadows, coniferous rain forests, glaciers, lakes, and streams characterize this area. The natl. park includes a separate 50-mi/80-km stretch of shoreline along the Pacific Ocean that contains scenic seascapes and wildlife. Center of park 50 mi/80 km W of Seattle. Temperate rain forests in valleys extending W toward Pacific Ocean; bounded on all sides by parts of Olympic Natl. Forest. Mt. Olympus at center of park. Jefferson and Clallam cos., extends S into Mason and Grays Harbor cos.

Olympic National Park (☐ 1,441 sq mi/3,732 sq km), NW Wash. Rain forests and glaciers in the Olympic Mts. Authorized 1938.

Olympic Peninsula, NW Wash., bounded E by Puget Sound and Hood Canal, W by Pacific Ocean, N by Strait of Juan de Fuca. Includes Olympic Mts., Olympic Natl. Park., and Olympic Natl. Forest. Clallam, Jefferson, parts of Mason and Grays Harbor cos. Kitsap Peninsula to E, across narrow Hood Canal; city of Port Angeles on N shore, main community on peninsula. Makah Indian Reservation at Cape Flattery, NW point; Quinault Indian Reservation in SW.

Olympus, Mount (10,132 ft/3,088 m), SW Alta., Canada, near B.C. border, in Rocky Mts., in Jasper Natl. Park, 50 mi/80 km SE of Jasper: 52°28′N 117°02′W.

Olyphant (O-li-fant), borough (1990 pop. 5,222), Lackawanna co., NE Pa., suburb 6 mi/9.7 km NE of Scranton, on Lackawanna R.; 41°27′N 75°34′W. Mfg. (lumber, wood prods., pharmaceuticals, consumer goods). Archbald Pothole State Park to NE; Moosic Mts. to SE; Bell Mt. to NW. Settled 1858, inc. 1877.

Omaha, city (1990 pop. 335,795), ⊙ Douglas co., E Nebr., on the W bank of the Missouri R., across the river from Council Bluffs (Iowa); 41°15′N 96°00′W. The largest city in the state, it is a busy port of entry and a major transportation center. It is also one of the largest livestock markets in the world and a market for agr. prods. Much of the city's industry is devoted to food processing, although it is a diverse mfg. center. Omaha is the home of many insurance companies, telecommunications firms, and a center for medical treatment and research. Founded when the Nebr. Territory was opened to settlement in 1854, it grew as a supply point for westward migration and became a thriving transportation and industrial center after the arrival of the Union Pacific RR in 1865, and its transcontinental linkup with the Central Pacific in 1869. It was the territorial capital from 1855 to 1867. A world's fair, the Trans-Mississippi and Internatl. Exhibition, was held here in 1898. Fort Omaha (built 1868) serves as hq. of the naval reserve and marine reserve training command. Boys Town is 9 mi/14.5 km to the W, and Offutt Air Force Base, hq. of the Strategic Command, is to the S. Some river and local flash flooding occured during floods of 1993. President Gerald Ford's birthplace, including his home and rose garden, is here. The city has noted park and school systems and is the seat of Creighton Univ., the Univ. of Nebr. at Omaha, Univ. of Nebr. Col. of Medicine, Nebr. Christian Col., and the Col. of St. Mary. Of interest are the Joslyn Art Mus., Western Heritage Mus., an aerospace mus., a Mormon cemetery, Fontenelle Forest, Henry Doorly Zoo, Rosenblatt Stadium, Coliseum. Omaha Home for Boys, Nebr. School for the Deaf, main airport is Epply Airfield 4 mi/6.4 km NE of downtown. Omaha Livestock Market in SE part of city (Union Stockyards). Barge dock on Missouri. R. Inc. 1857.

Omaha, town (1990 pop. 833), Morris co., NE Texas, c.45 mi/72 km WSW of Texarkana; 33°10′N 94°44′W. Watermelons; peanuts; poultry, cattle; timber.

Omaha 1 village (1990 pop. 207), Boone co., N Ark., 15 mi/24 km NNW of Harrison, near Mo. state line; 36°27′N 93°11′W. Mfg. (charcoal). Recreation area. Arm of Table Rock reservoir to W; Bull Shoals L. to E. **2** village (1990 pop. 116), Stewart co., SW Ga., 14 mi/23 km WNW of Lumpkin, near Chattahoochee R.; 32°09′N 85°01′W. **3** village (1990 pop. 273), Gallatin co., SE Ill., 16 mi/26 km NNW of Shawneetown; 37°53′N 88°17′W. In agr. area.

Omaha Reservation (1990 pop. c. 1,500), mainly in SE

Thurston co., Nebr. A patchwork of tribal and allotted land comprises the reservation. In 1855, the Omaha ceded extensive hunting grounds in exchange for a reservation. In 1865, the N ½ was sold to the Winnebago tribe through the U.S. govt. Following authorization by President Chester Arthur in 1882, c.76,000 acres/30,757 ha were allotted and 55,450 acres/22,441 ha were reserved for future generations. The remainder was given to whites. Subsequently, Omaha land has been much reduced, with little allotted land remaining (most of which is leased to non-Indians). Commonly the leases permit the Omaha family to live in a house on the land, and there is some acquired tribal land. The majority of the Omaha pop. live in villages, esp. Macy, where the Omaha agency is located. Many more live off the reservation, mainly in cities, some distant. The Omaha hold an annual powwow in Macy in late Aug.

Omak, town (1990 pop. 4 ,117), Okanogan co., N Wash., on Okanogan R. at mouth of Omak Creek, 4 mi/6.4 km NE of Okanogan; 48°25′N 119°32′W. Apples; lumber, wood prods.; mfg. (millwork, printing and publishing); logging. Fish hatchery. Omak L. (on No Name Creek) to SE; large Colville Indian Reservation to E, across river. St. Mary's Mission to SE. Inc. 1911.

Omao (O-MAH-o), town (1990 pop. 1,142), Kauai isl., Kauai co., Hawaii, 8 mi/12.9 km WSW of Lihue, 2 mi/3.2 km inland from S coast, on Omao Stream, on Kaumualii Highway; 21°55′N 159°29′W. Sugarcane, fruit. Lihue-Koloa Forest Reserve to N.

Omar, uninc. town (1990 pop. 800), Logan co., SW W.Va., 7 mi/11.3 km S of Logan. In coal region.

Omealca (o-me-AHL-kah), town (1990 pop. 3,339), Veracruz, E Mexico, in Sierra Madre Oriental foothills, on Blanco R., 14 mi/23 km SE of Córdoba; 18°45′N 96°46′W. Coffee, sugarcane, fruit.

Omega (o-MAI-guh), town (1990 pop. 912), Tift co., S central Ga., 9 mi/14.5 km SW of Tifton; 31°20′N 83°36′W. In farm area.

Omemee (o-MEE-mee), village (1991 pop. 1,099), S Ont., Canada, near S end of Pigeon L., 12 mi/19 km W of Peterborough; 44°18′N 78°33′W. Dairying; mixed farming.

Omemee (o-MEM-ee), village, Bottineau co., N N.Dak., 9 mi/14.5 km SSE of Bottineau; 48°41′N 100°20′W. RR junction.

Omena (o-MEE-nah), village, Leelanau co., NW Mich., 10 mi/16 km N of Traverse City, on W shore of Grand Traverse Bay; 45°03′N 85°35′W. Has Native Amer. cemetery. Resorts. Winery.

Omer (AH-mer), village (1990 pop. 385), Arenac co., E Mich., 7 mi/11.3 km NE of Standish, and on Rifle R. near its mouth on Saginaw Bay; 44°02′N 83°51′W. In farm area; fishing; mfg. (aluminum doors, concrete). Settled 1873, inc. as city 1903.

Ometepec (o-ME-te-pek), city (1990 pop. 11,474) and township, ⊙ Ometepec muncipio, Guerrero, SW Mexico, in Pacific lowlands, 100 mi/161 km E of Acapulco de Juárez; 16°41′N 98°24′W. Agr. center (cereals, sugarcane, tobacco, cotton, fruit; livestock).

Ometepec Bay (o-ME-te-pek), small inlet of Gulf of California, on NE coast of Lower California, NW Mexico, near mouth of Colorado R., 85 mi/137 km SE of Mexicali. Large deposits of sea salt.

Omitlán de Juárez (o-mee-TLAHN dai HWAH-res), town (1990 pop. 1,128), Hidalgo, central Mexico, 6 mi/9.7 km NE of Pachuca de Soto on Mexico Highway 105; 29°19′N 99°37′W. Corn, maguey, beans; livestock.

Ommaney, Cape, SE Alaska, S tip of Baranof Isl., on W shore of S entrance to Christian Sound, 7 mi/11.3 km S of Port Alexander; 56°10′N 134°40′W.

Ompompanoosuc River (AHM-pahm-pan-oo-suhk), c.25 mi/40 km long, E Vt.; rises in E Orange co.; flows S to the Connecticut near Norwich.

Omro (AHM-ro), town (1990 pop. 2,836), Winnebago co., E central Wis., on Fox R., and 10 mi/16 km W of Oshkosh; 44°02′N 88°44′W. Mfg. (business forms, polyethylene tubing). Settled 1845; inc. as village in 1857, as city in 1944.

Onaga (o-NAIG-uh), village (1990 pop. 761), Pottawatomie co., NE Kansas, on Vermillion Creek, 14 mi/23 km NE of Westmoreland; 39°29′N 96°10′W. Trade and shipping point in livestock and grain region. Mfg. (clothing).

Onakawana (o-nah-kuh-WAH-nuh), village, NE Ont., Canada, on Abitibi R., and 110 mi/177 km NNW of Cochrane. Lignite deposits.

Onalaska (AHN-uh-LAS-kah), city (1990 pop. 11,284), La Crosse co., W Wis., on Mississippi R. (Minn. state line), suburb 6 mi/9.7 km N of downtown La Crosse; 43°53′N 91°13′W. In farm and dairy area. Dairy prods.; mfg. (consumer goods, printing, printed circuit boards, machinery); summer resort. Hamlin Garland b. nearby. Lock and Dam No. 7 and La Crosse Airport to E. Interstate 90 bridge to Minn. Settled 1854, inc. 1887.

Onalaska, village (1990 pop. 728), Polk co., E Texas, 45 mi/72 km SSW of Lufkin, on NE shore of L. Livingston (Trinity R.); 30°48′N 95°06′W. Residential and recreational community in timber- and oil-producing area.

Onamia (o-NAI-mee-yuh), village (1990 pop. 676), Mille Lacs co., E central Minn., 30 mi/48 km SE of Brainerd, on Rum R., at its exit from L. Onamia, 4 mi/6.4 km S of Mille Lacs L.; 46°04′N 93°40′W. Agr. (grain; livestock, poultry; dairying); mfg. (lumber and wood chips, custom circuit hybrid mfg.); timber. Mille Lacs Kathio State Park and part of Mille Lacs Indian Reservation to NW; part of Rum R. Wildlife Area to W; Mille Lacs Wildlife Area to SE.

Onancock (o-NAN-kawk), town (1990 pop. 1,434), Accomack co., E Va., 4 mi/6.4 km W of Accomac, on Onancock R. estuary, arm of Chesapeake Bay; 37°42′N 75°44′W. Mfg. (seafood processing, commercial printing); trade center for farming region (vegetables, grain, fruit; poultry, livestock); timber (pine). Ferry to Tangier Isl. Founded 1680.

Onaping Lake (O-nuh-ping), SE central Ont., Canada, 40 mi/64 km NW of Sudbury; 35 mi/56 km long, 3 mi/5 km wide. Drains S into Wanapitei L.

Onaqui Mountains (O-nuh-kee), range (6,000 ft/1,829 m–9,000 ft/2,743 m) in Tooele co., W Utah; forms S extension of Stansbury Mts. The ranges (2) separated by Johnsons Pass (6,237 ft/1,901 m). Rush Valley to E.

Onarga (o-NAHR-gah), village (1990 pop. 1,281), Iroquois co., E Ill., 15 mi/24 km WSW of Watseka; 40°42′N 88°00′W. In rich agr. area (corn, wheat, soybeans; livestock; nursery stock); canned foods. Inc. 1867.

Onavas (o-NAH-vahs), town (1990 pop. 439), Sonora, NW Mexico, on Yaqui R., and 100 mi/161 km ESE of Hermosillo; 28°28′N 109°32′W. Cereals, fruit; livestock.

Onawa, city (1990 pop. 2,936), ⊙ Monona co., W Iowa, near the Miss. R., 37 mi/60 km SSE of Sioux City; 42°01′N 96°05′W. Trade center for grain. Agr. (livestock; dairying); mfg. (farm equip., leather goods). Lewis and Clark State Park is W. Inc. 1858.

Onawa (AHN-uh-wah), village, Piscataquis co., Maine, 14 mi/23 km NNW of Dover-Foxcroft, on Onawa L.

Onaway (AHN-ah-wai), town (1990 pop. 1,039), Presque Isle co., NE Mich., 20 mi/32 km WSW of Rogers City; 45°21′N 84°13′W. In lake-resort and farm area (livestock; grains, potatoes; dairy prods.). Fishing on nearby Black L. State forest nearby and Onaway State Park, on E end of Black L., to N. Settled c.1880; inc. as village 1899, as city 1903.

Onaway, village (1990 pop. 203), Latah co., N Idaho, 16 mi/26 km NNE of Moscow, borders Potlatch, near Palouse R.; 46°56′N 116°54′W. Timber; cattle, sheep. St. Joe Natl. Forest to N; Coeur d'Alene Indian Reservation to N.

One Hundred and Two River, c.90 mi/145 km long, in SW Iowa and NW Mo.; rises in S Iowa (S Adams co.); flows S to Little Platte R. 6 mi/9.7 km E of St. Joseph. Also called Hundred and Two.

O'Neals, uninc. village, Madera co., central Calif., 26 mi/42 km NNE of Fresno. Dairying; cattle, poultry; nuts, fruit, honey, grain. Mfg. (concrete). Sierra Natl. Forest to NE; Millerton L. reservoir and State Recreation Area to S.

Oneco (O-ni-ko), village, Windham co., E Conn., 20 mi/32 km NE of Norwich, near R.I. border. A postal sect. of Sterling.

Oneida 1 (o-NEI-duh), county (□ 1,201 sq mi/3,111 sq km; 1990 pop. 3,492), SE Idaho; ⊙ Malad City; 42°13′N 112°31′W. Mt. region bordering on Utah and crossed in SE by Malad R. and tributaries. Cattle; agr. (wheat, alfalfa, barley). Part of Caribou Natl. Forest in E; part of Sawtooth Natl. Forest in NW corner; part of Curlew Natl. Grassland in center of co. Formed 1864. **2** county (□ 1,257 sq mi/3,256 sq km; 1990 pop. 250,836), central N.Y.; ⊙ Rome and Utica; 43°14′N 75°26′W. Partly bounded W by Oneida L.; rises to the Adirondacks in E and NE; drained by Mohawk and Black rivers, and by Oneida, Oriskany, and West Canada creeks. Traversed by the Barge Canal. Extensive mfg. (variety of industrial wire prods., fishing tackle, silverware, ornamental ironwork, tools, dies and machinery) at Rome, Utica; dairying, livestock-raising, farming; limestone quarries and lime and lime prods. Year-round recreation on lakes and in Adirondacks. Formed 1798. **3** county (□ 1,236 sq mi/3,201 sq km; 1990 pop. 31,679), N Wis.; ⊙ Rhinelander; 45°42′N 89°31′W. Largely a resort area with numerous lakes; contains part of Amer. Legion State Forest in N and a sect. of Nicolet Natl. Forest in E corner. Lumbering; dairying and farming (mostly brans) on cutover forest land. Bearskin State Trail (N-S) in W part. Drained by Wisconsin R. Formed 1885.

Oneida 1 city (1990 pop. 723), Knox co., NW central Ill., 10 mi/16 km NE of Galesburg; 41°04′N 90°13′W. In agr. area. **2** city (□ 22 sq mi/57 sq km; 1990 pop. 10,850), Madison co., central N.Y.; 43°04′N 75°39′W. Silverware is its best-known prod.; factories also make cutlery, industrial wire and cable, paper and plastic goods. Nearby was the Oneida Community, a religious society of Perfectionists that was est. 1848 by John Humphrey Noyes. Members of the sect held all property in common and practiced complex marriage and common care of the children. The community prospered by making steel traps and silverware. In 1881 it was reorganized as a joint stock company, and the social experiments were abandoned. Inc. 1901.

Oneida 1 (o-NEI-duh), town (1990 pop. 49), Delaware co., E Iowa, 6 mi/9.7 km NE of Manchester; 42°32′N 91°20′W. **2** town (1990 pop. 3,502), Scott co., N Tenn., 50 mi/80 km NW of Knoxville, in the Cumberlands; 44°30′N 88°12′W. Ships coal, farm produce, livestock; mfg. of wood prods., textiles. Settled 1868; inc. 1914.

Oneida 1 (o-NEED-uh), village (1990 pop. 79), Nemaha co., NE Kansas, 7 mi/11.3 km E of Seneca; 39°52′N 95°56′W. Livestock; grain. **2** (o-NEI-duh), village, Butler co., SW Ohio.

Oneida Castle, village (1990 pop. 671), Oneida co., central N.Y., on Oneida Creek and just SE of Oneida; 43°04′N 75°37′W. Center of Oneida Territory, site of chief settlement of Oneida people.

Oneida Lake (□ c.80 sq mi/207 sq km), central N.Y., NE of Syracuse; 22 mi/35 km long, 1–5 mi/1.6–8 km wide; 43°12′N 75°55′W. The N.Y. State Barge Canal links the E end of the lake with the Mohawk R., and also follows part of the Oneida R., which flows from the W end of the lake c.20 mi/32 km into the Oswego R.

Oneida Territory, parcel of scrubby land (□ 5 sq mi/13 sq km), Oneida co., central N.Y., adjacent to Route 46 near Verona. Site of Turning Point gambling casino, this region is all that remains of millions of acres of land once owned by the Oneida, part of the six Nations of Iroquois Confederacy. In the late 18th cent., the U.S. govt. led by President George Washington, tried to settle land disputes with the entire Iroquois Confederacy, including the Oneida. In 1785 and 1788, however, before an agreement could be reached with the Federal govt., N.Y. state signed treaties with the Oneida that resulted in the tribe surrendering all rights to most of its land. In 1978, several Oneida groups filed suit, claiming that the state did not have the authority to make those treaties, and that they were invalid since the Federal govt. had not ratified them. They laid claim to 9,375 sq mi/24,281 sq km of land (equal to ⅕ of the state) bounded on the W by a meridional line just E of Syracuse and extending from the St. Lawrence R. to the N.Y.-Pa. border and on the E by another meridonal line. They also demanded fair rental payments from the state for the use of their property for the last 100 years. The claim affected all or part of 12 cos., the cities of Binghamton,

Norwich, and Watertown, numerous municipal corporations, and land owned by 60,000 individuals. N.Y. state offered the Oneida $8 million and title to Sampson State Park in Seneca and Cayuca cos., but they refused. In Nov. 1980 the case went to court, and in 1981 it was decided in favor of the state. The U.S. Court of Appeals upheld the decision in a 1988 hearing, and the Supreme Court refused to hear a further appeal, thus ending the Oneida claim to the land.

O'Neill, town (1990 pop. 3,852), ⊙ Holt co., N Nebr., 70 mi/113 km NW of Norfolk, and on Elkhorn R.; 42°27′N 98°39′W. Elev. 2,000 ft/610 m. RR terminus. Shipping point for grain and livestock region. Printing; concrete. Founded 1874.

Onekama (AHN-ah-KAH-mah), village (1990 pop. 515), Manistee co., NW Mich., 9 mi/14.5 km NNE of Manistee, on Portage L., and 3 mi/4.8 km E of L. Michigan; 44°22′N 86°12′W. Mfg. (electrical wire harnesses); resort.

Oneonta (o-nee-AHN-tah), city (□ 4 sq mi/10.4 sq km; 1990 pop. 13,954), Otsego co., E central N.Y., W of the Catskills, on the Susquehanna R.; 42°27′N 75°04′W. Mobile medical laboratories and clinics, plastic moldings, laboratory apparatus and glass, plasticware, and electronic items are produced. In a farm area. Oneonta grew after the coming of the RR in 1865; however, no vestiges of importance as a RR center exist today. Brotherhood of R.R. Brakemen founded here in 1883), which was renamed Brotherhood of RR Trainmen in 1889. Seat of the State Univ. of N.Y. Col. at Oneonta; Hartwick Col. Regional medical center. Natl. Soccer Hall of Fame. Settled c.1780, inc. as a city 1909.

Oneonta (o-nee-AHN-tah), town (1990 pop. 4,844), ⊙ Blount co., N central Ala., 35 mi/56 km NE of Birmingham. Vegetable area; clothing; millwork; meat packaging; tire rims; motor vehicle customizing.

Ong, village (1990 pop. 69), Clay co., S Nebr., 14 mi/ 23 km SE of Clay Center; 40°23′N 97°50′W.

Onida, town (1990 pop. 761), ⊙ Sully co., central S.Dak., 27 mi/43 km NNE of Pierre; 44°42′N 100°04′W. Ranching area.

Onley (ON-lee), town (1990 pop. 532), Accomack co., E Va., 3 mi/4.8 km SW of Accomac, on Delmarva Peninsula; 37°41′N 75°43′W. Mfg. (printing and publishing, concrete); agr. area (vegetables, grain; poultry, livestock).

Onondaga, county (□ 805 sq mi/2,085 sq km; 1990 pop. 468,973), central N.Y.; ⊙ Syracuse; 43°00′N 76°12′W. Situated in Finger Lakes region; drained by Seneca and Oswego rivers and by Onondaga and small Chittenango creeks; crossed by the N.Y. State Barge Canal. Includes Onondaga Indian Reservation. Resorts on Oneida and Skaneateles lakes. Dairying and farming area (poultry; corn, potatoes, hay), with extensive mfg. Formed 1794.

Onondaga (ahn-uhn-DO-guh), town (1991 pop. 1,519), SE Ont., Canada, 8 mi/13 km E of Brantford; 43°07′N 80°06′W. Mohawk Indian reserve here.

Onondaga Lake, brackish lake, central N.Y., NW of Syracuse; 5 mi/8 km long and 1 mi/1.6 km wide; 43°05′N 76°12′W. In 1654, Father LeMoyne, a missionary, was taken to salt springs along the lakeshore by the Onondagas. He showed them how to obtain salt from the water by boiling it. In 1795 the lake was purchased from the Native Americans by N.Y. state for its salt resources. The Salt Mus. on the lakeshore near Liverpool contains relics of the early salt industry, which thrived in the mid-19th cent. Due to industry pollution (including chemical mfg.), all normal lake recreational activities are precluded (with the exception of boating). Ranks as one of the nation's major Superfund sites.

Onota, Lake (uh-NO-duh), reservoir, Berkshire co., W Mass., on branch of Housatonic R., in the Berkshire Mts., 3 mi/4.8 km NW of Pittsfield; c.3 mi/4.8 km long; 42°28′N 73°16′W.

Onoway (AH-no wai), agr. village (1991 pop. 681), central Alta., W Canada, 30 mi/48 km WNW of Edmonton; 53°42′N 114°11′W.

Onset, Mass.: see WAREHAM.

Onslow (AHNZ-lo), county (□ 908 sq mi/2,352 sq km; 1990 pop. 149,838), E N.C., on the Atlantic; ⊙ Jacksonville; 34°42′N 77°24′W. Bounded S by Atlantic Ocean,

NE by White Oak R. Intracoastal Waterway channel parallels coast (SE). Drained by New R., New R. estuary indents co. from SE. Heavily forested and partly swampy tidewater area. Agr. area (tobacco, corn, wheat, cotton, soybeans, hay, sweet potatoes). Some mfg. at Jacksonville. Fishing. U.S. Camp Lejeune (Marine base) in SE. Catherine L. in NW; Hammocks Beach State Park on Atlantic in E; part of Hoffmann Forest in N; part of Topsail Isl, beach resort area in S. Formed 1734.

Onslow, town (1990 pop. 216), Jones co., E Iowa, 14 mi/ 23 km E of Anamosa; 42°06′N 91°00′W. In livestock and grain area; fertilizers; feeds.

Onslow Bay (AHNZ-lo), SE N.C., bay of the Atlantic from Cape Lookout (NE) to Cape Fear (SW); c.100 mi/ 161 km long, c.25 mi/40 km wide. Long curvature in Atlantic coastline.

Onsted (AHN-sted), village (1990 pop. 801), Lenawee co., SE Mich., 12 mi/19 km NW of Adrian; 42°00′N 84°11′W. In farm area. Mfg. (hardware).

Ontario (awn-TER-ree-o), province (□ 412,582 sq mi/ 1,068,587 sq km; 1991 pop. 10,084,885), E central Canada; ⊙ TORONTO, the largest metropolitan area in Canada; 50°00′N 86°00′W. Other important cities are OTTAWA, HAMILTON, KITCHENER, LONDON, WINDSOR, THUNDER BAY, and ST. CATHARINES. Ont., the 2d-largest Can. prov., is the most populous and the most important in terms of mineral, industrial, and agr. output and in terms of financial and other services. It is bounded on the N by Hudson Bay and James Bay; on the E by Que.; on the S by the St. Lawrence R., lakes Ontario, Erie, Huron, and Superior, and by the U.S.; and on the W by Man. The prov. has 3 main geographic regions. In the W and central portion is the Can. Shield, a region of mineral-rich rock covered with forests and broken by a labyrinth of rivers and lakes. In the N is the Hudson Bay Lowlands bordering on Hudson and James bays, an area consisting mainly of marshes, swampland, and forest. In the S and E is the Great Lakes–St. Lawrence lowlands, where 90% of the pop. lives and where industry and agr. are concentrated. Climate varies among the regions. The far N has subarctic conditions, while the W has a temperate climate. Around the Great Lakes the weather is moderate and summers are longer than in other parts of the prov. The St. Lawrence R. gives Ont. access to the Atlantic. Other important rivers are the Ottawa (which forms part of the boundary with Que.), the St. Clair, the Detroit, and the St. Marys. Several of the prov.'s rivers are used to generate hydroelectric power, among them the Niagara, with its famous falls. The most important economic activity in Ont. is mfg., and the Toronto-Hamilton region is the most highly industrialized sect. of the country. The area from Oshawa around to Niagara Falls is known as the "Golden Horseshoe." Major industrial prods. include motor vehicles and parts, iron, steel, and other metal prods., foods and beverages, electrical goods, machinery, chemicals, petroleum and coal prods., and paper prods. Ont. has attracted many high technology industries, esp. around Ottawa, and its service industries are 2d in importance only to mfg. Agr. is also important, with cattle, dairy prods., and hogs producing the most income. Other major crops are corn, wheat, potatoes, and soybeans. On the shores of the E Great Lakes are orchards and tobacco plantations. Mining is important in the Can. Shield region, where iron ore, copper, zinc, gold, silver, and uranium are found. The area around Sudbury is particularly rich in copper and nickel; Ont. produces ½ the world's nickel. Ont. is also a major producer of lumber and pulp and paper. With steady immigration by people from Italy, Germany, Portugal, the West Indies, India, and East Asia, Ont.'s ethnic composition is rapidly diversifying. People of Br. ancestry make up about ½ the prov.'s pop., and 10% are Fr. Over 80% of Ont.'s residents live in urban centers. Ont. has 4 natl. parks and numerous tourist attractions, 3 of the most notable being Niagara Falls, the annual Shakespeare Festival at Stratford, and the annual George Bernard Shaw Festival at Niagara-on-the-Lake. Among the prov.'s institutions of higher education are the Univ. of Toronto, the Univ. of Ottawa, McMaster Univ., Queen's Univ., the Univ. of

Western Ont., Brock Univ., Carleton Univ., Trent Univ., Univ. of Waterloo, Wilfred Laurier Univ., York Univ., and Ryerson Polytech Univ. Before the arrival of Europeans the area of Ont. was inhabited by several Algonquian (Ojibwa, Cree, and Algonquin) and Iroquoian (Iroquois, Huron, Petun, Neutral, Erie, and Susquehannock) tribes. Étienne Brulé explored S Ont. in 1610–1612. Henry Hudson sailed into Hudson Bay in 1611 and claimed the region for England. Within a few years Samuel de Champlain reached (1615) the E shores of L. Huron, and Fr. explorers, missionaries, and trappers had established posts at several points. However, settlement was long hindered by the presence of the Iroquois. In the late 17th cent. the British established trading posts in the Hudson Bay area, and the Anglo-Fr. struggle for control of Ont. began. The conflict was resolved by the Treaty of Paris of 1763, which gave Great Britain all of France's mainland N Amer. territory. In 1774 the British attached Ont. to QUEBEC, which had a predominantly Fr. culture. When many pro-Br. Loyalists migrated to Ont. after the Amer. Revolution, the desire for institutions and a govt. separate from those of Que. grew. The Constitutional Act of 1791 split Que. into Lower Canada (present-day Que.) and Upper Canada (present-day Ont.), with the Ottawa R. as the dividing line. During the War of 1812, Americans raided Upper Canada and burned Toronto (1813). After the war many Eng., Scottish, and Irish settlers came to the colony. Conflict developed bet. the conservative, aristocratic governing group, known as the Family Compact, and the reformers and radicals led by William Lyon Mackenzie. The radicals staged an armed uprising in 1837 but were easily suppressed. However, the rebellion occurred at the same time as a revolt in Lower Canada, and the Br. govt. sent over Lord Durham to study the situation in the N. Amer. colonies. He recommended the reunion of the 2 colonies (to place the French of Que. in a minority) and the granting of self-govt. Accordingly Upper and Lower Canada were joined in 1841 and became known, respectively, as Canada West and Canada East. Parliamentary self-govt. was not granted until 1849. However, conflict bet. French and English made the united prov. unworkable, and in 1867 when the confederation of Canada was formed, Ont. and Que. became separate provs. With the construction of the transcontinental RR in the 1880s, settlement increased in W Canada and Ont.'s commerce and industry flourished. The exploitation of the minerals in the Can. Shield region began in the early 20th cent. Ont. sends 24 senators and 99 representatives to the natl. parliament.

Ontario, county (□ 853 sq mi/2,209 sq km), S Ont., Canada, on L. Ontario and L. Simcoe; ⊙ Whitby; 44°15′N 79°05′W.

Ontario, county (□ 662 sq mi/1,715 sq km; 1990 pop. 95,101), W central N.Y.; ⊙ Canandaigua; 42°51′N 77°17′W. Situated in Finger Lakes region, and partly bounded E by Seneca L.; includes Canandaigua, Honeoye, and Canadice lakes. Drained by small Honeoye, Mud, and Flint creeks, and Canandaigua Outlet. Diversified mfg., esp. at Geneva, Canandaigua, Naples; fruit-growing area; nurseries; agr. (grain, hay, potatoes; dairy prods.; poultry). Formed 1789.

Ontario 1 city (1990 pop. 133,179), San Bernardino co., S Calif., suburb 35 mi/56 km E of downtown Los Angeles, and 20 mi/32 km W of San Bernardino; 34°03′N 117°37′W. In a region of vineyards. Also important to the economy are the mfg. of aircraft and aircraft parts, aerospace vehicle parts, sporting goods, leather goods, electrical equip., and plastics. The growing number of high-technological industries in the S Calif. area have added to Ontario's development. Founded in 1882, the city is the site of Chaffey Col., Ontario Internatl. Airport, and Ontario Motor Speedway in E part of city; Calif. Insts. for Men and Women (separate prison facilities) to S. It is also one of the fastest-growing U.S. cities, marked by a pop. increase of 50% bet. 1980 and 1990. San Gabriel Mts. and San Bernardino Natl. Forest to N; Angeles Natl. Forest to NW. Inc. 1891. **2** city (1990 pop. 9,392), Malheur co., E Oregon, on Snake R., at mouth of Malheur R., 45 mi/72 km NW of Boise,

Idaho; 44°01′N 116°58′W. Elev. 2,154 ft/657 m. RR, trade, and highway center for large irrigated area in Owyhee R. project. Agr. (sugar beets, potatoes, grain); dairy prods. Mfg. (printing, publishing; concrete). Site of Treasure Valley Community Col. Ontario State Park to N. Inc. 1914.

Ontario 1 village (1990 pop. 1,000), Wayne co., W N.Y., 16 mi/26 km ENE of Rochester; 43°15′N 77°19′W. In agr. area. **2** (awn-TER-ree-o), village (1990 pop. 407), Vernon co., SW Wis., on Kickapoo R., and 32 mi/51 km. ESE of La Crosse; 43°43′N 90°35′W. In farm and dairy area. Wildcat Mt. State Park to S.

Ontario, Lake (□ 7,540 sq mi/19,529 sq km), bet. SE Ont. and NW N.Y.; 193 mi/311 km long and 53 mi/85 km at its greatest width; smallest and lowest of the Great Lakes. It has a surface elev. of 246 ft/75 m above sea level and a max. depth of 778 ft/237 m. L. Ontario is fed chiefly by the waters of L. Erie by way of the Niagara R.; other tributaries are the Genesee, Oswego, and Black rivers in New York and the Trent R. in Ontario. The lake is drained to the NE by the St. Lawrence R. Oceangoing vessels reach the lake through the St. Lawrence Seaway and use the Welland Canal to bypass Niagara Falls and reach L. Erie; smaller craft (mostly pleasure boats) can travel the Rideau Canal bet. Kingston and Ottawa, and the Trent Canal bet. the Bay of Quinte and Georgian Bay. Navigation on the lake is not usually impeded by ice in winter. The chief Can. lakeshore cities are St. Catharines, Hamilton, Toronto, Oshawa, and Kingston; on the S shore are Rochester and Oswego, N.Y. Commercial fishing is important, but pollution has been a problem. A U.S.-Can. pact (1972) established that water quality would be improved and further pollution ended. Recreational facilities are provided at state and provincial parks. The 1st European to see (1615) L. Ontario was Étienne Brulé, the Fr. explorer; later that year Samuel de Champlain visited it.

Ontonagon (ahn-TAHN-ah-guhn), county (□ 3,741 sq mi/9,689 sq km; 1990 pop. 8,854), NW Upper Peninsula, Mich.; ⊙ Ontonagon. Bounded N by L. Superior; drained by Ontonagon R. and by small Iron and Firesteel rivers; 46°58′N 89°16′W. Lumber and agr. area (cattle; oats; hay; dairy prods.); fishing; resorts. Mfg. in Ontonagon. Boundary with Gogebic co. (S) and Iron co. (SE) coterminous with Central and Eastern time zone boundary. Ontonagon co. westernmost extension 89°50′W of Eastern time zone (extends further W in Ontario, lengthout 90°W). Porcupine Mts. are in NW, part of Porcupine Mts. State Park in W; part of Ottawa Natl. Forest in S ½ of co. and part of Gogebic L., on S boundary; Ontonagon Indian Reservation in NE. Organized 1848.

Ontonagon (ahn-TAHN-ah-guhn), town (1990 pop. 2,040), ⊙ Ontonagon co., NW Upper Peninsula, Mich., 40 mi/64 km SW of Houghton, on L. Superior at mouth of Ontonagon R.; 46°52′N 89°18′W. RR terminus; RR/ship transfer point. Mfg. (paperboard); shipping center; fishing. Resort. The Ontonagon boulder, a huge copper mass, was found near the river, and was moved to the Smithsonian Inst. Ontonagon Indian Reservation to NE; Porcupine Mts. State Park and Ski Area to W; Ottawa Natl. Forest to S. Established on site of Native Amer. village. Inc. 1885.

Ontonagon River (ahn-TAHN-ah-guhn), c.22 mi/35 km long, W Upper Peninsula, Mich.; formed by several branches uniting in Ontonagon co., c.6 mi/9.7 km SW of Mass.; flows NNW to L. Superior at Ontonagon. East Branch rises in Kunzie L., SE Houghton co.; flows c.35 mi/56 km NNW. Middle Branch rises in E Gogebic co., flows generally c.40 mi/64 km N past Watersmeet. South Branch rises at Wis. state line, flows c.55 mi/89 km NNE, past Ewen; 46°41′N 89°09′W. Victoria Dam (power) is on the South Branch just below the influx of West Branch (c.20 mi/32 km long), which flows from N end of Gogebic L. All generally flow through Ottawa Natl. Forest.

Onward, town (1990 pop. 63), Cass co., N central Ind., 10 mi/16 km ESE of Logansport; 40°41′N 86°12′W. In agr. area.

Ookala (o-O-KAH-lah), village, NE Hawaii isl., Hawaii

co., Hawaii, 23 mi/37 km NW of Hilo on Hamakua Coast. Manowaialee Forest Reserve to S; Hilo Forest Reserve to W; Hilo Forest Reserve to SE.

Oolitic, town, Lawrence co., S Ind., on Salt Creek, and 4 mi/6.4 km NNW of Bedford. Limestone quarries.

Oologah (OOL-uh-guh) or **Oolagah**, town, Rogers co., NE Okla., 25 mi/40 km NE of Tulsa. In stock-raising and agr. area. Will Rogers' birthplace to E. To S, on Verdigris R., is site of Oologah L. Dam, for flood control, hydroelectric power.

Oologah Lake, reservoir, Rogers and Nowate cos., NE Okla., on Verdigris R., 26 mi/42 km NE of Tulsa; 36°25′N 95°41′W. Max capacity 1,519,000 acre-ft. Formed by dam (137 ft/42 m high), built (1963) by Army Corps of Engineers for flood control; also used for water supply and navigation. Will Rogers Home near dam.

Ooltewah (OOL-te-wah), town (1990 pop. 4,903), Hamilton co., SE Tenn., 12 mi/19 km E of Chattanooga, 35°4′N 85°03′W.

Oostanaula River (oo-stuh-NAW-luh), c.45 mi/72 km long, NW Ga.; formed by confluence of Conasauga and Coosawattee rivers 3 mi/4.8 km NE of Calhoun; flows SSW to Rome, where it joins with Etowah R. to form the Coosa; 34°32′N 84°51′W.

Oostburg (OOST-buhrg), town (1990 pop. 1,931), Sheboygan co., E Wis., 10 mi/16 km SSW of Sheboygan; 43°37′N 87°47′W. In dairy and farm area; mfg. (dairy prods., canned vegetables, plastic prods.); fishing. Kohler-Andrae State Park (on L. Michigan) to NE (formerly called Terry-Andrae).

Ootsa Lake (OOT-suh) (□ 50 sq mi/130 sq km), W central B.C., Canada, on N boundary of Tweedsmuir Park, 120 mi/193 km WSW of Prince George. Drains ESE into Nechako R. by short Ootsa R.

Opal (O-puhl), village (1990 pop. 95), Lincoln co., SW Wyo., on Hams Fork, and 11 mi/18 km E of Kemmerer; 41°46′N 110°19′W. Elev. c.6,668 ft/2,032 m. Shipping point for sheep and wool. Agr. (barley, alfalfa, hay; cattle).

Opal Cliffs, uninc. town (1990 pop. 5,940), Santa Cruz co., SW Calif., residential suburb 3 mi/4.8 km E of downtown Santa Cruz, on W side of Soquel Cove, Monterey Bay, Pacific Ocean; 36°58′N 121°58′W. Capitola and New Brighton state beaches to W.

Opalescent River, N.Y.: see HUDSON RIVER.

Opa-Locka (o-puh-LAHK-uh), city (□ 4 sq mi/10.4 sq km; 1990 pop. 15,283), Dade co., 14 mi/23 km NW of Miami, SE Fla.; 25°53′N 80°15′W. There is some diverse light industry, and a large county airport. A U.S. Coast Guard station is located at the airport. Opa-Locka's city hall is patterned after a Moorish castle, and other bldgs. are of Arab. architecture. Inc. 1926.

Opechee Bay (O-puh-chee) Belknap co., central N.H., S extension of L. Winnipesaukee, in city of Laconia, continuation of larger Paugus Bay to NE, connected by narrow channel to E side of Opechee Bay; 2 mi/43.2 km long. Drains SW through Winnipesaukee R., 1 mi/1.6 km to Winnisquam L. Sometimes called Opechee L.

Opelika (ah-puh-LEE-kuh), city (1990 pop. 22,122), ⊙ Lee co., E Ala., c. 15 mi/24 km W of Chattahoochee R. (Ga. line), and c.23 mi/37 km NW of Phenix City. Trade center, with textile, lumber, paperboard (box), tires, sporting goods, magnetic recording tape, drilling equip., and metallurgical industries. Factory outlet mall here. Inc. 1854.

Opelousas (ah-puh-LOO-suhs), city (1994 pop. 19,305), ⊙ St. Landry parish, S central La., 20 mi/32 km N of Lafayette; 30°31′N 92°05′W. RR junction. Industries based chiefly on the agr. prods. and livestock of the surrounding region; printing and publishing, mfg. (water treating units, plasma, glass, cooking oil, sausage and food production, apparel, pipe fittings). Oil and gas nearby. Opelousas still retains some of its early Fr. and Span. flavor, and many antebellum structures remain. It was founded c.1765 by Fr. traders and served (1863) as state capital for a period during the Civil War. Boyhood home of James Bowie here. Antebellum homes in area. Inc. 1821.

Open Lake, Tenn. See: RIPLEY.

Opeongo Lake (o-pee-AHNG-go), S Ont., Canada, in Algonquin Provincial Park, 60 mi/97 km W of Pembroke; 20 mi/32 km long, 5 mi/8 km wide. Elev. 1,323 ft/403 m. Drained by Madawaska R.; 45°42′N 78°23′W.

Opheim, village (1990 pop. 145), Valley co., NE Mont., near Canada (Sask.) border, 48 mi/77 km N of Glasgow; 48°52′N 106°25′W. Opheim port of entry 10 mi/16 km N. Agr. (wheat, barley, oats, hay; cattle, sheep, hogs); mfg. potato lefse (pancakes).

Ophir 1 (O-fuhr), village, SW central Alaska, on Innoko R., and 30 mi/48 km WNW of McGrath. Trapping; placer gold mining. Airstrip. **2** village (1990 pop. 69), San Miguel co., SW Colo., in San Juan Mts., 5 mi/8 km S of Telluride, on Howard Fork Creek; 37°51′N 107°49′W. Elev. c.9,800 ft/2,987 m. Surrounded by Uncompahgre Natl. Forest. In gold-mining region. Ophir Loop (elev. 9,280 ft/2,829 m), 2 mi/3.2 km W, turnoff to Ophir. **3** village (1990 pop. 25), Tooele co., N central Utah, 12 mi/19 km S of Tooele, in Oquirrh Mts.; 40°22′N 112°15′W. Elev. 6,498 ft/1,981 m. Silver, gold, lead deposits; lead and silver still mined. Old mining town founded 1874, once had pop. of 6,000, pop. in 1959 was 199; semi-ghost town with general store.

Opichén (o-pee-CHEN), town (1990 pop. 3,300), Yucatán, SE Mexico on Mexico Highway 184, 33 mi/53 km SSW of Mérida; 20°56′N 89°41′W. Henequen, sugarcane, fruit.

Opiskoteo Lake (o-pis-KO-tee-o), E central Que., Canada, near Lab. border; 20 mi/35 km long, 15 mi/24 km wide; 53°10′N 68°10′W. Elev. 2,025 ft/617 m.

Opodepe (o-po-DAI-pai), town (1990 pop. 515), Sonora, NW Mexico, on San Miguel de Horcasitas R., and 60 mi/97 km NNE of Hermosillo; 29°56′N 110°38′W. Corn, beans; cattle.

Opp (AHP), city (1990 pop. 6,985), Covington co., S Ala., 15 mi/24 km E of Andalusia. Clothing, textiles; food processing; lumber. Douglas MacArthur State Technical Col. Inc. 1902.

Opportunity, uninc. city (1990 pop. 22,326), Spokane co., E Wash., a residential suburb 7 mi/11.3 km E of downtown Spokane; 47°39′N 117°14′W. It is a growing residential town.

Opportunity, locality, Deer Lodge co., SW Mont., within city of Anaconda (city and county boundries are coterminous), 6 mi/9.7 km ESE of Anaconda proper, near Silver Bow Creek, which becomes Clark Fork river 5 mi/8 km to NE. Former copper mining area, closed 1970. Tailings pond to N. Anaconda Stack State Park to W, 585 ft/178 m smokestack.

Opryland USA, theme park, in Davidson co., central Tenn., on the Cumberland R., 6 mi/10 km NE of Nashville; 36°12′N 86°41′W. Covers 120-acre/49-ha complex including an amusement park, a hotel, and performance theaters, including the Opryhouse. The Grand Ole Opry, a live country music program founded in 1925, is broadcast weekly from the Opryhouse

Optima (AWP-ti-muh), village (1990 pop. 92), Texas co., central Okla. Panhandle, 10 mi/16 km NE of Guymon, near North Canadian (Beaver) R.; 36°45′N 101°20′W. In wheat-growing area. Nearby is site of Optima L. reservoir, for flood control, irrigation; includes Optima Natl. Wildlife Refuge around lake.

Oquaga Lake (ok-WAH-gah), resort village, Broome co., S N.Y., near Pa. state line, 25 mi/40 km ESE of Binghamton, on small Oquaga L.; 42°02′N 75°27′W.

Oquawka (ok-WAW-kah), village (1990 pop. 1,442), ⊙ Henderson co., W Ill., on the Mississippi, and 11 mi/18 km NNE of Burlington, Iowa; 40°56′N 90°57′W. Summer resort; agr. (produce; livestock); limestone quarries.

Oquirrh Mountains (O-kuhr), NW Utah, extend c.30 mi/48 km S from Great Salt L., Salt Lake, Tooele, and Utah cos. Rise to c.11,000 ft/3,353 m. Copper, lead, zinc, gold and silver mined near Bingham Canyon; Kennecott Corp. Open Cut Copper Mine, largest in world. On boundary of Tooele (W) and Salt Lake and Utah cos. (E).

Oquitoa (o-kee-TO-ah), town (1990 pop. 370), Sonora, NW Mexico, on Altar R., and 60 mi/97 km SW of Nogales; 30°46′N 111°42′W. Wheat, corn, cotton, beans; cattle.

Oquossoc, Maine: see RANGELEY, village.

Oracabessa, town (1991 pop. 4,066), St. Mary parish, N Jamaica, banana port on fine Caribbean bay, 4 mi/6.4 km WNW of Port Maria; 18°28′N 76°56′W.

Oracle, uninc. town (1990 pop. 3,043), Pinal co., S central Ariz., 31 mi/50 km NNE of Tucson. Cattle, sheep; alfalfa. Black Hills to N; Santa Catalina Mts., in part of Coronado Natl. Forest, to S. Site of Biosphere 2 environmental living experiment to S, at Mt. Lemmon.

Oradell (or-RUH-del), residential borough (1990 pop. 8,024), Bergen co., NE N.J., on Hackensack R., at SW end of Oradell Reservoir, and 5 mi/8 km N of Hackensack; 40°57′N 74°01′W. Settled by Dutch before the Revolution, inc. 1894.

Oraibi (o-REI-bei), pueblo, Navajo co., N Ariz., on a mesa 55 mi/89 km N of Winslow, in Hopi Indian Reservation. It was built 1100 and was discovered in 1540 by Pedro de Tovar, a lieutenant of Coronado. The mission of San Francisco, established on the site in 1629, was destroyed in the Pueblo revolt of 1680. Oraibi was long the most important pueblo of the Hopi Indians, but because of economic disturbances and internal dissension many of the inhabitants left in 1907 to form the pueblos of Hotevilla and Bacavi. Also called Old Oraibi.

Oran (o-RAN), city (1990 pop. 1,164), Scott co., SE Mo., in Mississippi alluvial plain, 16 mi/26 km SSW of Cape Girardeau; 37°05′N 89°39′W. Corn, soybeans; livestock; some mfg. Platted 1869.

Orange 1 county (□ 790 sq mi/2,046 sq km; 1990 pop. 2,410,556), S Calif.; ⊙ Santa Ana; 33°40′N 117°47′W. Coastal plain and foothill region, drained by Santa Ana R.; rises to Santa Ana Mts. (over 5,000 ft/1,524 m) along E border. San Gabriel R. forms part of W boundary. Although statistically counted separately from Los Angeles, Orange co. is a direct continuation of the Los Angeles urbanized area. Urbanization in the co. increased after World War II, starting in NW, near Los Angeles, and encroaching SE. With the approach of the year 2000, the remaining gap bet. Los Angeles and San Diego, is being filled with large new cities. Agr. (beans, celery, avocados, artichokes, peppers, tomatoes, strawberries, oranges; livestock). Extensive petroleum and natural gas fields in N and offshore. Large packing, canning, and processing industries; oil refining. Coast has Huntington Beach, Newport Beach (includes Balboa), Laguna Beach, resort areas that have become extensions of the Los Angeles urbanized area. Disneyland theme park at Anaheim, in NW. Along coast, Bolsa Chica, Huntington, Doheny, Corona del Mar, and San Clemente state beaches, lagoons and marshes; part of Cleveland Natl. Forest, in Santa Ana Mts., in NE. County declared bankruptcy in 1995 as result of imprudent investments. Formed 1889. **2** county (□ 1,004 sq mi/2,600 sq km; 1990 pop. 677,491), central Fla., bounded E by St. Johns R.; ⊙ Orlando; 28°30′N 81°19′W. Heavily urbanized as result of recent growth of Orlando metro area. Hilly lake region in W includes part of L. Apopka; lowland in E. A major citrus fruit–growing area; also small-scale farming, dairying, poultry raising. Mfg. of high-tech electronics and food prods. Formed 1824. **3** county (□ 408 sq mi/1,057 sq km; 1990 pop. 18,409), S Ind.; ⊙ Paoli; 38°32′N 86°30′W. Drained by Lost and Patoka rivers and Lick Creek. Mainly agr. (corn, fruit; cattle, hogs, poultry; dairy prods.); stone quarrying. Mineral springs (notably French Lick) are resorts. Mfg. at Paoli. Lost R. runs E to W below surface in limestone karst topography c.18 mi/29 km in N part of co. Springs Valley State Fish and Wildlife Area, Tillery Hill and Jackson State Recreation Areas and Patoka L. all in SW part of co. Hoosier Natl. Forest in S, W, and NW. S and W parts of co. are hilly and heavily forested; N and E parts of co. are in karst plain. Formed 1816. **4** county (□ 838 sq mi/2,170 sq km; 1990 pop. 307,647), SE N.Y.; ⊙ Goshen; 41°23′N 74°18′W. Bounded E by the Hudson R., SW by N.J. and Pa. borders and Delaware R.; includes parts of the Hudson highlands, the Ramapos, and the Shawangunk range. Drained by small Wallkill and Ramapo rivers and by Shawangunk Kill. Now largely suburban with several major shopping malls, was once an important dairying region; farming (fruit, hay; poultry). Large farm migratory worker pop., mainly Hispanic. Many mts. and lakes. Includes West Point military reservation and part of Palisades Interstate Park. Mfg. at Newburgh, Middletown. Formed 1683. **5** county (1990 pop. 93,851), N central N.C.; ⊙ Hillsborough; 36°03′N 79°07′W. Bounded by Haw R., in SW corner, drained by Eno R. Piedmont area; agr. (tobacco, corn, dairying, wheat, oats, soybeans, hay, cattle, hogs), timber (pine, oak); mfg. of textiles, furniture; timber. Stone quarrying. Mfg. at Hillsborough. Eno River State Park on E boundary. Univ. L. reservoir in S. Formed 1753. **6** county (□ 379 sq mi; 1990 pop. 80,509), SE Texas; ⊙ Orange; 30°07′N 93°53′W. Deepwater port, industrial center. Bounded E by Sabine R. (here the La. line), W and SW by Neches R., S by Sabine L. Gulf coastal plains in S; wooded (chiefly pine; timber) in N. Livestock (cattle, horses, hogs); fish farming, aquaculture; honey. Hunting, fishing. Oil, natural gas wells; sand and gravel, clay. Part of Big Thicket Natl. Preserve in W. Formed 1852. **7** county (□ 691 sq mi/1,790 sq km; 1990 pop. 26,149), central and E Vt., bounded E by the Connecticut; ⊙ Chelsea; 44°00′N 72°22′W. Dairying, lumbering; mfg. (machinery, wood prods., paper); maple sugar; winter and summer resorts. Drained by White, Waits, and Ompompanoosuc rivers. Organized 1781. **8** county (□ 343 sq mi/888 sq km; 1990 pop. 21,421), N central Va.; ⊙ Orange; 38°14′N 78° 00′W. In the Piedmont region; bounded N by Rapidan R., S by North Anna R. (head of L. Anna reservoir in SE). Agr. (barley, wheat, corn, soybeans, grapes, fruit, legumes, sweet potatoes, tobacco, hay, alfalfa; cattle, sheep, poultry; dairying); oak timber. Many historic estates, including "Montpelier," SW of Orange in W center. Lake of the Woods reservoir in NE. Formed 1734.

Orange 1 city (1990 pop. 110,658), Orange co., S Calif., suburb 26 mi/42 km SE of downtown Los Angeles and 4 mi/6.4 km ESE of Anaheim; 33°49′N 117°49′W. City drained by Santa Ana R. and Santiago Creek. RR junction. Citrus fruits and nuts are packed, processed, and shipped; rubber prods., electronic components, plastics prods., aircraft parts, and industrial furnaces are manufactured in Orange. The growing city has been marked by a pop. increase of about 35% bet. 1970 and 1990. Orange was founded as Richland until it was renamed in 1875. Chapman Col. is there. Anaheim Stadium to W. Santiago Reservoir (Irvine L.) to E; Santa Ana Mts. and part of Cleveland Natl. Forest to E; large Chino Hills State Park to NE. Inc. 1888. **2** city (1990 pop. 29,925), Essex co., NE N.J. Orange and the surrounding municipalities of East Orange, West Orange, South Orange, and Maplewood are known as "The Oranges," a single suburb of Newark and N.Y. city. Although chiefly residential, Orange has some mfg. Settled c.1675, set off from Newark 1806, inc. as a city 1872. **3** city (1990 pop. 19,381), SE Texas, 18 mi/29 km NE of Port Arthur and 22 mi/35 km E of Beaumont; ⊙ Orange co.; 30°06′N 93°45′W. A deepwater port on the Sabine R. (La. boundary). The Intracoastal Waterway follows Sabine L. and River from Texas Coast (SW) to point 5 mi/8 km SSE of Orange, where it continues E across La. marsh, 22 mi/35 km inland. In the wet, lush country of the Gulf Coast, it is a port of entry, with shipyards, oil and gas wells, and major petrochemical plants. It also has facilities for processing paper, lumber, and rice. Cattle, hogs; honey; winery. Lamar Univ.–Orange Campus (2-year). The U.S. navy has a "mothball fleet" there. Settled c.1800, inc. 1858

Orange 1 town (1990 pop. 12,830), New Haven co., SW Conn.; 41°16′N 73°01′W. A residential suburb of New Haven; set off from Milford 1822. It is a major retail center. Mfg. of fabricated metal prods., furniture, electronic equip., food, transportation equip. A major retail shopping area has developed along U.S. Route 1 N of Interstate 95. The town's first house (1720) still stands. Settled 1720, inc. 1921. **2** town (1990 pop. 7,312), including Orange village, Franklin co., N Mass., on Millers R. and 15 mi/24 km E of Greenfield; 42°37′N 72°18′W. Fabricated metal prods. Settled c.1746, inc. 1810. **3** town (1990 pop. 237), Grafton co., W central N.H., 15 mi/24 km SW of Plymouth; 43°38′N 71°57′W. Mfg. (lumber); agr. (vegetables, apples, nursery crops; cattle, poultry; dairying); chalk, ochre deposits. Includes solitary Mt. Cardigan (3,121 ft/951 m) in Cardigan State Forest in E. **4** town (1990 pop. 915), Orange co., E central Vt., 5 mi/8 km SE of Barre; 44°09′N 72°23′W. **5** town (1990 pop. 2,582), N central Va., 25 mi/40 km NE of Charlottesville; ⊙ Orange co.; 38°15′N 78°06′W. RR junction; mfg. (fixtures, printing and publishing, apparel, wood prods.); trade center for agr. area. (grain, soybeans, tobacco; livestock; dairying). "Montpelier," home (built c.1760) of James Madison, is 4 mi/6.4 km W; Madison and his wife are buried nearby. James Madison Mus. to SW. Settled c.1810, inc. 1856.

Orange, village (1990 pop. 2,810), Cuyahoga co., N Ohio, a SE suburb of Cleveland; 41°26′N 81°28′W.

Orange Beach, town (1990 pop. 2,253), Baldwin co., SW Ala., 8 mi/12.9 km E of Gulf Shores, near Gulf State Park; 30°17′N 87°35′W. Manhole cover mfg. On Perdido Bay, just off Gulf of Mexico.

Orange City 1 town (□ 5 sq mi/13 sq km; 1990 pop. 5,347), Volusia co., E central Fla., 24 mi/39 km SW of Daytona Beach; 28°56′N 81°17′W. Known for its pure water, bottled here and shipped all over Fla. **2** town (1990 pop. 4,940), NW Iowa, 37 mi/60 km NNE of Sioux City; ⊙ Sioux co.; 43°00′N 96°03′W. Mfg. (aircraft, chemicals, apparel, printing and publishing, concrete, feeds, fertilizers). Sand and gravel pits nearby. Northwestern Col. is here. Holds annual Tulip Day. Founded 1869 by Dutch settlers; inc. 1884.

Orange Cove, city (1990 pop. 5,604), Fresno co., central Calif., 27 mi/43 km ESE of Fresno, in sheltered valley of Sierra Nevada foothills; 36°37′N 119°19′W. Citrus fruit, avocados, olives, grapes, almonds, vegetables; dairying. Sequoia Natl. Forest to NE, Sequoia Natl. Park to E. Inc. 1948.

Orange Grove, uninc. city (1990 pop. 15,676), Harrison co., SE Miss., residential suburb 6 mi/9.7 km N of Gulfport, near Bernard Bayou; 30°26′N 89°05′W. Cotton corn, citrus, pecans. Gulfport-Biloxi Regional Airport to S.

Orange Grove, town (1990 pop. 1,175), Jim Wells co., S Texas, 35 mi/56 km WNW of Corpus Christi, near Nueces R.; 27°57′N 97°56′W. In area producing oil, natural gas, vegetables; cotton; cattle; light mfg.

Orange Lake, c.16 mi/26 km long, Alachua co., N central Fla., 10 mi/16 km SE of Gainesville; drains into Oklawaha R. (E) via Orange Creek (c.6 mi/9.7 km long).

Orange Park, town (□ 5 sq mi/13 sq km; 1990 pop. 9,488), Clay co., NE Fla., on St. Johns R. and 12 mi/19 km SSW of Jacksonville; 30°10′N 81°42′W.

Orangeburg, county (□ 1,127 sq mi/2,919 sq km; 1990 pop. 84,803), S central S.C.; ⊙ Orangeburg; 33°26′N 80°47′W. Bounded SW by South Fork of Edisto R., NE by L. Marion reservoir; drained by North Fork of the Edisto. One of leading agr. cos. in the South. Sand, clay, limestone; apparel, textiles, wood prods., asphalt, chemicals, cement, concrete, food, lumber, printing and publishing. Agr. includes poultry prods., hogs, cattle, corn, wheat, rye, tobacco, sorghum, peanuts, pecans, cotton, watermelons, peaches. Formed 1785.

Orangeburg, city (1990 pop. 13,739), central S.C., 36 mi/58 km SSE of Columbia on the North Fork of the Edisto R.; ⊙ Orangeburg co.; 33°29′N 80°52′W. It is the trade and processing center of a cotton and agr. area with large textile and apparel industries and a variety of light industry including printing and publishing, food, asphalt, cement, and concrete prods., chemicals. Orangeburg was a planned settlement established by German-Swiss immigrants who had free grants of land. It is the seat of S.C. State Univ. Orangeburg-Calhoun Technical Col. and Claflin Col. Of interest are the Edisto gardens and the Donald Bruce House (c.1735). Settled 1732, inc. as a city 1883.

Orangeburg, village (□ 3 sq mi/7.8 sq km; 1990 pop. 3,583), Rockland co., SE N.Y., 3 mi/4.8 km SSW of Nyack; 41°02′N 73°57′W. Some mfg. Site of Rockland Children's Psychiatric Center. Pop. figure includes Rockland.

Orangetown, Du. *Oranjestad*, village, Neth. Antilles, West Indies, overlooking small bay; ⊙ Sint Eustatia Isl.; 17°28′N 62°59′W. Snorkeling, ruins of fort.

Orangeville, town (1991 pop. 17,921), S Ont., Canada, on Credit R. and 40 mi/64 km WNW of Toronto; ⊙ Dufferin co.; 43°55′N 80°05′W. Milling, dairying.

Orangeville, uninc. city (1990 pop. 26,266), Sacramento co., central Calif., residential suburb 16 mi/26 km NE of downtown Sacramento. Citrus, grain, nursery prods., dairying , poultry. Mfg. (machinery). Near American R., Folsom L. reservoir and State Recreation Area to NE.

Orangeville, town (1990 pop. 1,459), Emery co., central Utah, 2 mi/3.2 km NW of Castle Dale; 39°13′N 111°03′W. Elev. 5,790 ft/1,765 m. Alfalfa; cattle; coal mining. Manti-La Sal Natl. Forest to W. Settled 1877 on Cottonwood Creek, forms Joes Valley Reservoir to NW.

Orangeville 1 village (1990 pop. 451), Stephenson co., N Ill., near Wis. line, 11 mi/18 km N of Freeport; 42°28′N 89°38′W. In agr. area (dairying; corn, oats; cattle, hogs). **2** village, Orange co., S Ind., near Lost R. and 6 mi/9.7 km WSW of Orleans. In agr. area (cattle). Near rise of Lost R. Laid out 1849. **3** village (1990 pop. 253), Trumbull co., NE Ohio, 17 mi/27 km NE of Warren, and on Pymatuning Creek, at Pa. line; 41°20′N 80°31′W.

Orangeville, borough (1990 pop. 504), Columbia co., E central Pa., 6 mi/9.7 km NNE of Bloomsburg; 41°04′N 76°24′W. Light mfg.; agr. (grain; livestock, dairying). Covered bridges in area.

Oranjestad (aw-RAH-nyuh-STAHT), town, Du. West Indies, port on isl.'s W coast, 80 mi/129 km WNW of Willemstad, Curaçao; ⊙ Aruba; 12°32′N 70°03′W. Only 20 mi/32 km N of the Venezuela coast, it is an important petroleum transshipping and refining point, at which most of the isl.'s pop. is concentrated. The oil refineries are in NW outskirts.

Oranjestad (aw-RUH-nyuh-STAHT) or **Orange Town**, principal settlement of Saint Eustatius, Neth. Antilles, in the Leewards, 8 mi/12.9 km NW of St. Kitts, c.530 mi/853 km NE of Willemstad, Curaçao; 17°29′N 62°58′W. Yams, cotton, corn, livestock raised in vicinity. Has 2 old forts.

Orbisonia (OR-bi-SO-nee-ah), borough (1990 pop. 447), Huntingdon co., S central Pa., 10 mi/16 km S of Mount Union, on Blacklog Creek, adjoining Rockhill Furnace to W; 40°14′N 77°53′W. Mfg. (printing and publishing); agr. (corn, hay, alfalfa; livestock, dairying). Blacklog Mt., and Blacklog Gap, to E.

Orcas Island (OR-kuhs), San Juan co., NW Wash., in NE part of San Juan Isls., 14 mi/23 km long; 8 mi/12.9 km wide. Bounded E by Rosario Strait, N by Strait of Georgia, W by President and San Juan channels, S by Pole Pass, Harney Channel, Lopez Sound and Obstruction Pass. Isl. is deeply indented from S in 3 places: East Sound splits isl. into 2 main lobes, with town of Eastsound at N end, on isthmus, West Sound is in W, and Deer Harbor is at far W end. Moran State Park in E; 8 other state parks on small offshore isls. Mt. Constitution (2,408 ft/734 m) in E, highest pt. in San Juans. Other communities: West Sound, Deer Harbor, Olga. Fishing. Tourism.

Orchard, town (1990 pop. 93), Mitchell co., N Iowa, near Cedar R., 4 mi/6.4 km SSE of Osage; 43°13′N 92°46′W. Limestone quarries, sand and gravel pits in vicinity.

Orchard 1 village (1990 pop. 439), Antelope co., NE Nebr., 17 mi/27 km NW of Neligh; 42°20′N 14°98′W. Dairy center; grain, livestock; light mfg. **2** village (1990 pop. 373), Fort Bend co., SE Texas, 38 mi/61 km WSW of Houston, near Brazos R.; 29°36′N 95°58′W. Oil and natural gas; agr. area.

Orchard Beach, village, Anne Arundel co., central Md., 10 mi/16 km SE of downtown Baltimore, near Chesapeake Bay. Colonel Thomas Cresap built a fortified home here before pushing on to Oldtown.

Orchard Beach, N.Y.: see PELHAM BAY PARK.

Orchard City, town (1990 pop. 2,218), Delta co., W Colo., on branch of Gunnison R. and 9 mi/14.5 km NE of Delta; 38°48′N 107°57′W. Elev. c.5,800 ft/1,768 m. In dairying area. Light mfg. Post office name is Eckert. Grand Mesa Natl. Forest to N.

Orchard Hill, village (1990 pop. 239), Spalding co., W central Ga., 6 mi/9.7 km SE of Griffin; 33°11′N 84°13′W. Light mfg.

Orchard Lake, village (1990 pop. 2,286), Oakland co., SE Mich., suburb 1 mi/1.6 km SW of Pontiac; 42°34′N 83°22′W. In lake-resort and farm area. Seat of St. Mary's Col. Surrounds Orchard L., Upper Straits L. in W., borders Cass L. on N., other lakes in area.

Orchard Park, residential village (☐ 1 sq mi/2.6 sq km; 1990 pop. 3,280) in Orchard Park town (1990 pop. 24,632), Erie co., W N.Y., 10 mi/16 km SE of Buffalo; 42°45′N 78°45′W. Some mfg. Seat of Erie Co. Community Col. (S campus). NFL franchise at Rich Stadium (capacity 80,290), 2.5 mi/4 km to NW. Until 1934, called E. Hamburg. Inc. 1921.

Orchards, uninc. town (1990 pop. 3,500), Clark co., SW Wash., suburb 6 mi/9.7 km NE of Vancouver, Wash. Dairying; poultry; fruit, nuts, vegetables. Clark County Airport to NE.

Orcutt, uninc. village, Santa Barbara co., SW Calif., 6 mi/9.7 km S of Santa Maria. In oil field. Cattle; grain, fruit, vegetables.

Ord, town (1990 pop. 2,481), central Nebr. 55 mi/89 km NW of Grand Isl. and on North Loup R; ⊙ Valley co.; 41°36′N 98°55′W. RR terminus. Livestock, dairy, poultry, grain. Mfg. (printing and publishing). Ft. Hartsuff State Historical Park to NW. Surveyed 1874.

Ord, Fort, Calif.: see MONTEREY, city.

Ord, Mount (7,155 ft/2,181 m), on Maricopa/Gila co line, central Ariz., in Mazatzal Mts., c.50 mi/80 km NE of Phoenix, in Tonto Natl. Forest.

Orderville, village (1990 pop. 422), Kane co., SW Utah, 18 mi/29 km NNW of Kanab and near E Fork of Virgin R.; 37°16′N 112°37′W. Elev. 5,280 ft/1,609 m. Apples; cattle. Dixie Natl. Forest to N; Zion Natl. Park to W. Founded 1874 as Mormon economic experiment by United Order communal society; settled 1875.

Ordinary, uninc. town, Gloucester co., E Va., 21 mi/34 km N of Newport News, 4 mi/6.4 km N of Gloucester Point; 37°18′N 76°30′W. Light mfg; agr. (cattle; grain, soybeans). Coleman Swamp to SE.

Ordway, town (1990 pop. 1,025), SE central Colo., near Bob Creek, 45 mi/72 km E of Pueblo; ⊙ Crowley co.; 38°13′N 103°45′W. Elev. 4,312 ft/1,314 m. Melon shipping point in agr. region; alfalfa meal, dairy prods., sugar beets; turkeys. Small lake nearby. L. Meredith Reservoir to SE; L. Henry Reservoir to NE. Inc. 1900.

Ordway, village, Brown co., N S.Dak., 10 mi/16 km NNE of Aberdeen, near Elm Creek; 45°34′N 98°24′W.

Ore City, town (1990 pop. 898), Upshur co., NE Texas, 27 mi/43 km NW of Marshall; 32°47′N 94°43′W. Dairying; poultry; vegetables; timber; mfg. (food, lumber). L. O' the Pines to NE (Big Cypress Creek).

Oreana, village (1990 pop. 847), Macon co., central Ill., suburb 7 mi/11.3 km NE of downtown Decatur; 39°56′N 88°52′W. Agr. area; light mfg.

Orefield (OR-feeld), uninc. village, Lehigh co., E Pa., 6 mi/9.7 km WNW of Allentown on Jordan Creek; 40°38′N 75°35′W. Mfg. includes printing and publishing, food, fabricated metal prods., electronic equip. Agr. includes dairying, livestock, poultry; grain, apples. Covered bridges in area.

Oregon, state (☐ 98,386 sq mi/254,820 sq km 1995 est. pop. 3,140,585); NW U.S., in the Pacific Northwest; 44°07′N 120°21′W. Admitted 1859 as the 33d state. SALEM is ⊙ and the 3d largest city; the largest city is PORTLAND, followed by EUGENE. Oregon is bounded on the N by Wash.; most of N boundary, from N center W to Pacific Ocean, formed by Columbia R.; on the E by Idaho, with the Snake R. forming the boundary in the NE; on the S by Nev. and Calif.; and on the W by the Pacific Ocean. The state's contrasting physical features are characterized by great forested mt. slopes and treeless basins, rushing rivers and barren playas, lush valleys and extensive wastelands. The major determinant for these unusual climatic differences are the Cascade Range, a rugged mt. chain running N to S c.100 mi/160 km inland and the Coast Range. As the moist, warm E-moving air masses, cooled by the Calif. Ocean Current and blocked by mt. ranges, rise and cool precipitation occurs over the W ⅓ of Oregon, esp. autumn through spring. A dry continental climate prevails over the E ⅔ of the state, receiving little of the rainfall from the W. The W shoreline (c.300 mi/483 km) is bordered by narrow coastal plains of sandy beaches, luxuriant pastures, and occasional jutting promontories. About 25 mi/40 km inland, the rugged Coast Range rises to heights of 4,000 ft/1,219 m. The Willamette R., which flows N, in NW, is bounded W by Coast Range and E by Cascade Range. Its valley is the main artery of Oregon's economy and pop. Most of its agr. and mfg. is there. Portland, whose metropolitan area contains nearly ½ the state's pop., straddles the Willamette near its junction with the Columbia and extends to the Columbia R. Salem and Eugene lie S in the valley, which rises in the S in the low range of the Calapooia Mts. The snowcapped volcanic peaks of the Cascades include Mt. Hood in N of range, rising to the state's highest elev. (11,235 ft/3,424 m). Much of Oregon's timber resources are in several natl. forests: Ochoco and Malheur in E center; Umatilla and Wallow-Whitman in NE; Siskiyou and Siuslaw in W; Umpqua, Rogue R., Winema, Deschutes, and Fremont in S center; Willamette and Mt. Hood in N center. Two large state forests, Clatsop and Tillamook, are in NW. Eastward the Cascades level out into high plateaus drained in the N by the Deschutes and the John Day rivers. Area just E of the Cascades referred to as the High Desert Region. To the S a variegated pattern of marshland, intermittent lakes, and mt. merges in the E into the semiarid Harney Basin, part of the larger Great Basin, a large area, covering part of 6 states, that has no outlet to the oceans. There, little vegetation grows, and the absence of potable water makes habitation difficult. NE of this area rise the pine-covered Blue Mts. and Wallowa Mts., which in some places extend to the Snake R. to form precipitous gorges. Part of Hells Canyon (Grand Canyon of the Snake) Natl. Recreational Area in NE, extends into Idaho. Other parts of the region where the Snake cuts through the plateau are more level and have been made productive through irrigation. Oregon's irrigation projects include the Deschutes, the Umatilla, and the Vale; the Klamath, shared with Calif.; and the Boise and the Owyhee, shared with Idaho. The state's major sources of farm income are cattle and sheep, with large herds grazing on the plateaus E of the Cascades, dairying, and poultry. Fur farms in NW. Chief crops in terms of value are hay, wheat, pears, and onions. Oregon is one of the nation's leading producers of snap beans, peppermint, sweet cherries (orchards are particularly numerous in the N Willamette valley), broccoli, strawberries, and grass seed. Oregon has developed an important and growing wine industry (NW) since 1980. The state's c.30,700,000 acres/12,400,000 ha of rich forestlands (almost ½ the area of the state) comprise the country's greatest reserves of standing timber; large areas have been set aside for conservation. Oregon has been the nation's foremost lumber state since 1950, producing much of the nation's lumber and most of its plywood. It exports lumber in increasing amounts to Japan. Wood processing is Oregon's major industry. Douglas fir predominates in the Cascades and Ponderosa pine in the eastern regions. Other major prods. are food, paper and paper items, machinery, and fabricated metal prods. Printing and publishing are important businesses. Oregon is also home to many high-technology computer and electronics companies. Abundant, cheap electric power is supplied by numerous dams, most notably those on the Columbia R. — Bonneville Dam, The Dalles Dam, and McNary Dam. The John Day Dam is one of the largest hydroelectric generators in the world. The many dams provide locks for navigation. The Bonneville Dam, in the steep gorge through which the Columbia R. pierces the Cascades, enables large vessels to travel far inland, and although river traffic is not as vital as formerly, the Columbia R. cities still serve as transport centers for a vast hinterland to the E. Oregon's river resources are one of its greatest assets. Although commercial fishing has declined in recent decades, it remains an important part of the economy of Oregon's coastal counties. Lincoln co., on the middle coast (around Newport), is Oregon's largest fish producer; salmon, tuna, halibut, crabs, clams, and shrimp are important. Although mining is still relatively underdeveloped, Oregon leads the nation in the production of nickel. Sand and gravel, stone, and cement are also major sources of mineral income. Oregon's beautiful, long ocean beaches with dramatic rock formations on and off the coastline, and its lakes and mts., draw thousands of visitors annually, making tourism one of the state's largest industries. Major attractions are the Oregon Caves Natl. Monument (SW), Fort Clatsop Natl. Memorial (NW), and McLoughlin House Natl. Historic Site; Crater L. Natl. Park (SW center) is a vacationer's paradise. There are 13 natl. forests, 1 natl. grassland, and more than 220 state parks. Initial Eur. interest in the region was aroused by the search for the Northwest Passage. Span. seamen skirted the Pacific coast from the 16th to the 18th cent., hoping to claim the area. The Eng. may 1st have arrived in the person of Sir Francis Drake, who sailed along the coast in 1579, possibly as far as Oregon. Much later, in 1778, Capt. James Cook, seeking the award of £20,000 for the discovery of the Northwest Passage, charted some of the coastline. By this time the Russians were pushing S from posts in Alaska and the Br. fur companies were exploring the West. Oregon's furs promised to become an important factor in the rapidly expanding China trade, and the Oregon coast was soon active with the vessels of several nations engaged in fur trade with the Native Americans. Br. captains, among them John Meares and George Vancouver, made the coastal area known, but it was an American, Robert Gray, who 1st sailed up the Columbia R. (1792), thus establishing U.S. claim to the areas that it drained. Can. traders of the North West Company were approaching the Columbia R. country when the overland Lewis and Clark expedition arrived in 1805. David Thompson was already making his way to the lower river when John Jacob Astor's agents (in the Pacific Fur Company) founded Astoria, the 1st permanent settlement in the Oregon country. In the War of 1812 the post was sold (1813) to the North West Company, but in 1818 a treaty provided for 10 years of joint rights for the U.S. and Great Britain in Oregon (i.e., the whole Columbia R. area). This agreement was later extended. The North West Company merged with the Hudson's Bay Company in 1821, and soon the region was dominated by John McLoughlin at Fort Vancouver. In 1842 and 1843 enormous wagon trains began the "great migration" westward over the Oregon Trail. Trouble bet. the settlers and the Brtish followed. The Americans set out to form their own govt., and demanded the British be removed from the whole of the Columbia R. country up to lat. 54°40′N; one of the slogans of the 1844 election was "Fifty-four forty or fight." War with Britain was a threat momentarily, but diplomacy prevailed. In 1846 the boundary was set at the line of lat. 49°N. Soon afterward the Oregon Territory was created in 1848, embracing the area W of the Rockies from the 42d to the 49th parallel. The area was reduced with the creation of the Washington Territory in 1853, and Oregon became a state in 1859 with a constitution that prohibited slaveholding, but which also forbade free blacks from entering the state. Although the Calif. gold rush caused a temporary exodus of settlers, it also brought a new market for Oregon's goods, and the Oregon gold strike that followed attracted some permanent settlement to the E hills and valleys. Wheat farming prospered and in 1867–1868 a surplus crop was shipped to England, the beginning of Oregon's great wheat export trade. Cattle and sheep were driven up from Calif. to graze on the tall grass of the semiarid plateaus, and soon cattle barons, such as Henry Miller, acquired large herds. They dominated the industry until the late 19th cent., when sheepmen and homesteaders succeeded in reducing the cattle range. The 1850s, 1860s, and 1870s were plagued by Native Amer. uprisings, but by 1880 Native Amer. troubles were over, and the next few decades brought increasing settlement and internal improvements. During the 1880s, and largely under the management of Henry Villard of the Northern Pacific RR, transcontinental RR lines were completed to the coast and down the Willamette valley into Calif., bringing new trade and stimulating the beginnings of mfg. Lumbering, which had long been important, became a leading industry. Seemingly almost overnight logging camps and sawmills

were built in the W foothills. The huge stands of Douglas fir and cedar brought fortunes to the lumbering kings, and the threat to natural resources led ultimately to the creation of natl. forests. By the time of the Lewis and Clark Centennial Exposition at Portland in 1905, less than 50 years after statehood had been gained, the frontier era had passed. Most of the feuding on the E plateaus was over. In spring the Willamette valley was abloom with fruit blossoms, and the river cities were busy with trade and industry. Oregon has been a leader in social, environmental, and political reforms. It was the 1st state, for example, to institute initiative, referendum, and recall; and to initiate a ban against nonrecyclable containers. Several issues have divided conservative and liberal thought sharply. One has been the question of minority groups. In the 1880s the influx of Chinese threatened the labor market and brought violent anti-Chin. sentiment, and in the 20th cent. there was opposition to the Japanese. Feeling against minorities has never been universal, however, and large groups have vigorously opposed it. In the 1930s one of the most disputed issues was the question of public or private development of power. Today, however, it has to be recognized that the Federal power and irrigation projects have had a profound effect on the economy of the entire Pacific Northwest. Many acres have been opened to irrigated farming, and the tremendous industrial expansion of World War II was to a large extent dependent on Bonneville power. Environmental issues have dominated since the 1970s. The state's numerous hydroelectric dams are killing Pacific salmon. A major controversy was raised in the late 1980s over the spotted owl, which has been endangered as its forest habitat is cut down. The tension bet. preserving nature and maintaining the state's economic growth continues as many high-technology electronic and computer firms and individuals seeking to escape from crowding, migrate from Calif. to Oregon. Oregon still operates under its original constitution, drawn and ratified in 1857. Its executive branch is headed by a governor elected for a 4-year term. Its bicameral legislature has a senate with 30 members elected for 4-year terms and an assembly with 60 members elected for 2 years. The state elects 2 senators and 5 representatives to the U.S. Congress and has 7 electoral votes. Among the state's more prominent institutions of higher learning are the Univ. of Oregon at Eugene; Oregon State Univ. at Corvallis; Reed Col. and Portland State Univ. at Portland; and Willamette Univ. at Salem. Oregon has 36 cos.: BAKER, BENTON, CLACKAMAS, CLATSOP, COLUMBIA, COOS, CROOK, CURRY, DESCHUTES, DOUGLAS, GILLIAM, GRANT, HARNEY, HOOD RIVER, JACKSON, JEFFERSON, JOSEPHINE, KLAMATH, LAKE, LANE, LINCOLN, LINN, MALHEUR, MARION, MORROW, MULTNOMAH, POLK, SHERMAN, TILLAMOOK, UMATILLA, UNION, WALLOWA, WASCO, WASHINGTON, WHEELER, YAMHILL.

Oregon, county (□ 784 sq mi/2,031 sq km; 1990 pop. 9,470), S Mo.; ⊙ Alton; 36°41′N 91°24′W. In the Ozarks, borders Ark. on S, drained by Eleven Point R. and Spring R. Agr., hay, notably livestock (cattle, hogs); dairying; oak, hickory, walnut timber; mfg. at Thayer and Alton. Grand Gulf State Park in SW; Part of Mark Twain Natl. Forest in NE. Formed 1845.

Oregon **1** city (1990 pop. 3,891), N Ill., on Rock R. (bridged) and 21 mi/34 km SW of Rockford; ⊙ Ogle co.; 42°00′N 89°20′W. Trade and industrial center in rich agr. area (corn, soybeans, cattle, hogs; dairying); mfg. (machinery, glass). Nearby is Eagle's Nest Art Colony, founded 1898 by Lorado Taft and others; Taft's soldiers' monument is in the city, and his great *Black Hawk* statue is on bluff overlooking Rock R. White Pines State Forest and Lowden and Castle Rock state parks are nearby. Inc. 1843. **2** city (1990 pop. 935), NW Mo., near Missouri R., 22 mi/35 km NW of St. Joseph; ⊙ Holt co., 39°58′N 95°08′W. Corn, apples, wheat; hogs, cattle. Big L. State Park and Squaw Creek Natl. Wildlife Refuge to NW. Platted 1841. **3** city (1990 pop. 18,334), Lucas co., NW Ohio, a suburb adjacent to Toledo, on L. Erie; 41°40′N 83°25′W. It is a port with RR-owned and -operated docks. The city has industries producing oil, chemicals, and fabricated metal prods.

The majority of the city's area is open farmland, where tomatoes, soybeans, greenhouse vegetables, fruits, and grains are grown. Inc. 1958.

Oregon, town (1990 pop. 4,519), Dane co., S Wis., suburb 10 mi/16 km S of Madison; 42°55′N 89°22′W. In dairying and farming area (hogs; tobacco); creamery; light mfg. Settled 1842, inc. 1883.

Oregon Caves National Monument (488 acres/197 ha), S Josephine co., SW Oregon, 32 mi/51 km SW of Medford, 12 mi/19 km ESE of Cave Junction (its hq.), in Siskiyou Mts., bounded on all sides by Siskiyou Natl. Forest, 5 mi/8 km N of Calif. state boundary. Authorized by Presidential Proclamation, 1909. Intricate cave formations in marble bedrock.

Oregon City, city (1990 pop. 14,698), NW Oregon, suburb 11 mi/18 km S of downtown Portland, at falls (c.40 ft/12 m high), bypassed by locks of Willamette R., at mouth of Clackamas R.; ⊙ Clackamas co.; 45°20′N 122°35′W. RR junction. Mfg. (food, lumber, printing, publishing, fabricated metal prods.). End of the Oregon Trail. Territorial capital until late in 1851. Had 1st newspaper (*Oregon Spectator*, 1846) W of the Missouri R. Edwin Markham b. here (1852). McLoughlin House Natl. Historic Site (est. 1941; affiliated area administered but not owned by Natl. Park Service) preserves the home (1846–1857) of Dr. John McLoughlin, a prominent figure in the early development of the Pacific Northwest, who plotted the city and is considered to be the "Father of Oregon." Site of Clackamas Community Col. Laid out in 1842, inc. 1849.

Oregon Inlet, Dare co., E N.C., channel (c.1 mi/1.6 km wide) through the Outer Banks, 12 mi/19 km SSE of Manteo, c.40 mi/64 km N of Cape Hatteras and Bodie Isl. to N (lighthouse), Pea Isl. to S, including Peas Isl. Natl. Wildlife Refuge and Cape Hatteras Natl. Seashore; connects Pamlico Sound with the Atlantic.

Oregon River, U.S. and Canada: see COLUMBIA river.

Oregon Trail, natl. historic trail, runs through Mo., Kansas, Nebraska, Wyo., Idaho, Oregon, and Wash. It is an affiliated area of the Natl. Park Service, whose role it is to implement and manage the plan to preserve this primary route of the Oregon Trail (2,000 mi/3,219 km long), used by pioneer settlers during the 1840s, and 125 other associated historic sites.

Oregon Trail,, overland emigrant route in the United States from the Missouri R. to the Columbia R. country (all of which was then called Oregon) in the 1840s and 1850s. The pioneers by wagon train did not, however, follow any single narrow route. In open country the different trains might spread out over a large area, only to converge again for river crossings, mt. passes, and other natural constrictions. In time many cutoffs and alternate routes also developed. They originated at various places on the Missouri, although Independence and Westport (now part of Kansas City, Mo.) were favorite starting points, and St. Joseph had some popularity. Those starting from Independence followed the same route as the Santa fe Trail for some 40 mi/64 km, then turned NW to the Platte and generally followed that river to the junction of the North Platte and the South Platte. Crossing the South Platte, the main trail followed the North Platte to Fort Laramie, then to the present Casper, Wyo., and through the mts. by the broad, level South Pass to the basin of the Colorado R. The travelers then went SW to Fort Bridger, from which the Mormon Trail continued SW to the Great Salt L., while the Oregon Trail went NW across a divide to Fort Hall, on the Snake R. It then went along the Snake R. The California Trail branched off to the southwest, but the Oregon Trail continued to Fort Boise. From that point the travelers had to make the hard climb over the Blue Mts. Once the mts. were crossed, paths diverged somewhat; many went to Fort Walla Walla before proceeding down the south bank of the Columbia R., traversing the Columbia's gorge where it passes through the Cascade Mts. to the Willamette valley, where the early settlement centered. The end of the trail shifted as settlement spread. The Mountain Men were chiefly responsible for making the route known, and Thomas Fitzpatrick and James Bridger were renowned as guides. Capt. Benjamin de Bonneville 1st took wagons over South Pass in 1832. The 1st genuine emigrant train was that led by John Bidwell in 1841, half of which went to Calif., the rest proceeding from Fort Hall to Oregon on horses and mules. The 1st train of emigrants to reach Oregon was that led by Elijah White in 1842. In 1843 occurred the "great emigration" of more than 900 persons and more than 1,000 head of livestock. Four trains made the journey in 1844, and by 1845 the emigrants reached a total of over 3,000. Although it took the average emigrant train six months to traverse the c.2,000-mi/3,200-km route, the trail continued in use for many years. Travel upon the trail gradually declined with the coming of the RR, and it was abandoned in the 1870s.

Oreland (OR-luhnd), uninc. town (1990 pop. 5,695), Montgomery co., SE Pa., residential suburb 12 mi/19 km N of Philadelphia; 40°06′N 75°10′W. Mfg. includes printing and publishing, fabricated metal prods., industrial glass prods.

Orem, city (1990 pop. 67,561), Utah co., N central Utah, suburb 4 mi/6.4 km N of Provo, 36 mi/58 km SSE of Salt Lake City, near Utah L. Orem is located in an irrigated vegetable and fruit-growing area; 40°17′N 111°42′W. It has a large steel mill, and a variety of light industrial prods. are manufactured here (chemicals, food, furniture, fabricated metal prods., printing and publishing, electronic equip., steel, computer software); motion picture production. Uinta Natl. Forest, Bridal Veil Falls, and Sundance Ski Area to NE. Utah Valley Community Col. The city has been marked by growth, and its pop. more than doubled bet. 1970 and 1990. Originally named Provo Beach. Settled 1861, inc. 1919.

Orestes (aw-RES-tuhs), town (1990 pop. 458), Madison co., E central Ind., 2 mi/3.2 km W of Alexandria; 40°16′N 85°44′W. Agr. area; mfg. (food).

Orford (OR-fuhrd), town (1990 pop. 1,008), Grafton co., W N.H., 19 mi/31 km NNE of Lebanon; 43°53′N 72°04′W. Bounded W by Connecticut R., opposite Fairlee, Vt.; drained by Jacobs Brook. Orford Ridge, site of fine colonial and federal houses, in Orfrod Village. Appalachian Trail crosses E part. Smarts Mt. (3,240 ft/988 m) in SE corner.

Orfordville, town (1990 pop. 1,219), Rock co., S Wis., 12 mi/19 km WSW of Janesville; 42°37′N 89°15′W. In tobacco, dairying, and grain area.

Organ, uninc. village (1990 pop. 300), Dona Ana co., S N.Mex., 13 mi/21 km ENE of Las Cruces, W of San Agustin Pass (5,719 ft/1,743 m). Cattle, sheep. Light mfg. Organ Mts. to S; San Andres Mts. to N. At SW boundary of White Sands Missle Range. Aquirre Spring Natl. Recreation Area to SE.

Organ Cave, W.Va.: see RONCEVERTE.

Organ Mountains, S N.Mex., in Doña Ana co., just E of Rio Grande and Las Cruces. Prominent points: Organ Peak (8,872 ft/2,704 m), Organ Needle (8,990 ft/2,740 m). Just N is San Agustin Pass, separating range from San Andres Mts. and village of Organ, W of pass. Aguirre Springs Natl. Recreation Area in N; White Sands Missile Range to NE.

Organ Pipe Cactus National Monument (□ 516 sq mi/1,336 sq km), Pima co., S Ariz. Organ pipe cactus and other unique desert growth. Bounded by Mexico (Sonora) on S; by Ajo Range and Tohono O'odham (Papago) Indian Reservation on E; by Cabeza Prieta Natl. Wildlife Refuge on W; border village of Lukeville in S; Quitobaquito Springs in SW. Authorized 1937.

Órganos, Sierra de los (OR-guh-noz, see-AIR-uh dai los), mountain range, Pinar del Río prov., W Cuba, extending c.60 mi/97 km NE from Mantua to the Sierra del Rosario; rises to c.1,350 ft/411 m. Rich in copper and lumber. Sometimes considered to include the Sierra del Rosario.

Orient, city (1990 pop. 428), Franklin co., S Ill., 8 mi/12.9 km SSW of Benton; 37°55′N 88°58′W. In bituminous coal-mining and agr. area.

Orient 1 town (1990 pop. 376), Adair co., SW Iowa, 11 mi/18 km N of Creston; 41°12′N 94°25′W. In agr. region. **2** agr. town (1990 pop. 157), Aroostook co., E Maine, on Grand L. and 22 mi/35 km S of Houlton; 45°49′N 67°51′W. In recreational area.

Orient 1 resort village (1990 pop. 1,000), Suffolk co., SE N.Y., NE L.I., overlooking Orient Harbor (inlet of Gardiners Bay), 24 mi/39 km NE of Riverhead; 41°09′N 72°15′W. To E are Orient Point resort village, with ferry connections with New London, Conn.; Orient Point promontory at tip of N peninsula ("North Fork") of L.I.; and Orient Beach State Park (□ 342 acres/138 ha). **2** village (1990 pop. 59), Faulk co., N central S.Dak., 10 mi/16 km S of Faulkton; 44°53′N 99°05′W. L. Faulkton State Lakeside Use Area to N.

Orient Beach State Park, N.Y.: see ORIENT.

Orient Point, N.Y.: see ORIENT.

Oriental, town (1990 pop. 7,977), Puebla, central Mexico, on central plateau, 45 mi/72 km NE of Puebla; 19°24′N 97°40′W. Corn, maguey. RR junction.

Oriental, town (1990 pop. 786), Pamlico co., E N.C., on Neuse R. and 20 mi/32 km SE of New Bern; 35°01′N 76°40′W. Agr. inland (potatoes, grain, cotton, peanuts; hogs); mfg. (food).

Oriente (or-ee-AIN-tai), region and former province, E Cuba. Was the largest and most populous prov. of the isl., occupying its easternmost sect. Now subdivided into Granma, Guantánamo, Holguín, Las Tunas, and Santiago de Cuba provs.

Orillia (o-RIL-ee-uh), town (1991 pop. 25,925), SE Ont., Canada, on L. Couchiching; 44°36′N 79°25′W. Mfg. includes machinery, consumer goods, rubber prods. It is also a summer resort. A monument to Champlain, erected in 1925, commemorates his explorations. Canadian humorist Stephen Leacock had a summer home here.

Orinda, city (1990 pop. 16,642), Contra Costa co., W Calif., residential suburb 5 mi/8 km NE of downtown Oakland; 37°53′N 122°11′W. Mfg. (computer equip., light mfg.). Caldecott Tunnel to Oakland (Mt. Diablo Blvd.) to SW. Mokelumne Aqueduct passes to N, enters San Pablo Reservoir to NW, Briones Reservoir to N, Lafayette Reservoir to E; Berkeley Hills to SW; Briones Regional Park to NE.

Orion, town, Oakland co., Mich., suburb 10 mi/16 km W of Pontiac. Mfg. (electronic equip., transportation equip., machinery).

Orion, village (1990 pop. 1,821), Henry co., NW Ill., 12 mi/19 km WNW of Cambridge; 41°21′N 90°22′W. In agr. area.

Oriska (or-IS-kuh), village (1990 pop. 103), Barnes co., E N.Dak., 10 mi/16 km E of Valley City.; 46°55′N 97°47′W.

Oriskany (ah-RIS-kuh-nee), village (1990 pop. 1,450), Oneida co., central N.Y., near mouth of Oriskany Creek on Mohawk R., 7 mi/11.3 km NW of Utica; 43°09′N 75°19′W. Mfg. (transportation equip., fabricated metal prods.). Obelisk at Oriskany Battlefield (NW) marks site of an engagement (Aug. 6, 1777) of the Saratoga campaign, one of the bloodiest battles of the Amer. Revolution. Inc. 1914.

Oriskany Creek (ah-RIS-kuh-nee), c.30 mi/48 km long, central N.Y.; rises in Madison co. S of Oneida; flows S and NNE to Mohawk R. 6 mi/9.7 km NW of Utica.

Oriskany Falls (ah-RIS-kuh-nee), village (1990 pop. 795), Oneida co., central N.Y., on Oriskany Creek and 16 mi/26 km SW of Utica; 42°56′N 75°27′W. Mfg. of apparel.

Orizaba (o-ree-SAH-bah), city (1990 pop. 114,216) and township, Veracruz state, E central Mexi.co 18°51′N 97°08′W. It is the commercial center of a prosperous coffee and sugar growing region on Mexico Highway 150. The development of water power has stimulated mfg. industries, especially cotton and wool textile factories. Site of large brewery. Orizaba is a popular vacation spot. Mineral springs are nearby, and the majestic cone of Citlaltépetl rises in the distance. The city is also a cultural center noted for its fine-arts institute. The federal school in Orizaba houses murals by José Clemente Orozco. In 1862, Benito Juárez, seeking to forestall foreign intervention in Mexican affairs, called a conference at Orizaba of foreign representatives; his efforts failed. Fr. forces subsequently used the city as a base for their invasion of Mexico.

Orizaba, Mexico: see CITLALTÉPETL.

Orizatlán (o-ree-sah-TLAHN), town (1990 pop. 5,307), Hidalgo, central Mexico, in foothills of Sierra Madre Oriental, 13 mi/21 km WNW of Huejutla de Reyes; ⊙ San Felipe Orizatlán municipio; 21°10′N 98°36′W. Corn, rice, tobacco, coffee, fruit; cigars.

Orkney Springs, uninc. village, Shenandoah co., NW Va., near W.Va. state line, 25 mi/40 km N of Harrisonburg, in Allegheny Mt. foothills, in George Washington Natl. Forest; 38°47′N 78°48′W. Mineral springs; resort. Boyce Resort to N.

Orland, city (1990 pop. 5,052), Glenn co., N central Calif., in Sacramento Valley, 18 mi/29 km W of Chico; 39°45′N 122°11′W. Shipping, processing center; fruit, nuts, olives, rice, wheat, corn; nursery livestock; cattle, sheep; dairying; dried fruits and nuts. Hq. of U.S. Bureau of Reclamation irrigation project begun in 1910. Black Butte L. reservoir to W, Stony Gorge Reservoir to SW, both on Stony Creek. Tehama Colusa Canal passes to E and S. Orland Buttes (1,038 ft/316 m) to W. Founded 1881, inc. 1909.

Orland 1 town (1990 pop. 361), Steuben co., NE Ind., near Mich. line, 11 mi/18 km NW of Angola; 41°44′N 85°10′W. Mfg. (plastic prods., wire prods., food, transportation equip., fabricated metal prods.). Fawn R. State Fish Hatchery nearby to NW. Laid out 1838. **2** town (1990 pop. 1,805), Hancock co., S Maine, near Bucksport, 16 mi/26 km W of Ellsworth; 44°34′N 68°40′W. Settled 1764.

Orland Hills, village (1990 pop. 5,510), Cook co., NE Ill., residential suburb 23 mi/37 km SSW of downtown Chicago, 2 mi/3.2 km S of Orland Park; 41°35′N 87°50′W.

Orland Park, village (1990 pop. 35,720), Cook co., NE Ill., suburb 24 mi/39 km SW of downtown Chicago, 12 mi/19 km NE of Joliet; 41°36′N 87°50′W. Despite rapid urban growth, area still has some agr. (corn; dairying); light mfg.

Orlando, city (□ 71 sq mi/184 sq km; 1990 pop. 164,693), central Fla., in a lake region; ⊙ Orange co.; 28°30′N 81°22′W. It is a growing center of a high-tech mfg. region as well as one of the most visited vacation spots in the world. Orlando's economy focuses on the aerospace and electronics industries, but tourism brings in the largest revenues. Located 15 mi/24 km SW of Orlando is the famous Walt Disney World, with its many theme parks, which draw millions of visitors annually to the Orlando area. Hotels, restaurants, and tourist facilities abound in and around Orlando, which is noted for its subtropical climate. The Univ. of Central Fla. and Rollins Col. are in the metropolitan area.

Orlando, village (1990 pop. 198), Logan co., central Okla., 19 mi/31 km N of Guthrie; 36°08′N 97°22′W. Trade center for farming area. L. Carl Blackwell reservoir to E.

Orleans, community, SE Ont., Canada, suburb of Ottawa within city of Gloucester, part of Ottawa-Carleton Regional Municipality (1991 pop. 678,147), on S bank of Ottawa R. Residential area. Mixed farming.

Orleans, parish (□ 199 sq mi/515 sq km; 1990 pop. 496,938), SE La., coextensive with city of New Orleans; 30°04′N, 89°56′W. Home gardens, oysters, shrimp, crabs, finfish. Formed 1805.

Orleans 1 county (□ 817 sq mi/2,116 sq km; 1990 pop. 41,846), W N.Y.; ⊙ Albion; 43°22′N 78°13′W. Bounded N by L. Ontario; crossed by the N.Y. State Barge Canal; drained by Oak Orchard Creek. Diversified mfg. at Albion, Medina, Lyndonville. Fruit-growing area; also dairy prods. Formed 1924. **2** county (□ 720 sq mi/1,865 sq km; 1990 pop. 24,053), N Vt., on Can. (Que.) line; ⊙ Newport; 44°49′N 72°15′W. Dairying, lumbering; wood prods., furniture; maple sugar. Resorts on L. Memphremagog, L. Willoughby, and smaller lakes; winter sports. Drained by Barton, Missisquoi, Black, and Clyde rivers. Organized 1792.

Orleans 1 town (1990 pop. 2,083), Orange co., S Ind., near Lost R., 7 mi/11.3 km N of Paoli; 38°40′N 86°27′W. In agr. area (corn, cattle); mfg. (lumber, food, furniture). Karst topography. Settled 1815. **2** resort town (1990 pop. 560), Dickinson co., NW Iowa, on Spirit L., 2 mi/3.2 km NE of Spirit Lake; 43°27′N 95°05′W. Fish hatchery and Marble Beach State Park here. **3** town (1990 pop. 5,838), Barnstable co., SE Mass., near elbow of Cape Cod, 17 mi/27 km ENE of Barnstable; 41°46′N 69°58′W. Summer resort. Transatlantic cable to Brest,

France. Includes villages of East Orleans, Rock Harbor, South Orleans. Cape Cod Natl. Seashore just E; Nickerson State Park and Point of Rocks Beach nearby. Settled 1693, set off from Eastham 1797.
Orleans 1 village (1990 pop. 490), Harlan co., S Nebr., 6 mi/9.7 km WNW of Alma and on Republican R., near Kansas line; 40°07′N 99°27′W. RR junction. Grain. **2** village (1990 pop. 806) in Barton town, Orleans co., N Vt., 9 mi/14.5 km S of Newport and on Barton R.; 44°48′N 72°12′W. Settled c.1821.
Orléans, Île d' (dor-lai-AHN, eel) or **Orléans Island** (or-lai-AHN), 20 mi/32 km long and 5 mi/8 km wide, S Que., Canada, in the St. Lawrence NE of Que. It is connected with the mainland by a highway bridge. Settled (1651) by the French, it was the site of 1 of Wolfe's camps in his attack on Que. in 1759. It is a popular tourist attraction and a residential community for Quebec City. Potatoes, strawberries, cheese, and poultry are the chief prods.
Orlovista (or-luh-VIS-tuh), town (□ 1 sq mi/2.6 sq km; 1990 pop. 5,990), Orange co., central Fla., 5 mi/8 km WSW of Orlando; 28°32′N 81°27′W.
Orme (orm), town (1990 pop. 150), Marion co., S Tenn., near Ala. line, 29 mi/47 km W of Chattanooga; 35°00′N 85°48′W.
Ormiston (OR-mis-tuhn), village, S Sask., Canada, near small Shoe L., 45 mi/72 km S of Moose Jaw. Mfg. of chemicals.
Ormond Beach (OR-muhnd), resort and residential city (□ 26 sq mi/67 sq km; 1990 pop. 29,721), Volusia co., 5 mi/8 km NNW of Daytona Beach, E central Fla., on Halifax R. (a lagoon) and the Atlantic Ocean; 29°17′N 81°05′W. Inc. 1880.
Ormond-by-the-Sea (OR-muhnd), town (□ 1 sq mi/2.6 sq km; 1990 pop. 8,157), Volusia co., E central Fla., 12 mi/19 km NNW of Daytona Beach; 29°20′N 81°04′W.
Ormsby, village (1990 pop. 159), Martin and Watonwan cos., S Minn., 18 mi/29 km NW of Fairmont; 43°51′N 94°42′W. Agr. (grain, soybeans; livestock). Mfg. (fertilizers, lumber). Small lakes in area.
Ormsby, former county (□ 141 sq mi/365 sq km), W Nev. In July 1969 Carson City, ⊙ state and co., consolidated with the co. and replaced it, becoming an independent city. Formed 1854.
Ormstown, village (1991 pop. 1,577), S Que., Canada, on Châteauguay R., and 12 mi/19 km SE of Valleyfield; 45°08′N 74°00′W. Dairying.
Ornelas, Mexico: see SAN JOSÉ DE GRACIA, Michoacán.
Oro, El, Mexico: see EL ORO DE HIDALGO.
Oro Grande, uninc. village, San Bernardino co., S Calif., 34 mi/55 km N of San Bernardino, in Mojave Desert, on Mojave R. Mfg. asphalt; limestone quarrying in area.
Oro Valley, town (1990 pop. 6,670), Pima co., S Ariz., residential suburb 12 mi/19 km N of Tucson, on Oro R.; 32°25′N 110°57′W. Cattle. Coronado Natl. Forest to E; Catalina State Park to NE.
Orocovis (o-ro-KO-vis), town (1990 pop. 21,158), central P.R., in Cordillera Central, 23 mi/37 km SW of San Juan. Elev. 1,430 ft/436 m. Industrial and commercial area; light mfg. (electric items, apparel, furniture). Coffee-growing and processing. Artisanry.
Orofino, [Span.=pure gold], city (1990 pop. 2,868), ⊙ Clearwater co., N Idaho, on Clearwater R., near mouth of East Fork Clearwater R., and 40 mi/64 km E of Lewiston; 46°29′N 116°16′W. Elev. 1,027 ft/313 m. RR junction. Lumber-milling point and gateway to one of country's largest stands of white pine. Agr. (cattle; wheat, barley, alfalfa). Mfg. (wood prods., lumber). Limestone quarries nearby. In NE part of Nez Perce Indian Reservation, main center for reservation. Dworshak Dam, Reservoir, and State Park to N, Dworshak Natl. Fish Hatchery 1 mi/1.6 km N. Founded 1898 (c.25 mi/40 km from original site, established in gold rush of 1860), inc. 1906.
Oromocto (o-ro-MAHK-to), town (1991 pop. 9,325), S central N.B., Canada, on the St. John R.; 45°51′N 66°28′W. The town developed because of its proximity to Camp Gagetown, the largest (436 sq mi/1,129 sq km) military camp in Canada.

Oromocto Lake (□ 16 sq mi/41 sq km), SW N.B., Canada, 16 mi/26 km WSW of Fredericton; 8 mi/13 km long, 4 mi/6 km wide.
Oromocto River, 20 mi/32 km long, SW N.B., Canada; rises in 2 branches, one issuing from Oromocoto L., the other from South Oromocto L., joining 21 mi/34 km S of Fredericton; flows N to St. John R. at Oromocto.
Orono 1 (OR-uh-no), town (1990 pop. 10,573), including Orono village, Penobscot co., S Maine, on the Penobscot R., and 8 mi/12.9 km above Bangor; 44°52′N 68°42′W. Seat of main campus of Univ. of Maine. Settled c.1775, called Stillwater until inc. 1806, included Old Town until 1840. **2** (OR-no), town (1990 pop. 7,285), Hennepin co., E Minn., residential suburb 15 mi/24 km W of downtown Minneapolis, on N shore of L. Minnetonka, includes Big Isl. and several landlocked bays, N extension of lake; 44°58′N 93°35′W. Long L. in NE. Morris T. Baker Park Reserve on N boundary, in NW.
Orono (AH-ro-no), village, S Ont., Canada, 15 mi/24 km ENE of Oshawa. Food processing.
Oronoco (or-ruh-NO-ko), village (1990 pop. 727), Olmsted co., SE Minn., 10 mi/16 km NNW of Rochester; 44°09′N 92°32′W. In agr. area (grain, soybeans; livestock, poultry; dairying). Mfg. (signs). Parts of Richard J. Dorer Memorial Hardwood State Forest to NE and SW.
Oronogo (o-ruh-NO-go), city (1990 pop. 595), Jasper co., SW Mo., near Spring R., suburb 8 mi/12.9 km N of Joplin; 37°11′N 94°28′W. Agr. (wheat, soybeans; cattle). Former lead, zinc mines.
Orosi, uninc. town (□ 2 sq mi/5.2 sq km; 1990 pop. 5,486), Tulare co., S central Calif., in San Joaquin Valley, 15 mi/24 km N of Visalia; 36°33′N 119°17′W. Citrus, peaches, apples, plums, olives, nuts, grapes; cotton, nursery prods.; cattle, hogs, poultry.
Orovada (or-uh-VAH-duh), uninc. village (1990 pop. 200), Humboldt co., N Nev., 40 mi/64 km N of Winnemucca, 30 mi/48 km S of Oregon state boundary, E of Quinn R. Mercury, gold, silver. Cattle. Santa Rosa Mts. and Santa Rosa Peak (9,701 ft/2,957 m), in sect. of Humboldt Natl. Forest, to E. Parts of Fort McDermitt Indian Reservation to N and SW.
Oroville, city (□ 10 sq mi/26 sq km; 1990 pop. 11,960); ⊙ Butte co., N central Calif., 63 mi/101 km N of Sacramento on Feather R., in Sacramento Valley, at W base of the Sierra Nevada; 39°30′N 121°34′W. Diverse mfg. Agr. (citrus, olives, kiwi fruit, plums, peaches, walnuts, almonds, grain, nursery stock; cattle); timber. L. Oroville Reservoir and State Recreation Area to E (Feather R.); Feather R. Canyon and Feather Falls are to E; Plumas Natl. Forest to NE. Settled 1849 as gold camp (Ophir City), inc. 1857.
Oroville (OR-o-vil), town (1990 pop. 1,505), Okanogan co., N Wash., port of entry 4 mi/6.4 km S of Canada (B.C.) border, and 6 mi/9.7 km S of Osoyoos, B.C., 40 mi/64 km N of Okanogan, and on Okanogan R. at mouth of Similkamern R. (from W) and at S end of Osoyoos L. (extends into Canada); 48°57′N 119°26′W. RR terminus. Gold, silver; Agr. (timber, apples). Mfg. (wood prods.). Osoyoos L. State Park N of town; small sect. of Okanogan Natl. Forest to SE. Inc. 1908.
Oroville East, uninc. town (1990 pop. 8,462), Butte co., N central Calif., residential suburb 1 mi/1.6 km E of Oroville, near Feather R. L. Oroville reservoir, and State Recreation Area to NE; 39°31′N 121°29′W. Citrus, kiwi fruit, olives, almonds, grain, nursery stock; cattle.
Oroville, Lake, Butte co., N central Calif., on Feather R. (largest unit), 5 mi/8 km ENE of Oroville; c.17 mi/27 km long; 39°31′N 121°18′W. Elev. 899 ft/274 m. West, North (longest), Middle, and South Forks of the river form 4 large arms extending N and E. Formed by Oroville Dam (770 ft/235 m high, 7,600 ft/2,316 m long) built (1957–1968) to provide electric power, drinking water, and irrigation. Plumas Natl. Forest to NE; surrounded by L. Oroville State Recreation Area.
Orr, village (1990 pop. 265), St. Louis co., NE Minn., 43 mi/69 km N of Hibbing, on E end of Pelican L., Pelican R. exits to S, in Kabetogama State Forest area; 48°03′N 92°49′W. Resort area; timber. Mfg. (wood prods.). Nett L. Indian Reservation to W; Superior Natl. Forest to E; Voyageurs Natl. Park to N.

Orrick (O-rik), city (1990 pop. 935), Ray co., NW Mo., near Missouri R., 9 mi/14.5 km SW of Richmond; 39°12′N 94°07′W. Agr. (corn, wheat, soybeans; hogs). Mfg. (plastic molding). Plotted 1873.
Orrington, town (1990 pop. 3,309), Penobscot co., S Maine, on the Penobscot R., and 8 mi/12.9 km below Bangor; 44°43′N 68°46′W. Settled 1770, inc. 1788.
Orrs Island, Maine: see HARPSWELL.
Orrstown (ORS-toun), borough (1990 pop. 220), Franklin co., S Pa., 5 mi/8 km W of Shippensburg, on Conodoguinet Creek; 40°03′N 36°77′W. Agr. (grain; livestock, dairying). Light mfg. Letterkenny Army Depot to SW scheduled to close in late 1990s. Blue Mt. ridge to NW.
Orrum (OR-uhm), village (1990 pop. 103), Robeson co., SE N.C., 10 mi/16 km S of Lumberton; 34°28′N 79°00′W. Agr. (grain; sunflowers; livestock). Mfg. (ventilators). Lumber River State Park to SE.
Orrville, city (1990 pop. 7,712), Wayne co., N central Ohio, 20 mi/32 km W of Canton; 40°51′N 81°46′W. In agr. area; food and dairy prods. Mfg. (transportation equip., machinery, chemicals, wood prods., leather goods, mattresses). Settled c.1850, inc. 1864.
Orrville, town (1990 pop. 234), Dallas co., S central Ala., 15 mi/24 km SW of Selma. Mfg. (wooden church pews).
Orting, town (1990 pop. 2,106), Pierce co., W central Wash., 17 mi/27 km SE of Tacoma, and on Puyallup R. at mouth of Carbon R. to N; 47°05′N 122°13′W. RR junction. Agr. (bulbs; timber, fruit; dairy prods.). Mfg. (machinery, corrugated boxes). A fish hatchery is here. L. Kapowsin to S. Inc. 1889.
Ortiz, village, Conejos co., S Colo., on branch of Conejos R., in SE foothills of San Juan Mts., at N.Mex. state line, and 5 mi/8 km SSW of Antonito. Elev. c.8,000 ft/2,438 m. Rio Grande Natl. Forest to W; Carson Natl. Forest (N.Mex.) to S.
Ortiz Mountains (or-TEEZ), N central N.Mex., in Santa Fe co., E of Rio Grande, 25 mi/40 km SSW of Santa Fe. Highest point, Placer Peak (8,897 ft/2,712 m). Coal mines.
Ortley, village (1990 pop. 63), Roberts co., NE S.Dak. 24 mi/39 km SSW of Sisseton in Lake Traverse (Sisseton Wahpeton) Indian Reservation; 45°20′N 97°12′W.
Ortoire River (AWR-twahr), 31 mi/50 km long, SE Trinidad, Trinidad and Tobago; flows E to the Atlantic; 10°20′N 61°00′W. Not navigable. Formerly called Guataro R.
Ortonville, town (1990 pop. 2,205), ⊙ Big Stone co., W Minn., 67 mi/108 km WNW of Willmar, on S.Dak. state line, at S end of Big Stone L. (at outlet of Minnesota R.), opposite Big Stone City, S.Dak.; 45°17′N 96°26′W. Elev. 1,021 ft/311 m. Mfg. (fertilizer, soft drinks, printing and publishing); granite quarries nearby. Big Stone L. State Park to NW. Settled 1872, laid out 1873.
Ortonville, village (1990 pop. 1,252), Oakland co., SE Mich., 17 mi/27 km NNW of Pontiac; 42°51′N 83°26′W. In farm area. Diverse mfg. Ortonville State Recreational Area to N; Mt. Hilly and Pine Knob ski areas to SW.
Orwell, town (1990 pop. 1,114), Addison co., W Vt., on L. Champlain, 21 mi/34 km NW of Rutland, and 15 mi/24 km SSW of Middlebury; 43°48′N 73°17′W. Dairy prods., sheep.
Orwell 1 village (1990 pop. 400), Oswego co., N central N.Y., 27 mi/43 km NE of Oswego; 43°32′N 75°57′W. **2** village (1990 pop. 1,258), Ashtabula co., extreme NE Ohio, 25 mi/40 km S of Ashtabula; 41°32′N 80°51′W. In dairy, grain, and poultry area.
Orwell Bay, inlet S P.E.I., Canada, opening SE from Hillsborough Bay; 10 mi/16 km long, mouth 4 mi/6 km wide.
Orwigsburg (OR-wigs-buhrg), borough (1990 pop. 2,780), Schuylkill co., E central Pa., 5 mi/8 km ESE of Pottsville; 40°38′N 76°05′W. Mfg. (fabricated metal prods., pens and markers, machinery, wood prods., food prods., textiles, apparel). Agr. area (potatoes, corn, apples; livestock; dairying). Hawk Mt. Sanctuary and Appalachian Trail to E. Settled 1747, laid out 1796, inc. 1813.
Osage 1 (o-SAIJ), county (□ 719 sq mi/1,862 sq km; 1990

pop. 15,248), E Kansas; ⊙ Lyndon; 38°38′N 95°43′W. Gently rolling plains area, drained by Marais des Cygnes R. and Dragoon Creek. Agr. (hogs, cattle; soybeans, wheat, apples; sorghum, hay). Mfg. (paper prods., metal prods.). Osage State Fishing L. in N. Pomona L. Reservoir and Pomona State Park in E; Melvern L. Reservoir and Melvern State Park in SW. Formed 1859. **2** (O-saij), county (□ 601 sq mi/1,557 sq km; 1990 pop. 12,018), central Mo.; ⊙ Linn; 38°27′N 91°51′W. In Ozark region, on Missouri (N) and Osage (W) rivers; drained by Gasconade and Maries rivers. Agr. (corn, wheat, vegetables, hay; cattle, poultry; dairying; wineries). Fire-clay. Known for picturesque villages. Settled largely by Ger. immigrants beginning in the 1830s. Formed 1841. **3** (o-SAIJ), county (□ 2,303 sq mi/5,965 sq km; 1990 pop. 41,645), contiguous with Osage Indian Reservation, N Okla.; ⊙ Pawhuska, Osage agency hq; 36°37′N 96°24′W. Largest co. (land area) in Okla.; bounded N by Kansas state line, SW by Arkansas R. (forms Kaw L. in NW, Keystone L. in SE); drained by Caney R., Salt, Hominy, and Bird creeks; hilly in W. Co. includes part of city of Bartlesville in E, and part of city of Tulsa in SE corner. Cattle-ranching and oil- and natural gas–producing area, with some agr. (soybeans, sorghum, hay; cattle, horses). Mfg. (apparel, machinery, petroleum and coal prods., process control instruments). Includes Osage Hills State Park in E center; Bluestem L. reservoir in center; Skiatook L. reservoir in SE; Birch L. reservoir in E; Hulah L. reservoir and Wah-Sha-She State Park in NE; Walnut Creek State Park in S. Formed 1907.

Osage, city (1990 pop. 3,439), ⊙ Mitchell co., N Iowa, near Cedar R., and 22 mi/35 km ENE of Mason City; 43°16′N 92°48′W. Mfg. (textiles, apparel, paper prods., wood prods., lime, feed, food prods.). Limestone quarries, sand and gravel pits nearby. Settled 1853, inc. 1871.

Osage 1 (o-SAIJ) or **Osage City**, village (1990 pop. 163), Osage co., N Okla., 25 mi/40 km WNW of Tulsa, and on Arkansas R. (Keystone L.); 36°17′N 96°25′W. In agr. area. Walnut Creek State Park to SE. **2** village (1990 pop. 183), Monongalia co., N W.Va., 3 mi/4.8 km NW of Morgantown, on Scotts Run creek, near Monongahela R.; 39°39′N 80°00′W. Livestock; grain. **3** village, Weston co., NE Wyo., 14 mi/23 km NW of Newcastle. Elev. c.4,300 ft/1,311 m. Oil refining. Thunder Basin Natl. Grassland to N and W.

Osage Beach, town (1990 pop. 2,599), Miller co., central Mo., 35 mi/56 km SW of Jefferson City, at E end of the L. of the Ozarks, 5 mi/8 km S of Bagnell Dam (Osage R.). L. of the Ozarks State Park adjoins town on SE. Resort area; tourism. Mfg. (printing, medical prods., transportation equip., concrete, limestone prods., cut stone); sand and gravel processing.

Osage City (o-SAIJ), town (1990 pop. 2,689), Osage co., E Kansas, 25 mi/40 km NE of Emporia; 38°37′N 95°49′W. RR junction. Trade center for livestock, grain area. Mfg. (prefabricated wood bldgs.). Melvern L. reservoir and Melvern State Park to S. Settled 1865 near Santa Fe Trail inc. 1872.

Osage River, c.360 mi/579 km long (including lakes), Mo.; formed SE of Rich Hill, W Mo., by junction of Marais des Cygnes R. and Little Osage R.; flows SE and E, into the Ozarks, widening into Truman L. impounded by Harry S Truman Dam at Warsaw, then into the L. of the Ozarks impounded by Bagnell Dam (near Bagnell), then NE to Missouri R. E of Jefferson City. Power plants at the dams at Bagnell and Warsaw.

Osakis (o-SAI-kuhs), town (1990 pop. 1,256), Douglas and Todd cos., W Minn., at S end of L. Osakis, 11 mi/18 km E of Alexandria; 45°52′N 95°09′W. Agr. (grain; poultry; dairying). Mfg. (construction materials, diversified light mfg.).

Osakis, Lake (□ 10 sq mi/26 sq km), in Todd and Douglas cos., W Minn., 12 mi/19 km E of Alexandria; 8 mi/12.9 km long, 2 mi/3.2 km wide. Elev. 1,320 ft/402 m. Drains into small affluent of Long Prairie R. Fishing, boating, bathing.

Osawatomie (o-suh-WAHT-uh-mee), town (1990 pop. 4,590), Miami co., E Kansas, on the Marais des Cygnes R., 7 mi/11.3 km SW of Paola; 38°30′N 94°57′W. RR junction.The town, once a station on the Underground Railroad, has a memorial park that contains the cabin where John Brown lived in 1856; John Brown Mus. Founded 1855 by the New England Emigrant Aid Company, inc. 1883.

Osborn, Ohio: see FAIRBORN.

Osborne (AHZ-born), county (□ 894 sq mi/2,315 sq km; 1990 pop. 4,867), N central Kansas; ⊙ Osborne; 39°21′N 98°46′W. Smoky Hills region, drained by North and South forks of Solomon R. Cattle, hogs; wheat, rye, barley, sorghum). Mfg. (farm equip.); food processing. N arm of Waconda L. Reservoir in NE. Geodetic Center of U.S in SE (Meades Ranch). Formed 1871.

Osborne (AHZ-born), town (1990 pop. 1,778), ⊙ Osborne co., N Kansas, on South Fork of Solomon R., and 39 mi/63 km NNE of Russell; 39°26′N 98°42′W. Elev. 1,500 ft/457 m. RR junction. Shipping center for livestock and grain area. Mfg. (feeds, farm machinery, wood prods.). Founded 1871, inc. 1879.

Osborne (AHS-born), borough (1990 pop. 565), Allegheny co., SW Pa., residential suburb 11 mi/18 km NW of downtown Pittsburgh, on Ohio R; 40°31′N 80°10′W.

Osbornville, village, Ocean co., E N.J., 7 mi/11.3 km NNE of Toms River.

Osbourne Store, town (1991 pop. 3,390), Clarendon parish, S central Jamaica, 5 mi/8 km W of May Pen; 17°58′N 77°20′W. A highway junction along main road W of May Pen.

Osburn, town (1990 pop. 1,579), Shoshone co., N Idaho, 2 mi/3.2 km NW of Wallace, across highway (I-90) from Silverton; 47°31′N 116°00′W. Mfg. (concrete); silver mining. St. Joe Natl. Forest to S; Coeur d'Alene Natl. Forest to N.

Oscarville, village (1990 pop. 57), SW Alaska, near Bethel; 60°42′N 161°45′W.

Oscawana, village, Putnam co., SE N.Y., on Oscawana L. (2 mi/3.2 km long, c.1 mi/1.6 km wide), 8 mi/12.9 km NNE of Peekskill; 41°13′N 73°56′W. In dairying and farming area. Post office in Putnam Valley.

Osceola 1 (ah-see-O-luh), county (□ 1,506 sq mi/3,901 sq km; 1990 pop. 107,728), central Fla.; ⊙ Kissimmee; 28°03′N 81°09′W. Lowland area with many lakes (notably Kissimmee, Tohopekaliga, and E. Tohopekaliga), and streams of Kissimmee R. system. Agr. (citrus fruit, vegetables; cattle), lumber. Is sparsely settled except for its NE corner in suburban Orlando. Formed 1887. **2** county (□ 399 sq mi/1,033 sq km; 1990 pop. 7,267), NW Iowa, on Minn. line; ⊙ Sibley; 43°22′N 95°37′W. Rises to highest elev. (1,670 ft/509 m) in Iowa 6 mi/9.7 km NE of Sibley. Drained by Ocheyedan R. and Otter Creek. Prairie agr. area (hogs, cattle, poultry; corn, oats, soybeans). Iowa and Rush lakes in NE. Formed 1851. **3** (O-see-O-lah), county (□ 573 sq mi/1,484 sq km; 1990 pop. 20,146), central Mich.; ⊙ Reed City; 43°58′N 85°19′W. Intersected by Muskegon R. and drained by Pine R. Agr. (forage crops; cattle, hogs, poultry; wheat, oats, corn; dairy prods.). Some mfg. at Reed City. Resorts. Part of Manistee Natl. Forest in W and immediately beyond NW and SW corners of co. Organized 1869.

Osceola 1 (oh-see-OLE-uh), city (1990 pop. 4,164), ⊙ Clarke co., S Iowa, near Whitebreast Creek, c.40 mi/64 km SSW of Des Moines; 41°01′N 93°46′W. Mfg. (electrical equip., metal prods., transportation equip., apparel, dairy equip. and prods.). Stephens State Forest to SE. Settled 1850, inc. 1859. **2** (o-see-O-luh), city (1990 pop. 755), ⊙ St. Clair co., W Mo., on Osage R., arm of Truman L. (Harry S Truman Reservoir), and 85 mi/137 km SSE of Kansas City; 38°02′N 93°42′W. Agr. (cattle; wheat, sorghum). Recreational activities.

Osceola 1 (o-see-O-luh), town (1990 pop. 8,930), shares ⊙ functions with Blytheville, Mississippi co., NE Ark., 15 mi/24 km S of Blytheville, and on Mississippi R.; 35°42′N 89°59′W. In rich cotton and soybean area. Mfg. (consumer goods, construction materials, furniture, apparel, food prods., metal prods.). Inc. 1838. **2** town (1990 pop. 1,999), St. Joseph co., N Ind., 10 mi/16 km E of South Bend, and near St. Joseph R.; 41°40′N 86°04′W Light mfg. **3** (ahs-ee-O-lah), town (1990 pop. 2,075), Polk co., W Wis., on St. Croix R. (Minn. state line), and 19 mi/31 km NNE of Stillwater (Minn.); 45°19′N 92°42′W. In dairying and stock-raising area. Mfg. (wooden prods., metal prods., electrical equip., publishing, cheese). St. Croix Falls and Osceola Fish Hatcheries to NE.

Osceola (aw-see-O-luh), village (1990 pop. 879), ⊙ Polk co., E central Nebr., 20 mi/32 km SW of Columbus, and on branch of Big Blue R; 41°10′N 97°32′W. Livestock, poultry; grain. Founded c.1872.

Osceola Mills (AH-see-O-lah MILS), borough (1990 pop. 1,310), Clearfield co., central Pa., 25 mi/40 km NNE of Altoona, on Moshannon Creek; 40°51′N 78°16′W. Mfg. (apparel); surface bituminous coal, clay, timber in area. Agr. (grain; livestock, dairying). Laid out c.1857, inc. 1864.

Osceola, Mount (aw-see-YO-luh), peak (4,326 ft/1,319 m) in White Mts., Grafton co., central N.H., 6 mi/9.7 km ESE of North Woodstock, in White Mt. Natl. Forest.

Oscoda (ah-SKO-duh), county (□ 571 sq mi/1,479 sq km; 1990 pop. 7,842), NE central Mich.; ⊙ Mio; 44°40′N 84°07′W. Intersected by Au Sable R., and drained by Upper South Branch of Thunder Bay R. Agr. (grain; cattle, sheep; dairy prods., poultry). Mfg. (wood prods., metal prods.). Recreational area. Includes part of Huron Natl. Forest in S and several small lakes, especially N and S center; Mio Mt. Ski Area in center. Organized 1881.

Oscoda (ah-SKO-duh), village (1990 pop. 1,061), Iosco co., NE Mich., c.45 mi/72 km SE of Alpena, on L. Huron at mouth of Au Sable R.; 44°25′N 83°19′W. Trade center for resort and farm area (potatoes; cattle); fisheries. Mfg. (transportation equip., vinyl floor coverings). Paul B. Wurstmith Air Force Base to NW.

Oscura Peak (os-KOO-ruh) (9,650 ft/2,941 m), highest point in Sierra Oscura, on Lincoln co. and Socorro co. boundary, S central N.Mex., 29 mi/47 km W of Carrizozo. In Lincoln Natl. Forest.

Osgood 1 town (1990 pop. 1,688), Ripley co., SE Ind., 5 mi/8 km N of Versailles; 39°08′N 85°17′W. Farm trading center, with some mfg. (cement prods., shoes); grain milling, timber; limestone quarries. Laid out 1857. **2** town (1990 pop. 53), Sullivan co., N Mo., 12 mi/19 km W of Milan; 40°12′N 93°20′W.

Osgood, village (1990 pop. 255), Darke co., W Ohio, 18 mi/29 km NNE of Greenville; 40°20′N 84°29′W. In agr. area.

Osgood Mountains, N Nev., in E Humboldt co. Adam Peak (8,678 ft/2,645 m) 25 mi/40 km NE of Winnemucca, is highest point. Gold mining, tungsten deposits.

Osgoode Station, village, SE Ont., Canada, near Rideau R. and Rideau Canal, 20 mi/32 km S of Ottawa. Dairying, mixed farming.

O'Shaughnessy Dam, Calif.: see HETCH HETCHY VALLEY.

Oshawa (AHSH-uh-wuh), city (1991 pop. 129,344), SE Ont., Canada, on L. Ontario; 43°54′N 78°52′W. The production of motor vehicles, begun in 1907, is the leading industry, since Oshawa is the home site of General Motors of Canada. Other prods. include metals, glass, plastics, machine parts, furniture, leather and woolen goods, and electrical prods. On the site of a Fr. trading post; automobile mus.

Oshkosh (AWSH-kawsh), city (1990 pop. 55,006), ⊙ Winnebago co., E Wis., on L. Winnebago, where the Upper Fox R. enters; 44°01′N 88°32′W. Mfg. (apparel, transportation equip., wood prods., electrical equip., machinery). Summer resort. Father Allouez visited the site in 1670; Fr. explorers traveled there in the 18th cent.; and a Fr. fur-trading post was set up in the early 19th cent. Oshkosh grew as a lumber town. The downtown area was destroyed by fire in 1875. A branch of the Univ. of Wis. is here. Paine Art Center and Arboretum, Winnebago Mental Health Inst. to N, Experimental Aircraft Assn. Mus. and annual Fly-In in July at Whitman Field. Inc. 1846.

Oshkosh (AWSH-kawsh), town (1990 pop. 986), ⊙ Garden co., W Nebr., 37 mi/60 km NW of Ogallala, and on North Platte R; 41°24′N 102°20′W. In irrigated sugar-beet region; livestock, grain. Mfg. (wood furniture). Oregon Trail follows opposite side of river.

Osierfield (O-zhuhr-feeld), town, Irwin co., S central Ga., 8 mi/12.9 km ESE of Fitzgerald; 31°40′N 83°06′W.

Osisko Lake (o-SI-sko) W Que., Canada; 2 mi/3 km long, 2 mi/3 km wide. On W shore are mining centers of Rouyn and Noranda.

Oskaloosa, city (1990 pop. 10,632), ⊙ Mahaska co., SE Iowa, on the North and South Skunk rivers; 41°17′N 92°38′W. It is the trade and processing center of a rich farm and livestock area. Mfg. (machinery, feeds, egg prods.); steel fabrication. Coal has been mined here for over 100 years. A small fort was est. here in 1835, and it became a post on a much-traveled W trail. Pioneer Farm and Craft Mus., William Penn Col., and Vennard Col. are there. L. Keomah State Park to E. The city was settled (1844) by Quakers; inc. 1852.

Oskaloosa (ahs-kuh-LOO-suh), town (1990 pop. 1,074), ⊙ Jefferson co., NE Kansas, 23 mi/37 km NE of Topeka; 39°13′N 95°18′W. Trading point in grain, livestock, and dairy region. Perry Reservoir to W.

Osler (OS-luhr, OZ-), town (1991 pop. 634), central Sask., Canada, 18 mi/29 km NNE of Saskatoon. Mixed farming, dairying.

Oslo (AWS-lo), village (1990 pop. 362), Marshall co., NW Minn., 20 mi/32 km N of Grand Forks, N.Dak., on Red R. (N.Dak. state line); 48°11′N 97°07′W. Agr. (grain, potatoes, beans, sunflowers, sugar beets; livestock, poultry). Mfg. (fertilizer).

Osmond (AWZ-muhnd), village (1990 pop. 744), Pierce co., NE Nebr., 10 mi/16 km NNW of Pierce, and on branch of Elkhorn R, 42°21′N 97°35′W. In grain and livestock area; dairy and poultry prods. Mfg. (agr. equipment, irrigation systems).

Osnabrock (AHZ-nuh-brahk), village (1990 pop. 214), Cavalier co., NE N.Dak., 12 mi/19 km SE of Langdon; 48°40′N 98°09′W.

Osnaburgh House (AHZ-nuh-buhrg), village, NW Ont., Canada, in Patricia dist., on L. St. Joseph, 23 mi/37 km SSW of Pickle L., and 100 mi/161 km NE of Sioux Lookout; 51°08′N 90°16′W. Gold mining. Nearby is hydroelectric station.

Oso, Mount, peak (c.12,925 ft/3,940 m), in Rocky Mts., La Plata co., SW Colo., 25 mi/40 km NE of Durango.

Osoyoos (o-SOO-yuhs), town (1991 pop. 3,403), S B.C., Canada, near Wash. border, on Osoyoos L. (12 mi/19 km long), 30 mi/48 km S of Penticton; 49°02′N 119°28′W. In irrigated farming region (fruit, vegetables).

Osprey (AHS-spree), town (☐ 2 sq mi/5.2 sq km; 1990 pop. 2,597), Sarasota co., W central Fla., 10 mi/16 km S of Sarasota; 27°11′N 82°29′W. Mfg. (plastic prods., light mfg.).

Ossabaw Island (AH-suh-baw), one of the Sea Isls. (c.9 mi/14.5 km long, 7 mi/11.3 km wide), just off SE Ga. coast, in Chatham co., 15 mi/24 km S of Savannah; 31°48′N 81°05′W. Marshy. Ossabaw Sound (c.5 mi/8 km long and wide), at N end of isl., receives Ogeechee R. Extensive agr. in 19th cent., much of which has reverted to a natural state. Used by Creek Indians as hunting ground. Now administered by the Georgia Dept. of Natural Resources.

Osseo 1 (AH-see-yo), town (1990 pop. 2,704), Hennepin co., E Minn., industrial suburb 12 mi/19 km NNW of downtown Minneapolis, near Mississippi R.; 45°07′N 93°24′W. Mfg. (diversified mfg., printing and publishing, machining). Elm Creek Park Reserve to NW. **2** (AH-see-o), town (1990 pop. 1,551), Trempealeau co., W Wis., on Buffalo R., and 21 mi/34 km SE of Eau Claire; 44°34′N 91°13′W. In dairy, livestock, and poultry area; cheese. Mfg. (paint spray bottles, furniture). On Buffalo River State Trail. Settled 1851; inc. as village in 1893, as city in 1941.

Ossian 1 (OSH-en), town (1990 pop. 2,428), Wells co., E Ind., on small Longlois Creek, and 10 mi/16 km N of Bluffton; 40°53′N 85°10′W. Agr. area (soybeans, corn). Mfg. (food prods., transportation equip.); meat processing. Laid out 1850. **2** town (1990 pop. 810), Winneshiek co., NE Iowa, 11 mi/18 km S of Decorah; 43°08′N 91°45′W. In grain and dairy area. Limestone quarries nearby.

Ossineke (ah-SIN-e-kee), village (1990 pop. 1,091), Alpena co., NE Mich., on Thunder Bay of L. Huron, 10 mi/16 km S of Alpena; 44°54′N 83°25′W. Michigan Isls. Natl. Wildlife Refuge to ESE; Negwegon State Park to SE (Alcona co.).

Ossining, village (☐ 6 sq mi/15.5 sq km; 1990 pop. 22,582), Westchester co., SE N.Y., on the Hudson R.; 41°09′N 73°52′W. Mainly residential; some mfg. (medical instruments, pharmaceuticals). Ossining is the site of Sing Sing state prison (built 1825–1828). This prison was long known for its extreme discipline, but under Thomas Mott Osborne and Lewis Edward Lawes, notable reforms were introduced. By end of 19th cent., 2d-largest industrial center in Westchester. Brickyards produced bricks for Old Croton Aqueduct. Aqueduct Bridge in Ossining, one of most impressive parts of the aqueduct, is now part of the Osinning Urban Cultural Park. Maryknoll, the hq. of the Catholic Foreign Mission Society, is nearby. Settled c.1750, inc. 1813 as Sing Sing, renamed 1901.

Ossipee (AW-si-pee), town (1990 pop. 3,309), ⊙ Carroll co., E N.H., 28 mi/45 km N of Rochester; 43°43′N 71°09′W. Drained by Ossipee, Pine, Chocorua, and Lovell rivers. RR terminus at West Ossipee. Mfg. (plastic prods., printing and publishing, asphalt, lumber); timber; major source of sand and gravel for Boston. Agr. (nursery crops, vegetables; livestock, poultry; dairying). Covered bridge at village of West Ossipee, in NW (summer home of poet John Greenleaf Whittier). Resort area. Ossipee L. in NE; Ossipee L. and Heath Pond natural areas at S end of lake. Deer Cap Ski area in E. Mt. Shaw (2,975 ft/907 m) on SW boundary, in Ossipee Mts. Village of Center Ossipee in N. Inc. 1785.

Ossipee (AH-suh-pee), uninc. village, Alamance co., N central N.C., near Haw R., 7 mi/11.3 km NNW of Burlington. Tobacco, grain; chicken.

Ossipee Lake (AW-si-pee), N.H., fed by Pine R. (S), Lovell R. (W), Bearcamp R. (NW); 3.5 mi/5.6 km long, 2 mi/3.2 km wide; 43°07′N 71°08′W. Has 3 mi/4.8 km long E arm (Broad Bay), from which Ossipee R. drains into Maine. Ossipee L. and Heath Bog natural areas on S end.

Ossipee Mountain (AHS-uh-pee) (1,058 ft/322 m), York co., SW Maine, 7 mi/11.3 km N of Alfred. In Waterboro resort area.

Ossipee River (AW-si-pee), c.20 mi/32 km long, N.H.; rises in Ossipee L., E central Carroll co.; flows E through Broad Bay, past village of Effingham Falls, into SW Maine, past Kezar Falls (dam) to Saco R., 15 mi/24 km NW of Portland; 43°48′N 71°09′W.

Osterdock, town (1990 pop. 49), Clayton co., NE Iowa, on Turkey R., and 15 mi/24 km ESE of Elkader; 42°43′N 91°09′W. In dairying area.

Osterville, Mass.: see BARNSTABLE, town.

Ostrander 1 (AWS-tran-duhr), village (1990 pop. 276), Fillmore co., SE Minn., 28 mi/45 km S of Rochester, near Iowa state line; 43°36′N 92°25′W. Grain, soybeans; livestock, poultry; dairying. L. Louise State Park to SW. **2** village (1990 pop. 431), Delaware co., central Ohio, 7 mi/11 km WSW of Delaware; 40°16′N 83°13′W. Leather prods.

Ostrica (AH-strik-uh), village, Plaquemines parish, extreme SE La., on E bank (levee) of the Mississippi, and c.50 mi/80 km SE of New Orleans, in the delta. Oyster culture; hunting, fishing. Ostrica Canal, with lock through levee here, connects the Mississippi with Breton Sound (E). Oil and natural-gas wells in vicinity.

Ostuacán (os-too-ah-KAHN), town (1990 pop. 2,137), Chiapas, S Mexico, 45 mi/72 km NW of Tuxtla Gutiérrez; 17°25′N 93°18′W. Cacao, rice. Sometimes Usumacinta or Nuevo Usumacinta

O'Sullivan Dam, Wash.: see COLUMBIA BASIN PROJECT.

Osumacinta, town (1990 pop. 1,520), Chiapas, S Mexico, 10 mi/16 km NNE of Tuxtla; 16°54′N 93°05′W. Elev. 3,281 ft/1,000 m. Corn, fruit; livestock.

Oswayo (ahs-WAI-yo), borough (1990 pop. 156), Potter co., N Pa., on Oswayo R., and 10 mi/16 km N of Coudersport, on Oswayo Creek; 41°55′N 78°01′W. Agr. (corn, hay; dairying); timber. State fish hatchery.

Oswegatchie River (aks-wugh-GAH-chee), c.150 mi/241 km long, N N.Y.; rises in small lakes of the W Adirondacks; flows N, entering and issuing from Cranberry L., thence generally NW, past Gouverneur, beyond which it turns sharply SW and again NE in a bend, then continues NE and N to the St. Lawrence at Ogdensburg. West Branch (c.45 mi/72 km long) enters from S 7 mi/11.3 km SE of Gouverneur.

Oswego (ahs-WEE-go), county (☐ 1,312 sq mi/3,398 sq km; 1990 pop. 121,771), N central N.Y.; ⊙ Oswego and Pulaski; 43°28′N 76°12′W. Bounded NW by L. Ontario, S by Oneida L. and Oneida R.; crossed by the N.Y. State Barge Canal; drained by Oswego and Salmon rivers. Diversified mfg., esp. at Oswego. Dairying area; farming (strawberries); poultry, dairy cows. Limited shipping of bldg. cement, fuel oil, and limestone uses Barge Canal access to L. Ontario. Intensive recreational use of lakes and lakeshores. Formed 1816.

Oswego (ahs-WEE-go), city (☐ 11 sq mi/28 sq km; 1990 pop. 19,195), ⊙ Oswego co., N central N.Y., on L. Ontario and the Oswego R.; 43°27′N 76°30′W. The largest U.S. port on L. Ontario, it is a port of entry and a N terminus of the Barge Canal. The city's mfg. includes steel fabrication and rolled aluminum. A trading post est. here after the English founded Oswego (1722) became a vital outlet for the Albany fur trade. The strategic location prompted the bldg. of Fort Oswego (1727), Fort George (1755), and Fort Ontario (1755; an active U.S. army post until 1946, and a state historic site since 1951). These fortifications were much contested in the colonial wars. The city's importance as a lake port came with the completion of the Barge Canal (1917) and the St. Lawrence Seaway (1959). It is the seat of State Univ. Col. of Arts and Science at Oswego. Located NE of Oswego are 3 nuclear power plants. James A. Fitzpatrick (max. dependable capacity of 800 MW), 8 mi/12.9 km NE; and Nine Mile Point 1 (max. dependable capacity of 610 MW), and Nine Mile Point 2 (max. dependable capacity of 1,080 MW), both 6 mi/9.7 km NE. James Fenimore Cooper's novel *The Pathfinder* is set in the Oswego R. valley. Founded 1722, inc. as a city 1848.

Oswego (ahs-WEE-go), town (1990 pop. 1,870), ⊙ Labette co., extreme SE Kansas, on Neosho R., and 14 mi/23 km SSE of Parsons; 37°10′N 95°06′W. RR junction. Trading point in livestock, grain, and poultry area. Mfg. (pottery, construction machinery, cultured marble prods., truck and bus bodies). Sawmill. Founded 1865, inc. 1870.

Oswego (os-WEE-go), village (1990 pop. 3,876), Kendall co., NE Ill., on Fox R. (bridged here), and 4 mi/6.4 km SSW of Aurora, satellite community of Chicago; 41°42′N 88°19′W. Initial stages of urban growth occurring here. Dairying; mfg. (consumer goods, water softeners, telecommunications equip.).

Oswego River (ahs-WEE-go), 23 mi/37 km long, formed by the confluence of the Oneida and the Seneca rivers (referred to as Three Rivers), central N.Y., NW of Syracuse and flowing NW to L. Ontario at Oswego. It is a part of the state's canal-transportation system. As with Rochester and Buffalo, Oswego's Great Lakes port function has declined significantly with improvements in the St. Lawrence Seaway, development of the nation's system of superhighways and subsequent growth in trucking and, in Oswego's case, drop in demand for coal as an energy source.

Osyka (o-SAHK-ee), village (1990 pop. 483), Pike co., SW Miss., on Tangipahoa R., and 16 mi/26 km S of McComb, at La. state line; 31°00′N 90°28′W. Agr. (cotton, corn; cattle; dairying); mfg. (transportation equip.).

Otáez (o-TAH-es) or **Santa María de Otáez**, town (1990 pop. 712), Durango, N Mexico, in W foothills of Sierra Madre Occidental, 45 mi/72 km SW of Santiago Papasquiaro; 24°42′N 105°59′W. Corn, cotton, chickpeas.

Otatitlán (o-tah-tee-TLAHN), town (1990 pop. 4,679), Veracruz, SE Mexico, on Papaloapan R., and 9 mi/14 km NE of Tuxtepec. Sugarcane, coffee, fruit.

Otay, uninc. town, San Diego co., S Calif., residential suburb 12 mi/19 km SSE of downtown San Diego, on Otay R., S of Chula Vista. S end of San Diego Bay to NW; Tijuana Mts 4 mi/6.4 km to S.

Otay Mesa, uninc. town, San Diego co., S Calif., 16 mi/26 km SE of downtown San Diego and 4 mi/6.4 km

Cross references are shown in SMALL CAPITALS. The pronunciation key is on page xv. The dates of population figures are on page xii.

NE of Tijuana, Mexico. Brown Field Airport and U.S. Space Surveillance Station are here. Tijuana Internatl. Airport (Mexico) to S.

Otay River, c.25 mi/40 km long, intermittent stream, S Calif.; rises in SW San Diego co., 15 mi/24 km E of downtown San Diego, at San Miguel Mt.; flows first S through Upper and Lower Otay reservoirs, then W through San Ysidro section of San Diego, 3 mi/4.8 km N of Mex. border, to S end of San Diego Bay. Savage Dam (172 ft/52 m high, 750 ft/229 m long; completed 1919) impounds a water-supply reservoir for San Diego city.

Oteapan (o-te-AH-pan), town (1990 pop. 10,463), Veracruz, SE Mexico, on Isthmus of Tehuantepec, 8 mi/12.9 km W of Minatitlán, on RR; 18°00'N 94°39'W. Fruit; livestock; in petroleum-producing area.

Oteen (O-teen), uninc. town (1990 pop. 1,400), Buncombe co., W N.C., residential suburb 3 mi/4.8 km E of downtown Asheville, near Swannanoa R. Blue Ridge Parkway passes through town. Folk Art Center.

Otego (o-TEE-go), village (□ 1 sq mi/2.6 sq km; 1990 pop. 1,068), Otsego co., central N.Y., on the Susquehanna R., and 7 mi/11.3 km SW of Oneonta; 42°23'N 75°10'W. In dairying and grain-growing area.

Otero 1 (o-TER-o), county (□ 1,269 sq mi/3,287 sq km; 1990 pop. 20,185), SE Colo.; ⊙ La Junta; 37°53'N 103°42'W. Irrigated agr. area, drained by Purgatoire, Apishapa, and Arkansas (forms part of N boundary in W) rivers, also Horse and Timpas creeks. Cattle, poultry; wheat, hay, beans, corn, melons, vegetables, cantaloupes. Large part of Comanche Natl. Grassland in S; Horse Creek Reservoir on W boundary, in NE. Bent's Old Fort Natl. Historic Site in E. Formed 1889. **2** county (□ 6,627 sq mi/17,164 sq km; 1990 pop. 51,928), S N.Mex.; ⊙ Alamogordo; 32°37'N 105°43'W. Livestock-grazing area bordering Texas on S; small part of state line in SE corner of co. is Central-Mountain time zone boundary (N.Mex. and Hudspeth and El Paso cos., Texas, are in Mountain time zone). Gold, silver; cattle, sheep; fruit, nuts, pecans, hay, alfalfa, timber, some wheat. Part of large Fort Bliss Military Reserve in S ½ of co., extends N from El Paso, Texas; Mescalero Apache Indian Reservation in N; Sacramento Mts. in N and part of Guadalupe Mts. in SE; parts of Lincoln Natl. Forest in SE and center; part of White Sands Natl. Monument in W; Tularosa Valley, desert plain, in W, including White Sands Desert; Three Rivers Natl. Recreation Site in N; Oliver Lee State Park in N center. Formed in 1899.

Othello, town (1990 pop. 4,638), Adams co., SE Wash., 65 mi/105 km ENE of Yakima; 46°49'N 119°10'W. In Columbia basin agr. region; wheat, barley, oats, alfalfa, fruits, vegetables, peppermint; dairying; cattle, hogs; mfg. (fertilizers, food prods., printing and publishing). Scootenay Reservoir to SE; Eagle Lakes to S; large Potholes Reservoir and O'Sullivan Dam to NW. Columbia Natl. Wildlife Refuge to NW. U.S. Dept. of Energy Hanford Site to SW.

Otho, village (1990 pop. 529), Webster co., central Iowa, near Des Moines R., 5 mi/8 km S of Fort Dodge; 42°25'N 94°09'W.

Otis (O-tis), township (1990 pop. 355), Hancock co., S Maine, c.10 mi/16 km N of Ellsworth; 44°42'N 68°28'W. In recreational area.

Otis (O-dis), town (1990 pop. 1,073), Berkshire co., SW Mass., 19 mi/31 km SSE of Pittsfield; 42°13'N 73°05'W. Agr.; resort. Otis Ridge Ski Area nearby.

Otis 1 (O-tis), village (1990 pop. 451), Wash. co., NE Colo., 13 mi/21 km E of Akron; 40°08'N 102°57'W. Elev. 4,335 ft/1,321 m. Cattle; wheat, sunflowers; mfg. (construction materials). **2** village (1990 pop. 385), Rush co., central Kansas, 14 mi/23 km E of La Crosse; 38°31'N 99°02'W. In wheat area.

Otis Orchards, uninc. town (1990 pop. 3,200), Spokane co., E Wash., 14 mi/23 km ENE of Spokane, and 15 mi/24 km W of Coeur d'Alene, Idaho, 3 mi/4.8 km W of Idaho boundry. Agr. area; timber. Mfg. (wood prods., mining services). Newman L. reservoir to N; Liberty L. reservoir to S.

Otisco Lake (o-TIS-ko), easternmost of the 11 Finger Lakes, Onondaga co., central N.Y., 14 mi/23 km SW of Syracuse; 6 mi/9.7 km long, ½ mi/⁸⁄₁₀ km–1 mi/1.6 km wide; 42°52'N 76°17'W. Drains NE to Onondaga L. via Ninemile Creek.

Otisfield, town (1990 pop. 1,136), Cumberland co., SW Maine, bet. Crooked R. and Thompson L., c. 30 mi/48 km NNW of Portland; 44°05'N 70°32'W.

Otish Mountains, range in central Que., Canada, on N side of the Laurentian Plateau; c.50 mi/80 km long; 52°20'N 70°40'W. Rises to 3,700 ft/1,128 m. Eastmain, Peribonca, and Outardes rivers rise here. Range is part of the St. Lawrence–Hudson Bay watershed.

Otisville 1 village (1990 pop. 724), Genesee co., SE central Mich., 14 mi/23 km NE of Flint; 43°10'N 83°31'W. In farm area. Mfg. (fishing tackle). **2** village (1990 pop. 1,078), Orange co., SE N.Y., 7 mi/11.3 km WNW of Middletown, in the Shawangunk range; 41°28'N 74°32'W.

Otley, village, Marion co., S central Iowa, 10 mi/16 km NNE of Knoxville. In agr. area.

Oto, town (1990 pop. 118), Woodbury co., W Iowa, on Little Sioux R., and 31 mi/50 km ESE of Sioux City; 42°16'N 95°53'W. In livestock and grain area.

Otoe (AW-to), county (□ 619 sq mi/1,603 sq km; 1990 pop. 14,252), SE Nebr.; ⊙ Nebraska City; 40°38'N 96°08'W. Agr. and commercial region bounded E by Missouri R., forming Iowa and Mo. boundaries; drained by Little Nemaha R. and its branches. Mfg. at Nebraska City. Dairying; cattle, hogs; apples, corn, wheat, soybeans, sorghum. Arbor Lodge State Historical Park and Riverview Marina State Recreation Area at Nebraska City in E. Formed 1855.

Otoe, village (1990 pop. 196), Otoe co., SE Nebr., 13 mi/21 km W of Nebraska City, and on branch of Little Nemaha R; 40°43'N 96°07'W.

Otsego 1 (aht-SEE-go), county (□ 526 sq mi/1,362 sq km; 1990 pop. 17,957), N Mich.; ⊙ Gaylord; 45°01'N 84°36'W. Drained by Sturgeon and Black rivers, and by North Branch of Au Sable R. Agr. (cattle, hogs; potatoes, wheat, oats; dairy prods.); mfg. (wood prods., electronic equip.). Year-round resort area. Includes many small lakes and a state forest. Otsego State Park in SW; Tyrolean Hills Ski Area in E; Sylvan and Michawaye ski areas in center. Organized 1875. **2** county (□ 1,013 sq mi/2,624 sq km; 1990 pop. 60,517), central N.Y.; ⊙ Cooperstown; 42°37'N 75°02'W. Bounded W by Unadilla R.; drained by the Susquehanna R., issuing here from Otsego L. Mfg. at Oneonta, Unadilla, Worcester. Dairying area; also livestock; grain, hay. Canadarago and 14-mi/23-km-long Otsego lakes are physically the easternmost of the Finger Lakes. Mineral springs at Richfield Springs. Attractive region with many downstate residents' 2d homes. Formed 1791.

Otsego 1 (aht-SEE-go), town (1990 pop. 3,937), Allegan co., SW Mich., 9 mi/14.5 km ESE of Allegan, and on Kalamazoo R. (water power); 42°27'N 85°42'W. In agr. area; mfg. (plastic, paper, and metal prods.; machinery). Settled 1832; inc. as village 1865, as city 1918. **2** (aht-SEE-go), town (1990 pop. 5,836), Wright co., E Minn., 27 mi/43 km NW of Minneapolis, on Mississippi R., NE of mouth of Crow R.; 45°17'N 93°36'W. Residential community on NW fringe of Minneapolis–St. Paul (Twin Cities) urban area. Agr. includes dairying; poultry, livestock; grain, soybeans.

Otsego Lake 1 (aht-SEE-go), E central N.Y., SE of Utica, in a resort region; c.9 mi/14.5 km long; 42°45'N 74°54'W. The Susquehanna R. originates here at lake outlet from its S end at Cooperstown. State Univ. of N.Y. at Oneonta's Biological Field Station on the W shore is a major limnological research facility. The lake is the Glimmerglass of James Fenimore Cooper's tales and physically easternmost of a series of glacially derived "finger" lakes in N.Y. state. **2** Otsego co., N Mich.; 4 mi/6.4 km long; 44°57'N 84°41'W. At Send, 7 mi/11.3 km S of Gaylord, is Otsego Lake village (1990 pop. c.50). Resort with fine beaches. Otsego L. State Park is on E side.

Otselic River (aht-SIL-ik), c.45 mi/72 km long, central N.Y.; rises in S Madison co.; flows SW, past Cincinnatus, to Tioughnioga R. at Whitney Point.

Ottauquechee River (AWT-ah-KWEE-chee), c.40 mi/64 km long, E Vt.; rises in Green Mts. NE of Rutland, flows generally E, past Woodstock (dam here), to the Connecticut S of White R. Junction. Formerly Quechee R.

Ottawa 1 (AHT-uh-wah), county (□ 721 sq mi/1,867 sq km; 1990 pop. 5,634), N central Kansas; ⊙ Minneapolis; 39°07'N 97°39'W. Rolling prairie region, drained by Solomon R. and Salt Creek and in SW by Saline R. RR junction. Wheat, sorghum, alfalfa; cattle. Diversified mfg. Ottawa State Fishing L. near center of co. Rock sandstone formations in W center. Formed 1866. **2** county (□ 1,632 sq mi/4,227 sq km; 1990 pop. 187,768), SW Mich.; ⊙ Grand Haven; 42°55'N 86°13'W. Bounded W by L. Michigan; drained by Grand and Black rivers. Hogs, cattle, sheep, poultry; apples, cherries, onions, asparagus, grain; dairy prods.; tulip growing. Mfg. at Grand Haven, Holland, and Zeeland. Fisheries. Tourism; has resorts. Spring L., large backwater lake of L. Michigan, receives Grand R. in NW corner of co. Grand Haven Ski Bowl and Grand Haven State Park in NW; Holland State Park in SW. Organized 1837. **3** county (□ 263 sq mi/681 sq km; 1990 pop. 40,029), N Ohio; ⊙ Port Clinton; 41°32'N 83°06'W. Bounded NE by L. Erie; drained by Portage R. and small Toussaint and Packer creeks. Includes Perry's Victory and Internatl. Peace Memorial Natl. Monument. In the Lake Plains physiographic region. Agr. area (corn, soybeans; hogs); mfg. at Genoa, Oakharbor, Port Clinton (rubber and plastic prods., machinery). Limestone quarries; fisheries. Bass Isls. are resorts. Davis-Besse Nuclear Power Plant, 21 mi/34 km ESE of Toledo, uses cooling water from L. Erie, and has a max. dependable capacity of 918 MWe. The first electricity was generated on Aug. 28, 1977. Plant provides power to the city of Toledo and surrounding areas. The city was formed in 1840. **4** county (□ 484 sq mi/1,254 sq km; 1990 pop. 30,561), extreme NE Okla.; ⊙ Miami; 36°50'N 94°48'W. Bounded N by Kansas state line, E by Mo. state line; part of the Ozarks are in E. Drained by Neosho (headwaters of L. of the Cherokees) and Spring rivers; includes sect. of L. of the Cherokees (recreation). Contains part of lead- and zinc-mining region (centering on Picher) extending into Kansas and Mo. Also livestock raising, dairying, agr. (corn, wheat, hay, sorghum, soybeans); mfg. at Miami; timber. Spring River State Park in NE; Twin Bridges State Park near center. Formed 1907.

Ottawa (AHT-uh-wuh), city (1991 pop. 313,987), ⊙ Canada, SE Ont., at the confluence of the Ottawa and Rideau rivers; 45°25'N 75°42'W. Hull, Que., just across the Ottawa at the mouth of the Gatineau R., forms part of the metropolitan area. The Rideau Canal separates the city into upper and lower towns; along its banks and those of the rivers are many landscaped drives as well as much of the city's land area, which totals 1,500 acres/607 ha. Ottawa is not primarily an industrial center; however, it has industries that produce, among other goods, paper and paper prods., printed materials, telecommunications equip., and electronics. In the 1980s, Ottawa and its suburbs of Nepean and Kanata have become Canada's "Silicon Valley" with growth of high-technology industries. The area's industries utilize the hydroelectric power of the Ottawa (Chaudière Falls) and Gatineau valleys. Since 1940, the largest employer in Ottawa has been the federal govt. The Natl. Capital Commission, a developer of public works, has done much to redevelop the core of the city, removing old RR lines and building new parks (Confederation Square) and natl. bdgs. (Natl. Arts Center, Natl. Defence Bldg., Bank of Canada Bldg.). Development of natl. capital plan began with commissioning of Fr. architect Jacques Griber, 1937–1939. The Griber plan, which included broad boulevards, green spaces, and a regional dist. that took in both sides of Ottawa R. and city of Hull, Que., was adopted in 1950, and led to the establishment of the Natl. Capital Region (□ 4,662 sq mi/12,075 sq km; 2,719.5 sq mi/7,043.5 sq km in Ont., 1,942.5 sq mi/5,031.1 sq km in Que.). Gatineau N.C.C. Park, Que., was developed as part of the plan.

Several federal govt. offices and Can. Mus. of Civilization were relocated to Hull in 1970s and 1980s, as well as Natl. Gallery of Canada. In part because of these development projects, tourism has become Ottawa's 2d-largest industry, attracting about 4 million people annually. Ottawa proper was founded in 1827 by Col. John By, an engineer in charge of construction of the Rideau Canal. At first called Bytown, it was named after the Ottawa, an Algonquian-speaking people, in 1854. In 1858, Ottawa was chosen by Queen Victoria to be the capital of the United Provs. of Canada, and in 1867 it became the capital of the Dominion of Canada. The govt. bldgs., built bet. 1859 and 1865, were burned in 1916 but were immediately rebuilt on an enlarged scale. Other notable bldgs. are Rideau Hall, the residence of the Gov. General; the Anglican and R.C. cathedrals; the Bytown Mus.; the Can. Mus. of Nature; the Natl. Gallery; the Natl. Arts Centre; the Natl. Aviation Mus.; the Natl. Lib. and Public Archives Bldg.; the Natl. Mus. of Science and Technology; the Dominion Observatory; the Royal Mint; and the Rideau Centre complex. Univ. of Ottawa, St. Paul Univ., and Carleton Univ. are in the city. Ottawa is largely a bilingual city because federal govt. employees are required to know both Eng. and Fr.

Ottawa 1 (AHT-uh-wah), city (1990 pop. 17,451), ⊙ La Salle co., N central Ill., at the confluence of the Fox and Ill. rivers; 41°21′N 88°50′W. In a fertile farm area, the city has grain-oriented agr. and manufactures glass, tools, bldg. materials, and automobile parts. Points of interest include the site of the 1st Lincoln-Douglas debate (1858) and Fort Johnson (1832). Several state parks are in the area, and scenic attractions along the rivers draw many visitors. Inc. as a city 1853. **2** city (1990 pop. 10,667), ⊙ Franklin co., E Kansas, on the Marais des Cygnes R.; 38°36′N 95°16′W. The RR and industrial center of a farm area, it has a variety of light industries. The city is named for the Ottawa, who moved there (1832) after ceding their Ohio lands to the U.S.; they were subsequently removed (1867) to Okla. Ottawa Univ. is here. Inc. 1867.

Ottawa, village (1990 pop. 3,999), ⊙ Putnam co., NW Ohio, 18 mi/29 km N of Lima, and on Blanchard R.; 41°01′N 84°02′W. Mfg. of television equip., food and dairy prods., clay and wood prods. Oil wells, stone quarries. Founded 1833.

Ottawa, river, c.700 mi/1,130 km long, largest tributary of the St. Lawrence R., Canada; rises in the Laurentian Highlands, SW Que., and flows generally W through La Vérendrye Provincial Park to L. Timiskaming, then SE forming part of the Que.-Ont. border, past Ottawa, and into the St. Lawrence R. near Montreal. Its lower course has several expansions, known as the Allumette, Chats, and Deschênes lakes and L. of the Two Mountains. Among its chief tributaries are the Gatineau, Lièvre, and Coulonge rivers. Hydroelectric power stations at La Cave, Des Joachims, Bryson, Chenaux, Chats, Chaudière Falls, and Carillion have a combined generating capacity of about 1.5 million kw. The river is navigable for large vessels as far as Ottawa; it is connected with L. Ontario by the Rideau Canal system. There is some farming in the valley below Pembroke, but lumbering is the chief industry along the lower river. Samuel de Champlain, the Fr. explorer, was the 1st European to visit (1613–1615) the valley; the river, known then as the Grand R., later became an important highway for fur traders and missionaries.

Ottawa Hills, residential village (1990 pop. 4,543), Lucas co., NW Ohio, just W of Toledo; 41°40′N 83°39′W. Settled 1916, inc. 1924.

Ottawa Islands, SE Keewatin Dist., N.W.T., Canada, group of 24 small isls. and islets in Hudson Bay, off NW Ungava Peninsula; c.70 mi/113 km long, 50 mi/80 km wide; 60°00′N 80°00′W. Main isls. are Booth, Bronson, Gilmour (rises to over 1,800 ft/549 m), Perley, J. Gordon, Paltee, and Eddy.

Ottawa River, c.50 mi/80 km long, W Ohio; rises in Hardin co.; flows NW and W, past Lima, then N, past Elida, to Auglaize R. in Putnam co.; 40°59′N 84°14′W.

Otter Creek 1 30 mi/48 km long, S central Utah; rises in Fish L. Plateau in central Sevier co.; flows SSW, through Sevier Plateau, through Koosharem Reservoir, past Koosharem to Otter Creek Reservoir (5.5 mi/8.9 km long), formed by dam on East Fork of Sevier R. Creek is dammed near source to Sevier R. 13 mi/21 km ESE of Junction. **2** c.100 mi/161 km long, W Vt.; rises in Green Mts. near Dorset, flows generally NW, past Rutland, Proctor, Middlebury, and Vergennes, to L. Champlain near Ferrisburg. In upper course, flows bet. the Taconics (W) and Green Mts.

Otter Creek Recreational Area, Ky.: see MEADE.

Otter Lake 1 village (1990 pop. 474), Lapeer and Genesee cos., E Mich., 18 mi/29 km NE of Flint; 43°12′N 83°27′W. In farm and lake region. Mfg. (transportation equip., chemicals). **2** resort village (1990 pop. 460), Oneida co., central N.Y., in the W Adirondacks, on small Otter L., 35 mi/56 km N of Utica; 43°36′N 75°06′W.

Otter Lake, reservoir (□ 1 sq mi/2.6 sq km), Macoupin co., central Ill., on West Fork of Otter Creek, 30 mi/48 km NW of Springfield; 39°25′N 89°55′W. Max. capacity of 24,708 acre-ft. Formed by Otter L. Dam (71 ft/22 m high), built (1969) for water supply; also used for recreation.

Otter, Peaks of (Flat Top: 4,004 ft/1,220 m; Sharp Top: 3,870 ft/1,180 m), twin peaks, Bedford co., W central Va., 8 mi/12.9 km NW of Bedford, in Blue Ridge, in Jefferson Natl. Forest, immediately S of Blue Ridge Natl. Parkway.

Otter River, Mass.: see GARDNER.

Otter Tail, county (□ 2,225 sq mi/5,763 sq km; 1990 pop. 50,714), W Minn.; ⊙ Fergus Falls; 46°24′N 95°42′W. Extensively watered agr. area drained by Pelican, Pomme de Terre, and Otter Tail rivers, and numerous lakes. Alfalfa, hay, wheat, corn, oats, barley, soybeans, sugar beets, beans, sunflowers; hogs, sheep, cattle, poultry; dairying. Chief lakes are L. Lida in NW, and Dead L. and Otter Tail L. in center. Orwell Wildlife Area in SW on Orwell Reservoir; Maplewood State Park in NW center; Inspiration Peak (1,750 ft/533 m) State Park in S. Formed 1858.

Otter Tail Lake (□ 23 sq mi/60 sq km), Otter Tail co., W Minn., 17 mi/27 km ENE of Fergus Falls; 9 mi/14.5 km long, 3 mi/4.8 km wide; 46°24′N 95°39′W. Elev. 1,320 ft/402 m. Fed from NW and drained to SW by Otter Tail R. Fishing resorts.

Otter Tail River, 150 mi/241 km long, W central Minn.; rises in S part of Clearwater co., c.35 mi/56 km SW of Bemidji; flows S, through Elbow, Many Point, and Round lakes, through Tamarac Natl. Wildlife Refuge, past Frazee, through Rose and Long lakes, E through Mud, Little Pine, and Pine lakes, S through Pine, Rush, and Otter Tail lakes, then W, past Fergus Falls through Orwell Reservoir, to Breckenridge (opposite Wahpeton, N.Dak.), where it joins Bois de Sioux R. to form Red R. of the North; 47°01′N 95°32′W.

Otterbein, town (1990 pop. 1,291), Benton co., W Ind., 15 mi/24 km SE of Fowler; 40°29′N 87°05′W. Mfg. (bldg. components, transportation equip.). Agr. area (corn, soybeans; livestock). Laid out 1872.

Otterburne, village, SE Man., Canada, on Rat R., and 27 mi/43 km S of Winnipeg; 49°30′N 97°03′W. Grain; dairying.

Ottertail, village (1990 pop. 313), Otter Tail co., W Minn., just E of Otter Tail L., 27 mi/43 km NE of Fergus Falls; 46°25′N 95°33′W. Dairying; poultry; grain; mfg. (fur processing; concrete). Numerous lakes in area. Sometimes Otter Tail.

Otterville 1 town (1990 pop. 115), Jersey co., W Ill., 8 mi/12.9 km SSW of Jerseyville; 39°02′N 90°24′W. In apple-growing area. **2** town (1990 pop. 507), Cooper co., central Mo., near Lamine R., 12 mi/19 km E of Sedalia; 38°42′N 93°00′W. Cattle; corn, wheat; lumber.

Otterville, village, S Ont., Canada, on Otter Creek, and 16 mi/26 km SE of Woodstock; 42°55′N 80°36′W. Dairy prods.; tobacco (declining), fruit (cherries, peaches, apples, strawberries), peanuts, vegetables.

Ottine, uninc. village (1990 pop. 90), Gonzales co., S central Texas, on San Marcos R., and 10 mi/16 km NW of Gonzales. Health resort, with mineral springs. Site of Palmetto State Park, known for its semi-tropical plants.

Ottosen, town (1990 pop. 72), Humboldt co., N central Iowa, 15 mi/24 km NW of Dakota City; 42°53′N 94°22′W.

Ottoville, village (1990 pop. 842), Putnam co., NW Ohio, 18 mi/29 km NW of Lima, and on Auglaize R.; 40°56′N 84°20′W.

Ottumwa, city (1990 pop. 24,488), ⊙ Wapello co., SE Iowa, on both banks of the Des Moines R.; 41°01′N 92°25′W. A commercial and industrial center in a farm and coal area, Ottumwa's economy is based on its meat-packing plant and a farm-machinery industry, although it has a diverse variety of other mfg. In the center of the city is Ottumwa Park, which was developed from a reclaimed river bottom. Indian Hills Community Col. extension is 6 mi/9.7 km N, near airport. Inc. 1851.

Otumba de Gómez Farías (o-TOOM-bah dai GO-mes fah-REE-ahs), city (1990 pop. 6,565) and township, ⊙ Otumba municipio, Mexico state, central Mexico, 30 mi/48 km NE of Mexico city; 19°42′N 98°45′W. Maguey, corn; livestock. On nearby plains Cortés fought a fierce battle (1520) in which 20,000 Indians are said to have been slain.

Otway, village (1990 pop. 105), Scioto co., S Ohio, 13 mi/21 km WNW of Portsmouth; 38°52′N 83°11′W. Sawmills.

Otwell, village (1990 pop. 500), Pike co., SW Ind., 9 mi/14.5 km WNW of Jasper. Agr. (wheat, corn; cattle, hogs). Bituminous coal, old surface mines. Pike State Forest to SW.

Otzoloapan (ot-so-LO-AH-pahn), town (1990 pop. 1,302), in SW Mexico state, Mexico, 16 mi/25 km NW of Tejupilco de Hidalgo; 19°14′N 99°56′W. Elev. 5,906 ft/1,800 m. Agr. (sugarcane, peanuts), cattle raising.

Otzolotepec, Mexico: see VILLA CUAUHTÉMOC.

Ouachita (WAHSH-uh-tah), county (□ 739 sq mi/1,914 sq km; 1990 pop. 30,574), S Ark.; ⊙ Camden; 33°35′N 92°52′W. Drained by Ouachita R. (forms S part of E boundary); Little Missouri R. forms W part of N boundary, Two Bayou forms part of E boundary, Smackover Creek forms part of S boundary. Agr. (cattle, hogs). Mfg. at Camden. Oil and gas wells; timber; gravel, asphalt; lumbering. Poison Spring Battleground State Historical Monument in W center; part of Poison Springs Wildlife Management Area and White Oak L. State Park in NW. Formed 1844.

Ouachita (waw-shi-TAW), parish (□ 642 sq mi/1,663 sq km; 1990 pop. 142,191), NE central La.; ⊙ Monroe; 32°31′N, 92°05′W. Bounded E by Bayou Lafourche; intersected by Ouachita R. and Bayou D'Arbonne. Agr. (cotton, rice, soybeans, blueberries, peaches, sorghum, corn, home gardens, nursery crops, vegetables; cattle, horses, exotic fowl, alligators; dairying). Large natural-gas fields, gas pipelines. Logging, varied mfg., including food prods., apparel, paper prods., plastic prods., chemicals, electronic equip., industrial machinery, metal prods. Explored by Hernando de Soto in 1541. Formed 1807. Part of D'Arbonne Natl. Wildlife Refuge in N, Cheniere Brake Fish Preserve and lake at center, Ouachita and part of Russell Sage State Wildlife areas in E.

Ouachita, Lake (WAHSH-uh-tah), reservoir (□ 63 sq mi/163 sq km), W central Ala., on Ouachita R., mostly within Ouachita Natl. Forest, 7 mi/11.3 km NW of Hot Springs; 34°34′N 93°11′W. Max. capacity 3,760,000 acre-ft. Extends E-W into Garland and Montgomery cos. Formed by Blakely Mt. Dam (240 ft/73 m high), built (1953) by Army Corps of Engineers for power generation, flood control, and recreation.

Ouachita Mountains 1 (WAHSH-uh-tah), range of E-W ridges bet. the Arkansas and Red rivers, extending c.200 mi/320 km from central Ark. into SE Okla. Magazine Mt. (c.2,800 ft/850 m high) is the tallest peak. The Ouachita Mts. are geologically considered an outlier of the Appalachian Mts. They are composed of strongly folded and faulted sedimentary rocks. A whetstone industry is near Hot Springs, Ark. Mineral springs, lakes, and extensive wooded areas attract tourists. Several parts of the region have been set aside as

Cross references are shown in SMALL CAPITALS. The pronunciation key is on page xv. The dates of population figures are on page xii.

public parks or forest reservations. **2** (WAH-shuh-tuh), LeFlore, McCortain, Pushmataha, Atoka, and Latimer cos., S Okla. Range, formed by folding and faulting of resistant sedimentary rocks. Long, parallel ridges that run generally E-W. Ridges are as much as 1,500 ft/460 m above the adjacent valleys; greatest elev. is 2,666 ft/810 m. Farming in valleys; timber and grazing on slopes.

Ouachita River (WAHSH-uh-tah), c.600 mi/966 km long; rising in the Ouachita Mts., Polk co., W Ark., N of Mena; flows E, SE, and S through the Ouachita Mts. and the cotton-producing region of S Ark. and NE La. and into the Red R. system. It is joined by the Tensas R. at Jonesville, La., to form the Black R. Hot Springs, Ark., and Monroe, La., are the largest cities on the river; also important are Arkadelphia and Camden, Ark. The river is navigable for shallow-draft vessels below Arkadelphia. Three dams in the river near Hot Springs—Remmel (completed 1925), Carpenter (1931), and Blakeley Mt. (1955)—impound respectively L. Catherine, L. Hamilton, and L. Ouachita (63 sq mi/101 sq km, Ark.'s largest). Flows through Felsenthal Natl. Wildlife Refuge in S Ark. and Upper Ouachita Natl. Wildlife Refuge in N La. There is a hydroelectric power plant at Blakeley Mt. Dam. Felsenthal Dam in S Ark. impounds L. Jack Lee. The lakes, part of a Federal flood-control project, are the center of a popular recreation area.

Ouachita River, Texas and Okla.: see WASHITA river.

Ouanaminthe (wah-nah-MANGT), town (1982 pop. 7,276), Nord-Est dept., NE Haiti, on Massacre R. (Dominican Republic border), opposite Dajabón, 34 mi/55 km ESE of Cap-Haïtien; 19°33′N 71°44′W. Citrus fruits, sugarcane; sugar processing. Gold deposits nearby.

Ouest (WEST), department (1982 pop. 1,551,792), S central Haiti, bounded on N by Artibonite and Centre depts., E by Dominican Republic, W by Gulf of Gonaïves, S by Sud-Est dept.; ⊙ Port-au-Prince, both natl. and departmental; 18°40′N 72°20′W. Central part is the fertile Cul-de-Sac plain, bounded in N and S by mountains. Produces sugarcane, cotton, fruits, tobacco, sisal; has bauxite and manganese deposits.

Ouiatchouanish River (wee-uhch-WAH-nish), S central Que., Canada; outlet of Commissioners L.; flows N past Lac Bouchette to L. St. John at Val Jalbert. Just above its mouth are 236 ft/72 m falls.

Ouje-Bougoumou, village, central Que., Canada, on N shore of L. Opemisca, 10 mi/16 km N of Chapais. Planned Cree community est. 1989 to put end to 75 years of relocations of people by mining interests. Road terminus. Cultural center.

Ouray (YUR-ai), county (□ 542 sq mi/1,404 sq km; 1990 pop. 2,295), SW central Colo.; ⊙ Ouray; 38°09′N 107°46′W. Sheep-grazing and mining region, drained by Uncompahgre R. Gold, silver, lead, copper. Includes parts of Uncompahgre Natl. Forest in NW corner and S, small part of San Juan Forest on S boundary, and ranges of Rocky Mts. Ridgway State Park in center. Formed 1883.

Ouray (YUR-aī), town (1990 pop. 644), ⊙ Ouray co., SW central Colo., on Uncompahgre R., in San Juan Mts., and 85 mi/137 km SE of Grand Junction; 38°01′N 107°40′W. Elev. 7,706 ft/2,349 m. Health resort (Ouray Hot Springs) with mineral hot springs. Some agr. (grain, potatoes; livestock). Mfg. (printing and publishing). Gold, silver, lead, and copper mines in vicinity. Surrounded by Uncompahgre Natl. Forest. Wetterhorn Peak to E. Settled 1875; inc. 1884.

Ouray Peak (13,955 ft/4,253 m), Chaffer and Saquache cos., central Colo., in S tip of Sawatch Mts., 18 mi/29 km SW of Salida, E of Continental Divide.

Outagamie (out-a-GAIM-ee), county (□ 644 sq mi/1,668 sq km; 1990 pop. 140,510), E Wis.; ⊙ Appleton; 44°24′N 88°27′W. Drained by Wolf, Fox, and Embarrass rivers. Dairying and paper milling are principal industries. Some livestock raising (cattle, hogs, sheep, poultry) and farming (barley, oats, wheat, corn, soybeans, peas, beans, alfalfa, hay). Mfg. at Appleton, Kaukauna, Kimberly. Urbanized in S along Fox R. Part of Oneida Indian Reservation in E. Formed 1851.

Outaouais, suburban region, SW Que., Canada, opposite Ottawa, Ont., on Ottawa (Outaouais) R. It is the Que. portion of the Natl. Capital Region (□ 750 sq mi/1,942.5 sq km). Includes cities of Hull and Gatineau; Gatineau N.C.C. Park. Gatineau R. crosses region from N, enters Ottawa R. at Hull. Purpose of the Natl. Capital Commission region was to coordinate govt. activities; maintain quality of development, including limits to construction in vicinity of Parliament bldgs.; and establish greenways and parks. Federal govt. office bldgs. and the Canadian Mus. of Civilization were built in Hull in early 1980s. Inclusion of Que. portion of plan was seen as an attempt to appease separatist sentiments in the Fr.-speaking prov.

Outardes, Rivière aux (zoo-TAHRD, reev-YER o), 300 mi/483 km central Que., Canada, rises in Otish Mts., flows S, through Pletipi L., to the St. Lawrence 18 mi/29 km SW of Baie Comeau. Several waterfalls.

Outer Banks or **the Banks**, E N.C., SE Va., chain of sand barrier isls. and peninsulas paralleling the Atlantic coast enclosing several saltwater bodies called sounds, marked by 3 prominent capes, Cape Hatteras (E), Cape Lookout (SE), and Cape Fear (S). State Highway 12 runs length of banks in N and center. Known for shifting shoals and changing water depths, hazardous to shipping; also vulnerable to hurricanes. Banks are generally 1 mi/1.6 km wide or less. Includes Cape Lookout and Cape Hatteras Natl. Seashore in E, Pea Isl. Natl. Wildlife Refuge in NE. In S, banks are separated only by channel of Intracoastal Waterway, part natural, part man-made; farther N , the channel widens into Bogue and Core sounds (both 3 mi/4.8 km–5 mi/8 km wide); in center coast, channel widens further in Pamlico Sound (20 mi/32 km–30 mi/48 km wide), which is connected to Albermarle Sound in N by parallel Croatan (W) and Roanoke (E) sounds, then narrows in Currituck Sound, which extends into SE Va., as Back Bay; several large estuaries extend inland, especially Neuse R., Pamlico R., and Chowan R. N part of banks is attached to mainland at Virginia Beach, Va.

Outer Barrier, series of sandy barrier isls. or offshore bars, extending c.75 mi/121 km along the S shore of L.I., SE N.Y., from Rockaway Beach at the W-E end of Shinnecock Bay, and separating a series of lagoons (Great South Bay, Moriches Bay, Mecox Bay, and Shinnecock Bay) from the Atlantic Ocean. East Rockaway, Jones, Fire Isl., Moriches, Mecox Bay, and Shinnecock inlets pierce the barrier, forming the narrow, sandy isls. Includes the resort communities of Atlantic Beach, Long Beach, and Westhampton Beach, and Fire Isl. Natl. Seashore; Jones Beach State Park and other recreational areas are found here. The sparsely settled and largely undeveloped low-lying isls. suffer from wave erosion. During storms they are sometimes inundated and occasionally pierced. Strong littoral drift requires constant dredging of inlets for navigation by fishing and pleasure boats.

Outer Brewster Island, Mass.: see BREWSTER ISLANDS.

Outerbridge Crossing, N.Y. and N.J., highway bridge across Arthur Kill, bet. Tottenville, Staten Isl., and Perth Amboy, N.J.; 40°31′N 74°15′W. Completed 1928 by Port of N.Y. Authority, it is a cantilever structure; total length of truss spans is 2,100 ft/640 m, and main span is 750 ft/229 m long and 142 ft/43 m above water.

Outlook, town (1991 pop. 2,091), S central Sask., Canada, on South Saskatchewan R., and 50 mi/80 km SSW of Saskatoon; 51°30′N 107°03′W. Wheat.

Outlook, village (1990 pop. 109), Sheridan co., NE Mont., 13 mi/21 km NW of Plentywood; Canada (Sask.) border, 7 mi/11.3 km N; 48°54′N 104°47′W. Grain, hay, safflower, sunflower; sheep, hogs, cattle, exotic and game animals.

Outremont, city (1991 pop. 22,935), S central Que., Canada, residential suburb 1 mi/2 km W of downtown Montreal, on Montreal Isl.; 45°31′N 73°37′W. Bounded N, E, and S by city of Montreal, and on W by city of Mont-Royal. Mont-Royal Park to E; Univ. of Montreal campus to S.

Ouzinkie (oo-ZEEN-kee), village (1990 pop. 209), S Alaska, on Spruce Isl., in Gulf of Alaska, 9 mi/14.5 km NNW of Kodiak; 57°56′N 152°27′W. Salmon fishing and canning. Has an Orthodox church. Shipyard est. here by Russians c.1800. Also spelled Uzinki.

Ovando (uh-VAN-do), village (1990 pop. 100), Powell co., W Mont., on Warren Creek, near Blackfoot R., 41 mi/66 km ENE of Missoula. Timber, hay; cattle, sheep. Salmon L. State Park to W; Lolo Natl. Forest to N; Helena Natl. Forest and Lincoln State Forest to E; Lolo Natl. Forest and Clearwater State Forest to W.

Ovens Peninsula (3 mi/5 km long, 1 mi/2 km wide), SW N.S., Canada, 4 mi/6 km SSE of Lunenburg. Former gold-mining area.

Overbrook, village (1990 pop. 920), Osage co., E Kansas, 20 mi/32 km SSE of Topeka. Livestock; grain, feeds.

Overgaard, uninc. town (1990 pop. 750), Navajo co., E central Ariz., 43 mi/69 km S of Winslow, and 3 mi/4.8 km SE of Heber, in Apache-Sitgreaves Natl. Forest. Elev. c.6,000 ft/1,829 m. Timber. Fort Apache Indian Reservation and Mogollon Rim Escarpment to S.

Overland, residential city (1990 pop. 17,987), St. Louis co., E Mo., residential, business, and industrial suburb 10 mi/16 km WNW of downtown St. Louis; 38°42′N 90°22′W. Mfg. (machinery, chemicals, printing, signs, processed foods). U.S. military records center. Inc. 1939.

Overland Park, city (1990 pop. 111,790), 4th-largest city in Kansas, Johnson co., NE Kansas, a residential suburb 8 mi/12.9 km SSW of downtown Kansas City, Kansas; 38°54′N 94°40′W. Mfg. (printing and publishing, apparel, aircraft parts, cement, prepared foods, salt, chemicals, marine accessories, signs). It has profited from the regional growth and development in the burgeoning Kansas City area. Overland Park has become one of the fastest-growing U.S. cities, marked by a pop. increase of nearly 37% bet. 1980 and 1990. Inc. 1960.

Overland Trail, any of several trails of W migration in the U.S. The term is sometimes used to mean all the trails W from the Missouri to the Pacific and sometimes for the central trails only. Particularly, the term has been applied to a S alternate route of the OREGON TRAIL. It branched from the parent trail at the junction of the North Platte and South Platte rivers and followed the South Platte to present Julesburg, Colo., where it left the river and W overland to the North Platte, rejoining the parent trail east of Fort Laramie, Wyo. The term is also particularly applied to a route to Calif. that went W from Fort Bridger to the Great Salt L. (thus duplicating in part the Mormon Trail), then on to Sutter's Fort in Calif.; it was much used by immigrants bound for Calif.

Overlea (OH-ver-lee), village (1990 pop. 12,137), Baltimore co., central Md., 6 mi/9.7 km NE of downtown Baltimore; 39°22′N 76°31′W. One of Baltimore's earliest suburbs and mostly rowhouses, it (along with nearby Parkville) was once called Lavender Hill.

Overmountain Victory National Historic Trail, N.C., S.C., Tenn., Va., follows the path of Revolutionary patriots. It is 272 mi/438 km long and terminates in S at Kings Mt., S.C. Authorized 1980.

Overseas Highway, the 100 mi/161 km segment of U.S. 1 that links the Fla. Keys bet. Key Largo in the NE and Key West in the SW. Follows the route of Henry Flagler's "overseas railway," which reached Key West from Miami in 1912. When the great hurricane of 1935 destroyed the RR, its right-of-way and numerous bridges were rebuilt as a 2-lane highway that carries U.S. 1 to Key West.

Overton, county (□ 442 sq mi/1,145 sq km; 1990 pop. 17,636), N Tenn.; ⊙ Livingston, 36°20′N 85°17′W. In the Cumberlands; drained by affluents of Obey and Cumberland rivers. Includes part of Dale Hollow Reservoir. Agr. (corn, hay, tobacco, fruits; livestock, poultry); dairy prods. Coal mining, lumbering; mfg. at Livingston (clothing, auto parts). First commercial oil well in Tenn. was sunk here in 1866. Formed 1806.

Overton 1 (O-vuhr-tuhn), town (1990 pop. 1,111), Clark co., SE Nev., on Muddy R., near its mouth in N arm (Virgin R.) of L. Mead (L. Mead Natl. Recreation Area), and c.45 mi/72 km NE of Las Vegas. Overton Beach Marina, L. Mead 10 mi/16 km to SE. Cattle, poultry; hay. Lost City Mus. has Pueblo Indian relics. Moapa Indian Reservation to W. Valley of Fire State Park to SW. **2** town (1990 pop. 2,105), Rusk co., E Texas, 19 mi/31 km ESE of Tyler; an oil center in E Texas field; 32°16′N 94°58′W. RR junction; cattle; dairying; vegetables, watermelons; mfg. (natural-gas processing, metal fabrication, wood prods.). Boomed after oil discovery (1930).

Overton, village (1990 pop. 547), Dawson co., S central Nebr., 15 mi/24 km ESE of Lexington, near Platte R; 40°44′N 99°32′W. Grain; livestock.

Ovett (o-VET), uninc. village (1990 pop. 600), Jones co., SE Miss., 16 mi/26 km SSE of Laurel. Agr. (cotton, corn; cattle, poultry); timber; mfg. (pressure tanks). Oil-producing area. At W edge of De Soto Natl. Forest.

Ovid, town (1990 pop. 1,442), Clinton co., S central Mich., 10 mi/16 km E of St. Johns, and on Maple R.; 43°00′N 84°22′W. In agr. area; mfg. (metal-forming equip., dairy prods.). Plotted 1857; inc. 1869.

Ovid 1 village (1990 pop. 349), Sedgwick co., NE Colo., on S. Platte R., near Nebr. state line, 6 mi/9.7 km WSW of Julesburg; 40°57′N 102°23′W. Elev. 3,521 ft/1,073 m. Trade point in grain, cattle region; beet sugar. Mfg. (prepared foods). **2** uninc. village (1990 pop. 145), Bear Lake co., SE Idaho, 5 mi/8 km WSW of Montpelier; elev. 7,424 ft/2,263 m. Timber; cattle. Lumber. Cache Natl. Forest to W. **3** village (1990 pop. 660), ⊙ Seneca co., W central N.Y., 23 mi/37 km NW of Ithaca, bet. Seneca and Cayuga lakes; 42°40′N 76°49′W. In agr. area (vineyards; fruits, grain); dairy prods. Willard Correctional Facility is to W.

Oviedo (o-VEE-do), town (□ 13 sq mi/34 sq km; 1990 pop. 11,114), Seminole co., central Fla., 14 mi/23 km NE of Orlando, near L. Jessup; 28°39′N 81°10′W. Inc. 1925.

Ovilla, town (1990 pop. 2,027), Ellis and Dallas cos., N Texas, residential suburb 17 mi/27 km SSW of downtown Dallas; 32°32′N 96°53′W. Agr. area on fringe of large Dallas–Fort Worth urban area (cotton, nursery crops; cattle; dairying).

Owaneco (OH-wan-e-co), village (1990 pop. 260), Christian co., central Ill., 7 mi/11.3 km SE of Taylorville; 39°28′N 89°11′W. In agr. area. Near Taylorville Correctional Center.

Owasa, town (1990 pop. 37), Hardin co., central Iowa, 7 mi/11.3 km NW of Eldora; 42°25′N 93°12′W. In agr. area.

Owasco (o-WAS-ko), resort village (1990 pop. 400), Cayuga co., W central N.Y., in Finger Lakes region, bet. Owasco and Skaneateles lakes, 8 mi/12.9 km SE of Auburn; 42°53′N 76°29′W.

Owasco Lake (o-WAS-ko), one of the Finger Lakes, Cayuga co., W central N.Y., bet. Cayuga L. (W) and Skaneateles L. (E); extends c.11 mi/18 km SSE from Auburn, at its outlet; 42°50′N 76°31′W. Fillmore Glen State Park is near S end.

Owasso (o-WAH-so), city (1990 pop. 11,151), Tulsa co., NE Okla., suburb 11 mi/18 km NE of downtown Tulsa, near Bird Creek; 36°16′N 95°50′W. Mfg. (machining, plastics fabrication, electrical panels). Tulsa Internatl. Airport to S.

Owatonna (o-wuh-TAWN-uh), city (1990 pop. 19,386), ⊙ Steele co., SE Minn., 62 mi/100 km S of Minneapolis, on Straight R.; 44°05′N 93°13′W. RR junction. Mfg. (furniture, consumer goods, electronic equip., apparel, machinery, printing and publishing). Agr. (corn, oats, soybeans, peas, alfalfa; poultry, livestock; dairying). Rice L. State Park to E.

Owego (o-WEE-go), village (□ 2 sq mi/5.2 sq km; 1990 pop. 4,442), ⊙ Tioga co., S N.Y., on the Susquehanna R. at mouth of Owego Creek, and 18 mi/29 km W of Binghamton; 42°06′N 76°15′W. RR junction; mfg. (hardwood lumber, computers, RR items, iron castings); agr. (dairy prods.; poultry). Thomas C. Platt b. here. Settled 1787 and inc. 1827 on site of Native Amer. village destroyed (1779) in Sullivan campaign.

Owego Creek, c.35 mi/56 km long, S N.Y.; rises in S Cortland co.; flows generally SSW to the Susquehanna R. at Owego.

Owen 1 county (□ 387 sq mi/1,002 sq km; 1990 pop. 17,281), SW central Ind.; ⊙ Spencer; 39°19′N 86°50′W. Agr. (soybeans, corn, wheat, fruits; hogs, cattle; dairying). Mfg. at Spencer. Lumber milling; limestone quarrying; timber. Drained by West Fork of White R. and Mill Creek. McCormick's Creek State Park in E; Owen-Putnam State Forest and part of Lieber State Recreation Area on Cataract L. in N. Formed 1818. **2** county (□ 354 sq mi/917 sq km; 1990 pop. 9,035), N Ky.; ⊙ Owenton; 38°31′N 84°49′W. Bounded SW by Kentucky R., NW by Eagle Creek; drained in E by Eagle Creek. Rolling upland agr. area (burley tobacco, corn, hay, alfalfa; cattle, poultry; dairying), in Bluegrass region. Lead and zinc mines, limestone quarries. Twin Eagle Wildlife Management Area in NW, Kleber Wildlife Management Area in S; small Elmer Davis L. and Elk L. reservoirs in center of co. Formed 1819.

Owen, town (1990 pop. 895), Clark co., central Wis., on small Poplar R., and 45 mi/72 km W of Wausau; 44°57′N 90°34′W. RR junction. In dairying, livestock, and lumbering area; mfg. (cheese, wooden prods., drafting supplies). Settled c.1890; inc. as village 1904, as city 1925.

Owen, Mount, Wyo.: see GRAND TETON NATIONAL PARK.

Owen Sound, city (1991 pop. 21,674), SE Ont., Canada, on Owen Sound; 44°34′N 80°56′W. Port and RR terminal in a farming region, with large grain elevators; mfg. (tractor trailers, glass, paper, printing); fish processing.

Owendale, village (1990 pop. 285), Huron co., E Mich., 14 mi/23 km WSW of Bad Axe, near Saginaw Bay; 43°43′N 83°16′W.

Owens Lake, Calif.: see OWENS RIVER.

Owens River, c.120 mi/193 km long, Calif.; rises in the Sierra Nevada, SW Mono co., E Calif., c. 25 mi/40 km ESE of Yosemite Village, S of June L.; flows SSE through L. Crowley reservoir, past Bishop, Independence, and Lone Pine; enters Owens L. (dry), 25 mi/40 km SE of Mt. Whitney. At a point c.45 mi/72 km NW of Owens L., Los Angeles Aqueduct diverts tributary streams and river's water to Los Angeles, c.15 mi/24 km N of Independence and parallels river on W. Evaporation and ground absorption rates in Owens L. exceed in flow from Owens R. and other streams.

Owens Valley, Calif.: see OWENS RIVER.

Owensboro, city (1990 pop. 53,549), ⊙ Daviess co., W Ky., 82 mi/132 km WSW of Louisville, on the Ohio R. (bridged to Ind.); 37°45′N 87°07′W. Elev. 401 ft/122 m. It is an important tobacco market and a shipping point for a farm and oil region. Mfg. (limestone, whiskey, food processing, electrical motors, rubber gaskets, vinyl windows, coal and steel processing, office furniture, fertilizers, tobacco prods., metal stamping). Confederates attacked and burned part of the city, including the courthouse, in 1864. Owensboro-Daviess Co. Airport in SW part of city. Owensboro is home to Kentucky Wesleyan Col., Brescia Col., and Owensboro Community Col., to SE; the Mus. of Science and Industry, Mus. of Fine Arts, Owensboro Symphony, Owensboro Ice Arena. Carpenter and Kingfisher lakes (natural) to NE; Ben Hawes State Park to W; Lock and Dam No. 45 is here, on Ohio R. Settled 1798; inc. as city 1866.

Owensville, city (1990 pop. 2,325), Gasconade co., E central Mo., 40 mi/64 km SE of Jefferson City; 38°21′N 91°30′W. Corn; cattle, poultry; mfg. (printing, signs, store fixtures, hats); clay. Inc. 1900.

Owensville, town (1990 pop. 1,053), Gibson co., SW Ind., 9 mi/14.5 km SW of Princeton; 38°16′N 87°41′W. Agr.; gas and oil wells, bituminous-coal; timber; feed mill. Laid out 1817; inc. 1881.

Owensville, village (1990 pop. 1,019), Clermont co., SW Ohio, 20 mi/32 km E of Cincinnati; 39°07′N 84°08′W. Limestone quarry.

Owenton, town (1990 pop. 1,306), ⊙ Owen co., N Ky., 24 mi/39 km N of Frankfort; 38°32′N 84°50′W. In Bluegrass agr. area (burley tobacco, corn); mfg. (gas regulators, printing and publishing, lumber). Fishing nearby. Elmer Davis L. reservoir to S; Elk L. reservoir to SE; Twin Eagle Wildlife Management Area to W; Kleber Wildlife Management Area to S.

Owings, village, Laurens co., NW S.C., 12 mi/19 km NW of Laurens.

Owings Mills, village (1990 pop. 9,474), Baltimore co., N Md., 12 mi/19 km NW of downtown Baltimore; 39°25′N 76°47′W. Named after Samuel Owings, who established 3 grist mills in the mid-18th cent., it is now dominated by Rosewood State Hospital. He called the mills upper, lower, and middle and used the acronym for his house, Ulm, which has been restored as a restaraunt. Some of the Owings family are buried in the yard of St. Thomas Church (c.1742) in nearby Garrison.

Owingsville, town (1990 pop. 1,491), ⊙ Bath co., NE Ky., 28 mi/45 km ESE of Paris, in Bluegrass region; 38°08′N 83°45′W. Mfg. (apparel, printed circuit boards, wiring harnesses, fertilizer). To E are ruins of Slate Creek iron furnace (built 1790); to SE are Olympia Springs (used since 1791) in Daniel Boone Natl. Forest, once-famous mineral springs and baths for which co. is named. Cave Run L. reservoir to E.

Owl Creek Mountains, (highest point, 9,665 ft/2,946 m), central Wyo., a range of the Rockies, bet. Bridger Mts. (E), Absaroka Range (NW); bounds Bighorn Basin (N); range forms part of boundary between Hot Springs and Fremont cos., SW of Thermopolis. Entirely within Wind R. Indian Reservation.

Owl Head Mountain (3,425 ft/1,044 m), S Que., Canada, on W side of L. Memphremagog, near Vt. border, 30 mi/48 km SE of Granby.

Owls Head, resort and fishing town (1990 pop. 1,574), Knox co., S Maine, just S of Rockland on Owls Head peninsula; includes Ash Point village; 44°04′N 69°04′W. Lighthouse (1826) nearby.

Owosso (ah-WO-so), city (1990 pop. 16,322), Shiawassee co., S Mich., 3 mi/4.8 km WNW of Corunna, and on the Shiawassee R., 24 mi/39 km NE of Lansing, 27 mi/43 km W of Flint; 43°00′N 84°10′W. RR junction. Airport to NE. Mfg. (printing, bldg. materials, auto parts, corrugated containers, boats, auto seats, machinery); grain, soybeans; livestock. Thomas E. Dewey b. here. Inc. 1859.

Owsley (OUZ-lee), county (□ 198 sq mi/513 sq km; 1990 pop. 5,036), E central Ky., ⊙ Booneville, in the Cumberland Mts.; 37°24′N 83°41′W. Drained by South Fork of Kentucky R. and several creeks. Part of Daniel Boone Natl. Forest in NW, separate sect. bounds co. on S. Mt. agr. region (livestock; burley tobacco, hay); bituminous-coal mines, timber. Formed 1843.

Owyhee (oh-WEI-hee), county (□ 7,697 sq mi/19,935 sq km; 1990 pop. 8,392), SW Idaho; ⊙ Murphy; 42°34′N 116°10′W. Hilly region bordering on Oregon (W) and Nev. (S) and bounded N by Snake R. Irrigated areas are along Snake and in E along Bruneau R., and in SW along forks of Owyhee R. Sheep, cattle; dairying; agr. (hay, alfalfa; sugar beets, potatoes, beans; oats, barley, wheat); mining (gold, silver, zinc). Part of Duck Valley Indian Reservation is in S on Nev. state line. Pacific/Mountain time zone boundary follows S boundary and S part of W boundary. Bruneau Dunes State Park in N; Snake River Plain in N. Formed 1863.

Owyhee (O-wee-hee), uninc. village (□ 225 sq mi/583 sq km; 1990 pop. 908), Elko co., N Nev., on East Fork Owyhee R., near Idaho state line, and c.80 mi/129 km NNW of Elko; 41°54′N 116°11′W. Elev. 5,400 ft/1,646 m. Cattle, sheep. Wild Horse Reserve and State Recreation Area to SE. Part of Humboldt Natl. Forest to E and S.

Owyhee, river, c.200 mi/322 km long; rises in N Nev., S Idaho, SE Oregon. Main stream begins in SW Owyhee co., SW Idaho, at confluence of South and East forks, c.95 mi/153 km SSW of Boise; flows NW into Malheur co., Oregon, receiving North and Middle forks at Three Forks locality, continues NW, then NNE through 40-mi/64-km-long Owyhee Reservoir to Snake R. 5 mi/8 km S of Nyssa, Oregon, and 2 mi/3.2 km S of mouth of Boise R. Named in 1826 for 2 Hawaiian employees of the Hudson Bay Co. who were killed by Native Americans. After gold and silver were discovered in the region in 1863, there were many mining camps along the river. The Owyhee reclamation project of the U.S. Bureau of Reclamation irrigates a large area W of the Snake R. Owyhee Dam forms a reservoir 52 mi/84 km long.

Owyhee, Hawaii: see HAWAII.

Owyhee Reservoir (o-WEI-hee), Malheur co., SE Oregon, on Owyhee R., c. 50 mi/80 km W of Boise, Idaho, and 30 mi/48 km SSW of Ontario, Oregon; c.40 mi/64 km long, average width 1 mi/1.6 km; 43°38′N 117°15′W. Dry Creek enters from W. Formed by Owyhee Dam (417 ft/127 m high), built (1928–1932) for Owyhee Power and Irrigation Project. L. Owyhee State Park on NE shore.

Oxbow, town (1991 pop. 1,132), SE Sask., Canada, on Souris R., and 40 mi/64 km ENE of Estevan; 49°13′N 102°10′W. Grain elevators; livestock; dairying.

Oxbow, village, Oakland co., SE Mich., suburb 9 mi/ 14.5 km W of Pontiac on Oxbow L.; 42°38′N 83°28′W.

Oxbow, region (1990 pop. 69), Aroostook co., NE Maine, on the Aroostook, and 30 mi/48 km SW of Presque Isle; 46°25′N 68°30′W. Hunting, fishing.

Oxbow, reservoir (□ 2 sq mi/5.2 sq km), E Oregon (Baker co.)–W Idaho (Adams co.) border, on Snake R., 52 mi/84 km NW of Weiser; 44°58′N 116°50′W. Max. capacity 53,200 acre-ft. Formed by Oxbow Dam (175 ft/ 53 m high), built (1961) for power generation. Hells Canyon Natl. Recreation Area to NW; Payette Natl. Forest on E bank.

Oxbow Lake, S Hamilton co., E central N.Y., in the Adirondacks, 3 mi/4.8 km SW of L. Pleasant village; c.2 mi/3.2 km long; 43°27′N 74°28′W. Resort.

Oxchuc (OSH-chuk), town (1990 pop. 4,064), Chiapas state, S Mexico, 18 mi/29 km ENE of San Cristóbal de las Casas; 16°51′N 92°25′W. The majority of pop. is Tzeltal Maya Indians. Wheat, fruits. Also known as Media Luna, and Santo Tomás Oxchuc.

Oxford, county (□ 765 sq mi/1,981 sq km; 1991 pop. 92,888), S Ont., Canada, on Thames R.; ⊙ Woodstock; 43°05′N 80°50′W.

Oxford, town (1991 pop. 1,384), N N.S., Canada, on Philip R., and 20 mi/32 km ESE of Amherst; 45°44′N 63°52′W. Light mfg.

Oxford, county (□ 2,175 sq mi/5,633 sq km; 1990 pop. 52,602), W Maine, bordering on N.H. and Que., Canada; ⊙ South Paris; 44°29′N 70°45′W. Mfg. at Rumford (on the Androscoggin R.), Paris (on the Little Androscoggin R.), and Norway includes shoes, paper, wood prods.; lumber mills. Agr. includes dairying. Winter sports at Newry and Locke Mills; summer resorts in Rangeley Lakes region. Part of White Mt. Natl. Forest at N.H. state line. Formed 1805.

Oxford 1 city (1990 pop. 9,362), Calhoun co., E Ala., just S of Anniston. In farm area; poultry processing; mfg. (shirts, caskets; dairy prods.). Settled 1855. **2** city (1990 pop. 9,984), ⊙ Lafayette co., N central Miss.; 34°21′N 89°31′W. RR terminus. Agr. (cotton, corn, soybeans; cattle; dairying); mfg. (contract assembly, dairy prods., flower pots, apparel, bldg. materials, machinery, wire, printing and publishing, home appliances). Tourist center. Seat of Univ. of Miss. ("Ole Miss"), founded 1848. Although the town was burned by Union forces in 1864, many antebellum houses remain. Rowan Oak, antebellum home of novelist William Faulkner, is here, and the city was the setting for some of his works. In 1962, Oxford was the scene of rioting and conflict when the first Afr.-Amer. student, James Meredith, was enrolled in the univ. The Mary Buie Mus. houses one of the largest doll collections in the U.S. Holly Springs Natl. Forest to NE. Center for Study of Southern Culture. Sardis Waterfowl Area, on Sardis Reservoir, to NW. Inc. 1837. **3** city (1990 pop. 7,965), ⊙ Granville co., N N.C., 28 mi/45 km NE of Durham; 36°18′N 78°35′W. RR junction. Tobacco market and processing. Agr. area (tobacco, soybeans, grain; poultry, livestock; dairying). Mfg. (sheet metal; lumber, asphalt, and plastic prods.; consumer goods, textiles, and apparel). Settled 1760; laid out 1811; inc. 1816.

Oxford 1 town (1990 pop. 8,685), New Haven co., SW Conn., 14 mi/23 km NW of New Haven; 41°25′N 73°08′W. Agr. and light industry support the economy. Part of state forest here. Settled c.1680; inc. 1798. **2** town (1990 pop. 1,945), Newton co., N central Ga., 2 mi/ 3.2 km NNW of Covington; 33°37′N 83°52′W. Mfg. of concrete and lubricants. Oxford Col. of Emory Univ. located on original site of Emory. Col. listed on Natl. Register of Historic Places. **3** town (1990 pop. 1,273), Benton co., W Ind., 9 mi/14.5 km SSE of Fowler; 40°31′N 87°15′W. In agr. area (grain, soybeans, hybrid corn; livestock). Mfg. (plastic bottles, vertical blinds). **4** town (1990 pop. 663), Johnson co., E Iowa, 14 mi/ 23 km WNW of Iowa City; 41°43′N 91°47′W. In livestock and grain area. **5** town (1990 pop. 1,143), Sumner co., S Kansas, on Arkansas R., and 12 mi/19 km E of Wellington; 37°16′N 97°10′W. In wheat area; grain milling. **6** town (1990 pop. 3,705), Oxford co., SW Maine,

on Thompson L., and just S of South Paris; 44°08′N 70°28′W. Resorts; wood prods. Settled 1794; set off from Hebron and inc. 1829. **7** fishing town (1990 pop. 699), Talbot co., E Md., on Eastern Shore, 9 mi/14.5 km WNW of Cambridge, and on Tred Avon R.; 38°41′N 76°10′W. Rivaling Annapolis as an official port of entry into the colony from 1683 to the Revolutionary War, the town declined, and by 1825 muncipal govt. was suspended. Revived as an inc. town that year, it flourished as a shipbuilding, oystering, fishpacking, and resort community. The main street is named for Robert Morris (1734–1806), who came to Oxford in 1738 as the factor of Liverpool shipping firm and became the "Financier of the Amer. Revolution." The Tred Avon Ferry at the foot of Morris St., started by Elizabeth Skinner in 1760 with a rowed scow, still operates, carrying cars as well as passengers to Bellevue on the boat *Southside* every 15 min. until dusk. The remains of the Morris House (c.1774) have been inc. into the Robert Morris Inn. The Tred Avon Yacht Club holds an annual 3-day regatta here every Aug. 1–3. Wiley's Shipyard is more than 250 years old. Byberry, a shingled 1½ story house, is said to go back to 1695. **8** town (1990 pop. 12,588), Worcester co., S Mass.; 42°08′N 71°52′W. It is chiefly residential, with some light mfg. Clara Barton was b. here. Includes village of North Oxford. Settled 1687 by Fr. Protestants; inc. 1693. **9** town (1990 pop. 2,929), Oakland co., SE Mich., 14 mi/23 km N of Pontiac; 42°49′N 83°15′W. In lake and farm area (cattle; grain); mfg. (steel castings, urethane foam systems, plastic prods., dies, metal stampings); gravel pits; resort. Mt. Grampian Ski Area to E. Settled 1836; inc. 1876. **10** town (1990 pop. 949), Furnas and Harlan cos., S Nebr., 18 mi/29 km SW of Holdrege, and on Republican R.; 40°15′N 99°37′W. RR junction. Grain; mfg. (dairy prods., wooden pallets, fertilizers, auto parts). Inc. 1879.

Oxford 1 village (1990 pop. 562), Izard co., N Ark., 22 mi/ 35 km N of Melbourne; 36°12′N 91°55′W. **2** village (1990 pop. 44), Franklin co., SE Idaho, 17 mi/27 km NNW of Preston; 42°16′N 112°01′W. Caribou Natl. Forest to W. **3** village and township (1990 pop. 1,790), Warren co., NW N.J., on N slope of Scotts Mt., and 4 mi/ 6.4 km WSW of Belvidere; 40°48′N 75°00′W. Once an important iron-mining region. **4** village (□ 1 sq mi/ 2.6 sq km; 1990 pop. 1,738), in Oxford town (1990 pop. 4,075), Chenango co., central N.Y., on Chenango R., and 28 mi/45 km NE of Binghamton; 42°26′N 75°35′W. In agr. area (poultry); dairy prods. Site of N.Y. State Women's Relief Corps Home built in 1896 and now operated as the N.Y. State Veterans' Home. Settled 1788; inc. 1808. **5** village (1990 pop. 18,937), Butler co., SW Ohio, near the Ind. state line; 39°30′N 84°45′W. In farm area. Residential col. town and seat of Miami Univ. and the Western Col. State park and a pioneer farm (1835; now a mus.) nearby. Laid out 1810; inc. 1830. **6** village (1990 pop. 499), Marquette co., central Wis., on small Neenah Creek, and 17 mi/27 km NNW of Portage; 43°46′N 89°33′W. In livestock and dairy area; mfg. (bottled artesian water).

Oxford, borough (1990 pop. 3,769), Chester co., SE Pa., 17 mi/27 km SW of Coatesville, near Md. state boundary; 39°47′N 58°75′W. Mfg. (printing and publishing, fabricated metal prods., analytical instruments, communication systems, food prods., gas fuels, compost). Agr. area (grain, soybeans, mushrooms; poultry, livestock; dairying). Lincoln Univ. to NE; Oxford Airport to SW; Nottingham Park to SW; Octoraro L. reservoir to W; 3 covered bridges to SE. Inc. 1833.

Oxford Dam, N.C.: see LOOKOUT SHOALS LAKE.

Oxford Junction, town (1990 pop. 581), Jones co., E Iowa, near Wapsipinicon R., 20 mi/32 km ESE of Anamosa; 41°58′N 90°57′W. In livestock and grain area.

Oxford Lake, 38 mi/61 km long, 9 mi/14 km wide (□ 155 sq mi/401 sq km), NE central Man., Canada, on Hayes R.; 54°52′N 95°35′W.

Oxford, Mount, peak (14,153 ft/4,314 m) in Rocky Mts., Chaffee co., central Colo., in Collegiate Range; also includes mounts Columbia, Harvard, and Yale. San Isabel Natl. Forest, E of Continental Divide.

Oxkutzcab, town (1990 pop. 17,189), Yucatan state, SE

Mexico, and 10 mi/16 km SE of Ticul; 20°18′N 89°26′W. On RR. Agr. center (henequen, sugarcane, tobacco, corn, tropical fruits; timber). Remarkable Maya ruins are at Labná, 7 mi/11.3 km SW, and interesting grottoes are nearby.

Oxnard, city (□ 35 sq mi/91 sq km; 1990 pop. 142,216), Ventura co., S Calif., 53 mi/85 km WNW of Los Angeles, and 7 mi/11.3 km SE of Ventura, on the Pacific coast; 34°12′N 119°13′W. Its economy, formerly based on agr. and agr. processing, mining, and nearby military bases, has broadened to include large industrial and commercial operations. Mfg. (dairy prods., sporting goods, cosmetics, metal forging, prepared foods, paper mills, asphalt, pumps, aircraft parts, bldg. materials, uniforms, computer equip., concrete prods.); dairying, avocados, citrus fruits, vegetables, flowers, nursery products. There are also oil refineries. Point Mugu Naval Air Station to SE. Oxnard is the gateway for visitors to the Santa Barbara Isls. and to Los Padres Natl. Forest. The city has become one of the fastest growing in the U.S., and its population doubled bet. 1970 and 1990. Channel Isl. Natl. Area c.25 mi/40 km SW; Santa Monica Mts. Natl. Recreation Area to E; Oxnard Air Force Base to NE; Point Mugu State Park to S; McGrath State Beach to W; Oxnard Col. (2-year) is here. Inc. 1903.

Oxon Hill, village (1990 pop. 35,794), Prince Georges co., central Md., S suburb of Washington, D.C.; 38°48′N 76°59′W. Oxon Hill was dominated by large estates until the 1950s. Oxon Hill House, built in the mid-18th cent. by Thomas Addison, the great-great grandson of Col. John Addison, burned in 1895. It was once owned by the family of Sumner Welles (1892–1960), Franklin Roosevelt's undersecretary of state from 1937 to 1943. The Oxon Hill Farm is run by the Natl. Park Service as a 19th-cent. farm in which hand milking and horse plowing can be observed. Two 20-ton/22-metric-ton cannons, stone gun emplacements, and reinforced earthworks can still be seen in Fort Foote Park. The fort was built during the Civil War to protect the capital.

Oyen (OI-uhn), town (1991 pop. 1,019), SE Alta., Canada, near Sask. border, 60 mi/97 km W of Kindersley; grain elevators.

Oyens (OY-ens), town (1990 pop. 113), Plymouth co., NW Iowa, 6 mi/9.7 km ENE of Le Mars; 42°49′N 96°03′W. In livestock area.

Oyster, uninc. village, Northampton co., E Va., 5 mi/ 8 km E of Cape Charles town, on Mockhorn Bay, arm of Atlantic Ocean; 37°17′N 75°55′W. Mfg. (oyster processing); fish, oysters, clams.

Oyster Bay, uninc. area of Oyster Bay town (1990 pop. 6,687), Nassau co., SE N.Y., on N L.I., on L.I. Sound; 40°47′N 73°30′W. It is chiefly upper-income residential with many estates. Nearby is Theodore Roosevelt's estate, "Sagamore Hill," which was made a natl. shrine in 1953 and a Natl. Historic Site in 1963. Also of interest in Oyster Bay are several 18th-cent. houses, the Theodore Roosevelt Memorial Bird Sanctuary, a 12-acre/5-ha wildlife sanctuary owned by the Natl. Audubon Society, which adjoins Roosevelt's grave, and the Oyster Bay Natl. Wildlife Refuge (□ 5 sq mi/13 sq km). Settled 1653.

Oyster Bay, irregular inlet of L.I. Sound, SE N.Y., indenting N shore of W L.I., with entrance (c.2 mi/3.2 km wide) bet. Rocky Point (W) and Lloyd Point (E); 40°54′N 73°32′W. Cold Spring Harbor (c.3 mi/4.8 km long) is SE arm. Oyster Bay Harbor, with irregular branches, is W arm; Oyster Bay village is on its S shore.

Oyster Bay Cove, residential village (□ 4 sq mi/ 10.4 sq km; 1990 pop. 2,109), Nassau co., SE N.Y., on NW L.I., just ESE of Oyster Bay village; 40°51′N 73°30′W. In shore recreation area. Inc. 1931.

Oyster Creek, town (1990 pop. 912), Brazoria co., SE Texas, suburb 4 mi/6.4 km NE of Freeport, in Brazosport Area, on Oyster Creek; 29°00′N 95°19′W. Oil and natural gas. Mfg. (pump seals). Brazoria Natl. Wildlife Refuge to NE.

Oyster Creek Nuclear Power Plant, New Jersey: see OCEAN, CO.

Oyster Harbors, private island, Osterville, Mass., in

Barnstable town, Cape Cod. Summer estates and golf course.

Oyster River, c.12 mi/19 km long, Strafford co., SE N.H.; rises 9 mi/14.5 km W of Dover; flows ESE, in serpentine course, past Durham, to entrance of Great Bay into Little Bay.

Ozama River (o-ZAH-mah), c.65 mi/105 km long, S central and S Dominican Republic; rises in the Cordillera Central SE of Bonao; flows E and S to the Caribbean at Santo Domingo; 18°28′N 69°53′W. Navigable for c.15 mi/24 km upstream. Sometimes called Ozuma R.

Ozan (o-ZAN), village (1990 pop. 69), Hempstead co., SW Ark., 14 mi/23 km NNW of Hope; 33°51′N 93°43′W.

Ozark, county (□ 756 sq mi/1,958 sq km; 1990 pop. 8,598), S Mo.; ⊙ Gainesville, borders Ark. in S, in the Ozarks; drained by North Fork of White R.; 36°38′N 92°26′W. Hay; cattle; timber (cedar, oak, pine); tourism, canoeing, fishing. Parts of Mark Twain Natl. Forest in NE and NW corners. N end of Norfork L. in SE (dammed in Ark.); arms of Bull Shoals L. Reservoir in SW (also dammed in Ark.). Formed 1841.

Ozark 1 city (1990 pop. 12,922), ⊙ Dale co., SE Ala., c.20 mi/32 km NW of Dothan. Shipping center for agr. prods., such as nuts and timber; mfg. (aircraft, railcars, farm machinery, clothing, wood prods., fertilizer). The Ala. Aviation and Technical Col. is located in Ozark. Fort Rucker, the U.S. Army's aviation center, is nearby. Settled 1820; inc. 1870. **2** city (1990 pop. 4,243), ⊙ Christian co., SW Mo., in the Ozarks, near James R., 14 mi/23 km S of Springfield; 37°01′N 93°12′W. Fruits; cattle; dairying; mfg. (electric motors, boat trailers); limestone quarry.

Ozark (O-zahrk), town (1990 pop. 3,330), shares ⊙ functions with Charleston, Franklin co., NW Ark., 33 mi/53 km ENE of Fort Smith, and on Arkansas R. (here bridged); 35°30′N 93°50′W. Diversified agr. area. Mfg. (turkey processing [Cargill], concrete, shirts, air-conditioner parts). Ozark Natl. Forest to N; Ozark Jeta Taylor Lock and Dam (Arkansas R.) to SE; forms Ozark L. Settled 1836; inc. as city 1938.

Ozark Jeta Taylor Lock and Dam (O-zahrk), Franklin co., W Ark., on the Arkansas R., 1 mi/1.6 km SE of Ozark; 65 ft/20 m high; 35°27′N 93°48′W. Built (1969) by the Army Corps of Engineers for navigation and power generation. Forms Ozark L., a reservoir that is a raised navigation channel, with a max. capacity of 148,000 acre-ft.; extends c.45 mi/72 km to James W. Trimble Lock and Dam.

Ozark Mountains, Mo.: see OZARKS, THE.

Ozark National Scenic Riverways, 134 mi/216 km along the Current and Jacks Fork rivers, SE Mo. Covers 80,791 acres/32,695 ha. Authorized 1964 as the 1st natl. riverway; est. 1972. Many large springs flow into the rivers; Big Springs is the largest single-outlet spring in the U.S. Many large caves with interesting dripstone formations are found along the rivers. Forests cover about 75% of the riverways. Wildlife and fish are abundant in the area. Canoeing, floating, fishing. Park Headquarters at Van Buren.

Ozarks, Lake of the, Mo.: see LAKE OF THE OZARKS.

Ozarks, the or **Ozark Highland**, upland region, actually a dissected plateau, and sometimes called Ozark Mountains, c.50,000 sq mi/129,500 sq km, chiefly in S Mo. and N Ark., but partly in Okla. and Kansas, bet. the Arkansas and Missouri rivers. The Ozarks, which rise from the surrounding plains, are, in a few places, locally referred to as mts. Composed of igneous rock over 1 billion years old overlain mostly by limestone and dolomite, the anc. landform has been worn down by erosion. Summits (knobs) are found wherever there is a resistant igneous rock outcrop, as in the St. Francois Mts. of SE Mo. The Boston Mts. are the highest and most rugged sect., with several peaks more than 2,000 ft/610 m high. The Ozarks are metalliferous, esp. in lead, zinc, and iron, especially in the St. Francois Mts. and the Joplin areas. Cattle raising and wood prods. are major activities; fruit-growing areas are prevalent. Traditional household crafts have been maintained and promoted for the tourist industry. The Ozarks have many large lakes that were created by dams across numerous rivers; the dams generate electricity. The scenic Ozarks, with forests, caves, lakes, streams, and springs, are a popular tourist region, and the construction of summer homes and large retirement communities there has grown.

Ozaukee (o-ZAH-kee), county (□ 1,116 sq mi/2,890 sq km; 1990 pop. 72,831), E Wis.; ⊙ Port Washington; 43°15′N 87°30′W. Bounded E by L. Michigan; drained by Milwaukee R. Dairying, livestock, poultry, and vegetable farming area (barley, wheat, soybeans, peas), with dairy-prods. processing. Mfg. at Mequon, Cedarburg, and Port Washington. Fisheries. S part of co. has become urbanized, extension of Milwaukee metropolitan area. Huntington Beach State Park in NE, on L. Michigan. Formed 1853.

Ozona (O-zon-ah), town (1990 pop. 3,181), ⊙ Crockett co., W Texas, c.70 mi/113 km SW of San Angelo; 30°42′N 101°12′W. Trading center for oil and natural-gas and livestock region (sheep, Angora goats, cattle); mfg. (butane, propane, and natural-gas processing).

Ozone Park, S central section of borough of Queens, N.Y. city, SE N.Y., S of Atlantic Ave., NW of JFK Internatl. Airport, S of Woodhaven, a community from which it is virtually inseparable, both historically and culturally; 40°41′N 73°51′W. Both Ozone Park and Woodhaven began in June 1882 as the brainchild of Benjamin Hitchcock and Charles Denton, 2 real-estate developers. The idea, popular during the 1880s and 1890s, was to build 9 "parks" that could be pastoral residential areas for people who wanted to escape the older, crowded dists. of Manhattan, Brooklyn, and Queens. Ozone Park and Woodhaven flourished during the 1920s; though residential, they also attracted some light mfg. (pipes, hosiery, hats, corsets, and ice cream). Today the 2 communities are quiet, residential neighborhoods of unvarying frame and brick houses. The city's only racetrack, Aqueduct ("The Big A"), is here.

Ozuluama, Mexico: see OZULUAMA DE MASCAREÑAS.

Ozuluama de Mascareñas, city (1990 pop. 3,233) and township, ⊙ Ozuluama municipio, Veracruz state, E Mexico, in Gulf lowland, 38 mi/61 km S of Tampico; 21°40′N 97°54′W. Cereals, coffee, sugarcane, fruits; livestock.

Ozuma River, Dominican Republic: see OZAMA RIVER.

Ozumba de Alzate (o-ZOOM-bah dai ahl-SAH-te), town (1990 pop. 13,451), ⊙ Ozumba municipio, Mexico state, central Mexico, at W foot of Popocatépetl, and part of the Zona Metropolitana de la Ciudad de México, 35 mi/56 km SE of Mexico city; 19°03′N 98°48′W. Agr. center (cereals, fruits; livestock). Has old Franciscan church with 17th-cent. historical painting. Chimal Falls nearby.

P

Paauilo (pah-OU-EE-lo), village (1990 pop. 620), N Hawaii isl., Hawaii co., Hawaii, 28 mi/45 km NNW of Hilo, on Hamakua (NE) coast; 20°02′N 155°22′W. Macadamia nuts, cattle; fish, prawns. Hamakua Forest Reserve to S.

Pabellón de Arteaga (pah-be-YON de ahr-te-AH-gah), city (1990 pop. 18,364), in NW Aguascalientes, Mexico, on RR, 1 mi/2 km E of Mexico Highway 45, and 5 mi/8 km S of Rincón de Romos; 22°09′N 102°15′W.

Pablo (PAH-blo), town (1990 pop. 1,298), Lake co., NW Mont., near Flathead L., 6 mi/9.7 km SSE of Polson; 47°36′N 114°06′W. Agr. (cattle, sheep, llamas, hogs, oats, rape seed, corn, potatoes, hay); mfg. (lumber). Confederated Salish Kootenai Tribal Complex and Salish Kootenai Col. here. Mission Mts. Tribal Wilderness to E, in Flathead Indian Reservation; Pablo Reservoir and Natl. Wildlife Refuge to NW.

Pace (PAIS), town (□ 9 sq mi/23.3 sq km; 1990 pop. 6,277), Santa Rosa co., NW Fla., 12 mi/19 km N of Pensacola; 30°36′N 87°09′W. Mfg. includes fertilizers, boat interiors, industrial resins.

Pace, village (1990 pop. 354), Bolivar co., NW Miss., 29 mi/47 km NNE of Greenville. In cotton-growing area; corn, rice, soybeans; cattle.

Pachaug, Conn.: see GRISWOLD.

Pacheco, uninc. town (1990 pop. 3,325), Contra Costa co., W Calif., residential suburb 12 mi/19 km NE of downtown Oakland, 2 mi/3.2 km W of Concord; 38°00′N 122°04′W. Briones Regional Park to SW; John Muir Natl. Historic Site to NW.

Pachuca de Soto (pah-CHOO-kah de SO-to), city (1990 pop. 174,013) and township, ⊙ Hidalgo state, central Mexico, at the head of a ravine in Sierra de Pachuca; 20°07′N 98°43′W. Elev. 7,959 ft/2,426 m. Pachuca, one of Mexico's oldest and most famous mining towns, was founded in 1534 on the site of an anc. Toltec city. The region is extremely rich in ore deposits, especially silver, which has been mined since Aztec times. Pachuca is also a cultural and educational center, with a univ., a meteorological observatory, and a noted school of mining and metallurgy. Landmarks include a 16th-cent. convent and church and La Caja, built in 1670 as a storehouse to hold the royal tribute.

Pachuquilla (pah-choo-KEE-ya), town (1990 pop. 2,627), ⊙ Mineral de la Reforma municipio, Hidalgo, central Mexico, 3 mi/5 km SE of Pachuca de Soto on Mexico Highway 130; 20°04′N 98°42′W. Silver and gold mining inactive here, but still active in Pachuca de Soto, 5 mi/8 km N. Old mining center of Mineral de la Reforma is in the vacinity.

Pachuta (puh-CHOO-tuh), village (1990 pop. 268), Clarke co., E Miss., 25 mi/40 km SSW of Meridian; 32°02′N 88°52′W. Agr. (cotton, corn, cattle); mfg. (corrugated and paperboard boxes). L.C. Rhoden Mus.

Pacific, county (□ 1,223 sq mi/3,168 sq km; 1990 pop. 18,882), SW Wash.; ⊙ South Bend; 46°34′N 123°47′W. Bounded W by Pacific Ocean, S by Columbia R. (Oregon state boundary). Timber; dairying; fish, shellfish, crabs, oysters; hay. Grayland Beach State Park in NW; Leadbetter Point State Park in W; Fort Canby State Park, at Cape Disappointment, in SW; Fort Columbia State Park, on Columbia R., in SW. Shoalwater Indian Reservation in NW. Large Willapa Bay, arm of Pacific in W, separated from ocean by North Beach Peninsula; entrance in NW. Willapa Natl. Wildlife Refuge on Long Isl., in S end of bay, and at both sides of bay entrance. Astoria Bridge, 4 mi/6.4 km long, to Astoria, Oregon, crosses Columbia R. estuary in S. Formed 1851.

Pacific, city (1990 pop. 4,350), Franklin and St. Louis cos., E Mo., on Meramec R., and 25 mi/40 km W of St. Louis; 38°28′N 90°45′W. Silica sandstone mines (for sand for glass mfg.); mfg. (paper and cardboard prods.,

electronic components, consumer goods, silica prods.). Missouri Botanical Garden arboretum and Rockwoods Reservation (forest reserve) nearby Mo. state correctional facility to E. Laid out 1852.

Pacific, town (1990 pop. 4,622), King co., W central Wash., suburb 10 mi/16 km E of Tacoma and 26 mi/42 km S of Seattle, near White R.; 47°16′N 122°15′W. Berries. Dairying; poultry; mfg. (power cylinders, telephone equip., wiring devices, sheet-metal work). L. Tapps reservoir to SE.

Pacific Beach, uninc. town (1990 pop. 1,200), Grays Harbor co., W Wash., 21 mi/34 km NW of Hoquiam, on Pacific Ocean, at mouth of Joe Creek. Razor clams. Beach resort area. Timber. Quinault Indian Reservation to N.

Pacific Beach, suburban section of San Diego, San Diego co., S Calif., 8 mi/12.9 km NW of downtown San Diego, on Pacific Ocean. Mission Bay to SE; La Jolla area to N. Residential and beach resort area.

Pacific Beach, Calif.: see SAN DIEGO, city.

Pacific Grove, city (□ 3 sq mi/7.8 sq km; 1990 pop. 16,117), Monterey co., W central Calif., suburb 2 mi/3.2 km NW of Monterey, on Monterey Bay arm of Pacific Ocean; 36°37′N 121°56′W. Tourism; among the natural attractions of the area are the millions of Monarch butterflies that arrive each fall to spend the winter. Stanford Univ. has a marine laboratory here. Point Pinos Lighthouse to NW has been in operation since 1855. Several popular golf courses to S. Inc. 1889.

Pacific Highway, scenic inland route on W coast of N. Amer. Road (U.S. and Can. highway No. 99) extends c.1,675 mi/2,696 km N-S from Vancouver (B.C.) to Calexico (Calif.) at Mex. border.

Pacific Junction, town (1990 pop. 548), Mills co., SW Iowa, just SW of Glenwood; 41°01′N 95°47′W. Feed milling.

Pacific Margin, region, W sect. of the great N. Amer. Cordillera, W U.S. and W Canada, stretching from SW Alaska to S Calif. It is composed of a central lowland region (Central Valley, Willamette valley, Puget Sound lowlands) flanked by the COAST RANGES on the W and the SIERRA NEVADA, CASCADE RANGE, COAST MOUNTAINS, and ALASKA RANGE on the E. Another common reference to the geographical area is, more simply, the Pacific Mountains and Valleys.

Pacific Palisades, W residential district of Los Angeles city, Los Angeles co., S Calif., in Santa Monica Mts. (Santa Monica Mts. Natl. Recreation Area) above the Santa Monica Bay, Pacific Ocean, just NW of Santa Monica. Topanga Canyon to W; Topanga State Park and State Beach, J. Paul Getty Mus., and Will Rogers State Historic Park and State Beach are here.

Pacific Palisades, city (1990 pop. c.10,000), S Oahu isl., Honolulu co., Hawaii, residential suburb 10 mi/16 km W of downtown Honolulu, 2 mi/3.2 km NE of Pearl City. Pearl Harbor to S. Ewa Forest Reserve to NE.

Pacific Rim National Park (□ 60 sq mi/155 sq km), along the W coast of Vancouver Isl., near Ucluelet, SE B.C., Canada. The park includes Long Beach, several isls., the historic Life Saving Trail, and a variety of marine life. Est. 1971.

Pacifica, city (□ 12 sq mi/31 sq km; 1990 pop. 37,670), San Mateo co., W Calif., residential suburb 11 mi/18 km SSW of downtown San Francisco on the Pacific coast; 37°37′N 122°29′W. Mfg. (printing and publishing, light mfg.) Pacifica was formed by the consolidation of several communities in 1957. City sits almost directly astride San Andreas Fault which extends SSE overland and NNW on Continental Shelf in Pacific Ocean to Point Reyes (20 mi/32 km). Part of Golden Gate Natl. Recreation Area to E; Thornton State Beach to N. Inc. 1957.

Packwood 1 town (1990 pop. 208), Jefferson co., SE Iowa, 11 mi/18 km NW of Fairfield; 41°07′N 92°04′W. Livestock; grain; meat processing. **2** uninc. town (1990 pop. 1,010), Lewis co., W central Wash., 55 mi/89 km SE of Tacoma, on Cowlitz R., in Cascade Range. Timber. Resort area. Gifford Pinchot Natl. Forest surrounds area, including Goats Rocks Wilderness Area to

SE and Tatoosh Wilderness Area to N. Mt. Rainier Natl. Park to N.

Pacoima, uninc. suburban sect. of Los Angeles city, Los Angeles co., S Calif., 18 mi/29 km NNW of downtown Los Angeles, SE of San Fernando in San Fernando Valley, just SE of San Fernando. Diversified mfg. Nearby on Pacoima R. (an intermittent tributary of Los Angeles R.) is Pacoima or Reagan Dam (372 ft/113 m, high, 640 ft/195 m long; completed 1928; for flood control). Pacoima Reservoir to NE; San Gabriel Mts., Angeles Natl. Forest to NE.

Pacolet (PAK-o-let), town (1990 pop. 1,736), Spartanburg co., NW S.C., 10 mi/16 km ESE of Spartanburg; 34°53′N 81°46′W. Granite quarry. Just NE is Pacolet Mills village. Mfg. includes wood furniture, crushed stone, quarry prods., chrome plating. Agr. includes dairying, poultry, livestock, grain, soybeans, peaches, apples.

Pacolet Mills (PAK-o-let), town (1990 pop. 696), Spartanburg co., NW S.C., 11 mi/18 km E of Spartanburg and 3 mi/4.8 km NNE of Pacolet, on Pacolet R.; 34°55′N 81°45′W. Agr. area producing dairy prods., livestock, grain, soybeans, peaches.

Pacolet River (PAK-o-let), 50 mi/80 km long, NW S.C.; formed 10 mi/16 km NNE of Spartanburg by short North and South Pacolet rivers; flows SE past Pacolet Mills to Broad R. 4 mi/6.4 km N of Lockhart.

Pactolus (pak-TO-luhs), uninc. village, Pitt co., E N.C., 9 mi/14.5 km E of Greenville, near Tar R.

Pacula (pah-KOO-lah), town (1990 pop. 743), Hidalgo, central Mexico, 8 mi/12.9 km NW of Jacala; 21°03′N 99°18′W. Cereals, beans, sugar, stock.

Paddock Lake, town (1990 pop. 2,662), Kenosha co., SE Wis., 13 mi/21 km W of Kenosha; 42°34′N 88°05′W. Residential. Recreation area; small lakes to SW. Bong St. Rec. Area to N. Dairying, livestock, soybeans.

Paden 1 (PAID-uhn), village (1990 pop. 123), Tishomingo co., extreme NE Miss., 11 mi/18 km SSW of Iuka; 34°39′N 88°15′W. In timber and agr. area. On Tennessee-Tombigbee Waterway; Bay Springs L. reservoir to S. **2** village (1990 pop. 400), Okfuskee co., central Okla., 20 mi/32 km NNE of Seminole; 35°30′N 96°34′W. In agr. area; mfg. (storm windows and doors).

Paden City (PAID-uhn), town (1990 pop. 2,862), Tyler and Wetzel cos., NW W.Va., on the Ohio R., 35 mi/56 km SSW of Wheeling; 39°36′N 80°56′W. Agr. (corn); livestock; dairying. Mfg. (glass). Settled 1790.

Padilla, Mexico: see NUEVA VILLA DE PADILLA.

Padlei, trading post, S Keewatin dist., N.W.T., Canada, W of Maguse L.; 61°57′N 96°40′W.

Padloping Island, St. Franklin dist., N.W.T., Canada, in Merchants Bay of Davis Strait, off Cumberland Peninsula, SE Baffin Isl.; 4 mi/6 km long, 1 mi/2 km wide; 67°3′N 62°45′W. Site of Crystal III air base.

Padre Island, long, narrow, bow-shaped sand barrier isl., on W coast of Gulf of Mexico, S Texas; c.115 mi/185 mi long, less than 3 mi/4.8 km wide. Separated from mainland by Laguna Madre through which passes the Intracoastal Waterway. Small channel at N end separating it from Mustang Isl. has been filled; N end is opposite city of Corpus Christi (W), connected to it by causeway. Separated from Brazos Isl. on S end by Brazos Santiago Pass, 8 mi/12.9 km N of mouth of Rio Grande (Mex. border), Brownsville Shipping Channel enters Gulf through Pass. Causeway connects resort town of South Padre Isl. with Port Isabel, on mainland. Roads at opposite ends of Padre Isl. do not connect. About 35 mi/56 km N of S end is man-made Port Mansfield Channel, which splits the isl. in 2 and provides access to Gulf from Port Mansfield on mainland. S part sometimes called South Padre Isl. Padre Island Natl. Seashore extends 80.5 mi/129.5 km from c.15 mi/24 km SE of Corpus Christi S to Port Mansfield Channel; park hq. in N.

Padre Island National Seashore (□ 204 sq mi/528 sq km), Kleberg, Kenedy, and Willacy cos., S Texas, extending 80.5 mi/129.5 km from c.15 mi/24 km SE of downtown Corpus Christi, near N end of Padre Isl., S to Port Mansfield Shipping Channel, c.35 mi/56 km N of S end of isl. Narrow sand barrier isl. on W coast of

Gulf of Mexico characterized by large sand dunes, wide beaches and sparse vegetation. Explored by the Spanish in 1519, it became known as a ships' graveyard. In excess of 350 bird species, also small mammals, reptiles, marine life. Authorized 1962, est. 1968. See also Padre isl., Texas.

Padre Las Casas (PAH-dre las KAH-sahs), town (1993 pop. 7,419), Azua prov., SW Dominican Republic, 20 mi/32 km NW of Azua; 18°45′N 70°53′W. Tobacco- and coffee growing; lumbering. Until 1928, Túbano.

Paducah (puh-DOO-kuh), city (1990 pop. 27,256), ⊙ McCracken co., W Ky., 95 mi/153 km WSW of Owensboro, on the Ohio R. (bridged) near (W of) mouth of the Tennessee R.; 37°04′N 88°38′W. RR junction. It is a tobacco market, a farm trade and livestock shipping point, and a river port. It also has RR shops and boat yards; diversified mfg. During the Civil War, Paducah was held for the Union (1861) by Grant, and in 1864, it was the objective of a Confederate raid by Nathan Forrest. The city suffered serious floods in 1884, 1913, and 1937. Paducah Community Col. (Univ. of Ky.). Paducah Symphony Orchestra; Whitehaven Mansion (c.1866) to NW, is now state welcome center; Yeiser Art Center; Alben W. Barkley Mus., Amer. Quilters Society Mus., Barlow House Mus. (c.1905); Chief Paduke statue. Land Between the Lakes (Kentucky L. and L. Barkley reservoirs) to SE; Lock and Dam No. 52 is here; Players Bluegrass Downs to S. Est. 1827; inc. as a city 1856.

Paducah, town (1990 pop. 1,788), ⊙ Cottle co., NW Texas, in rolling plains 30 mi/48 km S of Childress; 34°00′N 100°17′W. Elev. 1,886 ft/575 m. RR spur terminus; grains, alfalfa; cotton; cattle, horses. Matador State Wildlife Management Area to NW. Settled 1885; est. 1892; inc. 1910.

Pagan River, c.10 mi/16 km long, SE Va.; tidal stream flowing NE through Isle of Wight co., past Smithfield (head of navigation), to James R.; 37°03′N 73°40′W.

Page 1 county (☐ 535 sq mi/1,386 sq km; 1990 pop. 16,870), SW Iowa, on Mo. state line; ⊙ Clarinda; 40°44′N 95°09′W. Prairie agr. area (corn, hogs, cattle, poultry) drained by Nodaway, East Nodaway, Tarkio, and East Nishnabotna rivers. Bituminous-coal deposits. Flooding occurred in 1993. Formed 1847. **2** county (☐ 314 sq mi/813 sq km; 1990 pop. 21,690), N Va.; ⊙ Luray; 38°36′N 78°28′W. In Shenandoah Valley; Massanutten Mt. in W, Blue Ridge in E; drained by South Fork of Shenandoah R. Some mfg. at Luray, Shenandoah; fertile valley agr. area (corn, barley, wheat, alfalfa, hay, apples, peaches; poultry, cattle, sheep, hogs; dairying); some timber. Includes part of Shenandoah Natl. Park in E, Luray Caverns in center; part of George Washington Natl. Forest in W, including Massanutten Visitor Center in SW. Mt. resorts. Formed 1831.

Page, city (1990 pop. 6,598), Coconino co., N Ariz., 125 mi/201 km NE of Flagstaff, on Colorado R., at E end of Glen Canyon Dam, forms L. Powell to N; 36°53′N 111°27′W. Tourism, recreation. Mfg. (boats, truck parts, steel rolling mill). Paria Canyon-Vermillion Cliffs Wildlife Area to W; large Navajo Indian Reservation to E and S. Glen Canyon Bridge S of dam; Navajo Bridge, spanning Marble Canyon of Colorado R., 12 mi/19 km SW (downstream). Glen Canyon Natl. Recreation Area to N; Rainbow Bridge Natl. Monument (Utah) to NE. N end of Marble Canyon extension of Grand Canyon Natl. Park to SW. Town is important embarkation point for boat trips and cruises on reservoir.

Page 1 village (1990 pop. 191), Holt co., N Nebr., 12 mi/19 km ESE of O'Neill; 42°23′N 98°25′W. **2** village (1990 pop. 266), Cass co., E N.Dak., 25 mi/40 km NW of Casselton; 47°09′N 97°34′W. RR junction to S. **3** uninc. village (1990 pop. 600), Fayette co., S central W.Va., 9 mi/14.5 km W of Fayetteville. Agr. (grain); livestock.

Pagedale, town (1990 pop. 3,771), St. Louis co., E Mo., suburb 8 mi/12.9 km WNW of downtown St. Louis; 38°40′N 90°18′W. Mfg. (sheet metal, swimming pool prods.). Served by Metrolink light RR. Inc. since 1940.

Pageland, town (1990 pop. 2,666), Chesterfield co., N S.C., 22 mi/35 km ENE of Lancaster, in the piedmont; 34°46′N 80°23′W. Mfg. includes porcelain lampholders,

rayon yarn, industrial valves, poultry production, upholstery fabrics, lumber, clothing. Agr. includes poultry, livestock, grain, tobacco, watermelons, peaches; granite. Timber.

Paget, parish (1991 pop. 4,877), central Bermuda, S of Hamilton; 32°16′N 64°46′W.

Paget Island, E Bermuda, at E entrance to St. George's Harbour; ⅔ mi/⁹⁄₁₀ km long, ⅕ mi/¹⁄₁₀ km wide; 32°22′N 64°39′W.

Pageton, uninc. village (1990 pop. 300), McDowell co., S W.Va., 9 mi/14.5 km SE of Welch. Bituminous-coal area. Anawalt Wildlife Management Area to SE.

Pagoda, mountain (13,497 ft/4,114 m), in Front Range, Boulder co., N Colo.; rises on SW slope of Longs Peak, 25 mi/40 km NW of Boulder; 40°14′N 105°37′W.

Pagosa Peak (12,640 ft/3,853 m), in San Juan Mts., Mineral co., SW Colo., 12 mi/19 km NNW of Pagosa Springs; 37°26′N 107°03′W. In San Juan Natl. Forest.

Pagosa Springs, town (1990 pop. 1,207), ⊙ Archuleta co., SW Colo., on San Juan R., in SW foothills of San Juan Mts., and 47 mi/76 km E of Durango; 37°16′N 107°01′W. Elev. 7,079 ft/2,158 m. Resort with mineral hot springs, also used as a heat source; sheep, cattle, mfg. (publishing, aircraft equip.). Pagosa Peak is 12 mi/19 km NNW. Chimney Rock, with ruins of anc. cliff dwellings, is 18 mi/29 km W, near Piedra R. Region is nearly surrounded by parts of San Juan Natl. Forest; Southern Ute Indian Reservation to SW. Wolf Creek Ski Area to NE. Plotted 1880; inc. 1891.

Paguate (pah-GWAH-te), uninc. village (1990 pop. 492), Cibola co., W central N.Mex., 20 mi/32 km E of Grants, in N part of Laguna Indian Reservation; 35°07′N 107°21′W. Sheep raising. Mt. Taylor (11,301 ft/3,445 m) to NW, in San Mateo Mts.

Pahala (PAH-HAH-lah), village (1990 pop. 1,520), S Hawaii, Hawaii co., Hawaii, 41 mi/66 km SW of Hilo, 4 mi/6.4 km inland from SE coast, on Mamalahoa Highway (Hawaii Belt Road); 19°11′N 155°28′W. Macadamia nuts. Cane-sugar processing ceased operation in 1996. Mauna Loa summit (13,677 ft/4,169 m) 18 mi/29 km NNW. Hawaii Volcanoes Natl. Park to NE; the Great Crack and Southwest Rift Zone to E; Kau Forest Reserve to NW; Turtle Cave to NE.

Pahoa (PAH-HO-ah), town (1990 pop. 1,027), E Hawaii isl., Hawaii co., Hawaii, 18 mi/29 km SSE of Hilo, inland, 12 mi/19 km W of Cape Kumukahi; 19°30′N 154°56′W. Geothermal power plant to E. Kupaianaha Vent, source of active lava flows to sea, 13 mi/21 km WSW. Parts of Nanawale Forest Reserve to E and NE; Malama-Ki Forest Reserve to SE; Puna Forest Reserve and Wao Kele O Puna Natural Area Reserve to SW; Lava Tree State Park to E.

Pahokee (puh-HO-kee), town (☐ 5 sq mi/13 sq km; 1990 pop. 6,822), Palm Beach co., SE Fla., c.40 mi/64 km WNW of West Palm Beach, on SE shore of L. Okeechobee; 26°49′N 80°39′W. Shipping center for large fruit and vegetable farming area. Inc. 1922.

Pah-rum Peak, Nev.: see LAKE RANGE.

Pahrump (puh-RUHMP), uninc. town (1990 pop. 7,424), Nye co., S Nev., 43 mi/69 km W of Las Vegas, 7 mi/11.3 km NE of Calif. state boundary, in Pahrump Valley; 36°15′N 116°01′W. One of Nevada's fastest-growing areas in 1980s and 1990s; influx of retired citizens has swelled pop. from about 250. Has Nevada's only winery. Toiyabe Natl. Forest to NE, including Charleston Peak (11,918 ft/3,633 m), in Springs Mts. Ash Meadows Wildlife Management Area to NW; Cathedral Canyon to SE.

Pahuatlán, Mexico: see PAHUATLÁN DE VALLE.

Pahuatlán de Valle (pah-wah-TLAHN dai VAH-ye), town (1990 pop. 3,674), ⊙ Pahuatlán municipio, Puebla, central Mexico, 8 mi/12.9 km NW of Huauchinango; 20°17′N 98°09′W. Corn, coffee, sugarcane, fruit.

Pahute Mesa (puh-HOOT MAI-suh), S Nev., tableland (6,000 ft/1,830 m–7,000 ft/2,130 m high) in S Nye co. Part used as bombing and gunnery range.

Paia (PAH-EE-ah), town (1990 pop. 2,091), E Maui, Maui co., Hawaii, 8 mi/12.9 km E of Wailuku, 1 mi/1.6 km SE of N coast; 20°54′N 156°22′W. Paia Sugar Mill. Maunaolu Col. to SE.

Paige, uninc. village (1990 pop. 225), Bastrop co., S central Texas, 37 mi/60 km E of Austin. In cattle-ranching, agr. area. L. Bastrop and Bastrop State Park to SW.

Pailolo Channel (PEI-LO-lo), Pacific Ocean, bet. Maui and Molokai isls., Maui co., Hawaii, 9.2 mi/14.8 km wide.

Paimiut (PAI-mee-yoot), Inuit village, W Alaska, on lower Yukon R., and 20 mi/32 km SW of Holy Cross; 61°43′N 165°45′W.

Paincourtville (pank-ur-VIL), uninc. town (1990 pop. 1,550), Assumption parish, La. 9 mi/14.5 km SW of Donaldsonville; 29°59′N 91°03′W. Elev. 10 ft/3 m. W bank of Bayou Lafourche; sugarcane area.

Painesdale, village, Houghton co., NW Upper Peninsula, Mich., 7 mi/11.3 km SW of Houghton, on Keweenaw Peninsula; 47°02′N 88°40′W.

Painesville, city (1990 pop. 15,699), ⊙ Lake co., NE Ohio, on the Grand R., in a farm area; 41°43′N 81°14′W. It has RR shops and plants that mfg. chemicals and machinery. L. Erie Col. is in Painesville. Laid out c.1805; inc. as a city 1902.

Paint, borough (1990 pop. 1,091), Somerset co., SW central Pa., 6 mi/9.7 km SSE of Johnstown, on Paint Creek; 40°14′N 78°50′W. Coal. Livestock, dairying.

Paint Creek, c.106 mi/171 km long, S central Ohio; rises in Madison co.; flows S, past Washington Court House and Greenfield, to Bainbridge, then E to Scioto R. just below Chillicothe; 39°17′N 82°56′W. Near its mouth, it receives North Fork (c.47 mi/76 km long). Rattlesnake Creek (c.43 mi/69 km long) enters 5 mi/8 km S of Greenfield.

Paint River, c.45 mi/72 km long, SW Upper Peninsula, Mich.; formed by 2 branches in Iron co.; flows SE, past Crystal Falls, to Brule R. 12 mi/19 km NW of Iron Mountain; 46°13′N 88°43′W.

Paint Rock, town (1990 pop. 214), Jackson co., NE Ala., on Paint Rock R., and 17 mi/27 km W of Scottsboro. Woodworking.

Paint Rock, village (1990 pop. 227), ⊙ Concho co., W central Texas, on Concho R., and 30 mi/48 km E of San Angelo; 31°30′N 99°55′W. Elev. 1,639 ft/500 m. Wool, mohair market, in sheep, goat, cattle ranching area; wheat; cotton; mfg. (wool prods.). Prehistoric rock paintings, hunting, fishing nearby. O. H. Ivie L. reservoir to E.

Paint Rock River, in S Tenn. and NE Ala.; rises in Franklin co., Tenn.; flows 65 mi/105 km S into Jackson co., Ala., entering Wheeler Reservoir, in Tennessee R., 13 mi/21 km NW of Guntersville.

Painted Canyon, Calif.: see MECCA.

Painted Desert, badlands NE of the Little Colorado R.; Coconino, Navajo, and Apache cos.; NE Ariz.; stretching c.200 mi/322 km SE from the Grand Canyon. Includes N part of Petrified Forest Natl. Park. Partly in Navajo and Hopi Indian Reservation. Striking bands of color result from irregularly eroded layers of red and yellow sediment and bentonite clay.

Painted Post, village (☐ 1 sq mi/2.6 sq km; 1990 pop. 1,950), Steuben co., S N.Y., at junction of Tioga and Cohocton rivers here forming Chemung R., 15 mi/24 km WNW of Elmira; 42°09′N 77°05′W. Some mfg. Settled before 1790; inc. 1893.

Painted Rock Dam, Maricopa co., S central Ariz., on Gila R., in Citrus Valley, 60 mi/97 km WSW of Phoenix; 141 ft/43 m high; 33°03′N 113°00′W. Built (1960) for flood control. Formed a (now dry) reservoir with a max. capacity of 4,834,600 acre-ft. Painted Rock Mts. to S.

Painter, town (1990 pop. 259), Accomack co, E Va., 11 mi/18 km SSW of Onancock; 37°35′N 75°46′W. Accomack Vineyards are here. Agr. (livestock, poultry; grain, vegetables).

Paintsville, town (1990 pop. 4,354), ⊙ Johnson co., E Ky., near Levisa Fork, 50 mi/80 km S of Ashland; 37°49′N 82°48′W. In mt. agr. area (livestock; burley tobacco); mfg. (plumbing fittings, lumber, printing and publishing); bituminous coal mines in area. Mayo Mansion (1912) houses Our Lady of the Mountains School. Old trading post called Paint Lick Station was here. Butcher Hollow, family home of Loretta Lynn to

SE at Van Lear, featured in movie "Coal Miner's Daughter." Paintsville L. reservoir and State Park to NW

Paisley (PAIZ-lee), village (1991 pop. 1,102), S Ont., Canada, on Saugeen R., at confluence of North and South Saugeen rivers, 25 mi/40 km SW of Owen Sound; 44°18′N 81°17′W. Dairying, flour and alfalfa milling, woodworking.

Paisley (PAIZ-lee), village (1990 pop. 350), Lake co., S Oregon, 35 mi/56 km NNW of Lakeview; 42°41′N 120°32′W. Elev. 4,369 ft/1,332 m. Agr. (wheat, barley, oats; sheep, cattle ranching). Summer L., with hot springs at S end to NW. L. Abert to E. Fremont Natl. Forest to SW, including Gearhart Mt. Wilderness Area. Chewaucan Marsh to SE.

Pajacuarán (pah-hah-kwah-RAHN), town (1990 pop. 8,653), Michoacán, central Mexico, 20 mi/32 km SE of Ocotlán; 20°07′N 102°34′W. Agr. center (cereals, fruit, vegetables, livestock).

Pajapan (pah-HAH-pahn), town (1990 pop. 5,384), Veracruz, SE Mexico, in Gulf lowland, on Isthmus of Tehuantepec, 19 mi/31 km NW of Coatzacoalcos; 18°15′N 94°42′W. Fruit, livestock.

Pajarito Peak, N.Mex.: see NACIMIENTO MOUNTAINS.

Pajarito Plateau (PAH-huh-ree-to pla-TO), high tableland (6,000 ft/1,830 m–8,000 ft/2,440 m) in N central N.Mex., Sandoval and Los Alamos cos., W of Santa Fe; extends 50 mi/80 km S from Rio Chama along W side of Rio Grande and forms E flank of Jemez Mts. Cut by numerous small canyons once occupied by Pueblo Indians. Parts of area included in Bandelier Natl. Monument.

Pajaro (pah-har-oh), uninc. town (□ 1 sq mi/2.6 sq km; 1990 pop. 3,332), Monterey co., W Calif., 1 mi/1.6 km S of Watsonville, on opposite side of Pajaro R. 4 mi/6.4 km E of Monterey Bay, Pacific Ocean; 36°54′N 121°45′W. Fruits, vegetables, nursery stock; dairying; cattle. Santa Cruz Mts to NE; Sunset State Beach to W; Moss Landing State Park to S.

Pajaro River (pah-har-oh), c.30 mi/48 km long, W Calif.; formed 7 mi/11.3 km S of Gilroy in Santa Clara co., by joining of San Benito (from S) and Pechaco Creek (from E); flows generally W past Watsonville to the Pacific 4 mi/6.4 km W of Watsonville. Applegrowing in valley. San Benito R., drains S part of Santa Clara Valley.

Pakala Village (PAH-kah-LAH), village (1990 pop. 565), S Kauai isl., Kauai co., Hawaii, on SW coast, 18 mi/29 km W of Lihue; 21°56′N 159°39′W. Mfg. (cane-sugar processing). Rus. Fort Elizabeth State Historical Park to NW. Also called Makaweli.

Pakenham (PA-kuhn-uhm), town (1991 pop. 1,782), SE Ont., on Mississippi R., and 28 mi/45 km W of Ottawa; 45°20′N 76°17′W. Dairying, lumbering, mixed farming.

Pala, uninc. village, San Diego co., S Calif., in Pala Indian Reservation, 21 mi/34 km NE of Oceanside; 09°22′N 14°54′E. Here are restored bldgs. of Mission San Antonio de Pala, founded 1816 as an *asistencia* of Mission San Luis Rey. Mission Indian Reservation to E.

Palacios (puh-LAY-shus), town (1990 pop. 4,418), Matagorda co., S Texas, on Matagorda Bay, Gulf of Mexico, and 25 mi/40 km SW of Bay City; 28°42′N 96°14′W. Elev. 17 ft/5 m. Fishing port and resort, in irrigated coastal farmland producing rice, cotton, cattle; seafood packing; natural gas, some oil. Military camp here was active in World War II. Settled 1903, inc. 1909.

Palacios, Los, Cuba: see LOS PALACIOS.

Palatine, village (1990 pop. 39,253), Cook co., NE Ill., NW of Chicago; 42°06′N 88°02′W. Primarily residential, the growing village produces a variety of prods., such as machine tools and industrial adhesives. William Rainey Harper Col. is in Palatine. Inc. 1869.

Palatine Bridge, village (1990 pop. 520), Montgomery co., E central N.Y., on Mohawk R. (bridged), opposite Canajoharie, and 20 mi/32 km W of Amsterdam; 42°54′N 74°34′W.

Palatka (puh-LAT-kuh), town (□ 6 sq mi/15.5 sq km; 1990 pop. 10,201), ☉ Putnam co., NE Fla., port on St. Johns R. (bridged here), and 26 mi/42 km SW of St.

Augustine; 29°38′N 81°39′W. Shipping and wood-processing center; lumber milling; mfg. of furniture and prefabricated bldgs. Citrus-fruit packing.

Palau (pah-LAH-oo), mining settlement (1990 pop. 16,364), Múzquiz muncipio, Coahuila, N Mexico, in Sabinas coal dist., E of Múzquiz on Mexico Highway 53; 27°55′N 101°25′W. Coal mines; coke oven; coal-tar prods.

Palawai Basin (PAH-LAH-WEI), basin, S central Lanai isl., Maui co., Hawaii, on S side of Lanaihale. Relatively level plain is central to Lanai's large pineapple industry. Lanai City at N end of basin; Lanai Airport at W end.

Palco (PAL-ko), village (1990 pop. 295), Rooks co., NW central Kansas, 14 mi/23 km W of Plainville; 39°15′N 99°33′W. In wheat and livestock area.

Palenque (pah-LEN-ke), city (1990 pop. 17,061), in NW Chiapas, Mexico, 70 mi/113 km SE of Villa Herkmosa at the foot of the Sierra hacandona, and on Mexico Highway 199; 17°30′N 91°58′W. Rich forest area with cattle, dairy farming, milk prods., meat and leather. RR 7 mi/11.3 km N. A few miles to S are Mayan ruins of Palenque.

Palenque (pah-LAIN-kai), small town, Guantánamo prov., SE Cuba, in center of Guaso Meseta; 20°22′N 74°58′W. Surrounded by coffee and cocoa production.

Palenque National Park (pah-LEN-kai) (□ 9 sq mi/23.3 sq km), in NE Chiapas, Mexico, 4.3 mi/7 km S of the town of Palenque, at the base of the Sierra Lacandona. One of the most beautiful and archaeologically important lowland Maya sites. The bldgs. indicate that the maximum development occurred between 600–700. The Temple of the Inscriptions housed sarcophagus of Pacal, one of the most powerful Mayan kings. The palace covers an area of 3,850 sq mi/9,972 sq km, has remnants of fine stucco work, and is believed to be an observatory. A small mus. is on the grounds. A paved road leads to the park. Previously known as Nachan. The site is partially reconstructed.

Palenville, resort village (1990 pop. 940), Greene co., SE N.Y., at E base of the Catskills, at entrance to Kaaterskill Clove, 8 mi/12.9 km WSW of Catskill; 42°10′N 74°01′W. Legendary home of Rip Van Winkle; Sleepy Hollow, where he reputedly slept for 20 years, is nearby.

Palermo 1 (pah-LER-mo), uninc. town (1990 pop. 5,260), Butte co., N central Calif., 5 mi/8 km S of Oroville, in Sacramento Valley; Feather R. is to W; 39°27′N 121°32′W. Walnuts, almonds, prunes, peaches, olives, kiwi fruit, rice, wheat; cattle. L. Oroville Reservoir and State Recreation Area to NE. **2** (puh-LER-mo), town (1990 pop. 1,021), Waldo co., S Maine, 20 mi/32 km W of Belfast; 44°23′N 69°25′W.

Palermo, village (1990 pop. 95), Mountrail co., NW central N.Dak., 7 mi/11.3 km E of Stanley; 48°20′N 102°13′W.

Palestine (PAL-es-steen), city (1990 pop. 18,042), ☉ Anderson co., E Texas, 43 mi/69 km SSW of Tyler; 31°45′N 95°39′W. Elev. 510 ft/155 m. It is a market, processing, and RR center for a rich oil area and for the vegetables, melons; cattle and other produce of the rolling red hills. It has meat-packing plants; other mfg. includes school supplies, crushed stone, aircraft hardware, concrete. The city has many old Victorian homes. Palestine-Rusk Texas State RR State Historical Park runs E to Rusk, in Cherokee co.

Palestine (PAL-es-tine), town (1990 pop. 1,619), Crawford co., SE Ill., near the Wabash, 7 mi/11.3 km E of Robinson; 39°00′N 87°36′W. In agr. area (livestock; wheat, corn); RR shops. Settled 1811, laid out 1816, inc. 1855.

Palestine 1 (PAL-uh-stein), village (1990 pop. 711), St. Francis co., E Ark., 7 mi/11.3 km WSW of Forrest City, on L'Anguille R.; 34°58′N 90°54′W. **2** village (1990 pop. 800), Kosciusko co., N central Ind., 6 mi/9.7 km SW of Warsaw, at W end of Palestine L. Recreation. Corn, soybeans; cattle. **3** village (1990 pop. 197), Darke co., W Ohio, 7 mi/11 km WSW of Greenville, near Ind. state line; 40°03′N 84°45′W.

Palestine, Lake, reservoir, E Texas, on Neches R. (Anderson and Cherokee co. line), 22 mi/35 km SSW of Tyler; extends N into Henderson and Smith cos.;

20 mi/32 km long; 32°03′N 95°25′W. Max. capacity 726,390 acre-ft. Formed by Blackburn Crossing Dam (55 ft/17 m high), built (1971) for water supply and irrigation; also used for recreation.

Palfrey Lake, Maine and Canada: see CHIPUTNETICOOK LAKES.

Palikea (PAH-lee-KEI-ah), peak (3,098 ft/944 m), W Oahu, Honolulu co., Hawaii, in Waianae Range, 18 mi/29 km NW of Honolulu; 21°20′N 15°74′W.

Palisade, town (1990 pop. 1,871), Mesa co., W Colo., on Colorado R., and 11 mi/18 km ENE of Grand Junction; 39°06′N 108°21′W. Elev. 4,727 ft/1,441 m. Fruit-shipping point in orchards of the Grand Valley, fruit, grapes, beans, wheat; cattle, sheep; marble; 4 wineries. Coal mines in vicinity Isl. Acres State Park to NE; Colorado River State Park to W; Grand Mesa Natl. Forest to SE. Powderhorn Ski Area to E.

Palisade 1 village (1990 pop. 144), Aitkin co., central Minn., on Mississippi R., and 16 mi/26 km NE of Aitkin; 46°42′N 93°29′W. Mfg. (industrial furnaces). **2** village (1990 pop. 381), Hitchcock and Hayes cos., S Nebr., 11 mi/18 km N of Trenton; 40°21′N 101°06′W. Livestock; grain. **3** village, Eureka co., N central Nev., on Humboldt R., and 27 mi/43 km SW of Elko. Elev. 4,850 ft/1,478 m. Ships livestock.

Palisades, cliffs along the W bank of the Hudson R., NE N.J. and SE N.Y., extending from N of Jersey City, N.J., to the vicinity of Piermont, N.Y. Elev. 350 ft/107 m–550 ft/168 m. The Palisades, rising vertically from close to the water's edge, are the margin of a sill of diabase, formed by the intrusion of molten material, which hardened into a great sheet. Slow cooling developed the columnar structure; uplift and faulting occurred, it is believed, at the close of the Triassic period, and cents. of erosion exposed the cliffs. A large part of the most scenic sect., lying N of Fort Lee, N.J., is embraced in Palisades Interstate Park (73 sq mi/189 sq km). The park was created when John D. Rockefeller Jr. bought the cliffs (to keep them from being mined and crushed for RR ballast) and subsequently turned them over to N.J. for permanent preservation. The park, lying along the W bank of the river, includes a chain of hilly, wooded recreational areas bet. Fort Lee, N.J., and Bear Mountain, N.Y. There are scenic roads, trails for hikers, campgrounds, and facilities for winter and summer sports.

Palisades Interstate Park, N.Y. and N.J.: see PALISADES.

Palisades Interstate Parkway, a 4-lane wooded highway, SE N.Y., extending from Ft. Lee, N.J. (at the George Washington Bridge) to Fort Montgomery, N.Y.; 42 mi/68 km long. Completed in Aug. 1958, it is named for the Palisades, a line of Triassic-period basaltic diorite and red sandstone cliffs rising along the W side of the Hudson R. As well as being a major commuter route into N.Y. city, the highway's primary role is to provide access to 17 state parks and 5 historic sites of the Palisades Interstate Park Region.

Palisades Nuclear Power Plant, Michigan: see VAN BUREN, CO.

Palisades Park, residential borough (1990 pop. 14,536), Bergen co., NE N.J., 3 mi/4.8 km SE of Hackensack; 40°51′N 74°00′W. Inc. 1899.

Palisades Reservoir (□ 25 sq mi/65 sq km), Bonneville co., SE Idaho, on S. Fork Snake R., bet. Targhee and Caribou natl. forests, 44 mi/70 km E of Idaho Falls; 43°20′N 111°13′W. Max. capacity 1,417,810 acre-ft. Extends SE to Wyo. state line. Formed by Palisades Dam (270 ft/82 m high), built (1957) by the Bureau of Reclamation for irrigation; also used for power generation, flood control, recreation, and as a fish and wildlife pond.

Palisadoes, The, peninsula, Kingston parish, SE Jamaica, a narrow spit (c.7 mi/11.3 km long) bounding Kingston Harbour; 17°56′N 76°46′W. On its W tip is the once prosperous town of Port Royal. In center, opposite Kingston, is the Norman Manley Palisadoes Internatl. airport. The peninsula is coextensive with Port Royal section of Kingston Harbour.

Palizada (pah-lee-SAH-dah), city (1990 pop. 2,577) and

township, Campeche, SE Mexico, on SW Yucatán Peninsulaon Río Palizada, a distributary channel of Río Usumacinta, 32 mi/51 km SSW of Carmen; 18°18'N 92°08'W. Corn, sugarcane, tobacco, henequen, fruit, livestock; dairying, furniture making.

Palm Bay, city (□ 66 sq mi/171 sq km; 1990 pop. 62,632), Brevard co., E central Fla., 5 mi/8 km SW of Melbourne; 27°59'N 80°39'W. Mfg includes aerospace and aircraft components, semiconductors, and optical instruments.

Palm Beach, county (□ 2,386 sq mi/6,180 sq km; 1990 pop. 863,518), SE Fla., on the Atlantic; ⊙ West Palm Beach; 26°38'N 80°26'W. Heavily urbanized for 10 mi/16 km inland along the Atlantic coast zone (E); fastest-growing portion of SE Fla. (Gold Coast) megalopolis. Everglades small-scale farming, dairy, and poultry area, with noted resort sect. (West Palm Beach, Palm Beach, Delray Beach), along coast. Mfg. of food and wood prods. Fishing. Includes L. Okeechobee (NW) and is crossed by several drainage canals from lake to the Atlantic. Formed 1909.

Palm Beach, town (□ 10 sq mi/26 sq km; 1990 pop. 9,814), Palm Beach co., SE Fla., on a barrier isl. bet. the Atlantic Ocean and West Palm Beach, which here lines L. Worth (a lagoon); 26°41'N 80°02'W. It is a well-known resort of the wealthy, with many fine estates, luxurious hotels, and yachting facilities. Worth Ave. retail dist. among finest shopping streets in the U.S. In the winter its pop. expands to much larger numbers. Inc. 1911.

Palm Beach Gardens, city (□ 26 sq mi/67 sq km; 1990 pop. 22,965), Palm Beach co., SE Fla., 10 mi/16 km N of West Palm Beach; 26°50'N 80°07'W. Industries include printing and publishing, diversified light mfg.

Palm Canyon, Calif.: see PALM SPRINGS.

Palm City, town (□ 3 sq mi/7.8 sq km; 1990 pop. 3,925), Martin co., E central Fla., 2 mi/3.2 km SW of Stuart; 27°09'N 80°16'W. Mfg. includes medical laboratory instruments, water chlorination equip., cable assemblies, resins.

Palm City, suburban section of San Diego city, San diego co., S Calif., in S extension of city, 12 mi/19 km SSE of downtown San Diego, on Otay R. Residential area.

Palm Coast, town (□ 20 sq mi/52 sq km; 1990 pop. 14,287), Flagler co., NE Fla., 23 mi/37 km SSE of St. Augustine; 29°34'N 81°12'W. Mfg. includes power-supply systems, electronic equip., fiberglass boats, and yachts.

Palm Coast, local name for the Atlantic coast of NE Fla., stretching from Daytona Beach on the S to metropolitan Jacksonville on the N.

Palm Desert, city (1990 pop. 23,252), Riverside co., S Calif., suburb 11 mi/18 km SE of Palm Springs, on Whitewater R.; 33°44'N 116°23'W. San Bernardino Natl. Forest and Santa Rosa Indian Reservation to SW; Agua Caliente Indian Reservation to NW. Cattle, dairying, fruit, avocados, flowers, nursery stock, grain. Seat of Col. of the Desert (2-year). Mfg. (printing and publishing, sand and gravel processing). Rapidly growing resort and retirement community, noted for its golf courses.

Palm Desert Country, uninc. town (1990 pop. 5,626), Riverside co., S Calif., residential suburb 11 mi/18 km SE of Palm Springs and 2 mi/3.2 km SSW of Palm Desert; 33°45'N 116°19'W. A rapidly growing resort and retirement community in irrigated agr. area.

Palm Harbor, city (□ 26 sq mi/67 sq km; 1990 pop. 50,256), Hillsborough co., W central Fla., 22 mi/35 km WNW of Tampa; 28°05'N 82°45'W. Diversified light mfg.

Palm Island, St. Vincent and the Grenadines, West Indies; 12°35'N 61°24'W. Just off Union Isl., privately leased by resort developer.

Palm Springs, city (□ 77 sq mi/199 sq km; 1990 pop. 40,181), Riverside co., S Calif., 50 mi/80 km ESE of Riverside; 33°47'N 116°32'W. Light mfg. It is a verdant desert oasis and a fashionable resort, site of many popular golf tournaments. It was known to the Spanish as early as 1774 as Agua Caliente because of its hot springs. By 1872 it was a regular stop on the stagecoach run bet. Prescott, Ariz., and Los Angeles. In Agua Caliente Indian Reservation; nearby are Mt. San Jacinto, (Mt. San Jacinto Wilderness State Park to W) with a cable run almost to the top, and Palm Canyon, containing stands of Washingtonia palms estimated to be over 1,000 years old; part of San Bernardino Natl Forest to W and S. Also in the area are the Joshua Tree Natl. Monument to NE, a community col., and a marine corps base. Palm Springs Municipal Airport. Founded 1876, inc. 1938.

Palm Valley, town (1990 pop. 1,199), Cameron co., extreme S Texas, residential suburb 5 mi/8 km W of Harlingen; 26°11'N 97°45'W. Irrigated Rio Grande Valley agr. region.

Palma, Río de la (PAHL-muh, REE-o dai lah), 47 mi/76 km long, river, Matanzas prov., W Cuba; rises S of Los Arabos; flows N to Santa Clara Bay. Drains 339 sq mi/878 sq km. Poor navigability.

Palma Soriano (PAHL-muh sor-ee-AHN-o), city (1981 pop. 55,851), Santiago de Cuba prov., SE Cuba, in the Cauto R. valley; 20°13'N 76°00'W. It is a road and RR hub and the commercial and processing center for a rich coffee and sugarcane area. Palma Soriano emerged in the early 19th cent. as the heart of a coffee-growing zone developed by Fr. emigrants from Haiti. Sugar mill Dos Ríos 2 mi/3.2 km N.

Palmar de Bravo (PAHL-mahr de BRAH-vo), town (1990 pop. 3,258), Puebla, central Mexico, 13 mi/21 km SSW of Ciudad Serdán; 18°50'N 97°34'W. Elev. 7,415 ft/2,260 m. Cereals, maguey, livestock.

Palmarito (pahl-mah-REE-to), town, Santiago de Cuba prov., E Cuba, on Cauto R., on RR, and 23 mi/37 km NNW of Santiago de Cuba; 20°19'N 75°57'W. Manganese mining. Now on shore of Mella Dam (created in 1980s). Sometimes called Palmarito de Cauto.

Palmdale, city (□ 77 sq mi/199 sq km; 1990 pop. 68,842), Los Angeles co., S Calif., in irrigated Antelope Valley (W Mojave Desert), suburb 35 mi/56 km NNE of downtown Los Angeles; 34°37'N 118°05'W. Near Little Rock Creek at the forming of L. Palmdale Reservoir. Mfg. (printing and publishing, power valves, screw machine prods.); agr. (onions, grain, peaches; dairying; cattle, poultry; eggs). Has airfield for jet-aircraft testing; chosen 1951 as site for mfg. of air-navigation systems, and aerospace vehicles, advanced aircraft design systems. Calif. Aqueduct runs E-W to S; San Gabriel Mts. (Angeles Natl. Forest to S); Edwards Air Force Base to NE; Saddleback Butte State Park to NE.

Palmdale East, uninc. town (1990 pop. 3,052), Los Angeles co., S Calif., residential suburb 3 mi/4.8 km E of Palmdale; 34°35'N 118°04'W. Fruit, nursery prods.; dairying, cattle. Palmdale Airport to N.

Palmer 1 town (1990 pop. 230), Pocahontas co., N central Iowa, 8 mi/12.9 km SSW of Pocahontas; 42°37'N 94°35'W. Livestock; grain. **2** town (1990 pop. 4,069), including Palmer village, Hampden co., S Mass., 14 mi/23 km ENE of Springfield; 42°10'N 72°19'W. Mfg. (paper prods., textiles, brushes, metal culverts); dairying, poultry; apples. Has state fish hatchery. Includes villages of Bondsville (1990 pop. 1,992), Thorndike, and Three Rivers (1990 pop. 3,006) at junction of Ware and Quaboag rivers (forming Chicopee R.). Settled 1716, inc. 1775. **3** town (1990 pop. 769), Grundy co., SE central Tenn., in the Cumberlands, 27 mi/43 km NW of Chattanooga; 35°21'N 85°34'W. In coal-mining region. **4** town (1990 pop. 1,659), Ellis co., N Texas, 25 mi/40 km SSE of Dallas; 32°25'N 96°40'W. Cotton; dairying; cattle; corn, wheat.

Palmer 1 village (1990 pop. 2,866), S Alaska, on Matanuska R., and 40 mi/64 km NE of Anchorage; 61°36'N 149°06'W. In Alaska RR spur, on Glenn Highway; market for Matanuska Valley agr. development. Airport. Hq. of Matanuska Valley Farmers' Cooperating Assn. Site of agr. experiment station of Univ. of Alaska and Mat-Su Community Col. Transportation Mus., Palmer Fair. **2** village (1990 pop. 275), Christian co., central Ill., 8 mi/12.9 km SW of Taylorville; 39°27'N 89°24'W. In agr. area. **3** village (1990 pop. 121), Washington co., N Kansas, 13 mi/21 km SSW of Washington; 39°37'N 97°08'W. Grain; livestock. **4** village, Marquette co., NW Upper Peninsula, Mich., 12 mi/19 km WSW of Marquette; 46°26'N 87°35'W. Terminus of RR spur; iron-ore mining. **5** village (1990 pop. 753), Merrick co., E central Nebr., 14 mi/23 km NW of Central City, near Loup R; 41°13'N 98°13'W. RR terminus. Dairying; grain; livestock.

Palmer Heights, uninc. town (1990 pop. 3,960), Northampton co., E Pa., residential suburb 3 mi/4.8 km W of Easton; 40°41'N 75°16'W.

Palmer Lake, town (1990 pop. 1,480), El Paso co., central Colo., on Monument Creek, in SE foothills of Front Range, 40 mi/64 km S of Denver, and 20 mi/32 km NNW of Colorado Springs; 39°07'N 104°54'W. Elev. 7,225 ft/2,202 m. Resort. Mfg. (wildflower growing kits, radio and television equip.). U.S. Air Force Acad. to S. Small lake nearby; Pike Natl. Forest to W.

Palmerston, town (1991 pop. 2,313), S Ont., Canada, 32 mi/51 km NW of Kitchener; 43°50'N 80°51'W. Mfg.; dairying.

Palmerton (PAHL-muhr-tuhn), borough (1990 pop. 5,394), Carbon co., E Pa., 15 mi/24 km NNW of Allentown, on Lehigh R., at mouth of Aquashicola Creek; 40°47'N 75°37'W. Mfg. (aluminum powder, apparel); sand quarries; agr. (soybeans, potatoes, grain; livestock, dairying). Little Gap Ski Area to E; Beltzville L. reservoir and Beltzville State Park to N; Lehigh Valley Tunnel (highway) through Blue Mt. ridge, to SW. Settled 1737, laid out 1898, inc. 1912.

Palmetto 1 (pal-MED-do), town (□ 3 sq mi/7.8 sq km; 1990 pop. 9,268), Manatee co., W central Fla., on Manatee R. near its mouth on Tampa Bay, and connected by bridge with Bradenton (3 mi/4.8 km to S); 27°31'N 82°34'W. Boating and fishing resort. **2** (pal-MET-o), town (1990 pop. 2,612), Fulton and Coweta cos., NW central Ga., 22 mi/35 km SW of Atlanta; 33°32'N 84°40'W. Mfg. of concrete, trusses, millwork, boat trailers. Inc. 1854.

Palmetto (PAWL-met-uh), village (1990 pop. 229), St. Landry parish, S central La., 16 mi/26 km NE of Opelousas; 30°43'N 91°59'W. In timber and agr. area.

Palmetto Point, town, central Bahama Isls., on E central shore of Eleuthera Isl., opposite Governor's Harbour, 75 mi/121 km E of Nassau; 25°10'N 76°09'E. Tomato growing.

Palmhurst, village (1990 pop. 326), Hidalgo co., S Texas, residential suburb 5 mi/8 km NW of McAllen; 26°15'N 98°17'W. Agr. area (citrus, vegetables, cotton).

Palmillas (pahl-MEE-yahs), town (1990 pop. 943), Tamaulipas, NE, Mexico, in Sierra Madre Oriental, 40 mi/64 km SW of Ciudad Victoria on Mexico Highway 101. Elev. 4,242 ft/1,293 m. Cereals; livestock.

Palmillas (pahl-MEE-yuhz), village, Matanzas prov., W Cuba, 10 mi/16 km ESE of Colón; 20°43'N 80°48'W. Fruit, honey; cattle. Sometimes Palmilla.

Palmira (pahl-MEE-ruh), town, Cienfuegos prov., central Cuba, on RR, and 7 mi/11.3 km NNE of Cienfuegos; 22°14'N 80°23'W. Sugar-growing center; 6 sugar mills within 12-mi/19-km radius.

Palms, SW residential sect. of Los Angeles city, Los Angeles co., S Calif., 9 mi/14.5 km W of downtown Los Angeles adjoining Culver City (SE).

Palms, Isle of, S.C.: see ISLE OF PALMS.

Palmview, town (1990 pop. 1,818), Hidalgo co., S Texas, residential suburb 8 mi/12.9 km W of McAllen; 26°13'N 98°22'W. Agr. area (citrus, vegetables, cotton). Bentsen–Rio Grande Valley State Park to S.

Palmyra (pahl-MEI-ruh), city (1990 pop. 3,371), ⊙ Marion co., NE Mo., on North R., near Mississippi R. and 10 mi/16 km NW of Hannibal; 39°47'N 91°31'W. Soybeans, corn, wheat; hogs, cattle; mfg. (agr. chemicals, magnesium die casting). Settled c.1819.

Palmyra 1 (pal-MEI-ruh), town (1990 pop. 621), Harrison co., S Ind., 14 mi/23 km NNE of Corydon; 38°25'N 86°07'W. Agr.; stone quarries; timber. **2** town (1990 pop. 1,867), Somerset co., central Maine, on the Sebasticook, and 18 mi/29 km ENE of Skowhegan; 44°51'N 69°22'W. **3** town (1990 pop. 1,539), Jefferson co., SE Wis., 26 mi/42 km NE of Janesville; 42°52'N 88°35'W. In agr. and resort region; mfg. (food supplements). Kettle Moraine State Forest (S unit) to SE.

Cross references are shown in SMALL CAPITALS. The pronunciation key is on page xv. The dates of population figures are on page xii.

Palmyra 1 village (1990 pop. 722), Macoupin co., SW central Ill., 13 mi/21 km NNW of Carlinville; 39°25′N 90°00′W. In agr. and coal area. **2** village (1990 pop. 545), Otoe co., SE Nebr., 17 mi/27 km ESE of Lincoln, and on branch of Little Nemaha R; 40°42′N 96°23′W. Gatling guns. **3** village (□ 1 sq mi/2.6 sq km; 1990 pop. 3,566), Wayne co., W N.Y., on the Barge Canal and 20 mi/32 km ESE of Rochester; 43°03′N 77°13′W. Mfg. (seals, gaskets and packings, machine parts; paper box mfg., milling); in fruit-growing area, agr. (dairy prods.; potatoes, fruit). Joseph Smith, founder and 1st president of the Mormon Church, lived and published *The Book of Mormon* here. Hill Cumorah Center, and pageant held each August atop the glacial drumlin where Smith buried his tablets; 4 mi/6.4 km S of villlage. **4** (pal-MEI-ruh), uninc. village, Halifax co., NE N.C., 15 mi/24 km NE of Tarboro, near Roanoke R. **5** uninc. village, ⊙ Fluvanna co., central Va., on Rivanna R., 16 mi/26 km SE of Charlottesville; 37°51′N 78°15′W. Light mfg.; agr. (livestock; grain, tobacco); timber. L. Monticello reservoir to NW.

Palmyra 1 (pal-MEI-ruh), borough (1990 pop. 7,056), Burlington co., SW N.J., on Delaware R. (bridged here) opposite Philadelphia, and 5 mi/8 km NE of Camden; 40°00′N 75°01′W. Mfg. (machinery, metal prods., electric signs). Inc. 1923. **2** (PAHL-mei-ruh), borough (1990 pop. 6,910), Lebanon co., SE central Pa., 14 mi/23 km ENE of Harrisburg; 40°18′N 76°35′W. Mfg. (food prods., flour, machinery, paperboard boxes, industrial aerators); limestone. Agr. (grain, soybeans, apples; livestock, poultry, dairying). Millard Airport to E; Memorial Lake State Park and Fort Indiantown Military Reserve to N (scheduled to close in late 1990's). Settled 1749, inc. 1913.

Palmyra (pahl-MEI-rah), not permanently inhabited atoll (2 sq mi/5.2 sq km), central Pacific, one of the Line Isls., c.1,100 mi/1,700 km SW of Honolulu. First visited by Americans in 1802, and later claimed by the Hawaiian kingdom (1862) and Great Britain (1889), it was annexed by the U.S. in 1898. Palmyra was under the jurisdiction of the city and county of Honolulu until Hawaii was granted statehood in 1959. The atoll is now under the control of the U.S. Dept. of the Interior.

Palo, town (1990 pop. 514), Linn co., E Iowa, on Cedar R. and 9 mi/14.5 km NW of Cedar Rapids; 42°03′N 91°47′W. In agr. area.

Palo (PAI-lo), village, W Sask., Canada, near Whiteshore L. (11 mi/18 km long), 40 mi/64 km S of North Battleford. Sodium-sulphate production; wheat, oats, rye, flax.

Palo Alto, county (□ 569 sq mi/1,474 sq km; 1990 pop. 10,669), NW Iowa; ⊙ Emmetsburg; 43°05′N 94°40′W. Prairie agr. area (cattle, hogs, poultry; corn, oats, soybeans) drained by West Des Moines R. Sand and gravel pits. Lost Island, Virgin, Silver and Rush lakes near W boundary; Five Island L. NE of Emmetsburg. General flooding occurred in 1993. Formed 1851.

Palo Alto, city (1990 pop. 55,900), Santa Clara co., W Calif., 12 mi/19 km WNW of San Jose and 27 mi/43 km SSE of San Francisco, near San Francisco Bay; bounded by San Francisquito Creek on NW (San Mateo co. line); 37°24′N 122°08′W. Nearby Stanford is the seat of Stanford Univ. Although primarily residential, Palo Alto has aerospace, electronics, and advanced research industries. The city's economic growth has been spurred as a result of regional developments in Silicon Valley technology. High tech mfg. A local attraction is "El Palo Alto," a tree that is more than 1,000 years old. Moffett Field Naval Air Station to E; Palo Alto Airport to N, on bay; Stanford Univ. to S; Dunbarton Bridge (separate highway and RR bridges) and Hetch Hetchy Aqueduct, which delivers water from Sierra Nevada to San Francisco, 4 mi/6.4 km to NE; both cross narrow point in lower San Francisco Bay. Inc. 1894.

Palo Alto (PA-lo AL-to), borough (1990 pop. 1,192), Schuylkill co., E central Pa., suburb 1 mi/1.6 km E of Pottsville, on Schuylkill R.; 40°40′N 76°10′W. RR junction. Silver Creek Reservoir to S. Laid out c.1844; inc. 1854.

Palo Alto Battlefield National Historic Site, Cameron co., S Texas, 8 mi/12.9 km N of Brownsville. Covers an area of 50 acres/20 ha. Site of the 1st of 2 major battles of the Mexican War fought on U.S. soil (May 8, 1846). The 2d major battle was fought the next day in Rosaca de la Palma Valley, in same general area. Authorized 1978.

Palo Duro Canyon (PAL-o DUHR-o), Randall and Armstrong cos. extreme N Texas, in the Panhandle, c.15 mi/24 km SE of Amarillo. A colorful gorge gashed in Caprock escarpment by Prairie Dog Town Fork of Red R., it reveals 4 geologic ages. Palo Duro Canyon State Park is located in upper (W) part of canyon (□ 16,402 acres/6,638 ha), with camping and other recreational facilities. Explored by Coronado's expedition, 1541; in 19th cent., Col. Charles Goodnight drove a herd through canyon to establish 1st Panhandle ranch.

Palo Duro Creek 1 (PAL-o DUHR-o), c.60 mi/97 km long, extreme N Texas, in the Panhandle; rises in W Deaf Smith co., at N.Mex. state line; flows generally E to join Tierra Blanca Creek near Canyon to form Prairie Dog Town Fork of Red R., whose scenic gorge, beginning just E of Canyon, is called Palo Duro Canyon. **2** starts as South Palo Duro Creek, intermittent stream, E of Dumas and 40 mi/64 km N of Amarillo, Moore co., extreme N Texas, flows ENE to Morse, then NE as Palo Duro Creek, through Palo Duro Reservoir (Hartford co.) into Texas co., in Okla. Panhandle, joins N. Canadian R. (Beaver R.) 25 mi/40 km E of Guymon.

Palo Pinto, county (□ 985 sq mi/2,551 sq km; 1990 pop. 25,055), N central Texas; ⊙ Palo Pinto; 32°45′N 98°18′W. Crossed NW-SE by Brazos R.; part of Possum Kingdom L. is in NW (Possum Kingdom State Park on W boundary). Palo Pinto Mts. (c.1,450 ft/442 m) in W. Agr., ranching, resort region (includes Mineral Wells); peanuts, oats, grain sorghum, wheat; cattle, horses. Oil, natural gas, clay, sand and gravel. Hunting, fishing. Timber (mainly juniper, locally called "cedar"). Span. for "Painted Stick." L. Palo Pinto reservoir in S. Formed 1856.

Palo Pinto, uninc. village (1990 pop. 350), ⊙ Palo Pinto co., N central Texas, 55 mi/89 km W of Fort Worth, near the Brazos. Elev. 1,043 ft/318 m. In farm, cattle-ranch area; peanuts, wheat.

Palo Pinto, Lake, reservoir (□ 31 sq mi/80 sq km), Palo Pinto co., central Texas, on Brazos R., 60 mi/96 km W of Fort Worth; 32°52′N 98°26′W. Max. capacity 570,200 acre-ft. Formed by Morris Sheppard Dam (154 ft/47 m high, 2,740 ft/835 m long), built (1941) for power generation.

Palo Seco (PAH-lo SAI-ko), village, SW Trinidad, Trinidad and Tobago, 15 mi/24 km SW of San Fernando. Petroleum wells.

Palo Verde, uninc. village, Imperial co., Calif., 13 mi/21 km SW of Blythe, near Colorado R. Cibola Natl. Wildlife Refuge (Ariz. and Calif.) to S. Irrigated agr. area.

Palo Verde 1, 2, and 3 Nuclear Power Plants, Arizona: see MARICOPA, CO.

Palo Verde Valley, SE Calif., irrigated desert basin in Imperial and Riverside cos., extending c.40 mi/64 km bet. Colorado R. (E) and low desert ranges (W). Blythe is chief town; in valley also are Midland (gypsum mining), Ripley, Palo Verde. Alfalfa, grain, cotton, fruit, vegetables, melons; dairying.

Palomar, Mount, peak (6,138 ft/1,871 m), San Diego co., S Calif., 48 mi/77 km NNE of San Diego, in Palomar Mt. State Park surrounded by Cleveland Natl. Forest; 33°21′N 116°50′W. It is the site of the Palomar Observatory, operated jointly by the Calif. Inst. of Technology and Carnegie Inst. It had the world's largest reflecting telescope (200 in/508 cm) until 1976, when Soviet scientists constructed a larger one. The increase in smog from S Calif. urban areas has reduced the clarity and reliability of the telescope.

Palos (PAHL-oz), town, La Habana prov., W Cuba, on RR, 45 mi/72 km SE of Havana, along N edge of the Meridional Karstic Plain, and 12 mi/19 km from Gulf of Batabanó; 22°49′N 81°44′W. In sugarcane-growing region.

Palos Heights (PAY-los), city (1990 pop. 11,478), Cook co., NE Ill., suburb 25 mi/40 km SW of downtown Chicago, on Calumet Sag Channel; 41°40′N 87°47′W. Light mfg. Trinity Christian Col. is here.

Palos Hills (PAY-los), city (1990 pop. 17,803), Cook co., NE Ill., suburb 25 mi/40 km SW of downtown Chicago; 41°42′N 87°49′W. Site of Moraine Valley Community Col. Light mfg. On Calumet Sog Channel.

Palos Park (PAY-los), village (1990 pop. 4,199), Cook co., NE Ill., SW suburb of Chicago, 15 mi/24 km NE of Joliet; 41°39′N 87°50′W.

Palos Verdes Estates, city (1990 pop. 13,512), Los Angeles co., S Calif., residential suburb 18 mi/29 km SW of downtown Los Angeles, on Pacific Ocean (Malaga Cove), at W base of Palos Verdes peninsula; 33°48′N 118°24′W. It is a residential community and suburb within the Los Angeles–Long Beach Metro area. City of Torrance to NE; Redondo State Beach to N; Flat Rock Point in SW. Inc. 1939.

Palos Verdes Hills, Los Angeles co., S Calif., low rolling range (1,300 ft/396 m) occupying Palos Verde peninsula. Sometimes called San Pedro Hills.

Palos Verdes Peninsula, Los Angeles co., S Calif., hilly land extension on Pacific Ocean coast bet. Santa Monica Bay (NW) and San Pedro Bay (E). Area of affluent suburbs developed in 1940s through 1970s. Includes communities of Palos Verdes Estates, Rolling Hills, Rolling Hills Estates, Rancho Palos Verdes and the San Pedro section of Los Angeles city. Marineland of the Pacific is at Point Vicente, in SW. Palos Verdes Point in W; Point Fermin in SE.

Palourde, Lake (puh-LOORD), SE La., just NE of Morgan City; c.6 mi/10 km long, 3 mi/5 km wide. Entered from N by Grand R.; joined by waterways to Grand L. (W) and L. Verret (N). Port Allen–Morgan City Canal to W. Bird sanctuary on NW shore.

Palouse (puh-LOOS), town (1990 pop. 915), Whitman co., SE Wash., 12 mi/19 km NNE of Pullman and on Palouse R., in the Palouse region, near Idaho state line; 46°55′N 117°04′W. RR junction. Barley, oats, lentils, wheat, peas; cattle, sheep, hogs; timber; mfg. (dry peas and lentils processing). Kamiak Butte (3,641 ft/1,110 m) to SW; St. Joe Natl. Forest (Idaho) to NE. Inc. 1889.

Palouse Falls, Wash.: see PALOUSE RIVER.

Palouse River, c.140 mi/225 km long, in N Idaho and SE Wash.; rises in E Latah co., Idaho; flows generally W, past Palouse and Colfax, Wash., to Snake R. 22 mi/35 km NW of Dayton. Drops over Palouse Falls (198 ft/60 m high) a few miles above mouth. Wheat, barley; livestock. Region, especially Wash., is generally referred to as the Palouse Country.

Paluxy Creek, 25 mi/40 km long, N central Texas; rises in several streams NE of Stephenville, c.50 mi/80 km SW of Fort Worth; flows generally ESE, past Glen Rose, to the Brazos R.

Pambrun, Mount (10,400 ft/3,170 m), SE B.C., Canada, in Selkirk Mts., 50 mi/80 km NE of Nelson; 50°06′N 116°35′W.

Pamlico (PAM-lik-o), county (□ 566 sq mi/1,466 sq km; 1990 pop. 11,372), E N.C.; ⊙ Bayboro; 35°08′N 76°40′W. Forested and swampy tidewater area; bounded by Pamlico Sound (E), Pamlico R. estuary (far NE), Neuse R. estuary; arm of Atlantic Ocean, (S). Agr. area (potatoes, corn, tobacco, wheat, soybeans, cotton, hogs), fish, crabs, shrimp; timber. Intracoastal Waterway crosses co. in E. Bay R. estuary indents co. in E, free ferry crosses Neuse R. (S). Formed 1872.

Pamlico River 1 (PAM-lik-o), estuary, N.C., lower reach of the Tar River where it enters Pamlico Sound. **2** (PAM-lik-o), estuary, Beaufort co., E N.C., W extension of Pamlico Sound, arm of Atlantic Ocean, receives Tar R. from W at Washington; 38 mi/61 km long, 1 mi/1.6 km–5 mi/8 km wide. Estuary has several arms, largest being Pungo R. estuary and Rose Bay, both on N side near entrance. Intracoastal Waterway crosses sound near its entrance and continues N through Pungo R.; ferry crossing at mid-course.

Pamlico Sound (PAM-lik-o), lagoon, E N.C., separated from the Atlantic Ocean by the Outer Banks, on E, a row of low, sandy barrier isls., Cape Hatteras on opposite side on barrier; largest lagoon along the U.S. East Coast; 80 mi/129 km long and 15 mi/24 km–30 mi/48 km wide. It receives the Neuse R. and Pamlico R. (estuary of Tar R.), from W and is linked on the N with Albemarle Sound through Roanoke and Croatan sounds (passages); Core Sound to S. Cape Hatteras Natl. Seashore is located on the barrier isls. (E and SE); Cape Lookout Natl. Seashore on Portsmouth Isl. (S). Along the coastal areas are numerous waterfowl nesting sites, and there is some commercial fishing in the waters. Including Pea Isl. Natl. Wildlife Refuge to NE, Swanquarter Natl. Wildlife Refuge on mainland in SW.

Pampa (PAM-pah), city (1990 pop. 19,959), ⊙ Gray co., extreme N Texas, 55 mi/89 km ENE of Amarillo; 35°32′N 100°57′W. Elev. 3,234 ft/986 m. This cow town on the Panhandle plains still ships cattle and wheat and packs meat; it is also an industrial center with refineries and other oil-based industries. Oil-drilling machinery, and chemicals are also mfg. in Pampa. McClellan Creek Natl. Grassland to S.

Pamplico (PAMP-luh-ko), town (1990 pop. 1,314), Florence co., E central S.C., 17 mi/27 km SE of Florence; 34°00′N 79°34′W. Mfg. of synthetic fabrics and lumber. Agr. includes cotton, grain; hogs, chickens. Logging and timber.

Pamplin City, town (1990 pop. 208), Appomattox and Prince Edward cos., S central Va., 27 mi/43 km ESE of Lynchburg; 37°15′N 78°40′W. RR junction; mfg. (clothing); agr. (grain, tobacco, soybeans; cattle; dairying).

Pamunkey River (pa-MUHN-kee), c.90 mi/145 km long, E Va.; formed c.20 mi/32 km N of Richmond by joining of North Anna and South Anna rivers; flows SE past Hanover, joins Mattaponi R. at West Point to form York R.; 37°48′N 77°24′W. Lower 50 mi/80 km navigable.

Pan de Guajaibón (pahn dai gwah-hei-BON), highest peak (2,293 ft/699 m) in the Sierra del Rosario, W Cuba, 35 mi/56 km NE of Pinar del Río; 22°48′N 83°21′W.

Pan de Matanzas (pahn dai mah-TAHN-zuhs), peak (1,250 ft/381 m), Matanzas prov., W Cuba, in hilly range, 6 mi/9.7 km W of Matanzas, near Matanzas–La Habana prov. border; 23°03′N 81°41′W.

Pana (PAI-nah), city (1990 pop. 5,796), Christian co., central Ill., 17 mi/27 km SE of Taylorville; 39°23′N 89°04′W. Shipping center for agr. area (grain); oil refinery; commercial rose growing. Inc. 1857.

Panabá (pah-nah-BAH), town (1990 pop. 5,040), Yucatán, SE Mexico, 12 mi/19 km NW of Tizimín; 21°20′N 88°16′W. Henequen, chicle.

Panacea (pan-uh-SEE-uh), town, Wakulla co., NW Fla., 31 mi/50 km SSW of Tallahassee. Mfg. includes crabmeat processing, concrete, septic tanks.

Panache, Lake (pa-NASH), SE central Ont., Canada, 20 mi/32 km SW of Sudbury; 20 mi/32 km long, 5 mi/8 km wide.

Panama 1 town (1990 pop. 201), Shelby co., W Iowa, on Mosquito Creek and 9 mi/14.5 km WNW of Harlan; 41°43′N 95°28′W. **2** town (1990 pop. 1,528), Le Flore co., E Okla., suburb 8 mi/12.9 km N of Poteau, on Poteau R.; 35°10′N 94°40′W. Agr. and timber area.

Panama 1 village (1990 pop. 294), in Bond and Montgomery cos., SW central Ill., 8 mi/12.9 km SSW of Hillsboro; 39°01′N 89°31′W. In agr. area (corn, wheat; dairy prods.). **2** village (1990 pop. 207), Lancaster co., SE Nebr., 16 mi/26 km SSE of Lincoln; 40°36′N 96°30′W. **3** village (□2 sq mi/5.2 sq km; 1990 pop. 468), Chautauqua co., extreme W N.Y., 13 mi/21 km W of Jamestown; 42°04′N 79°29′W. Lumber. Panama Rocks, a 25-acre/10-ha park with a 60-ft/18-m-high rock outcropping containing abundant early Paleozoic marine fossils, is 1 mi/1.6 km WSW.

Panama City (PAN-uh-maw), city (□21 sq mi/54 sq km; 1990 pop. 34,378), ⊙ Bay co., NW Fla., on St. Andrews Bay; 30°10′N 85°40′W. A Gulf Coast resort that draws visitors from all over the SE U.S. because of its amusement parks and excellent fishing. It is also a port of entry. The city's industries produce paper, clothing,

and chemicals. Tyndall Air Force Base and the U.S. Navy Mine Defense Laboratory are nearby. Inc. 1909.

Panama City Beach 1 (PAN-uh-maw), resort town (□5 sq mi/13 sq km; 1990 pop. 4,051), Bay co., NW Fla., on St. Andrew Bay, just W of Panama City; 30°12′N 85°50′W. **2** town (1990 pop. 4,051), Bay co., NW Fla., 8 mi/13 km W of Panama City; 30°12′N 85°50′W. Industries include lumber and light mfg.

Panamint Range, rugged mountains, SE Calif., near the Nev. state line. Telescope Peak (11,049 ft/3,368 m) is highest point; 36°26′N 117°21′W. The range is in W part of Death Valley Natl. Monument, overlooks Death Valley to E (−282 ft/86 m, lowest point in Western Hemisphere); to the W of the range is Panamint Valley.

Panasoffkee, Lake (pan-nah-SOF-kee), Sumter co., central Fla., 13 mi/21 km W of Leesburg; c.7 mi/11.3 km long, 1 mi/1.6 km wide. Shallow; has short outlet in W to Withlacoochee R.

Pandora (pan-DO-ruh), village (1990 pop. 1,009), Putnam co., NW Ohio, 16 mi/26 km NNE of Lima; 40°57′N 83°58′W. Diversified farming area; stone quarries.

Pangburn (PANG-buhrn), village (1990 pop. 630), White co., central Ark., 12 mi/19 km NNW of Searcy, and on Little Red R.; 35°25′N 91°50′W.

Pangnirtung (pang-nuhr-TUHNG), town, E Baffin Island, N.W.T., Canada; 66°08′N 65°45′W. Post of the Royal Can. Mounted Police and an arts and crafts co-op for Inuit artworks. Weaving shop; sealing, fishing, hunting (caribou, walrus); radio and TV stations. Scheduled air service. Major starting point and administrative center for Auyuittuq Natl. Park. Called the "Switzerland of the Arctic." Also called Pang.

Panguitch (PAIN-gwich), town (1990 pop. 1,444), ⊙ Garfield co., SW Utah, at junction of Panguitch and Assay creeks, which form Sevier R., and 32 mi/51 km SSE of Beaver; 37°49′N 112°26′W. Elev. 6,624 ft/2,019 m. Trading point for livestock and grain area; alfalfa, barley; cattle; timber; sawmill. Utah State Fish Hatchery 15 mi/24 km S. Part of Dixie Natl. Forest is just W, in Markagunt Plateau; separate units of Dixie Natl. Forest to E and W. Bryce Canyon Natl. Park to SE; Cedar Breaks Natl. Monument to SW. Name means "big fish" in Puinte Indian. Settled 1864 by Mormons, abandoned 1867, resettled 1871.

Panguitch Creek (PAIN-gwich), c.30 mi/48 km long, SW Utah; rises in Markagunt Plateau, SE Iron co., in Dixie Natl. Forest; flows generally NE, through Panguitch L. reservoir (1.5 mi/2.4 km long), and joins Assay Creek just N of Panguitch to form Sevier R.

Panhandle, town (1990 pop. 2,353), ⊙ Carson co., N Texas, in the Panhandle, 27 mi/43 km ENE of Amarillo; 35°21′N 101°22′W. Elev. 3,451 ft/1,052 m. RR junction; natural-gas and oil field; pipelines, oil wells; ships wheat, cattle, hay; mfg. (whirlpool baths, art supplies). L. Meredith Natl. Recreation Area and Alibates Flint Quarries Natl. Monument to NW. Became co. seat 1888, inc. 1909.

Panhandle, in U.S., name of narrow territorial extensions, such as those in FLORIDA, IDAHO, OKLAHOMA, TEXAS, WEST VIRGINIA, , and ALASKA.

Panindícuaro (pah-neen-DEE-kwah-no), town (1990 pop. 6,170), Michoacán, central Mexico, on central plateau, on RR and 42 mi/68 km WNW of Morelia; 19°59′N 101°45′W. Agr. center (grain, sugarcane; fruit; livestock).

Panna Maria, uninc. village (1990 pop. 96), Karnes co., S Texas, c.45 mi/72 km SE of San Antonio, on San Antonio R., at mouth of Cibolo Creek. Elev. 325 ft/99 m. Dairying; cattle; wheat. Located in area of Pol. settlement. Village of Cestohowa to NW. Est. Dec. 1854.

Panola 1 (puh-NO-luh), county (□705 sq mi/1,826 sq km; 1990 pop. 29,996), NW Miss.; ⊙ Batesville and Sardis; 34°21′N 89°57′W. Drained by Tallahatchie and Yocona rivers. Agr. (cotton, corn, hay, sorghum, soybeans, wheat; cattle, hogs). Timber; clay and gravel deposits. Part of Enid L. reservoir on Yocona R., in SE; John W. Kyle State Park at dam of Sardis L. reservoir on Tallahatchie R. in NE. Formed 1836. **2** county (□821 sq mi/2,126 sq km; 1990 pop. 22,035), E Texas; ⊙

Carthage; 32°09′N 94°18′W. Bounded E by La. line; drained by Sabine R. (forms part of N boundary); also by Martin Creek and Murvaul Bayou. Rolling wooded region (pine, gum, cypress; extensive lumbering). Huge natural-gas field is tapped by interstate pipelines; gas and some oil wells. Livestock (cattle, hogs, poultry). Lignite deposits. Martin Creek L. on W boundary; L. Murvaul in SW. Formed 1846.

Panola, village (1990 pop. 43), Woodford co., central Ill., 20 mi/32 km N of Bloomington; 40°47′N 89°01′W. In agr. area.

Panora (pa-NORE-uh), town (1990 pop. 1,100), Guthrie co., W central Iowa, near Middle Raccoon R., 8 mi/12.9 km E of Guthrie Center; 41°41′N 94°21′W. Livestock; grain; processed egg prods. Inc. 1872.

Panorama, Lake, reservoir, Guthrie co., W central Iowa, on Middle Raccoon R., 35 mi/56 km WNW of Des Moines; 6 mi/9.7 km long; 41°41′N 94°21′W. Max. storage capacity 23,700 acre-ft. Formed by Panorama Dam (58 ft/18 m high), built (1969) for water supply. Springbrook State Park to N.

Panorama Park, village (1990 pop. 127), Scott co., E Iowa, residential suburb 2.5 mi/4 km NE of downtown Bettendorf, in Quad Cities area, on bluff overlooking Mississippi R.; 41°33′N 90°27′W. Surrounded by city of Bettendorf. Scott Community Col. to W.

Panoroma City, suburb, Los Angeles co., S Calif., residential section 15 mi/24 km NW of downtown Los Angeles, in San Fernando Valley. Mfg. (truck bodies).

Panotla (pah-NOH-tlah), town (1990 pop. 6,188), Tlaxcala, central Mexico, 2.5 mi/4 km W of Tlaxcala. Elev. 7,326 ft/2,233 m. Grain, maguey, beans, livestock.

Pantego, town (1990 pop. 2,371), Tarrant co., N Texas, residential suburb 10 mi/16 km E of downtown Fort Worth, near Village Creek; 32°43′N 97°09′W. Town and neighboring Dalworthington Gardens are surrounded by city of Arlington.

Pantego (pan-TEE-go), village (1990 pop. 171), Beaufort co., E N.C., 22 mi/35 km E of Washington, near Pungo R.; 35°35′N 76°39′W. Tobacco, cotton, grain; livestock; timber. Mfg. (fertilizer; lumber).

Pantelhó (pahn-tel-HO), town (1990 pop. 4,356), Chiapas, S Mexico, 22 mi/35 km NNE of San Cristóbal de las Casas; 16°56′N 92°33′W. Elev. 4,331 ft/1,320 m. Cereals, fruit.

Pantepec 1 (PAHN-te-pek), town (1990 pop. 1,098), Chiapas, S Mexico, in Sierra Madre, 29 mi/47 km N of Tuxtla Gutierrez and just W of Mexico Highway 195. Elev. 4,856 ft/1,480 m. Cereals, fruit. Zoque-speaking area. **2** town (1990 pop. 2,167), Puebla, central Mexico, 25 mi/40 km NNE of Huauchinango. Coffee, sugarcane, tobacco, fruit. In Totnac Indian area.

Pantepec River, Mexico: see TUXPAN RIVER.

Panther Creek, c.35 mi/56 km long, NW Ky., formed SE of Owensboro by junction of North and South forks; flows generally W to Green R. 12 mi/19 km WSW of Owensboro. North Fork rises in SW Hancock co., flows c.22 mi/35 km generally W; South Fork rises in W Breckinridge co., flows c.40 mi/64 km SW and W.

Panther Mountain 1 peak (3,865 ft/1,178 m), in Hamilton co., NE central N.Y., in the Adirondacks, 35 mi/56 km SW of Mt. Marcy, and 7 mi/11.3 km WSW of Indian Lake village; 43°44′N 74°24′W. **2** peak (3,730 ft/1,137 m), in Ulster co., SE N.Y., in the Catskills, 22 mi/35 km WNW of Kingston; 42°07′N 74°24′W.

Panther Peak (4,442 ft/1,356 m), Essex co., NE N.Y., in the Adirondacks, 10 mi/16 km W of Mt. Marcy, and 14 mi/23 km SSW of Lake Placid village; 44°06′N 74°08′W.

Panton (PAN-tin), town (1990 pop. 606), Addison co., W Vt., on L. Champlain and 12 mi/19 km NW of Middlebury; 44°08′N 73°20′W. Burned by British in Revolution; site of grounding of Arnold's fleet (1776).

Pánuco, city (1990 pop. 6,254) and township, Veracruz, E Mexico, in Gulf lowland, on Pánuco R., and 23 mi/37 km SW of Tampico; 22°03′N 98°13′W. RR terminus; agr. center (corn, wheat, fruit, cattle). Petroleum production nearby.

Pánuco (PAHN-oo-ko), town (1990 pop. 779), Pánuco

muncipio, Zacatecas, N central Mexico, on interior plateau, 9 mi/14.5 km NNE of Zacatecas. Elev. 7,277 ft/ 2,218 m. Silver mining; agr. (maguey, corn; livestock).

Pánuco (PAHN-oo-ko), river, c.315 mi/507 km long, Mexico; rising as the Santa María R. in San Luis Potosí state, N central Mexico; flowing generally E to empty into the Gulf of Mexico near Tampico. It is navigable for small crafts for c.200 mi/322 km. Tributaries, including the Moctezuma, drain the ANÁHUAC region, sometimes by artificial means.

Pánuco de Coronado, Mexico: see FRANCISCO I. MADERO.

Paola (pai-O-luh), town (1990 pop. 4,698), ⊙ Miami co., E Kansas, 36 mi/58 km SSW of Kansas City, Kansas; 38°34′N 94°52′W. RR junction. Trade and RR center for grain, poultry, and livestock region. Mfg. (motor vehicle equip., forging). Ursuline Acad. here. Hillsdale L. Reservoir to N. Laid out 1855, inc. as city 1860.

Paoli 1 (1990 pop. 3,542), ⊙ Orange co., S Ind., on Lick Creek and 22 mi/35 km S of Bedford; 38°34′N 86°28′W. Trade center for agr. area; mfg. (furniture, wood prods., crushed limestone, electric motors); timber; mineral springs. Settled 1807, laid out 1816; inc. 1869. **2** (pai-O-lee), uninc. town (1990 pop. 6,703), Easttown and Tredyffrin townships, Chester co., SE Pa., suburb 17 mi/27 km WNW of downtown Philadelphia; 40°02′N 75°29′W. RR shops. Mfg. (electric motors, orthopedic instruments, transportation equip., photofinishing equip.). Some agr. in area (nursery stock, vegetables; livestock, dairying). Near here is birthplace of Gen. Wayne and scene of his defeat by British, 1777.

Paoli 1 (pai-O-lee), village (1990 pop. 29), Phillips co., NE Colo., on Frenchman Creek, near Nebr. state line, and 8 mi/12.9 km W of Holyoke; 40°36′N 102°28′W. Elev. 3,898 ft/1,188 m. Trade and supply point in grain region. Inc. 1930. **2** village (1990 pop. 574), Garvin co., S central Okla., 6 mi/9.7 km NNW of Pauls Valley, near Washita R.; 34°49′N 97°15′W. In agr. area.

Paonia, town (1990 pop. 1,403), Delta co., W Colo., on North Fork of Gunnison R., just W of West Elk Mts., and 27 mi/43 km ENE of Delta; 38°52′N 107°35′W. Elev. 5,674 ft/1,729 m. Fruit-shipping point; orchards, fruit, dairy prods. Coal mines nearby. Paonia State Park to NE (Gunnison co.), Grand Mesa Natl. Forest to NW, Gunnison Natl. Forest to SE. Inc. 1902.

Papaaloa (PAH-PAH-ah-LO-ah), village, NE Hawaii isl., Hawaii co., Hawaii, 19 mi/31 km NNW of Hilo, on Hamakua Coast (NE). Maulua Bay to E; Hilo Forest Reserve to SW; Laupahoehoe Beach Park is here.

Papaikou (PAH-pah-ee-KO), town (1990 pop. 1,634), E Hawaii isl., Hawaii co., Hawaii, on E coast at mouth of Kapue Stream, 3 mi/4.8 km N of Hilo, on coast; 19°47′N 155°05′W. Hilo Forest Reserve to W; Akaka Falls State Park to NW.

Papalotla 1 (pah-pah-LO-tlah), town (1990 pop. 2,195), Mexico state, central Mexico, 20 mi/32 km NE of Mexico City; 19°30′N 98°54′W. Maguey. **2** town (1990 pop. 14,854), ⊙ Papalotla de Xicohténcatl municipio, Tlaxcala, central Mexico, 8 mi/12.9 km N of Puebla on E slope of La Malinche Volcano. Cereals, alfalfa, beans; livestock.

Papalotla de Xicohténcatl, Mexico: see PAPALOTLA.

Papanoa Point (pah-pah-NO-ah), headland on Pacific coast of Guerrero, SW Mexico, 27 mi/43 km W of Tecpan de Galeana; 17°16′N 101°05′W. Lighthouse.

Papantla, Mexico: see PAPANTLA DE OLARTE.

Papantla de Olarte (pah-PAN-tlah de o-LAHR-te), town (1990 pop. 46,075), ⊙ Papantla municipio, Veracruz state, E central Mexico; 20°26′N 97°19′W. Elev. 961 ft/293 m. It is the commercial center of an agr. region and largest supplier of vanilla in the country; important oil production; orchards are also cultivated in the area. Papantla de Olarte is known for its proximity (4 mi/5.5 km) to the ruins of El Tajín. Totonac-speaking pop. in the area.

Paperville, Pa.: see MODENA.

Papillion (puh-PIL-ee-uhn), city (1990 pop. 10,372), ⊙ Sarpy co., E Nebr., suburb, 9 mi/14.5 km SW of downtown Omaha; 41°09′N 96°02′W. A suburb of Omaha.

Mfg. (wood cabinets, entertainment centers, processing equip. for hospitals, printing).

Papineau (PA-pin-o), county (□ 1,581 sq mi/ 4,095 sq km; 1991 pop. 19,526), SW Que., Canada, on Ont. border and on Ottawa R.; ⊙ Papineauville; 45°49′N 75°15′W.

Papineau, village (1990 pop. 142), Iroquois co., E Ill., 14 mi/23 km SSE of Kankakee; 40°58′N 87°43′W. In agr. area.

Papineau, Lake, S Que., Canada, 25 mi/40 km NW of Lachute; 8 mi/13 km long, 3 mi/5 km wide. Drains S into Ottawa R.

Papineauville (PA-pin-o-vil), village (1991 pop. 1,637), ⊙ Papineau co., SW Que., Canada, on Ottawa R., and 35 mi/56 km ENE of Ottawa; 45°37′N 75°01′W. Dairying, lumbering.

Papinsville (PA-pinz-vil), uninc. community, Bates co., W Mo., on Marais des Cygnes R., and 15 mi/24 km SSE of Butler. Farthest head of steamboat navigation in mid-19th cent. on the Osage R.

Paquette (pah-KEHT), village, S Que., Canada, on N.H. border, 30 mi/48 km SE of Sherbrooke. Dairying, lumbering, livestock raising.

Paquimé, Mexico: see CASAS GRANDES, historic site.

Paracho de Verduzco (pah-RAH-cho dai ver-DOOS-ko), town (1990 pop 14,322), ⊙ Paracho municipio, Michoacán, central Mexico, on central plateau, 18 mi/ 29 km N of Uruapan; 19°38′N 102°03′W. Corn, sugarcane, fruit, tobacco, livestock; mfg. of stringed instruments.

Parachute, village (1990 pop. 658), Garfield co., W Colo., on Colorado R., near mouth of Parachute Creek; 39°27′N 108°03′W. Elev. 5,095 ft/1,553 m. Sheep, cattle, oats, hay; mfg. of greeting cards. Grand Mesa Natl. Forest to SE.

Parácuaro (pah-RAH-kwah-ro), town (1990 pop. 3,310), Michoacán, W Mexico, 10 mi/16 km NE of Apatzingán. Sugarcane, rice, fruit.

Paradís, Dominican Republic: see PARAÍSO.

Paradise 1 city (1990 pop. 25,408), Butte co., N central Calif., 10 mi/16 km E of Chico, near Butte Creek, in the foothills of the Sierra Nevada range. It is mainly residential with a growing pop. Cattle, peaches, prunes, olives, walnuts, almonds, wheat, nursery stock; mfg. (printing and publishing). Gold was discovered nearby in 1859. Plumas Natl. Forest to E; L. Oroville reservoir State Recreation Area to SE. **2** uninc. city (1990 pop. 124,682), Clark co., S Nev., 4 mi/6.4 km SE of downtown Las Vegas, drained by Duck Creek; 36°04′N 115°07′W. It comprises the S unincorporated "half" of Las Vegas, generally S of Sahara Avenue. Nearly all of the gambling facilities and nightlife of Las Vegas Boulevard (The Strip), for which Las Vegas is noted, is S of this cross street where there are fewer regulations. Univ. of Nevada–Las Vegas, Las Vegas Convention Center, McCarran Internatl. Airport are all located here.

Paradise (PER-ah-deis), uninc. town (1990 pop. 1,043), Lancaster co., SE Pa., 10 mi/16 km ESE of Lancaster on Pequea Creek; 40°00′N 76°07′W. Mfg. includes wood prods., apparel, feeds, tool and die, crushed limestone. Agr. includes dairying, livestock, poultry; grain, soybeans; timber.

Paradise 1 village (1990 pop. 66), Russell co., N central Kansas, on small affluent of Saline R., and 16 mi/26 km NNW of Russell; 39°06′N 98°55′W. Livestock; wheat. **2** village (1990 pop. 325), Sanders co., W Mont., on Clark Fork R., 1 mi/1.6 km downstream (NW) from confluence of Flathead R. and the Clark Fork, 52 mi/ 84 km NW of Missoula. Flathead Indian Reservation to E; parts of Lolo Natl. Forest to W, N, and S. Village name derived from the "Pair o' Dice" Roadhouse. **3** village (1990 pop. 561), Cache co., N Utah, 10 mi/ 16 km NE of Brigham City on Little Bear R.; 41°34′N 111°49′W. Elev. c.4,500 ft/1,372 m. Raspberries, wheat, barley; dairying; cattle. Wasatch Natl. Forest to E, S, and W. Hyrum Reservoir and State Park to NW. Town site moved from Avon, 3 mi/4.8 km S; settled 1860.

Paradise Hills, uninc. town (1990 pop. 5,513), Bernalillo co., N central N.Mex., residential suburb 5 mi/8 km

NW of downtown Albuquerque, near Rio Grande; 35°12′N 106°41′W. Indian Petroglyph State Park to S.

Paradise Hills, suburban section of San Diego, San Diego co., S Calif., 6 mi/9.7 km ESE of downtown San Diego. Residential area in foothills of Coast Ranges.

Paradise Island, resort island, N central Bahama Isls., just NE of Nassau, to which it is linked by bridge; 4 mi/ 6.4 km long and ½ mi/⁹⁄₁₀ km wide; 25°05′N 77°18′W. Protects Nassau harbor. It was once called Hog Isl. because of the pig farms located on the isl. Since the 1950s, it has been developed as a major vacation center with luxury hotels, casinos, and shops. Has a popular beach.

Paradise, Lake, in Emmet and Cheboygan cos., N Mich., c.6 mi/9.7 km S of Mackinaw City; c.3 mi/ 4.8 km long, 1 mi/1.6 km wide; 45°40′N 84°45′W. Town of Carl Lake at W end. Formerly Carp L.

Paradise Valley, village (1991 pop. 147), E Alta., Canada, near Sask. border, 30 mi/48 km SW of Vermilion; 53°02′N 110°20′W. Mixed farming, grain; livestock.

Paradise Valley 1 town (1990 pop. 11,671), Maricopa co., central Ariz., residential suburb 8 mi/12.9 km NE of downtown Phoenix; 33°32′N 111°57′W. Adjoins Scottsdale on E. Scottsdale Municipal Airport to NE. Salt R. Indian Reservation to E. **2** uninc. city and small ranching community, Humboldt co., Nev., S of the Santa Rosa Range, NE of Winnemucca. For over 100 years, it has been a pivot of the range livestock industry of N central Nev. and historically was sometimes referred to as "the oasis of N Nevada." Est. 1866.

Paradox Lake, Essex co., NE N.Y., in the Adirondacks, just NE of Schroon L., and 14 mi/23 km W of Ticonderoga; c.4 mi/6.4 km long, ¼ mi/ km–1 mi/1.6 km wide; 43°53′N 73°44′W. State campsite.

Paragon, town (1990 pop. 515), Morgan co., central Ind., near West Fork of White R., 8 mi/12.9 km WSW of Martinsville; 39°23′N 86°34′W. Agr. area.

Paragonah (per-uh-GO-nah), village (1990 pop. 307), Iron co., SW Utah, in Parowan valley, 21 mi/34 km NE of Cedar City; 37°53′N 112°46′W. Alfalfa, barley; cattle, sheep. Dixie Natl. Forest to E and S. Settled 1850's.

Paragould (PAR-uh-goold), city (1990 pop. 18,540), ⊙ Greene co., NE Ark.; 36°03′N 90°30′W. The growing processing and trade center of the NE Ark. agr. region, Paragould also has a wide variety of mfg. Crowley's Ridge State Park to W. Inc. 1883.

Paraíso (pah-rah-EE-so), town (1993 pop. 4,761), Barahona prov., SW Dominican Republic, on the coast, 17 mi/27 km SSW of Barahona; 18°00′N 71°15′W. Coffee, sugarcane, timber. Formerly Paradís.

Paraíso (pahr-ah-EE-so), city (1990 pop. 18,313) and township, Tabasco, SE Mexico, on inlet of Gulf of Campeche, 32 mi/51 km NNW of Villahermosa; 18°26′N 93°10′W. Cacao-growing center.

Paraloma (par-uh-LO-muh), village, Sevier co., SW Ark., 11 mi/18 km NNE of Ashdown, on NW shore of Millwood L. Recreation.

Paramount, city (1990 pop. 47,669), Los Angeles co., S Calif.; 33°54′N 118°10′W. Originally a dairy region, it has become highly industrialized since the 1950s. The city grew in 1950s and 1960s. Mfg. (printing and publishing, pipe and pipe fittings, copper rolling, lawn and garden tractors, metal forgings, aerospace parts, cutting tools, rubber goods, metal plating). Bounded by Los Angeles R. on W. Inc. 1957.

Paramus (puh-RA-muhs), borough (1990 pop. 25,067), Bergen co., NE N.J.; 40°57′N 74°04′W. Large retail-trade center known for its expansive shopping malls, esp. the Garden State Plaza, one of the largest shopping centers in the U.S. An early Du. church and Bergan Community col. are here. Settled 1668, inc. 1922.

Parás (pah-RAHS), town (1990 pop. 685), Nuevo León, N Mexico, in alluvial plains of Rio Grande, 75 mi/ 121 km NE of Monterrey; 26°30′N 99°30′W. Cotton, corn, sugarcane, cactus fibers.

Parchment, town (1990 pop. 1,958), Kalamazoo co., SW Mich., residential suburb 3 mi/4.8 km NNE of Kalamazoo; 42°19′N 85°34′W. Mfg. (chemicals, paper processing). Founded 1909, inc. as city 1939.

Parco, Wyo.: see SINCLAIR.

Pardee Dam, Calif.: see PARDEE RESERVOIR.

Pardee Reservoir (☐ 3 sq mi/7.8 sq km), Amador and Calaveras cos., on Mokelumnee R., 30 mi/48 km NE of Stockton; 38°16′N 120°51′W. Max. capacity 215,000 acre-ft. Formed by Pardee Dam (345 ft/105 m high), built (1929) for power generation; also used for water supply and recreation. Camanche Reservoir downstream.

Pardeeville, town (1990 pop. 1,630), Columbia co., S central Wis., on Fox R., 8 mi/12.9 km E of Portage; 43°31′N 89°17′W. In farm area (livestock; melons); cheese and other dairy prods., canned foods; nursery stock; mfg. (electronic equip., molded plastics). Park L. to N. Inc. 1894.

Parent, Lac (pah-RAH, lahk), lake (32 mi/51 km long, 4 mi/6 km wide), W Que., Canada, extends NE from Senneterre. Elev. 990 ft/302 m. Drains N into Nottaway R.

Parham, village (1991 pop. 1,171), NE Antigua, Antigua and Barbuda Republic, West Indies, 5 mi/8 km E of St. John's. Near airport and U.S. Navy base.

Paria River (puh-REI-uh), c.75 mi/121 km long, in S Utah and N Ariz.; rises in Paunsaugunt Plateau N of Tropic, SW Garfield co., S central Utah, E of Bryce Canyon Natl. Park, flows SE through Paria Canyon–Vermilion Cliffs Wilderness Area (in Utah and Ariz.) to Colorado R. 9 mi/14.5 km downstream (S) of Glen Canyon Dam at N end of Marble Gorge, Ariz.

Parícutin (pah-REE-koo-teen), active volcano, Michoacán state, W central Mexico; 19°29′N 102°17′W. Elev. 7,382 ft/2,250 m. In one of the best-recorded eruptions of modern times, Parícutin burst forth from a cornfield on Feb. 20, 1943, and grew discontinuously until 1952, spewing forth over a billion tons of lava. It buried the town of San Juan Parangaricutiro and the village of Parícutin, whence its name. The cone is a remarkable example of volcanic growth, and its development was closely studied by internatl. scientific teams.

Paris, town (1991 pop. 8,600), S Ont., Canada, on Grand R., at mouth of Nith R., 7 mi/11 km NW of Brantford. In dairying, gypsum-quarrying region; mfg.

Paris 1 city (1990 pop. 8,987), ⊙ Edgar co., E Ill., 17 mi/27 km NW of Terre Haute, Ind.; 39°37′N 87°41′W. Trade, RR, and industrial center in agr. area; mfg. of farm machinery, aircraft parts; meatpacking. Lincoln practiced law here. Inc. 1853. **2** (PER-is), city (1990 pop. 1,486), ⊙ Monroe co., NE central Mo., on Middle Fork of Salt R., 38 mi/61 km WSW of Hannibal; 39°28′N 92°00′W. Soybeans, corn; cattle. Union Covered Bridge State Historic Site to SW. Laid out 1831. **3** city (1990 pop. 9,332), ⊙ Henry co., NW Tenn., 40 mi/64 km ESE of Union City; 36°18′N 88°19′W. A trade center for agr., clay, and timber-producing area; mfg. of motor vehicles, motors, power tools, and processed foods. Kentucky Reservoir is E. Laid out and inc. 1823. **4** city (1990 pop. 24,699), ⊙ Lamar co., E Texas, 95 mi/153 km NE of Dallas in the Red R. valley; 33°40′N 95°32′W. It is a RR junction and processing center for the rich farms of the blackland region, which produce cotton, grain, and cattle; peanuts; mfg. (food processing, paper prods.). The city developed after the arrival of the RR in 1876, and it was rebuilt after its destruction by fire in 1916. Paris Jr. Col. L. Crook and Pat Mayse L. to N; Sam Maxey House State Historic Site, Victorian historic structure. Settled 1824.

Paris 1 town (1990 pop. 3,674), ⊙ Logan co., W Ark., 38 mi/61 km E of Fort Smith, in Ouachita foothills; 35°17′N 93°43′W. Lumbering, farming, mfg. (charcoal, motor vehicle parts, apparel). Subiaco Col. and Abbey (Benedictine) are nearby. Ozark Natl. Forest to SE. Laid out 1874. **2** town (1990 pop. 8,730), ⊙ Bourbon co., central Ky., 18 mi/29 km NE of Lexington, on Stoner Creek, at mouth of Houston Creek, in Bluegrass region; 38°12′N 84°15′W. Agr. (bluegrass seed, burley tobacco; livestock) shipping point; mfg. (concrete, crushed limestone, lumber, fertilizer, apparel, fabricated aluminum prods., automotive parts); limestone quarries. Early distillery here (1790) was one of 1st in Ky.; its whiskey was called bourbon, after the co. Duncan Tavern and Duncan House, historic shrine. Nearby, to E, Cane Ridge Meeting House (1791) was scene of founding of Christian denomination of Disciples of Christ in 1804. Airport. City founded as Hopewell 1789; inc. 1893. **3** uninc. town (1990 pop, 900), Washington co., SW Pa., residential suburb 4 mi/6.4 km E of Weirton (W.Va.); 40°24′N 80°30′W. Agr. includes dairying, livestock; corn. **4** uninc. town, Greenville co., NW S.C., residential suburb 4 mi/6.4 km NW of Greenville, near Brushy Creek.

Paris, village (1990 pop. 581), ⊙ Bear Lake co., SE Idaho, 27 mi/43 km ENE of Preston; 42°14′N 111°24′W. Elev. 5,967 ft/1,819 m. Grain; cattle, sheep; dairying; mfg. (helmets). Cache Natl. Forest to W; Bear L. State Park and Natl. Wildlife Refuge to SE.

Paris, Maine: see SOUTH PARIS.

Paris Hill, Maine: see SOUTH PARIS.

Paris Mountain (2,020 ft/616 m), NW S.C., c.4 mi/6.4 km N of Greenville, in Paris Mt. State Park (☐ 1,275 acres/516 ha); 34°56′N 82°24′W. Forested recreational area (lakes, trails, picnic areas, and campgrounds).

Parish, village (☐ 1 sq mi/2.6 sq km; 1990 pop. 473), Oswego co., N central N.Y., 19 mi/31 km ESE of Oswego; 43°23′N 76°07′W. Agr. (dairy prods.; poultry; vegetables).

Park 1 county (☐ 2,210 sq mi/5,724 sq km; 1990 pop. 7,174), central Colo.; ⊙ Fairplay; 39°07′N 105°42′W. Mining and livestock-grazing region, drained by headwaters of South Platte R. (source is in N part of co.). Gold, silver, lead. Includes part of Park Range in W; part of Pike Natl. Forest in W, N, and E; part of Arapaho Natl. Forest along N boundary; Antero Reservoir and State Wildlife in SW; Spinney Mt. Reservoir and State Park in S center; Eleven-Mile Canyon Reservoir and Eleven-Mile State Park in SE; Tarryall State Wildlife Area in E center. Formed 1861. **2** county (☐ 2,666 sq mi/6,905 sq km; 1990 pop. 14,562) , S Mont.; ⊙ Livingston; 45°30′N 110°31′W. Agr. region drained by the Yellowstone and Shields rivers; borders on Wyo. on S. Wheat, barley, oats, hay, vegetables; cattle, sheep, hogs, horses; dairying; lumber, marble, coal. Part of Yellowstone Natl. Park in S; Paradise Valley (of Yellowstone R.) in SW part of co.; Cottonwood Reservoir in NW; Granite Park (elev. 12,799 ft/3,901 m), highest point in Mont., in extreme SE; part of Absaroka-Beartooth Wilderness Area in SE; part of Crazy Mts. in NE; Absaroka Range in S. Formed 1887; present boundaries est. 1929. **3** county (☐ 6,968 sq mi/18,047 sq km; 1990 pop. 23,178), NW Wyo.; ⊙ Cody; 44°29′N 109°33′W. Irrigated agr. area, bordering on Mont. on N and W. NW part of co. now includes N ½ and SE corner of Yellowstone Natl. Park (park was formerly independent of any co.). Watered by Yellowstone, Shoshone and Greybull rivers. Agr. (oats, barley, hay, sugar beets, alfalfa, corn, brans, beans; sheep, cattle); oil, coal, limestone. Shoshone Natl. Forest (including North Absaroka Winderness Area) and part of Absaroka Range in W center and S. E shore of Yellowstone L. forms part of W co. boundary. Gallatin Range in NW corner. Buffalo Bill Reservoir (Shoshone R.) and State Park at center of co. Formed 1909.

Park, village (1990 pop. 150), Gove co., W central Kansas, 12 mi/19 km NNE of Gove; 39°06′N 100°21′W.

Park City, city (1990 pop. 4,677), Lake co., NE Ill., residential suburb 36 mi/58 km NNW of Chicago, 4 mi/6.4 km WSW of Waukegan; 42°21′N 87°53′W. Mfg. of wood prods.

Park City 1 town (1990 pop. 5,050), Sedgwick co., S central Kansas, suburb 7 mi/11.3 km N of Wichita; 37°47′N 97°19′W. Residential. Agr. to N (wheat; cattle). **2** town (1990 pop. 4,468), Summit co., N central Utah, 20 mi/32 km ESE of Salt Lake City, in Wasatch Range; 40°39′N 111°29′W. Elev. 8,960 ft/2,731 m. Mfg. (metal fabrication, beverages); sheep. Former mining center (silver, gold, copper, lead, and zinc deposits), now mined out. Site of Winter Olympics, Alpine Events 2002. Largest ski center in state. Park City, Park West, and Deer Valley ski resorts in and around town. An elite suburb of Salt Lake City. Growth followed discovery of silver (1868). Wasatch Mt. State Park to S; Wasatch Natl. Forest to W; Jordanelle Reservoir and State Park to SE.

Park City 1 village (1990 pop. 549), Barren co., S Ky., 10 mi/16 km NW of Glasgow; 37°05′N 86°02′W. RR junction. A tourist center for Ky. limestone cave region. Agr. (tobacco, grain; livestock; dairying); mfg. (feeds). Diamond Caverns are here, Mammoth Cave Natl. Park to N, Crystal Onyx Cave to E; beautiful small caves are nearby. Until 1938, called Glasgow Junction. **2** village (1990 pop. 375), Stillwater co., S Mont., on Yellowstone R., 23 mi/37 km SW of Billings. Wheat, barley, sugar beets, hay; cattle, sheep, hogs; dairying. Big L. to N. Originally called Young's Point.

Park Cone, peak (12,100 ft/3,688 m) in Rocky Mts., Gunnison co., W central Colo., 24 mi/39 km NE of Gunnison; 38°47′N 106°36′W. Taylor Park Reservoir to N.

Park Falls, town (1990 pop. 3,104), Price co., N Wis., on Flambeau R., 50 mi/80 km SSE of Ashland, in wooded area; 45°55′N 90°27′W. Mfg. paper, steel prods., consumer goods, plywood, veneer. Nearby are resort lakes. E terminus of Tuscobia State Trail; large Turtle-Flambeau Flowage reservoir to NE; Chequamegon Natl. Forest to E; Flambeau State Forest to N and W. Inc. 1912.

Park Forest, village (1990 pop. 24,656), Cook and Will cos., NE Ill., S of Chicago; 41°28′N 87°41′W. Example of early planned commuter suburb. Inc. 1949.

Park Forest Village, uninc. town (1990 pop. 6,703), Centre co., central Pa., residential suburb 3 mi/4.8 km NW of State College; 40°47′N 77°54′W. Kolln Winery to N.

Park Hills 1 town (1990 pop. 3,321), Kenton co., N Ky., residential suburb 3 mi/4.8 km SW of Cincinnati (Ohio), 1 mi/1.6 km SW of Covington; 39°04′N 84°31′W. Mfg. (printing and publishing). Inc. 1927. **2** town (1990 pop. 7,886), St. Francois co., E Mo., 55 mi/89 km SSW of St. Louis, 7 mi/11.3 km NW of Farmington, on Flat R., S of its confluence with Big R. St. Joe State Park to S. Mineral Area Col. to E. Located in lead-mining belt, Park Hills was created in 1993 with the merger of towns of Flat River (1990 pop. 4,823), Elvins (1990 pop. 1,391), Rivermines (1990 pop. 459), and Esther (1990 pop. 1,071). Chickens, cattle, hogs; hay; lead, sand and gravel; mfg. (printing and publishing, glass prods., concrete prods.).

Park Place, uninc. town, Greenville co., NW S.C., 1 mi/1.6 km N of Greenville.

Park Range, part of the Rocky Mts., central Colo. and S Wyo., extending N from the Arkansas R. to and including Sierra Madre (Bridger Peak, 11,007 ft/3,355 m) in S Wyo.; Mt. Lincoln (14,286 ft/4,354 m) is the highest peak. Other peaks include Mt. Buckskin (13,865 ft/4,226 m), Mt. Sherman (14,036 ft/4,278 m), Mt. Democrat (14,148 ft/4,312 m), Mt. Bross (14,172 ft/4,320 m), Mt. Cameron (14,239 ft/4,340 m) and Quandary peak (14,265 ft/4,348 m).

Park Rapids, town (1990 pop. 2,863), ⊙ Hubbard co., central Minn., on Fish Hook R.; forms Fish Hook L. to N, and 55 mi/89 km NW of Brainerd; 46°55′N 95°03′W. Elev. 1,475 ft/450 m. Mfg. (candles, potato-processing equip., frozen foods, livestock trailers, diverse light mfg.); potatoes, oats, barley, rye, beans, sheep, timber. North Country Mus. of Arts here. L. Ithaca, 21 mi/34 km to NNW, source of Mississippi R. Itasca State Park to NW; Two Inlets State Forest to NW; Smoky Hills State Forest to W; Deer Town Theme Park to W. Municipal Airport to S. Founded 1880.

Park Ridge, city (1990 pop. 36,175), Cook co., NE Ill., suburb just NW of Chicago, on the Des Plaines R.; 42°00′N 87°50′W. It is chiefly residential. Several natl. and internatl. corporations have their hq. in Park Ridge. Nearby is O'Hare Internatl. Airport. Inc. 1873.

Park Ridge, village (1990 pop. 546), Portage co., central Wis., suburb 2 mi/3.2 km NE of Stevens Point; 44°31′N 89°32′W.

Park Ridge, borough (1990 pop. 8,102), Bergen co., NE N.J., near small Woodcliff L., 9 mi/14.5 km N of Hackensack; 41°02′N 74°02′W. Mfg. (office supplies, clothing). Largely residential. Settled c.1770, inc. 1894.

Park River, town (1990 pop. 1,725), Walsh co., NE

N.Dak., 15 mi/24 km W of Grafton and on South Branch of Park R.; 48°23′N 97°44′W. Trading center; mfg. (farm equip.); dairy prods., potatoes, grain. Homme Reservoir to W. Founded 1884.

Park River, 80 mi/129 km long, NE N.Dak.; formed by confluence of N and S branches in Walsh co.; 48°26′N 97°27′W. N branch rises in SE Cavalier co., flows SE 35 mi/56 km; S branch rises in S Cavalier co., flows SE 40 mi/64 km, through Homme Reservoir and past town of Park R.; the 2 join in E Walsh co. to form Park R.; flows 25 mi/40 km E, past Grafton, to Red R. of the North 6 mi/9.7 km S of Drayton.

Park Slope, residential section of Brooklyn borough of N.Y. city, SE N.Y., lying immediately W of Prospect Park; 40°40′N 73°58′W. Renovated brownstone bldgs. in historic dist. Pop. largely upper-income, young professional residents.

Parkchester, E section of borough of Bronx, N.Y. city, SE N.Y., between Tremont Ave. and Cross Bronx Expressway; 40°50′N 73°52′W. Created by the Metropolitan Life Insurance Company in 1941 on a large tract of land, it was a well-designed, high-density housing project which by 1950 had 40,000 residents and was the biggest such project in the U.S. This was the 1st planned high-rise community built in the E Bronx, which before World War II had been quiet and not densely populated. In 1950, it was a "city within a city" and N.Y. city's single largest taxpayer; it had its own subway to Manhattan, a branch of the N.Y. Public Lib., a theater, a post office, and many businesses.

Parkdale, village (1990 pop. 393), Ashley co., SE Ark., 23 mi/37 km E of Crossett, near Bayou Bartholomew; 33°07′N 91°32′W. Overflow Natl. Wildlife Refuge to W.

Parke, county (□ 450 sq mi/1,166 sq km; 1990 pop. 15,410), W Ind.; ⊙ Rockville; 39°47′N 87°13′W. Bounded W by Wabash R.; drained by Sugar and Raccoon creeks. Agr. and bituminous-coal-mining area, with some mfg. at Montezuma and Rockville. Corn, wheat, rye; hogs, cattle, sheep; timber, clay and gravel pits, mineral springs; maple syrup. The co. is known for its 31 covered bridges; an annual Covered Bridge Festival is held in Oct. Turkey Run State Park in N, part of Shades State Park in NE corner. Raccoon L. State Recreation Area and Mansfield Reservoir (also called Cecil M. Harden L.), in E; canoeing on Sugar Creek. Formed 1821.

Parker, county (□ 910 sq mi/2,357 sq km; 1990 pop. 64,785), N Texas; ⊙ Weatherford; 32°46′N 97°48′W. Partly hilly; drained by Brazos R. and Clear Fork of Trinity R. Rich, diversified agr. (peaches, peanuts, pecans; hay; beef cattle, horses); gas and oil; stone, clay, sand and gravel. L. Mineral Wells (recreation) is in W, L. Weatherford (recreation and residential) is in E. Processing, mfg. at Weatherford. Formed 1855.

Parker 1 or **Parker City**, city (1990 pop. 853), Armstrong co., W Pa., 20 mi/32 km NE of Butler, on Allegheny R. (bridged); 41°05′N 79°40′W. Light mfg.; oil; timber. Agr. area (corn, hay; dairying). Inc. as city 1873. Also called Parkers Landing. **2** uninc. city (1990 pop. 11,072), Greenville co., NW S.C., residential community 10 mi/16 km NNW of Greenville, near Saluda R.; 34°51′N 82°27′W.

Parker 1 town (1990 pop. 2,897), ⊙ La Paz co., W Ariz., on Colorado R. (on Calif. state line), 100 mi/161 km NNE of Yuma, in N part of Colo. R.; 34°01′N 114°13′W. Colorado R. Indian Reservation here. Trade center for grazing area, mfg. (fabricated metal prods.) and hq. of several Indian tribes (and reservations); Fort Yuma and Chemehuevi in Calif., Fort Mojave and Colorado R. in Calif. and Ariz., and Cocopah in Ariz. Parker Dam, on Colo. R., forms L. Havasu, 12 mi/19 km to NE; Buckskin Mts. and Buckskin Mt. State Park to NE. Inc. 1940. **2** town (1990 pop. 5,450), Douglas co., central Colo., suburb 18 mi/29 km SSE of Denver, on Cherry Creek; 39°30′N 104°45′W. Elev. 5,870 ft/1,789 m. Agr. area (cattle; wheat, sunflowers, oats, hay, nuts, fruits). Mfg. (food processing). **3** town (□ 2 sq mi/5.2 sq km; 1990 pop. 4,598), Bay co., NW Fla., 5 mi/8 km E of Panama City; 30°07′N 85°35′W. **4** town (1990 pop. 984), ⊙ Turner co., SE S.Dak., 23 mi/37 km SW of Sioux Falls,

on Vermillion R.; 43°23′N 97°08′W. In agr. region. Honey. Founded 1879. **5** town (1990 pop. 1,235), Collin co., N Texas, residential suburb 19 mi/31 km NE of Dallas, adjoining city of Plano on E, on Cottonwood Creek; 33°02′N 96°38′W. L. Lavon reservoir to E.

Parker 1 village (1990 pop. 288), Fremont co., E Idaho, 3 mi/4.8 km W of St. Anthony and on Henrys Fork R.; 43°58′N 111°46′W. Elev. 4,991 ft/1,521 m. Shipping point in agr. (potatoes; cattle, sheep); dairy area; mfg. (food-processing equip.). Sand dunes to N. **2** village (1990 pop. 256), Linn co., E Kansas, 11 mi/18 km S of Osawatomie; 38°19′N 94°59′W. In general farming area.

Parker, Cape, E extremity of Devon Isl., E Franklin dist., N.W.T., Canada, on Baffin Bay; 75°20′N 79°41′W.

Parker City, town (1990 pop. 1,323), Randolph co., E Ind., 12 mi/19 km W of Winchester; 40°11′N 85°12′W. In agr. area; mfg. (fabricated metal prods., fertilizers). Also called Parker. Laid out 1851.

Parker Dam, in NW Ariz. and SE Calif., on Colorado R. (Ariz.-Calif. state line), 60 mi/97 km S of Kingman, Ariz.; 320 ft/98 m high and 856 ft/261 m long; 34°16′N 114°07′W. Completed 1938. Forms Havasu L. Provides water for Los Angeles (carried by the Colorado R. Aqueduct) and San Diego; diverts water to Ariz. via Hayden-Rhodes Aqueduct.

Parker Head, Maine: see PHIPPSBURG.

Parker Pond, reservoir, Kennebec co. and on Franklin co. border, SW central Maine, 17 mi/27 km NW of Augusta; 4 mi/6.4 km long; 44°28′N 70°02′W. Drains S to Echo L.

Parkers Landing, Pa.: see PARKER.

Parkers Prairie, town (1990 pop. 956), Otter Tail co., W Minn., 37 mi/60 km ESE of Fergus Falls; 46°08′N 95°19′W. Mfg. (food-processing equip., seeds, animal feeds); grain; livestock; dairying. Small lakes in area; L. Milton to S; Inspiration Peak State Park to W.

Parkersburg, city (1990 pop. 33,862), ⊙ Wood co., NW W.Va., 70 mi/113 km N of Charleston, 12 mi/19 km SSW of Marietta (Ohio), on the Ohio R. (bridged), at mouth of Little Kanawha R.; 39°15′N 81°32′W. Industrial and shipping center in a coal region. Mfg. (metal fabrication, tools, packaging, printing and publishing, wooden prods., food and dairy processing). Agr. (grain, tobacco); livestock; poultry. Wood County Airport to NE. Ohio Valley Col. to N. Historic Blennerhassett Isl., in the Ohio R., is 5 mi/8 km to W. Blackwater Farms Zoo; Oil and Gas Mus; W.Va. Motor Speedway to S (at Mineral Wells); Pennsboro Speedway to E. W terminus of N. Bend State Trail to SE. Settled 1785, inc. 1820.

Parkersburg, town (1990 pop. 1,804), Butler co., N central Iowa, 24 mi/39 km WNW of Waterloo; 42°34′N 92°46′W. Shipping center (livestock; grain); mfg. (seed; agr. equip.). Inc. 1874.

Parkersburg 1 village (1990 pop. 211), Richland co., SE Ill., 10 mi/16 km S of Olney; 38°35′N 88°03′W. In agr. area (corn, wheat, apples; livestock). **2** village, Sampson co., S central N.C., 13 mi/21 km SW of Clinton near South R. Tobacco, grain; livestock.

Parkerton, village, Converse co., E central Wyo., on North Platte R., 18 mi/29 km E of Casper. Elev. 5,123 ft/1,561 m. Big Muddy oil field nearby.

Parkerville, village (1990 pop. 28), Morris co., E central Kansas, on headstream of Neosho R., 12 mi/19 km NW of Council Grove; 38°45′N 96°39′W. Grazing, agr.

Parkesburg (PAHRKS-buhrg), borough (1990 pop. 2,981), Chester co., SE Pa., 5 mi/8 km WSW of Coatesville; 39°57′N 75°55′W. Mfg. (capacitors, bldg. materials, machinery); stone quarries. Agr. area (grain, soybeans, apples; livestock; dairying). Chester County Carlson Airport. Inc. 1872.

Parkhill, town (1991 pop. 1,675), S Ont., Canada, on Parkhill R., 26 mi/42 km WNW of London; 43°10′N 81°41′W. Woodworking, lumbering; mfg.

Parkin, town (1990 pop. 1,847), Cross co., E Ark., 32 mi/51 km WNW of Memphis (Tenn.), on St. Francis R.; 35°15′N 90°32′W. In farm area (soybeans, corn, hay); mfg. of industrial machinery. Parkin Arch State Park to N.

Parkland, uninc. city (1990 pop. 21,600), Pierce co., W Wash., suburb 7 mi/11.3 km S of Tacoma. Services and

residential center for McChord Air Force Base, to W, and Fort Lewis Military Reservation, to S. Seat of Pacific Lutheran Univ.

Parkland, uninc. village, Middletown township, Bucks co., SE Pa., residential suburb 18 mi/29 km NE of Philadelphia, 6 mi/9.7 km NW of Bristol, on Nishaminy Creek; 40°09′N 74°55′W.

Parklawn, uninc. town, Fairfax co., NE Va., residential suburb 6 mi/9.7 km NW of Alexandria, 7 mi/11.3 km WSW of Washington, D.C.; 38°50′N 77°08′W. L. Barcroft reservoir to N.

Parkman, town (1990 pop. 790), Piscataquis co., central Maine, 10 mi/16 km WSW of Dover-Foxcroft; 45°06′N 69°27′W. In farming, lumbering area.

Parkman, village, Sheridan co., N Wyo., near Mont. line and Bighorn Natl. Forest to SW, 20 mi/32 km NW of Sheridan. Elev. c.4,300 ft/1,311 m. Supply point in ranching region. Large Crow Indian Reservation to N (in Mont.).

Parks 1 village, SW Alaska, on Kuskokwim R., 50 mi/80 km SE of Flat. **2** village (1990 pop. 400), St. Martin parish, S central La., 10 mi/16 km E of Lafayette, near Bayou Teche; 30°13′N 91°50′W. Mfg. (agr. equip.). Longfellow Evangeline State Commemorative Area to S.

Parksdale, uninc. town (1990 pop. 1,911), Madera co., S central Calif., residential community 13 mi/21 km NNW of Fresno, 10 mi/16 km ESE of Madera; 36°57′N 120°01′W. Cattle, poultry; dairying; nuts, citrus, vegetables, cotton, grain.

Parkside, borough (1990 pop. 2,369), Delaware co., SE Pa., residential suburb 13 mi/21 km SW of Philadelphia and 2 mi/3.2 km NW of Chester, near Ridley Creek; 39°52′N 75°22′W. Taylor Memorial Arboretum is here.

Parksley, town (1990 pop. 779), Accomack co., E Va., 6 mi/9.7 km N of Accomac, bet. Atlantic Ocean (E) and Chesapeake Bay (W); 37°47′N 75°39′W. Mfg. (food packaging, clothing, meat processing); agr. area (grain, fruit, vegetables; livestock).

Parkston, town (1990 pop. 1,572), Hutchinson co., SE S.Dak., 22 mi/35 km S of Mitchell; 43°23′N 97°59′W. In agr. area; mfg. (agr. equipment). Founded 1886.

Parksville, city (1991 pop. 7,306), SW B.C., Canada, on E Vancouver Isl., 20 mi/32 km NW of Nanaimo; 49°18′N 124°19′W. Farming, lumbering; suburban retirement community.

Parksville, town (1990 pop. 193), McCormick co., W S.C., 28 mi/45 km S of Greenwood, near Ga. line; 33°47′N 82°13′W. Timber production. Numerous state parks in area.

Parksville 1 village (1990 pop. 560), Boyle co., central Ky., 7 mi/11.3 km WSW of Danville, on North Rolling Fork R. In berry-growing region, also tobacco, grain; livestock; dairying. **2** resort village (1990 pop. 700), Sullivan co., SE N.Y., in the Catskills, 4 mi/6.4 km N of Liberty; 41°51′N 74°46′W.

Parksville Reservoir, Tenn., see OCOEE RIVER.

Parkton, village (1990 pop. 367), Robeson co., SE N.C., 13 mi/21 km SSW of Fayetteville near Big Swamp R.; 34°53′N 79°00′W. RR junction. Grain, soybeans, tobacco; cattle, hogs; dairying.

Parkview, village, Cuyahoga co., N Ohio, SW suburb of Cleveland. Former village absorbed into suburban development.

ParkView Peak (12,100 ft/3,688 m), in Front Range, bet. Grand and Jackson cos., N Colo., 20 mi/32 km NW of Granby; 40°19′N 106°08′W. Willow Creek Pass 3 mi/4.8 km ENE.

Parkville 1 uninc. city (1990 pop. 31,617), Baltimore co., N Md.; 39°23′N 76°33′W. An early rowhouse suburb of Baltimore, it (along with nearby Overlea) was once called Lavender Hill. **2** city (1990 pop. 2,402), Platte co., W Mo., suburb on Missouri R. and 10 mi/16 km NW of Kansas City; 39°12′N 94°40′W. Farming; tobacco. Park Col. here.

Parkville, uninc. town (1990 pop. 6,014), York co., S Pa., residential suburb 1 mi/1.6 km S of Hanover; 39°46′N 76°58′W.

Parkville, uninc. village, St. Louis co., NE Minn., 3 mi/ 4.8 km W of Virginia, in Mesabi Iron Range; 47°31′N 92°34′W. Mfg. (fabricated metal prods., electrical equip.). Superior Natl. Forest to N.

Parkwater, uninc. town (1990 pop. 4,300), Spokane co., E Wash., residential suburb 5 mi/8 km ENE of Spokane, on Spokane R. Felts Field Municipal Airport to NW.

Parkway, uninc. city (1990 pop. 31,903), Sacramento co., central Calif., residential suburb 6 mi/9.7 km SSE of Sacramento. Citrus, nursery stock; dairying; poultry. Also called South Sacramento; statistically reported as Parkway–South Sacramento.

Parkway Village, village (1990 pop. 707), Jefferson co., N Ky., suburb 3 mi/4.8 km SSE of Louisville; 38°12′N 85°44′W. Also called Parkway.

Parkwood 1 uninc. town (1990 pop. 1,659), Madera co., S central Calif., residential community 12 mi/19 km NNW of Fresno, 10 mi/16 km ESE of Madera; 36°56′N 120°02′W. Cattle, poultry; dairying; nuts, citrus, vegetables, cotton, grain. **2** uninc. town (1990 pop. 4,123), Durham co., central N.C., residential suburb 7 mi/ 11.3 km S of Durham; 35°53′N 78°54′W. Jordan L. reservoir (New Hope R.) to W. Research Triangle Park to E.

Parlier, city (1990 pop. 7,938), Fresno co., central Calif., in San Joaquin Valley, near Kings R., 17 mi/27 km SE of Fresno; 36°37′N 119°33′W. Agr. trade center. Citrus, nectarines, grain, cotton, tomatoes, sugar beets, grapes; dairying; winery.

Parma 1 (PAHR-muh), city (1990 pop. 995), New Madrid co., extreme SE Mo., in Mississippi R. alluvial plain, 22 mi/35 km SW of Sikeston; 36°36′N 89°49′W. Cotton, rice, corn, soybeans. Inc. 1906. **2** city (1990 pop. 87,876), Cuyahoga co., NE Ohio, suburb S of Cleveland; 41°23′N 81°43′W. Named for the Ital. city of Parma, it is residential with a large industrial research center. Mfg (automobile parts, metal fabrication). Pop. declined bet. 1970 and 1990, reflecting the pattern in conjunction with the greater N Ohio area. Parma has a junior col. Settled 1816, inc. 1924.

Parma, town (1990 pop. 1,597), Canyon co., SW Idaho, near Oregon state line, on Boise R., entrance into Snake R. 5 mi/8 km W and 15 mi/24 km NW of Caldwell; 43°48′N 116°57′W. In farming area served by Boise irrigation project. Ships fruit and agr. produce; mfg. (farming equip., fertilizers, firearms). Inc. 1904.

Parma, village (1990 pop. 809), Jackson co., S Mich., 10 mi/16 km W of Jackson; 42°15′N 84°35′W. In farm area (fruit; dairy prods.). Mfg. (motor vehicle parts, appliances).

Parma Heights, city (1990 pop. 21,448), Cuyahoga co., NE Ohio, residential suburb of Cleveland; 41°23′N 81°46′W. Surrounded on 3 sides by Parma. The 2 cities share the same school system and other municipal facilities. Settled 1818; set off from Parma and inc. 1912.

Parmachenee Lake (pahr-muh-CHEE-nee), N Oxford co., W Maine; c.3 mi/4.8 km long. Receives (N) and discharges (S) Magalloway R.

Parmele (PAHR-muh-lee), village (1990 pop. 321), Martin co., E N.C., 14 mi/23 km SE of Tarboro; 35°49′N 77°18′W. RR junction. Peanuts, tobacco, grain, cotton; chickens, cattle, hogs.

Parmer, county (□ 885 sq mi/2,292 sq km; 1990 pop. 9,863), W Texas; ⊙ Farwell, on N.Mex. line (W), and on Llano Estacado; 34°31′N 102°46′W. Elev. 3,800 ft/ 1,158 m–4,100 ft/1,250 m. Agr., esp. wheat; also grain sorghum, hay, barley, sunflowers, cotton; vegetables, sugar beets, beans, corn; cattle, hogs, sheep. Formed 1876.

Parnell (pahr-NEL), city (1990 pop. 157), Nodaway co., NW Mo., on Little Platte R., 14 mi/23 km NE of Maryville; 40°26′N 94°37′W. Corn, wheat, soybeans; hogs, cattle.

Parnell, town (1990 pop. 209), Iowa co., E central Iowa, 15 mi/24 km SSE of Marengo; 41°34′N 92°00′W. In agr. area.

Parole, village (1990 pop. 10,054), Anne Arundel co., central Md., 2 mi/3.2 km W of Annapolis; 38°59′N 76°33′W. Site of Camp Parole, which housed Federal

troops captured and paroled by the Confederates until they could return to duty.

Parowan (PER-uh-wawn), town (1990 pop. 1,873), ⊙ Iron co., SW Utah, 17 mi/27 km NE of Cedar City; 37°49′N 112°49′W. Elev. 5,990 ft/1,826 m. Timber; sheep, cattle; alfalfa, barley, potatoes; dairying. Tourism. Settled 1851 by Mormons, nominal capital of Utah Territory 1858–1859. Part of Dixie Natl. Forest is to E and S; Cedar Breaks Natl. Monument to S; Brian Head Ski Resort to S. Little Salt L. (dry) is N.

Parque Nacional Cabo de Samaná (PAHR-kai nah-see-o-NAHL dai sah-mah-NAH), natl. park, Samaná prov., Dominican Republic; located on Cabo Cabrón, a cape on the N edge of Cabo Samaná; 19°20′N 69°12′W. Features mangroves and exotic vegetation. Also called Cabo Cabrón National Park.

Parque Nacional Del Este (PAHR-kai nah-see-o-NAHL del AI-ste), natl. park, La Romana prov., Dominican Republic, on a cape SE of city of La Romana; 18°20′N 68°43′W. Includes offshore isl. of Isla Saona and features coastal habitats and mangroves.

Parque Nacional El Morro (PAHR-ke nah-see-o-NAHL el MOR-ro), natl. park, Monte Cristi prov., Dominican Republic, in far NW corner of the country, NE of Monte Cristi city. Features the mesa El Morro and its associated small hill La Granja [Span. = the farm]. Offshore, between El Morro and Punta Rucia, is a large reef in about 7 ft/2 km–10 ft/3 m of water; there are 10 known wrecks near Monte Cristi. The park also features magnificent views of the Atlantic Ocean, beaches, and exotic vegetation and bird life.

Parque Nacional Isla Cabritos (PAHR-ke nah-see-o-NAHL EES-lah kah-BREE-tos), natl. park, Independencia prov., Dominican Republic, on Isla Cabritos in Lago Enriquillo; 18°29′N 71°41′W. Crocodiles here. Also called Lago Enriquillo and Isla Cabritos Natl. Park.

Parque Nacional Jaragua (PAHR-ke nah-see-o-NAHL hah-RAH-gwah), natl. park (□ 520 sq mi/1,350 sq km), Pedernales prov., Dominican Republic; 17°49′N 71°41′W. Named for a Taino Indian chief, the park extends from Oviedo to Cabo Rojo in S Pedernales prov., including the isls. of Beata and Alto Velo and saltwater Lago de Oviedo, which has a rich variety of bird life. Access to the park is limited and requires a truck or jeep.

Parque Nacional Los Haitises (PAHR-kai nah see-o-NAHL los ai-TEE-ses), natl. park, San Cristóbal prov., Dominican Republic; at W end of Cordillera Oriental (N slopes); 19°02′N 69°30′W. Features exotic vegetation.

Parque Nacional Pico Duarte/Bermúdez y Ramírez (PAHR-ke nah-see-o-NAHL el DWAHR-te/ber-MOO-dez ee rah-MEE-rez), natl. park, Dominican Republic, in W Cordillera Central; 19°00′N 71°00′W. It encompasses 3 of the Dominican Republic's highest peaks (all over 10,000 ft/3,175 m): Duarte, La Rucilla, and La Pelona. The park's major attraction is climbing these mts., especially Pico Duarte (10,417 ft/3,175 m), starting from the village of La Ciénaga.

Parque Natural del Flamenco Mexicano, biological reserve, W Yucatán, Mexico, near the fishing village of Celestún, 60 mi/97 km W of Mérida. There is a surrounding wildlife refuge for a large colony of flamingos. They are most visible from Sept. through March when they are nesting. There are also herons, egrets, pelicans, and ducks.

Parque Natural Río Lagartos, biological reserve (□ 188 sq mi/487 sq km), NE Yucatán, Mexico, 62 mi/ 100 km N of Valladolid. Mexico's largest flamingo sanctuary, protected as a nature reserve, it contains a waterfowl habitat (local and migratory) and turtle nesting beaches.

Parque Natural San Felipe, biological reserve, NE Yucatán, Mexico, with the coastal village of San Felipe, 4.3 mi/7 km W of Río Lagartos. Swimming in sea, access to beach by boat. On a small isl. with ruins of Maya pyramid.

Parr Reservoir (□ 7 sq mi/18.1 sq km), on the border bet. New Berry and Fairfield cos., central S.C., on Broad R., 25 mi/40 km NW of Columbia; 34°16′N 81°20′W. Max. capacity 32,000 acre-ft. Extends N–S

through Sumter Natl. Forest. Formed by Parr Shoals Dam (46 ft/14 m high), built (1944) for power generation.

Parr Shoals Dam, S.C.: see PARR RESERVOIR.

Parral (PA-ruhl), village (1990 pop. 255), Tuscarawas co., E Ohio, 5 mi/8 km NNW of New Philadelphia; 40°34′N 81°29′W. Clay prods.

Parral, Mexico: see HIDALGO DEL PARRAL.

Parramore Island (PER-a-mor), Accomack co., E Va., off Atlantic shore, 10 mi/16 km SSE of Accomac; c.8 mi/12.9 km long; 37°32′N 75°37′W. Wachapreague Inlet, Cedar Isl. to N; Little Machipongo Inlet, Hog Isl. (Northumberland co.) to S.

Parras (PAH-rahs), city (1990 pop. 26,160) and township, Coahuila state, N Mexico; 25°30′N 102°11′W. On RR. Parras, an agr. center, has orchards and vineyards that make the city famous for wines and brandies. Cattle raising and cotton and flour milling are also important. Formerly called Parras de la Fuente.

Parris Island, S.C.: see SEA ISLANDS.

Parrish (PER-rish), town (1990 pop. 1,433), Walker co., NW central Ala., 7 mi/11.3 km S of Jasper. Explosives mfg.; coal mining.

Parrott (PER-uht), town (1990 pop. 140), Terrell co., SW Ga., 8 mi/12.9 km NW of Dawson; 31°53′N 84°31′W.

Parrottsville (PER-uhts-vil), town (1990 pop. 121), Cocke co., E Tenn., 7 mi/11 km NE of Newport; 36°00′N 83°05′W.

Parrsboro, town (1991 pop. 1,634), N N.S., Canada, port on the N shore of Minas Basin of the Bay of Fundy; 45°24′N 64°19′W. It is a local tourist center and an export point for lumber and plywood.

Parry, Cape, NW Mackenzie dist., N.W.T., Canada, N extremity of Parry Peninsula (50 mi/80 km long, 4 mi/ 6 km–30 mi/48 km wide), on Amundsen Gulf, bet. Franklin Bay (W) and Darnley Bay (E); 70°08′N 124°35′W.

Parry Islands, Canada: see QUEEN ELIZABETH ISLANDS, N.W.T.

Parry Sound, town (1991 pop. 6,125), S Ont., Canada, on Parry Sound, inlet of Georgian Bay of L. Huron; 45°20′N 80°02′W. It is an active port and the center of a popular vacation area.

Parryville (PER-ee-vil), borough (1990 pop. 488), Carbon co., E Pa., 3 mi/4.8 km NW of Palmerton, on Lehigh R. (bridged), at mouth of Pohopoco Creek; 40°49′N 75°40′W. Mfg. (concrete prods.); agr. (dairying).

Parshall (PAHR-shuhl), town (1990 pop. 943), Mountrail co., NW central N.Dak., 45 mi/72 km SW of Minot; 47°57′N 102°07′W. Dairy produce, grain, vegetables. Van Hook Arm, large bay of L. Sakakawea, reservoir on Missouri R. to W; located in N part of Fort Berthold Indian Reservation.

Parsippany (pah-SI-puh-nee), village, Morris co., N N.J., 6 mi/9.7 km NNE of Morristown, at S end of Parsippany Reservoir (c.2 mi/3.2 km long; formed by Boonton Dam in Rockaway R.), supplying water to Jersey City. Largely residential.

Parsippiny–Troy Hills (pah-SI-puh-nee–troi), township (1990 pop. 48,478), Morris co., N N.J., 5 mi/8 km NE of Morristown; 40°51′N 74°25′W. Major commercial center for region. Inc. 1928.

Parsnip, river, c.150 mi/240 km long, rising in central B.C., Canada, and flowing NW to join the Finlay R. at Williston L. and form the Peace R. Explored by Sir Alexander Mackenzie in 1793, it became, with the Peace R., an important fur-trading route.

Parsons, city (1990 pop. 11,924), Labette co., SE Kansas; 37°20′N 95°16′W. Major RR junction. It is a shipping point for dairy prods., grain, and livestock. Mfg. (ammunition, fabricated wire prods., paper prods., concrete, plastics, appliances, apparel). Labette Community Col. here. Neosho State Fishing L. to NE. Tri-City Airport 15 mi/24 km W. Inc. 1871.

Parsons 1 town (1990 pop. 2,033), Decatur co., W Tenn., 40 mi/64 km E of Jackson, near Kentucky Reservoir (Tennessee R.); 35°39′N 88°08′W. In timber, corn, and livestock area; limestone, sand, and gravel; clothing, appliances. **2** town (1990 pop. 1,453), ⊙ Tucker co., NE

W.Va., 25 mi/40 km SE of Grafton, at junction of Laurel Fork and Shavers Fork rivers, which form Cheat R.; 39°05′N 79°40′W. In Monongahela Natl. Forest, includes Fernow Experimental Forest to S. Timber. Agr. (grain); cattle, poultry. Mfg. (asphalt, charcoal, printing and publishing, footwear, fish processing). Battle of Corrick's (or Carrick's) Ford, a Union victory, was fought here in 1861. Inc. 1893.

Parsonsfield, town (1990 pop. 1,472), York co., SW Maine, on N.H. state line, 20 mi/32 km WNW of Alfred; 43°43′N 70°55′W. Includes villages of Kezar Falls, partly in Oxford co., and East Parsonsfield. Inc. 1785.

Partridge, village (1990 pop. 213), Reno co., S central Kansas, 11 mi/18 km SW of Hutchinson; 37°58′N 98°05′W. In wheat region.

Pas, the, Canada: see THE PAS.

Pasadena 1 city (1990 pop. 131,591), Los Angeles co., S Calif., suburb 9 mi/14.5 km NE of Los Angeles, city of Glendale to W, at the base of the San Gabriel Mts.; 34°10′N 118°08′W. Mfg. (plastics, paints, paper, machinery parts, electronics, printing and publishing, medical supplies, computers). Pasadena is the scene of the annual Tournament of Roses and of the postseason col. Rose Bowl football game held (Jan. 1) in the famous Rose Bowl stadium (capacity 100,000 spectators) in W part of city. The city is also the seat of the Calif. Inst. of Technology (with its noted NASA jet propulsion laboratory), Pasadena City Col., Pacific Oaks Col. It has a symphony orchestra, a community playhouse, the Huntington Lib. and Art Gall. (S of city), the noted Pasadena Art Mus., and several gardens noted for their rare flora. Mt. Wilson Observatory to NE. Angeles Natl. Forest to N, including San Gabriel Wilderness to NE. Drained by Arroyo Seco, forms Devils Gate Reservoir, in NW. Inc. 1866. **2** city (1990 pop. 119,363), Harris co., SE Texas, suburb 10 mi/16 km ESE of Houston, on Buffalo Bayou/Houston Ship Channel; 29°39′N 95°09′W. Drained by Armand Bayou. SE extension of city limits reaches Galveston Bay and Clear L. Located in a highly productive oil area. The city has oil refineries, chemical plants, meat-processing establishments, and factories that make oil-field equip., concrete, fishing equip., plastic prods. and packaging equip. NASA's Lyndon B. Johnson Manned Space Center is just S, on Clear L. The city was founded in 1895; the site was very near the old San Jacinto battlefield (April, 1836) where Santa Anna was captured. The San Jacinto Monument (built 1936–1939; 570 ft/174 m high), in the San Jacinto Battleground State Historical Park to NE, commemorates the event; also Battleship Texas State Historic Site next to it. Armand Bayou Nature Center (□ 1,900 acres/769 ha) to SE. Elllington Field airport to S, William P. Hobby Field airport to SW. The city is the seat of San Jacinto Col.–Pasadena (Deer Park) Campus and a chiropractic col. An annual rodeo is held here.

Pasadena, town (1986 pop. 3,268), W N.F., Canada, on shore of Deer Lake in Humber Valley, 16 mi/26 km E of Corner Brook. Originally mixed farming operation, now residential town for Corner Brook and provider of light industry and services for interior W region.

Pasadena Acres, uninc. town (1990 pop. 1,700), Spokane co., E Wash., residential suburb 6 mi/9.7 km ENE of Spokane, on Spokane R.

Pasadena Hills, town (1990 pop. 1,165), St. Louis co., E Mo., 8 mi/12.9 km NW of St. Louis; 38°42′N 90°17′W. Inc. 1937.

Pasadena Park, village (1990 pop. 532), St. Louis co., E Mo., 8 mi/12.9 km NW of St. Louis; 38°42′N 90°17′W.

Pascagoula (pas-kuh-GOO-luh), city (1990 pop. 25,899), ⊙ Jackson co.; 30°22′N 88°32′W, extreme SE Miss., 36 mi/58 km SW of Mobile (Ala.), 21 mi/34 km E of Biloxi. RR junction. A port of entry on Mississippi Sound, Gulf of Mexico, at the mouth of the Pascagoula R., it is a resort and a fishing and shipbuilding center; mfg. (steel fabrication, petroleum refining, concrete, lumber, catfish and seafood processing, plywood). It grew around the "Old Spanish Fort," built in 1718 and still extant and includes mus. Large quantities of lumber were shipped from Pascagoula in the late 19th cent. Pascagoula Naval Station on small isl. 2 mi/3.2 km SW of city; Scranton Floating Mus., on 70-ft/21-m shrimp boat; Grand Bay Natl. Wildlife Refuge to E; Miss. Sandhill Crane Natl. Wildlife Refuge to NW; Petit Bois Isl. 13 mi/21 km SSE; Horn Isl. 10 mi/16 km SSW, both part of Gulf Isls. Natl. Seashore.

Pascagoula River (pas-kuh-GOO-luh), c.90 mi/145 km long, SE Miss.; formed in N George co. by confluence of Leaf and Chickasawhay rivers, flows S through Pascagoula R. Wildlife Management Area to Mississippi Sound at Pascagoula and Gautier in several channels and bayous; partly navigable.

Pascalis (pahs-kah-LEE), village, W Que., Canada, 14 mi/23 km ENE of Val d'Or; 48°09′N 77°29′W. Gold mining.

Pasco (PAS-ko), county (□ 868 sq mi/2,248 sq km; 1990 pop. 281,131), W central Fla., on Gulf of Mexico (W); ⊙ Dade City; 28°18′N 82°26′W. Massive recent growth as Tampa metropolitan area has expanded from the S. Citrus fruit, poultry, and cattle area. Has many small lakes. Formed 1887.

Pasco (PAS-ko), city (1990 pop. 20,337), ⊙ Franklin co., SE Wash., 160 mi/257 km SE of Seattle, on the Columbia R. (L. Wallala reservoir) near its confluence with the Snake (downstream 4 mi/6.4 km E) and Yakima rivers; 46°15′N 119°08′W. RR junction. It is a trade and shipping center for the Columbia basin project. Wheat, alfalfa, potatoes, beans, grapes; cattle; mfg. (concrete, food processing, machine parts, winery, sheet metal, meatpacking, industrial equip.). Ice Harbor Dam, on Snake R. (forms L. Sacajawea) 10 mi/16 km E. One of the Tri-Cities, along with Kennewick (2 mi/3.2 km SW) and Richland (10 mi/16 km WNW). Pasco was an early RR division point. With Kennewick and Richland it forms the fast-growing Tri-City area that developed during World War II, when the Dept. of Energy's Hanford Works were constructed nearby. The completion (1956) of the McNary Dam (32 mi/51 km SW, on Oregon border) extended Columbia R. navigation to the mouth of the Snake R., thus making Pasco a river port. Sacajawea State Park and McNary Natl. Wildlife Refuge to SE; Juniper Dunes Wilderness Area to NE.

Pascoag, R.I.: see BURRILLVILLE.

Pascoag River (PAS-coge), c.6 mi/9.7 km long, NW R.I.; rises in W Glocester town, flows generally NE, through Burrillville town, joining Chepachet R. near Oakland to form Branch R. Dammed S of Pascoag village to form Pascoag Reservoir (c.2 mi/3.2 km long).

Pascola (pas-KO-luh), town (1990 pop. 120), Pemiscot co., in the bootheel of extreme SE Mo., 11 mi/18 km NW of Caruthersville; 36°16′N 89°49′W. Soybeans, cotton, corn.

Pascua Village, village, 10 mi/16 km WSW of Tucson, Pima co., SE Ariz., in Pascua Yaqui Indian Reservation. San Xavier Indian Reservation to S.

Pasley Bay, inlet, W Boothia Peninsula, S Franklin dist., N.W.T., Canada, on Franklin Strait, c.10 mi/16 km long; 70°35′N 96°32′W.

Paso de Ovejas (PAH-so dai oh-VE-has), town (1990 pop. 6,956), Veracruz, E Mexico, in Gulf lowland, 20 mi/32 km WNW of Veracruzon Mexico Highway 140. Fruit; livestock.

Paso de Sotos, Mexico: see VILLA HIDALGO, Jalisco state.

Paso del Macho (PAH-so del MAH-cho), town (1990 pop. 9,937), Veracruz, E Mexico, in Sierra Madre Oriental foothills, 15 mi/24 km ENE of Córdoba; 18°58′N 96°43′W. On RR; coffee, fruit. Formerly called Villa Jara.

Paso del Norte, El, Mexico: see JUÁREZ, city.

Paso Real de San Diego (pah-so rei-AHL dai sahn dee-AI-go), town, Pinar del Río prov., W Cuba, on RR, and 26 mi/42 km ENE of Pinar del Río; 22°39′N 83°19′W. Tobacco, fruit; livestock. Station for San Diego de los Baños spa, 8 mi/12.9 km NNE. Opening of Central Highway (1927–1932) made mineral springs and adjacent towns more accessible to all Cubans.

Paso Robles or **El Paso de Robles,** city (1990 pop. 18,583), San Luis Obispo co., SW Calif., on Salinas R., 25 mi/40 km N of San Luis Obispo; resort noted for its hot sulphur springs; 35°38′N 120°40′W. U.S. Camp Roberts, located nearby, was active in World War II. Grain, apples, avocados, strawberries, vegetables, nursery stock, flowers; cattle; mfg. (glass prods., electrical equip., printing and publishing, paper prods., fabricated metal prods., aircraft parts). San Miguel Arcangel Mission at San Miguel to N; Santa Lucia Range to SW; Nacimiento and San Antonio reservoirs to NW; Hunter-Liggett Military Reserve to NW. Inc. 1889.

Paspébiac (pahs-pai-BYAHK), village (1991 pop. 3,016), E Que., Canada, on S Gaspé Peninsula, on Chaleur Bay, 50 mi/80 km E of Dalhousie; 48°02′N 65°15′W. Fishing port, resort; lumbering.

Pasque Island, Mass.: see ELIZABETH ISLANDS.

Pasquotank (PAS-kwo-tank), county (□ 289 sq mi/749 sq km; 1990 pop. 31,298), NE N.C.; ⊙ Elizabeth City; 36°15′N 76°15′W. Bounded S by Albemarle Sound, including part of Dismal Swamp Natl. Wildlife Refuge in NW, E by Pasquotank R. SW in part by Little R. estuary. Forested tidewater area, partly in Dismal Swamp (N). Agr. area (soybeans, corn, sorghum, wheat, oats, potatoes, cotton, peanuts; hogs), fishing; mfg. at Elizabeth City. Formed 1672.

Pasquotank River (PAS-kwo-tank), c.50 mi/80 km long, NE N.C.; rises in Dismal Swamp, on line bet. Camden and Pasquotank cos.; flows SE past Elizabeth City, to Albemarle Sound, forms estuary mouth (3 mi/4.8 km–5 mi/8 km wide) at Elizabeth City. W branch of Intracoastal Waterway passes through estuary and Dismal Swamp Canal paralleling upper course of river.

Pass Christian, town (1990 pop. 5,557), Harrison co., SE Miss., 10 mi/16 km WSW of Gulfport, 55 mi/89 km ENE of New Orleans (La.), on Mississippi Sound, Gulf of Mexico; 3 mi/4.8 km E of entrance to Bay St. Louis (bridged); 30°19′N 89°14′W. Mfg. (oyster processing, plastics, titanium dioxide, concrete bldg. prods., apparel, paraffin wax). Settled in 18th cent.

Pass Island, S N.F., Canada, at entrance of Hermitage Bay, 70 mi/113 km E of Burgeo; 1 mi/1.6 km long; 47°30′N 56°13′W.

Pass Mountain, peak (11,400 ft/3,475 m) in Rocky Mts., Park co., central Colo.

Passaconaway, Mount, N.H.: see SANDWICH RANGE.

Passadumkeag (pas-uh-DUHM-keg), town (1990 pop. 428), Penobscot co., central Maine, on the Penobscot, at mouth of small Passadumkeag R., and c.28 mi/45 km above Bangor; 45°10′N 68°35′W. Hunting, fishing area.

Passagassawakeag River (pas-uh-gas-uh-WAH-keg), tidal stream, c.11 mi/18 km long, Waldo co., S Maine; flows SW to Belfast Bay to form part of harbor.

Pass-a-Grille Beach (PAS–sah–grill), resort town and residential suburb, Pinellas co., W central Fla., 8 mi/13 km SW of St. Petersburg, on Long Key; 27°37′N 82°45′W.

Passaic, county (□ 197 sq mi/510 sq km; 1990 pop. 453,060), N N.J., on N.Y. state line; ⊙ Paterson; 41°01′N 74°17′W. Highly industrialized in SE (steel, rugs, clothing, textiles, rubber goods, machinery, food, aircraft parts, communications equip., explosives, chemicals); agr. (poultry, vegetables). Residential in E. Includes part of Ramapo Mts. Many lakes (including Greenwood L., with state park) have resorts. Drained by Passaic, Ramapo, and Pequannock rivers; Wanaque Reservoir is here. Formed 1837.

Passaic, city (1990 pop. 58,041), Passaic co., NE N.J., a port on the Passaic R.; 40°51′N 74°07′W. Formerly a great textile center, its productions include rubber goods, factory equip., chemicals, plastics, and aluminum foil. The city was once the scene of considerable labor unrest; an Industrial Workers of the World strike occurred in 1912, and an important strike in protest against a wage cut and involving the right of assembly occurred in 1926. Settled 1678 by Du. traders as Acquackanonk, named Passaic 1854. Inc. as a city 1873.

Passaic, river, c.80 mi/129 km long, N.J.; rising near Morristown and flowing with a winding course NE then S past several industrial towns to Newark Bay. It is navigable by large vessels to the rapids above Passaic. At Paterson is the Great Falls of the Passaic (70 ft/21.3 m high), a natl. historic dist. and an area of channels that provided power to industrial mills. The river's power aided the growth of industry in NE N.J. that began in the late 18th cent.

Passamaquoddy Bay (pas-uh-muh-KWAHD-ee), inlet of the Bay of Fundy, bet. Maine and N.B., Canada, at the mouth of the St. Croix R. Most of it (including Campobello isl.) is within the Can. border. N.B. towns in the vicinity are St. Andrews and St. George; Maine towns are Eastport and Lubec (at the bay's entrance). A large hydroelectric project (frequently called the Quoddy project), which planned to make use of the bay's great tidal range (up to 25 ft/8m) and began (1935) in the U.S. sector with funds from the Public Works Administration, was suspended after Congress refused funds in 1936. The Franklin D. Roosevelt summer home on Campobello Isl. (N.B.) is an internatl. park.

Passumpsic (PAH-suhmp-sik), village of Barnet town, Caledonia co., NE Vt., just S of St. Johnsbury and on Passumpsic R.

Passumpsic River (PAH-suhmp-sik), c.40 mi/64 km long, NE Vt.; rises in N Caledonia co. and flows S, past St. Johnsbury, to the Connecticut R. at Barnet.

Pastelillo (pah-stel-EE-yo), end of small peninsula near port of Nuevitas, N coast of Camagüey prov., E central Cuba, 4 mi/6.4 km E of Nuevitas; 21°34′N 75°13′W. Oil storage facility ("farm") there.

Pastol Bay, W Alaska, on S Norton Sound, W Alaska, E of Yukon R. delta, 50 mi/80 km wide; 63°10′N 163°14′W. Pastolik village on S shore.

Pastolik, Inuit village, W Alaska, on Pastol Bay of Norton Sound, 50 mi/80 km SW of St. Michael. Important under Russians in 19th cent., now deserted.

Pastor Ortiz (pas-TOR or-TEES), town (1990 pop. 7,235), ⊙ José Sixto Verduzco municipio, Michoacán, central Mexico, on Lerma R. (Guanajuato border), 17 mi/27 km NNW of Puruándiro. Cereals; stock. Formerly called Zurumuato.

Pastora Peak (9,412 ft/2,869 m), NE Apache co., NE corner of Ariz., c.55 mi/89 km W of Farmington (N.Mex.), in Navajo Indian Reservation. Highest point in Carrizo Mts.

Patagonia, town (1990 pop. 888), Santa Cruz co., S Ariz., 18 mi/29 km NE of Nogales; 31°32′N 110°45′W. Elev. 4,044 ft/1,233 m. Ranching area, cattle; hay. Santa Rita Mts. are N, Patagonia Mts. S; Patagonia L. State Park to SW; parts of Coronado Natl. Forest to N and S.

Patagonia Mountains, W of Huachuca Mts., in sect. of Coronado Natl. Forest, Santa Cruz co., SE Ariz., N of Mex. border; rises to 7,300 ft/2,225 m in Ariz.; 31°24′N 110°43′W.

Patamsan, Cerro, Mexico: see URIPITIJUATA, CERRO.

Patapsco (puh-TAP-scoh), river, c.65 mi/105 km long, Md.; formed in the center of the state by the confluence of the North Branch (c.45 mi/70 km long) and the South Branch and flowing SE into Chesapeake Bay at Baltimore. The lower river is tidal and forms a wide estuary on which Baltimore's harbor installations and industrial suburbs (including Sparrows Point) are located. The Baltimore Harbor Tunnel (c.6,300 ft./1,920 m. long; opened 1957) carries vehicular traffic under the estuary; another tunnel, the I-95, was opened in the 1980s. Spanning the entire waterway is the Francis Scott Key Bridge, built in the 1970s. The valley of the Patapasco was Md.'s industrial center during the 19th cent., the river waters driving power wheels for mills and furnaces. Today, most of the valley is a park. Land acquisition begun in 1912 now encompasses 6 recreation areas over 8,000 acres/3,240 ha.

Pataskala (puh-TA-skuh-luh), village (1990 pop. 3,046), Licking co., central Ohio, 15 mi/24 km WSW of Newark, and on South Fork of Licking R.; 40°00′N 82°40′W. In fruit and dairy area.

Patch Grove, village (1990 pop. 202), Grant co., extreme SW Wis., 11 mi/18 km SE of Prairie du Chien; 42°56′N 90°58′W. Wyalusing State Park to W.

Patchogue (PA-chawg), village (1990 pop. 11,060), Suffolk co., SE N.Y., on L.I., on Great South Bay; 40°46′N 73°01′W. Former summer resort, now year-round residential area with some light mfg. Inc. 1893.

Patchogue Highlands (PA-chawg), village, Suffolk co., SE N.Y.; 40°45′N 73°01′W. Chiefly residential.

Pateros (puh-TER-ahs), village (1990 pop. 570), Okanogan co., N central Wash., 25 mi/40 km SSW of Okanogan, on Columbia R. (L. Pateros reservoir, formed by Wells Dam 6 mi/9.7 km S) at mouth of Methow and Columbia rivers; 48°03′N 119°54′W. In agr. region. Alta L. State Park and Okanogan Natl. Forest to W.

Pateros, Lake, reservoir (□ 15 sq mi/39 sq km), Okanogan, Douglas, and Chelan cos., N central Wash., on Columbia R., on W border of Okanogan Natl. Forest, 10 mi/16 km NE of Chelan; 47°58′N 119°53′W. Max. capacity 500,000 acre-ft. Formed by Wells Dam (160 ft/49 m high), built (1968) for power generation; also used for irrigation, recreation, and as a fish and wildlife pond. Chief Joseph Dam just upstream.

Paterson, city (1990 pop. 140,891), ⊙ Passaic co., NE N.J., at the falls of the Passaic R.; 40°54′N 74°09′W. Founded in 1791 by Alexander Hamilton and others of the Society for Establishing Useful Manufactures, Paterson was a planned attempt to promote industrial independence in the newly formed U.S. In 1792 and 1794 cotton-spinning mills, forerunners of the city's textile industry, were established. In 1835, Samuel Colt began the mfg. of the Colt revolver. Shortly thereafter the silk industry was established, beginning a silk boom which would earn Paterson the appellation "Silk City of the World." The iron industry, which initially supplied Paterson with textile machinery, was producing locomotives in great numbers by 1880. After World War I, the aeronautics industry moved to Paterson. Although the silk industry is gone, textiles and transportation equip. are still made, and there is a large garment industry. Among the many other mfg. are electronic equip., data processing services, paper and food prods., fabricated metals, rubber, and plastics. During the 1st half of the 20th cent., notably in 1912–1913, 1933, and 1936, many bitter strikes arose due to labor conditions in the silk industry. The city has gradually become an ethnic center, with significant black and Hispanic pops. High unemployment rates have marked Paterson since the 1970s. Of special interest here is the historic dist. that centers around the roaring falls of the river. Designated a natl. historic site in 1970, it is a unique display of industrial history, with old cobblestone streets and stone bridges; the abandoned houses of workmen and mill owners; and industrial works that include several locomotive factories (one dating back to 1830), the Colt gun factory (1835), and historic spinning mills and waterworks. Passaic County College is in downtown Paterson. Lou Costello of Abbot and Costello b. here. Inc. 1851.

Paterson, uninc. village (1990 pop. 100), Benton co., S Wash., 27 mi/43 km SW of Richland, on Columbia R. (L. Umatilla reservoir, formed by John Day Dam, 55 mi/89 km WSW); McNary Dam 13 mi/21 km upstream (E). Oregon state is across river. Wheat; cattle. Winery. Umatilla Natl. Wildlife Refuge to E and SW; Crow Butte State Park, on isl. in Columbia R., to SW.

Pathfinder Reservoir (□ 35 sq mi/91 sq km), Carbon and Natrona cos., central Wyo., on North Platte R., 36 mi/58 km SW of Casper; 20 mi/32 km long, max. 4 mi/6.4 km wide; 42°27′N 106°50′W. Max. capacity 1,070,000 acre-ft. Main reservoir of North Platte project. Formed by Pathfinder Dam (masonry; 214 ft/65 m high), built (1913) for irrigation. Immediately above dam is Sweetwater (R.) Arm, 12 mi/19 km long to W, 3 mi/4.8 km wide. Alcova Reservoir is downstream (NE); Kortes Dam is upstream (S) at headwaters of Pathfinder Reservoir; large Seminoe Reservoir 4 mi/6.4 km S of Kendrick. Pathfinder Bird Refuge here.

Pathfork, village, Harlan co., SE Ky., in the Cumberland Mts., 9 mi/14.5 km SW of Harlan. Bituminous coal.

Patillas (pah-TEE-yahs), town (1990 pop. 19,633), SE P.R., 6 mi/9.7 km E of Guayama. In irrigated area. Light mfg.; tourism, fishing.

Patoka, town (1990 pop. 704), Gibson co., SW Ind., on Patoka R., 4 mi/6.4 km N of Princeton; 38°25′N 87°35′W. Shipping center for fruit, grain, and vegetables; lumber. Oil wells. Settled 1789, laid out 1813.

Patoka, village (1990 pop. 656), Marion co., S central Ill., 12 mi/19 km NNW of Salem; 38°45′N 89°05′W. In oil-producing and agr. area.

Patoka Lake, reservoir, Dubois, Orange, and Crawford cos., SW Ind., 13 mi/21 km ENE of Jasper. Built on Patoka R. for flood control. Mostly surrounded by Hoosier Natl. Forest. L. has 4 state recreation areas.

Patoka River, 138 mi/222 km long, S Ind.; rises in SE Orange co., flows generally W, past Jasper, Winslow, and Patoka, to the Wabash opposite Mount Carmel (Ill.).

Paton (PAT-un), town (1990 pop. 255), Greene co., central Iowa, 12 mi/19 km NNE of Jefferson; 42°09′N 94°15′W. In agr. area.

Patricia, district, N portion of Kenora co., NW Ont., Canada, bounded by Manitoba (W) and Hudson Bay (N); drained by Severn, Winisk, and Attawapiskat rivers. There is abundant water power. Contains numerous lakes, including Big Trout, St. Joseph, and North Caribou lakes. Gold is mined in Pickle Crow and Central Patricia region. Formerly part of N.W.T., dist. was disputed bet. Man. and Ont. It was added to Ont. by the Ontario Boundaries Extension Act of 1912; named after Princess Patricia, daughter of the duke of Connaught, who was governor general at the time. Annexed 1927 for judicial purposes to Kenora co.

Patrick, county (□ 485 sq mi/1,256 sq km; 1990 pop. 17,473), S Va.; ⊙ Stuart; 36°40′N 80°17′W. Partly in Piedmont region; rises to Blue Ridge in W and NW; bounded S by N.C. state line; drained by North Mayo, South Mayo, Smith, and Dan rivers. Agr. (corn, hay, alfalfa, soybeans, tobacco, apples, peaches; cattle; dairying); timber. Fairy Stone Mt. (in Fairy Stone State Park) in NE; Pinnacles of Dan in W central; Philpott Reservoir (Smith R.) on boundary in NE corner. Blue Ridge Parkway, Appalachian Trail traverse co. Formed 1790.

Patrick, village (1990 pop. 368), Chesterfield co., N S.C., 35 mi/56 km NW of Florence; 34°34′N 80°02′W. Mfg. includes machine tools and clothing. Agr. includes livestock. Timber.

Patrie, La (pah-TREE, lah), village (1991 pop. 332), S Que., Canada, on Salmon R. (a tributary of St. Francis R.), 30 mi/48 km E of Sherbrooke, at foot of Megantic Mt. Dairying; livestock raising.

Patriot, town (1990 pop. 190), Switzerland co., SE Ind., on Ohio R., 14 mi/23 km NE of Vevay; 38°50′N 84°50′W. In agr. area; mfg. (fiberglass, motor vehicle parts). Sand and gravel. Suffered during flood of 1937. Laid out 1820.

Patsaliga Creek (pat-suh-LEE-guh), c.60 mi/97 km long, S Ala.; rises in S Montgomery co.;' flows S and SW to Conecuh R. 4 mi/6.4 km NNW of Andalusia.

Patten, town (1990 pop. 1,256), Penobscot co., E central Maine, 30 mi/48 km WSW of Houlton; 45°59′N 68°29′W. Lumbering, hunting, fishing area. Includes Patten village. Settled 1828, inc. 1841.

Patterson 1 city (1990 pop. 8,626), Stanislaus co., central Calif., 12 mi/19 km SW of Modesto; 37°28′N 121°08′W. In irrigated fruit-growing (melons), vegetables (pumpkins), poultry, grain, and dairying area. Mfg. (motor vehicles, frozen food). San Joaquin R. to NE; Delta Mendola Canal to SW; Diablo Range to SW, including Eylar Mt. (4,088 ft/1,246 m) to W. Inc. 1919. **2** city (1994 pop. 5,532), St. Mary parish, S La., 41 mi/66 km SSW of Baton Rouge, on Bayou Teche; 29°42′N 91°19′W. In sugarcane-growing area; catfish, crawfish; mfg. (tools, boats). Natural gas and oil. Settled in late 18th cent.; inc. 1907.

Patterson, town (1990 pop. 128), Madison co., S central Iowa, 13 mi/21 km E of Winterset; 41°21′N 93°52′W. In agr. area.

Patterson 1 village (1990 pop. 445), Woodruff co., E central Ark., 8 mi/12.9 km E of Augusta, on Cache R.; 35°15′N 91°14′W. Mfg. (fertilizer). **2** village (1990 pop. 626), Pierce co., SE Ga., 18 mi/29 km NE of Waycross; 31°23′N 82°08′W. **3** uninc. village, Lemhi co., E Idaho, 46 mi/74 km SSE of Salmon, near Big Creek. **4** village (1990 pop. 1,200), Putnam co., SE N.Y., 11 mi/18 km NW of Danbury (Conn.); 41°29′N 73°35′W. In dairying and farming area. Watchtower Educational Center, part

Cross references are shown in SMALL CAPITALS. The pronunciation key is on page xv. The dates of population figures are on page xii.

of physical and spiritual hq. of Watchtower Bible and Tract Society (Jehovah's Witnesses). Residents of center are Bethelites. Complex include livestock farm. **5** uninc. village, Caldwell co., W central N.C., 5 mi/8 km N of Lenoir on Yadkin R., on E edge of Pisgah Natl. Forest, in Blue Ridge Mts. Agr. area. Mfg. (packaging materials, furniture). **6** village (1990 pop. 145), Hardin co., W central Ohio, 10 mi/16 km NNE of Kenton; 40°47′N 83°31′W.

Patterson, township (1990 pop. 3,074), Beaver co., W Pa., residential suburb 1 mi/1.6 km WSW of Beaver Falls; 40°44′N 80°19′W. Includes the communities of Riverview, Steffens Hill, and Pleasantview.

Patterson Creek, 45 mi/72 km long, mostly in Eastern Panhandle, NE W.Va.; rises in E Grant co.; flows NNE along W base of Patterson Creek Mt. to North Branch of the Potomac R., 5 mi/8 km SSE of Cumberland, Md.

Patterson Creek Mountain, ridge, NE W.Va., in the Appalachian Mts., in Eastern Panhandle; from South Branch of the Potomac R. near Petersburg extends 31 mi/50 km NNE; highest point (2,774 ft/846 m) is 8 mi/12.9 km NNE of Petersburg.

Patterson Gardens, town, Monroe co., SE Mich., suburb 3 mi/4.8 km W of Monroe on S side of R. Raisin; 41°55′N 83°25′W.

Patterson Heights, borough (1990 pop. 576), Beaver co., W Pa., residential suburb 2 mi/3.2 km SSW of Beaver Falls, near Beaver R.; 40°44′N 80°19′W.

Patterson, Mount (10,490 ft/3,197 m), SW Alta., Canada, near B.C. border, in Rocky Mts., in Banff Natl. Park, 60 mi/97 km NW of Banff; 51°45′N 116°35′W.

Patterson Springs, village (1990 pop. 690), Cleveland co., S N.C., 3 mi/4.8 km SSE of Shelby; 35°13′N 81°31′W. Cotton, grain, soybeans; livestock.

Pattison, village (1990 pop. 327), Waller co., SE Texas, 38 mi/61 km W of Houston; 29°48′N 95°58′W. Oil and natural gas. Cotton, rice, cattle. Mfg. (oil field equip.).

Pattison State Park, Douglas co., extreme NW Wis., 15 mi/24 km S of Superior. Covers an area of 1,374 acres/556 ha; principal feature is Big Manitou Falls or Manitou Falls (165 ft/50 m high), highest in Wis., in Black R. Est. 1920.

Patton (PA-tuhn), borough (1990 pop. 2,206), Cambria co., W central Pa., 25 mi/40 km NE of Johnstown, on Chest Creek; 40°37′N 78°39′W. Mfg. (sawmill, printing and publishing). Agr. area (corn, potatoes; livestock; dairying); timber. Glendale L. reservoir in Prince Gallitzin State Park to NE.

Pattonsburg, city (1990 pop. 414), Daviess co., NW Mo., on Grand R., 42 mi/68 km NE of St. Joseph; 40°02′N 94°08′W. Corn, wheat, soybeans; cattle; mfg. (dairy prods.); lumber; limestone quarries. Located on a flood plain of the Missouri R., it was flooded out in 1993. Being relocated and rebuilt on higher ground.

Patuxent (puh-TUX-ent), river, c.100 mi/161 km long, rising in central Md. and flowing SE to Chesapeake Bay. The longest river entirely in the state, its estuary is a deepwater anchorage with important oyster beds. Upriver, 2 reservoirs supply the Wash., D.C. area, Tridelphia formed by Brighton Dam and Rocky Gorge formed by the Howard C. Duckett Dam. The Azalea Gardens at Brighton Dam on the Patuxent are the largest in Md.

Pátzcuaro (PAHTS-kwah-ro), city (1990 pop. 42,459) and township, Michoacán, central Mexico, on S shore of L. Pátzcuaro, 30 mi/48 km SW of Morelia; 19°32′N 101°37′W. Elev. 7,133 ft/2,174 m. Resort; fishing, processing, and agr. center (cereals, sugarcane, fruit, livestock); canning, tanning, flour- and sawmilling, liquor distilling; processing of forest prods. (resins). Known for native lacquer ware. Old Tarascan town, with 16th-cent. colonial character.

Pátzcuaro (PAHTS-kwah-ro), lake (□ c.100 sq mi/259 sq km), Michoacán state, W Mexico; 19°30′N 101°30′W. Elev. 6,726 ft/2,050 m. Its indented shores, dotted with Tarascan villages, green isls., and the curious native sailboats help make L. Pátzcuaro popular as a resort. The lake is rich in fish. Pátzcuaro is the chief town on the lake.

Paugus Bay (PAW-guhs), Belknap co., central N.H., just

N of Laconia; extends 4 mi/6.4 km S from SW side of L. Winnipesaukee, connected S through narrow channel to Opeche Bay, which drains 1 mi/1.6 km through Winnipesaukee R., through Laconia, to Winnisquam L. Sometimes called L. Paugus.

Paukaa (POU-KAH-ah), E Hawaii isl., Hawaii co., Hawaii, residential suburb (1990 pop. 495), 5 mi/8 km N of Hilo, on Hilo Bay, E coast, at mouth of Kapue Stream; 19°45′N 155°05′W.

Paul, town (1990 pop. 901), Minidoka co., S Idaho, 5 mi/8 km W of Rupert; 42°37′N 113°47′W. Elev. 4,200 ft/1,280 m. Beet-sugar processing; cattle, sheep; potatoes, beans; grain; dairying; mfg. (irrigation equip., concrete).

Paul Smiths, village, Franklin co., NE N.Y., on Lower St. Regis L., in the Adirondacks, 10 mi/16 km NNW of Saranac L. village; 44°26′N 74°15′W. Founded 1859 as one of the 1st wilderness resorts in region, it got its present name from successful entrepreneur Apollos ('Pol, then Paul) Smith, who had established himself by the time he died in 1912 at age 87 as the Adirondacks' most famous historical figure. Site of Paul Smith's Col. of Arts and Sciences, which was funded by the estate of Smith's son Phelps, who died in 1937.

Paulatuk, trading post (1991 pop. 255), N Mackenzie dist., N.W.T., Canada, at head of Darnley Bay (50 mi/80 km long, 23 mi/37 km–40 mi/64 km wide) of Amundsen Gulf; 69°23′N 123°59′W. Site of R.C. mission (est. 1935). School and power station constructed 1960, gave community permanence. Hunting, fishing, trapping, big-game outfitting. Weather station at Cape Parry. Scheduled air service.

Paulding 1 (PAWL-ding), county (□ 315 sq mi/816 sq km; 1990 pop. 41,611), NW Ga.; ⊙ Dallas; 33°55′N 84°52′W. Piedmont agr. (fruit); cattle, poultry; timber area; becoming a suburban bedroom community of W Atlanta. Mfg. at Dallas. Formed 1832. **2** county (□ 416 sq mi/1,077 sq km; 1990 pop. 20,488), NW Ohio; ⊙ Paulding; 41°07′N 84°35′W. Bounded W by Ind. line; drained by Maumee and Flatrock rivers. In the Lake Plains physiographic region. Agr. area (hogs, cattle; corn, soybeans, wheat); mfg. (glass, plastics, motor vehicle bodies). Formed 1839.

Paulding 1 (PAWL-ding), uninc. village, ⊙ Jasper co. (with Bay Springs), E central Miss., 30 mi/48 km SW of Meridian; 32°01′N 89°02′W. Claude Bennett State L. to N. **2** village (1990 pop. 2,605), ⊙ Paulding co., NW Ohio, 14 mi/23 km SW of Defiance; 41°07′N 84°35′W. Corn, wheat, oats; alfalfa milling; mfg.

Pauline, Lake, reservoir, Hardeman co., N Texas, on small S tributary of Red R., 5 mi/8 km SE of Quanah; 2 mi/3.2 km long; 34°13′N 99°32′W. Max. capacity c.7,000 acre-ft. Formed by power dam. Fishing; hunting nearby.

Paulins Kill, stream, c.35 mi/56 km long, NW N.J.; rising in Kittatinny Mt. ridge in NW Sussex co.; flows SW, past Blairstown, to the Delaware at Columbia (hydroelectric dam here). Dammed W of Newton to form Paulins Kill L. (c.3 mi/4.8 km long; recreation).

Paullina, town (1990 pop. 1,134), O'Brien co., NW Iowa, 17 mi/27 km NNW of Cherokee; 42°58′N 95°41′W. Mfg. (seed; feeds; concrete prods.; farm equip.; meat and poultry processing). Sand and gravel pits nearby. Mill Creek State Park just E. Inc. 1883.

Pauls Valley, town (1990 pop. 6,150), ⊙ Garvin co., S central Okla., 31 mi/50 km SW of Ada, and on Washita R.; 34°43′N 97°13′W. Elev. 876 ft/267 m. Mfg. (food; publishing and printing). Washita Valley Mus. Settled c.1887, inc. 1899.

Paulsboro, borough (1990 pop. 6,577), Gloucester co., SW N.J., on Mantua Creek, 10 mi/16 km SW of Camden, near the Delaware; 39°50′N 75°14′W. Oil refineries; mfg. (fertilizer, chemicals), agr. (vegetables, fruit; poultry). Fortified in the Revolution. Settled 1681, inc. 1904.

Paulus Hook, N.J.: see JERSEY CITY.

Paunsaugant Plateau (PAWN-suh-gant), high tableland, Garfield and Kane cos., SW Utah; extends S from Sevier Plateau along East Fork Sevier R., terminating in Pink Cliffs on S and E. Elev. 7,000 ft/2,134 m–

9,300 ft/2,835 m. Unusually dissected part of plateau and cliffs on E incl. in Bryce Canyon Natl. Park. Mostly within Dixie Natl. Forest.

Pavant Mountains (puh-VAHNT), Millard and Sevier cos., SW central Utah, in Fishlake Natl. Forest; extend c.45 mi/72 km N from Tushar Mts. along W bank of Sevier R. Rise to 10,020 ft/3,054 m at Mt. Catherine. Kanosh Indian Reservation on W slope.

Pavillion, village (1990 pop. 126), Fremont co., W central Wyo., on branch of Bighorn R., 28 mi/45 km N of Lander, at center of Wind River Indian Reservation; 43°14′N 108°41′W. Elev. 5,690 ft/1,734 m. Ocean L. to SE.

Pavlof or **Pavlof Harbor**, village, SW Alaska, on E shore of Pavlof Bay, on SW Alaska Peninsula; 55°29′N 161°29′W. Fishing. Nearby is Pavlof Volcano.

Pavlof Bay, inlet of N Pacific, SW Alaska, on SW Alaska Peninsula, 21 mi/34 km long, 10 mi/16 km wide at mouth; 55°24′N 161°36′W. On E shore is Pavlof village; Pavlof Volcano on W shore.

Pavlof Islands, group of 7 small islands, SW Alaska, off SW Alaska Peninsula, at entrance of Pavlof Bay; 55°06′N 161°38′W. Largest is Dolgoi Isl. (10 mi/16 km long, 7 mi/11.3 km wide).

Pavlof Volcano (8,600 ft/2,621 m), SW Alaska, at W end of Alaska Peninsula, on W shore of Pavlof Bay; 55°25′N 161°54′W. Active volcano.

Pavo (PAV-o), town (1990 pop. 774), Thomas and Brooks cos., S Ga., 17 mi/27 km ENE of Thomasville; 30°58′N 83°44′W. Light mfg.

Paw Paw, town (1990 pop. 3,169), ⊙ Van Buren co., SW Mich., 16 mi/26 km SW of Kalamazoo and on a branch of Paw Paw R.; 42°13′N 85°53′W. In fruit-growing area (peaches, grapes, apples); mfg. (canned juices, paper prods., grape, cherry, and apple concentrates, metal plating, rubber prods.); winery. Resort. Native Amer. earthworks nearby. Settled 1832; inc. 1859.

Paw Paw 1 village (1990 pop. 791), Lee co., N Ill., 20 mi/32 km SW of De Kalb; 41°41′N 88°58′W. In rich agr. area. **2** village (1990 pop. 538), Morgan co., NE W.Va., 27 mi/43 km WNW of Martinsburg, in Eastern Panhandle, on the Potomac R.; 39°31′N 78°27′W. (grain, apples); livestock. Mfg. (clothing). Site of main tunnel of Chesapeake and Ohio Canal Natl. Historic Park.

Paw Paw Lake, town (1990 pop. 3,782), Berrien co., extreme SW Mich., 13 mi/21 km NNE of St. Joseph, on Paw Paw L. (3 mi/4.8 km long); 42°12′N 86°16′W. Resort.

Paw Paw River, c.55 mi/89 km long, SW Mich.; formed in NE Van Buren co.; flows W and SW, past Lawrence, Hartford, Watervliet, and Coloma, to St. Joseph R. just above its mouth on L. Michigan at Benton Harbor; 42°15′N 85°55′W. West Branch rises in SE Van Buren co., flows N c.10 mi/16 km and past Paw Paw to enter main branch.

Pawcatuck, Conn.: see STONINGTON.

Pawcatuck River (PAW-cu-tuck), c.30 mi/48 km long, in R.I. and Conn.; rises in Worden Pond, S R.I.; flows W and SW, past Kenyon, Shannock, Carolina, and Bradford, then NW, W, and S, past Potter Hill and Westerly, forming part of state line, to Little Narragansett Bay 13 mi/21 km E of New London. Furnishes water power to several mfg. villages. Formerly called Charles R. bet. source and mouth of Wood R. NNE of Bradford.

Pawhuska (paw-HUHS-kuh), town (1990 pop. 3,825), ⊙ Osage co., N Okla., 39 mi/63 km NNW of Tulsa, on Bird Creek; 36°40′N 96°19′W. Elev. 879 ft/268 m. In oil- and natural-gas-producing, agr., cattle-ranching region. Oil and natural-gas wells. Mfg. (machinery, dairy prods., petroleum prods., apparel). Annual rodeo. The Osage Agency Mus. and Hq. here. Osage Hills State Park to NE; Bluestem L. reservoir to NW. Settled 1872; inc. 1906.

Pawik, Alaska: see NAKNEK.

Pawlet, town (1990 pop. 1,314), Rutland co., SW Vt., on Mettawee R., 20 mi/32 km SW of Rutland; 43°21′N 73°11′W. Slate, lumber. Settled in 1760s.

Pawleys Island, village (1990 pop. 176), Georgetown co.,

E S.C., on Grand Strand on Atlantic coast, 10 mi/16 km ENE of Georgetown; 33°25′N 79°07′W. Tourism is the main economic activity; mfg. of hammocks and furniture. Huntington Beach State Park to N. Small Pawleys Isl. is just offshore.

Pawling, village (□ 2 sq mi/5.2 sq km; 1990 pop. 1,974), Dutchess co., SE N.Y., 20 mi/32 km SE of Poughkeepsie; 41°33′N 73°35′W. Mfg. (plastics, rubber prods., tiles); in resort and diversified-farming area. Seat of Trinity-Pawling School. In 1937, Thomas E. Dewey, 3-term governor and 2-time nominee for U.S. president, purchased a 486-acre/197-ha farm here, although his legal address was the Roosevelt Hotel in N.Y. city. When he returned to legal practice after being governor, he resided at the World Trade Center. He and his wife are buried in Pawling Cemetery. Settled by Quakers c.1740; inc. 1893.

Pawnee 1 (paw-NEE), county (□ 754 sq mi/1,953 sq km; 1990 pop. 7,555), SW central Kansas; ⊙ Larned; 38°10′N 99°13′W. Rolling plain area, drained by Arkansas and Pawnee rivers. Wheat, sorghum, sugar beets, alfalfa; cattle. Formed 1872. **2** county (□ 432 sq mi/1,119 sq km; 1990 pop. 3,317), SE Nebr.; ⊙ Pawnee city; 40°07′N 96°14′W. Farm area bounded S by Kansas; drained by branches of North and South forks of Big Nemaha R. and Turkey Creek. Cattle, hogs; sorghum, corn, soybeans, dairying. Limestone. Burchard L. near center of co. Formed 1857. **3** county (□ 594 sq mi/1,538 sq km; 1990 pop. 15,575), N Okla.; ⊙ Pawnee; 36°18′N 96°42′W. Bounded NE by Arkansas R. with Cimarron R. (forms Keystone L. reservoir in SE corner); drained by Cimarron R. and small Black Bear Creek. Agr. area (soybeans, wheat, hay; cattle); some mfg. in Pawnee and Cleveland. Oil and natural-gas wells. Feyodi Creek State Park in E; part of Sooner L. reservoir in NW corner. Formed 1893.

Pawnee (paw-NEE), city (1990 pop. 2,197), ⊙ Pawnee co., N Okla., 18 mi/29 km NE of Stillwater; 36°20′N 96°47′W. Elev. 866 ft/264 m. RR junction. In grain, cattle area; mfg. (medical equip., fabricated metal prods., apparel, ground rock). The home and mus. of Pawnee Bill (Gordon W. Lillie), one of the Wild West show heroes and partner of Buffalo Bill Cody, is here. Founded c.1893 on site of trading post and Pawnee Tribal Hq.

Pawnee, village (1990 pop. 2,384), Sangamon co., central Ill., 13 mi/21 km SSE of Springfield; 39°35′N 89°34′W. In agr. and bituminous-coal area; grain; livestock. Inc. 1891.

Pawnee City, town (1990 pop. 1,008), ⊙ Pawnee co., SE Nebr., 55 mi/89 km SSE of Lincoln, near North Fork R., near Kansas state line, is on Turkey Creek; 40°06′N 96°09′W. Livestock; grain; animal foods; printing. Inc. 1858.

Pawnee Creek, NE Colo.; North Fork rises in N Weld co., flows c.20 mi/32 km SE. South Fork rises in S Weld co., flows NE, joining North Fork in E Weld co. to form main stream, flows c.35 mi/56 km SE to South Platte R. 6 mi/9.7 km S of Sterling.

Pawnee River (paw-NEE), c.100 mi/161 km long, SW central Kansas; rises in S central Finney co. E of Garden City and flows E, past Rozel, to Arkansas R. at Larned.

Pawnee Rock (paw-NEE), village (1990 pop. 367), Barton and Pawnee cos., central Kansas, 13 mi/21 km SW of Great Bend, near Arkansas R.; 38°16′N 98°58′W. In grain area. Pawnee Rock State Monument nearby.

Pawtuckaway River, N.H.: see NOTTINGHAM.

Pawtucket, city (□ 8 sq mi/20.7 sq km; 1990 pop. 72,644), Providence co., NE R.I., on the Blackstone R. at Pawtucket Falls; 41°52′N 71°22′W. Known as "the place by the waterfall" to Native Americans, it was settled by Europeans in 1671. The 4th-largest city in the state, Pawtucket has been a textile center since Samuel Slater built the nation's 1st successful water-powered cotton mill here in 1793. A dam built along the Blackstone R. in 1790 provides the electric power for the city, known as "the cradle of the U.S. textile industry." Mfg. includes textiles, wire, cable, and textile machinery. The area, deeded to Roger Williams in 1638, was a haven for religious freedom in New England. Pawtucket's 1st settler was an ironworker who est. (1671) a forge at the falls. Metalworks and sawmills sprang up, and after Slater erected his cotton mill on the banks of the river, the textile industry boomed. After World War II, when much textile mfg. moved S, Pawtucket shared the decline of many New England cities and towns. Of principal interest is the 1793 Slater mill, restored in 1995 and now a mus. Many tourist and recreational sites are in the area. Inc. 1885 after the E sect. (which was part of Mass. until 1862) was merged with the W sect. into a single town in R.I.

Pawtuxet River (paw-TUX-et), c.11 mi/18 km long, central R.I.; formed in West Warwick town by junction of Southwest Branch (8 mi/12.9 km long; drains Flat R. Reservoir) and North Branch (7 mi/11.3 km long; dammed to form Scituate Reservoir) at R. Point; flows generally NE, bet. Cranston and Warwick, furnishing water power for mfg. area, to Narragansett Bay at Pawtuxet village.

Pax (PAKS), village (1990 pop. 167), Fayette co., S central W.Va., 14 mi/23 km SW of Fayetteville; 37°54′N 81°15′W. Coal-mining and agr. region. Mfg. (coal processing). RR junction. Plum Orchard Wildlife Management Area to NE.

Paxico (PAKS-uh-ko), village (1990 pop. 174), Wabaunsee co., NE central Kansas, 26 mi/42 km W of Topeka; 39°04′N 96°10′W. In cattle and grain region.

Paxinos (pak-SEE-nos), uninc. village, Northumberland co., E central Pa., 4 mi/6.4 km N of Shamokin on Shamokin Creek; 40°51′N 76°34′W. Mfg. includes furniture parts, food prods., printing. Agr. includes dairying; livestock; grain.

Paxtang (PAKS-tang), borough (1990 pop. 1,599), Dauphin co., S central Pa., residential suburb 3 mi/4.8 km E of Harrisburg, on Spring Creek; 40°15′N 76°49′W. Limestone. Here occurred (1763) uprising of Paxtang (Paxton) Boys against Native Americans. County Prison to S.

Paxton, city (1990 pop. 4,289), ⊙ Ford co., E Ill., 24 mi/39 km NNE of Champaign; 40°27′N 88°05′W. In rich agr. area (corn, wheat, soybeans; livestock). Settled by Swedes in 1850s; inc. 1865.

Paxton, town (1990 pop. 4,047), Worcester co., central Mass., 7 mi/11.3 km WNW of Worcester; 42°19′N 71°57′W. Anna Maria Col. is here. Moore State Park nearby. Settled c.1749; inc. 1765.

Paxton 1 village (1990 pop. 33), E central Alaska, 70 mi/113 km S of Delta Junction, on Gulkana R. Elev. 2,650 ft/808 m. Tourism; fishing; machining. Located on Richardson Highway (Route 4), at E terminus of Denali Highway (Route 8). Trans-Alaska Pipeline runs N-S on E side of highway. Highway services center. **2** uninc. village, Plumas co., NE Calif., 8 mi/12.9 km N of Quincy, on Last Chance Creek, in Plumas Natl. Forest. Timber; cattle. L. Almanor reservoir to N. **3** village (1990 pop. 536), Keith co., SW central Nebr., 19 mi/31 km E of Ogallala, on South Platte R.; 41°07′N 101°21′W. Grain; livestock; mfg.

Paxtonia (PAKS-to-nee-ah), uninc. town (1990 pop. 4,862), Dauphin co., S Pa., residential suburb 6 mi/9.7 km NE of Harrisburg; 40°19′N 76°47′W.

Paxville, village (1990 pop. 218), Clarendon co., central S.C., 12 mi/19 km S of Sumter; 33°44′N 80°21′W. Agr. includes poultry, cattle; grain, cotton. Timber.

Payette, county (□ 410 sq mi/1,062 sq km; 1990 pop. 16,434), W Idaho; ⊙ Payette; 44°01′N 116°46′W. Farming region bounded W by Snake R. and Oregon, drained by irrigated by Payette R. Dairying, agr. (hay, alfalfa; sugar beets, vegetables, potatoes, apples, peaches, plums; sheep, cattle). Formed 1917.

Payette, city (1990 pop. 5,592), ⊙ Payette co., W Idaho, on Snake R. at mouth of Payette R., 50 mi/80 km NW of Boise, 5 mi/8 km NE of Ontario (Oregon); 44°05′N 116°56′W. Elev. 2,152 ft/656 m. RR junction, trade and shipping center for fruit, dairy, and poultry area in Boise irrigation project (Idaho) and in Vale project (Oregon). Food processing (meat prods., canned vegetables, beans), mfg. of wood prods. Settled 1883, inc. 1901.

Payette Lake, reservoir (□ 8 sq mi/20.7 sq km), Valley co., W central Idaho, on North Fork of Payette R., 90 mi/145 km N of Boise; 44°55′N 116°07′W. Max. capacity 41,000 acre-ft. Formed by Payette L. Dam, built (1944) for irrigation; also used for recreation. Bounded by Payette Natl. Forest; ski areas just N of reservoir.

Payette River, c.70 mi/113 km long, W Idaho; formed by confluence of North Fork and South Fork in NW corner of Boise co.; flows S, past Horseshoe Bend, then W through Black Canyon Dam, past Emmett, to Snake R. at Payette at Oregon line. North Fork, c.110 mi/177 km long; rises in Upper Payette L., NW Valley co.; flows S through Payette L. reservoir (6 mi/9.7 km long, 1 mi/1.6 km wide; just N of McCall), past Cascade, to junction with South Fork, to form main stream, at Banks. South Fork, 70 mi/113 km long; rises in E Custer co.; flows W. Black Canyon Dam, on main stream, and Cascade Dam, on North Fork, are units in Payette div. of Boise irrigation project.

Payne, county (□ 697 sq mi/1,805 sq km; 1990 pop. 61,507), N central Okla.; ⊙ Stillwater; 36°04′N 96°58′W. Intersected by Cimarron R. (forms part of SW boundary); drained by Stillwater Creek; forms L. Carl Blackwell. Cattle, poultry; dairying; diversified agr. (grain, corn). Mfg. at Stillwater and Cushing. Oil and gas fields. Okla. State Univ. at Stillwater. L. McMurray reservoir on NW boundary. Formed 1890.

Payne, city (1990 pop. 192), Bibb co., central Ga., just NW of Macon; 32°51′N 83°41′W.

Payne, village (1990 pop. 1,244), Paulding co. NW Ohio, on small Flatrock Creek, near Ind. line, 24 mi/39 km SW of Defiance; 41°04′N 84°43′W. Grain; livestock.

Payne Lake (□ 300 sq mi/777 sq km), NW Que., Canada, on Ungava Peninsula, 55 mi/89 km long, 10 mi/16 km wide; 59°25′N 74°W. Drained by Payne R. into Ungava Bay.

Payne River, NW Que., Canada; issues from Payne L.; flows 200 mi/322 km NNE and E to W side of Ungava Bay. Near its mouth is Payne Bay (60°02′N 70°02′W), Hudson's Bay Company trading post.

Paynesville, town (1990 pop. 2,275), Stearns co., S central Minn., on North Fork of Crow R., near L. Koronis, 26 mi/42 km SW of St. Cloud; 45°22′N 94°43′W. In agr. area (grain, alfalfa, soybeans, fruit; cattle, hogs, sheep, poultry); dairying; mfg. (dairy prods., fertilizer, apparel, printing and publishing, feeds). In area of natural lakes; L. Koronis to S; Rice L. to E. Inc. 1887.

Payson 1 town (1990 pop. 8,377), Gila co., E central Ariz., 70 mi/113 km NE of Phoenix, near East Verde R., in Tonto Natl. Forest; 34°14′N 111°19′W. Elev. 4,930 ft/1,503 m. Cattle; timber; mfg. (concrete prods., printing and publishing, candy). Holds annual rodeo. Tonto Natural Bridge State Park to NW; Mogollon Rim escarpment (faces S) to N; fish hatchery to NE, N of Kohls Ranch. **2** town (1990 pop. 9,510), Utah co., central Utah, near Utah L., 13 mi/21 km S of Provo; 40°01′N 111°43′W. Elev. 4,500 ft/1,372 m. RR junction. Trade center and egg-shipping point in agr. area (sugar beets, onions, alfalfa, fruit); dairying, mfg. (motor vehicle parts). Surrounding region served by irrigation works on Strawberry R. Annual Onion Days Festival in Sept. Uinta Natl. Forest to S; Utah L. to NW. Settled 1850 by Mormons, inc. 1865.

Payson, village (1990 pop. 1,114), Adams co., W Ill., 12 mi/19 km SE of Quincy; 39°49′N 91°14′W. In agr. area; limestone quarries.

Paz, La, Mexico: see LA PAZ.

Pe Ell (pee-EL), village (1990 pop. 547), Lewis co., SW Wash., 18 mi/29 km SW of Centralia; 46°34′N 123°18′W. Timber. Rainbow Falls State Park to N.

Pea Island, Dare co., c.18 mi/29 km SSE of Manteo, E N.C., sect. (c.8 mi/12.9 km long) of the Outer Banks, bet. Pamlico Sound (W) and the Atlantic Ocean (E); Oregon Inlet (bridged by Bodie Isl.) is at N end, joined to Hatteras Isl. at S end, once separated by New Inlet. Part of Cape Hatteras Natl. Seashore; Pea Isl. Natl. Wildlife Refuge extends from shore into Pamlico Sound.

Pea Patch Island, New Castle co., N Del., in Delaware R., 5 mi/8 km S of New Castle; c.1 mi/1.6 km long;

39°35′N 75°34′W. Site of U.S. Fort Delaware (1814), part of river and bay defenses. Entire isl. comprises Fort Delaware State Park.

Pea Ridge 1 town (1990 pop. 1,620), Benton co., extreme NW Ark., 8 mi/12.9 km N of Rogers, near Mo. line, near Pea Ridge in the Ozarks; 36°27′N 94°07′W. Mfg. (machinery). Battle of Pea Ridge (or battle of Elkhorn Tavern), principal Civil War engagement on Ark. soil, was fought here (March 7–8, 1862); victory of Union troops prevented Confederates from carrying war into Mo. Pea Ridge Natl. Military Park to E **2** uninc. town (1990 pop. 6,535), Cabell co., W W.Va., residential suburb 5 mi/8 km E of Huntington, on Guyandotte R.; 38°24′N 82°19′W.

Pea Ridge, chain of hills, NW Ark., near Mo. border, where the Civil War battle of Pea Ridge (or Elkhorn Tavern) was fought March 6–8, 1862. Earl Van Dorn, leading a large Confederate command, which included Sterling Price's retreating Mo. forces and Ben McCulloch's army, attacked the strongly entrenched Union army under Samuel Ryan Curtis. The Confederate wings, becoming separated, were crushed on successive days. Pea Ridge was the 1st decisive victory won by the Union army W of the Mississippi; not until Price's raid (1864) did the Confederates again try to carry the war to Mo. in force.

Pea Ridge National Military Park, Benton co., NW Ark., 12 mi/19 km NE of Rogers, near Mo. boundary. Authorized 1956; covers 4,300 acres/1,740 ha. Site of the Civil War battle of Pea Ridge, which kept Mo. in the Union. Town of Pea Ridge 6 mi/9.7 km to W.

Pea River, c.140 mi/225 km long, SE Ala.; rises in Bullock co., E of Union Springs; flows SW past Elba, then S and E to Choctawhatchee R. below Geneva.

Peabody (PEE-buh-dee), city (1990 pop. 47,039), Essex co., NE Mass., suburb of Boston, on the Danvers R.; 42°32′N 70°58′W. Its tanning industry dates from early in the 18th cent. Once called the "leather and tanning capital of the U.S.," now little is left. Retailing center. Leather goods, chemicals, electronic equip., precision instruments, plastics, and fabricated metals are also produced. The Peabody Inst. lib. contains much of the memorabilia of George Peabody, the philanthropist, for whom the city was named. Site of North Shore Mall, one of the largest shopping centers in U.S. Settled c.1633, inc. as South Danvers 1855, name changed 1868.

Peabody (PEE-bahd-ee), town (1990 pop. 1,349), Marion co., SE central Kansas, 15 mi/24 km NE of Newton; 38°10′N 97°06′W. RR junction. In grain and livestock area; dairy prods. Platted 1871, inc. 1878.

Peabody River, c.15 mi/24 km long, Coos co., N central N.H.; rises just E of Mt. Washington; flows E and NNE to the Androscoggin R. at Gorham.

Peace, river, 945 mi/1,521 km long, formed by the junction of the Finlay and Parsnip rivers at Williston L., N central B.C., Canada. It flows E through the Rocky Mts., then generally NE across N Alta. and onto the Northern Plains, where it meanders to the Slave R. at L. Athabasca. From the head of the Finlay R. the Peace R. is 1,195 mi/1,923 km long; it is one of the chief headstreams of the Mackenzie R. At the mouth of the Peace R. is Wood Buffalo Natl. Park. The valley of the middle Peace is fertile, with wheat the chief crop; it is the northernmost commercially important agr. region of Canada. Large natural-gas reserves are tapped along the river; oil, coal, salt, and gypsum deposits are also worked. Near Hudson Hope, B.C., W.A.C. Bennett Dam (625 ft/191 m high; opened 1967) impounds Williston L. (680 sq mi/1,761 sq km). The dam's power plant (present generating capacity 2.1 million kw), the 6th-largest in Canada, provides electricity for Vancouver. The Peace R. was probably visited (1775–1778) by Peter Pond, the Amer. fur trader, and 1st explored (1792–1793) by Sir Alexander Mackenzie, the Can. explorer. It was long an important route of fur traders. Settlement in the valley began in the early 1900s.

Peace Dale, industrial village in South Kingstown town, Washington co., S R.I., just N of Wakefield. Textiles, rubber fabrics.

Peace River, town (1991 pop. 6,717), W Alta., Canada, on Peace R., just below mouth of Smoky R., 250 mi/402 km NW of Edmonton; 56°14′N 117°17′W. Fur-trading center, distributing point for Great Bear L. mineral regions, and transportation center for the Far North. Industries include woodworking, lumbering, meat packing, brick and lime mfg., tar and sand extraction; dairying. Formerly site of Fort Fork, where Sir Alexander Mackenzie wintered (1792–1793).

Peace River, c.80 mi/129 km long, central and SW Fla.; rises in L. Hancock; flows S past Bartow and Arcadia, into Charlotte Harbor near Punta Gorda.

Peach, county (□ 151 sq mi/391 sq km; 190 pop. 21,189), central Ga.; ⊙ Fort Valley; 32°34′N 83°50′W. Bounded W by Flint R. Mfg. includes apparel, textiles, and chemicals; coastal plain peach-growing and timber area; also produces cotton, corn, soybeans, wheat, peanuts, pecans; cattle.

Peach Bottom 2 and 3 Nuclear Power Plants, Pa.: see YORK, CO.

Peach Creek, uninc. village (1990 pop. 500), Logan co., SW W.Va., 2 mi/3.2 km NNE of Logan, near Guyandotte R. Coal-mining region.

Peach Island, islet, S Ont., Canada, in SW part of L. St. Clair, 4 mi/6 km NE of Windsor.

Peach Lake, village (1990 pop. 1,499), Putnam and Westchester cos., SE N.Y., 19 mi/31 km ENE of Peekskill on E side of Peach L., near Conn. border; 41°22′N 73°35′W.

Peach Lake, SE N.Y., near Conn. line, 3 mi/4.8 km SE of Brewster, c.1.25 mi/2.01 km long; 41°22′N 73°35′W. Resort area.

Peach Orchard 1 village (1990 pop. 197), Clay co., extreme NE Ark., 19 mi/31 km NW of Paragould; 36°16′N 90°39′W. Dave Donaldson–Black R. Wildlife Management Area to NW. **2** uninc. rural community, Pemiscot co., E Mo., 11 mi/18 km NNE of Kennett. Cotton, rice, soybeans.

Peach Springs, uninc. town (1990 pop. 787), Mohave co., NW Ariz., 40 mi/64 km E of Kingman, in S part of Hualapai Indian Reservation. Elev. 4,791 ft/1,460 m. Located at head of Peach Springs Canyon, which leads into Grand Canyon of Colorado R. (14 mi/23 km N); includes W extension of Grand Canyon Natl. Park. Cattle, sheep.

Peacham (PEECH-uhm), town (1990 pop. 627), Caledonia co., NE Vt., 10 mi/16 km SW of St. Johnsbury; 44°19′N 72°12′W. Summer resort; agr.

Peachland, village (1991 pop. 3,459), S B.C., Canada, on W shore of Okanagan L., 20 mi/32 km NNW of Penticton; 49°46′N 119°45′W. Peach growing and packing.

Peachland, village (1990 pop. 384), Anson co., S N.C., 11 mi/18 km W of Wadesboro; 34°59′N 80°16′W. Grain, cotton, soybeans, tobacco; livestock. Mfg.

Peachtree City, city (1990 pop. 19,027), Fayette co., Ga., 20 mi/32 km NW of Griffin; 33°23′N 84°34′W. Planned city S of Atlanta. Known for golf communities and paved pathway system used by residents for off-road travel within the city; conference center. Hq. of the Atlanta offices of the Natl. Weather Service. Mfg. includes concrete, chemicals, paper prods., textiles, audio components, consumer goods. Founded 1959.

Peacock 1 village, Burlington co., W central N.J., c.15 mi/24 km E of Camden. **2** uninc. village (1990 est. pop. 125), Stonewall co., NW central Texas, 60 mi/97 km NW of Abilene, near Salt Fork of Brazos R. In cattle and agr. area (wheat). Inc. 1938.

Peak, town (1990 pop. 78), Newberry co., NW central S.C., on Board R., 25 mi/40 km NW of Columbia; 34°14′N 81°19′W.

Peaks Island, SW Maine, residential isl. off Portland; 717 acres/290 ha. Pioneer summer resort of Casco Bay area.

Peaks of Otter, Va.: see OTTER, PEAKS OF.

Peale, Mount, highest peak (12,721 ft/3,877 m) in La Sal Mts., NE San Juan co., E Utah, 20 mi/32 km SE of Moab, near Colo. line; 38°26′N 109°13′W. On boundary of Manti-La Sal Natl. Forest.

Peapack-Gladstone, residential borough (1990 pop. 2,111), Somerset co., N central N.J., 11 mi/18 km SW of Morristown; 40°43′N 74°39′W. Ski area to SW. Settled before 1776, inc. 1912.

Peard Bay, inlet of Chuckchi Sea, NW Alaska, 20 mi/32 km NE of Wainwright; 18 mi/29 km long, 8 mi/12.9 km wide; 70°48′N 158°30′W.

Pearisburg (PER-is-buhrg), town (1990 pop. 2,068), ⊙ Giles co., SW Va., in the Allegheny Mts., 19 mi/31 km WNW of Blacksburg, on New R.; 37°19′N 80°43′W. Mfg. (mining equip., clothing, fiberglass materials, printing and publishing); agr. (cattle, poultry; alfalfa, apples). RR junction to NW. Settled 1782; inc. 1914.

Pearl, city (1990 pop. 19,588), Rankin co. central Miss., suburb 5 mi/8 km ESE of Jackson, near Pearl R.; 32°16′N 90°06′W. Cotton, corn; poultry, cattle. Mfg. (steel prods., consumer goods, paper prods., furniture). Allen C. Thompson Airport to NE.

Pearl, village, (1990 pop. 177), Pike co., W Ill., on Illinois R., 15 mi/24 km SE of Pittsfield; 39°27′N 90°37′W. In agr. area.

Pearl, river, 485 mi/781 km long, Miss. and La.; rises in N Winston co., E central Miss.; flows SW past Carthage and through Ross Barnett Reservoir, then S past Jackson, Monticello and Columbia, Miss., and Bogalusa, La., to L. Borgne, arm of Gulf of Mexico. Lower course forms state boundary. bet. La. and Miss. Bogue Chitto Natl. Wildlife Refuge, La., S of Bogalusa, on W bank.

Pearl and Hermes Reef, atoll, N Pacific, part of Honolulu co., Hawaii, 1,230 mi/1,979 km NW of Honolulu, 300 mi/483 km N of Tropic of Cancer, 100 mi/161 km ESE of Midway Isl.; 27°50′N 175°55′W. Oblong with 7 sand islets; main isls. are North Isl., Southwest Isl., and Kittery Isl. (W); annexed 1857 by Hawaii. Now included in the city and co. of Honolulu.

Pearl City, city (1990 pop. 30,993), S Oahu, Honolulu co., Hawaii, suburb 9 mi/14.5 km NW of Honolulu, on N shore of Pearl Harbor, W of Waimalu Stream; 21°23′N 157°58′W. Mfg. (fruit and vegetable processing, metalworking, machinery). Pearl Harbor Naval Reservation to SW; Ewa Forest Reserve and Keaiwa Heiau State Recreational Area to NE.

Pearl City, village (1990 pop. 670), Stephenson co., N Ill., 10 mi/16 km W of Freeport; 42°16′N 89°49′W. In agr. area (corn, oats; cattle, hogs); dairy prods.

Pearl Harbor, inlet, on the S coast of Oahu isl., Hawaii, 5 mi/8 km W of Honolulu; one of the largest and best natural harbors in the Pacific Ocean; access to Pacific Ocean through 3-mi/4.8-km channel from Mamala Bay to S. Harbor channel splits in 2, leading NW to West Loch, which receives Waikele Stream from N, and N to main harbor area, which has 2 N lobes, Middle Loch and East Loch, and has Ford Isl. at its center; U.S.S. Arizona Natl. Monument E of isl., U.S.S. Utah Memorial W of isl.; Aiea, Waimalu, and Waimanu Streams enter E harbor from N. In the Pearl Harbor vicinity are many U.S. military installations, including the Pearl Harbor U.S. Pacific naval base; Hickam Air Force Base; and Camp H.M. Smith, hq. of the U.S. Pacific Marines Corps' Command. The U.S. 1st gained rights here in 1887, when the Hawaiian monarchy granted permission for the maintenance of a coaling and repair station. After the U.S. annexed Hawaii in 1900, Pearl Harbor was made a naval base. Harbor improvements and fortifications were later added, especially after the signing of the Berlin Pact in 1940 by the Axis nations. On Sunday Dec. 7, 1941, while negotiations were going on with Jap. representatives in Washington, Jap. carrier-based planes swept in without warning over Oahu and attacked (7:55 A.M. local time) the bulk of the U.S. Pacific fleet, moored in Pearl Harbor. A total of 19 naval vessels, including 8 battleships, were sunk or severely damaged; 188 U.S. aircraft were destroyed. Military casualties were 2,280 killed and 1,109 wounded; 68 civilians were also killed. On Dec. 8, the U.S. declared war on Japan. There were many charges of negligence against those responsible for Pearl Harbor's defense. A special investigatory commission appointed by President Franklin D. Roosevelt accused the army and navy commanders at Hawaii of dereliction of duty in a report on Jan. 24, 1942. Later Army and Navy investigations concluded that no valid grounds existed for court-martial. A joint congressional committee, formed in Sept. 1945, absolved the Army and Navy commanders in a formal report to Congress on July 16, 1946, but censured the War Dept. and the Dept. of the Navy. Pearl Harbor is now a natl. historic landmark; a memorial has been built over the sunken hulk of the USS *Arizona*. Most of the harbor's activity is military in nature; some commercial shipping from Aiea, on NE shore, and Waipahu, on W Loch. Most of Honolulu's commercial shipping is from Honolulu Harbor to E (not part of Pearl Harbor).

Pearl Island, W N.F., Canada, on N side of the Bay of Isls., 25 mi/40 km NW of Corner Brook, 3 mi/5 km long, 2 mi/3 km wide; 49°14′N 58°18′W.

Pearl River, county (□ 818 sq mi/2,119 sq km; 1990 pop. 38,714), SE Miss.; ⊙ Poplarville; 30°46′N 89°35′W. Bounded W by Pearl R. (La. state line); also drained by Hobolochitto and Catahoula creeks and by Wolf R. Agr. (cotton, corn, tung nuts, pecans, blueberries, blackberries; cattle; dairying); timber; sand and gravel. Part of De Soto Natl. Forest in NE; Old R. Wildlife Management Area in W. Formed 1890.

Pearl River 1 town (1994 pop. 1,839), St. Tammany parish, SE La., 36 mi/58 km NE of New Orleans, on West Pearl R.; 30°22′N 89°45′W. Mfg. (abrasives, bricks, lumber). Pearl R. Wildlife Area to E. **2** uninc. town (1990 pop. 2,136), Neshoba co., E central Miss., 9 mi/14.5 km WNW of Philadelphia, on Pearl R., in Mississippi Choctaw Indian Reservation; 32°47′N 89°14′W. Cotton, corn; cattle; dairying.

Pearl River, uninc. village (□ 7 sq mi/18.1 sq km; 1990 pop. 15,314), Rockland co., SE N.Y., near the N.J. border; 41°03′N 74°00′W. It is a residential suburb of N.Y. city. Computer and telecommunications research and development center. Hq. of Mercedes-Benz of N. Amer.

Pearland, city (1990 pop. 18,697), Brazoria and Harris cos., SE Texas, suburb 13 mi/21 km SSE of Houston, on Clear Creek; 29°33′N 95°16′W. Agr. to S and W (rice, cotton, soybeans, pecans). Oil and natural gas. Mfg. (welding equip., oil-field equip., concrete prods., steel prods., textiles, solvents).

Pearlington (PUHRL-ing-tuhn), uninc. town (1990 pop. 1,603), Hancock co., SE Miss., 30 mi/48 km NE of New Orleans (La.), 15 mi/24 km W of Bay St. Louis, on Pearl R.; 30°15′N 89°35′W. RR spur terminus. Mfg. (electrical equip., plastic prods., steel fabrication, boats). Stennis Space Center (NASA) to N.

Pearsall, town (1990 pop. 6,924), ⊙ Frio co., SW Texas, c.50 mi/80 km SW of San Antonio, near Frio R.; 28°53′N 99°05′W. Elev. 646 ft/197 m. A processing and trading center for irrigated winter agr. area (esp. peanuts, also melons, corn, vegetables); hogs, cattle ranches. Oil and natural gas fields nearby. Mfg. (natural gas processing, fertilizers). Settled 1881, inc. 1909.

Pearse Canal, natural waterway, SE Alaska and NW B.C. (Canada), running bet. mainland and Pearse Isl.; SW channel of Portland Canal; forms internatl. boundary bet. Alaska and Canada. Extends 25 mi/40 km NE from N end of Chatham Sound.

Pearse Island (□ 81 sq mi/210 sq km; 20 mi/32 km long), W B.C., Canada, in Portland Inlet, 35 mi/56 km N of Prince Rupert, 6 mi/10 km wide; separated from Alaska mainland by Pearse Canal (1 mi/2 km wide).

Pearson (PIR-suhn), town (1990 pop. 1,714), ⊙ Atkinson co., S Ga., 30 mi/48 km W of Waycross; 31°18′N 82°51′W. Mfg. of burlap, plastic and paper bags; lumber; mobile homes; clothing.

Peary Channel (PEE-ree), N Franklin dist., N.W.T., Canada, arm extending SE from the Arctic Ocean bet. Meighen Isl. (N) and Ellef Ringnes and Amund Ringnes isls. (S), 120 mi/193 km long, 60 mi/97 km wide; 79°00′N 96°00′W–80°N 104°00′W.

Pease (PEEZ), village (1990 pop. 178), Mille Lacs co., E Minn., 4 mi/6.4 km S of Milaca, bet. Rum R. (E) and its West Branch (W); 45°42′N 93°39′W. Dairying; grain; livestock.

Pease River, c.75 mi/121 km long, NW Texas; formed in NE Cottle co. by North Pease R. (c.80 mi/129 km long) and Middle Pease R. (c.70 mi/113 km long); flows generally E from their junction to Red R. 9 mi/14.5 km E of Vernon. Middle Pease R. receives South Pease R. (c.60 mi/97 km long) 17 mi/27 km WSW of its junction with the North Pease. All 3 branches rise as intermittent streams at face of Caprock escarpment in W Motley co.

Pebble Beach, village, Monterey co., W Calif., on S shore of Monterey Peninsula on Carmel Bay of Pacific Ocean, 3 mi/4.8 km SW of Monterey. Tourism. World-famous Pebble Beach Golf Course is here; other golf courses to N.

Pecan Bayou, c.100 mi/161 km long, central Texas; rises out of Clyde L., in Callahan co.; flows generally SE, through L. Brownwood, past Brownwood, to the Colorado R. 15 mi/24 km N of San Saba. L. Brownwood (200,000 acre-ft.) provides irrigation, recreation. L. Brownwood State Park is here.

Pecan Gap, village (1990 pop. 245), Delta co., NE Texas, 22 mi/35 km SW of Paris, near North Sulphur R.; 33°26′N 95°50′W. In agr. area.

Pecan Island (pee-KAHN), uninc. village, Vermilion parish, S La., on low ridge (chenier) of same name (c.18 mi/29 km long) surrounded by sea marshes, 42 mi/68 km SW of New Iberia; 29°38′N 91°27′W. Short canal leads to White L. (N), Gulf of Mexico 6 mi/10 km S. Oil and natural gas wells and pipeline; agr. (sugarcane; cattle); hunting, fishing, fur trapping. Indian mounds here have yielded many relics. Rockefeller State Refuge to SW.

Pecatonica (PEC-ah-ton-i-ca), village (1990 pop. 1,760), Winnebago co., N Ill., on Pecatonica R. (bridged here), 13 mi/21 km W of Rockford; 42°18′N 89°21′W. In agr. area (dairying); mfg. (consumer goods). Inc. 1869.

Pecatonica River, c.120 mi/193 km long, in S Wis. and N Ill.; rises near Cobb in Iowa co., Wis.; flows generally SE, past Darlington, to Freeport, Ill., then ENE to Rock R. at Rockton, Ill., 4 mi/6.4 km SW of Beloit, Wis. Receives short East Branch (c.50 mi/80 km), rises in E Iowa co., just W of Browntown.

Peck 1 village (1990 pop. 160), Nez Perce co., NW Idaho, 8 mi/12.9 km W of Orofino; 46°28′N 116°25′W. In Nez Perce Indian Reservation, near Clearwater R. **2** village (1990 pop. 558), Sanilac co., E Mich., 12 mi/19 km S of Sandusky; 43°15′N 82°49′W. In farm area. Mfg. (electrical equip.).

Peck Beach, SE N.J., along Atlantic bet. Great Egg Harbor Inlet (N) and Corsons Inlet (S); Ocean City at N tip. Separated from mainland by Great Egg Harbor Bay (bridged) and Intracoastal Waterway channel (bridged).

Peconic (pe-KAH-nik), village (□ 4 sq mi/10.4 sq km; 1990 pop. 1,100), Suffolk co., SE N.Y., on N peninsula of E L.I., 12 mi/19 km NE of Riverhead; 41°02′N 72°27′W. In summer-resort area.

Peconic Bay, N.Y.: see GREAT PECONIC BAY.

Peconic River (pe-KAH-nik), c.15 mi/24 km long, SE N.Y.; rises on E L.I. S of Wading R.; flows generally E, past Calverton and Riverhead, to Flanders Bay of Great Peconic Bay; navigable to Riverhead.

Pecos (PAI-kuhs), county (□ 4,765 sq mi/12,341 sq km; 1990 pop. 14,675), extreme W Texas; ⊙ Fort Stockton; 30°46′N 102°43′W. Elev. 2,200 ft/671 m–5,200 ft/1,585 m. The 2d-largest co. in state, extending from Glass Mts. (SW) to Pecos R. (NE boundary). Large-scale ranching (cattle, sheep, goats). Irrigated agr. (alfalfa, watermelons, vegetables, pecans, grapes; cotton) near Fort Stockton and in Pecos valley (water from Red Bluff L., c.85 mi/137 km NW). Large oil and natural gas production. Tourist trade. Imperial Reservoir in N near Pecos R. Formed 1871.

Pecos, city (1990 pop. 12,069), ⊙ Reeves co., W Texas, 75 mi/121 km WSW of Odessa, on the Pecos R., W mouth of Toyah Creek. Elev. 2,580 ft/786 m. It is an important RR and highway junction and the market for an extensive ranch and irrigated farm area. It is also a sulfur, sand and gravel, gas, and oil center. There are cattle feed lots and vegetable-packing houses. The annual rodeo, held here since 1883, was the world's 1st. L. Toyah to SE. Inc. 1903.

Pecos (PAI-kos), town (1990 pop. 1,012), San Miguel co., N central N.Mex., on Pecos R.; 35°34′N 105°40′W. Elev. 6,932 ft/2,113 m. Trading point in livestock-raising, dude-ranching region. Fish hatchery is here; area surrounded by Santa Fe Natl. Forest. Pecos Natl. Historical Park, 2 mi/3.2 km S, consists of ruins of 2 Span. missions; and 2 communal dwellings that once contained 585 and 517 rooms each. Pueblo founded c.1348; abandoned 1838 because of epidemics.

Pecos (PAI-kos), river, 926 mi/1,490 km long, rises in N N.Mex. in extreme SW Mora co., in Santa Fe Natl. Forest, 23 mi/37 km NE of Santa Fe, S of Truchas Peak, Sangre de Cristo Mts. Flows S past Pecos and Pecos Natl. Monument, then SE past Santa Rosa, through Sumner L., past Fort Sumner, then S past Roswell and Artesia, through L McMillan and Avalon reservoirs, past Carlsbad, enters Red Bluff L. reservoir on the border bet. N.Mex. and Texas (lowest point in N.Mex., at 2,842 ft/866 m), continues SE through Texas, past Pecos and Sheffield, entering Rio Grande in Amistad Natl. Recreation Area, upstream (NW of) Amistad Reservoir, on U.S.-Mexico border, 33 mi/53 km NW of Del Rio; drains c.38,300 sq mi/99,197 sq km. In N.Mex., dams at Sumner, Avalon, and McMillan serve the Carlsbad reclamation project (est. 1906), which irrigates c.25,000 acres/10,118 ha; in W Texas, Red Bluff Dam forms a reservoir on the Pecos. Long-standing interstate disputes about water use were settled in 1949, when a Federal bill provided for a compact bet. N.Mex. and Texas. Near Pecos, N.Mex., is Pecos Natl. Monument, which encloses the ruins of Pecos pueblo. In the heyday of ranching in W Texas, "west of the Pecos" was the term for the distinct and rugged region of the W tip of the state. Much of its course is used to irrigate farmland in its vicinity, especially in N.Mex.

Peculiar, town (1990 pop. 1,777). Cass co., W Mo., 8 mi/12.9 km NW of Harrisonville; 38°43′N 94°27′W. Corn, sorghum; cattle; mfg. (plumbing fixtures).

Peddocks Island (PE-duhks), E Mass., in Quincy Bay (part of Boston Harbor), just off W tip (Windmill Point) of Nantasket Peninsula and E of Quincy; c.1.5 mi/2.4 km long. Summer residents. Camping. Part of Boston Harbor Isls. State Park. Site of Fort Andrews, Span.-Amer., World War I, World War II fortifications.

Pedee River, N.C. and S.C.: see PEE DEE RIVER.

Pedernales (pe-der-NAH-les), province (□ 373 sq mi/967 sq km; 1993 pop. 16,975), SW Dominican Republic, on the Caribbean coast and border of Haiti; ⊙ Pedernales; 18°03′N 71°29′W. Much of the land is too dry for agr., but coffee is produced along the Pedernales R.

Pedernales (pe-der-NAH-les), town (1993 pop. 7,373), Barahona prov., SW Dominican Republic, on the coast, on Haiti border opposite Anse-à-Pitre, 40 mi/64 km WSW of Barahona; 18°05′N 71°36′W. In irrigated region yielding coffee, sugarcane, corn, tubers. Has a fort. Founded 1915.

Pedernales River (PER-duh-nal-iz), c.105 mi/169 km long, S central Texas; rises in springs on Edwards Plateau in W Gillespie co.; flows generally E to L. Travis in the Colorado R. WNW of Austin. Separate units of Lyndon B. Johnson (LBJ) Natl. Historic Site at Johnson City (boyhood home) and Stonewall (LBJ Ranch), both on the river.

Pedley, uninc. town (1990 pop. 8,864), Riverside co., S Calif., residential suburb 6 mi/9.7 km W of Riverside, on Santa Ana R.; 33°59′N 117°28′W. Riverside Municipal Airport to S.

Pedregal (ped-RE-gahl), lava field (□ c.15 sq mi/39 sq km), Federal dist., central Mexico, S of Church of El Carmen in Villa Obregón. Dates from eruption of Cerro Ajusco, c.150 A.D. Excavations have revealed archaeological remains believed to be contemporary with Cuicuilco pyramid (1.5 mi/2.4 km W of Tlalpan).

Pedregal River, Mexico: see TONALÁ RIVER.

Pedricktown, village, Salem co., SW N.J., near the Delaware, 3 mi/4.8 km NE of Penns Grove. In rapidly suburbanizing area.

Pedro Ascencio Alquisiras, Mexico: see IXCAPUZALCO.

Pedro Bank, Caribbean shoal, 40 mi/64 km SSW of Portland Point, Jamaica, extending W for nearly

100 mi/161 km. Fringed by coral reefs, the largest of which are the Pedro Cays.

Pedro Bay (PEED-ro), village (1990 pop. 42), SW Alaska, on NE shore of Iliamna L.; 59°46′N 154°09′W.

Pedro Betancourt (PAI-dro bai-tahn-KURT), town, Matanzas prov., W Cuba, on RR, 28 mi/45 km SE of Matanzas; 22°43′N 81°19′W. Agr. center (sugarcane, rice; cattle). Nearby are the refineries and sugar centrals of Cuba Libre (W) and Jaime López (NNW). Stone quarries in vicinity.

Pedro Cays, group of 4 Caribbean islets and a number of smaller reefs, dependency of Jamaica, 40 mi/64 km SSW of Portland Point, Clarendon. They are situated bet. 16°58′N 77°45′W–17°03′N 77°49′W. Include Northeast, Middle, Southwest, and South Cays (Southwest is the largest). Yield some guano and coconuts. They were occupied by the British in 1863 and made a Jamaican dependency in 1882. Uninhabited. Sometimes called, together with Morant Cays (120 mi/193 km ENE), Guano Isls.

Pedro Escobedo (PAI-dro es-ko-BAI-do), town (1990 pop. 6,219), E Quéretaro, Mexico, 16 mi/33 km SE of Quéretaro, on Mexico Highway 57; 20°30′N 100°08′W. Elev. 3,904 ft/1,190 m. RR. Temperate climate. Agr. (corn, wheat, alfalfa, fruits), dairy prods., poultry and cattle breeding.

Pedro Montoya, Mexico: see SAN CIRO DE ACOSTA.

Pedro Santana (PAI-dro sahn-TAH-nah), village (1993 pop. 1,098), Elían Piña prov., W Dominican Republic, on Haiti border, on Artibonito R., adjoining Bánica. Agr. (rice, cotton); goats.

Pedro Valley, Calif.: see SAN PEDRO VALLEY.

Pee Dee River or **Great Pee Dee**, c.200 mi/322 km long; rising in the Blue Ridge, W N.C., and flowing NE then SE to Winyah Bay, S.C. It is called the Yadkin until it is joined by the Uharie R. W of Troy, N.C. Formed by joining of Yadkin and Rocky rivers 14 mi/23 km N of Wadesboro, SSE through Blewett Falls L. reservoir, to W of Rockingham, N.C.; then flows past Cheraw and Pee Dee, S.C., joins Waccamaw R. in several channels, from 14 mi/23 km SW of Myrtle Beach to Georgetown, paralleling Waccamaw bet. these points. Receives Little Pee Dee R. from N 18 mi/29 km W of Myrtle Beach; enters Winyah Bay with Black R. at Georgetown. Several hydroelectric power plants are on the river in N.C. Sometimes spelled Pedee R.

Peebles, village (1990 pop. 1,782), Adams co., S Ohio, 26 mi/42 km WNW of Portsmouth, in agr. area; 38°57′N 83°24′W. Serpent Mound State Park is nearby.

Peekamoose Mountain (3,863 ft/1,177 m), Ulster co., SE N.Y., in the Catskills, 20 mi/32 km W of Kingston; 41°57′N 74°24′W.

Peekskill, city (☐ 5 sq mi/13 sq km; 1990 pop. 19,536), Westchester co., SE N.Y., on the Hudson R.; 41°17′N 73°55′W. Clothing, leather goods, lighting fixtures, and office equip. are made here. In the Amer. Revolution, Peekskill was attacked and burned (1777) by the British; after the war the city became a prominent trade center. In 19th cent. had foundries based on Putnam co. iron deposits. Peter Cooper and Henry Ward Beecher b. here. St. Peter's Church, dedicated in 1767, has been restored. Settled 1665, inc. as a village 1816, as a city 1940.

Peekskill, Lake, N.Y.: see LAKE PEEKSKILL.

Peel, county (☐ 469 sq mi/1,215 sq km), S Ont., Canada, on L. Ontario; ⊙ Brampton; 43°45′N 79°50′W.

Peel Point, NW Victoria Isl., SW Franklin dist., N.W.T., Canada, on Viscount Melville Sound, at N end of Prince of Wales Strait; 73°22′N 113°45′W.

Peel River, 365 mi/587 km long, N.W.T., Canada; rises in the Yukon near 65°30′N 140°00′W; flows E to 66°00′N 134°00′W, then generally N, crossing into Mackenzie dist., to Mackenzie R. 40 mi/64 km SSE of Aklavik. Its lower course is W boundary of Peel R. Preserve, game sanctuary (3,300 sq mi/8,547 sq km) on river, set up 1923.

Peel Sound, arm of the Arctic Ocean, S central Franklin dist., N.W.T., Canada, bet. Barrow (N) and Franklin straits (S), 110 mi/177 km long, 15 mi/24 km–50 mi/80 km wide; 73°00′N 97°00′W. Separates Somerset (E) and Prince of Wales isls. (W).

Peerless, village (1990 pop. 135), Daniels co., NE Mont., 19 mi/31 km W of Scobey. Wheat, barley, oats, safflower; cattle, hogs, exotic game. Fort Peck Indian Reservation to S.

Peerless Park, village (1990 pop. 33), St. Louis co., E Mo., mfg. suburb on S bank of Meramec R., 18 mi/29 km SW of St. Louis; 38°32′N 90°30′W. Mfg. (steel prods.); sand and gravel quarrying. Area flooded 1993.

Peetz, village (1990 pop. 179), Logan co., NE Colo., 24 mi/39 km NNE of Sterling and 14 mi/23 km SW of Sidney, Nebr., near Nebr. state line; 40°57′N 103°06′W. Elev. 4,432 ft/1,351 m. Wheat, corn, sunflowers; cattle. In oil- and gas-extraction region.

Peever, village (1990 pop. 195), Roberts co., NE S.Dak., 10 mi/16 km SSE of Sisseton; 45°32′N 96°57′W. In farming area.

Peggs, village, Cherokee co., E Okla., 14 mi/23 km NNW of Tahlequah. In farm area; mfg. (wood prods.).

Peggy's Cove, uninc. locality (1986 pop. 47), N.S., Canada, 27 mi/43 km S of Halifax. Popular tourist attraction is picturesque inlet on rugged granite coastline.

Peigneur, Lake (pen-YUR), Iberia parish, S La., 9 mi/14 km W of New Iberia; c.2 mi/3 km in diameter; 29°58′N 91°59′W. Jefferson Isl. (salt dome) is on E shore; dredged channel joins lake with Intracoastal Waterway to S. Scenic Gardens on NE end.

Pejepscot, Maine: see TOPSHAM.

Pekin (PEE-kin), city (1990 pop. 32,254), ⊙ Tazewell co., central Ill., port on the Illinois R., suburb 8 mi/12.9 km S of Peoria; 40°34′N 89°37′W. A processing, RR, and shipping point in agr. (corn, soybeans; cattle, hogs; dairying) area, Pekin has a large food industry, also mfg. (fabricated metal prods., chemicals, feeds, paper prods.). Pekin L. Conservation Area on river. Federal prison nearby. Inc. 1839.

Pekin 1 or **New Pekin**, village (1990 pop. 950), Washington co., S Ind., 9 mi/14.5 km SSE of Salem, on Blue R. Clark State Forest to E. Mfg. (plastic prods., wire prods., wood prods.). Cattle, poultry. Laid out 1831. **2** (PEEK-in), village (1990 pop. 101), Nelson co., E central N.Dak., 18 mi/29 km S of Lakota, near Sheyenne R.; 47°47′N 98°19′W. Stump L. to N.

Pelahatchie (pee-luh-HACH-ee), town (1990 pop. 1,553), Rankin co., central Miss., 23 mi/37 km E of Jackson; 32°19′N 89°47′W. Agr. (cotton, corn; poultry, cattle); timber; mfg. (bldg. equip.; chicken feed, automotive parts, apparel). Bienville Natl. Forest and Roosevelt State Park to E. Sometimes spelled Pelahatchee.

Pelée (puh-LAI), volcano (4,429 ft/1,350 m), on N Martinique isl., Fr. West Indies. On May 8, 1902, the day after the eruption of Soufrière on St. Vincent, Pelée also erupted, engulfing Saint-Pierre at its base and killing c.40,000 people in the city and adjacent area. Because the chemical composition of the volcanic ash prevents plant life, the thick layer deposited over a wide expanse is almost complete wasteland. Pelée also erupted in 1792 and 1851.

Pelee Island (PEE-lee) (☐ 18 sq mi/47 sq km), S Ont., Canada, in W L. Erie. Scudder is the chief town. Ferry service connects the isl. with the Can. and U.S. mainland. Middle Isl., off S Pelee, is the southernmost point of Canada.

Pelee, Point, Canada: see POINT PELEE.

Pelham, town (1986 pop. 12,137), Ont., Canada; bet. Niagara escarpment and Welland R., Niagara Peninsula. Vineyards, orchards, sand quarries.

Pelham 1 (PEL-uhm), town (1990 pop. 3,869), Mitchell co., SW Ga., 22 mi/35 km NNW of Thomasville; 31°08′N 84°09′W. Mfg. of apparel, textiles, wood prods. and veneers, cotton thread, motor vehicle parts. Settled 1870; inc. 1881. **2** town (1990 pop. 1,373), Hampshire co., W central Mass., 12 mi/19 km ENE of Northampton, near Quabbin Reservoir; 42°23′N 72°25′W. Lumbering. **3** town (1990 pop. 9,408), Hillsborough co., S N.H., 7 mi/11.3 km E of Nashua; 42°43′N 71°19′W. Drained by Beaver Brook; bounded S and SE by Mass. state line. Mfg. (fabricated metal prods., consumer goods, machining); agr. (fruit, vegetables, nursery crops, corn; livestock; dairying). Little Isl. Pond in E.

Pelham, upper-income residential village (1990 pop. 6,413) in Pelham town (1990 pop. 11.903), Westchester co., SE N.Y., just E of Mt. Vernon, in N.Y. city metropolitan area; 40°54′N 73°48′W. Some light mfg. (kitchen prods., map publishing). Settled in 17th cent.; inc. 1896.

Pelham, suburb (1990 pop. 9,765), Shelby co., N central Ala., 15 mi/24 km S of Birmingham; 33°18′N 86°48′W.

Pelham Bay Park (☐ 3 sq mi/7.8 sq km), in Bronx borough of N.Y. city, SE N.Y.; 40°52′N 73°49′W. Park is in 2 divs., connected by causeway across Eastchester Bay. Includes Rodman's Neck peninsula, Orchard Beach (bathing), Hunter's Isl., and small Twin Isls. Golfing, picnicking; sports stadium.

Pelham Manor, residential village (☐ 1 sq mi/2.6 sq km; 1990 pop. 5,443), part of town of Pelham, Westchester co., SE N.Y., on N shore of L.I. Sound, just N of the Bronx, in N.Y. city metropolitan area; 40°53′N 73°48′W. Settled in mid-17th cent.; inc. 1891.

Pelican City, village (1990 pop. 222), SE Alaska, on W part of Chichagof Isl., on Lisianski Inlet, 38 mi/61 km W of Hoonah; 57°57′N 136°12′W. Fishing center; sawmill, hydroelectric plant, cannery, cold-storage plant. Est. 1939. Also called Pelican.

Pelican Lake, village, Oneida co., N Wis., on E end of Pelican L., 15 mi/24 km SE of Rhinelander. In transitional farming and forest area. Mole L. Indian Reservation to E.

Pelican Lake 1 (☐ 15 sq mi/39 sq km), Crow Wing co., central Minn., 13 mi/21 km N of Brainerd; 5.5 mi/8.9 km long, 4 mi/6.4 km wide; 46°34′N 94°10′W. Drains E from N end through Pelican Brook to Pine R. Fishing resorts. Village of Breezy Point on NW shore. Crow Wing State Forest to E. **2** in NE Grant co., W Minn., 19 mi/31 km SE of Fergus Falls, fed by short stream from L. Christina to NE; 3.5 mi/5.6 km long, 2.5 mi/4 km wide; 46°03′N 95°48′W. Narrow 2-mi/3.2-km peninsula crosses N part of lake from E. Village of Ashby near N end. **3** W Minn., in NW Otter Tail co., near boundary of Becker co., 9 mi/14.5 km SW of Detroit Lakes city; 6 mi/9.7 km long, 2 mi/3.2 km wide; 46°41′N 96°01′W. Resorts. Drains S by Pelican R. to L. Lizzie. Fed from NE from L. Melissa through short stream and Little Pelican L. (to E). **4** (☐ 19 sq mi/49 sq km), St. Louis co., NE Minn., in Kabetogama State Forest, 43 mi/69 km N of Hibbing; 7 mi/11.3 km long, max. width 5.5 mi/8.9 km; 48°03′N 92°54′W. Elev. 1,288 ft/393 m. Includes small bay in SE and several small isls. Drains E into Pelican R. to Vermilion R. Orr village is on E shore.

Pelican, Lake, Codington co., E S.Dak., 1 mi/1.6 km SW of Watertown; 5 mi/8 km long, 1 mi/1.6 km wide; 44°53′N 97°09′W. Pelican State Recreation Area on S shore.

Pelican Lakes, Minn.: see BREEZY POINT.

Pelican Rapids, town (1990 pop. 1,886), Otter Tail co., W Minn., 19 mi/31 km N of Fergus Falls on Pelican R., forms Prairie L. to N; L. Lida to E; 46°34′N 96°05′W. Trade center and shipping point for grain and livestock; agr. (dairying; livestock; grain, alfalfa, sunflowers); mfg. (lumber, feeds, turkey prods.). "Minnesota man," human skeleton believed to be prehistoric, was found nearby in 1932. Numerous small lakes, especially to E and N; Maplewood State Park to SE. Inc. 1882.

Pelican River, c.60 mi/97 km long, W Minn.; rises in Pelican L., SW of Detroit Lakes city; drains L. Pelican and L. Lizzie; flows S through L. Lizzie and Prairie L., past Pelican Rapids town, to Otter Tail R. 3 mi/4.8 km W of Fergus Falls; 46°53′N 95°49′W. Crystal L. and L. Lida drain into L. Lizzie from E.

Pelion (PEE-lee-in), village (1990 pop. 336), Lexington co., central S.C., 20 mi/32 km SSW of Columbia; 33°46′N 81°15′W. Agr. area featuring dairying; livestock; grain, peaches.

Pell City, city (1990 pop. 8,118), St. Clair co., NE central Ala., 29 mi/47 km ENE of Birmingham. Mfg. (clothing, lumber, plastic prods., yarn; sausage).

Pella, city (1990 pop. 9,270), Marion co., S central Iowa, 16 mi/26 km NW of Oskaloosa; 41°24′N 92°55′W. Mfg. and trade center (bldg. equip.; Venetian blinds; plastic prods.; concrete; apparel; food; foundry; wood prods.). Ships coal and livestock. Central Col. is here. Sunset Ski Slope and Elk Rock State Park to W; Red Rock Dam and Reservoir to SW. Settled by Dutch in 1847; inc. 1855.

Pellston, village (1990 pop. 583), Emmet co., NW Mich., on small Maple R. and 15 mi/24 km NE of Petoskey; 45°32′N 84°46′W. Mfg. (fabricated aluminum prods., wire insulators). Airport here. Douglas L. to NE.

Pelly, village (1991 pop. 376), E Sask., Canada, near Man. border, 20 mi/32 km N of Kamsack; 51°52′N 101°55′W. Mixed farming.

Pelly, river, c.330 mi/530 km long, Canada; rising W of the Mackenzie Mts., S central Yukon Territory, and flowing generally NW to join the Yukon R. at Fort Selkirk. The Pelly receives the Ross and Macmillan rivers. It was explored (1840) by Robert Campbell of the Hudson's Bay Company.

Pelly Bay, village (1991 pop. 409) and R.C. mission station, N Keewatin dist., N.W.T., Canada, at head of Pelly Bay, inlet (75 mi/121 km long, 10 mi/16 km–40 mi/64 km wide) of the Gulf of Boothia; 68°24′N 89°12′W. Crafts; seal hunting, fishing. Radio, TV. Scheduled air service. Remains of R.C. church built of hand-quarried stone. Mission station est. 1935.

Pelly, Lake (□ 331 sq mi/857 sq km), NW Keewatin and NE Mackenzie dists., N.W.T., Canada, just W of L. Garry; 66°N 102°W; 60 mi/97 km long, 2 mi/3 km–23 mi/37 km wide. Drained E by Back R.

Pelly Mountains, N range of Rocky Mts., S Yukon, Canada; extends c.200 mi/322 km NW-SE bet. upper course of Liard R., near B.C. border NW of Watson L., and Pelly R. valley. Rises to c.9,500 ft/2,896 m (NW).

Peloncillo Mountains, in Graham and Greenlee cos., SE Ariz., S of Clifton, S of Gila R., near N.Mex boundary; rise to c.6,000 ft/1,829 m in N.

Pelto, Lake (PEL-to), bay, Terrebonne parish, S La., extension of Terrebonne Bay to E, lying bet. marshy coast and Isles Dernieres (S), c.12 mi/19 km long E-W, 5 mi/8 km wide; 29°05′N, 90°42′W. Oil wells in E part. Connected by passage to Caillou Bay (W).

Pelzer, village (1990 pop. 81), Anderson co., NW S.C., on Saluda R., 15 mi/24 km S of Greenville; 34°38′N 82°27′W. In agr. area; contiguous with West Pelzer. Mfg. of clothing.

Pemadumcook Lake (pem-uh-DUHM-kuk), Piscataquis and Penobscot cos., central Maine, 8 mi/12.9 km WNW of Millinocket; c.13 mi/21 km long. West Branch of Penobscot R. flows through.

Pemaquid (PEM-uh-kwid), peninsula, Lincoln co., S Maine, 16 mi/26 km E of Bath; site of town of Bristol. Gives name to fishing and resort villages of Pemaquid Beach; Pemaquid Harbor, Pemaquid Neck, Pemaquid Point (lighthouse here built 1827), and Pemaquid Pond, lake (5.5 mi/8.9 km long) near Bremen.

Pemberton, village (1990 pop. 228), Blue Earth co., S Minn., 15 mi/24 km SE of Mankato, near Little Cobb R.; 44°00′N 93°46′W. Dairying; livestock; corn, alfalfa; mfg. (feed and fertilizer).

Pemberton, borough (1990 pop. 1,367), Burlington co., central N.J., on Rancocas Creek, 6 mi/9.7 km E of Mt. Holly; 39°58′N 74°41′W. Textiles; poultry; wheat, dairy prods. Settled by Quakers before 1690. Site of Burlington County Col.

Pemberville, village (1990 pop. 1,279), Wood co., NW Ohio, 10 mi/16 km ENE of Bowling Green and on Portage R.; 41°24′N 83°27′W. Grain, food prods. Settled 1834, inc. 1876.

Pembina (PEM-bi-nuh), county (□ 1,124 sq mi/2,911 sq km; 1990 pop. 9,238), extreme NE N.Dak.; ⊙ Cavalier; 48°46′N 97°32′W. Agr. area drained by Tongue and Pembina rivers; bounded by Red R. of the North (Minn. boundary) and N by Man. (Canada). Farming; wheat, rye, sugar beets, potatoes; cattle, hogs; transportation equip. Earliest settled co. of N.Dak. Icelandic State Park in W; Pembina Historic Site in NE corner; Walhalla Historic Site in NW corner. Formed 1867.

Pembina (PEM-bi-nuh), village (1990 pop. 642), Pembina co., extreme NE N.Dak., 22 mi/35 km NE of Cavalier and on Red R. of the North, opposite St. Vincent

(Minn.), at mouth of Pembina R.; 48°58′N 97°15′W. Oldest community in N.Dak. Dairy prods.; livestock; grain, sugar beets; mfg. (motor vehicles). Can. border, port of entry. Oldest town in N.Dak.; lowest point in state (750 ft/229 m). Fur trade post in 1797, intermittent settlement to 1843, permanent settlement afterwards, inc. 1885. Pembina Historic Site and State Historical Society of N.Dak. Pembina Mus.

Pembina Mountains (PEHM-bi-nuh), range, S Man., Canada; extends c.60 mi/97 km NW-SE bet. Assiniboine R. and N.Dak. border. Rises to c.2,000 ft/610 m.

Pembina River, 350 mi/563 km long, Alta., Canada; rises in Rocky Mts. on E edge of Jasper Natl. Park; flows in a winding course generally NE to Athabaska R. 40 mi/64 km W of Athabaska.

Pembina River, c.275 mi/443 km long, in N.Dak. and Canada; rises in Turtle Mts. of N N.Dak. and in Drift Prairie of S Manitoba; flows NE, then SE, into N.Dak., near Walhalla then E to Pembina and Red R. of the North.

Pembroke (PEM-brok), parish (1991 pop. 11,507), central Bermuda, Hamilton city on S shore; 32°17′N 64°47′W.

Pembroke (PEHM-brok), town (1991 pop. 13,997), SE Ont., Canada, NW of Ottawa, on the Ottawa R.; 45°49′N 77°07′W. It is a lumbering center and also has mfg. (steel, electric prods.).

Pembroke, city (1990 pop. 1,503), ⊙ Bryan co., SE Ga., 31 mi/50 km W of Savannah, near Canoochee R.; 32°08′N 81°37′W. In agr. and timber area; sawmilling. Mfg. of clothing.

Pembroke 1 (PEM-bruk), town (1990 pop. 852), Washington co., NE Maine, 22 mi/35 km NE of Machias, near Eastport, on an inlet of Cobscook Bay; 44°56′N 67°10′W. Settled 1770, inc. 1832. **2** town (1990 pop. 14,544), Plymouth co., E Mass., on North R., 23 mi/37 km SE of Boston; 42°04′N 70°48′W. Resort. In suburbanizing area. Settled 1650, set off from Duxbury 1712. **3** town (1990 pop. 6,561), Merrimack co., S central N.H., 5 mi/8 km SE of Concord; 43°10′N 71°27′W. Bounded by Merrimack R. on SW; drained by Suncook and Soucook rivers (Soucook forms NW boundary). Mfg. (food processors, paper prods.); timber; agr. (apples, vegetables, nursery crops; livestock; dairying). Includes village of Suncook (1990 pop. 5,214). Plausawa Hill (978 ft/298 m) in N. Created 1727 as Suncook, inc. 1759 as Pembroke. **4** town (1990 pop. 2,241), Robeson co., SE N.C., 11 mi/18 km WNW of Lumberton, near Lumber R.; 34°40′N 79°12′W. RR junction. In agr. area (grain, tobacco, sunflowers, soybeans; cattle, hogs). Mfg. (apparel, motor vehicles, wooden boxes, cabinets). Lumber R. changes name from Drowning Creek about here. Seat of Pembroke State Univ. Native Amer. Resources (center on campus). **5** town (1990 pop. 1,064), Giles co., SW Va., in Allegheny Mts., 13 mi/21 km NNW of Blacksburg, on New R.; 37°19′N 80°38′W. Mfg. (metal fabrication); in agr. area (cattle, poultry; alfalfa, apples); timber. Mountain L. Resort to NE; Cascade Falls Recreation Area to N.

Pembroke (PEM-bruk), village (1990 pop. 640), Christian co., SW Ky., 9 mi/14.5 km SE of Hopkinsville; 36°46′N 87°21′W. Agr. (tobacco, grain; livestock; dairying); mfg. (fertilizers, ham). Jefferson Davis State Historic Site to NE.

Pembroke, Cape, NE extremity of Coats Isl., E Keewatin dist., N.W.T., Canada, on Hudson Bay; 62°55′N 81°54′W.

Pembroke Pines, city (□ 33 sq mi/85 sq km; 1990 pop. 65,452), Broward co., SE Fla., residential suburb located 10 mi/16 km SW of Ft. Lauderdale; 26°00′N 80°20′W. Has grown and urbanized rapidly since 1970; a major retirement community is here. Inc. 1961.

Pemigewasset River (PE-mi-ge-WAW-set), c.70 mi/113 km long, central N.H.; rises in Franconia Notch, in N central Grafton co.; flows generally S past North Woodstock and Plymouth, joins Winnipesaukee R. at Franklin to form Merrimack R. Its East Branch rises in NE Grafton co.; flows 16 mi/26 km to the Pemigewasset at North Woodstock. Franklin Falls Dam (136 ft/41 m high, 1,740 ft/530 m long; for flood control), completed

1943, is 2 mi/3.2 km N of Franklin center. White Mt. Natl. Forest on both sides of upper course.

Pemiscot (pe-mis-KAHT), county (□ 488 sq mi/1,264 sq km; 1990 pop. 21,921), in the bootheel of extreme SE Mo.; ⊙ Caruthersville; 36°12′N 89°46′W. On Mississippi R. Drainage channels of the Little R. Drainage Dist. Cotton, rice, corn, soybeans; mfg. at Caruthersville, Hayti, and Steele. Land surface and drainage modified by New Madrid earthquakes of 1811-1812. Formed 1861.

Pen Argyl (PEN AHR-gei-uhl), borough (1990 pop. 3,492), Northampton co., E Pa., 12 mi/19 km NNW of Easton; 40°52′N 75°15′W. Mfg. (apparel, slate and roofing materials); slate quarries; agr. (corn, hay; livestock; dairying). Appalachian Trail passes to N on Kittatinny Mt. Founded 1868, inc. 1882.

Pen Mar, uninc. village, Franklin co., S Pa. adjacent to Pen Mar, Washington co., N Md., at edge of South Mt. ridge, continuation of the Blue Ridge on Pa.-Md. state line, and 4 mi/6.4 km SE of Waynesboro, Pa.; 39°43′N 77°30′W. Appalachian Trail passes to E.

Peña Blanca (PAIN-yuh BLAHN-kuh), village (1990 pop. 300), Sandoval co., N central N.Mex., on Rio Grande, in Cochiti Pueblo land grant, 24 mi/39 km WSW of Santa Fe. Elev. c.5,100 ft/1,554 m. Grain; mfg. (goat cheese). Cochiti Pueblo and Cochiti L. reservoir to N; Bandelier Natl. Monument 9 mi/14.5 km N. Settled by Spaniards in early 17th cent.; part of Santa Fe Natl. Forest to NE; Santo Domingo Indian Reservation to S; Also spelled Peñablanca.

Peña Nevada (PE-nyah ne-VAH-dah), peak, Sierra Madre Oriental, N Mexico, on Nuevo León-Tamaulipas border, W of Ciudad Victoria; 23°49′N 99°51′W. Elev. 11,955 ft/3,644 m.

Penacook (PE-nuh-kuk), village, Merrimack co., S central N.H., in city of Concord, 6 mi/9.7 km NNW of Concord center, on Merrimack R., at mouth of Contoocook R. Mfg. (speedometers, mica processing, electrical equip., bldg. materials). Monument on isl. in the Merrimack commemorates Hannah Dustin's escape from Indian captors, 1697. Hannah Dustin Memorial State Historical Site.

Penal (PEE-nal), village, SW Trinidad, Trinidad and Tobago, on RR, and 7 mi/11.3 km S of San Fernando. Petroleum wells. Sometimes spelled Peñal.

Penalosa (pen-uh-LO-suh), village (1990 pop. 21), Kingman co., S Kansas, 12 mi/19 km WNW of Kingman; 37°43′N 98°19′W. Wheat. Kingman State Fishing L. to SE.

Peñamiller (pe-nyah-MEE-yer), town (1990 pop. 932), Peñamiller municipio, Querétaro, central Mexico, 25 mi/40 km ESE of Jalpan de Sierra; 21°02′N 99°51′W. Elev. 4,462 ft/1,360 m.

Peñasco (pin-YAH-sko), village (1990 pop. 648), Taos co., N N.Mex., in Picuris San Lorenzo Pueblo land grant, in Sangre de Cristo Mts., near Rio Grande, 25 mi/40 km SSW of Taos; 36°10′N 105°41′W. Elev. 7,685 ft/2,342 m. Agr., sheep raising; handicrafts. Part of Carson Natl. Forest to N, E, and S; Sipapu Ski Area to SE.

Penasse (pe-NA-see), village, in Lake of the Woods co., N Minn., in the Northern Angle region, 36 mi/58 km NNE of Warroad, 6 mi/9.7 km ENE of Angle Inlet village; 49°22′N 94°57′W. On small Penasse Isl., at entrance to Northwest Angle Inlet of Lake of the Woods; Canada (Ont.) border is immediately to N. Northernmost settlement in U.S. outside Alaska. In Northwest Angle State Forest.

Penbrook, borough (1990 pop. 2,791), Dauphin co., S central Pa., residential suburb 2 mi/3.2 km ENE of downtown Harrisburg; 40°16′N 76°50′W.

Pend d'Oreille, Idaho: see PEND OREILLE.

Pend Oreille (pahn-duh-RAI), county (□ 1,425 sq mi/3,691 sq km; 1990 pop. 8,915), NE Wash., on Idaho state line (E), Canada (B.C.) border (N); ⊙ Newport; 48°32′N 117°17′W. Drained by Pend Oreille R. Alfalfa, hay, oats; dairying; gold, silver, copper, lead. Includes Kalispell Indian Reservation in center; parts of Kaniksu (E and SW) and Colville (NE and NW) natl. forests. Formed 1911.

Pend Oreille, Lake (□ 148 sq mi/383 sq km), mainly in Bonner co. (Idaho), extends S into Kootenai co, N Idaho, in Panhandle of Idaho; 65 mi/105 km long, and 1,200 ft/366 m deep. Largest lake in Idaho and one of the largest and deepest lakes in the U.S. Fed by the Clark Fork, which flows from SE out of Mont. and enters E side of lake and drained by the Pend Oreille R., flows W from NW end, near Sandpoint, the only sizable community on lake, the lake, with the surrounding Coeur d'Alene (SE) and Kaniksu (NE) natl. forests, is a place of beauty and a landmark in a farming, lumbering, and mining region. Farragut State Park at S end.

Pend Oreille River (o-rai), c.130 mi/209 km long, in N Idaho, NE Wash., and SE B.C. (Canada); leaves NW end of Pend Oreille L. at Sandpoint, Bonner co., N Idaho; flows W, past Priest R., Idaho, past Newport, Wash., thence N, through Pend Oreille co., NE Wash. Bet. units of Kaniksu and Colville natl. forests, enters Canada at Nelway, B.C. (Canada), then turns W, entering Columbia R. at Waneta, B.C., just N of Boundary Wash.; Can. portion c.15 mi/24 km long. Sometimes considered as part of CLARK FORK, which enters Pend Oreille L. on E from Mont. Sometimes spelled Pend d'Oreille.

Pender (PEN-duhr), county (□ 932 sq mi/2,414 sq km; 1990 pop. 28,855), SE N.C.; ⊙ Burgaw; 34°30′N 77°53′W. Bounded SE by Atlantic Ocean, SW by Cape Fear R.; drained by Northeast Cape Fear R. (forms part of S boundary) and Black R. (forms part of W boundary). Includes SW part of Topsail Isl., long sand barrier isl. parallels coast. Intracoastal Waterway passes behind Topsail and smaller isls. Low marshy coastal plain; Angola Swamp in N, Holly Shelter Swamp in East Moores Creek Natl. Battlefield in W. Some mfg. at Burgaw. Beach resorts on coast. Agr. area (corn, wheat, soybeans, hay, sweet potatoes, peanuts, tobacco; turkeys, hogs).

Pender, town (1990 pop. 1,208), ⊙ Thurston co., NE Nebr., 70 mi/113 km NNW of Omaha, and on Logan Creek; 42°06′N 96°42′W. Farm implements. Mfg. (earth moving equip., steel fabrication). Located in W part of Omaha Indian Reservation, Winnebago Indian Reservation to N; primary town for both reservations. Mfg. (machinery). Inc. 1886.

Pender Island, North (□ 10 sq mi/26 sq km), Gulf Isls., SW B.C., Canada, in Strait of Georgia, bet. Saltspring Isl. (W) and Saturna Isl. (E), 25 mi/40 km N of Victoria; 7 mi/11 km long, 1 mi/2 km–3 mi/5 km wide; mixed farming. Tourism. South Pender Isl. (4 mi/6 km long) is just SE.

Pendergrass, village (1990 pop. 298), Jackson co., NE central Ga., 12 mi/19 km SE of Gainesville; 34°10′N 83°41′W. Mfg. (food and meat processing).

Pendleton 1 (PEND-uhl-tuhn), county (□ 281 sq mi/728 sq km; 1990 pop. 12,036), N Ky.; ⊙ Falmouth; 38°41′N 84°21′W. NE corner bounded by Ohio R. (Ohio state line); drained by Licking R. and its South Fork, also Fort Lick and South Fork Grassy creeks. Gently rolling upland agr. area (burley tobacco, hay, corn, alfalfa, soybeans; cattle, sheep, poultry; dairying), in N part Bluegrass region. Some mfg. at Falmouth. Kincaid L. State Park in E. Formed 1798. **2** county (□ 698 sq mi/1,808 sq km; 1990 pop. 8,054), E W.Va., in Eastern Panhandle; ⊙ Franklin; 38°40′N 79°21′W. Bounded E, S, and SW by Va.; Allegheny Front traverses in. in West Spruce Knob (4,861 ft/1,482 m) in W is highest point in W.Va. Shenandoah Mt. is on Va. state line in E. Drained by South Branch of the Potomac R., and its N and S forks (here flowing through the SMOKE HOLE). Includes Seneca Caverns in center, Smoke Hole Gorge and Seneca Rocks in N., and parts of George Washington Natl. Forest (E) and Monongahela Natl. Forests (W). Agr. (corn, potatoes, alfalfa, hay) and livestock (cattle; hogs; poultry; sheep); timber; mfg. at Franklin. Summer resorts. Formed 1788.

Pendleton, city (1990 pop. 15,126), ⊙ Umatilla co., NE Oregon, on the Umatilla R., 150 mi/241 km E of Portland, at mouth of McKay Creek, in the foothills of the Blue Mts.; 45°40′N 118°49′W. Elev. 1,068 ft/326 m. RR

junction. Mfg. (meat prods., flour milling, lumber, printing and publishing, construction materials, transportation equip.). A distribution and trade center for wheat, livestock, and timber region; woolen mills. Pendleton Roundup rodeo, dating from 1910, held annually in Sept. Site of Blue Mt. Community Col. Points of interest: Round-Up Hall of Fame and Crow's Shadow Art Inst. Columbia R. 20 mi/32 km NNW. McKay Creek Reservoir and Natl. Wildlife Refuge to S; Emigrant Springs State Park to SE. Hq. for Umatilla Natl. Forest (E and S), adjacent to the Umatilla Indian Reservation to E. Founded 1869 on the Old Oregon Trail; inc. 1889.

Pendleton 1 town (1990 pop. 2,309), Madison co., E central Ind., on small Fall Creek, and 7 mi/11.3 km SSW of Anderson; 40°00′N 85°44′W. In agr. area (livestock, dairy and poultry farms; grain); mfg. (metal prods.). Indiana Reformatory. Settled 1823; laid out 1830. **2** town (1990 pop. 3,314), Anderson co., NW S.C., 13 mi/21 km NW of Anderson; 34°38′N 82°46′W. Mfg. includes sprinkler systems, textiles, apparel, plastics prods., stairs and ladders; agr. area noted for its dairying, cattle, soybeans, grain, sorghum, hogs. Oldest settlement in S.C. piedmont; founded in late 18th cent.

Pendleton, Camp, Calif.: see OCEANSIDE.

Pendroy, village, Teton co., N Mont., 20 mi/32 km. N of Choteau. In irrigated region. Cattle. Oil fields to N and E.

Penelope, village (1990 pop. 210), Hill co., N central Texas, 25 mi/40 km NNE of Waco; 31°51′N 96°55′W. In cotton area.

Penetanguishene (pehn-uh-tang-guh-SHEEN), town (1991 pop. 6,643), S Ont., on Georgian Bay. The name is a Native Amer. word for "white rolling sands." Settled under the Fr. regime, it has many Fr.-speaking inhabitants. The town is a port and tourist center; mfg. (fiberglass boats and motor vehicle parts). It became a naval post in 1793 and had a role in the War of 1812. The hulls of the captured Amer. vessels *Tecumseh* and *Tigris* are in the mus.

Penfield, town, Greene co., NE central Ga., 7 mi/11.3 km N of Greensboro; 33°40′N 83°10′W. Sawmilling.

Penfield 1 village (1990 pop. 6,300), Monroe co., W N.Y., residential suburb on small Irondequoit Creek, S of Irondequoit Bay, and 7 mi/11.3 km ESE of Rochester; 43°09′N 77°27′W. **2** uninc. village, Hustone township, Clearfield co., central Pa., 14 mi/23 km NW of Clearfield; 41°12′N 78°34′W. Mfg. (veneer, machinery); surface bituminous coal. Village of Penfield is in Haverford township, Delaware co., SE Pa., a residential suburb 7 mi/11.3 km W of downtown Philadelphia on Cobbs Creek.

Pengilly (PEN-gi-lee), village, Itasca co., NE central Minn., 17 mi/27 km ENE of Grand Rapids, in Mesabi Iron Range; 47°19′N 93°11′W. Iron mines nearby. Hill Annex Mine State Park to W; Swan L. to SE.

Penguin Islands, group of 7 islets just off S N.F., Canada, 15 mi/24 km SW of Cape La Hune; 47°23′N 56°59′W. Largest is Harbour Isl.

Penhold (PEHN-hold), town (1991 pop. 1,590), S central Alta., near Red Deer R., 10 mi/16 km SSW of Red Deer; 52°08′N 113°52′W. Mixed farming.

Penikese Island, Mass.: see ELIZABETH ISLANDS.

Peninsula, village (1990 pop. 562), Summit co., NE Ohio, 10 mi/16 km N of Akron, and on Cuyahoga R.; 41°14′N 81°33′W.

Peninsula, Canada: see MARATHON.

Peninsula Point, Mich.: see BIG BAY DE NOC.

Peninsula State Park, Door co., NE Wis., on Door Peninsula, 3 mi/4.8 km W of Ephraim, on Green Bay of L. Michigan. Wooded, with bathing beaches; covers 3,388 acres/1,371 ha.

Penjamillo de Degollado (pen-hah-MEE-yo dai de-go-YAH-do), town (1990 pop. 4,173), ⊙ Penjamillo municipio, Michoacán, central Mexico, on central plateau, 18 mi/29 km SSE of La Piedad de Cabadas; 20°06′N 101°55′W. Elev. 5,397 ft/1,645 m. Cereals; livestock.

Pénjamo (PEN-hah-mo), city (1990 pop. 27,276) and township, Guanajuato, central Mexico, on central plateau, 30 mi/48 km SW of Irapuato; 20°28′N 101°44′W.

Agr. center (corn, wheat, alfalfa, beans, fruit, sugarcane, stock). RR station 4 mi/6.4 km SE. Founded 1542.

Penland, uninc. village, Mitchell co., W N.C., 3 mi/4.8 km NW of Spruce Pine on North Tar R. Mining nearby. Parts of Pisgah Natl. Forest to N and S.

Penn, borough (1990 pop. 511), Westmoreland co., SW Pa., suburb 2 mi/3.2 km W of Jeannette, on Brush Creek, and 5 mi/8 km NW of Greensburg; 40°19′N 79°38′W. Mfg. (aluminum railings); agr. (corn, hay, dairying). Bushy Run Battlefield historic site to N. Laid out 1859, inc. 1865.

Penn Hills, township (1990 pop. 51,430), Allegheny co., residential suburb 9 mi/14.5 km E of Pittsburgh and includes the communities of Rodi, Churchill Valley, and Penn Ridge; 40°28′N 79°49′W. Mfg. includes fabricated metal prods., signs.

Penn Lake Park, borough (1990 pop. 242), Luzerne co., NE central Pa., residential community 4 mi/6.4 km N of White Haven, near Lehigh R., Penn L. reservoir on Wright Creek at center; 41°06′N 75°46′W.

Penn Valley, uninc. town (1990 pop. 1,242), Nevada co., E central Calif., 7 mi/11.3 km W of Grass Valley, on Squirrel Creek, in Penn Valley; 39°12′N 121°11′W. Timber; cattle; hay. L. Wildwood reservoir to N.

Penn Wynne (PEN WIN), uninc. town, Montgomery co., SE Pa., residential suburb 6 mi/9.7 km WNW of Philadelphia; 39°59′N 75°16′W.

Penn Wynne, Pa.: see LOWER MERION.

Penn Yan (pen YAN), village (□ 2 sq mi/5.2 sq km; 1990 pop. 5,248), ⊙ Yates co., W central N.Y., in Finger Lakes region, on E arm of Keuka L., 15 mi/24 km SSW of Geneva; 42°39′N 77°02′W. Mfg. (transportation equip., salt for animal feeds and canning industry, flour milling, dielectrics); agr. (grain, grapes). Keuka Col. is at nearby Keuka Park. Named for Pennsylvanians and New Englanders ("Yankees") who settled here. Jemima Wilkinson established her short-lived "Jerusalem" near here in late-18th cent. Inc. 1833.

Pennant, village (1991 pop. 156), SW Sask., Canada, 26 mi/42 km NW of Swift Current. Wheat.

Penndel (PEN-del), borough (1990 pop. 2,703), Bucks co., SE Pa., suburb 18 mi/29 km NE of downtown Philadelphia, on Neshaminy Creek; 40°08′N 74°54′W. Mfg. (plastic prods., food prods., textiles, electronics). Philadelphia Park Racetrack to S. Formerly South Langhorne. Inc. 1889.

Pennell, Mount, Utah: see HENRY MOUNTAINS.

Pennesseewassee, Lake (pen-uh-see-WAH-see), Oxford co., W Maine, in summer resort area; c.3 mi/4.8 km long. Drains S, past Norway (town), to Little Androscoggin R.

Pennfield, town (1991 pop. 2,211), SW N.B., Canada, 18 mi/29 km ENE of St. Andrews; 45°08′N 66°45′W. Mfg machinery; mixed farming, blueberries. Site of airfield.

Pennington 1 county (□ 618 sq mi/1,601 sq km; 1990 pop. 13,306), NW Minn.; ⊙ Thief River Falls; 48°04′N 96°02′W. Agr. area drained by Red Lake and Thief rivers. Wheat, hay, alfalfa, oats, barley, sunflowers; dairying; poultry, sheep. County bounded by Red Lake Indian Reservation on W. Formed 1910. **2** county (□ 2,784 sq mi/7,211 sq km; 1990 pop. 81,343), SW S.Dak., borders Wyo. on W; ⊙ Rapid City; 44°00′N 102°49′W. Black Hills and Black Hills Natl. Forest in W; traversed E by Cheyenne R. Mfg. at Rapid City; farming (wheat) and ranching (cattle, livestock) region rich in minerals (gold, granite, timber). Tourist trade; places of interest include Harney Peak, Stratosphere Bowl (from which balloon ascents have been made) and Mt. Rushmore Natl. Memorial in SW, and Badlands Natl. Park and Buffalo Gap Natl. Grassland in SE. Ellsworth A.F.B. on N boundary, NE of Rapid City. Formed 1875.

Pennington, borough (1990 pop. 2,537), Mercer co., W N.J., 7 mi/11.3 km N of Trenton; 40°19′N 74°47′W. Pennington School for boys (1838) here. Settled 1708, inc. 1890.

Pennington Gap, town (1990 pop. 1,922), Lee co., extreme SW Va., in Cumberland Mts., near Ky. state line, 25 mi/40 km SW of Norton, near Powell R.; 36°45′N 83°01′W. RR junction; mfg. (furniture, crushed stone);

trade center for agr. area (grain, tobacco; cattle); timber; bituminous coal, limestone. Inc. 1891 or 1892.

Pennock (PE-nawk), village (1990 pop. 476), Kandiyohi co., SW central Minn., 7 mi/11.3 km W of Willmar; 45°08′N 95°10′W. Dairying; poultry, livestock; grain, sugar beets. Small natural lakes to E; Solomon L. to NE.

Pennock Island (PE-nawk), in Alexander Archipelago, SE Alaska, in Revillagigedo Channel bet. Annette Isl. (S) and Revillagigedo Isl. (N), just S of Ketchikan; 3 mi/4.8 km long. Fishing.

Penns Creek, uninc. village (1990 pop. 700), Snyder co., central Pa., 14 mi/23 km W of Sunbury on Penns Creek; 40°51′N 77°03′W. Mfg. of apparel and bakery prods; agr. (dairying; livestock, poultry; grain).

Penns Creek, c.75 mi/121 km long, central Pa.; rises in E central Centre co., 13 mi/21 km ENE of State College, at Penns Cave; flows E past New Berlin, and S past Selinsgrove to Susquehanna R. 3 mi/4.8 km S of Selinsgrove (40°53′N 77°36′W). Marker on its bank N of Selinsgrove commemorates massacre (1755) of settlers by Native Americans.

Penns Grove, residential borough (1990 pop. 5,228), Salem co., SW N.J., on Delaware R. opposite Williimington, Del. (ferry); 39°43′N 75°28′W. Mfg. (chemicals, apparel, lumber prods.); agr. (poultry; fruit, produce; dairy prods.). One of N.J.'s most economically depressed communities. Settled 1675, inc. 1894.

Pennsauken (pen-SAW-kin), suburban township (1990 pop. 34,738), Camden co., SW N.J., just NE of Camden; 39°57′N 75°03′W. Mfg. (beer, plastics, wire prods., machinery, packaging supplies, food and beverage processing, automotive engines, construction materials). Settled 1840, inc. 1892.

Pennsauken Creek (pen-SAW-kin), c.5 mi/8 km long, SW N.J.; rises E of Camden in North Branch (c.10 mi/16 km long) and South Branch (c.15 mi/24 km long), which join NW of Maple Shade; flows NW to Delaware R. 5 mi/8 km above Camden.

Pennsboro, town (1990 pop. 1,282), Ritchie co., NW W.Va., on North Fork of Hughes R., 30 mi/48 km E of Parkersburg; 39°16′N 80°58′W. Market, shipping, and trade center for agr. (livestock, poultry; corn), natural-gas, and oil region. Mfg. (apparel, glassware, vinyl and aluminum windows). Co. fairgrounds here. North Bend State Park to SW; North Bend State Trail passes E-W through town. Settled in early 1800s.

Pennsburg (PENS-buhrg), borough (1990 pop. 2,460), Montgomery co., SE Pa., 15 mi/24 km S of Allentown; 40°23′N 75°30′W. Mfg. (food prods., power transformers, wood prods., optical components). Agr. (grain, soybeans, apples; livestock; dairying). Green Lane Reservoir to S. Settled 1840, inc. 1887.

Pennsbury Village (PENS-buhr-ee), borough (1990 pop. 774), Allegheny co., W Pa., residential suburb 4 mi/6.4 km W of Pittsburgh on Chartiers Creek; 40°25′N 80°05′W.

Pennside, uninc. town (1990 pop. 2,920), Berks co., SE central Pa., residential suburb 2 mi/3.2 km E of Reading; 40°20′N 75°52′W.

Pennsville, residential village (1990 pop. 12,218), Salem co., SW N.J., on Delaware R., opposite New Castle, Del. (ferry), with bridge nearby; 39°39′N 75°30′W. Settled by Swedes after 1640.

Pennsylvania, state (□ 46,059 sq mi/119,293 sq km; 1995 est. pop. 12,071,842), NE U.S.; ⊙ HARRISBURG. A Middle Atlantic state and one of the original 13 Colonies. Bordered on the NW by L. Erie, N by N.Y.; E by the Delaware R.; S by Del., Md., and W.Va.; W by W.Va. and Ohio. The Great Lakes Plain meets the Appalachian Plateau in the extreme NW part of the state. The Appalachian Plateau covers the W and N sects. of Pa. and more than ½ the area of the state. The Allegheny Mts. line the E edge of the plateau and run SW to NE. The Jacks, Tuscarora, and Blue Mt. ridges, and others comprise a ridge and valley sect. with Great Valley (extension of Cumberland Valley of Va.) to the SE and E. The Piedmont Plateau gives way to the Atlantic Coastal Plain in the extreme SE portion of the state. Pa. is drained in E by the Delaware R. system, in the center by Susquehanna R. system; in the W by the Allegheny and the Monongahela rivers, which join at Pittsburgh to form the Ohio R. The center and NE parts of Pa. are crossed by long ridges running generally SW-NE, 2 mi/3.2 km–5 mi/8 km wide and some over 100 mi/161 km long, which are divided by deep river passes, called gaps, which have provided routes through the mt. system. Highest point is Mt. Davis (3,213 ft/979 m) in SW, near Md. state line (Somerset co.); lowest point is sea level on Delaware R., in SE. The great forests and lush vegetation that once covered the entire state were transformed during the Carboniferous period into deposits of anthracite coal in the NE and extensive bituminous beds in the W. In many areas, the coal deposits and quality of remaining supplies has declined; anthracite coal deposits around Wilkes-Barre/Scranton are nearly depleted. Large areas of woodland remain and, in some isolated sects., have retained an almost primitive wildness. Iron smelting became important in the 18th cent., made possible by abundant supplies of ore and hardwoods for the furnaces. In the 19th cent., after the Bessemer process required use of its great bituminous deposits to produce coke, Pa. quickly emerged as the nation's leading steel producer, but the industry has declined dramatically, and Pa. now ranks 3d in iron and steel production. Pa. also actively exploits a wide variety of other mineral resources, especially sand, gravel, and stone. Heavy industry has declined as well, but the state still has factories that manufacture metal prods., foodstuffs, machinery, electronic prods., and chemicals. Pa.'s economy is now dominated by service industries such as the retail and wholesale trade, insurance, banking, and health care; service employment accounts for the vast majority of the state's jobs. The PITTSBURGH and PHILADELPHIA metropolitan areas, situated at opposite ends of the state and dominating the commercial and industrial life of their regions, present startling contrasts in production and culture. Pittsburgh is Pa.'s window to the W. Philadelphia, on the Delaware R., is Pa.'s only seaport; ERIE, on L. Erie, is Pa.'s only Great Lakes port (accessible to Atlantic Ocean by St. Lawrence Seaway). Other leading cities include ALLENTOWN, BETHLEHEM, READING, SCRANTON, and WILKES-BARRE. Agr. is concentrated in the fertile cos. of the SE; here the Pa. Dutch (Ger.) farmer built a culture that is identified with the bountiful agrarian life. Principal agr. prods. include dairy prods., eggs, poultry, cattle, hay, corn, mushrooms, potatoes, vegetables and fruits. In the early 1600s the English, Dutch, and Swedes disputed rights to the region. Explorations were confined to the Delaware R. vicinity, and fur trading with the Native Americans was carried on. The original permanent settlement was made at TINICUM ISLAND (1643) in the Delaware R., SW of Philadelphia, by Johan Printz, governor of NEW SWEDEN, and was followed in the succeeding years by the neighboring colony of Uppland. Swed. jurisdiction was short-lived as the Dutch, operating from their stronghold in New Amsterdam, succeeded in gaining control of the Middle Atlantic region in 1655. In turn the Dutch were overpowered by the Br. forces of Col. Richard Nicolls, acting for the Duke of York (later James II), and in 1664 the British took over the Del. area. The Duke of York remained in control until 1681, when, in payment of a royal debt, William Penn was granted proprietary rights to almost the whole of what is now Pa., and, in addition, leased the 3 Lower Cos. (see DELAWARE). A devout Quaker who had suffered for his beliefs, Penn viewed his colony as a holy experiment, designed as an asylum for the persecuted under conditions of equality and freedom. In 1681 he sent William Markham as deputy to establish a govt. at Uppland and sent instructed commissioners to plot the City of Brotherly Love (Philadelphia), which was laid out a few miles N of the confluence of the Delaware and the Schuylkill rivers. Penn carefully constructed a constitution, known as the Frame of Govt., that gave Pa. the most liberal govt. in the colonies. Religious freedom was guaranteed to all who believed in God, a humane penal code was adopted, and the emancipation of slaves was encouraged. However, under the representative system that it established, the popular assembly was left in an inferior position in relation to the executive branches controlled by the proprietors. In 1682 Penn arrived at Uppland (renamed Chester). Shortly thereafter he met with the chiefs of the Del. tribes and a famous treaty was signed, which promoted long-lasting good will bet. the Native Americans and the Eur. settlers. After Penn's death in 1718 proprietary rights were held by his heirs. By this time Pa. had developed into a dynamic and growing colony, enriched by the continuous immigration of numerous different peoples. The Quakers, English, and Welsh were concentrated in Philadelphia and the E cos., where they acquired great commercial and financial power through foreign trade and where they achieved a political dominance that they held until the time of the Amer. Revolution. Philadelphia had by then become the finest city in the nation, a leader in the arts and the professions. The Germans (Pa. Du.) — largely of the persecuted religious sects of Mennonites (including Amish), Moravians, Lutherans, and Reformed — settled in the farming areas of SE Pa., where they retained their cohesion and to a considerable extent their language, customs, architecture, and superstitions. After 1718 the Scotch-Irish began colonizing in the Cumberland Valley and gradually pushed the frontiers toward W Pa. Their rugged independence and the peculiarities of their frontier problems made them rebellious against the established order. Throughout the prov. agr. was the chief occupation, although industry was spurred by abundant water power and resources. In the W settlement was hindered by a growing unrest among the Native Americans. Penn's heirs lacked both the good sense and the ethical values that prompted Penn's fair and considerate treatment. Resentful of encroachment on their lands and of the land purchase made by the Albany Congress (1754), the Native Americans allied themselves with the French, who were then fortifying positions in the Ohio valley. The frontier settlements were severely ravaged until, after several initial reverses, the French abandoned (1758) FORT DUQUESNE to Br. and Amer. forces under Gen. John Forbes. The power of the Native Americans was not completely broken until the suppression of the uprising of 1763. The inept defenses provided by the Quaker-controlled assembly during the crisis aroused bitter resentment and intensified efforts to overturn proprietary rule. The struggle bet. proprietary and antiproprietary parties was soon overshadowed, however, by the opposition to Br. imperial policy that culminated in the Amer. Revolution. Important Pennsylvanians of both parties emerged as leaders of the Revolutionary movement — Benjamin Franklin, Benjamin Rush, Joseph Reed, Thomas Mifflin, John Dickinson, Robert Morris, and Haym Salomon. In 1776 a provincial convention dominated by radical patriots created the Commonwealth of Pa. under one of the most democratic of the new state constitutions. In the postwar period, Pa.'s role as the geographical keystone of the new nation was strengthened by the resolution of boundary disputes that had persisted throughout the colonial period. Philadelphia, host to the First and Second Continental Congresses (1774, 1775–1781) and scene of the signing of the Declaration of Independence, was for many years the nation's leading city. Philadelphia was not, however, typical of the state as a whole. Western influence in state affairs increased as the rapid movement of settlers into the Ohio country created new markets, stimulated the growth of new industries, and assured the importance of Pittsburgh and Erie as commercial centers. In political life the Democratic party was generally dominant, and in 1857 Pa. gave the nation a Democratic president in James Buchanan. However, a split within the party over opposition to slavery and the desire for a high protective tariff for the state's growing industries led to a Republican victory in 1860 and began Pa.'s long affiliation with the Republican party. Because of Pa.'s location near the South, it was the scene of several battles in the Civil War, notably the Gettysburg Campaign of 1863. With the close of the war came the rapid emergence of the state as a mighty industrial commonwealth. Supported by the high protective tariffs, the industries found favorable markets and a constant supply of immigrant labor. The 1st oil well was dug at Titusville in 1859, and the Rockefeller fortune was founded on petroleum. But it was steel that became the basic industry, using iron ore from the Lehigh valley and the Bethlehem area and the native Pa. coal. Later the iron ore was brought in massive amounts across the Great Lakes. Under the manipulation of such men as Andrew Carnegie, Henry Frick, Charles Schwab, and J. Pierpont Morgan (1837–1913) numerous interests were merged into vast combines with state and natl. influence. In the face of this increasing concentration of power, labor struggled to achieve safer working conditions, higher wages, and shorter hours. The campaign brought bloodshed during the fight bet. mine owners and the radical Molly Maguires and reached a climax in the strike at Homestead in 1892. The miners, under the leadership of John Mitchell and aided by the intervention of Theodore Roosevelt, achieved a qualified victory in the anthracite strike of 1902, but the great steel strike of 1919 was broken. During the 1930s the Congress of Industrial Organizations (CIO) successfully promoted unionization in many new areas and somewhat weakened the strength of the American Federation of Labor. By 1941 the CIO had succeeded in organizing the steel industry, while the United Mine Workers acquired increasing strength in the coal fields. The powerful and corrupt political machine that had been built by Simon Cameron continued into the 20th cent. under the leadership of such bosses as Boies Penrose. Gifford Pinchot, a Progressive Republican, was governor for 2 terms (1923–1927, 1931–1935) and did much to repair govt. through a new administrative code, an improved budget system, and pioneer work in conservation. In 1979, an accident at the THREE MILE ISLAND nuclear facility near Harrisburg resulted in a partial meltdown. Pa.'s pop. has grown very little since the 1940s, when it was the 2d-largest state in the union; it was the 5th most populous state after the 1990 census. After losing hundreds of thousands of mfg. jobs in the 1980s, the state's economy shifted to the service sector. Such industries as biotechnology and pharmaceuticals have grown in recent years, largely in the suburbs of Philadelphia and Pittsburgh. Pa. is governed under the constitution adopted in 1873 and amended extensively since then, the last time in 1968. The governor serves a 4-year term and may succeed himself for 1 additional term. The state legislature, called the general assembly, consists of a senate of 50 members and a house of representatives of 203 members. Pa. sends 2 senators and 21 representatives to the U.S. Congress and has 23 electoral votes. Among many natl. historic sites and parks are Fort Necessity Natl. Battlefield in SW, Gettysburg Military Park in S, and Independence Natl. Historical Park at Philadelphia; Appalachian Natl. Scenic Trail extends from Delaware R. on E, passes N of Allentown and Harrisburg to Md. state line in S; part of Delaware Gap Natl. Recreation Area and Delaware and Upper Delaware natl. scenic rivers in E; there are numerous state forests, some covering large areas, esp. in center of state, an extensive state park system and extensive state game properties. Major reservoirs are Raystown L. in center, Allegheny Reservoir in NW, on N.Y. state line, Pymatuning Reservoir in NW, on Ohio state line, and L. Wallenpaupack in NE. The state enjoys a rich and varied cultural heritage beginning with the remarkable accomplishments of Benjamin Franklin and the eminent physician Benjamin Rush. The Pittsburgh Symphony Orchestra and the Philadelphia Orchestra have achieved nationwide recognition. In addition to the institutions of the state's extensive univ. system are Bryn Mawr Col., at Bryn Mawr; Bucknell Univ., at Lewisburg; Carnegie-Mellon Univ., the

Univ. of Pittsburgh, and Duquesne Univ., at Pittsburgh; Dickinson Col., at Carlisle; Drexel Univ., Temple Univ., the Univ. of Pa., Saint Joseph's Univ., and La Salle Col., at Philadelphia; Haverford Col., at Haverford; Lehigh Univ., at Bethlehem; Lincoln Univ., at Oxford; Pa. State Univ., mainly at Univ. Park; Swarthmore Col., at Swarthmore; Villanova Univ., at Villanova; Franklin and Marshall Col., at Lancaster; and Lafayette Col., at Easton. Pa. has 67 cos.: ADAMS, ALLEGHENY, ARMSTRONG, BEAVER, BEDFORD, BERKS, BLAIR, BRADFORD, BUCKS, BUTLER, CAMBRIA, CAMERON, CARBON, CENTRE, CHESTER, CLARION, CLEARFIELD, CLINTON, COLUMBIA, CRAWFORD, CUMBERLAND, DAUPHIN, DELAWARE, ELK, ERIE, FAYETTE, FOREST, FRANKLIN, FULTON, GREENE, HUNTINGDON, INDIANA, JEFFERSON, JUNIATA, LACKAWANNA, LANCASTER, LAWRENCE, LEBANON, LEHIGH, LUZERNE, LYCOMING, MCKEAN, MERCER, MIFFLIN, MONROE, MONTGOMERY, MONTOUR, NORTHAMPTON, NORTHUMBERLAND, PERRY, PHILADELPHIA, PIKE, POTTER, SCHUYLKILL, SNYDER, SOMERSET, SULLIVAN, SUSQUEHANNA, TIOGA, UNION, VENANGO, WARREN, WASHINGTON, WAYNE, WESTMORELAND, WYOMING, and YORK.

Pennsylvania Avenue Historic Site, Washington, D.C., authorized 1965. Portion of Pennsylvania Ave. and adjacent area bet. the Capitol and the White House. Two blocks in front of White House closed to vehicles in 1994 to improve presidential security.

Pennsylvania Turnpike, toll divided highway in Pa., parts of Interstate Highway Sysytem. Interstate Highway 76 for most of its length, from Norristown to Ohio; Interstate Highway 276 Delaware R. from Delaware R. to Norristown; Interstate Highway 70 coincides with part of 76 in W; extends E-W across the state from Delaware R., 19 mi/31 km NE of downtown Philadelphia, to Ohio line 12 mi/19 km WNW of New Castle; 40°54′N 75°29′W–41°28′N 75°41′W. Highway bypasses any cities near its route, passes N of Philadelphia, S of Reading and Harrisburg, and NE of Pittsburgh. First portion (with several long mt. tunnels) bet. Carlisle (E) and Irwin was completed 1940. E extension opened late 1950, W extension about a year later; total length 363 mi/584 km. Continues W as Ohio Turnpike; 6 mi/9.7 km E connection with N.J. Turnpike at the N.J. Turnpike interchange no. 6.

Pennville 1 town (1990 pop. 637), Jay co., E Ind., on Salamonie R., and 9 mi/14.5 km NW of Portland; 40°29′N 85°09′W. In agr. area; mfg. (food prods.). **2** uninc. town (1990 pop. 1,559), York co., S Pa., residential suburb 1 mi/1.6 km SW of Hanover on Plum Creek; 39°47′N 76°59′W.

Pennyroyal Plateau, Ky.'s largest physiographic region (□ 11,500 sq mi/29,785 sq km), S central Ky. Mississippian geologic era. Hilly in E, karstic caves and sinkholes in middle, flat to rolling topographic landscapes in W. Contains Mammoth Cave Natl. Park. Named for a member of the Mint family.

Penobscot (pe-NAHB-skaht), county (□ 3,556 sq mi/9,210 sq km; 1990 pop.146,601), S and central Maine; ⊙ Bangor; 45°23′N 68°38′W. Drained by Penobscot R. Agr.; mfg. (pulp, paper, wood prods., canoes) in S; lumbering, hunting, fishing and other outdoor recreation in N. Numerous lakes. Formed 1816.

Penobscot (pe-NAHB-skaht), town (1990 pop. 1,131), Hancock co., S Maine, on Penobscot Bay, and 15 mi/24 km WSW of Ellsworth; 44°28′N 68°43′W. In resort area.

Penobscot (pe-NAHB-skaht), river, 350 mi/563 km long; rising in numerous lakes in central Maine; flows generally E in 4 branches, uniting, then flowing S into Penobscot Bay; longest river in Maine. The river, navigable to Bangor, is an important source of power for pulpwood and paper mills. The Penobscot's upper course is in a wooded region famous for hunting, fishing, and canoeing. Pulpwood and paper prods. are the principal freight on the river. The Penobscot was 1st explored by the Eng. voyager Martin Pring in 1603; in 1604 the Fr. explorer Samuel de Champlain sailed up the course of the river.

Penobscot Bay (pe-NAHB-skaht), inlet of the Atlantic Ocean, 35 mi/56 km long and 27 mi/43 km wide, S Maine. The bay was entered by the Eng. explorer Martin Pring in 1603; the Fr. explorer Samuel de CHAMPLAIN claimed the area for France in 1604. An important shipbuilding center in the 19th cent., the bay has become a fishing and resort center.

Penobscot Lake (pe-NAHB-skaht), Somerset co., W Maine, 19 mi/31 km NNE of Jackman, near Que. (Canada) border; 3 mi/4.8 km long.

Penobsquis (peh-NAHB-skwis), village, SE N.B., Canada, on Kennebecasis R., and 8 mi/13 km NW of Sussex; 45°47′N 65°27′W. Gypsum quarrying.

Peñón Blanco (pe-NYON BLAHN-ko), town (1990 pop. 5,057), Durango, N Mexico, 65 mi/105 km NE of Durango; 24°47′N 104°02′W. Elev. 8,202 ft/2,500 m. Agr. center (corn, cotton, alfalfa, chickpeas).

Peñón del Rosario, Mexico: see ROSARIO, PEÑÓN DEL.

Penrose, uninc. town (1990 pop. 2,235), Fremont co., S central Colo., 13 mi/21 km E of Cañon City, near Arkansas R.; 38°25′N 105°00′W. Elev. 5,330 ft/1,625 m. Agr. (sheep; fruit, vegetables; irrigated area); oil and natural gas; mfg. of consumer goods, oil refining. Fort Carson Military Reservation to NE.

Pensacola (pen-suh-KO-luh), city (□ 39 sq mi/101 sq km; 1990 pop. 58,165), ⊙ Escambia co., extreme NW Fla., on Pensacola Bay; 30°26′N 87°11′W. It is a port of entry with a natural harbor and shipping and fishing industries. Leading mfg. center (synthetic fibers, chemicals, and naval stores) for NW Fla. Magnificent beaches on barrier isls. S of Pensacola are a major tourist attraction. Much of the life of the city is oriented around the U.S. naval air station, est. here in 1914. Eglin Air Force Base is nearby. The Univ. of W. Fla. and a community col. are here. Inc. 1822.

Pensacola (pen-suh-KO-luh), village (1990 pop. 69), Mayes co., NE Okla., 13 mi/21 km S of Vinita; 36°27′N 95°07′W. Pensacola Dam and Cherokee State Park c.5 mi/8 km E. Inc. 1938.

Pensacola Bay (pen-suh-KO-luh), inlet of the Gulf of Mexico, 13 mi/21 km long and c.2.5 mi/4 km wide, extreme NW Fla.; entered through a narrow channel bet. Santa Rosa Isl. and the mainland. The Escambia R. flows into the bay from the N, near the city of Pensacola.

Pensacola Dam, Okla.: see LAKE OF THE CHEROKEES.

Pensauken, N.J.: see PENNSAUKEN, township.

Pense (pehns), village (1991 pop. 556), S Sask. (Canada), 16 mi/26 km W of Regina. Wheat.

Pentagon Building, Va.: see ARLINGTON, CO.

Penticton, city (1991 pop. 27,258), S B.C., Canada, located where the Okanagan R. flows into Okanagan L.; 49°30′N 119°35′W. Service and trade center for the Okanagan valley, a resort and fruit-growing area. Canning plants and factories making wood and metal prods.

Pentwater, town (1990 pop. 1,050), Oceana co., W Mich., 7 mi/11.3 km WNW of Hart, and on L. Michigan at mouth of short Pentwater R.; 43°46′N 86°25′W. In resort and farm area; ships fruit; has fisheries. Mfg. (store displays). Charles Mears State Park, on L. Michigan, has sand dunes; Pentwater L. to SE. Inc. 1867.

Peñuelas (PAIN-wai-lahs), town (1990 pop. 22,515), S P.R., 7 mi/11.3 km WNW of Ponce. Petrochemicals industry and other related industries; petroleum center of P.R. Fishing. The Garzas Falls and hydroelectric plant are 2.5 mi/4 km N.

Penwell, uninc. village (1990 pop. 74), Ector co., W Texas, 15 mi/24 km SW of Odessa. An oilfield center; mfg. (portland cement).

Peoria, county (□ 630 sq mi/1,632 sq km; 1990 pop. 182,827), central Ill.; ⊙ Peoria; 40°47′N 89°45′W. Bounded E and S by Illinois R., L. Peoria, and Upper L. Peoria; drained by Spoon R. and Kickapoo Creek. Agr. (corn, soybeans, cattle, vegetables; dairy prods.). Bituminous coal mines; sand, gravel deposits. Diversified mfg., food processing and packing. Includes Jubilee Col. State Park and Historical Site. Formed 1825.

Peoria 1 city (1990 pop. 50,618), Maricopa co., central

Ariz., suburb 11 mi/18 km NW of Phoenix; 33°41′N 112°14′W. Drained by New R. (intermittent). Mfg. (sheet metal fabricating, textile prods., machinery parts). Training camps of Seattle Mariners and San Diego Padres baseball teams; Southwest Indian School is here; Glendale Municipal Airport to S. Settled 1897. **2** city (1990 pop. 113,504), ⊙ Peoria co., central Ill., on L. Peoria and the Illinois R.; 40°44′N 89°36′W. A busy port of entry, it is one of the state's oldest settlements and a regional trade and transportation point; grain, livestock, and coal from the area are marketed, processed, and shipped in Peoria. It has factories that produce numerous heavy and light industrial goods (fabricated metal prods., machinery, iron and steel, transportation equip., commercial printing, construction materials, medical equip. chemicals). Although it is an industrial city, Peoria is known for its scenic beauty and its many recreational activities associated with Lakeview Park, which also contains a planetarium, community theater, and arts and sciences center. La Salle established Fort Creve Coeur in the region in 1680, and the spot later became a Fr. trading post. The area was known as Fort Clark after 1813; the first permanent Amer. settlement was est. 1819. First bridge across Illinois R. opened here in 1849. Bradley Univ., St. Francis Col. of Nursing, and a U.S. Dept. of Agr. Northern Regional research laboratory are in the city. Jubilee Col. State Park and Historic Site 13 mi/21 km NW. Inc. as a city 1845.

Peoria (pee-OR-ee-uh), village (1990 pop. 136), Ottawa co., extreme NE Okla., 12 mi/19 km ENE of Miami, near Mo. line; 36°55′N 94°40′W. Lead and zinc reserves.

Peoria Heights, village (1990 pop. 6,930), Peoria co., central Ill., residential suburb 2 mi/3.2 km N of downtown Peoria, on Upper L. Peoria (Illinois R.); 40°45′N 89°33′W. Inc. 1898.

Peoria, Lake, at Creve Coeur, central Ill., on Illinois R. (Peoria/Tazewell co. border), 4 mi/6.4 km SSW of downtown Peoria; c.20 mi/32 km long, up to 2 mi/3.2 km wide above dam; 40°39′N 89°37′W. Peoria and Peoria Heights on W shore, East Peoria on SE shore.

Peosta, town (1990 pop. 128), Dubuque co., E Iowa, 9 mi/14.5 km WSW of Dubuque; 42°27′N 90°50′W. Mfg. (wood pallets, electric motors, plastics, high-pressure water machines, plant nursery supplies).

Peotone (PEE-ah-ton), village (1990 pop. 2,947), Will co., NE Ill., 19 mi/31 km SE of Joliet; 41°19′N 87°47′W. In agr. area; mfg. of steel prods. Inc. 1869. State hoping to build 3d major Chicago area to E of Peotone.

Pepacton Reservoir (puh-PAK-tuhn), artificial lake, SE N.Y., for water supply to N.Y. city; impounded in East Branch of Delaware R. near Downsville by Downsville Dam (2,450 ft/747 m long, 200 ft/61 m high; begun 1947); 18 mi/29 km long; 42°05′N 74°55′W. A 25-mi/40-km water tunnel leads to Rondout Reservoir, from which Delaware Aqueduct continues to N.Y. city.

Pepeekeo (pai-PAI-ai-KAI-o), town (1990 pop. 1,813), E Hawaii isl., Hawaii co., Hawaii, on E coast, 8 mi/12.9 km N of Hilo, 2 mi/3.2 km SE of Honomu; 19°49′N 155°06′W. Kohola Point to N. Hilo Forest Reserve to W.

Pepillo Salcedo (pe-PEE-yo sahl-SAI-do), town (1993 pop. 2,929), Monte Cristi prov., NW Dominican Republic, port on Manzanillo Bay of the Atlantic, at mouth of Massacre (Dajabón) R. (Haiti border), 12 mi/19 km SW of Monte Cristi; 19°40′N 71°40′W. Exports bananas. Renamed 1949 from Manzanillo. Includes Puerto Libertador or Libertador, a port developed 1945.

Pepin, county (□ 248 sq mi/642 sq km; 1990 pop. 7,107), W Wis., bounded SW by L. Pepin (Mississippi R.); ⊙ Durand; 44°36′N 92°00′W. Hilly region, drained by Chippewa R. Dairy and livestock area. Corn, soybeans; hogs. Fishing and resorts on L. Pepin (a widening of the Mississippi), natural lake formed by entrance of Chippewa R. from NE, its braided channels choked with glacial sediments. Smallest co. in Wis., formed 1858.

Pepin, town (1990 pop. 873), Pepin co., W Wis., on L. Pepin, 31 mi/50 km SSW of Menomonie; 44°26′N 92°09′W. In dairy and farm area; mfg. of agr. implements, dairy prods. processing; fishing and lake resort.

Pepin, Lake (PE-pin), Mississippi R., Wabasha and Goodhue cos., SE Minn., Buffalo and Pierce cos., W Wis., 5 mi/8 km NW of Wabasha, Minn.; 21 mi/34 km long, and c.3 mi/4.8 km wide; 44°26′N 91°19′W. Formed by alluvial deposits from Chippewa R., which joins Mississippi R. from N (Wis.). Much of the material is of glacial origin. Lake City on SW shore.

Pepper Pike, city (1990 pop. 6,185), Cuyahoga co., N Ohio, an E suburb of Cleveland; 41°28′N 81°28′W.

Pepperell (PE-per-el), town (1990 pop. 10,098), Middlesex co., N Mass., on Nashua R., near N.H. state line, and 14 mi/23 km W of Lowell; 42°40′N 71°37′W. Mfg. (paper, paper prods.). Settled 1720, inc. 1753. Includes East Pepperell village (1990 pop. 2,296).

Pepperell (PEP-puhr-rel), village, Lee co., E Ala., 3 mi/4.8 km SW of Opelika. Cotton milling.

Pepperton, town, Butts co., central Ga., just SE of Jackson; 33°17′N 83°56′W.

Pequabuck (pi-kwah-BUHK), village, Conn., c.8 mi/12.9 km N of Waterbury. A postal sect. of Plymouth.

Pequabuck River, c.25 mi/40 km long, W central Conn.; rises NW of Bristol; flows S, E, and NE, past Bristol and Plainville, to Farmington R. near Farmington.

Pequannock (pi-KUH-nuhk), township (1990 pop. 12,844), Morris co., N N.J., 15 mi/24 km NE Morristown; 40°57′N 74°17′W. Inc. 1798.

Pequannock River (pi-KUH-nuhk), c.20 mi/32 km long, NE N.J.; rises in E Sussex co.; flows generally ESE, forming part of Passaic-Morris co. line, joining Ramapo R. near Pompton Plains to form Pompton R. Near source, dams form Canistear and Oak Ridge reservoirs.

Pequest River (PEE-kwest), c.35 mi/56 km long, NW N.J.; rises SE of Newton; flows SW and W, bet. ridges of the Appalachians, to Delaware R. at Belvidere.

Pequonnock River (pe-KWAN-uhk), c.15 mi/24 km long, SW Conn.; rises near Monroe; flows generally S, past Trumbull, to L.I. Sound at Bridgeport. Navigable for 1.3 mi/2.1 km above Bridgeport harbor.

Pequop Mountains (PEE-kwuhp), NE Nev., in E Elko co., E of Ruby Mts., Spruce Mt. (11,062 ft/3,372 m) is in SW spur, c.50 mi/80 km ESE of Elko.

Pequot Lakes (PEE-kwawt), town (1990 pop. 843), Crow Wing co., central Minn., 18 mi/29 km NNW of Brainerd; 46°36′N 94°19′W. Dairying; poultry; oats, alfalfa; mfg. (chapel cabinets, candles, tool and die, steel docks). Pequot Lakes to SW; Pelican L. to E; Crow Wing State Forest to E. Known as Pequot until 1939.

Pérade, La, Canada: see SAINTE ANNE DE LA PÉRADE.

Peralta (puhr-AWL-tuh), uninc. town (1990 pop. 3,182), Valencia co., central N.Mex., 17 mi/27 km S of Albuquerque, on Rio Grande; 34°49′N 106°41′W. Cattle, sheep, dairying; corn, grain, alfalfa. Mfg. (wood moldings). Isleta Indian Reservation to N and E. Part of Cibola Natl. Forest to SE.

Peravia (pe-rah-VEE-ah), province (□ 626 sq mi/1,622 sq km; 1981 pop. 168,123), S central Dominican Republic, on the Caribbean coast; ⊙ Baní; 18°30′N 70°27′W. Mountainous, semiarid region in outliers of the Cordillera Central and Sierra de Ocoa. Has fertile, irrigated areas, where coffee, rice, sugarcane, and fruit are grown. San José de Ocoa is known for its tobacco. Has coal deposits. Salt is worked at small Calderas Bay. Also called Trujillo Valdés or Trujillo Valdez.

Percé (pehr-SAI), town (1991 pop. 4,028), ⊙ Gaspé East co., E Que., Canada, E Gaspé Peninsula, on the Gulf of St. Lawrence, 25 mi/40 km SSE of Gaspé, at foot of Percé Mt. (1,230 ft/375 m), opposite Bonaventure Isl.; fishing center.

Percé Rock (pehr-SAI), E Que., Canada, just off the tip of the Gaspé Peninsula. It is a massive rock (1,420 ft/433 m long; c.300 ft/90 m wide; and 290 ft/88 m at the highest point), rising sheer from the Atlantic. It takes its name from an arch 50 ft/15 m high near its seaward end. With nearby Bonaventure Isl., it is a well-known tourist attraction.

Perches (PERSH) or **Les Perches**, town (1982 pop. 1,358), Nord-Est dept., NE Haiti, 25 mi/40 km SE of Cap-Haïtien; 19°31′N 71°55′W. Citrus fruits; gold deposits nearby.

Percy, village, Randolph co., SW Ill., 14 mi/23 km NE of Chester; 38°00′N 89°37′W. In agr. and coal area.

Percy, N.H.: see STARK.

Percy Cobb Dam, Ark.: see ERLING, LAKE.

Perdido River (puhr-DEE-do), c.60 mi/97 km long, in Ala. and Fla.; rises 8 mi/12.9 km NW of Atmore, S Ala.; flows S, forming SW Ala.–NW Fla. stateline, to Perdido Bay (15 mi/24 km long, 1 mi/1.6 km–5 mi/8 km wide) of Gulf of Mexico, 11 mi/18 km WNW of Pensacola, Fla.

Perdue (PUHR-doo), village (1991 pop. 395), S central Sask., Canada, on small Van Scoy L., 40 mi/64 km W of Saskatoon; 52°03′N 107°33′W. Grain elevators; dairying.

Pere Marquette River (PER mahr-KET), c.50 mi/80 km long, W Mich.; rises as Little South Branch in N Newaygo co.; flows generally NW, past Scottville, to L. Michigan at Ludington. Middle Branch rises in SE Lake co., flows 15 mi/24 km W to join Little South Branch SE of Baldwin. Big South Branch rises in N Newaygo co. (Brookings L.) flows 30 mi/48 km NW joins main river near Custer.

Pere Marquette State Park, Ill.: see GRAFTON.

Pérez Island, Mexico: see ALACRÁN.

Perham 1 (PUHR-uhm), town (1990 pop. 395), Aroostook co., NE Maine, 15 mi/24 km NW of Presque Isle; 46°52′N 68°15′W. In agr. region. **2** town (1990 pop. 2,075), Otter Tail co., W Minn., 32 mi/51 km NE of Fergus Falls; 46°36′N 95°34′W. Grain, potatoes; livestock, poultry; mfg. (tortillas, licorice, cheese; fertilizer, concrete). Maplewood State Park to W; Rush L. to S; Little Pine L. to N; Big Pine L. to E. Municipal Airport to NW.

Peribán de Ramos (pe-ree-BAHN dai RAH-mos), town (1990 pop. 9,179), ⊙ Peribán municipio, Michoacán, central Mexico, at W foot of Sierra de los Tarascos, and on N slope of Tancítaro volcano, 33 mi/53 km WNW of Uruapan; 19°31′N 102°25′W. Sugarcane, tobacco, coffee, fruit, livestock.

Peribonca (peh-ri-BAHNG-kuh), river, c.280 mi/450 km long, Que., Canada; rises in the Otish Mts., central Que.; flows S through Peribonca L. to L. St. John. It is an important source of hydroelectric power.

Perico (pai-REE-ko), town, Matanzas prov., W Cuba, on Central Highway, and 40 mi/64 km ESE of Matanzas; 22°47′N 81°02′W. RR junction and sugar-growing center. Nearby are the sugar centrals of España Republicana (N), Sergio González (E).

Peridot, uninc. town (1990 pop. 957), Gila co., E central Ariz., 16 mi/26 km ESE of Globe, on San Carlos R., in San Carlos Indian Reservation. Cattle, hay. Coolidge Dam, on Gila R., 9 mi/14.5 km to SSW; forms San Carlos L., to S. Hayes Mts. to SW.

Peril Strait, SE Alaska, bet. Chichagof Isl. (N) and Baranof Isl. (S), extends c.50 mi/80 km from Salisbury Sound to Chatham Strait on the Pacific; 57°N 135°W.

Perimeter Center, suburban downtown, located astride the Fulton and DeKalb co. borders, Ga., N of Atlanta at the intersection of Ashford-Dunwoody road and the I-285 beltway. Leading corporate hq. location in the Atlanta region. Began as an office park and retail mall in the early 1970s. Served by Ga. 400 limited access highway and the Metropolitan Atlanta Rapid Transit Authority (MARTA) RR transit and bus system. Corporate hq. include Holiday Inn, Goldkist, and UPS.

Perkasie (PUHR-ka-see), borough (1990 pop. 7,878), Bucks co., SE Pa., 28 mi/45 km NNW of Philadelphia, on East Branch of Perkiomen Creek; 40°22′N 75°17′W. Agr. (grain, soybeans, apples; livestock; dairying); mfg. (printing and publishing, transportation fixtures, thermometers and thermostats, plastic prods., textiles, electricity testing equip., machinery). Penridge Airport to N. L. Nockamixon reservoir and Nockamixon State Park to NE. Inc. 1876.

Perkins 1 county (□ 884 sq mi/2,290 sq km; 1990 pop. 3,367), SW central Nebr.; ⊙ Grant; 40°50′N 101°39′W.

Cross references are shown in SMALL CAPITALS. The pronunciation key is on page xv. The dates of population figures are on page xii.

Agr. area bounded W by Colo. Wheat, corn, beans; cattle, hogs; dairying. Central and Mountain time zone border follows E boundary and E part of S boundary. Formed 1887. **2** county (□ 2,890 sq mi/7,485 sq km; 1990 pop. 3,932), NW S.Dak., on N.Dak. state line; ⊙ Bison; 45°30′N 102°28′W. Farming and ranching region drained by North Fork of Grand R., Moreau R., and several creeks. Lignite deposits and mines. Wheat, hay; cattle, sheep. Standing Rock Indian Reservation to E (Corson co.); Cheyenne River Indian Reservation to E (Ziebach co.). Shadehill Reservoir (?is)& State Rec. Area and Llewellyn Johns Memorial State Rec. Area in NE. Grand River Natl. Grassland (several units) in N. Formed 1908.

Perkins, town (1990 pop. 1,925), Payne co., N central Okla., 10 mi/16 km S of Stillwater, and on Cimarron R.; 35°58′N 97°01′W. Agr. (wheat, corn; dairying; cattle, sheep); mfg. (meat processing).

Perkins 1 village, Delta co., S Upper Peninsula, Mich., 17 mi/27 km N of Escanaba; 45°58′N 87°04′W. In farm and resort area. **2** uninc. rural community, Scott co., SE Mo., in Mississippi flood plain, 7 mi/11.3 km W of Oran.

Perkins, Maine: see SWAN ISLAND.

Perkins Peak (9,880 ft/3,011 m), SW B.C., Canada, in Coast Mts., 200 mi/322 km NNW of Vancouver; 51°48′N 125°05′W.

Perkinston, village, Stone co., SE Miss., 28 mi/45 km N of Gulfport. Mfg. (steel fabricating, sand and gravel processing). Miss. Gulf Coast Community Col. Part of De Soto Natl. Forest to S.

Perkinsville, Vt.: see WEATHERSFIELD.

Perkiomen Creek (puhr-kee-O-muhn), c.35 mi/56 km long, Pa.; rises in NE Berks co.; flows S past East Greenville, through Green Lane reservoir, past Schwenksville and Collegeville, to Schuylkill R. 6 mi/9.7 km WNW of Norristown; 40°26′N 75°35′W.

Perla, La, Mexico: see LA PERLA.

Perley (PUHR-lee), village (1990 pop. 132), Norman co., W Minn., on Red R., and 20 mi/32 km N of Fargo, N.Dak.; 47°10′N 96°47′W. Wheat, sugar beets, sunflowers, potatoes.

Perlican Island (PUHR-li-kuhn), islet on E side of Trinity Bay, SE N.F., Canada, just NW of Old Perlican; 48°5′N 53°01′W. Lighthouse.

Perote (pe-RO-te), city (1990 pop. 25,031) and township, Veracruz, E Mexico, at NW foot of Cofre de Perote, in Sierra Madre Oriental, 22 mi/35 km W of Xalapa Enríquez on RR, and on Mexico Highway 140; 19°32′N 97°16′W. Agr. center (corn, coffee, maguey); pulque distilling, sawmilling. Fortress of San Carlos de Perote (built 1770–1777) nearby; has been restored as military prison.

Perote, Cofre de, Mexico: see COFRE DE PEROTE NATIONAL PARK.

Perpetua, Cape (puhr-PET-yoo-uh), SW Lincoln co., W Oregon, coastal promontory 10 mi/16 km S of Waldport, 2 mi/3.2 km SW of Yachats, near mouth of Yachats R. Recreational area.

Perquimans (puhr-KWIM-uhns), county (□ 328 sq mi/850 sq km; 1990 pop. 10,447), NE N.C.; ⊙ Hertford; 36°10′N 76°24′W. Bounded S by Albermarle Sound; E in part by Little R. estuary, drained by Perquimans R., indented from SE by its estuary, drained by Perquimans R. Partly forested tidewater area, with part of Dismal Swamp in NE. Agr. area (wheat, soybeans, peanuts, cotton, corn; turkey, hay, chickens, cattle, hogs), fish, crabs. Formed 1672.

Perquimans River (puhr-KWIM-uhns), c.30 mi/48 km long, NE N.C.; rises in Dismal Swamp, in N Perquimans co.; flows S and SE to Albermarle Sound 14 mi/23 km SE of Hertford, widens into estuary at Hertford.

Perrine (puh-RYIN), uninc. city (□ 4 sq mi/10.4 sq km; 1990 pop. 15,576), Dade co., SE Fla., a residential suburb 12 mi/19 km SW of Miami, in a fruit- and vegetable-packing area; 25°36′N 80°20′W.

Perrinton, village (1990 pop. 393), Gratiot co., central Mich., 8 mi/12.9 km SSW of Ithaca; 43°10′N 84°40′W. In agr. and dairying area.

Perris, city (1990 pop. 21,460), Riverside co., S Calif., a suburb 16 mi/26 km SSE of Riverside, bet. San Jacinto Mts. (E) and Santa Ana Mts. (W); 33°48′N 117°13′W. Mfg. (concrete prods., feeds, prefabricated metal bldgs., plastics, furniture); fruit-growing, general farming. Plotted 1885; inc. 1911. March Air Force Base to N; Val Verde Tunnel (Colo.) Aqueduct runs E-W to N; L. Perris Reservoir State Recreational Area to NE; RR Canyon Reservoir to SW.

Perris Lake, Riverside co., SE Calif., on small stream (branch of Perris Valley Storm Drain), in Perris L. State Park, 14 mi/23 km ESE of Riverside; 3 mi/4.8 km long, 2 mi/3.2 km wide at dam; 33°50′N 117°10′W. Max. capacity 125,000 acre-ft. Formed by Perris Dam (120 ft/37 m high), built (1973) by the Calif. Department of Water Resources for water supply.

Perron (pe-RO), village, W Que., Canada, 11 mi/18 km ENE of Val d'Or; 48°09′N 77°34′W. Gold mining.

Perrot Island or **Ile Perrot** (eel peh-RO), suburban isl. (7 mi/11 km long, 3 mi/5 km wide), S Que., Canada, at W end of L. St. Louis, at confluence with St. Lawrence R., 18 mi/29 km SW of Montreal; 45°22′N 73°57′W. Agr.; mfg. (concrete). Bounded by channels of Ottawa R.; linked with Montreal Isl. and mainland by bridges.

Perry 1 county (□ 724 sq mi/1,875 sq km; 1990 pop. 12,759), W central Ala.; ⊙ Marion, 32°39′N 87°18′W. In the Black Belt; drained by Cahaba R. and Oakmulgee Creek. Soybeans, corn, hay; livestock. Part of Talladega Natl. Forest in NE. Formed 1819. **2** county (□ 560 sq mi/1,450 sq km; 1990 pop. 7,969), central Ark.; ⊙ Perryville; 34°56′N 92°58′W. Bounded NE by Arkansas R. Nimrod Dam in Fourche La Fave R. is on W boundary, drained by Fourche LaFave R. and its S Branch. Agr. (soybeans; cattle, hogs, poultry); lumber milling. Formed 1840. Part of Ouachita Natl. Forest in SW ½ of co.; Harris Brake Wildlife Management area near center. **3** county (□ 446 sq mi/1,155 sq km; 1990 pop. 21,412), SW Ill.; ⊙ Pinckneyville; 38°05′N 89°22′W. Bounded partly E by Little Muddy R.; drained by small Beaucoup and Galum creeks. Agr. area (corn, wheat; dairy prods.; livestock, poultry), with bituminous coal mining. Mfg. (textiles, metal prods., consumer goods, electronic equip.). Formed 1827. Includes Pyramid State Park and Du Quoir State Fair grounds. One of 17 Ill. cos. to retain Southern-style commission form of co. govt. **4** county (□ 386 sq mi/1,000 sq km; 1990 pop. 19,107), S Ind.; ⊙ Tell City; 38°05′N 86°38′W. Bounded S and partly E by Ohio R., here forming Ky. state line; drained by small Anderson R., a tributary of the Ohio. Agr. area (corn, soybeans, dairy prods.; poultry, cattle, hogs), with mfg. at Cannelton and Tell City. Timber; sandstone quarries. E ¾ of co. dominated by Hoosier Natl. Forest. Formed 1814. **5** county (□ 342 sq mi/886 sq km; 1990 pop. 30,283), SE Ky.; ⊙ Hazard, in the Cumberlands; 37°15′N 83°12′W. Drained by North Fork, Middle and Carr forks, Kentucky R., and Troublesome Creek. Important bituminous coal-mining area; oil and gas wells, timber; some agr. (burley tobacco; livestock). Mfg. at Hazard. Buckhorn L. reservoir and State Resort Park (on Middle Fork Kentucky R.) in NW. Formed 1820. **6** county (□ 650 sq mi/1,684 sq km; 1990 pop. 10,865), SE Miss.; ⊙ New Augusta; 31°10′N 88°59′W. Drained by Leaf R.; by Black, Thompsons, and Tallahala creeks, and Bogue Homa rivers. Agr. (cotton, corn; poultry); timber. Part of De Soto Natl. Forest covers S ½ of co., also bounds co. in N. L. Perry State Park in E. Formed 1820. **7** county (□ 476 sq mi/1,233 sq km; 1990 pop. 16,648), E Mo.; ⊙ Perryville; 37°42′N 89°50′W. Bounded E by Mississippi R. Corn, wheat, soybeans; hogs, cattle; lumber. Mfg. at Perryville. Area noted for its Ger. heritage, esp. Lutheran-Missouri Synod. NE area severely damaged in 1993 flood. Formed 1820. **8** county (□ 409 sq mi/1,059 sq km; 1990 pop. 31,557), central Ohio; ⊙ New Lexington, 39°44′N 82°14′W. Drained by small Rush, Sunday, Jonathan, and Moxahala creeks. Includes part of Buckeye L. (resort). In the Till Plains and the Unglaciated Plains physiographic regions. Agr. (livestock; grain, fruit, produce); mfg. at New Lexington and Crooksville (primarily metals industries and stone, clay, and glass prods.); coal mining, fire-clay quarrying. Formed 1817. **9** county (□ 555 sq mi/1,437 sq km; 1990 pop. 41,172), S central Pa.; ⊙ Bloomfield; 40°23′N 77°16′W. Bounded E by Susquehanna R., Tuscarora Mt. ridge along N boundary, Blue Mt. ridge along S boundary; drained by Juniata R. and Sherman Creek. Agr. (corn, hay, alfalfa, soybeans; poultry, cattle; dairying); limestone quarrying. Some mfg. at Duncannon. Appalachian Trail passes through SE; Big Spring and Fowlers Hollow state parks in SW; parts of Tuscarora State Forest in SW and N. Formed 1820. **10** county (□ 419 sq mi/1,085 sq km; 1990 pop. 6,612), W central Tenn.; ⊙ Linden; 35°39′N 87°52′W. Bounded W by Tennessee R.; drained by Buffalo R. Includes part of Kentucky Reservoir. Livestock raising, some agr. (corn, hay, soybeans); timber. Formed 1819.

Perry 1 city (1990 pop. 6,652), Dallas co., central Iowa, 30 mi/48 km NW of Des Moines, on N Raccoon R.; 41°50′N 94°05′W. RR junction. Processing and trade center, with meat- and poultry-packing plants, foundry, and RR shops; mfg. (ice cream; pork processing; shovels; fertilizers; farm-machinery blades; concrete; iron castings; tillage equip.). Widespread flooding occurred in 1993. Settled in 1860s. **2** city (1990 pop. 711), Ralls co., NE Mo., 25 mi/40 km SW of Hannibal; 39°25′N 91°40′W. Corn, soybeans; cattle, hogs; coal. Mark Twain L. to N.

Perry 1 town (□ 9 sq mi/23.3 sq km; 1990 pop. 7,151), ⊙ Taylor co., N central Fla., c.50 mi/80 km ESE of Tallahassee; 30°06′N 83°34′W. RR junction; sawmilling center (lumber; crates). **2** town (1990 pop. 9,452), ⊙ Houston co., central Ga., 26 mi/42 km S of Macon; 32°28′N 83°44′W. Located in diversified agr. and quarrying area, adjacent to I-95. Mfg. (cement, lumber, baskets, concrete, machinery, glass). Boyhood home of former U.S. senator Sam Nunn. The Ga. Natl. Fairgrounds and Agr. Center offers many antique and agr. shows. Settled c.1820; inc. 1824. **3** town (1990 pop. 758), Washington co., E Maine, on Passamaquoddy Bay, and 25 mi/40 km NE of Machias; 44°58′N 67°05′W. **4** town (1990 pop. 2,163), Shiawassee co., S central Mich., 18 mi/29 km NE of Lansing; 42°49′N 84°13′W. In farm area (livestock, oats, soy beans, grain, beans; dairy prods.). **5** town (1990 pop. 4,978), ⊙ Noble co., N Okla., 34 mi/55 km ESE of Enid, near Black Bear Creek; 36°17′N 97°17′W. RR junction. In agr. area; mfg. (cable and pipe locating systems, barbecue smokers, fabricated metal prods.). Oil and natural gas wells. Cherokee Strip Mus. Founded as a tent city 1893, inc. 1894. **6** town (1990 pop. 1,211), Box Elder co., N Utah, 3 mi/4.8 km S of Brigham City, near Willard Bay of Great Salt L., to W; 41°27′N 112°01′W. Elev. 4,315 ft/1,315 m. Cherries, peaches, sugar beets, barley, alfalfa; cattle sheep; dairying. Originally named Three Mile Creek. Wasatch Range and Natl. Forest to E.

Perry 1 village (1990 pop. 228), Perry co., central Ark., 20 mi/32 km W of Conway, near Arkansas R.; 35°02′N 92°47′W. **2** village (1990 pop. 491), Pike co., W Ill., 10 mi/16 km NNE of Pittsfield; 39°46′N 90°45′W. In agr. area. **3** village (1990 pop. 881), Jefferson co., NE Kansas, on Delaware R., near its mouth on Kansas R., and 14 mi/23 km E of Topeka; 39°04′N 95°23′W. Shipping point for grain and livestock. **4** village (□ 2 sq mi/5.2 sq km; 1990 pop. 4,219), Wyoming co., W N.Y., 27 mi/43 km SSE of Batavia, near Silver L.; 42°43′N 78°00′W. Summer resort. Letchworth State Park is just SE. Light mfg. Settled 1815, inc. 1830. **5** village (1990 pop. 1,012), Lake co., NE Ohio, 6 mi/10 km NE of Painesville, near L. Erie; 41°46′N 81°08′W. **6** village (1990 pop. 241), Aiken co., SW S.C., 23 mi/37 km ENE of Aiken and 28 mi/45 km SSW of Columbia; 33°37′N 81°18′W. Agr. includes livestock; grain, cotton, peanuts, peaches.

Perry, Camp, Ohio: see PORT CLINTON.

Perry Hall, village (1990 pop. 22,723), Baltimore co., N Md., 11 mi/18 km NE of downtown Baltimore; 39°25′N 76°29′W. The main block of Perry Hall was built in 1773 and sold to Harry Dorsey Gough (1745–1808), who added wings and pavilions after the Revolution. Methodist leaders Francis Asbury and Thomas Coke stayed here while the Methodist Church in Amer. was being organized in meetings held in Baltimore in 1784. A fire in 1824 reduced the size of the house in half. This is one of Baltimore's most rapidly growing areas.

Perry Lake, reservoir (□ 19 sq mi/49 sq km), Jefferson co., NE Kansas, on Delaware R., 15 mi/24 km ENE of Topeka; 39°07′N 94°26′W. Max. capacity 770,000 acreft. Formed by Perry Dam (121 ft/37 m high), built (1969) by Army Corps of Engineers for flood control; also used for water supply and recreation. Perry State Park near dam.

Perry Nuclear Power Plant, Ohio: see LAKE, CO.

Perry Point, Md.: see PERRYVILLE.

Perry River, trading post, NW Keewatin dist., N.W.T., Canada, on Queen Maud Gulf, at mouth of Perry R.; 67°48′N 101°40′W.

Perryman, village (1990 pop. 2,160), Harford co., NE Md., 26 mi/42 km ENE of Baltimore; 39°28′N 76°13′W. It was named Perrymansville by the Baltimore and Ohio RR for the Perryman family from which the RR bought land in the 1830s. Residents of the village which developed around the RR line shortened the name in 1880. Spesutie Church, organized in 1671, (c.1851) is built on the foundations of an earlier church dating back to 1760. The original vestry (c.1766) remains in the churchyard.

Perryopolis (PER-ee-ah-po-lis), borough (1990 pop. 1,833), Fayette co., SW Pa., 13 mi/21 km N of Uniontown, near Youghiogheny R.; 40°05′N 79°45′W. Agr. area (alfalfa; livestock; dairying). George Washington Grist Mill here.

Perry's Victory and International Peace Memorial, N Ohio, at Put-in-Bay on South Bass Isl. in L. Erie. Authorized 1936. Scene of the victory near Put-in-Bay of Oliver H. Perry in the War of 1812. The memorial stands 352 ft/107 m high and 45 ft/14 m in diameter at its base.

Perrysburg, city (1990 pop. 12,551), Wood co., NW Ohio, S suburb of Toledo, across Maumee R. from SW outskirts of Toledo; 41°33′N 83°37′W. Metal stampings, glass, furniture, playground equip., tile, meat prods. Laid out 1816.

Perrysburg, village (1990 pop. 404), Cattaraugus co., W N.Y., 18 mi/29 km E of Dunkirk; 42°27′N 79°00′W. Mfg. (wood prods., furniture).

Perrysville, town (1990 pop. 443), Vermillion co., W Ind., on the Wabash, and 11 mi/18 km SE of Danville, Ill.; 40°03′N 87°26′W. Agr. and bituminous-coal area.

Perrysville, village (1990 pop. 691), Ashland co., N central Ohio, 13 mi/21 km ESE of Mansfield, on Black Fork of Mohican R.; 40°39′N 82°19′W. Pleasant Hill Reservoir, on Clear Fork of Mohican R., is nearby. Machining industry.

Perryton, town (1990 pop. 7,607), ⊙ Ochiltree co., extreme N Texas, in high plains of the Panhandle, near Okla. line, 100 mi/161 km NNE of Amarillo; 36°23′N 100°47′W. Elev. 2,942 ft/897 m. Market center for rich wheat-producing co.; ships cattle, feed; mfg. (oil field storage tanks, livestock feed, plastic fittings). Founded 1919, inc. 1920.

Perryville, city (1990 pop. 6,933), ⊙ Perry co., E Mo., 34 mi/55 km NW of Cape Girardeau; 37°43′N 89°52′W. Agr. (corn, soybeans; cattle); mfg. (baked goods, insulation, barrel staves, plastic automotive prods.; printing); wood. St. Mary's Seminary (Catholic) nearby. Founded c.1821.

Perryville 1 town (1990 pop. 1,141), ⊙ Perry co., central Ark., 31 mi/50 km WSW of Conway, and on Fourche La Fave R.; 35°00′N 92°47′W. In livestock-raising and agr. area. Mfg. (plastic molding). Harris Brake Wildlife Management Area to SE; Ouachita Natl. Forest ot S. **2** town (1990 pop. 815), Boyle co., central Ky., 9 mi/14.5 km W of Danville, on Chaplin R.; 37°38′N 84°57′W. Agr. (burley tobacco, grain; livestock, poultry; dairying). To N is Perryville Battlefield State Historic Site, scene of Civil War battle (Oct. 8, 1862) bet. Confederates under Gen. Braxton Bragg and Union forces under Gen. D. C. Buell, involved 40,000 troops, stopped Confederate advance. Halfway Inn (built c.1792) and a Perryville Natl. Cemetery in vicinity. **3** town (1990 pop.

2,456), Cecil co., NE Md., at mouth of the Susquehanna R. (bridged 1940), opposite Havre de Grace; 39°34′N 76°04′W. RR shops. The Perry Point Mansion, believed to have been built in the late 17th cent., is on the grounds of Perry Point Veterans Hosp.

Perryville 1 village (1990 pop. 108), SW Alaska, on SE Alaska Peninsula, N of Kupreanof Point; 55°54′N 159°08′W. Fishing. Est. 1912 when natives from Katmai Volcano dist. were moved here. **2** village, in South Kingston town, Washington co., S R.I. Perryville State Trout Hatchery here.

Pershing (PUHR-shing), county (□ 6,067 sq mi/15,714 sq km; 1990 pop. 4,336), NW central Nev.; ⊙ Lovelock; 40°27′N 118°24′W. Mt. region crossed (N-S) by Humboldt R. Enters Humboldt Sink (Humboldt Wildlife Management) on S border. Rye Patch Reservoir State Recreation Area on Humboldt, in N center. Mining (mercury, tungsten, gold, silver, copper, diatomite). Agr. (barley); cattle, sheep raising, and dairying in Humboldt irrigation project (N of Lovelock). Chief ranges are Tobin in E, Humboldt in center, Seven Troughs and Trinity W. Part of Black Rock Desert is in NW. Winnemucca L. (dry) on W border in SW. Formed 1919.

Pershing 1 village, Marion co., S central Iowa, 6 mi/9.7 km SE of Knoxville. In agr. area. **2** village, Osage co., N Okla., 6 mi/9.7 km SSE of Pawhuska.

Persia, town (1990 pop. 312), Harrison co., W Iowa, on Mosquito Creek, and 12 mi/19 km ESE of Logan; 41°34′N 95°34′W.

Person (PUHRS-uhn), county (□ 404 sq mi/1,046 sq km; 1990 pop. 30,180), N N.C., on Va. line; ⊙ Roxboro; 36°23′N /8°58′W. In Piedmont region, drained by Hyco and Flat rivers. Mfg. at Roxboro. Agr. area (corn, wheat, oats, soybeans, sorghum, hay, tobacco; cattle, hogs); timber. Part of Hyco reservoir on Hyco R., in NW; Mayo reservoir in NE. Formed 1791.

Perth, county (□ 840 sq mi/2,176 sq km; 1991 pop. 69,976), S Ont., Canada, on Thames R.; ⊙ Stratford; 43°30′N 81°05′W.

Perth, town (1991 pop. 5,574), ⊙ Lanark co., SE Ont., Canada, on Tay R., and 45 mi/72 km SW of Ottawa. Milling, woodworking; light mfg. Resort area.

Perth, village, NW N.B., Canada, on St. John R., and 22 mi/35 km S of Grand Falls. Lumbering, woodworking.

Perth, village (1990 pop. 22), Towner co., N N.Dak., 20 mi/32 km NW of Cando; 48°42′N 99°27′W.

Perth Amboy, city (1990 pop. 41,962), Middlesex co., NE N.J., with a harbor on Arthur Kill at the mouth of the Raritan R., which is crossed here to Staten Isl., N.Y. by the Outerbridge Crossing (1928); 40°31′N 74°16′W. A port of entry, Perth Amboy is a shipping center with industries that include metal working; oil refining; printing; apparel; and chemical mfg. The city's name combines the old Native Amer. name *Amboy* with that of the Earl of Perth. It was the capital of East Jersey from 1684 until the union of East and West Jersey in 1702 and was the alternate capital with Burlington until 1790. Perth Amboy particularly grew after it became the tidewater terminal of the Lehigh Valley RR in 1876 and a coal-shipping point. Of interest are the former mansion of Gov. William Franklin, which Gen. William Howe used as his hq. in the Revolutionary War, and St. Peter's Church (1722; Episcopal). Settled 1683, inc. as a city 1718.

Peru 1 (puhr-OO), city (1990 pop. 9,302), La Salle co., N Ill., on Illinois R. (bridged), adjoining La Salle; 41°20′N 89°07′W. Ships grain by barge. Zinc smelters, foundry; mfg. (prefinished metals and vinyl laminates, auto parts, chemicals, educational materials, nails and screws). Bituminous coal mines; agr. (corn, wheat, soybeans, cattle in area). Founded 1835, inc. 1845. Illinois Valley Community Col. across river. **2** (puh-ROO), city (1990 pop. 12,843), ⊙ Miami co., N Ind., on the Wabash R.; 40°45′N 86°04′W. It is a trade, processing, and RR center for a fertile agr. area. Mfg. (furniture, plastic and metal prods., stationery, machinery, metal stampings, motor vehicle parts, bacon prods., food processing,

electrical equip.). The annual summer Circus City Festival commemorates the 7 circuses that once wintered there. Peru is the birthplace of Cole Porter. Grissom Air Base is to the South Miami State Rec. Area and Mississinewa. Reservoir to SE. Laid out 1834; inc. 1847.

Peru 1 (puhr-OO), town (1990 pop. 1,541), Oxford co., W Maine, on the Androscoggin R., and 20 mi/32 km N of South Paris; 44°28′N 70°27′W. In recreational area. Includes villages of East Peru, Worthley, Pond and West Peru. Settled 1793, inc. 1821. **2** rural town (1990 pop. 779), Berkshire co., W Mass., 11 mi/18 km E of Pittsfield; 42°26′N 73°03′W. Highest town in state (elev. 2,064 ft/629 m). **3** town (1990 pop. 1,110), Nemaha co., SE Nebr., 8 mi/12.9 km NE of Auburn, and on Missouri R; 40°28′N 95°43′W. Grain; livestock; dairy and poultry prods. Peru State Col. here. Indian mounds nearby. Inc. 1860. **4** town (1990 pop. 324), Bennington co., SW Vt., in Green Mt. Natl. Forest, 10 mi/16 km NE of Manchester; 43°15′N 72°54′W.

Peru 1 (puhr-OO), village (1990 pop. 206), Chautauqua co., SE Kansas, 5 mi/8 km SE of Sedan; 37°04′N 96°05′W. In livestock, grain, and oil producing area. **2** village (□ 1 sq mi/2.6 sq km; 1990 pop. 1,565), Clinton co., extreme NE N.Y., 8 mi/12.9 km SSW of Plattsburgh; 44°34′N 73°31′W. Lumber, wood prods.

Pescadero, uninc. village, San Mateo co., W Calif., near the Pacific Ocean, in canyon of short Pescadero Creek, 35 mi/56 km S of San Francisco. Artichokes, strawberries, flowers, ornamentals, Christmas trees, timber. Big Basin Redwoods State Park to SE; Pigeon Point to SW; Pescadero State Beach is here. Tourist area. Est. in 1856 by Port. and Ital. farmers.

Peshastin (puh-SHAS-tin), uninc. town (1990 pop. 900), Chelan co., central Wash., 17 mi/27 km NW of Wenatchee, on Wenatchee R., at entrance to Derby Canyon. Fruit-growing area (apples, pears). Wenatchee Natl. Forest to N, W, and S.

Peshtigo, city (1990 pop. 3,154), Marinette co., NE Wis., on Peshtigo R., 6 mi/9.7 km SW of Marinette, and 6 mi/9.7 km inland from Green Bay arm of L. Michigan; 45°03′N 87°45′W. In dairying and lumbering area; mfg. (paper, transportation equip., laminated timber, tools). Nearby is a memorial and mus. of the Oct. 8, 1871 fire (taking 1,182 lives), which occurred on the same night as the great Chicago fire (taking 250 lives). Inc. 1903.

Peshtigo River, c.100 mi/161 km long, NE Wis.; rises in Forest co., in Nicolet Natl. Forest; flows through forested area, past Crivitz and Peshtigo, to Green Bay 8 mi/12.9 km S of Marinette. Whitewater canoeing in Nicolet Natl. Forest.

Pesotum (pih-SO-tum), village (1990 pop. 558), Champaign co., E Ill., 13 mi/21 km S of Champaign; 39°54′N 88°16′W. In agr. area (corn, wheat, soybeans, oats, barley; dairying).

Pesqueira, Mexico: see VILLA PESQUEIRA.

Pesquería (pes-kee-REE-ah), town (1990 pop. 3,069), Nuevo León, N Mexico, on Pesquería R., and 18 mi/29 km ENE of Monterrey. Chickpeas, grain, cotton; livestock.

Pesquería River (pes-kee-REE-ah), 110 mi/177 km long, Nuevo León, N Mexico; rises in Sierra Madre Oriental W of Monterrey; flows E, past Apodaca, Pesquería, and Los Herreras, to San Juan R. 1 mi/1.6 km S of Doctor Coss. Receives Salinas R. Used for irrigation.

Pestel (pes-TEL), town, Sud dept., SW Haiti, on N coast of Jacmel Peninsula, 23 mi/37 km ESE of Jérémie; 18°32′N 73°48′W. Coffee growing; bauxite deposits nearby. Fishing port.

Petal, town (1990 pop. 7,883), Forrest co., SE Miss., suburb 1 mi/1.6 km NE of Hattiesburg on opposite side of Leaf R.; 31°20′N 89°15′W. Agr. (cotton, corn; poultry); mfg. (steel fabrication, aluminum satellite dishes, light mfg.). Checkers Hall of Fame, holds annual checkers championships. Power plant (1945) to N has guided tours.

Petaluma, city (1990 pop. 43,184), Sonoma co., W Calif., 32 mi/51 km NNW of San Francisco, on Petaluma R., 10 mi/16 km NW of San Pablo Bay; 38°14′N 122°38′W. Founded in 1833 by a colony of Mexicans, Petaluma is

---

a large dairy center that has grown into a full-fledged, upper income suburb since 1970. Its pop. has increased accordingly. Mfg. (printing and publishing; fabricated metal prods., baked goods, dairy prods., telephone apparatus, feeds, machinery, coated paper, prosthetic devices, ion etching systems). Dairying, poultry (calls itself "World's Egg Basket"); apples, grapes, grain; cattle, sheep. Petaluma Adobe State Park to SE. Inc. 1858.

Petatlán (pe-taht-LAHN), city (1990 pop. 18,044) and township, Guerrero, SW Mexico, in Pacific lowland, 100 mi/161 km NW of Acapulco; 17°31′N 101°16′W. Rice, sugarcane, tobacco, fruit; livestock; forest prods. (rubber, vanilla, resin).

Petawawa (peh-tuh-WAH-wuh), village (1991 pop. 5,793), SE Ont., Canada, on Ottawa R., and 10 mi/16 km NW of Pembroke; 45°54′N 77°17′W. Paper, pulp milling. Site of military camp.

Petenwell Lake, reservoir (□ 36 sq mi/93 sq km), Adams co., central Wis., on Wisconsin R., 30 mi/48 km SSW of Wisconsin Rapids, in Wisconsin Dells; 44°04′N 90°01′W. Max. capacity 386,000 acre-ft. Formed by Petenwell Dam (50 ft/15 m high), built (1949) for power generation; also used for recreation and flood control. Necedah Natl. Wildlife Refuge just W.

Peter Cooper Village, section of borough of Manhattan, N.Y. city, SE N.Y, adjacent to Stuyvestant Town, located bet. 1st Ave. on W, the East R. on E, E 23th St. on N, and E 20th St. on S. This was one of the many housing projects planned and built bet. the end of World War II and the mid-1950s that provided apartments for low- and middle-income residents of N.Y. city. This project, composed of a series of 15-story red brick bldgs. set amidst nicely landscaped, well-maintained grounds and playgrounds, was built by the Metropolitan Life Insurance Company, which was also responsible for the Stuyvesant Town project and the Parkchester project in the Bronx.

Peter Island, islet, B.V.I., 4 mi/6.4 km S of Tortola isl.; 18°20′N 65°35′W.

Peter Pond Lake (□ 302 sq mi/782 sq km), NW Sask., Canada, 200 mi/322 km N of North Battleford, on main headwater of Churchill R.; 40 mi/64 km long, 14 mi/23 km wide.

Peterborough, county (□ 1,415 sq mi/3,665 sq km; 1991 pop. 119,992), S Ont., Canada, on Buckhurst, Stony, and Rice lakes; ⊙ Peterborough; 44°30′N 78°10′W.

Peterborough, city (1991 pop. 68,371), SE Ont., Canada, NE of Toronto; 44°18′N 78°20′W. It is at the falls of the Otonabee R., which connects, through the Trent Canal, with lakes Ontario and Huron. Settled early in the 19th cent. as a lumber town, it has become a RR and industrial center and is the hq. of the Can. General Electric Co. Peterborough is also a resort for the Kawartha Lakes region. The lift-locks on the Trent-Severn waterway are the highest in the world. It is the seat of Trent Univ. Archaeologically valuable Native Amer. sites are nearby.

Peterborough (PEE-tuhr-buh-ro), town (1990 pop. 5,239), Hillsboro co., S N.H., 16 mi/26 km ESE of Keene; 42°53′N 71°56′W. Drained by Contoocook R. Resort. Mfg. (fabricated metal prods., business forms, printing and publishing, wooden prods., automated tools); agr. (fruit, vegetables, nursery crops; livestock, poultry; dairying). Seat of MacDowell Colony for creative artists, developed (1907) by Marian Nevins MacDowell in memory of Edward Macdowell who lived here from 1896. Ski trails. First free tax-supported public lib. in U.S. founded here 1833. Cranberry Meadow Pond in SE; Sheiling State Forest in center; Miller State Park in SE. Granted 1738, settled 1749, inc. 1760.

Peters Dome, mountain (10,600 ft/3,231 m), S central Alaska, in Alaska Range, in Mt. McKinley Natl. Park, 140 mi/225 km NNW of Anchorage; 63°08′N 151°12′W.

Peters Mountain, ridge, 50 mi/80 km long, in SE W.Va. and SW Va., in the Allegheny Mts. in Jefferson Natl. Forest; from gorge of New R. at Va.-W.Va. state line, extends NE to W Alleghany co., Va. Elev. 3,000 ft/914 m–4,000 ft/1,219 m; its SW continuation is East R. Mt.; 38°23′N 79°53′W.

Petersburg 1 city (1990 pop. 2,261), ⊙ Menard co., central Ill., on Sangamon R. (bridged here), and 16 mi/26 km NNW of Springfield; 40°00′N 89°50′W. Agr. area (corn, wheat, soybeans; livestock); mfg. Founded c.1836, inc. 1841. Ann Rutledge's grave is here. Lincoln's NEW SALEM (State Historic Site) is S. **2** city (1990 pop. 2,449), ⊙ Pike co., SW Ind., near White R., 19 mi/31 km SE of Vincennes; 38°29′N 87°17′W. Surface coal (bituminous) mines; oil wells; timber. Agr. area. Mfg. (steel fabrication). Electricity generation. Laid out 1817, inc. 1924. **3** independent city (□ 23 sq mi/60 sq km; 1990 pop. 38,386), SE Va., on Appomattox R., separate from adjacent Chesterfield, Dinwiddie, and Prince George cos.; 37°12′N 77°23′W. Port of entry, important tobacco market. Mfg. (chemicals, pharmaceuticals, furniture, structural steel fabrication, lumber, printing and publishing, paper goods, medical equip.); agr. area (grain, tobacco, peanuts, soybeans; livestock); tourism. Ft. Henry built here (1646) on Native Amer. village site, followed by a trading post and, in 1784, 3 villages—Petersburg, Blandford, and Pocahontas—were combined as Petersburg town. Petersburg, guarding S approaches to Richmond, was under siege during Civil War (June 15, 1864–April 3, 1865). Nearby Confederate victory of Battle of "The Crater" (July 30, 1864). Union victory at FIVE FORKS (April 1, 1865) led to a general assault on Confederate Petersburg lines; the city fell on April 3, 1865, the same day Union forces entered Richmond. Lee surrendered the remnants of his army at APPOMATTOX COURTHOUSE1 week later. Petersburg Natl. Battlefield (est. 1926), mainly in E part of the city, encompasses much of the battle scene; many old earthworks and tunnels are preserved, including "The Crater." Blandford Cemetery (30,000 Confederate dead); Blandford Church (1735–1737); Center Hill Mansion (1823; mus.); Gen. William Mahone's home, now part of the public lib.; Siege Mus.; historic Farmers Bank. Va. State Univ. to N in Ettrick; Richard Bland Col., Col. of William and Mary (2-year) to S. Poplar Green Natl. Cemetery to SW. Petersburg Airport to W. Ft. Lee Military Reservation to E. Inc. 1850.

Petersburg 1 town (1990 pop. 3,207), SE Alaska, on N tip of Mitkof Isl., Alexander Archipelago, 120 mi/193 km SSE of Juneau; 56°46′N 132°51′W. Major fishing and fish canneries. Municipally owned hydroelectric plant. Celebrates Nor. heritage on May 17th. Settled 1897 by Nor. fishermen; inc. 1910. **2** town (1990 pop. 1,201), Monroe co., extreme SE Mich., 17 mi/27 km W of Monroe, and on R. Raisin, in grain growing and dairying area; 41°53′N 83°42′W. Mfg. of auto parts. **3** town (1990 pop. 514), Lincoln and Marshall cos., S Tenn., 12 mi/19 km NNW of Fayetteville; 35°19′N 86°38′W. In timber and farm area. **4** town (1990 pop. 1,292), Hale co., NW Texas, on the Llano Estacado, 25 mi/40 km NE of Lubbock; 33°52′N 101°35′W. In agr. area (cotton; cattle); mfg. (agr. machinery); oil and gas. **5** town (1990 pop. 2,360), ⊙ Grant co., NE W.Va., 32 mi/51 km SSW of Keyser, in Eastern Panhandle on South Branch of the Potomac R.; 39°0′N 79°7′W. Trade center for agr. area (livestock; poultry; grain). Mfg. (plastic prods., poultry processing, lumber, apparel). RR terminus. State trout hatcheries here and to S at Dorcas. Holds annual co. rodeo. Monongahela Natl. Forest to SW; Smoke Hole Caverns to W; Appalachian Trail passes to SE. Settled c.1745.

Petersburg 1 uninc. village (1990 pop. 450), Boone co., N Ky., on the Ohio R., 2 mi/3.2 km SW of Lawrenceburg, and 8 mi/12.9 km NW of Burlington, Ky. Agr. (tobacco; livestock, poultry; dairying); mfg. (rock and sand processing, light mfg.). **2** village (1990 pop. 388), Boone co., E central Nebr., 12 mi/19 km N of Albion; 41°51′N 98°04′W. Livestock, grain; poultry prods. **3** village (1990 pop. 600), Rensselaer co., E N.Y., on Hoosic R., and 7 mi/11.3 km WNW of Williamstown (Mass); 42°46′N 73°20′W. **4** village (1990 pop. 219), Nelson co., E central N.Dak., 17 mi/27 km E of Lakota; 48°00′N 98°00′W.

Petersburg (PEE-tuhrs-buhrg), borough (1990 pop. 469), Huntingdon co., central Pa., 6 mi/9.7 km NNW of Huntingdon, on Juniata R., at mouth of Shaver Creek; 40°34′N 78°02′W. Agr. (grain, poultry, dairying); mfg. (bottled water, transformers, apparel). Indian Caverns to NW at Spence Creek; Whipple Dam State Park to NE; Rothrock State Forest to NW.

Petersburg, natl. battlefield (□ 4 sq mi/10.4 sq km), SE Va., Dinwiddie and Prince George cos. and independent cities of Petersburg and Hopewell; 37°14′N 77°24′W. Site of Civil War Battle of the Crater and a 10-month Union campaign (1864–1865) to seize PETERSBURG, Va., then a Confederate RR supply center. Authorized 1926.

Petersfield, town (1991 pop. 2,045), Westmoreland parish, SW Jamaica, 5 mi/8 km NE of Savanna-la-Mar; 18°15′N 78°04′W. Agr. (rice, sugarcane, breadfruit); livestock.

Petersfield, village, SE Man., Canada, near S end of L. Winnipeg, 30 mi/48 km NNE of Winnipeg. Grain; dairying.

Petersham (PEE-duhr-shuhm), town (1990 pop. 1,131), Worcester co., N central Mass., 19 mi/31 km NW of Worcester; 42°27′N 72°13′W. Site of Harvard Forest and research center.

Peterson, town (1990 pop. 390), Clay co., NW Iowa, on Little Sioux R., and 18 mi/29 km SSW of Spencer; 42°55′N 95°20′W. In livestock and grain area; sand and gravel pits.

Peterson, village (1990 pop. 259), Fillmore co., SE Minn., 18 mi/29 km SSW of Winona on Root R.; 43°47′N 91°49′W. Mfg. (wood specialty prods.); dairying, poultry, grain, soybeans. Surrounded by Richard J. Dorer Memorial Hardwood State Forest.

Peterson Bay or **Gjoa Haven**, trading post (1991 pop. 783), SE King William Isl., S Franklin dist., N.W.T., Canada, at junction of Simpson and Rae straits; 68°38′N 95°55′W. Site of winter quarters of Roald Amundsen's NW Passage expedition, 1903–1906.

Peterstown, village (1990 pop. 550), Monroe co., SE W.Va., at Va. state line, 19 mi/31 km SW of Union; 37°23′N 80°47′W. Agr. (grain); livestock, poultry. Mfg. (tool and die, bottled water). Bluestone L. reservoir and Wildlife Management Area to NW.

Petersville, locality, S central Alaska, 22 mi/35 km NW of Talkeetna, on Peters Creek. Located at terminus of Petersville Road, 40-mi/64-km spur from Trappers Creek, on George Parks Highway (Rt. 3). Mt. McKinley, in Denali Natl. Park and Preserve, 40 mi/64 km to N. Petersville was est. in 1920s as high-yielding gold mining camp. Although abandoned, mining and trapping activities continue in area.

Pétionville (pai-tyong-VEEL) or **Pétion-Ville**, town (1982 pop. 35,333), Ouest dept., S Haiti, on N hills of the Massif de la Selle, 3.5 mi/5.6 km ESE of Port-au-Prince; 18°31′N 72°17′W. Wealthy residential suburb and resort, where most of Haiti's economic and political elite live.

Petit Bois Island (pe-tee BOI), SE Miss., one of isl. chain in the Gulf of Mexico, partly sheltering Mississippi Sound (N), 13 mi/21 km SSE of Pascagoula; c.8 mi/12.9 km long. Horn Isl. to W; Dauphin Isl. (Ala.) to E. Part of Gulf Isls. Natl. Seashore (Miss. and Fla.).

Petit Caillou, Bayou (puh-TEE kah-YOO, BEI-yoo), SE La., navigable waterway extending 35 mi/56 km generally N-S, bet. Bayou Terrebonne c.3 mi/5 km SE of Houma, and L. Peltom W arm of Terrebonne Bay; navigable; partly channeled as a branch of Intracoastal Waterway. Houma Navigational Canal parallels Bayou on W side for c.15 mi/24 km in N, then crosses Bayou at a SE angle, to its entrance to Terrebonne Bay.

Petit Cul de Sac (puh-TEE kyoo duh SAHK), bay in S Guadeloupe, Fr. West Indies, bet. Basse-Terre and Grande-Terre, and linked by 04-mi/6.4-km-long Rivière Salée with Grand Cul de Sac; 16°12′N 61°33′W. At its head (NE) is Pointe-à-Pitre.

Petit Jean River (pet-ee JEEN), 113 mi/182 km long, W central Ark.; rises in Sebastian co.; flows E, past Booneville and Danville, to Arkansas R. 10 mi/16 km W of Morrilton. Impounded W of Danville by Blue Mt. Dam, for flood control; the dam (115 ft/35 m high, 2,800 ft/853 m long) forms Blue Mountain L. (7.5 mi/12.1 km long, 1 mi/1.6 km wide; flood-control storage,

233,000 acre-ft.), used for boating and fishing. Flows through Petit Jean Wildlife Management Area downstream from Danville. Petit Jean State Park S of confluence W Arkansas R.

Petit Jean State Park (pet-ee JEEN), recreational area, Conway co., central Ark., on Petit Jean Mt., c.10 mi/16 km W of Morrilton, S of confluence of Petit Jean and Arkansas rivers. Covers 3,621 acres/1,465 ha. Waterfalls, canyons, caves, lakes (bathing, boating, fishing), bridle and foot trails; cabins, lodge.

Petit Manan Island (puh-teet muh-NAN), Washington co., E Maine, small lighthouse isl. 3 mi/4.8 km SE of Petit Manan Point, W of entrance to Pleasant Bay.

Petit Manan Point, Washington co., E Maine, peninsula, c.30 mi/48 km SW of Machias, and on E side of Dyer Bay.

Petit Martinique, St. Vincent and the Grenadines: see PETITE MARTINIQUE.

Petit Nord Peninsula, Canada: see GREAT NORTHERN PENINSULA.

Petit Piton, St. Lucia: see PITONS, THE.

Petit Pré (puh-TEE PRAI), village, S Que., Canada, on the St. Lawrence, and 12 mi/19 km NE of Quebec. Mica mining.

Petit St. Vincent, islet, St. Vincent and the Grenadines, West Indies, S of Union Isl., and N of Petit Martinique; 12°32′N 61°23′W. Southernmost isl. in St. Vincent and the Grenadines; privately owned by exclusive resort.

Petit-Bourg (puh-tee-BOOR), town, E Basse-Terre, Guadeloupe, 5 mi/8 km SW of Pointe-à-Pitre. In agr. region (coffee, cacao); sugar milling, distilling.

Petit-Canal (puh-tee-kah-NAHL), town, W Grande-Terre, Guadeloupe, 10 mi/16 km NNE of Pointe-à-Pitre. In sugarcane region.

Petitcodiac (peh-tee-KO-di-ak), village (1991 pop. 1,342), SE N.B., Canada, on Petitcodiac R., and 22 mi/35 km WSW of Moncton; 45°56′N 65°10′W. Lumbering; dairying.

Petitcodiac River, 80 mi/129 km long, SE N.B., Canada; rises NE of Sussex; flows ENE to Moncton, then SSE, past Hillsborough, to Shepody Bay at Hopewell Cape. Navigable below Moncton, it carries the region's mineral resources. Bay of Fundy tidal bore ascends to Moncton.

Petit–de–Grat Island (puh-TEE-duh-GRAH), E N.S., Canada, off S Cape Breton Isl., just E of Madame Isl.; 3 mi/5 km long, 2 mi/3 km wide; 45°30′N 61°00′W.

Petite Martinique, islet (1991 est. pop. 720), S Grenadines, dependency of Grenada, West Indies, 3 mi/4.8 km E of Carriacou isl., 40 mi/64 km NE of St. George's; 12°21′N 61°23′W. Also known as Little Martinique; also spelled Petit Martinique.

Petite Terre (puh-teet TAHR), group of 2 small islets (□ 1.2 sq mi/3.1 sq km), Guadeloupe dept., Fr. West Indies, 27 mi/43 km ESE of Pointe-à-Pitre, Guadeloupe; 16°10′N 61°06′W. Consists of Terre-de-Bas and Terre-de-Haut. Lighthouse.

Petite-Anse (puh-tee–TAWNGS), village (1982 pop. 1,046), Nord dept., N Haiti, 2 mi/3.2 km SE of Cap-Haïtien; 19°38′N 73°09′W. Agr. (citrus fruits, sugarcane, tobacco); cattle. On nearby sandbank Columbus's flagship, the *Santa María*, was lost (Christmas Day, 1492). Here the navigator built La Navidad Fort.

Petite-Rivière-de-l'Artibonite (puh-teet–ree-VYER–duh–lahr-tee-bo-NEET), town (1982 pop. 10,099), Artibonite dept., central Haiti, on Artibonite R., and 14 mi/23 km E of Saint-Marc; 19°08′N 72°29′W. Agr. center (cotton, coffee, sugarcane, limes, tobacco, rice; cattle); sugar processing. Has old palace and fort.

Petite-Rivière-de-Nippes (puh-teet–ree-VYER–duh–NEEP), town (1982 pop. 1,284), Grande-Anse dept., SW Haiti, on the N coast of Jacmel Peninsula, 40 mi/64 km W of Léogâne; 18°29′N 73°15′W. In agr. region (cotton, rice, coffee, bananas, limes, sugarcane). Fishing port. Bauxite deposits nearby.

Petit-Goâve (puh-tee–GWAHV), town (1982 pop. 7,310), Ouest dept., S Haiti, port on S arm of the Gulf of Gonaïves, at N base of Jacmel Peninsula, 36 mi/58 km WSW of Port-au-Prince; 18°26′N 72°52′W. Coffee and cacao-shipping center. Trades also in other agr.

prods. (cotton, sweet potatoes, coconuts, oranges, mangoes, limes, sugarcane); sugar processing. Fishing port. Has wharf and customhouse.

Petit-Trou-de-Nippes (puh-tee–troo–duh–NEEP), town (1982 pop. 1,524), Grande-Anse dept., Haiti, 28 mi/45 km NE of Les Cayes; 18°32′N 73°31′W. Agr. (cotton, coffee, sugarcane growing); sugar processing. Fishing port.

Petlalcingo (pet-lahl-SEEN-go), town (1990 pop. 2,590), Puebla, central Mexico, on Inter-Amer. Highway, and 13 mi/21 km SE of Acatlán; 18°05′N 98°34′W. Sugarcane, fruit, corn; livestock.

Peto (PE-to), town (1990 pop. 14,421), Yucatán, SE Mexico, 70 mi/113 km SE of Mérida; 20°08′N 88°53′W. RR terminus. Agr. center (henequen, sugarcane, corn, fruit; timber).

Petoskey (pe-TAH-skee), town (1990 pop. 6,056), ⊙ Emmet co., NW Mich., on Little Traverse Bay of L. Michigan, and c.52 mi/84 km NE of Traverse City; 45°22′N 84°57′W. In lake and farm area (potatoes, apples). Mfg. (portland cement, food processing, wiring devices, construction materials, fasteners, plastics, wood prods.); lumber, limestone quarries; site of famous Petoskey stone for rock collectors; resort area. North Central Mich. Col. Petoskey Ski Area to SE; Petosky State Park 3 mi/4.8 km NE at Bay View. A winter carnival and summer Native Amer. pageant are held here. Settled c.1860; inc. as village 1879; city 1895.

Petrey (PET-ree), town (1990 pop. 80), Crenshaw co., S Ala., 10 mi/16 km NNE of Luverne.

Petrified Forest National Park, Apache and Navajo cos., 22 mi/35 km E of Holbrook, E Ariz. Adjoins Navajo Indian Reservation on N, Interstate highway 40 crosses park. Covers 93,533 acres/37,853 ha; authorized 1906, as a natl. park 1962. A part of the Painted Desert in N, it contains the largest known display of petrified wood in the world. There are 6 separate "forests," with great logs of jasper and agate lying on the ground surrounded by the varied colors of endless fragments and small chips. Dating from the Triassic period, these "stone trees" were killed by natural processes, such as fire, insect attacks, and fungus. The trees were deeply buried in mud and sand that contained silica-rich volcanic ash. The logs became petrified as the mineral, carried into the wood by groundwater, replaced the wood cells. As the surrounding material was eroded away, the petrified trees were exposed on the surface. Prehistoric Native Americans lived among the stone trees; ruins of their dwellings and their petroglyphs (anc. rock art) remain. Although the 1st known report of the petrified forests was made by Lt. Lorenzo Sitgreaves, an army officer who explored the area in 1851, it was virtually unknown until the late 1870s.

Petroglyph (PE-tro-glif), natl. monument, Bernalillo co., N.Mex., 8 mi/12.9 km W of downtown Albuquerque, N of Interstate highway 40. Covers 5,207 acres/2,107 ha. More than 15,000 prehistoric and historic Native Amer. and Hispanic petroglyphs and rock art carvings. Authorized 1990.

Petroleum, county (□ 1,674 sq mi/4,336 sq km; 1990 pop. 519), central Mont.; ⊙ Winnett; 47°07′N 108°16′W. Agr. area drained by Box Elder, Yellow Water, and Flatwillow creeks; bounded N by Missouri R. (Fort Peck L.); E by Musselshell R. Wheat, barley; hay, cattle, sheep. Petroleum, natural gas. Charles M. Russel Natl. Wildlife Refuge to N; 3 units of War Horse Natl. Wildlife Refuge protects War Horse and Wild Horse lakes in NW and Yellow Water Reservoir in SW. Formed 1925.

Petrolia (pe-TRO-lee-uh), town (1991 pop. 4,594), S Ont., Canada, on Bear Creek, and 15 mi/24 km ESE of Sarnia; 42°53′N 82°09′W. Oil production center, with refineries, tank farms; also dairying, fruitgrowing region. Clay quarries nearby.

Petrolia, town (1990 pop. 762), Clay co., N Texas, near Red R., 18 mi/29 km ENE of Wichita Falls, near Wichita R.; 34°00′N 98°13′W. In farm area (pecans, peaches; cotton; wheat; dairying).

Petrolia (puh-TRO-lee-ah), borough (1990 pop. 292), Butler co., W Pa., 15 mi/24 km NE of Butler, on South Branch Bear Creek; 41°01′N 79°43′W. Agr. (corn, hay;

livestock, dairying); mfg. (oil and grease refining). Former oil producing center.

Petros (PEE-trahs), village, Morgan co., NE central Tenn., 11 mi/18 km NW of Oak Ridge; 36°06′N 84°27′W. In a coal mining valley of the Cumberlands. Nearby are Frozen Head State Park and Natural Area, and a state prison.

Pettis, county (□ 679 sq mi/1,759 sq km; 1990 pop. 35,437), central Mo.; ⊙ Sedalia; 38°43′N 93°16′W. Corn, wheat, hay; cattle, horses, mules; mfg. at Sedalia; limestone quarries. Bothwell State Park N of Sedalia; State Fairgrounds at Sedalia. State Fair Com. Col. in Sedalia. Formed 1833.

Pettus, uninc. village (1990 pop. 400), Bee co., S Texas, 15 mi/24 km N of Beeville, on Medio Creek. Oil and gas; cattle, horses.

Petty's Island, Camden co., SW N.J., in Delaware R. just above Camden; c.1 mi/1.6 km long. Oil refinery.

Pevely (PEEV-lee), town (1990 pop. 2,831), Jefferson co., E Mo., on Mississippi R. and 10 mi/16 km NE of Hillsboro, suburb of St. Louis; 38°17′N 90°24′W. Mfg. (fabricated metal prods., steel castings, plastic foam insulation, glass prods.).

Pewamo (pe-WAH-mo), village (1990 pop. 520), Ionia co., S central Mich., 11 mi/18 km E of Ionia; 43°00′N 84°50′W.

Pewaukee (pee-WAW-kee), town (1990 pop. 4,941), Waukesha co., SE Wis., at E end of Pewaukee L. (c.4.5 mi/7.2 km long), suburb 17 mi/27 km W of Milwaukee, and 5 mi/8 km N of Waukesha; 43°05′N 88°15′W. In dairy and poultry farm area; farm trade center; resort (summer and winter lake sports); mfg. (personal computers, magazine printing, fencing and guard rails, candies, plywood). Waukesha County Area Technical Col. Inc. 1876.

Pewee Valley (PEE-wee), town (1990 pop. 1,283), Oldham co., N Ky., residential suburb 13 mi/21 km ENE of downtown Louisville, in N part of Bluegrass region; 38°18′N 85°29′W. Mfg. (counter tops). Confederate Cemetery.

Pfafftown (PAHF-tuhn), uninc. town (1990 pop. 900), Forsyth co., N central N.C., suburb 8 mi/12.9 km NW of downtown Winston-Salem. Agr. area (tobacco, grain; cattle). Mfg. (flexible packaging material).

Pfeiffer State Redwood Park, Calif.: see BIG SUR.

Pflugerville (FLOO-guhr-vil), town (1990 pop. 4,444), Travis co., S central Texas, suburb 14 mi/23 km NE of downtown Austin, on Gilleland Creek; 30°26′N 97°37′W. In cotton, grain, dairying, cattle, pecan area; mfg. (tool and die, metal stampings, wooden pallets, contact lenses, circuit board assemblies; printing).

Phaéton (fah-ai-TONG), village (1982 pop. 1,652), Nord-Est dept., NE Haiti, on inlet of the Atlantic, 4 mi/6.4 km W of Fort Liberté; 19°41′N 71°54′W. Limes, sugarcane; mfg. of sisal fibers.

Pharr (FAHR), city (1990 pop. 32,921), Hidalgo co., extreme S Texas, suburb 2 mi/3.2 km E of McAllen; 26°10′N 98°11′W. Elev. 107 ft/33 m. It is located in the irrigated region of the lower Rio Grande valley; mfg. (transportation equip., concrete blocks). Oil and natural gas wells are located in the city, which more than doubled in pop. bet. 1970 and 1990. Santa Ana Natl. Wildlife Refuge on Rio Grande (Mex. border) 8 mi/12.9 km SSE. Inc. 1916.

Pheba (FEE-buh), village, Clay co., E Miss., 17 mi/27 km W of West Point. Agr. (cotton, corn; cattle); mfg. (work gloves).

Phelps 1 county (□ 677 sq mi/1,753 sq km; 1990 pop. 35,248), central Mo.; ⊙ Rolla; 37°52′N 91°47′W. In the Ozarks, drained by Meramec and Gasconade rivers. Grapes, fruit; corn, hay; livestock, timber; fire-clay; wineries. Mfg. at Rolla and St. James. Part of Mark Twain Natl. Forest in SW; Meramec Spring Park SE of St. James. Univ. of Mo. campus at Rolla. Formed 1857. **2** county (□ 540 sq mi/1,399 sq km; 1990 pop. 9,715), S Nebr.; ⊙ Holdrege, located in Platte River valley; 40°30′N 99°24′W. Farm area bounded N by Platte R. Cattle, hogs; corn; dairy prods. Mfg. at Holdrege. Oregon Trail follows S side of river. Formed 1873.

Phelps (FELPS), town (1990 pop. 1,298), Pike co., E Ky., in the Cumberland Mts., 13 mi/21 km SSE of Williamson (W.Va.); 37°30′N 82°09′W. In bituminous coal-mining area; mfg. (treated wood).

Phelps 1 village (□ 1 sq mi/2.6 sq km; 1990 pop. 1,978), Ontario co., W central N.Y., in Finger Lakes region, on Canandaigua Outlet, and 7 mi/11.3 km NW of Geneva; 42°57′N 77°03′W. Mfg. (machinery, cement prods., hydraulic and pneumatic valves for the aerospace industry); sand and gravel pits, peat, stone quarries. Agr. (oats, vegetables, wheat). Inc. 1855. **2** village, Vilas co., N Wis., at E end of North Twin L., 33 mi/53 km NNE of Rhinelander. In wooded lake region of Nicolet Natl. Forest. Sawmilling. Near Mich. boundary (Ottawa Natl. Forest beyond boundary).

Phelps City, town (1990 pop. 32), Atchison co., NW Mo., near the Missouri R. 8 mi/12.9 km SSW of Rock Port; 40°23′N 95°35′W. Missouri R. bridge to Nebraska.

Phelps Lake, Washington and Tyrell cos., E N.C., 17 mi/27 km NE of Belhaven; c.7 mi/11.3 km long, 5 mi/8 km wide. Included in Pettigrew State Park. Drains NE to Bull Bay, in Albermarle Sound. Surrounded by East Dismal Swamp. Somerset Place State Historical Site near N shore.

Phenix, town (1990 pop. 260), Charlotte co., S Va., 31 mi/50 km SE of Lynchburg; 37°4′N 78°45′W. Mfg. (lamp sockets); agr. (dairying; livestock; grain, soybeans, tobacco). Red Hill-Patrick Henry Natl. Memorial to SW. Also spelled Phoenix. Inc. 1930.

Phenix (FEE-nix), village in West Warwick town, Kent co., central R.I., on North Branch of Pawtuxet R., and 10 mi/16 km SW of Providence. Lace goods, textile dyeing and finishing.

Phenix City (FEE-niks), city (1990 pop. 25,312), ⊙ Russell co., E Ala., on the Chattahoochee R. opposite Columbus, Ga. In a cotton area, textile mfg. here. In 1954 the state governor placed Phenix City under martial law for about 5 months—a result of the corruption that had long prevailed in the city. Chatahochee Valley State Community Col. here. Nearby is Fort Benning military reservation (in Ga.) as well as the site of Fort Mitchell (1811–1837) and Fort Mitchell Natl. Cemetery. Inc. 1883.

Phil Campbell, town (1990 pop. 1,317), Franklin co., NW Ala., 10 mi/16 km S of Russellville. Mfg. (apparel, furniture, mobile homes). Northwest-Shoals Community Col. here.

Philadelphia, county (□ 142 sq mi/368 sq km; 1990 pop. 1,585,577), SE Pa., ⊙ Philadelphia. City and co. of Philadelphia are coextensive; 40°00′N 75°07′W.

Philadelphia, city (1990 pop. 1,585,577), ⊙ Philadelphia co., SE Pa., city and co. of Philadelphia are coextensive, on the Delaware R., at mouth of Schuylkill R. (4 bridges), opposite (W of) Camden N.J. Bounded SW by Darby and Cobb creeks; drained and bounded NW by Schuylkill R.; bounded NE by Poquessing Creek; also drained by Pennypack, Tacony, Frankford, and Wissahickon creeks; 40°00′N 75°58′W. The 5th-largest city in the U.S. and a leading commercial and cultural center since the 18th cent. Has ocean port facilities on most of its Delaware R. frontage and SW to Del. state line. An important trading and mfg. hub even before the Revolution, it maintains a diverse industrial base. Mfg. includes printing and publishing, chemicals, fabricated metal prods., textiles, apparel, paper prods., food prods., machinery, electronics, transportation equip., plastic prods., instruments, and furniture. Prominent among the metropolitan area's newer tertiary industries is a concentration of growing health-care firms. Philadelphia is a major retailing, educational, insurance and banking center. The site was 1st occupied by Native Americans. In the 17th cent. there was a Swed. settlement; the land was soon claimed by the Dutch and then contested by the British. William Penn acquired it through a grant from Charles II of England and in 1682 founded Philadelphia, the "City of Brotherly Love," intended as a refuge for the peaceable Quakers—hence the nickname Quaker City. Its commercial, industrial, and cultural growth was rapid, and by 1774 it was 2d only to London as the largest Eng.-speaking city. It was the seat of the Continental Congress and served as the Amer. capital from 1777 to 1788, except during the Br. occupation (Oct. 1777–June 1778) after the battle of Brandywine. It was the capital of the new republic from 1790 to 1800, as well as the state capital (to 1799). The 2 Banks of the U.S. (1791–1811; 1816–1836) were here. The bank bldgs. are examples of Gr. revival architecture. A nucleus of Amer. culture in colonial times (among its prominent citizens at that time was the scientist and statesman Benjamin Franklin), Philadelphia is still the seat of many philosophical, artistic, dramatic, musical, and scientific societies. Among these are the Philadelphia. Academy of the Fine Arts (1805); the Academy of Natural Sciences (1812); the Amer. Philosophical Society (1743); and the Science Mus. of the Franklin Inst. (1824), which now includes the Benjamin Franklin Memorial (1933), an important unit of which is the Fels Planetarium. In nearby Merion is the Barnes Foundation, with an extraordinary collection of paintings. Musical activities flourish in the city, which has an outstanding symphony orchestra. In Fairmount Park, the largest city park in the U.S., are the Philadelphia Mus. of Art, zoological gardens, and many historic monuments and shrines. Many early historic shrines are also in Independence Natl. Historical Park (est. 1956). Among them are Independence Hall, where the Declaration of Independence was signed; the Liberty Bell; the neighboring Congress Hall, where Congress met from 1790 to 1800 and where George Washington gave his farewell address; and Carpenters' Hall, where the First Continental Congress met. City Hall, one of the nation's largest, is a conspicuous bldg. with a tower surmounted by a statue of William Penn. Also of interest are the Rodin Mus.; the Gloria Dei (Old Swedes') Church; and Christ Church (begun in 1727), a representative example of Colonial architecture. Near Elfreth's Alley, a narrow street that has retained its colonial air, is the Betsy Ross House, where, according to one story, the 1st Amer. flag was made. Edgar Allan Poe's house has also been preserved (Edgar Allen Poe Natl. Historic Site). The historic 18th-cent. houses in the Society Hill sect. are additional tourist attractions. The Revolutionary War Fort Mifflin has been restored. Amer. Swedish History Mus., Chin. Cultural Center, Thaddeus Kosciaszko Natl. Memorial commemorates Pol.-born patriot, Philadelphia Zoological Gardens, Philadelphia Maritime Mus., Pa. Convention Center in downtown. Philadelphia has more than 30 educational institutions, including the Univ. of Pa., Temple Univ., Drexel Univ., La Salle Col., Chestnut Hill Col., St. Joseph's Univ., Curtis Institute of Music, Academy of Music, Hahnemann Medical Col. and Hosp., Philadelphia Col. of Pharmacy and Science, Thomas Jefferson Univ., the Philadelphia Col. of Art, Moore Col. of Art and Design, Art Inst. of Philadelphia (2-year col.), the Philadelphia Col. of Textiles and Science, Academy of Natural Sciences, the Annenberg Inst. for Judaic and Near Eastern Studies, and Community Col. of Philadelphia. Site of Franklin Mills, one of the largest shopping centers in U.S. A sports complex in S Philadelpha comprises the Spectrum, home of the Natl. Basketball Association's Philadelphia Seventy-Sixers and the Natl. Hockey League's Flyers; Veteran's Stadium, home of Natl. Football League's Eagles and the Major League Baseball's Natl. League Phillies, as well as the the site of the annual Army-Navy football game. Installations of the U.S. Mint, the Federal Reserve System, and the Internal Revenue Service are in the city. The U.S. Naval Shipyard, the nation's oldest military shipyard and most prominent of Philadelphia's several military installations, had lost most of its building programs by the 1980s and was closed in 1991. Some of its facilities are redirected to building cruise ships. Despite an ambitious program of urban redevelopment initiated in the 1950s, the city experienced the decay of its economic base and a sharp decline in pop. through subsequent decades. Philadelphia Internatl. Airport at SW end, on Delaware R. (Philadelphia/Delaware cos.), Northeast Philadelphia Airport in NE. Benjamin Rush State Park in NE; John Heinz Natl. Wildlife Refuge in SW; Fairmont, Tacony Creek, and Pennypack parks follow city's streams. Longstanding tensions erupted in race riots in the 1960s. In the 1970s, Frank Rizzo, a former police commissioner often portrayed as a spokesman for the city's working-class whites, was elected mayor. Wilson Goode became Philadelphia's 1st black mayor in 1983. His administration was shaken by the controversial firebombing of a city block containing the home of an armed organization of black radicals. The decline of the central city was met in part by the construction of new office bldgs. downtown and development projects on the Delaware R. waterfront. Overall, attempts at gentrification in the inner city have fallen below expectation. The city govt. came close to bankruptcy in 1990. Meanwhile, the metropolitan area, long noted for its wealthy and exclusive suburbs (especially along the fabled Main Line), witnessed dramatic growth in the Delaware Valley region. Chartered 1701.

Philadelphia, town (1990 pop. 6,758), ⊙ Neshoba co., E central Miss., 34 mi/55 km NW of Meridian; 32°46′N 89°06′W. Agr. (cotton, corn; poultry, cattle; dairying; timber); mfg. (canvas, electronic equip., and wood prods., lumber, apparel, metal fabrication, printing and publishing, concrete). Seat of Choctaw Indian Agency; Choctaw Indian Reservation is W; smaller reservation to SE. Choctaw Mus. of the Southern Indian, Nanih Waiya Memorial State Historic Site, Choctaw burial mounds, to NE. Neshoba County Legion L. to SE.

Philadelphia, village (1990 pop. 1,478), Jefferson co., N N.Y., on Indian R., and 16 mi/26 km NE of Watertown; 44°08′N 75°42′W.

Philip, village (1990 pop. 1,077), ⊙ Haakon co., central S.Dak., 70 mi/113 km WSW of Pierre, and on Bad R.; 44°02′N 101°39′W. In farming and ranching area (dairy prods.; livestock; grain); mfg. (ironworkers' models). Buffalo Gap Natl. Grassland to S.

Philippi (FIL-uh-pee), city (1990 pop. 3,132), ⊙ Barbour co., N W.Va., on Tygart R., 13 mi/21 km S of Grafton; 39°08′N 80°02′W. Coal mines, gas and oil wells. Agr. (corn); livestock; poultry; dairying. Timber. Mfg. (apparel, coal processing, concrete). Alderson-Broaddus Col. here. Philippi Covered Bridge. Tygart L. State Park to N. Civil War battle (a Union victory) was fought here, June 3, 1861. Settled c.1780.

Philipsburg, town (1990 pop. 925), ⊙ Granite co., W Mont., 45 mi/72 km NW of Butte and on Flint Creek; 46°20′N 113°17′W. Restored 1880s mining town. Sapphire, silver; timber; cattle, hay; mfg. (bottled spring water). John Long Mts. to W; Flint Creek Range to E. Discovery Basin Ski Area to S; parts of Deerlodge Natl. Forest to E and N; Georgetown L. to S. Natl. Ghost Town Hall of Fame; Granite County Mus. Inc. 1890. Originally called Camp Creek.

Philipsburg (FI-luhps-buhrg), borough (1990 pop. 3,048), Centre co., central Pa., 14 mi/23 km SE of Clearfield, on Moshannon Creek; 40°53′N 78°12′W. Agr. (livestock); light mfg.; surface bituminous coal mining. Midstate Airport 7 mi/11.3 km to E. Moshanon State Forest and Black Moshanon State Park to E. Laid out 1797, inc. 1864.

Philipsburg, principal settlement of Du. sect. of SAINT MARTIN, in the Leewards, West Indies, part of Neth. Antilles, 3 mi/4.8 km SE of Marigot; 18°01′N 63°02′W. Tourism center; cruise ships, casinos, and duty-free shopping. Has good harbor. Jap. commercial fishing operation.

Philipsburg Manor, N.Y.: see PHILIPSE MANOR.

Philipse Manor, former colonial estate, SE N.Y., extending bet. Hudson and Bronx rivers from the present Sleepy Hollow (N) to the present Yonkers (S); 41°05′N 73°55′W. Chartered 1693, it was once the property of Frederick Philipse. At Yonkers is the S manor hall (c.1682), now state-owned, with historical collections; at N. Tarrytown is Castle Philipse (c.1683; restored; now a mus.), the N manor seat. Also called Philipsburg Manor.

Phillips 1 county (□ 727 sq mi/1,883 sq km; 1990 pop. 28,838), E Ark.; ⊙ Helena; 34°25′N 90°50′W. Bounded E by Mississippi R.; W in part by White R. drained by St. Francis R. and by Big Creek. Includes part of Crowley's Ridge. Agr. (cotton, rice, wheat, soybeans; hogs).

Mfg. at Helena and West Helena. Timber; gravel. Formed 1820. Louisiana Purchase State Historical Monument on NW corner; part of White River Natl. Wildlife Refuge in SW; part of small St. Francis Natl. Forest in NE. **2** county (□ 687 sq mi/1,779 sq km; 1990 pop. 4,189), NE Colo.; ⊙ Holyoke; 40°35'N 102°20'W. Agr. area, bordering on Nebr. on E; drained by Frenchman Creek. Cattle, poultry, wheat, hay, sorghum, beans, sunflowers, oats, corn, sugar beets. Formed 1889. **3** county (□ 894 sq mi/2,315 sq km; 1990 pop. 6,590), N Kansas; ⊙ Phillipsburg; 39°46'N 99°20'W. Rolling prairie region, bordering N on Nebr.; drained by North Fork of Solomon R. Corn, wheat, sorghum; hogs, cattle, livestock. Petroleum prods. Kirwin Reservoir and Natl. Wildlife Refuge in SE. Formed 1872. **4** county (□ 5,212 sq mi/13,499 sq km; 1990 pop. 5,163), N Mont.; ⊙ Malta; 48°16'N 107°55'W. Agr. area bordering N on Canada (Sask.); bounded S by Missouri R. (upper reach at Fort Peck L. reservoir); drained by Milk R. and Whitewater, Frenchman and Beaver creeks. Border forms Central and Mountain time zone boundary; Mont. is in Mountain time zone. Wheat, barley, oats, hay; cattle, sheep, hogs. Natural gas. Heawitt Lake Natl. Wildlife Refuge at center of co.; part of Fort Belknap Indian Reservation in W; part of Charles M. Russell Natl. Wildlife Refuge in S along shore of Fort Peck L.; UL Bend Natl. Wildlife Refuge in S center in sharp bend of Fort Peck L. Formed 1915.

Phillips 1 town (1990 pop. 1,148), Franklin co., W central Maine, on Sandy R., and 15 mi/24 km NW of Farmington; 44°50'N 70°22'W. In recreational area; mfg. (wood prods.). Diatomaceous earth found here. Settled 1791, inc. 1812. **2** uninc. town (1990 pop. 2,500), Hutchinson co., extreme N Texas, 25 mi/40 km NW of Pampa, and 2 mi/3.2 km NE of Borger. An oil-refining center in great Panhandle oil and natural gas region. **3** town (1990 pop. 1,592), ⊙ Price co., N Wis., 48 mi/77 km W of Rhinelander; 45°42'N 90°24'W. In wooded lake region; sawmilling, woodworking; dairying; mfg. (hardwood, plastic prods., Christmas decorations), Chequamegon Natl. Forest to NE, Flambeau State Forest to W. Settled 1874, inc. 1891.

Phillips 1 village (1990 pop. 316), Hamilton co., SE central Nebr., 7 mi/11.3 km E of Grand Isl., and on Platte R; 40°53'N 98°12'W. **2** village (1990 pop. 161), Coal co., S central Okla., 2 mi/3.2 km S of Coalgate, near Muddy Boggy Creek; 34°30'N 96°13'W. In agr. area.

Phillips Island, Beaufort co., S S.C., one of the Sea Isls., NE of entrance to Port Royal Sound; 6 mi/9.7 km long. St. Helena Isl to N., Pritchards Isl. to NE, Atlantic Ocean to SE.

Phillips Reservoir, Baker co., E Oregon, on Powder R., 11 mi/18 km SW of Baker City; 5 mi/8 km long; 44°40'N 118°01'W. Max. capacity 108,410 acre-ft. Formed by Mason Dam (159 ft/48 m high), built (1968) for irrigation and flood control. Surrounded by, but not within, Wallowa-Whitman Natl. Forest.

Phillipsburg 1 town (1990 pop. 2,828), ⊙ Phillips co., N Kansas, 60 mi/97 km N of Hays, 5 mi/8 km N of Solomon R.; 39°45'N 99°19'W. Elev. 1,940 ft/591 m. Corn; hogs, cattle. Mfg. (roofing prods., RR equip., natural gas facility). Old Ft. Bissell is here. Kirwin Reservoir and Kirwin Natl. Wildlife Refuge to SE. **2** town (1990 pop. 15,757), Warren co., NW N.J., on the Delaware R. opposite Easton, Pa.; 40°41'N 75°10'W. Settled 1739, inc. 1861. RR and industrial center in a farm area. Iron and steel works once dominated the economy; mfg. now includes electroplated parts and wire, metal pipes, and chemicals.

Phillipsdale, neighborhood, in East Providence city, Providence co., NE R.I. Formerly a mill village.

Phillipy (FI-li-pee), resort village, Lake co., extreme NW Tenn., on Reelfoot L., 15 mi/24 km W of Union City. Popular bird-watching area.

Philo 1 (FI-lo), uninc. town (1990 pop. 960), Mendocino co., NW Calif., 14 mi/23 km WSW of Ukiah, near Navarro R., in Anderson Valley. Fruit, grapes; dairying; poultry, cattle. Winery. Hendy Woods State Park to W. **2** town (1990 pop. 1,028), Champaign co., E central Ill., 7 mi/11.3 km SSE of Urbana; 40°00'N 88°09'W. Corn, soybeans; precision sheet metal fabricating.

Philomath (fi-LAM-uhth), town (1990 pop. 2,983), Benton co., W Oregon, 5 mi/8 km WSW of Corvallis, on Mary's R.; 44°32'N 123°21'W. Terminus of RR spur from Corvallis. Fruit, beans; cattle, poultry. Mfg. (lumber, particleboard, timber). Fish hatchery to SW. Siuslaw Natl. Forest to W; McDonald State Forest to N; William L. Finley Natl. Wildlife Refuge to S.

Philpot (FIL-paht), uninc. village (1990 pop. 700), Daviess co., NW Ky., 7 mi/11.3 km ESE of Owensboro, near Panther Creek. Tobacco, grain; livestock, dairying. Mfg. (storage tanks, light mfg.).

Phippsburg (FIPS-buhrg), town (1990 pop. 1,815), Sagadahoc co., S central Maine, just S of Bath, on peninsula with Casco Bay to W, and the Kennebec R. E; 43°46'N 69°49'W. Includes villages of Phippsburg, Parker Head, Popham Beach, West Point, and Sebasco. Popham Beach State Park, Morse Mt. Preserve (salt marsh and sandy beach) are here. Set off from Bristol in 1816.

Phoebus, former town, Elizabeth City co., SE Va., now part of independent city of Hampton.

Phoenicia (fuh-NEE-shuh), village, Ulster co., SE N.Y., in the Catskills, on Esopus Creek and 19 mi/31 km NW of Kingston; 42°05'N 74°19'W.

Phoenix, city (1990 pop. 983,403), ⊙ state and Maricopa co., S Ariz., on the Salt R.; 33°32'N 112°04'W. Largest city in Ariz, 9th largest city in the U.S., the hub of the rich agr. region of the Salt R. valley, and an important center for research and development, electronics, telecommunications, semiconductors, and the aerospace industry. Production of aircraft parts, electrical appliances, agr. chemicals, machinery, tools, plastic prods., cosmetics, food processing, wood prods., and leather goods remains central to its mfg. base. The city was founded on the site of anc. Native Amer. canals; hence its name, signifying a new town which had risen from the ruins of an old civilization. In 1868, pioneers developed what remained of the Native Amer. irrigation system; water was diverted from the Salt R., and farming began, supplemented by mining and ranching in the surrounding desert and mts. Modern-day irrigation and water supply canals and aquaducts lace the area. The completion (1911) of the Roosevelt Dam on the Salt R. brought power and abundant water to the community and opened a new era of farming in the valley. Phoenix grew as an important trade and distribution center. It boomed during World War II, when 3 airfields were opened, bringing thousands of servicemen into the area. The phenomenal growth continued after the war; veterans who had been stationed in Phoenix returned to make it their home (Ariz. Veterans Memorial Cemetery in N), and mfg. concerns moved there to utilize the large labor supply. Area has greatly expanded in 1970s–1990s with influx of retired citizens and businesses moving to Sun Belt. The expanding metropolitan area includes the suburbs of MESA, SCOTTSDALE, CHANDLER, TEMPE, and GLENDALE, all of which are among the fastest-growing cities in the U.S. At Papago Park in E are the Desert Botanical Gardens and Phoenix Zoo, McDowell Mt. Park is to NE; 16,000 acres/6,475 ha South Mt. Park is in S, has summit lookout at Dobbins Point. Among its mus. are Ariz. Society Mus., with anc. and pioneer relics; Heard Mus., with Indian exhibitions; the Ariz. Historical Mus.; the Phoenix Art Mus.; the Pueblo Grande Mus., containing the excavations of Indian ruins c.800 years old; and the State Dept. of Archives Mus. Another attraction is the Ariz. Center shopping complex and the Mystery Castle, built of native rock. Phoenix is the seat of Grand Canyon Univ., Phoenix Col., Phoenix Indian School, Gatway Community Col., Paradise Community Col., Rio Salado Community Col., and South Mt. Community Col. The city has a symphony orchestra and many sports and recreational facilities, including a coliseum. Several major league baseball teams (referred to as the Cactus League, and the one in Phoenix being the Oakland Athletics) hold their spring-training camps in the area. The Phoenix Suns play in the Natl. Basketball Association at the Amer. West Arena. The Cardinals of the Natl. Football League moved to Phoenix from St. Louis in 1988; they play at Ariz. State Univ.'s Sun Devil Stadium in suburban Tempe, to E. The Milwaukee Brewers of the Natl. League new spring training facility (Maryvale Stadium; scheduled to open in 1998), in Maryvale (formerly in Chandler), a lower income suburb of Phoenix, will open as a part of Maricopa County Stadium Dist. In the area are a number of Native Amer. communities and reservations, natl. monuments, and many state parks. Sky Harbor Internatl. Airport E of downtown; Salt R. and Fort McDowell Indian reservations to E; Pueblo Grande Ruins and Mus. in E; Phoenix Military Reservation to E; Tonto Natl. Forest to NE; Deer Valley Airport in N; Turf Paradise Race Track in N; Pioneer Ariz. Mus. to N; Gila R. Indian Reservation to S; Univ. of Ariz. Cotton Research Farm in S; Luke Air Force Base to W. Inc. 1881.

Phoenix, town (1990 pop. 3,239), Jackson co., SW Oregon, 5 mi/8 km SE of Medford on Bear Creek; 42°16'N 122°49'W. Agr. (plums, apples, pears, peaches, cherries, wheat; poultry, cattle). Millwork, timber. Parts of Rogue R. Natl. Forest to S and E.

Phoenix, Va.: see PHENIX.

Phoenix 1 village (1990 pop. 2,217), Cook co., NE Ill., S suburb of Chicago, just E of Harvey; 41°36'N 87°37'W. Inc. 1900. **2** village (□ 1 sq mi/2.6 sq km; 1990 pop. 2,435), Oswego co., central N.Y., on Oswego R. and the Barge Canal, and 15 mi/24 km NNW of Syracuse; 43°13'N 76°17'W. Mfg. (consumer goods, hunting and archery bows, conveyor systems, molded thermoplastics, specialized machinery, tools and dies); agr. (dairy prods.; vegetables). Inc. 1849.

Phoenix Lake–Cedar Ridge, uninc. town (1990 pop. 3,569), Tuolumne co., E central Calif., 5 mi/8 km NE of Sonora, on Sullivan Creek (forms Phoenix Reservoir to W), in Stanislaus Natl. Forest; 38°01'N 120°18'W.

Phoenix Mountains, Maricopa co., central Ariz., NE of Phoenix. Rise to 2,704 ft/824 m in CAMELBACK MOUNTAIN and 2,608 ft/795 m on Squaw Peak; 33°33'N 112°01'W.

Phoenixville (FEE-nuhks-vil), borough (1990 pop. 15,066), Chester co., SE Pa., suburb 22 mi/35 km NW of downtown Philadelphia, on the Schuylkill R.; 40°08'N 75°31'W. Mfg. (food prods., corrugated boxes, plastic prods., tool and die, adhesives, printing and publishing). Agr. to NW (apples, grain; livestock, dairying; nursery stock); Iron deposits in the region led to the early development of an iron industry and later (1886) to the mfg. of steel. Phoenixville was the westernmost point in the state reached (1777) by the British during the Revolutionary War. Several 18th-cent. stone houses are here. Valley Forge is a few miles to the SE. Seat of Valley Forge Christian Col. Gingrich Airport to NW. Valley Forge Army Hospital to W, Fox Meadow Farm winery to W. Valley Forge Natl. Historical Park to SE; Prickers Creek Reservoir to SE. Settled 1720, inc. 1849.

Piankatank River, estuary, SE Va., inlet of Chesapeake Bay, forms boundary of Middlesex (N), Mathews(S), and Gloucester (S) cos.; receives short stream (Dragon Run) from W; c. 7 mi/11.3 km long; 37°34'N 76°35'W.

Piapot (PI-uh-paht), village (1991 pop. 61), SW Sask., Canada, in the Cypress Hills, on Piapot Creek, and 17 mi/27 km ENE of Maple Creek; 49°59'N 109°07'W. Ranching, wheat growing.

Piarco (PEE-ah-ko), village, N central Trinidad, Trinidad and Tobago, 12 mi/19 km ESE of Port of Spain. Internatl. airport.

Piatt (PEI-at), county (□ 440 sq mi/1,140 sq km; 1990 pop. 15,548), central Ill.; ⊙ Monticello; 40°00'N 88°35'W. Agr. (corn, soybeans; livestock). Some mfg. (grain, mill prods.). Drained by Sangamon R. Formed 1841.

Piaxtla (pee-ASH-tlah), town (1990 pop. 1,650), Puebla, central Mexico, 30 mi/48 km SE of Izúcar de Matamoros. Corn, sugarcane, fruit; livestock.

Piaxtla River (per-ASH-tlah), c.150 mi/241 km long, W Mexico; rises on W slopes of Sierra Madre Occidental in Durango near Sinaloa border; flows SW through fertile coastal lowlands of Sinaloa, past San Ignacio, to the Pacific 45 mi/72 km NW of Mazatlán.

Picacho (pee-KAH-cho), uninc. town (1990 pop. 850), Pinal co., S central Ariz., 18 mi/29 km ESE of Casa Grande. Irrigated agr. area (cotton, grain, sugar beets; livestock). Picacho Reservoir to N; Picacho Mts. to NE; Picacho Peak State Park to SE.

Picacho (pee-KAH-cho), village, Lincoln co., S central N.Mex., 36 mi/58 km W of Roswell on Rio Hondo, E of Sacramento Mts. Elev. 4,980 ft/1,518 m. Trading point in cattle, sheep, alfalfa, hay, grain. Mescalero Indian Reservation, parts of Lincoln Natl. Forest to W and NW. Mescalero Apache Indian Reservation to SW.

Picacho Butte (7,168 ft/2,185 m), Yavapai co., NW central Ariz., 10 mi/16 km SE of Seligman.

Picatinny Arsenal, N.J.: see DOVER.

Picayune (pik-ee-YOON), city (1990 pop. 10,633), Pearl R. co., S Miss., 36 mi/58 km WNW of Gulfport, and 45 mi/72 km NNE of New Orleans, La., near the Pearl R. (La. state line); 30°31′N 89°40′W. It is the trade, processing, and shipping center. Agr. (cotton, corn, pecans; cattle; dairying); mfg. (elevators, chemicals, polyurethane, metal containers, computer equip., sand and gravel processing, plastics, lumber, transportations equip.). Stennis Space Center (NASA) to S. Old River Wildlife Management Area to NW. Inc. 1904.

Picher, town (1990 pop. 1,714), Ottawa co., extreme NE Okla., 6 mi/9.7 km NNE of Miami, near Kansas line; 36°59′N 94°49′W. A center of lead- and zinc-mining region extending into the 3 states.

Pichilinque Bay (pee-chee-LEEN-ke), small inlet of La Paz Bay, SE Baja California Sur, NW Mexico, 8 mi/12.9 km N of La Paz. Good deep-sea harbor. Ferries from mainland dock here.

Pichucalco (per-choo-KAHL-ko), city (1990 pop. 10,609) and township, Chiapas, S Mexico, in Gulf lowland, near Tabasco border, 35 mi/56 km SSW of Villahermosa; 17°30′N 93°04′W. Rubber- and cocoa-growing center. Petroleum deposits nearby.

Pick City, village (1990 pop. 203), Mercer co., central N. Dak., on Missouri R., and 17 mi/27 km NNE of Hazen; 47°30′N 101°27′W. W side of Garrison Dam and Power Station, opposite Riverdale, L. Sakakawea and Sakakawea State Park to N.

Pickaway (PI-kuh-wai), county (□ 507 sq mi/1,313 sq km; 1990 pop. 48,255) S central Ohio; ⊙ Circleville; 39°39′N 83°02′W. Intersected by Scioto R. and by Darby, Paint, and small Salt and Little Walnut creeks. In the Till Plains and the Unglaciated Plains physiographic regions. Agr. (hogs, cattle; corn, soybeans); mfg. (food prods., plastics, stone, clay, and glass prods., electric lamps); sand and gravel pits. Formed 1810.

Pickens 1 county (□ 890 sq mi/2,305 sq km; 1990 pop. 20,699), W Ala.; ⊙ Carrollton. In Black Belt, bordering on Miss.; drained by Tombigbee and Sipsey rivers. Soybeans, corn; poultry; lumber milling; crude oil and natural gas production. Formed 1820. **2** county (□ 233 sq mi/603 sq km; 1990 pop. 14,432), N Ga.; ⊙ Jasper; 34°28′N 84°28′W. Blue Ridge farming (corn, cotton, hay, fruit); cattle, poultry; marble quarrying, sawmilling. In resort area. Mt. Oglethorpe (NE). Formed 1853. **3** county (□ 511 sq mi/1,323 sq km; 1990 pop. 93,894), NW S.C.; ⊙ Pickens; 34°53′N 82°43′W. Bounded E by Saluda R., W by Keowee and Seneca rivers; borders N on N.C. Mfg. (textiles; limestone, granite and sand quarries); agr. (cotton, corn, poultry; timber). Summer-resort area; Highest spot in S.C. is Sassafras Mt. at 3,560 ft/1,085 m. Formed 1826. Part of the Blue Ridge Mts. is in N; also includes Table Rock State Park and part of Sumter Natl. Forest.

Pickens 1 town (1990 pop. 1,285), Holmes co., central Miss., 42 mi/68 km NNE of Jackson, and on Big Black R.; 32°53′N 89°58′W. Agr. (cotton, corn, sorghum; cattle; timber); mfg. (tissue paper). Casey Jones Mus. State Park to S, at Vaughan. Rob Morris' Little Red School House, former Masonic Col. **2** town (1990 pop. 3,042), ⊙ Pickens co., NW S.C., 17 mi/27 km W of Greenville; 34°52′N 82°42′W. Summer resort area in Blue Ridge Mts., state parks nearby. Mfg. (textiles, tools, apparel, lumber; printing and publishing); agr. (dairying; poultry, eggs; hogs; corn; timber). Settled 1868, inc. 1908. Nearby are sites of Old Pickens (1828–1868) and Fort Prince George (1753), the latter a center of conflict in the Cherokee War (1760–1762).

Pickerel Lake, W Ont., Canada, 100 mi/161 km W of Port Arthur; elev. 1,338 ft/408 m; 14 mi/23 km long, 4 mi/6 km wide. Drains SW into Rainy L.

Pickerel Lake, Emmet co., NW Mich., 10 mi/16 km ENE of Petoskey; c.2.5 mi/4 km long, 1 mi/1.6 km wide; 45°23′N 84°46′W. Resorts; fishing. Joined to Crooked L. (NW) by short stream.

Pickering, town (1991 pop. 68,631), S Ont., Canada, near L. Ontario, 20 mi/32 km NE of Toronto; 43°52′N 79°02′W. E expansion city for Toronto. Warehousing, mfg. (plastics, motor vehicles, machinery, wood and metal prods., pharmaceuticals), dairying, mixed farming. Pickering nuclear facility is here; in 1997, 4 of the units here were shut down at least until the year 2000 (and perhaps permanently).

Pickering, town (1990 pop. 171), Nodaway co., NW Mo., on One Hundred and Two R., and 7 mi/11.3 km N of Maryville; 40°27′N 94°50′W.

Pickerington, city (1990 pop. 5,668), Fairfield and Franklin cos., central Ohio, 13 mi/21 km ESE of Columbus; 39°54′N 82°46′W. Dairy prods.

Picket Wire River, Colorado: see PURGATOIRE RIVER.

Pickett, county (□ 174 sq mi/451 sq km; 1990 pop. 4,548), N Tenn.; ⊙ Byrdstown, 36°34′N 85°05′W. On Cumberland Plateau; bounded N by Ky.; drained by Obey and short Wolf rivers. Includes Pickett State Park, and parts of Dale Hollow Reservoir, and Big South Fork Natl. R. and Recreation Area. Lumbering (hardwood, pine), bituminous-coal mining; agr. (livestock, tobacco, corn). Formed 1879.

Pickford, village, Chippewa and Mackinac co., E Upper Peninsula, Mich., 24 mi/39 km S of Sault Ste. Marie, and on Munuscong R.; 46°09′N 84°21′W.

Pickle Crow, village, NW Ont., Canada, in Patricia dist., 6 mi/10 km ENE of Pickle L., and 130 mi/209 km NE of Sioux Lookout; 51°30′N 90°04′W. Gold mining.

Pickle Lake, town (1991 pop. 654), NW Ont., Canada, in Patricia dist., on Pickle L. (5 mi/8 km long), 120 mi/193 km NE of Sioux Lookout. Gold mining.

Pickle Street, locality, Lewis co., central W.Va., 12 mi/19 km W of Weston. Agr. (corn, potatoes); cattle.

Pickleville, uninc. village, Rich co., N Utah, near Idaho state line, on W shore of Bear Lake, 2 mi/3.2 km S of Garden City. Wasatch Natl. Forest to W.

Pickrell, village (1990 pop. 201), Gage co., SE Nebr., 7 mi/11.3 km N of Beatrice, and on branch of Big Blue R.; 40°22′N 96°43′W.

Pickstown, village (1990 pop. 95), Charles Mix co., S S.Dak., 7 mi/11.3 km S of L. Andes, near site of Fort Randall Dam on Missouri R. to NW; 43°04′N 98°31′W. In Yankton Indian Reservation.

Pickwick Lake, reservoir (□ 67 sq mi/174 sq km), SW Tenn., NE Miss., and NW Ala., on Tennessee R., 12 mi/19 km S of Savannah, Tenn.; c.55 mi/89 km long, max. 2 mi/3.2 km wide; 35°04′N 88°15′W. Max. capacity 1,091,400 acre-ft. Forms Miss.-Ala. state line; Wilson Dam (Ala.) at S tip. Bear R. forms 15-mi/24-km S arm (Miss.-Ala. state line). Formed by Pickwick Landing Dam (concrete construction; 113 ft/34 m high), built (1938) by TVA for flood control and power generation. Pickwick Landing State Park (Tenn.) at dam; J.P. Coleman State Park (Miss.) on SW shore.

Pico de Orizaba National Park (PEE-ko dai o-ree-ZAH-bah) (□ 77 sq mi/199 sq km), central Veracruz, Mexico, 20 mi/32 km N of the city of Orizaba. The chief feature of the park is Orizaba, the highest mt. in Mexico (18,898 ft/5,760 m) and the 3d highest in N. Amer. (after Mt. McKinley and Mt. Logan); 19°01′N 97° 11′W. The peak marks the border bet. Puebla and Veracruz. The volcanic eruptions took place in 1545, 1559, 1613, and 1687. A road to the park branches N of Mex. route 150. At the city of Orizaba the park is also known as Citlaltépetl.

Pico de Tancítaro (PEE-ko dai tahn-SEE-tah-ro), natl. park (□ 115 sq mi/298 sq km), in central Michoacán, Mexico, 13 mi/21 km E of Angahuan. Elev. 12,664 ft/3,860 m. The park includes Parícutin volcano. There are no tourist facilities. Rural roads leading NW from the town of Uruapan access the park. Est. in 1940.

Pico Peak (PEE-ko) (3,957 ft/1,206 m), in Green Mts., W central Vt., 7 mi/11.3 km NE of Rutland; 43°38′N 72°50′W. Major winter resort area; ski lifts and trails.

Pico Rivera, city (1990 pop. 59,177), Los Angeles co., SW Calif., 8 mi/12.9 km ESE of downtown Los Angeles on the San Gabriel, and Rio Hondo rivers; 34°00′N 118°05′W. Mfg. (furniture, machinery, exercise equip., metal doors, B-2 aircraft, wire springs, food preparations, wood prods.). Pio Pico State Historical Park to E. Inc. 1958 with the union of Pico and Rivera into one community

Picton, town (1991 pop. 4,373), ⊙ Prince Edward co., SE Ont., Canda, on Adolphus Reach (an arm of L. Ontario leading to Bay of Quinte), 16 mi/26 km SE of Belleville; 44°01′N 77°09′W. Fruit and vegetable processing center; dairying.

Picton Island, one of the Thousand Isls., Jefferson co., N N.Y., 3 mi/4.8 km NE of Clayton; 1 mi/1.6 km long; 44°17′N 76°04′W. Roughly dumbbell-shaped. Several abandoned quarries on NE side.

Pictou (PIK-to, -too, pik-TOO), county (□ 1,124 sq mi/2,911 sq km; 1991 pop. 49,651), N N.S., Canada, on Northumberland Strait; ⊙ Pictou; 45°40′N 62°42′W. Has declining coal deposits. Timber; lobster, scallops, crabs, fish; potatoes; dairying. Includes cluster of towns of New Glasgow, Trenton, Stellarton, and Westville. Ferries to P.E.I. and Pictou Isl. from Caribou.

Pictou (PIK-too, pik-TOO), town (1991 pop. 4,134), N N.S., Canada, on Pictou Harbour, an inlet of Northumberland Strait; 45°41′N 62°43′W. A lobster-fishing port; terminal of a ferry to P.E.I. and to Pictou Isl., 5 mi N at Caribou. Has lumbering and light industries; coal mines (declining) in the area. Pictou was settled (1763) by a group of colonists from Philadelphia and later received many settlers from the Scottish Highlands.

Pictou Island, Northumberland Strait, bet. N N.S., and SE P.E.I., Canada, 10 mi/16 km NE of Pictou; 5 mi/8 km long, 2 mi/3 km wide; 45°50′N 62°34′W.

Picture Butte, town (1991 pop. 1,559), S Alta., Canada, 14 mi/23 km N of Lethbridge. Coal mining, beet-sugar refining; wheat, flax; cattle.

Picture Rocks, borough (1990 pop. 660), Lycoming co., N central Pa., 17 mi/27 km ENE of Williamsport, on Muncy Creek; 41°16′N 76°42′W. Agr. (potatoes; livestock; dairying; timber); mfg. (wood prods., turkey calls). Tiadaghton State Forest to N.

Pictured Rocks National Lakeshore (□ 114 sq mi/295 sq km), N Mich.; 42 mi/68 km long, c. 5 mi/8 km wide; 46°33′N 86°19′W. Sandstone cliffs, sand dunes, beaches, marshes, waterfalls, and inland lakes along L. Superior; the 1st natl. lakeshore. Extends along lake from Grand Marais in E to South Bay, near Munising in W. Cruises from Munising. Rock formations include Minnie's Castle, Battleship Rock, Indian Colored Rocks. Lakes include Beaver, Grand Sable, Chapel, Noble, and Trappers. Area has rich history in logging, trapping, and maritime activities. Camping, fishing, and cross-country skiing. Munising Falls and Miners Falls. Authorized 1966.

Pie Island, W Ont., Canada, in L. Superior, at entrance of Thunder Bay, 10 mi/16 km SE of Fort William; 8 mi/13 km long, 4 mi/6 km wide.

Pie Town, uninc. village, Catron co., W N.Mex., 60 mi/97 km SW of Grants. Cattle, sheep, goats. Mfg. (goats' milk processing). Part of Cibola Natl. Forest to E; part of Apache-Sitgreaves Natl. Forest to SW. Continental Divide skirts village to N, E, and S.

Piedad, La, Mexico: see LA PIEDAD DE CABADAS.

Piedmont, generally rolling upland region (□ c.80,000 sq mi/207,200 sq km) of the E U.S., bordering the Older Appalachian Mts. (of which it is physiographically the non-mountainous part) on the E, from N.J. on the NE to central Ala. on the SW. Inner boundary is E base of the Blue Ridge, except in S Pa. and at SW end, where it directly adjoins the Great Appalachian Valley. Alt. of inner edge is low in N (under 300 ft. in

N.J.) and rises S to c.1,800 ft. in Ga. Its E boundary is the transition zone (the FALL LINE) where it meets the coastal plain. Piedmont soils, generally clayey, are moderately fertile, but have suffered much from erosion and over-cropping, particularly in S Piedmont (from central N.C. across S.C. and Ga.), where cotton is the chief crop. From central N.C. to central Va. tobacco dominates; N lies a belt producing fruit (especially apples), fine livestock (especially horses), and general farm crops; northernmost sect. (Md. and Pa.) has prosperous general farming and dairying.

Piedmont 1 city (1990 pop. 5,288), Calhoun co., NE Ala., 12 mi/19 km ESE of Gadsden; 33°55'N 85°37'W. In dairying and grain area; mfg. (transportation equip., cotton yarn and textiles, lumber). Iron mines nearby. Part of Talladega Natl. Forest just S. **2** city (1990 pop. 10,602), Alameda co., W Calif., a residential suburb 13 mi/21 km NE of downtown Oakland, bounded on all sides by city of Oakland; 37°49'N 122°14'W. Many of its homes and streets enjoy a spectacular view of the San Francisco Bay area. Inc. 1907. **3** city (1990 pop. 2,166), Wayne co., SE Mo., near Black R., 32 mi/51 km NW of Poplar Bluff; 37°08'N 90°42'W. Agr. center (cattle and fruit); lumber mills; mfg. (leather prods.). Clearwater Lake and Dam are W.

Piedmont 1 (PEED-mahnt), town, Lamar co., W central Ga., 6 mi/9.7 km WSW of Barnesville; 33°01'N 84°15'W. **2** town (1990 pop. 2,522), Canadian co., central Okla., residential suburb 17 mi/27 km NW of downtown Oklahoma City, and 12 mi/19 km NE of El Reno; 35°40'N 97°45'W. Agr. area (wheat; dairying; cattle); light mfg. **3** town (1990 pop. 1,094), Mineral co., NE W.Va., 5 mi/8 km WNW of Keyser, in Eastern Panhandle, on North Branch of the Potomac R. (bridged) opposite Westernport (Md.); 39°28'N 79°02'W. Agr. (grain, tobacco); livestock, poultry. Light mfg. Chartered 1856.

Piedmont (PEED-mahnt), village (1991 pop. 1,514), S Que., Canada, in the Laurentians, on the North R., and 40 mi/64 km NW of Montreal. Dairying; ski resort.

Piedmont 1 (PEED-mahnt), village (1990 pop. 4,143), Anderson and Greenville cos., NW S.C., on Saluda R., and 10 mi/16 km S of Greenville; 34°42'N 82°27'W. **2** village, Meade co., W S.Dak., 15 mi/24 km NW of Rapid City, at NE edge of Black Hills (?is)& Black Hills Natl. Forest; 44°13'N 103°23'W. Elev. 3,463 ft/1,056 m. Supply point for ranching region; tourist trade; wood fuel pellets. Petrified forest to E, and Crystal and Wonderland caves.

Piedmont Lake, reservoir (□ 3 sq mi/7.8 sq km), Belmont and Harrison cos., E central Ohio, on Stillwater Creek, 25 mi/40 km WNW of Wheeling (W.Va.); 40°11'N 81°13'W. Max. capacity 6,670 acre-ft. Formed by Piedmont Dam (45 ft/14 m high), built (1937) by Army Corps of Engineers for flood control; also used for recreation and as a fish and wildlife pond.

Piedmont Reservoir, Ohio: see STILLWATER CREEK.

Piedra Blanca (pee-AI-drah BLAHN-kah), village (1993 pop. 6,346), La Vega prov., central Dominican Republic, in the Cordillera Central, 9 mi/14.5 km SE of Bonao. In agr. region (tobacco, cacao, cereals). Manganese deposit nearby.

Piedras Blancas, Point, San Luis Obispo co., SW Calif., promontory on the Pacific Ocean, c.35 mi/56 km W of Paso Robles, 5 mi/8 km WNW of San Simeon. Lighthouse.

Piedras Negras, city (1990 pop. 96,178) and township, Piedras Negras municipio, Coahuila state, N Mexico, on the Rio Grande opposite Eagle Pass, Texas; 38°42'N 100°31'W. Commercial and processsing center for the surrounding agr. region. Founded in 1849, the city grew as an international shipping point. In 1888, Piedras Negras was renamed Ciudad Porfirio Díaz in honor of the dictator, but the old name was restored after his overthrow in 1911.

Piedrecitas (pee-ai-drai-SEE-tuhz), town, Camagüey prov., E Cuba, on RR, and 31 mi/50 km NW of Camagüey; 21°34'N 78°19'W. Sugarcane; cattle. Sugar mills República Dominicana (SSE) and Carlos Manuel de Céspedes (SE) nearby.

Pierce 1 (PIRS), county (□ 344 sq mi/891 sq km; 1990 pop. 13,328), SE Ga.; ⊙ Blackshear; 31°22'N 82°13'W. Bounded S by Satilla R., NE by Little Satilla R.; drained by small Alabaha R. Mfg. apparel and textiles. Coastal plain agr. (tobacco, cotton, soybeans, corn); cattle, hogs, poultry; eggs. Formed 1857. **2** county (□ 575 sq mi/1,489 sq km; 1990 pop. 7,827), NE Nebr.; ⊙ Pierce; 42°16'N 97°36'W. Agr. region drained by branches of Elkhorn R. Cattle, hogs; dairying; corn, alfalfa; dairy prods. Formed 1856. **3** county (□ 1,037 sq mi/2,686 sq km; 1990 pop. 5,052), N central N.Dak.; ⊙ Rugby; 48°15'N 99°58'W. Agr. area watered by numerous mid-sized lakes. Dairy prods.; wheat, barley, rye; cattle. Geographical center of North Amer. in N, S of Rugby; Round L. in NW. Formed 1887. **4** county (□ 1,807 sq mi/4,680 sq km; 1990 pop. 586,203), W central Wash.; ⊙ Tacoma; 47°03'N 122°07'W. E boundary formed by crest of Cascade Range. Drained by White (forms part of N boundary), Puyallup, Nisqually (forms most of S boundary), and Carbon rivers. Rich agr. area (berries, lettuce, hay, daffodil bulbs, fresh flowers); dairying; poultry, cattle. W part of co. around Tacoma (NW) and along Puget Sound is urbanized. Fort Lewis Military Reservation and McChord Air Force Base in SW. County includes SE part of Kitsap Peninsula (W boundary formed by Case Inlet), separated from remainder of co. by Puget Sound; also includes McNeil, Fox, and Anderson isls. in Puget Sound. Penrose Point State Park in W (Kitsap Peninsula); Crystal Mt. Ski Resort at E boundary. Includes most of Mt. Rainier Natl. Park and part of Mt. Baker–Snoqualmie Natl. Forest, both in E; latter includes Clearwater Wilderness Area and part of Norse Peak Wilderness Area. Formed 1852. **5** county (□ 591 sq mi/1,531 sq km; 1990 pop. 32,765), W Wis.; ⊙ Ellsworth; 44°43'N 92°25'W. Bounded W by St. Croix R., SW and S by the Mississippi (L. Pepin in S), all forming Minn. state line. Generally rugged terrain, with dairying and livestock raising (cattle, hogs, sheep) as chief industries; also barley, oats, corn, soybeans, hay; poultry; lumbering; mfg. at River Falls. Lock and Dam No. 3 on Mississippi R. in SW; Kinnickinnic State Park in NW. Formed 1853.

Pierce 1 town (1990 pop. 823), Weld co., N Colo., 15 mi/24 km N of Greeley; 40°37'N 104°45'W. Elev. 5,039 ft/1,536 m. In irrigated, sugar-beet area. Pawnee Natl. Grassland to NE. **2** town (1990 pop. 746), Clearwater co., N Idaho, 22 mi/35 km E of Orofino; 46°29'N 115°48'W. Cattle; alfalfa, barley; mfg. (cedar prods., logs); timber. Summer resort and outfitting point in elk hunting region. First Idaho gold discovery made here (1860). Bald Mt. Ski Area to NW; Clearwater Natl. Forest to E. **3** town (1990 pop. 1,615), ⊙ Pierce co., NE Nebr., 13 mi/21 km NNW of Norfolk, and on branch of Elkhorn R.; 42°12'N 97°31'W. Grain; livestock; dairy prods. Settled 1870.

Pierce Bridge, N.H.: see BETHLEHEM.

Pierce City (1990 pop. 1,382), Lawrence co., SW Mo., in the Ozarks, 30 mi/48 km ESE of Joplin; 36°57'N 94°00'W. Corn, wheat, fruit; dairying; cattle; lime prods. Founded c.1870.

Pierce, Mount, N.H.: see PRESIDENTIAL RANGE.

Pierceton, town (1990 pop. 1,030), Kosciusko co., N central Ind., 8 mi/12.9 km ESE of Warsaw; 41°12'N 85°43'W. Mfg. (fabricated metal prods.). Corn, soybeans; poultry, cattle; lumber. Resort lakes nearby to N.

Piermont (PEER-mawnt), town (1990 pop. 624), Grafton co., W N.H., 23 mi/37 km NNE of Lebanon; 43°59'N 72°01'W. Bounded W by Connecticut R. (Vt. state line); drained by Eastman Brook. Agr. (cattle, poultry; dairying; vegetables, nursery crops). Piermont Mt. (2,721 ft/829 m) in E.

Piermont, residential village (□ 1 sq mi/2.6 sq km; 1990 pop. 2,163), Rockland co., SE N.Y., on W bank of the Hudson R., and 3 mi/4.8 km S of Nyack; 41°02'N 73°55'W. Until the 1980s, mfg. (paperboard, silk ribbons). Site of Camp Shanks, which was operational during World Wars I and II. Pier (1 mi/1.6 km long) from which village takes its name was used for embarkation of troops. Site where 1983 Woody Allen movie *The Purple Rose of Cairo* was filmed. Tallman Mt. State Park nearby. Inc. 1847.

Pierpont, village (1990 pop. 173), Day co., NE S.Dak., 18 mi/29 km NW of Webster; 45°30'N 97°49'W. In agr. area (livestock, poultry; dairy prods.; grain).

Pierre (PIR) city (1990 pop. 12,906), state ⊙ (since 1889) and seat of Hughes co., central S.Dak., on E bank of Missouri R., opposite town of Fort Pierre; 44°22'N 100°19'W. Its economy is centered around agr. (chiefly grains and cattle), tourism, and the state govt. Mfg. (electrical equip., irrigation equip.; printing). Originally the fortified capital of the Aricara, Pierre served as the trade center of the middle Missouri R. from 1822 to 1855. From 1876 to 1885 it was the steamboat head for the Black Hills gold trade. The city boomed with the arrival of the RR (1880), becoming an important trading and shipping center for a farm and ranch area. In Central time zone; Mountain-Central time zone boundary follows Mo. R. S to Pierre/Ft. Pierre, then veers SW across land. A U.S. Native Amer. school is here. Oahe Dam, a major unit of the Missouri R. basin project, 6 mi/9.7 km NNW. Pierre Regional Airport; S.Dak. Cultural Heritage Center; S.Dak. Discovery Center and Aquarium. Farm Isl. State Rec. Area and Fort Pierre Natl. Grassland to S. Fort Pierre (1832) to W. Inc. 1883.

Pierre, Bayou (pee-YER, BEI-yoo), c.85 mi/137 km long, NW La., rises in city of Shreveport; flows generally SE, through Wallace L. reservoir (3 mi/5 km long), past Hanna and Powhatan, to Red R. c.5 mi/8 km N of Natchitoches. Formerly an auxiliary channel of Red R.

Pierre Bayou, c.50 mi/80 km long, SW Miss.; rises in N Lincoln co.; flows WSW, past Port Gibson, to the Mississippi R. in SW Claiborne co., 13 mi/21 km WSW of Port Gibson.

Pierre Part (Pierre Pass) (pee-YER), uninc. town (1990 pop. 3,053), Assumption parish, La., 11 mi/18 km NW of Napoleonville; 29°57'N 91°12'W. Crawfish ponds; oil and gas field nearby. Bayou Pierre Part is a small stream that empties into L. Verret. Fr.-speaking area. Ancestral center of Sp. moss collection.

Pierreville (PYER-vil), village (1991 pop. 1,074), S Que., Canada, on St. Francis R., near its mouth on the St. Lawrence R., 15 mi/24 km E of Sorel; 46°04'N 72°48'W. Lumbering, woodworking, dairying.

Pierron (PEER-ron), village (1990 pop. 554), in Bond and Madison cos., SW central Ill., 13 mi/21 km WSW of Greenville; 38°46'N 89°34'W. In agr. area (corn, wheat, soybeans, sorghum; dairy prods.; poultry).

Pierson 1 (PIR-suhn), town (□ 8 sq mi/20.7 sq km; 1990 pop. 2,988), Volusia co., E central Fla., near L. George, 27 mi/43 km W of Daytona Beach; 29°14'N 81°27'W. **2** town (1990 pop. 341), Woodbury co., W Iowa, 27 mi/43 km E of Sioux City; 42°32'N 95°52'W. Livestock; grain.

Pierson, village (1990 pop. 207), Montcalm co., central Mich., 26 mi/42 km NNE of Grand Rapids; 43°19'N 85°30'W. In lake and farm area.

Pierz (PIRZ), town (1990 pop. 1,014), Morrison co., central Minn., 14 mi/23 km E of Little Falls, on Skunk R., at mouth of Hillman Creek; 45°58'N 94°05'W. In agr. area; dairying; livestock; grain, potatoes, sunflowers; mfg. (redwood doors, concrete, feeds, fabricated metal prods.). Pierz L. to SW.

Pigeon, town (1990 pop. 1,207), Huron co., E Mich., 18 mi/29 km W of Bad Axe, and on small Pigeon R.; 43°49'N 83°16'W. Grain, beans, sugar beets; livestock; dairy prods. Mfg. (feeds; machining, steel casting, publishing).

Pigeon Cove, Mass.: see ROCKPORT.

Pigeon Creek 1 c.55 mi/89 km long, S Ala.; formed by confluence of several headstreams E of Greenville; flows SSW to Sepulga R. 13 mi/21 km W of Andalusia. **2** c.65 mi/105 km long, NE Ind. and S Mich.; rises in extreme NE Steuben co. near Mich. state line, flows SW, NW, and W, and widens into several small lakes, reaching Mongo Reservoir in N Lagrange co. Issues

Cross references are shown in SMALL CAPITALS. The pronunciation key is on page xv. The dates of population figures are on page xii.

from reservoir as Pigeon R., flows NW into Mich., to join St. Joseph R. near Ind. state line.

Pigeon Falls, village (1990 pop. 289), Trempealeau co., W Wis., 28 mi/45 km SSE of Eau Claire; 44°25'N 91°12'W. Dairying; poultry; corn, soybeans, alfalfa. Mfg. (consumer goods).

Pigeon Forge, city (1990 pop. 3,027), Sevier co., NE Tenn., on the Little Pigeon R., 7 mi/11 km SSE of Sevierville; 35°47'N 83°33'W. In scenic mtn. area; tourism, shops, crafts. Dollywood entertainment complex is located here. Great Smoky Mts. Natl. Park is nearby. Inc. 1961.

Pigeon Island, islet, connected by causeway (1970) to NW St. Lucia, 6 mi/9.7 km NNE of Castries; ½ mi/8/10 km long, ¾ mi/1.2 km wide; 14°06'N 60°58'W. Elev. 334 ft/102 m. Uninhabited, but a popular picnic resort. Historic point, from whence Rodney watched movements of the Fr. fleet. Now St. Lucia Natl. Trust Park with ruins of fortification, small mus. See RODNEY BAY.

Pigeon Island, tiny islet off S Jamaica, St. Catherine parish, at entrance of Old Harbour Bay, 22 mi/35 km SW of Kingston; 17°48'N 77°5'W. Covers roughly 50 acres/20 ha; formerly leased to U.S. in 1940.

Pigeon Lake, Kawartha Lakes, S Ont., Canada, 10 mi/16 km WNW of Peterborough; 18 mi/29 km long, 1 mi/2 km–5 mi/8 km wide. Drained E by Trent Canal.

Pigeon Point (PAI-jahn), headland, SW Tobago, Trinidad and Tobago, 12 mi/19 km W of Scarborough, 0.9 mi/1.5 km N of Store Bay and just N of Crown Point Airport; 11°10'N 60°50'W. Has isl.'s principal bathing beach. Public beach facilities, hotels.

Pigeon Point, coastal promontory, San Mateo co., W Calif., SW of Pescadero, 37 mi/60 km S of San Francisco. Lighthouse.

Pigeon River, 49 mi/79 km long, on U.S./Canada border, in Cook co., NE Minn. and Thunder Bay dist., W Ont.; rises in North and South Fork lakes, flows SE and E, through Partridge Falls and Pigeon Falls (near mouth) to L. Superior 6 mi/9.7 km NE of Grand Portage, Minn., and 30 mi/48 km SSW of Thunder Bay, Ont.; 48°02'N 89°49'W. Drains several small lakes in its course. Upper course forms N boundary of Grand Portage State Forest, lower course forms N boundary of Grand Portage Indian Reservation; Grand Portage Trail, historical Indian and fur-trading portage, reaches river below Partridge Falls. Partially in Grand Portage Indian Reservation.

Pigeon River, c.100 mi/161 km long, N.C. and Tenn.; rises in the Blue Ridge Mts., in S Haywood co., W N.C.; flows NNW, past Canton and through Waterville L. reservoir, bet. Great Smoky Mts. (SW) and Bald Mts (NE) and into Tenn. past Newport, then joins French Broad R. 4 mi/6.4 km N of Newport in upper reach of Douglas L. reservoir.

Pigeon River, Ind.: see PIGEON CREEK.

Piggott (PIG-uht), town (1990 pop. 3,777), ⊙ Clay co., extreme NE Ark., 28 mi/45 km NE of Paragould, on E slope of Crowley's Ridge; 36°22'N 90°12'W. In farm and orchard area. Mfg. (esp. wood prods.).

Pignon (pee-NYONG), town (1982 pop. 4,576), Nord dept., N central Haiti, in Massif du Nord, 31 mi/50 km SSE of Cap-Haïtien; 19°20'N 72°07'W. Agr. (coffee, oranges, limes); cattle; bee-keeping; timber.

Pihuamo (pee-WAH-mo), town (1990 pop. 8,325), ⊙ Pihuamo municipio, Jalisco, W Mexico, 23 mi/37 km E of Colima; 19°15'N 103°23'W. Corn, sugarcane, chickpeas, fruit.

Pijijiápan (pee-hee-hee-AH-pahn), city (1990 pop. 12,103) and township, Chiapas, S Mexico, in Pacific lowland, on RR, and 45 mi/72 km SE of Tonalá; 15°42'N 93°12'W. Cacao, sugarcane, tobacco, fruit; livestock.

Pike 1 county (□ 672 sq mi/1,740 sq km; 1990 pop. 27,595), SE Ala.; ⊙ Troy. Coastal plain drained by Conecuh R., Pea R., and Patsaliga Creek. Peanuts, corn, hay; poultry, cattle. Formed 1822. **2** county (□ 613 sq mi/1,588 sq km; 1990 pop. 10,086), SW Ark.; ⊙ Murfreesboro; 34°10'N 93°39'W. Bounded S in part by Little Missouri R.; on E in part by Antoine R., drained by Little Missouri in center, by Cadd R. in NE corner. Agr. (cattle, hogs, chickens). Manganese and quicksilver mines; diamond mines (now inactive); Crater of Diamonds State Park in S; only commercially viable diamond reserve in N. America. Gypsum quarries; lumbering. Large L. Greerson in W center, formed by Narrows Dam on Little Missouri R. L. Greerson Wildlife Management Area to W of lake; Daisy State Park on N shore; small part of Ouachita Natl. Forest on N boundary. Formed 1833. **3** county (□ 219 sq mi/567 sq km; 1990 pop. 10,224), W central Ga.; ⊙ Zebulon; 33°06'N 84°26'W. Bounded W by Flint R. Piedmont agr. (cotton, peaches, corn, soybeans, wheat); cattle, poultry; mfg. of food prods. In timber area; sawmilling. Formed 1822. **4** county (□ 848 sq mi/2,196 sq km; 1990 pop. 17,577), W Ill.; ⊙ Pittsfield; 39°37'N 90°53'W. Bounded W and SW by Mississippi R. and E by Illinois R.; drained by small Bay and McCraney creeks. Agr. (corn, wheat, hay, sorghum, apples, cattle, hogs). Some mfg. (flour; cheese and other dairy prods.). Includes Upper Mississippi Wildlife Refuge, on the Mississippi and Ray Norbut State Fish and Wildlife Area, on the Ill. Formed 1821. **5** county (□ 341 sq mi/883 sq km; 1990 pop. 12,509), SW Ind.; ⊙ Petersburg; 38°24'N 87°14'W. Bounded N by White R. and its East Fork; drained by Patoka R. Bituminous-coal mines, oil wells, clay pits; timber; agr. (grain, livestock); mfg. at Petersburg. Formed 1816. **6** county (□ 788 sq mi/2,041 sq km; 1990 pop. 72,583), E Ky., in the Cumberland Mts. Bounded NE by Tug Fork (W.Va. state line), SE by Va. state line, drained by Levisa and Russell fork rivers; ⊙ Pikeville; 37°28'N 82°23'W. Bituminous coal-mining region; one of the leading Ky. cos. in coal production; some agr. (livestock; hay); timber; some mfg. at Pikeville. Includes Breaks of Big Sandy R. (in Breaks Interstate Park) and part of Pine Mt. inpart of Jefferson Natl. Forest, both on Va. border in SE. Fishtrap L. reservoir in center. Largest co. in Ky. Formed 1821. **7** county (□ 410 sq mi/1,062 sq km; 1990 pop. 36,882), SW Miss.; ⊙ Magnolia; 31°10'N 90°24'W. Bordered S by La. state line; drained by the Bogue Chitto and Tangipahoa rivers. Agr. (cotton, corn; cattle; dairying; timber). Percy Quin State Park in W. Formed 1815. **8** county (□ 681 sq mi/1,764 sq km; 1990 pop. 15,969), E Mo.; ⊙ Bowling Green; 39°20'N 91°10'W. Bounded E by Mississippi R.; crossed by Salt R. Wheat, corn, soybeans, fruit (especially apples; cattle, hogs; limestone; mfg. at Bowling Green and Louisiana. Ted Shanks Conservation Area and DuPont Reservation at Ashburn. Amish community near Curryville. Formed 1818. **9** county (□ 443 sq mi/1,147 sq km; 1990 pop. 24,249), S Ohio; ⊙ Waverly; 39°04'N 83°04'W. Intersected by Scioto R. and small Sunfish and Beaver creeks. Includes L. White State Park (resort). In the Unglaciated Plains physiographic region. Agr. area (cattle, poultry; corn); hardwood timber; sawmilling, mfg. (wood prods., chemicals, transportation equip.). Formed 1815. **10** county (□ 566 sq mi/1,466 sq km; 1990 pop. 27,966), NE Pa.; ⊙ Milford; 41°19'N 75°01'W. Forested lake region, bounded NE and SE by Delaware R., which forms N.Y. state line (NE) and N.J. state line (SE). Agr. (hay; cattle; dairying); timber. Recreational area. Much of co. covered by sects. of Delaware State Forest; numerous small reservoirs and ponds throughout co., upon which are several residential developments; part of Delaware Water Gap Natl. Recreation Area in SE; Promised Land State Park in W. Formed 1814.

Pike, village (1990 pop. 384), Wyoming co., W N.Y., 17 mi/27 km S of Warsaw, and on small Wiscoy Creek; 42°33'N 78°09'W. In agr. area.

Pike, Ark.: see PIKE CITY.

Pike City, village, Pike co., SW Ark., 30 mi/48 km W of Arkadelphia. Formerly Pike.

Pike Creek, uninc. town (1990 est. pop. 10,163) New Castle co., N Del., 9 mi W of downtown Wilimington, 5 mi NE Newark; 39°44'N 75°42'W. Suburban residential community bet. Wilimington and Newark.

Pike, Fort orleans parish, SE La., old U.S. fortification built in early 19th cent., on bank of Rigolets pass, 30 mi/48 km ENE of downtown New Orleans; 30°09'N 89°44'W. Covers 94 acres/38 ha. Designated a state commemorative area.

Pikes Peak (14,110 ft/4,301 m), El Paso co., central Colo., in the Front Range of the Rocky Mts., 12 mi/19 km W of Colorado Springs, in Pike Natl. Forest; 38°50'N 105°02'W. Discovered by U.S. explorer Zebulon Pike in 1806. There are many higher peaks in the Rockies, but this is the best known and most conspicuous because of its location on the edge of the Great Plains. At its E base is Colorado Springs; to the N is Denver. Its summit, generally snow covered, is reached by a cog RR and a road. Visitors center at summit.

Pikesville, uninc. city (1990 pop. 24,815), Baltimore co., central Md., residential suburb NW of Baltimore; 39°23'N 76°42'W. It was named for Zeublon Pike, the discoverer of Pike's Peak, by Dr. James Smith. Smith himself introduced vaccination in America for which he was given the title U.S. Agent of Vaccination. A U.S. Arsenal here (c.1819) became a Confederate soldiers home in 1888, the only one outside the Confederate states. It now houses offices of the Md. State Police. Irvine Natural Science Center c.3 mi/4.8 km NE. Settled in the late 18th cent, this former suburb is now very urbanized.

Piketon, village (1990 pop. 1,717), Pike co., S Ohio, on Scioto R. and 18 mi/29 km S of Chilicothe; 39°04'N 82°59'W. Grain prods., lumber. Piketon Nuclear Regulatory Commission plant reprocesses military uranium stockpiles into nuclear reactor fuels.

Pikeville 1 town (1990 pop. 6,324), E Ky., in the Cumberland Mts., 120 mi/193 km ESE of Lexington, on Levisa Fork; ⊙ Pike co.; 37°28'N 82°30'W. Elev. 685 ft/209 m. Trade and shipping center for bituminous coal-mining and timber region; mfg. (printing and publishing, fabricated metal prods., concrete); coal mining. Pike County Airport to NW. Seat of Pikeville Col. (4-year). Hatfield and McCoy Historic Dist. Fishtrap L. reservoir to SE. **2** town (1990 pop. 1,771), central Tenn., on Sequatchie R. and 40 mi. N of Chattanooga; ⊙ Bledsoe co.; 35°36'N 85°11'W. In coal, timber, and farm region; mfg. of transportation equip.

Pikeville, village (1990 pop. 598), Wayne co., E central N.C., 7 mi/11.3 km N of Goldsboro; 35°30'N 77°58'W. Tobacco, grain, cotton, soybeans; poultry, livestock. Mfg. (apparel, food). Charles B. Aycock Birthplace State Historical Site to N.

Pikmiktalik, Inuit village, W Alaska, near Pastol Bay, 22 mi/35 km SW of St. Michael.

Pilate (pee-LAHT), town (1982 pop. 2,874), Nord dept., N Haiti, in the Massif du Nord, on Les Trois Riviéres and 23 mi/37 km WSW of Cap-Haïtien; 19°40'N 72°33'W. Agr. (coffee, tropical fruit, cacao).

Pilcaya (peel-KAH-yah), town (1990 pop. 3,599), Guerrero, SW Mexico, on S slope of central plateau, on Mexico state border, 13 mi/21 km NNW of Taxco de Alarcón; 18°13'N 98°42'W. Cereals, sugarcane, coffee, fruit.

Pile Bay, village, SW Alaska, on E shore of Iliamna L.; 59°43'N 154°04'W.

Pilger (PIL-juhr), village (1990 pop. 361), Stanton co., NE Nebr., 10 mi/16 km ENE of Stanton and on Elkhorn R.; 42°00'N 97°02'W. In hog-raising area; dairy, poultry prods., grain.

Pilgrim Nuclear Power Plant, Massachusetts: see PLYMOUTH, CO.

Pilgrim Springs, village, NW Alaska, on Seward Peninsula, 45 mi/72 km NNE of Nome. Airstrip.

Pillager (PI-luh-juhr), village (1990 pop. 306), Cass co., central Minn., 13 mi/21 km W of Brainerd, Crow Wing R.; 46°19'N 94°28'W. Dairying; poultry, cattle; oats, alfalfa, timber; light mfg. Gull L. to NE; Pillsbury State Forest to N; Camp Ripley Military Reserve to SE.

Pillar Point, Calif.: see HALF MOON BAY.

Pilley's Island (□ 17 sq mi/44 sq km), E N.F., Canada, in Notre Dame Bay, 40 mi/64 km W of Twillingate; 6 mi/10 km long, 4 mi/6 km wide; 49°32'N 55°43'W. Fishing.

Pillow, borough (1990 pop. 341), Dauphin co., E central Pa., on Mahantango Creek, 26 mi/42 km N of Harrisburg; 40°38'N 76°48'W. Agr. includes grain; poultry, livestock, dairying. Mahatango Mt. ridge to S.

Pillsbury, village (1990 pop. 31), Barnes co., E central N.Dak., 22 mi/35 km NNE of Valley City; 47°12′N 97°47′W. L. Ashtabula Reservoir to W (Sibley Crossing).

Pillsbury, Lake, reservoir (5 mi/8 km long), Lake co., NW Calif., on Eel R., in Coast Range, in Mendocino Natl. Forest, 25 mi/40 km N of Lakeport; 39°24′N 122°58′W. Has large N bay (2 mi/3.2 km long, 1.5 mi/2.4 km wide). Rice Fork R. enters from SE. Formed by Scott Dam. Gravelly Valley Airport at N end.

Pilón (pee-LON), small port town, Granma prov., SE Cuba, on Caribbean Sea; 19°54′N 77°20′W. Site of Luis Carracedo sugar mill.

Pilot Grove, city (1990 pop. 714), Cooper co., central Mo., 12 mi/19 km SW of Boonville; 38°52′N 92°54′W. Wheat, corn; cattle. Platted 1873.

Pilot Knob, town (1990 pop. 783), Iron co., SE central Mo., St. Francis Mts., just NNW of Ironton. Historic iron mine. Civil War battle of Pilot Knob, fought Sept. 27, 1864, resulted in reverse for Confederates under Sterling Price. Settled 1834, platted 1858; 37°37′N 90°38′W. Light mfg.

Pilot Mound, town (1990 pop. 199), Boone co., central Iowa, near Des Moines R., 10 mi/16 km NW of Boone; 42°09′N 94°01′W.

Pilot Mound, village (1991 pop. 747), S Man., Canada, in Pembina Mts., 60 mi/97 km SW of Portage la Prairie; 49°12′N 98°54′W. Grain elevators.

Pilot Mountain, town (1990 pop. 1,181), Surry co., NW N.C., 23 mi/37 km NNW of Winston-Salem; 36°22′N 80°28′W. Agr. area (tobacco, grain, soybeans, poultry, livestock, dairying); mfg. (textiles and apparel, rope, fabricated metal prods., lumber). Pilot Mt. State Park (2,440 ft/744 m), to S.

Pilot Point, town (1990 pop. 2,538), Denton co., N Texas, 18 mi/29 km NE of Denton; 33°23′N 96°57′W. In agr. area (cotton, wheat, peanuts; cattle); mfg. (wood prods., apparel); oil wells. L. Ray Roberts reservoir to W. Settled 1835, inc. 1906.

Pilot Point, village (1990 pop. 53), SW Alaska, on Alaska Peninsula, on Ugashik Bay, E arm (10 mi/16 km long) of Bristol Bay, 45 mi/72 km S of Egegik; 57°34′N 157°35′W. Fishing (cannery at Ugashik, 6 mi/9.7 km E).

Pilot Rock, town (1990 pop. 1,478), Umatilla co., NE Oregon, 13 mi/21 km S of Pendleton on Birch Creek, at mouth of E Birch Creek; 45°28′N 118°49′W. Apples, plums; sheep, cattle. Umatilla Indian Reservation and McKay Creek Natl. Wildlife Refuge and Reservoir to NE.

Pilot Station, village (1990 pop. 463), W Alaska, on lower Yukon R. and 90 mi/145 km NW of Bethel; 61°56′N 162°52′W. Also called Pilot Village.

Pilot Village, Alaska: see PILOT STATION.

Pilottown (PEI laht-toun), village, Plaquemines parish, extreme SE La., 75 mi/121 km SE of New Orleans and on E bank of the Mississippi R., in the delta just above Head of the Passes (junction of North, South, and Southwest Passes, the 3 mouths that take the Mississippi waters from its main channel into the Gulf); 29°10′N 89°15′W. Oil deposits, pipelines. Located in Delta Natl. Wildlife Refuge. Hunting, fur trapping, fishing nearby. Pass a Loutre State Wildlife Area to SE.

Piltzville, village (1990 pop. 500), Missoula co., W Mont., 7 mi/11.3 km E of Missoula, on Clark Fork R. Timber; cattle, horses; hay. Lolo Natl. Forest to N and S. Formerly called Plitz Addition.

Pim Island, NE Franklin dist., N.W.T., Canada, in Smith Sound, off Cape Sabine, E Ellesmere Isl.; 8 mi/13 km long, 4 mi/6 km wide; 78°44′N 74°40′W. Donald MacMillan here erected (1924) memorial tablet to members of Greely expedition who died at Cape Sabine, 1884.

Pima (PEE-mah), county (□ 9,189 sq mi/23,800 sq km; 1990 pop. 666,880), S Ariz.; ⊙ Tucson; 32°06′N 111°48′W. Mt. area bordering on Mexico (Sonora) on S. Santa Catalina Mts. and Santa Rita Mts. in NE, Growler Mts. in W, Baboquivari Mts. in S. Drained by Santa Cruz and Rillito rivers (intermittent) in E. Saguaro Natl. Monument is E of Tucson; Organ Pipe Cactus Natl. Monument in W; part of large Tohono O'Odham (Papago) Indian Reservation in W center. Irrigated farming (cattle; cotton, sugar beets, barley and lettuce) along Santa Cruz R. (NE); copper, gold, silver, lead mines near Ajo (NW); health resorts around Tucson. Kitt Park Observatory at center; San Xavier and Pascua Yaqui Indian reservations in E center; city of Tucson in NE center; parts of Coronado Natl. Forest in NE, E, and SE; Catalina State Park in NE; Saguaro Natl. Monument (2 units; Tucson Mt. and Rincon Mt.) in NE; Spencer Canyon Ski Area in NE; part of large Cabeza Prieta Natl. Wildlife Refuge in W, boundary overlaps Goldwater (formerly Luke) Air Force Range. Formed 1864; 14th largest co. in U.S.

Pima, town (1990 pop. 1,725), Graham co., SE Ariz., on Gila R. and 8 mi/12.9 km NW of Safford; 32°53′N 109°49′W. Mfg. (transportation equip.); agr. trade center. Part of Coronado Natl. Forest to S.

Pimentel (pee-men-TEL), town (1993 pop. 9,793), Duarte prov., E central Dominican Republic, in fertile La Vega Real valley, on RR and 13 mi/21 km SE of San Francisco de Macorís; 19°13′N 70°10′W. Cacao growing.

Pimería Alta (pee-me-REE-ah AHL-tah), region in the U.S. Southwest and N Mexico, chiefly in SW Ariz. and NW Sonora. It was inhabited by the Pima Indians and was the scene of the missionary labors of Father Eusebio Kino in the late 17th and early 18th cents.

Pimlico Race Track, Md.: see BALTIMORE.

Pimmit Hills, uninc. town, Fairfax co., NE Va., residential suburb 9 mi/14.5 km W of Washington, D.C., on Capital Beltway highway; 38°54′N 77°12′W.

Pinal (PEE-nal), county (□ 5,374 sq mi/13,919 sq km; 1990 pop. 116,379), S central Ariz.; ⊙ Florence; 32°54′N 111°20′W. Plateau and mesa region. San Carlos Reservoir (in NE) holds water from Gila and San Carlos rivers for irrigation. Cotton, alfalfa, hay, wheat, barley, citrus fruits, vegetables, sheep, hogs, cattle, poultry. Copper mining at Ray, S of Superior. Co. includes Ak-Chin Indian Reservation and part of Gila R. Indian Reservation; part of Tohono O'odham (Papago) Indian Reservation in SW, part of San Carlos Indian Reservation in NE. Casa Grande Natl. Monument is N of Coolidge, at center; McFarland State Historic Park in center, at Florence. Lost Dutchman State Park in N; part of Tonto Natl. Forest in N, includes Boyce Thompson State Arboretum; small part of Coronado Natl. Forest, including Santa Catalina Mts., in S; part of Table Top Wilderness Area on W boundary, part of Aravaipa Canyon Wilderness Area on E boundary. Formed 1875.

Pinal de Amoles, town (1990 pop. 1,401), Querétaro, Mexico, at E foot of Cerro Pingüicas, 12 mi/19 km SW of Jalpan de Sierra on Mexico Highway 120; 21°00′N 99°45′W. Cereals, sugar, tropical fruit, maguey. Also Amoles.

Pinal Mountains, Tonto Natl. Forest, Gila co., SE central Ariz., bet. Gila and Salt rivers; 33°16′N 110°49′W. Rise to 7,848 ft/2,392 m in Pinal Peak, 8 mi/12.9 km S of Globe. Also called Mescal Mts.

Pinaleno Mountains (PEE-nah-LAI-no), SE Ariz., range (40 mi/64 km long, 8 mi/12.9 km wide) in Graham co., SW of Safford, in part of Coronado Natl. Forest. Chief peaks: Merrill Peak (9,288 ft/2,831 m), Hawk Peak (10,627 ft/3,239 m), and Mt. Graham (10,717 ft/3,267 m; highest).

Pinar del Río (pee-NAHR dail REE-o), province (□ 4,170 sq mi/10,800 sq km; 1994 est. pop. 700,000), W Cuba, the westernmost prov. of Cuba; ⊙ Pinar del Río. The pop. density is just 65 inhab./sq. km. The prov., occupying a narrow area, has an irregular and swampy coast; it is mostly level, with 1 important mt. range, the Cordillera de Guaniguanico. Drained by the Cuyaguateje R., with 133,000 acres devoted to agr., Cuba's poorest prov.; primary activity is the growing some of the world's best tobacco on 9% of the land devoted to agr., cultivated in the Vuelta Abajo region. Tobacco mostly processed in Havana. Rice paddies draw on 1.1 trillion gallons of dam water for irrigation. Five sugar mills are located in E part of prov. Other agr. prods. are of limited importance; mining of zinc, lead, copper (mines at Minas de Matahambre), nickel, bauxite, and phosphorous. Prov. has no port facilities and no commercial airport. Major cities include: Pinar del Río, Consolación del Sur, Los Palacios, and San Cristóbal.

Pinar del Río (pee-NAHR dail REE-o), city (1994 est. pop. 118,000), W Cuba, on RR, and 100 mi/161 km SW of Havana; ⊙ Pinar del Río prov.; 22°25′N 83°42′W. Terminus of Central Highway and center of rich Vuelta Abajo tobacco-growing region. Has only military and agr. airstrips in vicinity. Mfg. of cigars, cigarettes, furniture, pharmaceuticals. Nearby is picturesque valley of Viñales with unusual karstic topography.

Pinardville (pi-NAHRD-vil), village (1990 pop. 4,654), Hillsborough co., S N.H., residential suburb 2 mi/3.2 km W of downtown Manchester, within town of Goffstown, on Piscataquog R.; 43°00′N 71°30′W. St. Anselm Col. here.

Pinawa (pin-AH-wuh), village (1991 pop. 1,806), SE Man., Canada, on Pinawa Channel, branch of Winnipeg R., bet. Natalie L. and Lac du Bonnet, 60 mi/97 km ENE of Winnipeg; 50°09′N 95°53′W. Hydroelectric power.

Pinch, uninc. town (1990 pop. 2,695), Kanawha co., W central W.Va., 9 mi/14.5 km NE of Charleston, near Elk R.; 38°24′N 81°28′W. Corn; poultry; cattle.

Pincher Creek, town (1991 pop. 3,660), SW Alta., Canada, on Pincher Creek and 50 mi/80 km WSW of Lethbridge; 49°29′N 113°57′W. Coal mining, lumbering, cattle raising.

Pinchi Lake (PIN-chee) (□ 17 sq mi/44 sq km), central B.C., Canada, just NE of Stuart L., 40 mi/64 km NNW of Vanderhoof; 14 mi/23 km long, 2 mi/3 km wide. Drains S into Stuart L. Mercury mining on NE shore.

Pinckard (PIN-kuhrd), town (1990 pop. 618), Dale co., SE Ala., 10 mi/16 km NW of Dothan.

Pinckney, village (1990 pop. 1,603), Livingston co., SE Mich., 16 mi/26 km NW of Ann Arbor; 42°27′N 83°57′W. In lake-resort and farm area (hay, soybeans, grain, corn, apples; livestock; dairy). Light mfg. Pinckney State Recreational Area to SW.

Pinckneyville (PEENK-nee-vil), city (1990 pop. 3,372), SW Ill., on Beaucoup Creek and 33 mi/53 km SSW of Centralia; ⊙ Perry co.; 38°04′N 89°22′W. RR junction. In bituminous coal (large strip mine) and agr. area (sorghum, wheat, corn, soybeans; dairying); mfg. (construction materials, compact discs). Pyramid State Park to S, created from reclaimed coal strip mines. Inc. 1861.

Pinconning (pin-KAHN-ing), town (1990 pop. 1,291), Bay co., E Mich., 18 mi/29 km NNW of Bay City, near Saginaw Bay; 43°51′N 83°57′W. Agr. trade center (sugar beets, grains, beans, cucumbers, soybeans, corn; livestock); food processing. Light mfg. Summer resort. Arenac County Saginaw Project, on Indian reservation, to NE. Settled c.1866; inc. as village 1877, as city 1931.

Pine, county (□ 1,434 sq mi/3,714 sq km; 1990 pop. 21,264), E Minn.; ⊙ Pine City; 46°08′N 92°44′W. Agr. area bounded E and SE (St. Croix R.) by Wis.; drained by Kettle R. Alfalfa, hay, oats, cattle, sheep, dairying, poultry, timber; sandstone quarries. Part of St. Croix Natl. Scenic Riverway, on St. Croix R., in SE. Several small natural lakes in co., especially in N, W, and far S; Sandstone Natl. Wildlife Refuge and Banning State Park in center; Nemadji State Forest in NE; St. Croix State Forest in E; part of Chengwatana State Forest in SE; large St. Croix State Park in SE. County formed 1856.

Pine Apple, town (1990 pop. 365), Wilcox co., S Ala., 20 mi/32 km ESE of Camden. Lumber.

Pine Barrens, coastal plain region, c.3,000 sq mi/7,770 sq km, S and SE N.J.; composed chiefly of sandy soils, swamp-edged streams, pine stands, and tracts of cranberries and blueberries. Originally a well-forested area of pine, cedar, and oak, its trees were indiscriminately cut for shipbuilding and charcoal-making until the 1860s, when they were nearly exhausted. Now second-growth forests are extensive. Several state forests and Fort Dix, a U.S. army base that was the largest training center in the U.S. and was closed as an active base in 1992, are here. Very lightly populated, its inhabitants, descendants of 18th- and 19th-cent. settlers, are called "Pineys." On the periphery of the Pine Barrens, suburban development has grown since the 1970s. Efforts to maintain the wilderness have increased as a result of environmentalist action, but the area continues to feel a great deal of pressure from residential development. See PINELANDS NATIONAL RESERVE.

Pine Beach, borough (1990 pop. 1,954), Ocean co., E N.J., on Toms R. and 2 mi/3.2 km SE of Toms River, in resort, fishing area; 39°56′N 74°10′W.

Pine Bluff, city (1990 pop. 57,140), S central Ark., on the Arkansas R. Drained by Bayou Bartholomew, Emmett Sanders Lock and Dam to E, L. Pine Bluff in N part of city, L. Langhofer, oxbow lake of Arkansas R. to NE; ⊙ Jefferson co.; 34°12′N 92°01′W. Mfg. (fabricated metal prods., machinery, electric equip., food prods., wood prods., paper prods., printing and publishing). It is also a research center and the seat of the Univ. of Ark., Pine Bluff. Of economic importance to the city is the huge Pine Bluff Arsenal (Natl. Center for Toxicological Research) to the N; established during World War II, it is the center of U.S. army chemical, biological, and toxicological research. Pine Bluff has an arts and science center and a civic complex designed by Edward Durell Stone. SE Ark. Livestock Showgrounds; women's correctional center here. Inc. 1839.

Pine Bluffs, town (1990 pop. 1,054), Laramie co., SE Wyo., on Lodgepole Creek, at Nebr. line, and 40 mi/64 km E of Cheyenne; 41°10′N 104°04′W. Elev. c.5,047 ft/1,538 m. Agr. (grain, sugar beets; cattle, sheep; dairying); mfg. (food). Site of Univ. of Wyo. archaeological dig (1995).

Pine Bush, village (□ 2 sq mi/5.2 sq km; 1990 pop. 1,445), Orange co., SE N.Y., on Shawangunk Kill and 13 mi/21 km NNE of Middletown; 41°36′N 74°17′W. Mfg. of textiles.

Pine Castle, town (□ 2 sq mi/5.2 sq km; 1990 pop. 8,276), Orange co., central Fla., 5 mi/8 km S of Orlando; 28°28′N 81°22′W.

Pine City, town (1990 pop. 2,613), E Minn., on Snake R., near Wis. state line (St. Croix R.), and 60 mi/97 km N of St. Paul; ⊙ Pine co.; 45°49′N 92°58′W. Elev. 946 ft/288 m. Mfg. (fabricated metal prods., electronic equip., food prods.); oats, alfalfa, dairying, poultry, livestock. North West Company Fur Post State Historical Site to W; St. Croix Natl. Scenic Riverway to E; Chengawatana State Forest to E; Cross L. to NE; Pokegama L. to W. Platted 1869, inc. 1881.

Pine Creek 1 75 mi/121 km long, in N Pa.; rises in NE central Potter co., 5 mi/8 km SW of Ulysses; flows SE past Galeton, then S through Pine Creek Gorge (c.1,000 ft/305 m deep; called Grand Canyon of Pa.), then to West Branch of Susquehanna R. bet. towns of Jersey Shore (E) and Avis (W); 41°51′N 77°49′W. **2** c.30 mi/48 km long, in NE Texas; rises in Lamar co., W of Paris; flows NE through L. Crook (920 acres/372 ha, owned by city of Paris), to Red R.

Pine Creek Lake, reservoir (13 mi/21 km long), McCurtain co., SE Okla., on Little R., 22 mi/35 km NW of Idabel; 34°05′N 95°04′W. Max. capacity 465,800 acre-ft. Formed by Pine Creek Dam (95 ft/29 m high), built (1969) by the Army Corps of Engineers for flood control and water supply.

Pine Falls, village, SE Man., Canada, on Winnipeg R. (waterfalls), near its mouth on L. Winnipeg, 60 mi/97 km NE of Winnipeg; 50°33′N 96°14′W. Hydroelectric power center; paper milling.

Pine Flat Dam, Calif.: see KINGS RIVER.

Pine Flat Lake, Fresno co., S Calif., on Kings R., 25 mi/40 km ENE of Fresno; 36°50′N 119°21′W. Extends NE; max. capacity of 1,113,000 acre-ft; 17 mi/27 km long; elev. 951 ft/290 m. Formed by Pine Flat Dam (424 ft/129 m high), built by the Army Corps of Engineers for flood control, irrigation and power generation.

Pine Flat Mountain, N.Mex.: see MIMBRES MOUNTAINS.

Pine Forest, village (1990 pop. 709), Orange co., SE Texas, residential suburb 8 mi/12.9 km NE of Beaumont; 30°10′N 94°01′W. Timber and agr. area.

Pine Forest Mountains, NW Nev., in NW Humboldt co., near Oregon state line. Highest point Duffer Peak (9,397 ft/2,864 m), 65 mi/105 km NW of Winnemucca.

Pine Grove, town (1990 pop. 701), Wetzel co., NW W.Va., 10 mi/16 km SE of New Martinsville, at confluence of N and S forks of Fishing Creek. Petroleum-producing and agr. region. Lewis Wetzel Wildlife Management Area to S.

Pine Grove, village, Shasta co., N Calif., near Shasta L., 8 mi/12.9 km NNE of Redding and 1 mi/1.6 km S of Project City.

Pine Grove, borough (1990 pop. 2,118), Schuylkill co., E central Pa., 13 mi/21 km SW of Pottsville, on Swatara Creek; 40°32′N 76°23′W. Mfg. (chemicals, plastic prods., construction materials, apparel); agr. (corn, hay; poultry; dairying). Pine Grove Airport to W; Swatara State Park to W; part of Weiser State Forest to NE; Appalachian Trail passes to S. Settled 1771, laid out 1830, inc. 1832.

Pine Grove Mills, uninc. town (1990 pop. 1,129), Centre co., 4 mi/6.4 km SSW of State College; 40°44′N 77°52′W. Light mfg. Agr. includes dairying, livestock, poultry; grain, vegetables. State forests and parks in area.

Pine Hall, uninc. village, Stokes co., N N.C., 18 mi/29 km NNE of Winston-Salem, on Dan R. Tobacco; grain; livestock. Light mfg. Belows L. reservoir to SE.

Pine Hill 1 town (1990 pop. 481), Wilcox co., SW Ala., near Alabama R., 17 mi/27 km W of Camden. Paper and lumber. **2** or **Pine Hills,** uninc. town (1990 pop. 2,947), Humboldt co., NW Calif., residential surburb SSW of Eureka, near Humboldt Bay; 40°44′N 124°09′W.

Pine Hill, resort village (1990 pop. 400), Ulster co., SE N.Y., in the Catskills, 28 mi/45 km NW of Kingston; 42°08′N 74°29′W. Belle Ayr Mt. (skiing) is nearby.

Pine Hill, borough (1990 pop. 9,854), Camden co., SW N.J., 14 mi/23 km SE of Camden; 39°47′N 74°59′W. Residential and light industry. Inc. 1929.

Pine Island, town (1990 pop. 2,125), Goodhue co., SE Minn., on Harkcom Creek, and 15 mi/24 km NW of Rochester; 44°12′N 92°39′W. Dairying; poultry, livestock; grain, soybeans; mfg. (fabricated metal prods., food). Dorer Memorial Hardwood State Forest to E. Settled 1854, inc. 1878.

Pine Island (1990 pop. 5,244), off coast of SW Fla., c.15 mi/24 km W of Fort Myers; c.15 mi/24 km long, 1 mi/1.6 km–3 mi/4.8 km wide; 26°05′N 80°16′W. Has causeway to mainland. Has rapidly suburbanized since 1980; resort and fishing villages of Pineland and St. James City. Isl. is bordered W by Pine Isl. Sound (c.15 mi/24 km long, 5 mi/8 km wide), sheltered from the Gulf of Mexico by a chain of barrier isls.: Lacosta, Captiva, Sanibel, and opening into Charlotte Harbor (N) and San Carlos Bay (S).

Pine Knoll Shores, town (1990 pop. 1,360), Carteret co., E N.C., residential community 8 mi/12.9 km WSW of Morehead City, on Bogue Isl. (Bogue Banks), on Atlantic Ocean (S) and Bogue Sound (N); 34°42′N 76°49′W. Theodore Roosevelt State Natural Area N.C. Aquarium to W.

Pine Knot, town (1990 pop. 1,549), McCreary co., SE Ky., 5 mi/8 km S of Whitley city; 36°39′N 84°26′W. Tobacco; cattle; timber. Mfg. (wood prods., lumber). Area surrounded by Daniel Boone Natl. Forest. Big South Fork Natl. R. and Recreation Area to W.

Pine Lake, town (1990 pop. 810), De Kalb co., NW central Ga., 10 mi/16 km E of Atlanta; 33°47′N 84°13′W. Suburb of Atlanta.

Pine Lake 1 Ind.: see LA PORTE. **2** Minn.: see BIG PINE LAKE.

Pine Lawn, town (1990 pop. 5,092), St. Louis co., E Mo., suburb 7 mi/11.3 km NW of downtown St. Louis; 38°42′N 90°16′W. Villages of Mary Ridge and Goodfellow Terrace absorbed by Pine Lawn. Inc. 1940.

Pine Level, town (1990 pop. 1,217), Johnston co., central N.C., 5 mi/8 km E of Smithfield; 35°30′N 78°15′W. Agr. area (tobacco, cotton, peanuts, grain, potatoes, sweet potatoes; poultry; livestock). Light mfg.

Pine Meadow, uninc. village, Litchfield co., Conn., 6 mi/9.7 km SSE of Winsted. A postal sect. of New Hartford. Much damage and loss of life in 1955 floods.

Pine Mountain, town (1990 pop. 875), Harris co., Ga.,

10 mi/16 km W of Warm Springs; 32°52′N 84°51′W. Mfg. (textiles). Many shops and galleries as well as food and lodging establishments catering to tourists visiting Callaway Gardens and Warm Springs.

Pine Mountain, ridge of the Cumberland Mts. (c.50 mi/80 km long), mostly in SE Ky., from Pineville (Cumberland R.) in SW to Elkhorn City, Ky., (Russell Fork). Rises to 2,100 ft/640 m–2,300 ft/701 m in SW, to 2,600 ft/792 m–2,800 ft/853 m in NE ½ with sects. rising above 3,000 ft/914 m; forms Va. (Ky. state line) in NE (c.40 mi/64 km). Extensive timber tracts and coal deposits. Trail of the Lonesome Pine (scenic highway) passes over part of ridge. Pound Gap (2,380 ft/725 m; U.S. highway 23) is in N sect., near Jenkins, Ky. Pine Mtn. Resort State Park (1,519 acres/615 ha), SW of Pineville, Ky., has annual mt. laurel festival (May). Central part in Daniel Boone Natl. Forest. Extension to SW into Tenn. also called Log Mts. and Kentucky Ridge.

Pine Mountain Valley, town (1990 pop. 950), Harris co., Ga., 23 mi/37 km NNE of Columbus. Light mfg.; poultry processing.

Pine Nut Mountains, W Nev., E of Carson City; extend c.35 mi/56 km S from Carson R. Rise to 9,450 ft/2,880 m in S, at Mt. Siegel. Lyon and Douglas cos. and Carson City (independent city).

Pine Park, town, Grady co., SW Ga., 7 mi/11.3 km ESE of Cairo; 30°51′N 84°06′W.

Pine Plains, village (□ 2 sq mi/5.2 sq km; 1990 pop. 1,312), Dutchess co., SE N.Y., 25 mi/40 km NE of Poughkeepsie; 41°58′N 73°39′W. In diversified agr. area.

Pine Point, town (1991 pop. 9), W N.W.T., Canada, 70 mi/113 km E of town of Hay River, S of Great Slave L. Built bet. 1962 and 1965 by Cominco, Ltd., as residential and service center for lead-zinc mine. Pop. exceeded 1700 in 1980. Mine closed, 1987; town dismantled, 1988.

Pine Prairie, town (1990 pop. 713), Evangeline parish, 11 mi/18 km NW of Ville Platte; 30°45′N 92°26′W. Oil and gas fields nearby.

Pine Ridge, town (1990 pop. 2,596), Shannon co., SW S.Dak., 80 mi/129 km SSE of Rapid City, near Nebr. line, and White Clay Creek, branch of White R.; hq. for Pine Ridge Indian Reservation, which consists of most of Shannon co. and over ⅓ of Jackson co, S.Dak., and small part of Sheridan co., Nebr. Wounded Knee Massacre site, 12 mi/19 km NE; 43°01′N 102°33′W.

Pine River, town (1990 pop. 871), Cass co., N central Minn., 27 mi/43 km NNW of Brainerd on Pine R., at mouth of Norway Brook, Whitefish L. to E; 46°43′N 94°24′W. Mfg. (lumber, wood prods.); livestock, poultry; dairying; oats, alfalfa; cattle, sheep. Numerous small lakes, esp. to N; Foothills State Forest to W.

Pine River 1 c.80 mi/129 km long, in central Mich.; rises in SW Isabella co.; flows SE into Gratiot co., then NE, past Alma and St. Louis, to Chippewa R. just W of Midland; 43°35′N 85°08′W; canoeing. **2** c.25 mi/40 km long, in NE Mich.; rises in central Alcona co., flows SE through Huron Natl. Forest, widening into Van Ettan L. (c.4 mi/6.4 km long) and 4 mi/6.4 km above its confluence with Au Sable R., at Oscoda. W and S branches converge S of Mikado; 44°35′N 83°26′W. **3** c.50 mi/80 km long, in N central Minn.; rises in lake region 10 mi/16 km S of Walker, in W Cass co.; flows S through Pine Mountain L., then E past Pine River town and through Upper and Lower Whitefish lakes, and SE, through Cross L. reservoir, to Mississippi R. near Crosby. Lower course is in Crow Wing State Forest. **4** c.30 mi/48 km long, in SW Wis.; formed by several streams rising N of Richland Center; flows generally S past Richland Center, to Wisconsin R. 12 mi/19 km NW of Spring Green.

Pine River, Colo. and N.Mex.: see LOS PINOS RIVER.

Pine River Reservoir (□ 21 sq mi/54 sq km), Crow Wing co., central Minn., on Pine R., 25 mi/40 km N of Brainerd; 46°40′N 94°07′W. Max. capacity 179,200 acre-ft. Formed by Pine R. Dam (23 ft/7 m high), built (1886) by Army Corps of Engineers for flood control; also used for water supply and recreation.

Pine Springs, village (1990 pop. 436), Washington co.,

E Minn., residential suburb 10 mi/16 km NE of downtown St. Paul; 45°02′N 92°57′W. Small lakes in vicinity; White Bear L. to NW.

Pine Tree Line, Canada: see DEW LINE.

Pine Valley, uninc. town (1990 pop. 1,297), San Diego co., S Calif., 37 mi/60 km E of San Diego; 32°52′N 116°30′W. Cuyapaipe Indian Reservation to E; La Posta and Manzanita Indian reservations to SE; Cuyamaca Rancho State Park to NW; Anza-Borrego Desert State Park to NE and E. Forest. Cattle; dairying; poultry.

Pine Valley, borough (1990 pop. 19), Camden co., SW N.J., 13 mi/21 km SE of Camden; 39°47′N 74°58′W. Largely residential.

Pine Valley 1 village (□ 3 sq mi/7.8 sq km; 1990 pop. 1,486), Suffolk co., SE N.Y., 1 mi/1.6 km S of Riverhead; 40°53′N 72°40′W. **2** village, Le Flore co., SE Okla., 28 mi/45 km SSW of Poteau, SE of Muse and on Kiamichi R., in the Ouachita Mts.

Pine Valley Mountains (rising to 10,324 ft/3,147 m.), in Pine Valley Mt. Wilderness Area, Dixie Natl. Forest, N Washington co., SW Utah, N of St. George.

Pine Village, town (1990 pop. 134), Warren co., W Ind., on small Big Pine Creek and 11 mi/18 km NNE of Williamsport; 40°27′N 87°15′W. Agr. area.

Pinebluff, town (1990 pop. 876), Moore co., central N.C., 6 mi/9.7 km SSW of Southern Pines; 35°06′N 79°28′W. Light mfg. Tobacco, grain, soybeans; poultry, livestock.

Pinecliff Lake, N.J.: see WEST MILFORD.

Pinecreek, village, Roseau co., NW Minn., 11 mi/18 km NNW of Roseau, on Pine Creek, 2 mi/3.2 km S of Canada (Man.) border, port of entry 3 mi/4.8 km to NW; 48°58′N 95°56′W. Roseau R. Wildlife Area to W; part of Isl. Beltrami State Forest to E. Sometimes Pine Creek.

Pinecrest, town (1990 pop. 3,821), Carter co., extreme NE Tenn., 3 mi/5 km SE of Johnson City; 36°09′N 82°48′W.

Pinecrest, residential suburb of Miami, Dade co., SE Fla., 10 mi/16 km SSW of Miami. Inc. 1995.

Pinedale 1 uninc. town, Fresno co., central Calif., residential suburb 7 mi/11.3 km N of Fresno on Joaquin R. Dairying; poultry; fruit, grain, sugar beets, almonds. Millerton L. Reservoir and State Recreational Area to NE. **2** town (1990 pop. 1,181), W Wyo., near New Fork R., and c.95 mi/153 km NNW of Rock Springs; ⊙ Sublette co.; 42°52′N 109°51′W. Elev. 7,175 ft/2,187 m. Resort; sheep, cattle; timber. Six reservoirs located in nearby mt. valleys: New Fork and Willow lakes (N), Fremont and Halfmoon lakes (NE), Burnt and Boulder lakes (E). Wind River Mts. and Bridger-Teton Natl. Forest to NE (Bridger Wilderness Area).

Pinehurst, city (1990 pop. 388), Dooly co., central Ga., 15 mi/24 km N of Cordele; 32°12′N 83°46′W.

Pinehurst 1 town (1990 pop. 1,722), Shoshone co., N Idaho, 27 mi/43 km ESE of Coeur d'Alene; 47°32′N 116°14′W. Timber. Coeur d'Alene Natl. Forest to N; St. Joe Natl. Forest to SE; Silver Mt. Ski Area to SE. **2** town (1990 pop. 5,103), Moore co., central N.C., suburb 5 mi/8 km W of Southern Pines Resort Area; 35°10′N 79°27′W. Noted for its golf courses and as a training center for horses. Tobacco, grain, soybeans; cattle, hogs, chickens. Mfg. of textiles. Sandhills Community Col. Pinhurst Southern Pines Airport to NE. Developed after 1895; chartered 1911. **3** town (1990 pop. 3,284), Orange co., SE Texas, suburb 2 mi/3.2 km WNW of Orange, on Adams Bayou; 30°11′N 95°42′W. Light mfg.

Pinehurst, village, Snohomish co., NW Wash., suburb 4 mi/6.4 km S of Everett and 24 mi/39 km NNE of Seattle.

Pinehurst, Mass.: see BILLERICA.

Pineland, town (1990 pop. 882), Sabine co., E Texas, c.45 mi/72 km ESE of Lufkin; 31°15′N 93°58′W. Timber; cattle, poultry; mfg. (wood prods.). At W edge of Sabine Natl. Forest; Sam Rayburn Reservoir to SW. Inc. after 1940.

Pineland, village, Jasper co., S S.C., 15 mi/24 km NW of Ridgeland. Timber.

Pinelands National Reserve, E N.J., authorized 1978 (1,562 sq mi/4,046 sq km). Large tract of undeveloped forest and wetlands. It is also a UNESCO coastal plain reserve.

Pinellas (pei-NEL-lus), county (□ 607 sq mi/1,572 sq km; 1990 pop. 851,569), W central Fla.; ⊙ Clearwater; 27°53′N 82°44′W. Largely a peninsula (Pinellas peninsula), bet. Gulf of Mexico (W) and Tampa Bay (E); bordered W by chain of barrier isls., including Long Key; has L. Butler in N. Tourist area, with canning, wood processing, and sponge-fishing industries. Former mfg. of nuclear weapons parts; converted to light industry. Formed 1911.

Pinellas Park (pei-NEL-lus), city (□ 14 sq mi/36 sq km; 1990 pop. 43,426), Pinellas co., W central Fla., 8 mi/12.9 km NW of St. Petersburg; 27°51′N 82°42′W. Mainly residential; some mfg. (electronic equip., plastics). Inc. 1915

Pineridge or **Pine Ridge**, town (1990 pop. 1,731), Lexington co., central S.C., residential suburb 7 mi/11.3 km SSW of downtown Columbia; 33°54′N 81°05′W. Styx State Fish hatchery is here; Columbia Municipal Airport to SW.

Pines, Isle of, Cuba: see JUVENTUD, ISLA DE LA.

Pinetop-Lakeside, town (1990 pop. 2,422), Navajo co., E central Ariz., 50 mi/80 km SSE of Holbrook, at upper (N) edge of Mogollon Rim escarpment, in Apache-Sitgreaves Natl. Forest; 34°08′N 109°58′W. Cattle, sheep, hogs; corn, alfalfa; timber; mfg. (machinery, glass). Fort Apache Indian Reservation to S.

Pinetops, town (1990 pop. 1,514), Edgecombe co., E central N.C., 13 mi/21 km SE of Rocky Mount; 35°47′N 77°38′W. In agr. area (tobacco, grain, cotton, peanuts, sweet potatoes; poultry, livestock). Light mfg.

Pinetown, uninc. village, Beaufort co., E N.C., 12 mi/19 km ENE of Washington. RR junction. Mfg. (furniture, food).

Pineview, town (1990 pop. 594), Wilcox co., S central Ga., 19 mi/31 km ENE of Cordele; 32°07′N 83°30′W.

Pineview Dam, Utah: see OGDEN RIVER.

Pineville, city (1990 pop. 12,251), Rapides parish, central La., on Red R., to NE of Alexandria, its sister city; 31°20′N 92°25′W. RR junction; mfg. (wood prods., electronic equip., fabricated metal prods.). Commercial fishing. La. Col., a natl. cemetery, a veterans hosp., and Central La. State Hosp. are here. Camp Livingston and U.S. Camp Beauregard to NE; L. Fort Buhlow to N. Settled in early 18th cent.; inc. 1878.

Pineville 1 town (1990 pop. 2,198), SE Ky., in the Cumberland Mts., on Cumberland R., and 11 mi/18 km N of Middlesboro; ⊙ Bell co.; 36°45′N 83°42′W. Elev. c.1,000 ft/305 m. RR junction. Resort and tourist center; bituminous-coal-mining area; light mfg. Clear Creek Baptist Bible Col. Holds annual (May) Cumberland valley music festival. Town settled on old Wilderness Road around tollgate (1797–1830) at gap (the Narrows) in Pine Mt. Pine Mt. State Resort Park and Ky. Ridge State Forest to SW (Spring Flower and Fern Fes tival at park); Cumberland Gap Natl. Historical Park to SE. **2** town (1990 pop. 580), extreme SW Mo., in the Ozarks, on Elk R., and 19 mi/31 km S of Neosho; ⊙ McDonald co.; 36°35′N 94°22′W. Resort and recreational area; fruit-growing region. Dairy, grain prods.; tourism. Plotted c. 1847. **3** town (1990 pop. 2,970), Mecklenburg co., SW N.C., 10 mi/16 km SSW of Charlotte, near S.C. line; 35°04′N 80°53′W. Mfg. (plastic prods., fabricated metal prods., printing and publishing, electronic equip., food). James K. Polk Memorial State Historical Site, birthplace of President Polk, to E. **4** town (1990 pop. 865), S W.Va., on Guyandotte R., 24 mi/39 km SW of Beckley; ⊙ Wyoming co.; 37°35′N 81°31′W. Trade center for coal-mining, timber, agr. (corn, potatoes; cattle) area. Light mfg.(coal processing). Twin Falls State Park to NE; W.D. Bailey reservoir and Wildlife Management Area to W.

Pinewood, village (1990 pop. 600), Sumter co., central S.C., 13 mi/21 km SSW of Sumter; 33°44′N 80°27′W. Agr. includes livestock; tobacco, cotton; grain, peanuts. State parks nearby.

Piney Fork, village, Jefferson co., E Ohio, 9 mi/14 km E of Cadiz. In coal-mining area.

Piney Green, uninc. town (1990 pop. 8,999), Onslow co., SE N.C., residential suburb 7 mi/11.3 km ESE of downtown Jacksonville; 34°45′N 77°19′W. On N boundary of Camp Lejeune Marine Corps Base.

Piney Point, resort, St. Marys co., S Md., on the Potomac, and 12 mi/19 km SE of Leonardtown. The 1st "Summer White House," James Madison's, was here until it was swept away in a 1933 gale. The Harry Luenberg School for Seaman has a collection of restored boats, including a yacht President John F. Kennedy sailed and a ferry boat that used to ply bet. Mt. Vernon and Marshall Hall. The lighthouse here was taken over by St. Marys co. in 1980.

Piney Point Village, town (1990 pop. 3,197), Harris co., SE Texas, residential suburb 9 mi/14.5 km W of downtown Houston, bounded S by Buffalo Bayou; 29°45′N 95°31′W. Surrounded by city of Houston.

Piney River, uninc. village, Nelson co., central Va., on small Piney R., 22 mi/35 km N of Lynchburg; 37°41′N 79°01′W. Agr. (apples, corn; cattle); mining of titanium ores, apatite.

Piney View, uninc. town (1990 pop. 1,085), Raleigh co., S W.Va., 5 mi/8 km NNE of Beckley; 37°51′N 81°08′W. Cattle; grain. Mfg. (fabricated metal prods.). New R. Gorge Natl. R. (includes Grandview Visitor Center) to E.

Pineyville, uninc. village (1990 pop. 212), Gaines co., E Texas, 50 mi/80 km NW of Houston. Elev. 325 ft/99 m. Agr. area (apples, plums, peaches, berries; cattle). Light mfg. Annual Renaissance Festival held here.

Pingree (PING-ree), village (1990 pop. 61), Stutsman co., central N.Dak., 21 mi/34 km NNW of Jamestown; 47°09′N 98°54′W. RR junction. Arrowwood Natl. Wildlife Refuge and Jamestown Reservoir (Jim L.) to E.

Pingree Grove, village (1990 pop. 138), Kane co., NE Ill., residential suburb of Elgin, satellite community c.40 mi/64 km WNW of Chicago; 42°04′N 88°24′W. In agr. area (dairy prods.; corn, soybeans).

Pingüicas, Cerro (peen-GWEE-kahs), peak (9,941 ft/3,030 m), in Querétaro, central Mexico, 3 mi/4.8 km WNW of Amoles; 21°10′N 99°42′W.

Pink, town (1990 pop. 1,020), Pottawatomie co., central Okla., 17 mi/27 km E of Norman, and 11 mi/18 km E of Norman, and 11 mi/18 km WSW of Shawnee; 35°13′N 97°06′W. Agr. area on urban fringe. Shawnee Reservoir to NE.

Pink Cliffs, SW Utah, series of rugged precipices (800 ft/244 m–2,000 ft/610 m high) of multicolored sandstone (primarily pink) extending in great U-shaped arc through parts of Garfield, Kane, and Iron cos.; form escarpments of Paunsaugunt Plateau on E and S sides of Markagunt Plateau on S. Unusually dissected areas in Garfield and Iron cos. now included in Bryce Canyon Natl. Park and Cedar Breaks Natl. Monument. Partly in Dixie Natl. Forest.

Pink Hill, village (1990 pop. 547), Lenoir co., E central N.C., 17 mi/27 km SSW of Kinston; 35°03′N 77°44′W. Tobacco, grain, cotton, sweet potatoes; poultry, hogs. Light mfg.

Pinkham Notch (PEENK-uhm), scenic pass (2,032 ft/619 m), N central N.H., in N Carroll co., near Coos co. line, in White Mts., running N-S bet. Presidential Range (W) and Carter-Moriah Range (E); Peabody R. flows N, Ellis R. S, from Notch. Area bought (1911) by U.S. as part of White Mt. Natl. Forest. Winter sports.

Pinkhams Grant (PEENK-uhmz), land grant, Coos co., N central N.H., 23 mi/37 km S of Berlin, in White Mt. Natl. Forest. Wildcat Mt. Ski Area and Gondola Lift are here. Crossed by Appalachian Trail.

Pinnacle Mountain (PIN-uh-kuhl), peak (c.2,860 ft/872 m) in Bell co., SE Ky., in the Cumberland Mts., near Va. line, just E of Middlesboro. Rises above N side of Cumberland Gap; Skyland Highway ascends mt. to Pinnacle Overlook (2,440 ft/744 m). Ruins of Fort Lyon, strategic Civil War point, are on mt.

Pinnacle Mountain, S.C.: see TABLE ROCK.

Pinnacles, village, San Benito co., W Calif., 25 mi/40 km SSE of Hollister in Bear Valley, in San Andreas Rift Zone. Pinnacles Natl. Monument is just SW.

Pinnacles, National Monument, San Benito and Monterrey cos., W Calif., authorized 1908, in Gabilon range of Coast Ranges, 8 mi/12.9 km E of Soledad, 30 mi/48 km SSE of Hollister; rock spires from 500 ft/152 m–1,200 ft/366 m high; caves.

Pinnacles of Dan, Va.: see PATRICK.

Pinola (pein-O-luh), village, Simpson co., S central Miss., 32 mi/51 km SSE of Jackson, near Strong R. Agr. (cotton, corn; poultry, cattle).

Pinola, Mexico: see LAS ROSAS.

Pinole, city (1990 pop. 17,460), Contra Costa co., W Calif., residential suburb 13 mi/21 km N of downtown Oakland and 5 mi/8 km NNE of Richmond, on San Pablo Bay, at mouth of Pinole Creek; 38°01′N 122°19′W. Primarily residential, mfg. includes concrete and chemicals. Inc. 1903.

Pinopolis (pei-NAH-puh-lis), village, Berkeley co., SE S.C., 30 mi/48 km N of Charleston, on L. Moultrie reservoir. Pinopolis Dam and hydroelectric plant E on Cooper R.

Pinopolis Dam, S.C.: see PINOPOLIS.

Pinos (PEE-nos), city (1990 pop. 3,278) and township, Zacatecas, N central Mexico, on interior plateau, 40 mi/64 km WNW of San Luis Potosí; 22°18′N 101°35′W. Silver- and gold-mining center.

Piños Altos (PEEN-yos AHL-tos), uninc. village (1990 pop. 250), Grant co., SW N.Mex., in Pinos Altos Mts., 7 mi/11.3 km NNE of Silver City. Elev. 6,997 ft/2,133 m. Historic gold and silver mines. Gila Natl. Forest to W, N and E; Black Peak to NE; on Continental Divide.

Piños Altos Mountains (PEEN-yos AHL-tos), in Grant co., SW N.Mex., near Gila R., N of Silver City, largely within Gila Natl. Forest; 32°51′N 108°14′W. Highest point, Black Peak (9,025 ft/2,751 m), on Divide. Silver and copper are mined. Continental Divide passes through NE-SW.

Pinos, Isla de, Cuba: see JUVENTUD, ISLA DE LA.

Pinos, Los, Cuba: see LOS PINOS.

Pinos, Mount (8,831 ft/2,692 m), N Ventura co., near Kean co. line, S Calif., a peak of the Coast Ranges, in S wall of San Joaquin Valley, 40 mi/64 km S of Bakersfield; 34°48′N 119°08′W. In Los Padres Natl. Forest.

Pinos, Point, Calif.: see MONTEREY PENINSULA.

Pinotepa de Don Luis (pee-noe-TE-pah de don-loo-EES), town (1990 pop. 4,877), in SW Oaxaca, Mexico, 8 mi/13 km NNE of Santiago Pinotilan Nacional, on the slopes of the Sierra Madre del Sur on unpaved road; 16°25′N 97°55′W. Hot climate. Cattle region. Agr. (corn, plantains, mango). Forestry.

Pinotepa Nacional, Mexico: see SANTIAGO PINOTEPA NACIONAL.

Pinson, village, Jefferson co., N central Ala., c.15 mi/24 km NE of Birmingham; 33°40′N 86°39′W. Mfg of plastic prods. Combined with the villages of Clay and Chalkville in 1 census dist. (1990 pop. 10,987).

Pinsonfork, village, Pike co., E Ky., 15 mi/24 km ENE of Pikeville, bet. McAndrews (N) and McVeigh (S). Coal mining. Also called Pinson.

Pintada Peak (13,176 ft/4,016 m), in San Juan Mts., Rio Grande co., S Colo., 12 mi/19 km SSW of Del Norte Rio Grande Natl. Forest; 37°29′N 106°24′W.

Pinto (PIN-to), village, SE Sask., Canada, on Souris R. and 15 mi/24 km ESE of Estevan, near N.Dak. border; coal.

Pinto, village, Allegany co, W Md., on North Branch of the Potomac. c.7 mi/11.3 km SSW above Cumberland. The town was presumably named for the pony of a mail rider. A famous geologic exposure of rock is near the Baltimore and Ohio track.

Pinto Butte, mountain (3,350 ft/1,021 m), SW Sask., Canada, near Mont. border, 70 mi/113 km SSE of Swift Current.

Pinware, locality, SE Lab., Canada, on Strait of Belle Isle, on coastal road and ferry. Pinware R. Provincial Park (168 acres/68 ha) nearby. Fishing.

Pioche (pee-OCH), uninc. village (1990 pop. 630), E Nev., 87 mi/140 km SSE of Ely; ⊙ Lincoln co. Elev. 6,100 ft/1,859 m. Perlite, sand and gravel; cattle. Echo Canyon State Recreation Area to E. Spinng Valley State Park to NE. Cathedral Gorge State Monument to S. Co. mus. Million Dollar Courthouse (1876) slated to

cost $16,000, ultimately cost $1,000,000. Pop. was c.12,000 by 1875; was one of most lawless towns in West.

Pioneer 1 town (1990 pop. 46), Humboldt co., N central Iowa, 12 mi/19 km E of Dakota City; 42°38′N 94°23′W. Livestock; grain. **2** town (1990 pop. 116), West Carroll parish, La., 9 mi/14.5 km SW of Oak Grove; 32°44′N 91°26′W. Purchased from a brother of President Taft in 1903 by the Pioneer Cooperage Co. In agr. (cotton, corn; cattle) area. Small farms.

Pioneer, village (1990 pop. 1,287), Williams co., extreme NW Ohio, near St. Joseph R. and Mich. line, 15 mi/24 km N of Bryan; 41°40′N 84°33′W. Light mfg.

Pioneer Memorial State Park, Ky.: see OLD FORT HARROD STATE PARK.

Pioneer Mine, village, SW B.C., Canada, in Coast Mts., on Cadwallader Creek, and 110 mi/177 km N of Vancouver; 50°46′N 122°46′W. Timber. Former gold mine.

Pioneer Mountains 1 in Blaine and Custer cos., S central Idaho, bet. Big Wood R. and Big Lost R. Include parts of Challis (NE) and Sawtooth (SW) natl. forests; 43°40′N 113°54′W. Sun Valley village and ski resort is on W slope. Chief peaks: Smiley Mt. (11,505 ft/3,507 m.), Ryan Peak (11,795 ft/3,595 m.), and Hyndman Peak (12,078 ft/3,681 m.), highest point in range. **2** in SW Mont., rise in NW part of Beaverhead co. as spur of Bitterroot Range of Rocky Mts.; extend N to Continental Divide. Bounded by the Big Hole R. (W, N, and E) by Grasshopper Creek (on S). Prominent peaks; Torrey Mt. (11,147 ft/3,398 m); Baldy Mt. (10,568 ft/3,213 m); Highboy Mt. (10,431 ft/3,171 m); Comet Mt. (10,212 ft/3,113 m).

Pipe Spring National Monument, NE Mohave co., 14 mi/23 km WSW of Fredonia, 8 mi/12.9 km S of Utah border, NW Ariz. Covers 40 acres/16 ha. Mormon homestead, Winsor Castle, with fortified courtyard between 2 strong houses, built 1870 astride spring, which continues to run through basement trough to pool outside. Surrounded by Kaibab Indian Reservation. Proclaimed 1923.

Piper (PEIP-uhr), Wyandotte co., NE Kansas, residential suburb 12 mi/19 km WNW of Kansas City, Kansas, and 7 mi/11.3 km S of Leavenworth, near Missouri R. Wyandotte Co. L. to E.

Piper City (PIE-per), village (1990 pop. 760), Ford co., E Ill., 30 mi/48 km SSW of Kankakee; 40°45′N 88°11′W. In agr. area (corn, soybeans; livestock); light mfg.

Piper Peak, Nev.: see SILVER PEAK MOUNTAINS.

Pipestone, village (1991 pop. 1,795), SW Man., Canada, 50 mi/80 km WSW of Brandon; 49°33′N 100°57′W. Grain; livestock.

Pipestone, county (□ 466 sq mi/1,207 sq km; 1990 pop. 10,491), SW Minn.; ⊙ Pipestone; 44°01′N 96°15′W. Agr. area bounded on W by S.Dak, drained by Rock R. Hogs, sheep, cattle, poultry; dairying; corn, oats. Pipestone Natl. Monument is just N of Pipestone in W center; Split Rock Creek State Park in SW. Includes part of Coteau des Prairies. Co. formed 1857.

Pipestone, town (1990 pop. 4,554), SW Minn., on Coteau des Prairies, 38 mi/61 km NE of Sioux Falls, S. Dak. on Pipestone Creek; ⊙ Pipestone co.; 44°00′N 96°18′W. Elev. 1,737 ft/529 m. Trade center for agr. area (grain, soybeans; livestock, poultry); dairying to N; granite, pipestone quarries; mfg. (transportation equip., concrete, printing and publishing). Municipal Airport to SE. Pipestone Natl. Monument to N; Split Rock Creek State Park to W.

Pipestone Bay or **Pipestone Lake**, extends 1 mi/1.6 km SE, then 6 mi/9.7 km SW; 1 mi/1.6 km wide, in Lake co., NE Minn., near Canada (Ont.) border, 10 mi/16 km NE of Ely, extension of Jackfish Bay of Basswood L., from near entrance to Jackfish Bay; 48°01′N 91°42′W. Fed from S by short stream from Newton L., through Newton Falls. In Boundary Waters Canoe Area of Superior Natl. Forest.

Pipestone Monument, Pipestone co., SW Minn., 1 mi/1.6 km N of Pipestone on Pipestone Creek. Covers 282 acres/114 ha. Quarry of pipestone rock that was a source for Native American ceremonial pipes; 44°00′N 96°19′W. Quarries were 1st described in print by painter George Catlin. Park includes Upper Midwest Indian

Cultural Center, crafts demonstration center. Authorized 1937.

Pippa Passes, uninc. village, Knott co., E Ky., 6 mi/9.7 km E of Hindman, in Cumberland foothills. Bituminous coal-mining; mfg. (printing and publishing). Seat of Alice Lloyd Col.

Piqua (PIK-wai), city (1990 pop. 20,612), Miami co., W Ohio, on the Miami R.; 40°08′N 84°15′W. It is an industrial city with diverse mfg. including transportation equip., steel and iron, paper, aluminum, wood, fabricated metal prods. Of special interest is a historical area just north of the city, the site of a number of old Native Amer. villages and of battles during the last conflict of the Fr. and Indian Wars. Settled 1797, chartered 1929.

Pirates' Well, town, SE Bahama Isls., on NW Mayaguana Isl., 10 mi/16 km NW of Abraham's Bay; 22°28′N 73°05′W. Salt panning, fishing, and farming. Sometimes Pirate Well.

Pirtleville, uninc. town, Cochise co., SE Ariz., 3 mi/4.8 km N of Mex. border, 2 mi/3.2 km NW of Douglas. Cattle; cotton, alfalfa, hay; grain, corn.

Piru, uninc. town (1990 pop. 1,157), Ventura co., S Calif., 27 mi/43 km NE of Oxnard and 40 mi/64 km NW of Los Angeles; 34°25′N 118°48′W. N of Piru R., L. Piru reservoir to N, to confluence with Santa Clara R. Oil fields; orange groves; avocadoes, vegetables. Santa Susana Mts. to S; Los Padres Natl. Forest to N, including Condor Refuge.

Pisaflores (pee-sah-FLO-res), town (1990 pop 1,378), Hidalgo, central Mexico, 18 mi/29 km NE of Jacala, on border with Querétaro; 29°11′N 99°00′W. Corn, sugar, coffee, fruit.

Piscadera Bay (pis-kah-DAI-rah), inlet and beach resort, W Curaçao, Neth. Antilles, 3 mi/4.8 km WNW of Willemstad.

Piscataqua (pi-SKA-duh-waw), navigable river, SE N.H., 12 mi/19 km long; formed by the junction of the Cocheco and the Salmon Falls rivers; flows SE to Portsmouth harbor, forming part of the N.H.-Maine border. The tidal harbor from Portsmouth to the Atlantic Ocean is one of the finest in the U.S. and is the site of Portsmouth Naval Shipyard (est. 1800).

Piscataquis (pis-KAT-uh-kwis), county (□ 4,377 sq mi/11,336 sq km; 1990 pop.18,653), N central Maine; ⊙ Dover-Foxcroft; 45°50′N 69°17′W. Agr., mfg. (wood prods.). Lumbering and wilderness recreational area of N has state's largest lake (Moosehead), highest mt. (Katahdin) and 200,000-acre/80,940-ha Baxter State Park; and the S part of Allagash Wilderness Waterway; hundreds of lakes are resort and camp sites for hunting, fishing, canoeing. Drained by Piscataquis and Pleasant rivers and West Branch of the Penobscot. Formed 1838.

Piscataquis River (pis-KAT-uh-kwis), c.78 mi/126 km long, central Maine; rises in 2 branches just S of Moosehead L.; flows S of E, past Dover-Foxcroft (water power), to the Penobscot at Howland.

Piscataquog River (pi-SKA-duh-kwawg), c.30 mi/48 km long, S N.H.; rises in N Hillsborough co. in Deering L.; flows 1st E through L. Horace and Everett L. reservoirs, then SE to the Merrimack just below (S of) downtown Manchester. South Branch rises in Pleasant Pond, N central Hillsborough co., flows 18 mi/29 km then enters river just W of Goffstown.

Piscataway (pis-KA-tuh-wai), village, Prince Georges co., S Md., 14 mi/23 km SSE of Washington, D.C. The principal dwelling place of Indians along the Potomac 14th cent. to 18th cent., the town was founded in 1707 by the colonists and named for the Piscataway Indian tribe. It was an important 18th-cent. shipping center until the Piscataway Creek filled with silt.

Piscataway (pis-KA-tu-wai), township (1990 pop. 47,089), Middlesex co., NE N.J., on Raritan R. opposite New Brunswick; 40°32′N 74°27′W. Mfg. (chemicals, fabricated metal prods., pharmaceuticals, electronic equip.). St. James Episcopal Church (1837), here, is reproduction of earlier church destroyed by tornado in 1835. Site of branch campuses of Rutgers Univ. Township inc. 1693.

Piscataway Park (6 sq mi/15.5 sq km; 1,091 acres/442 ha), Prince Georges co., S Md. Preserves the view

George Washington enjoyed—and wanted preserved—from across the river at Mt. Vernon. Authorized in 1961.

Piseco (pi-SEE-ko), village (1990 pop. 200), Hamilton co., E central N.Y., in the Adirondacks, on Piseco L., c.45 mi/72 km NE of Utica; 43°27′N 74°31′W. Has airport.

Piseco Lake (pi-SEE-ko), Hamilton co., E central N.Y., in the Adirondacks, 37 mi/60 km NW of Amsterdam; c.5 mi/8 km long, ½ mi/8⁄10 km–1 mi/1.6 km wide; 43°25′N 74°32′W. State campsite here.

Pisek (PEE-zek), village (1990 pop. 130), Walsh co., NE N.Dak., 16 mi/26 kmSW of Grafton; 48°18′N 97°42′W.

Pisgah 1 town (1990 pop. 652), Jackson co., NW Ala., 11 mi/18 km E of Scottsboro. **2** town (1990 pop. 268), Harrison co., W Iowa, on Soldier R. and 15 mi/24 km NNW of Logan; 41°49′N 95°55′W.

Pisgah (PIZ-ga), village, Charles co., S Md., 26 mi/42 km SSW of Washington, D.C. Nearby is Doncaster State Park and Myrtle Grove Wildlife Management Refuge.

Pisgah Forest (PIS-gah), uninc. town (1990 pop. 1,899), Transylvania co., W N.C., 24 mi/39 km SSW of Asheville and 3 mi/4.8 km NNE of Brevard, near French Broad R. Paper mill here is chief U.S. producer of cigarette paper (from flax). Tobacco, corn, vegetables; cattle, poultry. Mfg. (plastic prods., paper). Holmes Educational State Forest to E; Pisgah Natl. Forest to NW.

Pisgah, Mount 1 peak (10,081 ft/3,073 m), in Front Range, Clear Creek and Gilpin cos., central Colo. 4 mi/6.4 km W of Central City in Arapaho Natl. Forest; 39°48′N 105°34′W. **2** peak (3,365 ft/1,026 m) of the Catskills, Delaware co., S N.Y., 14 mi/23 km SW of Stamford; 42°14′N 74°44′W. **3** peak (2,885 ft/879 m) of the Catskills, Greene co., SE N.Y., 18 mi/29 km E of Stamford; 42°22′N 74°15′W. **4** peak (5,721 ft/1,744 m) of the Blue Ridge Mts., W N.C., 16 mi/26 km SW of Asheville, in Pisgah Natl. Forest on Buncombe/Haywood co. line; 35°25′N 82°45′W.

Pismo Beach, town (1990 pop. 7,669), San Luis Obispo co., SW Calif., on Pacific Ocean, 10 mi/16 km S of San Luis Obispo; 35°08′N 120°41′W. Fine beach area; clams, fish; strawberries, apples, avocadoes, vegetables, grain, flowers; nursery livestock, cattle. Oil and natural-gas fields nearby. Pismo State Beach is here. Inc. 1946.

Pistakee Highlands, uninc. village (1990 pop. 3,848), McHenry co., NE Ill., suburb 6 mi/9.7 km NE of McHenry; 42°23′N 88°12′W. Fox L. to E. Chain O'Lakes State Park to NE. Recreation area.

Pistakee Lake, Ill.: see CHAIN O' LAKES.

Pit River, NE Calif.; begins at joining of North and South forks of Alturas, W of Warner Mts., in E central Modoc co.; flows in a serpentine course generally WSW past Fall River Mills to Sacramento R. in Shasta L. reservoir (in Shasta Unit of Whiskeytown-Shasta-Trinity Natl. Recreation Area) 12 mi/19 km N of Redding. Lower 15 mi/24 km of river forms prominent E arm of Shasta L. South Fork rises in Moon L. in NE Lassen co., 28 mi/45 km SSE of Alturas, flows generally NNW c.40 mi/64 km to Alturas. North Fork rises 15 mi/24 km NNE of Alturas 5 mi/8 km S of Goose L., flows c.20 mi/32 km SSW to Alturas; prehistoric outflow of Goose L.

Pitcairn (PIT-kern), borough (1990 pop. 4,087), Allegheny co., SW Pa., residential suburb 12 mi/19 km E of downtown Pittsburgh, on Turtle Creek; 40°24′N 79°46′W. Light mfg. Laid out c.1890, inc. 1891.

Pitch Lake, pool of pitch (asphalt), c.114 acres/46 ha, SW Trinidad isl., Trinidad and Tobago, near La Brea. The lake is believed to be formed and supplied by the seepage of natural pitch, a form of petroleum, from the surrounding oil-rich region. The pitch, hard around the edges of the pool, becomes more viscous towards the center. The seemingly inexhaustible supply has yielded millions of tons of pitch since the 16th cent. Fossils of prehistoric animals have been found in Pitch L., which has also become a tourist attraction.

Pitiquito, town (1990 pop. 4,022), ⊙ Pitiquito municipio, Sonora, NW Mexico, on lower Magdalena R., and 80 mi/129 km SW of Nogales; 30°42′N 110°58′W. Elev. 965 ft/294 m. Agr. center (wheat, corn, fruit; cotton; cattle).

Pitkas Point, Inuit village (1990 pop. 135), W Alaska, on Yukon R., and 100 mi/161 km NW of Bethel; 62°01′N 163°16′W.

Pitkin, county (□ 972 sq mi/2,517 sq km; 1990 pop. 12,661), W central Colo.; ⊙ Aspen; 39°13′N 106°55′W. Continental Divide forms E border, Ruedi Reservoir (Fryingpan R.) on N border. Sheep-grazing and mining area, drained by Roaring Fork (of Colorado) R. Silver, lead. White R. Natl. Forest covers all but parts of NW and center of co. Part of Sawatch Mts. in E. Major tourism and 4 ski resort areas at Aspen and Snowmass Village, both at center of co. Formed 1881.

Pitkin, village (1990 pop. 53), Gunnison co., W central Colo., on Quartz Creek, in Sawatch Mts., and 23 mi/37 km ENE of Gunnison; 38°36′N 106°31′W. Elev. 9,241 ft/2,817 m. State fish hatchery to SW. Surrounded by Gunnison Natl. Forest.

Pitman, borough (1990 pop. 9,365), Gloucester co., SW N.J., 15 mi/24 km S of Camden; 39°43′N 75°07′W. Summer resort. Agr. (fruit, vegetables, dairy and nursery prods.) Mfg. (telecommunications). A growing residential area. Site of Lipari Landfill, one of nation's worst Federal Superfund sites. Cleanup completed in 1995, including draining L. Alsyon. Settled 1871 as place for Methodist camp meetings; inc. 1905.

Pitons, The (pee-TONZ), twin peaks, SW St. Lucia, on S Soufrière Bay, 13 mi/21 km SSW of Castries. Petit Piton (N) rises to 2,461 ft/750 m and Gros Piton to 2,619 ft/798 m. They form remarkable, pyramidical cones, detached from other mts.

Pitsburg, village (1990 pop. 425), Darke co., W Ohio, 11 mi/18 km SE of Greenville; 39°59′N 84°29′W. Also spelled Pittsburg.

Pitt, county (□ 654 sq mi/1,694 sq km; 1990 pop. 108,480), E central N.C.; ⊙ Greenville; 35°35′N 77°22′W. Bounded SW by Contentnea Creek, in S corner by Neuse R. Coastal plain, drained by Tar R. and Swift Creek. Diverse agr. area (corn, wheat, oats, barley, soybeans; hay, cotton, peanuts, tobacco; chickens, cattle, hogs, catfish). Stone quarrying. Formed 1760.

Pitt, Fort, Pa.: see FORT DUQUESNE; PITTSBURGH.

Pitt Island (□ 528 sq mi/1,368 sq km), W B.C., Canada, in Hecate Strait, separated from mainland by Grenville Channel; 56 mi/90 km long, 5 mi/8 km–14 mi/23 km wide; 53°30′N 130°W. Rises to 3,155 ft/962 m. Chino Hat Indian village on W coast. Lumbering; magnesite and iron deposits.

Pitt Lake, SW B.C., Canada, 20 mi/32 km ENE of Vancouver, on Pitt R. (52 mi/84 km long), which flows to the Fraser; 17 mi/27 km long, 1 mi/2 km–2 mi/3 km wide.

Pitt Meadows, town (1991 pop. 11,147), SW B.C., Canada, residential suburb 21 mi/34 km E of downtown Vancouver, on N bank of Fraser R., E of confluence of Pitt R.; 49°14′N 122°41′W. Logging, dairying; fruit, mixed farming.

Pitts, town (1990 pop. 214), Wilcox co., S central Ga., 13 mi/21 km E of Cordele; 31°57′N 83°32′W.

Pittsboro 1 town (1990 pop. 815), Hendricks co., central Ind., 18 mi/29 km NW of Indianapolis; 39°52′N 86°28′W. Agr. area (corn, soybeans; cattle, sheep, hogs). **2** town (1990 pop. 1,436), ⊙ Chatham co., central N.C., 31 mi/50 km WSW of Raleigh; 35°43′N 79°10′W. Agr. area (tobacco, grain, soybeans; dairying; poultry, livestock). Mfg. (pumps, transportation equip., wood prods., signs); lumber, poultry processing. Jordan L. reservoir, on Haw and New Hope rivers, Jordan L. State Recreation Area to E. Settled 1771.

Pittsboro, village (1990 pop. 277), ⊙ Calhoun co., N central Miss., 29 mi/47 km ENE of Grenada; 33°56′N 89°20′W. In agr. (cotton, corn, soybeans, sorghum; cattle; timber) area. Mfg. (furniture).

Pittsburg, county (□ 1,377 sq mi/3,566 sq km; 1990 pop. 40,581), SE Okla.; ⊙ McAlester; 34°55′N 95°45′W. Bounded N by Canadian R. (forms Eufaula L. reservoir); drained by small Gaines Creek; Ouachita Mts. are in SE corner; Arrowhead L., large S arm of Eufaula, is in NE. Agr. (vegetables, peanuts, soybeans, hay, wheat, oats; cattle). Mfg. (textiles, plastics prods., machinery, electronic equip.) at McAlester. Natural-gas and oil wells; coal reserves, timber. Arrowhead State Park in N. McAlester U.S. Army Ammunition Plant is in SW. Jack Fork Mts. (extension of Ouachita Mts.) in SE. Formed 1907.

Pittsburg 1 city (1990 pop. 47,564), Contra Costa co., W Calif., suburb 22 mi/35 km NE of downtown Oakland, on the NE edge of the San Francisco Bay area, W of the junction of the Sacramento and the San Joaquin rivers; E of Suisun Bay, extension of San Francisco Bay; 38°01′N 121°54′W. RR junction. Mfg. (packaging equip, construction materials, machinery, chemicals, industrial glass, printing). Coal was discovered here in 1855 and was mined until 1902. Mokelumne Aqueduct passes S of city. Los Medanos Col. (2 year). Laid out 1849; inc. 1903 **2** city (1990 pop. 17,775), Crawford co., SE Kansas, near the Mo. state line, 122 mi/196 km S of Kansas City, Kansas, and 25 mi/40 km NNW of Joplin, Mo.; 37°24′N 94°42′W. Elev. 944 ft/288 m. Major RR junction and center. It is a mining center near large coal deposits. Clay, limestone, zinc, lead, and oil are also found in the area. Mfg. (transportation equip.,printing and publishing, chemicals, electrical equip., machinery, paper prods., fabricated metal, limestone and clay prods., apparel, plastics prods.); coal. Pittsburg State Univ. here. Airport NW of city. Crawford State Fishing L. to N. Founded 1876 as a mining town and named for Pittsburgh, Pa.; inc. 1880.

Pittsburg 1 town (□ 291 sq mi/754 sq km; 1990 pop. 901), Coos co., N N.H., 41 mi/66 km NNW of Berlin; 45°08′N 71°13′W. Connecticut R. (Vt. state line) forms part of S border; bounded W and N by Can. (Quebec) border, E by Maine state line. Timber; agr. (hay; poultry, cattle; dairying). Village of Pittsburg in S on Connecticut R., at its exit from L. Francis. Hunting, fishing. Magalloway Mt. (3,360 ft/1,024 m) in SE; Connecticut R. forms L. Francis and First Connecticut, Second Connecticut, and Third Connecticut (at source) lakes, in ascending order; Connecticut Lakes State Forest in N; L. Francis State Park in S; 3 covered bridges; largest town in land area in N.H. Independent "Republic of Indian Stream" formed here by settlers in 1832; functioned until occupation by N.H. militia in 1835; inc. with N.H. in 1840. **2** town (1990 pop. 4,007), ⊙ Camp co., NE Texas, 45 mi/72 km NW of Marshall; 33°00′N 94°58′W. Elev. 398 ft/121 m. RR junction in agr. (peaches, blueberries; dairying; cattle), timber area. Oil and gas; mfg. (feed, apparel, waste water treatment equip.); food processing. L. Bob Sandlin reservoir (State Park) to NW. Indian artifacts found nearby. Settled 1854.

Pittsburg 1 village (1990 pop. 602), Williamson co., S Ill., 10 mi/16 km ESE of Herrin; 37°46′N 88°50′W. In bituminous-coal-mining and agr. area. **2** uninc. village (1990 pop. 700), Laurel co., SE Ky., 3 mi/4.8 km NNW of London. Agr. (tobacco, grain; livestock; dairying). Food processing. Wood Creek L. reservoir and Daniel Boone Natl. Forest to W. **3** village (1990 pop. 249), Pittsburg co., SE Okla., 17 mi/27 km SSW of McAlester; 34°42′N 95°50′W. In agr. area. Jack Fork Mts. to E.

Pittsburg, Ohio: see PITSBURG.

Pittsburg Landing, village, Hardin co., SW Tenn., on Tennessee R., and 45 mi/72 km SE of Jackson, at entrance to Shiloh Natl. Military Park.

Pittsburgh (PITS-buhrg), city (1990 pop. 369,879), ⊙ Allegheny co., W Pa., at the confluence of the Allegheny and the Monongahela rivers, which join in downtown Pittsburgh to form the Ohio R.; 40°26′N 79°58′W. A major river port, highway and RR center, and air transportation hub. Mfg. includes transportation equip., wooden prods., printing and publishing, aluminum prods., book binding, petroleum refining, plastic prods., textiles, chemicals, fabricated metal prods., paper prods., food prods., computers, glass prods., and programmable controls. The city was a leading industrial center in the 19th cent. Since the 1960s, as the number of those employed in the steel industry has declined, the city's economic base has undergone a dramatic shift from mfg. to service industries and commercial enterprises. As of the early 1990s, Pittsburgh ranked 3d among U.S. cities as a center for corporate hq. The city was founded on the site of the Native Amer. town of Shannopin, a late 17th-cent. fur-trading post with many canoe routes and trails. FORT DUQUESNE, built by the French in the middle of the 18th cent., later fell to the English and was renamed Fort Pitt. The village surrounding the fort was settled in 1760, and it prospered with the opening of the Northwest Territory. At the height of industrial development in the late 19th cent., Pittsburgh was a hotbed of labor unrest and union movements. The "Steel City" was once also called the "Smoky City," because of severe air and water pollution; the problem, however, gradually abated by the late 1970s as industrial production fell. Sprawled over a hilly area, Pittsburgh has become an attractive city. The city is divided into 3 sects., N, E, and S Pittsburgh, by the meeting of the "three rivers." Of note are 3 tunnels in the city's street and highway system, Fort Pitt and Liberty Tunnels S of downtown, and Squirrel Hill Tunnel to E. The business dist. was refurbished and marked by a construction boom in the 1980s. The triangular downtown area, situated in the wedge formed by the confluence of the Allegheny (N) and Monongahela (S) rivers, is known as the Golden Triangle. Point State Park at its tip, with its circular fountain and site of Fort Pitt (blockhouse preserved) and backdrop of high-rise bldgs., is the visual symbol for the region. Includes Gateway Center, a landscaped hub of office and hotel space. Pittsburgh is the seat of the Carnegie-Mellon Univ., the Univ. of Pittsburgh, Chatham Col., Duquesne Univ., Carlow Col., Community Col. of Allegheny Co. (4 campuses), Art Inst. of Pittsburgh (2-year), and an experiment station of the U.S. Bureau of Mines. The Pittsburgh Symphony Orchestra, Pittsburgh Opera, the Heinz Hall for the Performing Arts, the Carnegie Mus. (including Andy Warhol Mus.), and the Carnegie Lib. are noteworthy. On the Univ. of Pittsburgh campus is a memorial hall dedicated to songwriter Stephen Foster, who was born near Pittsburgh. The city has a fine park system, of which Schenley Park is the principal unit. Two botanical conservatories, a planetarium, Allegheny Observatory, Civic Arena (with a retractable dome), Natl. Aviary of Pittsburgh, Fort Pitt Mus., the Flag Plaza, Three Rivers Stadium, and the Pittsburgh Zoo are among the city's other features. Pittsburgh has professional football (Steelers), ice hockey (Penguins), and baseball (Pirates) teams. Many of the city's institutions benefited or were established by the donations of industrialist Andrew Carnegie (1835–1919), founder of U.S. Steel Corp.; also Henry Heinz (1844–1919), founder of food empire. Several regional parks in city's outskirts. Pittsburgh Internatl. Airport 12 mi/19 km WNW of downtown; Allegheny Co. Airport to S; Pittsburgh-Monroeville Airport to E. Inc. 1816.

Pittsfield 1 city (1990 pop. 4,231), ⊙ Pike co., W Ill., 32 mi/51 km WSW of Jacksonville; 39°36'N 90°48'W. In agr. area (corn, wheat, apples, hay; livestock). Mfg. (food prods.). Laid out 1833, inc. 1869. **2** city (1990 pop. 48,622), ⊙ Berkshire co., W Mass., bet. mt. ranges, on branches of the Housatonic R.; 42°27'N 73°16'W. The city is the metropolis of the Berkshire resort area. Once a farming area, it developed industrially in the 19th cent. as a result of plentiful water power. Mfg. (electrical prods., textiles, plastics, concrete, foundry prods.). Airport. Oliver Wendell Holmes lived nearby, and "Arrowhead" was Herman Melville's home here from 1850 to 1863. A community col. is in Pittsfield. Includes village of West Pittsfield. Ski resort. Berkshire Mus. and Historical Society. Hancock Shaker village of Shaker Religious Community nearby. Inc. as a town 1761, as a city 1889.

Pittsfield 1 town (1990 pop. 4,190), including Pittsfield village, Somerset co., central Maine, on the Sebasticook, and 16 mi/26 km E of Skowhegan; 44°46'N 69°25'W. Agr. trade center. Maine Central Inst. here. Settled 1794, inc. 1819 as Warsaw, renamed 1824. **2** town (1990 pop. 3,701), Merrimack co., S central N.H., 12 mi/19 km ENE of Concord; 43°17'N 71°18'W. Drained by Suncook R. Agr. (livestock, poultry; vegetables, corn, apples; dairying). Mfg. (apparel, labels, textiles). Settled 1768, inc. 1782. **3** town (1990 pop. 389), Rutland co., central Vt., 14 mi/23 km NE of Rutland, partly in Green Mt. Natl. Forest; 43°49'N 72°50'W.

Pittsford, town (1990 pop. 2,919), including Pittsford village, Rutland co., W central Vt., on Otter Creek, and 8 mi/12.9 km N of Rutland; 43°43'N 73°02'W. Marble, dairy prods., lumber. Includes village of East Pittsford. Fish hatchery here. Settled 1769; 2 forts here during Revolution.

Pittsford, residential village (1990 pop. 1,488), Monroe co., W N.Y., on the Barge Canal, just SE of Rochester; 43°05'N 77°31'W. Mfg. (filters, electrical equip., safes, testing and measuring equip.). Farming. Inc. 1827.

Pittsgrove, township (1990 pop. 8,121), Salem co., S N.J., 6 mi/9.7 km NW of Vineland; 39°32'N 75°07'W. Agr., vegetable farming. Inc. 1798.

Pittsound Island, E N.F., Canada, in Bonavista Bay; 5 mi/8 km long, 1 mi/2 km wide; 48°52'N 53°45'W.

Pittston (PITS-tuhn), city (1990 pop. 9,389), Luzerne co., NE Pa., suburb 6 mi/9.7 km NE of Wilkes-Barre and 10 mi/16 km SW of Scranton, on the Susquehanna R. (bridged); 41°19'N 75°47'W. It is a mining center for surface anthracite coal. Mfg. (fabricated metal prods., apparel, plastic prods., beverages, paper prods., printing, electrical equip.); mineral wool. Wilkes-Barre Scranton Internatl. Airport to NE. Settled c.1770 by the Susquehanna Company of Conn., inc. 1894 as a city.

Pittston, town (1990 pop. 2,444), Kennebec co., S Maine, on the Kennebec, just S of Augusta; 44°10'N 69°42'W. Settled c.1759, inc. 1779.

Pittsville 1 town (1990 pop. 602), Wicomico co., SE Md., 10 mi/16 km ENE of Salisbury; 38°23'N 75°25'W. In vegetable-farm area; tomato-packing plant. Named for William Pitts, president of the Wicomico and Pocomoke RR, it was once a major strawberry-growing area, but now is limited to pine-bark prods. and ornamental iron and collections of holly and evergreens in Dec. **2** town (1990 pop. 838), Wood co., central Wis., near Yellow R., 14 mi/23 km W of Wisconsin Rapids; 44°26'N 90°07'W. In dairy and farm area; cranberry bogs; cheese; pottery.

Pittsylvania, county (□ 978 sq mi/2,533 sq km; 1990 pop. 55,655), S Va.; ⊙ Chatham, independent city of Danville in S, separate from co.; 36°49'N 79°24'W. In Piedmont region; bounded S by N.C. state line, N by Roanoke R. (forms Leesville L., Smith Mt. L. reservoirs in NW): drained by Dan, Banister, Pigg, and Sandy rivers. Mfg. at Chatham, Hurt; agr. (rich tobacco-growing area; also hay, alfalfa, barley, wheat, soybeans, corn; cattle; dairying); timber. Formed 1767.

Piute (PEI-yoot), county (□ 765 sq mi/1,981 sq km; 1990 pop. 1,277), SW central Utah; ⊙ Junction; 38°20'N 112°07'W. Mt. and plateau area drained by Sevier R., East Fork Sevier R., and Otter Creek. Piute Reservoir, on Sevier R., is near Junction in SW; Piute State Park on N end. Parts of Fishlake Natl. Forest in W and center. Cattle, sheep; alfalfa, vegetables; dairying; gold, silver, antimony. Small part of Dixie Natl. Forest on S boundary; Otter Creek Reservoir and State Park in SE. Formed 1865.

Piute Reservoir, Utah: see SEVIER RIVER.

Pixley, uninc. town (1990 pop. 2,457), Tulare co., S central valley of Calif., 17 mi/27 km S of Tulare; 35°58'N 119°17'W. Agr. (cotton, alfalfa, grain, sugar beets; fruit, nuts, grapes, olives; cattle, hog, poultry). Pixley Natl. Wildlife Refuge to W.

Placedo, uninc. village (1990 pop. 515), Victoria co., S Texas, 13 mi/21 km SE of Victoria. RR junction in agr., cattle-raising area.

Placentia (pluh-SEHN-shuh), town (1991 pop. 1,954), SE N.F., Canada, on Placentia Bay; 47°14'N 53°58'W. Founded by the French in 1662 as Plaisance and was the Fr. hq. on N.F. until 1713.

Placentia, city (1990 pop. 41,259), Orange co., S Calif., suburb 25 mi/40 km SE of downtown Los Angeles and 5 mi/8 km NE of Anaheim; 33°53'N 117°51'W. Drained by Carbon Canyon Creek. Once a rural farming community, it has become a residential city with shopping centers. Mfg. (industrial prods., food prods., furniture, construction materials, electronic equip., machinery, plastics). Placentia has grown along with the continued development of the Orange co. area; the city's population doubled bet. 1970 and 1990. Abundant orange trees exist throughout the city. Carbon Canyon Dam (flood control) to NE; large Chino Hills State Park to NE. Inc. 1926.

Placentia Bay, SE N.F., Canada; c.100 mi/160 km long and up to 80 mi/129 km wide. Many fishing settlements and canneries along the shore. Placentia, site of a naval base since 1622, is the largest town.

Placentia Island, Maine: see LONG ISLAND.

Placer, county (□ 1,404 sq mi/3,636 sq km; 1990 pop. 172,796), central and E Calif.; ⊙ Auburn; 39°04'N 120°44'W. Narrow county extending E from Sacramento Valley, across foothills and crest of the Sierra Nevada (here reaching c.9,000 ft/2,743 m) to L. Tahoe, which forms point of E boundary (SE corner) on Nev. state line. Donner Pass is along N border. Drained by Bear R. (forms part of N border), Rubicon R., and Middle Fork of American R. Parts of Tahoe Natl. Forest in E ½ of co., small part of El Dorado Natl. Forest in E, along S border. Source of Trucker R. in E. Ghost towns like You Bet and Red Dog are reminders of region's rich yields during the gold rush. Winter sports (many ski resorts near L. Tahoe), hunting, fishing, camping in mts. Agr. (nursery prods., apiary prods., rice, walnuts, plum, kiwi fruit, wheat, oats, corn; cattle, sheep, turkeys). Mining and quarrying (clay, gold, sand, gravel); timber (pine, fir, cedar). SW corner of co. approaches Sacramento city, urbanized. Folsom L. reservoir and State Recreation Area (American R.) on SE boundary. Formed 1851.

Placerville, city (1990 pop. 8,355), ⊙ El Dorado co., E central Calif., c.40 mi/64 km ENE of Sacramento, in Sierra Nevada foothills, near South Fork of American R.; 38°44'N 120°48'W. Fruit-shipping center. Agr. (apples, grapes, walnuts; lamb, cattle, sheep, poultry). Mfg. (printing and publishing, diverse light mfg); lumber milling, logging; limestone quarrying. Gateway to sierra resorts (E). Hq. of El Dorado Natl. Forest. Gold mining in region. Discovery (1848) of gold at nearby Coloma, and soon after also on this site, made settlement one of largest and wealthiest in Calif. in 1850s. Its early inhabitants' celebrated exercise of frontier justice earned it the name "Hangtown." Marshall Gold Discovery State Park to NW; El Dorado Natl. Forest to E and W. Inc. as town in 1854, as city in 1903.

Placerville 1 village, San Miguel co., SW Colo., on San Miguel R., in NW foothills of San Juan Mts., and 14 mi/23 km WNW of Telluride. Elev. c.7,300 ft/2,225 m. Shipping point for cattle and sheep. Mining. Parts of Uncompahgre Natl. Forest to NW, E, and S. **2** village (1990 pop.14), Boise co., SW Idaho, 25 mi/40 km NNE of Boise; 43°57'N 115°57'W. Elev. 4,300 ft/1,311 m. In Boise Natl. Forest. Once important gold center.

Placetas (pluh-SAI-tuhz), city (1994 est. pop. 42,000), Villa Clara prov., central Cuba; 22°19'N 79°35'W. Tobacco processing is the city's chief industry. Located on a major highway; serves as a RR center. Nearby are sugar mills Juan Carbo (N), Hermanos Ameijeiras (E), and Benito Juárez (SE). Founded in 1867.

Placid, Lake, NE N.Y., in the Adirondack Mts., near Mt. Marcy; 4 mi/6.4 km long and c.1.5 mi/2.4 km wide; 44°19'N 73°59'W. The lake, with Lake Placid village at the S end, is a noted winter-sports center. It was the site of the 1980 Winter Olympics.

Placitas (pluh-SEE-tuhs), uninc. town (1990 pop. 1,611), Sandoval co., N central N.Mex., 7 mi/11.3 km E of Bernalillo, at N end of Sandia Mts. Cibola Natl. Forest to S, including Sandia Crest Recreation Area and Sandia Peak Ski Area; 35°19'N 106°28'W.

Plain, village (1990 pop. 691), Sauk co., S central Wis., 20 mi/32 km SW of Baraboo; 43°16'N 90°02'W. In dairy and livestock area; cheese prods. Natural Bridge State Park to NE.

Plain City, town (1990 pop. 2,722), Weber co., N Utah, suburb 9 mi/14.5 km NW of Ogden, on Weber R., near Great Salt L.; 41°17'N 112°04'W. Elev. 4,300 ft/1,311 m. Agr. (vegetables, fruit, barley alfalfa; cattle; dairying).

Willard Bay State Park to N; Harold S. Crane Waterfowl Management Area to NW. Settled 1859.

Plain City, village (1990 pop. 2,278), on Madison-Union co. line, central Ohio, 17 mi/27 km WNW of Columbus, and on Darby Creek; 40°06′N 83°16′W. In agr. area. Laid out 1818.

Plain Dealing (DEEL-eeng), town (1990 pop. 1,074), Bossier parish, NW La., near Ark. state line, 27 mi/43 km N of Shreveport; 32°55′N 93°42′W. In agr. area (cotton, hay; corn, wheat). Mfg. (cross ties, lumber, jackets); oil wells. Founded 1888.

Plain View, town, Scott co., E Iowa, 14 mi/23 km NW of Davenport.

Plainedge, uninc. area (□ 1 sq mi/2.6 sq km; 1990 pop. 8,739), Nassau co., SE N.Y., on central L.I.; 40°43′N 73°28′W. Chiefly residential, it is 1 of more than 30 communities that constitute the town of Oyster Bay.

Plaine-du-Nord (plen–dyoo–NOR), agr. town (1982 pop. 1,694), Nord dept., N Haiti, 6 mi/9.7 km SW of Cap-Haïtien; 19°41′N 72°16′W. Coffee, sugarcane, cacao, tobacco, tropical fruit; cattle.

Plainfield, city (1990 pop. 46,567), Union co., NE N.J.; 40°37′N 74°25′W. Formerly a residential city in the New York metropolitan area, it has become the urban center of 10 closely allied municipalities, with diversified industries, including printing and the mfg. of chemicals, machinery, electronic equip., and transportation equip. Among the several 18th-cent. bldgs. remaining are a Friends' meetinghouse (1788), the Martine house (1717), and the Nathaniel Drake House (1746), known as Washington's Hq. Nearby Washington Rock, overlooking the piedmont, is reputed to be the vantage point from which George Washington watched Br. troop movements. Settled 1684 by Friends, inc. as a city 1869.

Plainfield 1 town (1990 pop. 14,363), including Plainfield village, Windham co., E Conn., on Quinebaug R. (dammed here), and 15 mi/24 km E of Willimantic; 41°42′N 71°54′W. Includes Moosup village. Agr. (poultry, dairy prods.). Mfg. (textiles, wood prods., elastic prods., apparel, furniture) at villages of Wauregan and Central Village. Part of state forest here. Settled c.1690, inc. 1669. **2** town, Dodge co., S central Ga., 9 mi/14.5 km NE of Eastman; 32°17′N 83°06′W. **3** town (1990 pop. 10,433), Hendricks co., central Ind., on Whitelick Creek, and 7 mi/11.3 km SE of Danville; 39°42′N 86°23′W. Agr. area; lumber, dairy prods. Mfg. (metal prods., plastics, electrical prods.). Suburb of Indianapolis. Hq. Islamic Society of N. Amer.; Ind. Youth Center prison. Laid out 1839. **4** town (1990 pop. 455), Bremer co., NE Iowa, on Cedar R., and 10 mi/16 km N of Waverly; 42°50′N 92°32′W. Feed. Sand pit, limestone quarry nearby. **5** town (1990 pop. 571), Hampshire co., NW Mass., on headstream of Westfield R., and 18 mi/29 km ENE of Pittsfield; 42°31′N 72°56′W. **6** town (1990 pop. 2,056), Sullivan co., W N.H., 12 mi/19 km N of Claremont; 43°33′N 72°16′W. Bounded W by Connecticut R. (Vt. state line). Drained by Bloods Brook and Blow-me-down-Brook. Includes town of Meriden in E. Agr. (cattle, poultry; nursery crops; timber); light mfg. Site of bird sanctuary; 1st bird club in U.S. formed here 1910. **7** town (1990 pop. 1,302), Washington co., central Vt., just E of Montpelier; 44°15′N 72°24′W. Winter sports. Goddard Col. (founded 1938) is here. Plainfield village is partly in Marshfield town.

Plainfield 1 village (1990 pop. 4,557), Will co., NE Ill., on Du Page R. (bridged here), and 7 mi/11.3 km NW of Joliet; 41°37′N 88°12′W. In agr. area. Settled 1829 on site of a Native Amer. village and a trading post (est. 1790). **2** village (1990 pop. 178), Coshocton co., central Ohio, 9 mi/14 km ESE of Coshocton, and on Wills Creek; 40°12′N 81°43′W. **3** village (1990 pop. 839), Waushara co., central Wis., 21 mi/34 km SE of Wisconsin Rapids; 44°12′N 89°29′W. In agr. area (rye, potatoes); dairy prods.

Plains 1 town (1990 pop. 716), Sumter co., SW central Ga., 10 mi/16 km WSW of Americus; 32°02′N 84°23′W. Small agr. town in heart of peanut-growing area. Mfg. (wooden prods., pipes); peanuts. Home of Jimmy Carter, former President of the U.S. The Jimmy Carter Historic Site in town includes a visitor center, mus. in former Plains High School, the "Campaign HQ" depot, Billy Carter gas station, the Carter Home; state-run visitors center outside town. **2** town (1990 pop. 992), Sanders co., NW Mont., 61 mi/98 km NW of Missoula, and on the Clark Fork; 47°28′N 114°53′W. Agr. (hay; cattle, horses); forest industries, commercial greenhouses. Surrounded by units of Lolo Natl. Forest. Thompson R. State Forest to N. Originally called Horse Plains. **3** uninc. town (1990 pop. 4,694), Plains township, Luzerne co., NE central Pa., suburb 3 mi/4.8 km NE of downtown Wilkes-Barre, on Susquehanna R., in Wyoming Valley; 41°16′N 75°50′W. Mfg. (underground cable equip., textile prods., paper prods.). Pocono Downs Race Track is here. Includes communities of Hudson, Midvale, and Plainsville. **4** town (1990 pop. 1,422), ⊙ Yoakum co., NW Texas, on the Llano Estacado, 60 mi/97 km WSW of Lubbock; 33°11′N 102°49′W. Elev. 3,690 ft/1,125 m. In agr. (cotton; wheat, peanuts, sorghum; cattle) and oil region; gasoline refineries in area.

Plains, village (1990 pop. 957), Meade co., SW Kansas, 12 mi/19 km W of Meade; 37°15′N 100°35′W. In grain area; concrete.

Plains 1 Ohio: see THE PLAINS. **2** Va.: see THE PLAINS.

Plains of Abraham, Canada: see ABRAHAM, PLAINS OF.

Plainsboro, township (1990 pop. 14,213), Middlesex co., central N.J., near Millstone R., 12 mi/19 km NE of Trenton; 40°19′N 74°35′W. In rapidly suburbanizing area. Many corporate office parks have moved to the region.

Plainsville, Pa.: see PLAINS.

Plainview 1 uninc. city (□ 5 sq mi/13 sq km; 1990 pop. 26,207), Nassau co., SE N.Y., on L.I.; 40°46′N 73°28′W. It is chiefly residential. **2** city (1990 pop. 21,700), ⊙ Hale co., NW Texas, 40 mi/64 km NNW of Lubbock, on the Llano Estacado; 34°11′N 101°43′W. Elev. 3,366 ft/1,026 m. On White R. where it extends into Running Water Draw creek. The level plain, irrigated by shallow wells from a large underground water belt, yields wheat, grain sorghum, soybeans, cotton, and cattle raising. RR junction. Mfg. (food processing; hybrid seeds, farm equip.). Wayland Baptist Univ. is in the city. Inc. 1907.

Plainview 1 town (1990 pop. 2,768), Wabasha co., SE Minn., 17 mi/27 km NE of Rochester; 44°10′N 92°10′W. Agr. (grain; livestock, poultry; dairying). Mfg. (fertilizer, food prods., dairy prods.). Part of Richard J. Dorer Memorial Hardwood State Forest to N; Carley State Park to S; Whitewater Wildlife Area to E. Plotted 1857, inc. 1875. **2** town (1990 pop. 1,333), Pierce co., NE Nebr., 17 mi/27 km NW of Pierce; 42°21′N 97°47′W. Dairying; grain; livestock. Inc. 1880.

Plainview, village (1990 pop. 685), Yell co., W central Ark., 22 mi/35 km SSW of Russellville; 34°59′N 93°17′W. Mfg. (lumber). Nimrod L. Reservoir to S (Fourche La Fave R.); Ouachita Natl. Forest to N and S.

Plainville 1 town (1990 pop. 17,392), Hartford co., central Conn., in the sandy headwaters of the Quinnipiac R.; 41°40′N 72°51′W. Mfg. (metal prods., machinery, electrical prods.). The city park contains a restored portion of the New Haven–Northampton Canal, which operated here in the 1840s. Settled 1657, inc. 1869. **2** town (1990 pop. 444), Daviess co., SW Ind., 10 mi/16 km N of Washington; 38°48′N 87°09′W. Agr. area. Oil wells. **3** town (1990 pop. 2,173), Rooks co., NW central Kansas, 24 mi/39 km N of Hays; 39°13′N 99°17′W. Shipping point for wheat and livestock region. Mfg. (oil and natural gas, prefabricated wood bldgs.). Oil wells nearby. Rooks State Fishing L. to N. Settled 1877, inc. 1888. **4** town (1990 pop. 6,871), Norfolk co., SE Mass., near R.I. line, 4 mi/6.4 km NNW of Attleboro; 42°01′N 71°20′W. Mfg. (consumer goods, paper prods.); metal refining; dairying. Settled 1661, inc. 1905.

Plainville 1 village (1990 pop. 231), Gordon co., NW Ga., 12 mi/19 km NNE of Rome; 34°24′N 85°02′W. Mfg. (carpets and rugs, bricks). Clay mining. **2** village (1990 pop. 261), Adams co., W Ill., 16 mi/26 km SE of Quincy; 39°46′N 91°10′W. In agr. area.

Plainwell, town (1990 pop. 4,057), Allegan co., SW Mich., 11 mi/18 km NNW of Kalamazoo, on Kalamazoo R; 42°27′N 85°38′W. Agr. (apples, peaches; poultry, hogs; dairying). Mfg. (plastic prods., machining, paper, office equip., food prods.); ships produce. Settled 1836, inc. as city 1934.

Plaisance (ple-ZAWNGS), town (1982 pop. 2,823), Nord dept., N Haiti, in Massif du Nord, 21 mi/34 km SW of Cap-Haïtien; 19°36′N 72°28′W. Agr. (coffee, cacao, oranges); copper deposits nearby. Just S is village of Châtard.

Plaistow (PLAS-dou), town (1990 pop. 7,316), Rockingham co., SE N.H., 6 mi/9.7 km ENE of Salem, 4 mi/6.4 km NNW of Haverhill, Mass.; 42°50′N 71°05′W. Drained by Little R. Mfg. (electrical equip., printing and publishing, plastic prods., cryogenic equip., foods prods.). Agr. (vegetables, nursery crops; poultry, cattle; dairying).

Planada, uninc. town (1990 pop. 3,531), Merced co., central Calif., 9 mi/14.5 km E of Merced; 37°17′N 120°19′W. Dairying; poultry, cattle; alfalfa, grain, almonds, grapes, sugar beets, beans.

Plandome, village (1990 pop. 1,347), Nassau co., SE N.Y., on N shore of W L.I., on Manhasset Bay, just N of Manhasset; 40°48′N 73°42′W. Nearby are Plandome Heights (1990 pop. 854) and Plandome Manor (1990 pop. 788).

Plankinton, town (1990 pop. 604), ⊙ Aurora co., SE central S.Dak., 23 mi/37 km W of Mitchell; 43°43′N 98°28′W. In agr. region.

Plano 1 (PLAI-no), city (1990 pop. 5,104), Kendall co., NE Ill., near Fox R., 5 mi/8 km WNW of Yorkville; 41°39′N 88°31′W. Ships grain. Mfg. (plastics prods., fabricated metal prods.). Silver Springs State Park to S. Settled 1835, inc. 1865. **2** city (1990 pop. 128,713), Collin and Denton cos., N Texas, suburb 17 mi/27 km NNE of downtown Dallas; 33°02′N 96°45′W. Elev. 655 ft/200 m. Drained by White Rock, Pittman, and Rowlett creeks. RR junction in a farm and livestock area on the blackland prairie, Plano has become a booming city—a financial and commercial center and hq. for large natl. corporations. Mfg. (plumbing supplies, paper prods., medical prods., cable, metal prods., communication equip.). Large office complexes and housing developments have been constructed since the 1970s as the Dallas–Fort Worth metropolitan area has burgeoned. Plano has become one of the fastest-growing U.S. cities, marked by a pop. increase of nearly 78% bet. 1980 and 1990. The city was reached by RR in 1872; almost destroyed by fire in 1881. Site of Southfork Ranch (famous setting for "Dallas" television series); J.C. Penney Mus. recreated 1st store; hq. of retail chain; L. Lavor reservoir to E. Inc. 1873.

Plano, town (1990 pop. 75), Appanoose co., S Iowa, 9 mi/14.5 km W of Centerville; 40°45′N 93°02′W.

Plano, village (1990 pop.), Tulare co., central Calif., suburb 2 mi/3.2 km S of Porterville. Porterville State Hosp. to E.

Plant City, city (1990 pop. 22,754), Hillsborough co., W central Fla., 15 mi/24 km E of Tampa; 28°00′N 82°27′W. It is a processing, trade, and shipping center located in a growing suburban region at edge of metropolitan Tampa. The city is known esp. for its strawberries. Plant City was settled on the site of a Native Amer. village and developed with the coming of the RR in 1884. A large state farmers' market is here. Inc. 1885.

Plantagenet (plan-TA-jin-it), village (1991 pop. 949), SE Ont., Canada, on South Nation R. and 35 mi/56 km ENE of Ottawa. Agr. (dairying, mixed farming). Mineral springs nearby.

Plantain Garden River, c.20 mi/32 km long, St. Thomas parish, E Jamaica; rises in S slopes of Blue Mts.; flows E to Jamaica Channel at Holland Bay; 17°58′N 76°21′W. In its lower basin are sugar plantations and factories.

Plantation, city (□ 21 sq mi/54 sq km; 1990 pop. 66,692), Broward co., SE Fla., a residential suburb 7 mi/11.3 km W of Fort Lauderdale; 26°07′N 80°15′W. The city has grown rapidly; major housing developments and the presence of banking companies mark Plantation's urban boom. Inc. 1953.

Plantation, town (1990 pop. 830), Jefferson co., N Ky.,

residential suburb 8 mi/12.9 km ENE of downtown Louisville, near Ohio R.; 38°16′N 85°35′W.

Plantation Key, town (1990 pop. 4,405), Monroe co., upper Fla. Keys, 12 mi/19 km SW of Key Largo.

Plantersville, town (1990 pop. 1,046), Lee co., NE Miss., suburb 4 mi/6.4 km SSE of Tupelo, near East Fork Tombigbee R.; 34°12′N 88°40′W. Agr. (cotton, corn, soybeans; cattle, poultry; dairying). Mfg. (apparel, wood prods., plastic prods.).

Plantsville, Conn.: see SOUTHINGTON.

Plaquemine (PLA-kuh-min, or PLAK-min), city (1990 pop. 7,186), ⊙ Iberville parish, SE central La., 12 mi/19 km SSW of Baton Rouge, and on W bank (levee) of the Mississippi R. (toll ferry here); 30°17′N 91°14′W. Mfg. (chemicals, plastics, metal prods., machinery, food prods.); machine shops; lumber mills (cypress lumber), moss gins. In agr. area (rice, sugarcane, corn), commercial fisheries; oil wells, timber in region. Plaquemine Locks connect Port Allen–Morgan City Waterway with the Mississippi here. Inc. 1838.

Plaquemine, Bayou (PLA-kuh-min, BEI-yoo), Iberville parish, SE central La., formerly a distributary of the Mississippi at Plaquemine, whence it flowed SW to Grand R.; 30°13′N 91°19′W. Its dredged channel is now part of Plaquemine–Morgan City Waterway, connected with the Mississippi R. at Plaquemine by Plaquemine Locks (55 ft/17 m lift; completed 1909).

Plaquemine Brule, Bayou (PLA-kuh-min BROO-lee, BEI-yoo), c.75 mi/121 km long, S La.; rises in SW St. Landry parish; flows SW, passes N of Crowley, to Bayou des Cannes just above its junction with Bayou Nezpique to form Mermentau R.; 30°12′N 92°34′W. Navigable for 19 mi/31 km of lower course.

Plaquemine–Morgan City Waterway (PLA-kuh-min, or PLAK-min), c.55 mi/89 km long, S La.; connects Mississippi R. (through locks at Plaquemine) with Atchafalaya R. and main Intracoastal Waterway channel at Morgan City. All but the 1st 5 mi/8 km in N (from Plaquemine SW to Indian Village) has been incorporated into the newer PORT ALLEN–MORGAN CITY WATERWAY.

Plaquemines (PLA-kuh-minz), parish (□ 984 sq mi/2,549 sq km; 1990 pop. 25,575), extreme SE La., N part of New Orleans metro area; ⊙ Pointe a la Hache; 29°34′N 89°47′W. Occupies all of the central part of the delta of Mississippi R. below New Orleans and is the largest parish in the state; Barataria Bay and Gulf of Mexico are on W and S, Breton Sound and Gulf of Mexico on E. Bounded in part on NE by Bayou Terre Boeufs. In S, parish is chiefly swamp; the SE part of parish is a peninsula 10 mi/16 km–15 mi/24 km wide; the leveed Mississippi R. flows through it, radiating into 3 passes—North, South, and Southwest—as it enters the Gulf. The passes, or mouths, are bounded by narrow strips (levees) of land on both sides. Land mass is shrinking because of compaction, subsidence, and dredging. Numerous lakes and bayous in parish. Migratory waterflow refuge. Agr. (oranges, nursery crops, vegetables, tomatoes; cattle); oysters, shrimp, crabs, finfish, alligators. Natural gas, oil. Mfg. (chemicals, petroleum refining, electronic equip.; boatbuilding); food processing; hunting, fishing, fur (nutria) trapping. Includes Breton Isls. in Breton Sound, extension of Chandeleur Isls., and part of Breton Natl. Wildlife Refuge, Delta Natl. Wildlife Refuge, and Pass a Loutre State Wildlife Area in SE, at mouth of Mississippi R. Formed 1807.

Plasterco, uninc. village, Washington co., SW Va., near North Fork of Holston R., 3 mi/4.8 km SW of Saltville; 36°51′N 81°47′W. Gypsum mining and processing.

Platea (PLA-tee-ah), borough (1990 pop. 467), Erie co., NW Pa., 18 mi/29 km SW of Erie; 41°57′N 80°19′W. Agr. (grain, soybeans; livestock; dairying).

Plateado, El, Mexico: see GENERAL JOAQUÍN AMARO.

Plateau Mountain (3,855 ft/1,175 m), Greene co., SE N.Y., in the Catskills, 12 mi/19 km WNW of Saugerties; 42°09′N 74°11′W.

Platinum, village (1990 pop. 64), SW Alaska, at entrance to Goodnews Bay of Bering Sea, 120 mi/193 km W of Dillingham; 59°01′N 161°47′W. Platinum and osmiridium mining; 1st platinum strike made 1927. Airfield.

Plato (PLAI-do), village (1990 pop. 355), McLeod co., S Minn., 5 mi/8 km E of Glencoe, near Buffalo Creek; 44°46′N 94°02′W. Grain; dairying. Mfg. (cabinets).

Platón Sánchez (plah-TON SAHN-ches), town (1990 pop. 9,701), Veracruz, E Mexico, at foot of Sierra Madre Oriental, 11 mi/18 km SW of Tantoyuca; 21°18′N 98°21′W. Cereals, sugarcane, coffee, fruit.

Platt (PLAT), village, Washtenaw co., SE Mich., 4 mi/6.4 km SE of Ann Arbor. In farm area.

Platte 1 (PLAT), county (□ 414 sq mi/1,072 sq km; 1990 pop. 57,867), W Mo.; ⊙ Platte City; 39°22′N 94°46′W. Bounded S and W by Missouri R.; drained by Platte R. Kansas City suburbs include Parkville, Riverside, Weatherby Lake; urban growth area of Kansas City; Kansas City annexed into co. during 1960s. Agr. region (wheat, corn, tobacco); distillery at Weston; tobacco market at Weston (only one W of Mississippi R.). Weston Bend State Park. Kansas City Internatl. Airport in SE. Formed 1838. **2** county (□ 689 sq mi/1,785 sq km; 1990 pop. 29,820), E central Nebr.; ⊙ Columbus; 41°34′N 97°31′W. Agr. region bounded S by Platte R.; drained by Loup R. Mfg. at Columbus. Corn, alfalfa, soybeans, wheat; cattle, hogs; dairying. L. North and L. Babcock in SE. Formed 1855. **3** county (□ 2,111 sq mi/5,467 sq km; 1990 pop. 8,145), SE Wyo.; ⊙ Wheatland; 42°07′N104 °57′W. Watered by Chugwater Creek, North Platte (forms Guernsey and Glendo Reservoirs in N), and Laramie rivers. Agr. (corn, oats, wheat, hay, sugar beets, alfalfa, beans; cattle). Part of Laramie Mts. and small part of Medicine Bow Natl. Forest in W. Guernsey and Glendo state parks in N. Grayrocks Reservoir in E. Formed 1911.

Platte, town (1990 pop. 1,311), Charles Mix co., SE S.Dak., 40 mi/64 km SE of Chamberlain, near Platte Creek; 43°23′N 98°50′W. In dairying and agr. region (dairy prods., flour, cattle feed, corn). Co. fair held annually here. Settled 1882.

Platte, river, c.310 mi/499 km long, Nebr.; formed by the confluence of the North Platte (680 mi/1,090 km long) and South Platte (430 m/690 km) rivers at North Platte, Nebr.; flows generally E across S Nebr., past Kearney, Grand Island, and Columbus, to join the Missouri R. at Plattsmouth, Nebr. The river is too flood-prone in spring and too shallow and braided the rest of the year for navigation. Much of its water and the water of its tributaries is diverted for irrigation, municipal uses, and hydroelectric power production. Platte R., esp. W of Grand Island, is a major stop for migratory wild fowls and much visited by wildlife enthusiasts. The Platte valley was an important route to the West in the 19th cent.; the Mormon Trail followed the N bank, and the Oregon Trail followed the S bank. Continues as transportation route U.S. Highway 30, which follows Platte and South Platte length, from Fremont W past Ogallala; I-80 follows river from Grand Island W to Colo. boundary, I-76 continues along South Platte into Colo. as far as Fort Morgan. Extreme lower Platte affected by floods of 1993.

Platte Center, village (1990 pop. 387), Platte co., E central Nebr., 10 mi/16 km NW of Columbus, and on branch of Platte R.; 41°32′N 97°29′W. Irrigation pipe.

Platte City, city (1990 pop. 2,947), ⊙ Platte co., W Mo., on Platte R., and 23 mi/37 km NNW of downtown Kansas City; 39°21′N 94°46′W. Agr. (wheat, corn, tobacco; cattle). Destroyed by Union army during Civil War. Satellite community of Kansas City. Kansas City Internatl. Airport to SE. Plotted 1839.

Platte Lake 1 (PLAT), Benzie co., NW Mich., 4 mi/6.4 km N of Beulah, near L. Michigan; c.3.5 mi/5.6 km long, 1.5 mi/2.4 km wide. Resort area. Former Benzie State Park to N, now part of Sleeping Bear Dunes Natl. Lakeshore. **2** central Minn., largely in Crow Wing co., extends S into Morrison co., 25 mi/40 km NE of Little Falls; 3 mi/4.8 km long, 2 mi/3.2 km wide; 46°09′N 93°55′W. Narrow passage connects lake with Sullivan L., to SW, and Platte R.

Platte River 1 50 mi/80 km long, central Minn.; rises in Sullivan L., NE Morrison co., just W of passage to Platte L. (to NE); flows SW, through Rice L., where it receives Skunk R. from E, past Royalton to Mississippi R. 4 mi/6.4 km S of Royalton; 46°12′N 93°54′W. **2** c.35 mi/56 km long, Grant co., SW Wis.; rises c.15 mi/24 km W of Dodgeville; flows SW to the Mississippi, 7 mi/11.3 km N of Dubuque, Iowa.

Platte River, Iowa and Mo.: see LITTLE PLATTE RIVER.

Platte Woods, town (1990 pop. 444), Platte co., W Mo.; residential suburb 12 mi/19 km NNW of downtown Kansas City; 39°13′N 94°39′W.

Plattekill (PLA-tuh-kil), resort village (1990 pop. 1,400), Ulster co., SE N.Y., 8 mi/12.9 km NNW of Newburgh; 41°38′N 74°04′W.

Platteville, city (1990 pop. 9,708), Grant co., extreme SW Wis., on Little Platte R. (small branch of Platte R.), and 18 mi/29 km NNE of Dubuque, Iowa; 42°44′N 90°28′W. Trade center for dairying, farming; cheese. Mfg. (fluorescent and mercury ballasts for lighting, masks). Mining Mus. Seat of Univ. of Wis. Platteville. Wis.'s early territorial capitol bldg. (1836), now restored in First Capitol State Park to NE. W terminus of Pecatonica Trail. Founded 1827, inc. 1876.

Platteville, town (1990 pop. 1,515), Weld co., N Colo., on South Platte R., and 30 mi/48 km NNE of Denver, 16 mi/26 km SSW of Greeley; 40°13′N 104°49′W. Elev. 4,825 ft/1,471 m. Trade point in irrigated agr. area (poultry, eggs, cattle; sugar beets, fruit, beans). Mfg. (electronic equip., food processing, fertilizer). Reconstructed Fort Vasquez (state mus.), former adobe fur-trading post, is to S. Milton Reservoir to E; Barbour Ponds State Park to W.

Plattsburg, city (1990 pop. 2,248), ⊙ Clinton co., NW Mo., on Little Platte R., and 24 mi/39 km SE of St. Joseph; 39°34′N 94°27′W. Agr. (corn, wheat, soybeans; cattle, hogs); limestone. Mfg. (packaging, picture frames). Founded c.1835.

Plattsburgh, city (□ 6 sq mi/15.5 sq km; 1990 pop. 21,255), ⊙ Clinton co., NE N.Y., on L. Champlain; 44°42′N 73°27′W. It is a trade and distribution point, with plants making paper and plastics. A major source of employment has been the adjoining Plattsburgh Air Force Base, a Strategic Air Command installation, which was closed in 1993 by the Defense Base Closure and Realignment Commission. The city is also a summer vacation center, attracting Canadians as well as Americans. During the War of 1812 a makeshift Amer. fleet under Thomas Macdonough defeated the British in a pitched battle on L. Champlain near Plattsburgh, compelling an accompanying land-invasion force under Sir George Prevost to return to Canada. Seat of the State Univ. of N.Y. Col. at Plattsburgh, Clinton Co. Community Col.; Physicians' Hosp. is in the city. Settled 1767, inc. 1902.

Plattsmouth, town (1990 pop. 6,412), ⊙ Cass co., E Nebr., 15 mi/24 km S of Omaha, and on Missouri R., S of Platte R. mouth; 41°00′N 95°53′W. RR junction, trade center in grain, dairying region. Mfg. (furniture, lumber, machinery). Nearby bluffs along the Missouri contain deposits of clay, sand, and stone suitable for commercial use. Game refuge just N of city. Founded 1854–1855.

Plattsville, village, S Ont., Canada, on Nith R., and 14 mi/23 km NE of Woodstock. Flax and flour milling; dairying, mixed farming.

Plaucheville (PLO-shai-vil), village (1990 pop. 187), Avoyelles parish, E central La., 36 mi/58 km SE of Alexandria; 30°58′N 91°59′W. In agr. area (cotton, rice, sweet potatoes, soybeans).

Playa de Fajardo (PLAH-yah dai fah-HAHR-do), port of Fajardo, to its SE, NE P.R., opposite W of Culebra Isl., 33 mi/53 km ESE of San Juan. Major tourism center. Customhouse. E portion of Puerto Real.

Playa de Guayanilla, P.R.: see GUAYANILLA.

Playa de Humacao (PLAH-yah dai oo-mah-KOU), at Punta Santiago, village, E P.R., port for Humacao (5 mi/8 km WSW). Beach resort. Small Santiago Isl., on which the Univ. of P.R.'s Caribbean Primate Research Center maintains a monkey colony, is 1 mi/1.6 km off the coast.

Playa del Caimito (PLEI-yuh dail KEI-MEE-to), town,

on SE coast of La Habana prov., W Cuba, on N shore of Ensenada de la Broa, arm of Gulf of Batabanó; 22°41′N 81°53′W. Fishing.

Playa del Rey, suburban section of Los Angeles, Los Angeles co., S Calif., residential and beach resort area on Pacific Ocean, 12 mi/19 km WSW of downtown Los Angeles, 5 mi/8 km SSE of Santa Monica. Founded as resort 1903–1904; annexed 1911 by Venice (N), 1925 (with Venice) by Los Angeles. Loyola Marymount Univ. in E; Los Angeles Internatl. Airport in S; Marina del Rey on N, boat harbor; Dockwater State Beach is here.

Playa Dorada (PLAH-yah do-RAH-dah), beach resort zone, on N coast of Dominican Republic, E of Puerto Plata. Casinos, resort hotels.

Playa Girón (PLEI-yuh hee-RON), town, SE Matanzas prov., W central Cuba, at E entrance to Bahía de Cochinas (Bay of Pigs); 22°04′N 81°03′W. Landing site of abortive U.S.-directed counterrevolutionary invasion in 1961. Mus. and memorial site.

Playa Grande (PLAH-yah GRAHN-dai), locality, on Vieques isl., E P.R., 6 mi/9.7 km SW of Isabel Segunda. Former sugar-milling area.

Playa Rosario (PLEI-yuh ro-SAHR-ee-o), town, on SE coast of La Habana prov., W Cuba, on N shore of Ensenada de la Broa, arm of Gulf of Batabanó; 22°41′N 82°02′W. Fishing.

Playa Vicente (PLAH-yah vee-SEN-te), town (1990 pop. 7,438), Veracruz, SE Mexico, in N outliers of Sierra Madre del Sur, 37 mi/60 km S of Cosamaloapan; 17°50′N 95°49′W. Sugarcane, fruit.

Playas (PLEI-uhs), uninc. village, Hidalgo co., SW N.Mex., 25 mi/40 km S of Lordsburg. Cattle. Copper mining. Pyramid Mts. to W; Little Hatchet Mts. to E. Continental Divide to E, N, and W.

Playgreen Lake (□ 257 sq mi/666 sq km), central Man., Canada, N arm of L. Winnipeg; 62 mi/100 km long, 12 mi/19 km wide. Drains N into Nelson R.

Plaza, village (1990 pop. 193), Mountrail co., NW central N.Dak., 10 mi/16 km NE of Parshall; 48°01′N 101°57′W. Terminus of RR spur. Fort Berthold Indian Reservation to S.

Plaza de la Constitución (PLAH-zah dai lah kon-stee-too-see-ON), Span., *Zócalo*, city square, Mexico city, Mexico. This space has been the symbolic heart of Mexico since the founding of the Aztec empire. Before the Span. conquest it was part of the ceremonial center of Aztec Tenochtitlán; now it is the site of important natl. events such as independence day celebrations and presidential inaugurations. The Zócalo served as a public market place until the rule of Maximilian (1864–1867), when it was made into a formal park with trees, grass, sidewalks, and benches. The Zócalo was paved over early in this cent. and is now a vast, concrete-covered open space, the center of which is occupied during the day by a huge Mex. flag. The Metropolitan Cathedral is located on the N side of the plaza; begun in the 16th cent., but not completed until 1813, it is one of the largest cathedrals in Lat. Amer. E of the cathedral are the ruins of the principal Aztec temple, the Templo Mayor or Teocalli, buried after the conquest and rediscovered in 1978 during subway construction. An archaeological mus. adjoins the Templo Mayor on the E. The natl. palace occupies the former site of Moctezuma's palace E of the Plaza. This bldg. houses govt. offices and is noted for its famous murals by Diego Rivera. The Mexico city municipal palace (city hall) and other govt. bldgs. are on the S, and businesses are on the W side of the plaza.

Plaza Mayor, Mexico: see PLAZA DE LA CONSTITUCIÓN.

Pleasant Bay 1 Washington co., E Maine, branching inlet of the Atlantic, bet. Millbridge and Addison towns; 7 mi/11.3 km wide, 9 mi/14.5 km long. **2** E Mass., sheltered inlet of the Atlantic at SE elbow of Cape Cod, bet. Chatham and Orleans. Fishing and shellfishing.

Pleasant City, village (1990 pop. 419), Guernsey co., E Ohio, 9 mi/14 km SSE of Cambridge; 39°54′N 81°32′W. In agr. and coal area.

Pleasant Dale, village (1990 pop. 253), Seward co., SE Nebr., 13 mi/21 km SE of Seward, and on branch of Platte R; 40°47′N 96°55′W.

Pleasant Farms, uninc. town (1990 pop. 900), Ector co., W Texas, 10 mi/16 km S of Odessa. Ranching area (cattle, horses; pecans). Leading oil-producing area.

Pleasant Gap, uninc. town (1990 pop. 1,699), Spring township, Centre co., central Pa., 4 mi/6.4 km S of Bellefonte; 40°51′N 77°44′W. Light mfg. Agr. (corn, hay; livestock; dairying).

Pleasant Garden, uninc. town (1990 pop. 2,228), Gulford co., N central N.C., suburb 9 mi/14.5 km S of downtown Greensboro; 35°57′N 79°46′W. In agr. area (tobacco, grain, soybeans; poultry, livestock; dairying). Mfg. (bricks, air compressors).

Pleasant Green, uninc. rural community, Cooper co., central Mo., near Lamine R., 11 mi/18 km SSW of Boonville. Cattle; wheat, corn.

Pleasant Grove, city (1990 pop. 13,476), Utah co., N central Utah, suburb 10 mi/16 km NNW of Provo, 30 mi/48 km SSE of Salt Lake City, on Battle Creek, near Utah L. just W of Wasatch Range and the Uinta Natl. Forest; 40°22′N 111°43′W. Elev. 4,621 ft/1,408 m. Agr. (cattle, sheep; apples, cherries, berries) area; dairying. Mfg. (concrete, ranch equip., machinery, computer equip., motor vehicles). City is served by Provo R. irrigation project. Originally called Battle Creek. Timpanogos Cave Natl. Monument is nearby. Settled 1849 by Mormons, inc. 1855.

Pleasant Grove, suburb (1990 pop. 8,458), Jefferson co., N central Ala.; suburb 6 mi/9.7 km W of Birmingham; 33°29′N 86°58′W. Inc. 1933.

Pleasant Hill 1 city (1990 pop. 31,585), Contra Costa co., W Calif., suburb 11 mi/18 km NE of downtown Oakland, 2 mi/3.2 km SSW of Concord; 37°57′N 122°04′W. Mfg. (electronic equip., diverse light mfg.). Diablo Valley Community Col. Diablo State Park to SE; Mokelumne Aqueduct passes through city. Briones Regional Park to W. First settled in 1844, the area remained rural until the housing boom of World War II; inc. 1961. **2** city (1990 pop. 3671), Polk co., central Iowa, suburb 5 mi/8 km E of downtown Des Moines, on Des Moines R.; 41°35′N 93°30′W. Sawmill. **3** city (1990 pop. 3,827), Cass co., W Mo., 11 mi/18 km NNE of Harrisonville; 38°47′N 94°16′W. RR jct. Agr. Mfg.(treated lumber, wood prods., furniture). Laid out 1843.

Pleasant Hill 1 uninc. town (1990 pop. 1,114), Northampton co., N N.C., 10 mi/16 km NNE of Roanoke Rapids, at Va. state line; 36°15′N 80°53′W. Agr. area (peanuts, cotton, tobacco; poultry, livestock). **2** uninc. town (1990 pop. 1,659), Lebanon co., SE Pa., residential suburb 2 mi/3.2 km W of Lebanon on Quittapahilla Creek; 40°20′N 76°27′W. **3** town (1990 pop. 494), Cumberland co., E central Tenn., 9 mi/14 km WNW of Crossville; 35°59′N 85°12′W.

Pleasant Hill 1 village (1990 pop. 1,030), Pike co., W Ill., near the Mississippi, 12 mi/19 km SSW of Pittsfield; 39°26′N 90°52′W. In agr. area. **2** village (1990 pop. 824), Sabine parish, W La., 50 mi/80 km SSE of Shreveport; 31°49′N 93°31′W. Oil, natural gas. Agr. (poultry, exotic fowl, cattle; dairying); timber. Just N is Old Pleasant Hill, scene of Civil War battle (1864). **3** village (1990 pop. 1,066), Miami co., W Ohio, 9 mi/14 km SW of Piqua, and on Stillwater R.; 40°03′N 84°20′W. In agr. area.

Pleasant Hill, former Shaker settlement, Mercer co., central Ky., on Kentucky R., and 20 mi/32 km SW of Lexington. Last member of Shaker (religious group) colony here died 1925. Guest house, now a mus., contains relics. Settled 1805. Formerly Shakertown.

Pleasant Hill Lake, reservoir (□ 4 sq mi/10.4 sq km), Ashland co., N central Ohio, on Clear Fork Mohican R., 15 mi/24 km SE of Mansfield; 40°36′N 82°20′W. Max. capacity 87,700 acre-ft. Formed by Pleasant Hill Dam (113 ft/34 m high), built (1937) by Army Corps of Engineers for flood control; also used for recreation and as a fish and wildlife pond. Malabar Farm State Park at W end of reservoir.

Pleasant Hills, uninc. town (1990 pop. 1,650), Dauphin co., S Pa., residential suburb 6 mi/9.7 km NE of Harrisburg; 40°33′N 76°55′W.

Pleasant Hills, borough (1990 pop. 8,884), Allegheny co., SW Pa., residential suburb 7 mi/11.3 km S of downtown Pittsburgh; 40°19′N 79°57′W. Allegheny Co. Airport to NE; South Regional Park to SW. Inc. 1947.

Pleasant Hope, town (1990 pop. 360), Polk co., SW central Mo., 15 mi/24 km SSE of Bolivar; 37°27′N 93°16′W. Hay; cattle.

Pleasant Lake, village (1990 pop. 79), Stearns co., S central Minn., 8 mi/12.9 km SW of St. Cloud on small Pleasant L.; 45°30′N 94°16′W. Grain; dairying.

Pleasant, Lake, Maricopa co., S central Ariz., on Agua Fria R., 30 mi/48 km NNW of Phoenix; 5 mi/8 km long, 1 mi/1.6 km wide; 33°38′N 112°15′W. Max. capacity 856,400 acre-ft. Formed by New Waddell Dam (300 ft/91 m above the river bed; built 1986–1992) for irrigation and water storage from the Central Ariz. Project's Hayden-Rhodes Aqueduct during winter months. Earlier dam built (1927) for irrigation further upstream now submerged.

Pleasant, Lake, N.Y.: see LAKE PLEASANT.

Pleasant Mountain (2,007 ft/612 m), Oxford co., SW Maine, near Bridgton; 44°01′N 70°49′W. In resort area, developed ski area.

Pleasant Plain, town (1990 pop. 128), Jefferson co., SE Iowa, 11 mi/18 km NE of Fairfield; 41°08′N 91°51′W. In agr. area.

Pleasant Plain, village (1990 pop. 138), Warren co., SW Ohio, 24 mi/39 km ENE of downtown Cincinnati; 39°16′N 84°06′W.

Pleasant Plains 1 village (1990 pop. 256), Independence co., NE central Ark., 15 mi/24 km S of Batesville; 35°32′N 91°37′W. **2** village (1990 pop. 701), Sangamon co., central Ill., 15 mi/24 km WNW of Springfield; 39°52′N 89°55′W. Agr.; bituminous-coal mines; ships grain.

Pleasant Plains, sect. of Staten Isl. borough of N.Y. city, SE N.Y., on S Staten Isl.; 40°32′N 74°12′W. Outerbridge Crossing to N.J. is just W.

Pleasant Point, cape, SE Ont., Canada, on L. Ontario, on S side of entrance of Adolphus Reach, approach to the Bay of Quinte, 20 mi/32 km WSW of Kingston. Lighthouse.

Pleasant Pond, Kennebec co., S Maine, narrow lake (c.5 mi/8 km long) just SW of Gardiner. Drains NE into the Kennebec.

Pleasant Prairie, city, Kenosha co., SE Wis., suburb 3 mi/4.8 km S of Kenosha, and 12 mi/19 km N of Waukegan, Ill.; 42°31′N 87°52′W. Borders L. Michigan on E; Ill. on S. Mfg. (primary metals, metal prods.).

Pleasant Ridge, plantation (1990 pop. 91), Somerset co., central Maine, on the Kennebec R. just above Bingham; 45°06′N 69°59′W. Hunting, fishing.

Pleasant Ridge, city (1990 pop. 2,775), Oakland co., SE Mich., residential suburb 10 mi/16 km NW of downtown Detroit; 42°28′N 83°08′W. Mfg. (golf clubs). Detroit Zoological Park is to NW. Inc. as village 1919, as city 1928.

Pleasant River 1 c.22 mi/35 km long, central Maine; rises in 3 branches in central Piscataquis co.; flows SE to the Piscataquis E of Milo. The Gulf, gorge on W branch, is scenic feature. **2** c.25 mi/40 km long, Washington co., E Maine; rises in Pleasant L. near W boundary of co.; flows generally SE to Pleasant Bay below Columbia Falls.

Pleasant Run, uninc. village (1990 pop. 4,964), Hamilton co., extreme SW Ohio, a NNW suburb of Cincinnati, c.13 mi/21 km from downtown; 39°17′N 84°34′W.

Pleasant Unity, uninc. town (1990 pop. 900), Unity township, Westmoreland co., SW central Pa., 5 mi/8 km SE of Greensburg, on Sewickley Creek; 40°14′N 79°27′W. Corn, hay; dairying. Hillcrest Winery to W.

Pleasant Valley, town (1990 pop. 2,731), Clay co., W Mo., residential suburb 12 mi/19 km NE of downtown Kansas City, and 4 mi/6.4 km WSW of Liberty; 39°13′N 94°28′W.

Pleasant Valley 1 village, Scott co., E Iowa, on the Mississippi, 12 mi/19 km ENE of Davenport, immediately E of Bettendorf in Quad Cities area. Mfg. (machinery). Lock and Dam No. 14 to E. **2** village (□ 1 sq mi/2.6 sq km; 1990 pop. 1,688), Dutchess co., SE N.Y., 7 mi/11.3 km ENE of Poughkeepsie; 41°45′N

73°49′W. Light mfg. **3** village (1990 pop. 378), Wichita co., N Texas, residential suburb 6 mi/9.7 km WNW of downtown Wichita Falls, near Wichita R.; 33°56′N 98°35′W.

Pleasant Valley, Conn.: see BARKHAMSTED.

Pleasant View, town (1990 pop. 3,603), Weber co., N Utah, suburb 6 mi/9.7 km NNW of Ogden; 41°19′N 112°00′W. Wasatch Range and Natl. Forest to E. Hot springs nearby.

Pleasanton 1 city (1990 pop. 50,553), Alameda co., W Calif., a suburb 24 mi/39 km ESE of downtown Oakland on Arroyo de la Laguna; 37°40′N 121°54′W. RR junction. Mfg. (electronic equip., printing and publishing, computer equip., transporation equip., primary metals, medical supplies); stone quarrying. In a vineyard and dairy region; wine, cheese. Pop. tripled bet. 1970 and 1990. Pleasanton Ridge to W; Livermore Municipal Airport to E. Inc. 1894. **2** city (1990 pop. 1,231), Linn co., E Kansas, 22 mi/35 km N of Fort Scott, near Mo. state line; 38°10′N 94°42′W. In diversified agr. region; flour milling, poultry dressing. Civil War battle took place (1864) on site of city. Mus. Marais des Cygnes Waterfowl Refuge to N; Mine Creek Battlefield Park to S; Trading Post Mus. Complex 6 mi/9.7 km N. Inc. 1870.

Pleasanton 1 town (1990 pop. 58), Decatur co., S Iowa, near Mo. state line, 11 mi/18 km S of Leon; 40°34′N 93°44′W. **2** town (1990 pop. 7,678), Atascosa co., SW Texas, 32 mi/51 km S of San Antonio, and on Atascosa R.; 28°57′N 98°29′W. Elev. 374 ft/114 m. Agr. (cattle; vegetables, strawberries, peanuts; dairying), with oil and gas fields; light mfg. Est. 1858, inc. 1928.

Pleasanton, village (1990 pop. 372), Buffalo co., S central Nebr., 19 mi/31 km N of Kearney, and on South Loup R.; 40°58′N 99°05′W.

Pleasants, county (□ 135 sq mi/350 sq km; 1990 pop. 7,546), NW W.Va.; ⊙ St. Marys; 39°22′N 81°09′W. Bounded NW by Ohio R. (Ohio state line); drained by Middle Island Creek. Agr. (corn, wheat, alfalfa, hay); cattle. Coal mines, gas and oil wells. Formed 1851.

Pleasantville, residential and resort city (1990 pop. 16,027), Atlantic co., SE N.J., just W of Atlantic City; 39°23′N 74°31′W. It is the trade center of an area known as "the Mainland." Tourism, shellfishing, deep-sea fishing, and boatbuilding. Settled 1702, inc. 1888.

Pleasantville, town (1990 pop. 1,536), Marion co., S central Iowa, 8 mi/12.9 km NW of Knoxville; 41°23′N 93°16′W. In agr. area; feed mfg.

Pleasantville 1 residential village (□ 1 sq mi/2.6 sq km; 1990 pop. 6,592), Westchester co., SE N.Y.; 41°08′N 73°46′W. The village has well-known printing and publishing facilities; hq. of *Reader's Digest* is here. **2** village (1990 pop.926), Fairfield co., central Ohio, 27 mi/43 km ESE of Columbus; 39°48′N 82°31′W. In agr. area.

Pleasantville 1 (PLE-suhnt-vil), borough (1990 pop. 991), Bedford co., S Pa., 12 mi/19 km NNW of Bedford; 41°35′N 79°34′W. Diversified mfg. Agr. (apples, corn, oats, hay; dairying); timber. Covered bridge in area; Blue Knob State Park to N; Gallitzin State Forest to W. **2** borough (1990 pop. 215), Venango co., NW Pa., 5 mi/ 8 km SE of Titusville; 41°10′N 78°36′W. Oil; agr. (dairying). Oil Creek State Park to W; Pithole City Historic Site to S.

Pleasure Island, locality, New Hanover co., SE N.C., S tip extends into Brunswick co.; name given to S end of peninsula bet. Cape Fear R. estuary (W) and Atlantic Ocean (E), separated from mainland on N by 2-mi/ 3.2-km canal, part of Intracoastal Waterway (bridged), Cape Fear 5 mi/8 km to S on Bald Head Isl. Resort towns of Carolina Beach in N and Kure Beach in center.

Pleasure Ridge Park, uninc. city (1990 pop. 25,131), Jefferson co., N Ky., residential suburb 8 mi/12.9 km SSW of downtown Louisville; 38°08′N 85°50′W.

Pleasureville, town (1990 pop. 761), Henry and Shelby cos., N Ky., 18 mi/29 km NW of Frankfort, in Bluegrass region. Agr. (tobacco, grain; livestock; dairying). Also called South Pleasureville.

Plenty, village (1991 pop. 170), W Sask., Canada, near

Opuntie L. (7 mi/11 km long), 30 mi/48 km NE of Kindersley. Wheat.

Plentywood, town (1990 pop. 2,136), ⊙ Sheridan co., extreme NE Mont., on Big Muddy Creek, and 60 mi/ 97 km NW of Williston, N.Dak.; 48°46′N 104°33′W. Agr. (cattle, sheep, hogs, exotic game animals; wheat, barley, oats, safflower). An important center of communism in the 1920s and 1930s. Fort Peck Indian Reservation to SW. Inc. 1912.

Plessis, resort village (1990 pop. 320), Jefferson co., N N.Y., 5 mi/8 km SE of Alexandria Bay; 44°16′N 75°51′W. Lakes nearby.

Plessisville (PLEH-see-vil), village (1991 pop. 6,952), S Que., Canada, 24 mi/39 km WNW of Thetford Mines; 46°13′N 71°46′W. Milling, mfg. (maple prods.).

Pletipi Lake (pleh-tee-PEE), (□ 138 sq mi/357 sq km), central Que., Canada; 51°45′N 70°07′W. Fed and drained by R. aux Outardes; 28 mi/45 km long, 10 mi/ 16 km wide.

Plevna 1 (PLEV-nuh), village (1990 pop. 117), Reno co., S central Kansas, on North Fork Ninnescah R. and 21 mi/34 km WSW of Hutchinson; 37°58′N 98°18′W. Wheat. **2** village (1990 pop. 140), Fallon co., E Mont., on Sandstone Creek, at mouth of South Fork Sandstone Creek, 65 mi/105 km E of Miles City; 46°25′N 104°31′W. Wheat, oats, hay; cattle, sheep. South Sandstone Reservoir to SE.

Plonge, Lac la (PLOHZH, lak lah), lake (□ 64 sq mi/ 166 sq km), central Sask., Canada, 140 mi/225 km NNW of Prince Albert; 16 mi/26 km long, 10 mi/16 km wide. Drains N into Lac Île-à-Crosse and Churchill R. through Beaver R.

Plover 1 town (1990 pop. 101), Pocahontas co., N central Iowa, 10 mi/16 km N of Pocahontas; 42°52′N 94°37′W. Livestock; grain. **2** town (1990 pop. 8,176), Portage co., central Wis., 5 mi/8 km S of Stevens Point, on Wisconsin R.; 44°27′N 89°32′W. RR junction. Standing Rock Ski Area to E. Vegetables, potatoes; dairying. Mfg. (machinery, food).

Plover River, c.50 mi/80 km long, in central Wis.; rises in Langdale co.; flows SSW to Wisconsin R. 2 mi/ 3.2 km S of Stevens Point.

Plum, borough (1990 pop. 25,609), Allegheny co., SW Pa., residential suburb 13 mi/21 km ENE of downtown Pittsburgh, on the Allegheny R.; 40°30′N 79°45′W. Drained by Plum Creek. Bituminous coal area; also some agr. (apples; nursery livestock; dairying). Lock and Dam No. 3, on Allegheny R., in NW; Pittsburgh Monroeville Airport to SW; Boyce Regional Park and Ski Area in S. Founded 1788, inc. 1956.

Plum Beach, resort village, in North Kingstown, Washington co., R.I., on Narrangansett Bay, 20 mi/32 km S of Providence. Fine beach; sailing, fishing.

Plum Branch, village (1990 pop. 101), McCormick co., W S.C., 25 mi/40 km S of Greenwood; 33°51′N 82°15′W. Agr. includes timber; cattle, poultry; hay. On edge of Sumter Natl. Forest. J. Strom Thurmond L. reservoir to SW.

Plum City, village (1990 pop. 534), Pierce co., W Wis., 16 mi/26 km ENE of Red Wing, Minn.; 44°37′N 92°11′W. Dairying; livestock raising.

Plum Coulee (koo-LAI), village (1991 pop. 676), S Man., Canada, 55 mi/89 km SW of Winnipeg; 49°11′N 97°46′W. Mixed farming; grain; livestock.

Plum Creek (length with longest branch, c.40 mi/ 64 km.), central Colo.; rises in 2 branches in S Douglas co. West Plum formed by Bear and Gove creeks, flows N c.15 mi/24 km, East Plum rises in S Douglas co., flows N past Castle Rock then NW, c.35 mi/56 km, joining West Plum to form Plum Creek, flows NW c.15 mi/ 24 km to South Platte R. at Chatfield Reservoir, 5 mi/ 8 km SSW of Littleton.

Plum Island 1 in NE Mass., sandy island (¼ mi/ km– 1 mi/1.6 km wide) extending c.8 mi/12.9 km along coast, bet. Plum Isl. R. (bridged) and the Atlantic, from mouth of Merrimack R. (N) to Plum Isl. Sound (arm of Ipswich Bay) at mouth of Ipswich R. (S). Summer resort; lighthouse on N end. A state park is at S end. The W ½ of the isl. is largely a wildlife refuge. Plum Isl.

Beach, Plum Isl. State Park, Parker R. Natural Wildlife Sanctuary. **2** (c.2.5 mi/4 km long), SE N.Y., off Orient Point (NE tip of L.I.), at N side of entrance to Gardiners Bay; lighthouse (41°10′N 72°13′W). Site of old U.S. Fort Terry. Isl., owned by Suffolk co., is used as recreational area.

Plum River, c.55 mi/89 km long, in NW Ill.; rises in Jo Daviess co.; flows S and SW to the Mississippi at Savanna; 42°20′N 89°59′W.

Pluma Hidalgo (PLOO-mah hee-DAHL-go), town (1990 pop. 895), in S cental Oaxaca, Mexico, 14 mi/20 km NNE of San Pedro Pochutla; 15°55′N 96°25′W. Elev. 4,839 ft/1,475 m. Mountainous. Temperate climate. Agr. (coffee, corn, sugarcane, beans, pineapple, mangoes, lemons). On unpaved road.

Plumas, county (□ 2,554 sq mi/6,615 sq km; 1990 pop. 19,739), NE Calif., in the Sierra Nevada; ⊙ Quincy; 40°01′N 120°50′W. Mt. Ingalls (8,377 ft/2,553 m), parts of Plumas Natl. Forest in center, S and E parts of Lassen Natl. forest in NW and part of Lassen Volcanic Natl. Park in NW corner. L. Almanor (NW) (resorts), L. Davis and Frenchman L. (E), and other reservoirs are impounded by power dams. Drained by North, Middle, and South forks of Feather R., here formed by forks flowing in scenic canyons. All of co., except extreme SE, N, and SW corners, in natl. forest. Hunting, fishing; hot springs; winter sports. Timber (pine, fir, cedar), livestock grazing; alfalfa, hay, Christmas trees grown in mt. basins, largest of which is Sierra Valley (partly in co.). Mining of gold (since 1850), copper, silver; quarrying of sand and gravel. Formed 1854. Pacific Crest Natl. Scenic Trail crosses co. in SW; Plumas-Eureka State Park in S.

Plumas (PLOO-muhs), village, S central Man., Canada, 20 mi/32 km ENE of Neepawa.

Plumerville (PLUHM-uhr-vil), town (1990 pop. 832), Conway co., central Ark., 11 mi/18 km WNW of Conway, near Arkansas R.; 35°09′N 92°38′W. Mfg. (lumber). Brewer L. Reservoir to NE. Also spelled Plummerville.

Plummer, town (1990 pop. 804), Benewah co., N Idaho, 15 mi/24 km W of St. Maries; 47°20′N 116°53′W. Trade town in Coeur d'Alene Indian Reservation. Mfg. (lumber). Heyburn State Park to E.

Plummer, village (1990 pop. 277), Red Lake co., NW Minn., on Clearwater R., and 10 mi/16 km E of Red L. Falls; 47°55′N 96°02′W. RR junction. Grain, sugar beets, sunflowers, potatoes; cattle.

Plummer Island, Md.: see CABIN JOHN.

Plumstead, township (1990 pop. 6,005), Ocean co., E central N.J., 7 mi/11.3 km W of Lakehurst; 40°02′N 74°28′W. Inc. 1845.

Plumsteadville (PLUHM-sted-vil), uninc. town (1990 pop. 1,200), Berks co., SE Pa., 5 mi/8 km N of Doylestown; 40°23′N 75°08′W. Diverse mfg. Agr. includes dairying; livestock, poultry; grain, soybeans, apples.

Plumtree, village, Avery co., NW N.C., 28 mi/45 km NW of Morganton, on North Toe R., near edge of Pisgah Natl. Forest (W). Mica mining. Tobacco, hay; cattle. Mfg. (mica electrical components).

Plumville (PLUHM-vil), borough (1990 pop. 390), Indiana co., W central Pa., 12 mi/19 km N of Indiana, on North Branch of Plum Creek; 40°47′N 79°10′W. Agr. (corn, hay; dairying). Keystone L. reservoir to SW.

Plymouth, town, ⊙ Montserrat isl., B.W.I., port on W coast; 16°43′N 62°13′W. Administrative center on open roadstead in tropical setting. Exports cotton, citrus fruit, vegetable oil, lime juice, sugarcane, cattle. Has nearby hot springs, gypsum and sulphur deposits. Airport nearby. Ruins of Fort St. George built by French in 1782 during brief occupation. Amer. Univ. of the Caribbean Medical School located here.

Plymouth (PLAI-moth), town, SW Tobago, Trinidad and Tobago, on N coast 4 mi/6.4 km NW of Scarborough, overlooking Great Courland Bay. Coconut growing. Ruins of Fort St. James.

Plymouth 1 county (□ 864 sq mi/2,238 sq km; 1990 pop. 23,388), NW Iowa, on S.Dak. state line (W; formed here by Big Sioux R.); ⊙ Le Mars; 42°44′N 96°13′W. Prairie agr. area (cattle, hogs, poultry, sheep; corn, oats, barley), drained by Floyd R. and West Fork of Little Sioux R.; sand and gravel pits. Formed 1851. **2** county (□ 1,093 sq mi/2,831 sq km; 1990 pop. 435,276), SE Mass.; ⊙ Plymouth; 42°00′N 70°44′W. On Massachusetts Bay and Cape Cod Bay (E), Buzzards Bay (S). Its shore communities are popular summer resorts. Includes town of North Plymouth (1990 pop. 3,450). Some industry; agr. (cranberries, vegetables; poultry). Was 1st settled town in Mass. by Pilgrims (1620). Historical sites include: Plymouth Rock (1st landing of Pilgrims), Mayflower II, Plymouth Plantation, Cranberry World Visitor Center. Formed 1685. Pilgrim Nuclear Power Plant (initial criticality June 16, 1972) 4 mi/6.4 km SE of Plymouth; uses cooling water from Cape Cod Bay, and has a max. dependable capacity of 670 MWe.

Plymouth 1 city (1990 pop. 811), Amador co., central Calif., 35 mi/56 km E of Sacramento, on Dry Creek, in Sierra Nevada foothills; 38°29′N 120°51′W. Gold mining; grain, walnuts, grapes; cattle; wineries. **2** city (1990 pop. 8,303), ⊙ Marshall co., N Ind., on Yellow R., and 24 mi/39 km S of South Bend; 41°21′N 86°19′W. RR junction. Shipping and trading center in agr. area (cattle; dairy prods.; soybeans, corn). Highly diversified mfg. Popular resort lakes mainly to SW. The Potawatomi Indians had a village on this site. Laid out 1834, inc. 1872. **3** city (1990 pop. 9,560), Wayne co., SE Mich., suburb 22 mi/35 km WNW of downtown Detroit, and on the Middle R. Rouge, 42°22′N 83°28′W. Diversified mfg. Parkway along river. Settled 1825; inc. as village 1867, as city 1932. **4** city (1990 pop. 50,889), Hennepin co., SE Minn., a suburb 9 mi/14.5 km WNW of downtown Minneapolis; 45°01′N 93°27′W. Highly diversified mfg. A residential suburb, rapidly growing along with the development of the Minneapolis-St. Paul area. Several small lakes in city; Medicine L. in SE, drained by Bassett Creek. L. Minnetonka to SW. Inc. 1955.

Plymouth 1 town (1990 pop. 11,822), Litchfield co., W central Conn., near Naugatuck R., just N of Waterbury; 41°40′N 73°01′W. Mfg. (electronic equip.; fabricated metal prods.; consumer goods; wood, plastic, and metal prods.). Includes Terryville (1990 pop. 5,426) and Pequabuck villages. Settled 1728, inc. 1795. **2** town, Orange co., central Fla., 15 mi/24 km NW of Orlando, near L. Apopka; 28°43′N 81°33′W. Large citrus-fruit canneries. **3** town, Cerro Gordo co., N Iowa, on Shell Rock R., and 8 mi/12.9 km NE of Mason City. RR junction. Feed; sand and gravel pits. **4** town (1990 pop. 1,152), Penobscot co., S Maine, 23 mi/37 km WSW of Bangor; 44°46′N 69°13′W. In agr. area. **5** uninc. town (1990 pop. 45,608), ⊙ Plymouth co., SE Mass., on Plymouth Bay, 34 mi/55 km SE of Boston; founded 1620; 41°54′N 70°37′W. Various light mfg. is important to the economy. Wineries. The town, with summer resort facilities and major historic attractions, has a large tourist industry. Its harbor, now used by fishing boats and leisure craft, was the scene of the famous landing by the Pilgrims in 1620, and Plymouth was the 1st permanent Eur. settlement in New England (Plymouth Colony). Most famous of its many monuments is Plymouth Rock, returned to its original site in 1880; according to legend, the Pilgrims stepped on this boulder when disembarking from the *Mayflower.* The *Mayflower II,* a replica of the original ship, is moored here. The sites of the 1st houses are marked by tablets on Leyden St., the 1st street laid out by the Pilgrims. A number of 17th-cent. houses on nearby streets are maintained as museums. Cole's Hill and Burial Hill contain graves of many of the 1st settlers, and Pilgrim Hall has numerous valuable relics. Near the site of the original village is the 80-ft/24-m granite *National Monument to the Forefathers,* (1889) which is the largest granite monument in the U.S. Of great interest is nearby Pilgrim Village, Plymouth Plantation, a re-creation of the early settlement. The town also has a wax mus. and a marine mus. and aquarium. Myles Standish State Forest to S. Includes villages of Manomet and North Plymouth. Oldest Wooden courthouse in the U.S. (1749). Also Cranberry World Visitor Center and Pilgrim Nuclear Power Plant. Priscilla Beach, White Horse Beach, Manoticut Beach. **6** town (1990 pop. 5,811), Grafton co., central N.H., 18 mi/29 km NNW of Laconia; 43°44′N 71°43′W. Drained by Pemigewasset R. and Baker R. W of Squam L. Winter sports; mfg. (wood prods., wire, pillows); agr. (apples, nursery crops, vegetables; poultry; dairying). Plymouth State Col., state's oldest teachers col. (1871) is here. Nathaniel Hawthorne d. here (1864). Plymouth Mt. (2,187 ft/667 m) in S; Tenney Mt. (2,310 ft/704 m) in W. Covered bridge. Inc. 1763. **7** town (1990 pop. 4,328), ⊙ Wash. co., E N.C., 28 mi/45 km NE of Wash., on Roanoke R., near its entrance to Albermerle Sound; 35°51′N 76°45′W. RR junction. Timber; cotton, peanuts, tobacco, grain; poultry, livestock; hunting, fishing. Mfg. (apparel, wood prods., paper prods.). Founded late 18th cent.; inc. 1800. **8** town (1990 pop. 440), Windsor co., S central Vt., 10 mi/16 km SW of Woodstock; 43°31′N 72°43′W. Birthplace and grave of Calvin Coolidge here; Coolidge State Forest nearby. Includes Tyson, resort village on small Echo L. **9** town (1990 pop. 6,769), Sheboygan co., E Wis., on Mullet R. (tributary of Sheboygan R.), and a suburb 13 mi/21 km W of Sheboygan; 43°45′N 87°58′W. In dairy and grain area; cheese and dairy prods.; mfg. (consumer goods; food prods.; printing). Kettle Moraine State Forest to W. Inc. 1877.

Plymouth 1 village, Hancock co., W Ill., 15 mi/24 km ESE of Carthage; 40°17′N 90°55′W. In agr. area (grain; dairy prods.; livestock); oil refinery. **2** village (1990 pop. 455), Jefferson co., SE Nebr., NE of Fairbury; 40°17′N 96°59′W. Livestock trailers. Homestead Natl. Monument to E (in Gage co.). **3** village (1990 pop. 1,942), on Richland-Huron co. line, N central Ohio, 17 mi/27 km NNW of Mansfield; 40°59′N 82°36′W. Settled 1815, inc. 1838. **4** village (1990 pop. 267), Box Elder co., N Utah, 27 mi/43 km NNW of Brigham City, near Malad R.; 41°52′N 112°08′W. Elev. 4,400 ft/1,341 m. Wheat, barley, alfalfa, sugar beets; cattle, sheep. Caribou Natl. Forest to N.

Plymouth, borough (1990 pop. 7,134), Luzerne co., NE central Pa., residential suburb 4 mi/6.4 km W of Wilkes-Barre, on Susquehanna R. (bridged); 41°14′N 75°57′W. Mfg. (filament fibers, apparel, concrete; printing). State correctional facility to NW; part of Lackawanna State Forest to W; Larksville Mt. to NW. Inc. 1866.

Plymouth Bay, SE Mass., inlet of the Atlantic with entrance bet. Gurnet Point (N) and Rocky Point (S), NW of Cape Cod Bay; c.7 mi/11.3 km long, 4 mi/6.4 km wide. Plymouth Harbor is S arm, with Plymouth on its SW shore; Duxbury Bay is N arm, protected from the Atlantic by 5 mi/8 km sandbar with Gurnet Point (lighthouse here) at SE tip (42°00′N 70°36′W). Protected harbor discovered by Pilgrims in 1620 after stopping at Provincetown.

Plymouth Meeting, uninc. town (1990 pop. 6,241), Whitemarsh township, Montgomery co., SE Pa., suburb 12 mi/19 km NW of Downtown Philadelphia, and 2 mi/3.2 km NE of Conshohocken; 40°06′N 75°16′W. Diversified mfg. Wings Field Airport to N; Fort Washington State Park to NE. Has old meetinghouse built 1710–1712, rebuilt 1867.

Plymouth Rock, Mass.: see PLYMOUTH.

Plympton, town (1990 pop. 2,384), Plymouth co., SE Mass., 7 mi/11.3 km W of Plymouth; 41°58′N 70°49′W. Cranberries. Settled 1662, inc. 1707.

Plymptonville (PLIMP-tuhn-vil), uninc. town (1990 pop. 1,074), Lawrence township, Clearfield co., central Pa., residential suburb 2 mi/3.2 km N of Clearfield; 41°02′N 78°27′W.

Poanas, Mexico: see VILLA UNIÓN, Durango.

Poboktan Mountain (po-BAHK-tuhn) (10,920 ft/3,328 m), SW Alta., Canada, near B.C. border, in Rocky Mts., in Jasper Natl. Park, 50 mi/80 km SE of Jasper.

Poca (PO-kuh), town (1990 pop. 1,124), Putnam co., W central W.Va., 14 mi/23 km NNW of Charleston, on Pocatalico R., 1 mi/1.6 km E of its mouth on Kanawha R.; 38°28′N 81°48′W. Agr. (corn, tobacco); cattle, poultry; mfg.

Pocahontas 1 (po-kuh-HAHN-tuhs), county (□ 579 sq mi/1,500 sq km; 1990 pop. 9,525), N central Iowa; ⊙ Pocahontas; 42°43′N 94°40′W. Prairie agr. area (cattle, hogs, poultry; corn, oats, soybeans), with coal deposits in SE. Lizard L. in E; Kalsow Prairie State Preserve in S. Formed 1851. **2** county (□ 942 sq mi/2,440 sq km; 1990 pop. 9,008), E W.Va.; ⊙ Marlinton; 38°19′N 80°00′W. In the Allegheny Mts.; Allegheny Mt. extends along E border (Va. state line). Includes Droop Mt. Battlefield and Watoga state parks in S. Most of co. is in Monongahela Natl. Forest, except for SW and center. Drained by Greenbrier, Gauley, Cranberry, and Shavers Fork rivers. Agr. (corn, oats, potatoes, alfalfa, hay, apples); cattle, poultry, sheep; timber. Some mfg. at Marlinton. Elk R., Silver Creek, and Snowshoe ski areas in NW. Seneca State Forest in NE center; Cass Scenic RR State Park in N; Calvin Price State Forest in S; Greenbrier R. State Trail follows Greenbrier R. through center from S. Formed 1821.

Pocahontas 1 (po-kuh-HAHN-tuhs), town (1990 pop. 6,151), ⊙ Randolph co., NE Ark., 32 mi/51 km NNW of Jonesboro, on Black R.; 36°16′N 90°58′W. Historic riverport town, in diversified agr. area; mfg. (cut leather, shoes, transportation equip., fabricated metal prods., consumer goods). Old Davidsonville State Park to SW; Dave Donaldson–Black R. Wildlife Management Area to E. **2** town (1990 pop. 2,085), ⊙ Pocahontas co., N central Iowa, 30 mi/48 km WNW of Fort Dodge; 42°44′N 94°40′W. Ships livestock, grain; mfg. (concrete, machinery, feeds, fertilizers). Kalsow Prairie State Preserve to S. Inc. 1892. **3** town (1990 pop. 90), Cape Girardeau co., SE Mo., near Mississippi R., 8 mi/12.9 km N of Jackson; 37°30′N 89°38′W. **4** town (1990 pop. 513), Tazewell co., SW Va., in Allegheny Mts., near W.Va. state line, 4 mi/6.4 km NNW of Bluefield; 37°18′N 81°20′W. Agr. (livestock); bituminous coal. Founded 1882; inc. 1884.

Pocahontas, village (1990 pop. 837), Bond co., SW central Ill., 25 mi/40 km WSW of Vandalia; 38°49′N 89°32′W. In agr. area (corn, wheat, vegetables; livestock; dairy prods.). Formerly a stagecoach stop on old Natl. Road.

Pocasset, Mass.: see BOURNE.

Pocatalico (po-kuh-TAL-uh-ko), uninc. town, Kanawha co., W central W.Va., 12 mi/19 km N of Charleston, on Pocatalico R. Woodrum Wildlife Management Area to N.

Pocatalico River, c.75 mi/121 km long, W central W.Va.; rises in central Roane co.; flows generally SW, past Pocatalico and Poca, to Kanawha R., 1 mi/1.6 km W of Poca.

Pocatello, city (1990 pop. 46,080), ⊙ Bannock co., SE Idaho, 195 mi/314 km ESE of Boise, bet. mts. on the Portneuf R. near its junction with the Snake R. (forms American Falls Reservoir to NW); 42°53′N 112°28′W. A RR center since 1882, Pocatello is a major shipping and processing point for a livestock and farm area. It has an important mining industry (large phosphate deposits are nearby) and plants mfg. electronic equip., chemicals, metal prods., and asphalt and concrete. Tourism is significant; excellent skiing and water sport facilities are in the area. Idaho Mus. of Natural History, Pocatello Municipal Aiport. Pocatello is the seat of Idaho State Univ. and the hq. for Caribou Natl. Forest. Bannock Co. Fairgrounds to NE; Fort Hall Indian Reservation with its irrigation project to N and W; the site of Fort Hall (1834) is on the nearby Snake R.; Old Fort Hall Replica to S; Part of Caribou Natl. Forest to S; Pebble Creek Ski Area in E. Inc. 1889.

Pochutla, Mexico: see SAN PEDRO POCHUTLA.

Pocola (puh-KO-luh), town (1990 pop. 3,664), Le Flore co., E Okla., on Ark. border, suburb 10 mi/16 km SSW of Fort Smith, Ark., on Poteau R.; 35°14′N 94°28′W. Agr. and timber area near Ouachita Mts. Mfg. (furniture).

Pocomoke City or **Pocomoke**, town (1990 pop. 3,922), Worcester co., SE Md., on Delmarva Peninsula 20 mi/32 km S of Salisbury, and on Pocomoke R.; 38°04′N 75°34′W. River shipping point in vegetable farm and timber area; mfg. (clothing, lumber, flour, feed, fertilizer, fabricated metal prods.; vegetable canneries, meatpacking and poultry-dressing plants). Successively called Stevens, Warehouse, and Meeting-House Landing point in the early 18th cent., until it was laid out in 1780 and called Newtown; became Pocomoke City in 1878. Fires in 1888, 1892, and 1922 destroyed most of the old structures.

Pocomoke River, c.15 mi/24 km long, SE Md., an arm of Chesapeake Bay, crossed by Md.-Va. boundary; up to 10 mi/16 km wide. Above Pocomoke City, the river is not very accessible and remains a sanctuary for wildlife, esp. in Pocomoke State Forest and Milburn Landing and Shad Landing state parks.

Pocono Lake (PO-kah-no), uninc. village, Tobyhanna township, Monroe co., NE Pa., 17 mi/27 km NW of Stroudsburg, in Pocono Mts.; 41°06'N 75°28'W. Mfg. (printing and publishing); resort area. Pocono L. reservoir and Pocono L. Preserve (resort) to W; L. Naomi reservoir to E.

Pocono Manor (PO-kah-no), uninc. village, Pocono township, Monroe co., NE Pa., in Pocono Mts., 12 mi/19 km NW of Stroudsburg, and 2 mi/3.2 km S of Mount Pocono; 41°06'N 75°21'W. Resort area; skiing, golf.

Pocono Mountains (PO-kah-no), range of low hills (c.2,000 ft/610 m) in the Appalachian Mt. system, NE Pa.; 41°18'N 75°12'W–40°59'N 75°27'W. Forested and having many lakes and streams, the Poconos are a major resort area. There are year-round recreational facilities, including well-known ski areas. Since the 1970s, the area has experienced significant residential development, with homes owned by retirees and weekend commuters from N.Y. city and Philadelphia.

Pocono Pines (PO-kah-no), uninc. town (1990 pop. 824), Monroe co., NE Pa., in Pocono Mts., 15 mi/24 km NW of Stroudsburg; 41°07'N 75°27'W. Light mfg. L. Naomi reservoir at center of community, Pocono L. reservoir to W, both on Tobyhanna Creek. Pocono Internatl. Raceway to SW.

Pocono Springs (PO-kah-no), uninc. town, Wayne co., NE Pa., residential development 16 mi/26 km SE of Scranton on Pocono Peak L., the source of the Lehigh R.; 41°16'N 75°24'W.

Pocono Summit (PO-kah-no), uninc. town (1990 pop. 1,500), Monroe co., NE Pa., Tobyhanna and Coalbaugh townships, in Pocono Mts., 13 mi/21 km NW of Stroudsburg; 41°06'N 75°23'W. Surrounds Pocono Summit L. reservoir. Resort area. Mfg. (wooden cabinets and furniture, machinery). Pocono Mts. Municipal Airport to N; Stillwater L. reservoir to W.

Pocotalago (po-kuh-tah-LAI-go), town, Madison co., NE Ga., 17 mi/27 km NNE of Athens; 34°11'N 83°17'W.

Pocotopaug Lake (pe-ka-to-PAHG), reservoir, East Hampton town, Middlesex co., central Conn., on Pocotopaug R., 8 mi/12.9 km ENE of Middletown; 1.5 mi/2.4 km long; 41°35'N 72°30'W.

Pocumcus Lake (po-KUHM-kuhs), Wash. co., E Maine, in chain bet. Sysladobsis and Grand lakes, 32 mi/51 km W of Calais; 5 mi/8 km long.

Poge, Cape, Mass.: see CHAPPAQUIDDICK ISLAND.

Pogromni Volcano (6,568 ft/2,002 m), SW Alaska, on W Unimak Isl., 11 mi/18 km N of Unimak village; 54°34'N 164°42'W. Active.

Pohatcong Mountain (po-HAT-kuhng) (c.800 ft/244 m), NW N.J., ridge of the Appalachians extending NE from point E of Phillipsburg to vicinity of Hackettstown; NE part is called Upper Pohatcong Mtn.; 40°43'N 75°01'W. Agr., dairying region. W of Hackettstown is source of the Pohatcong River, which flows c.35 mi/56 km SW, along SE foot of the Pohatcongs, to Delaware R. above Riegelsville.

Poinciana Place Park (POIN-see-an-nah), town (□ 8 sq mi/20.7 sq km; 1990 pop. 3,618), Citrus co., W central Fla., 5 mi/8 km E of Inverness; 28°09'N 81°28'W.

Poinsett (POIN-set), county (□ 763 sq mi/1,976 sq km; 1990 pop. 24,664), NE Ark.; ⊙ Harrisburg; 35°34'N 90°39'W. Intersected by Crowley's Ridge; drained by St. Francis and L'Anguille rivers and Left Hand and Right

Hand Chutes of Little R. Agr. (cotton, rice, wheat, soybeans, alfalfa); hardwood timber. Mfg. at Marked Tree and Lepanto. Part of St. Francis Sunken Lands Wildlife Management Area in NE; Earl Bliss Bayou Deview Wildlife Management Area in NW; L. Poinsett State Park at center. Co. was formed 1838.

Poinsett, Lake, E S.Dak., 20 mi/32 km S of Watertown; 7 mi/11.3 km long, 3 mi/4.8 km wide at widest point; 44°33'N 97°04'W. On Hamlin/Kingsbury co. boundary. Two small streams flow from it to Big Sioux R. Recreation. L. Poinsett State Rec. Area on S side; other lakes nearby.

Poinsett State Park (poin-SET) (□ c.1.6 sq mi/0.6 sq km), Sumter co., central S.C., 14 mi/23 km SW of Sumter. Contains excellent selection of plants native to area. Manchester state forest to E.

Point, village (1990 pop. 645), Rains co., NE Texas, 55 mi/89 km ENE of Dallas; 32°55'N 95°52'W. Natural gas and oil. Agr. (cattle; vegetables, watermelons, wheat). Mfg. (fabricated metal prods.). L. Tawakoni reservoir (Sabine R.) to SW.

Point Agassiz (A-guh-see), cape, SE Alaska, c. 8 mi/12.9 km N of Petersburg; 57°00'N 133°00'W.

Point Arena, city (1990 pop. 407), Mendocino co., NW Calif., 28 mi/45 km WSW of Ukiah, on the Pacific Ocean; 38°55'N 123°42'W. Dairy center; livestock (sheep, cattle). Lighthouse at Point Arena, a promontory to NW. Manchester State Beach to NW.

Point Baker, village, SE Alaska, on NW shore of Prince of Wales Isl., on Sumner Strait, 50 mi/80 km WSW of Wrangell; 56°22'N 133°37'W. Fishing.

Point Barrow, northernmost point of Alaska, on the Arctic Ocean, separating Beaufort and Chukchi seas; 71°23'N 156°30'W. Visited in 1826 by Frederick W. Beechey, a Br. explorer, and named by him for the Br. geographer Sir John Barrow, it has since been the object of many expeditions and has figured prominently in arctic aviation. Navigation is open for only 2 or 3 months a year. To the SW is the village of Barrow. Farther S is a monument to Will Rogers and Wiley Post, who lost their lives here in an airplane crash in 1935.

Point Beach 1 and 2 Nuclear Power Plants, Wis.: see MANITOWOC, CO.

Point Chautauqua (shuh-TAW-kwuh), resort village (1990 pop. 150), Chautauqua co., extreme W N.Y., on Chautauqua L., 3 mi/4.8 km SE of Mayville; 42°14'N 79°28'W.

Point Clear, village (1990 pop. 2,125), Baldwin co., SW Ala., 17 mi/27 km SE of Mobile, on Mobile Bay; 30°29'N 87°54'W. Precision machine works and gaswell production.

Point Comfort, town (1990 pop. 956), Calhoun co., S Texas, 6 mi/9.7 km NE of Port Lavaca, on opposite side of Lavaca Bay, connected by causeway; 28°40'N 96°33'W. Mfg. (aluminum, chemicals, plastic prods., fertilizer).

Point Dume, uninc. town (1990 pop. 2,809), Los Angeles co., S Calif., 7 mi/11.3 km W of Malibu, at Point Dume, Pacific Ocean; 34°01'N 118°49'W. Point Dume State Beach is here; Santa Monica Mts. Natl. Recreation Area to N. Also called Malibu Riviera.

Point Edward, village (1991 pop. 2,336), S Ont., Canada, on St. Clair R., at foot of L. Huron; NW suburb of Sarnia, opposite Port Huron, Mich.; 43°00'N 82°24'W. Docks are part of port of Sarnia.

Point Fortin (FOR-tin), village, SW Trinidad, Trinidad and Tobago, on the Gulf of Paria, 16 mi/26 km WSW of San Fernando. Petroleum field with oil refinery and loading pier.

Point Grey, suburb of Vancouver, SW B.C., Canada. Site of the Univ. of B.C.

Point Harbor, uninc. village, Currituck co., NE N.C., 28 mi/45 km SE of Elizabeth City, on Albemarle Sound, at entrance to Currituck Sound. Wright Memorial Bridge crosses Currituck Sound to Kitty Hawk on Outer Banks, 3 mi/4.8 km E.

Point Hill, town (1991 pop. 3,651), St. Catherine parish, central Jamaica, 12 mi/19 km NW of Spanish Town; 18°05'N 77°06'W.

Point Hope, village (1990 pop. 639), NW Alaska, on

Point Hope headland, on Chukchi Sea; 68°20'N 166°45'W. Inuit settlement; hunting and fishing; formerly important whaling base. Airfield.

Point Judith, promontory extending into Block Isl. Sound and marking the SW entrance to Narragansett Bay, S R.I., in the town of Narragansett. Resort and recreational fishing area. A U.S. coast guard station (scheduled to close in the late 1990s), a ferry terminal, and a lighthouse are here. Fishing village of Galilee lies to W. Point Judith Harbor of Refuge immediately WSW.

Point Lake, expansion of Coppermine R., E central Mackenzie dist., N.W.T., Canada, ESE of Great Bear L.; 75 mi/121 km long, 1 mi/2 km–14 mi/23 km wide; 65°00'N 113°00'W.

Point Lay, Inuit village (1990 pop. 139), NW Alaska, on Chukchi Sea, 65 mi/105 km SW of Wainwright; 69°50'N 162°55'W. Fishing settlement; airfield. Coal deposits nearby.

Point Lisas (LEE-sahs), port, Trinidad, Republic of Trinidad and Tobago, on Lisas Bay, Gulf of Paria, N of San Fernando. Industrial port built on 1,500 acres/607 ha of former sugarcane and swamp land; project begun in 1977 and still in progress. Also hotel development area and residential development. Petrochemicals, iron, and steel.

Point Marion (ME-ree-uhn), borough (1990 pop. 1,344), Fayette co., SW Pa., 15 mi/24 km SW of Uniontown, and 8 mi/12.9 km NNE of Morgantown, W.Va., near W.Va. state line, on Monongahela R., at mouth of Cheat R. (Cheat L. reservoir, W.Va., to SE); 39°43'N 79°54'W. Mfg. (glassware and ceramics). Friendship Hill Natl. Historic Site to N. Laid out 1842.

Point of Pines, Mass.: see REVERE.

Point of Rocks, town, Frederick co., W Md., on the Potomac (bridged here to Va.), 12 mi/19 km S of Frederick. The Victorian Gothic RR station, on the Natl. Register of Historic Places, still serves a weekday commuter train in each direction. The scene of more Civil War–skirmishing than any other in Md., it is where Gen. George G. Meade received his command of the Army of the Potomac from President Lincoln just before the Battle of Gettysburg.

Point Pelee (PEE-lee), peninsula, c.10 mi/16 km long, extending into W L. Erie, S Ont., Canada, near Leamington. It is the southernmost part of the Can. mainland. Point Pelee Natl. Park, a wildlife sanctuary, is here.

Point Pelee National Park (□ 6 sq mi/15.5 sq km), SW Ont., Canada, 34 mi/55 km SE of Windsor. Occupies triangular peninsula on N shore of L. Erie, 7 mi/11 km long, 3 mi/5 km wide at base. Less than ⅓ of park is dry land. Cattail marsh and ponds, as well as woodland, are important bird and wildlife sanctuary, accessible to visitors by serpentine boardwalk. Group camping, day-use facilities, beaches. Est. 1918.

Point Pleasant 1 uninc. town, New Madrid co., in the bootheel of extreme SE Mo., on Mississippi R., and 7 mi/11.3 km E of Portageville. **2** town (1990 pop. 4,996), ⊙ Mason co., W W.Va., 35 mi/56 km NNE of Huntington, on the Ohio R. (RR bridge) at Kanawha R. (bridge S to Henderson); 38°51'N 82°07'W. Mfg. (steel fabricating; plastic and wood prods.). Agr. (grain, tobacco); livestock; dairying. In battle of Point Pleasant (1774), a large force of Indians was defeated by Andrew Lewis and frontiersmen. Point Pleasant Battlefield State Park. Clifton F. McClintic Wildlife Management Area to NE. Settled around Fort Blair (built 1774).

Point Pleasant, village, Clermont co., SW Ohio, on Ohio R., and 21 mi/34 km SE of Cincinnati. Has a replica of Ulysses S. Grant's birthplace; Grant Memorial State Park.

Point Pleasant, residential and resort borough (1990 pop. 18,177), Ocean co., E N.J., 11 mi/18 km NE of Toms River, near the Manasquan Inlet. Nearby Point Pleasant Beach (1990 pop. 5,112) is a summer seaside resort. Settled 1850, inc. 1920.

Point Pleasant Beach, resort borough (1990 pop. 18,177), Ocean co., E N.J., on the coast, at mouth of Manasquan R., just NE of Point Pleasant borough, and

12 mi/19 km NE of Toms River; 40°04′N 74°04′W. Inc. 1886.

Point Reyes National Seashore, National Seashore (□ 111 sq mi/287 sq km), Marin co., W Calif., 20 mi/32 km NW of downtown San Francisco, on Pacific Ocean. Coastal area with beaches, steep bluffs overlooking the Pacific Ocean, lagoons, and estuaries enclosed by sand dunes, rolling hills, and forests. On offshore rocks are bird rookeries and sea-lion herds. Diagonal valley and islets that nearly sever peninsula from mainland is a NW corner of the San Andreas Fault; there is a 15 ft/5 m–20 ft/6 m horizontal displacement of rock (a result of the 1906 earthquake). Sir Francis Drake probably stopped here (1579) to repair his ship, the *Golden Hinde,* before crossing the Pacific Ocean. Point Reyes extends c.10 mi/16 km W into Pacific; forms Drake's Bay on S of peninsula. Farallon Isls. Natl. Wildlife Refuge c.15 mi/24 km to S (San Francisco co.). Natl. Seashore authorized 1962.

Point Reyes Station, uninc. village, Marin co., W Calif., at head (SE end) of Tomales Bay, 17 mi/27 km WNW of San Rafael. Dairying. Point Reyes is 12 mi/19 km WSW. Village lies directly on San Andreas Fault. Point Reyes Natl. Seashore to W.

Point Roberts, uninc. town (1990 pop. 750), Whatcom co., NW Wash., on the Strait of Georgia on W side of Point Roberts peninsula near its tip, extending S from B.C. (Canada), and separated from Wash. mainland by Boundary Bay (E), 20 mi/32 km S of downtown Vancouver, B.C.; c.30 mi/48 km NW of Bellingham, Wash. Resort. Dairying; cattle; tourism; mfg. (machinery parts, electronic components). Point visited and named (1792) by Capt. George Vancouver. Can be reached overland from U.S. only by going through B.C. or by private boat. B.C. Ferry jetty at Tsawwassan 3 mi/4.8 km NW; ferries to Swartz Bay, on Vancouver Isl.

Point Salines (POIN suh-LEEN), Grenada, West Indies. Point Salines internatl. airport on SW peninsula. St. George's Medical School located at end of runway.

Point Shirley, Mass.: see WINTHROP.

Point Sur, rugged promontory on W coast of Monterrey co., Calif., 20 mi/32 km S of Monterey. Lighthouse (built 1889; 270 ft/82 m above sea). Site of Andrew Molera State Park.

Point Tupper, village, E N.S., Canada, SW Cape Breton Isl., on the Strait of Canso opposite Mulgrave; 45°36′N 61°22′W.

Point Whiteshed, village, S Alaska, on Point Whiteshed, 8 mi/12.9 km SW of Cordova. Also spelled Whitshed. Also called simply Whiteshed.

Pointe a la Hache (POINT uh luh HAHSH), uninc. village, ⊙ Plaquemines parish, extreme SE La., 31 mi/50 km SE of New Orleans, and on E bank of the Mississippi in the delta; 29°34′N 89°47′W. Deepwater port. Sugarcane, fruit; mfg. (furniture), oyster processing, fishing. Free ferry to West Pointe a la Hache. Recreation area.

Pointe au Chien, Bayou (POINT o shee-AN, BEI-yoo), c.45 mi/72 km long, boundary bet. Plaquemines and Terrebonne parishes, SE La.; flows from its source in N Terrebonne parish to L. Raccourci, arm of Gulf of Mexico.

Pointe au Pic (pweht o PEEK), village (1991 pop. 952), SE central Que., Canada, on the St. Lawrence, and 2 mi/3 km SSE of La Malbaie; 47°38′N 70°09′W. Resort.

Pointe Aux Barques (POINT O BAHRK), Huron co., E Mich., resort settlement at the Pointe Aux Barques (N tip of the Thumb), at SE side of entrance to Saginaw Bay, 17 mi/27 km N of Bad Axe, 2 mi/3.2 km NE of Port Austin; 44°03′N 82°57′W. Lighthouse and coast guard station here.

Pointe Claire (point KLER, Fr. pweht KLER), residential town (1991 pop. 27,647), S Que., Canada, on S shore of Montreal Isl., on L. St. Louis, 14 mi/23 km SW of Montreal; 45°26′N 73°45′W.

Pointe Coupee (POINT kuh-PEE), parish (□ 564 sq mi/1,461 sq km; 1990 pop. 22,540), SE central La.; ⊙ New Roads; 30°43′N 91°36′W. Bounded E by the Mississippi R., N by Old R. (former channel of Red R.), W by Atchafalaya R.; drained in S by Bayou Maringouin and Bayou Des Glaises. Agr. (cotton, corn, pecans, rice, soybeans, sugarcane, vegetables, wheat; cattle, hogs, horses), crawfish; logging. Some mfg. (primarily wood prods.), lumber. Has a number of antebellum homes including Parlange. False R., 13-mi/21-km-long oxbow lake, in E; part of Sherburne State Wildlife Area in SW, Atchafalaya Natl. Wildlife Refuge just beyond boundary in SW. Formed 1807.

Pointe du Bois (point doo-BWAH), village, SE Man., Canada, on Winnipeg R. (waterfalls), and 80 mi/129 km ENE of Winnipeg; 50°18′N 95°33′W. Hydroelectric power center.

Pointe Fortune (pweht fohr-TUHN), village (1991 pop. 413), SW Que., Canada, on Ottawa R., and 8 mi/13 km SSW of Lachute, on Ont. border. Dairying; potatoes.

Pointe-a-la-Croix, village (1991 pop. 1,755), E Que., Canada, SW Gaspé Peninsula, at head of Chaleur Bay, at mouth of Restigouche R., opposite Campbellton. Fishing port.

Pointe-à-Pierre (pee-AHR), village, W Trinidad, Trinidad and Tobago, landing on the Gulf of Paria, on RR, and 23 mi/37 km SSE of Port of Spain; 10°20′N 61°24′W. Oil-bunkering port and major refining center (with cracking plants, tanks, laboratories). Its oil-loading jetty is 1.5 mi/2.4 km offshore, linked by pipelines. In 1808 it was proposed to make the village the capital of Trinidad. Sometimes the name La Carrière, settlement just E with main petroleum installations, is used interchangeably for Pointe-à-Pierre.

Pointe-à-Pitre (pwang–tah–PEE-truh), city (1982 pop. 25,310), Guadeloupe, West Indies; 16°20′N 61°25′W. It is on Grande-Terre isl. at the S entrance of the Rivière Salée, the narrow, shallow ocean channel that separates Basse-Terre isl. from Grande-Terre. Pointe-à-Pitre is the largest city and leading port in the dept. with large transshipment facilities. Its chief exports are bananas and rum.

Pointe-Noire (pwangt–NWAHR), town, NW Basse-Terre isl., Guadeloupe, minor port 17 mi/27 km NNW of Basse-Terre city. Trading; cacao and vanilla growing; alcohol distilling.

Poipu (PO-ee-POO), town (1990 pop. 975), Kauai isl., Kauai co., Hawaii, on S coast, 8 mi/12.9 km SSW of Lihue; 21°52′N 159°27′W. Sugarcane, fruit; fish. Poipu Beach Park here. Makahuena Point to E; Puu Wanawana Crater to NE.

Pojoaque (po-WAH-kee), pueblo (□ 21 sq mi/54 sq km; 1990 pop. 1,037), Santa Fe co., N central N.Mex., 13 mi/21 km NNW of Santa Fe; small trading point bet. Sangre de Cristo Mts. and the Rio Grande; 35°53′N 106°01′W. Elev. 5,852 ft/1,784 m. Smallest of the 8 N pueblos. In Pojoaque Pueblo land grant. Inhabitants (chiefly Span. American) raise grain and chiles.

Pokagon State Park, Steuben co., NE Ind., 5 mi/8 km N of Angola. Popular winter sports park.

Pokegama Lake (po-ke-GAH-muh), reservoir (□ 35 sq mi/91 sq km), Itasca co., N central Minn., on Mississippi R., 4 mi/6.4 km SW of Grand Rapids; 13 mi/21 km long, 3 mi/4.8 km wide; 47°15′N 93°35′W. Elev. 1,274 ft/388 m; max. capacity 120,000 acre-ft. Drains N into Mississippi R. through short stream. Wendigo Arm, SW extension, 5 mi/8 km long. Formed by Pokegama L. Dam (16 ft/5 m high), built (1884) by Army Corps of Engineers for flood control; also used for water supply and recreation. Resort area. Forest History Center at N end of lake. Golden Anniversary State Forest nearby.

Poke-O-Moonshine Mountain (2,162 ft/659 m), Essex co., NE N.Y., in the Adirondacks, near L. Champlain, 7 mi/11.3 km S of Keeseville; 44°24′N 73°30′W. State campsite here.

Poland, town (1990 pop. 4,342), Androscoggin co., SW Maine, 10 mi/16 km W of Auburn; 44°02′N 70°23′W. Bottling works. Includes West Poland on Tripp L. and Poland Spring, summer resort long known for its mineral water (1st inn opened 1797). Range Ponds State Park is here. Settled c.1768, inc. 1795.

Poland 1 village (1990 pop. 444), Herkimer co., central N.Y., 13 mi/21 km NE of Utica; 43°13′N 75°03′W. **2** village (1990 pop. 2,992), Mahoning co., E Ohio, 7 mi/11 km S of downtown Youngstown; 41°01′N 80°37′W. Settled c.1799.

Poland Spring, Maine: see POLAND.

Pole (PO-lai), archaeological site, Mexico, on E coast of the Yucatan peninsula in Quintana Roo state, off Mexico Highway 307 near Puerto Carmen. Reported to have been the principal port for trade with Cozumel Isl. in pre-Columbian times, the ruins have not been reconstructed and are not developed for tourism. Also known as Xcaret.

Pole Creek Mountain, peak (13,716 ft/4,181 m), in San Juan Mts., Hinsdale co., SW Colo., 13 mi/21 km E of Silverton; 37°47′N 107°25′W.

Polk 1 (POK), county (□ 862 sq mi/2,233 sq km; 1990 pop. 17,347), W Ark.; ⊙ Mena; 34°28′N 94°13′W. Bounded W by Okla. state line; drained by Ouachita, Saline, Little Missouri, and Mountain Fork rivers; situated in the Ouachita Mts. Lumbering; agr. (cattle, hogs, chickens); dairying. Some mfg. at Mena. Part of Ouachita Natl. Forest in N and SE (recreation); Cossatot State Park in S; Queen Wilhelmina State Park in NW. Formed 1844. **2** county (□ 2,010 sq mi/5,206 sq km; 1990 pop. 405,382), central Fla., bounded E by Kissimmee R. and partly N by Withlacoochee R.; ⊙ Bartow; 27°57′N 81°42′W. Hilly lake region, swampy in N, drained by Peace R.; includes Lakes Hancock, Hamilton, Hatchineha, Weohyakapka, and Crooked. Contains Iron Mt. (elev. 325 ft/99 m). Major citrus-fruit-growing and phosphate-mining center. Also produces vegetables and fruit (esp. strawberries), corn; cattle, and poultry. Formed 1861. **3** county (□ 312 sq mi/808 sq km; 1990 pop. 33,815), NW Ga. on Ala. state line; ⊙ Cedartown; 34°00′N 85°11′W. Textile mfg. Valley and ridge agr. (cotton, corn, hay, sweet potatoes, fruit); cattle, poultry; timber; iron mining. Formed 1851. **4** county (□ 591 sq mi/1,531 sq km; 1990 pop. 327,140), central Iowa; ⊙ Des Moines; 41°41′N 93°35′W. Includes city of Des Moines (state capitol) and suburbs of West Des Moines, Urbandale, Johnston, and Ankeny. Drained by Des Moines, Raccoon, and Skunk rivers and by Beaver Creek. Agr. mainly in N and SE (hogs, cattle, poultry; corn, soybeans, oats). Mfg. at Des Moines, West Des Moines, and Ankeny. Bituminous-coal deposits mined in S. Large Saylorville Reservoir and Dam and Big Creek State Park in NW; Walnut Woods State Park in SW; Margo Frankel Woods State Park in N; Living History Farm in W. Extensive flood damage to city of Des Moines and adjacent areas in 1993. Formed 1846. **5** county (□ 1,997 sq mi/5,172 sq km; 1990 pop. 32,498), NW Minn.; ⊙ Crookston; 47°45′N 96°35′W. Agr. area bounded W by Red R. of the North (N.Dak. boundary) and drained by Poplar, Sand Hill, and Red L. rivers. Wheat, hay, alfalfa, oats, barley, sugar beets, soybeans, beans, sunflowers, potatoes; cattle, poultry, sheep, hogs; dairying. Large White Earth Indian Reservation bounds co. to SE. Formed 1858. **6** county (□ 642 sq mi/1,663 sq km; 1990 pop. 21,826), SW central Mo.; ⊙ Bolivar; 37°37′N 93°24′W. In the Ozarks, drained by Pomme de Terre R. and Little Sac R. Corn, wheat, sorghum, hay; cattle, horses, poultry; timber. Pomme de Terre L. on N border; Little Sac arm of Stockton L. in SW. Southwest Baptist Univ. at Bolivar. Mfg. at Bolivar. Formed 1835. **7** county (□ 441 sq mi/1,142 sq km; 1990 pop. 5,675), E central Nebr.; ⊙ Osceola; 41°11′N 97°32′W. Agr. area bounded N by Platte R.; drained by Big Blue R. in S. Cattle, hogs; corn, sorghum; dairying. Formed 1870. **8** county (□ 238 sq mi/616 sq km; 1990 pop. 14,416), SW N.C., in Piedmont region, bounded S by S.C. state line; ⊙ Columbus; 35°16′N 82°10′W. Agr. area (wheat, hay, peaches, corn; cattle); timber. L. Adger reservoir in N. Formed 1855. **9** county (□ 744 sq mi/1,927 sq km; 1990 pop. 49,541), NW Oregon; ⊙ Dallas; 44°54′N 123°25′W. Coast Range extends along W border, bounded E by Willamette R. Agr. (grapes, hops, apples, cherries, pears, plums, peaches, blackberries, corn, brans, wheat, oats, barley; hogs, sheep, cattle); dairy prods.; timber; nurseries; wineries. Small unit of Siuslaw Natl. Forest in center; Baskett Slough Natl. Wildlife Refuge in NE center; Holman State Wayside in NE;

Cross references are shown in SMALL CAPITALS. The pronunciation key is on page xv. The dates of population figures are on page xii.

Helmick State Park in SE. **10** county (□ 436 sq mi/ 1,129 sq km; 1990 pop. 13,643), SE Tenn.; ⊙ Benton; 35°08′N 84°31′W. Bounded E by N.C., S by Ga.; Unicoi Mts. in NE; drained by Hiwassee R. and Ocoee R. (with 3 TVA dams). Largely included in Cherokee Natl. Forest. In SE is copper-producing region, with mines and smelters. Lumbering (pine, oak), agr. (corn, hay, soybeans; livestock; dairy prods.). Whitewater recreation (rafting, kayaking) is a significant part of the local economy. Formed 1839. **11** county (□ 1,109 sq mi/ 2,872 sq km; 1990 pop. 30,687), E Texas; ⊙ Livingston; 30°48′N 94°49′W. Bounded SW by Trinity R., NE by Neches R. Lumbering (pine, hardwoods, Christmas trees); oil and natural gas fields; sand and gravel; agr. (peaches, blueberries, vegetables); some livestock (cattle, hogs, poultry). Hunting, fishing. Alabama-Coushatta Indian Reservation in E; part of Big Thicket Natl. Preserve in SE; L. Livingston State Park in SW. Formed 1846. **12** county (□ 956 sq mi/2,476 sq km; 1990 pop. 34,773), NW Wis., bounded W by St. Croix R. (Minn. boundary); ⊙ Balsam L.; 45°27′N 92°25′W. Dairying is principal industry; barley, wheat, corn, soybeans, beans, alfalfa, hay; cattle, hogs, sheep. Has numerous small lakes. Interstate State Park in W, part of Knowles State Forest in NW corner, Trollhaugen Ski Area in W; St. Croix Indian Reservation in E; St. Croix Falls and Osceola Fish Hatchery in W. Formed 1853.

Polk 1 village (1990 pop. 345), Polk co., E central Nebr., 15 mi/24 km SW of Osceola, near Platte R; 41°04′N 97°46′W. Livestock; poultry prods.; grain. **2** village (1990 pop. 355), Ashland co., N central Ohio, 7 mi/ 11 km NE of Ashland; 40°57′N 82°13′W. In agr. area; fireworks.

Polk, borough (1990 pop. 1,267), Venango co., NW Pa., 5 mi/8 km WSW of Franklin, on Sandy Creek; 41°22′N 79°55′W. Mfg. (machining). Agr. area (corn, hay; dairying). Pa. State Hosp. and School here. Settled c.1798, laid out 1839, inc. 1886.

Polk City 1 town (1990 pop. 1,439), Polk co., central Fla., 13 mi/21 km NE of Lakeland; 28°10′N 81°49′W. **2** town (1990 pop. 1,908), Polk co., central Iowa, near Des Moines R., 14 mi/23 km NNW of Des Moines, satellite community of Des Moines; 41°46′N 93°43′W. In agr. area. Saylorville Reservoir to SW; Big Creek L. and State Park to N.

Polk, Fort, La.: see LEESVILLE.

Polkton (POK-tuhn), village (1990 pop. 662), Anson co., S N.C., 7 mi/11.3 km WNW of Wadesboro; 35°00′N 80°12′W. Cotton, tobacco, grain, soybeans; poultry, livestock. Mfg. (sheet metal fabricating).

Polkville (POK-vil), town (1990 pop. 1,514), Cleveland co., S N.C., 11 mi/18 km NW of Shelby, on First Broad R.; 35°25′N 81°38′W. Cotton, grain, soybeans; poultry, livestock.

Polkville (POK-vil), village (1990 pop. 129), Smith co., S central Miss., 17 mi/27 km ESE of Brandon; 32°11′N 89°41′W. Timber; cotton; livestock. Bienville Natl. Forest to E; Roosevelt State Park to N.

Pollard (PAHL-uhrd), town (1990 pop. 100), Escambia co., S Ala., 8 mi/12.9 km SW of Brewton, near Conecuh R. and Fla. state line; 31°01′N 87°10′W.

Pollard, village (1990 pop. 229), Clay co., extreme NE Ark., 6 mi/9.7 km NW of Piggott, near Mo. state line; 36°25′N 90°16′W. Mfg. (wooden boxes).

Pollock (PAH-luhk), town (1990 pop. 330), Grant parish, central La., 15 mi/24 km N of Alexandria; 31°31′N 92°25′W. In agr. and lumber area; mfg. (anhydrous ammonia, veneer). Located in Kisatchie Natl. Forest.

Pollock 1 village (1990 pop. 379), Campbell co., N S.Dak., 23 mi/37 km NNE of Mobridge, near Missouri R., on L. Pocasse (Spring co.); 45°53′N 100°17′W. RR terminus. Grain; livestock, poultry; mfg. (cheese, whey protein). Pocasse Natl. Wildlife Refuge to E. **2** uninc. village (1990 pop. 300), Angelina co., E Texas, 11 mi/ 18 km NW of Lufkin, near Angelina R. Timber area. Mfg. (lumber). Davy Crockett Natl. Forest to SW.

Pollock Pines, uninc. town (1990 pop. 4,291), El Dorado co., E Calif., 11 mi/18 km E of Placerville; 38°45′N 120°34′W. Area surrounded by parts of El Dorado Natl. Forest. Jenkinson L. reservoir to S.

Pollocksville, village (1990 pop. 299), Jones co., SE N.C., 12 mi/19 km SW of New Bern, on Trent R.; 35°00′N 77°13′W. Grain, tobacco, peanuts, cotton; livestock. Mfg. (crushed rock, mops). Croatan Natl. Forest to E. Hoffman Forest to SW.

Polo 1 (PO-lo), city (1990 pop. 2,514), Ogle co., N Ill., 13 mi/21 km W of Oregon; 41°58′N 89°34′W. Trade center in dairy, livestock, and grain area; food prods.; nursery. Inc. 1857. **2** city (1990 pop. 539), Caldwell co., NW Mo., 31 mi/50 km SW of Chillicothe; 39°32′N 94°02′W. Corn, wheat; cattle, hogs.

Polotitlán (po-lo-teet-LAHN), town (1990 pop. 2,303), Mexico state, central Mexico, 16 mi/26 km SE of San Juan del Río; 20°13′N 99°49′W. Cereals; livestock. Formerly Polotitlán de la Ilustración.

Polotitlán de la Ilustración, Mexico: see POLOTITLÁN.

Polson, town (1990 pop. 3,283), ⊙ Lake co., NW Mont., at S end of Flathead L., at exit of Flathead R. just NW of Mission Range, 55 mi/89 km N of Missoula; 47°42′N 114°10′W. Main town in large Flathead Indian Reservation; resort; sawmill; dairying; honey; cattle, sheep, hogs; corn, rape seed, potatoes, fruit. Pablo Natl. Wildlife Refuge to S; Mission Mts. Tribal Wilderness to SE; Finley Point Unit of Flathead L. State Park to NE. To SW on Flathead R. is Kerr Dam (200 ft/61 m high, 350 ft/107 m long; for power and irrigation; completed 1938). Founded 1989. Inc. 1902. Polson-Flathead Historical Mus.; Miracle of Amer. Mus.

Pomaria (puh-MER-ee-uh), village (1990 pop. 267), Newberry co., NW central S.C., 27 mi/43 km NW of Columbia; 34°16′N 81°25′W. Agr. includes livestock, poultry; grain, soybeans. Logging and timber. Just E is Parr Reservoir on Broad R. Sumter Natl. Forest to N.

Pomeroy 1 town (1990 pop. 762), Calhoun co., central Iowa, 10 mi/16 km N of Rockwell City; 42°32′N 94°40′W. In agr. area. **2** (PAHM-uh-rai), town (1990 pop. 1,393), ⊙ Garfield co., SE Wash., 45 mi/72 km NE of Walla Walla; 46°28′N 117°36′W. RR terminus. Trade center for agr. area; apples, peas, alfalfa; hogs. Central Ferry State Park to NW; Umatilla Natl. Forest to S. Lower Granite Dam (Snake R.) to N. Inc. 1886.

Pomeroy, village (1990 pop. 2,259), ⊙ Meigs co., SE Ohio, on the Ohio R., and 18 mi/29 km NNE of Gallipolis; 39°01′N 82°02′W. Iron and steel foundries; mfg. of electronic equip., machinery. Coal and salt mines; hardwood timber. Settled in early 19th cent.; inc. 1840.

Pomfret 1 town (1990 pop. 3,102), Windham co., NE Conn., on Quinebaug R., and 20 mi/32 km NE of Willimantic; 41°51′N 71°58′W. Resorts. Agr., dairying; forestry; mfg. of cable, fiberoptics, and foods. Pomfret School (1894) here. State parks. Settled before 1700, inc. 1713. **2** town (1990 pop. 874), Windsor co., E Vt., just N of Woodstock; 43°42′N 72°30′W. Includes South Pomfret village.

Pomme de Terre Lake (pawm duh TER), reservoir (□ 25 sq mi/65 sq km), Hickory and Polk cos., SW Mo., on Pomme de Terre R., 45 mi/72 km N of Springfield; c.18 mi/29 km long; 37°53′N 93°19′W. Max. capacity 407,000 acre-ft. Lindley Creek forms 10-mi/16-km SE arm, joining main channel at dam. Formed by Pomme de Terre Dam (155 ft/47 m high), constructed by the Army Corps of Engineers (1963) for flood control and power generation. Pomme de Terre State Park on promontory opposite dam.

Pomme de Terre River 1 (pawm duh TER) [Fr. = potato], c.100 mi/161 km long, in W Minn.; rises in Stalker L., 12 mi/19 km ESE of Fergus Falls; flows S, through several small lakes, natural Ten Mile L., Pomme de Terre L. (4 mi/6.4 km long, 1 mi/1.6 km wide), Barrett L., North and Middle Pomme de Terre lakes (North Pomme de Terre L. is 18 mi/29 km S of Pomme de Terre L.) and Perkins L.; continues past Morris and Appleton, to Minnesota R. at SE end of Marsh L. at dam, 4 mi/6.4 km SW of Appleton; 46°11′N 95°51′W. Used to generate power at Appleton. **2** (puhm duh TAHR), 113 mi/182 km long, central Mo.; headwaters rise in Greene and Webster cos., joining S of Bolivar; flows N, through Ozark Mts., to Truman L. (Osage R.). Pomme de Terre Dam and L. S of Hermitage.

Pomona (puh-MO-nuh), city (1990 pop. 131,723), Los Angeles co., S Calif., 28 mi/45 km E of downtown Los Angeles, and 9 mi/14.5 km W of Ontario, at the foot of the San Gabriel Mts.; 34°04′N 117°46′W. RR junction. It is a residential, industrial, and commercial suburb of Los Angeles where citrus fruits and vegetables are canned and shipped. Mfg. (printing and publishing; foods, paper prods., chemicals, fabricated metal prods., plastic prods.; paper mills, aluminum foundry, iron foundry). Pomona, to W, is the seat of Calif. State Polytechnic Univ., Pomona and is the site of the largest fair in the state, the Los Angeles Co. Fair. It is one of the fastest-growing U.S. cities, marked by a pop. increase of 42% bet. 1980 and 1990. Pomona Col. and Claremont Col. Extension Center (multi-school) in neighboring Claremont, to NE; U.S. Naval Training Center is here; Brackett Field Airport is in N; Angeles Natl. Forest to N; Bonelli Regional Park to NW; Marshall Canyon Regional Park to N. Inc. 1888.

Pomona, town (1990 pop. 2,624), Atlantic co., N.J., 10 mi/16 km E of Atlantic City; 39°28′N 74°32′W. Site of Richard Stockton Col. of N.J.

Pomona 1 (puh-MO-nuh), village (1990 pop. 835), Franklin co., E Kansas, near Marais des Cygnes R., 10 mi/16 km W of Ottawa; 38°36′N 95°27′W. In livestock and grain region. **2** village (1990 pop. 2,611), Rockland co., SE N.Y., 8 mi/12.9 km NW of Nyack. Mfg. of chemicals.

Pomona Lake, reservoir (□ 6 sq mi/15.5 sq km), Osage co., E central Kansas, on Hundred and Ten Mile Creek (also called Dragoon R.), 35 mi/56 km NW of Emporia; 38°39′N 95°34′W. Max. capacity 254,600 acre-ft. Formed by Pomona L. Dam (110 ft/34 m high), built (1963) by Army Corps of Engineers for flood control; also used for water supply and recreation. Pomona L. State Park near dam.

Pompano Beach (PAWM-puh-no), city (□ 21 sq mi/ 54 sq km; 1990 pop. 72,411), Broward co., SE Fla., 12 mi/ 19 km N of Ft. Lauderdale, on the Atlantic coast and the Intracoastal Waterway; 26°14′N 80°07′W. It is a resort city with ocean beaches, excellent fishing, and a harness-racing track. Over 60% of the city's economy is based on tourism. Mfg. includes precision and electronic equip. and various technological supplies. Inc. 1908.

Pompanoosuc, Vt.: see NORWICH.

Pomperaug River (PAHM-puhr-ahg), c.25 mi/40 km long, W Conn.; rises near Bethlehem; flows S to the Housatonic R. in Southbury town.

Pompton Lakes (PAWMP-tuhn), borough (1990 pop. 10,539), Passaic co., NE N.J., 8 mi/12.9 kmNW of Paterson; 41°00′N 74°17′W. Settled 1682 by the Dutch. Chiefly residential. Mfg. ordnance and machinery. Several pre-Revolutionary houses remain. Inc. 1895.

Pompton Plains (PAWMP-tuhn), village, Morris co., N N.J., near Pequannock R., 3 mi/4.8 kmS of Pompton Lakes borough, on site of a prehistoric lake. Largely residential.

Pompton River (PAWMP-tuhn), c.8 mi/12.9 km long, NE N.J.; formed S of Pompton Lakes borough by junction of Ramapo R. (issues from Pompton L.) and Pequannock R.; flows S to Passaic R.

Ponaganset River (pon-ah-GAN-set), small stream, 10 mi/16 km long, N central R.I.; rises in W Glocester town, where dam forms Ponaganset Reservoir (c.1.5 mi/2.4 km long); flows generally SE, through Foster town (where it is drammed to form Barden Reservoir, c.2 mi/3.2 km long), to W arm of Scituate Reservoir in Scituate town. Formerly joined Moswansicut R. to form North Branch of Pawtuxet R. in area now flooded by reservoir.

Ponca (PAWN-kuh), town (1990 pop. 877), ⊙ Dixon co., NE Nebr., 15 mi/24 km WNW of Sioux City (Iowa), and on Missouri R.; 42°34′N 96°42′W. Livestock; grain. Ponca State Park to N.

Ponca City (PAWN-kuh), city (1990 pop. 26,359), Kay co., N Okla., on the Arkansas R., 65 mi/105 km NW of Tulsa; 36°43′N 97°04′W. It is a trade, processing, and shipping hub in a grain, livestock, and oil area. Mfg. (metal spinning; pellet mills; chemicals, fabricated metal prods., bldg. materials, machinery, carbon black). Many parks. Pioneer Women's Mus. and a Native Amer. mus.; also Marland Mansion, Ponca Tribal Hq. and Mus. L. Ponca to E; Kaw L. reservoir to NE. Nearby are several Native Amer. reservations. Founded 1893 with the opening of the Cherokee Strip, inc. 1899.

Ponca Creek, c.80 mi/129 km long, S S.Dak. and N Nebr.; rises in Tripp co. (S.Dak.); flows SE to Missouri R. NW of Niobrara (Nebr.); 43°13′N 99°45′W.

Ponce (PON-sai), city (1990 pop. 187,749), S P.R. The isl.'s 2d-largest city in area, 3d-largest in pop. One of Puerto Rico's most rapidly growing urban areas, it is the isl.'s chief Caribbean port. From 1820 to 1920, its port was a center for the coffee, sugar, and tobacco trade. In the 1950s–1970s it was an oil port (refinery was built nearby, but has since closed). Ponce is also an agr. trade and distribution center. Industries include the processing of agr. prods., sugar refining, liquor distilling, mfg. (cement, shoes, beverages, foods, coffee). Tourism is now an important industry. Founded in the early 16th cent., Ponce is one of the oldest cities in the Americas. Seat of the Catholic Univ. of P.R. (est. 1948) and a regional col. of the Univ. of P.R. Landmarks include a cathedral, an 18th-cent. fort, and many preserved old Span. homes and churches, major central plaza restoration. Site of Ponce Mus. of Art, the Firestation mus. (1883), and several other mus., Tibes Indian Ceremonial Center (oldest cemetery in Antilles). Airport.

Ponce de Leon (pahns duh LEE-on), village (□ 4 sq mi/10.4 sq km; 1990 pop. 406), Holmes co., NW Fla., 17 mi/27 km W of Bonifay; 30°43′N 85°56′W. Nearby are Ponce de Leon Springs, one of many named for the Span. explorer.

Ponce de Leon Inlet (pons duh LEE-on), break in E coast barrier beach, NE Fla., 13 mi/21 km SSE of Daytona Beach; connects S end of Halifax R. lagoon and N end of Hillsborough R. lagoon with the Atlantic Ocean.

Ponce Inlet (PAHNS), town (□ 14 sq mi/36 sq km; 1990 pop. 1,704), Volusia co., E central Fla., 14 mi/23 km SSE of Daytona Beach; 29°06′N 80°55′W.

Poncha Pass (9,010 ft/2,746 m), central Colo., on border bet. Suguache and Chaffee cos., in the N tip of the Sangre de Cristo Mts. One of the lowest mt. passes in Colo., it was often used in the 19th cent. by Native Americans, overland immigrants, and mt. men. Now crossed by U.S. Highway 285.

Poncha Springs, village (1990 pop. 244), Chaffee co., central Colo., South Arkansas R., 4 mi/6.4 km W of confluence, bet. Sangre de Cristo and Sawatch mts., and 4 mi/6.4 km W of Salida; 38°30′N 106°04′W. Elev. 7,469 ft/2,277 m. Livestock; textile area. Hot mineral springs here. Poncha Pass nearby. Arkansas Headwaters State Park to N; parts of Isabel Natl. Forest to S, W, and NE.

Ponchatoula (pahn-shuh-TOO-luh), city (1994 pop. 5,934), Tangipahoa parish, SE La., 45 mi/72 km E of Baton Rouge; 30°27′N 90°27′W. Ships strawberries, cattle, poultry, catfish, shrimp; mfg. (foods, water purification filters, feeds). Settled c.1830, inc. c.1860. Joyce State Wildlife Area to SE.

Poncitlán (pon-seet-LAHN), town (1990 pop. 10,863), Jalisco, central Mexico, on Santiago R., on RR, and 35 mi/56 km SE of Guadalajara, N of L. Chapala; 20°25′N 102°54′W. Wheat-growing center.

Pond Creek, town (1990 pop. 982), Grant co., N Okla., 19 mi/31 km N of Enid, and near Salt Fork of Arkansas R; 36°40′N 97°47′W. In wheat-producing area; cattle. Settled c.1889. Also spelled Pondcreek.

Pond Inlet, trading post (1991 pop. 974), N Baffin Isl., N.W.T., N Canada, opposite Bylot Isl. Govt. radio and TV stations and a post of the Royal Can. Mounted Police are located here. Seal and whale hunting, fishing, fox trapping. Hudson's Bay Company established post 1926. Scheduled air service. Bylot Isl. Bird Sanctuary across inlet.

Pond Island, Sagadahoc co., SW Maine, small lighthouse isl. at mouth of the Kennebec R.

Pond River, c.65 mi/105 km long, W Ky.; rises N of Elkton in central Todd co; flows NNW, passing E of Madisonville.

Ponder, village (1990 pop. 432), Denton co., N Texas, 10 mi/16 km WSW of Denton, near Denton Creek; 33°10′N 97°17′W. Agr. area (cotton, sorghum, peanuts, wheat; cattle, horses). Mfg. (transportation equip., electrical prods., apparel).

Pondera (pahn-DE-ruh), county (□ 1,639 sq mi/4,245 sq km; 1990 pop. 6,433), N Mont.; ⊙ Conrad; 48°14′N 112°13′W. Agr. area drained by L. Frances and Dupuyer and Birch creeks, and Two Medicine R. Marias R. forms part of N border, Continental Divide forms extreme W border. Wheat, barley, oats, hay; cattle, hogs, sheep; coal, oil. Part of large Blackfeet Indian Reservation in NW and W; part of Lewis and Clark Natl. Forest in W. Formed 1919.

Ponderay, village (1990 pop. 449), Bonner co., N Idaho, on L. Pend Oreille, 2 mi/3.2 km NNE of Sandpoint; 48°18′N 116°32′W. RR junction; mfg. (aircraft parts). Schweitzer Basin Ski Area to N.

Ponds, Island of, just off SE Lab., E Canada; 10 mi/16 km long, 9 mi/14 km wide; 53°26′N 55°54′W. At NE extremity is fishing settlement of Domino Harbour.

Poneto (puh-NET-o), town (1990 pop. 236), Wells co., E Ind., 7 mi/11.3 km SSW of Bluffton; 40°40′N 85°13′W. Agr. area.

Ponhook Lake (PAHN-huk), W N.S., E Canada, 16 mi/26 km WSW of Bridgewater; 6 mi/10 km long, 3 mi/5 km wide. Fed and drained by Medway R.

Ponoka (puh-NO-kuh), town (1991 pop. 5,861), S central Alta., W Canada, on Battle R., and 20 mi/32 km NNE of Red Deer; 52°41′N 113°34′W. Hog shipping center; lumbering; ranching, mixed farming (barley, oats); hogs, cattle; timber.

Pont Rouge (po ROOZH), village (1991 pop. 4,133), S Que., E Canada, on Jacques Cartier R., and 23 mi/37 km W of Quebec; 46°45′N 71°42′W. Dairying; livestock raising.

Pontchartrain, Lake (PAHN-chuh-train), shallow brackish-water lake (□ c.630 sq mi/1,630 sq km), SE La., N of New Orleans, an extension of the Gulf of Mexico; 41 mi/66 km long, 25 mi/40 km wide. Linked with L. Maurepas at its W end and with the gulf at its E end through L. Borgne. Tidal influenced. The Bonnet Carre Spillway can divert part of the floodwaters of the Mississippi R. during high floods into the lake at SW end; 2 causeways, each c.24 mi/40 km long, connect New Orleans (S) with Covington (N); the long, multispan Pontchartrain Causeway II, opened in 1969, allows for divided highway crossing, each span has 2 lanes for each direction of traffic. Popular resort and recreational region.

Ponteix (pahn-tuh-EHKS), town (1991 pop. 631), SW Sask., W Canada, 40 mi/64 km SSE of Swift Current; 49°45′N 107°29′W. Wheat.

Pontiac (PAHN-tee-ak), county (□ 9,560 sq mi/24,760 sq km), SW Que., E Canada, on Ont. border; 46°45′N 77°00′W.

Pontiac 1 city (1990 pop. 11,428), ⊙ Livingston co., central Ill., on Vermilion R., and 33 mi/53 km NE of Bloomington; 40°52′N 88°38′W. Trade, shipping, and mfg. center in agr. and bituminous-coal area; limestone quarries; corn, soybeans; livestock, poultry; dairy prods. Mfg. (machinery, fabricated metal prods., concrete prods.). A maximum security state penitentiary is here. Settled 1833, inc. 1857. **2** city (□ 20 sq mi/52 sq km; 1990 pop. 71,166), ⊙ Oakland co., SE Mich., 25 mi/40 km NW of downtown Detroit, on the Clinton R.; 42°38′N 83°17′W. Industries developed early and expanded after the RR came. Carriage making, important in the 1880s, gave way to the automobile industry and the mfg. of trucks, buses, and automotive parts. Pontiac still is an auto-mfg. center, but on a much smaller scale since the decline of the U.S. auto industry in the 1970s and 1980s. Mfg. (chemicals, ferrous and nonferrous metals, transportation equip., wood prods., electrical equip.; printing). Named for the Ottawa chief Pontiac, who is said to be buried nearby. Expanding development has virtually made Pontiac a Detroit suburb. Site

of the Pontiac Silverdome (built 1975), the sports complex that is currently home to the Detroit Lions Natl. Football League team (though the team is scheduled to relocate to downtown Detroit). Oakland Pontiac Airport to NW. Dodge Brothers State Park No. 4 to SW on Cass L.; Pontiac L. State Recreational Area to NW; Crystal L. in SW part of city; numerous lakes to W and S. Founded 1818 by promoters from Detroit, inc. as a city 1861.

Pontiac, uninc. village, Richland co., central S.C., 13 mi/21 km ENE of Columbia. Mfg. includes chain saws, coffee and tea prods. Fort Jackson Military Reservation to E.

Pontoon Beach, village (1990 pop. 4,013), Madison co., SW Ill., residential suburb 8 mi/12.9 km NE of downtown St. Louis (Mo.), 3 mi/4.8 km NE of Granite City; 38°43′N 90°02′W. Horseshoe L. State Park to S.

Pontoosuc, village (1990 pop. 264), Hancock co., W Ill., on the Mississippi R., and 5 mi/8 km E of Ft. Madison (Iowa); 40°37′N 91°12′W. In agr. area (corn, wheat, soybeans; cattle, hogs).

Pontoosuc Lake (pawn-TOO-suhk), reservoir, Berkshire co., W Mass., on Housatonic R. near its source, in the Berkshire Mts., 3 mi/4.8 km N of Pittsfield; 1.5 mi/2.4 km long; 42°29′N 73°15′W.

Pontotoc 1 (PAHN-tuh-tahk), county (□ 501 sq mi/1,298 sq km; 1990 pop. 22,237), N Miss.; ⊙ Pontotoc; 34°13′N 89°02′W. Drained by Skuna and Yocona rivers, and by Chiwapa Creek. Agr. (cotton, corn, soybeans, wheat; cattle; dairying; timber). clay and bauxite deposits. Mfg. at Pontotoc. Small part of Tombigbee Natl. Forest in SE corner, small part of Holly Springs Natl. Forest in NW corner; Traces State Park on E border; Natchez Trace (Natl.) Parkway crosses SE corner. Formed 1836. **2** county (□ 725 sq mi/1,878 sq km; 1990 pop. 34,119), S central Okla.; ⊙ Ada; 34°43′N 96°41′W. Bounded N by Canadian R.; drained by Clear Boggy Creek and Blue R. Agr. (wheat, oats, hay, sorghum; cattle, hogs; dairying). Mfg. at Ada. Oil and natural-gas fields; limestone, shale, silica, sand, and clay. Formed 1907.

Pontotoc (PAHN-tuh-tahk), town (1990 pop. 4,570), ⊙ Pontotoc co., N Miss., 16 mi/26 km W of Tupelo; 34°15′N 89°00′W. Trade and industrial center for agr. (cotton, grain, soybeans; cattle; dairying). Mfg. (textiles, furniture, consumer goods, transportation equip., fabricated metal prods., medical equip., apparel; pork processing). Has several notable antebellum houses. Inc. as town in 1837.

Pony, village (1990 pop. 150), Madison co., SW Mont., 39 mi/63 km W of Bozeman, on North Willow Creek, just E of Tobacco Root Mts. In gold-mining dist. Sheep; cattle; dairying; wheat, oats, potatoes, hay. Cataract Reservoir to SW; Deerlodge (W) and Beaverhead (SW) natl. forests nearby.

Poole 1 (POOL), uninc. village (1990 pop. 350), Webster and Henderson cos., W Ky., 14 mi/23 km SSW of Henderson. Burley and dark tobacco, grain; livestock. Mfg. (hand-blown glass). **2** village, Buffalo co., S central Nebr., 21 mi/34 km NNE of Kearney, and on South Loup R.

Pooler, town (1990 pop. 4,453), Chatham co., E Ga., 10 mi/16 km WNW of Savannah; 32°07′N 81°16′W. Lumber.

Pooles Island, N Md., low, wooded island, in Chesapeake Bay, 19 mi/31 km E of Baltimore; c.1.5 mi/2.4 km long, ½ mi/⅓ km wide.

Poolesville, town (1990 pop. 3,796), Montgomery co., central Md., 28 mi/45 km NW of Washington, D.C.; 39°08′N 77°25′W. The 1st house, made of logs by John Poole in 1793, is still standing, selling old-time prods. Frequently occupied by both Union and Confederate troops, Poolesville still has several houses from the 17th and 18th cents. clustered along the town square. The village itself is on the Register of Historic Places. Major residential growth is occuring in the area.

Poor Fork, c.45 mi/72 km long, SE Ky.; rises in the Cumberland Mts. in SE Letcher co.; flows WSW past Cumberland, joining Clover Fork 1 mi/1.6 km N of Harlan to form Cumberland R.

Poorman, village, W central Alaska, 45 mi/72 km S of Ruby.

Pope 1 county (□ 830 sq mi/2,150 sq km; 1990 pop. 45,883), N central Ark.; ⊙ Russellville; 35°27′N 93°02′W. Bounded S by Arkansas R., Dardenelle Lock and Dam at Russellville forms large L. Dardanelle to W; drained by Ill. Bayou and Big Piney Creek; situated in Ozark region. Part of Ozark Natl. Forest on N; L. Dardenelle State Park in SW, at Russellville; Galla Creek Wildlife Management Area and Holla Bend Natl. Wildlife Refuge (on S side of Arkansas R. bend separated from rest of co. by new river channel) in S. Diversified farming (wheat, soybeans; cattle, hogs, chickens). Coal mines, some natural gas wells; timber. Formed 1829. Nuclear power plants Arkansas 1 (initial criticality Aug. 6, 1974; max. dependable capacity of 836 MWe) and Akansas 2 (initial criticality Dec. 5, 1978; max. dependable capacity of 858 MWe) are 6 mi/9.7 km WNW of Russellville; both use cooling water from Dardanelle Reservoir. **2** county (□ 374 sq mi/969 sq km; 1990 pop. 4,373), extreme SE Ill.; ⊙ Golconda; 37°24′N 88°34′W. Bounded SE by Ohio R.; drained by Bay and Lusk creeks, small tributaries of the Ohio. All but S tip and SW corner of co. are in Shawnee Natl. Forest; Dixon Springs State Park here. Predominantly agr. area (grain; cattle; timber); wood prods.; fluorspar mining. Formed 1816. One of 17 Ill. counties to retain Southern-style commission form of co. govt. **3** county (□ 717 sq mi/ 1,857 sq km; 1990 pop. 10,745), W Minn.; ⊙ Glenwood; 45°35′N 95°27′W. Agr. area drained by Chippewa, Little Chippewa, and East Chippewa rivers and watered by numerous small lakes, with the larger L. Minnewaska at center. Wheat, corn, oats, barley, alfalfa, hay, soybeans, beans, honey; sheep, hogs, cattle, poultry; dairying. Glacial L. State Park in S center. Formed 1862.

Pope, village (1990 pop. 171), Panola co., NW Miss., 30 mi/48 km NNW of Grenada; 34°12′N 89°57′W. Agr. (cotton, grain; livestock); mfg. (beef and pork processing). Enid L. reservoir to SE.

Pope Air Force Base (1990 pop. 2,857), Cumberland co., S central N.C., near Fayetteville; 35°10′N 79°00′W.

Pope Creek, c.50 mi/80 km long, NW Ill.; rises NE of Galesburg; flows W through Mercer Co. to the Mississippi R. at Keithsburg; 41°09′N 90°13′W.

Popejoy, town (1990 pop. 92), Franklin co., N central Iowa, near Iowa R., 15 mi/24 km SW of Hampton; 42°35′N 93°25′W.

Popham Beach, Maine: see PHIPPSBURG.

Poplar 1 (PAHP-luhr), uninc. town (1990 pop. 1,901), Tulare co., S central Calif., 22 mi/35 km SSE of Visalia. Fruit, nuts, grain, cotton, sugar beets; cattle, hogs, poultry. **2** town (1990 pop. 881), Roosevelt co., NE Mont., on Missouri R., at mouth of Poplar R., and 20 mi/32 km E of Wolf Point; 48°07′N 105°12′W. Sheep, cattle, poultry; hay, wheat, barley, corn (maize), beans, potatoes. Mfg. (textiles, fabricated metal prods.). Hq. of Fort Peck Indian Reservation here, located on S border of reservation. Inc. 1916.

Poplar, village (1990 pop. 516), Douglas co., NW Wis., 16 mi/26 km ESE of Superior; 46°34′N 91°47′W. Food processing. American R. State Park to W.

Poplar Bluff, city (1990 pop. 16,996), ⊙ Butler co., SE Mo., in the Ozark Mts., on the low bluffs of the Black R. near the Ark. state line; 36°45′N 90°24′W. Trade, shipping, and medical center in a farming area. Mfg. (transportation equip., plastic prods., furniture, bldg. materials, flour, wood and paper prods., shoes, lumber). Three Rivers Community Col. and Veterans Hospital are here; Mark Twain Natl. Forest to N. Inc. 1870.

Poplar Grove 1 village, Phillips co., E Ark., 14 mi/23 km W of Helena. In farm area. **2** village (1990 pop. 743), Boone co., N Ill., 14 mi/23 km ENE of Rockford; 42°22′N 88°49′W. In agr. area.

Poplar Islands, three low, wooded islands named Poplar, Jefferson, and Coaches created out of erosion of 1 named Poplin's or Popeley's, Talbot co., E Md., on Chesapeake Bay at S entrance to Eastern Bay, 17 mi/ 27 km W of Easton. A local story has Charles Carroll, grandson of Charles Carroll of Carrollton, raising black cats here in 1847 to sell their pelts to China. But the cats presumably escaped when an ice bridge to the mainland formed that winter. A club on Jefferson Isl., visited by Presidents Roosevelt and Truman, burned in 1950. Now uninhabited and owned by the Smithsonian Inst., the isls. are used to study the great blue heron and osprey.

Poplar River, 167 mi/269 km long, W Canada (Sask.) and Mont.; rises in S Sask.; flows S, past Scobey (NE Mont.), to Missouri R. at Poplar.

Poplar Tent, uninc. town (1990 pop. 3,872), Cabarrus co., S central N.C., residential suburb 2 mi/3.2 km W of downtown Concord, on Poplar Tent road, near Buffalo Creek; 35°24′N 80°38′W. Concord Regional Airport to W; Charlotte Motor Speedway to SW.

Poplarville (PAHP-luhr-vil), town (1990 pop. 2,561), ⊙ Pearl River co., SE Miss., 36 mi/58 km SSW of Hattiesburg, near Wolf R.; 30°50′N 89°31′W. In agr. (cotton, corn, tung nuts, blueberries, blackberries) and timber area; mfg. (machinery, lumber, apparel). A junior col. and a state agr. experiment station are here. Part of De Soto Natl. Forest to NE. Inc. 1883.

Popo Agie River (po-po AG-ee), c.30 mi/48 km long, primarily in SW Fremont co., W central Wyo.; rises in 3 forks all in Shoshone Natl. Forest, in S part of Wind R. Range.; flows NE to join Wind R. at Riverton, forming the Bighorn R. North Fork rises at Continental Divide 23 mi/37 km W of Lander, flows NE c.30 mi/ 48 km. Middle Fork rises at the Divide in E edge 24 mi/ 39 km SW of Lander of Sublette co., flows c.35 mi/ 56 km E into Fremont co., then NE past Lander joining North Fork 2 mi/3.2 km N of Lander forming main stream of Popo Agie. The 3d Fork, the Little Popo Agie R., also in Fremont co., rises 22 mi/35 km SSW of Lander, flows NE c.45 mi/72 km joining main stream 3 mi/4.8 km N of Hudson. Middle Fork passes through Sinks Canyon State Park. At the "sinks," the river disappears into a cave reemerging at "the rise of the sinks," a pool filled with large trout which thrive on handouts from visitors.

Popocatépetl (po-po-kah-TE-petl) [Aztec = smoking mountain], volcano (17,887 ft/5,452 m), in the Cordillera de Anáhuac, central Mexico, on the border bet. Puebla and Mexico states; 19°02′N 98°38′W. The 2d-highest peak in Mexico. The normally snow-capped cone is symmetrical, and the large crater has practically pure sulfur deposits only partially exploited. The ascent, which is fairly easy, was probably 1st made by Europeans in 1519 by 1 of Cortés' men. Active during the 1st 2 cents. of Span. colonial times, the volcano erupted in 1994 and 1996.

Popof Island, Shumagin Isls., SW Alaska, off S coast of Alaska Peninsula, just E of Unga Isl.; 10 mi/16 km long, 5 mi/8 km wide; 55°19′N 160°24′W. Rises to 1,550 ft/ 472 m. Fishing, fish canning, big-game hunting. Sand Point village, E.

Popponesset, Mass.: see MASHPEE.

Poquonock (pah-KAH-nik), village (1990 pop. 2,770) in Windsor town, N Conn., on Farmington R., and 14 mi/ 23 km N of Hartford; 41°21′N 72°01′W.

Poquoson (pa-KO-sun), independent city (□ 10 sq mi/ 16 sq km), E Va., residential suburb 7 mi/11.3 km N of Hampton, separate from adjacent York co. and Hampton city; 37°08′N 76°17′W. Bounded S by Hampton city, SE by Back R. estuary, N by Poquson R. estuary, E by Salt Marsh (Plum Tree Isl. Natl. Wildlife Reserve), with Chesapeake Bay beyond it. Mfg. (clam processing, tool and die machining). Langley Air Force Base and NASA to S. Williamsburg–Newport News Internatl. Airport to W.

Poquott, village (1990 pop. 770), Suffolk co., SE N.Y., on N shore of L.I., on Port Jefferson Harbor, just E of Port Jefferson; 40°57′N 73°05′W.

Porcher Island (POHR-kuhr) (□ 210 sq mi/544 sq km), W B.C., W Canada, in Hecate Strait, 16 mi/26 km SSW of Prince Rupert, NW of Pitt Isl.; 22 mi/35 km long, 18 mi/29 km wide. S coat is deeply indented. Rises to over 2,000 ft/610 m. Villages are Jap Inlet (N), Refuge Bay (NW), and Oona R. (E); lumbering.

Porcupine, village, E Ont., central Canada, on Porcupine L., 8 mi/13 km ENE of Timmins. Gold and barite mining. Founded 1909 as mining camp, it gives its name to surrounding mining dist., which includes famous Dome and Hollinger mines, discovered 1909. Porcupine has been superseded by nearby South Porcupine.

Porcupine, river, 448 mi/721 km long, Yukon Territory and Alaska; rises in the Ogilvie Mts., NW Yukon Territory; flows in a great arc NE through the Eagle Plain, then W into Alaska and to the Yukon R. (of which it is a main tributary) at Fort Yukon. The river was explored (1842) by John Bell, a chief trader for the Hudson's Bay Co.

Porcupine Hills, SW Alta., W Canada, foothills of Rocky Mts., extend c.30 mi/48 km N-S 40 mi/64 km W of Lethbridge; rise to over 4,000 ft/1,219 m.

Porcupine Mountain, range, W Man., central Canada, extends 60 mi/97 km along Sask. border W of L. Winnipegosis. Highest point is Hart Mt. (2,700 ft/823 m), 27 mi/43 km NNW of Swan R.

Porcupine Mountains, Ontonago and Gogebic cos., NW Upper Peninsula, N Mich., WSW of Ontonagon, on L. Superior; 46°46′N 89°45′W. Mining of large copper deposits here began 1951 at White Pine Mine, 15 mi/ 24 km WSW of Ontonagon. Mine now closed. Contained within Porcupine Mts. State Park (□ 83 sq mi/ 215 sq km), a wilderness state park. Porcupine Mt. Ski Area within park. Government Peak (1,863 ft/568 m). Crossed by Carp, Little Carp, and Presque Isle rivers.

Porcupine Plain, town (1991 pop. 803), E central Sask., W Canada, 40 mi/64 km ESE of Tisdale; 52°36′N 103°15′W. Wheat; dairying.

Porcupines, the, small islands, Hancock co., S Maine, in Frenchman Bay just E of Bar Harbor. Individually known as Long Porcupine, Burnt Porcupine, Sheep Porcupine, and Bald Porcupine isls., and Rum Key.

Port Alberni (al-BUHR-nee), city (1991 pop. 18,403), SW B.C., W Canada, on Vancouver Isl., at the head of Alberni Canal and Barkley sound; 49°14′N 124°48′W. It is a fishing port with one of the largest forestry complexes in the world.

Port Alexander, village (1990 pop. 119), SE Alaska, on Chatham Strait, near S tip of Baranof Isl., 60 mi/97 km SSE of Sitka; 56°13′N 134°37′W. Fishing (cannery at Port Armstrong, 6 mi/9.7 km N).

Port Alfred, town, S central Que., E Canada, on Ha Ha Bay of the Saguenay R., 11 mi/18 km SE of Chicoutimi; 48°20′N 70°53′W. Lumbering; dairying; resort.

Port Alice, village (1991 pop. 1,371), SW B.C., W Canada, on N Vancouver Isl., on an inlet of Quatsino Sound, 27 mi/43 km WSW of Alert Bay; 50°23′N 127°26′W. Pulp milling; lumber-shipping port.

Port Allegany (A-luh-GAI-nee), borough (1990 pop. 2,391), McKean co., N Pa., 20 mi/32 km SSE of Olean (N.Y.), on Allegheny R., near mouth of Allegheny Portage Creek; 41°48′N 78°16′W. Mfg. (glass prods., thermal insulation); oil and gas fields nearby; timber; agr. (dairying). Lumber center in 1830s. Part of Susquehanna State Forest to S. Settled c.1816, inc. 1882.

Port Allen, city (1990 pop. 6,277), ⊙ West Baton Rouge parish, SE central La., on the Mississippi, opposite Baton Rouge (bridge); 30°27′N 91°13′W. In agr. area (sugarcane, rice, corn, cotton). Sugar and flour milling, printing, mfg. (chemicals, coffee, fabricated metal prods., machinery; galvanizing). Port Allen lock here; start of Port Allen–Morgan City Waterway. Laid out 1854, inc. 1923.

Port Allen, uninc. village (1990 pop. 700), Calhoun co., S Texas, 35 mi/56 km ESE of Victoria, on arm of Matagorda Bay, Gulf of Mexico. Fishing. Agr. (rice, cotton). Resort area.

Port Allen, commercial harbor, port of entry, Hanapepe Bay, S Kauai, Kauai co., Hawaii, 14 mi/23 km WSW of Lihue, on Kaumualii Highway. Sugarcane plantations to NE. Numila Cane Mill to E. Port Allen Airport (Burns Field) to SW, at Puolo Point.

Port Allen–Morgan City Waterway, canal, c.55 mi/ 89 km long, S La., shipping route that provides shortcut bet. Mississippi R. (N) and Gulf Intracoastal Waterway (S). Used by barges and other low-draft vessels. It starts in N at Port Allen, opposite Baton Rouge, heads W c.5 mi/8 km, connecting with the Plaquemine locks, then curves S and continues through E margin of Atchafalaya Basin, through West Baton Rouge, Iberville, Iberia, and St. Martin parishes, ending at Grand Lake, N of Morgan City, an inland port with access to offshore oil and natural gas facilities in Gulf of Mexico. Oil, gas, and chemical production plants located at both ends of canal. Also called Port Allen–Morgan City Alternate Shipping Route.

Port Angeles, city (1990 pop. 17,710), ⊙ Clallam co., NW Wash., on Strait Juan de Fuca opposite (20 mi/32 km S of) Victoria (B.C.), 62 mi/100 km NW of Seattle; 48°11′N 123°28′W. A port of entry with a good harbor, Port Angeles is a boating and fishing center and has pulp and paper mills; mfg. (wood prods., transportation equip.; printing and publishing); logging. Lower Elwha Indian Reservation to W; ferry to Victoria. Fairchild Internatl. Airport to W. Hurricane Ridge Alpine Ski Area to S, in Olympic Natl. Park; Dungeness Natl. Wildlife Refuge and Dungeness State Park (marine) to E. Parts of Olympic Natl. Forest to SW and SE. The city is also a resort and the hq. for Olympic Natl. Park. Peninsula Col. and a U.S. Coast Guard Station at end of Ediz Hook, narrow peninsula that forms Port Angeles Harbor. Inc. 1890.

Port Antonio, town (1991 pop. 13,118), ⊙ Portland parish, NE Jamaica, 3d-largest port of the isl., 27 mi/43 km NE of Kingston (linked by RR); 18°10′N 76°27′W. RR terminus, tourist resort, and trading center situated on spacious bay protected by small Navy Isl. Has 2 harbors and is divided into 2 sects., with Titchfield the residential sect. Once a leading banana port, it still ships tropical fruit (coconuts, bananas, cacao). Ice factory, bottling works; mfg. of sweets. Has govt. bldgs., old military barracks.

Port Aransas, town (1990 pop. 2,233), Nueces co., S Texas, on Aransas Pass (shipping channel to Corpus Christi Bay and harbor), and at N end of Mustang Isl. and part of Harbor Isl. (ferry), 22 mi/35 km E of Corpus Christi; 27°49′N 97°04′W. Resort area, tourism; fishing; light mfg. Intracoastal Waterway runs bet. isl. and mainland, Redfish Bay Causeway to NW connects town with mainland. Mustang Isl. State Park and Padre Isl. Natl. Seashore to S by road.

Port Armstrong, Alaska: see PORT ALEXANDER.

Port Arthur, Ont., Canada: see THUNDER BAY.

Port Arthur, city (1990 pop. 58,724), Jefferson co., SE Texas, 85 mi/137 km E of Houston; 29°49′N 93°55′W. On Sabine L., a widening of Sabine R., 18 mi/29 km from Gulf of Mexico; a S extension of city limits reaches to Texas Point on Sabine Pass on gulf. Twin city to Beaumont 18 mi/29 km NW. A deepwater port of entry on the Sabine-Neches Canal, it is an extensive oil port, with many large refineries, chemical plants, and oil rigs and ships. Natural-gas processing, printing and publishing, mfg. of bldg. materials and metal prods. Agr. (rice; soybeans; cattle). The Sabine region had already been visited and settled (livestock; rice) before Arthur E. Stilwell decided (1894) to found a RR terminus here. Amer. financier and promoter John Warne Gates ("Bet-a-Million Gates") also contributed to the early growth of the city. A ship channel was completed in 1899. Boomed after the discovery (1901) of oil at Spindletop, it is now a major oil-shipping port (23,000,000 tons/20,861,000 metric tons annually). Seat of Lamar Univ. (2-year). Sea Rim State Park to S, on coast; Sabine Battleground State Historic Site in S; Texas Point Natl. Wildlife Refuge in S, to W of point; McFadden Natl. Wildlife Refuge to SW, on coast. Inc. 1898.

Port Arthur Canal, Texas: see SABINE-NECHES WATERWAY.

Port au Choix National Historic Park, N N.F., E Canada, at Barbace Point, on Gulf of St. Lawrence, W side of Northern Peninsula, 120 mi/193 km N of Corner Brook. Site of Maritime Archaic Native Amer. burial ground, c.2340 B.C. Declared Federal historic park, 1970.

Port au Port (POR to POR), peninsula on the Gulf of St. Lawrence, SW N.F., E Canada, bet. St. George and Port au Port bays, W of Stephenville; 30 mi/48 km long, up to 10 mi/16 km wide; connected with mainland by narrow isthmus. On N shore of isthmus is fishing settlement of Port au Port, 45 mi/72 km SW of Corner Brook. From N end of peninsula a narrow spit of land projects 15 mi/24 km NE, enclosing Port au Port Bay (18 mi/29 km long, up to 12 mi/19 km wide). At W extremity of peninsula is Cape St. George.

Port Austin, town (1990 pop. 815), Huron co., E Mich., 16 mi/26 km N of Bad Axe, on L. Huron; 44°02′N 83°00′W. Mfg. (hand tools, thread rolling). Grindstone City to E, with 6-ft/1.8-m-diameter grindstones on beach produced at nearby quarries in pioneer days. Port Crescent State Park to W has petroglyphs in sandstone outcrops.

Port Authority of New York and New Jersey, SE N.Y., political subdivision of N.Y. and N.J. that plans, develops, and operates transportation facilities in the 2 states. Created in 1921 as a compact bet. N.Y. and N.J. and approved by Congress, it occupies a tract of land (☐ 1,500 sq mi/3,885 sq km) that encompasses both states. Centered on N.Y. Harbor, within which is an integrated system of marine terminals, airports, highways, RR lines, transit systems, and trade services. The 4 basic groupings of the authority's operations and facilities are air and marine terminals, an interstate transportation system, and economic development facilities. Operations encompass the oceanborne commerce of the Port of N.Y. and N.J., including motor vehicle, passenger ship, and maritime cargo terminals; JFK, Newark, and LaGuardia airports; Teterboro Airport in Bergen co., N.J.; Manhattan's World Trade Center; and heliports at 2 locations in Manhattan. Also included is the system of bridges, tunnels, and terminals linking N.Y. and N.J., such as the George Washington Bridge (bet. Bergen co., N.J., and Upper Manhattan), the Outerbridge Crossing, Goethals and Bayonne bridges (all 3 connect Staten Isl. with N.J.), and the Lincoln and Holland tunnels. The Port Authority's facilities and operations generate c.431,000 jobs for the region.

Port aux Basques (por to BASK), town, at SW tip of N.F., E Canada, on small bay, 310 mi/499 km W of St. John's (connected by RR), and 8 mi/13 km ESE of Cape Ray; 47°35′N 59°10′W. Terminal for ferry service across Cabot Strait from North Sydney (N.S.). Fishing port, with cold storage plants. Inc. 1945 with nearby Channel as a single municipality.

Port Barre (port BAH-ree), town (1990 pop. 2,144), St. Landry parish, S central La., 8 mi/13 km E of Opelousas, near Bayou Teche; 30°34′N 91°58′W. Wood prods. Oil and natural-gas fields nearby.

Port Bolivar, uninc. town (1990 pop. 1,200), Galveston co., S Texas, at tip of Bolivar Peninsula (coastal sand barrier isl.), across mouth of Galveston Bay, 2 mi/3.2 km NE of Galveston Isl. and city of Galveston (ferry service). Intracoastal Waterway passes on NW side of peninsula.

Port Burwell, village (1991 pop. 883), S Ont., central Canada, on L. Erie, at mouth of Otter Creek, 21 mi/34 km ESE of St. Thomas; 42°39′N 80°49′W. Fishing and port.

Port Byron 1 village (1990 pop. 1,002), Rock Island co., NW Ill., on the Mississippi R., and 15 mi/24 km NE of Rock Island; 41°37′N 90°19′W. In agr. area. **2** village (☐ 1 sq mi/2.6 sq km; 1990 pop. 1,359), Cayuga co., W central N.Y., in Finger Lakes region, 8 mi/12.9 km NNW of Auburn; 43°02′N 76°37′W. Mfg. of plastic prods.

Port Carbon, borough (1990 pop. 2,134), Schuylkill co., E central Pa., 2 mi/3.2 km NE of Pottsville, on Schuylkill R.; 40°42′N 76°10′W. Mfg. (fabric bleaching and dyeing, apparel, machinery, lumber); anthracite coal; agr. (grain; poultry, livestock; dairying). Laid out 1828, inc. 1852.

Port Carling, resort village, S Ont., central Canada, in Muskoka lake region, bet. lakes Rosseau (N) and Muskoka (S), 28 mi/45 km SE of Parry Sound.

Port Charlotte, uninc. city (☐ 23 sq mi/60 sq km; 1990 pop. 41,535), Charlotte co., SW Fla., on Charlotte Harbor (an inlet of the Gulf of Mexico), and the Peace and Myakka rivers; 26°59′N 82°06′W. It is a planned residential community—1 of several on a peninsula once owned by the Vanderbilt family. An important cultural center and large retired pop. are here. The town's pop. quadrupled bet. 1970 and 1990.

Port Chester, village (☐ 2 mi/3.2 km; 1990 pop. 24,728), Westchester co., SE N.Y., a suburb of N.Y. city, on L.I. Sound, at the mouth of the Byram R., and on the Conn. state line; 41°00′N 73°40′W. Primarily residential, it produces some household goods. Gen. Israel Putnam had his hq. here 1777–1778. Several Colonial-here homes remain. Previously called Saw Pits, village was renamed in 1837. Settled after 1660, inc. 1868

Port Chicago, village (1990 pop.), Contra Costa co., W Calif., 8 mi/12.9 km W of Pittsburg, 19 mi/31 km NNE of downtown Oakland, on S shore of Suisun Bay. Industrial port. Former site of U.S. Naval Magazine Pacific Ordnance depot. An explosion of ammunition vessels here during World War II killed 320. Depot since moved to Concord Naval Station. Port Chicago Natl. Memorial.

Port Chilkoot, Alaska: see CHILKOOT.

Port Clements, village (1991 pop. 483), W B.C., W Canada, on E central Graham Isl., on Masset Inlet, 23 mi/37 km S of Massett; 53°41′N 132°10′W. Lumbering. Ferry landing.

Port Clinton, city (1990 pop. 7,106), ⊙ Ottawa co., N Ohio, at mouth of Portage R., on L. Erie, 32 mi/51 km ESE of Toledo; 41°30′N 82°56′W. In fruit-growing area; makes transportation equip., boats, gypsum prods., canned goods; fisheries. Camp Perry (Natl. Guard) and Erie Ordnance Depot (at Lacarne) are nearby. Founded c.1828.

Port Clinton, borough (1990 pop. 328), Schuylkill co., E central Pa., 3 mi/4.8 km NW of Hamburg, on Schuylkill R., at mouth of Little Schuylkill R.; 40°34′N 76°01′W. Gap through Blue Mt. to SE; parts of Weiser State Forest to SW and NE; Appalachian Trail passes through town (NE-SW) from Blue Mt. to cross Schuylkill R.; Hawk Mt. Sanctuary to NE.

Port Clyde, Maine: see SAINT GEORGE.

Port Colborne (KOL-buhrn), town (1991 pop. 18,766), S Ont., central Canada, on L. Erie, at the S end of the Welland Ship Canal; 42°53′N 79°14′W. It is an important transshipment center bet. Montreal and points W. It has a nickel refinery, grain elevators, and a cement plant.

Port Conclusion, bay, SE Alaska, on Chatham Straight, near S tip of Baranof Isl., 4 mi/6.4 km SSW of Port Alexander; 56°00′N 134°00′W.

Port Coquitlam (ko-KWIT-luhm), city (1991 pop. 36,773), SW B.C., W Canada, in lower Fraser R. valley, on Coquitlam R., urban enclave 15 mi/24 km E of Vancouver; 49°16′N 122°46′W. Center of vegetable- and fruit-growing (cranberries) region. Meatpacking, mfg. (foods, fabricated metal, chemicals, electronic equip., elevators, machinery), shipbuilding; steelworks; mining services. Hydroelectric power.

Port Dalhousie (dal-HOO-zee), village, S Ont., central Canada, on L. Ontario, at N end of old Welland Canal, 3 mi/5 km N of St. Catharines, near N terminal of new Welland Ship Canal; 43°12′N 79°16′W. Port, with dry dock; food processing.

Port Daniel, village (1991 pop. 1,804), E Que., E Canada, SE Gaspé Peninsula, on the Gulf of St. Lawrence, 50 mi/80 km SE of Gaspé; 48°11′N 64°59′W. Fishing center.

Port Deposit, town (1990 pop. 685), Cecil co., NE Md., on the Susquehanna R., and 3 mi/4.8 km N of Havre de Grace; 39°36′N 76°07′W. Granite quarrying (since 1808) and shipping; makes fabricated steel prods. Col. Thomas Cresap operated a ferry here as early as 1729 and the town was known as Cresap's Ferry into the early 19th cent. The town came into existence in 1808 with the completion of the Susquehanna, or Md., Canal. Named Fort Deposit in 1813, it literally became a port of deposit for arks (or rafts) and sailing vessels. An iron foundry (1849) produced the popular Armstrong stove in the 1870s. The canal, unable to compete with the RR, closed in the 1890s, and quarrying remained the only industry until the Bainbridge Naval

Training Center was est. 1942. Washington Hall was built in 1894 to house the Tome Inst., a free school, financed by a $1.5-million bequest from millionaire lumber dealer Jacob Tome (1819–1898); closed in 1941, but the school's Adams Hall is now Town Hall. A successor institution, the Bainbridge Center (closed 1976), was a training center for WAVEs during World War II.

Port Dickinson, residential village (1990 pop. 1,785), Broome co., S N.Y., on Chenango R., just N of Binghamton; 42°08′N 75°53′W. Inc. 1876.

Port Dover, village, S Ont., central Canada, on L. Erie, 35 mi/56 km SW of Hamilton; 42°47′N 80°12′W. Fishing port; food processing.

Port Eads (EEDZ), village, Plaquemines parish, extreme SE La., on South Pass (a mouth of the Mississippi R.) near tip of the delta, c.85 mi/137 km SE of New Orleans. Pilot station and hq. for channel maintenance engineers. Lighthouse here (29°01′N 89°10′W). Natural-gas wells. Within Pass a Loutre State Game Area.

Port Edward, village (1991 pop. 739), W B.C., W Canada, on inlet of Chatham Sound of the Pacific Ocean, on Yellowhead Highway, and 7 mi/11 km S of Prince Rupert; 54°14′N 130°18′W. Pulp mill, fish canneries. Oldest cannery village on N coast; mus.

Port Edwards, town (1990 pop. 1,848), Wood co., central Wis., on Wisconsin R., and 4 mi/6.4 km SSW of Wisconsin Rapids; 44°21′N 89°50′W. RR junction in timber and dairy region; paper, caustic soda, potash mfg. Power dam. Inc. 1902.

Port Elgin, town (1991 pop. 6,857), S Ont., central Canada, on L. Huron, 25 mi/40 km WSW of Owen Sound. Fishing; dairying; light mfg.; resort; tree nurseries.

Port Elgin (EL-gin), village (1991 pop. 490), SE N.B., E Canada, on Baie Verte of Northumberland Strait, 35 mi/56 km E of Moncton. Fishing port (smelts, lobster).

Port Elizabeth, town, Bequia, St. Vincent and the Grenadines, West Indies, on Admiralty Bay; 13°01′N 61°14′W. Isl.'s commercial center and main port.

Port Essington, village, W B.C., W Canada, on Skeena R. estuary, 18 mi/29 km SE of Prince Rupert; 54°09′N 129°57′W. Salmon-canning center. Nearby are silver, gold, copper deposits.

Port Everglades, Fla.: see FORT LAUDERDALE.

Port Ewen (YOO-uhn), village (□ 2 sq mi/5.2 sq km; 1990 pop. 3,444), Ulster co., SE N.Y., near W bank of the Hudson R., just S of Kingston; 41°54′N 73°58′W.

Port Frederick, Alaska: see HOONAH.

Port Gamble, village (1990 pop. 380), Kitsap co., W Wash., on Hood Canal near Puget Sound, at mouth of Port Gamble Bay, 20 mi/32 km N of Bremerton. Fishing port; crabs, oysters, halibut, herring. Port Gamble Indian Reservation to E; Hood Canal Floating Bridge 1 mi/1.6 km to W.

Port Gibson, town (1990 pop. 1,810), ⊙ Claiborne co., SW Miss., 28 mi/45 km S of Vicksburg, near Bayou Pierre, and the Mississippi R.; 31°57′N 90°58′W. Agr. (cotton, corn, soybeans; cattle); mfg. (cable assemblies, paper prods., plastic prods., lumber, cottonseed oil). Alcorn Agr. and Mechanical Univ. to SW, at Alcorn. Founded in late 18th cent. A Civil War battle of Vicksburg campaign was fought near here, but the town was spared and many historic homes remain. Grand Gulf Military Park to NW, on Mississippi R., Grand Gulf Nuclear Power Station 10 mi/16 km to N. Miss. Cultural Crossroads.

Port Graham, village (1990 pop. 166), S Alaska, SW Kenai Peninsula, 8 mi/12.9 km SW of Seldovia; 59°21′N 151°50′W. Fishing; cannery.

Port Greville (GRE-vil), village, N N.S., E Canada, on N shore of Minas Channel, 35 mi/56 km SSW of Amherst; 45°25′N 64°33′W. Fishing port; shipbuilding.

Port Hadlock, Wash.: see HADLOCK.

Port Hammond or **Hammond**, village, SW B.C., W Canada, on Fraser R., urban enclave 20 mi/32 km E of Vancouver; 49°03′N 122°39′W. Lumbering; dairying; fruit, vegetables.

Port Hardy, village (1991 pop. 5,082), SW B.C., W Canada, on N Vancouver Isl., on Queen Charlotte Strait, 27 mi/43 km WNW of Alert Bay; 50°43′N 127°29′W.

Elev. 73 ft/22 m. N terminus of highway from Nanaimo, S terminus of Inside Passage ferry from Prince Rupert, start of Cape Scott Trail. Sawmill; logging, copper ore processing, fishing (salmon, prawns).

Port Harrison, village, NW Que., E Canada, on Hudson Bay; 58°28′N 78°07′W; Hudson's Bay Co. trading post.

Port Hastings, village, E N.S., E Canada, SW Cape Breton Isl., on Canso Strait, 4 mi/6 km NW of Port Hawkesbury; 45°38′N 61°24′W. Fishing; shipping.

Port Hawkesbury, town (1991 pop. 3,991), E N.S., E Canada, SW Cape Breton Isl., on the Strait of Canso, 30 mi/48 km E of Antigonish; 45°36′N 61°21′W. Port; fishing. Refineries, mills; forest prods.

Port Heiden, village (1990 pop. 119), SW Alaska, 160 mi/257 km S of Dillingham, N side of Alaska Peninsula, on Port Heiden bay, extension of Bristol Bay, Bering Sea; 56°57′N 158°35′W. Fishing.

Port Henry, resort village (□ 1 mi/1.6 km; 1990 pop. 1,263), Essex co., NE N.Y., on harbor on L. Champlain, 14 mi/23 km NNW of Ticonderoga; 44°02′N 73°27′W. In dairying area. Inc. 1869.

Port Herman, Md.: see CHESAPEAKE CITY.

Port Hill, village, W P.E.I., E Canada, near Malpeque Bay, 14 mi/23 km NW of Summerside. Mixed farming, dairying.

Port Hobron, small bay, N Sitkalidak Isl., S Alaska, on Gulf of Alaska, off SE Kodiak Isl., 50 mi/80 km SW of Kodiak. At head of bay is McCord village, former whaling station.

Port Hood, town, ⊙ Inverness co., E N.S., E Canada, on SW coast of Cape Breton Isl., on Northumberland Strait, at entrance to George Bay, 20 mi/32 km SW of Inverness; 46°02′N 61°32′W. Coal-mining region. Just W is Port Hood Isl.

Port Hood Island, in Northumberland Strait, E N.S., E Canada, at entrance to George Bay, 2 mi/3 km W of Port Hood, SW Cape Breton Isl.; 2 mi/3 km long, 1 mi/2 km wide.

Port Hope, town (1991 pop. 11,505), SE Ont., central Canada, on L. Ontario, E of Toronto; 43°57′N 78°18′W. Has a large plant for refining uranium ore. Summer resort.

Port Hope, village (1990 pop. 313), Huron co., E Mich., 17 mi/27 km ENE of Bad Axe, on L. Huron; 43°56′N 82°43′W. Glass prods. Resort.

Port Hope Simpson, village (1991 pop. 614), SE Lab., E Canada, on Alexis R., and 35 mi/56 km WNW of Battle Harbour; 52°31′N 56°18′W. Lumbering center.

Port Howe, town, central Bahama Isls., on S shore of Cat Isl., 11 mi/18 km SSE of The Bight; 24°14′N 75°18′W. Cattle and horse raising.

Port Hudson, village, East Baton Rouge parish, SE central La., on E bank of the Mississippi R., and 16 mi/26 km NNW of Baton Rouge; 30°40′N 91°16′W. Port Hudson State Commemorative Area, here, is site of strong Confederate earthen fortifications, besieged (May–July 1863) by Union troops under Gen. N. P. Banks, surrendered after fall of Vicksburg (Mus. and Natl. Cemetery).

Port Hueneme (wei-NEE-mee), city (1990 pop. 20,319), Ventura co., S Calif., suburb 3 mi/4.8 km S of Oxnard, on the Pacific Ocean coast; 34°10′N 119°12′W. Mfg. (fabricated metal prods.); flowers, nursery prods. It has an artificial, deep-sea harbor and is the site of a huge naval construction-battalion ("Seabee") center. Notable Seabee mus. Point Mugu Naval Air Station to E; Santa Monica Mts. Natl. Recreation Area to E; Channel Isls. Natl. Park to SW; Point Mugu State Park is here; McGrath State Beach to NW. Founded 1870, inc. 1948.

Port Huron (HYUHR-on), city (1990 pop. 33,694), ⊙ St. Clair co., S Mich., a natural, deepwater port of entry at the exit of the St. Clair R. from L. Huron; 42°59′N 82°25′W. RR junction and RR/ship transfer. It is a shipping center with RR shops. Mfg. includes transportation equip.; bldg. materials, machinery, salt, fabricated metal prods., paper prods., chemicals, machinery, consumer goods, electrical equip.; electroplating. The earliest Eur. settlement began (1686) with the Fr. fort, St. Joseph. The town grew after the building (1826) of Fort Gratiot Turnpike (bet. Port Huron and Detroit), ushering in a lumbering era. Local deposits of salt, oil, and

natural gas were developed. Connected by St. Clair RR tunnel and an internatl. bridge with Sarnia (Ont.). St. Clair Co. Community Col. The old Fort Gratiot lighthouse marks the St. Clair straits off Port Huron. Thomas Edison grew up here. Internatl. Airport to SW. Lakeport State Park to N. Inc. 1857.

Port Isabel, town (1990 pop. 4,467), Cameron co., extreme S Texas, on S end of Laguna Madre, at its entrance to South Bay and Gulf of Mexico, and 22 mi/35 km NE of Brownsville; 26°04′N 97°13′W. Deepwater port on Gulf Intracoastal Waterway and ship channel from Gulf of Mexico SW to Brownsville (terminus of Waterway). Ships petroleum, fish. Resort. Oil refining; pipeline terminus; mfg. (textiles; shrimp processing and shrimp boat rebuilding). Causeway and bridge connect town with S end of Padre Isl. (E) and community of South Padre Isl. Laguna Atascosa Natl. Wildlife Refuge to NW; Port Isabel Lighthouse (1835) State Historic Site; several lagoons to W, including Laguna Largo and Bahia Grande. Formerly called Point Isabel. In Mex. War was supply base for Gen. Zachary Taylor. Inc. 1928.

Port Ivory, a former industrial section of Staten Isl. borough of N.Y. city, SE N.Y., on NW Staten Isl.; 40°39′N 74°11′W.

Port Jefferson 1 residential village (1990 pop. 7,455), Suffolk co., SE N.Y., on N shore of L.I., on Port Jefferson Harbor (yachting), 19 mi/31 km E of Huntington; 40°57′N 73°03′W. In orchard and diversified-farming area; sand and gravel; boatyards. Ferry connections with Bridgeport (Conn.). Port Jefferson Station village, just SE, is terminus of North Shore line of L.I. RR. **2** village (1990 pop. 381), Shelby co., W Ohio, 5 mi/8 km NE of Sidney, and on Great Miami R.; 40°19′N 84°05′W.

Port Jefferson Harbor, inlet of L.I. Sound, SE N.Y., denting N shore of L.I.; c.2 mi/3.2 km long; 40°57′N 73°03′W. Port Jefferson is on its S shore. Setauket Harbor (c.1 mi/1.6 km long) is W arm.

Port Jefferson Station, unincorporated village (□ 2 sq mi/5.2 sq km; 1990 pop. 7,232), Suffolk co., L.I., SE N.Y., immediately S of Port Jefferson; 40°55′N 73°04′W. Mfg. (aerospace components, prefabricated bldgs.; publishing).

Port Jervis (JAHR-vuhs), resort city (□ 2 mi/3.2 km; 1990 pop. 9,060), Orange co., SE N.Y., on Delaware R. at mouth of Neversink R., near intersection of N.J., N.Y., and Pa. state lines; 41°22′N 74°41′W. Mfg. of glass, office and school supplies, rubber prods., apparel, chemcals, consumer goods, bldg. materials. At the terminus of the Port Jervis Branch of Metro-North commuter RR. Grew after opening (1828) of Delaware and Hudson Canal. It is one of the largest equestrian centers in nation. Settled before 1700, inc. 1907.

Port Kent, village (1990 pop. 250), Essex co., NE N.Y., on W shore of L. Champlain, 12 mi/19 km S of Plattsburgh; 44°32′N 73°24′W. Ferry to Burlington, Vt.

Port la Joie, P.E.I.: see CHARLOTTETOWN.

Port Lavaca, city (1990 pop. 10,886), ⊙ Calhoun co., S Texas, 27 mi/43 km SE of Victoria, on Lavaca Bay; 28°36′N 96°37′W. A RR terminus and a deepwater port of entry, it is a shipping point for an irrigated agr. (corn, rice; cattle; cotton) area. There are shrimp, crayfish, crab, and fishing industries, as well as related processing. Tourism is significant, and nearby gas and oil wells add to the economy. Mfg. of concrete, machinery, and chemicals. Port Lavaca Causeway State Recreation Park (State Fishing Pier), 3,202 ft/976 m of old causeway used for swimming, boating, fishing. Myrtle Foester Whitmire Div., Aransas Natl. Wildlife Refuge to SE. Nearby are a state park and Matagorda Air Force Base. Inc. 1907.

Port Leyden (LEI-duhn), village (1990 pop. 723), Lewis co., N central N.Y., on Black R., and 27 mi/43 km N of Rome; 43°34′N 75°20′W. Originally known as Kelsey's Mills, it was renamed in 1839 in anticipation of becoming a thriving port upon completion of the Black R. Canal.

Port Lions, village (1990 pop. 222), Kodiak isl., S Alaska, 9 mi/14.5 km W of Kodiak, on Kizhuyak Bay; 57°53′N

152°51′W. No roads; state ferry serves village from Kodiak and Kenai Peninsula. Surrounded by Kodiak Natl. Wildlife Refuge. Settlement was moved from nearby Afognak Isl., after sustaining heavy damage in 1964 Good Friday Earthquake, move subsidized by Lions Internatl. Fishing. Crab-processing plant.

Port Maitland 1 village, W N.S., E Canada, on the Atlantic Ocean, 10 mi/16 km N of Yarmouth. Dairying center; fishing. **2** village, SW Ont., central Canada, on L. Erie, at mouth of Grand R., 30 mi/48 km SSE of Hamilton.

Port Mann, village, SW B.C., W Canada, 4 mi/6 km E of New Westminister, across lower Fraser R.; 49°14′N 122°50′W. Part of city of Surrey and urban industrial enclave of Vancouver. River port; logging transfer point; gypsum processing.

Port Mansfield, uninc. town (1990 pop. 731), Willacy co., extreme S Texas, on Red Fish Bay (arm of Laguna Madre, Gulf of Mexico), 23 mi/37 km ENE of Raymondville. Dredged Port Mansfield Channel (1962), across Laguna Madre and through Padre Isl., gave direct access to gulf for shipping, fishing and pleasure craft. Ships oil, irrigated-agr. produce, canned goods. Intracoastal Waterway passes N-S through Laguna Madre near mainland (W) shore.

Port Maria, town (1991 pop. 7,196), ⊙ St. Mary parish, N Jamaica, seaport on protected Caribbean inlet, 29 mi/47 km NNW of Kingston; 18°23′N 76°55′W. Trading center and resort; ships bananas. Also produces logwood, coffee, coconuts, pimento, oranges.

Port Matilda, borough (1990 pop. 669), Centre co., central Pa., 28 mi/45 km NE of Altoona, on Bald Eagle Creek; 40°47′N 78°02′W. Sandstone; light mfg.; agr. (corn, hay; dairying). Midstate Airport to N; Moshannon State Forest and Black Moshannon State Park to N.

Port Mayaca (mei-YAH-kah), village, Martin co., E central Fla., 37 mi/60 km SW of Fort Pierce, on E shore of L. Okeechobee at entrance (lock here) on St. Lucie Canal; 27°00′N 80°33′W.

Port McNicoll, village (1991 pop. 1,786), S Ont., central Canada, on Georgian Bay, 22 mi/35 km NW of Orillia. Grain-transshipment port, with large elevators.

Port Medway, village, SW N.S., E Canada, on Medway Harbour, near mouth of Medway R., 10 mi/16 km NE of Liverpool. Fisheries; pulpwood exports.

Port Mellon, village, SW B.C., W Canada, on inlet of Howe Sound, 25 mi/40 km NW of Vancouver; 49°32′N 123°29′W. Pulp and paper milling. Opposite is Gambier Isl.

Port Menier (por muhn-YAI), village, E Que., E Canada, on SW Anticosti Isl., on the St. Lawrence R., and 70 mi/113 km N of Gaspé; 49°49′N 64°21′W. Lumber port.

Port Moller, village, SW Alaska, on Alaska Peninsula, at entrance of Port Moller, inlet (20 mi/32 km long) of Bristol Bay of Bering Sea; 56°00′N 160°31′W. Fishing, fish canning.

Port Monmouth, village (1990 pop. 3,558), Monmouth co., E N.J., on Raritan Bay, and 15 mi/24 km NE of Freehold; 40°25′N 74°05′W. Chiefly residential.

Port Moody, city (1991 pop. 17,712), SW B.C., W Canada, in lower Fraser R. valley, at W end of Burrard Inlet of the Strait of Georgia, urban enclave 11 mi/18 km E of Vancouver; 49°17′N 122°51′W. Elev. 813 ft/248 m. In lumbering region; oil refinery, winery.

Port Morant, town (1991 pop. 3,004), St. Thomas parish, SE Jamaica, port on Caribbean inlet, 31 mi/50 km ESE of Kingston; 17°56′N 76°51′W. In agr. region (bananas, sugarcane, coconuts, vegetables; livestock; ships bananas. Morant Point, easternmost cape of the isl., is 10 mi/16 km E.

Port Morien (MO-ree-uhn), village, NE N.S., E Canada, N Cape Breton Isl., on Morien Bay, 6 mi/10 km SE of Glace Bay; 46°08′N 59°53′W. Fisheries.

Port Neches, city (1990 pop. 12,974), Jefferson co., SE Texas, suburb 5 mi/8 km N of downtown Port Arthur, on the Neches R.; 29°58′N 93°56′W. Oil-shipping port on the deepwater Sabine-Neches Canal (Neches R.). Mfg. (synthetic rubber, chemicals, wood prods.); oil refining. Inc. 1927.

Port Nelson, village, N Man., central Canada, on Hudson Bay, at mouth of Nelson R., 12 mi/19 km W of York Factory; 57°04′N 92°36′W. Hudson's Bay Co. post since 1670; it was proposed terminus of Hudson Bay RR but was abandoned in favor of Churchill in 1927. Now minor port.

Port Norris, village (1990 pop. 1,701), Cumberland co., S N.J., near mouth of Maurice R., 10 mi/16 km S of Millville; 39°15′N 75°02′W. Oysters.

Port O'Connor, uninc. town (1990 pop. 1,184) Calhoun co., S Texas, on Matagorda Bay, 19 mi/31 km SE of Port Lavaca. Resort area; fishing; mfg. (seafood processing; fishing boats). Matagorda Isl. State Park to S, accessible by boats.

Port of Spain, city (1990 pop. 50,878), ⊙ Trinidad and Tobago, on the Gulf of Paria; 10°39′N 61°31′W. It is the industrial and commercial center of the country. From 1958 to 1962, Port of Spain was the capital of the dissolved Federation of the W.I. It is one of the major shipping hubs of the Caribbean, with exports of agr. prods. and asphalt. Bauxite from the Guianas and iron ore from Venezuela are transferred here for overseas shipment. Has attractive public bldgs. and botanical gardens; focal point of the tourist trade. Served by Piarco Internatl. Airport, 16 mi/25.5 km SE.

Port Orange, city (□ 22 sq mi/57 sq km; 1990 pop. 35,317), Volusia co., E central Fla., on Halifax R. lagoon, 2 mi/3.2 km S of Daytona Beach; 29°06′N 81°00′W. Shrimp, oysters; citrus. Est. 1861.

Port Orchard, town (1990 pop. 4,984), ⊙ Kitsap co., W central Wash., on an arm of Puget Sound, opposite Bremerton; 47°32′N 122°38′W. Timber; strawberries; crabs, fish, clams. Mfg. (wood prods., transportation equip.); gravel. Settled 1854.

Port Orford, town (1990 pop. 1,025), Curry co., SW Oregon, on Pacific Ocean, 45 mi/72 km SSW of Coos Bay; 42°45′N 124°30′W. Urchin processing. Dairy prods.; poultry, sheep, cattle. Fish hatchery to E, on Elk R. Humbug Mt. (1,748 ft/533 m) State Park to S; Cape Blanco State Park and Lighthouse to NW; Siskiyou Natl. Forest, including Grassy Knob Wilderness Area, to E.

Port Penn, uninc. village, New Castle co., E Del., 15 mi/24 km S of Wilmington, and on Delaware R.; 39°31′N 75°35′W. Reedy Isl. is offshore, as NE. Chesapeake and Delaware Canal Mus. is here. Augusta Wildlife Area and E entrance to Chesapeake and Delaware Canal to N; Silver Run Wildlife Area to S. Disincorporated after 1940. Site of Port Penn Mus.

Port Perry, village, S Ont., central Canada, on L. Scugog, 40 mi/64 km NE of Toronto; 44°06′N 78°56′W. Light mfg.; dairying.

Port Radium, mining village, N central N.W.T. , N Canada, on Great Bear L. The mines were discovered in 1930 and yielded deposits of pitchblende, from which much radium was produced. During World War II the mines were expropriated by the Can. govt. when scientists found that these ores contained a rich store of uranium oxide, a source of atomic energy. They were exhausted and closed in 1960.

Port Reading, N.J.: see WOODBRIDGE.

Port Renfrew (REN-froo), village, SW B.C., W Canada, on S Vancouver Isl., on Port San Juan inlet of Juan de Fuca Strait, 50 mi/80 km W of Victoria; 48°33′N 124°25′W. Lumber port.

Port Republic, city (1990 pop. 992), Atlantic co., S N.J., 12 mi/19 km NNW of Atlantic City; 39°32′N 74°29′W.

Port Republic, uninc. village, Rockingham co., NW Va., on South Fork of Shenandoah R., 10 mi/16 km SSE of Harrisonburg. Agr. (dairying; poultry, livestock; grain, apples). Civil War site of last battle of Confederate Gen. Stonewall Jackson's Shenandoah Valley campaign (June 8–9, 1862) nearby. Shenandoah Natl. Park to SE.

Port Richey, city (□ 2 sq mi/5.2 sq km; 1990 pop. 2,523), Pasco co., W central Fla., 27 mi/43 km NW of Tampa, near the Gulf of Mexico; 28°16′N 82°43′W.

Port Richmond, section of Staten Island borough of N.Y. city, SE N.Y., on N shore of Staten Isl., across Kill Van Kull (bridged) from Bayonne (N.J.); 40°38′N 74°08′W. Trade and mfg. center.

Port Robinson, village, S Ont., central Canada, on Welland Ship Canal and on Welland R., 8 mi/13 km S of St. Catharines. Dairying; fruit growing.

Port Rowan (RO-uhn), village, S Ont., central Canada, on L. Erie, 16 mi/26 km SW of Simcoe; 42°38′N 80°27′W. Lumbering; dairying; fruit, vegetables.

Port Royal, town (1991 pop. 1,261), ⊙ Kingston parish, SE Jamaica, on W tip of the Palisadoes peninsula (which encloses Kingston Harbour), 4 mi/6.4 km SW of Kingston; 17°56′N 76°51′W. Once one of the most prosperous towns in the W.I., it was destroyed by 1692 earthquake and partly buried by the sea. Remaining is Fort Charles (begun 1662), where Nelson commanded in 1779. St. Peter's Church (built 1725–1726) is still used. Port Royal was, in early colonial times, hq. of buccaneers. Port Royal (c.2 acres/0.8 ha) is coextensive with Palisadoes peninsula and is customarily considered part of Kingston parish, though retaining some administrative functions.

Port Royal 1 town (1990 pop. 2,985), Beaufort co., S S.C., on Port Royal Isl., and 5 mi/8 km S of Beaufort; 32°22′N 80°41′W. Tourist and fishing center (shrimp), with fine harbor. Ships cotton, phosphate, manganese using the Intracoastal Waterway. **2** town (1990 pop. 204), Caroline co., E Va., on Rappahannock R. (bridged), 17 mi/27 km SE of Fredericksburg; 38°10′N 77°11′W. Mfg. (apparel).

Port Royal, borough (1990 pop. 836), Juniata co., central Pa., 10 mi/16 km SE of Lewistown, on Juniata R. (bridged), at mouth of Tuscarora Creek; 40°31′N 77°23′W. Mfg. (playground and park equip., food prods.; printing and publishing). Agr. area (apples, soybeans, grain; poultry, livestock; dairying). Tuscarora State Forest to SE.

Port Royal, N.S.: see ANNAPOLIS ROYAL.

Port Royal Bay or **Little Sound**, W Bermuda, 2 mi/3.2 km SW of Hamilton, opens N on Great Sound; 2 mi/3.2 km long, 1 mi/1.6 km wide. On a spit of land in N is naval base on site leased to U.S. in 1941.

Port Royal Island, Ga.: see SEA ISLANDS.

Port Royal Sound, arm of the Atlantic Ocean, bet. St. Helena, Phillips, and Parris isls. (N) and Hilton Head Isl. (S), in Beaufort co., S S.C.; it receives the Broad R. The sound was named in 1562 by Fr. explorer Jean Ribaut, founder of a short-lived Huguenot settlement on Parris Isl. In Nov. 1861, during the Civil War, Union Commander Samuel F. Du Pont reduced the forts guarding the sound, and the area remained in Union hands for the rest of the war, becoming a major naval base.

Port Saint Joe, town (□ 3 sq mi/7.8 sq km; 1990 pop. 4,044), ⊙ Gulf co., NW Fla., 32 mi/51 km SE of Panama City, on inlet of Gulf of Mexico; 29°48′N 85°17′W. Mfg. includes chemicals, paper prods.; seafood and fish processing. Port of entry.

Port Saint Lucie (LOO-see), town (□ 77 sq mi/199 sq km; 1990 pop. 55,866), St. Lucie co., E central Fla., 8 mi/13 km NNW of Stuart. Mfg; 27°16′N 80°20′W. Mfg. includes fabricated metal prods.; trailer assembly, printing and publishing, stone processing.

Port Salerno (suh-LER-no), town (□ 4 sq mi/10.4 sq km; 1990 pop. 7,786), Martin co., E central Fla., 6 mi/9.7 km SE of Stuart; 27°08′N 80°11′W. Mfg. includes marine hardware, tuna boat towers, machinery.

Port San Juan (san WAHN), inlet of Juan de Fuca Strait, in S Vancouver Isl., B.C., W Canada, 50 mi/80 km W of Victoria; 4 mi/6 km long. In lumbering area. Port Renfrew, lumber port, is on SE shore.

Port Sanilac (SA-ni-LAK), village (1990 pop. 656), Sanilac co., E Mich., 14 mi/23 km E of Sandusky, on L. Huron; 43°25′N 82°32′W. Mfg. (motor vehicles; machining). Resort area.

Port Simpson, village, W B.C., W Canada, on Tsimpsean Peninsula, on Chatham Sound, 18 mi/29 km N of Prince Rupert; 54°33′N 130°25′W. Fishing port; lumbering; raspberry growing. Former site of post of Hudson's Bay Company.

Port Stanley, village (1991 pop. 2,223), S Ont., central Canada, on L. Erie, 8 mi/13 km S of St. Thomas; 42°40′N 81°13′W. Resort.

Port Sulphur, uninc. village (1990 pop. 3,523), Plaquemines parish, extreme SE La., on W bank (levee) of the Mississippi R., and 40 mi/64 km SE of New Orleans; 29°30′N 89°43′W. Mfg. (sulphur). Fishing, oysters, shrimp, crabs, crawfish. Est. 1933 for workers in sulphur mines of marshy L. Grande Ecaille, c.10 mi/16 km SW. Sulphur shipments from mines once reached deep-water wharf on the Mississippi here by canal (c.10 mi/16 km long). Oil and natural gas deposits. Seaplane base.

Port Sydney, village, S Ont., central Canada, in Muskoka lake region, on Mary L. (4 mi/6 km long), 14 mi/23 km NNE of Bracebridge. Resort.

Port Tobacco Village, village (1990 pop. 36), Charles co., S Md., on inlet of Potomac R. estuary, 27 mi/43 km S of Washington, D.C.; 38°31′N 77°01′W. The Native Amer. village here called Potobac was visited in 1608 by John Smith. Father Andrew White, the Jesuit priest who accompanied the 1st settlers, lived among the Natives for years and converted their queen to Christianity. It was Md.'s most important port from the mid-17th cent. until silting reduced ship traffic to small boats by 1775. Originally called Chandlers' Town for the 1st Eur. settler, John Chandler, it was re-named Charlestown in 1729 and Port Tobacco in 1829. An active Confederate underground operated here during the Civil War. After the courthouse burned in 1892, the co. seat was moved to La Plata in 1895. Chimney House, believed to predate the Revolution; Stagg Hall, late 18th cent.; the courthouse of 1820 completely rebuilt; and Chandler's Hope, started in 1639 and completed by 1790.

Port Townsend, town (1990 pop. 7,001), ⊙ Jefferson co., NW Wash., port 30 mi/48 km WNW of Everett, and on Admiralty Inlet of Puget Sound; 48°07′N 122°47′W. Ships lumber, wood pulp, salmon, halibut, herring, crabs, oysters. Mfg. (consumer goods, wood prods.; pulp mill); dairying. Marine Sciences Center; Coast Artillery Mus. here. Ferry to Fort Casey, on Whidbey Isl., to NE. Gateway to Olympic Natl. Park (SW). Popular retirement location. Nearby are Fort Flagler (at N end of Marrowstone Isl., to SE), Old Port Townsend (to S), and Fort Worden (to N) state parks. Inc. 1860.

Port Union, town (1991 pop. 638), SE N.F., E Canada, on N side of entrance of Trinity Bay, 10 mi/16 km S of Bonavista; 48°29′N 53°06′W. Fishing port.

Port Vincent, town (1990 pop. 446), Livingston parish, 8 mi/12.9 km NE of Gonzales; 30°20′N 90°51′W.

Port Vue (VYOO), borough (1990 pop. 4,641), Allegheny co., SW Pa., residential suburb 10 mi/16 km SE of downtown Pittsburgh, and 1 mi/1.6 km SW of McKeesport, on Youghiogheny R., 1 mi/1.6 km S of its mouth on the Monongahela R.; 40°20′N 79°52′W. Inc. 1892.

Port Walter, bay, SE Alaska, on SE Baranof Isl., 10 mi/16 km N of Port Alexander. Sometimes called Big Port Walter.

Port Washington, city (1990 pop. 9,338), ⊙ Ozaukee co., E. Wis., on L. Michigan, 24 mi/39 km N of Milwaukee; 43°23′N 87°52′W. In dairy and farm area; mfg. (shoes, chemicals, fabricated metal prods., wire forms, consumer goods, machinery). Huntington Beach State Park to NE, on L. Michigan. Settled before 1835, inc. 1882.

Port Washington, uninc. town (□ 5 sq mi/13 sq km; 1990 pop. 15,387), Nassau co., SE N.Y., a suburb of N.Y. city, on the N shore of L.I. and Manhasset Bay; 40°49′N 73°40′W. Extensive mfg., much of it reflecting its past association with the region's aircraft and aerospace industry, but also including machinery, electronic equip., bldg. materials. Initially important for extensive sand pits; center for seaplanes 1900–1920; early Col. of L.I. 1920–1930s.

Port Washington, village (1990 pop. 513), Tuscarawas co., E Ohio, 12 mi/19 km SSW of New Philadelphia, and on Tuscarawas R.; 40°19′N 81°31′W.

Port Weller, village, S Ont., central Canada, on L. Ontario, port at N end of Welland Ship Canal, 5 mi/8 km N of St. Catharines; 43°13′N 79°13′W.

Port Wentworth, town (1990 pop. 4,012), Chatham co., E Ga., NW suburb of Savannah; 32°11′N 81°11′W. Mfg. of paper prods., bldg. materials, chemicals, asphalt; sugar refining. Near Garden City, Ga. Ports Authority, port facilities.

Port William, village (1990 pop. 242), Clinton co., SW Ohio, 9 mi/14 km N of Wilmington; 39°33′N 83°47′W.

Port Wing, village (1990 pop. 434), Bayfield co., extreme N Wis., at mouth of Flag R. on L. Superior, 32 mi/51 km E of Superior; 46°45′N 91°20′W. Trade center for cooperative-farm area. Chequamegon Natl. Forest to SE.

Portage 1 county (□ 504 sq mi/1,305 sq km; 1990 pop. 142,585), NE Ohio; ⊙ Ravenna; 41°10′N 81°12′W. Intersected by Cuyahoga R. and tributaries of the Mahoning R. Has many small lakes. In the Glaciated Plain physiographic region. Agr. area (dairy prods.; sheep, lambs; fruit, corn). Mfg. mainly at Ravenna, Kent, Garrettsville (plastics, fabricated metal prods., rubber prods.; printing); sand and gravel pits, coal mines. **2** county (□ 822 sq mi/2,129 sq km; 1990 pop. 61,405), central Wis.; ⊙ Stevens Point; 44°28′N 89°30′W. Intersected by Wisconsin R. (impounded by Du Bay Dam near N border); also drained by Plover and small Waupaca rivers. Corn, peas, potatoes; cattle, hogs, sheep, poultry; dairying, and papermaking. Formed 1836.

Portage 1 city (1990 pop. 29,060), Porter co., NW Ind., a suburb of Gary, on L. Michigan; 41°35′N 87°11′W. A new port, accommodating ocean vessels, began operating here in the early 1970s (Burns Intl. Harbor). Mfg. includes steel, steel prods. Part of Port of Ind. Ind. Dunes State Park nearby to E. Inc. 1959. **2** city (1990 pop. 41,042), Kalamazoo co., SW Mich., suburb 4 mi/6.4 km SSW of Kalamazoo; 42°12′N 85°35′W. Growing twin city to Kalamazoo. Mfg. (printing; fabricated metal prods., plastic prods., chemcials, tool and die; motor vehicle assembly); world hq. for Pharmecia-Upjohn's. Kalamazoo Municipal Airport to NE. Austin L. in SE part; several lakes surround city. Inc. 1963. **3** city (1990 pop. 8,640), ⊙ Columbia co., central Wis.; 43°32′N 89°28′W. In 1673, Louis Jolliet and Father Marquette were the 1st Europeans to use the important portage link in the water route from the Great Lakes to the Mississippi R. The path has become a ship canal, and the city is an agr. trade center with some light mfg. industry; plastics mfg. Part of Fort Winnebago (1828) has been restored as a mus. Zona Gale and Frederick Jackson Turner b. here. Inc. 1854.

Portage (POR-tuhj), town, ⊙ Columbia co. S central Wis., 32 mi/51 km N of Madison. RR junction. Baraboo Mts. to SW; Wis. Dells to NW. Grain, soybeans, vegetables; livestock. Mfg. (dairy prods., machinery, fabricated metal prods., rubber prods., electronic goods, furniture). Silica sand quarry. Tourism.

Portage 1 or **Portage Junction**, village, S Alaska, 40 mi/64 km SE of Anchorage, and on highway and RR to Seward, at head of Turnagain Arm. Junction for car train to Whittier and ferry to Valdez. **2** village (1990 pop. 469), Wood co., NW Ohio, on Portage R., and 3 mi/5 km S of Bowling Green. Limestone quarrying. **3** village (1990 pop. 218), Box Elder co., N Utah, 35 mi/56 km NNW of Brigham City, and on Malad R., near Idaho state line; 41°58′N 112°14′W. Elev. 4,480 ft/1,366 m. Agr. (sugar beets, wheat, barley; cattle, sheep). Caribou Natl. Forest to E.

Portage, borough (1990 pop. 3,105), Cambria co., W central Pa., 14 mi/23 km ENE of Johnstown, on Little Conemaugh R.; 40°23′N 78°40′W. Mfg. (machinery, concrete prods.; printing); underground bituminous coal; timber; agr. (grain; livestock; dairying). Beaverdam Run Reservoir to S.

Portage, Maine: see PORTAGE LAKE.

Portage des Sioux (por-tij duh SOO), town (1990 pop. 503), St. Charles co., E Mo., 12 mi/19 km NE of St. Charles, and on Mississippi R.; 38°55′N 90°20′W. Settled by French c.1799, at 1 end of a portage bet. Mississippi and Missouri rivers. Important negotiations and treaties (1815) here, bet. U.S. commissioners and Native Amer. tribes. Corn, soybeans, vegetables. Damaged by flood of 1995.

Portage du Fort (por-TAHZH duh FOR), village (1991 pop. 295), SW Que., E Canada, on Ottawa R., and 45 mi/72 km WNW of Ottawa. Lumbering, dairying; livestock.

Portage Island (POR-tij), NE N.B., E Canada, in the Gulf of St. Lawrence, at entrance of Miramichi Bay, 22 mi/35 km ENE of Chatham; 3 mi/5 km long, 1 mi/2 km wide; 47°10′N 65°02′W. At S end are 2 lighthouses.

Portage la Prairie (por-tij luh PRER-ree), city (1991 pop. 13,186), S Man., central Canada; 49°58′N 98°18′W. Center of a mixed-farming region; diversified industries. Near the site of Fort La Reine, an important fur-trading post built (1738) by Vérendrye as a carrying point bet. the Assiniboine R. and L. Manitoba.

Portage Lake (POR-tij), town (1990 pop. 445), Aroostook co., NE Maine, on Portage L., and 23 mi/37 km WNW of Presque Isle; 46°47′N 68°29′W. In hunting, fishing region. Includes Portage village.

Portage Lake, inlet of Keweenaw Bay, N Mich., indenting the SE shore of Keweenaw peninsula; c.20 mi/32 km long, 2 mi/3.2 km wide. An old portage route connected it with L. Superior, it is now part of the Keweenaw Waterway that crosses base of Keweenaw Peninsula (SE to NW) past the ports of Houghton and Hancock.

Portage Lake, Maine: see FISH RIVER LAKES.

Portage Lakes, group of 7 reservoirs, Summit co., NE Ohio, on Tuscarawas R., extending from Long L. (41°01′N 81°33′W), 8 mi/12.9 km S of downtown Akron, S to Nimisila Reservoir (40°58′N 81°32′W), the largest lake. City of Portage Lakes, S suburb of Akron, in NE. Portage Lakes State park at W center.

Portage River, c.33 mi/53 km long, N Ohio; formed in Wood co. by North, Middle, and South branches; flows NW, past Pemberville, Woodville, and Oakharbor, to L. Erie at Port Clinton; 41°30′N 82°56′W. North Branch rises near Leipsic, flows c.40 mi/64 km N; Middle (c.35 mi/56 km long) and South (c.20 mi/32 km long) branches flow NE and join just before entering main stream.

Portageville (POR-tij-vil), city (1990 pop. 3,401), New Madrid co., in the bootheel of extreme SE Mo., near Mississippi R., 15 mi/24 km SW of New Madrid; 36°25′N 89°42′W. Cotton; timber processing, plastic prods. Inc. 1903.

Portageville, village, Wyoming co., W N.Y., on Genesee R., and 11 mi/18 km S of Perry, at S entrance to Letchworth State Park; 42°34′N 78°03′W.

Portal 1 (POR-tuhl), village (1990 pop. 522), Bulloch co., E Ga., 10 mi/16 km WNW of Statesboro; 32°32′N 81°56′W. **2** village (1990 pop. 192), Burke co., NW N.Dak., 20 mi/32 km NW of Bowbells, and on Can. border; 49°00′N 102°32′W. Port of entry.

Portales (por-TAL-uhs), city (1990 pop. 10,690), ⊙ Roosevelt co., E N.Mex., 19 mi/31 km SSW of Clovis, near the Texas state line, in the Llano Estacado; 34°10′N 103°20′W. Trade and processing center of an agr. area. Mfg. (food processing; printing and publishing; machinery, furniture, bldg. prods., feeds). Oil wells in the vicinity. Seat of Eastern N.Mex. Univ. Cannon Air Force Base (near Clovis), Blackwater Draw Natl. Archaeological Site, and Oasis State Park to N. Grulla Natl. Wildlife Refuge to SE; Muleshoe Natl. Wildlife Refuge (Texas) to E. Inc. 1910.

Port-à-Piment (POR–tah–pee-MAWNG), agr. town (1982 pop. 2,781), Sud dept., SW Haiti, on SW coast of Jacmel Peninsula, 25 mi/40 km W of Les Cayes; 18°15′N 74°06′W. Limes, tobacco; coffee growing; manganese deposits nearby. Fishing port.

Port-au-Prince (POR–to–PRANS), city (1987 est. pop. 800,000), ⊙ Haiti, SW Haiti, on a bay at the end of the Gulf of Gonâïves; 18°32′N 72°20′W. The country's chief seaport, it exports mainly coffee and sugar. The city has food-processing plants, soap, textile, and cement industries, and other light mfg., esp. electronics and sporting goods for export to the U.S. Has the country's main airport. It was founded in 1749 by Fr. sugar planters. In 1770 it replaced Cap-Haïtien as capital of the Fr. colony of Saint-Domingue (as Haiti was then called), and in 1804 it became the capital of newly independent Haiti. The city is laid out like an amphitheater, with business and commercial quarters along the water and residences on the hills above. Although Haiti is still dominantly rural, rural-to-urban migration, driven by rural poverty, has begun to swell the pop. of Port-au-Prince. Inadequate housing forces c.½ of the city's residents into squalid shantytowns. Unemployment and underemployment total at least 50% of the work force. Landmarks include the Fr.-built quay (1780), the Univ. of Haiti (est. 1944), the Natl. Palace, the Natl. Mus., and the Basilica of Notre Dame.

Port-de-Paix (POR–duh–PAI), city (1982 census pop. 15,540) ⊙ Nord-Ouest dept. (□ c.1,060 sq mi/ 2,745 sq km), NW Haiti, port on the Atlantic Ocean, opposite Tortuga Isl., 40 mi/64 km WNW of Cap-Haïtien; 19°57'N 72°50'W. In agr. region (coffee, limes, sisal, rice, cacao); beekeeping. Its fine harbor ships agr. produce, hides, logwood; essential-oils distillery. Fishing. An old historic site, where Columbus made a landing (Dec. 8, 1492). Fr. filibusters, founding the town in 1665, gained here their 1st foothold after being driven by the British from Tortuga Isl. In Port-de-Paix occurred (1679) 1st revolt of Afr. slaves.

Porter, county (□ 521 sq mi/1,349 sq km; 1990 pop. 128,932), NW Ind., on L. Michigan (N); ⊙ Valparaiso; 41°31'N 87°04'W. Bounded S by Kankakee R.; drained by Little Calumet and Grand Calumet rivers. Agr. (corn, fruit, grain; hogs, cattle, poultry; dairy prods.). Mfg. at Valparaiso and Portage. Resorts, Ind. Dunes Natl. Lakeshore and Ind. Dunes State Park are in picturesque dunes area along L. Michigan. Formed 1835.

Porter 1 town (1990 pop. 3,118), Porter co., NW Ind., near L. Michigan, 13 mi/21 km E of Gary. Mfg. (steel processing). Laid out 1855. **2** town (1990 pop. 1,301), Oxford co., W Maine, on the Ossipee R., and 35 mi/ 56 km SW of South Paris; 43°49'N 70°56'W. Settled c.1781, inc. 1807. **3** town (1990 pop. 1,448), Montgomery co., SE Texas, 27 mi/43 km NNE of Houston. Agr. area on fringe of Houston urbanized area. Mfg. (motor homes, concrete). L. Houston State Park to SE.

Porter 1 village (1990 pop. 210), Yellow Medicine co., SW Minn., 22 mi/35 km NW of Marshall, on North Branch of Yellow Medicine R., near S.Dak. state line; 44°38'N 96°10'W. Grain, soybeans, alfalfa, sugar beets; livestock. **2** village (1990 pop. 588), Wagoner co., E Okla., 11 mi/18 km NW of Muskogee, midway bet. Arkansas (S) and Verdigris (NE) rivers; 35°52'N 95°31'W. In agr. area; peaches.

Porter Springs, resort village, Lumpkin co., N Ga., 7 mi/ 11.3 km NNE of Dahlonega, in the Blue Ridge; 34°37'N 83°56'W.

Porterdale, town (1990 pop. 1,278), Newton co., N central Ga., 31 mi/50 km ESE of Atlanta, and on Yellow R.; 33°34'N 83°54'W. Mfg. of yarns and textiles. Developed around mills est. here in 1868.

Portersville (PORT-tuhrs-vil), borough (1990 pop. 307), Butler co., W Pa., 14 mi/23 km WNW of Butler; 40°55'N 80°08'W. Mfg. (plastic prods., valves, trailers; coal processing). Bituminous coal; agr. (corn, hay; dairying). L. Arthur reservoir, in Moraine State Park, to NE; McConnells Mill State Park to NW and W.

Porterville, city (1990 pop. 29,563), Tulare co., S central Calif., 23 mi/37 km SE of Visalia, on the Tule R.; 36°04'N 119°02'W. RR junction. The city is chiefly residential; olives, fruit, nuts, grapes, grain, sugar beets, nursery prods., cotton; cattle, hogs, turkeys. Mfg. (machinery, electrical equip.; publishing and printing). Hq. for Sequoia Natl. Forest. Porterville Col. (2 year) and a state hosp. are in the city. L. Success reservoir to E; Tule R. Indian Reservation and Sequoia Natl. Forest to E. Founded 1859 on the old Los Angeles–San Francisco stage route. Inc. 1902

Porthill, uninc. village (1990 pop. 65), Boundary co., N Idaho, port of entry at Can. (B.C.) border, on Kootenai R., and 21 mi/34 km NNW of Bonners Ferry, and 2 mi/ 3.2 km S of Creston (B.C.), opposite Rykerts (B.C.). Timber. Kaniksu Natl. Forest to E and W, Smiths Falls to W.

Portia (POR-shuh), village (1990 pop. 521), Lawrence co., NE Ark., 25 mi/40 km NW of Jonesboro, and near Black R.; 36°05'N 91°04'W. In agr. area.

Portis, village (1990 pop. 129), Osborne co., N Kansas, on North Fork Solomon R,. and 7 mi/11.3 km N of Osborne; 39°33'N 98°41'W. Livestock; grain.

Portland, parish (1991 pop. 75,493), Surrey co., NE Jamaica; ⊙ Port Antonio. Bounded on the S by St. Thomas, W by St. Mary, SSW by St. Andrew parishese. Extends from N slopes of the Blue Mts. to the ocean; watered by the Rio Grande. Its coastline is indented by many fine bays, on which lie its chief town, Port Antonio, St. Margaret's Bay, Hope Bay. Linked by RR with Kingston. Predominantly rainy and primarily agr. (coconuts, bananas, cacao, yams; horses). Tourism.

Portland 1 city (1990 pop. 6,483), ⊙ Jay co., E Ind., on Salamonie R., and 28 mi/45 km NE of Muncie; 40°26'N 84°59'W. In agr. area (livestock; dairy prods.; soybeans, grain); mfg. (transportation equip., harnesses, paper goods, foods and beverages, chemicals, fabricated metal prods., machinery, apparel, consumer goods: metallizing). Natural gas. Laid out 1837. Elwood Haynes b. here. **2** city (1990 pop. 64,358), ⊙ Cumberland co., SW Maine, on a small peninsula and adjacent land, with a large, deepwater harbor on Casco Bay; 43°40'N 70°12'W. The largest city in Maine, it is a port of entry (the nearest U.S. port to Europe), the commercial center of the state, and the RR, highway, shipping, and processing center for a vast farming, lumbering, and resort area. It is the E terminus of the Portland-Montreal (Que.) oil pipeline and a major receiving port for goods destined for Montreal. Has shipyards, canneries (esp. for fish), printing and publishing firms, foundries, and important lumbering, paper-milling, computer chips, fishing, chemical, and textile industries. Portland has an internatl. airport, scheduled ferry service to Yarmouth (N.S.), and Coast Guard base. The restored Old Port waterfront dist. is a tourist center. George Cleeve settled here to trade c.1632. His post grew in importance, and the settlement known as Falmouth developed; in the late 17th cent. it became a commercial center. It was almost completely destroyed by the British in 1775. Served as state capital 1820–1832. Maine's 1st newspaper, the Falmouth *Gazette*, was issued here in 1785. In 1866 a great fire destroyed much of Portland. Seat of the Univ. of Southern Maine and Westbrook Col. Numerous museums. Henry Wadsworth Longfellow (whose house is a landmark) and Robert E. Peary lived here. The old lighthouse at Cape Elizabeth nearby, est. 1791, is still in use. Settled c.1632, set off from Falmouth and inc. 1786. **3** city (1990 pop. 437,319), ⊙ Multnomah co., NW Oregon, on the Willamette and Columbia rivers; 45°32'N 122°39'W. The largest city in the state, it is a port of entry, a leading financial and industrial center, and an important deepwater port, with shipyards and a busy foreign trade. Mfg. includes lumber, wood prods., paper, metals, machinery, food items, textiles, clothing, computer parts, and furniture. Massive suburban growth has developed around Portland since the late 1970s, and even the central city pop. has increased. Founded in 1845, it was named for Portland, Maine. Its growth was rapid after 1850, when it served as a supply point for the Calif. goldfields, and continued with the coming of the RR (1883), the Alaska gold rush (1897–1900), and the Lewis and Clark Centennial Exposition (1905). An educational center, Portland is the seat of the Univ. of Portland, Concordia Col., Lewis and Clark Col., Reed Col., Warner Pacific Col., Portland State Univ., a community col., several theological schools, the Oregon Graduate Center, the Oregon Health Sciences Univ. (medical, nursing, and dental schools), and the Mus. Art School. Portland has an art mus., a mus. of science and industry, a planetarium, a forestry center, a zoo, a Jap. garden, and a symphony orchestra. The state historical society is here. Important annual events are the rose festival, Oregon Prods. Week, and the Pacific Internatl. Livestock Exposition and Rodeo. Near the city is an internatl. airport. The area is noted for its beautiful scenery, and the Columbia R. Gorge and Mt. Hood are easily accessible. Inc. 1851. **4** city (1990 pop. 12,224), San Patricio co., S Texas, on Corpus Christi (SE) and Nueces (SW) bays, suburb 10 mi/16 km N of Corpus Christi; 27°52'N 97°19'W. Fish; cattle; oil and gas; recreation; tourism; mfg. (concrete; natural gas processing). Bridge to Corpus Christi across mouth of Nueces Bay. Inc. after 1940.

Portland 1 town (1990 pop. 8,418), Middlesex co., central Conn., on the Connecticut R. (here bridged to Middletown); 41°36'N 72°35'W. Sandstone and feldspar quarries, mfg. (wire, paper and fiber prods., fabricated metal prods., machinery, tools, rubber and plastic prods., petroleum and coal distributors, fertilizer); agr. includes nursery prods.; boatyards for building, storage, and repair. Includes Gildersleeve village, site of early-18th-cent. shipyard. State park, state forest here. Settled c.1690, inc. 1841. **2** town (1990 pop. 3,889), Ionia co., S central Mich., 18 mi/29 km NW of Lansing, on Grand R., at confluence of Looking Glass R.; 42°52'N 84°54'W. Agr. area (corn, wheat, soybeans, apples, green beans; poultry, cattle, hogs; dairying); mfg. (bldg. materials, feeds, transportation equip., fabricated metal prods., chemicals). **3** town (1990 pop. 602), Traill co., E N.Dak., 2 mi/3.2 km W of Mayville, near Goose R.; 47°30'N 97°22'W. Terminus of 1 of 2 RR spurs; joins Mayville spur 4 mi/6.4 km N. **4** town (1990 pop. 5,165), Summer co., N Tenn., near Ky. state line, 32 mi/51 km NNE of Nashville; 36°35'N 86°31'W. Strawberry-shipping point; plastic, metal, and steel fabrication.

Portland 1 village (1990 pop. 560), Ashley co., SE Ark., 17 mi/27 km E of Hamburg, near Bayou Bartholomew; 33°14'N 91°30'W. In agr. area (cotton). Cut-off Creek Wildlife Management Area to N. **2** village, Fremont co., S central Colo., on Arkansas R., just NE of Wet Mts., and 5 mi/8 km E of Florence. Elev. 5,040 ft/1,536 m. In fruit-growing region. Cement, plaster; dairy and coal-mining area. **3** village, Ouray co., SW Colo., 5 mi/8 km NW of Ouray, on Uncompahgre R. Elev. 7,257 ft/ 2,212 m. Cattle, sheep.

Portland, borough (1990 pop. 516), Northampton co., E Pa., 7 mi/11.3 km SE of Stroudsburg, on Delaware R., opposite Columbia (N.J.); 40°55'N 75°05'W. Mfg. (wood prods., furniture, machinery, fabricated metal prods.); agr. (apples, potatoes, grain; livestock; dairying). Delaware Water Gap Natl. Recreation Area to N, includes Slateford Farm, 10-room, 19th-cent. farmhouse and slate quarry site

Portland Bight, S of St. Catherine parish and SE of Clarendon parish, Jamaica; 17°47'N 77°12'W. Scattered coral and algal reefs rise to form a number of cays in the Bight.

Portland Canal, navigable channel bet. extreme SE Alaska and SW Canada (B.C.), extending 70 mi/113 km N from Pearse Isl. to Hyder (Alaska) and Stewart (B.C.); 55°00'–56°00'N 130°00'W.

Portland Cays, SE Clarendon parish, group of tiny islets off S Jamaica, at SW entrance of Old Harbour Bay, 25 mi/40 km SW of Kingston; 17°42'N 77°07'W.

Portland Head, Maine: see COTTAGE, CAPE.

Portland Inlet, W B.C., W Canada, near S tip of Alaska panhandle, NE arm of Dixon Entrance and Chatham Sound; mouth is 26 mi/42 km NNW of Prince Rupert; 30 mi/48 km long, 4 mi/6 km–8 mi/13 km wide. Contains Pearse, Wales, and Somerville isls. Receives Nass R. at head, and is continued NNE by Portland Canal and NE by Observatory Inlet.

Portland Point, Clarendon parish, cape on Portland Ridge, S Jamaica, at southernmost sect. of the isl., 30 mi/48 km SW of Kingston; 17°42'N 77°10'W. Lighthouse at 17°44'N 77°10'W.

Portland Ridge, peninsula of low hills (525 ft/160 m), Clarendon parish, S Jamaica, southernmost part of the isl., 30 mi/48 km SW of Kingston; 77°45'N 77°10'W. Lighthouse as landmark. Has phosphate deposits. Its shoreline (c.19 acres/8 ha) was leased as naval base to U.S. in 1940.

Portlandville, village (1990 pop. 300), Otsego co., central N.Y., at N end of Goodyear L., 12 mi/19 km S of Cooperstown; 42°32'N 74°58'W. Hardwood milling and kiln-drying, and lumber produced in quantity, much for foreign export.

Portlock, former town, Norfolk co., now independent city of Chesapeake, SE Va., 4 mi/6.4 km S of Portsmouth, on South Branch Elizabeth R.; 36°46'N 76°16'W. Became city in 1963. Inc. as town in 1940.

Portlock, village, on S tip of Kenai Peninsula, S Alaska, 15 mi/24 km S of Seldovia. Fishing; cannery.

Port-Louis (pawr–LWEE), town, NW Grande-Terre, Guadeloupe, minor port on the Grand Cul de Sac, 14 mi/23 km N of Pointe-à-Pitre. Alcohol distilling, sugar milling, fishing.

Port-Margot (POR–mahr-GO), town (1982 pop. 2,087), Nord dept., N Haiti, near the Atlantic Ocean, 14 mi/23 km W of Cap-Haïtien; 19°45′N 72°26′W. Agr. (coffee, cacao, fruit).

Portmore, city (1991 pop. 93,799), St. Catherine parish, SE Jamaica, 6 mi/10 km W of Kingston; 17°58′N 76°52′W. Jamaica's 3d-largest city. Largely a residential suburb of Kingston. Historic 18th- and 19th-cent. homes in Port Henderson sect. Racetrack.

Portneuf (port-NUHF), county (□ 1,440 sq mi/3,730 sq km; 1991 pop. 43,179), S Que., E Canada, on the St. Lawrence R.; ⊙ Cap Santé; 47°00′N 72°00′W.

Portneuf (por-NUHF) or **Notre Dame de Portneuf** (no-truh DAHM duh por-NUHF), town (1991 pop. 1,393), S central Que., E Canada, on the St. Lawrence R., and 32 mi/51 km WSW of Quebec; 46°41′N 71°53′W. Paper milling, lumbering; dairying.

Portneuf River, 90 mi/145 km long, SE Idaho; rises in SE corner of Fort Hall Indian Reservation in NW Caribou co., 15 mi/24 km SE of Blackfoot; flows S through Portneuf Reservoir, then W at Lava Hot Springs and NW, through city of Pocatello, to Snake R., 7 mi/11.3 km NW of Pocatello. Dam in upper course forms Portneuf Reservoir (3.5 mi/5.6 km long, 1 mi/1.6 km wide), used for irrigation.

Porto Rico: see PUERTO RICO.

Portola, city (1990 pop. 2,193), Plumas co., NE Calif., in the Sierra Nevada, 40 mi/64 km NW of Reno (Nev.), on Middle Fork Feather R.; 39°48′N 120°28′W. Trade center for timber, cattle, and recreational region; winter sports. Plumas Eureka State Park to W; L. Davis reservoir to N; Plumas Natl. Forest to N; Tahoe Natl. Forest to S. Inc. 1946.

Portola Hills, uninc. town (1990 pop. 2,677), Orange co., S Calif., residential suburb 6 mi/9.7 km NE of Mission Viejo, at SW edge of Santa Ana Mts.; 33°41′N 117°38′W. Cleveland Natl. Forest to N and E.

Portola Valley, city (1990 pop. 4,194), San Mateo co., W Calif., residential suburb 30 mi/48 km S of downtown San Francisco, and 18 mi/29 km W of San Jose, in Santa Cruz Mts.; 37°22′N 122°13′W. Portola and Castle Rock state parks to S. Artichokes, brussels sprouts, flowers, ornamentals, Christmas trees, timber.

Port's Island, islet in Great Sound, Bermuda, 2.5 mi/4 km WSW of Hamilton; 900 ft/274 m long, 700 ft/213 m wide.

Port-Salut (POR–sah-LYOO), town (1982 pop. 755), Sud dept., SW Haiti, on the SW coast of Jacmel Peninsula, 14 mi/23 km SW of Les Cayes; 18°05′N 73°55′W. Basketmaking; fishing port.

Portsmouth, town (1991 pop. 3,621), NW Dominica, B.W.I., port on Prince Rupert Bay, 20 mi/32 km NNW of Roseau; 15°35′N 61°28′W. Limes, cacao, coconuts. Agr. demonstration center.

Portsmouth 1 city (1990 pop. 25,925), Rockingham co., SE N.H., 35 mi/56 km E of Manchester, on Piscataqua R. (tidal; Maine state line), at its entrance to Atlantic Ocean, opposite Kittery (Maine); 43°03′N 70°46′W. Great Bay is 6 mi/9.7 km W. RR terminus. Mfg. (fabricated steel prods., machinery, processed seafood, topsoil, glass prods., bldg. materials, paper prods.; printing and publishing). Pease Internatl. Tradeport, commerce center and airport, to W, formerly Pease Air Force Base. Portsmouth Naval Shipyard and commercial port facilities at Portsmouth Harbor. Portsmouth Children's Mus., Strawberry Banke Historic Mus., and Wenworth Coolidge Mansion here. **2** city (1990 pop. 22,676), ⊙ Scioto co., S Ohio, in a hilly area on the Ohio R. at the mouth of the Scioto R., across from South Portsmouth (Ky.); 38°23′N 82°57′W. Mfg. includes chemicals, plastics, and bricks. Completion of the Ohio Canal (1832), linking Portsmouth with Cleveland, and the discovery of iron ore in the area started the city's industrial growth. Of interest are the 1810 house; Mound Park, with anc. Native Amer. burial grounds; a civic center; and traces of the old Ohio R. Canal. A branch of Ohio Univ. and a state prison are here. Nearby are a Nuclear Regulatory Commission plant producing fissionable material as well as Shawnee State Forest, Wayne Natl. Forest, and Portsmouth State Park. Inc. 1814. **3** independent city (□ 46 sq mi/119 sq km; 1990 pop. 103,907), SE Va., on Hampton Roads Channel and Elizabeth R., 3 mi/4.8 km SW of Norfolk; 36°51′N 76°21′W. Bounded N by Hampton Roads harbor and Elizabeth R. estuary (Norfolk opposite), S and W by Chesapeake city (West and South Branches of Elizabeth R.), NW by Suffolk city; West Branch of Elizabeth R. separates West Norfolk sect. from rest of Portsmouth. A busy commercial seaport, RR center, with RR shops and terminals; mfg. (foods, furniture, chemicals, clothing, tool and die, electronic equip., plastic prods., machines; machining, scrap metal processing). This port of Hampton Roads forms, with Norfolk, one of world's largest operating naval installations. One of world's largest shipyards; huge naval hosp.; naval ammunitions dump; hq. of Fifth U.S. Coast Guard dist. Private shipyard built here (1767) served as Br. base in Amer. Revolution, after which it became U.S. base (U.S.S. *Chesapeake* built here). In the Civil War, occupied by Confederates 1861–1862; steamship *Merrimack* was converted into world's 1st ironclad. First U.S. battleship (*Texas*) built here (1892), 1st aircraft carrier (*Langley*, 1922). Trinity Episcopal Church (1762); Monumental Church (1772; Methodist); Naval Shipyard Mus., with model of *Merrimack;* U.S. Naval Hosp. (1830); Old Towne Historic Dist.; Va. Sports Hall of Fame; Children's Mus. of Va. Tidewater Community Col. (Portsmouth campus) to NW, in Suffolk. Craney Isl. Corps of Engineers (U.S. Army) Disposal Area, Craney Isl. U.S. Naval Station in NW. Connected to Norfolk by Midtown and Downtown tunnels under Elizabeth R. A floodwall also serves as pedestrian promenade along waterfront. Founded 1752 on Native Amer. village site, inc. 1858.

Portsmouth 1 town (1990 pop. 209), Shelby co., W Iowa, on Mosquito Creek, and 10 mi/16 km W of Harlan; 41°38′N 95°31′W. **2** town (1990 pop. 16,817), Newport co., SE R.I., on Rhode Isl. (Aquidneck); 41°36′N 71°17′W. It is mainly residential with some light industry and also serves as a summer resort. The Native Americans called this area Pocasset. Founded by William Coddington, John Clarke, Anne Hutchinson, and others in 1638, it was the 2d Eur. settlement in the state. An early fishing, shipping, and shipbuilding center, with some farming. The 1st general assembly of the new colony met here in 1647. The Br. general Richard Prescott was captured (1777) at his own hq. in the town by Amer. raiders, and the battle of R.I. was fought here (1778). Coal mining and guano factories were important in the 19th cent. The Mt. Hope (1929) and the Sakonnet (1956) bridges connect the town to Bristol and Tiverton, respectively. Inc. 1644.

Portsmouth Island, Carteret co., E N.C., 40 mi/64 km NE of Morehead City bet. Pamlico Sound (NW) and Raleigh Bay (SE), SW of Ocracoke Inlet, opposite Ocracoke Isl., and NE of Swash Inlet; 7 mi/11.3 km long. Part of Cape Lookout Natl. Seashore. Portsmouth, fishing village and resort is on NE end. Cape Hatteras Natl. Seashore to NE, across Ocracoke Inlet.

Portville, village (1990 pop. 1,040) in Portville town (1990 pop. 4,397), Cattaraugus co., W N.Y., on Allegheny R., near Pa. state line, and 6 mi/9.7 km SE of Olean; 42°02′N 78°20′W. Dairy prods.; grain, potatoes. Inc. 1895.

Porum (POR-uhm), town (1990 pop. 851), Muskogee co., E Okla., 27 mi/43 km S of Muskogee, near Canadian R.; 35°21′N 95°15′W. In agr. area; mfg. (pottery). Eufaula Dam and Reservoir to SW.

Porus, town (1991 pop. 5,095), Manchester parish, central Jamaica, on Jamaica RR, and 6 mi/9.7 km E of Mandeville; 18°02′N 77°25′W. In agr. region (tropical fruit and spices).

Posen 1 (PO-zen), village (1990 pop. 4,226), Cook co., NE Ill., S suburb of Chicago; 41°37′N 87°41′W. Settled 1893 by Pol. immigrants. Inc. 1900. **2** village (1990 pop. 263), Presque Isle co., NE Mich., 12 mi/19 km SSE of Rogers City; 45°15′N 83°42′W. RR junction to W. In farm area; mfg. (wood prods.).

Posey, county (□ 419 sq mi/1,085 sq km; 1990 pop. 25,968), extreme SW Ind., on Ill. (W; Wabash R.) and Ky. (S; Ohio R.) state lines; ⊙ Mount Vernon; 38°01′N 87°52′W. Drained by Big Creek. Agr. area (corn, wheat, melons; hogs, poultry), with mfg. of food prods.; petroleum fields. Harmonie State Park in W; New Harmony State Memorial at New Harmony. Hovey L. State Fish and Wildlife Area in extreme S. Ind.'s southernmost point and lowest elev. (320 ft/98 m) in Posey co. Formed 1814.

Poseyville, town (1990 pop. 1,089), Posey co., SW Ind., 17 mi/27 km NNE of Mt. Vernon; 38°10′N 87°47′W. Agr. area; feed milling.

Possum Kingdom Lake, reservoir, mainly in Palo Pinto co., N central Texas, in Brazos R., 60 mi/97 km WNW of Fort Worth. The meandering lake is generally Z-shaped. Impounded by Morris Sheppard Dam (1,300,000 acre-ft. capacity). Possum King State Park on SW end of lake.

Post, town (1990 pop. 3,768), ⊙ Garza co., NW Texas, 40 mi/64 km SE of Lubbock, just below Caprock escarpment; 33°11′N 101°22′W. Elev. 2,590 ft/789 m. Shipping point for agr. (cotton, grain, peanuts), eggs, poultry and cattle-ranching region; mfg. (machinery; meat processing). Founded 1907 by C. W. Post cereal manufacturer as balanced agr.-mfg. community.

Post Falls, town (1990 pop. 7,349), Kootenai co., N Idaho, on Spokane R., near Wash. state line, 8 mi/12.9 km WNW of Coeur d'Alene, and 21 mi/34 km E of Spokane (Wash.); 47°43′N 116°57′W. RR junction at center. Mfg. (machinery, furniture, wood prods. and lumber, chemicals, plastic prods.; aluminum recovery). Hauser L. to NW.

Postville, town (1990 pop. 1,472), Allamakee co., NE Iowa, 14 mi/23 km SSW of Waukon; 43°04′N 91°34′W. Mfg. (dairy prods., feed and fertilizer, concrete, plastic prods.), beef and poultry processing. Settled 1841, inc. 1873.

Potagannissing Bay, Mich.: see DRUMMOND.

Potash (PAHT-ash), uninc. village, Plaquemines parish, SE La., on the Mississippi R., 39 mi/63 km S of New Orleans, and 1 mi/2 km NW of Port Sulphur; 29°29′N 89°42′W. Oil and natural-gas deposits in vicinity.

Potato Lake, Hubbard co., NW central Minn., 4 mi/6.4 km N of Park Rapids; 4 mi/6.4 km long; 47°00′N 95°03′W. Drained S by Fishhook R. Small resorts.

Potato Lake, Minn.: see NORTH STAR LAKE.

Potato Peak (c.10,236 ft/3,120 m), Mono co., E Calif., 12 mi/19 km N of Mono L.

Potawatomi State Park (PAH-tah-WAH-to-mee) (□ 2 sq mi/5.2 sq km), Door co., NE Wis., 4 mi/6.4 km NW of city of Sturgeon Bay, on Door Peninsula. On wooded bluffs overlooking Sturgeon Bay, arm of Green Bay.

Poteau (PO-to), town (1990 pop. 7,210), ⊙ Le Flore co., SE Okla., 25 mi/40 km SSW of Fort Smith (Ark.), and on Poteau R., in Ouachita Mts.; 35°02′N 94°37′W. Elev. 497 ft/151 m. RR junction. In agr., lumbering, and resort area; mfg. (fabricated metal prods., plastic prods., foods). Coal mines, gas wells. Wister L. reservoir and State Park to SW. The Ouachita Mts. and Ouachita Natl. Forest are c.15 mi/24 km S; Heavener-Runestone State Park to S. Seat of Carl Albert State Col. (2-year). Inc. 1898.

Poteau River (PO-to), 128 mi/206 km long, in Ark. and Okla.; rises in the Ouachita Mts., in Scott co., W Ark.; flows W into Okla., where it is joined by the small Fourche Moline, then NNE, past Poteau, Shadypoint, and Panama, to Arkansas R. at Fort Smith (Ark.). Wister Dam (99 ft/30 m high, 8,700 ft/2,652 m long, including concrete spillway and earth-fill barrier and dike; completed 1949 by U.S. Army Engineers) is in middle course just S of Wister (Okla.); used for flood control; forms Wister Reservoir (15 mi/24 km long, max. width 1.5 mi/2.4 km; capacity 430,000 acre-ft.).

Poteet, town (1990 pop. 3,206), Atascosa co., SW Texas, 26 mi/42 km S of San Antonio; 29°02′N 98°34′W. Elev.

525 ft/160 m. Vegetables, strawberries; oil and gas; mfg. (wood prods.).

Poth, town (1990 pop. 1,642), Wilson co., S Texas, 34 mi/ 55 km SE of San Antonio, near San Antonio R.; 29°04′N 98°04′W. In agr. area (peanuts, sunflowers; vegetables, melons; dairying; cattle; mfg. (feed and fertilizer).

Potholes Reservoir (□ 54 sq mi/140 sq km), Grant co., E central Wash., on Lower Crab Creek, 10 mi/16 km S of Moses L.; 46°59′N 119°16′W. Max. capacity 566,300 acre-ft. Formed by O'Sullivan Dam (200 ft/ 61 m high), built by the Bureau of Reclamation for flood control; also used for irrigation, navigation, and power generation. Columbia Natl. Wildlife Refuge in former valley of Glacial Columbia R. is just S. Potholes State Park on W bank, near dam.

Potlatch, town (1990 pop. 790), Latah co., N Idaho, on Palouse R., and 15 mi/24 km N of Moscow; 46°55′N 116°54′W. Logging; mfg. (meatpacking). Coeur d'Alene Indian Reservation to N; St. Joe Natl. Forest to N.

Potlatch River, c.40 mi/64 km long, N Idaho; rises near Bovill, E Latah co.; flows SW to Clearwater R. ENE of Lewiston. In Nez Perce Indian Reservation.

Potomac (pah-TO-mak), village (1990 pop. 753), Vermilion co., E Ill., on Middle Fork of Vermilion R., and 13 mi/21 km NW of Danville; 40°18′N 87°47′W. In agr. and bituminous-coal area.

Potomac (puh-TO-muhk), residential suburb (1990 pop, 45,634), Montgomery co., central Md., near the Potomac R., 13 mi/21 km NW of Wash., D.C.; 39°02′N 77°12′W. One of the wealthiest communities in the Washington area. The Potomac Polo Club is nearby as well as the Congressional Co. Club (organized 1924), the Natl. Women's Country Club, and the Natl. Capital Horse-Show grounds.

Potomac (puh-TO-muhk), river, 285 mi/459 km long, E central U.S.; formed SE of Cumberland (Md.), by the confluence of its North and South branches; flows generally SE to Chesapeake Bay. Forms part of the border bet. Md. and W.Va. and then separates Va. from both Md. and D.C. The upper course of the Potomac has cut several gaps across the parallel ridges of the Appalachian Mts.; the water gap at Harpers Ferry (W.Va.) is the largest. The river passes over the Great Falls above Wash., D.C., where it is crossed by Arlington Memorial Bridge and others, and enters a tidal estuary below the city. It is navigable for large ships to Wash., D.C., and formerly many smaller boats went to Cumberland (Md.), via the CHESAPEAKE AND OHIO CANAL. Its principal tributary is the Shenandoah R., which it receives at Harpers Ferry. The river is noted for both its beauty and its historical associations. Mt. Vernon is on the Va. shore below Wash., D.C.

Potomac Heritage Scenic Trail (□ 1 sq mi/2.6 sq km), Md., along the Potomac R. Authorized 1983.

Potosi (puh-TO-see), city (1990 pop. 2,683), ☉ Washington co., SE central Mo., in the Ozark Mts., 55 mi/ 89 km SW of St. Louis; 37°56′N 90°46′W. Center of barite-mining area. Center of historic lead-mining area, 1720s–1960s. Mfg. (transportation equip., apparel, lumber, metal, limestone prods., shoes; barite processing). Potosi State Correctional Center (scene of Mo. executions). Settled c.1773 as Mine à Breton by French. Plotted 1814. Grave of Moses Austin, founder of 1st Amer. colony in Texas. Inc. c.1826.

Potosi (puh-TO-see), village (1990 pop. 654), Grant co., extreme SW Wis., near the Mississippi R., and near mouth of Grant R.; 10 mi/16 km S of Lancaster; 42°41′N 90°42′W. In agr. region; mfg. (machinery); smoked fish. Site of St. John Mine, the nation's oldest lead mine, now a mus.

Potowomut Peninsula, an exclave of Warwick city, Kent co., R.I., on Narragansett Bay. Goddard Memorial State Park here.

Potowomut River, R.I.: see HUNT RIVER.

Potrerillo, Pico (po-trai-REE-yo, PEE-ko), peak (3,054 ft/931 m), Sancti Spíritus prov., central Cuba, in the Escambray Mts., 6 mi/9.7 km N of Trinidad city; 21°53′N 80°01′W. At its W slope are scenic Topes de Collantes. Serves as Cuba's 3d-most important coffee-growing area.

Potrero, El, Mexico: see EL POTRERO.

Potsdam 1 village (□ 103 sq mi/267 sq km; 1990 pop. 10,251), St. Lawrence co., N N.Y. on Raquette R., and 25 mi/40 km E of Ogdensburg; 44°40′N 75°02′W. Paper, lumber; kilns. Agr. (dairy prods.; corn and hay); timber. Seat of State Univ. of N.Y. Col. at Potsdam and Clarkson Univ. Inc. 1831. **2** village (1990 pop. 250), Miami co., W Ohio, 12 mi/19 km SW of Troy; 39°58′N 84°25′W.

Pottawatomie 1 (pah-tuh-WAH-tuh-mee), county (□ 862 sq mi/2,233 sq km; 1990 pop. 16,128), NE Kansas; ☉ Westmoreland; 39°22′N 96°19′W. Gently rolling to hilly area, bounded S by Kansas R., W by Big Blue R. (large Tuttle Creek reservoir). Drained by Vermillion Creek in E. Cattle, hogs, poultry; corn, apples, wheat, hay. Mfg. of machinery. Pottawatomie State Fishing L. Numbers 1 (N) and 2 (SW). Part of Tuttle Creek State Park on shore of reservoir. Formed 1856, the year of John Brown's massacre of 5 pro-slavery adherents. **2** county (□ 793 sq mi/2,054 sq km; 1990 pop. 58,760), central Okla.; ☉ Shawnee; 35°12′N 96°56′W. Intersected by North Canadian, Canadian (forms S border), and Little rivers; E extremity of Oklahoma City limits; takes in L. Shawnee reservoir in NW. Agr. area (corn, peanuts; cattle; dairying). Mfg. at Shawnee. Oil and natural-gas wells. Formed 1891.

Pottawatomie Creek (pah-tuh-WAH-tuh-mee), river, 63 mi/101 km long, in E Kansas; rises in Franklin co. E of Waverly; flows ESE and NE, past Greeley and Lane, to Marais des Cygnes R. at Osawatomie.

Pottawatomie Park, town (1990 pop. 281), LaPorte co., NW Ind., residential suburb 3 mi/4.8 km E of Michigan City, 2 mi/3.2 km from L. Michigan.

Pottawattamie, county (□ 960 sq mi/2,486 sq km; 1990 pop. 82,628), SW Iowa, on Nebr. (W; Missouri R.) state line; ☉ Council Bluffs; 41°20′N 95°32′W. Part of Omaha, Nebr., metropolitan area. Prairie agr. area (oats, corn; cattle, hogs), with bituminous-coal deposits. Drained by West and East Nishnabotna rivers, and by Keg, Silver, and Walnut creeks. Includes L. Manawa State Park in SW; Wilson Isl. State Park in extreme NW corner. Major flooding of rivers occurred in 1993. Formed 1847; town of Carter Lake (Iowa), located on Nebr. side of Missouri R., cut off from rest of state by change in river course.

Potter 1 county (□ 1,081 sq mi/2,800 sq km; 1990 pop. 16,717), N Pa., on N.Y. (N) state line; ☉ Coudersport; 41°44′N 77°54′W. Agr. and forested region, source of Allegheny R. (N center) and of streams draining to Gulf of Mexico by Allegheny R. (including Oswayo Creek), to Chesapeake Bay by Susquehanna R. (Kittle and Sinnemahoning creeks), and to Gulf of St. Lawrence by Genesee R. (Pine Creek and Cowanesque R.). Mfg. at Coudersport. Agr. (corn, oats, hay, alfalfa, potatoes; cattle; dairying); timber. Part of Sinnemahoning State Park in SW; parts of Susquehannock State Forest in W, center, E, and SE; Ole Run State Park in SE; Sizerville State Park on SW border; Lyman Run and Denton Hill state parks in E center; Patterson, Prouty Place, and Cherry Springs state parks in center. Formed 1804. **2** county (□ 898 sq mi/2,326 sq km; 1990 pop. 3,190), N central S.Dak.; ☉ Gettysburg; 45°03′N 99°57′W. Irrigated agr. area, bounded W by Missouri R. (L. Oahe reservoir, also border bet. Mountain and Central time zones); drained by Swan and Okobojo creeks. Dairy prods.; corn, wheat, rye, oats, barley; cattle, hogs. Formed 1873. **3** county (□ 922 sq mi/ 2,388 sq km; 1990 pop. 97,874), extreme N Texas, in high plains of the Panhandle; ☉ Amarillo; 35°23′N 101°53′W. Drained by Canadian R. (forms L. Meredith in NE). Has helium field producing much of world's supply; also oil and gas wells and pipelines, deposits of clay, sand, and gravel. Cattle-ranching region. Agr. (oats, barley, grain sorghums, forage). Amarillo (partly in Randall co. to S) is commercial and industrial center of Panhandle area. Alibates Flint Quarries Natl. Monument and part of L. Meredith Natl. Recreation Area in NE. Formed 1876.

Potter 1 village, Atchison co., NE Kansas, on small Stranger Creek, and 9 mi/14.5 km S of Atchison. Poultry; apples; dairying. **2** village (1990 pop. 388), Cheyenne co., W Nebr., 18 mi/29 km W of Sidney, and on Lodgepole Creek; 41°13′N 103°18′W.

Potter Hill, mill village in Hopkinton and Westerly towns, Washington co., SW R.I., on Pawcatuck R., at Conn. state line. Woolens.

Potter Valley, uninc. village, Mendocino co., NW Calif., 12 mi/19 km NE of Ukiah. Grapes, fruit; cattle; timber. Mfg. (wood prods., food preparations). L. Pillsburg reservoir to E; Mendocino Natl. Forest to E.

Potters Fork, Ky.: see CROMONA.

Potters Village, town (1991 pop. 1,265), 2 mi/3.2 km E of Saint John's, Saint John Parish, N Antigua Isl., Antigua and Barbuda Republic; 17°07′N 61°49′W. Suburb of Saint John's.

Pottersville, resort village (1990 pop. 750), Warren co., E N.Y., in the Adirondack Mts., at S end of Schroon L., 29 mi/47 km NNW of Glens Falls; 43°44′N 73°49′W.

Potterville, town (1990 pop. 1,523), Eaton co., S central Mich., 12 mi/19 km SW of Lansing; 42°37′N 84°45′W. Satellite community of Lansing. Hogs, cattle, poultry; mfg. (plastic prods.).

Potts Camp, village (1990 pop. 483), Marshall co., N Miss. 12 mi/19 km SE of Holly Springs, in Holly Springs Natl. Forest; 34°38′N 89°18′W. Mfg. (lumber).

Potts Mountain, Va. and W.Va., ridge of Allegheny Mts., extends c.40 mi/64 km NE from Giles co. (Va.), partly along state line, to Alleghany co. (Va.), in Jefferson Natl. Forest (both states); elev. c.3,000 ft/914 m–4,000 ft/ 1,219 m high; 37°26′N 80°25′W.

Pottsboro, town (1990 pop. 1,177), Grayson co., N Texas, 9 mi/14.5 km N of Sherman; 33°46′N 96°40′W. In agr. area (cattle); recreation; mfg. (signs). Eisenhower State Park to N; large L. Texoma reservoir (Red R.; Okla. state line) to N; Hagerman Natl. Wildlife Refuge to W.

Pottsgrove (PAHTS-grov), uninc. town (1990 pop. 3,122), Northumberland co., E central Pa., 5 mi/8 km ENE of Lewisburg, near Chillisquaque Creek; 40°15′N 75°36′W. Anthracite coal in area. Agr. includes dairying; livestock, poultry.

Pottstown (PAHTS-toun), borough (1990 pop. 21,831), Montgomery co., SE Pa., 15 mi/24 km ESE of Reading, on the Schuylkill R.; 40°15′N 75°38′W. Mfg. (plastic prods., furniture, electronic equip., textiles, transportation equip., chemicals, fabricated metal prods., machinery, food prods., universal joints; electroplating; printing and publishing). The state's 1st ironworks were est. here in 1715. The Hill School, a preparatory school, is here. Other points of interest are Pottsgrove Manor, the home of John Potts (1754), colonial ironmaster and the community's planner, and Hopewell Furnace Natl. Historic Site. French Creek State Park to SW; Ringing Rocks to NE. Settled c.1700, inc. 1815.

Pottsville (PAHTS-vil), city (1990 pop. 16,603), ☉ Schuylkill co., E Pa., on the Schuylkill R., 27 mi/43 km NNW of Reading; 40°40′N 76°12′W. Anthracite-coal-mining region. Diverse mfg. including plastic prods., food prods., transportation equip., filters, apparel, beverages; steel processing, printing and publishing. Rallying place for the Molly Maguires, who were tried here in 1877. Locust L. State Park to NE. Inc. 1847.

Pottsville, town (1990 pop. 984), Pope co., N central Ark., 6 mi/9.7 km ESE of Russellville, near Arkansas R.; 35°14′N 93°03′W. Mfg. (wood prods.). Galla Creek Wildlife Management Area and Holla Bend Natl. Wildlife Refuge to S.

Potwin, village (1990 pop. 448), Butler co., SE central Kansas, 12 mi/19 km NW of El Dorado; 37°56′N 97°01′W. In cattle and grain region; shipping point for gasoline. Oil wells.

Pouce Coupé (poos KOO-pai), village (1991 pop. 832), E B.C., W Canada, near Alta. border, 5 mi/8 km SE of Dawson Creek; 55°43′N 120°08′W. Grain elevators; farming; livestock raising.

Poughkeepsie (puh-KIP-see), city (□ 5 sq mi/13 sq km; 1990 pop. 28,844), ☉ Dutchess co., SE N.Y., on the Hudson R.; 41°42′N 73°55′W. It is a trade center with

---

Cross references are shown in SMALL CAPITALS. The pronunciation key is on page xv. The dates of population figures are on page xii.

industries such as printing, lithography, computer assembly, and electronics research. Mfg. includes machinery, precision instruments, dairy equip., clothing, and chemicals. It became the temporary state capital in 1777, and the U.S. Constitution was ratified (1788) here. Seat of Vassar and Marist cols., and a community col. An annual intercollegiate regatta is held on the river here in June. Several historic 18th-cent. bldgs. still stand. The Mid-Hudson Bridge crosses the river here. At N end of the Hudson branch of Metro-North commuter RR. Hyde Park lies just N. Settled 1687 by the Dutch, inc. as a city 1854.

Poulan (PO-luhn), city (1990 pop. 962), Worth co., S central Ga., 15 mi/24 km W of Tifton; 31°31′N 83°47′W.

Poulsbo (PAWLZ-bo), town (1990 pop. 4,848), Kitsap co., W central Wash., 12 mi/19 km N of Bremerton and Liberty Bay of Puget Sound; 47°45′N 122°38′W. Mfg. (electronic equip., foods, beer); fish; timber; agr. Bangor U.S. Naval Station to W, on Hood Canal.

Poultney, town (1990 pop. 3,498), including Poultney village, Rutland co., W Vt., on Poultney R., and 15 mi/24 km SW of Rutland; 43°31′N 73°11′W. Quarry machinery; slate; dairy and maple prods. Resorts on L. St. Catharine. Seat of junior col. here. Settled 1771.

Poultney River, c.40 mi/64 km long, in Vt. and N.Y.; rises W of Wallingford in W central Vt.; flows NW, past Middletown Springs and Poultney, then SW to L. Champlain near Whitehall (N.Y.).

Pound, town (1990 pop. 995), Wise co., SW Va., 11 mi/18 km N of Wise, near North Fork Pound R.; 37°07′N 82°36′W. Agr. (tobacco, hay; cattle); timber. North Fork Pound L. Recreation Area to W. Inc. since 1940.

Pound, village (1990 pop. 434), Marinette co., NE Wis., 20 mi/32 km W of Marinette; 45°06′N 88°01′W. Trade center for dairying area; mfg. (fabricated metal prods., machinery).

Pound Gap, pass (c.2,380 ft/725 m), crosses Pine Mt. ridge in the Cumberland Mts., in Jefferson Natl. Forest, at Ky.-Va. state line, 2 mi/3.2 km SW of Jenkins (Ky.). Much used by Native Americans and pioneers; now traversed by U.S. highway 23.

Pounding Mill, uninc. village, Tazewell co., SW Va., 28 mi/45 km WSW of Bluefield, on Clinch R.; 37°04′N 81°42′W. Mfg. (machinery, bldg. materials); agr. (dairying; livestock; corn, tobacco); bituminous coal, limestone. Jefferson Natl. Forest to S.

Poverty Point State Commemorative Area (□ 1 sq mi/3 sq km), West Carroll parish, NE La., 5 mi/8 km NE of Epps, on Bayou Macon; 32°38′N 91°24′W. Remains of the main trade center and ceremonial grounds of a Native Amer. culture that flourished in area c.2000 B.C. Authorized 1988.

Povungnituk, village (1991 pop. 1,091), NW Que., E Canada, on E shore of Hudson Bay, W side of Ungava Peninsula; 59°47′N 77°19′W. Populated by Inuit people. Hunting, fishing, trapping. Scheduled air service.

Powassan (po-WAH-suhn), town (1991 pop. 1,150), SE central Ont., central Canada, 17 mi/27 km SSE of North Bay; 46°04′N 79°21′W. Sawmilling, brick making.

Poway, city (1990 pop. 43,516), San Diego co., S Calif., suburb 19 mi/31 km NNE of downtown San Diego; 33°00′N 117°01′W. Dairying; cattle, poultry; grain, citrus, avocadoes, flowers, ornamentals. Mfg. (electronic equip., computer equip., textiles, consumer goods; printing and publishing).

Powder River, county (□ 3,298 sq mi/8,542 sq km; 1990 pop. 2,090), SE Mont., on Wyo (S) state line; ⊙ Broadus; 45°23′N 105°38′W. Agr. area drained by Powder and Little Powder rivers and Pumpkin and Mizpah creeks. Wheat, oats, hay; cattle, sheep; oil and natural gas, coal. Part of Custer Natl. Forest in W. Formed 1919.

Powder River 1 c.110 mi/177 km long, W Baker co., NE Oregon; rises in Elkhorn Ridge, 20 mi/32 km W of Baker City; flows E through Phillips Reservoir, then N past Baker City, receives N Powder R., then turns ESE through Thief Valley Reservoir to Snake R. Forms Idaho state line S of Wallowa Mts. A dam (73 ft/22 m high, 390 ft/119 m long; completed 1932), in middle course 17 mi/27 km N of Baker City, forms small reservoir. Used for irrigation. **2** c.375 mi/603 km long, in Wyo. and Mont.; begins with joining of North, South, and Middle forks in foothills of Bighorn Mts. in S Johnson co., N central Wyo.; flows E, then generally N into SE Mont., past Broadus, to Yellowstone R. in Prairie co., near Terry 30 mi/48 km NE of Miles City. The North Fork rises at Powder R. Pass 35 mi/56 km SW of Buffalo; flows S then SE c.45 mi/72 km joining South Fork 7 mi/11.3 km SSE of Kaycee to form main stream; South Fork rises in W Natrone co. in Rattlesnake Range, flows NE c.95 mi/153 km to join North Fork; Middle Fork rises in SE corner at Washakie co., flows ENE 45 mi/72 km joining North Fork 3 mi/4.8 km E of Kaycee. Main tributaries are Little Powder R., in Wyo. and Mont.; Crazy Woman Creek, in Wyo.

Powder River Pass (9,666 ft/2,946 m), in Bighorn Mts., in Bighorn Natl. Forest, at S edge of Cloud Peak Wilderness Area, W Johnson co., N Wyo., 15 mi/24 km SSE of Cloud Peak, and 22 mi/35 km SW of Buffalo; crossed by U.S. Highway 16.

Powder Springs, town (1990 pop. 6,893), Cobb co., NW central Ga., 18 mi/29 km WNW of Atlanta; 33°52′N 84°41′W. Mfg. includes metal fabrication, plastics, bldg. materials; diversified light mfg.

Powderhorn, village, Gunnison co., SW central Colo., Cebolla Creek, at mouth of Powderhorn Creek, in foothills of San Juan Mts., and 20 mi/32 km SSW of Gunnison. Elev. 8,080 ft/2,463 m. Coal-mining area. Mineral hot springs here. Fishing, hiking. The Powderhorn primitive area is one of the biggest alpine tundra areas in the lower 48 states.

Powderly, town (1990 pop. 748), Muhlenberg co., W Ky., residential suburb 3 mi/4.8 km NNE of Greenville, 5 mi/8 km SSW of Central City; 37°14′N 87°09′W. Muhlenberg Co. Airport is here.

Powe (PO), uninc. rural community, Stoddard co., SE Mo., near St. Francis R., 8 mi/12.9 km W of Bernie. Cotton, rice, soybeans.

Powell 1 county (□ 180 sq mi/466 sq km; 1990 pop. 11,686), E central Ky.; ⊙ Stanton; 37°49′N 83°49′W. Drained by Red R. and several creeks. Hilly agr. area (corn, hay, burley tobacco; cattle); bituminous-coal mines, limestone quarries; timber. Mfg. at Stanton and Clay City. Includes part of Natural Bridge State Park near Slade, on E border, Red R. Gorge, in Red R. Natl. Geological Area, in NE corner; part of Daniel Boone Natl. Forest in E ½ of co. Formed 1852. **2** county (□ 2,332 sq mi/6,040 sq km; 1990 pop. 6,620), W central Mont.; ⊙ Deer Lodge; 46°51′N 112°57′W. Agr. and mining area, drained by Blackfoot, Little Blackfoot, Clark Fork, and South Fork Flathead rivers. Continental Divide forms SE border and extreme NE corner. Potatoes, hay; cattle, sheep; lumber; phosphate, lignite. Part of Flint Creek Range in SW; parts of Deerlodge Natl. Forest on SW and SE; parts of Helena Natl. Forest in E; parts of Lolo Natl. Forest in N center; part of Flathead Natl. Forest far N; part of Scapegoat and Bob Marshall wilderness areas in N; Grant-Kohrs Natl. Historical Site in S center, N of Deer Lodge. Formed 1901. Present borders est. 1915.

Powell 1 town (1990 pop. 7,534), Knox co., NE Tenn., 7 mi/11 km NW of Knoxville, 36°01′N 84°01′W. Plastics; dairy prods. **2** town (1990 pop. 5,292), Park co., NW Wyo., near Shoshone R. and Mont. state line, 22 mi/35 km NE of Cody; 44°47′N 108°44′W. Elev. 4,365 ft/1,330 m. Trade center for irrigated agr. region producing sugar beets, barley, alfalfa; mfg. (printing and publishing; bldg. materials, electronic equip., machinery). Hq. of Shoshone irrigation project. Gas and oil wells nearby; fossil beds in vicinity. Settled 1908, inc. 1910.

Powell, village (1990 pop. 2,154), Delaware co., central Ohio, 11 mi/18 km S of Delaware; 40°10′N 83°04′W. Inc. 1947.

Powell, Lake, NE Ariz. and SE Utah, on the Colorado R., 120 mi/193 km N of Flagstaff, at Page; 36°55′N 111°29′W. Extends c.186 mi/299 km upstream (NE). Navajo Indian Reservation on SE shore; remainder in Glen Canyon Natl. Recreation Area. Named after Amer. explorer John W. Powell who mapped and named the canyon in 1870. Formed by Glen Canyon Dam (710 ft/216 m high, 1,560 ft/475 m long; completed 1964), one of the world's largest concrete dams (larger in bulk, though not in ht., than Hoover Dam) and the key unit of the U.S. Bureau of Reclamation's Colorado R. Storage Project; regulates the flow of the upper Colorado and its tributaries and produces hydroelectricity. The Glen Canyon Bridge (1,271 ft/387 m long, 700 ft/213 m high), downstream (S) of dam, is one of the world's longest and highest steel-arch bridges.

Powell, Mount (13,398 ft/4,084 m), Summit and Engle cos., N central Colo., in Gore Range, 8 mi/12.9 km N of Vail; 39°25′N 106°20′W.

Powell Mountain, NE Tenn. and SW Va., ridge (1,500 ft/457 m–2,500 ft/762 m) in Great Appalachian Valley, bet. Powell and Clinch rivers; from Hancock co. (Tenn.) extends NE into Wise co. (Va.). In Va., Natural Tunnel through mt. attracts tourists.

Powell River, town (1991 pop. 12,991), SW B.C., W Canada, on the Strait of Georgia, at mouth of Powell R., near Powell L., and 80 mi/129 km NW of Vancouver; 49°52′N 124°33′W. Pulp- and newsprint-milling center and port; lumbering. Hydroelectric power.

Powell River, 150 mi/241 km long, in Va. and Tenn.; rises in central Wise co., SW Va., near Norton; flows SW past Big Stone Gap and Jonesville, into Tenn., joins Clinch R. in large Norris L. reservoir, c. 20 mi/32 km N of Knoxville; forms long NE arm of reservoir.

Powellhurst, uninc. city (1990 pop. 28,756), Multnomah co., NW Oregon, residential suburb 6 mi/9.7 km E of downtown Portland.

Powellsville, village (1990 pop. 103), Bertie co., NE N.C., 5 mi/8 km SSE of Ahoskie; 36°13′N 76°55′W. Cotton, peanuts, grain; livestock.

Powellton, uninc. town (1990 pop. 1,905), Fayette co., S central W.Va., 20 mi/32 km W of Fayetteville; 38°05′N 81°19′W. Mfg. (coal processing). Coal-mining region.

Power, county (□ 1,442 sq mi/3,735 sq km; 1990 pop. 7,086), SE Idaho; ⊙ American Falls; 42°42′N 112°51′W. Livestock-raising and agr. area (cattle, sheep; dairying; alfalfa; wheat, rye, potatoes, barley) drained by Snake R. and Bannock Creek, and lying partly in Snake R. Plain. American Falls Dam, at American Falls, is used in generation of power and forms American Falls Reservoir along N border. Pocatello Municipal Airport in NW corner. Part of Fort Hall Indian Reservation is in mt. region in NE. Part of Curlew Natl. Grassland in S; Massacre Rocks State Park in W; part of Sawtooth Natl. Forest in SW corner. Formed 1913.

Power, village (1990 pop. 120), Teton co., N central Mont., 25 mi/40 km NW of Great Falls, near Muddy Creek. RR Junction, wheat-shipping point. Wheat, hay; cattle, sheep.

Powers 1 village (1990 pop. 271), Menominee co., SW Upper Peninsula, N Mich., 23 mi/37 km WSW of Escanaba, and on Big Cedar R.; 45°41′N 87°31′W. RR junction. Mfg. (wood prods.; machining). Mich. Potawatomi Indian Reservation to E. **2** village (1990 pop. 682), Coos co., SW Oregon, on South Fork Coquille R., 21 mi/34 km SSE of Coquille; 42°53′N 124°04′W. RR terminus. Timber. Coquille Myrtle Grove State Park to NW; Siskiyou Natl. Forest, including Wild Rogue Wilderness Area, to S.

Powers Lake, village (1990 pop. 408), Burke co., NW N.Dak., 25 mi/40 km SW of Bowbells; 48°33′N 102°38′W. Powers L. to S; Lostwood Natl. Wildlife Refuge to E.

Powersville, town (1990 pop. 38), Putnam co., N Mo., 17 mi/27 km WNW of Unionville; 40°32′N 93°17′W.

Powerton Lake, reservoir, Tazewell Co., central Ill., on channel of Illinois R., which parallels lake to NW, 5 mi/8 km WSW of Pekin; 40°33′N 89°47′W. Max. capacity 15,600 acre-ft. Formed by dam (11 ft/3 m high), built (1972) for cooling effluent from Powerton electric power plant.

Poweshiek, county (□ 586 sq mi/1,518 sq km; 1990 pop. 19,003), central Iowa; ⊙ Montezuma; 41°41′N 92°31′W. Rolling-prairie agr. area (hogs, cattle, poultry; corn, oats, hay) drained by English R. and North Skunk R. Bituminous-coal deposits (S, W). Fun Valley Ski Area in S. Formed 1843.

Powhatan, county (□ 262 sq mi/679 sq km; 1990 pop. 15,328), central Va.; ⊙ Powhatan; 37°32′N 77°55′W. Bounded N by James R., S by Appomattox R. Agr. (esp. tobacco; corn, barley, wheat, hay, alfalfa, soybeans; cattle; dairying). Formed 1777.

Powhatan 1 (pou-uh-TAN), village (1990 pop. 51), one ⊙ Lawrence co., NE Ark., 28 mi/45 km NW of Jonesboro, and on Black R.; 36°04′N 91°07′W. Village formerly shared co. administration with Walnut Ridge; courthouse is now historical site (Powhatan Courthouse State Park). L. Charles State Park to W. **2** uninc. village, ⊙ Powhatan co., central Va., 25 mi/40 km W of Richmond; 37°32′N 77°55′W. Mfg. (lumber; printing and publishing); agr. (grain, tobacco, soybeans; cattle; dairying).

Powhatan Point (pou-HA-tuhn), village (1990 pop. 1,807), Belmont co., E Ohio, on the Ohio R., and 17 mi/27 km SSE of Saint Clairsville; 39°52′N 80°48′W. In coal-mining area. Settled 1819, inc. 1895.

Powhattan (pou-HAT-uhn), village (1990 pop. 111), Brown co., NE Kansas, 8 mi/12.9 km SW of Hiawatha; 39°45′N 95°37′W. In corn belt; livestock. Kickapoo Indian Reservation is just S.

Pownal 1 (POU-nuhl), town (1990 pop. 1,262), Cumberland co., SW Maine, 18 mi/29 km NNE of Portland; 43°53′N 70°10′W. Bradbury Mt. State Park here. Includes villages of Pownal Center and West Pownal. **2** town (1990 pop. 3,485), Bennington co., extreme SW Vt., on Hoosic R., just S of Bennington; 42°47′N 73°12′W. Limestone; dairy prods. Seat of Oak Grove Seminary. James Fisk b. here. First settled c.1720, permanently settled after 1760.

Poydras (POI-druhs), uninc. town (1990 pop. 4,029), St. Bernard parish, La.; 29°52′N 89°53′W. On E bank (levee) of Mississippi R. Poydras revetment.

Poygan, Lake (POI-gan), widening of Wolf R., in Winnebago and Waushara cos., E central Wis., 10 mi/16 km NW of Oshkosh; c.10 mi/16 km long, 3 mi/4.8 km wide. Its E arm (c.3 mi/4.8 km long) is called L. Winneconne; town of Winneconne at E end. Receives Willow Creek from W.

Poyner, village (1990 pop. 257), Henderson co., E Texas, 25 mi/40 km SW of Tyler. Oil and natural gas. Agr. area; mfg. (natural-gas processing).

Poynette (poi-NET), village (1990 pop. 1,662), Columbia co., S central Wis., on small Rowan Creek, and 22 mi/35 km N of Madison; 43°23′N 89°24′W. Agr.; cannery; mfg. (humidifiers; light mfg.). State environmental center and game farm to NE.

Poza Rica, Mexico: see POZA RICA DE HIDALGO.

Poza Rica de Hidalgo (PO-sah REE-kah dai ee-DAHL-go), city (1990 pop. 151,739), ⊙ Poza Rica de Hidalgo municipio, Veracruz, Mexico, on the Gulf Coastal Plain in La Huasteca, on Mexico Highways 130 and 180, 151 mi/244 km N of Veracruz; 20°33′N 97°27′W. Elev. 200 ft/61 m. One of Mexico's oldest and, for many years, its most important oil-production and -processing center. Area around city retains a fairly large Native Huastec pop. Tropical agr.; livestock. Formerly Poza Rica.

Prado Dam, Calif.: see SANTA ANA RIVER.

Prague (PRAIG), town (1990 pop. 2,308), Lincoln co., central Okla., 17 mi/27 km N of Seminole; 35°29′N 96°41′W. Trade center for agr. area (livestock; oats, soybeans, wheat); mfg. (quartz blanks, apparel). Settled by Czechs; inc. 1902.

Prague (PRAIG), village (1990 pop. 282), Saunders co., E Nebr., 12 mi/19 km NW of Wahoo, and on branch of Platte R.; 41°18′N 96°48′W.

Prairie 1 county (□ 675 sq mi/1,748 sq km; 1990 pop. 9,518), E central Ark.; ⊙ Des Arc and DeValls Bluff; 34°49′N 91°33′W. Drained by White R.; Bayou Des Arc and Cypress Bayou form part of N border; Two Prairie Bayou forms S part of W border. Peckerwood L. reservoir (LaGrue Bayou) in S. Agr. (rice, wheat, soybeans, hay; cattle, hogs); timber; lumber milling, commercial fishing. Formed 1846. Bayou Des Arc (N) and Wattensaw (center) wildlife management areas. **2** county (□ 1,742 sq mi/4,512 sq km; 1990 pop. 1,383), E Mont.; ⊙

Terry; 46°51′N 105°22′W. Agr. area drained by Yellowstone and Powder rivers, and O'Fallon Creek. Wheat, barley, oats, corn (maize), hay, sugar beets, beans; cattle, sheep, hogs, poultry; gravel, oil (though most, if not all, of the oil wells are said to be dry). Formed 1915.

Prairie, village, Monroe co., E Miss., 7 mi/11.3 km WSW of Aberdeen. Timber; mfg. (lumber and wood prods., chemicals).

Prairie City 1 town (1990 pop. 1,360), Jasper co., central Iowa, 12 mi/19 km SW of Newton; 41°36′N 93°14′W. Feed. **2** town (1990 pop. 1,117), Grant co., NE central Oregon, 65 mi/105 km SW of Baker City, on John Day R.; 44°27′N 118°42′W. Elev. 3,539 ft/1,079 m. Wood prods.; timber; poultry, sheep, cattle. Site of DeWitt Mus. Blue Mt. Hot Springs to SE. Malheur Natl. Forest to N, E, and S, including Strawberry Mt. Wilderness Area to S.

Prairie City, village (1990 pop. 497), McDonough co., W Ill., 15 mi/24 km NE of Macomb; 40°37′N 90°27′W. In agr. and bituminous-coal area.

Prairie Creek Redwoods State Park (□ 22 sq mi/57 sq km), Humboldt co., NW Calif., tract of redwood forest and meadows, 25 mi/40 km S of Crescent City, near the Pacific Ocean coast; follows 8 mi/12.9 km of U.S. Highway 101. Cabins, camp sites, recreational facilities. Revelation Trail designed for the blind. Fauna include Roosevelt elk.

Prairie Creek Reservoir, water supply reservoir, on Prairie Creek, Delaware co., E Ind., 6 mi/9.7 km SE of Muncie. Built by the Muncie Water Works Company.

Prairie Dog Creek, river, c.160 mi/257 km long, in NW Kansas and S Nebr.; rises in central Thomas co. at Colby (Kansas); flows ENE through Newton Reservoir, past Norton, into Harlan co. (Nebr.), entering Republican R. at Harlan Co. L. Reservoir, 6 mi/9.7 km ESE of Alma.

Prairie Dog Town Fork of Red River, c.120 mi/193 km long, in Texas and Okla.; formed in the Panhandle of Texas by junction of intermittent Palo Duro and Tierra Blanca creeks near Canyon, Randall co.; flows generally ESE, through scenic Palo Duro Canyon (State Park), past Newlin to junction with Okla. state line. Generally referred to as Red R. eastward.

Prairie du Chien (PRER-ee doo SHAIN), town (1990 pop. 5,659), ⊙ Crawford co., SW Wis., on Mississippi R. just above mouth of the Wisconsin R., and 53 mi/85 km S of La Crosse; 43°02′N 91°08′W. RR junction in agr. area (dairying; grain); farm trade center, with mfg. of chemicals, electronic prods., bldg. materials, lumber. City's strategic site on Fox-Wisconsin river route to the Mississippi made it a meeting point for explorers, missionaries, and traders in late 17th cent.; Nicolas Perrot erected Fort St. Nicolas here in 1686; Fr. settlers came c.1781, and an Amer. Fur Company trading post was built here before 1812. In War of 1812, Americans built Fort Shelby (1814), renamed Fort McKay soon after. Fort Crawford (1816; abandoned 1856) was scene of medical (surgery) experiments by Dr. William Beaumont. Wyalusing State Park to S. Inc. 1872.

Prairie du Rocher (PRER-ree doo RO-sher), village (1990 pop. 540), Randolph co., SW Ill., near the Mississippi R., 18 mi/29 km SSE of Waterloo; 38°04′N 90°05′W. Flour, wood prods. Settled by French in early 18th cent. A speculative land venture. Old fort (restored) is in Fort de Chartres (or Fort Chartres) State Historic Park, 4 mi/6.4 km W.

Prairie du Sac (PRER-ee doo SAK), town (1990 pop. 2,380), Sauk co., S central Wis., on Wisconsin R., 2 mi/3.2 km N of Sauk City, and 22 mi/35 km NW of Madison; 43°17′N 89°43′W. In dairying and farming area (corn; hogs); dairy prods.; winery; mfg. (chemicals, machinery, fabricated metal prods.). Agr. research station to N. Settled 1839, inc. 1885.

Prairie Farm, village (1990 pop. 494), Barron co., NW Wis., 38 mi/61 km NW of Eau Claire; 45°14′N 91°58′W. Dairying; mfg. (fabricated metal prods.).

Prairie Grove, town (1990 pop. 1,761), Washington co., NW Ark., 11 mi/18 km WSW of Fayetteville, near Illinois R., in the Ozark Mts.; 35°58′N 94°19′W. Trade center for agr. and timber area. Mfg. (galvanizing; printing;

machinery). Site of a Civil War battle (Dec. 7, 1862) here resulted in a Confederate retreat; Prairie Grove Battlefield State Park nearby.

Prairie Grove, village (1990 pop. 654), McHenry co., NE Ill., residential suburb 4 mi/6.4 km S of McHenry, on Thunderbird L.; 42°16′N 88°16′W. Light mfg.

Prairie Hill, uninc. community, Chariton co., N central Mo., near Chariton R., 13 mi/21 km NNE of Keytesville. Strip coal mines in area, closed 1980s.

Prairie Home, town (1990 pop. 215), Cooper co., central Mo., near Missouri R., 14 mi/23 km SE of Boonville; 38°48′N 92°35′W. Corn, soybeans; cattle.

Prairie Island 1 and 2 Nuclear Power Plants, Minn.: see GOODHUE.

Prairie Provinces, Canada: see MANITOBA LBERTAAN-ALBERTA.

Prairie River, c.45 mi/72 km long, SW Mich.; rises in small lakes in SE Branch co. near Ind. state line; flows NW, past Burr Oak and Centerville, to St. Joseph R. 2 mi/3.2 km S of Three Rivers; 41°48′N 85°00′W.

Prairie View, town (1990 pop. 4,004), Waller co., SE Texas, c.45 mi/72 km WNW of Houston; 30°04′N 95°59′W. Elev. 250 ft/76 m. Cattle; rice, corn; mfg. (concrete prods.). Seat of Prairie View Agr. and Mechanical Univ.

Prairie View, village (1990 pop. 111), Phillips co., N Kansas, 14 mi/23 km WNW of Phillipsburg; 39°49′N 99°34′W. In corn belt; livestock.

Prairie Village, city (1990 pop. 23,186), Johnson co., NE Kansas, 8 mi/12.9 km SW of Kansas City. Residential suburb 6 mi/9.7 km S of Kansas City. Inc. 1951.

Prairie Village, town (1990 pop. 3,680), Jefferson co., N Ky., residential suburb 10 mi/16 km SSW of downtown Louisville, on Pond Creek.

Prairieburg, town (1990 pop. 213), Linn co., E Iowa, near Buffalo Creek, 22 mi/35 km NE of Cedar Rapids; 42°14′N 91°25′W.

Prairies, Rivière des (prer-EE, reev-YER dai), branch of Ottawa R., 30 mi/48 km long, S Que., E Canada; flows from L. of the Two Mountains NE bet. Montreal and Jesus isls. to the St. Lawrence R.

Prairieville, uninc. village, Ascension parish, SE La., 15 mi/24 km SE of Baton Rouge; 30°18′N 90°58′W. In agr. area (sugarcane, peppers, strawberries, pecans). Mfg. (bldg. materials, fabricated metal prods., machinery, fabricated steel; valve repair).

Praise (PRAIZ) or **Elkhorn City,** village, Pike co., SE Ky., 12 mi/19 km SE of Pikeville, in the Cumberland Mts., near Va. state line, on Russell Fork. In bituminous-coal and timber region.

Pralls Island, small isl. in Arthur Kill, just W of Staten Isl., SE N.Y., in Staten Isl. borough of N.Y. city; 40°36′N 74°12′W.

Pratt, county (□ 735 sq mi/1,904 sq km; 1990 pop. 9,702), S Kansas; ⊙ Pratt; 37°38′N 98°44′W. Gently rolling plain, drained by South Fork Ninnescah R. and Chikaskia R. Wheat, sorghum; cattle, sheep. Small gas and oil fields in E. Formed 1879.

Pratt, city (1990 pop. 6,687), ⊙ Pratt co., S Kansas, on South Fork Ninnescah R., and c.75 mi/121 km W of Wichita; 37°38′N 98°44′W. RR junction. Trade and shipping center, for area producing wheat, sorghum, corn, alfalfa, hay; cattle, hogs; and oil. RR repair shops. Mfg. (hydraulic components, feeds, wood prods.). State Fish and Game Hq. Inc. 1884.

Pratt, village (1990 pop. 640), Kanawha co., W central W.Va., 18 mi/29 km SE of Charleston, on Kanawha R.; 38°12′N 81°23′W. Coal-mining region. Agr. (corn, tobacco); cattle, poultry. RR junction.

Prattsburg, village (1990 pop. 950), Steuben co., W central N.Y., 29 mi/47 km NNW of Corning; 42°31′N 77°18′W.

Prattsville, resort village (1990 pop. 600), Greene co., SE N.Y., in the Catskill Mts., on Schoharie Reservoir, 29 mi/47 km WNW of Catskill; 42°19′N 74°25′W.

Prattville, city (1990 pop. 19,587), ⊙ Autauga co., central Ala., 10 mi/16 km NW of Montgomery. Textile and related industries, automotive parts mfg., lumber, and a paper mill. Cotton gin mfg. here since 1838. A state game farm is here. Inc. 1872.

Praxedis G. Guerrero (prah-HE-dees ZHAI ger-RER-ro), town (1990 pop. 3,338), Chihuahua, N Mexico, on Rio Grande, and 38 mi/61 km SE of Juárez; 31°22′N 106°00′W. Cotton, grain; livestock. Formerly San Ignacio.

Preble (PRE-buhl), county (□ 428 sq mi/1,109 sq km; 1990 pop. 40,113), W Ohio, on Ind. (W) state line; ⊙ Eaton; 39°45′N 84°38′W. Drained by small Twin, Seven Mile, and Four Mile creeks and by East Fork of Whitewater R. Includes Fort St. Clair State Park near Eaton. Agr. area (livestock; tobacco, grain, fruit); mfg. at Eaton; limestone quarries; timber; nurseries. Formed 1808.

Preble, Fort, Maine: see SOUTH PORTLAND.

Prêcheur (pre-SHER), town, NW Martinique, at W foot of Mont Pelée, 26 mi/42 km NW of Fort-de-France. Minor port; cacao growing; mfg. of lime juice and rum. Heavily damaged by eruption of Pelée (1902).

Preeceville (town (1991 pop. 1,205), E Sask., W Canada, on Assiniboine R., and 50 mi/80 km NNW of Yorkton; 51°57′N 102°40′W.

Preissac (pre-SAK), village (1991 pop. 529), W Que., E Canada, near N end of Lac Preissac, 15 mi/24 km SW of Amos; 48°24′N 78°15′W. Gold, zinc, copper; molybdenite and bismuth mining.

Prelate, village (1991 pop. 191), SW Sask., W Canada, near South Saskatchewan R., 45 mi/72 km SSW of Kindersley. Wheat.

Premier, village, NW B.C., W Canada, on U.S. (Alaska) border, 100 mi/161 km ESE of Wrangell; 56°04′N 129°59′W. Former mining area. 30 mi/48 km road from Hyder (Alaska) and Stewart (B.C.). Ghost towns and mining sites used for movie scenes.

Premier Group, short range of high peaks of Rocky Mts., SE B.C., W Canada, 70 mi/113 km N of Jasper, overlooking Fraser R. valley. Highest elev. is Mt. Sir Wilfrid Laurier (11,750 ft/3,581 m).

Premium, uninc. village (1990 pop. 729), Letcher co., SE Ky., 5 mi/8 km W of Whitesburg, on North Fork of Kentucky R. Bituminous coal.

Premont, town (1990 pop. 2,914), Jim Wells co., S Texas, c.55 mi/89 km SW of Corpus Christi; 27°21′N 98°07′W. In agr. area (cotton, vegetables; cattle; dairying). Inc. 1938.

Prenter, uninc. village, Boone co., W central W.Va., 10 mi/16 km ESE of Madison. Coal mining. Mfg. (coal processing).

Prentice, village (1990 pop. 571), Price co., N Wis., 43 mi/69 km W of Rhinelander; 45°32′N 90°17′W. In wooded area. Dairy and farm prods.; mfg. (lumber, plywood, machinery; fuelwood processing). Has an airport. Separate units of Chequamegon Natl. Forest to SW and NE; Timms Hill (1,951.5 ft/594.8 m), highest point in Wis., 8 mi/12.9 km SE.

Prentiss, plantation (1990 pop. 245), Penobscot co., E central Maine, 57 mi/92 km NE of Bangor; 45°30′N 68°04′W. In lumbering area.

Prentiss, county (□ 418 sq mi/1,083 sq km; 1990 pop. 23,278), NE Miss.; ⊙ Booneville; 34°36′N 88°31′W. Drained by East Fork of the Tombigbee and Tuscumbia rivers. Agr. (cotton, corn, soybeans, wheat, hay; cattle; dairying; timber; clay deposits. Natchez Trace (Natl.) Parkway passes through SE corner; part of Bay Springs Reservoir, on Tennessee-Tombigbee Waterway, on E border; part of John Bell Williams Wildlife Management Area (canal sect.) in SE corner. Formed 1870.

Prentiss, town (1990 pop. 1,487), ⊙ Jefferson Davis co.; 31°36′N 89°52′W, S central Miss., 37 mi/60 km WNW of Hattiesburg. Agr. (cotton, corn; cattle, hogs, poultry; timber); mfg. (pork processing).

Presa Abraham González (PRAI-sah ah-brah-AHM gon-ZAH-lez), dam, in Chihuahua, Mexico, on Papagóchic R. (from the Yaqui R. basin), and 36 mi/58 km W of Cuantémoc. Also known as the Guadalupe Dam.

Presa Adolfo López Mateos (PRAI-sah ah-DOL-fo LO-pez mah-TAI-os), dam, in central Sinaloa, Mexico, 20 mi/33 km N of Culiacan Rosales, on the Humaya R. (from the Culiacán R. basin). Max. capacity 5,316 cu yd/4,064 cu m. Built for irrigation, flood control and

the generation of electricity (capacity 85,500 kw). Also known as El Humaya.

Presa Aguamilpa (PRAI-sah ah-wah-MEEL-pah), dam, in Nayarit, Mexico, on the lower Santiago (Grande) R. Capacity 9,156 cu yd/7,000 cu m, for hydroelectric generation, irrigation, and flood control. Generating cap. over 600,000 kw.

Presa Alvaro Obregón (PRAI-sah AHL-vah-ro o-brai-GON), dam, on the Yaquí R., in SW Sonora, Mexico, 22 mi/35 km NE of the city of Obregón. Max. capacity 4.2 million cu yd/3.2 million cu m. Built for irrigating the wheat, cotton, rice, corn, alfalfa, flax, sesame in the reclaimed 781 sq mi/2,023 sq km in the valley; and for the rechanneling of waterways and the generation of electricity. Also known as the Oviachic Dam.

Presa Belisario Domínguez (PRAI-sah bai-lee-SAH-ree-o do-MEEN-ges), dam, Chiapas, Mexico, 16 mi/25 km W of Venustiano Carranza, on the Grijalva R. Max. capacity 26,444 cu yd/20,217 cu m, for flood control and hydroelectric generation (capacity 900,000 kw). Also known as Presa la Angostura.

Presa Carlos Ramírez Ulloa (PRAI-sah KAHR-los rah-MEE-res oo-YO-ah), dam, Guerrero, Mexico, on Río Balsas, bet. Ciudad Altamirano and Chilpancingo de los Bravo; built for hydroelectric generation (max. capacity over 600,000 kw).

Presa El Tintero (PRAI-sah el teen-TAI-ro), dam, in N Chihuahua, Mexico, on the Santa María R. Used for irrigation and flood control.

Presa Francisco I. Madero (PRAI-sah frahn-SEES-ko EE mah-DAI-ro), dam, in W Chihuahua, Mexico, SW of the town of Delicias, across the San Pedro R. (tributary of the Conchos R. flowing from the Bravo R. basin). Max. capacity 555.8 million cu yd/425 million cu m capacity; built for irrigation. Also known as Las Virgenes.

Presa Francisco Zarco (PRAI-sah frahn-SEES-ko ZAHR-ko), in Durango, Mexico, on the Nazas R. Built for irrigation and flood control. Also known as Las Tórtolas.

Presa Ignacio Allende (PRAI-sah eeg-NAH-see-o ah-YEN-dai), dam, in E Guanajuato, Mexico, 3.1 mi/5 km W of San Miguel de Allende, on the Río Lajas (from Lerma R.). Built for flood control and for providing potable water. Also known as La Begoña Dam.

Presa Infiernillo (PRAI-sah een-fee-ER-no), dam, in S Michoacán, Mexico, W of the Guerrero state border, on the Balsas R. Max. capacity 15,513 cu yd/11,860 cu m. Built for generating electricity (1,012,000 kw) and flood contol.

Presa Juárez (PRAI-sah HWAH-rez), dam, in SE Oaxaca, Mexico, 22 mi/35 km NW of Santo Domingo Tehuantepec, on the Tehuantepec R. Used for irrigation. The official name is Presa Presidente Benito Juárez. Also known as El Marqués.

Presa la Angostura (PRAI-sah lah ahn-gos-TOO-rah), dam in NE Sonora, Mexico, 13 mi/21 km SE of Heroica Nogales, on the Río Bavispe (a Yaqui R. tributary). Built to irrigate and generate electricity.

Presa la Boquilla (PRAI-sah lah bo-KEE-yah), dam, in SW Chihuahua, Mexico, 18 mi/29 km S of the town of Camargo, on the Conchos R. (from the Bravo R. basin). Built for irrigation and the generation of electricity. Also known as Lago Toronto.

Presa Lázaro Cárdenas (PRAI-sah LAH-zah-ro KAHR-dai-nahs), dam, in N Durango, Mexico, 105 mi/170 km NNW of the city of Durango, built on the Nazas R. Used for irrigation and flood control. Also known as El Palmito.

Presa Luis L. León (PRAI-sah loo-EES lai-ON), dam, in E Chihuahua, Mexico, on the Conchos R. (from Bravo R. basin). Built for irrigation, flood control and to generate electricity. Also known as El Granero.

Presa Manuel Avila Camacho (PRAI-sah mahn-WEL ah-VEE-lah kah-MAH-cho), dam, in central Puebla, Mexico, 7 mi/11 km E of Atlixco, built on the Atoyac R. (from the Balsas R. basin). Max. capacity 554.5 million cu yd/424 million cu m. Built for irrigation. Also known as the Valsequillo Dam.

Presa Manuel M. Torres (PRAI-sah mahn-WEL TO-res), dam, Chiapas, Mexico, 12 mi/18 km N of Tuxtla Gutiérrez, on the Grijalva R. Max. capacity 15,543 cu yd/11,883 cu m. Built for hydroelectric generation (capacity over 1,000,000 kw). Also known as Presa Chicoasen.

Presa Marte R. Gómez (PRAI-sah MAHR-tai ER-rai GO-mez), dam, in N Tamaulipas state, Mexico, 6 mi/10 km S of Ciudad Camargo, on the Río Bravo del Norte. Also known as El Azúcar.

Presa Miguel de la Madrid Hurtado (PRAI-sah MEE-gel dai lah mah-DREED uhr-TAH-do), dam, in Oaxaca and Veracruz, Mexico, on the Santo Domingo R., 11 mi/17 km WSW of Tuxtepec. Max. capacity 7,037 cu yd/5,380 cu m. Built for hydroelectric generation and flood control. Also known as Presa Cerro de Oro.

Presa Miguel Hidalgo (PRAI-sah MEE-gel ee-DAHL-go), dam, in Sinaloa, Mexico, on the Fuerte R., 6 mi/10 km N of El Fuerte. Max. capacity 5,271 cu yd/4,030 cu m. Built for hydroelectric generation, flood control, irrigation, and domestic water supply. Also known as Presa El Mahone.

Presa Netzahualcóyotl (PRAI-sah net-zah-hwahl-KO-yo-tuhl), in W Chiapas, Mexico, 7 mi/12 km E of the Guerrero state border, and 9 mi/15 km NW of Tuxtla Gutiérrez, on the Grijalva R. Max. capacity 17 million cu yd/13 million cu m. Built for irrigation, controlling waterways, and generating electricity. Also known as Malpaso Dam.

Presa Penitas (PRAI-sah pen-NEE-tahs), dam, in Chiapas, Mexico, on lower Grijalva R. Hydroelectric generation; capacity over 210,000 kw.

Presa Plutarco Elías Calles (PRAI-sah ploo-TAHR-ko ai-LEE-ahs KAH-yes), dam, on Yaquí R., Sonora, Mexico. Used for irrigation and generating electricity (max. capacity 135,000 kw). Also known as El Novillo.

Presa Presidente Miguel Alemán (PRAI-sah mee-GEL ah-lai-MAHN), dam, in N Oaxaca, Mexico, 3.1 mi/5 km W of Temazcal, built on the Tonto R. (from the Papaloapan R. basin). Built for irrigation, flood control, and for generating electricity (max. capacity 720,000 kw). Also known as Temascal.

Presa Sanalona (PRAI-sah sah-nah-LO-nah), dam, in central Sinaloa, Mexico, 15 mi/24 km E of Culiacan Rosales, on the Tamazula R. (from the Culiacán R. basin). Built for irrigation and the generation of electricity.

Presa Venustiano Carranza (PRAI-sah vai-noos-tee-AH-no kah-RAHN-zah), dam, in Coahuila, Mexico, on the Salado R. (from the Bravo R. basin). Built for irrigation and flood control. Also known as the Don Martín Dam.

Presa Vicente Guerrero (PRAI-sah vee-SEN-tai gai-RAI-ro), dam, in central Tamaulipas, Mexico, 7 mi/12 km NE of Ciudad Victoria, on the Río Soto la Marina. Built for irrigation and flood control. Also known as Las Adjuntas.

Prescott (PRE-skuht), county (□ 494 sq mi/1,279 sq km), SE Ont., central Canada, on Ottawa, R., and on Que. border; ⊙ L'Orignal; 45°30′N 74°45′W. Part of United Co. of Prescott and Russell.

Prescott (PRES-kuht), town (1991 pop. 4,512), SE Ont., central Canada, on the St. Lawrence R., opposite Ogdensburg (N.Y.); 44°43′N 75°31′W. Fort Wellington, built during the War of 1812, is now a military mus. At nearby Windmill Point the British repulsed an Amer. attack in 1838.

Prescott 1 city (1990 pop. 26,455), ⊙ Yavapai co., 80 mi/129 km NNW of Phoenix, central Ariz.; 34°34′N 112°27′W. Elev. 5,389 ft/1,643 m. In a mineral-rich area; it is a mining and ranching center, a summer resort, and the hq. of Prescott Natl. Forest (parts of forest to S, W, and E). Cattle farming; timber, wheat, corn, alfalfa, hay and mining are the predominant economic activities, but light mfg. (waxes, earthenware; printing, publishing; sawmill) is developing in importance. Gold was discovered in the co. in 1863, and Prescott was built in 1864 near Fort Whipple. It was twice territorial capital (1864–1867, 1877–1889). Seat of Prescott Center (2 year) and Yavapai cols. Of note is a Smoki Native Amer. Mus., Sharlot Hall History Mus., Phippen Mus. of Western Art. Jerome State Historic Park to NE. Inc. 1883. **2** city (1990 pop. 3,243), Pierce co., W Wis., 3 mi/4.8 km E of Hastings (Minn.), at confluence of the St. Croix and the Mississippi rivers; 44°45′N 92°47′W. In livestock-raising and dairying area; warehouses, dairy plants; mfg. wood prods. Lower St. Croix Natl. Riverway along St. Croix R.; Kinnickinnic State Park to NE.

Prescott 1 town (1990 pop. 3,673), ⊙ Nevada co., SW Ark., c.45 mi/72 km NE of Texarkana; 33°47′N 93°23′W. RR junction. Mfg. (bldg. materials, lumber, apparel). Settled 1873. **2** town (1990 pop. 287), Adams co., SW Iowa, on East Nodaway R., and 7 mi/11.3 km ENE of Corning; 41°01′N 94°36′W. Feed.

Prescott 1 village (1990 pop. 301), Linn co., SE Kansas, near Mo. state line, 15 mi/24 km N of Fort Scott; 38°03′N 94°42′W. Agr. Mine Creek Battlefield Park to N. **2** village (1990 pop. 314), Ogemaw co., NE central Mich., 16 mi/26 km ESE of West Branch; 44°11′N 83°55′W. **3** village (1990 pop. 63), Columbia co., NW Oregon, on Columbia R., 15 mi/24 km NNW of St. Helens; 46°02′N 122°53′W. Site of Trojan Nuclear Power Plant (closed). **4** village (1990 pop. 267), Walla Walla co., SE Wash., 15 mi/24 km N or Walla Walla, and on Touchet R., at mouth of Whetstone Creek; 46°18′N 118°19′W. In agr. region; vegetables, wheat, potatoes; hogs.

Prescott Valley, town (1990 pop. 8,858), Yavapai co., W central Ariz., suburb 8 mi/12.9 km ENE of Prescott; 34°36′N 112°19′W. Cattle; wheat, corn, alfalfa, hay; mfg. (fabricated metal prods., machinery parts, wood prods.; steel foundry). Parts of Prescott Natl. Forest to S and NE.

Presho, town (1990 pop. 654), Lyman co., S central S.Dak., 34 mi/55 km SSE of Pierre, and on Medicine Creek; 43°54′N 100°03′W. In wheat area; grain; livestock. Lower Brule Indian Reservation to NE. Fort Pierre Natl. Grassland to NW.

Presidential Range, group of the White Mts., N N.H., so called from the names of its peaks. Mt. Washington (6,288 ft/1,917 m) is the highest peak in N.H. and highest point in NE U.S.; a meteorological station is at the summit. A year-round resort center, it was developed for tourists in the mid-1800s. Other peaks include Mt. Adams (5,798 ft/1,767 m), Mt. Jefferson (5,717 ft/1,743 m), Mt. Clay (5,535 ft/1,687 m), Mt. Monroe (5,385 ft/1,641 m), Mt. Madison (5,363 ft/1,635 m), Mt. Franklin (5,004 ft/1,525 m), Mt. Eisenhower (4,760 ft/1,451 m), Mt. Pierce (4,310 ft/1,314 m), Mt. Jackson (4,050 ft/1,234 m), and Mt. Webster (3,910 ft/1,192 m). In White Mt. Natl. Forest. Appalachian Trail follows crest of range, linking the summits. Famous for spring skiing in Tuckerman's Ravine (no lifts).

Presidio, county (□ 3,856 sq mi/9,987 sq km; 1990 pop. 6,637), extreme W Texas, on Mex. (W and S; Rio Grande) border; ⊙ Marfa; 30°00′N 104°13′W. State's 4th-largest co.; in the Big Bend. Drained by Cibolo and Chispa creeks. High broken plateau (elev. 2,400 ft/732 m–7,730 ft./2,356 m), with mts.: Sierra Vieja (NW), Chinati Mts. (W). RR terminus; large-scale ranching (cattle, horses); some irrigated agr. in Rio Grande valley (onions, vegetables, lettuce, peppers; hay); silver mines; sand and gravel. Scenery attracts tourists; hunting. Fort Leaton State Historic Site in S. Formed 1850.

Presidio, town (1990 pop. 3,072), Presidio co., extreme W Texas, on the Rio Grande, near mouth of Cibolo Creek, and opposite mouth of Conchos R., and opposite Ojinaga (Mex.), c.60 mi/97 km SSW of Marfa; 29°33′N 104°21′W. Elev. 2,594 ft/791 m. Internatl. port of entry; imports Mex. timber. In irrigated agr. (onions, cantaloupes, lettuce, peppers; hay) and ranching area (cattle, horses); sand and gravel. Span. mission founded here 1684. Fort Leaton State Historic Site to E; old adobe fortress (1848).

Presidio de Río Grande, Mexico: see GUERRERO.

Presidio of Monterey, Calif.: see MONTEREY.

Presidio of San Francisco, military base (□ 2 sq mi/5.2 sq km) in San Francisco, San Francisco co., Calif. Historic army garrison from Span. and Mex. periods. Opened as U.S. Army facility in 1846. Closed in large part in 1994, land now part of Natl. Park Service.

Presidio River (pre-SEE-dee-yo), c.100 mi/161 km long, Sinaloa, W Mexico; rises in Sierra Madre Occidental in Durango; flows SW through fertile coastal lowlands, past Concepción, Siqueros, and Villa Unión, to the Pacific Ocean, 12 mi/19 km SE of Mazatlán.

Presque Isle (PRESK EIL), county (□ 2,572 sq mi/6,661 sq km; 1990 pop. 13,743), NE Mich.; ⊙ Rogers City; 45°19′N 83°27′W. Bounded NE by L. Huron; drained by Black, Rainy, and short Ocqueoc rivers, and by the North Branch of Thunder Bay R. Dairying and agr. area (cattle, hogs, poultry; oats, beans). Mfg. at Rogers City and Onaway. Limestone quarries; fisheries. Resorts. Grand L. and part of Long L. in E end of co., and part of Black L. on W border, in NW. Co. has state forests; Onaway State Park in NW, on Black L.; P.H. Hoeft State Park in N on L. Huron. Organized 1875.

Presque Isle (PRESK EIL) [Fr. = peninsula], city (1990 pop. 10,550), Aroostook co., NE Maine; 46°41′N 67°59′W. It is the trade, tourist, and shipping (potatoes) center of the Aroostook valley. During World War II an important air base here served as a ferry point for planes to Great Britain. Northern Maine Regional Airport is here. Seat of the Univ. of Maine at Presque Isle. Inc. 1859.

Presque Isle (PRESK EIL), village, Presque Isle co., NE Mich., 16 mi/26 km N of Alpena on E side of Grand L., on narrow strip of land separating Grand L. (W) from L. Huron; 45°18′N 83°28′W. Lighthouse nearby.

Presque Isle (PRESK EIL), NW Pa., small peninsula in L. Erie, off NW Pa.; narrow neck of land connects peninsula to mainland on SW; encloses Presque Isle Bay to S, harbor of city of Erie, Pa.; 7 mi/11.3 km long, ⅛ mi/ km–1 mi/1.6 km wide; 42°09′N 80°06′W. Harbor entrance to SE. Reconstructed blockhouse here, commemorating fort built 1753 by French is in Presque Isle State Park (□ 6 sq mi/15.5 sq km), as is most of the peninsula. Lighthouse on NW shore; U.S. Coast Guard Station at SE end; recreation area for Erie and other lake shore cities; vehicular access via Peninsula Drive; formed by glacial moraine.

Presque Isle River (PRESK EIL), c.50 mi/80 km long, W Upper Peninsula, NW Mich.; rises in small lakes in N Vilas co. (Wis.); flows NNW, into Mich., past Marenisco, to L. Superior in N Gogebic co. Falls and through W end of Porcupine Mts. State Park, at its mouth; 46°21′N 89°41′W.

Presque Isle Stream (PRESK EIL), c.35 mi/56 km long, Aroostook co., NE Maine; rises N of Houlton; flows N and E to the Aroostook R. near Presque Isle.

Preston, county (□ 651 sq mi/1,686 sq km; 1990 pop. 29,037), N W.Va., on Pa. (N) and Md. (E) state lines; ⊙ Kingwood; 39°28′N 79°40′W. On Allegheny Plateau; includes part of Laurel Ridge and other mts. Drained by Cheat R. Includes a small part of Monongahela Natl. Forest in SE. Agr. (honey, corn, wheat, oats, barley, potatoes, alfalfa, hay, vegetables, apples, grapes, nursery crops); dairy prods.; poultry, cattle, hogs, sheep. Coal mining; limestone quarrying. Timber. Part of Coopers Rock State Forest in NW; Cathedral State Park in SE; Fairfax Stone State Monument (State Park) on SE corner; Upper Decker Creek Wildlife Management Area in W; Briery Mt. Wildlife Management Area in S center. Formed 1818.

Preston, city (1990 pop. 3,710), ⊙ Franklin co., SE Idaho, on small tributary of Bear R., and 60 mi/97 km SE of Pocatello, near Utah state line; 42°06′N 111°52′W. Elev. 4,718 ft/1,438 m. RR terminus and commercial center for cattle, sheep, and irrigated agr. area (sugar beets, peas, vegetables, wheat); beet sugar; dairy prods.; flour. Mfg. (printing and publishing; plastic prods.). Caribou (to W) and Cache (to E) natl. forests. Settled 1866 by Mormons, inc. 1913.

Preston 1 town (1990 pop. 5,006), New London co., SE Conn., on Quinebaug R., 6 mi/9.7 km E of Norwich; 41°31′N 72°00′W. Mfg. of brass. Farming; resorts. Amos L. to S. Settled c.1650, inc. 1687. **2** town (1990 pop. 1,052), Jackson co., E Iowa, 14 mi/23 km E of Maquoketa; 42°02′N 90°24′W. Mfg. (feed milling, meat processing; cheese, concrete). **3** town (1990 pop. 437), Caroline co., Md., 14 mi/23 km NE of Cambridge; 38°43′N 75°55′W. Originally a tiny settlement called Snow Hill, the named was changed to that of a Baltimore lawyer in 1856. It is now a vegetable-gardening and poultry-raising center best known as the site of Bethesda Chapel, one of the 1st Methodist churches in Amer. The Bethesda Methodist Church now occupies the site. **4** town (1990 pop. 136), Hickory co., central Mo., 5 mi/8 km W of Hermitage; 37°56′N 93°12′W.

Preston 1 village (1990 pop. 388), ⊙ Webster co., W Ga., on Kinchafoonee R., and 17 mi/27 km W of Americus; 32°04′N 84°32′W. Tool and die mfg. **2** village (1990 pop. 177), Pratt co., S Kansas, 13 mi/21 km NE of Pratt; 37°45′N 98°33′W. Elev. 1,880 ft/573 m. In wheat and grain region, natural gas. **3** village (1990 pop. 1,530), ⊙ Fillmore co., SE Minn., 31 mi/50 km SE of Rochester, on South Branch Root R., near Iowa state line; 43°40′N 92°04′W. Elev. 1,085 ft/331 m. Livestock-shipping point in diversified-farming area; grain, soybeans; poultry; dairying. Mfg. (lumber, wood prods.; packaging and assembly). Richard J. Dorer Memorial Hardwood State Forest to W and N; Forestville–Mystery Cave State Park to W. Courthouse built 1863. **4** village (1990 pop. 40), Richardson co., extreme SE Nebr., 4 mi/6.4 km ESE of Falls City, near Missouri R., and Kansas state line, on Big Nemaha R.; 40°01′N 95°31′W. At edge of Sac and Fox Indian Reservation.

Preston, Pa.: see HAVERFORD.

Preston, Cuba: see GUATEMALA.

Preston, Lake, Kingsbury co., E S.Dak.; 5 mi/8 km long, 1 mi/1.6 km wide. City of Lake Preston at S end.

Preston Peak, Calif.: see SISKIYOU MOUNTAINS.

Prestonsburg, town (1990 pop. 3,558), ⊙ Floyd co., E Ky., in Cumberland foothills, on Levisa Fork, and 20 mi/32 km NW of Pikeville; 37°40′N 82°46′W. RR junction. In bituminous-coal-mining and agr. (corn; livestock) area. Mfg. (printing and publishing; underground mining cars, concrete). Has airport. Civil War battle of Middle Creek was fought nearby, on Jan. 10, 1862; Union forces claimed the victory. Ky. Opry. Boone Salt Springs to SW; Jenny Wiley State Resort Park, on Dewey L. reservoir, to NE. Settled 1791; est. 1797.

Prestonville, village (1990 pop. 205), Carroll co., N Ky., 1 mi/1.6 km W of Carrollton, bet. mouths of Kentucky (E) and Little Kentucky (W) rivers; 38°40′N 85°12′W. Agr. (tobacco; livestock). Prestonville Community Col. (Univ. of Ky.).

Presumpscot River (pruh-SUHM-skaht), c.22 mi/35 km long, SW Maine; rises in Sebago L., Cumberland co.; flows SSE, past Westbrook (water power), then NE and E to the Atlantic Ocean at Falmouth.

Pretty Prairie, village (1990 pop. 601), Reno co., S Kansas, 18 mi/29 km SSW of Hutchinson; 37°46′N 98°01′W. In wheat area.

Prettyboy Reservoir, Baltimore co., N Md., on Gunpowder Falls R., 22 mi/35 km NNW of Baltimore; 9 mi/14.5 km long; 39°37′N 76°42′W. Formed by Prettyboy Dam (concrete; 167 ft/51 m high, 845 ft/258 m long), built (1933) for Baltimore water supply. Gunpowder Falls State Park below dam, to E.

Pribilof Islands, group of 4 volcanic islands, off SW Alaska in the Bering Sea, c.230 m/370 km N of the Aleutian Isls. Fishing port constructed in 1980s to service Bering Sea fisheries; tourism. Explored and named in 1786 by Gerasim Pribilof, a Rus. navigator. The larger isls., St. Paul (57°07′N 170°17′W) and St. George (56°35′N 169°35′W), are famous as the breeding place of the Alaska fur seal. The isls., part of the 1867 U.S. purchase of Alaska, became a seal reservation in 1868; they are administered by the U.S. Bureau of Fisheries. Prior to 1911, competition and ruthless hunting methods threatened extinction of the seals. At that time, the U.S., Great Britain, Japan, and Russia entered into the North Pacific Sealing Convention, giving the U.S. the right to enforce the provisions of the convention. Japan withdrew from the convention in 1941. Under protection, the seal herd has greatly increased. Blue and white fox are native to the isls. The Aleuts, brought to the isls. in the late 1700s by the Russians, made a living by processing the seal and fox furs, but this was prohibited in the 1980s. Air connections to St. Paul and St. George villages; large bird-nesting areas.

Price, county (□ 1,278 sq mi/3,310 sq km; 1990 pop. 15,600), N Wis.; ⊙ Phillips; 45°40′N 90°21′W. Drained by Flambeau and Jump rivers. Dairying; lumbering; barley. Contains sect. of Chequamegon Natl. Forest in NE, small part of Flambeau R. State Forest in NW; E part of Tuscobia State Trail in NW; Timms Hill (1,951.5 ft/594.8 m), highest point in Wis., in SE, 8 mi/12.9 km SE of Prentice, and several resort lakes. Formed 1879.

Price, city (1990 pop. 8,712), ⊙ Carbon co., central Utah, on Price R., and 100 mi/161 km SE of Salt Lake City; 39°36′N 110°47′W. Elev. 5,566 ft/1,697 m. Coal-mining center in agr. area (cattle; alfalfa) served by nearby irrigation works on Price R. Mfg. (apparel, machinery). Seat of Col. of Eastern Utah (2 year). Prehistoric Mus. Growth followed arrival of RR (in early 1880s) and discovery of coal. Settled 1879. Manti–La Sal Natl. Forest to W.

Price or **Priceville**, village (1991 pop. 1,962), SE Que., E Canada, on Metis R., near its mouth on the St. Lawrence R., 21 mi/34 km NE of Rimouski; 48°36′N 68°09′W. Lumbering center; hydroelectric station.

Price Island, Canada: see SWINDLE ISLAND.

Price River, 130 mi/209 km long, Utah; rises in Wasatch Range NW of Scofield, on border bet. Sanpete and Utah cos., central Utah; flows generally SE, past Price and through deep canyons, to Green River town 15 mi/24 km NNE of Green R. Scofield Dam (120 ft/37 m high, 575 ft/175 m long; completed 1946), near its source, is used for irrigation.

Pricedale (PREIS-dail), uninc. village (1990 est. pop. 1,500), Rostraver township, Westmoreland co., SW Pa., 13 mi/21 km S of McKeesport, and 2 mi/3.2 km SE of Monessen; 40°07′N 79°50′W. Agr. (hay, corn; dairying; livestock). Reported as Lynnwood-Pricedale (1990 pop. 2,664) by Census Bureau.

Priceville, town (1990 pop. 1,323), Morgan co., N Ala., 8 mi/12.9 km SE of Decatur, on Tennessee R.; 34°31′N 86°53′W. Wheeler Natl. Wildlife Refuge just N.

Priceville, Canada: see PRICE.

Prichard, city (1990 pop. 34,311), Mobile co., SW Ala., an industrial suburb N of Mobile. It developed as a vegetable-shipping point due to the local Mobile and Ohio RR track. Mfg. now includes rubber, lumber, and paper prods. Settled 1900, inc. 1925.

Prickly Bay, inlet, at L'Anse aux Epines, Grenada, W.I. Popular yachting anchorage.

Prickly Pear Creek, 32 mi/51 km long, SW central Mont.; rises in E Jefferson co. in Elkhorn Mts.; flows N, past E Helena, receives Tenmile Creek before entering L. Helena, forms outlet from L. Helena to Missouri R. Now an arm of Hauser L. reservoir. Drains mining and agr. region.

Prides Crossing, Mass.: see BEVERLY.

Prien (PREE-an), uninc. town (1990 pop. 6,448), Calcasieu parish, La., 6 mi/9.7 km SW of Lake Charles (city); 30°06′N 93°10′W. Suburb of Lake Charles.

Priest Lake, in mt. region of N Idaho, in NW Bonner co., 20 mi/32 km NW of Sandpoint, near Wash. state line; 24 mi/39 km long, 1 mi/1.6 km–4 mi/6.4 km wide. Center of resort area. Has several small isls. Fed by Upper Priest R., drained by Priest R. Roosevelt Grove Anc. Cedars, virgin stand of cedar, on W side.

Priest Rapids Lake, reservoir (□ 13 sq mi/34 sq km), Grant, Kittitas, and Yakima cos., S central Wash., on Columbia R., 27 mi/43 km E of Yakima; 46°46′N 119°59′W. Max. capacity 222,600 acre-ft. Formed by Priest Rapids Dam (96 ft/29 m high), built (1959) for power generation; also used for flood control. U.S. Military Reservation, Yakima Training Center just W.

Priest River, town (1990 pop. 1,560), Bonner co., N Idaho, 20 mi/32 km WSW of Sandpoint, and on Pend Oreille R., at mouth of Priest R. (90 mi/145 km long; rises in B.C., W Canada, as Upper Priest R., near Kostenay Pass, Selkirk Mts., 20 mi/32 km W of Creston, B.C.; flows S, through Upper Priest and Priest lakes; becomes Priest R. below lake); 48°11′N 116°55′W. Mfg. (lumber; light mfg.). Albeni Falls Dam to W; Round L. State Park to E. Settled 1889.

Priestly Lake, Piscataquis co., N Maine, 66 mi/106 km WSW of Presque Isle; 3 mi/4.8 km long. In wilderness recreational area.

Prim Point, cape on S coast of P.E.I., E Canada, on Northumberland Strait, at E side of Hillsborough Bay entrance, 15 mi/24 km SSE of Charlottetown; 46°03′N 63°02′W. Lighthouse.

Primera, town (1990 pop. 2,030), Cameron co., extreme S Texas, residential suburb 5 mi/8 km WNW of Harlingen; 26°13′N 97°45′W. Irrigated agr. area (vegetables, citrus, cotton).

Primero de Enero (pree-MER-o dai ai-NAI-ro), sugarmill town, Ciego de Ávila prov., E Cuba, on RR, and 17 mi/27 km SE of Morón; 21°56′N 78°26′W. Small airport just N. Formerly Violeta.

Primghar, town (1990 pop. 950), ⊙ O'Brien co., NW Iowa, 24 mi/39 km N of Cherokee; 43°05′N 95°37′W. In livestock and grain area. Sand and gravel pits nearby. Mill Creek State Park to S.

Primrose 1 town, Meriwether co., W Ga., 17 mi/27 km ENE of La Grange; 33°08′N 84°44′W. **2** uninc. town (1990 pop. 1,154), Cass township, Schuylkill co., E central Pa., 5 mi/8 km W of Pottsville; 40°41′N 76°16′W.

Primrose, village (1990 pop. 69), Boone co., E central Nebr., 12 mi/19 km WSW of Albion, and on Cedar R.; 41°37′N 98°14′W.

Primrose Lake (□ 181 sq mi/469 sq km), W Sask. and E Alta., W Canada, 110 mi/177 km N of Lloydminster; 26 mi/42 km long, 13 mi/21 km wide. Drains into Churchill R. through Beaver R.

Primrose Lake Air Weapons Range, W Sask. and E Alta., W Canada, 100 mi/161 km N of Lloydminster; 40 mi/64 km N-S, 110 mi/177 km E-W (60 mi/97 km in Sask., 50 mi/80 km in Alta.). Weapons testing area for Can. Armed Forces.

Prince, county (□ 778 sq mi/2,015 sq km; 1991 pop. 43,241), in NW part of P.E.I., E Canada; ⊙ Summerside.

Prince Albert, city (1991 pop. 34,181), central Sask., W Canada, on the North Saskatchewan R.; 53°12′N 105°45′W. Commercial and distribution center for a lumbering, gold- and uranium-mining, and mixed-farming area. Wood prods. and meatpacking industries. Founded in 1866 as a Presbyterian mission to the Native Amer. Cree. Gateway to Prince Albert Natl. Park, to the NW. Seat of Anglican and R.C. cathedrals and hq. of the Royal Can. Mounted Police for central and N Sask., as well as the site of the provincial penitentiary.

Prince Albert National Park (□ 1,496 sq mi/3,875 sq km), central Sask., W Canada, NW of Prince Albert, in a forested area. The numerous streams and lakes afford excellent fishing and canoeing. Sanctuary for moose, elk, deer, caribou, bear, pelican, and double-crested cormorant. Administration and tourist hq. are at Waskesiu, on L. Waskesiu. Est. 1927.

Prince Albert Peninsula, NW part of Victoria Isl., SW Franklin dist., N.W.T., N Canada, separated from Banks Isl. by Prince of Wales Strait; 150 mi/241 km long, 80 mi/129 km–150 mi/241 km wide; 72°00′N 115°00′W. Rises to c.1,500 ft/457 m on Adventure Mt. (NW).

Prince Albert Sound, inlet of Amundsen Gulf, off SW Victoria Isl., SW Franklin dist., N.W.T., N Canada; 170 mi/274 km long, 40 mi/64 km wide; 70°30′N 115°00′W.

Prince Edward, county (□ 390 sq mi/1,010 sq km; 1991 pop. 23,763), SE Ont., central Canada, on L. Ontario and on Bay of Quinte; ⊙ Picton; 44°00′N 77°15′W.

Prince Edward, county (□ 353 sq mi/914 sq km; 1990 pop. 17,320), central Va.; ⊙ Farmville; 37°13′N 78°26′W. Rolling agr. area, bounded N by Appomattox R. Mfg. at Farmville; agr. (wheat, barley, tobacco, hay, corn; hogs; dairying); some timber. Twin Lakes State Park, Gallion State Forest in SE. Formed 1753.

Prince Edward Island, province (□ 2,184 sq mi/5,657 sq km; 1991 pop. 129,765), E Canada, across Northumberland Strait from N.B. (linked by bridge) and N.S. (both to S); ⊙ CHARLOTTETOWN; 46°20′N 63°30′W. One of the Maritime provs. Canada's smallest prov., but also has Canada's highest pop. density. The generally low, level land is c.140 mi/225 km long and 5 mi/8 km–35 mi/56 km wide. Sandy beaches line the deeply indented N shore, and much of this favorite resort spot is now P.E.I. Natl. Park (est. 1937). Low, red sandstone cliffs rim the S shores. The tide reaches back into the headwaters of the isl.'s short rivers. With fertile and distinctive red soil and an agreeable climate, the isl. is known as the Garden of the Gulf. About 90% of the land is arable. Agr. and fishing dominate the economy. Since earliest settlement, fishing has been an important industry, yielding an abundance of lobsters, oysters, codfish, halibut, mackerel, and herring. Livestock, fruit, and vegetables are produced, and potatoes (dominant crop) are exported. Harvest of Irish moss seaweed important. Because of the lack of raw materials and cheap sources of power, mfg. is largely limited to food processing, such as the making of butter and cheese and the canning of pork and lobsters. Govt. programs to improve and diversify the economy have had limited success. The tourist industry has experienced the most growth. Traditionally islanders held a monopoly in the breeding of silver foxes from the beginning of the industry, in 1887, until 1912. The Native Amer. Micmac lived here before Europeans arrived. Jacques Cartier wrote enthusiastically about the isl. after landing here in 1534. Samuel de Champlain named it Île St. Jean in 1603, and it was known by that name, or Isle St. John, until 1799, when it was renamed after Edward, duke of Kent, who became the father of Queen Victoria. The 1st permanent settlement was made by the French in 1719 near present-day Charlottetown. The British gained permanent control under the Treaty of Paris in 1763. Many of the Fr. settlers were deported by the British (see ACADIA), but others remained and their descendants still live here. In 1803, Lord Selkirk's 1st colony of impoverished Scots settled here, and their descendants still constitute about 33% of the present inhabitants. In 1763, P.E.I. was annexed to N.S., but it became a separate colony in 1769. Responsible, or cabinet, govt. was granted in 1851. In 1864 delegates from the Maritime Provs. met in Charlottetown to discuss union—the 1st step toward the Can. confederation, achieved in 1867. However, P.E.I. did not join the confederation until 1873. Throughout the 20th cent. the isl.'s economy has been relatively stable, although its lack of energy and technology has caused it to lag behind the rest of Canada. The Conservatives and the Liberals are the only 2 parties to control the provincial govt. since 1873. The prov. sends 4 senators and 4 representatives to the natl. parliament. A musical version of *Anne of Green Gables*, from a book by local author Lucy Maud Montgomery, is performed every summer. The Univ. of P.E.I., the Atlantic Veterinary Col., and Holland Col. are here.

Prince Edward Island Bridge or **P.E.I. Bridge**, fixed link from Jourimain Isl., N.B., to Borden, P.E.I., E Canada, across Northumberland Strait of Gulf of St. Lawrence; 8 mi/13 km long. Sometimes referred to as Northumberland Strait Bridge. Replaced ferry service from Cape Tormentine (N.B.), to Borden. The isl. prov.'s 1st and only direct link to mainland. First (1957) proposal to construct rock-fill causeway was met with opposition from shipping interests and was replaced by bridge-causeway plan. Construction began in 1959, but was halted by Trudeau govt. in 1969 due to serious cost overruns. Only the bridge approaches and rights-of-way acquisition had been completed. In 1986, a proposal competition led to selection of 3, all of them bridge-only plans. Construction resumed in 1990, but was met with continued delay resulting from the sagging economy of Canada and the Maritime provs. and to opposition. The P.E.I. Tourist Board, trucking companies, and the isl. potato growers favored it. Most islanders opposed it, pointing out that the link would

Area in square miles is shown by the symbol □ capital city or county seat by ⊙

bring an increase in seasonal residents and traffic, raise property values, and put isl. businesses in direct competition with mainland concerns. In Dec. 1992, $60 million was appropriated by Can. govt. for the $800-million project. In June 1993, an additional $840 million was appropriated, making the project a certainty. Construction began on bridge approaches in 1995; piers in place on Borden, P.E.I., side. Pier and span sects. were preformed off-site, then placed upon bridge pier shafts. Completed in 1997.

Prince Edward Island National Park (□ 7 sq mi/18 sq km), NW P.E.I., E Canada, on the Gulf of St. Lawrence. Extends 25 mi/40 km along the coast and contains sand dunes, cliffs, salt marshes, and swimming beaches. Est. 1937.

Prince Frederick, village (1990 pop. 1,885), ⊙ Calvert co., S Md., 31 mi/50 km SSW of Annapolis; 38°33′N 76°35′W. In agr. area. Named after a son of George II and the co. seat since 1725, all its old bldgs. were burnt by the British in 1814 and by another fire in 1882. The present courthouse, built in 1916, was remodeled in 1948. Summer-resort area on Chesapeake Bay nearby. Greater accessability via the Patuxent R. bridge and road imputs have led to pop. increase.

Prince George, city (1991 pop. 69,653), central B.C., W Canada, at the confluence of the Fraser and Nechako rivers; 53°55′N 122°46′W. A RR division point and a distributing center for a lumber region. Sawmills, pulp mills, chemical plants, oil refinery; mfg. of paints, plywood, furniture. In 1807, Simon Fraser of the North West Company est. here, on the site the fur-trading post of Fort George, which was taken over (1821) by the Hudson's Bay Company. Settlement began c.1910 with the building of a RR via Fort George to Prince Rupert, and in 1915 the city was incorporated and the name was changed. Seat of Univ. of Northern B.C.

Prince George, county (□ 281 sq mi/728 sq km; 1990 pop. 27,394), E Va.; ⊙ Prince George; independent cities of Hopewell and Petersburg are separate from co.; 37°11′N 77°13′W. In Tidewater region; bounded NW by Appomattox R., N by James R.; source of Blackwater and Nottoway rivers. Agr. (peanuts, corn, wheat, barley, hay, soybeans, cotton, melons; poultry, cattle, hogs). Ft. Lee Military Reservation in NW. Includes part of Petersburg Natl. Battlefield in NW. Formed 1702.

Prince George, uninc. village, ⊙ Prince George co. (since 1785), SE Va., 6 mi/9.7 km E of Petersburg. Mfg. (steel fabrication; bldg. materials, lumber, fabricated metal prods.); agr. area (grain, tobacco, soybeans, melons; cattle). Merchant's Hope Church (1650s). Fort Lee Military Reservation to NW.

Prince Georges, county (□ 499 sq mi/1,292 sq km; 1990 pop. 729,268), central Md., on Va. (W; Potomac R.) state and D.C. line, ⊙ Upper Marlboro; 38°50′N 76°51′W. Bounded E and NE by Patuxent R., drained NW by Anacostia R. Rolling coastal plains, with NW part in the piedmont. Contains many residential suburbs of Washington; agr. sects. produce tobacco, truck, dairy prods., corn, wheat. Some mfg. (esp. machine tools, transportation equip., electronic equip., chemicals). Formed in 1695 and named for Prince George of Denmark, the husband of Queen Anne, it includes Univ. of Md. at College Park, Greenbelt (planned model town), some of the Natl. Capital Parks (W), part of Cedarville State Forest (S), U.S. Dept. of Agr. research center and Patuxent wildlife research center near Beltsville, U.S. Bureau of the Census and Navy Hydrographic Office at Suitland and Andrews Air Force Base, near Camp Springs. A marker on the lawn of the courthouse (started 1881, remodeled 1940–1973) commemorates John (1st Amer. R.C. archbishop) and Daniel (signer of the Declaration of Independence) Carroll born in a house that stood on the site.

Prince Gustav Adolph Sea, W Franklin dist., N.W.T., N Canada, arm, extending S from the Arctic Ocean bet. North and South Borden isls. (W) and Ellef Ringnes Isl. and the Findlay Isls. (E); 140 mi/225 km long, 60 mi/97 km wide; 77°00′–79°00′N 104°00′–109°00′W. Continued S by Byam Martin Channel. Maclean Strait (80 mi/129 km long, 70 mi/113 km wide) is SE arm of the sea. Hazen Strait extends SW.

Prince Leopold Island, central Franklin dist., N.W.T., N Canada, in Barrow Strait, off NE Somerset Isl.; 10 mi/16 km long, 4 mi/6 km wide; 74°00′N 90°00′W.

Prince of Wales, Cape, at the tip of the Seward Peninsula, NW Alaska, on the Bering Strait; westernmost point of N. Amer. Cape Dezhnev (Siberia, Russia) is only 55 mi/89 km to the W.

Prince of Wales Island (□ c.12,800 sq mi/33,150 sq km), N.W.T., N Canada, bet. Victoria and Somerset isls. The low tundra-covered isl. has an irregular coastline and is deeply indented by Ommanney and Browne bays.

Prince of Wales Island, island (□ 2,731 sq mi/7,073 sq km; 1990 pop. 3,278), off SE Alaska; largest isl. of the Alexander Archipelago, in Tongass Natl. Forest; 55°47′N 132°50′W. Heavily forested. Salmon industry brought permanent pop. to isl. in 1870s. Main towns are Hydaburg, Hollis, Craig, Klawock, and Thorne Bay, all connected by road. Many of the islanders left when the pearl shell industry, once profitable, declined after the 1950s. Third-largest isl. under U.S. sovereignty. Highest point, Copper Mt., 3,917 ft/1,194 m.

Prince of Wales Strait, SW Franklin dist., N.W.T., N Canada, arm of the Arctic Ocean, extending from Viscount Melville Sound (NE) to Amundsen Gulf (SW), separating Banks and Victoria isls.; 200 mi/322 km long, 10 mi/16 km–20 mi/32 km wide; 71°30′–73°30′N 115°00′–120°00′W.

Prince Patrick Island 1 (□ 6,696 sq mi/17,343 sq km), Parry Isls., W Franklin dist., N.W.T., N Canada, in the Arctic Ocean, separated from Banks Isl. (S) by McClure Strait, from Melville Isl. (E) by Fitzwilliam Strait; 150 mi/241 km long, 20 mi/32 km–50 mi/80 km wide; 75°43′–77°36′N 115°50′–124°05′W. Irregular SE coastline. Center of isl. is plateau over 1,000 ft/305 m high. At Mould Bay (SE; 76°05′N 119°45′W) is U.S.–Can. weather station. Discovered 1853 by Sir Francis McClintock. **2** (□ 6,119 sq mi/15,848 sq km), westernmost of Queen Elizabeth Isls., N.W.T., N Canada. Low elevation; dissected plateau.

Prince Regent Inlet, S Franklin dist., N.W.T., N Canada, arm of the Arctic Ocean, bet. Lancaster Sound and Barrow Strait (N) and the Gulf of Boothia (S); 150 mi/241 km long, 40 mi/64 km–90 mi/145 km wide; 73°00′N 92°00′W. Separates Somerset Isl. (W) from Brodeur Peninsula of NW Baffin Isl.

Prince Rupert, city (1991 pop. 16,620), W B.C., W Canada, on Kaien Isl., in Chatham Sound near the mouth of the Skeena R., S of the U.S. (Alaska) border; 54°19′N 130°19′W. A RR and highway terminus and an ice-free port, it serves the mining, lumber, and agr. areas of central and W B.C. It is a major fish-processing center, and there are wood-processing plants. The city's growth dates from the arrival (1914) of the RR. During World War II the city was a major supply base for U.S. forces in Alaska. Unstable muskeg has discouraged development; old bldgs. are sagging. Ferry terminus for B.C. and Alaska ferry and ferry to Queen Charlotte Isls.

Prince Rupert Bay, inlet of NW Dominica, B.W.I., 17 mi/27 km NNW of Roseau. Guarded by once strongly fortified hills. Portsmouth is on its NE shore. Site of naval battle (1805), where Rodney defeated the French.

Prince William, county (□ 349 sq mi/904 sq km; 1990 pop. 215,686), N Va.; ⊙ Manassas; independent cities of Manassas and Manassas Park, which adjoin each other, are separate from surrounding co.; 38°42′N 77°28′W. Bounded E by the Potomac R., NE and N by Occoquan and Bull Run rivers. Agr. (corn, wheat, barley, hay, alfalfa, soybeans, tobacco; cattle, sheep, hogs; dairying). Co. has become urbanized (esp. residential) in E since 1980s. Site of Potomac Mills, one of the largest shopping centers in U.S. Manassas Natl. Battlefield Park in N; Prince William Forest Park, a unit of Natl. Capital Parks system, in SE; Leesylvania State Park in E, on Potomac R. Part of Quantico Marine Corps Base in S. George Mason Univ. Prince William campus; Northern Va. Comm. Col. Manassas and Woodbridge campuses. Formed 1731.

Prince William Forest Park (□ 29 sq mi/75 sq km), Prince William co., N Va., 10 mi/16 km SE of Manassas, near Potomac R., in Quantico Creek watershed; 38°35′N 77°22′W. Woodland with 89 species of trees in pure stands. Part of Natl. Capital Parks system. Formerly Chopawamsic Recreation Area. Authorized 1936.

Prince William Sound, large, irregular, islanded inlet of the Gulf of Alaska, S Alaska, E of the Kenai peninsula. It has good harbors. Shipping is focused at the port of Valdez, which is the S terminus of the trans-Alaskan pipeline linked to Prudhoe Bay. Access to the interior of the sound is by highway and RR. Fishing, tourism, and some mining are prevalent activities in the area. Valdez and Cordova are the largest towns on the sound. On Mar. 24, 1989, the *Exxon Valdez* hit a reef nearby and spilled approximately 10 million gal/37,853,000 liters of oil into Prince William Sound. Clean-up efforts followed.

Prince's Bay, a sect. of Staten Isl. borough of N.Y. city, SE N.Y., on S Staten Isl.; 40°32′N 74°11′W. Frederick Law Olmsted worked a farm here in the years before he designed Central Park.

Prince's Lake, town (1990 pop. 1,055), Johnson co., central Ind., 10 mi/16 km SSW of Franklin. Atterbury Fish and Wildlife Area to E; Camp Atterbury military reserve to SE. Livestock; grain, vegetables. Timber.

Princes Town, town, W Trinidad, Trinidad and Tobago, 6 mi/9.7 km E of San Fernando. Trading and sugar-growing center. Formerly a Span. mission among Native peoples. Remarkable small mud volcanoes are nearby (SE).

Princess Anne, town (1990 pop. 1,666), ⊙ Somerset co., SE Md., on the Eastern Shore, 13 mi/21 km SSW of Salisbury, and on Manokin R.; 38°12′N 75°42′W. Processing, shipping center for fruit- and vegetable-farm area (potatoes, strawberries, tomatoes, beans); canneries, lumber and flour mills, clothing factories. Seat of the Univ. of Md., Eastern Shore, which grew out of Princess Anne Col. Laid out in 1733, it became the co. seat in 1742 when Somerset co. was carved out of Worcester co. Notable bldgs. include Washington Hotel (c.1744); Manokin Presbyterian Church (c.1765); St. Andrews Protestant Episcopal Church (c.1767); Beckford (c.1776); and East Glen or Johnston House (c.1800); the Handy Garden (1842).

Princess Marie Bay, E Ellesmere Isl., NE Franklin dist., N.W.T., N Canada, arm of Kane Basin, on N side of Bache Peninsula; 50 mi/80 km long, 8 mi/13 km–15 mi/24 km wide; 79°20′N 76°00′W. It was visited by the *Albert* and *Discovery* of the Nares expedition, 1875–1876; by Peary's *Windward* in 1899; and by Shackleton (1935).

Princess Royal Island (□ 876 sq mi/2,269 sq km), W B.C., W Canada, in Hecate Strait, 20 mi/32 km SE of Pitt Isl., and 1 mi/2 km off the mainland; 52 mi/84 km long, 7 mi/11 km–26 mi/42 km wide; 53°10′N 128°37′W. W coast is deeply indented. Rises to 5,500 ft/1,676 m. Lumbering. Surf Inlet village is N. On NE coast is Butedale village; fish canning. Home of rare white kermode bear, subspecies of black bear.

Princeton, town (1991 pop. 2,796), S B.C., W Canada, in Cascade Mts., on Similkameen R. at mouth of Tulameen R., and 45 mi/72 km W of Penticton; 49°27′N 120°31′W. Elev. 2,133 ft/650 m. Highway junction. Copper and lumbering region; cattle; tourism.

Princeton, village, S Ont., central Canada, 12 mi/19 km ENE of Woodstock. Dairying, mixed farming.

Princeton 1 city (1990 pop. 7,197), ⊙ Bureau co., N Ill., 45 mi/72 km N of Peoria; 41°22′N 89°28′W. In agr. area; nursery, greenhouses; fruit, corn, wheat, soybeans; livestock. Mfg. (food prods., machinery). Laid out 1833, inc. 1849. It was the home of abolitionist Owen Lovejoy. **2** city (1990 pop. 8,127), ⊙ Gibson co., SW Ind., 27 mi/43 km N of Evansville; 38°22′N 87°34′W. Oil and agr. area; oil refining; mfg. (machinery, electrical prods., food prods., fabricated metal prods., rubber prods., plastics; truck assembly). Bituminous-coal mines nearby. Settled c.1812, laid out 1814. **3** city (1990 pop. 6,940), ⊙ Caldwell co., W Ky., 40 mi/64 km E of Paducah; 37°06′N 87°52′W. RR junction (shops); trade and industrial center for agr. (burley tobacco, grain; livestock); mfg. (apparel, foods, lumber, crushed limestone, lumber, wood prods., fabricated metal prods.; meat processing). Princeton-Caldwell Airport to E. Adsmore Mus. (c.1857). Univ. of Ky. Research and Education Center, crop (esp. tobacco) and livestock research. Champion-Sheperdson House (1817). Mineral Mound State Park, on L. Barkley, to SW; Pennyrile Forest State Resort Park to E (on L. Beshear reservoir); Jones-Keeney and Tradewater wildlife management areas to NE. Ky. Reservoir is c.20 mi/32 km SW. Est. 1927; inc. as city after 1930. **4** city (1990 pop. 1,021), ⊙ Mercer co., N Mo., on Weldon R., and 22 mi/35 km N of Trenton; 40°23'N 93°35'W. Corn, soybeans; cattle, hogs. L. Paho to W. Calamity Jane b. here. Settled c.1840, inc. 1853.

Princeton 1 town (□ 7 sq mi/18.1 sq km; 1990 pop. 7,073), Dade co., SE Fla., 22 mi/35 km SW of Miami; 25°32'N 80°24'W. Packs vegetables, cans fruit. **2** town (1990 pop. 806), Scott co., E Iowa, on Mississippi R., 15 mi/24 km NE of Davenport; 41°40'N 90°21'W. **3** town (1990 pop. 973), Washington co., E Maine, near St. Croix R., 35 mi/56 km N of Machias; 45°11'N 67°32'W. Lake dist.; wood prods. Settled 1815, inc. 1832. **4** agr. town (1990 pop. 3,189), Worcester co., N central Mass., 13 mi/21 km NNW of Worcester; 42°27'N 71°53'W. Ski resort. State park here. Mt. Wachusett, highest mt. in central Mass. (2,006 ft/611 m) accessible by road. Settled 1743, inc. 1771. **5** town (1990 pop. 3,719), Mille Lacs co., E Minn., 28 mi/45 km E of St. Cloud, on Rum R. at mouth of West Branch Rum R.; 45°34'N 93°35'W. Shipping point in agr. area; grain, soybeans; livestock, poultry; dairying. Mfg. (fabricated metal prods., wood prods., transportation equip., plastic prods.; printing and publishing). Sherburne Natl. Wildlife Refuge and Sand Dunes State Forest to SW. Plotted 1856, inc. 1877. **6** town (1990 pop. 1,181), Johnston co., central N.C., 10 mi/16 km NW of Goldsboro; 35°28'N 78°09'W. Agr. area (tobacco, cotton, peanuts, grain, potatoes, sweet potatoes; poultry, livestock). Mfg. (clothing, fertilizer, wood prods., crushed stone). **7** town (1990 pop. 2,321), Collin co., N Texas, suburb 32 mi/51 km NE of downtown Dallas, and 7 mi/11.3 km E of McKinney, on urban fringe; 33°22'N 96°30'W. In corn, cotton area; mfg. (transportation equip., marble prods., store fixtures). L. Lavon reservoir to S. **8** town (1990 pop. 7,043), ⊙ Mercer co., S W.Va., 10 mi/16 km NE of Bluefield; 37°22'N 81°05'W. Trade center for bituminous-coal, timber, agr. area. Mfg. (beverages, signs, computers, wood prods., hardwood veneers, machinery, crushed limestone). Camp Creek State Forest to N. Settled 1826. **9** town (1990 pop. 1,458), Green L. co., central Wis., on Fox R., and 35 mi/56 km W of Fond du Lac; 43°51'N 89°07'W. In farm area (dairy prods.; livestock); mfg. hoisery, light mfg. Settled 1830; inc. as village in 1860, as city in 1920.

Princeton 1 village, Dallas co., S central Ark., 17 mi/27 km NW of Fordyce. **2** village (1990 pop. 275), Franklin co., E Kansas, 9 mi/14.5 km S of Ottawa; 38°29'N 95°16'W. Livestock; grain. **3** village, Laurens and Greenville cos., NW S.C., 26 mi/42 km SSE of Greenville, near Saluda R. Agr. includes poultry, livestock; grain; dairying.

Princeton, borough (1990 pop. 12,016), Mercer co., W central N.J.; 40°21'N 74°39'W. A leading education center, it is the seat of Princeton Univ., the Inst. for Advanced Study, Princeton Theological Seminary, Westminster Choir Col., St. Joseph's Col., and other institutions. Home to numerous natl. and internatl. corporate research centers and hq. The Educational Testing Service (ETS) is centered here. Settled late 1600s, called Stony Brook until 1724. In the Amer. Revolution, the British and, later, Colonial troops occupied Nassau Hall (of Princeton Univ.) as barracks. Shortly after the battle of Trenton, Princeton was the scene of a battle (Jan. 3, 1777) in which George Washington surprised and defeated a superior Br. force. Gen. Hugh Mercer was mortally wounded in the attack. A monument with sculptures by Frederick MacMonnies commemorates the battle. "Morven" (1701), home of Richard Stockton, was Cornwallis' hq. and a center of social and political life during and after the Revolution. The Continental Congress met in Nassau Hall June–Nov. 1783. William Bainbridge's birthplace is the hq. of a historical society. Palmer Square, a civic center on Nassau St., has bldgs. designed in Colonial style by Thomas Stapleton. Paul Robeson b. here and Albert Einstein spent the last 20 years of his life here. Inc. 1713.

Princeton, Mount (14,197 ft/4,327 m), central Colo., in Collegiate Range of Sawatch Mts., 9 mi/14.5 km SW of Buena Vista; 38°44'N 106°14'W.

Princeville, town (1991 pop. 3,914), S Que., E Canada, 28 mi/45 km W of Thetford Mines; 46°10'N 71°53'W. Meatpacking, mfg. of furniture, plastics; cattle market.

Princeville 1 town (1990 pop. 1,244), Kauai isl., Kauai co., Hawaii, 17 mi/27 km NNW of Lihue, on N coast, E side of Hanalei Bay, near mouth of Hanalei R.; 22°13'N 159°29'W. Tourism. Hanalei Natl. Wilderness Reserve to SE. Known for its Princeville Golf Course that overlooks Pacific Ocean at Kaweonui Point. **2** town (1990 pop. 1,652), Edgecombe co., E central N.C., suburb 1 mi/1.6 km SE of Tarboro, on Tar R. opposite Tarboro; 35°53'N 77°31'W. Agr. area (tobacco, grain, peanuts, cotton; poultry, livestock).

Princeville, village (1990 pop. 1,421), Peoria co., central Ill., 16 mi/26 km NNW of Peoria; 40°55'N 89°45'W. In agr. area.

Principe Channel (PRIN-si-pee), strait off B.C. coast, W Canada, bet. Pitt and Banks isls.; 50 mi/80 km long, 3 mi/5 km wide.

Principio Furnace (prin-SIP-ee-o), village, Cecil co., NE Md., 4 mi/6.4 km NE of Havre de Grace. The Principio Iron Works were started here in 1719 by Joseph Farmer with capital from England and an ironmaster, John England, who made it one of the most successful in the colonies by the 1740s, producing iron good enough to be sold in London. Thomas Russell, Jr., England's successor, produced cannonballs for the Continental Army during the Revolution. The works, destroyed by the British in 1814, were rebuilt and produced iron until 1925. Part of the stone furnace still remains on the site and is on the Natl. Register of Historic Places.

Prineville (PREIN-vil), town (1990 pop. 5,355), ⊙ Crook co., central Oregon, on Crooked R. at mouth of Ochoco Creek, 28 mi/45 km NE of Bend; 44°18'N 120°50'W. Elev. 2,860 ft/872 m. RR terminus. Mfg. (lumber, wood prods.; printing, publishing). Dairy prods.; grain; livestock. Ochoco State Wayside to W; Ochoco L. State Park to E; Prineville Reservoir and State Park 15 mi/24 km to SE; Crooked R. Natl. Grassland to NW. Hq. of Ochoco Natl. Forest, including Mill Creek Wilderness Area to NE. Settled 1868, inc. 1880.

Prineville Reservoir, Crook co., central Oregon, on Crooked Creek, 13 mi/21 km SSE of Prineville; 12 mi/19 km long; 44°06'N 120°46'W. Max. capacity 235,000 acre-ft. Bear Creek enters from S, near dam. Formed by Prineville Dam (182 ft/55 m high), built (1961) for irrigation and flood control. Prineville Reservoir State Park on N shore.

Pringle, village (1990 pop. 96), Custer co., SW S.Dak., 11 mi/18 km S of Custer; 43°36'N 103°35'W. In farming and ranching area; tourism. Located in Black Hills Natl. Forest near W entrance to Wind Cave Natl. Park.

Pringle, borough (1990 pop. 1,161), Luzerne co., NE central Pa., suburb 2 mi/3.2 km NNW of downtown Wilkes-Barre, on Huntsville Creek; 41°16'N 75°54'W. Inc. 1914.

Prinsburg (PRINZ-buhrg), village (1990 pop. 502), Kandiyohi co., S central Minn., 13 mi/21 km SW of Willmar, on Chetomba Creek; 44°56'N 95°11'W. Mfg. (plastic prods., fertilizers); agr. (grain, sugar beets, beans, alfalfa; poultry, livestock; dairying).

Prior Lake, city (1990 pop. 11,482), Scott co., SE central Minn., residential suburb 20 mi/32 km SSW of downtown Minneapolis; 44°43'N 93°25'W. Grain, soybeans; poultry, livestock; dairying. Mfg. (sand and gravel processing, machining, diverse light mfg.). Prior L. (4 mi/6.4 km long, 1 mi/1.6 km wide) crosses length of city; Spring L. SW of Prior L.

Pripet, Maine: see ISLESBORO.

Pritchett, village (1990 pop. 153), Baca co., SE Colo., 13 mi/21 km W of Springfield, near Bear Creek; 37°22'N 102°51'W. Elev. 4,827 ft/1,471 m. Cattle; wheat. Comanche Natl. Forest to S.

Procter, village, S B.C., W Canada, on Kootenay L., 17 mi/27 km NE of Nelson; 49°37'N 116°57'W. In lumbering and gold-mining (declining) region.

Proctor 1 town (1990 pop. 2,974), St. Louis co., NE Minn., residential suburb 7 mi/11.3 km SW of downtown Duluth, near St. Louis R.; 46°44'N 92°13'W. Agr. to W (vegetables, hay; poultry; dairying); light mfg. Spirit Mt. Ski Area to SW; Jay Cooke State Park to SW. Settled 1893. **2** town (1990 pop. 1,979), including Proctor village, Rutland co., W central Vt., on Otter Creek, just NW of Rutland; 43°38'N 73°02'W. Marble-quarrying and -finishing center since 19th cent. Large marble exhibit.

Proctor, uninc. village (1990 pop. 220), Comanche co., central Texas, near Leon R., 13 mi/21 km NE of Comanche, on E shore of L. Proctor reservoir (Leon R.). In agr., ranching area.

Proctor Lake, reservoir, Comanche co., central Texas, on Leon R., 24 mi/39 km SW of Stephenville; 12 mi/19 km long; 31°59'N 98°46'W. Max. capacity 433,000 acre-ft. Has 9-mi/14.5-km W arm. Formed by Proctor Dam (81 ft/25 m high), built (1965) by Brazos R. Authority for irrigation.

Proctorsville, Vt.: see CAVENDISH.

Proctorville 1 (PRAHK-tuhr-vil), village (1990 pop. 168), Robeson co., S N.C., 10 mi/16 km S of Lumberton; 34°28'N 79°02'W. Grain, tobacco; livestock. **2** village (1990 pop. 765), Lawrence co., S Ohio, on the Ohio R., 17 mi/27 km SE of Ironton; 38°26'N 82°23'W.

Profile Mountain, N.H.: see CANNON MOUNTAIN.

Progreso (pro-GRAI-so), city (1990 pop. 35,280) and township, ⊙ Progreso municipio, Yucatán, SE Mexico, on offshore bar in Gulf of Mexico, 23 mi/37 km N of Mérida; 21°18'N 89°39'W. Railhead; port of entry; minor seaport and beach resort. Port for Mérida (connected by RR).

Progreso 1 (pro-GRE-so), town (1990 pop. 637), Coahuila, N Mexico, 45 mi/72 km NE of Monclova, on Río Salado de Nadadores; 27°28'N 101°00'W. Cereals; candelilla wax; cattle. **2** (pro-GRAI-so), town (1990 pop. 14,467), ⊙ Progreso de Obregón municipio, Hidalgo, central Mexico, on Tula R., and 30 mi/48 km WNW of Pachuca de Soto; 20°20'N 99°12'W. RR terminus; agr. center (corn, wheat, beans, potatoes, fruit; livestock). Also Progreso de Álvaro Obregón.

Progreso (pro-GRAI-so), uninc. town (1990 pop. 1,951), Hidalgo co., S Texas, 20 mi/32 km ESE of McAllen, 2 mi/3.2 km N of Rio Grande (Mex. border); 26°06'N 97°57'W. Privately owned toll bridge to Mexico. Citrus, vegetables. Santa Ana Natl. Wildlife Refuge to W.

Progreso 1 Mexico: see EL PROGRESO INDUSTRIAL. **2** Mexico: see SAN JOSÉ DEL PROGRESO.

Progreso de Álvaro Obregón, Mexico: see PROGRESO.

Progreso de Zaragoza (pro-GRAI-son dai sah-rah-GO-sah), town (1990 pop. 2,170), ⊙ Coahuitlán municipio, Veracruz, E Mexico, in Sierra Madre Oriental, 29 mi/47 km WSW of Papantla; 20°17'N 97°43'W. Also known as El Plan Grande. Corn, sugarcane, fruit. In Totonac Native area.

Progreso, El, Mexico: see EL PROGRESO.

Progreso Industrial, El, Mexico: see EL PROGRESO INDUSTRIAL.

Progreso Lakes (pro-GRAI-so), village (1990 pop. 154), Hidalgo co., S Texas, residential suburb 21 mi/34 km ESE of McAllen, and 1 mi/1.6 km S of Progreso, on Rio Grande (Mex. border); 26°04'N 97°57'W. Toll bridge. Agr. area.

Progress, uninc. town (1990 pop. 9,654), Susquehanna township, Dauphin co., S central Pa., residential suburb 2 mi/3.2 km NE of downtown Harrisburg; 40°17'N 76°50'W.

Project City, uninc. village, Shasta co., N Calif., 8 mi/12.9 km NNE of Redding. Timber; irrigated agr. Shasta L. reservoir, in Whiskeytown-Shasta Natl. Recreation Area, to N; Shasta Dam 3 mi/4.8 km NW.

Promise City, town (1990 pop. 132), Wayne co., S Iowa, 6 mi/9.7 km E of Corydon; 40°45'N 93°09'W.

Area in square miles is shown by the symbol □ capital city or county seat by ⊙

Promontory, Utah, see: GOLDEN SPIKE.

Promontory Point (PRAH-men-tor-ee), Box Elder co., NW Utah, peninsula extending c.20 mi/32 km S into Great Salt L. from N shore and forming W shore of Bear R. Bay. Promontory Mts. rise to 7,075 ft/2,156 m in S. Salt is produced at hamlet in S tip. RR, crossing Great Salt L. E-W, passes through S end of peninsula. Indian Caves on W side.

Prompton, borough (1990 pop. 238), Wayne co., NE Pa., 4 mi/6.4 km W of Honesdale, on Lackawaxen R., which forms Prompton L. reservoir here; 41°35′N 75°19′W. Mfg. (wood prods., lumber, machinery). Agr. area (apples, grain; livestock; dairying).

Prophetstown, village (1990 pop. 1,749), Whiteside co., NW Ill., on Rock R. (bridged here), and 10 mi/16 km S of Morrison; 41°40′N 89°55′W. Trade and shipping center in agr. area. Settled on site of village of Native Amer. prophet White Cloud. Inc. 1859. State Park nearby.

Prospect 1 town (1990 pop. 7,775), New Haven co., SW Conn., 5 mi/8 km SE of Waterbury; 41°30′N 72°58′W. Rural residential. Inc. 1827. **2** town (1990 pop. 2,788), Jefferson co., N Ky., suburb 10 mi/16 km NE of downtown Louisville, on Ohio R.; 38°21′N 85°36′W. Mfg. (fiberglass prods., consumer goods., machinery; printing and publishing). **3** resort town (1990 pop. 542), Waldo co., S Maine, on the Penobscot R., and 14 mi/23 km NE of Belfast; 44°33′N 68°51′W. Site of Fort Knox State Park.

Prospect 1 village (1990 pop. 312), Oneida co., central N.Y., on West Canada Creek, and 15 mi/24 km N of Utica; 43°17′N 75°09′W. **2** village (1990 pop. 1,148), Marion co., central Ohio, 10 mi/16 km SSW of Marion, and on Scioto R.; 40°27′N 83°11′W. Settled 1832, inc. as village 1876.

Prospect, borough (1990 pop. 1,122), Butler co., W Pa., 8 mi/12.9 km WNW of Butler; 40°53′N 80°02′W. Agr. (apples; dairying). L. Arthur reservoir, in Moraine State Park, to NW and N.

Prospect Heights, city (1990 pop. 15,239), Cook co., NE Ill., suburb 37 mi/60 km NW of downtown Chicago, E of Arlington Heights; 42°06′N 87°55′W. Palwaukee Airport in E. Diversified light mfg.

Prospect Heights, village (1990 pop. 19), Fremont co., S central Colo., suburb 1.5 mi/2.4 km SW of Canon City, near Arkansas R.; 38°25′N 105°14′W. Elev. 5,403 ft/1,647 m.

Prospect Park 1 borough (1990 pop. 5,053), Passaic co., NE N.J., just N of Paterson. Mfg. (metal prods., textiles). Chiefly residential. Inc. 1901. **2** borough (1990 pop. 6,764), Delaware co., SE Pa., residential suburb 9 mi/14.5 km SW of downtown Philadelphia, near Darby Creek; 39°53′N 75°18′W. Light mfg. Morton Homestead, Finn.-Scandinavian home site (17th cent.). Inc. 1984.

Prospect Park, municipal park, W central Brooklyn, N.Y. city, SE N.Y., bounded on E by Washington and Ocean aves., S by Parkside Ave., W by Prospect Park SW, N by Flatbush Ave.; 40°40′N 73°59′W. A 562-acre/227-ha public park set on land acquired by the City of Brooklyn in 1855; one of the nation's finest landscaped parks. Designed by Frederick Law Olmstead and Calvert Vaux, who also designed Central, Morningside, and Riverside parks in N.Y. city, the State Reservation Park in Niagara Falls, and South Park in Chicago. Prospect Park has been called by some admirers their best creation. The designers had envisioned connecting Prospect and Central parks with a series of wide, tree-lined boulevards, but the plans never came to fruition. The 2d-largest of Brooklyn's many parks. Contains Lookout Hill, held by Continental Army against the British in 1776 Battle of L.I.; Soldier and Sailor's Memorial Arch; the Du.-style Lefferts Homestead (built 1783); Prospect Park Wildlife Center; Litchfield Villa (c.1860); and an old Quaker cemetery. Grand Army Plaza, Brooklyn Botanical Garden to N.

Prospect Point, N.Y.: see MANHASSET NECK.

Prosper, town (1990 pop. 1,018), Collin co., N Texas, suburb 31 mi/50 km N of downtown Dallas, in urban fringe; 33°14′N 96°47′W. Cotton, corn; mfg. (animal milk substitutes; egg packaging).

Prosperity 1 town (1990 pop. 1,116), Newberry co., NW central S.C., 7 mi/11.3 km SE of Newberry; 34°12′N 81°31′W. Dreher Isl. State Park to SE on L. Murray reservoir. Mfg. includes meat prods., paper and wood prods., clothing. Agr. includes livestock, poultry; grain, soybeans, sorghum. Logging and timber. **2** uninc. town (1990 pop. 1,322), Raleigh co., S W.Va., suburb 4 mi/6.4 km N of Beckley; 37°50′N 81°12′W. Agr. (grain, nursery crops); cattle; mfg. (machinery repair); bituminous coal.

Prosser (PRAH-suhr), town (1990 pop. 4,476), ⊙ Benton co., S Wash., at the falls of Yakima R., 30 mi/48 km W of Pasco; 46°13′N 119°46′W. Apples, peaches, pears, grapes, corn, sugar beets. Wineries. Mfg. (machinery, feeds). Benton Co. Historical Mus. here. Horse Heaven Hills to S. Inc. 1904.

Prosser (PRAW-suhr), village (1990 pop. 77), Adams co., S Nebr., 10 mi/16 km NW of Hastings, near Platte R.; 40°41′N 98°34′W.

Prosser Creek Reservoir, Nevada co., E Calif., on Prosser Creek, 3 mi/4.8 km NNE of Truckee, in Tahoe Natl. Forest; 2.5 mi/4 km long; 39°21′N 120°07′W. Max, capacity of 42,200 acre-ft. Formed by Prosser Dam (133 ft/41 m high), built (1962) by the Bureau of Reclamation for flood control.

Protection, village (1990 pop. 625), Comanche co., S Kansas, 9 mi/14.5 km SW of Coldwater; 37°12′N 99°28′W. Shipping point for wheat, livestock, and dairy area.

Protivin, town (1990 pop. 305), Howard co., NE Iowa, 10 mi/16 km S of Cesco; 43°13′N 92°05′W. Feed milling.

Prouts Neck (PROUTS), SW Maine, peninsula at mouth of Nonesuch R., 10 mi/16 km SSW of Portland; c.2 mi/3.2 km long. Prouts Neck village is in Scarborough town.

Provencal (PRO-vawn-sal), town (1990 pop. 538), Natchitoches parish, La., 10 mi/16 km SW of Natchitoches; 31°39′N 93°12′W. In timber area.

Providence, county (□ 416 sq mi/1,077 sq km; 1990 pop. 596,270), N R.I., on Conn. (W) and Mass. (N) state lines; ⊙ PROVIDENCE, ⊙ R.I.; 41°52′N 71°35′W. Largest city of state and industrial center. Resorts, recreational fisheries, gravel pits, agr. (dairy prods.; poultry). Includes Scituate, Smith and Sayles, and Pascoag reservoirs; drained by Blackstone (here becoming the Seekonk), Providence, Woonasquatucket, Moshassuck, Pawtuxet, and Ten Mile river systems. Inc. 1703.

Providence, city (1990 pop. 160,728), ⊙ state and of Providence co., NE R.I., a port at the head of Narragansett Bay; 41°49′N 71°25′W. The largest city in the state and one of the 3 largest in New England, it is a port of entry and a major trading center. The bay receives the Seekonk and other rivers, opens into Narragansett Bay, and forms an excellent harbor into which oil and other cargoes are shipped. Widely known as a silverware- and jewelry-mfg. and banking, insurance, and medical center. Textiles, machinery, metal prods., electronic equip., plastic goods, and machine tools are also made, and there are printing and publishing enterprises. Roger Williams chose this site in 1636 after he was exiled from Mass. He secured title to the land from Native Narragansett chiefs and named the place in gratitude for "God's merciful providence." The settlement grew as a refuge for religious dissenters. Many of its bldgs. were burned in King Philip's War (1675–1676). Prosperity came in the 18th cent. with foreign commerce, and after the Amer. Revolution, industrial development was rapid. The Brown brothers, John, Nicholas, and Moses, played leading roles in the growth of the town, prospering in foreign trade and fostering the textile and other industries. In 1842, Thomas W. Dorr led a rebellion that collapsed after an abortive assault on the armory here. The city became sole capital of R.I. in 1900 (Newport had been joint capital until then). In 1901 the state legislature began to meet in the impressive marble-domed capitol designed by McKim, Mead, and White. Seat of the noted R.I. School of Design and Mus. of Art, some of whose work is related to the city's famous silverware and jewelry industry; and of Brown Univ., Johnson and Wales Col. and Culinary Archives and Mus., Providence Col., R.I. Col., and the New England Inst. of Technology. It has several noted lib., including the John Carter Brown Lib. of Brown Univ. and the Athenaeum (1753), one of the oldest libraries in the U.S. Among the city's many historic structures are the old statehouse (where the general assembly met 1762–1900; now a courthouse), the old market bldg. (1773), Stephen Hopkins House (c.1755), John Brown House (1786), and the First Baptist Meetinghouse (1775; the congregation was organized in 1638). The city has monuments to Oliver Hazard Perry (1928) and Nathanael Greene (1931). On Prospect Terrace is Leo Friedlander's heroic statue of Roger Williams (1939). Another memorial to the founder is in Roger Williams Park, which contains a mus. of natural history and a natural amphitheater. Providence suffered severely in hurricanes in 1938 and 1954; a hurricane barrier was completed in 1966. Inc. as a city 1832.

Providence 1 town (1990 pop. 4,123), Webster co., W Ky., 15 mi/24 km WNW of Madisonville; 37°23′N 87°45′W. In bituminous-coal, timber, and agr. (tobacco, corn, hay; livestock) area. Mfg. (consumer goods, apparel, machinery, plastic goods; printing and publishing, coal processing, heavy steel bending). Providence–Webster Co. Airport to NE. **2** town (1990 pop. 3,344), Cache co., N Utah, just S of Logan; 41°42′N 111°48′W. Elev. 4,600 ft/1,402 m. Trading point in wheat, barley, vegetables, and fruit area; dairying. Mfg. paper goods. Limestone quarrying nearby. Settled 1859 by Mormons. Wasatch Natl. Forest to E.

Providence Bay, village, S central Ont., central Canada, on S Manitoulin Isl., on L. Huron, 28 mi/45 km SW of Little Current. Fishing; lumbering.

Providence, Cape, S Melville Isl., W Franklin dist., N.W.T., N Canada, on Viscount Melville Sound, at SE end of McClure Strait; 74°24′N 112°30′W.

Providence Channels, Bahama Isls.: see NORTHWEST PROVIDENCE CHANNEL or NORTHEAST PROVIDENCE CHANNEL.

Providence Forge, uninc. village, New Kent co., E Va., near the Chickahominy R., 23 mi/37 km ESE of Richmond; 37°26′N 77°02′W. Mfg. (wood prods., lumber); agr. (grain, soybeans; poultry, cattle). Iron foundry est. here in 1770. State game farm nearby.

Providence River, estuary, 8 mi/12.9 km long, E R.I.; receives Seekonk R. and small Woonasquatucket and Moshassuck rivers at Providence; extends S to head of Narragansett Bay; N part is harbor of Providence.

Providenciales, Turks and Caicos Isls.: see BLUE HILLS.

Province Lake, N.H.: see WAKEFIELD.

Provincetown (PRAW-vins-toun), resort town (1990 pop. 3,561), Barnstable co., SE Mass., on the tip of Cape Cod, with a harbor on Cape Cod Bay, and 24 mi/39 km NNE of Barnstable; 42°04′N 70°11′W. The principal industries are tourism and fishing. Airport; ferry service from Boston. The Pilgrims landed here in 1620 and stayed about a month before moving on to Plymouth. Permanent Eur. settlement was not made until c.1700. Fishing was always the town's staple industry, but whaling, salt making, rum running, and smuggling were also practiced. In the 20th cent. the town gained fame as a resort favored particularly by artists. Points of interest include the granite Pilgrim Monument and Mus. (1910); the Cape Cod Natl. Seashore's visitor center; whale watching; and the Provincetown Playhouse. Inc. 1727.

Provo (PRO-vo), city (1990 pop. 86,835), ⊙ Utah co., N central Utah, 40 mi/64 km SSE of Salt Lake City, on the Provo R. near Utah L., at mouth of Provo R.; 40°15′N 111°38′W. Elev. 4,490 ft/1,369 m. RR junction. It is a distribution, processing, and mfg. center in an extensive mining (silver, lead, copper, gold) and irrigated-farm and fruit-growing area. A major source of employment is a large steel mill nearby. Pop. grew by over 30% bet. 1970 and 1990. Mfg. includes electronic equip., apparel, concrete prods., herbal prods. and health supplements, fabricated metal prods., computer software; book publishing, coal tar refining, iron casting. Settled by Mormons in 1849 and successfully defended against Native Americans in a war (1865–1868). RR connections from Salt Lake City (1873) and Scofield (1878) made it a shipping point for the region's mines. Seat of Brigham Young Univ. and Utah Valley Community Col. in neighboring Orem (N). A Mormon temple and tabernacle are also located here. Nearby are the Uinta Natl. Forest (E), with hq. here; a state fish hatchery; a wild bird refuge; and Provo Peak (11,070 ft/ 3,374 m). Utah L. State Park, Provo Boat Harbor, and Provo Municipal Airport on lakefront. Bridal Veils Falls and Sundance Ski Area to NE, Rock Canyon in E part of city. Inc. 1851.

Provo River, c.70 mi/110 km long, Utah; rises in the Uinta Mts., Wasatch Natl. Forest, S Summit co., NE Utah; flows SW through Jordanelle and Deer Creek reservoirs, through Wasatch Range, past Provo and Orem to Utah L. It was early used for irrigation, but after Utah L. was badly depleted in the 1930s, the Bureau of Reclamation rehabilitated the old irrigation installations and built new ones centering on the Provo R. The project also gets water from the Weber R. by a canal (built 1929–1930; enlarged 1941–1947) and from the Duchesne R., a tributary of the Green R., by a tunnel (completed 1942) across the mt. divide. The water is used to irrigate the valley of Utah L. and to supply the needs of the towns there; in addition, Salt Lake City is served by the 42-mi/68-km Salt L. Aqueduct (completed 1951). The Deer Creek Dam (completed 1941; 40°19′N 111°30′W) is the chief dam on the Provo R.; it impounds a large reservoir and has a power plant.

Provost (PRO-vost), town (1991 pop. 1,776), E Alta., W Canada, near Sask. border, 40 mi/64 km SE of Wainwright; 52°21′N 110°16′W. Grain elevators.

Prowers, county (□ 1,644 sq mi/4,258 sq km; 1990 pop. 13,347), SE Colo., on Kansas (E) state line; ⊙ Lamar; 37°57′N 102°24′W. Irrigated agr. area drained by Arkansas R., also Two Buttes and Big Sandy creeks. Clay, wheat, hay, sorghum, barley, corn; cattle. Formed 1889.

Pruden (PROO-duhn), village, Bell co., SE Ky., in the Cumberland Mts. W of Middlesboro, on Tenn. state line. Bituminous coal.

Prudence Island, in Portsmouth town, SE R.I., in Narragansett Bay, 12 mi/19 km S of Providence; 6 mi/ 9.7 km long. Resort area; site of Prudence village. Revolutionary skirmishes fought here, 1776. Public fishing areas.

Prud'homme (PROO-duhm), village (1991 pop. 184), central Sask., W Canada, 35 mi/56 km ENE of Saskatoon. Wheat.

Prunedale, uninc. town (1990 pop. 7,393), Monterey co., W Calif,. 10 mi/16 km N of Salinas, 5 mi/8 km E of Monterey Bay, Pacific Ocean, in Gabilan Range; 36°48′N 121°40′W. Cattle; dairying; vegetables. Fremont Peak State Park to E.

Pryor (PREI-uhr) or **Pryor Creek**, town (1990 pop. 8,327), ⊙ Mayes co., NE Okla., 35 mi/56 km ENE of Tulsa; 36°17′N 95°19′W. Elev. 633 ft/193 m. Trade center for agr. area; mfg. (paper, wood, concrete, and metal prods., transportation equip., furniture, chemicals, dairy prods., machinery, bldg. materials, ceramic fiber, food prods.). A U.S. agr. experiment station and a state home for children are here. Snowdale and Salina state parks to E, on L. Hudson reservoir (Neosho R.). Settled 1872 on site of old trading post (1820).

Pryor, village (1990 pop. 654), Big Horn co., S Mont., 26 mi/42 km S of Billings, on Pryor Creek, in W part of Crow Indian Reservation; 45°25′N 108°32′W. Cattle; grain, hay, sugar beets, beans. Chief Plenty Coups State Park and Chief Plenty Coups Mus. to W, home and burial site of last great Crow war chief. Pryor Mts. and Custer Natl. Forest to S.

Ptarmigan Peak 1 (13,739 ft/4,188 m), in Park Range, Lake and Park cos., N central Colo., 8 mi/12.9 km SSE of Leadville; 39°09′N 106°10′W. **2** (12,498 ft/3,809 m), Summit and Grand cos., in Williams River Mts., N central Colo., 4 mi/6.4 km NE of Silverthorne; 39°41′N 106°01′W.

Puako (POO-ah-KO), village (1990 pop. 397), N Hawaii

isl., Hawaii co., Hawaii, on Kawaihae Bay, Kohala (NW) Coast, 50 mi/80 km NW of Hilo; 19°56′N 155°52′W. Cattle ranching to E. Resorts, golf courses. Hapuna Beach State Park to N. Puako Petroglyph Archaeological Reserve here. Whale watching in winter.

Pubnico (PUHB-ni-ko), village, W N.S., E Canada, at head of Pubnico Harbour (8 mi/13 km long) of the Atlantic Ocean, 19 mi/31 km SE of Yarmouth; 43°42′N 65°47′W. Fisheries; lobster packing. Pop. is of Acadian origin.

Puckaway, Lake, widening of Fox R., in Green Lake co., central Wis., SW of Green L., 33 mi/53 km W of Fond du Lac; c.7 mi/11.3 km long, c.2 mi/3.2 km wide.

Puckett, village (1990 pop. 294), Rankin co., central Miss., 26 mi/42 km SE of Jackson, near Strong R.; 32°04′N 89°46′W. Timber. Agr. area (cotton, corn; poultry, cattle). Natural gas. Mfg. (transportation equip.; natural-gas and sulphur processing). Bienville Natl. Forest to E.

Puebla (poo-E-blah), state (□ 13,126 sq mi/33,996 sq km; 1990 pop. 4,126,101), E central Mexico; ⊙ Heroica Puebla de Zaragoza; 17°53′N 96°46′W. The state is divided bet. high plateau in the W and rugged mts. in the N and E. N Puebla is dominated by the Sierra Madre Oriental, and the Transverse Volcanic Axis, which stretches across the central part of the state. Mexico's 3 highest peaks — CITLALTÉPETL in the E and POPO-CATÉPETL and IXTACIHUATL in the W — border on Puebla. The state's extreme NE sect. lies on the humid coastal plain of the Gulf of Mexico; the S part is in drier upland valleys. Differences in climate and elev. permit the cultivation of a variety of agr. prods., although corn and cereal grains are dominant. Livestock raising is also important. The majority of the state's pop. is engaged in agr. Puebla has a diverse industrial sector as well, including motor vehicles, textile, and various light mfg. The state's resources include gold, silver, copper, and lead, but mining is not significantly developed. Communications within the state are excellent.

Pueblo (PWEB-lo), county (□ 2,397 sq mi/6,208 sq km; 1990 pop. 123,051), S central Colo.; ⊙ Pueblo; 38°08′N 104°30′W. Industrial and irrigated agr. area; cattle; wheat, hay, beans, sorghum, corn. Mfg. (foods, machinery, transportation equip., electronic equip., bldg. prods., fabricated metal prods., plastic prods., fuel oil, beverages, vinyl prods., consumer goods; printing and publishing). Drained by Arkansas, St. Charles rivers at Pueblo. Apishapa R. in SE. Includes part of San Isabel Natl. Forest; Pueblo Reservoir and Pueblo State Park in W; part of Fort Carson Military Reserve in NW. Pueblo Ordnance Depot and U.S. Dept. of Transportation High Speed Test Center in NE. Formed 1861.

Pueblo, city (1990 pop. 98,640), ⊙ Pueblo co., S central Colo., c.40 mi/64 km SSE of Colorado Springs, on the Arkansas R. in the foothills of the Rockies; 38°16′N 104°37′W. Elev. 4,695 ft/1,431 m. Front Range to NW, Wet Mts. to SW. It is the center of shipping, retail, and industry for the irrigated Arkansas valley farm area, as are coalfields and abundant timber, cattle, wheat, beans, corn, sorghum. A trading post, called Pueblo, was est. here in 1842, followed by a temporary Mormon settlement (1846–1847). The city was laid out in 1860. After a severe flood in 1921, levees were constructed to control the Arkansas R.; a dam impounding Pueblo Reservoir and Pueblo State Park to W was also built. Construction on an ambitious Arkansas R. reclamation project, designed to serve irrigation, rediversion, and power purposes, began in 1964. Seat of the Univ. of Southern Colo. and the the hq. for San Isabel Natl. Forest. Fort Carson Military Reserve to NW; Pueblo Army Depot (chemical weapons) to E. U.S. Dept. of Transportation High Speed Test Center to NE. Colo. State Fair (Aug.). Pueblo Zoo, El Pueblo Mus., Sangre de Cristo Arts and Conference Center, Pueblo Community Col. here. Pueblo Municipal Airport to E. Inc. 1885.

Pueblo Nuevo (poo-AI-blo noo-AI-vo), city (1990 pop. 3,804) and township, Guanajuato, central Mexico, on

Lerma R., and 11 mi/18 km S of Irapuato. Grain, alfalfa, beans, sugarcane, fruit.

Pueblo Nuevo (PWAI-blo noo-AI-vo), town, Granma prov., E Cuba, 32 mi/51 km NW of Santiago de Cuba; 20°11′N 76°31′W. In fruit and sugar region.

Pueblo Nuevo (PWAI-blo noo-AI-vo), S residential sect. of Matanzas, Matanzas prov., W Cuba; 23°04′N 81°32′W.

Pueblo Nuevo 1 Mexico: see EL SALTO. **2** Mexico: see CUAUTITLÁN.

Pueblo Nuevo Solistahuacán (poo-AI-blo noo-AI-vo so-lees-tah-wah-KAHN), town (1990 pop. 4,964), Chiapas, S Mexico, in N spur of Sierra Madre, 32 mi/ 51 km NNE of Tuxtla Gutiérrez, on Mexico Highway 195; 17°06′N 92°53′W. Elev. 5,367 ft/1,636 m. Zoque, Tzotzil, and Maya-speaking pop. in rural area. Cereals, fruit.

Pueblo Reservoir (PWEB-lo) (□ 10 sq mi/26 sq km), Pueblo co., S central Colo., on Arkansas R., just W of Pueblo; 38°23′N 104°44′W. Max. capacity 489,116 acreft. Formed by Pueblo Dam (250 ft/76 m high), built (1975) by the Bureau of Reclamation for irrigation; also used for flood control and recreation. Pueblo State Park on N shore.

Pueblo Viejo, Mexico: see CIUDAD CUAUHTÉMOC.

Pueblo Viejo, Mexico: see CASAS GRANDES.

Pueblo West, village (1990 pop. 4,386), Pueblo co., S central Colo., 4 mi/6.4 km NW of downtown Pueblo; 38°21′N 104°43′W. Elev. 4,960 ft/1,512 m. Mfg. of wood prods., machinery; steel fabricating. Pueblo Reservation and State Park to SW.

Puente, Calif.: see LA PUENTE.

Puente de Ixtla (poo-EN-tai dai EESH-tlah), town (1990 pop. 17,815), Morelos, central Mexico, 22 mi/ 35 km SSW of Cuernavaca, on Mexico Highway 95, on RR; 18°32′N 99°36′W. Rice, sugarcane, fruit, vegetables.

Puente Nacional (PWEN-tai nah-see-o-NAHL), town (1990 pop. 422), E central Veracruz, Mexico, 13 mi/ 21 km NW of Veracruz, on RR, on Mexico Highway 140; 19°20′N 96°26′W. Mountainous terrain to the S with mostly plains in the E. Water from La Antigua R. Hot climate. Agr. (corn, beans, sugarcane, tropical fruits), woods; poultry breeding.

Puerca, Point (PWER-kah), easternmost cape of isl. of P.R., 7 mi/11.3 km SE of Fajardo; 18°14′N 65°36′W.

Puerta de Golpe (PWER-tah dai GOL-pai), town, Pinar del Río prov., W Cuba, on RR, and 9 mi/14.5 km ENE of Pinar del Río; 22°26′N 83°34′W. Tobacco, fruit, vegetables.

Puerto Angel (poo-ER-to AHN-hel), village, Oaxaca, S Mexico, minor sheltered port on the Pacific Ocean, 42 mi/68 km W of San Pedro Pochutla, 100 mi/161 km S of Oaxaca de Juárez; 15°40′N 96°32′W. Resort development. Air service.

Puerto Boniato (PWER-to bo-nee-AH-to), resort village, Santiago de Cuba prov., E Cuba, in hills 5 mi/ 8 km N of Santiago de Cuba, with noted view of Santiago de Cuba; 22°07′N 75°49′W. Sometimes Puerto de Boniato.

Puerto Escondido (PWER-to es-kon-DEE-do), port (1990 pop. 8,194), San Pedro Mixtepec municipio, Oaxaca, S Mexico, minor port on Pacific coast, 42 mi/ 68 km W of San Pedro Pochutla, on Mexico Highway 200. Resort development, air service.

Puerto Esperanza (PWER-to es-pai-RAHN-zuh), town, Pinar del Río prov., W Cuba, minor port on N coast, 24 mi/39 km N of Pinar del Río; 22°47′N 83°43′W. Swimming, fishing (esp. bonito and lobster). Also La Esperanza.

Puerto Jobos, P.R.: see JOBOS.

Puerto Libertador or **Libertador**, Dominican Republic: see PEPILLO SALCEDO.

Puerto México, Mexico: see COATZACOALCOS.

Puerto Padre (PWER-to PAH-drai), town, Las Tunas prov., E Cuba, on sheltered Puerto Padre Bay (Atlantic Ocean), and 30 mi/48 km NE of Holguín; 21°12′N 76°37′W. Sugar port and trading center for fertile, irrigated region (sugarcane, tobacco, fruit; livestock). In 1994 9.5% of Cuba's sugar exports came through here.

Port has facilities for bulk grain and liquid cargo handling. Sugar mills, tobacco factories, brick- and lumberyards. Nearby are the sugar mills Antonio Guiteras (2 mi/3.2 km E) and Jesús Menéndez (7 mi/11.3 km E). Saltworks NE; also asphalt deposits in vicinity.

Puerto Padre Bay (PWER-to PAH-drai), sheltered harbor, on Atlantic coast of E Cuba, Las Tunas prov., 30 mi/48 km NW of Holguín, linked with ocean by narrows; c.6 mi/9.7 km long, 2 mi/3.2 km wide; 21°13′N 76°36′W. At its head is the town of Puerto Padre. Adjoining E is larger Chaparra Bay.

Puerto Peñasco (PWER-to pain-YAHS-ko), town (1990 pop. 26,625), Sonora, NW Mexico, 56 mi/90 km SW of Sonoita; 31°19′N 113°12′W. Fishing port on the Gulf of California. One of Mexico's most important shrimp-fishing centers; tourism at resort of Cholla Bay.

Puerto Plata (PWER-to PLAH-tah), province (□ 809 sq mi/2,095 sq km; 1993 pop. 255,061), N Dominican Republic, on the Atlantic Ocean; ⊙ Puerto Plata; 19°45′N 70°45′W. Crossed by the Cordillera Central. Fertile agr. region: coffee, cacao, tobacco, sugarcane, rice, corn, tropical fruit. Also much dairying. Puerto Plata city is leading port on N coast. Other centers are Altamira, Imbert, and Luperón. Ruins of Isabela, reputedly 1st town settled by the Spanish in Americas, are 9 mi/14.5 km W of Luperón. Created 1875.

Puerto Plata (PWER-to PLAH-tah), city (1993 pop. 85,042), ⊙ Puerto Plata prov., N Dominican Republic, on the Atlantic Ocean. It is the major N port of the country, serving Santiago de los Caballeros and other inland towns. Dairy and cacao prods. are made here. The surrounding region contains among the largest deposits of amber in the world, with downtown amber mus. Tourism has become Puerto Plata's economic mainstay, and resort beaches at "Playa Durado" have been quickly developed. Nearby airport. Nearby are the ruins of Columbus' 1st settlement in the New World. Founded in 1895.

Puerto Ponce (PWER-to PON-sai), port section of Ponce, S P.R. Second-most important port of the isl., with fine harbor. Warehouses, docks. Adjoining beaches.

Puerto Príncipe, Santa Maria del, Cuba: see CAMAGÜEY.

Puerto Real 1 (PWER-to rai-AHL), village, SW P.R., on bay of Mona Passage, 8 mi/12.9 km SSW of Mayagüez. A prosperous port of entry in colonial era, it is now an important fishing center. Across the bay are the Cabo Rojo salt mines. **2** village, near SW coast of Vieques Isl., E P.R., 3 mi/4.8 km SW of Isabela Segunda. Tourism. Founded 1816 as a fort.

Puerto Real (PWER-to re-AHL), port for Playa de Fajardo, NE P.R.

Puerto Rico (PWER-to REE-ko), town, ⊙ Puerto Rico municipio, Caqueta dept., S Colombia, 31 mi/50 km NE of Florencia, in the Oriente. Sugarcane, corn, cassava; livestock.

Puerto Rico (POR-to REE-ko), island (□ 3,425 sq mi/8,871 sq km; 1990 pop. 3,522,037), W.I., c.1,000 mi/1,610 km SE of Miami, Fla.; ⊙ SAN JUAN. Officially known as the Commonwealth of P.R. (a self-governing entity in association with the U.S.), it includes the offshore isls. of Mona, Monito, Desecheo, Vieques, and Culebra. Important cities include San Juan, PONCE, CAGUAS, and MAYAGÜEZ. Smallest and easternmost of the Greater Antilles, P.R. is bounded by the Atlantic Ocean on the N and the Caribbean Sea on the S. Mona Passage to the W separates the isl. from the Dominican Republic, and the U.S. V.I. lie to the E. P.R. is crossed by mt. ranges, notably the Cordillera Central, which rises to 4,389 ft/1,388 m in the Cerro de Punta. Although rivers are short and unnavigable, some in the N or windward side of the mts. provide irrigation or hydroelectric power. The climate ranges from humid tropical in the N to tropical and dry in the SW. Hurricanes are likely to occur bet. Aug. and Oct. P.R.'s fertile soil supports one of the densest pops. in the world. Sugar milling has declined significantly, only 3 mills remain. Coffee, pineapples, and other fruits are other leading crops, and vegetable growing and canning are increasingly important. Reforestation has been undertaken to restore the tropical woods of the interior, where the Caribbean Natl. Forest is set apart. Heavy industry and mfg. have come to replace agr. as the greatest contributors to P.R.'s natl. income largely because of "Operation Bootstrap," which since the 1940s has attracted U.S. firms through the use of tax exemptions. Machinery mfg. and chemical industries, electrical and high-technology equip., and food processing are among the most important, along with oil refining (using crude oil from Venezuela) and the production of petrochemicals. Tourism is also a major industry. P.R.'s mineral resources are limited and not fully exploited. The U.S. is by far P.R.'s chief trading partner. The leading exports include apparel, pharmaceuticals and other petrochemical prods., machinery, and chemicals. Imports consist mainly of food prods. as well as such consumer items as motor vehicles and home appliances. Although P.R. is no longer dependent on a single-crop economy and has reduced its unemployment rate, overpopulation and insufficient jobs have contributed to social and economic problems and to heavy migration (mainly to N.Y.). The Puerto Ricans are descended from Span. colonists, and also from Taino and Carib Native Americans and Africans. Span. and Eng. are the official languages, although Span. is by far predominant. Roman Catholicism is the main religion. Before the Spanish arrived the isl. was inhabited by the Arawak people, who called the region Borinquén or Boriquén. Christopher Columbus visited the isl. in 1493 and named it San Juan Bautista [St. John the Baptist], but he sailed on to Hispaniola to plant a settlement. Juan Ponce de León began the actual conquest in 1508, landing at San Juan harbor, which he called P.R. [Span. = rich port]. As hardship, disease, and Span. massacres eliminated the Arawaks altogether, they were replaced as plantation workers by Afr. slaves, 1st introduced in 1513. In 1595, Sir Francis Drake unsuccessfully attacked San Juan. George Clifford, earl of Cumberland, held the city for 5 months in 1598, and the Dutch besieged the isl. in 1625. Spain's response was to build several fortresses (whose walls still stand) that made San Juan virtually impregnable. As part of a reform movement that extended to P.R., slavery was abolished in 1873, and the new Span. constitution of 1876 granted P.R. representation in Spain's parliament. A movement for self-govt., supported by liberal groups in Spain, grew in P.R. during the 1880s. Finally, in Feb. 1898, largely through the efforts of the P.R. statesman Luis Muñoz Rivera, Spain granted the isl. some autonomy. The new form of govt. had little chance to operate, however, for a few months later the Span.-Amer. War erupted. U.S. troops occupied the isl. without much difficulty. By the Treaty of Paris (Dec. 10, 1898), which ended the war, P.R. was ceded to the U.S. It remained under direct military rule until 1900, when the U.S. Congress passed the Foraker Act, setting up an administration with a U.S. governor, an upper legislative chamber appointed by the U.S. President, and an elected house of delegates; the U.S. Congress was given the right to review all legislation. Meanwhile, a movement for P.R. independence gained strength as pressures to define the isl.'s political status grew. In 1917 the Jones Act stipulated that P.R. was a U.S. territory whose inhabitants were entitled to U.S. citizenship. The act provided for election of both houses of the P.R. legislature, but the governor and other key officials were still to be appointed by the U.S. President, and the governor was empowered to veto any legislation. During World War I, U.S. holdings in P.R. increased, and the change to a 1-crop sugar economy was completed. The isl.'s territorial status gave P.R. sugar a ready market within U.S. tariff walls; however, large sugar corporations encroached on land where foods had been raised for subsistence, thus causing social upheaval in the countryside and necessitating greater food imports. Absentee ownership and 1-crop culture aggravated the ills of overpopulation. Sanitary and health improvements under the U.S. occupation further accelerated pop. growth. Many Puerto Ricans criticized the Amer. regime for its conflict with the Hispanic roots of P.R. culture. Criticism intensified when the sugar market dropped in the 1930s and many workers, always near the edge of starvation, became even more desperate. Recovery measures were taken during the presidency of Franklin Delano Roosevelt, when public works were launched, and esp. under the governorship (1941–1946) of Rexford G. Tugwell. Military activities related to World War II also aided the economy. The Popular Democratic party, headed by Luis Muñoz Marín, adopted a program based on economic reform and expansion, but other political parties were more concerned with U.S.-P.R. relations. The Conservative Republicans advocated statehood; the Independentists, led by Gilberto Concepción, and the Nationalists, headed by Pedro Albizu Campos, favored immediate independence. In 1946, the U.S. govt. granted P.R. increased local autonomy, exemplified by the appointment of the 1st native P.R. governor, Jesus T. Piñero. The right of popular election of the governor followed, and Muñoz Marín won the 1948 election. His administration undertook a program of agr. reform and industrial expansion called "Operation Bootstrap." On July 25, 1952, the Commonwealth of P.R. was proclaimed. The continuing Nationalist campaign for independence, however, was dramatized by an attempt to assassinate President Harry S. Truman in 1950 and by a shooting attack in the U.S. House of Representatives in 1954. Muñoz Marín was reelected in 1952, 1956, and 1960. Declining to run for reelection in 1964, he was succeeded by his Popular Democratic party's candidate, Roberto Sánchez Vilella. In the face of an increasingly active movement for statehood, the governor arranged for a plebiscite in 1967 in which Puerto Ricans could choose among independence, statehood, and maintenance of the commonwealth relationship. An overwhelming majority voted in favor of the commonwealth. P.R.'s status continues to be an important issue, with the citizens almost equally divided bet. the choices of statehood and remaining a commonwealth; a small percentage desire independence. P.R. would lose important tax shelters if it became a state and could be forced to adopt a much wider use of Eng. A 1991, isl.-wide vote rejected an amendment that would have "reviewed" commonwealth status. In 1992, New Progressive party (which advocates statehood) candidate Pedro Rosello was elected governor. P.R.'s governor and both legislative houses are popularly elected for 4-year terms. There are 27 senators and 51 representatives. An elected resident commissioner sits in the U.S. House of Representatives but cannot vote. The governor may serve an unlimited number of terms. On the local level, P.R. is divided into municipalities, each with its own mayor and assembly. Puerto Ricans in the isl. share all the rights and obligations of U.S. citizenship, including service in the armed forces; however, they do not pay Federal taxes and cannot vote in natl. elections. The U.S. govt. handles P.R.'s foreign affairs, and U.S. military installations are maintained here. Since P.R.'s relationship with the U.S. began, illiteracy has been greatly reduced. Although Span. is the medium of instruction, Eng. is a 2d language studied by all Puerto Ricans. By the late 1950s the commonwealth was able to provide a basic education for all children of elementary school age. The isl.'s rural vocational schools are exemplary. Institutions of higher learning include the Univ. of P.R. (with its main branch at Río Piedras), the Inter-Amer. Univ. at San Germán, the Catholic Univ. at Ponce, and a Catholic col. for women at San Juan. The industrial development of P.R. is presently facing serious problems as the U.S. Congress recently eliminated important tax incentives that for years attracted industries here. Formerly spelled Porto Rico.

Puerto Rico Trench, submarine trench in the Caribbean Sea, c.50 mi/80 km N of Puerto Rico, extending on the outerside of the Antillean Ridge from Hispaniola to the median part of the Lesser Antilles arc near Guadeloupe Isl.; c.220 mi/354 km E-W; c.20°00′N. The width of the floor does not exceed 4 mi/6.4 km. It is the deepest trench in the Atlantic Ocean and the 5th-deepest body of water in the world, with maximum depth of 28,232 ft/8,605 m in the W part.

Puerto Tarafa (PWER-to tah-RAH-fuh), N port of Nuevitas, Camagüey prov., E Cuba; 21°33'N 77°15'W. Pier c.7,000 ft/2,134 m long; served by RR and trucks. Able to handle 7 vessels at once, esp. machinery, fruit, cement, and general cargo.

Puerto Vallarta (PWER-to vah-YAHR-tah), city (1990 pop. 93,503) and township, Jalisco state, W Mexico; 20°36'N 105°15'W. Located on the Bahía de Banderas, Puerto Vallarta has been used since the 16th cent. as a stopover point for ships making long sails along the W coast. Today it is one of Mexico's largest resort developments, known for its sports fishing and luxurious facilities.

Puerto Viejo Lagoon, Mexico: see TAMPICO LAGOON.

Puffin Island, islet, E N.F., E Canada, on N side of Bonavista Bay, just SW of Greenspond; 49°03'N 53°35'W.

Puget Island (PYOO-jit), Wahkiakum co., SW Wash., in Columbia R.; c.5 mi/8 km long, up to 2 mi/3.2 km wide. Bridge from Cathlamet to NW; Puget Isl. Ferry S to Westport (Oregon). Agr.; dairying; herbs; fish.

Puget Sound (PYOO-jit), arm of the Pacific Ocean, NW Wash., connected to the Pacific by Strait of Juan de Fuca, main entrance to sound through the Admiralty Inlet bet. Quimper Reservoir, extension of Olympic Peninsula (Port Townsend) to SW, and Whidbey Isl., NE, and extending in 2 arms. Secondary entrance to N through Skagit Bay and Deception Pass, bet. Whidbey (S) and Fidalgo (N) isls. The main sound extends c.100 mi/161 km S to Olympia, Hood Canal extends c.50 mi/80 km SSW with a 15-mi/24-km NE hook at its end. The sound, which receives many streams from the Cascade Range, has numerous isls. and is navigable for large ships. Along its shores are important ports and commercial cities. The Puget Sound lowland, which extends W and E from the sound, is the most densely populated area of Wash.; major cities in the sound are Seattle and Tacoma, on E side, others include Olympia, Everett, and Bremerton; all are major shipping and fishing ports. Bainbridge Isl., opposite (W) from Seattle; Vashon Isl., SW of Seattle. Anderson, McNeil, Fox and Hartstene in S. Kitsap Peninsula separates Hood Canal from rest of Puget Sound. Olympic Peninsula, with Olympic Mts., is to W; Cascade Range to E and S. Discovered in 1787, the sound was explored and named by Eng. Capt. George Vancouver for his aide, Peter Puget, in 1792.

Pugwash, village, N N.S., E Canada, on Northumberland Strait, at mouth of Pugwash R., 40 mi/64 km NNW of Truro; 45°51'N 63°40'W. Resort; fisheries; mfg. (silverware). Site of Pugwash Conference (July 1957), series of meetings of scientists to discuss nuclear arms race and other world problems. The Pugwash Movement continues to pave the way for intl. arms agreements.

Puhi (POO-hee), town (1990 pop. 1,210), SE Kauai, Kauai co., Hawaii, 2 mi/3.2 km WSW inland from Lihue, on Kaumualii Highway, on Puhi Stream; 21°58'N 159°24'W. Kauai Community Col. here. Lihue-Koloa Forest Reserve and Kilohana Crater to NW; Huleia Natl. Wildlife Refuge to S.

Pukalani (POO-kah-LAH-nee), town (1990 pop. 5,879), central Maui isl., Maui co., Hawaii, 8 mi/12.9 km ESE of Kahului, inland 7 mi/11.3 km from N coast, in the "Up Country"; 20°50'N 156°20'W. Cattle; timber. Enchanting Floral Gardens of Kula Maui to S. Makawao and Koolau forest reserves to E. Olinda Prison Camp to E. Entrance to Haleakala Natl. Park 8 mi/12.9 km SE.

Pukaskwa National Park (PUHK-as-kwuh) (□ c.725 sq mi/1,890 sq km), central Ont., central Canada, near Marathon; stretching for c.50 mi/80 km along the N shore of L. Superior bet. the Pukaskwa and White rivers. Rugged terrain with many lakes, rivers, and waterfalls. Tip Top mt. (2,120 ft/650 m high), one of the highest points in Ont. Est. 1971.

Pukwana, village (1990 pop. 263), Brule co., S central S.Dak., 8 mi/12.9 km E of Chamberlain; 43°46'N 99°10'W.

Pulaski 1 (puh-LAS-kee), county (□ 807 sq mi/2,090 sq km; 1990 pop. 349,660), central Ark.; ⊙ Little Rock; 34°46'N 92°18'W. Intersected NW to SE by Arkansas R. (David D. Terry Lock and Dam in E, Murray Lock and Dam at center); drained by small Bayou Fourche Creek and Maumelle R. Center of co. is highly urbanized, agr. in SE and NE, wooded in W. Agr. (wheat, soybeans; cattle, hogs). Mfg. at Little Rock. Abandoned bauxite mines, oil and gas wells, stone quarries. Part of Camp Robinson Natl. Guard Training Area in N; Little Rock Air Force Base in NE. Pinnacles State Park in NW on large L. Maumelle reservoir. Formed 1818. **2** county (□ 250 sq mi/648 sq km; 1990 pop. 8,108), S central Ga.; ⊙ Hawkinsville; 32°14'N 83°28'W. Mfg. includes apparel and textiles. Coastal plain area intersected by Ocmulgee R. Agr. includes cotton, soybeans, peanuts, corn, wheat, fruit; cattle, hogs. Formed 1808. **3** (poo-LAS-kee), county (□ 203 sq mi/526 sq km; 1990 pop. 7,523), extreme S Ill.; ⊙ Mound City; 37°13'N 89°07'W. Bounded SE by Ohio R.; drained by and bordered on W by Cache R. Agr. area (grain, fruit; dairy prods.). Formed 1843. One of 17 cos. to retain Southern-style commission form of co. govt. **4** (puh-LAS-kei), county (□ 434 sq mi/1,124 sq km; 1990 pop. 12,643), NW Ind.; ⊙ Winamac; 41°02'N 86°41'W. Agr. (corn, soybeans; oats, rye) and livestock-raising (dairy prods.; poultry, hogs, cattle) area. Mfg. at Winamac. Drained by Big Monon Creek and Tippecanoe R. Tippecanoe R. State Park and Winamac State Fish and Wildlife Area in N; part of Jasper-Pulaski State Fish and Wildlife Area in NW corner. Formed 1835. **5** (puh-LAS-kee), county (□ 677 sq mi/1,753 sq km; 1990 pop. 49,489), S Ky.; ⊙ Somerset; 37°06'N 84°34'W. Bounded E by Rockcastle R.; drained by Cumberland R. (forms L. Cumberland reservoir in S and parts of S border) and by Fishing, Pitman, and Buck creeks. Hilly agr. area, partly in Cumberland foothills (burley tobacco, corn, hay, alfalfa, soybeans, wheat; cattle, hogs, poultry; dairying); bituminous-coal mines, oil wells, stone quarries; timber. Some mfg. at Somerset. Includes Mill Spring Natl. Cemetery; part of Daniel Boone Natl. Forest in E and SE. General Burnside State Park in S. Formed 1798. **6** county (□ 551 sq mi/1,427 sq km; 1990 pop. 41,307), central Mo.; ⊙ Waynesville; 37°49'N 92°12'W. In the Ozark Mts.; drained by Gasconade R. Corn, wheat, fruit; livestock. Mfg. at Waynesville. Part of Mark Twain Natl. Forest in S ½. Fort Leonard Wood Army basic training facility and airport in S; base services at St. Robert and Waynesville. Settled 1818. Formed 1833. **7** county (□ 329 sq mi/852 sq km; 1990 pop. 34,496), SW Va.; ⊙ Pulaski; 37°03'N 80°42'W. In Great Appalachian Valley, traversed by ridges; drained by New R., here dammed to form Claytor L. Mfg. at Pulaski and Dublin; agr., (hay, alfalfa, corn; cattle, sheep; dairying), timber; anthracite coal, iron, zinc mining. Has mineral springs. Includes part of Jefferson Natl. Forest in NW. Claytor L. State Park in center, New R. Trail State Park extends S from Pulaski town. Formed 1839.

Pulaski (pyoo-LAS-kee), city (1990 pop. 7,895), ⊙ Giles co., S Tenn., 28 mi/45 km S of Columbia, 35°12'N 87°12'W. In livestock, cotton, tobacco, vegetable-farming area. Mfg. motor vehicle parts, electronics, foods; lumber milling. Timber tracts, phosphate-rock quarries nearby. Seat of Martin Col. Settled 1807; inc. 1819.

Pulaski 1 (puh-LAS-kee), town (1990 pop. 221), Davis co., SE Iowa, 10 mi/16 km SE of Bloomfield; 40°42'N 92°16'W. In sheep-raising area. **2** town (1990 pop. 9,985), ⊙ Pulaski co., SW Va., 11 mi/18 km SW of Radford, on Peak Creek; 37°02'N 80°45'W. Mfg. (textiles and clothing, machinery, fabricated metal prods., furniture, lumber; printing and publishing); agr. (corn, alfalfa; livestock; dairying). N terminus of New R. Trail State Park (from Galax); Claytor L. reservoir to SE; Claytor L. State Park to E. Inc. 1886. **3** town (1990 pop. 2,200), Brown co., NE Wis., 16 mi/26 km NW of Green Bay; 44°40'N 88°14'W. In dairying and farming area; canning; mfg. (machinery).

Pulaski 1 (puh-LAS-kee), village (1990 pop. 264), Candler co., E central Ga., 12 mi/19 km WSW of Statesboro; 32°23'N 81°58'W. Mfg. of bldg. materials. **2** (poo-LAS-kee), village (1990 pop. 361), Pulaski co., extreme S Ill., 8 mi/12.9 km N of Mound City; 37°13'N 89°12'W. In agr. area. **3** (puh-LAS-kei), village (□ 3 sq mi/7.8 sq km; 1990 pop. 2,525), a ⊙ Oswego co., N central N.Y., on Salmon R., near L. Ontario, and 35 mi/56 km N of Syracuse; 43°34'N 76°07'W. Summer resort; mfg. (electronic equip., paper prods.). State park nearby. Prized coho salmon fishing in the Salmon R. Trout and salmon hatchery at Altman, 7 mi/11.3 km SE. Inc. 1832.

Pulaski, Fort, Ga.: see FORT PULASKI.

Pullman 1 former city, now a part of Chicago, in Cook co., NE Ill.; 41°41'N 87°36'W. Founded 1880 by G. M. Pullman as experimental model city for workers in his sleeping-car plant; annexed by Chicago in 1889 and part of Southside Chicago. Scene of famous strike, 1894. **2** city (1990 pop. 23,478), Whitman co., SE Wash., 8 mi/12.9 km W of Moscow (Idaho), and on South Fork of Palouse R., in the Palouse region; 46°44'N 117°10'W. Elev. 2,351 ft/717 m. RR junction. Commercial and shipping center for wheat, barley, oats, alfalfa, peas, lentils; sheep, hogs. Mfg. (electronic equip., machinery). Lower Granite Dam and Reservoir in Snake R. Canyon, to SW. Pullman Moscow Airport to NE. Seat of Wash. State Univ. Founded 1884, inc. 1888.

Pullman, village (1990 pop. 109), Ritchie co., NW W.Va., 5 mi/8 km ESE of Harrisville; 39°11'N 80°57'W.

Pulsatilla, Mount (puhl-suh-TI-luh) (10,060 ft/3,066 m), SW Alta., W Canada, near B.C. border, in Rocky Mts., in Banff Natl. Park, 23 mi/37 km NW of Banff.

Pultneyville, village (1990 pop. 400), Wayne co., W N.Y., on L. Ontario, 23 mi/37 km ENE of Rochester; 43°17'N 77°10'W.

Pumpkin Center, uninc. town (1990 pop. 2,857), Onslow co., E N.C., residential suburb 3 mi/4.8 km NE of downtown Jacksonville; 34°46'N 77°22'W. Hoffmann Forest to NE.

Puna (POO-nah), district, E part of Hawaii isl., Hawaii co., S of Hilo dist., Hawaii; c.25 mi/40 km long and wide. Camp Kumukahi at E extremity; Hawaii Volcanoes Natl. Park to SW. Along with the N Kona dist. in W Hawaii isl., Puna is the fastest-growing dist. in Hawaii co. because of proximity of jobs in Hilo and availability of low-cost land in the sprawling rural subdivisions around the former sugar-plantation towns of Pahoa, Keaau, Kurtistown, and Mountain View. Surface is mostly recent lava flows, mitigated by heavy rain, which makes farming of macadamia, papaya, orchids and other flowers possible in volcanic ash and pulverized lava. Thousands of acres were subdivided in 1960s and 1970s providing little more than a network of roads. Since 1980, lava flows from the NE rift of Kilauea volcano have extended the coastline over a kilometer in some places and obliterated most of Royal Gardens subdivision in S, the coastal town of Kalapana, and the well-known Black Sand Beach at Kaimu.

Punaluu (POO-nah-LOO-oo), village (1990 pop. 672), S Hawaii isl., Hawaii co., Hawaii, 45 mi/72 km SW of Hilo, 4 mi/6.4 km SW of Pahala, on SE coast of Punaluu Harbor; 21°35'N 157°54'W. Nursery prods.; cattle; fish. Punaluu Black Sand Beach Park to SW; Kau Forest Reserve to NW. Hawaii Volcanoes Natl. Park (coastal sect.) to NE.

Punchbowl, Hawaiian *Puowaina*, extinct volcanic crater, in the city of Honolulu, SE Oahu isl., Honolulu co., Hawaii, 1 mi/1.6 km NE of downtown. Elev. 500 ft/152 m. In the bowl-like crater at the summit (reached by a scenic drive) is the Natl. Memorial Cemetery of the Pacific, honoring those killed in World War II. Observation point on S rim.

Pungarabato, Mexico: see CIUDAD ALTAMIRANO.

Pungo River (PUHN-go), tidal estuary of Pamlico R. estuary, c.20 mi/32 km long, E N.C.; serpentine estuary (2 mi/3.2 km wide) runs SE, turns W, then S to Pamlico R. estuary, near its entrance to Pamlico Sound; Belhaven is on NW shore. Connected with Alligator R.

(NE) by Alligator–Pungo R. Canal, forming part of Intracoastal Waterway; waterway passes through most of estuary also connected to NE by channel to Alligator L. (natural); estuary forms part of border bet. Beaufort and Hyde cos. East Dismal Swamp to N.

Pungoteague (PUN-go-teeg), uninc. village, Accomack co., E Va., in Eastern Shore area, 9 mi/14.5 km SW of Accomac, near Chesapeake Bay; 37°37′N 75°48′W. Agr. (poultry; vegetables, grain); fish, seafood. Old St. George's Church nearby.

Punta Alegre (POON-tuh ah-LAI-grai), town, Ciego de Ávila prov., E Cuba, on N coast on Buena Vista Bay, 22 mi/35 km NW of Morón; 22°23′N 78°49′W. In sugar and cattle region. Produces salt and gypsum. Sugar mill Máximo Gómez is just E. N slope of Gypsum Hills (Lomas de Yeso).

Punta Arenas (POON-tah ah-RAI-nahs), cape on NW Vieques isl., E P.R., near westernmost point of the isl., 8 mi/12.9 km WSW of Isabel Segunda. Within U.S. Naval Reservation.

Punta Brava (POON-tuh BRAH-vuh), town, Ciudad de La Habana prov., W Cuba, on RR, on Natl. Highway, and 12 mi/19 km SW of Havana; 23°10′N 82°30′W. Tobacco, sugarcane, fruit.

Punta Cajón (POON-tuh kah-HON), point, extreme NW Guanahacabibes Peninsula, Pinar del Río prov., near westernmost part of Cuba, bet. Gulf of Guanahacabibes and Yucatan Straits; 21°55′N 84°55′W.

Punta Caleta (POON-tuh kah-LAI-tuh), beach, Guantánamo prov., extreme SE corner of Cuba; 20°04′N 74°18′W.

Punta Camarón Grande (POON-tuh kah-mah-RON GRAHN-dai), point in SE corner of Granma prov., SE Cuba, on Caribbean Sea, near Santiago de Cuba border; 19°53′N 77°05′W.

Punta Cana (POON-tah KAH-nah), beach resort area, on E tip of Dominican Republic, 27 mi/43 km E of Higuey.

Punta Cayo Mono (POON-tuh KEI-yo MO-no), extreme S point of small peninsula marking E entry into the Ensenada de Coloma, Pinar del Río, Cuba; 22°10′N 83°28′W. Large mangrove and swamp region.

Punta, Cerro de (POON-tah, SER-ro dai), peak (4,389 ft/1,338 m), W central P.R., highest point on the isl., in the Cordillera Central, 3 mi/4.8 km S of Jayuya; 18°10′N 66°35′W.

Punta de Inglés (POON-tuh dai een-GLAIS), southernmost point in Granma prov., SE Cuba, on Caribbean Sea; 19°50′N 77°40′W. Surrounded by tropical forest. Meseta de Cabo Cruz to the N.

Punta de los Barcos (POON-tuh dai los BAHR-kos), point, in far NW corner of Isla de la Juventud, off S coast of Cuba; 21°56′N 83°00′W.

Punta de Mulas (POON-tuh dai MOO-luhz), point, N shore of Holguín prov., E Cuba, 12 mi/19 km ENE of Banes, on Banes Bay; 21°01′N 75°35′W.

Punta de Tirry (POON-tuh dai TIR-ee), northernmost point of Isla de la Juventud, off S coast of Cuba; 21°57′N 82°58′W.

Punta del Este (POON-tuh dail ES-tai), town, Isla de la Juventud, off S coast of Cuba; 21°39′N 82°34′W. Only town in SE corner of isl.

Punta del Gato (POON-tuh dail GAH-to), point at mouth of Ensenada del Gato, Pinar del Río, Cuba, on Gulf of Batabanó; 22°15′N 83°19′W.

Punta del Quemado (POON-tuh dail kai-MAH-do), easternmost point in Guantánamo prov. and mainland Cuba, on Windward Passage; 20°12′N 74°08′W.

Punta Gorda (PUHN-tuh GOR-duh), point (□10 sq mi/26 sq km; 1990 pop. 10,747), ⊙ Charlotte co., SW Fla., on Charlotte Harbor (bridged here), near mouth of Peace R., 23 mi/37 km NW of Fort Myers; 26°53′N 82°03′W. Resort; shipping point for fish and vegetables; mfg. of shell novelties. Inc. 1901.

Punta Gorda (POON-tuh GOR-duh), SW residential suburb of Santiago de Cuba, at head of Santiago de Cuba Bay, Santiago de Cuba prov., E Cuba; 19°58′N 71°53′W.

Punta Ladrillo (POON-tuh lah-DREE-yo), beach, S

Sancti Spíritus prov., central Cuba, at mouth of Zaza R., on Caribbean Sea; 21°41′N 79°38′W.

Punta María Aguilar (POON-tuh mah-REE-uh ah-gee-LAHR), town, SW Sancti Spíritus prov., central Cuba, on Caribbean Sea, and 6 mi/9.7 km SSW of Trinidad; 21°45′N 80°02′W. Ancón tourist hotel 3 mi/4.8 km E.

Punta Mayarí (POON-tuh mei-yahr-EE), beach resort, Holguín prov., E Cuba, on E side of channel leading to Nipe Bay; 20°47′N 75°32′W.

Punta Mora (POON-tuh MOR-uh), point, on SE coast of La Habana prov., W Cuba, on Ensenada de la Broa, arm of Gulf of Batabanó, at mouth of Mayabeque R.; 22°40′N 82°04′W.

Punta Pasabanao (POON-tuh pah-suh-bah-NOU), point, S entrance of Júcaro Morón Plain, SE Sancti Spíritus prov., central Cuba, on Caribbean Sea; 21°33′N 79°11′W.

Punta Rasa (PUN-tah RAH-sah), fishing village (□ 4 sq mi/10.4 sq km; 1990 pop. 1,493), Lee co., SW Fla., at mouth of Caloosahatchee R. on San Carlos Bay, 12 mi/19 km SW of Fort Myers; 26°30′N 82°00′W.

Punta Santiago, P.R.: see PLAYA DE HUMACAO.

Punta Tabacal (POON-tuh tah-bah-KAHL), small village and growing beach resort, Santiago de Cuba prov., SE Cuba, on Caribbean Sea; 19°57′N 76°21′W.

Punxsutawney (PUHK-sah-TAW-nee), borough (1990 pop. 6,782), Jefferson co., W central Pa., 60 mi/97 km NE of Pittsburgh, on Mahoning Creek; 40°56′N 78°58′W. RR junction to E. Mfg. (construction materials, electronic components; printing and publishing, machining, food processing); subsurface- and surface- bituminous-coal mining. Agr. area (corn, hay; dairying). Home of Punxsutawney Phil, the official groundhog of Groundhog Day, Feb. 2. Punxsutawney Groundhog Zoo, habitat of Punxsutawney Phil. His prognostications on Gobbler's Knob in Sportsman's Park (to SE) are witnessed by many visitors each year. Punxsutawney Municipal Airport to NE. Settled 1772, laid out c.1818, inc. 1850.

Pupukea (POO-POO-KAI-ah), town (1990 pop. 4,111), N Oahu isl., Honolulu co., Hawaii, 24 mi/39 km NNW of Honolulu, 1 mi/1.6 km inland from N coast; 21°39′N 158°03′W. Puuomahuka State Monument to W; Waimea Falls Park to S; Pupukea Paumalu Forest Reserve to E; Pupukea Beach Park to NW at Waimea.

Purcell (puhr-SEL), city (1990 pop. 359), Jasper co., SW Mo., 12 mi/19 km N of Joplin, on Spring R.; 37°14′N 94°26′W. Wheat, soybeans, sorghum; cattle.

Purcell, town (1990 pop. 4,784), ⊙ McClain co., central Okla., 32 mi/51 km SSE of Oklahoma City, and on Canadian R. (bridged); 35°00′N 97°22′W. Elev. 1,102 ft/336 m. In agr. area (cotton, corn, fruit; dairying); mfg. (clutch assemblies).

Purcell, village, Weld co., N Colo., 15 mi/24 km NNE of Greeley. Elev. 5,010 ft/1,527 m. Grain- and cattle-shipping area. Sugar beets, sunflowers. Pawnee Natl. Grassland to N and E.

Purcell Mountains, interior B.C., W Canada, bet. Rocky Mt. Trench and East Kootenay L. Extend from U.S.-Can. border (S) to Trans-Canada Highway (N). Generally 984 ft/300 m–1,969 ft/600 m lower than Rockies.

Purcellville (PUHR-sel-vil), town (1990 pop. 1,744), Loudoun co., N Va., 8 mi/12.9 km W of Leesburg; 39°08′N 77°42′W. Mfg. (printing and publishing, roller skate wheels). In agr. area (apples, wheat; livestock; timber.

Purdin (PUHR-din), town (1990 pop. 217), Linn co., N central Mo., 6 mi/9.7 km N of Linneus, 39°57′N 93°10′W.

Purdon, village (1990 pop. 133), Navarro co., E central Texas, 13 mi/21 km SW of Corsicana, near Richland Creek. In farm area.

Purdy, city (1990 pop. 977), Barry co., SW Mo., in the Ozarks, 7 mi/11.3 km S of Monett; 36°49′N 93°55′W. Apples, peaches, vegetables; dairying; mfg. (drill bits).

Purépero de Echáiz (poo-RE-pe-ro de e-CHAH-ees), town (1990 pop. 12,902), ⊙ Purépero municipio, Michoacán, central Mexico, on central plateau, 19 mi/

31 km ESE of Zamora de Hidalgo; 19°50′N 102°00′W. Agr. center (corn, sugarcane, tobacco, fruit; livestock).

Purgatoire River, c.175 mi/282 km long, in SE Colo.; formed by confluence of its North Fork and Middle Fork in Culebra Range of Sangre de Cristo Mts.; flows first E through Trinidad Reservoir then (in canyon over 100 mi/161 km long) NE past part of Comanche Natl. Grassland to Arkansas R. 4 mi/6.4 km E of Las Animas, just above John Martin Reservoir. Drains coal-mining and agr. region. Dinosaur tracks have been found in rock bed of river. North Fork rises in NW corner of Las Animas co., flows SE c.25 mi/40 km (Middle Fork, formed by several creeks in W Las Animas, flows E c.20 mi/32 km, to form mainstream in N Fork); South Fork formed by creeks in SW Las Animas co. flows c.20 mi/32 km ENE joining Purgatoire at Weston. The informal spellings Picket Wire and Picketwire are sometimes used.

Purgatory Peak, Colo.: see SANGRE DE CRISTO MOUNTAINS.

Purial, Sierra de (poor-YAHL, see-ER-uh dai), small range, Guantánamo prov., E Cuba, near E tip of the isl. SW of Baracoa; extends c.25 mi/40 km SE from Toa R. to S coast; 20°11′N 74°35′W. On its slopes coffee, cacao, bananas, and coconuts are grown. Yields timber.

Purificación, Mexico: see VILLA PURIFICACIÓN.

Purísima de Bustos (poo-REE-see-MAN dai BOOS-tos), town (1990 pop. 12,486), ⊙ Purísima del Rincón municipio, Guanajuato, central Mexico, 15 mi/24 km SW of León. RR terminus. Cereals, alfalfa, beans, sugarcane; livestock. Also Purísima del Rincón.

Purísima del Rincón, Mexico: see PURÍSIMA DE BUSTOS.

Purísima, La, Mexico: see LA PURÍSIMA.

Purling, village (1990 pop. 300), Greene co., SE N.Y., in the Catskills, 9 mi/14.5 km NW of Catskill; 42°17′N 74°01′W.

Purple Peak (12,958 ft/3,950 m), in Rocky Mts., Gunnison co., W central Colo., 10 mi/16 km NW of Crested Butte, on boundary of White R. and Gunnison Natl. Forests; 38°54′N 107°07′W. Also known as Slate Peak.

Pursglove (PUHRS-gluhv), uninc. village (1990 pop. 500), Monongalia co., N W.Va., 4 mi/6.4 km NW of Morgantown, on Scotts Run Creek. Coal-mining region.

Purtuniq, village, N Que., E Canada, inland on Ungava Peninsula, 50 mi/80 km S of Cap de Nouveau-France. Asbestos mining site in 1950s. Asbestos Hill nearby.

Purúa, Mexico: see HEROICA ZITÁCUARO.

Puruándiro (poo-roo-AHN-dee-ro), city (1990 pop. 24,238) and township, Michoacán, central Mexico, on central plateau, 35 mi/56 km NW of Morelia; 20°06′N 101°32′W. Agr. center (cereals, vegetables, fruit); flour milling, tanning.

Purvis (1990 pop. 2,140), ⊙ Lamar co., SE Miss., 14 mi/23 km SSW of Hattiesburg; 31°08′N 89°24′W. In agr. (cotton, corn; poultry, cattle) and pine-timber area; mfg. (petroleum coke, wooden pallets, apparel, lumber). Paul B. Johnson State Park to E; De Soto Natl. Forest to SE.

Puryear (PUH-ree-uhr), city (1990 pop. 592), Henry co., NW Tenn., 10 mi/16 km N of Paris; 36°26′N 88°19′W.

Pushaw Lake (PUSH-aw), Penobscot co., S central Maine, 6 mi/9.7 km N of Bangor; 7.5 mi/12.1 km long.

Pushmataha (push-muh-TAH-hah), county (□ 1,422 sq mi/3,683 sq km), SE Okla.; ⊙ Antlers; 34°25′N 95°21′W. In the Ouachita Mts. (Kiamichi Mts. in NE, Jack Fork Mts. in NW); drained by Kiamichi and Little rivers. Wheat, corn; livestock. Some mfg. at Antlers; timber. Clayton L. and Sordis L. in N; Clayton L. State Park in N center; part of Sardis L. reservoir in N. Formed 1907.

Putah Creek, c.85 mi/137 km long; rises in the Coast Ranges, SW Lake co., W central Calif., 17 mi/27 km S of Clear L.; flows SE through L. Berryessa (Monticello Dam) and E past Winters and Davis, entering marshy area on W side of Sacramento R. c.10 mi/16 km SW of Sacramento; prevented from entering Sacramento R. by Sacramento Deep Water Canal. Forms part of border bet. Yolo and Solano cos.

Put-in-Bay, village (1990 pop. 141), Ottawa co., N Ohio, on Put-in-Bay harbor of South Bass Isl., in L. Erie, c.35 mi/56 km E of Toledo; 41°39′N 82°49′W. Tourist resort; has state and federal fish hatcheries, commercial fisheries. Perry's Victory and Internatl. Peace Memorial natl. monument (est. 1936), is near here; a granite column 352 ft/107 m high commemorates battle of L. Erie (1813), in which Admiral Perry's U.S. fleet defeated the British, and symbolizes century of peace bet. U.S. and Canada.

Putla de Guerrero, Mexico: see PUTLA VILLA DE GUERRERO.

Putla Villa de Guerrero (POO-tlah VEE-yah dai ge-RE-ro), town (1990 pop. 7,181), Oaxaca, S Mexico, on S slopes of Sierre Madre del Sur, 24 mi/39 km SW of Tlaxiaco, on Mexico Highway 125; 17°01′N 97°56′W. Cereals, sugarcane, coffee, fruit, vegetables; livestock; timber.

Putnam 1 county (□ 827 sq mi/2,142 sq km; 1990 pop. 65,070), NE Fla.; ⊙ Palatka; 29°36′N 81°44′W. Lake and swamp area drained by St. Johns R.; includes L. George and part of Crescent L. Agr. (corn, vegetables, peanuts, citrus fruit, poultry; livestock), forestry (lumber, naval stores), fishing, and mining (kaolin, peat, sand). Has resorts. Formed 1849. **2** county (□ 361 sq mi/935 sq km; 1990 pop. 14,137), central Ga.; ⊙ Eatonton; 33°19′N 83°22′W. Bounded E by Oconee R.; drained by Little R. Mfg. (lumber, wood prods., industrial machinery). Agr. includes peaches; cattle, dairying. Formed 1807. **3** county (□ 172 sq mi/445 sq km; 1990 pop. 5,730), N central Ill., bounded N and W by the great bend of Illinois R.; ⊙ Hennepin; 41°12′N 89°17′W. Agr. (corn, soybeans, wheat; livestock, poultry; dairy prods.). Mfg. (industrial chemicals, steel prods). Includes Senachwine and Sawmill lakes (bayous of the Ill.), with fishing resorts. Formed 1831, although 1825 often cited as date of formation. **4** county (□ 482 sq mi/1,248 sq km; 1990 pop. 30,315), W central Ind.; ⊙ Greencastle; 39°40′N 86°50′W. Drained by Walnut, Deer, Raccoon, and Mill creeks. Corn, soybeans, wheat; hogs, sheep, cattle; mfg. at Greencastle. Timber; limestone quarries. Lieber State Recreation Area and Cataract L. on S boundary. Ind. State Farm in SW near Putnamville. Formed 1821. **5** county (□ 518 sq mi/1,342 sq km; 1990 pop. 5,079), N Mo.; ⊙ Unionville, 40°29′N 93°01′W. Iowa on N. Bounded E by Chariton R. Corn, wheat, soybeans; sheep, cattle. Mfg. at Unionville. L. Thunderhead N of Unionville. Formed 1845. **6** county (□ 246 sq mi/ 637 sq km; 1990 pop. 83,941), SE N.Y.; ⊙ Carmel; 41°25′N 73°45′W. Bounded W by the Hudson R., E by Conn.; includes part of the Taconic Mts., here meeting the highlands of the Hudson R. Hilly region with many lakes (Mahopac, Peekskill, Carmel, Oscawana, Peach) and N.Y. city water-supply reservoirs of Croton R. system. Dairying and poultry raising, but increasingly suburban with light mfg. Traversed by Taconic State Parkway. Clarence Fahnestock Memorial State Park has skiing facilities. Named after Israel Putnam, officer who served in both Fr. and Indian War and Amer. Revolution. Charcoal from trees here fired foundries that produced the Parrott guns, locomotives, and machinery of the Civil War. Formed 1812. **7** county (□ 486 sq mi/ 1,259 sq km; 1990 pop. 33,819), NW Ohio; ⊙ Ottawa; 41°02′N 84°08′W. Intersected by Auglaize and Blanchard rivers. In the Till Plains physiographic region. Agr. area (livestock, poultry; corn, soybeans, wheat, sugar beets). Food processing and light mfg. at Ottawa, Leipsic, Columbus Grove. Clay pits, limestone quarries. Formed 1820. **8** county (□ 408 sq mi/1,057 sq km; 1990 pop. 51,373), central Tenn.; ⊙ Cookeville; 36°08′N 85°30′W. Hilly timber and farm region on Cumberland Plateau; drained by affluents of Cumberland R. Includes part of Center Hill Reservoir (Caney Fork R.). Agr. (small grains, tobacco, corn, apples, hay; poultry, cattle, hogs; lumbering; granite quarrying; oil and gas deposits. Diverse mfg. at Cookeville (motor vehicle parts, candy, wood prods.). Formed 1842. **9** county (□ 350 sq mi/907 sq km; 1990 pop. 42,835), W W.Va.; ⊙ Winfield; 38°30′N 81°54′W. Drained by Kanawha and Pocatalico rivers. Bituminous-coal mines; some natu-

ral-gas and oil wells. Corn, potatoes, alfalfa, hay, tobacco, vegetables, nursery crops; cattle, poultry. Mfg. at Poca and Hurricane. Formed 1848.

Putnam, textile city (1990 pop. 9,031) in Putnam town, a ⊙ (with Willimantic) of Windham co., NE Conn., on Quinebaug R., and 20 mi/32 km NE of Willimantic; 41°54′N 71°52′W. Mfg. (diverse textiles, metal prods., paper goods, apparel, optical goods, lumber, chemicals, furniture). Agr. (dairy prods., poultry, fruit). Has state park. Settled 1693, town set off from Killingly 1855, city inc. 1895.

Putnam 1 village (1990 pop. 44), Dewey co., W Okla., 23 mi/37 km N of Clinton; 36°00′N 99°13′W. In agr. and livestock-raising area. **2** village (1990 pop. 103), Callahan co., central Texas, 31 mi/50 km E of Abilene; 32°22′N 99°12′W. In agr. area; natural-gas and oil wells; natural-gas processing.

Putnam Valley, village (1990 pop. 1,960), Putnam co., SE N.Y., 4 mi/6.4 km NE of Peekskill, on L. Peekskill; 41°20′N 73°53′W. Pop. figure includes Oscawana.

Putnamville, village, Putnam co., W central Ind., near Deer Creek, and 5 mi/8 km S of Greencastle. Timber; cattle. Ind. State Farm located nearby to the W. Lieber State Recreation Area to the S. Laid out 1830.

Putney, town (1990 pop. 2,352), Windham co., SE Vt., on the Connecticut R., and 9 mi/14.5 km N of Brattleboro; 42°59′N 72°31′W. Lumber, wood prods., and paper; baskets. A resort area. Dairying in vicinity. Putney School (1935; co-educational) is near Putney village.

Puu Ka Pele (POO-oo KAH PAI-lai), peak (3,662 ft/ 1,116 m), W central Kauai, Kauai co., Hawaii, on W edge of Waimea Canyon, 21 mi/34 km WNW of Lihue; 22°05′N 159°40′W.

Puu Kukui (POO-oo koo-KOO-ee), mountain (5,788 ft/ 1,764 m), W Maui, Maui co., Hawaii, 8 mi/12.9 km W of Kahului; highest point near center of peninsula; in W Maui Mts. Eke Crater (4,480 ft/1,366 m), 1 mi/ 1.6 km to N; 20°53′N 156°35′W.

Puu Ohia (POO-oo O-HEE-ah), peak (3,575 ft/1,090 m), N Hawaii, Hawaii; 20°00′N 155°31′W.

Puu Ulaula (POO-oo OO-lah-OO-lah), peak (10,023 ft/ 3,055 m), SE Maui isl., Maui co., Hawaii, extinct volcano, highest point on Maui, located at SW rim of Haleakala Crater, SW corner of Haleakala Natl. Park; 19°32′N 155°28′W. Summit reached by Haleakala Crater Road from Waiakoa. Park visitor center ½ mi/⅘ km N. Also called Red Hill.

Puu Waawaa (POO-oo WAH-ah-WAH-ah), peak (3,967 ft/1,209 m), W Hawaii, Hawaii, in N Kona dist., 47 mi/76 km W of Hilo, 8 mi/12.9 km from W (Kona) coast; 19°46′N 155°50′W. Extinct volcanic vent; gives name to a large nearby ranch.

Puuc Hills (poo-OOK), a region, in W Yucatán, Mexico, trends NW–SE, roughly paralleled on N by Mexico Highway 184 bet. Maxanu and Tizukab. An area of rolling hills with many Mayan archaeological sites, including Uxmal, Kabáh, Sayil, and Labná. There is a Puuc style of architecture characterized by a stone sculpture arranged into designs and masks that form a mosaic veneer on bldgs., and by rows of short columns used as decoration.

Pu'uhonua o Honaunau National Historic Park (POO-oo-ho-NOO-ah O HO-NOU-NOU), SW Hawaii isl., Hawaii co., Hawaii, on Kona Coast, 2 mi/ 3.2 km W of Honaunau, 55 mi/89 km WSW of Hilo. Covers 182 acres/74 ha. Until 1819, was a place of refuge for defeated warriors, tabu breakers; park contains prehistoric house sites and royal fish ponds. Authorized as City of Refuge Natl. Historical Park in 1955; name changed in 1978.

Puukohola Heiau National Historic Site (PUU-oo-KO-ho-LAH HAI-OU), NW Hawaii isl., Hawaii co., Hawaii, 50 mi/80 km NW of Hilo, 9 mi/14.5 km W of Waimea, near Kawaihae Bay (W) on Kohala Coast. Covers 80 acres/32 ha. Authorized 1972, name means Hill of the Whale. Temple built (1791) by King Kamehameha the Great, who offered his son as a human sacrifice; site preserves temple ruins.

Puukolii (PU-oo-ko-LEE-ee), village, W Maui isl., Maui

co., Hawaii, 2 mi/3.2 km N of Lahaina, suburb 2 mi/ 3.2 km SSE of Kahului, 2 mi/3.2 km S of Kahului Bay, N coast on Mokulele Highway. Mfg. (sugarcane processing).

Puunene (PU-oo-NAI-NAI), town, N Maui, Hawaii, S of Kahului.

Puxico (PUHK-see-ko), city (1990 pop. 819), Stoddard co., SE Mo., near St. Francis R., 19 mi/31 km NE of Poplar Bluff; 36°57′N 90°09′W. Near Ozark Escarpment. Mfg. (apparel). Mingo Natl. Wildlife Refuge (wetlands) to W. Rice, soybeans, wheat, corn.

Puyallup (pyoo-A-luhp), city (1990 pop. 23,875), Pierce co., W Wash., suburb 8 mi/12.9 km SE of downtown Tacoma, on the Puyallup R.; 47°11′N 122°17′W. RR junction. It is located in a fertile farm valley noted for its berries and daffodil bulbs; vegetables; dairying; poultry. Mfg. (mining machinery; men's clothing, refrigeration equip., feeds, pallets, store fixtures, millwork, semiconductors; sheet metal and concrete prods.; printing and publishing, prefabricated wooden bldgs., food processing, wooden doors and cabinets; sand and gravel). Puyallup Fish Hatchery, on Clarks Creek, and a Wash. State Univ. agr. experiment station are here. Daffodil Festival; W Wash. Fairgrounds. Of interest is the mansion home (1890) of Ezra Meeker, the city's founder. Inc. 1890.

Puyallup River (pyoo-A-luhp), c.45 mi/72 km long, W central Wash.; rises on W slopes of Mt. Rainier, in Mt. Rainier Natl. Park, SW Pierce co.; flows generally NW, past Puyallup and through city of Tacoma, to Commencement Bay, Puget Sound, at Tacoma. Has hydroelectric plants. Rich valley of lower river produces berries, flower bulbs, hops; poultry; dairying.

Pyatt (PEI-uht), village (1990 pop. 185), Marion co., N Ark., 15 mi/24 km E of Harrison, in the Ozarks, on Crooked Creek; 36°15′N 92°50′W. Mfg. (butcher block squares).

Pymatuning Creek (pei-muh-TOO-ning), c.27 mi/ 43 km long, in Ohio and Pa.; rises in Ashtabula co., Ohio; flows SSE to Shenango R. just above Sharon, Pa.; 41°17′N 90°27′W.

Pymatuning Reservoir (PAI-mah-TOO-ning), (□ 23 sq mi/60 sq km), Crawford co., NW Pa., and Ashtabula co., NE Ohio; 16 mi/26 km long, 2.5 mi/4 km wide, 7 mi/11.3 km NNW of Greenville, Pa, and 6 mi/ 10 km ESE of Meadville (Pa.); 41°29′N 80°27′W. Formed (1932) by flood-control dam (50 ft/15 m high; built 1932) on Shenango R.; max. capacity 445,000 acre-ft. Forms part of Pa.-Ohio border. Used for recreation; Pymatuning State Park (Pa.) on S shore of NE arm; Pymatuning State Park (Ohio) on W shore.

Pyote (PEI-ot), village (1990 pop. 348), Ward co., extreme W Texas, 22 mi/35 km ENE of Pecos; 31°32′N 103°07′W. Oil and natural gas in area; natural-gas processing; livestock; cotton; alfalfa.

Pyramid Lake 1 (□ 188 sq mi/487 sq km), Washoe co., W Nev., 40 mi/64 km NNE of Reno. The Truckee R. flows into the S end of the lake; there is no outlet. Discovered in 1844 by U.S. explorer John Frémont, the lake was named for its large pyramidal rocks. It is located in Pyramid L. Indian Reservation. Anaho Isl. is in S Idaho Natl. Wildlife Refuge. **2** Los Angeles co., S Calif., on Piru Creek, 19 mi/31 km NW of Santa Clarita, in Angeles Natl. Forest; 3 mi/4.8 km long; 34°38′N 118°45′W. Elev. 2,579 ft/786 m. Max. capacity of 179,000 acre-ft. Formed by Pyramid Dam (358 ft/109 m high), built (1973) by the Calif. Department of Water Resources for water supply; W Branch Calif. Aqueduct diverts water to Castaic L. Reservoir (SE). Pyramid L. State Recreation Area on W side.

Pyramid Peak 1 mountain (9,984 ft/3,043 m) in El Dorado co., E Calif. in the Sierra Nevada, 12 mi/19 km SW of South L. Tahoe in Eldorado Natl. Forest; 38°50′N 120°09′W. **2** (14,018 ft/4,273 m) in Pitkin co., W central Colo., in Elk Mts., 10 mi/16 km SW of Aspen.

Pyramid Range, W Nev., part of Virginia Mts., in Washoe co., extending N from Truckee R. along W shore of Pyramid L. Rises to Virginia Peak (8,366 ft/ 2,550 m) in S.

Q

Quabbin Reservoir (KWAW-bin) (□ 39 sq mi/ 101 sq km), in Hamshire, Franklin, and Worcester cos., central Mass., on Swift R., 17 mi/27 km NE of Springfield; 42°16′N 72°20′W. Largest reservoir in Mass. Has 2 large N-S arms linked by 1 mi/1.6 km channel: W arm, on West Branch Swift R., is 12 mi/19 km long; E arm (many isls.), on East Branch Swift R., is 17 mi/ 27 km long. Formed by Windsor Dam for Boston water supply; water diverted E to Wachusett Reservoir through Quabbin Aqueduct (25 mi/40 km long). Managed by the Mass. Water Resource Authority.

Quaboag River (KWAI-bawg), c.30 mi/48 km long, in S central Mass.; rises in W Worcester co.; flows SW and W, joining Ware R. to form Chicopee R. in Palmer.

Quad Cities 1 and 2 Nuclear Power Plants, Illinois: see ROCK ISLAND, CO.

Quaddick Reservoir (KWAH-dik), extreme NE Conn., lake (c.2.5 mi/4 km long) near Thompson. Formed by dam in small Five Mile R. (tributary of Quinebaug R.). Quaddick village nearby.

Quadra Island (KWAH-druh) (□ 120 sq mi/311 sq km), SW B.C., Canada, in Discovery Passage, off NE Vancouver Isl., S of Sonora Isl., 23 mi/37 km NNW of Courtenay, opposite Campbell R.; 22 mi/35 km long, 1 mi/2 km–10 mi/16 km wide; 50°08′N 125°16′W. Gold mining, lumbering; cannery, salmon hatchery. Granite Bay (N) is chief village. Ferry from Campbell R. to Quathiaski Cove. Kwakiutl Mus.

Quail Valley, uninc. town (1990 pop. 1,937), Riverside co., S Calif., residential community 20 mi/32 km S of Riverside, on E side of Railroad Canyon Reservoir; 33°43′N 117°15′W.

Quake Lake or **Earthquake Lake**, Gallatin and Madison cos., SW Mont., on Madison R., in Madison R. canyon. Natural lake formed Aug. 17, 1959, by earthquake which caused mt. side to collapse, blocking river; 5 mi/8 km long, ½ mi/⁸⁄₁₀ km wide. Visitor center.

Quaker Bridge, village, Cattaraugus co., W N.Y., in Allegany Indian Reservation, 18 mi/29 km E of Jamestown. Dairy prods.

Quaker City, village (1990 pop. 560), Guernsey co., E Ohio, 16 mi/26 km SE of Cambridge; 39°58′N 81°17′W.

Quaker Hill, village, New London co., SE Conn., 4 mi/ 6.4 km N of New London. A postal section of Waterford.

Quakertown (KWAI-kuhr-toun), borough (1990 pop. 8,982), Bucks co., SE Pa., 13 mi/21 km SE of Allentown, near Tonockin Creek; 40°26′N 75°20′W. Apples, soybeans, grain; poultry, livestock; dairying. Diverse light mfg. L. Nockamixon reservoir and Nockamixon State Park to E. Settled c.1700, inc. 1855.

Quakish Lake (KWAIK-ish), reservoir, Penobscot co., central Maine, on West Branch Penobscot R., 2 mi/ 3.2 km S of Millinocket; c.3 mi/4.8 km long; 49°39′N 68°42′W.

Qualicum Beach (KWAH-lik-uhm), town (1991 pop. 4,418), SW B.C., Canada, E Vancouver Isl., on Strait of Georgia, 26 mi/42 km WNW of Nanaimo; 49°21′N 124°27′W. Farming, lumbering. Summer resort.

Quamba (KWAHM-buh), village (1990 pop. 124), Kanabec co., E Minn., 6 mi/9.7 km ENE of Mora, on Mud Creek; 45°55′N 93°10′W. Dairying; livestock; barley. Mud L. to S.

Quanah (KWAH-nuh), town (1990 pop. 3,413), ⊙ Hardeman co., N Texas, near Red R. (Okla. border), and 75 mi/121 km WNW of Wichita Falls; 34°17′N 99°44′W. Elev. 1,568 ft/478 m. RR junction in rich irrigated wheat, cotton, cattle area; mfg. (plasterboard, wallboard, cattle feed). L. Pauline (fishing, hunting), Medicine Mound (Native Amer. relics) to SE; L. Copper Breaks and Copper Breaks State Park to S. Founded 1886, inc. 1887.

Quandary Peak (14,265 ft/4,348 m), Summit co., central

Colo., in Park Range, 14 mi/23 km NE of Leadville; 39°23′N 106°06′W. Gold, silver, copper, lead, zinc, molybdenum mines in vicinity. In Arapahoe Natl. Forest; N of Continental Divide.

Quantico, town (1990 pop. 670), Prince William co., NE Va., on Potomac R., 29 mi/47 km SSW of Washington, D.C.; 38°31′N 77°17′W. Mfg. (printing and publishing). Contained within large Quantico U.S. Marine Corps base (mostly in W). Was Revolutionary service base for Colonial vessels. FBI Acad. located here. Prince William Forest Park is to NW. Inc. 1927; reinc. 1934.

Quantico (KWAHN-ti-koh), village, Wicomico co., SE Md., 8 mi/12.9 km W of Salisbury. Cannery nearby. Takes its name from Quantico [= dancing place] Creek.

Quapaw, town (1990 pop. 928), Ottawa co., extreme NE Okla., 18 mi/29 km WSW of Joplin (Mo.), near Kansas and Mo. state lines; 36°57′N 94°47′W. In zinc- and leadmining region; mfg. (germanium, gallium, and silica refining). Spring River State Park to NE.

Qu'Appelle (kah-PEHL), town (1991 pop. 671), S Sask., Canada, 30 mi/48 km ENE of Regina, S of Fort Qu'Appelle; 50°32′N 103°52′W. Dairying center; wheat.

Qu'Appelle (kah-PEHL), river, c.270 mi/430 km long; rises in S Sask., Canada, NW of Moose Jaw; flows generally E through Buffalo Pound L. and Fishing Lakes, past Fort Qu'Appelle to the Assiniboine R., just over the Manitoba border. Noted for whitefish.

Quaqtaq or **Notre-Dame-de-Koartac**, village (1991 pop. 236), N Que., Canada, on Hudson Strait, W side of entrance to Ungava Bay, NE end of Ungava Peninsula, at Cap Hopes Advance. Inuit community. Hunting, fishing, trapping. Scheduled air service.

Quarryville (KWAH-ree-vil), borough (1990 pop. 1,642), Lancaster co., SE Pa., 12 mi/19 km SE of Lancaster; 39°53′N 76°09′W. Mfg. (feeds, metal castings, farm equip., printing and publishing, plastic prods.); stone quarries. Agr. (grain, soybeans; poultry, livestock; dairying). Settled 1791, inc. 1892.

Quartier-Morin (kahr-TYAI–mo-RANG), town (1982 pop. 883), Nord dept., N Haiti, near the coast, 5 mi/ 8 km SE of Cap-Haïtien; 19°42′N 72°09′W. Sugar, fruit, cacao, tobacco; cattle; essential oils distillery.

Quartz Hill, uninc. city (1990 pop. 9,626), Los Angeles co., S Calif., residential suburb 41 mi/66 km N of Los Angeles, in Antelope Valley; 34°39′N 118°13′W. Irrigated agr. area (fruit, vegetables, nuts, cotton). Calif. Poppy Preserve to W. Calif. Aqueduct passes to SW.

Quartzsite, town (1990 pop. 1,876), La Paz co., W Ariz., 68 mi/109 km NNE of Yuma, on Tyson Wash, in La Posa Plain. Service center on Interstate Highway 10. Winter visitors crowd the area in cooler months. Kofa Natl. Wildlife Refuge to SE; Yuma Proving Ground to SW; Colorado R. Indian Reservation to NW.

Quasqueton, town (1990 pop. 579), Buchanan co., E Iowa, on Wapsipinicon R., and 9 mi/14.5 km SE of Independence; 42°23′N 91°45′W. In agr. area. Cedar Rock, designed by Frank Lloyd Wright, is here.

Quassapaug Pond (KWAH-se-pahg), reservoir, Middlebury, Litchfield and New Haven cos., W central Conn., on Eight Mile R., 6 mi/9.7 km WSW of Waterbury; c.1 mi/1.6 km long; 41°32′N 73°08′W. Seasonal residences; recreation.

Quatsino (kwaht-SEE-no), village, SW B.C., Canada, on N Vancouver Isl., port on Quatsino Sound, 30 mi/ 48 km W of Alert Bay; 50°32′N 127°36′W. Salmon fishing; pulp milling, lumbering.

Quatsino Sound, inlet of the Pacific on N Vancouver Isl., B.C., Canada, 22 mi/35 km W of Alert Bay; 50 mi/ 80 km long, 1 mi/2 km–7 mi/11 km wide. Main arms are Holberg Inlet (N), Neroutsos Inlet (SSE), and Rupert Inlet (E). Settlements at Port Alice and Quatsino. In fishing, copper mining, and lumbering area.

Quay (KWAI), county (□ 2,882 sq mi/7,464 sq km; 1990 pop. 10,823), E N.Mex.; ⊙ Tucumcari; 35°06′N 103°32′W. Watered by Canadian R., which forms Ute L. Reservoir (State Park) in N, and Tucumcari Creek; borders on Texas (E), Central/Mountain time zone boundary; N Mex. in Mountain time zone. Triticale area; cotton, sorghum, hay alfalfa, blue corn, wheat,

oats, barley, millet; sheep, cattle, some dairying. Formed 1903. Caprock Amphitheater in SE.

Quay, village (1990 pop. 59), on Pawnee-Payne co. line, N Okla., 13 mi/21 km NNE of Cushing; 36°09′N 96°42′W. In agr. area.

Quealy (KWEE-lee), village, Sweetwater co., SW Wyo., near Little Bitter Creek, 4 mi/6.4 km S of Rock Springs.

Quebec (kwuh-BEHK), Fr. *Québec* (kai-BEHK), province (□ 594,860 sq mi/1,553,637 sq km; 1991 pop. 6,895,963), E Canada; ⊙ QUEBEC; 54°00′N 72°00′W. MONTREAL is the largest city; other important centers are LAVAL, TROIS RIVIÈRES, GATINEAU, SHERBROOKE, and HULL. Bounded on the N by Hudson Strait and Ungava Bay, on the E by Lab. and the Gulf of St. Lawrence, on the S by N.B. and the U.S., and on the W by Ont., James Bay, and Hudson Bay. It is Canada's largest prov.; 3 times the size of France and 7 times the size of Great Britain. The Canadian Shield comprises the N 90% of the prov., relatively unexplored and uninhabited; the region has been planed by glacial action into a pattern of rounded hills, swiftly flowing rivers, and numerous lakes and bogs. Dense forests cover much of the surface, and the area is rich in minerals. S of the Canadian Shield lies the great St. Lawrence R. On both sides of the river S of Quebec city are the lowlands that are the centers of agr., commerce, and industry. Quebec city and Trois Rivières are on the N bank of the river and Montreal, the leading industrial center of Canada, is situated on an isl. where the Ottawa R. joins the St. Lawrence. In the SE sect. of the prov. are the Appalachian Highlands, which run parallel to the St. Lawrence. The Gaspé Peninsula, on the S bank of the St. Lawrence, borders on the Gulf of St. Lawrence. The climate is generally temperate, with variations among the regions. Tourism is important throughout the prov. during the summer season, and in the winter the Laurentian Mts. are a skiing attraction. Que. has vast resources of water power — Hydro-Quebec is the largest producer of electricity in Canada. The massive James Bay Project, however, was dealt a severe blow in 1992 when the N.Y. State Power Authority refused to sign a purchase contract for the next phase of the project. The forests of the N yield wood for the pulp, paper, and lumber industries, and throughout the N copper, iron, zinc, silver, and gold are mined. The iron ore deposits in the Ungava Bay region have been exploited in recent decades. Asbestos is found in the far N and, more importantly, in the Thetford Mines region of the Appalachian Highlands. At Jonquière, in the Saguenay valley, is one of the world's largest aluminum plants. The small farms of the lowlands yield dairy prods., sugar beets, and tobacco. Que. is 2d to Ont. among the Can. provs. in industrial production. Its main mfg. includes refined petroleum, food prods., beverages, motor vehicles, clothing, furniture, iron and steel, chemicals, and metal and paper prods. The fur and fishing trades are still important. The service sector has grown significantly since the 1970s, and now represents one of the largest sectors of the economy. Since many continental explorations began here, Que. has been called the cradle of Canada. In 1534, Jacques Cartier planted a cross on the Gaspé and the following year he sailed up the St. Lawrence. In 1608, Samuel de Champlain built a trading post on the site of present-day Quebec city, and from this and subsequent settlements Catholic missionaries, explorers, and fur traders penetrated the continent. In 1663 Louis XIV made the region, known as New France, a royal colony. The long struggle to protect the colony and the fur trade against the Iroquois and the British was effectively lost in 1759 when the British defeated the French on the Plains of Abraham. By the Treaty of Paris of 1763, Great Britain acquired New France. In an attempt to conciliate the Fr. inhabitants, the British passed the Quebec Act of 1774, under which the colony was allowed to continue its semifeudal system of land tenure and to retain its language, religion, legal system, and customs. After the Amer. Revolution, many Br. Loyalists came to settle in Que. By the Constitutional Act of 1791 the British detached the area W of the Ottawa R. and made it the colony of Upper Canada (now Ontario). Que. became known as Lower Canada, and in 1791 the 1st elective assembly was introduced. The resentment of leaders of the Fr. community against the British precipitated a revolt in 1837. Although the rebellion was crushed, the disturbances in Upper and Lower Canada caused the British to send the Earl of Durham to study conditions. His report led ultimately to internal self-govt. and the creation of the Can. confederation. Upper and Lower Canada were reunited in 1841, and Que. became known as Canada East. With the formation of the confederation of Canada in 1867, Canada East became the prov. of Que. Its special, traditional institutions were specifically written into the Can. constitution. Eng. and Fr. were made the official languages of both Que. and the Can. Parliament, and a dual school system was established within Que. But the coexistence of majority-Fr. and minority-Eng. cultures and Native Amer. cultures (Inuit, Cree, etc.) within the prov., and the reverse situation within Canada as a whole, has remained a source of tension. During the 20th cent. great economic growth in Que. was coupled with increasing determination to maintain and broaden provincial rights. In the 1960s separatist groups, advocating an independent Que., gained attention. In 1970 separatist terrorists kidnapped a Br. diplomat, James R. Cross, and the Que. Minister of Labour, Pierre Laporte. Cross was later released, but Laporte was found murdered. The incident led to the temporary curtailment on the part of the federal govt. of certain civil rights guaranteed in the Can. constitution. It was the 1st time such powers had been used by the federal govt. during peacetime. In 1974 Fr. was made the sole official language of the prov., and all children were required to attend Fr.-language school. In 1976 the Parti Québecois, a party of Fr.-Can. nationalists formed in 1970, won control of the provincial parliament under René Lévesque. The new govt. initiated a series of language and cultural reforms which caused a steady outmigration of Eng.-speaking people from the prov., mainly to Ont. In 1978 the Sun Life Assurance Co. moved its hq. from Montreal to Toronto, one of several large companies to leave Que. because of its language laws. However, Montreal did attract many high technology and financial services companies during the 1980s. In 1980 Lévesque's plan for an independent Que., called sovereignty-association, was defeated in a provincial referendum. The Parti Québecois was reelected in 1981, however, and in 1982 the provincial govt. refused to accept the new Can. constitution. Only after Liberal Robert Bourassa became premier in 1985 did there appear to be progress on the issue of Que. separatism, when the Meech Lake Accord was signed. The Accord was defeated on June 22, 1990, however, when N.F. and Man. failed to approve it. A package of constitutional reforms was drafted by the Can. govt. and presented to voters in a natl. referendum in Oct. 1992. Its defeat in Que. and several other provs. encouraged the separatist movement. However, in Oct. 1995, the separatists lost a provincial referendum by a narrow margin. There is sympathy across Canada to put the separatist issue to rest, but Que.'s separatism remains strong. In Que., 24 senators are appointed and 75 representatives are elected. Que. has many univs., including McGill Univ., Univ. de Montreal, Bishop's Univ., Concordia Univ., Univ. de Sherbrooke, and Lennoxville Univ.

Quebec (kwuh-BEHK), Fr. *Québec,* county (□ 2,745 sq mi/7,110 sq km), S Que., Canada, on the St. Lawrence; ⊙ Beauport; 47°30′N 72°00′W.

Quebec (kwuh-BEHK), Fr. *Québec,* city (1991 pop. 167,517), ⊙ Que. prov., S Que., Canada, at the confluence of the St. Lawrence and St. Charles rivers; 46°48′N 71°15′W. The pop. is largely Fr.-speaking, and the town is at the ideological core of Fr. Canada. An important port and an industrial, cultural, service, and tourist center. Part of the city is built on the waterfront and is called Lower Town; that part called Upper Town is on Cape Diamond, a bluff rising c.300 ft/91 m above the St. Lawrence. Winding, narrow streets link the 2 sects. The chief industries are shipbuilding and tourism, and the mfg. of pulp, paper, newsprint, leather prods., textiles, clothing, machinery, and foods and beverages. The site of Quebec was visited by Cartier in 1535, and in 1608 Champlain established a Fr. colony in the present Lower Town; this was captured (1629) by the English, who held it until 1632. In 1663, Quebec was made the capital of New France and became the center of the fur trade. The city was unsuccessfully attacked by the English in 1690 and 1711. Finally in 1759 Eng. forces defeated the French on the Plains of Abraham and captured Quebec. Quebec became capital of Lower Canada in 1791. After the union (1841) of Upper and Lower Canada, it was twice capital of the United Provinces of Canada (1851–1855 and 1859–1865). Much of historic Quebec is preserved, including the Ursuline Convent (1639); the Basilica of Notre Dame (1647); Quebec Seminary (1663); and parts of the fortifications enclosing Old Quebec. Nearby are Montmorency Falls, the Île d'Orléans, and the shrine of Ste Anne de Beaupré. Laval Univ. is a center for the city's largely francophone culture.

Quebradillas (ke-brah-DEE-yahs), town (1990 pop. 21,425), NW P.R., near the Atlantic, 14 mi/23 km W of Arecibo. Important coffee-growing area. In irrigated region (pineapples, plantains, vegetables); cattle, horses; dairying; light mfg. Tourism.

Quechee, Vt.: see HARTFORD.

Quechee River, Vt.: see OTTAUQUECHEE RIVER.

Quecholac (ke-cho-LAK), town (1990 pop. 6,014), Puebla, central Mexico, 37 mi/60 km ESE of Puebla. Cereals, maguey.

Quechultenango (ke-chool-te-NAN-go), town (1990 pop. 3,088), Guerrero, SW Mexico, in Sierra Madre del Sur, 18 mi/29 km SE of Chilpancingo de los Bravo; 17°25′N 99°13′W. Cereals, fruit, sugar.

Queen Anne, village (1990 pop. 250), Queen Annes co., E Md., 12 mi/19 km NNE of Easton and on Tuckahoe Creek; 38°55′N 75°57′W. Tuckahoe State Park nearby. The village lies partly in Talbot co.

Queen Annes, county (□ 509 sq mi/1,318 sq km; 1990 pop. 33,953) E Md.; ⊙ Centreville; 39°02′N 76°05′W. On the Eastern Shore, bounded E by Del. line, W by Chesapeake Bay. Eastern Bay and a narrow channel (bridged) lie bet. Chesapeake Bay shore and Kent Isl. Tidewater agr. area (vegetables, fruit, wheat, corn; dairy prods.; poultry); fishing, oystering; several canneries. Includes many historic structures. Formed in 1706. The courthouse in Centreville is one of only 2 built in the 18th cent. still standing in Md. Despite housing developments and business centers created by Bay Bridge traffic, it remains essentially agr. It is part of the Baltimore Metropolitan Statistical Area (MSA) according to the 1990 Census.

Queen Bess, Mount (10,700 ft/3,261 m), SW B.C., Canada, in Coast Mts., 150 mi/241 km N of Vancouver; 51°16′N 124°31′W.

Queen, Cape, SW extremity of Baffin Isl., SE Franklin Dist., N.W.T., Canada, at W end of Foxe Peninsula, on Foxe Channel; 64°43′N 78°30′W.

Queen Charlotte, village, W B.C., Canada, on SE Graham Isl., on Skidegate Inlet, 100 mi/161 km SW of Prince Rupert; 53°15′N 132°05′W. Port, trade center for lumbering, cattle raising, potato-growing region. Formerly called Queen Charlotte City.

Queen Charlotte Channel (10 mi/16 km long, 2 mi/3 km wide), SW B.C., Canada, E entrance of Howe Sound from Strait of Georgia, 10 mi/16 km NW of Vancouver, separating Bowen Isl. (W) from E shore of Howe Sound.

Queen Charlotte Islands, archipelago of several large and many small isls., off the coast of W B.C., Canada. The main isls. are Graham and Moresby. Masset on Graham Isl. is the main settlement. About 2,000 of the Isls.' 5,700 inhabitants are Haida, a native people whose anc. village, Ninstints, on Skungwai Isl., was named a World Heritage Site by the UN. Valuable timber, fishing resources, and several good harbors are here. Because they escaped glaciation, making them biologically unique, the Isls. attract many scientists and tourists. The archipelago was visited in 1774 by Juan Pérez and in 1778 by Capt. James Cook; in 1787 it was surveyed by Capt. George Dixon. Hecate Strait separates it from the mainland; Dixon Entrance lies bet. it and Alaska to the N; and Queen Charlotte Sound separates it from Vancouver Isl. to the S.

Queen Charlotte Sound, bay of the Pacific in B.C., Canada, bet. Vancouver Isl. (S) and Queen Charlotte Isls. (N). In the N it merges with Hecate Strait; in S it narrows to Queen Charlotte Strait (60 mi/97 km long, 16 mi/26 km wide), separating NE Vancouver Isl. from the mainland. The strait, part of the inland water route to Alaska, is joined to Strait of Georgia via Johnstone Strait and Discovery Passage.

Queen City, city (1990 pop. 704), Schuyler co., N Mo., near Chariton R., 9 mi/14.5 km S of Lancaster; 40°24′N 92°34′W. Soybeans, corn; sheep, hogs.

Queen City, town (1990 pop. 1,748), Cass co., NE Texas, 19 mi/31 km SSW of Texarkana; 33°08′N 94°09′W. Mfg. (military equip. plating).

Queen Creek, town (1990 pop. 2,667), Maricopa co., central Ariz., suburb 28 mi/45 km SE of downtown Phoenix, on Queen Creek; 33°14′N 111°38′W. Irrigated agr. region (fruit, vegetables, grain, cotton; livestock). Mfg. (cotton milling, plastics prods., agr. chemicals). Salt-Gila Aqueduct to E. Gila R. Indian Reservation to SW; Ariz. Boys Ranch to NW.

Queen Elizabeth Islands, N.W.T., Canada, a group of isls. (□ 164,093 sq mi/425,001 sq km, ⅕ covered with land ice), in Canadian Arctic Archipelago. Form triangle at N tip of Canada. Major isls.: Ellesmere, Devon, Cornwallis, Bathurst, Melville, and Prince Patrick. Named after Queen Elizabeth II in 1953.

Queen Mary, Mount (10,600 ft/3,231 m), SE B.C., Canada, near Alta. border, in Rocky Mts., 40 mi/64 km S of Banff.

Queen Maud Gulf, S Franklin dist., N.W.T., Canada, arm (140 mi/225 km long, 50 mi/80 km—100 mi/161 kmwide) of the Arctic Ocean, on Mackenzie-Keewatin dist. shore S of Victoria and King William isls. Connected (W) with Dease Strait and Coronation Gulf, N with Victoria Strait, E with Simpson Strait. At W end of gulf is Melbourne Isl.; other isls. in gulf are Jenny Lind Isl. and the Royal Geographical Society Isls. Queen Maud Gulf forms part of NW Passage through the Arctic Archipelago.

Queen River or **Queens River**, S R.I.; rises in West Greenwich town; flows c.15 mi/24 km S, past Usquepaug village, to Pawcatuck R. near Kenyon. Sometimes called Usquepaug R. below Usquepaug.

Queens 1 county (□ 1,373 sq mi/3,556 sq km; 1991 pop. 12,519), S central N.B., Canada, intersected by St. John R. and centered on Grand L.; ⊙ Gagetown. **2** county (□ 983 sq mi/2,546 sq km; 1991 pop. 12,923), SW N.S., Canada, on the Atlantic; ⊙ Liverpool. **3** county (□ 765 sq mi/1,981 sq km; 1991 pop. 67,196), in central part of P.E.I., Canada; ⊙ Charlottetown.

Queens, county (□ 177 sq mi/458 sq km; 1990 pop. 1,951,598), SE N.Y., coextensive with Queens borough of N.Y. city; 40°39′N 73°50′W.

Queens, borough of N.Y. city (□ c.147 sq mi/381 sq km; 1990 pop. 1,951,598), on the W portion of L.I., SE N.Y., coextensive with Queens co.; 40°39′N 73°50′W. Having the largest area of the city's boroughs, it extends from the junction of the East R. and L.I. Sound in the N, across L.I. to Jamaica Bay and the Atlantic Ocean in the S. It is connected with Manhattan by the Queensboro Bridge, the Queens–Midtown Tunnel, RR, and subway tunnels; with the Bronx and Manhattan by the Triborough Bridge; with the Bronx by the Hell Gate RR bridge, and by the Bronx–Whitestone and Throgs Neck bridges. The borough has c.200 mi/322 km of waterfront. It is industrialized in L.I. City; there and at Sunnyside are extensive RR yards. Astoria, Flushing, Queens Boulevard, Rego Park, and Jamaica (seat of St. John's Univ.) are industrial and commercial centers, though Jamaica has declined in the 1990s. Among the many residential communities are Flushing (Queens Col. is here), Forest Hills, and Kew Gardens. The Rockaways, on a peninsula bet. Jamaica Bay and the Atlantic

Ocean, is a popular beach area. The 1st settlements in the area were made by the Dutch in 1635. Queens co. was organized in 1683, the main settlements were Flushing, Jamaica, and Newtown (later Elmhurst). Several bldgs. of the 17th and 18th cents. remain. One of the 1st commercial nurseries in the country was est. c.1737, and the community's collection of trees still includes several rare species. In the Amer. Revolution, Br. troops held the area after the battle of L.I. (1776). The W portions of Queens co. voted to join N.Y. city in 1898; Nassau co. became the new name for the E sect. In the 20th cent., growth was spurred with the opening of the Queensboro Bridge (1909) and a RR tunnel (1910). After World War II there was a great increase in housing construction. Queens is the site of LaGuardia Airport and JFK Internatl. Airport. The 2d-most populous borough in N.Y. city, Queens has become the most ethnically diverse co. in the U.S., with large pops. of new immigrants. Early film studios in Astoria have been restored for TV and film production. Two N.Y. World's Fairs (1939–1940; 1964–1965) were held in Flushing Meadow Park. Also in the borough are Aqueduct racetrack and Shea Stadium, home of the N.Y. Mets (baseball), and the U.S. Open tennis tournament is held here annually. Parts of Jamaica Bay and the Rockaway Peninsula (including former U.S. Fort Tilden) are included in the Gateway Natl. Recreation Area. Settled by the Dutch 1635, est. as a borough of N.Y. city 1898.

Queens Channel, N.W.T., Canada: see WELLINGTON CHANNEL.

Queens River, R.I.: see QUEEN RIVER.

Queens Village, residential section of E Queens borough of N.Y. city, SE N.Y.; 40°44′N 73°46′W. Limited mfg. Creedmore Psychiatric Center is here.

Queensboro Bridge, cantilever bridge across East R. bet. midtown Manhattan and L.I. City dist. of Queens, N.Y. city, SE N.Y.; 40°46′N 73°57′W. Including approaches, c.7,450 ft/2,271 m long; longest span is 1,182 ft/360 m. Crosses Roosevelt Isl. Opened 1909.

Queens-Midtown Tunnel, vehicular tunnel under East R. bet. midtown Manhattan and L.I. City dist. of Queens, N.Y. city, SE N.Y.; 40°45′N 73°57′W. Twin 2-lane tubes, 3,055 ft/931 m long under the river, 95 ft/29 m below the surface. Built 1936–1940.

Queenston, village, S Ont., Canada, just N of Niagara Falls. Here the Br. defeated Amer. invaders in the battle of Queenston Heights (Oct. 13, 1812) in the War of 1812; 43°10′N 79°03′W. The Br. commanding general, Sir Isaac Brock, was killed in the fighting.

Queenstown, fishing town (1990 pop. 453), Queen Annes co., E Md., on the Eastern Shore, 16 mi/26 km NNW of Easton, and on Chester R. estuary; 38°59′N 76°10′W. Vegetable cannery, oyster-packing plant.

Queets River (KWEETS), c.60 mi/97 km long, Jefferson co., W Wash.; rises in Olympic Natl. Park SE of Mt. Olympus, and NW of Mt. Queets; flows SW. Receives Clearwater R., and flows through NW corner of Quinalt Indian Reservation before entering Pacific Ocean at Queets.

Quemada (ke-MAH-dah) or **La Quemada**, ruined Toltec center, N central Mexico, on central plateau, 33 mi/53 km SW of Zacatecas, NE of Villanueva. On anc. turquoise trade route. Ruins, of great value to archaeologists, were abandoned long before the arrival of Spaniards, who discovered them 1535.

Quemado 1 (ke-MAH-do), uninc. village, Catron co., W N.Mex., 78 mi/126 km SW of Grants, on Largo Creek, at mouth of Mangas Creek. Cattle, sheep, goats. Escondido Mt. (9,869 ft/3,008 m) and Quemado L., both in Apache Natl. Forest, to S. **2** uninc. village (1990 pop. 426), Maverick co., S Texas, 18 mi/29 km N of Eagle Pass, on Rio Grande (Mex. border). In irrigated Rio Grande valley (vegetables, pecans, wheat; cattle).

Quemado de Güines (kai-MAH-do dai GWEE-naiz), town, Villa Clara prov., central Cuba, on RR, and 11 mi/18 km W of Sagua la Grande; 22°48′N 80°15′W. In cattle-raising and sugar-growing region. Jerked-beef industry. Nearby are the centrals of Panchito Gómez Toro (WSW) and José Riquelme (NW).

Quemahoning Reservoir (KEE-mah-ho-neeng), Somerset co., SW Pa., lake (c.3 mi/4.8 km long) formed by dam in short Quemahoning Creek; flows NE to Stonycreek R., 9 mi/14.5 km S of Johnstown; 40°10′N 78°56′W.

Quenemo (KWIN-uh-mo), village (1990 pop. 369), Osage co., E Kansas, on Marais des Cygnes R., and 8 mi/12.9 km E of Lyndon; 38°34′N 95°31′W. Livestock; grain.

Quentin, village, Franklin co., SW Miss., 18 mi/29 km WSW of Brookhaven, in Homochitto Natl. Forest. Timber.

Queponco, Md.: see NEWARK.

Queréndaro (ke-REN-dah-ro), town (1990 pop. 8,350), Michoacán, S of L. Cuitzeo, and 22 mi/35 km ENE of Morelia; 19°48′N 100°53′W. Cereals, fruit, maguey; livestock.

Querétaro (ke-RE-TAH-ro), city (1990 pop. 385,503) and township, ☉ of Querétaro state, central Mexico, on RR, on Mexico highwrays 45 and 57; 20°38′N 100°23′W. It is a distribution center with industries producing machinery and farm implements; the city's cotton mills are among the most important in Mexico. Querétaro is also a popular tourist center. The conspiracy (1810) under Hidalgo y Costilla and Allende that led to the revolution against Spain was planned there. In 1867, Emperor Maximilian and his generals Miguel Miramon and Tomás Mejia were forced to surrender and then executed on Cerro de las Campanas outside the city. In 1917 the Mex. Constitution was written in Querétaro, which retains numerous colonial landmarks and is famous for its 18th-cent. aqueduct.

Querétaro Arteaga (ke-RE-tah-ro ahr-te-AH-gah), state (☐ 4,432 sq mi/11,479 sq km; 1990 pop. 1,061,236), central Mexico; ☉ QUERÉTARO; 20°01′N 99°03′W. With mountains in the N, plus valleys and plains in the S, the state raises a variety of agr. prods., especially grains. Extensive pasturelands make livestock breeding important. The state is famous for its opals; silver, iron, copper, and mercury are also mined. Although Querétaro is developing an industrialized economy, most mfg. remains concentrated in the capital. The territory of Querétaro was taken from the Chichimecs by the Spanish in 1531, but colonization did not begin until 1550. Later included in the intendancy of Guanajuato, Querétaro became a separate state in 1824.

Quesnel (kuh-NEHL), city (1991 pop. 8,179), S central B.C., Canada, on Fraser R. at mouth of Quesnel R., and 70 mi/113 km S of Prince George; 52°59′N 122°29′W. Dairying, mixed farming; lumbering, plywood mfg. Gold and diatomaceous earth are found in region.

Quesnel Lake (☐ 104 sq mi/269 sq km), E B.C., Canada, in Cariboo Dist., 120 mi/193 km SE of Prince George; 60 mi/97 km long, 1 mi/2 km–3 mi/5 km wide. Drained NW of Quesnel R. (64 mi/103 km long) into Fraser R. Just S is Horsefly L.

Questa (KWES-tuh), town (1990 pop. 1,707), Taos co., N N.Mex., on Red R., near its mouth on Rio Grande, in Sangre de Cristo Mts., and 22 mi/35 km N of Taos; 36°42′N 105°35′W. Elev. 7,461 ft/2,274 m. Agr. (alfalfa; cattle, sheep; timber); sawmill. Large molybdenum mine nearby. Part of Carson Natl. Forest to S and E; Latir Peak 9 mi/14.5 km NE. Settled 1829 as San Antonio del Rio Colorado; named Questa 1884. Wild Rivers Natl. Recreation Area and fish hatchery to SW, in Rio Grande Gorge.

Quetiquo Provincial Park (KWEH-ti-ko) (☐ 1,720 sq mi/4,455 sq km), NW Ont., Canada, on Minn. border, 80 mi/129 km W of Fort William; 55 mi/89 km long, 40 mi/64 km wide; wilderness area; contains numerous lakes e.g., Pickerel, Quetiquo, Kawnipi.

Queue de Tortue, Bayou (KWAI duh TOOR-tai, BEI-yoo), c.40 mi/64 km long, S La.; rises E of Rayne; flows SW of Mermentau R. just above L. Arthur; partly navigable.

Quick Creek Reservoir, Ind.: see HARDY LAKE.

Quicksand, uninc. village (1990 pop. 450), Breathitt co., E central Ky., 3 mi/4.8 km SE of Jackson, on North Fork Kentucky R. Agr. (tobacco; cattle; honey; timber).

Robinson Forest, Univ. of Ky., experimental and research forest, to SE.

Quidi Vidi (ki-tee VI-tee, kwei-tuh VEI-tuh), SE N.F., Canada, N residential suburb of St. John's; 47°35′N 52°42′W. Rennie's R. (reclaimed urban trout stream) flows through Quidi Vidi L. (1 mi/2 km long, 1 mi/2 km wide) before entering Quidi Vidi Harbour. In World War II, U.S. Army base was est. here. Signal Hill Natl. Historic Park to S.

Quiebra Hacha (kee-AI-bruh AH-chuh), town, La Habana prov., W Cuba, 4 mi/6.4 km WSW of Mariel; 22°57′N 82°49′W. Tobacco, sugarcane; livestock. Sugar mill Orlando Nodarse to SW.

Quilcene (KWIL-seen), uninc. town (1990 pop. 1,200), Jefferson co., NW Wash., 20 mi/32 km S of Port Townsend, on Quilcene Bay, extension of Hood Canal, at mouth of Quilcene Natl. Fish Hatchery, on Perry Creek, to SW. Mfg. (fresh and frozen seafood). Olympic Natl. Forest, including Buckhorn Wilderness Area, and Olympic Natl. Park to W.

Quill Lake, village (1991 pop. 464), S central Sask., Canada, near the Quill Lakes, 40 mi/64 km ESE of Humboldt; 52°04′N 104°15′W. Mixed farming, dairying.

Quill Lakes, 2 lakes (☐ 236 sq mi/611 sq km), S central Sask., Canada, 90 mi/145 km N of Regina, and just N of Wynyard. Larger lake is 19 mi/31 km long, 14 mi/23 km wide; smaller lake, just E, 18 mi/29 km long, 8 mi/13 km wide, drains E into Assiniboine R. through Whitesand R.

Quillayute River (kwil-ah-YOOT), c.6 mi/9.7 km long, Clallam co., NW Wash., short stream of Olympic Peninsula; formed by junction of Soleduck (Sol Duc) and Bogachiel rivers E of La Push; flows W to Pacific Ocean, in coastal section of Olympic Natl. Park, where its estuary is harbor of La Push. Quillayute Needles Natl. Wildlife Refuge extends S from La Push in offshore rocks and isls.

Quillingok, Alaska: see KWIGILLINGOK.

Quimby, town (1990 pop. 334), Cherokee co., NW Iowa, on Little Sioux R., and 9 mi/14.5 km SSW of Cherokee; 42°37′N 95°38′W. Rendering and feed-milling plants.

Quimixtlán (kee-mish-TLAHN), town (1990 pop. 1,270), Puebla, central Mexico, in Sierra Madre, 30 mi/48 km NE of Ciudad Serdán; 19°16′N 97°07′W. Elev. 6,627 ft/2,020 m. Cereals, maguey.

Quinault Lake (kwin-AWLT), Grays Harbor co., W Wash., in Olympic Natl. Forest (SW end borders Quinault Indian Reservation), 35 mi/56 km N of Hoquiam; c.4 mi/6.4 km long. Center of Quinault L. Recreational Area, in SW Olympic Natl. Park on NE and NW of Quinault. Resort village on SE shore, has Quinault Rain Forest Visitor Center. Receives from NE and discharges SW the Quinault R., c.75 mi/121 km long, rising SW of Mt. Anderson, and flowing SW through Quinault Indian Reservation to Pacific Ocean near Taholah. N. Fork rises S of Mt. Quects; flows S c.25 mi/40 km, entirely within park. Colonel Bob Wilderness Area to E.

Quinby, town (1990 pop. 865), Florence co., E central S.C., 4 mi/6.4 km NE of Florence, near Black Creek; 34°13′N 79°43′W. Mfg. of special machines; agr. includes cotton, tobacco, grain; poultry, livestock.

Quincy 1 (KWIN-see), city (1990 pop. 39,681), ☉ Adams co., W Ill., on a bluff above the Mississippi, c.90 mi/145 km W of Springfield; 39°55′N 91°23′W. It is a trade, industrial (steel parts), and distributing center in a grain and livestock area. The city and co. were named for John Quincy Adams. Quincy has a good harbor and was an important river port in the mid-19th cent. Before the Civil War it was the scene of several proslavery-abolitionist struggles. The 6th Lincoln-Douglas debate was held here on Oct. 13, 1858. Quincy Univ.; a state soldiers' and sailors' home; Gem City Col., and John Wood Community Col. are here. Inc. 1839. **2** city (1990 pop. 84,985), Norfolk co., E Mass., a suburb of Boston, on Boston Bay; 42°16′N 71°01′W. It has plants that make power transmissions, machinery, soaps, textile prods., detergents, chemicals, and printing and publishing. The Plymouth Colony broke up (1627) a trading post est. 1625 in the area by Thomas Morton, but a new settlement began in 1634. Ironworks began operation in 1644, and Quincy's famed granite started to be quarried in 1750. The 1st RR tracks in the U.S. were laid in Quincy in 1826. The city's large shipyard Fore R. was of great importance in both world wars. Presidents John Adams and John Quincy Adams were born in Quincy. They and their wives are buried in the First Parish Church (built 1828), and their homes and places of birth are natl. historic sites. John Hancock was also b. here. E. Nazarene Col. and a junior col. are in the city. Hq. of Natl. Fire Protection Inst. Includes villages of Merrymount, Squantum, Wollaston. Settled 1634, set off from Braintree 1792, inc. as a city 1888.

Quincy 1 (KWIN-see), uninc. town (1990 pop. 2,670), ⊙ Plumas co., NE Calif., 70 mi/113 km NW of Reno (Nev.), in the Sierra Nevada; timber, cattle. Mfg. (printing and publishing); winter sports. Hq. for Plumas Natl. Forest, which surrounds area. Statistically reported as Quincy–East Quincy (1990 pop. 4,271); East Quincy 5 mi/8 km E. Feather R. Community Col. (Dist.). **2** town (□ 6 sq mi/15.5 sq km; 1990 pop. 7,444), ⊙ Gadsden co., NW Fla., near Ga. state line, 20 mi/ 32 km WNW of Tallahassee; 30°34′N 84°34′W. Cigar mfg. and tobacco marketing center; mushrooms. **3** town (1990 pop. 1,680), Branch co., S Mich., 6 mi/ 9.7 km E of Coldwater near N end of Marble L.; 41°56′N 84°52′W. In farm area. Mfg. (aluminum and vinyl windows; gaskets and seals, freezer shelves; meat processing). Resort, with small lakes nearby. Settled 1833, inc. 1858. **4** town (1990 pop. 3,738), Grant co., central Wash., 15 mi/24 km SW of Ephrata; 47°14′N 119°51′W. In Columbia basin agr. region; apples, sugar beets, peppermint, spearmint, vegetables, potatoes, beans. Mfg. (frozen fruits and vegetables). Columbia R. 5 mi/8 km to W.

Quincy (KWIN-see), village (1990 pop. 697), Logan co., W central Ohio, 12 mi/19 km WSW of Bellefontaine, and on Great Miami R., in agr. area; 40°17′N 83°58′W.

Quincy Adams, Mount (13,560 ft/4,133 m), on Alaska–B.C., Canada, border, in Fairweather Range, 5 mi/8 km E of Mt. Fairweather, 120 mi/193 km WNW of Juneau; 58°54′N 137° 27′W.

Quincy Bay, Mass.: see BOSTON BAY.

Quincy Reservoir, Arapahoe co., N central Colo., on Toll Gate Creek, 12 mi SE of downtown Denver; 1 mi/ 1.6 km long; 39°39′N 104°46′W. Formed by Quincy Dam (68 ft/21 m high), built (1973) by the City of Aurora (to NNW) for water supply.

Quinebaug River (KWI-nuh-bawg), c.80 mi/129 km long, in Mass. and Conn.; rises in ponds NW of Sturbridge, Mass.; flows SE and S, through Conn., past Putnam, Danielson, Plainfield (dam here), and Jewett City, to Shetucket R. just NE of Norwich. On its upper reaches in Mass. are sites of East Brimfield Dam and Westville Dam, both for flood control.

Quinhagak, Alaska: see KWINHAGAK.

Quinlan, town (1990 pop. 1,360), Hunt co., NE Texas, 16 mi/26 km S of Greenville; 32°54′N 96°07′W. In agr. area (dairying; nursery crops; cotton, wheat). Mfg. (wooden house trim). L. Tawakoni reservoir to E, State Park to SE.

Quinlan, village (1990 pop. 23), Woodward co., NW Okla., 19 mi/31 km E of Woodward; 36°27′N 99°02′W. In livestock and grain area.

Quinn, village (1990 pop. 72), Pennington co., SW central S.Dak., 4 mi/6.4 km E of Wall; 43°59′N 102°07′W. At edge of Buffalo Gap Natl. Grassland.

Quinn River (KWIN), c.110 mi/177 km long, NW Nev.; rises in NE Humboldt co. near Oregon state line; flows generally SW through 2 units of Fort McDermitt Indian Reservation; receives King R. NE of Jackson Mts., at lower unit of Indian reservation, then through Jackson Mts., turning SSW to sink into Black Rock Desert c. 60 mi/97 km W of Winnemucca.

Quinnesec (KWIN-uh-sek), village (1990 pop. 1,254), Dickinson co., S Upper Peninsula, Mich., 4 mi/ 6.4 km SE of Iron Mountain, near Menominee R.; 45°47′N 88°00′W. Mfg. (pulp and paper mill).

Quinnipiac River (KWIN-e-pee-ak), c.50 mi/80 km long, Conn.; rises near New Britain; flows generally S, past Southington, Meriden, and Wallingford, to New Haven Harbor at New Haven.

Quinsam Lake (KWIN-suhm), on central Vancouver Isl., SW B.C., Canada, 25 mi/40 km SW of Campbell R.; iron mining.

Quinsigamond, Lake (kwin-SI-guh-muhnd), reservoir, Worcester co., central Mass., 5 mi/8 km SE of Worcester; c.7 mi/11.3 km long; 42°13′N 71°42′W. Drains through short stream to Flint Pond and Blackstone R. Quinsigamond State Park on NW shore.

Quintana, village (1990 pop. 51), Brazoria co., SE Texas, residential suburb 4 mi/6.4 km SE of Freeport, in Brazosport Area, bet. Gulf of Mexico (SE) and Intracoastal Waterway (NW); 28°55′N 95°19′W. Recreation area. Bryan Beach State Park to SW.

Quintana Roo (keen-TAH-nah ROO), state (□ 19,630 sq mi/50,842 sq km; 1990 pop. 493,277), SE Mexico, on the Caribbean; ⊙ Chetumal; 17°50′N 86°42′W. Occupying most of the E part of the YUCATÁN peninsula, it was, until recently, wild, sparsely settled, and populated almost entirely by the Mayas. In recent years large areas have been cleared for farming and pasture. It has a hot climate with high rainfall. The economy is dominated by tourism. The resorts of CANCÚN and COZUMEL are leading internatl. holiday spots. While Cozumel began drawing visitors in the 1960s, Cancún is an entirely planned resort city, begun in 1974. Scandalous episodes involving the wholesale purchase of Mayas for what amounted to slave labor in the chicle plantations tarnished the history of the territory in the late 19th and early 20th cent. Along the Caribbean coast is the famous Mayan archaeological site of Tulum. Quintana Roo's forest reserves suffered damage from a hurricane in 1988, and a major fire in 1989.

Quintana Roo (keen-TAH-nah ROO), town (1990 pop. 1,050), Yucatán, SE Mexico, 29 mi/47 km NW of Valladolid on RR; 20°52′N 88°38′W. Henequen, sugarcane.

Quinte, Bay of (KWIN-tee), arm of L. Ontario, S Ont., Canada, bet. the mainland and the peninsula of Prince Edward co. With its approach, Adolphus Reach, it is 60 mi/97 km long. The Trent R., which is the lower portion of the Trent Canal bet. L. Ontario and L. Huron, flows into the head of the bay. Belleville and Trenton are on the N shore.

Quinter (KWIN-tuhr), village (1990 pop. 945), Gove co., W central Kansas, 32 mi/51 km E of Oakley; 39°04′N 100°13′W. In grain and cattle region. Mfg. (honey, feeds, farm machinery).

Quinton, town (1990 pop. 1,133), Pittsburg co., SE Okla., 26 mi/42 km ENE of McAlester; 35°07′N 95°22′W. In agr. region, logging area. Mfg. (log home kits). Sanbois Mts. to SE; Robbers Cave State Park to S.

Quinton, township (1990 pop. 2,511), Salem co., SW N.J., on Alloway Creek, and 3 mi/4.8 km SE of Salem; 39°31′N 75°22′W. Monument marks Revolutionary battle site.

Quinwood, village (1990 pop. 559), Greenbrier co., SE W.Va., 22 mi/35 km NNW of Lewisburg; 38°3′N 80°42′W. Agr. (grain, tobacco); livestock. Monongahela Natl. Forest to NE.

Quinze, Lac des (KEHZ, lahk dai), lake (□ 55 sq mi/ 142 sq km), 35 mi/56 km long, SW Que., Canada; 80 mi/129 km N of North Bay.

Quinze, Rapide des (rah-PEED), torrential stream, 20 mi/32 km long, in W Que., Canada; issues from L. des Quinze at Angliers; flows W to L. Timiskaming. Along course are 15 waterfalls. Near Angliers is large barrage and hydroelectric station, supplying Rouyn-Noranda mining region.

Quiotepec, Mexico: see SAN JUAN QUIOTEPEC.

Quirauk Mountain, Pa. and Md.: see SOUTH MOUNTAIN.

Quiriego (kee-ree-E-go), town (1990 pop. 1,014), Sonora, NW Mexico, on affluent of Mayo R., and 41 mi/66 km E of Ciudad Obregón; 27°31′N 109°12′W. Livestock raising (cattle, hogs, horses).

Quiroga (kee-RO-gah), town (1990 pop. 11,765), Michoacán, central Mexico, on N shore of L. Pátzcuaro,

25 mi/40 km W of Morelia, on Mexico Highway 15. Resort; fishing and agr. center (corn, fruit; livestock).

Quirpon Island (KAHR-puhn), (□ 4 sq mi/10 sq km), just off NE extremity of N.F., Canada, 20 mi/32 km E of Cape Norman; 51°37′N 55°27′W. Isl. is 4 mi/6 km long, 2 mi/3 km wide; rises to 505 ft/154 m. Fishing. A N extremity is Cape Bauld, with lighthouse (51°39′N 55°26′W). On mainland, 2 mi/3 km WSW of isl., is fishing settlement of Quirpon.

Quispamsis, town (1986 pop. 7,185), N.B., Canada, 10 mi/16 km NE of Saint John. Summer community until 1960s. Now residential community of Saint John.

Quisqueya (kees-KAI-yah), locality (11,612), San Pedro de Macorís prov., SE Dominican Republic, 10 mi/16 km NW of San Pedro de Macorís. Sugar mill.

Quitaque (KIT-uh-kwai), village (1990 pop. 513), Briscoe co., NW Texas, 38 mi/61 km ENE of Plainview, just below Caprock escarpment (W); 34°22′N 101°02′W. Elev. 2,570 ft/783 m. Cotton; cattle; mfg. (saddle pads and horse blankets). Caprock Canyon State Park to W.

Quithlook, Alaska: see KWETHLUK.

Quitman 1 county (□ 161 sq mi/417 sq km; 1990 pop. 2,209), SW Ga.; ⊙ Georgetown; 31°52′N 85°01′W. Bounded W by Ala. state line, formed here by Chattahoochee R. Coastal plain agr. (cotton, corn, peanuts, pecans); cattle; in sawmilling area. Antebellum courthouse. Sheffield Camelia Garden named after famous local camellia gardener and developer of new varieties. Downtown historic dist. features early 20th-cent. storefronts. Formed 1858. **2** county (□ 406 sq mi/ 1,052 sq km; 1990 pop. 10,490), NW Miss.; ⊙ Marks; 34°15′N 90°17′W. In rich lowland cotton-growing area. Drained by Coldwater and Tallahatchie rivers. Agr. (cattle; cotton, rice, sorghum, soybeans, wheat); timber processing. O'Keefe Wildlife Management Area in center. Formed 1877.

Quitman 1 town (1990 pop. 5,292), ⊙ Brooks co., S Ga., 17 mi/27 km WSW of Valdosta; 30°47′N 83°34′W. A tobacco market and processing center. Mfg. (textiles, fertilizers, foods, clothing; wire harnesses, animal feed, canning); cotton milling, meat packing; lumber. Inc. 1859. **2** town (1990 pop. 2,736), ⊙ Clarke co.; 32°02′N 88°43′W, E Miss., 21 mi/34 km S of Meridian, and on Chickasawhay R. In agr. (cotton, corn; cattle) and timber area; mfg. (lumber, automotive parts, feeds, textiles, PVC pipe, wood prods., apparel). Clarkco State Park to NE; Bucatunna Wildlife Management Area to NE. **3** town (1990 pop. 47), Nodaway co., NW Mo., on Nodaway R., and 11 mi/18 km W of Maryville; 40°22′N 95°04′W. **4** town (1990 pop. 1,684), ⊙ Wood co., NE Texas, 31 mi/50 km NNW of Tyler; 32°47′N 95°26′W. Trade point in oil, agr. (dairying; cattle, chickens; vegetables; grain); timber area; mfg. (gas mixtures). L. Quitman to N, L. Fork Reservoir to NW; Governor Hogg Shrine State Historic Site is here.

Quitman 1 village (1990 pop. 632), Cleburne co., N central Ark., 24 mi/39 km NNE of Conway; 35°22′N 92°12′W. In agr. area. Mfg. (custom trailers). Woolly Hollow State Park to SW. **2** village (1990 pop. 162), Jackson parish, N central La., 38 mi/61 km WSW of Monroe; 32°21′N 92°43′W. In agr. and lumbering area; RR terminus; lumber. Jackson–Bienville State Wildlife Area to N and W.

Quitman Mountains, Hudspeth co., extreme W Texas, range extending SSE from point W of Sierra Blanca c.30 mi/48 km to the Rio Grande; highest point, 5,683 ft/1,732 m; 31°03′N 105°26′W. Fort Quitman to W.

Quitupan (kee-TOO-pahn), town (1990 pop. 2,203), Jalisco, central Mexico, 40 mi/64 km ENE of Ciudad Guzmán; 19°51′N 102°50′W. Grain, beans; livestock.

Quivicán (kee-vee-KAHN), town, La Habana prov., W Cuba, 20 mi/32 km S of Havana; 22°50′N 82°21′W. Processing and agr. center (sugarcane, yucca, rice, corn); mfg. of cigars, starch. Sugar mill Pablo Noriega 6 mi/ 9.7 km SW.

Quivira (kee-VEE-rah), name given to land sought and reached by Francisco Vásquez de Coronado in 1541 and explored by later Span. expeditions (1593 and 1601). The records do not make it entirely clear exactly where Quivira was located. It is generally identified with villages of the Wichitas, probably around Great Bend, Kansas; however, other sites have been suggested, including one in N Texas.

Qulin (KYOO-lin), town (1990 pop. 384), Butler co., SE Mo., 14 mi/23 km SE of Poplar Bluff; 36°36′N 90°15′W. Mfg. (concrete). Rice, wheat, corn.

Quoddy, Maine: see PASSAMAQUODDY BAY.

Quoddy Narrows (KWAHD-ee), Washington co., E Maine, strait lying bet. Lubec and Campobello Isl.; joins Passamaquoddy Bay to the Atlantic. Also known as Quoddy Bay, Quoddy Roads.

Quogue, summer-resort village (□ 6 sq mi/15.5 sqkm; 1990 pop. 898), Suffolk co., SE N.Y., on S shore of L.I., at W end of Shinnecock Bay, 13 mi/21 kmW of Southampton; 40°49′N 72°35′W. In shore-resort area.

Quonochontaug (KWON-o-chon-tawg), resort village in Charlestown town, Washington co., SW R.I., on the coast, at Quonochontaug Beach, resort on Block Isl. Sound, near inlet to Quonochontaug Pond (c.3 mi/4.8 km long; bay sheltered by dunes along Block Isl. Sound). Quonochontaug fishing area.

Quonset Point (KWON-set), blunt peninsula extending into Narragansett Bay, S R.I., in the town of North Kingstown, Washington co. Davisville Naval Construction Battalion Center was located here.

Quyon (KWEE-ahn, Fr. kuh-YOH), village, SW Que., Canada, on Ottawa R., and 25 mi/40 km WNW of Ottawa; 45°31′N 76°14′W. Lumbering; dairying.

R

Rabbit Ears Mountain, twin peak (10,654 ft/3,247 m) in Rocky Mts., on Continental Divide, Grand and Jackson cos.; 3 mi/4.8 km NNE of Rabbit Ears Pass, NW Colo., 12 mi/19 km ESE of Steamboat Springs; 40°25′N 106°36′W. Rabbit Ears Pass (W; 9,426 ft/2,873 m high), on Grand and Jackson co. border; Routt co. line 2 mi/3.2 km W.

Rabbit Hash, uninc. village, Boone co., N Ky., 7 mi/11.3 km SW of Burlington, on Ohio R. Historic village with general store, craft shop, and iron mill dating to 1831. Tourism.

Rabun (RAI-buhn), county (□ 377 sq mi/976 sq km; 1990 pop. 11,648), extreme NE Ga., on N.C. and S.C. state lines; ⊙ Clayton; 34°53′N 83°24′W. In Chattahoochee Natl. Forest and the Blue Ridge, rising here to 4,663 ft/1,421 m in Rabun Bald (NE); drained by Tallulah R. (dammed; forms lakes Burton and Rabun) and the Little Tennessee. Agr. (hay, potatoes, fruits); cattle, poultry; timber. Resort area. Formed 1819.

Rabun Gap (RAI-buhn), resort village, Rabun co., extreme NE Ga., 5 mi/8 km N of Clayton, on Little Tennessee R., and in Rabun Gap; 34°55′N 83°23′W. Highway and RR pass through Blue Ridge Mts. Mfg. includes meat processing, machining; yarns, crushed stone. Home of the *Foxfire* project that produced over 10 volumes of books documenting the folk traditions and history of people in NE Ga.

Rabun, Lake (RAI-buhn), reservoir (c.4 mi/6.4 km long), Rabun co., NE Ga., on Tallulah R., in Chattahoochee Natl. Forest, 13 mi/21 km NNW of Toccoa; 34°45′N 83°23′W. Formed by Rabun Dam, built for power generation.

Raccoon Creek 1 75 mi/121 km long, W Ind.; rises in SW Boone co.; flows SW, then turns NW near Rosedale, converging with the Wabash 8 mi/12.9 km W of Rockville. Sometimes called Big Raccoon Creek. Raccoon Creek flows into Raccoon L. (also known as Cecil M. Harden Reservoir or Mansfield Reservoir) NE of Mansfield. **2** c.25 mi/40 km, SW N.J.; rises SE of Glassboro; flows generally NW, past Swedesboro, to Delaware R. opposite Chester, Pa. Navigable for c.9 mi/14.5 km below Swedesboro. **3** c.100 mi/161 km, S Ohio; rises in Hocking co.; flows generally S, past Zaleski and Vinton, to the Ohio R. c.7 mi/11 km S of Gallipolis. **4** c.25 mi/40 km long, Licking co., central Ohio, W tributary of Licking R.; 40°02′N 82°24′W.

Raccoon Key, coast island, Charleston co., E S.C., c.30 mi/48 km NE of Charleston, just NE of Bulls Bay; c.7 mi/11.3 km long. Cape Romain lighthouse (now unused) is at E end.

Raccoon River, 200 mi/322 km, central Iowa; rises in Buena Vista co., NW Iowa; flows S and SE, past Sac City and Jefferson, to Des Moines R. at Des Moines. South Raccoon R. rises near Guthrie-Audubon co. line; flows c.50 mi/80 km SE, past Guthrie Center, to Raccoon R. near Van Meter. Middle Raccoon R. rises in NW Carroll co.; flows 76 mi/122 km SE, past Carroll City, to South Raccoon R. near Redfield. Raccoon R. was partially responsible (along with Des Moines R. and others) for severe flood damage in Des Moines and other areas along it, in 1993.

Raccourci, Lake (ra-KOOR-see), shallow inlet of the Gulf of Mexico, Lafourche parish, SE La., N arm of Tibalier Bay, lying just N of Timbalier Bay; c.7 mi/11 km long; 29°15′N 90°21′W. Bayou Pointe-aux-Chenes enters Timbalier Bay just W. Oyster beds; fishing. Oil and natural gas fields.

Race, Cape, flat-topped cliffs, SE extremity of N.F., Canada, at SE end of Avalon Peninsula, 65 mi/105 km SSW of St. John's; 46°40′N 53°05′W. Site of Loran C navigation system. Natl. historic site.

Race Course, town (1991 pop. 2,589), Clarendon parish, S central Jamaica, 8 mi/13 km SSW of May Pen; 17°50′N 77°17′W. Road junction.

Race Lake, SE Ont., Canada, 10 mi/16 km SE of Peterborough; 20 mi/32 km long, 3 mi/5 km wide. Drained E by Trent R.

Race Point, Provincetown, SE Mass., point on NW side of tip of Cape Cod. Has lighthouse (42°04′N 70°15′W). Provincetown Airport. Race Point Beach. Provincetown visitor center; part of Cape Cod Natl. Seashore.

Raceland 1 town (1990 pop. 2,256), Greenup co., NE Ky., residential suburb, 8 mi/12.9 km NW of Ashland, on Ohio R.; 38°32′N 82°43′W. Agr. (tobacco, corn, alfalfa; cattle). Horse racing. Ashland Regional Airport. Inc. 1920 as Chinnville; renamed 1930. **2** (RAS-luhnd), uninc. town (1990 pop. 5,564), Lafourche parish, SE La., on Bayou Lafourche, and 33 mi/53 km SW of New Orleans; 29°43′N 90°36′W. Elev. 14 ft/5 m. RR junction. In agr. area (sugarcane; cattle), crawfish, shrimp, crabs, fish, alligators; mfg. (plastic buoys, raw and refined sugar). Lake Fields to S.

Racine (rai-SEEN), county (□ 791 sq mi/2,049 sq km; 1990 pop. 175,034), SE Wis.; ⊙ Racine; 42°46′N 87°45′W. Bordered E by L. Michigan; drained by Fox and Root rivers. Urbanized in E. Farming area (wheat, corn, oats, soybeans; hogs, sheep); recreation. Extensive mfg. at Racine and Burlington. Small lakes in W. Formed 1836.

Racine (rai-SEEN), city (1990 pop. 84,298), ⊙ Racine co., SE Wis., 20 mi/32 km SSE of Milwaukee, on L. Michigan, at the mouth of the Root R.; 42°43′N 87°48′W. Together with Kenosha to S, Racine is part of an urbanized link bet. Chicago (S) and Milwaukee. It is a port of entry, and its manufactures include farm machinery, automobile parts, stitching machines, tools, corrugated containers, waxes and polishes, and electrical equip. The 1st permanent settlement was est. 1834. Improvement of the harbor (c.1844) and the coming of the RR (1855) brought industrial growth. Three bldgs. in Racine were designed by Frank Lloyd Wright, and the reliefs at the co. courthouse were designed by Carl Milles. Univ. of Wis.-Parkside campus to S. Inc. 1848.

Racine 1 (rai-SEEN), village (1990 pop. 288), Mower co., SE Minn., 17 mi/27 km S of Rochester, near Bear Creek; 43°46′N 92°28′W. Mfg. (agr. machinery); agr. (dairying; poultry; corn, soybeans, peas). Part of Richard J. Dorer Memorial State Forest to E. **2** village (1990 pop. 729), Meigs co., SE Ohio, on Ohio R., and 7 mi/11 km SE of Pomeroy; 38°58′N 81°55′W.

Racine, Canada: see CHUTE SHIPSHAW.

Rackliff Island, Knox co., S Maine, in Penobscot Bay, 3 mi/4.8 km NE of Tenants Harbor; 1.25 mi/2.1 km long.

Radburn, borough, N.J. One of 1st U.S. planned communities. Started in 1928, on 23 sq mi/60 sq km, 600 homes were built before bankruptcy in 1933. Natl. Registry of Historic Places. Now part of borough of Fair Lawn.

Radcliff, city (1990 pop. 19,772), Hardin co., N Ky., 30 mi/48 km SSW of Louisville, at SW edge of Fort Know Military Reserve, including U.S. Gold Bullion Depository to N. Agr. area (tobacco, grain; livestock; dairying). Mfg. (concrete, watch bands, business forms).

Radcliffe, town (1990 pop. 574), Hardin co., central Iowa, 15 mi/24 km E of Eldora; 42°19′N 93°25′W. Livestock; grain.

Radersburg, village (1990 pop. 60), Broadwater co., SW central Mont., 35 mi/56 km SE of Helena. Gold mines to W and SW. Elkhorn Mts., Deer Lodge Natl. Forest, and Helena Natl. Forest to NW; Canyon Ferry L. to NE. Also spelled Radersburgh.

Radford, independent city (□ 10 sq mi/26 sq km; 1990 pop. 15,940), SW Va., 35 mi/56 km WSW of Roanoke, on New R.; 37°08′N 80°33′W. RR junction. Mfg. (motors, iron castings, clothing and textiles, contract assembly, paper goods, paper boxes, construction panels); agr. (corn, alfalfa, apples; livestock; dairying). Radford Univ. Parts of Radford Army Ammunition Plant to W and N. Jefferson Natl. Forest to NW; Claytor L. State Park, on Claytor L. reservoir (New R.), to SW. New R. Valley Airport to W. Settled 1756; inc. as a city 1892.

Radisson, town (1991 pop. 390), central Sask., Canada,

near North Saskatchewan R., 40 mi/64 km NW of Saskatoon. Grain elevators.

Radisson, village (1990 pop. 237), Sawyer co., N Wis., 32 mi/51 km ESE of Spooner; 45°46′N 91°13′W. Lac Court Oreille Indian Reservation to NW. On Tuscobia State Tribal Timber area. Mfg. (lumber, wood cabinets).

Radium (RAI-dee-uhm), village (1990 pop. 47), Stafford co., S central Kansas, 14 mi/23 km NNW of St. John; 38°10′N 98°53′W. In wheat area.

Radium Hot Springs, resort village (1991 pop. 395), SE B.C., Canada, on slope of Rocky Mts., on Columbia R., and 50 mi/80 km SW of Banff; 50°37′N 116°06′W. Elev. 3,456 ft/1,053 m. Resort at edge of Kootenay Natl. Park.

Radium Springs, resort village, Dougherty co., SW Ga., just S of Albany; 31°31′N 84°08′W. Groundwater from radium springs comes from the largest natural springs in the state, which are part of the Floridian aquifer.

Radnor (RAD-nuhr), township (1990 pop. 28,703), Delaware co., SE Pa., suburb 12 mi/19 km NW of downtown Philadelphia; 40°01′N 75°22′W. Drained by Gulph and Darby creeks. Mfg. (industrial gases, printing and publishing). Gen. Anthony Wayne buried here. Campus of Villanova Univ. in NE. Includes villages of Radnor, St. David's, Garrett Hill, Willowburn, and Villanova. Settled c.1685 by Welsh, who built (1715) the extant St. David's Church.

Radom (RAI-dom), village (1990 pop. 174), Washington co., SW Ill., 7 mi/11.3 km SE of Nashville; 38°16′N 89°11′W. In agr. area.

Radville, town (1991 pop. 846), S Sask., Canada, 25 mi/40 km WSW of Weyburn; 49°28′N 104°17′W. RR divisional point; grain elevators; livestock.

Radway, village (1991 pop. 173), central Alta., Canada, on Namepi Creek, near its mouth on North Saskatchewan R., and 45 mi/72 km NE of Edmonton; 54°04′N 112°56′W. Wheat; livestock.

Rae Isthmus, N.W.T., Canada, land narrows (50 mi/80 km long) at base of Melville Peninsula, bet. head of Committee Bay of the Gulf of Boothia (NNW) and Repulse Bay (SSE); 67°00′N 86°30′W. At S end of isthmus is Repulse Bay trading post.

Rae, Mount (10,576 ft/3,224 m), SW Alta., Canada, near B.C. border, in Misty Range of Rocky Mts., 50 mi/80 km SE of Banff; 50°38′N 114°58′W.

Rae-Edzo (RAI–ED-zo), village (1991 pop. 1,521), S Mackenzie dist., N.W.T., Canada; Rae is on Marian L. (20 mi/32 km long, 4 mi/6 km wide) just N of head of North Arm of Great Slave L., 60 mi/97 km NW of Yellowknife; Edzo straddles isthmus bet. Marian L. and N arm of Great Slave L. at mouth of Marian R.; 62°50′N 116°03′W. Rae is an old Indian hunting spot and site of 2 trading posts. Edzo was est. 1965 on Yellowknife Highway, 15 mi/24 km away, to provide schools and essential services. Most residences are in Rae. Fur-trading post; radio and TV stations, Royal Can. Mounted Police post. Crafts; fishing, hunting, trapping. Float plane service.

Raeford (RAI-fuhrd), town (1990 pop. 3,469), ⊙ Hoke co., S central N.C., 20 mi/32 km WSW of Fayetteville; 34°58′N 79°13′W. In agr. area (tobacco, grain, cotton, soybeans; livestock, poultry). Mfg. (textiles, cosmetics, printing and publishing, transformers, rubber compounds, billboards). Large Fort Bragg Military Reserve to N.

Rafael Delgado (rah-fah-EL del-GAH-do), town (1990 pop. 6,153), Veracruz state, E Mexico, in Sierra Madre Oriental, 6 mi/10 km SE of Orizaba; 18°48′N 97°04′W. Coffee, fruits.

Rafael Freyre (rah-fah-EL FRAI-rai), town, Holguín prov., E Cuba, near N coast inlet, on RR, and 9 mi/14.5 km ESE of Gibara; 21°03′N 76°00′W. Sugar mill with same name.

Rafael J. García (rah-fah-EL gar-SEE-ah), town (1990 pop. 3,715), ⊙ Chilchotla municipio, Puebla state, central Mexico, in Sierra Madre, 27 mi/43 km NE of Ciudad Serdán; 19°15′N 97°10′W. Elev. 7,251 ft/2,210 m. Cereals, maguey, fruits; livestock. Also called Chilchotla.

Rafael Lara Grajales (rah-fah-EL LAH-rah grah-HAH-les) or **San Marcos**, town (1990 pop. 8,503), Puebla state, central Mexico, on Mexico highway 129, 29 mi/47 km NE of Puebla. Elev. 7,785 ft/2,373 m. RR junction; cereals, maguey.

Rafael Lucio (rah-fah-EL loo-SEE-o), town (1990 pop. 2,603), Veracruz state, E Mexico, in Sierra Madre Oriental, on RR, and 7 mi/11.3 km NW of Xalapa Enríquez; 19°35′N 96°58′W. Elev. 6,237 ft/1,901 m. Coffee, corn.

Raft River, c.60 mi/97 km long, in N Utah and S Idaho; rises in Raft R. Mts., NW Box Elder co., NW Utah; flows generally N, through Cassia co., Idaho, to Snake R. E of L. Walcott and 17 mi/27 km SW of American Falls.

Raft River Mountains (8,000 ft/2,438 m–10,000 ft/3,048 m), in Sawtooth Natl. Forest, NW Box Elder co., NW Utah; extend E-W along Idaho state line.

Ragan (RAI-guhn), village (1990 pop. 59), Harlan co., S Nebr., 10 mi/16 km SE of Holdrege; 40°18′N 99°17′W. Grain; livestock; poultry; dairy prods.

Ragged Island, in SW Maine, small island in Casco Bay off Phippsburg; the "Elm Island" of Elijah Kellogg's stories.

Ragged Island, Maine: see MATINICUS ISLE.

Ragged Island and Cays, archipelago and district (□ 5 sq mi/13 sq km; 1990 pop. 89), S Bahama Isls., at SE fringe of the Great Bahama Bank, SW of Long Isl., c.175 mi/282 km SE of Nassau, 70 mi/113 km N of Cuba. Consists of Great Ragged Isl. (or Ragged Isl.) and Little Ragged Isl., and is generally considered to include a chain of small cays stretching c.70 mi/113 km N. Group sometimes called Jumento Cays.

Ragged Lake, Piscataquis co., central Maine, 32 mi/51 km WNW of Millinocket, SW of Caribou L., to which it is joined by a stream; 6 mi/9.7 km long, 1.5 mi/2.4 km wide.

Ragged Mountain, Maine: see CAMDEN HILLS.

Ragland, town (1990 pop. 1,807), St. Clair co., E Ala., 9 mi/14.5 km SE of Ashville, near Coosa R.

Ragsdale, uninc. village, Dougherty co., SW Ga.

Rahway (RAW-wai), industrial city (1990 pop. 25,325), Union co., NE N.J., on the Rahway R.; 40°36′N 74°16′W. Plastics, clothing, pharmaceuticals, and electrical equip. are among the city's mfg. The British were routed in skirmishes here in 1777. One of the signers of the Declaration of Independence and 42 Revolutionary soldiers are buried in the Rahway cemetery. Settled c.1720 as part of Elizabethtown; inc. 1858.

Rahway River (RAW-wai), c.30 mi/48 km long, NE N.J.; rises in central Essex co.; flows S, past Rahway, then E to Arthur Kill N of Carteret; receives South Branch (c.10 mi/16 km long) near Rahway.

Raiford (RAI-fuhrd), village (1990 pop. 198), Union co., N central Fla., 29 mi/47 km NNE of Gainesville; 30°03′N 82°14′W. Corn, vegetables. Fla. State Prison nearby.

Railroad, borough (1990 pop. 317), York co., S Pa., 14 mi/23 km S of York; 39°45′N 76°42′W. Mfg. (plastic molds); agr. (grain; livestock; dairying).

Rain Water Basin, region (□ c.6,000 sq mi/15,540 sq km), S central Nebr. Also called the Loess Plain, the basin is roughly triangular in shape, with its base in the E overlooking the valley of Big Blue R., and extending to the low terraces of the Platte R. in the N and above the Republican Valley at the SW. The land generally slopes gradually to the SE. Much of the Loess Plain has no surface drainage; instead the moderate amount of precipitation is disposed of by evaporation and infiltration through the thick, silty soil. Water may remain on the land in shallow, wind-carved depressions; where the basins are deeper and infiltration slowed by nearly impenetrable claypan, rainwater basins such as ponds, lagoons, and marshes result. They are common in the more humid E part of the Loess Plain, esp. in Clay and Fillmore cos. The wetlands have been reduced from c.100,000 acres/40,470 ha to c.21,000 acres/8,499 ha through drainage and road building. Much of the wetland remaining is managed by the U.S. Fish and Wildlife Service, esp. for wildfowl. The Neb. Game and Parks Commission controls a smaller acreage.

Rainbow, uninc. town (1990 pop. 2,006), San Diego co., S Calif., 20 mi/32 km N of Escondido; 33°25′N 117°09′W. Cattle. Pala Indian Reservation to SE. Camp Pendleton Marine Corps Base to W.

Rainbow Bridge National Monument, San Juan co., S Utah, 28 mi/45 km ENE of Page, Ariz., in Navajo Indian Reservation. Covers 160 acres/65 ha. Rainbow Bridge, the largest natural bridge in the world, is a symmetrical pink sandstone arch, 309 ft/94 m high, 33 ft/10 m wide, with a 278 ft/85 m span. Located in one of the most rugged and remote regions of the U.S., it was discovered in 1909 by an expedition that set out to find the great stone arch rumored by the Native Americans. Authorized and est. 1910.

Rainbow City, city (1990 pop. 7,673), Etowah co., NE Ala., 5 mi/8 km S of Gadsden, on Coosa R.; 33°55′N 86°05′W. Lumber.

Rainbow Lake, town (1991 pop. 817), NW Alta., Canada, 160 mi/257 km NW of Peace River, 85 mi/137 km W of High Level. W terminus of Rte. 58. Rainbow oil field discovered here (1965); nearby Zama field discovered 1967. Oil from Norman Wells, N.W.T., piped to Zama for transfer to Edmonton refineries. Scheduled air service.

Rainbow Lake, resort village, Franklin co., NE N.Y., on Rainbow L. (c.3 mi/4.8 km long), in the Adirondacks, 10 mi/16 km N of Saranac Lake village; 44°28′N 74°10′W.

Rainbow Lake, Piscataquis co., central Maine, 19 mi/31 km NW of Millinocket; 4 mi/6.4 km long. In hunting and fishing area.

Rainbow Lakes Estates, town (1990 pop. 1,196), Marion and Levy cos., N central Fla., 15 mi/24 km W of Ocala; 26°33′N 80°07′W.

Rainelle (rai-NEL), town (1990 pop. 1,681), Greenbrier co., SE W.Va., 20 mi/32 km NW of Lewisburg; 37°58′N 80°46′W. Agr. (grain, tobacco); livestock, poultry; dairying. Timber. Coal mining. Mfg. (lumber, signs; contract sewing). RR junction.

Rainier 1 (rai-NIR), town (1990 pop. 1,674), Columbia co., NW Oregon, on Columbia R., c.40 mi/64 km NNW of Portland; 46°05′N 122°57′W. Highway bridge to Longview, Wash., 2 mi/3.2 km N. Berries, nuts; poultry, cattle; dairy prods. Salmon and smelt fisheries. Closed Trojan Nuclear Plant to SE. Part of Clatsop State Forest to S. Settled 1851; inc. 1885. **2** town (1990 pop. 991), Thurston co., W Wash., 14 mi/23 km SE of Olympia; 46°54′N 122°41′W. Blueberries; poultry; logging. Part of Fort Lewis Military Reservation to N.

Rainier, Mount, Wash.: see MOUNT RAINIER NATIONAL PARK.

Rains, county (□ 258 sq mi/668 sq km; 1990 pop. 6,715), NE Texas; ⊙ Emory; 32°52′N 95°47′W. Prairie in W, woodland in E; drained by Sabine R. (SW boundary forms L. Tawakoni in W). Agr. (watermelons, vegetables, wheat, hay); livestock (mainly cattle). Gas, oil, coal. Arm of Lake Fork Reservoir on E boundary. Formed 1870.

Rainsburg, borough (1990 pop. 175), Bedford co., S Pa., 8 mi/12.9 km S of Bedford, near Cove Creek, in Friends Cove valley; 39°53′N 78°31′W. Corn, oats; livestock; dairying.

Rainsford Island, E Mass., in Quincy Bay sect. of Boston Harbor, SE of downtown Boston. Part of Boston Harbor Isls. State Park.

Rainsville, city (1990 pop. 3,875), DeKalb co., NE Ala., 5 mi/8 km NW of Fort Payne; 34°30′N 85°51′W. Mfg. of clothing, church pews, structural steel, machinery. Northeast Ala. State Community Col. located here.

Rainy Lake, (□ c.345 sq mi/890 sq km), on the U.S.-Canada border in N Minn. and W Ont. The lake, irregular in shape and dotted with isls., is located in rough woodlands. Its outlet, Rainy R. (c.85 mi/140 km long), flows W along the internatl. border to L. of the Woods, passing Internatl. Falls (site of a power plant) and Baudette, Minn.

Rainy River, district (□ 7,276 sq mi/18,845 sq km; 1991 pop. 22,997), NW Ont., Canada, on Minn. border, and on Rainy R.; ⊙ Fort Frances; 48°30′N 93°00′W.

Rainy River, town (1991 pop. 968), NW Ont., Canada, on Rainy R. (bridge), and 50 mi/80 km W of Fort Frances, on Minn. border; 48°43′N 94°34′W. Dairying; lumbering, woodworking.

Rainy River, c.30 mi/48 km long, NE Mich.; rises in SW Presque Isle co., in Rainy L.; flows NNW, through forest and farm area, to SE end of Black L. in Presque Isle co.; Onaway State Park at its mouth; 45°15′N 84°03′W.

Rainy River, Minn. and Canada: see RAINY LAKE.

Raisin, River, 115 mi/185 km long, Mich.; rises in S Mich. in NW corner of Lenawee co. at Cement City; flows NE to Manchester, then S past Tecumseh and Palmyra, then E past Petersburg and Dundee, to L. Erie, at Monroe, Mich.; 42°03′N 84°15′W. After Detroit's surrender in the War of 1812, U.S. troops under Gen. James Winchester, sent to retake Frenchtown (the present Monroe), were crushed there by the British and their Native Amer. allies. The Native Americans, after promising protection, attacked and killed (Jan. 22, 1813) the remaining Americans, and "Remember the R. Raisin" became the Amer. rallying cry to the war's end.

Rajah, The, mountain (9,903 ft/3,018 m), W Alta., Canada, near B.C. border, in Rocky Mts., in Jasper Natl. Park, 33 mi/53 km NW of Jasper; 53°16′N 118°33′W.

Rake, town (1990 pop. 238), Winnebago co., N Iowa, near Minn. state line, 21 mi/34 km NW of Forest City; 43°28′N 93°55′W.

Raleigh, county (□ 609 sq mi/1,577 sq km; 1990 pop. 76,819), S W.Va.; ⊙ Beckley; 37°46′N 81°15′W. On Allegheny Plateau; bounded E by New R.; drained by Big Coal and Guyandotte rivers. Extensive mining of semibituminous coal; gas fields. Agr. (corn, oats, alfalfa, hay, nursery crops); cattle. Mfg. at Beckley. Part of New R. Gorge Natl. R. in E, includes Gandview Visitor Center; Tamarack State Crafts Center, Little Beaver State Park in E; Stephens L. reservoir in center. Formed 1850.

Raleigh 1 (RAW-lee), city, Meriwether co., W Ga., 6 mi/9.7 km N of Manchester; 32°56′N 84°38′W. **2** city (1990 pop. 212,092), ⊙ of state and of Wake co., central N.C.; city of Durham 22 mi/35 km to NW.; 35°49′N 78°39′W. Second-largest city in N.C. after Charlotte; the site was selected for the capital in 1788, and the city was laid out and inc. 1792. It is a political, cultural, trade, and industrial center. Raleigh has also become an air travel hub with the extension of the Raleigh-Durham Internatl. Airport to NW. Mfg. (printing and publishing; electrical, medical, electronic, and telecommunications equip.; apparel, soybean and dairy processing, corrugated boxes and paper packaging, food and beverage processing, pharmaceuticals, metal fabricating). A research center for textiles and chemicals, Raleigh is part of N.C.'s Research Triangle (est. 1959), an area and organization shared with Chapel Hill and Durham that utilizes the scientific talent of the 3 cities' univs. Research Triangle Park 12 mi/19 km to W. The cooperative has drawn numerous corporations to Raleigh, which has become one of the fastest-growing U.S. cities. Its pop. increased by more than 38% bet. 1980 and 1990. The 1st capitol (built 1792–1794) burned in 1831 and was replaced by the present bldg., completed in 1840. In the Civil War, Sherman occupied the city on April 14, 1865. Raleigh is the seat of N.C. State Univ., (N.C. State Univ. Farms to S), Shaw Univ., Meredith Col., St. Augustine's Col., St. Mary's Col., and Peace Col. It has lib., mus., a theater, and several 18th-cent. houses, including the birthplace of President Andrew Johnson, whose home is preserved as a historic site. Falls L. State Recreation Area to N; William B. Umstead State Park to NW. N.C. Mus. of Art; State Mus.; State Lib. Walnut Creek Amphitheatre to SE. Raleigh Natl. Cemetery. State fairgrounds in W.

Raleigh 1 (RAW-lee), town (1990 pop. 1,291), ⊙ Smith co., S central Miss., 33 mi/53 km NW of Laurel; 32°01′N 89°31′W. Trade center in agr. (cotton, corn; cattle, hogs, poultry) and timber area; mfg. (automotive and industrial engine starters, apparel, lumber). Bienville Natl. Forest to N. Inc. 1935. **2** uninc. town (1990 pop. 900), Raleigh co., S W.Va., 2 mi/3.2 km SE of Beckley, on Piney Creek. Coal-mining area.

Raleigh, village (1990 pop. 305), Saline co., SE Ill., 6 mi/9.7 km N of Harrisburg; 37°49′N 88°31′W. In bituminous-coal-mining and agr. area.

Raleigh Bay, E N.C., long curvature in the Atlantic coast line from Cape Hatteras (NE) to Cape Lookout (SW); c.75 mi/121 km long, c.10 mi/16 km wide. Separated from Pamlico Sound to NW by Outer Banks, sand barrier islands.

Raleigh, Fort, N.C.: see ROANOKE ISLAND.

Raleigh Hills, uninc. town (1990 pop. 6,066), Washington co., NW Oregon, residential suburb 5 mi/8 km WSW of downtown Portland, and 2 mi/3.2 km E of Beaverton, on Fanno Creek; 45°28′N 122°45′W.

Ralls, county (□ 478 sq mi/1,238 sq km; 1990 pop. 8,476), NE Mo. on Mississippi R.; drained by Salt R.; ⊙ New London; 39°31′N 91°31′W. Soybeans, corn, wheat; cattle, hogs. Clarence Cannon Dam and Mark Twain L. in W; Lock and Dam No. 22 on Miss. R. Formed 1820.

Ralls, town (1990 pop. 2,172), Crosby co., NW Texas, on Llano Estacado, 28 mi/45 km ENE of Lubbock; 33°40′N 101°22′W. Elev. 3,108 ft/947 m. In agr. area (cotton, wheat, vegetables; cattle, hogs, sheep); mfg. (irrigation pumps). Founded 1911; inc. 1921.

Ralston, city (1990 pop. 6,236), Douglas co., E Nebr., a suburb of Omaha, 5 mi/8 km SW of downtown; 41°12′N 96°02′W. Mfg. (polyurethane foam, veterinary pharmaceuticals, control panels).

Ralston, town (1990 pop. 119), on Carroll-Greene co. line, W central Iowa, 12 mi/19 km E of Carroll; 42°02′N 94°37′W. Soybean prods.

Ralston 1 village (1990 pop. 405), Pawnee co., N Okla., on Arkansas R., and 12 mi/19 km NNE of Pawnee; 36°30′N 96°44′W. **2** uninc. village, McIntyre township, Lycoming co., N central Pa., a 19 mi/31 km N of Williamsport; 41°30′N 76°57′W. Bituminous-coal area. Hunting and fishing nearby. Surrounded by Tiadaghton State Forest.

Ralston Creek, N central Colo.; rises in Front Range N of Blackhawk, Gilpin co.; flows c.30 mi/48 km E through Arvada to Clear Creek just NW of Denver. Ralston Dam (200 ft/61 m high; 1,150 ft/351 m long) is c.10 mi/16 km W of Denver; completed 1938 as unit in city's water-supply system.

Ram Island, Lincoln co., S Maine, small lighthouse isl. 3.5 mi/5.6 km SE of Boothbay Harbor.

Ramah, village (1990 pop. 94), El Paso co., E central Colo., 40 mi/64 km NE of Colorado Springs; 39°07′N 104°10′W. Elev. 6,094 ft/1,857 m. Wheat, cattle, greenhouse/nursery, sunflowers, oats. Ramah State Wildlife Area to SW, on Big Sandy Creek (Ramah Reservoir to W).

Ramah (RAH-muh) [Hebrew = high place], Cibola co., N.Mex., a small historic Mormon community, 45 mi/72 km SW of Grants.

Ramapo, village (1990 pop. 75), Rockland co., SE N.Y., in the Ramapos, on Ramapo R., just NW of Suffern; 41°08′N 74°06′W.

Ramapo Mountains (RA-muh-po), forested range of the Appalachian Mts., NE N.J. and SE N.Y. Elevations range from c.900 ft/274 m to 1,200 ft/366 m; many trails for hikers. In the E part of the range there is pressure from residential development.

Ramblewood, uninc. town (1990 pop. 1,104), Centre co., central Pa., 7 mi/11.3 km WSW of State Col.; 40°43′N 77°57′W. Agr. includes dairying; livestock; corn, hay, apples.

Ramea Islands (RA-mee-uh), group of isls. (□ 5 sq mi/13 sq km) just off S N.F., Canada. Main isl. is Ramea (2 mi/3 km long, 1 mi/2 km wide), 13 mi/21 km ESE of Burgeo; 47°32′N 57°23′W; site of lighthouse. Fishing. Just E is uninhabited Great Isl. (2 mi/3 km long, 1 mi/2 km wide); 47°32′N 57°20′W. Group is surrounded by several islets.

Ramey (RAI-mee), borough (1990 pop. 536), Clearfield co., central Pa., 22 mi/35 km N of Altoona; 40°47′N 78°24′W. Hay; livestock; dairying.

Ramón Santana (rah-MON sahn-TAH-nah), town (1993 pop. 1,513), San Pedro de Macorís prov., SE Dominican Republic, 10 mi/16 km NE of San Pedro de Macorís; 18°30′N 69°10′W. In sugar-growing region.

Ramona, uninc. city (1990 pop. 13,040), San Diego co., S Calif., a residential suburb 27 mi/43 km NE of downtown San Diego, in foothills of Coast Ranges; 33°02′N 116°52′W. Flowers, fruits, grain; dairying; poultry; mfg. (soft drinks, in vitro diagnostic substances). Barona Ranch Indian Reservation to S; parts of Cleveland Natl. Forest to N and E.

Ramona 1 village (1990 pop. 106), Marion co., central Kansas, 8 mi/12.9 km SW of Herington; 38°36′N 97°03′W. Grain; livestock. **2** village (1990 pop. 508), Washington co., NE Okla., 15 mi/24 km S of Bartlesville; 36°31′N 95°55′W. **3** village (1990 pop. 194), Lake co., E S.Dak., 10 mi/16 km NNW of Madison; 44°07′N 97°13′W.

Ramos, Mexico: see VILLA DE RAMOS.

Ramos Arizpe (RAH-mos ah-REES-pe), city (1990 pop. 16,796) and township, ⊙ Ramos Arizpe, Coahuila state, N Mexico, in Sierra Madre Oriental, 10 mi/16 km N of Saltillo, on Mexico Highway 40; 25°32′N 100°58′W. Elev. 4,590 ft/1,399 m. RR junction in agr. region (corn, beans, alfalfa, istle fibers; candelilla wax; cattle).

Ramos River (RAH-mos), c.125 mi/201 km long, Durango state, NW Mexico; rises in Sierra Madre Occidental 28 mi/45 km W of Victoria de Durango; flows N and NW, past Santiago Papasquiaro, joining Río Sextín to form Nazas R. in Lázaro Cárdenas reservoir. Upper course called Santiago R.

Rampart, village (1990 pop. 68), central Alaska, on Yukon R., and 85 mi/137 km NW of Fairbanks; 65°22′N 150°00′W. Site (1900–1925) of agr. experiment station. Airfield. Supply center in Klondike gold rush, when pop. was c.1,500.

Rampart House, village, on Alaska-Yukon border, on Porcupine R., and 130 mi/209 km NE of Fort Yukon. Est. c.1870 by Hudson's Bay Company; now deserted.

Rampart Reservoir, 2 mi/3.2 km long, El Paso co., central Colo., on W. Monument Creek, in Rocky Mt. foothills and in Pike Natl. Forest, 12 mi/19 km NW of Colorado Springs; 38°55′N 104°58′W. Max. capacity of 41,450 acre-ft. Formed by Rampart Dam (240 ft/73 m high), built (1970) by the city of Colorado Springs for water supply.

Ramsay, village, Gogebic co., W Upper Peninsula, Mich., 2 mi/3.2 km SE of Bessemer; 46°28′N 89°59′W. Mfg. (concrete). Indianhead Mt. Ski Area to E; Ottawa Natl. Forest to N.

Ramseur (RAM-suhr), town (1990 pop. 1,186), Randolph co., central N.C., 9 mi/14.5 km ENE of Asheboro on Deep R.; 35°43′N 79°39′W. Agr. area (tobacco, grain, soybeans; dairying; poultry; livestock). Mfg. (textiles and apparel, furniture, wooden furniture frames). Settled c.1850; inc. 1895.

Ramsey 1 (RAM-zee), county (□ 170 sq mi/440 sq km; 1990 pop. 485,765), E Minn.; ⊙ St. Paul (capital of state and twin city to Minneapolis, in Hennepin co.); 45°01′N 93°05′W. Industrial and residential area crossed in S by Mississippi R., forms parts of S and W boundaries. Urbanized co. in Minneapolis–St. Paul metropolitan area (Twin Cities). Numerous small lakes in co., esp. in N; White Bear L. on E boundary, in NE; Bald Eagle L. on N boundary, in NE. Other important communities include Roseville, Maplewood, and White Bear L. Formed 1849. **2** county (□ 1,248 sq mi/3,232 sq km; 1990 pop. 12,681), NE central N.Dak.; ⊙ Devils Lake, in Drift Prairie, large Devils L. forms S boundary; 48°15′N 98°43′W. Rich area with several lakes in W (Sweetwater, Chain, Dry, Irvine, and Alice, formerly Aux Mortes, lakes); Devils L. is largest. Wheat, sunflowers, barley, rye; cattle; dairy prods. Formed 1873. L. Alice Wildlife Refuge in W.

Ramsey, city (1990 pop. 12,408), Anoka co., E Minn., suburb 19 mi/31 km NNW of downtown Minneapolis, bounded by Mississippi R. on S, by Rum R. on E; 45°15′N 93°27′W. Mfg. (abrasives, athletic exercise equip., Easter prods., diverse light mfg.); agr. (alfalfa, rye; dairying). Gateway North Industrial Airport in N.

Ramsey, village (1990 pop. 963), Fayette co., S central Ill., 12 mi/19 km N of Vandalia; 39°08′N 89°06′W. Corn, wheat; dairy prods.; poultry, livestock. State park nearby.

Ramsey, residential borough (1990 pop. 13,228), Bergen co., NE N.J., 13 mi/21 km NNW of Hackensack; 41°03′N 74°09′W. Settled 1846; inc. 1908.

Ranburne, town (1990 pop. 447), Cleburne co., E central Ala., c.30 mi/48 km SE of Anniston, and 5 mi/8 km W of Bowdon, Ga.; 33°31′N 85°20W. Commercial trading center of local agr. (poultry, livestock) area.

Ranchester, village (1990 pop. 676), Sheridan co., N

Wyo., on Tongue R., near Mont. state line, and 15 mi/24 km NW of Sheridan; 44°54′N 107°09′W. Rural supply point for Tongue R. valley. Connor Battlefield State Historic Site is here. Large Crow Indian Reservation to N (in Mont.).

Rancho Boyeros (RAHN-cho bo-YER-oz), airport, in suburb in Ciudad de la Habana prov., W Cuba, 9 mi/14.5 km S of Havana; 23°03′N 82°22′W. Site of José Martí Internatl. Airport, warehouses, and a small biotechnology center.

Rancho Cordova, uninc. city (1990 pop. 48,731), Sacramento co., N Calif.; a suburb 12 mi/19 km ENE of downtown Sacramento on the American R.; 38°36′N 121°20′W. The town is marked by rapid growth in the 1970s–1990s. Nursery prods., citrus, grain; dairying; poultry. Mfg. (metal doors, electron tubes, RR equipment, industrial gases, machinery, plastic production, cabinets, diverse light mfg.).

Rancho Cucamonga, city (1990 pop. 101,409), San Bernardino co., S Calif., suburb 15 mi/24 km W of San Bernardino, and 5 mi/8 km NE of Ontario; 34°07′N 117°34′W. Citrus, avocados, vegetables, nursery prods. Mfg. (metal foundries, processed foods, resin, metal coatings, coated paper, wire drawing, hardware, plastic prods., aircraft parts, RR equip., structural metal work). San Gabriel Mts. and San Bernardino Natl. Forest (including Cucamonga Wilderness Area) to N. Seat of Cahffey Col. (2-year).

Rancho Dominques, uninc. town, Los Angeles co., S Calif., industrial suburb 12 mi/19 km S of downtown Los Angeles, and 3 mi/4.8 km S of Compton. Mfg. (adhesives, furniture, aircraft parts, motor vehicle parts, computers, sporting goods, cosmetics, toys, electronic components, plastics prods., brassware, printing, lighting fixtures). Rancho Domingues Hills to SW.

Rancho Mirage, city (1990 pop. 9,778), Riverside co., S Calif., suburb 9 mi/14.5 km SE of Palm Springs, on Whitewater R., in rapidly growing resort and retirement area; 33°46′N 116°26′W. Cotton, avocados, citrus, grain; poultry. San Bernardino Natl. Forest to SW.

Rancho Murieta, uninc. town (1990 pop. 2,336), Sacramento co., central Calif., 22 mi/35 km E of Sacramento; 38°31′N 121°04′W. Apples; grain; dairying; cattle, poultry. Rancho Murieta Airstrip to S.

Rancho Palos Verdes, city (1990 pop. 41,659), Los Angeles co., S Calif., residential suburb 22 mi/35 km SSW of downtown Los Angeles, and 10 mi/16 km W of Long Beach, on Pacific Ocean, at S end of Palos Verdes Peninsula; 33°46′N 118°22′W. Marineland of the Pacific, at Pt. Vicente, in SW. Royal Palms State Beach to E; S. Coast Botanical Gardens to N. Branch of Marymount Col. (2-year) is here.

Rancho Rinconada, uninc. town (1990 pop. 4,206), Santa Clara co., W Calif., residential suburb 8 mi/12.9 km WSW of downtown San Jose, on Calabazas Creek; 37°19′N 122°00′W.

Rancho San Diego, uninc. town (1990 pop. 6,977), San Diego co., S Calif., residential suburb 12 mi/19 km NE of downtown San Diego, SE of El Cajon; 32°45′N 116°56′W.

Rancho Santa Fe, uninc. village, San Diego co., S Calif., 21 mi/34 km N of San Diego, 5 mi/8 km NE of Pacific Ocean coast, on San Dieguito R.; residential; citrus fruits, avocado groves. L. Hughes reservoir to NE.

Rancho Santa Margarita, uninc. city (1990 pop. 11,390), Orange co., S Calif., suburb 5 mi/8 km ENE of Mission Viejo, near Santa Ana Mts.; 33°39′N 117°36′W. Mfg. (industrial valves, hardware, machinery parts, printing). Cleveland Natl. Forest to E.

Rancho Seco Nuclear Power Plant, California: see SACRAMENTO, CO.

Rancho Veloz (RAHN-cho vai-LOZ), town, Villa Clara prov., central Cuba, near the coast, on RR, and 20 mi/32 km WNW of Sagua la Grande; 22°54′N 80°24′W. Sugarcane, fruits, salt. The sugar mill of Quintín Banderas is 3 mi/4.8 km SE.

Rancho Viejo (RAN-cho vee-AI-ho), town (1990 pop. 835), Cameron co., extreme S Texas, residential suburb 10 mi/16 km NNW of Brownsville; 26°01′N 97°33′W. Irrigated agr. area. Palo Alto Battlefield Natl. Historic Site to E.

Ranchos de Taos (RAHN-chos de TOUS), uninc. town (1990 pop. 1,779), Taos co., N N.Mex., in Sangre de Cristo Mts., and 3 mi/4.8 km SSW of Taos; 36°21′N 105°35′W. Elev. 6,900 ft/2,103 m. Light mfg. Famous for St. Francis of Assisi Mission, adobe church (rebuilt c.1772; 120 ft/37 m long, with 6 ft/1.8 m wall); has many religious objects, including paintings of saints (or *santos*). Ponce de Leon hot springs, with swimming pools, nearby. Part of Pueblo de Taos Indian Reservation to NE and NW; part of Carson Natl. Forest to E; Kit Carson State Park to NE; Orilla Verde Natl. Recreation Area to SW.

Ranchuelo (rahnch-WAI-lo), town, Villa Clara prov., central Cuba, 12 mi/19 km WSW of Santa Clara; 22°22′N 80°10′W. Processing center in well-known tobacco belt. Mfg. of cigars, sweets; meatpacking. Nearby are centrals of Diez de Octubre (E) and Efraín Alonso (W).

Rancocas Creek (rang-KO-kuhs), c.30 mi/48 km long, Burlington co., SW N.J.; rises E of Browns Mills (here forming Mirror L.); flows W and NW, past Mt. Holly, to the Delaware at Riverside. Navigable c.9 mi/14.5 km above mouth. South Branch (c.15 mi/24 km long) enters creek W of Mt. Holly.

Rand, uninc. town, Kanawha co., W central W.Va., residential suburb 4 mi/6.4 km SE of downtown Charleston, on Kanawha R. Agr. (corn, tobacco); cattle; poultry.

Rand Mountains, San Bernardino and Kern cos., S Calif., range (over 4,000 ft/1,219 m) in the Mojave Desert, extending c.20 mi/32 km SW from Randsburg. The Rand, a rich mining dist. here, produces silver, tungsten, gold.

Rand, The, Calif.: see RAND MOUNTAINS.

Randalia, town (1990 pop. 88), Fayette co., NE Iowa, 8 mi/12.9 km SSW of West Union; 42°51′N 91°53′W. Limestone quarries nearby.

Randall, county (□ 922 sq mi/2,388 sq km; 1990 pop. 89,673), extreme N Texas; ⊙ Canyon; 34°58′N 101°54′W. On high plains of the Panhandle; elev. 3,000 ft/914 m–3,800 ft/1,158 m. Irrigated area (cattle, horses; sorghum, wheat). Drained by Tierra Blanca and Palo Duro creeks, here forming Prairie Dog Town Fork of Red R., Palo Duro Canyon State Park in E. Buffalo L. Natl. Wildlife Refuge is in SW. Formed 1876.

Randall, town (1990 pop. 161), Hamilton co., central Iowa, 20 mi/32 km SE of Webster City; 42°14′N 93°35′W.

Randall 1 village (1990 pop. 96), Jewell co., N Kansas, on small affluent of Republican R., and 20 mi/32 km WNW of Concordia; 39°38′N 98°02′W. Grain; livestock. Jamestown Waterfowl Management Unit to E. **2** village (1990 pop. 571), Morrison co., central Minn., 10 mi/16 km NW of Little Falls on Little Elk R., at mouth of South Branch Little Elk R.; 46°05′N 94°30′W. Grain, sunflowers, potatoes; poultry; dairying; mfg. (marble vanity tops). L. Alexander to N; Camp Ripley Military Reservation to NE.

Randall, Ill.: see EAST GALESBURG.

Randalls Island, N.Y. city, SE N.Y., in East R. at confluence with the Harlem R.; linked to Manhattan and Queens boroughs by Triborough Bridge; 40°48′N 73°56′W. Covers 194 acres/79 ha. Now a municipal park and sports center, with a large stadium; formerly occupied by city institutions for children.

Randallstown, suburban village (1990 pop. 26,277), Baltimore co., central Md., 11 mi/18 km WNW of downtown Baltimore; 39°22′N 76°48′W. Named for Thomas and Christopher Randall from England, who purchased land here in the early 18th cent. Located in a rapid growth corridor out from Baltimore.

Randleman (RAND-uhl-muhn), town (1990 pop. 2,612), Randolph co., central N.C., 9 mi/14.5 km N of Asheboro, and on Deep R.; 35°49′N 79°47′W. Agr. area (tobacco, grain, soybeans; dairying; poultry, livestock). Mfg. (medical devices, furniture, textiles and apparel, plastic and paper prods., wire cord, foam and cotton batting, brass valves, cushions). Richard Petty Mus. to N, race memorabilia.

Randles, uninc. rural community, Cape Girardeau co., SE Mo., 6 mi/9.7 km WSW of Chaffee.

Randlett, village (1990 pop. 458), Cotton co., S Okla., near Red R., 15 mi/24 km SW of Walters; 34°10′N 98°27′W. Trade center for agr. area.

Randolph 1 county (□ 584 sq mi/1,513 sq km; 1990 pop. 19,881), E Ala., on Ga. line; ⊙ Wedowee. Piedmont region drained by Tallapoosa and Little Tallapoosa rivers. Roanoke is processing center. Livestock, poultry; textiles, quarried prods. Formed 1832. **2** county (□ 656 sq mi/1,699 sq km; 1990 pop. 16,558), NE Ark.; ⊙ Pocahontas; 36°20′N 91°01′W. Bounded N by Mo. line by Spring R. on SW; drained by Black, Current, and Eleven Point rivers. Agr. (rice, wheat, soybeans; cattle, hogs); timber. Part of Dave Donaldson–Black R. Wildlife Management Area in E; Old Davidsonville State Park in S. Formed 1836. **3** county (□ 431 sq mi/1,116 sq km; 1990 pop. 8,023), SW Ga.; ⊙ Cuthbert; 31°46′N 84°47′W. Coastal plain agr. (wheat, sorghum, soybeans, cotton, corn, peanuts, fruits); cattle, hogs; timber. Formed 1828. **4** county (□ 597 sq mi/1,546 sq km; 1990 pop. 34,583), SW Ill.; ⊙ Chester; 38°02′N 89°49′W. Bounded SW by Mississippi R.; drained by Kaskaskia R. Agr. (wheat, corn, soybeans, sorghum; cattle, poultry; dairy prods.). Mfg. (textiles, aluminum prods., flour, industrial machinery). Bituminous coal mining. Fort Kaskaskia and Fort de Chartres state historic sites are here. Formed 1795. Includes Kaskaskia Isl. and village, 1st state capital of Ill., located on Mo. side of Mississippi R., separated from Ill. mainland in flood, accessible by bridge across Kaskaskia Slough from St. Mary's, Mo. One of 17 cos. to retain the Southern-style commission form of co. govt. **5** county (□ 453 sq mi/1,173 sq km; 1990 pop. 27,148), E Ind., bounded E by Ohio line; ⊙ Winchester; 40°09′N 85°01′W. Agr. area (corn, oats, wheat, soybeans; cattle, hogs, poultry; dairy prods.); mfg. at Union City and Winchester; stone quarrying. Drained by Mississinewa, Whitewater, and White rivers. Herbert Davis Forestry Farm (Purdue Univ. Agr. Center) in NW. Formed 1818. **6** county (□ 484 sq mi/1,254 sq km; 1990 pop. 24,370), N central Mo.; ⊙ Huntsville; 39°25′N 92°30′W. Drained by tributaries of Chariton and Salt rivers. Corn, wheat, oats, soybeans; cattle; mfg. at Moberly; bituminous coal, limestone quarries. Thomas Hill Dam and Reservoir in NW. Formed 1829. **7** county (□ 789 sq mi/2,044 sq km; 1990 pop. 106,546), central N.C.; ⊙ Asheboro; 35°42′N 79°48′W. Piedmont area, drained by Deep, Little, and Uwharrie rivers. Agr. area (tobacco, hay, corn, wheat, oats, soybeans; dairying; poultry; cattle, hogs); mfg. at Asheboro, Randleman, and Liberty, esp. furniture and hosiery. Stone quarrying. N.C. Zoological Park in center; part of Uwharrie Natl. Forest in SW. Formed 1779. **8** county (□ 1,040 sq mi/2,694 sq km; 1990 pop. 27,803), E central W.Va., at base of Eastern Panhandle; ⊙ Elkins; 38°46′N 79°52′W. On Allegheny Plateau; traversed N-S by Allegheny Front (E border), Rich Mt., Cheat Mt., Shaver's Mt., and other ridges. Large part of co. in Monongahela Natl. Forest in E and S. Drained by Elk and Tygart rivers, Shavers and Laurel forks of Cheat R., and Gandy Creek. Agr. (corn, oats, soybeans, potatoes, alfalfa, hay); cattle, hogs, poultry, sheep; dairying. Coal mining; timber; limestone quarries. Mfg. at Elkins. Kumbrabow State Forest in SW. Formed 1787.

Randolph 1 town (1990 pop. 243), Fremont co., SW Iowa, 10 mi/16 km NE of Sidney; 40°52′N 95°33′W. Livestock; grain. **2** residential town (1990 pop. 1,949), Kennebec co., S Maine, on the Kennebec just S of Augusta; 44°14′N 69°45′W. Inc. 1887. **3** town (1990 pop. 30,093), Norfolk co., E Mass.; 42°11′N 71°03′W. A chiefly residential, rapidly growing suburb of Boston. Industries include metal prods. and industrial tape. Settled c.1710; set off from Braintree and inc. 1793. **4** town (1990 pop. 983), Cedar co., NE Nebr., 25 mi/40 km N of Norfolk; 42°22′N 97°21′W. Livestock, poultry; grain; dairy prods. Settled 1886. **5** town (1990 pop. 371), Coos co., N central N.H., 8 mi/12.9 km SSW of Berlin; 44°23′N 71°19′W. Drained by Moose R. Agr. (poultry, livestock; dairying); timber. Trail center for Presidential Range. Parts of White Mt. Natl. Forest in North and South Crescent Range in center. **6** town (1990 pop. 4,764), including Randolph village, Orange co., central Vt., just SW of Chelsea; 43°56′N 72°36′W. The Morgan horse was 1st bred here. Vt. Technical Col. at Randolph Center village. Inc. 1783. Dairy prods.; winter sports.

Randolph, township (1990 pop. 19,974), Morris co., N N.J., 8 mi/12.9 km N of Morristown; 40°50′N 74°34′W. Mfg. (knives, metal parts, plastic package closures). Inc. 1806.

Randolph 1 village (1990 pop. 129), Riley co., NE Kansas, on Turtle Creek L., and 19 mi/31 km NNW of Manhattan; 39°25′N 96°45′W. In livestock and grain region. **2** village (1990 pop. 331), Dakota co., SE Minn., 30 mi/48 km S of St. Paul and 17 mi/27 km SW of Hastings, on Cannon R. (forms L. Byllesby reservoir to E) at mouth of Chub Creek; 44°31′N 93°01′W. In grain, livestock area. Small reservoir is just E. **3** village, Pontotoc co., N Miss., 11 mi/18 km WSW of Pontotoc. In agr., dairying, and timber area; mfg. (lumber, furniture). **4** **(East Kansas City)** village (1990 pop. 60), Clay co., W Mo., on left bank of Missouri R., industrial and commercial suburb 5 mi/8 km NE of downtown Kansas City, Mo. Mo. R. bridge. **5** village (□ 3 sq mi/7.8 sq km; 1990 pop. 1,298), Cattaraugus co., W N.Y., 14 mi/23 km ENE of Jamestown; 42°09′N 78°58′W. Mfg. (building materials, fabricated metal prods., furniture, machinery; printing); agr. (dairy prods.; poultry; grain). Randolph Children's Home, est. 1878 by the Western N.Y. Society for the Protection of Homeless and Dependent Children, is located here. Inc. 1867. **6** village (1990 pop. 488), ⊙ Rich co., N Utah, 35 mi/56 km E of Logan, bet. Little and Big creeks, near Bear R.; 41°39′N 111°10′W. Elev. 6,442 ft/1,964 m. In livestock (cattle, sheep) and grain (wheat, barley, alfalfa) area. Bear L. to NW; Wasatch Natl. Forest to W. Settled 1870. **7** village (1990 pop. 1,729), on Columbia-Dodge co. line, S central Wis., near Beaverdam L., 23 mi/37 km E of Portage; 43°32′N 89°00′W. RR junction in dairy and livestock region; seed warehouses; mfg. (can and bottle handling equipment, light mfg.). Settled 1844; plotted 1857; inc. 1870.

Random Island (□ 90 sq mi/233 sq km), just off SE N.F., Canada, in arm of Trinity Bay, 30 mi/48 km NW of Carbonear 20 mi/32 km long, 7 mi/11 km wide; 48°10′N 53°45′W. Rises to 843 ft/257 m. Numerous lakes. Bridge at W end to mainland. Has several fishing settlements, most connected by circular road. Snook's Harbour on NW coast.

Random Lake, town (1990 pop. 1,439), Sheboygan co., E Wis., on Random L. (resort), 35 mi/56 km N of Milwaukee; 43°32′N 87°57′W. In dairy and grain area; mfg. (tags, concrete prods., publishing).

Randsburg, uninc. village, Kern co., S central Calif., in Rand Mts., Mojave Desert, 45 mi/72 km NW of Barstow. Silver, tungsten. Named for the Rand gold-mining dist. of South Afr. Cuddeback L. (dry) to E.

Randville, village, Dickinson co., N Mich., on the Upper Peninsula, 11 mi/18 km N of Iron Mountain; 45°59′N 88°03′W. Iron ore treatment plant.

Range Ponds, reservoirs consisting of 3 small lakes, Androscoggin co., SW Maine, 7 mi/11.3 km SW of Auburn, and SE of Poland; combined length c.3 mi/4.8 km; 44°00′N 70°24′W. Resort area.

Rangeley (RAINJ-lee), town (1990 pop.1,063), Franklin co., W Maine, on Rangeley L., and 31 mi/50 km NW of Farmington; 44°58′N 70°43′W. Center of hilly, wooded Rangeley Lakes recreational region. Includes villages of Oquossoc, Haines Landing, and South Rangeley. Settled c.1825, inc. 1855.

Rangely, town (1990 pop. 2,278), Rio Blanco co., NW Colo., on White R., near Utah line, and 45 mi/72 km W of Meeker; 40°05′N 108°46′W. Elev. 5,224 ft/1,592 m. Supply point in coal, oil, and natural-gas, and cattle-grazing area. Sheep. Growth stimulated by oil boom of 1940s. Rangely Oil Field to NW. Colo. Northwestern Community Col. here. Dinosaur Natl. Monument to N. Founded 1880.

Ranger, town (1990 pop. 2,803), Eastland co., N central Texas, c.80 mi/129 km WSW of Fort Worth; 32°28′N 98°40′W. Elev. 1,429 ft/436 m. Supply center for oil field; oil refining, trade, processing point for agr. area (peanuts, cotton, livestock). Mfg. (athletic clothing, rebuilt RR cars, aircraft parts, hydrocarbon processing).

Seat of Ranger Junior Col. Founded 1881, inc. 1919; had c.50,000 pop. in boom following oil discovery, 1917.

Ranger, village (1990 pop. 153), Gordon co., NW Ga., 14 mi/23 km E of Calhoun; 34°30'N 84°43'W. Mfg. of household cleaners.

Rangerville, village (1990 pop. 280), Cameron co., extreme S Texas, residential suburb 7 mi/11.3 km SW of Harlingen, near Rio Grande (Mex. border); 26°06'N 97°44'W. Irrigated agr. region.

Ranier (ruh-NIR), village (1990 pop. 199), Koochiching co., N Minn., 4 mi/6.4 km NE of International Falls at outflow of Rainy R.; both river and lake form U.S.-Canada (Ont.) border; 48°36'N 93°20'W. Port of entry. Mfg. (fishing tackle). Voyageurs Natl. Park to E.

Rankin (RANG-kin), county (□ 806 sq mi/2,088 sq km; 1990 pop. 87,161), central Miss.; ⊙ Brandon; 32°15'N 89°57'W. Bounded W, NW, and N by Pearl R. (forms Ross Barnett Reservoir in NW); drained by Strong R. and tributaries. Agr. (cotton, corn; poultry, cattle; timber); natural-gas fields in SE (opened in 1930s). Mfg. at Pearl and Brandon. Co. is urbanized in W and center, areas adjacent to city of Jackson (to W), Miss.'s largest city. Formed 1828.

Rankin (RANG-kin), town (1990 pop. 1,011), ⊙ Upton co., W Texas, 55 mi/89 km S of Midland; 31°13'N 101°56'W. Elev. 2,595 ft/791 m. Oil- and gas-producing; sheep and cattle ranching. Cotton; pecans.

Rankin (RANG-kin), village (1990 pop. 619), Vermilion co., E Ill., 25 mi/40 km NNW of Danville; 40°27'N 87°54'W. Agr. (grain; livestock, poultry; dairy prods.).

Rankin, borough (1990 pop. 2,503), Allegheny co., SW Pa., on Monongahela R. (bridged), suburb 7 mi/11.3 km ESE of downtown Pittsburgh; 40°24'N 79°52'W. Mfg. (artificial trees, fabricated metal prods.); steel. Inc. 1892.

Rankin Inlet, village (1991 pop. 1,706), S central N.W.T., Canada, 300 mi/483 km NNE of Churchill, Man., on Rankin Inlet of Hudson Bay; 62°49'N 92°05'W. Nickel mining in 1950s attracted small pop. Mine closed in 1961, but Inuit residents remained. Crafts, fishing, hunting, sealing. Television and radio stations. Royal Can. Mounted Police post. Scheduled air service.

Ranlo, town (1990 pop. 1,650), Gaston co., S N.C., a residential suburb 3 mi/4.8 km E of Gastonia, near South Fork Catawba R.; 35°17'N 81°07'W.

Ranquitte (rawng-KEET), town (1982 pop. 946), Nord dept., N central Haiti, in Massif du Nord, 27 mi/43 km SSE of Cap-Haïtien; 19°25'N 72°05'W. Citrus fruit, coffee-growing.

Ranshaw (RAN-shaw), uninc. village, Coal township, Northumberland co., E central Pa., 19 mi/31 km NW of Pottsville; 40°47'N 76°31'W. Light mfg.

Ransom, county (□ 861 sq mi/2,230 sq km; 1990 pop. 5,921), SE N.Dak.; ⊙ Lisbon; 46°27'N 97°39'W. Rich prairie land drained by Sheyenne R. and Maple R. Cattle, hogs; soybeans; dairying; corn, wheat, barley, rye, hay, sunflowers. Formed 1873. Little Yellowstone Park, Fort Ransom State Park and Fort Ransom Historic Site all in NW.

Ransom 1 village (1990 pop. 438), La Salle co., N Ill., 17 mi/27 km SSE of Ottawa; 41°09'N 88°39'W. In agr. area. **2** village (1990 pop. 386), Ness co., W central Kansas, 13 mi/21 km N of Ness City; 38°38'N 99°55'W. Grain; livestock.

Ransomville, village (□ 6 sq mi/15.5 sq km; 1990 pop. 1,542), Niagara co., W N.Y., near L. Ontario, 13 mi/21 km NE of Niagara Falls city; 43°14'N 78°54'W. In fruit-growing area.

Ranson, town (1990 pop. 2,890), Jefferson co., NE W.Va., in Eastern Panhandle, 2 mi/3.2 km NW of Charles Town; 39°17'N 77°51'W. Mfg. (brass foundry prods., lumber). Agr. (grain, soybeans, apples); livestock; dairying. Leetown Natl. Fish Hatchery to NW. Inc. 1910.

Rantoul 1 (ran-TOOL), village (1990 pop. 17,212), Champaign co., E Ill., 14 mi/23 km N of Urbana; 40°17'N 88°09'W. In a rich blackland farm area that yields corn and soybeans. Chanute Air Force Base, now closed, was here. One of the oldest and largest technical training centers of the U.S. Air Force, first opened in 1917. Inc. 1868. **2** village (1990 pop. 200), Franklin co., E Kansas, near Marais des Cygnes R., 10 mi/16 km ESE of Ottawa; 38°32'N 95°05'W. In livestock and grain region.

Rapid City, town (1991 pop. 406), SW Man., Canada, on Minnesdosa R. (rapids), and 20 mi/32 km N of Brandon; 50°07'N 100°02'W. Dairying.

Rapid City, city (1990 pop. 54,523), ⊙ of Pennington co., SW S.Dak., on Rapid Creek, in an irrigated farm region served by the Bureau of Reclamation's Rapid Valley project. It is the trade and transportation center of an extensive lumbering, ranching, and mining (gold, silver, feldspar, bentonite, mica, and uranium) area. The growing city has flour mills and firms that make jewelry, cement, and lumber. Mfg. (wood millwork, wooden furniture; mat boards, sand and gravel; small arms ammunition and gun stocks; gold and silver jewelry; dairy prods., lumber, meat prods., display stands, packaging; concrete and steel fabrication, construction materials; doors; limestone prods.). Ellsworth Air Force Base to NE, a major air command installation, is a major source of employment. The city is also the tourist center of the Black Hills and the gateway to many attractions, including Mt. Rushmore Natl. Memorial & Custer State Park (to SW), the Badlands Natl. Park (to SE), and Wind Cave Natl. Park. S.Dak. School of Mines and Technology, and Mus. of Geology, 2 nursing schools, the Natl. Col. of Business, and the Sioux Indian mus. are in Rapid City. In June 1972, the city was struck by a severe flash flood after heavy rains, killing more than 200 people. Rapid City Regional Airport to SE. Creghorn Springs Fish Hatchery to SW; S.Dak. Natl. Guard Camp. Founded 1876 after the discovery of gold nearby, inc. 1882.

Rapid Creek, 86 mi/138 km long, S.Dak.; rises in the Black Hills in Pennington co., SW S.Dak.; flows E, past Silver City through Pacota Reservoir, through Rapid City, past Farmingdale to Cheyenne R., 13 mi/21 km SW of Wasta; 44°07'N 103°44'W. Castle Creek feeds into Rapid Creek above Silver City.

Rapid River, village, Delta co., S Upper Peninsula, Mich., 13 mi/21 km NNE of Escanaba, at mouth of small Rapid R. on Little Bay De Noc; 45°55'N 86°58'W. Mfg. of wood prods. and cedar log homes. In Hiawatha Natl. Forest.

Rapidan River, c.90 mi/145 km long, N Va.; rises in Blue Ridge on Madison-Greene co. line, 8 mi/12.9 km N of Stanardsville; flows SE, NE past Rapidan and E to Rappahannock R., 8 mi/12.9 km NW of Fredericksburg; 38°29'N 78°25'W. Receives Robinson R. from NW, 3 mi/4.8 km W of Rapidan.

Rapides (ra-PEEDZ), parish (□ 1,329 sq mi/3,442 sq km; 1990 pop. 131,556), central La.; ⊙ Alexandria; 31°17'N, 92°28'W. Bounded NE by Big Saline Bayou and Little R.; drained by Calcasieu and Red rivers. Includes part of Kisatchie Natl. Forest (NE and W), Claiborne Range Military Reservation (W center), and U.S. Camp Beauregard (NE). Agr. (cotton, corn, sorghum, hay; home gardens, nursery crops, rice, sugarcane, sweet potatoes, soybeans, vegetables; cattle, horses, poultry, exotic fowl; dairying), catfish, crawfish. Logging, varied mfg. including food, wood, metal, paper, and concrete prods.; chemicals. La. Seminary of Learning formed in 1860, later became La. State Univ. in Baton Rouge. Formed 1807. Part of Grand Cote Natl. Wildlife Refuge in SE; Alexander State Forest, including Indian Creek Recreational Area, at center; Cocodrie L. on S boundary; Kincaid Reservoir, Cotile L., and L. Rodemacher in NW.

Rapids City, village (1990 pop. 932), Rock Island co., NW Ill., on the Mississippi R., and 14 mi/23 km NE of Rock Island; 41°34'N 90°20'W. In agr. area.

Raponda, Lake (RAH-pawn-dah), c.1.5 mi/2.4 km long, S Vt., resort lake in Wilmington town, 12 mi/19 km W of Brattleboro Brattleboro. Formerly Ray Pond.

Rappahannock (rap-uh-HAN-uk), county (□ 266 sq mi/689 sq km; 1990 pop. 6,622), N Va.; ⊙ Washington; 38°41'N 78°10'W. In Piedmont region; rises (W, NW) to Blue Ridge; includes part of Shenandoah Natl. Park in W; Appalachian Trail follows NW boundary. Bounded NE by Rappahannock R., drained by Thornton R. and short Hughes R. Mainly agr. (hay, alfalfa, apples, peaches; cattle). Est. 1833 from Culpeper co.

Rappahannock River, 212 mi/341 km long, N and E Va.; rises in Blue Ridge Mts., N Va., in NW part of Fauquier/Rappahannock co. line; flows generally SE, passes SW of Warrenton, then passes Fredericksburg and Port Royal, where it becomes a tidal stream; continues SE past Tappahannock, widening into estuary and entering Chesapeake Bay, 38 mi/61 km N of Hampton, bet. Windmill Point (N) and Stingray Point. (S). Navigable to Fredericksburg. Receives Rapidan R. from W 8 mi/12.9 km NW of Fredericksburg. Area of much Civil War fighting.

Rappahannock Station, Va.: see REMINGTON.

Raquette Lake, resort village (1990 pop. 170), Hamilton co., NE central N.Y., in the Adirondacks, on Raquette L. (c.5 mi/8 km long, 1/2 mi/8/10 km–3 mi/4.8 km wide; drained by Raquette R.), c.55 mi/89 km NNE of Utica; 43°49'N 74°40'W. Located 4 mi/6.4 km S is Great Camp Sagamore–Adirondack Great Camp, former summer home of Vanderbilt family (built in 1897 by William West Durant), featuring 29 bldgs.

Raquette River, c.140 mi/225 km long, N N.Y.; issues from Raquette L. in the Adirondacks c.55 mi/89 km NNE of Utica; flows NE, entering and discharging from Long L., then N and NW, widening into irregular Raquette Pond near Tupper L. village; then NW, N, and NE, past Potsdam and Massena, to the St. Lawrence R. 3 mi/4.8 km W of Hogansburg.

Raritan (RA-ri-tuhn), town (1990 pop. 5,798), Somerset co., N central N.J., on Raritan R. (bridged here), just W of Somerville; 40°30'N 74°52'W. Mfg. (metal prods.). Largely residential. Inc. 1868.

Raritan (RA-ri-tuhn), river, 85 mi/137 km long N.J.; rises in N central N.J.; flows generally SE to Raritan Bay, an arm of Lower New York Bay, at Perth Amboy; known to be the only tidal river in N. Amer. Through pumping, the Raritan supplies water to the Spruce Run and Round Valley reservoirs. The Delaware and Raritan Canal once connected the Raritan and Delaware rivers.

Raritan Bay (RA-ri-tuhn), NE N.J. and SE N.Y., W arm of Lower New York Bay; situated S of Staten Isl., N.Y., and W of Point Comfort, Monmouth co., N.J. Arthur Kill joins Newark Bay (N) to dredged deep-water channel in Raritan Bay.

Raspberry Island (18 mi/29 km long, 3 mi/4.8 km–8 mi/12.9 km wide), S Alaska, E of Alaska Peninsula, bet. Afognak and Kodiak isls.; 58°03'N 153°10'W. Fishing, fish processing.

Raspberry Strait (20 mi/32 km long, 1 mi/1.6 km–2 mi/3.2 km wide), S Alaska, bet. Afognak Isl. and Raspberry Isl., connecting Gulf of Alaska and Shelikof Strait.

Rat Islands, Alaska: see ALEUTIAN ISLANDS.

Rat Rapids, village, NW Ont., Canada, in Patricia dist., at E end of L. St. Joseph, 100 mi/161 km NE of Sioux Lookout; 51°11'N 90°13'W. Hydroelectric station, supplying Pickle L. mining region.

Ratcliff, village (1990 pop. 180), Logan co., W Ark., 30 mi/48 km ESE of Fort Smith; 35°18'N 93°53'W. Mfg. (chocolate candies, lingerie).

Rathbun, town (1990 pop. 89), Appanoose co., S Iowa, 5 mi/8 km N of Centerville; 40°47'N 92°53'W.

Rathbun Lake, reservoir, Appanoose co., S Iowa, on Chariton R., 6 mi/9.7 km N of Centerville; c.12 mi/19 km long; 40°10'N 92°53'W. Has 2 arms. Max. capacity 552,000 acre-ft. Formed by Rathbun Dam (81 ft/25 m high), built (1972) by the Army Corps of Engineers for flood control, navigation, and water supply. Henry Creek State Park on N shore.

Rathdrum, town (1990 pop. 2,000), Kootenai co., N Idaho, 12 mi/19 km NW of Coeur d'Alene; 47°49'N 116°54'W. Trading point for irrigated agr. area (cattle; oats, alfalfa). Mfg. (cabinets, trailers); logging. Lead, silver, gold mines nearby. Twin Lakes and Spirit L. to N, Hauser L. to W.

Rathwell (RATH-wuhl), village, S Man., Canada, at N end of Pembina Mts., 25 mi/40 km SW of Portage la Prairie; grain, livestock.

Ratliff City, village (1990 pop. 157), Carter co., S Okla., 28 mi/45 km NW of Ardmore. Agr. and oil-producing region; 34°27'N 97°30'W. Mfg. (valves).

Raton (ruh-TON), town (1990 pop. 7,372), ⊙ Colfax co., NE N.Mex., near Colo. state line, in Raton Mts., 120 mi/193 km NE of Santa Fe, and 19 mi/31 km S of Trinidad, Colo.; 36°53'N 104°26'W. Elev. 6,400 ft/1,951 m. Trade center and resort in cattle, sheep, and mining, (molybdenum) region. Mfg. (metal doors and frames, portable bldgs.). State hosp., home for miners here. Raton Pass (7,834 ft/2,388 m) on state line to N; Capulin Volcano Natl. Monument, 27 mi/43 km ESE. Sugarite State Park and Ski Area near L. Maloya and state line to N; Johnson Mesa to NE; Natl. Rifle Assn. Whittington Center to SSW. Settled in 1870s on Santa Fe Trail, laid out 1880, inc. 1891.

Raton Mountains, E spur of Sangre de Cristo Mts. in Las Animas co., S Colo., and Colfax co., NE N.Mex. Includes Raton Mesa, 5 mi/8 km SSE of Trinidad, Colo., rising to 9,625 ft/2,934 m at Fishers Peak. Raton Pass (7,834 ft/2,388 m), just N of N.Mex. state line, carries road and RR. Coal is mined near Trinidad, Colo., and Raton, N.Mex. Laughlin Peak (8,820 ft/2,688 m), 20 mi/32 km SE of Raton.

Raton Pass (7,834 ft/2,388 m), in Raton Mts., on Colo.-N.Mex. state line, 12 mi/19 km S of Trinidad, Colo. Used by explorers and travelers in 18th and 19th cent.; now crossed by Interstate highway and RR.

Rattan (ruh-TAN), village (1990 pop. 257), Pushmataha co., SE Okla., 13 mi/21 km NNE of Hugo; 34°12′N 95°24′W. Agr. (wheat, cattle). Hugo L. reservoir to S.

Rattlesnake Creek, 122 mi/196 km long, S central Kansas; formed by confluence of several headstreams in Kiowa co., NE of Greensburg; flows NE through Quivira Natl. Wildlife Refuge before entering Arkansas R., 8 mi/12.9 km NW of Sterling.

Rattlesnake Creek, Ohio: see PAINT CREEK.

Rattlesnake Mountain (1,035 ft/315 m), Cumberland co., SW Maine, in resort area N of Sebago L.

Ratz, Mount (rats) (10,290 ft/3,136 m), NW B.C., Canada, near Alaska border, in Coast Mts., 65 mi/105 km N of Wrangell.

Raudales de Malpaso (rah-DAH-les dai mahl-PAH-so), village, Chiapas, S Mexico, Angel Albino Corzo municipio; site of Nezahualcóyotl Dam.

Ravalli (ruh-VAH-lee), county (□ 2,400 sq mi/6,216 sq km; 1990 pop. 25,010), W Mont.; ⊙ Hamilton; 46°05′N 114°07′W. Agr. region including fertile valley of Bitterroot R.; borders on Idaho (W and S); W part of boundary forms div. bet. Mountain and Pacific time zone; Continental Divide forms SE co. line. Wheat, barley, oats, potatoes, mint, apples, hay; cattle, sheep, hogs, llamas; forest industries, mining. Lost Trail Ski Area in SE; Fort Owen State Park (site of St. Mary's Mission), and Lee Metcalf Natl. Wildlife Refuge in N; Painted Rocks Reservoir and State Park in SW; parts of Selway-Bitterroot Wilderness Area in NW and SW. Bitterroot Range (W), in Bitterroot Natl. Forest, covers all of co. except Bitterroot Valley N–S through middle of co. E boundary formed by the Sapphire Mts. Formed 1893.

Ravanna (ruh-VAN-nuh), uninc. community, Mercer co., N Mo., near Weldon R., 7 mi/11.3 km ENE of Princeton.

Raven, uninc. town, Tazewell co., SW Va., residential community, 20 mi/32 km W of Tazewell, on Clinch R.; 37°05′N 81°51′W. Agr. (dairying, livestock; tobacco, grain); bituminous coal, limestone.

Ravena (□ 1 sq mi/2.6 sq km; 1990 pop. 3,547), Albany co., E N.Y., near the Hudson R., 12 mi/19 km S of Albany; 42°28′N 73°48′W. Mfg. (cement). Inc. 1914.

Ravenden (RAIV-en-den), village (1990 pop. 330), Lawrence co., NE Ark., 15 mi/24 km W of Pocahontas on Spring R.; 36°14′N 91°15′W. In agr area.

Ravenden Springs (RAIV-en-den), village (1990 pop. 131), Randolph co., NE Ark., 14 mi/23 km WNW of Pocahontas; 36°18′N 91°13′W. In agr. area. Mfg. (wooden pallets).

Ravenel (rav-en-EL), town (1990 pop. 2,165), Charleston co., S S.C., 17 mi/27 km W of Charleston; 32°46′N 80°13′W. Mfg. (fertilizers and signs). Agr. (tomatoes, sweet potatoes, vegetables; livestock; poultry). Formerly Ravenels.

Ravenna (ri-VA-nuh), city (1990 pop. 12,069), ⊙ Portage co., NE Ohio, in a lake and farm area; 41°09′N 81°14′W. Named after the Ital. city, Ravenna has diverse light mfg.; lamps. Settled 1799, inc. 1852.

Ravenna 1 (ruh-VE-nuh), town (1990 pop. 804), Estill co., E central Ky., 3 mi/4.8 km SE of Irvine, on Kentucky R., surrounded by Daniel Boone Natl. Forest;

37°41′N 83°57′W. Agr. (tobacco, soybeans; livestock). Mfg. (lumber, crushed limestone, fiberglass boats); oil wells, timber in region. Inc. 1921. **2** town (1990 pop. 1,317), Buffalo co., S central Nebr., at junction of Mud Creek and South Loup R., 23 mi/37 km NNE of Kearney; 41°01′N 98°54′W. Grain. Mfg. (egg prods., cheese, dehydrated food [chickens]). Ravenna L. State Recreation Area to N. Inc. 1886.

Ravenna 1 (ruh-VE-nuh), village (1990 pop. 919), Muskegon co., SW Mich., 17 mi/27 km ESE of Muskegon; 43°11′N 85°56′W. In dairying and agr. area; fruit growing. Mfg. (printing, metal patterns). **2** (rai-VE-nuh), uninc. village (1990 pop. 186), Fannin co., NE Texas, 7 mi/11.3 km NW of Bonham. In agr. area.

Ravenscrag (RAI-vuhnz-kraig), village, SW Sask., Canada, in the Cypress Hills, on Frenchman R., and 35 mi/56 km SE of Maple Creek. Elev. 3,127 ft/953 m; coal mining.

Ravenscroft, village, White co., central Tenn., 10 mi/16 km ENE of Sparta.

Ravenswood, town (1990 pop. 4,189), Jackson co., W W.Va., on the Ohio R. (bridged), 15 mi/24 km N of Ripley; 38°57′N 81°45′W. Agr. (grain, tobacco); cattle. Mfg. (plastic prods., printing and publishing). Gas wells. Sarvis Fork Covered Bridge to SE at Sandyville. Chartered 1852.

Ravenswood, village, Marion co., central Ind., suburb 8 mi/12.9 km N of downtown Indianapolis, on White R. Consolidated with Indianapolis in 1970.

Ravensworth, uninc. town, Fairfax co., NE Va., residential suburb 11 mi/18 km WSW of Washington, D.C.; 38°48′N 77°13′W. L. Accotink Park to S.

Ravenwood 1 town (1990 pop. 409), Nodaway co., NW Mo., on Florida R., and 10 mi/16 km E of Maryville; 40°21′N 94°40′W. Corn, wheat; cattle. **2** uninc. town, Fairfax co., NE Va., residential suburb 7 mi/11.3 km W of Washington, D.C.; 38°51′N 77°09′W. L. Barcroft reservoir to S.

Ravia (RAV-ee-uh), village (1990 pop. 404), Johnston co., S Okla., 5 mi/8 km W of Tishomingo, near Washita R. headwaters of N arm of L. Texoma; 34°14′N 96°45′W.

Ravinia, village (1990 pop. 79), Charles Mix co., SE S.Dak., 6 mi/9.7 km E of L. Andes; 43°08′N 98°25′W. L. Andes Natl. Wildlife Refuge to W.

Rawdon, village (1991 pop. 3,297), S Que., Canada, 35 mi/56 km N of Montreal; 46°02′N 73°42′W. Lumbering, dairying; tobacco, potatoes.

Rawlins, county (□ 1,069 sq mi/2,769 sq km; 1990 pop. 3,404), NW Kansas; ⊙ Atwood; 39°47′N 101°04′W. Gently rolling plain area, bordering N on Nebr.; watered by headstreams of Sappa, S Fork, Beaver, and Little Beaver creeks. Barley, wheats, corn, sorghum; cattle. Formed 1881.

Rawlins (RAW-luhnz), town (1990 pop. 9,380), ⊙ Carbon co., S Wyo., 90 mi/145 km WNW of Laramie; 41°46′N 107°13′W. Elev. 6,755 ft/2,059 m. RR and distribution center for mining; cattle and sheep region. Mfg. (computer peripherals); RR shops. Frontier State Prison to S, once in use (1903–1982), now open as a tourist attraction. Coal mines, oil wells, quarries nearby. Seminoe Reservoir and State Park to NE; Continental Divide and Great Divide Basin to W. Founded 1868.

Rawson 1 village (1990 pop. 9), McKenzie co., W N.Dak., 12 mi/19 km W of Watford City; 47°49′N 103°32′W. **2** village (1990 pop. 482), Hancock co., NW Ohio, c.9 mi/14 km SW of Findlay, in agr. region; 40°57′N 83°47′W.

Ray, county (□ 574 sq mi/1,487 sq km; 1990 pop. 21,971), W central Mo.; ⊙ Richmond; 39°21′N 93°59′W. Bounded S by Missouri R.; drained by Crooked R. Corn, wheat, soybeans; vegetable farming; hogs, cattle; former coal mines. Mfg. at Richmond and Henrietta. Formed 1820.

Ray 1 village, Pinal co., SE central Ariz., 18 mi/29 km SSW of Miami. Ray copper mine. **2** village (1990 pop. 603), Williams co., NW N.Dak., 26 mi/42 km NE of Williston; 48°20′N 103°09′W.

Ray Brook, town (1990 pop. 400), Essex co., N N.Y., 5 mi/8 km W of Lake Placid; 44°18′N 74°05′W. Hq. for Adirondack Park Agency, which administers and plans

development of Adirondack Park, the nation's largest state park. Adirondack Correctional Facility located here as well.

Ray, Cape, promontory at SW extremity of N.F., Canada, at entrance of the Gulf of St. Lawrence, 8 mi/13 km WNW of Port aux Basques; 47°37′N 59°22′W.

Ray City, village (1990 pop. 603), Berrien co., S Ga., 18 mi/29 km NNE of Valdosta; 31°04′N 83°12′W. Light mfg.

Ray Hubbard, Lake, reservoir, Kaufman, Dallas, Rockwell, and Collin cos., NE Texas, E. Fork Trinity R., 15 mi/24 km E of downtown Dallas; c.20 mi/32 km long; 32°48′N 96°31′W. Max. capacity 611,500 acre-ft. Formed by Forney Dam (53 ft/16 m high), built (1968) by City of Dallas for water supply. Dallas corporate limits extend E to lake; cities of Sunnyvale, Garland, and Rowlett on W shore, Rockwell on E shore.

Ray Mountains, central Alaska, S extension of Brooks Range, N of Tanana; 150–152°30′W at 65°45′N; rise to 3,500 ft/1,067 m.

Ray Pond, Vt.: see RAPONDA, LAKE.

Ray Roberts, Lake, reservoir (□ 46 sq mi/119 sq km), Denton and Cooke cos., N Texas, on Elk Fork of Trinity R., 40 mi/64 km NNW of Dallas; 33°16′N 97°03′W. Max. capacity 1,931,900 acre-ft. Formed by Ray Roberts Dam (141 ft/43 m high), built (1986) by Army Corps of Engineers for water supply; also used for recreation and power generation. Ray Roberts L. State Park near dam.

Rayland, village (1990 pop. 490), Jefferson co., E Ohio, on the Ohio, and 12 mi/19 km SSW of Steubenville, in coal-mining area; 40°11′N 80°42′W.

Rayle (RAI-lee), town (1990 pop. 107), Wilkes co., Ga., 11 mi/18 km NW of Washington; 33°47′N 82°55′W. Mfg. (log homes, wooden pallets).

Raymer or **New Raymer**, village (1990 pop. 98), Weld co., NE Colo., 45 mi/72 km ENE of Greeley; 40°36′N 103°50′W. Elev. 4,773 ft/1,455 m. Small trading point in oil-producing and agr. area. Pawnee Natl. Grassland to N.

Raymond, town (1991 pop. 3,130), S Alta., Canada, SE of Lethbridge; 49°28′N 112°40′W. In a sugar beet area. Sugar is refined, and honey is produced here. A provincial agr. col. is here.

Raymond 1 resort town (1990 pop. 3,311), Cumberland co., SW Maine, on Jordan Bay of Sebago L., and 20 mi/32 km NNW of Portland; 43°55′N 70°28′W. Nathaniel Hawthorne's boyhood home here. **2** town (1990 pop. 2,275), a ⊙ Hinds co. (seat shared with Jackson), W Miss., 14 mi/23 km WSW of Jackson; 32°15′N 90°25′W. In agr. (cotton, corn, soybeans; cattle, poultry) and timber area. Mfg. (automotive testing equip.). Hinds Community Col. Natchez Trace (Natl.) Parkway passes to NW. **3** town (1990 pop. 8,713), Rockingham co., SE N.H., 11 mi/24 km ENE of Manchester; 43°01′N 71°12′W. Drained by Lamprey R. Mfg. (ball valves, metal stampings, industrial machinery, plastic containers); agr. (vegetables, nursery crops; poultry, cattle; dairying). Pawtuckaway State Park to N. Inc. 1764. **4** town (1990 pop. 2,901), Pacific co., SW Wash., 20 mi/32 km SSE of Aberdeen, and on Willapa R., at mouth of South Fork Willapa R., near Willapa Bay 6 mi/9.7 km to N; 46°41′N 123°45′W. Alfalfa, hay; logging. Mfg. (wood flooring, lumber, dairy prods.). Willapa Harbor Airport to W. Willapa Fish Hatchery to SE. Inc. 1907.

Raymond 1 village (1990 pop. 820), Montgomery co., S central Ill., 13 mi/21 km NNW of Hillsboro; 39°19′N 89°34′W. In agr. area (corn, wheat, hay, soybeans, sorghum; cattle; dairy prods.). **2** village (1990 pop. 619), Blackhawk co., E central Iowa, suburb 7 mi/11.3 km E of Waterloo; 42°28′N 92°13′W. Corn; hogs, poultry. **3** village (1990 pop. 668), Kandiyohi co., SW central Minn., 12 mi/19 km SW of Willmar, near Hawk Creek; 45°01′N 95°14′W. Grain, sugar beets; poultry, livestock; dairying. Light mfg. **4** village (1990 pop. 35), Sheridan co., NE Mont., on McCoy Creek, 7 mi/11.3 km N of Plentywood. Port of Raymond (port of entry) on Can. (Sask.) border, 8 mi/12.9 km to N. Wheat; cattle. **5** village (1990 pop. 167), Lancaster co., E Nebr., 10 mi/16 km NNW of Lincoln and on branch of Platte R.; ⊙ 40°57′N 96°46′W. Branched Oak L. State Recreation

Area to W. **6** village (1990 pop. 96), Clark co., E central S.Dak., 10 mi/16 km W of Clark; 44°54′N 97°56′W.

Raymondville, city (1990 pop. 8,880), ⊙ Willacy co., extreme S Texas, 20 mi/32 km NNW of Harlingen; 26°28′N 97°46′W. Elev. 40 ft/12 m. Trade, shipping center for irrigated agr. area (sorghum, corn, sugarcane, cotton, vegetables; cattle, hogs, horses, goats). Mfg. (pork rinds and beef jerky, sweatshirts); some oil and gas. Tourist trade. Plotted 1904, inc. as city 1921.

Raymondville, town (1990 pop. 425), Texas co., S central Mo., 6 mi/9.7 km E of Houston; 37°20′N 91°50′W. Hay; cattle. Charcoal, wood prods.

Raymore, town (1991 pop. 668), S central Sask., Canada, at foot of Touchwood Hills, 30 mi/48 km SW of Wynyard; 51°24′N 104°32′W. Wheat; livestock.

Raymore, town (1990 pop. 5,592), Cass co., W Mo., residential suburb, 20 mi/32 km S of Kansas City; 38°48′N 94°27′W. Mfg. (automotive regulators).

Rayne (RAIN), city (1990 pop. 8,502), Acadia parish, S La., 6 mi/10 km NE of Crowley; 30°14′N 92°16′W. In rice and sugarcane area; sweet potatoes, fruit, vegetables, poultry. Mfg. (production chemicals, fitness equip.; seafood processing, gasoline refining); edible frog industry. Oil wells. Annual Frog Festival.

Raynham (RAI-nuhm), town (1990 pop. 9,867), Bristol co., SE Mass., on Taunton R., just NE of Taunton; 41°56′N 71°02′W. Ironworks est. here 1652. Inc. 1731. Includes East Taunton village.

Raynham (RAIN-uhm), village (1990 pop. 106), Robeson co., SE N.C., 12 mi/19 km WSW of Lumberton; 34°34′N 79°11′W. Grain, tobacco; livestock.

Raynolds Pass (RE-nuldz), (elev. 6,836 ft/2,084 m), SW Mont., on Continental Divide and on Madison co., Mont. (N) and Fremont co., Idaho (S) state line. Henrys L., NE Idaho, is 5 mi/8 km to SE. State Highway 87 (both states) passes through.

Rayón (rai-ON), city (1990 pop. 5,472) and township, San Luis Potosí, N central Mexico, in Sierra Madre Oriental, 23 mi/37 km ESE of Río Verde, 2 mi/3 km S of Mexico Highway 70. Grain, cotton, beans; livestock.

Rayón 1 (rai-ON), town (1990 pop. 3,594), Chiapas, S Mexico, in N spur of Sierra Madre, 30 mi/48 km NNE of Tuxtla Gutiérrez on Mexico Highway 195. Elev. 4,501 ft/1,372 m. Cereals, fruit, tobacco, sugarcane. **2** town (1990 pop. 1,468), Sonora, NW Mexico, on San Miguel de Horcasitas R. (irrigation), and 50 mi/80 km NNE of Hermosillo; 29°03′N 109°14′W. Elev. 1,837 ft/560 m. Wheat, corn, cotton, fruit. Copper mines nearby.

Rayones (rai-ON-es), town (1990 pop. 523), Nuevo León, N Mexico, 45 mi/72 km SSE of Monterrey in Sierra Madre Oriental; 25°00′N 100°08′W. Fruit; livestock.

Raysal (rai-SAL), uninc. village (1990 pop. 500), McDowell co., S W.Va., on Dry Fork, 13 mi/21 km WSW of Welch. Coal-mining and agr. area.

Raystown Branch, Pa.: see JUNIATA RIVER.

Raystown Lake, reservoir, Huntingdon and Bedford cos., S Pa., on Juniata R., bet. Allegrippus Ridge (W) and Terrace Mt. ridge (E), 4 mi/6.4 km S of Huntingdon; c.40 mi/64 km long; 40°25′N 78°01′W. Elev. 787 ft/240 m. Max. capacity 871,000 acre-ft. Formed by Raystown Dam (211 ft/64 m high), built (1973) by the Army Corps of Engineers for flood control. Trough Creek State Park, and Rothrock State Forest SE of lake center.

Raytown, city (1990 pop. 30,061), Jackson co., W central Mo., a residential suburb 10 mi/16 km SE of downtown Kansas City; 38°59′N 94°28′W. Mfg. (air-pollution filters, chain conveyors, wood accessories). Inc. 1950.

Rayville 1 (RAI-vil), town (1990 pop. 4,411), ⊙ Richland parish, NE La., 21 mi/34 km E of Monroe, near Boeuf R.; 32°28′N 91°46′W. In agr. area (cotton, vegetables, corn, rice, cattle). Mfg. (paper tubes, pulper parts, slacks and jeans); hunting, fishing. **2** town (1990 pop. 170), Ray co., NW Mo., on Crooked R., and 7 mi/11.3 km NW of Richmond; 39°21′N 94°03′W.

Razorback, mountain (10,667 ft/3,251 m), SW B.C., Canada, in Coast Mts., 170 mi/274 km NNW of Vancouver.

Rea (RAI), town (1990 pop. 62), Andrew co., NW Mo., near Platte R., 8 mi/12.9 km N of Savannah; 40°03′N 94°45′W. Corn, soybeans, wheat; cattle.

Read Island, SW Franklin dist., N.W.T., Canada, in Dolphin and Union Strait, just off SW Victoria Isl.; 5 mi/8 km long, 2 mi/3 km wide; 69°12′N 114°30′W.

Reader, town (1990 pop. 56), Ouachita co., S Ark., 20 mi/32 km NW of Camden, near Little Missouri R. at mouth of Caney Creek; 33°45′N 93°05′W. White Oak L. State Park and Poison Springs Wildlife Management Area to S.

Readfield (REED-feeld), town (1990 pop. 2,033), Kennebec co., S Maine, 10 mi/16 km NNW of Augusta; 44°22′N 69°57′W. In agr., resort, lumbering area; Maine Wesleyan Seminary (1821) is at Kents Hill village.

Reading 1 (RE-ding), city (1990 pop. 12,038), Hamilton co., extreme SW Ohio, a N suburb of Cincinnati; 39°13′N 84°26′W. Lithographing. Mfg. (chemicals, paperboard containers). Settled 1795; inc. as village in 1851, as city in 1930. **2** city (1990 pop. 78,380), ⊙ Berks co., SE Pa., 45 mi/72 km NW of Philadelphia, on the Schuylkill R., in the Pa. Du. region; 40°20′N 75°55′W. RR junction. Once an important industrial, commercial, and RR city, Reading has become a major factory discount retail center. Mfg. (food prods., semiconductors, plastic prods., textiles, fabricated metal prods., crushed stone, metal alloys, detergents, auto and truck frames; brass castings, auto batteries, dyes, coatings, and resins; paper and corrugated containers, printing, tool and die, overhead cranes, machinery). Beginning in the late 18th cent., Reading was an early iron-producing town; cannons were made here during the Amer. Revolution, and it was a Union ordnance center during the Civil War. The completion of the Philadelphia and Reading RR added to the city's economic growth, which was also spurred by the production of automobiles in the early 1900s. Reading is the seat of Albright Col., Alvernia Col., the Berks Campus of Pa. State Univ., and Reading Area Community Col. Also in the city are Reading Mus., Planetarium, and Art Gall., Reading Symphony Orchestra; Berks Co. Heritage Center (at Wyomissing); Mid-Atlantic Air Mus.; Nolde Forest Environmental Education Center to S; Daniel Boone Homestead, historic site to SE; observation tower and the Pagoda on Mt. Penn to E. Reading Regional Airport (Spaatz Field) to NW; Blue Marsh Ski Area to NW, on Blue Marsh L. reservoir (Blue Marsh L. State Recreation Area); L. Ontelaunee Reservoir to N. Laid out 1748, inc. as a city 1847.

Reading 1 (RE-ding), town (1990 pop. 22,539), Middlesex co., NE Mass., a suburb of Boston; 42°32′N 71°07′W. Printing is the major industry. A 17th-cent. tavern is in Reading. Settled 1639, set off from Lynn and inc. 1644. **2** (REE-ding), town (1990 pop. 1,127), Hillsdale co., S Mich., 8 mi/12.9 km SW of Hillsdale; 41°50′N 84°45′W. Livestock; agr. Small lakes in area. Mfg. (air-conditioning hoses and tubes). Settled 1840; inc. as village 1873; as city 1934. **3** (RE-ding), town (1990 pop. 614), Windsor co., E Vt., 8 mi/12.9 km W of Windsor; 43°29′N 72°35′W. Includes Felchville village. Talc and soapstone quarries.

Reading (RE-ding), village (1990 pop. 264), Lyon co., E central Kansas, on Marais des Cygnes R., and 15 mi/24 km ENE of Emporia; 38°31′N 95°57′W. Livestock; grain.

Readington, township (1990 pop. 13,400), Hunterdon co., N N.J., 7 mi/11.3 km NE of Flemington; 40°34′N 74°46′W. Inc. 1798.

Readland (REED-luhnd), village, Chicot co., extreme SE Ark., 25 mi/40 km SSW of Greenville, Miss., on Grand L., oxbow lake of Mississippi R.

Readlyn, town (1990 pop. 773), Bremer co., NE Iowa, 13 mi/21 km E of Waverly; 42°42′N 92°13′W. Dairy prods., feed.

Readsboro (REEDS-bor-o), town (1990 pop. 762), including Readsboro village, Bennington co., SW Vt., on Deerfield R., and 15 mi/24 km SE of Bennington, in Green Mts. at Mass. line; 42°47′N 72°58′W. Furniture, electronics. Harriman Dam on Deerfield R. is here. Granted 1764, settled c.1780.

Readstown, village (1990 pop. 420), Vernon co., SW Wis., on Kickapoo R., and 36 mi/58 km SE of La Crosse, in coulee country; 43°27′N 90°45′W. Cheese, butter. Mfg. (hydraulic equip.).

Reagan, county (□ 1,176 sq mi/3,046 sq km; 1990 pop. 4,514), W Texas; ⊙ Big Lake; 31°21′N 101°31′W. Elev. c.2,500 ft/762 m–2,800 ft/853 m. Broken prairies, at N edge of Edwards Plateau. Sheep, angora goats; some cattle; cotton, grains; oil, natural-gas wells. Source of Middle Concho R. Formed 1903.

Reagan, uninc. village (1990 pop. 200), Falls co., E central Texas, 31 mi/50 km SE of Waco. In cattle, cotton, corn area. Mfg. (air tools).

Reagan Dam, Calif.: see PACOIMA.

Real, county (□ 700 sq mi/1,813 sq km; 1990 pop. 2,412), SW Texas; ⊙ Leakey; 29°50′N 99°48′W. Elev. c.1,500 ft/457 m–2,400 ft/732 m. On Edwards Plateau, and drained by Nueces (forms part of W boundary) and Frio rivers. Ranching area (goats, sheep, cattle); little agr. (pecans); timber (mainly cedar). Hunting, fishing; guest ranches. Frio Canyon is vacation area. Formed 1913.

Real Campiña (rai-AHL kahm-PEEN-yuh), town, Cienfuegos prov., central Cuba, on RR, and 23 mi/37 km NW of Cienfuegos city; 22°20′N 80°48′W. Sugarcane growing; livestock; lumbering.

Real de Catorce (rai-AHL dai kah-TOR-sai), city, ⊙ Catorce municipio, San Luis Potosí, N central Mexico, in Sierra de Catorce, 15 mi/24 km W of Matehuala; 23°40′N 100°51′W. Elev. 9,045 ft/2,757 m. Situated in fabulously rich mining region, it once produced silver and antimony; also gold, lead, and copper deposits. Once a city of nearly 40,000 people, now nearly a ghost town. A popular tourist stop. Sometimes called Catorce.

Real Del Monte, Mexico: see MINERAL DEL MONTE.

Real del Oro, Mexico: see EL ORO DE HIDALGO.

Real Morelos, Mexico: see MORELOS.

Realitos, uninc. village (1990 pop. 250), Duval co., S Texas, 60 mi/97 km E of Laredo. In cattle-ranching area; cotton. Mfg. (natural-gas processing); oil and gas.

Reamstown, uninc. town (1990 pop. 2,649), Lancaster co., SE central Pa., 14 mi/23 km SW of Reading, on Cocalico Creek; 40°12′N 76°07′W. Rich agr. area (grain; poultry, livestock; dairying). Mfg. (aluminum sand castings, door hardware, commercial printing, apparel).

Reardan, village (1990 pop. 482), Lincoln co., E Wash., 22 mi/35 km W of Spokane; 47°40′N 117°53′W. Wheat, barley, oats, rye, alfalfa. Spokane Indian Reservation to N; Little Falls and Long Lake dams, both on Spokane R., to N.

Reasnor, town (1990 pop. 191), Jasper co., central Iowa, near Skunk R., 8 mi/12.9 km S of Newton; 41°34′N 93°01′W. In agr. area.

Rebecca, town (1990 pop. 148), Turner co., S central Ga., 14 mi/23 km WNW of Fitzgerald, near Alapaha R.; 31°49′N 83°29′W.

Reco (REE-ko), village, W Alta., Canada, in Rocky Mts., near E side of Jasper Natl. Park, 40 mi/64 km SSW of Edson. Coal mining; cattle.

Rector, town (1990 pop. 2,268), Clay co., extreme NE Ark., in St. Francis R. valley, 18 mi/29 km NE of Paragould; 36°15′N 90°17′W. In farm area. Mfg. (tool and die components; men's slacks).

Red Bank, uninc. town (1990 pop. 5,950), Lexington co., central S.C., residential suburb 12 mi/19 km WSW of Columbia; 33°55′N 81°13′W. Agr. area (poultry; dairy prods.; hogs; grain, peaches).

Red Bank, borough (1990 pop. 10,636), Monmouth co., E N.J., on the Navesink estuary, in a fertile farm area; 40°21′N 74°04′W. An early shipping center, it has become a summer and winter resort and residential suburb with some light industry. Landmarks include Old Christ Church (1769) and the Allen House (1667). Fort Monmouth to S. Count Basie b. here. Inc. 1908.

Red Bank Creek, c.75 mi/121 km long, W central Pa.; rises in NE Jefferson co., as North Fork Creek; flows SW, past Brookville, where it receives Sandy Lick Creek from E, and becomes Red Bank Creek; then W, past New Bethlehem, to Allegheny R., 11 mi/18 km N of Kittaning.

Red Bay, town (1990 pop. 3,451), Franklin co., NW Ala., 25 mi/40 km WSW of Russellville, at Miss. line; 34°26′N 88°08′W. Lumber. Mfg. (clothing, furniture, pet food, rubber hoses). Settled 1898, inc. 1908.

Red Bay, village (1991 pop. 288), S Lab., Canada, on the Strait of Belle Isle, 24 mi/39 km WNW of Cape Norman, N.F.; 51°44′N 56°25′W. Fishing port. Site of Basque whaling ships.

Red Bird, village, Wagoner co., E Okla., 16 mi/26 km NW of Muskogee, near Arkansas R. In agr. area.

Red Bluff, city (1990 pop. 12,363), ⊙ Tehama co., N Calif., 32 mi/51 km NW of Chico at head of navigation on Sacramento R., and 140 mi/225 km NNW of Sacramento; 40°10′N 122°14′W. Elev. 309 ft/94 m. Trading center for livestock; farm area. Almonds, walnuts, prunes, olives, grain, alfalfa, honey, beans. Mfg. (printing and publishing; light mfg.). N terminus of Tehana Colusa Canal, parallels R. on W; Kelly-Griggs House Mus.; William B. Ide Abode State Historical Park is here; Woodrow Bridge State Recreational Area to S; part of Lassen Natl. Forest to E; Shasta-Trinity Natl. Forest to W; salmon-viewing area at Red Bluff Diversion Dam to SE, on Sacramento R. Inc. 1876.

Red Bluff Lake, reservoir, Reeves-Loring co. border, W Texas, on Pecos R., c.40 mi/64 km NNW of Pecos; c.8 mi/12.9 km long; 31°55′N 103°53′W. Max. capacity c.300,000 acre-ft. Formed by Red Bluff Dam. Irrigates extensive farm area in Pecos R. valley to SE.

Red Boiling Springs, city (1990 pop. 905), Macon co., N Tenn., near Ky. line, 55 mi/89 km NE of Nashville, 36°32′N 85°51′W. Mineral springs.

Red Bud, city (1990 pop. 2,918), Randolph co., SW Ill., 13 mi/21 km SE of Waterloo; 38°12′N 90°00′W. In agr. area. Mfg. (fertilizer, wood prods., steel-coil handling equip.; concrete). Inc. 1867.

Red Cedar Lake, reservoir, Barron and Washburn cos., NW Wis., on Red Cedar R., 8 mi/12.9 km NE of Rice Lake; c.8 mi/12.9 km long, 1 mi/1.6 km wide; 45°34′N 91°35′W. Connected at S end to Hemlock L.

Red Cedar River 1 c.45 mi/72 km long, in S central Mich.; rises SW of Howell in Livingston co.; flows NW, past Fowlerville and East Lansing, to Grand R. at Lansing; 42°31′N 83°58′W. **2** c.85 mi/137 km long, in NW Wis.; rises in Red Cedar L. (Barron co.); flows S, past Rice L. and Menomonie, to Chippewa R. 12 mi/19 km S of Menomonie. Formerly important in lumbering industry.

Red Cedar River, in Minn. and Iowa: see CEDAR RIVER.

Red Chute, uninc. town (1990 pop. 5,431), Bossier parish, 8 mi/12.9 km NE of Bossier City; 32°33′N 93°36′W.

Red Cliff, village (1990 pop. 297), Eagle co., W central Colo., on Eagle R. at mouth of Homestake Creek, in Gore Range, and 18 mi/29 km N of Leadville; 39°30′N 106°22′W. Elev. 8,750 ft/2,667 m. Silver, lead, and zinc mines in vicinity. Surrounded by White River Natl. Forest.

Red Cloud, town (1990 pop. 1,204), ⊙ Webster co., S Nebr., 35 mi/56 km S of Hastings, and on Republican R., near Kansas line; 40°05′N 98°31′W. Grain, dairy, and poultry prods. RR junction to E. Willa Cather Pioneer Mus. (author of pioneer novels). Inc. 1872.

Red Creek, village (1990 pop. 566), Wayne co., W N.Y., 17 mi/27 km SW of Oswego; 43°15′N 76°43′W. Mfg. (wood flooring, clocks, tanks). Agr. (fruit).

Red Creek, c.75 mi/121 km long, SE Miss.; rises in S Lamar co.; flows SE to Pascagoula R. in N Jackson co., 1 mi/1.6 km S of mouth of Black Creek.

Red Deer, city (1991 pop. 58,134), S central Alta., Canada, on the Red Deer R.; 52°16′N 113°48′W. It developed as a trade and service center for a region of dairying and mixed farming. The discovery of oil and natural gas after World War II led to the growth of Red Deer's petroleum service industry, as well as the steady growth of the city itself. Red Deer is also in the center of a resort area that includes Sylvan L. and Gaetz L.

Red Deer, river, 385 mi/620 km long W Canada; rises in the Rocky Mts. in Banff Natl. Park, SW Alta., Canada; flows NE past Red Deer city, then SE and E across the plains to the South Saskatchewan R. just over the Sask. border.

Red Deer Lake, W Man., Canada, near Sask. border, 55 mi/89 km S of The Pas, and 10 mi/16 km W of N end of L. Winnipegosis; 14 mi/23 km long, 10 mi/16 km wide. Drains E into L. Winnipegosis by Red Deer R.

Red Hill, uninc. town (1990 pop. 6,112), Horry co., E S.C., residential suburb 2 mi/3.2 km SE of Conway, and 11 mi/18 km NW of Myrtle Beach, near Waccamaw R; 33°47′N 79°00′W.

Red Hill, borough (1990 pop. 1,794), Montgomery co., SE Pa., 16 mi/26 km S of Allentown; 40°22′N 75°28′W. Mfg. (store displays, textiles, metal stampings, paperboard prods.). Agr. (grain, soybeans, apples; livestock, dairying). Green Lane Reservoir (Perkiomen Creek) to W.

Red Hill, peak (10,023 ft/3,055 m), Maui isl., Maui co., Hawaii, highest point on Maui.

Red Hill Patrick Henry, Natl. Memorial, Charlotte co., S Va., 28 mi/45 km SE of Lynchburg, near Roanoke R. Covers 117 acres/47 ha. Law office and grave of Patrick Henry, at small plantation, his last home, now a mus. Affiliated area of Natl. Park system, owned by Patrick Henry Foundation. Authorized 1986.

Red Hook, village (□ 1 sq mi/2.6 sq km; 1990 pop. 1,794), Dutchess co., SE N.Y., 20 mi/32 km N of Poughkeepsie; 42°00′N 73°52′W. Mfg. (paper prods., soap, and soap-dispensing machines); in dairying and fruit-growing area.

Red Hook, section of SW Brooklyn borough, N.Y. city, SE N.Y., bounded on NE by Gowanus Expressway, on S by Gowanus Bay, on W by Upper N.Y. Bay, and on NW by Buttermilk Channel bet. Brooklyn shore and Governors Isl. and leading into SW entrance of East R.; 40°40′N 73°59′W. Part of former South Brooklyn. Settled in 1636 and named after the red soil and shape of the landform [Du. = *Roode Hock*]. A marshy backwater in colonial times, rapid industrial maritime and residential development began in 1850s centered on activity through and about Gowanus Canal (completed in 1864) and the Erie Basin. At the time, neighborhood was Ital. in character, but it was modified by a strong Middle Eastern contingent. Along with Brooklyn Heights, it had 1st row houses in Brooklyn. Red Hook Houses, built in 1936 for the families of dockworkers, was one of N.Y. city's 1st immense housing projects. Construction of Gowanus Expressway (1946) and completion of the Brooklyn-Battery Tunnel and its connection to the Belt Parkway (1950) had a severe negative impact on the neighborhood; it was cut off from the waterfront on 1 side and from the rest of the city on the other. Most of breakbulk shipping (the area's major employer) has moved to N.J. This port area was one of the world's busiest shipping centers from 1850s through World War II, and was the world's leading port 1900–1950. When the container port facilities were developed on the N.J. side in the 1960s, the Brooklyn sect. of the port declined precipitously, and many of the brick warehouses lining the wharf were abandoned or demolished. Some of the pier facilities are now being developed for light industrial use. The 79-acre/32-ha Red Hook Terminal (opened in 1981), a containerized cargo facility, has not compensated much for the loss of breakbulk shipping activity. Red Hook has lagged well behind the gentrification of brownstones that hasoccurred in surrounding neighborhoods. Principalthoroughfares are Atlantic Ave. and Court and Smith Streets. Ethnically the neighborhood is mostly Afr.-Amer. and Hispanic. Red Hook served as the setting for Elia Kazan's film *On the Waterfront.*

Red House, village (1990 pop. 25), Cattaraugus co., W N.Y., in Allegany Indian Reservation, 5 mi/8 km SW of Salamanca; 42°02′N 78°45′W. Main entrance to Allegany State Park is here.

Red Indian Lake (□ 70 sq mi/181 sq km), W central N.F., Canada, 5 mi/8 km S of Buchans; 35 mi/56 km long, 3 mi/5 km wide. Receives Lloyds R. (W) and Victoria R. (S); drained by Exploits R. (E). Near N shore is Halfway Mt. (1,400 ft/427 m).

Red Island 1 island (□ 9 sq mi/23 sq km), SE N.F., Canada, in Placentia Bay, 10 mi/16 km NW of Argentia; 4 mi/6 km long, 3 mi/5 km wide. Fishing. **2** island, S N.F., Canada, 6 mi/10 km ENE of Burgeo. Fishing.

Red Island, islet, SE Que., Canada, in the St. Lawrence, opposite mouth of Saguenay R.

Red Jacket, uninc. town (1990 pop. 760), Mingo co., SW W.Va., 7 mi/11.3 km ESE of Williamson; 37°38′N 82°07′W. Bituminous-coal region.

Red Jacket, Mich.: see CALUMET.

Red Lake, county (□ 432 sq mi/1,119 sq km; 1990 pop. 4,525), NW Minn.; ⊙ Red Lake Falls; 47°52′N 96°05′W. Agr. area drained by Red Lake, Poplar, and Clearwater rivers. Wheat, hay, alfalfa, oats, barley, sugar beets, sunflowers, potatoes; cattle. Formed 1896.

Red Lake, town (1991 pop. 2,268), NW Ont., Canada, in Patricia dist., on Red L. (30 mi/48 km long, 7 mi/11 km wide), 110 mi/177 km NW of Sioux Lookout; 51°02′N 93°50′W. Gold mining.

Red Lake, village, Beltrami co., NW Minn., 28 mi/45 km NNW of Bemidji, on S shore of Lower Red L., in S part of Red L. Indian Reservation; 47°52′N 95°01′W. Native Amer. school and reservation hq. are here.

Red Lake, reservoir (□ 430 sq mi/1,114 sq km), Beltrami co., SW shore forms boundary of Clearwater co., NW Minn., 25 mi/40 km N of Bemidji; c.40 mi/64 km long, 25 mi/40 km wide; 47°57′N 95°23′W. Elev. 1,175 ft/358 m. Max. capacity 3,985,000 acre-ft. Largest lake in Minn. Divided into Upper Red L., in NE (□ 184 sq mi/477 sq km; 21 mi/34 km long, 10 mi/16 km wide) and Lower Red L., in SW (□ 246 sq mi/637 sq km; 23 mi/37 km long, 12 mi/19 km wide); separated by 14-mi/23-km peninsula from E, connected by the Narrows passage. Drains W from lower lake through Red L. R. Once part of prehistoric glacial L. Agassiz. Formed by Lower Red L. Dam (10 ft/3 m), built (1951) by the Army Corps of Engineers for flood control. All of Lower lake and W part of Upper lake in Red L. Indian Reservation; Upper lake bounded by Lake Wildlife Area and Beltrami Isl. State Forest, on N; Red L. State Forest on E, Village of Red Lake on S shore.

Red Lake Falls, town (1990 pop. 1,481), ⊙ Red Lake co., NW Minn., on Red Lake R., and 18 mi/29 km NE of Crookston; 47°53′N 96°16′W. Elev. 1,036 ft/316 m. Terminus of RR spur from Dugdale (S). Resort. Agr. trading point; grain, sugar beets, sunflowers, potatoes; cattle. Mfg. (manufactured homes). Est. as fur-trading post before 1800; inc. as village 1881; as city 1898.

Red Lake River, c.200 mi/322 km long, NW Minn.; rises in Red. L., Beltrami co., exits W end of Lower Red L.; flows WNW through Red L. Indian Reservation to Thief River Falls town; then S and W, past Red L. Falls town and Crookston, to Red R. of the North at East Grand Forks, on N.Dak. border; 47°57′N 95°16′W. Receives Thief R. from N at Thief River Falls and Clearwater R. from E at Red Lake Falls. Assiniboine R. is principal tributary. Grand Marais R. flows NW out of river 9 mi/14.5 km W of Crookston, providing 2d outlet to Red R.; flows into Red R., 10 mi/16 km N of Grand Forks, N.Dak., c.25 mi/40 km long.

Red Level, town (1990 pop. 588), Covington co., S Ala., 10 mi/16 km NW of Andalusia; 31°23′N 86°36′W. Mfg. apparel.

Red Lion, borough (1990 pop. 6,130), York co., S Pa., suburb 8 mi/12.9 km SE of York; 39°53′N 76°36′W. Agr. area (soybeans, apples, grain; poultry, livestock, dairying). Mfg. (condenser coils, cardboard boxes, institutional furniture, cigars, flour, fabricated metal prods., communications equip., wooden prods., ammunition and military tanks; truck rims and wheels; cutting tools, computer floor panels, store fixtures). Inc. 1880.

Red Lodge, town (1990 pop. 1,958), ⊙ Carbon co., S Mont., on Rock Creek, NE of gateway to Yellowstone Natl. Park, and 55 mi/89 km SW of Billings; 45°11′N 109°15′W. Elev. 4,650 ft/1,414 m. Resort area; dairying, cattle, horses; vegetables, barley, oats, hay. Mfg. (portable chairs, camping equip.). Coal mines. Part of Custer Natl. Forest in Beartooth Range to SW, includes Absaroka-Beartooth Wilderness Area (to SW), and Red Lodge Mt. Ski Area (to W). Cooney Reservoir State Park to N. Carbon Co. Mus. Beartooth Nature Center and Petting Zoo. Inc. 1895.

Red Lodge Creek, c.50 mi/80 km long, S Mont.; rises in W Carbon co. at confluence of East and West Forks, (East Red Lodge, c.10 mi/16 km long, W Red Lodge c.15 mi/24 km long) 9 mi/14.5 km NNW of Red Lodge, in Beartooth Range; flows NE through Cooney Reservoir, past Boyd and Joliet, to the Clarks Fork of Yellowstone R., 10 mi/16 km. S of Laurel. Drains grain; livestock area.

Red Mountain, ridge (c.1,000 ft/305 m) of Great Appalachian Valley, central Ala., largely in Jefferson co. Extending SW–NE along right bank of Cahaba R., past Bessemer and Birmingham. Coal and iron mining. Statue of Vulcan is on crest of mt. in Vulcan Park, in S side of Birmingham.

Red Mountain Pass (11,018 ft/3,358 m), in San Juan Mts., SW Colo., 6 mi/9.7 km ESE of Telluride. Boundary bet. Ouray and San Juan cos., crossed by U.S. Highway 550.

Red Mountains, small mountain range in Rocky Mts. in S part of Yellowstone Natl. Park, Teton co., NW Wyo., 10 mi/16 km SW of Yellowstone L. Continental Divide runs between range and lake; 43°58′N 110°52′W. Highest point, Mt. Sheridan (10,308 ft/3,142 m).

Red Oak, city (1990 pop. 6,264), ⊙ Montgomery co., SW Iowa, on East Nishnabotna R. (hydroelectric plant), and 37 mi/60 km ESE of Council Bluffs; 41°00′N 95°13′W. RR junction. Mfg. (art calendars, calendar printing; advertising specialties; car-seat frames; dry cell batteries; lumber; furnaces; feeds; concrete; dairy prods.). Viking L. State Park to SE. Inc. 1869.

Red Oak, town (1990 pop. 3,124), Ellis co., N Texas, suburb 16 mi/26 km S of downtown Dallas; 32°31′N 96°48′W. Agr. area on S fringe of Dallas–Fort Worth Metroplex (cotton; cattle; dairying; wheat). Mfg. (wooden pallets, boat trailers).

Red Oak 1 village (1990 pop. 2,808), Nash co., NE central N.C., 8 mi/12.9 km NW of Rocky Mount; 36°02′N 77°54′W. Tobacco, cotton, peanuts, grain; chickens, cattle, hogs. **2** village (1990 pop. 602), Latimer co., SE Okla., 12 mi/19 km E of Wilburton; 34°57′N 95°04′W. Trade center for farm and recreation area. Ouachita Natl. Forest to SE. **3** uninc. village, Charlotte co., S Va., 17 mi/27 km ENE of South Boston; 36°43′N 79°11′W. Mfg. (lumber); agr. (grain, tobacco; cattle, dairying); timber.

Red Oak, suburb (1990 pop. 950), Fulton co., Ga., 9 mi/14.5 km SSW of Atlanta. Mfg. (wire display racks), steel fabricating, crushed stone

Red Peak, Colo.: see GORE RANGE.

Red River, parish (□ 413 sq mi/1,070 sq km; 1990 pop. 9,387), NW La.; ⊙ Coushatta; 32°01′N, 93°20′W. Bounded W by Bayou Pierre, E by Black L. Bayou (Black L. on SE); intersected by Red R. Agr. (cotton, peaches, berries, corn, wheat, hay, soybeans, vegetables, watermelons; cattle, horses, exotic fowl). Natural gas, oil fields. Logging, lumber milling. Formed 1871.

Red River, county (□ 1,057 sq mi/2,738 sq km; 1990 pop. 14,317), NE Texas; ⊙ Clarksville; 33°37′N 95°02′W. Bounded N by Red R. (Okla. boundary), S by Sulphur R. Diversified agr. (cotton; soybeans; wheat; hay); livestock (cattle, hogs, poultry); some dairying. Lumbering, lumber milling. Mfg., processing at Clarksville. Some oil and gas production. Formed 1836.

Red River, residential town, York co., N S.C., on Catawba R., and 4 mi/6.4 km NE of Rock Hill.

Red River, village (1990 pop. 387), Taos co., N N.Mex., 34 mi/55 km NE of Taos, in Carson Natl. Forest; 36°42′N 105°24′W. Red River and Enchanted Forest Ski Areas are here. Latir Peak (12,723 ft/3,878 m) and Latir Lakes to NE; Wheeler Peak (13,161 ft/4,011 m), highest point in N.Mex., to S, both in Sangre de Cristo Mts.

Red River or **Red River of the North**, 533 mi/858 km long, in U.S. and Canada, formed by confluence of Otter Tail and Bois de Sioux rivers at Wahpeton, N.Dak. (opposite Breckenridge, Minn.), flows N past Grand Forks, forming boundary bet. N.Dak. and Minn.; terminates in L. Winnipeg, Man. Used for irrigation. Drains Red R. Valley (bed of prehistoric L. Agassiz), rich wheat growing area in N.Dak. and Minn. Navigable in summer to Fargo. Chief tributaries are Sheyenne R., in N.Dak., Red L. R., in Minn., and Assiniboine R., in Man.

Red River 1 57 mi/92 km long, E central Ky.; rises in E Wolfe co.; flows generally W through Red R. Gorge, in Red R. Natl. Geological Area, past Stanton and Clay City, to Kentucky R. 11 mi/18 km SE of Winchester. **2** 56 mi/90 km long, in S Ky. and N. Tenn.; formed in S Logan co., Ky., by confluence of North and South forks; flows WSW to Cumberland R. at Clarksville, Tenn. North Fork rises at Ky.–Tenn. border, in SW Simpson co., S Ky.; flows WNW c.20 mi/32 km. South Fork rises in W Sumner co., N Tenn.; flows NW c.35 mi/56 km into S Ky. **3** c.40 mi/64 km long, in Taos co., N N.Mex.; rises near Wheeler Peak in Sangre de Cristo Mts., in Carson Natl. Forest; flows N and W, past Questa, to Rio Grande 8 mi/12.9 km N of Arroyo Hondo. **4** 1,290 mi/2,076 km long, southernmost of the large tributaries of the Mississippi R. It is generally referred to as Red R. from point where Prairie Dog Town Fork emerges from Texas Panhandle to join Okla.–Texas border. Main river is c.800 mi/1,287 km long. It rises in 2 branches in the Texas Panhandle and flows SE bet. Texas and Okla. and bet. Texas and Ark. to Fulton, Ark. It then turns S, enters La., and crosses SE to the Atchafalaya and the Mississippi rivers. In Texas, it flows rapidly through a canyon in semiarid plains, but later in its course, it spreads water into rich red-clay farm lands (whence the name Red). Dams on the river include the Denison Dam (completed 1943), which impounds L. Texoma, one of the largest reservoirs in the U.S. For many years navigation was difficult on the lower course of the Red R. due to fallen trees that floated downstream and collected behind obstructions, forming rafts. The Great Raft, a 160 mi/257 km log-jam built through the cents., was cleared from the river in the mid-1800s. The river is now navigable for small ships to maneuver above Natchitoches, La. There are many lakes along the lower part of the river, and reservoirs serve as flood-control units on its tributaries.

Red River Pass (9,852 ft/3,003 m), N N.Mex., on Taos–Colfax co. border, in Sangre de Cristo Mts., 23 mi/37 km, NE of Taos. State Highway 38 passes through.

Red River Settlement, agr. colony in present Man., Canada; N.Dak, and Minn. It was the undertaking of Thomas Douglas, 5th earl of Selkirk. Wishing to relieve the dispossessed and impoverished in Scotland and Northern Ireland, he secured enough control of the Hudson's Bay Company to obtain from it a grant of land called Assiniboia. This project met opposition, principally from the North West Company, but also from the fur traders in the Hudson's Bay Company Despite efforts to discourage the colony, Miles Macdonnell, a Selkirk man, brought a small group to the colony in 1812. The determined hostility of the North West Company mounted, esp. after the company men had won the half-breeds, or métis, entirely to their side. By cajolery and threat they persuaded settlers to desert, but a new group of settlers came, and the colony was restored in 1815. North West Company men and half-breeds resorted to violence, killing 22 in the massacre of Seven Oaks (June 19, 1816). On hearing the news of the massacre, Selkirk attacked the North West Company post, Fort William, and seized it. Other attacks followed. The result of these moves was a series of court charges and countercharges that impoverished Selkirk and helped to bring about the union (1821) of the Hudson's Bay Company and the North West Company Agr. had by this time been firmly established on the Western plains, and the Red R. settlements were to grow and flourish.

Red Rock or **Redrock**, village (1990 pop. 321), Noble co., N Okla., 13 mi/21 km NNE of Perry, on Red Rock Creek; 36°27′N 97°10′W. In agr. area. Sooner L. reservoir to E.

Red Rock Lake, reservoir, Marion Co., S Iowa, on Des Moines R., 8 mi/12.9 km NE of Knoxville; c.13 mi/21 km long; 41°22′N 92°59′W. Max. storage capacity of 1,830,000 acre-ft. Whitebreast Creek forms S arm. Formed by Red Rock Dam (79 ft/24 m high), built (1968) by the Army Corps of Engineers for flood control. Elk Rock State Park on N shore.

Red Rock Lakes, reservoirs, consisting of 2 connected lakes, Beaverhead co., SW Mont., on Red Rock R., c.30 mi/48 km W of W. Yellowstone, bet. Centennial Mts. (S; Idaho border and Continental Divide) and Gravelly Range (N). Upper Red Rock L. (3 mi/4.8 km long, 2 mi/3.2 km wide; 44°35′N 111°47′W) receives Red Rock Creek (from E), which flows to Lower Red Rock L. (7 mi/11.3 km long, max. 3 mi/4.8 km; 44°38′N 111°55′W) as Red Rock R. Lakes are 5 mi/8 km apart. Red Rock Pass (7,120 ft/2,170 m) to E on Divide and Idaho border, near source of Red Rock Creek.

Red Rock River, Mont.: see JEFFERSON RIVER.

Red Slate Mountain (13,163 ft/4,012 m), on Mono–Fresno co. border, E Calif., in the Sierra Nevada, c.25 mi/40 km S of Mono L. Inyo Natl. Forest to NE; Sierra Natl. Forest to SW; 37°30′N 118°52′W.

Red Springs, town (1990 pop. 3,799), Robeson co., SE N.C., 26 mi/42 km SW of Fayetteville; 34°48′N 79°10′W. Sulphur spring here. RR terminus. Agr. area (grain, tobacco, cotton; livestock, poultry). Mfg. (apparel, textile fabrics, rubber water-ski handles). Settled c. 1775.

Red Willow, county (□ 718 sq mi/1,860 sq km; 1990 pop. 11,705), S Nebr.; ⊙ McCook; 40°10′N 100°28′W. Fertile agr. area bounded S by Kansas; drained by Beaver, Red Willow, and Medicine creeks and Republican R. Dairying; corn, wheat, sorghum; cattle, hogs. Petroleum. Formed 1873.

Red Willow Dam, Nebr.: see HUGH BUTLER LAKE.

Red Wing, city (1990 pop. 15,134), ⊙ Goodhue co., SE Minn., 38 mi/61 km SE of St. Paul, on the Mississippi R. at the head of L. Pepin; 44°34′N 92°35′W. Elev. 750 ft/229 m. It is a commercial and mfg. center in the Hiawatha Valley farm area. Grain, alfalfa, soybeans; livestock, poultry; dairying. Mfg. (soft drinks, sunflower- and flax-processing; malt, bakery prods., leather tanning, machinery, industrial belts, printing and publishing, rollerskating shoes, kitchen cabinets, robotic systems). Site (1836–1840) of a Swiss mission to Native Americans Red Wing Vocational Technical School here. Lock and Dam No. 3 reservoir to NW; part of Richard J. Dorer Memorial Hardwood State Forest to S; Prairie Island Indian Reservation and Gores Pool No. 3 Wildlife Area to NW; Mt. Frontenac Ski Area to SE; Frontenac State Park to E. Inc. 1857.

Red Wing, village, Huerfano co., S Colo., on Huerfano Creek, headstream of Huerfano R., in E foothills of Sangre de Cristo Mts., and 28 mi/45 km WNW of Walsenburg. Elev. c.7,750 ft/2,362 m. Resort. Dude ranch nearby. Blanca Peak, 15 mi/24 km SW. Parts of San Isabel Natl. Forest to W and NE.

Redan (RED-uhn), suburb (1990 pop. 24,376), De Kalb co., Ga., 18 mi/29 km ENE of Atlanta. Mfg. (synthetic stucco insulation). Rapidly growing residential suburb E of Atlanta.

Redbud, uninc. village, Harlan co., SE Ky., in the Cumberland Mts., 8 mi/12.9 km E of Harlan. Bituminous coal.

Redby, uninc. village (1990 pop. 787), Beltrami co., NW Minn., 28 mi/45 km N of Bemidji, on S shore of Lower Red R., at mouth of Mud R., in Red L. Indian Reservation; 47°50′N 94°55′W. Mfg. (freshwater-fish processing, forest prods., landscape materials, docks, and pallets). Agr. (livestock, grain; fish; timber).

Redcliff, town (1991 pop. 3,768), SE Alta., Canada, near South Saskatchewan R., 6 mi/10 km NW of Medicine Hat; 50°05′N 110°47′W. Natural gas production; coal, shale, and clay mining; glass and pottery mfg.; livestock raising.

Redcloud Peak (14,034 ft/4,278 m), Hinsdale co., SW Colo., in San Juan Mts., 16 mi/26 km NE of Silverton.

Reddick 1 village (□ 1 sq mi/2.6 sq km; 1990 pop. 554), Marion co., N central Fla., 13 mi/21 km NNW of Ocala; 29°22′N 82°12′W. Small-scale farming; limestone quarrying. **2** village (1990 pop. 208), in Livingston and Kankakee cos., NE central Ill., 20 mi/32 km W of Kankakee; 41°06′N 88°15′W. In agr. area.

Redding, city (1990 pop. 66,462), seat of Shasta co., N central Calif., 140 mi/225 km NNW of Sacramento, on the Sacramento R., at far N end of Calif.'s Central Valley; 40°34′N 122°22′W. Elev. 555 ft/169 m. A principal tourist center for a mt. and lake region, it also has lumbering and food-processing industries. Timber, grapes, olives, strawberries, walnuts, plums, grain; cattle. Mfg. (valves and fittings; printing and publishing; measuring devices, concrete, plastics materials). Redding is one of the fastest-growing U.S. cities; its pop. quadrupled bet. 1970 and 1990. Shasta Community Col. is here. Lassen Volcanic Natl. Park 40 mi/64 km ESE; Shasta Natl. Forest to N and W; 3 sections of Whiskeytown-Shasta-Trinity Natl. Recreation Area to N, NW and W; L. Shasta reservoir and L. Shasta caverns to N; Whiskeytown L. reservoir to W; Redding Municipal Airport to SW. Inc. 1872.

Redding 1 residential town (1990 pop. 7,927), Fairfield co., SW Conn., on Saugatuck R., and 13 mi/21 km NW of Bridgeport; 41°17′N 73°23′W. Lib. here was gift of Mark Twain, a summer resident. Nearby Putnam Memorial Campground commemorates winter of 1778–1779, spent here by Gen. Putnam's Revolutionary troops. Joel Barlow b. here. Settled c. 1711, inc. 1767. **2** town (1990 pop. 119), Ringgold co., S Iowa, near Mo. line, 11 mi/18 km SW of Mount Ayr; 40°36′N 94°23′W.

Redfield 1 town (1990 pop. 1,082), Jefferson co., central Ark., 16 mi/26 km NNW of Pine Bluff, near Arkansas R.; 34°26′N 92°10′W. Lock and Dam No. 5 (Arkansas R.) to SE. Location of large electricity generator. **2** town (1990 pop. 883), Dallas co., central Iowa, on Middle Raccoon R., and 9 mi/14.5 km W of Adel; 41°35′N 94°12′W. Brick and tile plants; soybean prods. **3** town (1990 pop. 2,770), ⊙ Spink co., NE central S.Dak., 40 mi/64 km S of Aberdeen; 44°52′N 98°31′W. Resort. Mfg. of feeds. Twin Lakes to S; Cottonwood L. to SW; junction for spur to Frankfort.

Redfield, village (1990 pop. 143), Bourbon co., SE Kansas, 9 mi/14.5 km W of Fort Scott; 37°50′N 94°52′W. Dairying; general agr.

Redfield, Mount (4,606 ft/1,404 m), Essex co., NE N.Y., in the High Peaks sect. of the Adirondacks, 2 mi/3.2 km SW of Mt. Marcy, and 13 mi/21 km S of Lake Placid village; 44°06′N 73°57′W.

Redford Township, city, Wayne Co., SE Mich., suburb 13 mi/21 km NW of downtown Detroit; 42°23′N 83°17′W. Borders Detroit on E. Drained by Middle R. Rouge. Mfg. (metal stampings, steel forgings, diesel engines, ink, tools, fasteners, machining.)

Redgranite, town (1990 pop. 1,009), Waushara co., central Wis., on small Willow Creek, and 27 mi/43 km W of Oshkosh; 44°02′N 89°05′W. In agr. area. Mfg. (pickles, peppers, sauerkraut).

Redhook Point, E St. Thomas Isl., U.S.V.I., on Pillsbury Sound, and 5.5 mi/8.9 km E of Charlotte Amalie; 18°20′N 64°51′W. Ferry service to St. John.

Redings Mill, village (1990 pop. 204), Newton co., SW Mo., suburb 6 mi/9.7 km S of downtown Joplin; 37°01′N 94°31′W. Residential.

Redington Beach, town (□ 1 sq mi/2.6 sq km; 1990 pop. 1,626), Pinellas co., W central Fla., 10 mi/16 km WNW of St. Petersburg; 27°48′N 82°48′W.

Redington Shores, town (□ 1 sq mi/2.6 sq km; 1990 pop. 2,366) Pinellas co., W central Fla., 12 mi/19 km WNW of St. Petersburg; 27°49′N 82°49′W.

Redkey or **Red Key**, town (1990 pop. 1,383), Jay co., E Ind., 11 mi/18 km SW of Portland; 40°21′N 85°09′W. In agr. area.

Redlands, city (1990 pop. 60,394), San Bernardino co., S Calif., suburb 8 mi/12.9 km SE of San Bernadino, and 62 mi/100 km E of downtown Los Angeles in the San Bernardino Valley; 34°04′N 117°10′W. Mfg. (software research development, metal foil, furniture, cutting tools, sheet plastic, batteries, electrical industrial apparatus). Redlands, which is part of a regional residential-industrial complex, is surrounded by high peaks. The Univ. of Redlands is here, and Norton Air Force Base is nearby. Redlands Municipal Airport in NE; San Bernadino Mts., in San Bernadino Natl. Forest, to N; Green Valley Ski Areas to N; San Timoteo Canyon to SE. Inc. 1888.

Redmon, village (1990 pop. 201), Edgar co., E Ill., 8 mi/12.9 km WNW of Paris; 39°38′N 87°51′W. In agr. area.

Redmond, city (1990 pop. 35,800), King co., W Wash., a suburb 11 mi/18 km ENE of downtown Seattle, on N end of L. Sammamish at outlet of Sammamish R.; 47°40′N 122°07′W. Its rapidly-growing economy centers around research and development industries. Mfg. (computers, semiconductors, and electrical-measurement equip.; printed circuit boards, diagnostic substances, sporting goods, lighting equip., concrete prods., telephone apparatus, printing and printing machinery; prefabricated wood bldgs., furniture, medical instruments, men's clothing, folding paper boxes, asphalt, sheet metal, aerospace parts, industrial instruments, fresh and frozen seafood). Major center for computer software. Of interest are the preserved portions of the old brick Stevens Pass highway, and Marymoor Park, site of archaeological excavations and a historical mus. Velodrome, bicycle racing; wineries in area. Bridle Trails State Park to SW. Inc. 1912.

Redmond 1 town (1990 pop. 7,163), Deschutes co., central Oregon,16 mi/26 km NNE of Bend; 44°15′N 121°10′W. Elev. 2,996 ft/913 m. In irrigated agr. area. Agr. (clover, alfalfa seed, potatoes, wheat, oats, barley; poultry, sheep, cattle); dairy prods. Mfg. (meat processing; lumber, millwork, veneer). Cline Falls State Park to W; Smith Rock State Park, and Ogden Scenic State Wayside to N; Crooked R. Natl. Grassland to N. Inc. 1910. **2** town (1990 pop. 648), Sevier co., central Utah, 5 mi/8 km N of Salina and on Sevier R.; 39°00′N 111°51′W. Elev. 5,135 ft/1,565 m.

Redmond, village (1990 pop. 648), Sevier co., central Utah, 20 mi/32 km NE of Richfield, on Sevier R. Dairying; cattle; alfalfa, barley, wheat, sugar beets. Part of Fishlake Natl. Forest to SE.

Redonda, uninhabited island (0.5 sq mi/1.3 sq km), State of Antigua and Barbuda, West Indies, 30 mi/48 km SW of Antigua; 16°55′N 62°19′W.

Redonda Islands (ruh-DAHN-duh) (□ 108 sq mi/280 sq km), SW B.C., Canada, group of 2 isls. in NE arm of the Strait of Georgia, at entrance of Toba Inlet, 20 mi/32 km NE of Campbell R. W isl. is 14 mi/23 km long, 2 mi/3 km–8 mi/13 km wide; E isl. is 10 mi/16 km long, 1 mi/2 km–7 mi/11 km wide.

Redondo Beach, city (1990 pop. 60,167), Los Angeles co., S Calif., suburb 15 mi/24 km SW of downtown Los Angeles, 13 mi/21 km SSE of Santa Monica; 33°52′N 118°23′W. Beach resort area. Mfg. (aluminum foundry, printing and publishing, furniture, computer peripherals, diagnostic substances, laundry equip.). Bounded by city of Torrance on E; Redondo State Beach is here. Inc. 1892 (corporate limits extend to Pacific Ocean Coast).

Redondo Peak, N.Mex.: see VALLE GRANDE MOUNTAINS.

Redoubt, Mount (10,197 ft/3,108 m), active volcano, S Alaska, W of Cook Inlet, 110 mi/177 km WSW of Anchorage; 60°29′N 152°45′W.

Redstone Arsenal, U.S. rocket research and development center (61 sq mi/98 sq km), N Ala., SW of Huntsville; est. 1941. One of the state's largest industrial enterprises, it includes the Army Missile Command, responsible for the army's rocket and guided missile program; the Army Missile and Munitions Center and School; NASA's George C. Marshall Space Flight Center which researches and develops large boosters for space vehicles; and several private contractors.

Redvers (RED-vuhrs), town (1991 pop. 936), SE Sask., Canada, near Man. border, 40 mi/64 km S of Moosomin; 49°34′N 101°42′W. Mixed farming.

Redwater, town (1991 pop. 2,090), central Alta., Canada, 32 mi/51 km NE of Edmonton; 46°54′N 79°38′W. Oil production.

Redwater, town (1990 pop. 824), Bowie co., NE Texas, 12 mi/19 km WSW of Texarkana; 33°21′N 94°15′W. Cattle; wheat, rice, soybeans, vegetables. Wright Patman L. (Sulphur R.) to S.

Redwater, uninc. village (1990 pop. 289), Leake co., central Miss., 7 mi/11.3 km NNW of Carthage; 32°46′N 89°32′W. Cotton, corn; cattle, poultry; dairying.

Redwater River, c.110 mi/177 km long, E Mont.; rises in Big Sheep Mt. at N boundary of Prarie co.; flows NE, past Circle, to Missouri R., 4 mi/6.4 km S of Poplar.

Redway, uninc. town (1990 pop. 1,212), Humboldt co., NW Calif., 50 mi/80 km SSE of Eureka, on South Fork Eel R., Benbow L. St. Recreation Area to S; Humboldt Redwoods State Park to NW; 40°08′N 123°49′W. Timber; cattle, sheep.

Redwood, county (□ 881 sq mi/2,282 sq km; 1990 pop. 17,254), SW Minn.; ⊙ Redwood Falls; 44°23′N 95°15′W. Agr. area bounded N by Minnesota R., and drained by Redwood and Cottonwood rivers. Corn, oats, wheat, soybeans, alfalfa, sugar beets, peas; sheep, hogs, cattle, poultry; dairying. Lower Sioux Indian Reservation is in NE. Co. formed 1862.

Redwood, resort village (1990 pop. 600), Jefferson co., N N.Y., bet. Mud and Butterfield lakes (fishing), 6 mi/9.7 km ESE of Alexandria Bay; 44°18′N 75°48′W.

Redwood City, city (1990 pop. 66,072), ⊙ San Mateo co., W Calif., suburb 23 mi/37 km SSE of downtown San Francisco, at mouth of Redwood Creek, on San Francisco Bay; 37°31′N 122°13′W. The city underwent significant economic development in the 1980s. Diversified light mfg. (communications equip., electric and electronic equip., printing and publishing, medical equip., and biotechnology development). Large chrysanthemum industry here (from 1900). Cañada Col. (2 year) is here. Marine World and Afr. U.S.A., a large entertainment complex, is located nearby on several isls. in San Francisco Bay to NW at Belmont. San Carlos Airport to N; Bain Isl., other isls. to N, marshy area. Inc. 1868.

Redwood Falls, town (1990 pop. 4,859), ⊙ Redwood co., SW Minn., 35 mi/56 km NW of New Ulm on Redwood R. SW of its mouth in Minnesota R.; 44°32′N 95°06′W. Agr. area: soybeans, sugar beets; livestock, poultry; dairying. Mfg. (emergency rescue boards, hosp. equip., tallow and hides, commercial apartments, mobile homes, farm trailers and equip., computer components). Shipping point for farm produce and granite from nearby quarries. Lower Sioux Indian Reservation to E; Municipal Airport to E. Plotted 1865; inc. as village 1875, as city 1891.

Redwood National Park (□ 172 sq mi/445 sq km), along the Pacific coast, Humboldt and Del Norte cos., NW Calif. Backed by coastal bluffs, 40 mi/64 km of beach, lagoon, and rocky coast are preserved in their natural state; seals, sea lions, and birds live on offshore rocks. Inland, numerous stands of virgin Calif. redwood, many over 2,000 years old, are found; the world's tallest tree, 367 ft/112 m high, is located in the park. S part drained by Redwood R.; U.S. Highway 101 passes through length of park. Est. 1968

Redwood River, 80 mi/129 km long, SW Minn., just W of Ruthton; rises in NE Pipestone co.; flows NE and E, past Marshall, through Redwood L. reservoir, at Redwood Falls to Minnesota R. 2 mi/3.2 km NE of Redwood Falls; 44°10′N 96°10′W.

Ree Heights, village (1990 pop. 91), Hand co., central S.Dak., 10 mi/16 km W of Miller; 44°31′N 99°12′W.

Reed, plantation (1990 pop. 296), Aroostook co., E Maine, 31 mi/50 km SSW of Houlton; 45°42′N 68°07′W. In wilderness recreational area. Includes Wytopitlock village.

Reed City, town (1990 pop. 2,379), ⊙ Osceola co., central Mich., 12 mi/19 km N of Big Rapids, near Muskegon R.; 43°52′N 85°30′W. Livestock; dairy prods.; forage crops. Mfg. (computers, tube fabrication, yogurt, food prods.); oil refining. Resort. Manistee Natl. Forest to SW. Inc. as village 1875, as city 1932.

Reed Lake (□ 78 sq mi/202 sq km), central Man., Canada, 50 mi/80 km E of Flin Flon; 15 mi/24 km long, 10 mi/16 km wide. Drains N into Churchill R.

Reeder, village (1990 pop. 252), Adams co., SW N.Dak., 16 mi/26 km NW of Hettinger; 46°06′N 102°56′W.

Reedley, city (1990 pop. 15,791), Fresno co., central Calif., in San Joaquin Valley, 20 mi/32 km SE of Fresno, and on Kings R.; 36°36′N 119°27′W. RR junction. Citrus, almonds, nectarines, grapes, cotton, grain; dairying. Mfg. (feeds, packaging, machinery, glass prods.). Kings River Community Col. is here. Serves as gateway to Kings Canyon Natl. Park (c.30 mi/48 km E). Founded 1889, inc. 1913.

Reeds, town (1990 pop. 115), Jasper co., SW Mo., near Spring R., 9 mi/14.5 km SE of Carthage; 37°07′N 94°10′W.

Reeds Peak (10,015 ft/3,053 m), SW central N.Mex., in Black Range, 35 mi/56 km W of Truth or Consequences (Hot Springs), on Continental Divide, and Grant–Sierra co. border; 33°08′N 107°51′W. In Gila Natl. Forest.

Reeds Spring, town (1990 pop. 411), Stone co., SW Mo.,

in the Ozarks, near Table Rock L., 11 mi/18 km NNW of Branson; 36°45′N 93°22′W. Tourism. Mfg. (apparel, concrete prods.).

Reedsburg, town (1990 pop. 5,834), Sauk co., S central Wis., on Baraboo R., and 14 mi/23 km WNW of Baraboo; 43°31′N 90°00′W. RR terminus in timber and agr. area (dairy prods.; livestock). Mfg. (vegetable processing, prods. for infants, landscaping ties, seating for vehicles, lumber). Spring L. State Park to E; Redstone L. reservoir to NW. Inc. 1887.

Reedsport, town (1990 pop. 4,796), Douglas co., W Oregon, on Umpqua R. where it widens into Winchester Bay, its estuary to the Pacific Ocean, c.55 mi/89 km SW of Eugene; 43°42′N 124°06′W. Fisheries. Timber. Honey. Tourism. Pulp mill at Gardiner, 3 mi/4.8 km N. Parts of Siuslaw Natl. Forest to E and NE, including Elliott State Forest. Umpqua Wayside State Park to E; Umpqua Lighthouse State Park to SW; parts of Oregon Dunes Natl. Recreation Area to NW and SW. Tahkenitch L., behind dunes, to N. Inc. 1919.

Reedsville, uninc. town (1990 pop. 1,030), Mifflin co., central Pa., 5 mi/8 km NW of Lewistown, on Kishacoquillas Creek, NW of Jacks Mt. ridge; 40°39′N 77°35′W. Mfg. (amplifiers, medical diagnostic transducers, plastic molding). Agr. (corn, hay; poultry, livestock; dairying).

Reedsville 1 village (1990 pop. 482), Preston co., N W.Va., 10 mi/16 km SE of Morgantown; 39°30′N 79°47′W. Agr. (grain); livestock; poultry. Mfg. (glass fiber filters, packaging). Coal-mining area. Upper Decker Creek Wildlife Management Area to N. **2** village (1990 pop. 1,182), Manitowoc co., E Wis., 15 mi/24 km WNW of Manitowoc; 44°08′N 87°57′W. In grain belt; vegetable canning.

Reedville, uninc. village, Northumberland co., E Va., on Cockrell Creek estuary, arm of Chesapeake Bay, at tip of Northern Neck peninsula, 75 mi/121 km SE of Fredericksburg; 36°50′N 76°16′W. Port of entry; fishing port. Mfg. (fish, crabmeat, and herring processing; circuit board assembly, fish oil and meal). Agr. (grain, soybeans, tomatoes; poultry, cattle). Ferry from Fleeton (2 mi/3.2 km SSE) to Tangier Isl.

Reedy, village (1990 pop. 271), Roane co., W W.Va., 27 mi/43 km S of Parkersburg, on Reedy Creek; 38°53′N 81°25′W. Mfg. (mine and RR ties).

Reedy Island, E Del., in Delaware R., 1 mi/1.6 km NE of Port Penn; 1.5 mi/2.4 km long; 39°31′N 75°34′W. Intracoastal Waterway passes to E.

Reedy River, c.65 mi/105 km long, NW S.C.; rises in foothills of the Blue Ridge Mts. in N Greenwood co., N of Greenville; flows SSE, through Greenville, to Saluda R., 9 mi/14.5 km NE of Greenwood, where it forms a N arm of L. Greenwood reservoir.

Reelfoot Lake, 20 mi/32 km long, NW Tenn., near the Mississippi R.; 36°21′N 89°24′W. Designated a natl. natural landmark by the Natl. Park Service, it was formed when a depression created by the New Madrid earthquake in the winter of 1811–1812 was filled with Mississippi R. water. The lake is in a beautiful wooded area, which attracts fishermen and hunters. A state park and 2 natl. wildlife refuges are nearby.

Reese (REES), village (1990 pop. 1,414), Tuscola co., E Mich., 13 mi/21 km E of Saginaw; 43°27′N 83°41′W. In agr. area. RR junction. Mfg. (fertilizers, grain- and bean-milling).

Reese Air Force Base, Texas: see LUBBOCK.

Reese River (REES), c.150 mi/241 km long, central Nev.; rises in S Toiyabe Range, NW Nye co.; flows N, bet. Shoshone Mts. (W) and Toiyabe Range (E), past Austin; joins Humboldt R. at town of Battle Mt. Water used for irrigation.

Reeseville, village (1990 pop. 673), Dodge co., S central Wis., 12 mi/19 km S of Beaver Dam; 43°18′N 88°50′W. In dairying region.

Reeves, county (□ 2,642 sq mi/6,843 sq km; 1990 pop. 15,852), extreme W Texas; ⊙ Pecos; 31°19′N 103°40′W. Elev. c.2,500 ft/762 m–4,500 ft/1,372 m. Plains area, sloping to Pecos R. (NE boundary) from foothills of Davis Mts. (SW). Bounds N.Mex. for about 1 mi/1.6 km on N; drained by Toyah Creek (forms L. Toyah in N). Red Bluff L. reservoir (Pecos R.) on boundary in far N, near N.Mex. Cattle, sheep ranching; cotton, melons (esp. cantaloupes), vegetables (esp. onions and bell peppers) in irrigated sects. Some oil and natural gas production; gravel. Balmorhea L. in S. Formed 1883.

Reeves, village (1990 pop. 188), Allen parish, SW La., 22 mi/35 km NE of Lake Charles city and on tributary of Calcasieu R.; 30°31′N 93°02′W. In agr. area; timber. Oil field nearby.

Reevesville, village (1990 pop. 244), Dorchester co., S central S.C., c.6 mi/9.7 km WNW of St. George; 33°12′N 80°39′W. Agr. (poultry, livestock; cotton, grain).

Reform, town (1990 pop. 2,105), Pickens co., W Ala., 10 mi/16 km NNE of Carrollton; 33°22′N 88°01′W. Lumber. Mfg. (apparel and glass).

Reforma (rai-FOR-mah), a region of Mexico's major oil fields in Chiapas and Tabasco. In 1972, explorations for oil were initiated in the areas of Reforma, Chiapas, and Samaria, Tabasco, esp. in the camps of Sitio Grande and Cactus. The production in these new areas passed 440,000 barrels of oil a day. Total oil production for the country with this new zone went from 486,573 barrels a day in 1971 to 806,176 barrels a day in 1975. After 1975, exploration began on the continental shelf as well as promising exploration in Chihuahua, Coahuila, Nuevo León, Tamaulipas, and Campeche.

Reforma (rai-FOR-mah) or **La Reforma**, town (1990 pop. 19,068), Chiapas, S Mexico, 18 mi/29 km WSW of Villahermosa; 17°52′N 93°09′W. Cereals, rubber, fruit. Site of Reforma oil fields.

Reforma de Pineda (rai-FOR-mah dai pee-NE-dah), town (1990 pop. 2,826), in extreme SE Oaxaca, 53 mi/85 km ENE of the port of Salina Cruz; 16°24′N 94°28′W. Good road connections with Mexico Highway 200 and on RR. Agr.

Reforma, La, Mexico: see LA REFORMA.

Refugio (ruh-FYUHR-ee-o), county (□ 818 sq mi/2,119 sq km; 1990 pop. 7,976), S Texas; ⊙ Refugio; 28°19′N 97°10′W. Bounded N by San Antonio R., SW by Aransas R., SE by Copano Bay, NE by San Antonio Bay; drained by Mission R. and Copano Creek. A leading Texas oil and natural gas producing co. Ranching (cattle); some agr. (mainly cotton; grain sorghum, corn). Oil refineries, pipelines. Formed 1836.

Refugio (ruh-FYUHR-ee-o), town (1990 pop. 3,158), ⊙ Refugio co., S Texas, on Mission R., and 39 mi/63 km SW of Victoria; 28°18′N 97°16′W. Elev. 43 ft/13 m. Trade, shipping center for petroleum and natural gas; cattle; agr. area (cotton, grain); oil refineries; pipelines to Aransas Pass. Mfg. (lollipops, natural gas, and oil processing). Settled after 1829 around Span. mission that moved here in 1795; became pueblo in 1834. Captured (1836) by Mexicans in Texas Revolution and again occupied by Mexicans in 1842.

Regal, village (1990 pop. 51), Kandiyohi co., S central Minn., 22 mi/35 km NNE of Willmar on North Fork Crow R.; 45°24′N 94°50′W. Dairying. Small lakes to S.

Regal Mountain (13,845 ft/4,220 m), S Alaska, in Wrangell Mts., 130 mi/209 km NE of Cordova; 61°44′N 142°52′W.

Regan (REE-guhn), village (1990 pop. 51), Burleigh co., central N.Dak., 12 mi/19 km E of Wilton; 47°09′N 100°31′W. RR terminus. Florence L. Natl. Wildlife Refuge to NE.

Regent, village (1990 pop. 268), Hettinger co., SW N. Dak., 12 mi/19 km WNW of Mott and near Cannonball R.; 46°25′N 102°33′W.

Reger (REE-guhr), uninc. community, Sullivan co., N Mo., on Locust Cr., 6 mi/9.7 km SW of Milan. Corn, hay, cattle.

Regina (ri-JEI-nuh), city (1991 pop. 179,178), ⊙ Sask., Canada, S Sask., on Wascana Creek; 50°27′N 104°37′W. Distribution and service center for 1 of the world's largest wheat-growing plains. Industries include agr. processing, meat-packing, printing, oil refining, and the mfg. of communications equip. and bldg. materials. Regina was founded in 1882 when a RR line was constructed through the region. It was capital of the N.W.T. from 1883 to 1905, when it became capital of the newly created Sask. From 1892 to 1920, Regina was the hq. of the NW Mounted Police, and it is now W hq. of the Royal Can. Mounted Police, which maintains its crime detection laboratory here. The Univ. of Regina is located here.

Regina Beach, town (1991 pop. 921), S Sask., Canada, on Last Mountain L., 28 mi/45 km NW of Regina; resort.

Register, town (1990 pop. 195), Bulloch co., Ga., 10 mi/16 km SW of Statesboro; 32°22′N 81°53′W.

Regla (RAIG-luh), city and county, (1994 est. pop. 44,000), Ciudad de la Habana prov., W Cuba, a commercial and old industrial suburb of Havana, located in the S corner of Havana Bay. It is connected to Centro Habana and Habana Vieja by road and ferry service. It grew up around the hermitage of Nuestra Señora de Regla (est. 1690) and was officially founded in 1765. During the colonial period, Regla was a smuggling center for Havana.

Rego Park, a residential and commercial sect. of Queens borough of N.Y. city, SE N.Y.; 40°43′N 73°52′W. Named for the Rego Construction Company, which initiated the bldg. of the area.

Rehoboth (ri-HO-buhth), town (1990 pop. 8,656), Bristol co., SE Mass., 13 mi/21 km NNW of Fall River; 41°51′N 71°15′W. Enameling; foundries, concrete. Long called Seekonk or Seeconck; included present town of Seekonk until 1812. Settled 1636, inc. 1645.

Rehoboth (ri-HO-buhth), village, Somerset co., SE Md., 23 mi/37 km SSW of Salisbury and on Pocomoke R. Named for an early plantation.

Rehoboth Bay, lagoon, SE Del., 2 mi/3.2 km SW of Rehoboth Beach town; joined by channel to Indian R. Bay (S), which enters ocean through dredged passage; separated from the Atlantic by barrier beach; c.5 mi/8 km long, 3 mi/4.8 km wide; 38°40′N 75°06′W. Lewes and Rehoboth Canal enters at N end.

Rehoboth Beach (ri-HO-buhth), town (1990 pop. 1,234), Sussex co., SE Del., on Atlantic coast 5 mi/8 km SE of Lewes; Lewes and Rehoboth Canal passes to W; 38°43′N 75°04′W. Mfg. (boat construction; printing and publishing). Fishing, bathing. Resort is frequented by people from Wash., D.C. and Baltimore, and is called the "summer capital." Del. Seashore State Park to S; Cape Henlopen State Park to N: Rehoboth Bay to S. Settled c.1675, inc. 1873.

Reidsville, city (1990 pop. 12,183), Rockingham co., N N.C., 23 mi/37 km NNE of Greensboro; 36°21′N 79°40′W. Tobacco center. Mfg. (industrial gasses; metal, aluminum, and concrete prods.; cigarettes, textiles and apparel, thermostatic clad materials, poultry and paper processing, plastic containers, printing and publishing). Chinqua-Penn Plantations (1925). Settled c.1815, inc. 1873.

Reidsville (REEDZ-vil), town (1990 pop. 2,469), ⊙ Tattnall co., E central Ga., 32 mi/51 km SW of Statesboro; 32°05′N 82°07′W. Mfg. (metal picnic tables). Agr. area (tobacco, cotton, sweet potatoes). State penitentiary nearby; Gordonia-Alatamaha State Park in vicinity. Historic bldgs. Inc. 1838.

Reidville, uninc. village, Spartanburg co., NW S.C., 12 mi/19 km SW of Spartanburg near Tyger R. Agr. includes peaches, grain, poultry; livestock.

Reiffton (REIF-tuhn), uninc. town (1990 pop. 2,522), Berks co., SE central Pa., residential suburb, 3 mi/4.8 km ESE of Reading; 40°19′N 75°52′W. Agr. includes dairying, livestock, poultry; grain, apples, plums.

Reile's Acres (REIL-eez), village (1990 pop. 210), Cass co., E N.Dak., residential suburb 6 mi/9.7 km NW of Fargo; 46°55′N 96°51′W.

Reinbeck, town (1990 pop. 1,605), Grundy co., central Iowa, 10 mi/16 km E of Grundy Center; 42°19′N 92°35′W. Asparagus; animal feed. Inc. 1877.

Reindeer Depot, former trading post, NW Mackenzie dist., N.W.T., Canada, on E channel of Mackenzie R. delta, 50 mi/80 km S of its mouth, 35 mi/56 km NNW of Inuvik; 68°43′N 134°7′W. Located in Reindeer Grazing Reserve (□ 6,600 sq mi/17,094 sq km; 170 mi/274 km long, 50 mi/80 km wide) extends NE and includes Richards Isl. Reserve; est. 1935; in 1946 herd numbered c.4,000, and 10,000 in 1981.

Reindeer Lake, one of the largest lakes in Canada, 2,467 sq mi/6,390 sq km, NE Sask. and NW Man., Canada. The Reindeer R. drains it S to the Churchill R. The lake has many isls. and is noted for its commercial and sport fishing.

Reine, La (REN, lah), village (1991 pop. 473), W Que., Canada, on Ont. border, 50 mi/80 km NNW of Rouyn; gold, copper, zinc mining.

Reisterstown (REI-stuhrz-toun), residential suburb (1990 pop. 19,314), Baltimore co., N Md., 17 mi/27 km NW of Baltimore; 39°28'N 76°49'W. In agr. area; mfg. (radio equip.). Named for John Reister (b. 1715). Montrose School (a state training school for delinquent girls; chartered 1831) is nearby.

Relay, suburban village, Baltimore co., central Md., on Patapsco R., and 8 mi/12.9 km SW of Baltimore. The name comes from the days when Baltimore and Ohio horses were changed here before the introduction of steam locomotives. Patapsco State Park nearby.

Reliance, village (1991 pop. 10), SE Mackenzie dist., N.W.T., Canada, at head of McLeod Bay of Great Slave L.; 62°43'N 109°09'W. Trading post; Royal Can. Mounted Police post.

Reliance 1 village (1990 pop. 169), Lyman co., S central S.Dak., 13 mi/21 km E of Kennebec; 43°52'N 99°35'W. Lower Brule Indian Reservation to N and NE. **2** village, Sweetwater co., SW Wyo., near Bitter Creek, 5 mi/8 km N of Rock Springs. Terminus of RR spur from Rock Springs. Mfg. (metal prods.). Coal mines.

Rembert, village, Sumter co., central S.C., 12 mi/19 km SE of Camden. Cotton, soybeans, corn, wheat.

Rembrandt, town (1990 pop. 229), Buena Vista co., NW Iowa, 11 mi/18 km N of Storm Lake; 42°49'N 95°10'W. Animal feed.

Remedios (rai-MAI-dee-oz), town, Villa Clara prov., central Cuba, on RR, and 26 mi/42 km ENE of Santa Clara; 22°30'N 79°33'W. Trading and processing center in region known for its tobacco; also coffee, sugarcane, fruit. Cigars, liquor, sweets, soap, shoes, brooms. Stone quarrying. Sugar mill of Marcelo Salado is 3 mi/4.8 km ENE.

Remer (REE-muhr), village (1990 pop. 342), Cass co., N central Minn., 32 mi/51 km E of Walker, on Willow R., in Chippewa Natl. Forest; 47°03'N 93°54'E. Wild rice, oats; poultry, cattle, sheep; dairying; light mfg. Leech Lake Indian Reservation is to W. Remer State Forest to NE; Land O' Lakes State Forest to S; Schoolcraft State Park to N; Big Rice L. to S.

Remerton (REM-uhr-tuhn), suburb (1990 pop. 463), Lowndes co., Ga., 2 mi/3.2 km WNW of Valdosta; 30°50'N 83°19'W.

Remington 1 town (1990 pop. 1,247), Jasper co., NW Ind., 12 mi/19 km S of Rensselaer; 40°46'N 87°09'W. In grain and livestock area; mfg. (soy protein, carbon alloy forming). Laid out 1860. **2** town (1990 pop. 460), Fauquier co., N Va., on Rappahannock R., 13 mi/21 km S of Warrenton; 38°31'N 77°48'W. Mfg. (hardware, plastic bags); agr. (grain, soybeans, apples; livestock). Called Rappahannock Station during Civil War; site of Union victory (Nov. 1863).

Remmel Dam, Ark.: see CATHERINE, LAKE.

Remote Mountain (11,000 ft/3,353 m), SW B.C., Canada, in Coast Mts., 190 mi/306 km NW of Vancouver; 51°27'N 125°30'W.

Remsen, town (1990 pop. 1,513), Plymouth co., NW Iowa, 10 mi/16 km E of Le Mars; 42°48'N 95°58'W. Livestock; grain; feeds; apparel. A fire in 1936 destroyed many bldgs. Founded 1839.

Remsen, village (1990 pop. 518), Oneida co., central N.Y., 16 mi/26 km N of Utica; 43°19'N 75°11'W. Reconstructed log cabin of Baron von Steuben, drillmaster to Continental Army (state historic site) 2 mi/3.2 km W. Hinckley Reservoir E of village.

Remus (REE-mus), village, Mecosta co., central Mich., 18 mi/29 km W of Mt. Pleasant; 43°33'N 85°08'W. In agr. area (livestock, poultry; grain, apples; dairy prods.). Light mfg.

Rencontre East (RAHN-kahn-tuhr), village (1991 pop. 212), SE N.F., Canada, at head of Belle Bay, arm of Fortune Bay, 50 mi/80 km NE of Grand Bank; 47°39'N 55°13'W. Fishing port.

Rend Lake, reservoir, Franklin and Jefferson cos., S Ill., on Big Muddy R., 3 mi/4.8 km NNW of Benton; 14 mi/23 km long; 38°01'N 88°57'W. Max. capacity 608,000 acre-ft. Formed by Rend Lake Dam (earth-gravity construction), built (1971) for flood control. Causeway (3 mi/4.8 km long) crosses center of lake. Wayne Fitzgerald State Park and Rend L. Col. on E shore.

Rendville, village (1990 pop. 32), Perry co., central Ohio, 9 mi/14 km SE of New Lexington; 39°37'N 82°05'W. In coal-mining area.

Renfrew (REN-froo), county (□ 3,009 sq mi/7,793 sq km; 1991 pop. 91,685), SE Ont., Canada, on Ottawa R., and on Que. border; ⊙ Pembroke; 45°40'N 77°15'W.

Renfrew, town (1991 pop. 8,134), SE Ont., Canada, on Bonnechére R., and 50 mi/80 km W of Ottawa; 45°28'N 76°41'W. Woolen milling, woodworking, dairying; mfg. of machinery and appliances. Iron, mica, and graphite mining nearby.

Renfro Valley, uninc. village, Rockcastle co., central Ky., suburb 2 mi/3.2 km N of Mt. Vernon, near Roundstone R. Growing commercial area on Interstate Highway 75. Mfg. (candy). L. Linville reservoir to W. Renfro Valley Entertainment Center (country music).

Renfrow (REN-fro), village (1990 pop. 19), Grant co., N Okla., 10 mi/16 km NE of Medford; 36°55'N 97°39'W. In agr. area.

Renick (RE-nik), town (1990 pop. 195), Randolph co., N central Mo., 5 mi/8 km S of Moberly; 39°20'N 92°24'W. Moberly State Correctional Center (penitentiary).

Renick (RE-nik) or **Falling Spring**, village (1990 pop. 191), Greenbrier co., SE W.Va., on Greenbrier R., 13 mi/21 km NNE of Lewisburg. Light mfg. Droop Mt. Battlefield and Beartown state parks to NE; Watoga State Park and Calvin Price State Forest to NE; parts of Monongahela Natl. Forest to NW and SE.

Rennell, Cape, N extremity of Somerset Isl., central Franklin dist., N.W.T., Canada, on Barrow Strait; 74°11'N 93°15'W.

Rennert (REN-uhrt), village (1990 pop. 217), Robeson co., SE N.C., 13 mi/21 km NNW of Lumberton and 20 mi/32 km SSW of Fayetteville; 34°48'N 79°04'W. Grain, tobacco; poultry, livestock.

Reno (REE-no), county (□ 1,271 sq mi/3,292 sq km; 1990 pop. 62,389), S central Kansas; ⊙ Hutchinson; 37°57'N 98°05'W. Wheat-growing region, drained by Arkansas R. and North Fork Ninnescah R. Food processing, chemicals, industrial machinery, transportation equip. Mfg. and salt refining at Hutchinson. Poultry, cattle, hogs, sheep; strawberries, sorghum, alfalfa. Part of Quivira Natl. Wildlife Refuge in NW corner, salt marsh area. Formed 1872.

Reno (REE-no), city (□ 57 sq mi/148 sq km; 1990 pop. 133,850), ⊙ Washoe co., W Nev., on the Truckee R.; 39°32'N 119°49'W. Tourism has been developed into a major industry since gambling was legalized in Nev. in 1931. With its extensive resort facilities, night entertainment, and casinos, Reno is a year-round vacation spot. The city is known for its fast life and refers to itself as "the biggest little city in the world." It also serves as a major distributing and warehouse center for commercial goods. Mfg. (concrete, automated gaming systems and devices, printing and publishing, Western buckles and accessories, beverage dispensers, plastic prods., milled metal prods., valves and fittings, steel fabrication, alfalfa processing); mining (gold and silver); convention center. Reno is one of the fastest-growing U.S. cities, marked by a pop. increase of nearly 33% bet. 1980 and 1990. Reno-Tahoe Internatl. Airport in SE part of city. The site was once a popular campsite beside a ford on the Donner Pass route to Calif.; in 1860 a bridge was built. Once known as "divorce capital of the world" for liberal divorce laws. The name Lake's Crossing was changed to Reno when the Central Pacific RR arrived in 1868 and the town was laid out. Univ. of Nevada, with its school of mines mus. and Desert Research Instit.; Truckee Meadows Community Col. The city is also the hq. for the Toiyabe Natl. Forest. Pyramid L. and Pyramid L. Indian Reservation to NE. Parts of Toiyabe Natl. Forest to NW and SW. L. Tahoe is to SSW; ski resorts. Large suburb of Sparks adjoins city on E. Nev. Mus. of Art.; Natl. Automobile Mus.; Fleischmann Planetarium. Inc. 1903.

Reno 1 (REE-no), town, Grady co., SW Ga., 8 mi/12.9 km SSW of Cairo; 30°46'N 84°17'W. **2** town (1990 pop. 1,748), Lamar co., NE Texas, 5 mi/8 km E of Paris; 32°56'N 97°34'W. Agr. area (cattle; soybeans, cotton, peanuts).

Reno (REE-no), uninc. village, Venango co., NW central Pa., 2 mi/3.2 km SW of Oil City, on Allegheny R; 41°24'N 79°45'W. Light mfg.

Reno, Fort, Okla.: see EL RENO.

Reno, Lake, Pope co., W central Minn., extends NE into Douglas co. at its outflow to Maple L., 5 mi/8 km N of Glenwood; 4.5 mi/7.2 km long, 2 mi/3.2 km wide; 45°44'N 95°24'W. Source of Little Chippewa R.

Renova (re-NO-vuh), village (1990 pop. 636), Bolivar co., W Miss., 2 mi/3.2 km N of Cleveland; 33°46'N 90°43'W. RR terminus. Cotton, corn, rice, soybeans; cattle.

Renovo (re-NO-vo), borough (1990 pop. 1,526), Clinton co., N central Pa., 21 mi/34 km NW of Lock Haven, on West Branch Susquehanna R.; 41°19'N 77°45'W. Mfg. (chip wood, printing and publishing); bituminous coal; timber; livestock. Surrounded by Sproul State Forest. Kettle Creek State Park to NW; Hyner Run and Hyner View state parks to E. Laid out 1862, inc. 1866.

Rensselaer (ren-suh-LIR), county (□ 665 sq mi/1,722 sq km; 1990 pop. 154,429), E N.Y.; ⊙ Troy; 42°42'N 73°30'W. Bounded W by the Hudson R., E by Mass. and Vt.; includes part of Taconic Mts. in E. Drained by Hoosic R.; contains Tomhannock Reservoir and small lakes (resorts). Dairying, farming (hay, sweet corn, cauliflower, tomatoes, strawberries, apples, potatoes); poultry raising. The towns of Troy and Rensselaer are industrial and commercial centers. Includes Bennington Battlefield State Park at Hoosick Falls, site of successful capture of Burgoyne's raiding party (Aug. 16, 1777). Vital Burden Iron Works turned out horseshoes and iron plate for Union's ironclad warship *Monitor* during Civil War. At Eagle Bridge, septuagenarian Grandma Moses captured nation's attention with her simple paintings of rural life in early 20th cent. Formed 1791.

Rensselaer 1 (ren-suh-LIR), city (1990 pop. 5,045), ⊙ Jasper co., NW Ind., on Iroquois R., and 45 mi/72 km SSE of Gary; 40°56'N 87°09'W. Trade center for livestock and grain area; light mfg. Seat of St. Joseph's Col. (1889). Settled c.1836, laid out 1839, inc. 1897. **2** city (□ 3 sq mi/7.8 sq km; 1990 pop. 8,255), Rensselaer co., E N.Y., on the E bank of the Hudson R. opposite Albany; 42°38'N 73°44'W. Chemicals, textiles, leather goods. The city was formed by the union of several villages within the tract granted to Kiliaen Van Rensselaer by the chartered Du. West Indies Company. At the 17th-cent. Fort Crailo, now a mus., the Br. surgeon Richard Shuckburg is said to have written "Yankee Doodle." Settled 1630 by Dutch, inc. 1897.

Rensselaer (ren-suh-LIR), village (1990 pop. 94), Ralls co., NE Mo., 8 mi/12.9 km NW of New London. Corn, soybeans; hogs.

Rensselaer Falls (ren-suh-LIR), village (1990 pop. 316), St. Lawrence co., N N.Y., on Oswegatchie R., and 11 mi/18 km SE of Ogdensburg; 44°35'N 75°19'W. In dairy and poultry area.

Rentiesville (REN-teez-vil), village (1990 pop. 66), McIntosh co., E Okla., 17 mi/27 km SSW of Muskogee; 35°31'N 95°29'W. In agr. area.

Renton, city (1990 pop. 41,688), King co., W Wash., an industrial suburb 10 mi/16 km SSE of Seattle, at S end of L. Washington, at mouth of Cedar R. It is a freshwater port via the L. Washington Ship Canal. RR junction. Its clay works were est. in 1901 and its iron foundry in 1905; lumber; diverse mfg.; aircraft parts and aircraft. A Boeing aircraft plant began operation during World War II and has since greatly expanded. The city, marked by growth since the 1970s, has a municipal airport, 4 flying schools, and a seaplane base. Seattle-Tacoma (Sea-Tac) Internatl. Airport to SW. Inc. 1901.

Renton (REN-tuhn), uninc. village, Penhills township, Allegheny co., W Pa., 16 mi/26 km ENE of downtown Pittsburgh, near Plum Creek; 40°30'N 79°43'W.

Rentz, village (1990 pop. 364), Laurens co., central Ga., 12 mi/19 km SSW of Dublin; 32°23'N 82°59'W. Mfg. (feeds, kitchen cabinets).

Renville 1 county (☐ 987 sq mi/2,556 sq km; 1990 pop. 17,673), S Minn.; ⊙ Olivia; 44°43'N 94°57'W. Agr. area bounded S by Minnesota R. (flows NW to SE). Oats, corn, wheat, hay, alfalfa, soybeans, beans, sugar beets, peas; hogs, cattle, poultry, sheep; dairying; sand and gravel. Fort Ridgely State Park on S boundary in SE; Joseph R. Brown State Wayside in W, on Minnesota R.; small lake in NE corner. Formed 1855. **2** county (☐ 886 sq mi/2,295 sq km; 1990 pop. 3,160), N N.Dak.; ⊙ Mohall; 48°42'N 101°39'W. Agr. area drained by Souris R. (Mouse R.), borders Sask. (Canada) on N. Diversified farming (cattle; wheat, barley, rye; dairy prods.). Formed 1910.

Renville, town (1990 pop. 1,315), Renville co., S central Minn., 4 mi/6.4 km W of Olivia; 44°47'N 95°12'W. Grain, sugar beets, soybeans, beans; livestock, poultry; dairying; mfg. (feeds and fertilizers, beet sugar, tractor seats). Settled c.1863.

Renwick, town (1990 pop. 287), Humboldt co., N central Iowa, near Boone R., 14 mi/23 km NE of Dakota City; 42°49'N 93°58'W.

Repton, town (1990 pop. 293), Conecuh co., S Ala., 17 mi/27 km W of Evergreen.

Republic, county (☐ 720 sq mi/1,865 sq km; 1990 pop. 6,482), N Kansas; ⊙ Belleville; 39°49'N 97°39'W. Plains region, bordering N on Nebr., and drained by Republican R. Corn, wheat, strawberries, sorghum, alfalfa; hogs, cattle, sheep; plastics prods. Pawnee Indian Village across Republican R. from village of Rossville in NW. Jamestown Waterfowl Management Unit in SW corner. Formed 1868.

Republic, city (1990 pop. 6,292), Greene co., SW Mo., in the Ozarks, satellite town 12 mi/19 km SW of Springfield; 37°07'N 93°28'W. Dairying; fruits, vegetables; light mfg. Wilson's Creek Natl. Battlefield to E.

Republic 1 uninc. town (1990 pop. 1,603), Fayette co., SW Pa., 9 mi/14.5 km NW of Uniontown, on Dunlap Creek; 39°57'N 79°52'W. Light mfg.; bituminous coal; agr. (corn, hay, dairying). **2** town (1990 pop. 940), ⊙ Ferry co., NE Wash., 40 mi/64 km WNW of Colville, on Granite Creek, near Sanpoil R.; 48°39'N 118°44'W. Wheat, barley, oats, alfalfa; poultry; timber, lime; gold mines, silver; mfg. (meat prods., lumber). Co. historical mus. Parts of Colville Natl. Forest to N, E, and S; Okanogan Natl. Forest to W; Curlew L. reservoir and State Park to NE.

Republic 1 village (1990 pop. 177), Republic co., N Kansas, 12 mi/19 km NW of Belleville, near Republican R. and Nebr. state line; 39°55'N 97°49'W. Corn, wheat; livestock. Pawnee Indian Village Mus. nearby. **2** village, Marquette co., NW Upper Peninsula, Mich., 16 mi/26 km SW of Ishpeming, near Michigamme R.; 42°24'N 87°58'W. Its abandoned iron mine was one of the richest in Marquette Iron Range. **3** village (1990 pop. 611), Seneca co., N Ohio, 8 mi/13 km E of Tiffin; 41°07'N 83°01'W. In livestock and grain area.

Republican City, village (1990 pop. 199), Harlan co., S Nebr., 5 mi/8 km E of Alma, near Republican R., near Kansas state line, N of Harlan County L. Dam; 40°06'N 99°13'W. Grain; livestock.

Republican River, c.420 mi/676 km long, Nebr. and Kansas; formed by the junction of its North Fork and South Fork at Benkelman; flows E across the rolling grasslands of Nebr. then past McCook and Superior, SE across Kansas past Concordia, to join the Smoky Hill and form the Kansas R. at Junction City. Its broad channel traverses a rich agr. region. The river is included in the Missouri R. basin project. Many dams and reservoirs have been built for flood control, irrigation, and power. Milford L. reservoir N of Junction City; Harlan County L. reservoir near Alma, Nebr.; Swanson Reservoir at Treaton, Nebr.

Repulse Bay, trading post (1991 pop. 488), S Melville Peninsula, SE Franklin dist., N.W.T., Canada, at head of Repulse Bay, inlet (40 mi/64 km long, 19 mi/31 km–40 mi/64 km wide) of Foxe Channel; 66°32'N 86°15'W. Radio station. Fishing, hunting, trapping. Stone and bone carvings. Scheduled air service.

Requa, uninc. village, Del Norte co., NW Calif., near mouth of Klamath R., 2 mi/3.2 km E of the Pacific, 15 mi/24 km SE of Crescent City. Sport fishing. Redwood Natl. Park to W; Six Rivers Natl. Forest to E.

Resaca (ri-SAK-uh), village (1990 pop. 410), Gordon co., NW Ga., 13 mi/21 km S of Dalton, on Oostanaula R.; 34°35'N 84°56'W. Mfg. (carpets). Civil War battle in the Atlanta campaign occurred here, May 13–16, 1864.

Resaca de la Palma, valley, an abandoned bed of the Rio Grande, N of Brownsville, Texas, where the 2d battle of the Mex. War was fought, May 9, 1846. Mex. troops under Gen. Mariano Arista, retreating S after the battle of Palo Alto, were defeated by Amer. forces led by Gen. Zachary Taylor.

Res-delta, locality, S Mackenzie dist., N.W.T., Canada, on S shore of Great Slave L., at mouth of Slave R., 9 mi/14 km NNE of Fort Resolution; 61°17'N 113°35'W. River-lake transshipment point for Yellowknife mining region.

Research Triangle Park, Durham and Wake cos., N central N.C., research and business park (☐ 11 sq mi/28 sq km), 5 mi/8 km SSE of Durham, 10 mi/16 km E of Chapel Hill, and 15 mi/24 km NW of Raleigh; 6 mi/9.7 km long, 2 mi/3.2 km wide. Employs some 34,000 workers in a 3-county area with total pop. of 690,000. Est. in 1950s to boost state's spending in modern technology, developed through cooperation of Univ. of N.C. at Chapel Hill, N.C. State Univ. at Raleigh, and Duke Univ. at Durham. Such prods. as Astroturf, bar codes, and the drug AZT have been developed here. Mfg. (industrial gasses, printed circuit boards, cellular phones, computers, electronic measurement devices, medical prototypes, semiconductors, agr. chemicals, powdered metals). Referred to locally as R.T.P. Raleigh-Durham Internatl. Airport and William B. Umstead State Park to E.

Reseda, suburban sect. of Los Angeles, Los Angeles co., S Calif., in W San Fernando Valley, 19 mi/31 km NW of Los Angeles, on Los Angeles R. Food processing; light mfg. Van Nuys Airport to E. Area sustained damage in 1994 Northridge earthquake (Northridge to N).

Reserva Biológica Yuscarán (re-SER-vah bee-ah-LO-hee-ko yoos-kah-RAHN), small forest reserve, on the summit of Montserrat Peak (6,202 ft/1,891 m), 5 mi/8 km W of Yuscarán; 13°55'N 86°51'W.

Reserve, uninc. city (1990 pop. 8,847), St. John the Baptist parish, SE La., on E bank (levee) of the Mississippi, and 29 mi/47 km WNW of New Orleans; toll ferry to Edgard; 30°05'N 90°34'W. Refining and shipping center for sugarcane area; mfg. (plastic bottles, soft drinks, surfactants and emulsifiers).

Reserve 1 village (1990 pop. 108), Brown co., NE Kansas, near Nebr. border, and 9 mi/14.5 km N of Hiawatha; 39°58'N 95°34'W. In corn and dairy region. At entrance to Iowa Sac and Fox Indian Reservation (to E). **2** village (1990 pop. 319), ⊙ Catron co., W N.Mex., on San Francisco R., near Ariz. border, 70 mi/113 km NNW of Silver City, in Gila Natl. Forest; 33°42'N 108°45'W. Elev. 5,749 ft/1,752 m. Timber; agr.; cattle, sheep, goats. Apache Natl. Forest to W and N. Eagle Peak is 11 mi/18 km E.

Reserve, township (1990 pop. 3,866), Allegheny co., W Pa., residential suburb 3 mi/4.8 km N of Pittsburgh; 40°28'N 79°59'W.

Reserve Mines, town, NE N.S., Canada, on Cape Breton Isl., 4 mi/6 km W of Glace Bay; 46°11'N 60°01'W. Coal mining.

Resolute, settlement (1986 pop. 184), S coast of Cornwallis Isl., Franklin dist., N.W.T., Canada, on Barrow Strait; 74°42'N 94°34'W. U.S.-Can. high Arctic weather station. Inuit community.

Resolution Island (☐ c.390 sq mi/1,000 sq km), off SE Baffin Isl., N.W.T., Canada, at the E entrance of Hudson Strait.

Rest Haven, town (1990 pop. 176), Gwinnett co., N central Ga., 12 mi/19 km N of Lawrenceville; 34°08'N 83°59'W.

Restauración (res-too-rah-see-ON), town (1993 pop. 2,124), Dajabón prov., NW Dominican Republic, in the Cordillera Central, near Haiti border, 13 mi/21 km S of Dajabón; 19°18'N 71°35'W. Coffee, corn, fruit.

Resthaven Mountain (10,253 ft/3,125 m), W Alta., Canada, near B.C. border, in Rocky Mts. at N edge of Jasper Natl. Park, 70 mi/113 km NW of Jasper; 53°27'N 119°31'W.

Restigouche, Indian reservation (1986 pop. 896), N.B., Canada, on Gaspé Peninsula at mouth of Restigouche R. Bridge to Campellton. Site of last battle of Seven Years War bet. French and British (July 8, 1760). Mission site and Micmac reserve.

Restigouche (RE-sti-goosh), county (☐ 3,242 sq mi/8,397 sq km; 1991 pop. 38,760), N N.B., Canada, on Bay of Chaleur, and on Que. border; ⊙ Dalhousie.

Restigouche (RE-sti-goosh), river, c.130 mi/210 km long; rises in NW N.B., Canada, E of Edmundston; flows generally NE to the Matapedia R., then past Campbellton to Chaleur Bay at Dalhousie. Its lower course forms part of the border with Que. Noted for salmon fishing.

Reston, uninc. city (1990 pop. 48,556), Fairfax co., N Va., suburb 17 mi/27 km WNW of Washington, D.C.; 38°57'N 77°20'W. Mfg. (printing and publishing, machinery, instruments, sheet metal fabrication). Va.'s 2d largest business dist., with over 2,000 businesses, and hq. for several major U.S. corporations; electronics and computer development and research. Hq. of U.S. Geological Survey. Wolf Trap Farm Park for the Performing Arts (natl. parks unit) to E. Dulles Internatl. Airport to W.

Reston, village, SW Man., Canada, 55 mi/89 km WSW of Brandon, near Sask. border; 49°33'N 101°05'W. Grain elevators; livestock.

Resurrection Bay, inlet of Gulf of Alaska, in SE Kenai Peninsula, S Alaska; 15 mi/24 km long, 2 mi/3.2 km–7 mi/11.3 km wide; opening into Blying Sound at 60°00'N 149°23'W. At head of bay is Seward, S terminus of Alaska RR. Named by Baranov (1792); shipbuilding yard est. here 1794 by Russians.

Resurrection, Cape, on SE Kenai Peninsula, S Alaska, 15 mi/24 km S of Seward, at E entrance of Resurrection Bay; 59°32'N 149°17'W.

Retallack (ri-TA-lik), village, SE B.C., Canada, 40 mi/64 km N of Nelson, in Selkirk Mts.; 50°01'N 117°10'W. Silver, lead, zinc mining; timber.

Retsil, uninc. town (1990 pop. 1,524), Kitsap co., W Wash., on Sinclair Inlet, arm of Puget Sound, 2 mi/3.2 km SE of Bremerton.

Retsof, village (1990 pop. 500), Livingston co., W central N.Y., near Genesee R., 26 mi/42 km SW of Rochester; 42°50'N 77°53'W. Name is derived from spelling the name of the village's founder (Foster) backward. Site of largest salt mine (☐ 18 sq mi/47 sq km; 1,000 ft/305 m deep) in Western Hemisphere, which has been worked for over 100 years. Mine supplies most of the winter road salt for N.Y. state, N.Y. city, and New England. In March 1994, roof slabs fell to the mine floor at Cuylerville (3 mi/5 km S of Retsof), causing an earthquake measuring 3.6 on the Richter scale. No deaths resulted, but 9 sq mi/23.3 sq km of the Genesee R. valley sank 8 ft/3 m, and river water flooded miles of underground tunnels. As a result, sinkholes, disappearing structures, dry wells, and flares of explosive methane gas have been created.

Reubens, village (1990 pop. 46), Lewis co., W Idaho, 15 mi/24 km WNW of Nezperce; 46°19'N 116°32'W. Farming, livestock. In Nez Perce Indian Reservation.

Revelstoke (REV-uhl-stok), city (1991 pop. 7,729), SE B.C., Canada, on the Columbia R., at foot of Selkirk Mts.; 51°00'N 118°11'W. A RR division point; distribution center for mining and lumbering area. Gateway to Mt. Revelstoke Natl. Park.

Revelstoke Dam, on Columbia R., SE B.C., Canada, at Revelstoke. Built in 1984 under terms of Columbia R. Treaty bet. U.S. and Canada (1964) to generate hydroelectricity. Dam is designed to withstand water surges from potential rock slides. Reservoir runs N 84 mi/135 km to Mica Dam.

Revere (re-VIR), city (1990 pop. 42,786), Suffolk co., E Mass., a residential suburb of Boston, on Massachusetts Bay; 42°25'N 71°00'W. Revere Beach is a popular swimming beach. Much of Point of Pines, formerly a prosperous summer colony at the N end of Revere Beach, has been built up with apartment and housing complexes. Horatio Alger b. here. Settled c.1630, set off from Chelsea and named for Paul Revere 1871, inc. as a city 1914.

Revere (re-VIR), town (1990 pop. 133), Clark co., extreme NE Mo., near Des Moines R., and 6 mi/9.7 km NNE of Kahoka; 40°29′N 91°40′W.

Revere, village (1990 pop. 117), Redwood co., SW Minn., near Cottonwood R., and 26 mi/42 km SW of Redwood Falls; 44°13′N 95°21′W. Grain; livestock; dairying; feeds.

Reversing Falls, N.B., Canada: see SAINT JOHN, city.

Revillagigedo Channel (re-VI-luh-gi-GAI-do), in Alexander Archipelago, SE Alaska, bet. mainland (E), Revillagigedo Isl. (N), and Duke and Annette isls. (SW); extends c.35 mi/56 km NW from Dixon Entrance; forms part of Inside Passage to Ketchikan.

Revillagigedo Island (□ 1,120 sq mi/2,901 sq km), in Alexander Archipelago, SE Alaska, separated from mainland (E) by Behn Canal, and from Prince of Wales Isl. (W) by Clarence Strait; 55 mi/89 km long, 30 mi/48 km wide; center near 55°35′N 131°06′W. Rises to 4,592 ft/1,400 m on Mt. Reid (E). Ketchikan in S. Fishing, canning, logging. Visited by Rus., Eng., and Span. explorers and named (1793) for Count Revilla Gigedo, viceroy of Mexico (1789–1794).

Revillagigedo Islands (re-vee-yah-hee-HE-do) (□ 320 sq mi/829 sq km), archipelago of 3 volcanic isls. and several smaller adjoining rocks in the Pacific, c.450 mi/724 km W of Manzanillo, Mexico. Socorro (□ 110 sq mi/285 sq km) is the largest isl.; 24 mi/39 km long, 9 mi/14.5 km wide; rises to 3,707 ft/1,130 m; 19°19′N 110°49′W. A volcano on San Benedicto isl. rose suddenly in 1952. In 1957, a military base was established on Clarión. Fishing grounds. Guano deposits.

Revillo, village (1990 pop. 152), Grant co., E S.Dak., 15 mi/24 km S of Milbank; 45°00′N 96°34′W.

Rewey (ROO-ee), village (1990 pop. 220), Iowa co., SW Wis., 8 mi/12.9 km NNE of Platteville; 42°50′N 90°24′W. In dairy and livestock region. First Capitol State Park to SE at Leslie.

Rexburg, city (1990 pop. 14,302), ⊙ Madison co., E Idaho, on channel of lower Teton R., near Snake R., and 25 mi/40 km NE of Idaho Falls; 43°50′N 111°48′W. Elev. 4,861 ft/1,482 m. Trade center for cattle, sheep, poultry, and irrigated agr. area (sugar beets, potatoes); dairying. Light mfg. Teton Flood Mus.; area flooded June 5, 1976, killing 11 people, after Teton Dam collapse 18 mi/29 km ENE on Teton R. Kelly Canyon Ski Area to SE. Ricks Col. (1888) is here. Founded 1883 by Mormons.

Rexford 1 village (1990 pop. 171), Thomas co., NW Kansas, 17 mi/27 km ENE of Colby; 39°28′N 100°44′W. In agr. and cattle area. **2** village (1990 pop. 132), Lincoln co., NW Mont., 60 mi/97 km NW of Kalispell, on Koocanusa L. reservoir (Kootenai R.). Tourism. Timber. Bridge across lake 7 mi/11.3 km to SW. Canada (B.C.) border 6 mi/9.7 km to N. Kootenai Natl. Forest to W, S, and E.

Roxton, village (1986 pop. 926), southeasternmost N.B., Canada, at mouth of Richibucto R.; 46°38′N 64°52′W. Fishing and farming.

Reydon (RAID-uhn), village (1990 pop. 200), Roger Mills co., W Okla., 31 mi/50 km NW of Elk City, near Texas border, in Black Kettle Natl. Grassland; 35°38′N 99°55′W. In agr. area.

Reyes, Veracruz, Mexico: see LOS REYES.

Reyes de Juárez, Los, Mexico: see LOS REYES DE JUÁREZ.

Reyes Etla (RAI-yes ET-lah), town (1990 pop. 1,538) in central Oaxaca, Mexico, 12 mi/20 km NW of Oaxaca de Juárez, and 2 mi/3.2 km N of Mexico Highway 190 (Inter-Amer. Highway). Farming, mainly for subsistence.

Reyes, Los, Mexico: see LOS REYES.

Reyes, Point, bold promontory on coast of Calif., Marin co., 20 mi/32 km NW of San Francisco, at tip of peninsula W of Drakes Bay; lighthouse (294 ft/90 m above sea; est. 1870) here. Coast guard station nearby. See also POINT REYES NATIONAL SEASHORE.

Reyes, San Luis Potosí, Mexico: see VILLA DE REYES.

Reyno (RAI-no), town (1990 pop. 467), Randolph co., NE Ark., 14 mi/23 km ENE of Pocahontas, near Current R.; 36°21′N 90°45′W. Dave Donaldson–Black R. Wildlife Management Area to SE.

Reynolds, county (□ 822 sq mi/2,129 sq km; 1990 pop. 6,661), SE Mo.; ⊙ Centerville; 37°21′N 90°58′W. In the Ozarks; drained by Black R. Livestock raising, hay; pine and oak timber, granite in NE, lead in NW. Wood prods. Part of Mark Twain Natl. Forest in NW; Johnson Shut-ins State Park in NE (local term "shut-ins" refers to boulder-strewn stream bed caused by natural cut through hard rock); Clearwater Lake in SE. Formed 1845.

Reynolds 1 town (1990 pop. 1,166), Taylor co., W central Ga., 33 mi/53 km SW of Macon, near Flint R.; 32°34′N 84°06′W. Mfg. of leather goods. **2** town (1990 pop. 528), White co., NW central Ind., 6 mi/9.7 km W of Monticello; 40°45′N 86°52′W. RR junction in agr. area.

Reynolds 1 village (1990 pop. 583), in Rock Island co., NW Ill., 13 mi/21 km SSW of Rock Island; 41°19′N 90°40′W. In agr. area. **2** village (1990 pop. 104), Jefferson co., SE Nebr., 10 mi/16 km SW of Fairbury, and on branch of Little Blue R. near Kansas border; 40°03′N 97°20′W. **3** village (1990 pop. 299), on border bet. Traill and Grand Forks cos., E N.Dak., 18 mi/29 km SSW of Grand Forks; 47°40′N 97°06′W.

Reynoldsburg, city (1990 pop. 25,748), Franklin and Licking cos., central Ohio; 39°57′N 82°48′W. Growing residential suburb of Columbus; pop. doubled bet. 1970 and 1990. Inc. 1839, as city 1961.

Reynoldsville (RE-nuhlds-vil), borough (1990 pop. 2,818), Jefferson co., W central Pa., 11 mi/18 km NNE of Punxsutawney, on Sandy Lick Creek; 41°05′N 78°53′W. Metal cutting tools, gas meters and equip.; bituminous coal mining; timber. Agr. area (corn, hay, dairying). Kyle L. reservoir to NE. Settled c.1824, laid out 1873.

Reynosa (rei-NO-sah), city (1990 pop. 265,663) and township, Tamaulipas, NE Mexico, on the Rio Grande opposite Hidalgo (Texas), on RR, and 50 mi/80 km WNW of Matamoros; 26°05′N 98°18′W. On Mexico Highway 2 at terminus of Mexico Highway 40. Agr. center (cotton, sugarcane, corn; livestock); cotton ginning, sawmilling, maquiladoras. Oil refinery (E) serves nearby oil fields.

Rhame (RAIM), village (1990 pop. 186), Bowman co., SW N.Dak., 13 mi/21 km W of Bowman; 46°13′N 103°39′W. Gas wells, lignite mines; livestock; wheat, rye, flax. Highest town (elev. 3,184 ft/970 m) in state. Fort Dilts Historical Site to NW; Little Missouri Natl. Grassland to N.

Rhea (rai), county (□ 335 sq mi/868 sq km; 1990 pop. 24,344), E Tenn.; ⊙ Dayton; 35°38′N 84°55′W. Drained by Tennessee R., impounded (in N) by Watts Bar Reservoir. Fruit, corn, vegetables, hay; dairy prods.; livestock; bituminous coal mining. Some industry at Dayton, Spring City (textiles, stone prods.). Part of Chickamauga Reservoir (Tennessee R.) in S. Formed 1807.

Rheatown (RAI-toun), town, Greene co., NE Tenn., 8 mi/13 km ENE of Greeneville.

Rheems (REEMS), uninc. town (1990 pop. 1,044), Lancaster co., SE Pa., 2 mi/3.2 km SE of Elizabethtown; 40°07′N 76°34′W. Food processing, concrete, bulk feeds. Dairying; livestock, poultry; grain, vegetables, apples.

Rhein, village (1991 pop. 218), E Sask., Canada, 16 mi/26 km NE of Yorkton; 51°21′N 102°12′W. Grain, mixed farming.

Rhine (REIN), town (1990 pop. 466), Dodge co., S central Ga., 14 mi/23 km S of Eastman; 31°59′N 83°12′W.

Rhinebeck, village (□ 1 sq mi/2.6 sq km; 1990 pop. 2,725), Dutchess co., SE N.Y., in the foothills of the Berkshire Mts., near the Hudson R.; 41°55′N 73°54′W. It is the site of Beekman Arms, said to be the oldest hotel in the U.S., and of a pre-Revolutionary Du. Reformed church and cemetery. Unique collection of aircraft from before and during World War I at Old Rhinebeck Aerodrome. Tourism center. Settled before 1700, inc. 1834.

Rhineland, town (1990 pop. 157), Montgomery co., E central Mo., on Missouri R., 18 mi/29 km S of Montgomery City; 38°43′N 91°31′W. Soybeans, corn, wheat; cattle. River flooding in 1993 destroyed town; relocated onto adjacent bluffs.

Rhinelander, town (1990 pop. 7,427), ⊙ Oneida co., N Wis., on Wisconsin R., and 47 mi/76 km NNE of Wausau; 45°38′N 89°24′W. Elev. 1,554 ft/474 m. In dairying and farming area (potatoes, strawberries); trade center for resort area; paper milling, woodworking; light mfg. Has logging mus. Hq. of Nicolet Natl. Forest. Agr. research station to E and W. Amer. Legion State Forest to N. Surrounded by forests and numerous lakes.

Rhode Island, state (□ 1,214 sq mi/3,144 sq km; 1995 est. pop. 989,794), officially the *State of Rhode Island and Providence Plantations*, NE U.S., in New England, one of the 13 Colonies; ⊙ and the largest city PROVIDENCE; 41°41′N 71°35′W. Other cities of the state are WARWICK, CRANSTON, PAWTUCKET, EAST PROVIDENCE, WOONSOCKET, NEWPORT, , and CENTRAL FALLS. R.I. has 5 cos.: BRISTOL, KENT, NEWPORT, PROVIDENCE, WASHINGTON.,The smallest of the 50 states and the 2d most densely populated, R.I. is bounded on the N and the E by Mass., on the S by the Atlantic Ocean, and on the W by Conn. Off Napatree Point, in the extreme SW, there is a water boundary with New York State. The dominant physiographic feature of the state is the Narragansett basin, a shallow lowland area of Carboniferous sediments, extending into SE Mass. and, in R.I., being partly submerged as Narragansett Bay. The bay cuts inland c.30 mi/48 km to Providence, where it receives the Blackstone R.; it contains several isls., including Rhode Isl., the largest (and the site of historic Newport); Conanicut Isl., coterminous with JAMESTOWN; and Prudence Isl. The coastline bet. Point Judith and Watch Hill is marked by sand spits and barrier beaches, sheltering lagoons and salt marshes. Glaciation left many small lakes, and the rolling hilly surface of the state is cut by short, swift streams, with numerous falls. More than ½ the state is covered with forests, and agr. is of limited importance to the economy. Most of the land is used for farm nursery production, turf farming, and dairying. The state is known for its Rhode Island Red chickens. Principal crops include potatoes, hay, apples, wine grapes, and turf grass. Commercial fishing is an important but declining industry. Narragansett Bay is a source of shellfish; flounder and porgy are also caught. Minerals found in the state are sand and gravel, crushed stone, and limestone. Many of the products for which R.I. is famous are still being manufactured: jewelry, silverware, textiles, primary and fabricated metals, machinery, electrical equip., and rubber and plastic items. However, the state's traditional mfg. base has given way to an economy based on tourism, services, trade (retail and wholesale), and finance. R.I. attracts summer tourists. Its coast is lined with resorts noted for their fine swimming and boating facilities, and windswept Block Isl. is a favorite vacation spot. Narragansett Bay is famous for its sailboats and yachts. The America's Cup yacht race was first held at Newport in 1930 and many times since. The state also has many historic attractions. Its official name is the State of Rhode Island and Providence Plantations, and its familiar name is taken from Rhode Isl. The region was probably visited (1524) by Verrazano, and in 1614 the area was explored by the Dutchman Adriaen Block. Roger Williams, banished from the Massachusetts Bay colony, est. in 1636 the first settlement in the area, at Providence, on land purchased from the Narragansett tribe. In 1638, Puritan exiles bought the isl. of Aquidneck (now Rhode Isl.) from the Native Americans. There they established the settlement of Portsmouth (1638). Because of factional differences, Newport was founded (1639) on the SW side of the isl., but the 2 towns later combined governments (1640–1647). Warwick, on the W shore of Narragansett Bay, was settled in 1642. Williams, through influential friends, secured (1644) a parliamentary patent under which the 4 towns drew up a code of civil law and organized (1647) a govt. The liberal charter granted (1663) by Charles II ensured the colony's survival, although boundary difficulties with Mass. and Conn. continued well into the 18th cent. The early settlers were mostly Eng. Many of them were drawn to the colony by the guarantee of religious freedom, a cardinal principle with Williams, confirmed in the patent of 1644 and reaffirmed by the royal charter of 1663. The first Jewish families of R.I. settled in Newport in 1658, and Quakers followed in large numbers. All the early settlers owned land that, following Williams' practice, was bought from the Native Americans.

Fishing and trade supplemented the living won from the soil. The colony's religious freedom was viewed with mixed loathing and fear by the more powerful neighboring colonies, and it was never admitted to the New England Confederation. However, it bore equally the devastation of King Philip's War in 1675–1676. Bet. 1750 and 1770 there was bitter strife bet. Providence and Newport over control of the colony. Livestock from Narragansett co. (South co., later Washington co.), especially the famous Narragansett pacers, figured largely in early commerce, which developed rapidly in the late 17th cent. Until the Amer. Revolution, Newport was the commercial center of the colony, thriving especially on the triangular trade in rum, slaves, and molasses. R.I., like other colonies, objected to Br. mercantilist policies and consistently violated the Molasses Act of 1733 and the Navigation Acts. Narragansett Bay became a notorious haven for smugglers, and the Br. revenue cutter *Gaspee* was burned (1772) by patriots protesting the enforcement of revenue laws. After the start of the Amer. Revolution, R.I. militia under Nathanael Greene joined (1775) the Continental Army at Cambridge, and on May 4, 1776, the prov. renounced its allegiance to George III. Br. forces occupied parts of R.I. from 1776 to 1779, withdrawing before the arrival of the Fr. fleet. The Revolution won, R.I., jealous of its independence, refused to sanction a natl. import duty; it thus deprived the Continental Congress of a major source of revenue and became one of the states responsible for the failure of the Articles of Confederation. R.I. did not send delegates to the Constitutional Convention at Philadelphia and resisted ratifying the Constitution until the Federal govt. threatened to sever commercial relations with the state; even then, ratification passed (1790) by only 2 votes. The post-Revolutionary era brought bankruptcy and currency difficulties. Shipping, which continued to be a major factor in the state's economy until the 1820s, was hard hit by Jefferson's Embargo Act of 1807 and by the competition of larger ports such as New York and Boston. However, this post-Revolutionary period also marked the beginning of R.I.'s industrial greatness. Samuel Slater built his first successful cotton-textile mill in the U.S. at Pawtucket in 1790. An abundance of water power led to the rapid development of mfg., in which merchants and shipping magnates invested their capital. With the growth ofindustry the towns increased in pop., and Providence surpassed Newport as the commercial center of the state. Since suffrage had long been restricted to freeholders, increased urbanization resulted in the disenfranchisement of most townspeople. Frustrated in repeated attempts to amend the constitution, many Rhode Islanders joined Thomas Wilson Dorr in forcibly establishing an illegal state govt. in Providence in 1842. Dorr's Rebellion, though abortive, resulted in the adoption of a new constitution (1842) extending suffrage; however, the property qualification was not abolished until 1888. Antislavery sentiment was strong in R.I., and the state firmly supported the Union in the Civil War. Until well into the 20th cent., R.I.'s political and economic life was dominated by mill owners. (Nelson W. Aldrich was a power in the nation as well as the state.) The small mill towns, with their company houses, company store, and large foreign-born pop., were important elements in the social fabric. Eng., Irish, and Scottish settlers had begun arriving in large numbers in the first ½ of the 19th cent.; Fr.-Can. immigration commenced around the time of the Civil War; at the end of the 19th cent. and the beginning of the 20th there was a large influx of Poles, Italians, and Portuguese. Sporadic labor troubles in the 19th cent. had little effect on the state's economy. However, after World War I there was a long textile strike centering in the Blackstone valley; this, together with the gradual removal of the mills to states in the S—where labor was cheaper—led to a continuing decline in the cotton-textile industry. Nevertheless, the mfg. of textile products is still carried on and new industries such as high-technology electronics have been introduced. Since the 1970s the economy has shifted toward the service sector. This shift has coincided with major suburban growth. In 1969 the Claiborne Pell (Newport) Bridge, which spans Narragansett Bay, was completed. Politically, R.I. was generally controlled by Republicans until the 1930s, when the Democrats' insistence on reapportionment of representation (which had tended to favor small towns at the expense of urban areas) helped bring their party into power. The present constitution was adopted in 1842; it has been amended 36 times. The state's executive branch is headed by a governor elected for a 4-year term and eligible for reelection. The bicameral legislature has a senate with 50 members and a house with 100, all elected for 2-year terms. Local govt. is carried out on the city level: R.I.'s cos. have no political functions. The state sends 2 senators and 2 representatives to the U.S. Congress. It has 4 electoral votes. The state's leading educational institutions are Brown Univ., in Providence, and the Univ. of R.I., at Kingston.

Rhode Island, island, 15 mi/24 km long and 5 mi/8 km wide, S R.I., at the entrance to Narragansett Bay. It is the largest island in the state, with steep cliffs and excellent beaches. Known to the Native Americans and early colonials as Aquidneck, it was renamed (probably after the isle of Rhodes) in 1644. Newport, Middletown, and Portsmouth are on the isl.

Rhodell (ro-DEL), village (1990 pop. 221), Raleigh co., S W.Va., 13 mi/21 km SSW of Beckley; 37°36′N 81°17′W. Semibituminous coal region.

Rhodes, town (1990 pop. 272), Marshall co., central Iowa, 17 mi/27 km WSW of Marshalltown; 41°55′N 93°10′W. In agr. area. Formerly Edenville.

Rhodes Point, Md.: see SMITH ISLAND.

Rhodhiss (ROD-his), village (1990 pop. 638), Burke and Caldwell cos., W central N.C., 5 mi/8 km NW of Hickory, on Catawba R.; 35°46′N 81°25′W. Dam here forms L. Rhodhiss reservoir (c.15 mi/24 km long) to W; L. Hickory reservoir to E (both on Catawba R.).

Rhome, village (1990 pop. 605), Wise co., N Texas, 23 mi/37 km NNW of Fort Worth, near West Fork Trinity R.; 33°02′N 97°28′W. In agr. area (dairying; livestock; peanuts, grains). Mfg. (truck and van conversions, steel tanks, tank trailers). Eagle Mt. L. to SW.

Rhyolite (REI-o-leit), ghost town, Nye co., S Nev., near Calif. line, c.5 mi/8 km W of Beatty. Boomed 1905–1908 after gold finds; had pop. of 6,000 at that time; still has pop. of about 5 people. Some mines have been reopened.

Rhyolite Mountain (10,780 ft/3,286 m), peak in Front Range, Teller co., central Colo., 3 mi/4.8 km N of Cripple Creek; 38°46′N 105°09′W.

Rialto, city (1990 pop. 72,388), San Bernardino co., S Calif., a suburb 5 mi/8 km W of San Bernadino and 50 mi/80 km E of Los Angeles; 34°07′N 117°23′W. RR junction. The city has greatly expanded as a result of the economic and demographic growth of the S Calif. area; its pop. more than doubled bet. 1970 and 1990. Food and beverages, fabricated structural metal, travel trailers, concrete prods., roofing systems. Rialto Municipal Airport in NW; Colton Airport to S. Lytle Creek to N; Lytle Creek Ranger Station to NW; San Gabriel Mts., in San Bernadino Natl. Forest, to N; Cucamonga Wilderness Area to NW; Glen Helen Regional Park to N. Inc. 1911.

Rib Lake, village (1990 pop. 887), Taylor co., N central Wis., on small Rib L., 37 mi/60 km NW of Wausau; 45°19′N 90°12′W. Dairy prods.; lumber. Timms Hill (1,951.5 ft/594.8 m), 8 mi/12.9 km N, is highest point in Wis.

Rib Mountain, (1,924 ft/586 m), Marathon co., central Wis., near Wausau; 3d-highest point in state, it is a quartzite outcrop. Summit is a state park. Winter sports.

Rib River, c.45 mi/72 km long, in NE Taylor co., central Wis.; rises in small Rib L.; flows SE to Wisconsin R. near Wausau.

Ribbon Falls, Calif.: see YOSEMITE NATIONAL PARK.

Ribera (ri-BER-uh), uninc. village, San Miguel co., N central N.Mex., 30 mi/48 km SSW of Las Vegas, on Pecos R. Cattle, sheep; alfalfa, grain, peas. Mfg. (lamps). Sections of Santa Fe Natl. Forest to E, W, and N; Villanueva State Park to SE. Glorieta Mesa to W.

Rice 1 county (□ 728 sq mi/1,886 sq km; 1990 pop. 10,610), central Kansas; ⊙ Lyons; 38°21′N 98°12′W. Rolling plain region, drained by Little Arkansas and Arkansas rivers and Cow Creek. Wheat, alfalfa, sorghum; cattle, hogs. Oil and gas fields. Part of Quivira Natl. Wildlife Refuge and salt marshes in SW corner. Quivira relics archaeological site at co. center. Formed 1871. **2** county (□ 516 sq mi/1,336 sq km; 1990 pop. 49,183), SE Minn.; ⊙ Faribault; 44°21′N 93°17′W. Agr. area drained by Cannon and Straight rivers. Alfalfa, hay, soybeans, corn, oats; sheep, cattle, hogs, poultry; dairying. Nerstrand-Big Woods State Park in E; Sakatah L. State Park on W boundary in SW. Formed 1858.

Rice 1 village (1990 pop. 610), Benton co., central Minn., 12 mi/19 km N of St. Cloud, bet. Mississippi R. and Little Rock Creek; 45°45′N 94°13′W. Dairying; light mfg. Little Rock L. to SE. **2** village (1990 pop. 564), Navarro co., E central Texas, 10 mi/16 km N of Corsicana; 32°14′N 96°30′W. In farm area; mfg. (trailers).

Rice Lake, SE Ont., Canada, 12 mi/19 km S of Peterborough; drained E by Trent R.; 20 mi/32 km long, 3 mi/5 km wide; 47°42′N 82°08′W.

Rice Lake, town (1990 pop. 7,998), Barron co., NW Wis., on small Rice L. and Red Cedar R., and 50 mi/80 km NNW of Eau Claire; 45°30′N 91°44′W. Commercial center for dairying and cattle-raising area; cheese; light mfg. Has park containing Native Amer. mounds. Univ. of Wis. Speedway. Nearby are lake resorts. City grew as a lumbering town. W terminus of Tuscobia State Trail to N. Hardscrabble Ski Area to E. Inc. 1887.

Rice Lake, Aitkin co., E central Minn., 15 mi/24 km E of Aitkin, in Rice Lake Natl. Wildlife Refuge; 4 mi/6.4 km long, 2 mi/3.2 km wide; 46°35′N 98°08′W. Drains NE through short stream (paralleled by manmade channel) to Rice R. Also known as Big Rice L.

Rice Lake, Ill.: see BANNER.

Rice Point, cape on S coast of P.E.I., Canada, on Northumberland Strait, at W side of Hillsborough Bay entrance, 9 mi/14 km SW of Charlottetown; 48°08′N 63°13′W.

Riceboro, town (1990 pop. 745), Liberty co., SE Ga., 31 mi/50 km SW of Savannah; 31°44′N 81°26′W. Mfg. (water treatment chemicals, lumber).

Rices Landing, borough (1990 pop. 457), Greene co., SW Pa., 10 mi/16 km ENE of Waynesburg, on Monongahela R. at mouth of Pumpkin Run; 39°57′N 79°59′W. Subsurface bituminous coal mining; hay; sheep; dairying.

Riceville, town (1990 pop. 827), on border of Howard and Mitchell cos., NE Iowa, on Wapsipinicon R., and 15 mi/24 km NE of Osage; 43°21′N 92°32′W.

Rich, county (□ 1,086 sq mi/2,813 sq km; 1990 pop. 1,725), N Utah; ⊙ Randolph; 41°37′N 111°14′W. Agr. (alfalfa, barley, wheat) and livestock (cattle, sheep) area bordering on Idaho (N) and Wyo. (E), drained in E by Bear R. Part of Wasatch Natl. Forest and Wasatch Range in W, S half of Bear L. in N. On Bear L., Bear Lake State Park on W shore, Rendezvous Beach State Park on S end, Cisco Beach State Park on E shore. Neponset Reservoir in S. Formed 1864.

Rich Creek, town (1990 pop. 670), Giles co., SW Va., 5 mi/8 km NW of Pearisburg, on New R. at mouth of Rich Creek, in small pocket bounded NE, NW, SW by W. Va.; 37°22′N 80°49′W. Mfg. (mining prods., industrial prods., meat processing); agr. (cattle, poultry; alfalfa, apples); coal mining.

Rich Hill, city (1990 pop. 1,317), Bates co., W Mo., near Marais des Cygnes R., 12 mi/19 km S of Butler; 38°06′N 94°21′W. Corn, wheat, sorghum; cattle. Center of a former coal-mining region.

Rich Mountain 1 ridge, W Randolph co., E W.Va., 1 of 2 ridges of same name in Randolph co., in the Allegheny Mts. From Tygart R. bend W of Elkins, extends c.25 mi/40 km SSW toward Elk R., here merging into a high plateau; rises to Whitman Knob (3,930 ft/1,198 m) near S end. Laurel Ridge is its N continuation. On mt. W of Beverly was fought (July 11, 1861) Civil War battle of Rich Mt., a Union victory. **2** ridge, NE Randolph co., E W.Va., 1 of 2 ridges of same name in Randolph co., in the Allegheny Mts. It lies bet. Laurel Fork R. (W) and Gandy Creek (E) (headstreams of Cheat R.); from Tucker-Randolph co. line, extends

17 mi/27 km S through Randolph co., in Monongahela Natl. Forest; c.3,000 ft/914 m in N; up to 4,335 ft/1,321 m in S.

Rich Square, town (1990 pop. 1,058), Northampton co., NE N.C., 25 mi/40 km SE of Roanoke Rapids; 36°16′N 77°16′W. Mfg. (apparel).

Richard B. Russell Lake, reservoir (□ 42 sq mi/109 sq km), in Elbert co., NE Ga. and Abbeville co., S.C., on Savannah R., 52 mi/84 km NW of Augusta (Ga.); 34°02′N 82°34′W. Max. capacity 1,488,155 acre-ft. Formed by Richard B. Russell Dam (195 ft/59 m high), built (1985) by Army Corps of Engineers for power generation; also used for flood control and recreation. Richard B. Russell State Park on W bank.

Richard City, town, Marion co., S Tenn., on Ala. border, near Tennessee R., 23 mi/37 km W of Chattanooga. In farm area.

Richard Collinson Inlet, N Victoria Isl., SW Franklin dist., N.W.T., Canada, arm (80 mi/129 km long, 15 mi/24 km–30 mi/48 km wide) of Viscount Melville Sound; 73°00′N 113°00′W.

Richards, town (1990 pop. 106), Vernon co., W Mo., near Marmaton R., 12 mi/19 km WNW of Nevada; 37°54′N 94°33′W. Sorghum, wheat, corn, hay; cattle.

Richards Island, NW Mackenzie dist., N.W.T., Canada, in Beaufort Sea of the Arctic Ocean, at mouth of Mackenzie R. delta, 60 mi/97 km NNW of Inuvik; 50 mi/80 km long, 6 mi/9.7 km–25 mi/40 km wide; 69°30′N 134°30′W. Port Tuktoyaktuk to E. Isl. forms part of the Reindeer Grazing Reserve.

Richardson, county (□ 555 sq mi/1,437 sq km; 1990 pop. 9,937), extreme SE Nebr.; ⊙ Falls City; 40°07′N 95°43′W. Agr. area bordering on Kansas and Mo.; bounded E by Missouri R.; drained by Nemaha R. and its North and South Forks. Lowest point in Nebr. (840 ft/256 m) in SE. Agr. equip.; food processing, feed; corn, soybeans, wheat, sorghum; cattle, hogs; dairying. Indian Cave State Park in NE corner; Verdon L. State Recreation Area at center. Sac and Fox Indian Reservation and Iowa Indian Reservation in SE corner. Extensive flooding along Missouri R. in 1993. Formed 1854.

Richardson, city (1990 pop. 74,840), Dallas and Collin cos., N Texas, suburb 13 mi/21 km N of Dallas; 32°58′N 96°42′W. Drained by Pittman and Rowlett creeks. Mfg. (telecommunications network equip., bone growth stimulators, supercomputers, telephony equip., computer chips, fiber optics). Site of Univ. of Texas at Dallas and Texas A&M Research Center. Founded in the 1850s, inc. as city 1956.

Richardson, Fort, Texas: see JACKSBORO.

Richardson Highway, S Alaska, extends 266 mi/428 km bet. Delta (Alaska Highway, N) and Valdez (S). Runs through Chugach Mts. and Alaska Range. Trans-Alaska Pipeline follows entire highway route. Alaska's first road (1898) known as Valdez Eagle Trail; brought to highway standard in 1920s.

Richardson Lakes, reservoir (□ 12 sq mi/31 sq km), Oxford co., W Maine, on Rapid R., 25 mi/40 km NW of Rumford; 44°47′N 70°55′W. Max. capacity 130,738 acre-ft. Formed by Middle Dam (25 ft/8 m high), built (1883) for power generation.

Richardson, Mount 1 (10,125 ft/3,086 m), SW Alta., Canada, in Rocky Mts. near B.C. border, 32 mi/51 km NW of Banff, in Banff Natl. Park; 51°29′N 116°06′W. **2** (3,885 ft/1,184 m), E Que., Canada, in Shickshock Mts., on N side of Gaspé Peninsula, 65 mi/105 km W of Gaspé.

Richardson Mountains, Canada: see ROCKY MOUNTAINS.

Richardson Park, uninc. town (1990 pop. 1,100), New Castle co., N Del., residential suburb 2 mi/3.2 km SW of Wilmington, near Christina R.; 39°44′N 75°35′W.

Richardson Sound, Cape May co., S N.J., sheltered inlet of the Atlantic, 7 mi/11.3 km NE of Cape May. Joined to Grassy Sound (NE) and Jarvis Sound (S) by Intracoastal Waterway channel.

Richardson Springs, uninc. village, Butte co., N central Calif., in Sierra Nevada foothills, 9 mi/14.5 km NNE of Chico, near Rock Creek.

Richardton, village (1990 pop. 625), Stark co., W N.Dak., 23 mi/37 km E of Dickinson; 46°52′N 102°18′W. Assumption Abbey, with junior col., is here.

Richboro (RICH-buhr-o), uninc. town (1990 pop. 5,332), Bucks co., SE Pa., residential suburb 19 mi/31 km NNE of Philadelphia and 12 mi/19 km W of Trenton, N.J.; 40°13′N 75°00′W. Light mfg. Dairying; livestock, poultry; grain, apples, nursery stock. U.S. Naval Air Development Center to W. Springfield L. reservoir to SE; Tyler State Park to NE.

Richburg 1 village (1990 pop. 494), Allegany co., W N.Y., 14 mi/23 km E of Olean; 42°05′N 78°09′W. **2** village (1990 pop. 405), Chester co., N S.C., 12 mi/19 km E of Chester; 34°43′N 81°01′W. Mfg. (glass, plastics, linens, rolled steel). Timber; poultry, livestock; dairying; grain, sorghum.

Riche, Point (rish), promontory on Gulf of St. Lawrence, NW N.F., Canada, on S side of entrance of St. John Bay; 50°43′N 57°27′W. Lighthouse.

Richelieu (RISH-loo), county (□ 221 sq mi/572 sq km), S Que., Canada, on the St. Lawrence; ⊙ Sorel; 46°00′N 73°00′W.

Richelieu, town (1991 pop. 2,843), S Que., Canada, on Richelieu R., at S end of Chambly Basin, 16 mi/26 km E of Montreal; 45°27′N 75°15′W. Dairying; vegetables.

Richelieu (RISH-lee-uhr), river, c.75 mi/121 km long; issuing from the N end of L. Champlain, on the N.Y.-Que., Canada border; flows N across S Que. to the St. Lawrence R. at Sorel. It is a link in the waterway connecting the Hudson and St. Lawrence rivers. Visited (1609) by Samuel de Champlain, the Fr. explorer, the river was the route of early explorers. It was an important military corridor in the Fr. and Indian War, in the Amer. Revolution, and in the War of 1812. There are pulp and paper mills along its banks. Fort Lennox Natl. Historic Park is on Île-aux-Noix near St. Jean.

Richey, village (1990 pop. 259), Dawson co., E Mont., 40 mi/64 km W of Sidney; 47°38′N 105°04′W. Wheat, barley, oats, corn, beans, sugar beets, hay; cattle, sheep, hogs; oil. Kuester Reservoir to NE. Richey Historical Mus.

Richeyville, Pa.: see CENTERVILLE.

Richfield, city (1990 pop. 35,710), Hennepin co., SE Minn., a residential suburb 7 mi/11.3 km S of Minneapolis; 44°52′N 93°16′W. Zinc electroplating, printing and publishing, cabinets, diverse light mfg. Minneapolis–St. Paul Internatl. Airport on E. Fort Snelling State Park and Natl. Cemetery to E; Wood and Richfield lakes in W. Settled c.1851; inc. 1964.

Richfield, town (1990 pop. 5,593), ⊙ Sevier co., S central Utah, on Sevier R., and 140 mi/225 km S of Salt Lake City; 38°46′N 112°05′W. Elev. 5,482 ft/1,671 m. Service and trade center for agr. and livestock area; dairying; cattle; alfalfa, barley. Coal and gypsum mines nearby. Sections of Fishlake Natl. Forest SE; West Pavant Mts. to W. Settled 1863 by Mormons.

Richfield 1 village (1990 pop. 383), Lincoln co., S Idaho, 15 mi/24 km NE of Shoshone, and on Little Wood R.; 43°03′N 114°10′W. Elev. 4,280 ft/1,305 m. RR junction and trade center in irrigated area (cattle; dairying; oats, corn, barley); cheese and whey. **2** village (1990 pop. 50), ⊙ Morton co., SW Kansas, on North Fork Cimarron R., and 23 mi/37 km WNW of Hugoton; 37°16′N 101°46′W. Grain. Cimarron Natl. Grassland to S. **3** village (1990 pop. 535), Stanly co., S central N.C., 9 mi/14.5 km NNW of Albemarle; 35°28′N 80°15′W. Cotton, grain, soybeans; poultry, livestock; dairying. Mfg. (apparel). Tuckertown L. dam (Radkin R.) to NE; Uwharrie Natl. Forest to E. **4** village (1990 pop. 3,117), Summit co., NE Ohio, bet. Cleveland and Akron, on State Highway 176, and 1 mi/2 km off U.S. Interstate 77; 41°14′N 81°38′W. **5** village (1990 pop. 159), Washington co., E Wis., 20 mi/32 km NW of Milwaukee; 44°01′N 89°39′W. RR junction. In hilly area; winter sports; mfg. (die cast building). Carmelite church, cathedral, and monasteries nearby.

Richfield Springs, village (1990 pop. 1,565), Otsego co., central N.Y., near N end of Canadarago L., and 21 mi/34 km SE of Utica; 42°51′N 74°59′W. Mfg. (fishing tackle, leather sporting goods). In diversified farming area; health resort until mid 20th cent.; sulphur springs. Inc. 1861, reincorporated 1934.

Richford, town (1990 pop. 2,178), including Richford village, Franklin co., N Vt., on Missisquoi R. at Que. border, and 24 mi/39 km NE of St. Albans; 44°58′N 72°38′W. Port of entry. Maple-sugaring equip.; dairy prods. Settled 1795.

Richgrove, uninc. town (1990 pop. 1,899), Tulare co., S central Calif., 27 mi/43 km N of Bakersfield; 35°48′N 119°06′W. RR junction. Cotton, grain, fruit, nuts, olives, sugar beets; cattle, hogs.

Richibucto (ri-shuh-BUHK-to), town (1991 pop. 1,469), ⊙ Kent co., E N.B., Canada, near mouth of Richibucto R., 40 mi/64 km N of Moncton; 46°41′N 64°52′W. Fishing port (oysters, smelt); lumber trade.

Richibucto River, 50 mi/80 km long, in E N.B., Canada; flows ENE past Richibucto to Northumberland Strait 5 mi/8 km ENE of Richibucto.

Richland 1 county (□ 364 sq mi/943 sq km; 1990 pop. 16,545), SE Ill.; ⊙ Olney; 38°42′N 88°05′W. Bounded partly W by Little Wabash R.; drained by small Fox R. and by Bonpas Creek. Agr. (corn, soybeans, wheat, apples; cattle, poultry; dairying). Oil and natural gas deposits. Some mfg. (food processing, toys, transportation equip.). Formed 1841. **2** county (□ 2,103 sq mi/5,447 sq km; 1990 pop. 10,716), NE Mont.; ⊙ Sidney; 47°48′N 104°34′W. Agr. area bordering on N.Dak. to E; bounded N by Missouri R.; drained in SE by Yellowstone R. Wheat, barley, oats, corn, beans, sugar beets, hay; cattle, sheep, hogs. Oil, coal, limestone. Formed 1914; present boundaries est. 1919. **3** county (□ 1,449 sq mi/3,753 sq km; 1990 pop. 18,148), extreme SE N.Dak.; ⊙ Wahpeton; 46°16′N 96°57′W. Borders S. Dak. on S; Bois de Sioux R. and Red R. of the North form Minn. state line on E. Agr. area watered by Sheyenne and Wild Rice rivers. Corn, wheat, soybeans, sunflowers, sugar beets; poultry, cattle, hogs, sheep. Food processing, wood prods., metal stampings, industrial machinery, electrical equip. Fort Abercrombie Historic Site in E. A portion of (Sisseton) Wahpeton Indian Reservation is in SW. Formed 1873. **4** county (□ 499 sq mi/1,292 sq km; 1990 pop. 126,137), N central Ohio; ⊙ Mansfield; 40°47′N 82°33′W. Drained by forks of Mohican R. In the Till Plains and the Glaciated Plains physiographic regions. Livestock; grain, fruit, potatoes; dairy prods. Mfg. at Mansfield, Shelby, Plymouth. Greenhouses; sand and gravel pits. Formed 1813. **5** county (□ 771 sq mi/1,997 sq km; 1990 pop. 285,720), central S.C.; ⊙ Columbia; 34°01′N 80°54′W. In Sand Hills belt; partly bounded SW by Congaree R., E by Wateree R.; parts of L. Murray and Broad R. in W. Columbia is mfg. and trade center. Processing of sand, clay, shale, granite, kaolin. Eggs; hogs, cattle; corn, oats, hay. Fort Jackson Military Reservation; numerous state parks. Formed 1785. **6** county (□ 589 sq mi/1,526 sq km; 1990 pop. 17,521), S central Wis.; ⊙ Richland Center; 43°22′N 90°25′W. Bounded S by Wisconsin R.; drained by Pine and Kickapoo rivers. Dairying; corn, apples, alfalfa, hay; cattle, hogs, sheep; maple syrup. Eagle Cave in SW. Formed 1842.

Richland, parish (□ 576 sq mi/1,492 sq km; 1990 pop. 20,629), NE La.; ⊙ Rayville; 32°25′N 91°46′W. Bounded W by Bayou Lafourche, on far E by Bayou Macon, on SE by Big Creek. Intersected by Boeuf R. and many bayous. Agr. (cotton, corn, sorghum, hay, rice, soybeans, wheat, vegetables; cattle). Logging, cotton processing, aluminum rolling and drawing, boatbuilding; mfg. apparel, industrial machinery; hunting, fishing. Part of Russell Sage State Wildlife Area in W. Formed 1868.

Richland 1 city (1990 pop. 1,668), Stewart co., SW Ga., 33 mi/53 km SSE of Columbus; 32°05′N 84°41′W. Mfg. (wooden pallets, mobile homes, boat trailers). Inc. 1886. **2** city (1990 pop. 2,029), Pulaski co., central Mo., in the Ozarks, near Gasconade R., 19 mi/31 km NW of Lebanon; 37°51′N 92°24′W. Grain, hay; cattle; mfg. (boats, apparel). Founded c.1870. **3** city (1990 pop. 32,315), Benton co., S Wash., 150 mi/241 km SE of Seattle, on the Columbia R. at mouth of the Yakima R.; 46°17′N 119°17′W. In agr. area (vegetables, fruit, potatoes, alfalfa, wheat; cattle). Mfg. (concrete, structural metal, primary metal prods.). One of the Tri-Cities (a fast-growing metropolis) along with Pasco and Kennewick, both c.10 mi/16 km ESE. It is the hq. of the

U.S. Dept. of Energy Hanford Site (□ 620 sq mi/1,606 sq km), located to N; has visitors' center. The area was settled in 1910, and a small farming hamlet here was taken over (1942) by the U.S. govt. for an atomic bomb development plant. The city was built (1943–1945) to house employees of the project. Federal ownership and management of the city were gradually relinquished, and since 1961 the Hanford Works has been operated by an increasingly large number of private companies. In the 1980s controversy erupted over the issue of nuclear waste disposal at the site. Hanford Science Center. Horse Heaven Hills to SW. Inc. 1958.

Richland 1 town (1990 pop. 522), Keokuk co., SE Iowa, 15 mi/24 km SE of Sigourney; 41°11′N 91°59′W. In livestock and grain area. **2** town (1990 pop. 4,014), Rankin co., central Miss., suburb 4 mi/6.4 km SSE of Jackson, on Pearl R.; 32°13′N 90°09′W. Agr. area (cotton, corn, vegetables; poultry, cattle). Light mfg.

Richland 1 village (1990 pop. 465), Kalamazoo co., SW Mich., 9 mi/14.5 km NE of Kalamazoo; 42°22′N 85°27′W. In farm area. Light mfg. **2** village (1990 pop. 96), Colfax co., E Nebr., 8 mi/12.9 km W of Schuyler, near Platte R.; 41°26′N 97°12′W. **3** village, Atlantic co., S N.J., 8 mi/12.9 km WNW of Mays Landing. In agr. area; poultry. **4** village (1990 pop. 161), Baker co., NE Oregon, 32 mi/51 km E of Baker City, on Eagle Creek, near Powder R.; 44°46′N 117°10′W. Grain, potatoes; cattle; dairy prods. Umatilla Natl. Forest to N. Snake R. 7 mi/11.3 km to E. **5** village (1990 pop. 244), Navarro co., E central Texas, 11 mi/18 km S of Corsicana, near Richland Arm of Richland Chambers Reservoir; 31°55′N 96°25′W. In farm area.

Richland, borough (1990 pop. 1,457), Lebanon co., SE central Pa., 9 mi/14.5 km E of Lebanon, near Tulpehocken Creek; 40°21′N 76°15′W. Mfg. (truck parts, apparel); agr. (apples, soybeans, grain; poultry, livestock; dairying). Middle Creek Waterfowl Management Area to S. Inc. 1906.

Richland Balsam, N.C.: see BALSAM MOUNTAIN.

Richland Center, town (1990 pop. 5,018), ⊙ Richland co., S central Wis., on Pine R., and c.50 mi/80 km WNW of Madison; 43°20′N 90°22′W. Terminus of RR spur from Lone Rock. Center for dairying and livestock-raising region; dairy prods.; mfg. (maple syrup, yogurt, satellite antennas, iron castings). Frank Lloyd Wright b. here. Settled c.1849, inc. 1887.

Richland Chambers Lake, reservoir (□ 8 sq mi/20.7 sq km), Navarro co., NE Texas, on Richland Creek, 60 mi/96 km ESE of Dallas; 31°57′N 96°42′W. Max. capacity 323,879 acre-ft. Formed by Navarro Mills Dam (82 ft/25 m high), built (1963) by Army Corps of Engineers for water supply; also used for recreation and power generation. Also known as Richland Creek Reservoir and Navarros Mills L.

Richland Hills, town (1990 pop. 7,978), Tarrant co., N Texas, suburb 7 mi/11.3 km NE of Fort Worth, on Big Fossil Creek; 32°48′N 97°13′W. Mfg.

Richland Springs, village (1990 pop. 344), San Saba co., central Texas, 36 mi/58 km S of Brownwood; 31°16′N 98°57′W. In agr. and ranch area (peanuts, wheat; cattle).

Richlands 1 town (1990 pop. 996), Onslow co., E N.C., 14 mi/23 km NNW of Jacksonville, near New R.; 34°53′N 77°32′W. RR terminus. Hog production center in agr. area (tobacco, cotton, peanuts, grain; poultry). Hoffmann Forest to E; Catherine L. to S. **2** town (1990 pop. 4,456), Tazewell co., SW Va., in Allegheny Mts., on Clinch R., and 33 mi/53 km WSW of Bluefield; 37°06′N 81°47′W. RR junction. Mfg. (truck bodies, apparel, concrete, printing and publishing). Agr. (tobacco, corn; livestock; dairying); timber, bituminous-coal mining; limestone quarrying. Southwest Va. Community Col. Municipal Airport to W.

Richlandtown, borough (1990 pop. 1,195), Bucks co., SE Pa., 12 mi/19 km SE of Allentown; 40°28′N 75°19′W. Grain; poultry, livestock; dairying. L. Nockamixon reservoir and Nockamixon State Park to E.

Richlawn, village (1990 pop. 435), Jefferson co., N Ky., residential suburb 6 mi/9.7 km E of Louisville; 38°15′N 85°38′W.

Richmond 1 county (□ 489 sq mi/1,267 sq km; 1991 pop. 11,260), NE N.S., Canada, in SW part of Cape Breton Isl.; ⊙ Arichat. **2** county (□ 544 sq mi/1,409 sq km), S Que., Canada, on St. Francis R.; ⊙ Richmond; 45°40′N 72°00′W.

Richmond, city (1991 pop. 126,624), SW B.C., Canada, 6 mi/10 km S of Vancouver, on Lulu and Sea isls. in Fraser R. delta. Strait of Georgia to W. Includes localities of Eburne, on Sea Isl., and Steveston (historic port), on Lulu Isl. Bridges to Vancouver (N), New Westminster (NE), Delta (SE); tunnel to Ladner (S). E half of Lulu Isl. is marshy. Vancouver Intl. Airport on Sea Isl. Diversified mfg., shipbuilding, book publishing. Fruit growing, nurseries. Fishing.

Richmond 1 town (1991 pop. 4,037), SE Ont., Canada, 18 mi/29 km SW of Ottawa; 45°11′N 75°50′W. Located in Ottawa-Carleton regional municipality, immediately W of Nepean corporate limit. Dairying; mixed farming. **2** town (1991 pop. 3,123), ⊙ Richmond co., S Que., Canada, on St. Francis R., and 22 mi/35 km NNW of Sherbrooke. Copper, chrome, and steatite mining center; woodworking. In dairying region.

Richmond, village (1991 pop. 1,984), St. Mary parish, N Jamaica, in uplands, on RR, and 20 mi/32 km NNW of Kingston; 18°14′N 76°54′W. Fruit growing; livestock.

Richmond 1 county (□ 328 sq mi/850 sq km; 1990 pop. 189,719), E Ga.; ⊙ Augusta; 33°22′N 82°04′W. Bounded NE by S.C. state line, formed here by Savannah R. Coastal plain agr. (cotton, wheat, soybeans, peanuts, fruit, corn); cattle; dairy prods. Clay mining; timber; mfg. at Augusta. Fort Gordon Military Reservation occupies W part. Formed 1777. **2** county (□ 102 sq mi/264 sq km; 1990 pop. 378,977), SE N.Y., coextensive with the Staten Isl. borough of N.Y. city, and with isl. of Staten Isl.; 40°33′N 74°08′W. Formed 1683. **3** county (□ 479 sq mi/1,241 sq km; 1990 pop. 44,518), S N.C.; ⊙ Rockingham; 35°00′N 79°45′W. Bounded S by S.C., W by Pee Dee R. (Great Pee Dee) (forms Blewett Falls L. reservoir), NE by Drowning Creek. Drained in NW by Little R. Forested sand hills (E) and Piedmont region (W). Agr. area (tobacco, cotton, corn, wheat, soybeans, hay, sweet potatoes; poultry, cattle, hogs). Sand and gravel, timber. Sandhills Recreation Area in E. Formed 1779. **4** county (□ 216 sq mi/559 sq km; 1990 pop. 7,273), E Va.; ⊙ Warsaw; 37°56′N 76°43′W. On Northern Neck peninsula, bounded SW by Rappahannock R. Barley, wheat, hay, corn, soybeans; cattle; timber (pine); extensive fish and shellfish industries. Many historic bldgs., some dating from 18th cent. Formed 1692.

Richmond 1 city (1990 pop. 87,425), Contra Costa co., W Calif., 9 mi/14.5 km NNW of Oakland, on peninsula bet. San Francisco Bay (SW) and San Pablo Bay (NW). RR center and bulk transfer point. It is a deepwater commercial port and an industrial center with oil refineries and RR repair shops. Mfg. (machinery and instruments, fabricated metal prods., chemicals, motor vehicles, construction materials, baked goods), ship building, printing and publishing, and biotechnology development. Richmond–San Rafael Bridge to Marin co. crosses San Pablo Strait 4 mi/6.4 km W. Originally part of a Span. ranch on the site of Native Amer. shell mounds, it grew with the coming of the Santa Fe RR at the turn of the 20th cent. San Pablo Ridge to NE; Point San Pablo to NW. Inc. 1905. **2** city (1990 pop. 38,705), ⊙ Wayne co., E Ind., near the Ohio state line, and 35 mi/56 km SE of Muncie; 39°50′N 84°53′W. It is an industrial city in the fertile Whitewater R. valley. Fabricated metal prods., printing and publishing, construction materials, foods, animal feed, electronics and electrical prods., machinery; motor vehicle assembly, steel fabricating. Earlham Col., a branch of Indiana Vocational Technical Col. (Ivy Tech); and Indiana Univ. East are here. Highest point in Ind. (1,257 ft/383 m, unnamed) is 9 mi/14.5 km N. Settled 1806 by Quakers from N.C.; laid out 1816, inc. as city 1840. **3** city (1990 pop. 21,155), ⊙ Madison co., central Ky., 22 mi/35 km SSE of Lexington, in the Bluegrass region; 37°44′N 84°17′W. It is a tobacco and livestock (cattle and thoroughbred horses) market; diversified mfg. Madison Airport to S. Seat of Eastern Kentucky Univ. (includes Hummel Planetarium). Lexington–Bluegrass Army Depot (chemical weapons) to SE. Valley View Ferry to NW, on Kentucky R. Fort Boonesborough State Park to N; White Hall State Historic Site to NW. Inc. 1798. **4** city (1990 pop. 5,738), NW Mo., ⊙ Ray co., near Missouri R., 35 mi/56 km ENE of Kansas City; 39°16′N 93°58′W. Soybeans, corn, wheat; cattle, hogs; mfg. (nuts and candies, animal feeds, cement blocks). Former coal mines. Laid out 1827. **5** city (1990 pop. 9,801), ⊙ Fort Bend co., SE Texas, on Brazos R., and 27 mi/43 km WSW of Houston; 29°34′N 95°46′W. Shares twin-city status with Rosenberg, 3 mi/4.8 km WSW. In oil-producing, livestock, and agr. area (cotton, vegetables, rice, corn; nurseries); mfg. (steel castings, concrete, cottonseed oil). Here are graves of Erastus "Deaf" Smith (namesake of Deaf Smith co., Texas), Mirabeau B. Lamar. Brazos Bend State Park and George Observatory to SE. Town founded 1822. **6** independent city (□ 62 sq mi/161 sq km; 1990 pop. 203,056), ⊙ Va., separate from adjacent Henrico and Chesterfield cos., E Va., at head of navigation on James R.; 37°31′N 77°28′W. Port of entry and a financial, commercial, shipping, and distribution center, with a deepwater port. Major tobacco market. Highly diversified mfg. Extensive suburban growth has occurred since the 1970s. Trading post est. here in 1637. Fort Charles built in 1645. City laid out in 1737. Capital of Virginia in 1779, raided by Br. in 1781. During the Civil War, Richmond was the capital of the Confederacy and the constant objective of Federal forces. Much of the city was burned during the Confederate evacuation, April 3, 1865. Richmond Natl. Battlefield Park (and Cemetery) includes several of the battlefields to SE and NE. State Capitol bldg. (1785), designed by Thomas Jefferson; Washington Monument; Valentine Mus.; White House of the Confederacy, once home of Jefferson Davis and now Confederate Mus.; St. John's Church (1741), where Patrick Henry made his famous "Give me liberty, or give me death" speech; Edgar Allan Poe Shrine (oldest bldg., built c.1686); Edgar Allen Poe Mus.; Robert E. Lee House (1844); Monument Avenue, with statues of Confederate leaders and Afr. Amer. athlete, Arthur Ashe. Hollywood Cemetery (1847); Maggie L. Walker Natl. Historic Site; Science Mus.; Va. Mus. of Fine Arts. Univ. of Richmond, Va. Commonwealth Univ., Va. Union Univ., Union Theological Seminary, Presbyterian School of Christian Education, J. Sargeant Reynolds Community Col. Va. Deepwater Terminal to S, on James R.; Richmond Internatl. Airport (Byrd Field) to E, includes Va. Aviation Mus. Va. State Fairgrounds to N; Pocahontas State Forest and Park to SW. Swift Creek Reservoir to SW. Settled 1637, inc. as a city 1782.

Richmond 1 town (1990 pop. 3,072), including Richmond village, Sagadahoc co., SW Maine, on the Kennebec R., and 12 mi/19 km N of Bath; 44°07′N 69°49′W. Wood prods. Named for fort here (1719–1754), inc. 1823. **2** town (1990 pop. 1,677), Berkshire co., W Mass., in the Berkshires, 7 mi/11.3 km SW of Pittsfield, near N.Y. state line; 42°23′N 73°22′W. Resort area. **3** town (1990 pop. 965), Stearns co., S central Minn., 18 mi/29 km SW of St. Cloud, on Sauk R. (forms Cedar Island L. to S); 45°27′N 94°31′W. In agr. area; mfg. (meat processing, light mfg.). Granite quarries nearby. Small natural lakes in vicinity. **4** town (1990 pop. 877), Cheshire co., SW N.H., 12 mi/19 km S of Keene; 42°45′N 72°16′W. Bounded S by Mass. Little Monadnock Mt. (1,883 ft/574 m) on E boundary. Vegetables, nursery crops; cattle, poultry; dairying; timber. Mfg. (musical instrument accessories). **5** town (1990 pop. 5,351), Washington co., SW R.I., along Wood R., 26 mi/42 km SSW of Providence; 41°30′N 71°40′W. Dairying; farming; light mfg. Includes Wyoming village and parts of Carolina, Shannock, and Usquepaug villages. State park. Set off from Charlestown and inc. 1747. **6** town (1990 pop. 1,955), Cache co., N Utah, near Idaho state line, 13 mi/21 km N of Logan; 41°55′N 111°48′W. Elev. 4,638 ft/1,414 m. Dairying; wheat, barley, fruit, vegetables; cattle; food processing. Mt. Naomi Wilderness Area of Wasatch Natl. Forest to E. Settled by Mormons 1859. **7** town (1990 pop. 3,729), including Richmond village, Chittenden co., NW Vt., on Winooski R., and 12 mi/19 km SE of Burlington; 44°23′N 72°59′W. Dairy prods., lumber. Bolton Valley and Cochran ski areas are nearby. Has 16-sided church (1812), one of 1st U.S. community churches. Settled 1775, formed 1794.

Richmond 1 village (1990 pop. 1,016), McHenry co., NE Ill., on Wis. state line, satellite community of Chicago, 25 mi/40 km WNW of Waukegan, across from Genoa City, Wis.; 42°28′N 88°18′W. In agr. and dairying area; mfg. (plastics prods., hardware, laboratory prods.). **2** village (1990 pop. 528), Franklin co., E Kansas, 15 mi/24 km S of Ottawa; 38°23′N 95°15′W. In livestock and grain region. **3** village (1990 pop. 447), Madison parish, NE La., 1 mi/2 km SE of Tallulah; 32°23′N 91°11′W. In agr. area (cotton, soybeans, corn; cattle). **4** village (1990 pop. 4,141), Macomb co., SE Mich., 16 mi/26 km NE of Mt. Clemens; 42°48′N 82°45′W. Satellite community of Detroit, in dairying and grain-growing area. RR junction. Mfg. (tube bending, wooden trusses, machining). Settled 1836, inc. 1879. **5** village (1990 pop. 446), Jefferson co., E Ohio, 9 mi/14 km WNW of Steubenville; 40°26′N 80°46′W. In agr. area.

Richmond, Ohio: see GRAND RIVER, village.

Richmond Beach, uninc. town (1990 pop. 5,000), King co., W Wash., residential suburb 11 mi/18 km N of Seattle, on Puget Sound.

Richmond Great House (RICH-mun), estate, hamlet of Belle Garden, N coast, Tobago, Rep. of Trinidad and Tobago. Restored 18th-cent. house on cocoa and coconut plantation.

Richmond Heights 1 city (1990 pop. 10,448), St. Louis co., E Mo., suburb 7 mi/11.3 km W of St. Louis; 38°37′N 90°19′W. Significant commercial and office development spillover from neighboring Clayton to N; light mfg. **2** city (1990 pop. 9,611), Cuyahoga co., N Ohio, a NE suburb of Cleveland; 41°33′N 81°30′W.

Richmond Heights, town (1990 pop. 1 sq mi/2.6 sq km; 1990 pop. 8,583), Dade co., SE Fla., 12 mi/19 km SW of Miami; 25°37′N 80°22′W. Richmond Heights Coast Guard facility located here.

Richmond Highlands, uninc. city (1990 pop. 26,037), King co., W Wash., residential suburb 10 mi/16 km N of Seattle, bet. N end of L. Washington (E) and Puget Sound (W); 47°46′N 122°20′W. L. Ballinger to N.

Richmond Hill, suburban town (1991 pop. 80,142), S Ont., Canada, 14 mi/23 km N of Toronto; 43°52′N 79°27′W. Mfg. (radio and television equip., garden equip.; hardware, small appliances, optical instruments, pharmaceuticals), book publishing; copper and aluminum foundry.

Richmond Hill, town (1990 pop. 2,934), Bryan co., SE Ga., 15 mi/24 km SW of Savannah, near Ogeechee R.; 31°56′N 81°19′W. Cranes and hoists, cultured marble, kitchen equip., clocks. Located on site of Ways Station, developed as a planned community by Henry Ford, whose initiative led to improved educational and cultural opportunities for area African-Americans.

Richmond Hill, a residential sect. of central Queens borough of N.Y. city, SE N.Y.; 40°42′N 73°51′W. Some mfg. Pop. was predominantly German and Irish; since the 1970s, the area has seen a large influx of immigrants from the Caribbean and Latin America.

Richmond Island, SW Maine, in Casco Bay off Cape Elizabeth town; 1 mi/1.6 km long, 0.75 mi/1.2 km wide. There was a settlement and trading center here early in 17th cent.

Richmond National Battlefield Park (□ 306 sq mi/793 sq km), E central Va., in Henrico, Hanover, and Chesterfield cos., and city of Richmond. Comprises several Civil War battle sites, including Cold Harbor, Drewry's Bluff, Gaines Mill, and Beaver Dam Creek.

Richmond Valley, a sect. of Richmond co., Staten Isl. borough of N.Y. city, SE N.Y., on S Staten Isl.; 40°31′N 74°14′W.

Richmond–San Rafael Bridge, Contra Costa (E) and Marin (W) cos., W Calif., c.4 mi/6.4 km long, part of the network of bridges serving the San Francisco Bay area. Cantilever bridge. It provides an essential link bet. the east side of San Francisco Bay and the north coastal cos. on the west side of the bay. Crosses San Pablo Strait, passage from San Francisco Bay to San Pablo Bay, its N extension. Connects Richmond (E) with San Rafael (W). San Quentin State Prison immediately S of W end.

Richmondville, village (□ 1 sq mi/2.6 sq km; 1990 pop. 843), Schoharie co., E central N.Y., 40 mi/64 km W of Albany; 42°37′N 74°33′W. Apparel.

Richthofen, Mount, Colo.: see NEVER SUMMER MOUNTAINS.

Richton, town (1990 pop. 1,034), Perry co., SE Miss., 20 mi/32 km E of Hattiesburg, and on Thompsons Creek; 31°21′N 88°56′W. Cotton, corn; poultry; timber; lumber; light mfg. Parts of De Soto Natl. Forest to N and S.

Richton Park, village (1990 pop. 10,523), Cook co., NE Ill., suburb 28 mi/45 km SSW of Chicago; 41°28′N 87°43′W. Some agr.

Richview, village (1990 pop. 307), Washington co., SW Ill., 7 mi/11.3 km ENE of Nashville; 38°22′N 89°10′W. In agr. area.

Richville 1 village (1990 pop. 121), Otter Tail co., W Minn., 26 mi/42 km NE of Fergus Falls; 46°30′N 95°37′W. In small lakes region. Grain, potatoes; dairying. **2** village (1990 pop. 311), St. Lawrence co., N N.Y., on Oswegatchie R., and 20 mi/32 km SSE of Ogdensburg; 44°25′N 75°23′W. In dairying area.

Richwood 1 town (1990 pop. 2,808), Nicholas co., central W.Va., 63 mi/101 km E of Charleston, on Cherry R., in Monongahhela Natl. Forest; 38°13′N 80°32′W. In timber, livestock, and coal region. Hardwood lumber milling, printing and publishing. Corn, apples; cattle, poultry. Cranberry Glades to E (elev. 3,400 ft/1,036 m) in the Allegheny Mts., are noted for flora unusual in W.Va. Inc. as town 1901, as city 1921. **2** town (1990 pop. 1,253), Ouachita parish, NE central La., residential suburb 5 mi/8 km S of Monroe, near Ouachita R.; 32°27′N 92°04′W. In agr. area, Russell Sage State Wildlife Area to E; Ouachita State Wildlife Area to SE. **3** town (1990 pop. 2,732), Brazoria co., SE Texas, residential suburb 3 mi/4.8 km E of Lake Jackson, on Oyster Creek; 29°03′N 95°24′W.

Richwood, village (1990 pop. 2,186), Union co., central Ohio, 13 mi/21 km SW of Marion, near Richwood L.; 40°25′N 83°17′W. In agr. area. Food processing; metal prods.

Rickardsville, village (1990 pop. 171), Dubuque co., NE Iowa, 7 mi/11.3 km WNW of Dubuque; 42°34′N 90°52′W. Corn; hogs, cattle.

Ricketts, town (1990 pop. 105), Crawford co., W Iowa, 14 mi/23 km WNW of Denison; 42°07′N 95°34′W. In agr. area.

Rickreall (rik-ree-AHL), uninc. village (1990 pop. 700), Polk co., NW Oregon, 8 mi/12.9 km W of Salem, on Rickreall Creek. Fruit, grapes; dairying; poultry; wine. Baskett Slough Natl. Wildlife Refuge to NW.

Rico, village (1990 pop. 92), Dolores co., SW Colo., on Dolores R., in San Juan Mts., and 30 mi/48 km NNW of Durango; 37°41′N 108°01′W. Elev. 8,827 ft/2,690 m. Sheep grazing. Formerly a silver and gold mining center; now, nearly a ghost town. Scheduled for housing redevelopment. Surrounded by San Juan Natl. Forest.

Riddle, town (1990 pop. 1,143), Douglas co., SW Oregon, 17 mi/27 km S of Roseburg, on Cow Creek, at confluence with South Umpqua R.; 42°57′N 123°22′W. Nearby nickel deposits.

Riddlesburg, uninc. village, Broad Top township, Bedford co., S Pa., 16 mi/26 km NE of Bedford, on Raystown Branch of Juniata R.; 40°09′N 78°15′W. Bituminous coal in area.

Riddleville, town (1990 pop. 79), Washington co., E central Ga., 10 mi/16 km SE of Sandersville; 32°55′N 82°40′W.

Rideau Canal (ree-DO), 126 mi/203 km long, S Ont., Canada, connecting the Ottawa R. at Ottawa with L. Ontario at Kingston. The canal, which has 47 locks, follows the course of the Rideau R. It was built (1826–1832) by army engineers under the direction of Col. John By to provide access from the St. Lawrence to L. Ontario without exposure to attack by Amer. forces on the U.S. shore of the St. Lawrence. Little used as a commercial waterway, the canal system has become a popular recreation area and scenic attraction.

Rideau Lake, SE Ont., Canada, 45 mi/72 km SW of Ottawa; 20 mi/32 km long, 4 mi/6 km wide. Drained N to the Ottawa by Rideau R. and S to L. Ontario by Cataraqui R.; forms summit level (406 ft/124 m) of Rideau Canal.

Ridge Farm, village (1990 pop. 939), Vermilion co., E Ill.,

15 mi/24 km S of Danville; 39°53′N 87°39′W. In agr. and bituminous coal area; ships grain.

Ridge Manor, town (□ 4 sq mi/10.4 sq km; 1990 pop. 1,947), Hernando co., W central Fla., 15 mi/24 km E of Brooksville; 28°30′N 82°10′W.

Ridge Spring, town (1990 pop. 861), Saluda co., W S.C., 37 mi/60 km WSW of Columbia; 33°51′N 81°39′W. Fertilizer; poultry, cattle; grain, soybeans.

Ridgecrest, city (1990 pop. 27,725), Kern co., S central Calif., c.72 mi/116 km ENE of Bakersfield; 35°38′N 117°40′W. Mfg. related to Naval Air Weapons Station. Cattle in area. Cerro Coso Community Col. China L. (dry) to N; Searles L. (dry) to NE; Death Valley Natl. Monument c.60 mi/97 km NE.

Ridgecrest, town (1990 pop. 804), Concordia parish, E central La., 8 mi/13 km WNW of Natchez, Miss., near Mississippi R.; 31°36′N 91°32′W. In agr. area (rice, pecans, sorghum, wheat; cattle). Catfish.

Ridgedale, village (1991 pop. 122), central Sask., Canada, on Carrot R., and 23 mi/37 km ENE of Melfort. Wheat; livestock.

Ridgefield 1 residential town (1990 pop. 20,919), Fairfield co., SE Conn.; 41°18′N 73°30′W. Agr. in area; nurseries. Pharmaceuticals, electronic research. It has many colonial homes and is noted for its 18th-cent. charm. The battle of Ridgefield (April 27, 1777) was fought here in an effort to stop William Tryon's men from retreating after a raid on Danbury. Inc. 1709. **2** town (1990 pop. 1,297), Clark co., SW Wash., 14 mi/23 km N of Vancouver, and on Lake R., slough of Columbia R.; 45°49′N 122°45′W. Berries, lettuce, potatoes; mfg. (trucks, metal barrels, machinery parts); timber. Ridgefield Natl. Wildlife Refuge to W, in river bottoms; Paradise Point State Park to NF.

Ridgefield, , residential borough (1990 pop. 9,996), Bergen co., NE N.J., 4 mi/6.4 km SSE of Hackensack; 40°49′N 74°01′W. Several corporate hq. are located here. Inc. 1892.

Ridgefield Park, village (1990 pop. 12,454), Bergen co., NE N.J., on the Hackensack R., 3 mi/4.8 km SSE of Hackensack; 40°51′N 74°01′W. Paper goods. Chiefly residential. Inc. 1892.

Ridgeland, city (1990 pop. 11,714), Madison co., central Miss., suburb 10 mi/16 km NNE of Jackson, near Pearl R. (forms Ross Barnett Reservoir to E); 32°25′N 90°07′W. Agr. to W (cotton, corn, soybeans; cattle, poultry; dairying). Mfg. (steel fabrication, computer keyboards, printing, concrete and plastic prods., food processing equip.). Natchez Trace (Natl.) Parkway passes through city; 13 mi/21 km incomplete sect. WSW to Clinton.

Ridgeland, town (1990 pop. 1,071), ⊙ Jasper co., S S.C., 30 mi/48 km NNE of Savannah, Ga.; 32°28′N 80°58′W. Mfg. (asphalt, banjos and guitars; lumber); agr. (grain, soybeans). Savannah R. Natl. Wildlife Refuge to S.

Ridgeland, village (1990 pop. 246), Dunn co., W Wis., 22 mi/35 km N of Menomonie; 45°12′N 91°54′W. In dairying area; mfg. (recycling equip.). Hunting and state fishery.

Ridgeley, town (1990 pop. 779), Mineral co., NE W.Va., in Eastern Panhandle, on North Branch Potomac R. (bridged at sharp bend in river), opposite (1 mi/1.6 km S of) Cumberland, Md.; 39°38′N 78°46′W. Cumberland Municipal Airport (W.Va.) to SE. Settled 1747; Fort Ohio was est. here 1754.

Ridgely 1 town (1990 pop. 1,034), Caroline co., E Md., 16 mi/26 km NE of Easton; 38°57′N 75°53′W. Vegetable canneries, apparel mfg. The town was laid out in 1867 as a speculative venture. Univ. of Md. agr. substation here. Tuckahoe State Park nearby. **2** town (1990 pop. 1,775), Lake co., extreme NW Tenn., near the Mississippi, 8 mi/13 km S of Tiptonville; 36°15′N 89°28′W. Reelfoot L. to NNE.

Ridgeside, city (1990 pop. 400), Hamilton co., SE Tenn., E suburb of Chattanooga; 35°02′N 85°15′W.

Ridgetop, town (1990 pop. 1,132), on border of Davidson and Robertson cos., N Tenn.,16 mi/26 km N of Nashville; 36°24′N 86°46′W.

Ridgetown, town (1991 pop. 3,246), S Ont., Canada, 15 mi/24 km E of Chatham; 42°26′N 81°53′W. Agr. center; food processing. Has agr. school and experimental farm.

Ridgeville 1 town (1990 pop. 808), Randolph co., E Ind., on Mississinewa R., and 9 mi/14.5 km NNW of Winchester; 40°17′N 85°02′W. Livestock and grain area; mfg. (mobile homes); stone quarrying. Settled 1817, laid out 1837, inc. 1868. **2** town (1990 pop. 1,625), Dorchester co., SE central S.C., 9 mi/14.5 km NW of Summerville; 33°05′N 80°18′W. Lumber prods., graphite electrodes. Poultry, livestock; grain, cotton, soybeans. Givhans Ferry State Park to SW.

Ridgeway, city (1990 pop. 379), Harrison co., NW Mo., 10 mi/16 km NE of Bethany; 40°22′N 93°56′W. Corn, soybeans; cattle.

Ridgeway 1 town (1990 pop. 295), Winneshiek co., NE Iowa, 10 mi/16 km W of Decorah. In agr. area. **2** town (1990 pop. 752), Henry co., S Va., near N.C. state line, 7 mi/11.3 km S of Martinsville; 36°34′N 79°51′W. Mfg. (furniture, clocks, particleboard); agr. (tobacco; poultry, cattle).

Ridgeway 1 village (1990 pop. 378), on Hardin-Logan co. line, W central Ohio, 10 mi/16 km S of Kenton; 40°31′N 83°34′W. **2** village (1990 pop. 407), Fairfield co., N central S.C., 22 mi/35 km N of Columbia; 34°18′N 80°57′W. Textiles, gold and silver prods. Cattle; corn, hay. **3** village (1990 pop. 577), Iowa co., S Wis., 8 mi/12.9 km ENE of Dodgeville; 43°00′N 89°59′W. In dairy and livestock region. On Military Ridge State Trail.

Ridgewood, residential village (1990 pop. 24,152), Bergen co., NE N.J.; 40°58′N 74°06′W. It was the site of many Amer. and Br. camps in the Revolutionary War. Inc. 1876.

Ridgewood, a residential sect. of N Brooklyn and S Queens boroughs of N.Y. city, SE N.Y.; 40°42′N 73°55′W. Some mfg.

Ridgway 1 village (1990 pop. 423), Ouray co., SW central Colo., on Uncompahgre R., near San Juan Mts. to SE, and 10 mi/16 km NNW of Ouray; 38°09′N 107°45′W. Elev. 6,985 ft/2,129 m. Picturesque town and vicinity; site for filming of *True Grit.* Ridgway State Recreation Reservoir and Area to N; parts of Uncompahgre Natl. Forest to SE and NW; Uncompahgre Plateau to NW. **2** village (1990 pop. 1,103), Gallatin co., SE Ill., c.12 mi/19 km W of junction of Wabash and Ohio rivers, and 8 mi/12.9 km NNW of Shawneetown; 37°47′N 88°15′W. Agr. (corn, soybeans); coal, oil, and natural gas; mfg. (popcorn). Inc. 1886.

Ridgway (RIDHZH-wai), borough (1990 pop. 4,793), ⊙ Elk co., N central Pa., 9 mi/14.5 km W of St. Mary's, on Clarion R.; 41°25′N 78°43′W. Mfg. (pigments, tool and die, lumber, leather prods.; printing and publishing); natural gas; timber. Agr. (hay; livestock; dairying). Settled 1822, laid out 1833, inc. 1881.

Riding Mountain National Park, (□ 1,148 sq mi/2,973 sq km), SW Man., Canada, 10 mi/16 km S of Dauphin, and W of L. Manitoba; A wooded region with small glacial lakes, on the highest part of the Manitoba escarpment (Riding Mt. 2,200 ft/671 m), it is a recreation area and animal sanctuary. Est. 1929.

Ridley Park (RID-lee), borough (1990 pop. 7,592), Delaware co., SE Pa., suburb 10 mi/16 km SW of Philadelphia; 39°52′N 75°19′W. Mfg. (printing). Founded 1870, inc. 1888.

Ridott, village (1990 pop. 156), Stephenson co., N Ill., on Pecatonica R., and 7 mi/11.3 km E of Freeport; 42°17′N 89°28′W. In agr. area.

Riegelsville (REE-guhlz-vil), village, Warren co., NW N.J., on Delaware R., at mouth of Musconetcong R., and 7 mi/11.3 km S of Phillipsburg.

Riegelsville (REE-guhls-vil), borough (1990 pop. 912), Bucks co., E Pa., 7 mi/11.3 km S of Easton, on Delaware R. (bridged), opposite mouth of Musconetcong R. (N.J.); 40°36′N 75°12′W. Light mfg. Apples, soybeans, grain; poultry, livestock; dairying. Roosevelt State Park to SE.

Riegelwood (REE-guhl-wud), uninc. town (1990 pop. 1,090), Columbus co., SE N.C., 20 mi/32 km WNW of Wilmington, near Cape Fear R. Agr. area (tobacco, cotton, peanuts, grain; cattle, hogs); timber. Mfg. (lumber, industrial chemicals, paperboard and pulp).

Rienzi (REN-zee), village (1990 pop. 339), Alcorn co., NE Miss., 12 mi/19 km S of Corinth; 34°45′N 88°31′W. In agr. area (cotton, corn, soybeans; cattle); mfg. (apparel).

Riesel, town (1990 pop. 839), McLennan co., E central Texas, 13 mi/21 km ESE of Waco; 31°28′N 96°55′W. In agr. area (dairying; cattle; cotton, corn, wheat). Tradinghouse Creek Reservoir to N.

Rifle, town (1990 pop. 4,636), Garfield co., W Colo., on Colorado R. at mouth of Rifle Creek, and 24 mi/39 km W of Glenwood Springs; 39°32′N 107°46′W. Elev. 5,345 ft/1,629 m. Trading point in sheep, cattle, oats, hay area. Sodium bicarbonate, light mfg. Oil and gas wells in vicinity. Nearby Rifle Gap Park is scenic area with waterfalls and hydroelectric plant. Rifle Gap Reservoir and State Park and Rifle Falls State Park to NE; parts of White River Natl. Forest to N; Grand Mesa Natl. Forest to S. The U.S. Naval Oil Shale Reserve is to NW. Inc. 1905.

Rifle Gap Reservoir, Garfield co., W Colo., on Rifle Creek, in Rifle Gap State Park, 7 mi/11.3 km NNE of Rifle; 2 mi/3.2 km long E-W; 39°37′N 107°45′W. Max. capacity of 18,800 acre-ft. East Rifle Creek enters from E. Formed by Rifle Gap Dam (114 ft/35 m high; on S shore), built (1967) by the Bureau of Reclamation for irrigation and flood control.

Rifle Lake, reservoir, Lewis co., W Wash., on Cowlitz R., 28 mi/45 km ESE of Centralia; 15 mi/24 km long; 46°31′N 122°25′W. Max. capacity 1,713,252 acre-ft. Formed by Mossyrock Dam (363 ft/111 m high), built (1968) by Tacoma for power generation and flood control.

Rifle River, c.65 mi/105 km long, in NE and E Mich.; rises in small lakes in Ogemaw co., flows generally SSE past Omer to Saginaw Bay; 44°23′N 84°01′W. Known for its fishing. Its West Branch rises in Ogemaw co., flows c.15 mi/24 km SE past city of West Branch to main stream.

Rifton, village (1990 pop. 650), Ulster co., SE N.Y., in Hudson River Valley, 6 mi/9.7 km SSE of Kingston; 41°50′N 74°02′W. Site of Woodcrest, a 400-member Anabaptist community which makes wooden playground equip., furniture, and equip. for the disabled. The community has its own air charter service. Rifton is nicknamed "the explosive town" because it is the hq. of Lafflin and Rand Powder Company. In mid-1800s, a large number of mills were built here to exploit the area's water power potential. During Prohibition, the village was known for its top-quality applejack. Birthplace of anti-slavery orator Sojourner Truth (1797–1883).

Rigaud (ree-GO), suburb (1991 pop. 2,503) of Montreal, S Que., Canada, near L. of the Two Mountains, 35 mi/56 km W of Montreal; 45°29′N 74°18′W. Mfg. (frozen foods); in agr. region (apples).

Rigby, city (1990 pop. 2,681), ⊙ Jefferson co., E Idaho, 14 mi/23 km NNE of Idaho Falls, inside bend of Snake R. (to NE and W); 43°40′N 111°55′W. Elev. 4,949 ft/1,508 m. Shipping point for irrigated farming and dairying area; sugar beets, potatoes; logging; mfg. (vodka, log homes, animal feeds). Kelly Canyon Ski Area to E. Settled 1884 by Mormons, inc. as village 1903, as city 1915.

Riggins, village (1990 pop. 443), Idaho co., central Idaho, on Salmon R., and 37 mi/60 km SSW of Grangeville; 45°25′N 116°19′W. Elev. 1,800 ft/549 m. Mfg. (lodgepole furniture); logging; summer recreation; rafting. In mountain time zone; Pacific time zone across Salmon R. Part of Hells Canyon Natl. Recreation Area to SW; Nez Perce Natl. Forest to E and W; Golden Hump Wilderness Area to E.

Rigolet (ri-go-LEHT), settlement (1991 pop. 334), SE Lab., Canada, at head of Hamilton Inlet, at mouth of channel draining L. Melville; 54°11′N 58°25′W. Fishing, lumbering.

Rigolets, The (RI-guh-leez), navigable waterway, c.9 mi/14 km long, connecting L. Borgne (E) and L. Pontchartrain (W), SE La., 30 mi/48 km ENE of New Orleans; 30°09′N 89°37′W. Part of Intracoastal Waterway system, forms NE boundary of New Orleans. Fort Pike State Commemorative Area near W end.

Rikers Island (□ 0.6 sq mi/1.6 sq km), SE N.Y., in East R. bet. the Bronx (of which it is a part) and Queens boroughs of N.Y. city; 40°48′N 73°53′W. Site of main city prison since 1935.

Riley, county (□ 622 sq mi/1,611 sq km; 1990 pop. 67,139), NE Kansas; ⊙ Manhattan; 39°17′N 96°43′W. Level to rolling plain, bounded E by Tuttle Creek Reservoir, Big Blue R.; drained in S by Kansas R. Wheat, rye, corn, hay, apples, strawberries; cattle, sheep, hogs, poultry. Fort Riley Military Reserve in S. Formed 1855.

Riley, town (1990 pop. 232), Vigo co., W Ind., 8 mi/12.9 km SE of Terre Haute; 39°23′N 87°18′W. Meat processing; bituminous-coal mines. Laid out 1836.

Riley, village (1990 pop. 804), Riley co., NE Kansas, 15 mi/24 km WNW of Manhattan; 39°17′N 96°49′W. Grain-shipping point in agr. area.

Riley, Fort, Kansas: see FORT RILEY.

Rillito (ree-YEE-to), [Span. = little river], uninc. village, Pima co., S Ariz., 17 mi/27 km NW of Tucson. Cotton; cattle. Tucson Mt. Unit of Saguaro Natl. Monument to S.

Rimbey, town (1991 pop. 1,937), S central Alta., Canada, near Gull L., 30 mi/48 km NW of Red Deer; 52°38′N 114°13′W.

Rimersburg (REI-muhrs-buhrg), borough (1990 pop. 1,053), Clarion co., W central Pa., 13 mi/21 km SSW of Clarion; 41°02′N 79°30′W. Mfg. (cookies; lumber); bituminous coal, gas; timber; agr. (corn, hay, potatoes; livestock; dairying). Settled 1829; laid out 1839; inc. 1853.

Rimini (ruh-MI-nee), village, Lewis and Clark co., W central Mont., 12 mi/19 km SW of Helena, on Tenmile Creek. Continental Divide to W; in Helena Natl. Forest.

Rimouski (rim-OO-skee), county (□ 2,089 sq mi/5,411 sq km), E Que., Canada, on the St. Lawrence, and on N.B. border; ⊙ Rimouski; 48°15′N 68°30′W.

Rimouski (rim-OO-skee), town (1991 pop. 30,873), S Que., Canada, on the S shore of the St. Lawrence R., NE of Que.; 48°26′N 68°31′W. A major center for oceanographic research, the town is a health and social services center.

Rimrock Lake, reservoir, 6 mi/9.7 km long, Yakima co., S Wash., on Tieton R., in Cascade Range and in Mt. Baker–Snoqualmie Natl. Forest, c.30 mi/48 km W of Yakima; 46°39′N 121°07′W. Elev. 2,926 ft/892 m. Formed by Tieton Dam (c.230 ft/70 m high), built (1925) for irrigation. Tieton R. rises near Gilbert Peak in Snoqualmie Natl. Forest; flows 45 mi/72 km through Rimrock L.

Rinard, town (1990 pop. 71), Calhoun co., central Iowa, 9 mi/14.5 km SE of Rockwell City; 42°20′N 94°29′W.

Rincón (ring-KON), town, Ciudad de la Habana prov., W Cuba, 12 mi/19 km SSW of Havana; 22°56′N 82°25′W. RR junction in agr. region (sugarcane, tobacco; cattle). Shrine.

Rincón (ring-KON), town (1990 pop. 12,213), W P.R., on coast, 11 mi/18 km NW of Mayagüez; westernmost settlement of the isl. In fruit-growing region; light mfg., fishing, tourism. Recreation, popular surfing area; whale watching. Rincón Lighthouse and Maritime Mus. are part of El Faro Park. Former nuclear plant located in the NE.

Rincon (RING-kuhn), town (1990 pop. 2,697), Effingham co., E Ga., 17 mi/27 km NNW of Savannah; 32°17′N 81°14′W. Mfg. of paper prods., printing and publishing.

Rincon (ring-KON), uninc. village, Doña Ana co., S N.Mex., 5 mi/8 km E of Hatch. Fork in San Francisco RR: one line to El Paso, Tex., another line W to Deming, N.Mex.

Rincón de Romos (ring-KON dai RO-mos), city (1990 pop. 16,965) and township, Aguascalientes, N central Mexico, 24 mi/39 km NNW of Aguascalientes on Mexico Highway 45; 22°13′N 102°20′W. Agr. center (grain, beans, wine, fruits, vegetables; livestock).

Rincón, Lake (rin-KON), freshwater lake (4 mi/6.4 km long), Barahona prov., SW Dominican Republic, 7 mi/11.3 km NW of Barahona city.

Rincon Mountains, in sect. of Coronado Natl. Forest, Pima and Cochise cos., SE Ariz., E of Tucson. Mica Mt. (8,666 ft/2,641 m) is highest point. Rincon Peak (8,482 ft/2,585 m), in S end of range, is 27 mi/43 km ESE of Tucson. In sect. of Coronado Natl. Forest and E part of Saguaro Natl. Monument.

Rincon Peak (ring-KON) (11,600 ft/3,536 m), NW San Miguel co., N N.Mex., in Sangre de Cristo Mts., 23 mi/37 km ENE of Santa Fe. In Santa Fe Natl. Forest.

Rindge, town (1990 pop. 4,941), Cheshire co., SW N.H., 18 mi/29 km SE of Keene; 42°45′N 72°00′W. Bounded S by Mass. state line. Light mfg.; timber; agr. (nursery crops, vegetables; cattle, sheep, poultry; dairying). Franklin Pierce Col. In hilly lake region, notably Hubbard Pond (NE), Contoocook L. (on N boundary), and L. Monomonac (S boundary). Part of Annett State Forest in NE, including Woodbound Ski Touring Area; Cathedral of the Pines in NE

Rinfret, village, S Que., Canada, on North R., and 25 mi/40 km NW of Montreal. Mica mining.

Ringgold, county (□ 538 sq mi/1,393 sq km; 1990 pop. 5,420), S Iowa, on Mo. line (S); ⊙ Mount Ayr; 40°44′N 94°14′W. Rolling prairie agr. area (hogs, cattle, poultry; corn, oats) drained by Little Platte and East Fork Grand rivers. Bituminous-coal deposits; fish hatchery at center. Some flooding occurred in 1993. Formed 1847.

Ringgold 1 town (1990 pop. 1,675), ⊙ Catoosa co., NW Ga., 13 mi/21 km SE of Chattanooga, Tenn.; 34°55′N 85°07′W. Battle of Ringgold fought here in 1863 during the Civil War. Mfg. includes acetylene gas, lumber, carpets, printing and publishing, sawmill equip., office furniture, telephones. Inc. 1847. **2** town (1990 pop. 1,856), Bienville parish, NW La., 30 mi/48 km ESE of Shreveport; 32°20′N 93°17′W. In cotton, lumber, and general farming area (peaches, watermelons, squash; cattle; dairying); mfg., lumber milling; oil field nearby. L. Bistineau is W; L. Bistineau State Game and Fish Preserve to NW; Loggy Bayou State Wildlife Area to SW.

Ringgold, uninc. village (1990 pop. 100), Montague co., N Texas, 32 mi/51 km E of Wichita Falls, near Red R. In farm area.

Ringgold, Fort, Texas: see RIO GRANDE CITY.

Ringling, town (1990 pop. 1,250), Jefferson co., S Okla., 26 mi/42 km W of Ardmore; 34°10′N 97°35′W. In agr. area (grain; sheep, cattle).

Ringling, village (1990 pop. 70), Meagher co., S central Mont., on Sixteenmile Creek, and 44 mi/71 km NNE of Bozeman. Mfg. (ethyl alcohol [ethanol]); agr. (wheat, barley, oats, hay; cattle). Originally called Leader.

Ringsted, town (1990 pop. 481), Emmet co., NW Iowa, 18 mi/29 km ESE of Estherville; 43°17′N 94°30′W. Livestock, grain; pontoon and paddle boats.

Ringtown, borough (1990 pop. 853), Schuylkill co., E central Pa., 3 mi/4.8 km NNW of Shenandoah; 40°51′N 76°14′W. Mfg. (plastic prods., doors and windows); agr. (hay, potatoes; poultry; dairying).

Ringwood, borough (1990 pop. 12,623), Passaic co., N N.J., in the Ramapo Mts., 15 mi/24 km NNW of Paterson, and on the Wanaque R. near the N.Y. state line; 41°06′N 74°16′W. Iron was found nearby in 1730; mines and works were developed from 1764 by Peter Hasenclever, who made Ringwood Manor his hq. His successor, Robert Erskine, produced munitions during the Amer. Revolution. Other owners of the Ringwood properties included Peter Cooper and Abram S. Hewitt. Presented to the state in 1936, the estate (95 acres/38 ha) became (1939) a park and the manor house was converted into a mus. Ringwood Manor has been designated a natl. historic landmark.

Ringwood, village (1990 pop. 394), Major co., NW Okla., 20 mi/32 km W of Enid; 36°22′N 98°14′W. In agr. area (grain; livestock).

Rio 1 (REE-o), town (1990 pop. 1,054), Martin co., E central Fla., 2 mi/3.2 km N of Stuart across the St. Lucie R.; 27°13′N 80°14′W. **2** uninc. town, Albemarle co., N central Va., residential suburb 5 mi/8 km NE of Charlottesville, near Rivanna R.; 38°04′N 78°27′W.

Rio 1 village (1990 pop. 260), Knox co., NW Ill., 14 mi/23 km N of Galesburg; 41°06′N 90°24′W. Hogs, cattle; dairying; soybeans, corn. **2** village (1990 pop. 768), Columbia co., S central Wis., 13 mi/21 km SE of Portage; 43°27′N 89°14′W. In agr. area (grain, potatoes; dairying); lime works; light mfg.

Rio Arriba (REE-o uh-REE-buh), county (□ 5,896 sq mi/15,271 sq km; 1990 pop. 34,365), NW N.Mex.; ⊙ Tierra Amarilla; 36°30′N 106°42′W. Cattle and sheep grazing and agr. (chilis, hay, apples, alfalfa) region. Watered by Rio Grande, Rio Chama, and Rio Brazos; borders in N on Colo. Part of Jicarilla Indian Reservation extends W center; parts of Santa Fe Natl. Forest in S and SE; parts of Carson Natl. Forest in NW and NE; Continental Divide runs N-S through W center; San Juan Mts. in NE; range of Rocky Mts. in NE; Indian pueblos of Pueblo Indians in SE; also San Juan and part of Santa Clara Indian Reservation in SE. San Juan R. (Navajo L. Reservoir) borders co. in NW corner; Navajo L. State Park (Sims Unit) on shore. Heron L. and El Vado L. state parks in center. Ghost ranch visitor center located near Abiquiu. Formed 1852.

Río Azul, Mexico: see HONDO, RÍO.

Rio Blanco, county (□ 3,223 sq mi/8,348 sq km; 1990 pop. 5,972), NW Colo.; ⊙ Meeker; 39°58′N 108°12′W. Bordering on Utah; drained by White R. Sheep, cattle grazing region; hay. Has Colo's richest coal and oil fields. Small L. Avery Reservoir in E. Part of White R. Natl. Forest and Rocky Mts. in E; Piceance State Wildlife Area in N; parts of White River Natl. Forest in E; Routt Natl. Forest in NE. Formed 1889.

Río Blanco, Mexico: see TENANGO DE RÍO BLANCO.

Río Bravo (REE-o BRAH-vo), town (1990 pop. 67,092), N Tamaulipas, Mexico, on the Gulf coastal flatlands, 16 mi/25 km ESE of Reynosa, Mexico; 25°58′N 98°06′W. Located on highway and the RR. Subtropical climate. Agr. (corn, cotton).

Rio Bueno, town (1991 pop. 1,108), Trelawny parish, N Jamaica, at mouth of the small Rio Bueno, on river boundary bet. Trelawny and St. Ann parishes, 12 mi/19 km E of Falmouth; 18°31′N 77°27′W. Sugarcane, tropical fruits, spices. Old Fort Dundas (1778).

Rio Chama, river, c.140 mi/225 km long, Colo. and N.Mex.; rises at Continental Divide, near Banded Peak in San Juan Mts. at Archuleta-Conejos co. line, S Colo.; flows S, into N N.Mex., past Chana through El Vado Reservoir and Dam, and SSE through Abiquiu Reservoir, to Rio Grande 4 mi/6.4 km N of Española, just S of Chamita. Dam (completed 1934) is 175 ft/53 m high; 1,300 ft/396 m long; forms El Vado Reservoir (capacity 200,000 acre-ft.) SW of Tierra Amarilla.

Rio Claro (REE-o KLAH-ro), village, S central Trinidad, Trinidad and Tobago, 33 mi/53 km SE of Port of Spain. In cacao-growing region.

Rio Costilla, N.Mex. and Colo.: see COSTILLA CREEK.

Rio del Mar, uninc. town (1990 pop. 8,919), Santa Cruz co., W Calif., residential suburb E of downtown Santa Cruz, on Monterey Bay, Pacific Ocean; 36°58′N 121°53′W. Seacliff State Beach to NW.

Rio Dell, city (1990 pop. 3,012), Humboldt co., NW Calif., on Eel R., and 20 mi/32 km S of Eureka; 40°30′N 124°07′W. Timber; cattle, sheep. Humboldt Redwoods State Park to SE.

Rio Frio, village (1990 pop. 50), Real co., SW Texas, 28 mi/45 km N of Uvalde, and on Frio R. In goat, sheep, cattle ranching area. Scenic Frio Canyon here is vacation area; Garner State Park to S.

Rio Grande, county (□ 913 sq mi/2,365 sq km; 1990 pop. 10,770), S Colo.; ⊙ Del Norte; 37°36′N 106°23′W. Irrigated agr. and mining (gold, silver) region, source of San Juan R. in SW corner, drained by Rio Grande. Wheat, hay, oats, barley, potatoes; sheep, cattle. San Juan Mts. in W; Continental Divide passes through SW corner. Part of San Juan Natl. Forest in SW corner; part of Rio Grande Natl. Forest dominates ⅔ of co. Formed 1874.

Río Grande, city (1990 pop. 26,554) and township, Zacatecas state, N central Mexico, on central plateau, on RR, and 85 mi/137 km NNW of Zacatecas on Mexico Highway 49; 23°50′N 103°02′W. Agr. center (cereals, sugarcane, tobacco, maguey; livestock). Also called Ciudad de Río Grande.

Río Grande (REE-o GRAHN-dai), town (1990 pop. 45,648), NE P.R., near the coast, 19 mi/31 km ESE of San Juan. Industrial and tourism center. Mfg. (cement, plastic, electric, and pharmaceutical prods.). Several celebrated golf courses in area. Luquillo Forest and El Yunque Natl. Forest nearby.

Rio Grande (REE-o GRAND), village (1990 pop. 995), Gallia co., S Ohio, 10 mi/16 km WNW of Gallipolis; 38°53′N 82°22′W. Seat of Rio Grande Col.

Rio Grande, river, c.1,885 mi/3,034 km long; rises in E San Juan co., SW Colo. in the San Juan Mts. at the Continental Divide; flows S past Alamosa, Colo., then through the middle of N.Mex. past Taos, and South Cruz, through Cochita L. reservoir, past Albuquerque, through Elephant and Caballo reservoirs, past Las Cruces, N.Mex., to El Paso, Texas (forms Texas- N.Mex. state boundary c.20 mi/32 km above El Paso), then coursing generally SE as the U.S-Mexico border, bet. Texas and Mexican states of Chihuahua, Cauhuila, Nuevo Leon, and Tamaulipas, making a big bend (see BIG BEND NATIONAL PARK), and eventually emptying into the Gulf of Mexico at Brownsville, Texas, and Matamoros, Mexico. Other paired towns are Laredo, Texas, and Nuevo Laredo, Mexico; and El Paso, Texas, and Juárez, Mexico. Brownsville reached by ship canal that parallels river. From El Paso, Rio Grande flows SE, around Big Bend Natl. Park, through Amistad Reservoir, past Del Rio, Texas; Piedas Negras, Mexico; Laredo, Texas/Nuevo Laredo, Mexico; through Falcon Reservoir, past Reynosa, Mexico, finally past Brownsville, Texas, and Matamoras, Mexico. Pueblos were thriving on its banks N of Las Cruces, N.Mex., and the Native Americans were practicing irrigation of the arid country, when Span. explorer Francisco Vásquez de Coronado arrived (1540). Dams on the Rio Grande are used for irrigation, flood control, and regulation of the river flow. Elephant Butte Dam (completed 1916) and Caballo Dam (completed 1938) in N.Mex. create reservoirs that serve large areas. Further downstream N of Del Rio, Texas, is the Amistad Dam (completed 1969), it is 6 mi/9.7 km long and impounds a huge reservoir. Amistad Natl. Recreation Area is there. Below Laredo are Falcon Dam (completed 1954) and its large reservoir. Near the mouth of the Rio Grande is the citrus-fruit and vegetable-farm region commonly called the Rio Grande Valley and developed principally in the 1920s. An agreement bet. the U.S. and Mexico in 1945 provided for future projects to share the river's water. Shifts in the river's channel have led to border disputes bet. the U.S. and Mexico. Parts of its bed have been stabilized by canalization, and an internatl. border commission mediates disputes. The 114-year controversy over the location of the border at El Paso was finally settled in 1968 when the water of the Rio Grande was diverted into a concrete channel. The river is known to the Mexicans as Río Bravo del Norte. Shallow river makes easy illegal crossings by Latin American immigrants.

Río Grande, river, c.150 mi/241 km long, in Jalisco and Michoacán, W Mexico; rises in mts. SW of Jiquilpan near Jalisco-Michoacán border; flows S and E to the Río Balsas (Guerrero border) 25 mi/40 km S of La Huacana. Empties into Infiernillo Reservoir. Also called Río Tepalcatepec.

Rio Grande City, city (1990 pop. 9,891), Starr co., extreme S Texas, 37 mi/60 km WNW of McAllen, and on the Rio Grande (bridged) opposite Camargo, Mexico; 26°22′N 98°49′W. Elev. 190 ft/58 m. Port of entry and trade, shipping, distribution center for oil and gas, cattle, and irrigated agr. (vegetables, cotton, sorghum); sand and gravel; mfg. (concrete, wood moldings). Nearby is Fort Ringgold, dating from 1848 and made inactive 1944. Area settled by Spanish, c.1753; town founded 1847 as Rancho Davis.

Rio Grande Pyramid, peak (13,821 ft/4,213 m) in San Juan Mts., Hinsdale co., on Continental Divde, SW Colo., 18 mi/29 km SE of Silverton.

Rio Grande Reservoir, 5 mi/8 km long, Hinsdale co., SW Colo., on Rio Grande river, in Rio Grande Natl. Forest, 18 mi/29 km S of Lake City; 37°45′N 106°15′W. Max. capacity of 67,782 acre-ft.; intermittently dry. Formed by Rio Grande Dam (100 ft/30 m high), built (1972) by the San Luis Valley Irrigation Dist. for irrigation.

Rio Grande Wild and Scenic River (9,600 acres/3,885 ha), Brewster and Terrell cos., S Texas; 191.2 mi/307.7 km strip of land on the U.S. shore of the Rio Grande, in Chihuahuan Desert, from E boundary of Big Bend Natl. Park, E to Terrell–Val Verde co. line. Authorized 1978.

Rio Hondo, town (1990 pop. 1,793), Cameron co., extreme S Texas, 24 mi/39 km NW of Brownsville and on Arroyo, Colo.; 26°13′N 97°34′W. Elev. 35 ft/11 m. Barge channel joining Gulf Intracoastal Waterway. In rich irrigated agr. area (sugarcane, cotton, vegetables) of lower Rio Grande valley; mfg. (agr. fertilizer). Laguna Atascosa Natl. Wildlife Refuge to NE.

Rio Hondo (REE-o ON-do), river, c.90 mi/145 km long, SE N.Mex.; formed just E of Sacramento Mts. in S Lincoln co. by confluence of Rio Bonito and Rio Ruidoso; flows past Roswell, to Pecos R. 7 mi/11.3 km E of Roswell.

Río Lagartos (REE-o lah-GAHR-tos), town (1990 pop. 1,690), Yucatan state, SE Mexico, at entrance to channel leading to Lagartos Lagoon, 30 mi/48 km N of Tizimín; 21°36′N 88°08′W. In henequen- and chicle-growing area. Site of Rio Lagartos Natl. Park, sanctuary to a large nesting colony of flamingos.

Río Lagartos National Park, Mexico: see PARQUE NATURAL RÍO LAGARTOS.

Rio Linda, uninc. town (1990 pop. 9,481), Sacramento co., central Calif., residential suburb 9 mi/14.5 km NNE of downtown Sacramento; 38°42′N 121°28′W. Citrus, grain, nursery stock; dairying; poultry. Mfg (concrete blocks, bricks). McClellan Air Force Base to SE; Natomas Airport to SW.

Rio Nido, village, Sonoma co., W Calif., on Russian R., and 16 mi/26 km WNW of Santa Rosa. Winery to SE; Armstrong Redwoods State Reserve to NW.

Río Piedras (REE-o pee-AI-drahs), suburb of San Juan, P.R., with which it was merged in 1951. It is an important transportation hub as well as an industrial, service-oriented, and commercial trading center. The Univ. of P.R. main campus is here, also botanical garden and museum. Most important medical facilities in P.R. New cardiovascular center. Known as "University City," or Ciudad Universitaria.

Rio Puerco 1 (REE-o PWER-ko), river, 100 mi/161 km long, NW N.Mex.; rises c.25 mi/40 km ESE of Gallup in mt. region of McKinley co. at Continental Divide, N.Mex.; flows W, past Gallup, then SW into Apache co., Ariz., passing through the SE part of Navajo Indian Reservation and through center of Petrified Forest Natl. Monument, to Little Colorado R. 2 mi/3.2 km E of Holbrook, in Navajo co. Another Rio Puerco, which flows to the Rio Grande, is c.60 mi/97 km E of the source of this one. **2** river, c.170 mi/274 km long, N central N.Mex.; rises c.40 mi/64 km WNW of Los Alamos in mt. area of NW Sandoval co., near Continental Divide; flows S, past Cuba and bet. Nacimiento Mts. (E) and Sierra Chivato (W), through sections of Cañoncito and Isleta Indian reservations, W of Albuquerque, to Rio Grande 22 mi/35 km N of Socorro; intermittent in upper course. San Jose R. (Rio San Juan) enters from W in Isleta Indian Reservation.

Río Rancho (REE-o RAN-cho), city (1990 pop. 32,512), Sandoval and Bernalillo cos., N central N.Mex., suburb 8 mi/12.9 km N of downtown Albuquerque, on Rio Grande; 35°16′N 106°39′W. Area referred to locally as Silicon Mesa for its computer-based mfg. Mfg. (aerospace parts, laminated counter tops, computer equip., lighting equip., cable harnesses, printing). Coronado State Monument and State Park to N.

Río San Juan (REE-o sahn HWAHN), village (1993 pop. 6,849), Samaná prov., N Dominican Republic, on the coast at mouth of small San Juan R., 40 mi/64 km ESE of Puerto Plata; 19°35′N 70°03′W. Agr. (cacao, coffee, tropical fruits).

Río Tepalcatepec, Mexico: see RÍO GRANDE.

Rio Tinto (REE-o TIN-to), town, NE Nev., Elko co. Company-owned mining town near Mountain City. Mine still open.

Río Verde (REE-o VER-dai), c.180 mi/290 km long, N central Mexico; rises 15 mi/24 km S of Zacatecas; flows S and SW, across Aguascalientes state (there extensively used for irrigation), and into Jalisco to Santiago (Lerma) R. 6 mi/9.7 km NE of Guadalajara. Called Río San Pedro in Aguascalientes.

Rio Vista, city (1990 pop. 3,316), Solano co., central Calif., 28 mi/45 km SSW of Sacramento, and on Sacramento R. (bridged); forms Sacramento Deep Water Channel at this point; center of low-lying agr. area of

Sacramento delta; river port; 38°10′N 121°42′W. Almonds, fruits, grain, sugar beets, tomatoes, beans, sunflowers, safflowers, nursery prods. Natural gas field nearby. Founded 1857; inc. 1894.

Rio Vista, village (1990 pop. 541), Johnson co., N central Texas, 8 mi/12.9 km S of Cleburne, near Nolan Creek; 32°14′N 97°22′W. In cattle, wheat, dairy area. L. Pat Cleburne reservoir to NW.

Rion (REI-uhn), uninc. village, Fairfield co., central S.C., 23 mi/37 km NNW of Columbia. Granite; agr. includes cattle; corn, hay.

Ríoverde (REE-o-VER-dai), city (1990 pop. 42,073) and township, Rioverde municipio, San Luis Potosí, N central Mexico, on interior plateau, on Río Verde, and 65 mi/105 km ESE of San Luis Potosí, on Mexico Highway 70; 21°55′N 99°39′W. Elev. 3,251 ft/991 m. RR terminus. Agr. center (grain, cotton, fruits; livestock). Sometimes called Río Verde.

Rip Van Winkle Hollow, ravine in Greene co., SE N.Y., 21 mi/34 km SW of Catskill, 2.7 mi/4.3 km N of Palenville; 42°13′N 74°01′W. The spot where legendary Rip Van Winkle supposedly took his 20-year nap.

Riparius, resort village (1990 pop. 200), Warren co., E N.Y., in the Adirondacks, on Hudson R., and 27 mi/43 km NNW of Glens Falls; 43°40′N 73°54′W.

Ripley 1 county (□ 447 sq mi/1,158 sq km; 1990 pop. 24,616), SE Ind.; ⊙ Versailles; 39°06′N 85°16′W. Drained by small Laughery and Grahams creeks. Agr. (wheat, corn, tobacco); cattle, hogs; dairying. Limestone quarries; timber. Mfg., including farm-prods. processing, at Batesville and Osgood. Versailles State Park E of Versailles; part of Jefferson Proving Ground in SW. Formed 1816. **2** county (□ 639 sq mi/ 1,655 sq km; 1990 pop. 12,303), S Mo.; ⊙ Doniphan; 36°39′N 90°52′W. In the Ozarks, drained by Current and Little Black rivers. Hay; livestock; timber; rock quarries. Wood-products industries. Part of Mark Twain Natl. Forest in NW quarter. Mfg. at Doniphan and Naylor. Stream-related recreation. Tourism. Formed 1833.

Ripley, city (1990 pop. 6,188), ⊙ Lauderdale co., W Tenn., 22 mi/35 km SSW of Dyersburg; 35°45′N 89°32′W. In timber and farm area; cotton gins; makes wood-framed windows and doors, uniforms, castings. Inc. 1838; rechartered 1901. Open L. (fishing) and natl. wildlife refuge are to the NW.

Ripley 1 town (1990 pop. 445), Somerset co., central Maine, 23 mi/37 km NE of Skowhegan; 45°00′N 69°02′W. In farming region. **2** town (1990 pop. 5,371), ⊙ Tippah co., N Miss., 27 mi/43 km SW of Corinth; 34°43′N 88°56′W. Shipping center for agr., dairying, and timber area; mfg. (furniture, shoe soles and heels, boat oars, upholstery material, oil absorbants, apparel). Holly Springs Natl. Forest to W and NW; Tippah County State Lake to N. Plotted 1835; inc. 1837. **3** town (1990 pop. 3,023), ⊙ Jackson co., W W.Va., 33 mi/53 km SSW of Parkersburg; 38°49′N 81°42′W. Agr. (grain, tobacco, nursery crops); cattle. Gas wells; timber. Mfg. (lumber milling, prefabricated log homes, oil field equipment). Cedar L. State Camp, includes Staats Mill Covered Bridge (1887) to SE; Sarvis Fork Covered Bridge (1889) to W; Frozen Camp Wildlife Management Area to E.

Ripley, village (1991 pop. 635), S Ont., Canada, 8 mi/ 13 km SSE of Kincardine; 44°04′N 81°35′W. Dairying; mixed farming.

Ripley 1 uninc. village, Riverside co., S Calif., 6 mi/ 9.7 km SSW of Blythe, Colorado R. 5 mi/8 km to SE; irrigated desert area. Cotton, alfalfa, melons, grain. RR spur terminus. **2** village (1990 pop. 103), Brown co., W Ill., on La Moine R. (bridged here), and 8 mi/12.9 km ENE of Mt. Sterling; 40°01′N 90°38′W. In agr. area. **3** village (1990 pop. 1,189), Chautauqua co., extreme W N.Y., on L. Erie, 24 mi/39 km SW of Dunkirk; 42°14′N 79°41′W. Mfg. (wood prods., soft drinks); agr. (produce). Summer resort. **4** village (1990 pop. 1,816), Brown co., SW Ohio, on the Ohio, and 15 mi/24 km SSE of Georgetown; 38°44′N 83°51′W. Tobacco warehouses, shoe factory. Laid out 1812. The Rankin home, once a stop on the Underground Railroad, is a state

memorial. **5** village (1990 pop. 376), Payne co., N central Okla., 12 mi/19 km SE of Stillwater, and on Cimarron R; 36°01′N 96°54′W. Grain; livestock; mfg. (goat cheese).

Ripogenus Lake (rip-o-JEEN-uhs), 3 mi/4.8 km long, ½ mi/⅘ km wide, Piscataquis co., N central Maine, 26 mi/42 km NW of Millinocket; joined to S end of Chesuncook L. Ripogenus Dam, at SE end, releases waters into West Branch of Penobscot R.

Ripon, city (1990 pop. 7,455), San Joaquin co., central Calif., on Stanislaus R., a suburb 17 mi/27 km SE of Stockton, and 10 mi/16 km NW of Modesto; 37°45′N 121°08′W. Cattle; dairying; fruits, nuts, wheat, vegetables, nursery prods., grain, sugar beets; mfg. (nut processing, machinery, coffee processing, feeds, conveyors, paper mill). Caswell Memorial State Park to SW. Inc. 1945.

Ripon, town (1990 pop. 7,241), Fond du Lac co., E central Wis., on small Silver Creek, and 20 mi/32 km WNW of Fond du Lac; 43°51′N 88°50′W. RR junction in agr. area; mfg. (iron castings, travel bags, prepared foods, coin-operated washing machines and dryers, printing and publishing). Seat of Ripon Col. One of the meetings leading to formation of Republican party was held here in 1854. Carrie Chapman Catt was b. here. Green L. to W, Rush L. to N. Settled 1844 as Ceresco by Socialist Fourierists; inc. as Ripon in 1858.

Ripon (RI-puhn), village (1991 pop. 604), SW Que., Canada, 40 mi/64 km NNE of Ottawa; 45°47′N 75°06′W. Lumbering; dairying; livestock.

Rippey, town (1990 pop. 275), Greene co., central Iowa, 10 mi/16 km SE of Jefferson; 41°55′N 94°12′W. Mfg. (concrete blocks). Sand and gravel pits nearby.

Ripplemead, uninc. village, Giles co., SW Va., 16 mi/ 26 km WNW of Blacksburg, on New R., in Allegheny Mts.; 37°20′N 80°41′W. Mfg. (lumber, limestone processing); agr. (apples, alfalfa; poultry, cattle); limestone. Part of Jefferson Natl. Forest to N; Appalachian Trail passes to NW.

Rippowam River, c.20 mi/32 km long, in N.Y. and SW Conn.; rises in N.Y. N of Stamford, Conn.; flows S, through Conn., to L.I. Sound at Stamford; dams form 2 reservoirs.

Ripton, town (1990 pop. 444), Addison co., W central Vt., in Green Mts. just E of Middlebury; 44°00′N 72°58′W. Includes Bread Loaf Mtn. (3,823 ft/1,165 m) and Bread Loaf village, site of Middlebury Col. Bread Loaf Writers Conference.

Ririe, village (1990 pop. 596), Bonneville and Jefferson cos., SE Idaho, 15 mi/24 km NE of Idaho Falls, near Snake R.; 43°38′N 111°46′W. Elev. 4,965 ft/1,513 m. Grain, potatoes; dairying; mfg. (dehydrated paper prods.). Kelly Canyon Ski Area to E; Ririe Reservoir on Willow Creek, to S.

Risco, town (1990 pop. 434), New Madrid co., extreme SE Mo., 15 mi/24 km W of New Madrid; 36°32′N 89°49′W. Cotton gin.

Rising City, village (1990 pop. 341), Butler co., E Nebr., 9 mi/14.5 km WSW of David City, and on branch of Big Blue R; 41°12′N 97°17′W.

Rising Fawn, town (1990 pop. 390), Dade co., Ga., 32 mi/ 51 km W of Dalton. Furniture mfg. Popular clay pottery studio here.

Rising Star, town (1990 pop. 859), Eastland co., N central Texas, 25 mi/40 km N of Brownwood; 32°06′N 98°58′W. Oil and gas; vegetables, peanuts, cotton; cattle; mfg. (specialty caps). Settled 1880; inc. 1905.

Rising Sun, city (1990 pop. 2,311), ⊙ Ohio co., SE Ind., on Ohio R., and 30 mi/48 km NE of Madison; 38°57′N 84°52′W. Shipping point in agr. area (livestock; tobacco, vegetables). Founded 1814; inc. 1849.

Rising Sun, town (1990 pop. 1,263), Cecil co., NE Md. near Pa. state line, 28 mi/45 km W of Wilmington, Del.; 39°42′N 76°04′W. Trade center for agr. area; canned vegetables, work clothes. First called Summerhill or Summer Hill.

Rising Sun–Lebanon, uninc. town (1990 est. pop. 2,177) Kent co., central Del., 4 mi S of Dover; 39°06′N 75°30′W. Suburban community near Dover. Lebanon in 1850s was a busy boat-building and shipping center.

Risingsun, village (1990 pop. 659), Wood co., NW Ohio, 14 mi/23 km ESE of Bowling Green, in agr. area; 41°16′N 83°25′W.

Rison (REIZ-uhn), town (1990 pop. 1,258), ⊙ Cleveland co., S central Ark., 21 mi/34 km SSW of Pine Bluff; 33°57′N 92°11′W. Hay; sawmilling; mfg. (men's outerwear, treated wood).

Rita Blanca Creek (REE-tuh BLAHN-kuh) or **Mustang Creek**, in NE N.Mex. and extreme N Texas; rises as intermittent stream in central Union co., NE N.Mex., c.20 mi/32 km WNW of Clayton through sections of Kiowa (N.Mex) and Rita Blance (Texas) natl. grasslands, through Rita Blanca Reservoir, at Dalhart (Texas), to Canadian R. c.45 mi/72 km NW of Amarillo (Texas). Rita Blanca L. (c.2.5 mi/4 km long; capacity c.12,000 acre-ft.), is formed S of Dalhart by Rita Blanca Dam; irrigation.

Ritchey, town (1990 pop. 62), Newton co., SW Mo., in the Ozarks, 11 mi/18 km ENE of Neosho; 36°56′N 94°11′W.

Ritchie (RICH-ee), county (□ 454 sq mi/1,176 sq km; 1990 pop. 10,233), NW W.Va.; ⊙ Harrisville; 39°10′N 81°04′W. Drained by N and S forks of Hughes R. Agr. (corn, alfalfa, hay); cattle; poultry; sheep. Oil and natural-gas wells. Mfg. at Pennsboro and Harrisville. North Bend State Park in N; North Bend State Trail passes through W; Ritchie Mines Wildlife Management Area in SW; part of Hughes R. Wildlife Management Area in W. Formed 1843.

Ritchie, Camp, Md.: see SABILLASVILLE.

Rito Alto Peak (13,794 ft/4,204 m), S central Colo., in Sangre de Cristo Mts., Custer and Saguache cos., 10 mi/16 km W of Westcliffe; 38°06′N 105°39′W.

Ritter, Mount (13,156 ft/4,010 m), Madera co., E Calif., in the Ritter Range of Sierra Nevada, 19 mi/31 km SSW of Mono L., 4 mi/6.4 km SE of Yosemite Natl. Park; in Sierra Natl. Forest. Source of Middle Fork San Joaquin to NE; 37°41′N 119°11′W.

Rittman, city (1990 pop. 6,147), Wayne co., N central Ohio, 14 mi/23 km NE of Wooster; 40°58′N 81°47′W. In agr. area (fruits; livestock; dairying); mfg. of paper prods.

Ritzville, town (1990 pop. 1,725), ⊙ Adams co., SE Wash., 60 mi/97 km SW of Spokane; 47°08′N 118°23′W. In Columbia basin agr. region; wheat, barley, oats, corn, potatoes, beans, alfalfa, onions, asparagus, peppermint; lumber shipping and processing. Burroughs Wheatland Mus. Basaltic rock outcroppings in area referred to as the Channeled Scablands. Settled c.1878; inc. 1906.

Riva, Dominican Republic: see VILLA RIVAS.

Riva Palacio (REE-vah pah-LAH-see-o), town (1990 pop. 714), Chihuahua, N Mexico, in Sierra Madre Occidental, on RR, and 26 mi/42 km WSW of Chihuahua; 28°32′N 106°30′W. Corn, beans; cattle. Also called San Andrés.

Rivanna River, c.50 mi/80 km long, central Va.; formed in NW Albemarle co. by joining of North Fork Rivanna (formed in S Greene co. by joining of Parker Branch and Roach R.) and short South Fork Rivanna (formed by joining of Mechums and Moormans rivers); flows SE, past Charlottesville, to James R. at Columbia; 38°04′N 78°26′W. All headwaters rise in the Blue Ridge. L. Monticello reservoir on tributary 10 mi/16 km SE of Charlottesville, adjacent to Rivanna R.

River Bend, town (1990 pop. 2,408), Craven co., E N.C., residential suburb 7 mi/11.3 km WSW of New Bern, on Trent R.; 35°04′N 77°09′W. Croatan Natl. Forest to S. Agr. area (tobacco, cotton; peanuts; grain; poultry, livestock).

River Bend Nuclear Power Plant, La.: see WEST FELICIANA.

River Edge, residential borough (1990 pop. 10,603), Bergen co., NE N.J., on the Hackensack R., and 2 mi/3.2 km N of Hackensack; 40°55′N 74°02′W. Inc. 1894.

River Falls, city (1990 pop. 10,610), on Pierce–St. Croix co. line, W Wis., on small Kinnikinnic R. (tributary of St. Croix R.), and 24 mi/39 km ESE of St. Paul (Minn.); 44°51′N 92°37′W. In dairying and livestock-raising area; mfg. (sharpening equip., refrigerator equip., plastic molding). Grain elevator, poultry hatcheries. Univ. of Wisconsin, River Falls Campus is here. Kinnickinnic State Park to W; Lower St. Croix Natl. Riverway to W. Settled c.1850; inc. 1875.

River Falls, town (1990 pop. 710), Covington co., S Ala., on Conecuh R. (dammed nearby), and 5 mi/8 km NW of Andalusia; 31°21′N 86°32′W.

River Falls, village, Greenville co., NW S.C., in the Blue Ridge Mts., 20 mi/32 km N of Greenville. In summer resort region.

River Forest, village (1990 pop. 11,669), Cook co., NE Ill., a suburb W of Chicago, on the Des Plaines R.; 41°53′N 87°49′W. Seat of Rosary Col. and Concordia Univ. Several homes here were designed by Frank Lloyd Wright. A forest preserve is adjacent to the village. Inc. 1880.

River Grove 1 village (1990 pop. 9,961), Cook co., NE Ill., a suburb W of Chicago on the Des Plaines R.; 41°55′N 87°50′W. Mfg. of sports equip. and wire cables. Co. forest preserves and Triton Col. Inc. 1888. **2** village (1990 pop. 294), Clackamas and Washington cos., NW Oregon, residential suburb 8 mi/12.9 km SSW of downtown Portland, on Tualatin R. Agr. area.

River Hebert (HEE-buhrt) or **River Hébert**(ai-BER), town, N N.S., Canada, on Hebert R. (30 mi/48 km long), near its mouth on the Cumberland Basin of Chignecto Bay, 10 mi/16 km SW of Amherst; 45°41′N 64°23′W. Coal mining.

River Heights, town (1990 pop. 1,274), Cache co., N Utah, residential suburb 1 mi/1.6 km S of Logan; 41°43′N 111°49′W. Elev. 4,590 ft/1,399 m. Apples. Wasatch Natl. Forest to E.

River Hills, village (1990 pop. 1,612), Milwaukee co., SE Wis., on Milwaukee R., a suburb 7 mi/11.3 km N of downtown Milwaukee, near L. Michigan; 43°10′N 87°56′W.

River John, village, E N.S., Canada, near Northumberland Strait, 18 mi/29 km W of Pictou; 45°44′N 63°03′W. Dairying; mixed farming.

River Jordan, village, SW B.C., Canada, on S Vancouver Isl., on Juan de Fuca Strait, near mouth of small Jordan R., 30 mi/48 km W of Victoria; hydroelectric power plant, supplying Victoria. Sometimes called Jordan R.

River Oaks, town (1990 pop. 6,580), Tarrant co., N Texas, residential suburb 4 mi/6.4 km WNW of downtown Fort Worth, on W Fork Trinity R.; 32°46′N 97°24′W. L. Worth to NW; Carswell Air Force Base (closed) to W. Formerly called Castleberry. Inc. after 1940.

River Plaza, village, Monmouth co., E N.J., just across Navesink R. from Red Bank, 12 mi/19 km NE of Freehold.

River Point, village, of West Warwick town, Kent co., central R.I., on Pawtuxet R., and 10 mi/16 km SW of Providence. Textiles; textile soaps.

River Ridge, uninc. city (1990 pop. 14,800), Jefferson parish, SE La., suburb 6 mi/10 km WNW of New Orleans, near Mississippi R.; 29°58′N 90°13′W. City of Kenner is 2 mi/3 km W. Mfg. of school furniture.

River Road 1 uninc. town (1990 pop. 3,892), Beaufort co., E N.C., 4 mi/6.4 km SE of Washington, on Pamlico R. estuary; 35°30′N 76°59′W. Goose Creek State Park to SE. **2** uninc. town (1990 pop. 9,443), Lane co., W Oregon, residential suburb 3 mi/4.8 km NNW of downtown Eugene, on River Road, on Willamette R.; 44°04′N 123°07′W. RR yards; RR junction.

River Rouge, city (1990 pop. 11,314), Wayne co., SE Mich., an industrial suburb 5 mi/8 km SW of downtown Detroit, on the Detroit R. at mouth of R. Rouge, includes Zug Isls.; borders city of Detroit in N and W; 42°16′N 83°07′W. Mfg. (steel fabrication, paper and metallized films, lime, plasticboard). It is a port of entry, with automobile, shipbuilding, and marine engineering industries. The city grew in the 1920s with the expansion of the Ford Motor Company in the area; however, R. Rouge and its automobile industry have suffered since the early 1980s. Grant Lakes Steel Corp. is here. Settled c.1817; inc. 1899.

River Rouge, Mich.: see ROUGE RIVER, .

River Vale, township (1990 pop. 9,410), Bergen co., NE N.J., residential suburb of New York, 6 mi/9.7 km NE of Paterson; 41°00′N 74°00′W. Inc. 1906.

River View, Ala.: see VALLEY.

Riverbank, city (1990 pop. 8,547), Stanislaus co., central Calif., in San Joaquin Valley, a suburb 8 mi/12.9 km NE of Modesto, and on Stanislaus R.; 37°44′N 120°57′W. In irrigated agr. region (vegetables, melons; dairying; poultry; cattle). Mfg. (trusses, canned fruits and vegetables, wood cabinets, ordnance, metal cans, wood treating). Inc. 1922. Hetch Hetchy Aqueduct passes E-W to S.

Riverdale 1 town (1990 pop. 1,980), Fresno co., central Calif., in San Joaquin Valley, 22 mi/35 km SSW of Fresno, near Kings R.; 36°26′N 119°52′W. Ships fruits, vegetables, beans, sugar beets, grain; cattle. **2** town (1990 pop. 9,359), Clayton co., N central Ga., 14 mi/23 km S of Atlanta; 33°34′N 84°25′W. Suburb to the S of Atlanta near Hartsfield Internatl. Airport. Business parks and distribution facilities. Mfg. includes swimwear, steel fabrication, diversified light mfg. **3** town (1990 pop. 5,185), Prince Georges co., central Md., suburb NE of Washington, D.C.; 38°58′N 76°56′W. Makes machine tools, aircraft propellers. Inc. 1920. **4** town (1990 pop. 6,419), Weber co., N Utah, suburb 5 mi/8 km SSW of downtown Ogden, and 25 mi/40 km NNW of Salt Lake City, on Weber R.; 41°10′N 112°00′W. Elev. 4,235 ft/1,291 m. Settled 1850. Hill Air Force Base to S. Ogden Municipal Airport to N.

Riverdale 1 village (1990 pop. 13,671), Cook co., NE Ill., a suburb adjacent to Chicago, S of the city; 41°38′N 87°37′W. Its large steel mill closed with the natl. decline of the industry. On the Calumet-Sag Channel. Inc. 1892. **2** village (1990 pop. 433), Scott co., E Iowa, suburb 2 mi/3.2 km E of downtown Bettendorf, in Quad Cities area; 41°32′N 90°28′W. Borders Mississippi R. on S. Residential. Scott Community Col. in N part. **3** village (1990 pop. 208), Buffalo co., S central Nebr., 6 mi/9.7 km NW of Kearney, and on Wood R; 40°46′N 99°09′W. **4** village (1990 pop. 283) McLean co., central N.Dak., 58 mi/93 km NNW of Bismarck, on Missouri R., at E end of Garrison Dam, which forms the large L. Sakakawea reservoir to N. Sakakawea State Park to W. Fish hatchery; 47°30′N 101°22′W. Power station. Cattle. Honey production.

Riverdale, borough (1990 pop. 2,370), Morris co., N N.J., on Pequannock R., and 10 mi/16 km NW of Paterson; 41°00′N 74°18′W. Sand, gravel. Inc. 1923. Largely residential.

Riverdale, NW residential section of the Bronx borough of N.Y. city, SE N.Y., bet. the Hudson R. (W) and Van Cortlandt Park (E); 40°54′N 73°55′W. Affluent pop. Site of Manhattan Col., Col. of Mount St. Vincent, Fieldston School of the Ethical Culture Society, and Riverdale Country Day School. Henry Hudson Memorial here has a statue designed by Karl Bitter.

Riverdale, Mass.: see GLOUCESTER.

Riverdale Heights, town, Prince Georges co., central Md., suburb NE of Washington, D.C. Developed after Riverdale, Md., and is separated from it by the North east Branch of the Anacostia R.

Riverhead (□ 15 sq mi/39 sq km; 1990 pop. 8,814), ⊙ Suffolk co., SE N.Y., on Peconic R. near its mouth on Great Peconic Bay of E L.I., 21 mi/34 km ENE of Patchogue; 40°57′N 72°40′W. Mfg. (machinery components, capping machines); in resort and farm area (potatoes, sweet corn, cauliflower). Fishing, duck hunting. Mus. of Suffolk Co. Historical Society is here.

Riverhurst, village (1991 pop. 174), S Sask., Canada, near South Saskatchewan R., 60 mi/97 km NE of Swift Current; 50°55′N 106°51′W. Grain elevators.

Riverlea, suburban village (1990 pop. 503), Franklin co., central Ohio, just N of Columbus, and on Olentangy R.; 40°05′N 83°01′W.

Rivermines, Mo.: see PARK HILLS.

Rivermoor, Mass.: see SCITUATE.

Rivers, town (1991 pop. 1,076), SW Man., Canada, on Minnedosa R. and 18 mi/29 km NW of Brandon; 50°02′N 100°13′W. Grain, sand, gravel quarrying.

Riversdale, town (1991 pop. 2,791), St. Catherine parish, central Jamaica, on RR to Port Antonio, and 18 mi/29 km NW of Kingston; 18°09′N 76°58′W. In agr. region (citrus fruits, coffee; livestock).

Riverside, county (□ 7,303 sq mi/18,594 sq km; 1990 pop. 1,170,413), S Calif.; ⊙ Riverside; 33°44′N 115°59′W. Stretches c.190 mi/306 km E-W across state, from Colorado R. (Ariz. state line) to E to Santa Ana Mts. in W; SW corner comes within 10 mi/16 km of Pacific coast. San Jacinto and San Bernardino ranges (both over 10,000 ft/3,048 m) and Little San Bernardino Mts. cross center (NW-SE through center). Generally 40 mi/64 km wide N-S. E of center is part of COLORADO DESERT, including partially irrigated COACHELLA VALLEY in center and N part of SALTON SEA on S border (235 ft/72 m below sea level); part of PALO VERDE VALLEY (irrigated) is in extreme E at Blythe. Large part of JOSHUA TREE natl. monument in N center, extends N into San Bernardino co.; sections of Cleveland Natl. Forest in W and SW, part of San Bernardino Natl. Forests in W center. Cotton, peppers, nursery stock, avocados, tangerines, grapefruit, lemons, oranges, grapes, dates, melons, eggs, poultry, wheat, barley, oats, corn, beans. Working of limestone, gypsum, clay, sand, gravel, iron, salt deposits. Large packing and processing industries handle farm produce. Includes desert resorts (notably Palm Springs and Palm Desert), mt. recreational areas, L. Elsinore. Indian reservations: Pechanga in SW; Morongo, Soboba, Ramona, Cahuilla, Santa Rosa, Agua Caliente, and Cabazon in W center; part of Torrez Martinez Indian Reservation on S border, on Salton Sea; part of Colorado R. Indian Reservation in NE. Mt. Jacinto Wilderness State Park in W center; L. Perris reservoir and State Recreation Area in W center; part of Salton Sea State Recreation Area on S boundary. Colorado R. Aqueduct crosses co. E-W, San Diego Aqueduct branches to S in W. Part of extensive Anza-Borrego Desert State Park in S center. NW corner is within 25 mi/40 km of downtown Los Angeles, developed primarily 1960s–1980s, SW part of co. around Murrieta and Temecula, and desert area around Palm Springs, were developed in the 1990s. In land area it is 24th-largest in U.S. and 4th-largest in Calif. Formed 1893.

Riverside, city (1990 pop. 226,505), ⊙ Riverside co., S Calif., 45 mi/72 km ESE of downtown Los Angeles, and 10 mi/16 km SW of San Bernardino; Santa Ana R. bounds city on NW; 33°57′N 117°24′W. It is famous for its orange industry. Other industries include aircraft and aerospace components, aluminum, and machinery. Mfg. (aluminum prods., food and beverages, plastics prods., prefabricated wood and metal bldgs., medical equip., electronic components, motor vehicle parts, machinery parts, printing and publishing, sand and gravel, cosmetics). The navel orange was introduced here in 1873; the original tree, still producing, is a tourist attraction. Riverside is one of the fastest-growing U.S. cities, marked by a pop. increase of almost 33% bet. 1980 and 1990. The 1st marketing cooperative, organized in Riverside in 1892, led to the founding of the Calif. Fruit Growers Exchange. The city is also an education center and the seat of the Univ. of Calif. at Riverside (with Univ. of Calif. Experimental Station, est. 1907); La Sierra campus of Loma Linda Univ. in SW end of city; Calif. Baptist Col.; Riverside Community Col.; and a school for Native Americans. Mission Inn, a hotel in a unique mission setting, is in the city. March Air Force Base, hq. of the 15th U.S. Air Force and a major Strategic Air Command installation, is SE. L. Matthews Reservoir to S; L. Perris Reservoir to SE; Gage Aqueduct Canal runs N-S through city; Riverside Auto Race Track to E; Riverside Fla-Bob Airport to NW; Riverside Municipal Airport in NW part of city. Inc. 1883.

Riverside 1 town (1990 pop. 1,004), St. Clair co., NE central Ala., on Coosa R., and 6 mi/9.7 km E of Pell City; 33°36′N 86°12W. **2** town (1990 pop. 74), Colquitt co., S Ga., just W of Moultrie, on Ochlockonee R.; 31°11′N 83°49′W. **3** town (1990 pop. 824), Washington co., E central Iowa, 13 mi/21 km SSW of Iowa City, on English R.; 41°28′N 91°34′W. Corn; hogs, cattle. **4** town (1990 pop. 3,010), Platte co., W Mo., suburb 5 mi/8 km NNW of downtown Kansas City, Mo., on Missouri R. opposite Kansas City, Kansas (2 highway bridges). Bounded by Clay co. on E. Mfg. (pressure sensitive paper, automobile seats, cranes, foam cushions). **5**- uninc. town, Greenville co., NW S.C., residential suburb of Greenville near Reedy R., 2 mi/3.2 km NW of downtown Greenville.

Riverside 1 village (1990 pop. 8,774), Cook co., NE Ill., a residential suburb W of Chicago, on the Des Plaines R.; 41°49′N 87°49′W. It was planned as a model suburb by Frederick Law Olmsted and Calvert Vaux. The city has a number of bldgs. designed by Frank Lloyd Wright. The old water tower (late 19th cent.) is a natl. historic landmark. Inc. 1875. **2** summer resort village, Charles co., S Md., on the Potomac estuary c.50 mi/80 km below Washington, D.C. Small seafood industry. **3** village, suburb 2 mi/3.2 km N of Jackson, Jackson co., S. Mich. **4** village, Berrien co., SW Mich., 7 mi/11.3 km NE of Benton Harbor; 2 mi/3.2 km from L. Michigan; 42°11′N 86°22′W. Fruit-growing area (apples, cherries, grapes, peaches); hogs; soybeans; mfg. (nonferrous holding furnaces, corrugated cartons). **5** village (1990 pop. 585), Steuben co., S N.Y., just NW of Corning; 42°09′N 77°04′W. **6** village (1990 pop. 1,471), Montgomery co., W Ohio, just NE of Dayton, on Great Miami R.; 39°47′N 84°07′W. **7** village, in East Providence town, Providence co., R.I. **8** village (1990 pop. 451), Walker co., E central Texas, on Trinity R. at headwaters of L. Livingston reservoir, and 11 mi/18 km NE of Huntsville; 30°51′N 95°24′W. Mfg. (weight training equip.). **9** village (1990 pop. 223), Okanogan co., N Wash., 12 mi/19 km N of Okanogan, and on Okanogan R. at mouth of Johnson Creek; 48°30′N 119°31′W. Apples; timber. Parts of Okanogan Natl. Forest to E and W; Colville Indian Reservation to SE. **10** village (1990 pop. 85), Carbon co., S Wyo., on Encampment R., just E of the Sierra Madre, and 47 mi/76 km SSE of Rawlins, and 1 mi/1.6 km N of Encampment; 41°12′N 106°46′W. Elev. c.7,137 ft/2,175 m. Once a RR terminus and supply point. Parts of Medicine Bow Natl. Forest to SW and E.

Riverside, borough (1990 pop. 1,991), Northumberland co., E central Pa., 1 mi/1.6 km E of Danville, on Susquehanna R. (bridged), opposite Danville; 40°56′N 76°39′W. Agr. area (grain; livestock; dairying); mfg. (pharmaceuticals). Danville Airport to W.

Riverside, township (1990 pop. 7,974), Burlington co., SW N.J., on Delaware R., at mouth of Rancocas Creek, and 11 mi/18 km NE of Camden; 40°02′N 74°57′W. Mfg. (watch cases, clothing, metal prods., textiles, cement, boats); printing.

Riverside 1 Mass.: see GILL. **2** Mass.: see NEWTON.

Riverside Gardens, town (1990 pop. 760), Jefferson co., N Ky., residential suburb 7 mi/11.3 km SW of downtown Louisville, on Ohio R., near mouth of Mill Creek.

Riverside-Albert, amalgamated towns, SE N.B., Canada, on Crooked Creek, near Chignecto Bay, 23 mi/37 km S of Moncton. Mining district to NE. Fishing, logging, tourism. Separate towns merged in mid-1970s.

Riverton, city (1990 pop. 11,261), Salt Lake co., N central Utah, on Jordon R., and suburb 18 mi/29 km S of Salt L. City, on Jordan R.; 40°31′N 111°57′W. Mfg. modular bldgs. Camp Williams Military Reservation to SW. Inc. after 1940.

Riverton 1 town (1990 pop. 333), Fremont co., extreme SW Iowa, on East Nishnabotna R., and 6 mi/9.7 km SE of Sidney; 40°41′N 34°95′W. Livestock; grain. **2** town (1990 pop. 9,202), Fremont co., W central Wyo., at junction of Wind and Popo Agie rivers to form Bighorn R., 22 mi/35 km NE of Lander; 43°02′N 108°24′W. Elev. 4,956 ft/1,511 m. Main trade and industrial center for Wind R. Indian Reservation, located in SE part of reservation. Home of Shoshone and Arapaho nations. Trade and shipping point for irrigated Wind R. basin; cattle, sheep; sugar beets, potatoes, beans, hay; timber. Mfg. (meat prods., dairy prods., alfalfa prods., meat seasonings, printing and publishing, industrial chemicals, computer equip., pocket compasses, highway signs). Served by Riverton power and land-reclamation project, including Wind R. diversion dam, Bull L. and Pilot Butte dams, as well as the Pilot Butte power plant. Riverton Mus. here; Riverton Regional Airport to NW. Annual Mountain Man Rendezvous held since 1838. Gas Hills Uranium Mining Dist. 45 mi/72 km to E, petroleum exploration. Lost Wells Butte to N.

Riverton 1 village (1990 pop. 2,638), Sangamon co., central Ill., 6 mi/9.7 km NE of Springfield; 39°51′N 89°32′W. In agr. and bituminous coal area. Inc. 1873. **2** village (1990 pop. 122), Crow Wing co., central Minn., on Mississippi R., 11 mi/18 km NE of Brainerd; 46°27′N 94°02′W. Cuyuna Iron Range mining dist. to NE. Crow Wing State Forest to N. **3** village (1990 pop. 162), Franklin co., S Nebr., 8 mi/12.9 km E of Franklin, and on Republican R., near Kansas border; 40°05′N 98°45′W.

Riverton, Conn.: see BARKHAMSTED.

Riverton, residential borough (1990 pop. 2,775), Burlington co., SW N.J., on Delaware R., and 7 mi/11.3 km NE of Camden; 40°00′N 75°00′W. Ironworking. Inc. 1893.

Riverton Heights, uninc. city (1990 pop. 15,337), King co., W Wash., residential suburb 12 mi/19 km S of downtown Seattle. Seattle-Tacoma (Sea-Tac) International Airport to SW.

Riverview, city (1990 pop. 13,894), Wayne co., SE Mich., on the Trenton Channel of the Detroit R., a suburb 11 mi/18 km SSW of downtown Detroit; 42°10′N 83°11′W. Mfg. (plumbing fixtures, industrial chemicals, steel wheels). Rich limestone deposits, quarried as early as 1763, contributed to the city's growth. Tall bridge to N end of Grosse Ile. Inc. 1959.

Riverview, town (1991 pop. 16,270), SE N.B., Canada, S residential suburb of Moncton, on S bank of Petitcodiac R. Connected to Moncton by bridge and causeway.

Riverview, town (□ 9 sq mi/23.3 sq km; 1990 pop. 6,478), Hillsborough co., W central Fla., 12 mi/19 km SE of Tampa. Mfg. includes aluminum prods., solar electronics, phosphate fertilizers.

Riverview 1 village (1990 pop. 3,242), St. Louis co., E Mo., residential suburb 7 mi/11.3 km N of downtown St. Louis, on bluffs overlooking Mississippi R.; 38°44′N 90°12′W. **2** village, Greenville co., NW S.C., in the Blue Ridge Mts., 18 mi/29 km NNW of Greenville, in summer resort region.

Riverwood, village (1990 pop. 506), Jefferson co., Ky., residential suburb 6 mi/9.7 km ENE of downtown Louisville, near Ohio R.; 38°16′N 85°39′W.

Riverwoods, village (1990 pop. 2,868), Lake co., NE Ill., residential suburb 25 mi/40 km NNW of downtown Chicago, 6 mi/9.7 km W of Highland Park, on Des Plaines and N. Chicago rivers; 42°10′N 87°54′W. Law report printing.

Rives 1 (REEVZ), town (1990 pop. 89), Dunklin co., extreme SE Mo., in Mississippi alluvial plain, 10 mi/16 km S of Kennett. **2** town (1990 pop. 344), Obion co., NW Tenn., 5 mi/8 km S of Union City; 36°21′N 89°03′W.

Rivesville (REEVZ-vil), town (1990 pop. 1,064), Marion co., N W.Va., near the Monongahela R., 4 mi/6.4 km N of Fairmont; 39°31′N 80°07′W. Coal-mining region. Agr. (corn, apples); livestock. Mfg. (mining cable, millwork). Laid out 1837.

Riviera, uninc. village (1990 pop. 550), Kleberg co., S Texas, near head of Baffin Bay, 16 mi/26 km S of Kingsville, on Los Olmos Creek. Coast resort; mfg. (boats and boat motors).

Riviera Beach 1 (ri-vee-ER-rah), resort city (□ 9 sq mi/23.3 sq km; 1990 pop. 27,639), Palm Beach co., SE Fla., 5 mi/8 km N of West Palm Beach, on L. Worth (a lagoon); 26°46′N 80°04′W. Research and development firms are located in the growing city. Inc. 1922. **2** summer resort (1990 pop. 11,376), Anne Arundel co., central Md., on Patapasco R., 11 mi/18 km SE of Baltimore; 39°10′N 76°31′W. Summer houses here have become permanent and beaches private since the Bay Bridge opened.

Rivière à Pierre (ah PYER), village (1991 pop. 672), S Que., Canada, 50 mi/80 km WNW of Quebec; 46°59′N 72°11′W. Dairying; pigs, poultry.

Rivière Beaudette (bo-DET) or **River Beaudette**, agr. commuter suburb (1991 pop. 1,292) of Montreal, S Que., Canada, near L. St. Francis, 11 mi/18 km WSW of Valleyfield; 45°20′N 74°21′W. Mfg. (vehicle parts); dairying; pigs; potatoes.

Rivière Bleue or **Saint Joseph de la Rivière Bleue** (seh zho-ZEHF duh lah reev-YER BLUH), village (1991 pop. 1,643), SE Que., Canada, on St. Francis R., and 35 mi/56 km SE of Rivière du Loup; 47°26′N 69°02′W. Dairying; lumbering.

Rivière des Lacs, N.Dak.: see DES LACS RIVER.

Rivière du Loup (duh LOO), county (□ 723 sq mi/1,873 sq km), SE Que., Canada, on the St. Lawrence R.; ⊙ Rivière du Loup; 48°00′N 69°10′W.

Rivière du Loup (reev-YER duh loo), city (1991 pop. 14,017), E Que., Canada, on the S shore of the St. Lawrence R., NE of Quebec; 47°50′N 69°32′W. Commercial and industrial center in a lumbering and agr. region. Sawmills and paper mills; resort and tourist center. Settled in 1833. Originally called Fraserville.

Rivière Ouelle (WEL), village (1991 pop. 1,244), SE Que., Canada, on the St. Lawrence R., and 35 mi/56 km SW of Rivière du Loup. Dairying; pigs.

Rivière Salée (ree-VYER sah-LAI), narrow strait, Guadeloupe, Fr. West Indies, separating Guadeloupe into 2 isls., Basse-Terre (W) and Grande-Terre (E), and linking the bays Grand Cul de Sac (N) and Petit Cul de Sac (S); 4 mi/6.4 km long, 50 yd/46 m–120 yd/110 m wide. A tidal channel in mangrove swamps, it is navigable for vessels of light draught; spanned by a bridge. Pointe-à-Pitre is near S entrance.

Rivière Trois Pistoles (trwah pee-STOL), village, SE Que., Canada, on the St. Lawrence R., and 30 mi/48 km NE of Rivière du Loup. Agr.

Rivière-aux-Renard, village, E Que., Canada, on NE Gaspé Peninsula, on the St. Lawrence R., and 12 mi/19 km NNE of Gaspé. Fishing port; lumbering; dairying.

Rivière–Blanche, Canada: see SAINT ULRIC.

Rivière-Pilote (ree-VYER–pee-LAWT), town, S Martinique, 14 mi/23 km SE of Fort-de-France. Sugar plantations; limekiln; rum distillery.

Rivière-Salée (ree-VYER–sah-LAI), town, SW Martinique, 7 mi/11.3 km SE of Fort-de-France. Produces vanilla.

R. L. Harris Reservoir (□ 17 sq mi/44 sq km), Randoph co., E central Ala., on Tallapoosa R., 28 mi/45 km SSE of Anniston; 32°16′N 85°37′W. Max. capacity 426,000 acre-ft. Formed by R. L. Harris Dam (152 ft/46 m high), built (1982) for power generation; owned by Ala. Power Co. Extends NE from dam with 2d arm extending NW; several branches on each arm. Also called Harris L. and L. Wedowee.

Roa Bárcena, Mexico: see TEQUILA, town.

Roachdale, town (1990 pop. 902), Putnam co., W central Ind., 15 mi/24 km NNE of Greencastle; 39°51′N 86°48′W. In agr. area; dairy prods.; grain, soybeans; livestock. Laid out 1879.

Road Town, ⊙ and largest town (1991 pop. 3,983) of Tortola in the B.V.I.

Roan Cliffs, Utah and Colo.: see BOOK CLIFFS.

Roan High Knob, Tenn. and N.C.: see ROAN MOUNTAIN.

Roan Mountain (ron), on NE Tenn.–W N.C. line, in the Appalachians, 10 mi/16 km SE of Johnson City, Tenn.; its summit, called Roan High Knob, rises to 6,285 ft/1,916 m. Rhododendron festival every June.

Roan Plateau, high tableland (7,000 ft/2,134 m–9,000 ft/2,743 m), largely in Garfield co., W Colo. Forms E continuation of East Tavaputs Plateau, Utah. Bounded on S by Book Cliffs.

Roane 1 (ron), county (□ 375 sq mi/971 sq km; 1990 pop. 47,227), E Tenn.; ⊙ Kingston; 35°51′N 84°31′W. In Tennessee R. valley; here Clinch R. enters an arm of Watts Bar Reservoir of the Tennessee. Coal and iron mines; hardwood lumbering; fruit growing, agr. (tobacco, corn, wheat); livestock; dairying. Some industry at Harriman and Rockwood. Formed 1801. **2** (RON), county (□ 484 sq mi/1,254 sq km; 1990 pop. 15,120), W W.Va.; ⊙ Spencer; 38°43′N 81°21′W. Drained by Little Kanawha and Pocatalico rivers and Sandy, Reedy, and Mill creeks. Timber region. Agr. (corn, tobacco, potatoes, alfalfa, hay); cattle, poultry, sheep. Some mfg. at Spencer. Parts of Wallback Wildlife Management Area and B. J. Taylor Wildlife Management Area in SE. Formed 1856.

Roann, town (1990 pop. 447), Wabash co., NE central Ind., on Eel R., and 13 mi/21 km NE of Peru; 40°55′N 85°55′W. In agr. area. Laid out 1853.

Roanoke, county (□ 250 sq mi/648 sq km; 1990 pop. 79,332), SW Va.; independent cities of Salem and Roanoke separate from co.; ⊙ Salem; 37°16′N 80°04′W. In Great Appalachian Valley, drained by Roanoke R., traversed by ridges; Brush Mt. Ridge in NW and Blue Ridge (here cut by Roanoke R.) in SE. Rich agr. area (hay, alfalfa, apples, peaches; cattle and poultry raising). Includes part of Jefferson Natl. Forest. in NW; Blue Ridge Parkway passes through SE; Appalachian Trail passes through N. Formed 1838.

Roanoke 1 (ro-uh-NOK), city (1990 pop. 6,362), Randolph co., E Ala., near Ga. line, 13 mi/21 km SE of Wedowee. Apparel, textiles, lumber, fertilizers, beverages. Settled c.1835, inc. 1888. **2** independent city (□ 42 sq mi/109 sq km; 1990 pop. 96,397), SW Va., separate from surrounding Roanoke co., bet. Blue Ridge and Allegheny Mts., at S end of Shenandoah valley, 52 mi/84 km WSW of Lynchburg, on Roanoke R.; 37°16′N 79°57′W. RR junction with RR shops; mfg. (machinery, chemicals, fabricated metal prods., foods and beverages, concrete prods., fixtures, electronic equip., apparel, furniture, printing and publishing, plastic prods.). A tiny village until RR arrived in 1882, Roanoke has since developed into the region's commercial, transportation, and industrial center. Seat of Roanoke Valley Col. of Health Sciences; Va. Western Community Col.; Hollins Col. to N, at Hollins; Roanoke Col. to W, in Salem. Hq. of the Jefferson Natl. Forest, parts of forest to NW and NE. Va. Mus. of Transportation; Science Mus. of Western Va.; Art Mus. of Western Va.; Hopkins Planetarium. Dixie Caverns to W; Booker T. Washington Natl. Monument to SE; Roanoke Mtn. Recreation Area to S. Roanoke Regional Airport in N. Settled c.1740, inc. 1882.

Roanoke 1 town (1990 pop. 1,018), Huntington co., NE central Ind., on Little Wabash R. and 16 mi/26 km SW of Fort Wayne; 40°58′N 85°23′W. Agr. area; grain, dairy prods.; mfg. (transportation equip., concrete). Laid out 1850. **2** town (1990 pop. 1,616), Denton co., N Texas, suburb 18 mi/29 km NE of Fort Worth, in N fringe of large Dallas–Fort Worth metropolitan area; 33°00′N 97°13′W. In farm area (cotton; wheat; cattle, horses); mfg. (consumer goods, concrete, asphalt).

Roanoke 1 village (1990 pop. 1,910), Woodford co., central Ill., 22 mi/35 km ENE of Peoria; 40°47′N 89°12′W. In agr. area. Inc. 1874. **2** uninc. rural community, Randolph and Howard cos., N central Mo., 15 mi/24 km SW of Moberly.

Roanoke Island (RO-uh-nok), 12 mi/19 km long and 3 mi/4.8 km wide, Dare co., NE N.C., bet. mainland (W) and Outer Banks (E; Atlantic Ocean beyond) bounded E by Roanoke Sound (bridged), N by Albermarle Sound, W by Croatan Sound (bridged), S by Pamlico Sound. Manteo near N end is the chief town, and tourism and fishing are the principal industries of the isl. Wanchese is at S end. The Eng. navigators Philip Amadas and Arthur Barlowe, exploring for Sir Walter Raleigh in 1584, brought back such glowing accounts of the isl. that Raleigh immediately dispatched a colonizing expedition under Sir Richard Grenville and Sir Ralph Lane. The colonists landed on Roanoke Isl. in Aug., 1585, and built the "Citie of Ralegh" (or New Fort), but they returned to England the next year. In 1587 Raleigh sent out another group under John White. Forced to return to England for supplies, White was unable to come back to Roanoke until 1591. Upon his return he found the colonists gone and the letters CROATOAN carved on a tree. This gave rise to a theory that the settlers had moved to Croatoan Isl. or had joined the Croatoan or Hatteras Native Americans. In 1937 Paul Green's symphonic drama *The Lost Colony* was 1st presented to commemorate the 350th anniversary of the landing of White's colony. Fort Raleigh Natl. Historic Site is at N end; artifacts have been unearthed at site.

Roanoke Rapids (RO-uh-nok), city (1990 pop. 15,722), Halifax co., N N.C., 37 mi/60 km NNE of Rocky Mount, on the Roanoke R., forms Roanoke Rapids L. reservoir to W, L. Gaston reservoir farther to W, near the Va. state line; 36°27′N 77°39′W. Mfg. (textiles, transportation equip., lumber, printing and publishing). Founded 1893, inc. 1931.

Roanoke River, c.410 mi/660 km long, Va. and N.C.; rises along borders of E Montgomery, W Roanoke and NE Floyd cos.; formed by joining of North and South forks of Roanoke R., c.15 mi/24 km E of Christiansburg, SW Va.; flows in circular course, briefly NW, then E past Salem and Roanoke, through Blue Ridge Mts., then generally SE, through Smith Mt. L. and Leesville L. reservoirs, past Altavista, through Kerr Reservoir (Bugg Isl. L.), L. Gaston reservoir (where it enters NE N.C.), and Roanoke Rapids L. reservoir; flows past Roanoke Rapids city, Williamston, and Plymouth; turns briefly NE and enters Batchelor Bay sect. of Albemarle Sound, arm of Atlantic Ocean 7 mi/11.3 km NE of Plymouth and just S of mouth of Chowan R. Va. part also known as Staunton R. Lower river navigable for small craft.

Roanoke Sound (RO-uh-nok), passage, Dare co., E N.C., bet. Roanoke Isl. (W) and Outer Banks (peninsula at this point), bridged; Albemarle Sound (N) and Pamlico Sound (S). Croatan Sound on W side of Roanoke Isl.

Roaring Fork River, c.70 mi/113 km long, W central Colo.; rises at Continental Divide at Independence Pass, in Sawatch Mts., Pitkin co.; flows NW past Aspen and Carbondale, to Colorado R. at Glenwood Springs. Supplies water, via Twin Lakes tunnel under Sawatch Mts., to Twin Lakes Reservoir.

Roaring Gap, uninc. village, Alleghany co., NW N.C., 11 mi/18 km SE of Sparta, in the Blue Ridge Mts. Tobacco, grain; livestock; dairying. Blue Ridge Natl. Parkway passes to NW. Stone Mt. State Park to SW.

Roaring River, c.5 mi/8 km long, in St. Ann parish, N Jamaica, bet. St. Ann's Bay and Ocho Rios; 18°23′N 77°10′W. Along it are picturesque Roaring R. Falls, largest on the isl., used for hydroelectric power.

Roaring Spring, borough (1990 pop. 2,615), Blair co., S central Pa., 12 mi/19 km S of Altoona, on Halter Creek; 40°19′N 78°24′W. Agr. (grain, apples; livestock, dairying); mfg. (paper prods., chemicals, concrete prods., bottled water, feeds). Dunning Mt. ridge to W, Loop Mt. ridge to NE. Inc. 1888.

Roaring Springs, village (1990 pop. 264), Motley co., NW Texas, just below Caprock escarpment, c.50 mi/80 km SW of Childress and on South Pease R.; 33°53′N 100°51′W. Trade and recreational center, with springs (camping, swimming); light mfg.

Robb, village, W Alta., Canada, in Rocky Mts., near Jasper Natl. Park, 35 mi/56 km SW of Edson. Coal mining; cattle.

Robbins, city (1990 pop. 970), Moore co., central N.C., 22 mi/35 km SE of Asheboro; 35°25′N 79°34′W. Tobacco, grain; poultry, cattle, hogs. Mfg. (apparel, construction materials). Formerly Hemp. Inc. 1935.

Robbins 1 village (1990 pop. 7,498), Cook co., NE Ill., residential suburb 15 mi/24 km SSW of downtown Chicago; 41°38′N 87°42′W. On Calumet-Sag Channel. Inc. 1917. **2** village, Barnwell co., W S.C., near Savannah R., in Savannah River Nuclear Site.

Robbinsdale, city (1990 pop. 14,396), Hennepin co., E Minn., residential suburb 4 mi/6.4 km NW of downtown Minneapolis; 45°01′N 93°19′W. Mfg. (electronic equip.). Crystal L. at center. Platted 1887, inc. as city 1938.

Robbinston, town (1990 pop. 495), Washington co., E Maine, on St. Croix R., near its mouth at Passamaquoddy Bay, and 30 mi/48 km NE of Machias; 45°04′N 67°09′W.

Robbinsville, village (1990 pop. 709), W N.C., in Nantahala Natl. Forest, 20 mi/32 km NNE of Murphy, on Cheoah R., forms Santeetlah L. reservoir to NW.; ⊙ Graham co.; 35°19′N 83°48′W. Mfg. (apparel, furniture). Appalachian Trail passes to E. Joyce Kilmer Memorial Forest to W (part of Nantahal Natl. Forest).

Robeline (RO-buh-leen), village (1990 pop. 149), Natchitoches parish, NW central La., 14 mi/23 km SW of Natchitoches, on small Bayou Pedro; 31°42′N 93°18′W. In agr. area (cotton, corn); catfish, crawfish. Los Adaes State Commemorative Area to NW.

Roberdel (RAHB-uhr-del), uninc. village, Richmond co., S N.C., 3 mi/4.8 km NNE of Rockingham. Sometimes spelled Roberdell.

Robersonville (RO-buhr-suhn-vil), town (1990 pop. 1,940), Martin co., E central N.C., 16 mi/26 km NNE of Greenville; 35°49′N 77°15′W. RR junction to W. In agr. area (tobacco, cotton, peanuts, grain; poultry, livestock). Mfg. (food, apparel). Settled 1700s; inc. 1872.

Robert (raw-BER), town, E Martinique, minor port on an Atlantic bay, 9 mi/14.5 km ENE of Fort-de-France. Trading point in sugar-growing region; alcohol and rum distilling, sugar milling. Sometimes called Le Robert.

Robert Lee, town (1990 pop. 1,276), W Texas, 29 mi/47 km N of San Angelo and on Colorado R; ⊙ Coke co.; 31°53′N 100°28′W. Elev. 1,780 ft/543 m. In farm and ranch area (cattle; cotton; grains); oil and gas. Old Fort Chadbourne is 12 mi/19 km NE; large E.V. Spence Reservoir to W.

Robert Lee Dam, Texas: see E.V. SPENCE RESERVOIR.

Robert S. Kerr Lake, reservoir (c.30 mi/48 km long, max. 5 mi/8 km wide), on Sequoyah/Le Flore co. border and in Haskell and Muskogee cos., E Okla., on Arkansas R., 22 mi/35 km W of Fort Smith, Ark.; 35°19′N 94°47′W. Max. capacity 493,600 acre-ft. Webbers Falls Lock and Dam at NW tip. Sans Bois Creek forms 15-mi/24-km S arm; Illinois R. enters from N. Formed by Robert S. Kerr Lock and Dam (52 ft/16 m high), built (1971) by the Army Corps of Engineers in 1971 for navigation and power generation. Sequoyah Natl. Wildlife Refuge at NW end.

Roberta, town (1990 pop. 939), Crawford co., central Ga., 22 mi/35 km WSW of Macon; 32°43′N 84°01′W.

Roberts 1 county (□ 1,111 sq mi/2,877 sq km; 1990 pop. 9,914), NE S. Dak., bordering on N.Dak. and Minn.; ⊙ Sisseton; 45°37′N 96°57′W. Agr. area watered by numerous lakes and North Fork Whetstone R., bounded E by Big Stone L. (Minn. R.) and L. Traverse (Bois de Sioux R.) Coteau des Prairies plateau runs N-S; Lake Traverse (Sisseton Wahpeton) Indian Reservation extends through all but SE part of co. Corn, wheat, soybeans; cattle, hogs. Hartsford Branch and Big Stone L. State parks in SE. Formed 1883. **2** county (□ 924 sq mi/2,393 sq km; 1990 pop. 1,025), extreme N Texas; ⊙ Miami; 35°49′N 100°48′W. Elev. 2,500 ft/762 m–3,000 ft/914 m. On high plains of the Panhandle. Cattle-ranching area, also producing wheat, milo, corn, hay; cattle and hogs; oil and gas. Drained by Canadian R. and tributaries, source of Wichita R. in E. Formed 1876.

Roberts, town (1990 pop. 1,043), St. Croix co., W Wis., 25 mi/40 km E of St. Paul, Minn.; 44°59′N 92°32′W. Concrete prods.

Roberts 1 village (1990 pop. 557), Jefferson co., SE Idaho, 17 mi/27 km NNW of Idaho Falls, on Snake R.; 43°43′N 112°08′W. Elev. 4,773 ft/1,455 m. Trade center in irrigated agr. area (wheat, alfalfa, sugar beets, potatoes; sheep, cattle; dairying). Camas Natl. Wildlife Refuge to N. **2** village (1990 pop. 397), Ford co., E Ill., 13 mi/21 km NNW of Paxton; 40°36′N 88°10′W. Grain, hay; livestock, poultry; some mfg. **3** village (1990 pop. 320), Carbon co., S Mont., on Rock Creek and 12 mi/19 km NNE of Red Lodge. S of Cooney Reservoir State Park.

Roberts, Camp, Calif.: see PASO ROBLES.

Roberts Creek Mountain, Nev.: see ROBERTS MOUNTAINS.

Roberts Mountains, rise to 10,133 ft/3,089 m at Roberts Creek Mt., Eureka co., central Nev., SE of Cortez Mts., 30 mi/48 km NW of Eureka; 39°52′N 116°18′W.

Robertsdale, town (1990 pop. 2,401), Baldwin co., SW Ala., 24 mi/39 km S of Bay Minette. Vegetable and meat packing, lumber milling; furniture, apparel.

Robertson 1 county (□ 100 sq mi/259 sq km; 1990 pop. 2,124), N Ky.; ⊙ Mt. Olivet; 38°32′N 84°03′W. Bounded W and SW by Licking R., N in part by North Fork Licking R; drained by Johnson Creek. Gently rolling upland agr. area (dairying; cattle, poultry; burley tobacco, corn, hay, alfalfa), in Bluegrass region. Blue Licks Battlefield State Park in S; Johnson Creek Covered Bridge in S. Formed 1867. **2** county (1990 pop. 41,494), N Tenn.; ⊙ Springfield; 36°32′N 86°52′W. Bounded N by Ky.; drained by Red R. and its small affluents Carr Creek and Sulphur Fork. Rich agr. area (dairying; fruit growing, tobacco, grain; livestock); some mfg. at Springfield. Wild horse and burro adoption center near Cross Plains. Formed 1796. **3** county (□ 865 sq mi/2,240 sq km; 1990 pop. 15,511), E central Texas; ⊙ Franklin; 31°01′N 96°30′W. Bounded W by Brazos R., E by Navasota R. Rich, diversified, irrigated agr. area (cotton, sorghum, grain, hay, corn, watermelons; cattle, hogs, poultry; dairying). Oil, natural gas, lignite. L. Limestone in N corner of co.; Twin Oak Reservoir in N. Formed 1837.

Robertsonville, village (1991 pop. 1,832), S Que., Canada, 5 mi/8 km NE of Thetford Mines; 46°08′N 71°13′W. In asbestos-mining region.

Robertville, village, Jasper co., S S.C., 18 mi/29 km NW of Ridgeland. Named for family of Henry Martyn Robert, author of *Rules of Order*. Timber.

Roberval (RAH-buhr-vuhl), town (1991 pop. 11,628), S central Que., Canada, on SW Shore of L. St. John, 130 mi/209 km NW of Quebec; ⊙ Lac St. Jean Ouest co.; 48°31′N 72°13′W. In agr. region; mfg.; resort.

Robeson (RO-buh-suhn), county (□ 951 sq mi/2,463 sq km; 1990 pop. 105,179), SE N.C., ⊙ Lumberton; 34°38′N 79°06′W. Coastal plain; drained by Lumber R. forms SE border, (called Drowing Creek to W) and Big Swamp R., forms large part of E boundary. Bounded SW by S.C. state line. Textile and lumber mills. Agr. (corn, wheat, oats, soybeans, sorghum, hay, cotton, peanuts, tobacco; chickens, turkeys, cattle, hogs). Mfg. at Maxton and Lumberton. Lumber River State Park on SE boundary. Formed 1786.

Robesonia (RO-bah-SO-nee-ah), borough (1990 pop. 1,944), Berks co., SE central Pa., 11 mi/18 km W of Reading, on Furnace Creek; 40°21′N 76°08′W. Agr. (grain, soybeans; poultry, livestock, dairying); mfg. (chemicals, food prods., machinery, paper prods., furniture). Blue Marsh L. reservoir and State Recreation Area to NE. Founded 1855.

Robinette (rahb-in-ET), uninc. town, Logan co., SW W.Va., 12 mi/19 km ESE of Logan, Amherstdale 2 mi/3.2 km to W. Bituminous coal.

Robinhood, Maine: see GEORGETOWN.

Robins, town (1990 pop. 875), Linn co., E Iowa, 7 mi/11.3 km N of Cedar Rapids; 42°04′N 91°40′W. Livestock, grain.

Robins Air Force Base, located in Warner Robins, Ga., near Macon in Houston co. Local leaders pledged the original 3,108 acres/1,258 ha of this future air base to the U.S. govt. in 1941 to secure its designation. Building began in 1942 for its designation. Building began in 1942 for the Warner Robins Army Air Depot. By 1943 the city of Warner Robins was inc. The base became an important Cold War installation after World War II. The complex now also includes the Warn Robins Air Logistics Center and covers 8,790 acres/3,557 ha. Over 4,000 civilians and 16,000 military personnel are employed here. Mus. of aviation stands next to the air base.

Robins Island, SE N.Y., lying bet. Great Peconic and Little Peconic bays, bet. flukes of E L.I., 11 mi/18 km E of Riverhead; c.2 mi/3.2 km long, 40°58′N 72°28′W. Summer resort.

Robinson, city (1990 pop. 6,740), SE Ill., 24 mi/39 km NNW of Vincennes, Ind.; ⊙ Crawford co.; 39°00′N 87°44′W. Trade and mfg. center in agr. and oil-producing area; mfg. of pottery, plastic prods., fabricated metal prods., food; oil refinery. Poultry, livestock; corn, wheat. Lincoln Trail Col. and Robinson Correctional Center here. Inc. 1875.

Robinson, township (1990 pop. 10,830), Allegheny co., W Pa., residential suburb 8 mi/12.9 km W of Pittsburgh; 40°27′N 80°07′W. Drained by Montour Creek. Pittsburgh Internatl. Airport to W. Settlers Cabin Park to S.

Robinson, town (1990 pop. 7,111), McLennan co., E central Texas, residential suburb 7 mi/11.3 km S of downtown Waco; 31°26′N 97°07′W. Drained by Flat and Castleman creeks. Agr. to S and E (cattle, dairying; cotton, wheat).

Robinson 1 village (1990 pop. 268), Brown co., NE Kansas, on small affluent of Missouri R. and 7 mi/11.3 km ESE of Hiawatha; 39°48′N 95°24′W. Corn; livestock. Brown State Fishing L. to E. **2** village (1990 pop. 87), Kidder co., central N.Dak., 21 mi/34 km N of Steele; 47°08′N 99°46′W. Small lakes to SE.

Robinson 2 Nuclear Power Plant, S.C.: see HARTSVILLE.

Robinson Creek, uninc. town (1990 pop. 800), Pike co., E Ky., 7 mi/11.3 km SSW of Pikesville, on Robinson Creek. Bituminous coal. Mfg. (concrete prods.).

Roblin, town (1991 pop. 1,838), W Man., Canada, 60 mi/97 km W of Dauphin. Near group of small lakes; grain elevators; tanning, dairying, mixed farming.

Robson, Mount, Canada: see MOUNT ROBSON PROVINCIAL PARK.

Robstown, city (1990 pop. 12,849), Nueces co., S Texas, suburb 16 mi/26 km W of downtown Corpus Christi; 27°48′N 97°39′W. It is a RR junction and a packing and shipping center for a blackland region that produces cotton, sorghum, and oil. There is oil refining and related chemical industries; mfg. (fabricated metal prods, apparel); sand and gravel. In 1992 chemical cloud from butadiene plant precipitated class action suit. Primarily Mex.-Amer. pop. Nueces co. airport is here. Inc. 1912.

Roby, village (1990 pop. 616), NW central Texas, 20 mi/32 km N of Sweetwater; ⊙ Fisher co.; 32°45′N 100°22′W. Elev. 1,990 ft/607 m. In agr. (cotton; wheat, alfalfa) and cattle-ranching area; oil and gas; gypsum.

Roca, village (1990 pop. 84), Lancaster co., SE Nebr., 10 mi/16 km S of Lincoln and on branch of Platte R.; 40°39′N 96°39′W. Light mfg.

Roca Partida Point (ro-kah pahr-TEE-dah), cape in Veracruz, SE Mexico, on Gulf of Campeche, 19 mi/31 km N of San Andrés Tuxtla; 19°00′N 112°07′W.

Rocanville (RO-kuhn-vil), town (1991 pop. 842), SE Sask., Canada, near Man. border, 16 mi/26 km N of Moosomin; 50°23′N 101°42′W. Grain elevators; livestock.

Rochdale, village (1990 pop. 1,800), Dutchess co., SE N.Y.; 41°43′N 73°51′W.

Rochdale, Mass.: see LEICESTER.

Roche Percée (rahsh PUHR-see), village (1991 pop. 154), SE Sask., Canada, on Souris R. and 10 mi/16 km ESE of Estevan, near N.Dak. border. Coal mining.

Roche-à-Bateau (ro-shah-bah-TO), town (1982 pop. 1,210), Sud dept., SW Haiti, on Jacmel Peninsula, 15 mi/24 km W of Les Cayes; 18°11′N 74°00′W. Fruit growing; basketmaking.

Rochelle, city (1990 pop. 8,769), Ogle co., N Ill., 16 mi/26 km ESE of Oregon; 41°55′N 89°03′W. Trade, processing, and shipping center in rich agr. area; mfg. (textiles, food). Corn, wheat, soybeans; livestock; dairy prods. Inc. 1819.

Rochelle (ruh-SHEL), town (1990 pop. 1,510), Wilcox co., S central Ga., 17 mi/27 km E of Cordele; 31°57′N 83°28′W. Mfg. includes food, apparel, chemicals.

Rochelle 1 (RO-shel), uninc. village, Grant parish, central La., 34 mi/55 km N of Alexandria, and on Little R. just below its formation by junction of Dudgemona R. and Bayou Castor; 31°47′N 92°22′W. Timber. **2** uninc. village (1990 pop. 163), McCulloch co., central Texas, 10 mi/16 km NE of Brady. In farm area (cattle). **3** uninc. village, Madison co., N Va., 22 mi/35 km NNE of Charlottesville; 38°17′N 78°16′W. Mfg. (fixtures, chemicals); agr. (dairying, livestock; grain, apples); timber.

Rochelle Park (ro-SHEL), village in Rochelle Park township (1990 pop. 5,587), Bergen co., NE N.J., on Saddle R. and 5 mi/8 km E of Paterson; 40°54′N 74°04′W. Mfg. (fabricated metal prods., chemicals).

Rocheport, town (1990 pop. 255), Boone co., central Mo., on Missouri R. and 12 mi/19 km W of Columbia; 38°58′N 92°33′W. Winery. Access to Katy Trail State Park. Historic river port. Town is on the National Historic Register. Platted 1825.

Rochester, village, central Alta., Canada, on Tawatinaw R. and 50 mi/80 km N of Edmonton. Mixed farming; wheat; livestock.

Rochester 1 city (1990 pop. 5,969), N Ind., at NW end of L. Manitou (c.2 mi/3.2 km long) and 24 mi/39 km NNE of Logansport; ⊙ Fulton co.; 41°04′N 86°12′W. Tippecanoe R. to N. Agr. area (soybeans, grain; livestock); resort; mfg. (plastic prods., food prods., apparel, transportation equip., printing and publishing, fabricated metal prods.). Laid out 1835. **2** city (1990 pop.

70,745), ⊙ Olmsted co.; SE Minn., 68 mi/109 km SSE of St. Paul, on South Fork of Zumbro R., at mouth of Cascade Creek; 44°00′N 92°28′W. Elev. 1,006 ft/307 m. RR junction. It is a farm trade center. Mfg. (printing and publishing, food prods., machinery, fabricated metal prods., computers, construction materials, electronic equip.). The city is famous as the home of the Mayo Clinic, a combination of hospitals and hotels, founded (1889) by Dr. W. W. Mayo with his sons Charles Horace Mayo and William James Mayo. A state mental hosp. and a Bible col. are also here. Rochester has a symphony orchestra, a municipal band, and mus. of medical science, history, and antique vehicles. Seat of Rochester Community Col.; Rochester Vocational Technical Col.; Rochester Arts Center; Rochester Municipal Airport 7 mi/11.3 km S. Parts of Richard J. Dorer Memorial Hardwood State Forest to NW, N, and SW; Quarry Hills Park and Nature Center in E. Inc. 1858. **3** city (1990 pop. 26,630), Strafford co., SE N.H., 27 mi/43 km ENE of Concord and 8 mi/12.9 km NNW of Dover, bounded NE by Salmon Falls R. (Maine state border), drained by Cocheco R. and Isinglass R.; 43°17′N 70°58′W. Mfg. (electronic equip., apparel, fabricated metal prods., consumer goods); agr. in rural ouskirts (apples, vegetables, nursery crops; cattle; dairying). An annual agr. fair has been held here since 1875. In Rochester are an art gallery and an antique aircraft mus. The L. Winnipesaukee recreation area, with popular water sports and skiing facilities, is to NW. Includes East Rochester, 2 mi/3.2 km NE of city center on Salmon Falls R., also residential village of Gonic. Settled 1728, inc. as a city 1891. **4** industrial city (□ 37 sq mi/96 sq km; 1990 pop. 231,636), ⊙ Monroe co.; W N.Y., a port of entry on the Genesee R. and L. Ontario; 43°10′N 77°37′W. It is a leading center in the production of photographic, photocopying, optical, and dental equip., process control and recording instruments, and thermometers. Rochester also ranks high in the mfg. of electronics, machinery, transportation equip., fabricated metal prods., plastic prods. In a rich fruit-growing region. Permanent settlement by Col. Nathaniel Rochester and others began in 1812. During the Civil War, Rochester was a stop on the Underground Railroad. The Erie Canal gave impetus to Rochester's growth; flour milling became the 1st important industry. Seat of the Univ. of Rochester, Nazareth Col. of Rochester, the Rochester Inst. of Technology (est. 1829), Roberts Wesleyan Col., St. John's Fisher Col., and Monroe Community Col. The city's cultural features include the Rochester Philharmonic Orchestra and Eastman School of Music's Eastman Philharmonia, the Rochester Mus. and Science Center and Strasenburgh Planetarium, the Memorial Art Gall., N.Y. State Archeological Society, Seneca Park Zoo, and the Rundell Memorial Bldg., which houses the public lib. and an art gallery. Prominent residents have been Susan B. Anthony (her home is a Natl. Landmark and mus.), who is buried in the Mt. Hope Cemetery; Frederick Douglass; and George Eastman (his home is the Internatl. Mus. of Photography; also a Natl. Landmark and mus.). Numerous parks and nurseries have earned Rochester the name Flower City. Site of the Mall at Greece Ridge Center, one of the largest shopping centers in the U.S. Inc. 1817.

Rochester 1 town (1990 pop. 3,921), Plymouth co., SE Mass., near head of Buzzards Bay, 9 mi/14.5 km NE of New Bedford; 41°46′N 70°51′W. Agr., lumber mills. Settled c.1638, inc. 1686. **2** town (1990 pop. 7,130), Oakland co., SE Mich., suburb 24 mi/39 km NNW of downtown Detroit, 9 mi/14.5 km ENE of Pontiac, on Clinton R., in rapidly suburbanizing area; 42°41′N 83°07′W. Mfg. (transportation equip., pharmaceuticals, machinery, plastic prods.). Oakland Univ. is here. Meadow Brook Hall, 100 room Tudor mansion of auto baron John Dodge. Settled 1817, inc. 1869. **3** resort town (1990 pop. 1,181), Windsor co., central Vt., on White R. and 25 mi/40 km NW of Woodstock, in Green Mts.; 43°52′N 72°49′W. Winter sports; dairy prods. **4** uninc. town (1990 pop. 1,250), Thurston co., W Wash., 17 mi/27 km SW of Olympia, bet. Black and Chehalis rivers; 46°50′N 123°04′W. RR junction. Timber; blueberries, vegetables; cattle, poultry. Light mfg. Site of The Mall at Greeceridge Center (□ 1,700,000 sq ft/157,930 sq m), the 21st largest shopping center in U.S. Chehalis Indian reservation to W; Fort Henness Monument to E. **5** town (1990 pop. 978), Racine co., SE Wis., on Fox R. and 26 mi/42 km SW of Milwaukee; 42°44′N 88°13′W. In dairy region and recreation region; mfg. of aircrafts.

Rochester 1 village (1990 pop. 2,676), Sangamon co., central Ill., near South Fork of Sangamon R., 6 mi/9.7 km SE of Springfield; 39°45′N 89°32′W. In agr. and bituminous coal area. **2** village (1990 pop. 191), Butler co., W Ky., 11 mi/18 km W of Morgantown, on Green R., near mouth of Mud R.; 37°12′N 86°53′W. Agr. (tobacco; livestock). Toll ferry crosses Green R. **3** village (1990 pop. 206), Lorain co., N Ohio, 19 mi/31 km SSW of Elyria and on West Branch of Black R.; 41°07′N 82°18′W. **4** village (1990 pop. 458), Haskell co., NW central Texas, c.60 mi/97 km N of Abilene; 33°18′N 99°51′W. Irrigated agr. area (cotton, corn, peanuts, wheat; cattle).

Rochester, borough (1990 pop. 4,156), Beaver co., W Pa., 1 mi/1.6 km E of Beaver, on Ohio R., at mouth of Beaver R.; 40°42′N 80°16′W. Agr. (hay, corn; livestock, dairying); mfg. (food prods., wooden prods., chemicals). Shale and sandstone nearby. Originally an Indian town; early 19th-cent. river port. Settled 1799, laid out c.1835, inc. 1838.

Rochester Hills, city (1990 pop. 61,766), Oakland co., SE Mich., suburb 22 mi/35 km NNW of Detroit and 7 mi/11.3 km E of Pontiac; 42°40′N 83°09′W. Mfg. (transportation equip., plastic prods., fabricated metal prods.). Oakland Univ. (on W border with Auburn Hills) and Mich. Christian Col. are here. Rochester-Utica State Recreation Area to E; Stony Creek Metropark to NE.

Rock 1 county (□ 482 sq mi/1,248 sq km; 1990 pop. 9,806), extreme SW Minn.; ⊙ Luverne; 43°40′N 96°15′W. Agr. area bounded on W by S.Dak. and on S by Iowa; drained by Rock R. Corn, oats, hay, alfalfa, soybeans; hogs, cattle, sheep, poultry; dairying. Blue Mounds State Park in center. Formed 1857. **2** county (□ 1,011 sq mi/2,618 sq km; 1990 pop. 2,019), N Nebr., located in Sand Hills region; ⊙ Bassett; 42°25′N 99°27′W. Agr. area bounded N by Niobrara R. Cattle, hogs; corn; dairying. Several small natural lakes in S including Pony, Smith, and Long lakes. Formed 1888. **3** county (□ 726 sq mi/1,880 sq km; 1990 pop. 139,510), S Wis., on Ill. line (S); ⊙ Janesville. Drained by Rock and Sugar rivers and Turtle Creek. Rich agr. area (wheat, corn, soybeans, peas, beans; cattle, sheep, hogs; tobacco; dairy prods.). Diversified mfg. at Janesville and Beloit. Resorts at L. Koshkonong in NE. Formed 1836.

Rock City, village (1990 pop. 286), Stephenson co., N Ill., 11 mi/18 km NE of Freeport; 42°24′N 89°28′W. In agr. area.

Rock Creek, village, S B.C., Canada, near Wash. border, on Kettle R. and 24 mi/39 km W of Grand Forks; 49°06′N 118°58′W. Highway junction. Silver, lead, zinc mining (declining).

Rock Creek, town (1990 pop. 1,040), Pine co., E Minn., 5 mi/8 km S of Pine City, near Rock Creek. St. Croix R. to E; 45°45′N 92°54′W. Some mfg.; agr. (dairying; poultry, cattle, sheep; oats, alfalfa; timber). Chenwatana State Forest and St. Croix Natl. Scenic Riverway to E and NE; Rush L. to SW.

Rock Creek, village (1990 pop. 553), Ashtabula co., extreme NE Ohio, 6 mi/10 km SSW of Jefferson and on small Rock Creek; 41°40′N 80°51′W.

Rock Creek 1 c.45 mi/72 km long, NW Ill.; rises S of Lanark in Carroll co.; flows SSW past Morrison, to Rock R. below Prophetstown; 42°05′N 89°48′W. **2** c.30 mi/48 km long, in Md. and D.C.; rises just S of Laytonsville in Montgomery co., Md.; flows S past Garrett Park, Kensington, and Forest Glen in Md., and through Rock Creek Park and Natl. Zoological Park in Washington to the Potomac in Georgetown. **3** c.85 mi/137 km long, SE Wyo.; rises in N Medicine Bow Mts. in E Carbon co.; flows NE past Rock R. town, then W to Medicine Bow R. 3 mi/4.8 km E of Medicine Bow (town).

Rock Creek Butte, peak (9,097 ft/2,773 m), W Baker co., in Elkhorn Ridge, NE Oregon, 14 mi/23 km. W of Baker City; 44°25′N 118°02′W.

Rock Creek Park, upper NW Washington, D.C.; 38°57′N 77°03′W. In 1890 President Benjamin Harrison signed Congress' million-dollar endowment of Rock Creek Park, mandating the preservation of this rugged stretch, once the home of Algonquin Indians. D.C.'s largest and finest park, encompassing approximately 1,800 acres/728 ha (4 mi/6.4 km long, with an average 1 mi/1.6 km width), was purchased for public enjoyment. Another 2,700 acres/1,093 ha, Rock Creek Regional Park, falls within Montgomery co., Md. A wooded preserve with abundant wildlife and wildflowers. One of the largest urban parks in the nation, Rock Creek Park offers many outdoor recreational activities. The Natl. Zoological Park is here.

Rock Falls, city (1990 pop. 9,654), Whiteside co., NW Ill., on the Rock R. opposite Sterling, 17 mi/27 km SW of Dixon; 41°46′N 41°89′W. It is an industrial center in a farm region (corn, soybeans; cattle, hogs; dairying); mfg. (electronic equip., feeds, plastics). Restored Feeder canal for Ill. and Mississippi canal leaves Rock R. here. Inc. 1889.

Rock Falls, town (1990 pop. 130), Cerro Gordo co., N Iowa, on Shell Rock R. and 7 mi/11.3 km ENE of Mason City; 43°12′N 93°05′W. Sand and gravel pits nearby.

Rock Falls, village, Dunn co., W Wis., 12 mi/19 km SW of Eau Claire. In dairying and farming area.

Rock Fort, spa and township, Kingston parish, S Jamaica, in E outskirts of Kingston; 17°58′N 76°45′W. Has baths with curative waters. Site of old fort (built 1694). W along the coast is the former Bournemouth Bath.

Rock Hall, fishing and resort town (1990 pop. 1,584), Kent co., E Md., 10 mi/16 km SE of Chestertown; 39°08′N 76°14′W. A ferry plied to Annapolis here as a link in a main post road N and S. Ships oysters, crabs, fish; tomato cannery, shirt factory. Commercial fishermen fear being crowded out by pleasure craft since the Army Corps of Engineers rebuilt the jetties and upgraded the harbor in 1981.

Rock Harbor, Mass.: see ORLEANS.

Rock Hill, city (1990 pop. 41,643), York co., N S.C., 21 mi/34 km SSW of Charlotte, N.C., near Catawba R; 34°56′N 81°01′W. An important textile center, it also has industries producing paper, glass, fabricated metal prods., pharmaceuticals, chemicals, textiles, printing and publishing, food. A beautifully landscaped flower garden is in the center of the city. Rock Hill is the seat of Winthrop Univ. and a York Technical Col. The co. fair and a co. horse show are held here annually. A 25 mi/40 km long impoundment of the nearby Catawba R. provides water recreation. Mus. of York Co. to N. Andrew Jackson State Park lies to SE. Catawba Nuclear Power Plants 1 and 2 nearby to NW. Inc. 1870.

Rock Hill, town (1990 pop. 5,217), St. Louis co., E Mo., residential and commercial suburb 8 mi/12.9 km W of downtown St. Louis; 38°36′N 90°22′W. Light mfg. Inc. 1929.

Rock Island, town (1991 pop. 1,067), S Que., Canada, at the Vt. border; 45°00′N 72°06′W. It is the seat of Stanstead Col. Machinery, textiles.

Rock Island, county (□ 451 sq mi/1,168 sq km; 1990 pop. 148,723), NW Ill.; ⊙ Rock Island; 41°28′N 90°34′W. Bounded N and W by the Mississippi and partly E by Rock R.; drained by Rock R. Has Ill. portion of Quad Cities. Includes Black Hawk State Historic Site and Campbell's Isl. state parks and part of a natl. wildlife refuge. Mfg. (machinery, ordnance, apparel, wood prods.); agr. (cattle, hogs, poultry; corn, soybeans; dairy prods.). Nuclear power plants: Quad Cities 1 (initial criticality October 18, 1971) and Quad Cities 2 (initial criticality April 26, 1972) are 20 mi/32 km NE of Moline. Use cooling water from the Mississippi R., and each has a max. dependable capacity of 769 MWe. Rock Island (city) was spared flood damage in 1993 by flood wall, while Davenport, across river, was seriously affected. Formed 1831.

Rock Island, city (1990 pop. 40,552), NW Ill., on the Mississippi and Rock rivers, adjacent to Moline and opposite Davenport, Iowa; ⊙ Rock Island co.; 41°28′N

90°34'W. These 3 cities, with East Moline, are called the Quad Cities. Rock Isl. is a trade, transportation, and industrial center. Mfg. of machinery, metal and wood prods., apparel. RR maintenance is also an important industry. Rock Isl. is the seat of Augustana Col., and Black Hawk State Park adjoins the city. On a 1,000-acres/405-ha isl. in the Mississippi R. is a huge U.S. arsenal (est. 1862), one of the largest mfg. arsenals in the world and a major source of local employment. Arsenal Isl. was fortified by the British in the War of 1812 and by the Americans in 1816. In 1833, George Davenport built a palatial house here that still stands. During the Civil War, Arsenal Isl. was the site of a large northern military prison. A Confederate cemetery and a natl. cemetery are here. Bridges connect Arsenal Isl., Rock Isl., Davenport, and Moline. Inc. 1841.

Rock Island 1 village (1990 pop. 478), Le Flore co., E Okla., 12 mi/19 km NE of Poteau and 14 mi/23 km SSW of Fort Smith, Ark.; 35°10'N 94°28'W. Agr. and timber area in Ouachita Mts. **2** village (1990 pop. 524), Douglas co., central Wash., 8 mi/12.9 SE of Wenatchee and on Columbia R. (Rock Isl. Dam, downstream 3 mi/4.8 km SE) was completed 1931; 47°22'N 120°08'W. Wheat, barley, oats, alfalfa; some mfg. Mouth of Rock Isl. Creek to SE. RR junction across river to SW. Pangborn Airport to NW.

Rock Island, Wis.: see WASHINGTON ISLAND.

Rock Lake (c.3 mi/4.8 km long, c.3 mi/4.8 km wide), Jefferson co., S Wis., 20 mi/32 km E of Madison. Outlet to Crawfish R. Town of L. Mills is on E shore. At bottom of lake are large stone pyramids thought to have been built by prehistoric Indians. State wildlife and fish hatchery (bass and walleye). Glacial Drumlin State Trail passes along S shore.

Rock Point, summer-resort village, Charles co., S Md., on Wicomico R. near its mouth on the Potomac, 12 mi/19 km SW of Frederick and c.45 mi/72 km SSE of Washington. Once called Wood Land. Named for the rockfish (striped bass).

Rock Port, city (1990 pop. 1,438), NW Mo., near Missouri R., 55 mi/89 km NW of St. Joseph; ⊙ Atchison co.; 40°24'N 95°31'W. Corn, soybeans, wheat; hogs, cattle. Platted 1851.

Rock Rapids, city (1990 pop. 2,601), extreme NW Iowa, near Minn. line, on Rock R. and 26 mi/42 km ESE of Sioux Falls, S.Dak.; ⊙ Lyon co.; 43°25'N 96°10'W. Mfg. (apparel, food). Sand and gravel pits nearby. Inc. 1886.

Rock River, village (1990 pop. 190), Albany co., SE Wyo., on Rock Creek and 35 mi/56 km NNW of Laramie; 41°43'N 105°58'W. Elev. 6,892 ft/2,101 m. Trade and shipping center for livestock and oil. Como Bluff, large dinosaur fossil bed, to N.

Rock River 1 c.285 mi/459 km long, in SE Wis.; rises in SW Fond du Lac co.; flows S through Horicon Natl. Wildlife Refuge and Horicon Marsh State Wildlife Refuge, past Horicon, through Sinissippi L. It continues SW past Watertown and Fort Atkinson through L. Koshkonong and receives Yahara R. SW of Edgerton, then flows S through Janesville and Beloit, Wis., and Rockford Ill., then SW past Dixon and Sterling to join Mississippi R. at Rock Isl. **2** c.100 mi/161 km long, in Minn. and Iowa; formed in NE Pipestone co., SW Minn., c.13 mi/21 km NE of Pipestone; flows generally S, receives East Branch (c.15 mi/24 km long) from NNE, 7 mi/11.3 km E of Pipestone, flows past Edgerton and Luverne, Minn., continues S into Iowa, past Rock Rapids, receives Little Rock R. from NE, turns SW, flows past Rock Valley to Big Sioux R. 6 mi/9.7 km N of Hawarden; 44°07'N 96°07'W.

Rock Sound, town, central Bahama Isls., on inlet of S central Eleuthera Isl., 20 mi/32 km S of Governor's Harbour, 75 mi/121 km ESE of Nassau; 24°55'N 76°12'W. Pineapples, tomatoes.

Rock Springs, city (1990 pop. 19,050), Sweetwater co., SW Wyo., on Bitter Creek; 41°36'N 109°13'W. Elev. c.6,271 ft/1,911 m. Fourth-largest city in Wyo.; junction of RR spur to Reliance. It is a cattle and sheep shipping point and the center of large trona deposits, natural source of soda ash. Oil and gas production, electric-power distribution (Flaming Gorge Reservoir), a revived coal industry, and tourism are also important.

Mfg. (food, printing and publishing, chemicals). Rock Springs is the gateway to many recreational areas and natural wonders. It was settled around a trading post and stage station established on the Overland Trail in the 1860s. Western Wyo. Community Col. (2-year); Old City Hall Mus.; and an annual Red Desert Roundup Rodeo are there. Flaming Gorge Reservoir and Natl. Recreation Area to SW. Inc. 1888.

Rock Springs, village (1990 pop. 432), Sauk co., S central Wis., on Baraboo R. and 8 mi/12.9 km W of Baraboo; 43°28'N 89°55'W. In dairying region. Natural Bridge State Park to S. Until 1947, called Ableman.

Rock Valley, town (1990 pop. 2,540), Sioux co., NW Iowa, near S.Dak. line, on Rock R. and 21 mi/34 km NW of Orange City; 43°12'N 96°17'W. Ships sand and gravel; makes concrete blocks, dairy prods. Inc. 1888.

Rockaway, borough (1990 pop. 6,243), Morris co., N N.J., on Rockaway R. and 7 mi/11.3 km NNW of Morristown, on old Morris Canal; 40°53'N 74°30'W. In suburbanizing area. Mfg. (machinery, fabricated metal prods.); nursery prods. Settled 1739, inc. 1894.

Rockaway Beach (RAHK-uh-wai), town (1990 pop. 970), Tillamook co., NW Oregon, on Pacific Ocean, 12 mi/19 km NNW of Tillamook; 45°36'N 123°56'W. Resort. Nehalem Bay State Park to N. Inc. 1942.

Rockaway Beach, uninc. village, San Mateo co., W Calif., suburb on the Pacific Ocean, 11 mi/18 km S of downtown San Francisco. Part of Golden Gate Natl. Recreation Area to E.

Rockaway Beach, N.Y.: see ROCKAWAY PENINSULA.

Rockaway Inlet, passage connecting Jamaica Bay with the Atlantic Ocean, SE N.Y., at W tip of Rockaway Peninsula; 40°34'N 73°55'W.

Rockaway Peninsula, in Queens borough of N.Y. city, SW L.I., SE N.Y.; 40°35'N 73°50'W. A 10-mi/16-km, narrow finger of land extending SW from about 2 mi/3.2 km S of JFK Internatl. Airport. Densely pop. NE ½, with residential/resort communities of Far Rockaway, Edgemere, Arverne, Neponsit, Rockaway Park, Seaside, and Belle Harbor. The remainder is taken up by Fort Tilden and Jacob Riis Park, part of the Gateway Natl. Recreation Area. Rockaway Beach, along its SE shore, fronts on the open Atlantic Ocean. Marshlands of Jamaica Bay are contained bet. it and SE Brooklyn, and are accessed via the Gil Hodges Memorial Bridge-Flatbush Ave. and Cross Bay Bridge and Blvd.

Rockaway River, c.35 mi/56 km long, N N.J.; rises in NW Morris co.; flows E, SW, and SE past Dover and Boonton (here dammed to form Parsippany Reservoir), to Passaic R. W of Caldwell.

Rockbridge, county (□ 601 sq mi/1,557 sq km; 1990 pop. 18,350), NW Va., independent cities of Lexington and Buena Vista separate from co.; ⊙ Lexington; 37°48'N 79°27'W. N sect. is at S end of Shenandoah Valley, with Allegheny Mts. in NW, Blue Ridge in SE (cut by James R. in S); also drained by Murry R. Mfg. at Glasgow; agr. (hay, alfalfa, corn, soybeans, apples, peaches; cattle, sheep, hogs, horses; dairying); timber; limestone quarrying. Includes parts of George Washington Natl. Forest in NW and SE. Scenic mt. resort area; mineral springs, Natural Bridge in S. Formed 1778.

Rockbridge, village (1990 pop. 212), Greene co., SW central Ill., 12 mi/19 km E of Carrollton; 39°16'N 90°12'W. In agr. area (corn, wheat, soybeans, sorghum; cattle, hogs).

Rockcastle, county (□ 318 sq mi/824 sq km; 1990 pop. 14,803), central Ky.; ⊙ Mt. Vernon; 37°21'N 84°19'W. Bounded SE by Rockcastle R.; drained by Dix R. and Roundstone Creek. Hilly agr. area (burley tobacco, hay, alfalfa, corn; cattle, hogs, poultry; dairying); bituminous coal mines, limestone and sandstone quarries, oil wells; timber. Includes part of Daniel Boone Natl. Forest in E, including Great Saltpeter Cave. Formed 1810.

Rockcastle River, c.45 mi/72 km long, SE Ky., formed by joining of Middle and South forks, on Jackson/Laurel co. line, 13 mi/21 km N of London; flows SSW to Cumberland R., 14 mi/23 km ESE of Burnside. Middle Fork rises in SE Jackson co.; flows W c.20 mi/32 km. South Fork rises on Laurel/Clay co. line, flows NW c.25 mi/40 km.

Rockcliffe Park, residential village (1991 pop. 2,113), SE

Ont., Canada, on S shore of Ottawa R., just E of Ottawa; 45°27'N 75°41'W. Embassy residences here.

Rockdale, county (□ 132 sq mi/342 sq km; 1990 pop. 54,091), N central Ga.; ⊙ Conyers; 33°39'N 84°02'W. Piedmont area drained by Yellow and South rivers. Former agr. area now urbanizing rapidly as the Atlanta metropolitan area expands eastward. Site of Ga. Internatl. Horse Park equestrian competition during the 1996 summer Olympic Games. Agr. includes vegetables and fruit; cattle-raising; mfg. (textiles). Formed 1870.

Rockdale, town (1990 pop. 5,235), Milam co., central Texas, c.50 mi/80 km NE of Austin; 30°39'N 97°00'W. Market, processing center for cotton, corn, cattle, poultry area. Aluminium plant; lignite mine, some oil wells. Source of E Yegua Creek. Settled 1873, inc. 1874.

Rockdale 1 village, (1990 pop. 1,717), Will co., NE Ill., on Des Plaines R., suburb 2 mi/3.2 km SW of Joliet, satellite community of Chicago; 41°30'N 88°06'W. In agr. area; mfg. (construction materials). Illinois Youth Center is here. Inc. 1903. **2** village (1990 pop. 235), Dane co., S Wis., on small Koshkonong Creek and 18 mi/29 km ESE of Madison; 42°58'N 89°01'W. In dairying and tobacco-growing region.

Rockefeller Center, complex of bldgs., in central Manhattan, N.Y. city, bet. 48th and 51st Sts. and Fifth Ave. and the Ave. of the Americas (Sixth Ave.). Fourteen of the bldgs., including the 70-story GE (General Electric) Bldg., were built bet. 1931 and 1939. The Time-Life Bldg. (built 1960–1961), the most recent addition to the group, extended the center's boundaries W of the Ave. of the Americas. The bldgs. are occupied by offices, shops, restaurants, exhibition rooms, broadcasting studios, and the Radio City Music Hall. Five of the W bdgs. of Rockefeller Center in the broadcasting and entertainment sect. are known as Radio City. Many sculptors and painters are represented in the decoration of the bldgs. and grounds. Paul Manship designed the Prometheus of the central fountain, which overlooks an outdoor skating rink and mall.

Rocker, village, Silver Bow co., SW Mont., 4 mi/6.4 km W of Butte, on Silver Bow Creek. Hay, mining dist., service center.

Rocket Center, locality, Mineral co., NE W.Va., 7 mi/11.3 km SSW of Cumberland, Md., on N. Branch of Potomac R. Mfg. (rocket motors).

Rockfall, Conn.: see MIDDLEFIELD.

Rockfish Gap, pass (elev. 1,850/564 m) across the Blue Ridge, NW Va., on Augusta-Nelson co. line, crossed by interstate 64, 3 mi/4.8 km SE of Waynesboro; 38°01'N 78°51'W.

Rockfish River, c.40 mi/64 km long, central Va.; rises in N Nelson and W Albemarle cos.; flows S and SE to James R. 12 mi/19 km E of Lovingston; 37°54'N 78°50'W.

Rockford, city (1990 pop. 139,426), ⊙ Winnebago co. N Ill., on the Rock R. near the Wis. line; 42°16'N 89°03'W. It is the trade, processing, and shipping hub of an extensive agr. region as well as an important mfg. center. Agr. (corn, wheat, soybeans; cattle, hogs; dairying).; mfg. (transportation equip., machinery, electronics, furniture, printing and publishing, food prods.). The city's furniture business dates from the 1860s. Rockford was founded (1834) on the site of a battlefield of the Black Hawk War. It is the seat of Rockford Col. and Rock Valley Col., also Illinois Col. of Medicine. The city has an extensive park and recreational system, a symphony orchestra, and several mus., including the notable Time Mus. with its antique clocks and watches. Rockford also has a large riverfront recreational area, the Sinnissippi Park Sunken Gardens. Rock Cut State Park to NE. Inc. 1839 with the merger of 2 settlements on opposite sides of the river.

Rockford 1 town (1990 pop. 461), ⊙ Coosa co. E central Ala., 35 mi/56 km N of Montgomery. Lumber; yarn. **2** town (1990 pop. 863), Floyd co., N Iowa, on Shell Rock R. at mouth of Lime Creek, and 13 mi/21 km W of Charles City; 43°02'N 92°57'W. Brick and tile plant. **3** town (1990 pop. 3,750), Kent co., SW Mich., 12 mi/19 km NNE of Grand Rapids and on short Rogue R.; 43°07'N 85°33'W. In farm area (livestock; apples, potatoes, grain, hay); dairy prods.; mfg. (electronic equip., plastic prods., apparel). Resort. Pando Ski Area to E. Cannonsburg Ski Area to SE. Settled 1841; inc. as village 1871, as city 1933. **4** town (1990 pop. 2,665), Hennepin and Wright cos., S central Minn., on Crow R. and 25 mi/40 km WNW of Minneapolis; 45°05′N 93°44′W. Grain, soybeans; poultry; dairying; some mfg. Small natural lakes in area.

Rockford 1 village (1990 pop. 1,119), Mercer co., W Ohio, on St. Marys R. and 10 mi/16 km N of Celina; 40°42′N 84°39′W. In agr. region; tomato canneries; limestone quarries. **2** village (1990 pop. 481), Spokane co., E Wash., near Idaho line, 20 mi/32 km SE of Spokane, on Rock Creek; 47°27′N 117°08′W. Wheat, peas, oats, alfalfa; sheep, hogs. Coeur d'Alene Indian Reservation and Coeur d'Alene L. reservoir to E, in Idaho.

Rockglen, town (1991 pop. 507), S Sask., Canada, 32 mi/51 km S of Assiniboia, near Mont. border; 49°11′N 105°57′W. Wheat; in coal mining region.

Rockham, town (1990 pop. 48), Faulk co., NE central S.Dak., 17 mi/27 km SE of Faulkton; 44°54′N 98°49′W.

Rockhill, Pa.: see ROCKHILL FURNACE.

Rockhill Furnace, borough (1990 pop. 421), Huntingdon co., S central Pa., 10 mi/16 km S of Mount Union, adjoins Orbisonia, to E, on Blacklog Creek; 40°14′N 77°54′W. Agr. (hay; livestock; timber); mfg. of apparel. East Broad Toe RR, narrow gauge RR; Rockhill Trolly Mus. Also called Rockhill.

Rockingham 1 (RAW-keeng-ham), county (□ 794 sq mi/2,056 sq km; 1990 pop. 245,845), SE N.H.; ⊙ Exeter; 42°58′N 71°05′W. Bounded NE by Piscataqua R. (tidal; Maine state border), E by Atlantic Ocean, and S by Mass. state line. Mfg. at Portsmouth, Exeter, Hampton, Seabroook, Plaistow, Derry, Londonderry, Windham, and Salem; agr. (apples, nursery crops, vegetables, corn, beans; seafood, fish, lobster; cattle, poultry; dairying); shipping at Portsmouth; resorts on coast and lakes. Drained by Exeter, Piscassic, Hampton, Pawtuckaway, and Lamprey rivers. Seabrook nuclear power plant, initial criticality June 13, 1989; is 13 mi/21 km S of Portsmouth, uses cooling water from the Atlantic Ocean, and has a max. dependable capacity of 1150 MWe. Fort Constitution and Fort Stark state historic sites in NE; part of Bear Brook State Park on NW boundary; Pawtuckaway State Park in NW; Kingston State Park in S; Isles of Shoals (Maine/ N.H.) 7 mi/11.3 km off coast; numerous ponds in S; Massabesic L. on W boundary; Pawtuckaway L. in NW; on coast Odiorne Point, Wallis Sands, Rye Harbor, and Jenness Beach state parks in NE; Hampton State Park in SE. State's 1st settlement made 1623 near Portsmouth. Formed 1769. **2** county (□ 572 sq mi/1,481 sq km; 1990 pop. 86,064), N N.C., in Piedmont region; ⊙ Wentworth; 36°23′N 79°46′W. Bounded N by Va. state line. Agr. area (especially tobacco also corn, wheat, oats, soybeans, sorghum, hay; dairying; poultry, cattle, hogs); drained by Dan and Haw rivers. Mfg. at Riedsville and Eden. Parts of Belews L. reservoir in SW corner. Formed 1785. **3** county (□ 853 sq mi/2,209 sq km; 1990 pop. 57,482), NW Va.; independent city separate from co.; ⊙ Harrisonburg; 38°31′N 78°52′W. Partly in central Shenandoah Valley; bounded NW and NE, in part, by W.Va. state line; Allegheny Mts. in W and NW, Massanutten Mtn. ridge in E center, Blue Ridge along SE border. Drained by North R., which joins South R. to form South Fork of Shenandoah R., which flows through SE. Mfg. at Bridgewater, Dayton, Mount Crawford, Broadway, Timberville, and Elkton. Diversified agr. (hay, alfalfa, wheat, corn, soybeans, apples, peaches; poultry, cattle, sheep, hogs; dairying); timber; limestone quarrying; freshwater fish (trout). Parts of George Washington Natl. Forest in NW and S; part of Shenandoah Natl. Park along SE border; Appalachian Trail and Skyline Drive follow SE border. Limestone caves. Formed 1778.

Rockingham, city (1990 pop. 9,399), S N.C., 60 mi/97 km ESE of Charlotte, near Pee Dee (Great Pee Dee) R., forms Blewett Falls L. reservoir to NW.; ⊙ Richmond co.; 34°56′N 79°45′W. Agr. area (cotton, tobacco, grain, soybeans; hogs, poultry, cattle). Mfg. (textiles, apparel, asphalt, fabricated metal prods., printing and publishing, paper prods.). N.C. Motor Speedway to N. Settled c.1780; inc. 1887.

Rockingham, town (1990 pop. 5,484), Windham co., SE Vt., on the Connecticut R., and 20 mi/32 km N of Brattleboro; 43°10′N 72°30′W. Includes villages of Bellows Falls (furniture, paper prods., dairy prods.) and Saxtons R., seat of Vermont Acad., at mouth of small Saxtons R. (c.20 mi/32 km long). Has Congregational church, built 1787. Settled c.1753.

Rockingham Park, N.H.: see SALEM.

Rocklake, village (1990 pop. 221), Towner co., N N.Dak., 20 mi/32 km N of Cando, on S end of Rock L. (9 mi/14.5 km long, 1 mi/1.6 km wide); 48°47′N 99°14′W.

Rockland, county (□ 199 sq mi/515 sq km; 1990 pop. 265,475), SE N.Y.; ⊙ New City; 41°08′N 74°01′W. Bounded E by the Hudson R. (here widening into Tappan Zee), and SW and S by N.J. border; includes the part of the Ramapo Mts. of N.J. that extends into N.Y. and forms the border bet. Rockland and Orange cos. Drained by Hackensack and Ramapo rivers. Has many residential communities of N.Y. city commuters; former summer resort areas. Some farming (fruit), dairying; hothouse flowers and vegetables. Some mfg. at Haverstraw, Nyack, Pearl R., Spring Valley, Suffern. Contains several sects. of Palisades Interstate Park, including Bear Mt. recreational area. Formed 1798.

Rockland, city (1990 pop. 7,972), S Maine, on W shore of Penobscot Bay and 35 mi/56 km ESE of Augusta; ⊙ Knox co.; 44°07′N 69°07′W. Port of entry. Resort (with yacht harbor), trade center; fishing port, noted for lobsters, with a well-known lobster festival annually, the 1st weekend in August. Tourism. Coast Guard installations are here. Settled c.1770; town inc. 1848 as East Thomaston, city inc. 1854.

Rockland, town (1991 pop. 6,771), SE Ont., Canada, on Ottawa R. and 22 mi/35 km ENE of Ottawa; 45°33′N 75°19′W. Milling, woodworking.

Rockland, industrial town (1990 pop. 16,123), Plymouth co., E Mass.; 42°08′N 70°55′W. Some mfg. The naval air station in adjacent South Weymouth is scheduled to close. Settled 1673, set off from Abington and inc. 1874.

Rockland 1 village (1990 pop. 264), Power co., SE Idaho, 15 mi/24 km S of American Falls; 42°34′N 112°52′W. Elev. 4,671 ft/1,424 m. Wheat, alfalfa, barley; cattle, sheep. Fort Hall Indian Reservation to NE; Sawtooth Natl. Forest to SW; Curlew Natl. Grassland to S. **2** village in Rockland town (□ 95 sq mi/246 sq km; 1990 pop. 4,096), Sullivan co., SE N.Y., on Beaver Kill and 14 mi/23 km NW of Liberty; 41°57′N 74°47′W. Lakes nearby. **3** village (1990 pop. 509), La Crosse co., W Wis., 16 mi/26 km ENE of La Crosse; 43°54′N 90°55′W. In dairy and livestock area; mfg. of lumber. On La Crosse River State Trail.

Rockland Lake, village (1990 pop. 120), Rockland co., SE N.Y., on Rockland L. (1 mi/1.6 km long), 3 mi/4.8 km N of Nyack, near W bank of the Hudson R.; 41°08′N 73°56′W.

Rockledge (RAHK-lej), city (□ 11 sq mi/28 sq km; 1990 pop. 16,023), Brevard co., E central Fla., 7 mi/11.3 km SW of Cape Canaveral, on Indian R. (a lagoon); 28°19′N 80°43′W.

Rockledge (RAHK-lej), borough (1990 pop. 2,679), Montgomery co., SE Pa., residential suburb 9 mi/14.5 km NNE of downtown Philadelphia; 40°04′N 75°05′W. Light mfg. Pennycock Creek to NE. Settled 1880, inc. 1893.

Rockleigh, residential borough (1990 pop. 270), Bergen co., extreme NE N.J., at N.Y. line, 1 mi/1.6 km SE of Tappan, N.Y.; 41°00′N 73°56′W.

Rocklin, city (1990 pop. 19,033), Placer co., central Calif., 20 mi/32 km NE of Sacramento; 38°48′N 121°14′W. RR junction; timber; plums, kiwi fruit; grain; cattle, sheep, turkeys. Mfg. (fabricated metal prods., wood prods., plastic prods., computer equip., electronic equip.). Sierra Col. (2 year). Folsom L. State Recreation Area to E.

Rockmart, town (1990 pop. 3,356), Polk co., NW Ga., 19 mi/31 km SSE of Rome; 34°01′N 85°03′W. Many bldgs. built of locally quarried slate or locally produced bricks. Mfg. includes transportation equip., concrete, electronic equip., fabricated metal prods., food. Inc. 1872.

Rockne, uninc. village (1990 pop. 400), Bastrop co., S central Texas, 28 mi/45 km SE of Austin. Agr. area (cattle; corn, cotton, wheat, soybeans). Oil and natural gas.

Rockport, city (1990 pop. 2,315), SW Ind., on Ohio R. and 29 mi/47 km ESE of Evansville; ⊙ Spencer co.; 37°53′N 87°03′W. Agr. and oil- and natural gas-producing area; mfg. (construction materials, food prods.); clay pits. RR terminus. Lincoln Pioneer Village, a memorial with reconstructed pioneer homes, is here. Settled 1802.

Rockport 1 resort and fishing town (1990 pop. 2,854), Knox co., S Maine, on Penobscot Bay and just N of Rockland; 44°10′N 69°05′W. Includes villages of Rockville and Glen Cove. Tourism; boating. Settled 1769, set off from Camden 1891. **2** town (1990 pop. 7,482), including Rockport village, Essex co., NE Mass., on Cape Ann N of Gloucester; 42°40′N 70°36′W. Summer resort and artists' colony; ships granite; fishing. Includes resort village of Pigeon Cove. Halibut Point State Park. Settled 1690, set off from Gloucester 1840. **3** town (1990 pop. 4,753), S Texas, on Aransas Bay 26 mi/42 km NE of Corpus Christi; ⊙ Aransas co. Aransas Bay traversed by Gulf Intracoastal Waterway. RR terminus; tourist resort (beaches, fishing, duck hunting); fisheries (fish, shrimp, oysters); redfish hatchery; some mfg. Aransas co. airport to N. Copano Bay State Fishing Pier is to N. Founded 1868.

Rockport, village (1990 pop. 385), Ohio co., W Ky., on Green R. and 9 mi/14.5 km SW of Hartford; 37°20′N 86°59′W. Bituminous coal; agr. area (tobacco, grain; livestock; timber).

Rocksprings, town (1990 pop. 1,339), SW Texas, on Edwards Plateau, 61 mi/98 km NE of Del Rio; ⊙ Edwards co.; 30°01′N 100°12′W. Elev. 2,450 ft/747 m. In goat-, cattle-, and sheep-ranching region; important mohair market; tourist center. Settled 1887, inc. 1924; rebuilt after 1927 tornado.

Rockton 1 village (1990 pop. 2,928), Winnebago co., N Ill., at junction of Rock and Pecatonica rivers (both bridged here), 12 mi/19 km N of Rockford, near Wis. line; 42°27′N 89°04′W. Agr.; mfg. (wood prods.). Inc. 1847. **2** uninc. village, Fairfield co., N central S.C., 25 mi/40 km N of Columbia. Mfg. of granite monuments. Granite quarries located here. Agr. includes cattle; corn, hay.

Rockvale, village (1990 pop. 321), Fremont co., S central Colo., near Arkansas R., 30 mi/48 km WNW of Pueblo; 38°22′N 105°09′W. Elev. 5,350 ft/1,631 m. Coal mining. Part of San Isabel Natl. Forest to SW.

Rockville 1 city, N central Conn., in Vernon town, on Shenipsit L., at source of Hockanum R. (early water power); ⊙ Tolland co. Rockville General Hosp. Light mfg. Chartered 1889. **2** city (1990 pop. 44,835), W central Md., NW suburb of Washington, D.C.; ⊙ Montgomery co.; 39°05′N 77°09′W. Rockville was orginally called Hungerford's Tavern in honor of Charles Hungerford's establishment where local citizens met in 1774 to issue resolves against further trade with Great Britain. The name was changed to Montgomery Courthouse in 1776 when the co. was established and renamed Williamsburg in honor of a local developer in 1886. The origins of the current name, bestowed in 1803, are unknown. After the Civil War when the town was occupied by both Confederate and Union troops, several hotels were built near the RR line opened in 1873. One, the former Woodlawn, has been a sanitorium since 1908. It has several scientific and technical research and technology laboratories that focus on the aerospace, electronics, nuclear energy, and communications industries. The Food and Drug Administration (FDA) is here, as is a campus of Montgomery Col. The commercial center was destroyed in the early 1970s to make way for a shopping center, but several older bldgs. remain. Among them are the 3d courthouse (c.1891) near the present courthouse built in 1931; the RR station which is on the Natl. Register of Historic Places; and the Beall-Dawson House, home of the Montgomery Historical Society. F. Scott Fitzgerald, the novelist, and his wife, Zelda, are buried in a local Catholic cemetry. Settled in the 1760s.; inc. as a city in 1860. **3** city (1990 pop. 193), Bates co., W Mo., near Osage

R., 16 mi/26 km E of Rich Hill; 38°04′N 94°04′W. Corn, wheat, sorghum; cattle.

Rockville, town (1990 pop. 2,706), W Ind., 23 mi/37 km NNE of Terre Haute; ⊙ Parke co.; 39°46′N 87°14′W. Agr. and timber area; some mfg. Turkey Run State Park 8 mi/12.9 km N; center for Covered Bridge Festival, Oct. Laid out 1823, inc. 1854.

Rockville 1 village (1990 pop. 579), Stearns co., central Minn., on Sauk R. and 10 mi/16 km SW of St. Cloud; 45°28′N 94°20′W. Grain; poultry, livestock; dairying. Granite quarries here. Small natural lakes in area; Grand L. to S. **2** village (1990 pop. 87), Sherman co., central Nebr., 13 mi/21 km SSE of Loup City and on Middle Loup R; 41°07′N 98°49′W. **3** uninc. village, Susquehanna township, Dauphin co., S central Pa., 5 mi/8 km N of Harrisburg, on Susquehanna R., here crossed by Rockville Bridge, stone-arch RR bridge (3,798 ft/1,158 m long); 40°20′N 76°54′W. **4** village in Hopkinton town, Washington co., SW R.I., 4 mi/6.4 km N of Hopkinton village, near Conn. line. In agr. area. **5** village (1990 pop. 182), Washington co., SW Utah, 30 mi. NE of St. George, on Virgin R.; 37°08′N 113°03′W. Zion Natl. Park to N and E, near W main entrance to park. Tourism. **6** uninc. village, Hanover co., E central Va., 17 mi/27 km NW of Richmond, South Anna R. to N and Chickahominy R. to S; 37°43′N 77°40′W. Mfg. (crushed stone); agr. (dairying, cattle; grain); major limestone quarrying area.

Rockville, S.C.: see WADMALAW ISLAND.

Rockville Centre, residential village (□ 3 sq mi/7.8 sq km; 1990 pop. 24,727), Nassau co., SE N.Y., on SW L.I.; 40°39′N 73°38′W. Seat of Molloy Catholic Col. for Women. A state park is adjacent to the village. Inc. 1893.

Rockwall, county (□ 148 sq mi/383 sq km; 1990 pop. 25,604), NE Texas; ⊙ Rockwall; 32°53′N 96°24′W. Smallest Texas co. in land area; W margin of co. experiencing urban pressure from Dallas-Fort Worth area; drained by East Fork of Trinity R. Agr. (wheat, hay, sorghum); cattle; some timber. L. Ray Hubbard on W border. Named for extensive geological formation resembling masonry wall. Formed 1873.

Rockwall, city (1990 pop. 10,486), NE Texas, 21 mi/34 km NE of downtown Dallas, on E shore of L. Ray Hubbard (East Fork of Trinity R.); ⊙ Rockwall co.; 32°55′N 96°27′W. Elev. 596 ft/182 m. Trade, shipping point in agr. area (cotton; wheat, sorghum, hay); cattle, horses; mfg. (electronics, chemicals, fabricated metal prods.).

Rockwell 1 town (1990 pop. 1,008), Cerro Gordo co., N Iowa, 12 mi/19 km S of Mason City; 42°58′N 93°11′W. In agr. area; feeds, chemicals. Limestone quarry nearby. **2** town (1990 pop. 1,598), Rowan co., W central N.C., 9 mi/14.5 km SSE of Salisbury; 35°32′N 80°24′W. Grain, tobacco; poultry, livestock; dairying; mfg. (apparel, construction equip.).

Rockwell City, city (1990 pop. 1,981), central Iowa, 25 mi/40 km WSW of Fort Dodge; ⊙ Calhoun co.; 42°23′N 94°37′W. Mfg. (feeds). North Central Correctional Facility to S. Twin Lakes State Park to N. Inc. 1882.

Rockwood, village, S Ont., Canada, 7 mi/11 km NE of Guelph; 43°37′N 80°08′W. Dairying; mixed farming; limestone quarrying. Site of noted Rockwood Academy.

Rockwood, city (1990 pop. 5,348), Roane co., E Tenn., on Cumberland escarpment, near Tennessee R., 40 mi/64 km W of Knoxville; 35°52′N 84°41′W. In coal, iron, limestone, timber, farm area; mfg. of apparel, pharmaceuticals, steel; metal recycling. Settled c.1816.

Rockwood, town (1990 pop. 3,141), Wayne co., SE Mich., suburb 20 mi/32 km SSW of downtown Detroit, near Huron R.; 42°04′N 83°14′W. In farm area. Light mfg. Inc. 1926.

Rockwood 1 village (1990 pop. 45), Randolph co., SW Ill., on the Mississippi and 8 mi/12.9 km SE of Chester; 37°50′N 89°42′W. In agr. area. **2** resort village, Somerset co., W central Maine, on W shore of Moosehead L., c.60 mi/97 km N of Skowhegan.

Rockwood, borough (1990 pop. 1,014), Somerset co., SW Pa., 7 mi/11.3 km SW of Somerset, on Casselman R.; 39°55′N 79°09′W. Agr. (corn, oats; livestock; dairying);

mfg. (lumber); bituminous coal. Laid out 1857, inc. 1885.

Rocky, village (1990 pop. 181), Washita co., W Okla., 26 mi/42 km SSW of Clinton, and 10 mi/16 km SSW of Cordell; 35°09′N 99°03′W. Trade center for diversified farm area.

Rocky Bottom, uninc. village, Pickens co., NW S.C., 27 mi/43 km NW of Greenville near N.C. state line, in the Blue Ridge Mts.

Rocky Comfort, uninc. community, McDonald co., extreme SW Mo., in the Ozarks, 18 mi/29 km SE of Neosho. Settled c. 1860.

Rocky Face, town (1990 pop. 1,000), Whitfield co., Ga., 4 mi/6.4 km NW of Dalton. Mfg. of lumber and fixtures.

Rocky Ford 1 town (1990 pop. 197), Screven co., E Ga., 13 mi/21 km WSW of Sylvania, near Ogeechee R.; 32°40′N 81°50′W. **2** town (1990 pop. 4,162), Otero co., SE central Colo., on Arkansas R., and 50 mi/80 km ESE of Pueblo; 38°02′N 103°43′W. Elev. 4,178 ft/1,273 m. Trade and melon-shipping point in agr. area; mfg. (food, printing and publishing, concrete); cantaloupes; cattle, poultry; vegetables. Melon Day is celebrated annually in Sept. L. Meridith reservoir to N; Comanche Natl. Grassland to S. Inc. 1887.

Rocky Gap, uninc. village, Bland co., SW Va., 5 mi/8 km ESE of Bluefield, W. Va., near W.Va. state line, in Jefferson Natl. Forest; 37°14′N 81°06′W. Mfg. (electrical equip., fabricated metal prods.); agr. (livestock); timber; limestone.

Rocky Grove, uninc. town, (1990 est. pop. 2,000), Sugarcreek township, Venango co., NW Pa., 1 mi/1.6 km NE of Franklin, near mouth of French Creek, on Allegheny R.; 41°24′N 79°49′W.

Rocky Hill, town (1990 pop. 16,554), Hartford co., central Conn., a suburb of Hartford, on the Connecticut R.; 41°39′N 72°39′W. Chemicals, textiles. Rocky Hill was an important river port from 1700 to 1820. Of note are the Congregational Church (built in 1808) and Dinosaur Park. Settled c.1650, inc. 1843.

Rocky Hill, borough (1990 pop. 693), Somerset co., central N.J., 12 mi/19 km SW of New Brunswick; 40°23′N 74°38′W. Major source of terra cotta for facings on Manhattan building facades. Washington wrote his farewell address to the army here, 1783. A state historical site is here.

Rocky Mount, city (1990 pop. 49,961), Edgecombe and Nash cos., E N.C., 50 mi/80 km ENE of Raleigh, on the Tar R.; 35°57′N 77°48′W. The growing city is the commercial and distribution center of a rich agr. area (tobacco, cotton; peanuts, corn; chickens, hogs, cattle). Mfg. (construction materials, furniture, transportation equip., textiles, apparel, printing and publishing). Rocky Mount is also a large tobacco market and processing point. N.C. Wesleyan Col. is to N, near Battlesboro; Nash Community Col. to W; Rocky Mount-Wilson Airport to S. Rocky Mount Arts Center, occupies renovated water tank; Children's Mus. Stonewall Manor Estate. Settled by 1818, inc. 1867.

Rocky Mount 1 town, Meriwether co., W Ga., 22 mi/35 km ENE of La Grange; 34°09′N 84°40′W. **2** town (1990 pop. 4,098), S Va., in E foothills of Blue Ridge, 18 mi/29 km S of Roanoke, near Blackwater R.; ⊙ Franklin co.; 37°00′N 79°53′W. Mfg. (wood prods., lumber, construction materials, printing and publishing, machinery, furniture); agr. area (grain, tobacco, apples, peaches; cattle); timber. Booker T. Washington Natl. Monument, Smith Mt. L. reservoir and State Park to NE; Chateau Natural Vineyard to N. Philpott reservoir to SW. Inc. 1873.

Rocky Mountain House, town (1991 pop. 5,461), S central Alta., Canada, at the foot of the Rocky Mts. and the confluence of the North Saskatchewan and Clearwater rivers; 52°22′N 114°55′W. Founded in 1799 as a fortified post of the North West Co. in Blackfoot country and known as Blackfoot post, it was taken over (1821) and operated by the Hudson's Bay Company until 1875. It is now the gateway to a big-game hunting area.

Rocky Mountain National Park (□ 414 sq mi/1,072 sq km), Grand, Larimer, and Boulder cos., central

Colo. Scenic Rocky Mts. region on the Continental Divide (bisects park N-S); 45 mi/72 km NW of Denver. Many high snow-capped peaks. Longs Peak is the highest at 14,255 ft/4,345 m, and 76 are over 12,000 ft/3,658 m. Includes Hidden Valley Milner Pass (10,758 ft/3,279 m). The E slope is steeper and drier. Bounded by Roosevelt Natl. Forest, E and N, Arapahoe Natl. Forest, W and S. Arapahoe Natl. Recreation Area borders SW corner. Popular Trail Ridge Road winds its way across park from Estes Park to Grand Lake. Source of Colorado R. in NW corner of park. Authorized 1915.

Rocky Mountains, major mountain system of W N. Amer. and easternmost belt of the N. Amer. cordillera, extending more than 3,000 mi/4,800 km from central N.Mex. to NW Alaska; Mt. Elbert (14,433 ft/4,399 m) in Colo. is the highest peak. The Rockies are located bet. the Great Plains on the E (from which they rise abruptly for most of their length) and a series of broad basins and plateaus on the W. The mts. form the Continental Divide, separating rivers draining to the Atlantic and Arctic oceans from those draining to the Pacific. The major Atlantic-bound rivers rising in the Rockies include the Rio Grande, Arkansas, Platte, Yellowstone, Missouri, and Saskatchewan. Those draining to the Arctic include the Peace, Athabasca, and Liard rivers. Flowing to the Pacific Ocean are the Colorado, Columbia, Snake, Fraser, and Yukon rivers. The Rockies were formed in the Mesozoic and Early Cenozoic eras during the Cordilleran orogeny. They are geologically complex, with remnants of an ancestral Rocky Mt. system and evidence that uplift, which involved almost all mt.-building processes, occurred as a series of pulses over millions of years. The mts. have since been eroded to expose anc. crystalline cores flanked by thick upturned layers of sedimentary rocks. Glaciers and snowfields, which cover portions of the N ranges and the high peaks of the S, were at one time more extensive; throughout the system the erosional features of alpine glaciation are apparent. Topographically, the Rockies are usually divided into 5 sects.: the Southern Rockies, Middle Rockies, Northern Rockies (all in the U.S.), the Canadian Rockies, and Brooks Range in Alaska. The Wyoming Basin, the system's principal topographic break, is sometimes considered a 6th sect. The Southern Rockies, in N.Mex., Colo., and S Wyo., are dominated by 2 N-S belts of folded mts. that have been eroded to expose cores of Precambrian rocks rimmed by younger sedimentary rocks. The E belt comprises the Laramie, Medicine Bow, and Wet mts. and the Front Range. The principal ranges of the W belt are the Park, Gore, Mosquito, Sawatch, and Sangre de Cristo mts. Bet. the 2 belts are 3 basins known as the North, South, and Middle "Parks." To the SW are the San Juan Mts., a nonlinear group of uplands composed mainly of volcanic rocks. The Southern Rockies are the system's highest sect. and include many peaks above 14,000 ft/4,267 m, among them Mt. Elbert, Mt. Massive, and Mt. Harvard, all in the Sawatch Mts. The Middle Rockies, chiefly in NE Utah and W Wyo., lie N of the Southern Rockies and are separated from them by the Wyo. Basin. The ranges of this sect. are generally lower and less continuous than those to the S. The principal parts are the Wasatch and Teton ranges (which are both great tilted fault blocks), the Yellowstone Plateau and Absaroka Range (both developed on volcanic rocks), the Bighorn, Beartooth, Owl Creek, and Uinta mts., and the Wind River Range (all broad folded mts.). All of these component sections have been eroded down to their Precambrian cores and are rimmed by Paleozoic and Mesozoic sedimentary rocks. The highest peaks of the Middle Rockies are Gannet Peak (13,785 ft/4,202 m) in the Wind River Range and Grand Teton (13,766 ft/4,196 m) in the Teton Range. The Northern Rockies, in NE Wash., N and central Idaho, NW Wyo., and W Mont. extend N from YELLOWSTONE NATIONAL PARK to the U.S.–Can. border. They are composed of the Clearwater and Salmon River mts., the Sawtooth and Lost River ranges (all of which developed in the batholith of central Idaho), and the Bitterroot Range along the Idaho-Mont. state line. In the E are the Front Ranges of Mont. A series of N-S trending ranges separated by narrow trenches and valleys occupies most of N Mont. and the Idaho panhandle. Two especially distinctive trenches are the Rocky Mt. Trench, which extends NW from Flathead L., and the Purcell Trench, which extends N from Coeur d'Alene L. The Okanagan Highlands, in NE Wash., form the W edge of the Northern Rockies. The peaks of the Northern Rockies are generally lower than those to the S; among the highest are Borah Peak (12,662 ft/3,859 m) and Leatherman Peak (12,231 ft/3,728 m) in the Lost River Range. The Rocky Mt. system of Canada is composed of 2 major sections: the high rugged peaks of the Can. Rockies proper, to the E, and the Columbia Mts. group on the W. The Can. Rockies are located along the B.C.–Alberta border and include Mt. Robson (12,972 ft/3,954 m; highest peak of the Rocky Mts. in Canada), Mt. Columbia (12,294 ft/3,747 m), and Mt. Forbes (11,852 ft/3,612 m). The prominent, wide-floored Rocky Mt. Trench, W of the crest line, continues c.800 mi/1,290 km into Canada from Mont. and is drained by the headwaters of the Peace R. and by sections of the Fraser, Columbia, and Kootenay rivers. The Purcell Trench to the W also crosses into Canada and joins the Rocky Mt. Trench c.200 mi/320 km N of the border. Farther to the W is the Columbia Mts. group, which includes the Selkirk, Purcell, Monashee, and Cariboo mts. The Rockies continue into the Yukon Territory and N.W.T. as the Mackenzie, Richardson, and Franklin mts. In N Alaska, the Brooks Range, a cold and treeless region rising to Mt. Chamberlin (9,020 ft/2,749 m), forms the northernmost sect. of the Rocky Mts. Exploitable mineral deposits (lead, zinc, copper, silver, gold) are sparsely dispersed throughout the entire system. The principal mining centers are Leadville and Cripple Creek, Colo.; the Butte-Anaconda dist. of Mont.; Coeur d'Alene, Idaho; and the Kootenay Trail region of B.C. In the 1970s oil shale found in the Rocky Mt. area led to an oil industry that spurred city and state growth, especially in Colo.; by the mid-1980s, the industry was already in decline. The Rockies are a year-round recreational attraction and have seen a boon in vacation-housing construction—especially in Colo., which is most convenient to cross-country travel routes—and, thus, pop. increases since the late 1970s and 1980s. The U.S. natl. parks in the system include Rocky Mt., Yellowstone, Grand Teton, and Glacier natl. parks. In Canada are Jasper, Banff, Yoho, Glacier, Kootenay, Arctic and Kobuk Valley, North Yukon, Nahanni, and Mt. Revelstoke natl. parks. Vast forests, largely under govt. control and supervision, are a major natural resource. Lumbering and other forestry activities are limited mainly to Mont., Idaho, and B.C., where commercially valuable stands are most abundant and accessible. The Rockies have been traversed by W-bound pioneers; the principal U.S. pass across the mts. is South Pass (elev. c.7,550 ft/2,301 m) at the S end of the Wind River Range, SW Wyo., which links the Wyo. Basin and the Great Plains with the basins and plateaus W of the Rockies. This pass was followed by the Oregon, Mormon, and California trails; the Santa Fe Trail skirted the S end of the Rockies. In Canada the important passes are Kicking Horse (elev. 5,390 ft/1,643 m), which carries the Trans-Canada Highway; Crowsnest Pass (4,534 ft/1,382 m); and Yellowhead Pass (3,760 ft/1,146 m). Explorers of the U.S. Rockies have included Vasquez de Coronado (1540), Meriwether Lewis and William Clark (1804–1806), Zebulon Pike (1806–1807), Stephen Long (1819–1820), Benjamin Bonneville (1832–1835), John Frémont (1843–1844), Isaac Stevens (1853), John W. Powell (1868), and Ferdinand Hayden (1871). Leading Can. explorers were sieur de la Vérendrye (1738–1739), Sir Alexander Mackenzie (1792–1793), David Thompson (1799–1803), and Simon Fraser (1803–1807).

Rocky Point, town (1991 pop. 2,744), Clarendon parish, S central Jamaica, 12 mi/19 km S of May Pen; 17°46'N 77°16'W. Fishing center on S coast of Jamaica.

Rocky Point 1 village (☐ 10 sq mi/26 sq km; 1990 pop. 8,596), Suffolk co., SE N.Y., near N shore of L.I., 7 mi/11.3 km E of Port Jefferson; 40°55'N 72°55'W. In summer resort area. **2** uninc. village, Pender co., SE N.C., 14 mi/23 km N of Wilmington, near Northeast Cape Fear R.

Rocky Point, R.I.: see WARWICK.

Rocky Reach Dam, Wash.: see ENTIAT, LAKE.

Rocky Ridge, village (1990 pop. 425), Ottawa co., N Ohio, 15 mi/24 km W of Port Clinton, in agr. area; 41°32'N 83°13'W.

Rocky Ripple, town (1990 pop. 751), Marion co., central Ind., on West Fork of White R., suburb c.6 mi/9.7 km N of downtown Indianapolis; 39°51'N 86°10'W.

Rocky River, city (1990 pop. 20,410), Cuyahoga co., N Ohio, 8 mi/13 km W of downtown Cleveland, on L. Erie, at mouth of Rocky R.; 41°28'N 81°51'W. Novelties. Chiefly residential, noted for scenic atmosphere and quiet charm. Settled 1815, inc. 1903.

Rocky River, c.90 mi/145 km long, S N.C.; rises in S Iredell co.; flows SE of Mooresville, passes Kannapolis and Concord to SW, joins Yadkin R. 12 mi/19 km N of Wadesboro to form Pee Dee, or Great Pee Dee R.

Rockyford, village (1991 pop. 318), S Alta., Canada, 25 mi/40 km SW of Drumheller. Wheat.

Roda, uninc. village, Wise co., SW Va., 12 mi/19 km NW of Norton, in coal-mining region of Cumberland Mts., near Ky. state line, in Jefferson Natl. Forest; 36°58'N 82°49'W.

Rodas (RO-duhz), town, Cienfuegos prov., central Cuba, on Damují R., on RR and 37 mi/60 km W of Santa Clara; 22°20'N 80°34'W. In agr. region (sugarcane; cattle; honey). Catorce de Julio sugar mill is 8 mi/12.9 km SSE; that of Guillermo Moncada is 8 mi/12.9 km SSW.

Rodas River, Cuba: see DAMUJÍ RIVER.

Rodeo (ro-DAI-o), town (1990 pop. 3,569), Durango, N Mexico, on Nazas R. and 80 mi/129 km N of Victoria de Durango, on Mexico Highway 45; 25°12'N 104°35'W. Corn, cotton, wheat, alfalfa, chickpeas.

Rodeo, uninc. town (1990 pop. 7, 589), Contra Costa co., W Calif., suburb 12 mi/19 km N of downtown Oakland and 8 mi/12.9 km NE of Richmond, on San Pablo Bay; 38°03'N 122°14'W. In industrial area; mfg. (chemicals). Mare Isl. Naval Shipyard to N; Carquinez Channel and Bridge to NE.

Roderick Island (☐ 91 sq mi/236 sq km), SW B.C., Canada, in SE arm of Hecate Strait; 20 mi/32 km long, 3 mi/5 km–6 mi/10 km wide; 52°39'N 128°22'W. Just S is Susan Isl. (☐ 14 sq mi/36 sq km); 8 mi/13 km long, 2 mi/3 km–6 mi/10 km wide.

Rodessa (ro-DE-suh), village (1990 pop. 294), Caddo parish, extreme NW La., near Texas (W) and Ark. (N) lines, 34 mi/55 km NW of Shreveport; 32°58'N 94°00'W. Center of Rodessa oil and natural gas field (discovered 1935); some mfg. Black Bayou L. reservoir to SE.

Rodman, town (1990 pop. 56), Palo Alto co., NW Iowa, near West Des Moines R., 10 mi/16 km SE of Emmetsburg; 43°01'N 94°31'W.

Rodman Reservoir, Putnam and Marion cos., NE Fla., on Oklawaha R., 13 mi/21 km SSW of Palatka; c.20 mi/32 km long; 29°30'N 81°49'W. Max. capacity of 237,000 acre-ft. Bow shaped. Formed by Rodman Dam (38 ft/12 m high), built (1968) by the Army Corps of Engineers for navigation and recreation. Ocala Natl. Forest on S shore.

Rodney, town (1990 pop. 65), Monona co., W Iowa, near Little Sioux R., 15 mi/24 km NE of Onawa; 42°12'N 95°57'W.

Rodney, village (1991 pop. 1,087), S Ont., Canada, 28 mi/45 km ENE of Chatham; 42°34'N 81°41'W. Milling; vegetables, fruit.

Rodney Bay, large anchorage in NNW St. Lucia, 6 mi/9.7 km N of Castries; 14°05'N 60°58'W. Named after Br. admiral George Rodney, who based his fleet here during the Amer. Revolution and sailed from here in 1782 to decisively defeat the French at the Battle of the Saints. Now 2d-largest yachting and chartering center in the Caribbean. Hotels and time-share condominiums.

Rodney Village, uninc., town (1990 est. pop. 1,745), Kent co., central Del., 2 mi SSW of Dover; 39°08'N 75°32'W. Suburb of Dover.

Rodríguez Dam, Mexico: see TIJUANA RIVER.

Roe (RO), village (1990 pop. 135), Monroe co., E central Ark., 6 mi/9.7 km SW of Clarendon; 34°37'N 91°23'W. In farm area.

Roebling (RO-bling), industrial village, Burlington co., W N.J., on the Delaware and 7 mi/11.3 km S of Trenton. Founded as "company town" for Roebling steel-cable and wire works.

Roebuck, uninc. town (1990 pop. 1,966), Spartanburg co., NW S.C., 5 mi/8 km SSW of Spartanburg; 34°52'N 81°57'W. Mfg. includes chemicals, machinery, electrical equip. Agr. includes dairying; livestock, poultry; grains, soybeans, peaches, apples.

Roeland Park (RO-luhnd), city (1990 pop. 7,706), Johnson co., E Kansas, suburb of Kansas City, Kansas, 3 mi/4.8 km S of downtown; 39°02'N 94°38'W. Inc. after 1950.

Roes Welcome Sound, E Keewatin dist., N.W.T., Canada, NW arm of Hudson Bay, bet. Southampton Isl. and mainland; 180 mi/290 km long, 15 mi/24 km–70 mi/113 km wide; 65°00'N 88°00'W. Opens N on Repulse Bay.

Roff, town (1990 pop. 717), Pontotoc co., S central Okla., 13 mi/21 km SW of Ada; 34°37'N 96°50'W. In agr. area; mfg. (wood pallets, silica sand).

Roger Mills, county (☐ 1,146 sq mi/2,968 sq km; 1990 pop. 4,147), W Okla.; ⊙ Cheyenne; 35°41'N 99°42'W. Bounded W by Texas, N by Canadian R.; intersected by Washita R. Hilly region of Antelope Hills (elev. c.2,000 ft/610 m) lies in a great bend of the Canadian, in N. Wheat, oats; dairying; cattle; oil and gas (Anadarko Basin) boom 1970s–1980s. Black Kettle Natl. Grasslands in W and center. Formed 1891.

Roger Williams National Memorial, Providence, R.I., memorial to the founder of the Rhode Island colony and a pioneer of religious freedom. Authorized 1965.

Rogers, county (☐ 711 sq mi/1,841 sq km; 1990 pop. 55,170), NE Okla.; ⊙ Claremore; 36°22'N 95°35'W. Intersected by Verdigris R. (forms Oologah L. reservoir in N), small Bud Creek, and Caney R. Cattle, hogs, poultry; grain, fruit, corn, soybeans, hay; dairying. Mfg. (industrial machinery, auto parts) at Claremore. Coal and shale mining; mineral springs. Cherokee Plains in E. Part of Oolagah L. in N. Fair Oaks, Catoosa, and port of Catoosa in SW are suburbs of Tulsa. Formed 1907.

Rogers, city (1990 pop. 24,692), Benton co., extreme NW Ark., in the Ozarks; 36°19'N 94°07'W. In resort and fruit farm area. Diversified mfg. First Wal-Mart was opened here in 1962. Large Beaver L. reservoir (White R.) and Beaver L. State Park to E. Inc. 1881.

Rogers, town (1990 pop. 1,131), Bell co., central Texas, 13 mi/21 km SSE of Temple; 30°55'N 97°13'W. In cotton, corn, grain, wheat area; juniper (locally called cedar) timber; mfg. (hardwood moldings).

Rogers 1 village (1990 pop. 698), Hennepin co., E Minn., suburb 20 mi/32 km NW of Minneapolis, near Crow R., S of its confluence with Mississippi R.; 45°11'N 93°32'W. Grain, nursery crops; livestock; dairying; mfg. (machine tooling, metal stampings, steel fabrication, plastic packaging, lumber). Crow Hassan Regional Park to W. **2** village (1990 pop. 89), Colfax co., E Nebr., 7 mi/11.3 km E of Schuyler, and on Platte R.; 41°27'N 96°55'W. **3** village (1990 pop. 69), Barnes co., E central N.Dak., 14 mi/23 km NW of Valley City; 47°04'N 98°12'W. RR junction. **4** village (1990 pop. 247), Columbiana co., E Ohio, 10 mi/16 km ENE of Lisbon; 40°48'N 80°37'W. In agr. and coal area.

Rogers City, city (1990 pop. 3,642), ⊙ Presque Isle co., NE Mich., 30 mi/48 km NW of Alpena, on L. Huron; 45°25'N 83°48'W. Terminus of RR spur. In resort and farm area. Large limestone quarry to S (opened 1912) ships high calcium limestone from nearby port. Mfg. (auto parts); fisheries. P.H. Hueft State Park to NW on L. Huron; Ocquenoc Falls to W (largest falls on Lower Peninsula). Settled 1869; inc. 1877 as village, 1944 as city.

Rogers Dam Pond (☐ 1 sq mi/2.6 sq km), Mescota co., central Mich., on Muskegun R., 47 mi/76 km N of Grand Rapids; 43°37'N 85°29'W. Max. capacity 10,000 acre-ft. Formed by Rogers Dam (45 ft/14 m high), built (1906) for power generation; also used for recreation. Manistee Natl. Forest nearby.

Rogers Heights, village, Prince Georges co., central Md., suburb ENE of Washington, D.C.

Rogers, Mount (10,525 ft/3,208 m), SE B.C., Canada, in Selkirk Mts., in Glacier Natl. Park, 40 mi/64 km NE of Revelstoke; 51°22′N 117°32′W.

Rogers, Mount (5,729 ft/1,746 m), highest point in Va., bet. Smyth and Grayson cos., SW Va., in Iron Mts. of Appalachian Mts., 12 mi/19 km S of Marion, in Mt. Rogers Natl. Recreation Area of Jefferson Natl. Forest; 36°39′N 81°32′W. Appalachian Trail traverses mt. E-W.

Rogers Pass (4,341 ft/1,323 m), in Selkirk Mts., B.C., Canada. Canadian Pacific RR constructed overpass in 1885 at great expense. After much damage and loss of life from avalanches, the Connaught Tunnel (5 mi/8 km long) was built below pass.

Rogersville 1 town (1990 pop. 1,125), Lauderdale co., NW Ala., near Wheeler Reservoir (on Tennessee R.), 21 mi/34 km E of Florence. Lumber; apparel. Wheeler Dam 5 mi/8 km W. **2** town (1990 pop. 995), Webster co., S central Mo., in the Ozarks, near James R., 14 mi/23 km SE of Springfield; 37°07′N 93°03′W. Apples; dairying; cattle; light mfg. **3** town (1990 pop. 4,149), ⊙ Hawkins co., NE Tenn., near Holston R., 17 mi/27 km NE of Morristown; 36°24′N 83°01′W. In tobacco, timber, and limestone region. Mfg. (ball bearings, steering gears). Mineral springs nearby. Founded 1786.

Rogue (ROG), river, c. 200 mi/322 km long, Oregon; rises in the Cascade Range at Desert Ridge, at N boundary of Crater Lake Natl. Park; flows generally W through Rogue R. Natl. Forest and Lost Creek Reservoir, past town of Rogue River and Grants Pass, then through the Coast Range (Siskiyou Natl. Forest) to the Pacific at Gold Beach. The river and its tributaries irrigate lands noted for orchards around Grants Pass, Medford, and Ashland. River boating, rafting.

Rogue River (ROG), town (1990 pop. 1,759), Jackson co., SW Oregon, 17 mi/27 km WNW of Medford, on Rogue R., at mouth of Evans Creek; 42°26′N 123°10′W. Fruit, nuts, grain; timber; veneer. Site of Woodville Mus. Valley of the Rogue State Park to SE.

Rogue River (ROG), c.32 mi/51 km long, in W central and SW Mich., rises SE of Newaygo in Newaygo co.; flows S, E, and again S, past Rockford, to Grand R. just NE of Grand Rapids; 43°18′N 85°40′W.

Rohnert Park, city (1990 pop. 36,326), Sonoma co., W Calif., 6 mi/9.7 km S of Santa Rosa; 38°21′N 122°42′W. Dairying; poultry; apples, grapes, vegetables, nursery prods. Mfg. (electrical measurement equip., industrial instruments, furniture).

Rohnerville, uninc. village, Humboldt co., NW Calif., 15 mi/24 km S of Eureka. RR junction.

Rohrerstown (ROR-uhrs-toun), uninc. town (1990 pop. 1,170), East Hemphill township, Lancaster co., SE Pa., residential suburb 3 mi/4.8 km WNW of Lancaster, near Little Conestoga Creek; 40°03′N 76°21′W. Victorian wine cellars here.

Rojas de Cuauhtémoc (RO-hahs dai kwah-oo-TE-mok), town (1990 pop. 993), central Oaxaca, Mexico, 7 mi/12 km SE of Oaxaca de Juárez. Elev. 5,505 ft/1,678 m. Temperate climate. Largely subsistence farming.

Rojo, Cabo (ro-ho, KAH-bo), headland in Veracruz, E Mexico, on Gulf of Mexico; easternmost point of barrier isl. peninsula separating Tamiahua Lagoon from gulf, 55 mi/89 km SE of Tampico; 21°38′N 97°18′W.

Rojo, Cape (RO-ho), on SW coast of P.R., 19 mi/31 km S of Mayagüez; 17°55′N 67°11′W.

Roland 1 town (1990 pop. 1,035), Story co., central Iowa, 10 mi/16 km N of city of Nevada; 42°10′N 93°30′W. **2** town (1990 pop. 2,481), Sequoyah co., E Okla., 6 mi/9.7 km WNW of Fort Smith, Ark. and 15 mi/24 km E of Sallislaw; 35°25′N 94°30′W.

Roland, village (1991 pop. 968), S Man., Canada, 50 mi/80 km SW of Winnipeg; 49°22′N 97°57′W. Grain elevators, stockyards.

Roland, Lake, reservoir, Baltimore co., N Md., on Roland Run creek, in Robert E. Lee Park, 7 mi/11.3 km N of Baltimore; c.2 mi/3.2 km long; 39°22′N 76°38′W. Formed by dam built for Baltimore water supply.

Rolesville (ROLZ-vil), village (1990 pop. 572), Wake co., central N.C., 15 mi/24 km NE of Raleigh; 35°55′N 78°27′W. Agr. area (cotton, tobacco, grain; poultry, livestock); mfg. (chemicals, monuments).

Rolette (ro-LET), county (□ 912 sq mi/2,362 sq km; 1990 pop. 12,772), N N.Dak.; ⊙ Rolla; 48°46′N 99°50′W. Borders Man., Canada, on N. Prairie, drained by Willow, Wolf, and Ox creeks. Wheat, barley, rye; cattle. Mfg. (communications equip., truck trailers, watch parts). Turtle Mt. and Turtle Mt. Indian Reservation in N center of co.; Long and Island lakes in SE; Lords L. on W border; Willow and Carpenter lakes in NW; Internatl. Peace Garden and Internatl. Music Camp on U.S.–Can. border, 13 mi/21 km N of Dunseith (on U.S. Highway 281 and Man. Highway 10). Formed 1873.

Rolette (ro-LET), village (1990 pop. 623), Rolette co., N N.Dak., 17 mi/27 km SW of Rolla, between Ox and Wolf creeks; 48°39′N 99°50′W. Turtle Mt. Indian Reservation to N.

Rolfe, town (1990 pop. 721), Pocahontas co., N central Iowa, 10 mi/16 km NE of Pocahontas; 42°48′N 94°31′W. RR junction. Feed mill.

Rolla, village, E B.C., Canada, near Alta. border, near Alaska Highway, 11 mi/18 km NNE of Dawson Creek, and 180 mi/290 km NE of Prince George; 55°54′N 120°08′W. Lumbering; grain; livestock.

Rolla (RAHL-luh), city (1990 pop. 14,090), ⊙ Phelps co., S central Mo.; 37°57′N 91°46′W. Regional center for a livestock and general farming area of the Ozarks. Mfg. (apparel, roof and floor trusses, chemicals, cabinets, printing); limestone. Wineries nearby. The Univ. of Mo. (formerly Mo. School of Mines) has a campus here. U.S. Geological Survey Mid-Continent Mapping Center. Airport 11 mi/18 km N at Vichy. U.S. Forest Service (Mark Twain Natl. Forest) offices. Caves and springs abound in the area. Inc. 1861.

Rolla (RAH-luh), town (1990 pop. 1,286), ⊙ Rolette co., N N.Dak., 67 mi/108 km NW of Devils L., at E end of Turtle Mts.; 48°51′N 99°37′W. RR terminus. Grain; dairy prods.; livestock. Light mfg. (jewel bearings). Turtle Mt. Indian Reservation to W. Rolla View Ski Area to NW. Inc. 1907.

Rolla (RAH-luh), village (1990 pop. 387), Morton co., extreme SW Kansas, 39 mi/63 km W of Liberal; 37°07′N 101°37′W. In grain area. Cimarron Natl. Grasslands to W.

Rolleville, town, central Bahama Isls., on N Great Exuma Isl., 20 mi/32 km NW of George-Town; 23°41′N 76°W. In livestock-raising region (sheep, goats, hogs).

Rolling Fields, village (1990 pop. 593), Jefferson co., N Ky., residential suburb 5 mi/8 km ENE of Louisville; 38°16′N 85°40′W.

Rolling Fork, town (1990 pop. 2,444), ⊙ Sharkey co., W Miss., 38 mi/61 km N of Vicksburg, on Deer Creek; 32°54′N 90°52′W. Agr. (cotton, oats, corn, soybeans, rice, wheat; cattle; timber); light mfg. Indian mounds nearby. Indian Bayou Waterfowl Area to W; Delta Natl. Forest to SE. Settled c.1827.

Rolling Fork, river, c.115 mi/185 km long, in central Ky.; formed by joining of North Rolling Fork and Big South Fork in SE Marion co.; flows W and NW past New Haven to Salt R. in Fort Knox Military Reservation. North Rolling Fork R. rises in S Boyle co.; flows c.20 mi/32 km WSW. Big South Fork rises in N Casey co.; flows c.20 mi/32 km W.

Rolling Hills, city (1990 pop. 1,871), Los Angeles co., S Calif., residential suburb 20 mi/32 km SSW of Los Angeles and 8 mi/12.9 km W of Long Beach; 33°46′N 118°20′W. On Palos Verde peninsula, Pacific Ocean coast 3 mi/4.8 km S. South Coast Botanical Gardens is here.

Rolling Hills, town (1990 pop. 1,135), Jefferson co., N Ky., residential suburb 9 mi/14.5 km ENE of Louisville; 38°16′N 85°34′W.

Rolling Hills, village (1990 pop. 330), Converse co., E Wyo., 3 mi/4.8 km NNE of Glenrock, near North Platte R.; 42°53′N 105°50′W. Cattle, sheep; grain.

Rolling Hills Estates, city (1990 pop. 7,789), Los Angeles co., S Calif., residential suburb 20 mi/32 km SSW of Los Angeles, on Palos Verdes Peninsula; 33°47′N 118°21′W. Mfg. (printing and publishing). Torrance to N; Torrance Municipal Airport to NE. Botanicial gardens.

Rolling Meadows, city (1990 pop. 22,591), Cook co., NE Ill., a suburb 27 mi/43 km NW of Chicago; 42°04′N 88°01′W. Research and development firms and some light mfg. (office supplies, printing, electronic components). Some remnant agr. Inc. 1955.

Rolling Meadows, village (1990 pop. 291), Gregg co., E Texas, residential suburb 7 mi/11.3 km SW of Longview; 32°24′N 94°48′W. Cattle; oil, natural gas.

Rolling Prairie, village (1990 pop. 600), La Porte co., NW Ind., 6 mi/9.7 km NE of La Porte. Light mfg. Dairying; vegetables. Settled 1831, laid out 1853.

Rollingstone, village (1990 pop. 697), Winona co., SE Minn., 10 mi/16 km WNW of Winona near Mississippi R. (Lock and Dam No. 5 to N); 44°06′N 91°49′W. Grain; livestock, poultry; dairying; light mfg. Area surrounded by John A. Latch State Park; Richard J. Dorer Memorial State Forest to N.

Rollingwood, town (1990 pop. 1,388), Travis co., S Texas, residential suburb 2 mi/3.2 km W of Austin, near Colorado R.; 30°16′N 97°47′W. Barton Springs Park to E.

Rollins Reservoir, Nevada and Placer cos., E Calif., on Bear R., 9 mi/14.5 km SE of Grass Valley; 4 mi/6.4 km long; 39°07′N 12°57′W. Max. capacity 66,000 acre-ft. Formed by Rollins Dam built (1965) by the Bureau of Reclamation for irrigation and power generation. Chicago Park village on W shore.

Rollinsford (RAW-linz-ford), town (1990 pop. 2,645), Strafford co., SE N.H., 3 mi/4.8 km NE of Dover; 43°13′N 70°50′W. Bounded E by Piscataqua R. (tidal), NE by Salmon Falls R. (both on Maine border), SW by Cocheco R.; drained by Rollins and Twombley brooks; opposite South Berwick, Maine. Generally urbanized area. Light mfg.; nursery crops; cattle; dairying. Village of Salmon Falls within town limits. Part of Somersworth until inc. 1849.

Rollinsville, village, Gilpin co., N central Colo., in Front Range, 30 mi/48 km WNW of Denver. Elev. 8,420 ft/2,566 m. Placer mining for gold. Tourism. Eldora Ski Area to NW, surrounded by Roosevelt Natl. Forest. Golden Gate Canyon State Park to SE.

Roma, town (1990 pop. 8,059), Starr co., extreme S Texas, on the Rio Grande (bridged, toll) opposite Ciudad Aleman, Mexico, and 50 mi/80 km SSE of Laredo; 26°23′N 99°00′W. Port of entry and market center for ranching and irrigated Rio Grande valley agr. area (cattle; vegetables, cotton, sorghum); sand and gravel. Internatl. Falcon Reservoir and Falcon State Recreation Park to NW. Inc. 1937.

Romain, Cape, Charleston co., E S.C., SE tip of Cape Isl. (c.5 mi/8 km long), in the Atlantic near coast, 21 mi/34 km S of Georgetown; 33°00′N 79°24′W. Cape Romain lighthouse (now unused) is at E end of Raccoon Key (just W). Much of surrounding region of low marshy isls. is included in large Cape Romain Natl. Wildlife Refuge, which includes Cape and Bull isls., plus smaller surrounding isls.

Romaine River (ro-MAIN), 250 mi/402 km long, E Que., Canada; rises on Lab. border at 52°40′N 63°25′W; flows S, through Lac Long (20 mi/32 km long) and Burnt L. (20 mi/32 km long), to the St. Lawrence 10 mi/16 km WNW of Havre St. Pierre, opposite Mingan Isls. There are several rapids.

Roman Nose, mountain summit (3,140 ft/957 m) of the Alleghenies, Garrett co., extreme W Md., just S of Deep Creek L., and 5 mi/8 km N of Oakland; 39°30′N 79°19′W.

Romana, La, Dominican Republic: see LA ROMANA.

Romancoke, Md.: see KENT ISLAND.

Romano, Cape (ro-MAH-no), S point of sandy island just offshore in the Gulf of Mexico, SW Fla., c.7 mi/11.3 km S of Collier City; 25°50′N 81°40′W. Ten Thousand Isls. are just E.

Romano, Cayo (ro-MAHN-o KEI-o), coral island, off N coast of Camagüey prov., E central Cuba, in Old Bahama Channel, bet. Cayo Coco (NW) and Cayo Guajaba (SE), 50 mi/80 km N of Camagüey; 55 mi/89 km long NW-SE, 10 mi/16 km wide; 22°20′N 78°09′W. Salt panning, fishing. Part of Camagüey Archipelago. Connected to mainland by elevated causeway. New tourism development.

Romanzof Mountains, range, NE Alaska, in NE Brooks

Range, near 69°15′N 144°00′W. Rises to 8,855 ft/2,699 m on Mt. Michelson.

Rome 1 city (1990 pop. 30,326), ⊙ Floyd co., NW Ga., at the confluence of the Etowah and Oostanaula rivers to form the Coosa R.; 34°16′N 85°11′W. In a farm, timber, and quarry area. The city was 1st established as a cotton market and an industrial center, with textile and lumber mills, apparel factories, and foundries; now serves as a mfg. center (printing and publishing, concrete, transportation equip., crushed stone, plastics, electrical equip., metal prods., food). Rome was captured by Union forces in the Civil War; Sherman burned the city in Nov. 1864. Seat of Floyd Col., a unit of the Univ. System of Ga., and Shorter Col. The tall clock tower (1871) atop one of the city's hills is Rome's famous landmark. Berry Coll. located to the N. Est. 1834 on the site of a Cherokee village; inc. 1847. **2** industrial city (□ 75 sq mi/194 sq km; 1990 pop. 44,350), Oneida co., central N.Y., on the Mohawk R., and the N.Y. Barge Canal; 43°13′N 75°29′W. Rome is situated on Wood Creek, ½ mi/8/10 km from the Mohawk R. It became recognized for its copper and brass mfg. and was dubbed the "Copper City." Cooking utensils, machine tools, and strip steel are still among its prods. Laid out c.1786 on the site of Fort Stanwix. Because of its location bet. the Mohawk R. valley and the Great Lakes lowland, the city was a busy portage point, and it had great strategic importance during the Fr. and Indian War and in the Amer. Revolution. The 6 Nation Treaty of 1768 was concluded here. The unsuccessful Br. siege of the fort in the Amer. Revolution led to the Battle of Oriskany, site of one of the Revolution's bloodiest battles; Fort Stanwix is now within Rome's corporate limits. Construction on the Erie Canal began (1817) in Rome. Erie Canal Village, an 1840s reconstruction, occupies site of former Fort Bull, and a state school for the deaf. Nearby are realigned Griffiss Air Force Base and Rome Development Center, which remain open. Nearby are 2 state parks and a state trout hatchery. Inc. as a city 1870.

Rome 1 town (1990 pop. 124), Henry co., SE Iowa, near Skunk R., 7 mi/11.3 km W of Mount Pleasant; 40°58′N 91°40′W. Limestone quarries. Large Indian mound nearby. **2** town (1990 pop. 758), Kennebec co., S Maine, 18 mi/29 km NNW of Augusta; 44°34′N 69°52′W. In Belgrade Lakes recreational area.

Rome 1 uninc. village (1990 pop. 2,744), Peoria co., E Ill., 8 mi/12.9 km NE of Peoria; 40°52′N 89°30′W. **2** village, Sunflower co., NW Miss., 17 mi/27 km SSE of Clarksdale. In cotton-growing area. Parchman State Farm to SW. **3** village (1990 pop. 99), Adams co., S Ohio, on the Ohio, and 13 mi/21 km SE of West Union; 38°40′N 83°22′W. Also called Stout.

Rome, borough (1990 pop. 475), Bradford co., NE Pa., 8 mi/12.9 km NE of Towanda, on Wysox Creek; 41°51′N 76°20′W. Agr. (corn, hay, dairying).

Rome City, town (1990 pop. 1,138), Noble co., NE Ind., on Sylvan L. (c.2 mi/3.2 km long), 7 mi/11.3 km NNE of Albion; 41°29′N 85°22′W. Mfg. (electronic equip.). Gene Stratton Porter's 2d home (state memorial) is nearby to SW. Settled c.1837.

Romeo, town (1990 pop. 3,520), Macomb co., SE Mich., 15 mi/24 km NNW of Mt. Clemens; 42°47′N 83°00′W. In fruit-growing area. Mfg. (plastic prods., transportation equip.). Fishing nearby. Airport to E. Inc. 1838.

Romeo, village (1990 pop. 341), Conejos co., S Colo., in foothills of San Juan Mts., 21 mi/34 km SSW of Alamosa, in San Luis Valley; 37°10′N 105°59′W. Elev. 7,750 ft/2,362 m. Trading point in grain and potato region.

Romeoville, village (1990 pop. 14,074), Will co., NE Ill., on the Des Plaines R., with access to the Illinois and Mississippi Canal and the Chicago Sanitary and Ship Canal, 8 mi/12.9 km N of Joliet; 41°38′N 88°05′W. A suburb of the greater Chicago area. Mfg. (medical supplies); oil refineries, power-generating facility. Lewis Univ. here. Inc. 1901.

Romita (ro-MEE-tah), city (1990 pop. 16,535) and township, Guanajuato, central Mexico, on central plateau, 21 mi/34 km SE of León; 20°52′N 101°31′W. Agr. center (cereals, alfalfa, chickpeas, sugarcane, fruit, vegetables; livestock). Also Romita de Liceaga.

Romita de Liceaga, Mexico: see ROMITA.

Romney (RAHM-nee), town (1990 pop. 1,966), ⊙ Hampshire co., NE W.Va., 13 mi/21 km ESE of Keyser, in Eastern Panhandle, on South Branch of the Potomac R.; 39°21′N 78°45′W. Agr. (grain, apples, peaches, strawberries; livestock; poultry). Mfg. (apparel, leather shoes, metal prods., wine). Limestone quarries. Fort Mill Ridge Trenches historic site (Civil War battle) in town. Hopewell Indian Burial Mound (c.500–1000 A.D.) in Indian Mound Cemetery. Springfield Wildlife Management Area to N; Fort Mill Wildlife Management Area to SW, Nathanial Mt. Wildlife Management Area to S. Ice Mt., where ice is formed the year around, to E. One of 2 oldest towns in state; town changed hands 56 times during Civil War. Founded 1762.

Romney, village (1990 est. pop. 300), Tippecanoe co., W central Ind., 11 mi/18 km S of Lafayette. In agr. area (corn, soybeans; livestock). Mfg. (popcorn; wheat-, soybean-seed improvement). Founded c.1831.

Romoland, uninc. town (1990 pop. 2,319), Riverside co., S Calif., residential community 18 mi/29 km SSE of Riverside, near San Jacinto R.; 33°45′N 117°10′W. Railroad Canyon Reservoir to SW.

Romulus, city (1990 pop. 22,897), Wayne co., SE Mich., suburb 19 mi/31 km SW of downtown Detroit; 42°13′N 83°22′W. Mfg. (fiberglass and aluminum prods., machinery, dental supplies, chemicals, plastic prods.). Boundaries coterminus with Romulus township. City surrounds Detroit-Metropolitan-Wayne County Airport. Huron R. to SW and Lower Huron Metropark.

Romulus, village (1990 pop. 350), Seneca co., central N.Y., 49 mi/79 km N of Elmira; 42°43′N 76°49′W. Rich farming area (vegetables, sweet and field corn, hay; dairying). Seneca Army Depot (□ 16 sq mi/41 sq km) with airstrip capable of handling the largest military cargo aircraft. Cited by the Dept. of Defense as a storage facility for conventional munitions, hazardous materials, and pre-positioned reserve stocks, but the storage of tactical nuclear weapons at this site has never been officially confirmed. Scheduled for complete closure in July 2001 except as a caretaker depot for hazardous materials and ores.

Ronan (RO-nuhn), town (1990 pop. 1,547), Lake co., NW Mont., on Spring Creek, 10 mi/16 km SSE of Polson, in Flathead Indian Reservation; 47°32′N 114°06′W. In irrigated agr. region (cattle, sheep, llamas, hogs; potatoes, hay, rapeseed, corn). Mfg. (printing and publishing, electronic equip.). Ninepipe Reservoir and Kicking Horse Reservoir to S; both units of Ninepipe Natl. Wildlife Refuge and Wildlife Management Area; Lower Crow Reservoir to W; Mission Mts. Tribal Wilderness to E; Natl. Bison Range to SSE. Garden of the Rockies Mus. Settled 1910, inc. 1912.

Ronceverte (RAHN-suh-vuhrt), town (1990 pop. 1,754), Greenbrier co., SE W.Va., on Greenbrier R., 4 mi/6.4 km SSW of Lewisburg; 37°45′N 80°28′W. Trade center. Agr. (grain, apples, tobacco); livestock; poultry; dairy prods.; timber. Mfg. (wood prods., millwork, construction materials, machinery). Organ Cave, 3 mi/4.8 km SSE, attracts tourists. W.Va. State Fairgrounds to N. Greenbrier State Forest to E. Settled c.1800.

Ronda (RAHN-duh), village (1990 pop. 367), Wilkes co., NW N.C., on Yadkin R., 5 mi/8 km WSW of Elkin; 36°13′N 80°56′W. Agr. (tobacco, grain; chickens, hogs; dairying). Mfg. (machinery, cellulose prods.).

Ronde Island, islet, S Grenadines, dependency of Grenada, West Indies, 20 mi/32 km NNE of St. George's; 12°18′N 61°35′W.

Rondo (RAHN-do), village (1990 pop. 283), Lee co., E Ark., 16 mi/26 km NW of Helena; 34°39′N 90°49′W. In agr. area.

Rondout Creek, c.50 mi/80 km long, SE N.Y.; rises in the Catskills in W Ulster co.; flows SW, SE, and NE, past Napanoch, Kerhonkson, and Rosendale, to the Hudson R. at Kingston, where its lower ½ mi/8/10 km forms Rondout Harbor; receives small Wallkill R. below Rosendale. Merriman Dam (2,450 ft/747 m long, 200 ft/61 m high; earth fill) on upper course impounds Rondout Reservoir (8 mi/12.9 km long; filling began 1951). From reservoir, to which tunnels extend from Pepacton and Neversink reservoirs, Delaware Aqueduct runs to N.Y. city.

Ronge, Lac la (ROZH, lahk lah), lake (□ 450 sq mi/1,166 sq km), central Sask., Canada, 140 mi/225 km NNE of Prince Albert; 43 mi/69 km long, 30 mi/48 km wide. Drains NE into Churchill R. Region is rich in minerals. Recreation area; tourism. Town of La Ronge, with wild-rice processing plant, on W shore. Most of shoreline and large area to NE included in Lac La Ronge Provincial Park. Sport fishing is major industry. Fur trapping.

Ronkonkoma, residential village (□ 8 sq mi/20.7 sq km; 1990 pop. 20,391), Suffolk co., SE N.Y., central L.I., c.2 mi/3.2 km SSW of Lake Ronkonkoma village and L. Ronkonkoma; 40°47′N 73°07′W. In diversified-farming area.

Ronneby (RAW-ne-bee), village (1990 pop. 58), Benton co., central Minn., 17 mi/27 km ENE of St. Cloud, and 2 mi/3.2 km NE of Foley near St. Francis R.; 45°40′N 93°52′W. In grain and livestock area.

Roodhouse, city (1990 pop. 2,139), Greene co., W central Ill., 13 mi/21 km N of Carrollton; 39°28′N 90°22′W. In agr. area. Mfg. (paper prods.); RR shops. Inc. 1876.

Roof Butte (9,784 ft/2,982 m), NE Apache co., NE Ariz., in Chuska Mts., near N.Mex. state line, c.50 mi/80 km WSW of Farmington, N.Mex.; 36°27′N 109°05′W.

Rooks (RUKS), county (□ 895 sq mi/2,318 sq km; 1990 pop. 6,039), N central Kansas; ⊙ Stockton; 39°21′N 99°19′W. Smoky Hills region, drained by South Fork Solomon R. and Bow Creek. Agr. (rye; cattle). Mfg. (mobile home). Scattered oil fields. Formed 1872.

Roopville (ROOP-vil), town (1990 pop. 248), Carroll co., W Ga., 9 mi/14.5 km SSW of Carrollton; 33°28′N 85°08′W.

Roosevelt 1 county (□ 2,369 sq mi/6,136 sq km; 1990 pop. 10,999), NE Mont.; ⊙ Wolf Point; 48°18′N 105°02′W. Agr. area bordering N.Dak. on E; bounded S by Missouri R.; drained by Poplar R. and Big Muddy Creek (forms E boundary of Fort Peck Indian Reservation, also forms part of co. boundary in NE). State line on E forms Central/Mountain time zone boundary. Mfg. (textiles, fabricated metal prods.). Agr. (wheat, barley, oats, corn, beans, sugar beets, hay; cattle, hogs, sheep). Part of Medicine L. Natl. Wildlife Refuge (Homestead L. unit) in NE; part of Fort Union Trading Post Natl. Historical Site in SE corner, on N.Dak. boundary. Fort Peck Indian Reservation covers all of co. W of Big Muddy R. (approximately 75% of co.), extends into Daniels (N), and Valley (NW) cos. Formed 1919. **2** county (□ 2,455 sq mi/6,358 sq km; 1990 pop. 16,702), E N.Mex.; ⊙ Portales; 34°01′N 103°28′W. Agr. (triticale, blue corn, peanuts, potatoes, wheat, hay, alfalfa, oats, barley, millet, rye, sorghum, corn, cotton, green beans, pumpkins, melons; cattle, sheep; dairying) region bordering on Texas (E), Central/Mountain time zone boundary. Oasis State Park in N. Formed 1903. Grulla Natl. Wildlife Refuge in NE. In Llano Estacado plains region.

Roosevelt 1 uninc. residential town (□ 1 sq mi/2.6 sq km; 1990 pop. 15,030), Nassau co., SE N.Y., on L.I.; 40°40′N 73°34′W. A large retail business exists in Roosevelt, and the town has become the co.'s busiest economic area. Large Afr.-Amer. pop. Troubled school dist. was taken over by the State Dept. of Education in mid-1990s for restructuring and improvement. **2** town (1990 pop. 3,915), Duchesne co., NE Utah, 110 mi/177 km ESE of Salt Lake City, near Uinta Mts.; 40°17′N 110°00′W. Elev. 5,282 ft/1,610 m. Trading point for ranching and agr. area served by irrigation works on L. Fork. Agr. (dairying; flour; oil), natural gas. Mfg. (natural gas liquids). Gilsonite mines in vicinity. Area surrounded by parts of Uintah and Ouray Indian Reservation. Ashley Natl. Forest, Uinta Mts. to N. Settled 1905, inc. 1913.

Roosevelt 1 uninc. village, Gila co., central Ariz., near S end of Theodore Roosevelt Dam, forms Theodore Roosevelt Reservoir, 25 mi/40 km NW of Globe, in Tonto Natl. Forest. Many inhabitants being moved to higher locations as dam raised 77 ft/23 m (completed 1996). Tonto Natl. Monument is SE. **2** village (1990 pop. 180), Roseau co., NW Minn., 12 mi/19 km SE of Warroid, L. of the Woods to N; 48°48′N 95°05′W. Agr. (potatoes, grain, flax, sunflowers, alfalfa). Mfg. (custom boat tops). Beltrami Isl. State Forest to S. **3** village (1990 pop. 323), Kiowa co., SW Okla., 13 mi/21 km SSE of Hobart; 34°51′N 99°01′W. Trading point for farm area. Tom Steed L. reservoir and Great Plains State Park to S.

Roosevelt, borough (1990 pop. 884), Monmouth co., central N.J., 11 mi/18 km WSW of Freehold; 40°13′N 74°28′W. Founded 1933 as Jersey Homesteads by Federal Resettlement Administration as govt.-aided experiment in cooperative agr. and mfg. for garment workers; sold 1940, later renamed in honor of Franklin D. Roosevelt.

Roosevelt Campobello (□ 4 sq mi/10 sq km), national park–affiliated area, SW N.B., Canada authorized 1964. Summer home of President Franklin D. Roosevelt on Campobello Island; first internatl. park to be administered by a joint U.S.-Can. commission.

Roosevelt Dam, Ariz.: see SALT RIVER VALLEY.

Roosevelt Field Shopping Center, shopping mall, central Nassau co., SE N.Y., 20 mi/32 km E of Manhattan; bisected by Meadowbrook State Parkway connecting with the N. State and S. State Parkways; 40°44′N 73°36′W. Built in 1909 and originally called Hazelhurst, the field was renamed after Quentin Roosevelt (the son of Theodore Roosevelt), who was killed on a training flight here in 1917. Roosevelt Field was the place from which Charles E. Lindbergh launched his nonstop 1927 trans-Atlantic flight to Paris. At the beginning of World War II, it was world's largest private airport, but after the construction of La Guardia Airport, its importance markedly declined. The airfield was sold by the county to a private developer in 1950 and closed in 1951. Today, it is the site of Roosevelt Industrial Park and Roosevelt Field Shopping Mall, which, when it 1st opened in 1956, was the largest mall in the world. The mall continues to be one of the most successful on the E. Coast.

Roosevelt International Bridge, N.Y. and Ont., Canada: see ROOSEVELTOWN.

Roosevelt Island, borough of Manhattan, N.Y. city, SE N.Y., in East River opposite midtown Manhattan; 40°46′N 73°56′W. Isl. is 1.75 mi/2.82 km long and only 800 ft/244 m wide at its widest point; 147 acres/59 ha in area. In 19th and 20th cents., as city property, it housed a lunatic asylum, a poorhouse, a penitentiary, and hospitals for the chronically ill. In 1921, after investigation of notorious conditions at these institutions, the prison was moved to Rikers Isl., and the name was changed from Blackwell's Isl. to Welfare Isl. In 1971 the State's Urban Development Corp. decided to convert the isl. to a high-density residential community; severe fiscal and management problems caused only 2,138 housing units (less than half the number originally planned) to be built. Yet, the result has been a pleasing, successful project accessible by subway, by car from Ravenswood, Queens, via the Roosevelt Isl. Bridge (built 1955), and by an aerial tramway from a terminal at E 60th St. and 2d Ave. in Manhattan. In 1973 Welfare Isl. was renamed Franklin D. Roosevelt Isl. to honor one of the city's most renowned citizens.

Roosevelt Lake, Wash.: see GRAND COULEE DAM.

Roosevelt, Mount (9,500 ft/2,896 m), N B.C., Canada, in Rocky Mts.; 58°27′N 125°20′W.

Roosevelt Park, town (1990 pop. 3,885), Muskegon co., SW Mich., residential suburb 2 mi/3.2 km SW of Muskegon near L Michigan; 43°12′N 86°16′W. Inc. 1946.

Roosevelt Roads, U.S. naval reservation in E P.R., just SE of Ceiba, to the NW of Vieques Isl., and surrounding the fine harbor of Ensenada Honda. Airfield 2.5 mi/4 km SE; Fort Bundy on N shore.

Rooseveltown, village (1990 pop. 50), St. Lawrence co., N N.Y., 8 mi/12.9 km ENE of Massena; 44°58′N 74°45′W. Port of entry. Here is Roosevelt Internatl. Bridge (1934) across the St. Lawrence R. to Cornwall, Ont. Until 1934, called Nyando.

Root, Mount (12,860 ft/3,920 m), on Alaska-B.C. border, in Fairweather Range, 7 mi/11.3 km N of Mt. Fairweather; 58°59′N 137°30′W.

Root River 1 c.60 mi/97 km long, in SE Minn.; formed by confluence of North Branch and South Branch at Lanesboro; flows E, past Rushford, Houston, and Hokah to Mississippi R. opposite La Crosse, Wis. North Branch Root R., SE Minn.; rises c.25 mi/40 km SW of Rochester in central Mower co., near Dexter; flows NE past Stewartville (forms L. Florence reservoir here) then SE past Chatfield; receives Middle Branch (c.15 mi/24 km long) from SW, then joins South Branch (c.70 mi/113 km long). South Branch Root R., SE Minn; rises in E Mower co., c.25 mi/40 km SSW of Rochester; flows ENE past Mystery Cave/Forestville State Park and Preston and Lanesboro to North Branch (c.75 mi/121 km long); 43°48′N 92°10′W. **2** c.35 mi/56 km long, in SE Wis.; rises in E Waukesha co., near New Berlin; flows generally SE, past Greendale and Franklin, to L. Michigan at Racine.

Roper (ROP-uhr), village (1990 pop. 669), Washington co., E N.C., 7 mi/11.3 km E of Plymouth; 35°52′N 76°37′W. Cotton, peanuts, tobacco, grain; livestock; mfg. (lumber).

Ropesville, village (1990 pop. 494), Hockley co., NW Texas, 16 mi/26 km SE of Levelland; 33°24′N 102°09′W. Agr. (cattle; cotton); oil and gas.

Roque (RO-kai), village, Matanzas prov., W Cuba, on the Canal del Roque, on RR, and 21 mi/34 km SE of Cárdenas; 22°46′N 81°05′W. Sugarcane, fruits.

Roque Bluffs (ROK), town (1990 pop. 234), Washington co., E Maine, on Englishman Bay, and 7 mi/11.3 km S of Machias; 44°37′N 67°28′W.

Roque, Canal del (RO-kai, kah-NAHL dail), artificial waterway, c.30 mi/48 km long, Matanzas prov., W Cuba; fed by lagoon SW of Colón; flows N to E shore of Cárdenas Bay, joining small San Antonio R. in lower course. Built to prevent flooding during rainy season.

Roque Island (ROK), Washington co., E Maine, crescent-shaped isl. in Englishman Bay, 3 mi/4.8 km long, 10 mi/16 km SSW of Machias.

Rosales (ro-SAH-les), town (1990 pop. 4,383), Chihuahua, N Mexico, on San Pedro R., and 6 mi/9.7 km W of Delicias. Corn, cotton, beans, sugarcane; cattle. Sometimes called Santa Cruz de Rosales.

Rosales, Mexico: see VILLA UNIÓN, Coahuila.

Rosalia (ro-ZAI-lee-uh), village (1990 pop. 552), Whitman co., SE Wash., 28 mi/45 km S of Spokane, on Pine Creek; 47°14′N 117°22′W. RR junction. Barley, wheat; cattle, sheep; mfg. (feeds). Steptoe Battlefield Memorial State Park (Battle of Tohotonimme) to S.

Rosalie, village (1990 pop. 178), Thurston co., NE Nebr., 12 mi/19 km ESE of Pender, near Missouri R; 42°03′N 96°30′W. Grain; livestock. Located in S central part of Omaha Indian Reservation.

Rosalind, village (1991 pop. 192), S central Alta., Canada, 23 mi/37 km SE of Camrose; 52°47′N 112°27′W. Coal mining; oil and gas; wheat, flax, barley; cattle.

Rosamond, uninc. town (1990 pop. 7,430), Kern co., S central Calif., in Mojave Desert, 13 mi/21 km N of Lancaster; 34°52′N 118°12′W. Cattle; gold mines near. Rosamond L. (dry), c.5 mi/8 km in diameter, is E. Saddleback Butte State Park to SE; Edwards Air Force Base to E.

Rosamorada (ro-sah-mo-RAH-dah), town (1990 pop. 3,694), Nayarit, W Mexico, in Pacific lowland, 45 mi/72 km NW of Tepic, on RR, on Mexico Highway 15; 22°09′N 105°12′W. Corn, tobacco, sugarcane, beans, tomatoes, bananas; cattle.

Rosario, town (1990 pop. 2,735), Sonora state, NW Mexico, 95 mi/153 km E of Guaymas; 27°59′N 109°20′W. Cattle, hogs, horses. Also called Tezopaco.

Rosario 1 Mexico: see EL ROSARIO. **2** Mexico: see VALLE DEL ROSARIO.

Rosario, Canal del (ro-SAH-ree-o, kah-NAHL dail), Caribbean channel (c.2 mi/3.2 km wide), off S central Cuba, bet. the keys Cayo Rosario (E) and Cayo Cantiles (W); 21°38′N 81°57′W.

Rosario, Peñón del (ro-SAH-ree-o, pen-YON del), peak (11,214 ft/3,418 m), central Mexico, on Tlaxcala-Puebla border, 8 mi/12.9 km NW of Tlaxco; 19°40′N 98°11′W.

Rosario, Sierra del (ro-SAH-ree-o, see-ER-uh dail), mountain range, Pinar del Río prov., W Cuba; continuing the Sierra de los Órganos, it extends c.45 mi/72 km ENE. Rises in Pan de Guajaibón to 2,533 ft/772 m.

Rosario Strait, NW Wash., passage (c.25 mi/40 km long) through E part of San Juan Isls., linking Strait of Georgia (N) and Juan de Fuca Strait (turns to W); leads indirectly to Puget Sound to S. Forms boundary of San Juan (W), Skagit (E), and Whatcom (NE) cos.

Rosas, Las, Mexico: see LAS ROSAS.

Rosboro (RAHS-buhr-o), village, Pike co., SW Ark., 30 mi/48 km WSW of Hot Springs, 4 mi/6.4 km SE of Glenwood, near Caddo R.

Roscoe 1 town (1990 pop. 100), St. Clair co., W Mo., on Osage R., and 8 mi/12.9 km SW of Osceola; 37°58′N 93°48′W. **2** town (1990 pop. 1,446), Nolan co., W Texas, 6 mi/9.7 km W of Sweetwater; 32°26′N 100°32′W. RR junction in farm area (cattle, sheep; cotton, wheat); oil and gas; mfg. (plows). Recreation on nearby lakes. Inc. 1907.

Roscoe 1 village (1990 pop. 2,079), Winnebago co., N central Ill., suburb 12 mi/19 km NNE of downtown Rockford; 42°25′N 89°00′W. Mfg. (level controls, valve actuators, motion control systems). **2** village (1990 pop. 141), Stearns co., central Minn., 23 mi/37 km WSW of St. Cloud; 45°25′N 94°38′W. Grain; poultry; dairying; mfg. (organs). Natural lakes in area. **3** village (1990 pop. 900), Sullivan co., SE N.Y., in the Catskills, on Beaver Kill, and 13 mi/21 km NW of Liberty; 41°56′N 74°55′W. Light mfg.; stone quarrying. Lakes nearby. **4** village, Coshocton co., central Ohio, on Muskingum R., opposite Coshocton. Shops. Restored buildings from canal era; canal and canal boat. **5** village, Edmunds co., N S.Dak., 15 mi/24 km W of Ipswich; 45°26′N 99°20′W. In agr. and livestock area.

Roscoe (RAHS-ko), borough (1990 pop. 872), Washington co., SW Pa., 4 mi/6.4 km SSE of Charleroi, on Monongahela R.; 40°04′N 79°51′W. Agr. (corn, hay; livestock; dairying); mfg. (converted paper). Inc. 1892.

Roscoe, suburban section of Los Angeles city, Los Angeles co., S Calif., 13 mi/21 km NNW of downtown Los Angeles, in San Fernando Valley. Hollywood Burbank Airport to SE; Roscoe Park is here.

Roscommon (rahs-KAH-muhn), county (□ 579 sq mi/1,500 sq km; 1990 pop. 19,776), N central Mich.; ⊙ Roscommon, located near N border; 44°19′N 84°36′W. Drained by Muskegon R. and branches of Tittabawassee and Au Sable rivers. Forest area; mfg. automotive stampings; dairy prods; some farming (livestock). Resorts. Includes Houghton and Higgins lakes, and L. St. Helen; S Higgins L. State Park in N; N. Higgins L. State Park on N boundary, in NW corner. Organized 1875.

Roscommon (rahs-KAH-muhn), town (1990 pop. 858), ⊙ Roscommon co., N central Mich., c.45 mi/72 km NE of Cadillac, near N border of co., and on South Branch of Au Sable R.; 44°29′N 84°35′W. Trade center for resort and farm area (cattle; forage crops). Mfg. (transportation equip.). Starting point for Au Sable R. canoe trips. Forest fire experiment station nearby. Kirtland Community Col. here. Airport to SE. Higgins L. is W; North Higgins L. State Park to W; South Higgins L. State Park to SE.

Rose City 1 village (1990 pop. 686), Ogemaw co., NE central Mich., 11 mi/18 km NNE of West Branch, at edge of Huron Natl. Forest; 44°25′N 84°07′W. Mfg. (lumber, steel tools, auto parts, plastic toys). Huron Natl. Forest to N; Rifle R. State Park to SE. **2** village (1990 pop. 572), Orange co., SE Texas, suburb 4 mi/6.4 km NE of Beaumont, near Neches R.; 30°06′N 94°02′W. Mfg. (metal fabricating).

Rose Creek, village (1990 pop. 363), Mower co., SE Minn., on Rose Creek R., 9 mi/14.5 km SE of Austin; 43°36′N 92°49′W. Grain, soybeans; livestock, poultry; dairying; mfg. (hunting feed). St. Croix Natl. Scenic Riverway to E.

Rose Hall, village, St. James parish, NW Jamaica, 8 mi/12.9 km ENE of Montego Bay; 18°37′N 77°49′W. Once a flourishing sugar center; 18th-cent. estates and palatial houses.

Rose Hill, uninc. city, Fairfax co., NE Va., residential suburb 4 mi/6.4 km WSW of Alexandria , 9 mi/14.5 km SW of Washington, D.C. U.S. Coast Guard Radio Station to S; Huntley Meadows Park to S.

Rose Hill 1 town (1990 pop. 171), Mahaska co., S central Iowa, 10 mi/16 km E of Oskaloosa, bet. Skunk and North Skunk rivers; 41°19′N 92°27′W. In livestock area. State park is S. Limestone quarries nearby. **2** town (1990 pop. 1,287), Duplin co., E N.C., 36 mi/58 km S of Goldsboro; 34°49'N 78°01'W. Tobacco, cotton, sweet potatoes, grain, cucumbers, grapes; livestock. Hq. for the country's largest hog producer. Mfg. (wooden cabinets, wine, poultry processing, animal feed, satin bedding). Duplin Wine Cellars. **3** uninc. town, Lee co., SW Va., 13 mi/21 km W of Jonesville, near Martin Creek, near W.Va. state line; 38°47'N 77°06'W. Agr. (tobacco, corn; cattle); bituminous coal. Cumberland Mtn. to N.

Rose Hill, village (1990 pop. 78), Jasper co., SE Ill., 8 mi/12.9 km N of Newton; 39°06'N 88°09'W. In agr. area (wheat, corn, soybeans; cattle; dairying).

Rose Island, narrow islet (c.9 mi/14.5 km long), N central Bahama Isls., just E of New Providence Isl., 6 mi/9.7 km ENE of Nassau.

Rose Lynn, village, SE Alta., Canada, 19 mi/31 km SE of Hanna; 51°25'N 112°38'W. Coal mining; wheat; cattle.

Rose, Mount, Nev.: see CARSON RANGE.

Rose Peak, (8,786 ft/2,678 m), Greenlee co., E Ariz., highest in Blue Range, 25 mi/40 km N of Morenci, in Apache-Sitgreaves Natl. Forest; 33°26'N 109°22'W.

Rose Valley, town (1991 pop. 409), SE central Sask., Canada, near Ponass L. (12 mi/19 km long, 4 mi/6 km wide), 40 mi/64 km SSE of Tisdale. Wheat; dairying.

Rose Valley, borough (1990 pop. 982), Delaware co., SE Pa., residential suburb 12 mi/19 km WSW of downtown Philadelphia, and 2 mi/3.2 km SSE of Media, near Ridley Creek; 39°53'N 75°23'W.

Roseau (RO-zo), county (□ 1,678 sq mi/4,346 sq km; 1990 pop. 15,026), NW Minn., ○ Roseau; 48°46'N 95°47'W. Agr. area bounded NE by Muskeg Bay of L. of the Woods and N by Can. (Man.) border, drained by Roseau R. and its North and South forks. Wheat, hay, flax, barley, oats, alfalfa, sunflowers; cattle, sheep, poultry; dairying; timber; peat deposits. Hayes L. State Park in SE; parts of Beltrami Island State Forest in NE and SE; Roseau R. Wildlife Area in NW. Roseau Municipal Airport to E. County formed 1894.

Roseau (RO-zo), town (1991 pop. 15,853), ⊙ Dominica, Windward Isls., B.W.I., on SW coast of the isl., 370 mi/595 km SE of San Juan, P.R., and 50 mi/80 km NNW of Fort-de-France, Martinique; 15°17'N 61°23'W. Port on open roadstead; exports limes, lime juice, essential oils, tropical vegetables, spices. In a picturesque setting, it is situated on small Roseau R., with some of the highest mts. in the Lesser Antilles towering over it, with nearby waterfalls, thermal springs, and scenic plateaus. Has R.C. cathedral (built 1841), St. George's Church, Govt. House, Victoria Memorial Mus., and Botanic Gardens (est. 1891). Canefield Airport c.3 mi/4.8 km N. Formerly called Charlotte Town.

Roseau (RO-zo), town (1990 pop. 2,396), ⊙ Roseau co., NW Minn., 53 mi/85 km NNE of Thief River Falls on Roseau R.; port of entry 10 mi/16 km S of Can. (Man.) border; 48°51'N 95°45'W. Elev. 1,047 ft/319 m. Trade and shipping center for agr. area; grain, flax, sunflowers; cattle, sheep, poultry; dairying; mfg. (snowmobiles and all-terrain vehicles, fertilizers, shipping crates, concrete). Hayes L. State Park to SE; parts of Beltrami Island State Forest to NE and SE; Roseau River Wildlife Area to NW.

Roseau River (RO-zo), 140 mi/225 km long, formed by confluence of North and South forks in marshy area 6 mi/9.7 km S of Roseau, in Roseau co., NW Minn.; flows N, past Roseau, then W and NW, into Man., Canada, past Dominion City to Red R., 8 mi/12.9 km S of St. Jean Baptiste, Man.; 48°31'N 95°12'W. North Fork (c.45 mi/72 km long) and South Fork (c.35 mi/56 km long) rise at NW edge of Beltrami co., flow generally NNW.

Roseaux (ro-ZO), town (1982 pop. 3,499), Grande-Anse dept., SW Haiti, on NW coast of Jacmel Peninsula, 8 mi/12.9 km ESE of Jérémie; 18°43'N 71°56'W. In agr. region (sugarcane, coffee). Fishing port.

Rosebank, section of Staten Isl. borough of N.Y. city, SE N.Y., on E Staten Isl., on The Narrows; 40°37'N 74°04'W. Attractions include the Garibaldi-Meucci Mus. and Alice Austen House.

Roseboro, town (1990 pop. 1,441), Sampson co., S central N.C., 22 mi/35 km ESE of Fayetteville; 34°57'N 78°30'W. Tobacco, cotton, peanuts, grain, sweet potatoes; livestock. Mfg. (yarn, brick, plywood, plastic pipe, basesball uniforms).

Rosebud, village, S Alta., Canada, on Rosebud R., and 16 mi/26 km SW of Drumheller; 51°18'N 112°57'W. Coal; wheat; cattle. Badlands of Rosebud R.; fossil beds.

Rosebud, county (□ 5,026 sq mi/13,017 sq km; 1990 pop. 10,505), E central Mont.; ⊙ Forsyth; 46°14'N 106°43'W. Agr. region drained by Tongue and Yellowstone rivers; Big Porcupine, Rosebud, and Sandy creeks. Musselshell R. forms part of extreme W boundary. Wheat, barley, oats, hay, corn, beans, sugar beets; cattle, sheep; timber. Oil; large open-pit coal mine at Colstrip; in S center, bentonite. Part of Custer Natl. Forest in S; part of Northern Cheyenne Indian Reservation in S. Formed 1901; present boundaries est. 1919.

Rosebud 1 town (1990 pop. 380), Gasconade co., E central Mo., 7 mi/11.3 km NE of Owensville; 38°23'N 91°24'W. Corn, hay; cattle. Machine tools. Settled 1840s. **2** town (1990 pop. 1,638), Falls co., E central Texas, 35 mi/56 km SSE of Waco; 31°04'N 96°58'W. RR terminus. Cotton, corn; cattle; timber; mfg. (children's clothing, printing, fir wood processing). Settled 1890; inc. 1906.

Rosebud, village (1990 pop. 1,538), Todd co., S S.Dak., 10 mi/16 km SW of Mission near Little White R.; hq. for Rosebud and Yankton Indian reservations; 43°14'N 100°50'W. Sioux Indian Mus. to SW. Sinte Gleska Univ., only reservation-based tribal univ. in U.S., started as col. in 1975.

Roseburg, city (1990 pop. 17,032), ⊙ Douglas co., SW Oregon, 60 mi/97 km SSW of Eugene on South Umpqua R., at mouth of Deer Creek; 43°13'N 123°21'W. Elev. 479 ft/146 m. Lumbering industry important. Handles diversified products of nearby cattle ranches. Mfg. (soft drinks, uniforms, lumber, veneer, printing, publishing, asphalt, electronic connectors, dairy prods.); agr. (vineyards, wine; fruits). Tourism., fishing, hunting. Site of Umpqua Community Col., co. fairgrounds, and co. mus. Camas Mt. Wayside State Park to SW. Hq. for Umpqua Natl. Forest to E. Inc. 1872.

Rosecrans, Fort, Calif.: see LOMA, POINT.

Rosedale, town, S Alta., Canada, on Red Deer R., and 5 mi/8 km SE of Drumheller; 51°25'N 112°38'W. In coal-mining and grain-growing region; wheat, flax; cattle.

Rosedale, village, S B.C., Canada, near Fraser R., 7 mi/11 km E of Chilliwack; lumbering; fruits, hops.

Rosedale 1 uninc. town (1990 pop. 4,673), Kern co., S central Calif., residential suburb 7 mi/11.3 km W of Bakersfield, W of Greenacres, near Kern R.; 35°23'N 119°12'W. Cotton, grain; cattle; dairying. Oil and natural gas. **2** town (1990 pop. 783), Parke co., W Ind., near Raccoon Creek, 10 mi/16 km SSW of Rockville; 39°37'N 87°17'W. In agr. area; machine shop. Settled c.1819. **3** (ROZ-dail), town (1990 pop. 807), Iberville parish, SE central La., 16 mi/26 km W of Baton Rouge, near Bayou Maringouin; 30°27'N 91°28'W. In agr. area (sugarcane, cattle). Catfish, crawfish, alligators. **4** town (1990 pop. 2,595), ⊙ Bolivar co. (seat shared with Cleveland), W Miss., on the Mississippi R., and 30 mi/48 km N of Greenville; 33°51'N 91°01'W. RR terminus. In rich agr. area (cotton, corn, rice, soybeans; cattle; timber); ships fish; mfg. (furniture, structural steel fabrication). Great River Road State Park is here; L. Bolivar State Lake to E. Inc. as city since 1930.

Rosedale, village (1990 pop. 48), McClain co., central Okla., 12 mi/19 km SE of Purcell, near Canadian R.; 34°55'N 97°10'W. Inc. 1931.

Rosedale, residential section of SE Queens borough of N.Y. city, SE N.Y.; 40°39'N 73°45'W. Large Caribbean pop.

Roseland 1 uninc. town (1990 pop. 8,779), Sonoma co., W Calif., residential suburb 2 mi/3.2 km W of downtown Santa Rosa; 38°25'N 122°43'W. Santa Rosa Airport to S. Fruits, grain; dairying; cattle, poultry. **2** town (□ 2 sq mi/5.2 sq km; 1990 pop. 1,379), Indian River co., E central Fla., 15 mi/24 km NNW of Vero Beach; 27°50'N 80°29'W. Mfg. includes wire and cable, lead castings. **3** town (1990 pop. 706), St. Joseph co., N Ind., N suburb of South Bend; 41°43'N 86°15'W. **4** town (1990 pop. 1,093), Tangipahoa parish, SE La., 20 mi/32 km N of Ponchatoula, on Tangipahoa R.; 30°46'N 90°31'W. Timber and agr. area; catfish; mfg. (go carts). Founded 1888; inc. as village 1892; as town 1936. Sandy Hollow State Wildlife Area to NE.

Roseland 1 village (1990 pop. 98), Cherokee co., extreme SE Kansas, 7 mi/11.3 km N of Columbus; 37°16'N 94°50'W. In coal-mining and diversified agr. region. **2** village (1990 pop. 247), Adams co., S Nebr., 12 mi/19 km SW of Hastings; 40°28'N 98°33'W. **3** uninc. village, Nelson co., central Va., 6 mi/9.7 km W of Lovington; 37°44'N 78°58'W. Mfg. (wooden furniture); titanium ore.

Roseland, borough (1990 pop. 4,847), Essex co., NE N.J., 9 mi/14.5 km NW of Newark; 40°49'N 74°18'W. Electronic and photographic equip. Inc. 1908.

Roselawn, village, Newton co., NW Ind., 19 mi/31 km S of Crown Point. In agr. area. Resorts. Laid out 1882.

Roselle (ro-ZEL), village (1990 pop. 20,819), Du Page co., NE Ill., suburb 25 mi/40 km NW of downtown Chicago, and 10 mi/16 km ESE of Elgin; 41°58'N 88°04'W. Some agr.; mfg. (trade show exhibits, metal hoses, food cans). Schaumburg Airport to NW.

Roselle (ro-ZEL), borough (1990 pop. 20,314), Union co., NE N.J., just W of Elizabeth; 40°38'N 74°15'W. Chiefly residential, the borough has some industry. Thomas Edison had a laboratory here, and Roselle was the world's 1st community to have incandescent bulbs light its streets. Abraham Clark, a signer of the Declaration of Independence, b. here. Set off from Linden 1890; inc. 1894.

Roselle Park (ro-ZEL), borough (1990 pop. 12,805), Union co., NE N.J., just W of Elizabeth; 40°40'N 74°16'W. Mainly residential, the borough produces some light industrial goods, such as rugs and leather prods. Founded c.1700; inc. 1901.

Rosemead, city (1990 pop. 51,638), Los Angeles co., SW Calif., a suburb 9 mi/14.5 km E of downtown Los Angeles; 34°04'N 118°05'W. Mainly residential, Rosemead grew rapidly in the 1960s and 1970s. Mfg. (directory publishing, furniture, electronic components, printing). Founded 1867; inc. 1959.

Rosemont, uninc. city (1990 pop. 22,851), Sacramento co., central Calif., residential suburb 6 mi/9.7 km E of downtown Sacramento, near American R.; 38°33'N 121°21'W. Agr. to SE (fruits, nuts, vegetables; dairying; cattle, poultry).

Rosemont 1 (ROS-mahnt), village (1990 pop. 3,995), Cook co., NE Ill., suburb 13 mi/21 km NW of downtown Chicago, near entrance to O'Hare Airport (to W); 41°59'N 87°52'W. Mfg. (electronic ballast, paperboard cartons, aluminum extrusions, printed circuit boards). Major convention center. **2** uninc. village, Lower Merion township, Montgomery co., and Radnor township, Delaware co., SE Pa., 9 mi/14.5 km WNW of Philadelphia; 40°01'N 75°19'W. Mfg. (carbide and diamond industrial tools). Seat of Rosemont Col.

Rosemount, town (1990 pop. 8,622), Dakota co., SE Minn., suburb 14 mi/23 km S of downtown St. Paul, bounded by Mississippi R. (Spring L. reservoir) on NE corner; 44°45'N 93°04'W. RR junction. Agr. area to S (grain, soybeans; livestock; dairying); mfg. (concrete prods., plastic laminating, multiwall paper bags, weather strips, mats). Seat of Dakota County Technical Col. Small lakes to NW.

Rosenberg, city (1990 pop. 20,183), Fort Bend co., SE Texas, on the Brazos R., 30 mi/48 km WSW of Houston; 29°33'N 95°47'W. RR junction in an oil and natural gas area. Rosenberg and its sister city of Richmond (3 mi/4.8 km ENE) are physically one community. Rosenberg is the larger and more industrialized; it was founded with the coming of the RR in 1883 and grew as a farm-marketing and shipping center. Brazos Bend State Park and George Observatory to SE. Mfg. (plastic prods., concrete, oil rigs and equip., food processing, brooms and mops, engine and motor controls). Inc. 1902.

Rosendale, town (1990 pop. 186), Andrew co., NW Mo., on One Hundred and Two R., and 7 mi/11.3 km N of Savannah; 40°02'N 94°49'W.

Rosendale 1 village (1990 pop. 1,284), Ulster co., SE N.Y., on Rondout Creek, and 7 mi/11.3 km SW of Kingston; 41°51'N 74°04'W. Mfg. (injection-molded thermoformed plastics). Inc. 1890. **2** village (1990 pop. 777), Fond du Lac co., E central Wis., 10 mi/16 km W of Fond du Lac; 43°48'N 88°40'W. In farm area.

Rosenfeld, village, S Man., Canada, 50 mi/80 km SSW of Winnipeg; 49°12′N 97°33′W. Grain; livestock.

Rosenhayn (RO-zuhn-hain), village (1990 pop. 1,053), Cumberland co., SW N.J., 6 mi/9.7 km NE of Bridgeton; 39°28′N 75°08′W.

Rosepine (ROZ-pein), town (1990 pop. 1,135), Vernon parish, W La., 55 mi/89 km SW of Alexandria, near Texas line; 30°55′N 93°17′W. Cattle, poultry, hogs; dairying; timber. Kisatchie Natl. Forest to NE; Boise-Vernon State Wildlife Area to W.

Roseto (ro-SEE-to), borough (1990 pop. 1,555), Northampton co., E Pa., 1 mi/1.6 km N of Bangor; 40°52′N 75°13′W. Light mfg. Slate quarries. Appalachian Trail passes to N, on Kittatinny Mt. Inc. 1910.

Rosetown, town (1991 pop. 2,519), SW Sask., Canada, 70 mi/113 km SW of Saskatoon; 51°33′N 107°59′W. Wheat center; grain elevators.

Roseville 1 city (1990 pop. 44,685), Placer co., N central Calif., suburb 15 mi/24 km NE of downtown Sacramento, in the foothills of the Sierras; 38°46′N 121°17′W. RR junction and center. Marked by rapid growth since the 1970s. Agr. area (fruits, grain, esp. rice, walnuts; cattle, sheep, turkeys); mfg. (apiary prods., adhesives, printing and construction machinery, electronic components, lab instruments, computer equip., printing and publishing). Folsom L. State Recreation Area to E. Inc. 1909. **2** city (1990 pop. 51,412), Macomb co., SE Mich., a residential suburb 12 mi/19 km NE of downtown Detroit, near L. St. Clair; 42°30′N 82°56′W. Mfg. (machinery, metal plating, military electronics, auto trim, precast concrete, scrap metal processing, nonferrous metals foundry). Inc. as a village 1926; as a city 1958. **3** city (1990 pop. 33,485), Ramsey co., SE Minn., a suburb 5 mi/8 km NW of downtown St. Paul, and 6 mi/9.7 km ENE of downtown Minneapolis; Mississippi R. is to W; 45°01′N 93°09′W. Mfg. (plastic flower pots, metal fabrication, thermal remediation equip., graphics boards, metal finishing, school emblems, printing, bakery prods., computer systems). Inc. 1948.

Roseville, town (1990 pop. 1,151), Warren co., W Ill., 13 mi/21 km S of Monmouth; 40°43′N 90°39′W. Trade and shipping center in agr. area (corn, soybeans; cattle, hogs). Inc. 1875.

Roseville, village (1990 pop. 1,847), on Muskingum-Perry co. line, central Ohio, 10 mi/16 km SSW of Zanesville; 39°48′N 82°04′W.

Roseville (ROS-vil), borough (1990 pop. 230), Tioga co., N Pa., 17 mi/27 km SSW of Elmira, N.Y., on Mill Creek; 41°52′N 76°57′W. Agr. (hay; dairying).

Roseway River, 35 mi/56 km long, W N.S., Canada; rises from small Roseway L.; flows S to the Atlantic at Shelburne.

Rosewood 1 village, Humboldt co., NW Calif., just S of Eureka. **2** uninc. village, Muhlenberg co., W Ky., 8 mi/12.9 km SSE of Greenville. Agr. (tobacco; livestock). L. Malone reservoir and State Park to SE.

Rosewood Heights, uninc. village (1990 pop. 4,821), Madison co., SW Ill., residential suburb of St. Louis, bet. East Alton and Bethalto; 38°53′N 90°04′W. St. Louis Regional Airport to E.

Rosharon, uninc. village (1990 pop. 436), Brazoria co., SE Texas, 15 mi/24 km N of Angleton. Oil and natural gas region. Mfg. (oil field equip.).

Rosholt 1 (RAH-sholt), village (1990 pop. 408), Roberts co., extreme NE S.Dak., 21 mi/34 km NE of Sisseton, near N.Dak.-Minn. state line (Bois de Sioux R. to E); 45°52′N 96°43′W. In rich farming region. **2** village (1990 pop. 512), Portage co., central Wis., 15 mi/24 km NE of Stevens Point; 44°37′N 89°17′W. In dairying area.

Rosiclare, city (1990 pop. 1,378), Hardin co., SE Ill., on Ohio R., 3 mi/4.8 km SW of Elizabethtown; 37°25′N 88°20′W. Agr. (sorghum, corn); Mfg. fluorspar processing. Inc. as village 1874, as city 1932.

Rosier, Cape (ro-ZIR), Hancock co., S Maine, point on E side of Penobscot Bay, 20 mi/32 km SW of Ellsworth. Cape Rosier village is in Brooksville town.

Rosiers, Cape, E Que., Canada, at E end of Gaspé Peninsula, on the Gulf of St. Lawrence, 13 mi/21 km E of Gaspé; 48°51′N 64°12′W. Lighthouse.

Rosine (ro-ZEEN), uninc. village (1990 pop. 400), Ohio co., W Ky., 10 mi/16 km ENE of Beaver Dam. Bituminous cola. Tobacco, grain; livestock. Birthplace of Bill Monroe, the "Father of Bluegrass Music."

Rosita, Mexico: see NUEVA ROSITA.

Roslindale, Mass.: see BOSTON.

Roslyn, town (1990 pop. 869), Kittitas co., central Wash., 25 mi/40 km NW of Ellensburg; 47°14′N 121°06′W. On RR spur from Cle Elum. Potatoes; dairying; sheep, cattle; timber. Near Cle Elum R., Cle Elum L. reservoir to NW. Easton and Iron Horse state parks to W; Wenatchee Natl. Forest to N, W, and S and Alpine Lakes Wilderness to N and W. Several ski areas to NW. Inc. 1889.

Roslyn 1 residential village (1990 pop. 1,965), Nassau co., SE N.Y., on N shore of W L.I., at head of Hempstead Harbor, 4 mi/6.4 km N of Mineola; 40°47′N 73°39′W. Mfg. (printing equip., food prods., fabricated steel prods.). "Cedarmere," home of William Cullen Bryant, is here. As a part of the Defense Base Closure and Realignment Commission's decisions, the Roslyn Air Guard Station was closed in 1995 and its functions transferred to the Air Guard Station at Stewart Internatl. Airport in Newburgh. Inc. 1932. **2** village (1990 pop. 251), Day co., NE S.Dak., 11 mi/18 km N of Webster; 45°30′N 97°29′W.

Roslyn, Pa.: see ABINGTON.

Roslyn Estates, residential village (1990 pop. 1,184), Nassau co., SE N.Y., on N shore of W L.I., just SW of Roslyn; 40°47′N 73°39′W.

Roslyn Heights, uninc. residential village (□ 1 sq mi/2.6 sq km; 1990 pop. 6,405), Nassau co., SE N.Y., on L.I.; 40°46′N 73°38′W.

Rosman (RAHS-muhn), village (1990 pop. 385), Transylvania co., W N.C., 8 mi/12.9 km SSW of Brevard, near French Broad R.; 35°08′N 82°49′W. Timber; tobacco, corn; cattle. Mfg. (thread, pumps, furniture, fabricated metal prods.). Toxaway Falls (123 ft/37 m) and L. Toxaway reservoir to W. Pisgah Natl. Forest to W and NW. Sassafras Mt. (3,560 ft/1,085 m) highest point in neighboring S.C. to S.

Ross, county (□ 687 sq mi/1,779 sq km; 1990 pop. 69,330), S Ohio; ⊙ Chillicothe; 39°21′N 83°04′W. Intersected by Scioto R. and by Paint, Deer, and small Walnut and Salt creeks. Includes Mound City Group Natl. Monument. In the Glaciated Plains, Unglaciated Plains, and Till Plains physiographic regions. Farming (corn, soybeans); hog and cattle raising; dairying. Mfg. at Chillicothe (paper mills, motor vehicle bodies). Sand, gravel pits. Formed 1798.

Ross, city (1990 pop. 2,123), Marin co., W Calif., residential suburb 15 mi/24 km NNW of San Francisco, 2 mi/3.2 km W of San Rafael; in Ross Valley, on San Anselmo Creek; 37°58′N 122°34′W. L. Lagunitas Reservoir to W; Mt. Tamalpais State Park and Muir Woods Natl. Monument to S. Inc. 1908.

Ross (RAWS), township (1990 pop. 33,482), Allegheny co., W Pa., residential suburb 7 mi/11.3 km N of Pittsburgh; includes the communities of Perrysville, Laurel Gardens, and Berkeley Hills; 40°31′N 80°01′W.

Ross Barnett Reservoir (□ 52 sq mi/135 sq km), on border of Madison and Rankin cos., central Miss., on Pearl R., 5 mi/8 km NE of Jackson; 32°24′N 90°04′W. Extends NE-SW. Formed by Ross R. Barnett L. Dam (64 ft/20 m high), built for recreation; also used for flood control and water supply.

Ross Dam, Wash.: see SKAGIT, river.

Ross Lake, reservoir (□ 18 sq mi/47 sq km), Whatcom co., N central Wash., on Skagit R., in Cascade Mts., in Ross L. Natl. Recreational Area within North Cascades Natl. Park, 70 mi/113 km E of Bellingham; 48°45′N 121°04′W. Max. capacity 1,452,750 acre-ft. Extends N to Can. (B.C.) border. Formed by Ross Dam (542 ft/165 m high), built (1949) for power generation. Mt. Baker–Snoqualmie Natl. Forest and Pasayten Wilderness Area to E.

Ross Lake National Recreation Area (□ 184 sq mi/477 sq km), Whatcom co., N Wash. Includes Ross L. and Dam, and Diablo and Gorge dams downstream, in Skagit R. canyon; bounded by N and S units of North Cascades Natl. Park and by Mt. Baker–Snoqualmie Natl. Forest on E and SW. Extends to Canada (B.C.) border. Authorized 1968.

Ross River, Indian village (1991 pop. 324), S Yukon, Canada, on Pelly R. at mouth of Ross R., 120 mi/193 km NE of Whitehorse; 62°00′N 132°27′W. Fur-trading post.

Rossburg (RAHS-buhrg), village (1990 pop. 250), Darke co., W Ohio, 12 mi/19 km N of Greenville; 40°16′N 84°40′W.

Rossburn, village (1991 pop. 609), S Man., Canada, 40 mi/64 km NE of Brandon, near Riding Mt. Natl. Park; 50°40′N 100°49′W. Wheat; mixed farming.

Rosseau (RAH-so), village (1991 pop. 263), S Ont., Canada, on L. Rosseau, 20 mi/32 km ESE of Parry Sound, in Muskoka lake region. Lumbering; resort.

Rosseau, Lake, S Ont., Canada, in Muskoka lake region, 20 mi/32 km ESE of Parry Sound; 12 mi/19 km long, 5 mi/8 km wide. Drains into Georgian Bay.

Rosser, village (1990 pop. 366), Kaufman co., NE Texas, 28 mi/45 km SE of Dallas, near Trinity R.; 32°27′N 96°26′W. Agr. area (cattle, cotton, wheat, nurseries).

Rossford, city (1990 pop. 5,861), Wood co., NW Ohio, on Maumee R., just S of Toledo; 41°36′N 83°34′W. Large plate-glass plant; also mfg. of chemicals, bldg. materials, grain prods. Inc. 1939.

Rossie, town (1990 pop. 68), Clay co., NW Iowa, 9 mi/14.5 km SSW of Spencer; 43°00′N 95°11′W.

Rossignol, Lake (RAH-sig-nyol), W N.S., Canada, 16 mi/26 km NW of Liverpool, for which it is reservoir; 16 mi/26 km long, 10 mi/16 km wide. Drained by Mersey R.

Rossiter (RAW-si-tuhr), uninc. town (1990 pop. 900), Indiana co., W central Pa., 4 mi/6.4 km SE of Punxsutawney; 40°53′N 78°55′W. Agr. (corn, hay; dairying); timber.

Rossland, city (1991 pop. 3,557), SE B.C., Canada, near Wash. border, in Selkirk Mts., 5 mi/8 km WSW of Trail; 49°05′N 117°49′W. Elev. 5,150 ft/1,570 m. Fruit-growing, dairying, ranching center; residential town for Trail mining region (silver, lead, zinc).

Rosslyn, central business district of Arlington, Va.

Rosslyn Farms (ROS-i-lin), borough (1990 pop. 483), Allegheny co., SW Pa., residential suburb 5 mi/8 km W of Pittsburgh, on Chartiers Creek; 40°25′N 80°05′W.

Rossmoor, uninc. city (1990 pop. 9,893), Orange co., S Calif., residential suburb 20 mi/32 km SSE of Los Angeles; and 7 mi/11.3 km E of Long Beach, near San Gabriel R., 3 mi/4.8 km NE of Pacific Ocean; 33°48′N 118°05′W. Los Alamitos Naval Air Station to NE; Seal Beach Naval Weapons Station to SE.

Rossmore, uninc. village (1990 pop. 300), Logan co., SW W.Va., 3 mi/4.8 km S of Logan.

Rossmoyne (ROS-moin), uninc. town (1990 pop. 1,060), Cumberland co., S Pa., 5 mi/8 km W of Harrisburg; 40°11′N 76°56′W. Camp Hill State Correctional Inst. to NE.

Rossmoyne (rahs-MOIN), village, Hamilton co., extreme SW Ohio, 11 mi/18 km NE of Cincinnati.

Rossport, village, W central Ont., Canada, on L. Superior, 80 mi/129 km ENE of Thunder Bay; 48°50′N 87°31′W. Zinc mining.

Rosston, village (1990 pop. 54), Harper co., NW Okla., 17 mi/27 km W of Buffalo, near Canadian (Beaver) R.; 36°48′N 99°55′W. Grain; livestock area.

Rossville 1 (RAWS-vil), town (1990 pop. 3,601), Walker co., NW Ga., on Tenn. state line; industrial suburb of Chattanooga (Tenn.); 34°58′N 85°17′W. Named for Cherokee chief John Ross, who lived here. Mfg. includes twine, fabrics, thread, yarns, sports equip., plastics; vegetable processing. Chickamauga and Chattanooga Natl. Military Park and Fort Oglethorpe are nearby. **2** town (1990 pop. 1,175), Clinton co., central Ind., on a fork of Wildcat Creek, 10 mi/16 km NNW of Frankfort; 40°25′N 86°36′W. In agr. area; fertilizer blending. Laid out 1834. **3** town (1990 pop. 291), Fayette co., SW Tenn., on Wolf R., and 27 mi/43 km E of Memphis; 35°02′N 89°32′W.

Rossville 1 village (1990 pop. 1,334), Vermilion co., E Ill., on North Fork of Vermilion R., 17 mi/27 km N of Danville; 40°22′N 87°40′W. Agr. (corn, soybeans; cattle); mfg. (consumer goods). Platted 1857, inc. 1872. **2** village (1990 pop. 1,052), Shawnee co., NE Kansas, on small affluent of Kansas R., 15 mi/24 km WNW of Topeka; 39°08′N 95°57′W. Trading point in agr. region (grain; livestock); dairying.

Rossville, section of Staten Isl. borough of N.Y. city, SE N.Y., on W Staten Isl., on Arthur Kill; 40°33′N 74°12′W.

Rosthern (RAHS-thuhrn), town (1991 pop. 1,560), central Sask., Canada, 4 mi/6.5 km NNE of Saskatoon; 52°39′N 106°20′W. Site of govt. telephone center; experimental farm, grain elevators, flour mills, dairies.

Roswell 1 (RAHZ-wel), city (1990 pop. 47,923), Fulton co., NW central Ga., 18 mi/29 km N of Atlanta, near Chattahoochee R.; 34°02′N 84°22′W. Rapidly growing exclusive suburb of Atlanta on its affluent N side. Rapidly expanding professional white-collar employment base along Ga.'s 400 limited-access expressway. Major retail mall nearby. Historic town center originally a cotton town at water tower site on Chattahoochee R. Bulloch Hall (1839) is Theodore Roosevelt's mother's childhood home. Mfg. includes medical equip., computer circuit boards, furniture. Settled c.1837; inc. 1854. **2** city (1990 pop. 44,654), ⊙ Chaves co., SE N.Mex., 160 mi/257 km SE of Albuquerque on Rio Hondo near its confluence with the Pecos R.; 33°22′N 104°31′W. It is the trade, marketing, and RR center of an irrigated farm area. Mfg. includes food and beverages, fireworks, clothing, pipes, printing and publishing, concrete, motor vehicles. The city grew rapidly after the discovery (1891) of artesian wells, with the coming (1894) of the RR, and with the later discovery of oil. Eastern N.Mex. Univ. has a campus in Roswell; and N.Mex. Military Inst. is also here. Nearby are Bitter Refuge and the ranch of John S. Chisum, the 19th-cent. cattleman. Roswell Music and Art Center. Bitter L. Natl. Wildlife Refuge to NE; Bottomless Lakes State Park to SE; Dexter Natl. Fish Hatchery at L. Van to SE. Settled 1869 as a trading post; inc. 1903.

Roswell 1 village (1990 pop. 257), Tuscarawas co., E Ohio, 5 mi/8 km E of New Philadelphia, in agr. area; 40°28′N 81°20′W. **2** village (1990 pop. 19), Miner co., SE central S.Dak., 8 mi/12.9 km W of Howard; 44°00′N 97°42′W.

Rosyln Harbor, village (1990 pop. 1,114), Nassau co., SE N.Y., on W L.I., on Hempstead Harbor, S of Glen Cove; 40°49′N 73°38′W. In yachting area.

Rotan, town (1990 pop. 1,913), Fisher co., NW central Texas, 25 mi/40 km N of Sweetwater; 32°51′N 100°28′W. A trade, shipping, processing point for cattle, hogs, and Angora goats. Ranching; oil and gas; agr. region (cotton, alfalfa, hay); mfg. (wallboard). Gypsum plant. Inc. 1908.

Rothesay (RAHTH-see), residential and resort town (1991 pop. 1,647), S N.B., Canada, on Kennebecasis Bay, 9 mi/14 km NNE of St. John; 45°23′N 66°00′W.

Rothsay, village (1990 pop. 443), Wilkin co., W Minn., 17 mi/27 km NW of Fergus; 46°28′N 96°17′W. Grain; poultry, cattle, sheep; dairying; mfg. (fertilizer, meat processing). Rothsay Wildlife Area to NW.

Rothschild, town (1990 pop. 3,310), Marathon co., central Wis., on Wisconsin R., suburb 5 mi/8 km S of Wausau; 44°53′N 89°37′W. Mfg. (chemicals, bldg. materials). Dam, which forms L. Wausau, is here. Rib Mt. State Park to NW.

Rothsville (RAWTHS-vil), uninc. town (1990 pop. 2,097), Lancaster co., SE Pa., 8 mi/12.9 km NNE of Lancaster, on Cocalico Creek; 40°08′N 76°15′W. Agr. area (grain, soybeans; livestock; dairying).

Rothville, town (1990 pop. 100), Chariton co., N central Mo., 20 mi/32 km NNW of Keytesville; 39°38′N 93°03′W.

Rotonda (ro-TON-duh), town (□ 12 sq mi/31 sq km; 1990 pop. 3,576), Charlotte co., SW Fla., 9 mi/14.5 km SE of Englewood; 26°52′N 82°16′W.

Rotterdam, residential town (□ 36 sq mi/93 sq km; 1990 pop. 21,228), Schenectady co., E N.Y.; 42°48′N 74°00′W. Settled c.1670, inc. 1821.

Roubaix (ROU-bai), village, Lawrence co., W S.Dak., in Black Hills, 7 mi/11.3 km SE of Deadwood; 44°16′N 103°39′W. Elev. 5,392 ft/1,643 m. Gold mine here.

Rouge River, 150 mi/241 km long, SW Que., Canada; rises in Mont Tremblant Park, flows S to Ottawa R. 17 mi/27 km W of Lachute.

Rouge, River (roozh), c.30 mi/48 km long, Mich.; rises in S Michigan; winds S and SE to the Detroit R. at the city of River Rouge; 42°37′N 83°10′W. Dearborn and part of Detroit also lie on the river, which carries much of the raw material used by Detroit's industries.

Rougemont (roozh-MOH), village (1991 pop. 1,159), S Que., Canada, 20 mi/32 km E of Montreal. Dairying; vegetables, tobacco, maple sugar prods.

Rough River, 136 mi/219 km long, NW Ky.; rises in NW Hardin co.; flows generally WSW, past Hardin Springs, through Rough R. L. reservoir, past Hartford, to Green R. at Livermore.

Rough River Lake, reservoir (□ 80 sq mi/207 sq km), Breckinridge and Grayson cos., W Ky., on Rough R., 36 mi/58 km ENE from Elizabethtown; 37°37′N 86°30′W. Max. capacity 334,400 acre-ft. Has 2 E branches. Formed by Rough R. L. Dam (132 ft/40 m high), built (1959) by Army Corps of Engineers for flood control; also used for recreation and water supply. Rough Rider Dam State Park next to dam.

Rouleau (roo-LO), town (1991 pop. 480), S Sask., Canada, near Moosejaw Creek, 22 mi/35 km SW of Regina; 50°11′N 104°54′W. Grain elevators, oil depot, lumbering.

Roulette (ROO-let), uninc. town (1990 pop. 1,500), Potter co., N Pa., 7 mi/11.3 km W of Coudersport on Allegheny R.; 41°46′N 78°09′W. Mfg. includes lumber; agr. includes dairying; livestock; hay, potatoes; timber.

Round Bay, summer resort, Anne Arundel co., central Md., 7 mi/11.3 km NNW of Annapolis.

Round Butte Dam oregon: see BILLY CHINOOK, LAKE.

Round Hill, village, central Alta., Canada, 14 mi/23 km NE of Camrose; 53°10′N 112°37′W. Coal mining; oil and gas; wheat, barley, oats, flax; hogs.

Round Hill, town (1990 pop. 514), Loudoun co., N Va., 9 mi/18 km W of Leesburg, near W.Va. state line, in E foothills of Blue Ridge Mts.; 39°07′N 77°46′W. Mfg. (millwork); agr. (livestock; grain, apples); timber.

Round Island 1 in N Mich., in the Straits of Mackinac 6 mi/9.7 km SE of St. Ignace, bet. Mackinac and Bois Blanc isls.; c.2 mi/3.2 km long, 1 mi/1.6 km wide. **2** one of the Thousand Isls., Jefferson co., N N.Y., in the St. Lawrence R., near N.Y. shore, just NE of Clayton; c.1 mi/1.6 km long, 0.8 mi/1.3 km wide; 44°16′N 76°03′W. Resort.

Round Lake 1 village (1990 pop. 3,550), Lake co., NE Ill., 14 mi/23 km W of Waukegan, residential suburb 41 mi/66 km NW of Chicago, W of Round L.; 42°21′N 88°06′W. RR junction. In agr. area (grain; dairying); mfg. (signs, hosp. equip., industrial ovens and furnaces). Just N is Round Lake Beach village. Residential Round Lake Park village, is just SE of Round L. Volo Bog State Natural Area to W. **2** village (1990 pop. 463), Nobles co., SW Minn., near Iowa state line, 8 mi/12.9 km SE of Worthington; 43°32′N 95°28′W. Corn, soybeans; hogs; dairying; mfg. (candy and nuts). Near several small natural lakes of glacial origin, including Round L. to NE (Jackson co.). **3** residential village (□ 1 sq mi/2.6 sq km; 1990 pop. 765), Saratoga co., E N.Y., on small Round L., 11 mi/18 km NNE of Schenectady; 42°56′N 73°47′W. In agr. area.

Round Lake Beach, village (1990 pop. 16,434), Lake co., NE Ill., residential suburb 42 mi/68 km NW of Chicago, 14 mi/23 km W of Waukegan, on N side of Round L.; 42°22′N 88°04′W. Remnant agr.; mfg. (circuit boards, forklift equip.). Inc. 1937.

Round Lake Heights, village (1990 pop. 1,251), Lake co., NE Ill., residential suburb 44 mi/71 km NW of Chicago, 13 mi/21 km WNW of Waukegan; 42°22′N 88°05′W.

Round Lake Park, village (1990 pop. 4,045), Lake co., NE Ill., 12 mi/19 km WSW of Waukegan, residential suburb 38 mi/61 km NW of Chicago; 42°19′N 88°03′W. Mfg. (metal fabrication). Remnant agr. Campbell's Airport here. Inc. 1947.

Round Mountain, locality, Nye co., central Nev., 42 mi/68 km NNE of Tonopah, in Toquima Range, surrounded by Toiyabe Natl. Forest on S and E. Active gold-mining dist.

Round O, uninc. village, Colleton co., S S.C., 7 mi/11.3 km E of Walterboro. Mfg. of feeds; agr. includes livestock; grain, watermelons, vegetables.

Round Pond, lake (□ 21 sq mi/54 sq km), S N.F., Canada, 50 mi/80 km SSW of Grand Falls; 7 mi/11 km long, 7 mi/11 km wide; drains into Hermitage Bay.

Round Pond, Maine: see BRISTOL.

Round Rock, city (1990 pop. 30,923), Williamson and Travis cos., central Texas, suburb 17 mi/27 km N of Austin; 30°31′N 97°40′W. Elev. 720 ft/219 m. RR junction and market center in rich agr. area (cotton, dairying); lime kilns, limestone quarries; mfg. (bldg. materials, medical equip., electronic systems, pharmaceuticals). In 1878 Sam Bass, famous outlaw, was killed here by Texas Rangers. Palm House Mus.

Round Top 1 resort village (1990 pop. 600), Greene co., SE N.Y., in the Catskills, 9 mi/14.5 km. NW of Catskill; 42°16′N 74°02′W. Round Top mt. is nearby. **2** village (1990 pop. 81), Fayette co., S central Texas, 20 mi/32 km SW of Brenham; 30°03′N 96°42′W. In farm area. Round Top Acad. (1854–1861). Internatl. Festival Inst. has concert hall and 80-acre/32-ha campus. Est. 1835.

Round Valley Reservoir, at Lebanon, Hunterdon co., NW N.J., on Prescott Brook, in Round Valley State Recreation Area, 27 mi/43 km N of Trenton; 3 mi/4.8 km long, 2 mi/3.2 km wide; 40°37′N 74°49′W. Max. capacity 168,500 acre-ft. Formed by Round Valley Dam (165 ft/50 m high), built (1961) by the State of N.J. for flood control.

Roundup, town (1990 pop. 1,808), ⊙ Musselshell co., central Mont., on Musselshell R., 45 mi/72 km N of Billings; 46°27′N 108°32′W. Trade center for former coal-mining region; wheat, hay, cattle, sheep. L. Mason Natl. Wildlife Refuge to NW. Musselshell Valley Historical Mus. Inc. 1909.

Rouses Point (ROU-sez), resort village and port of entry (□ 2 sq mi/5.2 sq km; 1990 pop. 2,377), Clinton co., extreme NE N.Y., on L. Champlain (bridged to Vt.), near Que. (Canada) border, 20 mi/32 km N of Plattsburgh; 44°59′N 73°22′W. Paper packaging mfg. and pharmaceuticals; in agr. area. Inc. 1877.

Rouseville (ROOS-vil), borough (1990 pop. 583), Venango co., NW central Pa., 3 mi/4.8 km NNE of Oil City, on Pithole Creek; 41°28′N 79°41′W. Mfg. (machining, oil blending). Oil Creek State Park to N.

Rousseau, Lake, reservoir (□ 55 sq mi/142 sq km), Levy and Citrus cos., N Fla., on Witchlacoochee R., 13 mi/21 km N of Beverly Hills; 29°02′N 82°37′W. Max. capacity 33,600 acre-ft. Extends E to form Citrus co. N border with Levy and Marion cos. Formed by Inglis Dam (21 ft/6 m high), built (1909) for flood control.

Routt, county (□ 2,368 sq mi/6,133 sq km; 1990 pop. 14,088), NW Colo.; ⊙ Steamboat Springs; 40°28′N 106°59′W. Agr. and coal-mining area bordering on Wyo. on N; Continental Divide forms NE border, bounded E by Park Range; drained by Yampa R. Cattle, sheep; wheat, hay, barley. Part of Routt Natl. Forest in N and E; part of White R. Natl. Forest in SW; Steamboat L. and Pearl L. state parks in N; Stagecoach State Park in S center. Formed 1877.

Rouville (roo-VEEL), county (□ 243 sq mi/629 sq km; 1991 pop. 31,370), S Que., Canada, on Richelieu R.; ⊙ Marieville; 45°25′N 73°00′W.

Rouyn-Noranda (ROO-in–nuh-RAN-duh), city (1991 pop. 26,448), extreme SW Que., Canada. Created (1986) by an amalgamation of Rouyn and Noranda, it is the center of a gold-, copper-, and zinc-mining region. Noranda is the site of a large smelter.

Rouzerville, uninc. town (1990 pop. 1,188), Franklin co., S Pa., 3 mi/4.8 km ESE of Waynesboro, near Md. state line; 39°43′N 77°31′W. Agr. (grain, apples; livestock; dairying). Fort Richie Military Reservation (Md.) to SE. Michaux State Forest to N; Appalachian Trail passes to E.

Rowan 1 (ROU-uhn), county (□ 286 sq mi/741 sq km; 1990 pop. 20,353), NE Ky.; ⊙ Morehead; 38°11′N 83°25′W. Bounded SW by Licking R., forms Cave Run L. reservoir. Hilly clay-mining and agr. (burley tobacco, hay, alfalfa, soybeans, corn; cattle) area; sandstone quarries, timber. Mfg. at Morehead. Daniel Boone Natl. Forest covers most of co., in N, center and S. Formed 1856. **2** county (□ 523 sq mi/1,355 sq km; 1990 pop. 110,605), W central N.C.; ⊙ Salisbury; 35°38′N 80°31′W. Bounded E and N by Yadkin R., from High Rock and Tuckertown reservoirs on E, N by South Yadkin R. Piedmont region; farming (corn, wheat, hay, oats, barley, soybeans, cotton; chickens, cattle; dairying), textile mfg., granite quarrying, sawmilling. Mfg. at Salisbury. Spencer Shops State Historical Site in N, at Spencer. Formed 1753.

Rowan, town (1990 pop. 189), Wright co., N central Iowa, near Iowa R., 9 mi/14.5 km E of Clarion; 42°44′N 93°32′W.

Rowdy (ROU-dee), uninc. village, Perry co., SE Ky., 11 mi/18 km N of Hazard, on Troublesome R. Tobacco; livestock.

Rowe, town (1990 pop. 378), Franklin co., NW Mass., 16 mi/26 km WNW of Greenfield; 42°42′N 72°55′W. Agr. Yankee-Rowe Nuclear Plant, 1st nuclear power station in U.S., decommisioned in 1992.

Rowena, uninc. village (1990 pop. 466), Runnels co., W central Texas, 23 mi/37 km NE of San Angelo. In farm area; mfg. (feed; goat, lamb, and pork processing).

Rowes Run (ROS), uninc. town (1990 pop. 900), Redstone township, Fayette co., SW Pa., 9 mi/14.5 km NW of Uniontown, near Redstone Creek; 40°00′N 79°49′W. Agr. (hay; dairying).

Rowesville, village (1990 pop. 316), Orangeburg co., S central S.C., 9 mi/14.5 km S of Orangeburg; 33°22′N 80°50′W. Mfg. includes lumber; agr. includes timber; cotton, grain, peanuts.

Rowland (RO-land), town (1990 pop. 1,139), Robeson co., SE N.C., 17 mi/27 km SW of Lumberton, near S.C. state line; 34°32′N 79°17′W. Grain, soybeans, melons, tobacco; poultry, cotton, hogs. Mfg. (plastic prods., textiles, plywood, apparel).

Rowland Heights, uninc. city (1990 pop. 42,647), Los Angeles co., S Calif., residential suburb 18 mi/29 km ESE of Los Angeles, NE of Whittier, in Puente Hills; 33°59′N 117°54′W.

Rowlesburg (ROLZ-buhrg), village (1990 pop. 648), Preston co., N W.Va., on Cheat R., 17 mi/27 km E of Grafton; 39°21′N 79°40′W. Agr. and coal-mining area. Mfg. (lumber, flooring). Briery Mt. Wildlife Management Area to N. Tray Run Viaduct (1872). Chartered 1858.

Rowlett, city (1990 pop. 23,620), Dallas and Rockwall cos., N Texas, suburb 17 mi/27 km NE of Dallas, surrounds a W arm of L. Ray Hubbard reservoir (E Fork Trinity R.); bounds Rowlett Creek on W; 32°54′N 96°32′W. Mfg. (electronic components, sporting equip., concrete, machining, wire prods.).

Rowley, village, S Alta., Canada, 22 mi/35 km N of Drumheller. Coal mining; oil and gas; cattle, wheat.

Rowley 1 (ROU-lee), town (1990 pop. 272), Buchanan co., E Iowa, near Wapsipinicon R., 7 mi/11.3 km S of Independence; 42°22′N 91°50′W. **2** town (1990 pop. 4,452), Essex co., NE Mass., 6 mi/9.7 km S of Newburyport; 42°43′N 70°54′W. Has fine old houses. State forest. Settled 1638, inc. 1639.

Rowley Junction, uninc. village, Tooele co., NW Utah, 30 mi/48 km W. of Salt Lake City, near SW shore of Great Salt L. Elev. 4,226 ft/1,288 m. Cattle, grain; salt. Highway junction on I-80 on E edge of Great Salt Lake Desert. Small unit of Wasatch Natl. Forest to S; Timpie Springs Waterfowl Management Area to NE; Skull Valley Indian Reservation to S. Formerly called Timpie.

Roxana, village (1990 pop. 1,562), Madison co., SW Ill., near the Mississippi, and 15 mi/24 km N of East St. Louis, industrial suburb of St. Louis, within St. Louis metropolitan area; 38°50′N 90°02′W. Agr. area to E (wheat; cattle). Large oil refinery and storage. Inc. 1921.

Roxboro (RAHKS-buhr-o), town (1990 pop. 7,332), ⊙ Person co., N N.C., 27 mi/43 km N of Durham, near Va. state line; 36°23′N 78°58′W. Agr. area (grain, tobacco, soybeans, sorghum; cattle, hogs); mfg. (aluminum prods., construction equip., fertilizers, fabrics, concrete, lumber, motor vehicles, apparel, electronic components, yarn, fabricated copper). Hyco reservoir to NW; Mayo reservoir to NE.

Roxborough (RAWKS-buh-ro), village, NE Tobago, Trinidad and Tobago, 11 mi/18 km NE of Scarborough.

Roxbury 1 resort town (1990 pop. 1,825), Litchfield co., W Conn., on Shepaug R., 14 mi/23 km W of Waterbury; 41°32′N 73°17′W. Agr. Iron mined in 18th and 19th cents. Seth Warner (buried at Roxbury Center), Ethan Allen, and Remember Baker lived here. **2** town (1990 pop. 437), Oxford co., W Maine, on Swift R., 32 mi/51 km N of South Paris; 44°38′N 70°35′W. In lumbering area. **3** town (1990 pop. 248), Cheshire co., SW N.H., 4 mi/6.4 km E of Keene; 42°57′N 72°11′W. Agr. (nursery crops, vegetables; cattle, poultry; dairying). Woodward Pond in E. **4** (RAWKS-bah-ree), town (1990 pop. 575), Washington co., central Vt., 15 mi/24 km SW of Montpelier; 44°04′N 72°43′W. Agr.; marble; summer camps. Includes Roxbury State Forest.

Roxbury, resort village (1990 pop. 700), Delaware co., S N.Y., in the Catskills, on East Branch of Delaware R., 37 mi/60 km NW of Kingston; 42°17′N 74°32′W. John Burroughs's home is nearby.

Roxbury, township (1990 pop. 20,429), Morris co., N N.J., 10 mi/16 km NW of Morristown; 40°52′N 74°39′W. Inc. 1798.

Roxbury, Mass.: see BOSTON.

Roxie, village (1990 pop. 568), Franklin co., SW Miss., 18 mi/29 km E of Natchez; 31°30′N 91°04′W. Agr. (cotton, corn; timber); mfg. (lumber). Parts of Homochitto Natl. Forest to E and W.

Roxobel (RAHKS-uh-bel), village (1990 pop. 244), Bertie co., NE N.C., 29 mi/47 km SE of Roanoke Rapids; 36°12′N 77°14′W. Cotton, peanuts, tobacco, grain; livestock. Mfg. (textiles).

Roxton, village (1990 pop. 639), Lamar co., NE Texas, 12 mi/19 km SW of Paris, near N Sulphur R.; 33°32′N 95°43′W. In cotton, corn, peanuts, hay area; mfg. (consumer goods).

Roxton Falls, village (1991 pop. 1,336), SW Que., Canada, 20 mi/32 km E of St. Hyacinthe. Food processing, lumbering, woodworking, furniture mfg.

Roxton Pond or **Sainte Pudentienne** (set puh-dat-YEN), village (1991 pop. 969), SW Que., Canada, 16 mi/26 km SE of St. Hyacinthe. Dairying, lumbering, woodworking.

Roy, city (1990 pop. 24,603), Weber co., N Utah, near Great Salt L., suburb 5 mi/8 km SW of Ogden, and 26 mi/42 km NNW of Salt Lake City; 41°10′N 112°02′W. Elev. 4,350 ft/1,326 m. Mfg. (computer equip.). Many residents work at nearby Hill Air Force Base. Hill Air Force Base to SE. Ogden Municipal Airport to NE. Settled by Mormons 1877, inc. 1937.

Roy 1 village (1990 pop. 362), Harding co., NE N.Mex., 92 mi/148 km NNW of Tucumcari; 35°57′N 104°12′W. Elev. 5,888 ft/1,795 m. Cattle; grain, alfalfa. Carbon-dioxide fields nearby. Chicosa State Park to N; section of Kiowa Natl. Grasslands in N; Canadian R. Canyon is W. **2** village (1990 pop. 258), Pierce co., W central Wash., 18 mi/29 km S of Tacoma; 47°00′N 122°32′W. Flower bulbs; dairying; poultry; mfg. (apparel, metal fabrication). Bounded by Fort Lewis Military Reservation to N and W.

Roy Inks Dam, Texas: see INKS LAKE.

Royal, town (1990 pop. 466), Clay co., NW Iowa, 9 mi/14.5 km WSW of Spencer; 43°03′N 95°16′W. In livestock and grain area.

Royal, village (1990 pop. 81), Antelope co., NE Nebr., 15 mi/24 km NNW of Neligh; 42°19′N 98°07′W.

Royal Center, town (1990 pop. 859), Cass co., N central Ind., 11 mi/18 km NW of Logansport; 40°52′N 86°30′W. Agr. area; lumber; mfg. (machinery, wood prods.). Laid out 1846.

Royal City, town (1990 pop. 1,104), Grant co., E central Wash., 22 mi/35 km SW of Moses L.; 46°54′N 119°37′W. Irrigated agr. area (vegetables, peppermint, spearmint, sugar beets, beans, potatoes). Numerous small units of Columbia Natl. Wildlife Refuge to SW, S, and SE.

Royal Geographical Society Islands, group of 4 small islands and several islets, S Franklin dist., N.W.T., Canada, bet. S end of Victoria Strait and NE side of Queen Maud Gulf, bet. SE Victoria Isl. and SW King William Isl. near 68°50′N 100°15′W.

Royal Gorge, narrow canyon cut by the Arkansas R., Fremont co. 4 mi/6.4 km W of Cañon City, S central Colo.; 10 mi/16 km long. Often called the Grand Canyon of the Arkansas. The gorge was discovered in 1806 by an expedition led by U.S. explorer Zebulon Pike. Its near-vertical walls are more than 1,200 ft/366 m high in places. One of the world's highest suspension bridges (1,053 ft/321 m above the river) crosses the canyon, and a cable RR ascends the canyon wall.

Royal Island, central Bahama Isls., just N of Eleuthera Isl. and W of St. George's Cay, 40 mi/64 km NE of Nassau; c. 3.5 mi/5.6 km long; 25°32′N 76°50′W. Has fine harbor. Belongs to Spanish Wells dist.

Royal Lakes, village (1990 pop. 272), Macoupin co., SW Ill., 20 mi/32 km NE of Alton; 39°06′N 89°57′W. Residential community in agr. and coal-mining region.

Royal Mills, uninc. village, Wake co., central N.C., 1 mi/1.6 km NE of Wake Forest.

Royal Oak, city (1990 pop. 65,410), Oakland co., SE Mich., residential suburb 12 mi/19 km NNW of Detroit; 42°30′N 83°09′W. Mfg. (motor vehicle and computer parts, metal forging). Pop. decreased by nearly 28% bet. 1970 and 1990. Detroit Zoological Park is to S in Huntington Woods. Oakland Troy Airport to N. Settled c.1820, inc. as a city 1921.

Royal Palm Beach, town (□ 8 sq mi/20.7 sq km; 1990 pop. 14,589), Palm Beach co., SE Fla., 10 mi/16 km W of West Palm Beach; 26°42′N 80°13′W. Light mfg.

Royal Pines, uninc. town (1990 pop. 4,418), Buncombe co., W N.C., residential suburb 7 mi/11.3 km SSE of Asheville; 35°28′N 82°30′W. Blue Ridge Parkway to N.

Royal River, c.25 mi/40 km long, SW Maine; rises in N central Cumberland co., flows generally SSE to Casco Bay at Yarmouth.

Royale, Isle, Mich.: see ISLE ROYALE NATIONAL PARK.

Royalston, town (1990 pop. 1,147), Worcester co., N Mass., 21 mi/34 km WNW of Fitchburg; 42°41′N 72°11′W. Agr.

Royalton 1 town (1990 pop. 802), Morrison co., central Minn., 11 mi/18 km SSE of Little Falls, on Platte R. 4 mi/6.4 km N of its confluence with the Mississippi R.; Mississippi R. passes 2 mi/3.2 km to W; 45°49′N 94°17′W. Grain, potatoes; poultry; dairying; mfg. (dairy prods., boat docks). **2** town (1990 pop. 2,389), Windsor co., E central Vt., on White R., 15 mi/24 km N of Woodstock; 43°48′N 72°32′W. In agr. area; dairy prods., maple sugar. Includes South Royalton village (seat of Vt. Law School). Raid in 1780 by Indians and Tories is commemorated by a monument.

Royalton, village (1990 pop. 1,191), Franklin co., S Ill., 14 mi/23 km SW of Benton; 37°52′N 89°06′W. In agr. and bituminous-coal-mining area. Inc. 1907.

Royalton, borough (1990 pop. 1,120), Dauphin co., S Pa., residential suburb 1 mi/1.6 km SE of Middletown, on Susquehanna R., at mouth of Swatara Creek; 40°11′N 76°43′W. Three Mile Isl. Nuclear Plant 2 mi/3.2 km to S; Olmstead Air Force Base to SE.

Royersford (ROI-yuhrs-fuhrd), borough (1990 pop. 4,458), Montgomery co., SE Pa., 24 mi/39 km NW of Philadelphia, on Schuylkill R.; 40°11′N 75°32′W. Agr. (grain, soybeans, apples; livestock; dairying); mfg. (pumps and power tools, dairy prods., wire springs, plastics prods., printing and publishing). Settled 1839, inc. 1879.

Royse City, town (1990 pop. 2,206), Rockwall and Collin cos., NE Texas, 30 mi/48 km NE of Dallas; 32°58′N 96°19′W. Market point in agr. area (cotton; wheat; cattle, horses); mfg. (fabricated metal prods., medical equip.). Settled c.1886, inc. 1888.

Royston (ROI-stuhn), town (1990 pop. 2,758); Franklin, Hart, and Madison cos.; NE Ga., 27 mi/43 km NE of Athens; 34°17′N 83°07′W. Mfg. of metal shelving, textiles, baby prods., clothing, farm equip. Hometown of Ty Cobb.

Rozel (ruh-ZEL), village (1990 pop. 187), Pawnee co., central Kansas, on Pawnee R., 15 mi/24 km W of Larned; 38°12′N 99°24′W. Grain; livestock.

Rubicon River, c.60 mi/97 km long, E central Calif.; rises in Desolation Valley in the Sierra Nevada 11 mi/18 km WSW of South Lake Tahoe, in NE El Dorado co.; flows NW through small Rubicon Reservoir, turns SW at Hell Hole Reservoir, Placer co., forming part of El Dorado–Placer co. line, turns NW again to join Middle Fork of American R. 20 mi/32 km ENE of Auburn.

Rubidoux, uninc. city (1990 pop. 24,367), Riverside co., S Calif., residential suburb 3 mi/4.8 km NNW of Riverside, on Santa Ana R.; 34°00′N 117°25′W. Fla-Bob Airport is here.

Ruby 1 village (1990 pop. 170), W Alaska, on Yukon R. opposite mouth of Melozitna R., 100 mi/161 km WSW of Tanana; 64°43′N 155°31′W. Airfield. **2** village (1990 pop. 300), Chesterfield co., N S.C., 15 mi/24 km WNW of Cheraw, near N.C. state line; 34°44′N 80°10′W. Mfg. includes rubber prods., leather prods. Agr. includes livestock; grain, tobacco, watermelons, peaches. Carolina Sand Hills Natl. Wildlife Refuge to S.

Ruby, locality, Santa Cruz co., S Ariz., near Mex. border, 20 mi/32 km WNW of Nogales. Elev. 4,335 ft/1,321 m. Former mining dist., in sect. of Coronado Natl. Forest.

Ruby Lake, Elko and White Pine cos., NE Nev. Tule Marsh L. just E of S part of Ruby Mts.; 13 mi/21 km long, 2 mi/3.2 km wide. Ruby Natl. Wildlife Refuge here.

Ruby Mountains, largely in Elko co., NE Nev.; extend S into White Pine co., SE of Elko, and c.60 mi/97 km SSW from East Humboldt Range through part of Humboldt Natl. Forest; 40°37′N 115°28′W. Ruby Dune (11,387 ft/3,471 m) in NW, Pearl Peak (10,847 ft/3,306 m) in S. South Fork of Humboldt R. to W. Ruby Mt. Scenic Area in NW part of range. Ruby L. is just E, includes glaciated Lamoille Canyon.

Ruby Range, N extension of Snowcrest Mts. in Madison co., SW Mont., W of Ruby R., S of Sheridan. Rises to max. elev. of 9,391 ft/2,862 m at Ruby Peak.

Ruby River, 76 mi/122 km long, SW Mont.; rises in SW Madison co.; flows N between Gravelly Range (E) and Snowcrest Range (W), through Ruby R. Reservoir, turns NW between Ruby Range (SW) and Tobacco Root Mts. (NE), joining Beaverhead R. S of Twin Bridges. Beaverhead R. joins Big Hole R. 4 mi/6.4 km N to form Jefferson R.

Ruckersville, town, Elbert co., NE Ga., 6 mi/9.7 km NE of Elberton; 34°09′N 82°47′W.

Ruckersville, uninc. village, Greene co., N central Va., 15 mi/24 km NNE of Charlottesville; 38°13′N 78°22′W. Mfg. (wood flooring, consumer goods); agr. (grain; livestock; dairying); timber.

Rudd, town (1990 pop. 429), Floyd co., N Iowa, 12 mi/19 km WNW of Charles City; 43°07′N 92°54′W. In livestock area.

Rudolph, village (1990 pop. 451), Wood co., central Wis., 8 mi/12.9 km NNE of Wisconsin Rapids; 44°30′N 89°47′W. Dairying. Mfg. (cheese).

Rudy, village (1990 pop. 45), Crawford co., NW Ark., 13 mi/21 km NE of Fort Smith, on Frog Bayou; 35°31′N 94°16′W.

Rudyard (RUHD-yuhrd), village (1990 pop. 500), Hill co., N Mont., 41 mi/66 km W of Havre. Hogs, cattle; wheat, barley, oats, hay.

Ruedi Reservoir, Pitkin and Eagle cos., W Colo., on Fryingpan R., in White R. Natl. Forest, 12 mi/19 km N of Aspen; 4 mi/6.4 km long; 39°21′N 106°47′W. Max. capacity of 119,000 acre-ft. Formed by Ruedi Dam (281 ft/86 m), built (1968) by the Bureau of Reclamation for irrigation and flood control.

Rufus (ROO-fuhs), village (1990 pop. 295), Sherman co., N Oregon, 22 mi/35 km ENE of The Dalles, on Columbia R. (L. Celilo reservoir, formed by the Dalles Dam); 45°41′N 120°44′W. John Day Dam 2 mi/3.2 km ENE (upstream), forms L. Umatilla reservoir. Cattle, poultry; wheat, barley, oats.

Rufus Woods, Lake, reservoir (□ 13 sq mi/34 sq km), on border of Okanogan and Douglas cos., E Wash., on Columbia R., on S border of Colville Indian Reservation, 22 mi/35 km NE of Chelan; 48°00′N 119°38′W. Max. capacity 593,000 acre-ft. Formed by Chief Joseph Dam (230 ft/70 m high), built (1955) by Army Corps of Engineers for power generation; also used for recreation.

Rugby, town (1990 pop. 2,909), ⊙ Pierce co., N central N.Dak., 60 mi/97 km E of Minot; 48°22′N 99°59′W. Geographical center of N. Amer. to S. RR junction; dairy prods., sunflowers; grain; livestock. Round L. to NW. Platted 1886, inc. 1905.

Rugby, historic site, village, Morgan co., E Tenn., 15 mi/24 km SE of Jamestown. Preserved site of 19th-cent. utopian community (founded 1880), the last organized Eng. colonialization effort in America. Includes homes, churches, school. Listed on the Natl. Register of Historic Places. Big South Fork Natl. R. and Recreation Area is just N.

Ruger, Fort (ROO-ger), on Diamond Head, SE Oahu,

Honolulu co., Hawaii, 4 mi/6.4 km SE of downtown Honolulu, in caldera of extinct volcano. Hawaiian Natl. Guard Base. Diamond Head State Monument, on slopes of mt. to W and S. Fort Ruger City park to E.

Ruidoso (ree-uh-DO-so), town (1990 pop. 4,600), Lincoln co., S central N.Mex., 47 mi/76 km NE of Alamogordo, in Lincoln Natl. Forest; 33°22′N 105°38′W. Sheep, cattle; printing and publishing, other light mfg. Mescalero Apache Indian Reservation to S and W; Ski Apache Ski Area to NW near Sierra Blanca; Sierra Blanca (11,977 ft/3,651 m) to NW; Alto Reservoir to N; L. Mescalpro Reservoir to SW; Ruidoso Downs Racetrack to E, site of the All-Amer. Futurity Race, Labor Day.

Ruidoso Downs (ree-uh-DO-so), town (1990 pop. 920), Lincoln co., S central N.Mex., 4 mi/6.4 km E of Ruidoso, in Lincoln Natl. Forest; 33°19′N 105°35′W. Site of Ruidoso Downs Racetrack.

Ruiz (roo-ees), town (1990 pop. 12,532), Nayarit, W Mexico, on San Pedro R., on Pacific coastal plain, on RR, 35 mi/56 km NNW of Tepic. Agr. center (corn, sugarcane, tobacco, cotton, tomatoes, bananas).

Rule, town (1990 pop. 783), Haskell co., NW central Texas, c.50 mi/80 km N of Abilene; 33°10′N 99°53′W. In irrigated agr. area (cotton, corn; peanuts; cattle); oil wells. Inc. 1909.

Ruleville (ROOL-vil), town (1990 pop. 3,245), Sunflower co., W Miss., 24 mi/39 km NW of Greenwood, near Sunflower R.; 33°43′N 90°32′W. Agr. (cotton, corn, rice, soybeans; cattle); mfg. (ammunition, apparel) Amer. Costume Mus. Laid out 1898.

Rulo (ROO-lo), village (1990 pop. 191), Richardson co., extreme SE Nebr., 9 mi/14.5 km E of Falls City, and on Missouri R., near Kansas state line; 40°02′N 95°25′W. Iowa Indian Reservation to SE.

Rum Cay, island and district (□ 29 sq mi/75 sq km; 1990 pop. 53), central Bahama Isls., bet. Long Isl. (W) and San Salvador or Watling Isl. (NE), 185 mi/298 km SE of Nassau; 9.5 mi/15.3 km long, 5 mi/8 km wide; 23°40′N 74°55′W. Main industry is salt panning; also produces sisal and coconuts. Second isl. visited by Columbus, who landed here on Oct. 15, 1492, naming it Santa María de la Concepción, a name later applied to an islet, Conception Isl., 15 mi/24 km NW.

Rum River, c.140 mi/225 km long, E central Minn.; rises in Mille Lacs L. (Aitkin/Mille Lacs cos.); flows S through Ogechie, Shakopee, and Onamia lakes near its outflow from Mille Lacs L., past Milaca and Princeton, then generally E, in a very serpentine course, to Cambridge, then S past Isanti to Mississippi R. at Anoka, 16 mi/26 km NNW of Minneapolis; 43°07′N 93°46′W. Was important route for explorers and fur traders. Parts of Rum R. State Forest are to E and W of its outflow from Mille Lacs L.

Ruma, village (1990 pop. 256), Randolph co., SW Ill., 18 mi/29 km NNW of Chester; 38°07′N 90°00′W. In agr. area.

Rumford, town (1990 pop. 7,078), including Rumford Falls village, Oxford co., W Maine, 23 mi/37 km N of South Paris, at falls of the Androscoggin (water power), at influx of Swift R.; 44°31′N 70°37′W. Paper mills. Settled 1774, inc. 1800.

Rumford, neighborhood, in East Providence town, Providence co., R.I., on Conrail.

Rumney, town (1990 pop. 1,446), Grafton co., W central N.H., 7 mi/11.3 km WNW of Plymouth; 43°49′N 71°48′W. Drained by Baker R., and Stinson Brook; Stinson L. in N. Vegetables, nursery crops; cattle, poultry; dairying; timber. Light mfg. Part of White Mt. Natl. Forest.

Rumsey, village (1991 pop. 60), S Alta., Canada, 27 mi/43 km NNW of Drumheller; 51°51′N 112°51′W. Wheat, mixed farming.

Rumsey, uninc. village, McLean co., W Ky., 19 mi/31 km SW of Owensboro, on Green R. (bridged), opposite (S) Calhoun.

Rumson, resort borough (1990 pop. 6,701), Monmouth co., E N.J., bet. Navesink R. and Shrewsbury R. estuaries, near the Atlantic, 16 mi/26 km NE of Freehold; 40°21′N 74°00′W. Estate center; boating. Settled c.1700, inc. 1907.

Runaway Bay, town (1991 pop. 5,655), St. Ann parish, N Jamaica, 8 mi/12.9 km W of St. Ann's Bay, minor seaport and resort; 18°27′N 77°20′W. Here the last Span. governor embarked on his flight from Jamaica. At Dry Harbour, 5 mi/8 km W, Columbus made his 1st landing in Jamaica (1494), taking possession of the isl. for Spain.

Runge, town (1990 pop. 1,139), Karnes co., S Texas, c.60 mi/97 km SE of San Antonio, near San Antonio R.; 28°53′N 97°42′W. Corn, wheat; cattle, dairying; oil and gas; mfg. (natural-gas processing). Settled 1884, inc. 1913.

Runnells, town (1990 pop. 306), Polk co., central Iowa, near Des Moines R., 14 mi/23 km ESE of Des Moines; 41°30′N 93°21′W. In agr. area.

Runnels, county (□ 1,057 sq mi/2,738 sq km; 1990 pop. 11,294), W central Texas; ⊙ Ballinger; 31°49′N 99°58′W. Drained by Colorado R. and Oak Creek. A leading Texas agr. co. (cotton, wheat, grain sorghum); livestock raising (cattle, sheep, goats); wool marketed. Oil and natural-gas wells. Formed 1858.

Runnemede (RUH-ni-meed), residential borough (1990 pop. 9,042), Camden co., SW N.J., 6 mi/9.7 km SSE of Camden; 39°51′N 75°04′W. Settled 1683 by Friends (Quakers), originally called New Hope. Inc. 1926.

Running Springs, uninc. town (1990 pop. 4,195), San Bernardino co., S Calif., 10 mi/16 km ENE of San Bernardino, in San Bernardino Mts., near Deep Creek; 34°13′N 117°07′W. Recreation area; Green Valley and Snow Valley ski areas are here.

Rupert 1 (ROO-puhrt), town (1990 pop. 5,455), ⊙ Minidoka co., S Idaho, near Snake R., 8 mi/12.9 km NE of Burley; 42°37′N 113°40′W. Elev. 4,158 ft/1,267 m. RR junction and shipping center for farm produce (potatoes, sugar beets, peas, beans, alfalfa, wheat); cheese; potato processing and livestock grown on Minidoka irrigation project (on Snake R.). Minidoka Dam and Snake R., to NE. Laid out (1905) as model city by govt. engineers; inc. as village 1906, as city 1917. **2** town (1990 pop. 654), Bennington co., SW Vt., on N.Y. state line, 28 mi/45 km N of Bennington; 43°16′N 73°12′W. An early mint made coins here, at East Rupert, for independent State of Vt. in the 1780s. **3** town (1990 pop. 1,104), Greenbrier co., SE W.Va., 17 mi/27 km NW of Lewisburg, on Meadow R.; 37°58′N 80°41′W. Agr. (grain); livestock, poultry; dairying. Mfg. (coal processing). Parts of Meadow R. Wildlife Management Area to W and S.

Rupert House, village, NW Que., Canada, on James Bay of Hudson Bay, near mouth of Rupert R.; 51°30′N 78°46′W. Oldest post of Hudson's Bay Co., it was est. 1668; subsequently alternated bet. Fr. and Br. possession, until restored to Br. possession by Treaty of Utrecht, 1713.

Rupert River, 380 mi/612 km long, W Que., Canada; issues from L. Mistassini, flows W, through Nemiscau L., past Rupert House, to James Bay 3 mi/5 km W of Rupert House.

Rupert's Land, Can. territory held (1670–1869) by the Hudson's Bay Company, Canada, named for Prince Rupert, 1st gov. of the company. Under the charter granted (1670) to the company by Charles II, the region comprised the drainage basin of Hudson Bay. The area embraced what is today the provs. of Ont. and Que. N of the Laurentians and W of Lab.; all of Man.; most of Sask.; the S half of Alta.; the E part of the N.W.T.; and portions of Minn. and N.Dak. in the U.S. In 1869 the Hudson's Bay Company transferred Rupert's Land to Canada for £300,000 but retained certain blocks of land for trading and other purposes.

Rural Hall (RUHR-uhl), town (1990 pop. 1,652), Forsyth co., N central N.C., suburb 11 mi/18 km NNW of downtown Winston-Salem; 36°13′N 80°17′W. RR junction. Hanging Rock State Park to N. Agr. area (tobacco, grain, soybeans; poultry; cattle). Mfg. (furniture, textiles, metal fabricating, business forms, turbine blades, medical equip.).

Rural Retreat, town (1990 pop. 972), Wythe co., SW Va., 10 mi/16 km WSW of Wytheville; 36°53′N 81°16′W. Mfg. (clothing, plastic film, mining equip., brake

---

Cross references are shown in SMALL CAPITALS. The pronunciation key is on page xv. The dates of population figures are on page xii.

parts); agr. area (cabbage, grain, apples, soybeans; livestock; dairying).

Rural Valley (RUHR-ruhl), borough (1990 pop. 957), Armstrong co., W central Pa., 11 mi/18 km E of Kittanning, on Cowanshannock Creek; 40°47′N 79°18′W. Agr. (corn, hay; livestock; dairying); bituminous coal, gas. Keystone L. reservoir to SE.

Rush 1 county (□ 408 sq mi/1,057 sq km; 1990 pop. 18,129), E central Ind.; ⊙ Rushville; 39°37′N 85°28′W. Drained by Big Blue and Flatrock rivers. Wheat, soybeans, corn; livestock, poultry; dairying; stone quarrying. Mfg. at Carthage and Rushville. Soldiers' and Sailors' Children's Home 2 mi/3.2 km SSE of Knightstown. Formed 1821. **2** county (□ 718 sq mi/1,860 sq km; 1990 pop. 3,842), central Kansas; ⊙ La Crosse; 38°31′N 99°18′W. Agr. region, watered by Walnut Creek. Wheat; cattle, poultry. Formed 1874.

Rush Center, village (1990 pop. 177), Rush co., central Kansas, 5 mi/8 km S of La Crosse, on Walnut Creek; 38°27′N 99°18′W. Wheat; cattle; mfg. (fiberglass prods.).

Rush City, town (1990 pop. 1,497), Chisago co., E Minn., 50 mi/80 km N of St. Paul, on Rush R.; 45°40′N 92°58′W. In agr. region (grain; cattle, poultry; dairying); mfg. (printed circuit boards, plastic molds). St. Croix Natl. Scenic Riverway to E; part of Chengwatana State Forest to E; Rush L. to W; St. Croix R. to E. Settled before 1873.

Rush Creek, c.50 mi/80 km long, S Okla.; rises near Rush Springs in Grady co.; flows E, through Garvin co., to Washita R., just SE of town of Pauls Valley.

Rush Hill, town (1990 pop. 121), Audrain co., NE central Mo., 9 mi/14.5 km NE of Mexico; 39°12′N 91°43′W. Wheat, soybeans; cattle.

Rush Lake 1 Chisago co., E Minn., near Wis. state line, c.50 mi/80 km N of St. Paul; 45°41′N 93°03′W. Neck of land divides lake into 2 sections, connected by narrow channels; E arm is 4.5 mi/7.2 km long, W arm 3.5 mi/5.6 km long; average width 1 mi/1.6 km. Drains E from SE end by Rush Creek (c.10 mi/16 km long) to St. Croix R. Rush City is to E. **2** (□ 8 sq mi/20.7 sq km), Otter Tail co., W Minn., 38 mi/61 km NE of Fergus Falls; 5 mi/8 km long, max. width 3 mi/4.8 km; 46°29′N 95°31′W. Elev. 1,321 ft/403 m. Resort area. Fed from N and drained SW by Otter Tail R. **3** in Cavalier co., NE N.Dak., near Can. border; 5 mi/8 km long, 2 mi/3.2 km wide; 46°53′N 96°54′W. It is slowly receding. **4** in Winnebago co., E central Wis., 12 mi/19 km SW of Oshkosh; c.5 mi/8 km long, c.3 mi/4.8 km wide. In resort region.

Rush Springs, town (1990 pop. 1,229), Grady co., central Okla., 18 mi/29 km S of Chickasha, and on small Rush Creek; 34°46′N 97°57′W. Market and shipping center for agr. area; light mfg. (animal feed).

Rush Valley, village (1990 pop. 339), Tooele co., NW Utah, 16 mi/26 km SW of Tooele, in Rush Valley. Rush L. to NE; 40°21′N 112°27′W. Part of Wasatch Natl. Forest, incl. Deseret Peak Wilderness, to NW. Skull Valley Indian Reservation to W. Dugway Proving Grounds to SW.

Rushford, town (1990 pop. 1,485), Fillmore co., SE Minn., 15 mi/24 km S of Winona, on Root R. at mouth of Rush Creek; 43°48′N 91°45′W. Trade and shipping center for agr. area (feed); mfg. (composite materials, panels and switches). Surrounded by Richard J. Dorer Memorial Hardwood State Forest. Settled before 1854.

Rushford, village (1990 pop. 700), Allegany co., W N.Y., 23 mi/37 km NNE of Olean; 42°23′N 78°15′W. Maple syrup, dairy prods., apples.

Rushford Village, village (1990 pop. 705), Fillmore co., SE Minn., 16 mi/26 km S of Winona, and 1 mi/1.6 km S of Rushford, on Root R., surrounded by Richard J. Dorer Memorial Hardwood State Forest; 43°48′N 91°47′W. Municipality includes South Rushford. Corporate limits include all of surveyed township, excluding Rushford and Peterson.

Rushmere, uninc. town, Isle of Wight co., SE Va., 6 mi/9.7 km NNW of Smithfield, on James R.; 37°04′N 76°40′W. Agr. (grain, peanuts, soybeans, cotton; hogs, cattle).

Rushmore, village (1990 pop. 381), Nobles co., SW Minn., near Iowa state line, 11 mi/18 km W of Worthington; 43°37′N 95°47′W. Soybeans, grain; livestock, poultry; dairying; mfg. (fertilizers).

Rushmore, Mount, S.Dak.: see MOUNT RUSHMORE NATL. MEMORIAL.

Rushsylvania, village (1990 pop. 573), Logan co., W central Ohio, 8 mi/13 km NE of Bellefontaine, and on small Rush Creek; 40°28′N 83°40′W. Limestone quarry nearby.

Rushville 1 city (1990 pop. 3,229), ⊙ Schuyler co., W Ill., 24 mi/39 km SSE of Macomb; 40°07′N 90°34′W. Trade center in agr. area; livestock, corn, wheat; meatpacking plant. Lincoln pleaded cases and made a campaign speech here. Founded 1825, inc. 1839. **2** city (1990 pop. 5,533), ⊙ Rush co., E central Ind., on Flatrock R., and 40 mi/64 km ESE of Indianapolis; 39°37′N 85°27′W. Trade center in agr. area (wheat, corn, soybeans; hogs, cattle; lumber); mfg. (machinery, electronics, transportation equip., fabricated metal prods., furniture, animal feed; food processing). Stone quarry. Laid out 1822.

Rushville 1 town (1990 pop. 306), Buchanan co., NW Mo., near Missouri R., 15 mi/24 km SW of St. Joseph; 39°35′N 95°01′W. Corn, soybeans, oats; livestock. Lewis and Clark State Park 3 mi/4.8 km SW. **2** town (1990 pop. 1,127), ⊙ Sheridan co., NW Nebr., 30 mi/48 km ESE of Chadron; 42°42′N 102°28′W. Livestock, dairy and poultry prods.; grain. Founded c.1885; inc. as city 1932.

Rushville 1 village (1990 pop. 609), on Ontario-Yates co. line, W central N.Y., 15 mi/24 km SW of Geneva, in Finger Lakes region; 42°45′N 77°13′W. **2** village (1990 pop. 229), Fairfield co., central Ohio, 10 mi/16 km ENE of Lancaster, and on small Rush Creek; 49°46′N 82°26′W.

Rusk 1 county (□ 938 sq mi/2,429 sq km; 1990 pop. 43,735), E Texas; ⊙ Henderson; 32°06′N 94°45′W. Rolling wooded area (extensive timber). Bounded extreme NE by Sabine R. and Attoyac Bayou in SE. Source of Attoyac and Murvaul bayous and Martin Creek. A leading Texas petroleum co., with NW and W parts in rich E Texas oil field; also natural gas. Agr. (vegetables, watermelons, nursery crops), dairying; beef cattle, hogs, poultry, horses. Clay, lignite deposits. Mfg. at Henderson, Overton. L. Cherokee Reservoir on N boundary, part of L. Striker reservoir in SW, Martin Creek L. reservoir and State Park on NE border. Formed 1843. **2** county (□ 930 sq mi/2,409 sq km: 1990 pop. 15,079), N Wis.; ⊙ Ladysmith; 45°28′N 91°08′W. Drained by Chippewa and Flambeau rivers. Largely wooded, with many resort lakes. Barley; sheep, livestock; lumbering. Part of Flambeau R. State Forest in NE; Christie Mt. Ski Area in W. Formed 1901.

Rusk, town (1990 pop. 4,366), ⊙ Cherokee co., E Texas, 40 mi/64 km S of Tyler; 31°48′N 95°09′W. Elev. 489 ft/149 m. Vegetables, peaches; cattle; timber; oil; mfg. (caps, flowerpots, mulch); greenhouse plants. Jim Hogg State Historical Park to E; Rusk-Palestine and Texas State RR State Historical Park runs W to Palestine (Anderson co.). Settled 1846, inc. 1858.

Ruskin, village, SW B.C., Canada, on Fraser R. at mouth of Stave R., and 7 mi/11 km WNW of Mission; 49°12′N 122°28′W. Hydroelectric power station on Stave L. (hydro tunnel runs from Alouette L. to Stave L.); lumbering.

Ruskin, town (□ 7 sq mi/18.1 sq km; 1990 pop. 6,046), Hillsborough co., W central Fla., 18 mi/29 km S of Tampa, on E shore of Tampa Bay; 27°42′N 82°25′W. Ships vegetables (esp. tomatoes) and citrus fruit.

Ruskin, village (1990 pop. 187), Nuckolls co., S Nebr., 13 mi/21 km NE of Superior, near Kansas state line; 40°08′N 97°52′W. Livestock, grain.

Ruso (ROO-so), village (1990 pop. 8), McLean co., central N.Dak., 33 mi/53 km SSE of Minot; 47°50′N 100°55′W. Small lakes to SE.

Russell, county (□ 407 sq mi/1,054 sq km), SE Ont., Canada, on Ottawa R., and on Que. border; ⊙ L'Orignal; 45°25′N 75°10′W. Part of United County of Prescott and Russell.

Russell, town (1991 pop. 1,616), SW Man., Canada, 60 mi/97 km WSW of Dauphin; 50°47′N 101°17′W. Grain elevators; dairying.

Russell 1 county (□ 647 sq mi/1,676 sq km; 1990 pop. 46,860), E Ala.; ⊙ Phenix City. Coastal plain with Black Belt, bounded on E by Chattahoochee R. and Ga. Peanuts, corn, cotton; livestock; mfg. of textiles. Formed 1832. **2** county (□ 899 sq mi/2,328 sq km; 1990 pop. 7,835), central Kansas; ⊙ Russell; 38°55′N 98°46′W. Located in Smoky Hills region, sloping to gently rolling plain, drained by Saline and Smoky Hill rivers. Cattle, wheat, hay; transportation equip. Oil fields. Formed 1872. **3** county (□ 282 sq mi/730 sq km; 1990 pop. 14,716), S Ky.; ⊙ Jamestown; 36°59′N 85°03′W. Drained by Cumberland R. and Russell Creek. Hilly agr. area in Cumberland foothills (corn, burley tobacco, hay, alfalfa, soybeans, wheat; hogs, cattle, poultry; dairying). Mfg. at Jamestown and Russell Springs. L. Cumberland reservoir, on Cumberland R., dominated SE part of co., L. Cumberland State Resort Park on NW shore in S. Formed 1825. **4** county (□ 476 sq mi/1,233 sq km; 1990 pop. 28,667), SW Va.; ⊙ Lebanon; 36°56′N 82°05′W. In Allegheny Mts.; Clinch Mtn. along SE border; drained by Clinch R. and Copper Creek. Agr. area (cattle, sheep; tobacco, hay, alfalfa, corn; dairying); mining of bituminous-coal, some lead and zinc. Formed 1786.

Russell 1 city (1990 pop. 871), Barrow co., NE central Ga., just SE of Winder; 33°59′N 83°42′W. Home of former U.S. Senator Richard Russell, Jr. **2** city (1990 pop. 4,781), ⊙ Russell co., central Kansas, 24 mi/39 km E of Hays, bet. Saline and Smoky Hill rivers; 38°53′N 98°50′W. In oil-producing and agr. area; RR way-station; oil refining. Mus. Hometown of Sen. Robert Dole. Inc. 1872.

Russell 1 town (1990 pop. 531), Lucas co., S Iowa, near source of Cedar Creek, 6 mi/9.7 km ESE of Chariton; 40°58′N 93°12′W. In livestock-raising area. **2** town (1990 pop. 4,014), Greenup co., NE Ky., suburb 6 mi/9.7 km NW of Ashland, on Ohio R. (bridged) opposite Ironton, Ohio; 38°30′N 82°42′W. Mfg. (rebuilt freight cars). Ashland Regional Airport to NW. **3** town (1990 pop. 1,594), Hampden co., SW Mass., on Westfield R., and 16 mi/26 km WNW of Springfield; 42°10′N 72°52′W. Settled 1782, inc. 1792. Includes village of Woronoco (paper milling). **4** uninc. town (1990 pop. 1,000), Warren co., NW Pa., 7 mi/11.3 km N of Warren on Conewago Creek near N.Y. state line; 41°56′N 79°08′W. Light mfg.; agr. includes dairying; potatoes, corn, hay, apples; timber. Warren State Hosp. to S.

Russell 1 village (1990 pop. 180), White co., central Ark., 15 mi/24 km ENE of Searcy; 35°21′N 91°30′W. In agr. area; mfg. (plastic molding, wood molding). **2** village (1990 pop. 394), Lyon co., SW Minn., 12 mi/19 km SW of Marshall on Redwood R.; 44°19′N 95°57′W. Grain, soybeans, alfalfa; poultry, cattle, sheep, hogs; dairying. Camden State Park to NE. **3** village (1990 pop. 300), St. Lawrence co., N N.Y., on Grass R., and 25 mi/40 km SE of Ogdensburg; 44°23′N 75°08′W. **4** village (1990 pop. 14), Bottineau co., N N.Dak., 24 mi/39 km WSW of Bottineau; 48°40′N 100°54′W. J. Clark Salyer Natl. Wildlife Refuge to E.

Russell Cave, monument, NE Ala., 8 mi/12.9 km NW of Bridgeport. Cave containing a nearly continuous archaeological record of human habitation from about 6000 B.C. to A.D. 1650. Authorized 1961.

Russell Creek, c.70 mi/113 km long, S Ky.; rises in NW Russell co.; flows generally NW, past Columbia, to Green R. 2 mi/3.2 km S of Greensburg.

Russell Fiord, Alaska: see DISENCHANTMENT BAY.

Russell Fork, river, c.50 mi/80 km long, SW Va. and E Ky.; rises in E Dickenson co., Va.; flows generally NW, past Haysi, into Pike co., Ky., to Levisa Fork (of Big Sandy R.) 7 mi/11.3 km SE of Pikeville; 37°03′N 82°02′W. Breaks of Sandy in Breaks Interstate Park at state line, a 5-mi/8-km stretch of river's gorge at N end of Pine Mtn., falls and rapids descend 350 ft/107 m. Receives Pound R. from W (4 mi/6.4 km NW of Haysi).

Russell Island, central Franklin dist., N.W.T., Canada, in Barrow Strait, off N Prince of Wales Isl.; 40 mi/64 km long, 7 mi/11 km wide; 73°55′N 99°00′W.

Russell, Mount 1 (11,670 ft/3,557 m), S central Alaska, in Alaska Range, at SW corner of Mt. McKinley Natl. Park, 130 mi/209 km NW of Anchorage; 62°48′N

151°56′W. **2** (14,086 ft/4,293 m), E Calif., on Tulare-Inyo co. line, in the Sierra Nevada, just N of Mt. Whitney, on E boundary of Sequoia Natl. Park; 36°35′N 118°17′W.

Russell Point, E extremity of Banks Isl., SW Franklin dist., N.W.T., Canada, at junction of McClure Strait and Viscount Melville Sound, at N end of Prince of Wales Strait; 73°30′N 115°W.

Russell Springs, town (1990 pop. 2,363), Russell co., S Ky., in Cumberland foothills, 26 mi/42 km W of Somerset; 37°02′N 85°04′W. Agr. (burley tobacco, grain; livestock, poultry; dairying); mfg. (houseboats, steel wire, transportation equip., diverse light mfg.); resort with mineral springs. Creelsboro Arch, limestone formation (S). Inc. 1936.

Russell Springs, village (1990 pop. 29), Logan co., W Kansas, on Smoky Hill R., and 23 mi/37 km SW of Oakley; 38°54′N 101°10′W. Grain; livestock. Battlefield Trail Mus.; Logan State Fishing L. to W.

Russells Point, resort village (1990 pop. 1,504), Logan co., W central Ohio, on Great Miami R. at its source in Indian L., and 9 mi/14 km NW of Bellefontaine; 40°28′N 83°54′W.

Russellton (RUH-suhl-tuhn), uninc. town (1990 pop. 1,691), West Deer township, Allegheny co., W Pa., suburb 15 mi/24 km NE of downtown Pittsburgh, near Little Deer Creek; 40°36′N 79°50′W. Agr. area (hay; dairying); mfg. (household fixtures). West Penn Airport (E); Deer Lake Regional Park (NE).

Russellville 1 city (1990 pop. 7,812), ⊙ Franklin co., NW Ala., 20 mi/32 km S of Florence. Mfg. (transportation equip., pulleys, artificial plants, apparel; poultry processing and hatchery); stone quarries. Iron mines in vicinity. Settled c.1815. **2** city (1990 pop. 21,260), ⊙ Pope co., central Ark., on Arkansas R.; 35°16′N 93°08′W. Town of Dardanelle, opposite side of river. In an area yielding coal, timber, and diverse agr. prods. Dardanelle Lock and Dam is here, forms L. Dardenelle to W of city (recreational area). L. Dardanelle State Park within city limits. Mfg. (transportation equip., poultry processing). Ark. Technical Univ. and the hq. of the Ozark Natl. Forest are here. Mt. Nebo State Park to W; Galla Creek Wildlife Management Area and Holla Bend Natl. Wildlife Refuge to SE. Arkansas 1 and 2 Nuclear Power Plants are 6 mi/9.7 km WNW. Settled 1835, inc. 1870.

Russellville 1 town (1990 pop. 336), Putnam co., W central Ind., 16 mi/26 km NNW of Greencastle; 39°52′N 86°59′W. Agr. (grain; livestock); mfg. (wood prods., limestone prods., metal heat sinks); limestone quarries. Laid out 1828. **2** town (1990 pop. 7,454), ⊙ Logan co., S Ky., 27 mi/43 km WSW of Bowling Green; 36°50′N 86°53′W. In agr. (burley tobacco, corn; dairying; livestock, poultry), coal mining; limestone area. Mfg. (apparel, transportation equip., rolled aluminum, crushed limestone, plastic molding, fertilizer, poultry equip.). Airport to SE. Logan County Glade State Nature Preserve nearby; L. Herndon reservoir to NW. Advocates of state sovereignty passed Act of Secession here in 1861, declaring Ky. a Confederate state. Founded as Big Boiling Spring c.1790; inc. 1798. **3** town (1990 pop. 869), Cole co., central Mo., 15 mi/24 km WSW of Jefferson City; 38°30′N 92°26′W. Corn, hay; cattle.

Russellville 1 village (1990 pop. 133), Lawrence co., SE Ill., on the Wabash, and 10 mi/16 km NE of Lawrenceville; 38°49′N 87°31′W. In agr., oil, and natural-gas area. **2** village (1990 pop. 459), Brown co., SW Ohio, 6 mi/10 km E of Georgetown, in agr. area; 38°52′N 83°47′W. **3** uninc. village, Berkeley co., SE S.C., 40 mi/64 km N of Charleston, at NE end of L. Moultrie reservoir, on new channel of Santee R. Mfg. includes timber-related prods. of veneer and plywood, resins, lumber, particleboard. Francis Marion Natl. Forest to E.

Russian Mission, village (1990 pop. 246), W Alaska, on Yukon R., and 70 mi/113 km NNE of Bethel; 61°47′N 161°20′W.

Russian River, c.100 mi/161 km long, W Calif.; rises in Mendocino co.; flows S through L. Mendocino reservoir, past Ukiah and Healdsburg, then SW, through redwood groves and vineyards, to the Pacific Ocean at Jenner 20 mi/32 km W of Santa Rosa. Along its lower course are many resorts.

Russiaville (ROO-shuh-vil), town (1990 pop. 988), Howard co., central Ind., 8 mi/12.9 km SW of Kokomo; 40°25′N 86°16′W. Corn, soybeans; hogs; mfg. (energy management equip.); sawmill. Laid out 1845.

Rustbelt, economic region in the NE midwest quadrant of the U.S., focused on the Midwestern states of Ill., Ind., Mich., and Ohio, as well as Pa. The term gained wide use in the 1970s as the formerly dominant industrial region became noted for the abandonment of factories, unemployment, outmigration, the loss of electoral votes, and overall decline. Since the 1960s, mfg. cities throughout the Great Lakes region and in the Northeast have suffered a decline in pop. and economic strength as manufacturers relocated, primarily to the SUNBELT, overseas, or more recently, to Mexico. Region esp. hard-hit in steel and motor vehicle decline. New motor vehicle plants est. in mid-South and Calif. Meanwhile, the nation as a whole has shifted toward a service economy. Detroit, although still one of the world's largest mfg. centers, has been esp. hard hit and unable to reduce its dependence on the mfg. sector. Suburban flight induced by the decline of the central city has been dramatic in large cities such as St. Louis and Cleveland, as well as smaller cities like Gary, Ind., and Akron, Ohio. By the 1980s, the economy of some Rustbelt cities had noticeably improved through modernization of industries, such as motor vehicles, machine tools, chemicals, and the introduction or expansion of non-mfg. industries. Pittsburgh, initially devastated by cutbacks in its steel industry as early as the late 1950s, has since emphasized its role as a center for research and development and finance. In the 1990s, Cleveland's downtown seemed to be reviving thanks to the effort of a business-govt. partnership.

Rustburg, uninc. village, ⊙ Campbell co., SW central Va., 9 mi/14.5 km SSE of Lynchburg; 37°16′N 79°06′W. Mfg. (machining, furniture); agr. (tobacco, grain; livestock; dairying).

Rustico (RUH-sti-ko), fishing port, N P.E.I., E Canada, on small Rustico Bay of the Gulf of St. Lawrence, 15 mi/24 km NW of Charlottetown; 1st settled by Acadians 1710.

Ruston (RUHS-tuhn), city (1990 pop. 20,027), ⊙ Lincoln parish, N La., 27 mi/43 km W of Monroe; 32°32′N 92°39′W. Trading center of a natural-gas region; agr. (cattle, poultry; peaches, blueberries); logging, printing, mfg. (broom and mop handles, lamps and lighting fixtures, soft drinks, plywood). Home of the Dixie Jamboree and the La. Passion Play. La. Tech Univ. is here. Jackson-Bienville State Wildlife Area to SW. Settled 1884 as a RR town and inc. the same year.

Ruston, village (1990 pop. 693), Pierce co., W central Wash., on Dalco Passage of Puget Sound, suburb 5 mi/8 km NW of downtown Tacoma; 47°18′N 122°31′W. Historic Fort Nisqually, in Pt. Defiance Park, to NW. Ferry to Tahlequah, Vashon Isl., to N.

Ruth (ROOTH), town (1990 pop. 550), White Pine co., E Nev., 5 mi/8 km W of Ely in Egan Range. Elev. c.6,870 ft/2,094 m. Terminus of RR spur from Ely. Copper mining (large open pit). Part of Humboldt Natl. Forest to S.

Ruth, village (1990 pop. 366), Rutherford co., W N.C., 2 mi/3.2 km N of Rutherfordton; 35°22′N 81°57′W. Grain, soybeans; poultry, livestock. Called Hampton until 1939.

Ruther Glen, uninc. village, Caroline co., NE Va., 10 mi/16 km N of Ashland, near North Anna R.; 37°55′N 77°27′W. Mfg. (millwork, lumber, stone and gravel processing); agr. (grain, soybeans, tobacco; cattle); timber.

Rutherford 1 (RUH-thuhr-fuhrd), county (□ 565 sq mi/1,463 sq km; 1990 pop. 56,918), S N.C., bounded on S by S.C. state line; ⊙ Rutherfordton; 35°23′N 81°55′W. Piedmont agr. (cotton, corn, wheat, soybeans, hay; cattle, chickens, turkeys; dairying) and timber area; drained by Broad R. (forms L. Lure reservoir in NW) and source of First Broad R. in N. Textile and lumber mills; resorts. Mfg. at Forest City, Rutherfordton, and Spirdale. Formed 1779. **2** county (□ 630; 1990 pop. 118,570), central Tenn.; ⊙ Murfreesboro; 35°51′N 86°25′W. In central basin; drained by Stones R. Includes Stones R. Natl. Military Park. Agr. (corn, hay, wheat, cotton; livestock raising; dairying); lumbering; limestone quarries. Mfg. at Murfreesboro. Motor vehicle mfg. at Smyrna. Formed 1803.

Rutherford (RUH-thuhr-fuhrd), town (1990 pop. 1,303), Gibson co., NW Tenn., on headstream (South Fork) of the Obion, and 10 mi/16 km N of Trenton; 36°07′N 88°59′W. In clay, hardwoods, and farm area. David Crockett Cabin here.

Rutherford, uninc. village, Napa co., W Calif., in Napa R. valley; mfg. (wineries). Grapes, walnuts, nursery prods.; cattle; dairying. L. Berryessa reservoir to E; L. Hennesey reservoir (Conn Creek Dam) to N.

Rutherford (RUH-thuhr-fuhrd), borough (1990 pop. 17,790), Bergen co., NE N.J., a residential suburb of the N.Y. city–N N.J. metropolitan area, 5 mi/8 km SSW of Hackensack; 40°49′N 74°06′W. Seat of Fairleigh Dickinson Univ. Several pre-Revolutionary houses remain here. Inc. 1881.

Rutherford Heights (RUH-thuhr-fuhrd), uninc. town (1990 pop. 3,481), Dauphin co., S Pa., residential suburb 6 mi/9.7 km E of downtown Harrisburg; 40°16′N 76°46′W.

Rutherford Island, Maine: see SOUTH BRISTOL.

Rutherfordton (RUH-thuhr-fuhrd-tuhn), town (1990 pop. 3,617), ⊙ Rutherford co., W N.C., 36 mi/58 km SE of Asheville; 35°21′N 81°57′W. Diversified agr. grain, soybeans, sorghum; poultry, livestock; timber in region. Mfg. (aluminum die casting, furniture, lumber, corrugated containers, steel fabrication, chemicals, textiles, apparel, machinery). Founded 1779; inc. 1841.

Ruthford College (RUTH-fuhrd), town (1990 pop. 1,126), Burke co., W central N.C., 10 mi/16 km E of Morganton, and 11 mi/18 km W of Hickory. L. Rhodhiss reservoir (Catawba R.) to N (bridged). Grain; soybeans, chickens, hogs. Mfg. (textiles).

Ruthton, village (1990 pop. 328), Pipestone co., SW Minn., 17 mi/27 km NE of Pipestone on Redwood R.; 44°10′N 96°05′W. Grain, soybeans; poultry; dairying.

Ruthven, town (1990 pop. 707), Palo Alto co., NW Iowa, 11 mi/18 km W of Emmetsburg; 43°07′N 94°54′W. In livestock and grain area; summer resort.

Rutland (RAHT-lind), county (□ 944 sq mi/2,445 sq km; 1990 pop. 62,142), SW Vt., partly bounded W by L. Champlain and Taconic Mts., and rising to Green Mts. in E; ⊙ Rutland; 43°34′N 73°02′W. Marble and slate quarrying and finishing; agr. (dairying; fruit; poultry); mfg. (wood prods., textiles, tools, machinery); lumber; maple sugar. Mtn. and lake resorts, winter sports. Includes part of Green Mtn. Natl. Forest and Killington Peak. Drained by Otter Creek and Castleton, Poultney, and Clarendon rivers. Organized 1781.

Rutland (RAHT-lind), city (1990 pop. 18,230), ⊙ Rutland co., W Vt., at the junction of Otter and East creeks; 43°36′N 72°58′W. It is a trade and tourist center (summer and winter) with many small industries. Marble quarrying, which began c.1845, is still in area. The hq. of the Green Mountain Natl. Forest, Rutland is surrounded by mts., lakes, streams, and nearby skiing and recreational areas (Killington and Pico Peak). The Col. of St. Joseph the Provider is here. Settled c.1770; inc. as a city 1892.

Rutland 1 town (1990 pop. 149), Humboldt co., N central Iowa, on Des Moines R., and 5 mi/8 km NW of Dakota City; 42°45′N 94°17′W. Limestone quarries, sand pits nearby. **2** town (1990 pop. 4,936), including Rutland village, Worcester co., central Mass., 10 mi/16 km NW of Worcester; 42°23′N 71°58′W. Agr. (dairying; produce, poultry); mfg. (transportation equip.). Settled 1716, inc. 1722.

Rutland 1 village (1990 pop. 391), La Salle co., central Ill., 28 mi/45 km SSW of Ottawa; 40°58′N 89°02′W. In agr. area. **2** village (1990 pop. 212), Sargent co., SE N.Dak., 7 mi/11.3 km ESE of Forman; 46°02′N 97°30′W. (Sisseton) Wahpeton Indian Reservation to SE, including Tewaukon Natl. Wildlife Refuge, on L. Tewaukon. **3** village (1990 pop. 469), Meigs co., SE Ohio, 5 mi/8 km W of Pomeroy, in coal-mining area; 39°02′N 82°07′W.

Rutledge 1 (RUT-lij), town, Crenshaw co., S Ala., 2 mi/3.2 km NW of Luverne, near Patsaliga Creek; 31°43′N 86°17′W. **2** town (1990 pop. 74), Scotland co., NE Mo., near North Fabius R., 11 mi/18 km SSE of Memphis;

40°18′N 92°05′W. Amish community nearby. **3** town (1990 pop. 903), ⊙ Grainger co., E Tenn., 30 mi/48 km NE of Knoxville; 36°17′N 83°31′W. In timber and farm area; mfg. (textiles, apparel, transportation equip.; lumber milling). Marble quarrying. State fish hatchery, and wildlife management area nearby.

Rutledge 1 (RUHT-lij), village (1990 pop. 659), Morgan co., N central Ga., 27 mi/43 km SSW of Athens; 33°38′N 83°37′W. Mfg. (poultry processing and packaging). **2** village (1990 pop. 152), Pine co., E Minn., 50 mi/80 km SW of Duluth on Kettle R., at mouth of Pine R.; 46°15′N 92°52′W. Oats; livestock, poultry; dairying.

Rutledge (RUHT-ledhzh), borough (1990 pop. 843), Delaware co., SE Pa., residential suburb 10 mi/16 km WSW of downtown Philadelphia; 39°53′N 75°19′W.

Ryan 1 town (1990 pop. 382), Delaware co., E Iowa, 10 mi/16 km S of Manchester; 42°21′N 91°28′W. In livestock area. **2** town (1990 pop. 945), Jefferson co., S Okla., 10 mi/16 km SSE of Waurika, and on Beaver Creek near its mouth on Red R. (Texas state line); 34°01′N 97°57′W. In agr. area (grain, corn; livestock). Founded 1892.

Ryan Peak, Idaho: see PIONEER MOUNTAINS.

Ryans Slough, village, Humboldt co., NW Calif.

Rycroft (REI-kroft), village (1991 pop. 634), W Alta., Canada, near B.C. border, 40 mi/64 km N of Grande Prairie, 55°46′N 118°43′W. Tanning, lumbering, mixed farming (wheat).

Ryder, village (1990 pop. 121), Ward co., central N.Dak., 29 mi/47 km SW of Minot; 47°55′N 101°40′W.

Rye, city (□ 20 sq mi/52 sq km; 1990 pop. 14,936), Westchester co., SE N.Y., a suburb of N.Y. city, on L.I. Sound; 40°57′N 73°40′W. It is chiefly residential (upper-income pop.), with a cancer-research center, a hardware and locks mfg. company, and several corporate offices. In colonial times, Rye was the 1st stop on the Boston Post Road after N.Y. city. The old Square House, an inn where many Revolutionary notables stayed, is now a mus. Playland, a large co.-owned amusement park, is on the beach here. Chief Justice John Jay is buried in Rye. Settled 1660, inc. as a city 1942.

Rye, town (1990 pop. 4,612), Rockingham co., SE N.H., 4 mi/6.4 km S of Portsmouth; 43°00′N 70°44′W. Bounded E by Atlantic Ocean, NE by Little Harbor; also includes N.H. portion of Isles of Shoals 7 mi/11.3 km SE of Odiome Point. Town has 4 state parks, all on coast. Nursery crops; cattle, poultry; dairying; light mfg. First settled (1623) at Odiorne's Point by David Thomson; earliest settlement in N.H. Set off from New Castle 1726.

Rye, village (1990 pop. 168), Pueblo co., S Colo., in foothills of Wet Mts., 30 mi/48 km SW of Pueblo; 37°55′N 104°55′W. Elev c.6,900 ft/2,103 m. Farming town and resort. Cattle.

Rye Brook, suburban village (□ 3 sq mi/7.8 sq km; 1990 pop. 7,765), SE N.Y., E of Westchester on Conn. state line, 4 mi/6.4 km E of White Plains; 41°01′N 73°41′W. Upper-income pop. Corporate hq. for General Foods; other corporate hq. in area.

Rye Patch Dam, Nev.: see HUMBOLDT RIVER.

Rye Patch Reservoir, Pershing co., NW Nev., on Humboldt R., mostly in Rye Patch State Recreation Area, 45 mi/72 km SW of Winnemucca; c.15 mi/24 km long; 40°28′N 118°18′W. Humboldt R. drains S from dam to Carson Sink. Formed by Rye Patch Dam (63 ft/19 m high), built (1936) by the Bureau of Reclamation for irrigation and recreation.

Ryegate, town (1990 pop. 1,058), Caledonia co., NE Vt., on the Connecticut R., and 15 mi/24 km SSW of St. Johnsbury; 44°13′N 72°06′W. Granite. Includes villages of South Ryegate and East Ryegate (winter sports). Chartered 1763, settled 1773.

Ryegate, village (1990 pop. 260), ⊙ Golden Valley co., S central Mont., on Musselshell R., near mouth of Fish Creek, and 50 mi/80 km NW of Billings; 46°18′N 109°15′W. Wheat, alfalfa, grain; sheep, hogs, poultry. Mouth of Swimming Woman Creek to E; Deadman's Basin Reservoir and State Park to W. Prehistoric inscriptions W of town.

Ryland Heights (REI-luhnd), village (1990 pop. 279), Kenton co., N Ky., residential suburb 12 mi/19 km S of Cincinnati, Ohio, and 10 mi/16 km S of Covington, Ky., on Licking R.; 38°57′N 84°28′W. Dairying; cattle; tobacco.

Ryley, village (1991 pop. 432), central Alta., Canada, near Beaverhill L., 25 mi/40 km NE of Camrose. RR junction; mixed farming; dairying.

S

Saanich, city (1991 pop. 95,577), SW B.C., Canada, on S end of Vancouver Isl.; suburb immediately N of Victoria; 48°33′N 123°22′W. Haro Strait to E; Saanich Inlet to NW. Much of municipality is rural. Univ. of Victoria; Butchart Gardens; several regional parks. Mfg. (metal doors), dairying; fruit.

Saanich Inlet (SA-nich), arm of Strait of Georgia, SW B.C., Canada, SE Vancouver Isl., 10 mi/16 km NW of Victoria; 48°38′N 123°30′W. Entered from Stuart Channel.

Saba (SAH-bah), island (□ 5 sq mi/13 sq km; 1990 est. pop. 1,100), Neth. Antilles, along with St. Maarten and St. Eustatius, one of the Du. Windwards in the Leeward Isls.; 17°38′N 63°14′W. The rugged isl. is actually the cone of an extinct volcano rising to c.2,800 ft/853 m. Spiral roads winding up through steep cliffs and lush greenery make Saba a scenic isl., but there are no sheltered harbors; Fort Bay is a deep-water pier used for boat docking and scuba diving. The chief settlement, called The Bottom, is in the crater of the volcano. The Dutch settled the isl. in 1632.

Sabana Archipelago (sah-BAH-nuh), group of keys off Matanzas and Villa Clara provs., N central Cuba, forming S fringe of Nicholas Channel; extend c.60 mi/97 km WNW-ESE; 23°06′N 80°10′W.

Sabana de la Mar (sah-BAH-nah dai lah MAR), town (1993 pop. 10,792), Hato Mayor prov., E Dominican Republic, port on S shore of Samaná Bay, 31 mi/50 km NW of Seibo; 19°02′N 69°25′W. In agr. region (coffee, cacao, fruit; cattle).

Sabana Grande (sah-BAH-nah GRAHN-de), town (1990 pop. 22,843), SW P.R., at foot of Cordillera Central, 15 mi/24 km ESE of Mayagüez. Growing industrial area; light mfg.; dairying. Virgen del Pozo chapel 1.5 mi/ 2.4 km NE.

Sabana Grande de Boya (sah-BAH-nah GRAHN-dai dai BOI-yah), town (1993 pop. 14,001), San Cristóbal prov., S Dominican Republic, on the coast, 20 mi/ 32 km SW of Santo Domingo. In agr. region (rice, coffee, fruit, sugarcane).

Sabana Yegua (sah-BAH-nah YAI-gwah), town (1993 pop. 9,375), Azua prov., S Dominican Republic, 25 mi/ 40 km NW of Azua; 18°43′N 71°01′W. In agr. region. Hydroelectric facility nearby.

Sabaneta, town (1993 pop. 14,934), ☉ Santiago Rodríguez prov., NW Dominican Republic, in Cordillera Central, 32 mi/51 km SE of Monte Cristi. Principal prods. are tobacco, beeswax, fine wood, hides. Sometimes called Santiago Rodríguez or San Ignacio de Sabaneta.

Sabanilla (sah-bah-NEE-yah), town (1990 pop. 1,644), Chiapas, S Mexico, 40 mi/64 km NW of Ocosingo.

Sabattus (suh-BAT-uhs), township (1990 pop. 3,696), Androscoggin co., SW Maine, just E of Lewiston; 44°05′N 70°04′W. Light mfg., including rubber and plastic prods. Sabattus village and Sabattus Pond (4 mi/ 6.4 km long) are on NE edge of town. Webster Corner is on S border. Formerly called Burnt Meadows and, later, Webster.

Sabbath Day Point, resort (1990 pop. 100), Warren co., E N.Y., on W shore of L. George, 13 mi/21 km S of Ticonderoga; 43°40′N 73°30′W.

Sabbathday Lake, Maine: see NEW GLOUCESTER.

Sabetha (suh-BETH-uh), city (1990 pop. 2,341), Nemaha and Brown cos., NE Kansas, near Nebr. state line, 42 mi/68 km NW of Atchison; 39°53′N 95°47′W. Trading center for livestock and grain region; dairying. Mfg. (control systems, fabricated metal prods., food prods., machinery). Small L. Sabetha, 5 mi/8 km W, is used for water supply. Inc. 1874.

Sabillasville (sah-BIL-AZ-vil), resort village, Frederick co., N Md., in the Blue Ridge, 20 mi/32 km N of Frederick. Was 1st called Zollingers' Town after a developer

of the same name; he changed it to Servilla for his wife following her death. Over time, the pronunciation and the spelling changed. The Victor Cullen School for Delinquent Boys is named after the founder of the state's 1st tuberculosis hosp. here in 1908. Nearby are Catoctin Mt. Park and Camp Ritchie (W), named after Md. Gov. Albert G. Ritchie (1876–1936).

Sabin (SAI-bin), village (1990 pop. 495), Clay co., W Minn., 10 mi/16 km SE of Fargo, N.Dak., on South Buffalo R., in Red R. valley; 46°46′N 96°39′W. Grain, potatoes, sugar beets; livestock; dairying.

Sabina (suh-BEI-nuh), village (1990 pop. 2,662), Clinton co., SW Ohio, 11 mi/18 km ENE of Wilmington; 39°29′N 83°38′W.

Sabinal (SAB-in-ahl), town (1990 pop. 1,584), Uvalde co., SW Texas, near Sabinal R., 21 mi/34 km ENE of Uvalde; 29°19′N 99°28′W. In cattle, sheep, goat, and farm area; mohair, wool. Settled before 1870, inc. 1906.

Sabinal, Cayo (sah-bee-NAHL, KEI-yo), coral island off NE Cuba, at entrance of Old Bahama Channel, SE of Cayo Guajaba, just N of Nuevitas, and linked with main isl. by tidal marshes, 25 mi/40 km NW-SE, c.6 mi/ 9.7 km wide; 21°35′N 77°10′W. Charcoal burning.

Sabinal River (SAB-in-ahl), c.55 mi/89 km long, S central Texas; rises in springs on Edwards Plateau, flows generally S, through Sabinal Canyon and past Sabinal, to Frio R. 15 mi/24 km NE of Batesville.

Sabinas (sah-BEE-nahs), city (1990 pop. 42,567) and township, Coahuila, N Mexico, 160 mi/257 km NW of Monterrey and 70 mi/113 km SSW of Piedras Negras, on Mexico Highways 53 and 57; 27°50′N 101°09′W. RR junction and shipping center for rich coal-mining area; has coke ovens and other industries.

Sabinas Hidalgo (sah-BEE-nahs ee-DAHL-go), town (1990 pop. 26,123), ☉ Sabinas Hidalgo municipio, Nuevo León, N Mexico, on Inter-Amer. Highway, 60 mi/97 km N of Monterrey; 26°29′N 100°10′W. Mining center (silver, lead, gold); cereals, cactus fibers; livestock.

Sabinas River (sah-BEE-nahs), c.100 mi/161 km long, Coahuila, N Mexico; rises on NE slopes of Sierra del Carmen, flows SE, past Sabinas and San Felipe, to Venustiano Carranza Dam 23 mi/37 km NE of Progreso; from there usually called Río Salado, it flows to Rio Grande near Guerrero. Venustiano Carranza Dam irrigates large cotton-growing area in Coahuila and Nuevo León.

Sabine (suh-BEEN), parish (□ 1,029 sq mi/2,665 sq km; 1990 pop. 22,646), W La.; ☉ Many; 31°34′N 93°34′W. Bounded SW by Sabine R., Toledo Bend Reservoir (largest man-made body of water in the South), and Texas border; drained by tributaries of the Sabine, including Bayou Toro (forms part of SE boundary). Agr. (home gardens, vegetables; cattle, poultry, exotic fowl; dairying). Natural gas; oil fields; logging; timber. Part of Peason State Wildlife Area in SE; North Toledo Bend State Park in W; Sabine State Wildlife Area in W center; Fort Jesup State Commemorative Area in E center. Formed 1843.

Sabine, county (□ 576 sq mi/1,492 sq km; 1990 pop. 9,586), E Texas; ☉ Hemphill; 31°20′N 93°50′W. Bounded E by Sabine R. (Toledo Bend Reservoir; La. state line); most of co. (N, E, and S) is in Sabine Natl. Forest. Timber, lumber milling are chief industries; also agr. (vegetables, fruit); livestock (cattle, poultry). Hunting, fishing. Arm of Sam Rayburn Reservoir enters SW corner. About ¾ of land area is now either reservoir or natl. forest. Formed 1836.

Sabine, river, c.575 mi/925 km long, Texas and La.; rises on the prairies of Houston co., NE of Dallas, Texas; flows SE through L. Tawakoni reservoir, across Texas, then S to mark the Texas-La. state line, forming large Toledo Bend Reservoir. At Orange, Texas, it turns SW and forms Sabine L. (c.17 mi/27 km long, c.7 mi/ 11.3 km wide), a natural lake, then passes SE through Sabine Pass to the Gulf of Mexico. The Neches R. flows into the lake from NW. Port Arthur, Texas, is on Sabine L. The Intracoastal Waterway, which carries barge traffic 1 mi/1.6 km inland from Gulf Coast, joins Sabine

R. from Lake Charles, La., to E, and follows river and NW shore of Sabine L. before continuing SW.

Sabine, Cape (SA-bin), E Ellesmere Isl., NE Franklin dist., N.W.T., Canada, on Smith Sound; 78°43′N 74°20′W. Located 4 mi/6 km NW is cave which was hq. of Greely expedition in 1884; 18 members of expedition died here.

Sabine Crossroads (suh-BEEN), locality, De Soto parish, NW La., 3 mi/4.8 km SE of Mansfield, in Mansfield State Commemorative Area. In the Civil War, Union forces under Nathaniel P. Banks, advancing on Shreveport, were defeated here and driven back by Gen. Richard Taylor on April 8, 1864.

Sabine Lake, Texas and La.: see SABINE, river.

Sabine Pass, village, Jefferson co., SE Texas, 28 mi/ 45 km SE of Beaumont; part of city of Port Arthur. Oil port on W shore of Sabine Pass (deepwater channel). On April 8, 1863, at nearby Sabine (now a port of entry), a small Confederate force repulsed a Union invasion in battle of Sabine Pass; park, monument mark site.

Sabine Pass, La. and Texas: see SABINE, river.

Sabine-Neches Waterway, system of deepwater channels, SE Texas; leading N from Gulf of Mexico through Sabine Pass and Sabine L., then through 2 land cuts on W side of shallow Sabine L. Sabine R. arm continues NE to Orange, connecting just below Orange with Intracoastal Waterway. Neches R. (Beaumont–Port Arthur Canal) arm extends NW to Beaumont, Texas.

Sable, Cape, S extremity of N.S., Canada, on an islet just S of Cape Sable Isl., from which it is separated by tidal flat, off SW N.S.; 43°23′N 65°37′W. Lighthouse.

Sable, Cape, S end of Fla. peninsula, southernmost extremity of the U.S. mainland. It is part of Everglades Natl. Park, located 3 mi/4.8 km W of Flamingo.

Sable Island, low, sandy island, off N.S., Canada, SE of Halifax. It is the exposed part of a sand shoal that stretches NE-SW for more than 100 mi/160 km; isl. is 25 mi/40 km long and 1 mi/2 km wide. The isl. was known to mariners in the early 16th cent., and a small Fr. semimilitary colony was here from 1598 to 1603. Known as the "graveyard of the Atlantic," Sable Isl. is a major hazard to navigation and has been the scene of many shipwrecks; it now has a lighthouse, a lifesaving station, and a radio beacon. The isl. is also a breeding place for seals, which are protected by the govt.

Sabula, town (1990 pop. 710), Jackson co., E Iowa, on the Mississippi (bridged here with highway and RR bridges), 16 mi/26 km N of Clinton; 42°04′N 90°10′W. RR junction. Livestock and grain area; mfg. (transformers).

Sac, county (□ 578 sq mi/1,497 sq km; 1990 pop. 12,324), W Iowa; ☉ Sac City; 42°23′N 95°05′W. Prairie agr. area (cattle, hogs; corn, oats) drained by Raccoon and Boyer rivers. Gravel pits, coal deposits. Black Hawk L. State Park in S. Formed 1851.

Sac City, city (1990 pop. 2,492), ☉ Sac co., W Iowa, on Raccoon R., 18 mi/29 km SSE of Storm Lake; 42°25′N 95°00′W. Agr. trade and processing center and light mfg. (popcorn; animal feed). Sand and gravel pits nearby. Indian mounds in vicinity. Inc. 1856.

Sac River (SAK), 107 mi/172 km long, SW Mo.; headwaters rise in Lawrence and Greene cos., joining near Greenfield; flows N, through the Ozarks, to Osage R. just above Osceola. Stockton Dam at Stockton impounds Stockton L.

Sacajawea, Lake, reservoir (□ 13 sq mi/34 sq km), on the border bet. Franklin and Walla Walla cos., SE Wash., on Snake R. near its mouth at the Columbia R., 12 mi/19 km E of Pasco; 46°15′N 118°53′W. Formed by Ice Harbor Dam (208 ft/63 m high), built (1962) by Army Corps of Engineers for navigation; also used for power generation, flood control, irrigation, and recreation.

Sacajawea Peak (sak-uh-juh-WEE-uh) (9,839 ft/ 2,999 m), S Wallowa co., NE Oregon, in Wallowa Mts., near Wallowa L., c.40 mi/64 km E of La Grande, 7 mi/ 11.3 km SSW of Joseph; 45°14′N 117°17′W.

Sacalum (sah-kah-LOOM), town (1990 pop. 2,554), Yucatán, SE Mexico, 33 mi/53 km S of Mérida; 20°29′N 89°35′W. Henequen, sugar, fruit; timber.

Sacandaga (sa-kuhn-DAH-ga), resort village (1990 pop. 200), Fulton co., E central N.Y., on NW arm (bridged) of Sacandaga Reservoir, opposite Northville; 43°13′N 74°11′W. Also called Sacandaga Park.

Sacandaga Lake (sa-kuhn-DAH-ga), reservoir, Hamilton co., E central N.Y., in the Adirondack Mts., in Adirondack Park, 1 mi/1.6 km NW of L. Pleasant (joined by a stream), c.35 mi/56 km N of Johnstown; c.2 mi/3.2 km in diameter; 43°28′N 74°25′W. Town of Lake Pleasant bet. lakes.

Sacandaga Park, N.Y.: see SACANDAGA.

Sacandaga River (sa-kuhn-DAH-ga), c.12 mi/19 km long, NE N.Y.; formed in the Adirondacks S of Wells by East Branch (c.35 mi/56 km long) and West Branch (c.25 mi/40 km long); flows S to Great Sacandaga Lake (□ c.250 sq mi/648 sq km; c.27 mi/43 km long), which is impounded by dam at Conklingville (largest earthen dam in the state), then c.7 mi/11.3 km E to the Hudson opposite Lake Luzerne village.

Sacaton (saw-caw-ton), uninc. town, Pinal co., central Ariz., 32 mi/51 km SE of Phoenix, in Gila R. Indian Reservation, on Gila R. Hq. for Gila R., Fort McDowell, Ak-Chin, and Salt R. Indian reservations. Casa Grande Natl. Monument to SE.

Sachem Head, village, New Haven co., S Conn., 14 mi/23 km SE of New Haven, on bay of L.I. Sound, at Joshua Point.

Sachs Harbour, village (1991 pop. 125), NW N.W.T., Canada, on SW shore of Banks Isl., on Amundsen Gulf near Beaufort Sea; 71°59′N 125°12′W. Surrounded by bird sanctuary. Noted for white fox furs. Oil exploration began about 1980. Big game outfitting. Scheduled air service. Est. in 1953 with Royal Can. Mounted Police station.

Sachse, town (1990 pop. 5,346), Dallas and Collin cos., N Texas, suburb 16 mi/26 km NE of Dallas, near Rowlett Creek; 32°58′N 96°34′W. Mfg. L. Ray Hubbard reservoir to SE; L. Lavon reservoir to NE.

Sackets Harbor, village (□ 2 sq mi/5.2 sq km; 1990 pop. 1,313), Jefferson co., N N.Y., on Black R. Bay and Sackets Harbor (inlets of L. Ontario), 11 mi/18 km W of Watertown; 43°56′N 76°07′W. Summer resort. In 1809 a company of infantry was stationed here to enforce the Embargo Act and control smuggling. Following the outbreak of the War of 1812, it became the center of U.S. naval and military activity for Upper St. Lawrence Valley and L. Ontario. It expanded further as a base during the 1830s and 1840s due to the Patriots War in Canada. Ultimately its growth led to the development of Pine Camp (Fort Drum) near Watertown. Zebulon Pike is buried here. Settled c.1801, inc. 1814.

Sackville, town (1991 pop. 5,494), SE N.B., Canada, near the head of Chignecto Bay (an arm of the Bay of Fundy); 45°53′N 64°21′W. The early Fr. Acadian settlers diked and reclaimed the nearby Tantramar marshes, creating fertile agr. land. The 1st Baptist church in Canada was est. here in the 1770s. Sackville is the seat of Mt. Allison Univ.

Saco (SAH-ko), city (1990 pop. 15,181), York co., SW Maine, on the Saco R., opposite Biddeford; 43°32′N 70°27′W. The city has an industrial park and makes diverse prods., such as machinery, leather, and shoes. Thornton Acad. (1811) is located here. The York Inst. is a mus. with a fine-arts collection. Saco is named for the Sawatucke ethnic group and means "burnt pine." Settled 1631, inc. as Pepperellboro 1762; name changed to Saco 1805; inc. as a city 1867.

Saco (SAI-ko), village (1990 pop. 261), Phillips co., N Mont., on Beaver Creek, near Milk R., 25 mi/40 km ENE of Malta; 48°28′N 107°20′W. In irrigated region; wheat, barley, oats, hay; cattle. L. Bowdoin and Bowdoin Natl. Wildlife Refuge to SW; Saco Hot Springs to W; Nelson Reservoir and Hewitt L. Natl. Wildlife Refuge to NW; natural-gas wells in same area. Larb Hills to S. Sleeping Buffalo Rocks are glacial boulders that from a distance look like bison lying down. Huntley School, the 1-room school where Chet Huntley began his education (b. in Cardwell, W Mont., in 1911).

Saco (SAW-ko), river, c.105 mi/169 km long, in N.H. and Maine; rises in the White Mts., N central N.H., in NW extremity of Carroll co. at Crawford Notch, flows SE past Conway, Fryeburg, Standish, and Saco/Biddeford, Maine to the Atlantic Ocean 5 mi/8 km SE of Biddeford. The falls at Biddeford were source of power for the textile industry, since declined. Receives Ossipee R. from W, 8 mi/12.9 km NW of Standish.

Sacramento (sahk-rah-MEN-to), town (1990 pop. 1,888), Coahuila, N Mexico, in E outliers of Sierra Madre Oriental, 23 mi/37 km WNW of Monclova, on Mexico Highway 30. Cattle grazing.

Sacramento, county (□ 966 sq mi/2,502 sq km; 1990 pop. 1,041,219), central Calif.; ⊙ Sacramento; 38°27′N 121°21′W. At heart of Central Valley; bounded W by Sacramento R., S by San Joaquin and Consumnes rivers and Dry Creek; drained by Consumnes and American rivers (latter forms Folsom L. reservoir in NE corner). Co. is urbanized around Sacramento, in N part, especially E part of city. Dairying; cattle, turkeys; nursery stock, corn, rye, wheat. barley, oats, rice, tomatoes, pears, grapes, sugar beets, beans. Center of processing, packing, river and RR shipping, and mfg. for wide region; many towns have packing houses, canneries. A leading Calif. co. in natural gas production, gold dredging (American R.); also produces sand and gravel, stone, silver. Rancho Seco nuclear power plant, initial criticality September 16, 1974, is 25 mi/40 km SE of Sacramento, uses cooling water from the Folsom Canal, and has a max. dependable capacity of 873 MWe. It was closed for 31 days in June 1989 as a result of a public vote that called into question the further operation of the plant. Part of Folsom L. State Recreation Area in NE; Co. tapers to a narrow peninsula in San Joaquin–Sacramento delta in SW. Formed 1850.

Sacramento, city (1990 pop. 369,365), ⊙ Calif. and Sacramento co., central Calif., 70 mi/113 km NE of San Francisco, on the Sacramento R. at its confluence with the American R.; 38°34′N 121°28′W. A deepwater port via the 43-mi/69-km-long Sacramento Deep Water Channel to Suisun Bay (S) (opened 1963), it is the shipping, RR, processing, and marketing center for the fertile Sacramento valley; fruit, vegetables, corn, rice, sugar beets, beans, wheat; dairying; poultry, cattle. Food processing is a major industry; other mfg. includes printing and publishing, electronic components, glass, wood preserving, iron foundry, dairy prods., electrical instruments, wood prods., machinery, prefabricated metal bldgs., computers, semiconductors, bldg. materials, soaps, concrete, corrugated boxes. Aerospace and electronics industries and nearby military installations —Mather Air Force Base, McClellan Air Force Base (scheduled by Pentagon to be closed by year 2000 and land privatized) to NE, and Sacramento Army Depot in SE—contribute greatly to the city's economy and development. Sacramento is one of the fastest growing U.S. cities, marked by a pop. increase of 34% bet. 1980 and 1990. It lies on a part of a Mex. land grant that belonged to John A. Sutter, who in 1839 began a settlement called New Helvetia and in 1840 built a fort. The discovery of gold in 1848 at nearby Sutter's Mill (now Coloma) led to the plotting of the town, and its pop. soon reached 10,000. Sacramento was made the state capital in 1854. The city annexed adjacent North Sacramento in 1965. It is the seat of Calif. State Univ. at Sacramento and American River Col., Consumnes River Col., and Sacramento City Col. Sacramento also has a professional basketball team. Points of interest include the capitol bldg. in a beautiful park, the governor's mansion (occupied 1903–1968; now a mus.), Sutter's Fort State Historical Park and Old Sacramento State Historical Park, both historical parks in downtown area;, and Crocker Art Gall. The city is known for its camellias; a camellia festival is held annually along with the Calif. State Fair and Exposition. Folsom L. Reservoir and State Recreation Area to NE; Folsom State Prison to NE; State Industrial Mus.; Calif. Exposition. Settled 1839, inc. 1850.

Sacramento (sak-ruh-MEN-to), village (1990 pop. 563), McLean co., W Ky., 15 mi/24 km ENE of Madisonville; 37°25′N 87°16′W. In agr. (tobacco, grain; livestock); coal, and timber area.

Sacramento Mountains, S branch of Rocky Mts. in S central N.Mex., mainly Otero co.; extends SE into Chaves co., E of Alamogordo and Tularosa Valley; includes Sierra Blanca ranges in N; 32°47′N 105°49′W. Covered by part of Lincoln Natl. Forest in S, Mescalero Apache Indian Reservation in N.

Sacramento Pass, Nev.: see SNAKE RANGE.

Sacramento River, longest river of Calif., c.380 mi/612 km long; rises SW of Mt. Shasta, c.35 mi/56 km SSE of Yreka, S Siskiyou co., N Calif., flows NE for short distance, then S, thorugh Shasta L. reservoir, past Redding, Red Bluff, Colusa, and Sacramento. Then joins San Joaquin R. c.40 mi/64 km SSW of Sacramento and continues jointly with San Joaquin as an estuary 10 mi/16 km W to Suisha Bay, an arm of San Francisco Bay, c.30 mi/48 km NE of San Francisco, where it forms a large delta with the San Joaquin R. Its chief tributaries are the Pit, Feather, McCloud, and American rivers. Sacramento Deep Water Channel coincides with river's lower c.20 mi/32 km, then parallels river to W, from Cache Slough N to West Sacramento, giving Sacramento city port access. The valley saw the great gold strike of 1848, and many of the cities on or near the river and its tributaries sprang up in the gold rush; Sacramento is the largest. This N part of the Central Valley of Calif. has been developed as a fertile agr. region. The Central Valley Project has been developed to use the waters of the Sacramento with greater efficiency, particularly in the fertile but dry San Joaquin (S) part of the Central Valley. Shasta Dam on the Sacramento is a major unit of the project; it also generates electricity. Irrigated farming through much of river's course, from Redding S.

Sacramento Valley, Calif.: see SACRAMENTO RIVER.

Sacré Coeur Saguenay (SAH-krai kuhr sah-guh-NAI) or **Sacré Coeur de Jésus** (SAH-krai kuhr duh zhai-ZUH), village, SE Que., Canada, near Saguenay R., 8 mi/13 km NNW of Tadoussac; 48°14′N 69°49′W. In mica-mining region; dairying, lumbering. Airport.

Sacred Heart, village (1990 pop. 603), Renville co., SW Minn., 10 mi/16 km E of Granite Falls; 44°46′N 95°20′W. Grain, sugar beets, soybeans; livestock; dairying; light mfg. Joseph R. Brown State Wayside to S, on Minnesota R.

Sacrificios, Isla (sak-ree-FEE-see-yos, EES-lah), small island in Gulf of Mexico, 3 mi/4.8 km SE of Veracruz, Mexico; 19°10′N 96°05′W. Alleged place of Aztec human sacrifices.

Saddle Ball, mountain (3,238 ft/987 m), Mass., in Greylock State Forest; 42°37′N 73°11′W. Appalachian Trail goes over summit, just W of Maple Grove.

Saddle Brook, township (1990 pop. 13,296), Bergen co., NE N.J., upper-income residential suburb of N.Y. city, 4 mi/6.4 km E of Paterson. Inc. 1798.

Saddle River, borough (1990 pop. 2,950), Bergen co., NE N.J., on small Saddle R., and 8 mi/12.9 km NNE of Paterson; 41°01′N 74°05′W. Paper prods. Chiefly residential.

Saddle River, c.25 mi/40 km long, in SE N.Y. and NE N.J.; rises in small streams in Rockland co., SE N.Y., near N.J. line; flows S to Passaic R. opposite Passaic, N.J.

Saddle Rock, residential village (1990 pop. 832), Nassau co., SE N.Y., on Little Neck Bay; 40°47′N 73°45′W. Upper-income pop.

Saddleback Mountain 1 peak (4,116 ft/1,255 m) in Franklin co., W Maine, 5 mi/8 km E of Rangeley L.; 44°56′N 70°30′W. Saddleback Ski Area is in Sandy R. Plantation just S of Rangeley L. **2** peak (4,530 ft/1,381 m) of the High Peaks sect. of the Adirondacks, Essex co., NE N.Y., 2.5 mi/4 km ENE of Mt. Marcy, 11 mi/18 km SSE of Lake Placid village; 44°08′N 73°53′W.

Sadieville (SAID-ee-vil), village (1990 pop. 255), Scott co., N Ky., on Eagle Creek, 12 mi/19 km N of Georgetown, in the Bluegrass region; 38°23′N 84°32′W. Agr. (tobacco, grain; horses, cattle; dairying); mfg. (meat processing).

Sadler, village (1990 pop. 316), Grayson co., N Texas, 14 mi/23 km WNW of Sherman; 33°40′N 96°50′W. Agr.

area (cattle, poultry; wheat, peanuts). Hagerman Natl. Wildlife Refuge, on arm of L. Texoma (Red R.), to NE.

Sadorus (sah-DORE-us), village (1990 pop. 469), Champaign co., E Ill., near Kogkaskie R., 13 mi/21 km SW of Urbana; 39°58′N 88°20′W. In agr. area.

Saegertown (SAI-guhr-toun), borough (1990 pop. 1,066), Crawford co., NW Pa., 5 mi/8 km N of Meadville, on French Creek; 41°42′N 80°08′W. Agr. area (grain, soybeans; livestock; dairying); mfg. (metal fabrication, plastic prods.). Woodcock Creek L. reservoir to SE.

Safe Harbor, uninc. village, Conestoga township, Lancaster co., SE Pa., 9 mi/14.5 km SW of Lancaster; 39°55′N 76°22′W. Safe Harbor Dam in Susequehanna R. here, forms L. Clarke reservoir. Produces hydroelectric power in conjunction with small Holtwood Dam c.8 mi/12.9 km downstream.

Safety Harbor, city (□ 4 sq mi/10.4 sq km; 1990 pop. 15,124), Pinellas co., W central Fla., 15 mi/24 km W of Tampa, at head of Old Tampa Bay; 28°00′N 82°42′W.

Safford, town (1990 pop. 7,359), ⊙ Graham co., SE Ariz., on Gila R., 85 mi/137 km NE of Tucson; 32°49′N 109°42′W. Elev. 2,920 ft/890 m. Agr. area (livestock; grain, cotton); trade center; mfg. (sand and gravel, paper prods., machinery parts, printing and publishing); hq. for Coronado Natl. Forest. Pinaleno Mts. are SW, Gila Mts. N. San Carlos Indian Reservation to N; Gila Box Riparian Natl. Conservation Area to E; Roper L. State Park to S. Founded 1872, inc. 1901.

Sag Harbor, resort village (□ 2 sq mi/5.2 sq km; 1990 pop. 2,134), Suffolk co., SE N.Y., on SE peninsula of L.I., on Sag Harbor (inlet of Gardiners Bay), 9 mi/14.5 km NE of Southampton; 41°00′N 72°17′W. An important 19th-cent. whaling port. Natl. Historic Dist. The *Long Island Herald* (1791) was L.I.'s 1st local paper. The Whalers' Church and Whalers' Mus., noted for their architecture, are among its historic bldgs. Had 1st customhouse in N.Y., and 1st post office on L.I., est. 1794. The 187-acre/76-ha Morton Natl. Wildlife Refuge for migratory shorebirds is here. Summer vacation spot. Settled 1720–1730, inc. 1846.

Sagadahoc (SAG-uh-duh-hahk), county (□ 370 sq mi/ 958 sq km; 1990 pop. 33,535), SW Maine; ⊙ Bath (shipbuilding center, on the navigable Kennebec); 43°54′N 69°50′W. The 1st Eng. colony in New England was planted at Fort St. George (now Popham Beach) in 1607. Mfg. (wood prods.; bldg. supplies); fishing; agr.; dairying. Summer colonies on coast and isls. Androscoggin R. joins the Kennebec at Merrymeeting Bay, noted for duck hunting. Formed 1854.

Sagamore (SA-gah-mor), uninc. town (1990 pop. 850), Armstrong co., W Pa., 15 mi/24 km ESE of Kittanning, on North Branch of Plum Creek, forms Keystone L. reservoir to SW; 40°46′N 79°13′W. Agr. (hay; dairying).

Sagamore, Mass.: see BOURNE.

Sagamore Hill, historic site, Nassau co., SE N.Y., on N shore of L.I., overlooking Oyster Bay Harbor, 24 mi/ 39 km NE of Manhattan, N.Y. city; 40°53′N 73°30′W. Built by Theodore Roosevelt from 1884 to 1885 at a cost of $16,975; it remained his permanent home, and he died here (Jan. 1919) at age 60. One of the most famous homes in America. Originally named "Leeholm" for his 1st wife Alice Lee, it was later renamed after old Sagamore Mohannis, who as chief of his tribe had signed away rights to tribal land. The 23-room Victorian frame and brick structure includes the Gun Room, where Roosevelt entertained friends. In 1950, 2 years after the death of Roosevelt's 2d wife Edith, the nonprofit Theodore Roosevelt Association purchased the estate, its contents, and 383 acres/155 ha of the land. It was authorized as a natl. historic site in 1962. Roosevelt's gravesite and sanctuary, Memorial Park, and Old Orchard Mus. (built 1938), former home of Theodore Roosevelt Jr., are nearby.

Sagamore Hills, former village, Summit co., N Ohio, 15 mi/24 km N of Akron. Inc. 1931, disincorporated 1947.

Saganaga Lake (SA-guh-NAH-guh), on U.S.-Canada border, Cook co., NE Minn., and Rainy River and Thunder Bay dists., W Ont., Canada, in chain of lakes

on internatl. border; c.40 mi/64 km NW of Grand Marais; c.15 mi/24 km long, max. width 5 mi/8 km; 48°15′N 90°55′W. Has deeply indented shoreline, including Red Rock Bay in S, Cache Bay in SW, and several small isls. Minn. sect. of lake is in Superior Natl. Forest (Boundary Waters Canoe Area); W part in Ont. is in Quetico Provincial Park. Fed from S by Sea Gull R., by Granite R. from SE; outflow to SW to Knife L. Village of Saganaga Lake, Ont., on NE shore. Saganagons L. to NW.

Sagaponack, resort village (1990 pop. 1,850), Suffolk co., SE N.Y., on S peninsula of E L.I., just ESE of Bridgehampton; 40°55′N 72°16′W. Sagaponack L. (c.1.5 mi/ 2.4 km long) is nearby.

Sagavanirktok River (saw-gaw-va-NEERK-tok), c.180 mi/290 km long, NE Alaska; rises on N slope of Brooks Range near 68°35′N 147°00′W, flows NNW to Beaufort Sea at 70°13′N 147°50′W. Trans-Alaska Pipeline and Dalton Highway follow its valley, reaches Beaufort Sea near Prudhoe Bay.

Sage, Mount (1,781 ft/543 m), W Tortola isl., Br. Virgin Isls., 2.75 mi/4.2 km WSW of Road Town; 18°24′N 64°39′W.

Sagerton, uninc. village (1990 pop. 115), Haskell co., W central Texas, c.45 mi/72 km N of Abilene. In cotton, cattle area.

Sageville, town (1990 pop. 288), Dubuque co., E Iowa, near Mississippi R., 4 mi/6.4 km NW of Dubuque; 42°32′N 90°42′W

Saginaw, county (□ 815 sq mi/2,111 sq km; 1990 pop. 211,946), E central Mich.; ⊙ Saginaw; 43°19′N 84°02′W. Drained by Saginaw R. and its affluents; by Cass, Flint, Shiawassee, Bad, and Tittabawassee rivers; and by small Mistequay Creek. Agr. (sugar beets, soybeans, beans, wheat, oats, potatoes, cucumbers, corn; cattle, hogs, poultry; dairy prods.). Mfg. at Saginaw. Oil fields, salt. Tourism, esp. Ger. town of Frankenmuth, in SE. State game area in co. Apple Mt. Ski Area in N; Shiawassee Natl. Wildlife Refuge at center, S of Saginaw city. Organized 1835.

Saginaw, city (1990 pop. 69,512), ⊙ Saginaw co., S Mich., on the Saginaw R., 15 mi/24 km from its mouth on Saginaw Bay (an inlet of L. Huron); 43°25′N 83°57′W. RR junction. Situated in an extensive agr. area, Saginaw is also a port of entry with diversified industries. Mfg. (machinery, animal feeds, fabricated metal prods., automobile parts, food processing, concrete, electrical equip.). Nearby are major salt, coal, and oil deposits. Native Amer. trails once crossed the city's site, and local Native Amer. villages were abundant. Lewis Cass negotiated a treaty here (1819) with the indigenous groups, who ceded much of what is now Mich. to the U.S. Fur trade was followed by a great pine-lumbering industry, which thrived until about 1890. The old Schuch Hotel (1868) has an interesting collection of antiques. Airport E of city. Great Lakes Jr. Col. of Business. Saginaw Valley State Univ. Historical Mus.; Art Mus.; Rose Gardens. Apple Mt. Ski Area to NW; Shiawassee Natl. Wildlife Refuge to S. Settled 1816, inc. 1857.

Saginaw, town (1990 pop. 8,551), Tarrant co., N Texas, suburb 8 mi/12.9 km NNW of Fort Worth; 32°52′N 97°22′W. Mfg. (aluminum prods., canvas prods., paper prods., lumber, cooking oils). Meacham Field airport to S.

Saginaw (SA-gi-naw), uninc. village, St. Louis co., NE Minn., 17 mi/27 km WNW of Duluth, on W shore of Grand L.; 46°51′N 92°26′W. Mfg. (concrete, drilling equip.); agr. (dairying; poultry; hay).

Saginaw, river, 22 mi/35 km long, Mich.; formed by the confluence of 8 branches, SE Mich.; 43°23′N 83°57′W. The river basin drains a large area of lower Mich. It flows N past Saginaw, Zilwaukee, and Bay City into Saginaw Bay (c.60 mi/100 km long and 15 mi/24 km– 25 mi/40 km wide), an arm of L. Huron. Bay City has lake port facilities; river is navigable to Saginaw. Coal, iron, salt, and oil are transported on the river.

Saginaw Bay, SW arm of L. Huron, E Mich.; extends c.60 mi/97 km SW from its mouth bet. Au Sable Point (NW) and Pointe Aux Barques (SE); 15 mi/24 km– 25 mi/40 km wide; 43°45′N 83°40′W. Resorts; fishing.

Bay City, its chief port, is at its head, near mouth of Saginaw R. North, Heisterman, Manisou, and Middle Grounds isls. along E shore; Charity and Little Charity isls. at center of bay, near entrance.

Sagona Island (suh-GO-nuh), islet, SE N.F., Canada, on NW side of Fortune Bay, 20 mi/32 km N of Grand Bank.

Sagua de Tánamo (SAH-gwuh dai TAH-nah-mo), town (1994 est. pop. 22,000), Holguín prov., E Cuba, on Sagua de Tánamo R., 29 mi/47 km E of Mayarí; 20°35′N 70°15′W. In agr. region (tobacco, coconuts, bananas).

Sagua de Tánamo River (SAH-gwuh dai TAH-nuh-mo), 40 mi/89 km long, Holguín prov., E Cuba; rises at S foot of the Sierra del Cristal, flows N, past Sagua de Tánamo, to N coast just E of Tánamo Bay, Atlantic Ocean. Navigable in lower reaches for small boats. Drains 728 sq mi/1,174 sq km.

Sagua la Chica (SAH-gwuh luh CHEE-kuh), river, 57 mi/92 km long, in N Cuba; runs through Villa Clara prov., draining 407 sq mi/1,054 sq km and emptying into Atlantic Ocean. One of the longest rivers in this part of the country.

Sagua la Grande (SAH-gwuh luh GRAHN-dai), city (1994 est. pop. 50,000), Villa Clara prov., central Cuba, on the Sagua la Grande R.; 22°49′N 80°04′W. Road and RR hub; commercial and processing center for the surrounding area, where sugarcane and cattle are raised. Has primarily heavy industry, including a major steel foundry and industrial boiler factory. Founded in the 17th cent. Sugar mill Antonio Finalet to SE.

Sagua la Grande River (SAH-gwuh luh GRAHN-dai), 89 mi/144 km long, Villa Clara prov., central Cuba; rises S of Santa Clara; flows N, past Santo Domingo and Sagua la Grande, to Nicholas Channel at Isabela de Sagua. The 3d-longest river in Cuba, it is navigable 15 mi/24 km upstream for small vessels. The Sagua la Chica, rising near the Sagua la Grande, empties into ocean 25 mi/40 km SE of Isabela de Sagua.

Saguache (suh-WAHCH), county (□ 3,170 sq mi/ 8,210 sq km; 1990 pop. 4,619), S central Colo.; ⊙ Saguache; 38°04′N 106°17′W. Continental Divide crosses co. in NW. Irrigated agr. area, including N part of fertile San Luis Valley in E. Sheep, cattle; wheat, hay, oats, barley, potatoes, vegetables. Mining (gold, silver, copper). Includes ranges of Rocky Mts. and parts of Rio Grande Natl. Forest in E, N, and W center; Gunnison Natl. Forest in NW; part of Great Sand Dunes Natl. Monument in SE. Formed 1867.

Saguache (suh-WAHCH), village (1990 pop. 584), ⊙ Saguache co., S central Colo., on Saguache Creek, in S foothills of Sawatch Mts., W of Sangre de Cristo Mts., 32 mi/51 km SSW of Salida; 38°05′N 106°08′W. Elev. 7,697 ft/2,346 m. Trading point in livestock region. Mfg. (pottery; lumber). Gold, silver, copper, and lead mines in vicinity. Parts of Rio Grande Natl. Forest to N and W. Founded 1866, inc. 1891.

Saguache Creek (suh-WAHCH), c.75 mi/121 km long, SW Colo.; rises in San Juan Mts., SW Saguache co., flows NE and SE, past Saguache, to San Luis Creek in N part of San Luis Valley. SE of Saguache, Rio Grande Canal extends SSW to Rio Grande at Del Norte (irrigation canal).

Saguaro Lake, E Maricopa co., S central Ariz., on Salt R., 33 mi/53 km ENE of Phoenix, in Tonto Natl. Forest; 10 mi/16 km long; 33°20′N 111°32′W. Max. capacity of 69,800 acre-ft. Formed by Stewart Mt. Dam (207 ft/ 63 m high, 1,260 ft/384 m long; completed 1930), a concrete-arched dam and unit in Salt R. irrigation project; used for irrigation and power. Mormon Flat Dam (Canyon L.) upstream, to E.

Saguaro National Monument (suhg-WAH-ro) (□ 130 sq mi/337 sq km), Pima co., SE Ariz., Rincon Mt. Unit 15 mi/24 km E of Tucson, Tucson Mt. Unit 12 mi/19 km NW of Tucson. Mt. and desert area, with extensive stands of saguaro, a giant cactus (can reach up to 50 ft/ 15 m tall) with edible fruits, native to arid regions of SW U.S. and NW Mexico; its blossom is Ariz. state flower. Authorized 1933.

Saguenay (SA-guh-nai), county (□ 315,176 sq mi/ 816,306 sq km), SE Que., Canada, extending N from the St. Lawrence and lower course of Saguenay R.; ⊙ Tadoussac; 51°00′N 64°00′W.

Saguenay (SA-guh-nai), river, c.125 mi/200 km long, S Que., Canada; issues from L. St. John (□ c.375 sq mi/ 970 sq km) in 2 channels, the Grande Décharge and the Petite Décharge, separated by the Île d'Alma, and flows generally SE past St. Joseph d'Alma, Arvida, and Chicoutimi, to the St. Lawrence R. at Tadoussac. Navigable below Chicoutimi, it flows through a picturesque gorge whose banks rise to more than 1,500 ft/457 m at Eternity and Trinity capes. The Peribonca R. is its chief tributary. The Saguenay was 1st visited (1535) by Cartier, and Champlain explored its lower reaches in 1603. For more than 3 cents. it was a route traveled by explorers, missionaries, and fur traders; later it became a major lumber transportation route and the approach to noted hunting and fishing areas. In the 20th cent. pulp and paper mills and important hydroelectric stations (especially those at Shipshaw and Chute à Caron) were built on the banks of the river and some of its tributaries, and at Jonquière is one of the world's largest aluminum plants. Excursions up the Saguenay by steamer from Que. have long been a tourist attraction.

Sahuaripa (sah-wah-REE-pah), city (1990 pop. 3,898) and township, Sonora, NW Mexico, on Sahuaripa R. (affluent of the Yaqui), 105 mi/169 km E of Hermosillo; 29°03′N 109°13′W. Mining center (molybdenum, tungsten, silver, gold, lead, copper) in rich iron dist.; livestock raising.

Sahuayo de Morelos (sah-WEI-o dai mo-RE-los), town (1990 pop. 50,463), ⊙ Sahuayo municipio, Michoacán, central Mexico, on central plateau, near S shore of L. Chapala, 60 mi/97 km SE of Guadalajara, on Mexico Highways 15 and 110; 20°05′N 102°42′W. Agr. center (cereals, sugarcane, tobacco, beans, fruit; livestock; flour milling.

Sail Rock, Caribbean islet, U.S.V.I., halfway bet. Culebra Isl. (W) and St. Thomas isl. (E) in Virgin Passage; 18°17′N 65°06′W.

Sailor Springs, village (1990 pop. 136), Clay co., SE central Ill., 8 mi/12.9 km E of Louisville; 38°45′N 88°21′W. In agr., oil, and natural gas area.

Sain Alto (sah-REEN AHL-to), town (1990 pop. 4,592), ⊙ Sain Alto municipio, Zacatecas, N central Mexico, on interior plateau, 27 mi/43 km SW of Río Grande, 2 mi/3.2 km E of Mexico Highway 45; 23°34′N 103°13′W. Elev. 6,860 ft/2,091 m.

Saindon, Canada: see SAYABEC.

Saint Agapit (se tah-gah-PEET) or **Saint Agapitville** (se tah-gah-PEET-vil), village (1991 pop. 2,980), S Que., Canada, 20 mi/32 km SW of Quebec; 46°34′N 71°26′W. Dairying; lumbering; pig raising.

Saint Agatha, town (1990 pop. 919), Aroostook co., N Maine, 10 mi/16 km E of Fort Kent, and on Long L.; 47°14′N 68°19′W. Fishing resort. In Frenchville until inc. in 1899.

Saint Alban (OL-buhn), village (1991 pop. 621), S Que., Canada, on Ste. Anne R., 34 mi/55 km NE of Trois Rivières; 46°42′N 72°05′W. Agr.

Saint Albans 1 city (1990 pop. 7,339), ⊙ Franklin co., NW Vt., 24 mi/39 km N of Burlington; 44°48′N 73°04′W. Saint Albans town, on St. Albans Bay of L. Champlain, surrounds city, which is resort, RR, trade, shipping and mfg. center, and a port of entry. Produces textiles, metal, wood, and paper prods.; grain and feed, maple and dairy prods. Smugglers' base in early 19th cent.; scene of Confederate bank raid from Canada in 1864; gathering point (1866) for Fenians planning invasion of Canada. Became RR center, 1850. Seat of Bellows Free Acad. Town chartered 1763, organized 1788; St. Albans city inc. as village 1859, as city 1897. **2** city (1990 pop. 11,194), Kanawha co., W central W.Va., residential suburb 10 mi/16 km WNW of Charleston, on the Kanawha R., near the mouth of the Big Coal R.; 38°22′N 81°49′W. Mfg. (asphalt, masonry blocks, chemicals, windows; also diverse light mfg.) The Battle of Scary Creek (1861) was fought nearby. W.Va. State Col. is to E. Settled c.1790, inc. 1868.

Saint Albans (AWL-buns), town (1990 pop. 1,724), Somerset co., central Maine, 19 mi/31 km NE of Skowhegan, on Big Indian L.; 44°55′N 69°23′W. Agr.; wood prods. Settled 1800, inc. 1813.

Saint Albans, residential section of E Queens borough of N.Y. city, SE N.Y.; 40°42′N 73°45′W. Some mfg. Largely Afr.-Amer., middle-class community, with many residents from the Caribbean. In 1940s, neighborhood was popular with many prominent Afr.-Amer. musicians.

Saint Albert, city, central Alta., Canada, on Sturgeon R., suburb 7 mi/11 km NW of Edmonton; 53°38′N 113°38′W. Coal mining; grain; dairying.

Saint Alexandre de Kamouraska (se tah-lehk-SA-druh duh kah-moo-rahs-SKAH) or **Saint Alexandre** (se tah-lehk-SA-druh), village (1991 pop. 1,954), SE Que., Canada, near the St. Lawrence, 12 mi/19 km SSW of Rivière du Loup; 47°41′N 69°38′W. Dairying; pig raising.

Saint Alexandre d'Iberville (dee-ber-VEEL), village, S Que., Canada, 8 mi/13 km SE of St. Jean. Dairying.

Saint Alexis de la Grande Baie, Canada: see GRANDE BAIE.

Saint Alexis de Montcalm (se tah-lehk-SEES duh moh-KAHLM) or **Saint Alexis**, village (1991 pop. 477), S Que., Canada, 30 mi/48 km N of Montreal. Lumbering; dairying; tobacco, potatoes.

Saint Alexis des Monts (se tah-lehk-SEES dai MOH), village (1991 pop. 2,760), S Que., Canada, on Rivière du Loup, 30 mi/48 km WNW of Trois Rivières. Dairying; pig raising.

Saint Ambroise de Chicoutimi (se tah-BRWAHZ duh shee-KOO-tee-MEE), village, S central Que., Canada, on Rivière des Aulnets, 15 mi/24 km NW of Chicoutimi. Lumbering; dairying.

Saint André de Kamouraska (se tan-DRAI kah-moo-RAH-skah) or **Andréville** (an-DRAI-vil), village, SE Que., Canada, on the St. Lawrence, 15 mi/24 km SW of Rivière du Loup. Dairying, pig raising.

Saint Andrew, parish (1991 pop. 510,467), Surrey co., E Jamaica; ⊙ Half Way Tree; 18°00′N–18°01′N 76°54′W–76°39′W. Lies just N of Kingston, bounded on W by St. Catherine, N by St. Mary, NE by Portland along the Blue Mts. Range, and E by St. Thomas. Mangoes, cacao, peas, beans, sugarcane, coffee; cattle; dairy goods. Cigar and cigarette mfg. at Half Way Tree. Key interest areas are the Agr. School, Hope and Castleton botanical gardens, the Univ. of the West Indies, Col. of Arts, Science and Technology, with Mona reservoir adjoining S. The Governor General's Residence at King House and the Prime Minister's Residence, modern commercial New Kingston Complex, Bob Marley's Mus., and the Natl. Sports Stadium.

Saint Andrew, county (□ 282.74 sq mi/732.3 sq km; 1990 pop. 34,471), E Trinidad, Trinidad and Tobago, bordering on the Atlantic; 10°35′N 61°10′W. Forms (together with St. David, Nariva, and Mayaro) the administrative dist. of Eastern Cos. Pop. figure includes St. David.

Saint Andrew Bay, irregular arm of the Gulf of Mexico, with which it is connected by narrow channel (c.5 mi/ 8 km long) bet. barrier beaches, Bay co., NW Fla.; c.35 mi/56 km long E-W; bay has 3 arms (East, West, and North bays). Chief port is Panama City. Linked by Gulf Intracoastal Waterway to Apalachicola Bay (SE), Choctawhatchee Bay (NW).

Saint Andrew Channel, arm of Great Bras d'Or, NE N.S., Canada, in Cape Breton Isl., opening on the Atlantic, 22 mi/35 km long, 3 mi/5 km wide. Forms SE side of Boularderie Isl.

Saint Andrews, town (1991 pop. 1,652), ⊙ Charlotte co., SW N.B., Canada, on headland in Passamaquoddy Bay, 50 mi/80 km WSW of St. John, just E of Maine border. Fishing and golfing resort, retirement community; haddock, pollock, herring fisheries; lobster market. Formerly important lumber shipping port, trading with Great Britain and the West Indies. Fisheries Canada research station.

Saint Andrews, uninc. city (1990 pop. 25,692), Richland co., central S.C., 6 mi/9.7 km NW of Columbia, between Broad and Saluda rivers. Harrison State Forest to N.

Saint Andrews, uninc town (1990 pop. 5,600), Charleston co. SE S.C., residential suburb 2 mi/3.2 km W of Charleston, on Ashley R. at mouth of Wappoo Creek; 34°02′N 81°05′W. James Isl. to S. Chalres Towne Landing State Park to N. Magnolia Gardens and Middleton Place Gardens, former plantations, to NW.

Saint Andrews East, village, S Que., Canada, on North R., near its mouth on Ottawa R., 7 mi/11 km S of Lachute. Dairying.

Saint Anicet (se tah-nee-SAI), village (1991 pop. 2,215), S Que., Canada, on the St. Lawrence, 15 mi/24 km SW of Valleyfield; 45°08′N 74°21′W. Dairying; cattle, pigs.

Saint Ann, parish (1991 pop. 146,983), Middlesex co., central and N Jamaica; ⊙ St. Ann's Bay; 18°28′N–18°12′N 77°28′W–77°W. Bounded on W by Trelawny, S by Clarendon and St. Catherine, E by St. Mary along White R. It is the 2d-largest parish of the isl. Its narrow, indented coastal strip and picturesque uplands (Dry Harbour Mts., Mt. Diablo) are noted for their limestone caves. Rich in agr. prods. (limes, corn, oranges, pimento, coffee, ginger, sweet potatoes, yams, annatto, coconuts; cattle, horses, hogs). Trading centers are St. Ann's Bay, Brown's Town, and Ocho Rios, with tourist attractions at Dunns R. This region is noted for historical associations. At Dry Harbour, Columbus made his 1st landing (May 4, 1494), taking possession of the isl. for Spain. Seville or Sevilla Nueva, founded 1509 upon orders of his son Diego, was 1st capital of Jamaica.

Saint Ann, city (1990 pop. 14,449), St. Louis co., E Mo., residential suburb 13 mi/21 km NW of St. Louis. Lambert–St. Louis Internatl. Airport to NE. Site of Northwest Plaza, one of the largest shopping centers in U.S. Inc. 1948.

Saint Ann Bay, inlet of the Atlantic, NE N.S., Canada, on NE Cape Breton Isl., 15 mi/24 km W of North Sydney; extends 12 mi/19 km SW inland, 4 mi/6 km wide at entrance. On E side of entrance is Cape Dauphin (46°21′N 60°25′W). SW part of bay is called St. Ann's Harbour.

Saint Anne, village (1990 pop. 1,153), Kankakee co., NE Ill., 11 mi/18 km SE of Kankakee; 41°01′N 87°43′W. In agr. area; tile; food prods. Founded by Fr. settlers in 1852; inc. 1872.

Saint Ann's, residential suburb, NW Trinidad, Trinidad and Tobago, just N of Port of Spain; 10°41′N 61°28′W.

Saint Ann's Bay, town (1991 pop. 10,961), ⊙ St. Ann parish, N Jamaica, Caribbean port 40 mi/64 km NW of Kingston; 18°25′N 77°12′W. Principal prods. (fruit, pimento, coffee, dyewood, coconuts) exported through its unprotected harbor; vessels anchor offshore. Mfg. of essential oils. Also bathing and fishing resorts. Just W is the now defunct Seville or Sevilla Nueva, the 1st capital of Jamaica, founded upon orders of Diego Columbus in 1509. The site of St. Ann's Bay was named Santa Gloria by Columbus on his 2d voyage (1494). Fort, built 1777, is still seen.

Saint Anselme (se tah-SELM), village (1991 pop. 1,861), SE Que., Canada, on Etchemin R., 18 mi/29 km SE of Quebec; 46°37′N 70°58′W. Dairying; pig raising.

Saint Ansgar, town (1990 pop. 1,063), Mitchell co., N Iowa, near Cedar R., 9 mi/14.5 km NW of Osage; 43°22′N 92°55′W. Crushed rock, agr. limestone; feed. Sand and gravel pits nearby.

Saint Anthony, town, NE N.F., Canada, on small inlet near N side of Hare Bay; 51°22′N 55°35′W. Fishing; port for Labrador missions; lumbering. Site of hosp. established by Grenfell mission.

Saint Anthony 1 town (1990 pop. 3,010), ⊙ Fremont co., E Idaho, on Henrys Fork, and 40 mi/64 km NE of Idaho Falls; 43°58′N 111°41′W. Elev. 4,970 ft/1,515 m. Shipping and flour-milling point in irrigated agr. area (seed peas, potatoes, grain, sugar beets; cattle, sheep); mfg. (sawmill prods., chokecherry syrup); timber; hq. Targhee Natl. Forest (NE). State industrial school here. Crystal Falls Cave (with frozen river and waterfall) is 24 mi/39 km NNW; sand dunes to NW. Founded 1890 near site of Fort Henry (fur-trading post; 1810), inc. as city 1905. **2** town (1990 pop. 112), Marshall co., central Iowa, 15 mi/24 km WNW of Marshalltown; 42°07′N 93°12′W.

Saint Anthony 1 village (1990 pop. 470), Dubois co., SW Ind., 6 mi/9.7 km SE of Jasper. Mfg. (furniture). Cattle, poultry; corn. **2** village, Hennepin and Ramsey cos., E Minn., suburb 4 mi/6.4 km NE of Minneapolis. Light mfg. Silver L. in N. **3** village (1990 pop. 7,727), Stearns co., central Minn., 23 mi/37 km WNW of St. Cloud; 45°01′N 93°13′W. Grain; livestock; dairying. Birch L. State Forest to NW.

Saint Anthony Falls, Minn.: see MINNEAPOLIS.

Saint Antoine (se taht-WAHN), town (1991 pop. 10,232), S Que., Canada, on the St. Lawrence, 20 mi/32 km SW of Quebec. Dairying; pigs, cattle.

Saint Antoine sur Richelieu (se taht-WAHN suhr reesh-LYUH), village (1991 pop. 1,576), S Que., Canada, on Richelieu R., 16 mi/26 km NW of St. Hyacinthe. Dairying.

Saint Armand's Key (AHR-mundz), small island, Sarasota co., W central Fla., adjacent to downtown Sarasota, just S of Longboat Key. Wealthy resort and beach suburb containing upscale retail dist.

Saint Aubert (se to-BER), village (1991 pop. 1,275), SE Que., Canada, on Trois Saumons R., 3 mi/5 km SE of St. Jean Port Joli. Dairying; lumbering; pig raising.

Saint Augustin (se to-guhs-TE), village (1991 pop. 534), S Que., Canada, 20 mi/32 km WNW of Montreal; 51°14′N 58°39′W. Dairying; vegetables.

Saint Augustine (o-GUHS-tin), village, NW Trinidad, Trinidad and Tobago, 8 mi/12.9 km E of Port of Spain. Imperial Col. of Tropical Agr. (est. 1921) with research station. St. Augustine campus of Univ. of the West Indies located here.

Saint Augustine (AW-gus-steen), town (□ 9 sq mi/ 23.3 sq km; 1990 pop. 11,692), ⊙ St. Johns co., NE Fla.; 29°53′N 81°18′W. Located on a peninsula bet. the Matanzas and San Sebastian rivers, it is separated from the Atlantic Ocean by Anastasia Isl.; the Intracoastal Waterway passes through the city. Fort Matanzas, now a natl. monument, was built by the Spanish on the S tip of Anastasia Isl. in the 1740s to guard the S approach to the city. St. Augustine is a port of entry, a shrimping and commercial fishing center, and a popular year-round resort. The economic mainstay is tourism, supplemented with revenues from small industries. The oldest city in the U.S., it was founded in 1565 by the Span. explorer Pedro Menéndez de Avilés. Inc. 1824.

Saint Augustine, village, Knox co., NW central Ill., 15 mi/24 km S of Galesburg; 40°43′N 90°24′W. In agr. area.

Saint Augustine Beach (AW-gus-steen), town (□ 1 sq mi/2.6 sq km; 1990 pop. 3,657), St. Johns co., NE Fla., 45 mi/72 km SSE of Jacksonville; 29°50′N 81°16′W.

Saint Augustine Shores (AW-gus-steen), town (□ 3 sq mi/7.8 sq km; 1990 pop. 4,411), St. Johns co., NE Fla., 5 mi/8 km S of St. Augustine; 29°48′N 81°18′W.

Saint Barbe Islands (se BAHRB) or **Horse Islands**, group of 2 isls. at entrance of White Bay, NE N.F., Canada; 50°13′N 55°50′W. Eastern Isl. (6 sq mi/ 16 sq km), 20 mi/32 km NW of Cape St. John, is 4 mi/ 6 km long, 2 mi/3 km wide; rises to 550 ft/168 m. Western Isl., 2 mi/3 km W, is 3 mi/5 km long; rises to 500 ft/ 152 m.

Saint Barnabé Nord (se bahr-nah-BAI NOR), village, S Que., Canada, 16 mi/26 km W of Trois Rivières. Dairying; pig raising.

Saint Barthélémi (se bahr-tai-lai-MEE), village, S Que., Canada, 11 mi/18 km N of Sorel; 46°11′N 73°07′W. Dairying; grain, potatoes.

Saint Benedict, hamlet, Marion co., NW Oregon, 14 mi/23 km NE of Salem. Fruit.

Saint Benedict, Mount (BE-nai-dik), hill (c.800 ft/ 244 m), NW Trinidad, Trinidad and Tobago, 6 mi/ 9.7 km E of Port of Spain. Tourist site known for its view. Benedictine monastery on summit.

Saint Benoît (se buhn-WAH), village, S Que., Canada, 25 mi/40 km W of Montreal. Dairying; vegetable growing.

Saint Benoît Joseph Labre, Canada: see AMQUI.

Saint Bernard, parish (□ 510 sq mi/1,321 sq km; 1990 pop. 66,631), extreme SE La.; ⊙ Chalmette; 29°57′N 89°58′W. Just SE of New Orleans; mainland portion bounded N by L. Borgne, E by Chandeleur Sound, S by Breton Sound, W by the Mississippi R. Includes Chandeleur Isl., 25 mi/40 km to E in Gulf of Mexico. Industrial communities near New Orleans have sugar refineries, oil refineries, stockyards, industrial machinery, diversified mfg. Oil and natural gas extraction. Agr. (home gardens, nursery crops, vegetables, tomatoes, exotic fowl), oysters; hunting, fishing. Mississippi R. Gulf Outlet, canal, branch of Intracoastal Waterway, runs SE from New Orleans nearly the length of the parish. Once named Terre aux Boeufs for its wild oxen. Among earliest settlers were the Islenos from the Canary Isls. St. Bernard State Park in W; Jean Lafitte Natl. Historic Park, Chalmette Unit, is at Chalmette; Biloxi State Wildlife Area in E; part of Breton Natl. Wildlife Refuge in Chandeleur Isls. in far E of parish. Formed 1807. All localities within parish are incorporated, including Chalmette.

Saint Bernard, city (1990 pop. 5,344), Hamilton co., extreme SW Ohio, within but politically independent of Cincinnati; 39°10′N 84°29′W. Soap, fertilizer. Settled 1794; inc. as village in 1878, as city in 1912.

Saint Bernard, uninc. village, St. Bernard parish, extreme SE La., 15 mi/24 km SE of New Orleans, near E bank of the Mississippi R.; 29°52′N 89°51′W. Mfg. (canned oysters, boats). Site of St. Bernard State Park.

Saint Bernice, village (1990 pop. 950), Vermillion co., W Ind., 8 mi/12.9 km NW of Clinton, near Ill. border. Corn, wheat; cattle. Laid out 1905.

Saint Bonaventure (bo-nuh-VEN-chuhr), village (1991 pop. 1,079), S Que., Canada, 22 mi/35 km ESE of Sorel. Dairying; pig raising.

Saint Boniface (se BAH-ni-fais), former city and historic community, SE Man., Canada, on the Red R. opposite Winnipeg; 49°54′N 97°06′W. Now part of Winnipeg, it is an industrial center, with large stockyards and meat-packing plants, oil refineries, flour mills, and breweries. Many of the inhabitants are Fr.-speaking. An R.C. cathedral is here, as is St. Boniface Col., affiliated with the Univ. of Man. St. Boniface was founded in 1818 as an R.C. mission.

Saint Boniface de Shawinigan (se BAH-ni-fais duh shuh-WI-ni-guhn) or **Boniface**, village (1991 pop. 3,813), S Que., Canada, on branch of Yamachiche R., 6 mi/10 km SW of Shawinigan Falls. Dairying; cattle.

Saint Bonifacius (bah-ni-FAI-shuhs), village (1990 pop. 1,180), Hennepin co., E Minn., suburb 24 mi/39 km W of Minneapolis; 44°53′N 93°45′W. Agr. (grain; livestock); mfg. (cosmetics, tools, plastic prods., ordnance, millwork). L. Waconia to SW; L. Minnetonka to NE.

Saint Bride, Mount (10,875 ft/3,315 m), SW Alta., Canada, near B.C. border, in Rocky Mts., in Banff Natl. Park, 30 mi/48 km NW of Banff; 51°32′N 115°58′W.

Saint Bruno (se bruh-NO), village (1991 pop. 2,628), S central Que., Canada, 6 mi/10 km S of St. Joseph d'Alma. Dairying; pig raising.

Saint Canut (se kah-NUH), village, S Que., Canada, on North R., 27 mi/43 km WNW of Montreal. Quartz mining.

Saint Casimir (se kah-zee-MEER), village (1991 pop. 1,331), S Que., Canada, on Ste. Anne R., 23 mi/37 km NE of Trois Rivières; 46°40′N 72°08′W. Lumbering; mfg. of agr. implements; agr.

Saint Casimir Est (se kah-zee-MEER EST), village, S Que., Canada, on Ste. Anne R., 23 mi/37 km NE of Trois Rivières, opposite St. Casimir. Dairying; cattle, pigs.

Saint Catharines, city (1991 pop. 129,300), S Ont., Canada, on the Welland Ship Canal; 43°10′N 79°14′W. An industrial center in a rich fruit-growing region, it has canneries and wineries as well as textile and paper mills; motor vehicle parts, machinery, electrical prods., and farm implements are mfg. Brock Univ. (1964) is in the city. The Royal Henley Regatta is held annually in Port Dalhousie, part of St. Catharines since 1961. Founded in 1790.

Saint Catherine, parish (1991 pop. 369,247), Middlesex co., S central Jamaica, ⊙ Spanish Town; 18°15′N 77°12′W–17°50′N 76°52′W. Bounded W by Clarendon, N by St. Ann, NE by St. Mary, E by St. Andrew, and S by the Caribbean Sea. Largest parish of the isl.; Cobre R., widely used for irrigation. Principal settlements are all located along the river. Spanish Town, Bog Walk, and Linstead are linked by RR to Port Antonio in the NE. Spanish Town, formerly the Jamaican capital, remains isl.'s leading communication center, with many historical bldgs. dating back to the 15th cent. Agr. includes sugar, bananas, rice, citrus, cocoa and tobacco; dairy prods.; fish farming. The famous Georgian Sq. comprises govt. records offices, the old House of Assembly (1872), courthouses (1819) still in use, and relics of Kings House, residence of Jamaica's governors for 100 yrs. St. James Cathedral (erected 1525), the oldest ecclesiastical structure in the Br. Empire, is still in use. Passage Fort marks the point at which the English from Barbados and St. Kitts landed in 1642 to plunder Spanish Town and the 1655 landing of the 36-ship Eng. expedition ending 161 yrs. of Span. rule. Private development of the Portmore area extending from Waterford through Bridgeport to Port Henderson has expanded accommodation for the Greater Kingston overflow.

Saint Catherine, Lake, in towns of Wells and Poultney, Rutland co., W Vt., on branch of Mettawee R., 15 mi/ 24 km SW of Rutland; 5 mi/8 km long; 43°25′N 73°12′W. Drains S through Little Pond, 1 mi/1.6 km E of N.Y. state border. Resorts.

Saint Catherine, Mount (2,749 ft/838 m), N Grenada, West Indies, 8 mi/12.9 km NE of St. George's. Highest point on the isl.

Saint Catherines Island, one of the Sea Isls., Liberty co., SE Ga., just off the coast, bet. Ossabaw and Sapelo isls.; c.10 mi/16 km long, 2 mi/3.2 km–4 mi/6.4 km wide; 31°39′N 81°09′W. Small St. Catherines Sound at N end. Privately owned, undeveloped, and most unspoiled of the barrier isl. in Ga. Wildlife sanctuary for Bronx Zoo.

Saint Catherine's Point, northernmost point of Bermuda, on St. George's Isl.; 32°23′N 64°40′W.

Saint Célestin (se sai-les-TE), village (1991 pop. 737), S Que., Canada, 12 mi/19 km SSE of Trois Rivières. Dairying; pig raising.

Saint Césaire (se sai-ZER), town (1991 pop. 2,907), S Que., Canada, on Yamaska R., 30 mi/48 km E of Montreal; 45°24′N 73°00′W. Woodworking, food processing.

Saint Charles 1 village, S Man., Canada, on Assiniboine R., 8 mi/13 km WSW of Winnipeg. Grain; livestock. **2** village (1991 pop. 979), S Que., Canada, on Richelieu R., 14 mi/23 km WNW of St. Hyacinthe. Dairying; pig raising. A center of the Lower Canada Rebellion (1837); the Confederation of the Six Cos. was proclaimed here Oct., 1837. Subsequently Br. troops here defeated the insurgents and burned the village, which was later rebuilt.

Saint Charles, parish (□ 304 sq mi/787 sq km; 1990 pop. 42,437), SE La.; ⊙ Hahnville; 29°58′N 90°25′W. Bounded N by L. Pontchartrain, SE by Salvador and Cataouatche lakes, SW by Bayou and Lac Des Allemands; intersected by the Mississippi R. Agr. (nursery crops, sugarcane, vegetables; cattle, horses, exotic fowl); alligators, catfish, crabs. Oil and natural gas production and refining; other mfg. Among earliest settlers were Germans from Ark., which gave the name Ger. Coast to the area. Waterford nuclear power plant (opened March 4, 1985; max. capacity of 1,075 MW) is 20 mi/ 32 km W of New Orleans, uses cooling water from the Mississippi R. Bonnet Carre Spillway in NW carries floodwaters from Mississippi R. NE to L. Pontchartrain. Salvador State Wildlife Area to S. Formed 1807.

Saint Charles, county (□ 561 sq mi/1,453 sq km; 1990 pop. 212,907), E Mo.; ⊙ St. Charles; 38°46′N 90°40′W. Bounded E and N by Mississippi R., S by Missouri R., which enters the Mississippi here. Area bounded by I-70, U.S. Highway 40, and Missouri R., referred to as "Golden Triangle." Part of St. Louis Metro Area. Rich agr. region (corn, soybeans, hay); mfg. at St. Charles, St. Peters, Wentzville, and O'Fallon. One of Missouri's 5 original cos. Very rapid residential and commercial growth since 1960s. Large automobile plant at Wentzville (NE of town) built c.1980, replacing aging facility in N St. Louis. Large cities include St. Charles, St. Peters, O'Fallon, Lake St. Louis, Wentzville. August A. Busch and Weldon Spring Conservation Areas in S; Daniel Boone Home N of Augusta; wineries at Augusta and St. Charles. Extensive flooding often occurs on low-lying alluvial peninsula bet. Mo. and Miss. rivers. Serious flood damage occurred 1993 in E part of co., especially NE of St. Charles on flood plain. Settled late 1700s. Formed 1812.

Saint Charles 1 city (1990 pop. 22,501), Du Page and Kane cos., NE Ill., on the Fox R., satellite community of Chicago, 2 mi/3.2 km N of Geneva; 41°55'N 88°17'W. In agr. area (corn, soybeans); mfg. (aluminum prods., plastic prods., communications equip., food processing, printing). Inc. 1839. **2** city (1990 pop. 54,555), ⊙ St. Charles co., E Mo., on the low bluffs along the N bank of the Missouri R., an old city, now a suburb 18 mi/29 km NW of St. Louis and fully incorporated into the St. Louis metropolitan region; 38°47'N 90°31'W. City had rapid urban growth beginning in 1960s; has waged ongoing land-grab battle with neighboring St. Peters. Known for historic Main Street shops, restaurants, winery; casino riverboats and showboat. Mfg. (clothing, shoes, metal prods., electronic equip., computer equip., wood cabinets, concrete, metal fabrication, machining). The city served as the state capital from 1821 to 1826. The Lindenwood Col. and the Sacred Heart Convent (1818) are here. St. Charles Community Col. Of interest is the old capitol bldg. Settled by Fr. traders 1769, inc. as a city 1849.

Saint Charles 1 town, Coweta co., W Ga., 7 mi/11.3 km S of Newnan; 33°16'N 84°46'W. **2** town (1990 pop. 357), Madison co., S central Iowa, 12 mi/19 km ESE of Winterset; 41°17'N 93°48'W. **3** town (1990 pop. 2,144), Saginaw co., E central Mich., 13 mi/21 km SW of Saginaw; 43°17'N 84°09'W. Coal mines. Mfg. (cosmetics, wood crates, fiberglass boats). **4** town (1990 pop. 2,642), Winona co., SE Minn., 20 mi/32 km E of Rochester; 43°58'N 92°03'W. Agr. (grain; livestock; dairying); mfg. (turkey prods., animal feeds, seeds). Whitewater State Park to N; Whitewater Wildlife Area to NE. Plotted 1854, inc. 1870. **5** town (1990 pop. 206), Lee co., extreme SW Va., in Cumberland Mts., near Ky. state line, 25 mi/40 km WSW of Norton; 36°47'N 83°03'W. Mfg. (coal processing); bituminous coal mining.

Saint Charles 1 village (1990 pop. 169), Arkansas co., E central Ark., 25 mi/40 km ESE of Stuttgart, and on White R.; 34°22'N 91°07'W. The large White R. Natl. Wildlife Reservoir is to E and SE. **2** village (1990 pop. 189), Bear Lake co., SE Idaho, 8 mi/12.9 km S of Paris on NW shore of Bear L.; 42°07'N 111°23'W. Elev. 5,944 ft/1,812 m. Bear L. State Park and Bear L. Natl. Wildlife Refuge to E; Cache Natl. Forest and Minnetonka Cave to W; Wasatch Natl. Forest to SW (Utah). **3** village (1990 pop. 316), Hopkins co., W Ky., 11 mi/18 km SSW of Madisonville; 37°11'N 87°33'W. Bituminous coal.

Saint Charles Bay, Texas: see ARANSAS BAY.

Saint Charles, Cape, at E extremity of Lab., Canada, at N end of Strait of Belle Isle, 22 mi/35 km NW of Misery Point, Belle Isle; 52°13'N 55°40'W. Site of fishing settlement of Cape Charles.

Saint Charles de Bellechasse (se shahrl duh bel-SHAS), village, S Que., Canada, 14 mi/23 km ESE of Quebec. Lumbering; dairying; fruit growing; mfg. of maple prods.

Saint Charles de Caplan (se shahrl duh kah-PLAH), village, E Que., Canada, S Gaspé Peninsula, on Chaleur Bay, 33 mi/53 km E of Dalhousie. Fishing port.

Saint Charles des Grondines, Canada: see GRONDINES.

Saint Christopher-Nevis: see SAINT KITTS AND NEVIS.

Saint Chrysostôme (se kri-SAH-stuhm), village (1991 pop. 902), S Que., Canada, 22 mi/35 km ESE of Valleyfield. Dairying.

Saint Clair 1 county (□ 653 sq mi/1,691 sq km; 1990 pop. 50,009), NE central Ala.; ⊙ Ashville. Hilly area bounded E by Coosa R. Hay; livestock; mfg. of textiles. Deposits of iron ore, limestone. Formed 1818. **2** county (□ 673 sq mi/1,743 sq km; 1990 pop. 262,852), SW Ill.; ⊙ Belleville; 38°28'N 89°55'W. Bounded NW by Mississippi R.; also drained by Kaskaskia R. and Silver Creek. Includes part of St. Louis metropolitan area; highly industrialized in sect. centered at East St. Louis. RR and highway junction, river shipping; bituminous coal, clay, limestone; timber; agr. (wheat, barley, soybeans, sorghum, apples; dairy prods.; hogs, poultry). Includes part of Cahokia Mounds State Historic Site. Major communities are Belleville, East St. Louis, O'Fallon, Cahokia, Fairview Heights. Formed 1790 (was the 1st co. in Ill.). **3** county (□ 832 sq mi/2,155 sq km; 1990 pop. 145,607), E Mich.; ⊙ Port Huron. Bounded E by L. Huron and St. Clair R., S by L. St. Clair, which forms border with Ont. (Canada); drained by Belle and Black rivers, and by short Mill Creek; 42°55'N 82°40'W. Cattle, hogs, poultry; agr. (corn, wheat, oats, sugar beets, soybeans); dairy prods. Mfg. at Port Huron and Marysville. Salt mines; fisheries. Border crossings at Port Huron (bridge), Algonac (ferry), and Marine City (ferry). Resorts. St. Clair Co. Internatl. Airport SW of Port Huron. Lakesport State Park in NE on L. Huron. Organized 1821. **4** county (□ 699 sq mi/1,810 sq km; 1990 pop. 8,457), W Mo.; ⊙ Osceola; 38°02'N 93°46'W. Drained by Osage and Sac rivers. Corn, sorghum, hay, pecans; cattle, poultry; coal, sand, and gravel. Schell-Osage Conservation Area (part) in W. Osage arm of Truman L. extends SW to Roscoe. Formed 1841.

Saint Clair 1 town (1990 pop. 5,116), St. Clair co., E Mich., 11 mi/18 km SSW of Port Huron, on St. Clair R.; 42°49'N 82°29'W. Salt processing; mfg. (salt, plastics). Laid out 1818; inc. as village 1850, as city 1858. **2** town (1990 pop. 3,917), Franklin co., E central Mo., near Meramec R., 7 mi/11.3 km S of Union; 38°21'N 90°58'W. Mfg. (rubber prods., wood prods., metal fabrication, tools, and motor vehicle bodies). Meramac State Park and Robertsville State Park nearby. Settled 1840s.

Saint Clair, village (1990 pop. 633), Blue Earth co., S Minn., on Le Sueur R., 9 mi/14.5 km SE of Mankato; 44°04'N 93°51'W. Dairy prods.; corn, soybeans; hogs, cattle, sheep. Rice L. to S.

Saint Clair, borough (1990 pop. 3,524), Schuylkill co., E central Pa., 3 mi/4.8 km N of Pottsville; 40°43'N 76°11'W. Agr. (grain; livestock; dairying); mfg. (medical equip., motor vehicles, paper prods.); anthracite coal. Laid out 1831, inc. 1850.

Saint Clair, Lake (□ c.490 sq mi/1,270 sq km), on the U.S.-Can. border, bet. SW Ont. (Canada) and SE Mich.; 27 mi/43 km long. The St. Clair R. flows into the lake from L. Huron; the Detroit R. drains it S into L. Erie. The lake is one of the busiest sects. of the Great Lakes Waterway. The lake region is a popular vacation area in summer. Anchor Bay, Mich. is N arm.

Saint Clair River, outlet of L. Huron, c.40 mi/64 km long, bet. SE Mich. and S Ont. (Canada); flows S, bet. Port Huron (Mich.) and Sarnia (Ont.), which are linked by bridge and tunnel, and past Marysville and Marine City (Mich.), to L. St. Clair, from which Detroit R. flows to L. Erie; forms internatl. boundary; 43°00'N 82°25'W. At its mouth is a delta (St. Clair Flats) containing a number of isls. (resorts), largest of which are Walpole (Ont.) and Harsens (Mich.).

Saint Clair Shores, city (1990 pop. 68,107), Macomb co., SE Mich., residential suburb 12 mi/19 km NW of Detroit, on L. St. Clair; 42°29'N 82°53'W. Mfg. (jewelry, fabricated metal prods., welding equip.). Selfridge Air Natl. Guard Base to NE. Jefferson Beach in S; Venice Beach in W. Marinas and minor port facilities; boating center. The surrounding lake region is popular with summer vacationers. Settled 18th cent. by the French, inc. 1925.

Saint Clairsville (KLERZ-vil), city (1990 pop. 5,162), ⊙ Belmont co., E Ohio, near Ohio R., 10 mi/16 km W of Wheeling (W.Va.); 40°04'N 80°54'W. Trade center for coal mining and dairying area; oil and gas wells. Laid out 1801.

Saint Clairsville (KLERZ-vil), borough (1990 pop. 88), Bedford co., S Pa., 10 mi/16 km N of Bedford; 40°09'N 78°30'W. Agr. (hay, corn, oats; dairying).

Saint Clements Island, Md.: see BLAKISTON ISLAND.

Saint Clet (se KLAI), village (1991 pop. 1,388), S Que., Canada, 8 mi/13 km NW of Valleyfield. Dairying; pigs, potatoes.

Saint Cloud, city (1990 pop. 48,812), ⊙ Stearns co., extends E into Benton and Sherburne cos., central Minn., on the Mississippi R., S of mouth of Sauk R.; 45°32'N 94°10'W. Elev. 1,003 ft/306 m. RR junction. Agr. (dairying; poultry, sheep, hogs, cattle; grain, soybeans, beans, alfalfa); mfg. (paper prods., machinery, concrete, meat processing, optical goods, beverages, printing and publishing, medical equip., furniture, granite prods.). Granite has been quarried here since 1868, and granite finishing is still a leading industry. Seat of St. Cloud State Univ., St. Cloud Technical Col. Minn. State Reformatory (1887) is here. Sherburne Natl. Wildlife Refuge to E; small natural lakes to W and SW; Powder Ridge Ski Area to S. Inc. 1856.

Saint Cloud, town (□ 7 sq mi/18.1 sq km; 1990 pop. 12,453), Osceola co., central Fla., 22 mi/35 km SSE of Orlando, near E. Tohopekaliga L.; 28°14'N 81°17'W. Trade center for cattle area.

Saint Cloud, village (1990 pop. 494), Fond du Lac co., E Wis., near Sheboygan R., 14 mi/23 km ENE of Fond du Lac; 43°49'N 88°10'W. In dairying and mixed-farming region; cheese. Carriage Mus. Wade House State Historical Park to SE; wildlife area.

Saint Coeur de Marie, Canada: see DÉLISLE.

Saint Columbans, village, Sarpy co., E Nebr., 15 mi/24 km S of Omaha, on Missouri R. at confluence of Platte R.

Saint Côme, Canada: see LINIÈRE.

Saint Croix (KROI), river, 75 mi/121 km long, Canada; rising in the Chiputneticook Lakes; flowing SE to Passamaquoddy Bay, forming part of the U.S.-Can. border; navigable to Calais, Maine. The river is used for power and to float logs downstream. In 1604, Fr. explorer Samuel de Champlain helped establish a colony on St. Croix Isl. (now a natl. monument) near the river's mouth; it was abandoned in 1605.

Saint Croix (KROI), county (□ 735 sq mi/1,904 sq km; 1990 pop. 50,251), W Wis.; ⊙ Hudson; 45°02'N 92°27'W. Bounded W by St. Croix R. (Minn. border); drained by Eau Galle R. Dairying; barley, oats, wheat, corn, soybeans, beans, alfalfa, hay; cattle, sheep, hogs, poultry; some mfg. of wood prods. Willow R. State Park in W; Snow Crest Ski Area in NW; Eau Galle Dam Recreation Area (Army Corps of Engineering) on S boundary, in SE; numerous small lakes. Formed 1840.

Saint Croix (KROI), island (□ 80 sq mi/207 sq km; 1990 pop. 55,139), the largest of the U.S.V.I., in the West Indies. Christiansted (1980 pop. 2,856), on the NE coast, is the isl.'s leading town. St. Croix suffered enormous damage from a hurricane in Sept. 1989 and was again damaged by hurricane in 1995. Has one of the world's largest oil refineries. Flat terrain with abundant vegetation in N, tropical forests in W, and flat plains in S well suited to sugar growing. Was 1st settled in 1625, after 1733 was under Dan. control, and became the richest sugar isl. in the Caribbean. In the 19th cent., the decline of sugar industry, along with political and geological turbulence, devastated the economy. Purchased by the U.S. in 1917; post–World War II tourism provided economic growth. Alexander Hamilton Airport; Marine Corps airfield here.

Saint Croix (KROI), river, 164 mi/264 km long, Wis.; rises out of Upper St. Croix L., Douglas co., NW Wis. and flowing generally SW then S to the Mississippi R. at Prescott, Wis., 20 mi/32 km SE of St. Paul (Minn.). Lower c.125 mi/201 km forms part of the Wis.-Minn. line. The Dalles of the St. Croix, a scenic gorge, is located in Interstate Park. A hydroelectric plant at St. Croix Falls supplies power to the Minneapolis–St. Paul metropolitan area. Lower St. Croix Scenic Riverway on lower 27 mi/43 km, both sides, St. Croix Natl. Scenic Riverway on upper river below St. Croix Flowage (15 mi/24 km below source) and Namekagon R, its main branch.

Saint Croix Falls (KROI), town (1990 pop. 1,640), Polk co., NW Wis., on St. Croix R., opposite Taylors Falls

(Minn.), 40 mi/64 km NE of St. Paul (Minn.); 45°24'N 92°37'W. In dairying and farming area; has large St. Croix Falls Trout Hatchery; mfg. (printing presses, plastic prods., bookbinding, knit trim). Hydroelectric plant supplies power to St. Paul and Minneapolis. Interstate Park to SW; part of the Ice Age Natl. Scientific Reserve and hq. for the St. Croix Natl. Scenic Riverway are here. Canoeing. Settled 1837, an early lumbering center. Inc. 1888.

Saint Croix Island (KROI), islet in St. Croix R., Washington co., E Maine, 6 mi/9.7 km NW of St. Andrews, N.B. (Canada), and below Calais, Maine; c.7 acres/ 2.8 ha. Has lighthouse (45°08'N 67°08'W). The first settlement in Acadia was made here (1604) by de Monts and Champlain; abandoned 1605 because of scurvy, settlement was moved to Port Royal. In dispute bet. U.S. and Britain, isl. was assigned (1798) to U.S. Originally St. Croix Isl., name was officially Dochet or Dochet's Isl. for many years. In 1949, a natl. monument here was authorized as an internatl. historic site.

Saint Croix, Lake, Minn. and Wis.: see SAINT CROIX, river.

Saint Croix National Scenic Riverway (KROI) (□ 42.9 sq mi/111.1 sq km), NW Wis. and E central Minn., c.50 mi/80 km NNE of St. Paul. Covers 24 sq mi/ 62 sq km in Minn. and 81 sq mi/210 sq km in Wis. Includes both sides of upper St. Croix R. below the dam at St. Croix Flowage (c.15 mi/24 km below its source) and lower Namekagon R., its main tributary, from Namekagon Reservoir, near its source. Canoeing, fishing. Limited facilities. Est. 1969.

Saint Croix Stream (KROI), c.20 mi/32 km long, Aroostook co., E Maine; rises in St. Croix L., flows NW to the Aroostook.

Saint Cuthbert, village (1991 pop. 1,645), S Que., Canada, 9 mi/14 km NNW of Sorel. Dairying; livestock.

Saint Cyrille de Wendover (se see-REEL duh WEN-do-vuhr), village (1991 pop. 3,682), S Que., Canada, 5 mi/ 8 km NE of Drummondville. Dairying; cattle, pigs.

Saint David, county (□ 79 sq mi/204 sq km; 1990 pop. 34,471), NE Trinidad, Trinidad and Tobago, bordering on the Caribbean (N) and the Atlantic (W); 10°35'N 61°10'W. Forms, together with St. Andrew, Nariva, and Mayaro, the administrative dist. of Eastern Cos. Pop. figure includes St. Andrew.

Saint David, village (1990 pop. 603), Fulton co., W central Ill., 8 mi/12.9 km NNE of Lewiston; 40°29'N 90°02'W. In agr. and bituminous coal area.

Saint David, Maine: see MADAWASKA.

Saint David d'Yamaska (se dyuh-MA-skuh), village, S Que., Canada, on small tributary of Yamaska R., 14 mi/ 23 km ESE of Sorel. Dairying; pig raising.

Saint David's Island, NE Bermuda, bct. St. George's Harbour and Castle Harbour, 8 mi/12.9 km E of Hamilton, 1 mi/1.6 km S of St. George; 3.5 mi/5.6 km long, 0.75 mi/1.2 km wide. Leased (1941) to the U.S. for 99 years as naval base and airfield. Causeways join it with neighboring isls. Area of the isl. has been increased by fill after becoming a U.S. base. Site of Bermuda's internatl. airport.

Saint Denis (se duh-NEE), village (1991 pop. 1,038), S Que., Canada, on Richelieu R., 15 mi/24 km NW of St. Hyacinthe. Dairying, lumbering.

Saint Denis, uninc. town (1990 pop. 2,400), Jefferson co., N Ky., residential suburb 5 mi/8 km SW of Louisville, near Ohio R.

Saint Dominique (se do-mee-NEEK), village (1991 pop. 2,103), SW Que., Canada, 6 mi/10 km SE of St. Hyacinthe. Dairying; cattle, pigs.

Saint Donat de Montcalm (se do-NAH duh mo-KAHLM), village, S Que., Canada, in the Laurentians, on L. Archambault (elev. 1,281 ft/390 m), 20 mi/32 km NNE of Ste. Agathe des Monts; 46°19'N 74°13'W. Dairying; skiing resort.

Saint Donatus (don-AI-shus), village (1990 pop. 145), Jackson co., E Iowa, 12 mi/19 km SSE of Dubuque, near Mississippi R.; 42°21'N 90°32'W. Historic and picturesque Luxembourger village dominated by the Chapel on the Mount. Cattle, hogs; corn.

Saint Edward, village (1990 pop. 822), Boone co., E central Nebr., 10 mi/16 km SE of Albion, and on Beaver Creek; 41°34'N 97°51'W. Livestock, grain; poultry prods., livestock equip.; printing.

Saint Elias, Cape, S extremity of Kayak Isl., S Alaska, 30 mi/48 km S of Katalla; 59°48'N 144°36'W. Named 1741 by Bering.

Saint Elias, Mount (i-LEI-uhs) (18,008 ft/5,489 m), in the St. Elias Mts. on the U.S.-Can. border bet. SW Yukon Territory and SE Alaska; 4th-highest peak of N. Amer. It was 1st seen by Dan. explorer Vitus Bering on July 16, 1741; the duke of the Abruzzi, an Ital. explorer, was the 1st (1897) to climb it. Malaspina Glacier rises here.

Saint Elias Mountains, section of the Coast Ranges, SW Yukon Territory (Canada) and SE Alaska, rising to 19,850 ft/6,050 m at Mt. Logan, Canada's highest peak. Kluane Natl. Park is here.

Saint Elizabeth, parish (1991 pop. 144,842), Cornwall co., SW Jamaica; ⊙ Black River; 18°15'N 77°56'W– 17°51'N 77°34'W. Watered by Black R., largest and only navigable river of the isl. Bounded W by Westmoreland, N by St. James and Trelawny, E by Manchester. Has fertile plains for agr. (cassava, corn, peas, beans, pimento, ginger, annatto, tobacco, cacao, coffee, fruit). Considerable livestock raising (goats, sheep, hogs, cattle, horses). Logwood is exported through Black R. The govt. here runs a sisal plantation and factory for relief of unemployment. Traversed by Jamaica RR.

Saint Elizabeth, town (1990 pop. 257), Miller co., central Mo., 10 mi/16 km E of Tuscumbia; 38°15'N 92°16'W. Hay; cattle. Mfg. (apparel).

Saint Elmo, city (1990 pop. 1,473), Fayette co., S central Ill., 14 mi/23 km ENE of Vandalia; 39°01'N 88°50'W. In oil-producing and agr. area (corn, wheat; dairy prods.; poultry); RR shops, oil refineries. Settled 1830, inc. 1896.

Saint Elmo, village, Chaffee co., W central Colo., on Chalk Creek, in Sawatch Mts., 22 mi/35 km NW of Salida. Elev. 10,012 ft/3,052 m. Mt. Shavano 7 mi/ 11.3 km SE.

Saint Emilien, Canada: see DESBIENS.

Saint Éphrem de Beauce (se tai-FREM duh BOS), village (1991 pop. 1,262), S Que., Canada, 14 mi/23 km SW of Beauceville. Dairying.

Saint Étienne des Grès (se tai-TYEN dai GRE), village (1991 pop. 3,575), S Que., Canada, on St. Maurice R., and 14 mi/23 km NW of Trois Rivières. Dairying; pigs; potatoes.

Saint Eustache (se tuhs-TAHSH), town, S Que., Canada, on L. of the Two Mountains, 15 mi/24 km W of Montreal; 45°34'N 73°54'W. Dairying; food processing; resort.

Saint Eustatius (yoos-TAI-shuhs), Du. *Sint Eustatius*, island (□ 8 sq mi/20.7 sq km; 1989 pop. 1,861), Neth. Antilles, one of the Leeward Isls.; 17°30'N 62°58'W. The mountainous isl. is not very prosperous, although there is a developing tourist industry; it also possesses facilities for petroleum transshipment. Oranjestad, the chief port, has a colorful history. Settled by the Dutch in 1632, it became a center of contraband trade with the Amer. colonies before and during the Amer. Revolution. According to tradition, it was the 1st foreign port to salute (1776) the Amer. flag. The isl. has changed hands frequently. During the 18th cent. pirates and smugglers made it one of the leading trade centers of the West Indies. The isl. is called Statia by its inhabitants.

Saint Faustin Station (se fos-TE), village, S Que., Canada, in the Laurentians, 11 mi/18 km NW of Ste. Agathe des Monts. Elev. 1,254 ft/382 m. Dairying; ski resort.

Saint Félicien (se fai-lees-YE), town (1991 pop. 9,340), S central Que., Canada, on Ashuapmuchuan R., near its mouth on L. St. John, 15 mi/24 km NW of Roberval; 48°39'N 72°27'W. Dairying center; lumbering. Nearby are the Salmon Falls (20 ft/6 m high).

Saint Félix de Valois (se fai-LEEKS duh vahl-WAH), village (1991 pop. 1,625), S Que., Canada, 10 mi/16 km N of Joliette; 46°10'N 73°25'W. Dairying; lumbering; tobacco, potatoes; poultry.

Saint Ferdinand (se fer-dee-NAH) or **Bernierville** (BEHR-nyai-vil), village (1991 pop. 1,907), S Que., Canada, on L. William (4 mi/6 km long), 15 mi/24 km W of Thetford Mines. Dairying; cattle, pigs.

Saint Flavien (se flahv-YE), village (1991 pop. 728), S Que., Canada, 25 mi/40 km SW of Quebec. Dairying; lumbering; pig raising.

Saint Francis, plantation (1990 pop. 683), Aroostook co., N Maine, on St. John R., opposite mouth of St. Francis R., 16 mi/26 km WSW of Fort Kent; 47°08'N 68°53'W. Wood prods., lumber.

Saint Francis, county (□ 642 sq mi/1,663 sq km; 1990 pop. 28,497), E Ark.; ⊙ Forrest City; 35°01'N 90°45'W. Intersected by Crowley's Ridge; drained by St. Francis and L'Anguille rivers. Mississippi R. is just beyond SE corner. Agr. (cotton, rice, wheat, sorghum). Mfg. at Forrest City. Timber; sand, gravel. Formed 1827.

Saint Francis, city (1990 pop. 9,245), Milwaukee co., SE Wis., residential suburb 4 mi/6.4 km SE of Milwaukee on L. Michigan; 42°58'N 87°52'W. A power plant; mfg. (steel and plastic prods., meat prods., fabricated metal prods.). St. Francis Seminary, and St. Francis De Sales College in Milwaukee. General Mitchell Field airport to SW in Milwaukee. Inc. 1951.

Saint Francis 1 town (1990 pop. 1,495), ⊙ Cheyenne co., NW Kansas, on South Fork of Republican R., 31 mi/50 km N of Goodland; 39°46'N 101°47'W. Elev. 3,291 ft/1,003 m. Trade and shipping center in agr. area; grain milling. Founded 1885, inc. 1903. **2** town (1990 pop. 2,538), Anoka co., E Minn., suburb 20 mi/40 km N of Minneapolis, on Rum R.; 45°23'N 93°23'W. Mfg. (machine parts); agr. (dairying; poultry, livestock; grain, alfalfa. Small lakes in area.

Saint Francis 1 village (1990 pop. 201), Clay co., extreme NE Ark., 6 mi/9.7 km NE of Piggott and on St. Francis R., near Mo. line; 36°27'N 90°08'W. **2** village (1990 pop. 815), Todd co., S S.Dak., 15 mi/24 km SW of Mission; 43°08'N 100°54'W.

Saint Francis, river, c.470 mi/760 km long, Mo. and Ark.; rising in the St. Francis Mts. of SE Mo. and flowing S through the Ozarks and the Mississippi alluvial plain of NE Ark. to join the Mississippi R. near Helena, Ark. The river forms part of the Ark.-Mo. border. Wappapello Dam (completed 1941), near the Ozark Escarpment N of Poplar Bluff, Mo., forms L. Wappapello. The river in the Ozarks is popular for recreational activities, esp. canoeing, kayaking, fishing.

Saint Francis, Canada: see SAINT FRANÇOIS.

Saint Francis, Cape, promontory, SE N.F., Canada, on Avalon Peninsula, on E side of entrance to Conception Bay, 18 mi/29 km NNW of St. John's; 47°49'N 52°47'W.

Saint Francis, Lake, expansion of the St. Lawrence R., SE Ont. and S Que., Canada, SW of Montreal, extending bet. Cornwall and Valleyfield. It is part of the St. Lawrence Seaway.

Saint Francis Mountains, Mo.: see SAINT FRANCOIS MOUNTAINS.

Saint Francisville, city (1990 pop. 851), Lawrence co., SE Ill., on the Wabash, 9 mi/14.5 km S of Lawrenceville; 38°35'N 87°39'W. In agr., oil, and natural gas area; mfg. (popcorn, cabinets). Mt. Carmel Airport to W. Inc. 1843.

Saint Francisville, town (1990 pop. 1,700), ⊙ West Feliciana parish, SE central La., 26 mi/42 km NW of Baton Rouge, on the Mississippi R.; 30°47'N 91°23'W. Pulp and paper milling, mfg. (concrete). Toll ferry crosses river to New Roads. Noted for antebellum houses in area, including Greenwood, the Myrtles, Catalpa, Rosedown, and Oakley. Hosts the Festival of St. Francis. Audubon State Commemorative Area to E; Locust Grove State Commemorative Area to N, historic cemetery (1 acre/0.5 ha). Tunica Hills Wildlife Management Area 14 mi/23 km NW.

Saint Francois (FRAN-sis), county (□ 457 sq mi/ 1,184 sq km; 1990 pop. 48,904), E Mo.; ⊙ Farmington; 37°48'N 90°27'W. Partly in St. Francois Mts.; drained by Big R. to the N and St. Francis R. to the S. Corn, wheat, hay; livestock; timber. Formerly a region of great mining importance, especially lead, zinc, nickel, iron. Lead mining began in early 1800s and ceased in 1960s.

Cross references are shown in SMALL CAPITALS. The pronunciation key is on page xv. The dates of population figures are on page xii.

Center of the "Lead Belt," the nation's leading lead producer. Mfg. at Bonne Terre, Desloge, Park Hills, and Farmington. The co. has 3 large residential developments (retirement and commuters); semi-urban growth in 1980s. St. Francois State Park in N; St. Joe State Park at center; part of Mark Twain Natl. Forest in extreme E. Formed 1821.

Saint François 1 (san frahn-swah) or **Saint Francis**, river, 165 mi/266 km long, Que., Canada; rising in Lac St. François, SE Que., and flowing SW through Lac Aylmer to Sherbrooke, then NW past Drummondville to Lac St. Pierre of the St. Lawrence R. There are several hydroelectric stations on its course. **2** or **Saint Francis**, river, c.60 mi/100 km long, Que., Canada; rising in the Notre Dame Mts., SE Que., and flowing generally SE to the St. John R. It forms part of the Quebec and New Brunswick boundary with N Maine.

Saint François du Lac (se frahn-sah duh LAHK), village (1991 pop. 912), S Que., Canada, on St. Francis R. opposite Pierreville, 14 mi/23 km E of Sorel; 46°04′N 72°50′W. Dairying; pig raising. Mineral springs nearby.

Saint François, Lake, Canada: see SAINT FRANCIS, LAKE.

Saint Francois Mountains (FRAN-sis), range, SE Mo., consisting of isolated knobs rising above Ozark highland, bet. Park Hills (N) and Piedmont (S). Taum Sauk Mt. (1,772 ft/540 m), W of Ironton, is highest point in Mo. An outcrop of igneous rocks, mts. are center of mining region yielding iron, lead, barite, zinc, silver, manganese, cobalt, nickel, granite, and limestone. Sometimes erroneously spelled St. Francis.

Saint Frédéric (se frai-dai-REEK), village (1991 pop. 1,008), S Que., Canada, 40 mi/64 km SSE of Quebec. Lumbering, dairying; cattle, pigs.

Saint Froid Lake, Maine: see FISH RIVER LAKES.

Saint Gabriel, uninc. village, Iberville parish, SE La., 12 mi/19 km SSE of Baton Rouge, on Mississippi R.; 30°15′N 91°05′W. In agr. area (sugarcane, pecans, strawberries, peppers). Mfg. (machinery, chemicals). Hansen's Disease Center to SW. Area noted for its antebellum homes.

Saint Gabriel de Brandon, village (1991 pop. 2,155), S Que., Canada, on L. Maskinonge, 22 mi/35 km NW of Sorel. Lumber; dairying.

Saint Gédéon (se zhai-dai-O), village (1991 pop. 1,707), S central Que., Canada, on E shore of L. St. John, 8 mi/13 km SE of St. Joseph d'Alma; 48°29′N 71°47′W. Dairying; pigs.

Saint George, parish (□ 9 sq mi/23 sq km; 1991 pop. 4,473), N central Antigua isl., Antigua and Barbuda Republic; 17°08′N 61°47′W. Site of V.C. Bird Internatl. Airport, and U.S. Naval and Air stations.

Saint George, town (1985 est. pop. 1,700), on St. George's Isl., Bermuda; 32°23′N 64°40′W. It was the capital of Bermuda until 1815, when it was replaced by Hamilton. During the Amer. Civil War it harbored Confederate blockade-runners.

Saint George, town (1991 pop. 1,345), SW N.B., Canada, on Magaguadavic R. estuary, 5 mi/8 km E of its mouth on Passamaquoddy Bay, 40 mi/64 km WSW of St. John; 45°08′N 66°49′W. Fishing port (sardines, herring, quahaug, pollock); ships pulp and lumber. Has pulp mills, hydroelectric station. Nearby are airport and granite quarries.

Saint George, village, S Ont., Canada, 8 mi/13 km N of Brantford. Sawmilling; dairying; mixed farming.

Saint George, county (□ 355 sq mi/919 sq km; 1990 pop. 425,385), NW Trinidad, Trinidad and Tobago, bordering on the Caribbean and the Gulf of Paria, encompassing greater Port of Spain and St. George mt. range; 10°40′N 61°25′W.

Saint George, city, ⊙ Washington co., SW Utah, on Virgin R., at mouth of Santa Clara R., 45 mi/72 km SW of Cedar City, near Ariz. line, 255 mi/410 km SSW of Salt Lake City. Elev. 2,880 ft/878 m. Trade and tourist center in diversified-farming area (cattle; alfalfa, barley). Copper, iron mines nearby. Seat of Dixie Col., Mormon temple (completed 1877), and Mormon tabernacle made of red sandstone (completed 1871). Dixie Natl. Forest is N, Zion Natl. Park c.30 mi/48 km ENE. Beaver Dam Wilderness Area to SW; Shivwits Indian

Reservation to NW; Snow Canyon State Park to NW; Quail Creek Reservoir and State Park to NE. Settled in 1861 as cotton center.

Saint George 1 town (1990 pop. 2,261), Knox co., S Maine, on peninsula S of Rockland; 43°54′N 69°13′W. Includes villages of St. George, Port Clyde, and Tenants Harbor. Fishing, resorts, granite quarries. Area was visited 1605, trading post c.1630. Fort St. George (1809) fell to British in War of 1812. **2** town (1990 pop. 2,077), ⊙ Dorchester co., S central S.C., 45 mi/72 km NW of Charleston; 33°11′N 80°34′W. Mfg. includes apparel, lumber, consumer goods. Trading center for agr. area (grain, cotton; livestock; timber). Methodist campgrounds nearby. Settled 1788. **3** town (1990 pop. 705), Chittenden co., NW Vt., 8 mi/12.9 km SE of Burlington; 44°22′N 73°07′W.

Saint George 1 village (1990 pop. 397), Pottawatomie co., NE Kansas, on Kansas R., 13 mi/21 km S of Westmoreland; 39°11′N 96°25′W. Livestock; grain. Home to St. George Geographical Society. Pottawatomie State Fishing L. No. 2 to NW. **2** village (1990 pop. 1,270), St. Louis co., E Mo., residential suburb 10 mi/16 km SSW of St. Louis; 38°32′N 90°18′W. Surrounded by Affton (uninc.). **3** village, ⊙ Richmond co., SE N.Y., and seat of borough hall of Richmond borough of N.Y. city, on NE Staten Isl., 5 mi/8 km SSW of tip of Manhattan; 40°39′N 74°05′W. Terminus of ferries to Manhattan and isl.'s chief business and transportation center. Here are hq. and mus. of Staten Isl. Inst. of Arts and Sciences. Fort Hill was site of Br.-held fort in the Revolution.

Saint George Bay, SW N.F., Canada; 60 mi/97 km long, 40 mi/64 km wide at mouth; 48°00′N 59°00′W. Entrance is bet. Cape Anguille (S) and Cape St. George (N); N shore is bounded by Port au Port Peninsula. Anguille Mts. extend along SE shore. There are several fishing settlements, including St. George's and Stephenville.

Saint George, Cape, promontory on the Gulf of St. Lawrence, SW N.F., Canada, at W end of Port au Port peninsula, on N side of entrance to St. George Bay, 70 mi/113 km SW of Corner Brook; 48°28′N 59°18′W. Lighthouse.

Saint George Island 1 Pribilof Isls., SW Alaska, in Bering Sea; 12 mi/19 km long, 2 mi/3.2 km–7 mi/11.3 km wide; 56°35′N 169°35′W. Rises to 946 ft/288 m at Ulakaia Hill. Port to service fishing vessels. Former center of fur sealing. St. George village is in NE. Air service. **2** narrow wooded barrier isl., NW Fla., in the Gulf of Mexico, S and SE of Apalachicola, bet. Dog (NE) and St. Vincent (W) isls.; c.20 mi/32 km long. Partly shelters Apalachicola Bay and St. George Sound. **3** in S Md., in the Potomac near mouth of St. Mary's R., 14 mi/23 km SE of Leonardstown; c.3 mi/4.8 km long, 1 mi/1.6 km wide. Bridge to left bank. In July 1776, a Br. fleet under Lord Dunsmore used the isl. as a base for attacking the mainland; the 1st naval action of the Revolution took place nearby. Fishing, oystering; also a summer resort.

Saint George Lake, Waldo co., S Maine, in L. St. George State Park (□ 8 sq mi/20.7 sq km), 13 mi/21 km WSW of Belfast; 2 mi/3.2 km long.

Saint George, Point, promontory on Pacific Ocean coast, Del Norte co., NW Calif., NW of Crescent City. Site of govt. radio station. Lighthouse just offshore.

Saint George River, c.30 mi/48 km long, S Maine; rises in S Waldo co., flows SE and S to Thomaston, where it becomes 12-mi/19-km inlet (½ mi/⅘ km–1 mi/1.6 km wide) opening into Muscongus Bay bet. St. George and Cushing.

Saint George Sound, arm of the Gulf of Mexico in Franklin co., NW Fla., partly sheltered by St. George and Dog isls., c.25 mi/40 km long, 5 mi/8 km wide; connects with Apalachicola Bay (SW). W part is traversed by Gulf Intracoastal Waterway.

Saint George's, parish (1991 pop. 58,460), NE Bermuda; 32°21′N 64°40′W. Includes all isls. E and S of Castle Harbour and the SE part of Bermuda Isl. called Tucker's Town.

Saint George's, town (1991 pop. 1,678), SW N.F., Canada, on SE side of St. George Bay, 9 mi/14 km SE of Stephenville; 48°26′N 58°30′W. Fishing.

Saint George's, town (1991 pop. 4,439), ⊙ Grenada, in the West Indies; 12°03′N 61°44′W. A port town on a deep and beautiful harbor, it is the administrative hq. of the country and a growing tourist center. Chief exports are cacao, nutmeg, and mace. St. George's was the capital of the former Br. colony of the Windward Isls. St. George's Univ. School of Medicine is located here and is still in operation after the U.S. invasion of 1983, which had the stated mission of protecting the U.S. students studying at the school during a military coup. The school was founded in 1977 and has c.400 students, mostly from the U.S.

Saint Georges, uninc. village, New Castle co., N central Del., 14 mi/23 km SSW of Wilmington, on Chesapeake and Delaware Canal (bridged here); 39°33′N 75°39′W. Canal Natl. Wildlife Refuge follows canal; Lums Pond State Park to W; Fort Dupont State Park to E. Founded before 1730. Disincorporated after 1940.

Saint Georges, Canada: see SAINT GEORGES DE CHAMPLAIN.

Saint George's Cay, islet, central Bahama Isls., just N of Eleuthera Isl., 50 mi/80 km NE of Nassau; 25°34′N 76°45′W. On it is Spanish Wells village. Produces tomatoes, coconuts, pineapples; fishing. The British here defeated (1798) the Spanish, marking end of Span. claims in what was then Br. Honduras.

Saint Georges de Beauce (se zhohrzh duh BOS) or **Saint Georges Est** (se zhohrzh EST), village (1991 pop. 2,990), S Que., Canada, on Chaudière R., 55 mi/89 km SE of Quebec. Mfg.; dairying. Service center for region.

Saint Georges de Champlain or **Saint Georges**, village (1991 pop. 3,933), S Que., Canada, on St. Maurice R., opposite Grand'Mére. Mfg.; dairying; lumbering.

Saint George's Island, one of principal isls. of Bermuda, in NE part of the isl. group, 7 mi/11.3 km ENE of Hamilton; 3 mi/4.8 km long, ¼ mi/ km–1 mi/1.6 km wide; 32°23′N 64°40′W. Tourist center, with numerous fine beaches. Town and port of St. George is on S shore. Linked by road and RR with the other isls.

Saint Germain de Grantham (se zher-ME duh GRAN-thuhm) or **Saint Joseph de Grantham** (se zho-ZEF duh GRAN-thuhm), town (1991 pop. 1,594), S Que., Canada, 24 mi/39 km NE of St. Hyacinthe; 45°38′N 72°56′W. In dairying, livestock-raising region.

Saint Guillaume d'Upton (se gee-YOM DUHP-tuhn), village, S Que., Canada, 20 mi/32 km NE of St. Hyacinthe; 45°53′N 72°46′W. Dairying; pigs.

Saint Hedwig, town (1990 pop. 1,443), Bexar co., S central Texas, satellite community 19 mi/31 km E of San Antonio, near Cibolo Creek; 29°25′N 98°12′W. Agr. area (wheat, corn, peanuts, vegetables; cattle). Oil and natural gas.

Saint Helen Island, islet, S Que., Canada, in the St. Lawrence opposite Montreal. It became crown property 1812 and for many years was Br. garrison.

Saint Helen, Lake, Roscommon co., N central Mich., 12 mi/19 km NW of West Branch, in forest area; c.4 mi/6.4 km long, 1.5 mi/2.4 km wide; 42°21′N 84°27′W. Resort; fishing. Source of South Branch of Au Sable R. Village of St. Helen at E end.

Saint Helena (huh-LEE-nuh), parish (□ 420 sq mi/1,088 sq km; 1990 pop. 9,874), SE La.; ⊙ Greensburg; one of the Florida parishes; 30°50′N 90°40′W. Bounded W by Amite R., N by Miss. line; intersected by Tickfaw R. Agr. (vegetables, hay; cattle, poultry; dairying); logging. Formed 1810.

Saint Helena, town (1990 pop. 4,990), Napa co., W Calif., on Napa R., 12 mi/19 km ENE of Santa Rosa; 38°30′N 122°28′W. Center of chief wine-growing dist. of Napa R. valley. Mfg. (wineries, lumber, printing and publishing); grapes, walnuts, nursery prods.; dairying; cattle.

Saint Helena 1 village, industrial suburb 5 mi/8 km ESE of Baltimore, Baltimore co., central Md. Makes chemicals. **2** (huh-LEEN-uh), village (1990 pop. 321), Pender co., SE N.C., 19 mi/31 km N of Wilmington. Strawberries, grain, sweet potatoes, tobacco, peanuts; livestock.

Saint Helena Island (HE-luh-nuh), Beaufort co., S S.C., one of the Sea Isls., c.12 mi/19 km long and c.10 mi/16 km wide. Bounded SW by Port Royal Sound, W by Intracoastal Waterway, Port Royal Isl. opposite, N by Coosaw R., NE by St. Helena Sound, SE by Atlantic Ocean. Smaller Hunting, Fripp, Pritchards, and Phillips Isls. bet. isl. and Atlantic Ocean.

Saint Helena, Mount, peak (4,343 ft/1,324 m), W Calif., at meeting of Napa, Lake, and Sonoma co. lines, 7 mi/11.3 km N of Calistoga in Coast Ranges; 38°40′N 122°37′W. Volcanic origin. Robert Louis Stevenson Monument State Historical Park marks site where he lived in 1880.

Saint Helena Sound (HE-luh-nuh), coastal inlet, S S.C., Beaufort and Colleton cos., E of Beaufort, bet. Edisto Isl. and Hunting Isl.; 7.5 mi/12.1 km wide. Receives Combahee from NW and Edisto and Ashepos rivers from N; Coosaw R. connects its N end with Broad R. channel (W). Crossed by Intracoastal Waterway. St. Helena Isl to W.

Saint Helens, town (1990 pop. 7,535), ⊙ Columbia co., NW Oregon, on the Columbia R., opposite the mouth of Lewis R. (Wash.), 25 mi/40 km NNW of Portland; 45°51′N 122°48′W. River port. Mfg. (lumber, veneer, printing and publishing, fertilizers, ceiling prods.). Mt. Saint Helens Volcano (Wash.) c. 30 mi/48 km to NE. Ridgefield Natl. Wildlife Refuge (Wash.) to SE. Small unit of Clatsop State Forest to W. Closed Trojan Nuclear Power Plant to N. Founded 1847–1848, inc. 1889.

Saint Helens, Mount, volcanic peak (8,366 ft/2,550 m), Skamania and Cowlitz cos., SW Wash., in the Cascade Range. Dormant since 1857, Mt. Saint Helens erupted on May 18, 1980, after months of ominous activity, in one of the largest volcanic explosions in N. Amer. history. After a fissure appeared along the N side of the mt. and swelling occurred in the crater, a great portion of the rock facing fell, followed by an enormous blast of stone, ash, and poison gas. Landslides ensued, leveling entire forests in a radial pattern away from the blast and carrying debris over 20 mi/32 km. A blanket of ash was broadcast downwind (E) to Yakima, Wenatchee, Ellensburg, and other cities, 75 mi/121 km–100 mi/161 km away, creating snowlike drifts that remained for weeks, and coloring the skies of the Midwestern states. The mt. also lost 1,311 ft/400 m of its elev. The disaster took 60 lives, wiped out substantial populations of elk, deer, bears, and coyotes, and destroyed miles of vegetation. The outflow of Spirit L., on NE side, into North Toutle R., was permanently blocked. Mud and melted snow descended into the river valleys; esp. affected was Toutle R., to W, and its parent stream, the Cowlitz R. A 2d eruption occurred a week later, on May 25, and then again on April 11, 1981. Entire area is now protected by Mt. Saint Helens Natl. Volcanic Monument. The high summit of Mt. Saint Helens was replaced by a horseshoe-shaped crater c.2,461 ft/750 m deep; the volcano lost a total about 3,773 ft/1,150 m of elev. from the old peak to the new crater floor. The volcano became and still remains a prime subject of study for geologists and vulcanologists, providing evidence and a working model for predicting volcanic eruptions. Scientists predict future eruptions in the early 21st cent.

Saint Helens National Volcanic Monument, Mount, Wash., see MOUNT SAINT HELENS NATIONAL VOLCANIC MONUMENT.

Saint Henri, village (1991 pop. 3,886), S Que., Canada, on Etchemin R., 12 mi/19 km SE of Quebec; 46°41′N 71°04′W. Dairying.

Saint Henry, village (1990 pop. 1,907), Mercer co., W Ohio, 10 mi/16 km SSW of Celina; 40°25′N 84°38′W. Lumber milling.

Saint Hilaire (se tee-LER), village, S Que., Canada, on Richelieu R., 16 mi/26 km E of Montreal; 45°34′N 73°12′W. Food processing; in agr. region.

Saint Hilaire (hi-LER), village (1990 pop. 298), Pennington co., NW Minn., on Red Lake R., 7 mi/11.3 km S of Thief River Falls; 48°00′N 96°12′W. Terminus of

RR spur from Thief River Falls. Agr. (grain, potatoes, sunflowers; sheep); mfg.

Saint Hilarion (se tee-lah-ree-O), village (1991 pop. 1,185) SE central Que., Canada, 10 mi/16 km NE of Baie St. Paul; 47°34′N 70°24′W. Lumbering; dairying.

Saint Hugues (se UHG), village (1991 pop. 1,281), S Que., Canada, near Yamaska R., 12 mi/19 km NNE of St. Hyacinthe. Lumbering; dairying; cattle, pigs.

Saint Hyacinthe (HEI-uh-suhnth), county (□ 278 sq mi/720 sq km), S Que., Canada, on Yamaska R.; ⊙ St. Hyacinthe; 45°40′N 73°00′W.

Saint Hyacinthe (HEI-uh-suhnth), city (1991 pop. 38,292), S Que., Canada, on the Yamaska R., NE of Montreal; 45°38′N 72°56′W. It is an industrial center, with textile mills and plants mfg. rubber and paper prods., furniture, shoes, and leather goods. The famous Casavant organ factory (est. c.1860) is here. Institutions for religious education and schools of dairy husbandry, textile technology, and veterinary medicine.

Saint Ignace (IG-nis), town (1990 pop. 2,568), ⊙ Mackinac co., SE Upper Peninsula, Mich., on the Straits of Mackinac, opposite Mackinaw City (S); 45°52′N 84°43′W. Resort and fishing center, with ferry and freight docks; passenger ferry to Mackinac Isl. to E. Agr. (cattle, grain). The grave of Father Marquette is here. Father Marquette Natl. Memorial and Mus. Its early history is that of Mackinac region. Hiawatha Natl. Forest to N; Straits State Park W of bridge. Inc. as village in 1882, as city in 1883.

Saint Ignace, Isle (IG-nnlis), W Ont., Canada, in L. Superior, at entrance of Nipigon Bay, 60 mi/97 km ENE of Port Arthur; 17 mi/27 km long, 7 mi/11 km wide. Rises to over 1,000 ft/305 m. Just E is Simpson Isl.

Saint Ignatius (ig-NAI-shuhs), town (1990 pop. 778), Lake co., W Mont., on Mission Creek, 31 mi/50 km N of Missoula; 47°19′N 114°06′W. Cattle, horses, sheep, hogs; hay, corn, rapeseed, potatoes. Mission Reservoir to E, in Flathead Indian Reservation; Natl. Bison Range to W; Ninepipe Reservoir and Natl. Wildlife Refuge to N; Mission Mts. Tribal Wilderness to E. St. Ignatius Mission founded here in 1854. Flathead Indian Mus. and Trading Post. Inc. 1938.

Saint Inigoes (IN-ih-goz), hamlet, St. Marys co., S Md., near the Potomac, 17 mi/27 km SE of Leonardtown. Nearby is Cross Manor, once considered to be the oldest house in Md., now known to have been built in the late 18th cent. Also nearby is the site of St. Indigoes Manor, where Jesuits under Rev. Thomas Copley (1594–1653) bought land directly from the Indians and asserted freedom from secular law. St. Ignatius Church (c.1785) was built on the foundations of an earlier church built in the 1630s.

Saint Isidore (I-zuh-dohr), village (1991 pop. 833), SE Que., Canada, 18 mi/29 km SSE of Quebec. Dairying; lumbering; pig raising.

Saint Jacob, village (1990 pop. 752), Madison co., SW Ill., 22 mi/35 km ENE of East St. Louis; 38°43′N 89°46′W. Dairying.

Saint Jacobs, village, S Ont., Canada, on Conestoga R., 7 mi/11 km NNW of Kitchener. Milling; dairying; mixed farming. Mennonite cultural center.

Saint Jacques (seh ZHAHK), village (1991 pop. 2,251), S Que., Canada, 30 mi/48 km N of Montreal. Tobacco growing and processing; dairying.

Saint James, parish (1991 pop. 148,587), Cornwall co., NW Jamaica; ⊙ Montego Bay; 18°31′N 77°59′W–18°13′N 77°44′W. Bounded W by Hanover Parish, SW by Westmoreland Parish, S by St. Elizabeth Parish, E by Trelawny Parish. Largely hilly, it has fertile valleys along its small rivers, where bananas are principally grown. Produces also sugarcane, honey; goats. Montego Bay, 3d-largest city of the isl. and home of the Sangster Inn, is the leading cruise-shipping port and trading and processing center in the W. Its many seaside resorts creating a thriving tourism industry. Doctor's Cave is known for its curative effects. Other centers are Montpelier, Cambridge, Catadupa, and Anchovy, all along Jamaica RR.

Saint James, parish (□ 249 sq mi/645 sq km; 1990 pop.

20,879), SE central La.; ⊙ Convent; 30°01′N 90°49′W. Divided by the Mississippi R., drained in N by Blind R. Chemical production area. Agr. (sugarcane, vegetables; cattle, horses), crawfish. This is the only place in the world that grows perique tobacco. Sunshine Bridge crosses Mississippi R. in NW, only bridge crossing bet. Baton Rouge and New Orleans area. Formed 1807.

Saint James 1 city (1990 pop. 4,368), ⊙ Watonwan co., S Minn., 34 mi/55 km WSW of Mankato; 43°58′N 94°37′W. Shipping and food-processing center for farming area; agr. (grain, alfalfa, soybeans; livestock); mfg. (poultry prods., meat processing, printing and publishing, metal fabrication, fertilizer). Small St. James L. to SW. Plotted 1870, inc. as village 1871, as city 1899. **2** city (1990 pop. 3,256), Phelps co., central Mo., near the Meramec R. in the Ozarks, 10 mi/16 km ENE of Rolla; 38°00′N 91°36′W. Mfg. (apparel, packaging, transformers). Hay, grapes; cattle; ships agr. prods.; lumber mills, wineries. Mo. Veterans' Home here. Maramec Spring Park and historic iron furnace to E. Founded c. 1857.

Saint James, uninc. town (□ 4 sq mi/10.4 sq km; 1990 pop. 12,703), Suffolk co., SE N.Y., on L.I.; 40°52′N 73°09′W.

Saint James, Mich.: see BEAVER ISLAND.

Saint James, Cape, W B.C., Canada, S extremity of Kunghit Isl. and of the Queen Charlotte Isls.; 51°56′N 131°01′W. Lighthouse.

Saint James Islands (□ 0.7 sq mi/1.8 sq km), group, U.S.V.I., just off E tip of St. Thomas isl., on Pillsbury Sound, 8 mi/12.9 km ESE of Charlotte Amalie; 18°18′N 64°49′W.

Saint Jean Baptiste (seh zhah bahp-TEEST), village, S Man., on Red R., 45 mi/72 km SSW of Winnipeg; 47°07′N 70°11′W. Grain; livestock.

Saint Jean de Boischatel, Canada: see SAINT JEAN D'ORLÉANS.

Saint Jean de Matha (se zhah duh mah-TAH), village (1991 pop. 3,260), S Que., Canada, near L'Assomption R., 16 mi/26 km NNW of Joliette; 46°13′N 73°32′W. Dairying; potatoes; poultry.

Saint Jean d'Orléans (se zhah dor-lai-AH) or **Saint Jean de Boischatel** (se zhah duh bwah-shah-TEL), village (1991 pop. 3,878), S Que., Canada, on SE shore of Ile d'Orléans, on the St. Lawrence, 16 mi/26 km ENE of Quebec. Dairying; vegetables, fruit.

Saint Jean Port Joli (se zhah por zho-LEE), village (1991 pop. 3,369), ⊙ L'Islet co., SE Que., Canada, on the St. Lawrence, 50 mi/80 km ENE of Quebec; 47°12′N 70°16′W. Woodcarving center; furniture mfg.; dairying. Founded 1721.

Saint Jean-Sur-Richelieu (sahn zhahn–suhr–RISH-uh-loo), city (1991 pop. 37,607), S Que., Canada, on the Richelieu R., SE of Montreal. It is an industrial center with textile and hosiery mills and mfg. such as sewing machines, bricks, and wood prods. A fort was built on the site in the 17th cent. A later post, Fort St. Jean, changed hands several times during the Amer. Revolution. The city was the terminus of the 1st Can. RR (1836) from Laprairie. It was the seat of a bilingual military school, the Collège Militaire Royal de Saint Jean.

Saint Jérome (sahn zhai-ROM), city (1991 pop. 23,384), S Que., Canada, on the North R., NW of Montreal; 45°46′N 74°00′W. It is an industrial center with woolen and paper mills. Rubber and wood prods. are also manufactured. Saint Jérome is a commercial center for the Laurentian resort area.

Saint Jérôme, Canada: see METABETCHOUAN.

Saint Jo, town (1990 pop. 1,048), Montague co., N Texas, 58 mi/93 km ESE of Wichita Falls; 33°42′N 97°31′W. Elev. 1,146 ft/349 m. Near source of Elm Fork of Trinity R. In ranch, farm area (cattle; dairying; wheat, watermelons, cantaloupes, peanuts); oil and gas wells. Est. 1856 at crossing of California Trail and Chrisholm Trail.

Saint Joe, town (1990 pop. 452), DeKalb co., NE Ind., on St. Joseph R., 8 mi/12.9 km SE of Auburn; 41°19′N 84°54′W. Agr. area; mfg. (steel prods., food, furniture, feed). Laid out 1875.

Saint Joe, village, Searcy co., N Ark., 21 mi/34 km SE of Harrison, in the Ozarks. Mfg. (wood prods.). Buffalo Natl. R. to S and SE.

Saint Joe River, c.130 mi/209 km long, N Idaho; rises in SE Shoshone near Mont. line in N ½ of Bitterroot Range, in St. Joe Natl. Forest; flows generally W, past St. Maries, where it receives St. Maries R., to S tip of Coeur d'Alene L. at Heyburn State Park, in Coeur d'Alene Indian Reservation. Passes through rugged canyon and has many small falls. Navigable for 32 mi/51 km above mouth.

Saint John, parish (□ 29 sq mi/75 sq km; 1991 pop. 35,635), NW Antigua isl., Antigua and Barbuda Republic; 17°08′N 61°50′W. The most populous and urbanized parish. St. John's (the republic capital) and its nearby suburbs are located here.

Saint John, county (□ 611 sq mi/1,582 sq km; 1991 pop. 81,462), S N.B., Canada, on the Bay of Fundy; ⊙ St. John; 45°18′N 66°00′W.

Saint John, city (1991 pop. 74,969), S N.B., Canada, at the mouth of the St. John R. on the Bay of Fundy; 45°16′N 66°04′W. A major year-round port, it has an excellent harbor, large dry docks, and terminal facilities and maintains extensive shipping connections with Europe, N. and S. Amer., and the West Indies. The city is the commercial, mfg., and transportation center of N.B., though it is being challenged by Moncton. It has pulp and paper mills, oil and sugar refineries, and food-processing plants. Lumbering and fishing are important. The site was visited (1604) by Champlain, and a fort and trading post were built (1631–1635) by Charles de la Tour. In the struggle bet. France and England for possession of Acadia, the fort was captured and recaptured several times, finally becoming Br. in 1758. Growth of the city dates from 1783, when a large party of Loyalists from the U.S. established themselves here on land grants. The settlement was called Parr Town and in 1785 was inc. with Carleton and named St. John, becoming the 1st inc. city in Canada. Benedict Arnold lived and conducted a business here from 1786 to 1791. Much of the old city was destroyed by fire in 1877. Among notable features are Market Slip (1783), the old Loyalist Burying Ground (1783), Martello Tower (fortification; built 1812), the old court house (1830), the R.C. cathedral and bishop's residence (1853), the New Brunswick Mus., and the Reversing Falls rapids. The Univ. of New Brunswick at St. John is here.

Saint John, city (1990 pop. 7,466), St. Louis co., E Mo.; suburb 12 mi/19 km NW of St. Louis; 38°42′N 90°20′W. Inc. 1940. Sometimes referred to as St. Johns.

Saint John 1 town (1990 pop. 4,921), Lake co., extreme NW Ind., 6 mi/9.7 km WNW of Crown Point; 41°27′N 87°29′W. Satellite community of Chicago and Gary. Settled 1830s, laid out 1881. **2** town (1990 pop. 1,357), ⊙ Stafford co., S central Kansas, 22 mi/35 km S of Great Bend, near Rattlesnake Creek; 38°00′N 98°45′W. Trade center for wheat area. Mfg. (machinery). Plotted 1879, inc. 1885.

Saint John 1 village (1990 pop. 368), Rolette co., N N.Dak., 9 mi/14.5 km NW of Rolla, near Can. border; 48°56′N 99°42′W. Port of entry. Turtle Mt. Indian Reservation to S. **2** village (1990 pop. 499), Whitman co., SE Wash., 17 mi/27 km NW of Colfax, near Cottonwood Creek, in the Palouse country; 47°05′N 117°35′W. RR junction. In agr. region; ships wheat, barley, rye; cattle.

Saint John, plantation (1990 pop. 274), Aroostook co., N Maine, on St. John R., 10 mi/16 km WSW of Fort Kent; 47°08′N 68°46′W.

Saint John, island (□ 19 sq mi/49 sq km; 1990 pop. 3,400), one of the U.S.V.I. More than ½ the land and offshore area is U.S. Natl. Park, including the 3 peaks, Camelberg, Mamey, and Bordeaux. Cruz Bay is main town. Subtropical forest on NW slopes, arid land and salt ponds on E end. Danish took control in 1694 and it became a prosperous colony until the collapse of the sugar economy. The U.S. took control in 1917. Wildlife, feral donkeys; ecotourism.

Saint John, Antigua and Barbuda Republic: see SAINT JOHN'S

Saint John Bay, shallow inlet of Gulf of St. Lawrence, W N.F., Canada, bet. Ferolle Point (N) and Point Riche (S); 10 mi/16 km long, 25 mi/40 km wide at entrance; 50°55′N 57°10′W. Contains several isls., largest of which is St. John Isl.

Saint John, Cape, E N.F., Canada, bet. White Bay (N) and Notre Dame Bay (S); 49°58′N 55°29′W.

Saint John Island (□ 9 sq mi/23 sq km), W N.F., Canada, in St. John Bay, 10 mi/16 km NE of Point Riche; 50°49′N 57°15′W.

Saint John, Lake 1 SE N.F., Canada, on Terra Nova R., 40 mi/64 km S of Gander; 4 mi/6 km long, 3 mi/5 km wide; 48°23′N 54°41′W. **2** (□ 375 sq mi/971 sq km), S central Que., Canada, c.110 mi/177 km NNW of Quebec, W of Chicoutimi; 28 mi/45 km long, 18 mi/29 km wide. Fed by Ashuapmuchuan, Mistassini, and Peribonca rivers, drained by Saguenay R. Riparian towns are Roberval, Chambord, and Metabetchouan. Saguenay R. leaves lake by Grande Décharge (hydroelectric station) and Petite Décharge, channels enclosing Île d'Alma.

Saint John, Lake, Canada: see SAGUENAY, river.

Saint John, Lake, Concordia parish, E central La., oxbow lake formed by a cutoff of the Mississippi R., 7 mi/11 km NE of Ferriday; c.7 mi/11 km long. Fishing.

Saint John River, 418 mi/673 km long; rises in NW Maine; flows NE to N.B., Canada, then SE below Edmundston, past St. Leonard, Grand Falls, Woodstock, and Fredericton to the Bay of Fundy at St. John. It forms part of the border bet. Maine and N.B. Its chief tributaries are the Allagash, Aroostook, and Tobique rivers. At Grand Falls the river drops 75 ft/23 m in a great cataract. At its mouth, within the city of St. John, are the Reversing Falls Rapids, caused by the strong tides of the Bay of Fundy, which force the river to reverse its flow at high tide. The river was visited (1604) by the Fr. explorers Samuel de Champlain and Sieur de Monts. In the 17th and 18th cents. it was an important route for Fr., Indian, and Eng. traders, and several trading posts were established on its banks. It later became a major lumber transportation route. There are major hydroelectric power plants at Grand Falls, Beechwood, and Mactaquac. The river is navigable to Fredericton. The valley of the St. John is fertile, and potatoes are raised here. The sect. bet. Baker L. and Allagash village is a wilderness canoe area.

Saint John the Baptist, parish (□ 225 sq mi/583 sq km; 1990 pop. 39,996), SE La.; ⊙ Edgard; 30°02′N 90°34′W. Bounded N by L. Maurepas and Pass Manchac, E by L. Pontchartrain, S and E partly by L. Des Allemands; divided by the Mississippi R. Oil- and chemical-refining area along river. Agr. (soybeans, sugarcane, vegetables; cattle), catfish, crawfish, alligators. Mfg. (food prods., sugar processing, chemicals, petroleum refining, plastic prods., steel prods.). Natural gas, oil. Manchac State Wildlife Area in NE. Commonly referred to as St. John parish. Formed 1807.

Saint John's, city (1991 pop. 21,514), on Antigua isl., in the West Indies, ⊙ Antigua and Barbuda Republic; 17°07′N 61°51′W. St. John's, at the head of a harbor formed by an inlet, is the commercial center of the country. Tourism is important. The harbor has been dredged to accommodate deep-draft vessels. In the 18th cent. St. John's served as a hq. for the Royal Navy in the West Indies.

Saint John's, city (1991 pop. 95,770), ⊙ N.F., SE N.F., Canada, on the NE coast of the Avalon Peninsula; 47°33′N 52°40′W. Built on hills overlooking a fine harbor, it is the commercial and industrial center of the prov. and the base of its great fishing fleet. The city's industries are chiefly related to fishing and include shipbuilding, the mfg. of fishing equip. and marine engines, and the storing, preserving, and processing of fish. Cod industry is at a standstill (mid-1990s); shellfish, herring, other fishing still viable. Also mfg. beverages, machinery, brewing, meat packing, petroleum refining. The city is mainly a service center, however, that relies heavily on civil service jobs for its stability. Although the exact date of its 1st settlement is not known, St. John's is one of the oldest settlements in N.

Amer. In 1583, Sir Humphrey Gilbert took possession of the region for England. Since that time fishing boats from many countries have based here. The settlement was captured and recaptured by France and England, becoming permanently British in 1762 and serving as a naval base during the Amer. Revolution and in the War of 1812. It was at St. John's that Marconi heard (1901) the 1st transatlantic wireless message and from here that the 1st nonstop transatlantic flight was made in 1919. The city has been partially destroyed by fire several times. It is the site of the provincial govt. offices, of R.C. and Anglican cathedrals, of the N.F. Mus., and of Memorial Univ. of N.F.

Saint Johns, county (□ 821 sq mi/2,126 sq km; 1990 pop. 83,829), NE Fla., bounded by St. Johns R. (W) and the Atlantic (E); ⊙ St. Augustine; 29°54′N 81°24′W. Lowland area, partly swampy, with Anastasia Isl. (barrier beach) and Matanzas R. (lagoon). Agr. (corn, potatoes, vegetables; poultry; dairy prods.), fishing, and some forestry (naval stores, lumber). Formed 1821.

Saint Johns 1 town (1990 pop. 3,294), ⊙ Apache co., E Ariz., 53 mi/85 km SE of Holbrook, on Little Colorado R. (forms Zion Reservoir to NW and Lyman L Reservoir to S); 34°30′N 109°22′W. Elev. 5,725 ft/1,745 m. Cattle, sheep; sorghum, hay. Small dam forms reservoir here. Lyman L. State Park to S; Zuni Indian Reservation to NW; Petrified Forest Natl. Park to NW. Inc. 1940. **2** town (1990 pop. 7,284), ⊙ Clinton co., S central Mich., 19 mi/31 km N of Lansing; 43°00′N 84°33′W. In farm area (hogs, cattle; wheat, corn, apples, soybeans, peppermint); mfg. (machinery, tools). Inc. as village 1857, as city 1904.

Saint Johns, village (1990 pop. 262), Perry co., SW Ill., 1 mi/1.6 km N of Du Quoin; 38°01′N 89°14′W. In agr. area (wheat, sorghum; dairying).

Saint Johns, Mo.: see SAINT JOHN.

Saint Johns River, 285 mi/459 km long, E central Fla.; rising N of L. Okeechobee; flowing N to Jacksonville, where it turns abruptly E and enters the Atlantic Ocean 28 mi/45 km away. It passes through 8 lakes and receives many tributaries; the Oklawaha R. is the most important. The dredged river is navigable c.170 mi/274 km upstream. The lower ⅓ of the river forms part of the Intracoastal Waterway.

Saint Johns River, Calif.: see KAWEAH RIVER.

Saint Johnsbury, town (1990 pop. 7,608), ⊙ Caledonia co., NE Vt., on Passumpsic and Moose rivers, 29 mi/47 km NE of Montpelier; 44°27′N 72°00′W. It is known for its maple sugar. Other mfg. includes tools, fabrics, wood prods., feed; dairy prods. Winter sports. Burke Mt. Ski Area is NE. Points of interest are St. Johnsbury Acad. (1842), Maple Mus., Fairbanks Mus. of Natural Hist., war monument by Larkin G. Mead. Settled 1786. Includes St. Johnsbury village.

Saint Johnsville, village (1990 pop. 1,825), Montgomery co., E central N.Y., on Mohawk R. and the Barge Canal, 28 mi/45 km ESE of Utica; 43°00′N 74°40′W. Textile milling, apparel. Settled c.1775, inc. 1868.

Saint Jones River, c.25 mi/40 km long, E central Del.; rises in NW Kent co. 8 mi/12.9 km WNW of Dover, flows E and SE through Silver L. and Moors L., through city of Dover (head of navigation), to Delaware Bay just N of Bowers (Bowers Beach). Fishing, bird hunting in marshes along lower course.

Saint Joseph, village (1991 pop. 2,174), W Dominica, B.W.I., 6 mi/9.7 km NNW of Roseau; 15°24′N 61°26′W. Cacao, coconuts, limes.

Saint Joseph, town, NW Trinidad, Trinidad and Tobago, on RR, 6 mi/9.7 km E of Port of Spain. In cacao-growing region. Has anc. colonial church. Founded as San José de Oruña (1577–1584), it is the oldest town of the isl., of which it was capital until 1783. Sir Walter Raleigh destroyed it in 1595. At adjoining Valsayn, site of govt. stock farm, the last Span. governor signed treaty of capitulation (Feb. 18, 1797). Now residential development.

Saint Joseph 1 county (□ 460 sq mi/1,191 sq km; 1990 pop. 247,052), N Ind., bounded N by Mich. state line; ⊙ South Bend; 41°37′N 86°17′W. Agr. (dairy prods.; corn, grain, fruit, mint; livestock); mfg. at South Bend and Mishawaka. Lake resorts. Drained by St. Joseph, Yellow, and Kankakee rivers. Potato Creek State Park in SW; Twin Branch State Fish Hatchery in NE. Formed 1830. **2** county (□ 521 sq mi/1,349 sq km; 1990 pop. 58,913), SW Mich.; ⊙ Centerville; 41°55′N 85°31′W. Bounded S by Ind. state line; drained by St. Joseph R. and its affluents. Cattle, hogs, sheep, poultry; wheat, soybeans, corn; dairy prods. Mfg. at Sturgis, Three Rivers, and White Pigeon. Small lakes (resorts) distributed throughout co., especially on St. Joseph R. Formed and organized 1829.

Saint Joseph 1 city (1990 pop. 9,214), ⊙ Berrien co., SW Mich., 48 mi/77 km WSW of Kalamazoo, on L. Michigan at the mouth of the St. Joseph R.; 42°06′N 86°29′W. Twin city with Benton Harbor, to NE. Fruit-growing area; mfg. (auto parts, machinery, printing, swimming pools, publishing). Household appliances, auto parts, and rubber goods supplement the tourist industry. A resort with beaches and mineral springs, it is also a port with good harbor facilities. Western Mich. Univ. extension. Native-Amer. villages, a Jesuit mission, Fort Miami (1679), and a fur-trading post occupied this site before permanent Amer. settlement began c.1830. Inc. 1834. **2** city (1990 pop. 71,852), ⊙ Buchanan co., NW Mo., on the Missouri R.; 39°45′N 94°49′W. It is the trade center of a rich agr. and farming area. The city is a large market for livestock and grain, and has meat-packing and food-processing plants and stockyards. Corn, oats, wheat, soybeans, tobacco (SW); cattle, hogs. Mfg. (electrical prods., machinery, chemicals, clothing, soybean prods., animal medicines, bldg. materials, leather processing, pet food, wire, paper prods., printing). St. Joseph–Rosencrans Airport is located across the Missouri R., N of Elwood, but is in Mo., cut off from rest of state by a new river channel. The city was laid out c.1843 on the site of a trading post founded (1826) by Joseph Robidoux. In the 1840s and 1850s it was a major jumping-off place for settlers bound for Calif., Oregon, and Colo. In 1860, St. Joseph became the E terminus of the Pony Express. The city was also an early, important RR center until bypassed by the transcontinental RR. Its economy was built on livestock and grain. At one time it was the world's 5th-largest livestock market and 10th-largest flour producer. Both activities have declined significantly. Of interest are the Pony Express stables (now a mus.), the poet Eugene Field's home, and the city mus. with noted Native Amer. relics. Mo. Western Col. and a state mental hosp. are here. Commonly referred to as "Saint Joe." Inc. 1845.

Saint Joseph 1 town (1990 pop.1,517), ⊙ Tensas parish, E La., near the Mississippi, 36 mi/58 km SW of Vicksburg (Miss.); 31°55′N 91°14′W. In cotton-growing area; rice, soybeans, peanuts. Fine antebellum houses in area. L. Bruin (horseshoe lake of Mississippi R.) and state park to N. **2** town (1990 pop. 3,294), Stearns co., central Minn., near Mississippi R., 7 mi/11.3 km W of St. Cloud; 45°34′N 94°19′W. In farming area. Dairying; livestock; grain, soybeans. Mfg. (metal fabrication, canvas prods.). Several small natural lakes to W.

Saint Joseph, village (1990 pop. 2,052), Champaign co., E Ill., 8 mi/12.9 km E of Urbana; 40°06′N 88°02′W. In agr. area; corn, wheat, soybeans.

Saint Joseph, river, 210 mi/338 km long, Mich. and Ind.; rising near Baw Beee L. in Hillsdale co., S Mich.; flows generally W past Hillsdale and Three Rivers, Mich.; Elkhart and South Bend, Ind; Niles and Berrien Springs, Mich., in wide curves. Flows into L. Michigan at Benton Harbor and St. Joseph, Mich.; 41°54′N 84°36′W. River was an important link to the Ohio R. and L. Erie for pioneer travelers.

Saint Joseph Bay, arm of the Gulf of Mexico, in Gulf co., NW Fla.; sheltered S and W from the gulf by a sandspit extending 4 mi/6.4 km W from the mainland to Cape San Blas and then 17 mi/27 km N to St. Joseph Point; c.13 mi/21 km long, 3 mi/4.8 km–6 mi/9.7 km wide. The bay, 20 ft/6 m–35 ft/11 m deep, forms an excellent harbor for Port St. Joe.

Saint Joseph d'Alma (se zho-ZEF DAHL-muh), town,

⊙ Lac St. Jean Est co., S central Que., Canada, on Saguenay R., near L. St. John, 130 mi/209 km NW of Quebec. Wool carding, lumbering, mfg. of paper prods., bricks.

Saint Joseph de Beauce (se zho-ZEF duh BOS), village (1991 pop. 3,111), S Que., Canada, on Chaudière R., 40 mi/64 km SSE of Quebec; 46°18′N 70°52′W. Lumbering; dairying; marble quarrying; mfg. of shoes, furniture, powdered milk.

Saint Joseph de Grantham, Canada: see SAINT GERMAIN DE GRANTHAM.

Saint Joseph de la Rive (se zho-ZEF duh lah REEV), village (1991 pop. 225), SE central Que., Canada, on the St. Lawrence, 6 mi/10 km E of Baie St. Paul, opposite Île aux Coudres. Dairying; vegetables. Hydroelectric station.

Saint Joseph de la Rivière Bleue, Canada: see RIVIÈRE BLEUE.

Saint Joseph de Sorel (se zho-ZEF duh suh-REL), town (1991 pop. 2,069), S Que., Canada, on the St. Lawrence, at mouth of Richelieu R. opposite Sorel; 46°02′N 73°08′W. Dairying; fruit growing.

Saint Joseph Island, central Ont., Canada, at W extremity of North Channel, in NW L. Huron, 18 mi/29 km SE of Sault Ste. Marie; 20 mi/32 km long, 12 mi/19 km wide.

Saint Joseph Island, barrier isl., S Texas, bet. Aransas Bay and Gulf of Mexico; c.23 mi/37 km long, 1 mi/1.6 km–5 mi/8 km wide. Separated by broad pass from Mud and Harbor isls. (SW), by a narrow channel from Matagorda Isl. (NE).

Saint Joseph, Lake (□ 187 sq mi/484 sq km), Patricia dist., NW Ont., Canada, 70 mi/113 km NE of Sioux Lookout; 52 mi/84 km long, 12 mi/19 km wide. Elev. 1,218 ft/371 m. Drained by Albany R. into James Bay.

Saint Joseph, Lake, Tensas parish, E La., oxbow lake formed by a cutoff of the Mississippi R., extends 14 mi/23 km SE from Newellton. Fishing.

Saint Joseph River, c.100 mi/161 km long, in Mich., Ohio, and Ind.; rises in Hillsdale co., S Mich., SW of Hillsdale, near source of NW-flowing St. Joseph R. of Mich. and Ind. Flows SE into Williams co. in NW Ohio, then SW, past Montpelier and Edgerton (Ohio) and through De Kalb and Allen cos. (Ind.), joining St. Marys R. to form the Maumee at Fort Wayne. East Branch rises in Hillsdale co., near Osseo, flows SE, then SW c.20 mi/32 km to join main river in Williams co. (Ohio).

Saint Jovite (se zho-VEET), town (1991 pop. 4,118), S Que., Canada, in the Laurentians, 16 mi/26 km WNW of Ste. Agathe des Monts; 46°07′N 74°35′W. Dairying; ski resort.

Saint Kitts and Nevis, Federation of, island state (□ 120 sq mi/311 sq km; 1991 est. pop. 40,300), West Indies, in the Leeward Isls.; ⊙ Basseterre on St. Kitts; 17°20′N 62°45′W. The state consists of the isls. of St. Kitts, also called St. Christopher (□ 68 sq mi/176 sq km), Nevis (□ 50 sq mi/130 sq km), and Sombrero (□ 2 sq mi/5.2 sq km). The chief settlement on Nevis is Charlestown, the birthplace of Alexander Hamilton. A narrow strait (c.2 mi/3.2 km wide) separates the 2 larger isls., which are volcanic in origin, mountainous, and renowned for their scenery. Sugar, molasses, cotton, and coconuts are exported. Tourism is an important part of the economy, and a limited degree of mfg. has been developed. St. Kitts and Nevis were visited by Columbus in 1493, but Eur. settlement did not begin until the British arrived on St. Kitts in 1623. Fr. settlers came to the isl. 2 years later. Nevis was 1st settled by the British in 1628. The Treaty of Paris of 1783 granted the isls. to Britain. They were part of the colony of the Leeward Isls. (1871–1956) and of the West Indies Federation (1958–1962). In 1967, together with Anguilla, they became a self-governing state in association with Great Britain. Anguilla seceded later that year; it was placed under direct control of Great Britain and was formally separated from St. Kitts and Nevis in 1980. In 1983 the 2 isls. gained full independence, with provisions that allow for them to separate if approved by a referendum. In recent years, there has been strong sentiment on

Nevis for independence. Recently, export-processing industrialization has been encouraged and tourist development occurred, in the S of St. Kitts.

Saint Lambert (LAM-buhrt), city (1991 pop. 20,976), S Que., Canada, on the St. Lawrence R.; 45°29′N 73°30′W. Residential suburb of Montreal.

Saint Landry, parish (□ 929 sq mi/2,406 sq km; 1990 pop. 80,331), S central La.; ⊙ Opelousas; 30°31′N 92°05′W. Bounded E by Atchafalaya R., Bayou des Cannes forms extreme W boundary; drained by Bayou Teche and other bayous. Most inhabitants are descendants of the Acadians. Fertile agr. area (cotton, peaches, corn, sorghum, hay, rice, sugarcane, sweet potatoes, vegetables, wheat; cattle, horses, sheep, hogs; dairying); crawfish, catfish. Mfg. at Opelousas and Eunice, logging. Natural gas fields. Annual Yambilee Festival. Thistlethwaite State Wildlife Area at center. Formed 1805.

Saint Laurent (se lo-RAH), village (1991 pop. 1,115), S Man., Canada, on L. Manitoba, 50 mi/80 km NW of Winnipeg. Resort; fishing.

Saint Lawrence, SE residential suburb of Bridgetown, SW Barbados, B.W.I. Tourist hotel enclave.

Saint Lawrence, county (□ 2,821 sq mi/7,306 sq km; 1990 pop. 111,974), N N.Y.; ⊙ Canton; 44°30′N 75°04′W. Bounded NW by the St. Lawrence R.; drained by St. Regis, Indian, Grass, Oswegatchie, and Raquette rivers, which are all tributaries of the St. Lawrence. Plains area along the St. Lawrence; rises to the Adirondacks in SE. A leading U.S. dairying co.; also farming, timber harvesting, saw-timber mills, maple-sugar production. Lead, zinc, limestone, talc deposits. Diversified mfg. concentrated at Massena. Sizable hydroelectric power generation facilities have attracted the major aluminum companies to the co.; aluminum smelting and refining. Seasonal residences and recreational facilities can be found on the St. Lawrence R. and on Black and Cranberry lakes. Formed 1802.

Saint Lawrence or **Great Saint Lawrence**, town (1991 pop. 1,743), SE N.F., Canada, on SW shore of Placentia Bay, on Burin Peninsula, 22 mi/35 km ESE of Grand Bank; 46°54′N 55°24′W. Fluospar mining center. Just NE is Little St. Lawrence, site of hydroelectric station.

Saint Lawrence, village (1990 pop. 223), Hand co., central S.Dak., 2 mi/3.2 km E of Miller; 44°31′N 98°56′W. In dairying region.

Saint Lawrence, borough (1990 pop. 1,542), Berks co., SE central Pa., residential suburb 3 mi/4.8 km ESE of Reading, on Antietam Creek; 40°19′N 51°75′W. Mfg. (millwork).

Saint Lawrence, one of the principal rivers of N. Amer., 744 mi/1,197 km long. It issues from the NE end of L. Ontario and flows NE, 1st along the U.S.-Can. border, then into S Que., past Montreal and Quebec city, to the Gulf of St. Lawrence, N of Cape Gaspé. It is the outlet of the Great Lakes and together with them forms a c.2,300-mi/3,700-km waterway from the W end of L. Superior to the Atlantic Ocean. The river is an integral part of the St. Lawrence Seaway (opened 1959). In its upper course the river cuts through a part of the Can. Shield; here, just downstream from L. Ontario, are the Thousand Isls. Below Cornwall, Ont., the river widens into L. St. Francis. Shortly it widens again into L. St. Louis, then descends through the Lachine Rapids to Montreal, head of navigation for very large oceangoing vessels. Bet. Sorel and Trois Rivières is L. St. Peter. Below the city of Quebec the river is tidal. It gradually increases in width to c.90 mi/140 km at its mouth. The river's principal tributaries are the Richelieu (linking the St. Lawrence with L. Champlain and the Hudson R.), St. Francis, Ottawa, St. Maurice, and Saguenay rivers. The St. Lawrence R. is an important source of hydroelectric power; one of the world's largest facilities is the Beauharnois power plant near Montreal. Agreements bet. the U.S. and Canada govern power distribution and navigation in the internatl. sect. of the river. Canals have been constructed around the rapids, making the entire river navigable; however, the upper part is unnavigable during the winter months because of ice accumulation. The most important cities and ports along the St. Lawrence are Ogdensburg, N.Y.; Kingston,

Brockville, and Cornwall, Ont.; and Montreal, Sorel, Trois Rivières, Quebec city, and Lévis, Que. The many bridges that cross the St. Lawrence R. include the Thousand Isls. Internatl. Bridge (1938), the Roosevelt Internatl. Bridge (1934), and the Seaway Skyway Bridge (1960), all bet. Ont. and N.Y.; the Victoria Bridge (remodeled 1898) at Montreal; and the Quebec Bridge (1917), near Quebec. The St. Lawrence valley is an agr. region; potatoes, grains, hay, vegetables, and dairy cattle are raised.

Saint Lawrence, Cape, N extremity of Cape Breton Isl., NE N.S., Canada, on Gulf of St. Lawrence, 65 mi/105 km NNW of Sydney; 47°03′N 60°35′W.

Saint Lawrence, Gulf of, arm (□ c.100,000 sq mi/259,000 sq km) of the Atlantic Ocean, SE Canada, extending c.250 mi/400 km from the mouth of the St. Lawrence R. to N.F. on the E. At its greatest width (NE-SW) it is c.500 mi/800 km. It is bounded by N.S., N.B., and Que.; in the Gulf are P.E.I., Anticosti Isl., the Magdalen Isls., and numerous small isls. near its N shore. Chaleur Bay, a W inlet, lies bet. the Gaspé Peninsula and N.B. The Strait of Belle Isle, Cabot Strait, and the Strait of Canso lead to the Atlantic. The gulf is subject to frequent fog and is closed to navigation due to ice from early December to mid-April. It was visited by explorers before the 16th cent., and it has important fishing grounds, esp. for cod.

Saint Lawrence Island, W Alaska, in the Bering Sea; c.90 mi/145 km long, 8 mi/12.9 km–22 mi/35 km wide; 63°30′N 170°30′W. A treeless isl., it is inhabited by Inuit engaged in fishing and walrus hunting. Highest point, Atok Mt. (2,070 ft/631 m). Main villages are Gambell (63°46′N 171°46′W) on NW tip and Savoonga (63°42′N 170°27′W) on N central coast. It was visited by Dan. explorer Vitus Bering on St. Lawrence's Day, 1728. Formed by an enormous shield volcano.

Saint Lawrence Islands National Park (□ 1.6 sq mi/4 sq km), S Ont., Canada, in the Thousand Isls. It includes 17 wooded Can. isls. and some adjacent mainland bet. Kingston and Brockville. It is popular with summer campers. Est. 1904.

Saint Lawrence Seaway, internatl. waterway of NE U.S. and SE Canada, 360 mi/579 km long; it is the portion of the St. Lawrence–Great Lakes Waterway System from Montreal, Que., on the St. Lawrence R., to Port Colborne, Ont., on L. Erie, at S end of Welland Canal. Includes series of 7 locks and dams on St. Lawrence R. that lift oceangoing ships from 20 ft/6 m to L. Ontario's surface elev. of 246 ft/75 m. The locks are St. Lambert, Montreal; Cote Ste. Catherine, Montreal (L. St. Louis); Lower Beauharnois, Upper Beauharnois, both at Beauharnois, Que. (L. St. Francis); Snell, Cornwall, Ont.; Eisenhower (Moses Saunders Power Dam), Massena, N.Y.; Iroquois, Prescott, Ont.–Ogdensburg, N.Y. The dams are also used to generate electricity. The Welland Canal, which connects L. Ontario and L. Erie, is also part of the Seaway. It parallels the Niagara R. 10 mi/16 km–15 mi/24 km to the W and overcomes the 326 ft/99 m Niagara Escarpment, the most formidable barrier on the entire waterway network, to L. Erie's 572 ft/174 m. The Seaway allows a min. depth of 27 ft/8 m, allowing ships having a max. draught of 25 ft/8 m to pass in and out of the Great Lakes. Construction began on the Seaway in 1954 after more than a decade of negotiations, agreements, and planning. It was formally opened on April 25, 1959. The Welland Canal was originally built in 1829 and its present course established bet. St. Catherines and Port Colbourne in 1833. A series of improvements followed, the latest being in 1973, which straightened, widened, and deepened an 8 mi/12.9 km sect. Completion of the Seaway allowed ships from the Atlantic Ocean to reach such distant inland lake ports as Chicago, on L. Michigan, and Duluth, on L. Superior. Despite its advantages, there have been difficulties.

Saint Lawrence–Great Lakes Waterway, 1,865 mi/3,001 km long, SE Canada and NE U.S.; stretches from Sept-Iles, Que., to Duluth, Minn.; includes St. Lawrence R., the St. Lawrence Seaway, the Great Lakes, and their connecting rivers, canals, and locks. Ocean- and lakegoing vessels use the waterway to reach the inland ports of the Great Lakes and to travel in and out of the Atlantic Ocean through the St. Lawrence. The waterway was made complete with the opening of the St. Lawrence Seaway in 1959, allowing ships to reach L. Ontario (elev. 326 ft/99 m) through a series of 7 locks and dams on St. Lawrence R., and L. Erie (elev. 572 ft/174 m), through the Welland Canal and its 8 locks, from St. Catherines to Port Colbourne, Ont. Creation of a shipping channel through the Detroit R., L. St. Clair, and St. Clair R., completed during WWII, allowed ships to reach the 578-ft/176-m level of lakes Huron and Michigan. The Soo Canal and Locks (4 parallel locks on U.S. side constructed 1855–1968; one on Can. side constructed 1895) on St. Mary's R. at Sault Ste. Marie, Mich.-Ont., allow ships to reach L. Superior (elev. 602 ft/183 m), from L. Huron. Completion of seaway allowed lampreys to enter lake system from Atlantic Ocean, devastating the lake fishing industry. Other problems include pollution and ship traffic jams at locks. The waterway allows the transfer of manufactured goods from such lake ports as Chicago, Milwaukee, Cleveland, Detroit, Toronto, Hamilton, and Buffalo, and of raw materials such as iron ore, wheat, corn, timber. The waterway ties into other canal and river systems—the Ottawa R.–Rideau Canal; the Trent and Murray Canal, bet. L. Ontario and Georgian Bay, L. Huron; the N.Y. State (Erie) Canal and Hudson-Mohawk R.; and the Ill. and Mich. Canal and Mississippi R. system—creating a waterway network that serves the E ½ of N. Amer.

Saint Leo, town (□ 1 sq mi/2.6 sq km; 1990 pop. 1,009), Pasco co., W central Fla., 29 mi/47 km NE of Tampa; 28°20′N 82°15′W.

Saint Leo, village (1990 pop. 111), Yellow Medicine co., SW Minn., 26 mi/42 km WSW of Granite Falls; 44°43′N 96°02′W. Mfg. (fertilizer); agr. (grain; livestock).

Saint Leon, town (1990 pop. 493), Dearborn co., SE Ind., 15 mi/24 km NNW of Lawrenceburg; 39°17′N 84°58′W. In agr. area.

Saint Leonard, town (1991 pop. 1,545), NW N.B., Canada, on St. John R., 24 mi/39 km SE of Edmundston, on Maine border. Potato-growing region.

Saint Léonard d'Aston (seh lai-oh-NAHR DA-stuhn), village (1991 pop. 1,006), S Que., Canada, on Nicolet R., 14 mi/23 km SE of Nicolet. Dairying; lumbering.

Saint Liboire (se leeb-WAHR), village (1991 pop. 904), ⊙ Bagot co., S Que., Canada, 9 mi/14 km ENE of St. Hyacinthe. Dairying; cattle, pigs.

Saint Libory (li-BOR-ee), village (1990 pop. 525), St. Clair co., SW Ill., 18 mi/29 km SE of Belleville; 38°21′N 89°42′W. In agr. area.

Saint Lin, Canada: see LAURENTIDES.

Saint Louis 1 (LOO-is), county (□ 6,860 sq mi/17,767 sq km; 1990 pop. 198,213), NE Minn.; ⊙ Duluth; 47°34′N 92°27′W. Extensively watered area drained by St. Louis (forms part of SE boundary), Little Fork, Whiteface, Vermilion, and numerous other rivers. Bounded N by Canada (Ont.) border; W-E by Rainy L., Namakan L., Loon R., Loon L., Lac La Croix, Iron L., and Crooked L.; SE by L. Superior. Agr. (potatoes, hay, oats; dairying; poultry); timber; tourism. Vermilion Iron Range, in NE, and Mesabi Iron Range, extending E-W through central area, have immensely productive mines. Numerous lakes and reservoirs, especially in N; chief lakes are Burntside, in NE, Trout and Vermilion, in N, and Pelican and Kabetogama, in NW. Parts of Superior Natl. Forest in N ½ of co.; part of Fond du Lac Indian Reservation in S; parts of Fond du Lac and Savanna state forests in SW; Kabetogama State Forest and Sturgeon R. State Forest in NW; most of Voyageurs Natl. Park in NW; parts of Boundary Waters Canoe Area in NE; Whiteface R. State Forest in S; Cloquet Valley State Forest in SE; Lake Jeanette, Burntside, and part of Bear Isl. state forests are in NE; McCarthy Beach State Park in NW; Bear Head L. and Soudan Underground Mine state parks in N center. Formed 1855. **2** county (□ 497 sq mi/1,287 sq km; 1990 pop. 993,529), E Mo.; ⊙ Clayton; 38°38′N 90°26′W. Bounded by Mississippi R. (E), Missouri R. (NW), and Meramec R. (SE, SW). Agr. (corn, wheat, hay, horticulture; dairy); limestone, shale, and clay; lumber prods. Generally referred to as "the County" as opposed to "the City." When the city of St. Louis separated from St. Louis co. in 1876 to become independent, it had all the advantages of industry, commerce, and transportation. St. Louis co. was basically rural, with a scattering of small towns such as Kirkwood, Ballwin, and Florissant. The 1904 World's Fair in Forest Park helped spur the growth of the co.'s 1st suburbs, University City, Clayton, and Webster, all W of St. Louis city. The establishment of the St. Louis Municipal Airport (1920s) in the NW part of the co., and the construction of new highways and Manchester Road (W), esp. U.S. Route 66 to SW and U.S. Route 40 to NW, boosted the economy of the co. World War II and McDonnell Aircraft Corp. (now McDonnell-Douglas) brought the 1st significant industry to the co. The "baby boom" after World War II brought with it a flurry of new home construction in the late 1940s and 1950s, esp. around the airport. Because St. Louis could not annex land in the co. beyond its 1876 limits to keep abreast of spreading urbanization, dozens of municipalities were created to form a mosaic of about 90 total. The original small towns grew into larger cities, while small villages were created to counter annexation by larger municipalities. An office and hotel bldg. boom occurred in the co. seat of Clayton in the 1960s, creating a 2d downtown for the St. Louis area. The construction of I-270 (the "Circumferential Highway" as it is called) in the 1960s replaced Lindbergh Blvd. as the co.'s Main Street. Glass office bldgs., hotels, shopping centers, and hosps. now line the interstates. Large office and industrial parks have been built in Fenton (Chrysler plant), Maryland Heights, Chesterfield, Earth City, and Hazelwood. Some built-up areas, such as Affton, Mehlville, and Spanish Lakes, remain uninc. In the mid-1990s, only the extreme W remains undeveloped, but even here, low-density housing is being constructed among the deeply wooded hills (the city of Wildwood, bordering Franklin co., voted to incorporate in 1995). Heading toward the year 2000, what happened to "the City" was happening to "the County"; development has moved on to adjacent cos., esp. St. Charles, and the inner ring of suburbs are losing pop. noticeably. St. Louis co.'s pop. is almost 3 times the size of St. Louis city. In 1993, flood damage occurred in Lemay and Bellefontaine Neighbors (backwater from Mississippi R.), in the Chesterfield Airport and industrial area along Mississippi R. (Chesterfield Valley) and in Valley Park, on Meramec R. Babler State Park in W; Castlewood State Park and Rockwoods Reservation (nature reserve) in SW. Chesterfield Airport serves W co. corporations and private aircraft. Jefferson Barracks Park (former army base) and Natl. Cemetery in Lemay. Riverport Amphitheatre in Maryland Heights (opened 1992). Grants Farm and Ulysses S Grant Home, Affton (Grantwood Village). Univ. of Missouri–St. Louis at Bellerive; Washington Univ. in Clayton. Several other private and public cols. and seminaries. Metrolink light RR system, using mainly existing RR track, opened 1993; links Lambert–St. Louis Internatl. Airport with downtown St. Louis and East St. Louis, Ill. Six Flags Mid-America and Hidden Valley Ski Resort, Eureka. Formed 1812 as one of Mo's original cos.

Saint Louis 1 (LOO-is), city (1990 pop. 3,828), Gratiot co., central Mich., 34 mi/55 km W of Saginaw and 4 mi/6.4 km NE of Alma, on Pine R.; 43°24′N 84°37′W. In oil-bearing and agr. area (livestock; dairy prods.; grain, sugar beets, cucumbers). Petroleum refining. Mfg. (food prods., fertilizer, chemicals); poultry hatcheries. Mineral springs (health resort). Settled 1849, inc. as city 1891. **2** independent city (1990 pop. 396,685), with a status similar to a co., E Mo., on the Mississippi R. below the mouth of the Missouri R.; 38°38′N 90°14′W. The heart of the largest metropolitan area within 250 mi/402 km, St. Louis has long been a major industrial, commercial, and transportation hub. It is the nation's 2d-largest inland river port and the 3d-largest RR center. It is also a natl. trucking and air-travel center. It has widely diversified industries, producing chemicals, consumer goods, motor vehicles and parts, electronic components, food prods., textiles, shoes, and beer. Other mfg. includes paper prods., paints, coffee, publishing, plastic prods., fabricated metal prods., soap and detergents, hardware, dairy prods., pharmaceuticals, and apparel. Aircraft, spacecraft, and heavy industry across the river in Ill. are often said to be in St. Louis city as well, although they are actually in the suburbs. St. Louis is also a wholesale, banking, and financial center. St. Louis was the nation's 4th-largest city at the end of the 19th cent. The city had its largest pop. (c.900,000) immediately following World War II. Bet. 1950 and 1990 the city pop. decreased by more than ½, and industry has significantly declined since 1970, much of it moving to suburbs or to Southern and Southwestern states. While many of the outlying suburbs grew steadily and developed industries, some, such as EAST SAINT LOUIS, Ill., have been marked by high unemployment and poverty. St. Louis' status as an independent city, set by the Mo. constitution, prevents it from annexing beyond its current limits (set in 1876), making it unable to balance inner-city statistics with suburban. The site of the city was chosen (1763) by Pierre Laclède for a fur-trading post. To honor Louis XV of France, it was named for his "name" saint, Louis IX of France. Transferred to the Spanish in 1770, it was retroceded to France in the time of Napoleon I and then sold to the U.S. along with the other lands of the Louisiana Purchase. St. Louis, the gateway to the Missouri valley and the West, was the market and supply point for fur traders, mountain men, and explorers (including Lewis and Clark). The town grew rapidly after the War of 1812, when immigrants began to come in numbers to settle the West. St. Louis grew to be one of the greatest U.S. river ports; even after the RR arrived in the 1850s, the river steamers remained important. Commercial barge traffic has replaced the steamboats. Eads Bridge (1867–1874) was the 1st bridge to span the Mississippi below its junction with the Missouri R. The city and surrounding area have a noted symphony orchestra, a municipal opera, and more than 30 educational institutions, including St. Louis Univ., Washington Univ., 3 theological seminaries, and a branch of the Univ. of Mo. It has a state mental hosp. and a state regional mental health center. The city's large Forest Park has an open-air theater, a recognized art mus., a zoo, a planetarium, and the Jefferson memorial bldg., which recalls the Louisiana Purchase Exposition of 1904 (the "St. Louis Fair"), the same year St. Louis hosted the 1st Olympic games outside Europe. St. Louis has a major league baseball team, the Cardinals, as well as a professional ice hockey team. A professional football team, the Rams, occupy an indoor stadium (built 1996) adjacent to expanded convention center on N side of downtown. Poet Eugene Field was born in St. Louis; his house is a mus. Other St. Louisans in the field of literature include Sara Teasdale and T.S. Eliot. New Cathedral is one of the largest R.C. cathedrals in the country. The Jefferson Natl. Expansion Memorial Natl. Historic Site was est. in 1935 to preserve such historical bldgs. as the old courthouse (1839–1864), where the famous Dred Scott case was tried. The city's major attraction is Gateway Arch (erected in 1965), a giant stainless steel arch, 630 ft/192 m high, designed by Eero Saarinen. Standing on the banks of the Mississippi, it and the Mus. of the West beneath it symbolize St. Louis as the gateway to the West. Inc. as a city 1822.

Saint Louis (LOO-is), village (1990 pop. 181), Pottawatomie co., central Okla., 18 mi/29 km SSE of Shawnee; 35°04′N 96°50′W. In agr. area.

Saint Louis Bay (LOO-is), inlet of Mississippi Sound, Hancock and Harrison cos., S Miss., c.10 mi/16 km W of Gulfport; c.5 mi/8 km long N-S, c.6 mi/9.7 km wide. Town of Bay St. Louis is on W shore, town of Pass Christian near E shore. Highway and RR bridges at its entrance. Wolf R. enters from NE, Jordan R. from W.

Saint Louis Bay, Minn.: see SAINT LOUIS RIVER.

Saint Louis de Kent, village (1991 pop. 1,009), E N.B., Canada, on Kouchibouguac R., 7 mi/11 km NW of Richibucto, in Acadian dist.; 46°44′N 64°58′W. Agr. Landscaped grounds and replica of shrine at Lourdes, France. Kouchibouguac Natl. Park is NE.

Saint Louis, Lake (LOO-ee), expansion (□ 57 sq mi/148 sq km) of the St. Lawrence, S Que., Canada, 8 mi/13 km SW of Montreal; 18 mi/29 km long, up to 7 mi/11 km wide. Bounded N by Montreal Isl. Receives Ottawa R. (W), through 2 channels on either side of Perrot Isl., and Châteauguay R. (S).

Saint Louis Park, city (1990 pop. 43,787), Hennepin co., SE Minn., suburb 5 mi/8 km WSW of Minneapolis; 44°57′N 93°21′W. Mfg. (printing and publishing, machining, rubber, food, furniture). Settled 1854, inc. 1886.

Saint Louis River, 160 mi/257 km long, Minn.; rises in Small Cujkin L. in W Lake co., NE Minn, 80 mi/129 km NNE of Duluth; 47°30′N 91°49′W. Flows generally SW, through Seven Beaver L., passes S of Mesabi Iron Range, turns SE at Floodwood; flows past Cloquet and Carlton and Jay Cooke State Park; becomes Minn.-Wis. state border, flows through Spirit L. as it turns NE and enters St. Louis Bay and L. Superior, which forms Duluth Harbor. Largely navigable. Its estuary (called St. Louis Bay) is c.1 mi/1.6 km wide and forms part of the harbor for the twin ports of Duluth and Superior. Drains part of Superior Natl. Forest in upper course, passes through picturesque gorge in Jay Cooke State Park, just W of Duluth. Dammed for power at Carlton, forms small Thomson Reservoir. Important tributaries are Cloquet R., above Cloquet, and Whiteface R., above Floodwood, both from NE.

Saint Louisville (LOO-is-vil), village (1990 pop. 372), Licking co., central Ohio, 7 mi/11 km N of Newark, on North Fork Licking R.; 40°10′N 82°25′W. In agr. area.

Saint Lucas, town (1990 pop. 174), Fayette co., NE Iowa, 10 mi/16 km NNW of West Union; 43°04′N 91°55′W. In agr. area.

Saint Lucia (LOO-shuh), island state (□ 238 sq mi/616 sq km; 1991 pop. 133,308), West Indies, one of the Windward Isls.; ⊙ CASTRIES; 13°55′N 60°59′W. Morne Gimie (3,145 ft/959 m) and the twin pyramidal cones known as the Pitons are the most imposing landmarks, near town of Soufrière. Much of isl. is heavily forested with rugged terrain. The economy used to center around sugar production, but with that industry's collapse in the 1950s, it is now largely based on other agr. (bananas and other tropical prods. are exported) and tourism. Saint Lucia has diversified its industrial base and possesses oil storage and transshipment facilities, but bananas still account for 80% of export earnings. Exports to the UK and EU receive tariff and quota protection. Columbus may have sighted the isl. on his 1502 voyage. The British failed in their 1st attempts at colonization in the early 17th cent. The isl. was often used as a pirate base until it was settled by the French, who signed a treaty with the local Caribs in 1660. Thereafter Saint Lucia was much contested by the 2 Eur. powers until the British regained it in 1814. In 1958 it joined the short-lived Federation of the West Indies and formed part of the Br. Windward Isls. colony until 1959, when the colony was dissolved. In 1967, Saint Lucia became one of the 6 Associated States of the West Indies, with internal self-govt., and in 1979 it gained full independence. The isl. was badly damaged in 1980 and 1994 by hurricanes and has also suffered from significant political unrest and economic problems due to a drop in banana prices in world markets.

Saint Lucia Channel (LOO-shuh), SE West Indies, bet. Martinique (N) and St. Lucia (S); c.20 mi/32 km wide.

Saint Lucie (LOO-see), county (□ 688 sq mi/1,782 sq km; 1990 pop. 150,171), E central Fla., on the Atlantic (E); ⊙ Fort Pierce; 27°22′N 80°26′W. Largely a swampy lowland area, with towns along coast; bordered E by a barrier beach enclosing Indian R. lagoon. Rapid urban growth since 1980 as part of Fla.'s booming "Treasure Coast." Citrus-fruit and agr. region, with some fishing; cattle, poultry. Formed 1905.

Saint Lucie (LOO-see), village (1990 pop. 584), St. Lucie

co., E central Fla., 3 mi/4.8 km N of Fort Pierce; 27°30′N 80°20′W.

Saint Lucie Canal (LOO-see), Martin co., E central Fla., extends c.30 mi/48 km ENE from L. Okeechobee at Port Mayaca to St. Lucie R. near Stuart on the Atlantic Ocean; has 2 locks and is crossed by bridges.

Saint Lucie Inlet (LOO-see), narrow passage through barrier beach, E central Fla., 5 mi/8 km ESE of Stuart, connects mouth of St. Lucie R. and S end of Indian R. lagoon (part of Intracoastal Waterway) with the Atlantic.

Saint Lucie River (LOO-see), c.35 mi/56 km long, E central Fla.; rises in swamp c.10 mi/16 km WSW of Fort Pierce; flows E and S into the Atlantic through St. Lucie Inlet at S end of Indian R. lagoon. Its lower course, an estuary, receives the St. Lucie Canal near Stuart.

Saint Ludger (suhnt LUH-juhr), village (1991 pop. 180), S Que., Canada, on Chaudière R., 15 mi/24 km NE of Megantic; 45°45′N 70°42′W. Dairying; lumbering.

Saint Malo (se mah-LO), village, S Man., Canada, on Rat R., 40 mi/64 km S of Winnipeg; 45°12′N 71°30′W. Dairying; grain.

Saint Marc des Carrières (se mahrk dai kah-ree-ER), village (1991 pop. 2,844), S Que., Canada, 33 mi/53 km NE of Trois Rivières; 46°41′N 72°02′W. Limestone quarrying; lumbering; dairying.

Saint Margaret's Bay, town, Portland parish, E Jamaica on N coast, on RR, 5 mi/8 km WNW of Port Antonio; 18°12′N 76°31′W. In fruit-growing region (bananas, coconuts, cacao).

Saint Marie, Ill.: see SAINTE MARIE.

Saint Maries, town (1990 pop. 2,442), ⊙ Benewah co., N Idaho, SE of Coeur d'Alene L., at confluence of St. Joe and St. Maries rivers, 45 mi/72 km SE of Spokane, Wash.; 47°19′N 116°34′W. Elev. 2,216 ft/675 m. Lumber town; mfg. Hq. St. Joe Natl. Forest, units of St. Joe Natl. Forest to E and S. At edge of Coeur d'Alene Indian Reservation. Named for mission founded here (1842) by Father De Smet. Settled 1888, inc. 1902.

Saint Maries River, c.50 mi/80 km long, N Idaho; rises in SW corner of Shoshone co., flows NW to St. Joe R. at St. Maries.

Saint Marks, town, Meriwether co., W Ga., 13 mi/21 km NE of La Grange; 33°07′N 84°49′W.

Saint Martin, parish (□ 738 sq mi/1,911 sq km; 1990 pop. 43,978), S La.; ⊙ St. Martinville; 30°07′N 91°50′W. Divided into 2 sects., separated by part of Iberia parish; traversed by Atchafalaya and Grand rivers and Bayou Teche; contains several lakes, L. Palourde on boundary in extreme SE corner. Much of parish is in the Atchafalaya Basin, esp. in E and S. Agr. (rice, soybeans, sugarcane, sweet potatoes, cabbage, peppers; cattle, horses, hogs, exotic fowl), crawfish, catfish, alligators; logging, mfg. (food prods., apparel, chemicals); natural gas, oil; fur trapping. Includes Longfellow-Evangeline State Commemorative Area N of St. Martinsville; part of Allakanas Island State Wildlife area in W of S section. Formed 1807 as Attakapas parish; name changed to St. Martin in 1811.

Saint Martin, uninc. town (1990 pop. 6,349), Jackson co., SE Miss., residential suburb 3 mi/4.8 km NNE of Biloxi and 2 mi/3.2 km E of D'Iberville, on Biloxi Bay; 30°26′N 88°52′W.

Saint Martin 1 village (1990 pop. 274), Stearns co., central Minn., 25 mi/40 km WSW of St. Cloud, near Sauk R.; 45°30′N 94°39′W. Agr. (grain, soybeans; livestock; dairying); mfg. **2** village (1990 pop. 141), Brown co., SW Ohio, 15 mi/24 km W of Hillsboro; 39°13′N 83°53′W.

Saint Martin (sang mahr-TANG), Du. *Sint Maarten*, island (□ 37 sq mi/96 sq km), Fr. West Indies, one of the Leeward Isls.; 18°04′N 63°04′W. Since its occupation in 1648 by the Dutch and the French, it has been divided. The N part (□ 20 sq mi/52 sq km; 1982 pop. 8,072), with the ⊙ at Marigot, is administered by Guadeloupe, which is an overseas dept. of France; the S part (□ 17 sq mi/44 sq km; 1989 est. pop. 29,500) belongs to the Neth. Antilles (see CURAÇAO); ⊙ Philipsburg. Nearby Maho Beach and Mullet Bay are adjacent resort-casinos. Both Marigot and Philipsburg are free ports. A hilly, scenic isl. provided with good harbors, including Mullet Bay, it is a popular tourist resort. Isl. devastated by Hurricane Luis (Sept. 1995), which demolished the airport (now again operational) on the Fr. side near Grande Case.

Saint Martin Bay, inlet of L. Huron, SE Upper Peninsula, Mich., lying N of Mackinac Isl.; bounded N by Mackinac co., E by peninsula terminating at St. Martin Point; c.7 mi/11.3 km long, 5 mi/8 km wide; 46°00'N 84°37'W. Small St. Martin Isls. are in bay. Receives Carp R.

Saint Martins, village (1991 pop. 411), S N.B., Canada, on the Bay of Fundy, 26 mi/42 km ENE of St. John; 45°21'N 65°32'W. Fishing (lobster, clams, sardines, declining cod). Former shipbuilding center. Manganese deposits nearby.

Saint Martins, village (1990 pop. 717), Cole co., central Mo., commuting suburb 8 mi/12.9 km W of Jefferson City; 38°36'N 92°19'W. Residential.

Saint Martinville, city (1994 pop. 8,063), ⊙ St. Martin parish, S La., on navigable Bayou Teche, 13 mi/21 km ESE of Lafayette; 30°07'N 91°50'W. In agr. area; mfg. (food prods., concrete, apparel, asphalt); commercial fisheries (catfish, crawfish, alligators); oil wells. Hosts annual Zydeco Festival. Settled c.1760, it became a resort during steamboat era. Supposedly the site of the Evangeline romance, commemorated by Longfellow Evangeline State Commemorative Area, just N. Le Peptit Paris Mardis Gras Mus. La Fausse Pointe State Park to SE.

Saint Mary, parish (□ 23 sq mi/60 sq km; 1991 pop. 5,303), SW Antigua isl., Antigua and Barbuda Republic; 17°03'N 61°52'W. Mountainous parish with agr. (sweet potatoes, fruit); cattle. Beach resorts.

Saint Mary, parish (1991 pop. 107,502), Middlesex co., N Jamaica; ⊙ Port Maria; 18°09'N 77°03'W–18°24'N 76°42'W. Situated bet. Portland (E) and St. Ann (W) parishes. Watered by Wag Water R. Several bays along coast, with ports of Port Maria, Annotto Bay, and Oracabessa mainly shipping bananas. Other prods. include coconuts, cacao, coffee, citrus fruit, vegetables, breadfruit, pimento, annatto; livestock; logwood. Crossed by Kingston–Port Antonio RR. Lighthouse at Galina Point; 18°25'N 76°55'W.

Saint Mary, parish (□ 605 sq mi/1,567 sq km; 1990 pop. 58,086), S La.; ⊙ Franklin; 29°48'N 91°31'W. On the Gulf of Mexico Coast, and bounded W and S by West Cote Blanche, East Cote Blanche, and Atchafalaya bays, and NE by Grand L. (widening of Atchafalaya R.); crossed by Intracoastal Waterway; drained by Atchafalaya R.; part of L. Palourde in NE corner, Grand L. in NE (former channel of Atchafalaya) and Bayou Teche. Agr. (soybeans, sugarcane; cattle, hogs). Salt mines near coast. Natural gas, oil; fisheries (crawfish, oysters, crabs, alligators). Seafood canning, sugar refining, mfg. (carbon black, minerals, structural metal); shipbuilding; sport fishing, hunting. Includes Belle Isle and Cote Blanche Isl. (salt domes), and Chitimacha Indian Reservation in N, near L. Fausse Pointe. Part of Cypremont Point State Park in W; part of Allakanas State Wildlife Area in NE; Atchafalaya Delta State Wildlife Area off S coast. Formed 1811.

Saint Mary, city (1990 pop. 461), Ste. Genevieve co., E Mo., near Mississippi R., 9 mi/14.5 km SE of Ste. Genevieve. Grain mills; bridge to Kaskaskia Isl., Heavily damaged by flood of 1993. Often referred to as St. Marys.

Saint Mary, village (1990 pop. 225), Marion co., central Ky., 6 mi/9.7 km W of Lebanon. Agr. (tobacco, grain; livestock). Seat of St. Mary's Col.

Saint Mary Bay, inlet of the Atlantic, W N.S., Canada, 5 mi/8 km SE of Digby; 35 mi/56 km long, 4 mi/6 km–12 mi/19 km wide. NW shore of bay is formed by Digby Neck, Long Isl., and Brier Isl. On mainland shore is Weymouth.

Saint Mary, Cape 1 promontory, SE N.F., Canada, on SE side of entrance of Placentia Bay, at SW extremity of Avalon Peninsula, 33 mi/53 km SSW of Argentia; 46°50'N 54°12'W. Lighthouse. **2** W extremity of N.S. mainland, Canada, at entrance to St. Mary Bay, 18 mi/29 km NNW of Yarmouth; 44°05'N 66°13'W. Lighthouse.

Saint Mary Lake, Mont.: see GLACIER NATIONAL PARK.

Saint Mary River, 25 mi/40 km long, E N.S., Canada; rises in 2 branches in Cobequid Mts. East R. St. Mary, 50 mi/80 km long, rises 7 mi/11 km S of New Glasgow, flows ESE; West R. St. Mary, 50 mi/80 km long, rises 20 mi/32 km SW of New Glasgow, flows E. Branches unite 10 mi/16 km NNW of Sherbrooke, and St. Mary R. flows SSE, past Sherbrooke, to the Atlantic 10 mi/16 km SE of Sherbrooke.

Saint Mary River, c.150 mi/241 km long, in NW Mont. and SW Alta.; rises at Gunsight Mt., at Continental Divide, W Galcier co., NW Mont., at center of Glacier Natl. Park; flows NE, through Gunsight L., near its source, then through St. Mary L., exits Glacier Natl. Park, passes village of St. Mary and through lower St. Mary L., crosses into Alta., Canada, continues past Cardston and through St. Mary Reservoir and Dam to Oldman R., 6 mi/9.7 km SW of Lethbridge. Forms E boundary of Blood Indian Reserve from Cardston to its mouth.

Saint Mary-of-the-Woods, village (1990 pop. 850), Vigo co., W Ind., suburb 4 mi/6.4 km NW of Terre Haute. Site of Saint Mary-of-the-Woods Col. Village called St. Marys.

Saint Marys, town (1991 pop. 5,496), S Ont., Canada, on North Thames R., 11 mi/18 km SW of Stratford. Woodworking; dairying; lumbering; cement making.

Saint Mary's, village (1991 pop. 637), SE N.F., Canada, on E side of St. Mary's Bay, 60 mi/97 km SW of St. John's. Fishing; lumbering.

Saint Marys, county (□ 764 sq mi/1,979 sq km; 1990 pop. 75,974). S Md.; ⊙ Leonardtown; 38°13'N 76°32'W. Tidewater peninsula, bounded NE by Patuxent R., E by Chesapeake Bay, S by Potomac (forms Va. line here); S tip is Point Lookout. Tidewater agr. area (chiefly tobacco), with some lumbering and commericial fishing; SE portion, suffering from soil erosion, is sparsely settled and little cultivated. Small resorts; hunting, water sports. Includes Patuxent Naval Air Test Center at Cedar Point. As 1st (March 1634) region of settlement in Md., it was named in honor of Virgin Mary by the colonists who had landed on the Feast of the Assumption (1634). Many points of historic interest (notably St. Marys City). Much of its land is still held under patents of the Lords Baltimore. Formed in 1637.

Saint Marys 1 city (1990 pop. 8,187), Camden co., extreme SE Ga., 30 mi/48 km S of Brunswick, on St. Marys R. (forms Fla. state line here), near the Atlantic; 30°46'N 81°35'W. Mfg. includes pulp and paper milling, plastics, shrimp canning; lumber. Kings Bay Submarine Base is E and led to rapid growth in the area in the 1980s. Southernmost town in U.S. when Fla. was still a Span. possession. Access point to Cumberland Isl. Natl. Seashore. Inc. 1802. **2** city (1990 pop. 1,791), Pottawatomie co., NE Kansas, on Kansas R., 22 mi/35 km WNW of Topeka; 39°11'N 96°04'W. In livestock and grain area. Here is St. Mary's Seminary, outgrowth of R.C. mission (est. 1848) to Pottawatomie Indians. Pottawatomie Indian Reservation to NE (Jackson co.). Laid out as town in 1866, inc. as city in 1869. **3** city (1990 pop. 8,441), Auglaize co., W Ohio, 19 mi/31 km SW of Lima, on St. Marys R., near Grand L.; 40°32'N 84°23'W. Lake resort. Mfg. (food prods., rubber goods, furniture, plastics, paper prods.). State fish hatchery.

Saint Marys 1 town (1990 pop. 113), Warren co., S central Iowa, 10 mi/16 km WSW of Indianola; 41°18'N 93°43'W. In agr. area. **2** town (1990 pop. 2,148), ⊙ Pleasants co., NW W.Va., 21 mi/34 km NE of Parkersburg, on the Ohio R. (bridged), at mouth of Middle Isl. Creek; 39°23'N 81°12'W. Agr. (grain); cattle. Coal and natural gas area. Mfg. (oil refining, lumber, printing and publishing). Settled c.1850.

Saint Marys, borough (1990 pop. 5,511), Elk co., N central Pa., 36 mi/58 km S of Bradford, on Elk Creek; 41°25'N 78°33'W. Agr. area (hay; livestock; dairying); mfg. (lumber, graphite prods., electrical equip., printing and publishing, wooden prods., machinery, industrial gases, carbon prods.). Bendigo and Elk state parks to N; parts of Elk State Forest to SE and N, Moshannon State Forest to S, Elk State Forest to N. Settled 1842 by Ger. Catholics, laid out 1844, inc. 1848.

Saint Marys, river, c.175 mi/282 km long, Ga. and Fla.; rises in the Okefenokee Swamp, SE Ga.; flows with a great S bend, E to the Atlantic Ocean; 30°25'N 82°12'W. It forms part of the Ga.-Fla. state line. The lower river is dredged for navigation.

Saint Mary's Bay, inlet of the Atlantic, SE N.F., Canada, on S coast of Avalon Peninsula, 50 mi/80 km SW of St. John's; 40 mi/64 km long, 25 mi/40 km wide at entrance; 46°55'N 53°45'W. Contains Colinet Isls. On shore are several fishing settlements.

Saint Marys City, village (1990 pop. 3,200), St. Marys co., S Md., on St. Marys R. Eng. colonists, after purchasing a small village from Native Americans, renamed it St. Marys and built Fort St. George. The 1st state assembly met here in 1635, and the village was the colonial capital until the govt. was moved to Annapolis in 1695. The original capitol bldg. was converted to a courthouse, and later, to a chapel. In 1829, it was dismantled and the original bricks used to build Trinity Chapel. This is the location of the oldest Catholic parish in Eng.-speaking N. Amer. Site of St. Mary's Col. Est. 1634 as Md.'s 1st town.

Saint Mary's Park, residential section of S Bronx borough of N.Y. city, SE N.Y.

Saint Mary's Point, village (1990 pop. 339), Washington co., E Minn., residential suburb 14 mi/23 km ESE of St. Paul, 1 mi/1.6 km NE of Afton, on St. Croix R. (St. Croix L.); 44°54'N 92°45'W.

Saint Marys River 1 c.22 mi/35 km long, in S Md.; rises in SE St. Marys co.; flows SE, past St. Marys City c.8 mi/12.9 km above its mouth. Its estuary is c.2 mi/3.2 km wide at the mouth. **2** c.100 mi/161 km long, in W Ohio and E Ind.; rises in Auglaize co., Ohio; flows NW, past St. Marys, Mendon, Rockford, and Willshire (Ohio) into Ind., past Decatur, to Fort Wayne, where it joins St. Joseph R. to form the Maumee; 41°05'N 85°07'W. **3** 63 mi/101 km long; flowing generally SE from L. Superior to L. Huron and forming part of the U.S.-Can. border. The cities of Sault Sainte Marie, Mich., and Sault Sainte Marie, Ontario, are on the river. The rapids here are circumvented by the Sault Sainte Marie Canals. The r. and canal are frozen for about 5 months each year.

Saint Matthew Island, W Alaska, in Bering Sea, 170 mi/274 km WNW of Nunivak Isl.; 22 mi/35 km long, 1 mi/1.6 km–3 mi/4.8 km wide; 60°22'N 172°25'W. Rocky and uninhabited isl. is game sanctuary; rises to 1,500 ft/457 m.

Saint Matthews, city (1990 pop. 15,800), Jefferson co., N Ky., residential suburb 5 mi/8 km E of Louisville; 38°15'N 85°38'W. Mfg. (printing). Bowman Field airport to S. Inc. 1950.

Saint Matthews, town (1990 pop. 2,345), ⊙ Calhoun co., central S.C., 13 mi/21 km NNE of Orangeburg; 33°39'N 80°46'W. Mfg. includes machinery, automotive parts, plastic prods.; agr. area for vegetables, cotton, grain, soybeans, pecans; livestock. L. Marion reservoir to E. Settled in early 18th cent.

Saint Maurice (se mo-REES), county (□ 1,820 sq mi/4,714 sq km), S Que., Canada, extends NW from the St. Lawrence; ⊙ Yamachiche; 47°00'N 73°30'W.

Saint Maurice (se mo-REES), river, c.325 mi/520 km long, Que., Canada; rises in the Laurentian Mts. and flows SE and S to the St. Lawrence R. at Trois Rivières. It passes La Tuque, Grand' Mère, and Shawinigan Falls, where waterfalls furnish hydroelectric power. The river is important for the transportation of lumber.

Saint Meinrad, village, Spencer co., SW Ind., on small Anderson R., 24 mi/39 km NE of Rockport. Mfg. (printing). Seat of a Benedictine archabbey and seminary.

Saint Michael, village, central Alta., Canada, 40 mi/64 km ENE of Edmonton. Mixed farming; dairying.

Saint Michael 1 town (1990 pop. 2,506), Wright co., E Minn., on Crow R., 26 mi/42 km NW of Minneapolis and 11 mi/18 km E of Buffalo; 45°12'N 93°39'W. Dairy prods.; mfg. (fabricated metal prods.). Crow Hassan

Park Reserve to SE; Pelican L. to W. **2** uninc. town (1990 pop. 900), Adams township, Cambria co., W central Pa., 8 mi/12.9 km E of Johnstown, on South Fork of Little Conemaugh R.; 40°20′N 78°46′W. Agr. (hay; dairying). Johnstown Flood Natl. Memorial 1 mi/1.6 km to NW.

Saint Michael, village (1990 pop. 295), W Alaska, on SE shore of Norton Sound, 110 mi/177 km NE of mouth of Yukon R., on a deltaic peninsula (of Nunavulnuk R.), and 120 mi/193 km SE of Nome; 63°29′N 162°02′W. Has school. Had Amer. army fort in 1867. Was port for the Yukon R. prior to completion of Alaska RR in 1923. Est. 1831 by Wrangel as trading post of Rus. Amer. Company.

Saint Michaels, town (1990 pop. 1,301), Talbot co., E Md., on the Eastern Shore, 17 mi/27 km NNW of Cambridge, on narrow neck bet. Miles R. and inlet of Choptank R.; 38°47′N 76°13′W. Oyster dredging and fishing center; summer resort, with yachting. Named for St. Michael's Protestant Episcopal Church (built in the 1660s), it was a shipbulding center until timber became scarce and Baltimore increased in importance during the 1800s. The armed barge *Experiment* was outfitted here in 1781 to protect the bay. As Br. ships approached in 1813, lights were placed as decoys on trees so cannonballs passed harmlessly over the town; for this reason, town was nicknaned "the town that fooled the British." Maritime mus.

Saint Michel de Bellechasse (se mee-SHEHL duh behl-SHAHS), village, S Que., Canada, on the St. Lawrence, opposite Île d'Orléans, 16 mi/26 km ENE of Quebec. Lumbering; dairying; pigs.

Saint Moïse (se mo-EEZ), village (1991 pop. 667), E Que., Canada, at base of Gaspé Peninsula, 25 mi/40 km SW of Matane; 48°32′N 67°51′W. Lumbering; dairying.

Saint Nazianz, village (1990 pop. 693), Manitowoc co., E Wis., 14 mi/23 km WSW of Manitowoc; 44°00′N 87°55′W. Mfg. (farm equip.). Seat of Salvatorian Seminary (R.C.). Settled 1854 by colony of Ger. Christian communists.

Saint Nicolas, Cape (sang nee-ko-LAH), NW Haiti, on Windward Passage, 2.5 mi/4 km SW of Môle-Saint-Nicolas; 19°48′N 73°25′W.

Saint Norbert (se nor-BAIR), village, S Man., Canada, on Red R., 10 mi/16 km S of Winnipeg. Farming; grain; livestock; honey processing. Site of Trappist monastery of Notre Dame des Prairies.

Saint Octave (se tok-TAHV), village, E Que., Canada, near the St. Lawrence, 23 mi/37 km NE of Rimouski. Lumbering; dairying.

Saint Olaf, town (1990 pop. 111), Clayton co., NE Iowa, 6 mi/9.7 km N of Elkader; 42°55′N 91°23′W. In agr. and dairying region; feed milling.

Saint Ours (se TOOR), town (1991 pop. 560), S Que., Canada, on Richelieu R., 12 mi/19 km S of Sorel; 45°53′N 73°09′W. Mfg., woodworking, milling; market in dairying region.

Saint Pacôme (seh pah-KOM), village (1991 pop. 1,880), SE Que., Canada, near the St. Lawrence, 35 mi/56 km SSW of Rivière du Loup; 47°25′N 69°57′W. Dairying; lumbering; pigs.

Saint Paris, village (1990 pop. 1,842), Champaign co., W central Ohio, 11 mi/18 km W of Urbana; 40°07′N 83°57′W. Honey, grain. Settled 1813.

Saint Pascal (se pahs-KAHL), town (1991 pop. 2,578), ⊙ Kamouraska co., SE Que., Canada, near the St. Lawrence, 25 mi/40 km SSW of Rivière du Loup; 47°31′N 69°49′W. Dairying; lumbering; pigs.

Saint Patrick, county (☐ 260.8 sq mi/675.5 sq km; 1990 pop. 121,358), SW Trinidad, Trinidad and Tobago, bordering on the Gulf of Paria (N) and the Serpent's Mouth (S); 10°10′N 61°35′W.

Saint Patrick Channel, arm of Great Bras d'Or, NE N.S., Canada, in central part of Cape Breton Isl.; 20 mi/32 km long, up to 4 mi/6 km wide. On N side of entrance is village of Baddeck.

Saint Paul (se pol) or **Saint Paul de Métis** (se pol duh mai-TEE), town (1991 pop. 4,881), E Alta., Canada, near small Upper Therien L., 50 mi/80 km NNW of Vermilion. Grain elevators, fruit canning, lumbering; dairying; mfg. of chemicals, castings.

Saint Paul, parish (☐ 19 sq mi/49 sq km; 1991 pop. 6,117), S Antigua isl., Antigua and Barbuda Republic; 17°02′N 61°46′W. Agr. areas (vegetables; cattle). Location of Eng. Harbour historic and tourist sites.

Saint Paul, city (1990 pop. 272,235), ⊙ Minn. and Ramsey co., E Minn., on bluffs along the Mississippi R., 8 mi/12.9 km ESE of Minneapolis; 44°57′N 93°05′W. RR hub. Mfg. (electrical equip., fabricated sheet metal, construction equip., paper prods., printing and publishing, storage tanks, medical equip., food, motor vehicles, consumer goods, plastic prods., oil refining); financial center. At a large E-W bend in the Mississippi (river flows through S part of city): major river port facilities in SE, on downstream of river. Bounded by city of Minneapolis to W, forming the Twin Cities metropolitan area. Minnesota R. enters Mississippi R. to SW, St. Croix R. to SE. St. Croix and Lower St. Croix Natl. Scenic Riverway to E, on St. Croix R. (Wis. state border). A fur-trading post was est. (early 1800s) at the confluence of the Mississippi and Minnesota rivers in what is now the historic village of Mendota (6 mi/9.7 km SW of St. Paul), and Fort Snelling was built here. Traders, missionaries, and explorers were the 1st inhabitants; settlers came from the E after treaties with the Native Americans officially opened the area to farming and lumbering. By 1823 the landing at the head of navigation on the Mississippi was an important debarkation point and trading port. In 1841, Father Galtier established St. Paul Church, from which the city (plotted along the river in 1846) took its name. St. Paul became territorial capital in 1849 and state capital when Minnesota was admitted to the Union in 1858. It was a booming river port and transportation center, esp. after the arrival of the RR in 1862. Later it became the center of the RR empire of James J. Hill. Like many of the upper Mississippi R. towns, St. Paul's oldest streets are narrow and crooked, conforming to the hills and to the river frontage. Keller-Phalen (NE); Como Regional Park (NW); Battle Creek Regional Park (E); Pigs Eye Park with Pigs Eye L., backwater of Mississippi R. (SE); numerous natural lakes, especially to N; Como Park Zoo in NW; Minnesota Zoo in suburban Apple Valley, 12 mi/19 km to S; Afton Alps Ski Area to E. A Native Amer. mounds park is here. An annual Winter Carnival is held in the city, and the state fairgrounds are in the Midway dist., near Falcon Heights, bet. St. Paul and Minneapolis. The capitol, completed in 1904 and designed by Cass Gilbert, was modeled after St. Peter's in Rome. Near the capitol are the Cathedral of St. Paul and the St. Paul Arts and Science Center. In the concourse of the city hall and county courthouse (1932) is a notable peace monument. Other points of interest in the area are Fort Snelling State Park, at mouth of Mississippi R., the Sibley House Mus. (1835), home of the 1st territorial governor, Minn. Transportation Mus., Minn. Historic Center, and Ordway Music Theatre. St. Paul's many educational institutions include Metro State Univ. Technical Vocational Inst., Bethel Col., The Col. of St. Catherine, Univ. of St. Thomas, Concordia Col., Hamline Univ., Macalester Col., William Mitchell Col. of Law, several theological seminaries, and a branch of the Univ. of Minnesota. Minneapolis–St. Paul Internatl. Airport to SW; St. Paul Downtown (Holman Field) in S part of city. Inc. 1854.

Saint Paul 1 town, on co. line bet. Decatur and Shelby cos., SE central Ind., on the Flatrock R., 10 mi/16 km SE of Shelbyville. In agr. area; mfg. (meat packing, crushed stone). **2** town (1990 pop. 120), Lee co., SE Iowa, 15 mi/24 km NW of Madison; 40°46′N 91°31′W. In livestock area. **3** town (1990 pop. 2,009), ⊙ Howard co., E central Nebr., 20 mi/32 km N of Grand Isl., near confluence of North Loup and Middle Loup rivers; 41°12′N 98°27′W. Trade and shipping center for agr. area; grain; livestock; dairy and poultry prods. North Loup State Wayside Area to N. Founded 1871. **4** town (1990 pop. 1,007), Russell and Wise cos., SW Va., on Clinch R., 17 mi/27 km E of Norton; 36°54′N 82°18′W. RR junction; mfg. (furniture, clothing, beverages, limestone processing); agr. area (tobacco, alfalfa; livestock; dairying); coal area, limestone quarrying.

Saint Paul 1 village (1990 pop. 88), Madison co., NW Ark., 26 mi/42 km SE of Fayetteville, on White R. in the Ozarks; 35°49′N 93°45′W. Mfg. (wooden prods.). Ozark Natl. Forest to S. **2** village (1990 pop. 687), Neosho co., SE Kansas, on Neosho R., 14 mi/23 km NNE of Parsons; 37°31′N 95°10′W. Shipping point for livestock-raising and farming area. Gas wells nearby. Neosho Waterfowl Refuge to E; Neosho State Fishing L. to SW. **3** village (1990 pop. 322), Marion co., NW Oregon, 18 mi/29 km N of Salem, near Willamette R.; 45°12′N 122°58′W. Agr. (grain, fruit, nuts, berries; poultry); dairy prods. Champoeg State Park to NE. **4** village (1990 pop. 415), Collin co., N Texas, residential suburb 23 mi/37 km NE of Dallas, 10 mi/16 km E of Plano, near SW shore of L. Lavon reservoir; 33°02′N 96°32′W. Urban growth area. Recreation.

Saint Paul de Métis, Canada: see SAINT PAUL.

Saint Paul du Nord (se pol duh NOR), village (1991 pop. 789), E Que., Canada, on the St. Lawrence, 30 mi/48 km WNW of Rimouski; 48°34′N 69°14′W. Lumbering center.

Saint Paul Island, in Cabot Strait, bet. the Atlantic and the Gulf of St. Lawrence, off NE N.S., Canada, 16 mi/26 km NE of Cape North, Cape Breton Isl.; 3 mi/5 km long, 1 mi/2 km wide; 47°12′N 60°09′W.

Saint Paul Island, Pribilof Isls., SW Alaska, in Bering Sea; 14 mi/23 km long, 2 mi/3.2 km–8 mi/12.9 km wide; 57°11′N 170°16′W. Rises to 665 ft/203 m. St. Paul village in S.

Saint Paul Park, town (1990 pop. 4,965), Washington co., E Minn., on Mississippi R. (bridged), suburb 9 mi/14.5 km SSE of St. Paul; 44°50′N 92°59′W. RR junction. Oil refinery in area; mfg. (gasoline and jet fuel, boat accessories, food).

Saint Paulin (se po-LE), village (1991 pop. 1,556), S Que., Canada, 23 mi/37 km W of Trois Rivières. Dairying; pigs.

Saint Pauls, town (1990 pop. 1,992), Robeson co., SE N.C., 18 mi/29 km S of Fayetteville, near Big Swamp R.; 34°48′N 78°58′W. Agr. area (grain, tobacco, soybeans; cattle, hogs; dairying); mfg. (yarn and textile prods., apparel, turkey processing).

Saint Paul's Church, historic site, Manhattan, SE N.Y. Authorized 1943, 18th-cent. church associated with the events leading to the arrest of John Peter Zenger; link in Amer. architectural history.

Saint Pete Beach, town (☐ 19 sq mi/49 sq km; 1990 pop. 9,200), Pinellas co., W central Fla., 7 mi/11.3 km SW of St. Petersburg; 27°42′N 82°46′W.

Saint Peter, parish (☐ 13 sq mi/34 sq km; 1991 pop. 3,622), NE Antigua isl., Antigua and Barbuda Republic; 17°05′N 61°45′W. Largely an agr. area (fruits, vegetables).

Saint Peter, town (1990 pop. 9,421), ⊙ Nicollet co., S Minn., on Minnesota R., 11 mi/18 km N of Mankato; 44°19′N 93°57′W. Agr. (grain, soybeans, peas; livestock; dairying); mfg. (aluminum prods., printing and publishing, electronic prods.). Gustavus Adolphus Col. and state mental hosp. are here. Traverse des Sioux State Historic Marker to NW, on site of which treaty was signed (1851) with Sioux Indians. Numerous small lakes to SE. Municipal airport to N. Settled 1853, inc. 1865.

Saint Peter, village (1990 pop. 353), Fayette co., S central Ill., 15 mi/24 km ESE of Vandalia; 38°52′N 88°50′W. In agr. area.

Saint Peter, Lake (☐ 130 sq mi/337 sq km), S Que., Canada, expansion of the St. Lawrence, extending 30 mi/48 km ENE from Sorel almost to Trois Rivières; 9 mi/14 km wide. Receives St. Francis, Yamaska, Nicolet, and several smaller rivers. At SW end of lake are several isls.

Saint Peter, Point, cape at E end of Gaspé Peninsula, E Que., Canada, on the Gulf of St. Lawrence, on S side of Gaspé Bay, 20 mi/32 km SE of Gaspé; 48°37′N 64°10′W. Lighthouse.

Saint Peters 1 village, E N.S., Canada, S Cape Breton Isl., on canal (bridge) linking Bras d'Or L. and the Atlantic, 23 mi/37 km E of Port Hawkesbury. Fishing port. In early 17th cent. it was fishing and trading station, later a fort. **2** or **Saint Peters Bay**, village (1991 pop.

284), NE P.E.I., Canada, at head of St. Peters Bay of the Gulf of St. Lawrence, 30 mi/48 km ENE of Charlottetown. Fisheries.

Saint Peters, city (1990 pop. 45,779), St. Charles co., E Mo., 7 mi/11.3 km W of St. Charles; 38°46′N 90°36′W. Grew from small town to sprawling residential city during 1970s. This quiet village with Catholic church sitting on a hill was transformed into a sprawling urban mass "overnight," competing with neighboring towns, especially St. Charles, for land to annex. Mfg. (fabricated metal prods., household prods., foam prods.). Regional shopping mall. Hosp.

Saint Peters Bay, Canada: see SAINT PETERS, P.E.I.

Saint Peter's Island, islet in the Atlantic, E N.S., Canada, off S Cape Breton Isl., 7 mi/11 km SE of St. Peters.

Saint Peters Island, islet at entrance of Hillsborough Bay, S P.E.I., Canada, 8 mi/13 km SSW of Charlottetown; 46°07′N 63°11′W. Lighthouse.

Saint Petersburg, city (□ 132 sq mi/342 sq km; 1990 pop. 238,629), Pinellas co., W central Fla., on Tampa Bay and the Gulf of Mexico, at the S end of the Pinellas peninsula; 27°45′N 82°38′W. A port of entry with a large harbor, it is a popular winter resort and year-round residential community. It is also one of Fla.'s largest retirement centers. Mfg. includes boats, motor vehicles, appliances, and electronic equip.; citrus-fruit and commercial-fishing industries. Eckerd Col., the Stetson Univ. Col. of Law, a junior col., a campus of the Univ. of Southern Fla., and a military acad. are here, as well as an airport and a U.S. Coast Guard base. Bridges cross the bay to Tampa and the Sunshine Skyway Bridge links the peninsula to Bradenton. Settled in the mid-1800s, inc. 1892.

Saint Petersburg, borough (1990 pop. 349), Clarion co., W central Pa., 18 mi/29 km S of Oil City, bet. Clarion R. (S) and Allegheny R. (W); 41°09′N 79°39′W. Agr. (corn, hay, potatoes; livestock; dairying).

Saint Philip, Fort, La.: see TRIUMPH.

Saint Phillip, parish (□ 17 sq mi/44 sq km; 1991 pop. 2,964), E Antigua isl., Antigua and Barbuda Republic; 17°03′N 61°42′W. Agr. areas (fruits, vegetables) around Willikies. Beach resorts along SE coast.

Saint Pie (se PEE), village (1991 pop. 2,083), S Que., Canada, on tributary of Yamaska R., 9 mi/14 km SSE of St. Hyacinthe; 45°30′N 72°54′W. Woodworking, dairying; cattle, pigs.

Saint Pie de Guire (se pee duh GIER), village (1991 pop. 500), ⊙ Yamaska co., S Que., Canada, near St. Francis R., 18 mi/29 km ESE of Sorel. Dairying; pigs.

Saint Pierre and Miquelon (se pyer and mee-kuh-lon), Fr. territorial collectivity (□ 93 sq mi/242 sq km; 1993 est. pop. 6,277), consisting of 9 small isls., S of Newfoundland, Canada, in the Gulf of St. Lawrence; ⊙ St. Pierre. St. Pierre is c.180 mi/290 km WSW of St. John's, Newfoundland (and is separated from N.F. by a c.15 mi/24 km wide channel). Because of the influence of the Gulf Stream, St. Pierre's port is free of ice throughout the year. St. Pierre isl. has 7 islet dependencies: Grand Colombier and Petit Colombier just NE; Île aux Marins (E); Île aux Pigeons; Île aux Vainqueurs (Lazaret); Île aux Moules; and Île aux Massacres. Miquelon (□ 83 sq mi/215 sq km) is the largest isl. Ownership of Île Verte (lighthouse) is shared with Canada. The pop. consists mainly of fishermen, most of whom live in or near the capital. St. Pierre is an important cod-fishing station (canning and salting); and is connected by cable with Amer. mainland and Europe. The isls. are barren, rocky, and often fog-bound, but their proximity to the Grand Banks makes them a valuable base for fishermen. Probably 1st settled by Basques, they were colonized by France in 1604. They were taken by the British (1713) but returned to France in 1763; twice retaken by the British, they were restored to France in 1814, with the provision that they be unfortified. They were granted local autonomy in 1935, became an overseas dept. in 1976, and reclassified as a territorial collectivity in 1985 to comply with EC trade regulations. The offshore limits to fishing rights have been a source of diplomatic dispute bet. France and Canada since the early 1960s.

Saint Pierre d'Orléans (se pyer dor-lai-A), village, S Que., Canada, on NW shore of the Île d'Orléans, on the St. Lawrence, 10 mi/16 km NE of Quebec. Dairying; vegetables; poultry.

Saint Pierre-Jolys (se pyer–zho-LEE), village, SE Man., Canada, on Joubert Creek, 30 mi/48 km SSE of Winnipeg. Dairying; grain.

Saint Polycarpe (se po-lee-KAHRP), village (1991 pop. 1,640), S Que., Canada, 10 mi/16 km WNW of Valleyfield. Dairying; pigs; potatoes.

Saint Prime (se PREEM), village (1991 pop. 2,522), S central Que., Canada, on W shore of L. St. John, at mouth of Ashuapmuchuan R., 8 mi/13 km NE of Roberval; 48°36′N 72°20′W. Dairying; pigs.

Saint Quentin, village (1986 pop. 2,264), N N.B., Canada, bet. Restigouche and Miramichi rivers. Sawmills and forest-related industries.

Saint Raphael (se rah-fah-EL), village (1991 pop. 1,285), ⊙ Bellechasse co., S Que., Canada, 22 mi/35 km E of Quebec; 46°47′N 70°45′W. Lumbering; dairying.

Saint Raymond (se rai-MO), town (1991 pop. 3,373), S Que., Canada, on Ste. Anne R., 30 mi/48 km W of Quebec; 46°53′N 71°50′W. Paper milling, lumbering; brick mfg.; dairying.

Saint Rédempteur (se rai-damp-TUHR), residential town (1991 pop. 5,862), S Que., Canada, on Chaudière R., opposite Charny, 9 mi/14 km SW of Quebec.

Saint Règis (se REE-jis), village, S Que., Canada, on the St. Lawrence, at mouth of St. Regis R., opposite Cornwall, on N.Y. border. Formerly important Iroquois village, it still has predominantly Indian pop.

Saint Regis (se REE-juhs), village (1990 pop. 650), Mineral co., W Mont., at the confluence of the Clark Fork and St. Regis rivers; 61 mi/98 km WNW of Missoula. Timber. Area surrounded by Lolo Natl. Forest.

Saint Regis Falls, village (1990 pop. 950), Franklin co., N N.Y., on St. Regis R., 18 mi/29 km SW of Malone; 44°41′N 74°32′W. In agr. area.

Saint Regis Indian Reservation (□ 22 sq mi/57 sq km), in Franklin co., N N.Y., and Que. and Ont., Canada, astride the St. Lawrence R., partly in Canada and partly in N.Y.; 44°59′N 74°38′W. The area on the U.S. side is drained by the St. Regis and Racquette rivers. One of 10 Native Amer. reservations in N.Y. state, it is owned by the Mohawk, one of the 6 Nations of the Iroquois Confederacy. The Can. and U.S. sides choose their own separate tribal councils by popular vote. During Prohibition, liquor was funneled into the U.S. via the St. Lawrence R., then known as "Smuggler's Alley." In the early 1990s, the reservation clashed with the state and federal govts. when the Mohawks' 6 gambling casinos here was declared illegal. Several violent clashes ensued bet. the Mohawk and the state police, and 2 Mohawks died. In May 1993 Gov. Mario Cuomo urged the creation of an indigenous police force on the reservation to enforce state law, and in Oct. he agreed to allow casino operation on the reservation similar to the Turning Stone casino near Verona, but under the control of the N.Y. State Race and Wagering Board. The Mohawk approved the pact in Nov., but many issues continue to be unresolved. The reservation is called Akwesasne by the Mohawk.

Saint Regis Park, town (1990 pop. 1,756), Jefferson co., N Ky., residential suburb 7 mi/11.3 km ENE of Louisville; 38°13′N 85°36′W.

Saint Regis River, c.80 mi/129 km long, N N.Y.; rises in the Adirondacks NW of Saranac Lake village; flows generally NW and N, past St. Regis Falls, to the St. Lawrence just N of Hogansburg. Receives West Branch (c.65 mi/105 km long) near Brasher Falls; East Branch (c.35 mi/56 km long) joins above St. Regis Falls. River's headstreams drain Upper St. Regis L. (c.2 mi/3.2 km long, ½ mi–⁸⁄₁₀ km wide), Lower St. Regis L. (1.25 mi/2.01 km long, ½ mi/⁸⁄₁₀ km wide), St Regis Pond (c.2 mi/3.2 km long), and other Adirondack lakes.

Saint Rémi (se rai-MEE), town (1991 pop. 5,768), S Que., Canada, 16 mi/26 km S of Montreal; 45°15′N 73°36′W. In dairying, vegetable-growing region; lumbering; food processing.

Saint Rémi d'Amherst (se rai-MEE DAM-huhrst), village, S Que., Canada, 23 mi/37 km WSW of Ste. Agathe des Monts; 46°01′N 74°46′W. Quartz mining; dairying; poultry raising.

Saint Rémi de Tingwick (se rai-MEE duh TING-wik), village (1991 pop. 443), S Que., Canada, 9 mi/14 km NE of Asbestos. Asbestos mining.

Saint Robert, town (1990 pop. 1,730), Pulaski co., central Mo., 3 mi/4.8 km SE of Waynesville, at N entrance to Fort Leonard Wood army base; 37°49′N 92°09′W. Service center for base. Mark Twain Natl. Forest to S and E. Mfg. (publishing). Tanning and massage parlors; houses of prostitution.

Saint Romuald (se rom-WAHLD), town (1991 pop. 9,830), ⊙ Lévis co., S Que., Canada, on the St. Lawrence, 5 mi/8 km SSW of Quebec. Milling; lumbering. Site of Trappist monastery.

Saint Rosa, village (1990 pop. 75), Stearns co., central Minn., 26 mi/42 km NW of St. Cloud; 45°43′N 94°43′W. Dairying; grain. Birch L. State Forest to NW.

Saint Rose, village, NE N.S., Canada, W Cape Breton Isl., on Gulf of St. Lawrence, 10 mi/16 km NE of Inverness. Coal mining.

Saint Sauveur des Monts (se so-VUHR dai MO), village (1991 pop. 2,545), SW Que., Canada, in the Laurentians, 40 mi/64 km NW of Montreal; 45°54′N 74°10′W. Dairying; skiing resort.

Saint Sébastien de Beauce (se sai-bahs-TYE duh BOS), village, SE Que., Canada, 15 mi/24 km NNW of Megantic. Dairying; lumbering.

Saint Siméon (se see-mai-O), village (1991 pop. 1,020), SE central Que., Canada, on the St. Lawrence, 18 mi/29 km NE of La Malbaie. Lumbering; dairying; vegetables; resort.

Saint Simon de Bagot (se see-MO duh bah-GO), village, S Que., Canada, near Yamaska R., 9 mi/14 km NE of St. Hyacinthe. Dairying; pigs.

Saint Simon de Rimouski (se see-MO ri-MOO-skee), village, SE Que., Canada, on the St. Lawrence, 40 mi/64 km NE of Rivière du Loup; 48°12′N 69°01′W. Dairying; lumbering; pigs.

Saint Simons Island, one of the Sea Isls. (1990 pop. 12,026), Glynn co., SE Ga., just off the coast, at mouth of Altamaha R.; c. 13 mi/21 km long, 3 mi/4.8 km–7 mi/11.3 km wide; 31°13′N 81°21′W. Most developed and 2d-largest of the Ga. Barrier Isls. At S end is resort village of St. Simons Isl., connected by causeway and bridges to Brunswick, 7 mi/11.3 km W on the mainland. Mfg. includes textiles, printing, publishing, and seafood processing. On W coast of isl. is Fort Frederica Natl. Monument (74.5 acres/30.2 ha), est. 1945, including ruins of Eng. fort built (1736–1754) by Oglethorpe. The Battle of Bloody Marsh (1742), fought on SE side of St. Simons Isl. and won by the British, was the decisive engagement in struggle with Spain for control of what is now SE U.S.

Saint Stanislas de Champlain (se stah-nees-LAHS duh sha-PLEH) or **Deux Riviéres** (duh reev-YAIR), village, S Que., Canada, on Batiscan R., 15 mi/24 km E of Grand'Mère. Dairying; lumbering.

Saint Stephen, town (1991 pop. 4,931), SW N.B., Canada, on the St. Croix R. opposite Calais, Maine; 45°12′N 67°16′W. The 2 towns, connected by an internatl. bridge, form virtually a single community. St. Stephen was founded by Loyalists after the Amer. Revolution.

Saint Stephen or **Saint Stephens**, town (1990 pop. 1,697), Berkeley co., E S.C., 37 mi/60 km W of Georgetown; 33°23′N 79°55′W. Mfg. of paper, felt, apparel; agr. includes timber, cotton, tobacco, grain; livestock. Located at NW edge of Francis Marion Natl. Forest.

Saint Stephens **1** former town, Washington co., SW Ala., on the Tombigbee, c.60 mi/97 km N of Mobile. Here, on the original settlement of a Span. fort (built 1789) and a trading post (1803), the 1st territorial legislature of Ala. met in 1818. **2** uninc. town (1990 pop. 8,734), Catawaba co., W central N.C., residential suburb 4 mi/6.4 km NE of Hickory; 35°45′N 81°16′W. L. Hickory reservoir (Catawba R.) to N.

Saint Stephens, village (1990 pop. 607), Stearns co., central Minn., near Mississippi R., 10 mi/16 km NNW of St. Cloud; 45°42′N 94°16′W. Agr. (grain; livestock; dairying); mfg. (optical equip., machinery).

Saint Sylvestre (se seel-VE-struh), village (1991 pop. 353), S Que., Canada, 30 mi/48 km S of Quebec; 46°22′N 71°14′W. Dairying; cattle, pigs.

Saint Tammany (TAM-uh-nee), parish (□ 908 sq mi/ 2,352 sq km; 1990 pop. 144,508), SE La.; ⊙ Covington; 30°29′N 90°07′W. Bounded S by L. Pontchartrain, extreme SE by L. Borgne, E by Pearl R. (here forming Miss. line); drained by the Bogue Chitto, Bogue Falaya, and Tchefuncte R. Resorts on lakes. In the piney woods sect. of La., often called the Ozone Belt. Agr. (blueberries, hay, sorghum, vegetables; cattle, horses, exotic animals; dairying); catfish, shrimp, crabs, alligators. Varied mfg. (food prods., apparel, concrete, machinery, shipbuilding). Named after a Delaware Indian chief. Part of Florida Parishes of La., former Br. colony of W Florida. L. Ramsey State Wildlife Area in NW; Fairview-Riverside State Park in SW; Fontainbleu State Park and St. Tammany State Refuge in S; Bogue Chitto Natl. Wildlife Refuge in NE; Pearl R. State Wildlife Area in SE. Formed 1810.

Saint Thomas, city (1991 pop. 29,990), S Ont., Canada, S of London; 42°47′N 81°11′W. The city is located in a rich agr. area, and has automobile plants and other factories.

Saint Thomas, parish (1991 pop. 83,749), Surrey co., E Jamaica; ⊙ Morant Bay; 18°05′N 76°40′W–17°52′N 76°11′W. Bounded N by Portland, along the grand ridge of the Blue Mts., on the W by St. Thomas. Crossed by Plantain Garden R. Predominantly agr. (bananas, coconuts, copra, sugarcane, coffee, mangoes, peas and beans, honey; livestock). Morant Bay and Port Morant are its main trading and shipping points. Bowden, served by narrow-gauge RR, is banana port. Bath has thermal springs. Lighthouse at Morant Point; 17°55′N 76°12′W.

Saint Thomas 1 town (1990 pop. 444), Pembina co., NE N.Dak., 14 mi/23 km N of Grafton; 48°37′N 97°27′W. 2 uninc. town (1990 pop. 850), Franklin co., S Pa., 7 mi/ 11.3 km W of Chambersburg; 39°55′N 77°47′W. Agr. area (grain, apples; livestock; dairying; timber); mfg. (wooden prods., dairy prods.). Buchanan State Forest to N.

Saint Thomas, island (□ 32 sq mi/83 sq km; 1990 pop. 48,166), U.S. V.I., 40 mi/64 km N of St. Croix and 3 mi/ 4.8 km W of St. John. Max. elev. 1,500 ft/457 m. Charlotte Amalie is main town and capital of U.S. Virgin Isls. Hilly terrain, largely denuded with no primary rain forest remaining; over 40 beaches. Was 1st settled by Danish in 1666 for agr.; after abolition of slavery in 1848, became arms supply depot en route to S. Amer.; during late 19th cent. became coaling depot for Eur. steamship companies. U.S. Navy took possession of the isl. in 1917; since the end of World War II tourism is the main economic activity. Cyril E. King Airport. Hardest hit of the U.S. V.I. during 1995 hurricane season, with considerable damage to hotels, offshore reefs, and the airport; large-scale reconstruction is underway. Has Marine Corps airfield.

Saint Thomas-ye-Vale, interior valley; St. Catherine parish, in E central Jamaica, along upper Cobre R., c.20 mi/32 km NW of Kingston; 18°12′N 75°35′W. Tropical fruit grown extensively. Main towns of Linstead, Bog Walk, and Ewarton are linked by RR. Also known as St. Thomas in the Vale.

Saint Tite (se TEET), town (1991 pop. 2,654), S Que., Canada, 10 mi/16 km NE of Grand'Mère; 46°43′N 72°34′W. Mfg.; lumbering; dairying.

Saint Ubalde (se tuh-BAHLD), village (1991 pop. 1,552), S Que., Canada, 22 mi/35 km NE of Grand'Mère. Dairying; livestock.

Saint Ulric (se tuhl-REEK) or **Rivière Blanche** (reev-YAIR BLAHSH), village (1991 pop. 768), E Que., Canada, on the St. Lawrence, 9 mi/14 km WSW of Matane; 48°47′N 67°42′W. Lumbering; dairying; fishing.

Saint Urbain de Charlevoix (se tuhr-BE duh shahrl-VWAH), village, SE central Que., Canada, 19 mi/31 km ESE of La Malbaie. Titanium mining; dairying; lumbering.

Saint Victor de Beauce or **Saint Victor de Tring**, village (1991 pop. 1,183), S Que., Canada, 20 mi/32 km ENE of Thetford Mines. Dairying; pigs.

Saint Victor de Tring, Canada: see SAINT VICTOR DE BEAUCE.

Saint Vincent, village (1990 pop. 116), Kittson co., extreme NW Minn., on Red R. of the North, 19 mi/31 km NW of Hallock, opposite Pembina (N.Dak.), 2 mi/ 3.2 km S of Canada (Man.) border; 48°58′N 97°13′W. Agr. (grain, sugar beets, potatoes).

Saint Vincent and the Grenadines, island state (□ 150 sq mi/389 sq km; 1990 est. pop. 115,000), West Indies, in the Windward Isls.; ⊙ KINGSTOWN; 13°05′N 61°12′W. It comprises the isl. of St. Vincent (□ 140 sq mi/363 sq km) and about ⅔ of the small Grenadine isls. to the S. St. Vincent isl. is mountainous, rising to 4,048 ft/1,234 m at Soufrière volcano, which erupted in 1902 and 1979, causing considerable damage to the isl. The climate is well suited to agr., which is an important part of St. Vincent's economy. Bananas, arrowroot, and copra are the chief exports, followed by other agr. prods. such as sea-island cotton; farmers here have also begun growing marijuana. Tourism is also economically important. Presumably visited by Columbus in 1498, St. Vincent remained uncolonized by Europeans until a Br. settlement was made in 1762. The French captured it in 1779 but it was restored to Britain in 1783. Attempts in overwhelming the native Caribs failed; the British deported most of them in 1797. Port. and East Indian laborers were introduced here in the 19th cent. after the emancipation of black Africans, who had been brought to the isl. earlier as slaves. St. Vincent was part of the Br. colony of the Windward Isls. (1880–1958) and of the West Indies Federation (1958–1962). In 1979 it gained full independence.

Saint Vincent Island, barrier island in the Gulf of Mexico, off Franklin co., NW Fla., W of St. George Isl., 7 mi/11.3 km SW of Apalachicola; 9 mi/14.5 km long, 4.5 mi/7.2 km wide. Shelters St. Vincent Sound (c.2 mi/ 3.2 km wide), which connects with Apalachicola Bay (E).

Saint Vincent Island, West Indies: see SAINT VINCENT AND THE GRENADINES.

Saint Vincent Passage, channel, SE West Indies, bet. St. Lucia and St. Vincent and the Grenadines; c.25 mi/ 40 km wide.

Saint Vrain Creek, N Colo.; rises in both North and South St. Vrain creeks at Continental Divide, NW Boulder co. North St. Vrain, c.25 mi/40 km long, in Rocky Mt. Natl. Park; South St. Vrain, c.30 mi/48 km long, in Roosevelt Natl. Forest. They meet at Lyons, flows 30 mi/48 km E past Longmont and then NE to South Platte R. 5 mi/8 km N of Milliken.

Saint Walburg (WAL buhrg), town (1991 pop. 746), W Sask., Canada, 70 mi/113 km NNW of North Battleford; 53°38′N 109°12′W. Grain.

Saint Zotique (se zo-TEEK), village (1991 pop. 2,515), S Que., Canada, on L. St. Francis, 7 mi/11 km W of Valleyfield; 45°14′N 74°15′W. Dairying; pigs; potatoes.

Saint-Barthélemy (sang–bahr-tai-luh-MEE), island (□ 9.5 sq mi/24.6 sq km), dependency of Guadeloupe, Fr. West Indies, in Leeward Isls., 12 mi/19 km SE of St. Martin and 125 mi/201 km NW of Guadeloupe; ⊙ Gustavia; 17°54′N 62°52′W. Mountainous and of irregular shape, 11 mi/18 km long (W-E), up to 2.5 mi/4 km wide; rises to 990 ft/302 m. While of little economic importance, it produces some cotton, tropical fruit, livestock, fishing, salt panning, mfg. of fiber hats. Has small lead and zinc deposits, relies on tourism and free-port status. Exclusive, high-end tourist destination; yachting, cruise ships, and small luxury hotels. Settled by the French, the isl. was ceded to Sweden (1784) but was returned to France by 1877 treaty.

Saint-Claude (sang–KLOD), town, S Basse-Terre isl., Guadeloupe, 2 mi/3.2 km NE of Basse-Terre. Agr. (coffee, cacao, bananas, honey); mfg. of alcohol. Also a health resort, with adjoining Matouba thermal springs.

Sainte Adèle (se tah-DEL), town (1991 pop. 4,916), SW Que., Canada, in the Laurentians, 10 mi/16 km SE of Ste. Agathe des Monts; 45°57′N 74°09′W. Dairying; skiing resort.

Sainte Agnès de Charlevoix (se tahn-YES duh shahrl-VWAH), village, SE central Que., Canada, 6 mi/10 km NW of La Malbaie. Dairying, lumbering center; mica mining.

Sainte Angèle de Laval (se tah-ZHEL duh lah-VAHL) or **Laval** (lah-VAHL), town (1991 pop. 314,398), S Que., Canada, on the St. Lawrence, opposite Trois Rivières (fErry); 46°19′N 72°31′W. Dairying.

Sainte Angèle de Rimouski (se tah-ZHEL duh ree-moo-SKEE) or **Sainte Angèle de Mérici** (se tah-ZHEL duh mai-ree-SEE), village (1991 pop. 1,168), E Que., Canada, on Mitis R., 20 mi/32 km ENE of Rimouski. Dairying; pigs.

Sainte Anne de Beaupré (se TAN duh bo-PRAI), village (1991 pop. 3,146), S Que., Canada, on the St. Lawrence R. NE of Quebec; 47°01′N 70°56′W. It is the site of a famous shrine est. in 1620 by sailors who had been shipwrecked. A chapel was built in 1658 and a large church in 1876. Burned in 1922, the church was magnificently rebuilt; it houses relics and is one of Canada's foremost pilgrim resorts. Many miraculous cures are ascribed to prayers at the shrine. Mts., a river, and falls near the village are also named for the saint.

Sainte Anne de Bellevue (se TAN duh bel-VOO), town (1991 pop. 4,030), S Que., Canada, on Montreal Isl., SW of Montreal; 45°29′N 73°54′W. The town has woodworking plants and a publishing house. In fur-trading days it was the point of departure for canoes going W, and it is referred to in Thomas Moore's "Canadian Boat Song." The agr. faculty of Macdonald Col., McGill Univ., is here.

Sainte Anne de Chicoutimi (se TAN duh shee-koo-tee-MEE), village, S central Que., Canada, on Saguenay R., opposite Chicoutimi; 48°27′N 71°04′W. Lumbering; dairying.

Sainte Anne de la Pérade (se TAN duh lah pai-RAHD) or **La Pérade** (lah pai-RAHD), village (1991 pop. 2,213), S Que., Canada, on Ste. Anne R., near its mouth on the St. Lawrence, 23 mi/37 km NE of Trois Rivières. Dairying; lumbering.

Sainte Anne de la Pocatière (se TAN duh lah pokaht-YAIR), village (1991 pop. 1,824), SE Que., Canada, on the St. Lawrence, 40 mi/64 km SE of Rivière du Loup; 47°22′N 70°02′W. In dairying, wheat- and flax-growing region; furniture mfg., woodworking. Has agr. col., experimental farm, and acad.

Sainte Anne de Portneuf, Canada: see HAMILTON COVE.

Sainte Anne des Chênes (se TAN dai SHAIN), village, SE Man., Canada, on Seine R., 27 mi/43 km SE of Winnipeg. Grain; dairying.

Sainte Anne des Monts (se TAN dai MO), town (1991 pop. 5,652), ⊙ Gaspé West co., E Que., Canada, on the St. Lawrence, on N side of Gaspé Peninsula, 50 mi/ 80 km ENE of Matane; 49°07′N 66°29′W. Dairying; lumbering.

Sainte Anne River 1 (se TAN), 90 mi/145 km long, S Que., Canada; rises in S part of Laurentides Provincial Park, flows past St. Raymond and St. Casimir, to the St. Lawrence at Ste. Anne de la Pérade. 2 60 mi/97 km long, S Que., Canada; rises in SE part of Laurentides Provinicial Park, flows SW to the St. Lawrence 3 mi/ 5 km NE of St. Anne de Beaupré.

Sainte Croix (set KRWAH), village (1991 pop. 1,650), ⊙ Lotbinière co., S Que., Canada, on the St. Lawrence, 28 mi/45 km WSW of Quebec; 46°37′N 71°44′W. Lumbering; dairying; pig raising.

Sainte Famille (set fah-MEE), village (1991 pop. 942), S Que., Canada, on NW shore of Île d'Orléans; 46°58′N 70°57′W. Dairying; vegetables, fruit. Founded 1661, it has church built 1742.

Sainte Genevieve (se GEN-uh-veev), county (□ 500 sq mi/1,295 sq km; 1990 pop. 16,037), E Mo.; ⊙ Ste. Genevieve, on Mississippi R. (NE); 37°53′N 90°11′W. Agr. region (grapes, corn, wheat, hay; cattle; pigs); wineries; limestone for hydrated lime and pulverized calcium carbonate; limestone for marble stone. Part of Mark Twain Natl. Forest in S; Hawn State Park in SW. Flood of 1993 affected E part of co. Area noted for its

Fr. history and sites; tourism. Formed 1812; one of Mo.'s original 5 cos.

Sainte Genevieve (se GEN-uh-veev), city (1990 pop. 4,411), ⊙ Ste. Genevieve co., E Mo., on Mississippi R., 45 mi/72 km S of St. Louis; 37°58′N 90°02′W. Trade center for farm area; mfg. (bldg. materials, apparel, hydrated lime and other lime prods., vinyl prods., crushed stone); limestone (marble) quarries nearby. Important tourist destination for historic architecture and ambience. Founded before 1750, it was earliest permanent white settlement in Mo.; early lead-shipping port. Town relocated after flood of 1785. Town center is filled with historic homes dating from late 1700s and other bldgs., most relating to Fr. heritage. Town center is a Natl. Landmark and a Natl. Historical Dist. Felix Valle State Historic Site. Great River Road Interpretive Center. Le Grande Champ, a common field divided into long lots, is on the S side of town. Intense sandbagging efforts spared most of historical town from floods of 1993 and 1995.

Sainte Hélène de Bagot (se tai-LEN duh bah-GO), village (1991 pop. 1,454), S Que., Canada, 14 mi/23 km NE of St. Hyacinthe. Dairying; livestock raising.

Sainte Hénédine (se tai-nai-DEEN), village (1991 pop. 1,225), ⊙ Dorchester co., S Que., Canada, 20 mi/32 km SE of Quebec; 46°34′N 70°59′W. Dairying.

Sainte Irénée (se tee-rai-NAI), village (1991 pop. 363), SE central Que., Canada, on the St. Lawrence, 7 mi/11 km SSW of La Malbaie; 47°34′N 70°12′W. Lumbering; dairying; resort.

Sainte Julie de Verchéres (set zhuh-LEE duh ver-SHAIR), village, S Que., Canada, 15 mi/24 km NE of Montreal. Dairying; pig raising.

Sainte Julienne (set zhuhl-YEN), village (1991 pop. 6,092), ⊙ Montcalm co., S Que., Canada, 32 mi/51 km N of Montreal. Lumbering; dairying; tobacco, potatoes.

Sainte Justine, Canada: see LANGEVIN.

Sainte Madeleine (set mahd-LEN), village (1991 pop. 2,181), S Que., Canada, 8 mi/13 km WSW of St. Hyacinthe. Dairying.

Sainte Madeleine, village, W Trinidad, Trinidad and Tobago, 3 mi/4.8 km E of San Fernando. Rum distilling and sawmilling.

Sainte Marguerite (set mahr-guh-REET) or **Lac Masson** (lahk mah-SO), village (1991 pop. 1,571), SW Que., Canada, in the Laurentians, on small L. Masson (elev. 1,102 ft/336 m), 11 mi/18 km E of Ste. Agathe des Monts. Dairying; skiing center.

Sainte Marie (set mah-REE) or **Sainte Marie Beauce** (set mah-REE BOS), village, S Que., Canada, on Chaudiére R., 28 mi/45 km SSE of Quebec. Textiles; dairying; woodworking; mfg. of shoes, furniture.

Sainte Marie, village (1990 pop. 281), Jasper co., SE Ill., 8 mi/12.9 km ESE of Newton; 38°55′N 88°01′W. In agr. area (livestock; redtop seed, fruit). Also spelled Saint Marie.

Sainte Marie Beauce, Canada: see SAINTE MARIE.

Sainte Marthe (set MAHRT), village (1991 pop. 1,056), SW Que., Canada, 14 mi/23 km NW of Valleyfield. Dairying; potatoes.

Sainte Martine (set mahr-TEEN), village (1991 pop. 2,228), ⊙ Châteauguay co., S Que., Canada, on Châteauguay R., 20 mi/32 km SSW of Montreal. Dairying.

Sainte Pétronille (set pai-tro-NEE) or **Beaulieu** (bol-YUHL), village (1991 pop. 1,128), S Que., Canada, at SW end of Île d'Orléans, on the St. Lawrence, 5 mi/8 km NE of Quebec. Dairying; fruit, vegetables.

Sainte Pudentienne, Canada: see ROXTON POND.

Sainte Rose de Lima (set ROZ duh lee-MAH) or **Templeton**, village, SW Que., Canada, near Ottawa R., 8 mi/13 km NE of Hull. Mica, silica mining.

Sainte Rose du Lac (set roz duh LAHK), village (1991 pop. 1,008), SW Man., Canada, 24 mi/39 km ESE of Dauphin. Wheat; mixed farming.

Sainte Scholastique (set sko-lahs-TEEK), village, ⊙ Deux Montagnes co., S Que., Canada, 25 mi/40 km WNW of Montreal. Dairying; vegetables. Scene of 2 battles in 1837 revolt.

Sainte Thècle (se TAI-kluh), village (1991 pop. 2,766),

S Que., Canada, 16 mi/26 km NE of Grand' Mère. Dairying; lumber.

Sainte Thérèse (set tai-REZ), city (1991 pop. 24,158), S Que., Canada, on the St. Lawrence R., NW of Montreal. It has factories producing automobile parts, pianos, furniture, plywood, and plastics.

Sainte-Agathe (se-tah-GAHT), village (1991 pop. 694), S Que., Canada, 30 mi/48 km SSW of Quebec; 46°23′N 71°24′W. Dairying, lumbering, mfg. (furniture); pigs. Also called Ste-Agathe-de-Lotbiniére.

Sainte-Agathe-des-Monts (se-tah-GAHT-dai-mon), town (1991 pop. 5,452), S Que., Canada, on the North R., NW of Montreal, at E end of Lac des Ecorces; 46°03′N 74°17′W. NW terminus of Laurentian Autoroute. It is a resort center, popular ski resort in Laurentian Highlands; fishing, hunting. Mfg. (apparel). Its hotels were popularly known as the "Canadian Borscht Belt" during the 1950s and 1960s.

Sainte-Anne 1 (sang-TAHN), town, S Grande-Terre, Guadeloupe, 9 mi/14.5 km E of Pointe-à-Pitre. In sugar-growing region; rum distilling. Resort area. **2** town, SE Martinique, 17 mi/27 km SE of Fort-de-France. Sugarcane growing, distilling; seaside resorts.

Sainte-Foy, city (1991 pop. 71,133), S central Que., Canada, residential suburb 5 mi/8 km WSW of Quebec city, near St. Lawrence R.; 46°47′N 71°18′W.

Sainte-Marie (sangt-mah-REE), town, E Martinique, 13 mi/21 km NNE of Fort-de-France. Agr. (cacao, pineapples); fruit canning; limekiln.

Sainte-Rose (sangt-RAWZ), town, N Basse-Terre, Guadeloupe, minor port 13 mi/21 km WNW of Pointe-à-Pitre. Sugar growing; distilling.

Saint-Esprit (sang-te-SPREE), town, S Martinique, 10 mi/16 km ESE of Fort-de-France. Bananas, coffee. Sometimes called Le Saint-Esprit.

Sainte-Suzanne (sang-syoo-ZAHN), town, Nord dept., N Haiti, on the Plaine du Nord, 15 mi/24 km SE of Cap-Haïtien; 19°35′N 72°05′W. Cacao, citrus fruits, coffee.

Saint-Eustache, town (1991 pop. 37,278), S Que., Canada, on Lake of the Two Mountains, suburb 15 mi/24 km W of Montreal; 45°34′N 73°53′W. Dairying; mfg. (photographic equip., medical equip., metal fabrication), publishing; resort. Also called Saint-Eustache-sur-le-Lac.

Saint-Évariste (se-tai-vah-REEST), village, Que., Canada, 26 mi/42 km N of Megantic, 1 mi/2 km SSW of La Guadalupe. Dairying; mfg. (apparel, motor vehicles).

Saint-François (sang-frawng-SWAH), town, SE Grande-Terre, Guadeloupe, 17 mi/27 km E of Pointe-à-Pitre. In agr. region (sugarcane, cotton). Tourist development and internatl. resort, casino, and marina.

Saint-Gaudens National Historic Site (GAW-duhns), Sullivan co., N N.H., 9 mi/14.5 km N of Claremont, in town of Cornish, on Blow-Me-Down Brook, near Connecticut R. Memorial (148 acres/60 ha) to the Amer. sculptor Augustus Saint-Gaudens; contains his home, studios, gardens, and 2 galleries. Covered bridge to N. Authorized 1964, est. 1977.

Saint-Georges-Ouest, town, S central Que., Canada, on SW bank of Chaudiere R., opposite St.-Georges; 46°07′N 70°41′W. Farming region; dairying; potatoes.

Saint-Jean (sang-ZHAWNG) or **Saint-Jean-du-Sud** (sang-ZHAWNG-duh-SOOD), town (1982 pop. 400), Sud dept., SW Haiti, on SW coast of Jacmel Peninsula, 9 mi/14.5 km SW of Les Cayes; 18°05′N 73°49′W. Fruit growing; basket making. Fishing port.

Saint-Jean-du-Sud, Haiti: see SAINT-JEAN.

Saint-Joseph (sang-zho-SEF), town, central Martinique, 5 mi/8 km NNW of Fort-de-France. Agr. center (bananas, pineapples, cacao, coffee, vanilla).

Saint-Laurent, city (1991 pop. 72,402), S Que., Canada, suburb 5 mi/8 km W of Montreal, on Montreal Isl., near Prairies R., S of Laurentian Autoroute. Cartierville Airport (S); Montreal Internatl. Airport at Dorval (4 mi/6 km SW). Residential area.

Saint-Leonard, city (1991 pop. 73,120), S central Que., Canada, residential suburb 5 mi/8 km N of Montreal, on Montreal Isl., near Prairies R., bounded by city of

Montreal on S and E, Montreal-Nord on W, Anjou on E.

Saint-Louis (sang-LWEE), town, on NW coast of Marie-Galante isl., Guadeloupe.

Saint-Louis-du-Nord (sang-LWEE-dyoo-NOR), town (1982 pop. 7,203), Nord-Ouest dept., N Haiti, fishing port on the Atlantic, 8 mi/12.9 km E of Port-de-Paix; 19°56′N 72°43′W. Agr. (cacao, coffee, rice); copper deposits nearby.

Saint-Louis-du-Sud (sang-LWEE-dyoo-SYOOD), town (1982 pop. 1,113), Sud dept., SW Haiti, on Jacmel Peninsula, on the Caribbean, 7 mi/11.3 km NE of Les Cayes; 18°16′N 73°33′W. Agr. (coffee, fruits, sugarcane). Fishing port.

Saint-Luce (sang-LYOOS), town, S Martinique, 13 mi/21 km SE of Fort-de-France. In sugar-growing region; distilling. Beaches, resort.

Saint-Marc (sang-MAHRK), town (1982 pop. 24,165), Artibonite dept., W Haiti, port on Gulf of Gonaïves, 45 mi/72 km NW of Port-au-Prince; 19°07′N 72°42′W. Together with Gonaïves (23 mi/37 km N), it is outlet for fertile Artibonite Plain, shipping cotton, coffee, bananas, precious wood. Agr. (cotton, sugarcane, coffee growing). Sugar processing, cotton, sisal, and rice milling, essential oils distilling, vegetable-oil extracting; mfg. of soap and lard. Bauxite deposits nearby. Sisal plantations in vicinity. Fishing port.

Saint-Michel-de-l'Atalaye (sang-mee-SHEL-duh-lah-tah-LAI), town (1982 pop. 7,559), Artibonite dept., N central Haiti, in Massif du Nord, 24 mi/39 km ESE of Gonaïves; 19°22′N 72°20′W. Cotton, sugarcane, and tobacco growing; copper deposits nearby. Sometimes called Saint-Michel-du-Nord.

Saint-Michel-du-Nord, Haiti: see SAINT-MICHEL-DE-L'ATALAYE.

Saint-Michel-du-Sud (sang-mee-SHEL-dyoo-SYOOD), village, Sud dept., SW Haiti, 34 mi/55 km WSW of Léogâne; 18°22′N 73°07′W. Coffee growing.

Saint-Pierre (sang-PYER), town (1990 est. pop. 5,550), Martinique, West Indies, 12 mi/19 km NNW of Fort-de-France. Founded by Esnambuc in 1635 and once the chief commercial city of the isl., it was engulfed by a mass of flame, lava, and ash in the eruption (1902) of Pelée. Of the city's c.28,000 inhabitants, only one person survived, and many thousands more were killed in the surrounding region. The town's present activity revolves around tourists visiting the ruins.

Saint-Raphaël (sang-rah-fah-EL), town (1982 pop. 3,889), Nord dept., N central Haiti, in Massif du Nord, 23 mi/37 km S of Cap-Haïtien; 19°26′N 72°12′W. Agr. (sugarcane, tobacco, citrus fruits, coffee).

Saint-Romuald, city (1991 pop. 9,830), S central Que., Canada, suburb 5 mi/8 km S of Quebec city, on SE shore of St. Lawrence R., E of Pierre-LaPorte Bridge. Mfg. (plastic prods., sheet metal, fabricated metal prods.); agr.

Sakakawea, Lake, reservoir, at Pick City, W central N.Dak. and Mont., on Missouri R., 55 mi/89 km NNW of Bismarck, N.Dak.; c.190 mi/306 km long; 47°29′N 101°26′W. Has many arms, including Yellowstone R. (c.20 mi/32 km long; extends into Mont.); Van Hook (N center) and Little Missouri (S center) bays. Formed by Garrison Dam (210 ft/64 m high), built (1956) by Army Corps of Engineers for power generation and irrigation. Surrounded by Fort Berthold Indian Reservation, Audubon Natl. Wildlife Refuge, and various state parks and recreation areas. Formerly called Garrison Reservoir.

Sakami Lake (sah-kah-MEE), NW Que., Canada, bet. Fort George R. (N) and Eastmain R. (S); 55 mi/89 km long, 20 mi/32 km wide; 53°N 76°45′W. Elev. 640 ft/195 m.

Sakonnet (sa-KON-net), resort village in Little Compton town, Newport co., SE R.I., 6 mi/9.7 km E of Newport and on Sakonnet Point (peninsula on Atlantic coast E of mouth of Sakonnet R.). Yacht club basin and harbor.

Salada Beach, Calif.: see SHARP PARK.

Salada, Laguna (sah-LAH dah, lah-GOO-nah), salt lake (☐ c.250 sq mi/648 sq km), Baja California Norte, NW

Mexico, 18 mi/29 km SW of Mexicali, 25 mi/40 km W of Colorado R., bet. Sierra de Juárez (W) and Sierra de los Cocopás (E); c.25 mi/40 km long, c.6 mi/9.7 km wide. Size varies widely, depending on overflow of Colorado R. Imperial Valley, irrigated farming area, to NE.

Salado, uninc. town (1990 pop. 1,216), Bell co., central Texas, 15 mi/24 km SW of Temple; 30°56′N 97°31′W. In farm area. Was seat of Salado Col. (1860–c.1890). Inc. 1867.

Salado, El, Mexico: see EL SALADO.

Salado, Río 1 (sah-LAH-do, REE-o) river, c.110 mi/177 km long, N Mexico, continuation of Sabinas R. from Venustiano Carranza Dam on Coahuila-Nuevo León border; flows SE, partly along Nuevo León-Tamaulipas border, past Ciudad Guerrero, to the Rio Grande at Falcon Reservoir opposite Zapata, Texas. Used to irrigate cotton-growing area. **2** (sah-LAH-do, REE-o), river, c.40 mi/64 km long, Colima, W Mexico; rises at S foot of Colima volcano; flows SSE to Tuxpan R. Used for irrigation.

Salahkai Mesa (c.7,000 ft/2,134 m–8,000 ft/2,438 m), tableland in Navajo Indian Reservation, NW Apache co., NE Ariz., c.75 mi/121 km NE of Winslow, SW of Chinle.

Salamanca (sah-lah-MAHN-kah), city (1990 pop. 6,566) and township, ⊙ Salamanca municipio, Guanajuato state, W central Mexico; 20°34′N 101°11′W. Elev. 5,646 ft/1,721 m. Chiefly an oil-refining center, it also serves as the commercial and distribution point for the surrounding agr. region. The city lies on Mexico Highways 43 and 45, on RR. The first important battle bet. liberals and conservatives in the 19th-cent. War of the Reform (see MEXICO) was fought here.

Salamanca (sal-uh-MAIN-kuh), city (□ 5 sq mi/13 sq km; 1990 pop. 6,566), Cattaraugus co., W N.Y., on both sides of the Allegheny R., and 10 mi/16 km NW of Olean; 42°09′N 78°43′W. In Allegany Indian Reservation. Allegany State Park is just S. Furniture, plastic and wood prods.; printing. Most of the city is built on land that is leased from the Seneca Nation's Allegany Indian Reservation. Settled in 1860s; inc. as city 1913.

Salamonia, town (1990 pop. 138), Jay co., E Ind., near Salamonie R., and 7 mi/11.3 km SE of Portland; 40°23′N 84°52′W. In agr. area.

Salamonie Lake, reservoir, Wabash and Huntington cos., NE central Ind., on Salamonie R., 8 mi/12.9 km E of Wabash; 10 mi/16 km long; 40°48′N 85°40′W. Max. capacity of 263,600 acre-ft. Formed by Salamonie Dam (114 ft/35 m high), built (1966) by the Army Corps of Engineers for flood control. Lost Bridge and Salamonie state recreation areas border the reservoir.

Salamonie River, 82 mi/132 km long, E and NE central Ind.; rises near Salamonia in E Jay co.; flows NW, past Portland and Montpelier, to the Wabash opposite Lagro.

Salcedo (sahl-SAI-do), province (□ 205 sq mi/533 sq km; 1993 pop. 99,965), N central Dominican Republic, ⊙ Salcedo; 19°25′N 70°20′W. CORDILLERA SEPTENTRIONAL occupies N sect.; Cibao Valley, the S. Agr. (cacao, peanuts).

Salcedo (sahl-SAI-do), town (1993 pop. 12,531), Espaillat prov., N Dominican Republic, 6 mi/9.7 km E of Moca; ⊙ Salcedo prov.; 19°25′N 70°23′W. Agr. center (cacao, coffee, corn).

Sale City (SAIL), town (1990 pop. 324), Mitchell co., SW Ga., 12 mi/19 km E of Camilla; 31°16′N 84°01′W.

Salée, Rivière, Guadeloupe: see RIVIÈRE SALÉE.

Salem (SAI-luhm), county (□ 350 sq mi/907 sq km; 1990 pop. 65,294), SW N.J., bounded W by Delaware R.; ⊙ Salem. Mfg. (chemicals and allied prods., glass containers, food prods., women's clothing, floor coverings, electronic connectors); dairying; agr. (produce, fruit; soybeans; poultry). N.J.'s least densely populated county and one of its poorest. Includes Parvin State Park. Drained by Maurice and Salem rivers and Oldmans, Alloway's, and Stow creeks. Nuclear power plants: Hope Creek (initial criticality June 28, 1986; max. dependable capacity 1,031 MWe) is 18 mi/29 km SE of Wilmington, Delaware. Salem 1 (initial criticality December 11, 1976) and Salem 2 (initial criticality August 8, 1980) are 18 mi/29 km S of Wilminton, Delaware, and each has a max. dependable capacity of 1,106 MWe. All 3 use cooling water from the Delaware R. Formed 1681.

Salem 1 (SAI-luhm), city (1990 pop. 7,470), ⊙ Marion co., S central Ill., 12 mi/19 km NE of Centralia; 38°37′N 88°57′W. RR junction. Mfg. (concrete pipes and culverts, livestock bldgs., grinding wheels, bags and packing materials). Oil wells. Agr. (fruit, corn, wheat; dairy prods.; livestock). William Jennings Bryan was b. here. Inc. 1837. **2** city (1990 pop. 5,619), ⊙ Washington co., S Ind., on Blue R., and 27 mi/43 km SE of Bedford; 38°36′N 86°06′W. Trade center for agr. area; mfg. (furniture, wood prods., appliances, hats and caps, mallets, concrete, transportation equip., machinery, lumber); limestone quarries; timber. John Hay b. here. Laid out 1814; inc. as town 1815, as city 1933. **3** city (1990 pop. 38,091), ⊙ Essex co., NE Mass., on an inlet of Massachusetts Bay; 42°32′N 70°52′W. Its once famous harbor has silted up. Salem has electronic, leather, and machinery industries, and tourists are drawn to its many historical landmarks. In 1626, Roger Conant led a group from Cape Ann to this site, called Naumkeag by the Native Americans. Salem's early history was darkened by the witchcraft trials of 1692, in which Samuel Sewall was a judge. From colonial days through the clipper ship era, Salem was world famous as a port and a wealthy center for the China trade. It was a privateering base in the Amer. Revolution and in the War of 1812. Nathaniel Hawthorne was overseer of the port from 1846 to 1849. Shipping declined after the War of 1812, and the city turned to mfg. Many colonial bldgs. remain. Hawthorne's birthplace dates from the 17th cent. The House of Seven Gables (1668) is preserved. Also of interest are Pioneer Village, a reproduction of early Salem; the Witch House (1642), where witch trials were held; Halloween is a high-profile holiday here. The Peabody Maritime Mus., founded in 1868; and Salem Maritime Natl. Historic Site. The Essex Inst. (est. 1848) has an excellent lib. and historical collections. Salem State Col. is here. North Shore Medical Center and Children's Hosp. Electric power plant on harbor. Inc. 1629. **4** city (1990 pop. 4,486), ⊙ Dent co., SE central Mo., in the Ozarks, 75 mi/121 km SE of Jefferson City; 37°38′N 91°31′W. Elev. 1,182 ft/360 m. Agr. (wheat, hay); cattle; mfg. (apparel, cheese, charcoal, caps, lumber). Former iron mines. Tourist center for large region of the Ozarks; Indian Trail State Forest to NE; Montauk State Park to SW. Inc. 1860. **5** city (1990 pop. 6,883), ⊙ Salem co., SW N.J., on Salem R., c.3 mi/4.8 km above its mouth on the Delaware, and 16 mi/26 km NW of Bridgeton; 39°34′N 75°28′W. Market center for agr. region; glass-making center, mfg. (floor coverings, canned foods). Noted for its colonial bldgs. Salem Oak (30 ft/9 m in circumference, 80 ft/24 m high) stands in Quakers' burial ground. Settled 1675 by Quakers; inc. 1858. **6** city (1990 pop. 12,233), Columbiana co., NE Ohio; 40°54′N 80°51′W. In a coal region. Tools and dies, industrial machinery, appliances, and pumps are among its many diverse manufactures. Settled (1803) by Quakers, Salem was an early abolitionist center and an important station on the Underground RR. A branch of Kent State Univ. is here. Inc. 1806. **7** city (1990 pop. 107,786), ⊙ Oregon and of Marion co., extends W into Polk co. (W Salem), NW Oregon, on the Willamette R.; 44°55′N 123°01′W. A growing city, Salem has numerous food-processing plants, a paper mill, wood, metal, and cloth industries. RR junction. Wineries. Agr. (pears, apples, peaches, plums, grapes, berries, nuts, grain). Mfg. (poultry processing, food and beverage processing, bakery prods., draperies, lumber, millwork, cabinets, prefabricated wood homes, corrugated boxes, printing, publishing, paints, concrete, sheet metal, treated poles for data equip., traffic control equip., silicon wafers, boats, navigational equip.). Salem is the site of Willamette Univ., Chemekta Community Col. (NE of city), Western Baptist Bible Col., Gilbert House Childrens Mus., various state and federal govt. bldgs., state hosps., and the state penitentiary (E of city). Of note is the Neoclassic state capitol bldg. (1937). Ankeny Natl. Wildlife Refuge to S; Baskett Slough Natl. Wildlife Refuge to W; Holman State Wayside to W; Willamette Mission and Maud Williamson State Parks to N; Silver Falls State Park to E. Municipal airport and state fairgrounds in SE. Founded 1840–1841; inc. 1857. Founded by Methodist missionaries, it became the capital of Oregon Territory in 1851 and remained the capital when Oregon became a state in 1859. **8** independent city (□ 14 sq mi/36 sq km; 1990 pop. 23,756), ⊙ Roanoke co., SW Va., 5 mi/8 km W of downtown Roanoke, smaller twin city of Roanoke and separate from Roanoke co., on Roanoke R., bet. Blue Ridge and Allegheny Mts.; 37°17′N 80°03′W. RR junction; mfg. (machinery, heat exchangers, earth moving equip., automated teller machines, steel foundry, apparel, tool and die, lumber, brick, furniture, tires; printing and publishing, prefabricated home kits, meat processing, fire sprinklers). Dixie Caverns 6 mi/9.7 km W. Roanoke Col. First inc. 1806, inc. as a city 1967.

Salem 1 (SAI-luhm), town (1990 pop. 1,474), ⊙ Fulton co., N Ark., c.40 mi/64 km NNW of Batesville, near Mo. state line; 36°22′N 91°49′W. Ships, cattle, hogs; mfg. (metal polishers, rubber regulating wheels, apparel). **2** town (1990 pop. 3,310), New London co., SE Conn., 14 mi/23 km NW of New London; 41°28′N 72°16′W. Summer homes; rural residential community. Part of Gardner L. here. **3** town (1990 pop. 453), Henry co., SE Iowa, 8 mi/12.9 km SSW of Mount Pleasant; 40°51′N 91°37′W. In livestock and grain area. **4** town (1990 pop. 770), Livingston co., W Ky., 10 mi/16 km WSW of Marion; 37°16′N 88°14′W. Agr. area (burley tobacco, sorghum, grain; livestock; dairying). Mfg. (horse saddles). **5** town (1990 pop. 25,746), Rockingham co., SE N.H., 18 mi/29 km SE of Manchester and 6 mi/9.7 km NNW of Lawrence, Mass.; drained by Spicket R. and Policy Brook; 42°47′N 71°13′W. It is a marketing and distributing center. Mfg. (computers, electronics, polyethylene, software, machinery, laminated cable; printing and publishing). Canobie Lake Amusement Park and Rockingham Park Race Track. Canobie L. on W boundary. Of interest is Mystery Hill, or America's Stonehenge, site of large stone structures believed to date from 2000 B.C., which is 3 mi/4.8 km N. Includes village of NORTH SALEM. Arlington Mill Reservoir in N. World End Pond in SE. Settled 1652; inc. 1750. **6** (SAI-luhm), uninc. town (1990 pop. 2,271), Burke co., W central N.C., residential suburb 3 mi/4.8 km SE of Morganton; 35°42′N 81°42′W. South Mts. State Park to S. **7** town (1990 pop. 1,289), ⊙ McCook co., SE S.Dak., 35 mi/56 km WNW of Sioux Falls; 43°43′N 97°23′W. In agr. area. Mfg. (farm machinery; printing). Settled 1880, inc. 1885. **8** town (1990 pop. 2,284), Utah co., central Utah, 3 mi/4.8 km E of Payson and 12 mi/19 km S of Provo; 40°02′N 111°40′W. Elev. c.5,000 ft/1,524 m. Precious metal jewelry, medicinals, botanicals; dairying; agr. (apples, cherries, alfalfa, cattle). Settled 1956 as Pond Town. Parts of Uinta Natl. Forest to S and NE. **9** town (1990 pop. 2,063), Harrison co., N W.Va., 12 mi/19 km W of Clarksburg, on Salem Fork of Tenmile Creek; 39°16′N 80°34′W. Agr., coal, gas, and oil region. Agr. (corn); cattle; poultry. Mfg. (glass factories). Salem-Teikyo Univ. is near. On North Bend State Trail. Settled 1790. **10** town, Kenosha co., SE Wis., 15 mi/24 km W of Kenosha. Lakes dist.; recreation. Residential. Wheat, soybeans.

Salem 1 (SAI-luhm), village, Franklin co., W central Maine, on branch of Carrabassett R., and 17 mi/27 km NW of Farmington. **2** village, Dorchester co., E Md., 12 mi/19 km ESE of Cambridge. A Biblical name meaning peace. Methodists built a church here in 1800. Linkwood Wildlife Management Center nearby. **3** village (1990 pop. 160), Richardson co., SE Nebr., 7 mi/11.3 km W of Falls City and inside confluence of N and S Forks of Big Nemaha R., near Kansas state line; 40°04′N 95°43′W. **4** village (□ 2 sq mi/5.2 sq km; 1990 pop. 958), Washington co., E N.Y., near Vt. border, 24 mi/39 km ENE of Saratoga Springs; 43°10′N 73°19′W. Mfg. of apparel, textiles, feed, paper prods.; lumber milling; slate quarrying. Small lakes (resorts) nearby. Settled 1764, inc. 1803. **5** village (1990 pop. 192), Oconee co., NW S.C., 10 mi/16 km NNE of Walhalla; 34°53′N 82°58′W. Mfg. of bottled water, sawmills; timber; livestock; grain. Sumter Natl. Forest to NW. Devils Fork State Park at Jocassee Dam to N. Keowee Toxaway State Park to E on L. Keowee reservoir.

Salem 1 and 2 Nuclear Power Plants, N.J.: see SALEM co.

Salem Church, Va.: see CHANCELLORSVILLE, battlefield.

Salem Maritime Historic Site, NE Mass., wharf and bldgs. important during Salem's seafaring days. Salem Custom House Natl. Historic Site managed by Natl. Park Service. Authorized 1938.

Salem River (SAI-luhm), c.30 mi/48 km long, SW N.J.; rises in E Salem co.; flows W and S, past Woodstown and Salem (head of navigation), to Delaware R. near Salem.

Salemburg (SAI-luhm-buhrg), village (1990 pop. 409), Sampson co., S central N.C., 22 mi/35 km ESE of Fayetteville; 35°00′N 78°30′W. Tobacco, cotton, peanuts, sweet potatoes, grain; poultry, livestock. Seat of N.C. Justice Academy.

Salesville, village (1990 pop. 84), Guernsey co., E Ohio, 12 mi/19 km ESE of Cambridge; 39°58′N 81°20′W.

Salida 1 uninc. town (1990 pop. 4,499), Stainslaus co., central Calif., in San Joaquin Valley, 6 mi/9.7 km NW of Modesto, near Stanislaus R.; 37°43′N 121°05′W. Wine making; ships fruit, hay, grain, vegetables, almonds, grapes, melons; dairying, poultry; mfg. (farm machinery). Hetch Hetchy Aqueduct runs E-W to S. **2** town (1990 pop. 4,737), Chaffee co., central Colo., on Arkansas R., bet. Sangre de Cristo and Sawatch mts., and 80 mi/129 km WNW of Pueblo; 38°31′N 106°00′W. Elev. 7,036 ft/2,145 m. Resort, trade center, and RR division point in grain, mineral, and livestock region; some agr. in valley. Mfg. (printing and publishing; chemicals, light mfg.). Repair shops and hosp. maintained by RR. Monarch Ski Area to W; Arkansas Headwaters State Park to NW. Nearby are hot springs and part of San Isabel Natl. Forest to NE and SW, for which city is hq. Founded by RR c.1880 as an outlet for Leadville's mines; inc. 1891.

Salina (suh-LEI-nuh), city (1990 pop. 42,303), ⊙ Saline co., central Kansas, on the Smoky Hill R., 67 mi/108 km WSW of Manhattan; 38°49′N 97°37′W. Elev. 1,229 ft/375 m. Major RR junction. It is a marketing and shipping center. Mfg. (flour milling, aircraft, industrial gases, printing, houseboats, electronic control panels, corrugated packaging, foundry, soft drinks, plastics prods., machinery, aluminum prods., office supplies, frozen foods). Kansas Wesleyan Univ., Marymount Col., Kansas State Univ.-Salina, and St. Johns Military School are here. Smoky Hill Mus. Nearby are prehistoric Native Amer. burial grounds to E along river. Ottawa State Fishing L. to N. Founded 1858 by antislavery settlers, inc. 1870.

Salina 1 (suh-LEI-nuh), town (1990 pop. 1,153), Mayes co., NE Okla., 9 mi/14.5 km E of Pryor, near Neosho R. (L. Hudson reservoir; Markham Dam nearby); 36°17′N 95°09′W. Recreation. Settled on site of the 1st Okla. trading post, founded in early 19th cent. by Jean Pierre Chouteau. Chouteau Mus., and Salina State Park here. Snowdale State Park to W. **2** town (1990 pop. 1,943), Sevier co., central Utah, on Salina Creek, near Sevier R., 18 mi/29 km NE of Richfield, W of Wasatch Plateau; 38°57′N 111°51′W. Elev. 5,147 ft/1,569 m. Shipping point for cattle, sheep, poultry; sugar beets, alfalfa; dairying, turkey processing. Coal, salt mining. Parts of Fishlake Natl. Forest to E and W. Salina Canyon to E, link in Span. Trail. Settled 1863, abandoned during Indian troubles (1866), resettled 1871.

Salina, village, Boulder co., N Colo., on Fourmile Creek, in E foothills of Front Range, and 6 mi/9.7 km WNW of Boulder. Elev. c.6,581 ft/2,006 m. Gold mining. In Roosevelt Natl. Forest.

Salina Cruz (sah-LEE-nah krooz), city (1990 pop. 61,656) and township, Oaxaca, S Mexico, on Pacific coast, 12 mi/19 km S of Santo Domingo Tehuantepec on Mexico Highway 49; 16°11′N 95°12′W. RR terminus; major Pacific coast oil port. Fishing, lumber milling, fruitgrowing. Linked by oil pipeline with Minatitlán.

Salinas, city (1990 pop. 108,777), seat of Monterey co., W Calif., 45 mi/72 km S of San Jose, near Salinas R., 7 mi/11.3 km SE of Monterey Bay, Pacific Ocean; 36°41′N 121°39′W. It is the shipping and processing center of a fertile valley famous for its grain, lettuce. Fruits, artichokes, vegetables, nurseries; cattle; dairying; strawberries; spices, candy; wines; mfg. (fabricated wire prods., fertilizers, food preparations; canned fruits and vegetables, power transformers, industrial trucks, printed circuit boards, soft drinks, packaging paper, jams and jellies, corrugated boxes; printing and publishing). The pop. of this growing city almost doubled bet. 1970 and 1990. The Alisal area (formerly called East Salinas), which was annexed by Salinas in 1964, was settled (1933) principally by migratory farm workers. The city is the scene of an annual rodeo and the seat of a community col. John Steinbeck was born and buried in Salinas, and his home is open to tourists. Hartnell Col. (2 year). Fort Ord Military Reserve to SW; Freemont Peak State Park to NE; Pinnacles Natl. Monument to SE; part of Los Padres Natl. Forest to S. Inc. 1874.

Salinas (sah-LEE-nahs), town (1990 pop. 28,335), S P.R., near the coast (adjoining is the port Playa Salinas), 12 mi/19 km W of Guayama. Industrial and commercial area; light mfg. Fishing. Has a training center for Olympic athletes. Airport just W. Many caves with Indian relics in vicinity. U.S. Army Training Area nearby (N).

Salinas de Hidalgo, city (1990 pop. 10,334) and township, ⊙ Salinas municipio, San Luis Potosí, N central Mexico, on interior plateau, on RR, and 55 mi/89 km NW of San Luis Potosí; 22°37′N 101°43′W. Elev. 6,886 ft/2,099 m. Salt- and cinnabar-mining center.

Salinas Peak (suh-LEE-nahs) (8,958 ft/2,730 m), in San Andres Mts., Sierra co., SW N.Mex., c.45 mi/72 km NW of Alamogordo, in White Sands Missile Range; 33°17′N 106°31′W.

Salinas National Monument (suh-LEE-nahs PWEB-lo) (1.7 sq mi/4.4 sq km), Torrance and Socorro cos., central N.Mex., proclaimed 1909 as Gran Quivion Natl. Monument; current name adopted in 1988. Ruins of 3 Native Amer. Pueblos (villages) of Pueblo Indians, abandoned c.1670s. Also preserves 4 of 6 surviving 17th-cent. Franciscan mission churches. Abo Pueblo Ruins Unit 8 mi/12.9 km WSW of Mountainair, Quarai; Pueblo Ruins Unit 3 mi/4.8 km NNW of Mountainair (both in W Torrance co.). Gran Quivia Pueblo Ruins Unit 23 mi/37 km SSE of Mountainair in NE Socorro co.

Salinas River (sah-LEE-nahs), c.150 mi/241 km long, N Mexico; rises in Coahuila in Sierra Madre Oriental near Saltillo; flows N and E, past Hidalgo, Carmen, Salinas Victoria, Ciénaga de Flores, and General Zuazua (all in Nuevo León), to Pesquería R. 5 mi/8 km E of Pesquería Chica.

Salinas River, c.150 mi/241 km long, S Calif.; rises in the Santa Lucia Mts., c. 20 mi/32 km E of San Luis Obispo; flows NW through Salinas Reservoir, past Atascadero, King City, Paso Robles, and Salinas to Monterey Bay 8 mi/12.9 km NW of Salinas. The irrigated valley is highly productive and is one of the chief lettuce and artichoke producing regions in the U.S.

Salinas Victoria (sah-LEE-nahs veek-TO-ree-ah), town (1990 pop. 4,674), ⊙ Salinas Victoria municipio, Nuevo León, N Mexico, on Salinas R., on RR, and 20 mi/32 km N of Monterrey; 25°57′N 100°18′W. Elev. 1,522 ft/464 m. Agr. center (cotton, corn, sugarcane; livestock).

Saline 1 (suh-LEEN), county (□ 730 sq mi/1,891 sq km; 1990 pop. 64,183), central Ark.; ⊙ Benton; 34°38′N 92°40′W. Drained by Saline R. and its tributaries. Agr. (cotton, corn; cattle, hogs). Abandoned bauxite mines. Gravel and clay pits; timber. Industries at Bauxite, Benton. Part of Ouachita Natl. Forest in NW (including L. Winona reservoir). Formed 1835. **2** county (□ 386 sq mi/1,000 sq km; 1990 pop. 26,551), SE Ill.; ⊙ Harrisburg; 37°45′N 88°32′W. Agr. (grain, fruit; cattle). Extensive bituminous coal fields, oil. Mfg. (textiles, hats). Drained by Saline R.; includes part of Shawnee Natl. Forest in S. Southeastern Ill. Col. here. Formed 1847. **3** county (□ 721 sq mi/1,867 sq km; 1990 pop. 49,301), central Kansas; ⊙ Salina; 38°46′N 97°39′W. Partially located in Smoky Hills region, intersected by Smoky Hill, Saline, and Solomon rivers. Wheat, alfalfa, sorghum; cattle, hogs; food processing, electronic and transportation equip. Coronado Heights, campsite of Span. explorers, in S. Formed 1859. **4** county (□ 759 sq mi/1,966 sq km; 1990 pop. 23,523), central Mo.; ⊙ Marshall; 39°08′N 93°12′W. Bounded N and E by Missouri R.; drained by Blackwater R. Agr. (corn, wheat, soybeans, sorghum; cattle, hogs; dairy prods.); mfg. at Marshall and Sweet Springs. Arrow Rock State Historical Site at Arrow Rock. Grand Pass Wildlife Area and Van Meter State Park in N. Formed 1829. **5** county (□ 576 sq mi/1,492 sq km; 1990 pop. 12,715), SE Nebr.; ⊙ Wilber; 40°31′N 97°08′W. Fertile loess plain. Farming region drained by Big Blue R. and its West Fork (in N). Mfg. (flour, tools, animal feed); agr. (cattle, hogs; corn, wheat, soybeans, sorghum; dairying). Formed 1867.

Saline, town (1990 pop. 6,660), Washtenaw co., SE Mich., 8 mi/12.9 km SSW of Ann Arbor, on Saline R.; 42°10′N 83°46′W. In diversified farm area (corn, wheat, apples; dairying); mfg. (sheet metal doors, machinery, bulk publishing, cutting machine tools, industrial microcomputers). Ann Arbor Municipal Airport to NE. Cooperative Saline Valley Farms nearby. Settled 1824; inc. as city 1931.

Saline (suh-LEEN), village (1990 pop. 272), Bienville parish, NW La., 50 mi/80 km ESE of Shreveport, and near Saline Bayou; 32°10′N 92°58′W. In farming region (squash, watermelons, sweet potatoes, peaches; cattle; dairying). Mill Creek Reserve to W; Kisatchie Natl. Forest to S.

Saline Lake 1 (suh-LEEN), reservoir, on Avoyelles–La Salles parish border, on Big Saline Bayou, 15 mi/24 km N of Marksville; 4 mi/6 km long, 1 mi/2 km wide; 31°20′N 92°02′W. Saline State Wildlife Area bounds it on N. **2** reservoir, on Winn-Natchitoches parish border, central La., on Saline R., in NW La. Game and Fish Preserve, 17 mi/27 km WSW of Winnfield; 31°51′N 92°54′W.

Saline River 1 (suh-LEEN), c.300 mi/483 km long, in S central Ark.; rises in the Ouachita Mts. (Saline co.), W of Little Rock; flows past Benton and Warren, SSE to Ouachita R. at L. Jack Lee reservoir (in Felsenthal Natl. Wildlife Refuge), 10 mi/16 km W of Crossett. **2** c.25 mi/40 km long, in SE Ill.; formed near Equality by confluence of South Fork (c.50 mi/80 km long) and North Fork (c.50 mi/80 km long); flows generally SE to Ohio R. 9 mi/14.5 km below Shawneetown; 37°41′N 88°27′W. Middle Fork (c.30 mi/48 km long) enters South Fork c.7 mi/11.3 km W of Equality. Name originated with early salt deposits near Equality. **3** c.240 mi/386 km long, Kansas; starts as intermittent stream in SW Thomas co., NW Kansas; flows E past Oakley, to the N of Hays and Russell, through Wilson L. Reservoir, and past Lincoln, to Smoky Hill R. 6 mi/9.7 km E of Salina. **4** c.65 mi/105 km long, NW La.; rises in N Bienville parish; flows S to Saline L. (c.6 mi/10 km long; backward L shaped), then SSW to Red R., 7 mi/11 km E of Natchitoches; flows through or bounds Kisatchie Natl. Forest for most of its course. Lake is part of NW La. State Game and Fish Preserve.

Salines, Pointe des (sah-LEEN, pwangt dai), headland, SE Martinique, 19 mi/31 km SE of Fort-de-France; 14°24′N 60°53′W.

Salineville (suh-LEEN-vil), village (1990 pop. 1,474), Columbiana co., E Ohio, 11 mi/18 km SSW of Lisbon, in coal-mining area; 40°37′N 80°50′W. Confederate raiders, under Gen. John Morgan, were captured near here in 1863.

Salisbury, village (1991 pop. 1,805), SE N.B., Canada, on Petitcodiac R., and 14 mi/23 km WSW of Moncton; 46°02′N 65°03′W. Dairying.

Salisbury 1 (SALZ-berry), city (1990 pop. 20,592), ⊙ Wicomico co. (since 1867), SE Md., c.55 mi/89 km S of Dover (Del.), at head of navigation in Wicomico R.;

38°22′N 75°35′W. Water, RR, and trade center for wide area of the Eastern Shore; a center for poultry-raising industry; produce farms, timber tracts in region. Mfg. (clothing, machine tools, machinery, boats, construction materials, fertilizer); food-processing plants. Historic bldgs. include Pemberton Hall, the home of Isaac Hardy (c.1741), and Popular Hill Mansion (c.1795), built during the Revolution. Salisbury State Univ.; medical center of the Lower Peninsula with 2 state hosps., a large general hosp., and nursing home facilities. The Wildfowl Mus., opened in 1976, has an extensive collection of carved birds, including prairie falcolns, doves, and ducks. Hunting nearby. **2** (SAWLZ-ber-ee), city (1990 pop. 1,881), Chariton co., N central Mo., near Missouri R., 19 mi/31 km W of Moberly; 39°25′N 92°47′W. Agr. (corn, wheat, soybeans; cattle, hogs); mfg. (air pollution filters, metal fabrication, flour, feed); former coal mines. Settled 1877, inc. 1891. **3** (SAHLZ-buhr-ee), city (1990 pop. 23,626), ⊙ Rowan co., W central N.C., in the Piedmont region; 35°40′N 80°28′W. RR junction. Mfg. (machinery; food processing; furniture; electrical equip.; bldg. materials; textiles and apparel; aluminum processing; chemicals; stone, wood, and paper prods.; medical equip.). Agr. area (grain, tobacco, soybeans, sorghum; livestock; dairying). Salisbury is the seat of Catawba Col. and Rowan Cabbarus Community Col. The city has a number of 18th and 19th-cent. bldgs., churches, and homes. The Salisbury Natl. Cemetery was the site of one of the largest Confederate prison camps during the Civil War; approximately 11,700 Federal soldiers are buried there. Boone's Cave State Park to N; High Rock L. reservoir to E; Spencer Shops State Historical Site, including N.C. Transportation Mus., to N at Spencer. Inc. 1770.

Salisbury 1 (SAHLS-buh-ree), resort town (1990 pop. 4,090), Litchfield co., NW Conn., in Taconic Mts., on N.Y. and Mass. state lines, and 20 mi/32 km NW of Torrington; 41°58′N 73°25′W. Patent medicines, cutlery, handles; agr. (dairy prods., poultry); skiing. Includes villages of Lakeville on L. Wononskopomuc, Salisbury (with Salisbury School for boys, 1901), Taconic, and Lime Rock (site of race track). Bear Mt., state's highest peak, and Twin Lakes, resort on small Twin Lakes here. Old iron mines and forges made Revolutionary munitions here. Settled c.1720, inc. 1741. **2** town (1990 pop. 6,882), Essex co., extreme NE Mass., on coast, 4 mi/6.4 km N of Newburyport, at mouth of Merrimack R.; 42°51′N 70°52′W. State park on coast. Includes resort of Salisbury Beach (state park here). Settled 1638, inc. 1640. **3** town (1990 pop. 1,061), Merrimack co., S central N.H., 15 mi/24 km NNW of Concord; 43°22′N 71°45′W. Drained by Blackwater R., forms Blackwater Reservoir in W. Mfg. (novelties); agr. (vegetables, apples, nursery crops; poultry; dairying). Daniel Webster Birthplace in NE; N.H. State Forest Nursery in E; part of Winslow State Park in W. **4** (SAHLZ-bah-ree), town (1990 pop. 1,024), Addison co., W Vt., on L. Dunmore, and 8 mi/12.9 km S of Middlebury, in Green Mts.; 43°55′N 73°06′W. Resorts, state fish hatchery.

Salisbury (SALS-buhr-ee), borough (1990 pop. 716), Somerset co., SW Pa., 17 mi/27 km S of Somerset near Md. state line; 39°45′N 79°04′W. Mt. Davis (3,213 ft/979 m; highest point in Pa.) is here.

Salisbury Beach, Mass.: see SALISBURY.

Salisbury Island (☐ 490 sq mi/1,269 sq km), SE Franklin dist., N.W.T., Canada, at W entrance of Hudson strait, off SW Baffin Isl., E of Nottingham Isl; 32 mi/51 km long, 12 mi/19 km wide; 63°30′N 77°00′W.

Salisbury Mills, uninc. community, Orange co., SE N.Y., 7 mi/11.3 km SW of Newburgh, in dairying area; 41°26′N 74°07′W.

Salix 1 (SAL-iks), town (1990 pop. 367), Woodbury co., W Iowa, 15 mi/24 km SSE of Sioux City; 42°18′N 96°17′W. In agr. area. **2** uninc. town (1990 pop. 1,257), Cambria co., W central Pa., 8 mi/12.9 km E of Johnstown; 40°17′N 78°45′W. Mfg. (ice rinks). Agr. (dairying; livestock; hay).

Salkehatchie River, S S.C.; rises 5 mi/8 km NNW of Barnwell, S.C.; flows SE to join Little Salkehatchie R. to form Combahee R.

Salkehatchie River, S.C.: see COMBAHEE RIVER.

Salladasburg (SAL-lah-dahs-buhrg), borough (1990 pop. 301), Lycoming co., N central Pa., 10 mi/16 km WNW of Williamsport, on Larrys Creek; 41°16′N 77°13′W. Agr. (grain; livestock; dairying); mfg. (food prods.). Parts of Tiadaghton State Forest to NW and NE.

Salley, town (1990 pop. 451), Aiken co., W central S.C., 24 mi/39 km E of Aiken; 33°34′N 81°17′W. Known for its Chitlin Festival.

Sallis (SAL-is), village (1990 pop. 139), Attala co., central Miss., 11 mi/18 km WSW of Kosciusko; 33°01′N 89°45′W. Agr. area.

Sallisaw (SAL-uh-saw), city (1990 pop. 7,122), ⊙ Sequoyah co., E Okla., 22 mi/35 km W of Fort Smith (Ark.), in hilly region; 35°27′N 94°48′W. Elev. 526 ft/160 m. RR junction. Center of farm area (corn, soybeans, grain; cattle); mfg. (polystyrene, machinery). Coal mines, salt deposits nearby. Brushy Creek State Park in town. Horse racetrack nearby. Site of Short Mt. Reservoir. Arkansas R. is S; Sallisaw State Park to N; Sequoyah Natl. Wildlife Refuge to W; Robert S. Kerr Dam and Reservoir to S. Founded c.1886.

Salluit or **Sugluk**, village (1991 pop. 823), N Que., Canada, on S shore of Hudson strait, on Sugluk Inlet, N end of Ungava Peninsula. Inuit community. Hunting, fishing, trapping. Scheduled air service.

Salmo (SAL-mo), village (1991 pop. 1,069), S B.C., Canada, on Salmo R. at mouth of Beaver Creek, and 20 mi/32 km S of Nelson; 49°12′N 117°17′W. Elev. 2,210 ft/674 m. Salmo Ski Hill and oldest telephone booth in the world are here.

Salmon, town (1990 pop. 2,941), ⊙ Lemhi co., E Idaho, on Salmon R. at confluence of Lemhi R., 160 mi/257 km NE of Boise; 45°11′N 113°54′W. Elev. 4,003 ft/1,220 m. Distributing center for gold-mining, stock-raising, agr. area; dairy prods.; mfg. (laminated beams, cheese and butter). Ships cobalt ore from Forney (SW). U.S. fish hatchery; co. mus.; hq. Salmon Natl. Forest are here, forest nearly surrounds area. Fort Lemhi to SE. Referred to as the White Water Capital of the World; outfitting for white water rafting on Salmon R., also known as River of No Return. Continental Divide and Mont. state line, on crest of Bitterroot Range, to E. Founded (1867) as Salmon City after discovery of gold here (1866); name changed 1869.

Salmon, Indian village, E Alaska, near Yukon border on upper Black R., and 75 mi/121 km E of Fort Yukon.

Salmon, river, c.425 mi/684 km long, central Idaho; rises in NW Blaine co., in the Sawtooth Range (White Cloud Peaks), in Sawtooth Natl. Forest and Salmon R. mts.; flows NE past Challis and is joined, at Salmon, by the Lemhi R.; then W through Frank Church River of No Return Wilderness Area (also forms Pacific [N] and Mountain [S] time zone boundary from here to its mouth), where it is joined by the Middle Fork and the South Fork, then turns N at Riggins then W again to join the Snake R., 35 mi/56 km S of Lewiston. The river's canyon, c.1 mi/1.6 km deep and 10 mi/16 km wide in some places, threads through a wilderness preserve. In 1935 a party sponsored by the Natl. Geographic Society explored the canyon. Though navigable downstream, the swift waters and rapids of most of the river's course make it impossible to return; thus, Lewis and Clark named it River of No Return. Later renamed for the salmon, which travel up the river to spawn. One of longest free-flowing rivers in N. Amer.

Salmon Arm, city, S B.C., Canada, on Salmon Arm of Shuswap L., 30 mi/48 km N of Vernon; 50°42′N 119°17′W. Dairying; lumbering; fruit growing; resort.

Salmon Arm, ENE arm of Seechelt Inlet, SW B.C., Canada, 35 mi/56 km NW of Vancouver; 14 mi/23 km long, 1 mi/1.6 km–2 mi/3.2 km wide. In lumbering area. Receives small Clowham R. at head.

Salmon Creek, uninc. town (1990 pop. 2,100), Clark co., SW Wash., residential suburb 5 mi/8 km N of Vancouver, Wash., on Salmon Creek. Commercial and agr. center. Dairying; poultry; vegetables, fruit. Columbia R. to SW.

Salmon Creek, NW suburb of Juneau, SE Alaska; 58°00′N 139°00′W.

Salmon Creek Reservoir (☐ 5 sq mi/13 sq km), Twin Falls co., extreme S central Idaho, on Salmon Falls Creek, 22 mi/35 km S of Twin Falls, and 6 mi/9.7 km N of Nev. state line; 42°13′N 114°44′W. Max. capacity 230,650 acre-ft. Formed by Salmon Falls Dam (also Salmon Dam; 217 ft/66 m high), built (1912) for water supply; also used for irrigation.

Salmon Dam, Idaho: see SALMON FALLS CREEK.

Salmon Falls Creek, 100 mi/161 km long, rises in Elko co., NE Nev.; flows E, then N past Jackpot, Nev., into Twin Falls co., S Idaho, through Salmon Creek Reservoir; entering Snake R. 10 mi/16 km NNW of Buhl. Salmon Dam (230 ft/70 m high, 480 ft/146 m long), in Idaho 15 mi/24 km N of Nev. state line, forms Salmon Creek Reservoir (11 mi/18 km long, 1 mi/1.6 km wide), used for irrigation.

Salmon Falls River, in Maine and N.H.; rises in N.H. near Great East L.; flows SSE, forming c.28 mi/45 km of state line, joining Cocheco R. to form Piscataqua R. at Dover, N.H. Furnishes water power at Salmon Falls and Somersworth, N.H., and Berwick, Maine.

Salmon River, reservoir (☐ 6 sq mi/15.5 sq km), Oswego co., N central N.Y., on Salmon R., 35 mi/56 km NNE of Syracuse; 43°33′N 75°55′W. Max. capacity 75,430 acre-ft. Formed by dam (35 ft/10 m high), built (1914) for power generation; also used for flood control and recreation.

Salmon River 1 c.18 mi/29 km long, in E central Conn.; rises near Hebron; flows SW, through summer-resort area, to the Connecticut just NW of East Haddam. Power dam near Leesville village. **2** c.45 mi/72 km long, in N.Y. and Que. (Canada); rises in lakes in E Franklin co., NE N.Y.; flows NNW, past Malone (water power) and Fort Covington, to the St. Lawrence in Que., 10 mi/16 km E of Cornwall, Ont. **3** c.30 mi/48 km long, in N and central N.Y.; rises in Lewis co.; flows generally W to L. Ontario 4 mi/6.4 km below Pulaski. Dam 5 mi/8 km NE of Altmar impounds Salmon Reservoir (c.7 mi/11.3 km long). Famed for coho salmon fishing.

Salmon River Mountains, in E Idaho, occupies parts of Custer, Lemhi, Valley, and Idaho cos., and bounded on S, E, and N by Salmon R. Includes sections of Challis and Salmon natl. forests and much of Salmon R. primitive area, includes part of Frank Church River of No Return Wilderness Area. Chief peaks: Bald Mt. (10,313 ft/3,143 m), Twin Peaks (10,341 ft/3,152 m). N extension of range is Yellowjacket Mts.

Salt Cay, islet (☐ 4 sq mi/10.4 sq km; 1990 pop. 208), Turks and Caicos Isls., crown colony of Great Britain, West Indies, 7 mi/11.3 km SW of Grand Turk isl.; 21°20′N 71°12′W. Large resort hotel. Formerly center of salt panning.

Salt Creek 1 c.100 mi/161 km long, in central Ill.; rises in McLean co.; flows SW and W to Sangamon R. 8 mi/12.9 km N of Petersburg; 40°25′N 88°34′W. Forms Clinton L. in De Witt Co. **2** c.45 mi/72 km long, in S central Ind.; rises in Brown co. in small streams that join SE of Bloomington; flows SW and S to East Fork of White R. 3 mi/4.8 km SW of Bedford. Monroe Reservoir is located on Salt Creek about halfway bet. the headwaters and its mouth. **3** 88 mi/142 km long, in SE Nebr.; rises in Lancaster co.; flows NE, to Platte R. near Ashland. **4** c.50 mi/80 km long, in central Wyo.; rises in NE Natrona co.; flows N, past Teapot Dome and towns of Midwest and Edgerton, through Salt Creek oil field, to Powder R. 16 mi/26 km E of Kaycee.

Salt Fork of Arkansas River or **Salt Fork**, 192 mi/309 km long, in S Kansas and N Okla.; formed by confluence of several headstreams in Comanche co. in S Kansas; flows SE into Okla. to Alva; then E, past Pond Creek city, to Arkansas R. 7 mi/11.3 km S of Ponca City. Not navigable. Great Salt Plains Dam (69 ft/21 m high, 5,700 ft/1,737 m long; completed 1948 by U.S. Army Engineers) is in stream 12 mi/19 km E of Cherokee, Okla.; used for flood control; forms Great Salt Plains Reservoir (capacity 259,000 acres-ft) in salt-encrusted plains area. Part of reservoir serves as wildlife refuge.

Agr. and livestock raising are leading activities in river basin. Gas and oil fields are in E.

Salt Fork of Red River, c.140 mi/225 km long, in N Texas and SW Okla.; rises in intermittent streams in Armstrong co., Texas; flows E through Greenbelt Reservoir, then into SW Okla., past Mangum then S to join Red R. (Texas-Okla. state line) 10 mi/16 km S of Altus, Okla.

Salt Island, islet, B.V.I., 6 mi/9.7 km E of Tortola isl., bet. Peter Isl. (W) and Cooper Isl. (E); 18°22'N 64°30'W. Has salt ponds.

Salt Key, Bahama Isls.: see CAY SAL.

Salt Lake, county (□ 807 sq mi/2,090 sq km; 1990 pop. 725,956), N central Utah; ⊙ Salt Lake City; 40°40'N 111°55'W. Tableland area drained by Jordan R.; bounded NW by Great Salt L. Wasatch Range is in E. Mfg. at Salt Lake City. Copper, salt; sand and gravel, limestone, magnesium salt; cattle, sheep, wheat, barley, alfalfa, sugar beets, fruit, vegetables. Salt Lake City Internatl. Airport No. 1 in N; Salt Lake City Municipal Airport No. 2 in center. Highly urbanized from Salt Lake City in N, S through Jordan Valley, rapid growth occurred 1980s and 1990s. Agr. remains important. Kennecott Corp. Brigham open-cut copper mine in SW, largest in world. Part of Camp Williams military reservation in SW. Solitude, Brighton, Alta, and Snowbird ski areas in SE. Great Salt L. (S shore) State Park in W. Jordan R. Parkway State Park in N (in Salt Lake City); part of Wasatch Natl. Forest in E. Formed 1850.

Salt Lake City, city (1990 pop. 159,936); ⊙ state and Salt Lake co., N central Utah, on the Jordan R. and near the Great Salt L., at the W foot of the Wasatch Range; 40°46'N 111°55'W. Elev. c.4,330 ft/1,320 m. The largest city in the state, it is a great regional center, world hq. of the Church of Jesus Christ of Latter Day Saints (Mormon), and the processing point for prods. of an irrigated farm region that is rich in minerals. Major industries include tourism, medical research, food processing; silver, lead, copper, zinc, and iron smelting; the mfg. of computers and electronic equip.; oil refining; and, since 1970, warehousing. The city's outlying suburbs grew rapidly in the 1980s. Founded in 1847 by Brigham Young as the capital of the Mormon community, the city achieved greatness as its economic hub. The prominence of the gigantic Temple (built 1853–1893) on Temple Sq. at the city's heart reflects the Mormon nature of Salt Lake City. After 1849, Salt Lake City was and still remains a supply point for overland travel to Calif. and was connected with the first transcontinental RR by a line built (1869–1870) by Brigham Young to Ogden. It is the seat of the Univ. of Utah, Westminster Col., and Salt Lake Community Col. Bldgs. of interest include the state capitol (1914), Brigham Young's home (the "Beehive House"; restored to its 1877 appearance), the Brigham Young Monument (1897), and a planetarium. Also in the city are the Univ. of Utah and Fort Douglas, which was founded in 1862. Pioneer Trail State Park on E edge of city; Jordan Valley Parkway State Park in city W of downtown. Salt Lake City Internatl. Airport No. 1 in W part of city; municipal airport No. 2 to S. Has Internatl. Peace Garden, Hogle Zoo. Site for the Winter Olympics in 2002. Inc. 1851.

Salt Lick, village (1990 pop. 342), Bath co., NE Ky., 10 mi/16 km WSW of Morehead, near Licking R. at N edge of Daniel Boone Natl. Forest; 38°07'N 83°37'W. Agr. (tobacco; cattle; timber); mfg. (machining, wood flooring). Clear Creek Furnace (early 1800s) to S; Cave Run L. reservoir to SE.

Salt River 1 200 mi/322 km long, in central Ariz.; formed in plateau region of E Ariz. by confluence of Black and White rivers c.40 mi/64 km NE of Globe, where it forms, with Black R., boundary bet. Fort Apache (N) and San Carlos (S) Indian reservations, then it flows generally W, to Gila R. 15 mi/24 km WSW of Phoenix, through Salt R. Canyon and Tonto Natl. Forest, where it passes through Theodore Roosevelt L. reservoir and dam, Apache L. (Horse Mesa Dam), Canyon L. (Mormon Flat Dam), and Saguaro L. (Stewart Mt. Dam), and through Granite Reef Dam, which diverts water to canals to irrigate Phoenix area, in close succession, then forms S boundary of Salt River Indian Reservation, then flows past Mesa, Tempe, and Scottsdale, and through city of Phoenix, S of downtown. Sierra Ancha and Mazatzal mts. are N of river's mid-course; Salt River Mts. S of lower course in Phoenix. Was used for irrigation centuries ago by Indians and in 19th cent. by early settlers. Valley is now served by Salt R. irrigation project, 1st major undertaking in U.S. reclamation program. Important dams built on river as units in project are ROOSEVELT DAM, HORSE MESA DAM, MORMON FLAT DAM, STEWART MOUNTAIN DAM, , and Granite Reef Dam (small, concrete weir, completed 1908, c.25 mi/40 km ENE of Phoenix). Cave Creek Dam (109 ft/33 m high, 1,648 ft/502 m long; completed 1923; used for flood control) is on small, intermittent tributary and N of Phoenix. BARTLETT DAM and Horseshoe Dam are on Verde R., chief tributary of Salt R. Water is distributed through more than 1,000 mi/1,609 km of irrigation canals; cotton, alfalfa, fruit, and vegetables are raised. Favorable climate makes river valley popular as resort area. **2** 125 mi/201 km long, in N Ky.; rises in Boyle co., W of Danville; flows N past Harrodsburg, then W through Taylorsville L. reservoir, past Taylorsville and Shepherdsville (head of navigation of small craft), through Fort Knox Military Reservation to Ohio R. at West Point, 12 mi/19 km W of Shepherdsville. Main tributaries: Rolling Fork (and its tributary Beech Fork), enters from SE in Fort Knox, Floyds Fork enters from NE 2 mi/3.2 km E of Shepherdsville. **3** c.200 mi/322 km long, NE Mo.; North Fork, rises in Schuyler co., Middle Fork in Macon co., and South Fork in Audrain co. The three forks merge in Monroe co. E of Paris. The river (using North Fork) flows SE and E to Mississippi R. above Louisiana. Mark Twain L. and Clarence Cannon Dam S of Monroe City. **4** c.40 mi/64 km long, mainly in W Wyo.; rises in several branches in N central Lincoln co.; flows N, between Salt R. Range, Wyo. (E), and Caribou Range, Idaho (W), to Snake R. (Palisades Reservoir) on Idaho-Wyo. state line. Drains part of Star Valley, rich grain and dairy region (c.50 mi/80 km long, 5 mi/8 km–7 mi/11.3 km wide) in Wyo. and Idaho.

Salt River Mountains, Maricopa co., S central Ariz., bet. Gila and Salt rivers, in S part of city of Phoenix, rise to 2,612 ft/796 m in W tip; 33°34'N 110°55'W. Include Phoenix South Mt. Park. Gila R. Indian Reservation to S.

Salt River Range, in Rocky Mts. of W Wyo., just E of Idaho state line; extends c.70 mi/113 km N-S bet. Salt R. (W) and Greys R. (E). Prominent peaks: Virginia Peak (10,143 ft/3,092 m), Prater Mt. (10,105 ft/3,080 m). Range includes part of Bridger-Teton Natl. Forest.

Salt River Valley, Maricopa co., central Ariz, at Phoenix. Irrigated region around the lower course of the Salt R., which rises in mt. streams near the Mogollon Rim of the Mogollon Plateau and flows SW to join the Gila R. in S central Ariz. Native Americans used the Salt R. for irrigation here many cent. ago. In the 19th cent., Amer. settlers began irrigated farming in the valley, and the Mormons used some of the old Native Amer. canals at Mesa, Ariz. The Salt River project, the 1st large irrigation scheme undertaken under the Federal Reclamation Act of 1902, is one of the most economically successful projects in N. Amer. It began in 1903 when construction started on the Roosevelt Dam in a canyon E of Phoenix. The dam, forming Roosevelt L. behind it, impounded enough water to irrigate fields for about 2 years even if no rain falls. Roosevelt Dam raised 77 ft/23 m, completed 1996. Other dams were built bet. 1922 and 1946 to supply water and power. The region is a rich producer of citrus fruits, lettuce, melons, and other crops. A major factor in the Salt R. project's success is the long season without frost; the climate also makes this area an attractive winter resort.

Salt Springs Dam, Calif.: see MOKELUMNE RIVER.

Salt Sulphur Springs, locality, Monroe co., SE W.Va., in the Allegheny Mts., 21 mi/34 km SW of White Sulphur Springs. A health resort (5 mineral springs) since 1820s.

Saltabarranca (sahl-tah-bah-RAHN-kah), town (1990 pop. 3,329), Veracruz, SE Mexico, in Sotavento region, 23 mi/37 km WNW of San Andrés Tuxtla; 18°36'N 95°32'W. Fruit, cattle.

Saltair, village, Salt Lake co., N Utah, suburb 12 mi/19 km W of Salt Lake City, on Great Salt L. Bathing resort (water here c.25% salt), Great Salt L. (S shore) State Park is here. Saltair Resort built 1893.

Saltaire, N.Y.: see FIRE ISLAND.

Saltcoats, town (1991 pop. 545), SE Sask., Canada, on small Anderson L., 18 mi/29 km SE of Yorkton; 51°02'N 102°10'W. Grain elevators, lumbering.

Salters, uninc. village, Williamsburg co., E central S.C., 5 mi/8 km S of Kingstree, near Black R. Mfg. (billiard tables and lumber); agr includes timber.

Saltese (sahl-TEEZ), village (1990 pop. 70), Mineral co., W Mont., 80 mi/129 km WNW of Missoula, and on St. Regis R., near Idaho state line. Silver, gold; timber. Lookout Pass (4,725 ft/1,440 m) to W, on Idaho border. Area surrounded by Lolo Natl. Forest. Originally called Silver City.

Salt-Gila Aqueduct, S central Ariz., in Maricopa, Pinal, and Pima cos., a S continuation of Hayden-Rhodes Aqueduct. Begins at Granite Reef Dam on Salt R., 22 mi/35 km E of Phoenix; runs S c.100 mi/161 km in serpentine course past Florence and Picacho Mts. to Santa Cruz R. 18 mi/29 km NW of Tucson. Delivers water from Colorado R. (via Hayden-Rhodes Aqueduct) and upper Salt R. systems to the intermittent Santa Cruz R. system for irrigated farming and urban use.

Saltillo (sahl-TEE-yo), city (1990 pop. 420,947) and township, ⊙ Coahuila state, N Mexico; 25°25'N 100°59'W. Elev. 5,246 ft/1,599 m. It is located in an alluvial valley almost surrounded by mts. Saltillo is a commercial and industrial center with heavy and light mfg. and has grown rapidly. Founded in 1575, the city was known in colonial times for its annual fair, at which imports from Spain and the Philippines were exchanged for prods. made in Mexico. RR junction; on Mexico Highways 40, 54, and 57. The city has a univ. and other institutions of higher learning.

Saltillo (sahl-TEE-yo), town (1990 pop. 1,219), ⊙ Lafragua municipio, Puebla, central Mexico, 24 mi/39 km NNE of Ciudad Serdán. Cereals, maguey; livestock.

Saltillo 1 (sahl-TIL-o), town (1990 pop. 117), Washington co., S Ind., 11 mi/18 km NW of Salem; 38°40'N 86°18'W. In agr. area. **2** town (1990 pop. 1,782), Lee co., NE Miss., 8 mi/12.9 km N of Tupelo; 34°22'N 88°41'W. Agr. (cotton, grain, soybeans, honey; poultry, cattle; dairying); mfg. (furniture, corrugated containers).

Saltillo (sal-TI-lo), borough (1990 pop. 347), Huntingdon co., S central Pa., 19 mi/31 km S of Huntingdon, on North Spring Branch Creek; 40°12'N 78°00'W. Bituminous coal. Agr. includes dairying, livestock, poultry; grain.

Salto de Agua (sahl-to dai AH-gwah), town (1990 pop. 3,802), Chiapas, S Mexico, on affluent of Grijalva R., in Gulf lowland, 45 mi/72 km SE of Villahermosa; 18°35'N 92°20'W. Fruit.

Salto, El 1 Mexico: see EL SALTO DURANGO. **2** Mexico: see EL SALTO JALISCO.

Salton Sea, saline lake (□ 370 sq mi/958 sq km), N part of the Imperial Valley, Riverside and Imperial cos., SE Calif.; 235 ft/72 m below sea level. Salton Sea was formed as the Colorado R. delta grew across the Gulf of Calif., severing the river's N part. The area was a salt-covered depression known as Salton Sink until 1905, when a flood on the Colorado broke through an irrigation gap in its levee; the river flowed into the sink for two years before being checked. The Salton Sea's water level has gradually risen due to runoff from surrounding mts. and irrigation systems, thus flooding out some settlements and natural formations along its shores. The Salton Sea is a major S Calif. recreation and fishing area. Whitewater R. enters from NW; San Felipe R. enters from W; New R. and Alamo R. enter from S; Coachella Canal parallels lake to NE; Torrez Martinez Indian Reserve at NW end; Salton Sea State Recreation Area on NE shore; Salton Sea Natl. Wildlife Refuge in S part of lake.

Saltonstall, Lake, reservoir, on East Haven/Branford town border, New Haven co., S Conn., on channel of Farm Brook, 3 mi/4.8 km E of New Haven, and 2 mi/ 3.2 km N of L.I. Sound; 3 mi/4.8 km long; 41°16′N 72°51′W.

Saltrou (sahl-TROO), agr. town (1982 pop. 2,048), Sud-Est dept., S Haiti, fishing port on the Caribbean, 28 mi/ 45 km SE of Port-au-Prince; 18°14′N 72°04′W. Coffee, cacao, construction wood. Sometimes called Belle-Anse.

Saltsburg (SALTS-buhrg), borough (1990 pop. 990), Indiana co., SW Pa., 12 mi/19 km W of Latrobe, at confluence of Conemaugh R., and Loyalhanna Creek, which form Kiskiminetas R.; 40°29′N 79°27′W. Agr. (grain, soybeans; livestock, dairying); mfg. (vinyl windows); bituminous coal. Keystone State Park to SE; Beaver Run Reservoir to W. Laid out 1817, inc. 1838.

Saltspring Island, largest (□ 70 sq mi/181 sq km) of Gulf Isls., B.C., Canada, in Strait of Georgia just off SE Vancouver Isl., 7 mi/11 km E of Duncan, 25 mi/40 km N of Victoria; 16 mi/26 km long, 2 mi/3 km–7 mi/11 km wide. Tourism; lumbering, dairying, poultry raising, sheep raising, fruit growing. Chief settlements: Ganges on E central shore, Fulford Harbour on SE shore. Formerly Admiral Isl.

Saltville, town (1990 pop. 2,300), Smyth and Washington cos., SW Va., 14 mi/23 km W of Marion, on North Fork of Holston R.; 36°52′N 81°45′W. RR spur terminus; mfg. (hoists, phosphates, steel rims, gypsum wallboard, insulated wires); salt and gypsum mines. Saltmaking began in 1788; saltworks destroyed in Civil War by Union forces (1864), but reestablished later. Inc. 1894.

Salud, La, Cuba: see LA SALUD.

Saluda (suh-LOO-duh), county (□ 460 sq mi/ 1,191 sq km; 1990 pop. 16,357), W central S.C.; ⊙ Saluda; 34°00′N 81°43′W. Bounded N by Saluda R.(forms L. Murray reservoir in NE); includes part of Sumter Natl. Forest. Mfg. in town of Saluda. Sparsely settled agr. area that produces chickens, eggs, turkeys, cattle, corn, wheat, soybeans, sorghum, hay, peaches, timber. Formed 1895.

Saluda (suh-LOO-duh), town (1990 pop. 2,798), ⊙ Saluda co., W central S.C., 45 mi/72 km W of Columbia; 34°00′N 81°46′W. Mfg. includes paperboard, apparel, textiles, processed meats; agr. includes poultry, livestock, grain, cotton, peaches; timber. L. Murray reservoir to NE and Sumter Natl. Forest to W.

Saluda 1 (suh-LOO-duh), village (1990 pop. 543), Polk co., W N.C., 8 mi/12.9 km SE of Hendersonville, in the Blue Ridge foothills, near North Saluda R.; 35°14′N 82°20′W. Grain, sweet potatoes; poultry, cattle. L. Summit reservoir to W. **2** uninc. village, ⊙ Middlesex co., E Va., near Rappahannock R., 12 mi/19 km ENE of West Point; 37°36′N 76°35′W. Mfg. (lumber); agr. (tobacco, grain; livestock); timber. Rappahannock Community Col. (Glenns Campus) is 3 mi/4.8 km to S.

Saluda River (suh-LOO-duh), c.200 mi/322 km long, N.C. and S.C.; rises in Mountain L. reservoir in N Greenville co., near N.C. state line, in the Blue Ridge Mts., W S.C.; flows SE across the Piedmont region past Ware Shoals town through L. Greenwood and Murray L. reservoirs, joining the Broad R at Columbia to form the Congaree R. The Saluda Dam (completed 1930) impounds L. Murray, created Dreher Isl. State Park; its hydroelectric power plant has a large capacity.

Salunga (SAL-uhng-ga), uninc. town (1990 pop. 920), Lancaster co., SE Pa., 8 mi/12.9 km NW of Lancaster; 40°06′N 76°25′W. Mfg. includes machinery. Covered bridges in area. Landisville is 1 mi/1.6 km SE.

Salvador Alvarado, Mexico: see GUAMÚCHIL.

Salvador Escalante, Mexico: see SANTA CLARA DEL COBRE.

Salvador, Lake (SAL-vuh-dor), St. Charles, Jefferson, and Lafourche parishes, SE La., 10 mi/16 km SW of

New Orleans, receives Bayou Des Allemands in SW; c.12 mi/19 km long, 6 mi/10 km wide; 29°40′N 90°10′W. Shallow; joined by other waterways to L. Cataouatche and the Mississippi R. (N), and to the Intracoastal Waterway, passing near lake on S and SE. Salvador State Wildlife Area on NW shore; Jean Lafitte Natl. Historic Park, Barataria Unit, on E shore.

Salvage Head (sal-VAJ), cape, SE N.F., Canada, on NW side of Trinity Bay, 2 mi/3 km SE of Trinity; 48°22′N 53°22′W.

Salvaleón de Higuey (sahl-vah-lai-ON dai ee-GWAI), **Higüey**, or **Higüei**, town (1993 pop. 50,127), ⊙ La Altagracia prov., SE Dominican Republic, 23 mi/37 km ESE of Seibo; 18°42′N 68°40′W. In agr. region (cacao, corn, rice; cattle); dairy prods. Known for its shrine of the Virgin, with magnificent altar, attracting many pilgrims from the isl. Town was founded 1502 by Juan Ponce de León. Airport nearby.

Salvatierra (sahl-vah-tee-E-rah), city (1990 pop. 33,520) and township, Guanajuato, central Mexico, on Lerma R., and 23 mi/37 km SSW of Celaya on Mexico Highway 51; 20°12′N 100°53′W. Elev. 5,738 ft/1,749 m. On RR; agr. center (cereals, sugarcane, alfalfa, cotton, fruit; livestock); mfg. of cotton goods; lumber works. Founded 1643.

Salyersville (SAL-yuhrz-vil), town (1990 pop. 1,917), ⊙ Magoffin co., E Ky., on Licking R., and 36 mi/58 km N of Hazard, in the Cumberland Mts.; 37°45′N 83°03′W. Agr. (burley tobacco, corn; cattle); coal; mfg. (machinery, lumber, coal processing, outdoor furniture). Settled as Adamsville; renamed 1860.

Sam Houston, Fort, Texas: see SAN ANTONIO.

Sam Rayburn Reservoir, E Texas, on Angelina R., 12 mi/19 km NNW of Jasper, in Jasper, Angelina, San Augustine, Nagadoches, and Sabine cos.; c.50 mi/ 80 km long; 31°04′N 94°05′W. Max. capacity 5,610,000 acre-ft. Has 2 N arms, 1 extending from dam (13 mi/21 km), 1 on Attoyac Bayou in upper reach (20 mi/32 km). Formed by Sam Rayburn Dam (113 ft/ 34 m high), built (1965) by the Army Corps of Engineers for water supply and flood control. Partly in Rayburn Natl. Forest.

Samahil (sah-mah-EEL), town (1990 pop. 2,048), Yucatán, SE Mexico, 18 mi/29 km WSW of Mérida; 20°53′N 89°53′W. Henequen.

Samaná (sah-mah-NAH), province (□ 840 sq mi/ 2,176 sq km; 1993 pop. 73,094), NE Dominican Republic, on the Atlantic; ⊙ Samaná; 19°15′N 69°27′W. Consists of little-settled Samaná Peninsula and fertile E sect. of Cibao valley. Watered by Yuna R. Agr. (cacao, coconuts, coffee, rice, tobacco, corn, beeswax); cattle; tropical hardwood. Fishing along the coast. Sánchez, at head of sheltered Samaná Bay, is linked by RR with La Vega. Other trading and agr. centers are Samaná, Matanzas, Julia Molina, Cabrera. Formed 1908 from part of Seibo.

Samaná (sah-mah-NAH), town (1993 pop. 8,197), ⊙ Samaná prov., NE Dominican Republic, port on S coast of Samaná Peninsula, on Samaná Bay, 60 mi/97 km NE of Santo Domingo; 19°13′N 69°20′W. Trades in precious wood, cacao, coconuts, rice. Tanning. Beach resort. Founded 1756 by settlers from Canary Isls., followed by freed Afr.-Amer. slaves from Philadelphia and Baltimore in 1825. Also known as Santa Bárbara de Samaná.

Samaná Bay (sah-mah-NAH), Atlantic inlet on NE coast of Dominican Republic, bounded N by Samaná Peninsula; 19°10′N 69°25′W. Deep, well-protected bay, c.30 mi/48 km long (W-E), 10 mi/16 km wide. Sánchez is at its head, Samaná on N shore. Into it flows Yuna R. Tourist and fishing site. Discovered by Columbus on his 1st voyage.

Samaná, Cape (sah-mah-NAH), headland, NE Dominican Republic, easternmost point of Samaná Peninsula, 14 mi/23 km NE of Samaná; 19°18′N 69°08′W.

Samana Island, islet, SE Bahama Isls., 22 mi/35 km NE of Acklins Isl.; 10 mi/16 km long, up to 2 mi/3.2 km wide; 23°05′N 73°45′W. Produces cascarilla bark. Also known as Atwood Cay.

Samaná Peninsula (sah-mah-NAH), on NE coast of Dominican Republic, bet. Samaná Bay (S) and Escocesa Bay (NW); 30 mi/48 km long from Sánchez, at its base, to Cape Samaná; c.6 mi/9.7 km wide. On its coast are grown cacao, coffee, and coconuts. Rich in tropical hardwood. Samaná on S shore.

Sambro, Cape (SAM-bro), on Sambro Harbour, small inlet of the Atlantic, S N.S., Canada, 12 mi/19 km S of Halifax; 44°28′N 63°36′W.

Samburg, town (1990 pop. 374), Obion co., extreme NW Tenn., on Reelfoot L., 22 mi/35 km N of Dyersburg; 36°23′N 89°21′W.

Sammamish Lake (suh-MAH-mish), resort lake, King co., W central Wash., 10 mi/16 km E of Seattle, c.8 mi/ 12.9 km long. Surrounded by suburban developments. Fed and drained by Sammamish R., flowing another c.15 mi/24 km N from N end of Sammamish L. and W past Woodinville and Bothell to N end of L. Washington. L. Sammamish State Park at SE end. City of Bellevue on W shore; Redmond at N end.

Samoa, uninc. village, Humboldt co., NW Calif., on sandspit just across Humboldt Bay from Eureka. Terminus of RR spur from Arcata; site of large redwood mill; mfg. (sawmill, pulp and paper). Samoa Cookhouse Mus.; bridge access to Eureka.

Samoset (SAM-uh-set), town (□ 1 sq mi/2.6 sq km; 1990 pop. 3,119), Manatee co., W central Fla., 2 mi/ 3.2 km SE of Bradenton; 27°28′N 82°32′W. Quarrying (dolomite, limestone).

Sampit River, c.25 mi/40 km long, SE S.C.; rises in swampy region of W Georgetown co.; flows E to Winyah Bay at Georgetown. Partly navigable by small crafts.

Sampson, county (□ 947 sq mi/2,453 sq km; 1990 pop. 47,297), SE central N.C.; ⊙ Clinton; 34°59′N 78°22′W. Bounded W and SW by South R.; drained by Black R. and Great Coharrie and Six Run creeks. Coastal plain agr. (wheat, oats, barley, soybeans, peanuts, sorghum, hay, potatoes, sweet potatoes, tobacco, corn, cotton; chickens, turkeys, hogs, cattle); timber (pine, gum) area. Mfg. at Clinton. Formed 1784.

Sampson, park, Seneca co., W central N.Y., on E shore of Seneca L., 12 mi/19 km S of Geneva; 42°44′N 76°55′W. Former Air Force base and training center here, which had been built 1942 as a naval training station, functioned for a time after 1946 as Sampson Col., a state emergency col. for veterans of World War II. It now is Sampson Naval Mus. and state park.

Sam's Point, N.Y.: see SHAWANGUNK MOUNTAIN.

Samson, town (1990 pop. 2,190), Geneva co., SE Ala., 12 mi/19 km NW of Geneva, near Fla. state line and Pea R. Lumber, peanuts, plastic pipe mfg. Conecuh Natl. Forest is W. Settled 1895, inc. 1906.

Samsonville, resort village (1990 pop. 150), Ulster co., SE N.Y., in the Catskills, 15 mi/24 km W of Kingston; 41°53′N 74°18′W. High Point mt. is just N.

Samsula (sam-SOO-luh), town (1990 pop. 3,331), Volusia co., E central Fla., 6 mi/9.7 km W of New Smyrna Beach.

San Agustín, Mexico: see ELOXOCHTLÁN.

San Agustín Amatengo (sahn ah-goos-TEEN ah-mah-TEN-go), town (1990 pop. 2,229), in S Oaxaca, Mexico, 6 mi/9.7 km SW of Ejutla de Crespo; 16°30′N 96°47′W. Elev. 4,429 ft/1,350 m. Temperate climate in Valle Grande on Atoyac R. Farming, mainly for subsistence. A Zapotec-speaking community.

San Agustín Atenango (sahn ah-goos-TEEN ah-ten-AHN-go), town (1990 pop. 1,658) in NW Oaxaca, Mexico, 22 mi/35 km SW of Huajuapam de León, 1 mi/ 1.6 km off paved road to Huajuapam de León. Elev. 5,495 ft/1,675 m. Agr. (beans, corn, aguardiente; cattle), woven straw textiles.

San Agustín Chayuco (sahn ah-goos-TEEN chah-YOO-ko), town (1990 pop. 193), in SW Oaxaca, Mexico, 8 mi/12.9 km N of Santiago Jamiltepec. In a valley of la Arena R.; 16°25′N 97°48′W. Elev. 820 ft/250 m. Hot climate. Pop. consists of blacks and mulattoes. Agr. (corn, beans, coffee, sugarcane, and tropical fruits). Access to Mexico Highway 200 by unpaved road.

San Agustín de las Juntas (sahn ah-goos-TEEN dai

lahs HOON-tahs), town (1990 pop. 2,646), in central Oaxaca, Mexico, 6 mi/10 km S of Oaxaca de Juárez; 17°00′N 96°42′W. Elev. 5,144 ft/1,568 m. Temperate climate with summer rain. Farming. A Zapotec community.

San Agustín Etla (sahn ah-goos-TEEN ET-lah), town (1990 pop. 2,819), in central Oaxaca, Mexico, 7 mi/12 km N of Oaxaca de Juárez, 2 mi/3.2 km E off Inter-Amer. Highway; 17°12′N 96°46′W. Elev. 5,440 ft/1,658 m. Total pop. lives here in capital of the municipality. Farming. A Zapotec community.

San Agustín Loxicha (sahn ah-goos-TEEN lo-SHE-chah), town (1990 pop. 1,955), in S central Oaxaca, Mexico, 22 mi/35 km S of Mianuatlán de Porfirio Díaz; 16°02′N 96°37′W. Elev. 6,184 ft/1,885 m. On unpaved road in rugged mt. area. In the S part of the state, high quality coffee and corn are produced on a large scale. A Zapotec community.

San Agustín Metzquititlán, Mexico: see METZQUITI-TLÁN.

San Agustín Tlacotepec (sahn ah-goos-TEEN tlah-KO-te-pek), town (1990 pop. 245), in W Oaxaca, Mexico, 11 mi/18 km ESE of Tlaxiaco; 17°93′N 97°32′W. Elev. 5,709 ft/1,740 m. Agr. (corn, beans, wheat, mezcal, fruits); mfg. (wood prods. and woven textiles). On unpaved road. A Mixtec town.

San Agustín Tlaxiaca (sahn ah-goos-TEEN tlah-hee-AH-kah), town (1990 pop. 6,982), ⊙ San Agustín Tlaxiaca municipio, Hidalgo, central Mexico, on RR, and 10 mi/16 km W of Pachuca de Soto; 20°07′N 98°53′W. Elev. 7,782 ft/2,372 m. Cereals, beans, maguey; livestock. Also known as Tlaxiaca.

San Agustín Yatareni (sahn ah-goos-TEEN yah-tah-RE-nee), town (1990 pop. 2,687), in central Oaxaca, Mexico, 5 mi/8 km NE of Oaxaca de Juárez, on Mexico Highway 175. Elev. 5,472 ft/1,668 m. Agr. is the main industry. Prods. are sold in the state capital (Oaxaca de Juárez.) A Zapotec town.

San Andreas, uninc. town (1990 pop. 2,115), ⊙ Calaveras co., central Calif., 38 mi/61 km NE of Stockton; 38°11′N 120°40′W. Gold mining; grapes, walnuts, olives, oats, honey, cattle. In 1849 Gold Rush Region. New Hogan Reservoir to W; Pardee Reservoir to NW.

San Andreas, reservoir (□ 1 sq mi/2.6 sq km), San Mateo co., central Calif., on tributary of San Mateo Creek, along San Andreas Rift Zone, in San Francisco State Game and Fish Refuge, 4 mi/6.4 km W of Burlingame; 37°35′N 122°25′W. Max. capacity 22,985 acre-ft. Formed by San Andreas Dam (107 ft/33 m high), built (1870) for water supply; owned by city and co. of San Francisco.

San Andreas Fault, large rift in the earth's crust in coastal Calif. It is the principal fault of an intricate network of faults extending more than 600 mi/966 km from NW Calif. to the Gulf of California. The San Andreas fault, a strike-slip fault, also extends vertically at least 20 mi/32 km into the earth. It is located on the boundary bet. 2 sects. of the earth's crust—the N. Amer. plate and the Pacific plate—and separates SW Calif. from remainder of the N. Amer. continent. The Pacific plate is moving NW in relation to the N. Amer. plate, and it is believed that the total displacement along the fault since its formation more than 30 million years ago has been about 350 mi/563 km. Movement along the fault causes earthquakes; several thousand occur annually, although only a few are of moderate or higher magnitude. The destructive San Francisco earthquake of 1906 was caused by a movement in which land surfaces on either side of the fault were displaced horizontally up to 21 ft/6 m. The rift is most noticeable on surface at Upper and Lower Crystal Springs reservoirs and San Andreas Reservoir, in San Mateo co., S of San Francisco; the reservoirs are aligned SE-NW with the fault. It continues NW beneath Pacific Ocean and reemerges at Point Reyes Peninsula, Monterey co., where it nearly separates peninsula from mainland.

San Andrés, Mexico: see RIVA PALACIO.

San Andrés Ahuatlán, Mexico: see AHUATLÁN.

San Andrés Cabecera Nueva (sahn ahn-DRAIS kah-be-SE-rah noo-AI-vah), town (1990 pop. 394), in W Oaxaca, Mexico, 20 mi/32 km SE of Putla de Guerrero; 16°53′N 97°41′W. Elev. 5,709 ft/1,740 m. A mountainous region in the Verde R. drainage. Temperate climate. There is little level land available for agr. use by the pop. Forestry, mezcal. A Mixtec town.

San Andrés Calpan (sahn ahn-DRAIS KAHL-pahn), town (1990 pop. 8,828), Puebla, central Mexico, on E slope of Iztaccihuatl volcano, 16 mi/26 km WNW of Puebla; 19°06′N 98°27′W. Agr. center (cereals, vegetables, maguey; livestock).

San Andrés Chiautla (sahn ahn-DRAIS chee-OUT-lah), ⊙ town (1990 pop. 4,417), Chiautla municipio, Mexico state, central Mexico, 17 mi/27 km NE of Mexico city, and in the Zona Metropolitana de la Ciudad de Mexico; 19°30′N 98°13′W. Cereals, maguey; livestock. Sometimes called Chiautla.

San Andrés Cholula (sahn ahn-DRAIS cho-LOO-lah), town (1990 pop. 18,259), Puebla, central Mexico, 6 mi/9.7 km W of Puebla. Cereals, fruit; livestock.

San Andrés Dinicuiti (sahn ahn-DRAIS dee-nee-KWEE-tee), town (1990 pop. 884), in NW Oaxaca, Mexico, 9 mi/15 km SSE of Huajuapam de León; 17°40′N 97°44′W. Elev. 4,265 ft/1,300 m. Temperate climate colder at higher elevs. Agr. (corn, beans, wheat), cattle raising, and mezcal processing. There is a road to Huajuapam de León.

San Andrés Huaxpaltepec (sahn ahn-DRAIS hwaks-PAHL-te-pek), town (1990 pop. 3,533), in SW Oaxaca, Mexico, on Mexico Highway 200, 7 mi/11.3 km NW of Santiago Jamiltepec; 16°20′N 97°55′W. Very hot climate. Agr. (corn, beans, sugarcane, and tropical fruits).

San Andrés Huayapam (sahn ahn-DRAIS hwah-yah-PAHM), town (1990 pop. 2,355), in central Oaxaca, Mexico, 3.1 mi/5 km NE of Oaxaca de Juárez; 17°06′N 96°40′W. A Zapotec community.

San Andrés Ixtlahuaca (sahn ahn-DRAIS eeks-tlah-HWAH-kah), town (1990 pop. 841), in central Oaxaca, Mexico, 5 mi/8 km W of Oaxaca de Juárez; 17°04′N 96°49′W. Elev. 5,413 ft/1,650 m. In the Oaxaca Valley near the Atoyac R. Temperate climate. Agr. (corn, beans, wheat, fruits), pottery, and woven textiles. A Zapotec community.

San Andrés Jaltenco, Mexico: see JALTENCO.

San Andrés Lagunas (sahn ahn-DRAIS lah-GOO-nahs), town (1990 pop. 339), in NW Oaxaca, Mexico, 24 mi/39 km SE of Huajuapam de León; 17°34′N 97°32′W. Elev. 7546 ft/2,300 m. Mountainous. Temperate climate. Agr. (corn, beans, wheat, fruits), woods, mezcal, and cattle.

San Andrés Larrainzar, Mexico: see LARRAINZAR.

San Andres Mountains (san AN-druhs), S N.Mex., in Sierra and Doña Ana cos., paralleling Rio Grande on E, extend N from Organ Mts. and San Agustin Pass to Sierra Oscura (Socorro co.); 32°40′N 106°32′W. Highest point, Salinas Peak (8,958 ft/2,730 m; N). White Sands Natl. Monument is just E. Mts. are almost entirely in White Sands Missile Range.

San Andrés Nuxiño (sahn ahn-DRAIS noo-HEEN-yo), town (1990 pop. 180), in central Oaxaca, Mexico, 29 mi/47 km NW of Oaxaca de Juárez; 17°05′N 97°06′W. Elev. 5,938 ft/1,810 m. Agr. (cereals, fruits, mezcal), woods, and pottery. Near the Inter-Amer. Highway (190). A Mixtec-speaking community.

San Andrés Paxtlán (sahn ahn-DRAIS PASH-tlahn), town (1990 pop. 927), in SE Oaxaca, Mexico, 10 mi/16 km SE of Miahuatlan de Porfirio Díaz; 16°13′N 96°29′W. Elev. 5,413 ft/1,650 m. Agr. Just W of Mexico Highway 175. Temperate climate. Some farming. A Zapotec community.

San Andrés Sinaxtla (sahn ahn-DRAIS see-NAKS-tlah), town (1990 pop. 492), in NW Oaxaca, Mexico, on Inter-Amer. Highway (190), 40 mi/65 km SE of Huajuapam de León; 17°28′N 97°17′W. Elev. 7,054 ft/2,150 m. In Rio Grande valley; cool climate. Agr. (cereals and fruits), straw textiles, and wood. Mixtec community.

San Andrés Solaga (sahn ahn-DRAIS so-LAH-gah), town (1990 pop. 865), in central Oaxaca, Mexico, 37 mi/60 km NE of Oaxaca de Juárez; 17°17′N 96°13′W. Elev.

5,610 ft/1,710 m. A mountainous region with a temperate climate. Agr. (cereals and fruits), forestry, and cattle. In Zapotec-speaking area.

San Andrés Tenejapan (sahn ahn-DRAIS te-ne-HAH-pahn), town (1990 pop. 481), W central Veracruz, Mexico, 3.7 mi/6 km S of Orizaba; 18°47′N 97°05′W. Elev. 4,462 ft/1,360 m. Rugged terrain with water from tributaries that form the Blanco R. Temperate rainy climate. Agr. (corn, beans, coffee, sugarcane, fruits), wood, cattle, and poultry raising.

San Andrés Teotilalpam (sahn ahn-DRAIS te-o-tee-lahl-PAHM), town (1990 pop. 1,215), in N Oaxaca, Mexico, 38 mi/61 km NNE of Tuxtepec; 17°57′N 96°40′W. Elev. 2,297 ft/700 m. Hot climate. A region of steep terrain irrigated by the Santo Domingo R., as it flows to the Papaloapan R. Agr. (corn, beans, fruits), lumber, and cattle. A Mixtec community.

San Andrés Tepetlapa (sahn ahn-DRAIS te-pet-LAH-pah), town (1990 pop. 585), in extreme NW Oaxaca, Mexico, 43 mi/70 km SW of Huajuapam de León; 17°37′N 98°22′W. Elev. 4,921 ft/1,500 m. Bordering the state of Guerrero. Mild climate. Small farming, mainly subsistence. In the Mixteca Baja.

San Andrés Tuxtla (sahn ahn-DRAIS TOOSH-tlah), city (1990 pop. 49,658), Veracruz, SE Mexico, at S foot of Tuxtla Volcano, 80 mi/129 km SE of Veracruz; 18°26′N 95°11′W. RR terminus; on Mexico Highway 180. Agr. center (fruit, high-grade tobacco); cigar making. Formerly called Los Tuxtlas.

San Andrés Yaá (sahn ahn-DRAIS YAH-ah), town (1990 pop. 687), in E Oaxaca, Mexico, 43 mi/70 km NE of Oaxaca de Juárez; 17°20′N 96°09′W. Elev. 5,512 ft/1,680 m. Temperate climate. Forestry (woods, pine, cypress, white cedar).

San Andrés Zabache (sahn ahn-DRAIS zah-BAH-che), town (1990 pop. 1,074), in central Oaxaca, Mexico, 31 mi/50 km SSW of Oaxaca de Juárez; 16°36′N 96°50′W. Small farming, mainly for subsistence. On Atoyac R. A Zapotec community.

San Andrés Zautla (sahn ahn-DRAIS zah-OO-tlah), town (1990 pop. 1,693), Oaxaca, Mexico, 12 mi/19 km NW of Oaxaca de Juárez; 17°13′N 96°49′W. Elev. 5,528 ft/1,685 m. A mountainous region on the Atoyac R. Temperate climate. Agr., cattle, poultry breeding, and textile industry for local artisans. A Zapotec community.

San Angelo, city (1990 pop. 84,474), ⊙ Tom Green co., W Texas, 80 mi/129 km SW of Abilene, where North, South, and Middle forks join to form the Concho R.; 31°26′N 100°27′W. Elev. 1,847 ft/563 m. It is an important wool and mohair market and a trade and shipping point for a wide area of sheep, goat, and cattle ranches, irrigated farms (cotton; wheat, sorghum, sesame), and oil and natural gas fields. Mfg. (meat and dairy prods., shoes, leather goods, surgical sutures, and stone, fiberglass, and metal prods.). Founded beside a border military post, Fort Concho (1867; restored as a mus., now a Natl. Historical Landmark), San Angelo was a rough frontier town of cattle trails and overland traffic in the 1870s; it grew after the coming of the RR in 1888. Angelo State Univ. is there. Mathis Field airport to SW; Goodfellow Air Force Base is in SE part of the city and O. C. Fisher L. reservoir on NW side of city, large park area on SW shore. L. Nasworthy reservoir and Twin Buttes Reservoir to SW. Est. 1867, inc. 1903.

San Angelo Dam, Texas: see O.C. FISHER LAKE.

San Anselmo, city (1990 pop. 11,743), Marin co., W Calif., a residential suburb 15 mi/24 km NNW of downtown San Francisco; 37°59′N 122°34′W. San Francisco Theological Seminary (1871) is there. Point Reyes Natl. Seashore to W; Mt. Tamalpais State Park and Muir Woods Natl. Monument to S; San Anselmo Creek (Ross Valley). Inc. 1907.

San Antonio, sugar-mill village, Guantánamo prov., E Cuba, 8 mi/12.9 km E of Guantánamo. Also called Río Seco.

San Antonio (sahn ahn-TO-nyo), town (1990 pop. 387), NE San Luis Potosí, Mexico, 29 mi/46 km ESE of Ciudad Valles. At base of Sierra Madre Oriental. On

Río Coy, tributary of Tampaón R. Resources are cattle and agr. Some Huastec-speaking residents.

San Antonio (sahn ahn-TO-nyo), village (1990 pop. 15), Comondu municipio, Baja California Sur, NW Mexico, on Mexico Highway 1, 30 mi/48 km S of La Paz; 23°50′N 110°00′W. Silver, lead, gold mining.

San Antonio (san an-TO-nee-o), city (1990 pop. 935,933), ⊙ Bexar co., S central Texas, 190 mi/306 km W of Houston, at the source of the San Antonio R.; 29°27′N 98°30′W. Elev. 750 ft/229 m. It is one of the nation's largest military centers; Fort Sam Houston and Air Force Aerospace Medical Center are in the city, and nearby are Lackland and Randolph air force bases, both training command centers; Brooks Air Force Base, an aerospace medical hq.; Camp Bullis Military Reservation to N; and Kelly Air Force Base (to be closed), an air material and security service post. San Antonio is also the industrial, commercial, and financial center of a large agr. area. Its manufactures include sunglasses, computerized mapping equip., snack foods, air conditioners, aircraft parts, beer, textile finishing, picante sauce, and draperies and curtains. Tourism is also an important industry. The tree-lined river meandering through the downtown, the huge Mex. quarter, the Franciscan missions, and the warm climate attract thousands of tourists annually. The pop. of San Antonio increased by nearly 45% bet. 1970 and 1990, and its outlying suburban area developed and expanded significantly in those two decades. The site had been visited by the Spanish long before the expedition under Martín de Alarcón founded a mission (San Antonio de Valero, "The Alamo") and a presidio (San Antonio de Béjar or Béxar) there in 1718. Other missions were opened along the river—San José (1719), Concepción (1731), San Francisco de la Espada (1731), and San Juan Capistrano (1731)—and the neighboring town of San Fernando (now the heart of San Antonio) was founded in 1731. San Antonio was the most important Texas settlement in Span. and Mex. days. During the Texas revolution it was captured by the Texans (Dec. 1835) and was the scene of the ALAMO (now downtown) in March 1836. Later a group of Comanche were killed (1840) in the "council house fight," and in 1842, San Antonio was taken and held briefly by Mexicans. After the Civil War and especially after the coming of the first RR in 1877, San Antonio prospered as a roaring cow town with a Span. flavor, which it still retains. San Antonio Internatl. Airport in N part. Points of interest include the Alamo; La Villita, the reconstruction of a 250-year-old Span.-speaking settlement; the Span. governor's palace (c.1749); the Paseo del Río, the River Walk, along San Antonio R.; the Hertzberg Circus Collection; San Antonio Zoo; San Fernando Cathedral (1738); Joe Freeman Coliseum; the Alamodome sports center; and numerous old homes. The Hemisfair Plaza, site of the 1968 World's Fair, contains the Inst. of Texan Cultures and the 750 ft/229 m Tower of the Americas. Among San Antonio's educational institutions are Trinity Univ., St. Mary's Univ., Incarnate Word Col., Our Lady of the Lake Col., San Antonio Col., Natl. Univ. of Mexico, Palo Alto Col. (2-year), and the Univ. of Texas at San Antonio. The Southwest Research Inst. is notable for its research into the technical problems of the SW region. San Antonio Missions Natl. Historical Park has 4 Span. missions (La Espada, San Jose, Capistrano, and Concepción); San Jose and Navarro House state historic sites within city. The city has artists' colonies, a symphony orchestra, McNay Inst., and numerous mus., including Cowboy Mus. Area reservoirs include Calaveras and Branning lakes (SE), Mitchell and Blue Wing lakes (S). Inc. 1837.

San Antonio (san an-TO-nee-o), uninc. village (1990 pop. 359), Socorro co., W central N.Mex., and 10 mi/16 km S of Socorro, on Rio Grande, and part of Cibola Natl. Forest to W. Elev. 4,500 ft/1,372 m. In irrigated alfalfa region; cattle, sheep; chiles, dairying, wheat. Trading point for ranches. Nogal Canyon (300 ft/91 m–1,000 ft/305 m deep) nearby. Fort Craig Natl. Historic Site to SW; Jornada del Muerto plain to SE, including part of White Plains Missile Range. Early home of Conrad Hilton.

San Antonio Acutla (sahn ahn-TO-nyo ah-KOOT-lah), town (1990 pop. 105), NW Oaxaca, Mexico, 22 mi/35 km ESE of Huajuapam de León; 17°39′N 97°26′W. Elev. 7,218 ft/2,200 m. Temperate climate. In the Mixteca Alta. Farming, mainly for subsistence.

San Antonio Bay, S Texas, 27 mi/43 km SSE of Victoria, an inlet sheltered from Gulf of Mexico by Matagorda Isl.; c.19 mi/31 km long NW-SE, c.19 mi/31 km wide. A NW arm is called Hynes Bay. Receives Guadalupe R. in N. Joins Aransas Bay (SW) and Espiritu Santo Bay and thence to Matagorda Bay (NE); Intracoastal Waterway crosses mouth of the bay. Aransas Natl. Wildlife Refuge to SW.

San Antonio Cañada (sahn ahn-TO-nyo kahn-YAH-dah), town (1990 pop. 1,882), SE Puebla, Mexico, 7 mi/11 km NE of Tehuacán; 18°30′N 92°17′W. Elev. 5,810 ft/1,771 m. A mountainous region on the ridges of the Sierra Zongolica in Río Salado drainage. Agr. (cotton, barley, corn, sugarcane, rice, beans, fruits), various woods. Unmined coal, slate quarries, marble, and granite. Poor access by road.

San Antonio, Cape, W extremity of Cuba, Pinar del Río prov., on Guanahacabibes Peninsula, facing Yucatan Peninsula (Mexico), 190 mi/306 km SW of Havana; 21°52′N 84°57′W. Lighthouse.

San Antonio Castillo Velasco (sahn ahn-TO-nyo kahs-TEE-yo ve-LAHS-ko), town (1990 pop. 4,337), in central Oaxaca, Mexico, adjoins Ocotlán de Morelos on NW, on Mexico Highway 175; 16°47′N 96°41′W. Temperate climate. Agr. (castor oil plants, corn, beans). Previously known as Ocotlán San Antonio.

San Antonio Cuaxomulco, Mexico: see CUAXOMULCO.

San Antonio de la Cal (sahn ahn-TO-nyo dai lah KAHL), town (1990 pop. 7,941), central Oaxaca, Mexico, 5 mi/8 km S of Oaxaca de Juarez; 20°45′N 99°55′W. Elev. 5,197 ft/1,584 m. In the Valle Grande arm of the Oaxaca Valley. Temperate climate. Agr. (corn, beans, fruits); pottery; cattle and poultry breeding. Good road access to Oaxaca de Juárez.

San Antonio de las Vegas, town, Ciudad de la Habana prov., W Cuba, on RR, and 10 mi/16 km S of Havana, on N slope of Lomas del Cacahual; 22°57′N 82°23′W. Dairying; sugar growing.

San Antonio de las Vueltas (sahn ahn-TO-nyo dai lahs VWAIL-tahs), town, Villa Clara prov., central Cuba, 15 mi/24 km ENE of Santa Clara, in Remedios tobacco-growing region; 20°32′N 79°43′W. Also raises sugarcane, fruit, cattle, hogs. Mfg. of cigars. The Luis Arcos Bergnes sugar mill is 5 mi/8 km W.

San Antonio de los Baños (sahn ahn-TO-nyo dai los BAHN-yos), city, La Habana prov., W Cuba, on small San Antonio de los Baños R., on RR, and 19 mi/31 km SSW of Havana; 22°53′N 82°30′W. Popular health resort with thermal springs. Also produces high-quality tobacco, pineapples, sugarcane. Mfg. of cigars, yeast, apparel. Military base, Natl. Film School and sugar central nearby.

San Antonio de Padua, Mission, Calif.: see JOLON.

San Antonio de Río Blanco, Cuba: see SAN ANTONIO DEL RÍO BLANCO.

San Antonio del Río Blanco (sahn ahn-TO-nyo dail REE-o BLAHN-ko), town, La Habana prov., W Cuba, on RR, 2.5 mi/4 km NE of Jaruco; 23°06′N 81°58′W. Sugarcane, fruit. Also called San Antonio de Río Blanco or San Antonio de Río Blanco del Norte.

San Antonio el Alto (sahn ahn-TO-nyo el AHL-to), town (1990 pop. 639), in central Oaxaca, Mexico, 24 mi/39 km W of Ocotlán de Morelos; 16°49′N 97°02′W. Elev. 5,669 ft/1,728 m. Agr. (mainly subsistence farming). Temperate climate. In Mixteca area.

San Antonio el Tule, Mexico: see EL TULE.

San Antonio Eloxochitlán, Mexico: see ELOXOCHITLÁN DE FLORES MAGÓN.

San Antonio Heights, uninc. town (1990 pop. 2,935), San Bernardino co., S Calif., residential suburb 35 mi/56 km ENE of downtown Los Angeles, and 6 mi/9.7 km N of Ontario, in S foothills in N, including Cucamonga Wilderness Area and Mt.; 34°09′N 117°40′W. Baldy Ski area.

San Antonio Huitepec (sahn ahn-TO-nyo HWEE-te-pek), town (1990 pop. 1,244), central Oaxaca, Mexico, 28 mi/45 km WSW of Oaxaca de Juárez; 16°56′N 97°08′W. Elev. 7,874 ft/2,400 m. A mountainous region with a temperate climate. Agr. and livestock; mezcal processing, pottery. In the Mixteca area.

San Antonio la Isla, town (1990 pop. 7,309), Mexico state, central Mexico, 11 mi/18 km SSE of Toluca; 19°04′N 99°34′W. Elev. 8,383 ft/2,555 m. Grain, livestock. Also called La Isla.

San Antonio Missions National Historical Park, S central Texas. Covers 477 acres/193 ha; 4 missions situated on or near the San Antonio R.: Mission Nuestra Señora de la Purisma Concepción (Mission Concepción), Mission San Francisco de la Espada (Mission la Espada), Mission San Jose y San Miguel de Aguayo (Mission San Jose), Mission San Juan Capistrano (Mission Capistrano). In S part of San Antonio; important examples of Span. cultural influence. Authorized 1978, est. 1983.

San Antonio Monte Verde (sahn ahn-TO-nyo MON-tai VER-dai), town (1990 pop. 1,021), NW Oaxaca, Mexico, 16 mi/26 km W of San Pedro y San Pablo Teposcoluca; 17°33′N 97°44′W. Elev. 7,382 ft/2,250 m. A mountainous region of the Mixteca Alta. Temperate climate. Agr. (cereals, mezcal) and woods. An unpaved road in San Pedro y San Pablo Teposcolula.

San Antonio, Mount (10,064 ft/3,068 m), on Los Angeles/San Bernardino co. line, S Calif., highest point in San Gabriel Mts., 23 mi/37 km NW of San Bernardino; 34°17′N 117°38′W. Popularly called Old Baldy or Mt. Baldy. Source of San Gabriel R. to N; Angeles Natl. Forest (W); San Bernadino Natl. Forest (E); Mt. Baldy Ski Area is here; scenic road to summit from S.

San Antonio Nanahuatipam (sahn ahn-TO-nyo nah-nah-hwah-tee-PAHM), town (1990 pop. 1,023), in extreme N Oaxaca, Mexico, on the border with the state of Puebla; 18°07′N 97°06′W. Elev. 2,805 ft/855 m. On RR. Connected to Teotitlán and Mexico Highway 131 by unpaved road. In Nahuatl-speaking area.

San Antonio Reservoir 1 Monterey co., SW Calif., on San Antonio R., at San Luis Obispo co. line, 40 mi/64 km NNW of San Luis Obispo; 13 mi/21 km long, 1 mi/1.6 km wide; 35°47′N 12°52′W. Max. capacity 348,000 acre-ft. Mostly in San Antonio Reservoir County Recreation Area. Formed by San Antonio Dam (179 ft/55 m high), built by Monterey city for water supply and debris control. **2** Alameda co., W central Calif., on the San Antonio Creek, in La Costa Valley, 9 mi/14.5 km E of Fremont; 2.5 mi/4 km long; 37°33′N 121°51′W. Extends E; max. capacity 50,000 acre-ft. Formed by James H. Turner Dam (175 ft/53 m high), built (1964) by the City of San Francisco for water supply.

San Antonio River, c.195 mi/314 km long, Texas; rises from springs in San Antonio city; flows SE to Guadalupe R. just above its mouth on San Antonio Bay. Receives Medina R., 5 mi/8 km E of Elmendorf and Cibolo Creek, 6 mi/9.7 km NNE of Karnes City. Los Olmos Creek, in N part of San Antonio, is a continuation of river. Known for the River Walk, which in San Antonio is lined with cafes, shops, and parks.

San Antonio Sinacahua (sahn ahn-TO-nyo see-nah-KAH-hwah), town (1990 pop. 483), in W Oaxaca, Mexico, 13 mi/21 km SE of Tlaxiaco; 17°09′N 97°34′W. Elev. 5,869 ft/1,789 m. Farming, mainly for subsistence. A Mixtec community.

San Antonio Tepetlapa (sahn ahn-TO-nyo te-pet-LAH-pah), town (1990 pop. 2,116), in extreme SW Oaxaca, Mexico, on the border with the state of Guerrero, 14 mi/22 km N of Santiago Pinotepa Macronac; 16°33′N 98°05′W. Elev. 6,542 ft/1,994 m. In coastal lowland on tributary of Cortijos R. Hot climate. Agr. (sugarcane, coffee, corn, beans, tropical fruits), woods. Poor roads.

San Augustin Pass (san aw-guh-STEEN), Doña Ana co., S N.Mex., 13 mi/21 km NE of Las Cruces, bet. Organ Mts. and San Andres Mts. Elev. 5,719 ft/1,743 m. Crossed by U.S. Highway 70.

San Augustin, Plains of (san aw-guh-STEEN), mostly Catron co., extends NE into Socorro co., W N.Mex. Bounded by Datil and Gallo Mts. (NW), Tularosa Mts. (W), Black Range and San Mateo Mts. (SE); 75 mi/121 km long (NE-SW), 15 mi/24 km–20 mi/32 km wide. Continental Divide encircles valley N, W, and S. Natl. Radio Observatory and Very Large Array (V.L.A.) telescope in NE end of plains.

San Augustine, county (□ 592 sq mi/1,533 sq km; 1990 pop. 7,999), E Texas; ⊙ San Augustine; 31°23′N 94°10′W. Bounded W by Attoyac Bayou, and Attoyac Arm of Sam Rayburn Reservoir, SW by Angelina R. (Sam Rayburn Reservoir). Includes part of Angelina Natl. Forest in SW and part of Sabine Natl. Forest in NE. Timber (pine, hardwoods) is important. Agr. (corn, vegetables, watermelons), beef cattle, horses, poultry. Hunting, fishing. Formed 1836.

San Augustine, town (1990 pop. 2,337), ⊙ San Augustine co., E Texas, on small Ayish Bayou, and 32 mi/51 km ESE of Nacogdoches; 31°31′N 94°06′W. Elev. 304 ft/93 m. Center of pine lumbering area. Region was site of a Span. mission (1716–1719; 1721–1773); a fort here (1756–1773) protected Span.-Fr. border. Settled 1818 by Anglo-Americans. Poultry, esp. chickens; cattle; watermelons, vegetables; mfg. (wood chips, fiberglass boats and tanks, RR ties). Sabine Natl. Forest to E, Angelina Natl. Forest to SW.

San Baltazar Chichicapam (sahn bahl-tah-SAHR chee-chee-kah-PAHM), town (1990 pop. 3,309), in central Oaxaca, Mexico, 34 mi/54 km SE of Oaxaca de Juárez; 16°45′N 96°29′W. Elev. 5,577 ft/1,700 m. Linked to Ocotlán de Morelos by unpaved road. Agr. and cattle. Zapotec community.

San Baltazar Loxicha (sahn bahl-tah-SAHR lo-SHE-chah), town (1990 pop. 1,987), in extreme S central Oaxaca, Mexico, 22 mi/36 km SW of Miahuatlán de Porfirio Díaz; 16°04′N 96°48′W. Elev. 1,837 ft/560 m. Linked to Miahuatlán de Porfirio Díaz. Unpaved road. Agr. (coffee, corn, fruit), wood, and fabricating. A coastal Zapotec community.

San Baltazar Yatzechi el Bajo 1 (sahn bahl-tah-SAHR yaht-ZET-chee el BAH-ho), town, Oaxaca, Mexico, 35 mi/56 km ENE of Oaxaca de Juárez; 17°13′N 96°13′W. Elev. 4,921 ft/1,500 m. A Zapotec community. Farming, mainly for subsistence. Access by dirt track. **2** town (1990 pop. 266), in central Oaxaca, Mexico, 34 mi/55 km NE of Oaxaca de Juárez. Elev. 5,545 ft/1,690 m. Agr. (cereals, fruits); woods, fabrics, mezcal. A Zapotec town.

San Bartolo, Mexico: see GENERAL SIMÓN BOLÍVAR.

San Bartolo Coyotepec (sahn bahr-TO-lo ko-YO-te-pek), town (1990 pop. 2,354), ⊙ San Bartolo Coyotepec municipio, Oaxaca, S Mexico, in Sierra Madre del Sur, 9 mi/15 km S of Oaxaca de Juárez; 16°58′N 96°42′W. Elev. 5,174 ft/1,577 m. Noted for black pottery. A Zapotec community.

San Bartolo Morelos (sahn bahr-TO-lo mo-RE-los), town (1990 pop. 1,534), ⊙ Morelos municipio, Mexico state, central Mexico, 43 mi/70 km NW of Mexico city; 19°41′N 99°40′W. Cereals, fruit, maguey; livestock.

San Bartolo Soyaltepec (sahn bahr-TO-lo so-YAHL-te-pek), town (1990 pop. 155), in NW Oaxaca, Mexico, 16 mi/25 km NNE of San Pedro y San Pablo Teposcolula; 17°34′N 97°20′W. Elev. 5,289 ft/1,612 m. Agr. (cattle and poultry). Process mezcal. In Mixteca Alta.

San Bartolo Tutotepec (sahn bahr-TO-lo too-TO-te-pek), town (1990 pop. 1,791), Hidalgo, central Mexico, 40 mi/64 km ENE of Pachuca de Soto; 20°25′N 98°12′W. Cereals, sugarcane, coffee, tobacco, fruit.

San Bartolo Yautepec (sahn bahr-TO-lo yah-OO-te-pek), town (1990 pop. 155), in SE Oaxaca, Mexico, 50 mi/80 km WNW of port Salina Cruz, 6 mi/9.7 km W of Mexico Highway 190, on unpaved road; 16°26′N 95°59′W. Farming, mainly for subsistence. Zapotec community.

San Bartolomé, Mexico: see VENUSTIANO CARRANZA.

San Bartolomé Ayautla (sahn bahr-TO-lo-MAI ah-yah-OO-tlah), town (1990 pop. 2,169), in N central Oaxaca, Mexico, 36 mi/58 km W of Textepec; 18°02′N 96°40′W. Elev. 2,133 ft/650 m. A mountainous region on the Santo Domingo R. Warm climate. Agr. (corn, wheat, beans, fruits), woods. On unpaved road. Mazatec-speaking area.

San Bartolomé Loxicha (sahn bahr-TO-lo-MAI lo-SHE-chah), town (1990 pop. 1,185), in S central Oaxaca, Mexico, 22 mi/36 km NW of San Pedro Pochutla; 15°58′N 96°43′W. Elev. 4,100 ft/1,250 m. Rough terrain. Temperate climate. Agr. (coffee, corn, beans, fruits); forest. Dirt track. Coastal Zapotec town.

San Bartolomé Quialana (sahn bahr-TO-lo-MAI kee-ah-LAH-nah), town (1990 pop. 2,510), in central Oaxaca, Mexico, 4 mi/6.4 km S of Tlacolula de Matamoros. Elev. 5,840 ft/1,780 m. Farming, mainly for subsistence. Zapotec community.

San Bartolomé Yucuañe (sahn bahr-TO-lo-MAI yoo-KWAHN-yai), town (1990 pop. 575), in central Oaxaca, Mexico, 16 mi/25 km E of Tlaxiaco; 17°14′N 97°27′W. Linked by unpaved road to Mexico Highway 125 (16 mi/25 km). Farming, mainly for subsistence. Mixtec community.

San Bartolomé Zoogocho (sahn bahr-TO-lo-MAI zo-o-GO-cho), town (1990 pop. 716), in central Oaxaca, Mexico, 33 mi/54 km ENE of Oaxaca de Juárez; 17°14′N 96°15′W. Elev. 5,512 ft/1,680 m. Zapotec community.

San Benedicto Island, Mexico: see REVILLAGIGEDO ISLANDS.

San Benito, county (□ 1,390 sq mi/3,600 sq km; 1990 pop. 36,697), W Calif.; ⊙ Hollister; 36°37′N 121°05′W. San Benito R. flows through San Benito Valley bet. Gabilan Range (W) and Diablo Range (E). Lewis Creek forms part of S boundary. Pajaro R. forms part of S boundary. San Benito Mt. (5,239 ft/1,597 m) in Diablo Range is c.20 mi/32 km NNW of Coalinga. Part of PINNACLES NATIONAL MONUMENT in SW. San Juan Bautista State Historical Park in NW. Nursery prods.; lettuce, peppers, onions, lettuce, grapes, eggs, poultry, wheat, barley, oats; granite, sand, gravel, mercury, limestone. Formed 1874. Upper part of Santa Clara Valley in N; Hollister Hills State Park in NW.

San Benito, city (1990 pop. 20,125), Cameron co., extreme S Texas, suburb 5 mi/8 km SE of Harlingen, and 18 mi/29 km NW of Brownsville; 26°08′N 97°38′W. San Benito is chiefly a processing center for citrus fruit and vegetables grown in the irrigated region of the lower Rio Grande valley. Mfg. (blue jeans, meat processing, fire retardant coverings, concrete). San Benito is also a retirement and winter tourist center. Municipal Airport (E). Inc. 1911.

San Benito Mountain, Calif.: see DIABLO RANGE.

San Benito River, c.70 mi/113 km long, San Benito co., W Calif.; rises in Diablo Range in SE San Benito co., just S of San Benito Mt., 18 mi/29 km NW of Coalinga; flows NW, bet. Gabilan (W) and Diablo (E) ranges, past Hollister to Pajaro R. 9 mi/14.5 km WNW of Hollister.

San Bernard River, c.120 mi/193 km, S Texas; rises in N Colorado co.; flows generally SSE to Gulf of Mexico 7 mi/11.3 km SW of Freeport.

San Bernardino, county (□ 20,062 sq mi/51,961 sq km; 1990 pop. 1,418,380), S Calif.; ⊙ San Bernardino; 34°50′N 116°11′W. Co. is over 200 mi/322 km E-W and over 120 mi/193 km N-S; largest co. in U.S. The SW corner (San Bernardino Valley), which lies S and W of San Gabriel Mts. and San Bernardino Mts. (both over 11,000 ft/3,353 m), is agr. area, which has been largely displaced by urban development, is continuation of Los Angeles urban area (to W), and has most of co.'s pop. Mojave Desert dominates remainder of co., to N and NE; bounded on E by Nev. and Ariz. state lines (the latter formed by Colorado R.), is part of COLORADO DESERT. SW border comes within 25 mi/40 km of Pacific Ocean. Mfg. (plastics prods., printing machinery, sand and gravel, printing and publishing, millwork, prefabricated structural metal, baked goods, industrial glass, apparel, filter aids, diverse light mfg.). In desert are ranches and some irrigated agr. (esp. S) (at irrigated dists. Victorville, Barstow, Needles): dairying, cattle, eggs, chickens, alfalfa, strawberries, oranges, grapefruits, oriental vegetables, nursery prods., barley. Mines and quarries (potash, borax, iron, sand and gravel, gold, talc, bentonite, clay, lead, zinc, limestone, salt). Shipping of farm prods. San Manuel Indian Reservation in SW (near San Bernadino); Twentynine Palms Indian Reservation in S; part of Fort Mojave, Chimehueri, and Colorado River Indian reservations in SE. Twentynine Palms Marine Corps Base in S; Fort Irwin Military Reservation in N; 2 parts of Chino Lake Naval Weapons Center in NW; part of Edwards Air Force Base in W; Norton Air Force Base in SE. About 75% of co. is publicly owned lands: part of San Bernardino Natl. Forest in SW, part of JOSHUA TREE NATIONAL MONUMENT in S, part of DEATH VALLEY NATIONAL MONUMENT in N. Mt. summer and winter resorts (notably Arrowhead and Big Bear lakes). Mojave Natl. Scenic Area and Providence Mts. State Recreation Area in NE; part of Chino Hills State Park in SE; Sherwood L. State Recreation area and Heart Bar State Park in SW. Formed 1853.

San Bernardino, city (1990 pop. 164,164), seat of San Bernardino co., S Calif., 55 mi/89 km E of downtown Los Angeles, and 10 mi/16 km at the foot of the San Bernardino Mts.; 34°08′N 117°17′W. Satellite city of Los Angeles. Drained by Lytle Creek. RR junction. It is the center of a thriving metropolitan area that includes the rapidly expanding cities of Ontario and Riverside. San Bernardino is one of the fastest-growing U.S. cities, marked by a pop. increase of more than 38% bet. 1980 and 1990. Among the mfg. is steel, iron, and related prods.; aerospace, electronic, and electrical goods; and food items. The adjacent Norton Air Force Base to SE is a major employer. The area was visited (1772), named (1810), and 1st settled by Span. explorers. A colony of Mormons arrived in the early 1850s and plotted the present city. It is the seat of Calif. State Univ., San Bernardino, and San Bernardino Valley Col. (2-year). San Manuel Indian Reservation on E edge of city. Tri-City Airport to S; Colton Airport to SW. The city is also the hq. of the San Bernardino Natl. Forest, which is on city's N boundary; San Bernardino Mts. to NE. Resort and recreational areas are nearby. San Gabriel Mts. to NW; Snow Valley and Green Valley ski areas to NE; Natl. Orange Show Grounds in S; Waterman Canyon to N; Arrowhead Hot Springs on N edge of city. Inc. 1854.

San Bernardino Contla, Mexico: see CONTLA, town.

San Bernardino Mountains, part of the Tranverse Ranges, San Bernardino co., S Calif., extending c.60 mi/97 km E-W N of San Bernardino, continuation of San Gabriel Mts. to W; 34°07′N 116°54′W. Notable peaks are San Bernardino Mt. (10,864 ft/3,311 m) and Mt. San Gorgonio (11,490 ft/3,502 m). This region embraces the mt. resort and recreational areas around Gregory, Arrowhead, and Big Bear lakes, in San Bernardino Natl. Forest. Mojave Desert is to N and E.

San Bernardino Valley, Calif.: see SAN BERNARDINO, co.

San Bernardo (sahn ber-NAHR-do), town (1990 pop. 884), Durango, N Mexico, on Sextín R., and 65 mi/105 km N of Santiago Papasquiaro; 25°59′N 105°28′W. Elev. 6,070 ft/1,850 m. Fluorspar and antimony mining.

San Bernardo Mixtepec (sahn ber-NAHR-do MEESH-te-pek), town (1990 pop. 1,895), in central Oaxaca, Mexico, 15 mi/24 km W of Ocotlán de Morelos; 16°49′N 96°54′W. Elev. 5,709 ft/1,740 m. Located 6 mi/9.7 km off Mexico Highway 131 on unpaved road. Agr. (corn, beans, wheat, potatoes, mezcal, fruits), cattle.

San Blas, town (1990 pop. 8,433), Nayarit, W Mexico, minor port on the Pacific, on narrow ocean inlet, S of mouth of Santiago R., 23 mi/37 km W of Tepic; 21°35′N 105°20′W. Corn, tobacco, coffee, cotton, bananas. Once important shipping point, esp. in viceregal times, when it had pop. of c.30,000. Harbor has gradually silted up.

San Blas Atempa (sahn blahs ah-TEM-pah), town (1990 pop. 8,370), in SE Oaxaca, Mexico, part of Santo Domingo Teuantepec, which it adjoins on NE. Hot climate. Agr. (corn, beans, coffee, fruits; cattle), woods; textiles. On Inter-Amer. Highway (190). In Zapotec area.

San Blas, Cape (san-BLAHS), Gulf co., NW Fla., on Gulf of Mexico, 12 mi/19 km SW of Port St. Joe, at SW point of sandspit enclosing St. Joseph Bay.

San Bruno, city (1990 pop. 38,961), San Mateo co., W Calif., residential suburb 10 mi/16 km S of downtown San Francisco, on San Francisco Bay; 37°37'N 122°26'W. Skyline Col. (2-year), a natl. archives and records center, and a U.S. Marine Corps reserve base are in the city. Mfg. (communications equip., plastic bags, publishing, printed circuit boards, petroleum refining). San Francisco Internatl. Airport adjoins it to E on bay shore. Part of Golden Gate Natl. Recreation Area to W; San Francisco State Fish and Game Refuge to SW, including San Andreas L. reservoir, on San Andreas Fault. Inc. 1914.

San Buenaventura (sahn bwai-nah-ven-TOO-rah), town (1990 pop. 17,511), Coahuila, N Mexico, 15 mi/24 km NW of Monclova, on Mexico Highway 30; 27°04'N 101°32'W. Agr. center (corn, wheat, fruit; cattle, sheep).

San Buenaventura, Calif.: see VENTURA, city.

San Buenaventura Nealtican (sahn bwai-nah-ven-TOO-rah ne-ahl-TEE-kahn), town (1990 pop. 8,380), ⊙ Nealtican municipio, Puebla, central Mexico, 16 mi/26 km W of Puebla; 19°03'N 98°25'W. Agr. center (cereals, sugarcane, fruit, maguey).

San Carlos (sahn KAHR-los), town (1990 pop. 1,258), central Tamaulipas, Mexico, 14 mi/22 km NNE of Ciudad Victoria in the Sierra de San Carlos; 24°35'N 98°56'W. Elev. 1,417 ft/432 m. Agr. (forestry, mezcal processing, cattle); lead and silver mines. On unpaved road.

San Carlos (sahn KAHR-los), resort, in SW Sonora, Mexico, 7 mi/11 km NW of Guaymas. Developed in the 1980s as a coastal vacation and retirement center.

San Carlos, Mexico: see MANUEL BENAVIDES.

San Carlos, city (1990 pop. 26,167), San Mateo co., W Calif., suburb 19 mi/31 km SSE of downtown San Francisco; 3 mi/4.8 km SW of San Francisco Bay, marshy area along shore; 37°30'N 122°16'W. Mfg. (plastic bags, printing and publishing, hardware, machinery parts, plastics prods., bookbinding, telephone apparatus, paints, signs, electron tubes, aerospace missile parts, fiber mill, coated paper). Hetch Hetchy Aqueduct to S; San Carlos Airport to E; San Francisco State Fish and Game Refuge to W; Marine World/Afr. U.S.A. to N. Inc. 1925.

San Carlos, town, Gila co., SE central Ariz., on San Carlos R., in San Carlos Indian Reservation, and 18 mi/29 km E of Globe. Hq. and trading point for reservation. Cattle, sheep. San Carlos Reservoir, at confluence of San Carlos with Gila rivers, is 10 mi/16 km S.

San Carlos, Lake, SE Ariz., on Gila-Pinal co. border, on Gila R., in San Carlos Indian Reservation, 95 mi/153 km ESE of Phoenix; c.13 mi/21 km long, 1.5 mi/2.4 km wide; 33°10'N 110°31'W. Extends E into Graham co. Receives San Carlos R. (N). Formed by Coolidge Dam (249 ft/76 m high, 920 ft/280 m long; built 1927–1928), which irrigates c.100,000 acres/40,470 ha.

San Carlos Park, town (□ 6 sq mi/15.5 sq km; 1990 pop. 11,785), Lee co., SW Fla., 15 mi/24 km S of Fort Myers; 26°28'N 81°49'W.

San Carlos River, c.40 mi/64 km long, SE Ariz.; formed by confluence of 2 forks near Gila Mts.; flows W and S, past San Carlos village, to San Carlos Reservoir (in Gila R.). Near Natanes Peak (7,590 ft/2,313 m) near Gila-Graham co. line, forms co. line to its confluence. Drains San Carlos Indian Reservation.

San Carlos Yautepec (sahn KAHR-los yah-OO-te-pek), town (1990 pop. 580), Oaxaca, S Mexico, in Sierra Madre del Sur, 11 mi/17 km SW of Inter-Amer. Highway (190) at El Camarón; 16°30'N 96°06'W. Elev. 3,281 ft/1,000 m. Cereals, sugarcane, coffee, fruit, vegetables; livestock. On unpaved road. In Zapotec-speaking area.

San Ciro de Acosta (sahn SEE-ro dai ah-KOS-tah), town (1990 pop. 6,400), San Luis Potosí, N central Mexico, in outliers of Sierra Madre Oriental, near Guanajuato border, 23 mi/37 km SE of Río Verde; 21°40'N 99°50'W. Agr. center (grain, beans, cotton, fruit; livestock). Formerly called Pedro Montoya.

San Clemente, city (1990 pop. 41,100), Orange co., S Calif., suburb 54 mi/87 km SE of downtown Los Angeles, and 14 mi/23 km SE of Laguna Beach on the Pacific coast; 33°27'N 117°37'W. Mfg. (plastics prods., printing and publishing, electrical industrial apparatus, diverse light mfg); irrigated agr. Camp Pendleton, a large U.S. marine base, adjoins the city to E, which is chiefly residential. San Clemente is a popular vacation spot, with several missions, a state park and state beach, and Cleveland Natl. Forest c.10 mi/16 km NE. Former President Richard Nixon maintained a "Western White House" summer residence here. San Clemente State Beach is here. Telega Canyon to NE in Santa Margarita Mts.; Doheny State Beach to NW; San Onofre State Beach to SE; Mission San Juan Capistrano to NE. Inc. 1928.

San Clemente Island, Los Angeles co., S Calif., c.60 mi/97 km SSW of Long Beach; 23 mi/37 km long NW-SE, max. 5 mi/8 km wide. Southernmost in isl. chain. Separated from Santa Catalina Isl. to N by Outer Santa Barbara Passage. Highest point 1,965 ft/599 m. Sparsely inhabited.

San Cosme, Mexico: see XALOZTOC.

San Cristóbal (sahn krees-TO-bahl), town, Pinar del Río prov., W Cuba, on small San Cristóbal R., on Central Highway, on RR, and 45 mi/72 km ENE of Pinar del Río; 22°43'N 83°03'W. Agr. and processing center (tobacco, sugar, coffee, fruit; cattle); apiculture. Sugar mill José Martí 3 mi/4.8 km SSE.

San Cristóbal (sahn krees-TO-bahl), province (□ 604 sq mi/1,564 sq km; 1993 pop. 409,301), S central Dominican Republic; ⊙ San Cristóbal; 18°33'N 70°12'W. Agr. (sugarcane, rice, coffee). Formerly included MONTE PLATA prov.; sometime called Trujillo.

San Cristóbal (sahn krees-TO-bahl), city (1993 pop. 88,376), S Dominican Republic, on a Caribbean coastal plain; ⊙ San Cristóbal prov; 18°25'N 70°08'W. The city was founded in the late 16th cent. The 1st Dominican constitution was signed in San Cristóbal in 1844. The dictator Rafael Trujillo was b. here in 1891. Nearby is an agr. institute.

San Cristóbal Amatlán (sahn krees-TO-bahl ah-maht-LAHN), town (1990 pop. 2,771), in central Oaxaca, Mexico, 12 mi/19 km E of Miahuatlán de Porfirio Díaz; 16°19'N 96°24'W. Elev. 5,512 ft/1,680 m. Agr. (coffee, sugarcane, corn, chile, beans, fruits), woods. Access to Miahuatlan via dirt road. A Zapotec community.

San Cristóbal Amoltepec (sahn krees-TO-bahl ah-MOL-te-pek), town (1990 pop. 559), in W Oaxaca, Mexico, 7 mi/12 km E of Tlaxiaco; 17°17'N 97°35'W. Elev. 5,761 ft/1,756 m. Agr. and livestock industry. Temperate climate. In the Mixtec area.

San Cristóbal de la Barranca (sahn krees-TO-bahl dai lah bahr-AHN-kah), town (1990 pop. 913), in N central Jalisco, Mexico, 26 mi/42 km N of Guadalajara on unpaved road; 21°03'N 103°26'W. Near the confluence of the Santiago and Juchipila rivers. Agr. (corn, beans, sugarcane, wheat, fruit), livestock, and some local crafts.

San Cristóbal de las Casas (sahn krees-TO-bahl dai lahs KAH-sahs) or **Ciudad de las Casas**, city (1990 pop. 73,388) and township, Chiapas, S Mexico, in Sierra de Hueytepec, 32 mi/51 km E of Tuxtla Gutiérrez on Inter-Amer. Highway (190); 16°45'N 92°40'W. Elev. c.7,000 ft/2,134 m. Processing, trading, and agr. center (cereals, fruit, sugarcane; livestock); tanning, alcohol and liquor distilling, flour milling, fruit canning, lumbering, mfg. of native footwear. Famous for silver saddles. Has theater, institute of arts and sciences, cathedral, church of Santo Domingo (begun 1547). Founded c.1530 as Ciudad Real. Later named for Bartolomé de las Casas, protector of Indians and 1st bishop of diocese. Was state capital until 1891. In Teotzil Maya-speaking area.

San Cristóbal Lachirioag (sahn krees-TO-bahl lah-chee-ree-O-ahg), town (1990 pop. 1,475), in central Oaxaca, Mexico, 1.9 mi/3 km from San Ildefonso Villa Alta, and 35 mi/57 km NE of Tlacolulu de Matamoros; 17°20'N 96°10'W. Elev. 5,659 ft/1,725 m. On unpaved road. Farming, mainly for subsistence. Zapotec-speaking area.

San Cristóbal Suchixtlahuaca (sahn krees-TO-bahl soo-cheeks-tlah-WAH-kah), town (1990 pop. 353), in NW Oaxaca, Mexico, 34 mi/55 km ESE of Huajuapam de León; 17°42'N 97°19'W. On unpaved road. Farming, mainly for subsistence. Temperate climate. Undeveloped roads.

San Cristóbal Tepeojuma, Mexico: see TEPEOJUMA.

San Diego, county (□ 4,205 sq mi/10,891 sq km; 1990 pop. 2,498,016), S Calif., bounded W by the Pacific, S by Mexico border (Baja California Norte); ⊙ San Diego; 33°01'N 116°46'W. Rolling coastal plain (W), Coast Ranges (center), COLORADO DESERT (E). Cuyamaca Peak (6,515 ft/1,986 m) is 35 mi/56 km ENE of San Diego; Mt. Palomar (astronomical observatory) at Palomar Mt. State Park is 45 mi/72 km NNE of San Diego. Includes part of Cleveland Natl. Forest (N-S, through NW center, including Pacific Coast Trail; S terminus at Mex. border). Cabrillo Natl. Monument is at San Diego; Anza-Borrego Desert State Park takes up E quarter of co., extends into Imperial and Riverside cos. Drained by Santa Margarita, San Luis Rey, Sweetwater, Otay, Tijuana, and San Diego rivers (nearly all intermittent) and Cottonwood Creek. Dairying; eggs, cattle, carnations, roses, avocadoes, cucumbers, tomatoes, oranges, lemons, strawberries, grain. Mfg. (esp. aircraft) in San Diego metropolitan area; processing industries in smaller towns. Ocean fisheries (from San Diego) are important. There are 17 small Indian reservations scattered N-S through hills E and NE of San Diego, including Capitan Grande and Los Coyotes. Camp Pendleton Marine Corps Base in NW. Coast and mt. resorts, hot springs, sport fishing, scenery attract vacationers; equable coast climate has made it a winter resort area. Nuclear power plants: San Onofre 1 (initial criticality June 14, 1967; max. dependable capacity of 436 MWe; closed 1992), San Onofre 2 (initial criticality July 26, 1982; max. dependable capacity of 1,070 MWe), and San Onofre 3 (initial criticality August 29, 1983; max. dependable capacity of 1,080 MWe) are 5 mi/8 km SE of San Clemente; they use cooling water from the Pacific Ocean. Ocotillo Wells State Recreation Area in far E; Cuyamaca Rancho State Park in center. Several state beaches on Pacific Coast: (N-S) San Onofre, Carlsbad, South Carlsbad, Torrey Pines (and Reserve), and Silver Strand; Border Field State Park in SW corner. Formed 1850.

San Diego, city (1990 pop. 1,110,549), ⊙ San Diego co., S Calif., 110 mi/177 km SSE of Los Angeles on San Diego Bay; 32°49'N 117°08'W. It is the 2d-largest city in Calif. and has an excellent natural harbor. Hot, dry climate modified by ocean currents from N and W. It is an important port of entry; a shipping and receiving point for S Calif., Ariz., N.Mex., and Mexico's Baja California; and hq. for the 11th U.S. naval dist. Major Navy and Marine Corps training bases are located there. In addition to military personnel and dependents, many military people retire here and establish permanent residency. San Diego has large aerospace, electronic, and shipbuilding industries, and is an important center for biomedical research and oceanography. It is also a leading high-tech center, with mfg. of software, telecommunications, and bio-tech and medical industries. Other mfg. includes industrial instruments and machinery, envelopes, printed circuit boards, electronic connectors, apparel, semiconductors, canned seafood, shipbuilding, machinery parts, frozen food specialties, soft drinks, binders, navigation systems, calculators, computers, electrical equip., desalination systems, fans and blowers, compressors, electronic components, computer peripherals, service industry machinery, paints, aerospace missiles, electrical measuring equip., industrial chemicals, writing pens, magnetic recording media, aircraft parts, biological prods., business machines, ophthalmic goods, electrical measurement devices, refrigerators, turbines, audio/visual equip., and transformers. It is also a distributing and processing point for a highly productive agr. area. Tourism is an important element in San Diego's economy; the city's delightful climate, its 17 mi/27 km of ocean beaches, and many historic attractions, as well as its proximity to Mexico, draw visitors, convention groups, artists, and retirees. It is the site of the 1st Eur. settlement in Calif. Juan Rodríguez Cabrillo sailed into San Diego Bay in 1542 and claimed the land for Spain. In 1769 Junípero Serra, a Franciscan missionary, established Mission San Diego de Alcalá and dedicated the Presidio, the 1st Span. fort in Calif. By 1830 most of the people were living in what is now Old Town. It was under Mex. jurisdiction from 1822, when Mexico won independence from Spain, until 1846, when it was captured by a U.S. naval force. The city's pop. surged when the Santa Fe RR arrived in 1884. San Diego became an important U.S. naval base during World War I; later, other branches of the military established bases there. In the 1950s, this concentration of military installations gave rise to San Diego's booming aerospace industry, which has experienced some decline since the 1970s but remains central to the local economy. The diversification of San Diego's economic base contributed to its rapid growth during the 1980s, when its downtown witnessed an urban revitalization effort that included Horton Plaza, an expansive shopping mall that won acclaim for its dramatic architecture. The 1st line of an extensive trolley system opened in 1986. San Diego is a cultural, educational, and medical center. U.S. Space Surveillance Station to SE. Its many health facilities include large naval and veterans hosps. It is the seat of the Univ. of Calif. at San Diego, San Diego State Univ., U.S. Internatl. Univ., the Univ. of San Diego, Electronic Technical Inst., Scripps Inst. of Oceanography (Univ. of Calif.), the Salk Inst. for Biological Sciences, Point Loma Nazarene Col., Christian Heritage Col., and 4 community cols.: Kelsey Jenney Community Col., San Diego City Col., San Diego Mesa Col., and San Diego Miramar Col. Balboa Park contains a fine art gallery, several museums (including an aerospace mus.), and the world-famous San Diego zoo. Some bldgs. from the Panama-Calif. Internatl. Exposition (1915–1916) and the Calif. Pacific Internatl. Exposition (1935–1936) remain, and there is also Sea World, at Mission Bay, to NW. Also of interest are Cabrillo Natl. Monument, 6 mi/9.7 km WSW of downtown, at Point Loma, and Mission San Diego de Alcalá, 5 mi/8 km NE of downtown (restored). Parts of Old Town are now a state historical park (Old Town San Diego State Historical Park). Jack Murphy Stadium is home for the city's professional baseball (San Diego Padres) and football (San Diego Chargers) teams. Site of the Mission Valley Center, one of the largest shopping centers in U.S. The San Diego Yacht Club, representing the U.S., won the Amer.'s Cup in 1987 and successfully defended it in 1992. San Diego Internatl. Airport (Lindbergh Field) 2 mi/3.2 km NW of downtown, on harbor. U.S. Marine Corps Recruit Depot W of airport. Several smaller Naval stations and other installations. Coronado Naval Amphibious Base S of downtown; Miramar Naval Air Station to N; North Isl. Naval Air Station W of downtown. The city of San Diego includes the suburban communities of LA JOLLA, San Ysidro, and Encanto. Neighboring cities include CORONADO on North Isl., Chulavista, Natl. City, and El Cajon across the Bay. South annexation (12 mi/19 km long) through San Diego Bay to Mex. border includes San Ysidro; Border Field State Beach to SW; Silver Strand State Beach to W. Torrey Pine State Beach and Reserve to NW. Inc. 1850.

San Diego, town (1990 pop. 4,983), ⊙ Duval co., on E border, S Texas, 10 mi/16 km W of Alice; 27°45′N 98°14′W. A trade center for area producing oil, natural gas, salt, cattle, cotton. Inc. 1935.

San Diego Aqueduct, c.80 mi/129 km long, S Calif., Riverside and San Diego cos.; S branch of Colorado R. Aqueduct, which delivers water from Davis Dam, Colorado R., to Los Angeles. San Diego Aqueduct diverts a portion of the water to San Diego, from a point 3 mi/4.8 km N of San Jacinto, S past Temecula, Escondido, and Poway, terminating at San Vicente Reservoir, 20 mi/32 km NE of San Diego.

San Diego Bay, San Diego co., S Calif., natural harbor (12 mi/19 km long, 1 mi/1.6 km–3 mi/4.8 km wide) of San Diego city, sheltered from the Pacific by 10 mi/16 km long Silver Strand Peninsula, which terminates at North Isl. (Naval Air Station) at harbor entrance, and the shorter 5 mi/8 km Point Loma (Cabrillo Natl. Monument), opposite North Isl.

San Diego Country Estates, uninc. town (1990 pop. 6,874), San Diego co., S Calif., residential suburb 27 mi/43 km NW of downtown San Diego, and 2 mi/3.2 km SE of Ramona; 33°01′N 116°47′W.

San Diego de Alejandria (sahn dee-AI-go dai ah-lai-hahn-DREE-ah), town (1990 pop. 3,516), Jalisco, central Mexico, near Guanajuato border, 22 mi/35 km SW of León; 20°59′N 101°59′W. Elev. 6,004 ft/1,830 m. Grain, beans; livestock.

San Diego de la Unión (sahn dee-AI-go dai lah oo-nee-ON), city (1990 pop. 5,464) and township, Guanajuato, central Mexico, 21 mi/34 km N of Dolores Hidalgo; 21°27′N 100°52′W. Elev. 6,824 ft/2,080 m. Corn, wheat, sugarcane, vegetables; livestock.

San Diego de los Baños (sahn dee-AI-go dai los BAHN-yos), town, Pinar del Río prov., W Cuba, resort at S foot of Sierra del Rosario, 26 mi/42 km NE of Pinar del Río; 22°39′N 83°23′W. Sulphurous springs.

San Diego del Valle (sahn dee-AI-go dail VEI-yai), town, Villa Clara prov., central Cuba, on RR, and 12 mi/19 km NW of Santa Clara; 23°33′N 80°06′W. Sugarcane, tobacco; cattle.

San Diego Islands (san dee-AI-go), 2 islets off NW Trinidad, Trinidad and Tobago, in the Gulf of Paria, 6 mi/9.7 km N of Port of Spain. Consists of Carrera Isl. (E), a prison, and Cronstadt Isl. (W), a bathing resort.

San Diego River, 55 mi/88 km long, Pinar del Río prov., W Cuba; rises in the Sierra del Rosario; flows S to the Gulf of Batabanó.

San Diego River, 52 mi/84 km long, San Diego co., S Calif.; rises in Cleveland Natl. Forest c.25 mi/40 km E of Escondido; flows SW through El Capitan L. reservoir and through city of San Diego N of downtown to Mission Bay arm of Pacific Ocean, 5 mi/8 km NW of downtown San Diego. On upper course is El Capitan Dam (270 ft/82 m high; 1,200 ft/366 m long; completed 1935; for water supply). On San Vicente Creek, a short tributary, is San Vicente Dam (199 ft/61 m high, 980 ft/299 m long; completed 1943; for water supply).

San Dimas, Mexico: see TAYOLTITA.

San Dimas, city (1990 pop. 32,397), Los Angeles co., S Calif., suburb 23 mi/37 km ENE of downtown Los Angeles at base of San Gabriel Mts.; 34°07′N 117°49′W. Citrus fruit groves; nurseries; plastics. Mfg. (electronic components, machinery, consumer goods, pharmaceuticals, space technology). Pacific Coast Baptist Col.; LaVerne Col.; Calif. State Polytechnic Univ., Pomona, to S. Frank G. Bonelli Regional Park, including Puddingstone Reservoir, in SE. Angeles Natl. Forest to N. Inc. 1960.

San Dionisio del Mar (sahn dee-o-NEE-syo del MAHR), town (1990 pop. 2,716), in extreme SE Oaxaca, Mexico, on the Pacific coast W of Mar Muerto Inferior, 19 mi/30 km SE of Juchitán de Zaragoza; 16°20′N 94°45′W. Rich fishing resources. Agr. (cereals, fruits). On unpaved road, near RR. Huave Indian community.

San Dionisio Ocotepec (sahn dee-o-NEE-syo o-KO-te-pek), town (1990 pop. 3,959), in central Oaxaca, Mexico, 31 mi/50 km SE of Oaxaca de Juarez, and 14 mi/22 km S of Tlacolula de Matamoros; 16°48′N 96°24′W. Elev. 5,377 ft/1,639 m. Mountainous region with a temperate climate. Agr. (corn, wheat, beans, chile), cattle and dairy farming.

San Dionisio Ocotlán (sahn dee-o-NEE-syo o-kot-LAHN), town (1990 pop. 903) in S central Oaxaca, Mexico 6 mi/9.7 km S of Ocotlán de Morelos; 16°45′N 96°40′W. In the Valle Grande arm of Valley of Oaxaca; farming, mainly for local markets.

San Dionisio Yauhquemehcan, Mexico: see YAUHQUE-MEHCAN.

San Elizario, uninc. town (1990 pop. 4,385), El Paso co., extreme W Texas, suburb 18 mi/29 km SE of downtown El Paso, and on the Rio Grande; 31°34′N 106°15′W. In irrigated farm area (dairying, cattle; cotton; pecans). One of oldest communities in Texas, founded in early 1680s as a presidio town; scene of Salt War violence (1877), a confrontation bet. the town and a private citizen over ownership of nearby salt lakes. From 1850 to 1876, San Elizario was capital of El Paso co. Once the seat was removed to Ysleta, San Elizario's importance declined considerably.

San Emigdio Mountains, Kern and Ventura cos., S central Calif., short range (c.4,000 ft/1,219 m–7,000 ft/2,134 m), part of S wall of San Joaquin Valley, linking Temblor Range (NW) with Tehachapi Mts. (E); 34°52′N 119°10′W.

San Esteban, Mexico: see VILLA UNIÓN, Durango.

San Esteban Atatlahuca (sahn es-TAI-bahn aht-lah-HOO-kah), town (1990 pop. 500), W Oaxaca, Mexico, 16 mi/25 km E of Putla de Guerrero; 17°04′N 97°40′W. Elev. 5,741 ft/1,750 m. Uneven rough terrain. Temperate climate. Agr. (corn, beans, wheat, mezcal, fruits), woods, and fabric. Paved roads. Mixtec community.

San Esteban Cuautempan (sahn es-TAI-bahn kwah-wah-TEM-pahn), town (1990 pop. 2,788), ⊙ Cuautempan municipio, Puebla, central Mexico, 10 mi/16 km E of Zacatlán; 19°54′N 97°51′W. Corn, coffee, sugarcane, fruit; vanilla, wood. In Popoloca Indian area.

San Felipe (sahn fai-LEE-pai), town, La Habana prov., W Cuba, 20 mi/32 km S of Havana; 22°50′N 82°20′W. RR junction; sugarcane, vegetables, cattle.

San Felipe (sahn fai-LEE-pai), city (1990 pop. 20,624) and township, Guanajuato, central Mexico, at intersection of Mexico Highways 37 and 51, 31 mi/50 km NE of Dolores Hidalgo. Agr. center (corn, wheat, barley, potatoes, maguey); tequila and mescal distilling. Formerly called San Felipe; changed to Ciudad González (until 1938); changed again to Doctor Hernández Álvarez.

San Felipe (sahn fai-LEE-pai), town (1990 pop. 1,254), Yucatán, SE Mexico, on bar offshore, 30 mi/48 km NNW of Tizimín; 21°34′N 88°12′W. Henequen-growing dist.

San Felipe, Mexico: see SAN FELIPE DE JESÚS.

San Felipe (san fuh-LEE-pai), pueblo (1990 pop. 1,557), Sandoval co., N central N.Mex., 10 mi/16 km NNE of Bernalillo, on the Rio Grande, in San Felipe Indian Reservation; 35°25′N 106°25′W. Founded early 18th cent. The inhabitants are Pueblo of the Keresan linguistic family. Ceremonial dances are held there in spring and winter.

San Felipe, village (1990 pop. 618), Austin co., S Texas, on Brazos R., and 45 mi/72 km W of Houston; 29°48′N 96°06′W. Founded 1823 as hq. of Steven F. Austin's colony. Conventions (of 1832 and 1833; consultation of 1835) held here before and during Texas revolution; burned 1836, later rebuilt. Stephen F. Austin State Park and monument here commemorate Austin and town's history. Also called San Felipe de Austin.

San Felipe Bay, shallow inlet of Gulf of California, in NE Baja California, NW Mexico, 120 mi/193 km SSE of Mexicali; 10 mi/16 km long, c.3 mi/4.8 km wide. Salt deposits.

San Felipe, Cayos de (sahn fai-LEE-pai, KEI-yos dai), chain of 8 islets and several other islets, bet. Gulf of Batabanó off SW Cuba and Caribbean Sea, 19 mi/31 km NW of Isla de la Juventud, 30 mi/48 km S of Pinar del Río; c.20 mi/32 km long; 21°56′N 83°30′W.

San Felipe de Jesús (sahn fai-LEE-pai dai hai-SOOS), town (1990 pop. 463), Sonora, NW Mexico, 80 mi/129 km SSE of Nogales; 27°20′N 106°02′W. Livestock; wheat. Mining (lead, zinc). Formerly called San Felipe.

San Felipe del Progreso (sahn fai-LEE-pai dai pro-GRE-so), town (1990 pop. 1,818), Mexico state, central Mexico, 55 mi/89 km WNW of Mexico city; 19°43′N 99°52′W. Cereals; livestock.

San Felipe Ixtacuixtla, Mexico: see VILLA MARIANO MATAMOROS.

San Felipe Jalapa de Diaz (sahn fai-LEE-pai hah-LAH-pah dai DEE-ahz), town (1990 pop. 7,886), N Oaxaca, Mexico, 41 mi/66 km W of Tuxtepec, on the SE slopes of Sierra Mazateca; 18°04′N 96°33′W. Elev. 1,969 ft/600 m. Paved road. Hot climate. Agr. with the primary prod. being coffee. In Mazatec-speaking area.

San Felipe Maderas, Mexico: see NICOLÁS BRAVO.

San Felipe Orizatlán, Mexico: see ORIZATLÁN.

San Felipe Tejalapam (sahn fai-LEE-pai te-hah-lah-PAHM), town (1990 pop. 1,837), in central Oaxaca, Mexico, 6 mi/10 km NW of Oaxaca de Juárez; 17°06′N 96°51′W. Elev. 5,266 ft/1,605 m. In Etla arm of Oaxaca Valley. Agr. (corn, beans, fruits; cattle and poultry), forestry. Mezcal processing and local crafts. On unpaved road connecting with Mexico Highway 190.

San Felipe Teotlalcingo (sahn fai-LEE-pai te-o-tlahl-SEEN-go), town (1990 pop. 5,029), Puebla, central Mexico, 23 mi/37 km NW of Puebla; 19°14′N 98°29′W. Corn, wheat, maguey.

San Felipe Tepatlán (sahn fai-LEE-pai te-paht-LAHN), town (1990 pop. 466), Puebla, central Mexico, in Sierra Madre Oriental, 17 mi/27 km ESE of Huauchinango; 20°06′N 97°49′W. Sugarcane, coffee, fruit. Poor road access. Sometimes called Tepatlán.

San Felipe Tepemaxalco (sahn fai-LEE-pai te-pe-mah-HAHL-ko), town (1990 pop. 715), ⊙ Tepemaxalco municipio, Puebla, central Mexico, 17 mi/27 km SW of Atlixco; 18°44′N 98°36′W. Corn, wheat, sugar.

San Felipe Usila (sahn fai-LEE-pai oo-SEE-lah), town (1990 pop. 4,342), N central Oaxaca, Mexico, 12 mi/19 km S of San Felipe Jalpa de Díaz; 17°53′N 96°33′W. A mountainous region in the Papaloapan R. drainage area. Elev. 656 ft/200 m. Hot climate. Agr. (corn, beans, rice, coffee, sugarcane, fruits), woods, cattle, dairy and poultry farming. On unpaved road. Chinantec-speaking community.

San Ferdinand, Mo.: see FLORISSANT.

San Fernando (sahn fer-NAHN-do), city (1990 pop. 20,737) and township, Tamaulipas, NE Mexico, on San Fernando R., on Gulf plain, and 85 mi/137 km SSW of Matamoros on Mexico Highway 180; 24°50′N 98°10′W. Cereals, sugar; cattle. Sometimes called San Fernando de Presas.

San Fernando (sahn fer-NAHN-do), town (1990 pop. 6,787), Chiapas, S Mexico, in Sierra Madre, 10 mi/16 km NW of Tuxtla Gutiérrez; 16°52′N 93°13′W. Cereals, sugarcane, fruit; livestock. A Zoque Indian community.

San Fernando, city (1990 pop. 30,092), Trinidad and Tobago, on the Gulf of Paria; 10°17′N 61°28′W. It is the country's 2d-largest city and a commercial center for S Trinidad.

San Fernando, city (1990 pop. 22,580), Los Angeles co., S Calif., 20 mi/32 km NNW of downtown Los Angeles, surrounded by city of Los Angeles, in the San Fernando valley; 34°17′N 118°26′W. Industries include apparel and electronics. Mfg. (cutting tools, chemicals, glass prods., aircraft parts, plastics prods., metal plating, electronic connectors, printed circuit boards, industrial controls, frozen food specialties, soft drinks, industrial instruments, fabricated rubber goods). The valley, 1st entered by Europeans in 1769, was early used for journeys to N Calif. Gold was found in 1842 before the big gold strike. Founded in 1874, San Fernando is the oldest city in the valley. Los Angeles Mission Col., opened in 1975, is there. San Fernando Airport and Whitman Airport in E; San Fernando Mission (1797) is SW. Santa Susana Mts. to NW; San Gabriel Mts., in Angeles Natl. Forest, to NE; Pacoima Reservoir to NE; Van Norman Lakes in W. Inc. 1911.

San Fernando de Camarones (sahn fer-NAHN-do dai kah-muh-RON-aiz), town, Villa Clara prov., central Cuba, 24 mi/39 km WSW of Santa Clara; 22°15′N 80°18′W. Sugarcane, fruit; livestock. Nearby (NW) is the sugar mill Espartaco.

San Fernando River, Mexico: see CONCHOS RIVER, Tamaulipas.

San Fernando Valley, Los Angeles co., S Calif., fertile basin (□ c.260 sq mi/673 sq km) NW of downtown Los Angeles, in NW part of city of Los Angeles, and walled by Santa Monica Mts. (S), Simi Hills (W), Santa Susana Mts. (N), San Gabriel Mts. (NE); communicates with Los Angeles basin via Cahuenga Pass (S) to Hollywood, and drained by intermittent Los Angeles R., which exits valley to SE. Once an area of irrigated small farms, orchards, and poultry ranches mingled with residential suburbs, the valley became fully urbanized 1950s–1970s; San Fernando (in N) is chief independent city. Although much of the valley was annexed (1915) by Los Angeles city, after construction here of terminal reservoir of Los Angeles Aqueduct, which delivers water from N (Sierra Nevada, near Sequoia Natl. Park) to Van Normova Lakes and Sepulveda Flood Control Basin (Los Angeles Reservoir), many communities, though officially part of Los Angeles, retain their identity: among them are North Hollywood, Sherman Oaks, Woodland Hills, Tarzana, Encino, Van Nuys (seat of municipal govt. branch offices), Canoga Park, Chatsworth, Pacoima, Reseda, Roscoe, Sepulveda, Sunland, Sylmar, Tujunga, Northridge.

San Francique, Trinidad and Tobago: see ERIN.

San Francisco 1 Mexico: see SOYANIQUILPAN. **2** Mexico: see ANGAMACUTIRO DE LA UNIÓN.

San Francisco, county (□ 232 sq mi/601 sq km; 1990 pop. 723,959), W Calif., at N end of San Francisco–Santa Cruz Peninsula; 37°48′N 122°33′W. Calif.'s smallest co., with 47 sq mi/121 sq km in land area, with remainder 185 sq mi/480 sq km in water area. Fish, nursery prods. Co. is coterminous with the city of San Francisco, but the 2 are politically separate, having separate functions. Bounded by Pacific Ocean on W, Golden Gate Strait on N, San Francisco Bay on E; San Mateo co. on S. Co. and city include Alcatraz, Treasure and Yerba Buena Isls. in San Francisco Bay, and the Farlallon Isls. (Natl. Wildlife Refuge) 25 mi/40 km to W, in Pacific. Includes part of Golden Gate Natl. Rec. Area on W shore and Alcatraz Isl.; Fort Point Natl. Historical Site in N. L. Merced reservoir in SW.

San Francisco, city (1990 pop. 723,959), coextensive with and ⊙ San Francisco co., W Calif., on the N end of a peninsula bet. the Pacific Ocean (W) and San Francisco Bay (E), separated from Marin Peninsula (Marin co.) by Golden Gate Strait, 6 mi/9.7 km W of downtown Oakland; 37°48′N 122°33′W. The city is the heart of the San Francisco Bay region and with Oakland and San Jose comprise the 4th-largest metropolitan area in the U.S. Mfg. (printing and publishing, food processing, mining services, apparel, textile processing, petroleum refining, computers, chemicals, communications equip., machinery). Tourism is the economic mainstay, with service industries supporting the large number of annual visitors. For most of its history, San Francisco has been the financial center of the West Coast, but since the early 1970s the city has had to compete with Los Angeles for this distinction. Finance remains one of the most important activities; the city is still hq. to 3 of the country's largest commercial banks as well as a Federal Reserve bank and the Pacific Stock Exchange. More than 600 insurance companies are based here. San Francisco is also the marketplace for a large agr. and mining region and the focus of many transportation routes. Along with the busy port of Richmond across the bay to E, and Oakland Harbor (San Leandro Bay) to E, San Francisco and the Bay Area form one of the largest ports on the West Coast and are a major center of trade with East Asia, Australia, S. Amer., Mexico, Canada, Hawaii, and Alaska. Although mfg. in San Francisco has declined, the clothing and food-processing industries remain important. Tourism is also very important. The area's transportation needs are served by an extensive highway and RR network. The interurban Bay Area Rapid Transit (BART) system began operating in 1972 bet. San Francisco and East Bay communities. The city was founded in 1776, when a Span. presidio and a mission were established at a location chosen by Juan Bautista de Anza. The little settlement called Yerba Buena was still a village when the Mex.-Amer. War broke out and a naval force under Commodore John D. Sloat took it (1846) in the name of the U.S. It was then renamed San Francisco. When gold was discovered in Calif. in 1848, San Francisco had a pop. of c.800; 2 years later it was inc. (1850) with a pop. of c.25,000. The rush of gold seekers, adventurers, and settlers brought a period of lawlessness, when the BARBARY COAST wharf dist. flourished. The city took on a cosmopolitan air, with newcomers arriving from all over the world. In this period the 1st Chinese settled in the city, and San Francisco's legendary Chinatown is among the largest communities of Chinese in the U.S. In the years after the gold rush, San Francisco continued to grow as Calif. became linked overland with the East, by the pony express in 1860 and by the transcontinental RR in 1869. On the morning of April 18, 1906, the great San Andreas fault, which extends up and down the Calif. coast, at this point lying submerged just W of the city's Pacific coast, shifted violently, and San Francisco was shaken by an earthquake which, together with the sweeping 3-day fire that followed, all but destroyed the city. Earthquakes have since continued to plague the city and its environs; in Oct. 1989, a severe earthquake hit the Bay Area, wreaking most damage on Oakland, the Bay Bridge, and local highways. The opening of the Panama Canal, a boon to the city's trade, was celebrated by the Panama-Pacific Exposition of 1915. The city was connected to Oakland (E) by the SAN FRANCISCO–OAKLAND BAY BRIDGE in 1936 (Interstate 80), and to Marin co. (N) by the spectacular GOLDEN GATE BRIDGE (U.S. Highway 101) in 1937. By the time of the Golden Gate Internatl. Exposition (1939–1940) the whole Bay Area was heavily industrialized; it had become the leading commercial center of the West Coast. During World War II, San Francisco was the major mainland supply point and port of embarkation for the war in the Pacific. The UN Charter (1945) was drafted at San Francisco, and the Jap. Peace Treaty (1951) was signed here. San Francisco's natural beauty and mild climate make it attractive as a residential city. It is split bet. very wealthy sects., and many areas of urban impoverishment; the latter have increased since the 1970s. Among the more well-known contemporary neighborhoods are Haight-Ashbury, famous in the 1960s and 1970s for its youth ("flower children"), music, and drug cultures; and a large homosexual community that has principally grown around Castro St. In 1978, George Moscone, the city's mayor, and Harvey Milk, the city supervisor, both proponents of gay rights, were assassinated at city offices. The city is renowned for its all-encompassing fogs; soaring bridges; cable cars (Cable Car Barn and Mus. on Washington St.); busy Market St., with its department stores and office bldgs.; the Embarcadero, crowded with docks, ships, and cargoes; Fisherman's Wharf, with its fishing fleet, seafood restaurants, and the center of the city's seafood industry; Chinatown, with its Asian architecture, tearooms, and temples; Telegraph Hill; Russian Hill; and Nob Hill, a neighborhood of millionaires. Other points of interest are Mission Dolores (1782; initially called San Francisco de Asís); many old mansions built by RR and mining kings; Golden Gate Park in W, where the Calif. Acad. of Sciences has 2 natural history museums, an aquarium, and a planetarium; the Cliff House and Palace of the Legion of Honors art mus. on Point Lobos, overlooking the Pacific and offshore rocks, 100 ft/30 m, habitated by sea lions; the San Francisco Zoological Gardens; and the civic center, with a distinctive Renaissance-style city hall, a public lib., and the municipally owned opera house, where performances of the symphony orchestra and ballet and opera companies are held. Other art museums include the San Francisco Mus. of Art, the M. H. De Young Memorial Mus., and the Asian Art Mus. Institutions of higher learning in the city include San Francisco State Univ., the Univ. of San Francisco, the Hastings Col. of Law, the Univ. of Calif., San Francisco, Lone Mountain Col. (formerly San Francisco Col. for Women), and several theological seminaries and community cols., such as the City Col. of San Francisco. The Presidio of San Francisco, the largest (1,542 acres/624 hectares) military encampment within the confines of an Amer. city, was the hq. of the Sixth U.S. Army, as well as the site of Letterman General Hosp.; it was decommissioned in 1994, and turned over to the Natl. Park Service as part of Golden Gate Natl. Recreation Area. Hunter's Point Naval Shipyard (closed) in SE. Treasure Isl. Naval Air Station, on Treasure and Yerba Buena isls. (linked by land), crossed on S by Bay Bridge.

Cross references are shown in SMALL CAPITALS. The pronunciation key is on page xv. The dates of population figures are on page xii.

San Francisco Internatl. Airport to S, on San Francisco Bay at San Bruno; Metro Oakland Internatl. Airport to E, at Oakland. Candlestick Park baseball stadium (1960) in SE. Cow Palace convention center, site of 1964 Republican Convention, immediately to S in Daly City. Farallon Isl. Natl. Wildlife Refuge off W coast. City includes Alcatraz Isl. to N, with prison (closed). Part of Golden Gate Natl. Recreation Area is W and N, including Alcatraz Isl., extends into Marin co; Fort Point Natl. Historical Site in N, E of Golden Gate Bridge.

San Francisco Bay, W Calif.; entered through the Golden Gate, a strait bet. San Francisco (S) and Marin (W) peninsulas; crossed by Golden Gate Bridge; 50 mi/ 80 km long, from 3 mi/4.8 km–13 mi/21 km wide. Bay's depth is up to 100 ft/30 m, with a channel 50 ft/15 m deep maintained through the sand bar off the Golden Gate. City of San Francisco is on the S peninsula; on the N peninsula are the residential suburbs of Marin co., while on the E shore of the crescent-shaped bay is Oakland and smaller cities of Alameda, Berkeley, and Richmond. The Santa Clara Valley extends SSE from S end of bay. San Jose is S of bay's S end; on bay's SW shore is Silicon Valley, which has large computer-technology-based economy, including Palo Alto, San Mateo, Menlo Park, and other communities. Angel Isl., Alcatraz, and Yerba Buena Isl. are in the bay. San Pablo Bay is the major N extension of San Francisco Bay, connected by San Pablo Strait, N of Richmond–San Rafael Bridge, including Hamilton Air Force Base on W side and Marr Isl. Naval Shipyard at Vallejo at NE end; bay extends further from San Pablo Bay E through narrow Carquinez Strait to Suisun Bay. Shipping channels continue from Suisun Bay N to W Sacramento and E to Terminow, 12 mi/19 km W of Lodi. Suisun Bay receives Sacramento and San Joaquin rivers. SE end is marshy, entered by Coyote and Guadalupe creeks. On those secondary bays and on Carquinez Strait, which connects them, are the cities of Vallejo, Benicia, Martinez, and Pittsburg. The bay is crossed by the San Francisco–Oakland Bay Bridge in N; the Richmond–San Rafael Bridge in N at entrance to San Pablo Bay, N extension of San Francisco Bay; the San Mateo Bridge; and the Dunbarton Bridge in S. The Trans-Bay Tube, a tunnel 3.5 mi/5.6 km long bet. San Francisco and Oakland, is one of the longest underwater rapid transit tubes in the world. The tunnel was esp. constructed to absorb earthquake tremors. Several U.S. Navy facilities are located in the region. The Eng. navigator Sir Francis Drake visited the bay in 1579; the Spanish explored it more fully in the late 18th cent. Angel Isl. State Park in N, ferry from Tiburon, Marin co.

San Francisco Cahuacuá (sahn frahn-SEES-ko kah-wah-koo-AH), town (1990 pop. 325), in W Oaxaca, Mexico, 37 mi/60 km WSW of Oaxaca de Juárez; 16°54′N 97°18′W. Elev. 5,906 ft/1,800 m. Mountainous with temperate climate. Agr. (corn, beans, coffee, fruit), fine woods and lumber, mezcal and rustic woven fabrics. Sometimes spelled Cahuaca.

San Francisco Cajonos (sahn frahn-SEES-ko kah-HO-nos), town (1990 pop. 329), in central Oaxaca, Mexico, 34 mi/55 km ENE of Oaxaca de Juárez; 17°11′N 96°16′W. Elev. 7,218 ft/2,200 m. Paved roads. Farming, mainly for subsistence.

San Francisco Chapulapa (sahn frahn-SEES-ko chah-LOO-pah), town (1990 pop. 340), in N Oaxaca, Mexico; 17°56′N 96°44′W. Elev. 2,001 ft/610 m. Mountainous with temperate humid climate. Unpaved roads.

San Francisco Chindúa (sahn frahn-SEES-ko cheen-DOO-ah), town (1990 pop. 719), in W Oaxaca, Mexico, 5 mi/8 km WSW of Asunción Nochixtlán; 17°25′N 97°19′W. Elev. 6,070 ft/1,850 m. Mountainous. Temperate climate. Agr. (wheat, fruits); woods and cattle. Unpaved road connects to the NE with Nochixtlán.

San Francisco de Asís, Calif.: see SAN FRANCISCO.

San Francisco de Borja (sahn frahn-SEES-ko dai BOR-hah), town (1990 pop. 1,353), Chihuahua, N Mexico, in Sierra Madre Occidental, on San Pedro R., and 65 mi/ 105 km SW of Chihuahua; 27°35′N 106°41′W. Elev. 7,041 ft/2,146 m. Grain, cotton; cattle.

San Francisco de Conchos (sahn frahn-SEES-ko dai KON-chos), town (1990 pop. 727), Chihuahua, N Mexico, on Conchos R., near La Boquilla Dam, on RR, and 13 mi/21 km SW of Camargo; 27°38′N 105°18′W. Corn, cotton, beans, tobacco, cattle; timber.

San Francisco de los Adame, Mexico: see LUIS MOYA.

San Francisco de Macorís (sahn frahn-SEES-ko dai mah-ko-REES), city (1993 pop. 96,503), N Dominican Republic; ⊙ Duarte prov; 19°18′N 70°12′W. It is the commercial and processing center for an agr. region. Its port is Sanchez.

San Francisco de Paula, town, Ciudad de la Habana prov., W Cuba, 6 mi/9.7 km SE of Havana; 23°05′N 82°19′W. Dairying, sugar growing. Home and mus. of Ernest Hemingway.

San Francisco de Solano, Mission, Calif.: see SONOMA, city.

San Francisco del Mar (sahn frahn-SEES-ko del MAHR), town (1990 pop. 3,016), in extreme SE Oaxaca, Mexico, 40 mi/65 km E of the port of Salina Cruz; 16°14′N 94°39′W. On S shore of Maz Muerto Inferior, on Barrier Isl. Good fishing resources; agr., cattle. Unpaved roads connect with RR and the Pan-Amer. Highway. Huave Indian community.

San Francisco del Mezquital (sahn frahn-SEES-ko del mes-KEE-tahl), town (1990 pop. 1,678), ⊙ Mezquital municipio, Durango, N Mexico, on Mezquital R. (upper San Pedro R.), and 45 mi/72 km SE of Victoria de Durango; 23°30′N 104°10′W. Grain, sugarcane, fruit, vegetables, tobacco.

San Francisco del Oro (sahn frahn-SEES-ko del O-ro), town (1990 pop. 8,505), San Francisco del Oro municipio, Chihuahua, N Mexico, in E outliers of Sierra Madre Occidental, 12 mi/19 km SW of Hidalgo del Parral; 26°52′N 105°50′W. Elev. 6,532 ft/1,991 m. On RR spur line. Silver, gold, lead, copper, and zinc mining.

San Francisco del Rincón (sahn frahn-SEES-ko del reen-KON), city (1990 pop. 52,291) and township, Guanajuato, central Mexico, on central plateau, 14 mi/ 23 km SW of León; 21°01′N 101°51′W. Elev. 5,781 ft/ 1,762 m. RR terminus; agr. center (grain, sugarcane, fruit, vegetables; livestock); flour mills; chicle, straw hats.

San Francisco Huehuetlán (sahn frahn-SEES-ko woo-e-woo-et-LAHN), town (1990 pop. 268), in N Oaxaca, Mexico, 9 mi/15 km NE of Teotitlán de Flores Magón, on unpaved road; 18°11′N 96°56′W. Elev. 8,219 ft/ 2,505 m. Agr. (cereals, fruits), woven straw textiles. In Mazatec-speaking area.

San Francisco Ixhuatán (sahn frahn-SEES-ko eeks-hwah-TAHN), town (1990 pop. 5,634), SE Oaxaca, Mexico, 9 mi/14.5 km S of Mexico Highway 200 on unpaved road; in the S part of the Isthmus of Tehuantepec on the bank of the Ostuta R., which flows to Laguna Oriental. Hot climate. Agr. (corn, sesame, mango), livestock.

San Francisco Jaltepetongo (sahn frahn-SEES-ko hahl-te-pe-TON-go), town (1990 pop. 185), in W Oaxaca, Mexico, 7 mi/12 km SSW of Asunción Nochixtlán; 17°27′N 97°27′W. Elev. 5,715 ft/1,742 m. A mountainous region; temperate climate. Agr. (corn, beans, fruits, wheat); pottery, straw textiles, cattle, and woods.

San Francisco Lachigoló (sahn frahn-SEES-ko lah chee-go-LO), town (1990 pop. 1,282), in central Oaxaca, Mexico, 12 mi/20 km ESE of Oaxaca de Juárez, off the Inter-Amer. Highway; 17°01′N 96°36′W. Farming.

San Francisco Logueche 1 (sahn frahn-SEES-ko lo-GWE-che), town, ⊙ San Francisco Logueche municipio, Oaxaca, Mexico, 17 mi/27 km E of Mihuatlán de Porfirio Díaz, on unpaved road; 16°21′N 96°22′W. Elev. 6,234 ft/1,900 m. Agr., small farming, mainly for subsistence. **2** (sahn frahn-SEES-ko lo-GE-che), town (1990 pop. 817), in S central Oaxaca, Mexico, 17 mi/ 27 km E of Miahuatlán de Porfirio Díaz; 16°21′N 96°22′W. Unpaved roads. Coastal Zapotec community.

San Francisco Maritime, natl. historical park, in city of San Francisco, San Francisco co., near Municipal Pier on N shore of San Francisco, W Calif., 2 mi/3.2 km NW of downtown, W of Fisherman's Wharf, E of Golden Gate Bridge. Covers 50 acres/20 ha. Largest collection of historic ships in the U.S.; mus. with exhibits and photographs on maritime history. Fort Point Natl. Historical Site to NW. Authorized 1988.

San Francisco Mixtla (sahn frahn-SEES-ko MEESH-tlah), town (1990 pop. 1,056), ⊙ Mixtla municipio, Puebla, central Mexico, 23 mi/37 km ESE of Puebla; 18°54′N 97°53′W. Cereals, vegetables.

San Francisco Mountains, Coconino co., N Ariz., N of Flagstaff, consisting of Mt. Humphreys (12,643 ft/ 3,854 m, highest point in Ariz.), Mt. Agassiz (12,340 ft/ 3,761 m), and Mt. Fremont (11,940 ft/3,639 m); 35°20′N 111°40′W. In Coconino Natl. Forest.

San Francisco Nuxaño (sahn frahn-SEES-ko nook-SAHN-yo), town (1990 pop. 477), in W Oaxaca, Mexico, 12 mi/20 km SW of Asunción Nochixtlán. Elev. 5,988 ft/1,825 m. Agr. Unpaved road to Asunción Nochixtlán.

San Francisco–Oakland Bay Bridge, double-decked structure, San Francisco–Alameda cos., W Calif.; built 1933–1936. It has a total length of 8.25 mi/13.28 km. From San Francisco it crosses the bay E to Yerba Buena Isl. (access to Yerba Buena and Treasure isls.), where a tunnel passes through upper elevations of isl. then continues as a bridge to Oakland and Berkeley. The bridge sustained damage in the severe Oct. 1989 earthquake that hit the bay area. Interstate Highway 80 crosses bridge.

San Francisco Ozolotepec (sahn frahn-SEES-ko o-zo-LO-te-pek), town (1990 pop. 838), in S central Oaxaca, Mexico, 31 mi/50 km NE of San Pedro Pochutla; 16°05′N 96°13′W. Elev. 5,545 ft/1,690 m. Mountainous; temperate climate. Agr. (cereals, fruits), woods, and cattle. Access by dirt track. Zapotec-speaking area.

San Francisco River, c.160 mi/257 km long, in E Ariz. and W N.Mex.; rises in S part of Apache co., E Ariz., at Big Creek, Catron co.; flows E into N.Mex., then S and W through Apache and Gila natl. forests, reentering Ariz. in Greenlee co., in Apache Natl. Forest, where it is joined by Blue R., from N, then S, joining Gila R. 7 mi/11.3 km SW of Clifton.

San Francisco Sola (sahn frahn-SEES-ko SO-lah), town (1990 pop. 599), in S central Oaxaca, Mexico, 17 mi/28 km W of Ejutla de Crespo, on Mexico Highway 131; 16°31′N 96°58′W. Elev. 5,348 ft/1,630 m. Mountainous; temperate climate. Agr. (corn, beans, coffee, fruits), fine wood, lumber, mezcal and pottery. A high percentage of the pop. is indigenous. Also called San Francisco Sola de Vega.

San Francisco Telixtlahuaca (sahn frahn-SEES-ko te-leesh-tlah-WAH-kah), town, ⊙ San Francisco Telixtlahuaca municipio, Oaxaca, Mexico, 22 mi/35 km NW of Oaxaca, on Mexico Highway 131, on RR, at upper end of Etla Arm of the Oaxaca Valley, on Atoyac R., near the Continental Divide; 17°18′N 96°54′W. Elev. 5,741 ft/1,750 m. Agr., small farming, mainly for subsistence; graphite mines.

San Francisco Teopan (sahn frahn-SEES-ko te-O-pahn), town (1990 pop. 353), NW Oaxaca, Mexico, 22 mi/35 km E of Huajuapam de León, bordering the state of Puebla; 17°49′N 97°28′W. Elev. 7,381 ft/2,750 m. Temperate climate. On unpaved road. Farming.

San Francisco Tepeyanco (sahn frahn-SEES-ko te-pe-YAHN-ko), town (1990 pop. 2,844), ⊙ Tepeyanco municipio, Tlaxcala, central Mexico, 5 mi/8 km S of Tlaxcala; 19°15′N 98°15′W. Cereals, maguey; livestock. Thermal springs nearby.

San Francisco Tlapancingo (sahn frahn-SEES-ko tlah-pahn-SIN-go), town (1990 pop. 733), extreme W Oaxaca, Mexico, 41 mi/66 km SW of Huajuapam de León, near Guerrero state border. Elev. 5,512 ft/1,680 m. Process mezcal and produce straw textiles. Temperate climate. Access by dirt road.

San Francisco Xonacatlán, Mexico: see XONACATLÁN DE VICENCIO.

San Gabriel, Mexico: see CIUDAD VENUSTIANO CARRANZA.

San Gabriel, city (1990 pop. 37,120), Los Angeles co., SW Calif., suburb 8 mi/12.9 km ENE of downtown Los Angeles; 34°05′N 118°06′W. Mfg. (fabric mills, furniture, paper prods., cutting tools, aircraft parts, measuring devices). An annual 3-day fiesta celebrates the founding (1771) of the San Gabriel Arcángel mission, which was partly rebuilt after an earthquake in 1812. Inc. 1913.

San Gabriel Chilac (sahn gah-bree-AIL chee-LAK), town (1990 pop. 8,916), Puebla, central Mexico, 10 mi/ 16 km S of Tehuacán; 18°20′N 97°24′W. Agr. center (corn, rice, sugar, fruit; livestock). In Popoloca Indian area. Sometimes called Chilac.

San Gabriel Mixtepec (sahn gah-bree-AIL MEESH-te-pek), town (1990 pop. 2,435), SW Oaxaca, Mexico, 36 mi/58 km WSW of Miahuatlan de Porfirio Díaz; 16°05′N 97°06′W. Elev. 2,297 ft/700 m. Mountainous area on Pacific slope of Oaxaca highlands. Hot climate. Agr. (coffee, sugarcane, corn, beans, fruits); woods and cattle. On unpaved road to Miahuatlán de Porfirio Díaz.

San Gabriel Mountains, Los Angeles and San Bernardino cos., S Calif., E and NE of Los Angeles, running c.50 mi/80 km W from Cajon Pass. San Antonio Peak (10,064 ft/3,068 m) is the highest of the range. S foothills and beyond are in highly urbanized Los Angeles metropolitan area; 34°14′N 118°05′W. Crossed N-S in W by Los Angeles Aqueduct. San Bernardino Mts. continue to E.

San Gabriel River 1 c.75 mi/121 km long, in Los Angeles co., S Calif., intermittent stream formed in San Gabriel Mts. NE of Los Angeles by 3 forks; flows SSW from their junction, through San Gabriel and Morris reservoirs and Santa Fe Flood Control Basin, past Baldwin Park, Pico Rivera, Lakewood, and Long Beach, spreading in a broad wash at base of the mts., to Alamitos Bay on E end of Long Beach. Subject to torrential floods, it has extensive control works (levees, dams): on West Fork is San Gabriel No. 2 Dam (290 ft/88 m high, 620 ft/189 m long; completed 1935); on upper main stream are San Gabriel No. 1 Dam (381 ft/116 m high, 1,540 ft/469 m long; completed 1938) and Morris Dam (328 ft/100 m high, 780 ft/238 m long; completed 1934; water-supply reservoir for Pasadena). On lower course is Santa Fe flood-control basin, formed by Santa Fe Dam (92 ft/28 m high, c.2,400 ft/732 m long). West Fork rises 8 mi/12.9 km N of Pasadena; flows E c.20 mi/ 32 km through Cogswell Reservoir, receives North Fork before joining East Fork at San Gabriel Reservoir. East Fork rises c.20 mi/32 km N of Pomona; flows S, then W to San Gabriel reservoir. North Fork rises c.15 mi/ 24 km N of Azusa; flows S c.10 mi/16 km. **2** c.50 mi/ 80 km long, in central Texas; formed at Georgetown by N and S forks rising in Burnet co.; flows generally E to Little R. 6 mi/9.7 km S of Cameron, in Milan co. Forms L. Georgetown, 28 mi/45 km N of Austin, and L. Granger, 35 mi/56 km NNE of Austin.

San Germán (sahn her-MAHN), town (1990 pop. 34,962), SW P.R. Commercial and industrial area; mfg. (medicines, electric appliances, fruit candies, clothing). The original village was founded in 1511, but it was early raided by the French; the fleeing residents established a new settlement in the nearby hills. The town is a center for art and needlework, and retains a colonial atmosphere. It is the site of the 17th-cent. Porta Coeli Convent, one of the oldest churches in the Americas (now a mus.). San Germán is the seat of the Inter-Amer. Univ. of P.R.

San Gorgonio, Mount, peak (11,489 ft/3,502 m) of San Bernardino Mts., highest point in S Calif., c.80 mi/ 129 km E of Los Angeles, 25 mi/40 km E of San Bernardino; 34°06′N 116°49′W.

San Gorgonio Pass (2,616 ft/797 m), Riverside co., S Calif., mt. pass 15 mi/24 km ESE of San Bernardino, connecting N end of Coachella Valley with San Bernardino Valley. Mt. San Gorgonio (in San Bernardino Mts.) is N, Mt. San Jacinto (San Jacinto Mts.) is S. Broad floor of pass (3 mi/4.8 km–4 mi/6.4 km wide) is orchard region. Interstate Highway 10, RR, and Colorado R. Aqueduct pass through. Major windpower site along with Altamont and Tehachapi passes.

San Gregario, uninc. village, San Mateo co., W Calif., 31 mi/50 km S of downtown San Francisco, and 27 mi/ 43 km W of San Jose, on Pacific Ocean, at mouth of San Gregorio Creek. Santa Cruz Mts. to NE. Tourist area. Ornamentals, flowers, Christmas trees, vegetables. San Gregario State Beach is here.

San Gregorio Atzompa (sahn grai-GOR-yo aht-SOM-pah), town (1990 pop. 2,963), Puebla, central Mexico, on RR, and 10 mi/16 kmW of Puebla; 19°02′N 98°20′W. Cereals, fruit; livestock. Sometimes called Atzompa.

San Hipólito Soltepec, Mexico: see SOLTEPEC.

San Ignacio (sahn eeg-NAH-see-o), city (1990 pop. 3,135) and township, Sinaloa, NW Mexico, in W outliers of Sierra Madre Occidental, on Piaxtla R., and 50 mi/80 km N of Mazatlán; 23°55′N 106°25′W. Elev. 9,843 ft/3,000 m. Gold and silver mining; construction lumber and fine woods.

San Ignacio, Mexico: see PRAXEDIS G. GUERRERO.

San Ignacio Island (sahn eeg-NAH-see-o) (☐ 19 sq mi/ 49 sq km), barrier island just off coast of Sinaloa, NW Mexico, in Gulf of California, 20 mi/32 km S of Los Mochis; 15 mi/24 km long, c.1.5 mi/2.4 km wide. Alluvial.

San Ildefonso (san il-duh-FAWN-so), pueblo (1990 pop. 447), Santa Fe co., N central N.Mex., on the Rio Grande, 15 mi/24 km NNW of Santa Fe, at center of San Ildefonso pueblo land grant (reservation; 1990 pop. 1,499); 35°53′N 106°07′W. The inhabitants speak a Tanoan language. The pueblo is famous for its excellent pottery and paintings, and many of its artists have won individual fame. On Jan. 23, the day of fiesta, ceremonial dances (e.g., the buffalo and Comanche dances) are performed. Est. early 1700s.

San Ildefonso Amatlán (sahn eel-dai-FON-so ahmaht-LAHN), town (1990 pop. 1,128), S Oaxaca, Mexico, 7 mi/12 km E of Miahuatlán de Porfirio Díaz; 16°20′N 96°30′W. Elev. 5,512 ft/1,680 m. Mountainous. Temperate climate. Agr. (corn, beans, coffee, fruits) and woods. Dirt road connects with the town of Miahuatlan.

San Ildefonso Sola (sahn eel-dai-FON-so SO-lah), town (1990 pop 182), S Oaxaca, Mexico, 1 mi/1.6 km N of San Miguel Sola de Vega, off Mexico Highway 131; 16°32′N 96°58′W. Elev. 4,757 ft/1,450 m. Farming, mainly for subsistence.

San Ildefonso Villa Alta (sahn eel-dai-FON-so VEE-yah AHL-tah), town (1990 pop. 1,117), Oaxaca, S Mexico, 40 mi/64 km NE of Oaxaca; 17°21′N 96°09′W. Elev. 9,937 ft/1,200 m. On unpaved road. Farming, mainly for subsistence.

San Isidro de las Cuevas, Mexico: see MATAMOROS.

San Isidro de Zaragoza, Mexico: see ZARAGOZA.

San Jacinto (san juh-SIN-to), county (☐ 627 sq mi/ 1,624 sq km; 1990 pop. 16,372), E Texas; ⊙ Coldspring; 30°34′N 95°09′W. Bounded N and E by Trinity R., and by Peach Creek on SW; drained by W Fork San Jacinto R. Contained within Sam Houston Natl. Forest (except E and N ends). Timber (including pulpwood) is chief industry; also livestock (cattle, hogs, horses); hay. Oil and gas wells; iron ore. Hunting, fishing. Formed 1869.

San Jacinto (san juh-SIN-to), city (1990 pop. 16,210), Riverside co., S Calif., suburb 26 mi/42 km SE of Riverside on San Jacinto R., at base of Mt. San Jacinto; 33°48′N 116°58′W. Fruit growing; mfg. (printing and publishing, electric housewares, electrical industrial apparatus, mobile homes, transformers). Mt. Jacinto Col. (2 year). With nearby Hemet, holds annual Ramona Pageant. Gilman Hot Springs to N, Soboba Hot Springs, and Soboba Indian Reservation to E. Colorado River Aqueduct runs E-W to N, San Diego Aqueduct branches S from it, to W; part of San Bernardino Natl. Forest to E. Inc. 1888.

San Jacinto (san juh-SIN-to), battlefield, Harris co., S Texas, c.16 mi/26 km E of Houston, NE of city of Deer Park, bet. Houston Ship Channel (Buffalo Bayou) and San Jacinto R. San Jacinto Battleground State Historic Site here (c.1,003 acres/406 ha), with monument 570 ft/ 174 m high, marks site of battle of San Jacinto (April 1836), in which Gen. Sam Houston's Texan troops defeated Mexicans under Santa Anna and won the decisive engagement of the Texas revolution, assuring the independence of the Republic of Texas and paving the way for its annexation by the U.S. Mus. of Texas History; park and picnic grounds. Battleship *Texas* (State Historic Site) moored beside park in San Jacinto R., pre-World War I dreadnought, also served as flagship on D-Day, 1944, World War II.

San Jacinto (san juh-SIN-to), river, c.130 mi/209 km long, SE Texas; rising as the West Fork, flowing S to Galveston Bay. Its chief tributary is Buffalo Bayou; both the lower bayou and the lower river are used for the Houston Ship Channel. East Fork rises in N San Jacinto co., flows c.50 mi/80 km, joining W Fork at L. Houston in Sam Houston Natl. Forest. San Jacinto Battleground State Historic Site, is on the river, near the mouth of Buffalo Bayou and E of Houston. The USS *Texas* is moored next to the park. Dams on San Jacinto include L. Houston Dam, 20 mi/32 km NE of downtown Houston, completed in 1953 (capacity 154,000 acre-ft) and the Conroe Dam, 50 mi/80 km NNW of Houston, completed in 1973 (capacity 780,000 acre-ft).

San Jacinto Amilpas (sahn hah-SEEN-to ah-MEEL-pahs), town (1990 pop. 1,514), central Oaxaca, Mexico, 3.1 mi/5 km NW of Oaxaca de Juárez; 17°04′N 96°45′W. Essentially a suburb of Oaxaca.

San Jacinto Bay, Texas: see GALVESTON BAY.

San Jacinto, Mount, Calif.: see SAN JACINTO MOUNTAINS.

San Jacinto Mountains (san yuh-SIN-to), Riverside co., S Calif., range extending c.30 mi/48 km SSE from San Gorgonio Pass (separating range from the San Bernardinos) to N end of Santa Rosa Mts.; 33°48′N 116°40′W. At N end is Mt. San Jacinto or San Jacinto Peak (10,804 ft/3,293 m); at peak's E base is Palm Springs. Mt. San Jacinto State Park (c.13,714 acres/ 5,550 ha) has trails, camp sites (at Idyllwild, a resort c.20 mi/32 km E of Hemet), tracts of desert and timberland. Pacific Crest Trail passes through the range.

San Jacinto Tlacotepec (sahn hah-SEEN-to tlah-KO-te-pek), town (1990 pop. 524), SW Oaxaca, Mexico, 56 mi/90 km SW of Oaxaca de Juárez; 16°29′N 97°22′W. Elev. 4,912 ft/1,500 m. Temperate climate. In Mixteca Alta. Farming for subsistence. On dirt track.

San Javier (sahn hah-vee-ER), town (1990 pop. 304), SE Sonora, Mexico, 12 mi/19 km SE of Hermosillo; 28°36′N 109°44′W. Mining town, isolated; access by dirt trail.

San Jerónimo (sahn he-RO-nee-mo), officially **San Jerónimo de Juárez** (sahn he-RO-nee-mo dai HWAH-res), town (1990 pop. 6,964), ⊙ Benito Juárez municipio, Guerrero, SW Mexico, in Pacific lowland, 40 mi/ 64 km WNW of Acapulco de Juárez on Mexico Highway 200; 17°05′N 100°28′W. Rice, sugarcane, fruit; livestock.

San Jerónimo Coatlán (sahn he-RO-nee-mo), town (1990 pop. 826) S central Oaxaca, Mexico, 20 mi/33 km WSW of Miahuatlan de Porfirio Díaz; 16°21′N 96°52′W. Elev. 5,479 ft/1,670 m. Rough terrain near the Atoyaco Verde R. Temperate climate. Agr. (corn, beans, coffee, sugarcane, fruits); woods. On unpaved road to Miahuatuán.

San Jerónimo Ixtepec, Mexico: see CIUDAD IXTEPEC.

San Jerónimo Silacayoapilla (sahn he-RO-nee-mo see-lah-kah-yo-ah-PEE-yah), town (1990 pop. 1,067), NW Oaxaca, Mexico, 6 mi/10 km W of Huajuapam de León; 17°49′N 97°50′W. Elev. 5,545 ft/1,690 m. Mountainous; temperate climate. Agr.; processing of aguardiente and local straw textiles. Gravel road to Huajuapam de León.

San Jerónimo Sosola (sahn he-RO-nee-mo so-SO-lah), town (1990 pop. 248), W Oaxaca, Mexico, 30 mi/48 km NW of Oaxaca de Juárez; 17°19′N 97°01′W. Elev. 5,249 ft/1,600 m. Mountainous area; temperate climate. Agr. (corn, beans, chilies, fruits); processing aguardiente and straw textiles. Linked to Inter-Amer. Highway (190) by gravel road.

San Jerónimo Taviche (sahn he-RO-nee-mo tah-VEE-che), town (1990 pop. 1,297), S central Oaxaca, Mexico, on RR, on gravel road 7.5 mi/12 km SE of Ocotlán de Morelos; 16°44′N 96°35′W. Elev. 6,004 ft/1,830 m. Temperate climate. Lead mine; former silver and gold mining. Agr. (wheat, potatoes, corn).

San Jerónimo Tecoatl (sahn he-RO-nee-mo te-KWAH-tul), town (1990 pop. 920), N central Oaxaca, Mexico,

2.5 mi/4 km E of the Puebla state border, and 12 mi/20 km to the E of Teotitlán de Flores Macón by a paved road; 18°09′N 96°55′W. Elev. 8,465 ft/2,580 m. Rugged terrain. Agr. (cereals, fruits), woods, straw textiles. Cold climate.

San Jerónimo Tecuanipan (sahn he-RO-nee-mo te-kwah-NEE-pahn), town (1990 pop. 1,825), Puebla, central Mexico, 13 mi/21 km W of Puebla; 19°01′N 98°24′W. Cereals, fruit, maguey. Sometimes called Tecuanipan.

San Jerónimo Tlacochahuaya (sahn he-RO-nee-mo tlah-ko-chah-WAH-yah), town (1990 pop. 2,049), Oaxaca, S Mexico, in Sierra Madre del Sur, 10 mi/16 km ESE of Oaxaca; 17°00′N 96°34′W. Elev. 5,249 ft/1,600 m. Fruit; livestock. Has pre-Columbian ruins with notable carvings; municipal palace, 16th-cent. church, 17th-cent. convent. Formerly called Tlacochahuaya de Morelos.

San Jerónimo Xayacatlán (sahn he-RO-nee-mo hah-yah-kah-TLAHN), town (1990 pop. 1,068), Puebla, central Mexico, 7 mi/11.3 km ENE of Acatlán on gravel road; 18°14′N 97°55′W. Agr. center (corn, rice, fruit; livestock). Xayacatlán de Bravo is 3 mi/4.8 km W.

San Joaquin (san wah-KEEN), county (□ 1,399 sq mi/3,623 sq km; 1990 pop. 480,628), central Calif.; ⊙ STOCKTON; 37°56′N 121°16′W. Level San Joaquin Valley, touching Coast Ranges (Diablo Range) in SW and foothills of Sierra Nevada in E; marshy delta (partly reclaimed) of San Joaquin R. in W. Drained by San Joaquin, Mokelumne, Columnes, and Calaveras rivers. N boundary formed by Dry Creek and San Joaquin R. (in extreme W); S border formed in part by Stanislaus R. Cattle; dairying; apples, pumpkins, cherries, almonds, walnuts, grapes, cauliflowers, onions, cucumbers, tomatoes, asparagus, celery, nursery prods., wheat, barley, oats, corn, sugar beets, beans. Extensive packing and processing industries (wineries, canneries, beet-sugar refineries); Stockton is inland seaport and a mfg. center. Sand, gravel, clay, stone, limestone quarrying; natural-gas wells. Mokelumne Aqueduct passes E-W through center of co.; also crossed N-S by Delta Mendota Canal. Caswell Memorial State Park in S. Formed 1850.

San Joaquin (san wah-KEEN), city (1990 pop. 2,311), Fresno co., central Calif., near San Joaquin R., 25 mi/40 km W of Fresno; 36°37′N 120°11′W. Grain, cotton, alfalfa, flax, sugar beets, cotton, fruit, vegetables, beans.

San Joaquín (sahn hwah-KEEN), town (1990 pop. 1,220), NE Querétaro, Mexico, 14 mi/23 km SSW of Jalpan; 20°55′N 99°34′W. Elev. 7,119 ft/2,170 m. Rugged terrain in the Sierra Gorda. Cool climate. Agr. (corn, beans), cattle raising; zinc and silver mines. A dirt track connects to neighboring municipalities.

San Joaquin River (san wah-KEEN), c.320 mi/515 km long, S central Calif.; rises in the Sierra Nevada, NE Madera co., E Calif.; flows SW then NW past Newman and Stockton, then W through Mammoth Pool Reservoir and Millerton L. Reservoir (Friant Dam) into Central Valley, and past Fresno to form a large delta with the Sacramento R. near Suisun Bay, an arm of San Francisco Bay. The San Joaquin is navigable c.40 mi/64 km for oceangoing vessels to within 15 mi/24 km (to NW) of Stockton. The Mokelumne, Tuolumne, Merced, and Fresno are its chief tributaries. The wide S part of the basin bet. the Sierra Nevada and the Coast Range is usually called the San Joaquin Valley, although it includes other rivers such as the Kings and the Kern. Bet. Stockton in the N and Bakersfield in the S are many cities, notably Fresno, Modesto, and Merced. The CENTRAL VALLEY PROJECT, undertaken largely to bring water from the N to make the San Joaquin Valley more productive, has as one of its units Friant Dam on the San Joaquin; the San Luis Dam is on the San Luis R.; Delta Mendota Canal parallels lower river to W.

San Jon (san HON), village (1990 pop. 277), Quay co., E N.Mex., 30 mi/48 km ESE of Tucumcari, near Texas state line; 35°06′N 103°19′W. Elev. 4,022 ft/1,226 m. In cattle and sheep ranching area. Caprock Amphitheater to S.

San Jorge Nuchita (sahn HOR-hai noo-CHEE-tah),

town (1990 pop. 2,254), in NW Oaxaca, Mexico, 17 mi/28 km E of the Guerrero state border, and 24 mi/39 km WSW of Huajuapan de León; 17°38′N 98°06′W. Elev. 5,052 ft/1,540 m. In the Mixteca Baja, a Mixtec Indian community. Temperate climate. Agr. (corn, beans, wheat, sugarcane); mezcal processing, cattle raising, and pottery making.

San Jose (san ho-ZAI), city (1990 pop. 782,248), ⊙ Santa Clara co., W central Calif., 40 mi/64 km SE of San Francisco, 38 mi/61 km SSE of Oakland, 10 mi/16 km SE of S end of San Francisco Bay; 37°18′N 121°51′W. In Santa Clara Valley, drained by Coyote, Guadalupe, and Los Gatos creeks. Along with San Francisco and Oakland the city comprises the 4th-largest metropolitan area in the U.S. Mfg. (computers, electronics and electrical equip., machinery, metal fabrication, medical equip., rubber and plastic prods., communications equip., transportation equip., paper prods., food and beverage processing, printing and publishing, semiconductor processing equip., chemicals). San Jose lies in a rich fruit-growing area and has wineries and a large number of food-processing industries. Diverse agr. to S and E, including fruits, vegetables, nursery prods.; dairying; poultry; eggs; grain, strawberries. Aerospace and commercial supply industries are in the vicinity, as is the Silicon Valley high-technology and computer-mfg. center, which extends NW through Santa Clara, Palo Alto, other communities. Industrial production developed significantly after World War II and growth has since been rapid and extensive in San Jose. The city's pop. increased by more than 70% bet. 1970 and 1990. The 1st state legislature (1849) met here, and San Jose was the state capital from 1849 to 1851. Among the city's parks are Alum Rock Park, with mineral springs; Kelley Park, with a zoo and a Jap. garden and tea house; and Rosicrucian Mus. and Planetarium, with an Egyptian mus., a science mus., and a planetarium. San Jose State Univ., San Jose City Col. (2 year), and Evergreen Valley Col. (2 year) are in the city. To the N lies Mission San Jose de Guadalupe (1797) and to the W is Mission Santa Clara de Asís (1777). San Jose Municipal Airport in N; Reid Hillview Airport in E. Moffett Field Naval Air Station to NW. Santa Cruz Mts. to SW; Santa Clara Co. Fairgrounds; Henry W. Coe State Park to SE; Frontier Village Theme Park to SE; Great Amer. Theme Park to NW. Founded 1777; inc. 1850.

San Jose (san JOZ), village (1990 pop. 519), in Logan and Mason cos., central Ill., 18 mi/29 km S of Pekin; 40°18′N 89°35′W. In agr. area; ships seeds.

San José Acateno (sahn ho-SAI ah-kah-TE-no), town (1990 pop. 2,873), Puebla, central Mexico, in Gulf lowlands, 22 mi/35 km SSE of Papantla de Olarte; 20°88′N 97°12′W. Sugarcane, coffee, fruit. Also called Acateno.

San José Allende, Mexico: see VILLA DE ALLENDE.

San José Ayuquila (sahn ho-SAI ah-yoo-KWEE-lah), town (1990 pop. 856), NW Oaxaca, Mexico, 16 mi/25 km NW of Huajuapan de León; 17°58′N 97°57′W. Elev. 5,085 ft/1,550 m. In a high valley in Mixteco R. drainage area. Temperate climate. Agr. (corn, beans, rice, sugarcane); poultry raising and local straw textiles. On gravel road.

San José Chiapa (sahn ho-SAI chee-AH-pah), town (1990 pop. 3,434), ⊙ San José de Chiapa, Puebla, central Mexico, on RR, and 32 mi/51 km NE of Puebla; 19°15′N 97°46′W. On Mexico Highway 129. Cereals, maguey.

San José Chiltepec (sahn ho-SAI CHEEL-te-pek), town (1990 pop. 2,836), NE Oaxaca, on Mexico Highway 125, 11 mi/18 km SW of Tuxtepec; 17°57′N 96°11′W. In Chinantec-speaking area.

San José de Gracia 1 (sahn ho-SAI dai GRAH-see-ah), town (1990 pop. 3,339), in NW Aguascalientes, Mexico, 3.1 mi/5 km SW of Villa General José Manuel Arteaga. Also known as Colonia Calles. **2** town (1990 pop. 7,242), ⊙ Marcos Castellanos municipio, in extreme NW Michoacán, Mexico, S of Lake Chapala in the NW region of state, very close to Jalisco, 21 mi/32 km WSW of Sahuayo de Morelos, on Jalisco border. Agr. (corn, wheat, beans) and livestock. Also known as Ornelas.

San Jose de Guadalupe, Mission, Calif.: see MISSION SAN JOSE.

San José de la Isla, Mexico: see GENARO CODINA.

San José de las Lajas (sahn ho-SAI dai lahs LAH-hahs), town (1994 est. pop. 33,000), La Habana prov., W Cuba, on Natl. Highway, and at RR junction 17 mi/27 km SE of Havana; 22°46′N 82°10′W. Commercial center in dairying and sugar-growing region. Has thermal springs. The Cotilla Caves are nearby.

San José de las Matas (sahn ho-SAI dai lahs MAH-tahs), town (1993 pop. 8,158), Santiago prov., N central Dominican Republic, 17 mi/27 km SW of Santiago; 19°20′N 71°05′W. Agr. (tobacco, chickpeas). Lumbering and gold washing in vicinity.

San José de los Ramos (sahn ho-SAI dai los RAH-mos), town, Matanzas prov., W Cuba, on RR, and 33 mi/53 km ESE of Cárdenas; 22°48′N 80°47′W. Sugarcane, fruit.

San José de Ocoa (sahn ho-SAI dai o-KO-ah), town (1993 pop. 18,899), Peravia prov., S Dominican Republic, in the Sierra de Ocoa, on Ocoa R., and 21 mi/34 km NW of Baní; 18°38′N 70°30′W. Tobacco-growing center. Coal deposits nearby.

San José de Oruña, Trinidad and Tobago: see SAINT JOSEPH.

San José del Cabo (sahn ho-SAI del KAH-bo), town (1990 pop. 14,892), ⊙ Los Cabos municipio, Baja California Sur, NW Mexico, near SE tip of peninsula, 85 mi/137 km SSE of La Paz; 23°03′N 109°41′W. Important beach resort, which emerged in 1970s, along with neighboring Cabo de San Lucas (20 mi/30 km away). Internatl. airport.

San José del Peñasco (sahn ho-SAI pen-YAHS-ko), town (1990 pop. 722), S Oaxaca, Mexico, 7 mi/12 km E of Miahuatlán de Porfirio Díaz; 16°26′N 96°31′W. Corn, coffee, beans; livestock. No all-weather road access.

San José del Progreso (sahn ho-SAI del pro-GRE-so), town (1990 pop. 2,013), in S central Oaxaca, Mexico, 16 mi/25 km E of Ejutla de Crespo; 16°36′N 96°31′W. Isolated community in Oaxaca highland, with no access by all-weather road. Temperate climate. Agr. (corn, wheat, beans, mezcal), cattle and poultry raising. Formerly called Progreso.

San José Estancia Grande (sahn ho-SAI es-TAHN-see-ah GRAHN-dai), town (1990 pop. 853), SW Oaxaca, Mexico, 14 mi/23 km W of the Guerrero state border, and 14 mi/23 km W of Santiago Pinotepa Nacional, on Mexico Highway 200; 16°51′N 98°12′W. Amusgo Indian community.

San José Independencia (sahn ho-SAI een-de-pen-DEN-see-ah), town (1990 pop. 841), N central Oaxaca, Mexico, 38 mi/62 km WNW of Tuxtepec; 18°14′N 96°40′W. Elev. 2,133 ft/650 m. A mountainous region near President Miguel Aleman Reservoir. Hot climate. Agr. (corn, beans, sugarcane, coffee, fruits), woods. Cattle and poultry breeding and raising. No road access. Mazatec-speaking community.

San José Island (□ 83 sq mi/215 sq km), in Gulf of California, off SE coast of Baja California Sur, NW Mexico, 50 mi/80 km N of La Paz; 20 mi/32 km long, 3 mi/4.8 km–7 mi/11.3 km wide; 24°52′N 111°00′W. Rises to 2,461 ft/750 m. Of volcanic origin; barren, uninhabited. Within Islas del Golfo de California Special Biosphere Reserve.

San José Iturbide (sahn ho-SAI ee-toor-BEE-de), city (1990 pop. 12,094), and township, Guanajuato, central Mexico, 29 mi/466 km N of Querétaro; 21°03′N 100°23′W. Elev. 6,627 ft/2,020 m. Cereals, sugar, alfalfa, fruit; livestock. Formerly called Álvaro Obregón.

San José Lachiguirí (sahn ho-SAI lah-chee-gee-REE), town (1990 pop. 1,443), S central Oaxaca, Mexico, 17 mi/28 km ENE of Miahuatlán de Porfirio Díaz; 16°23′N 96°20′W. Elev. 5,577 ft/1,700 m. A mountainous region. Temperate climate. Agr. (corn, beans, coffee, fruits), woods. On a dirt road.

San José Miahuatlán (sahn ho-SAI mee-ah-waht-LAHN), town (1990 pop. 5,762), Puebla, central Mexico, 13 mi/21 km SSE of Tehuacán; 18°17′N 97°17′W. Elev. 3,675 ft/1,120 m. Agr. center (corn, sugarcane, fruit; livestock). In Popoloca Indian area. Also called Miahuatlán.

San José Miahuatlán, Mexico: see MIAHUATLÁN.

San José Olintla, Mexico: see OLINTLA.

San José Purua, Mexico: see HEROICO ZITÁCUARO.

San Jose River (san ho-ZAI) or **Rio San Jose** (REE-o san ho-zai), c.90 mi/145 km long, S Mckinley co., just W of Thoreau, at Continental Divide, W N.Mex.; rises in Zuñi Mts.; flows ESE, bet. sects. of Cibola Natl. Forest and sects. of Acoma, Laguna, and Cañoncito Indian Reservations, past Bluewater, Grants, and Laguna, to Rio Puerco 22 mi/35 km N of Socorro (in Isleta Indian Reservation). Dam on headstream, 8 mi/12.9 km WNW of Bluewater, forms Bluewater Reservoir (4 mi/6.4 km long, 1 mi/1.6 km wide).

San José Tenango (sahn ho-SAI te-NAHN-go), town (1990 pop. 1,032), N central Oaxaca, Mexico, 6 mi/10 km E of the Puebla state border, and 24 mi/38 km E of Teotitlán de Flores Magón on the W side of the President Alemán dam (Presa Presidente Alemán); 18°09′N 96°44′W. Elev. 2,625 ft/800 m. In the Sierra Mazateca. In Mazatec-speaking area. Agr. (corn, wheat, potatoes, sugarcane, fruit), mezcal processing, wood, cattle and poultry breeding. Gravel road connects to Huautla.

San Juan (sahn HWAHN), interior province (□ 1,344 sq mi/3,481 sq km; 1993 pop. 247,029), W Dominican Republic, ⊙ San Juan; 18°50′N 71°15′W. Comprises fertile, irrigated San Juan valley; bounded by Cordillera Central (N, Pico Duarte is on the border) and Sierra de Neiba (S), watered by the Yaque del Sur. Main crops include rice, corn, coffee, bananas, potatoes, chickpeas, sugarcane. Lumbering. Prov., formerly part of Azua prov., was est. 1938. Elías Piña prov. was separated from it in 1942. Formerly called Benefactor.

San Juan (sahn HWAHN), city (1993 pop. 61,278), ⊙ San Juan prov., W Dominican Republic, in San Juan Valley, on affluent of the Yaque del Sur, on highway, and 90 mi/145 km WNW of Santo Domingo; 18°48′N 71°15′W. Agr. center (rice, coffee, corn, fruit, tubers). Founded 1504, became the capital of the prov. in 1938. Officially known as San Juan de la Maguana.

San Juan (SAN WAHN), town, NW Trinidad, Trinidad and Tobago, 4 mi/6 km E of Port of Spain. Market town (sugarcane, coconuts).

San Juan, Mexico: see LANDERO Y COSS.

San Juan (san WAHN), pueblo (1990 pop. 1,821), Rio Arriba co., N N.Mex., 27 mi/43 km N of Santa Fe, on the Rio Grande. Mfg. (food processing). Settled 1598 by Juan de Oñate. A Franciscan mission was later est. here. It was the home of Popé, the medicine man who led the Native Americans in the Pueblo revolt of 1680. The inhabitants are Pueblo who speak a language of the Tanoan family and produce art and handicrafts.

San Juan 1 (san WAHN), county (□ 5,538 sq mi/14,343 sq km; pop. 91,605), extreme NW N.Mex.; ⊙ Aztec; 36°30′N 108°19′W. Drained by Animas, Chaco La Plata, and San Juan (farms, Navajo L. on NE boundary) rivers. Livestock (cattle, sheep) grazing area; dairying; agr. (pumpkins, potatoes, apples, peanuts, blue corn, hay, alfalfa, wheat, barley, oats) in San Juan valley; oil and natural gas, near Shiprock, to W in Navajo Indian Reservation. Chaco Canyon Natl. Monument in SE; Aztec Ruins Natl. Monument in NE; Chuska Mts. in SW, including several small lakes. NW corner is only point in U.S. common to 4 states (Colo., Ariz., Utah, N.Mex.); bounded N by Colo., W by Ariz., touches Utah, NW. De-Na-Zin and Bisti Wilderness areas, both along Hunter Wash, in SE center; Angel Peak Natl. Recreation Area in E; Navajo L. State (Pine Unit) in NE, on Navajo L. Reservoir, San Juan R; part of large Navajo Indian Reservation (N. Mex., Ariz., Utah), more than ½ the co., is W; part of Ute Mt. Indian Reservation (N.Mex., Colo.) in N. Indian crafts, pottery are important industries. Formed 1887. **2** county (□ 388 sq mi/1,005 sq km; 1990 pop. 745), SW Colo.; ⊙ Silverton; 37°46′N 107°40′W. Mining and livestock-grazing region, drained by Animas R. Crossed in E by Continental Divide. Source of Rio Grande E of Divide; source of Uncompahgre R. in N. Lead, silver, gold, copper, zinc. San Juan Mts. and San Juan Natl. Forest throughout. Part of San Juan Natl. Forest in S and W; part of Rio Grande Natl. Forest in E; small part of Uncompahgre Natl. Forest in N. Formed 1876. **3** county (□ 7,933 sq mi/20,546 sq km; 1990 pop. 12,621), SE Utah; ⊙ Monticello. Mt. and plateau area bordering Colo. (E) and Ariz. (S), bounded on W by Colorado R. (L. Powell reservoir, formed by Glen Canyon Dam), crossed in S by San Juan R.; 37°37′N 109°48′W. Four Corner Area in SE, only point common to 4 states in U.S. Includes part of large Navajo Indian Reservation in S (which extends into Ariz. and N.Mex.). Abajo Mts. are W of Monticello, La Sal Mts. in NE, both lying in sects. of Manti–La Sal Natl. Forest in center and NE corner. Natural Bridges Natl. Monument is W of Blanding in center of W; Rainbow Bridge Natl. Monument is in SW; part of Hovenweep Natl. Monument is in SE. Timber; oil, natural gas, uranium mining (Blanding); wheat, cattle are raised in irrigated region near Blanding. Grand Gulch Primitive Area in S center; Dark Canyon Primitive Area in NW. Large part of Canyonlands Natl. Park in NW; part of Glen Canyon Natl. Recreational Area in W and SW, along Colorado R.; Newspaper Rock State Park in N center; Dead Horse Point State Park on N boundary. Formed 1880. **4** county (□ 621 sq mi/1,608 sq km; 1990 pop. 10,035), NW Wash.; ⊙ Friday Harbor; 48°34′N 122°58′W. Bounded N by Strait of Georgia, E by Rosario Strait, S by Strait of Juan de Fuca, W by Haro Strait; Canada (B.C.) border is to N and W. Co. includes the main isls. (SAN JUAN, Lopez, and Orcas; interconnected by ferry; ferry to Anacortes) of the SAN JUAN Isls., an archipelago SW of Bellingham, at N end of Puget Sound. Hay; dairying; cattle; fish, oysters, crabs, prawns; lime. Co. has 17 state parks, most important ones are Moran State Park, on Orcas Isl.; Lime Kiln Point, on San Juan Isl.; Spencer Spit, on Lopez Isl. All others are marine parks on small offshore isls. Parts of San Juan Isls. Natl. Wildlife Refuge scattered throughout group. Junes Isl. Natl. Wildlife and Migratory Bird Refuge at center; San Juan Isl. Natl. Historical Park in 3 units on San Juan Isls. Formed 1873.

San Juan 1 (sahn HWAHN), city (1990 pop. 437,745); ⊙ P.R. and largest city in pop., and chief port and commercial center of P.R., NE P.R. on Atlantic Ocean. It is the financial, tourism, social, and cultural center of isl. San Juan's industries include brewing, distilling, and publishing; mfg. includes metal prods., cement, and apparel. The city remains the isl.'s financial center and has many internatl. banks and business corporations. San Juan is serviced by an internatl. airport located to its W in Carolina and cruise ship docks. As the city's metropolitan area is home to nearly 35% of Puerto Rico's pop. as of the 1980s, the govt. has attempted, with limited success, to reverse pop. migration to San Juan's outlying areas. The city's old sect., situated on 2 rocky islets guarding one of the best harbors in the Caribbean, is linked by bridges with the mainland. The bay was named P.R. [=rich port] by Ponce de León, who in 1508 founded a settlement at nearby Caparra. In 1521 the settlement was moved across the bay to San Juan's present site. Strongly fortified, it withstood attacks by Eng. buccaneers in 1595, but succumbed for a few months in 1598 to George Clifford, earl of Cumberland, and was sacked by the Dutch in 1625. San Juan's port gained increasing importance during the 18th and 19th cents. U.S. troops occupied the city during the Span.-Amer. War in 1898. In the old city, whose narrow streets, small shops, and houses with overhanging balconies recall a colonial atmosphere, there are impressive historic bldgs.: El Morro castle (begun 1539), which commands the harbor entrance and is a natl. monument; San Cristóbal castle (begun 1631), originally a Span. fort; and La Fortaleza (begun 1529), a former fort now used as the governor's official residence. Other San Juan landmarks include San José Church (founded c.1523), the oldest church in continuous use in the Western Hemisphere; Casa Blanca (1523); and the Cathedral of San Juan Bautista, which contains the tomb of Ponce de León. Also in the city are the Univ. of P.R. and its School of Tropical Medicine, the Col. of the Sacred Heart, and a campus of the InterAmer. Univ. of P.R. Nearby are several resort beaches (notably the Condado and Isla Verde), which attract tourists from N. Amer. Sabana Seca Communications Center (U.S. Army) is W. **2** (san WAHN), city (1990 pop. 10,815), Hidalgo co., extreme S Texas, suburb 5 mi/8 km E of McAllen, in lower Rio Grande valley; 26°11′N 98°09′W. Elev. 102 ft/31 m. Trade, shipping center in irrigated fruit, vegetable, cotton area; mfg. (leather goods, concrete).

San Juan, river, c.400 mi/644 km long, Colo., N.Mex., and Utah; rises at Continental Divide in the San Juan Mts. to SW corner of Rio Grande co., SW Colo.; flows generally SW through Pagosa Springs, N.Mex., W through Navajo Reservoir, past Farmington and Shiprock, then NW through Navajo Indian Reservation, through extreme SW corner of Colo., into Utah (the Four Corners Area), continues W, forming N boundary of Navajo Indian Reservation, and S border of E extension of Glen Canyon Natl. Recreation Area. The lower 40 mi/64 km forms separate arms of L. Powell reservoir; joins Colorado R. 38 mi/61 km ENE of Page, Ariz., and Utah to L. Powell on the Colorado R. NAVAJO DAM, part of the upper Colorado R. storage project, is on the river, which is unnavigable. Its chief tributaries are the Animas, Los Pinos, La Plata, Piedra, and Mancos rivers. The San Juan is used for irrigation; vegetables, fruits, and grains are grown in the river valley in NW N.Mex.

San Juan, Calif.: see SAN JUAN BAUTISTA, town.

San Juan Achiutla (sahn HWAHN ah-chee-OOT-lah), town (1990 pop. 553), W Oaxaca, Mexico, 12 mi/19 km NE of Tlaxiaco; 17°20′N 97°31′W. Elev. 6,693 ft/2,040 m. Cold climate. Gravel road to Tlaxiaco connects with Mexico Highway 125. In the Mixteca Alta.

San Juan, Alturas de (sahn HWAHN, ahl-TOOR-ahs dai), low range, Cienfuegos prov., central Cuba, W of the Sierra de Trinidad, and part of larger Escambray Mts. massif; 12 mi/19 km long E-W. Rises in the Pico San Juan to 3,793 ft/1,156 m.

San Juan Atenco (sahn HWAHN ah-TEN-ko), town (1990 pop. 2,045), Puebla, central Mexico, 45 mi/72 km E of Puebla; 19°05′N 97°32′W. On Mexico Highway 144. Cereals, maguey. Sometimes called Atenco.

San Juan Atepec (sahn HWAHN AH-te-pek), town (1990 pop. 1,823), central Oaxaca, Mexico, 29 mi/47 km NNE of Oaxaca de Juárez; 17°25′N 96°32′W. Elev. 7,808 ft/2,380 m. A mountainous region in the banks of the Río Grande drainage area. Agr. (corn, beans, wheat), wool textile industry. Gravel road connects 3 mi/4.8 km to Mexico Highway 175.

San Juan Atzompa (sahn HWAHN aht-SOM-pah), town (1990 pop. 591), Puebla, central Mexico, 24 mi/39 km SE of Puebla; 18°45′N 98°05′W. Cereals; livestock. Sometimes called Atzompa or San Juan Atzompah.

San Juan Bautista (san WAHN bah-TEES-tah), city (1990 pop. 1,570), San Benito co., W Calif., near San Benito R.; 36°51′N 121°33′W. Vegetables, grapes, grain; poultry; nursery prods. San Juan Bautista State Historical Park has largest of the Calif. missions, San Juan Bautista (1797), which still functions as parish church; park also includes historic Plaza Hotel, other bldgs.

San Juan Bautista Atatlahuca (sahn HWAHN bou-TEE-stah ah-taht-lah-HOO-kah), town (1990 pop. 727), N central Oaxaca, Mexico, 35 mi/56 km NNW of Oaxaca de Juárez; 17°32′N 96°49′W. Farming, mainly for subsistence. Zapotec Indian community. Access by dirt road.

San Juan Bautista Coixtlahuaca (sahn HWAHN bou-TEE-stah koiks-tlah-HWAH-kah), town (1990 pop. 1,023), NW Oaxaca, Mexico, 17 mi/27 km ENE of Tamazulapan del Progresso; 17°43′N 97°19′W. Elev. 6,562 ft/2,000 m. Cool climate. A gravel road connects to the Inter-Amer. Highway (190).

San Juan Bautista Cuicatlán (sahn HWAHN bou-TEE-stah kwee-kaht-LAHN), town (1990 pop. 3,469),

⊙ Cuicatlán municipio, Oaxaca, S Mexico, on RR, and 53 mi/86 km NNW of Oaxaca de Juárez off Mexico Highway 131; 17°49′N 96°59′W. Cereals, vegetables, sugarcane, fruit, corn; livestock; mfg. (dairy prods., wood prods., ceramics). Founded 1530. Church built 1600.

San Juan Bautista Guelache (sahn HWAHN bou-TEE-stah ge-LAH-che), town (1990 pop. 946), central Oaxaca, Mexico, 11 mi/18 km NW of Oaxaca de Juárez off the Inter-Amer. Highway; 17°13′N 96°47′W. Elev. 5,545 ft/1,690 m. Temperate climate.

San Juan Bautista Jayacatlán (sahn HWAHN bou-TEE-stah hah-yah-kaht-LAHN), town (1990 pop. 1,500), N central Oaxaca, Mexico, 26 mi/42 km NNW of Oaxaca de Juárez. Elev. 4,265 ft/1,300 m. In Río Grande drainage area. Temperate climate. Agr. (corn, beans, fruit), wood, cattle and poultry raising, artisan textiles. Access to Inter-Amer. Highway by gravel road.

San Juan Bautista lo de Soto (sahn HWAHN bou-TEE-stah lo dai SO-to), town (1990 pop. 2,341), extreme SW Oaxaca, Mexico, on the Guerrero state border, 9 mi/14 km NW of Santiago Pinotepa Nacional; 16°31′N 98°18′W. In the coastal lowlands on Cortijos R. Hot climate. Agr. (corn, beans, coffee, sugarcane, fruits). Connections to Mexico Highway 200.

San Juan Bautista Suchitepec (sahn HWAHN bou-TEE-stah soo-CHEE-te-pek), town (1990 pop. 385), NW Oaxaca, Mexico, 14 mi/22 km NNE of Huajunpam Jr. León, and 3.1 mi/5 km E of the Puebla state border; 17°58′N 97°42′W. Moderately rainy climate. Off Mexico Highway 125 on gravel road.

San Juan Bautista Tlachichilco (sahn HWAHN bou-TEE-stah tlah-chee-CHEEL-ko), town (1990 pop. 820), NW Oaxaca, Mexico, in the Silacayoapan judicial dist., 9 mi/14 km E of the Guerrero state border, and 9 mi/14 km SW of Huajuapan de León; 17°34′N 98°21′W. In the R. Balsas basin. Temperate climate. Agr. (corn, beans, aguardiente), straw and sisal textiles.

San Juan Bautista Tlacoatzintepec (sahn HWAHN bou-TEE-stah tlah-kwaht-ZEEN-te-pek), town (1990 pop. 928), N central Oaxaca, Mexico, 12 mi/19 km S of San Felipe Jalapa de Díaz; 17°50′N 96°33′W. Elev. 2,362 ft/720 m. Mountainous terrain; temperate climate. Resources are cattle and agr. No access by road. A Chinahtec-speaking community.

San Juan Bautista Tuxtepec (sahn HWAHN bou-TEE-stah TOOKS-te-pek) or **Tuxtepec**, city (1990 pop. 62,788), extreme N Oaxaca, Mexico; 18°06′N 96°05′W. On the Santo Domingo R.; on Mexico Highway 175, and RR line. Near sea level; very hot climate. Agr. (coffee, tobacco, sugarcane, coconut milk, beans, rice, plantains, mangoes), cattle raising; precious woods (cedar, mahogany). Major urban center of the Papaloapan basin. Near President Miguel Aleman Dam (SW) and the Temazcal Hydroelectric plant. Both of these have helped expand the local economy. One of the largest paper manufacturers in the country is here.

San Juan Bautista Valle Nacional (sahn HWAHN bou-TEE-stah VAH-yai nah-see-o-NAHL), town (1990 pop. 5,525), N Oaxaca, Mexico, on Highway 175, 26 mi/42 km SSW of Textepec; 17°47′N 96°19′W. Elev. 328 ft/100 m. Partly mountainous terrain on Valle Nacional R. and its tributaries; hot climate. Agr. (corn, beans, rice, coffee, sugarcane, tropical fruits, mezcal) wood, cattle, and dairy prods. On Mexico Highway 175. Chinantec-speaking pop. Also called Valle Nacional.

San Juan Cacahuatepec (sahn HWAHN kah-kah-HWAH-te-pek), town (1990 pop. 3,116), extreme SW Oaxaca, Mexico, on the Guerrero state border, 20 mi/32 km NNW of Santiago Pinotepa Nacional; 16°36′N 98°10′W. Elev. 820 ft/250 m. Slightly mountainous; hot climate. Agr. (corn, beans, sugarcane, rice, tropical fruits). On Mexico Highway 125.

San Juan Cancuc (sahn HWAHN kahn-KOOK), town, in NW central Chiapas, Mexico, 21 mi/34 km NE of San Cristóbal de las Casas; 16°55′N 92°29′W. Elev. 4,429 ft/1,350 m. Farming, mainly subsistence.

San Juan, Cape (sahn HWAHN), Span. *Cabezas de San Juan*, headland on NE coast of P.R., 34 mi/55 km ESE of San Juan; 18°23′N 65°37′W. On cape is 316-acre/128-ha nature reserve representative of isl.'s ecosystems.

San Juan Capistrano (san WAHN kah-pi-STRAH-no), city (1990 pop. 26,183), Orange co., S Calif., residential suburb 46 mi/74 km SE of downtown Los Angeles, and 7 mi/11.3 km ESE of Laguna Beach, on San Juan Creek, at mouth of Arroyo Trabuco; 33°30′N 117°39′W. San Juan Capistrano has a small industrial park. Mfg. (aircraft parts, printing, electromedical apparatus). Boatbuilding at Dana Point. Irrigated agr. The economy is based chiefly on tourism. Padre Junípero Serra founded a mission here in 1776 and named it after St. John of Capistrano, a Crusader. The mission church, completed in 1806, was ruined by an earthquake in 1812, but the chapel is still in daily use. Swallows come to the ruins of the church every March 19, the Feast Day of St. Joseph, and depart on Oct. 23, the death date of St. John of Capistrano. An annual fiesta celebrates the arrival of the swallows. Pacific Ocean and Doheny State Beach 3 mi/4.8 km S; Historic Mission Viejo to NE; Capistrano Airport to S. Inc. 1961.

San Juan Chicomezúchil (sahn HWAHN chee-ko-me-ZOO-cheel), town (1990 pop, 406), central Oaxaca, Mexico, 22 mi/36 km NE of Oaxaca de Juárez; 17°17′N 96°29′W. Elev. 6,280 ft/1,914 m. Connected by gravel road to Mexico Highway 175.

San Juan Chilateca (sahn HWAHN chee-lah-TE-kah), town (1990 pop. 1,302), S central Oaxaca, Mexico, 17 mi/28 km SSE of Oaxaca de Juárez, and 2.2 mi/3.5 km N of the city of Ocotlán; 16°49′N 96°40′W. Elev. 5,085 ft/1,550 m. On Mexico Highway 175.

San Juan Chiquihuitlán (sahn HWAHN chee-kwee-WEET-lahn), town (1990 pop. 2,256), in the state of Oaxaca, Mexico, 25 mi/40 km ESE of Teotitlán de Flores Magón; 17°59′N 96°48′W. Elev. 3,609 ft/1,100 m in the Cuicatlán judicial dist. Located to the N of the Sierra de Juárez in the valley of the Santo Domingo R. Connected by unpaved road to Inter-Amer. Highway (190). Hot climate. The region produces primarily corn, sugarcane, and mangoes. In Mazatepec-speaking area. Formerly Chiquihuitlán de Benito Juárez.

San Juan Cieneguilla (sahn HWAHN see-e-nai-GEE-yah), town (1990 pop. 882), extreme NW Oaxaca, Mexico, 2.5 mi/4 km W of the Puebla state border, and 34 mi/55 km W of Huajuapam de León; 17°50′N 98°15′W. Elev. 5,479 ft/1,670 m. Temperate climate. On gravel road. Farming, mainly for sustenance. In Mixtec area.

San Juan Coatzospam (sahn HWAHN kwaht-zo-SPAM), town (1990 pop. 1,213), N Oaxaca, Mexico, near the Puebla state border SW of the Alemán Dam [Presa Presidente Alemán], and 27 mi/36 km ESE of Teotitlán de Flores Magón; 18°03′N 96°46′W. Elev. 6,306 ft/1,922 m. In Mazantec-speaking area. Temperate climate. Agr. and cattle raising. On gravel road. Also known as San Juan Coatzospan.

San Juan Coatzospan, Mexico: see SAN JUAN COATZOSPAM.

San Juan Colorado (sahn HWAHN ko-lo-RAH-do), town (1990 pop. 4,471), SW Oaxaca, Mexico, 5.6 mi/9 km E of the Guerrero state border, and 11 mi/17 km NE of Santiago Pinotepa Nacional, on Pacific lowland; 16°27′N 97°57′W. Hot climate. Agr. (corn, beans, sugarcane, coffee, fruits), and the mfg. of machetes. On gravel road.

San Juan Comaltepec (sahn HWAHN ko-MAHL-te-pek), town, NE Oaxaca, Mexico, 56 mi/91 km NE of Oaxaca de Juárez on secondary road; 17°18′N 95°59′W. Elev. 2,625 ft/800 m. Hot climate. Agr. (sugarcane, corn, beans, coffee, tropical fruits), cattle and poultry breeding. A Chinantec-speaking community.

San Juan Cotzocón (sahn HWAHN kot-zo-KON), town (1990 pop. 441), NE Oaxaca, Mexico, S of the Veracruz state border, and 50 mi/80 km ENE of Tlacolula de Matamoros; 17°10′N 95°47′W. Steep terrain in the Papaloapan R. basin. Agr. (sugarcane, corn, beans, coffee, fruits); woods; cattle and poultry breeding. No road access.

San Juan Cuautlancingo (sahn HWAHN kwou-tlahn-SEEN-go), town (1990 pop. 10,437), ⊙ Cuautlancingo municipio, Puebla, central Mexico, on RR, and 5 mi/8 km NW of Puebla; 19°05′N 98°16′W. Grain, maguey; livestock.

San Juan de Guadalupe (sahn HWAHN dai wah-dah-LOO-pai), town (1990 pop. 2,114), ⊙ San Juan de Guadalupe municipio, Durango, N Mexico, near Zacatecas border, 75 mi/121 km SE of Torreón; 24°37′N 102°45′W. Elev. 4,987 ft/1,520 m.

San Juan de la Maguana, Dominican Republic: see SAN JUAN.

San Juan de la Punta, Mexico: see CUITLÁHUAC.

San Juan de Lima Point, cape on Pacific coast of Michoacán, W Mexico, 6 mi/9.7 km SSE of mouth of Tuxpan R.; 18°37′N 103°49′W.

San Juan de los Cues (sahn HWAHN dai los KWES), town (1990 pop. 1,452), NW Oaxaca, Mexico, 7 mi/11 km S of Teotitlán de Flores Magón; 18°13′N 97°03′W. Elev. 2,900 ft/884 m. Mountainous; warm climate. Agr. (corn, beans); woods. Road to Teotitlán de Flores Magón; RR to Oaxaca de Juárez.

San Juan de los Lagos (sahn HWAHN dai los LAH-gos), city (1990 pop. 34,415) and township, Jalisco, central Mexico, 76 mi/123 km NE of Guadalajara, on Mexico Highway 80; 21°15′N 102°20′W. Corn-growing center; wheat, beans; livestock.

San Juan de los Yeras (sahn HWAHN dai los YAI-rahs), town, Villa Clara prov., central Cuba, on RR, and 10 mi/16 km SW of Santa Clara; 22°20′N 80°07′W. Sugarcane, tobacco, fruit; livestock; mfg. of cigars. Osvaldo Herrera (sugar mill) is SE.

San Juan de Mezquital, Mexico: see JUAN ALDAMA.

San Juan de Najasa River, Cuba: see NAJASA RIVER.

San Juan de Sabinas, Mexico: see NUEVA ROSITA.

San Juan del Estado (sahn HWAHN del es-TAH-do), town (1990 pop. 2,346), central Oaxaca, Mexico, 16 mi/25 km NNW of Oaxaca de Juárez; 17°16′N 96°47′W. Elev. 5,479 ft/1,670 m. A mountainous region in the Atoyac R. basin. Temperate climate. Agr. (cereals, fruit), woods. On gravel road.

San Juan del Rio (sahn HWAHN del REE-0), city (1990 pop. 61,652) and township, ⊙ San Juan del Rio municipio, Querétaro, central Mexico, on central plateau, on RR, and 79 mi/127 km SE of Querétaro; 20°23′N 99°59′W. Elev. 6,490 ft/1,978 m. Famous for its opals, mined at nearby La Trinidad, it is also an agr. center (corn, wheat, sugarcane, beans, alfalfa, fruit; livestock).

San Juan del Río (sahn HWAHN del REE-0), town (1990 pop. 1,509), SE Oaxaca, Mexico, 23 mi/37 km ESE of Tlacolula de Matamoros; 16°34′N 96°16′W. Elev. 5,020 ft/1,530 m. On gravel road. Agr. (corn, beans, wheat, mezcal, fruits). Poultry raising and processing of mezcal.

San Juan del Río, Mexico: see SAN JUAN DEL RÍO DEL CENTUARIO DEL NORTE.

San Juan del Río del Centauro del Norte (sahn HWAHN del REE-0 del sen-TOU-ro del NOR-tai), town (1990 pop. 2,816), ⊙ San Juan del Río municipio, Durango, N Mexico, on affluent of Nazas R., and 55 mi/89 km NNE of Victoria de Durango; 24°45′N 104°26′W. Elev. 5,577 ft/1,700 m. Grain, cotton, fruit; silver and lead deposits.

San Juan Diuxi (sahn HWAHN dee-OOK-see), town (1990 pop. 1,676), NW Oaxaca, Mexico, 20 mi/32 km SSW of Asunción Nochistlán; 17°15′N 97°22′W. Elev. 6,070 ft/1,850 m. Mountainous; temperate climate.

San Juan Epatlán (sahn HWAHN e-paht-TLAHN), town (1990 pop. 2,141), Puebla, central Mexico, 9 mi/14.5 km ENE of Izúcar de Matamoros; 17°38′N 96°22′W. Elev. 4,593 ft/1,400 m. Cereals, sugarcane; livestock.

San Juan Evangelista (sahn HWAHN ai-vahn-he-LEES-tah), town (1990 pop. 4,285), Veracruz, SE Mexico, on Isthmus of Tehuantepec, on San Juan R., and 16 mi/26 km WSW of Acayucan, off Mexico Highway 145; 17°52′N 95°08′W. Fruit; livestock.

San Juan Evangelista, Mexico: see ZACAPALA.

San Juan Evangelista Analco (sahn HWAHN ai-vahn-he-LEES-tah ah-NAHL-ko), town (1990 pop. 608), central Oaxaca, Mexico, 2 mi/3.2 km off Mexico Highway 175, 26 mi/42 km NNE of Oaxaca de Juárez; 17°24′N 96°32′W. Agr. (corn, beans, wheat, fruits).

San Juan Guelavía (sahn HWAHN ge-lah-VEE-ah),

town (1990 pop. 2,992), central Oaxaca, Mexico, 14 mi/
22 km SE of Oaxaca de Juárez, and 6 mi/10 km W of
Tlacolula de Matamoros; 16°57′N 96°33′W. Elev.
5,495 ft/1,675 m. Near RR and Inter-Amer. Highway
(190). Agr. (corn, beans); woven textiles; cattle prods.

San Juan Guichicovi (sahn HWAHN gee-chee-KO-
vee), town (1990 pop. 3,318), SE Oaxaca, Mexico, 9 mi/
14 km NW of Matías Romero, in the Coatzacoalcos R.
basin; 16°58′N 95°06′W. Hot climate. Agr. (corn, coffee,
sugarcane, beans, fruits), straw textiles, pottery, precious woods, and construction lumber. Good roads
connect to the Transisthmus Highway (185) and with
the RR. A Mixe Indian community.

San Juan Hill, Santiago de Cuba prov., E Cuba, near the
city of Santiago de Cuba. It was the scene (July 1898)
of a battle in the Span.-Amer. War, in which Theodore
Roosevelt and the Rough Riders took part.

San Juan Historic Site (sahn HWAHN), NE P.R., oldest
fortification within the limits of U.S. territory, built
(16th cent.) by the Spanish to protect the harbor guarding the sea lanes to the New World. Authorized 1949.

San Juan Ihualtepec (sahn HWAHN ee-HWAHL-te-
pek), town (1990 pop. 706), extreme NW Oaxaca, Mexico, 3.1 mi/5 km E of the Guerrero state border, and
37 mi/60 km WSW of Huajuapam de León; 17°45′N
98°17′W. Elev. 5,413 ft/1,650 m. Farming, mainly subsistence. Mixtec Indian community.

San Juan Island (san HWAHN), San Juan co., NW
Wash., in W part of San Juan Isls.; 11 mi/18 km long,
8 mi/12.9 km wide. Bounded E by San Juan Channel,
N by Spieden Channel, W by Haro Strait, S by Strait
of Juan de Fuca. Middle Bank extends SW from isl.
Friday Harbor, on N side, is largest town in the isl.
group and capital of San Juan co. Village of Roche Harbor is on NW. Dairying; fruit, hay; fishing. Limestone.
Tourism. Lime Kiln Point State Park on W side; Turn
Isl. State Park off E shore; Posey Isl. and Stuart Isl. state
parks off NW end. Three units of San Juan Natl. Historic Park are at Friday Harbor, at Wescott Bay (Eng.
Camp Unit) in N, and at Cattle Point (Amer. Camp
Unit) in S. Ferries to Lopez and Orcas isls. and Anacortes. Highest point, Cody Mt., in N (892 ft/272 m).

San Juan Island National Historical Park (□ 3 sq mi/
7.8 sq km), NW Wash. Commemorates the period
1853–1872 during which the N boundary of Oregon territory was established, which includes the clash on San
Juan Isl. bet. Eng. and Amer. forces known as the Pig
War. Park is now dedicated to the peaceful coexistence
of U.S. and Canada. Three units include Friday Harbor
unit (in E), Eng. Camp Unit on Wescott Bay N, and
Amer. Camp Unit (on Cattle Point S). Authorized 1966.

San Juan Islands, archipelago of 172 isls. constituting
San Juan co., NW Wash., E of Vancouver Isl. Bounded
by Strait of Georgia (N); Rosario Strait (E); Strait of
Juan de Fuca (S); Haro Strait (W). The isls. were visited
and named c.1790 by Span. explorers. They were the
subject of the San Juan border dispute bet. Great Britain and the U.S.; their ownership was decided in 1872.
The 3 main isls. are San Juan, Orcas, and Lopez. Main
town is Friday Harbor, San Juan Isl.; highest point is
Mt. Constitution (2,408 ft/734 m). Other important
isls. include Shaw (center); Blakely and Decatur (E);
Waldron, Stuart, and Spieden (N). Hay, fruit; dairying;
fish, oysters, crabs, clams.

San Juan Islet, NE P.R., between San Juan Bay and the
Atlantic Ocean. Its W portion is the walled city of Old
San Juan, with Puerta de Tierra to its E. Connected by
3 bridges to the main isl. Important tourist and cargo
port facilities and recreational areas. The most important govt. offices are located here, including the Capitol
of P.R. and the P.R. Supreme Court. Major renovation
of piers and waterfront facilities to the S.

San Juan Ixcaquixtla (sahn HWAHN eesh-kah-
KEESH-tlah), town (1990 pop. 3,676), Puebla, central
Mexico, on central plateau, 50 mi/80 km SE of Puebla;
18°27′N 97°94′W. Corn, sugarcane, fruit; livestock. In
Popoloba Indian area. Pre-Columbian ruins nearby.

San Juan Ixtenco, Mexico: see IXTENCO.

San Juan Jonotla, Mexico: see JONOTLA.

San Juan Juquila Mixes (sahn HWAHN joo-KWEE-
lah MEEK-ses), town (1990 pop. 1,925), E Oaxaca, Mexico, 38 mi/61 km E of Tlacolula de Matamoros; 16°58′N
95°55′W. Elev. 6,496 ft/1,980 m. Steep terrain. Temperate climate. Agr. (corn, bean, wheat, mezcal, fruits),
woods, and cattle raising. Pop. consists primarily of
Mixe-speakers.

San Juan Juquila Vijanos (sahn HWAHN joo-KWEE-
lah vee-HAH-nos), town (1990 pop. 627), NE Oaxaca,
Mexico, 12 mi/19 km E of Ixtlan de Juárez; 17°20′N
96°14′W. Elev. 3,031 ft/924 m. Agr. (cereals, fruits, mezcal), woods, cotton and woolen textiles. On unpaved
road.

San Juan Lachao (sahn HWAHN lah-CHAH-o), town
(1990 pop. 947), SW Oaxaca, Mexico, 27 mi/43 km N
of Puerto Escondido on the Pacific slope of Oaxaca
highland; 17°17′N 95°54′W. Elev. 5,577 ft/1,700 m. On
gravel road. Hot climate. Resources are agr. and cattle.

San Juan Lachigalla (sahn HWAHN lah-chee-GAH-
yah), town (1990 pop. 867), S central Oaxaca, Mexico,
13 mi/21 km ENE of Ejutla de Crespo; 16°35′N 96°33′W.
Elev. 4,862 ft/1,482 m. Temperate climate. Agr. (corn,
beans, coffee, sugarcane); cattle and dairy prods. Unimproved roads connect with Ejutla.

San Juan Lajarcia (sahn HWAHN lah-hahr-SEE-ah),
town (1990 pop. 679), SE Oaxaca, Mexico, 50 mi/80 km
WNW of Santo Domingo Tehuantepec, and 3.1 mi/
5 km S of Inter-Amer. Highway (190); 16°30′N 95°55′W.
Elev. 3,609 ft/1,100 m. Steep terrain in the Tehuantepec
R. basin. Hot climate. Agr. (cereals, mezcal), hand-woven textiles.

San Juan Lalana (sahn HWAHN lah-LAH-nah), town
(1990 pop. 262), NE Oaxaca, Mexico, 48 mi/77 km SSE
of Textepec on dirt track; 17°28′N 95°53′W. Elev. 1,312 ft/
400 m. Rough terrain in the Papaloapan R. basin. Hot
climate. Agr. (corn, sugarcane, beans, coffee, pineapple,
plantains); cattle and poultry breeding. A Chinantec-
speaking community. Also known as San Juan de la
Lana.

San Juan Mazatlán (sahn HWAHN mah-zaht-LAHN),
town (1990 pop. 936), E Oaxaca, Mexico, 29 mi/46 km
WNW of Matías Romero; 17°02′N 95°25′W. Elev.
4,921 ft/1,500 m. Mountainous; temperate climate. Agr.
(corn, beans, coffee, fruits, mezcal), woods; cattle. In
Mixe-speaking area.

San Juan Mixtepec 1 (sahn HWAHN MEESH-te-pek),
town, Oaxaca, S Mexico, in Oaxaca highlands, 20 mi/
33 km ESE of Miahuatlán de Porfirio Díaz; 16°17′N
96°22′W. On unpaved road. Farming. Important antimony deposits at Los Tecojotes, mined during 1930s
and 1940s. Also called Mixtepec. **2** town (1990 pop.
11,273), ⊙ San Juan Mixtepec municipio, Oaxaca, Mexico, 11 mi/17 km from Santa María Asunción Tlaxiaco,
on gravel road; 17°18′N 97°51′W. Elev. 5,741 ft/1,750 m.
Agr., small farming, mainly for subsistence.

San Juan Mountains, range of Rocky Mts., SW Colo.,
and N N.Mex., lying W of San Luis Valley, S of Gunnison R.; extend SSE toward Rio Chama, N.Mex.
Prominent points include Handies Peak (14,048 ft/
4,282 m), Sunshine Peak (14,001 ft/4,268 m), Wetterhorn Peak (14,015 ft/4,272 m), Redcloud Peak (14,034 ft/
4,278 m), Mt. Eolus (14,083 ft/4,292 m), Windom Peak
(14,082 ft/4,292 m), Mt. Sneffels (14,150 ft/4,313 m), San
Luis Peak (14,014 ft/4,271 m), Uncompahgre Peak
(14,309 ft/4,361 m). Range includes much of San Juan
Natl. Forest; drained by branches of San Juan R. and
headwaters of Rio Grande and San Juan R. Wolf Creek
Pass (10,850 ft/3,307 m), bet. Mineral and Archuleta
cos., is crossed by highway. Cumbres Pass in Colo.
(10,022 ft/3,055 m.; near N.Mex. state line) was used by
Span. explorers in 16th and 17th cents. and is also
crossed by State Highway 17. Range is of volcanic origin; gold, silver, lead, copper mined in vicinity of Silverton, Ouray, and Telluride. Telluride is a popular ski
resort.

San Juan Numí (sahn HWAHN nyoo-MEE), town (1990
pop. 496), W Oaxaca, Mexico, 28 mi/45 km S of Huajuapam de León, and 9 mi/15 km NW of Tlaxiaco;
17°36′N 97°49′W. Elev. 6,365 ft/1,940 m. Agr. (corn,

beans, sugarcane, mezcal); cattle; dairy prods., and
straw textiles.

San Juan Ozolotepec (sahn HWAHN o-zo-LO-te-pek),
town (1990 pop. 715), NE Oaxaca, Mexico, 12 mi/19 km
SW of the Veracruz state border, and 48 mi/78 km NW
of Matías Romero; 17°17′N 95°36′W. Elev. 6,234 ft/
1,900 m. Mountainous terrain. Temperate to hot climate. Farming, mainly for subsistence. Connected to
Mexico Highway 147 by unpaved road. Mixe-speaking
community.

San Juan Parangaricutiro, Mexico: see NUEVO SAN
JUAN PARANGARICUTIRO.

San Juan Petlapa (sahn HWAHN pet-LAH-pah), town
(1990 pop. 600), NE Oaxaca, Mexico, 17 mi/28 km SW
of the Veracruz state border, and 48 mi/78 km NE of
Tlacolula de Matamoros; 17°27′N 96°05′W. Elev.
6,824 ft/2,080 m. On NE slope of Cordon Cempoal-
tepetl. Hot climate. Agr. (coffee, sugarcane, corn,
beans, fruits), woods. Chinantec-speaking community.
No roads.

San Juan Quiahije (sahn HWAHN kee-ah-EE-he), town
(1990 pop. 1,076), SW Oaxaca, Mexico, 6 mi/10 km NW
of Santa Catarina, on Pacific slope of Oaxaca highlands; 16°17′N 97°20′W. Elev. 5,305 ft/1,617 m. A flat
region in the Verde R. basin. Hot climate and cool at
higher elev.

San Juan Quiotepec (sahn HWAHN kee-O-te-pek),
town (1990 pop.1,822), N Oaxaca, Mexico, 38 mi/61 km
NNE of Oaxaca de Juárez; 17°55′N 96°59′W. Elev.
4921 ft/1,500 m. Mountainous region; temperate climate. Farming for subsistence. Chinantec-speaking
community.

San Juan River, c.20 mi/32 km long, Matanzas prov., W
Cuba; flows to Matanzas Bay at Matanzas.

San Juan River 1 c.75 mi/121 km long, N Mexico;
formed in Nuevo León NE of Montemorelos by several
headstreams rising in Sierra Madre Oriental; flows N
and NE, past China, General Bravo, Doctor Coss, and
Los Aldamas, into Tamaulipas, and past Camargo, to
Rio Grande 2 mi/3.2 km SE of Rio Grande City, Texas.
Receives Pesquería R. Used for irrigation. **2** c.160 mi/
257 km long, in Veracruz, SE Mexico; rises at foot of
Zempoaltépetl (Oaxaca); flows NE and NW, past San
Juan Evangelista, to Papaloapan R. at Tlacotalpan.
Navigable by shallow-draft vessels.

San Juan Sayultepec (sahn HWAHN sah-YOOL-te-
pek), town (1990 pop. 471), W Oaxaca, Mexico, 3.1 mi/
5 km W of Asunción Nochixtlán, and 2 mi/3.2 km S
of Inter-Amer. Highway (190). Elev. 6,001 ft/1,829 m.
Steep terrain; temperate to cold climate. Agr. (cereals,
fruits), fine woods, construction lumber, and palm textiles.

San Juan Tabaá (sahn HWAHN tah-bah-AH), town
(1990 pop. 1,195), NE Oaxaca, Mexico, 20 mi/32 km E
of Ixtlán de Juárez; 17°18′N 96°12′W. Elev. 5,719 ft/
1,743 m. Farming.

San Juan Tamazola (sahn HWAHN tah-mah-ZO-lah),
town (1990 pop. 134), W Oaxaca, Mexico, 24 mi/38 km
S of Asunción Nochixtlán; 17°11′N 97°03′W. Elev.
6,890 ft/2,100 m. Steep terrain in Río Grande drainage
area. Access by dirt roads.

San Juan Teita (sahn HWAHN te-EE-tah), town (1990
pop. 722), W Oaxaca, Mexico, 31 mi/50 km SE of Tlaxiaco; 17°05′N 97°25′W. Elev. 5,479 ft/1,670 m. Unpaved
roads. Steep rough terrain; farming.

San Juan Teitipac (sahn HWAHN te-EE-tee-pak), town
(1990 pop. 2,970), central Oaxaca, Mexico, 12 mi/19 km
SE of Oaxaca de Juárez in Tlacolulu arm of Oaxaca Valley. On gravel road. Temperate climate. Agr. (corn,
beans, figs); cattle and pigs.

San Juan Tepeuxila (sahn HWAHN te-pe-ooks-ZEE-
lah), town (1990 pop. 575), N Oaxaca, Mexico, 10 mi/
16 km SE of San Juan Bautista Cuicatlán, 6 mi/9.7 km
off Mexico Highway 131; 17°48′N 96°51′W. Hot climate.
Agr. (corn, beans, sugarcane, fruits); wood; cattle.

San Juan Teposcolula, town (1990 pop. 548), ⊙ San
Juan Teposcolula municipio, Oaxaca, S Mexico, on
Mexico Highway 125, in Mixteca Alta, and 18 mi/29 km
NW of Asunción Nochixtlán; 17°33′N 97°26′W. Elev.

5,938 ft/1,810 m. Cereals, coffee, sugarcane, fruit; livestock.

San Juan Totolac, Mexico: see TOTOLAC.

San Juan Valley (sahn HWAHN), W Dominican Republic, bet. the Cordillera Central (N) and Sierra de Neiba (S), extends c.50 mi/80 km E from Haiti border to the Yaque del Sur. Agr. (bananas, chickpeas, rice, corn, coffee, sugarcane). Main centers: San Juan, Las Matas, and Elías Piña.

San Juan Valley, Calif.: see SANTA CLARA VALLEY.

San Juan Xiutetelco (sahn HWAHN hee-oo-te-TEL-ko), town (1990 pop. 4,982), ⊙ Xiutetelco municipio, Puebla, central Mexico, on Veracruz border, on Mexico Highway 129, 2 mi/3.2 km ESE of Teziutlán; 19°48'N 97°20'W. Corn, coffee, tropical fruit. Anc. pyramids are nearby.

San Juan y Martínez (sahn HWAHN ee mahr-TEE-naiz), town, Pinar del Río prov., W Cuba, on RR, and 12 mi/19 km SW of Pinar del Río, on San Juan y Martinez R. Tobacco-growing center in rich Vuelta Abajo region. Tobacco experiment station.

San Juan Yaé (sahn HWAHN yah-AI), town (1990 pop. 856), NE Oaxaca, Mexico, 16 mi/25 km NE of Ixtlán de Juárez; 17°26'N 96°17'W. Elev. 5,512 ft/1,680 m. Mountainous. Agr. and cattle raising. On unpaved road.

San Juan Yatzona (sahn HWAHN yaht-ZO-nah), town (1990 pop. 487), NE Oaxaca, Mexico, 22 mi/35 km ENE of Ixtlán de Juárez; 17°24'N 96°11'W. Elev. 5,840 ft/1,780 m. Temperate climate. Farming. On unpaved road.

San Juan Yucuita (sahn HWAHN yoo-KWEE-tah), town (1990 pop. 544), N Oaxaca, Mexico, 3.1 mi/5 km NW of Asunción Nochixtlán; 17°01'N 97°46'W. Elev. 5,846 ft/1,782 m. Steep terrain. Temperate climate. Agr. (cereals, fruits); woods. A gravel road connects with Asunción Nochixtlán.

San Juanito, Mexico: see ANTONIO ESCOBEDO.

San Juanito Island, Mexico: see TRES MARÍAS, LAS.

San Julián (sahn hoo-lee-AHN), town (1990 pop. 10,244), Jalisco, central Mexico, in Sierra Madre Occidental, 18 mi/29 km SE of San Juan de los Lagos; 21°01'N 102°10'W. Corn, beans; livestock.

San Leandro, city (1990 pop. 68,223), Alameda co., W Calif., suburb 7 mi/11.3 km SE of downtown Oakland on San Francisco Bay, and on San Leandro Creek, which forms L. Chabot to E, in Anthony Chabot Regional Park.; 37°42'N 122°10'W. Mfg. (metal prods., chemicals, leather goods, soft drinks, wood prods., medical equip., coffee, paper prods., cereals, baked goods, dairy prods., lighting fixtures; steel foundry). Nursery prods., greenhouse plants. Settled by José Joaquin Estudillo in 1837, it was co. seat from 1854 to 1871. Metropolitan Oakland Internatl. Airport to W, on Bay; Hayward Municipal Airport to SE. Knowland State Park and Arboretum to NE, in Oakland. Inc. 1872.

San Leon, uninc. town (1990 pop. 3,328), Galveston co., SE Texas, suburb 7 mi/11.3 km N of Texas City, and 30 mi/48 km SW of Houston, on Galveston Bay. Fish, crabs, oysters, shrimp. Mfg. (stringwound filters; oyster processing).

San Lorenzo (sahn lo-REN-so), town (1990 pop. 1,557), extreme SW Oaxaca, Mexico, 9 mi/14.5 km NW of Santiago Jamiltepec. On Pacific coastal lowlands. Hot climate. Agr. (corn, beans, sugarcane, coffee, fruit); woods. On dirt road.

San Lorenzo 1 Mexico: see DOCTOR BELISARIO DOMÍNGUEZ. **2** Mexico: see YANGA.

San Lorenzo (sahn lo-REN-so), town (1990 pop. 35,163), E P.R., in outliers of the Cordillera Central, 22 mi/35 km SSE of San Juan. Mfg. and commercial area. Agr. (sugarcane, plantains, tobacco, fruit, coffee).

San Lorenzo (san lo-REN-zo), pueblo (□ 23 sq mi/60 sq km), Taos co., N N.Mex. in Sangre de Cristo Mts., E of the Rio Grande, 7 mi/11.3 km N of Española. Elev. 7,320 ft/2,231 m. Agr.; livestock; pottery making, weaving. Important holiday is San Lorenzo's day (Aug. 10), accompanied by Mass in San Lorenzo de Picuris Church (c.1692), followed by traditional dances. Mission est. 1598 by Juan de Oñate. Village participated in general Pueblo revolt of 1680.

San Lorenzo (san luh-REN-zo), uninc. city (1990 pop. 19,987), Alameda co., W Calif., suburb 12 mi/19 km SE of downtown Oakland, bet. San Leandro (NW) and Hayward (SE); 37°41'N 122°08'W. Mfg. (prepared meats, metal doors, transportation equip., corrugated boxes, textiles). San Mateo Bridge crosses San Francisco Bay to San Mateo, to SW; Hayward Municipal Airport to S.

San Lorenzo Albarradas (sahn lo-REN-so ahl-bah-RAH-dahs), town (1990 pop. 1,592), S central Oaxaca, Mexico, 15 mi/24 km ESE of Tlacolula de Matamoros; 16°56'N 96°15'W. Mountainous; temperate climate. Resources are agr., cattle, and handmade textiles. Gravel road connects with Tlacolula.

San Lorenzo Cacaotepec (sahn lo-REN-so kah-lah-O-te-pek), town (1990 pop. 4,545), N Oaxaca, Mexico, 8 mi/12 km NNW of Oaxaca de Juárez; 17°10'N 96°48'W. Elev. 5,020 ft/1,530 m. In Etla arm of Oaxaca valley. Temperate climate. Agr. (corn, beans, fruit; cattle, poultry); wood. Off the Inter-Amer. Highway (190) and near RR.

San Lorenzo Chiautzingo (sahn lo-REN-so chee-out-SEEN-go), town (1990 pop. 5,362), ⊙ Chiautzingo municipio, Puebla, central Mexico, 20 mi/32 km NW of Puebla; 19°12'N 98°28'W. Corn, wheat, maguey.

San Lorenzo Creek, c.15 mi/24 km long, W. Calif.; rises in N Alameda co., c. 15 mi/24 km ESE of Oakland; flows WSW past Hayward, Castro Valley, and San Lorenzo, S suburbs of Oakland, to San Francisco Bay, arm of Pacific Ocean, W of San Lorenzo.

San Lorenzo Cuaunecuiltitla (sahn lo-REN-so kwou-ne-kweel-TEET-lah), town (1990 pop. 670), NW Oaxaca, Mexico, 12 mi/19 km NE of Teotitlán de Flores Magón; 18°10'N 96°56'W. In Sierra Mazateca (elev. 8,957 ft/2,730 m). Steep rough terrain; no road access.

San Lorenzo River, 72 mi/116 km long, NW Mexico; formed in Durango by headstreams (c.75 mi/121 km long) rising in Sierra Madre Occidental; flows WSW into Sinaloa, past Santa Cruz and Quilá, to Gulf of California at its mouth on the Pacific.

San Lorenzo River, c.25 mi/40 km long, W Calif.; rises in NW Santa Cruz co., 13 mi/21 km WSW of San Jose; flows SSE, through Santa Cruz Mts., to Monterey Bay, Pacific Ocean, at Santa Cruz. Agr. in valley.

San Lorenzo Texmelucan (sahn lo-REN-so teks-me-LOO-kahn), town (1990 pop. 877), SW Oaxaca, Mexico, 16 mi/25 km WNW of San Miguel Solada Vega; 16°35'N 97°11'W. Elev. 26.2 ft/8 m. Hot climate. Agr. (corn, beans, coffee, sugarcane, fruits); woods. On unpaved road.

San Lorenzo Victoria (sahn lo-REN-so veek-TOR-ee-ah), town (1990 pop. 805), NW Oaxaca, Mexico, 9 mi/14 km E of the Guerrero state border, and 25 mi/40 km SW of Huajuapam de León in the Mixta Baja. Elev. 5,545 ft/1,690 m. Agr. (corn, beans); mezcal processing, and woven textiles. On unpaved road. Mixtec Indian community.

San Lucas 1 (sahn LOO-kahs), town (1990 pop. 14), Chiapas, S Mexico, at S foot of Sierra de Hueytepec, 12 mi/18 km SW of San Cristóbal de las Casas. Cereals, fruit; livestock. Tzotzil Maya community. Also known as El Zapotal. **2** town (1990 pop. 4,649), Michoacán, central Mexico, 8 mi/12.9 km SE of Huetamo, on Mexico Highway 51. Sugarcane, coffee, cereals, fruit.

San Lucas Camotlán (sahn LOO-kahs kah-mo-TLAHN), town (1990 pop.1,797), E Oaxaca, Mexico, 53 mi/85 km E of Tlacolula de Matamoros; 16°57'N 95°47'W. Elev. 5,545 ft/1,690 m. Mountainous. Temperate climate. Agr. (corn, beans, wheat, potatoes, fruits); woods; cattle. On gravel road. High percentage of Mixte-speaking Indian population.

San Lucas, Cape, S extremity of Baja California peninsula, Mexico, at entrance to Gulf of California; 22°50'N 109°55'W.

San Lucas Ojitlán (sahn LOO-kahs o-heet-LAHN), town (1990 pop. 5,041), N Oaxaca, Mexico, 2.5 mi/4 km S of the President Miguel Aleman Dam [Presa Presidente Miguel Alemán], and 19 mi/31 km E of Tuxtepec; 18°04'N 96°23'W. Warm climate. Agr. (corn, sugarcane), fine woods, and lumber. Historically important

because the Plan de Tuxtepec, which was key to giving Porofirio Díaz the presidency, was proclaimed here in 1876. Chimantic Indian community.

San Lucas Quiaviní (sahn LOO-kahs kee-ah-vee-NEE), town (1990 pop. 2,156), SE Oaxaca, Mexico, 3.1 mi/5 km S of Tlacolula de Matamoros; 16°54'N 96°28'W. Elev. 5,938 ft/1,810 m. Agr. Temperate climate.

San Lucas Zoquiapam (sahn LOO-kahs zo-kee-ah-PAHM), town (1990 pop. 703), SE Oaxaca, Mexico, 11 mi/18 km E of Teotitlán de Flores Magón; 18°05'N 96°55'W. Elev. 8,501 ft/2,591 m. Gravel roads. Agr. (corn, beans, coffee, sugarcane, wheat, potatoes, chilies); cattle and poultry raising.

San Luis 1 (sahn loo-EES), town, Pinar del Río prov., W Cuba, on RR, and 10 mi/16 km SSW of Pinar del Río; 22°17'N 83°46'W. Tobacco-growing center. **2** town, Santiago de Cuba prov., E Cuba, 12 mi/19 km N of Santiago de Cuba; 20°11'N 75°56'W. RR junction, processing and trading center (sugarcane, coffee, fruit); coffee roasting. Manganese deposits. Sugar mills Rafael Reyes (NNE) and Paquito Rosales (NE) nearby.

San Luis 1 town (1990 pop. 800), ⊙ Costilla co., S Colo., in W foothills of Sangre de Cristo Mts., on Culebra Creek, on E slope of San Luis Valley, 30 mi/48 km SE of Alamosa; 37°12'N 105°25'W. Elev. 7,965 ft/2,428 m. Irrigation farming and logging. Vegetables, potatoes, wheat, oats, barley; sheep, cattle. Sanchez Reservoir to S. Oldest settlement in the state. Established by Mex. land grant settlers. **2** town (1990 pop. 4,212), Yuma co., SW Ariz., port of entry at Mex. border, opposite San Luis, Sonora state; 17 mi/27 km SW of Yuma, near Colorado R., to W; 32°29'N 114°46'W. Mfg. (apparel). Cocopah Indian Reservation to N and NE.

San Luis Acatlán (sahn loo-EES ah-kaht-LAHN), town (1990 pop. 5,171), Guerrero, SW Mexico, in Pacific lowland, 65 mi/105 km E of Acapulco de Juárez; 16°48'N 98°55'W. Sugarcane, coffee, cotton, fruit; livestock. On unpaved road.

San Luis Amatlán (sahn loo-EES ah-maht-LAHN), town (1990 pop. 1,004), S Oaxaca, Mexico, 8 mi/12 km NE of Miahuatlán de Porfirio Díaz; 16°30'N 96°33'W. Elev. 5,495 ft/1,675 m. In Miahuatlán Valley. Temperate climate. Agr. (corn, beans, coffee, fruits); woods. Unpaved road connects to Miahuatlán.

San Luis Creek, 65 mi/105 km long, S Colo.; rises in NE Saguache co., bet. Sawatch and Sangre de Cristo mts., near Poncha Pass (9,010 ft/2,746 m); flows SSE, past Villa Grove and Moffat, receives Saguache Creek, 8 mi/12.9 km S of Moffat, in N part of San Luis Valley. Flows into San Luis Lakes, 13 mi/21 km SE of confluence (San Luis Lakes State Park), NE Alamosa co.

San Luis de la Paz (sahn loo-EES dai la PAHS), city (1990 pop. 32,229) and township, Guanajuato, Mexico, in Sierra Madre Occidental, 50 mi/80 km ENE of Guanajuato on Mexico Highway 110; 21°17'N 100°30'W. Elev. 6,627 ft/2,020 m. RR junction; agr. center (cereals, sugarcane, wine, oranges, vegetables; livestock); alcohol distilling, wine and liquor making.

San Luis del Cordero (sahn loo-EES del kor-DE-ro), town (1990 pop. 1,880), Durango, NW Mexico, on interior plateau, 55 mi/89 km W of Torreón; 25°26'N 104°18'W. Elev. 4,921 ft/1,500 m. Corn, wheat, chickpeas; livestock.

San Luis Obispo, county (□ 3,305 sq mi/8,560 sq km; 1990 pop. 217,162), SW Calif., borders the Pacific; ⊙ San Luis Obispo; 35°23'N 120°27'W. Santa Lucia Range in W along coast, Temblor and La Panza ranges in E. Drained by Salinas R. Southern border formed by Cuyama (forms Twitchell Reservoir) and Santa Maria rivers. Agr. (peas, celery, beans, cauliflower, peppers, avocadoes, lettuce, broccoli, Oriental vegetables, apples, strawberries, flowers, nursery prods., grapes, wheat, barley, oats); cattle. Oil and natural gas field; Morro Bay town ships oil. Clay, sand, gravel quarrying; chromite, mercury mining. Coast resorts (Pismo Beach, Morro Bay); mineral springs at Paso Robles. Old missions at San Miguel, San Luis Obispo. Nuclear power plants: Diablo Canyon 1 (initial criticality April 29, 1984; max. dependable capacity of 1,073 MWe) and Diablo

---

Area in square miles is shown by the symbol □   capital city or county seat by ⊙

Canyon 2 (initial criticality August 20, 1985; max. dependable capacity of 1,087 MWe) are 12 mi/19 km WSW of San Luis Obispo; use cooling water from the Pacific Ocean. Carrizo Plain (part of Central Valley) in E, including Soda L. (dry); Morro Bay State Park, Montana de Oro State Park, and Atascadero State Beach in W; San Simeon State Beach and Hearst San Simeon State Historical Monument in NW; Los Osas Oaks State Reservoir in W center; Pismo Beach in SW; parts of Los Padres Natl. Forest in W center and S. Nacimiento Reservoir in NW; Santa Margarita Reservoir in center. Formed 1850.

San Luis Obispo, city (1990 pop. 41,958), ⊙ San Luis Obispo co., S Calif., 8 mi/12.9 km NE of San Luis Obispo Bay, 10 mi/16 km SE of Morro Bay, and 92 mi/148 km W of Bakersfield; 35°16′N 120°40′W. Elev. 234 ft/71 m. Mfg. (printing and publishing, machinery, medical goods, electronic equip., computers). In 1846, John Frémont seized the city for the U.S. To escape torrential rains he quartered in the Franciscan mission, San Luis Obispo de Tolosa (1772), which is now a state landmark. Many historic bldgs. are preserved in the mission plaza. Co. Historical Mus. The city is the seat of Calif. Polytechnic State Univ.; Cuesta Col. (2 year). Los Padres Natl. Forest and Santa Lucia Range lie to the NE; Los Osos Oaks State reserve to S, 700-year-old oaks. Moro Bay State Park, Atascadero State Beach, and Montana De Oro State Park to W. Inc. 1856.

San Luis Peak (14,014 ft/4,271 m), Saguache co., SW Colo., in San Juan Mts., 9 mi/14.5 km N of Creede, N of Continental Divide; 37°59′N 106°55′W. Gunnison Natl. Forest.

San Luis, Point, San Luis Obispo co., SW Calif., headland 10 mi/16 km SW of San Luis Obispo; bounds San Luis Obispo Bay on W. Lighthouse.

San Luis Potosí (sahn loo-EES po-to-SEE), state (1990 pop. 2,003,187), 24,417 sq mi/63,240 sq km, central Mexico; ⊙ SAN LUIS POTOSÍ; 21°10′N 98°21′W. Most of the state lies on the E basins and ranges of Mexico's central plateau. Except in the humid tropical Pánuco R. valley in the extreme E, near the Gulf of Mexico, the climate is mild and dry. The high basins (average elev. 6,000 ft/1,829 m) are separated by spurs of the Sierra Madre Oriental; it is largely desert in the N. Rainfall is generally light, and rivers are few; thus, despite fertile soil, agr. is practiced mainly for subsistence except where irrigation is available. Large crops of sugarcane, however, are cultivated in the E lowlands. San Luis Potosí has rich silver, gold, copper, zinc, and bismuth deposits and is one of Mexico's leading mining states. Industry is limited, yet diverse; basic metal mfg. comprises the largest sector.

San Luis Potosí, city (1990 pop. 489,238), ⊙ San Luis Potosí state, central Mexico; 22°09′N 100°58′W. Elev. 6,158 ft/1,877 m. Situated on a plain almost entirely surrounded by low mts., the city is a mining and agr. distribution center, on Mexico Highways 49, 57, 70, and 80, and a RR junction. Industries include foundries, smelters, and factories that produce apparel, leather goods, and beverages. Founded in 1576, San Luis Potosí was strategically important in colonial times and during the wars of the republican period. The patriot Francisco I. Madero, who was briefly imprisoned in the city in 1910, later named his revolutionary call to arms the Plan of San Luis Potosí. The city center has narrow cobbled streets and solid colonial architecture, but outlying areas are modern. Among its major landmarks are the San Francisco convent and Carmelite churches.

San Luis Reservoir (□ 20 sq mi/52 sq km), Merced co., central Calif., on San Luis Creek, in San Luis Reservoir State Recreational Area, 15 mi/24 km W of Los Banos; 37°04′N 121°04′W. Max. capacity 2,063,510 acre-ft. Formed by B. F. Sisk Dike (382 ft/116 m), built (1967) by the Bureau of Reclamation for irrigation.

San Luis Reservoir, Calif.: see CENTRAL VALLEY.

San Luis Rey, uninc. village, San Diego co., S Calif., 4 mi/6.4 km NE of Oceanside and Pacific Ocean, on San Luis Rey R. Mission San Luis Rey or San Luis Rey de Francia (est. 1798; restored) is here. Mfg. (horseshoes). Camp Pendleton Marine Corps Base to N.

San Luis Rey River, c.65 mi/105 km long, San Diego co., SW Calif.; rises in Coast Ranges c.45 mi/72 km NE of San Diego in N San Diego co.; flows NW through Henshaw reservoir and S of Mt. Palomar, through La Jolla, Rincon, and Pala Indian reservations, then SW past San Luis Rey village, to the Pacific at Oceanside. Dam impounds L. Henshaw (Henshaw Reservoir), c.6 mi/9.7 km long, in upper course. Lower valley is rich agr. area.

San Luis Río Colorado (sahn loo-EES REE-o ko-lo-RAH-do), city (1990 pop. 95,461) and township, Sonora, NW Mexico, on Colorado R., on U.S.-Mex. border, 42 mi/68 km ESE of Mexicali, and 16 mi/26 km SSW of Yuma, Ariz.; 32°29′N 114°48′W. Citrus fruit, wheat, corn, rice, beans.

San Luis Teolocholco, Mexico: see TEOLOCHOLCO.

San Luis Valley, in S Colo. and N N.Mex., irrigated area, extending S from E Saguache co., through Alamosa, Conejos, and Cortilla cos. (Colo.), into Taos co. (N.Mex.); 125 mi/201 km long, average width 50 mi/80 km. Elev. 7,500 ft/2,286 m–8,000 ft/2,438 m. Bounded E by Sangre de Cristo Mts., N by Sawatch Mts., W by San Juan Mts.; watered by Saguache and San Luis creeks in N and by Rio Grande, which flows S through middle of valley. Once formed bottom of extensive lake; now used for agr. (potatoes, grain, vegetables; sheep, cattle). Underlain by large ground water body. Chief valley towns: Monte Vista and Alamosa, Colo.; Taos, N.Mex.

San Manuel (sahn mahn-WEL), town, Las Tunas prov., E Cuba, on RR, and 28 mi/45 km NW of Holguín; 21°09′N 76°38′W. Sugarcane; livestock.

San Manuel (san man-WEL), uninc. mining town (1990 pop. 4,009), Pinal co., S central Ariz., 33 mi/53 km NE of Tucson near San Pedro R. RR terminus. Copper, gold, silver; agr. (cattle, sheep; alfalfa); mfg. (industrial chemicals). Santa Catalina Mts., in part of Coronado Natl. Forest, to SW.

San Marcial Ozolotepec (sahn mahr-see-AHL o-so-LO-te-pek), town (1990 pop. 580), S Oaxaca, Mexico, 25 mi/41 km N of San Pedro Pochutla; 16°05′N 96°24′W. Elev. 7,546 ft/2,300 m. Rugged steep terrain. Temperate climate. Agr. (coffee, sugarcane, corn, beans), woods. On unimproved road.

San Marcos 1 (sahn MAHR-kos), town (1990 pop. 11,732), Guerrero, SW Mexico, in Pacific lowland, 35 mi/56 km E of Acapulco de Juárez on Mexico Highway 200; 16°45′N 99°22′W. Rice, sugarcane, coffee, fruit, cotton; livestock. **2** town (1990 pop. 2,815), Jalisco, W Mexico, 18 mi/29 km NNW of Ameca; 20°20′N 103°33′W. On Laguna San Marcos; grain, sugarcane, beans, alfalfa; livestock.

San Marcos, Mexico: see RAFAEL LARA GRAJALES.

San Marcos 1 city (1990 pop. 38,974), San Diego co., S Calif., suburb 30 mi/48 km N of downtown San Diego, 10 mi/16 km E of Pacific Ocean; 33°08′N 117°10′W. Seat of Palomar Col. (2-year). Citrus, avocados, flowers, ornamental plants; dairying; poultry, cattle. Mfg. (metal prods., computer equip., electronic equip., consumer goods, metal fabrication, machinery, wire drawing, medical equip., botanical prods., plastic prods., printed circuit boards). **2** city (1990 pop. 28,743), ⊙ Hays co., S central Texas, 45 mi/72 km NE of San Antonio, and 32 mi/51 km SSW of Austin, on the San Marcos R.; 29°52′N 97°55′W. Elev. 581 ft/177 m. RR junction; mfg. (metal prods., plastic prods., business forms, machinery, transportation equip., lighting equip.); farm-related industries; and tourism support the economy. The city is situated on the Balcones fault zone, where prehistoric earthquakes split the earth, releasing spring water to the surface (the San Marcos R. was thus formed) and creating underground caves. Attractions include Aquarena Springs, with glass-bottomed boats, and Wonder World Cave. San Marcos is the seat of Southwest Texas State Univ. and San Marcos Baptist Acad. Inc. 1877.

San Marcos Acteopan, Mexico: see ACTEOPAN.

San Marcos Arteaga (sahn MAHR-kos ahr-te-AH-gah), town (1990 pop. 1,181), NW Oaxaca, Mexico, 4.3 mi/7 km SW of Huajuapam de León. Near Yosocuta Dam. Elev. 4,921 ft/1,500 m. Temperate to hot climate. Agr. and palm textiles. On paved secondary road.

San Marcos Island (□ 12 sq mi/31 sq km; 1990 pop. 590), Mulegé municipio, Baja California Sur, NW Mexico, in Gulf of California, 10 mi/16 km SE of Santa Rosalía; 6 mi/9.7 km long, c.2 mi/3.2 km wide; 30°29′N 116°07′W. Gypsum mines.

San Marcos River, c.90 mi/145 km long, S central Texas; rises at San Marcos city in huge San Marcos Springs; flows generally SE, past Luling, to Guadalupe R. at Gonzales. Recreational areas. Receives Blanco R. from NW 1 mi/1.6 km downstream from its source.

San Marino, city (1990 pop. 12,959), Los Angeles co., S Calif., residential suburb 9 mi/14.5 km NE of downtown Los Angeles; 34°07′N 118°07′W. Of interest are the Henry E. Huntington Lib. and Art Gall. Inc. 1913.

San Martin, uninc. town (1990 pop. 1,713), Santa Clara co., W Calif., 23 mi/37 km SSE of San Jose, on Llagas Creek, in Santa Clara Valley; 37°05′N 121°37′W. Agr. (cattle, poultry; dairying; grain, fruit, vegetables, grapes, mushrooms); timber. Santa Cruz Mts. to SW. Coyote Reservoir to E, Anderson Reservoir to N, both on Coyote Creek. H. W. Coe State Park to NE.

San Martín Atexcal (sahn mahr-TEEN ah-tesh-KAHL), town (1990 pop. 786), Puebla, central Mexico, 23 mi/37 km WSW of Tehuacán; 18°20′N 97°40′W. Elev. 6,184 ft/1,885 m. Corn, sugar; livestock. In Popoloca Indian zone. Sometimes called Atexcal.

San Martín Chalchicuautla (sahn mahr-TEEN chal-chee-KWOU-tlah), town (1990 pop. 2,973), San Luis Potosí, E Mexico, in fertile Gulf plain, 55 mi/89 km SW of Pánuco; 21°22′N 98°40′W. Agr. center (tobacco, sugarcane, coffee, rice, fruit; livestock).

San Martín de Bolaños (sahn mahr-TEEN dai bol-AHN-yos), town (1990 pop. 1,870), Jalisco, W Mexico, on Bolaños R., and 70 mi/113 km NW of Guadalajara; 21°29′N 103°58′W. Elev. 5,118 ft/1,560 m. Grain; livestock.

San Martín de las Pirámides (sahn mahr-TEEN dai pee-RAH-mee-des), town (1990 pop. 8,427), Mexico state, central Mexico, 27 mi/43 km NE of Mexico city; 19°42′N 98°50′W. Cereals, maguey; livestock. Near Teotihuacan archaeological site and in the Zona Metropolitana de la Ciudad de México.

San Martín de los Cansecos (sahn mahr-TEEN dai los kahn-SAI-kos), town (1990 pop. 784), Oaxaca, S Mexico, in Valle Grande arm of Oaxaca Valley, 10 mi/16 km SSW of Ocotlán de Morelos, on Mexico Highway 175; 16°40′N 96°44′W. Elev. 4,987 ft/1,520 m. Silver and gold deposits.

San Martín Hidalgo (sahn mahr-TEEN ee-DAHL-go), town (1990 pop. 6,858), Jalisco, W Mexico, 12 mi/19 km SE of Ameca; 20°28′N 103°58′W. Agr. center (sugarcane, corn, beans, chickpeas, alfalfa; livestock).

San Martín Huamelulpam (sahn mahr-TEEN hwah-me-lool-PAHM), town (1990 pop. 136), W Oaxaca, Mexico, 11 mi/17 km NNE of Tlaxiaco on Mexico Highway 125; 17°24′N 97°36′W. Elev. 7,277 ft/2,218 m. Farming, mainly subsistence. In Mixteca Alta.

San Martin Huamelulpan, Mexico: see SAN MARTÍN HUAMELULPAM.

San Martín Itunyoso (sahn mahr-TEEN ee-toon-YO-so), town (1990 pop. 630), NW Oaxaca, Mexico, 11 mi/18 km SE of Santiago Juxtlahuaca; 17°04′N 97°54′W. Elev. 5,774 ft/1,760 m. Temperate climate. Agr. (corn, beans, chilies, fruits); forestry. In Mixteca Alta.

San Martín Lachilá (sahn mahr-TEEN lah-chee-LAH), town (1990 pop. 1,350), SW Oaxaca, Mexico, 9 mi/14.5 km WNW of Ejutla de Crespo, on Atoyac R. near Mexico Highway 131; 16°37′N 96°51′W. Elev. 4,846 ft/1,477 m. In the Valle Grande arm of Oaxaca Valley.

San Martín Peras (sahn mahr-TEEN PE-rahs), town (1990 pop. 1,928), extreme W Oaxaca, Mexico, 15 mi/24 km W of Santiago Juxtlahuaca; 17°19′N 98°15′W. Elev. 8,530 ft/2,600 m. Rough uneven terrain; cold climate. Farming, mainly for subsistence. Former gold-mining area. On gravel road.

San Martín Texmelucan de Labastida (sahn mahr-TEEN tesh-me-LOO-kahn dai lah-bahs-TEE-dah), city

(1990 pop. 57,519) and township, ⊙ San Martín Texmelucan municipio, Puebla, central Mexico, on RR, on Inter-Amer. Highway (190), and 22 mi/35 km NW of Puebla; 19°13′N 98°26′W. Processing (cotton mills, flour mills, wine and liquor distilleries) and agr. center (corn, wheat, maguey, cotton; livestock). Has Franciscan and Carmelite convents. Sometimes known as Texmelucan.

San Martín Tilcajete (sahn mahr-TEEN teel-kah-HE-tai), town (1990 pop. 1,600), central Oaxaca, Mexico, 5 mi/8 km NNW of Ocotlán de Juárez. Elev. 5,085 ft/1,550 m. Farming.

San Martín Totoltepec (sahn mahr-TEEN to-TOL-te-pek), town (1990 pop. 676), SW Puebla, Mexico, 5.6 mi/9 km NE of Izúcar de Matamoros; 18°40′N 98°21′W. Elev. 5,249 ft/1,600 m. Farming, mainly for subsistence.

San Martín Toxpalan (sahn mahr-TEEN toks-pah-LAHN), town (1990 pop. 15,081), extreme N Oaxaca, Mexico, 3.1 mi/5 km S of the Puebla state border, and 2.5 mi/4 km S of Teotitlán de Flores Magón; 18°05′N 97°02′W. Elev. 3,602 ft/1,098 m. Just off Mexico Highway 131. Agr. and cattle raising.

San Martín Tuxtla Volcano, Mexico: see TUXTLA VOLCANO.

San Martín Xaltocan, Mexico: see XALTOCAN.

San Martín Zacatepec (sahn mahr-TEEN zah-KAH-te-pek), town (1990 pop. 871), NW Oaxaca, Mexico, 17 mi/28 km W of Huajuapam de León. Elev. 4,354 ft/1,327 m. Steep rugged terrain; temperate to hot climate. Agr. (corn, beans, rice, sugarcane, textiles from palm); cattle. In Mixteca Baja.

San Mateo (san muh-TAI-o), village, SW B.C., Canada, on SW Vancouver Isl., on Barkley Sound, near mouth of Alberni Canal, 23 mi/37 km SSW of Port Alberni. Fishing port; fish packing.

San Mateo (san muh-TAI-o), county (□ 449 sq mi/1,163 sq km; 1990 pop. 649,623), W Calif.; ⊙ Redwood City; 37°26′N 122°22′W. On San Francisco–San Mateo peninsula; bounded W by Pacific Ocean, E by San Francisco Bay; San Francisquito Creek forms SE border; San Mateo and Dunbarton bridges cross San Francisco Bay to Alameda co., to E; includes many S suburbs of San Francisco (industrial South San Francisco; residential San Mateo, Burlingame, Hillsborough, San Bruno, Atherton, Menlo Park, all on Bay side). Redwood City (residential, industrial) is a port. Santa Cruz Mts. divide low-lying suburban area along San Francisco Bay in E from rugged Pacific coast, indented by bays (notably Half Moon Bay). Timber, Christmas trees, ornamentals, flowers, artichokes, beans, brussel sprouts, oats, barley. Cement mfg. (from oyster shell); salt evaporating; extraction of magnesium from sea water; quarrying of stone, sand, gravel, salt. Redwoods in mts. Part of Golden Gate Natl. Recreation Area in N; Coyote Point Mus. for Environmental Science, to N; San Francisco State Fish and Game Refuge in center, including Upper and Lower Crystal Springs reservoirs and San Andreas Reservoir, all 3 nestled lengthwise in San Andreas Fault. Part of Big Basin Redwoods State Park on S border; Portola State Park in SE; several state beaches on Pacific coast. Formed 1856 from San Francisco co.

San Mateo (san muh-TAI-o), city (1990 pop. 85,486), San Mateo co., W Calif., residential suburb 15 mi/24 km SSE of downtown San Francisco on San Francisco Bay at mouth of San Mateo Creek; 37°34′N 122°19′W. It is a commercial and retail center with some high-technology mfg. (printing and publishing, electronic capacitors, wood prods., computer equip.). San Mateo [Span. = St. Matthew], was named by a Span. expedition in 1776. The area was a Mex. colony from 1822 to 1846. San Mateo's main growth dates from the start of RR service in 1863. Refugees from the 1906 San Francisco earthquake greatly increased San Mateo's pop. The city has a junior col. and a race track. San Mateo Bridge spans San Francisco Bay to E. Bay Meadows Racetrack to SW; Crystal Springs Dam to SW, forms lower Crystal Springs Reservoir; Lower and Upper Crystal Springs reservoirs are on San Andreas Fault line; San Francisco State Fish and Game Refuge to SW. Coyote Point to N. Inc. 1894.

San Mateo (san muh-TAI-o), uninc. village, Cibola co., W N.Mex., 16 mi/26 km NE of Grants, just N of San Mateo Mts. Elev. 7,298 ft/2,224 m. Trading point in sheep region. Ruins of Pueblo Alto, part of Cibola Natl. Forest nearby. Nearly surrounded by Cibola Natl. Forest; Mt. Taylor (11,301 ft/3,445 m) to S.

San Mateo Atenco (sahn mah-TAI-o ah-TEN-ko), town (1990 pop. 36,227), Mexico state, central Mexico, 9 mi/14.5 km E of Toluca de Lerdo; 19°15′N 99°40′W. Agr. center (cereals, fruit; livestock); dairying. Sometimes called Atenco.

San Mateo Cajonos (sahn mah-TAI-o kah-HO-nos), town (1990 pop. 588), E central Oaxaca, Mexico, 36 mi/58 km E of Oaxaca de Juárez; 17°09′N 96° 13′W. Elev. 5,610 ft/1,710 m. On gravel road. Temperate climate.

San Mateo del Mar (sahn mah-TAI-o del mar), town (1990 pop. 4,555), SE Oaxaca, Mexico, in the extreme S of the Isthmus of Tehuantepec on a sand spit separating Mar Muerto Superior from the Pacific; 16°12′N 95°00′W. Road connection to Salina Cruz. Very hot climate. Prosperous from great fishing resources, shrimp, bass, and many different species of fish. Agr. and salt works. A Huave Indian community.

San Mateo Eloxochitlán, Mexico: see SAN MATEO YOLOXOCHITLÁN.

San Mateo Etlatongo (sahn mah-TAI-o et-lah-TON-go), town (1990 pop. 511), NW Oaxaca, Mexico, 5 mi/8 km SW of Asunción Nochixtlán. Elev. 6,070 ft/1,850 m. Temperate climate. Agr. (beans, corn, wheat, fruits), woods.

San Mateo Mountains 1 (san muh-TAI-o), in W central N.Mex., in Socorro and Sierra cos., W of the Rio Grande. Chief peaks: San Mateo Peak and Mt. Wittington (10,115 ft/3,083 m) in N. In part of Cibola Natl. Forest. **2** in NW N.Mex., in Cibola, McKinley, and Sandoval cos., just N of San Jose R. Highest at Mt. Taylor (11,301 ft/3,445 m). NE extension of range is Sierra Chivato, sometimes known as Cebolleta Mts. Range lies partly within sect. of Cibola Natl. Forest.

San Mateo Nejapam (sahn mah-TAI-o ne-hah-PAHM), town (1990 pop.1,065), NW Oaxaca, Mexico, 22 mi/36 km NW of Silacayorpan, on the Guerrero state border; 17° 34′N 98°22′W. Elev. 5,184 ft/1,580 m. In the Mixteca Baja. Temperate climate. Gravel road connects with San Andrés Tepetlapa to NW and San Juan Bautista Tlachichilco to SE. Agr.

San Mateo Peak (san muh-TAI-o) (10,141 ft/3,091 m), in San Mateo Mts., SW Socorro co., SW central N.Mex.; c.45 mi/72 km SW of Socorro; 33°33′N 107°26′W.

San Mateo Peñasco (sahn mah-TAI-o pen-YAHS-ko), town (1990 pop. 727), W Oaxaca, Mexico, 13 mi/21 km SE of Tlaxiaco. Elev. 5,541 ft/1,689 m. Resources are agr.; cattle; mezcal processing; mfg. (handwoven textiles). Rugged terrain and temperate climate.

San Mateo Piñas (sahn mah-TAI-o PEEN-yahs), town (1990 pop. 655), S Oaxaca, Mexico, 20 mi/33 km NNE of San Pedro Pochutla on the Pacific coast; 15°59′N 96°20′W. Elev. 4,757 ft/1,450 m. Very mountainous. Agr. (corn, beans, coffee, sugarcane, fruit), wood. Temperate climate. Gravel road connects with Mexico Highway 175.

San Mateo Point, promontory, San Diego co., near Orange co. line, S Calif., 2 mi/3.2 km SE of San Clemente, in Camp Pendleton Marine Corps Base.

San Mateo Río Hondo (sahn mah-TAI-o REE-o HON-do), town (1990 pop. 934), S Oaxaca, Mexico, 22 mi/43 km N of San Pedro Pochutla; 16°10′N 96°27′W. Elev. 5,709 ft/1,740 m. Mountainous with temperate climate. On Pacific slope of Oaxaca highland. Agr. (corn, beans, fruits, medicinal herbs, coffee, sugarcane), precious woods and lumber. On gravel road leading to Mexico Highway 175.

San Mateo Sindihui (sahn mah-TAI-o seen-dee-HWEE), town (1990 pop.1,457), W Oaxaca, Mexico, 39 mi/63 km E of Putla de Guerrero; 17°00′N 97°20′W. Elev. 5,577 ft/1,700 m. Agr.; farming, mainly subsistence. In the Mixteca Alta.

San Mateo Tepetitla, Mexico: see TEPETITLA.

San Mateo Texcalyacac (sahn mah-TAI-o tesh-kahl-YAH-kak), town (1990 pop. 2,961), ⊙ Texcalyacac municipio, Mexico state, central Mexico, 15 mi/24 km SE of Toluca de Lerdo; 19°10′N 99°28′W. Elev. 8,383 ft/2,555 m. Cereals; livestock.

San Mateo Tlapiltepec (sahn mah-TAI-o tlah-PEEL-te-pek), town (1990 pop. 261), W Oaxaca, Mexico, 29 mi/46 km E of Huajuapam de León; 17°46′N 97°25′W. Elev. 6,398 ft/1,950 m. On unpaved road.

San Mateo Yoloxochitlán (sahn mah-TAI-o yo-loks-o-cheet-LAHN), town (1990 pop 1,986), N Oaxaca, Mexico, 11 mi/17 km E of Teotitlán de Flores Magón; 18°09′N 96°51′W. On Puebla state border. Agr. Mazatec-speaking community. Formerly called San Mateo Eloxochitlán.

San Matías Tlalancaleca (sahn mah-TEE-ahs tlah-lahn-kah-LE-kah), town (1990 pop. 8,356), Puebla, central Mexico, 27 mi/43 km NW of Puebla; 19°19′N 98°29′W. Elev. 8,038 ft/2,450 m. Cereals, maguey.

San Melchor Betaza (sahn MEL-chor be-TAH-sah), town (1990 pop. 261), central Oaxaca, Mexico, 23 mi/37 km ESE of Ixtlán de Juárez; 17°15′N 96°09′W. Elev. 5,571 ft/1,698 m. Farming, mainly for subsistence. On unpaved road.

San Miguel, Mexico: see MITONTIC.

San Miguel 1 (san mee-GEL), county (□ 1,288 sq mi/3,336 sq km; 1990 pop. 3,653), SW Colo., borders Utah on W; ⊙ Telluride; 38°00′N 108°25′W. Mining and livestock-grazing region, drained by Dolores and San Miguel rivers. Gold, silver, lead, uranium. Some agr. (sheep, cattle; wheat). Includes part of San Miguel Mts. in SE; Uncompahgre Natl. Forest in E and center; Miramonte State Wildlife Area in S center. **2** county (□ 4,735 sq mi/12,264 sq km; 1990 pop. 25,743), NE N.Mex.; ⊙ Las Vegas; 35°28′N 104°49′W. Agr. area watered E by Canadian R., center by Conchas R., W by Pecos R. and Gallinas R. Cattle, sheep; gold; hay, alfalfa, corn, peas, oats, barley. Parts of Santa Fe Natl. Forest and Sangre de Cristo Mts. in W; Conchas Reservoir in E center, at confluence of Conchas and Canadian rivers (Conchas L. State Park). Pecos Natl. Historic Park (formerly Natl. Monument). In W Villanveva State Park in SW; Las Vegas Natl. Wildlife Refuge and Storrie L. State Park in W. Formed 1862.

San Miguel, uninc. town (1990 pop. 1,123), San Luis Obispo co., SW Calif., 9 mi/14.5 km N of Paso Robles on Salinas R.; 35°45′N 120°42′W. Cattle; grain, apples, avocados, vegetables, flowers, nursery stock. Well preserved Mission San Miguel Arcángel (founded 1797) is here, still in use. Hunter Liggett Military Reserve to NW; Nacimiento Reservoir to W; San Antonio Reservoir to NW.

San Miguel Achiutla (sahn mee-GEL ah-chee-OO-tlah), town (1990 pop. 950), W Oaxaca, Mexico, 20 mi/33 km SW of Asunción Nochixtlán; 17°18′N 97°29′W. Elev. 6,565 ft/2,001 m. Mountainous terrain with a cold climate. In Mixteca Alta. Agr. (cereals, fruits); wood. On unpaved road.

San Miguel Ahuehuetitlan (sahn mee-GEL ah-wai-wai-TEET-lahn), town (1990 pop. 1,736), extreme NW of Oaxaca, Mexico, 38 mi/62 km WSW of Huajuapam de León; 17°40′N 98°19′W. Elev. 2,723 ft/830 m. Agr. (corn, beans) straw textiles. On unpaved road. Farming, mainly for subsistence. Hot climate. In the Mixteca Baja.

San Miguel Aloapan (sahn mee-GEL ah-lo-AH-pahn), town (1990 pop. 1,813), N central Oaxaca, Mexico, 24 mi/39 km N of Oaxaca de Juárez; 17°25′N 96°41′W. Elev. 7,218 ft/2,200 m. Steep terrain with a temperate climate. On gravel road.

San Miguel Amatitlán (sahn mee-GEL ah-mah-tee-TLAHN), town (1990 pop. 547), extreme NW Oaxaca, Mexico, 19 mi/30 km WNW of Huajuapam de León; 17°55′N 98°01′W. Elev. 5,052 ft/1,540 m. Irregular rugged terrain. On unpaved road. Agr. (corn, beans, sugarcane, sesame, medicinal herbs). Straw weaving and pottery industries.

San Miguel Amatlán (sahn mee-GEL ah-mah-tee-TLAHN), town (1990 pop. 333), N central Oaxaca,

Mexico, 4 mi/7 km S of Ixtlán de Juárez; 17°17′N 96°30′W. Elev. 8,530 ft/2,600 m on the N slope of Cugimoloyas. Cool climate. Agr. (corn, potatoes, beans, wheat and fruit); wood. Mining on a small scale. On gravel road.

San Miguel Atlautla, Mexico: see ATLAUTLA DE VICTORIA.

San Miguel Chicahua (sahn mee-GEL chee-KAH-wah), town (1990 pop. 229), NW Oaxaca, Mexico, 12 mi/19 km N of Asunción Nochixtlán; 17°37′N 97°11′W. Elev. 7,218 ft/2,200 m. Mountainous with cool climate. Agr. (corn, wheat, beans, potatoes, chilies, fruits); wood. On gravel road to Nochistlán. In the Mixteca Alta.

San Miguel Chimalapa (sahn mee-GEL chee-mah-LAH-pah), town (1990 pop. 1,269), far E Oaxaca, Mexico, 25 mi/40 km NE of Juchitán de Zaragoza; 16°43′N 94°41′W. Elev. 7,218 ft/2,200 m. Mountainous. Agr. (corn, beans, coffee, sugarcane, fruits); precious woods and lumber. Textiles by local artisans, pottery and mezcal processing. On gravel road. Zoqua-speaking community.

San Miguel Coatlán (sahn mee-GEL ko-aht-LAHN), town (1990 pop. 926), in S central Oaxaca, Mexico, 11 mi/18 km SW of Miahuatlán de Porfirio Diáz; 16°10′N 96°40′W. Elev. 6,201 ft/1,890 m. Rugged terrain. Temperate climate. Agr. Unpaved roads.

San Miguel Cozumel, Mexico: see COZUMEL.

San Miguel de Allende (sahn mee-GEL dai ah-YEN-dai) or **Allende** (ai-YEN-dai), city (1990 pop. 48,935), Guanajuato, central Mexico, on central plateau, on RR, and 33 mi/53 km ESE of Guanajuato, on Mexico Highway 51; 20°56′N 100°48′W. Agr. center (beans, cereals, sugarcane, fruit; livestock); flour and textile (cotton) milling, tanning. Artist colony; tourist center. Founded 1542. Birthplace of revolutionary hero Ignacio Allende.

San Miguel de Horcasitas (sahn mee-GEL dai or-kah-SEE-tahs), town (1990 pop. 651), Sonora, NW Mexico, on San Miguel R., and 33 mi/53 km NE of Hermosillo; 28°20′N 105°50′W. Corn, wheat, beans, fruit; livestock. Sometimes Horcasitas.

San Miguel de los Baños (sahn mee-GEL dai los BAHN-yos), spa, Matanzas prov., W Cuba, 20 mi/32 km SE of Matanzas; 22°56′N 81°20′W. Resort in hilly country, with sulphurous springs. Also called San Miguel.

San Miguel de Mezquital, Mexico: see MIGUEL AUZA.

San Miguel del Padrón (sahn mee-GEL del pah-DRON), town, Ciudad de la Habana prov., W Cuba, 5 mi/8 km SE of Havana. Suburban residences and some dairying, sugar growing.

San Miguel del Puerto (sahn mee-GEL del PWER-to), town (1990 pop. 697), extreme S central Oaxaca, Mexico, on Pacific slope of Oaxaca highland, 23 mi/37 km NE of Puerto Angel; 15°55′N 96°10′W. Elev. 2,788 ft/850 m. Hot climate. Agr. (coffee, corn, beans, tropical fruits); woods; cattle. On gravel road.

San Miguel del Rio (sahn mee-GEL del REE-o), town, (1990 pop. 410), central Oaxaca, Mexico, 22 mi/35 km NNE of Oaxaca de Juárez, 3.7 mi/6 km from San Pablo Guelatao, birthplace of Benito Juarez; 17°19′N 96°33′W. Mountainous; elev. 4,593 ft/1,400 m. Agr. and woven straw textiles. A Zapotec community.

San Miguel Ejutla (sahn mee-GEL e-HOO-tlah), town (1990 pop. 730), S central Oaxaca, Mexico, 2 mi/3.2 km N of Ejutla de Crespo, on Mexico Highway 175; 16°35′N 96°44′W. Elev. 5,509 ft/1,679 m. In Valle Grande arm of Oaxaca Valley. Farming.

San Miguel el Alto (sahn mee-GEL el AHL-to), city (1990 pop. 17,500) and township, Jalisco, central Mexico, 17 mi/27 km SSW of San Juan de los Lagos; 21°01′N 102°21′W. Agr. center (corn, wheat, beans, fruit, livestock).

San Miguel el Grande (sahn mee-GEL el GRAHN-dai), town (1990 pop. 760), W Oaxaca, Mexico, in Mixteca region, 22 mi/35 km E of Putla de Guerrero, on gravel road; 17°02′N 97°37′W. Elev. 8,530 ft/2,600 m. Agr. (corn and beans); cattle; gypsum.

San Miguel Huautla (sahn mee-GEL wou-TLAH), town (1990 pop. 987), NW Oaxaca, Mexico, 19 mi/30 km ESE

of Teotitlán de Flores Magón; 18°06′N 96°48′W. Elev. 8,104 ft/2,470 m. Steep rugged terrain in the Papaloapan R. basin. Cold climate. Agr. (corn, beans, wheat, potatoes, fruit); precious woods, lumber; and cattle. Poultry raising. Also known as San Miguel Huautepec.

San Miguel Island, Calif.: see SANTA BARBARA ISLANDS.

San Miguel Ixtlán (sahn mee-GEL eesh-TLAHN), town (1990 pop. 724), Puebla, central Mexico, 24 mi/39 km SE of Acatlán; 18°00′N 97°46′W. Corn, sugarcane; livestock.

San Miguel Mixtepec (sahn mee-GEL MEESH-te-pek), town (1990 pop. 483), central Oaxaca, Mexico, 19 mi/30 km W of Ocotlán de Morelos, on dirt track; 16°47′N 96°57′W. Elev. 5,840 ft/1,780 m. Mountainous region in Atoyac R. basin. Temperate climate.

San Miguel Mountain, N.Mex.: see NACIMIENTO MOUNTAINS.

San Miguel Mountains, SW Colo., W spur of San Juan Mts., between San Miguel and Dolores cos.; 37°46′N 107°51′W. Highest points are Dolores Peak (13,290 ft/4,051 m) and Mt. Wilson (14,246 ft/4,342 m).

San Miguel Panixtlahuaca (sahn mee-GEL pah-neesh-tlah-WAH-kah), town (1990 pop. 3,222), SW Oaxaca, Mexico, 48 mi/78 km WSW of Miahuatlán de Porfirio Díaz; 16°15′N 97°23′W. Elev. 3,937 ft/1,200 m. Climate of tropical rain forest. On Pacific slope of Oaxaca highland. On unpaved secondary road.

San Miguel Peras (sahn mee-GEL PE-rahs), town (1990 pop. 1,316), Oaxaca, Mexico, 24 mi/39 km WNW of Ocotlán de Morelos; 16°57′N 97°00′W. Elev. 6,726 ft/2,050 m. On gravel road. Farming, mainly for subsistence.

San Miguel Piedras (sahn mee-GEL pee-AI-drahs), town (1990 pop. 355), W Oaxaca, Mexico, 31 mi/50 km W of Oaxaca de Juárez; 17°00′N 97°13′W. Elev. 5,971 ft/1,820 m. Poor roads. Agr. (cereals and fruits), woods, woven palm textiles.

San Miguel Quetzaltepec (sahn mee-GEL ket-SAHL-te-pek), town (1990 pop. 2979), E central Oaxaca, Mexico, 68 mi/110 km E of Oaxaca de Juárez; 16°58′N 95°49′W. Elev. 6,037 ft/1,840 m. Mountainous region with temperate climate. Agr. resources are cereals, woods, and cattle. High percentage of Mixe-speaking pop. Poor roads.

San Miguel River, c.130 mi/209 km long, in Sonora, NW Mexico; rises SW of Cananea in outliers of Sierra Madre Occidental; flows S, past Rayón, to Sonora R. 7 mi/11.3 km NE of Hermosillo; 21°13′N 102°33′W. Gold and silver deposits along course.

San Miguel River, c.90 mi/145 km long, SW Colo.; rises in San Juan Mts. SE of Telluride; flows NW, past Placerville and Nucla, to Dolores R. 15 mi/24 km E of Utah state line.

San Miguel Santa Flor (sahn mee-GEL SAHN-tah FLOR), town (1990 pop. 820), N central Oaxaca, Mexico, 62 mi/100 km N of Oaxaca de Juárez, on gravel road; 17°50′N 96°47′W. Elev. 2,034 ft/620 m. Farming, mainly subsistence.

San Miguel Sola, Mexico: see SAN MIGUEL SOLA DE VEGA.

San Miguel Sola de Vega (sahn mee-GEL SO-lahm dai VAI-gah), town 1990 pop. 1,525), Oaxaca, S Mexico, in Sierra Madre del Sur, on Sola de Vega R., affluent of Atoyac R., and 59 mi/95 km SSW of Oaxaca de Juárez, on Mexico Highway 131; 16°31′N 96°58′E. Elev. 4,429 ft/1,350 m. Cereals, sugarcane, coffee, vegetables, fruit. Formerly Villa Sola de Vega.

San Miguel Suchixtepec (sahn mee-GEL soo-CHEESH-te-pek), town (1990 pop. 1,507), S Oaxaca, Mexico, 19 mi/30 km SSE of Miahuatlán de Porfirio Díaz, on Mexico Highway 175; 16°05′N 96°28′W. Elev. 9,324 ft/2,842 m. Mountainous region with cool or temperate climate depending on elevation.

San Miguel Talea de Castro (sahn mee-GEL tah-LE-ah dai KAH-stro), town (1990 pop. 2,094), N central Oaxaca, Mexico, 37 mi/60 km NE of Oaxaca de Juárez, on gravel road; 17°22′N 96°15′W. Elev. 5,512 ft/1,680 m. Mountainous region with temperate climate. Agr.; some cattle, and wood.

San Miguel Tecomatlan (sahn mee-GEL te-ko-mah-TLAHN), town (1990 pop. 273), Oaxaca, Mexico, 5 mi/8 km SSW of Asunción Nochixtlán; 17°22′N 97°16′W. Elev. 6,293 ft/1,918 m. Cold climate and infertile soil. Main industries are woven textiles; agr. and some cattle raising.

San Miguel Tenango (sahn mee-GEL te-NAHN-go), town (1990 pop. 526), SE Oaxaca, Mexico, 27 mi/43 km WNW of Salina Cruz, on gravel road; 16°16′N 95°36′W. Elev. 4,921 ft/1,500 m. Mountainous with mild climate. Agr. (corn, beans, coffee, fruits).

San Miguel Tequixtepec (sahn mee-GEL te-KEESH-te-pek), town (1990 pop. 604), NW Oaxaca, Mexico, 25 mi/40 km W of San Juan Bautista Cuicatlán; 17°48′N 97°20′W. Elev. 6,496 ft/1,980 m. In an upland valley. Temperate to cold climate. Agr. (corn, beans, wheat, potatoes, mezcal, fruits); wood. Gravel roads. In Mixta Alta.

San Miguel Tilquiapam (sahn mee-GEL tee-kee-ah-PAHM), town (1990 pop 3,183), S central Oaxaca, Mexico, 7 mi/11 km E of Ocotlán de Morelos, on secondary road; 16°47′N 96°35′W. Elev. 5,512 ft/1,680 m. Farming, mainly subsistence.

San Miguel Tlacamama (sahn mee-GEL tlah-kah-MAH-mah), town (1990 pop. 1,554), extreme SW Oaxaca, Mexico, 6 mi/9.7 km NNW of Santiago Pinotepa Nacional, 2 mi/3.2 km from Mexico Highway 175; 16°25′N 98°04′W. Near sea level. Hot climate. Agr. (corn, beans, sugarcane, coffee, fruits). Processing mezcal and unrefined sugar

San Miguel Tlacotepec (sahn mee-GEL tlah-KO-te-pek), town (1990 pop 1,824), W Oaxaca, Mexico, 29 mi/47 km SSW of Huajuadam de León; 17°28′N 98°01′W. Elev. 4,593 ft/1,400 m. Mountainous with temperate climate. Main industries are agr.; cattle; and minerals. On paved road.

San Miguel Totolapan (sahn mee-GEL to-to-LAH-pahn), town (1990 pop. 3,403), ⊙ San Miguel Totolapan municipio, Guerrero, SW Mexico, on the Río Balsas, and 23 mi/37 km SE of Ciudad Altamirano; 16°40′N 96°18′W. Cereals, sugarcane, fruit; cattle.

San Miguel Tulancingo (sahn mee-GEL too-lahn-SEEN-go), town (1990 pop. 373), NW Oaxaca, Mexico, 24 mi/38 km ESE of Huatuapam de León, and 68 mi/110 km NW of Oaxaca de Juárez; 17°44′N 97°26′W. Elev. 6,496 ft/1,980 m. In mountainous region, in Mixteco R. drainage area. Cold climate. On unpaved road.

San Miguel Xoxtla (sahn mee-GEL HO-tlah), town (1990 pop. 7,478), N central Puebla, Mexico, 5 mi/8 km N of Ocotlán; 19°11′N 98°18′W. In the Puebla-Tlaxcla Basin. Temperate climate. Agr. (cereals, fruits), wood, horticulture. On RR, on Mexico Highway 150.

San Miguel Yotao (sahn mee-GEL YO-tah-o), town (1990 pop. 514), NE Oaxaca, Mexico, 11 mi/17 km ENE of Ixtlán de Juárez; 17°20′N 96°19′W. Elev. 5,906 ft/1,800 m. No road access. Poor agr. resources. Predominantly Zapotec pop.

San Miguel Zinacantepec, Mexico: see ZINACANTEPEC.

San Nicolás, town, La Habana prov., W Cuba, on RR, and 38 mi/61 km SE of Havana; 22°48′N 81°54′W. Agr. center (sugar, rice, tomatoes). Sugar milling at central Héctor Molina (SE). Fishing, hunting at nearby lagoons.

San Nicolás 1 (sahn nee-ko-LAHS), town (1990 pop. 118), ⊙ San Nicolás municipio, Tamaulipas, NE Mexico, in Sierra de San Carlos, 50 mi/80 km ESE of Linares; 24°41′N 98°49′W. Elev. 2,402 ft/732 m. A mining center (lead, silver). **2** town (1990 pop. 918), S Oaxaca, Mexico, 12 mi/19 km NW of Miahuatlán de Porfirio Díaz, in Miahuatlán R. valley, 3 mi/5 km off Mexico Highway 125; 16°25′N 96°45′W. Elev. 5,397 ft/1,645 m. Temperate to hot climate. Agr. (corn, beans, sugarcane, fruits); precious wood and lumber.

San Nicolás Citlaltépec, Mexico: see CITLALTÉPETL.

San Nicolás de Buenos Aires (sahn nee-ko-LAHS dai BWE-nos EI-res), town (1990 pop. 3,276), ⊙ San Nicolás Buenos Aires municipio, Puebla, central Mexico, 45 mi/72 km ENE of Puebla, 4 mi/6.4 km E of Mexico

Highway 140; 19°10′N 97°34′W. Cereals, maguey. Malpaís or San Nicolás Malpaís until 1941.

San Nicolás de Carretas, Mexico: see GRAN MORELOS.

San Nicolás de los Garza (sahn nee-ko-LAHS dai los GAHR-sah), city (1990 pop. 436,603), Nuevo León state, N Mexico; 25°45′N 100°18′W. A working-class suburb of Monterrey, on N side of city.

San Nicolás de los Ranchos (sahn nee-ko-LAHS dai los RAHN-chos), town (1990 pop. 6,832), Puebla, central Mexico, 18 mi/29 km W of Puebla; 19°04′N 98°29′W. Elev. 8,287 ft/2,526 m. Corn, wheat, maguey.

San Nicolás Hidalgo 1 (sahn nee-ko-LAHS ee-DAHL-go), town, Nuevo León, N Mexico, on RR, on Salinas R., and 23 mi/37 km NW of Monterrey; 25°29′N 100°27′W. Grain; livestock. Sometimes Hidalgo. **2** town (1990 pop. 1,036), in NW Oaxaca, Mexico, 25 mi/40 km W of Huajuapam de León; 17°48′N 98°09′W. Elev. 5,184 ft/1,580 m. On gravel road. Farming, mainly for subsistence. In the Mixteca Baja, a Mixtec community.

San Nicolas Island, Calif.: see SANTA BARBARA ISLANDS.

San Nicolás Malpaís, Mexico: see SAN NICOLÁS DE BUENOS AIRES.

San Nicolás Tolentino (sahn nee-ko-LAHS to-len-TEE-no), town (1990 pop. 740), San Luis Potosí, N central Mexico, 27 mi/43 km ENE of San Luis Potosí, on San Nicolás R.; 22°16′N 100°34′W. Elev. 5,249 ft/1,600 m. Grain, beans; livestock.

San Nicolás Totolapan (sahn nee-ko-LAHS to-to-LAH-pahn), urban area, Federal dist., central Mexico, 12 mi/19 km SSW of Mexico city, and a part of La Magdalena Contreras delegation. A suburb of the city.

San Onofre 1, 2, and 3 Nuclear Power Plants, Calif.: see SAN DIEGO.

San Pablo, city (1990 pop. 25,158), Contra Costa co., W Calif., residential suburb 10 mi/16 km NNW of downtown Oakland, and 2 mi/3.2 km N of Richmond near San Pablo Bay; 37°58′N 122°20′W. Drained by San Pablo and Wildcat creeks; in a farm region. Mfg. (mineral wool, metal barrels, light mfg.). One of the oldest Span. settlements in the region, the city is a commercial and medical center. Contra Costa Col. (2-year). San Pablo Ridge and San Pablo Reservoir to E. Inc. 1948.

San Pablo, reservoir (□ 1 sq mi/2.6 sq km), Contra Costa co., central Calif., on San Pablo Creek, 25 mi/40 km NNE of Berkeley; 37°56′N 122°16′W. Max. capacity 57,103 acre-ft. Formed by San Pablo Dam (170 ft/52 m high), built (1920) for water supply; owned by East Bay Municipal Utility Dist. Wildcat Canyon and Charles Lee Tilden regional parks to W.

San Pablo, Mexico: see CHALCHIHUITÁN.

San Pablo Amicano (sahn PAH-blo ah-mee-KAH-no), town (1990 pop. 1,385), ⊙ San Pablo Anicano township, Puebla, central Mexico, 6 mi/9.7 km SSW of Acatlán; 18°15′N 98°15′W. Elev. 3,291 ft/1,003 m. Sugar, corn, fruit; livestock.

San Pablo Balleza, Mexico: see BALLEZA.

San Pablo Bay, Calif.: see SAN FRANCISCO BAY.

San Pablo Coatlan (sahn PAH-blo ko-ah-TLAHN), town (1990 pop. 969), S central Oaxaca, Mexico, 12 mi/19 km SW of Miahuatlán de Porfirio Díaz; 16°13′N 96°47′W. Elev. 5,906 ft/1,800 m. On gravel road. Temperate climate. Agr. (corn, coffee, sugarcane, beans, fruits); precious woods, lumber; mezcal processing.

San Pablo Cuatro Venados (sahn PAH-blo KWAH-tro vai-NAH-dos), town (1990 pop. 143), W Oaxaca, Mexico, 13 mi/21 km SW of Oaxaca de Juárez; 17°58′N 96°53′W. Elev. 7,198 ft/2,194 m. On unpaved road. Agr. resources are cereals, mezcal, and fruit.

San Pablo de las Tunas (sahn PAH-blo dai lahs TOO-nahs), town (1990 pop. 4,040), ⊙ General Felipe Ángeles municipio, central Puebla, Mexico, 5 mi/8 km ENE of Acatzingo, just off Mexico Highway 140; 18°59′N 97°42′W. On a gentle slope; farming. Temperate climate. Agr. (cereals, horticulture, fruits); woods.

San Pablo del Monte, Mexico: see VILLA VICENTE GUERRERO.

San Pablo Etla (sahn PAH-blo ET-lah), town (1990 pop. 1,902), ⊙ San Pablo Etla municipio, Oaxaca, S Mexico, near RR and Inter-Amer. Highway (190), and 6 mi/9.7 km NNW of Oaxaca de Juárez; 17°13′N 96°49′W.

Elev. 5,200 ft/1,585 m. Agr. (cereals, coffee, tobacco, sugarcane, fruit; livestock); mfg. (ceramics, arts and crafts). Market center. Onyx deposits nearby. Place of pilgrimage (to sanctuary of Our Lord of the Mountain). Old Indian town; it has an anc. aqueduct.

San Pablo Huitzo (sahn PAH-blo WEET-so), town (1990 pop. 4,413), Oaxaca, Mexico, at end of Etla arm of Oaxaca Valley, on the banks of the Atoyac R., 20 mi/32 km NW of city of Oaxaca de Juárez; 17°15′N 96°52′W. Elev. 5,669 ft/1,728 m. At junction of Inter-Amer. Highway (190) with Mexico Highway 131; on RR. Temperate climate. Main industries are cattle raising and agr. (corn, beans, wheat, castor oil plant); important mica resources.

San Pablo Huixtepec (sahn PAH-blo WEESH-tai-pek), town (1990 pop. 8224), S Oaxaca, Mexico, 7 mi/11 km W of Ocotlán de Morelos; 16°50′N 96°46′W. Elev. 5,249 ft/1,600 m in Valle Grande. Agr. (castor oil plants, corn, beans, sugarcane). Processing of unrefined sugar is a major industry.

San Pablo Macuiltianguis (sahn PAH-blo man-kweel-tee-AHN-gwees), town (1990 pop. 665), N central Oaxaca, Mexico, 37 mi/60 km N of Oaxaca de Juárez off Mexico Highway 175; 17°34′N 96°34′W. Elev. 7,759 ft/2,365 m. Mountainous in Rio Grande area. Cold climate. Agr. (corn, beans, wheat, beans). Predominantly indigenous, Zapotec-speaking pop.

San Pablo Tijaltepec (sahn PAH-blo tee-HAHL-tai-pek), town (1990 pop. 212), W Oaxaca, Mexico, 22 mi/35 km SE of Tlaxiaco, on gravel road; 17°01′N 97°31′W. Elev. 5,512 ft/1,680 m. Main industries are agr.; cattle; processing mescal, woven wool, straw textiles.

San Pablo Villa de Mitla (sahn PAH-blo VEE-yah dai MEE-tlah), town (1990 pop. 7,021) S Oaxaca, Mexico, 26.9 mi/43.3 km SE of city of Oaxaca de Juárez; 16°55′N 96°24′W. Elev. 5,249 ft/1,600 m. On paved road, 3 mi/5 km off Inter-Amer. Highway (190). Agr. (corn, beans, castor oil plant). Famous for the processing of mezcal, tequila, and woolen textiles made locally. Tourist and commercial center with the prehispanic ruins of Mitla at N end of town.

San Pablo Yaganiza (sahn PAH-blo yah-gah-NEE-sah), town (1990 pop. 947), central Oaxaca, Mexico, 33 mi/53 km ENE of Oaxaca de Juárez; 17°08′N 96°14′W. Elev. 4,593 ft/1,400 m. Temperate climate. Farming, mainly subsistence. Paved roads.

San Pasqual, hamlet, San Diego co., S Calif., 7 mi/11.3 km E of Escondido; part of NE extension of San Diego. San Pasqual Battlefield State Historical Monument marks site where an engagement of Mex.-Amer. War took place in Dec. 1846 bet. Gen. Stephen W. Kearny and Andrés Pico.

San Patricio, county (□ 707 sq mi/1,831 sq km; 1990 pop. 58,749), S Texas; ⊙ Sinton; 28°00′N 97°31′W. Bounded E by Redfish Bay, sheltered from Gulf of Mexico by St. Joseph (Aransas co.) and Mustang (Nueces co.) isls., S by Nueces R., Nueces and Corpus Christi bays, N in part by Aransas R. Intracoastal Waterway follows mainland shore in Redfish Bay. A leading Texas oil- and natural-gas-producing co.; also petroleum and gas processing. Aransas Pass is deepwater port. Agr. (cotton, grain, sorghum, corn, fruit; flax); livestock; fish. Resort area (beaches, fishing). Includes part of L. Corpus Christi (in W). Ingleside Naval Station in SE corner of co. Formed 1836.

San Patricio 1 (san puh-TREE-see-o), uninc. village (1990 pop. 300), Lincoln co., central N.Mex., 45 mi/72 km W of Roswell, on Rio Ruidoso near its confluence with Rio Bonito, forming Rio Hondo. Cattle, sheep; alfalfa. Mfg. (meatpacking). Parts of Lincoln Natl. Forest to N and W. **2** village (1990 pop. 369), San Patricio co., S Texas, 27 mi/43 km WNW of Corpus Christi, on Nueces R.; 27°58′N 97°46′W. Oil and natural gas; cattle; sorghum, cotton. L. Corpus Christi reservoir to NW.

San Pedro (san PAI-dro), city (1990 pop. 40,371) and township, Coahuila, N Mexico, in Laguna dist., 33 mi/53 km NE of Torreón; 25°45′N 102°59′W. On RR; agr. center (cotton, cereals, grapes, fruit, vegetables); cotton

ginning, flour milling, vegetable-oil distilling, tanning. Formerly known as San Pedro de las Colonias.

San Pedro 1 Mexico: see CERRO DE SAN PEDRO. **2** Mexico: see CAMOCUAUTLA. **3** Mexico: see CHENALHÓ. **4** Mexico: see TLAQUEPAQUE. **5** Mexico: see JANTETELCO.

San Pedro (san PEE-dro), section of Los Angeles, Los Angeles co., S Calif., in extreme S extension of city, at Point Fermin, E side of Palos Verdes Peninsula, on Los Angeles Harbor and San Pedro Bay, adjacent to Wilmington, and 22 mi/35 km S of downtown Los Angeles. Handles much of harbor's commerce (mainly exports), and has shipyards, dry docks; mfg. (boatbuilding, diverse light mfg.). On Point Fermin are U.S. Fort MacArthur Military Reservation and a park. Cabrillo Beach (park; bathing, amusements) is near tip of point. Long Beach Naval Shipyard and container port to E. Royal Palms State Beach is here. Ferries to Santa Catalina Isl. Laid out 1882 on San Pedro Bay, it early became a port, despite bay's shallowness and exposed position; inc. as city in 1888; in 1909, it was annexed (together with Wilmington) by Los Angeles city, and development of modern harbor was begun.

San Pedro Amuzgos (sahn PAI-dro ah-MOOS-gos), town (1990 pop. 3,460), SW Oaxaca, Mexico, on Mexico Highway 125, 22 mi/33 km N of Santiago Pinotepa Nacíonal, on Pacific slope of Oaxaca highland; 16°35′N 93°06′W. Hot climate. Agr. (corn, coffee, beans, sugarcane, fruits); woods.

San Pedro Apóstol (sahn PAI-dro ah-PO-stol), town (1990 pop. 1,634), central Oaxaca, Mexico, 6 mi/9.7 km SW of Ocotlán de Morelos; 16°44′N 96°44′W. On RR; access to Mexico Highway 175. Temperate climate. Agr. (castor oil plants, corn, beans, and sugarcane). Processing of unrefined sugar, cattle, and pork.

San Pedro Atoyac (sahn PAI-dro ah-TO-yahk), town (1990 pop. 2,399), SW Oaxaca, Mexico, 11 mi/18 km N of Santiago Pinotepa Nacional on unpaved road; 16°30′N 97°59′W. Elev. 656 ft/200 m. Hot climate. Agr. (corn, beans, sugarcane, fruits); wood; cattle; and poultry raising.

San Pedro Bay, Los Angeles co., S Calif., broad bay sheltered on W by Palos Verdes Hills and Point Fermin. On its shores are San Pedro and Wilmington (S sects. of city of Los Angeles), city of Long Beach, and manmade Los Angeles and Long Beach harbors. Los Angeles and San Gabriel rivers enter from N.

San Pedro Cajonos (sahn PAI-dro kah-HO-nos), town (1990 pop. 1,283), E central Oaxaca, Mexico, 33 mi/54 km ENE of Oaxaca de Juárez; 17°10′N 96°17′W. Elev. 5,551 ft/1,692 m. On unpaved road. Agr.; mezcal processing, and wood cutting.

San Pedro Cántaros Coxcaltepec (sahn PAI-dro KAHN-tah-ros kosh-KAHL-te-pek), town (1990 pop. 407), NW Oaxaca, Mexico, 6 mi/9.7 km NE of Asunción Nochixtlán, on unpaved road; 17°30′N 97°08′W. Elev. 7,382 ft/2,250 m. Steep rugged terrain. Temperate climate with cold at high elevations. Agr. (cereals and fruits); wood and ceramics are major resources.

San Pedro Caro, Mexico: see VENUSTIANO CARRANZA, Michoacán.

San Pedro Channel, off S Calif., passage bet. Santa Catalina Isl. and S Los Angeles co. (San Pedro dist. of Los Angeles); c.20 mi/32 km wide. Santa Monica Bay is NW, Gulf of Santa Catalina to SE. Often called Catalina Channel. Crossed by passenger ferries from Los Angeles and Newport Beach to Avalon, on Santa Catalina.

San Pedro Cholula, Mexico: see CHOLULA DE RIVADABIA.

San Pedro Comitancillo (sahn PAI-dro ko-mee-tahn-SEE-yo), town (1990 pop 3,616), SE Oaxaca, Mexico, 13 mi/21 km NE of Santo Domingo Tehuantepec; 16°30′N 95°04′W. Has RR station; on paved road. Agr., local crafts; cattle and dairy prods.

San Pedro Cuayuca (sahn PAI-dro kwah-YOO-kah), town (1990 pop. 1,114), ⊙ Cuayuca de Andrade municipio, S Puebla, Mexico, 22 mi/35 km SE of Izúcar de Matamoros; 18°28′N 98°11′W. Elev. 5,928 ft/1,807 m. Mountainous terrain. Mild climate. Agr. (cereals, sugarcane, fruits), woods. In Popolocal Indian area.

San Pedro de la Cueva (sahn PAI-dro dai la KWEI-vah), town (1990 pop. 1,188), Sonora, NW Mexico, in W outliers of Sierra Madre Occidental, on Plutarco Elias Calles Reservoir, 74 mi/120 km ENE of Hermosillo; 29°18′N 109°44′W. Corn, wheat; livestock. Sometimes Cuevas.

San Pedro de Macorís (sahn PAI-dro dai mah-ko-REES), province (□ 520 sq mi/1,347 sq km; 1993 pop. 212,886), SE Dominican Republic, on the Caribbean; ⊙ San Pedro de Macorís; 18°30′N 69°20′W. Its fertile tropical lowlands are the republic's main sugar-growing region. Produces also cattle; tropical fruit; timber. San Pedro de Macorís city is a leading sugar port and processing center. Prov. was set up 1908.

San Pedro de Macorís (sahn PAI-dro dai mah-ko-REES), city (1993 pop. 123,987), SE Dominican Republic, on the Caribbean Sea at the mouth of the Higuamo R.; ⊙ San Pedro de Macorís prov.; 18°33′N 69°15′W. It is the nation's leading sugar port. Textiles and alcohol are produced here.

San Pedro del Cotorro, Cuba: see COTORRO.

San Pedro del Gallo, town (1990 pop. 874), Durango, N Mexico, 55 mi/89 km W of Torreón; 25°33′N 104°18′W. Elev. 5,545 ft/1,690 m. Silver, gold, and lead mining.

San Pedro Ecatzingo, Mexico: see ECATZINGO DE HIDALGO.

San Pedro el Alto (sahn PE-dro el-AHL-to), town (1990 pop. 663), SW Oaxaca, Mexico, 23 mi/37 km SSE of Miahuatlán de Porfirio Díaz, off Mexico Highway 175; 16°01′N 96°28′W. Elev. 6,037 ft/1,840 m. Agr. (corn, beans, coffee, sugarcane, unrefined sugar, fruits); wood.

San Pedro Hills, Calif.: see PALOS VERDES HILLS.

San Pedro Huamelula (sahn PE-dro wah-me-LOO-lah), town (1990 pop. 1,897), SE Oaxaca, Mexico, 37 mi/60 km WSW of port of Salina Cruz, off Mexico Highway 200; 16°02′N 95°40′W. Flat region near the coast. Agr. (coffee, fruits); arts and crafts and cattle are primary resources.

San Pedro Huanusco, Mexico: see HUANUSCO.

San Pedro Huilotepec (sahn PE-dro wee-LO-te-pek), town (1990 pop. 2,236), SE Oaxaca, Mexico, 5 mi/8 km NE of port of Salina Cruz; 16°14′N 95°09′W. Near Gulf of Tehuantepec and Mar Muerto Superior.

San Pedro Ixcatlan (sahn PE-dro eesh-kat-LAHN), town (1990 pop. 2,739), N Oaxaca, Mexico, on the S shore of Presidente Miguel Alemán Reservoir; 18°09′N 96°30′W. Mountainous in the Papaloapan R. basin. Hot climate. Agr. (corn, beans, coffee, sugarcane, medicinal plants), precious woods, and lumber. Unpaved roads. A Mazatec-speaking community.

San Pedro Ixtlahuaca (sahn PE-dro eesh-tlah-WAH-kah), town (1990 pop. 1,985), central Oaxaca, Mexico, 5.6 mi/9 km W of Oaxaca de Juárez, and 3.1 mi/5 km N to ruins of Monte Albán; 17°03′N 96°48′W. Elev. 6,234 ft/1,900 m. In Oaxaca Valley. Temperate climate. Area ecologically suited to the cultivation of corn, beans, and wheat.

San Pedro Jaltepetongo (sahn PEI-dro hal-pe-TON-go), town (1990 pop. 728), NW Oaxaca, Mexico, 9 mi/15 km SSW of San Juan Bautista Cuicatlán; 17°14′N 97°02′W. Elev. 8,530 ft/2,600 m. Gravel road connects town with RR and Inter-Amer. Highway 190.

San Pedro Jicayan (sahn PE-dro hee-KAH-yahn), town (1990 pop. 3,733), SW Oaxaca, Mexico, 8 mi/8 km N of Santiago Pinotepa Nacional; 16°25′N 98°02′W. Relatively flat land, near Ixcapa R. Hot climate. Agr. (corn, coffee, sugarcane, fruits); handmade textiles. Unpaved roads.

San Pedro Jocotipac (sahn PE-dro ho-ko-TEE-pak), town (1990 pop. 1,159), NW Oaxaca, Mexico, 8 mi/13 km W of San Juan Bautista Cuicatlán; 17°46′N 92°04′W. Elev. 5,971 ft/1,820 m. Majority pop. is Mixtec Indians. Temperate climate. Agr. growing mainly fruits is major activity.

San Pedro Juchatengo (sahn PE-dro hoo-chah-TEN-ko), town (1990 pop. 1,292), SW Oaxaca, Mexico, 33 mi/54 km W of Miahuatlán de Porfirio Díaz, on Mexico Highway 131; 16°21′N 97°05′W. Elev. 4,921 ft/1,500 m.

Temperate climate. Mountainous region on Atoyac R. Farming, mainly for subsistence.

San Pedro Lagunillas (sahn PE-dro lah-goo-NEE-yahs), town (1990 pop. 3,584), Nayarit, W Mexico, 28 mi/45 km SSE of Tepic; 21°13′N 104°46′W. On toll road. Corn, beans, sugarcane; cattle.

San Pedro Mártir (sahn PE-dro MAHR-tir), town (1990 pop. 1,727), S central Oaxaca, Mexico, 6 mi/9.7 km SSW of Ocotlán de Morelos. Elev. 5,085 ft/1,550 m. In the Atoyac R. basin. Temperate climate. Farming and livestock raising.

San Pedro Mártir Quiechapa (sahn PE-dro MAHR-tir kee-e-CHAH-pah), town (1990 pop. 836), S central Oaxaca, Mexico, 25 mi/40 km ENE of Miahuatlán de Porfirio Díaz; 16°25′N 96°14′W. Elev. 6,234 ft/1,900 m. Access by dirt track. Temperate climate.

San Pedro Mártir, Sierra (sahn PE-dro MAH-tir, see-EH-rah), central range of Baja California, NW Mexico, c.90 mi/145 km long; 30°45′N 115°13′W. Mostly barren; rich in minerals (copper, silver, gold, lead); has some fertile, flat valleys. N sector in San Pedro Mártir National Park. Rises to 9,843 ft/3,000 m in Cerro La Encantada.

San Pedro Mártir Yucuxaco (sahn PE-dro MAHR-tir yoo-koo-HAH-ko), town (1990 pop. 407), W Oaxaca, Mexico, 12 mi/20 km NNE of Tlaxiaco, off Mexico Highway 125; 17°25′N 97°45′W. Elev. 6,037 ft/1,840 m. Agr.; cattle; and processing of mezcal are major resources.

San Pedro Mixtepec 1 (sahn PED-ro MEESH-te-pek), town (1990 pop. 11,273), ⊙ San Pedro Mixtepec municipio, Oaxaca, Mexico; 16°00′N 97°07′W. **2** town (1990 pop. 1,383), Oaxaca, Mexico; 16°17′N 96°17′W.

San Pedro Molinos (sahn PE-dro mo-LEE-nos), town (1990 pop. 416), W Oaxaca, Mexico, 15 mi/24 km SE of Tlaxiaco; 17°06′N 97°33′W. Elev. 4,839 ft/1,475 m. Temperate climate.

San Pedro Nopala (sahn PE-dro no-PAH-lah), town (1990 pop. 509), NW Oaxaca, Mexico, 16 mi/25 km E of Huajuapam de León. Elev. 4,839 ft/1,475 m. Mountainous in the Mixteca Alta. Temperate climate. Unpaved roads. Straw textiles, processing mezcal, and agr. are main resources.

San Pedro Ocopetatillo (sahn PE-dro o-ko-pe-tah-TEE-yo), town (1990 pop. 900), N central Oaxaca, Mexico, 12 mi/18 km ENE of Teotitlán de Flores Magón, in Sierra Mazateca; 18°10′N 96°54′W. Elev. 5,741 ft/1,750 m. Steep terrain with temperate climate. On gravel road.

San Pedro Ocotepec (sahn PE-dro o-KO-te-pek), town (1990 pop. 863), E Oaxaca, Mexico, 43 mi/70 km E of Tlacolula de Matamoros; 16°55′N 95°50′W. Elev. 5,709 ft/1,740 m. Mountainous with temperate climate. Agr. (cereals, mezcal, and fruits); woods and handmade straw textiles. Unpaved roads. Mixte-speaking community.

San Pedro Piedra Gorda (sahn PE-dro pee-aid-rah GOR-dah), town (1990 pop. 6,242), ⊙ Cuauhtémoc municipio, Zacatecas, N central Mexico, on interior plateau, 26 mi/42 km ESE of Zacatecas; 22°30′N 102°20′W. Elev. 6,847 ft/2,087 m. Main industry is agr. Also Ciudad Cuauhtémoc.

San Pedro Pochutla (sahn PE-dro po-CHOO-tlah), town (1990 pop. 8,518), ⊙ San Pedro Pochutla municipio, Oaxaca, S Mexico, in Pacific coast lowland, 95 mi/153 km SSE of Oaxaca de Juárez, at junction of Mexico Highways 175 and 200; 15°44′N 96°27′W. Elev. 535 ft/163 m. Coffee-growing center. Airport.

San Pedro, Point, Calif.: see SAN PEDRO VALLEY.

San Pedro Quiatoni (sahn PE-dro kee-ah-TO-nee), town (1990 pop. 1,008), E Oaxaca, Mexico, 31 mi/51 km ESE of Tlacolula de Matamoros, 37 mi/60 km E of Oaxaca de Juarez; 16°51′N 96°08′W. Elev. 5,906 ft/1,800 m. Mountainous with temperate climate. Access by dirt roads. Agr. (corn, beans, wheat, chilies, fruits, mezcal); woods; cattle and livestock; and handmade textiles.

San Pedro Remate, Mexico: see BELLA VISTA.

San Pedro River (sahn PAI-dro), c.55 mi/89 km long,

Camagüey prov., E Cuba; formed just S of Camagüey; flows SW and W to the Caribbean Sea.

San Pedro River, c.170 mi/274 km long, N Mexico and S Ariz.; intermittent stream rising in Sonora (state), Mexico; flows N, past Benson, to Gila R. near Hayden, Ariz.

San Pedro River, Mexico: see MEZQUITAL RIVER.

San Pedro Sochiapam (sahn PE-dro SOE-chee-ah-pahm), town (1990 pop. 1,008), N central Oaxaca, Mexico, 20 mi/32 km E of San Juan Bautista Cuicatlán; 17°45′N 96°47′W. Elev. 5,741 ft/1,750 m. Mountainous region in the Papaloapan R. drainage area. Hot climate. Agr. (corn, beans, coffee, sugarcane, mezcal, fruits); woods; and textiles. Cattle and poultry. No access by road. Chinantec-speaking community.

San Pedro Tapanatepec (sahn PE-dro tah-pah-NAH-te-pek), town (1990 pop. 5,389), extreme SE Oaxaca, Mexico, 58 mi/93 km E of Juchitán de Zaragoza; 16°21′N 94°12′W. A major junction of Inter-Amer. Highway (190) and Mexico Highway 200. Very hot climate. Agr. (corn, beans, coffee, fruits, cacao), precious woods and lumber, cattle and poultry breeding are main industries.

San Pedro Taviche (sahn PE-dro tah-VEE-che), town (1990 pop. 743), S central Oaxaca, Mexico, 14 mi/23 km of Ocotlán de Morelos on dirt road; 16°38′N 96°32′W. Elev. 5,951 ft/1,814 m. Farming, mainly for subsistence.

San Pedro Teozacoalco (sahn PE-dro te-o-zah-lo-AHL-ko), town (1990 pop. 470), W central Oaxaca, Mexico, 42 mi/67 km W of Oaxaca de Juárez; 17°01′N 97°16′W. Elev. 5,659 ft/1,725 m. Main resources are agr., straw textiles, pottery, and poultry breeding.

San Pedro Teutila (sahn PE-dro te-oo-TEE-lah), town (1990 pop. 1,497), N central Oaxaca, Mexico, 22 mi/35 km NE of San Juan Bautista Cuicatlán in the Papaloapan R. basin; 17°55′N 96°43′W. Elev. 3,445 ft/1,050 m. Warm climate. Mining, agr., cattle, and textiles are main resources.

San Pedro Tidaá (sahn PE-dro te-da-AH), town (1990 pop. 1,002), W Oaxaca, Mexico, 16 mi/25 km SW of town of Asunción Nochixtlán; 17°20′N 97°23′W. Gravel road to Nochixtlán. Agr.

San Pedro Topiltepec (sahn PE-dro to-PEEL-te-pek), town (1990 pop. 238), W Oaxaca, Mexico, 8 mi/13 km WSW of Asunción Nochixtlán; 17°27′N 97°21′W. Elev. 5,840 ft/1,780 m. Partly mountainous with temperate climate. Agr. (corn, wheat, potatoes, beans, mezcal, fruits); straw textiles and woods are main resources.

San Pedro Totolapa (sahn PE-dro to-to-LAH-pah), town (1990 pop. 2,044), SE central Oaxaca, Mexico, 29 mi/47 km SSE of Tlacolula de Matamoros on Inter-Amer. Highway (190); 16°40′N 96°18′W. Elev. 3,983 ft/1,214 m. Warm climate. Agr. (corn, beans, sugarcane, coffee, tropical fruits) and, in the more temperate climate, woods, mezcal, and textiles. Formerly San Pedro Totolapan.

San Pedro Tututepec (sahn PE-dro too-TOO-te-pek), town (1990 pop. 2,593), SW Oaxaca, Mexico, 3 mi/4.8 km off Mexico Highway 200, 36 mi/58 km ESE of Santiago Pinotepa Nacional with coasts on the Pacific Ocean; 16°09′N 97°38′W. Agr. (coffee, sugarcane, sesame, corn, beans, rice, tropical fruits); precious woods and lumber. Livestock and poultry raising.

San Pedro Valley, village, San Mateo co., W Calif., near the Pacific, c.12 mi/19 km SSW of downtown San Francisco on San Pedro Creek, in fertile San Pedro Valley. Artichokes and ornamental flowers. Point San Pedro juts into the Pacific to W; Puatola Historical Monument to W; Montana Mt. to SE.

San Pedro y San Pablo Ayutla (sahn PE-dro ee sahn PAHB-lo ah-YOOT-lah), town (1990 pop. 1,369), W central Oaxaca, Mexico, 29 mi/46 km ENE of Tlacolula de Matamoros; 17°00′N 96°05′W. Elev. 6,562 ft/2,000 m. Mountainous with temperate climate. Agr. (corn, beans, fruit, mezcal); woods. A Mixe-speaking community.

San Pedro y San Pablo Etla, Mexico: see VILLA DE ETLA.

San Pedro y San Pablo River, c.40 mi/64 km long, in SE Mexico, distributary channel of lower Usumacinta

R.; branches off 12 mi/19 km NNW of Jonuta in Tabasco; flows NW to Gulf of Campeche 15 mi/24 km NE of Álvaro Obregón; 18°39'N 92°28'W.

San Pedro y San Pablo Teposcolula (sahn PED-ro ee sahn PAHB-lo te-pos-ko-LOO-lah), town (1990 pop. 3,694), Oaxaca, Mexico; 17°31'N 97°29'W.

San Pedro y San Pablo Tequixtepec (sahn PE-dro ee sahn PAHB-lo te-KEEKS-te-pek), town (1990 pop. 703), NW Oaxaca, Mexico, 20 mi/32 km N of Huajuapam de León, 3 mi/4.8 km W of Mexico Highway 125; 18°03'N 97°42'W. Elev. 6,168 ft/1,880 m. Temperate to hot climate. Agr. (corn, beans, sugarcane, fruits, rice); woods, processing mezcal, pottery, and straw textiles.

San Pedro Yaneri (sahn PE-dro yah-NE-ree), town (1990 pop. 438), NE Oaxaca, Mexico, 37 mi/60 km NE of Oaxaca de Juárez; 17°24'N 96°31'W. Elev. 3,937 ft/1,200 m. Mountainous terrain. Temperate climate. Agr. (corn, beans, coffee, yucca, and fruits). Unpaved roads. Pop. mostly Zapotec-speaking.

San Pedro Yeloixtlahuacán (sahn PE-dro ye-lo-eesh-tlah-wah-KAHN), town (1990 pop. 727), ⊙ San Pedro Yeloixtlahuaca municipio, Puebla, central Mexico, 6 mi/9.7 km SSW of Acatlán; 18°07'N 98°05'W. Elev. 4,856 ft/1,480 m. Sugarcane, corn, fruit; livestock.

San Pedro Yólox (sahn PE-dro YO-loks), town (1990 pop. 988), N central Oaxaca, Mexico, 40 mi/65 km NNE of Oaxaca de Juárez; 17°37'N 96°34'W. Elev. 7,326 ft/2,233 m. Agr. (corn, beans, wheat, potatoes, mezcal, fruits). Unpaved roads. Chinantec-speaking community.

San Pedro Yucunama (sahn PE-dro yoo-koo-NAH-mah), town (1990 pop. 236), NW Oaxaca, Mexico, 4 mi/6.4 km N of San Pedro y San Pablo; 17°33'N 97°29'W. Elev. 7,940 ft/2,420 m. Temperate climate.

San Perlita, village (1990 pop. 512), Willacy co., extreme S Texas, 23 mi/37 km N of Harlingen; 26°30'N 97°38'W. Irrigated agr. area. Oil and natural gas.

San Pitch River, c.70 mi/113 km long, central Utah; rises in Wasatch Range N of Fairview, N Sanpete co.; flows SSW, through Sanpete Valley, past Manti, through Gunnison and Nine Mile reservoirs, past Gunnison to Sevier R. 2 mi/3.2 km W of Gunnison. Dammed for irrigation 6 mi/9.7 km SW of Manti.

San Quentin, uninc. village, Marin co., W Calif., suburb 12 mi/19 km N of downtown San Francisco, on a small peninsula of same name on San Francisco Bay at entrance to San Pablo Strait, just SE of San Rafael. Ferry to Richmond (E). San Quentin State Prison is here. W terminus of Richmond–San Rafael Bridge.

San Quentin, peninsula extending into San Francisco Bay, Marin co., W Calif., at entrance to San Pablo Strait.

San Rafael, Dominican Republic: see ELÍAS PIÑA.

San Rafael (sahn ra-FAH-ehl), town (1990 pop. 16,578), Talmanalco municipio, Mexico state, central Mexico, at NW foot of Ixtaccihuatl, 30 mi/48 km SE of Mexico city; 19°12'N 98°46'W. RR terminus; paper-milling center.

San Rafael, city (1990 pop. 48,404), ⊙ Marin co., W Calif., a suburb 13 mi/21 km NNW of downtown San Francisco, on the W shore of San Francisco Bay; in N part of bay, at San Pablo Island, San Pablo Bay to NE; 37°59'N 122°31'W. Several large companies have their regional hq. here; various light mfg. The city is the seat of the restored Mission San Rafael Arcángel (est. 1817) and the Dominican Col. of San Rafael. The co. civic center here was designed by Frank Lloyd Wright. Hamilton Air Force Base to N; China Camp State Park to NE; Mt. Tamalpais State Park and Muir Woods Natl. Monument to SW; W terminus of Richmond–San Rafael Bridge from Contra Costa co. (E). Inc. 1913

San Rafael (san rah-fei-EL), village, Cibola co., W N.Mex., near San Jose R., just SE of Zuni Mts., 4 mi/6.4 km S of Grants. Elev. 6,509 ft/1,984 m. Bandera Volcano and Ice Caves, parts of Cibola Natl. Forest to W and NE. El Malpais Natl. Monument in the Malpais lava field, to E and SE.

San Rafael del Yuma (sahn rah-fah-EL del YOO-mah), village (1993 pop. 3,848), La Altagracia prov., SE Dominican Republic, on small Yuma R., and 36 mi/58 km SE of Seibo; 18°23'N 68°40'W. In fruit and cattle region. Formerly Yuma.

San Rafael Mountains, Santa Barbara co., SW Calif., one of the Coast Ranges, beginning at Cuyama R. at SE end of Santa Lucia Range, and curving c.50 mi/80 km SE to merge with other ranges near Santa Barbara–Ventura co. line; 34°42'N 119°48'W. San Rafael Mt. (6,593 ft/2,010 m) is 22 mi/35 km NNW of Santa Barbara; Big Pine Mt. (6,880 ft/2,097 m) is 20 mi/32 km N of Santa Barbara.

San Rafael River (SAN ra-FEL), c.90 mi/145 km long, Emery co., E central Utah; formed by confluence of headstreams (Huntington, Cottonwood, and Ferron creeks), all of which converge 5 mi/8 km SE of Castle Dale, in NW Emery co.; flows generally SE, past San Rafael Swell (mts.), to Green R. 15 mi/24 km S of Green River city. Headwaters are tapped by 2 diversion tunnels passing through Wasatch Plateau and used to supplement irrigation in Sanpete Valley.

San Rafael Swell, mountains, in central Emery co., E central Utah, W of San Rafael R.; 38°48'N 110°51'W. Uranium, vanadium deposits. San Rafael Knob (7,934 ft/2,418 m) is highest point.

San Ramon, city (1990 pop. 35,303), Contra costa co., W Calif., suburb 13 mi/21 km ESE of downtown Oakland; 37°46'N 121°57'W. High tech mfg. Rocky ridge and Las Trampas Regional Park to NW; Crow Canyon to W; Diablo State Park to NE.

San Raymundo Jalpan (sahn rai-MOON-do HAHL-pahn), town (1990 pop. 1,429), S central Oaxaca, Mexico, 6 mi/9.7 km S of Oaxaca de Juárez; 16°57'N 96°44'W. Elev. 4,967 ft/1,514 m. Steep terrain with temperate climate. On RR.

San Saba, county (□ 1,138 sq mi/2,947 sq km; 1990 pop. 5,401), central Texas; ⊙ San Saba; 31°09'N 98°48'W. On NE Edwards Plateau, bounded N and E by Colorado R., with part of L. Buchanan in SE; drained by San Saba R. and Brady Creek. Ranching, agr. (cattle; pecans, peanuts; wheat). Hunting, fishing; stone quarrying. Colorado Bend State Park in SE. Formed 1856.

San Saba, town (1990 pop. 2,626), ⊙ San Saba co., central Texas, on Edwards Plateau, 55 mi/89 km W of Killeen, on San Saba R.; 31°11'N 98°43'W. Elev. 1,210 ft/369 m. Ships pecans, peanuts; cattle, horses, hogs, poultry. Tourist trade; hunting, fishing nearby; mfg. (shelled pecans, architectural stone, baseball caps). Colorado Bend State Park to SE. Settled 1854.

San Saba River, c.110 mi/177 km long, W central Texas; rises in Schleicher co., on Edwards Plateau W of Menard; flows generally ENE past Menard and San Saba, to the Colorado R. 8 mi/12.9 km NE of San Saba.

San Salvador (sahn sal-vah-DOR), town (1990 pop. 1,477), Hidalgo, central Mexico, 23 mi/37 km NW of Pachuca de Soto; 20°17'N 99°01'W. Corn, maguey; livestock.

San Salvador, island (1990 pop. 465), in the Bahamas, West Indies; 24°02'N 74°28'W. Many historians believe that it was the 1st land sighted by Columbus in the New World in 1492. The indigenous pop. called it Guanahani, and it has also been named Watling or Watlings Isl. It was formerly confused with what is known as Cat Isl. (1990 pop. 1,698).

San Salvador 1 Mexico: see EL SALVADOR, Zacatecas. **2** Mexico: see TZOMPANTEPEC.

San Salvador Atenco (sahn sal-vah-DOR ah-TEN-ko), town (1990 pop. 10,625), Mexico state, central Mexico, 16 mi/26 km NE of Mexico city; 19°35'N 98°55'W. Cereals, maguey; livestock.

San Salvador El Seco (sahn sal-vah-DOR el SE-ko), town (1990 pop. 12,378), Puebla, central Mexico, 38 mi/61 km ENE of Puebla, on Mexico Highway 140; 19°08'N 97°39'W. Agr. center (cereals, beans, maguey). Sometimes El Seco.

San Salvador El Verde (sahn sal-vah-DOR el VER-de), town (1990 pop. 1,840), Puebla, central Mexico, 24 mi/39 km NW of Puebla; 19°16'N 98°31'W. Wheat, corn, maguey.

San Salvador Huixcolotla (sahn sal-vah-DOR weesh-ko-LO-tlah), town (1990 pop. 6,733), Puebla, central Mexico, 30 mi/48 km ESE of Puebla; 18°55'N 97°46'W.

Elev. 6,791 ft/2,070 m. Cereals, maguey, fruit. Sometimes Huitzcolotla.

San Sebastián (sahn se-bahs-tee-AHN), town (1990 pop. 38,799), W P.R., on Culebrinas R., and 13 mi/21 km NE of Mayagüez. Agr. center (sugarcane, coffee, plantains, bananas, oranges, fruit; cattle); dairying. La Plata sugar mill is here. Mfg. (metal and cement prods., clothing). Artisanry (hammocks, religious items, musical instruments). Airfield.

San Sebastián, Mexico: see GÓMEZ FARÍAS, Jalisco.

San Sebastian Abasolo (sahn se-bahs-tee-AHN ah-bah-SO-lo), town (1990 pop. 1,697), S central Oaxaca, Mexico, 11 mi/17 km SE of Oaxaca de Juárez; 16°55'N 96°35'W. Elev. 5,413 ft/1,650 m. In central Oaxaca Valley; temperate climate. Livestock and poultry breeding are main activities. Zapotec community.

San Sebastián Coatlán (sahn se-bahs-tee-AHN ko-aht-LAHN), town (1990 pop. 1,180), S central Oaxaca, Mexico, 18 mi/29 km SW of Miahuatlán de Porfirio Díaz; 16°12'N 96°50'W. Elev. 5,801 ft/1,768 m in the Atoyac R. basin. Cereals, fruits, and wood are main resources.

San Sebastián del Oeste (sahn se-bahs-tee-AHN), town (1990 pop. 568), Jalisco, W Mexico, in coastal foothills, 22 mi/35 km NNW of Mascota. Sugarcane, cotton, tobacco, fruit, chilies. Formerly San Sebastián Ex Decimo Cantón.

San Sebastián Ixcapa (sahn se-bahs-tee-AHN eeks-KAH-pah), town (1990 pop. 1,393), extreme SW Oaxaca, Mexico, 16 mi/25 km NNW of Santiago Pinotepa Nacional on Mexico Highway 125, in Pacific coastal lowlands; 16°32'N 98°06'W. Hot climate. Agr. (corn, beans, coffee, sugarcane, tropical fruits) and woods are main resources.

San Sebastián Nicananduta (sahn se-bahs-tee-AHN nee-kah-nahn-DOO-tah), town (1990 pop. 1,751), Oaxaca, Mexico, 12 mi/19 km W of San Pedro y San Pablo Teposcolula, on unpaved road; 16°31'N 97°42'W. Elev. 6,070 ft/1,850 m. Woods, cereals, and fruits are main resources.

San Sebastián Río Hondo (sahn se-bahs-tee-AHN REE-o HON-do), town (1990 pop. 582), S central Oaxaca, Mexico, 14 mi/22 km SE of Miahuatlán de Porfirio Díaz; 16°10'N 96°12'W. Elev. 6,135 ft/1,870 m. Temperate climate. Agr. (coffee, cacao, sugarcane, corn, fruits); precious woods and lumber. Gravel road connects town with Mexico Highway 175.

San Sebastián Tecomaxtlahuaca (sahn se-bahs-tee-AHN te-ko-mahks-tlah-HWAH-kah), town (1990 pop. 2,028), W Oaxaca, Mexico, 25 mi/40 km WNW of Tlaxiaco; 17°21'N 98°02'W. Elev. 5,906 ft/1,800 m. Temperate to cold climate. Mining, forestry, and agr. (corn, beans, chilies, potatoes, fruits). Unpaved roads.

San Sebastián Teitipac (sahn se-bahs-tee-AHN te-EE-tee-pahk), town (1990 pop. 2,032), S central Oaxaca, Mexico, 9 mi/14 km W of Tlacolula de Matamoros; 16°56'N 96°36'W. Elev. 5,381 ft/1,640 m. Agr., processing mezcal, woolen textiles, and poultry breeding are main resources. Temperate climate.

San Sebastián Tutla (sahn se-bahs-tee-AHN TOOT-lah), town (1990 pop. 2,302), central Oaxaca, Mexico, 2.5 mi/4 km E of Oaxaca de Juárez, on Inter-Amer. Highway (190); 17°45'N 97°36'W. Elev. 5,138 ft/1,566 m in the Oaxaca valley. Agr. (cereals, fruits); pottery and handmade textiles. Temperate climate.

San Sebastián Zinacatepec, town (1990 pop. 11,156), ⊙ Zinacatepec municipio, Puebla, central Mexico, on RR, and 13 mi/21 km SE of Tehuacán, on Mexico Highway 131; 18°19'N 97°14'W. Elev. 3,638 ft/1,109 m. Agr. center (corn, sugarcane, fruit; livestock).

San Simeon, uninc. village, San Luis Obispo co., SW Calif., on Pacific Ocean, 30 mi/48 km W of Paso Robles. Cattle; flowers, nursery stock, fruit, vegetables. William Randolph Hearst estate (Hearst San Simeon State Historical Monument; 161 acres/65 ha) to N. San Simeon State Beach is here; Santa Lucia Range to NE.

San Simón Almolongas (sahn see-MON ahl-mo-LON-gahs), town (1990 pop. 1,204), S cenral Oaxaca, Mexico, 10 mi/16 km NW of Miahuatlán de Porfirio Díaz, off

Mexico Highway 175; 16°24′N 96°93′W. Elev. 5,587 ft/ 1,703 m. Temperate climate. Agr. (corn, beans, coffee, fruit of all types); fine wood and lumber; cattle and poultry breeding.

San Simon Creek (sahn see-MON), c.80 mi/129 km long, intermittent stream, SW N.Mex. and SE Ariz.; rises in W edge of Hidalgo co., SW N.Mex.; flows NW in Ariz., past San Simon to Gila R. W of Solomonsville.

San Simón de Guerrero (sahn see-MON de ge-RE-ro), town (1990 pop. 1,333), Mexico state, central Mexico, 33 mi/53 km SW of Toluca de Lerdo; 18°58′N 101°01′W. Sugarcane, coffee, fruit; livestock.

San Simón Zahuatlán (sahn see-MON zah-waht-LAHN), town (1990 pop. 1,646), extreme NW Oaxaca, Mexico, 16 mi/26 km W of Huajuapam de León, on gravel road; 17°50′N 98°00′W. Elev. 6,955 ft/2,120 m. Mountainous in the Mixteca Alta region. Temperate climate. Also known as San Simón Zihuatlán.

San Telmo Point, cape on Pacific coast of Michoacán, W Mexico, 40 mi/64 km SSW of Coalcomán; 18°20′N 103°31′W.

San Toribio Xicohtzingo, Mexico: see XICOTZINGO.

San Vicente (sahn vee-SAIN-tai), spa, Pinar del Río prov., W Cuba, 5 mi/8 km N of Viñales; 22°41′N 83°43′W. Sulphurous springs.

San Vicente, Mexico: see SAN VICENTE TANCUAYALAB.

San Vicente Chicoloapan, Mexico: see CHICOLOAPAN DE JUÁREZ.

San Vicente Coatlán (sahn vee-SEN-tai ko-aht-LAHN), town (1990 pop. 3,006), S Oaxaca, Mexico, in the Atoyac R. basin, 15 mi/24 km SSW of Ejutla de Crespo; 16°23′N 96°50′W. Elev. 4,856 ft/1,480 m. Agr. (cereals, fruits, mezcal); woods. Unpaved roads. The pop. is mostly Zapotec Indian.

San Vicente Coyotepec (sahn vee-SEN-tai ko-YO-tepek), town (1990 pop. 1,357), ⊙ Coyotepec municipio, Puebla, central Mexico, 30 mi/48 km W of Tehuacán; 18°26′N 97°51′W. Rice, corn, sugarcane, fruit; livestock. A Popoloca Indian community.

San Vicente Creek, Calif.: see SAN DIEGO RIVER.

San Vicente Lachixío (sahn vee-SEN-tai lah-cheek-SEE-o), town (1990 pop. 961), SW Oaxaca, Mexico, 12 mi/19 km NW of San Miguel Sola de Vega and 32 mi/51 km SW of Oaxaca de Juárez; 16°42′N 97°01′W. Elev. 5,610 ft/1,710 m. Temperate climate. Unpaved roads. Also known as San Vicente Lachixo.

San Vicente Nuñú (sahn vee-SEN-tai noon-YOO), town (1990 pop. 392), NW Oaxaca, Mexico, 5 mi/8 km SE of San Pedro y San Pablo Teposcolula; 17°27′N 97°27′W. Elev. 6,201 ft/1,890 m. Resources are agr., poultry breeding, and processing mezcal. Temperate climate.

San Vicente Tancuayalab (sahn vee-SEN-tai tahn-koo-ah-yah-LAHB) or **San Vicente**, town (1990 pop. 4,843), San Luis Potosí, E Mexico, in fertile Gulf plain, near Pánuco R., 35 mi/56 km SW of Pánuco; 21°44′N 98°34′W. Corn, sugarcane, tobacco, cotton, rice, fruit; livestock. Some Huastec speakers in municipio.

San Xavier del Bac, Ariz.: see TUCSON.

San Ygnacio, uninc. village (1990 pop. 895), Zapata co., extreme S Texas, on the Rio Grande (Mex. border) and 33 mi/53 km S of Laredo. In ranch area (cattle). Settled in 18th cent.; nearby are ruins of old fort.

San Ysidro (san i-SID-ro), village (1990 pop. 233), Sandoval co., N New Mexico, 23 mi/37 km NNW of Bernalillo; 35°33′N 106°46′W. Cattle, sheep, chilies. Crafts. Parts of Zia Indian Reservation to W and SE; part of Jemez Indian Reservation to N, with Sante Fe Natl. Forest beyond it. Jemez State Monument and Fenton L. State Park to N.

San Ysidro, suburban section of San Diego city, San Diego co., extreme S Calif., 15 mi/24 km SSE of downtown San Diego; drained by Tijuana R. and Otay R.; port of entry on Mexico border just N of Tijuana (Baja California Norte). Mfg. (onyx and marble prods., fans and blowers, wiring devices, aircraft parts, knit outerwear). Brown Field Airport and Space Surveillance Station to E.

Sanahcat (sah-nah-KAHT), town (1990 pop. 1,482), Yucatan, SE Mexico, 29 mi/47 km ESE of Mérida; 20°45′N 89°13′W. On RR; paved road. Henequen, citrus fruit.

Sanak, village, NW Sanak Isl., SW Alaska, E of Unimak Isl., 45 mi/72 km SSW of King Cove. Cod fishing and canning.

Sanak Island, Aleutian Isls., SW Alaska, 30 mi/48 km SE of Unimak Isl.; 13 mi/21 km long, 4 mi/6.4 km wide; 54°26′N 162°40′W. Rises to 1,740 ft/530 m. Devoid of bushes and trees. Cod fishing, fish processing. Surrounded by several small isls., it is largest of Sanak Isls. group.

Sanatoga (SA-nah-TO-gah), uninc. town (1990 pop. 5,534), Montgomery co., SE Pa., residential suburb 2 mi/3.2 km E of Pottstown; 40°14′N 75°35′W.

Sanborn, county (☐ 570 sq mi/1,476 sq km; 1990 pop. 2,833), SE central S.Dak.; ⊙ Woonsocket; 44°01′N 98°05′W. Agr. area watered by James R. and Sand Creek. Corn, soybeans; dairy produce; cattle, hogs, poultry; honey. Twin Lakes State Lakeside Use Area in SW. Formed 1883.

Sanborn, town (1990 pop. 1,345), O'Brien co., NW Iowa, 6 mi/9.7 km N of Primghar; 43°10′N 95°39′W. Concrete prods. Founded 1878, inc. 1880.

Sanborn 1 village (1990 pop. 459), Redwood co., SW Minn., on Cottonwood R., and 23 mi/37 km S of Redwood Falls; 44°12′N 95°07′W. Agr. (grain, soybeans, alfalfa; livestock, poultry; dairying); mfg. (meat processing, light mfg.). RR junction to E. **2** village (1990 pop. 164), Barnes co., E central N.Dak., 10 mi/16 km W of Valley City; 46°56′N 98°13′W. RR junction.

Sanbornton (SAN-born-tuhn), town (1990 pop. 2,136), Belknap co., central N.H., 1 mi/1.6 km NE of Franklin; 43°31′N 71°35′W. Bounded W in part by Pemigewasset R, E by L. Winnisquam. Hersey Mt. (2,005 ft/611 m) on NW boundary. Nursery crops, vegetables, apples; cattle, poultry; dairying; mfg. (baskets, food prods.).

Sanbornville (1990 pop. 970), Carroll co., SE N.H., 16 mi/26 km N of Rochester, in town of Wakefield, 1 mi/1.6 km S of town center, at NW end of Lovell L. Agr. area; mfg. (rubber rollers).

Sánchez (SAHN-chez), town (1993 pop. 9,537), Samaná prov., E Dominican Republic, port at head of Samaná Bay, near mouth of Yuna R., 18 mi/29 km W of Samaná; 19°10′N 69°37′W. RR terminus, trading and shipping point for E sect. of fertile Cibao region (cacao, rice, coffee, tobacco, beeswax; timber; cattle). RR shops, sawmills. Also bathing and fishing. Vessels anchor offshore.

Sánchez Ramírez, province (☐ 453 sq mi/1,174 sq km; 1993 pop. 158,218), central Dominican Republic, ⊙ Cotui; 19°00′N 70°10′W. Rich agr. region (cacao, rice, beans) drained by the Yuna R.

Sancti Spíritus (SAHNK-tee SPEE-ree-tus), province (☐ 2,062 sq mi/6,740 sq km), central Cuba; ⊙ Sancti Spíritus. Bounded N by Buena Vista Bay, S by the Gulf of Ana María (arm of Caribbean Sea), E by Ciego de Ávila prov., W by Cienfuegos and Villa Clara provs. Created in 1975 out of portions of old Camagüey and Las Villas provs. Over 75% of its land in agr. use. Possesses complex reservoir system which can hold 345 billion gal/1.3 billion cu m of water. Irrigation canals feed sugarcane and rice fields. Agabama and Zaza dams. Important centers are Sancti Spíritus (pop. 86,000), Trinidad (pop. 38,000), and Cabaiguán. Siguaney cement factory produces 15% of nation's total output. Lacking good ports, it ships through Cienfuegos and Caibarien.

Sancti Spíritus (SAHNK-tee SPEE-ree-tus), city (1994 est. pop. 86,000), ⊙ Sancti Spíritus prov., central Cuba, on Central Highway and RR, on the Yayabo R., and 45 mi/72 km SE of Santa Clara, 20 mi/32 km N of Tunas de Zaza; 21°56′N 79°26′W. Commercial and processing center of an area that raises sugarcane, tobacco, coffee, and cattle. Founded in 1514 by Diego Velázquez as 1 of 7 orig. towns, the city was moved to its present site in 1522. It experienced frequent pirate attacks in its early years. During the 19th cent., it became one of Cuba's most aristocratic cities. Sancti Spíritus was the 1st important city to be captured by Fidel Castro's guerrilla forces (late 1958). Declared a historic monument on its 450th anniversary, the city retains some of its colonial atmosphere; landmarks include a 16th-cent.

bridge over the Yayabo R., a 16th-cent. church, and a theater dating back to 1839.

Sancti-Spíritus, Alturas de (SAHNK-tee SPEE-ree-tus, ahl-TUR-uhz dai), small mountain range, Sancti Spíritus prov., central Cuba, 7 mi/11.3 km SW of Sancti Spíritus city; 10 mi/16 km long NW-SE. Rises to 2,785 ft/849 m (Loma de Banao); 21°52′N 79°38′W. Yields tropical timber.

Sanctórum (sahnk-TO-ruhm), town (1990 pop. 3,604), ⊙ Sanctórum de Lázaro Cárdenas municipio, Tlaxcala, central Mexico, 20 mi/32 km NW of Tlaxcala, and 2 mi/3.2 km S off Mexico Highway 136; 19°30′N 98°28′W. Maguey, grain; livestock.

Sanctórum de Lázaro Cárdenas, Mexico: see SANCTÓRUM.

Sand City, city (1990 pop. 192), Monterey co., W Calif., 1 mi/1.6 km N of Seaside, on Monterey Bay, Pacific Ocean; 36°39′N 121°51′W. Mfg. (industrial machinery). Fort Ord Military Reservation To E.

Sand Coulee, village (1990 pop. 275), Cascade co., W central Mont., 8 mi/12.9 km. SE of Great Falls. Wheat, barley, oats; hay, cattle, sheep; coal. Originally called Griffin.

Sand Creek, Kiowa co., on Big Sandy Creek, Colorado, 30 mi/48 km N of Lamar, site of a massacre (1864) of Cheyenne by Col. John M. Chivington and his Colo. Volunteers. The Cheyennes, led by their chief, Black Kettle, had offered to make peace with the white men and, at the suggestion of military personnel, had encamped at Sand Creek near Fort Lyon while awaiting word from the governor of the territory. There they were attacked in a surprise dawn raid on Nov. 29, 1864. Chivington and his men, choosing to ignore the white flag Black Kettle had raised over his tent, indiscriminately slaughtered and mutilated hundreds of men, women, and children. The atrocity has been the subject of much controversy.

Sand Fork, village (1990 pop. 196), Gilmer co., central W.Va., 5 mi/8 km ESE of Glenville, on Kanawha R.; 38°55′N 80°45′W. Agr. (grain); livestock; poultry.

Sand Hill, uninc. town (1990 pop. 2,307), Lebanon co., SE Pa., residential suburb 1 mi/1.6 km N of Lebanon; 40°21′N 76°25′W.

Sand Hill River, 80 mi/129 km long, NW Minn.; rises in Sand Hill in SE Polk co., 5 mi/8 km S of Fosston (47°30′N 95°44′W); flows generally W, past Winger, Fertile, and Beltrami to Red R. near Climax, c.15 mi/24 km SW of Crookston. Channelized in lower course.

Sand Lake, village (1990 pop. 456), Kent and Montcalm cos., SW Mich., 24 mi/39 km NNE of Grand Rapids; 43°17′N 85°31′W. Mfg. (concrete); trade center for lake-resort region.

Sand Lake, Itasca co., N Minn., in Leech L. Indian Reservation and Chippewa Natl. Forest, 30 mi/48 km NW of Grand Rapids; 6 mi/9.7 km long, max. 2 mi/3.2 km wide; 47°36′N 94°00′W. Has fishing resorts. Fed (from Bowstring L., S) and drained (into Little Sand and Rice lakes, N) by Bowstring R.

Sand Mountain, dissected plateau (c.1,500 ft/457 m), largely in De Kalb co., NE Ala., and partly in Dade co., extreme NW Ga. Extends 80 mi/129 km SW from Walden Ridge, near Chattanooga, Tenn., parallel to Lookout Mt. Part of Cumberland Plateau.

Sand Point, village (1990 pop. 878), on E Popof Isl., Shumagin Isls., SW Alaska; 55°19′N 160°32′W. Fishing; fish canning; supply point for fishermen and big-game hunters.

Sand Shoal Inlet, Va.: see COBB ISLAND.

Sand Springs, city (1990 pop. 15,346), Tulsa co., NE Okla., an industrial suburb of Tulsa, on the Arkansas R.; 36°08′N 96°07′W. Mfg. (food prods., pressure vessels, chemicals, construction materials); oil and natural-gas wells. Keystone L. reservoir (Arkansas R.) to W. Founded 1907.

Sand Tank Mountains, S Maricopa co., S Ariz., SE of Gila Bend in E part of Barry M. Goldwater (formerly Luke) Air Force Range; 32°43′N 112°26′W. Rise to c.4,000 ft/1,219 m.

Sandborn, town (1990 pop. 455), Knox co., SW Ind.,

24 mi/39 km NE of Vincennes. In agr. and bituminous-coal area (surface mines).

Sanders, county (□ 2,790 sq mi/7,226 sq km; 1990 pop. 8,669), NW Mont.; ⊙ Thompson Falls; 47°40′N 115°08′W. Agr. region bordering on Idaho (W). State line also serves as Mountain-Pacific time zone boundary; W of Mont. is in Mountain time zone. Drained by the Clark Fork, Thompson and Flathead (forms part of E boundary) rivers. Cattle, sheep; hay, barley; timber; antimony. Clark Fork forms Cabinet Gorge Reservoir (Cabinet Gorge Dam in Idaho) and Noxon Reservoir (Noxon Rapids Dam), both in NW. Thompson Falls State Park at center of co.; Cabinet Mts. and Cabinet Natl. Forest in NW; part of Flathead Indian Reservation in E and SE; much of remainder of co. is in natl. forests; parts of Lolo in E and center, part of Kaniksu in W; part of Kootenai in NW. Formed 1905.

Sanders, uninc. town (1990 pop. 900), Apache co., E Ariz., 38 mi/61 km SE of Gallup, N.Mex., on Puerco R. Elev. c.5,800 ft/1,768 m. Sheep, cattle. Indian crafts. Area surrounded by parts of large Navajo Indian Reservation; main part of reservation to N.

Sanders, village (1990 pop. 231), Carroll co., N Ky., on Eagle Creek, and 13 mi/21 km E of Carrollton; 38°38′N 84°57′W. Agr. (tobacco, grain; livestock).

Sanderson, town (1990 pop. 1,128), ⊙ Terrell co., extreme W Texas, near the Rio Grande, on Del Rio–El Paso highway, and c.75 mi/121 km ESE of Alpine; 30°08′N 102°24′W. Elev. 2,980 ft/908 m. In sheep-, goat-, cattle-ranching region; also oil and gas. Rio Grande Wild and Scenic R. (Natl. Park System) to S.

Sandersville 1 town (1990 pop. 6,290), ⊙ Washington co., E central Ga., c.50 mi/80 km ENE of Macon; 32°59′N 82°49′W. Mfg. of kaolin clay prods., clothing, concrete, printing and publishing. Founded 1796; inc. 1812. **2** town (1990 pop. 853), Jones co., SE Miss., 9 mi/14.5 km NE of Laurel; 31°47′N 89°02′W. Agr. (cotton, corn; cattle, poultry; dairying); mfg. (steel fabrication, petroleum refining); oil and natural gas. L. Bogue Homa State lake to SE.

Sandgate, town (1990 pop. 278), Bennington co., SW Vt., on N.Y. state line, 20 mi/32 km N of Bennington; 43°08′N 73°11′W.

Sandhills, Mass.: see SCITUATE.

Sandhills, SE U.S., belt of sandy, low (to c.500 ft/152 m) hills extending along inner border of the coastal plain, from central Ga. on SW, across S.C. to central N.C. on NE; 20 mi/32 km–40 mi/64 km wide. Native vegetation is mainly pine, oak; cotton and peaches are grown, and several areas (esp. Southern Pines and Pinehurst, N.C., Aiken and Camden, S.C.) are noted winter resorts, with generally mild and sunny winter climate.

Sandia (san-DEE-uh), pueblo (□ 39 sq mi/101 sq km; 1990 pop. 3,971), Sandoval and Bernalillo cos., central N.Mex. Sandia Pueblo (village) is on E bank of the Rio Grande and 12 mi/19 km N of Albuquerque, in Sandia land grant (Indian reservation); 35°15′N 106°33′W. Elev. 5,038 ft/1,536 m. In irrigated region. Annual fiesta and dance June 13 honors Our Lady of Sorrows. Ruins of 17th-cent. mission and monastery are here. Present village settled c.1740. Sandia Mts. in Cibola Natl. Forest.

Sandia, village (1990 pop. 215), Jim Wells co., S Texas, 32 mi/51 km WNW of Corpus Christi, near Nueces R. In area producing oil, natural gas; cattle; sorghum; vegetables; mfg. (metal radio towers). L. Corpus Christi dam to NW; site of Lipantitlan State Park.

Sandia Mountains (san-DEE-uh), Bernalillo and Sandoval cos., N central N.Mex., E of the Rio Grande, immediately NE of Albuquerque, largely within part of Cibola Natl. Forest. Highest point in range is Sandia Crest (10,678 ft/3,255 m). Sandia Crest Recreation Area; Sandia Peak Ski Area; South Sandia Peak is highest point in S part of the mt. range (9,702 ft/2,957 m).

Sandisfield, rural town (1990 pop. 667), Berkshire co., SW Mass., in the Berkshires, 24 mi/39 km SSE of Pittsfield, near Conn. state line; 42°06′N 73°08′W. Varied agr. West Branch of Farmington R. skirts township on E. Includes state forests, villages of Montville, New Boston, West New Boston, South Sandisfield. Resort area.

Sandon, village, S B.C., Canada, in Selkirk Mts., 30 mi/48 km N of Nelson; 49°58′N 117°12′W. Silver, lead, zinc mining; timber.

Sandoval (san-do-vahl), county (□ 3,714 sq mi/9,619 sq km; 1990 pop. 63,319), NW central N.Mex.; ⊙ Bernalillo; 35°41′N 106°50′W. Drained by Rio Grande, Rio Puerco, and Jemez rivers. Cattle, sheep; dairying; apples, corn, chilies, hay alfalfa, Christmas trees; gypsum and pumice. Part of Santa Fe Natl. Forest and Bandelier Natl. Monument in NE; part of Jicarilla Apache Indian reservation in NW; Continental Divide runs NE-SW through NW part; part of Laguna Indian reservation in SW; part of Sandia land grant (Indian reservation) in S; San Felipe and Santa Domingo Indian reservations (E), Zia , Jemez, and Santa Ana Indian reservations (central), and part of Santa Clara Indian Reservation (NE corner) are all in Sandoval co. Ranges of Rocky Mts. (Nacimento and Jemez mts.) in N. Formed 1903. Part of co. (□ c.100 sq mi/259 sq km) in NE was used to form (1949) part of Los Alamos co. Valle Grande Volcano and Mts. in NE; parts of Cibola Natl. Forest in SW and SE; Fenton L. State Park and Jemez State Monument in N center.

Sandoval, village (1990 pop. 1,535), Marion co., S central Ill., 10 mi/16 km W of Salem; 38°36′N 89°07′W. In oil- and natural-gas-producing, and agr. area. Inc. 1859.

Sandown, town (1990 pop. 4,060), Rockingham co., SE N.H., 14 mi/23 km ESE of Manchester; 42°55′N 71°10′W. Drained by Exeter R. Phillips Pond in S. Nursery crops, vegetables, apples; cattle, poultry; dairying.

Sandpoint, town (1990 pop. 5,203), ⊙ Bonner co., N Idaho, on NW shore of Pend Oreille L. (here spanned by 2 mi/3.2 km bridge), 42 mi/68 km NNE of Coeur d'Alene; 48°17′N 116°34′W. RR junction. Tourism; mfg. (salad dressings and dips, meat processing, wood prods., clothing, encoders, lumber). Bonner Co. Mus. Parts of Kaniksu Natl. Forest to NW, N, and E; Coeur d'Alene Natl. Forest to SE; Schweitzer Basin Ski Area to N. Laid out 1898, inc. 1900. Center for white supremacist groups.

Sands Point, upper-income residential village (□ 5 sq mi/13 sq km; 1990 pop. 2,477), Nassau co., SE N.Y., on N shore of L.I., on Manhasset Neck, c.4 mi/6.4 km NNW of Roslyn; 40°51′N 73°42′W. Sands Point promontory (lighthouse) is at tip of Manhasset Neck, NW of village.

Sandspit, village, W B.C., Canada, on NE Moresby Isl., at entrance to Skidegate Channel, 11 mi/18 km ESE of Skidegate, 10 mi/16 km E of Alliford Bay ferry landing (ferry from Skidegate); 53°14′N 131°50′W. Lumbering; fishing (salmon); cattle, sheep.

Sandston, uninc. town, Henrico co., E central Va., a suburb 7 mi/11.3 km E of downtown Richmond; 37°31′N 77°18′W. Diversified mfg. Richmond Internatl. Airport; Va. Aviation Mus.; Seven Pines Natl. Cemetery to E.

Sandstone, town (1990 pop. 2,057), Pine co., E Minn., on Kettle R., and c.57 mi/92 km SW of Duluth; 46°07′N 92°51′W. Agr. (livestock, poultry; dairying; oats, alfalfa); mfg. (construction supplies, govt. printing); sandstone quarries nearby. Banning State Park to NE; Sandstone Natl. Wildlife Refuge to SE. Numerous small lakes to W. Settled 1885, when quarries were opened.

Sandusky (suhn-DUH-skee), county (□ 410 sq mi/1,062 sq km; 1990 pop. 61,963), N Ohio; ⊙ Fremont; 41°21′N 83°08′W. Bounded NE by Sandusky Bay of L. Erie; intersected by Sandusky and Portage rivers and small Muddy and Green creeks. Has state park with home and tomb of Rutherford B. Hayes. In the Lake Plains physiographic region. Agr. (largest Ohio producer of sugar beets; also corn, soybeans, vegetables); mfg. at Fremont and Clyde (preserved fruits and vegetables, plastic foam prods., primary nonferrous metals, cutlery, hand and edge tools, batteries, motor vehicle parts and accessories); limestone quarries. Formed 1820.

Sandusky (suhn-DUH-skee), industrial city (1990 pop. 29,764), ⊙ Erie co., N central Ohio, a port of entry on Sandusky Bay of L. Erie; 41°27′N 82°43′W. Its natural harbor has coal-loading docks, and sand, gravel, and salt are also shipped. Sandusky has a fishing industry and many assorted mfg. Plastics mfg. (vehicle trim), auto chassis systems. It has been a tourist center since the 1880s. Nearby are Cedar Point, a summer resort with a large amusement park; Kelleys Isl. and numerous other small isls.; Blue Hole Spring; Crystal Rock Caves; and Marblehead Peninsula. Inc. 1824.

Sandusky (san-DUH-skee), town (1990 pop. 2,403), ⊙ Sanilac co., E Mich., 37 mi/60 km NW of Port Huron; 43°25′N 82°49′W. In farm area (poultry, livestock; grain; dairy); mfg. (metal prods., machinery, culvert pipe, air valves, fabicated rubber prods., lumber). Airport. Inc. as village 1885, as city 1905.

Sandusky, river, c.120 mi/193 km long, Ohio; rises in N Ohio; flows W through Bucyrus, then N past Tiffin to Sandusky Bay, an arm of L. Erie; 41°26′N 83°00′W. This landlocked bay, 18 mi/29 km long, is one of the best harbors on the lake.

Sandusky Bay, N Ohio, landlocked arm of L. Erie at mouth of Sandusky R.; c.18 mi/29 km long, 5 mi/8 km wide; 41°28′N 82°50′W. Sandusky is on harbor near its mouth. Marblehead Peninsula shelters bay on N, and small Cedar Point peninsula (site of Cedar Point, summer resort) extends from SE shore partly across its mouth.

Sandwich, district, Ont., Canada, part (since 1935) of the city of Windsor.

Sandwich, city (1990 pop. 5,567), De Kalb co., N Ill., 17 mi/27 km WSW of Aurora; 41°38′N 88°37′W. Mfg. (quartz crystals, zinc and aluminum castings); agr. (corn, soybeans, wheat; hogs; dairy prods.). Inc. 1859.

Sandwich 1 town (1990 pop. 15,489), including Sandwich village, Barnstable co., SE Mass., on Cape Cod Bay, at base of Cape, 11 mi/18 km WNW of Barnstable; 41°43′N 70°29′W. Summer resort; agr. (cranberries). State game farms, fish hatcheries, forest preserves here. Famous for glass made 1825–1888; local mus. has glass collection. Hoxie House dates partly from 1637. Heritage Plantation Park; grist mill. Includes villages of East Sandwich (1990 pop. 3,171), Forestdale (1990 pop. 2,833). Settled 1636, one of earliest settlements on Cape; inc. 1639. **2** town (1990 pop. 1,066), Carroll co., E central N.H., 18 mi/29 km NNE of Laconia; 43°50′N 71°26′W. Drained by Bearcamp and Cold rivers; source of Beebe R. in NW; Squam L. on boundary in SW corner. Includes villages of Center Sandwich, mfg. (handwoven apparel, log cabins), and North Sandwich, mfg. (wooden boats). Part of White Mt. Natl. Forest in N; part of Squam Mts. in W. Mt. Israel (2,630 ft/802 m) at center; part of Sandwich Range in N. Covered bridge in E. Nursery crops, vegetables, apples; livestock, poultry; dairying; timber.

Sandwich Bay, inlet, SE Lab., Canada; 30 mi/48 km long, 10 mi/16 km wide at entrance; 53°40′N 57°15′W. In entrance are Huntington Isl. and Earl Isl. On shore are several lumbering settlements, largest of which is Cartwright.

Sandwich Islands: see HAWAII.

Sandwich Range, E central N.H., in Grafton and Carroll cos., range of White Mts. NE of Plymouth and W of Conway, in SE part of White Mt. Natl. Forest; 43°54′N 71°29′W. Principal peaks: Sandwich Mt. (3,993 ft/1,217 m), Mt. Whiteface (4,015 ft/1,224 m), Mt. Passaconaway (4,060 ft/1,237 m), and Mt. Chocorua (3,475 ft/1,059 m). Sandwich Notch pass (1,776 ft/541 m) in W.

Sandy or **Sandy City**, city (1990 pop. 75,058), Salt Lake co., N central Utah, suburb 10 mi/16 km S of Salt Lake City, N central Utah, 10 mi/16 km S of downtown Salt Lake City, near Jordan R., just W of Wasatch Range; 40°34′N 111°50′W. Elev. 4,451 ft/1,357 m. Diversified mfg.; cut stone, sand and gravel, natural gas and oil. Settled 1871. Was ore-shipping and smelting center in late 19th cent. Little Cottonwood Canyon recreational area to E; in Wasatch Natl. Forest (Twin Peaks Wilderness Area to NE, Lone Peak Wilderness Area to SE).

Sandy 1 town (1990 pop. 4,152), Clackamas co., NW Oregon, 20 mi/32 km ESE of Portland, on Sandy R. Mt. Hood 27 mi/43 km E; 45°23′N 122°16′W. Agr. (fruit, nuts; poultry); wineries; timber; dairy prods. Fish hatchery to E. Columbia R. 10 mi/16 km to N. **2** uninc. town (1990 pop. 1,795), Clearfield co., central Pa., residential suburb 1 mi/1.6 km S of Du Bois; 41°06'N 78°46'W.

Sandy Bay, town (1991 pop. 4,476) and seaside resort, Hanover parish, NW Jamaica, on coast, 12 mi/19 km W of Montego Bay; 18°27'N 78°06'W. Bananas, rice, yams.

Sandy Bay, village (1989 est. pop. 3,305), N St. Vincent, West Indies, 15 mi/24 km NNE of Kingstown, on lower slopes of the Soufrière. Arrowroot growing. A Carib settlement, it was removed, because of floods, to adjoining site (1947). Sometimes called New Sandy Bay.

Sandy Creek 1 village (□ 1 sq mi/2.6 sq km; 1990 pop. 793), Oswego co., N central N.Y., near L. Ontario, 25 mi/40 km NE of Oswego; 43°38'N 76°05'W. Dairying. **2** village (1990 pop. 243), Brunswick co., SE N.C., 15 mi/24 km WNW of Wilmington; 34°16'N 78°09'W. Tobacco, grain, sweet potatoes; livestock.

Sandy Creek, c.90 mi/145 km long, SW central Wyo.; rises near Wind R. Peak in S part of Wind R. Range in SE Sublette, co.; flows generally SW through Big Sandy Reservoir to Green R. 30 mi/48 km NW of Rock Springs. Also called Big Sandy Creek. Eden Valley Reservoir SE of Big Sandy on small tributary. Little Sandy Creek rises in SE Sublette co. and flows SSW c.50 mi/80 km joining Sandy Creek 4 mi/6.4 km N of Eden.

Sandy Falls, waterfalls (34 ft/10 m), NE Ont., Canada, on Mattagami R., and 6 mi/10 km NW of Timmins. Hydroelectric station.

Sandy Hook 1 village (1990 pop. 548), ⊙ Elliott co., NE Ky., 40 mi/64 km SW of Ashland, on Little Sandy R.; 38°05'N 83°07'W. In mt. timber and agr. (tobacco, corn, hay; cattle) area; mfg. (cabinets, lumber). Daniel Boone Natl. Forest is to W; Grayson L. reservoir and State Park to NE; Laurel Gorge to NE. **2** uninc. village, Marion co., S Miss., 14 mi/23 km S of Columbia. Pearl R. to E, La. state line to S. Agr. area; timber; mfg. (lumber, wood chips, feeds; meat processing).

Sandy Hook, low, sandy peninsula, NE N.J., projecting 5 mi/8 km N toward N.Y., and separating Sandy Hook Bay from the Atlantic Ocean. At the N end is Fort Hancock, which was built to protect N.Y. harbor and was once used as a proving ground for heavy artillery. The Sandy Hook Lighthouse (85 ft/25.9 km high; built 1763) is a Natl. Historic Landmark and the oldest lighthouse still in use. Henry Hudson's team explored this region in 1609. The British held the peninsula during the Amer. Revolution. Sandy Hook is part of Gateway Natl. Recreation Area.

Sandy Hook Bay, NE N.J., triangular S arm of Lower New York Bay, off N shore of Monmouth co., protected from the Atlantic by Sandy Hook peninsula (E); 0.5 mi/0.6 km–4 mi/6.4 km wide, c.5 mi/8 km long. Passage at S end connects with Navesink R. and Shrewsbury R. estuaries.

Sandy Lake, borough (1990 pop. 722), Mercer co., NW Pa., 8 mi/12.9 km W of Polk, on Sandy Creek; 41°21'N 80°04'W. Agr. area (corn, hay, potatoes; dairying); mfg. (wooden prods., steel siding and roofing, electrical equip.). L. Wilhelm reservoir, in M. K. Goddard State Park to N.

Sandy Lake 1 (□ 49 sq mi/127 sq km), W central N.F., Canada, just NE of Grand L. (with which it is connected), 40 mi/64 km ENE of Corner Brook; 15 mi/24 km long, 5 mi/8 km wide. **2** (□ 270 sq mi/699 sq km), NW Ont., Canada, in Patricia dist., near Man. border; 48 mi/77 km long, 8 mi/13 km wide; 53°00'N 93°00'W. Drained E by Severn R.

Sandy Lake, Minn.: see BIG SANDY LAKE.

Sandy Point, town, N Bahama Isls., on SW shore of Great Abaco Isl., on NW Providence Channel, 65 mi/105 km N of Nassau; 26°02'N 77°–24'W.

Sandy Point, town, NW St. Kitts, West Indies, 8 mi/12.9 km WNW of Basseterre (in agr. region (sugarcane, sea-island cotton, fruit).

Sandy Point, point of land, Anne Arundel co., central Md., on Chesapeake Bay at S side of Magothy R.; 7 mi/11.3 km ENE of Annapolis. Here are a state park, the

W terminus of Chesapeake Bay Bridge and a lighthouse. Nearby is Whitehall (c.1765), one of the most famous mansions in Amer., designated a Natl. Historic Landmark in 1960. Built by Horatio Sharpe (1718–1790), governor of Md. from 1753 to 1769, the elaborately decorated structure overlooking lawns toward Chesapeake Bay was designed as a fortified castle on 1 side and a pastoral temple on the other.

Sandy Ridge, irregular mountain crest, Va., runs c.30 mi/48 km SW to NE in Camberland Mts. forming portions of the boundary bet. Dickenson and Wise and Russell cos., and bet. Buchanan and Russell and Tazewell cos. Part of Tennessee-Ohio R. drainage divide.

Sandy River 1 plantation (1990 pop. 64), Franklin co., W Maine, at E end of Rangeley L., 25 mi/40 km NW of Farmington; 44°53'N 70°33'W. Sandy R. rises here. Organized 1905. **2** c.60 mi/97 km long, in W Maine; rises in Franklin co., near Rangeley L.; flows generally SE, past Farmington, then NE to the Kennebec above Norridgewock. **3** E Clackamas co., NW Oregon; rises in glaciers of Mt. Hood; flows c.50 mi/80 km generally NW past Sandy and Troutdale to Columbia R., 14 mi/23 km E of Portland.

Sandy Springs, uninc. village, Anderson co., NW S.C., 8 mi/12.9 km NNW of Anderson. Mfg. includes packaging machinery, rubber prods.

Sandy's, parish (1991 pop. 6,437), W Bermuda, including W tip of Bermuda Isl., and Somerset and Ireland isls.; 32°17'N 64°52'W.

Sandyville, town (1990 pop. 59), Warren co., S central Iowa, 5 mi/8 km E of Indianola; 41°22'N 93°23'W. In agr. area.

Sanford 1 city (□ 20 sq mi/52 sq km; 1990 pop. 32,387), ⊙ Seminole co., central Fla., 22 mi/35 km N of Orlando, on L. Monroe and the St. Johns R.; 28°47'N 81°16'W. It is an agr. center where citrus fruit and vegetables are processed; mfg. (electronic equip., boats, clothing). S terminus of Amtrak's Auto Train that connects to N Va. suburbs of Washington D.C. Inc. 1877. **2** city (1990 pop. 14,755), ⊙ Lee co., central N.C., c.45 mi/72 km SW of Raleigh; 35°28'N 79°10'W. It is a diversified mfg. center in a rich agr. region (tobacco, cotton, grain, sweet potatoes; chickens, cattle, hogs). The city has a large tobacco market and is also a major brick-mfg. center. Stone and sand quarrying. Central Carolina Community Col. Inc. 1874.

Sanford 1 town (1990 pop. 750), Conejos co., S Colo., on Conejos R., E of San Juan Mts., and 14 mi/23 km S of Alamosa, in San Luis Valley; 37°15'N 105°54'W. Elev. 7,603 ft/2,317 m. Vegetables, potatoes; cattle, sheep. **2** industrial town (1990 pop. 20,463), York co., SW Maine, on the Mousam R. and just SW of Alfred; 43°25'N 70°45'W. Once a textile-mfg. center, there are now diversified industries, including aircraft parts. The town includes the uninc. village of Springvale (1990 pop. 3,542). Nearby ocean beaches and recreational facilities attract summer vacationers. Inc. 1768.

Sanford, village (1990 pop. 218), Hutchinson co., extreme N Texas, 38 mi/61 km NNE of Amarillo, at S end of Sanford Dam, which impounds large L. Meredith, Canadian R. to W; 35°42'N 101°31'W. Agr. (cattle; wheat, corn, soybeans). Recreation. L. Meredith Natl. Recreational Area surrounds lake.

Sanford Dam, Texas: see MEREDITH LAKE, .

Sanford Lake, c.3 sq mi/4.8 sq km, Essex co., NE N.Y., in the Adirondacks, 8 mi/12.9 km SW of Mt. Mercy and 18 mi/29 km SSW of L. Placid; 44°01'N 74°03'W. Resort. Titanium mining. Drains S through outlet to a tributary of the Hudson.

Sanford, Mount (16,237 ft/4,949 m), S Alaska, highest peak of Wrangell Mts., 100 mi/161 km NE of Valdez; 62°14'N 144°08'W. It was 1st climbed in 1938.

Sangamon (SANG-ah-mun), county (□ 877 sq mi/2,271 sq km; 1990 pop. 178,386), central Ill.; ⊙ Springfield; 39°45'N 89°39'W. Agr. (corn, sorghum, soybeans; cattle, hogs, poultry; dairying). Bituminous-coal mining; oil, sand, gravel deposits. Mfg. at Springfield. Drained by Sangamon R. and its South Fork; and by Spring, and small Brush and Sugar creeks. Includes artificial L. Springfield (water supply and resort). Formed 1821.

Sangamon River, c.250 mi/402 km long, central Ill., formed by headstreams in NW Champaign co.; flows SW to Decatur, where dam impounds L. Decatur, then W and NW to Illinois R. N of Beardstown, 40°26'N 88°44'W. Receives South Fork (c.65 mi/105 km long) E of Springfield.

Sangchris Lake, reservoir (□ 4 sq mi/10.4 sq km), Christian co., central Ill., on tributary of South Fork Sangamon R., 15 mi/24 km SE of Springfield; 39°40'N 89°30'W. Max. capacity 73,000 acre-ft. Formed by Sangchris L. Dam (55 ft/17 m high), built (1967) for water supply; also used for recreation.

Sanger, city (1990 pop. 16,839), Fresno co., S central Calif., suburb 11 mi/18 km ESE of Fresno, in the San Joaquin Valley; 36°42'N 119°33'W. Inc. 1911. It is an expanding shipping and processing center for a variety of agr. prods. Mfg. (sheet metal work; wineries; wire drawing, packaging machinery, corrugated boxes). Citrus, nectarines; dairying; cattle; grain, cotton, sugar beets. Pine Flat L. reservoir to NE; Sequoia Natl. Forest to NE.

Sanger, town (1990 pop. 3,508), Denton co., N Texas, c.45 mi/72 km N of Fort Worth; 33°21'N 97°10'W. RR junction in farm area (cattle, horses; cotton; wheat, peanuts); mfg. L. Ray Roberts to NW (dam and State Park to E).

Sangerfield, village (1990 pop. 400), S Oneida co., central N.Y., 15 mi/24 km SW of Utica; 42°53'N 75°22'W. Region of dairy farming; feed mills; mobile homes.

Sangerville (SANG-ulu-vil), town (1990 pop. 1,398), Piscataquis co., central Maine, on the Piscataquis, and just W of Dover-Foxcroft; 45°07'N 69°18'W. Agr. Settled 1801, inc. 1814.

Sangre de Cristo Mountains, part of the S Rocky Mts., extending c.220 mi/354 km from S central Colo. into N central N.Mex to S of Santa Fe. Noted peaks in Colo. are Blanca Peak (14,345 ft/4,364 m), the highest and lying in the Sierra Blanca sect.; Kit Carson Peak (14,165 ft/4,298 m); Purgatory Peak (13,719 ft/4,182 m), and Horn Peak (13,450 ft/4,100 m). N.Mex. peaks include Truchas Peak (13,102 ft/3,993 m) and Santa Fe Baldy (12,622 ft/3,847 m). Most of the range is included in Carson and Santa Fe Natl. Forest, N.Mex., and San Isabel and Rio Grande Natl. Forest, Colo. The Culebra Range is in Colo.'s southernmost part of the Sangre de Cristo Mts.

Sangre Grande (SAHN-gree GRAN-dee), town, N Trinidad, Trinidad and Tobago, 27 mi/43 km ESE of Port of Spain. Market center for cacao-growing region. Prospered after opening (1941) of U.S. army base Fort Read, just W (now closed).

Sangudo (san-GOO-do), village (1991 pop. 405), central Alta., Canada, on Pembina R., and 65 mi/105 km WNW of Edmonton; 53°53'N 114°54'W. Mixed farming, lumbering.

Sanibel (SAN-i-bel), resort town (□ 33 sq mi/85 sq km; 1990 pop. 5,468), Lee co., SW Fla., 16 mi/26 km SW of Fort Myers; 26°26'N 82°05'W. Main settlement on Sanibel Isl., a leading tourist area of SW Fla.

Sanibel Island (SAN-i-bel), narrow barrier island, SW Fla., in Gulf of Mexico, c.20 mi/32 km SW of Fort Myers; c.12 mi/19 km long; 26°26'N 82°05'W. Partly shelters San Carlos Bay and Pine Isl. Sound. Lighthouse and Sanibel village, a resort and beach suburb of Fort Myers, at SE end. Causeway connects it to mainland. The beach here is popular with shell collectors.

Sanikiluaq, village (1986 pop. 422), N.W.T., Canada, on Belcher Isl. in Hudson Bay. Trapping, fishing, soapstone carving.

Sanilac (SA-ni-LAK), county (□ 1,590 sq mi/4,118 sq km; 1990 pop. 39,928), E Mich.; ⊙ Sandusky. Bounded E by L. Huron; drained by Black and Cass rivers; 43°27'N 82°38'W. Agr. (beans, sugar beets, apples; cattle, hogs, poultry; corn, wheat, oats, barley; dairy prods.). Mfg. at Sandusky. Fisheries. Resorts. Sanilac State Park in NE, on L. Huron. Organized 1849.

Sanish, village, Mountrail co., N N.Dak., 24 mi/39 km SSW of Stanley and 2 mi/3.2 km W of New Town, and on Missouri R.; 47°58'N 102°32'W. Resort; fisheries;

timber; livestock. Located in Fort Berthold Indian Reservation. Four Bears State Recreation Area to W; community col. to E

Sankaty Head (SAIN-kuh-dee), headland, E Nantucket, Mass. Lighthouse in village of Siasconset.

Sankertown (SAN-kuhr-toun), borough (1990 pop. 770), Cambria co., W central Pa., residential suburb 1 mi/1.6 km NW of Cresson; 40°28′N 78°35′W. Mt. Aloysius Jr. Col. to S.

Sanpete, county (□ 1,602 sq mi/4,149 sq km; 1990 pop. 16,259), central Utah; ⊙ Manti; 39°22′N 111°34′W. Mt. area crossed N-S by Wasatch Plateau, in E watered by Sevier and San Pitch rivers. Includes irrigated Sanpete Valley (San Pitch R.; extending N-S); part of Manti–La Sal Natl. Forest in E. Cattle, sheep, poultry, hogs; alfalfa, barley, wheat, sugar beets, fruit, vegetables; rock salt, gypsum, sand, gravel; timber. Formed 1850. Part of Uinta Natl. Forest in NW. Fish hatchery in NW. Part of Sevier Bridge Reservoir, with Painted Rock and Yuba state parks, in W; Palisade State Park in S center.

Sanpete Valley, Sanpete co., central Utah, just W of Wasatch Plateau, along San Pitch R. Sanpete irrigation project (completed 1939) brings water to the valley from headstream of San Rafael R. Alfalfa, hay, grain, vegetables, fruit; sheep, cattle, hogs, and turkey raising. Principal towns: Mt. Pleasant, Ephraim, Fairview, Moroni, Spring City, Manti. Manti–La Sal Natl. Forest on E side; Uinta Natl. Forest on W side.

Sanpoil River (SAN-poil), c.70 mi/113 km long, NE Wash.; rises in N Ferry co. in Colville Natl. Forest; flows 1st W, then through Curlew L. reservoir past Republic, receives West Fork then flows through Colville Indian Reservation, to Columbia R. (Franklin D. Roosevelt L.), c.20 mi/32 km above Grand Coulee Dam. West Fork rises in E Okanogan co., flows generally SE c.30 mi/48 km.

Sans Souci (san-SOO-see), uninc. town (1990 pop. 7,612), Greenville co., NW S.C., a residential suburb 2 mi/3.2 km NW of downtown Greenville, on Reedy R; 34°53′N 82°25′W.

Sans Souci, Mich.: see HARSENS ISLAND.

Sans Toucher, Mont (sawng too-SHAI, mong), dormant volcano (4,855 ft/1,480 m), Guadeloupe, Fr. West Indies, 7 mi/11.3 km NNE of Basse-Terre city, just N of the Soufrière.

Sansom Park Village, town (1990 pop. 3,928), Tarrant co., N Texas, residential suburb 5 mi/8 km NW of downtown Fort Worth; 32°47′N 97°24′W. Meacham Field airport to NE. L. Worth reservoir to SW. Inc. since 1940.

Santa Ana, town, Matanzas prov., W Cuba, 8 mi/12.9 km S of Matanzas; 22°55′N 81°36′W. Sugarcane; livestock.

Santa Ana (SAHN-tah AH-nah), city (1990 pop. 8,971), N Sonora, Mexico, 106 mi/170 km N of Hermosillo, at intersection of Mexico Highways 2 and 15; 30°32′N 111°07′W. Elev. 2,254 ft/687 m. On the banks of the Magdalena R., a tributary of the Concepción R. On the RR. Hot dry climate. Resources are wheat, cotton, and cattle.

Santa Ana (SAHN-tah AH-nah), town (1990 pop. 1,682), S Oaxaca, Mexico, 9 mi/14.5 km W of Miahuatlán de Porfirio Diáz; 16°20′N 96°42′W. Elev. 5,381 ft/1,640 m. In Miahuatlán R. valley. Agr. Gravel roads. Also Santa Ana Miahuatlán.

Santa Ana, city (1990 pop. 293,742), ⊙ Orange co., S Calif., suburb 26 mi/42 km SE of downtown Los Angeles and 15 mi/24 km ESE of Long Beach in the fertile Santa Ana valley; drained by Santa Ana R. and Santiago Creek; 33°45′N 117°53′W. Varied light and heavy mfg. It began as a farm trade and processing center for the surrounding region and was connected to Los Angeles in 1878 by the Southern Pacific RR. The city grew industrially after World War II. Light mfg. is prevalent in Santa Ana, which is part of the large Anaheim–Santa Ana–Garden Grove metropolitan area. Insurance companies are also major employers. Santa Ana is one of the fastest- growing U.S. cities, marked by a pop. increase of 44% bet. 1980 and 1990. Santa Ana has a junior col. and a mus. that displays early Native Amer. and Span. artifacts. El Toro Marine Corps Air Station is to the S. Orange Coast Col. (2-year) in Costa Mesa, to S; U.S. Navy Helicopter Field to W; John Wayne (Orange co.) Airport S; Pacific Ocean coast 6 mi/9.7 km to SW. Inc. 1886.

Santa Ana, pueblo (□ 101 sq mi/262 sq km; 1990 pop. 593), central N.Mex., 23 mi/37 km N of Albuquerque, on the Jemez R., in Santa Ana Indian Reservation; 35°25′N 106°35′W. The inhabitants are Pueblo Indians of the Keresan linguistic stock. Their church, Santa Ana de Alamillo, dates from 1692.

Santa Ana Ateixtlahuaca (SAHN-tah AH-nah ah-te-eeks-tlah-HWAH-kah), town (1990 pop.152), extreme N Oaxaca, Mexico, 14 mi/23 km NE of Teotitlán de Flores Magón, in Sierra Mazateca, on the Puebla state border; 18°12′N 96°24′W. Elev. 8,399 ft/2,560 m. Moderately rainy climate. Farming (mainly subsistence).

Santa Ana Chiautempan, Mexico: see CHIAUTEMPAN.

Santa Ana Cuauhtémoc (SAHN-tah AH-nah kwah-hou-TE-mok), town, (1990 pop. 632), E Oaxaca, Mexico, 18 mi/29 km NE of San Juan Bautista Cuicatlán; 17°59′N 96°48′W. Elev. 4,921 ft/1,500 m. Unpaved road. Agr. Mostly Mixtex Indian pop. Formerly known as Santa Ana Chiquihuitlán.

Santa Ana del Valle (SAHN-tah AH-nah del VAH-ye), town (1990 pop. 2,220), SE Oaxaca, Mexico, 2.5 mi/4 km N of Tlacolula de Matamoros; 16°59′N 96°28′W. Elev. 5,840 ft/1,780 m. Temperate climate. Good roads.

Santa Ana Jilotzingo (sahn-tah AH-nah hee-lot-SEEN-go), town (1990 pop. 380), Mexico state central Mexico, 17 mi/27 km NE of Toluca ded Lerdo, and part of the Zona Metropolitana de la Ciudad de México; 19°32′N 99°24′W. Farming.

Santa Ana Maya (SAHN-tah AH-nah MAH-yah), town (1990 pop. 5,787), Michoacán, central Mexico, on N shore of L. Cuitzeo, 23 mi/37 km NNE of Morelia; 20°00′N 101°01′W. Cereals, fruit; livestock; fishing.

Santa Ana Mountains, S Calif., running 35 mi/56 km SW from Santa Ana R., along Orange-Riverside co. line to Santa Margarita R. Santiago Peak (5,687 ft/1,733 m), 20 mi/32 km E of Santa Ana, is highest point. Most of range is in sect. of Cleveland Natl. Forest. Santa Margarita Mts. to SW. Chino Hills at N end of range.

Santa Ana River, c.90 mi/145 km long, SW Calif.; rises in San Bernardino Mts., c.30 mi/48 km E of San Bernardino; flows generally SW, past San Bernardino and Riverside through Prado Flood Control Basin, past Anaheim and Santa Ana, to the Pacific just NW of Newport Beach at boundary of Huntington Beach. Prado Dam, an earth-fill flood-control dam (106 ft/32 m high, 2,280 ft/695 m long), was completed 1941 near Corona.

Santa Ana Tavela (SAHN-tah AH-nah tah-VE-lah), town (1990 pop. 1,351), SE Oaxaca, Mexico, 45 mi/72 km SE of Tlacolula de Matamoros; 11°38′N 95°54′W. Elev. 2,133 ft/650 m. On gravel road. Farming (mainly subsistence).

Santa Ana Tlapacoyan (SAHN-tah AH-nah tlah-pah-KO-yahn), town (1990 pop. 1,650), S central Oaxaca, Mexico, 12 mi/19 km WSW of Ocotlán de Morelos, in Valle Grande arm of Oaxaca Valley, on Atoyac R.; 16°44′N 96°50′W. Elev. 5,266 ft/1,605 m. Temperate climate. Agr. (corn, beans, wheat, chilies, coffee, mezcal and figs); woods; cattle. Mostly Zapotec indian.

Santa Ana Yareni (SAHN-tah AH-nah yah-RE-nee), town (1990 pop. 1,234), E central Oaxaca, Mexico, 9 mi/14.5 km NW of Ixtlán de Juárez; 17°23′N 96°37′W. Elev. 7,598 ft/2,316 m. Farming (mainly subsistence).

Santa Ana Zegache (SAHN-tah AH-nah ze-GAH-che), town (1990 pop. 2,555), in S central Oaxaca, Mexico, 7 mi/12 km WNW of Ocotlán de Morelos. Elev. 5,085 ft/1,550 m. Agr. In Valle Grande arm of Oaxaca Valley.

Santa Anita, Calif.: see ARCADIA.

Santa Anna, town (1990 pop. 1,249), Coleman co., central Texas, at foot of Santa Anna Mt. (2,000 ft/610 m), 19 mi/31 km W of Brownwood. RR junction in farm area (cattle, sheep, goats, horses; wheat, oats; cotton; mesquite); oil and gas.

Santa Anna Mountain, Texas: see SANTA ANNA.

Santa Bárbara (SAHN-tah BAHR-bah-rah), city (1990 pop. 12,746) and township, Chihuahua, N Mexico, in E outliers of Sierra Madre Occidental, 13 mi/21 km SW of Hidalgo del Parral; 26°48′N 105°49′W. Elev. 6,460 ft/1,969 m. Important mining center with metallurgy industry (silver, gold, copper, lead, and zinc) Rich mineral deposits known since early colonial days.

Santa Barbara, village, S Curaçao, Neth. Antilles, 6 mi/9.7 km E of Willemstad. Phosphate deposits. Linked by cableway with New Port on coast, where phosphates are shipped.

Santa Barbara, county (□ 2,739 sq mi/7,094 sq km; 1990 pop. 369,608), SW Calif.; ⊙ Santa Barbara; 34°33′N 120°02′W. On coast (here Channel Isls.; part of Channel Isls. Natl. Park , off coast to S. Point Conception and Point Arguello are W. From coastal plain (agr.) rise the Santa Ynez Mts. (c.2,000 ft/610 m–4,000 ft/1,219 m) and San Rafael Mts. (over 6,500 ft/1,981 m). Drained by intermittent Sisquoc and Santa Ynez rivers; bounded on N by Santa Maria and Cuyama rivers (latters forms Twitchell Reservoir). Cauliflower, broccoli, celery, squash, carrots, peas, cabbages, spinach, tomatoes, lettuce, avocadoes, strawberries, lemons, grapes, flowers; cattle; wheat, barley, oats, beans. Includes part of Los Padres Natl. Forest in center to E; U.S. Camp Cooke; Santa Ynez, La Purisima Concepcion, and Santa Barbara missions. Oil and natural-gas fields (Santa Maria and Summerland dists.); diatomite mining (a leading co. in Calif.); asphalt, clay also produced. Vandenburg Air Force base in W; La Purisima Mission State Historical Park in W; Carpenteria State Beach in SW; Gaviota and Refugio state beaches and El Capitan State Park in S; Chumash Painted Cave State Historical Park in S. Formed 1850.

Santa Barbara, city (1990 pop. 85,571), ⊙ Santa Barbara co., S Calif., c.85 mi/137 km WNW of Los Angeles, on the Pacific Ocean; 34°26′N 119°43′W. Diversified mfg. A beautiful residential and resort city with many recreational facilities, it also has electronics and aerospace research and development firms, and an orchid industry. Oil fields are in the area and offshore. The region was discovered by Juan Cabrillo in 1542 and explored and named in 1602. A Span. presidio, remnants of which remain, was founded here in 1782. The Span. mission (est. in 1786; present bldg. completed in 1820) is a major tourist attraction. Santa Barbara is known for its prevalent Span. architecture. Points of interest include a "street in Spain" shopping area, an undersea aquarium, and many parks and gardens. Santa Barabar City Col. (2-year) is here, and the Univ. of Calif. at Santa Barbara (8 mi/12.9 km to W) and Westmont Col. are just outside the city limits. Santa Barbara is hq. of the Los Padres Natl. Forest in the Santa Ynez Mts., which rise behind the city. In Feb. 1942, oil tanks in Santa Barbara harbor were the object of a Jap. submarine attack. In Jan. 1969, an oil leak in an offshore drilling platform in the Santa Barbara Channel brought great destruction to the city's harbor and beaches. Santa Barbara Municipal Airport to W; Chumash Caves State Historical Park to W; Los Padres Natl. Forest to N. Inc. 1850.

Santa Barbara Channel, strait bet. coast of S Calif. (here trending almost E-W) and Santa Barbara Isls.; c.20 mi/32 km–30 mi/48 km wide, c.70 mi/113 km long. U.S. navy speed-testing course; popular for yachting, fishing.

Santa Bárbara de Samaná, Dominican Republic: see SAMANÁ.

Santa Barbara Island, Santa Barbara co., S Calif., small isl. in Channel Isls., Pacific Ocean, 46 mi/74 km SW of Santa Monica. Part of Channel Isl. Natl. Park.

Santa Barbara Islands or **Channel Islands**, chain of 8 rugged isls. and many islets, Santa Barbara and Los Angeles cos., SW Calif., extending c.150 mi/241 km off S Calif. coast from S of Point Conception to W of San Diego. San Miguel, Santa Rosa, Santa Cruz, and the Anacapa group are in NW; Santa Barbara, San Nicolas, Santa Catalina, and San Clemente are widely dispersed in S and SE. The isls. were visited in 1542 by Juan Rodriguez Cabrillo, a Port. explorer in the service of Spain. They are located 13 mi/21 km–68 mi/109 km W of the

Area in square miles is shown by the symbol □ capital city or county seat by ⊙

mainland. Santa Cruz is the largest isl. (98 sq mi/254 sq km) of the chain; sheep and cattle are raised here. San Miguel Isl. is uninhabited and has been badly eroded. On its W point are large sea-elephant and sea-lion herds. Anacapa and Santa Barbara, the smallest isls. in the chain, constitute Channel Isls. Natl. Park est. 1938 as a natl. monument; est. 1980 as a natl. park. Channel Isls. Natl. Park includes all but Santa Catalina, San Clemente, and San Nicolas isls. (in S and SE). Santa Catalina Isl. is the most economically developed of the isls. and is a popular tourist center. In 1969 leakage from an oil well in the Santa Barbara Channel created an 800-sq-mi/2,072-sq-km oil slick that destroyed much aquatic life.

Santa Catalina or **Catalina Island**, Los Angeles co., S Calif., off Huntington Beach, 30 mi/48 km SSW of Long Beach; 22 mi/35 km long and 1 mi/1.6 km–8 mi/12.9 km wide. It is a resort isl. with a picturesque, irregular coastline dotted with coves and beaches. It was explored in 1542 by Juan Rodríguez Cabrillo, and given its present name by Vizcaíno in 1602. In 1919, William Wrigley bought the isl. and constructed vacation and sports facilities. Avalon, the only town on the isl., and in the isl. group, is the center of activities. No motorized vehicles are allowed. Passenger ferries from Los Angeles and Newport Beach. Of interest on Santa Catalina are a seal colony and submarine gardens. Commonly referred to as Catalina Isl.

Santa Catalina, Gulf, S Calif., reach of the Pacific lying bet. San Clemente and Santa Catalina isls. (W) and the coast N of San Diego. Communicates via San Pedro Channel with Santa Monica Bay to NW; Outer Santa Barbara Channel passes W bet. the 2 isls.

Santa Catalina Mountains, Pima and Pinal cos., SE Ariz., NE of Tucson, in sect. of Coronado Natl. Forest, Mt. Lemmon (9,157 ft/2,791 m) is highest point, Mt. Lemmon Ski Valley. Site of Biosphere 2, greenhouse-like environmental living structure and expressions (1994–1995).

Santa Catalina Quieri (SAHN-tah kah-tah-LEE-nah kee-E-ree), town (1990 pop. 1,239), SE central Oaxaca, Mexico, 22 mi/35 km E of Miahuatlán de Juárez, on unpaved road; 16°18'N 96°17'W. Elev. 5,971 ft/1,820 m. Farming, mainly for subsistence. Temperate climate.

Santa Catarina (SAHN-tah kah-tah-REE-nah), city (1990 pop. 893) and township, Guanajuato, central Mexico, 30 mi/48 km ESE of San Luis de la Paz; 21°08'N 100°04'W. Elev. 7,211 ft/2,198 m.

Santa Catarina 1 (SAHN-tah kah-tah-REE-nah), town (1990 pop. 162,707), Nuevo León, N Mexico, in foothills of Sierra Madre Oriental, 10 mi/16 km W of Monterrey on Mexico Highway 40; 25°44'N 100°30'W. **2** town (1990 pop. 239), SE San Luis Potosí, Mexico, 37 mi/60 km ESE of the town of Río Verde; 21°40'N 99°30'W. Elev. 4,551 ft/1,387 m. Mountainous terrain in Sierra Amapola. Temperate climate. Agr.; cattle; and straw textiles. Gravel roads only. Pames Indian center.

Santa Catarina Cuixtla (SAHN-tah kah-tah-REE-nah KWEEKS-tlah), town (1990 pop. 1,922), S central Oaxaca, Mexico, 4 mi/6.4 km SW of Moiahuatlán de Porfirio Díaz; 16°18'N 96°39'W. Elev. 5,348 ft/1,630 m. Temperate climate. in Miahuatlán R. valley. Agr. resources are cereals, fruits (mainly oranges and lemons).

Santa Catarina Ixtepeji (SAHN-tah kah-tah-REE-nah eeks-te-PE-hee), town (1990 pop. 861), N central Oaxaca, Mexico, 8 mi/13 km SW of Ixtlán de Juárez, and 22 mi/35 km NE of Oaxaca de Juárez; 17°16'N 96°34'W. A mountainous region drained by streams which flow into Río Grande. Temperate climate. Agr. (corn, beans, wheat, potatoes, fruits); local woolen textiles. Near Mexico Highway 175. A Zapotec community.

Santa Catarina Juquila (SAHN-tah kah-tah-REE-nah hoo-KEE-lah), town (1990 pop 3,102), Oaxaca, S Mexico, in Sierra Madre del Sur, 70 mi/113 km SW of Oaxaca de Juárez; 16°15'N 97°20'W. Cereals, sugar, coffee, fruit, vegetables; livestock. Sometimes Juquilla.

Santa Catarina Lachatao (SAHN-tah kah-tah-REE-nah lah-chah-TAH-o), town (1990 pop. 235), NE Oaxaca, Mexico, 6 mi/10 km S of Ixtlán de Juárez; 17°15'N 96°28'W. Elev. 6,358 ft/1,938 m. A mountainous region with poor soil. Temperate climate. Predominantly Zapote Indian pop. A gravel road connects to the W with Mexico Highway 175.

Santa Catarina Loxicha (SAHN-tah kah-tah-REE-nah lok-SEE-chah), town (1990 pop. 2,046), S Oaxaca, Mexico, 21 mi/34 km SSW of Miahuatlán de Porfirio Díaz; 16°04'N 96°46'W. Elev. 4,101 ft/ 1,250 m. Agr. prods. are corn, beans, coffee, and sugarcane.

Santa Catarina Mechoacán (SAHN-tah kah-tah-REE-nah me-cho-ah-KAHN), town, (1990 pop. 3,663), SW Oaxaca, Mexico, 16 mi/25 km E of Santiago Pinotepa Nacional, 3 mi/4.8 km off Mexico Highway 200 on gravel road; 16°20'N 97°50'W. Hot climate. Agr. resources are coffee, sugarcane, corn, beans, and fruits.

Santa Catarina Minas (SAHN-tah kah-tah-REE-nah MEE-nahs), town (1990 pop.1,449), central Oaxaca, Mexico, 4 mi/6.4 km E of Octlán de Morelos, in Valle Grande arm of Oaxaca valley; 16°47'N 96°37'W. Elev. 5,571 ft/1,698 m. Agr. (corn, beans, wheat, fruits), forestry, and handmade textiles.

Santa Catarina Quiané (SAHN-tah kah-tah-REE-nah kee-ah-NE), town (1990 pop. 1,660), S central Oaxaca, Mexico, 11 mi/18 km S of Oaxaca de Juárez; 16°53'N 96°44'W. Elev. 4,984 ft/1,519 m. In Valle Grande arm of Oaxaca Valley. In densely settled area. Farming; crafts; tourism.

Santa Catarina Quioquitani (sahn-tah kah-tah-REE-nah kee-o-kee-TAH-nee), town (1990 pop. 618), in SE Oaxaca, Mexico, 20 mi/32 kmE of Miahuitlán de Porfirio Díaz; 16°15'N 96°15'W. No all-season roads. Agr. prods. are corn, beans, sugarcane, rice, and cacao. Formerly Quioquitani.

Santa Catarina Tayata (SAHN-tah kah-tah-REE-nah tah-YAH-tah), town (1990 pop. 89), N central Oaxaca, Mexico, 10 mi/16 km NE of Tlaxiaco; 17°21'N 97°34'W. Elev. 6,965 ft/2,123 m. Steep terrain on Mixteca Alta. Temperate climate. Agr. Unpaved roads.

Santa Catarina Ticuá (SAHN-tah kah-tah-REE-nah tee-koo-AH), town (1990 pop. 442), W Oaxaca, Mexico, 15 mi/24 km SE of Tlaxiaco; 17°04'N 97°33'W. Elev. 5,709 ft/1,740. Temperate climate.

Santa Catarina Tlaltempan, town (1990 pop. 683), Puebla, central Mexico, 26 mi/42 km E of Izúcar de Matamoros; 18°37'N 98°05'W. Elev. 4,951 ft/1,509 m. Corn, sugarcane, fruit.

Santa Catarina Yosonotú (SAHN-tah kah-tah-REE-nah yo-so-no-TOO), town (1990 pop. 271), W Oaxaca, Mexico, 19 mi/30 km S of Tlaxiaco; 16°59'N 97°39'W. Elev. 7,425 ft/2,263 m. Activities are cattle and agr. cultivation. Also known as Santa Catarina Yaosonotu.

Santa Catarina Zapoquila (SAHN-tah kah-tah-REE-nah zah-po-KEE-lah), town (1990 pop. 423), NW Oaxaca, Mexico, near the Puebla state border, and 24 mi/38 km NNE of Huajuapam de León; 18°04'N 97°35'W. Elev. 9,505 ft/2,897 m. A mountainous region in the basin of the Mixteco R. Agr. (corn, beans, fruits, mezcal); textiles.

Santa Clara, city (1994 est. pop. 217,000), ⊙ Villa Clara prov., central Cuba; 22°24'N 79°58'W. Communications and commercial center at major RR and highway junctions; airport. Mfg. (household appliances, textiles; military plant). Cattle raising was the traditional industry until the 19th cent., when sugarcane became important. Tobacco processing and trading are carried on here. Captured by Castro's guerrilla forces in late 1958. Founded 1689.

Santa Clara (SAHN-tah KLAH-rah), town (1990 pop. 4,358), Durango, N Mexico, on affluent of Aguanaval R., and 90 mi/145 km ENE of Victoria Dr. Durango; 24°29'N 103°20'W. Grain, cotton, vegetables; livestock.

Santa Clara, county (□ 1,291 sq mi/3,344 sq km; 1990 pop. 1,497,577), W Calif.; ⊙ SAN JOSE; 37°14'N 121°42'W. Includes N part of rich fruit and vegetable growing SANTA CLARA VALLEY, extending SE from San Francisco Bay bet. Diablo Range (E; includes Mt. HAMILTON) and Santa Cruz Mts. (W). Drained by Coyote, Los Gatos, and Guadalupe creeks. San Francisquito Creek forms NW boundary. Grapes, peppers, lettuce, tomatoes, Oriental vegetables, onions, garlic, beans, nursery prods., mushrooms, flowers, strawberries, cherries; dairying; cattle; eggs, poultry; wheat, barley, oats, corn, and other tree fruits; mfg. of magnesium, agr. machinery, canning and packing equip., chemicals, printing, computer circuits. Working of cement, clay, sand and gravel, quicksilver deposits. Palo Alto (Stanford), Santa Clara (Santa Clara Univ.) are educational centers. Henry W. Coe State Park in SE; part of Castle Rock State Park on W boundary. Formed 1850.

Santa Clara, pueblo (□ 2 sq mi/5.2 sq km; 1990 pop. 1,156), Rio Arriba co., N N.Mex., 21 mi/34 km NNW of Santa Fe, on the Rio Grande in E end of Santa Clara Indian Reservation; 35°58'N 106°05'W. Its inhabitants are Pueblo of the Tanoan linguistic family. Having their own elected govt., the residents farm, raise cattle, or work at nearby Los Alamos. Some are noted painters and pottery makers. Near Santa Clara are Puye ruins, consisting of the remains of a pueblo (abandoned c.1700) with intricate architecture. The 1990 pop. of reservation is 10,193; pueblo, or village is only part of total.

Santa Clara 1 city (1990 pop. 93,613), Santa Clara co., W Calif., suburb 2 mi/3.2 km WNW of downtown San Jose and adjoining San Jose; 37°22'N 121°58'W. At SE end of the Silicon Valley high-tech mfg. complex, the city produces a variety of goods; diversified mfg. Santa Clara was developed as a fruit-processing center, and some agr. still remains important. Points of interest include the Santa Clara de Asís Mission, founded in 1777; and Great Amer. amusement park is in N. The Univ. of Santa Clara (1851), the oldest univ. in Calif., is in the city. Moffett Field Naval Air Station to N. Inc. 1852. **2** uninc. city (1990 pop. 12,834), Lane co., W Oregon, residential suburb 4 mi/6.4 km NNW of Eugene, on Willamette R.; 44°06'N 123°07'W. RR yards. Poultry; dairying; nurseries; grain, berries, fruit, grapes. Mahlon Sweet Airport to NW. Fern Ridge L. reservoir to W.

Santa Clara, town (1990 pop. 2,322), Washington co., SW Utah, 4 mi/6.4 km NW of St. George, and on Santa Clara R.; 37°07'N 113°39'W. Elev. 2,800 ft/853 m. Cattle; orchards. Settled 1854 as cotton-growing center. Shivwits Indian Reservation to W; Snow Canyon State Park to N; Beaver Dam Wilderness Area to SW.

Santa Clara Bay, inlet, NW Cuba, Matanzas prov., 15 mi/24 km E of Cárdenas, and flanked N by the Cayos de las Cinco Leguas; 15 mi/24 km long, 4 mi/6.4 km wide; 23°05'N 80°30'W.

Santa Clara del Cobre (SAHN-tah KLAH-rah DEL KO-bre), town (1990 pop. 9,852), ⊙ Salvador Escalante municipio, Michoacán, central Mexico, 9 mi/14 km S of Pátzcuaro; 19°24'N 101°34'W. Agr. center (cereals, coffee, tropical fruit, sugarcane). Formerly Villa Escalante.

Santa Clara Huitziltepec (SAHN-tah KLAH-rah weet-SEEL-te-pek), town (1990 pop. 2,041), Puebla, central Mexico, 29 mi/47 km SE of Puebla; 18°46'N 97°52'E. Cereals, vegetables.

Santa Clara Ocoyucan (SAHN-tah KLAH-rah o-ko-YOO-kahn), town (1990 pop. 3,321), Puebla, central Mexico, 8 mi/12.9 km SW of Puebla; 18°58'N 98°17'E. Cereals, fruit; livestock.

Santa Clara River 1 c.65 mi/105 km, Los Angeles and Ventura cos., S Calif.; rises in N central Los Angeles co., at Soledad Pass (3,225 ft/983 m), c.30 mi/48 km N of Los Angeles; flows W and SW bet. San Gabriel Mts. (S) and Sierra Madre (N), past Fillmore and Santa Paula, to the Pacific 3 mi/4.8 km SW of Ventura. Flow is intermittent. Its wide delta plain is chief agr. area of Ventura co.; upper valley has citrus-fruit groves, oil and gas fields. **2** c.50 mi/80 km, SW Utah; rises in N Washington co., in Dixie Natl. Forest; flows SSW through Gunlock Reservoir, then SE past Santa Clara town, joins Virgin R. at St. George, near Ariz. state line.

Santa Clara River, Mexico: see CARMEN RIVER.

Santa Clara River Valley, Calif.: see SANTA CLARA RIVER.

Santa Clara Valley, in Santa Clara and San Benito cos., W Calif., S extension of San Francisco Bay depression, stretching c.75 mi/121 km SE from bay shore, bet. Santa Cruz Mts. and Gabilan Range (W) and Diablo Range

(E), to point where ranges converge; 15 mi/24 km wide in N. Drained by Coyote Creek and short Guadalupe Creek in N; S of Gilroy, where Pajaro R. valley breaks mt. barrier to W separating Santa Cruz (N) and Gabilan (S) ranges; valley's S sect. is given local names (San Juan Valley, San Benito Valley). Fertile irrigated agr. region; tree fruits, vegetables, strawberries, grapes, nursery prods.; dairying; poultry, cattle. Better known now as Silicon Valley because of concentration of computer industry.

Santa Clarita, city (1990 pop. 110,642), Los Angeles co., S Calif., suburb 30 mi/48 km NW of downtown Los Angeles, on Santa Clara R.; 34°25′N 118°31′W. Includes areas of North Oaks, Newhall, Solemint and Mint Canyon. Dairying; cattle, poultry; nursery prods. Mfg. (lighting fixtures, motor homes). Seat of Col of the Canyons (2-year.).

Santa Claus 1 (SAN-tuh klaws), town (1990 pop. 154), Toombs co., Ga., 6 mi/9.7 km SE of Vidalia; 32°10′N 82°20′W. **2** town (1990 pop. 927), Spencer co., SW Ind., 16 mi/26 km NNE of Rockport; 38°07′N 86°56′W. Mfg. (television cabinets, office furniture). Its post office annually postmarks and remails large quantities of Christmas letters and parcels. Laid out 1846.

Santa Cruz, town (1991 pop. 8,144), St. Elizabeth parish, SW Jamaica, 29 mi/47 km W of May Pen; 18°04′N 77°43′W. Elev. 1,500 ft/457 m–3,000 ft/914 m. In agr. region (corn, spices; livestock).

Santa Cruz (SAHN-tah KROOS), town (1990 pop. 741), Sonora, NW Mexico, on Santa Cruz R., on RR, and 23 mi/37 km ESE of Nogales; 26°48′N 109°43′W. Livestock raising; beans, wheat.

Santa Cruz, Mexico: see VALLE DEL ROSARIO.

Santa Cruz 1 county (□ 1,238 sq mi/3,206 sq km; 1990 pop. 29,676), S Ariz., on Mex. border; ⊙ Nogales; 31°31′N 110°50′W. Agr. (cattle; hay, alfalfa, cotton); lead, zinc, stone. Patagonia Mts. are in S, part of Santa Rita Mts. in N. Irrigated farming area along Santa Cruz R. Tumacacori Natl. Monument and Tubac Presidio State Historic Park are in W sects. of Coronado Natl. Forest in W, N, and SE, including over ½ of co. land area; Smithsonian Astrophysical (Mt. Hopkins) Observatory W of Mt. Wrightson (9,453 ft/2,881 m), in N. Patagonia L. State Park is in center. Formed 1899, smallest co. in Ariz. **2** county (□ 446 sq mi/1,155 sq km; 1990 pop. 229,734), W Calif.; ⊙ Santa Cruz; 37°02′N 122°01′W. At base of San Francisco–Mateo peninsula, in Santa Cruz Mts.; bounded SW by Pacific Ocean and S by Monterey Bay and Pajaro R. Drained by San Lorenzo R. and short Soquel Creek. Pajaro R. valley produces 90% of county's crops. Co. produces blackberries, raspberries, strawberries, artichokes, cauliflower, lettuce, flowers, apples, mushrooms, nursery prods., celery, and brussel sprouts. Mostly shipped from Watsonville. Farm-prods. packing and processing industries (one of country's leading frozen food processors); fisheries; cement, clay, sands, granite, gravel, limestone quarrying. Contains beach, mt. resorts; New Brighton State Beach in S; Sunset State Beach in SE; Big Basin Redwoods State Park in NW; Forrest of Nisene Marks State Park in NE. Formed 1850.

Santa Cruz, city (1990 pop. 49,040), ⊙ Santa Cruz co., W Calif., 23 mi/37 km SSW of San Jose, on the N shore of Monterey Bay, Pacific Ocean; 36°58′N 122°02′W. Surrounded by hills and redwoods, the city is a seaside city with many fine beaches. The huge municipal wharf (built in 1913) is one of its most popular attractions. Diversified mfg. Points of interest include a replica of a mission est. here in 1791. The Univ. of Calif. at Santa Cruz is here. The city sustained much damage as a result of the 1989 earthquake that hit N Calif. New Brighton State Beach is here. Forest of Nisene Marks to NE; Big Basin Redwoods State Park to NW. Also Santa Cruz Beach Boardwalk theme park. Inc. 1866.

Santa Cruz, uninc. town (1990 pop. 2,504), Santa Fe co., N N.Mex., 21 mi/34 km NNW of Santa Fe, on Rio Grande; 35°59′N 106°01′W. Sangre de Cristo Mts. to E in Santa Clara Pueblo land grant; elev. 5,652 ft/1,723 m. Fruit; cattle, sheep; corn, wheat, alfalfa, oats, millet, barley, chilies. Santa Cruz Reservoir to E; Nambe and Pojoaque pueblos to SE; parts of Santa Fe Natl. Forest to E and W. Formed by Diego de Vargas in 1695. It was the 2d "villa" formally decreed by Spain, the 1st was in Santa Fe.

Santa Cruz, U.S. V.I.: see SAINT CROIX, isl.

Santa Cruz Acatepec (SAHN-tah KROOS ah-KAH-te-pek), town (1990 pop. 898), N Oaxaca, Mexico, 14 mi/22 km ENE of Teotitlán de Flores Magón, on paved road; 18°10′N 96°55′W. Elev. 8,432 ft/2,570 m. Mountainous terrain. Temperate climate.

Santa Cruz Amilpas (SAHN-tah KROOS ah-MEEL-pahs), town (1990 pop. 4,154), central Oaxaca, Mexico, N suburb of Oaxaca de Juárez. Elev. 5,427 ft/1,654 m. Temperate climate. Agr. Good roads.

Santa Cruz Atizapán (SAHN-tah KROOS ah-tee-sah-PAHN), town (1990 pop. 4,540), ⊙ Atizapán municipio, Mexico state, central Mexico, 13 mi/21 km SE of Toluca de Lerdo. Cereals; livestock. Sometimes Atizapán.

Santa Cruz de Barahona (SAHN-tah KROOS dai bah-rah-HO-nah), city (1993 pop. 61,600), SW Dominican Republic, on Neiba Bay, an arm of the Caribbean Sea; 18°10′N 71°15′W. Provincial capital and a port. It has a sugar industry and is a commercial and processing center for an agr. region.

Santa Cruz de Bravo (SAHN-tah kroos de BRAH-vo), town (1990 pop. 521), extreme W Oaxaca, Mexico, on the Guerrero state border, 34 mi/55 km SW of Huajuapam de León; 17°35′N 98°15′E. Elev. 4,265 ft/1,300 m. Temperate climate. Agr. (fruits, mezcal); handmade textiles. Undeveloped roads. The total pop. of the municipality live here.

Santa Cruz de Bravo, Mexico: see FELIPE CARRILLO PUERTO.

Santa Cruz de Galeana, Mexico: see SANTA CRUZ DE JUVENTINO ROSAS.

Santa Cruz de Juventino Rosas (SAHN-tah KROOS de hoo-ven-TEE-no RO-sahs), city (1990 pop. 29,828) and township, ⊙ Santa de Cruz de Juventino Rosas, Guanajuato, central Mexico, on central plateau, 14 mi/23 km NW of Celaya; 20°38′N 100°59′W. Agr. center (wheat, corn, alfalfa, beans, sugarcane, cotton, fruit; livestock). Santa Cruz de Galeana until 1938. Sometimes Juventino Rosas.

Santa Cruz de Rosales, Mexico: see ROSALES.

Santa Cruz del Norte (SAHN-tuh KROOS dail NOR-tai), town (1990 pop. 1,735), La Habana prov., N Cuba, on the Straits of Florida, on RR, and 27 mi/43 km E of Havana; 23°11′N 81°56′W. Sugar milling and refining, distilling, sunflower-oil pressing. Airfield. The sugar mill Camilo Cienfuegos is 2 mi/3.2 km SSW.

Santa Cruz del Seibo, Dominican Republic: see SEIBO.

Santa Cruz del Sur (SAHN-tah KROOS dail SOOR), town, Camagüey prov., E Cuba, minor port on the Gulf of Guacanayabo (arm of the Caribbean Sea), 45 mi/72 km S of Camagüey; 20°43′N 78°00′W. Fishing, fish-canning, and lumbering center. Ships mainly timber (mahogany, cedar). In agr. region (sugarcane, oranges; cattle; beeswax, honey). Sugar centrals are nearby. Destroyed by 1932 hurricane, it was rebuilt just N of its former site. Just W of mouth of Najasa R.

Santa Cruz Island (□ 6 sq mi/15.5 sq km), in Gulf of California, 13 mi/21 km off SE coast of Lower California, NW Mexico, 85 mi/137 km NNW of La Paz; 4 mi/6.4 km long, 1.5 mi/2.4 km wide; 25°19′N 110°42′W. Rises to 1,509 ft/460 m. Part of Islas del Golfo de California Special Biosphere Reserve.

Santa Cruz Island, Calif.: see SANTA BARBARA ISLANDS.

Santa Cruz Itundujia (SAHN-tah kroos ee-toon-doo-HEE-ah), town (1990 pop. 563), SW Oaxaca, Mexico, 22 mi/35 km SE of Putla de Guerrero; 16°52′N 97°39′W. Elev. 7,956 ft/2,425 m. A mountainous region with a cool climate. Agr. (corn, beans, wheat, potatoes, chilies, fruits); woods.

Santa Cruz Mixtepec (SAHN-tah kroos MEEKS-te-pek), town (1990 pop. 1,261), SW Oaxaca, Mexico, 22 mi/35 km SW of Oaxaca de Juárez, and 11 mi/17 km W of Ocotlán de Morelos, in the Valle Grande arm of Oaxaca Valley, on paved road; 16°38′N 96°52′E. Elev.

6,086 ft/1,855 m. Temperate to cold climate. Agr.; wood; pottery; and cattle raising.

Santa Cruz Mountains, W Calif., one of the Coast Ranges, near Pacific Ocean, extending c.70 mi/113 km NW from Pajaro R. at N end of Gabilan Range, along W side of Santa Clara Valley, and up San Francisco–San Mateo peninsula to N San Mateo co. Mt. Bielawski (3,232 ft/985 m) in center. Montana Mt. is NW extension of range, S of San Francisco. San Andreas Fault parallels range on E side.

Santa Cruz Nundaco (SAHN-tah kroos noon-DAH-ko), town (1990 pop. 964), W Oaxaca, Mexico, 9 mi/15 km SSW of Tlaxiaco and 62 mi/100 km NW of Oaxaca de Juárez; 17°10′N 97°44′W. Steep rugged terrain. Temperate to cold climate. Agr. (corn, beans, wheat, mezcal); woods; handmade textiles.

Santa Cruz Papalutla (SAHN-tah kroos pah-pah-LOOT-lah), town (1990 pop. 1,735), SE Oaxaca, Mexico, 9 mi/14 km SE of Oaxaca de Juárez and 9 mi/14 km W of Tlacolula de Matamoros. Elev. 5,427 ft/1,654 m. Agr. (corn, beans, fruits); local textiles; mezcal processing, and poultry breeding.

Santa Cruz River, in Ariz. and Mexico; rises in Patagonia, SE Santa Cruz Mts., S Ariz.; flows S into Sonora, NW Mexico, then N, re-entering Ariz. near Nogales and continuing N past Green Valley to Tucson, where it turns NW, passes S of Casa Grande joining Gila R. 20 mi/32 km S of Phoenix, in Gila R. Indian Reservation. Stream is intermittent. Used for irrigation in Pima co.

Santa Cruz Tacache de Mina (SAHN-tah kroos tah-KAH-che de MEE-nah), town (1990 pop. 2,262), extreme NW Oaxaca, Mexico, 25 mi/40 km W of Huajuapam de León; 17°51′N 98°07′W. Elev. 3,222 ft/982 m. In the Mixteco Bajo, a Mixtec community. Cattle and agr., local handmade textiles and mezcal. No paved roads.

Santa Cruz Tacahua (SAHN-tah kroos tah-KAH-hwah), town (1990 pop. 396), central Oaxaca, Mexico, 53 mi/85 km WSW of Oaxaca de Juárez; 16°56′N 97°30′W. Agr. (cereals, fruits, mezcal); wood; straw textiles.

Santa Cruz Tayata (SAHN-tah kroos tah-YAH-tah), town (1990 pop. 299), N Oaxaca, Mexico 59 mi/95 km NW of Oaxaca de Juárez and 9 mi/15 km NE of Tlaxiaco; 17°22′N 97°34′W. Elev. 7,031 ft/2,143 m. In the Mixteca Alta. Temperate climate. Paved roads.

Santa Cruz Tepexpan (SAHN-tah KROOS te-PESH-pahn), village (1990 pop. 6,455), Jiquipilco municipio, Mexico state, central Mexico, 35 mi/56 km NW of Mexico city; 17°50′N 96°26′W. Cereals; livestock. Here, in the Valley of Mexico, a skull and skeleton of a late Pleistocene-age woman was unearthed in 1948. Sometimes called Tepexpan.

Santa Cruz Tlaxcala (SAHN-tah KROOS tlaks-KAH-lah), town (1990 pop. 6,666), Tlaxcala, central Mexico, on RR, and 6 mi/9.7 km NE of Tlaxcala. Corn, wheat, alfalfa, maguey; livestock.

Santa Cruz Xitla (SAHN-tah kroos ZEE-tlah), town (1990 pop. 2,766), S central Oaxaca, Mexico, 6 mi/9 km W of Miahuatlán de Porfirio Díaz, at W edge of Miahuatlán R. valley; 16°19′N 96°40′W. Elev. 5,938 ft/1,810 m. Temperate climate. Agr. (corn, coffee, sugarcane, beans, fruits); wood. A gravel road connects to the Mexico Highway 125.

Santa Cruz Xoxocotlán (SAHN-tah kroos sho-sho-kot-LAHN), town (1990 pop. 26,849), central Oaxaca, Mexico, 1.2 mi/2 km SW of Oaxaca de Juárez; 17°01′N 96°44′W. Elev. 5,177 ft/1,578 m. Essentially part of Oaxaca de Juárez. Temperate climate. Active commerce with pottery and local textiles.

Santa Cruz Zenzontepec (SAHN-tah kroos zen-ZON-te-pek), town (1990 pop. 438), SW Oaxaca, Mexico, 62 mi/100 km SW of Oaca de Juárez and 31 mi/50 km W of San Miguel Sola de Vega; 16°33′N 97°30′W. Elev. 4,921 ft/1,500 m. Located in the S of the Mixteca region in the Río Verde drainage basin. Cuananá which form the Verde River. Undeveloped roads. A dirt road connects with San Miguel. Temperate climate. Agr. (corn, beans, mangoes).

Santa Elena (SAHN-tah e-LAI-nah), town (1990 pop. 2,516), Yucatán, SE Mexico, 6 mi/9.7 km SW of Ticul; 20°20'N 89°39'W. Henequen, citrus fruits, timber.

Santa Elena, Mexico: see BANAMICHI.

Santa Elena Canyon, Texas and Mexico: see BIG BEND NATIONAL PARK.

Santa Eulalia, Mexico: see AQUILES SERDÁN.

Santa Fe (SAHN-tah FAI), locality, San Pedro de Macorís prov., SE Dominican Republic, 3 mi/4.8 km NE of San Pedro de Macorís city. Sugar mill.

Santa Fe, county (□ 1,910 sq mi/4,947 sq km; 1990 pop. 98,928), N central N.Mex.; ⊙ Santa Fe; 35°30'N 105°58'W. Livestock grazing and agr. (corn, hay, alfalfa, apples, chilies, wheat, oats, barley, millet); pumice, sand and gravel; timber; gypsum; mining (lead, zinc, coal, gold, silver) in vicinity of Santa Fe. Drained NW by the Rio Grande. Includes parts of Santa Fe Natl. Forest in NW and NE; part of Sangre de Cristo Mts. in NE; Pueblo Indian area in N; part of Bandelier Natl. Monument in NW; El Cuervo Butte (6,947 ft/2,117 m) in SE corner; Pojoaque, Nambe, San Ildefonso, and Tesuque pueblos in N; Hyde Memorial State Park in NE; Part of Glorieta Mesa in E. Formed 1852. Part of co. (□ 13 sq mi/34 sq km) was used to form (1949) part of Los Alamos co.

Santa Fe, city (1990 pop. 55,859), ⊙ N.Mex. and of Santa Fe co., N N.Mex., 59 mi/95 km NE of Albuquerque, at the foot of the Sangre de Cristo Mts.; 35°40'N 105°57'W. Elev. 7,000 ft/2,134 m. It is an administrative, tourist, and resort center, and a shipping point for farm prods. and Native Amer. wares; mfg (printing and publishing, furniture, food prods., machinery, concrete, apparel, lumber, sand and gravel, textiles, custom wood doors, soy-based food prods.). Terminus of RR spur from Lamy to S. Founded c.1609 as the 1st Span. "villa," on the site of prehistoric Native Amer. ruins. It was a center of Span. trade with local ethnic groups for over 200 years. A seat of govt. since its founding, it is the oldest capital city in the U.S. In the Pueblo revolt of 1680, the Span. colonists were driven out; in 1692 they returned under Diego de Vargas. Shortly after Mexico gained independence from Spain (1821), extensive commerce with the U.S. developed by way of the Santa Fe Trail. In 1846, the region became a prov. of the U.S. The RR reached Lamy (the station for Santa Fe, 16 mi/26 km distant) in 1879. The seat of an archbishopric since 1875, the city, with its many churches, is a R.C. center. Points of interest are the Palace of the Governors (c.1610), which houses a state mus. and fine arts mus.; Laboratory of Anthropology; Inst. of Amer. Indian Arts, Mus. of Internatl. Folk Art, and Mus. of Indian Arts and Culture. Also in the city are artists' and writers' colonies, an opera house, St. John's Col., the Col. of Santa Fe, a Native Amer. school, and a state school for the deaf. The city is the hq. for the Santa Fe Natl. Forest as well as regional hq. for the Natl. Park Service. Parts of Santa Fe Natl. Forest to E and W; San Miguel Mission Natl. Historic Landmark; Hyde Memorial State Park to NE; Santa Fe Ski Area at Santa Fe Baldy Peak in NE; St. Francis Cathederal; Santa Fe Opera to N; Santa Fe Downs Racetrack and Santa Fe Co. Municipal Airport to SW; Santa Fe R. State Park in city; children's mus.; Rodeo grounds in SW.

Santa Fe, town (1990 pop. 8,429), Galveston co., SE Texas, suburb 11 mi/18 km W of Texas City, and 30 mi/48 km SSE of Houston; 29°22'N 95°05'W. Drained by Highland Bayou. Oil and natural gas. Agr. (cattle; soybeans, rice). Mfg. (valves and well head equip., boat trailers, wooden doors).

Santa Fe (SAN-tuh FAI), uninc. rural community, Monroe co., NE central Mo., on South Fork of Salt R., and 12 mi/19 km SE of Paris. Mark Twain State Park to N; Mark Twain L. to N.

Santa Fe Affiliated Area (san-tuh FAI), national park, Mo., Kansas, Okla., Col., N.Mex. Authorized 1987. Traces route of famous Sante Fe Trail.

Santa Fe Baldy, peak (12,622 ft/3,847 m), in SW Sangre de Cristo Mts., NE Santa Fe co., N central N.Mex., 15 mi/24 km NE of Santa Fe, in Santa Fe Natl. Forest; 35°49'N 105°45'W. Also called Baldy Peak.

Santa Fe Dam, Calif.: see SAN GABRIEL RIVER.

Santa Fe Lake (san-tah FAI), c.5 mi/8 km long, N central Fla., on Alachua-Bradford co. line, 15 mi/24 km ENE of Gainesville. Source of Santa Fe R.

Santa Fe Railroad, chartered in 1863 as the Atchison, Topeka, and Santa Fe RR; opened to traffic in 1864. Construction continued and, in 1880 it reached Santa Fe, N.Mex., essentially following the historic Santa Fe Trail and displacing it; the following year the RR connected with the Southern Pacific RR to form the country's 2d transcontinental line. The RR acquired several small lines, and further construction followed; by the early 1890s the Santa Fe, with its 9,000 mi/14,484 km of track and connections to Chicago and Los Angeles, became one of the world's longest RR systems. Poor management and a reckless dividend policy combined with the depression of 1893, however, to bankrupt the RR company, which in 1895 was reorganized as the Atchison, Topeka and Santa Fe RR Company. In the 20th cent. the RR increased its holdings. Santa Fe has since merged with Burlington Northern.

Santa Fe River (san-tah-FAI), c.65 mi/105 km long, N central Fla.; rises in Santa Fe L. on Alachua-Bradford co. line; flows generally W to Suwannee R.

Santa Fe Springs, city (1990 pop. 15,520), Los Angeles co., SW Calif., suburb 13 mi/21 km SE of downtown Los Angeles; 33°56'N 118°04'W. Inc. 1957. The city lies in a growing and developing oil and natural-gas region. Diversified mfg.

Santa Fe Trail, important caravan route of the W U.S., extending c.780 mi/1,255 km from Independence, Mo., SW to Santa Fe, N.Mex. Independence and Westport, Mo., were the chief points where wagons, teams, and supplies were obtained. From there, the trail led 150 mi/241 km SW to Council Grove, Kansas, which was the main wagon train organization point. Crossing the Kansas plains to the Arkansas R., the trail then followed the river to its fork near Dodge City, Kansas. The Mountain Div. of the trail in the N continued to hug the river W to Bents Fort (now a natl. historic site); turning S, it passed over its most rugged part, including the Raton Pass. The Cimarron or Cutoff Div. of the trail in the S, a more direct route, crossed the Great Plains from the Arkansas R. to Fort Union, N.Mex., where it rejoined the N route. Although less rugged, the S route was dry, with poor grass and little wildlife. By the early 19th cent. small trapping parties had reached Santa Fe, then under Span. rule; but they were forbidden to trade. In Nov. 1821, William Becknell, a trader, returned with news that Mexico was free and Santa Fe welcomed trade. Early in 1822 he left Mo. for Santa Fe with the 1st party of traders. From then on, annual wagon caravans, usually leaving in early summer, made the 40–60-day trip over the trail and returned after a 4–5-week stay in Santa Fe. An increasing amount of goods was taken to Santa Fe each year. In 1850 a monthly stage line was started bet. Independence and Santa Fe over the N route. In 1880 the Santa Fe RR reached Santa Fe, which marked the death of the trail.

Santa Gertrudis (SAHN-tah her-TROO-dees), town (1990 pop. 2,745), S central Oaxaca, Mexico, 22 mi/35 km SW of Oaxaca de Juárez, in the Valle Grande arm of Oaxaca Valley, on Mexico Highway 131; 16°46'N 96°46'W. Elev. 5,249 ft/1,600 m. Temperate climate. Agr. (corn, beans, coffee, sugarcane, fruits, mezcal); woods.

Santa Inés Ahuatempan (SAHN-tah ee-NES ah-wah-TEM-pahn), town (1990 pop. 3,360), ⊙ Ahuatempan municipio, Puebla, central Mexico, on central plateau, 45 mi/72 km SSE of Puebla; 18°25'N 98°01'W. Elev. 5,938 ft/1,810 m. Corn, sugarcane, fruit; livestock. A Native Popoluca community. Sometimes Ahuatempan.

Santa Inés de Zaragoza (SAHN-tah ee-NES de zah-rah-GO-zah), town (1990 pop. 142), W Oaxaca, Mexico, 31 mi/50 km WNW of Oaxaca de Juárez; 17°16'N 97°05'W. Steep terrain. Temperate climate. Resources are agr. and cattle raising. No paved roads. Formerly Zaragoza.

Santa Inés del Monte (SAHN-tah ee-NES del MON-te), town (1990 pop. 765), S central Oaxaca, Mexico, at the edge of the Valle Grande arm of Oaxaca Valley; 16°56'N 96°51'W. Elev. 7,874 ft/2,400 m. Farming, mainly for subsistence.

Santa Inés Yatzeche (SAHN-tah ee-NES yaht-ZE-che), town (1990 pop. 1,325), E Oaxaca, Mexico, on RR, 6 mi/9 km W of Ocotlán de Morelos, in the Valle Grande arm of the Oaxaca Valley; 17°13'N 96°13'W. Elev. 5,495 ft/1,675 m. Farming, mainly for subsistence.

Santa Inés Zacatelco, Mexico: see ZACATELCO.

Santa Isabel, Cuba: see COLORADOS, LOS.

Santa Isabel, Mexico: see GENERAL TRÍAS.

Santa Isabel (SAHN-tah ee-sah-BEL), town (1990 pop. 19,318), S P.R., near the coast, 14 mi/23 km ESE of Ponce. Beach resort, tourism. Airport just E.

Santa Isabel Cholula (SAHN-tah ee-sah-BEL cho-LOO-lah), town (1990 pop. 1,577), Puebla, central Mexico, 13 mi/21 km WSW of Puebla; 19°00'N 98°22'W. Cereals; livestock.

Santa Isabel Tetlatlahuca, Mexico: see TETLATLAHUCA.

Santa Lucía Chico, Arroyo (SAHN-tah loo-SEE-ah CHEE-ko, ah-ROI-o), river, 70 mi/113 km long, Florida dept., S central Uruguay; rises in the Cuchilla Grande Interior 2 mi/3.2 km W of Cerro Colorado; flows SW and S, past Florida, to Santa Lucía R. 7 mi/11.3 km NNE of Santa Lucía (34°21'S 56°20'W).

Santa Lucía del Camino (SAHN-tah loo-SEE-ah del kah-MEE-no), town (1990 pop. 27,611), central Oaxaca, Mexico, 3.1 mi/5 km E of Oaxaca de Juárez; 16°17'N 96°33'W. Elev. 5,151 ft/1,570 m. Once a separate town, now incorporated within Oaxaca de Juárez.

Santa Lucía Miahuatlán (SAHN-tah loo-SEE-ah mee-ah-waht-LAHN), town (1990 pop. 1,012), S central Oaxaca, Mexico, 10 mi/16 km S of Miahuatlán de Porfirio Díaz; 16°17'N 96°33'W. Temperate climate. Agr. (coffee, cacao, sugarcane, corn, beans, fruits); wood.

Santa Lucía Monteverde (SAHN-tah loo-SEE-ah mon-te-VER-de), town (1990 pop. 263), W central Oaxaca, Mexico, 21 mi/34 km S of Tlaxiaco and 20 mi/32 km ESE of Putla de Guerrero; 16°57'N 97°40'W. Elev. 8,458 ft/2,578 m. A mountainous region with a cold climate. Agr. (corn, beans, potatoes, chilies, wheat, fruits); woods. Dirt road access.

Santa Lucía Ocotlán (SAHN-tah loo-SEE-ah o-kot-LAHN), town (1990 pop. 2,846), SE Oaxaca, Mexico, 3 mi/5 km S of Ocotlán de Morelos, on Mexico Highway 175. Elev. 5,085 ft/1,550 m. Temperate climate. Agr. (cereals, fruits, mezcal); woods; cattle.

Santa Lucia Range, Monterey and San Luis Obispo cos., W Calif., in the Coast Ranges, extending c.140 mi/225 km SE along Pacific Ocean coast from SE of Carmel Bay to Cuyama R. and N end of San Rafael Mts. For c.60 mi/97 km in N, it rises steeply from the Pacific; narrow coastal plain boarders S part. Range is W wall of Salinas Valley. Junipero Serra (hoo-nee-PER-o SER-rah) Peak (5,862 ft/1,787 m), 17 mi/27 km W of King City, is highest point. Mt. Carmel (4,417 ft/1,346 m) is 15 mi/24 km SSE of Carmel.

Santa Lucrecia, Mexico: see JESÚS CARRANZA.

Santa Magdalena Jicotlán (SAHN-tah mahg-dah-LAI-nah hee-kot-LAHN), town (1990 pop. 157), in NW Oaxaca, Mexico, 22 mi/35 km E of Huajaupam de León; 17°48'N 97°28'W. Elev. 7,382 ft/2,250 m. Agr. with some fertile soil. Formerly Magdalena Jicotlán.

Santa Margarita, uninc. village, San Luis Obispo co., SW Calif., 9 mi/14.5 km N of San Luis Obispo, near Salinas R. Cattle; fruit, grain, vegetables, flowers, nursery stock. Sect. of Los Padres Natl. Forest, in Santa Lucia Range, to SW; Santa Margarita Reservoir to SE.

Santa Margarita Island (□ 85 sq mi/220 sq km), off Pacific coast of Lower California, NW Mexico, sheltering Magdalena Bay, 47 mi/75 km WNW of Ciudad Constitución; 24 mi/39 km long NW-SE, 2 mi/3.2 km–5 mi/8 km wide. Uninhabited, barren; rises to 1,858 ft/566 m. Magnesite deposits. Sometimes Margarita Isl.

Santa Margarita River, c.50 mi/80 km long, S Calif.; rises in SW Riverside co. c.15 mi/24 km ENE of Temecula; flows SW past Temecula and through Camp Pendleton Marine Corps Base to the Pacific 3 mi/4.8 km NW of Oceanside. Flow is intermittent.

Santa Maria, city (1990 pop. 61,284), Santa Barbara co., S Calif., 52 mi/84 km NW of Santa Barbara, on Santa Maria R., 12 mi/19 km E of Pacific Ocean, near San Luis Obispo Bay; 34°57′N 120°27′W. Elev. 216 ft/66 m. Mfg. (machinery, electronic components, telephone apparatus); vegetables, grain, avocadoes, fruit; cattle; strawberries. A growing city, its pop. nearly doubled bet. 1970 and 1990. The economy is based largely on agr. and oil. Santa Maria, founded in 1874 as Central City, received its present name in 1882. Allan Hancock Col. (2-year) is in the city. Vandenberg Air Force Base is 15 mi/24 km SSW. Twitchell Reservoir to E; Sierra Madre Mts. and Los Padres Natl. Forest to E; Santa Maria Historical Society Mus. is here. Inc. 1905.

Santa Maria, uninc. town, Maricopa co., central Ariz., residential suburb 7 mi/11.3 km WSW of downtown Phoenix, on Salt R. Gila R. Indian Reservation to S.

Santa Maria, uninc. village (1990 pop. 210), Cameron co., extreme S Texas, 25 mi/40 km WNW of Brownsville. In irrigated agr. area, S end of Willacy Canal.

Santa María, Mexico: see CUAJINICUILAPA.

Santa María Alotepec (SAHN-tah mah-REE-ah ah-LO-te-pek), town (1990 pop. 911), E central Oaxaca, Mexico, 44 mi/72 km ENE of Tlacoluch de Matamoros; 17°05′N 45°51′W. Elev. 8,858 ft/2,700 m. Steep terrain in the Papaloapan R. drainage basin. Cool climate. Agr. (cereals, fruits), woods. No paved roads. A Mixe-speaking community.

Santa María Apazco (SAHN-tah mah-REE-ah ah-PAHS-ko), town (1990 pop. 617), NW Oaxaca, Mexico, on a gravel road, 15 mi/24 km NNE of Asunción Nochistlan, and 43 mi/70 km NW of Oaxaca de Juárez; 17°38′N 97°07′W. Elev. 5,978 ft/1,822 m. A mountainous region. Subsistence farming.

Santa María Asunción Tlaxiaco, Mexico: see HEROICA CIUDAD DE TLAXIACO.

Santa María Atzompa (SAHN-tah mah-REE-ah aht-ZOM-pah), town (1990 pop. 3,345), S central Oaxaca, Mexico, 4 mi/7 km NW of Oaxaca de Juárez; 17°06′N 96°47′W. Farming community increasingly impacted by expansion of Oaxaca urban area.

Santa María Ayoquezco, Mexico: see AYOQUEZCO DE ALDAMA.

Santa María Azompa, Mexico: see SANTA MARÍA ATZOMPA.

Santa María Camotlán (SAHN-tah mah-REE-ah kahmot-LAHN), town (1990 pop.1,693), NW Oaxaca, Mexico, 9 mi/15 km NE of Huajuapam de León, and just off Mexico Highway 125; 17°54′N 97°41′W. Elev. 4,626 ft/1,410 m. Temperate climate. Agr. (corn, beans, sugarcane, fruits, mezcal); woods; cattle, and poultry raising.

Santa María, Cayo (SAHN-tah mah-REE-ah, KEI-yo), narrow key, off Villa Clara prov., N Cuba, 26 mi/42 km ENE of Caibarién; 8 mi/12.9 km long; 23°39′N 79°00′W.

Santa María Chachoapam (SAHN-tah mah-REE-ah chah-cho-ah-PAHM), town (1990 pop.466), NW Oaxaca, Mexico, 50 mi/80 km NW of Oaxaca de Juárez and 6 mi/9 km NW of Asunción Nochixtlán; 17°33′N 97°18′W. Elev. 5,906 ft/1,800 m. Temperate climate. Agr. (coffee, wheat, corn, beans and fruits); forestry and pottery. Unpaved roads.

Santa María Chigmecatitlán, Mexico: see CHIGMECATITLÁN.

Santa María Chilapa de Díaz (SAHN-tah mah-REE-ah chee-LAH-pah de DEE-ahs), town (1990 pop. 1,457), NW Oaxaca, Mexico, 19 mi/30 km SE of Huajuapam de León; 17°31′N 97°41′W. Elev. 5,709 ft/1,740 m. A mountainous region in Mixteco R. drainage basin. Temperate climate. Agr. resources are cereals, processing mezcal, and woods.

Santa María Chilchotla (SAHN-ta mah-REE-ah chee-CHO-tlah), town (1990 pop. 780), far N central Oaxaca, Mexico, 17 mi/28 km NE of Teotitlán de Flores Magín; 18°14′N 96°50′W. Agr. (corn, beans, wheat, potatoes, fruits, vegetables); woods; cattle and poultry raising. Temperate to cold climate. Unpaved roads. In Mazatec-speaking area.

Santa María Chimalapa (SAHN-tah mah-REE-ah chee-MAHL-pah), town (1990 pop. 2,272), far E Oaxaca, Mexico, 24 mi/38 km E of Matias Romero; 16°55′N 94°41′W. Steep rugged terrain. Hot climate. A large municipio, mainly in the Coatzacoalcos R. basin. Resources are agr. and forestry. Gravel roads go the SW connecting with the Trans-Isthmian Highway (185). A Zoque-speaking community.

Santa María Cohetzala (SAHN-tah mah-REE-ah ko-et-SAH-lah), town (1990 pop. 701), ⊙ Cohetzala municipio, Puebla, central Mexico, on affluent of Atoyac R., and 37 mi/60 km SW of Izúcar Matamoros; 18°11′N 98°49′W. Corn; livestock.

Santa María Colotepec (SAHN-tah mah-REE-ah ko-LO-te-pek), town (1990 pop. 947), extreme S Oaxaca, Mexico, 9 mi/15 km ENE of Puerto Escondido on the Pacific coast, in Pacific Coastal Lowlands, on Colotemec R., 7 mi/12 km N of Mexico Highway 200; 15°53′N 96°55′W. Elev. 328 ft/100 m. Hot climate. On gravel road. Subsistence farming.

Santa María Coronango (SAHN-tah mah-REE-ah ko-ro-NAHNG-go), town (1990 pop. 9,229), ⊙ Coronango municipio, Puebla, central Mexico, on RR, and 8 mi/12.9 km NW of Puebla; 19°07′N 98°17′W. Elev. 7,283 ft/2,220 m. Cereals, maguey; livestock.

Santa María Cortijo (SAHN-tah mah-REE-ah kor-TEE-ho), town (1990 pop. 935), extreme SW Oaxaca, Mexico, on Pacific Coastal Lowland, 6 mi/10 km W of the border of the state of Guerrero, 17 mi/28 km WNW of Santiago Pinotepa Nacional, and 3 mi/5 km from Mexico Highway 200; 16°26′N 98°14′W. Elev. is near sea level. A tropical dry forest with a hot and seasonally humid climate. Subsistence farming. Also known as Santa María Cortijos.

Santa María Coyomeapan (SAHN-tah mah-REE-ah ko-yo-me-AH-pahn), town (1990 pop. 1,566), Puebla, central Mexico, in Sierra Madre, 30 mi/48 km SE of Tehuacán; 18°16′N 96°59′W. Corn, sugarcane, fruit; livestock.

Santa María Coyotepec (SAHN-tah mah-REE-ah ko-YO-te-pek), town (1990 pop. 877), central Oaxaca, Mexico, 7 mi/12 km S of Oaxaca de Juárez; 16°57′N 96°41′W. Agr.

Santa María de la Asunción Tlaxiaco, Mexico: see HEROICA CIUDAD DE TLAXIACO.

Santa María de los Ángeles (SAHN-tah mah-REE-ah dai los AHN-he-les), town (1990 pop. 841), Jalisco, W Mexico, on N affluent of Santiago R., and 4 mi/6.4 km N of Colotlán; 22°11′N 103°14′W. Elev. 5,725 ft/1,745 m. Grain, vegetables; livestock.

Santa María de Otáez, Mexico: see OTÁEZ.

Santa María del Monte (SAHN-tah mah-REE-ah DEL MON-tai), town (1990 pop. 1,550), ⊙ Vicente Guerrero municipio, Puebla, E Mexico, in Sierra Madre, 13 mi/21 km NE of Tehuacán; 19°17′N 99°50′W. Elev. 8,399 ft/2,560 m. Cereals, sugarcane; livestock.

Santa María del Oro 1 (SAHN-tah mah-REE-ah DEL O-ro), town (1990 pop. 5,151), ⊙ El Oro municipio, Durango, N Mexico, 60 mi/97 km N of Santiago Papasquiaro; 25°56′N 105°19′W. Elev. 6,135 ft/1,870 m. Livestock; silver, gold, lead, copper mining; metallurgical plants. **2** town (1990 pop. 3,024), Nayarit, W Mexico, near Pacific coast, 20 mi/32 km ESE of Tepic. Corn, beans, sugarcane; cattle, hogs. Silver deposits nearby.

Santa María del Oro, Mexico: see MANUEL M. DIÉGUEZ.

Santa María del Río (SAHN-tah mah-REE-ah del REE-0), city (1990 pop. 9,598) and township, San Luis Potosí, N central Mexico, in Sierra Madre Oriental, on Mexico Highway 57, 30 mi/48 km SE of San Luis Potosí; 21°48′N 100°44′W. Elev. 5,587 ft/1,703 m. Agr. center (grain, cotton, fruit; livestock). Cinnabar deposits.

Santa María del Rosario (SAHN-tah mah-REE-ah del ro-SAHR-ee-o), town, Ciudad de la Habana prov., W Cuba, on Natl. Highway, and 8 mi/12.9 km SE of Havana; 23°05′N 82°16′W. Dairying, sugar growing. Has asphalt deposits and mineral springs. Noted for its richly decorated church.

Santa María del Rosario (SAHN-tah mah-REE-ah del ro-SAH-ree-o), town (1990 pop. 108), W Oaxaca, Mexico, 8 mi/13 km NNE of Tlaxiaco, just E of Mexico

Santa María del Tule (SAHN-tah mah-REE-ah DEL TOO-lai), town (1990 pop. 6,028), Oaxaca, S Mexico, in Oaxaca Valley, 7 mi/11 km E of Oaxaca, on Inter-Amer. Highway (190); 17°02′N 96°37′W. Elev. 5,151 ft/1,570 m. Cereals, fruit, sugarcane. Famous for its great cypress tree (*Taxodium mucronatum*), reputed to be world's largest tree, c.131 ft/40 m in ht. and 138 ft/42 m in circumference; was worshipped by Zapotecs as god of growth.

Santa María Ecatepec (SAHN-tah mah-REE-ah ek-AH-te-pek), town (1990 pop. 578), SW Oaxaca, Mexico, 48 mi/78 km WNW of the port of Salina Cruz; 16°07′N 95°53′W. Elev. 5,545 ft/1,690 m. A mountainous dry region. Temperate to hot climate. Agr. (corn, beans, fruits); woods. Gravel road connects to the Inter-Amer. Highway (190).

Santa María Guelacé (SAHN-tah mah-REE-ah ge-lah-SE), town (1990 pop. 656), central Oaxaca, Mexico, in Tlaconuca arm of Oaxaca Valley, on RR, 10 mi/16 km SE of the city of Oaxaca de Juárez; 17°00′N 96°37′W. Elev. 5,413 ft/1,650 m. Agr. Also Santa María Guelaxé.

Santa María Guienagati (SAHN-tah mah-REE-ah gee-e-nah-GAH-tee), town (1990 pop. 947), E Oaxaca, Mexico, on gravel road, 29 mi/47 km N of Santo Domingo Tehuantepec; 16°44′N 95°21′W. Elev. 2,789 ft/850 m. Resources are agr. and cattle raising and breeding.

Santa María Huatulco (SAHN-tah mah-REE-ah hwah-TOOL-ko), town (1990 pop. 1,939), far S Oaxaca, Mexico, on the Pacific coast, 24 mi/38 km ENE of San Pedro Pochutla; 15°51′N 96°19′W. Bahias de Huatulco resort development to SE; airport nearby. Formerly a quiet Zapotec town, now a rapidly growing satellite of nearby resorts.

Santa María Huazolotitlán (SAHN-tah mah-REE-ah hwah-zo-lo-teet-LAHN), town (1990 pop. 4,514), SW Oaxaca, Mexico, 7 mi/12 km ESE of Santiago Pinotepa Nacional, off Mexico Highway 200; 16°18′N 97°55′W.

Santa María Ipalapa (SAHN-tah mah-REE-ah ee-pah-LAH-pah), town (1990 pop. 1,321), SW Oaxaca, Mexico, 11 mi/18 km E of the Guerrero state border, 19 mi/30 km N of Santiago Pinotepa Nacional, and 3 mi/5 km off Mexico Highway 125; 16°38′N 98°02′W. Agr. (corn, beans, coffee, sugarcane, fruits); woods. A mountainous region with a hot climate.

Santa María Ixcatlán (SAHN-tah mah-REE-ah eeks-kaht-LAHN), town (1990 pop. 719), NW Oaxaca, Mexico, 21 mi/35 km SW of Teotitlán de Flores Magón; 17°51′N 97°11′W. Elev. 7,635 ft/2,327 m.

Santa María Jacatepec (SAHN-tah mah-REE-ah hah-KAH-te-pek), town (1990 pop. 958), NE Oaxaca, Mexico, on the Valle Nacional R., in Papaloapan Basin, 17 mi/28 km SSW of Tuxtepec, on Mexico Highway 175; 17°52′N 96°14′W. Elev. 328 ft/100 m. Agr. (corn, beans, lemons, coffee, pineapples, coconuts); cattle and poultry raising. In Chinantec-speaking area.

Santa María Jalapa del Marqués (SAHN-tah mah-REE-ah hah-LAH-pah del mahr-KES), town (1990 pop. 7,686), SE Oaxaca, Mexico, on Benito Juárez Reservoir, 17 mi/28 km WNW of Santo Domingo Tehuantepec, on the Inter-Amer. Highway (190); 16°25′N 95°27′W. Agr. (coffee, corn, beans, fruits); woods.

Santa María Jaltianguis (SAHN-tah mah-REE-ah hahl-tee-AHN-gees), town (1990 pop. 7,686), N central Oaxaca, Mexico, on 4 mi/6 km NW of Ixtlán de Juárez and 5.6 mi/9 km from San Pablo Guelatao, the birthplace of Benito Juárez; 17°22′N 96°32′W. Elev. 2,920 ft/890 m. Temperate climate. Agr.

Santa María Jiotes, Mexico: see SANTA MARÍA LA ASUNCIÓN.

Santa María la Asunción (SAHN-tah mah-REE-ah lah ah-soon-see-ON), town (1990 pop.1,880), ⊙ Oaxaca municipio, far W Oaxaca, Mexico, 12 mi/20 km NNW of Putla de Guerrero; 18°07′N 96°49′W. In the Mixteca Baja. Agr. (cereals, fruits); woods and straw textiles. Also called Santa Maria Jiotes.

Santa María Lachixío (SAHN-tah mah-REE-ah lah-CHEEK-see-o), town (1990 pop. 772), SW Oaxaca,

Mexico, 23 mi/37 km WSW of Ocotlán de Morelos; 16°44′N 97°01′W. Elev. 5,840 ft/1,780 m. A mountainous region with poor soil. Temperate climate. Paved roads.

Santa María, Lake (☐ 30 sq mi/78 sq km), in Chihuahua, N Mexico, 60 mi/97 km SW of Ciudad Juárez (U.S. border); 15 mi/24 km long, 2 mi/3.2 km–4 mi/6.4 km wide. An intermittently dry lake. Receives Santa María R.

Santa María Mixistlán, Mexico: see MIXISTLÁN DE LA REFORMA.

Santa María Mixtequilla (SAHN-tah mah-REE-ah meeks-te-KEE-yah), town (1990 pop. 3,432), in SE Oaxaca, Mexico, on Tehuantepec R., 3.1 mi/5 km N of Santo Domingo Tehuantepec (linked by paved road); 16°22′N 95°18′W. Agr. (corn, beans, coffee, fruits, mezcal); woods and cattle.

Santa María Natívitas 1 (SAHN-tah mah-REE-ah nah-TEE-vee-tahs), town (1990 pop. 8,886), ⊙ Natívitas municipio, Tlaxcala, central Mexico, 8 mi/12.9 km SW of Tlaxcala; 19°20′N 99°47′W. Elev. 6,644 ft/2,025 m. Cereals; livestock. **2** town (1990 pop. 312), NW Oaxaca, Mexico, 14 mi/23 km NNE of San Pedro y San Pablo Teposcolula, and 28 mi/45 km SE of Huajuapam de León; 17°39′N 97°20′W. Elev. 6,644 ft/2,025 m. In the Mixteca Alta. Cold climate. Agr. (corn, beans, wheat, potatoe, mezcal, fruits); cattle and poultry raising. On gravel road.

Santa María Nduayaco (SAHN-tah mah-REE-ah dwah-YAH-ko), town (1990 pop.194), far NW Oaxaca, Mexico, on unpaved road, 16 mi/25 km NE of Tlaxiaco; 17°24′N 97°30′W. Elev. 7,674 ft/2,339 m. Cold to temperate climate. Agr. (corn, beans, wheat, potatoes, fruits, mezcal); handmade fabrics and cattle raising.

Santa María Ozolotepec (SAHN-tah mah-REE-ah o-zo-LO-te-pek), town (1990 pop. 572), S central Oaxaca, Mexico, on the Pacific slope of the Oaxaca Highland, 28 mi/45 km NNE of San Pedro Pochutla; 16°08′N 96°21′W. Elev. 7,349 ft/2,240 m. Temperate to cool climate. Agr. (corn, beans, sugarcane, coffee, lemon, tropical fruits); fine woods and lumber. A gravel road connects to Mexico Highway 175.

Santa María Pápalo (SAHN-tah mah-REE-ah PAH-pah-lo), town (1990 pop. 1,283), NW Oaxaca, Mexico, on unpaved road, 11 mi/17 km ESE of San Juan Bautista Cuicatlán; 17°46′N 96°46′W. Elev. 3,281 ft/1,000 m. RR here. In Río Grande drainage basin. Hot climate. Agr. (corn, beans, coffee, fruits), and woods. Cuicatec-speaking pop.

Santa María Peñoles (SAHN-tah mah-REE-ah pen-YO-les), town (1990 pop. 379), central Oaxaca, Mexico, on Peñoles R., 19 mi/30 km W of Oaxaca de Juárez; 17°05′N 97°00′W. Elev. 6,562 ft/2,000 m. Temperate climate. Agr. (corn, wheat, beans, fruits, mezcal); woods; cattle. Textiles. Access by dirt road.

Santa María Petapa (SAHN-tah mah-REE-ah pe-TAH-pah), town, E Oaxaca, Mexico, 7 mi/11 km SW of Matías Romero; 16°41′N 93°29′W. In the Coatzacoalcos R. drainage basin. Agr. (corn, beans, fruit, coffee); woods. Access by paved road to the RR and the Trans-Isthmian Highway (185).

Santa María Quiegolani (SAHN-tah mah-REE-ah kee-e-go-LAH-nee), town (1990 pop. 888), SE Oaxaca, Mexico, 38 mi/61 km E of Miahuatlán de Porfirio Díaz, and 47 mi/75 km NE of San Pedro Pochutla; 16°15′N 96°02′W. Elev. 5,971 ft/1,820 m. Agr. resources, handmade fabrics, and wood. Access by dirt track.

Santa María Rayón (SAHN-tah mah-REE-ah rai-ON), town (1990 pop. 5,502), Mexico state, central Mexico, on RR, and 12 mi/19 km SSE of Toluca de Lerdo, on Mexico Highway 55; 19°04′N 99°32′W. Cereals; livestock.

Santa María River 1 (SAHN-tah mah-REE-ah), c.200 mi/322 km long, in Chihuahua, N Mexico; rises in Sierra Madre Occidental SW of Bachíniva; flows N, past Namiquipa, Buenaventura, and Galeana, to L. Santa María 70 mi/113 km SW of Juárez. Lower course often dry. Dammed for irrigation N of Cruces (El Tintero Dam). **2** c.200 mi/322 km long, N central and E Mexico; rises in Sierra Madre Oriental S of San Luis

Potosí near Guanajuato border; flows E, past Villa de Reyes and Santa María del Río, near San Luis Potosí–Querétaro border before joining Pánuco R. in fertile La Huasteca plains 50 mi/80 km SW of Tampico. Used for irrigation. Called Tampoán (tahm-po-AHN) in lower course. Receives Río Verde.

Santa Maria River 1 c.50 mi/80 km long, W central Ariz.; intermittent headstream which rises near Sheridan Mt., Prescott Natl. Forest, mt. region W of Prescott in Yavapai co.; flows SW to point near S end of Hualapai Mts., where it joins Big Sandy R. to form Bill Williams R. **2** c.30 mi/48 km, in SW Calif.; formed by joining of Cuyama and Sisquoc rivers, 6 mi/9.7 km SE of Santa Maria, on Santa Barbara–San Luis Obispo co. line; flows NW and W forming co. line, passes Santa Maria to N, to the Pacific Ocean 11 mi/18 km W of Santa Maria. Its valley (c.30 mi/48 km long; up to 10 mi/16 km wide) is oil-producing and has varied farming, including nursery stock and flowers. Santa Maria is chief center.

Santa María Sola (SAHN-tah mah-REE-ah SO-lah), town (1990 pop. 647), SW central Oaxaca, Mexico, in the Sola de Vega judicial dist., 20 mi/32 km W of Ejutla de Crespo and 40 mi/65 km SW of Oaxaca de Juárez. Elev. 5,308 ft/1,618 m; 16°34′N 97°00′W. A mountainous region in the Verde R. basin. Temperate climate. Agr. (cereals, fruits, mezcal); woods; cattle. Textiles, pottery.

Santa María Tataltepec (SAHN-tah mah-REE-ah tah-TAHL-te-pek), town (1990 pop. 494), NW Oaxaca, Mexico, 22 mi/36 km NW of Tlaxiaco; 17°08′N 97°24′W. Elev. 4,101 ft/1,250 m. Mountainous terrain in the Mixteca Alta. Unpaved roads. Agr. (cereals, fruits); wood.

Santa María Tecomavaca (SAHN-tah mah-REE-ah te-ko-mah-VAH-kah), town (1990 pop. 1,558), NW Oaxaca, Mexico, on Salado R., 12 mi/20 km S of Teotitlán de Flores Magón, on Mexico Highway 131 and RR; 17°57′N 97°01′W. Elev. 2,165 ft/660 m. Hot climate. Agr. and straw textiles.

Santa María Temaxcalapa (SAHN-tah mah-REE-ah te-mahks-kah-LAH-pah), town (1990 pop. 885), NE Oaxaca, Mexico, 22 mi/35 km E of Ixtlán de Juárez, and 5 mi/8 km from Villa Alta; 17°23′N 96°10′W. Elev. 3,609 ft/1,100 m. Temperate climate. Agr. Unpaved roads.

Santa María Temaxcaltepec (SAHN-tah mah-REE-ah te-mahks-KAHL-te-pek), town (1990 pop.755), SW Oaxaca, Mexico, 24 mi/38 km NW of Puerto Escondido; 16°10′N 97°13′W. Elev. 3,937 ft/1,200 m. Steep rugged terrain. Warm climate. Agr. (coffee, corn, beans, tropical fruits); cattle; fine woods and lumber. Access by dirt track.

Santa María Teopoxco (SAHN-tah mah-REE-ah te-o-POSH-ko), town (1990 pop. 660), far N Oaxaca, Mexico, 6 mi/9 km NE of Teotitlán de Flores Magón; 18°10′N 96°57′W. Elev. 7,382 ft/2,250 m. Agr.; cattle, and straw textiles. Cool climate.

Santa María Tepantlali (SAHN-tah mah-REE-ah te-pahn-LAH-lee), town (1990 pop. 724), 31 mi/50 km E of Tlacolula de Matamoros; 16°58′N 96°02′W. Elev. 6,102 ft/1,860 m. A mountainous region with a temperate climate. Agr. (corn, beans, wheat, chilies, fruits); woods. Cattle and poultry raising. Unpaved roads. Mixe-speaking community.

Santa María Texcatitlán (SAHN-tah mah-REE-ah teks-kah-teet-TLAHN), town (1990 pop. 1,096), N Oaxaca, Mexico, 9 mi/15 km SW of San Juan Bautista; 17°40′N 97°09′W. Elev. 4,757 ft/1,450 m. Warm climate. Agr.

Santa María Tlahuitoltepec (SAHN-tah mah-REE-ah tlah-wee-TOL-te-pek), town (1990 pop. 2,187), in E central Oaxaca, Mexico, 30 mi/48 km ENE of Tlacolula de Matamoros; 17°04′N 96°03′W. Elev. 7,218 ft/2,200 m. Unpaved roads. Temperate climate. Agr. (corn, beans, potatoes); cattle; forestry. Mixe-speaking community.

Santa María Tlalixtac (SAHN-tah mah-REE-ah tlah-LEEKS-tahk), town (1990 pop. 715), N Oaxaca, Mexico, 27 mi/43 km SE of Teotitlán de Flores Magón; 17°55′N 96°45′W. Elev. 3,775 ft/1,150 m. Unpaved roads. Agr.

Santa María Tocatlán, Mexico: see TOCATLÁN.

Santa María Tonameca (SAHN-tah mah-REE-ah to-nah-ME-kah), town (1990 pop. 955), extreme S Oaxaca, Mexico, 9 mi/15 km NW of Puerto Angel, on the Pacific coast; 15°44′N 96°33′W. Hot climate. Agr.

Santa María Totolapilla (SAHN-tah mah-REE-ah to-to-lah-PEE-yah), town (1990 pop. 929), E Oaxaca, Mexico, in the Tehuantepec R. basin, 28 mi/45 km NW of Santo Domingo Tehuantepec; 16°33′N 95°38′W. Elev. 1,411 ft/430 m. Hot, seasonally humid climate with a dry summer. Access by dirt track.

Santa María Tultepec (SAHN-tah mah-REE-ah TOOL-te-pek), town (1990 pop. 29,524), ⊙ Tultepec municipio, Mexico state, central Mexico, 17 mi/27 km N of Mexico city, and within the Zona Metropolitana de la Ciudad de México; 19°41′N 99°07′W. Elev. 7,221 ft/2,201 m. Grain, maguey; livestock.

Santa María Xadani (SAHN-tah mah-REE-ah zah-DAH-nee), town (1990 pop. 4,871), SE Oaxaca, Mexico, on the Laguna Superior (Gulf of Tehuantepec), 5 mi/8 km S of Juchitán de Zaragoza; 15°56′N 96°04′W. Produce agr. and fishing prods. Operate saltworks. Hot climate.

Santa María Yalina (SAHN-tah mah-REE-ah yah-LEE-nah), town (1990 pop. 403), central Oaxaca, Mexico, 32 mi/54 km NE of Oaxaca de Juárez, and 11 mi/17 km SW of San Ildefonso Villa Alta; 17°15′N 96°16′W. Elev. 5,577 ft/1,700 m. Temperate climate.

Santa María Yavesía (SAHN-to mah-REE-ah yah-ve-SEE-ah), town (1990 pop. 702), central Oaxaca, Mexico, 22 mi/35 km NE of Oaxaca de Juárez, and 8 mi/13 km SSE of Ixtlán; 17°14′N 96°24′W. Elev. 6,955 ft/2,120 m. Agr.

Santa María Yolotepec (SAHN-tah mah-REE-ah yo-LO-te-pek), town (1990 pop. 299), W Oaxaca, Mexico, 30 mi/48 km SSE of Tuaxiaco; 16°53′N 97°30′W. Elev. 6,037 ft/1,840 m. Unpaved roads. Produce agr. and cattle.

Santa María Yosoyúa (SAHN-tah mah-REE-ah yo-so-YOO-ah), town (1990 pop. 611), W Oaxaca, Mexico, 15 mi/24 km SE of Tlaxiaco; 17°10′N 97°38′W. Elev. 5,866 ft/1,788 m. Unpaved roads. In the Mixteca Alta. Temperate climate.

Santa María Yucuhiti (SAHN-tah mah-REE-ah yoo-koo-HEE-tee), town (1990 pop. 417), W Oaxaca, Mexico, 11 mi/18 km E of Putla de Guerrero; 17°01′N 97°46′W. Elev. 5,902 ft/1,799 m. Temperate to hot climate. Agr. (fruits, cereals, mezcal); woods and hand-woven fabrics. Unpaved roads. The pop. is mostly Mixtec Indian.

Santa María Zaachila, Mexico: see VILLA DE ZAACHILA.

Santa María Zacatepec (SAHN-tah mah-REE-ah zah-KAH-te-pek), town (1990 pop. 3,746), far W Oaxaca, Mexico, on Mexico Highway 125, 19 mi/30 km SW of Putla de Guerrero; 16°46′N 97°59′W. Elev. 1,312 ft/400 m. Mountainous terrain. Agr. (corn, beans, coffee, tropical fruits), fine woods and lumber; cattle and dairy prods.; fabrics, and pottery.

Santa María Zaniza (SAHN-tah mah-REE-ah sah-NEE-sah), town (1990 pop. 857), W Oaxaca, Mexico, 51 mi/82 km SW of Oaxaca de Juárez; 16°39′N 97°20′W. Elev. 5,853 ft/1,784 m. Unpaved roads, in one of the most isolated parts of the Oaxaca highland.

Santa María Zoquitlán (SAHN-tah mah-REE-ah so-keet-LAHN), town (1990 pop. 1,997), in S Oaxaca, Mexico, 45 mi/72 km SE of Oaxaca de Juárez; 16°33′N 96°23′W. Elev. 4,324 ft/1,318 m. Mountainous terrain. Temperate to hot climate, depending on the elevation. Agr. (corn, beans, fruits, mezcal); textiles.

Santa Monica, city (1990 pop. 86,905), Los Angeles co., S Calif., 12 mi/19 km W of downtown Los Angeles, on Santa Monica Bay, Pacific Ocean; 34°01′N 118°30′W. Mfg. center. Santa Monica Col. (2-year) and the J. Paul Getty Mus. are located here. Santa Monica Municipal Airport in E. The city has a 3-mi/4.8-km oceanfront beach. Will Rogers State Historical Park and State Beach and Topanga State Park and State Beach to W (both in Pacific Palisades dist.); Santa Monica State Beach in S; Venice City Beach (state beach) to S; Santa Monica Mts. Natl. Recreation Area to W and N; 20th

Century Fox Studios, Beverly Hills, and Hollywood to NE. Inc. 1886.

Santa Mónica Ario, Mexico: see ARIO DE RAYÓN.

Santa Monica Mountains (c.1,000 ft/300 m–3,000 ft/ 915 m), S Calif., an E-W range; c.40 mi/64 km long, c.10 mi/16 km wide. Mts. closely parallel N shore of Santa Monica Bay, Pacific Ocean from Oxnard E to Santa Monica, where they continue inland to Los Angeles R. valley, which connects Los Angeles basin (S of range) with San Fernando Valley (N). Most of range is on Santa Monica Mts. Natl. Recreation Area.

Santa Monica Mountains Natl. Recreation Area (□ 234 sq mi/606 sq km), Los Angeles and Ventura cos., S Calif. Large, rugged landscape with beaches, canyons. Habitats for eagles, hawks, cougars, bobcats. Wildflowers in Spring. Only 10% of park is Federally owned; remainder is comprised of state and co. parks and privately owned land. Authorized 1978.

Santa Paula, city (1990 pop. 25,062), Ventura co., S Calif., on the Santa Clara R. at mouth of Santa Paula Creek; 34°21′N 119°04′W. In a fertile valley that yields citrus fruits, avocados, vegetables, flowers, nursery prods., and walnuts. Fruit packing and oil production are major industries. Mfg. (concrete prods., oil field services, lingerie; paperboard mill). The Union Oil Company, founded in Santa Paula in 1890, operates a notable oil mus. here. Los Padres Natl. Forest to N. Laid out 1875, inc. 1902.

Santa Rita, Mexico: see VILLA HIDALGO, Zacatecas.

Santa Rita, uninc. village (1990 pop. 600), Grant co., SW N.Mex., in foothills of Pinos Altos Mts., 12 mi/ 19 km E of Silver City. Elev. 6,482 ft/1,976 m. Santa Rita Open-Pit Copper Mine engulfed townsite. Once worked by Span. convict labor, was rediscovered 1800. Molybdenum also mined. Black Peak (9,025 ft/2,751 m) is 9 mi/14.5 km NW, Gila Natl. Forest just N.

Santa Rita Mountains, Pima and Santa Cruz cos., SE Ariz., N of Nogales. Mt. Wrightson (9,453 ft/2,881 m) is highest point. Most of range is in sect. of Coronado Natl. Forest.

Santa Rita Tlahuapan (SAHN-tah REE-tah tlah-WAH-pahn), town (1990 pop. 5,198), ⊙ Tlahuapan municipio, Puebla, central Mexico, 30 mi/48 km NW of Puebla; 19°20′N 98°34′W. Cereals, beans, maguey.

Santa Rosa, Mexico: see CIUDAD MENDOZA.

Santa Rosa, county (□ 1,155 sq mi/2,991 sq km; 1990 pop. 81,608), NW Fla., bet. Ga. state line (N) and Gulf of Mexico (S), and bounded W by Escambia R.; ⊙ Milton; 30°41′N 87°01′W. Includes part of Pensacola Bay and Santa Rosa Sound in S. Rolling agr. area (corn, peanuts, cotton, vegetables; livestock), drained by Blackwater and Yellow rivers; also forestry (lumber, naval stores). Formed 1842.

Santa Rosa, city (1990 pop. 113,313), ⊙ Sonoma co., W Calif., 46 mi/74 km NNW of San Francisco and 20 mi/ 32 km NE of Pacific Ocean; 38°27′N 122°42′W. Elev. 169 ft/52 m. RR junction. It is an industrial city and a retail, financial, and medical center for the fertile Sonoma Valley. Diversified light and heavy mfg.; dairying; sheep, poultry; grapes, apples, vegetables, grain, nursery prods. The city's large retail business serves the growing number of residents. Santa Rosa is one of the fastest-growing U.S. cities, marked by a pop. increase of more than 37% bet. 1980 and 1990. Luther Burbank lived here, and his gardens are preserved as a monument. Also of interest is the Church of One Tree, built (1874) from a single redwood, and now housing the Robert L. Ripley Memorial Mus. Sonoma co. Airport to NW. Santa Rosa Junior Col. is in the city and Sonoma State Univ. is to S at Rohnert Park. Codding Mus. of Natural History. In the vicinity are the Jack London "Wolf House" and memorial mus., Armstrong Redwoods State Park and Austin Creek State Recreational Area to NW, and many other state parks and historic and natural attractions. Bothe-Napa Valley State Park to NE; Sugarloaf Ridge State Park to E; Point Reyes Natl. Seashore c.25 mi/40 km to S. Inc. 1868.

Santa Rosa 1 town (1990 pop. 2,263), ⊙ Guadalupe co., E central N.Mex., on Pecos R. and 59 mi/95 km WSW of Tucumcari; 34°56′N 104°40′W. Elev. 4,615 ft/1,407 m.

Light mfg. Shipping point for wool and livestock; trade center; grain, beans, fruit. Copper mines and deposit of asphalt rock in vicinity. Billy the Kid Mus. and U.S. fish hatchery is here. Settled c.1865. Santa Rosa L. State Park to N; Sumner L. Reservoir and State Park (Pecos R.) to SE; site of Coronado's Bridge to S, crossing point on Pecos R. of Coronado Expedition 1542–1545. **2** town (1990 pop. 2,223), Cameron co., extreme S Texas, 34 mi/ 55 km NW of Brownsville, near Willacy Canal. In irrigated agr. area; mfg. (raw sugar processing). Los Palmas State Wildlife Management Area to N.

Santa Rosa, uninc. rural community, De Kalb co., NW Mo., near Grand R., 10 mi/16 km NE of Maysville.

Santa Rosa de Mulegé, Mission, Mexico: see MULEGÉ.

Santa Rosa Island, narrow barrier beach bet. the Gulf of Mexico and Santa Rosa Sound, NW Fla., in the vicinity of Pensacola, extending c.50 mi/80 km parallel to the coast. It is the site of Fort Pickens and of a missile-launching station. The isl. has magnificent beaches and is also a resort area.

Santa Rosa Island, Calif.: see SANTA BARBARA ISLANDS.

Santa Rosa Lake, reservoir (□ 26 sq mi/67 sq km), Guadalupe co., E central N.Mex., on Pecos R., 50 mi/ 80 km SW of Tucumcari; 35°02′N 104°41′W. Max. capacity 719,000 acre-ft. Formed by Santa Rosa Dam (214 ft/65 m high), built (1979) by Army Corps of Engineers for irrigation and debris control. Sumner Lake State Park near dam; grave of Billy the Kid just SW.

Santa Rosa Mountains, S Calif., range along W side of Coachella Valley, extends c.30 mi/48 km SE from S end of San Jacinto Mts. Rises to 3,716 ft/1,133 m at Toro Peak, 22 mi/35 km S of Palm Springs. S part is in Anza-Borrego Desert State Park. Salton Sea to E.

Santa Rosa Range, N Nev., in NE Humboldt co., near Oregon state line, N of Humboldt R.; 41°34′N 117°40′W. Rises to 9,732 ft/2,966 m at Granite Peak, its highest point, and 9,701 ft/2,957 m at Santa Rosa Peak, c.40 mi/ 64 km N of Winnemucca. N ½ is in Humboldt Natl. Forest. Gold is mined; ranching near Paradise Valley. Quinn R. to W. Little Humboldt R. to E.

Santa Rosa Sound, lagoon in NW Fla., sheltered from the Gulf of Mexico by Santa Rosa Isl. (S), opens into Choctawhatchee (E) and Pensacola (W) bays; c.35 mi/ 56 km long, up to 2 mi/3.2 km wide. Forms part of Gulf Intracoastal Waterway.

Santa Rosalía (SAHN-tah ro-sah-LEE-ah), city (1990 pop. 10,190), Baja California Sur, ⊙ Mulegé municipio, NW Mexico, 95 mi/153 km SW of Guaymas across Gulf of California; 27°20′N 112°20′W. Former copper-mining and -smelting center (mines closed in 1985; smelter still operates); fruit growing (dates, figs). Gypsum deposits nearby. Noted for Fr.-influenced architecture.

Santa Susana Mountains, S Calif., short E-W range lying W of San Gabriel Mts., from which it is separated by Newhall Pass, and bet. San Fernando Valley (S) and valley of Santa Clara R. (N).

Santa Teresa, uninc. community, Dona Ana co., S N.Mex., suburb on development with golf and tennis club, 8 mi/12.9 km NW of downtown El Paso, Texas, on Rio Grande (Texas state boundary here) and 3 mi/ 4.8 km N of Mexico (Chihuahua) border. Irrigated agr. area. Mfg. (polyurethane foam, medical instruments, oil field equip.).

Santa Ventia, uninc. town (1990 pop. 3,362), Marin co., W Calif., residential suburb 17 mi/27 km N of downtown San Francisco, at mouth of Gallinas Creek, on San Pablo Bay; 38°01′N 122°30′W. China Camp State Park to E, on Bay. Hamilton Air Force Base to N.

Santa Ynez, uninc. town (1990 pop. 4,200), Santa Barbara co., SW Calif., near Santa Ynez R. (forms L. Cachuma reservoir to E), 25 mi/40 km WNW of Santa Barbara; 34°37′N 120°06′W. Site of Mission Santa Ynez (est. 1804), still in use as a church. Fruit, avocadoes, grain; cattle; vegetables, flowers.

Santa Ynez Mountains, Santa Barbara co., extends E into Ventura co., S Calif., E-W coastal range (c.2,000 ft/ 610 m–4,000 ft/1,219 m) bordering the Pacific (Santa Barbara Channel) for c.75 mi/121 km from Point Arguello (W) to Ventura R. (E), including part of Los Padres Natl. Forest; 34°31′N 119°58′W. Santa Ynez R.

and Lompoc Valley runs E-W along N base. Gaviota Pass (918 ft/280 m) is in W center.

Santa Ynez River, c.75 mi/121 km long, SW Calif.; rises in SE Santa Barbara co., 15 mi/24 km ENE of Santa Barbara, at Ventura co. line; flows W, along N base of Santa Ynez Mts. and through Lompoc Valley, through Jameson, Santa Barbara, and Cochuma reservoirs and past Lompoc to the Pacific Ocean 10 mi/16 km WNW of Lompoc N of Point Arguello and S of Vandenberg Air Force Base. Flow is intermittent. Reservoir formed by Gibraltar Dam (185 ft/56 m high, 1,100 ft/335 m long; completed 1920), which supplies water to Santa Barbara city. Cachuma Dam and reservoir are a U.S. Bureau of Reclamation project.

Santa Ysabel (ee-sah-bel), uninc. village, San Diego co., S Calif., 38 mi/61 km NE of San Diego. Cattle, grain. Mfg. (baked goods). Santa Ysabel Indian Reservation to N, Mesa Grande Indian Reservation to W, Inaja-Cosmit Indian Reservation to S. Anza-Borrego Desert State park to E; parts of Cleveland Natl. forest to W and S.

Santander Jiménez (sahn-tahn-DER her-ME-nes), town (1990 pop. 5,120), ⊙ Jiménez municipio, Tamaulipas, NE Mexico, 55 mi/89 km NE of Ciudad Victoria on Mexico Highway 101; 24°11′N 98°29′W. Cereals, sugarcane, beans; livestock.

Santander River, Mexico: see SOTO LA MARINA RIVER.

Santanoni Peak (4,621 ft/1,408 m), Essex co., NE N.Y., in the High Peaks sect. of the Adirondacks, 11 mi/18 km W of Mt. Marcy, and 16 mi/26 km SW of Lake Placid village; 44°05′N 74°08′W.

Santaquin (SAN-tuh-kwin), town (1990 pop. 2,386), Utah co., central Utah, 19 mi/31 km SSW of Provo; 39°58′N 111°46′W. Elev. 5,280 ft/1,609 m. In cattle and sheep and agr. (cherries, apples, alfalfa, wheat) area irrigated by water from Utah L. (NW) and Strawberry R. Mfg. apple juice; limestone. Settled 1851 by Mormons. Inc. 1931. Mona Reservoir to SW; Mt. Nebo Wilderness Area to S; Uinta Natl. Forest to SE

Santaren Channel, strait in the West Indies, S of Florida, bet. Clay Sal Bank (W) and Great Bahama Bank (E), linking the Straits of Florida (N) with Old Bahama Channel (S) off N Cuba; c.125 mi/201 km long; 24°00′N 79°30′W.

Santee, city (1990 pop. 52,902), San Diego co., S Calif., suburb 15 mi/24 km NE of downtown San Diego, near San Diego R.; 32°52′N 116°59′W. Mfg. (electrical equip., printing and publishing., construction materials, textiles, biological prods.). Gillespie Field Airport to S. Mission Trails Regional Park to W.

Santee 1 (san-TEE), village (1990 pop. 365), Nebr., 60 mi/97 km NNW of Norfolk, on Lewis and Clark L. on Missouri R., on N edge of Santee Sioux Reservation. Santee tribal powwow here in late June. Santee pop. on reservation c.425. **2** village (1990 pop. 638), Orangeburg co., S central S.C., near L. Marion, 22 mi/35 km E of Orangeburg; 33°28′N 80°29′W. Mfg. includes roof trusses and concrete. L. Marion reservoir to NE. Santee State Park to N.

Santee River, 143 mi/230 km long, central S.C.; formed by the confluence of the Congaree and Wateree rivers; flows SE to the Atlantic Ocean. The Santee-Wateree-Catawba system (c.440 mi/710 km long) is the chief waterway of S.C. A navigable canal (built 1792–1800) connects the Santee with the Cooper R. The Santee has been extensively developed for power and navigation. Santee Dam (48 ft/14.6 m high; c.8 mi/12.9 km long) impounds L. Marion. Pinopolis Dam, impounding L. Moultrie, has a large capacity.

Santeetlah (san-TEET-luh), village (1990 pop. 47), Graham co., W N.C., 4 mi/6.4 km NNW of Dobbinsville, on E shore of Santeetlah L. reservoir (Cheoah R.), in Nantahala Natl. Forest; 35°21′N 83°52′W.

Santeetlah Lake (san-TEET-luh), reservoir, Graham co., W N.C., c.40 mi/64 km S of Knoxville, Tenn. on Cheoah R., in Nantahala Natl. Forest, and just SW of Great Smoky Mts. Natl. Park; 5 mi/8 km long, 1 mi/ 1.6 km wide. Formed by Santeetlah Dam (200 ft/61 m high, 1,150 ft/351 m long; completed 1928; used for power) in Cheoah R. Boating and fishing. Joyce Kilmer Memorial Forest to W.

Santiago, Cuba: see SANTIAGO DE CUBA.

Santiago (sahn-tee-AH-go), province (□ 1,367 sq mi/ 3,541 sq km; 1993 pop. 690,548), N and NW central Dominican Republic; ⊙ Santiago or Santiago de los Caballeros; 19°25′N 70°55′W. An interior prov. in the most fertile and populous region (Cibao) of the Republic, intersected by the Yaque del Norte; bounded by the Cordillera Septentrional (N) and Cordillera Central (S). Main crops: tobacco, cacao, coffee, rice, corn, vegetables, tropical fruit; cattle. Much lumbering and gold washing. Regional airport. Prov. created 1845.

Santiago (sahn-tee-AH-go), town (1990 pop. 784), Los Cabos municipio, Baja California Sur, NW Mexico, in valley 60 mi/97 km SSE of La Paz; 23°30′N 109°40′W. Elev. 1,207 ft/368 m. Sugarcane and fruit (coconuts, dates, figs, grapes).

Santiago, town, Nuevo León, N Mexico, in foothills of Sierra Madre Oriental, on Inter-Amer. Highway (85) and 20 mi/32 km SE of Monterrey; 25°25′N 100°08′W. Fruit, chickpeas, grain; livestock.

Santiago Amoltepec (sahn-tee-AH-go ah-MOL-te-pek), town (1990 pop. 577), SW Oaxaca, Mexico, 40 mi/ 65 km SE of Putla de Guerrero; 16°37′N 97°30′W. Access by dirt track. Farming, mainly for subsistence.

Santiago Apoala (sahn-tee-AH-go ah-po-AH-lah), town (1990 pop. 262), NW Oaxaca, Mexico, 16 mi/ 25 km SW of San Juan Bautista Cuicatlán; 17°39′N 97°09′W. Elev. 5,315 ft/1,620 m. A mountainous region with a temperate climate. Agr. (corn, beans, wheat, chilies, fruits); woods. Access by dirt tracks. Archaeological site nearby.

Santiago Apóstol (sahn-tee-AH-go ah-POS-tol), town (1990 pop. 4,513), S central Oaxaca, Mexico, 3 mi/ 4.8 km W of Ocotlán de Morelos and 16 mi/25 km S of Oaxaca de Juárez. Elev. 5,085 ft/1,550 m. Agr. (corn, beans, wheat, sugarcane, fruits, mezcal); cattle.

Santiago Astata (sahn-tee-AH-go ah-STAH-tah), town (1990 pop. 1,988), far S Oaxaca, Mexico, 6 mi/ 10 km N of the Pacific coast and 34 mi/55 km SW of the port of Salina Cruz on Mexico Highway 200; 15°59′N 95°40′W. In coastal lowlands on Huemelula R. Hot climate. Agr. (coffee, tropical fruits, corn, beans); woods.

Santiago Atitlán (sahn-tee-AH-go ah-teet-LAHN), town (1990 pop. 450), NE Oaxaca, Mexico, in the Mixe judicial dist., 50 mi/80 km E of Oaxaca de Juárez; 17°06′N 95°55′W. Elev. 3,281 ft/1,000 m. Hot to temperate climate. Agr. (corn, beans, fruits, mezcal); wood; cattle. Unpaved roads. A Mixe Indian town.

Santiago Atzitzihuacán (sahn-tee-AH-go aht-SEET-see-wah-KAHN), town (1990 pop. 1,069), Puebla, Atzitzihuacán municipio, central Mexico, 30 mi/48 km SW of Puebla; 18°48′N 98°40′W. Cereals, sugar, vegetables.

Santiago Ayuquililla (sahn-tee-AH-go ah-yoo-kee-LEE-yah), town (1990 pop. 1,458), NW Oaxaca, Mexico, 5 mi/8 km from the Puebla state border and 16 mi/ 25 km NW of Huajuapa de León; 17°57′N 97°58′W. Elev. 5,341 ft/1,628 m. Mountainous terrain the Mixteco R. drainage. Temperate climate. Agr. (cereals, fruits, mezcal); woods, textiles.

Santiago Cacaloxtepec (sahn-tee-AH-go kah-kah-LOKS-te-pek), town (1990 pop. 1,161), NW Oaxaca, Mexico, 6 mi/10 km SE of Huajuapam de León. Activities are farming and livestock.

Santiago Camotlán (sahn-tee-AH-go kah-mot-LAHN), town (1990 pop. 709), NE Oaxaca, Mexico, 22 mi/35 km ENE of Ixtlán de Juárez; 17°28′N 96°12′W. Elev. 4,199 ft/1,280 m. Mountainous terrain. Temperate to hot climate. Agr. (corn, beans, fruits); woods; processing mezcal.

Santiago Chazumba (sahn-tee-AH-go chah-ZOOM-bah), town (1990 pop. 1,458), NW Oaxaca, Mexico, 3.1 mi/5 km E of the Puebla state border; 18°12′N 97°40′W. Elev. 4,580 ft/1,396 m. Mountainous terrain. Temperate to hot climate. On the headstream of the Mixteco River. Agr. (corn, beans, sugarcane, fruits, mezcal), woods. Cattle and poultry raising.

Santiago Choápam (sahn-tee-AH-go cho-AH-pahm), town (1990 pop. 960), Oaxaca, S Mexico, 48 mi/77 km NE of Tlacolula de Matamoros; 17°20′N 95°57′W. Elev. 2,953 ft/900 m. Cereals, sugarcane, coffee, fruit; livestock.

Santiago Comaltepec (sahn-tee-AH-go ko-MAHL-te-pek), town (1990 pop. 1,125), N Oaxaca, Mexico, 2 mi/ 3 km off Mexico Highway 175 and 40 mi/65 km ENE of Oaxaca de Juárez; 17°36′N 96°34′W. Elev. 8,793 ft/ 2,680 m. Very mountainous terrain with infertile soil. Agr. (cereals, fruits); forestry.

Santiago de Anaya (sahn-tee-AH-go dai ah-NAH-yah), town (1990 pop. 1,615), Hidalgo, central Mexico, 23 mi/ 37 km NW of Pachuca de soto; 17°36′N 96°34′W. Corn, maguey; livestock.

Santiago de Cuba (sahn-tee-AH-go dai KOO-buh), province (1995 est. pop. 1,080,000), SE Cuba; ⊙ Santiago de Cuba. Bordered N by Holguín prov., S by Caribbean Sea, E by Guantánamo prov., and W by Granma prov. Drained by Baconao, Cauto, and Mayarí rivers. Sierra Maestra in S. Until 1975, part of old Oriente prov. Eight sugar mills work c. 240,000 acres/ 82,500 ha. Pasture, citrus, and coffee are also important. With a pop. of 1.08 million, it has c. 10% of nation's total. Important centers are Santiago de Cuba (pop. 420,000), Palma Soriano (pop. 70,000), San Luís (pop. 33,000), and Contramaestra (pop. 30,000).

Santiago de Cuba (sahn-tee-AH-go dai KOO-buh), city (□ 2,450 sq mi/6,345 sq km; 1994 est. pop. 385,000), ⊙ Santiago de Cuba prov., SE Cuba; 20°03′N 75°49′W. Cuba's 2d-largest city, situated on a cliff overlooking a bay. Trade and industry dominate its economy. One of Cuba's most comprehensive port facilities with a capacity of handling over 3,000,000 tons/ 2,721,000 metric tons of containers, bulk grain, or liquid cargo. Founded in 1514 by Diego de Velázquez and moved to its present site in 1588, Santiago served as the capital of Cuba until the mid-16th cent. In its early days, it was captured by Fr. and Eng. buccaneers and was a center of the smuggling trade with the B.W. I. Frenchmen fleeing the slave revolt in Haiti in the early 19th cent. settled in Santiago and heavily influenced the city's development. It remained isolated until reached by the central RR and highway. During the Span.-Amer. War of 1898, U.S. ships established a blockade in Santiago's harbor; when the Span. admiral Pascual Cervera y Topete, bottled up in the harbor, made a desperate attempt to escape, his fleet was destroyed. Heavy fighting preceded the city's surrender. Fidel Castro began his revolutionary struggle against Fulgencio Batista by attacking the Moncada army garrison in Santiago on July 26, 1953. The city retains many colonial landmarks, notably its cathedral (the largest in Cuba) and the crumbling forts that stand on high cliffs above the harbor. It also has a univ. Linked to rest of country by the 2-lane Central Highway. Administrative center of 5 free zones in E Cuba. Port facilities are good and able to handle bulk grains, liquids, and containers. In the early 1990s, 13,000 ft/3,962 m of runway were added to Antonio Maceo Internatl. Airport, just S. The 2 thermoelectric plants and an oil refinery are backbone of local and regional industry.

Santiago de las Vegas, town, Ciudad de la Habana prov., W Cuba, on RR, 10 mi/16 km S of Havana and adjacent to José Martí Internatl. Airport; 22°56′N 82°23′W. Processing and agr. center (tobacco, sugarcane, citrus fruit, potatoes); mfg. of cigars, shoes, paint, pottery; tanning. Has agr. station.

Santiago de los Caballeros (sahn-tee-AH-go dai los kah-bah-YAI-ros), city (1993 pop. 364,859), ⊙ Santiago prov., N Dominican Republic, on the Yaque del Norte R., 85 mi/137 km NW of Santo Domingo; 19°28′N 70°42′W. The 2d-most important city in the country, it is a RR and road junction in the center of the fertile region known as the Cibao lowland. The region produces subsistence crops, sugarcane, tobacco, coffee, and cotton. Tobacco prods. and some light mfg. are the dominant economic activities. Cigar factories in duty-free zones; in 1997 it was the world's leading exporter of premium hand-made cigars. Santiago is the commercial center and distribution point for the most densely populated part of the country. It was founded in 1495 and in 1844 was the site of a decisive battle in the Dominican Republic's war of independence.

Santiago de Tequila, Mexico: see TEQUILA.

Santiago del Río (sahn-tee-AH-go del REE-o), town (1990 pop. 689), far NW Oaxaca, Mexico, 28 mi/45 km SW of Huajuapam de León; 17°26′N 98°05′W. Elev. 2,861 ft/872 m. Hot climate. Activities are agr., straw textiles, processing mezcal. Unpaved roads.

Santiago Huajolotitlán (sahn-tee-AH-go wah-ho-lo-teet-LAHN), town (1990 pop. 1,414), NW Oaxaca, Mexico, on Mexico Highway 125, 5 mi/8 km NW of Huajuapan de León; 17°49′N 97°44′W. Elev. 3,386 ft/ 1,032 m. Resources are agr., cattle, and handmade textiles.

Santiago Huauclilla (sahn-tee-AH-go wah-oo-KLEE-yah), town (1990 pop. 410), NW Oaxaca, Mexico, 11 mi/ 17 km E of Asunción Nochixtlán; 17°27′N 97°05′W. Elev. 4,790 ft/1,460 m. Agr. (corn, beans, wheat, potatoes, fruits); woods and cattle. No paved roads. Mountainous terrain. Temperate climate.

Santiago Ihuitlán Plumas (sahn-tee-AH-go ee-weet-LAHN PLOO-mahs), town (1990 pop. 320), NW Oaxaca, Mexico, 25 mi/40 km E of Huajuapam de León, on unpaved road. Elev. 6,562 ft/2,000 m. Agr. (corn, beans, wheat, potatoes, chilies, mezcal). Cool climate.

Santiago Island (sahn-tee-AH-go) or **Cayo Santiago**, small islet off E P.R., 1 mi/1.6 km off Playa de Humacao. The Caribbean Primate Research Center of the Univ. of P.R. here, maintains a monkey colony. The Natl. Inst. of Health is also involved.

Santiago Ixcuintepec (sahn-tee-AH go eeks-KWEEN-te-pek), town (1990 pop. 753), E Oaxaca, Mexico, 41 mi/ 66 km W of Matías Romero; 16°57′N 95°38′W. Elev. 5,610 ft/1,710 m. Temperate climate. Resources are agr. and livestock. Unpaved road. A Mixe-speaking community.

Santiago Ixcuintla (sahn-tee-AH-go eesh-KWEEN-tlah), city (1990 pop. 19,249) and township, Nayarit, W Mexico, on Pacific coastal plain, on lower Santiago R. and 30 mi/48 km NW of Tepic; 21°50′N 105°11′W. Processing and agr. center (corn, tobacco, beans, tomatoes, bananas); mfg. (tobacco prods., soap, vegetable oil, steel furniture). Gold placers nearby.

Santiago Ixtayutla (sahn-tee-AH-go eeks-tah-YOOT-lah), town (1990 pop. 1,171), SW Oaxaca, Mexico, 31 mi/ 50 km NE of Santiago Pinotepa Nacional, on Río Verde; 16°36′N 97°39′W. Elev. 2,297 ft/700 km. Farming, mainly for subsistence. Access by dirt track.

Santiago Jamiltepec, town (1990 pop. 8,181), Oaxaca, S Mexico, in Pacific coast lowland, 17 mi/28 km ESE of Santiago Pinotepa Nacional on Mexico Highway 200; 16°18′N 97°51′W. Elev. 1,312 ft/400 m. Cereals, sugarcane, coffee, cotton, fruit, vegetables, timber.

Santiago Jocotepec (sahn-tee-AH-go ho-KO-te-pek), town (1990 pop. 543), NE Oaxaca, Mexico, 68 mi/ 110 km NE of Oaxaca de Juárez. Elev. 6,890 ft/2,100 m. Mountainous terrain in the Papaloapan R. drainage. Temperate to hot climate. No paved roads. In Chinantec-speaking area. Also Monte Negro or Montenegro.

Santiago Juxtlahuaca (sahn-tee-AH-go HOOSH-tlah-WAH-kah), town (1990 pop. 5,195), W Oaxaca, Mexico, 36 mi/58 km SSW of Huajuapam de León; 17°20′N 98°00′W. Elev. 5,413 ft/1,650 m. In the Mixteca Baja on the banks of the Juxtlahuaca R. Connected by paved road (19 mi/30 km) to Mexico Highway 125 near Putla. Temperate climate. Agr. (corn, beans), livestock, and gypsum deposits. The most important industries are the processing of tequila and mezcal and local woolen textiles.

Santiago Lachiguirí (sahn-tee-AH-go lah-chee-gee-REE), town (1990 pop. 911), SE Oaxaca, Mexico, 31 mi/ 50 km NW of Santo Domingo Tehuantepec; 16°41′N 95°32′W. Elev. 6,890 ft/2,100 m. Mountainous terrain in the Tehuantepec R. basin. Agr. (coffee, corn, beans, cacao, sugarcane). Gravel roads.

Santiago Lalopa (sahn-tee-AH-go lah-LO-pah), town

(1990 pop. 543), the NE Oaxaca, Mexico, in the Villa Alta judicial dist., 43 mi/70 km E of Oaxaca de Juárez; 17°25′N 96°15′W. Elev. 4,593 ft/1,400 m. A mountainous terrain in the S of Ixtlán. Temperate climate. The Santo Domingo R. provides water. Undeveloped roads. The total pop. of the municipality lives here.

Santiago Laollaga (sahn-tee-AH-go lah-o-YAH-gah), town (1990 pop. 2,306), SE Oaxaca, Mexico, 16 mi/ 25 km NW of Juchitán de Zaragoza; 16°05′N 95°12′W. Hot climate. Agr. (corn, beans, fruits), straw textiles and forestry. On paved road.

Santiago Laxopa (sahn-tee-AH-go la-HO-pah), town (1990 pop. 878), NE Oaxaca, Mexico, 40 mi/65 km NE of Oaxaca de Juárez and 24 mi/38 km ESE of Ixtlán de Juárez; 17°13′N 96°18′W. Elev. 6,562 ft/2,000 m. Mountainous terrain. Temperate climate. Resources are cereals and wood. Access by dirt track.

Santiago Llano Grande (sahn-tee-AH-go YAH-no GRAHN-dai), town (1990 pop. 1,809), in extreme SW Oaxaca, Mexico, 26 mi/42 km WNW of Santiago Pinotepa Nacional, 6 mi/9.7 km off Mexico Highway 200, near the Pacific coast and the Guerrero state border; 16°29′N 98°15′W. The primary resource is agr.

Santiago Maravatío (sahn-tee-AH-go mah-rah-vah-TEE-o), city (1990 pop. 4,723), in S central Guanajuato, Mexico, 35 mi/56 km SW of Celaya; 20°10′N 100°00′W. Irrigation from Alto Lerma R. creates prosperous agr. zone excellent for growing beans and wheat.

Santiago Matatlán (sahn-tee-AH-go mah-taht-LAHN), town (1990 pop. 3,053), SW Oaxaca, Mexico, in the Tlacolula judicial dist., 28 mi/45 km SE of Oaxaca de Juárez on the Inter-Amer. Highway (190); 16°52′N 96°23′W. Elev. 5,440 ft/1,658 m. Agr.; cattle; the processing of mescal, and woven straw and woolen textiles.

Santiago Miahuatlán (sahn-tee-AH-go mee-ah-waht-LAHN), town (1990 pop. 8,182), Puebla, central Mexico, on RR and 7 mi/11.3 km NW of Tehuacán; 18°34′N 97°26′W. Elev. 5,840 ft/1,780 m. Agr. center (corn, rice, sugarcane, fruit; livestock). Sometimes Miahuatlán.

Santiago Miltepec (sahn-tee-AH-go MEEL-te-pek), town (1990 pop. 384), NW Oaxaca, Mexico, 14 mi/ 23 km N of Huajuapan de León, on Mexico Highway 125; 17°59′N 97°41′W. Mountainous terrain in the Mixteca Alta. Agr.

Santiago Minas (sahn-tee-AH-go MEE-nahs), town (1990 pop. 454), SW Oaxaca, Mexico, 25 mi/40 km WSW of San Miguel Sola de Vega, 34 mi/55 km NE of Río Grande; 16°26′N 97°10′W. Elev. 1,312 ft/400 m. Steep terrain. Hot climate. Resources are livestock and agr.

Santiago Mountains, Brewster co., extreme W Texas, in the Big Bend, extend c.35 mi/56 km; 29°50′N 103°24′W. SE from region SE of Alpine to NW end of Sierra del Carmen range runs through NE edge of Big Bend Natl. Park. Highest point is Santiago Peak (6,521 ft/1,988 m).

Santiago Nacaltepec (sahn-tee-AH-go nah-KAHL-te-pek), town (1990 pop. 884), N Oaxaca, Mexico, 31 mi/ 50 km NNW of Oaxaca de Juárez and 30 mi/48 km S of San Juan Bautista Cuicatlán; 17°31′N 96°56′W. Elev. 4,921 ft/1,500 m. Agr. (corn, beans, coffee, sugarcane, mezcal, fruits); woods; cattle raising.

Santiago Nejapilla (sahn-tee-AH-go ne-hah-PEE-yah), town (1990 pop. 335), W Oaxaca, Mexico, 10 mi/16 km WSW of Asunción Nochixtlán; 17°25′N 97°22′W. Elev. 6,037 ft/1,840 m. In the Mixteca Alta. Temperate climate. Agr. Unpaved roads.

Santiago Niltepec (sahn-tee-AH-go NEEL-te-pek), town (1990 pop. 3,477), in SE Oaxaca, Mexico, on RR, 32 mi/52 km ENE of Juchitán de Zaragoza on Mexico Highway 190–200, on Pacific coastal plain, on the Niltepec R.; 16°33′N 94°38′W. Hot climate. Agr.(corn, beans, coffee, rice, cacao, sugarcane, fruit), mezcal, cattle and poultry raising, and local textiles.

Santiago Nundiche (sahn-tee-AH-go noon-DEE-che), town (1990 pop. 173), W Oaxaca, Mexico, 4.3 mi/7 km N of Tlaxiaco, 2 mi/3.2 km off Mexico Highway 125; 17°21′N 97°40′W. Elev. 5,938 ft/1,810 m. Mountainous terrain in the Mixteca Alta. Temperate climate. Agr.

Santiago Nuyoó (sahn-tee-AH-go noo-yo-O), town (1990 pop. 621), W Oaxaca, Mexico, 12 mi/20 km E of Putla de Guerrero and 31 mi/50 km SW of Tlaxiaco; 17°01′N 97°45′W. Elev. 5,617 ft/1,712 m. Mountainous terrain in the Verde R. basin. Temperate climate. Resources are agr., cattle raising, processing mezcal, and the mfg. of woolen and straw textiles.

Santiago Oxtempan, Mexico: see SANTIAGO, Mexico state.

Santiago Papasquiaro (sahn-tee-AH-go pah-pahs-kee-AH-ro), city (1990 pop. 16,002) and township, Durango, N Mexico, on E slope of Sierra Madre Occidental, on Ramos R., and 85 mi/137 km NW of Victoria de Durango, on RR; 25°02′N 105°25′W. Elev. 5,630 ft/ 1,716 m. Grain, alfalfa, chickpeas; livestock; mineral resources.

Santiago Peak 1 Calif.: see SANTA ANA MOUNTAINS. **2** Texas: see SANTIAGO MOUNTAINS.

Santiago Pinotepa Nacional (sahn-tee-AH-go pee-no-TE-pah nah-see-yo-NAHL), city (1990 pop. 19,818) and township, Oaxaca, S Mexico, in Pacific coast lowland, 16 mi/26 km WNW of Santiago Jamiltepec, on Mexico Highway 200; 16°19′N 98°03′W. Cereals, sugarcane, fruit; livestock. Also Pinotepa Nacional.

Santiago, Río Grande de, Mexico: see LERMA.

Santiago River, Mexico: see RAMOS RIVER.

Santiago Rodríguez (sahn-tee-AH-go rod-REE-gez), province (□ 394 sq mi/1,020 sq km; 1993 pop. 60,015), NW Dominican Republic. S part is in Cordillera Central, N part in fertile Cibao valley; 19°25′N 71°20′W. Agr. (tobacco, beeswax, fine wood, hides).

Santiago Suchilquitongo (sahn-tee-AH-go soo-cheel-kee-TON-go), town (1990 pop. 4,686), central Oaxaca, Mexico, 17 mi/27 km NW of Oaxaca de Juárez; 17°15′N 96°53′W. Mountainous terrain. Temperate climate. Agr. (corn, beans, wheat, mezcal, fruits); woods; cattle raising and dairy prods. On the Inter-Amer. Highway (190) and on RR. At N end of Etla arm of Oaxaca Valley.

Santiago Tamazola (sahn-tee-AH-go tah-mah-ZO-lah), town (1990 pop. 1,915), NW Oaxaca, Mexico, 31 mi/50 km WSW of Huajuapam de León; 17°39′N 98°18′W. Elev. 5,856 ft/1,785 m. Resources are agr., straw textiles, and the processing of mezcal. Unpaved roads. Temperate climate. In the Mixteca Baja.

Santiago Tangamandapio (sahn-tee-AH-go tahn-gah-mah-dah-PEE-o), town (1990 pop. 8,638), ⊙ Tangamandapio municipio, Michoacán, central Mexico, 10 mi/16 km WSW of Zamora; 19°57′N 102°26′W. Cereals, sugarcane, fruit; livestock.

Santiago Tapextla (sahn-tee-AH-go tah-PEKS-lah), town (1990 pop. 1,515), extreme SW Oaxaca, Mexico, 16 mi/25 km W of Santiago Pinotepa Nacional and 3.1 mi/5 km E of the Guerrero state border with coasts on the Pacific Ocean; 16°19′N 98°23′W. Hot and humid climate. Agr. (corn, beans, sugarcane, coffee, mangoes, lemons); wood, cattle raising and fishing. No paved roads.

Santiago Tejupan, Mexico: see VILLA TEJUPAM DE LA UNIÓN.

Santiago Tenango (sahn-tee-AH-go te-NAHN-go), town (1990 pop. 444), N central Oaxaca, Mexico, 25 mi/ 41 km NW of Oaxaca de Juárez; 17°17′N 96°58′W. Elev. 5,381 ft/1,640 m. Mountainous terrain with a temperate climate. Agr. (cereals, fruits, mexcal), woods, and cattle raising.

Santiago Teopantlán, Mexico: see TEOPANTLÁN.

Santiago Teotongo, Mexico: see TEOTONGO.

Santiago Tepetlapa (sahn-tee-AH-go te-pet-LAH-pah), town (1990 pop. 108), NW Oaxaca, Mexico, 22 mi/35 km E of Huajuapam de León; 17°40′N 97°27′W.

Santiago Tequixquiac (sahn-tec-AH-go te-keesh-KEE-ahk), town (1990 pop. 14,315), ⊙ Tequixquiac municipio, Mexico state, central Mexico, on central plateau, on RR and 33 mi/53 km N of Mexico city; 19°54′N 99°08′W. Elev. 7,415 ft/2,260 m. Agr. center (cereals, maguey, fruit; livestock). Site of tunnel linking Cuautitlán R., and thus L. Texcoco and L. Zumpango, with Pánuco R. system. Formerly Tequixquiac.

Santiago Tetepec (sahn-tee-AH-go TE-te-pek), town

(1990 pop.1,108), SW Mexico, 5 mi/8 km NE of Santiago Jamiltepec, off Mexico Highway 200; 16°20′N 97°45′W. Hot climate in the Verde R. basin. Agr. (coffee, corn, beans, coconut, citrus); woods.

Santiago Texcalcingo (sahn-tee-AH-go teks-kahl-SEEN-go), town (1990 pop. 1,686), N Oaxaca, Mexico, on the Puebla state border, 9 mi/15 km NE of Teotitlán de Flores Magón; 18°12′N 96°57′W. Agr. (corn, beans, coffee, sugarcane, fruits); cattle raising.

Santiago Texcaltitlán, Mexico: see TEXCALTITLÁN.

Santiago Textitlán (sahn-tee-AH-go teks-teet-LAHN), town (1990 pop. 453), SW Oaxaca, Mexico, 23 mi/37 km NW of San Miguel Sola de Vega, on gravel road; 16°35′N 97°18′W. Elev. 4,554 ft/1,388 m. The pop. consists of primarily Mixtec Indians who live by farming.

Santiago Tilantongo (sahn-tee-AH-go tee-lahn-TON-go), town (1990 pop. 409), Oaxaca, S Mexico, in Sierra Madre del Sur, 24 mi/38 km E of Tlaxiaco; 17°17′N 97°21′W. Elev. 5,709 ft/1,740 m. Cereals, sugarcane, fruit. Archaeological site nearby.

Santiago Tillo (sahn-tee-AH-go TEE-yo), town (1990 pop. 342), NW Oaxaca, Mexico, 6 mi/9.7 km W of Asunción Nochixtlán, 2 mi/3.2 km off Inter-Amer. Highway (190) on granite road; 17°27′N 97°19′W. Elev. 6,342 ft/1,933 m. Mountainous terrain in the Mixteca Alta. Temperate climate. Agr. Undeveloped roads.

Santiago Tlazoyaltepec (sahn-tee-AH-go tlah-zo-YAHL-te-pek), town (1990 pop. 177), central Oaxaca, Mexico, 16 mi/25 km W of Oaxaca de Juárez; 17°02′N 96°59′W. Elev. 4,780 ft/1,457 m. In the Mixteca region on the W face of Sierra Peñoles on N border of the Valley of Oaxaca. On gravel road. Temperate climate. Agr. (corn and beans).

Santiago Tulantepec (sahn-tee-AH-go too-LAHN-te-pek), town (1990 pop. 12,089), ⊙ Santiago Tulantepec de Lugo Guerrero municipio, Hidalgo, central Mexico, RR junction, and 26 mi/42 km SE of Pachuca de Soto; 20°02′N 98°21′W. Grain, maguey; livestock.

Santiago Tuxtla (sahn-tee-AH-go TOOSH-tlah), city (1990 pop. 14,163) and township, Veracruz, SE Mexico, at SE foot of Tuxtla Volcano, 6 mi/9.7 km WNW of San Andrés Tuxtla, on Mexico Highway 180; 18°27′N 95°16′W. Agr. center (tobacco, coffee, sugarcane, fruit; livestock).

Santiago Xanica (sahn-tee-AH-go hah-NEE-kah), town (1990 pop.626), S Oaxaca, Mexico, 25 mi/40 km NE of San Pedro Pochutla; 16°00′N 96°14′W. Elev. 5,741 ft/1,750 m. Temperate climate. Agr. (coffee, cacao, sugarcane, corn, beans, fruits); woods. No paved roads.

Santiago Xiacuí (sahn-tee-AH-go hee-ah-KWEE), town (1990 pop. 767), E Oaxaca, Mexico, 7 mi/12 km from Ixtlán de Juárez and 50 mi/80 km NE of Oaxaca de Juárez; 17°17′N 96°26′W. Elev. 6,447 ft/1,959 m. A mountainous region with a cold climate. Agr. (corn, beans, wheat, potatoes, mezcal, fruits); woods.

Santiago Yaitepec (sahn-tee-AH-go yah-EE-te-pek), town (1990 pop. 1,609), SW Oaxaca, Mexico, 28 mi/ 45 km NW of Puerto Escondido on the Pacific coast and 2.5 mi/4 km E of Santa Catarina Juquila; 16°14′N 97°14′W. Elev. 6,562 ft/2,000 m. Resources are agr. and cattle. On hard-surface secondary road.

Santiago Yaonahuac, Mexico: see YAONÁHUAC.

Santiago Yaveo (sahn-tee-AH-go yah-VE-o), town (1990 pop. 812), NE Oaxaca, Mexico, 56 mi/90 km NW of Matias Romero; 17°19′N 95°42′W. Elev. 3,281 ft/ 1,000 m. Located in the Papaloapan R. drainage. Hot climate. Agr. (corn, beans, coffee, fruits); wood; processing mezcal. No paved roads.

Santiago Yolomécatl (sahn-tee-AH-go yo-lo-ME-kahtl), town (1990 pop. 1,453), in NW Oaxaca, Mexico, in the Teposcolula judicial dist., 27 mi/43 km SE of Huajuapan de León and 5 mi/8 km SW of the town of San Pedro y San Pablo Teposcolula, on Mexico Highway 125; 17°28′N 97°34′W. Elev. 6,991 ft/2,131 m. Cold climate. Resources are agr., cattle raising, and the processing of mezcal.

Santiago Yosundúa (sahn-tee-AH-go yo-sun-DOO-ah), town (1990 pop. 755), W Oaxaca, Mexico, 29 mi/ 47 km SSE of Tlaxiaco and 48 mi/78 km NE of Santiago

Pinotepa Nacional; 16°53′N 97°34′W. Elev. 5,840 ft/ 1,780 m. A mountainous terrain with a temperate to cold climate. Agr. (corn, beans, wheat, mezcal, fruits); woods; handmade fabrics. Unpaved roads.

Santiago Yucuyachi (sahn-tee-AH-go yoo-koo-YAH-chee), town (1990 pop. 807), NW Oaxaca, Mexico, 26 mi/42 km E of Tlapa de Comonfort (Guerrero) and 25 mi/40 km SW of Huajuapam de León; 17°35′N 98°10′W. Elev. 5,479 ft/1,670 m. In the Mixteca Baja. Resources are processing of mezcal and the mfg. of straw textiles. The agr. resources are poor. A Mixtec-speaking town.

Santiago Zacatepec (sahn-tee-AH-go zah-KAH-te-pek), town (1990 pop. 2,234), E Oaxaca, Mexico, 42 mi/ 68 km NE of Tlacolula de Matamoros; 17°11′N 95°51′W. Elev. 4,593 ft/1,400 m. Steep terrain in the Papaloapan R. drainage. Activities are cattle raising and agr. On hard surface road.

Santiago Zautla (sahn-tee-AH-go sah-OO-tlah), town (1990 pop. 468), ⊙ Zautla municipio, Puebla, central Mexico, 25 mi/40 km SE of Zacatlán; 19°42′N 97°41′W. Farming.

Santiago Zoochila (sahn-tee-AH-go so-on-CHEE-lah), town (1990 pop.436), E Oaxaca, Mexico, 28 mi/45 km NE of Oaxaca de Juárez, 19 mi/31 km ESE of Extlán de Juárez; 17°13′N 96°14′W. Rlev. 5,577 ft/1,700 m. Access by dirt roads.

Santiago Zoquiápam, Mexico: see NUEVO ZOQUIAPAM.

Santiaguillo, Laguna de (sahn-tee-ah-GEE yo), lake in Durango, N Mexico, on interior plateau, at E foot of Sierra Madre Occidental, 45 mi/72 km N of Victoria de Durango; 30 mi/48 km long, 1 mi/1.6 km wide. Elev. 6,400 ft/1,951 m. Lowest part of Guatimapí marsh.

Santiam Pass (san-tee-AM) (4,817 ft/1,468 m), on Linn-Jefferson co. line, W central Oregon, in Cascade Range, 35 mi/56 km NW of Bend. Crossed by U.S. Highway 20.

Santiam River (san-tee-AM), c.10 mi/16 km long, Linn co., W Oregon; formed 3 mi/4.8 km S of Jefferson by North Santiam R. (c.90 mi/145 km long) and South Santiam R. (c.60 mi/97 km long), which rise in Cascade Range; flows W to Willamette R. below Albany. North Santiam R. rises in NE Linn co., flows W through Detroit L. Reservoir, past Mill City and Stayton. South Santiam R. rises in SE Linn co., flows W to Foster Reservoir where it receives Middle Santiam R. from NE, then flows NW past Sweet Home and Lebanon. Middle Santiam R. rises in E Linn co., flows c. 35 mi/56 km SW through Green Peter Reservoir to Foster Reservoir. Detroit Dam (448 ft/137 m high, 1,580 ft/482 m long; for flood control) is on the North Santiam R.

Santo Cerro (SAHN-to SER-ro), village and hill, La Vega prov., central Dominican Republic, 4 mi/6.4 km N of La Vega city. Site of 16th-cent. church and shrine of Our Lady of Las Mercedes, where Columbus fought a battle against the Indians and the Virgin appeared to him.

Santo Domingo (SAHN-to do-MEEN-go), town, Villa Clara prov., central Cuba, on Sagua la grande R., on RR and Central Highway, 20 mi/32 km WNW of Santa Clara; 22°03′N 80°15′W. Agr. center (sugarcane, tobacco, corn, fruit, vegetables; cattle). The sugar mills George Washington is 4 mi/6.4 km W and Veintiseis de Julio is 3 mi/4.8 km SE.

Santo Domingo (SAHN-to do-MEEN-go), district (□ 548 sq mi/1,419 sq km; 1993 pop. 2,134,779), S Dominican Republic, on the Caribbean; ⊙ Santo Domingo. A narrow coastal strip where sugarcane and tropical fruit are grown and cattle raised. Boca Chica, 19 mi/ 31 km E, is a beach resort with sugar refinery. Fishing along the coast. It was set up as a natl. dist. in 1935 out of former Santo Domingo prov. Also referred to as the Natl. Dist.

Santo Domingo (SAHN-to do-MEEN-go), ⊙ city (1993 pop. 1,55,656), S Dominican Republic, on the Caribbean Sea, at the mouth of the Ozama R.; 18°35′N 69°50′W. It is the country's largest city, leading port, and primary commercial center. Founded Aug. 4, 1496, by Bartholomew Columbus, brother of Christopher Columbus, it is the oldest continuously inhabited Eur.

settlement in the Western Hemisphere. Shortly after its founding it became the base from which Diego de Velázquez set out to conquer Cuba. Prior to the conquest of Mexico and Peru, Santo Domingo was the seat of Spain's colonial administration in the New World. The city was sacked by Sir Francis Drake in 1586. Santo Domingo was almost totally destroyed by a hurricane in 1930 but was rebuilt and renamed Ciudad Trujillo, after dictator Rafael Leonidas Trujillo; the original name was restored in 1961 after his death. Although replete with historic sites, Santo Domingo today is a city of broad avenues and modern bldgs. The cathedral, begun in 1514, is the oldest in the Western Hemisphere; until 1990 it contained the reputed tomb of Christopher Columbus, which was then moved to the Columbus Memorial Lighthouse.

Santo Domingo (sahn-to do-MEEN-go), town (1990 pop. 552), San Luis Potosí, N central Mexico, on interior plateau, 95 mi/153 km NW of San Luis Potosí, on Mexico Highway 80; 23°20′N 101°45′W. Elev. 6,466 ft/ 1,971 m.

Santo Domingo 1 Mexico: see SANTO DOMINGO INGENIO. **2** Mexico: see FILOMENO MATA.

Santo Domingo, pueblo (□ 2 sq mi/5.2 sq km; 1990 pop. 2,866), Sandoval co., N central N.Mex., 26 mi/42 km WSW of Santa Fe, on the Rio Grande; 35°31′N 106°22′W. Founded c.1700 after earlier pueblos were destroyed by floods. Its inhabitants are Pueblo of the Eastern Keresan linguistic family. Its principal ceremony, a magnificent Green Corn (or Busk) dance, is held in August. 1990 pop. of reservation was 2,992; pueblo is in W part; reservation includes village of Domingo at center.

Santo Domingo (SAHN-to do-MEEN-go), island, former Span. colony on the isl. of HISPANIOLA. The name is also given to the DOMINICAN REPUBLIC, and in early days it applied to HAITI. Columbus visited the isl. in 1492 and established a settlement on the N coast, but when he returned in 1493, the settlers had vanished. He administered a new colony here until complaints against his rule caused him to be replaced (1500) by Francisco de Bobadilla. In 1509, Columbus's son Diego became governor. Failing to find mineral wealth in quantity, the colonists became farmers; the work was done for them under the encomienda system by the native Caribs. Before the adoption (1542) of the New Laws urged by Bartolomé de las Casas for protection of the Caribs, most of them had perished and the importation of black Afr. slaves had been sanctioned. Santo Domingo was subject to frequent raids by Eng. and Fr. buccaneers. Although Spain nominally owned the whole isl., Eur. colonization had not been undertaken in the W; Fr. buccaneers used the ports here (in present Haiti) as a rendezvous, and later Fr. planters were able to establish settlements. In the late 18th cent. sugarcane was introduced, and sugar plantations became dominant. Unable to enforce its claims to the whole isl., Spain ceded (1697) the W part (then called Saint-Domingue) to France and in 1795 gave up the whole isl. Span. rule was restored in the E when the inhabitants, aided by the British, rebelled against the French in 1808–1809. The Spanish themselves were ousted in 1821; in 1822 the Haitians extended their rule over the entire isl. The Haitians were driven out in 1844 and the Dominican Republic was proclaimed. Tourism flourished in the 1980s and 1990s, generating over 12% of the GDP by 1990, with over 1.5 million visitors per year in the mid-1990s.

Santo Domingo Albarradas (SAHN-to do-MEEN-go ahl-bah-RAH-dahs), town (1990 pop. 763), central Oaxaca, Mexico, 17 mi/27 km ENE of Tlacolula; 17°02′N 96°13′W. Elev. 5,840 ft/1,780 m. Mountainous terrain. Temperate climate. Agr. (corn, beans, potatoes, fruits); woods and textiles. On hard surface road.

Santo Domingo Armenta (SAHN-to do-MEEN-go ahr-MEN-tah), town (1990 pop. 2,738), SE Oaxaca, Mexico, 23 mi/37 km W of Santiago Pinotepa Nacional, on Pacific coastal lowlands; 16°18′N 98°20′W.

Santo Domingo Cay, islet, S Bahama Isls., on S fringe

of Columbus Bank, 40 mi/64 km N of Cuba, 32 mi/ 51 km S of Great Ragged Isl.; 21°42′N 75°46′W.

Santo Domingo Chihuitán (SAHN-to do-MEEN-go chee-wee-TAHN), town (1990 pop. 1,311), SE Oaxaca, Mexico, 16 mi/26 km NW of Juchitan de Zaragoza; 16°35′N 95°10′W. Agr.; livestock (cattle).

Santo Domingo de Morelos (SAHN-to do-MEEN-go dai mo-RE-los), town (1990 pop. 1,071), S Oaxaca, Mexico, 16 mi/26 km NE of san pedro Pochutla; 15°48′N 96°41′W. Elev. 656 ft/200 m. On Pacific slope of Siera Madre del Sur. Agr. (coffee, corn, beans, fruits, mezcal), wood, cattle raising, and fabrics.

Santo Domingo del Valle, Mexico: see VILLA DÍAZ ORDAZ.

Santo Domingo Huehuetlán (SAHN-to do-MEEN-go wai-wai-TLAHN), town (1990 pop. 2,038), ⊙ Huehuetlán El Grande municipio, Puebla, central Mexico, 21 mi/34 km S of Puebla; 18°44′N 98°10′W. Cereals, sugarcane, fruit; livestock.

Santo Domingo Ingenio (SAHN-to do-MEEN-go een-HEN-ee-o), town (1990 pop. 5,541), SE Oaxaca, Mexico, 20 mi/32 km NE of Juchitan de Zaragoza on the Inter-Amer. Highway (190); 16°35′N 95°46′W. Elev. 164 ft/ 50 m. Formerly Santo Domingo.

Santo Domingo Ixcatlán (SAHN-to do-MEEN-go eeks-kaht-LAHN), town (1990 pop. 143), W Oaxaca, Mexico, 26 mi/42 km SSE of Tlaxiaco; 16°55′N 97°32′W. Elev. 5,627 ft/1,715 m. Agr.; mfg. (textiles, mezcal).

Santo Domingo Nuxaá (SAHN-to do-MEEN-go noo-hah-AH), town (1990 pop. 194), NW Oaxaca, Mexico, 20 mi/32 km SE of Asunción Nochixtlán and 29 mi/ 47 km NW of Oaxaca de Juárez; 17°12′N 97°15′W. Elev. 5,906 ft/1,800 m. Agr. (corn, beans, wheat, potatoes, chilies, fruits); woods; processing of mezcal. A gravel road connects to Nochixtlán.

Santo Domingo Ozolotepec (SAHN-to do-MEEN-go o-zo-LO-te-pek), town (1990 pop. 705), SW Oaxaca, Mexico, 24 mi/39 km SE of Miahuatlán de Porfirio Daáz; 16°22′N 96°12′W. Elev. 6,201 ft/1,890 m. Temperate climate.

Santo Domingo Petapa (SAHN-to do-MEEN-go pe-TAH-pah), town (1990 pop. 3,993), E Oaxaca, Mexico, 10 mi/16 km SW of Matias Romero; 16°49′N 95°09′W. It is in the Isthmus of Tehuantepec region in Coatzacoalcos R. drainage. Hot climate. Agr. (corn, beans, coffee, pineapples, citrus), woods, and cattle raising. A paved road connects the town with Highway 185 (Trans-Isthmian Highway).

Santo Domingo River, c.120 mi/193 km long, Oaxaca, S Mexico; rises in Sierra Madre del Sur SE of Asuncíon Nochixtlán; flows N, E, and NNE, past San Juan Baustita Cuicatlán and Tuxtepec, to Papaloapan R. at Veracruz border 4 mi/6.4 km N of Tuxtepec. Dammed near Tuxtepec by Miguel de la Madrid Dam. Called Río San Antonio in middle course.

Santo Domingo Roayaga (SAHN-to do-MEEN-go ro-ah-YAH-gah), town (1990 pop. 544), NE Oaxaca, Mexico, 28 mi/45 km E of Ixtlán de Juárez; 17°20′N 96°07′W. Elev. 6,234 ft/1,900 m. Mountainous terrain with poor agr. resources. Unpaved roads.

Santo Domingo Tehuantepec (SAHN-to do-MEEN-go te-wahn-te-pek), city (1990 pop. 33,445) and township, Oaxaca state, S Mexico, on a wide bend of the Tehuantepec R. not far from the Gulf of Tehuantepec; 16°16′N 95°14′W. The town is on the Isthmus of Tehuantepec. The climate is hot and humid. The pop. is largely Zapotec. Tehuantepec is the commercial and social rival of Juchitán. De Zaragoza, also a largely Zapotec city.

Santo Domingo Teojomulco (SAHN-to do-MEEN-go te-o-ho-MOOL-ko), town (1990 pop. 1,994), Oaxaca, S Mexico, 17 mi/27 km W of San Miguel Soga de Vega; 16°36′N 97°14′W. Sometimes called Teojomulco.

Santo Domingo Tepuxtepec (SAHN-to do-MEEN-go te-POOKS-te-pek), town (1990 pop. 1,839), E central Oaxaca, Mexico, 30 mi/48 km E of Tlacolula de Matamoro; 16°58′N 96°10′W. Elev. 6,562 ft/2,000 m. Small farming, mainly for subsistence.

Santo Domingo Tlatayapam (SAHN-to do-MEEN-go

Cross references are shown in SMALL CAPITALS. The pronunciation key is on page xv. The dates of population figures are on page xii.

tlah-TAH-yah-pahm), town (1990 pop. 175), NW Oaxaca, Mexico, 12 mi/19 km SE of Teposcolula; 17°24'N 97°21'W. Mountainous terrain. Small farming.

Santo Domingo Tomaltepec (SAHN-to do-MEEN-go to-MAHL-te-pek), town (1990 pop. 2,353), Oaxaca, Mexico, 6 mi/9.7 km E of Oaxaca de Juárez, in Oaxaca valley; 17°04'N 96°37'W. Elev. 5,249 ft/1,600 m. Small farming.

Santo Domingo Tonalá (SAHN-to do-MEEN-go to-nah-LAH) town (1990 pop. 2,512), Oaxaca, S Mexico, 18 mi/29 km SW of Huajuápam; 17°41'N 97°56'W. Potteries.

Santo Domingo Tonaltepec (SAHN-to do-MEEN-go to-NAHL-te-pek), town (1990 pop. 133), NW Oaxaca, Mexico, 11 mi/18 km NE of San Pedro y San Pablo Teposcolua; 17°34'N 97°26'W. Elev. 5,453 ft/1,662 m. Reources are agr. and cattle raising.

Santo Domingo Xagacía (SAHN-to do-MEEN-go zahgah-SEE-ah), town (1990 pop. 1,132), E central Oaxaca, Mexico, 21 mi/34 km of Tuacolula de Matamoros; 17°08'N 96°17'W. Elev. 5,709 ft/1,740 m. Hot climate. Agr. Small farming mainly for subsistence. On gravel road.

Santo Domingo Yanhuitlán (SAHN-to do-MEEN-go yahn-hweet-LAHN), town (1990 pop. 989), NW Oaxaca, Mexico, 10 mi/16 km NW of Asunción Nochixtlán on Inter-Amer. Highway (190); 17°03'N 97°21'W. Elev. 7,041 ft/2,146 m. Resources are agr.; cattle raising; textiles; mezcal processing.

Santo Domingo Yodohino (SAHN-to do-MEEN-go yodo-EE-no), town (1990 pop. 521), NW Oaxaca, Mexico, 16 mi/25 km SE of Huajuapam de León; 17°36'N 97°43'W. Elev. 3,274 ft/998 m. Mixteca-Alta Mixtec-Indian pop. Unpaved. Poor agr.

Santo Domingo Zanatepec (SAHN-to do-MEEN-go zah-NAH-te-pek), town (1990 pop. 6,338), extreme SE Oaxaca, Mexico, 52 mi/84 km E of Juchitán de Zaragoza on Mexico Highway 200; 16°29'N 94°21'W. Elev 164 ft/50 m. Hot climate. Agr. (corn, sesame); livestock (pigs, goats); fine woods and construction lumber.

Santo, El, town, Villa Clara prov., central Cuba, near N coast, 18 mi/29 km NW of Caibarién, on Sagua la Chica R.; 22°45'N 79°41'W. Sugarcane, fruit.

Santo Tomás (SAHN-to to-MAHS), village (1990 pop. 320), Ensenada Municipio, Baja California, NW Mexico, in irrigated valley 23 mi/37 km SE of Ensenada on Mexico Highway 1; 31°32'N 116°26'W. Fruit growing (grapes, olives, peaches, figs, quinces).

Santo Tomás Hueyotlipan (SAHN-to to-MAHS waiyo-TLEE-pahn), town (1990 pop. 3,800), Puebla, central Mexico, 25 mi/40 km ESE of Puebla; 18°54'N 97°51'W. Cereals, vegetables.

Santo Tomás Jalieza (SAHN-to to-MAHS hah-lee-E-zah), town (1990 pop. 773), central Oaxaca, Mexico, 17 mi/27 km SW of Oaxaca de Juárez, and 4 mi/6.4 km N of Ocotuán de Morrlos; 16°54'N 96°27'W. Elev. 5,085 ft/1,550 m. Temperate climate. Agr. resources are corn, beans, wheat, sugarcane, fruits, mezcal. Cattle raising. A well-known weaving center.

Santo Tomás Mazaltepec (SAHN-to to-MAHS mah-ZAHL-te-pek), town (1990 pop. 1,954), central Oaxaca, Mexico, 12 mi/19 km NW of Oaxaca de Juárez and 7 mi/12 km W of San Pedro y San Pablo Etla; 17°09'N 96°52'W. Elev. 5,906 ft/1,800 m. Agr. A Zapotec town.

Santo Tomás Ocotepec (SAHN-to to-MAHS o-KO-te-pek), town (1990 pop. 450), W Oaxaca, Mexico, 11 mi/18 km SSW of Tlaxiaco; and 2 mi/3.2 km off Mexico Highway 125; 17°11'N 97°47'W. Elev. 5,577 ft/1,700 m. Resources are agr., cattle raising, mezcal processing, handmade textiles.

Santo Tomás Tamazulapam (SAHN-to to-MAHS tahmah-SOO-lah-PAHM), town (1990 pop. 1,149), S central Oaxaca, Mexico, 4 mi/6.4 km S of Miahuatlán, Mirhuatlán valley. De Porfirio Díaz on Highway 175; 16°17'N 96°35'W. Elev. 5,906 ft/1,800 m. Temperate climate.

Santos Reyes Nopala (SAHN-tos RE-yes no-PAH-lah), town (1990 pop. 120), in SW Oaxaca, Mexico, 41 mi/66 km NNW of Puerto Escondido; 16°06'N 97°08'W. In a rugged area on Nopala R. Hot climate. Agr. (corn,

beans, coffee, coconut, pineapples, lemons, oranges, mezcal); woods, and textiles. No roads.

Santos Reyes Pápalo (SAHN-tos RE-yes PAH-pah-lo), town (1990 pop. 1,916), N central Oaxaca, Mexico, 24 mi/38 km SSE of Teotitlán de Flores Magón; 17°49'N 96°51'W. Elev. 6,890 ft/2,100 m. Hot climate. Pop. is mostly Mixtec Indian. Resources are agr., and artesan crafts. No road access.

Santos Reyes Tepejillo (SAHN-tos RE-yes te-pe-HEE-yo), town (1990 pop. 1,542), NW Oaxaca, Mexico, 29 mi/47 km SSW of Huajuapam de León, in Mixteca Alta; 16°52'N 97°41'W. Elev. 8,136 ft/2,480 m. Cold climate. Resources are agr. and cattle raising.

Santos Reyes Yucuná (SAHN-tos yoo-koo-NOO), town (1990 pop. 300), NW Oaxaca, Mexico, 17 mi/27 km W of Huajuapam de León. Elev. 4,035 ft/1,230 m.

Santurce (sahn-TOOR-se), S residential sect. of San Juan, NE P.R., on mainland. Modern housing developments. Commercial area. Mus. of Contemporary Puerto Rican Art. R. Rout born here. Fine Arts Center. Marketplace with fresh produce.

Saona Island (sah-O-nah), just off SE Dominican Republic, 20 mi/32 km SE of La Romana; 15 mi/24 km long, 2 mi/3.2 km–3 mi/4.8 km wide; 18°09'N 68°40'W.

Sapello (sah-PAI-yo), uninc. village, (1990 pop. 600), San Miguel co., N central N.Mex., in Sangre de Cristo Mts., 13 mi/21 km N of Las Vegas. Cattle, sheep; grain; small trading point in wheat and alfalfa area. Morphy L. State Park to NW; Storrie L. State Park to S; Santa Fe Natl. Forest to W.

Sapelo Island (SAP-uh-lo), one of the Sea Isls., in McIntosh co., SE Ga., just off the coast, bet. St. Catherines and St. Simons isls.; c.10 mi/16 km long, 5 mi/8 km wide; 31°28'N 81°14'W. Small Sapelo Sound at N end. Owned by state of Ga. Sapelo Isl. Natl. Estuarine Research Reserve. Significant research facilities operated by the Univ. of Ga. Gray's reef located 18 mi/29 km off the coast is a natl. marine sanctuary. Hog Hammock is a small Afr.-Amer. community on the isl.

Sapinero, village, Gunnison co., W central Colo., on on the Blue Mesa Reservoir of the Gunnison R., just N of San Juan Mts., and 21 mi/34 km WSW of Gunnison. Elev. c.7,600 ft/2,316 m. Resort. Coal mining. Black Canyon of the Gunnison begins here. Curecanti Natl. Recreation Area surrounds both reservoirs. Blue Mesa Dam to W. Morrow Point Recreation downstream from it. Gunnison Natl. Forest to N.

Sappa Creek (SAP-uh), river, 100 mi/161 km long, NW Kansas and S Nebr.; formed by confluence of North Fork (90 mi/145 km long) and South Fork (70 mi/113 km long) near Oberlin in Kansas; flows ENE into Furnas co. in Nebr., to Beaver Creek 10 mi/16 km E of Beaver City.

Sapphire, uninc. village, Transylvania co., W N.C., in the Blue Ridge Mts., 16 mi/26 km SW of Brevard. Resort area. Sapphire L. to W, L. Toxaway reservoir to NE; large L. Jocassee reservoir (S.C.) to S. Toxaway Falls (123 ft/37 m) to E; Rainbow Falls (200 ft/61 m) to S; Whitewater Falls (upper cascade 441 ft/134 m) highest falls in E U.S., to SW, on S.C. boundary.

Sapphire Mountains, range of Rocky Mts. in W Mont., rise SE of Missoula and S of the Clark Fork; runs along Granite-Ravalli co. line, extending N in to Missoula co.; extend S bet. Flint Creek (E), and Bitterroot R. (W), to Anaconda Range. Elevations of 7,000 ft/2,134 m–9,000 ft/2,743 m. Deposits of silver, sapphires, and phosphates. Skalkaho Pass (c.7,250 ft/2,210 m), crossed by State Highway 38, is 20 mi/32 km E of Hamilton.

Sapulpa (suh-PUHL-puh), city (1990 pop. 18,074), ⊙ Creek co., E central Okla., suburb 13 mi/21 km SE of downtown Tulsa; 36°00'N 96°05'W. It is the trade center of a farm and oil region. Mfg. (furniture, zinc alloys, dinnerware, aluminum recycling, glass containers, publishing and printing, floor and deck coatings). Heyburn Reservoir and State Park to W. Inc. 1898.

Saragosa, uninc. village (1990 pop. 185), Reeves co., extreme W Texas, 28 mi/45 km S of Pecos, near NE base of Davis Mts. In irrigated agr. area (cotton, hay, cantaloupes).

Sarahsville, village (1990 pop. 162), Noble co., E Ohio,

8 mi/13 km NNE of Caldwell; 39°48'N 81°28'W. In agr. area.

Saraland, city (1990 pop. 11,751), Mobile co., SE Ala., 10 mi/16 km N of Mobile; 30°49'N 88°05'W. Petroleum refining, paper mill.

Saranac (SER-ah-NAK), village (1990 pop. 1,461), Ionia co., S central Mich., 8 mi/12.9 km SW of Ionia and on Grand R.; 42°55'N 85°12'W. In farm area (cattle; corn, soybeans, apples); mfg. (egg processing; plastic moldings, prepared food). Ionia State Park to NE.

Saranac Lake, village (□ 3 sq mi/7.8 sq km; 1990 pop. 5,377), Essex and Franklin cos., N N.Y., in the Adirondacks; 44°19'N 74°07'W. Situated on either side of Flower L., a 2-mi/3.2-km extension of Osetah L., S of the village; both lakes are in reality enlarged portions of the Saranac R. channel. Settled c.1819 as a lumbering town, inc. 1892. It is a year-round resort community; tourism is the main industry. It developed as a health center after Edward L. Trudeau founded a tuberculosis sanatorium here in 1884 (it closed in 1954). North Country Community Col. is in the village, which has noted skiing facilities.

Saranac Lakes, reservoirs, including 3 resort lakes, Franklin co., NE N.Y., on Saranac R., in the Adirondack Mts., in Adirondack Park, c.50 mi/80 km SW of Plattsburgh and W of Saranac Lake town. Consists of Upper Saranac L. (c.8 mi/12.9 km long; 44°17'N 74°19'W), Middle Saranac L. (c.2.5 mi/4 km long; 44°15'N 74°15'W), and Lower Saranac L. (c.3.5 mi/5.6 km long; 44°18'N 74°10'W). River drains E from lower lake to Oseetah L. Fish hatchery.

Saranap, village, Contra Costa co., W Calif., residential suburb 10 mi/16 km NE of downtown Oakland, 2 mi/3.2 km S of Walnut Creek.

Sarasota (sa-rah-SO-tuh), county (□ 725 sq mi/1,878 sq km; 1990 pop. 277,776), W central Fla., on Gulf of Mexico (W); ⊙ Sarasota; 27°11'N 82°32'W. Lowland area, drained by Myakka R.; coastal sect. bordered by barrier beaches and Sarasota Bay. Heavily urbanized in W coastal zone. Small-scale farming; also citrus-fruit growing, fishing, cattle raising, and quarrying (coquina, dolomite, limestone). Tourist region. Formed 1921.

Sarasota (sa-rah-SO-tuh), city (□ 25 sq mi/65 sq km; 1990 pop. 50,961), ⊙ Sarasota co., W central Fla., on Sarasota Bay; 27°20'N 82°32'W. It is a yachting and fishing resort with varied light mfg. and packing houses handling the citrus fruit, celery, and beef raised in the area. Urban growth has been prevalent since 1970. Sarasota is the former winter home of the Ringling Brothers and Barnum and Bailey Circus and is the site of the John and Mable Ringling Mus. of Art. New Col. is here. Nearby, on the keys off the Gulf of Mexico, are many beautiful white-sand beaches and wealthy communities. Settled c.1884, inc. 1914.

Saratoga, county (□ 843 sq mi/2,183 sq km; 1990 pop. 181,276), E N.Y.; ⊙ Ballston Spa; 43°06'N 73°52'W. Partly in the S Adirondacks, bounded E by the Hudson, S by Mohawk R. Includes Saratoga Natl. Historical Park, Saratoga Springs (noted spa, and summer recreation vacation area), Saratoga L., and part of Sacandaga Reservoir. Dairying; farming (corn, hay); poultry and livestock raising. Mfg. at Ballston Spa, Corinth, Mechanicville, Schuylerville, South Glens Falls, Saratoga Springs, Waterford. Formed 1791.

Saratoga, city (1990 pop. 28,061), Santa Clara co., W Calif., residential suburb 8 mi/12.9 km SW of San Jose, in the foothills of the Santa Cruz mts.; 37°16'N 122°01'W. Inc. 1956. Mfg. (navigation systems; light mfg.). The Montalvo Center for the Arts, former home of the late Senator James Phelan, is a cultural center; its extensive facilities include art galleries, theaters, and gardens. West Valley Col. (2-year). Castle Rock and Portola state parks to W; Santa Cruz Mts. to W and SW; Big Basin Redwoods State Park to SW.

Saratoga 1 town (1990 pop. 266), Randolph co., E Ind., 6 mi/9.7 km NE of Winchester; 40°14'N 84°55'W. In agr. area; mfg. (farm gates, steel tubing). Laid out 1875.
2 uninc. town (1990 pop. 1,000), Hardin co., SE Texas, 28 mi/45 km WNW of Beaumont, near Pine Isl. Bayou,

at W edge of Big Thicket Natl. Preserve. Elev. 83 ft/25 m. Timber area. Big Thicket Mus. is here. Settled 1850s; oil discovered 1901. **3** town (1990 pop. 1,969), Carbon co., S Wyo., on North Platte R., bet. the Sierra Madre (SW) and Medicine Bow Range (E), and 33 mi/53 km SE of Rawlins; 41°27′N 106°48′W. Elev. 6,786 ft/2,068 m. Terminus of RR spur from Walcott. Supply point for hunters, fishermen, and ranchers; livestock; grain; mfg. (lumber, concrete); logging. Saratoga Hot Springs are here. Parts of Medicine Bow Natl. Forest to SW and E.

Saratoga 1 village, Howard co., SW Ark., 19 mi/31 km WNW of Hope. Millwood L. reservoir to W. **2** village (1990 pop. 342), Wilson co., E central N.C., 9 mi/14.5 km SE of Wilson; 35°38′N 77°46′W. Tobacco, cotton, peanuts, grain; poultry, livestock. Mfg. (bottled water). Inc. 1939.

Saratoga, historical park (□ 5 sq mi/13 sq km), E N.Y., 25 mi/40 km NNE of Albany; 43°01′N 73°39′W. Authorized 1938. Scene of a famous battle during the Amer. Revolution.

Saratoga Lake (□ c.7 sq mi/18.1 sq km), Saratoga co., E N.Y., 23 mi/37 km N of Albany and just SE of Saratoga Springs; c.5 mi/8 km long; 43°01′N 73°45′W. Drains through outlet from its N end to the Hudson (E).

Saratoga Springs, resort and residential city (□ 29 sq mi/75 sq km; 1990 pop. 25,001), Saratoga co., E N.Y.; 43°04′N 73°46′W. Skidmore Col. is the largest source of employment, but the city also has light mfg. State Univ. of N.Y.–Empire State Col. is here. The last battle of the Saratoga campaign was fought near the city in 1777. The nearby Saratoga Natl. Historical Park embraces the battlefield. After the Amer. Revolution, as the fame of its carbonated mineral waters spread, the village became a health resort. In the 19th cent., Saratoga Springs was one of the most popular social and sporting centers in Amer. thoroughbred horse racing, which continues to be one of its major attractions, was begun after 1863. Of interest are the racing mus. and many old bldgs. and homes, including the Casino (1867), a former gambling house that now houses 2 museums. An elaborate state-owned spa (1935) preserves and utilizes the waters and offers curative baths. Saratoga Spa State Park, and the Saratoga Performing Arts center, summer home of the Philadelphia Orchestra and the N.Y. City Ballet with performances by the N.Y. City Opera, is S of the city. To the N is the cottage on Mt. McGregor where President Ulysses S. Grant completed his memoirs and spent the last weeks of his life. Inc. as a village 1826, as a city 1915. See also Yaddo.

Sarcoxie (sahr-KOK-see), city (1990 pop. 1,330), Jasper co., SW Mo., near Spring R., 21 mi/34 km E of Joplin; 37°04′N 94°07′W. Apples, peaches, vegetables, wheat, hay; dairying; cattle; mfg. (boots, furniture panels). Laid out 1834.

Sardinia 1 village (1990 pop. 550), Erie co., W N.Y., on Cattaraugus Creek and 30 mi/48 km SE of Buffalo; 42°32′N 78°32′W. **2** village (1990 pop. 792), Brown co., SW Ohio, 17 mi/27 km SW of Hillsboro, and on small White Oak Creek; 39°00′N 83°48′W.

Sardis, village, SW B.C., Canada, in lower Fraser valley, on Chilliwack R., and 3 mi/5 km S of Chilliwack. Dairying; livestock, fruit, hops, tobacco.

Sardis 1 (SAHR-dis), town (1990 pop. 1,116), Burke co., E Ga., 17 mi/27 km SE of Waynesboro; 32°58′N 81°46′W. Mfg. of clothing, tote bags. **2** (SAHR-duhs), town (1990 pop. 2,128), ⊙ Panola co. (seat shared with Batesville), NW Miss., c.50 mi/80 km S of Memphis, Tenn.; 34°25′N 89°54′W. Trade center for agr. (cotton, corn, soybeans; livestock) and timber area; mfg. (fishing lures, molded pallets, plastics prods., apparel). Heflin House Mus. John W. Kyle State Park, on Sardis L. reservoir, to E. Founded 1836. **3** (SAHR-dis), town (1990 pop. 305), Henderson co., W Tenn., 32 mi/51 km ESE of Jackson; 35°26′N 88°17′W.

Sardis (SAHR-dis), village (1990 pop. 171), Mason co., NE Ky., 12 mi/19 km SW of Maysville, in N part of Bluegrass region; 38°31′N 83°57′W. Agr. (tobacco, grain; livestock).

Sardis City, town (1990 pop. 1,301), Etowah co., NE Ala., 12 mi/19 km NNW of Gadsden; 34°47′N 86°07′W.

Sardis Dam, Miss.: see TALLAHATCHIE RIVER.

Sardis Lake 1 (SAHR-duhs), reservoir (□ 17 sq mi/44 sq km), Lafayette and Panola cos., N Miss., on Little Tallahatchie R., 9 mi/14 km NE of Batesville; 34°24′N 89°47′W. Max. capacity 3,016,000 acre-ft. Formed by Sardis Dam (107 ft/33 m high), built (1940) by Army Corps of Engineers for flood control. John W. Kyle State Park near dam. **2** reservoir (□ 22 sq mi/57 sq km), Pushmatahah co., SE Okla., on Jack Fork Creek, 35 mi/56 km SE of McAlester; 34°38′N 95°21′W. Max. capacity of 792,100 acre-ft. Formed by Sardis Dam (80 ft/24 m high), built (1982) by Army Corps of Engineers for flood control; also used for water supply and recreation. Choctow Council House on SE shore.

Sardis Reservoir, Miss.: see TALLAHATCHIE RIVER.

Sarepta (suh-REP-tuh), town (1990 pop. 856), Webster parish, La., 8 mi/12.9 km S of Springfield; 32°53′N 93°26′W. Oil field nearby.

Sargasso Sea, part of the N Atlantic Ocean, lying roughly bet. the West Indies and the Azores and from about 20°00′N to 35°00′N, in the Horse Latitudes. The relatively still sea is the center of a great swirl of ocean currents and is a rich field for the marine biologist. Noted for the abundance of gulfweed or Sargassum (a genus of brown algae) on its surface. The Bermuda Isls. are in the NW part of the sea.

Sargeant, village (1990 pop. 78), Mower co., SE Minn., 13 mi/21 km NE of Austin; 43°48′N 92°47′W. Grain; livestock; dairying.

Sargent, county (□ 852 sq mi/2,207 sq km; 1990 pop. 4,549), SE N.Dak.; ⊙ Forman; 46°06′N 97°37′W. Agr. area drained by Wild Rice R. Wheat, rye, soybeans; cattle, hogs; dairying, Formed 1883. L. Traverse (Sisseton) Wahpeton Indian Reservation and Tewaukon Natl. Wildlife Refuge on L. Tewaukon in SE.

Sargent, town (1990 pop. 850), Coweta co., Ga., 5 mi/8 km SW of Newnan; 33°26′N 84°26′E. Mfg. of bed sheets and pillow cases.

Sargent, village (1990 pop. 710), Cluster co., central Nebr., 20 mi/32 km NE of Broken Bow, in Loess Hills, and on Middle Loup R.; 41°38′N 99°22′W. Shipping point for grain and livestock region; soy meal and livestock feed.

Sargents Purchase, land purchase, Coos co., N central N.H., 16 mi/26 km SSW of Berlin, in White Mt. Natl. Forest. Crossed by Appalachian Trail. Mt. Washington (6,288 ft/1,917 m), highest point in NE U.S., on N boundary, in Mt. Washington State Park.

Sargentville, Maine: see SEDGWICK.

Sáric (SAH-reek), town (1900 pop. 701), Sonora, NW Mexico, 30 mi/48 km SW of Nogales; 31°06′N 111°23′W. Elev. 2,867 ft/874 m. Wheat, corn; livestock.

Sarita, uninc. village (1990 pop. 185), ⊙ Kenedy co., extreme S Texas, 21 mi/34 km S of Kingsville. Elev. 34 ft/10 m. In cattle-ranching area, horses; watermelons; oil and gas. Baffin Bay, arm of Laguna Madre (Gulf of Mexico) to NE.

Sarles, village (1990 pop. 86), Cavalier and Towner cos., N N.Dak., 32 mi/51km WNW of Langdon, near Can. border; 48°57′N 99°00′W. RR terminus; dairy prods.; livestock; grain. Port of entry.

Sarnia, city (1991 pop. 74,376), S Ont., Canada, on the St. Clair R., at the S end of L. Huron and opposite Port Huron, Mich.; 42°58′N 82°24′W. The 2 cities are connected by a RR tunnel, and there is a bridge bet. Port Huron and Point Edward, just N of Sarnia. The city is a port and handles a large volume of freight for transshipment from RRs to lake steamers. There are grain elevators, machinery plants, oil refineries, and chemical and synthetic-rubber industries.

Saronville (SER-uhn-vil), village (1990 pop. 38), Clay co., S Nebr., 7 mi/11.3 km NE of Clay Center; 40°36′N 97°56′W.

Sarpy (SAR-pee), county (□ 247 sq mi/640 sq km; 1990 pop. 102,583), E Nebr.; ⊙ Papillion; 41°06′N 96°06′W. Formerly agr. region, fast becoming part of Omaha metropolitan area with major military installation and mfg., esp. in Bellevue, bounded E by Missouri R. and Iowa, W and S by Platte R. Textiles, concrete prods.; food processing, feed, fertilizer, computer cable, printing, cattle, hogs, corn, fruit, dairying. Mfg. at Papillion and Bellevue. La Vista, residential suburb of Omaha. Flooding occurred along major rivers in flood of 1993. Formed 1857; lost territory (1943) to Pottawatamie co., Iowa. part of Omaha metropolitan area.

Sarrail, Mount (10,400 ft/3,170 m), SW Alta., Canada, near B.C. border, in Rocky Mts., 45 mi/72 km SSE of Banff; 50°35′N 115°10′W.

Sarre, La (SAHR, lah), town (1991 pop. 8,513), W Que., Canada, 40 mi/64 km NNW of Rouyn. Gold and copper mining, lumbering, pulpwood milling, dairying.

Sartell (sahr-TEL), town (1990 pop. 5,393), Stearns co., extends into Benton co., central Minn., on Mississippi R.; 45°37′N 94°12′W. Agr. (grain; livestock, poultry; dairying); mfg. (papers for magazine publishing, castings, valves).

Sarthe (sahr-tuh), department (□ 2,396 mi/3,856 km; 1990 pop. 514,600), in old prov. of Maine, W France; ⊙ Le Mans. Generally level region with low hilly ranges in N and NW; drained by the Sarthe and its tributaries (Huisne and Loir). Chiefly agr. (wheat, potatoes, apples, peas), with stock-raising (Percheron draft horses and cattle) growing in importance. Industries include paper milling, wood and metalworking (Le Mans, Sablé-sur-Sarthe), and mfg. of electrical and electronic prods. Principal towns are Le Mans, La Flèche, and La Ferté-Bernard. About 40% of pop. is concentrated in Le Mans urban area. The dept. forms part of the Pays de la Loire administrative region.

Sasabe, uninc. village, Pima co., S Ariz., port of entry at Mex. border, 35 mi/56 km WNW of Nogales. Elev. 3,598 ft/1,097 m. In S end of Buenos Aires Natl. Wildlife Refuge. Part of Coronado Natl. Forest to E; Tohono O'odham (Papago) Indian Reservation to W.

Sasakwa (suh-SAHK-wuh), village (1990 pop. 169), Seminole co., central Okla., 13 mi/21 km S of Wewoka, bet. Little R. (N) and Canadian R. (S); 34°57′N 96°31′W. In agr. area.

Saskatchewan (suhs-KACH-uh-wuhn), province (□ 251,700 sq mi/ 651,903 sq km; 1991 pop. 988,928), W Canada, ⊙ REGINA, largest city; 54°00′N 106°00′W. Other important cities are PRINCE ALBERT, SASKATOON, and MOOSE JAW. Sask. is bounded on the N by the N.W.T., on the E by Man., on the S by N.Dak. and Mont., and on the W by Alberta. Its N ⅓ is part of the Laurentian Plateau. The principal rivers are the Churchill, the North and South Saskatchewan, and the Qu'Appelle. Bet. the Saskatchewan and Churchill rivers lies a mixed forest belt containing much marketable timber; a sect. is reserved as Prince Albert Natl. Park. Only in S Sask. has there been any substantial settlement or development. Except for a semiarid sect. in the SW used for grazing and an area in the E and central portion given over to mixed farming and dairying, the land is devoted to the raising of hard wheat. Sask. normally produces 66% of Canada's wheat. The vast expanses of unbroken plain are well-suited to large-scale mechanized farming. Oats, barley, rye, rapeseed, and flax are also grown throughout this region. Sask. is rich in minerals. Oil and natural gas, found in the prairie land, are by far the prov.'s most important minerals. The region N of L. Athabaska has been exploited for ores yielding uranium. The region around Flin Flon, in the NE, is mined for copper, zinc, and gold. Coal is mined in the SW. Potash mining was begun in the 1950s near Saskatoon and Esterhazy, and Canada is now a leading producer of this mineral. Most of the prov.'s industries process raw materials. A steel mill was opened in Regina in 1960. The historic occupation of fur trapping is still practiced. Original inhabitants include tribes of 3 linguistic groups: the Athapaskan, Algonquian, and Siouan. Henry Kelsey of the Hudson's Bay Co. was probably the 1st European to see the area of Sask. (c.1690). The earliest trading posts were est. by the French (c.1750), but the 1st permanent settlement was made at Cumberland House in 1774 by the Hudson's Bay Co. Subsequently many other posts were set up by Br. fur traders along the region's waterways. In 1870 the Hudson's Bay Co., which had merged with the North West Co. in 1821, ceded its rights to the Can. govt., and the area became part of the N.W.T. The construction of a RR line (1882) brought many settlers from E Canada and later from Europe and opened up trade through the Great Lakes ports. Most Native Americans in the N.W.T. sold their lands to the govt. in the 1870s and were placed on reservations. Other Sask. Native Americans and Métis, people of mixed Fr. and Native Amer. ancestry, led by Louis Riel, rebelled in 1884–1885 and were suppressed. Sask. became a prov. in 1905. In the early 20th cent. Sask. farmers formed cooperative organizations to stabilize grain marketing. During the drought and depression of the 1930s the prov.'s pop. declined as immigration almost stopped and many families left the area. Conservation programs and the increased demand for grain during World War II revived the economy. Sask. sends 6 senators and 14 representatives to the natl. parliament. The Univ. of Sask. at Saskatoon and the Univ. of Regina are the leading higher educational institutions.

Saskatchewan, river, c.340 mi/550 km long, formed by the confluence of the North Saskatchewan (c.760 mi/1,220 km long) and the South Saskatchewan (c.550 mi/890 km long) rivers near Prince Albert, central Sask., Canada; flows generally E past Nipawin, across the Man. line, then past The Pas and through Cedar L. to L. Winnipeg. The system drains most of the Can. prairie provs. The North Saskatchewan R. rises in the Columbia ice field at the foot of Mt. Saskatchewan, SW Alta., and flows generally E past Edmonton, into Sask. prov., and then past North Battleford to Prince Albert. Its chief tributaries are the Clearwater, Brazeau, Vermillion, and Battle rivers. The South Saskatchewan R. is formed in S Alta. by the junction of the Bow and Oldman rivers. It flows E past Medicine Hat, then NE into Sask. prov., past Saskatoon, to Prince Albert; it receives the Red Deer R. The Bow–South Saskatchewan–Saskatchewan system is c.1,200 mi/1,930 km long. Completion (1967) of the Gardiner and Qu'Appelle Valley dams, major elements of the South Sasketchewan R. Project, impound L. Diefenbaker, a huge reservoir. The dams and reservoir provide hydroelectric power and irrigation for a large region S of Saskatoon. The Saskatchewan R. and its branches were once important thoroughfares for explorers and trappers.

Saskatchewan, Mount (10,964 ft/3,342 m), SW Alta., Canada, in Rocky Mts., in Banff Natl. Park, 70 mi/113 km SE of Jasper, overlooking North Saskatchewan R.

Saskatoon (sas-kuh-TOON), city (1991 pop. 186,058), S central Sask., on the South Saskatchewan R.; 52°08'N 106°40'W. The largest city in the prov, it is the chief mfg. and distributing center for central and N Sask. Grain elevators, grain and flour mills, stockyards, meat-packing plants, oil refineries, potash-processing plants, and various light mfg. Saskatoon was settled in 1883 and grew rapidly after the coming of the RR (1890). The Univ. of Sask. with its affiliated col. is here, and a dominion forestry station is nearby. The name derives from a Cree word for a berry found in the area.

Saspamco, village, Wilson co., S Texas, near San Antonio R., 17 mi/27 km SE of San Antonio. Mfg. (clay sewer pipes and fittings).

Sassafras (SAS-uh-fras), uninc. town (1990 pop. 950), Knott co., E Ky., 8 mi/12.9 km ESE of Hazard, on Carr Fork of Kentucky R. Bituminous coal. Carr Fork L. reservoir to E.

Sassafras Mountain (SA-suh-fras), peak (3,560 ft/1,085 m), Pickens co., S.C., and Transylvania co. N.C. NW S.C., in the Blue Ridge Mts., on the N.C. state line, 25 mi/40 km NW of Greenville, S.C. It is the highest point in S.C.

Sassafras River (SASS-ah-fras), c.20 mi/32 km long, NE Md., on the Eastern Shore; rises just over Del. state line in New Castle co.; flows W through Md., forming Cecil-Kent co. line, to Chesapeake Bay at Betterton.

Sasser (SAS-uhr), village (1990 pop. 335), Terrell co., SW Ga., 14 mi/23 km NW of Albany; 31°43'N 84°21'W. Mfg. of fertilizer.

Satanta (suh-TANT-uh), town (1990 pop. 1,073), Haskell co., SW Kansas, 26 mi/42 km N of Liberal; 37°26'N 100°59'W. RR junction. In grain area. Gas processing. Gas wells nearby.

Satartia (suh-TAHR-shee-uh), village (1990 pop. 59), Yazoo co., W central Miss., 15 mi/24 km SSW of Yazoo City and on Yazoo R.; 32°40'N 90°32'W. No Mistake Plantation (c.1833).

Satellite Beach, town (□ 3 sq mi/7.8 sq km; 1990 pop. 9,889), Brevard co., E central Fla., 7 mi/11.3 km N of Melbourne; 28°10'N 80°35'W.

Satevó (sah-te-VO), town (1990 pop. 447), Chihuahua, N Mexico, in E outliers of Sierra Madre Occidental, and 50 mi/80 km S of Chihuahua; 27°58'N 106°08'W. Elev. 4,488 ft/1,368 m. Grain, tobacco, beans; cattle.

Saticoy, uninc. village, Ventura co., S Calif., on Santa Clara R. and 8 mi/12.9 km E of Ventura. Avocados, flowers, nursery prods., vegetables, dairying; mineral springs nearby.

Satilla River (suh-TIL-uh), c.200 mi/322 km long, SE Ga.; rises near Fitzgerald; flows generally E, past Woodbine, to the Atlantic 10 mi/16 km S of Brunswick. Lower course dredged. Receives Little Satilla R. (c.70 mi/113 km long) 8 mi/12.9 km NE of Nahunta.

Satsop (SAT-suhp), uninc. village (1990 pop. 350), Grays Harbor co., Wash., 28 mi/45 km W of Olympia, on Satsop R. near its confluence with Chehalis R. Site of mothballed nuclear power plant. Timber.

Satsop River (SAT-suhp), c.6 mi/9.7 km long, Grays Harbor co., W Wash.; formed NE of Montesano by West Fork (c.45 mi/72 km long) and East Fork (c.40 mi/64 km long); flows S to Chehalis R., 2 mi/3.2 km S of Satsop. West Fork rises in Olympic Natl. Forest, NE Grays Harbor co., flows S; East Fork rises in central Mason co., flows SW.

Satsuma, city (1990 pop. 5,194), Mobile co., SW Ala., 12 mi/19 km N of Mobile, near Mobile R. Chemical pressure valves mfg.

Saturna Island (□ 11 sq mi/28 sq km), SW B.C., Canada, Gulf Isls., in Strait of Georgia, 30 mi/48 km S of Vancouver; 7 mi/11 km long, 1 mi/2 km–3 mi/5 km wide. Tourism; lumbering, farming. Just E is Wash. boundary line.

Saucillo (sah-oo-SEE-yo), city (1990 pop. 10,213) and township, Chihuahua, N Mexico, on Conchos R. (irrigation area), and 65 mi/105 km SE of Chihuahua on Mexican Highway 45; 28°00'N 105°18'W. Elev. 3,935 ft/1,199 m. On RR. Mining (silver, gold, lead) and agr. center (corn, cotton, beans, tobacco; livestock).

Saugatuck (SAW-guh-tuk), village (1990 pop. 954), Allegan co., SW Mich., 9 mi/14.5 km SW of Holland, on L. Michigan at mouth of Kalamazoo R.; 42°39'N 86°12'W. Mfg. (boats, frozen pies, tools). Resort; Bed and breakfast. Area contains large sand dunes. Saugatuck State Park on L. Mich.

Saugatuck, Conn.: see WESTPORT.

Saugatuck River, c.30 mi/48 km long, SW Conn.; rises S of Danbury; flows SE and S to Long Isl. Sound, forming harbor of Westport.

Saugeen Peninsula (SO-GEEN), S Ont., Canada, extends 60 mi/97 km NNW into L. Huron from Owen Sound toward Manitoulin Isl., forming SW side of Georgian Bay.

Saugeen River, c.100 mi/161 km long, S Ont., Canada; rises in several branches S of Owen Sound; main headstreams (North and South Saugeen rivers) unite 15 mi/24 km SSE of Southampton to form Saugeen R., which flows N to L. Huron at Southampton.

Saugerties (SAW-guhr-teez), village (□ 2 sq mi/5.2 sq km; 1990 pop. 3,915), Ulster co., SE N.Y., at foot of the Catskills, on Esopus Creek near its mouth on the Hudson, and 11 mi/18 km N of Kingston; 42°04'N 73°57'W. Former summer resort. Mfg. (canvas, wire and cable, fire hose fittings and valves, wrapping paper); limestone, shale quarries. Inc. 1831.

Sauget (soh-ZHAI), village (1990 pop. 197), St. Clair co., SW Ill., near the Mississippi, industrial suburb of St. Louis, just S of East St. Louis and within St. Louis metropolitan area; 38°35'N 90°10'W. Zinc and copper processing, mfg., chemicals, petroleum additives; steel foundry. Popular night club area. Formerly called Monsanto.

Saugstad, Mount (SUHG-stad) (10,000 ft/3,048 m), W B.C., Canada, in Coast Mts., 50 mi/80 km E of Ocean Falls, S of Tweedsmuir Park; 52°15'N 126°31'W.

Saugus 1 (SAW-guhs), uninc. town, Los Angeles co., S Calif., suburb 30 mi/48 km NW of downtown Los Angeles, on Santa Clara R. Dairying, poultry, nursery stock, grain. Mfg. (lab cleaners, machinery parts, resins). San Gabriel Mts. to S; Bouquet Canyon to NE. RR junction. **2** town (1990 pop. 25,549), Essex co., NE Mass., a suburb 6 mi/9.7 km NNE of Boston on the Saugus R. near the Atlantic Ocean; 42°28'N 71°01'W. Mainly residential, the town has some light mfg. The Saugus Ironworks Historic Site (1646–c.1670; restored 1954) were the 1st successful enterprise of the kind in the colonies. Includes villages of Cliftondale, East Saugus. Settled before 1637, set off from Lynn and inc. 1815.

Saugus Iron Works Historic Site, Saugus, E Mass. Reconstruction of the 17th-cent. colonial ironworks. Managed by Natl. Park Service. Authorized 1968.

Sauk (SAWK), county (□ 848 sq mi/2,196 sq km; 1990 pop. 46,975), S central Wis.; ⊙ Baraboo; 43°25'N 89°56'W. Bounded NE and S by Wisconsin R., Wis. Dells in NE; drained by Baraboo R. and tributaries of the Wisconsin. In Baraboo Mts. Dairying; grains, peas, beans, soybeans, alfalfa, hay; livestock, poultry; lumbering; some mfg. Has several lake resorts; Devils L. State Park is in E, Natural Bridge State Park at center, Mirror L. and Rocky Arbor state parks in NE; Dutch Hollow and Redstone lakes in NW; Devils Head Ski Area in E. Formed 1840.

Sauk Centre (SAWK), town (1990 pop. 3,581), Stearns co., central Minn., 37 mi/60 km WNW of St. Cloud on Sauk R., at S end of Sauk L.; 45°44'N 94°57'W. Resort; trading point in grain and livestock; agr. (dairying; poultry; grain, soybeans, beans, alfalfa); mfg. (printing and publishing, diversified light mfg). State industrial school for girls is here. City was birthplace of Sinclair Lewis, who used it as setting for *Main Street.* Sinclair Lewis Interpretive Center here. Municipal airport to S. Settled 1856, platted 1863, inc. as village 1876, as city 1889.

Sauk City (SAWK), town (1990 pop. 3,019), Sauk co., S central Wis., on Wisconsin R., adjoining Prairie du Sac, and 21 mi/34 km NW of Madison; 43°16'N 89°43'W. In timber, dairying, and farming area (corn, hogs; dairy); farm trade center, with mfg. (hand tools, agr. equip., frozen corn and peas); winery at Prairie du Sac. Resort. Haraszthy de Mokcsa settled here in 1840, and other liberal Eur. refugees followed. Natural Bridge State Park to NW. Founded 1838, inc. 1854.

Sauk Lake (SAWK), Stearns and Todd cos., central Minn., town of Sauk Centre at S end; 7 mi/11.3 km long, ½ mi/⅘ km wide. Fishing and bathing resorts. Fed and drained in S by Sauk R.

Sauk Rapids (SAWK), town (1990 pop. 7,825), Benton co., central Minn., suburb 2 mi/3.2 km N of St. Cloud on E bank of Mississippi R., opposite mouth of Sauk R.; 45°35'N 94°10'W. Agr. (dairy prods., flour); mfg. (fishing boats, electric signs, urethane foam fixtures flotation prods., ophthalmic lenses). Granite quarries nearby. Plotted 1851, inc. 1881.

Sauk River 1 (SAWK), 90 mi/145 km long, Minn.; rises in in L. Osakis, on Todd-Douglas co. line, W Minn. (45°53'N 95°05'W); flows E through Guernsey, Little Sauk, and Juergens lakes, then S through Saulk L. and past Sauk centre, SE past Melrose and Richmond, then NE through Cedar Isl. and Zumwalde lakes, past Cold Spring and Waite Park to Mississippi R., 2 mi/3.2 km N of St. Cloud. Drains small lakes in Stearns co. **2** c.45 mi/72 km long, in NW Wash.; formed by joining of North and South forks in Cascade Range W of Glacier Peak in E Snohomish co.; flows NW to Skagit R. c.10 mi/16 km above (SE of) Concrete. South Fork c.10 mi/16 km long; North Fork c.15 mi/24 km long.

Sauk Village, village (1990 pop. 9,926), Cook co., NE

Ill., 27 mi/43 km S of downtown Chicago, near Ind. state line on E; 41°29′N 87°34′W. Mfg. (steel cutting).

Saukville (SAWK-vil), town (1990 pop. 3,695), Ozaukee co., E Wis., on Milwaukee R. and 23 mi/37 km N of Milwaukee and 3 mi/4.8 km W of Port Washington; 43°22′N 87°56′W. In dairy and farm area; mfg. (electronic transformers, metal castings).

Saulsbury, town (1990 pop. 106), Hardeman co., SW Tenn., 50 mi/80 km E of Memphis, near Miss. state line; 35°02′N 89°05′W.

Sault au Mouton (SOO o moo-TO), village (1991 pop. 702), E Que., Canada, on the St. Lawrence, at mouth of Sault au Mouton R., and 35 mi/56 km WNW of Rimouski. Lumbering center.

Sault Sainte Marie (soo saint muh-REE), city (1991 pop. 81,476), S Ont., on the St. Marys R. opposite Sault Ste. Marie, Mich.; 46°30′N 84°20′W. A bridge connects the 2 cities. Sault Ste. Marie is an important port and mfg. center. Iron and steel, lumber, pulp and paper prods., and chemicals are made here. It is a tourist center and the gateway to hunting and fishing resorts in nearby lake and forest regions. A fur-trading post was built on the site in 1783, and a canal and lock to bypass the St. Marys rapids was constructed by 1898. Americans destroyed the post and lock during the War of 1812; a new lock was opened in 1895. There are 2 forest research stations.

Sault Sainte Marie (SOO SAINT), city (1990 pop. 14,689), ⊙ Chippewa co., N Mich., Upper Peninsula, a port of entry on the St. Marys R. opposite Sault Ste. Marie, Ont ; 46°28′N 84°22′W. Elev. 615 ft/187 m. RR terminus; ship-RR transfer point. A variety of light manufactured goods are produced (publishing, special alloys and plastics, veneer, plastic prods., fly wheel assemblies), but the city's economy is principally based on tourism and lake shipping. The famous "Soo" locks on the St. Marys R. draw annual visitors to watch heavy-laden ocean vessels and Great Lakes freighters pass through the intricate system that links lakes Superior and Huron. Particularly impressive is the 21 ft/6 m lift to the level of L. Superior. The region was 1st explored (1615) by Etienne Brulé, and Father Jacques Marquette est. a Jesuit mission here in 1668. Fr. occupation ended in 1763. The British remained in control until 1783, when the area was ceded to the U.S. in the Treaty of Paris. Fort Brady was built in 1822. The discovery of great mineral deposits in the NW stimulated the construction (1853–1855) of the Sault Ste. Marie Canal to facilitate the flow of ore; the locks have since been enlarged. An internatl. highway bridge connects Sault Ste. Marie with its Can. counterpart. Chippewa County Airport 15 mi/24 km to S. L. Superior State Col. (1946) in the city occupies the historic site of Fort Brady. Bay Mills (E Unit) Indian Reservation to SE, on Sugar Isl.; ferry to Sugar Isl.; Brimley State Park to SW. Only U.S.-Can. border crossing bet. Sarnia, Mich., 250 mi/402 km SSE, and Grand Portage, Minn., 250 mi/402 km WNW; major embarkment point for sport hunting and fishing tourism to Canada and Upper Peninsula.

Sault Sainte Marie Canals (SOO SAINT), 2 ship canals bypassing the rapids on the St. Marys R. bet. L. Superior and L. Huron, at the cities of Sault Ste. Marie, Mich. and Ont. (Canada). The Can. canal (1.4 mi/2.3 km long and 60 ft/18 m wide), which has 1 lock, was opened in 1895. It follows the route of the 1st canal constructed around the rapids (1797–1798) by a fur company. The U.S. canal (1.6 mi/2.6 km long and 80 ft/24 m wide) was constructed (1853–1855) by the state of Mich. and has since been reconstructed by the Federal govt. to accommodate larger vessels; it has 4 locks. Although closed by ice during the winter, the toll-free canals are among the country's busiest and are a vital link in the Great Lakes Waterway. Most of the ships pass through the larger and deeper U.S. canal. The waterways are popularly called the Soo Canals.

Saumâtre, Étang (so-MAH-truh, ai-TAWNG), lake (□ c.65 sq mi/168 sq km) SE Haiti, bordering on Dominican Republic, 18 mi/29 km E of Port-au-Prince, on

fertile Cul-de-Sac plain; 18 mi/29 km long, up to 6 mi/9.7 km wide; 18°35′N 72°00′W.

Saunders, county (□ 758 sq mi/1,963 sq km; 1990 pop. 18,285), E Nebr.; ⊙ Wahoo; 41°13′N 96°37′W. Farm area bounded E and N by Platte R, includes Todd Valley (former valley of Platte R.). Feed, food processing and other industries, cattle, hogs, corn, soybeans, sorghum, alfalfa, vegetables; dairying. Limestone. Pioneer State Wayside Area in S; Memphis L. State Recreation Area in SE. Formed 1867.

Saunderstown, R.I.: see NORTH KINGSTOWN.

Saundersville, Mass.: see GRAFTON.

Saunemin (SAWN-ah-min), village (1990 pop. 399), Livingston co., E central Ill., 11 mi/18 km E of Pontiac; 40°53′N 88°24′W. In agr. area.

Sauquoit (suh-KWOIT), village (1990 pop. 930), Oneida co., central N.Y., 7 mi/11.3 km S of Utica; 43°00′N 75°16′W.

Sausalito, city (1990 pop. 7,152), Marin co., W Calif., residential suburb 6 mi/9.7 km NW of downtown San Francisco on San Francisco Bay; 37°52′N 122°30′W. Richardson Bay to N; Golden Gate Strait to S; inc. 1893. RR junction. Mfg. (printing and publishing, light mfg.). Golden Gate Bridge to S; Golden Gate Natl. recreation Area to W and S; Mt. Tamalpais Game Refuge to N.

Saut-d'Eau (SO–DO), town, Ouest dept., Haiti, 20 mi/32 km NE of Port-au-Prince; 18°28′N 72°03′W. Cotton, citrus fruit growing.

Sauteurs (suhr-TYERS), town, N Grenada, West Indies, on Sauteurs Bay, 13 mi/21 km NE of St. George's; 12°13′N 61°38′W. Coconuts, cacao. Scene of Carib massacre by French (1650). Nearby is the crater lake Antoine.

Savage, town (1990 pop. 9,906), Scott co., S Minn., suburb 14 mi/23 km SSW of downtown Minneapolis, on Minnesota R.; 44°45′N 93°21′W. Agr. (corn, oats, barley; livestock, poultry; dairying); mfg. (cans, bandsaws, stock prods., asphalt, diversified light mfg.). Murphy Hanrahan Park Reserve in SE; James W. Wilke Regional Park to NW.

Savage 1 village, Howard co., central Md., at confluence of Middle and Little Patuxent rivers and 16 mi/26 km SW of Baltimore. Named after the financer of a mill here built here in 1750, which dominated the community for 130 years producing cotton prods. A row of identical houses built by the company which finally closed in 1951 still stand. **2** village (1990 pop. 300), Richland co., NE Mont., 20 mi/32 km SSW of Sidney and on Yellowstone R., near N.Dak. state line. Junction of RR spur to coal mines 5 mi/8 km W. Cattle, hogs, sheep, hay, beans, corn, barley. Elk Isl. Wildlife Management Area to NE.

Savage Dam, Calif.: see OTAY RIVER.

Savage River, c.25 mi/40 km long, NW Md.; rises in Garrett co., just S of Pa. line; flows SW and SE to North Branch of the Potomac at Luke. Savage R. Dam (175 ft/53 m high; begun 1939) is c.5 mi/8 km above mouth. The Army Corps. of Engineers releases water from a dam upstream, this creating the wild, fast flow needed for Olympic kayak racing trials.

Savage's Station, locality, Henrico co., E central Va., c.8 mi/12.9 km E of Richmond. Here was fought (June 29, 1862) one of Seven Days Battles.

Savana Island, islet (□ c.0.5 sq mi/1.5 sq km), U.S. Virgin Isls., in Virgin Passage, 2 mi/3.2 km off W tip of St. Thomas Isl.; 18°20′N 65°05′W.

Savanette (sah-vah-NET), town, Ouest dept., E Haiti, near Dominican Republic border, 35 mi/56 km NE of Port-au-Prince; 18°41′N 72°03′W. Coffee, timber; cattle.

Savanna (sah-VAN-ah), city (1990 pop. 3,819), Carroll co., NW Ill., on the Mississippi (bridged here) at mouth of Plum R., and 9 mi/14.5 km W of Mt. Carroll; 42°05′N 90°08′W. Trade and shipping center in rich agr. area (corn, wheat, livestock, poultry; dairy prods.); RR shops. U.S. Army's Savanna Ordnance Depot is 8 mi/12.9 km to NW. Mississippi Palisades State Park (c.800 acres/324 ha) is just N on cliffs above river. Settled 1828, inc. 1874.

Savanna, town (1990 pop. 869), Pittsburg co., SE Okla.,

9 mi/14.5 km SSW of McAlester; 34°49′N 95°50′W. In agr. region. At entrance to McLoster Army Amunition Plant.

Savannah 1 (suh-VAN-uh), city (1990 pop. 137,560), ⊙ Chatham co., SE Ga., a port of entry on the Savannah R. 18 mi/29 km upstream from its mouth; 32°01′N 81°08′W. A RR, fishing, and industrial center, it is a leading Southern port for the import and export of a wide variety of goods. The port of Savannah is connected by RR and interstate roads to the rest of the country. A 985 acres/399 ha container berth terminal was available to shipping in 1996 at the Garden City Terminal. The Ocean Terminal is a 208 acres/84 ha facility. Tourism is becoming increasingly important as a major industry of Savannah. Savannah is Georgia's oldest city; it was founded by James Oglethorpe in 1733 and served as the colonial capital. During the Amer. Revolution the British took Savannah on Dec. 29, 1778, and held it until July 1782. A land-sea force of French and Americans tried to retake the city in 1779, first by siege and then by direct assault (on Oct. 9), but failed dismally. Savannah was the state capital 1782–1785. With the growth of trade, and esp. after the invention of the cotton gin and the construction of RRs extending to the cotton fields of central Ga., the city became a rival of Charleston as a commercial center. The first steamship to cross the Atlantic, the *Savannah*, sailed from there to Liverpool in 1819. In the Civil War, Fort Pulaski, on Cockspur Isl. near the mouth of the Savannah R., was captured by Federals in 1862, but the city did not fall until Dec. 21, 1864, when Sherman entered. The original design of the city included a series of public squares surrounded by homes and important bldgs. (churches, mansions, schools). This area now forms the largest historic district in the U.S. on the Natl. Register. Adjacent to the historic district lies the Victorian district, a neighborhood experiencing rejuvenation; many of these homes are multi-family rental properties. Despite devastating fires in 1796 and 1820, many old homes and bldgs. remain, including the Pirates' House (1754), an old seaman's inn mentioned in Stevenson's *Treasure Island*; the Herb House (1734), the oldest existing bldg. in Georgia; and the Pink House (1789), site of Georgia's 1st bank. The mansion birthplace of Juliette Gordon Low (built 1819–1821) is owned and operated by the Girl Scouts of Amer. as a memorial to their founder. Savannah's historic dist. was designated a natl. historic landmark in 1966; many of its 18th- and 19th-cent. homes have been restored. The monument and grave of Nathanael Greene are in Johnson Square. The many churches include the Lutheran Church of Ascension (dating from 1741); the Independent Presbyterian Church (1890s), a replica of an earlier church destroyed by fire and the scene of Woodrow Wilson's marriage to Ellen Axson; and the Cathedral of St. John the Baptist (1876), one of the largest R.C. churches in the South. Monterey Square provovided the setting for the best-selling novel *Midnight in the Garden of Good and Evil*, which increased tourism and general interest in the city in the mid-1990s; in the center of Monterey Square, the statue of Revolutionary War hero Casimir Pulaski has been restored. Savannah is the seat of Savannah State Univ. and Armstrong Atlantic State Univ. (both units of the Univ. System of Ga.), Savannah Col. of Art and Design, several mus., the Telfair Acad. of Arts and Sciences, and the King-Tisdell Cottage and Mus. featuring displays of Savannah's Afr.-Amer. heritage and other important history of the city. An air force base and a U.S. coast guard station are here. Savannah served as the host city for the 1996 Summer Olympics sailing competition. Several beach and isl. resorts as well as a wildlife refuge are nearby. Internatl. airport to the W. Inc. 1789. **2** city (1990 pop. 4,352), ⊙ Andrew co., NW Mo., near Missouri R., 12 mi/19 km N of St. Joseph; 39°56′N 94°49′W. Corn, wheat, soybeans; hogs, cattle; poultry, produce farming; crushed limestone. Laid out 1842. **3** city (1990 pop. 6,547), ⊙ Hardin co., SW Tenn., on the Tennessee R., and 40 mi/64 km SE of Jackson, 35°14′N 88°15′W. In rough-timber and farm area; mfg. of shoes, clothing, mobile homes, handles. Pickwick Landing Dam and Shiloh Natl. Military Park are nearby.

Savannah 1 village (1990 pop. 700), Wayne co., W N.Y.,14 mi/23 km NW of Auburn; 43°04'N 76°45'W. Potato growing, storage, and shipping center. **2** village (1990 pop. 363), Ashland co., N central Ohio, 7 mi/11 km NNW of Ashland, in agr. area; 40°58'N 82°22'W.

Savannah (suh-VAN-uh), river, 314 mi/505 km long; formed by the confluence of the Tugaloo and Seneca rivers; flowing SE to the Atlantic Ocean; with the Tugaloo it forms the entire S.C.-Ga. state line; 34°26'N 82°51'W. Savannah, Ga., the largest port on the river, is the head of navigation for oceangoing ships. Clark Hill Dam (completed 1954) and Hartwell Dam (1961) above Augusta, Ga., are part of the Savannah R. basin development plan; the U.S. Atomic Energy Commission's Savannah R. plant is also on the river in S.C. The lower 25 mi/40 km of the river are dredged by the U.S. Corps of Engineers to maintain access by container ships to Port of Savannah in Garden City.

Savannah River Site, nuclear plant and nuclear fuel reprocessing facility (□ c.325 sq mi/842 sq km), W central S.C., bordered SW by the Savannah R. Est. 1950 by the Atomic Energy Commission to produce nuclear materials for defense, medical, and space-mission purposes and for reprocessing spent nuclear fuel. The fuel-production facilities and 5 productions reactors are no longer in use, though the reprocessing facility still provides nuclear material for NASA. The mission of the Savannah R. Site is shifting to environmental management, though it remains a major defense installation. Has radioactive waste disposal site. Village of Snelling is at main entrance.

Savanna-la-Mar, town (1991 pop. 16,340), ⊙ Westmoreland parish, SW Jamaica, port 90 mi/145 km WNW of Kingston; 18°13'N 78°08'W. Trading center on open bay; exports sugar, coffee, cacao, ginger, annatto, pimento, dyewood, rum. Ice factory; mfg. of aerated water. Frequently damaged by hurricanes.

Savant Lake, NW Ont., Canada, in Patricia dist., 60 mi/97 km ENE of Sioux Lookout; 25 mi/40 km long, 5 mi/8 km wide. Elev. 1,306 ft/398 m. Drains N into Albany R.

Savona, village (□ 1 sq mi/2.6 sq km; 1990 pop. 974), Steuben co., S N.Y., on Cohocton R. and 12 mi/19 km. NW of Corning; 42°16'N 77°13'W. Flour, wood prods.

Savonburg (SAV-uhn-buhrg), village (1990 pop. 93), Allen co., SE Kansas, 17 mi/27 km ENE of Chanute; 37°45'N 95°08'W. Livestock, grain.

Savoonga, Inuit village (1990 pop. 519), on N St. Lawrence Isl., W Alaska, in Bering Sea, 40 mi/64 km E of Gambell; 63°40'N 170°28'W. Whaling.

Savoy 1 town (1990 pop. 634), Berkshire co., NW Mass., 15 mi/24 km NE of Pittsfield; 42°35'N 73°01'W. Savoy Mt. State Forest is just N, in Hoosac Range. **2** town (1990 pop. 877), Fannin co., NE Texas, 11 mi/18 km W of Bonham; 33°36'N 96°22'W. In agr. area. Mfg. (textiles, consumer goods).

Savoy (sa-VOI), village (1990 pop. 2,674), Champaign co., E central Ill., suburb 4 mi/6.4 km S of Champaign; 40°04'N 88°15'W. Near source of Embarras R.

Sawatch Mountains, range of Rocky Mts. in central Colo., extending c.100 mi/161 km S from Eagle R. to Saguache town; bounded E by Arkansas R. (its source is in NE part of range), W by Elk Mts. Prominent peaks include Ouray Mt. (13,971 ft/4,258 m), Mt. of the Holy Cross (14,005 ft/4,269 m), Grizzly Mt. (13,723 ft/4,183 m), Shavano Peak (14,229 ft/4,337 m), Mt. Antero (14,269 ft/4,349 m), La Plata Peak (14,361 ft/4,377 m), Mt. Massive (14,421 ft/4,396 m), Mt. Elbert (14,433 ft/4,399 m.; highest point in Colo.). Part of range just N of St. Elmo, is known as Collegiate Range; includes Mt. Yale (14,196 ft/4,327 m), Mt. Princeton (14,197 ft/4,327 m), and Mt. Harvard (14,420 ft/4,395 m). Independence Pass (12,095 ft/3,687 m), near Mt. Massive, is crossed by highway, as is Hagerman Pass (11,925 ft/3,635 m), bet. Lake and Pitkin cos. Monarch Pass (11,312 ft/3,448 m) is W of Salida and crossed by highway. Marshall Pass (10,846 ft/3,306 m) is SW of Salida and serves RR. Range is penetrated 10 mi/16 km W of Leadville by Busk-Ivanhoe Tunnel (9,394 ft/2,863 m long), constructed as RR tunnel (1890) and now used by state road. Twin Lakes Tunnel, near Twin Lakes village, is unit in water-diversion project. Covered mainly by San Isabel, White R. and Gunnison natl. forests.

Sawmill Bay, locality, central Mackenzie dist., N.W.T., Canada, on E shore of Great Bear L., 35 mi/56 km SW of Port Radium; 65°44'N 118°55'W.

Sawmill Bay, S Alaska, small inlet on E side of Evans Isl., Prince William Sound, 4 mi/6.4 km W of Latouche; 60°3'N 148°2'W. Site of fish wharves; supply point for fishing in Prince William Sound.

Sawmills, town (1990 pop. 4,088), Caldwell co., W central N.C., 7 mi/11.3 km SE of Lenoir. L.; 35°49'N 81°28'W. Rhodhiss reservoir (Catawba R.) to S. Agr. area (tobacco, grain, poultry, livestock); timber.

Sawpit, village (1990 pop. 36), San Miguel co., SW Colo., 12 mi/19 km WNW of Telluride, on San Miguel R.; 37°59'N 108°00'W. Elev. 7,554 ft/2,302 m. Timber. Parts of Uncompahgre Natl. Forest to E and SW.

Sawtelle, Calif.: see WEST LOS ANGELES.

Sawtooth Mountains, in S central Idaho, NE of Boise, at head of Salmon R. and of its Middle Fork and South Fork. Include parts of Sawtooth, Challis, Payette, and Boise natl. forests. Prominent point is Castle Peak (11,820 ft/3,603 m). Sawtooth Range (rising to 10,704 ft/3,263 m) is largely in Elmore co., in S part of system. Deposits of gold, silver, lead, zinc, and copper. Source of Salmon and Payette river systems. Highest part (E) is referred to as the White Cloud Peaks. Sawtooth Wilderness Area (W) and Sawtooth Natl. Recreation Area (E) are at center of range.

Sawyer, county (□ 1,350 sq mi/3,497 sq km; 1990 pop. 14,181), N Wis.; ⊙ Hayward; 45°53'N 91°08'W. Drained by Chippewa, Namekagon, Thornapple, and Flambeau rivers. Generally forested area, with many lakes, the largest being L. Chippewa at center. Lumbering. Contains Lac Court Oreilles Indian Reservation in NE, former Ojibwa State Park (now a co. park) at center, part of Chequamegon Natl. Forest in NE, part of Flambeau R. State Forest in E; St. Croix Natl. Scenic Waterway follows Namekagon R. in NW; Tuscobia State Trail crosses co. from E to SW. Formed 1883.

Sawyer 1 (SOI-yuhr), village (1990 pop. 183), Pratt co., S Kansas, 11 mi/18 km SSE of Pratt; 37°30'N 98°40'W. In wheat region. **2** village (1990 pop. 319), Ward co., central N.Dak., 15 mi/24 km SE of Minot and on Souris R. (Mouse R.); 48°05'N 101°02'W.

Sawyer Island (SAW-yuhr), S Maine, in Sheepscot R., just W of Boothbay, to which it is bridged; c.75 mi/1.2 km in diameter.

Sawyerville, village (1991 pop. 900), S Que., Canada, on Eaton R., a tributary of St. Francis R. and 17 mi/27 km ESE of Sherbrooke. Dairying, livestock raising.

Saxapahaw (SAKS-uh-pah-haw), uninc. town (1990 pop. 1,178), Alamance co., N central N.C., 23 mi/37 km WSW of Durham, on Haw R.; 35°57'N 79°19'W. Tobacco, grain, soybeans, dairying.

Saxis, town (1990 pop. 367), Accomack co., E Va., 13 mi/21 km SW of Pocomoke City, Md. on Saxis Isl., on Chesapeake Bay (separated from mainland by marshes of the Saxis Waterfowl Management. Area); 37°55'N 75°43'W. Agr. (vegetables, grain; livestock; poultry); fish, shellfish.

Saxman, fishing village (1990 pop. 369), SE Alaska, on S coast of Revillagigedo Isl., 2 mi/3.2 km SE of Ketchikan; 55°19'N 131°35'W.

Saxon, uninc. town (1990 pop. 4,002), Spartanburg co., NW S.C., residential suburb 2 mi/3.2 km W of Spartanburg; 34°57'N 81°58'W. Spartanburg Methodist col. here.

Saxon, village, Iron co., N Wis., 23 mi/37 km ESE of Ashland. Trade center in submarginal farm area. Fishing, skiing. Superior Falls (90 ft/27 m) drops into Montral R. near Saxon Harbor to N; Whitecap Mt. Ski Area to S; Bad River Indian Reservation to W.

Saxonburg (SAKS-suhn-buhrg), borough (1990 pop. 1,345), Butler co., W Pa., 9 mi/14.5 km SSE of Butler, near Thorn Creek; 40°45'N 79°49'W. Agr. area (corn, hay, dairying); mfg. (ceramics, iron and steel processing, metals purifying, concrete, semiconductors).

Saxton (SAKS-tuhn), borough (1990 pop. 838), Bedford co., S Pa., 23 mi/37 km SW of Huntingdon, on Raystown Branch of Juniata R.; 40°12'N 78°15'W. Agr. (corn, oats, apples; livestock, dairying); timber; mfg. (lumber, apparel); bituminous coal. Warrior Path State Park to S; Raystown L. reservoir to N, Trough Creek State Park to NE. Inc. 1867.

Saxtons River, Vt.: see ROCKINGHAM.

Sayabec (SAI-behk, Fr. sah-yah-BEHK) or **Saindon** (seh-DOH), village (1991 pop. 2,088), SE Que., Canada, on L. Matapedia, 22 mi/35 km SSW of Matane; 48°33'N 67°41'W. Lumbering, dairying.

Saybrook, Conn.: see DEEP RIVER and OLD SAYBROOK.

Saybrook, village (1990 pop. 767), McLean co., E central Ill., 24 mi/39 km E of Bloomington; 40°25'N 88°31'W. Grain, livestock, poultry. On Sorgamon R.

Saybrook Point, Conn.: see OLD SAYBROOK.

Sayil (sah-YEEL), historic site, in SW Yucatán, Mexico, 3.1 mi/5 km S of Kabah off Mexico Highway 261 on paved road; 20°14'N 89°13'W. Sayil is representative of Puuc style architecture.

Saylesville, village in Lincoln town, Providence co., NE R.I., on Moshcassuck R. and 5 mi/8 km N of Providence. Formerly a center for textiles, textile dyeing and finishing.

Saylorsburg (SAI-luhrs-buhrg), uninc. village, Ross and Hamilton townships, Monroe co., NE Pa., 9 mi/14.5 km SW of Stroudsburg, surrounds small Saylors L.; 40°53'N 75°19'W. Mfg. of apparel. Cherry Valley Winery to S.

Saylorville Lake, reservoir (□ 9 sq mi/23.3 sq km), Polk co., central Iowa, on Des Moines R., 9 mi/14 km N of Des Moines; 41°42'N 93°41'W. Max. capacity 670,000 acre-ft. Formed by Saylorville Dam (120 ft/37 m high), built (1976) by Army Corps of Engineers for flood control; also used for recreation.

Sayre (SAI-uhr), town (1990 pop. 2,881), ⊙ Beckham co., W Okla., on North Fork of Red R., and 16 mi/26 km WSW of Elk City; 35°17'N 99°37'W. Elev. 1,816 ft/554 m. In agr. area (grain, cotton, peanuts; cattle). Natural gas fields nearby. RR shops. Seat of Sayre Jr. Col. Settled 1901; inc. as town 1903, as city 1910.

Sayre (SER), borough (1990 pop. 5,791), Bradford co., NE Pa., 17 mi/27 km ESE of Elmira, on Susquehanna R. Chemung R. on W; 41°59'N 76°31'W. Agr. area (hay; livestock, dairying); mfg. (printing and publishing, furniture, food prods., laundry detergents). Chemung Valley Airport in W part of town. Laid out 1871, inc. 1891.

Sayreville (SER-vil), borough (1990 pop. 34,986), Middlesex co., E N.J., on the Raritan R.; 40°28'N 74°19'W. Inc. 1919. Mfg. includes chemicals, plastics, steel, steel reinforcing, adhesives.

Sayula (sah-YOO-lah), city (1990 pop. 21,575) and township, Jalisco, central Mexico, near S shore of L. Sayula, on R and 45 mi/72 km N of Colima on Mexico Highway 54; 19°52'N 103°36'W. Processing and agr. center (grain, sugarcane, alfalfa, cotton, tobacco, livestock); flour milling, lumbering, sugar refining, vegetable-oil pressing, tanning.

Sayula, Mexico: see SAYULA DE ALEMÁN.

Sayula de Alemán (sai-OO-lah de ah-le-MAHN), town (1990 pop. 9,230), Veracruz, SE Mexico, on Isthmus of Tehuantepec, 29 mi/47 km WSW of Minatitlán at junction of Mexico Highways 145 and 185; 17°41'N 95°01'W. Fruit. In Popoluca-speaking area. Formerly Sayula.

Sayula, Lake (sai-oo-lah) (□ 79 sq mi/205 sq km), in Jalisco, central Mexico, on central plateau, SW of L. Chapala and 40 mi/64 km SSW of Guadalajara; 2 mi/3.2 km–6 mi/9.7 km wide, 16 mi/26 km long NNE-SSW. Elev. 4,511 ft/1,375 m. Town of Sayula near S shore.

Sayville, village (□ 5 sq mi/13 sq km; 1990 pop. 16,550), Suffolk co., SE N.Y., on S shore of L.I., on Great South Bay, 8 mi/12.9 km. E of Bay Shore; 40°45'N 73°05'W. Yachting center; oysters; flower growing. Mfg. (waxes and related prods., furniture, marble and mica prods.). Seafront recreational area.

Sayward, village (1991 pop. 406), SW B.C., Canada, on NE Vancouver Isl., on Johnstone Strait, at mouth of small Salmon R., 50 mi/80 km ESE of Alert Bay; 50°21′N 125°55′W. Lumbering and farming area. Just S is Hkusam, Indian village.

Scales Mound, village (1990 pop. 388), Jo Daviess co., extreme NW Ill., near Wis. line, 11 mi/18 km ENE of Galena; 42°28′N 90°15′W. In agr. area. Nearby is Charles Mound (1,235 ft/376 m), highest point in state.

Scalp Level, borough (1990 pop. 1,158), Cambria co., SW central Pa., residential suburb 6 mi/9.7 km SSE of Johnstown, on Paint Creek, at mouth of Little Paint Creek, adjoins Windber to SE; 40°15′N 78°50′W. Agr. area (corn, hay; dairying). Univ. of Pittsburgh-Johnstown Campus to N. Part of Gallitzin State Forest to SE. Inc. 1898.

Scammon (SKAM-muhn), village (1990 pop. 466), Cherokee co., extreme SE Kansas, 11 mi/18 km SW of Pittsburg; 37°16′N 94°49′W. In diversified agr. area. Mfg. (fabricated pipe and fittings).

Scammon Bay, Inuit village (1990 pop. 343), W Alaska, on Bering Sea, 60 mi/97 km SW of Akulurak; 61°51′N 165°34′W.

Scandia (SKAN-dee-uh), village (1990 pop. 421), Republic co., N Kansas, on Republican R., and 8 mi/12.9 km WSW of Belleville; 39°47′N 97°46′W. RR junction. In grain region.

Scandinavia, village (1990 pop. 298), Waupaca co., central Wis., 20 mi/32 km ESE of Stevens Point; 44°27′N 89°09′W. In timber and farm area; lumbering. Tourism.

Scanlon, town (1990 pop. 878), Carlton co., NE Minn., residential suburb 16 mi/26 km WSW of Duluth and 2 mi/3.2 km SE of Cloquet, on St. Louis R.; 46°42′N 92°25′W. Agr. (dairying; poultry; oats, alfalfa). Fond du Lac Indian Reservation to W.

Scantic, Conn.: see EAST WINDSOR.

Scantic River (SKAN-tik), c.35 mi/56 km, Mass. and Conn.; rises SSE of Springfield, Mass.; flows generally SW, through Conn., to the Connecticut near South Windsor.

Scappoose (skuh-POOS), town (1990 pop. 3,529), Columbia co., NW Oregon, 20 mi/32 km NW of Portland, near Columbia R.; 45°45′N 122°52′W. Multnomah Channel separates mainland from Sauvie Isl., Oregon. Mfg. (fishing waders, drysuits, boots). Berries, nuts; dairy prods.; poultry, sheep, cattle. State-operated gambling. Ridgefield Natl. Wildlife Refuge (Wash.) to N.

Scarborough, city (1991 pop. 524,598), borough of Metropolitan Toronto, S central Ont., Canada, 7 mi/11 km E of downtown Toronto; 43°45′N 79°12′W. Borders L. Ontario on S. MacDonald-Cartier Freeway (Highway 401) runs E-W. Metro. Toronto Zoo in NE. Diversified industry; mfg. (paper prods., chemicals, electrical machinery, cosmetics, electronic components, knitwear, apparel, shoes, lighting fixtures, furniture, signs, ventilation systems, records and compact discs).

Scarborough (SKAHR-buhr-o), town (1990 pop. 12,518), Cumberland co., SW Maine, just S of Portland, at mouth of Nonesuch R., includes villages of Dunstan and Prouts Neck; 43°34′N 70°21′W. Fishing and resort area. Scarborough Downs racetrack and Scarborough Marsh Nature Center (largest Maine salt marsh) are here. Rufus King b. here. Settled in 1630s, inc. 1658.

Scarborough, village, Westchester co., SE N.Y., 2 mi/3.2 km S of Ossining; 41°08′N 73°52′W. Seat of Scarborough School.

Scarborough Beach, R.I.: see NARRAGANSETT.

Scarbro (SKAHR-bro), uninc. village (1990 pop. 600), Fayette co., S central W.Va., 15 mi/24 km S of Fayetteville, in coal region. Plum Orchard Wildlife Management Area to W.

Scarsdale, village (□ 6 sq mi/15.5 sq km; 1990 pop. 16,987), Westchester co., SE N.Y., a residential suburb of N.Y. city; 40°59′N 73°46′W. Scarsdale is often considered typical of upper-class suburban communities. Settled c.1701, inc. 1915.

Scarville, town (1990 pop. 92), Winnebago co., N Iowa, near Minn. line, 14 mi/23 km N of Forest City; 43°28′N 93°37′W. Feed. Sand and gravel pits nearby.

Scatari Island, NE N.S., off E Cape Breton Isl., 15 mi/24 km SE of Glace Bay; 6 mi/10 km long; 46°2′N 59°47′W.

Sceptre, village (1991 pop. 168), SW Sask., Canada, near South Saskatchewan R., 40 mi/64 km S of Kindersley. Wheat; livestock.

Schaefferstown (SCHAI-fuhrs-toun), uninc. town (1990 pop. 950), Lebanon co., SE Pa., 8 mi/12.9 km ESE of Lebanon; 40°17′N 76°17′W. Agr. (grain; poultry, livestock; dairying); mfg. (wooden prods., metal prods.). Keller Brothers Airport to W. Mill Creek Waterfowl Management Area to SE.

Schaghticoke (SKAH-duh-kok) village (1990 pop. 794), Rensselaer co., E N.Y., on Hoosic R., and 13 mi/21 km NNE of Troy; 42°53′N 73°35′W. In dairying area.

Schaller, town (1990 pop. 768), Sac co., W Iowa, 16 mi/26 km WNW of Sac City; 42°30′N 95°17′W. Popcorn, feed.

Schaumburg, village (1990 pop. 68,586), Cook co., NE Ill., suburb 26 mi/42 km WNW of downtown Chicago, 10 mi/16 km E of Elgin; 42°01′N 88°04′W. Mfg. (plastic molding, food processing, machining, magnesium die casting, metal fabrication, communication systems, rubber printing plates). Hq. for Motorola. Site of Woodfield, one of the largest shopping centers in U.S., as well as other large shopping malls.

Schefferville, town (1991 pop. 303), E central Que., Canada, on the Lab. border; 54°48′N 66°49′W. With the closure of the Iron Ore Co. in 1983, the town shut down almost completely.

Schell City, town (1990 pop. 292), Vernon co., W Mo., near Osage R., 18 mi/29 km NE of Nevada; 38°01′N 94°07′W. Soybeans, wheat, hay; cattle. Schell-Osage Conservation Area (wetlands) to NE.

Schell Creek Range (SHEL), (12,000 ft/3,650 m–13,000 ft/3,960 m), E Nev., in White Pine co., E of Ely, W of Snake Range. Part of Humboldt in central part of range. Highway crosses range in S at Connors Pass (6,997 ft/2,133 m; also spelled Conners Pass). North Schell Peak (11,883 ft/3,622 m) at center.

Schellsburg (SCHELS-buhrg), borough (1990 pop. 245), Bedford co., S Pa., 8 mi/12.9 km WNW of Bedford; 40°02′N 78°38′W. Agr. (corn, oats; livestock; dairying). Shawnee L. reservoir and Shawnee State Park to S.

Schenectady (skuh-NEK-tuh-dee), county (□ 209 sq mi/541 sq km; 1990 pop. 149,285), E N.Y.; ☉ Schenectady; 42°38′N 74°04′W. Bounded N by Schoharie Creek; intersected by Mohawk R., and the N.Y. State Barge Canal. Dairying, fruit growing, general farming. Formed 1809.

Schenectady (skuh-NEK-tuh-dee), city (□ 10 sq mi/26 sq km; 1990 pop. 65,566), ☉ Schenectady co., E central N.Y., on the Mohawk R., and the Barge Canal; 42°47′N 73°55′W. Mfg. includes gas turbines, electric transmission systems; RR equip. It was the home of the huge General Electric Co., est. here in 1886. Several other companies make a variety of electrical equip., and the production of chemicals is also important. Destroyed (1690) in a Native Amer. attack, the village grew again, prospering as a stopping place for traders and settlers traveling W on the Mohawk R. The city's growth was particularly spurred by the opening (1820s) of the Erie Canal and the bldg. (1830s) of the RRs. The mfg. of locomotives, begun in 1848, was long an important industry. Schenectady is the seat of Union Col. and Univ. and Schenectady Co. Community Col. A science mus. is maintained by the state in the former home and laboratory of Charles P. Steinmetz. Notable among Schenectady's historic bldgs. are the homes in the old stockade area, which date from the early 1700s. Founded 1661 by Arent Van Curler, inc. 1798.

Schenevus (skuh-NEE-vus), village (1990 pop. 513), Otsego co., central N.Y., 12 mi/19 km SSE of Cooperstown, in the Catskills; 42°32′N 74°49′W. Small Schenevus L. is nearby.

Schererville, town (1990 pop. 19,926), Lake co., extreme NW Ind., 8 mi/12.9 km NW of Crown Point, near Ill. line; 41°29′N 87°27′W. Mfg. (scrap metal processing, foil and decals, water treatment chemicals, pipe coatings, steel fabricating). Laid out 1866.

Schertz, city (1990 pop. 10,555), Guadalupe, Comal and Bexar cos., S central Texas, suburb 17 mi/27 km NE of downtown San Antonio, on Cibolo Creek; 29°33′N 98°15′W. Agr. area (cattle, cotton, peanuts, nursery, crops). Mfg. (concrete, steel fabricating, industrial fans).

Schiller Park, village (1990 pop. 11,189), Cook co., NE Ill., a residential suburb W of Chicago; 41°57′N 87°52′W. Inc. 1914. O'Hare Internatl. Airport is to the W, and the co. forest preserve is to the E.

Schist Lake, village, W Man., Canada, on Schist L. (9 mi/14 km long), 8 mi/13 km SE of Flin Flon; 54°40′N 101°47′W. Copper mining.

Schlater (SLAI-tuhr), village (1990 pop. 404), Leflore co., W central Miss., 12 mi/19 km NW of Greenwood, near Quiver R.; 33°38′N 90°20′W. Cotton, grain; cattle. Mfg. (cotton gins).

Schleicher, county (□ 1,310 sq mi/3,393 sq km; 1990 pop. 2,990), W Texas; ☉ Eldorado; 30°53′N 100°32′W. On Edwards Plateau; elev c.2,100 ft/640 m–2,500 ft/762 m. Drained by San Saba R. (source) and Buckhorn Draw, headstream of Devil's R. Sheep ranching region; also cattle, goats; ships wool, mohair. Some agr. (hay, milo; oats, wheat, cotton). Some oil, natural gas. Hunting in East Fort McKavett State Historic site near E co. line. Formed 1887.

Schleisingerville, Wis.: see SLINGER.

Schleswig, town (1990 pop. 851), Crawford co., W Iowa, 11 mi/18 km NNW of Denison; 42°09′N 95°25′W.

Schley (SHLEI), county (□ 168 sq mi/435 sq km; 1990 pop. 3,588), W central Ga.; ☉ Ellaville; 32°16′N 84°19′W. Mfg. of leather and metal prods. Coastal plain agr. (cotton, corn, peanuts, wheat, pecans, peaches); poultry, hogs, cattle. Formed 1857.

Schlusser (SCHLLITS-suhr), uninc. town (1990 pop. 4,728), Cumberland co., central Pa., residential suburb 2 mi/3.2 km NNE of Carlisle on Conodoquinet Creek; 40°14′N 77°10′W.

Schnecksville (SCHNEKS-vil), uninc. town (1990 pop. 1,780), Lehigh co., E Pa., 8 mi/12.9 km NW of Allentown; 40°40′N 75°37′W. Agr. includes dairying, livestock, poultry; grain, apples. Seat of Lehigh Co. Community Col. Trexler-Lehigh co. Game Preserve to W.

Schneider, town (1990 pop. 310), Lake co., NW Ind., near Kankakee R., 16 mi/26 km SSW of Crown Point; 41°11′N 87°27′W. Agr. area. LaSalle State Fish and Wildlife Area nearby to SW.

Schoelcher (shuhl-KAI), town, W Martinique, 2 mi/3.2 km NW of Fort-de-France; 14°37′N 61°06′W. Agr. (cacao, coffee, and sugar); residential suburb. Univ. of the Fr. West Indies, and the Schoelcher Lib., ornate structure shipped from France in honor of Fr. abolitionist Victor Schoelcher.

Schoenbrunn Village State Memorial (SHAIN-bruhn), E Ohio, S of New Philadelphia. Site of the first town in Ohio, est. 1772 by Moravian missionary David Zeisberger and his Native Amer. converts. During the Amer. Revolution, the town was abandoned; later it was burned by Native Americans. Restoration of the site to its original appearance began in 1923. Mus. here.

Schoenchen (SHUHN-chuhn), village (1990 pop. 128), Ellis co., W central Kansas, on Smoky Hill R., and 11 mi/18 km S of Hays; 38°42′N 99°19′W. Grain; livestock.

Schofield (SKO-feeld), town (1990 pop. 2,415), Marathon co., central Wis., on L. Wausau reservoir at confluence of Wisconsin and Eau Claire rivers, suburb 2 mi/3.2 km S of Wausau; 44°55′N 89°36′W. Sawmilling; mfg. (glass prods., fiberglass, machinery, metal stampings, wire prods.). Wausau Airport to NW. Settled c.1849, inc. 1904.

Schofield Barracks (1990 pop. 19,597), central Oahu isl., Honolulu co., Hawaii, 16 mi/26 km NW of Honolulu; 21°30′N 158°03′W. Large U.S. army military post (est. 1909) on central plateau. City of Wahiawa outside E end of base. Schofield Military Firing Range to E of Wahiawa.

Schoharie (skuh-HER-ee), county (□ 626 sq mi/1,621 sq km; 1990 pop. 31,859), E central N.Y.; ☉ Schoharie; 42°35′N 74°26′W. Partly in the Catskills; traversed by the Helderbergs; drained by Schoharie Creek and its tributaries (impounded to create Schoharie Reservoir and the Blenheim Gilboa pumped storage project's reservoirs) and SE by Catskill Creek. Dairying, farming (hay, fruit, potatoes), poultry raising. Many recreational facilities and summer homes in the Catskills; includes several scenic caverns. Formed 1795.

Schoharie (skuh-HER-ee), village (□ 1 sq mi/2.6 sq km; 1990 pop. 1,045), ⊙ Schoharie co., E central N.Y., on Schoharie Creek, and 28 mi/45 km W of Albany; 42°40′N 74°18′W. Trade center in rich farming area; light mfg. Has 18th-cent. bldgs. (including Old Stone Fort; 1772), now a mus. Inc. 1867.

Schoharie Creek (skuh-HER-ee), c.85 mi/137 km long, E central N.Y.; rises in the Catskills in Greene co.; flows E and N, past Prattsville and Middleburg, to Mohawk R. 5 mi/8 km W of Amsterdam. At Gilboa, Gilboa Dam impounds Schoharie Reservoir, which supplies water to N.Y. city via Shandaken Tunnel to Ashokan Reservoir, and then through Catskill Aqueduct. Downstream is the Blenheim Gilboa pumped storage reservoirs used for hydroelectric power generation.

Schoharie Reservoir, at North Blenheim village, Schoharie, Greene, and Delaware cos., E central N.Y., on the Schoharie Creek, 35 mi/56 km SW of Albany; 10 mi/16 km long; 42°23′N 74°26′W. Formed by Blenheim Lower Dam (95 ft/29 m high) and Gilboa Upper Dam (105 ft/32 m high; 5 mi/8 km upstream), both built (1973) by the Power Authority of the State of N.Y. for power generation. Mine Kill State Park on W shore of lower reservoir.

Schomberg (SHOHM-buhrg), village, S Ont., Canada, 28 mi/45 km NW of Toronto. Dairying, mixed farming.

Schoodic Island (SKOO-dik), Hancock co., S Maine, small isl. just SE of Schoodic Peninsula, off entrance to Frenchman Bay.

Schoodic Lake (SKOO-dik), Piscataquis co., central Maine, 17 mi/27 km NE of Dover-Foxcroft; 9 mi/ 14.5 km long.

Schoodic Peninsula (SKOO-dik), Hancock co., S Maine, extending into the Atlantic at E side of Frenchman Bay; terminates at Schoodic Head (elev. 440 ft/ 134 m) just off which lies small isl. whose seaward tip is Schoodic Point. Peninsula is partly in ACADIA NATIONAL PARK.

Schoolcraft, county (□ 1,883 sq mi/4,877 sq km; 1990 pop. 8,302), S Upper Peninsula, Mich.; ⊙ Manistique; 46°01′N 86°11′W. Bounded S by L. Michigan; drained by Indian R. and by Manistique R. and its affluents. Cattle and agr. area (forage crops). Some mfg. at Manistique. Lumbering. Resorts. Fish hatchery. Palms Brook and Indian L. state parks on Indian L. in SW; Seney Natl. Wildlife Refuge dominates E central part of co.; part of Hiawatha Natl. Forest in W; McDonald and Gulliver lakes in SE; numerous small lakes in W and far N. Organized 1871.

Schoolcraft, town (1990 pop. 1,517), Kalamazoo co., SW Mich., 13 mi/21 km S of Kalamazoo; 42°07′N 85°37′W. RR junction. Mfg. (plastic molds, aircraft parts, marble bath prods.); cattle; forage crops.

Schooleys Mountain (SKOO-leez), village, Morris co., NW N.J., on Schooleys (or Schooley) Mtn., 17 mi/ 27 km W of Morristown. Mtn. (elev. c.1,000 ft/305 m) is flat-topped ridge of the Appalachians, extending NE-SW bet. valleys of Musconetcong R. and South Branch of the Raritan. Recreation.

Schottegat (SKHAW-tuh-gaht), lagoon, S Curaçao, Neth. Antilles; 3 mi/4.8 km long, 1.5 mi/2.4 km wide. Deep, sheltered inlet just N of Willemstad, and linked with the Caribbean through Sint Anna Bay. Harbor, dry dock and oil refinery.

Schram City, village (1990 pop. 692), Montgomery co., S central Ill., just NE of Hillsboro; 39°09′N 89°27′W. In agr. area.

Schreiber (SHREI-buhr), village, W Ont., Canada, on L. Superior, 90 mi/145 km ENE of Thunder Bay. Gold mining.

Schroon Lake (skroon), resort village (1990 pop. 1,100), Essex co., NE N.Y., in the Adirondacks, 37 mi/60 km NNW of Glens Falls; 43°51′N 73°46′W. At N end of Schroon L. (□ c.6.5 sq mi/16.8 sq km) , a widening of

Schroon R., which rises in E Essex co.; flows c.60 mi/ 97 km generally S to the Hudson just below Warrensburg.

Schuermann Heights (SHUHR-muhn), town, St. Louis co., E Mo. Merged into Woodson Terrace 1980.

Schulenburg, town (1990 pop. 2,455), Fayette co., S central Texas, 31 mi/50 km NNE of Yoakum, near Navidad R.; 29°40′N 96°54′W. Elev. 344 ft/105 m. In agr. area (poultry, cattle; dairying; corn, sorghum, peanuts, pecans); mfg. (smoked meats, pressure tanks, dairy prods., toys, leather goods). Inc. 1873.

Schulter (SHUHL-tuhr), village, Okmulgee co., E central Okla., 7 mi/11.3 km S of Okmulgee, and 5 mi/8 km N of Henryetta.

Schultz Lake (□ 110 sq mi/285 sq km), central Keewatin dist., N.W.T., Canada; 35 mi/56 km long, 11 mi/18 km wide; 64°42′N 97°30′W. Drained E by Thelon R.

Schumacher (SHOO-ma-kuhr), town, NE Ont., Canada, 2 mi/3 km E of Timmins, in gold mining region; 48°28′N 81°17′W.

Schurz (SHUHRTS), uninc. village (1990 pop. 617), Mineral co., W Nev., 18 mi/29 km ESE of Yerington, on Walker R., N of Walker L.; 38°59′N 118°49′W. Elev. 4,126 ft/1,258 m. Cattle. Headquarters of Walker R. Indian Reservation, located in SW point of reservation. Wassuk Range to W.

Schuyler 1 (SKY-ler), county (□ 441 sq mi/1,142 sq km; 1990 pop. 7,498), W Ill.; ⊙ Rushville; 40°09′N 90°36′W. Bounded SE by Illinois R.; drained by La Moine R. Agr. (livestock, dairy, and meat prods.; corn, soybeans, wheat, fruit). Formed 1825. **2** (SKEI-luhr), county (□ 306 sq mi/793 sq km; 1990 pop. 4,236), N Mo.; ⊙ Lancaster; 40°28′N 92°31′W. Bounded by Iowa on N, W by Chariton R.; drained by North Fabius R. Corn, wheat, soybeans; sheep, hogs, cattle, poultry. Formed 1845. **3** county (□ 346 sq mi/896 sq km; 1990 pop. 18,662), W central N.Y.; ⊙ Watkins Glen; 42°23′N 76°52′W. Situated in Finger Lakes region; includes S end of Seneca L., and Lamoka and Cayuta lakes. Drained by Cayuta and Catherine creeks. Fruit-growing and general-farming area (grain; poultry, livestock; hay; dairy prods.). Diversified mfg. at Watkins Glen and Montour Falls. Contains scenic Watkins Glen State Park, and several waterfalls and gorges. Formed 1854.

Schuyler (SHEI-luhr), town (1990 pop. 4,052), ⊙ Colfax co., E Nebr., 17 mi/27 km E of Columbus and on Platte R., on fertile low terraces of Platte Valley in prairie region; 41°27′N 97°3′W. RR and trade point for agr. region; grain, livestock; dairying. Mfg. (cattle slaughtering, meat processing, printing, plastic exhaust fans). Founded 1869.

Schuyler (SKEI-luhr), uninc. village, Nelson co., central Va., on Rockfish R., 20 mi/32 km SSW of Charlottesville; 37°47′N 78°41′W. Mfg. (stone processing); agr. (apples, corn; cattle); soapstone quarrying.

Schuyler, Fort, N.Y.: see FORT SCHUYLER.

Schuylkill (SKOOL-kil), county (□ 782 sq mi/ 2,025 sq km; 1990 pop. 152,585), E central Pa.; ⊙ Pottsville; 40°42′N 76°12′W. Mountainous region drained by Schuylkill R. Agr. (corn, wheat, oats, hay, alfalfa, soybeans, potatoes, apples; chickens, hogs, cattle, dairying); anthracite coal; limestone. Mfg. at Tamaqua, Orwigsburg, and Pottsville. Appalachian Trail follows most of S state line, on Blue Mt. ridge; part of Swatara State Park, SW; Tuscarora and Locust L. state parks, NE central; parts of Weiser State Forest, S and NW. Formed 1811.

Schuylkill (SKOOL-kil) [Du. = hidden creek], river, c.130 mi/209 km long; rises in NE Schuylkill co., E central Pa. (40°46′N 76°01′W); flows SW to Pottsville, then generally SE past Hamburg, Reading, Pottstown, Phoenixville, and Norristown and through city of Philadelphia, passes W of downtown, enters Delaware R., 5 mi/ 8 km S of downtown Philadelphia.

Schuylkill Haven (SKOOL-kil HAI-vuhn), borough (1990 pop. 5,610), Schuylkill co., E central Pa., 4 mi/ 6.4 km SSE of Pottsville, on Schuylkill R.; 40°37′N 76°10′W. RR junction. Agr. (hay, apples; poultry, livestock, dairying); mfg. (apparel, coal stokers, electrical wire and cable, heating equip., shoes); anthracite coal.

Penn. State Univ.-Schuylkill Campus (2-year) here. Part of Weiser State Forest to NW. Settled 1748, laid out 1829, inc. 1840.

Schwenksville (SCWENKS-vil), borough (1990 pop. 1,326), Montgomery co., SE Pa., on Perkiomen Creek, 11 mi/18 km NW of Norristown; 40°15′N 75°28′W. Agr. (grain, apples, soybeans; livestock; dairying); mfg. (tool and die). Pa. State Correctional Inst. to SE. Sunrise Mill Historic Site to NW; Pennypacker Mill Historic Site to SE.

Science Hill, village (1990 pop. 628), Pulaski co., S Ky., in Cumberland foothills, 6 mi/9.7 km NNW of Somerset; 37°10′N 84°38′W. Agr. (tobacco, grain; livestock; dairying; timber); mfg. (wood cabinets, wooden furniture, wooden pallets).

Scio 1 (SEI-o), village (1990 pop. 800), Allegany co., W N.Y., 4 mi/6.4 km NW of Wellsville; 42°08′N 78°00′W. **2** village (1990 pop. 856), Harrison co., E Ohio, 9 mi/ 14 km NNW of Cadiz and on small Conotton Creek; 40°23′N 81°05′W. **3** village (1990 pop. 623), Linn co., NW Oregon, on Thomas Creek; 44°42′N 122°50′W. Fruit; poultry, cattle. Timber. Fish hatchery to SE.

Sciota, village (1990 pop. 68), McDonough co., W Ill., 8 mi/12.9 km NNW of Macomb; 40°33′N 90°45′W. In agr. and bituminous coal area.

Scioto (sei-O-tuh), county (□ 609 sq mi/1,577 sq km; 1990 pop. 80,327), S Ohio; ⊙ PORTSMOUTH; 38°48′N 82°59′W. Bounded S by Ohio R., here forming Ky. state line; intersected by Scioto and Little Scioto rivers. Includes Shawnee State Forest and Roosevelt Game Preserve. In the Unglaciated Plains physiographic region. Agr. area (lambs, dairy prods., corn, soybeans, fruit); mfg. at Portsmouth (food and beverages, gray and ductile iron foundries, industrial organic chemicals). Formed 1803.

Scioto (sei-O-tuh), river, 237 mi/381 km long; rising in W Ohio near Indian L.; flows E, then turning S to pass through Columbus and Chillicothe and enter the Ohio R. at Portsmouth; 38°43′N 83°00′W. It receives numerous tributaries and has many multipurpose dams.

Scipio (SI-pee-o), village (1990 pop. 291), Millard co., W central Utah, 25 mi/40 km ESE of Delta; 39°15′N 112°05′W. Elev. 5,305 ft/1,617 m. Cattle, alfalfa, wheat, barley. Settled 1861. Scipio Reservoir 10 mi/16 km S. Sevier Bridge Reservoir and Yuba State Park, at N end, to NE; Pavant and Valley Mts. and Natl. Forests nearby.

Scituate 1 (SI-choo-wuht), town (1990 pop. 16,786), Plymouth co., SE Mass., 19 mi/31 km SE of Boston, on the Atlantic coast about midway bet. Boston and Plymouth; 42°13′N 70°45′W. Residential community and summer resort. Includes villages of Egypt, Greenbush, Minot, North Scituate (1990 pop. 4,891), Rivermoor, Sandhills, Shore Acres. **2** (SI-tu-it), town (1990 pop. 9,796), Providence co., central R.I., on North Branch of Pawtuxet R. (here dammed in 1920s to form Scituate Reservoir), and 11 mi/18 km W of Providence; 41°48′N 71°37′W. Includes villages of Hope and North Scituate (administrative center). In Amer. Revolution, cannon cast at Hope Furnace ironworks here. Stephen and Esek Hopkins b. in here. Set off from Providence in 1731; town inc. in 1739.

Scituate Reservoir (SI-tu-it), central R.I., 9 mi/14.5 km W of Providence, owned and operated by city of Providence, supplies water to more than ½ the state's residents. Kent (or Scituate) Dam (180 ft/55 m high, 3,200 ft/975 m long; completed 1928) impounds North Branch of Pawtuxet R.; reservoir receives Ponaganset R. in W arm (c.5 mi/8 km long) and short Moswansicut R. in N arm (c.7 mi/11.3 km long).

Scobey, town (1990 pop. 1,154), ⊙ Daniels co., NE Mont., 47 mi/76 km NNE of Wolf Point on Poplar R.; 48°48′N 105°25′W. Port of entry on Canada (Sask.) border 14 mi/23 km N. Wheat, barley, oats, hay; hogs, cattle, exotic game animals. Mfg. (meat prods.). Daniels Co. Mus. Association. Inc. 1919. Formerly called East Scobey.

Scofield, village (1990 pop. 43), Carbon co., central Utah, 20 mi/32 km NW of Price, in mt. region; 39°43′N 111°09′W. Elev. 7,702 ft/2,348 m. Cattle. Scofield Reservoir and State Park to N, on Price R. Coal deposits nearby. Manti-La Sal Natl. Forest to W.

Scofield Dam, Utah: see PRICE RIVER.

Scooba (SKOO-buh), village (1990 pop. 541), Kemper co., E Miss., 32 mi/51 km NNE of Meridian, near Ala. state line; 32°49′N 88°28′W. Agr. (cotton, corn; cattle; timber); mfg. (lumber, steel pipe, catfish processing). East Miss. Community Col.

Scotch Plains, residential village (1990 pop. 21,160), Union co., NE N.J., 9 mi/14.5 km W of Elizabeth; 40°37′N 74°22′W. Light mfg. Settled 1684 by Scotch Presbyterians and Quakers.

Scotia 1 (SKO-shuh), uninc. village, Humboldt co., NW Calif., 22 mi/35 km S of Eureka and on Eel R.; a company town built around large redwood-lumber mill. Timber, cattle. Rainbow Ridge to SW. **2** village (1990 pop. 318), Greeley co., central Nebr., 10 mi/16 km SW of Greeley and on North Loup R; 41°28′N 98°42′W. Grain, livestock. **3** village (□ 1 sq mi/2.6 sq km; 1990 pop. 7,359), Schenectady co., E N.Y., on Mohawk R. and the Barge Canal (bridged), opposite Schenectady; 42°49′N 73°57′W. Scotia Naval Supply Depot closed and replaced by small industries. Settled before 1660, inc. 1904. **4** village (1990 pop. 182), Hampton co., SW S.C., c.45 mi/72 km N. of Savannah, Ga.; 32°40′N 81°14′W. Agr. includes peanuts, cotton, grain, watermelons, livestock. James W. Webb Game Management Area and Wildlife Center to S.

Scotland, hilly moorland district, central Barbados, 4 mi/6.4 km E of Speightstown.

Scotland, village, S Ont., Canada, 10 mi/16 km SW of Brantford. Dairying, mixed farming.

Scotland 1 county (□ 441 sq mi/1,142 sq km; 1990 pop. 4,822), NE Mo.; ⊙ Memphis; 40°27′N 92°09′W. Iowa on N. Drained by North Fabius R. and North and South Wyaconda rivers. Corn, soybeans; cattle, sheep, hogs. Mfg. at Memphis. Formed 1841. **2** county (□ 320 sq mi/829 sq km; 1990 pop. 33,754), S N.C.; ⊙ Laurinburg; 34°50′N 79°28′W. Coastal plain and sand hills region; bounded SW by S.C. state line, E by Drowning Creek (extension of Lumber R.). Agr. area (cotton, tobacco, corn, wheat, soybeans, hay, chickens, hogs), mfg. at Laurinburg. Formed 1899.

Scotland, city (1990 pop. 244), Telfair and Wheeler cos., S central Ga., 5 mi/8 km E of McRae, and on Little Ocmulgee R.; 32°03′N 82°49′W.

Scotland 1 town (1990 pop. 1,215), Windham co., E Conn., near Little R., 7 mi/11.3 km E of Willimantic; 41°42′N 72°04′W. Agr. (dairy prods., poultry); summer resort. Has 18th-cent. houses, including birthplace of Samuel Huntington. **2** uninc. town (1990 pop. 900), Franklin co., S Pa., 4 mi/6.4 km NE of Chambersburg, on Conococheague Creek; 39°58′N 77°35′W. Agr. (grain, potatoes; livestock; dairying). **3** town (1990 pop. 968), Bon Homme co., SE S.Dak., 25 mi/40 km NW of Yankton, near James R.; 43°08′N 97°43′W. Diversified farming; dairy prods., grain; mfg. (chemicals). Founded 1879.

Scotland 1 village (1990 pop. 490), Archer co., N Texas, 16 mi/26 km S of Wichita Falls, near Little Wichita R., at SW end of L. Arrowhead reservoir; 33°38′N 98°27′W. Cattle, dairying, wheat. Oil and natural gas. Light mfg. **2** uninc. village, Surry co., SE Va., 4 mi/6.4 km NE of Surry, on James R. (ferry to Jamestown) opposite Jamestown Isl.; 37°11′N 76°47′W. Agr. (peanuts, grain, soybeans, melons; livestock).

Scotland Neck, town (1990 pop. 2,575), Halifax co., NE N.C., 25 mi/40 km NE of Rocky Mount; 36°07′N 77°25′W. Timber; tobacco, cotton, cattle, peanuts, grain, poultry, hogs. Mfg. (apparel, lumber, furniture). Settled 1722.

Scotlandville (SKAHT-luhnd-vil), city (1990 pop. 15,113), East Baton Rouge parish, SE central La., on E bank (levee) of the Mississippi, and suburb 5 mi/8 km N of Baton Rouge; 30°31′N 91°10′W. RR junction. Seat of Southern Univ. and Agr. and Mechanical Col. (A&M). Port of Baton Rouge to NW.

Scotstown, town (1991 pop. 625), S Que., Canada, on Salmon R., a tributary of St. Francis R., and 30 mi/48 km ENE of Sherbrooke; 45°32′N 71°17′W. In dairying, livestock-raising region.

Scott, town (1991 pop. 118), W Sask., Canada, 35 mi/56 km SW of North Battleford; wheat.

Scott 1 county (□ 898 sq mi/2,326 sq km; 1990 pop. 10,205), W Ark.; ⊙ Waldron; 34°52′N 94°02′W. In Ouachita Mts., and bounded W by Okla. line; drained by Poteau and Fourche La Fave rivers. Lumbering; agr. (cattle, hogs, poultry, hay). Entire co. except for 3 small pockets in center (including Waldron), N and E within Ouachita Natl. Forest. Formed 1883. **2** county (□ 252 sq mi/653 sq km; 1990 pop. 5,644), W central Ill.; ⊙ Winchester; 39°39′N 90°28′W. Bounded W by Illinois R.; drained by small Sandy and Mauvaise Terre creeks. Agr. (corn, wheat, soybeans; livestock). One of 17 cos. to retain southern-style commission form of co. govt. Formed 1839. **3** county (□ 192 sq mi/497 sq km; 1990 pop. 20,991), SE Ind.; ⊙ Scottsburg; 38°41′N 85°44′W. Bounded N by Muscatatuck R., and drained by its small tributaries. Agr. (grain, livestock, poultry); timber. Mfg. at Scottsburg and Austin. Hardy L. State Recreation Area in NE; Clark State Forest in SW; Pigeon Roost State Memorial in S. Formed 1820. **4** county (□ 468 sq mi/1,212 sq km; 1990 pop. 150,979), E Iowa; ⊙ Davenport; 41°38′N 90°38′W. Quad Cities area. Bounded E and S by Mississippi R. (forms Ill. state line here), and N mainly by Wapsipinicon R. Prairie agr. area (hogs, cattle, poultry, corn, oats), with mfg. at Davenport and Bettendorf; coal deposits (SW), limestone quarries. Buffalo Bill Cody Homestead in rural area in NE. Lock and Dam No. 15 at Davenport; Lock and Dam No. 14 below Le Claire. Severe flood damage occurred along rivers, esp. in downtown Davenport, in 1993. Formed 1837. **5** county (□ 717 sq mi/1,857 sq km; 1990 pop. 5,289), W Kansas; ⊙ Scott City; 38°28′N 100°54′W. Sloping to rolling plains region. Drained by Ladder Creek in N and White Woman Creek in SW, which flows into White Woman Basin, near center of co. which has no outlet. Wheat, cattle, hogs, sorghum, corn. El Cuartelejo Pueblo Ruins and Scott State Park in N. Formed 1886. **6** county (□ 285 sq mi/738 sq km; 1990 pop. 23,867), N Ky.; ⊙ Georgetown; 38°18′N 84°34′W. Bounded SW by Elkhorn Creek; drained by Eagle Creek and North Elkhorn Creek, in Bluegrass region. Gently rolling upland agr. area (burley tobacco, corn, hay, alfalfa; hogs, cattle); limestone quarries. Mfg. at Georgetown. First "bourbon" whiskey made here 1789, then part of Bourbon county, Va. Formed 1792. **7** county (□ 368 sq mi/953 sq km; 1990 pop. 57,846), SE central Minn., ⊙ Shakopee; 44°38′N 93°31′W. Bounded on N and W by Minnesota R. On SW fringe of Minneapolis-St. Paul urbanized area. Agr. (hay, corn, soybeans, oats, alfalfa; hogs, cattle, poultry; dairying); limestone; sand and gravel. Minnesota Valley State Park and Trail in NW. Prior L. Indian Reservation in N. Several small lakes in county. **8** county (□ 610 sq mi/1,580 sq km; 1990 pop. 24,137), central Miss.; ⊙ Forest; 32°23′N 89°32′W. Bounded by Pearl R. in extreme NW corner; drained by Strong and Leaf rivers and Pelahatchie Creek. Agr. (cotton, corn, soybeans; poultry, cattle); timber. Cotton research station is here. Golden Memorial State Park in NE, Roosevelt State Park in SW; part of Bienville Natl. Forest covers much of co., in S, center, and NW. Formed 1833. **9** county (□ 418 sq mi/1,083 sq km; 1990 pop. 39,376), SE Mo.; ⊙ Benton; 37°04′N 89°34′W. On Mississippi R. (E); drainage channels. Grows and processes corn, wheat, soybeans, melons, pumpkins, hay; lumber. Mfg. at Sikeston, Chaffee, Oran. Formed 1821. **10** county (□ 549; 1990 pop. 18,358), N Tenn.; ⊙ Huntsville; 36°26′N 84°31′W. Bordered N by Ky.; a rugged region of the Cumberlands; drained by South Fork Cumberland R. and small New R. Lumbering, coal and clay mining, oil fields; farming (corn, tobacco, hay, livestock, vegetables). Includes part of Big South Fork Natl. R. and Recreation Area. Formed 1849. **11** county (□ 538 sq mi/1,393 sq km; 1990 pop. 23,204), SW Va.; ⊙ Gate City; 36°43′N 82°35′W. Partly in Allegheny Mts.; bounded S by Tenn. state line; parts of Clinch Mtn. and Powell Mtn. ridges in W; Natural Tunnel State Park in W center. Drained by Clinch R. and North Fork of Holston R. Mfg. at Duffield; agr. (tobacco, corn, hay, alfalfa; cattle, sheep; dairying); timber; bituminous-coal mining. Includes part of Jefferson Natl. Forest in N, Bark Camp Recreation Area in NE. Formed 1814.

Scott 1 town, Johnson co., E central Ga., 14 mi/23 km E of Dublin; 32°33′N 82°40′W. **2** town (1994 pop. 5,641), Lafayette parish, S La., suburb 4 mi/6 km W of Lafayette; 30°14′N 92°05′W. In agr. area (sugarcane, rice, vegetables; cattle; dairying); some mfg. Oil and natural gas fields. Pecans grow nearby.

Scott, village (1990 pop. 339), on Van Wert-Paulding co. line, W Ohio, 8 mi/13 km N of Van Wert, in agr. area; 40°59′N 84°35′W.

Scott, township (1990 pop. 17,118), Allegheny co., W Pa., residential suburb 5 mi/8 km SW of Pittsburgh; 40°23′N 80°04′W. Chartiers Creek is W boundary.

Scott Air Force Base, Ill.: see BELLEVILLE.

Scott, Cape, SW B.C., Canada, NW extremity of Vancouver Isl.; 50°47′N 128°26′W. Lighthouse.

Scott Channel (7 mi/11 km wide), in the Pacific, SW B.C., Canada, separates Scott Isls. from NW tip of Vancouver.

Scott City, city (1990 pop. 4,292), Scott co., SE Mo., near Mississippi R., 6 mi/9.7 km S of Cape Girardeau; 37°13′N 89°31′W. Formed by merger of Fornfelt and Illmo (IL-mo). In agr. area. Melons, corn, soybeans, cotton. Some mfg. RR junction.

Scott City, town (1990 pop. 3,785), W Kansas, 34 mi/55 km N of Garden City; ⊙ Scott co.; 38°28′N 100°54′W. RR junction. Trade and shipping center for agr. and livestock-raising area. Last battle (1878) with Native Americans in Kansas was fought in nearby canyon. Lake Scott State Park (N) has remains of Taos Indian pueblo. El Cuartelejo Pueblo Ruins, later became first white settlement in Kansas. Inc. 1887.

Scott Dam, Calif.: see PILLSBURY, LAKE.

Scott Depot, uninc. village, Putnam co., W central W.Va., 17 mi/27 km WNW of Charleston. Agr. (corn, tobacco; livestock, poultry); mfg. (machinery, computers, fabricated metal prods., food, chemicals). Mus. in the Community is here.

Scott Jonction, village, S Que., Canada, on Chaudière R. and 22 mi/35 km SSE of Quebec. Lumbering. In agr. region.

Scottdale (SKAHT-dail), borough (1990 pop. 5,184), Westmoreland co., SW Pa., 31 mi/50 km SE of Pittsburgh; 40°06′N 79°35′W. Agr. (corn, hay, apples, dairying); mfg. (lumber, fabricated metal prods., printing and publishing, electrical equip.); bituminous coal. Mt. Pleasant-Scottdale Airport to E. Laid out 1872, inc. 1874.

Scottdale, suburb (1990 pop. 8,636), De Kalb co., Ga., 2 mi/3.2 km NE of Decatur. Old mill town located in E suburbs of Atlanta. Former mfg. base now replaced by business services and antique stores.

Scotts Bluff, county (□ 745 sq mi/1,930 sq km; 1990 pop. 36,025), W Nebr.; ⊙ Gering; 41°51′N 103°42′W. Irrigated agr. area bounded W by Wyo.; drained by L. Minatare and North Platte R. Wildcat Hills, highest at Wildcat Mt. (5,038 ft/1,536 m), in SE. Scotts Bluff Natl. Monument is near Scottsbluff, commercial center of co. Mfg. of machinery, food; Agr. includes cattle, hogs, corn, alfalfa, beans, potatoes, dairying. Mfg. at Scottsbluff and Gering. Oil. Old Oregon Trail crosses co. along S side of Platte R. from SE to NW. Scotts Bluff Natl. Monument (on 800 ft/244 m in promontory) at center of co., SW of Scottsbluff; Wildcat Hills State Recreation Area on S boundary; Minature L. State Recreation Area; L. Minature, Winters Creek L. and L. Alier in NE, all part of N Platte Natl. Wildlife Refuge. Co. airport E of Scottsbluff. Formed 1888.

Scotts Hill, town (1990 pop. 594), on Decatur-Henderson co. line, W Tenn., 8 mi/13 km SW of Decaturville; 35°31′N 88°15′W.

Scotts Mills, village (1990 pop. 283), Marion co., NW Oregon, 20 mi/32 km ENE of Salem, on Butte Creek.

Scotts Mountain (1,000 ft/305 m–1,150 ft/351 m), of the Appalachians, NW N.J., extending SW from Oxford (on its N slope) to point NE of Phillipsburg; 40°44′N 75°05′W.

Scotts Valley, city (1990 pop. 8,615), Santa Cruz co., W Calif., 4 mi/6.4 km N of Santa Cruz; 37°04′N 122°01′W.

Berries, apples, artichokes, vegetables, flower, nursery prods. Mfg. (computer equip., electronic equip.). Forest of Nisene Marks State Park to E.

Scottsbluff, city (1990 pop. 13,711), Scotts Bluff co., W Nebr., on the North Platte R. near the Wyo. line; 41°52′N 103°39′W. Elev. 3,885 ft/1,184 m. It is the market, distribution, and processing point of an irrigated farm region; also some mfg. Tourism is also important. The city is named for a nearby butte, Scotts Bluff (elev. 4,649 ft/1,417 m), a landmark to travelers on the Oregon and Mormon trails. In 1864, Fort Mitchell was est. there as an outpost of Fort Laramie. Western Nebr. Community Col., Scottsbluff Campus here. Veteran's Home. Oregon Trail Mus. is in Scotts Bluff Natl. Monument (SW), and Agate Fossil Beds Natl. Monument is 40 mi/64 km to the N. Wildcat Hills State Recreation Area to S; North Platte Natl. Wildlife Refuge and Minature L. State Recreation Area to NE. Larger twin city with Gering, across Platte R. to S. Oregon Trail follows S side of river. Co. airport to E. Inc. 1900.

Scottsboro, city (1990 pop. 13,786), NE Ala., near Tennessee R., at edge of Cumberland Plateau, 30 mi/48 km E of Huntsville; ⊙ Jackson co. Mfg. of apparel, lumber; limestone. Scene of famous Scottsboro Case, *cause célèbre* in which conviction (1931) of 9 Afr.-Amer. young males for rape was fought for years by liberals who felt the conviction was a miscarriage of justice infringing upon the civil rights of the accused. The Supreme Court reversed the convictions in 1932 due to lack of adequate defense counsel (Powell v. Ala.) and in 1935 because of lack of Afr.-Amer. representation on jury (Norns v. Ala.); 4 of the 9 were reconvicted; the last surviving 1 was pardoned at age 64 by Gov. George C. Wallace in 1976.

Scottsburg, city (1990 pop. 5,334), SE Ind., 28 mi/45 km N of New Albany; ⊙ Scott co.; 38°41′N 85°47′W. In agr. area (grain; livestock, poultry); mfg. (plastics, rubber prods., lumber). Laid out 1871.

Scottsburg, town (1990 pop. 152), Halifax co., S Va., 8 mi/12.9 km E of Halifax; 36°45′N 47°78′W. Agr. (grain, soybeans, tobacco; cattle). Staunton R. State Park, on Buggs Isl. L. reservoir, to SE.

Scottsdale, city (1990 pop. 130,069), Maricopa co., central Ariz., a suburb 8 mi/12.9 km ENE of downtown Phoenix; 33°41′N 111°52′W. The city extends 20 mi/32 km N-S. It is a resort and retirement center in the rapidly expanding Phoenix area. Electronic equip. is an important manufacture that is being extensively produced and developed in the state. Other mfg. includes chemicals, plastic prods., pharmaceuticals, furniture, transportation equip. Agr. is grown in the surrounding area, watered by canals (Hayden-Rhodes aqueduct crosses city) of the Salt R. project. Scottsdale is one of the fastest-growing U.S. cities, marked by a pop. increase of of nearly 47% bet. 1980 and 1990. The Taliesin West Home and School, School of Architecture founded by Frank Lloyd Wright, is to the N of the city; training camp of San Francisico Giants baseball team; Scottsdale Municipal Airport in N part of city. Adjoins Gila R. Indian Reservation to E, including Scottsdale Community Col. on reservation. Phoenix Military Reserve to SW, Fort McDowell Mt. Park to NE; Fort McDowell Indian Reservation to E; Tonto Natl. Forest to E and NE; Papago Park to SW, including Phoenix Zoo. Settled in 1895 by Winfield Scott, inc. 1951.

Scottsville 1 town (1990 pop. 4,278), S Ky., 20 mi/32 km SE of Bowling Green; ⊙ Allen co.; 36°45′N 86°12′W. Agr. (dairying; livestock, poultry; burley tobacco); timber; mfg. (lumber, electronic equip., printing and publishing). Allen County Historical Mus. Barren River L. reservoir and State Park to NE. **2** town (1990 pop. 239), Albemarle and Fluvanna cos., central Va., 16 mi/26 km S of Charlottesville, on James R.; 37°47′N 78°29′W. Mfg. (lumber); agr. (dairying; livestock; grain, apples); timber.

Scottsville 1 village (1990 pop. 26), Mitchell co., N Kansas, 10 mi/16 km NE of Beloit; 39°32′N 97°57′W. Grain, livestock. **2** residential village (□ 1 sq mi/2.6 sq km; 1990 pop. 1,912), Monroe co., W N.Y., on Genesee R. and 12 mi/19 km SSW of Rochester; 43°01′N 77°45′W. **3** village (1990 pop. 283), Harrison co., NE Texas, suburb 5 mi/8 km E of Marshall; 32°32′N 94°14′W. Timber; cattle; oil and natural gas. Light mfg.

Scottville, town (1990 pop. 1,287), Mason co., W Mich., 9 mi/14.5 km E of Ludington and on Pere Marquette R.; 43°57′N 86°16′W. In dairying and agr. area (vegetables, apples, cherries, livestock; dairying); mfg. (food). Native American mounds nearby. West Shore Community Col. Manistee Natl. Forest to E and N. Settled 1876; inc. as village 1889, as city 1907.

Scottville, village (1990 pop. 165), Macoupin co., SW central Ill., 18 mi/29 km NW of Carlinville; 39°28′N 90°05′W. In agr. (cattle, hogs, corn, wheat, sorghum, soybeans) and bituminous coal area.

Scranton (SKRAN-tuhn), city (1990 pop. 81,805), NE Pa., 105 mi/169 km NNW of Philadelphia, and 16 mi/26 km NE of Wilkes-Barre, its smaller twin city; ⊙ Lackawanna co.; 41°23′N 75°40′W. In a mt. region, on the Lackawanna R. Named for its founder George W. Scranton, a member of the Guilford-Madison, Conn. family also responsible for that area's settlement. It is a commercial and industrial center of the surrounding anthracite-coal region of NE Pa. Iron was 1st forged here in 1797, and in the 19th cent. produced most of the U.S. iron rails (the city was once served by five RRs). Mfg. (food prods., electrical equip., cigars, apparel, textiles, printing and publishing, ordnance, plastic prods., concrete prods., fabricated metal prods.). Early prods. were coal-mining machinery, locomotives, and rails. Anthracite-coal production declined after World War II; the unemployment that resulted was largely offset by a successful citizens' program that developed service industries. Univ. of Scranton, Marywood Col., Pa. State Univ.-Worthington-Scranton Campus (2-year), the Internatl. Correspondence Schools Center for Degree Studies (2-year), and a state school for the deaf are here. In Nay Aug Park are the Everhart Mus. of Natural History, Science, and Art and Anthracite Mus. and Lackawanna Coal Mine Tour. Also of interest are a large Masonic temple-Scottish rite cathedral, Steamtown Natl. Historic Site with collection of locomotives, and Scranton Iron Furnaces (1848). Wilkes-Barre Scranton Internatl. Airport 5 mi/8 km to SW. Lackawanna State Forest to S; Archbald Pothole State Park to NE; L. Scranton reservoir to SE. Settled in the 1700s, inc. 1866.

Scranton 1 town (1990 pop. 583), Greene co., central Iowa, 10 mi/16 km W of Jefferson; 42°01′N 94°32′W. Light mfg. Sand and gravel pits nearby. **2** town (1990 pop. 802), Florence co., NE central S.C., 18 mi/29 km S of Florence; 33°55′N 79°44′W. Agr. includes poultry, livestock, grain, tobacco, cotton, soybeans.

Scranton 1 village (1990 pop. 218), Logan co., W Ark., 23 mi/37 km W of Russellville, near Arkansas R. (Lake Dardanelle); 35°21′N 93°32′W. Light mfg. **2** village (1990 pop. 674), Osage co., E Kansas, 19 mi/31 km SSW of Topeka; 38°46′N 95°44′W. Shipping and marketing point in livestock and grain region. **3** village (1990 pop. 294), Bowman co., SW N.Dak., 13 mi/21 km E of Bowman. Lignite mines; grain; dairy prods.; 46°08′N 103°08′W. Bowman Haley Reservoir to S.

Screven (SKREV-uhn), county (□ 656 sq mi/1,699 sq km; 1990 pop. 13,842), E Ga.; ⊙ Sylvania; 32°45′N 81°37′W. Bounded E by S.C. state line (formed here by Savannah R.) and SW by Ogeechee R. Drained by Brier Creek. Coastal plain agr. (cotton, corn, soybeans, tobacco, potatoes, peanuts; cattle, hogs). In timber area. Formed 1793.

Screven (SKREV-uhn), town (1990 pop. 819), Wayne co., SE Ga., 11 mi/18 km SW of Jesup, near Little Satilla R.; 31°29′N 82°01′W. Light mfg.

Screven, Fort, located on Tybee Isl., E Ga. Former fort closed after World War II. Military fortifications now being used as a mus. and for housing. Adjacent to Zybee Isl.

Screw Auger Falls, Maine: see BEAR RIVER.

Scrub Island, islet, Br. Virgin Isls., 4 mi/6.4 km E of Tortola isl.; 18°29′N 64°30′W.

Scugog, Lake, SE Ont., Canada, 36 mi/58 km NE of Toronto, in Kawartha lake region; 16 mi/26 km long, 7 mi/11 km wide. Contains Scugog Isl. (9 mi/14 km long, 3 mi/5 km wide). Drained N into Sturgeon L. by Scugog R. On shore are several resorts.

Scullin (SKUHL-in), village, Murray co., S Okla., 6 mi/9.7 km E of Sulphur.

Scuppernong River (SKU-puhr-nahng), 15 mi/24 km long, in SE Wis.; rises in SW Waukesha co.; flows generally W to Bark R. 4 mi/6.4 km N of Whitewater.

Scuppernong River, N.C.: see COLUMBIA.

Scurry, county (□ 907 sq mi/2,349 sq km; 1990 pop. 18,634), NW central Texas; ⊙ Snyder; 32°45′N 100°55′W. Rolling plains (elev. 2,000 ft/610 m–3,000 ft/914 m.); drained by Colorado R. Agr., dairying, cattle-ranching, oil-producing region; cotton, grain sorghum, wheat, hay, silage, pecans; sheep, hogs, poultry. Leading U.S. oil-producing co. (1994–1995), natural gas, limestone. Formed 1876.

Sea Bright, resort borough (1990 pop. 1,693), Monmouth co., E N.J., bet. Shrewsbury R. inlet and the Atlantic, 18 mi/29 km NE of Freehold, in estate area; 40°21′N 73°58′W.

Sea Cliff, residential village (□ 1 sq mi/2.6 sq km; 1990 pop. 5,054), Nassau co., SE N.Y., on N shore of W L.I., on Hempstead Harbor, just S of Glen Cove; 40°51′N 73°39′W. Inc. 1883.

Sea Girt, resort borough (1990 pop. 2,099), Monmouth co., E N.J., on the coast, and 16 mi/26 km SE of Freehold; 40°07′N 74°01′W. Chiefly residential.

Sea Gull Lake, Cook co., NE Minn., near Ont. line, c.45 mi/72 km ENE of Ely; 6 mi/9.7 km long, 2 mi/3.2 km wide; 48°08′N 90°56′W. Sea Gull R. drains lake N into Saganaga L. Lies within Superior Natl. Forest, on edge of Boundary Water Canoe Area. Threemile Isl. at L. center.

Sea Island, one of the Sea Isls., in Glynn co., SE Ga., just off the coast of and connected by a causeway to St. Simons Isl.; c.5 mi/8 km long, 2 mi/3.2 km wide; 31°12′N 81°20′W. Near S end is the Sea Island Resort, an exclusive vacationing spot. Brunswick, the closest mainland town, is 8 mi/12.9 km W.

Sea Islands, chain of more than 100 low islands off the Atlantic coast of S.C., Ga., and N Fla., extending from the Santee R. to the St. Johns R. The ocean side of the isls. is generally sandy; the side facing the mainland is marshy. The isls. have a humid, subtropical climate, with hot summers, warm winters, and rain throughout the year. Some isls. remain uninhabited; others are resorts and wildlife sanctuaries. The Intracoastal Waterway passes through the Sea Isls. The Span. explored and were the first to inhabit the isls., setting up missions and garrisons in the 16th cent. These were abandoned as the English steadily advanced in the area. James Oglethorpe, founder of the Georgia colony, built Fort Frederica on St. Simons Isl. bet. 1736 and 1754, during the Eng.-Span. struggle for control of the SE U.S. The ruins of the fort are a natl. monument. The Sea Isls. were the first important cotton-growing area in N. Amer. In the early 19th cent., St. Helena and Port Royal Isl. became the seats of large plantations that grew long-staple, Sea-Isl. cotton. The Union invasion in the Civil War and the distribution of land by the Federal govt. to newly freed slaves after the war effected the wealth of the planters. With the coming of the boll weevil (c.1920), cotton culture gave way to diversified farming, including the growing of corn, potatoes, and peanuts; poultry raising, oyster gathering, and fishing are also important. Morris Isl., Fort Sumter, and other isls. lie in and around Charleston harbor. Beaufort (1990 pop. 9,576), on Port Royal Isl., is the main city of the Sea Isls. and is a center of menhaden fishing. Parris Isl. is the Atlantic coast recruit-training center for the U.S. marine corps; the area was visited by Fr. Huguenot explorer Jean Ribault in 1564. St. Simons Isl., Sea Isl., and Jekyll Isl. (also called the Golden Isles), near Brunswick, Ga., are popular resorts. St. Simons is joined to the mainland at Brunswick by a causeway. Jekyll Isl., once the site of a club for N millionaires, is now a state park. Cumberland Isl., largest of the Sea Isls., c.22 mi/35 km long and from 1 to 5 mi (1.6–8 km) wide, has been designated a natl. seashore. Other notable isls. are the Isle of Palms, Johns, Edisto, and Hilton Head, which is a major resort.

Sea Isle City, resort city (1990 pop. 2,692), Cape May co., SE N.J., on Ludlam Beach, and 20 mi/32 km SW of Atlantic City; 39°08'N 74°42'W. Printing and publishing.

Sea View, Mass.: see MARSHFIELD.

Seaboard, town (1990 pop. 791), Northampton co., NE N.C., 12 mi/19 km E of Roanoke Rapids; 36°29'N 77°26'W. Grain, tobacco, cotton, peanuts, poultry, livestock. Mfg. (lumber).

Seabrook 1 (SEE-bruk), town (1990 pop. 6,503), Rockingham co., SE N.H., 13 mi/21 km S of Portsmouth and 6 mi/9.7 km N of Newburyport, Mass.; 42°53'N 70°51'W. Bounded by Atlantic Ocean on E, by Mass. state line on S, by Hampton Falls R. on N. Mfg. (chemicals, machinery, plastic prods.); agr. (nursery crops; poultry, cattle; dairying); seafood. S part of Hampton Harbor in E. Seabrook Greyhound Race Track in W. Site of Seabrook Nuclear Power Plant. Resort area at Seabrook Beach. Settled 1638, inc. 1768. **2** town (1990 pop. 6,685), Harris co., SE Texas, suburb 24 mi/39 km SE of downtown Houston and on Galveston Bay; 29°34'N 94°59'W. Bounds Taylor L. and Bayou on W, Clear L. on S. Beach recreation area; light mfg. In area referred to as Clear Lake City. NASA Johnson Space Center to W.

Seabrook, village (1990 pop. with Lanham 16,792), Prince Georges co., central Md., 12 mi/19 km ENE of Washington, D.C.

Seabrook Island, c.5 mi/8 km long, Charleston co., SE S.C., one of Sea Isls., at E side of North Edisto R. mouth to SW (Edisto Isl. is opposite), 13 mi/21 km SW of Charleston; 32°34'N 80°10'W. Town of Seabrook Isl. (1990 pop. 948), formerly Seabrook Landing, on NE part of isl. Antebellum Sea Isl. Cotton Plantations here.

Seabrook Landing, S.C., see SEABROOK ISLAND.

Seabrook Nuclear Power Plant, N.H.: see ROCKINGHAM, CO.

Seadrift, town (1990 pop. 1,277), Calhoun co., S Texas, on Hynes Bay (an arm of San Antonio Bay), 33 mi/53 km SE of Victoria; 28°24'N 96°43'W. RR terminus to NW; fishing (crayfish, shrimp, crabs); rice; cotton; mfg. (food, chemicals).

Seaford 1 town (1990 pop. 5,689), Sussex co., SW Del., 13 mi/21 km W of Georgetown and at head of navigation on Nanticoke R.; 38°38'N 75°37'W. RR junction. Mfg. (machinery, chemicals); agr. area (fruit, vegetables; poultry, livestock; dairying). The largest nylon production plant in the U.S. is here. Founded 1799; inc. 1865. **2** uninc. town, York co., SE Va., 11 mi/18 km NNW of Hampton, on neck of land bet. Back Creek (N) and Chisman Creek (S), inlets of Chesapeake Bay; 36°11'N 76°26'W. Mfg. (food, machinery); fish, scallops, oysters, crabs. Historic Yorktown, in Colonial Natl. Historical Park; U.S. Coast Guard Training Center to NW.

Seaford, uninc. urban community (□ 2 sq mi/5.2 sq km; 1990 pop. 15,597), Nassau co., SE N.Y., on the S shore of L.I., on Great South Bay; 40°40'N 73°29'W. It is a residential suburb of N.Y. city and a resort village, with marinas and boatyards. The co. mus. of natural history is here. Settled 1643

Seaforth, town (1991 pop. 2,312), S Ont., Canada, on Bayfield R., and 24 mi/39 km NW of Stratford. Light mfg.

Seaforth, town (1991 pop. 4,108), St. Thomas parish, SE Jamaica, 20 mi/32 km ESE of Kingston; 17°56'N 76°27'W. Agr. market center.

Seaforth, village (1990 pop. 87), Redwood co., SW Minn., on Redwood R., and 11 mi/18 km WSW of Redwood Falls; 44°28'N 95°19'W. Grain area.

Seagate, uninc. town (1990 pop. 5,444), New Hanover co., SE N.C., residential suburb 5 mi/8 km E of downtown Wilmington; 34°12'N 77°50'W. On Bradley Creek estuary, 1 mi/1.6 km NW of Intracoastal Waterway; Atlantic Ocean 2 mi/3.2 km to SE. Airlie Gardens to NE; Univ. of N.C., Wilmington to NW.

Seagoville, town (1990 pop. 8,969), Dallas and Kaufman cos., N Texas, suburb 17 mi/27 km SE of downtown Dallas; 32°39'N 96°32'W. On SE fringe of Dallas-Fort Worth Metroplex. Bounded in E by E Fork Trinity R.

In agr. area (cotton, peaches, vegetables); sand, gravel pits; oil and gas; light mfg. Seagoville Correctional Inst.

Seagraves, town (1990 pop. 2,398), Gaines co., NW Texas, on S Llano Estacado, 60 mi/97 km SW of Lubbock, near N.Mex. line; 32°56'N 102°33'W. RR terminus, market, shipping center for cattle-ranching and oil-producing region, with some agr. (cotton, corn, vegetables); mfg. (chemicals). Inc. 1928.

Seagrove, village (1990 pop. 244), Randolph co., central N.C., 12 mi/19 km S of Asheboro; 35°32'N 79°46'W. Agr. area (tobacco, grain; poultry, livestock). Mfg. (pottery, lumber, food prods., furniture, plastic prods.). Uwharrie Natl. Forest to W; N.C. Zoological Park to N; Pisgah Covered Bridge to W. Potters Mus. Area known for its pottery (over 70 potteries).

Seahorse Point, E extremity of Southampton Isl., E Keewatin dist., N.W.T., Canada, on Hudson Bay, at S end of Foxe Channel; 63°46'N 80°09'W.

Seahurst, uninc. town (1990 pop. 1,900), King co., W Wash., residential suburb 10 mi/16 km SSW of downtown Seattle, on Puget Sound.

Seal Beach, city (1990 pop. 25,098), Orange co., S Calif., suburb 22 mi/35 km SSE of downtown Los Angeles, 5 mi/8 km E of Long Beach, at mouth of San Gabriel R. on Anaheim Bay of the Pacific Ocean; 33°46'N 118°05'W. Mfg. (concrete, transportation equip., aerospace prods.). It is a beach city with an active art colony. Seal Beach U.S. Naval Weapons Station is to E; Los Alamitos Naval Air Station to NE. Alamito Bay and Long Beach Marina immediately to W Inc. 1915.

Seal Harbor, Maine: see MOUNT DESERT.

Seal Island, off SW N.S., Canada, 30 mi/48 km SSE of Yarmouth; 2 mi/3 km long; 43°25'N 66°01'W.

Seal Island, Maine: see MATINICUS ISLE.

Seale (SEEL), town, Russell co., E Ala., 15 mi/24 km S of Phenix City. Mfg. of chemicals.

Sealy, town (1990 pop. 4,541), Austin co., S Texas, 47 mi/76 km W of Houston, near the Brazos R.; 29°46'N 96°09'W. RR junction; cotton; corn, rice peanuts. Mfg. (construction materials, food, trucks). Stephen F. Austin State Park to E. Inc. after 1940.

Seaman, village (1990 pop. 1,013), Adams co., S Ohio, 11 mi/18 km NNW of West Union, in agr. area; 38°56'N 83°34'W.

Searchlight, uninc. village (1990 pop. 500), Clark co., SE Nev., 49 mi/79 km SSW of Las Vegas. A partial ghost town spared only by its crossroads location near to Las Vegas, named for a once popular brand of sulphur matches. In 1907, the town had 5,000 people, 44 gold mines and 12 saloons. Searchlight Historical Mus. Cottonwood Cove Marina, on L. Mohave reservoir (Colorado R.), in L. Mead Natl. Recreation Area to E. Highland Range Crucial Bighorn Habitat Area to N.

Searcy (SUHR-see), county (□ 668 sq mi/1,730 sq km; 1990 pop. 7,841), N Ark.; ⊙ Marshall; 35°55'N 92°42'W. Intersected by Buffalo R.; drained by Middle Fork of Little Red R.; situated in Ozark region. Agr. (cattle, hogs). Timber. Buffalo Natl. R. crosses N part from W to NE; separates units of Ozark Natl. Forest in NE corner and SW; part of Gene Rush-Buffalo R. Wildlife Management Area in W. Formed 1838.

Searcy (SUHR-see), city (1990 pop. 15,180), central Ark., c.45 mi/72 km NE of Little Rock, near Little Red R.; ⊙ White co.; 35°14'N 91°43'W. Shipping point in strawberry-growing area; mfg. (fabricated metal prods., leather prods., food, consumer goods, furniture). Seat of Harding Univ. Inc. 1854.

Searight, town, Crenshaw co., S Ala., on Conecuh R. and 18 mi/29 km SW of Luverne.

Searles, uninc. village, Kern co., S Calif., 9 mi/14.5 km S of Ridgecrest in Mojave Desert. Cattle.

Searles Lake, Calif.: see TRONA.

Searles Valley, uninc. town (1990 pop. 2,740), San Bernardino co., S Calif., 16 mi/26 km NE of Ridgecrest, in Mojave Desert, incl. localities of Argus, Trona and Pioneer Point. Searles L. (dry) to E; 35°46'N 117°24'W. Cattle. Salt. Part of China L. Naval Weapons Center to W.

Searsboro, town (1990 pop. 164), Poweshiek co., central Iowa, 20 mi/32 km N of Oskaloosa; 41°34'N 92°42'W. In agr. area.

Searsburg, town (1990 pop. 85), Bennington co., SW Vt., on Deerfield R. and 12 mi/19 km. E of Bennington, in Green Mts.; 42°53'N 72°57'W.

Searsmont, town (1990 pop. 938), Waldo co., S Maine, 8 mi/12.9 km SW of Belfast; 44°21'N 69°11'W. In agr., recreational area; wood prods.

Searsport, town (1990 pop. 2,603), Waldo co., S Maine, on W shore of Penobscot Bay, near Belfast; 44°28'N 55°68'W. Terminus of Bangor and Aroostook RR. Chemical and fertilizer plants. Village of Searsport, now resort, flourished in sailing-ship days as shipbuilding center; maritime mus. opened in 1936. Set off from Belfast 1845.

Seashore State Park, SE Va., in Virginia Beach (independent city), recreational area (2,570 acres/1,040 ha) near Cape Henry, 14 mi/23 km ENE of Norfolk; 36°54'N 76°W. Bounded NW by Chesapeake Bay, Broad Bay (backwater l.) in SW. Beaches, sand dunes, cypress and live-oak forests, many bays, small lakes; recreational facilities. Ft. Story Military Reservation bet. park and cape, to NE.

Seaside, city (1990 pop. 38,901), Monterey co., W Calif., 10 mi/16 km WSW of Salinas on Monterey Bay; 36°37'N 121°49'W. Its economy is based upon tourism and U.S. Fort Ord Military Reserve to E. Fruit, vegetables, dairying. Monterey Peninsula to W; Monterey Peninsula Airport to S; Monterey State Beach to W. Founded 1887, inc. 1954.

Seaside, planned resort community on Gulf of Mexico, Walton co., NW Fla., 30 mi/48 km NW of Panama City. Built in mid-1980s according to Neo-traditional 19th cent. house-construction and community-layout principles to foster social interaction. Considered to be the pioneering landmark in the "new urbanism" movement led by architect-planners Andres Duany and Elizabeth Plater-Zyberk.

Seaside, town (1990 pop. 5,359), Clatsop co., NW Oregon, on the Pacific, 13 mi/21 km SSW of Astoria, at mouth of Necanicum R.; 45°59'N 123°55'W. RR terminus. Fish processing. Resort; tourism. Saddle Mt. State Park to E; Ecola State Park to S. Seaside State Airport to NE. Inc. 1899.

Seaside, a sect. of S Queens borough of N.Y. city, SE N.Y., on Rockaway Peninsula; 40°35'N 73°50'W.

Seaside Heights, resort borough (1990 pop. 2,366), Ocean co., E N.J., on peninsula (here bridged to mainland) bet. Barnegat Bay and the Atlantic, and 7 mi/11.3 km E of Toms River; 39°56'N 74°04'W. Boatyards, recreational facilities. Has 1 mi/1.6 km long boardwalk.

Seaside Park, resort borough (1990 pop. 1,871), Ocean co., E N.J., on peninsula bet. Barnegat Bay and the Atlantic, just S of Seaside Heights, 7 mi/11.3 km ESE of Toms River; 39°55'N 74°04'W. Includes Berkeley village.

Seat Pleasant, city (1990 pop. 5,359), Prince Georges co., central Md., E of Wash., D.C.; 38°54'N 76°54'W. Formerly named Chesapeake Junction because a RR ran here from Chesapeake Beach between 1900 and 1935, the name was changed in 1906. The Addison Chapel of St. Matthews Episcopal Church was built in 1809 on the site of 2 smaller churches. Inc. 1931.

SeaTac (SEE-tak), city (1990 pop. 22,830), King co., W Wash., commercial suburb 13 mi/21 km S of downtown Seattle and 14 mi/23 km NE of downtown Tacoma. Surrounds Seattle-Tacoma (SeaTac) Internatl. Airport. Large concentration of hotels and office bldgs.

Seaton, village (1990 pop. 221), Mercer co., NW Ill., 8 mi/12.9 km SSW of Aledo; 41°06'N 90°47'W. In agr. area (cattle, hogs, corn, soybeans).

Seatonville, village (1990 pop. 259), Bureau co., N Ill., 11 mi/18 km E of Princeton; 41°21'N 89°16'W. In agr. area.

Seattle, city (1990 pop. 516,259), W Wash., built on 7 hills, bet. Puget Sound (W) and L. Washington (E); ⊙ King co.; 47°37'N 122°21'W. Downtown Seattle fronts on Elliott Bay. L. Union N of downtown; Wash. Ship Canal and Locks connect it with L. Washington and Puget Sound. Seattle, the largest city in Wash. and the Pacific NW, is the region's commercial, financial, transportation, and industrial hub and a major port of entry, important in Far Eastern, Alaskan, and Canadian

---

trade. A center of aircraft mfg. and shipbuilding since World War II, the city is hq. for the Boeing Co., primarily based in Renton, to S, and Everett, to N, which employs a significant number of people in Seattle and adjacent cities. There are also major computer services, electronics, banking, insurance, biomedical, food-processing, and lumber industries. Mfg. (steel, electronic equip., shipbuilding, apparel, fabricated metal prods., printing and publishing, concrete, glass prods., aircraft, beer, food prods., plastics, textiles, biological prods.). Settled in 1851–1852, Seattle remained a small lumber town until the coming of the Great Northern RR in 1893. The city became a boom town with the 1897 Alaska gold rush and developed into the nation's chief link with Alaska. It grew further with the Alaska-Yukon-Pacific Exposition (1909), the opening of the Panama Canal (1914), and the completion (1917) of a canal and locks connecting L. Washington with Puget Sound, making the city both a saltwater and a freshwater port. Aiding its industrial growth was the presence of coal in the area and the development of hydroelectric power. Long a center of radical labor movements, Seattle was the scene of a major general strike (1919) led by the Industrial Workers of the World. During the 1960s, Seattle's port expanded enormously; it now has 18 major terminals, 4 smaller piers, a 600-boat fisherman's terminal, and huge marinas for private boats. The city, situated bet. the majestic Cascade Range to E and Olympic Mts. on Olympic Peninsula to W, with Mt. Rainier to the SE, Mt. Baker to the NE, and others, snowcapped extinct volcanoes that rise majestically above the surrounding Cascade Range, is accessible to many natl. and state parks and recreation areas. Seattle is a cultural center with numerous mus. and art galleries, a variety of theater and musical organizations, aquarium, an arboretum, a zoo, and a modern public lib. The city also has professional baseball, basketball, and football teams; Seattle Kingdome. During the 1980s and 1990s, Seattle became known for its art galleries, pubs, and espresso coffee bars (the latter becoming a nationwide trend during the mid-1990s). It is the seat of the Univ. of Washington, Seattle Univ. (including Burke Mus.), Seattle Pacific Univ., and Seattle Central Community Col. Site of Westlake Center and Southcenter, two of the largest shopping centers in U.S. Seattle was the site of the 1962 world's fair, the Century 21 Exposition. The Space Needle symbol of that fair — a 600–ft/183–m tower with revolving restaurant and viewing deck — now serves as Seattle's key skyline landmark, to N of downtown. Another remnant of the fair is the Monorail, the 1st publicly operated monorail in the U.S., which still operates downtown. Also remaining from the fair are the Pacific Science Center and a cultural and recreational park. Ferries connect Seattle with Kitsap Peninsula, Vashon, and Brinbrise Islands to W, and to Victoria on Vancouver Isl., B.C. (S terminus of Alaska State Ferry Systems, formerly at Seattle, is now at Bellingham to N). Its rapidly growing E side suburbs include several inc. private gated communities. Seattle-Tacoma (SeaTac) Internatl. Airport 10 mi/16 km S of downtown. Boeing Field (King County Internatl. Airport) in S part of city. Inc. 1869.

Seattle, Mount (10,070 ft/3,069 m), on Yukon-Alaska border, in St. Elias Mts., 150 mi/241 km WSW of Whitehorse, 40 mi/64 km NNE of Yakutat; 60°05′N 139°12′W.

Seavey's Island (SEE-veez), SW Maine, in Piscataqua R. bet. Kittery, Maine, and Portsmouth, N.H. U.S. navy submarine repair installations.

Seaview, uninc. village (1990 pop. 600), Pacific co., SW Wash., 15 mi/24 km NW of Astoria, Oregon, 4 mi/6.4 km N of mouth of Columbia R. Beach resort; tourism. Mfg. (food).

Seaway Trail, 454-mi/731-km-long scenic motor route from Ripley, N.Y. (in Chatauqua co., SW N.Y.) to Rooseveltown (in St. Lawrence co., N N.Y.) on Can. border. Longest Natl. Recreation Trail in U.S. follows historic shipping route through lowland along L. Erie, the Niagara R., L. Ontario, and the St. Lawrence R.

Seawell, airfield, E Barbados, B.W.I., 8 mi/12.9 km ESE of Bridgetown; 13°04′N 59°29′W. Now renamed Grantley Adams Internatl. Airport.

Sebago (suh-BAI-go), resort town, Cumberland co., SW Maine, on Sebago L. and 28 mi/45 km NW of Portland.

Sebago Lake (suh-BAI-go), c.12 mi/19 km long and from 1 mi/1.6 km to 8 mi/12.9 km wide, SW Maine, in a resort area. It is the 2d-largest lake in Maine and is the source of Portland's water supply. Sebago State Park is on the lake.

Sebago Lake, village, Maine: see STANDISH

Sebasco, Maine: see PHIPPSBURG.

Sebascodegan Island, Maine: see HARPSWELL.

Sebastian (suh-BAS-chuhn), county (☐ 546 sq mi/1,414 sq km; 1990 pop. 99,590), W Ark.; ⊙ Fort Smith and Greenwood; 35°12′N 94°16′W. Bounded W by Okla. line, N by Arkansas R.; source of Petit Jean R in S; Ouachita Mts. in S (part of Ouachita Natl. Forest). Large Fort Chaffee Military Reservation crosses N part of co., from Fort Smith E into Franklin co.; James W. Trimble Lock and Dam on Arkansas R. E of Fort Smith. Coal-mining region; also agr. (cattle, hogs, fruit; dairying; poultry raising). Mfg. at Fort Smith. Formed 1851.

Sebastian 1 (se-BAS-styuhn), resort town (☐ 13 sq mi/34 sq km; 1990 pop. 10,205), Indian R. co., E central Fla., 14 mi/23 km NNW of Vero Beach, on Indian R. lagoon; 27°47′N 80°28′W. Large retired pop. and much growth since 1980. **2** uninc. town (1990 pop. 1,598), Willacy and Cameron cos., extreme S Texas, 12 mi/19 km NNW of Harlingen; 26°20′N 97°47′W. Irrigated agr. area (citrus, cotton, vegetables).

Sebastian, Cape (suh-BAS-chen), Curry co., SW Oregon, promontory c. 712 ft/217 m high, 8 mi/12.9 km S of Gold Beach. Site of Cape Sebastian State Park.

Sebastián Vizcaíno Bay (se-bahs-tee-AHN VEES-kah-EE-no), large inlet of the Pacific on W coast of Baja California, NW Mexico; c.60 mi/97 km in diameter, 40 mi/64 km wide. Bounded W by Cedros Isl. Eugenia Point at SW entrance. El izcaíno Biosphere Reserve is on S shore.

Sebasticook Lake (suh-BAS-tuh-kuk), 4 mi/6.4 km long, Penobscot co., S central Maine, resort lake near Newport, 22 mi/35 km WNW of Bangor.

Sebasticook River (suh-BAS-tuh-kuk), c.40 mi/64 km long, central Maine; rises in SE Somerset co.; flows S and SW to the Kennebec at Winslow.

Sebastopol, city (1990 pop. 7,004), Sonoma co., W Calif., a suburb 5 mi/8 km W of Santa Rosa; 38°24′N 122°50′W. Fruit (esp. apples; also grapes), vegetables. Inc. 1902.

Sebastopol (suh-BAS-tuh-pool), town (1990 pop. 281), Scott co., central Miss. 39 mi/63 km WNW of Meridian; 32°34′N 89°19′W. RR spur terminus. Mfg. (food, apparel). Golden Memorial State Park to W.

Sebec (suh-BEK), resort town (1990 pop. 554), Piscataquis co., central Maine, on Piscataquis R., and Sebec L. and 9 mi/14.5 km NE of Dover-Foxcroft; 45°14′N 69°06′W.

Sebec Lake, Piscataquis co., central Maine, 4 mi/6.4 km N of Dover-Foxcroft; 11 mi/18 km long, ½ mi/⁸⁄₁₀ km–3 mi/4.8 km wide. Resort center. Source of Sebec River, which flows c.9 mi/14.5 km E and SE to the Piscataquis.

Sebec Lake, village, Maine: see WILLIMANTIC.

Sebeka (se-BEE-kuh), village (1990 pop. 662), Wadena co., W central Minn., on Redeye R. and 14 mi/23 km N of Wadena; 46°37′N 95°05′W. Agr. (Grain; livestock, poultry; dairying). Mfg. (printing and publishing, ceramics). Lyons State Forest to SE; Huntersville State Forest to NE; numerous small lakes to NE.

Sebewaing (SEE-buh-wing), town (1990 pop. 1,923), Huron co., E Mich., 23 mi/37 km NE of Bay City, on Saginaw Bay; 43°43′N 83°27′W. In farm area (grain, beans, sugar beets, corn, wheat, poultry; dairy prods.); Mfg. (fabricated metal prods., food). Settled 1835, inc. 1879.

Seboeis Lake (suh-BOI-uhs), Piscataquis co., central Maine, on W. Branch Seboeis R., 15 mi/24 km SW of Millinocket; 7 mi/11.3 km long, 1 mi/1.6 km wide; 45°27′N 68°49′W. Flows E to Endless L. Recreational

area. There is also a Grand L. Seboeis in N Penobscot co., Maine, 45 mi/72 km NNE.

Seboeis River (suh-BOI-uhs), c.20 mi/32 km long, in Penobscot co., central Maine; rises in Seboeis L.; flows S to East Branch of Penobscot R.

Seboomook (suh-BOO-muk), township (1990 pop. 19), Somerset co., W central Maine, at N end of Moosehead L., 32 mi/51 km NE of Jackman; 46°06′N 70°00′W. Hunting, fishing area.

Seboomook Lake (suh-BOO-muk), reservoir, Somerset co., NW Maine, on W. Branch Penobscot R. and at junction of North and South branches of Penobscot R., 52 mi/84 km WNW of Millinocket, just NW of Moosehead L.; 11 mi/18 km long; 45°54′N 69°44′W.

Sebree (SEE-bree), town (1990 pop. 1,510), Webster co., W Ky., 16 mi/26 km S of Henderson, near Green R.; 37°36′N 87°31′W. In agr. (tobacco, corn, wheat; cattle, hogs, horses) and timber area. Some mfg. Settled c.1850; inc. 1872.

Sebring (SEE-bring), town (☐ 10 sq mi/26 sq km; 1990 pop. 8,900), S central Fla., c.50 mi/80 km SE of Lakeland, on L. Jackson (c.3 mi/4.8 km long); ⊙ Highlands co.; 27°29′N 81°27′W. Citrus-fruit packing, mfg. of chemicals. Founded 1912 by George Sebring. Major automobile racing track/speedway.

Sebring, village (1990 pop. 4,848), Mahoning co., E Ohio, 5 mi/8 km E of Alliance; 40°55′N 81°01′W.

Sebringville (SEE-bring-vil), village, S Ont., Canada, 5 mi/8 km NW of Stratford; milling, leather mfg., dairying.

Secaucus (see-KAW-kuhs), town (1990 pop. 14,061), Hudson co., NE N.J., on the Hackensack R., adjoining Jersey City; 40°46′N 74°03′W. Once known as a pig farm center, it has emerged as a retail center and an area of industrial development, esp. in the high-technology fields. Some mfg. Secaucus has benefited economically from the construction in the 1970s of the professional Meadowlands Sports Complex. The town has become the site of many corporate hq. Inc. 1917.

Sechelt (SEE-shehlt), village, SW B.C., Canada, at base of Seechelt Peninsula, 33 mi/53 km WNW of Vancouver; 49°28′N 123°46′W. Resort; shingle milling. Nearby is Sechelt Indian village.

Seco (SEE-ko), village, Letcher co., SE Ky., in the Cumberland Mts., on North Fork Kentucky R.; and 5 mi/8 km NE of Whitesburg. Bituminous coal. Jefferson Natl. Forest to SE.

Second College Grant, land grant, Coos co., N N.H., 30 mi/48 km NNE of Berlin. Bounded E by Maine state boundary. Wilderness area drained by Dead Diamond and Swift Diamond rivers.

Second Connecticut Lake, N.H.: see CONNECTICUT LAKES.

Second Mesa, uninc. town (1990 pop. 929), Navajo co., NE central Ariz., 75 mi/121 km NE of Flagstaff, at center of Hopi Indian Reservation. Elev c.6,000 ft/1,829 m. Sheep; crafts. Polacca Wash to SE. Several Hopi villages in area.

Second Roach Pond, Piscataquis co., central Maine, 20 mi/32 km NE of Greenville; 3 mi/4.8 km long, ½ mi/⁸⁄₁₀ km wide. In recreational area. Joined by stream to First Roach Pond.

Seconesett, Mass.: see MASHPEE.

Secor (SEE-core), village (1990 pop.389), Woodford co., central Ill., 19 mi/31 km NNW of Bloomington; 40°44′N 89°08′W. In agr. area. Near Panther Creek.

Secret Caverns, N.Y.: see HOWES CAVE.

Secretary, fishing town (1990 pop. 528), Dorchester co., E Md., c.10 mi/16 km NE of Cambridge, on Choptank R.; 38°37′N 75°57′W. Clothing factory, oyster-packing plant.

Section, town (1990 pop. 777), Jackson co., NW Ala., 7 mi/11.3 km SSE of Scottsboro.

Security Bay, fishing village, SE Alaska, on NW shore of Kuiu Isl., 15 mi/24 km SW of Kake; 56°52′N 134°20′W.

Security-Widefield, uninc. city (1990 pop. 23,822), El Paso co., central Colo., suburb SSE of downtown Colorado Springs (Security 7 mi/11.3 km SSE; Widefield

10 mi/16 km SSE), on Fountain Creek, at main entrance to Fort Carson Military Reservation (to W); 38°44′N 104°42′W. Elev. 5,730 ft/1,747 m. Some mfg. Colorado Springs Municipal Airport to N.

Sedalia, city (1990 pop. 19,800), W central Mo.; ⊙ Pettis co.; 38°42′N 93°13′W. An agr. shipping and distribution center, and regional service and shopping center. Agr. (corn, soybeans, sorghum, wheat, cattle). Mfg. (apparel, consumer goods, printing and publishing, electronic equip., ordnance, fabricated metal prods.). The city was formerly an important RR center with RR stops for two different RRs. Sedalia is the site of the Mo. State Fair (since 1899); State Fair Community Col. Whiteman Air Force Base is W of the city. Bothwell State Park to N. Access to Katy Trail State Park. Scott Joplin memorial. Plotted 1857. Inc. 1864.

Sedalia (sed-AIL-yuh), village (1990 pop. 325), Graves co., W Ky., near Mayfield Creek and 8 mi/12.9 km S of Mayfield. Agr. (tobacco, grain; livestock, poultry).

Sedalia, Ohio: see MIDWAY.

Sedan (si-DAN), town (1990 pop. 1,306), SE Kansas, 30 mi/48 km WNW of Coffeyville; ⊙ Chautauqua co.; 37°07′N 96°10′W. Elev. 850 ft/259 m. In livestock-grazing area. Oil wells nearby. Founded 1875, inc. 1876.

Sedan (suh-DAN), village (1990 pop. 63), Pope co., W Minn., 9 mi/14.5 km SE of Glenwood; 45°34′N 95°15′W. Dairying; light mfg.

Sedco Hills, uninc. town (1990 pop. 3,008), Riverside co., S Calif., residential suburb 24 mi/39 km S of Riverside; 33°39′N 117°17′W. Cattle, dairying, poultry, grain. L. Elsinore (State Park) to W; Cleveland Natl. Forest to SW.

Sedge Garden (SEJ), uninc. town (1990 pop. 2,784), Forsyth co., central N.C., residential suburb 3 mi/4.8 km E of downtown Winston-Salem and 4 mi/6.4 km SW of Kernersville; 36°05′N 80°08′W.

Sedgewick, town (1991 pop. 874), E Alta., Canada, 35 mi/56 km W of Wainwright; 68°52′N 139°05′W. Food mfg., mixed farming.

Sedgewickville, town (1990 pop. 138), Bollinger co., SE Mo., on Whitewater R., and 16 mi/26 km N of Marble Hill; 37°31′N 89°54′W. Light mfg.

Sedgwick 1 (SEJ-wik), county (□ 549 sq mi/1,422 sq km; 1990 pop. 2,690), extreme NE Colo.; ⊙ Julesburg; 40°52′N 102°20′W. Bordering Nebr. on NE; watered by South Platte R. Irrigated agr. area; sugar beets, cattle, poultry, wheat, sunflowers, beans, oats, corn. Julesburg Reservoir on W boundary. Formed 1889. **2** county (□ 1,009 sq mi/2,613 sq km; 1990 pop. 403,662), S Kansas; ⊙ Wichita; 37°40′N 97°27′W. Flint Hills region in E. Sloping to gently rolling plain, drained by Arkansas and Little Arkansas rivers. Wheat, sorghum, hay, soybeans, cattle, hogs, sheep, poultry, strawberries, peaches; food, furniture, plastic prods., fabricated metal prods., chemicals, machinery. Scattered oil and gas fields. Industries at Wichita. Formed 1870.

Sedgwick 1 (SEJ-wik), town (1990 pop. 183), Sedgwick co., NE Colo., on South Platte R., mouth of Cottonwood Creek to W, near Nebr. line, and 13 mi/21 km WSW of Julesburg; 40°55′N 102°31′W. Shipping point in cattle area. Julesburg Reservoir to W. **2** town (1990 pop. 1,438), Harvey co., S central Kansas, on Little Arkansas R. and 16 mi/26 km NNW of Wichita; 37°55′N 97°25′W. Grain shipping point. **3** town (1990 pop. 905), Hancock co., S Maine, on Penobscot Bay and 20 mi/32 km SSW of Ellsworth; 44°19′N 68°39′W. Includes village of Sargentville.

Sedgwick (SEJ-wik), village (1990 pop. 86), Lawrence co., NE Ark., 13 mi/21 km NW of Jonesboro; 35°58′N 90°51′W.

Sedley, village (1991 pop. 342), S Sask., Canada, 35 mi/56 km SE of Regina. Wheat.

Sedley, uninc. village, Southampton co., SE Va., 8 mi/12.9 km NNW of Franklin; 36°46′N 76°59′W. Mfg. (machinery, food); agr. (grain, peanuts, cotton, melons; livestock).

Sedona, city (1990 pop. 7,720), Coconino co., N Ariz., 22 mi/35 km SSW of Flagstaff, in Coconino Natl. Forest; 34°51′N 111°47′W. Elev. 4,240 ft/1,292 m. Timber;

tourism; mfg. (electronic equip., printing and publishing). Red Rock State Park to SW; Slide Rock State Park to N; Prescott Natl. Forest to W and S.

Sedro-Woolley (SEE-dro WUL-ee), city (1990 pop. 6,000), Skagit co., NW Wash., 20 mi/32 km SE of Bellingham and near Skagit R.; 48°31′N 122°14′W. In rich agr. region; fruits and vegetables; dairying; poultry; mfg. (food, electronic equip., wood prods., lumber). Sedro and Woolley, founded separately, were consolidated in 1898. Snowcapped Mt. Baker (10,775 ft/3,284 m) to NE (Mt. Baker-Snoqualmie Natl. Recreation Area on S slopes); parts of Mt. Baker Natl. Forest to NE and SE.

Seechelt Inlet (SEE-shehlt), SW arm of Jervis Inlet, SW B.C., Canada, bet. Seechelt Peninsula (W) and mainland (E), in lumbering and fishing area; 22 mi/35 km long, 1 mi/2 km–2 mi/3 km wide. Sechelt village at S end. Narrows Arm and Salmon Arm branch off (W).

Seekong River, R.I.: see BLACKSTONE RIVER.

Seekonk (SEE-kawnk), town (1990 pop. 13,046), Bristol co., SE Mass., at the R.I. state line, 12 mi/19 km NW of Fall River; 41°51′N 71°19′W. It is chiefly residential. Settled 1636, set off from Rehoboth 1812.

Seeley, uninc. town (1990 pop. 1,228), Imperial co., S Calif., 6 mi/9.7 km W of el Centro, on New R., in Imperial Valley, 20 mi/32 km S of Salton Sea, 10 mi/16 km N of Mexico (Baja Calif. [Baja Calif. Norte]) border; 32°48′N 115°41′W. Vegetables, fruit, cotton, sugar beets, wheat, cattle, sheep. El Centro Naval Air Facility to N; Natl. Parachute Test Range to NW. Painted Gorge to W.

Seeley Lake, town (1990 pop. 870), Missoula co., W Mont., 32 mi/51 km NE of Missoula, at S end of Seeley L., exit of Clearwater R. Tourism. Mfg. (lumber). Clearwater State Forest to S; Lolo Natl. Forest to N and W; Placid L. State Park to SW; Salmon L. State Park to SE.

Seeley Lake, Missoula co., W Mont., just E of Mission Range, on Clearwater R., 32 mi/51 km NE of Missoula; 4 mi/6.4 km long, ½ mi/⅘ km wide; 47°10′N 113°31′W. Town of Seeley Lake at S end. Surrounded by Lolo Natl. Forest; S end in Clearwater State Forest; Seeley Lake Game Preserve at N end. Largest in chain of lakes.

Seelyville, town (1990 pop. 1,090), Vigo co., W Ind., suburb 8 mi/12.9 km ENE of Terre Haute; 39°29′N 87°16′W. In agr. and bituminous-coal area. Laid out 1871.

Seffner, town (□ 3 sq mi/7.8 sq km; 1990 pop. 5,371), Hillsborough co., W central Fla., 12 mi/19 km E of Tampa; 28°00′N 82°16′W. Mfg. includes fixtures, concrete prods., printing and publishing.

Seguam Island (SEE-gwawm), Aleutian Isls., SW Alaska, at E end of the Andreanof Isls., 180 mi/290 km WSW of Umnak; 13 mi/21 km long, 8 mi/12.9 km wide; 52°20′N 172°25′W. Rises to 3,458 ft/1,054 m on Pyre Peak (center).

Seguin (SUH-geen), city (1990 pop. 18,853), S central Texas, on the Guadalupe R.; ⊙ Guadalupe co.; 29°34′N 97°58′W. Elev. 520 ft/158 m. Mfg. of textiles, construction materials, plastic prods., steel, food, printing and publishing. The city was founded (1831) by members of the Texas Rangers and named after Colonel Juan Seguin, a hero of the Texas Revolution. L. McQueeney to NW; Sebastopol House State Historic Site. Texas Lutheran Col. is here. Inc. 1853.

Seguin Island (suh-GWIN), Sagadahoc co., SW Maine. At mouth of the Kennebec, with lighthouse built 1795, rebuilt 1857.

Segundo, village, Las Animas co., S Colo., on Purgatoire R. and 12 mi/19 km WSW of Trinidad. Elev. 6,480 ft/1,975 m. Coal mines nearby.

Seibert, village (1990 pop. 181), Kit Carson co., E Colo., 32 mi/51 km W of Burlington; 39°17′N 102°52′W. Elev. 4,710 ft/1,436 m. Cattle, wheat, corn, sunflowers, oats. Flagler State Wildlife Area to W.

Seibo (SAI-bo), lowland, SE Dominican Republic, extensive fertile plain stretching E c.100 mi/161 km along the Caribbean from Ozama R. near Santo Domingo to Mona Passage; c.20 mi/32 km wide. Mainly a sugar-growing region; other prods. include cacao, rice, corn, coffee, tobacco, tropical fruit; cattle. Also known as El Seibo.

Seibo, El (SAI-bo, el), province (□ 1,287 sq mi/3,333 sq km; 1993 pop. 94,244), E Dominican Republic; ⊙ Seibo; 18°48′N 69°03′W. Borders N on Samaná Bay; crossed W-E by the Cordillera Central. Fertile agr. region (Seibo lowland), yielding coffee, cacao, sugarcane, rice, corn, tropical fruit; also cattle raising, dairying. Main trading and processing centers are Seibo, Hato Mayor, and port of Sabana de la Mar. Prov., was set up 1845; in 1944 La Altagracia prov. was formed from it.

Seibo, El (SAI-bo, el), officially Santa Cruz del Seibo, city (1993 pop. 16,309), E Dominican Republic, in interior valley, on Soco R., and 60 mi/97 km ENE of Santo Domingo; ⊙ Seibo prov.; 18°45′N 69°02′W. Agr. center (cacao, coffee, sugarcane, corn; cattle; beeswax; medicinal plants). Has notable church. Founded 1502. Also called Seibo.

Seigling (SIG-ling), village, Allendale co., SW S.C., 3 mi/4.8 km N of Allendale. Agr. includes watermelons, cotton, peanuts, grain.

Seiling (SEEL-ing), town (1990 pop. 1,031), Dewey co., W Okla., 33 mi/53 km SE of Woodward, near North Canadian R.; 36°08′N 98°55′W. In agr. area (wheat, cotton); light mfg.

Seine River (sain), 150 mi/241 km long, W Ont., Canada; issues from Lac des Milles Lacs; flows SW through the lake region N of Minn. border to Rainy L.

Selah (SEE-luh), town (1990 pop. 5,113), Yakima co., S Wash., suburb 5 mi/8 km NNW of Yakima and on Yakima R. (Roza Diversion Dam to N), at mouth of Naches R.; 46°40′N 120°32′W. Vegetables, fruit, potatoes; dairying; poultry; cattle; mfg. (transportation equip., food prods., machinery); timber. Large U.S. Military Reservation/Yakima Training Center and Firing Range to E.

Selawik, Inuit village (1990 pop. 596), NW Alaska, on Selawik L., 70 mi/113 km ESE of Kotzebue, on Arctic Circle; 66°35′N 160°01′W. Fishing, hunting.

Selawik Lake, NW Alaska, SE arm of Hotham Inlet, 60 mi/97 km ESE of Kotzebue, on Arctic Circle; 45 mi/72 km long, 5 mi/8 km–20 mi/32 km wide; Selawik village, E. Mouth of Selawik R.

Selby, town (1990 pop. 707), N S.Dak., 80 mi/129 km N of Pierre; ⊙ Walworth co.; 45°30′N 100°01′W. In farming and cattle-raising area (livestock, dairying, poultry, grain). L. Hiddenwood to NE; Bangor Monument to S.

Selby, uninc. village, Contra Costa co., W Calif., 23 mi/37 km N of downtown Oakland at W end of Carquinez Strait, opposite Vallejo.

Selbyville, town (1990 pop. 1,335), Sussex co., SE Del., near Md. state line, 20 mi/32 km SE of Georgetown; 38°27′N 75°13′W. Mfg. (food); agr. area (fruit, vegetables; poultry, cattle, hogs; dairying). Cypress Swamp to W.

Selden 1 village (1990 pop. 248), Sheridan co., NW Kansas, 15 mi/24 km NW of Hoxie; 39°32′N 100°34′W. In agr. and livestock region. **2** uninc. village (□ 4 sq mi/10.4 sq km; 1990 pop. 20,608), Suffolk co., SE N.Y., on L.I.; 40°52′N 73°02′W. It is chiefly residential with some mfg. Suffolk Co. Community Col. Ammerman Campus is here.

Seldovia, village (1990 pop. 316), S Alaska, on Kachemak Bay, S Kenai Peninsula, 90 mi/145 km SW of Seward; 59°26′N 151°42′W. Fishing, fish processing; undeveloped coal deposits nearby. Orthodox church.

Selfridge, village (1990 pop. 242), Sioux co., S N.Dak., 15 mi/24 km WSW of Fort Yates, inside Standing Rock Indian Reservation; 46°02′N 100°55′W. Wheat, livestock, dairy prods. Mountain/Central Time Zone boundary to E.

Seligman, uninc. village, Yavapai co., NW central Ariz., 67 mi/108 km W of Flagstaff, near Big Chino Wash. Elev. 5,242 ft/1,598 m. Trade and shipping center for mining, ranching area (cattle; alfalfa, hay); highway service center. Juniper Mts. to SW, Prescott Natl. Forest to S, Kaibab Natl. Forest to E.

Selinsgrove (SEL-ins-grov), borough (1990 pop. 5,384), Snyder co., central Pa., 6 mi/9.7 km SW of Sunbury, on Susquehanna R. (RR bridge); 40°47′N 76°52′W. Drained by Penss Creek. RR junction. Agr. area (hay, apples; poultry, livestock, dairying). Mfg. (electrical prods., construction materials, textiles, apparel, flour, wood prods.). Susquehanna Univ. here. Penn Valley Airport to N. Middle Creek L. reservoir to S. Settled 1755, laid out 1790, inc. 1827.

Selkirk, town (1991 pop. 9,815), SE Man., Canada, on the Red R., just S of L. Winnipeg.Port for prods. from N Man.; steel mills, foundries, and shipyards. It is named for the 5th earl of Selkirk, who est. (1812) the Red River Settlement in the region.

Selkirk, village, S Ont., Canada, near L. Ontario, 27 mi/43 km SE of Brantford. Dairying, mixed farming.

Selkirk, Canada; see FORT SELKIRK.

Selkirk Mountains, rugged range of the Rocky Mts., SE B.C., Canada, near the Alta. border, and extending NW c.200 mi/320 km from the U.S. border. Mt. Sir Sanford (11,590 ft/3,533 m) is the highest peak. The range is almost encircled by the Columbia R., which loops around the N edge.

Selle, Massif de la (SEL, mah-SEEF duh lah), range in SE Haiti, just S of Port-au-Prince; extends c.50 mi/80 km E to Dominican Republic border; rises in Mont la Selle to 8,793 ft/2,680 m, the highest peak in Haiti; 18°21'N 72°17'W.

Sellers, village (1990 pop. 358), Marion and Dillon cos., NE S.C., 18 mi/29 km ENE of Florence; 34°16'N 79°28'W. Mfg. (construction materials). Agr. (livestock; grain, tobacco, cotton, sorghum).

Sellersburg, town (1990 pop. 5,745), Clark co., SE Ind., near small Silver Creek, 8 mi/12.9 km N of Jeffersonville; 38°23'N 85°46'W. Agr. area. Diversified mfg. Laid out 1846.

Sellersville (SEL-luhrs-vil), borough (1990 pop. 4,479), Bucks co., SE Pa., 27 mi/43 km NNW of Philadelphia, on East Branch Perkiomen Creek; 40°21'N 75°18'W. Agr. (grain, soybeans, apples; livestock, poultry, dairying). Mfg. (machinery, pharmaceuticals, hand bells and chimes); sandstone quarrying. Settled c.1730, inc. 1874.

Sells, uninc. town, Pima co., S Ariz., 57 mi/92 km SW of Tucson in E center of Tohono O'odham (Papago) Indian Reservation, 19 mi/31 km NE of Mex. (Sonora) border. Hq. and trade center for Gila Bend, Tohono O'odham (Papago), and San Xavier Indian reservations. Kitt Peak (6,875 ft/2,096 m) and Kitt Peak Observatory 18 mi/29 km E, in E part of reservation.

Selma 1 city (1990 pop. 23,755), ⊙ Dallas co., S central Ala., on the Alabama R., c.40 mi/64 km WNW of Montgomery; 32°25'N 87°01'W. In a fertile Black Belt farm area, where cotton farming has collapsed save for some big growers. Mfg. (machinery, paper prods., construction materials, transportation equip., furniture, textiles, apparel); dairy prods., lumber. A Confederate arsenal and supply point, Selma was ravaged in 1865; however, a number of antebellum houses remain, notably Sturdivant Hall (1853). Sen. William Rufus King, who named the town, lived and is buried here. Selma Univ., Concordia Col., and Wallace Community Col. Selma located here. A Civil War enactment takes place annually. Nearby is Cahaba, capital of Ala. from 1819 to 1826. In 1965, Selma was the center of a voter registration drive led by Dr. Martin Luther King, Jr. Inc. 1820. **2** city (1990 pop. 14,757), Fresno co., central Calif., a suburb 15 mi/24 km SE of Fresno, in irrigated San Joaquin Valley; 36°34'N 119°37'W. Mfg. (concrete block, fabricated metal prods., food, printing and publishing). Agr. (grapes, nectarines, citrus, cotton; dairying, cattle, poultry, sugar beets, rice, wheat); wineries in area. Inc. 1893.

Selma 1 town (1990 pop. 800), Delaware co., E Ind., 6 mi/9.7 km E of Muncie; 40°11'N 85°16'W. Agr. area. Mfg. (wire prods.). Laid out 1852. **2** town (1990 pop. 4,600), Johnston co., central N.C., suburb 4 mi/6.4 km NE of Smithfield, near Nuese R.; 35°32'N 78°17'W. RR junction. Agr. area (tobacco, peanuts, cotton, grain; poultry, livestock). Mfg. (consumer goods, feeds, textiles, electrical equip., fabricated metal prods.). **3** uninc. town, Allegheny co., NW Va., 2 mi/3.2 km SW of Clifton Forge, on Jackson R., in Allegheny Mts., in George Washington Natl. Forest; 37°48'N 79°50'W.

Selma, village (1990 pop. 520), Bexar, Guadalupe, and Comal cos., S central Texas, industrial suburb 16 mi/26 km NE of San Antonio, dissected by Cibolo Creek; 29°35'N 98°19'W. Elev. 875 ft/267 m. Agr. area. Mfg. (commercial dessicant systems, fabricated metal prods.); nut processing.

Selmer, town (1990 pop. 3,838), ⊙ McNairy co., SW Tenn., 33 mi/53 km SSE of Jackson; 35°10'N 88°36'W. In clay, timber, cotton, soybean, and corn area. Mfg. (shoes, electrical equip., wood prods., apparel).

Selway River, 100 mi/161 km long, N central Idaho; rises 1 mi/1.6 km SE Idaho co., in N ½ of Bitterroot Range, near Continental Divide and Mont. state line, flows N and W, through Selway-Bitterroot Wilderness Area of Nez Perce Natl. Forest, joining Luchsa R. at Lowell to form Middle Fork Clearwater R., 22 mi/35 km ESE of Kamiah. River is entirely within Idaho co.

Semans (SEE-muhnz), village (1991 pop. 333), S central Sask., Canada, 65 mi/105 km N of Regina; 51°24'N 104°44'W. Wheat, livestock.

Semichi Islands (se-MEE-chee), group of 3 small isls. of Aleutian Isls., SW Alaska, 20 mi/32 km ESE of Attu; 52°43'N 174°01'E. Consists of Shemya Island, Nizki Isl., and Alaid Isl.

Seminary, town (1990 pop. 231), Covington co., S central Miss., 20 mi/32 km NNW of Hattiesburg; 31°33'N 89°30'W. Agr. (cotton, corn; poultry, cattle). Mfg. (pottery, apparel).

Seminoe Reservoir (SEM-uh-no) (□ 32 sq mi/83 sq km), Carbon co., S central Wyo., on North Platte R., 30 mi/48 km NE of Rawlins; 25 mi/40 km long, average 2 mi/3.2 km wide; 42°09'N 106°53'W. Max. capacity 1,017,000 acre-ft. Medicine Bow R. forms 10-mi/16-km–long E arm. Formed by Seminoe Dam (concrete; 295 ft/90 m high), built (1939) for power generation and irrigation. Seminoe State Park on NW shore.

Seminole 1 (SEM-i-nol), county (□ 344 sq mi/891 sq km; 1990 pop. 287,529), central Fla.; ⊙ Sanford; 28°42'N 81°13'W. N and E boundaries formed by St. Johns R., including lakes Monroe and Harney. Contains L. Jessup and many smaller lakes. Major suburban growth since 1980 as N edge of expanding metropolitan Orlando. Agr. (celery, citrus fruit, corn; poultry, livestock). Some wood- and food-processing plants. Formed 1913. **2** (SEM-uh-nol), county (□ 257 sq mi/666 sq km; 1990 pop. 9,010), extreme SW Ga.; ⊙ Donalsonville; 30°56'N 84°52'W. Bounded W by Ala. and Fla. state lines (formed here by Chattahoochee R.) and E by Spring Creek. Mfg. (apparel, textiles), industrial machining. Coastal plain agr. (cotton, corn, vegetables, soybeans, wheat, almonds, peanuts; cattle, hogs); sawmilling area. Formed 1920. **3** county (□ 640 sq mi/1,658 sq km; 1990 pop. 25,412), central Okla.; ⊙ Wewoka; 35°10'N 96°36'W. Bounded S by Canadian R., N by North Canadian R.; drained by Little R. L. Konowa (recreation) in SW corner. Agr. area (corn, peanuts, fruit; cattle, poultry). Mfg. at Seminole and Wewoka. Oil and natural gas fields. Formed 1907.

Seminole 1 (SEM-i-nol), town (□ 2 sq mi/5.2 sq km; 1990 pop. 9,251), Pinellas co., W central Fla., 9 mi/14.5 km S of Clearwater; 27°50'N 82°47'W. **2** (SEM-uh-nol), town (1990 pop. 7,071), Seminole co., central Okla., 15 mi/24 km SE of Shawnee; 35°14'N 96°39'W. Largest town in co. In oil- and natural gas–producing and agr. area. Mfg. (machinery, apparel). Seat of Seminole Jr. Col. Settled 1890; inc. as town 1908, as city 1926. **3** town (1990 pop. 6,342), ⊙ Gaines co., NW Texas, on S Llano Estacado, 75 mi/121 km SW of Lubbock, on Seminole Draw, near N.Mex. state line; 32°43'N 102°39'W. Elev. 3,315 ft/1,010 m. Retail center for oil and natural gas, cattle, sheep, and hog ranching region. Agr. (vegetables, peanuts; cotton). Mfg. (machinery), gas processing. Founded 1908, inc. 1936.

Seminole, Lake (SEM-uh-nol), reservoir, Ga., Fla., and Ala., on Apalachicola R., where the river flows S into Fla., 40 mi/64 km WNW of Tallahassee, Fla.; 30°49'N 84°51'W. Chattahoochee R. (Ga. border with Ala. and Fla.) extends c.45 mi/72 km NNW; Chickasawhatchee R. enters from NE, forms arm c.30 mi/48 km long, joins lake just above dam. Max. capacity 406,200 acre-ft. Formed by Jim Woodruff Lock and Dam (53 ft/16 m high), built (1952) by the Army Corps of Engineers for navigation, power generation, and flood control. State parks on NE (Ga.) and W (Ala.) shores and at dam (Fla.).

Semisopochnoi Island (se-mei-suh-PAWCH-noi) [= Island of 7 Volcanoes], Rat Isls., Aleutian Isls., SW Alaska, 35 mi/56 km NE of Amchitka Isl.; 12 mi/19 km long, 10 mi/16 km wide; 51°57'N 179°38'E. Uninhabited; important as landmark for vessels sailing down the Aleutian chain.

Senado (sai-NAH-do), village, Camagüey prov., E Cuba, on RR, and 23 mi/37 km ENE of Camagüey; 21°34'N 77°35'W. Sugar mill Noel Fernández just S.

Senath (SEE-nuth), city (1990 pop. 1,622), Dunklin co., in boot heel of extreme SE Mo., near St. Francis R., 10 mi/16 km SW of Kennett; 36°07'N 90°09'W. Cotton, rice, soybeans. Founded 1882.

Senatobia (see-nuh-TO-bee-uh), town (1990 pop. 4,772), ⊙ Tate co., NW Miss., 35 mi/56 km S of Memphis, Tenn.; 34°37'N 89°58'W. In agr. (cotton, grain, soybeans), stock-raising, and timber area. Mfg. (aluminum prods., chemicals, furniture, printing, concrete, apparel). Has Northwest Miss. Community Col., Arkabutla L. reservoir to NW; John W. Kyle State Park, on Sardis L. reservoir to SE. Founded 1856; burned by Union troops in Civil War.

Seneca 1 county (□ 390 sq mi/1,010 sq km; 1990 pop. 33,683), W central N.Y.; ⊙ Ovid and Waterloo; 42°47'N 76°49'W. In Finger Lakes region, bounded E by Cayuga L. and Seneca R., partly W by Seneca L.; crossed by the N.Y. State Barge Canal in NE. Dairying and farming area (fruit, wheat, potatoes, hay, beans). Diversified mfg. Formed 1804. **2** county (□ 551 sq mi/1,427 sq km; 1990 pop. 59,733), N Ohio; ⊙ Tiffin; 41°07'N 83°07'W. Drained by Sandusky R. and tributaries. Bisected by the Lake Plains and Till Plains physiographic regions. Agr. area (livestock, poultry, dairy prods.; corn, soybeans). Limestone quarries, clay pits; mineral springs (resort). Mfg. at Fostoria and Tiffin (furniture and fixtures, pottery, fabricated metal prods., transportation equip., machinery, electronics). Formed 1824.

Seneca (SEN-i-kuh), city (1990 pop. 1,885), Newton co., SW Mo., in the Ozarks, 17 mi/27 km S of Joplin, next to Okla. state line; 36°50'N 94°36'W. Agr. (wheat, corn, hay, fruit). Mfg. (dairy prods., batteries). Tripoli mine and mill. Plotted c.1869.

Seneca 1 (SEN-i-kuh), town (1990 pop. 2,027), ⊙ Nemaha co., NE Kansas, on South Fork Nemaha R., and 55 mi/89 km NNW of Topeka; 39°50'N 96°04'W. Shipping point for hogs, poultry, corn, oats region; millwork; grain storage. Mfg. (machinery, furniture, wood prods.). Fort Markley and Indian Village tourist attraction. Nemaha State Fishing L. to SE. Laid out 1857. **2** uninc. town (1990 pop. 1,029), Venango co., NW Pa., suburb 3 mi/4.8 km S of Oil City; 41°22'N 79°42'W. Mfg. (machinery, dairy prods., electronic equip.). Agr. (dairying, livestock; grain). **3** town (1990 pop. 7,726), Oconee co., NW S.C., 34 mi/55 km WSW of Greenville; 34°41'N 82°57'W. Mfg. (textiles, plastic prods., metal prods., transportation equip., printing and publishing, apparel). Agr. (dairying; wheat, soybeans, apples, corn). Founded 1874.

Seneca 1 (SE-nuh-kuh), village (1990 pop. 1,878), La Salle co., N Ill., on Illinois R., and 13 mi/21 km ESE of Ottawa; 41°17'N 88°36'W. In agr. area. Was a shipbuilding center (barges) during World War II. **2** village (1990 pop. 78), Thomas co., central Nebr., 13 mi/21 km WNW of Thedford and on Middle Loup R; 42°02'N 100°49'W. Immediately E of Central/Mountain time zone boundary. **3** village (1990 pop. 191), Grant co., NE central Oregon, 37 mi/60 km N of Burns, on Silvies R., at mouth of Bear Creek; 44°07'N 118°58'W. Area surrounded by Malheur Natl. Forest. Timber; cattle, sheep. **4** village (1990 pop. 81), Faulk co., N central S.Dak., 20 mi/32 km W of Faulkton; 45°03'N 99°30'W. Diversified farming (grain).

Seneca Army Depot, N.Y.: see ROMULUS.

Seneca Caverns, Pendleton co., E W.Va., in the Allegheny Mts., 9 mi/14.5 km NNW of Franklin, in Monongahela Natl. Forest. Two series of underground caves, with varied rock formations; tourist attraction. State fish hatchery is here.

Seneca Caverns, Ohio: see BELLEVUE.

Seneca Falls, village (□ 4 sq mi/10.4 sq km; 1990 pop. 7,370), Seneca co., W central N.Y., in Finger Lakes region, on Seneca R. (water power), and 9 mi/14.5 km E of Geneva; 42°54′N 76°47′W. Mfg. (fabricated metal prods., transportation equip., machinery, electrical equip., textiles). Cayuga L. (with state park). Elizabeth Cady Stanton lived here and helped organize 1st women's rights convention in U.S., held here in 1848. Women's Rights Natl. Historic Park and Mus., located in the restored Elizabeth Cady Stanton House, and the Natl. Women's Hall of Fame are here. Immediately N of the village is the 10-sq-mi/26-sq-km Montezuma Natl. Wildlife Refuge on the E N. Amer. flyway for migratory waterfowl. Settled 1787, inc. 1831.

Seneca Gardens (SEN-i-kuh), village (1990 pop. 684), Jefferson co., N Ky., suburb 4 mi/6.4 km E of downtown Louisville; 38°13′N 85°40′W. Bowman Field airport to NE.

Seneca Lake, largest (□ c.67 sq mi/174 sq km) and 2d longest of the Finger Lakes, W central N.Y., lying bet. Keuka and Cayuga lakes, and extending 35 mi/56 km S from Geneva to Watkins Glen (site of scenic Watkins Glen State Park) at its head; 42°40′N 76°55′W. Its outlet is Seneca R. Linked to N.Y. State Barge Canal system by Cayuga and Seneca Canal. Seasonal and permanent homes ring its shores. Naval training base (at Sampson) was here in World War II.

Seneca Oil Spring, N.Y.: see CUBA, village.

Seneca River 1 c.65 mi/105 km long, in W central N.Y., issues from N end of Seneca L.; flows NE, supplying water power at Waterloo and Seneca Falls, to N end of Cayuga L., thence generally NE and E, traversing Cross L., and receiving outlets of the E Finger Lakes, and joining Oneida R. to form Oswego R. near Phoenix, at junction called Three Rivers. Sect. connecting Cayuga and Seneca lakes is canalized (Cayuga and Seneca Canal) as part of N.Y. State Barge Canal system. **2** 50 mi/ 80 km long, in NW S.C.; rises in N Oconee co., in the Blue Ridge Mts.; flows SSE through large L. Keowee reservoir, where it receives Keowee R. from N, past Clemson as large N arm of Hartwell L. reservoir joins Tugaloo R. WNW of Anderson to form Savannah R. in Hartwell L.

Seneca Rocks, Pendleton co., E W.Va., 14 mi/23 km N of Franklin. Castlelike rock formation (c.900 ft/274 m) in the Allegheny Mts.; on North Fork South Branch of Potomac R., in Monongahela Natl. Forest; trail to summit.

Senecaville, village (1990 pop. 434), Guernsey co., E Ohio, 9 mi/14 km SE of Cambridge; 39°56′N 81°27′W. Dam nearby impounds Senecaville Lake (capacity 88,500 acre-ft; for flood control) in a tributary of Wills Creek.

Senecaville Lake, reservoir (□ 6 sq mi/15.5 sq km), Noble and Guernsey cos., E central Ohio, on Seneca Fork of Wills Creek, 10 mi/16 km SE of Cambridge; 39°56′N 81°27′W. Max. capacity 88,500 acre-ft. Formed by Senecaville Dam (45 ft/14 m high), built (1937) by Army Corps of Engineers for flood control; also used for recreation and as a fish and wildlife pond.

Seney (SEE-nee), village, Schoolcraft co., S Upper Peninsula, Mich., 31 mi/50 km NE of Manistique; 46°20′N 85°56′W. Sawmill. Was a notoriously wild lumber camp in 1880s and 1890s. W entrance to Pictured Rocks Natl. Lakeshore 25 mi/40 km N of Grand Marais. Large Seney Natl. Wildlife Refuge is to SW.

Senguio (sen-GEE-o), town (1990 pop. 1,731), Michoacán, central Mexico, 45 mi/72 km E of Morelia; 19°44′N 100°21′W. Elev. 6,660 ft/2,030 m. Cereals.

Senneterre (sehn-TER), town (1991 pop. 3,563), W Que., Canada, at S end of L. Parent, 30 mi/48 km NE of Val d'Or; 48°24′N 77°15′W. Gold mining; trout fishing center.

Senneville (SEH-ni-vil), suburban resort (1991 pop. 961), S Que., Canada, on W shore of Montreal Isl.,

on L. of the Two Mountains, 20 mi/32 km WSW of Montreal.

Senoia (suh-NOI-ah), town (1990 pop. 956), Coweta co., W Ga., 15 mi/24 km ESE of Newnan; 33°19′N 84°33′W. Mfg. includes textile, polyethylene film extrusions.

Sentinel, town (1990 pop. 960), Washita co., W Okla., 13 mi/21 km SW of Cordell; 35°09′N 99°10′W. In agr. area (grain, cotton, alfalfa, peanuts; livestock); oil and gas. Settled 1901, inc. 1906.

Sentinel Butte, village (1990 pop. 79), Golden Valley co., W N.Dak., 8 mi/12.9 km E of Beach; 46°55′N 103°50′W. Lignite mines nearby. Camel Hump Reservoir to NE; Theodore Roosevelt Natl. Park (South Unit) to E; Little Missouri Natl. Grassland to E; Sentinel Butte to S (3,428 ft/1,045 m).

Sentinel Ridge, Wis.: see WYALUSING STATE PARK.

Separation Point, settlement, SE Lab., Canada, at head of Sandwich Bay; 53°36′N 57°27′W. Lumbering.

Septentrional, Cordillera (sep-ten-tree-o-NAHL, kor-dee-YER-rah), range, N Dominican Republic, parallel to the Cordillera Central, and along the Atlantic coast, extending c.120 mi/193 km ESE from Monte Cristi to Escocesa Bay; 19°35′N 70°45′W. Rises to 4,003 ft/ 1,220 m.

Sept-Îles (seh–TEEL), city (1991 pop. 24,848), E Que., Canada, on the St. Lawrence R. near its mouth; 50°12′N 66°23′W. S terminus of RR from Schefferville and Labrador City iron mines. Iron ore, aluminum production. It is a major port exporting iron ore. Ferry across St. Lawrence to Ste.-Anne-des-Monts. The harbor was visited by Jacques Cartier in 1535, and a trading post was built on the site in 1650.

Sepulga River (se-PUL-guh), c.50 mi/80 km long, S Ala.; rises in N Conecuh co.; flows SE and S to Conecuh R. 18 mi/29 km SW of Andalusia.

Sepulveda, suburban section of Los Angeles city, Los Angeles co., S Calif., in San Fernando Valley, 16 mi/ 26 km NW of downtown Los Angeles; centered on Sepulveda Blvd., one of the longest streets in U.S., c.50 mi/80 km long. Mfg. (machinery, transportation equip., plastics prods.). Van Nuys Airport and Busch Gardens theme park are here.

Sequatchie (suh-WAH-chee), county (□ 273; 1990 pop. 8,863), SE central Tenn.; ⊙ Dunlap; 35°22′N 85°25′W. Partly in the Cumberlands; Walden Ridge in SE; drained by Sequatchie R. Coal mining. Lumbering. Agr. (livestock, feed crops, tobacco). Some mfg. at Dunlap. Formed 1857.

Sequatchie River (suhk-WAH-chee), c.80 mi/129 km long, E Tenn.; rises in Crab Orchard Mts. in S Cumberland co.; flows SSW past Pikeville and Dunlap, to Tennessee R. 3 mi/5 km S of Jasper; 35°01′N 85°38′W. Its valley separates Cumberland Plateau and Walden Ridge.

Sequim (SKWIM), town (1990 pop. 3,616), Clallam co., NW Wash., 15 mi/24 km E of Port Angeles, near Dungeness (to W); 48°05′N 123°07′W. Trade center for agr. area (alfalfa, hay). Mfg. (furniture, textile prods., printing and publishing, winery). Dungeness Natl. Wildlife Refuge on Dungeness Spit, and Dungeness State Park to NW. Olympic Natl. Park to SW; part of Olympic Natl. Forest to S, including Buckhorn Wilderness Area; Sequim Bay State Park to E.

Sequoia National Park, Tulare co., E central Calif., c.55 mi/89 km ESE of Fresno; covers 402,482 acres/ 162,884 ha. In the park are 35 groves of giant sequoias, spectacular granite mts., and deep canyons. The General Sherman Tree, 272 ft/83 m high and 37 ft/11 m in diameter at its widest point, is the largest and one of the oldest living things in the world, est. to be more than 3,500 years old. Within the area are Mt. Whitney (14,494 ft/4,418 m), the highest point in the U.S. States outside of Alaska, on E boundary of park; the Great Western Divide in center of park, and Great Basin Divide (Sierra Nevada crest) on E boundary, separates Pacific Ocean Watershed (W) from Great Basin (E). Marble Falls drops 2,000 ft/610 m) in 7 cascades. Kings Canyon Natl. Park adjoins Sequoia Natl. Park to N; General Grant Grove Section adjoining to NW is separate unit of Kings Canyon Park. Mineral King Valley and Kern Canyon R. Est. 1890.

Sequoyah (suh-KWOI-uh), county (□ 714 sq mi/ 1,849 sq km; 1990 pop. 33,828), E Okla.; ⊙ Sallisaw; 35°30′N 94°45′W. Hilly region (Boston Mts.), bounded E by Ark. state line, S by Arkansas R., forming Robert S. Kerr L. in SW; drained by Illinois R. Agr. (vegetables, fruit, soybeans, corn, potatoes; poultry, cattle). Farm prods. processing, some mfg. at Sallisaw; some oil and gas, limestone quarries. Recreation. Part of Sequoyah Natl. Wildlife Refuge in W; Tenkiller State Park, on SE shore of Tenkiller L. in NW; Sallisaw and Brushy Creek state parks at center. Formed 1907.

Sequoyah Nuclear Power Plants, Tenn., see HAMILTON, county.

Serbin, uninc. village (1990 pop. 76), Lee co., S central Texas, 6 mi/9.7 km SW of Giddings. Wends (a Slavic people) settled the community in 1855. Old Wendish church and mus.

Serdán, Mexico: see CIUDAD SERDÁN.

Sergeant Bluff, town (1990 pop. 2,772), Woodbury co., W Iowa, near Missouri R., residential suburb 6 mi/ 9.7 km SSE of Sioux City; 42°23′N 96°21′W. Mfg. (food prods., construction materials, chemicals). Agr. (livestock, grain). Town is immediately E of Sioux City Municipal Airport.

Serpent Mound, park, Adams co., S Ohio, 20 mi/32 km NNE of West Union. Prehistoric Indian mound c.1,330 ft/405 m long, representing a serpent swallowing an egg. With adjacent mounds, it is now in a state park (trails, picnic grounds, and a mus.).

Serpentine Mountains, ridge (2,240 ft/683 m) in N central N.B., Canada, 40 mi/64 km ENE of Grand Falls.

Sesquicentennial State Park, S.C.: see COLUMBIA.

Sesser, city (1990 pop. 2,087), Franklin co., S Ill., 10 mi/ 16 km NW of Benton; 38°05′N 89°02′W. Livestock, dairy prods., corn, wheat. Inc. 1906. Near Rend L.

Setauket, village (1990 pop. 3,300), Suffolk co., SE N.Y., on N shore of L.I., on Setauket Harbor (W arm of Port Jefferson Harbor), 2 mi/3.2 km W of Port Jefferson village; 40°57′N 73°07′W. Caroline Church (1729) is one of oldest on L.I.

Seth, uninc. town (1990 pop. 800), Boone co., W central W.Va., 11 mi/18 km ENE of Madison, on Big Coal R. Coal-mining and agr. region.

Seton Lake (SEE-tuhn), SW B.C., Canada, in Coast Mts., 3 mi/5 km WSW of Lillooet, just E of Anderson L.; 14 mi/23 km long, 1 mi/2 km wide. Drains E into Fraser R.

Setting Lake (□ 65 sq mi/168 sq km), central Man., Canada, 70 mi/113 km N of L. Winnipeg; 28 mi/45 km long, 3 mi/5 km wide. Drains N into Nelson R.

Seul, Lac (SUHL, lac), lake (□ 416 sq mi/1,077 sq km), NW Ont., Canada; 50°30′N 92°W. Elev. 1,172 ft/357 m. Drained W by English R. Near SE shore is Sioux Lookout.

Seven Brothers Mountain (8,690 ft/2,649 m), SW N.Mex., in Mimbres Mts., 30 mi/48 km ENE of Silver City, on Grant-Sierra co. line, in Gila Natl. Forest; 32°51′N 107°45′W.

Seven Corners, uninc. city, Fairfax co., NE Va., residential and commercial suburb 6 mi/9.7 km SW of Wash., D.C., 6 mi/9.7 km NW of Alexandria. L.; 38°52′N 77°08′W. Barcroft reservoir to SW.

Seven Devils, village (1990 pop. 117), Watauga and Avery cos., NW N.C., 9 mi/14.5 km SW of Boone, in Pisgah Natl. Forest; 36°08′N 81°48′W. Blue Ridge Parkway passes to SE. Ski resort area.

Seven Devils Mountains, in Adams and Idaho cos., W Idaho, in Payette Natl. Forest (S); extend N-S and form E wall of Hells Canyon of the Snake R. (part of Oregon line). The chief peak is He Devil Mountain (9,393 ft/ 2,863 m).

Seven Falls, El Paso co., E central Colo, 5 mi/8 km SSW of downtown Colorado Springs, on S Cheyenne Creek, at edge of Pike Natl. Forest. Best viewed from Eagle's Nest by elevator or stairs. Night illumination.

Seven Fields, borough (1990 pop. 556), Butler co., W Pa., residential suburb 17 mi/27 km NNW of and 3 mi/ 4.8 km NNE of Bradford Woods; 40°41′N 80°03′W. Agr. area in urban fringe.

Seven Harbors, village, Oakland co., SE Mich., unincorporated residential suburb 15 mi/24 km WNW of Pontiac bet. Duck (W) and White (E) lakes; 43°40′N 83°34′W. Highland State Recreation Area to S.

Seven Hills, city (1990 pop. 12,339), Cuyahoga co., N Ohio, a residential suburb of Cleveland, in a hilly area; 41°22′N 81°40′W. Inc. as a city 1961. Part of its city hall is an old schoolhouse, built in 1861.

Seven Hundred Acre Island (□ c.2 sq mi/5.2 sq km), Waldo co., S Maine, in Penobscot Bay off Lincolnville.

Seven Islands, Canada: see SEPT ÎLES.

Seven Islands, group of 7 islets in the St. Lawrence R., E Que., Canada, off Sept Îles city, opposite Gaspé Peninsula, at entrance at Seven Islands Bay; 50°11′N 66°22′W. High, steep, and rocky; rise to 500 ft/152 m.

Seven Islands Bay, shallow inlet (10 mi/16 km long, 12 mi/19 km wide at mouth) of the Atlantic, NE Lab., Canada, at entrance of Kangalaksiorvik Fiord (extends 10 mi/16 km W inland); 59°25′N 63°40′W. Contains several isls. and islets; largest are Avigalik or Whale Isl. and Amiktok Isl. Bay is surrounded by high mts.

Seven Lakes, uninc. town (1990 pop. 2,049), Moore co., central N.C., residential community 10 mi/16 km NW of Southern Pines; 35°15′N 79°35′W. Tobacco growing area.

Seven Mile, village (1990 pop. 804), Butler co., extreme SW Ohio, 6 mi/10 km N of Hamilton and on small Seven Mile Creek; 39°28′N 84°33′W.

Seven Mile Beach, beach, Grand Cayman Isl., West Indies. Actually c.5.5 mi/8.9 km long, this beach area on the W coast is the busiest tourist area of the Cayman Isls. Many resort hotels and restaurants.

Seven Mile Beach, S N.J., barrier isl. bet. Great Sound and the Atlantic, off Cape May Peninsula; c.7 mi/11.3 km long. Site of Avalon and Stone Harbor resorts; 2 bridges to mainland.

Seven Oaks, uninc. city (1990 pop. 15,722), Lexington co., central S.C., residential suburb 7 mi/11.3 km NW of downtown Columbia on Saluda R.; 34°02′N 81°09′W. Harbison State Forest to NW; Saluda Dam forms L. Murray on Saluda R. to W.

Seven Pines, locality, Henrico co., E central Va., suburb 8 mi/12.9 km E of Richmond; 37°31′N 77°18′W. Site of Civil War Battle of Fair Oaks, which is sometimes called Battle of Seven Pines. Richmond Internatl. Airport to SW. Seven Pines Natl. Cemetery.

Seven Points, village (1990 pop. 723), Henderson co., E Texas, 45 mi/72 km SE of Dallas; 32°19′N 96°12′W. Oil and natural gas. Agr. area. Mfg. (concrete, sportswear). Recreation. Cedar Creek Reservoir to E.

Seven Sisters, mountain (9,140 ft/2,786 m), W B.C., Canada, in Coast Mts., 100 mi/161 km ENE of Prince Rupert.

Seven Sisters Falls, waterfalls, SE Man., Canada, on Winnipeg R., at N end of Natalie L., 50 mi/80 km ENE of Winnipeg; hydroelectric power center.

Seven Springs, village (1990 pop. 163), Wayne co., E central N.C., 13 mi/21 km SE of Goldsboro, on Neuse R.; 35°13′N 77°50′W. Tobacco, cotton, peanuts, grain; poultry, livestock. Mfg. (corn meal, machining, wooden cabinets). Cliffs of the Nuese State Park to NW.

Seven Springs, borough (1990 pop. 22), Somerset co., SW Pa., 11 mi/18 km W of Somerset on Laurel Hill Ridge; 40°01′N 79°17′W. Ski resort area. Forests and state parks in area. Seven Springs Airport to SW.

Seven Troughs Range, NW Nev., in Pershing co., SE of Black Rock Desert. Rises to 7,474 ft/2,278 m in Seven Troughs Mt., 27 mi/43 km NW of Lovelock; 40°28′N 118°49′W. Small scale mining (chiefly gold and silver). Seven Troughs and Vernon, farmer mining district.

Seven Valleys, borough (1990 pop. 483), York co., S Pa., 8 mi/12.9 km S of York, on South Fork Codorus Creek; 39°51′N 76°46′W. Agr. area (grain, apples; poultry, livestock, dairying); mfg. (electrical prods., apparel).

Severance 1 village (1990 pop. 106), Weld co., N Colo., 10 mi/16 km NW of Greeley, on Gress reservoir; 40°31′N 104°50′W. Elev. 4,886 ft/1,489 m. In irrigated grain area; sugar beets, cattle, wheat, barley, oats, sunflowers. **2** village (1990 pop. 98), Doniphan co., NE Kansas, 8 mi/12.9 km W of Troy; 39°46′N 95°15′W. Agr. (apples, corn, hogs).

Severn (SEV-uhrn), village (1990 pop. 260), Northampton co., NE N.C., 7 mi/11.3 km NW of Murfreesboro, near Meherrin R. and Va. state line; 36°30′N 77°11′W. Tobacco, grain, peanuts, cotton, livestock. Mfg. (resins, peanut processing).

Severn 1 (SE-vuhrn), river, c.420 mi/680 km long, Canada; rising in W Ont.; flowing NE through Severn L. to Hudson Bay. Fort Severn, a Hudson's Bay Company trading post established (1689) at the mouth of the river, was captured (1690) by Pierre le Moyne, sieur d'Iberville. The post was rebuilt in 1759 and has been in continuous operation since. **2** river, c.20 mi/30 km long, Canada; rising from the N end of L. Couchiching, S Ont.; flowing NW to Georgian Bay of L. Huron. It drains L. Couchiching and L. Simcoe and forms part of the inland waterway system linking Georgian Bay with L. Ontario via the Trent Canal. There are 2 large hydroelectric stations on its course.

Severn River (SEH-vern), c.15 mi/24 km long, central Md., estuary entering Chesapeake Bay in Anne Arundel co.; 39°08′N 76°41′W. Annapolis (site of the U.S. Naval Acad.) is on the right bank, at head of deep water channel. The radio towers of the Naval Ship Research and Development Center on the other bank can reach any naval vessel in the world and are visible 30 mi/48 km out to sea.

Severna Park (SEH-vernah), resort village (1990 pop. 25,879), Anne Arundel co., central Md., on Severn R. c.7 mi/11.3 km above Annapolis; 39°05′N 76°34′W. Suburban growth has been rapid in a community that was once only a collection of summer homes served by the Baltimore and Annapolis RR. The original RR station now belongs to the Severna Park model RR club.

Severy (SEV-uhr-ee), village (1990 pop. 357), Greenwood co., SE Kansas, 14 mi/23 km SSE of Eureka; 37°37′N 96°13′W. In grain and livestock region. Oil wells nearby

Sevier 1 (suh-VIR), county (□ 581 sq mi/1,505 sq km; 1990 pop. 13,637), SW Ark.; ⊙ De Queen; 33°59′N 94°15′W. Bounded W by Okla., S by Little R., E by Saline R. (Dierks L. Reservoir in NE corner); drained by small Rolling Fork and Cossatot R. Cattle, hogs, poultry; timber. Mfg. at De Queen. DeQueen L. Reservoir in NW; part of Millwood L. Reservoir (Little R.) in SE corner. Formed 1828. **2** county (□ 603 sq mi/1,562 sq km; 1990 pop. 51,043), E Tenn.; ⊙ Sevierville; 35°47′N 83°31′W. Bounded S and SE by N.C. Great Smoky Mts. along S border, with Clingmans Dome (6,643 ft/2,025 m; highest point in state), Mt. Guyot (6,621 ft/2,018 m; on N.C. state line), and Mt. Le Conte (6,593 ft/2,010 m). Drained by French Broad R. and small Little Pigeon R. Includes Douglas Dam and part of Douglas Reservoir. Lumbering; livestock; fruit, tobacco, corn, hay. Mfg. at Sevierville. Gatlinburg and Pigeon Forge are tourist centers. Formed 1794. **3** (SUH-veer), county (□ 1,918 sq mi/4,968 sq km; 1990 pop. 15,431), central Utah; ⊙ Richfield; 38°44′N 111°46′W. Mt. and plateau region crossed N-S by Sevier R. Sections of Fishlake Natl. Forest in E center, S, and W account for ⅔ of co. land area. Cattle, alfalfa, barley, hay, sugar beets, fruit, vegetables; dairying; gypsum, coal. Utah State Fish Hatchery (Glenwood) in W center. Fremont Indian State Park in SW; small part of Capitol Reef Natl. Park in SE corner. Fish L. and Johnson Reservoir in S. Formed 1865.

Sevier Bridge Reservoir (□ 17 sq mi/44 sq km), Juab co., central Utah, on Sevier R., 28 mi/45 km SSW of Nephi; 39°22′N 112°02′W. Max. capacity 362,165 acre-ft. Formed by Sevier Bridge Dam (92 ft/28 m high), built (1914) for irrigation. Yuba State Park near dam.

Sevier Lake (SUH-veer), intermittent salt lake in Great Basin, Millard co., W Utah, 35 mi/56 km SW of Delta; lake bed is 24 mi/39 km long, 9 mi/14.5 km wide. Receives Sevier R. from NE.

Sevier Plateau (SUH-veer), in Sevier, Piute, and Garfield cos., S Utah, extends N-S along E bank of Sevier R. through parts of Fishlake (N) and Dixie (S) natl. forests. Mt. Dutton (11,037 ft/3,364 m) is S of East Fork Sevier R. (crossing plateau E-W). Signal Peak (11,223 ft/3,421 m) and Monroe Peak (11,227 ft/3,422 m) are in N ½ of plateau.

Sevier River (SUH-veer), c.280 mi/450 km long, formed in Great Basin, SW Utah by the junction of Panguitch Creek and Asay Creek at Panguitch, in W Garfield co. It flows N through Piute Reservoir, past Richfield and Salina, NW through Sevier Bridge Reservoir, then turns SW past Delta and through the Sevier Desert to the intermittent Sevier L. Extensive diversion of the river's water for irrigation has diminished the volume of Sevier L.

Sevierville (suh-VIR-vil), town (1990 pop. 7,178), ⊙ Sevier co., E Tenn., on the Little Pigeon R., 22 mi/35 km ESE of Knoxville; 35°52′N 83°34′W. Trade center for timber and farm area; textiles, apparel, auto parts; lumber and flour milling. Great Smoky Mts. Natl. Park is S, Douglas Dam (French Broad R.) is N. Laid out 1795.

Sevilla Nueva, Jamaica: see SAINT ANN'S BAY.

Sevilla River (sai-VEE-yuh), 57 mi/92 km long, in Camagüey prov., E Cuba; rises just E of Hatuey; flows S to the Punta Sevilla in Las Tunas prov., on Gulf of Guacanayabo, opposite small Sevilla keys. Drains an area of 287 sq mi/743 sq km.

Seville, historic site, St. Ann parish, Jamaica, 1 mi/1.6 km W of SAINT ANN'S BAY; 18°26′N 77°13′W. First Span. capital in 1509.

Seville (suh-VIL), town, Wilcox co., S central Ga., 11 mi/18 km E of Cordele; 31°57′N 83°36′W.

Seville, village (1990 pop. 1,810), Medina co., N Ohio, 9 mi/14 km S of Medina, and on small Chippewa Creek; 41°01′N 81°52′W. In agr. area.

Sewall Point, point of land on S side of Hampton Roads estuary, arm of Chesapeake Bay, SE Va., bet. Elizabeth R. estuary (W) and Willoughby Bay (NE), in Norfolk, in Norfolk Naval Base; 36°57′N 76°19′W.

Sewalls Point (SOO-ullz), town (1990 pop. 1,588), St. Lucie co., E central Fla., 5 mi/8 km E of Stuart; 27°11′N 80°11′W.

Sewanee (suh-WAH-nee, SWAH-nee), village, Franklin co., S Tenn., 35 mi/56 km WNW of Chattanooga, near edge of Cumberland Plateau. Univ. of the South (1857) is here.

Seward 1 (SOO-uhrd), county (□ 640 sq mi/1,658 sq km; 1990 pop. 18,743), SW Kansas; ⊙ Liberal; 37°11′N 100°50′W. In plains region, bordered S by Okla.; drained by Cimarron R. Wheat, sorghum, corn; cattle; meat packing. Formed 1886. **2** county (□ 575 sq mi/1,489 sq km; 1990 pop. 15,450), SE Nebr.; ⊙ Seward; 40°52′N 97°08′W. Agr. area drained by Big Blue R. and its branches. Wood prods., transportation equip.; corn, wheat, soybeans, sorghum; dairy and poultry prods. Limestone. Blue Valley State Wayside Area at center. Formed 1865.

Seward 1 (SOO-uhrd), city (1990 pop. 2,699), Kenai Peninsula borough, S Alaska, on Kenai Peninsula at the head of Resurrection Bay; 60°06′N 149°26′W. Its airfield and ice-free harbor make it an important shipping and supply center for the Alaskan interior. It has a seafood cannery, fisheries, and freezer plant and a sawmill; coal terminal, cargo port. Tourism is also important. Seward was almost completely devastated by an earthquake in 1964 (90% of its waterfront industry was destroyed). Maximum security prison. Univ. of Alaska Maritime Educational Center. An annual salmon derby is held, and a race up nearby Mt. Marathon (3,022 ft/921 m) every July 4th attracts athletes from a wide area. Ferry service to Kodiak Isl. and Prince William Sound communities. Ranger office for Chugach Natl. Forest; Kenai Fjords Natl. Park to SW. Founded in 1903 as the ocean terminus of the Alaska RR (built 1915–1923); inc. 1912. **2** city (1990 pop. 5,634), ⊙ Seward co., SE Nebr., 20 mi/32 km WNW of Lincoln, on Big Blue R.; 40°54′N 97°05′W. RR junction on productive Loess Plain in prairie region. Cattle, hogs; dairying; corn, wheat, soybeans; mfg. (printing, automotive exhaust systems, electrical equip.). Concordia Teachers Col. here. City founded 1868, inc. 1874.

Seward 1 (SOO-uhrd), village (1990 pop. 71), Stafford co., S central Kansas, 13 mi/21 km S of Great Bend;

38°10′N 98°47′W. In wheat region. **2** village, Logan co., central Okla., 7 mi/11.3 km SW of Guthrie.

Seward (SOO-wahrd), borough (1990 pop. 522), Westmoreland co., SW central Pa., 9 mi/14.5 km NW of Johnstown, on Conemaugh R. (bridged); includes former village of Hooverville in W; 40°24′N 79°01′W. Agr. (corn, hay; livestock; dairying); mfg. (machinery). Gallitzin State Forest to E; Laurel Ridge State Park to SE.

Seward Glacier, SE Alaska (U.S.) and SW Yukon (Canada), in St. Elias Mts. glacier system, S of Mt. Logan. S arm flows to Malaspina Glacier; 60°00′N 140°00′W.

Seward Highway, 120 mi/193 km long, in S Alaska, it links Anchorage with Seward, on Kenai Peninsula to S. It begins in downtown Anchorage, a continuation of Alaska Route 1 and an extension of the Glen Highway from NE. It follows the N shore of Turnagain Arm of Cook Inlet and the Alaska RR SE to Portage. It then turns SW into interior of Kenai Peninsula, intersecting road to Hope and Sterling Highway to Soldotna, Kenai, and Homer. Seward Highway continues S to Seward as Route 9, rejoining the Alaska RR and passing the E end of Kenai L. State ferry system continues out from Seward to Gulf of Alaska communities. Paved.

Seward Mountain (4,404 ft/1,342 m), Franklin co., NE N.Y., in the High Peaks sect. of the Adirondacks, 14 mi/ 23 km SW of L. Placid village; 44°10′N 74°12′W.

Seward Peninsula, W Alaska, projecting c.200 mi/ 320 km into the Bering Sea bet. Norton Sound, Bering Strait, Chukchi Sea, and Kotzebue Sound, just below the Arctic Circle; 210 mi/338 km long, 90 mi/145 km– 140 mi/225 km wide. The region is mostly high brush and perpetually frozen muskeg tundra, rising to 4,720 ft/1,439 m in the SW. Gold mining, trapping are the chief occupations. Nome is on the S coast. Cape Prince of Wales, the westernmost point of North Amer., is located at the W tip. Contains York, Kigluaik, Bendeleben mts. Has lead, tin, and other metals.

Sewaren (SEE-wuh-ruhn), village (1990 pop. 2,569) in Woodbridge township, Middlesex co., E N.J., on Arthur Kill, just E of Woodbridge; 40°32′N 74°15′W. Chemicals and petroleum prods.; large power plant.

Sewickley (suh-WIK-lee), borough (1990 pop. 4,134), Allegheny co., W Pa., suburb 12 mi/19 km NW of Pittsburgh, on Ohio R. (bridged), near mouth of Little Sewickley Creek; 40°32′N 80°10′W. Agr. to NE (hay; livestock; dairying). Mfg. (steel rods and bolts, activated carbon, pumps). Dashfields Lock and Dam, on Ohio R., to NW. Inc. 1853.

Sewickley Heights (suh-WIK-lee), borough (1990 pop. 784), Allegheny co., W Pa., residential suburb 11 mi/ 18 km NW of Pittsburgh; 40°33′N 80°09′W.

Sewickley Hills (suh-WIK-lee), borough (1990 pop. 622), Allegheny co., W Pa., residential suburb 12 mi/ 19 km NW of Pittsburgh on Little Sewickley Creek; 40°33′N 80°07′W. Agr. and dairying.

Sexsmith, town (1991 pop. 1,260), W Alta., Canada, near B.C. border, 13 mi/21 km N of Grande Prairie; 55°21′N 118°47′W. Lumbering; wheat, mixed farming.

Sextin River, Mexico: see NAZAS, river.

Seyé (se-YAI), town (1990 pop. 6,277), Yucátan, SE Mexico, 18 mi/29 km SE of Mérida, and on RR; 20°50′N 89°22′W. Henequen, sugar, corn.

Seymour 1 (SEE-mor), city (1990 pop. 15,576), Jackson co., SE Ind., near East Fork White R., and 17 mi/27 km S of Columbus; 38°58′N 85°53′W. RR junction. A shipping center for a farm area, it also has diversified mfg. Muscatatuck Natl. Wildlife Refuge to E. Inc. 1864. **2** city (1990 pop. 1,636), Webster co., S central Mo., in the Ozarks, 30 mi/48 km E of Springfield; 37°08′N 92°46′W. Timber; apparel, sheet metal. Amish community nearby. **3** city (1990 pop. 2,782), Outagamie co., E Wis., 15 mi/24 km W of Green Bay; 44°30′N 88°19′W. Dairy prods., flour, food processing; mfg. (generators). Oneida Indian Reservation to E. Settled 1871, inc. 1879.

Seymour 1 (SEE-mor), town (1990 pop. 14,288), New Haven co., SW Conn., on the Naugatuck R.; 41°22′N 73°05′W. Metallurgical mfg. Settled c.1678, inc. 1850. **2** town (1990 pop. 869), Wayne co., S Iowa, near Mo. state line, 13 mi/21 km WSW of Centerville; 40°40′N 93°07′W. In livestock-raising area. Light mfg. Inc. 1874.

3 town (1990 pop. 7,026), Sevier and Blount cos., E Tenn., 10 mi/16 km SE of Knoxville; 35°53′N 83°43′W. **4** town (1990 pop. 3,185), ☉ Baylor co., N Texas, on Brazos R., and c.45 mi/72 km SW of Wichita Falls; 33°36′N 99°15′W. Elev. 1,291 ft/393 m. Trade and shipping center for cotton, cattle, wheat area; some irrigation; mfg. (corrugated metal culverts); oil and gas. L. Kemp reservoir to N, Millers Creek Reservoir to SW, and Diversion L. reservoir to NE. Settled 1878 at crossing of Dodge City and California trails; inc. 1906.

Seymour Canal, N-S inlet on E side of Admiralty Isl., Alexander Archipelago, SE Alaska; c.45 mi/72 km long; 57°00′N 134°00′W.

Seymour Lake, in town of Morgan, Orleans co., NE Vt., 9 mi/14.5 km E of Newport and 7 mi/11.3 km S of Can. (Que.) border; c.3 mi/4.8 km long; 46°54′N 71°57′W. Drains S through Echo Pond to Clyde R. In hunting, fishing area.

Seymour, Mount (4,120 ft/1,256 m), Franklin co., NE N.Y., in the High Peaks sect. of the Adirondacks, 13 mi/ 21 km SW of L. Placid village; 44°09′N 74°10′W.

Seymour Narrows, Canada: see DISCOVERY PASSAGE.

Shabbona (SHA-boe-nah), village (1990 pop. 897), De Kalb co., N Ill., 18 mi/29 km SSW of Sycamore; 41°45′N 88°52′W. In rich agr. area.

Shackelford, county (☐ 915 sq mi/2,370 sq km; 1990 pop. 3,316), N central Texas; ☉ Albany; 32°43′N 99°20′W. Drained by Clear Fork Brazos R. A leading cattle-ranching co. of Texas; also horses, hogs, some sheep; agr. in E and NE (wheat, cotton, grain, sorghum; mesquite). Oil, natural-gas wells. Fort Griffin State Park in NE. Formed 1856.

Shackleford Banks (SHAK-uhl-fuhrd), Carteret co., E N.C., sect. of the Outer Banks, extends 8 mi/12.9 km W from behind Core Banks 4 mi/6.4 km W of Cape Lookout to Beaufort Inlet (entrance to Beaufort Harbor). Faces Atlantic Ocean to S; Core Sound to N. Part of Cape Lookout Natl. Seashore.

Shacklefords, uninc. village, King and Queen co., E Va., 20 mi/32 km N of Williamsburg, near York R. estuary. Mfg. (printing, lumber pallets); agr. (cattle; grain, soybeans, tomatoes); oysters.

Shackleton, Mount (10,800 ft/3,292 m), SE B.C., Canada, near Alta. border, in Rocky Mts., in Hamber Provincial Park, 50 mi/80 km S of Jasper; 52°11′N 117°54′W.

Shade Gap, borough (1990 pop. 113), Huntingdon co., S central Pa., 14 mi/23 km S of Mt. Union, on Shade Creek; 40°10′N 77°52′W. Corn, hay, alfalfa; poultry, livestock; dairying; timber; mfg. (lumber). Covered bridge to South Tuscarora Tunnel, through Tuscarora Mts., on Pa. Turnpike 6 mi/9.7 km SSE. Shade Gap, pass in Shade Mt. ridge, to W.

Shade Mountain, ridge (1,800 ft/550 m–2,000 ft/610 m), central Pa., runs c.30 mi/48 km WNW-ESE from Juniata R. just E of Lewistown in SE Mifflin co., as a continuation of Blue Mt. ridge (separate from the longer Blue Mt. ridge to SE) to S of Middleburg in central Snyder co.; generally 4 mi/6.4 km wide.

Shadehill Reservoir (☐ 19 sq mi/49 sq km), Perkins co., NW S.Dak., on North Fork Grand R., 70 mi/112 km W of Mobridge; 45°45′N 102°12′W. Max. capacity 468,585 acre-ft. Formed by Shadehill Dam (145 ft/44 m high), built (1951) by the Bureau of Reclamation for irrigation; also used for flood control and recreation. Standing Rock Indian Reservation to E; Shadehill State Recreational Area near dam.

Shadeland, town, Tippecanoe co., W central Ind., 5 mi/ 8 km SW of Lafayette. Agr. area. Laid out 1824.

Shadow Mountain Lake, reservoir, Grand co., N Colo., on Colorado R. bet. Grand L. (NE) and L. Granby (S), in Arapaho Natl. Recreation Area, 10 mi/16 km NNE of Granby; 3 mi/4.8 km long; 40°12′N 105°50′W. Grand Lake town at N end. Formed by Shadow Mountain Dam (78 ft/24 m high, 3,100 ft/945 m long) built (1946) as unit in Colorado–Big Thompson project. Water-diversion canal bypasses Colorado R. to L. Granby; Alva B. Adams Tunnel delivers water across Continental Divide to Thompson R. basin, 14 mi/23 km NE.

Shadwell, locality, Albemarle co., central Va., suburb 4 mi/6.4 km ESE of Charlottesville, on Rivanna R.;

38°00′N 78°23′W. Nearby is Shadwell estate, birthplace of Thomas Jefferson; Monticello, Jefferson's home, to W.

Shady Cove, town (1990 pop. 1,351), Jackson co., SW Oregon, 18 mi/29 km N of Medford, on Rogue R.; 42°36′N 122°49′W. Timber; tourism. Fish hatchery to NE. Casey and Stewart state parks to NE; Rogue R. Natl. Forest to N and E; Crater Lake Natl. Park to NE.

Shady Dale, village (1990 pop. 180), Jasper co., central Ga., 9 mi/14.5 km NE of Monticello; 33°24′N 83°35′W. Wooden pallets, egg processing.

Shady Grove, uninc. village, Franklin co., S Pa., 3 mi/ 4.8 km ESE of Greencastle; 39°46′N 77°40′W. Dairying; livestock; grain, apples. Light mfg.

Shady Point, village (1990 pop. 597), Le Flore co., SE Okla., residential suburb 6 mi/9.7 km N of Poteau, and on Poteau R.; 35°08′N 94°39′W. Grew from early Choctaw settlement nearby.

Shady Side, village (1990 pop. 4,107), Anne Arundel co., central Md., on inlet of Chesapeake R., 10 mi/16 km S of Annapolis; 38°48′N 76°31′W. The original public resort has become a community of private homes and beaches. Sometimes spelled Shadyside.

Shady Spring, uninc. town (1990 pop. 1,929), Raleigh co., S W.Va., 7 mi/11.3 km SE of Beckley; 37°42′N 81°05′W. Grain, nursery crops; cattle. Little Beaver State Park to N.

Shadyside, village (1990 pop. 3,934), Belmont co., E Ohio, on the Ohio R., and 13 mi/21 km SE of St. Clairsville; 39°58′N 80°45′W. Mfg. (caskets). Inc. 1913.

Shafer (SHAI-fuhr), village (1990 pop. 368), Chisago co., E Minn., 35 mi/56 km NNE of St. Paul, and 5 mi/8 km E of Lindstrom; 45°23′N 92°45′W. Agr. (dairying; poultry, cattle; grain); mfg. (plastic coatings, electronic subassembly).

Shafer, Lake, reservoir, White co., NW central Ind., on Tippecanoe R., 2 mi/3.2 km N of Monticello; c.12 mi/ 19 km long; 40°46′N 86°45′W. Receives Big Monon Creek from NNW, forms 6 mi/9.7 km arm.

Shafter, city (1990 pop. 8,409), Kern co., S central Calif. valley, 17 mi/27 km NW of Bakersfield; 35°30′N 119°16′W. Mfg. (concrete pipe); potatoes, vegetables, melons, citrus, plums, apples, pistachios, almonds, grapes, sugar beet, tomatoes, beans, grain; dairying; cattle. Calloway Canal to E; Tule State Elk Reserve and Buena Vista L. irrigation reservoir to S. Inc. 1938.

Shafter, village (1990 pop. 31), Presidio co., extreme W Texas, 37 mi/60 km SSW of Marfa, in Chinati Mts. Elev. c.3,900 ft/1,189 m. Silver mines are shut down.

Shafter, Fort, Honolulu, S Oahu isl., Hawaii, 3 mi/ 4.8 km NW of Honolulu; length of military base runs parallel to Kalihi Stream to SE.

Shafter Lake, Texas: see ANDREWS.

Shaftsbury (SHAFZ-buhr-ee), town (1990 pop. 3,368), Bennington co., SW Vt., on N.Y. border, just N of Bennington; 42°58′N 73°12′W. Chartered 1761, settled 1763.

Shag Harbour, village, SW N.S., Canada, on the Atlantic, 30 mi/48 km SE of Yarmouth. Fisheries. Trading post est. here by De Monts.

Shagawa Lake (SHA-guh-waw), St. Louis co., NE Minn., in Superior Natl. Forest; 4 mi/6.4 km long, 2 mi/3.2 km wide; 47°54′N 91°52′W. Fed in W by Burntside R. (from W end of Burntside L.); drained to E by Shagawa R. to Fall L. Resorts. Ely is on its S shore.

Shageluk, village (1990 pop. 139), W Alaska, on Innoko R., and 30 mi/48 km N of Holy Cross; 62°40′N 159°34′W.

Shaker Heights, city (1990 pop. 30,831), Cuyahoga co., NE Ohio, a residential suburb of Cleveland; 41°28′N 81°32′W. Founded (1905) as a suburban development, it takes its name from a Shaker community that existed here (1822–1889). It is a beautiful city of imposing houses, squares, and wide boulevards, part of "the Heights" area, which also includes the cities of Beachwood, Cleveland Heights, South Euclid, and University Heights. Shaker mus. Inc. 1912.

Shakertown, Ky.: see PLEASANT HILL.

Shakopee (SHAW-kuh-pee), city (1990 pop. 11,739), ☉ Scott co., SE central Minn., suburb 18 mi/29 km SW of Minneapolis, on Minnesota R.; 44°46′N 93°28′W.

Cross references are shown in SMALL CAPITALS. The pronunciation key is on page xv. The dates of population figures are on page xii.

Trading and mfg. center (industrial gases and chemicals, sheet metal fabrication, crushed limestone, barley malt, landscape timbers; printing and publishing); farming area (livestock, poultry; grain, soybeans; dairying). Has Shakopee Reformatory for women. Amusement park and Canterbury Downs Racetrack are here. Minnesota Valley State Trail SW. James J. Walke Regional Park in NE; numerous small lakes in area, N and SE; Prior L. Indian Reservation in S. Settled 1851, inc. 1870.

Shaktolik, Inuit village, at E end of Norton Sound, W Alaska, 130 mi/209 km E of Nome. Sometimes spelled Shaktoolik.

Shalalth, village, S B.C., Canada, on Seton L., 13 mi/21 km W of Lillooet; 50°44′N 122°14′W. In lumbering and mining (gold, silver) region.

Shaler (SHAL-luhr), township (1990 pop. 30,533), Allegheny co., SW Pa., residential suburb 7 mi/11.3 km N of Pittsburgh; 40°31′N 79°57′W. Includes communities of Glenshaw, Wittmer, and Elfinwild. Mfg. (aluminum anodizing, welding and cutting equip., sheet metal fabrication).

Shallotte (SHAL-uht) or **Shallotte City**, town (1990 pop. 965), Brunswick co., SE N.C., 33 mi/53 km SW of Wilmington and on short Shallotte R., which flows S into Shallotte Inlet, arm of Atlantic Ocean; 33°58′N 78°23′W. Fish, oysters. Tobacco, grain, cotton; hogs. Mfg. (printing and publishing, machining, oyster processing). Green Swamp to N.

Shallow Lake, village (1991 pop. 505), S Ont., Canada, on small Shallow L., 8 mi/13 km WNW of Owen Sound. Dairying; mixed farming, fruit growing.

Shallowater, town (1990 pop. 1,708), Lubbock co., NW Texas, on the Llano Estacado, 10 mi/16 km NW of Lubbock, on Yellow Horse Draw; 33°41′N 101°59′W. In agr. region (cattle; cotton); oil and natural gas; mfg. (audiocassettes, irrigation prods., cotton gin components).

Shambaugh, town (1990 pop. 190), Page co., SW Iowa, on West Nodaway R., and 5 mi/8 km S of Clarinda; 40°39′N 95°02′W. Farm equip.

Shamokin (SHA-mo-ken), city (1990 pop. 9,184), Northumberland co., E Pa., 38 mi/61 km NNE of Harrisburg, on Shamokin Creek; 40°47′N 76°32′W. Mfg. (printing and publishing, carbon filters); anthracite coal. Agr. (corn, hay; dairying). Shamokin State Hosp. to N. Settled c.1835, inc. 1864.

Shamokin Dam (SHA-mo-ken), borough (1990 pop. 1,690), Snyder co., E central Pa., 2 mi/3.2 km SW of Sunbury, on Susquehanna R. (bridged); 40°51′N 76°49′W. Mfg. (apparel, meat processing). Agr. (grain, apples; livestock, poultry; dairying). Shamokin Dam on Susquehanna R.; mouth of West Branch Susquehanna R. 3 mi/4.8 km NNE. Shikellamy State Park to NE.

Shamong, township (1990 pop. 5,765), Burlington co., S N.J., 12 mi/19 km NW of Barnegat; 39°46′N 74°43′W. Inc. 1852.

Shamrock 1 town (1990 pop. 2,286), Wheeler co., extreme N Texas, near North Fork Red R., in E part of Panhandle, c.50 mi/80 km SE of Pampa; 35°13′N 100°15′W. Elev. 2,310 ft/704 m. Shipping, commercial, mfg. center for petroleum, oil, gas area; cotton, wheat; cattle, ostrichs. Tourism. Oil discovered 1926. Settled 1901, inc. 1911. **2** uninc. town, Logan co., SW W.Va., residential suburb 2 mi/3.2 km W of Logan.

Shamrock, village (1990 pop. 95), Creek co., central Okla., 28 mi/45 km WSW of Sapulpa; 35°54′N 96°34′W. In agr. and oil-producing area. Boom town which once had a pop. of 10,000.

Shamrock Lake, town, Blackford co., Ind., 5 mi/8 km SW of Hartford City. In agr. area.

Shandaken (shan-DA-kuhn), village (1990 pop. 500), Ulster co., SE N.Y., in the Catskills, on Esopus Creek, and 25 mi/40 km NW of Kingston; 42°04′N 74°21′W.

Shandaken Tunnel (shan-DA-kuhn), S Schoharie and N Ulster cos., E N.Y. Conveys water of N-flowing Schoharie Creek over drainage divide separating it from S-flowing Esopus Creek, thence to Askokan Reservoir; intake 3 mi/4.8 km N of Prattsville; outlet just S of Allaben. Horseshoe-shaped tunnel is 18.1 mi/29.1 km long, 11.5 ft/3.5 m high, and 10.2 ft/3.1 m wide; it has 7 shafts as air vents and slopes uniformly 4.4 ft/1.3 m per mile. Capable of conducting 650 million gals/2,460 million liters per day. Part of N.Y. city water system; built 1917–1924.

Shanesville (SHAINZ-vil), village, Tuscarawas co., E Ohio, 11 mi/18 km W of New Philadelphia. In Amish country.

Shangri-La, Md.: see CAMP DAVID.

Shaniko (SHAN-uh-ko), hamlet (1990 pop. 26), Wasco co., N Oregon, 45 mi/72 km SE of The Dalles; 45°00′N 120°45′W. Elev. 3,340 ft/1,018 m.

Shanks Village, Rockland co., N.Y., 3 mi/4.8 km SSW of Nyack; 41°02′N 73°56′W. During World War II, Camp Shanks (2 sq mi/5.2 sq km), with a capacity of 160,000 soldiers, was one of the largest embarkation ports for U.S. troops on the East Coast. Known then as "Last Stop, U.S.A.," this was the jumping-off point for 1.3 million soldiers heading out for the North Afr. and Eur. theaters of war. Ital. and Ger. POWs were also housed here. With no further value to the U.S. Army, and with a severe housing shortage after the war, 416 barracks were converted into housing and renamed Shanks Village. Veterans going to college in N.Y. city and their families were given preference. In 1954 the facility was closed and auctioned off. Title to a 500 ft/152 m right-of-way through the site was deeded to the Palisades Interstate Parkway. Today, only vestige left is a re-created barracks mus. near intersections of Routes 303 and 340.

Shanksville (SHAINKS-vil), borough (1990 pop. 235), Somerset co., SW Pa., 9 mi/14.5 km E of Somerset, on Stonycreek R.; 40°01′N 78°54′W. Agr. (corn, oats; livestock; dairying). L. Stonycreek and Indian L. reservoirs to NE.

Shannock (SHAN-nuhk), village in Charlestown and Richmond towns, Washington co., SW R.I., on Pawcatuck R., and 11 mi/18 km ENE of Westerly.

Shannon 1 county (□ 999 sq mi/2,587 sq km; 1990 pop. 7,613), S Mo.; ⊙ Eminence; 37°09′N 91°24′W. In the Ozark Mts.; drained by Current R. Cattle; hay; lumber mills. Former copper mines. Mfg. at Birch Tree; tourism and recreation. Parts of Mark Twain Natl. Forest in SE and NE corners. Ozark Natl. Scenic Riverways (natl. park) follow Current and Jacks Fork rivers; includes Big Spring, Alley Spring, and Round Spring (all former state parks). Canoeing, floating, hiking, fishing, hunting. Mo. State Forest portions throughout co. Formed 1841. **2** county (□ 2,096 sq mi/5,429 sq km; 1990 pop. 9,902), SW S.Dak., on Nebr. state line (S); 43°19′N 102°32′W. All of co. except large S extension of Badlands Natl. Park in N (added 1968) is within Pine Ridge Indian Reservation, which also includes large part of Jackson co., and small part of Sheridan co. (Nebr.). Drained by White R. and Medicine Rock, Porcupine, Wounded Knee, and White Clay creeks. Mixed grain; cattle. Administratively attached to Fall River co. to W. Oglala Lakota Col. in E, S of Kyle.

Shannon 1 town, Floyd co., NW Ga., 8 mi/12.9 km NNE of Rome; 34°20′N 85°04′W. **2** town (1990 pop. 1,419), Lee co., NE Miss., 10 mi/16 km S of Tupelo; 34°06′N 88°41′W. In agr. area (cotton, corn, soybeans; cattle, poultry; dairying); mfg. (furniture, woodworking equip., fabricated metal prods., steel processing).

Shannon, village (1990 pop. 887), Carroll co., NW Ill., 14 mi/23 km ENE of Mount Carroll; 42°08′N 89°44′W. In rich agr. area.

Shannon City, town (1990 pop. 97), on border of Ringgold and Union cos., S Iowa, on Grand R., and 12 mi/19 km SSE of Creston; 40°53′N 94°15′W. In livestock and grain area.

Shannon, Lake, reservoir (□ 3 sq mi/7.8 sq km), Skagit co., NW Wash., on Baker R., 23 mi/37 km NNE of Sedro Wolley; 48°32′N 121°46′W. Max. capacity 162,590 acre-ft. Formed by Lower Baker Dam (277 ft/84 m high), built (1927) for power generation; also used for recreation.

Shannontown, village, Sumter co., central S.C., just S of Sumter. Residential, industrial (woodworking plants).

Shanor-Northvue (SHA-nuhr–NORTH-vyoo), uninc. town (1990 pop. 3,517), Butler co., W. Pa., residential suburb 2 mi/3.2 km N of Butler; 40°54′N 79°55′W. Includes the communities of Shanor Heights and Windward Heights.

Shapleigh (SHAP-lee), town (1990 pop. 1,911), York co., SW Maine, 8 mi/12.9 km NW of Alfred; 43°32′N 70°50′W.

Sharbot Lake (SHAHR-buht), village, SE Ont., central Canada, on Sharbot L. (5 mi/8 km long), 40 mi/64 km NNW of Kingston; 44°46′N 76°41′W. Dairying, farming; resort.

Shark River, c.7 mi/11.3 km long, E N.J.; rises in E Monmouth co.; flows SE to irregularly shaped Shark R. Inlet, estuary (c.2 mi/3.2 km long) opening into the Atlantic Ocean bet. Belmar and Avon by the Sea; has improved harbor for yachts, fishing boats. Short North Branch enters river just above estuary.

Sharkey, county (□ 434 sq mi/1,124 sq km; 1990 pop. 7,066), W Miss.; ⊙ Rolling Fork; 32°52′N 90°48′W. Bordered SE by Yazoo R.; Indian Bayou forms part of W border; drained by Sunflower and Little Sunflower rivers and Deer Creek. Agr. (cotton, corn, oats, rice, soybeans, sorghum, wheat; timber). Much of SE part of co. is in Delta Natl. Forest. Formed 1876.

Sharon, city (1990 pop. 17,493), Mercer co., NW Pa., 12 mi/19 km NE of Youngstown (Ohio), and 2 mi/3.2 km N of Farrell, its smaller twin city, on the Shenango R., near the Ohio state line; 41°13′N 80°30′W. RR junction. An industrial city, mfg. (textiles, food prods., plastic prods., steel prods., electronic goods; printing and publishing). Pa. State Univ.–Shenango Campus (2-year) is here. Sharon Airport to SE. Shenango River L. reservoir to N. Settled c.1800, inc. as a city 1920.

Sharon 1 resort town (1990 pop. 2,928), Litchfield co., NW Conn., in Taconic Mts., bet. N.Y. state line and the Housatonic R., 19 mi/31 km WNW of Torrington; 41°51′N 73°27′W. State park, state forest, Audubon Center here. Industry in medical field; hosp. here. Noah Webster wrote his *Spelling Book* while teaching here. Inc. 1739. **2** residential town (1990 pop. 15,517), Norfolk co., E Mass., 9 mi/14.5 km WNW of Brockton; 42°07′N 71°11′W. Formerly popular lake resort, now rapidly growing suburb of Boston. Whaling mus. Settled c.1650, inc. 1775. Includes Sharon village. **3** town (1990 pop. 299), Hillsboro co., S N.H., 22 mi/35 km WNW of Nashua; 42°47′N 71°56′W. Vegetables, fruit; livestock, poultry; dairying; timber. Part of Annett State Forest in SW. Woodbound Ski Touring Area on SW border. **4** town (1990 pop. 1,047), Weakley co., NW Tenn., 7 mi/11 km S of Martin, 36°14′N 88°50′W. In farm area. **5** town (1990 pop. 1,211), Windsor co., E Vt., on White R., 29 mi/47 km NE of Rutland, and 11 mi/18 km NNE of Woodstock; 43°47′N 72°26′W. Joseph Smith, founder of Mormonism, b. here. **6** town (1990 pop. 1,250), Walworth co., SE Wis., on Ill. state line, 16 mi/26 km E of Beloit; 42°30′N 88°43′W. In agr. area; dairy prods.; mfg. (machinery, fabricated metal prods.); concrete burial vaults.

Sharon 1 village (1990 pop. 94), Taliaferio co., NE Ga., 6 mi/9.7 km E of Crawfordville; 33°34′N 82°48′W. Meatpacking. **2** village (1990 pop. 256), Barber co., S Kansas, on small affluent of Salt Fork of Arkansas R., and 9 mi/14.5 km ESE of Medicine Lodge; 37°15′N 98°25′W. Grain; cattle. **3** village (1990 pop. 119), Steele co., E N.Dak., 7 mi/11.3 km N of Finley; 47°36′N 97°54′W. **4** village, Trumbull co., NE Ohio, on Pa. (E) state line, 12 mi/19 km NE of Youngstown, and adjacent to Sharon (Pa.). **5** village (1990 pop. 108), Woodward co., NW Okla., 11 mi/18 km SSE of Woodward; 36°16′N 99°20′W. In livestock and grain area; mfg. (transportation equip.). **6** village (1990 pop. 270), York co., N S.C., 6 mi/9.7 km WSW of York; 34°57′N 81°20′W. Mfg. of apparel and pewter pins; agr. includes cotton, grains, soybeans; dairying; poultry, livestock.

Sharon Hill, borough (1990 pop. 5,771), Delaware co., SE Pa., suburb 6 mi/9.7 km SW of downtown Philadelphia, near Darby Creek; 39°54′N 75°16′W. Mfg. (concrete, laboratory equip., industrial insulations, bldg. materials, apparel). Inc. 1890.

Sharon Springs, town (1990 pop. 872), ⊙ Wallace co., W Kansas, 31 mi/50 km S of Goodland, near S Fork

Smoky Hill R.; 38°53′N 101°45′W. Elev 3,442 ft/1,049 m. Trading center for livestock and grain region; prepared foods. Highest point (4,039 ft/1,231 m) in Kansas is 18 mi/29 km NW, on Colo. state line.

Sharon Springs, village (□ 1 sq mi/2.6 sq km; 1990 pop. 543), Schoharie co., E central N.Y., 24 mi/39 km WSW of Amsterdam; 42°47′N 74°37′W. Former health resort, with sulphur springs.

Sharonville, city (1990 pop. 13,153), Hamilton co., SW Ohio; 39°17′N 84°24′W. Primarily residential suburb of Cincinnati. Mfg. of motor vehicle parts. Surveyed 1796, inc. 1911.

Sharp, county (□ 606 sq mi/1,570 sq km; 1990 pop. 14,109), N Ark.; ⊙ Ash Flat, on Mo. (N) state line; 36°08′N 91°28′W. Drained by Strawberry and Spring rivers. Agr. (hay; chickens, cattle, hogs); timber. Resorts (fishing). Formed 1868. Harold E. Alexander Wildlife Management Area at center.

Sharp, Cape, on Minas Channel, N N.S., E Canada, 4 mi/6 km SW of Parrsboro, at entrance to Minas Basin.

Sharp Park, suburban area, San Mateo co., W Calif., on the Pacific Ocean, just S of Pacifica. Sharp Park Regional Park, Salada Beach.

Sharp Top, Va.: see OTTER, PEAKS OF.

Sharpe, Lake, reservoir (□ 94 sq mi/243 sq km), Hughes, Lyman, and Buffalo cos., central S.Dak., on Missouri R., in Lower Brule and Crow Creek Indian reservations, 45 mi/72 km SE of Pierre; 44°02′N 99°27′W. Max. capacity 1,900,000 acre-ft. Formed by Big Bend Dam (95ft/29 m high), built (1963) by Army Corps of Engineers for flood control; also used for power generation, irrigation, navigation, and recreation. West Bend State Recreation Area on N shore; Fort Pierre Natl. Grass Lands in W; Fort Defiance Historic Site on S shore.

Sharpes, town (□ 6 sq mi/15.5 sq km; 1990 pop. 3,348), Brevard co., E central Fla., 6 mi/9.7 km N of Cocoa; 28°26′N 80°45′W. Mfg. includes rock and coquina mining and processing.

Sharps, uninc. village, Richmond co., E Va., on Rappahannock R., 55 mi/89 km SE of Fredericksburg; 37°49′N 76°42′W. Mfg. (oyster processing).

Sharps Island, islet, Talbot co., E Md., in Chesapeake Bay just off mouth of Choptank R., 16 mi/26 km WNW of Cambridge. Sharps Isl. Lighthouse is 1 mi/1.6 km NNW.

Sharpsburg 1 town (1990 pop. 116), Taylor co., SW Iowa, 10 mi/16 km NE of Bedford; 40°47′N 94°38′W. In agr. region. **2** town (1990 pop. 659), Washington co., W Md., 13 mi/21 km S of Hagerstown; 39°28′N 77°45′W. Named for Horatio Sharp, royal governor (1753–1768). The Civil War Battle of Antietam (or Sharpsburg) was fought here along Antietam Creek on Sept. 14, 1862, in which 12,410 Federal and 10,700 Confederate soldiers died; about 5,000 Federal dead (1,836 unidentified) are buried in The Natl. Cemetery at Sharpsburg and Confederate dead lie in churchyards all over the area. Antietam Natl. Battlefield Site (810 acres/328 ha; est. 1933). **3** town (1990 pop. 1,536), Nash, Edgecombe, and Wilson cos., E central N.C., a suburb 5 mi/8 km S of Rocky Mount; 35°52′N 77°49′W. Mfg. (sheet metal fabricating, machining; clothing). Agr. area (tobacco, cotton, peanuts, grain, sweet potatoes; chickens, cattle, hogs). Rocky Mount–Wilson Airport to SW.

Sharpsburg 1 village (1990 pop. 224), Coweta co., W Ga., 9 mi/14.5 km ESE of Newman; 33°20′N 84°39′W. Mfg. includes machining; cleaning systems. **2** village (1990 pop. 315), Bath co., NE central Ky., 8 mi/12.9 km N of Mount Sterling; 38°12′N 83°55′W. Agr. (burley tobacco; cattle; dairying).

Sharpsburg, borough (1990 pop. 3,781), Allegheny co., SW Pa., residential suburb 5 mi/8 km NE of downtown Pittsburgh, on Allegheny R. (bridged); 40°29′N 55°79′W. Lock and Dam No. 2 here. Inc. 1842.

Sharpsville, town (1990 pop. 769), Tipton co., central Ind., 8 mi/12.9 km SSE of Kokomo; 40°23′N 86°05′W. Agr. area; mfg. (commercial seeds; meat processing). Laid out 1850.

Sharpsville, borough (1990 pop. 4,729), Mercer co., W Pa., residential suburb 1 mi/1.6 km NE of Sharon, on

Shenango R.; 41°15′N 80°28′W. Mfg. (furniture, electronic goods, dairy prods.). Settled 1798, inc. 1874.

Sharptown, town (1990 pop. 609), Wicomico co., E Md., 14 mi/23 km WNW of Salisbury, and on Nanticoke R.; 38°32′N 75°43′W. Has a small park for fishing and swimming in the Nanticoke R. here.

Shasta (SHAS-tuh), county (□ 3,785 sq mi/9,803 sq km; 1990 pop. 147,036), N Calif.; ⊙ Redding; 40°46′N 122°02′W. S border formed in part by Cottonwood R. and its Middle Fork, and Battle Creek. Largely mountainous; Klamath Mts. (W) here meet Cascade Range (E) (connected by Trinity Mt. in NW) at N end of the irrigated Central Valley and is drained by Sacramento, Pit, and McCloud rivers. In SE is Lassen Peak (10,457 ft/3,187 m; active volcano), in LASSEN VOLCANIC NATIONAL PARK, most of which is in SE corner. Parts of Shasta Natl. Forest in N; part of Lassen Natl. Forest in SE; part of Trinity Natl. Forest in SW corner. Part of Castle Crags State Park on N border, in NW and McArthur–Burney Falls State Park in NE. Parts of Whiskeytown-Shasta-Trinity Natl. Recreation Area: Whiskeytown Unit in SW, (Whiskeytown Reservoir), Shasta Unit in W center (L. Shasta reservoir), Trinity unit in Trinity co., to W. Timber; cattle; apiary prods., walnuts, olives, strawberries; wheat, barley, oats; sand and gravel. Processing of farm prods. are principal industries. Tourism: hunting, fishing, camping attract vacationers. Formed 1850.

Shasta Lake (SHAH-tuh), reservoir (□ 46 sq mi/119 sq km), Shasta co., N Calif., on Sacramento R., 9 mi/14.5 km NNW of Redding; 40°50′N 122°23′W. Elev. 1,066 ft/325 m. Sacramento R. arm extends 19 mi/31 km N, Pit R. arm 21 mi/34 km E, McCloud R. arm 13 mi/21 km NNE, and Squaw Creek arm 7 mi/11.3 km NE. Formed by Shasta Dam (602 ft/183 m high, 3,460 ft/1,055 m long) built 1938–1945 as a major unit in the Central Valley Project for flood control, irrigation, and power generation. Within Shasta Unit of Whiskeytown-Shasta-Trinity Natl. Recreational Area. L. Shasta Caverns on N shore, E of McCloud Arm.

Shasta, Mount (SHAS-tuh), volcanic peak (14,162 ft/4,317 m), S Siskiyou co., N Calif., 56 mi/90 km N of Redding, in the Cascade Range, and in Shasta Natl. Forest; 41°24′N 122°11′W. Visited c.1827 by Peter Skene Ogden, a Br. fur trader and explorer, Mt. Shasta has long been dormant except for hot sulphurous springs near the top. The resort town of Mt. Shasta is 10 mi/16 km to SW. Source of Shasta R. to W.

Shasta River (SHAS-tuh), c.40 mi/64 km long, Siskiyou co., N Calif.; rises in S Siskiyou co., W of Mt. Shasta, 10 mi/16 km S of Weed; flows N, past Weed and through L. Shastina, past Montague, where it is joined by the Little Shasta R. from E, to Klamath R. c.10 mi/16 km N of Yreka.

Shattuck, town (1990 pop. 1,454), Ellis co., NW Okla., 12 mi/19 km NNW of Arnett, near Wolf Creek and Texas (W) state line; 36°16′N 99°52′W. In agr. area (livestock; dairy prods.); mfg. (paper prods.). Settled 1904, inc. 1906.

Shattuckville, Mass.: see COLRAIN.

Shaunavon (SHO-nuh-vuhn), town (1991 pop. 1,913), SW Sask., W Canada, in the Cypress Hills, 55 mi/89 km SW of Swift Current; 49°39′N 108°25′W. Elev. 3,012 ft/918 m. Coal mining. Grain elevators, cold storage plant, flour mills.

Shavano Park, town (1990 pop. 1,708), Bexar co., S central Texas, residential suburb 11 mi/18 km NNW of downtown San Antonio, on Salado Creek; 29°34′N 98°33′W. Camp Bullis Military Reservation to N.

Shavano Peak (14,229 ft/4,337 m), Chaffee co., central Colo., in S end of Sawatch Mts., 14 mi/23 km WNW of Salida; 38°37′N 106°14′W. Melting snow in fissures on peak creates figure known as Angel of Shavano. In San Isabel Natl. Forest.

Shaver Lake, reservoir, Fresno Co., S Calif., on Stevenson Creek, 38 mi/61 km NE of Fresno; 3 mi/4.8 km long, 2 mi/3.2 km wide; 37°09′N 119°17′W. Elev. 5,371 ft/1,637 m. Max. capacity 135,283 acre-ft. Formed by Shaver L. Dam (179 ft/55 m high). Built by Southern

Calif. Edison Company for power generation. Shaver Lake village at SW end.

Shavers Fork (SHAI-vuhrs), river, 83 mi/134 km long, E W.Va.; rises in N Pocahontas co. W of Cass; flows NNE bet. Cheat (W) and Shavers (E) mts., turns briefly W near Elkins to cross Cheat Mt., then NNE, joins Laurel Fork at Parsons to form Cheat R.

Shavers Mountain (SHAI-vuhrs), ridge, E W.Va., the Allegheny Mts.; from Laurel Fork of Cheat R. in S Tucker co., extends c.50 mi/80 km SSW, parallel to course of Shavers Fork (W), through Randolph and Pendleton cos., into NW Pocahontas co. Rises to 4,860 ft/1,481 m in Bald Knob, just N of Cass.

Shavertown, uninc. town (1990 pop. 2,010), Luzerne co., NE central Pa., suburb 6 mi/9.7 km NW of Wilkes-Barre, on Toby Creek. Agr. includes dairying; corn, hay, potatoes, apples. Huntsville Reservoir to W; Frances Slocum State Park to E.

Shaw (1990 pop. 2,349), Bolivar co., W Miss., 22 mi/35 km NE of Greenville; 33°36′N 90°46′W. In rich agr. area (cotton, corn, wheat, rice, soybeans; cattle); mfg. (screen printing).

Shaw, residential and commercial section in NW Washington, D.C., centered around Georgia and Rhode Island aves., and 1.5 mi/2.4 km NNE of the White House; 38°55′N 77°02′W. Howard Univ. is just N. Long the business and cultural center of the city's Afr.-Amer. community, Shaw was hit hard by riots in the late 1960s; since rebuilt, the area has attracted increasing investment and is now linked by subway to other areas.

Shaw Air Force Base, S.C.: see SUMTER.

Shawangunk Kill (shuh-WAWNG-guhnk), stream, c.35 mi/56 km long, SE N.Y.; rises in Orange co. E of Port Jervis; flows generally E, along E base of the Shawangunk range, to Wallkill R. just W of Gardiner.

Shawangunk Mountain (shuh-WAWNG-guhnk), SE N.Y., range (mainly a single ridge) of the Appalachians, extending SW from Rondout Creek near Kingston to junction with Kittatinny (ki-TA-tuh-nee) Mt. ridge in Orange co. near Port Jervis on N.J. state line; c.45 mi/72 km long; 41°35′N 74°27′W. Max. elev. 2,289 ft/698 m; Sam's Point (2,255 ft/687 m), in Ice Caves Mt., is best-known peak. Resort area, with small, natural lakes. A tilted crust of quartz-rich rubble (Silurian-age, Shawangunk conglomerate or "Shawangunk grit") rests atop 2,000 ft/610 m of underlying soft black Ordovician-age Martinsburg shale. Both rock sequences represent shore deposits of anc. inland sea. Upper slopes and summits covered with blueberry bushes, dwarf pitch pine, and birch. Area used to produce large commercial volume of wild blueberries, but no longer. A natl. natural landmark and tourist attraction. Colloquially known as "The Gunks."

Shawano, county (□ 909 sq mi/2,354 sq km; 1990 pop. 37,157), E central Wis.; ⊙ Shawano; 44°47′N 88°15′W. Drained by Wolf and Embarrass rivers. Generally forested area, with sawmills and agr. (barley, oats, corn, beans, potatoes, alfalfa, hay; cattle, sheep, hogs; granite and marble. Stockbridge Indian Reservation in N, Memominee Indian Reservation comprises all of Menominee co. to N; Navarino Ski Area in S; largest of several lakes in co. (nearly in E) is Shawano L. Formed 1853.

Shawano, city (1990 pop. 7,598), ⊙ Shawano co., NE Wis., on Wolf R., and 35 mi/56 km NW of Green Bay; 44°46′N 88°35′W. RR junction and trade center for lumbering and agr. area; mfg. (dairy prods., fabricated metal prods., wood prods.). Menominee Indian Reservation to N, Shawano L. to NE; Navarino Ski Area to S. Settled c.1840, it was an early lumbering center. Inc. 1874.

Shawano Lake, Shawano co., NE Wis., 3 mi/4.8 km E of Shawano; c.5 mi/8 km long, c.3 mi/4.8 km wide. Drained by small stream entering Wolf R. Village of Cecil on E end.

Shawbridge, village, S Que., E Canada, on North R., and 35 mi/56 km NW of Montreal; 45°52′N 74°05′W. Dairying.

Shawinigan (shuh-WI-ni-guhn), city (1991 pop. 19,931), S Que., E Canada. on the St. Maurice R.; 46°33′N

72°44′W. Just N are the falls of the St. Maurice, 150 ft/46 m high, with a hydroelectric station supplying power for the city's pulp and paper mills and plants that produce aluminum, abrasives, chemicals, cellulose, and textiles. Most of the inhabitants speak Fr.

Shawmut, Ala.: see VALLEY.

Shawnee (shaw-NEE), county (☐ 556 sq mi/1,440 sq km; 1990 pop. 160,976), NE Kansas; ⊙ Topeka; 39°02′N 95°45′W. Dissected plain, drained by Kansas R. and Soldier Creek and Wakarusa R in S. Cattle; corn, wheat, soybeans, hay, strawberries; general agr. Food processing, publishing, and printing. Industries at Topeka. Shawnee State Fishing L. in N. Formed 1855.

Shawnee 1 (shaw-NEE), city (1990 pop. 37,993), Johnson co., NE Kansas, a primarily residential suburb 9 mi/14.5 km WSW of downtown Kansas City; 39°01′N 94°47′W. RR junction. Mfg. (consumer goods, lumber, honey, concrete and terra cotta, fabricated metal prods., machinery); farm and dairy prods. are shipped. Original site of the Shawnee Indian Methodist Mission (1830). The re-creation of an old Shawnee town is in Bluejacket Park; Old Shawnee Town includes Kansas' 1st jail and other original bldgs. Area often referred to as Shawnee-Mission. Founded 1857, inc. 1922. **2** city (1990 pop. 26,017), ⊙ Pottawatomie co., central Okla., 30 mi/48 km ESE of Oklahoma City, on the North Canadian R.; 35°22′N 96°58′W. Elev. 1,055 ft/322 m. RR junction. The trade and RR center for a rich farm, dairy, and oil area; corn, peanuts; mfg. (electronic goods, machinery, apparel, chemicals, fabricated metal prods.). Shawnee boomed with the discovery of oil here in 1926. Seat of Okla. Baptist Univ. and St. Gregory's Col. Potawatomie Indian Mus. here. Jim Thorpe was born nearby. Inc. 1894.

Shawnee 1 village, Park co., central Colo., in Front Range, 35 mi/56 km SW of Denver; on North Fork of South Platte R. Elev. 8,150 ft/2,484 m. Resort. Christ of the Rockies, 52-ft/16-m figure, is nearby. Surrounded by Pike Natl. Forest. **2** village (1990 pop. 742), Perry co., central Ohio, 7 mi/11 km S of New Lexington; 39°37′N 82°12′W. **3** village, Converse co., E Wyo., 18 mi/29 km E of Douglas. Elev. c.5,000 ft/1,525 m. RR junction. Coal and oil nearby.

Shawnee Hills, village (1990 pop. 423), Delaware co., central Ohio, 14 mi/23 km NNW of Columbus, on Scioto R.

Shawnee State Forest (☐ c.94 sq mi/243 sq km), Scioto co., S Ohio, W of Portsmouth; largest forest area in Ohio. Small lakes; fishing, camping. Roosevelt Game Preserve is adjacent.

Shawneetown (SHAW-nee-toun), city (1990 pop. 1,575), ⊙ Gallatin co., SE Ill., near Ohio R. (bridge here), and 20 mi/32 km E of Harrisburg; 37°42′N 88°10′W. Trade center in agr. and bituminous-coal-mining area; wheat, corn; livestock; food prods. Shawneetown State Historical Site nearby, at old Shawneetown.

Shawnigan Lake (SHAW-ni-guhn), village, SW B.C., W Canada, on SE Vancouver Isl., on Shawnigan L. (5 mi/8 km long), 20 mi/32 km NW of Victoria. Lumbering; mixed farming, fruit growing.

Shawsheen Village, Mass.: see ANDOVER.

Shawsville, uninc. town, Montgomery co., SW Va., 8 mi/12.9 km ENE of Christiansburg; 37°20′N 80°14′W. Mfg. (crushed stone); agr. (grain, apples; livestock); stone quarrying.

Shawville, village (1991 pop. 1,591), SW Que., E Canada, near Ottawa R., 40 mi/64 km WNW of Ottawa; 45°36′N 76°29′W. Dairying; lumbering; brick and tile mfg.

Shea Stadium, Flushing Meadows, borough of Queens, N.Y. city, SE N.Y., S of Northern Blvd., bet. Grand Central Parkway and Van Wyck Expressway, at S end of Flushing Bay; 40°45′N 73°52′W. Home field of the N.Y. Mets Natl. League baseball team. Occupies part of the land purchased in 1935 as the site for the 1939 World's Fair. (Part of the fairgrounds, just E of the stadium, also hosted the 1984 World's Fair.) Opened April 17, 1964, stadium (capacity 55,601) was originally going to be called Flushing Meadow Park, but instead it was named after attorney William A. Shea, who was the driving force in acquiring a new baseball team for New York following the 1958 move to the West Coast of the Brooklyn Dodgers and N.Y. Giants. It was 1st stadium to accommodate both baseball and football (the N.Y. Jets played here for a while). Shea Stadium is the noisiest stadium in the major leagues because of nearby La Guardia Airport.

Sheakleyville (SHEEK-lee-vil), borough (1990 pop. 145), Mercer co., NW Pa., 14 mi/23 km SSW of Meadville; 41°26′N 80°12′W. Agr. (hay; dairying). M.K. Goddard State Park, on L. Wilhelm reservoir to E.

Shebandowan Lake, NW Ont., Canada, 40 mi/64 km WNW of Thunder Bay, 10 mi/16 km S of Lac des Milles Lacs; 25 mi/40 km long, 3 mi/5 km wide. Elev. 1,474 ft/449 m. Drains E into L. Superior.

Sheboygan, county (☐ 1,271 sq mi/3,292 sq km; 1990 pop. 103,877), E Wis.; ⊙ Sheboygan; 43°43′N 87°39′W. Bordered E by L. Michigan; drained by Sheboygan and Onion rivers. One of the leading dairying and cheese-producing areas in U.S.; barley, oats, wheat, soybeans, peas, alfalfa, hay; cattle, hogs, poultry. Diversified mfg. (esp. enamel, porcelain, and wood prods.) in Sheboygan, Kohler, Sheboygan Falls, and Plymouth. Includes Kohler Andrae State Park in E, N part Kettle Moraine State Forest (N unit) in W; Old Wade House State Historical Park in W; Sheboygen L. in NW. Formed 1836.

Sheboygan, city (1990 pop. 49,676), ⊙ Sheboygan co., E Wis., 50 mi/80 km NNE of Milwaukee; 43°45′N 87°43′W. A port of entry on L. Michigan at the mouth of the Sheboygan R. Plastics, stainless-steel prods., orthodontic prods., paper goods, enamelware, furniture, and lighting equip. are manufactured here. Dairying (cheese) and beer brewing are also important industries. Permanent settlement began c.1835, and Sheboygan grew into a shipping and industrial center. A Univ. of Wisconsin extension center and Lakeland Col. are located here. A Native Amer. mound park featuring a great number of prehistoric burial mounds just S of the city; Kohler Andrae State Park to S. Inc. 1853.

Sheboygan Falls, town (1990 pop. 5,823), Sheboygan co., E Wis., at falls of Sheboygan R., a suburb 5 mi/8 km W of Sheboygan; 43°43′N 87°49′W. In dairy and grain area; mfg. (furniture, fixtures, food processing, machinery, aluminum die castings, chemicals). Sheboygan County Airport to NW. Inc. as village in 1854, as city in 1913.

Sheboygan River, E Wis., c.70 mi/113 km long; rises in Fond du Lac co.; flows generally N through Sheboygan L., then SE, past Plymouth and Sheboygan Falls, to L. Michigan at Sheboygan. Navigable c.2.5 mi/4 km by small craft. Upper half of river flows around N end of large Kettle Moraine, formed from glacial debris.

Shediac (SHEHD-ee-ak), town (1991 pop. 4,343), SE N.B., Canada, on Northumberland Strait; 46°13′N 64°32′W. It is a resort and has lobster, oyster, and smelt fisheries.

Sheenjik River, c.200 mi/322 km long, NE Alaska; rises in Davidson Mts. near 68°30′N 143°20′W; flows S to Porcupine R. at 66°44′N 144°32′W.

Sheep Mountain 1 peak (12,350 ft/3,764 m) in Rocky Mts., N Park co., central Colo., 6 mi/9.7 km WSW of Fairplay; 39°11′N 106°06′W. Lesser Lamb Mt. to W. **2** peak (13,168 ft/4,014 m), SW Gunnison co., W central Colo., 12 mi/19 km NW of Lake City in Rocky Mts.; 38°09′N 107°27′W. **3** peak (13,292 ft/4,051 m), E San Juan co., SW Colo., in San Juan Mts., 7 mi/11.3 km E of Silverton, just E of Continental Divide; 37°47′N 107°31′W.

Sheep Range, SE Nev., in N Clark co., N of Las Vegas. Rises to Hayford Peak (8,912 ft/2,716 m) and Sheep Peak in S; c.50 mi/80 km long N-S; 35°45′N 115°17′W. Entirely in E part of Desert Natl. Wildlife Range.

Sheepscot Bay (SHEEPS-kaht), SW Maine, bet. Georgetown and Southport; c.5 mi/8 km wide; receives Sheepscot R.

Sheepscot River (SHEEPS-kaht), c.30 mi/48 km long, S Maine; rises in Sheepscot Pond, SW Waldo co., near Palermo; flows SW to Sheepscot Bay.

Sheepshead Bay, residential area in S Brooklyn borough of N.Y. city, SE N.Y., on N side of Sheepshead Bay; 40°35′N 73°57′W. It was once famous for its horse and automobile races and as a resort center. The bay is an anchorage for commercial and pleasure fishing craft; the Sheephead Bay Fishing Fleet still docks daily along Emmons Ave., selling fish. A number of restaurants specialize in seafood.

Sheerness, village, SE Alta., Canada, 15 mi/24 km SE of Hanna; 51°30′N 111°41′W. Coal mining; cattle, wheat.

Sheet Harbour, village, SE N.S., on Sheet Harbour, at mouth of a stream, 60 mi/97 km ENE of Halifax; 44°56′N 62°32′W. Site of major hydroelectric power station; pulp milling. Nearby is extensive game sanctuary.

Sheffield, city (1990 pop. 10,380), Colbert co., NW Ala., on Tennessee R. (bridged) opposite Florence. In iron and coal area. Metalworking center, with boat connections; aluminum prods. (ingots, wire, sheets, tubing, roofing), metals, structural castings, rolled rubber, motor vehicle transmission parts. Large Listerhill aluminum plant (built 1941) is E. Industries stimulated by construction of Wilson Dam (4 mi/6.4 km ENE) and development of TVA. Sheffield founded 1883, inc. 1885.

Sheffield 1 town (1990 pop. 1,174), Franklin co., N central Iowa, 18 mi/29 km S of Mason City; 42°53′N 93°12′W. Mfg. (grain drying and handling equip.); brick, tile; hybrid seed corn. Clay and gravel pits nearby. Inc. 1876. **2** resort town (1990 pop. 2,910), Berkshire co., SW Mass., in the Berkshires, on Housatonic R., and 22 mi/35 km S of Pittsfield; 42°06′N 73°22′W. Settled 1726, inc. 1733. Includes village of Ashley Falls. **3** uninc. town (1990 pop. 1,294), Warren co., NW Pa., 11 mi/18 km SE of Warren, on West Branch Tionesta Creek; 41°42′N 01°79′W. Agr. (livestock); timber; mfg. (transportation equip., lumber, corrugated boxes); oil and natural gas to N. Allegheny Reservoir to NE; surrounded by Allegheny Natl. Forest; Hears Content Scenic Area to W. Founded 1864. **4** town (1990 pop. 541), Caledonia co., NE Vt., 15 mi/24 km NNW of St. Johnsbury; 44°38′N 72°07′W. Dairy prods.

Sheffield 1 village (1990 pop. 951), Bureau co., N Ill., 14 mi/23 km W of Princeton; 41°21′N 89°44′W. In agr. area (corn, soybeans; cattle, hogs). Hennepin Canal State Trail to N. **2** village (1990 pop. 1,943), Lorain co., N Ohio, 4 mi/6 km N of Elyria; 41°27′N 82°05′W. Inc. 1933. **3** uninc. village (1990 pop. 600), Pecos co., extreme W Texas, on the Pecos R., and c.65 mi/105 km E of Fort Stockton. Trading point in cattle and sheep ranching region; cotton; vegetables, pecans. Fort Lancaster State Historic Site to E.

Sheffield Lake, city (1990 pop. 9,825), Lorain co., N Ohio, near L. Erie, 4 mi/6 km ENE of Lorain; 41°29′N 82°05′W. Inc. 1920.

Sheffield Lake (☐ 9 sq mi/23 sq km), W central N.F., Canada, 15 mi/24 km E of Sandy L. (into which it drains); 5 mi/8 km by 3 mi/5 km.

Shefford, county (☐ 567 sq mi/1,469 sq km), S Que., Canada, on upper Yamaska R.; ⊙ Waterloo; 45°27′N 72°32′W.

Sheho (SHEE-ho), village (1991 pop. 212), SE central Sask., Canada, near small Sheho L., 40 mi/64 km NW of Yorkton; 51°35′N 103°13′W. Mixed farming.

Shelbiana (shel-bee-AN-uh), uninc. village (1990 pop. 625), Pike co., E Ky., 3 mi/4.8 km S of Pikeville, on Russell Fork river. RR junction. Bituminous coal; mfg. (mining bits). Fishtrap L. reservoir to E.

Shelbina (shel-BEI-nuh), city (1990 pop. 2,172), Shelby co., NE Mo., near North Fork of Salt R., 36 mi/58 km W of Hannibal; 39°41′N 92°02′W. Agr. (corn, soybeans; dairying; cattle, horses); mfg. (copper tubes). Founded 1857.

Shelburn, town (1990 pop. 1,147), Sullivan co., SW Ind., 6 mi/9.7 km N of Sullivan; 39°11′N 87°24′W. Grain; livestock. Mfg. (blow molding); bituminous-coal mines; timber. Laid out 1855, inc. 1872.

Shelburne, county (☐ 979 sq mi/2,536 sq km; 1991 pop. 17,343), SW N.S., Canada, on the Atlantic; ⊙ Shelburne.

Shelburne 1 town (1991 pop. 2,245), ⊙ Shelburne co., SW N.S., Canada, at head of Shelburne Harbour (10 mi/16 km-long inlet of the Atlantic) at mouth of

Roseway R., 40 mi/64 km E of Yarmouth. Shipbuilding, fish curing and packing, lumbering; mfg. of boxes and barrels. Granite is quarried nearby. **2** town (1991 pop. 3,436), S Ont., Canada, 14 mi/23 km NNW of Orangeville. Dairying, milling, sandstone quarrying.

Shelburne 1 town (1990 pop. 2,012), Franklin co., NW Mass., on Deerfield R., and 4 mi/6.4 km W of Greenfield; 42°36'N 72°42'W. Includes part of Shelburne Falls village. Resort area; state forest nearby. Settled c.1756, seperated from Deerfield 1768. **2** town (1990 pop. 437), Coos co., NE N.H., 7 mi/11.3 km SE of Berlin; 44°23'N 71°04'W. Bounded E by Maine state boundary, drained by Androscoggin R. Livestock, poultry; dairying; timber. Part of White Mt. Natl. Forest in S; part of Mahoosuc Range in N. Appalachian Trail crosses N-S. Famous stance of birch trees along main highway. **3** town (1990 pop. 5,871), Chittenden co., NW Vt., on L. Champlain and 7 mi/11.3 km S of Burlington; 44°22'N 73°15'W. Lumber, dairying. Resorts; ski equip. Shelburne Mus. is here. Macdonough's fleet wintered here in War of 1812. Granted 1763, 1st settled 1768, organized 1787.

Shelburne Falls, village, Buckland and Shelburne towns, Franklin co., NW Mass., on both banks of Deerfield R., and 7 mi/11.3 km W of Greenfield, near crest of Mohawk Trail. Makes cutlery, tools. Resort area.

Shelby 1 county (□ 809 sq mi/2,095 sq km; 1990 pop. 99,358), central Ala.; ⊙ Columbiana; 33°16'N 86°40'W. Hilly agr. region lying bet. Coosa and Cahaba rivers. Agr. (cotton, corn, hay; livestock); coal, limestone, and iron ore. Formed 1818. **2** county (□ 768 sq mi/1,989 sq km; 1990 pop. 22,261), central Ill.; ⊙ Shelbyville; 39°24'N 88°47'W. Agr. (wheat, corn, hay, soybeans, sorghum; dairy prods.; hogs, cattle). Mfg. (construction machinery, paper prods.). Drained by South Fork of Sangamon R., and by Kaskaskia and Little Wabash rivers. Formed 1827. Includes L. Shelbyville; Eagle Creek and Wolfcreek state parks on opposite sides of lake. **3** county (□ 413 sq mi/1,070 sq km; 1990 pop. 40,307), central Ind.; ⊙ Shelbyville; 39°31'N 85°47'W. Part of Indianapolis metro area. Drained by Big Blue, Little Blue, and Flatrock rivers and by Sugar Creek. Rich farming and dairying region; corn, hay, wheat, soybeans; hogs, cattle. Mfg. at Morristown and Shelbyville. Formed 1821. **4** county (□ 591 sq mi/1,531 sq km; 1990 pop. 13,230), W Iowa; ⊙ Harlan; 41°41'N 95°20'W. Prairie agr. area (cattle, hogs, poultry; corn, alfalfa) drained by West Nishnabotna R. and by Keg, Silver, and Mosquito creeks; bituminous-coal deposits. Formed 1851. **5** county (□ 385 sq mi/997 sq km; 1990 pop. 24,824), N Ky.; ⊙ Shelbyville; 38°12'N 85°11'W. Drained by Beech, Plum, Clear, and Guist creeks. Gently rolling upland agr. area (burley tobacco, corn, wheat, soybeans, alfalfa, hay; hogs, cattle, poultry; dairying), in Bluegrass region. Mfg. at Shelbyville and Simpsonville. Guist Creek L. reservoir in E center. Formed 1792. **6** county (□ 502 sq mi/1,300 sq km; 1990 pop. 6,942), NE Mo.; ⊙ Shelbyville; 39°47'N 93°05'W. Drained by North and Salt rivers. Agr. (corn, wheat, hay, soybeans; cattle, hogs; dairying); limestone; lumber. Formed 1835. **7** county (□ 409 sq mi/1,059 sq km; 1990 pop. 44,915), W Ohio; ⊙ Sidney; 40°19'N 84°11'W. Intersected by Great Miami R. and Loramie Creek; L. Loramie is in W. In the Till Plains physiographic region. Agr. area (cattle, poultry; dairying; corn, soybeans); mfg. at Sidney and Jackson Center (preserved fruits and vegetables, transportation equip., apparel, plastic prods., machinery, aluminum foundries); gravel pits. Formed 1819. **8** county (□ 751 sq mi/1,945 sq km; 1990 pop. 826,330), extreme SW Tenn.; ⊙ MEMPHIS; 35°11'N 89°54'W. Bounded S by Miss. state line, W by Mississippi R. and Ark.; drained by Loosahatchie and Wolf rivers. Cotton, pecans, soybeans, wheat; dairying; livestock raising. Memphis is an important commercial and mfg. center of Tenn. and adjoining states. Includes 2 state parks, a bottomlands forest, and the U.S. Naval Air Station. Formed 1819. **9** county (□ 834 sq mi/2,160 sq km; 1990 pop. 22,034), E Texas; ⊙ Center; 31°47'N 94°08'W. Bounded E by Sabine R. (here the La. state line), W by Attoyac Bayou; includes part of Sabine Natl. Forest in E. Hilly, wooded area (pine, hardwood); lumbering is chief industry. Also natural gas wells, some oil; agr. (vegetables, watermelons), beef and dairy cattle, poultry (chickens, eggs). Hunting, fishing. Formed 1836.

Shelby 1 city (1990 pop. 14,669), ⊙ Cleveland co., W N.C., 43 mi/69 km W of Charlotte, near First Broad R.; 35°17'N 81°32'W. In a fertile Piedmont region, agr. area (mostly cotton; also grain, soybeans; cattle, hogs, poultry; dairying); mfg. (printing and publishing, dairy processing, machining; plastic and metal prods., upholstered furniture, textiles, apparel, chemcials, hydraulic tools, industrial parts, wooden panels and trusses, truck beds). Gardner-Webb Univ. to SW at Boiling Springs. Inc. 1843. **2** city (1990 pop. 9,564), Richland co., N central Ohio, 11 mi/18 km NW of Mansfield, and on Black Fork of Mohican R.; 40°53'N 82°40'W. In rich agr. region (livestock, poultry; corn); mfg. (steel tubing, cutlery, bicycles).

Shelby 1 town (1990 pop. 637), Shelby co., W Iowa, 10 mi/16 km SSW of Harlan; 41°30'N 95°27'W. Grain, livestock. **2** town (1990 pop. 1,871), Oceana co., W Mich., 27 mi/43 km NNW of Muskego; 43°36'N 86°22'W. In fruit growing and dairying area; mfg. (lumber, wood prods., optical crystals, canned fruits and vegetables). Wildlife sanctuary. Silver L. State Park to W; Manistee Natl. Forest to E. Inc. 1885. **3** town (1990 pop. 2,806), Bolivar co., NW Miss., 20 mi/32 km SSW of Clarksdale; 33°57'N 90°46'W. In rich cotton-growing area; agr. (corn, rice, soybeans; cattle); mfg. (automotive equip., die castings). **4** town (1990 pop. 2,763), ⊙ Toole co., N Mont., near Marias R. (S), 75 mi/121 km NNW of Great Falls; 48°31'N 111°52'W. RR junction. Oil and gas wells. Wheat, barley, oats; cattle, hogs. Discovery of oil (1921) to N was important factor in growth of town. Est. 1891; inc. 1914. Marias Mus. of History and Art. L. Elwell (Tiber Reservoir) to SE.

Shelby 1 uninc. village (1990 pop. 700), Lake co., NW Ind., 7 mi/11.3 km SSE of Lowell, on Kankakee R. RR junction. Dairying. **2** village (1990 pop. 690), Polk co., E central Nebr., 6 mi/9.7 km E of Osceola; 41°11'N 97°25'W. Dairying; grain; livestock, poultry.

Shelby Township, city, Macomb Co., SE Mich., suburb 23 mi/37 km N of downtown Detroit. Mfg. (plastic molding, machinery, transportation equip., accoustical enclosures, concrete prods.). Rochester-Utica State Recreation Area in SW; Stony Creek Metropark in NW; Berz-Macomb Airport to E.

Shelbyville 1 city (1990 pop. 4,943), ⊙ Shelby co., central Ill., on Kaskaskia R., and 30 mi/48 km SSW of Decatur; 39°24'N 88°47'W. Mfg. (machinery, metal prods.); agr. (soybeans, corn, wheat, hay; livestock; dairy prods.). Inc. 1839. **2** city (1990 pop. 15,336), ⊙ Shelby co., central Ind.; 39°31'N 85°47'W. It is a trading and mfg. center, in an agr. area. Agr. (corn, wheat, hogs, cattle); mfg. (motor vehicle glass prods., furniture, transportation equip., machinery, consumer goods, aluminum die castings, metal goods, plastic prods., chemicals, paper feed systems, fiberglass insulation, wire prods.). Plotted 1822, inc. as a city 1860. **3** city (1990 pop. 582), ⊙ Shelby co., NE Mo., near North Fork of Salt R., 36 mi/58 km WNW of Hannibal; 39°48'N 92°02'W. Corn, wheat; cattle, hogs; lumber. Plotted 1835. **4** city (1990 pop. 14,049), ⊙ Bedford co., central Tenn., on the Duck R., c. 53 mi/85 km SSE of Nashville; 35°29'N 86°30'W. In a farm and timber area. Mfg. (wood prods., apparel, plastics, transportation equip.); poultry processing. Surrounding region is noted for the breeding of the Tennessee Walking Horse. The Tennessee Walking Horse Mus. is here, and a natl. competition is held every Aug. One of the country's early planned cities, Shelbyville retains many of its 19th-cent. bldgs. Inc. 1819.

Shelbyville, town (1990 pop. 6,238), ⊙ Shelby co., N Ky., 30 mi/48 km E of Louisville, on Clear Creek, in Bluegrass region; 38°13'N 85°13'W. Agr. (livestock; corn, burley tobacco; dairying); mfg. (ethyl alcohol, metal prods., structural foam, consumer goods, staple wire, transportation equip., machinery, chemicals; printing and publishing). Science Hill School (for girls, 1825–1939; built c.1790). Stanley-Casey House (1867). Guist Creek L. reservoir to E. City founded 1792.

Shelbyville, uninc. village (1990 pop. 215), Shelby co., E Texas, 8 mi/12.9 km SE of Center. In vegetable farming area; timber; oil wells; sand and gravel. Toledo Bend Reservoir (Sabine R.) to E; Sabine Natl. Forest immediately E.

Shelbyville, Lake, reservoir, c.40 mi/64 km long, at Shelbyville, in Shelby and Moultrie cos., central Ill., on Kaskaskia R.; 39°24'N 88°46'W. Okaw R. forms 3-mi/4.8-km N arm. Max. capacity of 1,035,900 acre-ft. Formed by Shelbyville Dam (earth-gravity construction; 108 ft/33 m high), built (1970) for flood control, navigation, and water supply. Eagle Creek (W shore) and Wolfcreek (E shore) state parks here; Shelbyville Wildlife Management Area at NE end.

Sheldahl, town (1990 pop. 315), on Boone-Polk-Story co. line, central Iowa, 18 mi/29 km N of Des Moines; 41°51'N 93°42'W.

Sheldon, city (1990 pop. 4,937), O'Brien co., NW Iowa, on Floyd R., and 14 mi/23 km NW of Primghar; 43°10'N 95°50'W. RR junction; concrete prods., feed, beverages. Sand and gravel pits nearby. Has a community col. Inc. 1876.

Sheldon 1 town (1990 pop. 464), Vernon co., W Mo., 13 mi/21 km S of Nevada; 37°39'N 94°17'W. Wheat, sorghum, soybeans; cattle. **2** uninc. town (1990 pop. 1,653), Harris co., SE Texas, residential suburb 18 mi/29 km ENE of downtown Houston, on San Jacinto R. (forms L. Houston to N); 29°51'N 95°07'W. Sheldon State Wildlife Management Area to W. **3** town (1990 pop. 1,748), Franklin co., NW Vt., on Missisquoi R., and 8 mi/12.9 km NE of St. Albans; 44°53'N 72°55'W. Includes Sheldon Springs village. Granted 1763, settled 1789–1790, organized 1791.

Sheldon 1 village (1990 pop. 1,109), Iroquois co., E Ill., 9 mi/14.5 km E of Watseka, near Ind. state line; 40°46'N 87°34'W. Ships grain. Founded 1860; inc. 1901. **2** village (1990 pop. 149), Ransom co., SE N.Dak., 13 mi/21 km NE of Lisbon; 46°35'N 97°29'W. RR junction to SW. **3** village (1990 pop. 268), Rusk co., N central Wis., 13 mi/21 km SSE of Ladysmith; 45°18'N 90°57'W. Dairying. Concrete.

Sheldon's Point, village (1990 pop. 109), W Alaska, near Yukon R. delta; 62°31'N 164°53'W.

Shelikof Bay, SE Alaska, on W side of Kruzof Isl., on Gulf of Alaska, 20 mi/32 km W of Sitka; 4 mi/6.4 km long, 5 mi/8 km wide.

Shelikof Strait (130 mi/209 km long, 30 mi/48 km wide), S Alaska, bet. Alaska Peninsula (NW) and Kodiak and Afognak isls. (SE); connects Gulf of Alaska and its Cook Inlet (NE) with N Pacific (SW). Fishing villages on SE shore. Katmai Natl. Park and Preserve on NW coast.

Shell Creek, E central Nebr.; rises in Boone co.; flows 74 mi/119 km SE and E, past Newman Grove, to Platte R. near Schuyler.

Shell Lake, town (1990 pop. 1,161), ⊙ Washburn co., NW Wis., on W shore of Shell L., 5 mi/8 km S of Spooner; 45°44'N 91°54'W. In dairying and farming area (corn, peas, potatoes). Boat construction; fiberglass prods. Cheese processing.

Shell Point, uninc. town (1990 pop. 2,885), Beaufort co., S S.C., residential community, 6 mi/9.7 km SE of Beaufort on Port Royal Sound; 32°22'N 80°45'W. Parris Isl. Marine Corps Base to SE.

Shell Point, village, Contra Costa co., W Calif., near Pittsburg.

Shell River (4 mi/6.4 km long, 1.5 mi/2.4 km wide); in E central Becker co., W Minn.; rises in Shell L.; flows 40 mi/64 km SE to Blueberry L., N of Menahga, continuing NE to receive Fish Hook R. from N, S short distance to Upper Twin and Lower Twin lakes; then E to Crow Wing R., 10 mi/16 km ENE of Menagha; 46°56'N 95°24'W.

Shell Rock, town (1990 pop. 1,385), Butler co., N central Iowa, on Shell Rock R., and 13 mi/21 km ESE of Allison; 42°42'N 92°34'W. In agr. area; feed. Limestone quarries; sand and gravel pits nearby.

Shell Rock River, 102 mi/164 km long; in S Minn. and

N Iowa; 43°36′N 93°17′W. Rises in Albert Lea L. reservoir (fed from NW by Bancroft Creek through Fountain L. reservoir); flows SSE into Iowa, past Northwood and Clarksville, to Cedar R., 10 mi/16 km NW of Waterloo.

Shellbrook, town (1991 pop. 1,173), central Sask, Canada, 26 mi/42 km W of Prince Albert; 53°13′N 106°24′W. Grain elevators, flour mills, dairying.

Shelley, town (1990 pop. 3,536), Bingham co., SE Idaho, on Snake R., and 8 mi/12.9 km SSW of Idaho Falls; 43°23′N 112°07′W. Elev. 4,627 ft/1,410 m. Potato-shipping point. In cattle, sheep, and agr. area (potatoes, grain, poultry); sugar beets. Mfg. (honey, dehydrated potato prods., cabinets). Settled 1884, inc. 1904.

Shellman, town (1990 pop. 1,162), Randolph co., SW Ga., 11 mi/18 km E of Cuthbert; 31°46′N 84°37′W. Mfg. of agr. equip., furniture. Settled 1837.

Shellsburg, town (1990 pop. 765), Benton co., E central Iowa, 13 mi/21 km NW of Cedar Rapids; 42°05′N 91°52′W. Corn cannery. Limestone quarries nearby.

Shelly, village (1990 pop. 225), Norman co., NW Minn., 39 mi/63 km N of Fargo, N. Dak., on Marsh R., E of its confluence with Red R.; 47°27′N 96°49′W. Wheat, potatoes, sugar beets. Mfg. (fertilizers).

Shelmerdine (SHEL-muhr-deen), uninc. village, Pitt co., E N.C., 13 mi/21 km SSE of Greenville. Tobacco, livestock.

Shelocta (SHE-lok-tah), borough (1990 pop. 108), Indiana co., W central Pa., 8 mi/12.9 km WNW of Indiana, on Crooked Creek; 40°39′N 79°17′W. Bituminous coal.

Shelter Island (□ 27 sq mi/70 sq km; 1990 pop. 2,263), bet. the 2 peninsulas of E L.I. in SE N.Y.; 7 mi/11.3 km long and 6 mi/9.7 km wide; 41°04′N 72°19′W. Settled in the 17th cent. by Eng. colonists, the isl. has been a summer resort since the 1870s. Its irregular coastline provides harbors for small boats.

Shelton 1 city (1990 pop. 35,418), Fairfield co., SW Conn., on the Housatonic R. opposite Derby; 41°17′N 73°08′W. Mfg. (metal prods., furniture, and electronic equip.). A state park is nearby. Settled 1697, set off from Stratford 1789, inc. as a city 1915. **2** city (1990 pop. 7,241), ⊙ Mason co., W Wash., 15 mi/24 km NW of Olympia, and on Oakland Bay, at end of Hammersley Inlet of Puget Sound; 47°13′N 123°07′W. RR junction. Dairying; poultry; timber. Mfg. (computer peripheral equip.; aircraft parts, metal heat treating, millwork; textile prods., lumber, cutting tools). Squaxin Isl. Indian Reservation and State Park to E; Twanoh State Park to NE; Schafer State Park to SW; Skokomish Indian Reservation and Potlatch State Park to N; Olympic Natl. Forest to NW. Inc. 1889.

Shelton, town (1990 pop. 954), Buffalo co., S Nebr., 20 mi/32 km ENE of Kearney; 40°46′N 98°43′W. Grain, stock, potatoes. Mfg. (brooms and mops).

Shelton, village, Fairfield co., N central S.C., on Broad R., and 20 mi/32 km WNW of Winnsboro, in Sumter Natl. Forest; mineral springs.

Shemya Island (4 mi/6.4 km long, 2 mi/3.2 km wide), Semichi Isls., W Aleutian Isls., SW Alaska, 150 mi/241 km WNW of Kiska Isl., and 50 mi/80 km ESE of Attu Isl.; 58°00′N 154°00′W. Airport has been important air force station and emergency landing field on N air route bet. U.S. and the Far East (1,450 mi/2,333 km from Anchorage; 2,050 mi/3,299 km from Tokyo). Main mission during Cold War was to monitor former Soviet Union missile tests. On NW side is Alcan Harbor, anchorage with breakwater.

Shenandoah, county (□ 512 sq mi/1,326 sq km; 1990 pop. 31,636), NW Va.; ⊙ Woodstock; 38°51′N 78°34′W. In Shenandoah Valley; bounded NW by W.Va. state line and Allegheny Mts., SE by Massanutten Mt. ridge; drained by North Fork of Shenandoah R. and Cedar Creek. Mfg. at Strasburg, Mount Jackson, and New Market; diversified agr. (wheat, corn, barley, alfalfa, soybeans, hay, apples, peaches; poultry, dairy and beef cattle, sheep, hogs); timber; limestone quarrying. Mineral springs and resorts; parts of George Washington Natl. Forest in NW and SE; Shenandoah Caverns in S.

Strasburg and Woodstock are trade, processing centers. Formed 1772.

Shenandoah, city (1990 pop. 5,572), Page and Fremont cos., SW Iowa, on East Nishnabotna R., and 24 mi/39 km ENE of Nebraska City; 40°45′N 95°22′W. Nebr. RR junction, and a major shipping center for large nurseries, seed houses, and poultry hatcheries. Also has feed mills, bottling works, rendering plant, RR shops. Mfg. (horse trailers and flat beds; heavy duty transmissions, veterinary pharmaceuticals; windows and doors; dairy prods., packed poultry, neon signs, paint, chemicals; outerwear clothing). Flooding in area in 1993. Inc. 1871.

Shenandoah, town (1990 pop. 2,213), Page co., N Va., 22 mi/35 km NNE of Harrisonburg, on South Fork of Shenandoah R., bet. Massanutten Mt. (W) and Blue Ridge (E); 38°29′N 78°37′W. Mfg. (garage door openers, machine parts, louvered doors, clothing, food processing). Agr. area (dairying; livestock, poultry; apples, peaches, grain); timber. Inc. 1884.

Shenandoah (SHE-nan-DO-ah), borough (1990 pop. 6,221), Schuylkill co., E central Pa., 9 mi/14.5 km N of Pottsville, on Shenandoah Creek; 40°49′N 76°12′W. Agr. (grain, soybeans; livestock, poultry; dairying). Mfg. (frozen food specialties, bakery prods.; structural metals; apparel, printing and publishing, industrial cloths); anthracite coal. Settled 1835, laid out 1862, inc. 1866.

Shenandoah Caverns, Va.: see MOUNT JACKSON.

Shenandoah Heights (SHE-nan-DO-ah HEITS), uninc. town (1990 pop. 1,386), Schuylkill co., E central Pa., residential suburb 1 mi/1.6 km N of Shenandoah; 40°49′N 76°12′W.

Shenandoah Mountains, in Va. and W.Va., ridge of Allegheny Mts.; from Bath co., Va., extends 80 mi/129 km NW, partly along state border, into Hardy co., W.Va.; rises to over 4,400 ft/1,341 m W of Harrisonburg, Va.; 38°46′N 79°03′W. In George Washington Natl. Forest (both states); Shenandoah Valley to E.

Shenandoah National Park (□ 305 sq mi/790 sq km), N Va., extending 80 mi/129 km along crest of Blue Ridge; Skyline Drive, a N-S highway, extends for 105 mi/169 km through the park, continues as Blue Ridge Parkway from S end of park to Great Smoky Mts. Natl. Park (N.C.-Tenn.). Blue Ridge, Shenandoah Valley, Massanutten Mt., and Allegheny Mts. can be viewed from 75 overlooks on the drive. Park elevations range from 595 ft/181 m at Front Royal to 4,049 ft/1,234 m at the top of Hawksbill Mt. Heavily forested, the park contains a series of ridges and valleys, hollows, small hills, numerous streams, waterfalls, and trout-filled pools. The Appalachian Trail follows the crest. Accommodations at Skyland Lodge and Big Meadows Lodge. Est. 1935.

Shenandoah River, c.150 mi/241 km long, Va.; rises in 2 forks on either side of Massanutten Ridge. The North Fork rises in Rockingham co. W of Massanutten; flows through Timberville and Strasburg; South fork rises in Augusta co. as the union of the North, Middle, and South rivers and flows through Elkton and Shenandoah. The two branches unite near Front Royal, then flow NE to enter the Potomac R. at Harpers Ferry, W. Va.

Shenandoah Valley, N Va., part of Great Valley of the Appalachians, c.150 mi/241 km long, bet. Blue Ridge and Allegheny Mts. through which Shenandoah R. flows. Divided into 2 parts by Massanutten Mt., a ridge c.45 mi/72 km long and c.3,000 ft/914 m high. Shenandoah R., c.150 mi/241 km long; rises in 2 forks on either side of Massanutten Mt., uniting near Front Royal, Va.; flows NE to enter Potomac R. at Harpers Ferry, W.Va. Shenandoah Valley 1st explored in early 1700s. An important corridor in westward pioneer movement, it became a rich agr. area with farmland, orchards, and pastures. During the Civil War, the valley served as one of the principal Confederate storehouses. Shenandoah figured in Stonewall Jackson's "valley campaign" in 1862; Lee retreated through here after defeats at Antietam (1862) and Gettysburg (1863). Principal cities are Winchester, Front Royal, Staunton, and

Waynesboro. Recreational areas include Shenandoah Natl. Park, in the surrounding uplands to E. Valley is noted for its caves, including Luray, Endless, Shenandoah, and Grand Caverns.

Shenango River (she-NAN-go), c.100 mi/161 km long, NW Pa. and NE Ohio; rises in group of small lakes in W central Crawford co., Pa.; flows NW through Pymatuning Swamp to large Pymatuning Reservoir, on Pa./Ohio border, where it turns SSE into Pa.; flows past Jamestown and Greenville; turns W into Shenango River L. reservoir and receives Pymatuning Creek from NW; turns SW, flows past Sharon, Pa., and briefly enters Ohio; turns SSE again into Pa., and flows past Farrell, West Mahoning R. 3 mi/4.8 km SW of New Castle to form Beaver R.; 41°33′N 80°25′W.

Shenango River Lake, reservoir (□ 6 sq mi/15.5 sq km), in NW Pa. (Mercer co.) and NE Ohio (Trumbel co.), on Sharon R., 2 mi/3 km NE of Sharon; 41°16′N 80°28′W. Max. capacity 351,000 acre-ft. Has 2 branches. Formed by Shenango Dam (68 ft/21 m high), built (1965) by Army Corps of Engineers for flood control.

Shenipsit Lake (shin-ip-SIT), reservoir, at Rockville, in Elling, Tolland, and Vernon towns, Tolland co., N Conn., on Hockanum R., 14 mi/23 km NE of Hartford; 2 mi/3.2 km long; 41°52′N 72°25′W.

Shepaug River (she-PAHG), c.35 mi/56 km long, W Conn.; rises W of Goshen; flows generally S, forming Shepaug Reservoir near Warren, to the Housatonic 9 mi/14.5 km NE of Danbury.

Shepherd 1 town (1990 pop. 1,413), Isabella co., central Mich., 6 mi/9.7 km SE of Mt. Pleasant; 43°31′N 84°41′W. In livestock, dairying, and agr. area. **2** town (1990 pop. 1,812), San Jacinto co., E Texas, 55 mi/89 km NNE of Houston; 30°29′N 95°00′W. Timber; cattle, horses. Oil and natural gas. Mfg. (plastic coatings, eyeglass lenses). Sam Houston Natl. Forest to W; unit of Big Thicket Natl. Preserve to E; L. Livingston reservoir to N.

Shepherd, village (1990 pop. 275), Yellowstone co., S Mont., 12 mi/19 km NE of Billings, near Yellowstone R. Irrigated agr. area (cattle, sheep; hay, wheat, barley, oats; sugar beets, beans). Mfg. (racetrack betting forms).

Shepherdstown, town (1990 pop. 1,287), Jefferson co., NE W.Va., in E Panhandle on the Potomac R. (bridged), 10 mi/16 km N of Charles Town; 39°25′N 77°48′W. Mfg. (hardwood mulch, soap, commercial printing). Consists largely of retirees, commuters to Wash., D.C. and Md., artists, small shopkeepers. Shepherd Col. is here. Picturesque 18th and 19th cent. buildings are a mix of federal, colonial, and Victorian architecture. James Rumsey State Historic Monument (Rumsey demonstrated his steamboat here in 1787). The *Potomac Guardian* (started here 1790) was 1st newspaper in what is now W.Va. One of 2 oldest towns in state; est. in 1730s as Meachlenburg.

Shepherdsville, town (1990 pop. 4,805), ⊙ Bullitt co., N Ky., near Salt R., 16 mi/26 km S of Louisville; 37°59′N 85°42′W. In agr. area (tobacco, grain; livestock; dairying). Mfg. (crushed stone, materials handling equip., panic devices and door controls; magazine printing and publishing). Bernheim Arboretum and Research Forest to SE. Fort Knox Military Reservation to SW.

Shepody Bay (SHEH-puh-dee), NW arm (10 mi/16 km long, up to 5 mi/8 km wide) of Chignecto Bay of the Bay of Fundy, SE N.B., Canada, 20 mi/32 km SSE of Moncton. Receives Petitcodiac and Memramcook rivers.

Shequaga Falls, N.Y.: see MONTOUR FALLS.

Sherborn (SHUHR-born), town (1990 pop. 3,989), Middlesex co., E Mass., near Charles R., 5 mi/8 km SE of Framingham; 42°14′N 71°22′W. Settled 1652, inc. 1674.

Sherbrooke, county (□ 238 sq mi/616 sq km), S Que., Canada, on St. Francis R.; ⊙ Sherbrooke.

Sherbrooke, city (1991 pop. 76,429), S Que., Canada, at the confluence of the Magog and the St. François rivers, E of Montreal; 45°24′N 71°54′W. It is the commercial and market center for the surrounding farm and mining region; it is an industrial city, with textile mills and plants producing mining machinery, rubber prods., and leather goods. The Univ. of Sherbrooke (1954) is in the city.

Sherbrooke, village, SE N.S., Canada, on St. Mary R., and 45 mi/72 km SE of New Glasgow; 45°08′N 61°59′W. Lumbering; pulpwood shipping point. Founded 1662 as French post. Historic village reconstruction.

Sherbrooke Lake, W N.S., Canada, 18 mi/29 km N of Bridgewater. Drains into Lahave R.; 8 mi/13 km long, 2 mi/3 km wide.

Sherburn, town (1990 pop. 1,105), Martin co., S Minn., 14 mi/23 km W of Fairmont near Iowa state line; 43°38′N 94°43′W. Grain, soybeans; livestock. Mfg. (lawn equip.). Small lakes nearby, Fox L. to NE; East Fork Des Moines R. to SW. Also spelled Sherburne.

Sherburne, county (□ 451 sq mi/1,168 sq km; 1990 pop. 41,945), central Minn.; ⊙ Elk River; 45°26′N 93°46′W. Bounded W and S by Mississippi R., and drained by Elk R. Agr. area (corn, oats, rye, alfalfa, potatoes, soybeans; hogs); sand and gravel. Sherburne Natl. Wildlife Refuge and Sand Dunes State Forest in E center. Formed 1856.

Sherburne, town (1990 pop. 738), Rutland co., S central Vt., in Green Mts., 10 mi/16 km ENE of Rutland; 43°39′N 72°47′W. Wood prods. Winter resort, Killington and Pico Peak ski areas are here. Killington Peak is here.

Sherburne 1 (SHER-buhrn), uninc. village, Bath co., NE Ky., on Licking R., and 10 mi/16 km SSW of Flemingsburg, in Bluegrass region. **2** village (□ 1 sq mi/2.6 sq km; 1990 pop. 1,531), Chenango co., central N.Y., on Chenango R., and 33 mi/53 km SSW of Utica; 42°40′N 75°30′W. Mfg. (pet foods, metalworking, hosp. supplies, computer circuit boards, art supplies); in dairying area. Former summer resort. Rogers Environmental Education Center occupies a former state game farm nearby. Settled 1793, inc. 1830.

Sheridan 1 county (□ 896 sq mi/2,321 sq km; 1990 pop. 3,043), NW Kansas; ⊙ Hoxie; 39°21′N 100°26′W. Rolling plain area drained by South Fork of Solomon R. and Saline R., North Fork Solomon R, Bow Creek. Wheat, barley, corn, cattle, sheep, hogs. Sheridan State Fishing L. in E. Formed 1880. **2** county (□ 1,706 sq mi/4,419 sq km; 1990 pop. 4,732), extreme NE Mont.; ⊙ Plentywood; 48°44′N 104°30′W. Well-watered agr. area bordering on Canada (Sask.) N, and N.Dak. (E); both boundaries form Central-Mountain time zone boundary; Mont. is in Mountain time zone. Drained by Big Muddy and Lake creeks. Wheat, barley, oats, hay, sugar beets, cattle, hogs, sheep; oil, coal. Part of Fort Peck Indian Reservation in SW. Numerous lakes in SE, E, and NE. Medicine L. Natl. Wildlife Refuge in SE, includes Homestead L. on S boundary. Formed 1913. Present boundaries est. 1920. **3** county (□ 2,470 sq mi/6,397 sq km; 1990 pop. 6,750), NW Nebr.; ⊙ Rushville, in Sand Hills region. Agr. area bounded N by S.Dak.; drained by Niobrara R. and Snake R. Corn, wheat, alfalfa, cattle, hogs; dairying. Numerous small natural lakes scattered throughout S ⅓ of co., also in extreme NE corner. Small segment of Pine Ridge Indian Reservation on N boundary (remainder occupies most of Shannon and part of Jackson cos., S.Dak.). Walgren L. State Recreation Area in W. Formed 1885. **4** county (□ 998 sq mi/2,585 sq km; 1990 pop. 2,148), central N.Dak.; ⊙ McClusky, in Drift Prairie; 47°34′N 100°20′W. Agr. area watered by Sheyenne R. Dairy prods., wheat, barley, rye; cattle. Formed 1908. McClusky Canal, built for irrigation, connects Sheyenne R. to L. Audubon/L. Sakakawea (Missouri R.) in McLean co.; Kruegen and other small lakes in NW; Sheyenne L. in NE on Sheyenne R. **5** county (□ 2,527 sq mi/6,545 sq km; 1990 pop. 23,562), N Wyo.; ⊙ Sheridan; 44°47′N 106°52′W. Irrigated agr. and coal-mining area, bordering on Mont.; watered by Little Bighorn (source in NW corner), Tongue, and Powder rivers. Agr. (barley, oats, hay, alfalfa, corn, wheat, sugar beets, beans; cattle). Part of Bighorn Natl. Forest and Bighorn Mts. in W. Connor Battlefield State Historic Site in N. Formed 1888.

Sheridan, city (1990 pop. 13,900), ⊙ Sheridan co., N Wyo., 135 mi/217 km NNW of Casper, on Goose Creek E at mouth of Little Goose Creek of the Bighorn Mts.; 44°47′N 106°57′W. Elev. 3,745 ft/1,141 m. RR junction. In a mineral, livestock, and irrigated farm region. It is a regional trade and market hub with diverse mfg. (dairy prods.; feeds; rope; lumber; printing and publishing; saddles; concrete; aircraft protective coverings; irrigation supplies). Sheridan is also a tourist center and the hq. for the Bighorn Natl. Forest located to SW. A rodeo and a Native Amer. celebration are held annually. Sheridan Inn, built by Buffalo Bill Cody (1893) is a natl. historic landmark. Sheridan Col. (2-year) and a historical mus. are in the city; Wyo. Girls School S of town. Nearby are a reproduction of Fort Phil Kearny (a post in the 1860s) to S; and the Brinton Memorial Ranch to SW, which commemorates W art and culture. Inc. 1884.

Sheridan 1 town (1990 pop. 3,098), ⊙ Grant co., central Ark., 23 mi/37 km WNW of Pine Bluff; 34°18′N 92°24′W. In timber and farm area. Mfg. (laminated trailer floors, printing ink, metal wall panels, aircraft engine cowls, disposable paper bags, water faucets). Jenkins Ferry Battleground State Historical Monument to SW. **2** town (1990 pop. 4,976), Arapahoe co., N central Colo.; residential suburb 7 mi/11.3 km SSW of downtown Denver, on S Platte R., at mouth of Bear Creek; 39°38′N 105°01′W. Elev. 5,307 ft/1,618 m. Site of Englewood Speedway. Fort Morgan Mental Health Center to W (in Denver). **3** town (1990 pop. 2,046), Hamilton co., central Ind., 13 mi/21 km NW of Noblesville; 40°08′N 86°13′W. Agr. area (grain; livestock; dairying). Mfg. (animal feeds, screw-machine prods., computers). Laid out 1860. **4** town (1990 pop.174), Worth co., NW Mo., Platte R., and 11 mi/18 km NW of Grant City; 40°31′N 94°36′W. Corn, wheat, soybeans; cattle. Plotted 1887. **5** town (1990 pop. 3,979), Yamhill co., NW Oregon, on South Yamhill R., 20 mi/32 km NW of Salem; 45°06′N 123°24′W. Agr. (grain, berries, apples, plums, pears, cherries, peaches; poultry); dairy prods. Mfg. (flour milling, wood preserving). Part of Siuslaw Natl. Forest to W; Erratic Rock Wayside State Park to NE; Baskett Slough Natl. Wildlife Refuge to SE. Settled 1847, inc. 1880.

Sheridan 1 village (1990 pop. 1,288), La Salle co., N Ill., on Fox R. (bridged here), and 16 mi/26 km NNE of Ottawa; 41°31′N 88°41′W. In agr. area. Sheridan Correctional Center here. **2** village (1990 pop. 730), Montcalm co., central Mich., 6 mi/9.7 km S of Stanton; 43°12′N 85°04′W. In farm area. Mfg. (injection molded plastics). **3** village (1990 pop. 652), Madison co., SW Mont., on Mill Creek, and 40 mi/64 km SSE of Butte; 45°28′N 112°11′W. Cattle, sheep, horses, oats, potatoes, hay. Silver, lead, gold mined in Tobacco Root Mts. to NE. Beaverhead Natl. Forest to NE; Ruby Range to S. Robbers Roost to SE. **4** village (1990 pop. 400), Chautauqua co., extreme W N.Y., 5 mi/8 km E of Dunkirk; 42°29′N 79°14′W. Canned foods, paving material. **5** uninc. village, Millcreek township, Lebanon co., SE central Pa., 11 mi/18 km E of Lebanon, on Mill Creek; 40°21′N 76°13′W. **6** uninc. village (1990 pop. 225), Colorado co., S Texas, 17 mi/27 km SW of Columbus. Oil and natural gas center. Agr. area (cotton, soybeans, peanuts). Mfg. (gasoline processing).

Sheridan Beach, uninc. town (1990 pop. 6,518), King co., W Wash., residential suburb, 10 mi/16 km NNE of downtown Seattle, at N end of L. Washington, at mouth of McAleer Creek; 47°45′N 122°17′W.

Sheridan, Cape, NE extremity of Ellesmere Isl., NE Franklin dist., N.W.T., Canada, on Lincoln Sea of the Arctic Ocean, at NW entrance of Robeson Channel; 82°27′N 61°27′W. The *Alert* of the Nares expedition wintered here 1875–1876; Peary's expedition vessel, the *Roosevelt*, wintered here 1905–1906 and again 1908–1909. Notes left by Peary (1906) in a cairn were found by U.S. icebreakers in 1948.

Sheridan, Mount, Wyo.: see RED MOUNTAINS.

Sherman 1 county (□ 1,056 sq mi/2,735 sq km; 1990 pop. 6,926), NW Kansas, on Colo. (W) state line; ⊙ Goodland; 39°21′N 101°43′W. Gently rolling agr. area; watered by North Fork Smoky Hill R. (S) and by headstreams of Beaver and Sappa creeks. Wheat, corn; cattle. Border bet. Mountain and Central time zones follows N and E co. boundaries. Sheridan State Fishing L. in S. **2** county (□ 571 sq mi/1,479 sq km; 1990 pop. 3,718), central Nebr.; ⊙ Loup City; 41°13′N 98°58′W. Farming region drained by Middle Loup R. Corn, alfalfa; cattle, hogs, dairying. Sherman Reservoir and State Recreation Area in NE; Bowman L. State Recreation Area at center. Formed 1873. **3** county (□ 831 sq mi/2,152 sq km; 1990 pop. 1,918), N Oregon; ⊙ Moro; 45°24′N 120°41′W. Bounded on N by Columbia R. (forms Wash. state boundary), on W by Deschutes R., on E by John Day R. Agr. (wheat, oats, barley; poultry, cattle). Part of Deschutes R. State Recreation Area in W; part of John Day State Scenic Waterway in E. Columbia R. forms L. Celilo Reservoir up to John Day Dam, which forms L. Umatilla Reservoir. Formed 1889. **4** county (□ 923 sq mi/2,391 sq km; 1990 pop. 2,858), extreme N Texas; ⊙ Stratford; 36°16′N 101°53′W. Elev. c.3,100 ft/945 m–3,800 ft/1,158 m. In high Panhandle plains, and bounded N by Okla. border. Drained by N Canadian R. (Beaver), and Coldwater and Frisco creeks (all streams intermittent). Large-scale grain farming; beef cattle; silage, corn, sorghum, wheat, pinto beans. Natural-gas wells; some oil. Formed 1876.

Sherman, city (1990 pop. 31,601), ⊙ Grayson co., N Texas, 58 mi/93 km NNE of Dallas, near the Red R.; 33°37′N 96°36′W. Elev. 728 ft/222 m. Originally on a stagecoach route, it is a highway and RR junction. Mfg. (electronic equip.; meat and food processing, military equip.; metal prods.). Austin Col. is in Sherman, Grayson Community Col. to N. Hagerman Natl. Wildlife Refuge to NW (on arm of L. Texoma). Est. 1846, site moved E, 1848. Inc. 1858.

Sherman 1 town (1990 pop. 2,809), Fairfield co., W Conn., bet. N.Y. line and L. Candlewood, 13 mi/21 km N of Danbury; 41°34′N 73°30′W. Agr. **2** town (1990 pop. 1,027), Aroostook co., E central Maine, 34 mi/55 km SW of Houlton, in Molunkus Stream valley; 45°53′N 68°21′W. Farming, lumbering, hunting, fishing. Includes villages of Sherman Mills. **3** town (1990 pop. 528), Pontotoc and Union cos. border, N Miss., 12 mi/19 km NE of Pontotoc; 34°21′N 88°50′W. Agr. (cotton, corn, soybeans; cattle; dairying; timber). Mfg. (plastic prods., furniture, foam fabrication). **4** town (1990 pop. 66), Minnehaha co., E S.Dak., 20 mi/32 km NE of Sioux Falls, near Minn. line, on Pipestone Creek; 43°45′N 96°28′W.

Sherman 1 village (1990 pop. 2,080), Sangamon co., central Ill., suburb 7 mi/11.3 km NNE of Springfield, on Sangamon R.; 39°53′N 89°36′W. Agr. area; light mfg. **2** village (1990 pop. 694), Chautauqua co., extreme W N.Y., 19 mi/31 km WNW of Jamestown; 42°09′N 79°35′W.

Sherman Air Force Base, NE Kansas; the oldest military post in continuous operation (since 1827) W of the Mississippi R. Adjoins Leavenworth, a federal penitentiary. Mus. with artifacts.

Sherman, Mount, peak (14,036 ft/4,278 m) in Park Range, Park and Lake cos., central Colo., 7 mi/11.3 km ESE of Leadville; 39°13′N 106°10′W. Mosquito Pass (13,186 ft/4,019 m) to N.

Sherman Oaks, suburban residential sect., Los Angeles co., S Calif., in San Fernando Valley, 14 mi/23 km NW of downtown Los Angeles. Light mfg. Santa Monica Mts. Natl. Recreation Area to SW; Stone Canyon Reservoir to S; Encino Reservoir and Los Encinos State Historical Park to W.

Sherrard, village (1990 pop. 697), Mercer co., NW Ill., 12 mi/19 km SSE of Rock Island; 41°19′N 90°30′W. In agr. area.

Sherridon, town, W Man., Canada, on Kississing L., 40 mi/64 km NE of Flin Flon; 55°07′N 101°05′W. Copper-mining center, largely replaced in early 1950s by Lynn L. copper-nickel center, 120 mi/193 km N.

Sherrill, city (□ 1 sq mi/2.6 sq km; 1990 pop. 2,864), Oneida co., central N.Y., near Oneida Creek, 12 mi/19 km SSW of Rome; 43°04′N 75°35′W. Mfg. (pumps). Inc. 1916.

Sherrill, town (1990 pop. 148), Dubuque co., E Iowa, 8 mi/12.9 km NW of Dubuque; 42°36′N 90°46′W.

Sherrill, village (1990 pop. 55), Jefferson co., central Ark.,

11 mi/18 km NNE of Pine Bluff; 34°22′N 91°57′W. Tucker Correctional Unit, 5 mi/8 km to NE.

Sherrils Ford (SHER-uhls), uninc. town (1990 pop. 3,185), Catawba co., W central N.C., 14 mi/23 km ESE of Newton, near W shore of L. Norman reservoir (Catawba R.); 35°34′N 80°59′W. Agr. area (grain, soybeans, sorghum; chickens, cattle, hogs, dairying). Recreation area. Mfg. (car-washing equip., signs).

Sherrodsville, village (1990 pop. 284), Carroll co., E Ohio, 21 mi/34 km SSE of Canton, and on small Conotton Creek and Leesville L.; 40°29′N 81°14′W.

Sherwood, city (1990 pop. 18,893), Pulaski co., central Ark., suburb 5 mi/8 km NE of downtown adjacent to North Little Rock; 34°49′N 92°12′W. Mfg. (boats, metal chimney caps, labels). Camp Joseph T. Robinson Natl. Guard Training Base to NW.

Sherwood 1 town (1990 pop. 3,093), Washington co., NW Oregon, suburb 13 mi/21 km SW of Portland; 45°21′N 122°50′W. Agr. (vegetables, nuts, berries; poultry); dairy prods. Mfg. (walnut and filbert processing, pallets, hide tanning, wood-fired boilers). **2** town (1990 pop. 837), Calumet Co., E Wis., 6 mi/9.7 km SE of Appleton, on L. Winnebago; 44°10′N 88°16′W. Dairying, grain, vegetables, fruit. High Cliff State Park to SW.

Sherwood 1 village (1990 pop. 320), Branch co., S Mich., 13 mi/21 km NW of Coldwater; 42°00′N 85°14′W. In farm area. **2** village (1990 pop. 286), Renville co., N N.Dak., port of entry, 15 mi/24 km N of Mohall, near Can. border; 48°57′N 101°37′W. **3** village (1990 pop. 828), Defiance co., NW Ohio, on Maumee R., and 10 mi/16 km W of Defiance in farming area; 41°17′N 84°33′W. **4** village, Franklin co., S Tenn., 34 mi/55 km W of Chattanooga, in the Cumberlands, 35°05′N 85°56′W. **5** uninc. village (1990 est. pop. 73), Texas, Irion co., 23 mi/37 km SW of San Angelo, 2 mi/3.2 km NE of Mertzon. Livestock region. Historic courthouse here. Co. seat 1889–1936.

Sherwood Forest, village, Anne Arundel co., central Md., on Severn R., 5 mi/8 km NW of Annapolis.

Sherwood, Lake, reservoir, Ventura co., S Calif., on Malibu Creek, 2 mi/3.2 km SW of Thousand Oaks, at N edge of Santa Monica Mts. Natl. Recreation Area; 34°08′N 118°50′W.

Shetek, Lake (she-TEK), Murray co., SW Minn., 8 mi/12.9 km NNE of Slayton; 7 mi/11.3 km long, 2 mi/3.2 km wide; 44°06′N 94°41′W. Fed from NE and drained to SE by Des Moines R. Summer resorts. L. Shetek State Park on E shore.

Shetucket River, E Conn., formed at Willimantic by junction of Willimantic and Natchaug rivers; flows c.25 mi/40 km SE and S to the Thames at Norwich; receives Quinebaug R. 4 mi/6.4 km NE of mouth.

Shevlin (SHEV-lin), village (1990 pop. 157), Clearwater co., NW Minn., 18 mi/29 km W of Bemidji, and 7 mi/11.3 km E of Bagley, near Clearwater R.; 47°31′N 95°15′W. Dairying; livestock; grain.

Sheyenne (shei-AN), village (1990 pop. 272), Eddy co., central N.Dak., 11 mi/18 km N of New Rockford, and on Sheyenne R.; 47°49′N 99°07′W. Devils L. Sioux Indian Reservation just N.

Sheyenne River (shei-AN), 325 mi/523 km long; N.Dak.; rises in Sheridan co. in central N.Dak.; flows E through Sheyenne L., past Harvey, forms S boundary of Devils L. Sioux Indian Reservation then S through L. Ashtabula Reservoir, past Valley City and Lisbon, where it turns NE past Kindred and West Fargo to the Red R. of the North, 10 mi/16 km N of Fargo; 47°41′N 100°25′W.

Shiawassee (shee-uh-WAH-see), county (□ 540 sq mi/ 1,399 sq km; 1990 pop. 69,770), S central Mich.; 42°57′N 84°08′W; ⊙ Corunna. Drained by Shiawassee, Maple, and Looking Glass rivers. Agr. (beans, corn, potatoes; cattle, hogs, sheep, poultry; dairy prods.). Mfg. at Owosso. Organized 1837.

Shiawassee River (shee-uh-WAH-see), c.85 mi/137 km long, S central and E central Mich.; rises in NW Oakland co.; flows NW, past Holly, Fenton, and Owosso, then NNE, past Chesaning, to its confluence with the Tittabawassee to form Saginaw R. just SW of Saginaw

city; 42°43′N 83°30′W. Shiawassee Natl. Wildlife Refuge immediately upstream from Saginaw.

Shickley, village (1990 pop. 360), Fillmore co., SE Nebr., 10 mi/16 km SW of Geneva; 40°25′N 97°43′W. Mfg. (feed supplements).

Shickshinny (SHIK-shi-nee), borough (1990 pop. 1,108), Luzerne co., NE central Pa., 16 mi/26 km WSW of Wilkes-Barre, on Susquehanna R. at mouth of Shickshinny; 41°08′N 76°09′W. Agr. (dairying). Shickshinny Mt. to NE. Shickshinny L. reservoir to NW. Inc. 1861.

Shickshock Mountains, range of the Appalachian system, E Que., Canada, a continuation of the Notre Dame Mts., extending c.100 mi/160 km E-W near the N coast of the Gaspé Peninsula. Tabletop Mt., or Mt. Jacques Cartier (4,160 ft/1,268 m), is the highest point in SE Canada.

Shidler (SHEID-luhr), village (1990 pop. 487), Osage co., N Okla., 20 mi/32 km WNW of Pawhuska, on Salt Creek; 36°46′N 96°39′W. Oil and gas wells; petroleum prods.

Shillington (SHIL-ing-tuhn), borough (1990 pop. 5,062), Berks co., SE central Pa., residential suburb 3 mi/4.8 km SW of Reading; 40°17′N 75°58′W. Light mfg.; limestone. Nolde Forest Environmental Education Center. Founded 1860, inc. 1908.

Shilo, Can. Forces Base (1986 pop. 1,183), Canada, located on W boundary of Spruce Woods Provincial Park, 121 mi/195 km W of Winnipeg, Man. NATO artillery training.

Shiloh 1 (SHEI-lo), town (1990 pop. 329), Harris co., Ga., 7 mi/11.3 km W of Warm Springs; 32°49′N 84°42′W. Mfg. (lumber). **2** uninc. town (1990 pop. 8,245), York co., S Pa., residential suburb 4 mi/6.4 km NW of York on Conewago Creek; 39°58′N 76°47′W. Agr. (dairying, livestock, poultry; grain, apples).

Shiloh 1 village (1990 pop. 2,655), St. Clair co., SW Ill., residential suburb of St. Louis, 6 mi/9.7 km NE of Belleville, W of Scott Air Base; 38°32′N 89°54′W. In agr. area (soybeans, wheat, sorghum, hogs; dairying). Bituminous coal in area. **2** village (1990 pop. 778), Richland co., N central Ohio, 17 mi/27 km NNW of Mansfield, and on West Branch of Huron R.; 40°58′N 82°36′W.

Shiloh (SHEI-lo), borough (1990 pop. 408), Cumberland co., SW N.J., 4 mi/6.4 km NW of Bridgeton, in agr. region; 39°27′N 75°17′W.

Shiloh National Military Park (SHEI-lo) (□ 5 sq mi/ 13 sq km), Hardin co., SW Tenn., authorized 1894. Site of the Civil War battle of Shiloh, April 6–7, 1862, which left nearly 24,000 soldiers dead, and left central and W Tenn. in Federal hands. Shiloh Natl. Cemetery is here.

Shiner, town (1990 pop. 2,074), Lavaca co., S Texas, 11 mi/18 km N of Yoakum; 29°25′N 97°10′W. Elev. 350 ft/107 m. In cattle, milo, rice, corn, cotton area; brewery. Mfg. (wine prods., tool and die). Settled 1887, inc. 1890.

Shingle Springs, uninc. town (1990 pop. 2,049), El Dorado co., E central Calif., 30 mi/48 km ENE of Sacramento, near Sawmill Creek; 38°40′N 120°57′W. Timber; cattle, sheep, lambs. Mfg. (lumber).

Shinglehouse (SHING-guhl-haus), borough (1990 pop. 1,243), Potter co., N Pa., 15 mi/24 km NW of Coudersport, on Oswayo Creek; 41°58′N 78°11′W. Agr. (corn, potatoes; dairying); timber. Mfg. (lumber, concrete blocks); gas and oil wells. Settled 1808, inc. 1902.

Shinnecock Bay (SHIN-nuh-kak), inlet of the Atlantic indenting SE shore of L.I., SE N.Y., W of Southampton; c.12 mi/19 km E-W; max. width c.2.5 mi/4 km; 40°51′N 72°29′W. Sheltered from ocean by barrier beach, which is pierced by Shinnecock Inlet 6 mi/9.7 km WSW of Southampton. Connected with Great Peconic Bay (N) by Shinnecock Canal (c.1 mi/1.6 km long; partly a land cut; crossed by highway bridges). Resort area; yachting; duck hunting.

Shinnecock Hills (SHIN-nuh-kak), low rolling region of SE L.I. (□ 6 sq mi/15.5 sq km; 1990 pop. 2,847), Suffolk co., SE N.Y., bet. Great Peconic Bay (N) and Shinnecock Bay, c.4 mi/6.4 km W of Southampton; 40°53′N 72°27′W. Shinnecock Indian Reservation is here.

Shinnston (SHIN-stuhn), town (1990 pop. 2,543), Harrison co., N W.Va., on the West Fork R., 8 mi/12.9 km N of Clarksburg; 39°23′N 80°17′W. Bituminous coal; gas; oil. Mfg. (concrete, mining equip., meat processing, crushed stone, stainless steel fabricating). Agr. (corn); cattle; poultry. Settled 1818.

Shiocton (shi-AWK-tuhn), town (1990 pop. 913), Outagamie co., E Wis., on Wolf R., and 15 mi/24 km NW of Appleton; 44°27′N 88°34′W. Vegetable canning (sauerkraut and sauerkraut juice).

Ship Bottom, resort borough (1990 pop. 1,352), Ocean co., E N.J., on Long Beach isl. (here bridged to mainland), and 20 mi/32 km S of Toms River; 39°38′N 74°10′W.

Ship Island, Harrison co., SE Miss., in the Gulf of Mexico, in isl. chain (Gulf Isls.) lying bet. Mississippi Sound (N) and Chandeleur Sound (S), 11 mi/18 km S of Biloxi; c.8 mi/12.9 km long. A lighthouse (30°13′N 88°58′W), old Fort Massachusetts (built just before Civil War; later destroyed and rebuilt), and a former quarantine station are here. Surfing, swimming, boating. Was a port of entry for Fr. and Span. vessels from end of 17th cent. to 1720s. Isl. was held alternately by Union and Confederate forces in Civil War. To W is deepwater channel (Ship Isl. Pass) connecting the gulf (passenger ferries) with harbors of Biloxi, Gulfport, and other ports. Part of Gulf Islands Natl. Seashore.

Ship Island, islet, E N.F., Canada, on W side of Bonavista Bay, 25 mi/40 km WNW of Cape Bonavista; 48°45′N 53°39′W.

Ship Shoal Island, barrier isl., Northampton co., E Va., off Atlantic Coast of Delmarva (E Shore) peninsula, 12 mi/19 km ESE of Cape Charles town; 3 mi/4.8 km long, 1 mi/1.6 km wide. New Inlet and Wreck Isl. to N, Ship Shoal Inlet and Myrtle Isl. to S, South Bay to W.

Shipley, village, Anne Arundel co., central Md., 7 mi/11.3 km SSW of downtown Baltimore. Also called Shipley Heights.

Shipman 1 village (1990 pop. 624), Macoupin co., SW Ill., 17 mi/27 km NNE of Alton; 39°07′N 90°02′W. Agr. (cattle, hogs; corn, wheat, soybeans, sorghum); bituminous coal. **2** uninc. village, Nelson co., central Va., 3 mi/4.8 km SSE of Lovingston; 37°43′N 78°50′W. Mfg. (wooden ties). Agr. (apples, grain; cattle).

Shippensburg (SHI-pens-buhrg), borough (1990 pop. 5,331), Cumberland and Franklin cos., S Pa., 11 mi/ 18 km NE of Chambersburg; 40°02′N 77°31′W. RR junction. Agr. area (grain, soybeans, apples; poultry, livestock; dairying). Mfg. (wooden, plastic, and food prods.; printing and publishing; fertilizers, iron castings, apparel, heavy construction equip.; vacuum pumps, crushed limestone). Seat of Shippensburg Univ. of Pa. Shippensburg Airport to E. Letterkenny Army Depot to SW. Appalachian Trail, in Michaux State Forest to SE. Settled 1733, inc. 1819.

Shippenville (SHI-pen-vil), borough (1990 pop. 474), Clarion co., W central Pa., 5 mi/8 km NW of Clarion, on Deer Creek; 41°15′N 79°27′W. Agr. (dairying). Mfg. (utility trailers, mobile homes, fiber drums, lumber); bituminous coal.

Shippigan (SHI-pi-guhn), town (1991 pop. 2,760), NE N.B., Canada, fishing port on Shippigan Sound, bet. the Gulf of St. Lawrence and Chaleur Bay, 45 mi/72 km ENE of Bathurst, opposite Shippigan Isl.; 47°44′N 64°42′W. Cod, herring, mackerel, lobster. Also spelled Shippagan or Shippegan.

Shippigan Island, in the Gulf of St. Lawrence at entrance of Chaleur Bay, just off NE N.B., Canada, across narrow Shippigan Sound; 13 mi/21 km long, 8 mi/13 km wide; 47°47′N 64°36′W. Just N is Miscou Isl. Fishing industries: clam, lobster, mackerel, herring, and cod fisheries, and oyster beds.

Shippingport (SHI-ping-port), borough (1990 pop. 227), Beaver co., W Pa., 8 mi/12.9 km WSW of Beaver, on Ohio R.; 40°37′N 80°25′W. Agr. (corn, hay; livestock, dairying). Nuclear power plant to NE.

Shiprock, city (1990 pop. 7,687), San Juan co., extreme NW N.Mex., 24 mi/39 km W of Farmington, on San Juan R., Chuska Mts. to SW, in Navajo Indian Reservation; 36°47′N 108°42′W. Oil, coal, and natural-gas fields in vicinity. Shiprock Peak (7,178 ft/2,188 m), prominent rock mass that rises 1,400 ft/427 m above landscape, is 10 mi/16 km SW. Ute Mt. Indian Reservation (Colo., N.Mex.) to N and NE; 15 mi/24 km S of Colo. state border; 18 mi/29 km E of Ariz. state border; Four Corners, common point to 4 states (N.Mex., Ariz., Colo., Utah) 23 mi/37 km to NW.

Shipshaw River (SHIP-shoh), S Que., Canada; flows c.100 mi/161 km S to the Saguenay near Kenogami. Hydroelectric plant.

Shipshewana, town (1990 pop. 524), Lagrange co., NE Ind., 9 mi/14.5 km WNW of Lagrange; 41°40′N 85°35′W. In farm area. Mfg. (transportation equip.; livestock feed). Laid out 1888.

Shipwreck Point, cape on NE coast of P.E.I., Canada, on the Gulf of St. Lawrence, 12 mi/19 km NW of Souris; 46°28′N 62°26′W.

Shiremanstown (SHEI-uhr-muhns-toun), borough (1990 pop. 1,567), Cumberland co., S central Pa., residential suburb, 5 mi/8 km WSW of Harrisburg; 40°13′N 76°57′W. Mfg. (highway signs). Camp Hill State Correctional Inst. to S. Navy Shops Parts Control Center to W.

Shirley 1 town (1990 pop. 817), on Hancock-Henry co. border, E central Ind., 12 mi/19 km WSW of New Castle; 39°53′N 85°35′W. In agr. area. Mfg. (gas turbine engine parts, flour). Laid out 1890. **2** town (1990 pop. 6,118), including Shirley Village, Middlesex co., N Mass., on Nashua R., and 8 mi/12.9 km ESE of Fitchburg; 42°34′N 71°39′W. Mfg. (adhesives). Shaker community est. here 1793. State Prison. Settled c.1720, inc. 1753.

Shirley, village (1990 pop. 363), Van Buren co., N central Ark., c.40 mi/64 km N of Conway, and on Middle Fork of Little Red R.; 35°38′N 92°18′W. In farm area. Mfg. (sunscreen prods.).

Shirley City, Ind.: see WOODBURN.

Shirley Mills, town, Piscataquis co., central Maine, 22 mi/35 km NW of Dover-Foxcroft. Lumbering.

Shirleysburg (SHIR-lees-buhrg), borough (1990 pop. 140), Huntingdon co., S central Pa., 6 mi/9.7 km S of Mount Union, near Aughwick Creek; 40°17′N 77°52′E. Timber. Mfg. (lumber); brick clay. Mount Union Airport to N.

Shishaldin Volcano, (9,372 ft/2,857 m), on central Unimak Isl., SW Alaska, 44 mi/71 km NE of Unimak village; 54°45′N 163°58′W. Mildly active for at least 150 years; several eruptions recorded in recent years.

Shishmaref, village (1990 pop. 456), NW Alaska, on small Sarichet Isl., at entrance of Shishmaref Inlet, NW Seward Peninsula, on Chukchi Sea; 66°09′N 166°08′W. Inuit settlement.

Shishmaref Inlet, bay, NW Alaska, on NW Seward Peninsula, on Chukchi Sea; 10 mi/16 km long, 9 mi/14.5 km wide; 66°09′N 165°49′W. Inuit settlers in region. Shishmaref village on Sarichet Isl. at entrance of bay.

Shively (SHEIV-lee), city (1990 pop. 15,535), Jefferson co., N central Ky., residential suburb, 5 mi/8 km SW of downtown Louisville; 38°12′N 85°48′W. Mfg. (wine and vinegar). Settled c.1885, inc. 1938.

Shivwits Plateau, Mohave co., NW Ariz., N of Colorado R., W of Uinkaret Plateau, and E of Nevada border; tableland c.7,000 ft/2,134 m high. W escarpment is Grand Wash Cliffs.

Shoal Bay, Canada: see THURLOW ISLANDS.

Shoal Creek 1 c.75 mi/121 km long, in SW Ill.; formed SW of Greenville by junction of East Fork (c.40 mi/64 km long) and Middle Fork (c.45 mi/72 km long), both rising in SW central Ill.; flows S and SW to Kaskaskia R. 8 mi/12.9 km SE of New Baden; 39°05′N 89°32′W. West Fork (c.30 mi/48 km long) enters Middle Fork S of Hillsboro. **2** c.75 mi/121 km long, in Tenn. and Ala.; rises in Lawrence co., S Tenn., meanders generally S past Lawrenceburg, into NW Ala., to L. Wilson 5 mi/8 km NE of Wilson Dam.

Shoal Creek Drive, village (1990 pop. 296), Newton co., SW Mo., residential suburb 5 mi/8 km S of Joplin; 37°02′N 94°31′W. Inc. 1958.

Shoal Lake, village (1991 pop. 784), SW Man., Canada, on Shoal L. (6 mi/10 km long), 50 mi/80 km NW of

Brandon; 50°26′N 100°35′W. Grain elevators; lumbering; dairying. Resort.

Shoal River, c.45 mi/72 km long, NW Fla.; rises 12 mi/19 km N of De Funiak Springs in Walton co.; flows WSW to Yellow R. 8 mi/12.9 km SW of Crestview in Okaloosa co.

Shoals, town (1990 pop. 853), ⊙ Martin co., SW Ind., on East Fork of White R., 21 mi/34 km E of Washington; 38°40′N 86°47′W. Forested area; lumber milling; gypsum; mfg. of plaster and wallboard. Marlin State Forest and Hoosier Natl. Forest nearby; Hindostan Falls State Fishing Area to SW. Settled 1816, inc. c.1845.

Shoals, Isles of, Maine and N.H.: see ISLES OF SHOALS.

Shoemakersville (SHOO-mai-kuhrs-vil), borough (1990 pop. 1,443), Berks co., E central Pa., 11 mi/18 km NNW of Reading, on Pigeon Creek, near Schuylkill R.; 40°30′N 75°58′E. Agr. (grain, soybeans; livestock; dairying); mfg. (bricks, furniture, electrical equip., apparel, and textiles). Founded 1833.

Shokan (SHO-kuhn), resort village (1990 pop. 680), Ulster co., SE N.Y., in the Catskills, on Ashokan Reservoir, 12 mi/19 km WNW of Kingston; 41°58′N 74°13′W.

Sholes, village (1990 pop. 22), Wayne co., NE Nebr., 15 mi/24 km WNW of Wayne; 42°20′N 97°17′W.

Shongaloo (SHAWN-guh-loo) [Choctaw = cypress tree], town (1990 pop. 161), Webster parish, La., 10 mi/16 km SE of Springhill; 32°56′N 93°18′W. Oil and gas field nearby.

Shooters Hill, village, Manchester parish, S central Jamaica, 20 mi/32 km WNW of May Pen; 18°05′N 77°28′W. Spice processing.

Shooters Island, at entrance to Newark Bay from Kill Van Kull, just off N shore of Staten Isl., Richmond co., SE N.Y.; part of Staten Isl. borough of N.Y. city; 40°39′N 74°09′W.

Shore Acres, Mass.: see SCITUATE.

Shoreacres, village, S B.C., Canada, on Kootenay R. at mouth of Slocan R., 12 mi/19 km WSW of Nelson; 49°26′N 117°32′W. In lumbering and mining (gold, silver, tungsten) region.

Shoreacres, town (1990 pop. 1,316), Harris co., SE Texas, residential suburb 18 mi/29 km SE of Houston, on Galveston Bay; 29°37′N 95°00′W. Recreation.

Shoreham (SHOR-uhm), town (1990 pop. 1,115), Addison co., W Vt., on L. Champlain, 12 mi/19 km SW of Middlebury; in agr. area known for apples; 43°53′N 73°18′W. Levi P. Morton b. here. Chartered 1761, settled after Amer. Revolution.

Shoreham 1 (shah-ruhm), village (1990 pop. 737), Berrien co., extreme SW Mich., suburb 2 mi/3.2 km SW of St. Joseph, on L. Michigan; 42°03′N 86°30′W. **2** village (1990 pop. 540), Suffolk co., SE N.Y., near N shore of L.I., 8 mi/12.9 km E of Port Jefferson; 40°57′N 72°54′W. In summer recreational shore area. Agr. includes vegetables and poultry. Just N is Shoreham Beach, resort village.

Shoreham Beach, N.Y.: see SHOREHAM.

Shoreham Nuclear Power Facility, Suffolk co., SE N.Y., N shore of L.I., 60 mi/97 km E of Manhattan; 40°57′N 72°53′W. Plant proposed in 1960, built 1973–1984, but a dispute between owner/operator L.I. Lighting Company (LILCO) and the co. and state over emergency evacuation plans led to the plant being closed before it ever went into commercial operation. In 1992, after years of legal and political wrangling, LILCO sold the facility to N.Y. state, which bought it with the intention of making sure it never opened. It took 2 years and $185 million to deactivate the site—the 1st commercial reactor in the U.S. to be dismantled—and 353 truckloads and 5 million pounds/2.3 million kg of radioactive waste were shipped to burial and reprocessing sites in S.C. and Tenn. With transmission lines in place, and a saltwater harbor nearby, Shoreham has the potential for producing thermal electricity, but nothing has yet been decided.

Shoreline Park, uninc. town (1990 pop. 2,775), Hancock co., SE Miss., residential suburb 6 mi/9.7 km NW of Bay St. Louis, near Jordan R.; 30°19′N 89°24′W. Cotton, corn, pecans.

Shoreview, city (1990 pop. 24,587), Ramsey co., SE

Minn., suburb 7 mi/11.3 km NW of St. Paul and 8 mi/12.9 km NE of Minneapolis; 45°04′N 93°08′W. Drained by Rice Creek in NW. Mfg. (furniture, machinery, metal prods., light mfg.). Developed around 7 natural lakes, includes Turtle L. in N, L. Owasso on S boundary. Its pop. more than doubled bet. 1970 and 1990. Numerous small lakes in vicinity. Settled 1850, set off from Mounds View and inc. 1957.

Shorewood, city (1990 pop. 14,116), Milwaukee co., SE Wis., bet. the Milwaukee R. and L. Michigan, suburb 3 mi/4.8 km NE of Milwaukee; 43°05′N 87°53′W. Univ. of Wis. immediately S. It is mostly residential. Settled c. 1835, inc. 1900.

Shorewood, town (1990 pop. 5,917), Hennepin co., E Minn., residential suburb 17 mi/27 km WSW of Minneapolis, on S shore of L. Minnetonka; 44°55′N 93°34′W. Christmas L. to SE.

Shorewood, village (1990 pop. 6,264), Will co., suburb 3 mi/4.8 km W of Joliet, on Du Page R.; 41°31′N 88°12′W. Agr. area; mfg. (medical equip., concrete, electronic equip.).

Shorewood Hills, village (1990 pop. 1,680), Dane co., S Wis., suburb 3 mi/4.8 km W of Madison, on L. Mendota; 43°04′N 89°27′W. At W end of Univ. of Wis. campus. Residential. Inc. 1927.

Short Beach, village, New Haven co., S Conn., 6 mi/9.7 km SE of New Haven. A postal dist. of Branford.

Short Hills 1 N.J.: see MILLBURN. **2** Pa. and Md.: see SOUTH MOUNTAIN.

Shortsville, village (1990 pop. 1,485), Ontario co., W central N.Y., 25 mi/40 km SE of Rochester, in Finger Lakes region; 42°57′N 77°13′W. Light mfg. Inc. 1889.

Shoshone, county (□ 2,635 sq mi/6,825 sq km; 1990 pop. 13,931), N Idaho; ⊙ Wallace; 47°21′N 115°54′W. Mining and lumbering area bounded on E by Mont., boundary formed by Bitterroot Range, also forms boundary bet. Pacific and Mountain time zones, and crossed by Coeur d'Alene (source of North Fork of Clearwater R. in SE corner) and St. Joe rivers. Includes Coeur d'Alene mining dist., in Coeur d'Alene Mts., and parts of Coeur d'Alene (N) and St. Joe (center S and SE) natl. forests. Lead, silver, zinc, copper; little agr., some cattle. Silver Mt. Ski Area in W corner; Hobo Cedar Grove Botanical Area in SW. Formed 1858.

Shoshone, town (1990 pop. 1,249), ⊙ Lincoln co., S Idaho, on Little Wood R., 25 mi/40 km N of Twin Falls, in valley of Snake R.; 42°57′N 114°24′W. Elev. 3,968 ft/1,209 m. RR junction. Wool-shipping point in irrigated farming area (cattle, sheep; alfalfa, corn, barley, oats). Founded (1882) with coming of RR. At first a cattle town. After construction (1907) of Magic Dam and development of Minidoka irrigation project, village became trade center for productive agr. region. Shoshone Ice Caves and Magic Reservoir to N.

Shoshone Dam, Wyo.: see SHOSHONE RIVER.

Shoshone Falls, in the Snake R., at Twin Falls, on line bet. Jerome and Twin Falls cos., S Idaho; 212 ft/65 m high, 900 ft/274 m wide. Once a great spectacle, the flow of the falls has been reduced by irrigation projects upstream. Known as the "Niagara Falls of the West."

Shoshone Project (shuh-SHO-nee), NW Wyo., near the Mont. line and in the Shoshone R. basin E of Yellowstone Natl. Park. Developed by the U.S. Bureau of Reclamation, it irrigates a large portion of land and has 4 divs. The project is supplied by diversion dams and canals and by Buffalo Bill Dam (325 ft/99 m high; completed 1910), which has a power plant. The power system is integrated with the Missouri River Basin Project.

Shoshone Range (shuh-SHO-nee), central Nev.; mostly in Lander co., extends S into Nye co., W of Toiyabe Range and Reese R., in Toiyabe Natl. Forest; 40°43′N 116°50′W. Gold, silver mines. North Shoshone Peak (10,313 ft/3,143 m) and South Shoshone Peak (10,052 ft/3,064 m) are chief elevs. Shoshone Range continues NNE across Reese R. Includes Mt. Lewis (9,683 ft/2,951 m).

Shoshone River (shuh-SHO-nee), NW Wyo.; rises in 2 branches in Absaroka Range. North Fork, c.55 mi/89 km long; rises in E part of Yellowstone Natl. Park, Park co., Wyo.; flows E to Buffalo Bill Reservoir. South

Fork rises in SW Park co., flows NE c.65 mi/105 km (joining North Fork at reservoir); main river flows c.80 mi/129 km NE, past Cody and Lovell, to Bighorn R (Bighorn L. reservoir) 10 mi/16 km E of Lovell, near Mont. line. Chief crops in river valley are sugar beets, grain, beans. Shoshone power and irrigation project on river includes 161,654 acres/65,421 ha. Consists of system of canals and dams; Buffalo Bill (formerly Shoshone) Dam is largest; concrete dam 325 ft/99 m high, 200 ft/61 m long; finished 1910; forms Shoshone Reservoir (c.10 mi/16 km long, 4 mi/6.4 km wide). Project serves Cody, Powell, and Lovell.

Shoshoni (shuh-SHO-nee), village (1990 pop. 497), Fremont co., central Wyo., near Bighorn R. (site of Boysen Reservoir), 42 mi/68 km NE of Lander; 43°14′N 108°05′W. Elev. 4,820 ft/1,469 m. Sheep. Large Wind R. Indian Reservation 1 mi/1.6 km to W; Boysen State Park to N.

Show Low, town (1990 pop. 5,019), Navajo co., E Ariz., 45 mi/72 km S of Holbrook, in Apache-Sitgreaves Natl. Forest; 34°14′N 110°02′W. Elev. 6,331 ft/1,930 m. Cattle, sheep, hogs; corn, alfalfa; mfg. (farm fencing, printing and publishing, sawmills, concrete); timber. Fish hatchery to NE; Show Low L. to S; N of Mogollon Rim escarpment; Fort Apache Indian Reservation to S.

Shreve (shreev), village (1990 pop. 1,584), Wayne co., N central Ohio, 9 mi/14 km SSW of Wooster; 40°41′N 82°01′W. In gas and oil producing area.

Shreveport (SHREEV-port), city (1990 pop. 198,525),⊙ Caddo parish, NW La., 180 mi/290 km NW of Baton Rouge and 175 mi/282 km ESE of Dallas, Texas, on the Red R. near the Texas and Ark. state lines; 32°28′N 93°48′W. The 3d-largest city in the state, it is a regional oil and natural gas center, with important metal, cotton, and lumber manufactures. Mfg. (plastic injections, tools, telephones and equip., concrete and plastic prods., pumps, pipe prods., airfoil fans, fabricated steel plate, aluminum castings, gas compressors, vehicle assembly plant, pharmaceuticals, bldg. materials, pasta), printing and publishing. Downtown Airport N of downtown and Shreveport Regional Airport 5 mi/8 km SW of downtown. The city was founded after the Red R. was laboriously cleared (1833–1836) of logs and driftwood, using specially designed snag boats invented by Henry Shreve, which rendered it navigable. The city became the Confederate capital of La. in 1863. The discovery of oil in 1906 provided the greatest impetus for Shreveport's growth. It is the seat of Centenary Col., Southern Univ. at Shreveport, La. State Univ. in Shreveport, the La. State Univ. School of Medicine in Shreveport, and the state fairgrounds. Annual events include the La. State Fair and State Exhibit Mus. Of interest are the ruins of Confederate Fort Humbug, which was defended with fake cannons; Pioneer Heritage Center; Meadow Mus. of Indochinese Art; Norton Art Gallery. Barksdale Air Force Base, hq. of the 2d U.S. Air Force and a strategic command installation, is just across the river, to E in Bossier City (twin city to Shreveport). Cross L., in NW part of city, has parks and recreational facilities. Inc. 1839. Formerly called Shreve Town and Shreve's Landing.

Shrewsbury (SHROOZ-ber-ee), city (1990 pop. 6,416), St. Louis co., E Mo., suburb 7 mi/11.3 km SW of downtown St. Louis; 38°35′N 90°19′W. Mfg. (ink, drilling rigs). Kenrick Seminary; majority of the large seminary campus was developed into commercial and residential area in early 1980s.

Shrewsbury 1 (SHROOZ-buh-ree), uninc. town, Jefferson parish, SE La., suburb 7 mi/11 km NW of New Orleans, between Mississippi R. (S) and L. Pontchartrain (N); 29°58′N 90°08′W. **2** town (1990 pop. 24,146), Worcester co., suburb, Worcester, central Mass.; 42°17′N 71°43′W. Plastic goods, furniture, candy, fire alarm systems, and textiles are manufactured. Gen. Artemas Ward was b. here. Skiing. Site of Spags Store, regional landmark. Lake Quinsigamond State Park nearby. Inc. 1727. **3** town (1990 pop. 1,107), Rutland co., central Vt., 9 mi/14.5 km SE of Rutland; 43°32′N

72°50′W. Dairy prods.; winter sports center. Includes Cuttingsville village.

Shrewsbury 1 (SHROOZ-BE-ree), borough (1990 pop. 3,096), Monmouth co., E N.J., near head of Shrewsbury estuary, 12 mi/19 km NE of Freehold; 40°19′N 74°03′W. Has 18th-cent. church. Settled 1665, inc. 1926. Chiefly residential. **2** (SHROOS-buh-ree), borough (1990 pop. 2,672), York co., S Pa., 14 mi/23 km SSE of York; 39°46′N 76°40′W. Agr. area (grain, apples, soybeans; livestock; poultry; dairying); mfg. (electrical components, concrete, printing and publishing).

Shrewsbury River (SHROOZ-BE-ree), NE N.J., short stream entering navigable estuary (c.8 mi/12.9 km long) that extends ENE from Oceanport (head of navigation) to junction with Navesink R. estuary at entrance to passage to Sandy Hook Bay (N). Monmouth Beach, Sea Bright, and other resorts are on sandy peninsula sheltering estuary from the Atlantic.

Shrine Pass, Colo.: see GORE RANGE.

Shubenacadie (shoo-beh-NA-kuh-dee), village, central N.S., Canada, on Shubenacadie R., and 20 mi/32 km SSW of Truro; 45°05′N 63°24′W. Dairying and lumbering center. Center of Micmac Indian settlements of central N.S.

Shubenacadie Lake (7 mi/11 km long, 2 mi/3 km wide), S central N.S., Canada, 16 mi/26 km N of Halifax. Drained by Shubenacadie R.

Shubenacadie River, central N.S., Canada; issues from Shubenacadie L. 16 mi/26 km N of Halifax; flows 45 mi/72 km N to Cobequid Bay 12 mi/19 km WSW of Truro.

Shubert, village (1990 pop. 237), Richardson co., SE Nebr., 13 mi/21 km N of Falls City, near Missouri R.; 40°14′N 95°40′W. Grain.

Shubuta (shuh-BOO-tuh), village (1990 pop. 577), Clarke co., E Miss., 35 mi/56 km S of Meridian, and on Chickasawhay R.; 31°51′N 88°42′W. Agr. (cotton, corn; cattle); mfg. (laminated wooden beams, weight scales).

Shueyville, village (1990 pop. 223), Johnson co., E central Iowa, 8 mi/12.9 km S of Cedar Rapids; 41°51′N 91°39′W. Coralville Reservoir to SE. Hogs, cattle; corn.

Shuksan, Mount (SHUHK-sin), peak (9,127 ft/2,782 m), Whatcom co., N Wash., in Cascade Range, in North Cascades Natl. Park, c.40 mi/64 km ENE of Bellingham; 10 mi/16 km ENE of Mt. Baker; 11 mi/18 km S of Can. (B.C.) border; 48°49′N 121°36′W.

Shulaps Peak (SHOO-laps) (9,450 ft/2,880 m), S B.C., Canada, in Coast Mts., 120 mi/193 km NNE of Vancouver.

Shullsburg, town (1990 pop. 1,236), Lafayette co., S Wis., on a branch of Galena R., and 23 mi/37 km ENE of Dubuque (Iowa); 42°34′N 90°13′W. In dairy-farming area; cheese. Charles Mound, highest point in Illinois (1,235 ft/376 m) 6 mi/9.7 km S. Inc. 1889.

Shumagin Islands, SW Alaska, group of c.20 isls. and islets in N Pacific off S coast of Alaska Peninsula; 54°54′–55°20′N 159°15′–160°45′W. Largest isls. are Unga, Popof, and Nagai. Covered by low scrub alder and willow; mild, damp climate. Cod fishing and canning. Explored by Vitus Bering in 1741.

Shumway, village (1990 pop. 243), Effingham co., SE central Ill., 7 mi/11.3 km NW of Effingham; 39°10′N 88°39′W. In agr. area.

Shungnak (SHOOG-nak), village (1990 pop. 223), NW Alaska, on Kobuk R.; 66°54′N 157°08′W.

Shungopavi, Indian pueblo, Navajo co., NE Ariz., on high mesa, 55 mi/89 km N of Winslow, in Hopi Indian Reservation. Elev. 6,560 ft/1,999 m. Also spelled Shungopavy or Shongopovi.

Shuqualak (SHUG-uh-lahk), village (1990 pop. 570), Noxubee co., E Miss., 9 mi/14.5 km S of Macon; 32°58′N 88°34′W. Agr. (cotton, grain, soybeans; cattle; dairying); mfg. (lumber, work gloves).

Shushanna Junction, Alaska: see MCCARTHY.

Shushartie (shoo-SHAHR-tee), village, SW B.C., Canada, on extreme N Vancouver Isl., on Queen Charlotte Strait, 45 mi/72 km WNW of Alert Bay; 50°51′N 127°51′W. Lumbering.

Shuswap Lake (SHOOS-wahp) (□ 123 sq mi/ 319 sq km), S B.C., Canada, 35 mi/56 km W of Revelstoke; 87 mi/140 km long, including Seymour and Anstey arms (NE) and Salmon Arm (S); 1 mi/2 km–3 mi/ 5 km wide. Receives Shuswap R. (SE); drained W by South Thompson R.

Shuswap River, S B.C., Canada, 160 mi/257 km long; rises in Selkirk Mts. SW of Revelstoke; flows in a wide arc SSE and then N to Mabel L., thence W to Enderby, where it turns N, through Mara L., to Shuswap L. at Sicamous.

Shutesbury, town (1990 pop. 1,561), Franklin co., W central Mass., 12 mi/19 km SE of Greenfield, near Quabbin Reservoir; 42°27′N 72°25′W. Lumber.

Siasconset, Mass.: see NANTUCKET, isl.

Sibanicú (see-bah-nee-KOO), town, Camagüey prov., E Cuba, on Central Highway, and 27 mi/43 km ESE of Camagüey; 21°14′N 77°33′W. Cattle; sugarcane.

Sibley, county (□ 600 sq mi/1,554 sq km; 1990 pop. 14,366), S Minn.; ⊙ Gaylord; 44°34′N 94°13′W. Bounded E by Minnesota R.; drained by Rush R. and High Island Creek. Agr. area (corn, oats, wheat, soybeans, hay, alfalfa, sugar beets, peas; sheep, hogs, cattle, poultry; dairying). Several small lakes in co., esp. N center and NE. Formed 1853.

Sibley, city (1990 pop. 2,815), ⊙ Osceola co., NW Iowa, near Minn. line, 34 mi/55 km NW of Spencer, 17 mi/ 27 km SW of Worthington, Minn.; 43°23′N 95°44′W. RR junction. Highest point in Iowa (1670 ft/509 m) is 6 mi/9.7 km to NE. In livestock, dairy, and farm area; center for some of the chief Iowa cooperatives. Mfg. (powered milk prods.; printing; paper bags and packaging). Named 1872, inc. 1875.

Sibley (SIB-lee), town (1990 pop. 997), Webster parish, NW La., 27 mi/43 km E of Shreveport; 32°33′N 93°17′W. RR junction. In agr. (vegetables; cattle; dairying) and natural gas area; logging; mfg. (gases, propellants). L. Bistineau reservoir to SW (state park).

Sibley, village (1990 pop. 359), Ford co., E central Ill., 18 mi/29 km NW of Paxton; 40°35′N 88°22′W. In rich agr. area.

Sibley Lake (SIB-lee), reservoir, 33 mi/53 km long, Natchitoches parish, W central La., on Cane R., former channel (until 1834) of Red R., 4 mi/6.4 km W of Natchitoches; 31°44′N 93°06′W. Extends SE. Catfish farming.

Siboney (see-bo-NAI), town, Santiago de Cuba prov., E Cuba, on the Caribbean Sea, 9 mi/14.5 km ESE of Santiago de Cuba; 19°54′N 77°42′W. One of the points where Amer. troops disembarked (July 1898) in Span.-Amer. War. Name derived from indigenous group and rich part of Cuban folklore. Beach, swimming.

Sicamous (SI-kuh-moos), village (1991 pop. 2,501), S B.C., Canada, on Shuswap L. at mouth of Shuswap R., 35 mi/56 km WSW of Revelstoke; 50°50′N 119°00′W. Elev. 1,172 ft/357 m. Dairying; lumbering; fruit growing. Just S is Mara L.

Sichomovi, Hopi Indian pueblo, Navajo co., NE Ariz., on a mesa in Hopi Indian Reservation, c.65 mi/105 km NNE of Winslow, W of Polacca. Elev. c.6,200 ft/ 1,890 m. Sometimes spelled Sichomivi or Schomoir.

Sicily Island (SIS-i-lee), village (1990 pop. 421), Catahoula parish, E La., 25 mi/40 km NW of Natchez, Miss; 31°51′N 91°40′W. Called an isl. because of its location on high ground in often-flooded area. Sicily Isl. Hills State Wildlife Area to W.

Sideling Hill, NE-SW ridge (1,600 ft/488 m–2,000 ft/ 610 m), N Md. and S Pa., runs from Potomac R. in W part of Washington co., Md., c.65 mi/105 km NE of Juniata R. just above Mapleton, Pa. Sideling Hill Wildlife Management Area is on the W slope.

Sidell, village (1990 pop. 584), Vermilion co., E Ill., near Little Vermilion R., 17 mi/27 km SSW of Danville; 39°54′N 87°49′W. In agr. and bituminous coal area.

Sidney, village, S Man., Canada, 35 mi/56 km WSW of Portage la Prairie; livestock; grain.

Sidney, town (1991 pop. 10,082), SW B.C., Canada, on SE Vancouver Isl., on Haro Strait, 15 mi/24 km N of Victoria; 48°39′N 123°24′W. Center of lumbering, dairying, and agr. (fruits; poultry; bees) region; boat-building, fruit, salmon, and clam canning, mfg. (bricks, cement, woodworking machinery, paper industry machinery, fabricated metal prods.). Tourism, resort. Victoria Intl. Airport is here. Site of experimental farm and research station, Inst. of Ocean Sciences, and Butchart Gardens. Nearby are fox fur farms. Car ferries to Anacortes, Wash., and Tsawwassan, B.C.

Sidney, city (1990 pop. 18,710), ⊙ Shelby co., W central Ohio, on the Great Miami R.; 40°17′N 84°10′W. In a farm area. Refrigerator parts and machinery are among the items produced here. Founded 1811, inc. 1834.

Sidney 1 town (1990 pop. 167), Kosciusko co., N Ind., 11 mi/18 km SE of Warsaw; 41°06′N 85°44′W. In agr. area. **2** town (1990 pop. 1,253), ⊙ Fremont co., extreme SW Iowa, c.15 mi/24 km W of Shenandoah; 40°45′N 95°38′W. In livestock and corn area; meat processing. Annual championship rodeo held here (Aug.). Waubonsie State Park to SW. Inc. 1870. **3** town (1990 pop. 5,217), ⊙ Richland co., NE Mont., on Yellowstone R., near N.Dak. line, and 49 mi/79 km NNE of Glendive; 47°43′N 104°10′W. Trade center for irrigated agr. area: sugar beets, beans, wheat, barley, corn, hay; cattle, sheep. Mfg (refined beet sugar, horseback riding gear). Little Missouri Natl. Grassland (N.Dak.) to E. Nearby is Three Buttes, colorful scenic spot on edge of badlands region. Mondak Heritage Center and Art Gallery. Inc. 1911. Originally called Eureka. **4** town (1990 pop. 5,959), ⊙ Cheyenne co., W Nebr., 60 mi/97 km SE of Scottsbluff, on Lodgepole Creek, bet. North Platte and South Platte rivers; 41°07′N 102°58′W. RR junction. Trade and shipping center in Great Plains region; grain, potatoes; livestock, poultry; dairy prods. Mfg. (trailer hitches, natural extract, communications cable, aprons, printing). High Plains Agr. Lab. (USDA and Univ. of Nebr.). Fort Sidney Commanders Post Home Historical Site here. I-80 Golden Link SW of town, final link in construction of highway (N.Y. city to San Francisco). Has Community Col. Founded 1867 by Union Pacific RR, city grew around Fort Sidney (1867–1894) and was a supply station during Black Hills gold rush (1876–1877).

Sidney 1 village (1990 pop. 271), Sharp co., N Ark., 15 mi/24 km N of Batesville; 36°00′N 91°39′W. **2** village (1990 pop. 1,027), Champaign co., E Ill., 10 mi/16 km SE of Urbana; 40°01′N 88°04′W. Agr. (corn, soybeans, alfalfa). On Salt Fork of Vermilion R. **3** uninc. village (1990 pop. 500), Pike co., E Ky., 6 mi/9.7 km SW of Williamson, in Cumberland Mts. Coal mining area. Mfg. (coal processing, lumber). Flag Knob (1,658 ft/505 m) to NW. **4** village, Montcalm co., central Mich., 3 mi/4.8 km SW of Stanton; 43°15′N 85°07′W. Small lakes in area. Agr. area (potatoes, apples; dairying). Montcalm Community Col. located here. **5** village (□ 2 sq mi/5.2 sq km; 1990 pop. 4,720) in Sidney town (1990 pop. 6,667), Delaware co. S N.Y., in the Catskills, on Susquehanna R., and 30 mi/48 km NE of Binghamton; 42°18′N 75°24′W. Mfg. (calendars, aerospace and military electronic components); timber; bluestone quarrying. Inc. 1888.

Sidney, township (1990 pop. 2,593), Kennebec co., S Maine, bet. Kennebec R. and Messalonskee L., just N of Augusta; 44°26′N 69°45′W.

Sidney Lanier, Lake, reservoir (□ 74 sq mi/192 sq km), Forsyth, Dawson, Law, and Banks cos., N central Ga., on Chattahoochee R., 17 mi/27 km NE of Atlanta; 34°10′N 84°04′W. Max. capacity 2,554,000 acre-ft. Extends NE-SW. Fed by Chestatee R. Formed by Buford Dam (24 ft/7 m high), built (1958) by Army Corps of Engineers for flood control; also used for power, recreation, irrigation, water supply, and as a fish and wildlife pond.

Sidon (SEI-duhn), village (1990 pop. 596), Leflore co., W central Miss., 8 mi/12.9 km S of Greenwood, and near Yazoo R.; 33°24′N 90°12′W. Agr. (cotton, grain, soybeans; cattle). Mathews Brake Natl. Wildlife Refuge to SW.

Sierra 1 county (□ 958 sq mi/2,481 sq km; 1990 pop. 3,138), NE Calif.; ⊙ Downieville; 39°36′N 120°30′W. In the Sierra Nevada, here crossed by Yuba Pass (6,701 ft/2,042 m) in center of co.; rises to 8,615 ft/2,626 m at Sierra Buttes. Bounded E by Nev. state line. Drained by Yuba R. and tributaries. Parts of Tahoe Natl. Forest throughout co., and Plumas Natl. Forest along N boundary. Gold L., other lakes (fishing) in N. Gold mining (rich quartz lodes have yielded since 1850s); some gold, lead, and silver mining, sand and gravel quarrying. Timber (pine, fir, cedar); cattle and sheep; hay, alfalfa, field crops. Old mining camps, hunting, fishing, winter sports attract vacationers. Pacific Crest Natl. Scenic Trail passes N-S through center of co. Formed 1852. **2** county (□ 4,236 sq mi/10,971 sq km; 1990 pop. 9,912), SW N.Mex.; ⊙ Truth or Consequences (Hot Springs); 33°08′N 107°11′W. Cattle, some sheep; dairying; hay, alfalfa, chilis, cabbage, onions, lettuce, pecans, wheat, apples. Drained by Rio Grande, forms Elephant Butte and Caballo reservoirs (in center) and Alamosa R. Placer mining for gold. Part of Gila Natl. Forest in W; part of Cibola Natl. Forest in NW; parts of Black Range and Mimbres Mts. in W; part of Sierra Caballo in S; part of San Andres Mts., in part of White Sands Missile Range in E; Fra Cristobal Range in N; Caballo L. and Percha Dam state parks in S; Elephant Butte L. State Park in N center; part of Jornada del Muerto plain in NE. Formed 1884.

Sierra Ancha, mountain range, Gila co., central Ariz., N of Theodore Roosevelt Reservoir; rises to 7,694 ft/2,345 m at Aztec Mt. in S. In Tonto Natl. Forest; Sierra Ancha Experimental Forest near Aztec Mt. Also called Sierra Anchas.

Sierra Blanca, village (1990 pop. 700), ⊙ Hudspeth co., extreme W Texas, c.80 mi/129 km SE of El Paso, and c.15 mi/24 km from Mex. border. Elev. 4,512 ft/1,375 m. In ranching, mining, tourist region. Imports sludge from urban centers and applies it to grazing lands. Sierra Blanca Mt. is 7 mi/11.3 km NW; Quitman Mts. are SW. Est. 1881 at RR junction.

Sierra Blanca, peak (6,891 ft/2,100 m), Hudspeth co., extreme W Texas, 7 mi/11.3 km NW of Sierra Blanca village.

Sierra Blanca 1 range of Sangre de Cristo Mts., in parts of Alamosa, Huerfano, and Costilla cos., S Colo. Highest points are Ellingwood Point and Mt. Lindsey (both: 14,042 ft/4,280 m) and Blanca Peak (c.14,345 ft/4,372 m). **2** range of Sacramento Mts. in Lincoln and Otero cos., in S central N.Mex. Iron-ore deposits, softcoal mines. Chief peaks: Nogal Peak (9,957 ft/3,035 m), Sierra Blanca (11,977 ft/3,651 m; 33 mi/53 km NNE of Alamogordo; highest point in Sacramento Mts.). Range extends through part of Mescalero Apache Indian Reservation and parts of Lincoln Natl. Forest. Tularosa Valley to W; site of Ski Apache Ski Resort.

Sierra Buttes, Sierra co., NE Calif., jagged twin peaks of the Sierra Nevada, 10 mi/16 km ENE of Downieville; the higher summit is 8,615 ft/2,626 m; 39°35′N 120°38′W. Gold-bearing quartz mines here have yielded since 1850s.

Sierra Chivato, N.Mex.: see SAN MATEO MOUNTAINS.

Sierra City, uninc. village, Sierra co., NE Calif., 45 mi/72 km W of Reno, Nev., on North Yuba R., at S foot of Sierra Buttes; in Tahoe Natl. Forest. Winter sports area nearby. Yuba Pass is E. Pacific Crest Trail passes to E.

Sierra de la Laguna (see-ER-rah dai lah lah-GOO-nah), mountain range in S Baja California Sur, Mexico; 24°00′N 109°45′W. Max. elev. (7,096 ft/2,163 m) at Picacho La Laguna Peak. Site of proposed Sierra de la laguna Natural Park.

Sierra del Caballo Muerto, Texas: see CARMEN, SIERRA DEL.

Sierra del Carmen, Texas: see CARMEN, SIERRA DEL.

Sierra Diablo (see-ER-rah dee-AHB-lo), mountain group extending E and N from point NE of Sierra Blanca, Hudspeth-Culberson cos., extreme W Texas. Max. elev. c.6,600 ft/2,012 m. Forms part of S and E boundary of Diablo Bolson.

Sierra Estrella (es-TRAI-yah), mountain range, Maricopa and Pinal cos., SW central Ariz., near Gila R., SW of Phoenix. Rises to 4,337 ft/1,322 m at Montezum Peak.

Sierra Madre, city (1990 pop. 10,762), Los Angeles co., S Calif., suburb 13 mi/21 km NE of downtown Los Angeles and E of Pasadena, at the foot of Mt. Wilson (to N). There is some light mfg. Bounded by Angeles Natl. Forest on N. Inc. 1907.

Sierra Madre (see-ER-rah MAHD-rai), chief mountain system of Mexico, consisting of the Sierra Madre Oriental, the Sierra Madre Occidental, and the Sierra Madre del Sur and forming the dissected edges of the vast central Mexican plateau; a volcanic belt along the plateau's S edge links the 3 sierras. Extending from NW to SE through Mexico from the U.S. border, the rugged Sierra Madres, 6,000 ft/1,830 m–12,000 ft/3,660 m high, with deep, steep-sided canyons (barrancas), have long been a barrier to E-W travel. The terrain ranges from permanently snow-covered peaks to hot, tropical valleys; and from the humid, thickly vegetated seaward slopes to the dry, largely barren interior-facing slopes. Agr. prods. vary according to the climate. Lumbering is done in the N Sierra Madre Occidental. The Sierra Madres have a great wealth of minerals including iron ore, lead, silver, and gold. The mts. are sparsely populated, with settlement limited to mining towns and agr. communities. The Sierra Madres hold good potential for hydroelectric power development, and several stations have been built in the N ranges.

Sierra Madre del Sur (see-ER-rah MAHD-rai del SOOR), mountain range, S Mexico; 17°00′N 99°00′W. A poorly defined mountainous region. The Sierra Madre del Sur physiographic prov. lies between the Transverse Volcanic Axis and the Isthmus of Tehuantepec. It includes most of the states of Guerrero and Oaxaca and a large portion of Michoacán. This prov. is characterized by old crystalline rock that is highly mineralized in parts (gold, silver, lead, nickel, iron, asbestos). The Sierra Madre del Sur physiographic prov. includes some of the most rugged land in Mexico. The Sierra Madre del Sur range is a rugged, mountainous region within the Sierra Madre del Sur physiographic prov. which extends from NW-SE through S Guerrero state between the Balsas and Mezcala river valleys and the Pacific coast.

Sierra Madre Occidental (see-ER-rah MAHD-rai okssee-den-TAHL), mountain range, W Mexico, extending parallel to the Gulf of California for some 700 mi/1,130 km, roughly between 32°00′N and 22°00′N. The W escarpment of the Mexican Plateau, the Sierra Madre Occidental is composed mainly of basalt flows and other extrusive volcanic materials and reaches average elevations of 7,000 ft/2,130 m–8,000 ft/2,440 m with maximum elevations over 10,000 ft/3,050 m. The sierra is traversed by several rivers that flow from the W plateau surface to the Gulf of California through deep canyons, the most notable of which is Copper Canyon (Barranca del Cobre) in W Chihuahua state. Few highways and only one RR (the Chihuahua Pacific RR) have been built across this rugged area.

Sierra Madre Oriental (see-ER-rah MAHD-rai o-reeen-TAHL), mountain range, E Mexico, extending for approx. 700 mi/1,130 km between 29°00′N and 19°00′N. The Sierra Madre Oriental is divided into 2 sections. The N section extends S from Boquillas Canyon in Big Bend Natl. Park (U.S.) nearly to Monterrey. This sector of the sierra is formed by a series of discrete, parallel, fault-block ranges, some of which also show evidence of volcanic activity. The S sector, which is more rugged and higher than the N, comprises the E escarpment of the Mexican Plateau and is composed mainly of folded limestone ridges that rise from the coastal plain in a series of increasingly higher steps to the plateau surface at an elevation of 7,000 ft/2,130 m–8,000 ft/2,440 m. Maximum elevations in the Sierra Madre Oriental reach about 13,000 ft/3,960 m.

Sierra Maestra (see-ER-rah MAIS-trah), rugged mountain range, in Granma and Santiago de Cuba provs., SE Cuba, rising abruptly from the coast and surrounding Santiago de Cuba city on all but S side. Geologically related to the Bartlet Sea Trough (25,200 ft/7,680 m deep), it consists of connecting ranges with local names and is the highest system of Cuba. It extends 158 mi/254 km and is 22 mi/35 km across at its widest part. Lacking roads and full of thick forests, the slopes show striking vertical bioclimatic zoning. Rich in minerals, especially copper, manganese, chromium, and iron. Pico Turquino (6,470 ft/1,972 m) is the highest point. In the 1950s Fidel Castro had his base of operations in the mts. In the late 1980s, the govt. began Plan Turquino, to enhance roads and infrastructure and to halt local out-migration.

Sierra Mojada (see-ER-rah mo-HAH-dah), town (1990 pop. 592), Coahuila state, N Mexico, at foot of Sierra Mojada, on RR, and 120 mi/193 km N of Torreón; forms part of the E side of the Bolsón de Mapimí; 27°17'N 103°42'W. Elev. 4,121 ft/1,256 m.

Sierra Morena (see-ER-rah mo-RAIN-ah), town, Villa Clara prov., central Cuba, near N coast, 30 mi/48 km WNW of Sagua la Grande; 22°56'N 80°32'W. Sugarcane, fruits; cattle.

Sierra Nevada, mountain range, c.400 mi/644 km long and from c.40 mi/64 km to 80 mi/129 km wide, mostly in E Calif., E side of range extends into W Nev. It rises to 14,494 ft/4,418 m in Mt. Whitney, the highest peak in the United States outside Alaska. The mts. extend NW from Tehachapi Pass SE of Bakersfield, Calif., to about the North Fork Feather R., NE of Chico. The Cascade Range continues N beyond this, and includes Lassen Peak. A tilted fault-block structure (the largest in the United States), the Sierra Nevada's E front rises sharply from the Great Basin, while its W slope descends gradually to the hills bordering the Central Valley of California. Heavy winter precipitation is economically important to the surrounding areas and to metropolitan areas; also vital to winter recreation activities, the only viable industry for 6 months a year; snow-fed streams supply irrigation water to the Central Valley and to W Nev. and also generate hydroelectric power. Water from Sierra reservoirs transported by aqueduct to San Francisco, Los Angeles, and other cities. High, rugged, and frequently snowbound in winter, the mts. are a formidable barrier to overland travel. Donner Pass (elev. 7,089 ft/2,161 m), the principal pass across the mountains, was used by thousands of California-bound gold-seekers and pioneers on the Emigrant Trail in the middle and late 1800s. The Sierra Nevada are known as popular tourist area, for their magnificent scenery (especially in the High Sierra S of L. Tahoe and in Yosemite, Sequoia, and Kings Canyon natl. parks to S) and for their year-round resorts. Ski areas. L. Tahoe, on Calif.-Nev. state line, central to Sierra Nevada tourism; gambling casinos on Nev. side.

Sierra Oscura (see-ER-rah os-KOO-rah), mountain range, Socorro and Lincoln cos., S central N.Mex., S extension of Chupadera Mesa, just NE of San Andres Mts., E of Rio Grande. Highest at Oscura Peak (8,732 ft/2,662 m), on Socorro-Lincoln co. line. First atomic bomb was exploded (July 16, 1945) in desert region just W at Trinity site. Tularosa Valley to E; Jornada del Muerto to W.

Sierra Prieta, small mountain range, just W of Prescott, Yavapai co., central Ariz.; highest point is Granite Mountain (7,700 ft/2,347 m). In Prescott Natl. Forest.

Sierra San Pedro Mártir (see-ER-rah sahn PE-dro MAHR-tir), national park (157,500 acres/63,740 ha), central Baja California, Mexico, 124 mi/200 km S of the Calif. state border with Mexico. The 2 highest elevs. are found at La Encantada and Picacho del Diablo (10,157 ft/3,096 m).

Sierra Valley, Plumas and Sierra cos., NE Calif., mountain basin (c.20 mi/32 km long, up to 10 mi/16 km wide; elev. c.5,000 ft/1,524 m), largest in the Sierra Nevada, c.25 mi/40 km NW of Reno, Nev. Some dairying; some cattle, sheep; alfalfa, hay. Loyalton is chief settlement. Middle Fork Feather R. rises here. Beckwourth Pass across Sierra Nevada crest is E.

Sierra Vieja, mountains, Jeff Davis and Presidio cos., extreme W Texas, generally parallel to the Rio Grande (W), c.35 mi/56 km to W and NW of Marfa; c.30 mi/48 km long; rise to 6,467 ft/1,971 m. Sometimes called Tierra Vieja or Vieja Mountains.

Sierra Vista, city (1990 pop. 32,983), Cochise co., SE Ariz., 56 mi/90 km SE of Tucson; 31°34'N 110°19'W. Elev. 4,620 ft/1,408 m. Cattle; mfg. (machine tools, lumber, printing and publishing, motors, concrete blocks, hydraulic cement, machinery parts, plumbing supplies, roofing materials). Tourism and convention center. City extends SW into Huachuca Mts. San Pedro Riparian Natl. Conservation Area to E, on San Pedro R. Coronado Natl. Monument to S, on Mex. border. Part of Coronado Natl. Forest to SW.

Siesta Key (see-ES-tah), island (□ 3 sq mi/7.8 sq km; 1990 pop 7,772), Sarasota co., W central Fla., 5 mi/8 km S of Sarasota; 27°16'N 82°32'W.

Sigel (SIG-EL), town (1990 pop. 344), Shelby co., central Ill., 21 mi/34 km SE of Shelbyville; 39°13'N 88°30'W. Grain, soybeans; livestock; dairy prods.

Signal Hill, city (1990 pop. 8,371), Los Angeles co., S Calif., a residential suburb 16 mi/26 km SSE of downtown Los Angeles and 2 mi/3.2 km NE of downtown Long Beach, 2 mi/3.2 km N of San Pedro Bay, Pacific Ocean; surrounded by city of Long Beach; 33°48'N 118°10'W. Covered with many oil wells (1st gusher in 1921) within municipality. Long Beach Airport (Daugherty Field) to N. Inc. 1924.

Signal Mountain, town (1990 pop. 7,034), Hamilton co., SE Tenn., 8 mi/13 km N of Chattanooga, on slope of Signal Mt. (1,400 ft/427 m; S spur of Walden Ridge); 35°07'N 85°20'W. Scene of Civil War fighting in Chattanooga campaign; battlefield area now included in Chickamauga and Chattanooga Natl. Military Park. Settled 1911, inc. 1919.

Signal Peak (11,223 ft/3,421 m), in Sevier Plateau, S Sevier co., SW central Utah, 6 mi/9.7 km E of Monroe; 38°37'N 112°00'W. In Fishlake Natl. Forest.

Sigourney (SIG-ur-knee), city (1990 pop. 2,111), ⊙ Keokuk co., SE Iowa, 23 mi/37 km E of Oskaloosa; 41°19'N 92°12'W. In livestock and grain area; mfg. (feed, concrete blocks). Limestone quarries nearby. Inc. 1868.

Sigsbee Deep, Mexico: see MEXICO, GULF OF.

Sigurd, village (1990 pop. 385), Sevier co., central Utah, 8 mi/12.9 km NE of Richfield, and on Sevier R.; 38°51'N 111°58'W. Elev. 5,220 ft/1,591 m. Agr. (alfalfa, barley; cattle); dairying; mfg. gypsum prods. Settled 1873. Separate units of Fishlake Natl. Forest to W, E, and S.

Sikanni Chief River (si-KA-nee), c.275 mi/443 km long, NE B.C., Canada; rises in Stikine Mts. near 57°15'N 124°40'W; flows in a wide arc ENE and NE to confluence with Muskwa R. at Fort Nelson, forming Fort Nelson R.

Sikes (SEIKS), village (1990 pop. 120), Winn parish, N central La., 15 mi/24 km NE of Winnfield; 32°05'N 92°30'W. In agr. and timber area.

Sikeston (SEIKS-tuhn), city (1990 pop. 17,641), New Madrid and Scott cos., SE Mo., in the Mississippi alluvial plain; 36°52'N 89°34'W. Shipping, marketing, and processing center of a cotton, wheat, and soybean region. Mfg. (rope, vending machines,processed foods, printing, apparel, steel fabrication, wire). Interstate truck and service center. Large thermal electric power plant. Inc. 1874.

Silacayoapam (see-lah-kah-yo-ahn-PAHM), town (1990 pop. 2,470), Oaxaca state, S Mexico, in Sierra Madre del Sur, 35 mi/56 km NW of Tlaxiaco; 17°30'N 93°09'W. Elev. 5,643 ft/1,720 m. Cereals, sugarcane, fruits; livestock. In the Mixteca Baia. Formerly spelled Silacayoápan.

Silacayoapan, Mexico: see SILACAYOAPAM.

Silao (see-LAH-o), city (1990 pop. 50,828) and township, Guanajuato, central Mexico, on affluent of Lerma R., and 13 mi/21 km WSW of Guanajuato, on Mexico Highway 45-110, in the Bajío; 20°56'N 101°25'W. Elev. 5,830 ft/1,777 m. RR junction; motor vehicle assembly plant; agr. center (corn, wheat, alfalfa, beans, chili, sugarcane; livestock). Mineral springs nearby. Founded 1537.

Silas (SEI-luhs), town (1990 pop. 245), Choctaw co., SW Ala., 29 mi/47 km S of Butler; 31°46'N 88°19'W. Logging, lumber.

Silbert (seel-BER), town, Ouest dept., Haiti, 4 mi/6.4 km N of Port-au-Prince. Agr. (sisal, citrus fruits, sugarcane, tobacco); thermal springs nearby.

Silene, Mount (5,000 ft/1,524 m), NE Lab., Canada, near head of Nachvak Fiord; 58°58'N 64°02'W.

Siler City (SEI-luhr), town (1990 pop. 4,808), Chatham co., central N.C., 30 mi/48 km SE of Greensboro, near Rocky R.; 35°43'N 79°27'W. Timber; tobacco, grain, soybeans; poultry, cattle, hogs; dairying. Mfg. (industrial machinery, metal fabricating, poultry processing, furniture, food processing equip., textiles, processed meat prods., steel parts, lumber). Settled 1855, inc. 1885.

Silerton (SEI-luhr-tuhn), town (1990 pop. 59), Hardeman co., SW Tenn., 19 mi/31 km S of Jackson; 35°20'N 88°47'W. In pine-timber and farm area.

Siletz (suh-LITZ), town (1990 pop. 926), Lincoln co., W Oregon, 9 mi/14.5 km NE of Newport, on Siletz R. (c.70 mi/113 km long; flows SW past Suletz, then NW to Pacific Ocean, S of Lincoln City); 44°43'N 123°55'W. Poultry, sheep, cattle. Parts of Siuslaw Natl. Forest to N and S. Fish hatchery to N.

Silex (SEI-lex), town (1990 pop. 197), Lincoln co., E Mo., on N. Fork of Cuivre R., and 11 mi/18 km; 39°07'N 91°03'W. NNW of Troy.

Sill, Fort, Okla.: see FORT SILL.

Sillery, city (1991 pop. 12,519), S central Que., Canada, suburb 3 mi/5 km SW of Quebec City, on NW side of St. Lawrence R.; 46°46'N 71°15'W. Residential area. Laval Univ. campus here.

Silo (SEI-lo), village (1990 pop. 249), Bryan co., S Okla., 5 mi/8 km NW of Durant; 34°02'N 96°28'W. Agr. area. Washita Arm of L. Texoma to W.

Siloah (SEI-lo), town (1991 pop. 2,701), St. Elizabeth parish, SW Jamaica, 15 mi/24 km NW of Mandeville; 18°10'N 77°43'W. Rum factory nearby.

Siloam (SEI-luhm), town (1990 pop. 329), Greene co., NE central Ga., 6 mi/9.7 km ESE of Greensboro; 33°32'N 83°05'W.

Siloam Springs (SEI-lom), town (1990 pop. 8,151), Benton co., extreme NW Ark., 22 mi/35 km WNW of Fayetteville, near Okla. line, in the Ozarks; 36°10'N 94°32'W. Trade, shipping center for fruit, livestock, poultry area. Mfg. (vegetable canning, machinery parts, plastic prods., electrical prods., motor vehicle parts, food prods.). Health resort, with mineral springs. Seat of John Brown Univ. Laid out and inc. 1880. Small unit of Ozark Natl. Forest to SE.

Silsbee, town (1990 pop. 6,368), Hardin co., SE Texas, near Neches R., 20 mi/32 km N of Beaumont; 30°20'N 94°10'W. Elev. 85 ft/26 m. RR junction; trade center in agr. (cattle; egg prods.); oil wells; timber; cattle; RR shops; sawmill; mfg. (wood prods., particleboard, paper tubes, industrial sand). Main unit Big Thicket Natl. Preserve to S and E. Information station to NW. Founded c.1892; inc. as town 1906; as city 1938.

Silt, town (1990 pop. 1,095), Garfield co., W Colo., on Colorado R., and 18 mi/29 km W of Glenwood Springs; 39°32'N 107°39'W. Elev. c.5,432 ft/1,656 m. Shipping point for cattle and feed. Harvey Gap State Park to N.

Siltepec (SEEL-te-pek), town (1990 pop. 1,662), Chiapas state, S Mexico, in Sierra Madre, 45 mi/72 km N of Tapachula; 15°39'N 92°17'W. Sugarcane.

Siluria (suh-LUH-ree-uh), village, Shelby co., central Ala., 20 mi/32 km S of Birmingham. Lime and cement.

Silvana (sil-VAIN-uh), uninc. village (1990 pop. 160), Snohomish co., NW Wash., 14 mi/23 km N of Everett, on Stillaguamish R., opposite mouth of Pilchuck Creek. Dairying; poultry; berries; mfg. (concrete).

Silver Bank, shoal (c.35 mi/56 km wide) with reefs, in the West Indies, 55 mi/89 km NE of Puerto Plata (Dominican Republic), separated by 20-mi/32-km-wide Silver Bank Passage from Mouchoir Bank (W).

Silver Bay, town (1990 pop. 1,894), Lake co., NE Minn., 27 mi/43 km NE of Two Harbors, 53 mi/85 km NE of Duluth, on L. Superior; 47°17'N 91°16'W. Terminus of Reserve Mining Company RR from nearby Babbitt, in Mesabi Iron Range to N. Mfg. of iron ore pellets. Superior Natl. Forest to NW; Tettegouche State Park to NE; Split Rock Lighthouse and Gooseberry Falls state parks to SW; Finland State Forest to N.

Silver Bay, resort village (1990 pop. 250), Warren co., E N.Y., on W shore of L. George, 12 mi/19 km SSW of Ticonderoga; 43°42'N 73°30'W.

Silver Beach, Mass.: see FALMOUTH.

Silver Bell, uninc. town (1990 pop. 900), Pima co., S Ariz., 31 mi/50 km WNW of Tucson, near NE edge of Tohomo O'odham (Papago) Indian Reservation. Cattle. Part of Sauaro Natl. Monument to SE.

Silver Bow, county (□ 718 sq mi/1,860 sq km; 1990 pop. 33,941), SW Mont.; ⊙ Butte; 45°54′N 112°40′W. Mt. region crossed by Continental Divide also forms most of E boundary; bounded SW by Big Hole R., drained by Silver Bow Creek. Copper, zinc, lead, gold, silver, manganese, phosphorus. Dairying; cattle; hay. Parts of Deerlodge Natl. Forest in N, SW, and SE. Formed 1881. City of Butte coterminous with co. of Silver Bow except for Walkerville.

Silver City 1 town (1990 pop. 252), Mills co., SW Iowa, near Silver Creek, 7 mi/11.3 km NE of Glenwood; 41°06′N 95°38′W. In agr. area. **2** town (□ 8 sq mi/20.7 sq km; 1990 pop. 10,683), ⊙ Grant co., SW N.Mex., in foothills of Pinos Altos Mts., near Ariz. state line, 112 mi/180 km WNW of Las Cruces; 32°46′N 108°16′W. Elev. 5,938 ft/1,810 m. Health resorts; retirement area; trade and shipping center for irrigated agr. and livestock area: cattle; grain, alfalfa. Mfg. (meatpacking, printing and publishing, concrete prods., steel tanks). RR terminus; RR spurs to mine to S and E. Copper, zinc, and silver mines in vicinity. Western N.Mex. Univ.; Gila Natl. Forest to N and E, hq is here. Grew as silver and gold mining camp. Gila Cliff Dwellings Natl. Monument is 44 mi/71 km N. Silver City Grant Co. Airport to SE; Santa Rita Open Pit Copper Mine to E; City of Rocks State Park to SE. Founded 1870; inc. 1878. **3** uninc. town (1990 pop. 1,343), Hoke co., S central N.C., residential suburb 1 mi/1.6 km N of Raeford; 35°00′N 79°13′W. Fort Bragg Military Reserve to N.

Silver City 1 uninc. village, Owyhee co., SW Idaho, 48 mi/77 km SW of Boise, on Reynolds Creek. Elev. 6,179 ft/1,883 m. Referred to as the "Queen of Idaho Ghost Towns," some 70 bldgs. remain intact from silver boom years, including 50-room Idaho Hotel, Wells Fargo office, and Idaho Avalanche newspaper hq. Old Schoolhouse Mus. **2** village (1990 pop. 348), Humphreys co., W Miss., on the Yazoo R., and 6 mi/9.7 km S of Belzoni; 33°06′N 90°30′W. In agr. region (cotton, corn, rice); catfish. **3** uninc. village (1990 pop. 150), Lyon co., W Nev., 4 mi/6.4 km S of Virginia City in Virginia Range. Elev. c.5,060 ft/1,542 m. Formerly great silver producer (near Comstock Lode); mines mostly inactive. Tourism.

Silver Cliff, village (1990 pop. 322), ⊙ Custer co., S central Colo., bet. Sangre de Cristo and Wet mts., 45 mi/72 km WSW of Pueblo, 1 mi/1.6 km E of Westcliffe; 38°07′N 105°24′W. Elev. 7,982 ft/2,433 m. Boomed as silver camp in 1881.

Silver Creek 1 village, Floyd co., NW Ga., 5 mi/8 km S of Rome; 34°10′N 85°09′W. **2** village (1990 pop. 190), Lawrence co., S central Miss., 25 mi/40 km E of Brookhaven; 31°36′N 90°00′W. Agr. (cotton, corn; livestock; timber); mfg. (lumber). **3** village (1990 pop. 513), Newton co., SW Mo., residential suburb 5 mi/8 km SE of downtown Joplin; 37°02′N 94°28′W. **4** village (1990 pop. 625), Merrick co., E central Nebr., 17 mi/27 km WSW of Columbus, and on Platte R.; 41°19′N 97°40′W. Livestock; grain. **5** village (□ 1 sq mi/2.6 sq km; 1990 pop. 2,927), Chautauqua co., extreme W N.Y., on L. Erie, 10 mi/16 km NE of Dunkirk; 42°32′N 79°10′W. Light mfg.; in agr. area (grapes, cherries, tomatoes); summer resort. Annual grape festival held here in Oct. Inc. 1848.

Silver Creek 1 in SW Ill.; rises near Mount Olive; flows c.75 mi/121 km generally S to Kaskaskia R. opposite New Athens; 39°03′N 89°43′W. **2** in SW Iowa; rises near Westphalia in Shelby co.; flows c.70 mi/113 km S to West Nishnabotna R. 4 mi/6.4 km S of Malvern.

Silver Grove, town (1990 pop. 1,102), Campbell co., N Ky., a suburb 7 mi/11.3 km SE of downtown Cincinnati, Ohio, on the Ohio R.; 39°02′N 84°24′W. Agr. (tobacco, corn, soybeans; cattle); mfg. (cabinets).

Silver Islet, village, W Ont., Canada, on L. Superior, 20 mi/32 km E of Fort William; 48°20′N 88°49′W. Silver mining.

Silver Lake 1 town (1990 pop. 528), Kosciusko co., N Ind., 11 mi/18 km S of Warsaw; 41°04′N 85°53′W. Agr. area; mfg. (fabricated steel prods.). Resort lakes (fishing) nearby. Laid out 1859. **2** town (1990 pop. 764), McLeod co., S central Minn., 7 mi/11.3 km W of Hutchinson, on N side of Silver L.; 44°53′N 94°12′W. Grain, peas; livestock, poultry; dairying. Small lakes nearby. **3** uninc. town (1990 pop. 4,071), New Hanover co., SE N.C., residential suburb 5 mi/8 km SSE of downtown Wilmington; 34°08′N 77°55′W. **4** town (1990 pop. 1,801), Kenosha co., extreme SE Wis., on Silver L., 17 mi/27 km WSW of Kenosha; 42°32′N 88°10′W. Mfg. underwater weed cutters. Small lakes in area; recreation.

Silver Lake 1 village (1990 pop. 1,390), Shawnee co., NE Kansas, 10 mi/16 km WNW of Topeka; 39°06′N 95°51′W. In fertile agr. valley of Kansas R. Shawnee State Fishing L. to N. **2** village, in Tewksbury and Wilmington towns, Middlesex co., NE Mass., 8 mi/12.9 km SE of Lowell. Once a summer resort, now largely residential. Also called Nonantum. **3** resort village (1990 pop. 600), Wyoming co., W N.Y., on Silver L. (c.3 mi/4.8 km long), c.40 mi/64 km SSW of Rochester; 43°42′N 78°01′W. Site of a Methodist Church institute. **4** village (1990 pop. 3,052), Summit co., NE Ohio, 6 mi/10 km NE of downtown Akron, near Cuyahoga R.; 41°09′N 81°27′W. **5** uninc. village, Lake co., S central Oregon, 65 mi/105 km SSE of Bend, on Silver Creek. Elev. 4,345 ft/1,324 m. Silver L., a dry lake bed, is to E. Paulina Marsh to NE. Fort Rock State Monument to N. Fremont Natl. Forest to W and S. Thompson Valley Reservoir to S.

Silver Lake 1 Kent co., central Del., just N of downtown Dover; drained by St. Jones R. Delaware State Univ. at N end; c.2 mi/3.2 km long; 39°10′N 75°31′W. Silver L. Recreation Area at SE end. **2** Clinton co., extreme NE N.Y., in the Adirondacks, 24 mi/39 km SW of Plattsburgh; c.2.5 mi/4 km long, ½ mi/⁸⁄₁₀ km–1 mi/1.6 km wide; 44°31′N 73°52′W.

Silver Lake, reservoir, Amador co., E Calif., on Silver Fork American R., in the Sierra Nevada Mts., and in Eldorado Natl. Forest, 20 mi/32 km SSW of S. Lake Tahoe; 2 mi/3.2 km long; 38°38′N 120°05′W. Elev. 7,260 ft/2,213 m; Treasure Isl. in S center of lake.

Silver Lake 1 N.H.: see MADISON. **2** N.Y.: see STATEN ISLAND.

Silver Peak, uninc. village, Esmeralda co. (1990 pop. 100), W Nev., in E foothills of Silver Peak Mts., 30 mi/48 km SW of Tonopah. Elev. 4,270 ft/1,301 m. Formerly important silver-mining center (silver still mined; lithium); cattle.

Silver Peak Range, W Nev., in Esmeralda co., near Calif. state line. Chief peaks: Magruder Mt. (9,046 ft/2,757 m), 25 mi/40 km SW of Goldfield, and Piper Peak (9,450 ft/2,880 m), c.15 mi/24 km WSW of Silverpeak town; 37°44′N 117°47′W.

Silver Plume, town (1990 pop. 134), Clear Creek co., N central Colo., on headstream of Clear Creek, in Front Range, and 40 mi/64 km W of Denver, 2 mi/3.2 km W of Georgetown; 39°42′N 105°43′W. Elev. c.9,118 ft/2,779 m. At E end of Eisenhower Memorial Tunnel (I-70), highest stretch on U.S. Interstate system. Mining; mfg. (beer [micro-brewery]); major ski center; tourism; granite quarry nearby. Grays Peak 6 mi/9.7 km SW. With its neighbor, Georgetown, Silver Plume was the main silver dist. from 1864 to 1878, when Leadville's deposits were discovered. Silver Plume is on the Georgetown Loop Historic Mining Area train tour. Surrounded by Arapaho Natl. Forest.

Silver Sands, beach, 6 mi/9.7 km SSE of Bridgetown, near southernmost point of Barbados. Tourist center and location of world windsurfing championships.

Silver Spring, uninc. city (1990 pop. 76,046), Montgomery co., W central Md., a residential suburb of Washington, D.C.; 39°01′N 77°01′W. Silver Springs is a major suburban office center that has burgeoned since the 1970s. If it were incorporated, it would be the 2d-largest city in Md., after Baltimore. A large naval ordnance laboratory as well as several research laboratories (for the development of defense materials and of electronic and prosthetic equip.) are here as well as a plant making precision instruments. The city takes its name from the mica flakes gleaming on the bottom of a nearby spring.

Silver Springs, uninc. town (1990 pop. 2,253), Lyon co., W Nev., 33 mi/53 km NE of Carson City, near Carson R.; 39°22′N 119°12′W. Elev. 4,209 ft/1,283 m. Cattle, sheep, poultry; dairying; hay, vegetables, potatoes; mfg. (feeds, utility poles). Lahontan Reservation (Carson R.) and State Recreation Area to E; Fort Churchill State Historic Park to S. Virginia Mts. to NE.

Silver Springs 1 village (1990 pop. 900), Marion co., N central Fla., 3 mi/4.8 km NE of Ocala; 29°12′N 82°04′W. Mfg. includes sand and silica processing. **2** village (1990 pop. 852), Wyoming co., W N.Y., 24 mi/39 km SSE of Batavia; 42°39′N 78°04′W.

Silver Springs, mineral spring, N central Fla., source of Silver R. The Span. explorer Hernando De Soto was probably 1st European to visit spring (1539). Town of Silver Springs nearby.

Silver Springs Shores, town (□ 4 sq mi/10.4 sq km; 1990 pop. 6,421), Marion co., N central Fla., 6 mi/9.7 km SE of Ocala; 29°06′N 82°00′W.

Silver Zone Pass, Nev.: see TOANO MOUNTAINS.

Silverbow (SIL-vuhr BO), village, Silver Bow co., SW Mont., 8 mi/13 km W of Butte on Silver Bow Creek. Mining; cattle. Founded 1869.

Silverdale, uninc. town (1990 pop. 1,100), Kitsap co., W Wash., 6 mi/9.7 km NNW of Bremerton, at N end of Dyes Inlet, arm of Puget Sound, on narrow neck of land in Kitsap Peninsula. Dairying; poultry. Fishing. Timber. Mfg. (rubber goods). Hood Canal is 3 mi/4.8 km to W. Bangor U.S. Naval Station to N.

Silverdale (SIL-vuhr-dail), borough (1990 pop. 881), Bucks co., SE Pa., 26 mi/42 km NNW of Philadelphia, 2 mi/3.2 km SE of Perkasie; 40°21′N 75°16′E. Agr. area (grain, soybeans, apples; livestock; dairying).

Silverheels, Mount (13,822 ft/4,213 m), in Rocky Mts., NW Park co., central Colo., 7 mi/11.3 km N of Fairplay; 39°20′N 106°00′W.

Silverhill, farming town (1990 pop. 556), Baldwin co., SW Ala., 25 mi/40 km S of Bay Minette; 30°33′N 87°45′W. Cabinet and office furniture mfg.

Silvermine, Conn.: see NORWALK.

Silverstreet, village (1990 pop. 156), Newberry co., NW central S.C., 6 mi/9.7 km SW of Newberry; 34°13′N 81°42′W. Mfg. of hardwood and pine chips; agr. includes timber; livestock, poultry; grain. Near Saluda R.

Silverthorne, town (1990 pop. 1,768), Summit co., central Colo., 3 mi/4.8 km WNW of Dillon, on Blue R., downstream (N) from Dillon Reservoir; 39°38′N 106°04′W. Elev. 8,790 ft/2,679 m. Surrounded by Arapaho Natl. Forest. Tourism; mfg. of concrete, gravel processing. Eisenhower Memorial Tunnel and Continental Divide to E.

Silverthrone, Mount (13,220 ft/4,029 m), S central Alaska, in Alaska Range, in Mt. McKinley Natl. Park, 130 mi/209 km N of Anchorage, 10 mi/16 km ENE of Mt. McKinley; 63°07′N 150°40′W.

Silverthrone, Mount (9,700 ft/2,957 m), SW B.C., Canada, in Coast Mts., 210 mi/338 km NW of Vancouver.

Silverton, village (1991 pop. 231), SE B.C., Canada, in Selkirk Mts., on Slocan L., 30 mi/48 km N of Nelson. Silver, lead, zinc mining.

Silverton, city (1990 pop. 5,859), Hamilton co., extreme SW Ohio, a NE residential suburb of Cincinnati; 39°11′N 84°24′W. Inc. 1904.

Silverton 1 uninc. town (1990 pop. 800), Shoshone co., N Idaho, 2 mi/3.2 km NW of Wallace, across highway (I-90) from Osburn. Silver-mining dist. Tourism; timber. Coeur d'Alene Natl. Forest to N; St. Joe Natl. Forest to S. **2** town (1990 pop. 5,635), Marion co., NW Oregon, 12 mi/19 km ENE of Salem, on Silver Creek; 45°00′N 122°46′W. Agr. (fruits, nuts, vegetables; poultry, cattle); mfg. (dairy prods., printing and publishing). Silver Falls State Park to SE on Silver Creek. Founded c.1853; inc. 1891. **3** town (1990 pop. 779), ⊙ Briscoe co., NW Texas, on Llano Estacado, 30 mi/48 km NE of Plainview, near Caprock escarpment; 34°28′N 101°17′W. Elev. 3,278 ft/999 m. Trade center for farm, ranch area (wheat, cotton; cattle; dairying); some mfg. MacKenzie Reservoir to NW.

Silverton, village (1990 pop. 716), ⊙ San Juan co., SW Colo., in San Juan Mts., on Animas R., and 39 mi/ 63 km NNE of Durango; 37°48′N 107°39′W. Elev. 9,318 ft/2,840 m. N terminus of Durango and Silverton Narrow Gauge RR. Tourist and trade center. Lead, silver, copper, gold mines in vicinity. Mfg. (publishing and printing). San Juan Natl. Forest to S and W; Rio Grande Natl. Forest to E. Founded 1874; inc. 1885.

Silvertown, industrial city, Upson co., W central Ga., just N of Thomaston; 32°54′N 84°20′W. Founded 1926 around the Silver tire fabric plant. Inc. 1929.

Silverwood Lake, 3 mi/4.8 km long, San Bernardino co., SE Calif., on West Branch Mojave R., 8 mi/12.9 km S of Hesperia; 34°17′N 117°18′W. Extends SW; max. capacity of 157,000 acre-ft. Formed by Mojave Dam (204 ft/62 m high), built (1971) by the Army Corps of Engineers for flood control. Surrounded by Silverwood Lake State Recreation Area.

Silvies River (SIL-veez), c. 90 mi/145 km long, E central Oregon; rises c. 45 mi/72 km NNW of Burns, near Strawberry Range in Malheur Natl. Forest; flows generally S, past Seneca and Burns to Malheur L. (no outlet).

Silvis, city (1990 pop. 6,926), Rock Island co., NW Ill., suburb of Rock Island–Moline; 41°30′N 90°24′W. Mfg. (rebuilt locomotives and parts); agr. in area (corn, soybeans; cattle). Inc. 1906.

Simcoe (SIM-ko), county (□ 1,663 sq mi/4,307 sq km; 1991 pop. 288,684), S Ont., central Canada, bet. Georgian Bay and L. Simcoe; ⊙ Barrie; 44°25′N 79°50′W.

Simcoe, town (1991 pop. 15,539), S Ont., central Canada, on the Lynn R. SW of Hamilton; 42°50′N 80°18′W. Market center for a region producing fruit and vegetables. Once well known for tobacco. Food-processing and canning plants.

Simcoe Island, SE Ont., central Canada, one of the Thousand Isls., at head of L. Ontario, near entrance to the St. Lawrence R., opposite Kingston, and just W of Wolfe Isl.; 4 mi/6 km long, 1 mi/2 km wide.

Simcoe, Lake (□ 539 sq mi/1,396 sq km), S Ont., central Canada, bet. Georgian Bay and L. Ontario. Cook and Kempenfelt bays and L. Couchiching are arms of the lake. Drains N through the Severn R. to Georgian Bay and forms part of the Trent Canal system. Orillia, Barrie, and several small resorts are on the lake.

Simeonof Island (SI-mee-yuh-nawf), SW Alaska, 55 mi/ 89 km ESE of Unga; 4 mi/6.4 km long, 3 mi/4.8 km wide; 54°54′N 159°15′W. Fishing.

Simi Valley (SEE-mee), city (1990 pop. 100,217), Ventura co., SW Calif., suburb 40 mi/64 km NW of Los Angeles, and 20 mi/32 km ENE of Oxnard; 34°16′N 118°45′W. In an oil, fruit, and farm region (vegetables, strawberries, flowers, nursery prods.). Highly residential, with light mfg. (electric and electronic prods. and equip., clothing, computer equip., filter aids, medical equip., fabricated metal prods., plastics prods., furniture). The pop. doubled bet. 1970 and 1990 because of its close proximity to the burgeoning Los Angeles area, reflecting the boom in the city's metropolitan area and in S Calif. in general. Santa Susana Mts. to N. Laid out 1887, inc. 1969.

Similkameen River (si-MIL-kuh-meen), 140 mi/225 km long, N Wash. and SW Canada (B.C.); rises in N Cascade Range in Manning Provincial Park (S B.C.), c.15 mi/24 km N of internatl. border and N of Allison Pass (4,436 ft/1,352 m); flows SE, then N, receives Pasayten R. from S (Wash.), turns SE again at Princeton, crossing into Wash. 35 mi/56 km S of Penticton; then flows in winding course E along Wash. side of border, flows through Enloe Dam (diversion dam) before entering Okanogan R. at Oroville. River lends its name to the region of B.C. that it flows through (the Similkameen).

Simla, village (1990 pop. 481), Elbert co., E central Colo., on Big Sandy Creek, and 45 mi/72 km NE of Colorado Springs; 39°08′N 104°04′W. Elev. 6,029 ft/1,838 m. Cattle; wheat, oats, sunflowers.

Simmesport (SIMZ-port), town (1990 pop. 2,092), Avoyelles parish, E central La., 45 mi/72 km SE of Alexandria, and on Atchafalaya R.; 30°59′N 91°49′W. In agr. area (cotton, rice, sugarcane); mfg. (aluminum prods.).

Simmonsville, village, in Johnston town, Providence co., central R.I., 5 mi/8 km W of Providence.

Simms, village, S central Bahama Isls., on N Long Isl., 31 mi/50 km NNW of Clarence Town; 23°27′N 75°15′W. Livestock; sisal.

Simms, village (1990 pop. 200), Cascade co., W central Mont., on Sun R., and 31 mi/50 km W of Great Falls. In irrigated region; wheat, barley, oats, hay; cattle, sheep, poultry; dairying.

Simms, N.C.: see SIMS.

Simojovel de Allende (see-mo-ho-VEL dai ah-YEN-dai), city (1990 pop. 6,340) and township, ⊙ Simojovel municipio, Chiapas, S Mexico, 37 mi/60 km NE of Tuxtla Gutiérrez; 18°14′N 92°40′W. Cereals, sugarcane, fruit. A Tzotzil Maya community.

Simon Peak (10,899 ft/3,322 m), W Alta., W Canada, on B.C. border, in Rocky Mts., in Jasper Natl. Park, 18 mi/ 29 km SW of Jasper; 52°40′N 118°17′W.

Simonton, village (1990 pop. 717), Fort Bend co., SE Texas, 37 mi/60 km W of Houston, near Brazos R.; 29°40′N 96°00′W. Agr. area (rice, cotton, vegetables; nurseries). Oil and natural gas.

Simoom Sound (si-MOOM), village, SW B.C., W Canada, on Queen Charlotte Strait, opposite N Vancouver Isl., 25 mi/40 km NE of Alert Bay; 50°45′N 126°29′W. Lumbering.

Simpson, village (1991 pop. 212), S Sask., W Canada, 16 mi/26 km S of Watrous; 51°27′N 105°27′W. Wheat; livestock.

Simpson 1 county (□ 236 sq mi/611 sq km; 1990 pop. 15,145), S Ky., on Tenn. state line (S); ⊙ Franklin; 36°44′N 86°34′W. Drained by West Fork of Drakes Creek. Rolling agr. area (dark and burley tobacco, strawberries, barley, wheat, corn, soybean, hay, alfalfa; hog, cattle, poultry; dairying; timber); limestone quarries. Mfg. at Franklin. Formed 1819. **2** county (□ 590 sq mi/1,528 sq km; 1990 pop. 23,953), S central Miss.; ⊙ Mendenhall; 31°55′N 89°55′W. Bounded W by Pearl R.; drained by Strong R. and Okatoma Creek. Agr. (cotton, corn; poultry, cattle; timber). Simpson Co. Legion L. (state lake) in E. Formed 1824.

Simpson (SIMP-suhn), uninc. town (1990 pop. 1,670), Fell township, Lackawanna co., NE Pa., 16 mi/26 km NE of Scranton, and 2 mi/3.2 km NE of Carbondale; 41°35′N 75°29′W. Mfg. (bldg. materials, safety lenses); former anthracite coal center.

Simpson 1 village (1990 pop. 61), Johnson co., S Ill., 8 mi/12.9 km ENE of Vienna; 37°28′N 88°45′W. In fruit-growing region. Next to Shawnee Natl. Forest. **2** village (1990 pop. 107), Cloud and Mitchell cos., N central Kansas, on Solomon R., and 11 mi/18 km ESE of Beloit; 39°23′N 97°55′W. Grain; livestock. **3** village (1990 pop. 536), Vernon parish, W La. 30 mi/48 km W of Alexandria, near Calcasieu R.; 31°16′N 93°01′W. In agr. area (sweet potatoes, watermelons; cattle, hogs, poultry; dairying). Timber. **4** village (1990 pop. 410), Pitt co., E central N.C., on Tar R., and 6 mi/9.7 km ESE of Greenville, near Tar R.; 35°34′N 77°16′W. Tobacco, cotton, peanuts, grain; chickens, livestock.

Simpson Island, W Ont., central Canada, in L. Superior, at entrance of Nipigon Bay, 70 mi/113 km ENE of Thunder Bay, just E of Isle St. Ignace; 10 mi/16 km long, 6 mi/10 km wide. Just E are small Salter, Silson, and Copper isls.

Simpson Strait, S Franklin and N Keewatin dists., N.W.T., N Canada, arm of the Arctic Ocean, bet. King William Isl. (N) and Adelaide Peninsula of mainland (S); 40 mi. long, 2 mi/3.2 km–10 mi/16 km wide; 68°25′N 97°30′W. Opens W on Queen Maud Gulf.

Simpsonville, city (1990 pop. 11,708), Greenville co., NW S.C., 12 mi/19 km SE of Greenville, near Reedy R.; 34°43′N 82°15′W. Mfg. includes textiles, electrical goods, machinery, plastic prods.; clothing, chemicals,

ribbon cables. Agr. includes grain, tomatoes, soybeans, sorghum, peaches; cattle, hogs, poultry.

Simpsonville, town (1990 pop. 907), Shelby co., Ky., 25 mi/40 km E of Louisville, on Plum Creek, in Bluegrass region; 38°13′N 85°20′W. Mfg. (furniture, hardware; sausage processing).

Sims 1 (SIMZ), village (1990 pop. 338), Wayne co., SE Ill., 9 mi/14.5 km W of Fairfield; 38°21′N 88°31′W. In agr. area; oil wells. **2** village (1990 pop. 124), Wilson co., E central N.C., 8 mi/12.9 km WNW of Wilson; 35°45′N 78°03′W. Mfg. (wood prods., concrete). Sometimes spelled Simms.

Simsboro (SIMZ-buhr-o), village (1990 pop. 634), Lincoln parish, N La., 7 mi/11 km W of Ruston; 32°32′N 92°47′W. In agr. and timber area. Mfg. (glass prods., wood prods., treated lumber). Jackson-Bienville State Wildlife Area to S.

Simsbury, town (1990 pop. 22,023), Hartford co., N Conn.; 41°52′N 49°72′W. Although the town is mainly residential, it produces ordnance, machinery, and chemicals. Agr. and insurance offices. The Westminster and the Ethel Walker schools are here. Became home to many Olympic skaters from the former Soviet Union in the early 1990s with the opening of the Internatl. Skating Center. Gifford Pinchot, the forester and public official, b. here. Includes village of Tariffville (1990 pop. 1,477). Inc. 1670.

Sinai, village (1990 pop. 120), Brookings co., E S.Dak., 13 mi/21 km WSW of Brookings; 44°15′N 97°02′W.

Sinai, Mount (SEI-nei), peak (2,329 ft/710 m), S Grenada, W.I., 4 mi/6.4 km ENE of St. George's; 12°04′N 61°41′W.

Sinaloa (see-nah-LO-ah), state (□ 22,582 sq mi/ 58,487 sq km; 1990 pop. 2,204,054), W Mexico, on the Gulf of California and the Pacific Ocean; ⊙ CULIACÁN ROSALES 22°31′N 105°24′W. A long, narrow territory lying bet. the ocean and the Sierra Madre Occidental, Sinaloa has low, hot, humid plains and numerous marshes. The varying elev., many rivers, and fertile valleys contribute to the variety of crops grown under irrigation, including grains, tomatoes, cotton, sugarcane, and rice. The state's industry is mostly related to the processing of agr. prods. Fishing and livestock breeding are economically important. Sinaloa lies in a rich mining region where gold, silver, zinc, and copper are mined. Its forest prods.—fine woods—are not widely exploited. The state has numerous mineral springs. Sinaloa's coast has many sheltered harbors, but only MAZATLÁN is a major port. Sinaloa was joined with Sonora during the Span. period; it became a separate state in 1830.

Sinaloa, Mexico: see SINALOA DE LEYVA.

Sinaloa de Leyva (see-nah-LO-ah de LEI-vah), city (1990 pop. 3,435) and township, ⊙ Sinaloa municipio, Sinaloa, NW Mexico, on Sinaloa R., and 90 mi/145 km NW of Culiacán Rosales; 25°15′N 08°14′W. Agr. center (corn, chickpeas, tomatoes, sugarcane, fruit).

Sinaloa River (see-nah-LO-ah), c.200 mi/322 km long, NW Mexico; rises as Mohinora R. in Sierra Madre Occidental near border bet. Chihuahua and Sinaloa states; flows SW through fertile coastal lowlands, past Sinaloa and Guasave, to Gulf of California 20 mi/32 km S of Guazaub; 25°10′N 108°29′W.

Sinanché (see-nahn-CHAI), town (1990 pop. 2,617), Yucatán, SE Mexico, 30 mi/48 km NE of Mérida, on Mexico Highway 281; 21°13′N 89°11′W. Henequen.

Sinclair, village (1990 pop. 500), Carbon co., S Wyo., 7 mi/11.3 km E of Rawlins; 41°46′N 107°07′W. Elev. c.6,592 ft/2,009 m. Petroleum prods. Refinery processes oil from Lost Soldier field. Fort Steele Historic Site to E; Seminoe Reservoir and State Park to NE. Town named Parco until 1943.

Sinclair, Lake, reservoir, Baldwin, Hancock, and Putnam cos., NE central Ga., on Oconee R., 4 mi/6.4 km NNE of Milledgeville; 33°08′N 83°12′W. Main channel extends c.25 mi/40 km NNE from dam; Little R. joins 5 mi/8 km above dam, forms 5-mi/8-km arm. Max. capacity of 370,000 acre-ft. Formed by Wallace Dam

(107 ft/33 m high), built (1974) by the Ga. Power Company for power generaion. Oconee Natl. Forest along W arm.

Sinclairville, village (□ 1 sq mi/2.6 sq km; 1990 pop. 708), Chautauqua co., extreme W N.Y., 12 mi/19 km N of Jamestown; 42°15′N 79°15′W. Canned foods; dairy prods.; lumbering.

Sinepuxent Bay (SI-nah-PUHK-suhnt), narrow lagoon, c.12 mi/19 km long, SE Md., protected from the Atlantic Ocean by Assateague Isl. (E); communicates directly with Chincoteague Bay (S), and with ocean through Ocean City Inlet, at N end of bay.

Sing Sing, N.Y.: see OSSINING.

Singac, N.J.: see LITTLE FALLS.

Singers Glen, uninc. village, Rockingham co., NW Va., in Shenandoah Valley, c.8 mi/12.9 km NNW of Harrisonburg; 38°33′N 78°54′W.

Singuilucan (seen-gee-LOO-kahn), town (1990 pop. 2,918), Hidalgo, central Mexico, 19 mi/31 km SE of Pachuca de Soto; 19°58′N 98°31′W. Elev. 8,284 ft/2,525 m. Grain, maguey; livestock.

Sinissippi Lake, Wis.: see HUSTISFORD.

Sinking Spring, village (1990 pop. 189), Highland co., SW Ohio, 28 mi/45 km SW of Chillicothe; 39°04′N 83°23′W. Nearby are Fort Hill and Serpent Mound, prehistoric earthworks.

Sinking Spring, borough (1990 pop. 2,467), Berks co., SE central Pa., suburb 5 mi/8 km W of Reading, on Cacoosing Creek; 40°19′N 76°01′E. RR junction Mfg. (feeds, crushed stone, paints, plastics, fabricated steel and metal prods., paper prods.; printing and publishing). Settled 1793, laid out 1831, inc. 1913.

Sinnemahoning Creek (SI-nah-ma-HO-ning), 15 mi/24 km long, N central Pa.; formed by joining of Driftwood and Bennett branches of Sinnemahoning Creek, in S central Cameron co., 13 mi/21 km SSE of Emporium, at Driftwood; flows E through Bucktail State Park to West Branch Susquehanna R., 9 mi/14.5 km WSW of Renovo; 41°20′N 78°08′W. Receives First Fork 3 mi/4.8 km ESE of Driftwood. Bennett Branch rises in NW Clearfield co., 5 mi/8 km NE of DuBois, flows c.50 mi/80 km NE. Driftwood Branch rises in NE Elk co., 10 mi/16 km NNE of St. Marys flows c.45 mi/72 km SE past Emporium and through Bucktail State Park. First Fork Sinnemahoning Creek rises in central Potter co., flows c.40 mi/64 km generally S through George B. Stevenson reservoir, in Sinnemahoning State Park, to Sinnemahoning Creek.

Sinsinawa, village, Grant co., extreme SW Wis., 6 mi/9.7 km E of Dubuque (Iowa). Livestock raising. Native Amer. burial mound here.

Sint Anna Bay or **Santa Anna Bay**, harbor of Willemstad, W Curaçao isl., Neth. Antilles. A narrow, deep channel c.1 mi/1.6 km long, 331 ft/101 m–974 ft/297 m wide. The city is built on both sides; along it stretch several wharves. The bay widens into Schottegat, a deep lagoon.

Sint Christoffelberg (SINT KRI-staw-fuhl-BERKH), highest elev. (1,220 ft/372 m) on Curaçao isl., Neth. Antilles, 20 mi/32 km NW of Willemstad; 12°20′N 69°08′W.

Sint Eustatius, Neth. Antilles: see SAINT EUSTATIUS.

Sint Maarten, Fr. West Indies: see SAINT MARTIN.

Sintaluta (sin-tuh-LOO-tuh), town (1991 pop. 185), SE Sask., W Canada, 50 mi/80 km E of Regina; 50°29′N 103°26′W. Grain elevators.

Sinton, town (1990 pop. 5,549), ⊙ San Patricio co., S Texas, 19 mi/31 km NNW of Corpus Christi; 28°01′N 97°30′W. RR junction, shipping, trade center in cotton, cattle, sorghum, oil area; oil refining; mfg. (printing, concrete). Settled c.1892, inc. 1916.

Sioux 1 (SOO), county (□ 768 sq mi/1,989 sq km; 1990 pop. 29,903), NW Iowa, on S.Dak. state line (formed here by Big Sioux R.); ⊙ Orange City; 43°04′N 96°10′W. Prairie agr. area (hogs, cattle, poultry; corn, oats, hay) drained by Rock, Floyd, and West Branch Floyd rivers. Formed 1851. **2** county (□ 2,067 sq mi/5,354 sq km; 1990 pop. 1,549), extreme NW Nebr., on S.Dak. (N) and Wyo. (W) state lines; ⊙ Harrison;

42°28′N 103°46′W. In Pine Ridge grazing region; drained by branches of White and Niobrara rivers. Cattle, hogs; corn, alfalfa, beans, sugar beets. Agate Fossil Beds Natl. Monument at center; Fort Robinson State Park on E border; Oglala Natl. Grasslands in N, including Toadstool Park badlands with its moon-like landscape. Formed 1877. **3** county (□ 1,102 sq mi/2,854 sq km; 1990 pop. 3,761), S N.Dak.; ⊙ Fort Yates; 46°06′N 101°02′W. N border formed by Cedar Creek and Cannonball R. Cattle; wheat; dairying. Standing Rock Indian Reservation includes entire co. and Corson co. (S.Dak.) to S; hq. at Fort Yates. Formed 1914. Sitting Bull Burial Site at Fort Yates; SE corner, including Fort Yates, is in Central time zone, remainder in Mountain time zone (Missouri R. forms border in NE).

Sioux Center, town (1990 pop. 5,074), Sioux co., NW Iowa, 9 mi/14.5 km NW of Orange; agr. trade center with several cooperatives; 43°04′N 96°10′W. Mfg. (electric prods., machinery, food, bldg. materials, medical supplies, feeds, dressed poultry; pork processing). Inc. 1891. Many people of Du. descent in the area.

Sioux City, city (1990 pop. 80,505), ⊙ Woodbury co., NW Iowa, at the junction of the Big Sioux and the Floyd rivers with the Missouri R.; 42°30′N 96°23′W. RR junction and center. Shipping, wholesale trade, and industrial center for an extensive agr. and livestock area (including nearby states). It has a huge, central livestock market, a leading hog market, meatpacking houses, and processing plants for popcorn, poultry, and honey. Mfg. (chemicals and fertilizers, electric and electronic goods, consumer goods, feeds, apparel, machinery, transportation equip., power supplies, food and beverages, paper prods., computer equip., communication towers, fabricated metal prods., seed; printing, architectural millwork). Named for the ethnic group of a Native Amer. chief, Chirp War Eagle (his grave is in the W part of city at mouth of the Big Sioux), who aided the area's early pioneers. Seat of Morningside, Briar Cliff, and Western Iowa Technical Community cols. Nearby are Stone State Park in NW corner of city and Browns L. State Park to S. A monument commemorating the death and burial in 1804 of Sgt. Charles Floyd of the Lewis and Clark expedition is located in Floyd Park, overlooking river. Inc. 1857.

Sioux Falls, city (1990 pop. 100,814), ⊙ Minnehaha co., and includes N. Lincoln co., SE S.Dak., on the Big Sioux R. First settled in 1856, then abandoned in 1862 because of Native Amer. raids, but with the establishment (1865) of Fort Dakota it was resettled. Named for the falls on the Big Sioux R. (which furnish power), Sioux Falls is the largest city in the state and the commercial, industrial, and shipping center of an extensive agr. area. It has an important livestock market (one of the largest in the U.S.) as well as meat-processing plants. Electronics and machinery are among the principal manufactures. Sandstone ("Sioux Falls granite") is quarried nearby. Mfg. (signs, bldg. materials, computers, hot air balloons, plastic prods., consumer goods, sheet metal, paper prods., machinery, foods, apparel, transportation equip., electronic goods, storage bins, wood prods.; printing; sawmill). Seat of Univ. of Sioux Falls, Augustana Col., N. Amer. Baptist Seminary, and School for the Hearing Impaired. Also in the city are the S.Dak. Penitentiary (?is)& State Prison Farm (?is)& Joe Foss Field, Sioux Falls Regional Airport in N part, Pettigrew Mus. (?is)& Old Courthouse Mus.; W. H. Lyons Fairgrounds, and the Great Plains Zoo. Siouxland Heritage Mus.; Battleship U.S.S. *South Dakota* Memorial. Jim Savage Western Art Gall. (?is)& Historical Center. EROS data Center is 15 mi/24 km NE. Great Bear Ski Valley in NE. Highway Crossroads (I-90, E-W; I-29, N-S). Inc. as a village 1877, as a city 1883.

Sioux Lookout (SOO), town (1991 pop. 3,311), NW Ont., central Canada, on Pelican L. (4 mi/6 km long), near Lac Seul, 180 mi/290 km NW of Thunder Bay; 50°06′N 91°55′W. Elev. 1,198 ft/365 m. Gold-mining and lumbering center; creosote works. Distributing point for surrounding region.

Sioux Rapids (SOO), town (1990 pop. 761), Buena Vista co., NW Iowa, on Little Sioux R., and 16 mi/26 km N of Storm Lake; 42°53′N 95°09′W. Mfg. of metal prods. Sand pits nearby. Plotted 1858, replotted 1869.

Siparia (si-pah-REE-ah), village, SW Trinidad, Trinidad and Tobago, RR terminus 10 mi/16 km S of San Fernando; 10°09′N 61°28′W. In cacao-growing region. Formerly a Span. mission; has a church, founded by Capuchins (1758), with shrine to Black Virgin. Petroleum wells nearby.

Sipsey, village (1990 pop. 568), Walker co., NE Ala., on Mulberry Fork, and 10 mi/16 km E of Jasper. Coal mine. In agr. area.

Sipsey Creek, c.35 mi/56 km long, NW Ala. and NE Miss.; rises in NW Marion co. (Ala.); flows SW to Buttahatchee R. 15 mi/24 km ENE of Aberdeen (Miss.).

Sipsey Fork, river, c.60 mi/97 km long, NW Ala.; rises in Lawrence co.; flows SE to Mulberry Fork of Black Warrior R. 12 mi/19 km E of Jasper. Feeds Lewis Smith L. on SE side of William B. Bankhead Natl. Forest.

Sipsey River, c.100 mi/161 km long, W Ala.; rises in SE Marion co.; flows S and SW to Tombigbee R. 8 mi/12.9 km S of Aliceville.

Sir Alexander, Mount (10,740 ft/3,274 m), E B.C., W Canada, in Rocky Mts., 100 mi/161 km E of Prince George.

Sir Douglas, Mount (11,174 ft/3,406 m), SW Alta., W Canada, near B.C. border, in Rocky Mts., 35 mi/56 km SSE of Banff.

Sir Francis Drake's Channel, small strait in Br.V.I., bet. S and E Tortola isl. and E Virgin Gorda isl, and islets to its SW.

Sir James McBrien, Mount (9,049 ft/2,758 m), SW Mackenzie dist., N.W.T., N Canada, in Mackenzie Mts.; 62°07′N 127°45′W.

Sir John Abbott, Mount (11,250 ft/3,429 m), E B.C., W Canada, in Premier Group of Rocky Mts., 75 mi/121 km W of Jasper.

Sir John Thompson, Mount (11,250 ft/3,429 m), E B.C., W Canada, in Premier Group of Rocky Mts., 70 mi/113 km W of Jasper; 52°45′N 119°39′W. The large Thompson Icefield extends ESE of the peak.

Sir Mackenzie Bowell, Mount (11,000 ft/3,353 m), E B.C., W Canada, in Premier Group of Rocky Mts., 70 mi/113 km W of Jasper; 52°52′N 119°46′W.

Sir Sandford, Mount (11,590 ft/3,533 m), SE B.C., W Canada, in Selkirk Mts., on edge of Hamber Provincial Park, 55 mi/89 km NNW of Revelstoke; 51°39′N 117°52′W.

Sir Wilfrid Laurier, Mount (11,750 ft/3,581 m), E B.C., W Canada, in Premier Group of Rocky Mts., 70 mi/113 km W of Jasper; 52°48′N 119°45′W.

Sir Wilfrid, Mount (2,569 ft/783 m), SW Que., E Canada, in the Laurentians, 10 mi/16 km NNW of Mont Laurier; 46°42′N 75°35′W. Named for Sir Wilfrid Laurier.

Siren, town (1990 pop. 863), Burnett co., NW Wis., 16 mi/26 km E of Grantsburg; 45°46′N 92°22′W. Mfg. (furniture, fencing). St. Croix Indian Reservation to NE on Big Sand L.

Sisal (see-SAHL), port (1990 pop. 1,460), Hunucmá municipio, Yucatán, SE Mexico, on bar off N coast, 29 mi/47 km NW of Mérida; 21°10′N 90°01′W. Fishing village with fine beaches. Has colonial church, monastery.

Siskiwit Bay (SIS-ki-wit), large inlet, SE side of Isle Royale, L. Superior, N Mich., 12 mi/19 km long, 3 mi/4.8 km wide, separated from lake by small peninsula and isl. chain, in Isle Royale Natl. Park; 47°54′N 88°55′W. Also known as Siskiwit L.

Siskiyou, county (□ 6,287 sq mi/16,283 sq km; 1990 pop. 43,531), N Calif., on Oregon (N) state line; ⊙ Yreka; 41°36′N 122°32′W. In W, Klamath Mts. (peaks up to c.9,000 ft/2,743 m) are drained by Klamath R. and tributaries; in E center is part of Cascade Range, here rising to 14,162 ft/4,317 m at Mt. Shasta in S center, whose glacier-fed springs are sources of Shasta, Sacramento, and McCloud rivers, all in S. Wheat, barley, oats, potatoes, onions, sugar beets; cattle, lambs; mining and quarrying (sand, gravel). To E of the Cascades lies a semiarid farming and lumbering region (partly irrigated) of volcanic soils and lava beds (including Lava Beds Natl. Monument) in NE; Tule L. and Lower Klamath L. natl. wildlife refuges in NE. Marble Mts. Wilderness Area in W; part of Shasta Natl. Forest in S; part of Klamath Natl. Forest in center and W; part of Modoc Natl. Forest on E border. Part of Castle Crags State Park on S border. Mt. scenery, hunting, fishing attract vacationers. Formed 1852.

Siskiyou Mountains, N Calif. and SW Oregon, a range of Klamath Mts. extending NE from Calif. coast S of Crescent City, into Josephine and Jackson cos., Oregon; mark divide bet. Rogue (N) and Klamath (S) rivers. Chief peaks in Oregon are Mt. Ashland (7,533 ft/ 2,296 m), Dutchman Peak (7,555 ft/2,303 m), and Siskiyou Peak (7,147 ft/2,178 m), all S of Medford. Preston Peak (7,309 ft/2,228 m), is in Calif., c.30 mi/48 km E of Crescent City. Oregon Caves Natl. Monument attracts tourists. Logging (pine, fir, spruce), hunting, fishing. Fruit growing (esp. pears) and agr. in Rogue R. valley.

Sisquoc River, c.50 mi/80 km long, SW Calif.; rises in E Santa Barbara co., c.20 mi/32 km NNE of Santa Barbara; flows W past village of Sisquoc to Cuyama R. SE of Santa Maria; flow is intermittent.

Sisseton (SIS-suh-ton), town (1990 pop. 2,181), ⊙ Roberts co., NE S.Dak., 70 mi/113 km ENE of Aberdeen, 10 mi/16 km W of L. Traverse; 45°39′N 97°02′W. Trade center for diversified farming region; agency hq. for L. Traverse (Sisseton) Indian Reservation. Cattle feed, dairy prods.; livestock, poultry. Small lakes to W. Community Col. (?is)& Sisseton Agency Village to S. Fort Sisseton, 20 mi/32 km W, is historic military outpost est. 1864. Inc. 1892.

Sisson, Calif.: see MOUNT SHASTA.

Sissonville (SIS-uhn-vil), uninc. town (1990 pop. 4,290), Kanawha co., W central W.Va., 14 mi/23 km N of Charleston; 38°30′N 81°38′W. Agr. (corn, tobacco); cattle, poultry. Woodrun Wildlife Management Area to N.

Sister Bay, village (1990 pop. 675), Door co., NE Wis., on inlet of Green Bay, on Door Peninsula, 27 mi/43 km NE of Sturgeon Bay; 45°11′N 87°07′W. Dairying; cherry growing; light mfg. Tourism. Offshore are small Sister Isls.

Sisters, village (1990 pop. 679), Deschutes co., central Oregon, 20 mi/32 km NW of Bend, near Squaw Creek, in Cascade Range; 44°17′N 121°32′W. Elev. 3,182 ft/ 970 m. Prefabricated homes, lumber. Tourism; outfitting point for hunting, fishing. Corbett State Park and springs of the Metolius R. to NW. Surrounded by Deschutes Natl. Forest. Three Sisters peaks and Wilderness Area to SW; Mt. Washington Wilderness Area to W. Fish hatcheries to NW.

Sisters, the, group of 3 islets, S Ont., central Canada, and NE Ohio, at W end of L. Erie, 10 mi/16 km–25 mi/ 40 km W of Pelee Isl.; East Sister Isl. and Middle Sister Isl. belong to Ont., West Sister Isl. to Ohio.

Sistersville, town (1990 pop. 1,797), Tyler co., NW W.Va., 10 mi/16 km SW of New Martinsville, on the Ohio R. (ferry to Fly, Ohio); 39°33′N 81°0′W. Mfg. (chemicals; machining; printing and publishing). Wells Inn Hotel (1894). Settled 1802.

Sitalá (see-tah-LAH), town (1990 pop. 1,057), in N central Chiapas, Mexico, 28 mi/45 km NE of San Cristóbal de Las Casas; 17°05′N 92°27′W. Agr. produces corn, sugarcane, beans, and fruits. The climate is hot and humid with tropical forests. In Tzeltal Maya area.

Sitgreaves Mountain (sit-greevz) (9,388 ft/2,861 m), N central Ariz., 22 mi/35 km WNW of Flagstaff, 35°20′N 112°00′W.

Sitio de Xitlapehua (SEE-tee-o dai zee-TLAH-PAI-hwah), town (1990 pop. 485), S Oaxaca, Mexico, 4 mi/ 6.4 km E of Miahuatuán de Porfirio Diaz, in the Miahuatlán valley; 16°19′N 96°32′W. Elev 5,085 ft/1,550 m. On hard surface road.

Sitka (SIT-kuh), city (1990 pop. 8,588), Sitka census div., SE Alaska, in the Alexander Archipelago, on Baranof Isl.; 57°05′N 135°14′W. Tourism; fishing (salmon, halibut, red snapper, crab, herring, abalone, and clams).

There are also canneries. Old Sitka, now at Old Harbor ferry landing, was founded (1799) by Aleksandr Baranov. Destroyed by Tlingits in 1802, the Rus. port was rebuilt at its present site and became the flourishing capital of Rus. Amer. Here, in 1867, the U.S. officially took possession of Alaska from Russia, and Sitka remained the capital until 1900. Points of interest include Sitka Natl. Historical Park, scene of a decisive battle (1804) bet. the Russians and the Tlinglits; the Rus. Orthodox Cathedral of St. Michael (1844–1848); Sheldon Jackson Mus.; and Castle Hill, site of the transfer of Alaska to the U.S., which is commemorated by the annual Alaska Day Festival in Oct. Sitka Natl. Cemetery (1924); state logging championships are also held here. The city has Sheldon Jackson Col. (Presbyterian) and a Univ. of Alaska campus; Alaska Police Acad. Mt. Edgecumbe (3,201 ft/976 m), on an isl. to the W, can be seen from Sitka's harbor. Bridge to Japonsky isl. and airport. Inc. 1971.

Sitka (SIT-kuh), borough (□ 2,882 sq mi/7,464 sq km; 1990 pop. 8,588), SE Alaska, on Pacific Ocean (W), including Baranof, Kruzof, and part of Chichagof isls. Main town is Sitka. Sitka Natl. Historical Park in W center; most of borough in Tongass Natl. Forest. Borough bisected by Peril Strait. Tourism. Fishing; timber.

Sitka Dam, Greater Sitka borough, extreme SE Alaska, on Baranof isl. and on Medvetcha R.; 210 ft/64 m high; 56°54′N 135°04′W. Built (1961) by the City of Sitka for hydroelectric power and water supply; multi-arch construction. The reservoir created has a max. capacity of 185,000 acre-ft.

Sitka Historical Park, SE Alaska; 57°04′N 135°13′W. Covers 107 acres/43 ha. Proclaimed Sitka Natl. Monument 1910, declared Natl. Historic Park 1972; site of the Tlingit peoples' defeat by Russians in 1804. Only battle bet. Native Americans and Europeans in Alaska's history. Authentic totem poles.

Sitka Sound, SE Alaska, on W side of Baranof Isl., Alexander Archipelago; entrance to Sitka from Gulf of Alaska; washes SE shore of Kruzof Isl.

Sitkalidak Island, S Alaska, in Gulf of Alaska, off SE Kodiak Isl., 50 mi/80 km SW of Kodiak; 23 mi/37 km long, 3 mi/4.8 km–6 mi/9.7 km wide; 57°07′N 153°10′W. Port Hobron bay (N) was formerly site of whaling station.

Siuslaw River (sei-YOO-slaw), 110 mi/177 km long, W Oregon; rises in Coast Range S of Eugene, 5 mi/8 km SW of Cottage Grove; flows WNW and W to the Pacific Ocean at Florence. Lower course passes through Siuslaw Natl. Forest.

Siwhe Mountain (9,280 ft/2,829 m), SW B.C., W Canada, in Coast Mts., 80 mi/129 km N of Chilliwack.

Six Men's Bay, NW Barbados, 2 mi/3.2 km N of Speightstown. Dotted with small fishing villages.

Six Mile, village (1990 pop. 562), Pickens co., NW S.C., 9 mi/14.5 km SSW of Pickens, and 24 mi/39 km W of Greenville; 34°48′N 82°49′W. Mfg. includes machining; agr. includes dairying; poultry, hogs; corn.

Six Mile Run, Pa.: see COALDALE.

Sixtymile, village, W Yukon, W Canada, near U.S. (Alaska) border, 40 mi/64 km W of Dawson. Gold mining.

Siyeh, Mount, Mont.: see LEWIS RANGE.

Skagit (SKA-jit), county (□ 1,920 sq mi/4,973 sq km; 1990 pop. 79,555), NW Wash.; ⊙ Mount Vernon. 48°29′N 121°47′W. Bounded W by Rosario Strait, SW by Skagit Bay (Puget Sound); E by crest of Cascade Range. Drained by Skagit, Sark, Baker, Cascade, and South Fork Nooksack rivers. Swinomish Indian Reservation in W; parts of Mt. Baker–Snoqualmie Natl. Forest in E, S, and N. Berries, peas, carrots, potatoes, wheat, barley, oats, alfalfa, hay, tulips; dairying; fish, oysters; cattle, poultry. Lower Baker Dam, forms Shannon L., and Upper Baker Dam (on co. line, forms Baker L.) both on Baker R. in N center. Rockport State Park in E; parts of North Cascade Natl. Park and part of Ross L. Natl. Recreation Area (in Skagit R.) in NE. W part of co. includes Fidalgo Isl., with city of Anacortes, connected to mainland by bridges. Bay View State Park in W; Saddlebag Isl. State Park, in Padilla Bay, Skagit

Isl. and Hope Isl. state parks, in Skagit Bay, all in W. Formed 1883.

Skagit (SKA-jit), river, c.150 mi/240 km long, B.C., W Canada and Wash.; rises in the Cascade Range, B.C.; flows SW through Wash. into Puget Sound. Gorge High, Diablo, and Ross dams provide electricity for Seattle. The lakes formed behind the dams are in a 40-mi/64-km stretch of river canyon that makes up Ross L. Natl. Recreation Area. Ross L., 24 mi/39 km long, extends to the Can. border.

Skagway (SKAG-wai), city (1990 pop. 692), Skagway-Yakutat census div., SE Alaska, in the Panhandle, at the head of Lynn Canal; 59°28′N 135°19′W. It is an ice-free port of entry; a trade and tourist center; the coastal terminus of the White Pass and Yukon RR, which halted passenger service in 1982 but continues as a passenger tourist train to White Pass summit and L. Bennett; and the northernmost terminal of the state ferry system from Prince Rupert (B.C.). During the gold rush of 1897–1898 it was a major disembarking point to the Klondike. Pop. reached 20,000 in 1898, but declined in 1899 after gold rush. Reid Falls (295 ft/90 m) is nearby. Tourism is main industry. Historic Main Street has original false-front bldgs., boardwalks. Klondike Gold Rush Natl. Historical Park in and NE of town. Founded 1897, inc. 1900.

Skalkaho Pass, Mont.: see SAPPHIRE MOUNTAINS.

Skamania (skuh-MAIN-yuh), county (□ 1,676 sq mi/ 4,341 sq km; 1990 pop. 8,289), SW Wash., on Oregon state line; ⊙ Stevenson; 46°02′N 121°55′W. Bounded S by Columbia R. (forms Bonneville reservoir, SE). Mt. area watered by Lewis and Cispus rivers. Lumber; cattle; dairying; fruit, nuts. Part of Gifford Pinchot Natl. Forest, in center and N, dominates most of co., including Indian Heaven and Trapper Creek wilderness areas in center, part of Mt. Adams Wilderness Area in NE. Beacon Rock State Park in S. Mt. Saint Helens (8,366 ft/2,550 m) and main part of Mt. Saint Helens Natl. Volcanic Monument in NW, including Spirit L.; Swift Reservoir, Lewis R., in W. Formed 1854.

Skaneateles (ski-nee-AT-luhs), resort village (□ 1 sq mi/2.6 sq km; 1990 pop. 2,724), Onondaga co., central N.Y., in Finger Lakes region, at outlet and N end of Skaneateles L., 16 mi/26 km SW of Syracuse; 42°56′N 76°25′W. Mfg. (machinery, transportation equip., consumer goods, wood prods., medical instruments); agr. (hay, oats, wheat). Village in a Historic Dist. Settled before 1800, inc. 1833.

Skaneateles Lake, N.Y.: see FINGER LAKES.

Skanee (SKAH-nee), village, Baraga co., NW Upper Peninsula, N Mich., 15 mi/24 km NE of L'Anse, on Huron Bay, L. Superior; 46°52′N 88°12′W. Ships apples, potatoes, dairy prods. NE of L'Anse Indian Reservation.

Skedee (skuh-DEE), village (1990 pop. 96), Pawnee co., N Okla., 6 mi/9.7 km NE of Pawnee, near Black Bear Creek; 36°22′N 96°42′W. In agr. area.

Skeena (SKEE-nuh), river, c.360 mi/580 km long, B.C., W Canada; rises in the Stikine Mts., W B.C.; flows S and SW to the Pacific Ocean near Prince Rupert. Navigable for c.100 mi/161 km upstream. There are fish-processing plants near the mouth of the river. The Bulkley R. is its chief tributary.

Skegemog, Lake, Mich.: see ELK LAKE.

Skellytown, village (1990 pop. 664), Carson co., extreme N Texas, 12 mi/19 km WNW of Pampa; 35°34′N 101°10′W. RR spur terminus. Oil and natural gas. Cattle; wheat, corn, hay.

Skiatook (SKEI-uh-took), town (1990 pop. 4,910), Osage and Tulsa cos., NE Okla., 15 mi/24 km N of Tulsa, and on Bird Creek; 36°22′N 96°02′W. In agr. area; oil wells; mfg. (process and duct burners; light mfg). Skiatook L. reservoir to W (on Hominy Creek). Settled 1886, inc. 1907.

Skiatook Lake, reservoir (□ 16 sq mi/41 sq km), Osage co., NE Okla., on Hominy Creek, in Osage Indian Reservation, 20 mi/32km N of Tulsa; 36°21′N 96°05′W. Max. capacity 893,000 acre-ft. Formed by Skiatook L. Dam (143 ft/44 m high), built (1984) by Army Corps of Engineers for flood control; also used for water supply and recreation.

Skidaway Island (SKI-duh-wai), one of the Sea Isls., in Chatham co., SE Ga., just off the coast, 10 mi/16 km SSE of Savannah; bet. 2 distributaries of Savannah R.; c.10 mi/16 km long and wide; 31°56′N 81°01′W. Marshy. Residential suburb of Savannah and site of the Skidaway Inst. of Oceanography, operated by the Univ. System of Ga. Skidaway Isl. State Park.

Skidegate (SKI-duh-git), village, W B.C., W Canada, on SE Graham Isl., on Skidegate Inlet, 3 mi/5 km E of Queen Charlotte; 53°15′N 132°00′W. Lumbering; livestock; potatoes. Adjoining is a Haida village.

Skidegate Inlet, arm of Hecate Strait, W B.C., W Canada, bet. Graham (N) and Moresby (S) isls.; 16 mi/26 km long, 1 mi/2 km–7 mi/11 km wide. In lumbering and cattle-raising area. Queen Charlotte village is on N shore; Skidegate Channel (18 mi/29 km long) joins inlet with the Pacific Ocean.

Skidmore, city (1990 pop. 404), Nodaway co., NW Mo., on Nodaway R., and 12 mi/19 km SW of Maryville; 40°17′N 95°04′W. Corn, wheat, soybeans; cattle, hogs.

Skidmore, uninc village (1990 pop. 500), Bee co., S Texas, 12 mi/19 km SSE of Beeville. RR junction, in agr. area; oil and gas.

Skiff Lake (□ 3 sq mi/8 sq km), SW N.B., E Canada, near U.S. (Maine) border, 22 mi/35 km S of Woodstock; 3 mi/5 km long, a mi/3 km wide.

Skihist Mountain (9,660 ft/2,944 m), S B.C., W Canada, in Coast Mts., 70 mi/113 km N of Chilliwack.

Skilak Lake (SKEE lak), S Alaska, central Kenai Peninsula, 30 mi/48 km WNW of Seward; 15 mi/24 km long; 60°24′N 150°22′W. Game fishing, hunting. Drained WNW by Kenai R.

Skillet Fork, c.100 mi/161 km long, Marion co., S Ill.; rises NE of Salem; flows SE to Little Wabash R. 5 mi/8 km above Carmi; 38°48′N 88°43′W.

Skippack (SKI-pak), uninc. town (1990 pop. 2,042), Montgomery co., SE Pa., 7 mi/11.3 km NNW of Norristown, on Skippack Creek; 40°13′N 75°24′W. Mfg. of valves and paving materials. Agr. includes dairying; livestock; poultry; grain, soybeans, apples.

Skokie (SKO-kee), village (1990 pop. 59,432), Cook co., NE Ill., an industrial suburb 13 mi/21 km NNW of downtown Chicago; 42°02′N 87°44′W. Mfg. includes communications, computer, and electrical equip.; rubber prods.; tools; iron and steel prods. Also important are the printing and publishing industries; one of the largest publishers in the U.S. has its internatl. hq. in Skokie. Hebrew Theological Col. (1922) was moved here from Chicago in 1958, Natl. Jewish Theater. Site of Old Orchard Shopping Center, one of the largest shopping centers in the U.S. Inc. 1888.

Skokomish River (sko-KO-mish), c.10 mi/16 km long, W Wash.; formed NW of Shelton by North Fork (c.25 mi/40 km long) and South Fork (c.25 mi/40 km long), both rising in Olympic Mts.; flows E and NE to S end of Hood Canal; 47°20′N 123°10′W. L. Cushman reservoir is on North Fork.

Skookumchuck River (SKOO-kuhm-chuhk), c.45 mi/72 km long, W Wash.; rises in sect. of Mt. Baker–Snoqualmie Natl. Forest, N central Lewis co.; flows NW, then generally W, through Skookumchuck Reservoir, past Bucoda, entering Chehalis R. at Centralia.

Skookumchuk Reservoir, Thurston co., W Wash., on Skookumchuk R., 12 mi/19 km ENE of Centralia; 4 mi/6.4 km long; 46°48′N 122°43′W. Max. capacity 42,000 acre-ft. Formed by Skookumchuck Dam (150 ft/46 m high), built (1971) by the Pacific Power and Light Company for power generation. Skookumchuck Fish Hatchery below dam.

Skowhegan (skou-HEE-guhn), town (1990 pop. 8,725), ⊙ Somerset co., central Maine, on the Kennebec R., above Waterville; 44°45′N 69°40′W. Mfg. (shoes and wood prods.); supply point for resort areas. Holds annual agr. fair that dates from 1818. Lakewood, resort 5 mi/8 km N on Hayden L., has summer theater (opened 1901). Name is Abnaki word meaning "place to catch salmon." Includes Skowhegan village. Settled

1771, set off from Canaan as Milburn 1823, renamed 1836.

Skuna River (SKOON-uh), c.75 mi/121 km long, N central Miss.; rises in Pontotoc co.; flows SW, past Bruce, to Yalobusha R. 6 mi/9.7 km E of Grenada, in Grenada L. reservoir (forms N arm of reservoir).

Skunk River, 264 mi/425 km long, central and SE Iowa; rises in NE Hamilton co.; flows SE, past Ames, to the Mississippi R. 7 mi/11.3 km S of Burlington. Main tributary is North Skunk R., rising in Marshall co., flowing c.100 mi/161 km SE to Skunk R. 11 mi/18 km SE of Sigourney. The flood of 1993 affected the Skunk and all its tributaries, causing widespread damage to crops, businesses, and residences.

Skwentna, village, S Alaska, 70 mi/113 km NW of Anchorage, on Yentna R., at mouth of the Skwentna. Airfield.

Skwentna River, 55 mi/89 km long, S Alaska; rises in Mt. Gerdine glacier system near 61°40′N 152°45′W; flows in an arc N and E to Yentna R. at 61°58′N 151°10′W.

Sky Valley, town (1990 pop. 187), Rabun co., Ga.,11 mi/18 km NE of Clayton in extreme NE Ga.; 34°59′N 83°20′W.

Skykomish (skei-KO-mish), village (1990 pop. 273), King co., W central Wash., in Cascade Range, 45 mi/72 km E of Seattle, and on Skykomish R.; 47°43′N 121°22′W. Timber. Area surrounded by Mt. Baker–Snoqualmie Natl. Forest, including Alpine Lakes Wilderness Area to SE; Alpine Falls and Stevens Pass to E; 8-mi/12.9-km Cascade Tunnel (RR) to E, pass and tunnel cross crest of Cascades.

Skykomish River (skei-KO-mish), c.30 km long, NW Wash.; formed near Index by North (c.30 mi/48 km long) and South (c.35 mi/56 km long) forks, both rising in Snoqualmie Natl. Forest, in Cascade Range, E King co.; flows W past Sultan, where it receives Sultan R. from N, and Monroe, to junction with Snoqualmie R., forming Snohomish River 3 mi/4.8 km SW of Monroe.

Skyland, uninc. village, Buncombe co., W N.C., suburb 6 mi/9.7 km S of Asheville, near French Broad R. Mfg. (textiles, consumer goods, machinery).

Skylight, Mount (4,920 ft/1,500 m), peak in High Peaks sect. of the Adirondack Mts., Essex co., NE N.Y., just S of Mt. Marcy, and 13 mi/21 km S of Lake Placid village; 44°06′N 73°56′W.

Skyline, village (1990 pop. 272), Blue Earth co., S Minn., residential suburb 3 mi/4.8 km SW of Mankato, on Blue Earth R., 2 mi/3.2 km S of its confluence with Minnesota R.; 44°08′N 94°02′W.

Skyline, suburban section of San Diego, San Diego co., S Calif., 8 mi/12.9 km ESE of downtown San Diego, in hills overlooking city. Sweetwater Reservoir to E.

Skyline Caverns, Va.: see FRONT ROYAL.

Skyline Drive, Va.: see SHENANDOAH NATIONAL PARK.

Skyline View, uninc. town (1990 pop. 2,370), Dauphin co., W Pa., residential suburb 9 mi/14.5 km NE of Harrisburg; 40°20′N 76°43′W. Agr. includes dairying; livestock, poultry; grain, soybeans, apples. Blue Ridge Mts. to N. Pa. Natl. Race Course (horse racing) to NE.

Skytop, uninc. village, Barrett township, Monroe co., NE Pa., in Pocono Mts., 16 mi/26 km N of Stroudsburg, on Mountain L. reservoir; 41°13′N 75°14′W. Elev. 1,575 ft/480 m. Recreation center.

Skyway, uninc. town (1990 pop. 8,500), King co., W Wash., residential suburb 9 mi/14.5 km SSE of downtown Seattle, 2 mi/3.2 km W of Renton, on Duwamish R. Renton Municipal Airport to NE.

Slab Fork, uninc. village (1990 pop.150), Raleigh co., S W.Va., 10 mi/16 km SW of Beckley. Coal-mining region. Mfg. (steel fabricating). Twin Falls State Park to SW.

Slade, uninc. village, Powell co., E central Ky., in Daniel Boone Natl. Forest, 10 mi/16 km ESE of Stanton. Tourist resort; gateway to Natural Bridge State Resort Park to S; Red R. Gorge, in Red R. Natl. Geological Area, to N.

Slana, village (1990 pop. 63), E central Alaska, 50 mi/80 km SW of Tok, on Slana R., on Glenn Highway, at

junction of Nabesna Road; 62°42′N 143°59′W. Located on N edge of Wrangell–St. Elias Natl. Park and Preserve.

Slate Islands, group of 11 islands in L. Superior, W Ont., central Canada, 100 mi/161 km E of Thunder Bay. Largest is Patterson Isl. (5 mi/8 km long, 3 mi/5 km wide).

Slate Peak, Colo.: see PURPLE PEAK.

Slate River, c.40 mi/64 km long, W central Colo.; rises in Elk Mts., N Gunnison co.; flows SE, past Crested Butte town, joining Taylor R. at Almont to form Gunnison R. Gunnison Natl. Forest.

Slate Spring, village (1990 pop. 118), Calhoun co., N central Miss., 23 mi/37 km E of Grenada; 33°44′N 89°22′W. Mfg. (apparel). Also Slate Springs.

Slater, city (1990 pop. 2,186), Saline co., central Mo., near Missouri R., 10 mi/16 km NE of Marshall; 39°13′N 93°03′W. Corn, wheat, soybeans; cattle; mfg. (flour, apparel, filters, concrete); rock quarry.

Slater, town (1990 pop. 1,268), Story co., central Iowa, 15 mi/24 km SSW of Nevada; 41°52′N 93°40′W. Mfg. (feed; signs).

Slater, village (1990 pop. 2,245), Greenville co., NW S.C., 13 mi/21 km NNW of Greenville; 35°01′N 82°29′W. Mfg. includes fiberglass prods. Reported as Slater-Marietta by Census Bureau.

Slatersville, R.I.: see NORTH SMITHFIELD.

Slatersville Reservoir, R.I.: see BRANCH RIVER.

Slatington (SLAI-teeng-tuhn), borough (1990 pop. 4,678), Lehigh co., E Pa., 12 mi/19 km NNW of Allentown, on Lehigh R.; 40°45′N 36°75′W. Agr. (grain, apples, soybeans; poultry, livestock; dairying), mfg. (slate prods., apparel, textiles); slate quarrying. Appalachian Trail on Blue Mt. ridge, to N. Settled 1737, inc. 1864.

Slaton, town (1990 pop. 6,078), Lubbock co., NW Texas, near Caprock escarpment of Llano Estacado, 15 mi/24 km SE of Lubbock, near N Fork Double Mt. Fork of Brazos R; 33°26′N 101°38′W. Elev. 3,250 ft/991 m. RR div. point; grain elevator, cottonseed oil mills; mfg. (apparel, fabricated metal prods., feeds; sand and gravel processing). Buffalo Springs L. reservoir to NW.

Slaughter, town (1990 pop. 827), East Feliciana parish, SE central La., 19 mi/31 km N of Baton Rouge; 30°43′N 91°08′W. RR junction. In agr. and timber area; wood preserving, mfg. (dragline buckets).

Slaughter Beach, resort town (1990 pop. 114), Sussex co., E Del., 7 mi/11.3 km E of Milford and on Delaware Bay, 3 mi/4.8 km S of mouth of Mispillion R.; 38°54′N 75°17′W. Fishing, swimming. Prime Hook Natl. Wildlife Refuge to SE.

Slaughters, uninc. village (1990 pop. 235), Webster co., W Ky., 12 mi/19 km N of Madisonville; 37°29′N 87°30′W. Agr. (tobacco, grain; livestock). Also known as Slaughtersville.

Slaughterville, town (1990 pop. 1,843), Cleveland co., central Okla., 10 mi/16 km SE of Norman, satellite community of Oklahoma City (N), near Canadian R.; 35°06′N 97°16′W. Agr. area.

Slave, river, c.310 mi/500 km long, Fort Smith region, N.W.T., N Canada. It comprises the middle sects. of the Mackenzie R. system. The river channels the waters of L. Athabasca and the Peace R. into Great Slave L. at Fort Resolution. It is navigable for steamers except for the rapids bet. Fort Fitzgerald and Fort Smith, where it breaks through the Cariboo Hills. A wagon road portage (16 mi/26 km long) around the rapids.

Slave Falls, waterfalls, SE Man., on Winnipeg R., and 75 mi/121 km ENE of Winnipeg. Hydroelectric power center.

Slayden (SLAI-duhn), town (1990 pop. 111), Dickson co., N central Tenn., 40 mi/64 km WNW of Nashville; 36°17′N 87°28′W. In timber and farm area.

Slayton, town (1990 pop. 2,147), ⊙ Murray co., SW Minn., 28 mi/45 km E of Pipestone, on Beaver Creek; 43°59′N 95°45′W. Elev. 1,559 ft/475 m. Trade center in agr. area (grain, soybeans; livestock, poultry; dairying); mfg. (consumer goods, gravel; printing and publishing). L. Shetek State Park on Des Moines R. to NE. Settled 1881.

Sledge, town (1990 pop. 577), Quitman co., NW Miss.,

12 mi/19 km N of Marks; 34°25′N 90°13′W. In agr. (cotton, soybeans, grain; cattle) area.

Sleeper, uninc. town, Laclede co., S central Mo., in the Ozark Mts., near Gasconade R., 7 mi/11.3 km NE of Lebanon.

Sleeper Islands, SE Keewatin dist., N.W.T., N Canada, group of c.30 small isls. and islets in Hudson Bay, off W Ungava Peninsula; 57°30′N 79°45′W. Group extends 60 mi/97 km N-S.

Sleeping Bear Dunes National Lakeshore (□ 11 sq mi/28 sq km), Leelanau and Benzie cos., W central Mich.; 44°53′N 86°03′W. Sect. of the L. Michigan shoreline and the North and South Manitou isls.; beaches, sand dunes (elev. 460 ft/140 m), forests, and lakes. Acreage includes former D. H. Day (Leelanau co.) and Benzie (Benzie co.) state parks. Passenger ferry to isls. from Leland. Includes preserved fishing village of Glen Haven. Primitive camping on isls. Beech and maple forests, birch-lined streams. Est. 1977.

Sleepy Eye, town (1990 pop. 3,694), Brown co., S Minn., 14 mi/23 km W of New Ulm, near Cottonwood R.; 44°17′N 94°43′W. Grain, soybeans, sugar beets, peas; livestock, poultry; dairying. Mfg. (feeds, advertising specialties, canned vegetables, house kits; spray drying, printing and publishing). Fort Ridgely State Park to N, on Minnesota R.; Sleepy Eye L. on N end, Sleepy Eye Creek 5 mi/8 km to W. Plotted 1872.

Sleepy Hollow 1 village (1990 pop. 3,241), Kane co., NE Ill., residential suburb 4 mi/6.4 km NNW of Elgin, near Fox R.; 42°05′N 88°18′W. Agr. to W. **2** residential village, Westchester co., SE N.Y., on E bank of the Hudson R., just N of Tarrytown; 41°05′N 73°52′W. Originally called Beekmanton, name was changed to North Tarrytown in 1874. In 1996, name was changed again to Sleepy Hollow in honor of Washington Irving's famous short story "Legend of Sleepy Hollow," which was set here. Many sites in town are associated with the story. In 1900, some of the nation's 1st autos, including the Walker Steamer and the Maxwell gas-powered vehicle, began to be produced at a site along the Hudson R. In 1914, Chevrolet production began. General Motors Corp. produced 11 million cars, trucks, and minivans at this plant until it closed on June 28, 1996. Site of historic Phillipsburg Manor (c.1683) with collections relating to Irving (who lived nearby and is buried here) and John D. Rockefeller, Sr. (KyKuit, Rockefeller family estate, also here). Old Du. Reformed Church with 311-year-old bell and cemetery. Capture here of the Br. spy John André revealed Benedict Arnold's clandestine pro-Br. efforts in the Amer. Revolution.

Sleepy Hollow, residential suburb of Washington, D.C., Fairfax co., NE Va., 6 mi/9.7 km W of city center; 38°52′N 77°09′W. During the Civil War, Lincoln reviewed troops here.

Sleetmute, village (1990 pop. 106), W Alaska, on Kuskokwim R., at mouth of Holitna R., 90 mi/145 km ESE of Holy Cross; 61°43′N 157°10′W. Also river and portage to Yukon R. In 19th cent., Sleetmute R. was main winter route bet. St. Michael's, port for the Yukon, and Nuleto. Sometimes spelled Sleitmut.

Sleitmut, Alaska: see SLEETMUTE.

Slick, village (1990 pop. 124), Creek co., central Okla., 20 mi/32 km WNW of Okmulgee; 35°46′N 96°16′W. In agr. and oil-producing area.

Slickville (SLIK-vil), uninc. town (1990 pop. 1,066), Salem township, Westmoreland co., SW Pa., 11 mi/18 km N of Greensburg; 40°27′N 79°31′W. Agr. (corn, hay; livestock; dairying); timber; mfg. (lumber). Beaver Run Reservoir to W.

Slide Mountain (4,204 ft/1,281 m), Ulster co., SE N.Y., highest peak of the Catskill Mts., c.18 mi/29 km W of Kingston; 42°00′N 74°23′W.

Slidell (slei-DEL), city (1994 pop. 29,669), St. Tammany parish, SE La., 25 mi/40 km NW of downtown New Orleans, near L. Pontchartrain; 30°17′N 89°47′W. Here crossed by a bridge to New Orleans; RR junction. A shipbuilding and mfg. town in a farm and timber region, it serves primarily as a bedroom community for the aerospace industry that has developed (1960s) in the surrounding area. Large NASA computer complex

in town; Pearl R. NASA Test Site 13 mi/21 km NE (in Miss.). Also seafood; printing and publishing, mfg. (furniture, chemicals; boats and dredges, concrete, apparel, meat prods., machinery). Inc. 1888. Pearl R. Wildlife Refuge to E.

Sligo, borough (1990 pop. 706), Clarion co., W central Pa., 9 mi/14.5 km SW of Clarion, on Licking Creek; 41°06′N 30°79′W. Agr. (corn, hay, potatoes; livestock; dairying); mfg. (asphalt prods., wood prods.); bituminous coal.

Slinger, town (1990 pop. 2,340), Washington co., E Wis., 13 mi/21 km SW of West Bend; 43°19′N 88°17′W. Mfg. (electrical goods, cylinder sleaves, fabricated metal prods., industrial wheels); skiing. Nearby are Pike and Big Cedar lakes (resort). Speedway; Pike L. State Park to W. Formerly Schleisingerville.

Slippery Rock, borough (1990 pop. 3,008), Butler co., W Pa., 16 mi/26 km NW of Butler, near Slippery Rock Creek; 41°04′N 80°03′W. Agr. (potatoes, alfalfa; livestock; dairying); timber; mfg. (crushed stone, chemicals; printing and publishing); bituminous coal. Seat of Slippery Rock Univ. of Pa. Flying Acres Airport to NW. Moraine State Park, including L. Arthur reservoir to S. Inc. 1851.

Sloan, town (1990 pop. 938), Woodbury co., W Iowa, 21 mi/34 km SSE of Sioux City; 42°13′N 96°13′W. Feed milling.

Sloan, suburban village (1990 pop. 3,830), Erie co., W N.Y., just E of Buffalo; 42°53′N 78°47′W. RR shops. Commercial-residential community. Inc. 1896.

Sloatsburg, suburban village (□ 2 sq mi/5.2 sq km; 1990 pop. 3,035), Rockland co., SE N.Y., on Ramapo R., in the Ramapo Mts., near N.J. state line, 4 mi/6.4 km NW of Suffern; 41°09′N 74°11′W. Settled before 1775, inc. 1929.

Slocan (slo-KAN), village (1991 pop. 263), SE B.C., W Canada, on Slocan R., at S end of Slocan L., and 21 mi/34 km NNW of Nelson; 49°46′N 117°28′W. Silver, lead, zinc mining (declining).

Slocan Lake (□ 24 sq mi/62 sq km), S B.C., W Canada, 22 mi/35 km NNW of Nelson; 25 mi/40 km long, 1 mi/2 km–2 mi/3 km wide. At S end is Slocan. Drained by S by Slocan R.

Slocan River, 35 mi/56 km long, S B.C., W Canada; issues from S end of Slocan L. at Slocan; flows SSW to Kootenay R. at Shoreacres, 12 mi/19 km WSW of Nelson.

Slocomb (SLO-kuhm), town (1990 pop. 1,906), Geneva co., SE Ala., 18 mi/29 km ENE of Geneva, near Fla. state line. Farming; mfg. clothing. Settled 1884, inc. 1900.

Slocum, village, in North Kingstown town, Washington co., R.I. On Amtrak RR line. Turf and horticultural production.

Slope, county (□ 1,224 sq mi/3,170 sq km; 1990 pop. 907), SW N.Dak., on Mont. state line (W); ⊙ Amidon; 46°27′N 103°27′W. Elev. 3,468 ft/1,057 m. Extensive lignite deposits. Drained by Little Missouri and Cannonball rivers and Deep Creek. Cattle; wheat. White Butte, highest point in the state (elev. 3,506 ft/1,069 m), is in center of state. Created 1915. Little Missouri Natl. Grassland is in W ½ of co.; N.Dak. Badlands run N-S through co.; Fort Dilts Historic Site on S border; Burning Coal Vein and Columnar Cedars in N.

Slovan (SLO-vahn), uninc. town (1990 pop. 900), Smith township, Washington co., SW Pa., 20 mi/32 km WSW of Pittsburgh, on Burgetts Fork Creek; 40°21′N 80°23′W. Agr. (corn, hay; livestock; dairying); coal. Cross Creek Co. Park to S.

Sluiskin Falls (SLOO-skuhn), W central Wash., waterfall (300 ft/91 m high), on S slope of Mt. Rainier, Mt. Rainier Natl. Park, on headstream of Paradise Creek branch of Nisqually R.

Smackover (SMAK-o-vuhr), town (1990 pop. 2,232), Union co., S Ark., 12 mi/19 km NNW of El Dorado, on Smackover Creek; 33°21′N 92°43′W. Oil wells, refinery. Smackover oil and gas field nearby. Arka. Oil/Brine Mus. State Historic Site is here. Inc. 1922.

Smale (SMAIL), village, Monroe co., E central Ark., 11 mi/18 km E of Clarendon.

Small, Cape, SW Maine, peninsula marking NE edge of Casco Bay. Summer colony. Small Point and Bald Head are seaward extensions.

Smarr (SMAHR), town (1990 pop. 275), Monroe co., Ga., 15 mi/24 km NW of Macon; 32°59′N 83°53′W. Mfg. of hardwood lumber, wood prods.

Smarts Mountain, peak (3,240 ft/988 m), Grafton co., W N.H., 6 mi/9.7 km ENE of Lyme; 43°49′N 72°01′W. Appalachian Trail passes to W.

Smeaton (SMEE-tuhn), village (1991 pop. 225), central Sask., W Canada, 45 mi/72 km ENE of Prince Albert. Dairying; wheat.

Smelterville, village (1990 pop. 464), Shoshone co., N Idaho, 5 mi/8 km W of Kellogg; 47°32′N 116°11′W. Former site of Bunker Hill smelter complex. In mining (lead, zinc) dist.; tourism; mfg. (polymers, plastic molding, pottery). Coeur d'Alene (N) and St. Joe (SE) natl. forests; Silver Mt. Ski Area to S.

Smethport (SMETH-port), borough (1990 pop. 1,734), ⊙ McKean co., N Pa., 18 mi/29 km S of Olean (N.Y.), on Potato Creek, at mouth of Marvin Creek; 41°48′N 78°26′W. Agr. (hay; dairying); mfg. (machinery, wood prods., wax, consumer goods, chemicals, petroleum prods., lumber, clay). Kinzua Bridge State Park to SW. Laid out 1807, inc. 1853.

Smicksburg (SMIKS-buhrg), borough (1990 pop. 76), Indiana co., W central Pa., 11 mi/18 km WSW of Punxsutawney, on Little Mahoning Creek; 40°52′N 79°10′W. Agr. (livestock; dairying); timber; mfg. (food prods., wine, lumber).

Smiley, village (1990 pop. 463), Gonzales co., S central Texas, c.55 mi/89 km ESE of San Antonio; 29°16′N 97°38′W. Poultry hatching and shipping center; cattle; peanuts; mfg. (poultry feed).

Smiley Mountain, Idaho: see PIONEER MOUNTAINS.

Smith or **Mirror Landing**, village, central Alta., W Canada, on Athabaska R., at mouth of Lesser Slave R., and 45 mi/72 km NW of Athabaska; 55°10′N 114°02′W. Mixed farming (wheat); livestock.

Smith 1 county (□ 896 sq mi/2,321 sq km; 1990 pop. 5,078), N Kansas, on Nebr. (N) state line; ⊙ Smith Center; 39°50′N 98°45′W. Corn-belt region; drained by North Fork Solomon R. Corn, hay, wheat; cattle, hogs; sorghum, alfalfa. Geographic center of continental U.S. (lower 48 states) is 2 mi/3.2 km NW of Lebanon (39°50′N 98°35′W). Formed 1872. **2** county (□ 637 sq mi/1,650 sq km; 1990 pop. 14,798), S central Miss.; ⊙ Raleigh, 32°01′N 89°30′W. Drained by Leaf and Strong rivers and Oakhay Creek; includes part of Bienville Natl. Forest in N. Agr. (corn, cotton; poultry, cattle, hogs; timber); bentonite mining. L. Ross Barnett State L. to SW. Formed 1833. **3** county (□ 325 sq mi/842 sq km; 1990 pop. 14,143), N central Tenn.; ⊙ Carthage, 36°15′N 85°58′W. In central basin; drained by Cumberland R. and its tributaries. Livestock raising; dairying; lumbering; agr. (tobacco, soybeans, grain, corn); zinc mines, limestone quarries. Formed 1799. **4** county (□ 949 sq mi/2,458 sq km; 1990 pop. 151,309), E Texas; ⊙ Tyler; 32°22′N 95°16′W. Bounded N by Sabine R., W by Neches R. Diversified irrigated agr.; rose growing; livestock raising, dairying; oil and natural gas; clay, stone, sand and gravel, mining (iron ore, salt, silica, lignite, clays). Horticultural crops; fruit (esp. watermelons), vegetables, pecans; a leading Texas mule-raising co.; also cattle, hogs. Some timber. Formed 1846.

Smith and Sayles Reservoir, R.I.: see CHEPACHET RIVER.

Smith Bay, N Alaska, inlet of Beaufort Sea, 60 mi/97 km SE of Point Barrow; 20 mi/32 km wide; 70°54′N 153°50′W.

Smith Center, town (1990 pop. 2,016), ⊙ Smith co., N Kansas, 63 mi/101 km N of Russell; 39°46′N 98°46′W. Elev. 1,810 ft/552 m. In livestock and corn region; grain storage; mfg. (travel trailers). Founded 1871, inc. 1886.

Smith Creek, uninc. town (1990 pop. 7,461), New Hanover co., NE N.C., residential suburb 5 mi/8 km ENE of downtown Wilmington, on Smith Creek; 34°15′N 77°51′W. New Hanover Internatl. Airport to NW.

Smith Hill, town, Bibb co., central Ala., 14 mi/23 km N of Centreville.

Smith Island, Canada: see CAPE SMITH.

Smith Island, low-lying marshy archipelago, SE Md. and E Va., consisting of islets divided by narrow creeks, in Chesapeake Bay 8 mi/12.9 km W of Crisfield (ferry); S tip is in Va.; c.8 mi/12.9 km long, 4 mi/6.4 km wide. Most remote of Md. isls. and named for Capt. John Smith, the 3 small villages on the isl.—Ewell, Tylertown, and Rhodes Point—are separated by marshes. The people, who speak an archaic Eng. in which triple as well as double negatives are used, have made their living here from oystering and crabbing for over 300 years. Methodism, which reached here during the Great Revival, helped create a peaceful culture, in which there is no jail, no police, and no town govt. The most prominent landmarks are the steeples of the 3 Methodist churches.

Smith Island 1 Brunswick co., SE N.C., 3 mi/4.8 km SE of Southport; 5 mi/8 km long, 3 mi/4.8 km wide. Corncake Inlet, Cape Fear R. estuary to W, Atlantic Ocean to E; separated on S from Bald Head Isl. (Cape Fear) by narrow channel. **2** Northampton co., E Va., low sandy island just SE of Cape Charles, extends c.7 mi/11.3 km NE from entrance to Chesapeake Bay; isl. breached near middle. Cape Charles lighthouse on S isl. Fisherman's Isl. to SW, Myrtle Isl. to N.

Smith Mountain Lake, reservoir, on border bet. Pittsylvania and Bradford cos., S central Va., on Roanoke (Staunton) R., c.30 mi/48 km SE of Roanoke; c.25 mi/40 km long; 37°02′N 79°32′W. Max. capacity 1,142,000 acre-ft. Formed by Smith Mountain Dam (207 ft/63 m high), built (1963) by Appalachian Power Company for power generation. Blackwater R. enters from W to form c.19-mi/31-km arm. Smith Mountain L. State Park on NE shore. Smith Mt. ridge at SE end, on both sides of dam.

Smith Point, Northumberland co., E Va., low promontory in Chesapeake Bay, at S side of entrance to Potomac R. estuary; 37°53′N 76°14′W. Lighthouse. Ferry from Smith Point village to Smith Isl. (Md. and Va.) to NE.

Smith River, uninc. village, Del Norte co., NW Calif., near mouth of Smith R. 3 mi/4.8 km E of Pacific Ocean, 12 mi/19 km N of Crescent City. Trade center for lumbering, dairying area. Pelican State Beach to N, on Oregon state line, 5 mi/8 km N. Six Rivers Natl. Forest to E.

Smith River, trading post, N B.C., W Canada, near Yukon border, on Smith R. (tributary of Liard R.), on branch of Alaska Highway; 59°55′N 126°24′W. Airfield.

Smith River 1 20 mi/32 km long, Del Norte co., NW Calif.; formed by its South and Middle forks 8 mi/12.9 km NE of Crescent City; flows NNW to the Pacific Ocean just below Smith River village. Middle Fork rises in NE Del Norte co., 30 mi/48 km ENE of Crescent City, flows SW c.25 mi/40 km. South Fork rises in S Del Norte co., c.25 mi/40 km SE of Crescent City, flows N c.20 mi/32 km. **2** c.100 mi/161 km long, W central Mont.; rises in the Castle Mts. in S Meagher co.; flows NW, past White Sulphur Springs and past Smith R. State Park, then NNW to Missouri R. 12 mi/19 km SW of Great Falls. **3** c.20 mi/32 km long, central N.H.; rises in W part of Grafton; flows SE and E, past Danbury, to the Pemigewasset R., 8 mi/12.9 km NNW of Franklin. **4** 70 mi/113 km long, Oregon; rises in Douglas co., in Coast Ranges 20 mi/32 km SSW of Eugene; flows W to Umpqua R. near its entrance to Winchester Bay, Pacific Ocean. **5** c.70 mi/113 km long, Va. and N.C.; rises in N Patrick co., SW Va.; flows NE, then SE through Philpott Reservoir, past Bassett and Martinsville, into N.C., to Dan R. at Eden; 36°45′N 80°20′W.

Smith Town, uninc. village (1990 pop. 500), McCreary co., SE Ky., in the Cumberland Mts., 3 mi/4.8 km SW of Whitley City, in Daniel Boone Natl. Forest. Big South Fork Natl. R. and Recreation Area to W and SW.

Smith Village, village (1990 pop. 34), Oklahoma co., central Okla., residential suburb 5 mi/8 km E of downtown Oklahoma City, near North Canadian R.; 35°27′N 97°27′W.

Smithboro, village (1990 pop. 201), Bond co., S central Ill., 14 mi/23 km WSW of Vandalia; 38°53′N 89°20′W. RR junction. In agr. area (corn, wheat, barley, sorghum).

Smithers, town (1991 pop. 5,029), W central B.C., W Canada, on Bulkley R., and 130 mi/209 km ENE of Prince Rupert; 54°46′N 127°10′W. RR div. point; lumbering, fur trapping.

Smithers, town (1990 pop. 1,162), Fayette co., S central W.Va., 20 mi/32 km SE of Charleston, on Kanawha R. (bridged); 38°10′N 81°18′W. Coal-mining region. Agr. (grain); livestock, poultry. Mfg. (rebuilt mining equipment; gears). Inc. 1938.

Smithfield 1 resort town (1990 pop. 865), Somerset co., S Maine, 10 mi/16 km SSW of Skowhegan; 44°38′N 69°48′W. In Belgrade Lakes resort area. **2** town (1990 pop. 7,540), ⊙ Johnston co., central N.C., 25 mi/40 km SE of Raleigh, on Neuse R.; 35°30′N 78°20′W Agr. area (tobacco, peanuts, cotton, grain, potatoes, sweet potatoes; poultry, cattle, hogs). Mfg. (wood prods., textiles, furniture, electrical and electronic equip., air filters, lumber, tobacco prods., machinery; meat processing, printing and publishing, tool and die). Ava Gardner Mus. commemorates hometown actress (1922–1990). Settled before 1746; inc. 1777. **3** uninc. town (1990 pop. 2,495), Smithfield township, Huntingdon co., S central Pa., suburb 1 mi/1.6 km SW of Huntingdon, on Juniata R.; 40°28′N 77°59′W. **4** town (1990 pop. 19,163), Providence co., N R.I. ; 41°54′N 71°32′W. Long a textile town, it now has diversified industries. Seat of Bryant Col. Settled early in the 18th cent., mainly by Friends. Set off from Providence and inc. 1731. **5** town (1990 pop. 5,566), Cache co., N Utah, suburb 6 mi/9.7 km N of Logan, near Idaho state line, and on Summit Creek near Bear R., in Cache Valley; 41°50′N 111°49′W. Elev. 4,595 ft/1,401 m. Irrigated agr. area; cheese processing. Settled 1859. Wasatch Natl. Forest includes Mt. Naomi Wilderness Area to E. **6** town (1990 pop. 4,686), Isle of Wight co., SE Va., 11 mi/18 km W of Newport News, on Pagan R. (head of navigation), near James R.; 36°58′N 76°37′W. Mfg. (meat processing); agr. area (grain, soybeans, cotton, peanuts, melons; livestock). St. Luke's Church, one of the oldest Protestant churches in Amer. to SE. (at Benns Church); Bacon's Castle (1655), fortified (1676) in Bacon's Rebellion to NW. Settled c.1633; inc. 1752.

Smithfield 1 village (1990 pop. 277), Fulton co., W central Ill., 9 mi/14.5 km NW of Lewiston; 40°28′N 90°17′W. In agr. and bituminous-coal area. **2** village (1990 pop. 115), Henry co., N Ky., 26 mi/42 km NE of Louisville, on Little Kentucky R.; 38°23′N 85°15′W. Agr. (burley tobacco; livestock; timber); mfg. (wood veneer, lumber; hazardous industrial chemical recycling). **3** village (1990 pop. 53), Gosper co., S Nebr., 7 mi/11.3 km ESE of Elwood; 40°34′N 99°44′W. **4** village (1990 pop. 722), Jefferson co., E Ohio, 10 mi/16 km SW of Steubenville; 40°16′N 80°46′W. In coal-mining area. **5** village (1990 pop. 205), Wetzel co., N W.Va., on South Fork of Fishing Creek, 19 mi/31 km SE of New Martinsville; 39°30′N 80°33′W. Oil, gas, and agr. area. Lewis Wetzel Wildlife Management Area to W.

Smithfield, borough (1990 pop. 1,000), Fayette co., SW Pa., 8 mi/12.9 km SW of Uniontown, on Georges Creek; 39°47′N 79°48′W. Agr. (hay; livestock; dairying); mfg. (lumber, wood prods.).

Smithland, town (1990 pop. 235), Woodbury co., W Iowa, on Little Sioux R., and 30 mi/48 km SE of Sioux City; 42°13′N 95°55′W.

Smithland, village (1990 pop. 384), ⊙ Livingston co., W Ky., 12 mi/19 km ENE of Paducah, on Ohio R., at mouth of Cumberland R.; 37°08′N 88°24′W. In agr. area (burley tobacco, corn); mfg. (limestone processing). Smithland Lock and Dam (Ohio R.) to N; Ky. (Tenn. R.) and Barkley (Cumberland R.) dams to SE; Ky. Dam Village State Resort Park to S. Est. 1842.

Smithonia (smith-O-nee-uh), town, Oglethorpe co., NE Ga., 13 mi/21 km ENE of Athens; 34°00′N 83°10′W.

Smith's, parish (1991 pop. 5,261), central Bermuda, on Bermuda Isl.; 32°18′N 64°44′W.

Smiths, village (1990 pop. 3,456), Lee co., E Ala., 7 mi/11.3 km NW of Phenix City; 32°32′N 85°05′W.

Smiths Falls, town (1991 pop. 9,396), SE Ont., central Canada, on Rideau R., and 40 mi/64 km SSW of Ottawa; 44°54′N 76°01′W. RR center; mfg.; resort.

Smiths Grove, town (1990 pop. 703), Warren co., S Ky., 14 mi/23 km ENE of Bowling Green; 37°02′N 86°12′W. In agr. area (burley tobacco, grain; livestock, poultry; dairying); mfg. (fertilizers; meat processing). Mammoth Cave Natl. Park to N.

Smith's Island, NE Bermuda, at entrance of St. George's Harbour, just N of St. David's Isl.; 3/4 mi/1.2 km long, 1/4 mi/ km wide; 32°22′N 64°39′W.

Smithsburg, town (1990 pop. 1,221), Washington co., W Md., at W base of South Mt., 8 mi/12.9 km E of Hagerstown; 39°40′N 77°35′W. The founder, Christopher Smith (1750–1821), commonly known as "Stuffle" Smith, is buried in an unknown grave in the Lutheran Churchyard. Printing plant nearby.

Smithton, town (1990 pop. 532), Pettis co., central Mo., 8 mi/12.9 km E of Sedalia; 38°40′N 93°05′W. Dairy prods. Former mule center.

Smithton, village (1990 pop. 1,587), St. Clair co., SW Ill., 8 mi/12.9 km S of Belleville; 38°24′N 89°59′W. In bituminous-coal and agr. area.

Smithton, borough (1990 pop. 338), Westmoreland co., SE Pa., on Youghiogheny R., 24 mi/39 km SSE of Pittsburgh; 40°08′N 79°44′W. Agr. (corn, apples; livestock; dairying); mfg. (beer).

Smithtown 1 residential village (□ 12 sq mi/31 sq km; 1990 pop. 25,638), Suffolk co., SE N.Y., on Nissequogue R., and just W of Smithtown Branch; 40°51′N 73°12′W. Fast-growing area; diversifed light mfg. includes vinyl prods., military and aerospace electronic equip., chemicals, fabricated metal prods., machinery and machinery parts. **2** uninc. village, Yadkin co., NW N.C., 20 mi/32 km NW of Winston-Salem, near Yadkin R. Tobacco; livestock.

Smithtown Bay, open bight on N shore of L.I., SE N.Y., bet. Eatons (W) and Crane (E) necks, 3 mi/4.8 km N of Smithtown; c.8.5 mi/13.7 km wide; 40°57′N 73°13′W. Receives Nissequogue R. in SW. Stony Brook Harbor (c.2.5 mi/4 km long) is shallow SE arm.

Smithtown Branch, residential village, Suffolk co., SE N.Y., on central L.I., 13 mi/21 km ESE of Huntington; 40°51′N 73°11′W. Mfg. (apparel).

Smithville, village, S Ont., central Canada, on Twenty Mile Creek, and 19 mi/31 km SE of Hamilton; 43°06′N 79°32′W. Dairying, milling; fruit.

Smithville 1 town (1990 pop. 804), Lee and Sumter cos., SW central Ga., 12 mi/19 km S of Americus; 31°54′N 84°16′W. **2** town (1990 pop. 2,525), Clay co., W Mo., on Little Platte R., and 14 mi/23 km NW of Liberty; 39°22′N 94°34′W. Wheat, corn, fruit; livestock, poultry. Smithville Dam and L. on E side. **3** town (1990 pop. 3,791), ⊙ De Kalb co., central Tenn., 19 mi/31 km N of McMinnville, in the Cumberlands, 35°58′N 85°49′W. Mfg. of clothing, motor vehicle parts; fruit tree nurseries. Center Hill Dam and an Appalachian crafts center nearby. **4** town (1990 pop. 3,196), Bastrop co., S central Texas, on Colorado R., and 38 mi/61 km ESE of Austin; 30°00′N 97°09′W. Elev. 324 ft/99 m. RR junction. Cattle; cotton, soybeans. Mfg. (marine closures, consumer goods, apparel). Buescher State Park to N. Settled 1827, inc. 1895.

Smithville 1 village (1990 pop. 500), Monroe co., S central Ind., 9 mi/14.5 km S of Bloomington. Monroe Reservoir and Hoosier Natl. Forest to E; Fairfax State Recreational Area to S. Cattle; timber. Recreation. **2** village (1990 pop. 871), Monroe co., E Miss., 23 mi/37 km SE of Tupelo, near Ala. state line, and near Tombigbee R.; 34°04′N 88°24′W. Agr. (cattle; corn, soybeans; dairying); mfg. (apparel, furniture). Lock B, on Tennessee-Tombigbee Waterway is here. **3** village (1990 pop. 1,354), Wayne co., N central Ohio, 6 mi/10 km NE of Wooster; 40°52′N 81°51′W. **4** village (1990 pop. 111), McCurtain co., extreme SE Okla., 28 mi/45 km N of Broken Bow, in Ouachita Mts., on Mountain Fork R., near Ark. state line; 34°28′N 94°39′W. Part of Ouachita Natl. Forest to N; McCurtain Co. Wilderness and Broken Bow L. reservoir to S. **5** uninc. village, Ritchie co., NW W.Va., 9 mi/14.5 km SSW of Harrisville, on South Fork Hughes R. Agr. (corn); livestock, poultry. Mfg.

(aluminum and steel fabricating, rubber fabricating; lifeboats). Ritchie Mines Wildlife Management Area to W.

Smithville Reservoir (□ 11 sq mi/28 sq km), Clay and Clinton cos., NW Mo., on Little Platte R., 15 mi/24 km N of Kansas City; 39°24'N 94°56'W. Max. capacity 246,500 acre-ft. Formed by Smithville Dam (75 ft/23 m high), built (1979) by Army Corps of Engineers for flood control; also used for water supply and recreation. Jesse James b. nearby.

Smoaks (SMOKS), town (1990 pop. 142), Colleton co., S central S.C., 16 mi/26 km NNW of Walterboro; 33°05'N 80°49'W. Mfg. includes clothing. Agr. includes livestock, poultry; grain, watermelons; timber.

Smock, uninc. town (1990 pop. 950), Franklin township, Fayette co., SW Pa., 7 mi/11.3 km NNW of Uniontown, on Redstone Creek; 39°59'N 79°47'W. Agr. (dairying); bituminous coal.

Smoke Creek Desert, Washoe co., NW Nev., N of Pyramid L., W of Gerlach, near Calif. state line; SW extension (c.40 mi/64 km long) of Black Rock Desert.

Smoke Hole, Grant and Pendleton cos., NE W.Va., wooded gorge (c.16 mi/26 km long) of South Branch of the Potomac R., just E of the Allegheny Front, and 10 mi/16 km WSW of Petersburg, in Monongahela Natl. Forest; traversed by road. Smoke Hole village is here. Hunting, fishing; has spectacular rock formations and caves, including Smoke Hole Caverns in N, whose use by pioneers gave region its name.

Smokemont, uninc. village, Swain co., W N.C., 12 mi/19 km NNE of Bryson City, in Great Smoky Mts. Natl. Park at S entrance. Oconaluftre Visitor Center.

Smoky, river, c.250 mi/400 km long, Alta., W Canada; rises in Jasper Natl. Park, W Alta.; flows generally NE to the Peace R. It receives the Wapiti and Little Smoky rivers. It was explored (1792) by Alexander Mackenzie.

Smoky Hill River, c.560 mi/901 km long, Colo. and Kansas; rises on the Great Plains, Cheyenne co., central E Colo., Cheyenne co., 10 mi/16 km W of Cheyenne Wells; flows ENE into Kansas past Sharon Springs, and Russell Springs, through Cedar Bluff Reservoir, past Ellsworth, through Kanopolis Reservoir, past Lindsberg, Salina (where it receives Salina R. from W), and Abilene to Junction City, where it joins the Republican R. to form the Kansas (or Kaw) R. The Saline R. is its chief tributary. The Smoky Hill basin is included in the Missouri R. Basin Project. Kanopolis (completed 1948) and Cedar Bluff (1951) dams are used for irrigation and flood control.

Smoky Lake, town (1991 pop. 1,057), central Alta., W Canada, near Smoky L. (10 mi/16 km long), and near North Saskatchewan R., 60 mi/97 km NE of Edmonton; 54°07'N 112°28'W. Wheat; cattle, poultry.

Smooth Rock Falls, town (1991 pop. 2,043), E Ont., central Canada, on Mattagami R. (28-ft/9-m falls), and 30 mi/48 km NW of Cochrane; 49°17'N 81°38'W. In mining region; mixed farming.

Smoothstone Lake (□ 110 sq mi/285 sq km), central Sask., W Canada, 110 mi/177 km NNW of Prince Albert; 16 mi/26 km long, 11 mi/18 km wide. Drains N into Snake L. and Churchill R.

Smuggler's Notch, ski resort, Lamoille co., NW Vt., in the Green Mts., near village of Jeffersonville, Cambridge town, c.22 mi/35 km NE of Burlington. Also mt. pass between Mt. Mansfield and Spruce Peak nearby.

Smuttynose Island, Maine: see ISLES OF SHOALS.

Smyer, village (1990 pop. 442), Hockley co., W central Texas, 16 mi/26 km W of Lubbock; 33°35'N 102°09'W. Oil and natural gas. Cotton; cattle.

Smyrna (SMUHR-nuh), city (1990 pop. 30,981), Cobb co., NW Ga., a residential suburb of Atlanta; 33°52'N 84°31'W. Mfg. includes computer equip., bldg. materials, plastics, ordnance, chemicals; printing and publishing. Originally a religious camping ground, the city grew with the coming of the RR. It has a bird sanctuary and is noted for its jonquils. The city was almost totally destroyed during the Civil War. New town center municipality bldgs. opened in 1990s. Inc. 1872.

Smyrna 1 (SMUHR-nuh), town (1990 pop. 5,231), Kent and New Castle cos., central Del., 12 mi/19 km NNW of Dover, on Smyrna R.; 39°17'N 75°36'W. In agr. region (fruit, grain; poultry; dairying); mfg. (steel foundry; printing and publishing). Woodland Beach (to NE) and Bombay Hook (to E) natl. wildlife refuges nearby; L. Como (fishing) is S. Inc. 1859. **2** town (1990 pop. 13,647), Rutherford co., central Tenn., 18 mi/29 km SE of Nashville, 35°59'N 86°31'W. Wood prods., fabricated metal prods., chemicals, electrical prods., motor vehicles. Nearby are home and grave of Sam Davis, Confederate hero.

Smyrna 1 (SMUHR-nuh), village (1990 pop. 211), Chenango co., central N.Y., 32 mi/51 km SW of Utica; 42°41'N 75°34'W. In dairying and lumbering area. **2** village (1990 pop. 57), York co., N S.C., 10 mi/16 km WNW of York; 35°02'N 81°24'W. Mfg. includes screen printing. Agr. includes cotton, grain; livestock, poultry.

Smyrna Mills (SMUHR-nuh), agr. town, Aroostook co., E Maine, on East Branch of Mattawamkeag R., and 14 mi/23 km W of Houlton.

Smyrna River, c.15 mi/24 km long, central Del.; rises in NW Kent co, 6 mi/9.7 km W of Smyrna, near Md. state line; flows ENE, past Smyrna to Del. Bay N of Bombay Hook Isl. 6 mi/9.7 km NE of Smyrna. Navigable for c.10 mi/16 km in lower course.

Smyth (SMITH), county (□ 452 sq mi/1,171 sq km; 1990 pop. 32,370), SW Va.; ⊙ Marion; 36°50'N 81°31'W. In Great Appalachian Valley; Walker Mt. in N, part of Iron Mts. in S, including Mt. Rogers (5,729 ft/1,746 m); highest peak in Va. on S border; drained by North, Middle and South forks of Holston R. Mfg. at Marion, Atkins, and Chilhowie; agr. (tobacco, hay, alfalfa, corn, vegetables, fruit; cattle, sheep; dairying); timber; salt and gypsum mining, limestone quarrying. Includes Hungry Mother State Park in N center; parts of Jefferson Natl. Forest in N, E, and S, including parts of Mt. Rogers Natl. Recreation Area; crossed in SE by Appalachian Trail. Formed 1832.

Snag, village, W Yukon, NW Canada, near U.S. (Alaska) border, on White R., and 120 mi/193 km S of Dawson; 62°24'N 140°28'W. Trading post, services. Record low temp. of −81°F/-63°C was recorded here, Feb. 1947.

Snake Lake, N central Sask., W Canada, expansion of the Churchill R., 150 mi/241 km N of Prince Albert; 34 mi/55 km long, 10 mi/16 km wide.

Snake Mountain (5,518 ft/1,682 m), in the Appalachian Mts., on Tenn.-N.C. state line, 8 mi/13 km N of Boone (N.C.); 35°44'N 83°14'W.

Snake Range, E Nev., in White Pine co., E of Schell Creek Range, near Utah state line; extends N-S through 2 sects. of Humboldt Natl. Forest. Rises to 12,067 ft/3,678 m in Mt. Moriah and 13,063 ft/3,982 m in Wheeler Peak. Great Basin Natl. Park, including Lehman Caves, former natl. monument at Mt. Wheeler to S. U.S. Highway 6/50 crosses range at Sacramento Pass (c.7,154 ft/2,181 m).

Snake River 1 80 mi/129 km long, E Minn.; rises in marshy area of SE Aitkin co., E of Mille Lacs L.; 46°17'N 93°06'W; flows S, past McGrath, through Snake R. State Forest, receives Knife R. from NNW, flows past Mora, then E, past S end of Pokegama L., past Pine City and through Cross L. to St. Croix R. (on Wis. state line) in Pine co., 9 mi/14.5 km E of Pine City. **2** c.70 mi/113 km long, in NW Minn.; rises in marshy area of Marshall co., c.20 mi/32 km NW of Thief River Falls, just S of Middle R.; flows S and W, past Warren, then NNW, past Alvarado, to Red R. (N.Dak. state line), 35 mi/56 km N of Grand Forks (N.Dak.); 47°59'N 91°25'W. **3** 1,038 mi/1,670 km long, NW U.S., the chief tributary of the Columbia R.; rises in NW Wyo., in Yellowstone Natl. Park; flows through Jackson L. in Grand Teton Natl. Park, then S and W into Idaho and NW to its junction with the Henrys Fork R. The combined stream runs SW, then NW, crossing S Idaho through the Snake R. Plain; there are several notable falls. The Snake makes a bend into Oregon and turns N to form the Idaho-Oregon and Idaho-Wash. state lines (receiving several tributaries, including the Boise and Salmon rivers), then turns at Lewiston (Idaho; at the mouth of the Clearwater R.), and flows generally W to join the Columbia R. near Pasco (Wash.). Hell's Canyon, sometimes called Grand Canyon of the Snake R., is the greatest of the Snake's many gorges and one of the deepest in the world; extends c.125 mi/201 km N along the Oregon-Idaho state line; max. depth c.7,900 ft/2,408 m. The Snake was explored by the Lewis and Clark expedition (1803–1806) and was of major importance in U.S. expansion into the Pacific Northwest. The river is a major source of electricity, having numerous hydroelectric power plants. The upper and middle courses of the Snake and its tributaries are much used for irrigation by private projects (one of the most notable being at Twin Falls) and by projects of the U.S. Bureau of Reclamation, including the Minidoka, Boise, Palisades, and Owyhee projects. Four navigation and hydroelectric power projects along the lower Snake provide slack water navigation from the mouth of the Snake 140 mi/225 km upstream to Lewiston, Idaho. The projects are linked with the navigation system on the Columbia R., which extends 342 mi/550 km to the Pacific Ocean from its confluence with the Snake. Formerly called the Lewis R.

Snake River Plain, S Idaho, crescent-shaped lava tableland (elev. c.3,000 ft/914 m–5,000 ft/1,524 m) traversed by Snake R., from Wash. to Wyo. state line, mainly N of river; separates Northern Rocky Mts. (N) from the Great Basin and Middle Rocky Mts. (S). Irrigation has made parts of it cultivable, esp. near river, where most of Idaho's famous potato crop is grown (also sugar beets, fruit, vegetables). Broad central part of plain, N of river, has aquifer which carries water from Big and Little Lost rivers, 100 mi/161 km WSW to Thousand Springs, on Snake R.

Sneads (SNEEDZ), town (□ 4 sq mi/10.4 sq km; 1990 pop. 1,746), Jackson co., NW Fla., near Ga. state line, 19 mi/31 km ESE of Marianna; 30°42'N 84°55'W.

Sneads Ferry (SNEEDS), uninc. town (1990 pop. 2,031), Onslow co., E N.C., 38 mi/61 km N of Wilmington, and on New R estuary, at Intracoastal Waterway, 3 mi/4.8 km NW of Atlantic Ocean; 34°32'N 77°22'W. Mfg. (commercial boats and fishing equip.). Camp Lejeune Marine Base to N.

Sneedville, town (1990 pop. 1,446), ⊙ Hancock co., NE Tenn., on the Clinch R., 23 mi/37 km N of Morristown, 36°32'N 83°13'W. In mt. farm area.

Sneffels, Mount (14,150 ft/4,313 m), Ouray co., SW Colo., in San Juan Mts., 5 mi/8 km N of Telluride; 38°00'N 107°47'W. Uncompahgre Natl. Forest.

Snelling, village (1990 pop. 125), Barnwell co., W S.C., 26 mi/42 km SSE of Aiken, at main entrance of Atomic Energy Commission's Savannah R. Site (nuclear facility); 33°14'N 81°27'W.

Snelling, Fort, Minn.: see FORT SNELLING.

Snellville, city (1990 pop. 12,084), Gwinnett co., N central Ga., 22 mi/35 km ENE of Atlanta; 33°52'N 84°01'W. Commercial printing and light mfg. Rapidly expanding retail, medical, and service center in suburban Atlanta.

Snipatuit Pond (SNI-puh-TOO-wit), reservoir, Plymouth co., SE Mass., on Mattapoisett R., 8 mi/12.9 km N of its mouth on Buzzards Bay, 9 mi/14.5 km NNE of New Bedford; 1.25 mi/2.1 km long; 41°46'N 70°51'W.

Snohomish (sno-HO-mish), county (□ 2,196 sq mi/5,688 sq km; 1990 pop. 465,642), NW Wash.; ⊙ Everett; 48°02'N 121°43'W. Bounded E by crest of Cascade Range, W by Puget and Possession sounds, Port Susan and Skagit bays. Drained by Skykomish, Sauk, Stillaguamish, and Snoqualmie rivers. Co. is highly urbanized in SW, an extension of Seattle urbanized area. RR junction. Timber; gold, silver, copper, nickel; granite quarrying. Berries, peas, hay; dairying; cattle, poultry; salmon, crabs, oysters, herring, prawns. Glacier Peak in NE; Mukeltio and Wenberg state parks in W; Wallace Falls State Park in S center; E part of co. is in Mt. Baker–Snoqualmie Natl. Forest; and also includes Boulder R. Wilderness Area (N center); parts of Glacier Peak and Henry M. Jackson wilderness areas in E. Tulalip Indian Reservation (W); Cascade Range is in E. Formed 1861.

Snohomish (sno-HO-mish), town (1990 pop. 6,499), Snohomish co., NW Wash., suburb 7 mi/11.3 km SE of

Everett, and 24 mi/39 km NNE of Seattle, on Snohomish R.; 47°55′N 122°05′W. Vegetables, berries; dairying; cattle, poultry. Mfg. (feeds, lumber and wood prods., machinery; textiles; printing and publishing); sand and gravel. L. Stevens to N. Blackman Mus. here. Settled in 1850s, inc. 1890.

Snohomish River (sno-HO-mish), c.25 mi/40 km long, NW Wash.; formed 3 mi/4.8 km SW of Monroe in Snohomish co. by junction of Snoqualmie and Skykomish rivers; flows NW past Snohomish to Possession Sound at Everett.

Snook, village (1990 pop. 489), Burleson co., S central Texas, 15 mi/24 km S of Bryan; 30°29′N 96°28′W. Cattle, hogs; cotton, grain. Mfg. (sausage processing).

Snoqualmie (sno-KWAHL-mee), town (1990 pop. 1,546), King co., W central Wash., 25 mi/40 km E of Seattle, and on Snoqualmie R.; 47°31′N 121°49′W. Dairying; poultry; timber; mfg. (lumber). Mt. Baker–Snoqualmie Natl. Forest to E and S; Snoqualmie Falls to N, downstream is Snoqualmie R. Snoqualmie Pass and Ski Area to SE, at crest of Cascade Range.

Snoqualmie Falls, Wash.: see SNOQUALMIE RIVER.

Snoqualmie Pass (sno-KWAHL-mee) (3,021 ft/921 m), on border bet. King and Kittitas cos., W central Wash., highway passes (I-90, Burlington Northern RR) at crest of Cascade Range, c.45 mi/72 km SE of Seattle. Winter sports areas. Snoqualmie Ski Area on W side of pass.

Snoqualmie River (sno-KWAHL-mee), c.45 mi/72 km long, W central Wash.; formed near Snoqualmie by junction of North (c.30 mi/48 km long), Middle (c.35 mi/56 km long), and South (c.40 mi/64 km long) forks, rising in Cascade Range E of Seattle; flows W and NW past Carnation and Duvall to junction with Skykomish R., forming Snohomish R. near Monroe. Snoqualmie Falls (c.270 ft/82 m) N of Snoqualmie is power-plant site.

Snow Basin, Utah: see OGDEN.

Snow Dome, mountain (11,340 ft/3,456 m), on border bet. Alt. and B.C., W Canada, in Rocky Mts., on S edge of Jasper Natl. Park, 60 mi/97 km SE of Jasper; 52°11′N 117°19′W.

Snow Hill 1 town (1990 pop. 2,217), ⊙ Worcester co., SE Md., 18 mi/29 km SE of Salisbury, on Pocomoke R.; 38°10′N 75°23′W. Ships produce; vegetable canneries; makes wood prods., clothings, textiles, fertilizer. Patented by Col. William Stevens in 1676 and settled by Presbyterians Scots from N Ireland, the Makaemie Memorial Presbyterian Church has been the town's central bldg. since 1687. The present church was built in 1890. All Hallows Protestant Episcopal Church (c.1755) was remodeled in the 1890s and has a Bible printed (1701) in London given to the church by Queen Anne. An active trading port with England and the Barbadoes, many Loyalists hid out here in the swamps during the Revolution although the Assn. of Freemen was formed on July 26, 1775, and several rebel battalions were raised in the area. A center of Confederate sympathy during the Civil War, Snow Hill declined as Baltimore prospered and fires in 1834 and 1893 burned out most older bldgs. Many, however, remain, including Whitehill (c.1814), Chanceford (late 18th cent.; known for its elaborate woodwork), as well as Whaley House, 207 Ironshire, 109 Federal, Seltzer Cottage, Timmons House, Mansion House, and Mt. Ephraim (all 18th-cent.). **2** town (1990 pop. 1,378), ⊙ Greene co., E central N.C., 14 mi/23 km NNW of Kinston, on Contentnea Creek; 35°27′N 77°40′W. Agr. area (tobacco, cotton, peanuts, grain; poultry, hogs). Mfg. (rubber prods., electrical prods., apparel, textiles, hard hats). Founded 1799; inc. 1855.

Snow Lake, town (1991 pop. 1,598), W Man., central Canada, 70 mi/113 km E of Flin Flon. Gold-mining center.

Snow Lake, village, Desha co., SE Ark., c.40 mi/64 km SW of Helena, near the Mississippi (E) and White (W) rivers. Community is isolated from remainder of co. White R. Natl. Wildlife Refuge to W.

Snow Shoe, borough (1990 pop. 800), Centre co., central Pa., 12 mi/19 km NW of Bellefonte; 41°01′N 77°57′W.

Agr. (livestock); mfg. (clay refractory prods.); clay, bituminous coal; natural gas.

Snowbank Lake, Lake co., NE Minn., 20 mi/32 km ENE of Ely, and 3 mi/4.8 km S of Can. (Ont.) border, in Superior Natl. Forest, E and N part of lake in Boundary Waters Canoe Area; 4.5 mi/7.2 km long, 3 mi/4.8 km wide. Fed at S end from NE through chain of lakes, starting with Adventure L., flowing through Jitterbug, Ahsub, Disappointment, and Parent lakes; drains NE then NW through Boot, Ashigan, Splash, and Sucker lakes to Basswood L., connected by short stream.

Snowbird Mountains, W N.C., E extension of Unicoi Mts., in Appalachian Mts., along border bet. Cherokee and Graham cos., bet. Haw Knob and Nantahala R.; rise to 4,716 ft/1,437 m in Teyahalee Bald, 4 mi/6.4 km N of Andrews; 35°13′N 83°57′W. Joyce Kilmer Memorial Forest to N. In Nantahal Natl. Forest.

Snowcrest Mountains, range of Rocky Mts. in SW Mont., Madison and Beaverhead cos.; rise W of Ruby R., N of Red Rock R., near Idaho state line; extend c.45 mi/72 km NE; 45°00′N 112°00′W. Largely within Beaverhead Natl. Forest. Highest peaks are Hogback Mt. (10,605 ft/3,232 m), Sunset Peak (10,581 ft/3,225 m).

Snowdrift, trading post (1991 pop. 286), S Mackenzie dist., N.W.T., N Canada, on E side of Great Slave L., at mouth of Snowdrift R.; 62°24′N 110°45′W. Radio station. Trapping, hunting, fishing; crafts. Scheduled air service. Northernmost Chipewyan settlement. Est. 1927 when the tribe moved into area.

Snowflake, town (1990 pop. 3,679), Navajo co., E central Ariz., on Silver Creek, and 25 mi/40 km S of Holbrook; 34°31′N 110°04′W. Elev. 5,582 ft/1,701 m. Cattle, sheep; corn, alfalfa. Mfg. (concrete, wood prods.; pulp mill); timber. Apache-Sitgreaves Natl. Forest to S.

Snowmass, village, Pitkin co., central Colo., 13 mi/21 km NW of Aspen, on Roaring Fork R., at mouth of Snowmass Creek. Elev. 6,880 ft/2,097 m. Mfg. of machinery. Site of Rocky Mt. Inst., research institute. Snowmass Village, ski resort town, 7 mi/11.3 km S. Parts of White R. Natl. Forest to E and SW.

Snowmass Mountain (14,092 ft/4,295 m), Pitkin co., W central Colo., in Elk Mts., 13 mi/21 km WSW of Aspen; 39°07′N 107°03′W. In White R. Natl. Forest; ski resort town of Snowmass village to NE.

Snowmass Village, town (1990 pop. 1,449), Pitkin co., central Colo., 8 mi/12.9 km W of Aspen, on Snowmass Creek; 39°12′N 106°56′W. Elev. 8,975 ft/2,736 m. Popular ski resort in Elk Mts.; tourism. Village of Snowmass 7 mi/11.3 km N.

Snows, The, Mich.: see LES CHENEAUX ISLANDS.

Snowville, village (1990 pop. 251), Box Elder co., NW Utah, near Idaho state line, 46 mi/74 km NW of Brigham City; 41°58′N 112°42′W. Elev. 4,544 ft/1,385 m. Dairying; cattle. Spring Bay of Great Salt L. 15 mi/24 km SW, includes Locomotive Springs Waterfowl Management Area.

Snowy Mountain (3,903 ft/1,190 m), Hamilton co., NE central N.Y., in the Adirondack Mts., just W of Indian L., and 6 mi/9.7 km SW of Indian Lake village; 43°42′N 74°23′W.

Snug Corner, town, S Bahama Isls., on central Acklins Isl., c.250 mi/402 km SE of Nassau; 22°33′N 73°52′W. Cascarilla bark, aloe vera.

Snyder, county (□ 332 sq mi/860 sq km; 1990 pop. 36,680), central Pa.; ⊙ Middleburg; 40°46′N 77°04′W. Bounded E by Susquehanna R., S in part by West Branch Mahantango Creek; drained by Penns and Middle creeks. Agr. (corn, wheat, oats, hay, alfalfa, apples; poultry, cattle; eggs and dairying). Mfg. at Selinsgrove and Middleburg Jacks Mt. runs NE-SW across NW part. Parts of Bald Eagle State Forest in NW, center and SW. Formed 1855.

Snyder, city (1990 pop. 12,195), ⊙ Scurry co., NW Texas, 70 mi/113 km WNW of Abilene; 32°42′N 100°55′W. Elev. 2,316 ft/706 m. In a prairie and mesquite region. Oil production is the area's main industry; natural gas is also refined and processed. Cattle ranching and farming are important; cotton, wheat, sorghum, pecans are chief crops. Mfg. (feeds, apparel, machinery; printing, natural-gas processing). Western Texas Col. L. J. B. Thomas reservoir to SW. Inc. 1907.

Snyder, town (1990 pop. 1,619), Kiowa co., SW Okla., 22 mi/35 km E of Altus, and SW of Wichita Mts.; 34°39′N 98°57′W. RR junction. In agr. (grain; cattle, sheep) area; light mfg. Great Plains State Park on S end of Tom Steed L., to N. 1903.

Snyder, village (1990 pop. 280), Dodge co., E Nebr., 25 mi/40 km NW of Fremont, and on branch of Elkhorn R.; 41°42′N 96°47′W. Grain; mfg. (frozen meats, machinery).

Snydertown (SNEI-duhr-toun), borough (1990 pop. 416), Northumberland co., E central Pa., 6 mi/9.7 km E of Sunbury; 40°52′N 76°40′W. Agr. (grain; livestock, poultry; dairying); anthracite coal.

Soap Lake, town (1990 pop. 1,149), Grant co., central Wash., 7 mi/11.3 km NNE of Ephrata, near S end of the Grand Coulee, on Soap L.; 47°23′N 119°29′W. Vegetables, sugar beets, wheat, apples; poultry. L. Lenore Caves to N.

Sobieski (so-bee-YES-kee), village (1990 pop. 199), Morrison co., central Minn., 7 mi/11.3 km SW of Little Falls, on Swan R.; 45°55′N 94°28′W. Grain, potatoes; livestock, poultry; dairying. Charles A. Lindbergh State Park to E.

Soboba Hot Springs, Calif.: see SAN JACINTO.

Socastee (SAW-kuh-stee), uninc. city (1990 pop. 10,426), Horry co., E S.C., 6 mi/9.7 km W of Myrtle Beach, on Intracoastal Waterway; 33°41′N 79°00′W. Myrtle Beach Civil Jet Port to El Socastee Yacht Basin is here. Resort area.

Sochiapa (so-chee-AH-pah), town (1990 pop. 860), Veracruz, E Mexico, in Sierra Madre Oriental, 30 mi/48 km SE of Tuxtepec; 17°41′N 95°45′W. Elev. 4,396 ft/1,340 m. Fruit. Also Xochiapa.

Social Circle, town (1990 pop. 2,755), Walton co., N central Ga., 10 mi/16 km S of Monroe; 33°40′N 83°43′W. Located on the rural fringe of Atlanta. Mfg. includes foods, fabricated metal prods., rubber prods. Inc. 1831.

Society Hill, village (1990 pop. 686), Darlington co., NE S.C., 25 mi/40 km N of Florence near Great Pee Dee R.; 34°30′N 79°50′W. Mfg. includes fabrics and the dyeing and finishing of fabrics. Agr. includes poultry, livestock; dairying; grain, sorghum.

Socoltenango (so-kol-te-NAHN-go), town (1990 pop. 3,967), Chiapas, S Mexico, in Sierra Madre, 16 mi/26 km W of Comitán de Domínguez; 16°13′N 92°15′W. Cereals, sugarcane, fruit; livestock.

Soconusco (so-ko-NOOS-ko), region, in SE Chiapas, Mexico; 15°19′N 92°44′W. The Pacific slope of the Span. conquest bet. Pijijiapan and Ayutla (Guatemala). Sierra de Chiapas and adjacent coastal plain in SE Mexico and SW Guatamela. Pre-Columbian tributary state of the Aztec empire and a major supplier of cacao (chocolate), the region continued to produce cacao during the 16th cent. Today it is a center of coffee production and also produces other tropical crops.

Soconusco (so-ko-NOOS-ko), town (1990 pop. 4,284), Veracruz, SE Mexico, on Isthmus of Tehuantepec, 2 mi/3.2 km ENE of Acayucan; 17°58′N 94°52′W. Fruit; livestock.

Socorro (suh-KO-ro), county (□ 6,649 sq mi/17,221 sq km; 1990 pop. 14,764), central N.Mex.; ⊙ Socorro; 34°01′N 106°55′W. Cattle, sheep; dairying; chilies, corn, hay, alfalfa, wheat, barley, oats. Grain and livestock grazing area watered by Rio Grande, which flows through Elephant Butte Reservoir in South Magdalena Mts., are W of Socorro, San Mateo Mts. in SW, part of Gallinas Mts. in NW, parts of 3 sects. of Cibola Natl. Forest in W. Part of White Sands Missile Range, including Trinity Site (site of 1st atomic bomb explosion, July 16, 1945) is SE; Fort Craig Natl. Historic Site and Bosque del Apache Natl. Wildlife Refuge in S center; Sevilleta Natl. Wildlife Refuge in N center; part of Jornada del Muerto plain in S; Natl. Radio Observatory and Very Large Array (V.L.A.) telescope on W border; Gran Quivira Pueblos Ruins unit of Salinas Pueblo Missions Natl. Monument in NE; Alamo Band Apache Tribe reservation to NW. Formed 1852.

Socorro, uninc. city (1990 pop. 22,995), El Paso co., extreme W Texas, on the Rio Grande, and suburb 13 mi/21 km SE of downtown El Paso; 31°38′N 106°16′W. In irrigated farm area. One of oldest communities in Texas, founded in early 1680s around Span. missions of Concepción del Socorro (1682) and Concepción del Carmen (1681; rebuilt from ruins).

Socorro (suh-KO-ro), town (1990 pop. 8,159), ⊙ Socorro co., W central N.Mex., on Rio Grande, E of Magdalena Mts., and 78 mi/126 km S of Albuquerque; 34°03′N 106°54′W. Elev. 4,582 ft/1,397 m. In dairying, grain, livestock region. Mfg. (perlite ore, stone prods., jewelry, jewelers' tools); agr. (alfalfa, grapes). On site of Piro Pueblo, visited (1598) by Juan de Oñate. Church of San Miguel (part of which dates back to same year) and N.Mex. School of Mines here. Fort Craig Natl. Historic Site to SW; Bosque del Apache Natl. Wildlife Refuge to S; Sevilleta Natl. Wildlife Refuge to N; part of Cibola Natl. Forest, including Magadlena Mts. to W; Los Piña Mts. to NE; White Sands Missile Range, including Trinitity site (atomic bomb test site, 1945) to SE.

Socorro Island, Mexico: see REVILLAGIGEDO ISLANDS.

Soda Lake, Calif.: see MOJAVE RIVER.

Soda Springs, town (1990 pop. 3,111), ⊙ Caribou co., SE Idaho, 50 mi/80 km ESE of Pocatello, on Bear R.; 42°40′N 111°35′W. Elev. 5,779 ft/1,761 m. RR junction in mining (phosphates), agr., grazing area; dairying; mfg. (chemicals, fertilizers). Phosphorus plant (just N) begun 1951. Carbonic acid-charged springs. Blackfoot Reservoir to N; Caribou (to E) and Cache (to S) natl. forests in area. Settled 1863, laid out 1870 by Brigham Young.

Soda Springs, village, Nevada co., E Calif., in the Sierra Nevada, near Donner Pass, 10 mi/16 km W of Truckee. Elev. c.6,700 ft/2,042 m. Summer, winter resort. In Tahoe Natl. Forest; Sugarbowl Ski Area to E.

Sodaville, village (1990 pop. 192), Linn co., NW Oregon, 15 mi/24 km SE of Albany; 44°28′N 122°52′W.

Soddy-Daisy, city (1990 pop. 8,240), Hamilton co., SE Tenn., near Chickamauga Reservoir (Tennessee R.), bet. communities of Soddy (N) and Daisy (S), 18 mi/29 km N of Chattanooga, 35°15′N 85°11′W.

Sodus (SO-duhs), resort village (1990 pop. 1,904), Wayne co., W N.Y., near L. Ontario, 28 mi/45 km ENE of Rochester; 43°14′N 77°03′W. Mfg. of electronic equip., machinery, foods. Agr. (fruit). Marinas and summer homes. The lotuses of nearby Sodus Bay are famous. Inc. 1918.

Sodus Bay (SO-duhs), inlet of L. Ontario, W N.Y., indenting N shore of Wayne co., 32 mi/51 km E of Rochester; c.5 mi/8 km long; 43°15′N 76°57′W. Summer homes; has noted lotus beds.

Sodus Point (SO-duhs), resort village (□ 1 sq mi/2.6 sq km; 1990 pop. 1,190), Wayne co., W N.Y., on L. Ontario, at entrance of Sodus Bay, 33 mi/53 km ENE of Rochester; 43°15′N 76°59′W. Port of entry. Fired upon by British in War of 1812.

SoHo (SO-ho), a section of Lower Manhattan, N.Y. city, SE N.Y., a c.20-block area bet. Houston (N) and Canal (S) streets; 40°43′N 73°59′W. Name "SoHo" is an acronym for "south of Houston St.," and has no relation to London's Soho dist. E and W borders are not fixed, as galleries and upscale businesses have spread into Little Italy (E), Chinatown (SE), and the Printing Dist. (W). Through the 1950s it was a light industrial dist. (furriers, doll-makers, and box mfg.). The area was known as Hell's Hundred Acres due to the recurring warehouse fires. As mfg. left, artists began to move in, attracted by low rents and large warehouse lofts. In 1972, the city, attempting to maintain a mfg. presence in this part of Manhattan, passed a zoning ordinance that permitted only artists who have been certified as such by the Dept. of Cultural Affairs to live and work here. Treeless streets, soot-covered factory bldgs., and the absence of schools and other basic amenities, coupled with the bohemian urban lifestyle of the residents and high rents all lend an inverse snob-ambience to the area. Once described as N.Y. city's "commercial slum number 1," this trendy neighborhood contains the city's finest urban, commercial architecture. Now a historic dist., the neighborhood contains the world's largest concentration of Palladian and Italianate warehouses

and factories, many with full or partial intricate cast-iron facades. Site of Guggenheim Soho Mus., the Open Center of N.Y. Major retail and gallery throroughfares include Broadway, West Broadway, and Spring and Prince streets.

Sointula (swahn-TOO-luh), village, SW B.C., W Canada, on Malcolm Isl., just off NE Vancouver Isl., 170 mi/274 km NW of Nanaimo; 50°38′N 127°01′W. Fishing port; lumbering.

Solana (suh-LAH-nuh), town (□ 1 sq mi/2.6 sq km; 1990 pop. 1,128), Charlotte co., SW Fla., 5 mi/8 km SE of Port Charlotte; 26°56′N 82°01′W.

Solana Beach, city (1990 pop. 12,962), San Diego co., S Calif., on the Pacific coast, a suburb 20 mi/32 km N of downtown San Diego; 33°00′N 117°116′W. Mfg. (lab equip., computers; diverse light mfg.); flowers, citrus fruit, nursery prods., vegetables.

Solano, county (□ 828 sq mi/2,145 sq km; 1990 pop. 340,421), central and W Calif.; ⊙ Fairfield; 38°16′N 121°57′W. Bounded far SW by San Pablo Bay, S by Carquinez Strait (bridged) and Suisun Bay (and Grizzly Bay, N extension of Suisun Bay), SE by Sacramento R. N border formed by Putah Creek, Monticello Dam in NW corner (forms L. Berryessa reservoir). Low ranges in NW; rest of co. generally level; large marshy area in S, along bay. Rich low-lying delta lands near the Sacramento are protected by levees. Safflower, beans, sugar beets, tomatoes, sunflowers, nursery prods., almonds, apricots, pears, prunes, grapes; cattle, lambs; wheat, barley, oats, corn; clay; natural gas wells. Shipbuilding (Mare Isl. Naval Shipyard in SW, at Vallejo). U.S. Travis Air Force Base near Fairfield in center of co. Waterfowl hunting. Formed 1850.

Solano, Mission San Francisco de, Calif.: see SONOMA.

Soldier, town (1990 pop. 205), Monona co., W Iowa, on Soldier R., and 16 mi/26 km ESE of Onawa; 41°58′N 95°46′W.

Soldier, village (1990 pop. 135), Jackson co., NE Kansas, on small affluent of Kansas R., and 13 mi/21 km WNW of Holton; 39°32′N 95°57′W. Livestock; grain.

Soldier River, c.80 mi/129 km long, W Iowa; rises in Ida co.; flows SW to Missouri R. near Mondamin.

Soldier Summit, village (1990 pop. 12), Wasatch co., central Utah, in mt. region, 40 mi/64 km SE of Provo, on divide bet. Great Basin and Colorado R. drainage system. Elev. 7,477 ft/2,279 m. Sheep, cattle; timber. Uinta Natl. Forest to N.

Soldiers Grove, village (1990 pop. 564), Crawford co., SW Wis., on Kickapoo R., and 37 mi/60 km SE of La Crosse; 43°23′N 90°46′W. In agr. area (tobacco, corn; dairy).

Soldotna (sol-DAWT-nuh), town (1990 pop. 3,482), Kenai Peninsula, S Alaska, 65 mi/105 km SW of Anchorage, on Kenai R., near Cook Inlet; 60°29′N 151°03′W. Elev. 115 ft/35 m. Located on Sterling Highway at junction of Kenai Spur Road. Residential and service center for Cook Inlet oil development. Tourism; fishing. Airstrip. Kenai Community Col. of Univ. of Alaska. Kenai and Capt. Cook State Recreation Area to N. Inc. as city, 1967.

Soledad, city (1990 pop. 7,146), Monterey co., W Calif., in Salinas valley, 23 mi/37 km SE of Salinas; 36°26′N 121°19′W. Grapes, strawberries, vegetables; dairying. Ruins of Soledad (or Nuestra Señora de la Soledad) Mission (1791) nearby. Pinnacles Natl. Monument to NE; Sierra de Salinas to SW; Gabilan Range to NE. Soledad State Prison to NW.

Soledad Atzompa (so-lai-DAHD aht-SOM-pah), town (1990 pop. 599), Veracruz, E Mexico, in Sierra Madre Oriental, 7 mi/11.3 km SW of Orizaba; 18°45′N 97°09′W. Elev. 5,554 ft/1,693 m. Coffee, fruit. Sometimes Atzompa.

Soledad de Doblado (so-lai-DAHD dai do-BLAH-do), city (1990 pop. 11,409) and township, Veracruz, E Mexico, in Gulf lowland, on RR, and 20 mi/32 km SW of Veracruz; 19°02′N 96°25′W. Agr. center (coffee, tobacco, fruit, vanilla).

Soledad de Graciano Sánchez (so-lai-DAHD dai GRAH-see-AH-no SAHN-ches), city (1990 pop.

123,943) and township, San Luis Potosí, N central Mexico, on interior plateau, 4 mi/6.4 km. NE of San Luis Potosí; 25°11′N 112°03′W. Primarily an agr. community. Formerly Soledad Díez Gutiérrez, or Soledad Diez Gutiérrez.

Soledad Diez Gutiérrez, Mexico: see SOLEDAD DE GRACIANO SÁNCHEZ.

Soledad Etla (so-lai-DAHD ET-lah), town (1990 pop. 2,083), central Oaxaca, Mexico, 9 mi/14.5 km N of Oaxaca de Juárez, in Etla arm of Oxaco Valley, near the Inter-Amer. Highway 190 and RR. Elev. 5,381 ft/1,640 m. Temperate climate. Agr. (corn, beans, wheat, sugarcane, mezcal); cattle; dairy prods.; woods.

Soleduck River (SOL-duhk) or **Sol Duc River**, c.70 mi/113 km long, NW Wash.; rises in Olympic Natl. Park NW of Mt. Carrie; flows NW past Sol Duc Hot Springs and through Olympic Natl. Forest, then SW to junction with Bogachiel R., forming Quillayute R. E of La Push.

Solomon, town (1990 pop. 939), Dickinson co., central Kansas, on Smoky Hill R. at mouth of Solomon R., and 8 mi/12.9 km W of Abilene; 38°55′N 97°22′W. RR junction. Shipping point for agr. region; mfg. (transformers).

Solomon 1 village (1990 pop. 6), W Alaska, on S Seward Peninsula, on N shore of Norton Sound, 30 mi/48 km E of Nome; 64°34′N 164°30′W. Gold mining. **2** uninc. village, Graham co., SE Ariz., 4 mi/6.4 km E of Safford, on Gila R., at mouth of San Simon R. Cotton, alfalfa, corn. Settled 1876. Formerly Solomonsville. Gila Box Riparian Natl. Conservation Area to NE; Roper L. State Park to SW.

Solomon River, c.140 mi/225 km long, Kansas; formed 17 mi/27 km W of Beloit in N Kansas by confluence of the North and South forks, at Waconda L. Reservoir; flows SE, past Beloit, to Smoky Hill R. at Solomon. North Fork rises in Thomas co. SW of Colby, NW Kansas, flows c.165 mi/266 km generally E, past Logan through Kirwin Reservoir, where it is joined by Bow Creek from SW and Gaylord; South Fork rises in E Sherman co. only c.5 mi/8 km W of source of North Fork, and flows c.150 mi/241 km generally E, past Hill City through Webster Reservoir and past Stockton.

Solomons, town, Calvert co., S Md., on Solomons Isl. (causeway to mainland) in Patuxent R., and 17 mi/27 km SSE of Prince Frederick. Fishing resort and yachting center. Commercial fishing, oyster-packing, boatbuilding. Marine life of the bay and pollution problems have been studied at the Chesapeake Biological Laboratory run by the Natural Resources Inst. of the Univ. of Md. since 1922. Nearby Rouseby Hall, burned by the British in 1780 and replaced by the present structure was built by John Rouseby (c.1750). The Calvert Co. Maritime Mus. has displays of models, paintings, and tools.

Solomonsville, Ariz.: see SOLOMON.

Solon (so-luhn), city (1990 pop. 18,548), Cuyahoga co., NE Ohio, a suburb 15 mi/24 km SE of downtown Cleveland; 41°23′N 81°26′W. Mfg. includes metal prods., machinery, electrical prods. and equip., tools, and chemicals. Founded 1820, inc. as a city 1960.

Solon 1 (SO-luhn), town (1990 pop. 1,050), Johnson co., E Iowa, 10 mi/16 km N of Iowa City; 41°47′N 91°29′W. In agr. area. **2** town (1990 pop. 916), Somerset co., central Maine, on the Kennebec R., and 14 mi/23 km NNE of Skowhegan; 44°56′N 48°69′W. Wood prods.

Solon Springs, village (1990 pop. 575), Douglas co., NW Wis., 26 mi/42 km SSE of Superior; 46°21′N 91°49′W. In timber area. Nearby is the co. bird sanctuary, state hunting grounds; Lucius Woods State Park, on upper St. Croix L.; Brule R. State Forest to NE.

Solosuchiapa, Mexico: see SOLUSUCHIAPA.

Solsberry, village, Greene co., SW Ind., 10 mi/16 km ENE of Bloomfield. Forested area; cattle. Mfg. (beef processing). Large RR trestle nearby to W. Laid out 1848.

Soltepec (SOL-te-pek), town (1990 pop. 5,972), Puebla, central Mexico, 33 mi/53 km ENE of Puebla; 19°07′N 97°42′W. Elev. 7,940 ft/2,420 m. Cereals, maguey; livestock. Also San Hipólito Soltepec.

Solusuchiapa (so-lo-soo-chee-AH-pah), town (1990

---

pop. 1,534), Chiapas, S Mexico, 40 mi/64 km SSW of Villahermosa, and near Mexico Highway 195; 17°26′N 93°03′W. Elev. 1,066 ft/325 m. Fruit. Azoque town. Formerly Solosuchiapa.

Solvang, city (1990 pop. 4,741), Santa Barbara co., SW Calif., on Santa Ynez R., and 27 mi/43 km WSW of Santa Barbara; 34°36′N 120°08′W. Est. 1912 by Danes, it has preserved many Dan. customs. Mfg. (printing and publishing). Fruits, vegetables, flowers; cattle. L. Cachuma reservoir to E.

Solvay (SAHL-vai), village (□ 1 sq mi/2.6 sq km; 1990 pop. 6,717) in town of Geddes, Onondaga co., central N.Y., just W of Syracuse; 43°03′N 76°12′W. In the 20th cent., after earlier exploited salt springs had lost their deposits, brine wells provided basis for mfg. of chlorines, caustic soda, and bicarbonate of soda, and Solvay became a leading mfg. center of the area. Former heavy-mfg. and chemical-mfg. area have disappeared, mainly due to stricter environmental-quality standards. Major retail shopping centers occupy many former industrial sites. Inc. 1894.

Solway (SAWL-wai), village (1990 pop. 74), Beltrami co., NW Minn., 12 mi/19 km WNW of Bemidji; 47°31′N 95°07′W. Grain; dairying; timber; mfg. (wood prods. and pulpwood).

Sombrerete (so-brai-RAI-tai), city (1990 pop. 15,754) and township, Zacatecas, N central Mexico, on interior plateau, 90 mi/145 km NW of Zacatecas; 23°37′N 103°38′W. Elev. 7,713 ft/2,351 m. RR terminus. Mining center (silver, gold, lead, copper).

Sombrero, islet, dependency of St. Kitts and Nevis, separated from Br. V.I. by Anegada Passage, and 100 mi/161 km NW of Basseterre, St. Kitts. The bare rock rises to 40 ft/12 m at 18°36′N 63°29′W. Lighthouse. Phosphate of lime used to be quarried here. Belonged formerly to the Br. V.I.

Somerdale (SUH-muhr-dail), borough (1990 pop. 5,440), Camden co., SW N.J., 9 mi/14.5 km SE of Camden; 39°51′N 75°01′W. Chiefly residential. Inc. 1929.

Somerfield (SUH-muhr-feeld), uninc. village, former borough, Somerset co., SW Pa., 24 mi/39 km SW of Somerset, near Md. state line; 39°45′N 79°23′W. Original site inundated by reservoir dammed (1944) in Youghiogheny R., residential community now 1 mi/1.6 km to E of lake (bridged).

Somers 1 (SUH-muhrs), town (1990 pop. 9,108), Tolland co., N Conn., at Mass. state line, on Scantic R., and 19 mi/31 km NE of Hartford; 42°00′N 72°27′W. Agr. and diversified industry. Dairying. Site of a state prison. Organized 1734 as Mass. town, transferred to Conn. 1749. **2** town (1990 pop. 161), Calhoun co., central Iowa, 11 mi/18 km E of Rockwell City; 42°22′N 94°25′W. **3** town (1990 pop. 800), Flathead co., NW Mont., at N end of Flathead L., 10 mi/16 km SSE of Kalispell. RR terminus; tourism and recreation; timber; barley, potatoes, hay; cattle. Lake mouth of Flathead R. 5 mi/8 km E. Part of Flathead Natl. Forest to W. **4** town, Kenosha co., SE Wis., suburb 5 mi/8 km NW of Kenosha, on Pike R. Residential. Univ. of Wis. (Parkside Campus) to E. Kenosha Airport to S.

Somers, village (1990 pop. 620), N Westchester co., SE N.Y., on border of Putnam co. (N) and Conn. (E) state line; 41°19′N 73°44′W. Formerly rural, summer lake community, it is now a metropolitan N.Y. city exurb. IBM has hq. here; also beverage and perfume bottling. Has large condominium complex for retirees. Reservoir. Early Du. settlement, it was inc. 1778 as Stephentown. Renamed Somerstown for U.S. naval hero Capt. Richard Somers.

Somers Islands: see BERMUDA.

Somers Point (SUH-muhrz), city (1990 pop. 11,216), Atlantic co., SE N.J., 2 mi/3.2 km NW of Ocean City, on Great Egg Harbor Bay; 39°19′N 74°36′W. Boat-repair facility. Settled c.1695, inc. 1886.

Somerset 1 (SUH-muhr-set), county (□ 4,095 sq mi/10,606 sq km; 1990 pop. 49,767), central and W Maine, on Can. (Que.) border; ⊙ Skowhegan; 45°30′N 69°57′W. Resorts in Belgrade Lakes region along Kennebec co. border. Mfg. (shoes, paper, pulp, and wood prods.) at Skowhegan, Madison, Fairfield, Norridgewock on the Kennebec R., and Pittsfield on the Sebasticook R.; farming, dairying. Moosehead L. and Jackman-Moose R. regions are known for hunting, canoeing, and excellent fishing. In NW are lumber camps. The Kennebec is dammed at Bingham and furnishes power to several towns along its course. Formed 1809. **2** county (611 sq mi/1,582 sq km; 1990 pop. 23,440), SE Md. on peninsula on Eastern Shore; ⊙ Princess Anne; 38°05′N 75°52′W. Bounded SE by Pocomoke R., S by Pocomoke Sound (forms Va. state line here), W by Tangier Sound of Chesapeake Bay. Shores indented by Wicomico, Manokin, Big Annemessex river estuaries. In bay are Smith and South Marsh isls. Sandy, partly marshy tidewater area; agr. dists. produce fruit (esp. strawberries), white potatoes, vegetables; poultry; dairy prods. Timber; large seafood industry (esp. at Deal Isl.); some vegetable and seafood canneries, lumber mills, fishing equip., and clothing factories. Formed in 1666, it was named for Mary Somerset, sister-in-law of Cecilus, 2d Lord Baltimore **3** county (□ 307 sq mi/795 sq km; 1990 pop. 240,279), N central N.J., bounded NE by Passaic R.; ⊙ Somerville; 40°33′N 74°36′W. Dairying; agr. (vegetables, fruit, grain; poultry; dairy); mfg. (textiles, plastics, rubber goods, clothing, and metal prods.). NE part of co. is residential. Estate region in N includes Bedminster and Far Hills. Appalachian ridges in NW; part of Watchung Mts., in NE. Drained by Millstone R. and North and South branches of Raritan R. Raritan Valley Community Col. is here. Formed 1688. **4** county (□ 1,081 sq mi/2,800 sq km; 1990 pop. 78,218), SW Pa., on Md. state line (S); ⊙ Somerset; 39°58′N 79°01′W. Bounded SW by Youghiogheny R. (forms Youghiogheny R. L. reservoir); part of N border formed by Stonycreek R. and Paint Creek; drained by Casselman R., on SW border. Agr. (corn, wheat, oats, barley, hay, alfalfa, soybeans, potatoes; sheep, hogs, cattle; dairying; timber). Bituminous coal; sand and gravel; limestone. Mfg. at Somerset. Allegheny Mts. in E, Laurel Hill along W border; Mt. Davis (3,213 ft/979 m) in S, highest point in Pa. Parts of Laurel Ridge State Park in NW and W, on Laurel Hill ridge. Laurel Hill and Kooser state parks in NW. Formed 1795.

Somerset, city (1990 pop. 10,733), ⊙ Pulaski co., S Ky.; 37°04′N 84°36′W. Elev. 975 ft/297 m. In a farm, coal, and limestone area of the Cumberland foothills RR center. Agr. (burley tobacco, corn, wheat; cattle, hogs, poultry; dairying); diversified mfg. (jewelry, fabricated metal prods., bldg. materials, glass prods., wood prods., lumber, granite monuments, machinery). Somerset-Pulaski Airport to S. Somerset Community Col. (Univ. of Ky.). Mill Spring Natl. Cemetery to W. Daniel Boone Natl. Forest to SE; General Burnside State Park to S; L. Cumberland reservoir on Cumberland R., to S. Inc. 1801.

Somerset 1 residential town (1990 pop. 993), Montgomery co., central Md., just NNW of Washington, D.C.; 38°58′N 77°06′W. Founded in 1890 on a farm named Friendship by a group of govt. scientists. **2** residential town (1990 pop. 17,655), Bristol co., SE Mass., on the Taunton R., 3 mi/4.8 km N of Fall River; 41°45′N 71°10′W. Varied mfg. (including varnishes). Settled 1677, set off from Swansea and inc. 1790. **3** town (1990 pop. 1,144), Bexar co., S central Texas, 16 mi/26 km SW of San Antonio; 29°13′N 98°39′W. In oil field; agr. area (cattle; wheat, peanuts, vegetables). **4** town, Windham co., S Vt., in the Green Mts., 15 mi/24 km ENE of Bennington. Mt. Snow Ski Area partly here and in West Dover. **5** town (1990 pop. 1,065), St. Croix co., W Wis., on Apple R., and 11 mi/18 km NNE of Hudson; 45°07′N 92°40′W. In dairying and livestock-raising area; mfg. (machinery, consumer goods, plastic prods.). Snow Crest Ski Area to E.

Somerset, village (1991 pop. 496), S Man., central Canada, in Pembina Mts., 45 mi/72 km SW of Portage la Prairie. Grain elevators, flour mills; dairying.

Somerset 1 uninc. village, El Dorado co., E central Calif., 8 mi/12.9 km SE of Placerville. Timber; cattle; hay, grapes. Wineries (4). El Dorado Natl. Forest to E. **2** village (1990 pop. 1,390), Perry co., central Ohio, 18 mi/29 km WSW of Zanesville; 39°48′N 82°18′W. In agr. area. Oil wells in area. Laid out 1810. **3** uninc. village, Orange co., N Va., 5 mi/8 km SW of Orange. Mfg. (bldg. materials); agr. (dairying; livestock; grain, soybeans). "Montpelier," home of James Madison to E.

Somerset, uninc. area (1990 pop. 22,070), Somerset co., N N.J., 2 mi/3.2 km W of New Brunswick. Mfg. (electrical and electronic prods., computers, cosmetics, plastics, paint primers).

Somerset, borough (1990 pop. 6,454), ⊙ Somerset co., SW Pa., 65 mi/105 km SE of Pittsburgh; 40°00′N 79°04′W. Agr. (corn, oats, potatoes; livestock; dairying). Mfg. (hose nozzles, transportation equip., fabricated metal prods., chemicals, tool and die, china prods.; printing and publishing). Co. airport to NE. Dressler Center for the Arts; Somerset Historic Center; L. Somerset reservoir to NE; Hidden Valley Ski Area to W; Laurel Hill State Park to W; part of Forbes State Forest to W. Settled 1771, laid out 1787, inc. 1804.

Somerset Dam, Vt.: see SOMERSET RESERVOIR.

Somerset Island, W Bermuda, on Great Sound, 5 mi/8 km W of Hamilton, separated from Bermuda Isl. (S) by narrow channel; 2 mi/3.2 km long, ½ mi/8/10 km–1 mi/1.6 km wide; 32°17′N 64°52′W. Road connection with neighboring isls.

Somerset Island (□ 9,594 sq mi/24,848 sq km), central Franklin dist., N.W.T., N Canada, in the Arctic Ocean, separated from Boothia Peninsula (S) by Bellot Strait, from Prince of Wales Isl. (W) by Peel Sound, from Cornwallis Isl. (N) and Devon Isl. (NE) by Barrow Strait, and from Baffin Isl. (E) by Prince Regent Inlet; 160 mi/257 km long, 22 mi/35 km–105 mi/169 km wide; bet. 71°57′N–74°10′N and 90°10′W–95°45′W. Creswell Bay in SE; E coast has steep cliffs, backed by hills rising to c.2,500 ft/760 m. At SE extremity is Fort Ross trading post. Discovered 1819 by Sir William Parry.

Somerset Reservoir (SUHM-uhr-set) (□ c.3 sq mi/7.8 sq km), in towns of Somerset and Stratton, Windham co., S Vt., on E. Branch Deerfield R., 20 mi/32 km WNW of Brattleboro; 4 mi/6.4 km long; 42°58′N 72°54′W. Formed by Somerset Dam (104 ft/32 m high), built (1913) for power generation.

Somerstown, N.Y.: see SOMERS.

Somersworth (SUH-muhrz-wuhrth), city (1990 pop. 11,249), Strafford co., SE N.H., 4 mi/6.4 km N of Dover, opposite Berwick (Maine); 43°15′N 70°52′W. Mfg. (machining; fabricated metal prods., rubber prods., chemicals, electrical prods., consumer goods). Cotton mills 1st est. here 1822. Part of Dover (S) until 1729, known as Great Falls until 1893.

Somerton, town (1990 pop. 5,282), Yuma co., extreme SW Ariz., Colorado R. 5 mi/8 km to W, and 10 mi/16 km SSW of Yuma; 32°36′N 114°42′W. Shipping point for vegetables in irrigated agr. area. Parts of Cocopah Indian Reservation to E and W; Mexico border to W and S.

Somervell, county (□ 191 sq mi/495 sq km; 1990 pop. 5,360), N central Texas; ⊙ Glen Rose; 32°13′N 97°46′W. Wooded, hilly region (elev. c.600 ft/183 m – 1,250 ft/381 m), drained by Brazos R. and Paluxy and Squaw creeks. Scenic resort area; some agr. (grains, peanuts; hay), cattle; dairying; sand and gravel. Dinosaur Valley State Park in N, known for its dinosaur fossils, wildlife center; part of Squaw Creek L. reservoir on N border. Formed 1875. Comanche Peak 1 nuclear power plant (initial criticality April 3, 1990) is 4.5 mi/7.2 km N of Glen Rose; uses cooling water from the Sqaw Creek Reservoir, and has a max. dependable capacity of 1150 MW.

Somerville (SUHM-uhr-vil), plantation (1990 pop. 458), Lincoln co., S Maine, on Sheepscot R., and 24 mi/39 km NNE of Wiscasset; 44°17′N 69°29′W. Lumber mills.

Somerville (SUH-muhr-vil), city (1990 pop. 76,210), Middlesex co., E Mass., a residential and industrial suburb of Boston, on the Mystic R.; 42°23′N 71°06′W. Diverse light mfg., including chemicals. Historical attractions include the Old Powder House, used in the Amer.

Revolution; Prospect Hill Tower, where Gen. Israel Putnam raised the 1st flag of the united colonies (1776) and which served as a prison camp in the Civil War; and Ploughed Hill, one of the fortified hills used in the siege of Boston (1775). Settled 1630, set off from Charlestown 1842, inc. as a city 1871.

Somerville 1 (SUH-muhr-vil), town (1990 pop. 223), Gibson co., SW Ind., 12 mi/19 km SE of Princeton; 38°17'N 87°23'W. Agr. and bituminous-coal area. **2** town (1990 pop. 2,047), ⊙ Fayette co., SW Tenn., on Loosahatchie R., and 37 mi/60 km ENE of Memphis; 35°15'N 89°21'W. In timber, cotton, corn, soybeans, hay, livestock area; makes furniture, clothing, textiles. Founded 1825. **3** town (1990 pop. 1,542), Burleson co., S central Texas, near Yegua Creek at Somerville L. dam, c.70 mi/113 km ESE of Austin; 30°21'N 96°31'W. Elev. 250 ft/76 m. Junction and trade center in cotton, corn, cattle area; mfg. (prefabricated metal bldgs.). L. Somerville State Park to W. Est. 1883.

Somerville (SUH-muhr-vil), residential borough (1990 pop. 11,632), ⊙ Somerset co., N central N.J., on the Raritan R., 10 mi/16 km NW of New Brunswick; 40°34'N 74°36'W. Electronic parts and pharmaceuticals. Of interest are the Wallace House (residence of George Washington 1778–1779) and the old Du. parsonage (1751; now a mus.). Settled 1683, inc. as a borough 1909.

Somerville (SUH-muhr-vil), village (1990 pop. 279), Butler co., extreme SW Ohio, 12 mi/19 km NNW of Hamilton; 39°34'N 84°38'W.

Somerville Lake, reservoir, on border bet. Burleson and Washington cos. and in Lee co., SE central Texas, on Yegua R., 27 mi/43 km SSW of Bryan; 12 mi/19 km long; 30°19'N 96°31'W. Max. capacity 1,028,800 acre-ft. Formed by Somerville Dam (75 ft/23 m high), built (1967) by the Army Corps of Engineers for water supply and flood control. L. Somerville State Park on N shore.

Somes Sound, Maine: see MOUNT DESERT ISLAND.

Somonauk (SOM-ah-nok), village (1990 pop. 1,263), De Kalb and La Salle cos., N Ill., 20 mi/32 km WSW of Aurora; 41°37'N 88°40'W. Agr. (corn; soybeans, hogs, sheep; dairying); mfg. (fabricated metal prods., furniture).

Songo River (SAHNG-o), SW Maine, short navigable stream with several locks; links Long and Sebago lakes, Cumberland co.

Sonoita (so-no-EE-tah), town (1990 pop. 1,241), ⊙ General Plutarco Elias Calle municipio, NW Sonora, Mexico, 62 mi/100 km NE of Puerto Peñasco at intersection of Mexico Highways 8 and 2, and 2 mi/3 km from U.S. border. Customs station at border. Jesuit mission est. here in 1701. Municipio formed from a part of Puerto Peñasco in 1989.

Sonoita (so-NO-YEE-tah), village, Santa Cruz co., S Ariz., 27 mi/43 km NNE of Nogales, near Cienega Wash. Elev. 4,865 ft/1,483 m. Agr. (cattle; hay). Parts of Coronado Natl. Forest to S, W and NE; Mt. Wrightson to W.

Sonoma (suh-NO-muh), county (☐ 1,576 sq mi/4,082 sq km; 1990 pop. 388,222), W Calif., on Pacific coast; ⊙ Santa Rosa; 38°31'N 122°56'W. In the Coast Ranges; Mt. St. Helena is on E border. Bounded S in part by San Pablo Bay and Petaluma R., bounded W by Pacific Ocean; drained by Russian R. and short coastal streams. Large poultry industry centered at Petaluma. Sheep, turkeys, chickens; dairying; nursery prods., vegetables, apples, grapes, wheat, oats, corn; urchins, fish; very large wine industry; stone quarries. Redwood groves; some timber. Many vacation resorts along lower Russian R.; hot springs, geyser fields, petrified forest, on and near E border. Processing industries, mfg. at Santa Rosa, Sonoma, Petaluma, Healdsburg. Sonoma Coast State Beach in SW; Fort Ross and Salt Point state parks in W, on coast; Armstrong Redwoods State Park and Austin Creek State Recreation Area in W center; Petaluma Adobe and Sonoma State historical parks in SE; Bothe-Napa Valley and Sugar Loaf Ridge state parks on E border. Formed 1850.

Sonoma (suh-NO-muh), city (1990 pop. 8,121), Sonoma co., W Calif., 9 mi/14.5 km W of Napa; 38°17'N 122°28'W. Trade center of grape growing and wineries for Sonoma Valley; grapes, apples, vegetables, grain, nursery prods.; poultry; dairying. Mfg. (screw machine prods., pumps, cheese; printing and publishing). Founded 1835 by Gen. M. G. Vallejo on site of Serra's Mission San Francisco de Solano (1823; now restored). Bear Flag of the Calif. republic was raised here in 1846. Mission and the home of Gen. Vallejo are at Sonoma State Historical Park. Hot springs (resorts) nearby.

Sonoma, Lake, reservoir (☐ 6 sq mi/15.5 sq km), Sonoma co., N Calif., on Dry Creek, 9 mi/14.5 km NW of Healdsburg; 38°43'N 123°00'W. Extends NW-SE. Formed by Warm Springs Dam (381 ft/116 m), built (1982) by Army Corps of Engineers for flood control.

Sonoma Range (suh-NO-muh), Humboldt and Pershing cos., N Nev., SE of Winnemucca; 25 mi/40 km long N-S; 40°51'N 117°36'W. Sonoma Peak (9,396 ft/2,864 m) is at N end. Pleasant Valley Fault, a 25-mi/40-km, 15-ft/5-m vertical displacement caused by an earthquake (1915), runs along W side of range.

Sonora (so-NO-rah), state (☐ 70,484 sq mi/182,554 sq km; 1990 pop. 1,823,606), NW Mexico, on the Gulf of California, S of Arizona; ⊙ HERMOSILLO 27°30'N 109°15'W. Sonora is mostly mountainous, with vast desert stretches; along the gulf are low, broad coastlands. Irrigation projects on the Yaqui, Sonora, Mayo, and other rivers have opened large areas to agr. The most extensively irrigated of all Mex. states, Sonora is a leading natl. producer of cotton and wheat; other cereals and vegetables are also grown. Agr. is highly mechanized and export-oriented. Cattle raising and fishing are important, and large quantities of shrimp are exported to the U.S. Gold, silver, copper, and other metals are mined in Sonora. Power plants at Hermosillo and Guaymas have aided Sonora's rapid industrialization. Food processing and textile mfg. are major industries, and numerous maquiladoras, low-cost foreign-owned plants which finish prods. for export to the U.S., exist throughout the region. Nogales is the chief point of entry from the U.S. Systematic Span. exploration of Sonora, principally by Cristóbal de Oñate, began after Francisco Vásquez de Coronado's expedition in 1540. Span. missionaries, notably Eusebio Francisco Kino, were active in colonizing the territory during the 17th cent. Originally part of Nueva Viscaya, which also included the present-day states of Chihuahua and Durango, Sonora was later united with Sinaloa; they became separate states in 1830. Sonora played a key role in the Mex. Revolution that began in 1910.

Sonora, city (1990 pop. 4,153), ⊙ Tuolumne co., central Calif., 37 mi/60 km E of Modesto, in the Mother Lode gold-mining country; 37°59'N 120°23'W. Limestone quarrying; apples, hay; timber; cattle in area. Mfg. (lumber, automation machine tools, toys). Site of Big Bonanza mine; hq. for Stanislaus Natl. Forest (forest to NE). Old gold town of Columbia is 4 mi/6.4 km N. Sonora Pass across the Sierra Nevada is c.50 mi/80 km NE. New Melones L. reservoir to W. Founded 1848, inc. 1851.

Sonora, town (1990 pop. 2,751), ⊙ Sutton co., W Texas, on intermittent Dry Fork of Devil's R., and 70 mi/113 km S of San Angelo; 30°34'N 100°38'W. Elev. 2,120 ft/646 m. Retail point for ranching (sheep, goats, cattle) region; wheat; oil and natural gas; mfg. (gasoline). Co. is leading wool and mohair producer; hunting nearby. Caverns of Sonora, to W, have intricate crystalline formations. Settled 1888, inc. 1917.

Sonora (suh-NOR-uh), village (1990 pop. 295), Hardin co., central Ky., 11 mi/18 km S of Elizabethtown; 37°31'N 85°53'W. Agr. (tobacco, grain; livestock; dairying); mfg. (fiberglass prods., wood prods.).

Sonora Pass, mountain pass (c.9,625 ft/2,934 m), on border bet. Mono and Tuolumne cos., E Calif., across the Sierra Nevada, N of Yosemite Natl. Park and c.50 mi/80 km NE of Sonora. State Highway 108 passes through.

Sonora Peak (11,459 ft/3,493 m), E Calif., in the Sierra Nevada, on border bet. Mono and Alpine cos., 35 mi/56 km NW of Mono L.; 38°21'N 119°38'W.

Sonora River (so-NO-rah), c.250 mi/402 km long, Sonora, NW Mexico; rises on plateau near Cananea close to U.S. border; flows S and SW, past Arizpe, Banámichi, Ures, and Hermosillo, to Gulf of California opposite Tiburón Isl. Receives San Miguel R. Used for irrigation, esp. in Hermosillo dist. and in fertile delta, where cereals, vegetables, and subtropical fruit are grown. Reaches ocean only in years of heavy rain.

Soo Junction, village, Luce co., NE Upper Peninsula, N Mich., 12 mi/19 km SSE of Newberry; 46°20'N 85°15'W. Departure point for excursions to Tahquamenon Falls in Tahquamenon R.

Soo locks, The, Mich.: see SAULT SAINTE MARIE.

Sooke (SOOK), village, SW B.C., W Canada, on SE tip of Vancouver Isl., on Sooke Harbour of Juan de Fuca Strait, 18 mi/29 km W of Victoria; 48°23'N 123°44'W. Farming; fishing; lumbering.

Sopchoppy, village (☐ 1 sq mi/2.6 sq km; 1990 pop. 367), Wakulla co., NW Fla., 31 mi/50 km SSW of Tallahassee; 30°03'N 84°29'W.

Soper (SO-puhr), village (1990 pop. 305), Choctaw co., SE Okla., 11 mi/18 km W of Hugo, near Muddy Boggy Creek; 34°01'N 95°42'W. In rich farming area.

Soperton (SO-puhr-tuhn), town (1990 pop. 2,797), ⊙ Treutlen co., E central Ga., 22 mi/35 km ESE of Dublin; 32°23'N 82°35'W. Mfg. includes textiles, clothing.

Soperton (SAH-puhr-tuhn), village, Forest co., Wis., suburb of Wabeno. In Nicollet Natl. Forest.

Sophia, town (1990 pop. 1,182), Raleigh co., S W.Va., 6 mi/9.7 km SSW of Beckley; 37°42'N 81°15'W. Semi-bituminous-coal region. Mfg. (machinery, portable storage bldgs.). Agr. (grain); cattle. Inc. 1912.

Sophia, uninc. village, Randolph co. central N.C., 10 mi/16 km NNE of Asheboro. Tobacco., grain; poultry, livestock; timber. Mfg. (furniture and wood prods.).

Sopris Peak, Colo.: see ELK MOUNTAINS.

Soquel (so-KWEL), uninc. town (1990 pop. 9,188), Santa Cruz co., W Calif., in Soquel Creek canyon, 5 mi/8 km E of Santa Cruz, 1 mi/1.6 km N of Monterey Bay; 37°00'N 121°57'W. Bulb gardens; flowers, nursery prods., vegetables, apples; granite quarry.

Sorcerer Mountain (10,387 ft/3,166 m), SE B.C., W Canada, in Selkirk Mts., 30 mi/48 km NNE of Revelstoke.

Sorel (so-REL), city (1991 pop. 18,786), S Que., E Canada, at the confluence of the St. Lawrence and Richelieu rivers; 46°03'N 73°07'W. It is a grain-shipping center with an important shipbuilding industry. Mfg. (iron and steel, metal prods., textiles, furniture, plastics). On the site of Fort Richelieu, built by Pierre de Saurel in 1665.

Sorento, village (1990 pop. 596), Bond co., SW central Ill., 12 mi/19 km NW of Greenville; 39°00'N 89°34'W. RR junction. In agr. area (corn, wheat, soybeans, sorghum; dairy prods.).

Soroa (sor-O-uh), village, Pinar del Río prov., W Cuba; 22°48'N 83°01'W. Small town in tobacco-growing region in valley at foothills of Sierra del Rosario mts.; nearby cascades.

Sorrento 1 (suh-REN-to), town, Lake co., central Fla., 25 mi/40 km NW of Orlando; 28°48'N 81°35'W. Mfg. includes egg processing, cedar chest mfg., and printing and publishing. **2** town (1990 pop. 1,119), Ascension parish, La., 5 mi/8 km SE of Gonzales; 30°11'N 90°52'W. Oil and gas field nearby; sawmills, formerly exporting cypress. Boucherie Festival. **3** fishing and resort town (1990 pop. 295), Hancock co., S Maine, on Frenchman Bay, just NE of Mt. Desert Isl., and 14 mi/23 km ESE of Ellsworth; 44°28'N 68°10'W.

Soso (SO-so), village (1990 pop. 366), Jones co., SE Miss., 8 mi/12.9 km WNW of Laurel; 31°45'N 89°16'W. Agr. (cotton, corn, honey; cattle, poultry; dairying); light mfg.

Sosúa (so-SOO-ah), village (1993 pop. 8,685), Puerto Plata prov., N Dominican Republic, on the Atlantic Ocean, 11 mi/18 km E of Puerto Plata; 19°43'N 70°28'W. In agr. region (coffee, cacao, rice, bananas; cattle). Fishing and swimming resort. On Trujillo's invitation, on the eve of and during World War II, 22,230 acres/8,996 ha were set aside for agr. development for Jewish refugees from Europe. Although 5,000 visas were issued, only 700 persons actually settled or passed through Sosúa by 1947, and only ½ in agr. About 20 families still remain; local sausage factory.

Sotavento (so-tah-VEN-to), lowlands in Veracruz, SE Mexico, on Gulf of Campeche, around port of Alvarado, and along upper Papaloapan R. Noted cattle-raising country; sugarcane, coffee, fruit, timber; a part of Mexico's Gulf Coast oil-production region.

Soteapan (so-tai-AH-pahn), town (1990 pop. 3,115), Veracruz, SE Mexico, 29 mi/47 km WNW of Coatzacoalcos; 18°13′N 94°52′W. Tobacco, fruit.

Soto la Marina (SO-to la mah-REE-nah), town (1990 pop. 6,765), Tamaulipas, NE Mexico, on Gulf plain, on Soto la Marina R., and 60 mi/97 km E of Ciudad Victoria, on Mexico Highway 180; 23°44′N 98°10′W. Sugarcane, corn; livestock.

Soto la Marina River (SO-to lah mah-REE-nah), c.160 mi/257 km long, in Tamaulipas, NE Mexico; rises in Sierra Madre Oriental at Nuevo León border SW of Linares; flows E, past Padilla and Soto la Marina, to Gulf of Mexico 30 mi/48 km E of Soto la Marina. Irrigates fertile Gulf plains. Mouth barred by sand banks. Sometimes Santander R.

Sotuta (so-TOO-tah), town (1990 pop. 4,782), Yucatán, SE Mexico, 45 mi/72 km SE of Mérida; 20°36′N 89°0′W. RR terminus. Henequen, sugarcane, citrus fruit. Grotto and Maya ruins nearby.

Soucook River (SOO-kuk), c.30 mi/48 km long, S central N.H.; rises in ponds SW of L. Winnipesaukee; flows SW to the Merrimack R. below Concord.

Soudan (soo-DAN), village, St. Louis co., NE Minn., on Vermilion Iron Range, 25 mi/40 km NE of Virginia; 47°48′N 92°14′W. Its mine has been rich source of iron ore since 1884. Vermilion L. is just N; Soudan Underground Mine State Park to N.

Souderton (SOU-duhr-tuhn), borough (1990 pop. 5,957), Montgomery co., SE Pa., suburb, 24 mi/39 km NNW of downtown Philadelphia; 40°18′N 75°19′W. Agr. (grain, soybeans, apples; livestock; dairying); mfg. (electric and electronic equip., fabricated metal prods., furnaces, food; printing). Settled 1860, inc. 1887.

Soufrière (soo-FRER), village (1991 pop. 1,003), SW Dominica, B.W.I., on Soufrière Bay, 5 mi/8 km SSE of Roseau; 15°14′N 61°22′E. Cacao, limes.

Soufrière (soo-free-YER), active volcano (4,813 ft/1,467 m), on Basse-Terre, Guadeloupe, in the Caribbean Sea. Called also La Grande Soufrière, it is the highest mt. in the Lesser Antilles. The volcano erupted in 1976 with no loss of life, as the area had been safely evacuated.

Soufrière (soo-FRER), volcanic hill (2,999 ft/914 m), S Montserrat, Leeward Isls., B.W.I., just E of Plymouth; 16°42′N 62°11′W.

Soufrière (soo-free-ER), town (1991 pop. 3,041), SW St. Lucia, at head of beautiful Soufrière Bay, 11 mi/18 km SSW of Castries; 13°51′N 61°02′W. In agr. region (coconuts, limes, vegetables); fishing. Soufrière volcano with *solfataras* in collapsed cone is tourist attraction just above the town. Outside the town are the Ventine mineral springs (2.5 mi/4 km SE), the properties of which are said to be identical with those of Aix-les-Bains, in botanical garden. Soufrière Bay is flanked (SE) by famed The Pitons twin peaks, pyramidical cones rising from the sea.

Soufrière, volcano (4,048 ft/1,234 m), on St. Vincent isl., St. Vincent and the Grenadines; 13°20′N 61°11′W. On May 7, 1902, the day before the great eruption of Pelée on Martinique isl., Soufrière erupted, laying waste ⅓ of St. Vincent, killing more than 1,000 people, and scattering a heavy fall of ash on Barbados isl., c.75 mi/121 km E.

Souhegan River (so-HEE-guhn), c.35 mi/56 km long, N Mass. and S N.H.; rises just W of Ashby (Mass.); flows NE and E, into N.H., past Wilton and Milford, to Merrimack R. near Merrimack.

Soulanges (soo-LAWNZH), county (☐ 136 sq mi/352 sq km), S Que., E Canada, on the St. Lawrence R., and on Ont. border; ⊙ Coteau Landing; 45°17′N 74°13′W.

Soulanges (soo-LAWNZH), village, S Que., E Canada, on the St. Lawrence R., at NE end of L. St. Francis, 3 mi/5 km W of Valleyfield, and at W end of Soulanges Canal. Hydroelectric center, supplying Montreal.

Soulanges Canal (soo-LAWNZH), S Que., E Canada, extends 14 mi/23 km bet. lakes St. Francis (W) and St. Louis (E), on N side of the St. Lawrence R., bypassing rapids. Completed 1899, with 5 locks, it superseded original Beauharnois Canal, on S side of the St. Lawrence. Earlier canal on same route was opened 1783, enlarged 1848. Canal is now used for power purposes only.

Soulsbyville, uninc. town (1990 pop. 1,732), Tuolumne co., central Calif., 6 mi/9.7 km E of Sonora; 38°00′N 120°16′W. Timber; cattle; hay, apples. Stanislaus Natl. Forest to E.

Sound Island (☐ 6 sq mi/16 sq km), SE N.F., E Canada, at head of Placentia Bay, 35 mi/56 km NNW of Argentia; 3 mi/5 km long, 3 mi/5 km wide; 47°49′N 54°10′W. Fishing.

Sour Lake, town (1990 pop. 1,547), Hardin co., E Texas, 20 mi/32 km WNW of Beaumont, near Pine Isl. Bayou; 30°08′N 94°24′W. In oil field; oil pipeline station and storage point. Main unit of Big Thicket Natl. Preserve to N. Settled 1836, inc. 1939.

Sourdnahunk Lake, Maine: see NESOWADNEHUNKLAKE.

Sourdough, village, S Alaska, on Gulkana R., and 100 mi/161 km NNE of Valdez, on Richardson Highway. Sports hunting and fishing.

Souris (SUHR-is), town (1991 pop. 1,662), SW Man., central Canada, on Souris R., and 21 mi/34 km SW of Brandon. RR shops, foundries, grain elevators; dairying. Resort.

Souris (SOOR-is), river, c.450 mi/720 km long, central Canada and N central U.S.; rises in S Sask. (Canada); flows SE with a great loop into N.Dak. (passing Minot), then N and NE back into Canada, to the Assiniboine R. in SW Man.

Souris (SOR-is), village (1990 pop. 97), Bottineau co., N N.Dak., 12 mi/19 km WNW of Bottineau, near branch of Souris R.; 48°54′N 100°40′W.

Souris East, town (1991 pop. 1,333), NE P.E.I., E Canada, on the Gulf of St. Lawrence. Settled in 1748 by Acadians, it is a fishing port.

South Acton, Mass.: see ACTON.

South Amboy, city (1990 pop. 7,863), Middlesex co., E N.J., opposite Perth Amboy, with a harbor at mouth of Raritan R. (bridged here); 40°29′N 74°16′W. Mfg. (steel prods., rubber and plastic goods); clay (dug here since early 19th cent.); transships coal. Terminal (1832) of the Camden and Amboy, state's 1st RR; became an important coal port. Settled 1651; inc. as borough 1888, as city 1908. Damaged (1950) by explosion of munitions.

South Amherst (A-muhrst), village (1990 pop. 1,765), Lorain co., N Ohio, 7 mi/11 km W of Elyria; 41°21′N 82°14′W. Large sandstone quarries are just N.

South Anna River, c.85 mi/137 km long, central Va.; rises in NW Louisa co., c.15 mi/24 km E of Charlottesville; flows SE and E, joins North Anna R. c.20 mi/32 km N of Richmond to form Pamunkey R.; 38°10′N 78°13′W.

South Ardmore, Pa.: see HAVERFORD.

South Aulatsivik Island, NE Lab., E Canada, at entrance of Webb's Bay on the Atlantic Ocean; 22 mi/35 km long, 12 mi/19 km wide. Contains several lakes. At N end is Mt. Thoresby (3,007 ft/917 m); 56°54′N 61°28′W.

South Baldy, peak (10,783 ft/3,287 m) in Magdalena Mts., Socorro co., W central N.Mex., 17 mi/27 km WSW of Socorro, in sect. of Cibola Natl. Forest; 33°59′N 107°11′W.

South Barre, Mass.: see BARRE.

South Barrington, village (1990 pop. 2,937), Cook co., NE Ill., residential suburb, 31 mi/50 km NW of downtown Chicago, 7 mi/11.3 km ENE of Elgin; 42°05′N 88°09′W.

South Bass Island, largest of Bass Isls., N Ohio, in L. Erie, 15 mi/24 km NNW of Sandusky; c.3 mi/5 km long, 1 mi/2 km wide; 41°39′N 82°49′W. It is site of Put-in-Bay village and natl. monument commemorating

Perry's victory in battle of L. Erie. Extensive vineyards, wineries.

South Bay, town (☐ 1 sq mi/2.6 sq km; 1990 pop. 3,558), Palm Beach co., SE Fla., at SE tip of L. Okeechobee; 26°40′N 80°43′W. Highways run S and E from here to West Palm Beach and Miami.

South Beach, Art Deco tourist and entertainment district (☐ 6 sq mi/15.5 sq km; 1990 pop. 2,754) of Miami Beach, Dade co., SE Fla.; 27°35′N 80°20′W. Area marked by restored 1930s-era hotels along beachfront Ocean Drive and adjoining streets in SE corner of Miami Beach.

South Beach, a shore-residential sect. of Staten Island borough of N.Y. city, SE N.Y., along E shore of Staten Isl., SW of Fort Wadsworth, bet. the Verrazano Narrows Bridge (N) and Great Kills Natl. Recreation Area (S); 40°35′N 74°04′W. A 19th-cent. seaside resort, it is little used now due to pollution. Residential development was spurred by the opening of the Verrazano Bridge in the 1960s. Nearby, to the SW, are Midland, New Dorp, and Oakwood beaches.

South Belmar, resort borough (1990 pop. 1,482), Monmouth co., E N.J., on the Atlantic coast, 14 mi/23 km ESE of Freehold; 40°10′N 74°01′W.

South Beloit (BEL-oit), industrial city (1990 pop. 4,072), Winnebago co., N Ill., on Rock R. (bridged here), suburb of Beloit (Wis.) but within Rockford metro area; 42°28′N 89°01′W. Agr. (corn; cattle, hogs; dairying). Mfg. (fabricated metal prods., high-speed cutting tools, concrete prods., foods, bldg. materials, chemicals). Inc. 1917.

South Bend, city (1990 pop. 105,511), ⊙ St. Joseph co., N Ind., on the great S bend of the St. Joseph R.; 41°41′N 86°16′W. In a farming and mint-growing region. An industrial city; mfg. (fabricated metal prods., transportation equip., plastics and plastic prods., consumer goods, tool and die, steel wire and wire harnesses, electric and electronic prods., wood prods., machinery, chemicals, motor vehicles, asphalt, dental prods., paper prods., glass prods., foods and food flavorings, bldg. materials; precious metal recycling, steel processing, custom embroidering, printing, meat processing). The Studebaker mfg. corporation, founded here in 1852, was a major producer of automobiles in the 20th cent. until production ceased in 1963. Robert LaSalle, the Fr. explorer, camped in the area in 1679. Settled c.1823 (laid out 1831) as a post of the Amer. Fur Company on the site of a Fr. mission and trading post. The old St. Joseph Co. Courthouse (1855) houses a mus. Seat of the Univ. of Notre Dame, with its famous football team, athletic facilities, art gallery, and huge lib. Shares twin city status with Mishawaka to E; general area is referred to as Michiana. Michiana Regional Airport in NW part of city. St. Mary's Col., Ind. Univ. at South Bend, and Bethel Col. (in neighboring Mishawaka) are also here. Potato Creek State Park nearby to SW. Inc. as a city 1865.

South Bend, town (1990 pop. 1,551), ⊙ Pacific co., SW Wash., 21 mi/34 km S of Aberdeen, on Willapa R., 3 mi/4.8 km upstream (SE) from mouth, at end of Willapa Bay, arm of Pacific Ocean; 46°40′N 123°48′W. RR terminus. Dairying; alfalfa. Fishing. Mfg. (fresh and frozen seafood). Co. mus. Willapa Harbor Airport to NW.

South Bend 1 village, Lincoln co., SE Ark., near Arkansas R., 34 mi/55 km ESE of Pine Bluff. **2** village (1990 pop. 93), Cass co., SE Nebr., 20 mi/32 km W of Plattsmouth, and on Platte R; 41°0′N 96°15′W. Platte R. State Park nearby.

South Berwick (BUHR-wik), town (1990 pop. 3,877), including South Berwick village, York co., SW Maine, on Salmon Falls R., and 18 mi/29 km S of Alfred; 43°14′N 70°45′W. Light mfg. Seat of Berwick Acad. (founded 1791). Sarah Orne Jewett birthplace is preserved. Settled 1623, set off from Berwick 1814.

South Bethany, resort town (1990 pop. 148), Sussex co., central Del., on Atlantic Ocean, 2 mi/3.2 km S of Bethany; 38°31′N 75°03′W. Fenwick Isl. State Park to the S.

South Bethelehem (BETH-luh-hem), borough (1990 pop. 479), Armstrong co., W Pa., 15 mi/24 km NE of

Kittaning, on Redbank Creek, opposite New Bethlehem; 41°00′N 79°20′W. Agr. (grain; livestock; dairying).

South Bimini, Bahama Isls.: see BIMINI ISLANDS.

South Bloomfield, village (1990 pop. 900), Pickaway co., S central Ohio, 17 mi/27 km S of Columbus, near Scioto R.; 39°43′N 82°59′W.

South Borden Island, Canada: see BORDEN ISLANDS.

South Boston, town (□ 5 sq mi/13 sq km; 1990 pop. 6,997), Halifax co., S Va., 28 mi/45 km ENE of Danville, on Dan R.; 36°42′N 78°54′W. RR junction; mfg. (electrical equip., bldg. materials, textiles, clothing, flour, lumber, foundry prods., beverages, dairy prods.; printing and publishing); agr. area (tobacco, grain, soybeans; cattle); important tobacco market. William M. Tuck Airport to E. Staunton R. State Park, on Buggs Isl. L. (Kerr Reservoir) to E. Chartered 1796; inc. as independent city (separate from surrounding co.) 1884. Reverted to town in 1995

South Boston, Mass.: see BOSTON.

South Bound Brook, industrial borough (1990 pop. 4,185), Somerset co., N central N.J., on Raritan R. opposite Bound Brook; 40°32′N 74°31′W. Baron von Steuben had hq. here, 1778–1779. Inc. 1907.

South Braintree, Mass.: see BRAINTREE.

South Bristol, resort town (1990 pop. 825), Lincoln co., S Maine, partly on Rutherford Isl., on Johns Bay, and c.10 mi/16 km S of Damariscotta; 43°53′N 69°33′W. Includes villages of Walpole, with church built 1772, and Christmas Cove.

South Brooklyn, former section of Brooklyn borough of N.Y. city, SE N.Y., along shore of Upper New York Bay, including what are now Red Hook, Carroll Gardens, Cobble Hill, and (sometimes) Gowanus, Boerum Hill, and Park Slope; 40°40′N 73°59′W. Its port area included Erie and Atlantic shipping basins, N.Y. State Barge Canal terminal, and Red Hook sect. (partly residential). With the decline of the waterfront businesses and pop. loss, the term acquired a negative cachet; developers and community groups in the gentrifying neighborhoods further inland dropped the name in favor of both older ones (Carroll Gardens) and newer inventions (or, more precisely, reinventions, such as Cobble HIll).

South Brother Island, part of Manhattan borough, N.Y. city, SE N.Y., in East R. bet. Rikers and North Brother isls; 40°48′N 73°54′W. Consists of 7 acres/2.8 ha.

South Brother Mountain (3,951 ft/1,204 m), Piscataquis co., N central Maine, 25 mi/40 km NW of Millinocket, in Katahdin State Game Preserve; 45°56′N 69°00′W.

South Brownsville, Pa.: see BROWNSVILLE.

South Brunswick, township (1990 pop. 25,792), Middlesex co., N N.J., 8 mi/12.9 km SW of New Brunswick; 40°22′N 74°31′W. Printing and plastics industries. Inc. 1798.

South Burlington, city (1990 pop. 12,809), Chittenden co., NW Vt., on L. Champlain; 44°27′N 73°13′W. Some mfg., including electronic equip., skiing equip., and medical instruments. Burlington Internatl. Airport is here. Inc. 1971.

South Byfield, Mass.: see NEWBURY.

South Caicos, island (□ 9.4 sq mi/24.3 sq km, 1990 pop. 1,198), Turks and Caicos Isls., crown colony of Great Britain, W.I., at SE end of the Caicos Isls., on Turks Isl. Passage; 21°30′N 71°30′W. Former salt-panning center. Has an airfield at S end and best harbor in Caicos chain at Cockburn Harbor. Sailing, sport fishing, scuba diving, and tourism are main economic activities. Spiney lobster harvested and processed for export.

South Cairo, resort village (1990 pop. 950), Greene co., SE N.Y., on Catskill Creek, and 6 mi/9.7 km NW of Catskill, in Catskill Mts.; 42°17′N 73°58′W.

South Canaan, Conn.: see CANAAN.

South Carolina, state (□ 32,007 sq mi/82,898 sq km; 1995 est. pop. 3,673,287), SE U.S., 1 of the 13 Colonies; ⊙ COLUMBIA; 34°01′N 80°54′W. Columbia is the largest city; CHARLESTON and GREENVILLE are other major cities. Roughly triangular in shape, S.C. is bounded on the N by N.C., on the SW and NW tip by Ga. (with the SAVANNAH R. and its tributaries, the TUGALOO RIVER and CHATTOOGA RIVER in NW, forming the state line), and on the SE by the Atlantic Ocean. The coast is even for c.50 mi/80 km in NE, called the Grand Strand. N of GEORGETOWN it is lined with beautiful sand beaches, and includes resort city of MYRTLE BEACH. In contrast, center and S part of coast is marshy, crossed by a network of channels, rivers, and creeks, creating the SEA ISLANDS. The coastal climate is humid subtropical, with long, hot summers and short, mild winters. Coastal areas are vulnerable to hurricanes, which often turn NW and run directly into S.C.'s SE-facing coastline, as did Hurricane Hugo (1989), or brush past the coast as Agnes did (1972). In this area are found cypress swamps, Span. moss draped live oaks, beautiful flowering gardens, antebellum plantations, and the quaint historic seaports of Georgetown, BEAUFORT, and Charleston, the latter one of the chief ports of entry in the Southeast. The fall line, where falls are the head of navigation and have traditionally generated power for textile mills, separates the Coastal Plain from the rolling Piedmont plateau of the upcountry and runs generally parallel to the coast, passing through Columbia. The INTRACOASTAL WATERWAY follows natural and manmade channels inland from coast. Inland, the climate is temperate, becoming progressively cooler as the elev. increases. In the extreme NW are the BLUE RIDGE mts.; they occupy only c.500 sq mi/1,295 sq km in the state, with SASSAFRAS MOUNTAIN (3,560 ft/1,085 m), on N.C. state border, the highest point and only part of Appalachian Mts. in S.C. Rainfall is abundant and well distributed throughout S.C. The GREAT PEE DEE RIVER (or Pee Dee), SANTEE RIVER, EDISTO RIVER, and Savannah river systems drain the state, flowing W-E, creating rapids at the fall line. Large reservoirs include Thurmond, Russell, and Hartwell lakes in Savannah R., in SW, L. Murray in center, and the Santee-Cooper lakes connected by manmade channels in SE center. This abundant source of hydroelectric power is one of S.C.'s most important natural resources. Several nuclear plants operate in the state as well, although the Savannah R. plant near Aiken was found to be unsafe and was closed in 1988. Nuclear reprocessing and waste storage remains important. Mfg. is easily the largest sector of the state's economy, accounting for almost 27% of the Gross State Prod. in 1986. While mfg. has become more diversified, the leading industries are based largely on the state's agr. prods.—the huge textile and fabric mills and clothing and carpeting industries, centered in the Piedmont, and logging and related enterprises (such as the mfg. of pulp and paper) on the c.12,500,000 acres/5,058,750 ha of forestland that cover the state; the longleaf and loblolly pine are prevalent, and pine lumber is an important prod. S.C. has been successful in attracting foreign mfg. investment including foreign-owned tire and motor vehicle plants. Other leading mfg. includes chemicals and machinery. S.C. has considerable mineral resources, but not all can be profitably mined, and their importance in the state's economy is not great. Principal minerals are nonmetallic—cement, stone, clays, and sand and gravel; also gold and silver mines in N center. In agr., tobacco and soybeans have surpassed cotton as S.C.'s chief crops; the state ranks 3d (1990) in the nation in tobacco production. Cotton lint and cattle are economically important, and peanuts, pecans, soybeans, sweet potatoes, and peaches are grown in abundance. Fishing is a major commercial enterprise; the chief catches are blue crabs and shrimp; also oysters and clams. S.C. also benefits economically from the significant number of military installations in the state. The tourist industry is steadily increasing and today ranks as one of the state's chief sources of income. Thousands of vacationers are attracted to famous Myrtle Beach, to the Sea Isl. resorts, and to Charleston's stately homes and gardens. The state's historical places of interest include Fort Sumter Natl. Monument (SE), Kings Mt. Natl. Military Park and Cowpens Natl. Battlefield (NW), and Congaree Swamp Natl. Monument in center. Cape Romain Natl. Wildlife Refuge in SE, Pinckney Isl. and Savannah R. Natl. Wildlife Refuge in S. S.C. has 2 natl. forests, Sumter (NW center, W, and far NW) and Francis Marion near coast in SE. Also important is Sand Hills State Forest and neighboring Carolina Sandhills Natl. Wildlife Refuge in NE. At an unknown coastal site in the region that is now the Carolinas, what may have been the 1st Eur. settlement in N. Amer. was founded (1526; not permanent) by an expedition under the Span. explorer Lucas Vásquez de Ayllón. The Frenchman Jean Ribaut established (1562) a short-lived Huguenot settlement on Parris Isl. in Port Royal Sound, but Fr. colonizing ambitions were thoroughly thwarted by Pedro Menéndez de Avilés. Span. missions soon extended N from Fla. almost to the site of present-day Charleston, and they remained until the arrival of the English. Charles I asserted England's claim as early as 1629 by granting the territory from 36°00′N to 31°00′N (later named Carolina for Charles I) to Sir Robert Heath, but because no settlements were made, Heath's charter was forfeited. In 1663, Charles II awarded the area to 8 of his prominent supporters, the most active of whom was Anthony Ashley Cooper (Lord Ashley, later 1st Earl of Shaftesbury). The N and S sects. of Carolina developed separately. The 1st permanent colony was est. 1670 at Albemarle Point under William Sayle. To govern it, John Locke wrote (at Lord Ashley's behest) the Fundamental Constitutions (1669), which granted some popular rights but at the same time retained feudal privileges and limitations. The settlers refused to ratify it. Actual govt. consisted of a powerful council, of which ½ was appointed by the proprietors in England; a governor, also appointed by the proprietors; and a relatively weak assembly, elected by all freemen. In 1680 the colony moved across the river to Oyster Point, which was better suited for defense. There the colonists established their capital, called Charles Town (later Charleston), which was to become the chief center of culture and of wealth in the South. The 1680s saw the beginnings of prosperity. Wealthy colonists set up plantations worked by indentured servants and Afr. and Native Amer. slaves, while freemen (many of them former indentured servants) cultivated the 50 acres/20 ha granted them by the proprietors. On plantations and small farms alike, corn, livestock, and some cotton were raised, and some tobacco was cultivated. Forests yielded rich timber and naval stores. The fur trade (esp. in deerskins) with the Creek and other tribes prospered, and it was the leading exponent for the colony's 1st 40 years. But conflict with the Spanish and French increased, and the encroachment of the 2 countries dramatized the proprietors' lack of concern and their inability to defend the distant colony. Popular antagonism to proprietary rule was spurred by the parceling of much of the land into a few large grants, by the quitrent system, and most important by the issue of religion. Several religious groups had freely practiced their faith in the colony until the early 18th cent.; these included Anglicans, dissenters from Britain, and Fr. Huguenots. In 1704 the Anglicans, without opposition from the proprietors, managed to deprive the other groups of their religious liberty, and it was not until the Eng. govt. took action (1706) that religious toleration was restored. The colony was divided into N.C. and S.C. in 1713. In 1715–1716 the settlers were attacked by the Yamasee, who had become resentful of exploitation by the Carolina traders. The uprising was finally quelled after much loss of life and property. These attacks further revealed the lack of protection afforded by the proprietors, and in 1719 the colonists rebelled and received royal protection. The crown sent Francis Nicholson as provincial royal governor in 1720, and S.C. formally became a royal colony in 1729 when the proprietors finally accepted terms. Conditions were now in many respects improved. Pirates such as Blackbeard who had infested the coast had been hanged or dispersed. In addition the founding (1733) of Ga. to the S provided a buffer against the Spanish. Rice, experimented with as early as 1680, flourished in the marshy tidewater area and became the leading plantation style in the 1710s. Loss of territory and some of the colony's fur trade to Ga. was more than compensated for when indigo, supported by Br. bounty, became (1740s) the colony's 2d staple. To counterbalance the vast number of Afr. slaves being imported for plantation labor, Eur. immigration was encouraged. Germans and Swiss, arriving in the 1730s and 1740s, and Scotch-Irish and other migrants from Va. and Pa., arriving in the 1760s, settled the colony's lower middle country and uplands. Regional antipathies were generated by economic and social differences; the small, self-sufficient farmer of the up-country, demanding courts, roads, and defense against outlaws and the Cherokee, elicited little sympathy from the powerful plantation lords of lower Carolina. In the late 1760s discontent culminated in the formation of the Regulator movement. Finally the legislature was impelled to grant certain up-country demands, including the establishment of courts in the region. S.C.'s long friendship with the mother country was reflected in trade benefits resulting from the Navigation Acts and in protection by the strong Br. navy. However, public sentiment in the colony was transformed by the Stamp Act, the Townshend Act, and Br. political claims. South Carolinians—Christopher Gadsden, Henry Laurens, and Arthur Middleton—were leaders in the movement for independence, and in March 1776, an independent govt. of S.C. was set up with John Rutledge as president. In the Amer. Revolution the British failed to take Charleston in June 1776 (see FORT MOULTRIE), but Sir Henry Clinton successfully besieged the town in 1780. In the ensuing Carolina campaign the British were ultimately forced to retreat, although they held Charleston until Dec. 1782. In 1786 the site of Columbia was chosen for the new capital; its central location mollified the up-country pop. S.C. ratified the Federal Constitution in May 1788 and replaced the royal charter with a state charter in 1790. Complete religious liberty was established, and primogeniture was abolished, but property qualifications for voting and office holding ensured planter control of the legislature. The constitutional amendment known as the compromise of 1808 somewhat alleviated the sectional antagonism by reapportioning representation. Preceded by the introduction of long-staple Sea Isl. cotton in the 1790s, Eli Whitney's cotton gin had enabled short-staple cotton plantations to spread far into the Piedmont; thus the planters continued to dominate state policies. In the late 1820s cotton from the fertile W states (e.g., Miss., Ala.) glutted the market, and prosperity declined in S.C. Discontent was aggravated by natl. tariff policies that were unfavorable to S.C.'s agrarian economy. In 1832 the state passed its nullification act, declaring the tariff laws null and void and not binding upon S.C. citizens. President Andrew Jackson acted firmly for the Union in this crisis, and in 1833 S.C. repealed its act. Tariff reform that same year brought relief, but the possibility of secession had been broached and was subsequently renewed in reaction to abolitionist attacks and further economic grievances. John C. Calhoun became the acknowledged leader of the whole South with his defense of the states' rights doctrine; his political philosophy was later to form the intellectual basis for the Confederacy. Some of the state's apologists for slavery, notably Robert B. Rhett, equaled the most radical abolitionists in their zeal. After Lincoln's election S.C. was the 1st state to secede (Dec. 20, 1860) from the Union. Gov. Francis W. Pickens immediately demanded all Federal property within the state, including FORT SUMTER, which was held by Union men under Major Robert Anderson. The firing on Sumter by Confederate batteries on April 12, 1861, precipitated the Civil War. In Nov. 1861, a Union naval force under Samuel F. Du Pont took the forts of Port Royal Sound, but Charleston's forts withstood severe bombardments in 1863, and the state was saved from heavy military action until early in 1865. Then Gen. William T. Sherman, commanding the army that had marched through Ga., crossed the Savannah R. and advanced N through the state. Because S.C. was viewed as the birthplace of secession, it was difficult to restrain many of the Union soldiers, and the deliberate devastation, culminating in the burning of Columbia, was appalling. The Reconstruction period that followed the war was no less disastrous. S.C. was selected for President Andrew Johnson's moderate program, but the program had only a brief trial before the radical Republicans took over. For a decade the state was ruled by carpetbaggers and scalawags, with the support of Afr.- Amer. votes. The constitution of 1868, which established universal male suffrage and ended property qualifications for office holding, gained the state readmittance (June 1868) to the Union. Between 1868 and 1874 accomplishments such as the building of schools and RRs were offset by waste and corruption in the state govt. and by high taxation. Many of these abuses were corrected by the honest administration of Gov. Daniel H. Chamberlain (1874–1876). The Democratic party regained vitality in 1876, and S.C.'s war hero, Wade Hampton, was selected as candidate for governor. The election of 1876 was marked by irregular practices on both sides, and although Hampton gained a majority, Chamberlain refused to accept defeat. Thus there existed 2 state govts. until 1877, when President Rutherford B. Hayes removed all Federal troops from the South, and Chamberlain, bereft of the support that had made Republican rule possible, withdrew. Hampton attempted moderation on race issues, but, despite his efforts, by 1882 the vast majority of Afr. Americans had lost the vote; white political supremacy was assured. The wartime destruction and the abolition of slavery had nearly ruined the state's basic agr. economy. Although some vigorous planters and merchants managed to recoup their fortunes, the lack of capital and farm tenancy (replacing the old plantation system) held most of the state's farmers in economic bondage. The Panic of 1873 was followed by 2 decades of agrarian hard times. The rice plantations, which had already begun to decline, were hardest hit. Popular discontent was not ameliorated until the election (1890) of Benjamin Tillman, leader of the up-country farmers, as governor. Tillmanites wrested control of the Democratic party from the conservative element (the tidewater "Bourbon aristocracy"), reapportioned taxes and representation, expanded public education, and established preliminary labor reform laws. Reflecting another aspect of Tillman's policies, the constitution of 1895 initiated "Jim Crow laws" and adopted voting qualifications that excluded virtually all Afr. Americans from the crucial Democratic primaries. Renewed agrarian prosperity after 1900 was accompanied by political stagnation that lasted until the governorship (1914–1918) of Richard I. Manning; progressive trends already evident in other parts of the country were now belatedly manifested here in the passage of education and labor laws. Agr. again suffered a setback in the 1920s. Contributing factors were the destruction of the Sea Isls. cotton crop by the boll weevil and the erosion of the land as a result of long adherence to the 1-crop system. Industry, esp. the textile industry (which had been increasing in importance since the turn of the cent.), also suffered in the Great Depression of the 1930s. New Deal legislation and the state road-building program provided S.C. with some relief. During World War I the position of Afr. Americans had been improved through war work and service in the armed forces; however, in the 1920s the renewed power of the Ku Klux Klan had again brought oppression, and black migration began on a scale sufficient to bring the whites into the majority in the state by 1930. World War II and the postwar period brought great changes. A state court decision in 1947 opened the Democratic primaries to allow blacks to vote. Under the governorship (1951–1955) of the nationally prominent James F. Byrnes, the poll tax was abolished as a voting requirement, steps were taken to curb Ku Klux Klan activities, and the educational system was greatly expanded. Integration of the schools after the 1954 U.S. Supreme Court decision met opposition, but in 1963 South Carolinians accepted token integration of Clemson Col. without incident, and desegregation began in the Charleston schools. By 1970 all of the public school dists. were technically in compliance with Federal desegregation requirements. That year 4 Afr. Americans were elected to the previously all-white state legislature. In the 1970s and 1980s, S.C. experienced economic growth similar to other Sunbelt states. S.C.'s low tax rates and large nonunion workforce have attracted many firms from the other states as well as foreign countries. In 1989, Hurricane Hugo struck S.C., killing 26 and causing more than $5 billion in damage. Politically, S.C. has been strongly Democratic since the end of Reconstruction, although since the late 1960s Republicans have gained strength in both state and natl. elections. The executive branch is headed by a governor elected for a 4-year term. All governors were Democratic from 1876 to 1975, when James B. Edwards, a Republican, took office. S.C.'s bicameral legislature has a senate with 46 members elected for 4-year terms and a house of representatives with 124 members elected for 2 years. The state sends 2 senators and 6 representatives to the U.S. Congress and has 8 electoral votes. In the early 1970s the state's 1895 constitution was extensively revised. Military installations include Parris Isl. Marine Base in S, Charleston Naval and Air Force bases in SE, Fort Jackson Military Reservation E of Columbia in center. Among S.C.'s institutions of higher education are The Citadel (The Military Col. of S.C.), at Charleston; Clemson Univ., at Clemson; S.C. State Univ., at Orangeburg; and the Univ. of S.C., at Columbia. S.C. has 46 cos.: ABBEVILLE, AIKEN, ALLENDALE, ANDERSON, BAMBERG, BARNWELL, BEAUFORT, BERKELEY, CALHOUN, CHARLESTON, CHEROKEE, CHESTER, CHESTERFIELD, CLARENDON, COLLETON, DARLINGTON, DILLON, DORCHESTER, EDGEFIELD, FAIRFIELD, FLORENCE, GEORGETOWN, GREENVILLE, GREENWOOD, HAMPTON, HORRY, JASPER, KERSHAW, LANCASTER, LAURENS, LEE, LEXINGTON, MCCORMICK, MARION, MARLBORO, NEWBERRY, OCONEE, ORANGEBURG, PICKENS, RICHLAND, SALUDA, SPARTANBURG, SUMTER, UNION, WILLIAMSBURG, YORK.,

South Carrollton, village (1990 pop. 202), Muhlenberg co., W Ky., on Green R., 3 mi/4.8 km N of Central City; 37°20′N 87°08′W. Bituminous coal-mining; agr. (tobacco, grain; livestock; timber); mfg. (lumber, mine timbers).

South Casco, Maine: see CASCO.

South Charleston, city (1990 pop. 13,645), Kanawha co., W central W.Va., suburb, 6 mi/9.7 km W of downtown Charleston, on the Kanawha R. (bridged); 38°21′N 81°42′W. A highly industrialized area and chemical-mfg. center. Mfg. (machinery, electrical prods., chemicals, transportation equip., foods, dental equip.; commercial printing). A large Native Amer. mound (built by Adena people, 1st. cent. A.D.) is in the city. Kanawha State Forest to SE. Charleston Ordnance Center to W. Settled 1782, inc. 1917.

South Charleston, village (1990 pop. 1,626), Clark co., W central Ohio, 11 mi/18 km ESE of Springfield; 39°49′N 83°39′W. Founded 1815.

South Chatham, Mass.: see CHATHAM.

South Chicago Harbor, Ill.: see CALUMET HARBOR.

South Chicago Heights, residential village (1990 pop. 3,597), Cook co., NE Ill., suburb, 30 mi/48 km S of downtown Chicago, near Ind. state line; 41°28′N 87°38′W. In industrial area. Drained by Little Calumet R. Mfg. (steel fabricating, tool and die, millwork; wood prods., food containers). Inc. 1907.

South China, Maine: see CHINA.

South Cle Elum (klee E-luhm), village (1990 pop. 457), Kittitas co., central Wash., 1 mi/1.6 km S of CLE ELUM across Yakima R., mouth of Cle Elum R. 2 mi/3.2 km W; 47°11′N 120°57′W. Fruit, potatoes; dairying; sheep, cattle; timber. Wenatchee Natl. Forest to N and S; Easton and Iron Horse state parks to W.

South Coatesville (KOTS-vil), borough (1990 pop. 1,026), Chester co., SE Pa., residential suburb, 1 mi/1.6 km S of Coatesville, on West Fork Bradywine Creek; 39°58′N 75°49′W. Inc. 1921.

South Coffeyville, town (1990 pop. 791), Nowata co., NE Okla., suburb, 2 mi/3.2 km S of Coffeyville (Kansas), and 23 mi/37 km NE of Bartlesville; 36°59′N 95°37′W. RR junction.

South Congaree (KAHNG-uh-ree), town (1990 pop. 2,406), Lexington co., central S.C., residential suburb, 8 mi/12.9 km SW of downtown Columbia; 33°54′N 81°08′W. Columbia Municipal Airport to N.

South Connellsville (KAH-nuhls-vil), borough (1990 pop. 2,204), Fayette co., SW Pa., on Youghiogheny R., 2 mi/3.2 km S of Connellsville, and 8 mi/12.9 km NE of Uniontown; 39°59′N 79°34′W. Agr. (corn, hay; dairying); mfg. (glass prods., fabricated metal prods.).

South Corning, village (1990 pop. 1,025), Steuben co., S N.Y., just S of Corning; 42°07′N 77°02′W.

South Coventry, Conn.: see COVENTRY.

South Creek, uninc. village, Beaufort co., E N.C., 26 mi/42 km SE of Washington, and on Pamlico R.

South Dakota, state (□ 77,121 sq mi/199,743 sq km; 1995 est. pop. 729,034), N central U.S., admitted to the Union in 1889 simultaneously with N.Dak. (they are the 40th and 39th states); ⊙ PIERRE. The largest cities are SIOUX FALLS and RAPID CITY. Bounded N by N.Dak., E by Minn. (with the Minnesota R. forming part of the state line) and Iowa (from which it is separated by the Big Sioux R.), S by Nebr. (with the Missouri R. forming part of the state line), and W by Wyo. and Mont. S.Dak. shows some of the earliest geologic history of the continent in the rock formations of the anc. Black Hills and in the Badlands. At their extreme bet. the White R. and the S fork of the Cheyenne R., the Badlands display in their deeply eroded clay gullies not only colorful, fantastic shapes but also a wealth of easily accessible marine and land fossils (the Badlands Natl. Monument preserves the area for its startling scenery and geologic interest). The whole of S.Dak. has a continental climate; summer brings a succession of hot, cloudless days, and in the winter blizzards sweep across bare hillsides, filling the coulees with deep snow. The average annual rainfall is low and declines from E to W across the state, and in years of drought summer winds blow away acres of topsoil in "black blizzards." From E to W the state rises some 6,000 ft/1,829 m to Harney Peak (7,242 ft/2,207 m) in the Black Hills, highest point in the U.S. E of the Rockies. Through the center of the state the Missouri R. cuts a wide valley S; other principal rivers include the James and Big Sioux to the E, and the Cheyenne, Belle Fourche, the Moreau, the Grand, and the White rivers to the W. Almost ⅓ of the region W of the Missouri R., a semiarid, treeless plain, belongs to Native Americans, most of whom live on reservations such as Cheyenne R., Pine Ridge, Rosebud, and Standing Rock. Much of the remaining area is divided into large ranches; there cattle and sheep ranching provide the major source of income, with soybeans and wheat growing secondary. In the more productive region E of the Missouri, livestock and livestock prods. comprise the primary source of income. Corn, hay, soybeans, and wheat are S.Dak.'s chief cash crops; oats, flaxseed, and barley are also grown. Although there is a certain amount of diversified industry in the main cities of Sioux Falls and Rapid City, meatpacking and food processing constitute by far the major industries of the state. Gold is S.Dak.'s most important mineral, and the town of Lead in the Black Hills is among the country's leading gold-mining centers. In 1988 the state ranked 3d in the nation in gold production. Stone, sand and gravel, and cement are also important minerals. At the time of Eur. exploration, S.Dak. was inhabited by Native Americans of the agr. Arikara and the nomadic Dakota Sioux. By the 1830s the Dakota Sioux had driven the Arikara from the area. Part of the region that is now S.Dak. was explored in the mid-18th cent. by sons of the sieur de la Vérendrye. The U.S. acquired the region as part of the Louisiana Purchase, and it was partially explored by Lewis and Clark in their Missouri R. expedition of 1804–1806. Later explorers became well acquainted with the Sioux, who continued to dominate the region during the period of the fur trade down to the mid-19th cent. Individual traders from the time of Pierre Dorion in the late 18th cent. made the region their home, and the posts founded by Pierre Chouteau and the Amer. Fur Company were the 1st bases for settlement (Fort

Pierre was est. 1817.). It was not until land speculators and farmers moved W from Minn. and Iowa in the 1850s that any real settlement developed. Two land companies were est. 1856 at Sioux Falls, and in 1859 Yankton, Bon Homme, and Vermillion were laid out. A treaty with the Sioux opened the land bet. the Big Sioux and the Missouri, and in 1861 Dakota Territory was set up, embracing not only present-day N.Dak. and S.Dak. but also E Wyo. and E Mont. Yankton was the capital. Settlers were discouraged by droughts, conflict with the Native Americans, and plagues of locusts; however, by the time the RR pushed to Yankton in 1872, the region had received the 1st of the Eur. immigrants who later came in great numbers, contributing significant Ger., Scandinavian, and Rus. elements to the Dakotas. Rumors of gold in the Black Hills, confirmed by a military expedition led by George A. Custer in 1874, excited natl. interest, and Americans began to pour into the area. However, much of the Black Hills region had been granted (1868) to the Sioux by treaty, and when they refused to sell either mining rights or the reservation itself, warfare with the Sioux again broke out. The defeat (1876) of Custer and his men by Sitting Bull, Crazy Horse, and Gall in the battle of Little Bighorn (in what is now Mont.) did not prevent the whites from gradually acquiring more and more Native Amer. land, including the gold-lined Black Hills. Near extinction of the buffalo herds as well as Sitting Bull's death (1890) at the hands of army-trained Native Amer. police and the subsequent massacre of Big Foot's band at WOUNDED KNEE Creek were factors leading to the permanent end of Native Amer. resistance here. Tribal organization was weakened by the Dawes Act of 1887 (although the Indian Reorganization Act of 1934 attempted to restore tribal ownership of repurchased lands, the younger generations have been moving to the cities in increasing numbers). During the 1870s the gold fever mounted; Deadwood had its day of gaudy glory, Wild Bill Hickok and Calamity Jane created frontier legends, and the town of Lead began its long, productive career. Although gold did not make the fortune of S.Dak., it laid the foundation by stimulating cattle ranching — herds of cattle were 1st brought to the grasslands of W S.Dak. partly to supply food for the miners. Settlement in the E also increased, and the period from 1878 to 1886, following the resumption of RR building after the financial depression earlier in the decade, was the time of the great Dakota land boom, when pop. increased threefold. Agitation for statehood developed; in 1888 the Republican party adopted the statehood movement as a campaign issue, and in 1889 Congress passed an enabling act. The Dakotas were divided; S.Dak. became a state with Pierre as capital. The new state was affected by the unusually severe winter of 1886–1887, which had destroyed huge herds of cattle in the W, ruining the great bonanza ranches and promoting among the ranchers the trend — since dominant — of having smaller herds with provisions for winter shelter and feeding. Cattle grazed on public domain and were rounded up only for branding and shipment to market. Recurrent droughts added to the difficulties of the farmers, who sought relief in the cooperative ventures of the Farmers' Alliance and political action in the Populist party, which won a resounding victory in 1896. Initiative and referendum were adopted (1898; S.Dak. was the 1st state to adopt them) and other progressive measures of the day were enacted, but prosperity quickly returned S.Dak. to political conservatism and the Republican party. The extension of RRs (particularly the Milwaukee, which was the only transcontinental line passing through S.Dak.) encouraged further expansion of agr., but new droughts (esp. that of 1910–1911) brought a brief period of emigration. Many new farmsteads were abandoned, and a turn toward political radicalism developed. The Progressive party, led by Peter Norbeck (governor 1917–1921) and operating as a branch of the Republican party, revived the attempts of Populist reform programs to regulate RR rates and raise assessments of corporate property and entered in experiments in state ownership of business.

New prosperity-depression cycles occurred after the boom of World War I. The combination of droughts and the Great Depression brought widespread calamities in the late 1920s and early 1930s, and the state's pop. declined by 50,000 bet. 1930 and 1940. Vigorous measures of relief were instituted under the New Deal, and higher farm prices during World War II and the ensuing years brought a new era of optimism. The 1950s inaugurated a period of Democratic strength in state politics. George McGovern was elected to the House in 1956 and to the Senate in 1962, 1968, and 1974. In 1972 McGovern ran unsuccessfully for President. In 1973, a militant Native Amer. group occupied a courthouse at Custer and the resulting gun battle with Federal marshals and related conflicts at Wounded Knee highlighted the Native Amer. resentment of broken treaties with the U.S. govt. In the postwar period adoption of improved farming techniques resulted in a steady increase in agr. and livestock production. This was accompanied, however, by the consolidation of small farms into large units and the displacement of many small farmers. Irrigation projects, extension of hydroelectric power, and protective measures against wind and water erosion have been pushed to avoid the threat of new disasters. In 1981, a major N.Y. bank relocated its credit card operations to Sioux Falls, marking the beginning of a shift toward service, finance, and trade industries as well as significant economic growth. Some casino gambling was legalized in 1989 as tourism continues to be one of the state's top sources of income. S.Dak. is governed under its 1889 constitution. The legislature consists of 35 senators and 70 representatives, all elected for 2-year terms. The governor is elected for 4 years. George Mickelson, a Republican, was elected in 1986 and reelected in 1990. He was killed in an airplane crash in 1993. The state chooses 1 U.S. representative and 2 senators and has 3 electoral votes. Among the state's attractions are Wind Cave Natl. Park, Jewel Cave and Badlands natl. monuments, and the famous mammoth carvings of the Mt. Rushmore Natl. Memorial. Institutions of higher learning include Augustana Col., at Sioux Falls; S.Dak. School of Mines and Technology, at Rapid City; S.Dak. State Univ., at Brookings; the Univ. of S.Dak., at Vermillion; and Northern State Col., at Aberdeen. S.Dak. has 66 cos.: ARMSTRONG, AURORA, BEADLE, BENNETT, BON HOMME, BROOKINGS, BROWN, BRULE, BUFFALO, BUTTE, CAMPBELL, CHARLES MIX, CLARK, CLAY, CODINGTON, CORSON, CUSTER, DAVISON, DAY, DEUEL, DEWEY, DOUGLAS, EDMUNDS, FALL RIVER, FAULK, GRANT, GREGORY, HAAKON, HAMLIN, HAND, HANSON, HARDING, HUGHES, HUTCHINSON, HYDE, JACKSON, JERAULD, JONES, KINGSBURY, LAKE, LAWRENCE, LINCOLN, LYMAN, MCCOOK, MCPHERSON, MARSHALL, MEADE, MELLETTE, MINER, MINNEHAHA, MOODY, PENNINGTON, PERKINS, POTTER, ROBERTS, SANBORN, SHANNON, SPINK, STANLEY, SULLY, TODD, TRIPP, TURNER, UNION, WALWORTH, YANKTON, ZIEBACH.,

South Dartmouth, Mass.: see DARTMOUTH.

South Dayton, village (□ 1 sq mi/2.6 sq km; 1990 pop. 601), Cattaraugus co., W N.Y., 16 mi/26 km SE of Dunkirk; 42°21′N 79°02′W.

South Daytona (dai-TO-nuh), town (□ 4 sq mi/10.4 sq km; 1990 pop. 12,482), Volusia co., E central Fla., 5 mi/8 km SE of Daytona Beach; 29°09′N 81°00′W.

South Deerfield, Mass.: see DEERFIELD.

South Dennis, Mass.: see DENNIS.

South Dos Palos, town (1990 pop. 1,214), Merced co., central Calif., in San Joaquin Valley, 2 mi/3.2 km SSW of Dos Palos; 36°58′N 120°39′W. Dairying; poultry; grain, alfalfa, fruit, almonds, tomatoes, sweet potatoes.

South Durham, Fr. *Durham-Sud*, village, S Que., E Canada, 11 mi/18 km W of Richmond; 45°40′N 72°20′W. Dairying; cattle, pigs.

South Duxbury, Mass.: see DUXBURY.

South East Point, cape at E extremity of Jamaica, on Jamaica Channel, just S of Morant Point, and 40 mi/64 km E of Kingston; 17°54′N 76°12′W.

South Edisto River, S.C.: see EDISTO RIVER.

South Eel River, Calif.: see EEL RIVER.

South Egremont, Mass.: see EGREMONT.

South El Monte, city (1990 pop. 20,850), Los Angeles co., S Calif., suburb, 12 mi/19 km E of downtown Los Angeles, in the San Gabriel Valley; 34°03′N 118°03′W. Mfg. (transportation equip., tool and die, electrical prods., clothing, textiles, labels, machinery, furniture, plastic prods.; poultry processing, printing and publishing). San Gabriel R. to E. Inc. 1958.

South Elgin (EL-jin), village (1990 pop. 7,474), Kane co., NE Ill., on Fox R. (bridged here), just S of Elgin; 42°00′N 88°17′W.

South Eliot, Maine: see ELIOT.

South English, town (1990 pop. 224), Keokuk co., SE Iowa, near South Fork English R., 10 mi/16 km NE of Sigourney; 41°27′N 92°05′W. Livestock; grain.

South Essex, Mass.: see ESSEX.

South Euclid (YOO-klid), city (1990 pop. 23,866), Cuyahoga co., NE Ohio, a suburb of Cleveland; 41°31′N 81°31′W. It is mostly residential and is the site of Notre Dame Col., a R.C. school for women. Inc. as a city 1940.

South Fabius River, Mo.: see FABIUS RIVER.

South Fallsburg, resort village (□ 6 sq mi/15.5 sq km; 1990 pop. 2,115), Sullivan co., SE N.Y., 5 mi/8 km NE of Monticello; 41°43′N 74°37′W.

South Farmingdale, uninc. town (□ 2 sq mi/5.2 sq km; 1990 pop. 15,377), Nassau co., SE N.Y., on L.I.; 40°43′N 73°27′W. It is chiefly residential.

South Floral Park, residential village (1990 pop. 1,478), Nassau co., SE N.Y., on W L.I., just S of Floral Park; 40°42′N 73°42′W. Until 1931 called Jamaica Square.

South Fork, village (1990 pop. 390), Rio Grande co., S Colo., 43 mi/69 km WNW of Alamosa, on Rio Grande, at mouth of South Fork R. Elev. 8,180 ft/2,493 m. Surrounded by Rio Grande Natl. Forest except on E. Timber; mfg. of wood prods.

South Fork, borough (1990 pop. 1,197), Cambria co., SW central Pa., 7 mi/11.3 km ENE of Johnstown, on Little Conemaugh R.; 40°21′N 78°47′W. Agr. (hay; dairying); mfg. (clothing, ribbons). Break in South Fork Dam, 1 mi/1.6 km to S (Johnstown Flood Natl. Memorial), 1889, caused Johnstown Flood, killing 2,200 people. Part of Allegheny Portage Natl. Historic Site to W.

South Fork or **South Fork Malheur River**, c.45 mi/72 km long, SE Oregon; rises in NE Harney co.; flows in a circuitous course S then NE, joining Malheur R. 3 mi/4.8 km SE of Warm Springs Dam.

South Fork Cumberland River, 77 mi/124 km long, N Tenn. and S Ky.; formed in Scott co., Tenn., by confluence of several headstreams; flows N into McCreary co., Ky., to Cumberland R. at Burnside. Sometimes known as Big South Fork.

South Fork Musselshell River, S central Mont.; rises in Castle (and Crazy) Mts., SE Meagher co.; flows NE, joining North Fork to form main stream, near Martinsdale.

South Fork Owyhee River, c.140 mi/225 km long, in Nev., Idaho, and Oregon; rises in W central Elko co., N Nev.; flows generally NW, through Owyhee Desert and into Owyhee co., SW corner of Idaho. Receives Little Owyhee R. from S before joining East Fork; c.100 mi/161 km long.

South Fork Republican River, 151 mi/243 km long, Colo., Kansas, and Nebr.; rises in central Lincoln co. (E Colo.); flows ENE through Bonny Reservoir (1948), into NW Kansas, past St. Francis (NW Kansas) to Republican R. at Benkelman (S Nebr.), just N of Kansas state line.

South Fort Smith, village, Sebastian co., W Ark., suburb, 5 mi/8 km S of Fort Smith, part of city of Fort Smith.

South Fox Island, Mich.: see FOX ISLANDS.

South Fulton (FUL-tuhn), city (1990 pop. 2,688), Obion co., NW Tenn., on Ky. state line adjacent to Fulton (Ky.),11 mi/18 km NE of Union City, 36°30′N 88°52′W. Dairying.

South Gardiner, Maine: see GARDINER.

South Gastonia (gas-TON-yuh), uninc. town (1990 pop. 5,487), Gaston co., S N.C., residential suburb, 3 mi/4.8 km S of Gastonia; 35°12′N 81°12′W.

South Gate, city (1990 pop. 86,284), Los Angeles co., S

Calif., an industrial suburb, 7 mi/11.3 km SSE of downtown Los Angeles; 33°57′N 118°11′W. Bounded E by Los Angeles R. It has diverse manufactures that have developed along with the expanding S Calif. area (fabricated metal prods., consumer goods, electrical prods., machinery, foods, chemicals, paper prods., cutting tools, rubber goods, furniture; publishing and printing; iron foundry). Pop. increased by nearly 50% bet. 1970 and 1990. Inc. 1923.

South Gifford, town (1990 pop. 64), Macon co., N central Mo., on Chariton R., and 22 mi/35 km NW of Macon; 40°01′N 92°40′W.

South Glens Falls, village (□ 1 sq mi/2.6 sq km; 1990 pop. 3,506), Saratoga co., E N.Y., on the Hudson R. (bridged), opposite Glens Falls; 43°17′N 73°38′W. Some mfg. Inc. 1895.

South Gorin (GO-rin), town (1990 pop. 130), Scotland co., NE Mo., near North Fabius R., 10 mi/16 km SE of Memphis; 40°21′N 92°01′W. The town's post office is officially Gorin. The U.S. Census Bureau recognizes the town as South Gorin.

South Grand River, c.125 mi/201 km long, W Mo.; rises 30 mi/48 km S of Kansas City; flows SE to a W arm of Truman L. (Osage R.) in Benton co. South Grand is used to distinguish the river from the larger Grand R. in N Missouri.

South Greenfield, town (1990 pop. 112), Dade co., SW Mo., near Stockton L., just S of Greenfield; 37°22′N 93°50′W. Wheat, corn, hay; dairying; cattle.

South Greensburg, borough (1990 pop. 2,293), Westmoreland co., SW central Pa., residential suburb, 2 mi/3.2 km S of Greensburg, on Sewickley Creek; 40°16′N 79°32′W. Inc. 1891.

South Greenwood, uninc. village, Greenwood co., W S.C., a suburb, 2 mi/3.2 km S of Greenwood; part of the town of Greenwood.

South Hadley, residential town (1990 pop. 16,685), Hampshire co., W Mass., on the Connecticut R., near the Holyoke Range, 3 mi/4.8 km SE of Northhampton; 42°16′N 72°35′W. Its paper industry dates from the early 19th cent. Electronic equip., machinery, fabricated metal prods., and concrete prods. are also made, although the area has suffered from a decline in mfg. The 1st navigable canal in the U.S. began operation here in 1795. Seat of Mount Holyoke Col. Settled 1684, inc. 1775.

South Hampton, town (1990 pop. 740), Rockingham co., SE N.H., on Mass. (S) state line, 16 mi/26 km SW of Portsmouth; 42°53′N 70°58′W. Nursery crops; poultry, cattle; dairying. Mfg. (software). Powwow R. State Forest on center.

South Harriman, village, Roane co., E Tenn.

South Harwich, Mass.: see HARWICH.

South Haven, town (1990 pop. 5,563), Van Buren co., SW Mich., 21 mi/34 km WNW of Benton Harbor, on L. Michigan, at mouth of Black R.; 42°23′N 86°16′W. Has sand beach. Port of entry; supply center for resort and fruit-growing area (fruits and vegetables; poultry; dairying). Mfg. (food, paper, and rubber prods., plastic prods., glass prods., pulleys and belts, dairy prods., electrical prods., chemicals); fisheries. Mich. State Univ. maintains a horticultural experiment station here. Airport to SE. Palisades Nuclear Power Plant to S on L. Mich. Van Buren State Park, on L. Mich., to S; L. Michigan Maritime Mus. Settled before 1840; inc. as village 1869, as city 1902.

South Haven 1 village (1990 pop. 420), Sumner co., S Kansas, on small affluent of Chikaskia R., and 14 mi/23 km S of Wellington; 37°02′N 97°24′W. Wheat. **2** village (1990 pop. 193), Wright co., S central Minn., 19 mi/31 km W of St. Cloud; 45°17′N 94°13′W. Corn, oats; livestock; poultry; dairying. Clearwater L. to E.

South Head, promontory, W N.F., E Canada, on S side of entrance of the Bay of Islands, 25 mi/40 km NW of Corner Brook; 49°09′N 58°23′W. Lighthouse.

South Heights, borough (1990 pop. 647), Beaver co., W Pa., 3 mi/4.8 km SSE of Aliquippa, on Ohio R. opposite (W of) Ambridge; 40°34′N 80°14′W. Power plant. Pittsburgh Internatl. Airport 4 mi/6.4 km to S.

South Henderson, uninc. town (1990 pop. 1,374), Vance

co., N N.C., residential suburb, 1 mi/1.6 km S of Henderson; 36°17′N 78°24′W.

South Hero, town (1990 pop. 1,404), Grand Isle co., NW Vt., on S end of Grand Isle, in L. Champlain (bridge to mainland), and 15 mi/24 km S of North Hero; 44°37′N 73°18′W. Orchards; summer recreation.

South Hill, town (1990 pop. 4,217), Mecklenburg co., S Va., 55 mi/89 km SW of Petersburg, near Meherrin R.; 36°43′N 78°07′W. Mfg. (bldg. materials, concrete, wire harnesses, chemicals, transportation equip., textiles; printing and publishing); agr. (tobacco, peanuts, cotton, grain; livestock, poultry; dairying. Inc. 1901.

South Hingham, Mass.: see HINGHAM.

South Holland, village (1990 pop. 22,105), Cook co., NE Ill., a S suburb of Chicago; 41°36′N 87°35′W. South Suburban Col. of Cook Co. here. Settled 1846 by Dutch, inc. 1894.

South Hooksett (HUK-suht), village (1990 pop. 3,638), Merrimack co., S central N.H., in town of Hooksett, residential suburb, 3 mi/4.8 km NNE of downtown Manchester, and 4 mi/6.4 km S of Hooksett village, near Merrimack R.; 43°01′N 71°25′W.

South Houston, city (1990 pop. 14,207), Harris co., SE Texas, an industrial suburb, 9 mi/14.5 km SE of downtown Houston; 29°39′N 95°13′W. Mfg. (transportation equip., machinery, asphalts). William P. Hobby Field airport to W. Inc. 1911.

South Huntington, village (□ 3 sq mi/7.8 sq km; 1990 pop. 9,624), Suffolk co., SE N.Y.; 40°49′N 73°23′W. Katherine Gibbs School is in nearby Melville, 1 mi/1.6 km W of village.

South Hutchinson, town (1990 pop. 2,444), Reno co., S central Kansas, on right bank of Arkansas R., suburb, 2 mi/3.2 km S of Hutchinson; 38°01′N 97°56′W. Mfg. (meat prods.).

South International Falls, S suburb of International Falls, Koochiching co., N Minn., now part of International Falls; 48°35′N 93°23′W.

South Island, S.C.: see WINYAH BAY.

South Jacksonville, village (1990 pop. 3,187), Morgan co., W central Ill., adjacent to Jacksonville; 39°42′N 90°13′W.

South Jamesport, village (1990 pop. 600), Suffolk co., SE N.Y., on NE peninsula of L.I., on Great Peconic Bay, 4 mi/6.4 km E of Riverhead; 40°56′N 72°35′W. In summer-resort area.

South Jordan, city (1990 pop. 12,220), Salt Lake co., N central Utah, suburb, 12 mi/19 km S of downtown Salt Lake City, on Jordan R.; 40°33′N 111°58′W. Elev. 4,450 ft/1,356 m. Mfg. dental instruments. Large Kennecott Bingham open-cut copper mine to W. Settled 1857, inc. 1935.

South Kent, Conn.: see KENT.

South Kingstown, town (1990 pop. 24,631), ☉ Washington co., S R.I.; 41°25′N 71°33′W. Includes the villages of Kingston and Wakefield, birthplace (now a mus.) of Oliver Hazard Perry. Mfg. of computer power systems. Seat of the Univ. of R.I. The Narragansetts were attacked and dispersed at nearby Great Swamp in 1675 during King Philip's War. Settled 1641, inc. 1674 as Kings Towne, divided into South and North Kingstown 1723.

South Lake, uninc. town (1990 pop. 1,059), Kern co., S central Calif., 6 mi/9.7 km E of Lake Isabella; 35°38′N 118°22′W. Timber; cattle; hay. L. Isabella reservoir to NW. Area is surrounded by Sequoia Natl. Forest.

South Lake Tahoe, city (1990 pop. 21,586), El Dorado co., E Calif., 83 mi/134 km ENE of Sacramento, and 40 mi/64 km SSW of Reno (Nev.), at S end of L. Tahoe, on Nev. state line, opposite Stateline (Nev.) to E; 38°57′N 119°59′W. Desolation Wilderness Area to W. Emerald Bay State Park to W. Heavenly Valley Ski Area to SE. Lake Tahoe Airport to SW. Seat of Lake Tahoe Community Col.

South Lancaster, Mass.: see LANCASTER.

South Langhorne, Pa.: see PENNDEL.

South Lebanon, uninc. town (1990 pop. 1,764), Lebanon co., residential suburb, 2 mi/3.2 km S of Lebanon; 40°19′N 76°24′W.

South Lebanon (LE-buh-nuhn), village (1990 pop.

Cross references are shown in SMALL CAPITALS. The pronunciation key is on page xv. The dates of population figures are on page xii.

2,696), Warren co., SW Ohio, 24 mi/39 km NE of Cincinnati, and on Little Miami R.; 39°22′N 84°13′W. Chemicals.

South Lee, Mass.: see LEE.

South Lineville, town (1990 pop. 40), Mercer co., N Mo., near Weldon R., 13 mi/21 km NNE of Princeton, on Iowa state line across from Lineville (Iowa); 40°34′N 93°31′W.

South Loup River, Nebr.: see LOUP RIVER.

South Lyon (LEI-yuhn), city (1990 pop. 5,875), Oakland co., SE Mich., 13 mi/21 km NNE of Ann Arbor, satellite community, 35 mi/56 km WNW of downtown Detroit; 42°27′N 83°39′W. In farm area; mfg. of steel tubing. Island L. State Recreation Area to NW; several small lakes to W. Inc. as village 1873, as city 1930.

South Manchester, Conn.: see MANCHESTER.

South Manistique Lake, Mich.: see MANISTIQUE LAKE.

South Manitou Island, Mich.: see MANITOU ISLANDS.

South Mansfield, village (1994 pop. 540), De Soto parish, NW La., suburb, 1 mi/2 km S of Mansfield; 32°01′N 93°43′W. In agr., oil, and timber area.

South Marsh Island, low, marshy island, Somerset co., SE Md., in Chesapeake Bay, 12 mi/19 km NW of Crisfield, across Tangier Sound; c.5 mi/8 km long, 3 mi/ 4.8 km wide. South Marsh Isl. Wildlife Management Area is here.

South Miami, town (□ 2 sq mi/5.2 sq km; 1990 pop. 10,404), Dade co., SE Fla., a suburb, 6 mi/9.7 km SW of Miami; 25°42′N 80°17′W. Commercial and retail development in center of South Miami, which serves neighboring Coral Gables. Settled 1899, inc. 1926.

South Mills, uninc. village, Camden co., NE N.C., 11 mi/ 18 km NNW of Elizabeth City, on Dismal Swamp Canal. Area surrounded by Great Dismal Swamp. Grain, cotton, peanuts; cattle.

South Milwaukee, city (1990 pop. 20,958), Milwaukee co., SE Wis., a suburb, 7 mi/11.3 km S of downtown Milwaukee, on L. Michigan; 42°54′N 87°51′W. Draglines, machinery, consumer goods, electrical equip., and leather prods. are among the city's manufactures. An annual music festival is held here. Settled 1835, inc. 1897.

South Monroe, town (1990 pop. 5,266), Monroe co., SE Mich., suburb, 1 mi/1.6 km SW of Monroe; 41°53′N 83°25′W.

South Montrose (MAHN-tros), uninc. village, Susquehanna co., NE Pa., suburb, 1 mi/1.6 km SSW of Montrose; 41°47′N 75°53′W. Light mfg.

South Moresby National Park Reserve (□ 233 sq mi/ 603 sq km), W B.C., W Canada, on S ½ of Moresby Isl. and adjacent Queen Charlotte Isls., bet. Hecate Strait on E and Pacific Ocean on W. Other isls. include Kunghit, Burnaby, Lyell, Tanu. Preserves the most remote of what are referred to as "Canada's Galapagos," for its unique flora, fauna. Moss-draped rain forests; tufted puffin, auklet, petrel. Primitive camping, hiking. No facilities.

South Mount Vernon, village, Knox co., central Ohio.

South Mountain, ridge, in S Pa. and NW Md., northernmost sect. of the BLUE RIDGE; begins in S Cumberland co., SE of Carlisle (Pa.), extends c.65 mi/105 km SW, across Md., and into N Va., follows W.Va. state line (here called Short Hills) and joins with Blue Ridge; 39°56′N 77°25′W–40°02′N 77°21′W. The Potomac R. flows through gap in ridge E of Harpers Ferry (W.Va.). Lowest (c.1,000 ft/305 m) in S; rises to 2,145 ft/654 m at Quirauk Mt. (Md.), just S of Md.-Pa. state line. In Md., South Mt. splits into 2 arms embracing Middletown Valley; E arm is Catoctin Mt. Has deposits of quartz, manganese-iron ore, sandstone, dolomite, clay. Civil War battle of South Mt., fought near Burkittsville (Md.), Sept. 14, 1862, was a victory for McClellan over Lee's rear guard of Confederates.

South Nahanni River, c.250 mi/402 km long, SW Mackenzie dist., N.W.T., N Canada; rises in mts. on Yukon prov. border; flows SE to Liard R.; Virginia Falls (316 ft/ 96 m) are on it.

South Naknek (NAK-nek), village (1990 pop. 136), S Alaska, on Alaska Peninsula, on Naknek R., near its mouth on Bristol Bay, opposite Naknek; 58°41′N 156°58′W. Fishing, fish processing.

South Natick, Mass.: see NATICK.

South Negril Point, westernmost cape of Jamaica, Westmoreland parish, 33 mi/53 km WSW of Montego Bay; 18°16′N 78°23′W. The town Negril is just N. North Negril Point is 6 mi/9.7 km N. Subdivided areas for thriving internatl. tourism. Lighthouse.

South Nelson, village, NE N.B., E Canada, on Miramichi R., opposite Newcastle; 46°59′N 65°33′W. Lumbershipping port.

South New Castle, borough (1990 pop. 805), Lawrence co., W Pa., residential suburb, 2 mi/3.2 km S of New Castle, on Shenango R.; 40°58′N 80°20′W.

South Norfolk, former independent city, SE Va., 2 mi/ 3.2 km S of Norfolk, on South Branch Elizabeth R. City merged with Norfolk co. in 1963 to form independent city of Chesapeake. Inc. 1921–1963.

South Nyack (NEI-yak), residential suburban village (□ 1 sq mi/2.6 sq km; 1990 pop. 3,352), Rockland co., SE N.Y., on W bank of the Hudson R., just S of Nyack; 41°04′N 73°55′W. A state park is nearby. Inc. 1878.

South Ogden (AWG-duhn), city (1990 pop. 12,105), Weber co., N Utah, residential suburb, 4 mi/6.4 km S of downtown Ogden, and 26 mi/42 km N of Salt Lake City; 41°10′N 111°57′W. Elev. 4,600 ft/1,402 m. Drained by Burch Creek. Weber State Univ. to E, in Ogden. Wasatch Range and Natl. Forest to E. Settled 1848 by Mormons. Inc. 1936.

South Orange, village (1990 pop. 16,390), Essex co., NE N.J., 3 mi/4.8 km W of Newark; 40°45′N 74°15′W. Mostly residential; light industry. Seat of Seton Hall Univ. Inc. 1869.

South Orleans, Mass.: see ORLEANS.

South Oromocto Lake (oh-ro-MOHK-to) (□ 4 sq mi/ 10 sq km; 4 mi/6 km long), SW N.B., E Canada, 28 mi/ 45 km WNW of St. John.

South Oroville, uninc. town (1990 pop. 7,463), Butte co., N central Calif., residential suburb, 1 mi/1.6 km S of Oroville; 39°29′N 121°32′W. Fruit, nuts, olives; dairying; cattle.

South Padre Island, town (1990 pop. 1,677), Cameron co., extreme S Texas, 24 mi/39 km NE of Brownsville, at S end of Padre Isl., sand barrier on W coast of Gulf of Mexico; 26°06′N 97°10′W. Mfg. (candy). Resort area with high-rise hotels. Large Laguna Madre, separating isl. from mainland, is to W. Padre Isl. Natl. Seashore to N, no road access from S.

South Palm Beach, town (1990 pop. 1,480), Palm Beach co., SE Fla., 8 mi/12.9 km S of Palm Beach, on the Atlantic Ocean; 26°35′N 80°01′W.

South Paris, town (1990 pop. 2,320), ⊙ Oxford co., W Maine, on the Little Androscoggin R., and 17 mi/27 km NW of Auburn; 44°13′N 70°30′W. Mfg. (wood prods.). Township of Paris (1990 pop. 4,492) includes West Paris and Paris Hill (Hannibal Hamlin b. here). Settled 1779, inc. 1793.

South Park 1 uninc. village (1990 pop.), Sonoma co., W Calif., 2 mi/3.2 km SE of Santa Rosa. **2** village, Kane co., NE Ill., just S of Aurora., now part of Aurora and Montgomery; 41°44′N 88°18′W. **3** village, St. Clair co., E Mich., just S of Port Huron; 42°56′N 82°27′W.

South Park, township (1990 pop. 14,292), Allegheny co., W Pa., residential suburb, 10 mi/16 km S of Pittsburgh, and 3 mi/4.8 km E of Bethel Park; 40°17′N 79°59′W. U.S. Bureau of Mines Experimental Mine is here.

South Pasadena, city (1990 pop. 23,936), Los Angeles co., S Calif., a suburb, 7 mi/11.3 km NE of downtown Los Angeles, and 2 mi/3.2 km S of Pasadena; 34°07′N 118°10′W. Chiefly residential. Mfg. (medical supplies, clothing, transportation equip., electronic equip.). Inc. 1888.

South Pasadena (pa-suh-DEE-nuh), town (□ 1 sq mi/ 2.6 sq km; 1990 pop. 5,644), Pinellas co., W central Fla., 7 mi/11.3 km W of St. Petersburg; 27°45′N 82°44′W.

South Pass, broad, level valley (elev. c.7,550 ft/2,301 m), SW Wyo., cutting across the Rocky Mts. An important part on the Oregon Trail, it served for many years as a gateway for immigration to the Far West. South Pass has been designated a natl. historic landmark. Continental Divide passes to W.

South Pass, La.: see MISSISSIPPI RIVER.

South Pass City, village, Fremont co., W central Wyo., on Willow Creek, in foothills of Wind R. Range, 26 mi/ 42 km S of Lander. Elev. 7,805 ft/2,379 m. Gold dredging. Town built 1867 after discovery of gold; town is now a state historic site. South Pass City Historic Site is here. South Pass, a natl. historic landmark, once a major feature on Oregon Trail, is to SW. Shoshone Natl. Forest to N.

South Patrick, town (□ 3 sq mi/7.8 sq km; 1990 pop. 10,249), Brevard co., E central Fla., just S of Patrick Air Force Base, 10 mi/16 km S of Cape Canaveral, on the Atlantic Ocean; 28°11′N 80°36′W.

South Pekin (PEE-kin), village (1990 pop. 1,184), Tazewell co., central Ill., 4 mi/6.4 km S of Pekin; 40°30′N 89°39′W. Agr. (corn, soybeans; cattle, hogs; dairying). Inc. 1917.

South Philipsburg (FI-lips-buhrg), borough (1990 pop. 438), Centre co., central Pa., residential suburb, 1 mi/ 1.6 km SSE of Philipsburg, on Moshannon Creek; 40°53′N 78°13′W.

South Pittsburg, city (1990 pop. 3,295), Marion co., S Tenn., on the Tennessee R., and 22 mi/35 km W of Chattanooga; 35°01′N 85°42′W. In timber, coal-mining, agr. area; mfg. of hosiery, cooking utensils, wood prods., textiles.

South Plainfield, borough (1990 pop. 20,489), Middlesex co., NE N.J.; 40°34′N 74°25′W. Seat of several research and consulting firms; mfg. includes chemicals, plastics, spices and flavorings, cosmetics, rubber prods., pigments, electrical machinery, and structural steel. Inc. 1926.

South Plains, Texas: see LLANO ESTACADO.

South Platte (PLAT), river, c.450 mi/724 km long, Colo.; rises in the Rocky Mts. in many branches, main branch rising NW Park co., at Continental Divide, near mounts Democrat and Lincoln; flows SE through Pinney Mt. and Eleven Mile Canyon reservoir, then NNE through Chesman and Chatfield reservoirs, through of Denver to Greeley, then E and NE past Fort Morgan, Sterling and Julesburg, into Nebr., past Ogallala, joining North Platte R at town of North Platte, forming Platte R. Lower 80 mi/129 km nearly parallels North Platte. Grazing and irrigated agr. are important. The river basin has many private irrigation dams. The upper course of the South Platte is part of the Bureau of Reclamation's Colorado–Big Thompson project.

South Pleasureville, Ky.: see PLEASUREVILLE.

South Point, village (1990 pop. 3,823), Lawrence co., S Ohio, on Ohio R., opposite Catlettsburg (Ky.), and 9 mi/14 km SE of Ironton; 38°25′N 82°34′W. Makes chemicals.

South Pomfret, Vt.: see POMFRET.

South Porcupine, town, NE Ont., central Canada, on Porcupine L., 7 mi/11 km E of Timmins; 48°28′N 81°12′W. Gold- and barite-mining center.

South Portland, city (1990 pop. 23,163), Cumberland co., SW Maine, on the Fore R., and Casco Bay, part of the Portland metropolitan area; 43°37′N 70°17′W. Ships have been built here since the 17th cent. The city also produces varied light manufactures and is a wholesale and retail trade center. Fort Preble was built here before the War of 1812. Seat of the Univ. of Southern Maine. The area was settled by Europeans c.1633; inc. 1898.

South Portsmouth, village (1990 pop. 600), Greenup co., NE Ky., the Ohio R. (bridged) opposite Portsmouth (Ohio). In agr. area. On site of Lower Town, 1st colonial settlement in Ky.; established by Fr. traders with help of Native Shawnees in early 18th cent. and abandoned during Fr. and Indian Wars.

South Pottstown (PAHTS-toun), uninc. town (1990 pop. 1,966), North Coventry township, Chester co., SE Pa., residential suburb, 1 mi/1.6 km S of Pottstown, on Schuylkill R., opposite Pottstown; 40°14′N 75°39′W. French Creek State Park to W; Hopewell Furnace Natl. Historic Site to SW.

South Prairie, village (1990 pop. 180), Pierce co., W central Wash., 18 mi/29 km SE of Tacoma, and 3 mi/4.8 km

WSW of Buckley; 47°08′N 122°05′W. RR junction. In agr. region; berries, flowers; dairying; poultry; mfg. (cabinets).

South Raccoon River, Iowa: see RACCOON RIVER.

South Range, village (1990 pop. 745), Houghton co., NW Upper Peninsula, N Mich., 6 mi/9.7 km SW of Houghton, on Keweenaw Peninsula; 47°04′N 88°38′W. Mfg. (sawmill; wood prods.).

South Rangeley, Maine: see RANGELEY.

South Renovo (RE-no-vo), borough (1990 pop. 579), Clinton co., N central Pa., ½ mi/⅘ km S of Renovo, on West Branch of Susquehanna R.; 41°19′N 77°44′W. Sproul State Forest surrounds area.

South River, village (1991 pop. 1,141), S Ont., central Canada, on South R., and 33 mi/53 km S of North Bay; 45°51′N 79°22′W. Lumbering.

South River, borough (1990 pop. 13,692), Middlesex co., E N.J.; 40°27′N 74°22′W. Mfg includes clothing, furniture, and handkerchiefs. Settled 1720, inc. 1898.

South River 1 c.50 mi/80 km long, N central Ga.; rises near Atlanta; flows SE to Jackson L., 8 mi/12.9 km NE of Jackson; 33°40′N 84°26′W. **2** 53 mi/85 km long, S central Iowa; rises in NW Clarke co.; flows NE to Des Moines R. 16 mi/26 km SE of Des Moines. Flooded in 1993. **3** c.10 mi/16 km long, E central N.J.; rises in S Middlesex co.; flows NE and N, past Old Bridge and South R., to Raritan R. above Sayreville. **4** c.75 mi/121 km long, SE N.C.; rises in NE Harnett co., near Angier; flows generally SSE to Black R. 30 mi/48 km NW of Wilmington. **5** c.50 mi/80 km long, NW Va.; rises in S Augusta co.; flows NE, past Stuarts Draft and Waynesboro, joins North R. near Port Republic to form South Fork of Shenandoah R.; 37°56′N 79°10′W.

South River Peak (13,149 ft/4,008 m), Mineral co., SW Colo., in San Juan Mts., 19 mi/31 km SSW of Creede, on Continental Divide; 37°34′N 106°58′W.

South Rockwood, village (1990 pop. 1,221), Monroe co., SE Mich., 12 mi/19 km NNE of Monroe, suburb, 21 mi/34 km SW of downtown Detroit, and on Huron R., near L. Erie; 42°03′N 83°15′W. Mfg. (consumer goods).

South Rosemary, uninc. town (1990 pop. 1,965), Halifax co., N N.C., residential suburb, 2 mi/3.2 km W of Roanoke Rapids; 36°27′N 77°42′W. Roanoke Rapids L. reservoir (Roanoke R.) to N.

South Roxana, town (1990 pop. 1,961), Madison co., SW Ill., suburb, 14 mi/23 km NE of downtown St. Louis (Mo.), 1 mi/1.6 km S of Roxana; 38°49′N 90°03′W. Residential community in oil-refining area. Mfg. of air compressors.

South Roxton, village, S Que., E Canada, 10 mi/16 km NE of Granby; 45°29′N 72°36′W. Woodworking; dairying.

South Royalton, Vt.: see ROYALTON.

South Russell, village (1990 pop. 3,402), Geauga co., NE Ohio, 19 mi/31 km ESE of downtown Cleveland; 41°26′N 81°20′W.

South Ryegate, Vt.: see RYEGATE.

South Saint Paul, city (1990 pop. 20,197), Dakota co., SE Minn., a suburb, 5 mi/8 km SSEof downtown St. Paul, on the Mississippi R. (bridged); 44°53′N 93°02′W. It is known for its large stockyards and meatpacking industries. Its 75-acre/30-ha public livestock market on the banks of the Mississippi is one of the nation's largest. Mfg. (parachute saftey systems, awards, fabricated metal prods., hydrants and valves; pork processing, cowhide processing). Settled in 1853 on the site of a Native Amer. village. Its first stockyard opened in 1887. South St. Paul Municipal Airport in S. Inc. 1887.

South Salem (SAI-luhm), village (1990 pop. 227), Ross co., S Ohio, 17 mi/27 km W of Chillicothe; 39°20′N 83°18′W.

South Salt Lake, city (1990 pop. 10,129), Salt Lake co., N Utah; residential suburb, 4 mi/6.4 km S of downtown Salt Lake City, on Jordan R., at mouth of Mill Creek; 40°42′N 111°54′W. Inc. 1938.

South San Diego, suburban section of San Diego, San Diego co., S Calif., residential area 12 mi/19 km S of downtown San Diego, S extension of city bet. S end of San Diego Bay and Mex. (Baja California Norte) border. San Ysidro sect. of city to SE.

South San Francisco, city (1990 pop. 54,312), San Mateo co., W Calif., suburb, 8 mi/12.9 km S of downtown San Francisco, on San Francisco Bay, at mouth of Colma Creek; Pacific Ocean 5 mi/8 km to W; 37°40′N 122°19′W. Inc. 1908. Mfg. (medical supplies and equip., foods, paints, paper goods, consumer goods, clothing, cable prods.; textile finishing, printing and publishing). The city's founding and growth were spurred in the late 19th cent. by the cattle-ranching and meatpacking industries. San Francisco Internatl. Airport to SE on bay shore. Unit of Golden Gate Natl. Recreation Area to SW; Montana Mt. to SW; Tanforan Racetrack to S; San Bruno Mts. to N; Point San Bruno to E.

South San Gabriel, uninc. town (1990 pop. 7,700), Los Angeles co., S Calif., residential suburb, 8 mi/12.9 km E of downtown Los Angeles, and 2 mi/3.2 km S of San Gabriel; 34°03′N 118°06′W. Whittier Narrows Flood Control Basin to SE.

South San Jose Hills, uninc. city (1990 pop. 17,814), Los Angeles co., S Calif., residential suburb, 18 mi/29 km E of downtown Los Angeles, and 3 mi/4.8 km SSE of West Covina, in S end of San Jose Hills; 34°01′N 117°54′W.

South Sandia Peak, N.Mex.: see SANDIA MOUNTAINS.

South Sandisfield, Mass.: see SANDISFIELD.

South Santa Cruz, uninc. town (1990 pop. 4,128), Sonoma co., W Calif., residential suburb, 4 mi/6.4 km SSW of Santa Cruz. Dairying; cattle, poultry; grain, fruit, grapes. Santa Cruz Airport to NW.

South Saskatchewan, Sask.: see SASKATCHEWAN.

South Shore 1 town (1990 pop. 1,318), Greenup co., NE Ky., on Ohio R., opposite and 1 mi/1.6 km S of Portsmouth (Ohio), at mouth of Tygarts Creek; 38°43′N 82°57′W. Tobacco, alfalfa, soybeans, corn; cattle. Mfg. (bldg. materials, medical supplies; natural gas processing). Bennett's Mill Covered Bridge to S on Tygarts Creek. **2** town (1990 pop. 260), Codington co., E S.Dak., 16 mi/26 km NE of Watertown; 45°06′N 96°55′W. In agr. area.

South Sioux City (SOO), city (1990 pop. 9,677), Dakota co., NE Nebr., on W bank of the Missouri R., suburb, 1 mi/1.6 km S of Sioux City (Iowa); 42°28′N 96°24′W. In rich agr. region; dairy prods., vegetables, grain. Mfg. (iron foundry; printing, oat processing; consumer goods, chemicals, feeds, fabricated metal prods., foods, lumber, bldg. materials, transportation equip., signs and advertising specialties). Founded 1887.

South Solon (SO-luhn), village (1990 pop. 379), Madison co., central Ohio, 13 mi/21 km SW of London; 39°44′N 83°37′W. In livestock-raising and farming area.

South Streator (STREE-tuhr), uninc. village, Livingston co., E central Ill., just S of Streator; 41°07′N 88°49′W. In agr. area.

South Sudbury, Mass.: see SUDBURY.

South Sumter, uninc. town (1990 pop. 4,371), Sumter co., central S.C., residential suburb, 4 mi/6.4 km SSE of downtown Sumter, near Pocotaligo R.; 33°53′N 80°20′W.

South Superior, village, S of Superior, Sweetwater co., SW Wyo. Elev. c.6,900 ft/2,103 m. Coal mines.

South Swansea, Mass.: see SWANSEA.

South Taft, uninc. town (1990 pop. 2,170), Kern co., S central Calif., residential suburb, 1 mi/1.6 km S of Taft, 29 mi/47 km WSW of Bakersfield; 35°08′N 119°27′W. Irrigated agr. area.

South Tamworth, N.H.: see TAMWORTH.

South Temple, uninc. town (1990 pop. 1,400), Berks co., SE central Pa., residential suburb, 4 mi/6.4 km N of Reading; 40°23′N 75°55′W.

South Tent, peak (11,300 ft/3,444 m) in Wasatch Plateau, E Sanpete co., central Utah, 17 mi/27 km NE of Manti, in Manti–La Sal Natl. Forest; 39°23′N 111°21′W.

South Texas 1 and 2 Nuclear Power Plants, Texas: see MATAGORDA.

South, the, region of the U.S. embracing the SE and S central parts of the country. Traditionally, all states S of the MASON-DIXON LINE and the Ohio R. (except W.Va.) make up the South—Del., Md., Va., N.C., S.C., Ga., Fla., Ky., Tenn., Ala., Miss., Ark., La., Okla., and Texas. The contemporary South, however, is generally regarded to be those states mentioned above, exclusive of Md., Va., Texas, and Okl. The South has long been a region apart, even though it is not isolated by any formidable natural barriers and is itself subdivided into many distinctive areas: the coastal plains along the Atlantic Ocean and the Gulf of Mexico; the Piedmont; the ridges, valleys, and high mts. bordering the Piedmont, esp. the Great Smoky Mts. in N.C. and Tenn.; areas of bluegrass, black-soil prairies, and clay hills W of the mts.; bluffs, flood plains, bayous, and delta lands along the Mississippi R.; and W of the Mississippi, the interior plains and the Ozark Plateau. The humid subtropical climate, however, is 1 unifying factor. Winters are neither long nor very cold, and no month averages below freezing. The long, hot growing season (9 months at its peak along the Gulf) and the fertile soil (much of it overworked or ruined by erosion) have traditionally made the South an agr. region where such staples as tobacco, rice, and sugarcane have long flourished; citrus fruits, livestock, soybeans, and timber have gained in importance. Cotton, once the region's dominant crop, is now mostly grown in Texas, the Southwest, and Calif. In the post-World War II period, the South became increasingly industrialized. High-technology (such as aerospace and petrochemical) industries have boomed, and there has been impressive growth in the service, trade, and finance sectors. There has also been growth in motor vehicle mfg. in the mid-South (Ky. and Tenn.) and S.C. The chief cities of the South are Atlanta (Ga.), New Orleans, Charlotte (N.C.), Miami, Memphis (Tenn.), and Jacksonville (Fla.). The basic agr. economy of the Old South, which was abetted by the climate and the soil, led to the introduction (1617) of Africans as a source of cheap labor under the twin institutions of the plantation and slavery. Slavery might well have expired had not the invention of the cotton gin (1793) given it a firmer hold, but even so there would have remained the problem of racial tension. Issues of race have been central to the history of the South. Slavery was known as the "peculiar institution" of the South (despite its prevalence in such colonies as N.Y. in the 18th cent.) and was protected by the Constitution of the U.S. The Missouri Compromise (1820–1821) marked the rise of Southern sectionalism, rooted in the political doctrine of States' Rights, with John C. Calhoun as its greatest advocate. When differences with the North, esp. over the issue of the extension of slavery into the Federal territories, ultimately appeared insoluble, the South turned (1860–1861) the doctrine of states' rights into secession (or independence), which in turn led inevitably to the Civil War. Most of the major battles and campaigns of the war were fought in the South, and by the end of the war, with slavery abolished and most of the area in ruins, the Old South had died. The period of Reconstruction following the war set the South's political and social attitude for years to come. During this difficult time radical Republicans, "carpetbaggers, scalawags," and Afr. Americans, ruled the South with the support of Federal troops. The white Southerners, objecting to this rule, resorted to terrorism and violence and, with the aid of such organizations as the Ku Klux Klan, drove the Reconstruction govts. from power. The breakdown of the plantation system during the Civil War gave rise to sharecropping, the tenant-farming system of agr. that still exists in areas of the South. The last ½ of the 19th cent. saw the beginning of industrialization in the South, with the introduction of textile mills and various industries. The troubled economic and political life of the region in the years bet. 1880 and World War II was marked by the rise of the Farmers' Alliance, Populism, and Jim Crow laws and by the careers of such Southerners as Tom Watson, Theodore Bilbo, Benjamin Tillman, Huey Long, Sam Rayburn, and Lyndon Johnson. During the 1930s and 1940s, thousands of blacks migrated from the South to Northern industrial cities. Since World War II the South has been experiencing profound political, economic, and social change. Southern reaction to the policies of the New Deal, the Fair Deal, the New Frontier, and the

Great Society caused the emergence of a genuine 2-party system here. Also, many conservative Southern Democrats (such as Strom Thurmond) became Republicans because of disagreements over civil rights, the Vietnam War, and other issues. Although there are still Southern Democratic strongholds, Republicans are well-represented in most Southern states. During the 1950s and 1960s the Civil Rights movement, several key Supreme Court decisions, and Federal legislation ended the legal segregation of public schools, univs., transportation, businesses, and other establishments here, and helped Afr. Americans achieve more adequate political representation. The process of integration was often met with bitter protest and violence. Patterns of residential segregation still exist in much of the South, as they do throughout the country. Since the 1980s, however, increasing numbers of Afr. Americans — both of working and retirement age — have been moving here from other regions of the U.S. The influx of new industries into the region after World War II made the economic life of the South more diversified and more similar to that of the rest of the U.S. The portions of the South included in the SUNBELT have experienced dramatic growth since the 1970s. Fla.'s pop. almost doubled bet. 1970 and 1990 and Ga., N.C., and S.C. have also grown considerably. Economically, the leading metropolitan areas of the South have become popular destinations for corporations seeking favorable tax rates, and the region's relatively low union membership has attracted both foreign and U.S. mfg. companies. In much of the rural South, however, poverty, illiteracy, and poor health conditions still prevail. From William Byrd (1674–1744) to William Faulkner and Toni Morrison, the South has always had a strong regional literature. Its principal subject has been the Civil War, reflected in song from Paul Hamilton Hayne to Allen Tate and in novels from Thomas Nelson Page to Margaret Mitchell.

South Thomaston (TAHM-uh-stuhn), town (1990 pop. 1,227), Knox co., S Maine, on Weskeag R. inlet, and just S of Rockland; 44°02′N 69°08′W. Resorts; fishing. Includes Spruce Head village.

South Toms River, borough, Ocean co., E N.J., on Toms R., opposite Toms River.

South Torrington, village, S of Torrington, Goshen co., SE Wyo., on North Platte R.

South Truro, Mass.: see TRURO.

South Tucson (TOO-sawn), town (1990 pop. 5,093) and residential suburb, 2 mi/3.2 km S of downtown Tucson, Pima co., SE Ariz., near Santa Cruz R., surrounded by city of Tucson; 32°12′N 110°58′W. Inc. 1939.

South Twin Lake (□ 14 sq mi/36 sq km), central N.F., E Canada, 20 mi/32 km W of Botwood; 10 mi/16 km long, 2 mi/3 km wide; drains into Exploits R.

South Uniontown, village, Fayette co., SW Pa., part of Uniontown; 39°53′N 79°44′W.

South Venice (VE-nis), town (□ 6 sq mi/15.5 sq km; 1990 pop. 11,951), Sarasota co., W central Fla., 4 mi/6.4 km S of Venice; 27°02′N 82°24′W.

South Vernon, Mass.: see NORTHFIELD.

South Vienna or **Vienna** (both: vee-E-nuh), village (1990 pop. 550), Clark co., W central Ohio, 11 mi/18 km E of Springfield; 39°55′N 83°37′W. In agr. area.

South Wadesboro (WAIDZ-buhr-o), uninc. village, Anson co., S N.C., suburb, 1 mi/1.6 km S of Wadesboro.

South Wareham, Mass.: see WAREHAM.

South Warren, uninc town (1990 pop. 1,780), Warren co., NW Pa., residential suburb, 2 mi/3.2 km WSW of Warren; 41°49′N 79°10′W.

South Waverly, borough (1990 pop. 1,049), Bradford co., NE Pa., on Chemung R., 1 mi/1.6 km NW of Sayre, and 1 mi/1.6 km S of Waverly (N.Y.); 42°00′N 76°32′W. Inc. 1878.

South Wayne, village (1990 pop. 478), Lafayette co., S Wis., near Pecatonica R., 12 mi/19 km W of Monroe; 42°34′N 89°52′W. In dairy-farming area; cheese.

South Weber (WEE-buhr), town (1990 pop. 2,863), Davis co., N Utah, suburb, 7 mi/11.3 km SSE of Ogden, and 23 mi/37 km N of Salt Lake City, on Weber R.;

41°07′N 111°55′W. Elev. 4,200 ft/1,280 m. Settled 1851. Hill Air Force Base to SW; Wasatch Range and Natl. Forest to E.

South Webster, village (1990 pop. 806), Scioto co., S Ohio, 14 mi/23 km ENE of Portsmouth; 38°49′N 82°43′W. In agr. area; makes refractories.

South Weldon, uninc. town (1990 pop. 1,640), Halifax co., N N.C., 1 mi/1.6 km SSW of Weldon; 36°23′N 77°37′W.

South Wellfleet, Mass.: see WELLFLEET.

South Wellington, village, SW B.C., W Canada, on SE Vancouver Isl., suburb, 5 mi/8 km SSE of Nanaimo; 49°06′N 123°53′W. Coal mining; mixed farming. Pulp mill at Harmac.

South West City, town (1990 pop. 600), McDonald co., in the extreme SW corner of Mo., in the Ozark Mts., near Elk R., 13 mi/21 km SSW of Pineville; 36°31′N 94°36′W. Corn, hay; cattle, poultry.

South Weymouth, Mass.: see WEYMOUTH.

South Whitley, town (1990 pop. 1,482), Whitley co., NE Ind., on Eel R., and 9 mi/14.5 km SW of Columbia City; 41°05′N 85°38′W. In grain and livestock area; ships grain; mfg. (machinery, musical instruments, fabricated metal prods., electrical equip., paper goods, mobile office bldgs.). Laid out 1837.

South Whittier, uninc. city (1990 pop. 49,514), Los Angeles co., S Calif., residential suburb, 12 mi/19 km SE of downtown Los Angeles, and 2 mi/3.2 km SW of Whittier; 33°56′N 118°02′W.

South Williamson, town (1990 pop. 1,016), Pike co., E Ky., on Tug Fork of the Big Sandy R., opposite (SW of) Williamson (W.Va.; linked to bridged). Coal mining; mfg. (concrete).

South Williamsport, borough (1990 pop. 6,496), Lycoming co., N central Pa., suburb, 1 mi/1.6 km S of Williamsport; 41°13′N 77°00′W. Mfg. (fabricated metal prods., food prods., paper prods.). Peter J. McGovern Little League Mus. is here. Allenwood Federal Prison Camp to SE. Susquehanna State Park to W; part of Tiadaghton State Forest to SE; Bald Eagle Mt. ridge to S. Inc. 1886.

South Willington, Conn.: see WILLINGTON.

South Wilmington, village (1990 pop. 698), Grundy co., NE Ill., 26 mi/42 km SSW of Joliet; 41°10′N 88°16′W. In agr. area (corn, soybeans; dairying).

South Windham (WIND-uhm), village, in Windham and Gorham towns, Cumberland co., SW Maine, 10 mi/16 km NW of Portland.

South Windham, Vt.: see WINDHAM.

South Windsor, town (1990 pop. 22,090), Hartford co., N Conn.; 41°49′N 72°34′W. Chiefly residential. Oliver Wolcott, a signer of the Declaration of Independence, b. here. Set off from Windsor 1845.

South Yarmouth, Mass.: see YARMOUTH.

South Yuba City, uninc. town (1990 pop. 8,816), Sutter co., N central Calif., residential suburb, 2 mi/3.2 km SW of Yuba City; 39°07′N 121°39′W. Nursery prods., rice, corn, melons, walnuts, alfalfa, safflower.

South Zanesville (ZAINZ-vil), village (1990 pop. 1,969), Muskingum co., central Ohio, just S of Zanesville, on small Jonathan Creek near its mouth on Muskingum R.; 39°54′N 82°01′W. Lumber.

Southampton, parish (1991 pop. 5,804), W Bermuda, on Bermuda Isl.; 32°15′N 64°51′W.

Southampton, county (□ 603 sq mi/1,562 sq km; 1990 pop. 17,550), SE Va., on N.C. (S) state line; ⊙ Courtland; independent city of Franklin in E is separate from co.; 36°43′N 77°06′W. In Tidewater region; bounded W by Meherrin R., E by Blackwater R.; drained by Nottoway R. Diversified agr. (hay, peanuts, wheat, cotton, corn, soybeans, melons; cattle, hogs); timber. Set off 1748 from 1 of original Va. shires (formed 1634) and renamed Southampton.

Southampton, uninc. city (1990 pop. 16,076), Bucks co., SE Pa., suburb, 15 mi/24 km NNE of Philadelphia; 40°10′N 75°02′W. Drained by Mill Creek. Mfg. includes printing and publishing; environmental systems, transportation equip., paper goods, machinery, plastic prods. Springfield L. Reservoir to NE.

Southampton, town (1991 pop. 3,118), S Ont., central Canada, on L. Huron, at mouth of Saugeen R., 22 mi/35 km WSW of Owen Sound. Lumbering; furniture mfg.

Southampton (sou-THAM-tuhn), agr. town (1990 pop. 4,478), Hampshire co., W central Mass., 8 mi/12.9 km SSW of Northampton; 42°14′N 72°45′W. Hampton Ponds State Park nearby. Settled 1732, inc. 1775.

Southampton, township (1990 pop. 10,202), Burlington co., S N.J., 10 mi/16 km SE of Mount Holly; 39°54′N 74°43′W. Mfg. machine tools. Inc. 1845.

Southampton, residential village (□ 6 sq mi/15.5 sq km; 1990 pop. 3,980), Suffolk co., SE N.Y., on SE L.I., 14 mi/23 km ESE of Riverhead; 40°52′N 72°24′W. Some light mfg.; in rapidly shrinking potato-farming area. Affluent summer resort known for its many fine estates and celebrity residents. Parrish Memorial Art Mus. is here, as is Southampton Col. of L.I. Univ. Shinnecock Indian Reservation is W. Settled 1640 as 1st Eng. settlement in state, inc. 1894.

Southampton, Cape, SW extremity of Coats Isl., E Keewatin dist., N.W.T., N Canada, on Hudson Bay; 62°09′N 83°42′W.

Southampton Island (□ c.15,700 sq mi/40,700 sq km), Keewatin region, N.W.T., N Canada, at the entrance to Hudson Bay. Separated from the mainland by Ross Welcome Sound and Frozen Strait. With lowlands in the W, the tundra-covered isl. rises to c.2,000 ft/610 m in the E. Coral Harbour, a trading post and airfield, is at the head of South Bay.

Southard (SOU-thurd), village, Blaine co., W central Okla., 15 mi/24 km NNW of Watonga. Mfg. (gypsum prods., wallboard).

Southaven, city (1990 pop. 17,949), De Soto co., NW Miss., suburb, 10 mi/16 km S of downtown Memphis (Tenn.), on Tenn. state line; 34°58′N 90°00′W. Mfg. (printing and publishing; bldg. materials, motor vehicles, aircraft). Memphis Internatl. Airport to NE. Elvis Presley's Graceland Mansion to N.

Southboro or **Southborough**, town (1990 pop. 6,628), Worcester co., E central Mass., 15 mi/24 km E of Worcester. Chiefly residential; dairying. Includes villages of Cordaville (1990 pop. 1,530) and Fayville. Settled 1660, inc. 1727.

Southbridge, town (1990 pop. 17,816), Worcester co., S Mass., on the Quinebaug R.; 42°04′N 72°02′W. Textiles were the original chief manufactures, succeeded by specialized chemicals. Industries include tools, fabricated metal prods., clothing. Settled 1730, inc. 1816.

Southbury, residential town (1990 pop. 15,818), New Haven co., SW Conn., on the Housatonic R., at mouth of Pomrepaug R., and 10 mi/16 km SW of Waterbury; 41°28′N 73°13′W. In summer resort area. Industry includes the mfg. of plastic parts, screw machine prods., and ice cream. Southbury Training School for Mentally Retarded, the last such residential institution in the state; Heritage Hills (retirement communty). Settled 1673, set off from Woodbury 1782.

Southeast, township (1990 pop. 14,927), SE Putnam co., SE N.Y.; 44°24′N 73°36′W. The Tilly Foster Iron Mine (est. 1790), located on a 128-acre/52-ha farm owned by Tilly Foster, was the largest of a number of mines in the area. The town was named after this mine. For a time high-grade iron ore was shipped from here to Pa. Became open-pit mine in 1889, closed in 1897 after an avalanche. Today town is a center of mfg. (pharmaceuticals, dairy equip.).

Southern Indian Lake (□ 1,200 sq mi/3,108 sq km), N Man., central Canada, on Churchill R.; 105 mi/169 km long, 16 mi/26 km wide; 57°00′N 99°00′W.

Southern Pines, town (1990 pop. 9,129), Moore co., central N.C., 28 mi/45 km WNW of Fayetteville; 35°10′N 79°24′W. RR junction. Area famous for its golf courses; resort area. Tobacco, grain, soybeans; chickens, livestock. Mfg. (hand tools, consumer goods, machinery and parts, textiles; printing and publishing). Fort Bragg Military Rerserve to E. Weymouth Woods State Park (Sandhills Nature Preserve) to S. Pinehurst-Southern Pines Airport to N. Settled 1885, inc. 1887.

Area in square miles is shown by the symbol □   capital city or county seat by ⊙

Southern Shops, uninc town (1990 pop. 3,378), Spartanburg co., NW S.C., residential and commercial suburb, 5 mi/8 km WNW of downtown Spartanburg, at intersection of Interstates 26 and 85; 34°59′N 81°59′W.

Southern Shores, town (1990 pop. 1,447), Dare co., NE N.C., residential community, 32 mi/51 km ESE of Elizabeth City, on Currituck Sound (bridged), near its entrance to Albermarle Sound, on Outer Banks, W of Atlantic Ocean; 36°07′N 75°43′W. Beach resort area.

Southern View, village (1990 pop. 1,906), Sangamon co., central Ill., residential suburb, 3 mi/4.8 km S of downtown Springfield; 39°45′N 89°39′W. RR junction. In agr. and bituminous-coal area.

Southey (SOU-thee), town (1991 pop. 693), S Sask., W Canada, 35 mi/56 km N of Regina; 50°56′N 104°30′W. Wheat.

Southfield, city (1990 pop. 75,728), Oakland co., SE Mich., a suburb, 14 mi/23 km NW of downtown Detroit and immediately N of Detroit, on the Rouge R.; 42°28′N 83°15′W. Mfg. (electronic research, meat processing, printing; plastic prods., fabricated metal prods., chemicals, transportation equip., rubber prods., wood prods., machinery). It is the center of the retail and office industries in the Detroit metropolitan area. Many well-known companies have offices here. The growing city also has varied light mfg. and a warehousing industry. Duns Scotus Col., Lawrence Technological Univ., and an extension center of Wayne State Univ. are here. Site of Northland Shopping Center, one of the largest shopping centers in U.S. Laid out 1817, inc. as a city 1958.

Southfield, town (1991 pop. 2,671), St. Elizabeth parish, SW Jamaica, 15 mi/24 km SW of Mandeville; 17°53′N 77°40′W. Scenic "Lover's Leap" cliffs nearby.

Southfield, Mass.: see NEW MARLBORO.

Southfields, village (1990 pop. 550), Orange co., SE N.Y. on Ramapo R., and 9 mi/14.5 km NNW of Suffern; 41°15′N 74°10′W. Light mfg. Bear Mt. recreational area is just E.

Southgate, city (1990 pop. 30,771), Wayne co., SE Mich., a residential suburb, 10 mi/16 km SSW of downtown Detroit; 42°12′N 83°12′W. Mfg. (transportation equip.; publishing). Settled 1840–1860, inc. 1958.

Southgate, town (1990 pop. 3,266), Campbell co., N Ky., near the Ohio R., a suburb, 3 mi/4.8 km SE of downtown Cincinnati (Ohio), near Licking R.; 39°03′N 84°28′W. Mfg. (wood prods.).

Southhampton, town (1990 pop. 13,020), Suffolk co., SE N.Y., 13 mi/21 km SE of Riverhead, on S shore of L.I.; 40°53′N 72°24′W. Pop. figure includes Tuckahoe and Hampton Park.

Southington (SOU-thing-tuhn), town (1990 pop. 38,518), Hartford co., central Conn., 17 mi/27 km SSW of Hartford; settled 1696, inc. 1779; 41°36′N 72°52′W. Mfg. began in Southington in the 1770s, and its thriving machine-tool industry was spurred by inventions made there before 1840. Chemicals, primary and fabricated metals, and electrical and transportation equipment are among the town's other manufactures. Winter skiing nearby. Includes Milldale, Plantsville.

Southlake, town (1990 pop. 7,065), Tarrant co., N Texas, residential suburb, 17 mi/27 km NE of downtown Fort Worth, on Big Bear Creek (S); 32°57′N 97°09′W. Mfg. (machinery, prefab metal bldgs., electronic equip.). Grapevine L. reservoir to NE.

Southland 1 village, Jackson co., S Mich., unincorporated suburb, 3 mi/4.8 km S of Jackson; 41°43′N 83°46′W. **2** uninc. village (1990 pop. 168), Garza co., NW Texas, 20 mi/32 km SE of Lubbock. In cattle and agr. area; mfg. (metal fabrication).

Southmayd, village (1990 pop. 643), Grayson co., N Texas, 8 mi/12.9 km W of Sherman; 33°37′N 96°43′W. Oil and natural-gas. Cattle; peanuts. Hagerman Natl. Wildlife Refuge to N.

Southminster, village, W Sask., W Canada, on Alta. border, 5 mi/8 km SSE of Lloydminster. Elev. 2,086 ft/ 636 m. Oil and natural-gas production.

Southmont (SOUTH-mahnt), borough (1990 pop. 2,415), Cambria co., W central Pa., residential suburb,

2 mi/3.2 km SW of Johnstown; 40°18′N 78°55′W. Mill Creek Reservoir to W.

Southold, summer-resort village (□ 11 sq mi/28 sq km; 1990 pop. 5,192), Suffolk co., SE N.Y., on N peninsula of E L.I., 16 mi/26 km NE of Riverhead; 41°03′N 72°25′W. In declining agr. area (potatoes, vegetables); boatyards.

Southport, city (1990 pop. 1,969), Marion co., central Ind., 8 mi/12.9 km SSE of downtown Indianapolis; 39°40′N 86°07′W. Laid out 1852.

Southport 1 town, Bay co., NW Fla., 7 mi/11.3 km NNE of Panama City. Mfg. includes fishing boats, jewelry. **2** uninc. town, SE La., Jefferson parish, suburb, 3 mi/ 5 km W of downtown New Orleans; 29°57′N 90°08′W. **3** fishing and resort town (1990 pop. 645), Lincoln co., SW Maine, on isl. just S of Boothbay, and 10 mi/16 km SE of Bath; 43°49′N 69°40′W. Includes Squirrel Isl. resort community. **4** town (1990 pop. 2,369), ⊙ Brunswick co., S N.C., 22 mi/35 km SSW of Wilmington, on Atlantic coast, on Cape Fear R. estuary (entrance to S), W of Corncake Inlet, on Pleasure Isl.; 33°55′N 78°01′W. Toll ferry across Cape Fear R. to Kure and Carolina beaches 2 mi/3.2 km to NE. Fish, shrimp, crabs. Mfg. (citric acids; crab meat processing). Beach resort area. Sunny Point Ordinance Depot to N. Fort Johnston (built 1764, destroyed 1776, rebuilt after 1794) is preserved. Founded 1792.

Southside, city (1990 pop. 5,580), Etowah co., NE Ala., 8 mi/12.9 km S of Gadsden, near Coosa R.; 33°54′N 86°01′W.

Southside Place, town (1990 pop. 1,392), Harris co., SE Texas, residential suburb, 5 mi/8 km SW of downtown Houston, surrounded by city of Houston; 29°42′N 95°26′W. Site of Shell Oil Production Laboratory.

Southwest, Cape, SW extremity of Axel Heiberg Isl., N Franklin dist., N Canada, on Norwegian Bay; 78°11′N 92°10′W.

Southwest Gander River, headstream of Gander R., 50 mi/80 km long, E central N.F., E Canada; rises 50 mi/80 km SSE of Grand Falls; flows NE to Gander L.

Southwest Greensburg, borough (1990 pop. 2,456), Westmoreland co., SW central Pa., residential suburb, 1 mi/1.6 km W of Greensburg; 40°17′N 79°32′W. Inc. 1890.

Southwest Harbor, town (1990 pop. 1,952), Hancock co., S Maine, resort on S Mt. Desert Isl., 19 mi/31 km SSE of Ellsworth; 44°15′N 68°19′W. Boatyards. Set off from Tremont 1905.

Southwest Miramichi River, N.B.: see MIRAMICHI.

Southwick, town (1990 pop. 7,667), Hampden co., SW Mass., 11 mi/18 km WSW of Springfield; 42°03′N 72°47′W. Tobacco, potatoes. Inc. 1770.

Soyaló (so-yah-LO), town (1990 pop. 2,785), Chiapas, S Mexico, in spur of Sierra Madre, 17 mi/27 km NE of Tuxtla, on Mexico highway 195; 16°55′N 92°55′W. Elev. 3,740 ft/1,140 m. A Tzotzil Maya community.

Soyaniquilpan (so-yah-nee-KEEL-pahn), town (1990 pop. 989), ⊙ Soyaniquilpan de Juárez municipio, 34 mi/55 km SE of San Juan del Río, off Mexico Highway 57; 19°59′N 99°30′W. Small farming. Also San Francisco.

Soyopa (so-YO-pah), town (1990 pop. 282), Sonora, NW Mexico, on Yaqui R., and 85 mi/137 km ESE of Hermosillo; 28°45′N 109°38′W. Livestock; coal mining.

Space Coast, local name for the upper middle Atlantic coast of Fla. centered on Cape Canaveral's John F. Kennedy Space Center, bet. Melbourne (S) to Daytona Beach (N).

Spalding (SPAWL-ding), county (□ 200 sq mi/ 518 sq km; 1990 pop. 54,457), W central Ga.; ⊙ Griffin; 33°16′N 84°17′W. Bounded W by Flint R. Piedmont agr. (cotton, corn, peppers, wheat, soybeans, fruit); cattle, hogs, poultry. Timber area. Formed 1851. Rapidly urbanizing Atlanta suburb.

Spalding, village (1991 pop. 287), S central Sask., W Canada, 28 mi/45 km ENE of Humboldt. Wheat; livestock.

Spalding 1 uninc. village (1990 pop. 150), Nez Perce co., W Idaho 10 mi/16 km ENE of Lewiston, on Clearwater

R., in NW corner of Nez Perce Indian Reservation. RR junction. Cattle; grain, vegetables, alfalfa. Nez Perce Natl. Historic Park (Spalding Area Unit) located here, including Spalding Mission, 1836. **2** village (1990 pop. 592), Greeley co., E central Nebr., 13 mi/21 km NE of Greeley, and on Cedar R. RR terminus. Livestock; grain; mfg. (electronic prods., signs).

Spaldings, town (1991 pop. 2,865), Clarendon parish, central Jamaica, partly in Manchester parish, 22 mi/ 35 km NW of May Pen; 18°9′N 77°21′W. Agr. center (sugarcane, ginger, tropical fruit; livestock); exports honey.

Spanaway, uninc. city (1990 pop. 15,001), Pierce co., W Wash., suburb, 10 mi/16 km S of downtown Tacoma; 47°07′N 122°26′W. Agr. area to E (dairying; poultry; vegetables, berries). Timber. Mfg. (lumber, veneer, wood prods.). McChord Air Force Base to W; Fort Lewis Military Reservation to SW.

Spangle, village (1990 pop. 229), Spokane co., E Wash., 15 mi/24 km S of Spokane, on Spangle Creek; 47°26′N 117°23′W. In wheat-growing region; mfg. (furniture). Turnbull Natl. Wildlife Refuge here.

Spangler (SPANG-gluhr), borough (1990 pop. 2,068), Cambria co., W central Pa., 23 mi/37 km NNE of Johnstown, and 1 mi/1.6 km SSE of Barnesboro, on West Branch of Susquehanna R.; 40°38′N 78°46′W. Agr. (corn, hay; dairying); bituminous coal. Inc. 1893.

Spaniard's Bay, town (1991 pop. 2,198), SE N.F., E Canada, on SW side of Conception Bay, N Avalon Peninsula, 6 mi/10 km SW of Harbour Grace; 47°37′N 53°18′W. Fishing; lumbering.

Spanish, river, c.150 mi/240 km long, S Ont., central Canada; issuing from Spanish L., NW of Sudbury; flows generally S through Biskotasi and Agnew lakes to L. Huron opposite Manitoulin isl. Several hydroelectric stations.

Spanish America, collective term referring in its present usage to the Span.-speaking countries of LATIN AMERICA, thus including Mexico, Central Amer. (except Belize), S. Amer. (except Brazil and the Guianas), Cuba, the Dominican Republic, and generally also P.R. Hispanic Amer. is also used. As a historic concept Span. Amer. sometimes applies to all the areas settled by the Spanish in colonial times, including what are now Fla., Calif., Nev., N.Mex., Ariz., and parts of several other states.

Spanish Fork or **Spanish Fork City**, city (1990 pop. 11,272), Utah co., N central Utah, suburb, 8 mi/12.9 km S of Provo, at foot of Wasatch Range, near Spanish Fork R. and Utah L.; 40°06′N 111°38′W. Elev. 4,580 ft/ 1,396 m. Processing center for cattle, sheep, and agr. area (sugar beets, grain, fruit) irrigated by water from Strawberry R. Mfg. (ordnance, transportation equip., aluminum extrusion, paper prods., clothing, herbs and food supplements, pet food; meat processing, printing); sand, gravel. Spanish Fork Peak (10,192 ft/3,107 m) is 7 mi/11.3 km E, in Wasatch Range (Uinta Natl. Forest). Spanish Fork Airport to N. Settled 1850, inc. 1855.

Spanish Fork, stream, 48 mi/77 km, SE Utah co., N central Utah; rising in Wasatch Range; flows WNW past Spanish Fork city to Utah L. Receives water from Strawberry Reservoir (on Strawberry R.). Used for irrigation and hydroelectric power.

Spanish Fort, village (1990 pop. 3,732), Baldwin co., SW Ala., on E side of Mobile Bay, across from Mobile; 30°40′N 87°53′W. Lumber; gas exploration; vending machine mfg.

Spanish Peaks, S Colo., in Sangre de Cristo Mts., on border bet. Huerfano and Las Animas cos., c.25 mi/ 40 km NW of Trinidad. West Spanish Peak (13,626 ft/ 4,153 m) is 4 mi/6.4 km WSW of East Spanish Peak (12,683 ft/3,866 m); both are of volcanic origin.

Spanish Town, city (1991 pop. 110,379), ⊙ St. Catherine parish, SE Jamaica, on the Cobre R.; 17°59′N 76°57′W. The commercial and processing center of a rich agr. region, as well as the main RR and highway communications hub for traffic to and from Kingston and other parts of Jamaica. Founded c.1525 and formerly called Santiago de la Vega, Spanish Town was Jamaica's leading city after the destruction of Port Royal by earthquake in 1692. In 1872 Kingston became the capital city. Historic bldgs. enclosing the Spanish Town Square are Old Kings House, previous Governor's residence for 100 years, famous Fr. 1782 Rodney Memorial, 1819 Circuit Court Bldgs., and St. James Cathedral of 1525, oldest ecclesiastical structure of the Br. Empire.

Spanish Town, village, S Anegada, Br. V.I., 13 mi/21 km E of Road Town, Tortola; 18°25′N 64°25′W. Charcoal burning; livestock; vegetables.

Spanish Wells, settlement and district (□ 1/2 sq mi/ 1.3 sq km; 1990 pop. 1,372), central Bahama Isls., comprising 3 small islets — Royal Isl., Egg Isl., and St. George's Cay (on which is Spanish Wells village) — just off N tip of Eleuthera Isl., 50 mi/80 km NE of Nassau. Fruit, vegetables; fish. Spanish Wells was burned by an Amer. vessel during War of 1812.

Sparkill, village (1990 pop. 1,100), Rockland co., SE N.Y., near W bank of the Hudson R., 4 mi/6.4 km S of Nyack; 41°02′N 73°55′W. Lumber; sand, gravel. A state park is nearby.

Sparkman, village (1990 pop. 553), Dallas co., S central Ark., 19 mi/31 km SE of Arkadelphia, near Ouachita R.; 33°55′N 92°50′W. Mfg. (lumber).

Sparks, city (1990 pop. 53,367), Washoe co., W Nev., suburb 3 mi/4.8 km E of downtown Reno, on Truckee R.; 39°32′N 119°44′W. RR center. Mfg. (medical supplies, modular structures, machinery, transportation equip., concrete prods., paper prods., millwork, wood prods., electric and electronic equip., restaurant equip.; printing and publishing, minerals exploration, machining); tourism. Marked by rapid residential growth, its pop. doubled bet. 1970 and 1990. Pyramid L. and Pyramid L. Indian Reservation to N; points of interest include a planetarium and a monument honoring the Chin. immigrant laboreres who built the Southern Pacific RR.

Sparks, town (1990 pop. 1,205), Cook co., S Ga., 19 mi/ 31 km E of Moultrie; 31°10′N 83°26′W. In agr. area. Mfg. (chemicals, fiberglass boats).

Sparks, village (1990 pop. 202), Lincoln co., central Okla., 6 mi/9.7 km SSE of Chandler, near Deep Fork of Canadian R.; 35°36′N 96°49′W. In agr. area.

Sparland, village (1990 pop. 412), Marshall co., N central Ill., on Illinois R. (bridged here), opposite Lacon, and 23 mi/37 km NNE of Peoria; 41°01′N 89°26′W. In agr. area.

Sparlingville, town (1990 pop. 1,974), St. Clair co., E Mich., suburb, 4 mi/6.4 km W of Port Huron; 42°57′N 82°31′W. St. Clair Co. Internatl. Airport to S.

Sparrow Bush, resort village (1990 pop. 1,200), Orange co., SE N.Y., on the Delaware R., and 2 mi/3.2 km NW of Port Jervis; 41°24′N 74°44′W.

Sparrows Point, industrial district in Baltimore co., central Md., on navigable Patapasco R., and 9 mi/14.5 km SE of downtown Baltimore. Blast furnaces have been operating here since 1889. The giant steel mill and shipyard was acquired by the Bethlehem Steel Corp. in 1916 and steadily expanded. In full production, the facility could employ 22,000. Foreign and domestic ore as well as finished steel prods. are shipped out of the deep water ore docks and RR lines. The land was originally deeded to Thomas Sparrow by Lord Baltimore in 1666. His son, Solomon, built the 1st house called Sparrow's Nest.

Sparta 1 (SPAHR-tuh), city (1990 pop. 4,853), Randolph co., SW Ill., 16 mi/26 km NNE of Chester; 38°08′N 89°43′W. Mfg. of clothing; RR shops. Agr. (corn, wheat; dairy prods.; livestock, poultry); bituminous coal mines. Inc. 1847. **2** city (1990 pop. 4,681), ⊙ White co., central Tenn.,15 mi/24 km S of Cookeville, on Cumberland Plateau; 35°56′N 85°28′W. In coal, limestone, timber region; makes wood prods., clothing, consumer goods, electrical goods. Great Falls and Center Hill dams in Caney Fork of the Cumberland, and numerous state parks, are nearby. Founded 1809.

Sparta 1 (SPAHR-tuh), town (1990 pop. 1,710), ⊙ Hancock co., E central Ga., c.50 mi/80 km NE of Macon; 33°17′N 82°58′W. Mfg. of clothing and furniture. Inc. 1805. **2** town (1990 pop. 3,968), Kent co., SW Mich.,

14 mi/23 km NNW of Grand Rapids; 43°09′N 85°42′W. In dairy and fruit-farming area; mfg. (transportation equip., paper prods., structural wood, plastic prods.). Airport here. Plotted 1869, inc. 1883. **3** town (1990 pop. 751), Christian co., SW Mo., in the Ozark Mts., 8 mi/ 12.9 km E of Ozark; 37°00′N 93°04′W. Plotted 1885. **4** town (1990 pop. 1,957), ⊙ Alleghany co., NW N.C., 23 mi/37 km NW of Elkin, in the Blue Ridge Mts.; 36°30′N 81°07′W. Tobacco; grain; cattle; dairying. Mfg. (apparel, textiles, paper prods., consumer goods, bldg. materials). Blue Ridge (Natl.) Parkway passes to S and SE. **5** town (1990 pop. 7,788), ⊙ Monroe co., W central Wis., on La Crosse R., and 23 mi/37 km ENE of La Crosse; 43°56′N 90°48′W. In agr. area (tobacco; dairy prods.; poultry). Creameries, tobacco warehouses. Mfg. (machinery, fabricated metal prods., plating and spray painting, plastics, consumer goods). Seat of state school for children. U.S. Camp McCoy Military Reservation to NE. On La Crosse State Trail. Settled c.1850, inc. 1883.

Sparta 1 (SPAHR-tuh), village (1990 pop. 133), Gallatin and Owen cos., N Ky., 35 mi/56 km SW of Covington, on Eagle Creek; 38°40′N 84°54′W. Agr. (tobacco; livestock); timber; nurseries. Mfg. (knives). **2** village, Sussex co., NW N.J., at N end of L. Mohawk, 6 mi/9.7 km E of Newton. In recretional area. Has reproductions of historic colonial houses. **3** village (1990 pop. 201), Morrow co., central Ohio, 12 mi/19 km W of Mount Vernon; 40°23′N 82°42′W.

Spartanburg, county (□ 819 sq mi/2,121 sq km; 1990 pop. 226,800), NW S.C., on N.C. (N) state line; ⊙ Spartanburg; 34°55′N 81°59′W. Mfg. in several of the co.'s towns includes textiles and apparel, motor vehicles; granite, sand and gravel production. Vermiculite also produced. Agr. includes peaches, wheat, oats, soybeans, sorghum, hay, apples; hogs, chickens; eggs; dairying. Formed 1785.

Spartanburg, city (1990 pop. 43,467), ⊙ Spartanburg co., NW S.C., in Piedmont near the N.C. state line; 34°56′N 81°55′W. The city is noted for its textile mills. It is an important commercial, transportation, and trade focus in an agr., and livestock region. Mfg. includes textiles and sewing materials, machinery, chemicals, plastics, wood, metal, clay, transportation equip., paper prods.; printing and publishing). Agr. includes dairying; poultry, hogs; grain, peaches, apples. In the Amer. Revolution, 11 major battles were fought in the area. City and cou. were named for the "Spartan" regiment of Revolutionary troops recruited in the area. In the Civil War the city was a busy supply-mfg. point. Spartanburg is the seat of Wofford, Converse, Spartanburg Technical, and Spartanburg Methodist cols., 2 junior cols., and a branch of the Univ. of S.C. In the vicinity is a state school for the Deaf and Blind (est. 1849). Home of James F. Byrnes. Cowpens Natl. Battlefield and a state park are nearby. Inc. 1831.

Spartansburg (SPAHR-tuhns-buhrg), borough (1990 pop. 403), Crawford co., NW Pa., 7 mi/11.3 km SSW of Corry, on East Branch Oil Creek (forms Clear L. here); 41°49′N 79°40′W. Agr. (dairying); timber; mfg. (lumber).

Sparwood, town (1991 pop. 4,211), SE B.C., W Canada, in Rocky Mts., 20 mi/32 km NE of Fernie, on Elk R. at confluence of Flathead R.; 49°45′N 114°50′W. Commercial and service center for coal-mining region. Cattle, sheep; logging; tourism.

Spaulding, Lake, Calif.: see YUBA RIVER.

Spavinaw (SPA-vuh-naw), village (1990 pop. 432), Mayes co., NE Okla., 16 mi/26 km ENE of Pryor; 36°23′N 95°02′W. Spavinaw L. and Spavinaw State Park area here. Inc. 1930.

Spavinaw Lake, reservoir, at Spavinaw, Delaware and Mayes cos., NE Okla., on Spavinaw R., 18 mi/29 km NE of Pryor; c.10 mi/16 km long; 36°21′N 94°55′W. Formed by Spavinaw Dam, built for water supply. Recreation area. Upper Spavinaw Dam (36°21′N 94°55′W), 7 mi/11.3 km upstream from Spavinaw Dam, forms L. Eucha (or Upper Spavinaw L.); together referred to as Spavinaw Lakes. L. Eucha (formerly Upper Spavinaw) State Park at E end of L. Eucha.

Spear, Cape, E extremity of N.F., E Canada, on Avalon

Peninsula, 7 mi/11.3 km SE of entrance to St. John's Harbour; 47°32′N 52°38′W. Elev. 246 ft/75 m. Lighthouse. Easternmost point of N. Amer. Prime landfall for transatlantic navigators; natl. historical park.

Spearfish, town (1990 pop. 6,966), Lawrence co., W S.Dak., 10 mi/16 km NW of Lead, and on Spearfish Creek, at N edge of Black Hills; 44°29′N 103°50′W. Elev. 3,647 ft/1,112 m. Mfg. (paper prods., sand and gravel, jewelry, lumber). Tourist center. Seat of Black Hills State Univ. Black Hills Natl. Forest to S; Spearfish Canyon Natl. Scenic Highway to S (U.S. Highway 14A). Site of Black Hills Passion Play; McHenry State Fish Hatchery to NW of Richwater R.; D. C. Booth State Fish Hatchery S of town.

Spearman, town (1990 pop. 3,197), ⊙ Hansford co., extreme N Texas, in high grassy plains of the Panhandle, 80 mi/129 km NNE of Amarillo; 36°12′N 101°11′W. Elev. 3,105 ft/946 m. Storage, shipping point for wheat, sorghum, corn, and cattle area; oil and gas. Palo Duro Reservoir to N. Inc. 1921.

Spearsville (SPIRZ-vil), village (1990 pop. 132), Union parish, N La., 25 mi/40 km N of Ruston; 32°57′N 92°36′W. In agr. and timber area. Pulp mill.

Spearville, village (1990 pop. 716), Ford co., SW Kansas, 16 mi/26 km ENE of Dodge City; 37°51′N 99°45′W. Grain; livestock. Publishing.

Spectacle Island, E Mass., in Dorchester Bay sect. of Boston Harbor, SE of downtown Boston, between Castle and Long isls. (SE), in Boston Harbor Isls. State Park; c.½ mi/⁸⁄₁₀ km long. Two drumlins connected by low sandbars. Long an eyesore, site for city garbage disposal plant until 1959. Later became rendering plant. Being reclaimed and enlarged due to Harbor tunnel spoil and fill from Deer Isl.

Speculator, resort village (1990 pop. 400), Hamilton co., E central N.Y., in the Adirondack Mts., at N end of L. Pleasant, c.50 mi/80 km NE of Utica; 43°34′N 74°22′W. In winter (skiing)- and summer-resort area; lumbering.

Spednik Lake, Maine and N.B.: see CHIPUTNETICOOK LAKES.

Speed 1 village (1990 pop. 650), Clark co., S Ind., 9 mi/ 14.5 km N of Jeffersonville. Agr. area; mfg. (cement). Laid out c.1854. **2** village (1990 pop. 64), Phillips co., N Kansas, on North Fork of Solomon R., and 8 mi/ 12.9 km SW of Phillipsburg; 39°40′N 99°25′W. Corn; livestock. **3** village (1990 pop. 88), Edgecombe co., E central N.C., 7 mi/11.3 km NE of Tarboro; 35°58′N 77°26′W. Tobacco, grain; livestock.

Speedway, town (1990 pop. 13,092), Marion co., central Ind., suburb, 4 mi/6.4 km WNW of downtown Indianapolis; 39°47′N 86°15′W. Mfg. (beverages and flavorings, fabricated metal prods.). Municipality not included in 1970 consolidation of Marion co. with Indianapolis. The Indianapolis Motor Speedway, site of the annual Indianapolis 500 car race, is located here. Laid out 1912, inc. 1926.

Speers (SPIRS), borough (1990 pop. 1,284), Washington co., SW Pa., 2 mi/3.2 km SE of Charleroi, on Monongahela R., (bridged) opposite and SW of North Belle; 40°07′N 79°52′W.

Speightstown (SPEIS-toun), town, NW Barbados, B.W.I., 11 mi/18 km N of Bridgetown. Market for flying-fish catch. Formerly an important shipping place. Its old Denmark Fort is now an almshouse. Two famous landmarks are Arlington House and St. Peter's Parish Church.

Spelter, uninc. village (1990 pop. 400), Harrison co., N W.Va., on the West Fork R., 5 mi/8 km NNE of Clarksburg. Coal-mining region. Mfg. (zinc-dust processing).

Spelterville, village (1990 pop. 500), Vigo co., W Ind., suburb 4 mi/6.4 km N of Terre Haute, near Wabash R.

Spence Bay, village (1991 pop. 580), N central N.W.T., N Canada, on W side of Boothia Peninsula isthmus, on Spence Bay of Rae Strait; 69°32′N 93°32′W. Est. 1947 when people were removed from Fort Ross, on S end of Somerset Isl., because of severe ice conditions there. Noted for its parka and wool clothing mfg. Hunting, trapping, fishing. Radio and TV stations; Royal Can. Mounted Police post. Scheduled air service.

Spencer 1 county (□ 401 sq mi/1,039 sq km; 1990 pop.

19,490), SW Ind., on Ky. (S) state line (Ohio R.); ⊙ Rockport; 38°01′N 87°01′W. Drained by small Anderson R. and Little Pigeon Creek. Soybeans, corn, wheat; dairying; hogs, cattle. Mfg. at Rockport and Troy. Lincoln State Park and Lincoln Boyhood Natl. Memorial (200 acres/81 ha), the farm where Abraham Lincoln spent his boyhood years, in N part of co. Town of Santa Claus in NE. Formed 1818. **2** county (☐ 191 sq mi/495 sq km; 1990 pop. 6,801), N central Ky.; ⊙ Taylorsville; 38°01′N 85°19′W. Rolling upland agr. area (hay, alfalfa, soybeans, wheat, corn, burley tobacco; hogs, cattle, poultry; dairying); mfg. at Taylorsville. In Bluegrass region; drained by Salt R. (forms Taylorsville L. reservoir in E) and several creeks. Taylorsville L. State Park in E center. Formed 1824.

Spencer, city (1990 pop. 11,066), ⊙ Clay co., NW Iowa, on the Little Sioux R.; 43°08′N 95°09′W. In a fertile farm area. Beef processing; mfg. of clothing, machinery, prefabricated bldgs., fabricated metal prods.; printing, scrap metal processing. Numerous natural lakes, part of Iowa Lakes Dist., to E and N. A famous co. fair is held here every Sept. Inc. 1880.

Spencer 1 town (1990 pop. 2,609), ⊙ Owen co., SW central Ind., on West Fork of White R., and 15 mi/24 km NW of Bloomington; 39°17′N 86°46′W. Agr. area (corn, fruit; livestock). Mfg. (medical equip., electrical prods., food prods.; publishing). McCormick's Creek State Park to E. Settled c.1815. Poet and dramatist William Vaughn Moody b. here. **2** town (1990 pop. 11,645), suburb including Spencer village, Worcester co., central Mass., 10 mi/16 km W of Worcester; 42°15′N 72°00′W. Dairying; poultry. Spencer State Forest. Settled 1721, inc. 1775. **3** town (1990 pop. 3,219), Rowan co., W central N.C., 2 mi/3.2 km NE of Salisbury; 35°41′N 80°25′W. Grain, soybeans, barley; poultry, cattle; dairying. Mfg. (chemicals; fabric finishing, steel fabricating). High Rock L. reservoir (Yadkin R.) to E. Spencer (RR) Shops State Historic Site, including N.C. Transportation Mus. **4** town (1990 pop. 3,972), Oklahoma co., central Okla., residential suburb, 9 mi/14.5 km ENE of downtown Oklahoma City, near North Canadian R.; 35°30′N 97°22′W. **5** town (1990 pop. 317), McCook co., SE S.Dak., 10 mi/16 km W of Salem; 43°43′N 97°35′W. In farming region; bldg. stone and crushed rock quarries. **6** town (1990 pop. 1,125), ⊙ Van Buren co., central Tenn., 12 mi/19 km S of Sparta, in the Cumberland Mts., 35°44′N 85°28′W. Livestock raising; coal mining. **7** town (1990 pop. 2,279), ⊙ Roane co., W W.Va., 35 mi/56 km SSE of Parkersburg; 38°47′N 81°21′W. Agr. (corn, tobacco, potatoes); livestock. Natural-gas and oil area. Mfg. (wood and rubber prods., knitwear). State hosp. here. Inc. 1858. **8** town (1990 pop. 1,757), Marathon co., central Wis., 9 mi/14.5 km NW of Marshfield; 44°45′N 90°17′W. Makes cheese. RR junction.

Spencer 1 village (1990 pop. 11), Clark co., E Idaho, 13 mi/21 km N of Dubois; 44°23′N 112°11′W. Sheep; timber. Targhee Natl. Forest and Continental Divide to N. U.S. Sheep Experimental Station to S. **2** village (1990 pop. 536), Boyd co., N Nebr., 8 mi/12.9 km ESE of Butte, and on Ponca Creek, near S.Dak. state line; 42°52′N 98°42′W. Grain. Spencer Dam (built for flood control) to S. **3** village (☐ 1 sq mi/2.6 sq km; 1990 pop. 815), Tioga co., S N.Y., 18 mi/29 km NE of Elmira; 42°13′N 76°29′W. In agr. area (dairy prods.; poultry; grain). Small Spencer L. (resort) is 3 mi/4.8 km N. **4** village (1990 pop. 726), Medina co., N Ohio, 13 mi/21 km WSW of Medina; 41°05′N 82°07′W. In agr. area.

Spencer, Cape, SE Alaska, on Gulf of Alaska, on N shore of ocean entrance to Cross Sound, 80 mi/129 km W of Juneau; 58°13′N 136°40′W.

Spencer Lake, reservoir, Somerset co., W Maine, on Dead R., 18 mi/29 km SSW of Jackman; 6 mi/9.7 km long; 45°22′N 70°17′W. Recreation area. Spencer Mt. (2,400 ft/732 m) near W shore. Also Spencer Pond.

Spencer Mountain, village (1990 pop. 135), Gaston co., S N.C., 5 mi/8 km NE of Gastonia, on South Fork Catawba R., at mouth of Long Creek; 35°18′N 81°06′W.

Spencerport, village (☐ 1 sq mi/2.6 sq km; 1990 pop. 3,606), Monroe co., W N.Y., on the Barge Canal, and 10 mi/16 km W of Rochester; 43°11′N 77°48′W. Site of John T. Trowbridge's boyhood home. Inc. 1867.

Spencerville, village, SE Ont., central Canada, on South Nation R., and 9 mi/14 km N of Prescott. Dairying, mixed farming.

Spencerville 1 village, DeKalb co., NE Ind., on St. Joseph R., and 9 mi/14.5 km SE of Auburn. In agr. area (grain). Mfg. (grain trailers, fabricated metal prods.). Settled c.1828, laid out 1842. **2** village (1990 pop. 2,288), Allen co., W Ohio, 13 mi/21 km W of Lima; 40°42′N 84°21′W. Trade center in agr. area (dairy prods.; livestock; grain, soybeans); mfg. (furniture, metal prods., cement, tile). Oil wells. Laid out 1844–1845, inc. 1866.

Spences Bridge, village, S B.C., W Canada, on Thompson R., and 50 mi/80 km WSW of Kamloops; 50°25′N 121°21′W. Fruit, vegetables; lumbering.

Speonk, village (1990 pop. 1,000), Suffolk co., SE N.Y., near S shore of L.I., 16 mi/26 km E of Patchogue; 40°59′N 72°42′W. Poultry. Beaches.

Sperry, town (1990 pop. 937), Tulsa co., NE Okla., 10 mi/16 km N of Tulsa, near Bird Creek; 36°17′N 95°59′W. In agr. area; light mfg.

Sperryville, uninc. village, Rappahannock co., N Va., on Thornton R., 19 mi/31 km NW of Culpeper; 38°39′N 78°13′W. Agr. (apples, grain; cattle). Gateway to Shenandoah Natl. Park to W, including Thornton Gap (2,300 ft/700 m).

Speyside (SPAI-seid), village, NE Tobago, Trinidad and Tobago, 16 mi/26 km NE of Scarborough, overlooking Tyrrel's Bay. Cacao, coconuts; fishing, tourism. Departure point for Little Tobago isl. offshore.

Spiceland, town (1990 pop. 757), Henry co., E central Ind., 8 mi/12.9 km SSW of New Castle; 39°50′N 85°26′W. Agr. area; mfg. (shades and projection screens). Settled 1820s, laid out 1850.

Spicer, town (1990 pop. 1,020), Kandiyohi co., S central Minn., 10 mi/16 km NE of Willmar, at SW end of Green L.; 45°13′N 94°56′W. Grain, sugar beets, beans; livestock, poultry; dairying; light mfg. Nest L. to NW

Spickard or **Spickardsville**, city (1990 pop. 326), Grundy co., N Mo., on Weldon R., and 12 mi/19 km N of Trenton; 40°14′N 93°35′W. Corn, wheat; cattle.

Spillville, town (1990 pop. 387), Winneshiek co., NE Iowa, on Turkey R., and 10 mi/16 km SW of Decorah; 43°12′N 91°57′W. Meat processing. Here in this Czech community Antonín Dvořák spent the summer of 1893 and composed part of his symphony, *From the New World*. His house later became a mus. of famous clocks.

Spindale, town (1990 pop. 4,040), Rutherford co., S N.C., 22 mi/35 km ENE of Shelby; 35°21′N 81°55′W. Grain, soybeans; poultry, livestock. Mfg. (flour and cornmeal, plastic prods., valves, textiles and fabrics).

Spink, county (☐ 1,510 sq mi/3,911 sq km; 1990 pop. 7,981), NE central S.Dak.; ⊙ Redfield; 44°56′N 98°20′W. Agr. area drained by James R. and Snake, Mud, Timber, Turtle, and Wolf creeks. Corn, wheat, soybeans, hay; cattle, hogs, sheep; dairy prods. Formed 1873.

Spinney Mountain, reservoir (☐ 4 sq mi/10.4 sq km), Park co., central Colo., on South Platte R., 50 mi/80 km WNW of Colorado Springs; 38°58′N 105°37′W. Max. capacity 83,300 acre-ft. Formed by Spinney Mt. Dam (95 ft/29 m high), built (1982) for water supply and recreation.

Spiral Tunnels, SE B.C., W Canada, 2 tunnels on Can. Pacific RR transcontinental line, in Rocky Mts., in Yoho Natl. Park, bet. Hector and Field; tunnels are 3,255 ft/992 m and 2,922 ft/891 m long; in each, the RR line almost completes a circle.

Spirit Lake 1 town (1990 pop. 3,871), Kootenai co., N Idaho, near Wash. state line, 35 mi/56 km NE of Spokane (Wash.), and at NE end of Spirit L. Resort activities; logging. **2** town, ⊙ Dickinson co., NW Iowa, 19 mi/31 km N of Spencer, bet. Big Spirit (N) and East Okoboji (S) lakes, and NE of West Okoboji L. Mfg., farm-trade, and resort center; mfg. (consumer goods, wood prods., machinery, food prods., beverages, chemicals, boats, paper prods., bldg. materials, hardware). Sand and gravel pit nearby. Several state parks in vicinity; fish hatchery to N. Settled 1856, inc. 1879.

Spirit Lake 1 Kootenai co., N Idaho, freshwater lake, c.30 mi/48 km NE of Spokane (Wash.); 5 mi/8 km long, 1 mi/1.6 km wide. Resort town of Spirit Lake is on NE shore. Twin Lakes to S. **2** Skamania co., SW Wash., at NE base of Mt. Saint Helens, in Mt. Saint Helens Natl. Volcanic Monument; formerly the source of North Fork Toutle R., currently has no outlet. Once part of an ideal picture-postcard setting, with Spirit L. in foreground and snowcapped Mt. Saint Helens as a backdrop, the scene at Spirit L. changed dramatically on May 18, 1980, when the Mt. Saint Helens volcano erupted after being dormant for 123 years, sending a deep blanket of ash upon the lake and its environs, destroying the tranquil scene. Despite warnings of the impending eruption, a defiant Harry Truman, proprietor of the rustic Spirit L. Lodge, opted to ride out the threat with his dogs. He and his lodge were subsequently entombed by a mt. of debris beyond any chance of rescue. Harry's Ridge, on W side of lake, is named for him.

Spirit River, town (1991 pop. 1,016), W Alta., W Canada, near B.C. border, 40 mi/64 km N of Grande Prairie; 55°47′N 118°50′W. Lumbering; furniture mfg. Mixed farming, wheat. In oil-bearing region.

Spiritwood, town (1991 pop. 973), central Sask., W Canada, near Witchekan L. (10 mi/16 km long, 3 mi/5 km wide), 75 mi/121 km W of Prince Albert; 53°22′N 107°31′W. Grain; lumbering.

Spiro, town (1990 pop. 2,146), Le Flore co., SE Okla., near Arkansas R., 15 mi/24 km SW of Fort Smith, and 12 mi/19 km N of Poteau; 35°14′N 94°37′W. In agr. area (potatoes, corn). Site of Spiro Indian Mounds. Founded c.1895 near site of old Fort Coffee (1834).

Spitler Wood State National Area, Ill.: see DECATUR.

Spivey (SPEI-vee), village (1990 pop. 88), Kingman co., S Kansas, on Chikaskia R., and 12 mi/19 km S of Kingman; 37°27′N 98°09′W. Wheat.

Splendora, town (1990 pop. 745), Montgomery co., SE Texas, 35 mi/56 km NNE of Houston, on Peach Creek; 30°13′N 95°09′W. Located in timber region. Mfg. (lumber processing; ornamental fences). Sam Houston Natl. Forest to N.

Split, Cape, on S side of Minas Channel, NW N.S., E Canada, at entrance to Minas Basin, 18 mi/29 km N of Kentville; 45°20′N 64°29′W.

Split Lake, N Man., central Canada, on Nelson R.; 34 mi/55 km long, 10 mi/16 km wide; 56°10′N 96°W.

Split Peak (9,601 ft/2,926 m), SE B.C., W Canada, near Alta. border, in Rocky Mts., on SE edge of Kootenay Natl. Park, 25 mi/40 km SW of Banff; 50°53′N 115°56′W.

Split Rock Reservoir (☐ 1 sq mi/2.6 sq km), Morris co., N N.J., on Beaver Brook, 5 mi/8 km W of Pompton Lakes; 40°58′N 74°28′W. Max. capacity 9,517 acre-ft. Formed by Split Rock Pond Dam (39 ft/12 m), built (1948) for water supply; owned by Jersey City Dept. of Water. Farney State Park on W shore.

Spofford, village (1990 pop. 68), Kinney co., SW Texas, 31 mi/50 km ESE of Del Rio; 29°10′N 100°24′W. RR junction in ranching area (sheep, goats, cattle).

Spofford Lake (SPAW-fuhrd), Cheshire co., SW N.H., resort lake in Chesterfield, 8 mi/12.9 km W of Keene; 2 mi/3.2 km long.

Spokane (spo-KAN), county (☐ 1,780 sq mi/4,610 sq km; 1990 pop. 361,364), E Wash., on Idaho (E) state line; ⊙ SPOKANE; 47°40′N 117°25′W. Drained by Spokane R. (forms Long L. reservoir in NW). Timber; lettuce, alfalfa, hay, barley, oats; dairying; sheep, hogs; gypsum, limestone. Mt. Spokane (5,851 ft/1,783 m) State Park and Ski Area, in NE; Turnbull Natl. Wildlife Refuge in SW. Fairchild Air Force Base in W. Formed 1858.

Spokane (spo-KAN), city (1990 pop. 177,196), ⊙ Spokane co., E Wash., 280 mi/448 km E of Seattle, at the spectacular falls of the Spokane R. It is a port of entry and the commercial, transportation, and industrial center of a productive region known as the Inland Empire, comprising E Wash., N Idaho, W Mont., NE Oregon, and S B.C. (Canada). The irrigated farms of the Columbia basin project contribute to the city's prosperity. The area has mineral deposits (tungsten, clay, magnesium, uranium) and cattle ranches and yields wheat, dairying, and other farm prods. Mfg. (bldg. materials, electrical and electronic goods, transportation equip., canvas prods., machinery, food and beverages, chemicals, lumber, plastics, wood prods., lumber, computers, paper, fabricated metal prods., feeds, millwork, aluminum, consumer goods, concrete prods.; meat processing, printing and publishing). Spokane Raceway Park and Spokane Polo Club to W; Playfair Race Track E of downtown. Spokane Interstate Fairgrounds E of city. Cowles Mus., of Eastern Wash. Historical Society; Spokane Valley Pioneer Mus. John A. Finch Arboretum. Spokane Internatl. Airport and Air Natl. Guard Facility SW of city. A trading fort was est. here in 1810; settlement began in 1871. In 1889 a great fire destroyed most of the town, but it was rapidly rebuilt. Spokane is a focus of cultural and educational activities and also has several parks. Seat of Gonzaga Univ., Whitworth Col. (at Country Homes, to N), Fort Wright Col., and Spokane and Spokane Falls community cols. Riverside State Park to NW, on Spokane R.; Mt. Spokane State Park and Ski Area to NE. Spokane is a gateway to 2 natl. forests, recreational areas, numerous lakes, and several nearby resorts. The city hosted the EXPO '74. The large Fairchild Air Force Base contributes significantly to the economy (c.5,000 jobs). Inc. 1881.

Spokane, Mount (spo-KAN) (5,851 ft/1,783 m), Spokane co., E Wash., peak c.25 mi/40 km NE of Spokane; 47°55′N 117°06′W. Mt. Spokane Ski Resort and State Park here. Road to summit from SW.

Spokane River, c.100 mi/161 km long, Idaho and Wash.; rises in Coeur d'Alene L., at Coeur d'Alene, Kootenai co. (N Idaho); flows W into Spokane co. (NE Wash.), continues W past Millwood, through city of Spokane, then NW, receiving Little Spokane R. from NE, and W through Long L. reservoir and dam and Little Falls Dam; entering Columbia R. 45 mi/72 km WNW of Spokane. Farming, lumbering, and fishing are important in the valley.

Spoon River, c.160 mi/257 km long, NW central Ill.; rises in SW Bureau co.; meanders S, SW, and SE, to Illinois R. opposite Havana; 41°08′N 89°46′W. Celebrated in Edgar Lee Masters' *Spoon River Anthology.*

Spooner, town (1990 pop. 2,464), Washburn, co., NW Wis., on Yellow R., and 60 mi/97 km S of Superior; 45°49′N 91°53′W. In woods and lake region. RR junction; trade and shipping center for farming and dairying area; mfg. (explosives, light mfg.). Spooner State Fish Hatchery and agr. research station are nearby; Nest of Eagles Ski Area to E; Namekagon R. branch of St. Croix Natl. Scenic Riverway to N; Spooner L. to E. Settled c.1883, inc. 1909.

Sportsman Acres, village (1990 pop. 181), Mayes co., NE Okla., 5 mi/8 km SE of Pryor; 36°15′N 95°15′W. Residential and recreational community on Neosho R., on upper reach of Fort Gibson L. reservoir.

Spotswood, borough (1990 pop. 7,983), Middlesex co., E N.J., 8 mi/12.9 km SE of New Brunswick; 40°23′N 74°23′W. In rapidly suburbanizing area. Site of Revolutionary ironworks. Inc. 1908.

Spotsylvania, county (□ 412 sq mi/1,067 sq km; 1990 pop. 57,403), NE Va.; ⊙ Spotsylvania (independent city of Fredericksburg in N, separate from co.); 38°10′N 77°39′W. Bounded NE by Rappahannock and Rapidan rivers, on S by North Anna R. (forms L. Anna reservoir); drained by Mattaponi R. Agr. (soybeans, wheat, corn, hay, alfalfa, barley; cattle; dairying). Formerly part of estate of Alexander Spotswood, Va. colonial governor. Scene of several major Civil War engagements, including Battles of the Wilderness, Chancellorsville, and Spotsylvania Courthouse; sites now part of Fredericksburg-Spotsylvania Memorial Natl. Park; L. Anna state Park in SW. Formed 1720.

Spotsylvania, uninc. town (1990 pop. 2,694), ⊙ Spotsylvania co., NE Va., 10 mi/16 km SW of Fredericksburg; 38°12′N 77°35′W. Mfg. (lumber, wine). Site (then called Spotsylvania Courthouse) of indecisive Civil War engagement (May 1864). Battleground is now a unit of Fredericksburg Spotsylvania Co. Memorial Natl. Military Park. L. Anna State Park on L. Anna reservoir to SW.

Spotted Islands, island and settlement, just off SE Lab., E Canada; 4 mi/6 km long, 4 mi/6 km wide; 53°28′N 55°47′W. Fishing port and seaplane anchorage.

Sprague 1 (SPRAIG), town (1990 pop. 3,008), New London co., E Conn., on Shetucket R., and 6 mi/9.7 km N of Norwich; 41°37′N 72°04′W. Mfg. includes lithographing and engraving; agr. Includes mfg. villages of Baltic, Hanover, and Versailles. Inc. 1861. **2** uninc. town (1990 pop. 2,090), Raleigh co., S W.Va., suburb, 1 mi/1.6 km N of Beckley. Coal-mining area.

Sprague 1 (SPRAIG), village (1990 pop. 157), Lancaster co., SE Nebr., 12 mi/19 km S of Lincoln, and on branch of Platte R.; 40°37′N 96°45′W. RR junction. Bluestem L. State Recreation Area to W. **2** village (1990 pop. 410), Lincoln co., E Wash., 35 mi/56 km SW of Spokane; 47°18′N 117°58′W. In Columbia basin agr. region; wheat, hay, oats, barley, alfalfa. Sprague L. (formerly Colville L.) to SW, 6 mi/9.7 km long, is recreational area.

Sprague River (SPRAIG), c.75 mi/121 km long, SE Klamath co., S Oregon; formed in Cascade Range 35 mi/56 km ENE of Klamath Falls, at confluence of North and South Forks (both of which are c.30 mi/48 km long); flows W to join Williamson R., at Chiloquin, which flows S into Upper Klamath L.

Spragueville, town (1990 pop. 118), Jackson co., E Iowa, 12 mi/19 km E of Maquoketa; 42°04′N 90°25′W.

Spragueville, village, in Smithfield town, Providence co., N central R.I., 8 mi/12.9 km NW of Providence.

Spranger, Mount (9,920 ft/3,024 m), E B.C., W Canada, in Cariboo Mts., 75 mi/121 km E of Quesnel; 52°54′N 120°44′W.

Spray 1 uninc. village, Rockingham co., N N.C., adjacent to Leaksville, 12 mi/19 km NNW of Reidsville, near Va. state line. Merged with Leaksville, 1 mi/1.6 km SW, during late 1960s (1960 pop. 4,565). **2** village (1990 pop. 149), Wheeler co., N central Oregon, 35 mi/56 km SSW of Heppmer, on John Day R.; 44°49′N 119°47′W. Part of Umatilla Natl. Forest to NE.

Spreckels, uninc. village, Monterey co., W Calif., suburb, 3 mi/4.8 km S of Salinas on Salinas R.; a "company town" for large beet-sugar refinery. Terminus of RR spur from Salinas.

Spreckelsville, village, N Maui, Maui co., Hawaii, on N coast 4 mi/6.4 km ENE of Kahului. Named after Claus Spreckles, 19th-cent. sugar tycoon. Kahului Airport to SW; H. P. Baldwin Beach Park to E.

Spring, uninc. city (1990 pop. 33,111), Harris co., SE Texas, suburb 26 mi/42 km N of downtown Houston, near Spring Creek; 30°03′N 95°22′W. RR junction. Mfg. (fiberglass prods., hardware; biotechnology). Houston Intercontinental Airport to SE.

Spring Arbor, village (1990 pop. 2,010), Jackson co., S Mich., 11 mi/18 km WSW of Jackson; 42°12′N 84°33′W. Spring Arbor Col. Mfg. (molds, fasteners, machinery).

Spring Bay, village (1990 pop. 439), Woodford co., central Ill., on L. Peoria (widening of Illinois R.), 10 mi/16 km NNE of Peoria; 40°49′N 89°31′W. In agr. area.

Spring Brook, village (1990 pop. 29), Williams co., W N. Dak.,11 mi/18 km NE of Williston; 48°15′N 103°27′W.

Spring City, town (1990 pop. 2,199), Rhea co., E Tenn., at head of arm of Watts Bar Reservoir, 50 mi/80 km NE of Chattanooga, in Tennessee valley, 35°42′N 84°52′W. Mfg. of textiles; lumbering.

Spring City, borough (1990 pop. 3,433), Chester co., SE Pa., 26 mi/42 km NW of downtown Philadelphia, on Schuylkill R.; 40°10′N 75°32′W. Agr. area (grain, apples, vegetables; poultry, livestock; dairying; nursery crops). Mfg. (fiberglass prods., hydraulic components, concrete prods., dairy prods., apparel, fabricated metal prods.). Inc. 1867 as Springville; renamed 1872.

Spring City, village (1990 pop. 715), Sanpete co., central Utah, 17 mi/27 km NNE of Manti; 39°28′N 111°29′W. Elev. 5,826 ft/1,776 m. In irrigated agr. area. Settled 1852, originally named Canal. Manti–La Sal Natl. Forest to E.

Spring Creek, uninc. town (1990 pop. 5,866), Elko co., N central Nev., 9 mi/14.5 km SE of Elko; 40°44′N 115°35′W. Cattle, sheep; tourism. South Fork Indian Reservation to S; part of Humboldt Natl. Forest to SE, including Ruby Mt. Scenic Area.

Spring Creek 1 c.75 mi/121 km long, SW Ga.; rises W of Edison; flows S, past Colquitt, to Flint R. near its junction with the Chattahoochee R. at the Fla. state line. **2** c.40 mi/64 km long, in E Ill.; rises N of Paxton; flows generally NNE to Iroquois R. 6 mi/9.7 km NW of Watseka; 40°28′N 88°01′W. **3** c.60 mi/97 km long, W central N.Dak.; rises in Dunn co.; flows E through L. Ilo Natl. Wildlife Refuge, past Golden Valley and Zap, to Knife R. near Beulah; 47°24′N 102°57′W.

Spring Garden, uninc. rural community, Miller co., central Mo., near Osage R. 6 mi/9.7 km ESE of Olean. Dairying; cattle, poultry.

Spring Glen, resort village (1990 pop. 650), Ulster co., SE N.Y., near W base of the Shawangunk range, 4 mi/6.4 km SSW of Ellenville; 41°40′N 74°26′W.

Spring Green, town (1990 pop. 1,283), Sauk co., S central Wis., 32 mi/51 km WNW of Madison, on Wisconsin R.; 43°10′N 90°04′W. Tower Hill State Park to S. Frank Lloyd Wright's home, Taliesin, to S. Wintergreen Ski Area to SW. Dairying; poultry; soybeans, grain, vegetables. Mfg. (glass prods., electronic equip., furniture, wire harnesses).

Spring Grove 1 town (1990 pop. 420), Wayne co., E Ind., suburb, c.1 mi/1.6 km N of downtown Richmond. **2** town (1990 pop. 1,153), Houston co., extreme SE Minn., 25 mi/40 km SW of La Crosse Wis., near Iowa state line; 43°33′N 91°38′W. Grain, soybeans; livestock, poultry; dairying. Mfg. (fertilizers, consumer goods, hardwood timber, crushed limestone). Richard J. Dorer Memorial Hardwood State Forest to N and E.

Spring Grove, village (1990 pop. 1,066), McHenry co., NE Ill., near Fox L., 20 mi/32 km WNW of Waukegan; 42°26′N 88°14′W. In agr. and lake-resort area.

Spring Grove, borough (1990 pop. 1,863), York co., S Pa., 9 mi/14.5 km SW of York; 39°52′N 76°51′W. RR junction. Agr. area (grain, soybeans, apples; livestock, poultry; dairying); mfg. (pulp and paper). York Airport to N. L. Marburg reservoir and Codorus State Park to S. Laid out 1747, inc. 1882.

Spring Hill 1 town (1990 pop. 86), Warren co., S central Iowa, 5 mi/8 km NW of Indianola; 41°24′N 93°39′W. In agr. area. **2** town (1990 pop. 2,191), Johnson co., E Kansas, 25 mi/40 km SSW of Kansas City (Kansas); 38°45′N 94°49′W. Dairying; agr.; mfg. (glass, ordnance, feeds). Satellite community of Kansas City. Hillsdale L. Reservoir to SW. **3** uninc. town (1990 pop. 1,014), Portage township, Cambria co., W central Pa., 15 mi/24 km ENE of Johnstown, and 1 mi/1.6 km S and W of Portage, near Little Conemaugh R.; 40°22′N 78°40′W. **4** town (1990 pop. 1,464), Maury and Williamson cos., central Tenn., 28 mi/45 km SSW of Nashville, 35°45′N 86°56′W. In timber, livestock, farm area, boosted economicaly by motor-vehicle mfg. plant.

Spring Hill 1 village (1990 pop. 86), Warren co., S central Iowa, 11 mi/18 km S of Des Moines, on Middle R. Cattle; corn. **2** village (1990 pop. 77), Stearns co., central Minn., 33 mi/53 km W of St. Cloud; 45°31′N 94°49′W. Grain; livestock. George L. to W.

Spring Hill, uninc. residential W suburb of Mobile, Ala. Spring Hill Col. is here.

Spring Hope, town (1990 pop. 1,221), Nash co., NE central N.C., 17 mi/27 km W of Rocky Mount, near Tar R.; 35°56′N 78°06′W. RR terminus. In agr. area (cotton, tobacco, peanuts, grain, sweet potatoes; chickens, cattle, hogs). Mfg. (insulation, textiles, fiberboard, apparel, cable assemblies; meat processing, metal fabricating). Settled 1886; inc. 1989.

Spring House, uninc. town (1990 pop. 2,782), Montgomery co., SE Pa., suburb, 16 mi/26 km N of Philadelphia; 40°10′N 75°13′W. Mfg. includes industrial controls, book publishing; chemicals. Seat of Gwynedd Mercere Col.

Spring Lake 1 town, Hancock co., Ind., on Sugar Creek, and 4 mi/6.4 km W of Greenfield. Suburb of Indianapolis. Agr. area. Settled 1884, laid out 1912. **2** town (1990 pop. 2,537), Ottawa co., SW Mich., suburb 1 mi/1.6 km NE of Grand Haven, across bridge over Spring L. from Ferrysburg, and 12 mi/19 km SSE of Muskegon, at mouth of Grand R. on Spring L. (c.3 mi/4.8 km long; drains SW through short outlet of L. Michigan); 43°04′N 86°11′W. Resort and shipping point for orchard (apples) and farm area (poultry); mfg. (furniture, marine instruments, display cases, metal prods.). Native Amer. mounds nearby. Inc. 1869. **3** town (1990 pop. 7,524), Cumberland co., S central N.C., suburb, 8 mi/12.9 km NNW of downtown Fayetteville, near Little R.; 35°10′N 78°58′W. Service center for Fort Bragg Military Reserve, to E, S and W, and Pope Air Force Base to W. Mfg. (wood prods., consumer goods).

Spring Lake, borough (1990 pop. 3,499), Monmouth co., E N.J., near the Atlantic Ocean, 5 mi/8 km S of Asbury Park; 40°06′N 74°00′W. Upscale residential community. Small lakes nearby. St. Catharines R.C. Church here was built by Margaret and Martin Maloney as a tribute to their 16-year-old daughter Catharine Maloney, who died of T.B. in 1900 (all 3 buried in the church). The church is an example of Roman Renaissance and baroque architecture modeled after the Santa Marie del Popolo in Rome. Inc. 1892.

Spring Lake Heights, borough (1990 pop. 5,341), Monmouth co., E N.J., just W of Spring Lake; 40°08′N 74°01′W. Inc. 1927.

Spring Mill, uninc. village, Montgomery co., SE Pa., suburb 11 mi/18 km NW of downtown Philadelphia, and 2 mi/3.2 km E of Conshohocken, on Schuylkill R.; 40°04′N 75°16′W.

Spring Mill State Park, Ind.: see MITCHELL.

Spring Mills, uninc. village, Gregg township, Centre co., central Pa., 16 mi/26 km ENE of State College, on Penns Creek; 40°51′N 77°34′W. Mfg. (medical supplies); logging. Penns Cave to NW.

Spring Mount, uninc. town (1990 pop. 1,365), Montgomery co., SE Pa., 10 mi/16 km ENE of Pottstown, on Perkiomen Creek; 40°16′N 75°28′W. Light mfg. Agr. includes dairying; livestock, poultry; grain, apples, nursery stock.

Spring Mountains, SE Nev., in W Clark co., near Calif. state line, in Nevada Natl. Forest. Gold, silver, platinum, vanadium deposits; tourism. Rises to 11,910 ft/3,630 m in Charleston Peak, 32 mi/51 km W of Las Vegas.

Spring Park, town (1990 pop. 1,571), Hennepin co., E Minn., 17 mi/27 km WSW of downtown Minneapolis, on neck of land bet. West Arm (N) and Spring Park Bay (S) of L. Minnetonka; 44°56′N 93°37′W. Mfg. (custom bottling; foods).

Spring Place, town, Murray co., NW Ga., 8 mi/12.9 km E of Dalton; 34°45′N 84°49′W.

Spring River 1 c.100 mi/161 km long, S Mo. and N Ark.; rises in Howell and Oregon cos.; flows S and SE through Ozark Mts. to Black R. above Black Rock (Ark.). At Mammoth Spring (Ark.), receives flow of large springs. **2** 120 mi/193 km long, in Mo., Kansas, and Okla.; rises in the Ozark Mts. in Lawrence co., Mo.; flows W into SE Kansas, then S to Grand L. of the Cherokees E of Miami, Okla.

Spring Valley 1 uninc. city (1990 pop. 55,331), San Diego co., SW Calif., residential suburb, 10 mi/16 km ENE of downtown San Diego; 32°43′N 117°00′W. It is a rapidly growing residential community, with some light industrial production (transportation equip., paper prods., fabricated metal prods.). The Bancroft Ranch House Mus. (1856) is a natl. historic landmark. Sweetwater Reservoir to S. **2** city (1990 pop. 5,246), Bureau co., N Ill., on Illinois R. (bridged here), 15 mi/24 km WNW of Peru; 41°19′N 89°12′W. In agr. and mineral area (sand, gravel). Inc. 1886. **3** uninc. city (1990 pop. 51,726), Clark co., SE Nev., residential suburb, 6 mi/9.7 km WSW of downtown Las Vegas; 36°06′N 115°14′W.

Spring Valley 1 town (1990 pop. 2,461), Fillmore co., SE Minn., 23 mi/37 km S of Rochester, on Spring Valley Creek; 43°41′N 92°23′W. Trade center for agr. area (dairying; poultry; grain, soybeans); mfg. (cheese; printing and publishing). Richard J. Dorer Memorial Hardwood State Forest to E; Forestville Mystery Cave State Park to E, area noted for its karst topography. Settled 1855, inc. 1856. **2** town (1990 pop. 3,392), Harris co., SE Texas, residential suburb, 9 mi/14.5 km WNW of downtown Houston; 29°47′N 95°30′W. Surrounded by city of Houston. **3** uninc. town, Wayne co., W W.Va., residential suburb, 4 mi/6.4 km WSW of downtown Huntington. Veterans Administration Medical Center. **4** town (1990 pop. 1,051), Pierce co., W Wis., on Eau Galle R., below Eau Galle Dam (Army Corps of Engineering Recreation Area), 14 mi/23 km WSW of Menominie; 44°51′N 92°14′W. In dairying, poultry-raising, and lumbering area; light mfg. Crystal Cave State Trail.

Spring Valley 1 residential village (□ 2 sq mi/5.2 sq km; 1990 pop. 21,802), Rockland co., SE N.Y., near the N.J. state line; 41°06′N 74°02′W. Fast-growing suburb with office complexes and shopping malls. Inc. 1902. **2** village (1990 pop. 507), Greene co., S central Ohio, 6 mi/10 km SW of Xenia; 39°37′N 84°00′W. In fruit and farming area; mineral water bottled here.

Springboro, city (1990 pop. 6,590), Warren co., SW Ohio, 14 mi/23 km S of Dayton; 39°34′N 84°14′W.

Springboro (SPRING-buhr-o), borough (1990 pop. 471), Crawford co., NW Pa., 27 mi/43 km SW of Erie; 41°48′N 80°22′W. Agr. (corn, hay; livestock; dairying); mfg. (tool forgings; sand and gravel processing).

Springbrook, town (1990 pop. 116), Jackson co., E Iowa, 13 mi/21 km ENE of Maquoketa; 42°10′N 90°28′W. In agr. area.

Springdale, city (1990 pop. 29,941), Washington and Benton cos., NW Ark., 55 mi/89 km NNE of Fort Smith, 10 mi/16 km S of Rogers, and 10 mi/16 km N of Fayetteville; 36°10′N 94°09′W. Poultry-processing center. Mfg. (vegetable canning, printing; air-conditioning ducts, fabricated metal prods., carbide rock bits, machinery, hand tools, transportation equip., recycling containers, paper prods., textiles). There is also varied light mfg. The surrounding Ozark Mts. draw many tourists. An annual rodeo is held here. North Ark. Vocational Technical School. Small unit of Ozark Natl. Forest to W. Inc. 1878.

Springdale 1 town (1990 pop. 1,010), Jefferson co., N Ky., residential suburb, 8 mi/12.9 km ENE of downtown Louisville. **2** uninc. town (1990 pop. 2,643), Lancaster co., N S.C., 3 mi/4.8 km W of Lancaster; near Catawba R.; 34°41′N 80°47′W. Textile milling. **3** town (1990 pop. 3,226), Lexington co., central S.C., residential suburb, 4 mi/6.4 km SW of downtown Columbia; 33°57′N 81°06′W. Columbia Municipal Airport to S.

Springdale, borough (1990 pop. 3,992), Allegheny co., W central Pa., suburb, 13 mi/21 km NE of downtown Pittsburgh, on Allegheny R.; 40°32′N 79°46′W. Agr. area (dairying); mfg. (bldg. materials, chemicals, plastic prods., fabricated metal prods.). Inc. 1906.

Springdale 1 village (1990 pop. 275), Washington co., SW Utah, 33 mi/53 km E of St. George; 37°10′N 113°00′W. Elev. 3,800 ft/1,158 m. W gateway to Zion Natl. Park. Tourism. Settled 1862. East and North Forks Virgin R. join here to form Virgin R. **2** village (1990 pop. 260), Stevens co., NE Wash., 32 mi/51 km NNW of Spokane, and on Sheep Creek (headstream of Colville R.); 48°04′N 117°45′W. Dairying; hay, potatoes; lumber. Loon L. reservoir to E; Spokane Indian Reservation to SW.

Springer, town (1990 pop. 1,262), Colfax co., NE N.Mex., Cimarron R., near its confluence with Canadian R. (smaller of 2 Cimarron rivers in region; source of Cimarron R. c.50 mi/80 km to NE), near Sangre de Cristo Mts., and 39 mi/63 km SSW of Raton; 36°22′N 104°35′W. Elev. 5,832 ft/1,778 m. Trade center and shipping point in sheep and cattle region; agr. (alfalfa, grain). Miami L. Reservoir to W; sects. of Kiowa Natl. Grasslands to SE. Inc. 1910.

Springer, village (1990 pop. 485), Carter co., S Okla., 10 mi/16 km N of Ardmore; 34°17′N 97°07′W. In agr. and livestock-raising area; mfg. (trailers). Arbuckle Mts. to NW; Chickasaw Natl. Recreation Area on Arbuckle Reservoir, to NE.

Springer Mountain (3,820 ft/1,164 m), N Ga., the southernmost peak of the Blue Ridge Mts. and the S terminus of the Appalachian Trail; 34°37′N 84°11′W.

Springerton, village (1990 pop. 166), White co., SE Ill., 12 mi/19 km NW of Carmi; 38°10′N 88°20′W. In agr. area.

Springerville, town (1990 pop. 1,802), Apache co., E Ariz., on Little Colorado R., and 25 mi/40 km S of St. Johns, and 2 mi/3.2 km N of Eager; 34°09′N 109°17′W. Elev. 6,965 ft/2,123 m. Cattle, sheep, poultry; sorghum, hay; timber. Apache-Sitgreaves Natl. Forest to S, Lyman L. State Park to N.

Springetts Manor-Yorklyn (SPRING-gets), uninc. residential suburb (1990 pop. 3,433), York co., S Pa., 3 mi/4.8 km NE of York; 39°59′N 76°39′W.

Springfield, village (1991 pop. 627), S Ont., central Canada, 14 mi/23 km ENE of St. Thomas; 44°38′N 64°51′W. Dairying; farming, fruit growing.

Springfield 1 city (1990 pop. 105,227), ⊙ Sangamon co. and of Ill., central Ill., on the Sangamon R.; 39°46′N 89°38′W. Paddlewheel boats once brought commerce up Sangamon R. In a rich agr. region, it is a wholesale trade, retail, and distribution center. Agr. (sorghum, corn; cattle; dairying). Mfg. (consumer goods, flour, transportation equip., parking meters, bldg. materials, machinery, electrical and electronic prods.; book publishing). Oil and natural-gas field to S. Abraham Lincoln, who was instrumental in having Springfield made the state capital in 1839, lived and practiced law here from 1837 to 1861. He is buried nearby, with his wife and 3 of their children, in a tomb and monument designed by L. G. Mead and dedicated in 1874. Lincoln's home is preserved as a natl. historic site. Other places of interest include the capitol (1867–1887), built in the Renaissance style; the old capitol (1837), where Lincoln made his "House Divided" speech and which contains the state historical lib.; several Lincoln mus., including the Depot Mus., where Lincoln made his farewell address (1861); the governor's mansion (1853–1857); the state art gallery; and the state fairgrounds. Vachel Lindsay b. here; his house is a mus. Seat of Springfield Col. in Illinois, Sangamon State Univ., a theological seminary, and Lincoln Land Community Col. Nearby are Lincoln's New Salem Historic Site, Camp Butler Natl. Cemetery, and L. Springfield (S). Convention center here. Settled 1818, inc. as a city 1840. **2** industrial city (□ 33 sq mi/85 sq km; 1990 pop. 156,983), ⊙ Hampden co., SW Mass., on the Connecticut R.; 42°07′N 72°32′W. Mass.' 3d-largest city and major business center of W Mass. Port of entry. Has significant printing and publishing industries. Mfg. includes ordnance, chemicals, plastics, machinery, electrical equip., paper and metallurgical goods, and clothing. Settled (1636) by Puritans under William Pynchon, and was one of the scenes in Shays' Rebellion (1786–1787) and a station on the Underground RR. Site of the 1st U.S. automobile production company (1896). The U.S. Armory, which operated here from 1794 to 1966, was famous for the development of the Springfield and the Garand army rifles; it now contains an arms mus., a natl. historic site. The 1st U.S.-made projection planetarium was designed and built (1937) by Frank Korkosz for the city's science mus., which also contains an aquarium. Saint-Gaudens's *Puritan* is in Merrick Park. Also in the city are Forest Park (which has a zoo) and several additional mus. Seat of Springfield Col. (with a Basketball Hall of Fame tracing the game's development since its invention here in 1891 by Dr. James Naismith), Amer. Internatl. Col., West New England Col., and a technical col. Includes village of Indian Orchard. Inc. 1641. **3** city (1990 pop. 140,494), ⊙ Greene co., SW Mo., in the Ozark Mts.; 37°12′N 93°17′W. It is the industrial, trade, service and shipping center of a large agr. area producing dairy prods., livestock, poultry; grains, and fruit. Mfg. (fabricated metal prods., transportation equip., foods, machinery, electronics prods., wood prods., apparel, motor vehicles, machinery, paper prods., feeds, artificial flowers; printing). Site of last television factory in U.S. (closed in 1995; moved to Mexico). Seat of Drury Col., Southwest Mo. State Univ., Evangel Col. and Baptist Bible and Central Bible cols. Internatl. hq. for the Assemblies of God church. In the Civil War, Springfield was taken by Confederate forces after the local battle (1861) of Wilson's Creek;

nearby are the battlefield and a natl. cemetery for both Confederate and Union soldiers. "Wild Bill" Hickok lived here. Major tourist center and "Gateway to Ozarks." Sport fishing area (bass, crappie, catfish, trout) of streams and large lakes to N and S. Bass Pro Shop attracts tourists and fishermen and produces programs on sport fishing. Dept. of Justice Medical Center houses Federal prisoners requiring hospitalization. Municipal airport to NW. Annual Ozark Empire Fair. Settled 1830, inc. 1846. **4** city (1990 pop. 70,487), ⊙ Clark co., W central Ohio, on the Mad R.; 39°55′N 83°48′W. A mfg. center in a rich farm area, it is esp. known for its production of farm machinery and truck mfg. Other goods made are machinery, tools, and a variety of metal (iron and steel) prods. The city grew with the building of the Natl. Road (1838), the arrival of the RRs (mid-1800s), and the establishment of farm-machinery plants (late 1800s). Wittenberg Univ. and a technical col. are here. Nearby is George Rogers Clark Park. Settled 1799, inc. as a city 1850. **5** city (1990 pop. 44,683), Lane co., W central Oregon, 65 mi/105 km S of Salem, on Willamette R., and immediately E of twin city of Eugene; 44°02′N 122°58′W. Near the forested foothills of the Cascade Range. Bounded N by McKenzie R. Confluence of Middle and Coast forks of Willamette R. to S. RR junction. Agr. (berries, hazelnuts, filberts; poultry); dairy prods. Nurseries. Mfg. (smoked fish, lumber, millwork, plywood, veneer, chemicals, silicon metal alloy). Fish hatchery to E, on McKenzie R. Nearby are Armitage (N), Hendricks Bridge (E), and Elijah Bristow (SE) state parks; Willamette Natl. Forest to E. Inc. 1885. **6** city (1990 pop. 11,227), ⊙ Robertson co., N Tenn., suburb, 24 mi/39 km N of Nashville, 36°31′N 86°53′W. In tobacco, timber area; an important tobacco market; mfg. of wood prods., textiles, fabricated steel; flour milling; stone quarries. Founded c.1798. **7** uninc. city (1990 pop. 23,706), Fairfax co., NE Va., suburb, 8 mi/12.9 km WSW of Alexandria, 12 mi/19 km SW of Washington, D.C.; 38°47′N 77°10′W. Mfg. (foods, papare prods., transportation equip., concrete prods., medical equip., machinery, computers, furniture; steel fabrication, printing and publishing). It has grown extensively since the 1970s with the D.C. area. Ft. Belvoir Military Reservation to S. L. Accotink Park to NW.

Springfield 1 town (1990 pop. 1,475), ⊙ Baca co., SE Colo., 65 mi/105 km SE of La Junta; 37°24′N 102°37′W. Elev. 4,365 ft/1,330 m. RR junction. Cattle; wheat, barley, corn, sorghum. Two Buttes Reservoir and State Fishing L. to N; Comanche Natl. Forest to SW. Inc. 1889. **2** town (□ 4 sq mi/10.4 sq km; 1990 pop. 8,715), Bay co., NW Fla., suburb, 8 mi/12.9 km E of Panama City; 30°10′N 85°36′W. **3** town (1990 pop. 1,415), ⊙ Effingham co., E Ga., 24 mi/39 km NNW of Savannah; 32°22′N 81°19′W. Mfg of lumber and clothing. **4** town (1990 pop. 2,875), ⊙ Washington co., central Ky., 25 mi/40 km W of Danville; 37°41′N 85°13′W. Trade center for Bluegrass agr. region (livestock, poultry; dairying; burley tobacco, corn, wheat). Mfg. (dairy prods., apparel, wood prods., plastic prods., textiles; tobacco drying). Courthouse (1816) contains marriage certificate of Thomas Lincoln and Nancy Hanks (Abraham Lincoln's parents). Lincoln Homestead State Park to N, with reproduction of home (original 1782) of Lincoln's paternal grandmother and a memorial to Nancy Hanks; St. Rose Church and Priory (Dominican school founded 1806; attended 1816–1818 by Jefferson Davis; church built 1855); St. Catharine Col. (1931; 2-year); St. Catharine Convent (1820) to NW. Mt. Zion Covered Bridge to N; Lebanon-Springfield Airport to S. Founded 1793. **5** uninc. town (1990 pop. 439), Livingston parish, 7 mi/11.3 km SW of Hammond, on Natalbany R.; 30°25′N 90°33′W. One of shipping centers in La. history; possessed a fort during the Colonial period. In 1763 known as Bookter's Landing. **6** town (1990 pop. 406), Penobscot co., E central Maine, 50 mi/80 km NE of Bangor; 45°23′N 68°09′W. In hunting, fishing area. **7** town (1990 pop. 5,582), Calhoun co., S Mich., suburb, 2 mi/3.2 km W of downtown Battle Creek; 42°19′N 85°14′W. Surrounded by city, adjacent to Kalamazoo R. Mfg. (electrical equip., asphalt, furniture). W.K. Kellogg Regional Airport to S. Fort Custer State Park to SW. **8** town (1990 pop. 2,173), Brown co., SW Minn., 26 mi/42 km W of New Ulm, on Cottonwood R., E of mouth of Coal Mine Creek; 44°14′N 94°58′W. Trading point in agr. area; mfg. (machinery, fertilizers, feeds, butter; meat processing). Municipal Airport to SW. Boise L. to E. Plotted 1877, inc. as village 1881, as city 1923. **9** town (1990 pop. 788), Sullivan co., W N.H., 13 mi/21 km NE of Newport; 43°29′N 72°02′W. Mfg. (lumber); agr. (nursery crops, hay, corn, apples; poultry, cattle); timber. Gile State Forest in E. Several small ponds in town. **10** town (1990 pop. 834), Bon Homme co., SE S.Dak., 10 mi/16 km SSW of Tyndall, and on Missouri R. (Lewis & Clark L.); 42°51′N 53°97′W. State correction facility. Mfg. (rubber seals). Springfield State Recreation Area to NE. **11** town (1990 pop. 9,579), Windsor co., SE Vt., on Connecticut and Black rivers, and 25 mi/40 km S of Woodstock; 43°17′N 72°28′W. Mfg. (machinery, machine tools, computer components, metal prods., bldg. materials); agr. (dairy prods.). Winter sports. Settled before Amer. Revolution and chartered in 1761. Includes industrial Springfield village.

Springfield 1 village (1990 pop. 1,426), Sarpy co., E Nebr., 15 mi/24 km SW of Omaha, near Platte R.; 41°4′N 96°07′W. Grain; livestock. **2** village (1990 pop. 13,420), Union co., NE N.J., 7 mi/11.3 km W of Newark; 40°02′N 74°42′W. Mfg. (chemicals, laboratory equip., electronic prods., rubber goods). Largely residential. Settled c.1717. Church and several other bldgs. burned by British, 1780; Bret Harte's poem *Caldwell of Springfield* commemorates Chaplain James Caldwell's aid to defenders. Present church was built 1791. **3** village (1990 pop. 523), Orangeburg co., W central S.C., 24 mi/39 km W of Orangeburg; 33°30′N 81°16′W. Mfg. of wood prods. Agr. includes poultry, livestock; grain, peaches, pecans, cotton, peanuts, tobacco.

Springfield, township (1990 pop. 24,160), Delaware co., SE Pa., suburb, 9 mi/14.5 km WSW of Philadelphia, on Darby Creek; 39°55′N 75°20′W. Mfg. includes electronic equip., dairy prods.; light mfg.

Springfield Armory Historic Site, Springfield, Hampden co., W Mass. Large weapons mus. housed in former arsenal. Authorized 1974.

Springfield Gardens, a mostly residential section of SE Queens borough of N.Y. city, SE N.Y.; 40°40′N 73°45′W. Because of its proximity to JFK Internatl. Airport, area is the hq. of several air cargo companies. Pop. largely Afr.-Amer. and immigrant Caribbean.

Springfield, Lake, reservoir (□ 7 sq mi/18.1 sq km), Sangamon co., central Ill., on Sugar Creek, just S of Springfield; 39°46′N 89°36′W. Max. capacity 101,205 acre-ft. Formed by Spaulding Dam (48 ft/15 m high), built (1933) for water supply; also used for recreation. N end of reservoir in SE Springfield suburbs; Univ. of Ill. at Springfield on W bank, Henson Robinson Zoo on E bank.

Springhill, city (1990 pop. 5,668), Webster parish, NW La., near Ark. state line, 38 mi/61 km NE of Shreveport; 33°00′N 93°28′W. In agr. area (cotton, vegetables, sweet potatoes; dairying). Lumber, pulp, and paper milling, mfg. (tall oil, concrete, paper prods.). Inc. 1922. Bodcau State Wildlife Area to SW.

Springhill, town (1991 pop. 4,373), N N.S., E Canada; 45°39′N 64°03′W. In a region of mixed farming, lumbering, mfg. (plastic prods.), it was formerly an active coal-mining center. Site of major coal mine disaster in 1958; closed mines for good. Town has begun tapping geothermal heat from water-filled mine shafts.

Springlee, village (1990 pop. 451), Jefferson co., N Ky., residential suburb, 6 mi/9.7 km E of downtown Louisville; 38°14′N 85°38′W. Bowman Field Airport to SW.

Springport, town (1990 pop. 194), Henry co., E Ind., 8 mi/12.9 km N of New Castle; 40°03′N 85°23′W. In agr. area.

Springport, village (1990 pop. 707), Jackson co., S Mich., 17 mi/27 km NW of Jackson; 42°22′N 84°42′W. In agr. area; mfg. of metal stampings.

Springtown, town (1990 pop. 1,740), Parker co., N central Texas, 25 mi/40 km NW of Fort Worth; 32°58′N 97°40′W. A satellite community of Dallas–Fort Worth urbanized area. Agr. (cattle, horses; peaches, pecans, peanuts). Oil and natural gas. Mfg. (natural gas processing).

Springtown, village, Benton co., extreme NW Ark., 20 mi/32 km NW of Fayetteville, in the Ozark Mts. Unit of Ozark Natl. Forest to S.

Springvale, town, Randolph co., SW Ga., 6 mi/9.7 km NW of Cuthbert; 31°49′N 84°52′W.

Springvale, Maine: see SANFORD.

Springview, village (1990 pop. 304), ⊙ Keya Paha co., N Nebr., 20 mi/32 km N of Ainsworth, near S.Dak. state line, and near Nebraska R.; 42°49′N 99°45′W. Trade center; grain; livestock; dairy and poultry prods.

Springville, city (1990 pop. 13,950), Utah co., N central Utah, suburb 5 mi/8 km SSE of Provo, on Hobble Creek, near Utah L.; 40°09′N 111°36′W. Elev. 4,563 ft/1,391 m. RR junction. Fruit-shipping point in agr. area (sugar beets, fruit; cattle, sheep) irrigated by water from Strawberry R.; dairying. Mfg. (transportation equip., foods, wood prods., fabricated metal prods). Settled 1849 by Mormons. Has Springville Mus. of Art presenting work by Utah artists. Fish hatcheries nearby. Uinta Natl. Forest to E. Spanish Fork Airport to SW.

Springville 1 town (1990 pop. 1,910), St. Clair co., N central Ala., 13 mi/21 km WSW of Ashville. Mfg. of truck trailers. **2** town (1990 pop. 1,068), Linn co., E Iowa, 12 mi/19 km ENE of Cedar Rapids; 42°03′N 91°26′W.

Springville 1 village, Lawrence co., S Ind., 9 mi/14.5 km NW of Bedford. Limestone quarries. Mfg. (plastic prods., crushed stone, agr. lime, asphalt prods.). Laid out 1832. **2** village (□ 3 sq mi/7.8 sq km; 1990 pop. 4,310), Erie co., W N.Y., 28 mi/45 km SSE of Buffalo; 42°30′N 78°40′W. Mfg. (lightning protection devices, plastic prods., machine parts, machinery); lumbering. Dairy and poultry farms. Settled 1807, inc. 1834.

Springwater, village (1990 pop. 650), Livingston co., W central N.Y., 22 mi/35 km N of Hornell; 42°37′N 77°34′W.

Sproat Lake (□ 19 sq mi/49 sq km), SW B.C., W Canada, on S central Vancouver Isl., 5 mi/8 km W of Port Alberni; 14 mi/23 km long, 1 mi/2 km wide; 49°16′N 125°03′W. Fishing.

Spruce Creek, uninc. village, Huntingdon co., central Pa., 7 mi/11.3 km SE of Tyrone, on Little Juniata R., at mouth of Spruce Creek; 40°36′N 78°08′W. Rothrock State Forest to E, Indian Caverns to NE.

Spruce Island, S Alaska, in Gulf of Alaska, 6 mi/9.7 km N of Kodiak Isl.; 6 mi/9.7 km long, 2 mi/3.2 km–3 mi/4.8 km wide; 57°55′N 152°26′W. Fishing, canning. Inhabitants primarily Russian and Aleut; settled by Russians c.1800. Uzinki village in W.

Spruce Knob, peak (4,861 ft/1,482 m) of the Allegheny Mts., in W Pendleton co., E W.Va., 23 mi/37 km SE of Elkins, in Monongahela Natl. Forest; 38°41′N 79°31′W. Highest point in W.Va. Big Spruce Knob (4,673 ft/1,424 m), is SW, in Pocahontas co.

Spruce Mountain 1 Nev.: see PEQUOP MOUNTAINS. **2** W.Va.: see BIG SPRUCE KNOB.

Spruce Pine, town (1990 pop. 2,010), Mitchell co., W N.C., 35 mi/56 km NE of Asheville, in the Blue Ridge Mts.; 35°55′N 82°04′W. Mica, flint, kaolin, feldspar mines. Mfg. (wood prods., concrete, industrial minerals, apparel, ceramic prods., wood and gas stoves; quartz and feldspar processing, insulating material fabricating, motor vehicle assembly). Settled c.1908.

Spruce Run Reservoir (□ 2 sq mi/5.2 sq km), Hunterdon co., NW N.J., on Spruce Run R., 15 mi/24 km E of Easton (Pa.); 40°39′N 74°55′W. Max. capacity 33,670 acre-ft. Formed by Spruce Run Reservoir Dam (93 ft/28 m high), built (1964) for water supply. Spruce Run State Recreational Area just N.

Spry (SPREI), uninc. town (1990 pop. 4,271), York co., S Pa., residential suburb, 4 mi/6.4 km SSE of York; 39°54′N 76°41′W.

Spur, town (1990 pop. 1,300), Dickens co., NW Texas, on plains just below Caprock escarpment, c.55 mi/89 km

E of Lubbock; 33°28′N 100°50′W. Market, shipping, processing point for cattle ranching and goat ranching and agr. area (cotton. peanuts). Has state agr. experiment station. Hq. for large Spur Ranch, which once included this site. Settled 1909, inc. 1911.

Spurgeon 1 (SPUHR-jen), town (1990 pop. 149), Pike co., SW Ind., 17 mi/27 km S of Petersburg; 38°16′N 87°16′W. In agr. and bituminous-coal-mining area (surface mining). Laid out 1860. **2** town (1990 pop. 3,149), Sullivan and Washington cos., NE Tenn., 7 mi/11 km SSE of Kingsport, on Holston R., bet. Fort Patrick Henry L. and Boone Reservoir. Boone Dam is just E.

Spurr, Mount (11,070 ft/3,374 m), S Alaska, in Alaska Range, W of upper Cook Inlet, 80 mi/129 km W of Anchorage; 61°18′N 152°15′W.

Spuyten Duyvil Creek, N.Y.: see HARLEM RIVER.

Squa Pan Lake (SKWAH pan), narrow V-shaped lake, Aroostook co., NE Maine, 13 mi/21 km SW of Presque Isle; c.16 mi/26 km long.

Squam Lake (SKWAWM), irregularly shaped lake, central N.H., in Carroll, Gradton, and Belknap cos., 14 mi/23 km NNW of Laconia; c.7 mi/11.3 km long. In resort area; Squam Brook drains SW through Little Squam L. into Pemigewasset R. Town of Holderness at W end. Location of movie *On Golden Pond*. Also known as Asquam L.

Squamish (SKWAW-mish), village, SW B.C., W Canada, at head of Howe Sound, at mouth of Squamish R., 30 mi/48 km N of Vancouver; 49°42′N 123°09′W. Pulp and lumber milling; hydroelectric power. In mining (gold, silver) region. Tourism; ski resorts; gateway to recreation region.

Squannacook River (SKWAW-nuh-kuk), c.25 mi/40 km long, N Mass.; rises in region N of Fitchburg; flows E and SE to Nashua R. NW of Ayer.

Squantum, Mass.: see QUINCY.

Square Island, in St. Michael's Bay, SE Lab., E Canada; 4 mi/6 km long, 3 mi/5 km wide; 52°45′N 55°53′W. On S coast is fishing settlement of Square Isl. Harbour.

Square Lake, Maine: see FISH RIVER LAKES.

Squaw Harbor, village, SW Alaska, on E coast of Unga Isl.

Squaw Lake, village (1990 pop. 139), Itasca co., N Minn., 36 mi/58 km ENE of Bemidji, in N part of Leech L. Indian Reservation, bet. Squaw (NE) and Round (W) lakes; 47°37′N 94°08′W. Cattle, sheep, poultry; oats, wild rice; timber. Also in Blackduck State Forest and part of Chippewa Natl. Forest (boundaries overlap).

Squaw Mountain, peak (11,486 ft/3,501 m) in Front Range, Clear Creek co., N central Colo., 4 mi/6.4 km SSE of Idaho Springs; 39°40′N 105°29′W. Squaw Pass (9,807 ft/2,989 m), 1 mi/1.6 km E.

Squaw Valley, uninc. town (1990 pop. 2,565), Placer co., NE Calif., in the Sierra Nevada, 8 mi/12.9 km SE of Truckee, 5 mi/8 km NW of L. Tahoe in Tahoe Natl. Forest, in valley of Squaw Creek (a W side-valley of Truckee R.); 36°42′N 119°11′W. A well-known ski and winter recreational resort, it was the site of the 1960 Winter Olympics. Ski lifts and trails are on Squaw Peak (8,885 ft/2,708 m high). Squaw Valley State Recreation Area and Squaw Valley Ski Area are here; Alpine Meadows Ski Area to S.

Squire, uninc. village (1990 pop. 600), McDowell co., S W.Va., 12 mi/19 km S of Welch, near Va. state line. Coal. Berwind L. Wildlife Management Area to W.

Squirrel Island, Maine: see SOUTHPORT.

Stack Island, Mississippi midriver sand island, Issaquena Co., Miss., E of Lake Providence (La.); c.2 mi/3 km long; 32°49′N 91°08′W. Formerly in East Carroll parish (La.). State ownership under dispute for many years, awarded to Miss. by a Supreme Court decision in 1995.

Stacy, town (1990 pop. 1,081), Chisago co., 32 mi/51 km N of St. Paul, on W shore of Mud L., at inflow of West Branch Sunrise R.; 45°23′N 92°59′W. Cattle, poultry; grain; dairying. Mfg. (sawmill; concrete prods.; electrical prods; machining). Parts of Carlos Avery Wildlife Area to E and SW.

Stacyville 1 town (1990 pop. 481), Mitchell co., N Iowa,

near Minn. state line, on Little Cedar R., and 10 mi/16 km N of Osage; 43°26′N 92°46′W. Sand and gravel pits nearby. **2** township (1990 pop. 480), Penobscot co., central Maine, 18 mi/29 km NE of Millinocket; 45°54′N 68°29′W.

Stadacona (stuh-DAH-ko-nuh), district of Quebec city, S Que., E Canada, on the St. Lawrence R. Former Native Amer. village.

Stafford 1 county (□ 794 sq mi/2,056 sq km; 1990 pop. 5,365), S central Kansas; ☉ Saint John; 38°02′N 98°43′W. Gently rolling area, watered by Rattlesnake Creek and North Fork Ninnescah R. Cattle; wheat, soghum, soybeans, alfafla. Part of Quivira Natl. Wildlife Refuge in NE. Formed 1879. **2** county (□ 279 sq mi/723 sq km; 1990 pop. 61,236), NE Va., on Potomac R. (E: Md. state line); ☉ Stafford; 38°24′N 77°27′W. Bounded SW and S by Rappahannock R.; drained by Aquia Creek. Agr. (wheat, corn, soybeans, hay, tobacco; cattle, poultry). Part of Fredricksburg and Spotsylvania Co. Memorial Natl. Military Park in S, at Falmouth. Part of Quantico Marine Corps Base in N. Gold formerly mined here. Formed 1664.

Stafford 1 town (1990 pop. 11,091), Tolland co., NE Conn., c.8 mi/12.9 km N of Willington, on Mass. state line, and Willimantic R.; 41°59′N 72°18′W. Agr.; mfg. of electrical goods, print goods; textiles at Stafford Springs and West Stafford. Staffordville village, near L. Stafford (1.5 mi/2.4 km long) is resort. Settled and inc. 1719, Stafford Springs borough inc. 1873. Pop. figure includes Stafford Springs borough (1990 pop. 4,100). **2** town (1990 pop. 1,344), Stafford co., S central Kansas, 23 mi/37 km NNE of Pratt; 37°57′N 98°35′W. In wheat area; grain storage. Growth stimulated by discovery (1938) of oil nearby. Quivira Natl. Wildlife Reserve to NE. Inc. 1885. **3** town (1990 pop. 8,397), Fort Bend and Harris cos., SE Texas, exurb, 15 mi/24 km SW of downtown Houston; 29°37′N 95°33′W. Oil and natural gas. Agr. to S. Mfg. (paper goods, safety valves, food supplements, electronic equip., machinery, fabricated metal prods., hose couplings and fittings, motor vehicles, consumer goods, plastic prods., computer equip.; printing, poultry processing). **4** uninc. town, ☉ Stafford co. (since 1715), NE Va., near Potomac R., 9 mi/14.5 km NNE of Fredericksburg; 38°25′N 77°24′W. Mfg. (lumber; diverse light mfg.); in agr. area (tobacco, grain; cattle, poultry). Quantico Marine Corps Base and Quantico Natl. Cemetery to N.

Stafford, village (1990 pop. 89), Monroe co., E Ohio, 19 mi/31 km SSW of Barnesville; 39°43′N 81°16′W.

Stafford, township (1990 pop. 13,325), Ocean co., E central N.J., 5 mi/8 km S of Barnegat; 39°42′N 74°15′W. Inc. 1798.

Stafford Springs, Conn.: see STAFFORD.

Staffordsville, uninc. village (1990 pop. 700), Johnson co., E Ky., 3 mi/4.8 km NW of Paintsville. Coal, oil; agr. (tobacco; livestock). Paintsville L. reservoir and State Park to NW.

Staffordville, Conn.: see STAFFORD.

Stafore Estates (STA-for), uninc. town (1990 pop. 1,130), Northampton co., E Pa., residential suburb, 3 mi/4.8 km NNW of Bethlehem; 40°39′N 75°24′W. Agr. includes dairying; livestock; grain. Lehigh Valley Internatl. Airport to SW. Allentown State Farm to NW.

Stagecoach, uninc. village, Lyon co., W Nev., 23 mi/37 km NE of Carson City, near Carson R. Elev. 4,218 ft/1,286 m. Cattle, sheep; dairying. Virginia Mts. to N.

Staked Plain, Texas and N.Mex.: see LLANO ESTACADO.

Staley (STAI-lee), village (1990 pop. 204), Randolph co., central N.C., 23 mi/37 km SSE of Greensboro, near Rocky R.; 35°47′N 79°32′W. Tobacco, grain; poultry, livestock; dairying. Mfg. (furniture, crushed stone and gravel).

Stalin, Mount (9,500 ft/2,896 m), N B.C., W Canada, in Rocky Mts.; 58°15′N 124°45′W.

Stallings, town (1990 pop. 2,152), Union co., S N.C., suburb 14 mi/19 km SE of downtown Charlotte; 35°04′N 80°41′W. Agr. area (cotton, grain; poultry, livestock; dairying). Mfg. (machinery, wood prods.).

Stallworthy, Cape, N extremity of Axel Heiberg Isl., N

Franklin dist., N.W.T., N Canada, on the Arctic Ocean; 81°20′N 93°00′W.

Stambaugh (stam-baw), town (1990 pop. 1,281), Iron co., SW Upper Peninsula, N Mich., 1 mi/1.6 km SE of and opposite Iron River, in Menominee range, and 15 mi/24 km W of Crystal Falls; 46°04′N 88°37′W. Settled c.1878; inc. as village 1895, as city 1923.

Stamford, city (1990 pop. 108,056), Fairfield co., SW Conn., on L.I. Sound; 41°06′N 73°32′W. A variety of light industrial goods are produced here, such as machinery, fabricated metal prods., and chemicals. Since the 1970s, Stamford has become home to numerous corporation hq. that moved here from N.Y. city, providing a boon to the local economy. It is also a residential community for many N.Y. city commuters. Cummings Park is on the sound. The sanctuary of the First Presbyterian Church was designed by Wallace K. Harrison and built (1958) in the shape of a whale. The Stamford Mus. has a nature center and an observatory. A branch of the Univ. of Conn. is in the city. Settled 1641, inc. 1893 as a city within the town of Stamford (the 2 were consolidated in 1949).

Stamford 1 town (1990 pop. 3,817), Jones co., W central Texas, 34 mi/55 km N of Abilene; 33°01′N 99°38′W. Elev. 1,614 ft/492 m. In cotton, cattle area; oil, natural-gas wells. Mfg. (textiles; meat processing). Has annual Cowboy Reunion. L. Stamford reservoir to NE (Haskell co.). Founded 1900, inc. 1901. **2** town (1990 pop. 773), Bennington co., SW Vt., in Green Mts., on Mass. state line, 10 mi/16 km SE of Bennington; 42°46′N 73°04′W.

Stamford 1 village (1990 pop. 188), Harlan co., S Nebr., 12 mi/19 km W of Alma, and on Beaver Creek; 40°7′N 99°35′W. Livestock; grain. **2** summer-resort village (□ 1 sq mi/2.6 sq km; 1990 pop. 1,211), Delaware co., S N.Y., in the Catskill Mts., on West Branch of Delaware R., and 24 mi/39 km ESE of Oneonta; 42°24′N 74°37′W. Mt. Utsayantha (3,213 ft/979 m), a prominent local peak, is just SE. Inc. 1870.

Stampede Reservoir, Sierra Co., N Calif., on Little Truckee R., 11 mi/18 km NNE of Truckee, and 5 mi/8 km W of Nevada state line, in Tahoe Natl. Forest; 5 mi/8 km long; 39°27′N 120°05′W. Max. capacity 280,000 acre-ft. Formed by Stampede Dam (225 ft/69 m high), built (1970) by the Bureau of Reclamation for flood control.

Stamping Ground, village (1990 pop. 698), Scott co., N Ky., 12 mi/19 km ENE of Frankfort near North Elkhorn Creek; 38°16′N 84°41′W. Mfg. (tool and die); grain, tobacco; livestock; dairying.

Stamps, town (1990 pop. 2,478), Lafayette co., SW Ark., 31 mi/50 km E of Texarkana, near Bodcaw Creek; 33°21′N 93°30′W. RR junction; oil and gas field; mfg. (fabricated metal prods., furniture). Writer Maya Angelou b. here; setting of her book *I Know Why The Caged Bird Sings*.

Stanaford (STAN-uh-fuhrd), uninc. town (1990 pop. 1,706), Raleigh co., S W.Va., 4 mi/6.4 km NE of Beckley, on Piney Creek; 37°49′N 81°09′W. Agr. (grain, nursery crops); cattle.

Stanardsville, town (1990 pop. 257), ☉ Greene co., N central Va., 18 mi/29 km N of Charlottesville; 38°17′N 78°26′W. Light mfg.; agr. area (grain, alfalfa, tobacco; livestock; dairying).

Stanberry (STAN-be-ree), city (1990 pop. 1,310), Gentry co., NW Mo., near Grand R., 35 mi/56 km NE of St. Joseph; 40°13′N 94°32′W. Corn, soybeans; hogs; cattle; light mfg.

Standard, village (1991 pop. 329), S Alta., W Canada, 27 mi/43 km SSW of Drumheller; 51°07′N 112°59′W. Coal mining; wheat, flax; cattle.

Standard, uninc. village, Mt. Pleasant township, Westmoreland co., SW Pa., suburb, 1 mi/1.6 km N of Mt. Pleasant; 40°09′N 79°32′W.

Standard City, village (1990 pop. 128), Macoupin co., SW central Ill., 7 mi/11.3 km NE of Carlinville; 39°21′N 89°46′W. In agr. and bituminous-coal area.

Standing Pine, uninc. village (1990 pop. 346), Leake co., central Miss., 5 mi/8 km ESE of Carthage, near Pearl R.; 32°40′N 89°27′W. Cotton, corn; cattle, poultry.

Standish 1 town (1990 pop. 7,678), Cumberland co., SW

Maine, 12 mi/19 km NW of Portland, and on Sebago L.; 43°47′N 70°34′W. Mfg. (wood prods.). Includes resort village of Sebago L. (1990 pop. 1,259). Seat of St. Joseph's Col. **2** town (1990 pop. 1,377), ⊙ Arenac co., E Mich., 26 mi/42 km NNW of Bay City, and on South Branch of Pine R.; 43°58′N 83°57′W. Trade and shipping center for farm area. Mfg. (fire sprinklers, machinery). Recreation. Inc. as city 1903.

Standley Lake, reservoir, Jefferson co., N central Colo., on Big Dry Creek, 10 mi/16 km NW of downtown Denver, NW of Arvada; 1.5 mi/2.4 km long; 39°52′N 105°03′W. Max. capacity 48,441 acre-ft. Formed by Standley L. Dam (113 ft/34 m high, c.1 mi/1.6 km long), built (1973) for irrigation and water supply purposes. Co. park on S shore.

Stanfield, town (1990 pop. 1,568), Umatilla co., N Oregon, 21 mi/34 km WNW of Pendleton, on Umatilla R.; 45°47′N 119°13′W. Agr. (wheat, vegetables, potatoes, apples, plums, peaches; hogs, sheep, cattle). RR junction to NW. Cold Springs Reservoir and Natl. Wildlife Refuge to NE. Umatilla Ordnance Depot to NW.

Stanfield, village (1990 pop. 517), Stanly co., S central N.C., 15 mi/24 km SW of Albermarle, and 2 mi/3.2 km S of Locust; 35°14′N 80°25′W. Grain, cotton; poultry, cattle; dairying. Mfg. (furniture, clothing, fabricated metal prods., textiles, lumber, consumer goods, machinery).

Stanford, uninc. city (1990 pop. 18,097), Santa Clara co., W Calif., residential suburb, 12 mi/19 km WNW of downtown San Jose, and 27 mi/43 km SSE of downtown San Francisco, on San Francisquito Creek (border bet. San Mateo and Santa Cruz cos.); 37°25′N 122°10′W. Santa Crux Mts. to W. Stanford Univ. in W part of city.

Stanford, town (1990 pop. 2,686), ⊙ Lincoln co., central Ky., 11 mi/18 km SE of Danville; 37°31′N 84°39′W. In S part of Bluegrass region; mfg. (apparel, ceramic prods., transportation equip., concrete, stone fixtures, hats). Harvey Helm Mus. and Lib.; Isaac Shelby State Historical Site to NW; William Whitley House (c.1785) State Historical Site to SE; Stanford Reservoir to S. Founded 1786 by Va. legislature.

Stanford 1 village (1990 pop. 620), McLean co., central Ill., 11 mi/18 km WSW of Bloomington; 40°25′N 89°13′W. In rich agr. area. **2** village (1990 pop. 529), ⊙ Judith Basin co., central Mont., 57 mi/92 km. SE of Great Falls; 47°09′N 110°13′W. Shipping point for hay, wheat, barley, cattle, sheep, poultry; timber. Little Belt Mts. and part of Lewis and Clark Natl. Forest to SW. Founded in 1882.

Stanhope, town (1990 pop. 447), Hamilton co., central Iowa, 12 mi/19 km S of Webster City; 42°17′N 93°47′W. In agr. area.

Stanhope (STAN-hop), borough (1990 pop. 3,393), Sussex co., NW N.J., on old Morris Canal, near L. Hopatcong, and 11 mi/18 km SSE of Newton; 40°54′N 74°42′W. Mfg. (metal and stone prods.), agr. (poultry; dairy prods.). Produced iron in Amer. Revolution. Hopatcong State Park nearby. Waterloo Village, restored colonial village and site of a summer musical festival, 5 mi/8 km to W. Settled 1714, inc. 1904.

Staniard Creek, town, W Bahama Isls., on NE shore of Andros Isl., 40 mi/64 km WSW of Nassau; 24°51′N 77°54′W. Fishing, lumbering.

Stanislaus, county (□ 1,495 sq mi/3,872 sq km; 1990 pop. 370,522), central Calif.; ⊙ Modesto; 37°34′N 121°00′W. Level land in San Joaquin Valley, bordered by Coast Ranges (W); watered by San Joaquin, Tuolumne, and Stanislaus rivers. Stanislaus R. forms part of N border. Co. is crossed E-W by Modesto Main Canal and Hetch Hetchy Aqueduct, N-S by Delta Mendota Canal, among others. Irrigation water supplied by Modesto, Turlock, Don Pedro reservoirs. Catfish; cattle, chickens, turkey; eggs; dairying; almonds, walnuts, peaches, grapes, melons, tomatoes, beans, broccoli, cauliflower, onions, peas, peppers, spinach, pumpkins, wheat, barley, oats, rice. Working of gypsum and clay. Rapid urban growth has occurred since 1970s around Modesto and Turlock. Turlock L. State Recreation Area in E. Formed 1854.

Stanislaus Peak (11,233 ft/3,424 m), Alpine co., E Calif., in the Sierra Nevada, c.40 mi/64 km SSE of Lake Tahoe; 38°23′N 119°39′W.

Stanislaus River, c.65 mi/105 km long, central Calif.; formed by its North and South forks c.50 mi/80 km ENE of Stockton; flows SW through New Melones and Tullock reservoirs, past Oakdale and Ripon to San Joaquin R. 13 mi/21 km W of Modesto. About 7 mi/11.3 km W of Sonora is New Melones Dam (and Tulloch Dam) of Central Valley project. North Fork Stanislaus R. rises in SW Alpine co., 15 mi/24 km SW of Markleeville; flows c. 45 mi/72 km SW. Middle Fork Stanislaus R. rises in S Alpine co. at Sonora Pass, 27 mi/43 km S of Markleeville; flows c.55 mi/89 km NW, then SW through Donnelle and Beardsley reservoirs to North Fork c.10 mi/16 km NE of Angels Camp. South Fork Stanislaus R. rises in NE Tuolumne co., 30 mi/48 km S of Markleeville; flows c.40 mi/64 km SW through Pinecrest L. reservoir and N of Twain Harte to join North Fork.

Stanley, county (□ 1,517 sq mi/3,929 sq km; 1990 pop. 2,453), central S.Dak.; ⊙ Fort Pierre; 44°23′N 100°45′W. Bounded N by Cheyenne R. (W arm of L. Oahe), E by Missouri R. (L. Oahe reservoir to Oahe Dam, N of Pierre), and drained by Bad R. Livestock; wheat, barley, flax, oats, alfalfa. Border bet. Mountain and Central time zones follows Missouri R. S to Ft. Pierre, then crosses over land SW into Jones co. All but SE portion is in Mountain time zone; Ft. Pierre is in Central. Part of Fort Pierre Natl. Grassland and part of Lower Brule Indian Reservation in SE. Farm Isl. State Recreation Area in E. Formed 1873.

Stanley 1 town (1990 pop. 116), Buchanan co., E Iowa, 12 mi/19 km NNE of Independence; 42°38′N 91°48′W. **2** town (1990 pop. 2,823), Gaston co., S N.C., 17 mi/27 km NW of Charlotte; 35°21′N 81°05′W. Agr. area (cotton, grain; cattle). Mfg. (ropes, apparel, furniture, hardware, machinery, textiles, electrical prods., paper prods., fabricated metal prods.). Settled 1840; inc. 1879. **3** town (1990 pop. 1,371), ⊙ Mountrail co., NW central N. Dak., 51 mi/82 km WNW of Minot; 48°19′N 102°23′W. RR junction, in fertile farm area. Lignite mines; oil fields. Dairy prods.; wheat, flax, corn. Inc. 1909. **4** town (1990 pop. 1,186), Page co., N Va., in Shenandoah Valley, 7 mi/11.3 km S of Luray; 38°34′N 78°30′W. Mfg. (wood prods.; poultry processing); agr. (apples, grain; poultry, cattle; dairying). **5** town (1990 pop. 2.011), Chippewa co., W central Wis., 29 mi/47 km ENE of Eau Claire; 44°57′N 90°56′W. In dairying and farming area; produces cheese, chemicals, and fabricated metal prods. Settled c.1881, inc. 1898.

Stanley 1 village (1990 pop. 71), Custer co., central Idaho, 40 mi/64 km WSW of Challis, on upper reach of Salmon R; 44°13′N 114°57′W. Elev. 6,260 ft/1,908 m. In Sawtooth Natl. Recreation Area, surrounded by Challis Natl. Forest; Sawtooth Wilderness Area to SW. Nearby is Sawtooth fish hatchery; Stanley L. to NW, Redfish and Hells Roaring lakes to S, (Redfish L. visitor's center). **2** uninc. village (1990 pop. 350), Daviess co., NW Ky., 8 mi/12.9 km WNW of Owensboro, S of Ohio R., and NE of Green R. Tobacco, soybeans, grain; livestock. Mfg. (whiskey bottling; fertilizer).

Stanley Baldwin, Mount (10,900 ft/3,322 m), E B.C., W Canada, in Premier Group of Rocky Mts., 65 mi/105 km W of Jasper.

Stanley Bridge, village, N P.E.I., E Canada, on New London Bay, 16 mi/26 km ENE of Summerside; 46°27′N 63°27′W. Fisheries.

Stanley Draper, Lake, reservoir, Cleveland co., S central Okla., on East Elm Creek, within Oklahoma City limits, 12 mi/19 km SE of downtown; 4 mi/6.4 km long; 35°17′N 97°38′W. Max. capacity c.100,000 acre-ft. Formed by Draper Dam (90 ft/27 m high), built (1962) by the City of Oklahoma City for water supply. Aqueduct delivers water to L. Thunderbird reservoir to SE. Residential area; city park.

Stanley Peak (10,351 ft/3,155 m), on border bet. Alta. and B.C., W Canada, in Rocky Mts., on W edge of Banff Natl. Park, 20 mi/32 km W of Banff; 51°10′N 116°02′W.

Stanleytown, uninc. town, Henry co., S Va., 6 mi/9.7 km NW of Martinsville, on Smith R.; 36°45′N 79°57′W. Mfg. (furniture); agr. (tobacco; poultry; cattle). Bassett, furniture-making town, 2 mi/3.2 km to NW.

Stanleyville, uninc. town (1990 pop. 4,779), Forsyth co., N central N.C., residential suburb, 8 mi/12.9 km NNW of downtown Winston-Salem; 36°12′N 80°16′W. Agr. area to N and W (tobacco, grain; cattle).

Stanly, county (□ 404 sq mi/1,046 sq km; 1990 pop. 51,765), S central N.C.; ⊙ Albemarle; 35°18′N 80°15′W. In Piedmont region; bordered by Yadkin (E) and Rocky (S) rivers, which join in SE corner to form Pee Dee (Great Pee Dee) R. Agr. area (cotton, corn, wheat, barley, oats, soybeans, hay; chickens, turkeys, cattle; dairying); timber (pine, oak). Mfg. at Albermarle, Stanfield, Norwood, and Oakboro. Morrow Mt. State Park in E; Badin L. and L. Tillery reservoir (Yadkin R.) on E border. Formed 1841.

Stannard, town (1990 pop. 148), Caledonia co., NE Vt., 13 mi/21 km NW of St. Johnsbury; 44°32′N 72°12′W.

Stannard Rock, island with a lighthouse in L. Superior, N Mich., off Upper Peninsula, 30 mi/48 km SE of Keweenaw Point, and 45 mi/72 km NNE of Marquette.

Stansbury Mountains, in Wasatch Natl. Forest, Tooele co., NW Utah; extend N from Onaqui Mts. to S shore of Great Salt L. Rise to 11,031 ft/3,362 m in Deseret Peak. S ⅔ in small unit of Wasatch Natl. Forest includes Deseret Peak Wilderness Area.

Stanstead, county (□ 432 sq mi/1,119 sq km; pop.), S Que., E Canada, on U.S. (Vt.; S) border; ⊙ Coaticook; 45°07′N 72°12′W.

Stanstead or **Stanstead Plain**, village (1991 pop. 1,059), S Que., E Canada, 30 mi/48 km SSW of Sherbrooke, near Rock Island, at U.S. (Vt.) border. Dairying; granite quarrying.

Stanton 1 county (□ 680 sq mi/1,761 sq km; 1990 pop. 2,333), SW Kansas, on Colo. (W) state line; ⊙ Johnson City; 37°33′N 101°46′W. Sloping to rolling plain. Drained by Bear and Sandy Arroyo creeks. Grain (wheat, sorghum), soybeans, alfalfa; cattle. Stanton L. and Bear Creek in W. In Central time zone; border of Mountain time zone follows N and W borders. Formed 1887. **2** county (□ 431 sq mi/1,116 sq km; 1990 pop. 6,244), NE Nebr.; ⊙ Stanton; 41°55′N 97°11′W. Farming region in Loess Hills drained by Elkhorn R. Cattle, hogs; corn, alfalfa, soybeans; dairying. Formed 1867.

Stanton, city (1990 pop. 30,491), Orange co., SW Calif., suburb 21 mi/34 km ESE of downtown Los Angeles, and 4 mi/6.4 km WSW of Anaheim; 33°48′N 118°00′W. The city's pop. grew markedly during the 1970s. Mfg. (electrical and electronics goods, signs, computer equip., bldg. materials, plastic prods., tool and die; metal processing). Inc. 1956.

Stanton 1 uninc. town (1990 pop. 5,028), New Castle co., N Del., suburb 5 mi/8 km WSW of Wilmington, on White Clay Creek; 39°43′N 75°39′W. Mfg. (wood prods.). Del. Technical and Community Col. (Stanton-Wilmington campus). Del. Park Race Track here. Goldey-Beacom Col. to NW. **2** town (1990 pop. 692), Montgomery co., SW Iowa, on Tarkio R., and 7 mi/11.3 km ESE of Red Oak; 40°58′N 95°05′W. Grain. **3** town (1990 pop. 2,795), ⊙ Powell co., E central Ky., on Red R., 37 mi/60 km ESE of Lexington; 37°51′N 83°51′W. In agr. area (tobacco, corn; cattle); timber. Mfg. (machinery, wood prods., transportation equip, bldg. materials); oil wells, coal mines, clay pits, limestone quarries. Daniel Boone Natl. Forest to E and S. Red R. Gorge, in Red R. Natl. Geological Area, to E; Natural Bridge State Park to SE. **4** town (1990 pop. 1,504), ⊙ Montcalm co., central Mich., 38 mi/61 km NE of Grand Rapids; 43°17′N 85°04′W. In farm area (livestock; grain, potatoes, fruit, apples, soybeans, beans; dairy prods.). Mfg. (wood prods., consumer goods). Montcalm Community Col. to SW, at Sidney. **5** town (1990 pop. 1,549) ⊙ Stanton co., NE Nebr., 12 mi/19 km SE of Norfolk, and on Elkhorn R.; 41°57′N 97°13′W. Dairying; livestock. Inc. 1871. **6** town (1990 pop. 487), Haywood co., W Tenn., 11 mi/18 km SW of Brownsville; 35°28′N 89°24′W. In timber and farm area.

7 town (1990 pop. 2,576), ⊙ Martin co., W Texas, 20 mi/32 km SW of Big Spring; 32°07′N 101°47′W. Elev. 2,664 ft/812 m. In cattle-ranching and agr. region (grain, sorghum); mfg. (oil and gas processing; electrical equip.). Oil fields to E. Settled 1881, inc. 1925.

Stanton, village (1990 pop. 517), ⊙ Mercer co., central N. Dak.,12 mi/19 km ENE of Hazen, and on Missouri R., at mouth of Knife R.; 47°19′N 101°22′W. Knife R. Indian Village Natl. Historic Site is here; Fort Clark Historic Site to SE.

Stantonsburg (STAN-tuhns-buhrg), town (1990 pop. 782), Wilson co., E central N.C., 10 mi/16 km SSE of Wilson; 35°36′N 77°49′W.

Stanwix, Fort, N.Y.: see FORT STANWIX.

Stanwood 1 town (1990 pop. 646), Cedar co., E Iowa, 9 mi/14.5 km N of Tipton; 41°53′N 91°09′W. In agr. area. **2** town (1990 pop. 1,961), Snohomish co., NW Wash., 20 mi/32 km NW of Everett, near mouth of Stillaguamish R., near Port Susan Bay (to SW), and SE of Skagit Bay. Bridge to Camano Isl. (W). Berries, vegetables, peas; dairying; cattle, poultry. Mfg. (wood prods., foods; meatpacking, printing and publishing). Wenberg State Park and Tulalip Indian Reservation to S.

Stanwood, village (1990 pop. 174), Mecosta co., central Mich., 9 mi/14.5 km S of Big Rapids; 43°34′N 85°27′W. In farm area. Manistee Natl. Forest to W.

Staplehurst, village (1990 pop. 281), Seward co., SE Nebr., 6 mi/9.7 km NW of Seward, and on Big Blue R.; 40°58′N 97°10′W.

Staples, town (1990 pop. 2,754), Todd co., central Minn., near Crow Wing R., 30 mi/48 km W of Brainerd; 46°21′N 94°47′W. RR junction. Trade center for agr. area (grain, potatoes, beans; livestock, poultry; dairying). Mfg. (machining, printing and publishing). Hayden L. to SE. Settled 1881, plotted 1885, inc. 1906.

Stapleton 1 village (1990 pop. 330), Jefferson co., E Ga., 32 mi/51 km WSW of Augusta; 33°13′N 82°28′W. Mfg. of clothing and consumer goods. **2** village (1990 pop. 299), ⊙ Logan co., central Nebr., 25 mi/40 km NNE of North Platte, and on South Loup R; 41°28′N 100°30′W. Livestock; grain.

Stapleton, a port and industrial section of Staten Isl. borough of N.Y. city, SE N.Y., on NE Staten Isl., S of St. George; 40°38′N 74°04′W. The 1st U.S. foreign trade zone (free port, est. 1936) and a U.S. marine hosp. are here. Light industrial and brewery area from the late 19th to the mid-20th cents. Mfg. (nonferrous metals and fabricated metal prods., electronic goods, chemicals; machining and metal fabrication). In 1983, more than $200 million of Federal funds spent to create Staten Isl. Homeport here as 1 of 21 in nation for U.S. Navy fleets. Facility has been decommissioned as part of series of base closings nationwide.

Star, town (1990 pop. 775), Montgomery co., central N.C., 21 mi/34 km S of Asheboro, near Little R.; 35°23′N 79°46′W. RR junction. Cotton, grain, sweet potatoes; chickens, cattle, hogs. Mfg. (apparel, lumber, wood prods.).

Star, uninc. village, Ada co., SW Idaho, suburb, 12 mi/19 km WNW of downtown Boise, on Boise R. Irrigated agr. area (dairying; grain, vegetables; cattle, sheep). Mfg. (transportation equip.).

Star City, town (1991 pop. 507), central Sask., W Canada, 65 mi/105 km ESE of Prince Albert; 52°52′N 104°20′W. Grain; lumbering.

Star City 1 town (1990 pop. 2,138), ⊙ Lincoln co., SE Ark., 22 mi/35 km SSE of Pine Bluff; 33°56′N 91°50′W. Agr. (cotton, rice, fruit, watermelons, vegetables). Mfg. (wood prods., plastic prods., apparel). Cane Creek State Park to E. **2** town (1990 pop. 1,251), Monongalia co., N W.Va., on Monongahela R. (bridged), suburb, 3 mi/4.8 km NW of downtown Morgantown; 39°39′N 79°59′W. Coal-mining, gas-, and oil-producing area. Agr. (grain, strawberries); livestock, poultry. Inc. 1907.

Star City, village, Pulaski co. NW Ind., 7 mi/11.3 km SSE of Winamac. In agr. area (corn, soybeans; livestock). Mfg. (feed milling, grain grinding and mixing). Laid out 1859.

Star Island, Minn.: see CASS LAKE.

Star Island, N.H.: see ISLES OF SHOALS.

Star Junction, uninc. town (1990 pop. 1,200), Fayette co., SW Pa., 12 mi/19 km NNW of Uniontown; 40°03′N 79°45′W. Agr. (grain; livestock; dairying).

Star Lake, resort village (1990 pop. 1,092), St. Lawrence co., N N.Y., in the Adirondack Mts., on Star L. (c.1 mi/ 1.6 km long), 31 mi/50 km ENE of Carthage; 44°09′N 75°02′W.

Star Lake, Otter Tail co., W Minn., 18 mi/29 km NE of Fergus Falls; 6 mi/9.7 km long, 3 mi/4.8 km wide; 46°31′N 95°48′W. Drains through short stream into Dead L., just SE. Fishing and swimming resorts. Narrow peninsula from W separates lake from 3 mi/4.8 km long S arm. Numerous small lakes in area.

Star Prairie, village (1990 pop. 507), St. Croix co., W Wis., 19 mi/31 km NE of Hudson; 45°12′N 92°31′W. Dairying; trout farm. Numerous small lakes in area.

Star Valley, Wyo. and Idaho: see SALT RIVER.

Starbuck, village, S Man., central Canada, 22 mi/35 km WSW of Winnipeg. Grain; livestock.

Starbuck, town (1990 pop. 1,143), Pope co., W Minn., 8 mi/12.9 km WSW of Glenwood, at W end of L. Minnewaska, at outflow of Outflow Creek; 45°36′N 95°31′W. Poultry, livestock; grain, soybeans, beans; dairying. Mfg. (fabricated metal prods., ferilizers, feeds).

Starbuck, village (1990 pop. 170), Columbia co., SE Wash., on Tucannon R., near Snake R., and 33 mi/ 53 km NNE of Walla Walla; 46°31′N 118°07′W. In wheat growing region. Little Goose Dam 6 mi/9.7 km ENE, forms L. Bryan. Palouse Falls and Lyons Ferry state parks to NW.

Stargo, uninc. town (1990 pop. 10,580), Greenlee co., E Ariz., 4 mi/6.4 km W of Clifton. RR terminus. Coal, wheat, barley, alfalfa. Copper, molybdenum, gold, silver. Apache-Sitgreaves Natl. Forest to N; San Carlos Indian Reservation to NW; Gila-Box Riparian Natl. Conservation Area to S.

Stark 1 county (☐ 288 sq mi/746 sq km; 1990 pop. 6,534), N central Ill.; ⊙ Toulon; 41°05′N 89°47′W. Agr. (corn, soybeans, wheat; livestock). Bituminous coal. Mfg. Drained by Spoon R. and small Indian Creek. Formed 1839. Includes Rock Island State Trail. **2** county (☐ 1,316 sq mi/3,408 sq km; 1990 pop. 22,832), W N.Dak.; ⊙ Dickinson; 46°48′N 102°39′W. Agr. area drained by Heart and Green rivers and Antelope Creek. Rich in oil, lignite and clay. Cattle, hogs; wheat, barley, hay. Food processing; wood prods., machinery, transportation equip. Formed 1879. Patterson L. in W; Little Missouri Natl. Grassland beyond W border. **3** county (☐ 580 sq mi/1,502 sq km; 1990 pop. 367,585), E central Ohio; ⊙ CANTON; 40°49′N 81°22′W. Intersected by Tuscarawas R. and small Nimishillen, Sandy, and Sugar creeks. Includes Fort Laurens State Park. In the Glaciated Plains physiographic region. Agr. (poultry; corn, fruit; dairy prods.). Mfg. at Canton, Massillon, Alliance (meat prods., millwork, rubber goods, tiles, metal cans, machinery, transportation equip., fabricated metal prods., electrical equip., consumer goods; nonferrous foundries). Coal mining; limestone quarries, sand and gravel pits. Oil and gas extraction; petroleum refining. Formed 1808.

Stark, town (1990 pop. 518), Coos co., N N.H., 14 mi/23 km NE of Lancaster; 44°36′N 71°24′W. Drained by Upper Ammonoosuc R. Mfg. (rock salt); agr. (livestock, poultry; dairying); timber. Covered bridge. Part of White Mt. Natl. Forest in S; North Road State Forest and part of Nash Stream State Forest in N; South Pond State Park in SE. Percy village, near Christine L. (2 mi/3.2 km long), is summer resort.

Stark, village (1990 pop. 79), Neosho co., SE Kansas, 15 mi/24 km E of Chanute; 37°41′N 95°08′W. Livestock raising; general agr.

Stark City, town (1990 pop. 127), Newton co., SW Mo., in the Ozark Mts., 10 mi/16 km E of Neosho; 36°51′N 94°11′W.

Starke, county (☐ 312 sq mi/808 sq km; 1990 pop. 22,747), NW Ind.; ⊙ Knox; 41°17′N 86°39′W. Bounded NW by Kankakee R.; drained by Yellow R. and other tributaries of the Kankakee. Rich agr. area, producing large mint and onion crops. Corn, soybeans; cattle, hogs, poultry; some mfg. at Knox. Bass L. State Beach and Fish Hatchery in SE; Kankakee State Fish and Wildlife Area on NW border. Formed 1850.

Starke, town (☐ 6 sq mi/15.5 sq km; 1990 pop. 5,226), ⊙ Bradford co., N central Fla., 23 mi/37 km NE of Gainesville; 29°56′N 82°06′W. Agr. produce; timber, and naval-stores area. State prison.

Starks, town (1990 pop. 508), Somerset co., W central Maine, 13 mi/21 km WSW of Skowhegan; 44°44′N 69°57′W.

Starksboro, town (1990 pop. 1,511), Addison co., W central Vt., 16 mi/26 km NNE of Middlebury; 44°13′N 73°00′W. Dairying.

Starkville, city (1990 pop. 18,458), ⊙ Oktibbeha co., E Miss., 21 mi/34 km W of Columbus; 33°27′N 88°49′W. In a livestock, dairy, and agr. (cotton, corn, soybeans) area. Mfg. (bldg. materials, apparel, wood prods., beverages, consumer goods, aircraft, electrical and electronic equip., machinery; printing and publishing). Miss. State Univ. to SE. Originally called Boardtown because of its sawmills. Renamed in honor of Gen. John Stark of the Revolutionary War. Starr Forest Wildlife Mangement Area and Noxubee Natl. Wildlife Refuge to S; Oktibbeha Co. State L. to NW. Inc. 1837.

Starkville, village (1990 pop. 104), Las Animas co., S Colo., 5 mi/8 km S of Trinidad, near N.Mex. state line; 37°07′N 104°31′W. Elev. 6,360 ft/1,939 m. Cattle; wheat, hay, sorghum. Trinidad Reservoir and State Park to NW.

Starkweather, village (1990 pop. 197), Ramsey co., NE N.Dak., 24 mi/39 km N of Devils Lake; 48°27′N 98°52′W.

Starlight, village, Clark co., SE Ind., 10 mi/16 km NW of New Albany. Mfg. (wood prods.).

Starr, county (☐ 1,229 sq mi/3,183 sq km; 1990 pop. 40,518), extreme S Texas, on Mex. border (S and SW; Rio Grande); ⊙ Rio Grande City; 26°34′N 98°43′W. Irrigated Rio Grande valley produces vegetables, cotton, sorghum. Uplands have large ranches (cattle). Oil, natural gas wells; sand and gravel. Falcon State Recreation Park on W boundary; Internatl. Falcon Reservoir in W corner of co. Formed 1848.

Starr, village (1990 pop. 164), Anderson co., NW S.C., 10 mi/16 km S of Anderson; 34°22′N 82°42′W. Mfg. of insulation, textiles. Agr. includes poultry, livestock; grain. Hartwell L. reservoir and Sadlers Creek State Park to W.

Starr King, Mount 1 peak (9,092 ft/2,771 m) of the Sierra Nevada, NE Mariposa co., E Calif., in Yosemite Natl. Park, 5 mi/8 km SE of Yosemite Village; 37°42′N 119°31′W. There is a Mt. Clarence King in Kings Canyon Natl. Park. **2** peak (3,913 ft/1,193 m) of White Mts., S Coos co., N.H., in town of Jefferson, 7 mi/11.3 km SE of Lancaster, in White Mt. Natl. Forest; 44°26′N 71°26′W.

Starrett City (STA-ret), planned residential development, Spring Creek, SE sect. of borough of Brooklyn, N.Y. city, SE N.Y., N of Shore (Belt) Parkway, S of East N.Y., and W of Canarsie. Centered on lower Pennsylvania Ave. Middle-income, Mitchell-Lama housing project begun in 1972, opened for occupation in 1974; originally known as Twin Pine Project. Situated on 153 acres/62 ha, it consists of 46 residential bldgs. containing 5,881 apartment units with nearly 20,000 residents, most of whom are employed as blue-collar, office, and city workers. Other facilities include 8 parking garages, an outdoor parking lot, a shopping center with 25 business enterprises, 4 schools, a power plant, and a recreation center. This housing project was one of many constructed during N.Y. city's building boom after World War II, spurred on by the Natl. Housing Act of 1949 and Title I Slum Clearance provisions. Recently the target of a discrimination suit whose plaintiffs claimed that the management company maintained "white" and "black" lists of new tenants in an effort to maintain a genuine racial balance among residents.

Starrucca (stahr-RUK-ah), borough (1990 pop. 199), Wayne co., NE Pa., 36 mi/58 km NNE of Scranton;

Cross references are shown in SMALL CAPITALS. The pronunciation key is on page xv. The dates of population figures are on page xii.

41°53′N 75°27′W. Agr. (grain; livestock; dairying). Numerous small lakes to S. Also spelled Starucca.

Startex, uninc. town (1990 pop. 1,162), Spartanburg co., NW S.C., 9 mi/14.5 km W of Spartanburg; 34°55′N 82°05′W. Mfg. of cotton cloth; agr includes poultry, livestock; dairying; grain, soybeans, peaches.

Starucca, Pa.: see STARRUCCA.

Starvation Cove, locality, N Adelaide Peninsula, N Keewatin dist., N.W.T., N Canada, on Simpson Strait; 68°10′N 97°01′W. Here c.40 skeletons and other relics of Franklin expedition (1847–1848) have been found.

Starvation Peak (9,300 ft/2,835 m), SE B.C., W Canada, near Alta. and U.S. (Mont.) borders, in Rocky Mts., 50 mi/80 km SE of Fernie; 49°02′N 114°16′W.

Starvation Reservoir, Duchesne co., E Utah, on Strawberry R., 3 mi/4.8 km NW of Duchesne; 6 mi/9.7 km long; 40°11′N 110°25′W. Max. capacity 189,000 acre-ft. Has 3-mi/4.8-km N arm. Formed by Starvation Dam (156 ft/48 m high), built (1970) by the Bureau of Reclamation for irrigation, water supply, and flood control.

Starved Rock, cliff (140 ft/43 m), overlooking the Illinois R., bet. La Salle and Ottawa, N Ill.; 41°19′N 88°59′W. Legend says that in the 18th cent. the Ottawas drove a band of Illinois onto the cliff, where they died of thirst and starvation. Later, brigands and outlaws found refuge nearby in canyons and caves that were included in Starved Rock State Park (est. 1912). Starved Rock has been designated a natl. historic landmark.

State Center, town (1990 pop. 1,248), Marshall co., central Iowa, 14 mi/23 km W of Marshalltown; 42°01′N 93°10′W. Feeds. Laid out 1865, inc. 1867.

State College, borough (1990 pop. 38,923), Centre co., central Pa., 60 mi/97 km NW of Harrisburg; 40°47′N 77°51′W. Surrounded by farmland. Mfg. (electronic prods., food prods., chemicals, bottled water; printing and publishing). Agr. area (grain, vegetables; livestock; dairying). Univ. Park Airport to N. Seat and main campus of Pa. State Univ. (includes Mus. of Art and Frost Entomological Mus.). Rothrock State Forest and Whipple Dam State Park to S, Black Moshannon State Park to NW; Tussey Mt. Ski Area to E; Colyer L. Recreation Area to E. Settled 1859, inc. 1896.

State Line 1 town (1990 pop. 182), Warren co., W Ind., on Ill. state line, 8 mi/12.9 km NE of Danville (Ill.); 40°12′N 87°32′W. Agr. area. Also called State Line City. Laid out 1857. **2** uninc. town (1990 pop. 1,253), Franklin co., S Pa., 5 mi/8 km N of Hagerstown (Md.), at Md. state line; 39°43′N 77°43′W. Agr. includes dairying; livestock, poultry; grain, potatoes, apples. Washington Co. Regional Airport (Md.) is 1 mi/1.6 km to SW. Greencastle Military Reservation to N.

State Line 1 village (1990 pop. 26), Kootenai co., N Idaho, on Wash. state line, 14 mi/23 km W of Coeur d'Alene, and 16 mi/26 km E of Spokane (Wash.); 47°43′N 117°02′W. Stateline Stadium and Speedway, Coeur d'Alene Greyhound Park. Hauser L. to N. **2** village (1990 pop. 395), Greene and Wayne cos., SE Miss., 41 mi/66 km ESE of Laurel, at Ala. state line; 31°26′N 88°28′W. Agr. (cotton, corn; cattle, poultry; timber). De Soto Natl. Forest to W.

State Line, Mass.: see WEST STOCKBRIDGE.

Stateburg, village, Sumter co., central S.C., near Wateree R., 15 mi/24 km NE of Sumter. Founded by Revolutionary War Gen. Sumter in 1786. One of sites considered for state capital.

Stateline, uninc. town (1990 pop. 1,379), Douglas co., E Nev., 16 mi/26 km SW of Carson City, on SE shore of L. Tahoe, on Calif. state line, opposite South Lake Tahoe (Calif.); 38°58′N 119°56′W. Gambling resort. Toiyabe Natl. Forest to NE and SE; Tahoe Natl. Forest (Calif.) to S. Heavenly Valley Ski Area to S.

Staten Island (STA-tuhn) (□ 102 sq mi/264 sq km; 1990 pop. 378,977), SE N.Y., in N.Y. Bay, SW of Manhattan, forming Richmond co. of N.Y. state and the borough of Staten Isl. of N.Y. city; 40°33′N 74°08′W. It is separated from N.J. by Kill Van Kull and Arthur Kill, which are crossed by bridges (Goethals, Bayonne, Outerbridge Crossing, and a RR-lift bridge). Ferries connect the isl. with Manhattan, and the Verrazano-Narrows Bridge links it with Brooklyn. The hills of NE Staten Isl. rise to 410 ft/125 m at Todt Hill, the highest point along the Atlantic coast S of Maine. The industrial area of Staten Isl. is located in the N, where docks (now mostly abandoned, but Howland Hook Marine Terminal was reopened in 1994) line the N and E shores. The availability of open space has made the isl. the site of large container-handling facilities. Centers of trade include St. George (Borough Hall) and Port Richmond, as well as Hylan Boulevard (Clove Road to Tysens Lane) and the Staten Isl. Mall. Beaches and parks, including part of Gateway Natl. Recreation Area, are found along the SE coast. The isl. was visited by Henry Hudson in 1609 and was called *Staaten Eylandet* by the Dutch. The native pop. drove off the 1st Eur. settlers, but by 1661 a permanent settlement had been founded. Though there was considerable industrial activity here in the 19th cent., its predominant character was semi-rural, something which had not changed when it became a borough of N.Y. city in 1898. The turning point in its recent history was the completion of the Verrazano-Narrows Bridge (1964). Since then Staten Isl. has had an influx of new residents and industries, including Staten Isl. Teleport and a containerboard-recycling plant. Changes in the 1980s in the structure of N.Y. city's govt. led many Staten Islanders to believe their voting strength was being diminished, and by the 1990s a movement to secede from the city had gathered considerable strength. In 1993, a referendum endorsing Staten Isl.'s independence from N.Y. city received 65% of voter approval. An independent city, opposed by the N.Y. city govt., is unlikely because the state govt. must approve such a change. Staten Isl. is the only outer borough with its own newspaper, the Staten Isl. *Advance.* Among the extant bldgs. of the 17th–19th cent. is the Billopp, or Conference, House (built before 1688), in which an unsuccessful Amer. Revolution peace conference was held in 1776. The Richmondtown Restoration, an example of 18th- and 19th-cent. life on the isl., includes Voorlezer's House (built c.1695). Other points of interest include several old churches, Sailor's Snug Harbor, the Garibaldi-Meucci Memorial Mus., Fort Wadsworth, the Staten Isl. Zoo, the Alice Austen House, and the Jacques Marchais Center for Tibetan Art. Seat of Wagner Col., Col. of Staten Isl. (of the City Univ. of N.Y.), Silver L. Reservoir and Park, and a branch of St. John's Univ. Also on Staten Isl. is the Fresh Kills Landfill.

Statenville (STA-tuhn-vil), village, ⊙ Echols co., S Ga., 17 mi/27 km ESE of Valdosta, and on Alapaha R., near Fla.state line; 30°42′N 83°01′W.

Statesboro (STAITS-buhr-o), city (1990 pop. 15,854), ⊙ Bulloch co., E Ga.; 32°26′N 81°47′W. Mfg. includes foods, fertilizers, fabricated metal prods., paper prods., clothing; lumber and concrete processing. Ga. Southern Univ., a unit of the Univ. System of Ga., is here. Founded 1803, inc. 1902.

Statesville, city (1990 pop. 17,567), ⊙ Iredell co., W central N.C., 45 mi/72 km SW of Winston-Salem, on a plateau in the Blue Ridge foothills; 35°47′N 80°53′W. RR junction. Major commercial and industrial center. Agr. area (tobacco, grain, soybeans; chickens, cattle). Mfg. (transportation equip., machinery, concrete, furniture, hot air balloons, flour, feeds, textiles and apparel, lumber, paper; wood, plastic, and metal prods., mobile homes, glass prods., consumer goods; printing and publishing). Fort Dobbs (1795) State Historic Site to N. Duke Power State Park on L. Norman reservoir (Catawba R.) to SW. Mitchell Community Col. Statesville Arts and Science Center. Founded 1789, inc. 1847.

Statham (STAI-tuhm), town (1990 pop. 1,360), Barrow co., NE central Ga., 13 mi/21 km W of Athens; 33°58′N 83°36′W. Mfg. of potting soil and batteries.

Statia, Neth. Antilles: see SAINT EUSTATIUS.

Statue of Liberty National Monument, national historic site, SE N.Y., Upper Bay of N.Y. Harbor, 2 mi/3.2 km SW of S tip of Manhattan, on Liberty Isl.; 40°41′N 74°01′W. The Statue of Liberty was a gift from France to the U.S. symbolizing alliance and friendship bet. the 2 nations; dedicated Oct. 28, 1886, on the site of what was then called Bedloe's Isl., it was proclaimed a natl. monument in 1924. The site was chosen and the statue designed by Fr. sculptor Frederic-Augusta Bertholdi; Gustave Eiffel designed the statue supports, and American Richard Morris Hunt designed the Neo-Grecian base. It has become an internationally known landmark with particular significance with regard to immigrants coming to the U.S. The tip of the statue's torch is 305 ft/93 m above the waters of N.Y. Harbor. Enlargement of the base to accommodate the Mus. of Amer. Immigration, begun in 1956, was completed in 1972. In 1965, nearby Ellis Isl. became part of the natl. monument. A major, $150-million refurbishment of the statue and landscaping around it (1984–1986) was financed by donations by individuals and corporations. The statue is also known as Lady Liberty.

Staunton 1 city (1990 pop. 4,806), Macoupin co., SW Ill., 19 mi/31 km SSE of Carlinville; 39°00′N 89°47′W. Trade center for agr. and bituminous-coal mining area. Settled 1817, laid out 1835, inc. 1859. **2** independent city (□ 19 sq mi/49 sq km; 1990 pop. 24,461), ⊙ surrounding Augusta co., NW Va., in Shenandoah Valley; 38°09′N 79°03′W. RR junction. Trade and industrial center; mfg. (feeds and fertilizer, crushed limestone, beverages, furniture, fabricated metal prods., bldg. materials, textile prods., clothing, machinery; machining, printing and publishing). Agr. area (known for its poultry, livestock; apples, grain, soybeans; dairying). Civil War Confederate supply base; twice occupied by Federal forces. Origin of city manager form of govt. (1908). President Woodrow Wilson's Birthplace (natl. shrine since 1941) and Mus.; Mus. of Amer. Frontier Culture; many historic colonial houses. Mary Baldwin Col.; Va. School for the Deaf and Blind (est. 1838); Western State Hosp.; Staunton Correctional Center. Natural Chimneys Regional Park to N. Settled 1732, inc. as a city 1871.

Staunton, town (1990 pop. 592), Clay co., W Ind., 4 mi/6.4 km SW of Brazil; 39°29′N 87°11′W. Agr. and bituminous-coal area (surface mines). Founded 1851.

Staunton River, Va.: see ROANOKE RIVER.

Stave Falls, village, SW B.C., W Canada, on Stave R. at S end of Stave L., and 7 mi/11 km NNW of Mission. Site of dam and hydroelectric plant; lumbering.

Stave Lake (□ 24 sq mi/62 sq km), SW B.C., W Canada, 35 mi/56 km E of Vancouver; 18 mi/29 km long, 1 mi/2 km–5 mi/8 km wide. Elev. 270 ft/82 m. Drained S by short Stave R. into Fraser R.

Stavely, town (1991 pop. 478), S Alta., W Canada, 55 mi/89 km SSE of Calgary. Mixed farming (wheat, flax); cattle.

Stayner (STAI-nuhr), town (1991 pop. 3,458), S Ont., central Canada, near Georgian Bay, 45 mi/72 km ESE of Owen Sound; 44°25′N 80°05′W. Stockyard, cider mills.

Stayton, town (1990 pop. 5,011), Marion co., NW Oregon, on North Santiam R.,15 mi/24 km SE of Salem; 44°47′N 122°47′W. Agr. (fruit, vegetables, berries, nuts; poultry); dairy prods. Mfg. (foods, mobile homes, bldg. materials, aluminum prods.). Inc. 1891.

Steamboat or **Steamboat Springs**, uninc. village, Washoe co., NW Nev., 13 mi/21 km N of Carson City. Hot springs known for their mineral deposition processes. Reno bedroom community.

Steamboat Rock, town (1990 pop. 335), Hardin co., central Iowa, on Iowa R., and 4 mi/6.4 km NNE of Eldora; 42°24′N 93°04′W. Lumber. Steamboat Rock State Park nearby.

Steamboat Springs, town (1990 pop. 6,695), ⊙ Routt co., NW Colo., on Yampa R., just W of Park Range, and 110 mi/177 km NW of Denver; 40°28′N 106°49′W. Elev. 6,725 ft/2,050 m. Resort and skiing center. Cattle, sheep; wheat, barley, hay. Mfg. (publishing and printing, diversified light mfg.; consumer goods). Has hot mineral springs. Coal mines in vicinity. Hahns Mining Dist. to N. Hq. of nearby Routt Natl. Forest (to E). Howelsen Ski Area to W; Steamboat Ski Area to SE. Pearl Lake and Steamboat L. state parks to N; Stagecoach State Park to S. Founded 1875, inc. 1907.

Steamburg, village (1990 pop. 900), Cattaraugus co., W

N.Y., 17 mi/27 km E of Jamestown, near Allegany Indian Reservation; 42°07′N 78°54′W. Dairy prods.

Steamtown National Historic Site, Lackawanna co., NE Pa., in city of Scranton, on Lackawanna R., immediately W of downtown. A RR yard containing largest collection of steam era locomotives in the U.S., dedicated to the nation's RR heritage. Authorized 1986.

Stearns (STUHRNZ), county (□ 1,389 sq mi/3,598 sq km; 1990 pop. 118,791), central Minn.; ⊙ St. Cloud; 45°32′N 94°36′W. Bordered by Mississippi (E) and Clearwater (SE) rivers; watered by Sauk R. Agr. area (corn, oats, barley, wheat, rye, alfalfa, hay, soybeans, beans; sheep, hogs, cattle, poultry, mink; dairying); granite. Has numerous small lakes, esp. in S; L. Koronis on S border; Clearwater L. on SE border. Part of Birch L. State Forest on N border. Formed 1855.

Stearns (STUHRNZ), town (1990 pop. 1,550), McCreary co., SE Ky., in the Cumberland Mts., 29 mi/47 km SSE of Somerset; 36°41′N 84°28′W. Shipping point for coal and timber area; mfg. (transportation equip., wood prods., textiles, apparel). Big South Fork Natl. River and Recreation Area to W; Big South Fork Scenic RR runs W to Blue Heron community. Surrounded by Daniel Boone Natl. Forest.

Stebbins (STEE-binz), village (1990 pop. 400), W Alaska, on SE shore of Norton Sound, 7 mi/11.3 km WNW of St. Michael; 63°28′N 162°13′W.

Stedman, village (1990 pop. 577), Cumberland co., S central N.C., 10 mi/16 km ESE of Fayetteville; 35°00′N 78°42′W. Timber; cotton, tobacco, grain, peanuts; poultry, livestock. Mfg. (chemicals, wood prods.).

Steele 1 county (□ 432 sq mi/1,119 sq km; 1990 pop. 30,729), SE Minn.; ⊙ Owatonna; 44°01′N 93°13′W. Drained by Straight R. Agr. area (corn, oats, alfalfa, hay, soybeans, peas; hogs, sheep, cattle, poultry; dairying). Rice L. State Park on E border. Formed 1855. **2** county (□ 710 sq mi/1,839 sq km; 1990 pop. 2,420), E N.Dak.; ⊙ Finley; 47°27′N 97°43′W. Farming area watered by Goose R. Wheat, rye, potatoes, flax; cattle; dairy prods. Formed 1883. Red R. Valley in E.

Steele, city (1990 pop. 2,395), Pemiscot co., in the bootheel of extreme SE Mo., near Mississippi R., 12 mi/19 km SW of Caruthersville; 36°04′N 89°50′W. Rice, soybeans; cotton. RR shops. Mfg. of apparel. Inc. 1901.

Steele, town (1990 pop. 762), ⊙ Kidder co., central N.Dak., 40 mi/64 km E of Bismarck; 46°51′N 99°55′W. Grain elevators; shipping center for livestock; wheat, barley, rye; dairying. Long L. Natl. Wildlife Refuge to SW; Chaska Historic Site to WNW.

Steele City, village (1990 pop. 101), Jefferson co., SE Nebr., 11 mi/18 km SE of Fairbury, and on Little Blue R.; 40°02′N 97°01′W.

Steele, Mount (16,644 ft/5,073 m), in the St. Elias Mts., SW Yukon Territory, W Canada, in Kluane Natl. Park near the U.S. (Alaska) border; one of Canada's tallest peaks.

Steeles Tavern, uninc. village, Augusta co., W Va., 17 mi/27 km SSW of Staunton, near South R.; 37°55′N 79°12′W. Walnut Grove Farm, where Cyrus McCormick perfected his grain reaper is nearby. Also known as Midway Village.

Steeleville, village (1990 pop. 2,059), Randolph co., SW Ill., 12 mi/19 km NE of Chester; 38°00′N 89°39′W. Agr. (grain; poultry; dairying); bituminous-coal mines. Mfg. (fabricated metal prods., food prods.). Inc. 1851.

Steelton (STEEL-tuhn), borough (1990 pop. 5,152), Dauphin co., S central Pa., suburb, 4 mi/6.4 km SE of Harrisburg, on Susquehanna R.; 40°13′N 76°49′W. Limestone. Capital City Airport to S (across river). Site of Oberllin Gardens. First practical production of Bessemer steel in U.S. here, 1867. Once a steel-producing center, now has a steel minimill. Settled 1865.

Steelville, city (1990 pop. 1,465), ⊙ Crawford co., E central Mo., in the Ozark Mts., near Meramec R., 75 mi/121 km SW of St. Louis; 37°58′N 91°21′W. Hay, grapes; cattle; winery. Tourism; canoeing, floating, fishing. Mfg. (glue). Former iron-mining dist. to S. Remolded as 19th-cent. town. Founded 1835. U.S. center of pop. (1990) 9.7 mi/15.6 km SE of Steelville.

Steen, village (1990 pop. 176), Rock co., extreme SW Minn., 10 mi/16 km SSW of Luverne, near Iowa state line; 43°30′N 96°15′W. Grain; livestock, poultry; dairying.

Steens Mountain (9,670 ft/2,947 m), Harney co., SE Oregon, c. 60 mi/97 km S of Burns, ridge 40 mi/64 km long N-S. Alvord Desert to E.

Steep Rock Lake, SW Ont., central Canada, W of Lac des Mille Lacs; 4 mi/6.4 km long, 3 mi/5 km wide. Site of important iron-ore mining. Part of the lake was drained to facilitate the mining, and the flow of the Seine R. was diverted.

Steeples, The, mountain (9,100 ft/2,774 m), SE B.C., W Canada, in Rocky Mts., 16 mi/26 km E of Cranbrook, overlooking the Kootenay valley; 49°34′N 115°25′W.

Steese Highway, highway, 162 mi/261 km long, N central Alaska. Starts northbound as Alaska Route 2 from intersection of Alaska and George Parks highways on SE side of Fairbanks. At a point 10 mi/16 km to N, the Chena Hot Springs Road branches E 57 mi/92 km to hot springs resort. At village of Fox, Route 2 continues NW with the Elliot Highway; the Steese Highway turns NE and continues as Route 6, following the Chatanika R. for much of its length. It passes through Eagle Summit Pass (3624 ft/1105 m), then through village of Central, where it intersects the Circle of Hot Springs Road from SE, then terminates at village of Circle, on Yukon R., c.50 mi/80 km S of Arctic Circle.

Steger (STE-ger), village (1990 pop. 8,584), in Cook and Will cos., NE Ill., near Ind. state line, suburb, 31 mi/50 km S of downtown Chicago; 41°28′N 87°37′W. Agr. (corn; cattle; dairying); light mfg. Inc. 1896.

Steilacoom (STI-luh-kuhm), town (1990 pop. 5,728), Pierce co., W central Wash., on Puget Sound, and suburb, 7 mi/11.3 km SW of downtown Tacoma; 47°10′N 122°35′W. Mfg. (paper mill). Has historic landmarks. Ferry to Anderson and McNeil (Federal Penitentiary) isls. Has mus. and parks. Fort Lewis Military Reservation to S. Founded 1850; inc. 1854; oldest incorporated settlement in the state.

Steinauer (STIN-ou-uhr), village (1990 pop. 92), Pawnee co., SE Nebr., on Turkey Creek, 7 mi/11.3 km NNW of Pawnee City; 40°12′N 96°13′W.

Steinbach, town (1991 pop. 8,213), SE Man., central Canada, 27 mi/43 km SE of Winnipeg; 49°31′N 96°41′W. Commuter suburb. About 7,000 Mennonites from Russia settled in area, 1874–1880. Mennonite Heritage Village replicates settlement era. Mixed farming (wheat); dairying. Lumbering; boat mfg., publishing.

Stella, town (1990 pop. 132), Newton co., SW Mo., in the Ozark Mts., 12 mi/19 km SE of Neosho; 36°45′N 94°11′W.

Stella, village (1990 pop. 248), Richardson co., SE Nebr., 15 mi/24 km NW of Falls City, near Missouri R.; 40°13′N 95°46′W. Grain; livestock; dairy and poultry prods.

Stellarton (STE-luhr-tuhn), town (1991 pop. 5,237), N N.S., E Canada, 3 mi/5 km S of New Glasgow; 45°34′N 62°40′W. Coal mining (mainly for power-generating plants), mfg. of steel prods. (declining), soft drinks, apparel; large RR shops. Agr. area.

Stellaville (STE-luh-vil), town, Jefferson co., E Ga., 27 mi/43 km SW of Augusta; 33°11′N 82°19′W.

Steller, Mount (10,617 ft/3,236 m), S Alaska, in Chugach Mts., N of Bering Glacier, 90 mi/145 km E of Cordova; 60°31′N 143°05′W.

Stelton, village, Middlesex co., NE N.J., 2 mi/3.2 km NE of New Brunswick. Settled by Baptists before 1700.

Stem, village (1990 pop. 249), Granville co., N N.C., 17 mi/27 km NE of Durham; 36°12′N 78°43′W. Tobacco, grain; poultry, livestock. Camp Butner Natl. Guard Base to SW.

Stenen (STE-nuhn), agr. village (1991 pop. 120), E Sask., W Canada, near Assiniboine R., 50 mi/80 km N of Yorkton; 51°54′N 102°21′W.

Stephen, village, SE B.C., W Canada, on Alta. border, in Rocky Mts., in Yoho Natl. Park, at W end of Kicking Horse Pass, 35 mi/56 km NW of Banff; 51°27′N 116°18′W. Elev. 5,337 ft/1,627 m. Lumbering.

Stephen, village (1990 pop. 707), Marshall co., NW Minn., 19 mi/31 km NNW of Warren, on Tamarac R.; 48°27′N 96°52′W. Potatoes, sugar beets, beans, wheat; cattle, sheep; mfg. (agr. equip.).

Stephen, Mount (10,494 ft/3,199 m), SE B.C., W Canada, near Alta. border, in Rocky Mts., in Yoho Natl. Park, 40 mi/64 km WNW of Banff; 51°24′N 116°26′W.

Stephens 1 (STEE-vuhnz), county (□ 184 sq mi/477 sq km; 1990 pop. 23,257), NE Ga., on S.C. (E) state line (Tugaloo R.); ⊙ Toccoa; 34°34′N 83°17′W. Drained by headstreams of Broad R. Mfg. (textiles, furniture, metal prods.); agr. (cotton, corn, hay, sweet potatoes); cattle; stone quarrying. W part in Chattahoochee Natl. Forest. Formed 1905. **2** county (□ 891 sq mi/2,308 sq km; 1990 pop. 42,299), S Okla.; ⊙ Duncan; 34°28′N 97°51′W. Drained by Wildhorse Creek; includes small Comanche and Duncan lakes near center. Agr. (wheat, corn, oats, fruit, melons, peanuts; poultry, livestock; dairying). Oil and natural-gas fields; mfg. (concrete prods., machinery, medical supplies). Famed Chisolm Trail intersected co. Part of Waurika L. (Beaver Creek) in SW corner. Formed 1907. **3** county (□ 921 sq mi/2,385 sq km; 1990 pop. 9,010), N central Texas; ⊙ Breckenridge; 32°44′N 98°50′W. Drained by Clear Fork of Brazos R. and Sandy, Hubbard and Gonzales creeks. Diversified agr. (wheat, oats, grain sorghum, peanuts, pecans; cotton); livestock raising (cattle, goats, sheep, hogs, horses). Oil, natural-gas wells. Part of Possum Kingdom L. (recreation) is in NE, Possum Kingdom State Park on E border; Hubbard Creek Reservoir in W, L. Daniel reservoir in S. Formed 1858; renamed from Buchanan, 1861.

Stephens (STEE-vuhnz), town (1990 pop. 1,137), Ouachita co., S Ark., 18 mi/29 km SW of Camden; 33°25′N 93°04′W. In cotton-growing area. Oil refinery; mfg. (chemicals, textiles). Oil and gas wells in area.

Stephens City, town (1990 pop. 1,186), Frederick co., N Va., in Shenandoah Valley, 8 mi/12.9 km SSW of Winchester; 39°6′N 78°13′W. Light mfg.; agr. (apple-growing region; also grain; livestock; dairying).

Stephens Passage, channel, 105 mi/169 km long, SE Alaska, bet. Admiralty Isl. and mainland, S of Juneau; part of Inside Passage to Alaska.

Stephenson (STE-vin-son), county (□ 564 sq mi/1,461 sq km; 1990 pop. 48,052), N Ill., on Wis. (N) state line; ⊙ Freeport; 42°21′N 89°40′W. Dairying and agr. area (livestock; corn, wheat, oats, nursery prods.); mfg. of textiles, hardware. Drained by Pecatonica R. and small Yellow and Richland creeks. Formed 1837.

Stephenson, village (1990 pop. 904), Menominee co., SW Upper Peninsula, N Mich., 21 mi/34 km N of Menominee, and on Little Cedar R.; 45°24′N 87°36′W. In dairying and agr. area.

Stephenson, Miss.: see CROSBY.

Stephenville, city (1990 pop. 13,502), ⊙ Erath co., N central Texas, on Bosque R., and c.60 mi/97 km SW of Fort Worth; 32°13′N 98°13′W. Elev. 1,283 ft/391 m. Processing center in agr. area (cotton, peanuts, grain, pecans; dairy prods.); state's leading milk-production region (many farmers of Du. origin); feed milling; poultry hatcheries; nursery stock. Mfg. (electrical equip., sandpaper, fertilizers, transportation equip., fabricated metal prods.; printing). Seat of Tarleton State Univ. Founded 1850, inc. 1888.

Stephenville, town (1991 pop. 7,621), SW N.F., E Canada, on N shore of St. George Bay, 40 mi/64 km SW of Corner Brook; 48°32′N 58°36′W. Fishing port. Site of Harmon Field, U.S. air base built 1941; transport and ferrying field during World War II, is now town airport. Dairying and cattle and poultry raising in region.

Stepney, village, SW Conn., 5 mi/8 km NW of Trumbull, on Pequonnock R.

Stepovak Bay, 17 mi/27 km long, 17 mi/27 km wide at mouth, SW Alaska, in S coast of Alaska Peninsula, N of Shumagin Isls.; 55°45′N 159°49′W. Deep, sheltered anchorage.

Sterco (STUHR-ko), village, W Alta., W Canada, in Rocky Mts., near E side of Jasper Natl. Park, 40 mi/64 km SW of Edson. Coal mining; cattle. Also known as Coal Valley.

Sterling, county (□ 923 sq mi/2,391 sq km; 1990 pop. 1,438), W Texas; ⊙ Sterling City; 31°49′N 101°02′W.

Elev. c.2,000 ft/610 m–2,600 ft/792 m. In rolling prairies, drained by North Concho R. Ranching region (sheep, goats, beef cattle); wheat; wool, mohair marketed; some agr; oil and natural gas. Organized 1891.

Sterling 1 city (1990 pop. 10,362), ⊙ Logan co., NE Colo., on the South Platte R.; 40°37′N 103°12′W. Elev. 3,939 ft/1,201 m. RR junction. It is the trading and shipping center of an agr. area (grain; cattle). Mfg. (fabricated metal prods., machinery, farm implements; printing and publishing). Oil was discovered nearby in the 1950s, and oil-related industries developed here. Northeastern Junior Col. here. Pawnee Natl. Grassland to W; Sterling Reservoir and North Sterling State Park to NW; Summit Springs Battlefield to S. Inc. 1884. **2** city (1990 pop. 15,132), Whiteside co., NW Ill., on the Rock R., opposite Rock Falls; 41°47′N 89°41′W. It is an industrial center in a farm region. Fabricated metal prods., machinery. Inc. 1841. **3** uninc. city, Loudoun co., N Va., suburb 23 mi/37 km WNW of Washington, D.C., 10 mi/16 km SE of Leesburg; 39°00′N 77°24′W. Mfg. (duct work, computers, electronic prods. and equip., foods, furniture, bldg. materials, transportation equip.; printing and publishing, steel fabricating, machining). Northern Va. Community Col. (Loudoun Campus). Dulles Internatl. Airport to S, Natl. Weather Service to SW.

Sterling 1 town (1990 pop. 2,357), Windham co., E Conn., on Moosup R., near R.I. state line, and 17 mi/27 km NE of Norwich; 41°42′N 71°49′W. In hilly region; agr. (poultry and dairy farming). Mfg. of monuments; granite quarrying. Set off from Voluntown 1974. **2** town (1990 pop. 2,115), Rice co., S central Kansas, 18 mi/29 km NW of Hutchinson, near Arkansas R.; 38°12′N 98°12′W. RR junction. In wheat region. Mfg. (machinery, feeds). Salt mines and oil wells nearby. Seat of Sterling Col. Inc. 1876. **3** residential town (1990 pop. 6,481), Worcester co., central Mass., 12 mi/19 km N of Worcester; 42°26′N 71°46′W. Apple orchards; dairying. Suburban housing developments. Settled 1720, inc. 1781.

Sterling 1 village (1990 pop. 520), Arenac co., E Mich., 4 mi/6.4 km NW of Standish; 44°01′N 84°01′W. In farm area; sawmills. **2** village (1990 pop. 451), Johnson co., SE Nebr., 30 mi/48 km SSE of Lincoln, and on North Fork of Big Nemaha R.; 40°27′N 96°22′W. Grain; livestock, poultry. **3** village (1990 pop. 684), Comanche co., SW Okla., 16 mi/26 km NE of Lawton, on Beaver Creek; 34°45′N 98°10′W. In agr. area. **4** village (1990 pop. 191), Sanpete co., central Utah, 5 mi/8 km SSW of Manti, and near San Pitch R.; 39°11′N 111°41′W. Settled 1881. Gunnison Reservoir to N, Nine Mile Reservoir to SW. Palisade State Park to E; Manti–La Sal Natl. Forest to E.

Sterling City, town (1990 pop. 1,096), ⊙ Sterling co., W Texas, 40 mi/64 km NW of San Angelo, and on North Concho R.; 31°50′N 100°59′W. Elev. 2,294 ft/699 m. In ranching region (cattle, sheep, goats); wheat. Mfg. (natural-gas processing). Large E. V. Spence Reservoir to NE.

Sterling Heights, city (1990 pop. 117,810), Macomb co., SE Mich., suburb, 16 mi/26 km N of downtown Detroit, on Clinton R.; 42°34′N 83°01′W. Mfg. (transportation equip., machinery, plastic prods., wood prods.; machining). Aerospace center. Site of Lakeside, one of the largest shopping centers in U.S. Rochester-Utica State Recreation Area to N; Dodge Bros. State Park No. 8 in city.

Sterling Highway, 136 mi/219 km long, Kenai Peninsula, S Alaska; begins at intersection of Seward Highway at Tern Lake Junction, 45 mi/72 km S of Anchorage, a continuation of Alaska Route 1 from NE. It runs W across peninsula through Cooper Landing, connects on N to Kenai and Sterling to Soldotna, near Cook Inlet, where it turns SW. After passing Kasilof, it follows the Cook Inlet shore for the remainder of its length, turning SE at Anchor Point, continuing at or near the shore to Homer. This is the southernmost point in the Alaska highway system outside the Alaska Panhandle. Homer Spit Road extends 5 mi/8 km SE of Homer on a narrow strip of land separating Kechamak Bay from Cook Inlet. The state ferry system operates from the terminal at the SE end of the spit, serving communities on Kenai Peninsula, Kodiak Isl. and Prince William Sound. Paved.

Sterling Park, uninc. town (1990 pop. 1,700), San Mateo co., W Calif., residential suburb, 7 mi/11.3 km SW of downtown San Francisco, and 1 mi/1.6 km S of Daly City. San Bruno Mts. to E.

Sterling Reservoir (□ 5 sq mi/13 sq km), Logan co., NE Colo., on Cedar Creek (also known as Two Mile Creek), 15 mi/24 km N of Sterling; 40°47′N 103°16′W. Max. capacity 113,600 acre-ft. Formed by Point of Rocks Dam (86 ft/26 m high), built (1948) for irrigation. North Sterling State Park on N shore.

Sterlington (STUHR-ling-tuhn), town (1990 pop. 1,140), Ouachita parish, NE central La., 13 mi/21 km N of Monroe, near Ouachita R.; 32°42′N 92°04′W. In agr. (cotton, sorghum, vegetables, fruit) and natural-gas area; logging. Mfg. (fabricated structural steel, chemicals). D'Arbonne Natl. Wildlife Refuge to SW.

Stetson, town (1990 pop. 847), Penobscot co., S central Maine, 20 mi/32 km WNW of Bangor; 44°52′N 69°06′W.

Stetsonville, village (1990 pop. 511), Taylor co., N central Wis., 5 mi/8 km S of Medford; 45°04′N 90°18′W. Hardwoods, fertilizers.

Stettler, town (1991 pop. 4,947), S central Alta., W Canada, 50 mi/80 km E of Red Deer; 52°20′N 112°41′W. Grain elevators, flour and grist mills; dairying; mfg. of cereal foods. In coal-mining region.

Steuben 1 (STOO-buhn), county (□ 322 sq mi/834 sq km; 1990 pop. 27,446), extreme NE Ind., on Mich. (N) and Ohio (E) state lines; ⊙ Angola; 41°38′N 85°00′W. Drained by Pigeon Creek. Resort lakes. Wheat, hay, corn; hogs, sheep, cattle, poultry; dairying. Over 15 small lakes, glacial in origin, dispersed throughout co.; largest is L. James, in North Pokagon State Park (on E shore); part of Pigeon R. State Fish and Wildlife Area in W. Fawn R. State Fish Hatchery in NW corner. Formed 1835. **2** county (□ 1,404 sq mi/3,636 sq km; 1990 pop. 99,088), S N.Y., on Pa. (S) state line; ⊙ Bath; 42°15′N 77°23′W. Extends N into Finger Lakes region; includes part of Keuka L. Drained by Canisteo, Cohocton, Tioga, and Chemung rivers. Dairying, and potato- and grape-growing area, with diversified mfg. at Corning, Hornell, Bath, Canisteo, Hammondsport. World-famous Steuben glass produced at Corning. Timber; sand and gravel pits. Also grows grain, hay. Formed 1796.

Steuben (STOO-ben), fishing town (1990 pop. 1,084), Washington co., E Maine, on inlet of the Atlantic Ocean, and 29 mi/47 km WSW of Machias; 44°27′N 67°55′W. Lumbering; resorts.

Steuben (STOO-buhn), village (1990 pop. 161), Crawford co., SW Wis., on Kickapoo R., and 17 mi/27 km NE of Prairie du Chien; 43°10′N 90°51′W.

Steubenville (STOO-buhn-vil), city (1990 pop. 22,125), ⊙ Jefferson co., E central Ohio, on the Ohio R., across from W. Va.; 40°22′N 80°39′W. It is one of the oldest communities in the state. Its major steel industry has declined; mfg. includes tin, metals, chemicals, and paper goods. Bituminous coal is also mined. Of interest is the birthplace of Edwin M. Stanton. The Col. of Steubenville and a technical institute are here. The City of Murals, downtown, is a series of 19 bldgs. with historical scenes depicted on large murals. Laid out c.1797, inc. as a city 1851.

Stevens 1 county (□ 727 sq mi/1,883 sq km; 1990 pop. 5,048), SW Kansas, on Okla. (S) state line; ⊙ Hugoton; 37°12′N 101°19′W. Gently rolling plain; crossed in NW by Cimarron R. Cattle; wheat, sorghum, corn, alfalfa. Formed 1886. **2** county (□ 575 sq mi/1,489 sq km; 1990 pop. 10,634), W Minn.; ⊙ Morris; 45°34′N 96°00′W. Drained by Pomme de Terre R. Agr. area (wheat, corn, oats, barley, soybeans, alfalfa, beans, sunflowers; hogs, sheep, cattle). Several small lakes scattered throughout co. Formed 1862. **3** county (□ 2,540 sq mi/6,579 sq km; 1990 pop. 30,948), NE Wash., on Canada (N; B.C.) border; ⊙ Colville; 48°24′N 117°51′W. Watered by Columbia (Franklin D. Roosevelt reservoir with Kettle R. in NW, forms W border), and Colville rivers. Bounded S by Spokane R., has Little Falls and Long L. dams; arm of Roosevelt reservoir extends to Little Falls Dam. Mining (copper, gold, silver, zinc, marble, magnesium); agr. (alfalfa, hay, wheat, barley, oats; hogs; dairying); magnesite and cement processing; stone quarries. Forty-Nine Degrees North Ski Area in E; small part of Kaniksa Natl. Forest along E border; Little Pend Oreille Natl. Wildlife Refuge in E; Crystal Falls State Park in E; parts of Colville Natl. Forest in NW, NE, and E; Spokane Indian Reservation in SW; Coulee Dam Natl. Recreation Area extends along outer shore of Roosevelt Reservoir, including Spokane R. portion. Part of Selkirk Mts. in E. Formed 1863.

Stevens Pass (4,061 ft/1,238 m), on border bet. King and Chelan cos., central Wash., highway pass (U.S. Highway 2) through crest of Cascade Range, 55 mi/89 km ENE of Seattle. Cascade Tunnel (RR) 8 mi/12.9 km long, beneath pass.

Stevens Point, city (1990 pop. 23,006), ⊙ Portage co., central Wis., on the Wisconsin R., N of mouth of Plover R.; 44°31′N 89°33′W. The major industries are insurance and the mfg. of wood prods., cheese, furniture, and fishing equip. The Univ. of Wis. at Stevens Point is here. Inc. 1858.

Stevens Pottery, village, Baldwin co., central Ga., 9 mi/14.5 km SSW of Milledgeville; 32°58′N 83°17′W.

Stevens Village, village (1990 pop. 102), N central Alaska, on Yukon R., and 90 mi/145 km NNW of Fairbanks; 66°00′N 149°03′W. Airfield.

Stevenson 1 town (1990 pop. 2,046), Jackson co., NE Ala., on inlet of Tennessee R., and 19 mi/31 km NE of Scottsboro. Mfg. (clothes, textiles, paper prods., lumber). **2** town (1990 pop. 1,147), ⊙ Skamania co., SW Wash., 35 mi/56 km ENE of Vancouver, and on Columbia R. (Bonneville reservoir), near Cascade foothills; 45°42′N 121°54′W. Wheat, fruit; timber; dairying; poultry; salmon. Mfg. (consumer goods). Bonneville Dam 5 mi/8 km SW. Gifford Pinchot Natl. Forest to N. Bridge of the Gods, 2 mi/3.2 km SSW (to Cascade Locks, Oregon).

Stevenson, village, Fairfield co., SW Conn., 12 mi/19 km N of Bridgeport. Site of Stevenson Dam on Housatonic R. Eagle observation site. A postal sect. of Monroe.

Stevensville (STEE-vuhns-vil), town (1990 pop. 1,221), Ravalli co., W Mont., 25 mi/40 km S of Missoula, and on Bitterroot R., at mouth of Burnt Fork Creek, on Idaho (W) state line; 46°31′N 114°05′W. Bitterroot Range to W, Sapphire Mts. to E. Mfg. (consumer goods). Potatoes, mint, hay; cattle. Parts of Bitterroot Natl. Forest to E and W; Selway-Bitterroot Wilderness Area to W; Lee Metcalf Natl. Wildlife Refuge to N. St. Mary's Mission is here; consists of small church and mus. containing mementos of religious settlement est. here (1841) by Father Pierre DeSmet; Stevensville Mus. Fort Owen (1850), 1 m/ 1.6 km to NW (state park).

Stevensville, village (1990 pop. 1,230), Berrien co., extreme SW Mich., 6 mi/9.7 km SSW of St. Joseph, near L. Michigan; 42°00′N 86°31′W. Fruit growing. Mfg. (fabricated metal prods., plastic prods.).

Stevensville, Md.: see KENT ISLAND.

Steveston (STEEVS-tuhn), town, SW B.C., W Canada, on the Strait of Georgia, at mouth of S arm of Fraser R. delta, on Lulu Isl., 10 mi/16 km SSW of Vancouver; 49°06′N 123°09′W. Part of city of Richmond. Fishing port; vegetables, small fruit. Steveston Heritage Fishing Village and Mus. here.

Steward, village (1990 pop. 282), Lee co., N Ill., on Steward Creek (bridged here), and 23 mi/37 km E of Dixon; 41°51′N 89°01′W. In rich agr. area.

Stewardson, village (1990 pop. 660), Shelby co., central Ill., 15 mi/24 km SE of Shelbyville; 39°15′N 88°37′W. Grain.

Stewart 1 county (□ 463 sq mi/1,199 sq km; 1990 pop. 5,654), SW Ga., on Ala. state line (W) (Chattahoochee R.); ⊙ Lumpkin, 32°05′N 84°50′W. Mfg. of mobile homes and electronic equip. Coastal plain agr. (cotton, corn, peanuts, fruit); cattle, poultry, hogs; sawmilling. Formed 1830. **2** county (□ 484; 1990 pop. 9,479), NW Tenn., on Ky. state line (N); ⊙ Dover, 36°30′N 87°51′W. Bordered W by Tennessee R. (Kentucky Reservoir);

drained by Cumberland R. Livestock; dairying; agr. (corn, fruit, hay, tobacco). Includes Fort Donelson Natl. Military Park and Fort Henry, and part of Land Between the Lakes Recreation Area. Formed 1803.

Stewart, village, W B.C., W Canada, on U.S. (Alaska) border, at head of Portland Canal, at mouth of Bear R., 120 mi/193 km N of Prince Rupert; 55°56'N 129°59'W. Elev. 10 ft/3 m. Port; mining (gold, silver) center. Fishing (salmon, herring). Historical mines. Ski resort. Time zone border runs bet. here and Hyder (Alaska).

Stewart 1 village (1990 pop. 566), McLeod co., S Minn., 17 mi/27 km WSW of Glencoe; 44°43'N 94°29'W. Agr. area (poultry; grain, soybeans; dairying); mfg. (feeds; metal polishing). **2** village, Montgomery co., central Miss., 17 mi/27 km E of Winona, near Big Black R.

Stewart, locality and independent city, Carcon City, W Nev., 4 mi/6.4 km S of downtown Carson City, in valley of Carson R. Pop. in 1960, c.900. Became part of Carson City in 1969.

Stewart, river, 331 mi/533 km long, Yukon Territory, W Canada; rises in the Mackenzie Mts., central Yukon Territory; flows generally W to the Yukon R. S of Dawson. Navigable for most of its length; transportation route for lead ore from its upper reaches. It was explored (1850) by Robert Campbell of the Hudson's Bay Company.

Stewart Air Force Base, N.Y.: see STEWART INTERNATIONAL AIRPORT.

Stewart International Airport orange co., E N.Y., 3 mi/4.8 km W of Newburgh, in the lower Hudson Valley, 65 mi/105 km N of N.Y. city; 41°30'N 74°06'W. Occupies the former site of Stewart Air Force Base (closed 1970; then bought, along with dozens of surrounding farms, by the Metropolitan Transportation Authority of N.Y city). During the big-project era of Gov. Nelson Rockefeller's administration, the intention was to create the city's 4th jetport, which was supposed to outstrip JFK Internatl. Airport in size and passenger volume. But even today, Stewart handles only 400,000 passengers and 73,000 tons of cargo per year, and processes only 1 internatl. flight per week. Now owned by N.Y. state Dept. of Transportation, the airport (with the capacity to handle 1 million passengers per year) serves Dutchess, Orange, Putnam, Sullivan, and Rockland cos.; it has easy access to I-84, the N.Y. State Thruway, and the Tappan Zee bridge.

Stewart Manor, residential village (1990 pop. 2,002), Nassau co., SE N.Y., on W L.I., bet. Garden City and Floral Park; 40°43'N 73°41'W. Laid out 1926, inc. 1927.

Stewart, Mount (10,871 ft/3,313 m), SW Alta., W Canada, in Rocky Mts., near NE edge of Banff Natl. Park, 70 mi/113 km SE of Jasper; 52°13'N 116°57'W.

Stewart Mountain Dam, Ariz., see SAGUARO LAKE.

Stewart Peak (13,983 ft/4,262 m), in Rocky Mts., SW Saguache co., S central Colo., c.15 mi/24 km N of Creede; 38°01'N 106°55'W.

Stewart River, village, W Yukon, W Canada, on Yukon R. at mouth of Stewart R., and 50 mi/80 km S of Dawson; 63°19'N 139°25'W. Trading post, transshipment point for Mayo Landing mining region.

Stewart Town, town, Trelawny parish, N Jamaica, 15 mi/24 km ESE of Falmouth; 18°22'N 77°27'W. Fruit, sugarcane; livestock. Settled by Germans, 1836–1842.

Stewartstown, town (1990 pop. 1,048), Coos co., NW N.H., 40 mi/64 km NNW of Berlin, on Vt. (W and NW) state line (Connecticut R.); 44°57'N 71°24'W. Separated from Canada (Que.) border by ½-mi/⅘-km strip of land belonging to Vt. Mfg. (paper); agr. (hay; poultry, cattle; dairying); timber. West Stewartstown village, 2 mi/3.2 km SW of town center, is its commercial center. Inc. 1795 and 1799.

Stewartstown, borough (1990 pop. 1,308), York co., S Pa., 17 mi/27 km SSE of York. Agr. area (soybeans, grain, apples, grapes; poultry, livestock; dairying); mfg. (fruit processing; wine, plastic prods.); 39°45'N 76°35'W. Naylor Winery to N.

Stewartsville, city (1990 pop. 732), De Kalb co., NW Mo., 18 mi/29 km E of St. Joseph; 39°45'N 94°30'W. Corn, wheat, soybeans; cattle.

Stewartville, town (1990 pop. 4,520), Olmsted co., SE Minn., 11 mi/18 km S of Rochester, on North Branch Root R., forms L. Florence reservoir on W side of town; 43°51'N 92°29'W. Grain; livestock; mfg. (feeds, fertilizers, signs, wood prods. medical supplies; mechanical assembly). Rochester Municipal Airport 3 mi/4.8 km to N. Part of Richard J. Dorer Memorial Hardwood State Forest to NE. Settled 1858.

Stewiacke (STOO-yahk), town (1991 pop. 1,306), central N.S., E Canada, on Stewiacke R., and 16 mi/26 km SSW of Truro; 45°08'N 63°21'W. Agr. market in dairying region; furniture mfg.

Stibnite, uninc. village, Valley co., central Idaho, in mt. region c.45 mi/72 km NE of Cascade, on East Fork of South Fork, Salmon R. Elev. 5,270 ft/1,606 m. Former site of World War II strategic tungsten-mine project. In Payette Natl. Forest; Rainbow Peak (9,329 ft/2,843 m) to N. Occupied in summer only, as mining camp for gold.

Stickney 1 village (1990 pop. 5,678), Cook co., NE Ill., W suburb of Chicago; 41°49'N 87°46'W. Inc. 1913. On Chicago Sanitary and Ship Canal. **2** village (1990 pop. 323), Aurora co., S S.Dak., 8 mi/12.9 km S of Plankinton; 43°35'N 98°26'W. In agr. area.

Stidham (STI-duhm), village (1990 pop. 48), McIntosh co., E Okla., 8 mi/12.9 km NW of Eufaula; 35°22'N 95°42'W. Mfg. (asparagus and other vegetables).

Stigler (STIG-luhr), town (1990 pop. 2,574), ⊙ Haskell co., E Okla., 35 mi/56 km SSE of Muskogee; 35°15'N 95°07'W. Elev. 583 ft/178 m. In area yielding soybeans and cattle; mfg. (furniture). Robert S. Kerr reservoir (Arkansas R.) to NE.

Stikine (sti-KEEN), river, 335 mi/539 km long, W Canada (B.C.) and Alaska; rises in the Stikine Mts., NW B.C.; flows in an arc W and SW, crossing SE Alaska, to the Pacific Ocean N of Wrangell Isl. Navigable for c.130 mi/210 km upstream. It has cut deep gorges in the Coast Mts. The Stikine was one of the routes during the Klondike gold rush (1897–1898). It is now a chief route to the Cassiar mining region of N B.C. Noted salmon stream.

Stikine Mountains, range of the Rocky Mts., NW B.C., W Canada, extending c.250 mi/400 km NW-SE and rising to 8,200 ft/2,500 m in Mt. Witt. The Stikine, Skeena, and Finlay rivers rise here.

Stikine Strait, SE Alaska, in Alexander Archipelago, bet. Zarembo (N) and Etolin (S) isls., SW of Wrangell; extends N from Clarence Strait; part of Inside Passage.

Stilesville, town (1990 pop. 298), Hendricks co., central Ind., on Mill Creek, and 12 mi/19 km WSW of Plainfield; 39°38'N 86°38'W. In agr. area (corn, soybeans; hogs, cattle). Laid out 1828.

Still River 1 c.30 mi/48 km long, SW Conn.; rises W of Danbury; flows generally NE, past Danbury and Brookfield, to the Housatonic R. S of New Milford. **2** c.15 mi/24 km long, NW Conn.; rises near Torrington; flows generally N, past Winsted (water power), to West Branch Farmington R. at Riverton.

Still River, Mass.: see HARVARD.

Stillaguamish River (stil-ah-GWAH-mish), c.20 mi/32 km long, NW Wash.; formed near Arlington by North Fork (c.35 mi/56 km long; rises 15 mi/24 km N of Darrington) and South Fork (c.30 mi/48 km long; rises c.20 mi/32 km SSE of Darrington); flows E to Port Susan bay of Puget Sound, S of Stanwood. On South Fork, near town of Granite Falls, is 350-ft/107-m waterfall.

Stillhouse Hollow Lake, reservoir, Bell co., central Texas, on Lampasas R., 15 mi/24 km SW of Temple; c.20 mi/32 km long; 31°01'N 97°31'W. Max. capacity 1,013,300 acre-ft. Formed by Stillhouse Hollow Dam (195 ft/59 m high), built (1968) by the Army Corps of Engineers for flood control and water supply.

Stillman Valley, village (1990 pop. 848), Ogle co., N Ill., 12 mi/19 km NE of Oregon; 42°06'N 89°10'W. In rich agr. area.

Stillmore, village (1990 pop. 615), Emanuel co., E central Ga., 12 mi/19 km SE of Swainsboro; 32°26'N 82°13'W. Poultry processing.

Stillwater, county (□ 3 sq mi/7.8 sq km; 1990 pop. 6,536), S Mont.; ⊙ Columbus; 45°40'N 109°23'W. Irrigated agr. region drained by Yellowstone and Stillwater rivers. Sugar beets, beans, wheat, barley, hay; cattle, sheep, hogs; coal. Big L. (intermittent) in N. Haistone and Halfbreed natl. wildlife refuges in N; part of Custer Natl. Forest in SW, includes part of Absaroka-Beartooth Wilderness Area. Formed 1913.

Stillwater 1 city (1990 pop. 13,822), ⊙ Washington co., E Minn., suburb 15 mi/24 km ENE of downtown St. Paul, on the St. Croix R., at head of L. St. Croix (bridged), opposite Houlton (Wis.); 45°03'N 92°49'W. Mfg. (boxes, fabricated metal prods., signs, computer supplies, molding and tools, electronic goods; printing and publishing). A convention here drew up (1848) the petition to Congress for Minn.'s territorial organization. The Minn. State Prison was est. here in 1851; Minn. State Correctional Facilities to S at Oak Park Heights and Bagport. Lower St. Croix Natl. Scenic Riverway; small natural lakes in city and area. Inc. 1854. **2** city (1990 pop. 36,676), ⊙ Payne co., N central Okla., 16 mi/26 km NE of Guthrie, and 42 mi/68 km NNE of Oklahoma City, on Stillwater Creek; 36°07'N 97°04'W. Elev. 913 ft/278 m. SW RR terminus of spur from Pawnee. The market and processing center of a wheat and cattle area; mfg. (textiles, clothing, transportation equip., bldg. materials; publishing and printing). Gas wells in the area. Seat of Okla. State Univ., which was established during the 1st year of settlement and was responsible for the city's growth. Natl. Wrestling Hall of Fame here. L. McMurtry and L. Carl Blackwell reservoirs to W. Inc. 1899.

Stillwater 1 village (□ 1 sq mi/2.6 sq km; 1990 pop. 1,531), Saratoga co., E N.Y., on W bank of the Hudson R. opposite its confluence with Hoosic R., and 12 mi/19 km SE of Saratoga Springs; 42°57'N 73°38'W. In dairying area. The Amer. Revolutionary battles (Sept. 19, 1777, and Oct. 7, 1777) fought near here are commemorated by Saratoga Natl. Historical Park, 9 mi/14.5 km SE of Saratoga Springs. **2** village, in Smithfield town, Providence co., N central R.I., on Stillwater Reservoir, 8 mi/12.9 km NNW of Providence.

Stillwater, borough (1990 pop. 223), Columbia co., E central Pa., 12 mi/19 km NNE of Bloomsburg, on Fishing Creek; 41°08'N 76°22'W. Agr. (grain; livestock; dairying); mfg. (wood prods., asphalt). Covered bridges in area.

Stillwater, Maine: see OLD TOWN.

Stillwater Creek 1 c.60 mi/97 km long, E Ohio; rises in Belmont co.; flows N, past Freeport and Uhrichsville, to join the Tuscarawas R. at Midvale. Flood-control dam impounds Piedmont Reservoir (capacity 65,000 acre-ft.) just SE of Freeport. **2** c.40 mi/64 km long, N central Okla.; rises in SW Noble co.; flows SE, past Stillwater, to Cimarron R. N of Ripley. Dam impounds L. Carl Blackwell (c.6.5 mi/10.5 km long; recreation area) c.7 mi/11.3 km W of Stillwater.

Stillwater Reservoir (□ 10 sq mi/26 sq km), Herkimer co., N N.Y., on Beaver R., in Adirondack State Park, 45 mi/72 km S of Watertown; 43°54'N 75°03'W. Max. capacity 180,000 acre-ft. Formed by Stillwater North and South dams, built (1924) by Army Corps of Engineers for power generation; also used for flood control and recreation.

Stillwater River 1 c.70 mi/113 km long, S Mont.; rises near Wyo. state line in SE Park co., near NE corner of Yellowstone Natl. Park; flows generally NE, bet. Absaroka (W) and Beartooth (E) ranges, past Absarokee, to Yellowstone R. at Columbus. **2** c.65 mi/105 km long, W Ohio; rises in Darke co. near Ind. state line; flows SE, past Ansonia, to confluence with Greenville Creek at Covington, then S to the Great Miami R. at Dayton; 39°46'N 84°12'W. Flood-control dam at Englewood.

Stilwell, town (1990 pop. 2,663), ⊙ Adair co., E Okla., near Ark. state line, c.40 mi/64 km E of Muskogee; 35°48'N 94°37'W. Elev. 1,112 ft/339 m. Resort in Ozark Mts. producing vegetables, fruit; livestock. Mfg. (food prods., electrical equip., consumer goods, fabricated metal prods.). Adair State Park to NW.

Stimson, Mount, Mont.: see LEWIS RANGE.

Stinesville, town (1990 pop. 204), Monroe co., S central

Cross references are shown in SMALL CAPITALS. The pronunciation key is on page xv. The dates of population figures are on page xii.

Ind., 11 mi/18 km NW of Bloomington; 39°18′N 86°39′W. In agr. area; old limestone quarries. McCormick's Creek State Park nearby to W. Laid out 1855.

Stinnett, town (1990 pop. 2,166), ⊙ Hutchinson co., extreme N Texas, in high plains of the Panhandle, c.50 mi/80 km NNE of Amarillo, near Canadian R.; 35°49′N 101°26′W. Elev. 3,153 ft/961 m. RR terminus; oil and natural-gas wells, refineries. Ships cattle, wheat, sorghum. L. Meredith Natl. Recreation Area to SW. Est. 1901.

Stinson Beach, uninc. village (1990 pop.), Marin co., W Calif., on the Pacific Ocean, 5 mi/8 km W of Mill Valley. Fishing. Mt. Tamalpais State Park and Muir Woods Natl. Monument to SE; Point Reyes Natl. Seashore to NW; Golden Gate Natl. Recreation Area to SE.

Stirling 1 village (1991 pop. 799), S Alta., W Canada, on Stirling L. (5 mi/8 km long), 19 mi/31 km SE of Lethbridge. RR junction; mixed farming, ranching. **2** village (1991 pop. 2,140), SE Ont., central Canada, 12 mi/19 km NW of Belleville. Dairying; woodworking.

Stirling, village, Morris co., N central N.J., 8 mi/12.9 km S of Morristown, near Passaic R. Mfg. (metal prods., clothing, clay prods.).

Stirling City, uninc. village (1990 pop.), Butte co., N central Calif., in foothills of the Sierra Nevada, near Butte R., 20 mi/32 km NW of Chico. Cattle; grain, fruit, nuts; timber. Plumas Natl. Forest to E.

Stites, village (1990 pop. 204), Idaho co., central Idaho, 15 mi/24 km NE of Grangeville, and on South Fork Clearwater R., S of its confluence with Middle Fork; 46°05′N 115°59′W. RR terminus; center of agr. area; mfg. (wood prods.). In SE corner of Nez Perce Indian Reservation.

Stockbridge 1 town (1990 pop. 3,359), Henry co., N central Ga., 17 mi/27 km SSE of Atlanta; 33°33′N 84°14′W. Mfg. of concrete; pipe machining; granite quarrying. Suburb of Atlanta. **2** resort town (1990 pop. 2,408), Berkshire co., W Mass., on the Housatonic R., in the Berkshire Mts.; 42°18′N 73°20′W. It is a year-round tourist resort with nearby lake, ski, and recreational areas. Founded (1734) as a mission for the Muhhekanuks (Mohicans), the town was originally offered by Eng. settlers to what became known as the Stockbridge Indians, in reward for their defense of the English against Fr. forces and other tribes. Increased Eur. settlement in the area whittled down the size of the town and, despite Mohican assistance during the Amer. Revolution, the remaining Native Americans here were pressured into leaving for reservations and settlements in N.Y. and Wis. The mission house, restored as a mus., was built in 1739. The Berkshire Playhouse, a leading summer theater; a large art colony; and several galleries and mus. are here. The annual Berkshire Festival is held at Tanglewood, a former estate largely in the town of Stockbridge. Also of interest are the studio of sculptor Daniel Chester French and the Norman Rockwell Mus. The Boston Symphony Orchestra maintains a music school here. Includes villages of Glendale, Interlaken. Inc. 1739. **3** town (1990 pop. 1,202), Ingham co., S central Mich., 18 mi/29 km NE of Jackson; 42°27′N 84°10′W. In farm area (dairy prods.; grain, soybeans; poultry). Mfg. (machinery; machining). **4** town (1990 pop. 618), Windsor co., central Vt., on White R., and 16 mi/26 km NE of Rutland; 43°45′N 72°44′W. Partly in Green Mt. Natl. Forest.

Stockbridge, village (1990 pop. 579), Calumet co., E Wis., near L. Winnebago, 20 mi/32 km NNE of Fond du Lac; 44°04′N 88°19′W. In dairying and grain-growing area; mfg. (transportation equip., machining). High Cliff State Park to N. Settled in 1820s by Stockbridge Indians (Mohicans), after having lost their traditional lands in New England to Amer. settlers. Here, they were able to maintain some of their customs and way of life.

Stockdale, town (1990 pop. 1,268), Wilson co., S Texas, 34 mi/55 km ESE of San Antonio, near Cibolo Creek; 29°13′N 97°57′W. Vegetables, melons, peanuts. Mfg. (fabricated metals and metal prods.).

Stockdale, borough (1990 pop. 630), Washington co.,

SW Pa., 4 mi/6.4 km SE of Charleroi, on Monongahela R.; 40°04′N 79°50′W. Agr. (hay; livestock; dairying).

Stockdale, Mount (10,100 ft/3,078 m), SE B.C., W Canada, in Selkirk Mts., 65 mi/105 km SW of Banff; 50°33′N 116°35′W.

Stockertown, borough (1990 pop. 641), Northampton co., E Pa., 5 mi/8 km NNW of Easton, on Bushkill Creek; 40°45′N 75°15′W. Agr. (grain; livestock; dairying). Sandy L. on N side of town, L. Wilhelm reservoir in M. K. Goddard State Park to N.

Stockett, village (1990 pop. 175), Cascade co., W central Mont., near Missouri R., 12 mi/19 km. SSE of Great Falls. Wheat, barley, oats; cattle, sheep. Coal; logging.

Stockham, village (1990 pop. 64), Hamilton co., SE central Nebr., 10 mi/16 km S of Aurora, and on West Fork of Big Blue R.; 40°43′N 97°56′W.

Stockholm, village (1991 pop. 391), SE Sask., W Canada, 40 mi/64 km SSE of Yorkton. Wheat; livestock.

Stockholm, town (1990 pop. 286), Aroostook co., NE Maine, on Little Madawaska R., and 25 mi/40 km NNW of Presque Isle; 47°04′N 68°07′W. Settled 1870 by Swed. immigrants, inc. 1911.

Stockholm 1 village (1990 pop. 89), Grant co., NE S.Dak., 12 mi/19 km SW of Milbank; 45°06′N 96°47′W. **2** village (1990 pop. 89), Pepin co., W Wis., on L. Pepin (Mississippi R.), 14 mi/23 km ESE of Red Wing (Minn.); 44°28′N 92°15′W.

Stockport, town (1990 pop. 260), Van Buren co., SE Iowa, 12 mi/19 km SSE of Fairfield; 40°51′N 91°49′W. Livestock; grain.

Stockport, village (1990 pop. 462), Morgan co., E central Ohio, on the Muskingum R., and 7 mi/11 km SSE of McConnelsville; 39°33′N 81°48′W.

Stockton 1 city (1990 pop. 210,943), ⊙ San Joaquin co., central Calif., 48 mi/77 km E of Oakland, and 45 mi/72 km S of Sacramento, on the San Joaquin R.; 37°58′N 121°19′W. RR junction. It is an inland seaport located at the head of the San Joaquin delta; its harbor has been developed to accommodate oceangoing vessels. It is also a processing and distributing point for farm prods. and wines from the San Joaquin and Central valleys. Mfg. (signs, millwork, fabricated metal and metal prods., wood prods., electrical and electronic goods, foods, feeds, transportation equip., furniture, apparel; printing and publishing, meat processing, canning, wood processing, pepper processing). Dairying; cattle; fruit, nuts, vegetables, sugar beets, tomatoes, peppers, grapes, grain. Stockton is one of the fastest-growing U.S. cities, marked by a pop. increase of over 42% bet. 1980 and 1990. The city was an outfitting center in the gold-rush days. It has a historical mus., an art gallery, and an impressive civic auditorium. The Univ. of the Pacific, Humphreys Col., and San Joaquin Delta Col. (2-year) are here. A U.S. naval communications station is on a nearby isl. Sharpe General Depot to S. Caswell Memorial State Park to S. Inc. 1850. **2** city (1990 pop. 1,579), ⊙ Cedar co., W Mo., on Sac R., 42 mi/68 km NW of Springfield; 37°42′N 93°47′W. Corn, soybeans, wheat; cattle. Mfg. (walnuts and walnut shell processing; feeds, gear boxes). Stockton Dam on E side of city. Stockton L. to S. Stockton State Park to SW.

Stockton 1 town (1990 pop. 187), Muscatine co., SE Iowa, 15 mi/24 km NE of Muscatine; 41°35′N 90°51′W. **2** town (1990 pop. 1,507), ⊙ Rooks co., N Kansas, on South Fork Solomon R., and 36 mi/58 km N of Hays; 39°26′N 99°16′W. Elev. 1,820 ft/555 m. Shipping point for grain and livestock area. Oil wells nearby. Kansas-Nebr. Fair takes place here annually in Aug. Rooks State Fishing L. to SW; Webster Reservoir and State Park to W. Settled 1872, inc. 1880. **3** town (1990 pop. 426), Tooele co., NW central Utah, 5 mi/8 km SSW of Tooele; 40°27′N 112°21′W. Elev. 5,068 ft/1,545 m. Gold, silver, and lead.

Stockton 1 village, Baldwin co., SW Ala., 10 mi/16 km NW of Bay Minette, and on Tensaw R. Wood prods. **2** village (1990 pop. 1,871), Jo Daviess co., NW Ill., 19 mi/31 km WNW of Freeport; 42°21′N 90°00′W. Trade center in agr. area; dairy prods. Inc. 1890. **3** village, Worcester co., SE Md., 25 mi/40 km SSE of

Salisbury. RR-shipping point for Chincoteague Bay oysters. The name may come from the fact it was an assembly point for cattle herded to N cities. **4** village (1990 pop. 529), Winona co., SE Minn., 7 mi/11.3 km W of Winona; 44°01′N 91°46′W. Dairying; poultry; livestock; grain. Mfg. (tool and die). Surrounded by Richard J. Dorer Memorial Hardwood State Forest.

Stockton, borough (1990 pop. 629), Hunterdon co., W N.J., on Delaware R., and 17 mi/27 km NW of Trenton; 40°24′N 74°58′W.

Stockton Lake, reservoir (□ 99 sq mi/256 sq km), Cedar and Dade cos., SW Mo., on Sac R., 40 mi/64 km NW of Springfield, and 2 mi/3.2 km E of Stockton; c.30 mi/48 km long; 37°36′N 93°44′W. Max. capacity 1,674,000 acre-ft. Little Sac R. eners from SE, forming 17-mi/27-km arm. Formed by Stockton Dam (earth and rockfill; 153 ft/47 m high), built (1973) by the Army Corps of Engineers for flood control power generation. Stockton State Park on promontory where 2 arms meet.

Stockton Plateau, Texas: see EDWARDS PLATEAU.

Stockton Springs, town (1990 pop. 1,383), Waldo co., S Maine, on Penobscot R., and 8 mi/12.9 km NE of Belfast; 44°29′N 68°50′W. Includes village of Sandy Point.

Stockville, village (1990 pop. 32), ⊙ Frontier co., S Nebr., 25 mi/40 km NE of McCook, and on Medicine Creek; 40°31′N 100°22′W. Sites of prehistoric Native Amer. villages nearby. Medicine Creek Reservoir State Recreation Area to SE (Harry D. Strunk L.).

Stoddard, county (□ 837 sq mi/2,168 sq km; 1990 pop. 28,895), SE Mo., ⊙ Bloomfield; 36°51′N 89°57′W. On St. Francis R. (W); drained by lower Castor R. and drainage channels of the Little R. Rice, corn, soybeans, wheat, cotton (grown and processed); lumber. Mfg. at Dexter and Bloomfield. Mingo Natl. Wildlife Refuge on NW border. Generally flat alluvial plain. Crowleys Ridge runs SW to NE through center. Formed 1835.

Stoddard, town (1990 pop. 622), Cheshire co., SW N.H., 13 mi/21 km NE of Keene; 43°04′N 72°07′W. Agr. (nursery crops, apples, vegetables; sheep, poultry, cattle; dairying). Highland L. (5 mi/8 km long) extends from N border to center. Island Pond in S center; Pitcher Mt. (2,163 ft/659 m) in NW.

Stoddard, village (1990 pop. 775), Vernon co., SW Wis., on small Coon Creek, near the Mississippi R., and 10 mi/16 km S of La Crosse; 43°39′N 91°19′W. Fishing. Mt. La Crosse Ski Area to N.

Stokes, county (□ 455 sq mi/1,178 sq km; 1990 pop. 37,223), N N.C., on Va. (N) state line; ⊙ Danbury; 36°24′N 80°13′W. In Piedmont region; agr. area (tobacco, corn, wheat, soybeans, hay; cattle); timber. Drained by Dan R. Parts of Belews L. reservoir in SE corner; Hanging Rock State Park in center. Formed 1798.

Stokes, uninc. village, Pitt co., E central N.C., 10 mi/16 km NE of Greenville. Tobacco.

Stokes State Forest, recreational area (□ c.20 sq mi/52 sq km), NW N.J., on Kittatinny Mt., c.10 mi/16 km N of Newton.

Stokesdale, town (1990 pop. 2,134), Guilford and Rockingham cos., N central N.C., 15 mi/24 km NW of Greensboro; 36°14′N 79°58′W. Belews L. reservoir to NW. Tobacco, grain, soybeans; poultry, livestock; dairying. Mfg. (apparel, fabricated metal prods., feeds).

Stone 1 county (□ 609 sq mi/1,577 sq km; 1990 pop. 9,775), N Ark.; ⊙ Mountain View; 35°51′N 92°09′W. Bounded NE by White R.; drained in SW by Middle Fork Little Rock R.; in Ozark region. Agr. (cattle, poultry; hay). Some mfg. at Mountain View. Pine, hardwood timber. Blanchard Springs Caverns, Ozark Folk Center, and part of Ozark Natl. Forest in N. Formed 1873. **2** county (□ 448 sq mi/1,160 sq km; 1990 pop. 10,750), SE Miss.; ⊙ Wiggins; 30°47′N 89°07′W. Drained by Biloxi R. and Red and Black creeks. Agr. (cotton, corn, honey; tung and pecan groves; poultry; timber); sand and gravel. Part of De Soto Natl. Forest in S and E, also borders co. on N. Flint Creek Reservoir in N. Formed 1916. **3** county (□ 509 sq mi/1,318 sq km; 1990 pop. 19,078), SW Mo.; ⊙ Galena; 36°44′N 93°28′W. In the Ozark Mts.; drained by White and James rivers. Vegetables, fruit; corn, hay; cattle. Mfg. at

Crane. Major recreation and tourism area in S (caves, springs). Retirement communities. Table Rock L. crosses S part of co.; bridge S of Kimberling City. Mark Twain Natl. Forest in S part. Formed 1851.

Stone, uninc. town (1990 pop. 900), Pike co., E Ky., in the Cumberland Mts., 6 mi/9.7 km S of Williamson (W.Va.). Bituminous coal.

Stone City, village, Jones co., E Iowa, on Wapsipinicon R., and 4 mi/6.4 km W of Anamosa. Limestone quarries nearby.

Stone Creek, village (1990 pop. 181), Tuscarawas co., E Ohio, 9 mi/14 km SW of New Philadelphia; 40°23'N 81°33'W.

Stone Harbor, resort borough (1990 pop. 1,025), Cape May co., S N.J., on Seven Mile Beach isl. (bridged to mainland), bet. Great Sound and the Atlantic Ocean, and 4 mi/6.4 km ESE of Cape May Court House; 39°02'N 74°46'W. Yachting center; seafood. Bird Sanctuary and the Wetlands Inst., a research and education center on tidal ecology, are here.

Stone Mountain, city (1990 pop. 6,494), De Kalb co., NW central Ga., 12 mi/19 km ENE of Atlanta; 33°48'N 84°10'W. Mfg. includes printing and publishing; chemicals, electronic equip., machinery, fiber optics, wood prods., medical supplies. Historic village stores in center of town refurbished for 1996 Summer Olympic Games. Gateway to Stone Mt. Park.

Stone Mountain Memorial, historic site, memorial to the Confederacy, consisting of the equestrian figures of Robert E. Lee, Stonewall Jackson, and Jefferson Davis carved on the N face of Stone Mt., a granite dome 650 ft/198 m high in NW Ga., NE of Atlanta, in Stone Mt. Park. The memorial was commissioned by the Daughters of the Confederacy in 1916 and was designed and partially executed by Gutzon Borglum. In 1925, sculptor Augustus Lukeman took charge of the project. Work stopped in 1930 and was not resumed until 1963, when the state of Ga. purchased the mt. and established a state park. Walter Hahock completed the sculpture, which was dedicated in 1970.

Stone Mountains, range of the Appalachians along the border bet. Tenn. and N.C., paralleling Iron Mts. (W); from Watauga R. extend c.30 mi/48 km NE to White Top Mt. (Va.). Max. elev. 4,000 ft/1,219 m. Sometimes considered a range of Unaka Mts. Included in Cherokee and Pisgah natl. forests.

Stone Park, village (1990 pop. 4,383), Cook co., NE Ill., W suburb of Chicago; 41°53'N 87°52'W. Inc. 1939.

Stoneboro, borough (1990 pop. 1,091), Mercer co., NW Pa., 9 mi/14.5 km W of Polk; 41°20'N 80°06'W. Dairying; hay, corn, potatoes. Inc. 1866.

Stonefort, village (1990 pop. 311), in Saline and Williamson cos., S Ill., 13 mi/21 km SW of Harrisburg; 37°37'N 88°42'W. In agr. area. Until 1934, called Bolton. Ruins of prehistoric stone fort nearby. Shawnee Natl. Forest nearby.

Stonega (sto-NAI-gah), uninc. village, Wise co., SW Va., 7 mi/11.3 km WNW of Norton, in Jefferson Natl. Forest; 36°57'N 82°47'W. Junction of coal-mine RR spurs; timber; coal.

Stoneham 1 (STO-nuhm), township (1990 pop. 224), Oxford co., W Maine, 20 mi/32 km W of South Paris, in White Mt. Natl. Forest; 44°16'N 70°54'W. **2** town (1990 pop. 22,203), Middlesex co., NE Mass., residential suburb of Boston; 42°28'N 71°06'W. Site of Stoneham Zoo. Settled 1645, set off from Charlestown and inc. 1725.

Stones River, 39 mi/63 km long, central Tenn.; formed 9 mi/14 km N of Murfreesboro by confluence of East and West forks; meanders NNW to Cumberland R. 8 mi/13 km E of Nashville, 36°11'N 86°39'W. Stones R. Natl. Military Park is near the West Fork, 3 mi/5 km NW of Murfreesboro; includes site of Battle of Stones R. (Dec. 31, 1862–Jan. 2, 1863), a major Civil War battle that initiated Federal campaign to trisect Confederacy; Union troops, led by Gen. William Rosecrans, forced retreat of Confederates under Gen. Braxton Bragg and captured Murfreesboro. Stones R. Natl. Cemetery (20 acres/8 ha; est. 1865) is in park.

Stones River Battlefield, natl. historic site, central Tenn.; 35°52'N 86°22'W. Site of Stones R. Natl. Cemetery. Authorized 1927.

Stoneville, town (1990 pop. 1,109), Rockingham co., N N.C., 16 mi/26 km NW of Reidsville; 36°28'N 79°54'W. Tobacco, grain; livestock; dairying. Mfg. (apparel, wood prods., lumber, chemicals, textiles, consumer goods; glass fabricating).

Stoneville, Mass.: see AUBURN.

Stonewall, town (1991 pop. 2,997), SE Man., central Canada, 20 mi/32 km NNW of Winnipeg; 50°08'N 97°19'W. Dairying; grain. Dolomitic limestone is quarried.

Stonewall, county (☐ 920 sq mi/2,383 sq km; 1990 pop. 2,013), NW central Texas; ⊙ Aspermont; 33°10'N 100°15'W. Rolling plains, with hilly areas and mesquite woodlands; drained by Salt and Double Mt. forks of Brazos R., joining in NE to form the Brazos R. Cattle-ranching and farm area, with most of agr. in E (peanuts, wheat; hay); some sheep, hogs, goats. Oil and natural-gas wells; gypsum. Formed 1876.

Stonewall 1 town (1990 pop. 1,266), De Soto parish, NW La., 15 mi/24 km SSW of Shreveport, near Bayou Pierre (forms Wallace L. to NE); 32°16'N 93°49'W. In agr. area (cotton; cattle; dairying); timber. Processing of meat prods. **2** town (1990 pop. 1,148), Clarke co., E Miss., near Chickasawhay R., 17 mi/27 km SSW of Meridian; 32°08'N 88°47'W. Agr. (cotton, corn; cattle); mfg. (textiles). Clark Co. State park to SE; Bucatunna Wildlife Management Area to E.

Stonewall 1 village (1990 pop. 279), Pamlico co., E N.C., 1 mi/1.6 km SE of Bayboro, on Bay R. estuary; 35°08'N 76°44'W. Cotton, peanuts, grain; hogs. **2** village (1990 pop. 519), Pontotoc co., S central Okla., 12 mi/19 km SE of Ada, near Clear Boggy Creek; 34°38'N 96°31'W. In agr. area; mfg. (transportation equip.). **3** uninc. village (1990 pop. 245), Gillespie co., S central Texas, 13 mi/21 km ESE of Fredericksburg, on Pedernales R. Elev. 1,312 ft/400 m. Agr. area with cattle ranches, peach orchards. Wineries. Mfg. (marble and granite prods.). Part of L.B.J. Natl. Historic Site (L.B.J. Ranch, which was known as the Texas White House when Lyndon B. Johnson was President) and State Historic Site are here. Est. 1870.

Stonewall Jackson Lake, reservoir, Lewis co., central W.Va., on West Fork, 22 mi/35 km WSW of Clarksburg; 39°00'N 80°28'W. Max. capacity 145,000 acre-ft. Formed by Stonewall Jackson Dam (95 ft/29 m high), built (1986) for flood control; also used for water supply and recreation. Stonewall Jackson L. State Park near dam.

Stonewood, town (1990 pop. 1,996), Harrison co., N W.Va., 2 mi/3.2 km SE of Clarksburg; 39°15'N 80°18'W. Agr. (corn); cattle, poultry; dairying. Mfg. (consumer goods, clothing; steel fabricating). Inc. after 1940.

Stoney Creek, town (1991 pop. 49,968), SE Ont., central Canada, suburb of Hamilton; 43°13'N 79°45'W. Site of a Br. victory (1813) in the War of 1812.

Stonington 1 (STO-ning-tuhn), town (1990 pop. 16,919), New London co., extreme SE Conn., on a peninsula jutting into L.I. Sound; 41°22'N 71°54'W. Fishing and mfg. of precision tools, boats, and textiles are leading industries. The Old Lighthouse Mus. is just S. Stonington borough attracts many tourists to its narrow streets and quaint shops; the borough also is home port for Conn.'s only commercial fishing fleet. Stonington town also includes part of the village of Mystic. The town was attacked by Br. naval forces in the Amer. Revolution and in the War of 1812. Includes village of Pawcatuck (1990 pop. 5,289). Settled 1649 from Plymouth, inc. 1662. **2** town (1990 pop. 1,252), Hancock co., S Maine, port on S shore of Deer Isl., in Penobscot Bay, and 30 mi/48 km SSW of Ellsworth; 44°09'N 68°38'W. Fishing, resort center. Inc. 1897.

Stonington, village (1990 pop. 1,006), Christian co., central Ill., 8 mi/12.9 km NE of Taylorville; 39°38'N 89°11'W. In agr. and bituminous-coal-mining area. Inc. 1885.

Stono River (STO-no), tidal channel SW of Charleston, SE S.C.; runs SW to NE bet. mainland (NW) and Wadmalaw and Johns isls. (SE), from North Edisto channel through S bet. Johns (W) and James (E) isls.; Intracoastal Waterway runs through SW-NE sect.

Stony Brook, residential village (☐ 6 sq mi/15.5 sq km; 1990 pop. 13,726), Suffolk co., SE N.Y., on N shore of L.I., on Stony Brook Harbor (SE arm of Smithtown Bay), 15 mi/24 km E of Huntington; 40°54'N 73°07'W. Wood prods. Restored 1941 to resemble 18th-cent. village. State Univ. of N.Y. at Stony Brook, one of the univ.'s 4 graduate centers, and the State Univ. of N.Y. Health Science Center are here.

Stony Creek, town (1990 pop. 271), Sussex co., SE Va., 18 mi/29 km S of Petersburg; 36°57'N 77°24'W. Mfg. (lumber, concrete prods.); agr. (tobacco, peanuts, grain; poultry, livestock).

Stony Creek 1 village, New Haven co., Conn., 9 mi/14.5 km ESE of New Haven. A postal sect. of Branford. **2** resort village (1990 pop. 250), Warren co., E N.Y., in the Adirondack Mts., on a tributary of the Hudson R., and 16 mi/26 km NW of Glens Falls; 43°25'N 74°01'W. Lakes nearby.

Stony Creek, c.80 mi/129 km long, N central Calif.; rises in the Coast Ranges at joining of North, Middle, and South forks (each c.10 mi/16 km long) 35 mi/56 km WNW of Colusa at border bet. Glenn and Colusa cos.; flows E to receive Little Stony Creek from SW (forms East Park reservoir), then flows N through Stony Gorge Reservoir, NE through Black Butte Reservoir, then ESE, past Orland, crosses Tehana Colusa Canal, joins Sacramento R. 5 mi/8 km W of Chico, flows NE, N, and E, to the Sacramento near Hamilton City; flow is intermittent in lower course. Orland irrigation project is served by reservoirs impounded by Stony Gorge Dam (139 ft/42 m high, 868 ft/265 m long; completed 1928) and East Park Dam (137 ft/42 m high, 249 ft/76 m long, completed 1910). Plans of Central Valley project call for construction of Black Butte Reservoir for additional irrigation.

Stony Creek Mills, uninc. town (1990 pop. 2,550), Berks co., SE central Pa., residential suburb 3 mi/4.8 km E of Reading, on Antietam Creek; 40°20'N 75°52'W.

Stony Hill, town (1991 pop. 8,244), St. Andrew parish, E Jamaica, in W foothills of Blue Mts., 8 mi/12.9 km N of Kingston; 18°05'N 76°47'W. Industrial school and transmission station (Coopers Hill); dairying.

Stony Island, Jefferson co., N N.Y., in E part of L. Ontario, 8 mi/12.9 km WSW of Sackets Harbor village; c.4 mi/6.4 km long, ½ mi/⁸⁄₁₀ km–1 mi/1.6 km wide; 43°55'N 76°25'W.

Stony Lake, Kawartha Lakes, S Ont., central Canada, 18 mi/29 km NNE of Peterborough; 10 mi/16 km long, 1 mi/2 km–3 mi/5 km wide; drains S into the St. Lawrence R. Clear L. (5 mi/8 km long) is SW arm.

Stony Man Mountain, peak (4,010 ft/1,222 m) of Blue Ridge, N Va., at corner of Rappahannock, Madison, and Page cos., in Shenandoah Natl. Park, 22 mi/35 km S of Front Royal; 38°35'N 78°22'W.

Stony Mountain, village, SE Man., central Canada, 14 mi/23 km NNW of Winnipeg; 50°04'N 97°13'W. Grain; dairying. Site of Man. Penitentiary.

Stony Plain, town (1991 pop. 7,226), central Alta., W Canada, 20 mi/32 km W of Edmonton, in Cree Indian reservation; 53°32'N 114°00'W. Grain elevators.

Stony Point, uninc. town (1990 pop. 1,286), Alexander co., W central N.C., 10 mi/16 km NW of Statesville, near South Fork Yadkin R.; 35°52'N 81°02'W. Tobacco, grain, soybeans; poultry, livestock; dairying. Mfg. (textiles, duct tape).

Stony Point, village (☐ 6 sq mi/15.5 sq km; 1990 pop. 10,587), Rockland co., SE N.Y., on W bank of the Hudson R., and 5 mi/8 km SW of Peekskill; 41°13'N 74°00'W. Nearby is Stony Point Mus. (1936) in battlefield reservation (part of Palisades Interstate Park), commemorating storming of Stony Point by "Mad" Anthony Wayne's Continental forces in July 1779.

Stony Rapids, village, N central Sask., W Canada, 95 mi/153 km ESE of Uranium City, on S bank of Fond du Lac R.; 59°16'N 105°50'W. Connected by road to village of Baker Lake, 14 mi/23 km SE. Airstrip. Sport fishing and hunting. Furs. Sometimes spelled Stoney Rapids.

Cross references are shown in SMALL CAPITALS. The pronunciation key is on page xv. The dates of population figures are on page xii.

Stony River, village (1990 pop. 51), W Alaska, on Kuskokwim R., at mouth of Stony R., and 65 mi/105 km SE of Flat; 61°47′N 156°34′W.

Stony River, stream, 170 mi/274 km long, W Alaska; rises on W slope of Alaska Range near 61°17′N 153°48′W; flows generally WNW to Kuskokwim R. at Stony River (village).

Stonybrook, uninc. town (1990 pop. 1,500), York co., S Pa., residential suburb 4 mi/6.4 km ENE of York; 39°59′N 76°38′W.

Stonycreek River, c.45 mi/72 km long, SW Pa.; rises in Stonycreek township, E Somerset co.; flows N through L. Stonycreek reservoir, past Hooversville and Ferndale to join Little Conemaugh R. at Johnstown to form Conemaugh R.; 39°55′N 78°57′W.

Storden (STOR-duhn), village (1990 pop. 283), Cottonwood co., SW Minn., 15 mi/24 km NW of Windom; 44°02′N 95°19′W. Grain, soybeans; livestock; mfg. (bins). Small lakes in area; Augusta L. to SE.

Storey (STO-ree), county (□ 263 sq mi/681 sq km; 1990 pop. 2,526), W Nev.; ⊙ Virginia City; 39°27′N 119°31′W. Bounded N by Truckee R. Site of famous Comstock Lode, at Mt. Davidson in SW. Diatomite, gold, silver; cattle, poultry; dairying; hay. Formed 1861.

Storm King, mountain (1,355 ft/413 m), SE N.Y., on the W shore of the Hudson R. near West Point; 41°25′N 73°59′W. Included in the Palisades Interstate Park.

Storm Lake, city (1990 pop. 8,769), ⊙ Buena Vista co., NW Iowa, on N side of Storm L. (c.4 mi/6.4 km long), 52 mi/84 km WNW of Ft. Dodge; 42°38′N 95°12′W. Summer resort. Pork and poultry packing, turkey processing; mfg. (printing; agr. storage bins, hydrants). Buena Vista Col. and local parks around glacial lake are here. Small but growing Hispanic and Lao pop. Inc. 1873.

Storm Mountain (10,372 ft/3,161 m), on border bet. Alta. and B.C., W Canada, in Rocky Mts., on SW edge of Banff Natl. Park, 20 mi/32 km W of Banff; 51°12′N 116°00′W.

Stormont (STOR-muhnt), county (□ 412 sq mi/ 1,067 sq km), SE Ont., central Canada, on the St. Lawrence R., and on U.S. (N.Y.) border; ⊙ Cornwall; 45°10′N 75°00′W. Part of United Co. of Stormont, Dundas, and Glengarry.

Stornoway (STOR-nuh-wai), village, S Que., E Canada, 18 mi/29 km NW of Megantic. Dairying; lumbering; pigs.

Storrs (STORZ), community (1990 pop. 12,198), a part of the town of Mansfield, Tolland co., NE Conn.; 41°48′N 72°15′W. Seat of the Univ. of Conn.

Story, county (□ 573 sq mi/1,484 sq km; 1990 pop. 74,252), central Iowa; ⊙ Nevada; 42°02′N 93°28′W. Prairie agr. area (hogs, cattle, poultry; corn, oats, soybeans) drained by Skunk R. Mfg. at Ames and Nevada. Limestone quarries, sand and gravel pits, bituminouscoal deposits. State Forest Nursery S of Ames. General flooding occurred in 1993. Formed 1846.

Story, village, Sheridan co., N Wyo., on Piney Creek, just E of Bighorn Mts., and 16 mi/26 km SSE of Sheridan. Elev. 4,960 ft/1,512 m. Summer resort. Agr. (barley, alfalfa, wheat, oats, corn; cattle). Just S is reproduction of Fort Phil Kearny (est. 1866); to NE is site of Fetterman Massacre, in which Native American band killed some U.S. soldiers (1866).

Story City, town (1990 pop. 2,959), Story co., central Iowa, near Skunk R., 11 mi/18 km N of Ames; 42°11′N 93°35′W. Mfg. (dairy prods.; plastic prods.; cement prods.; concrete, paper prods., transportation equip.; machining). Little Wall L. to N. Has pioneer schoolhouse. Inc. 1881.

Story Military Reservation, Fort, Va.: see HENRY, CAPE.

Stotesbury, town (1990 pop. 42), Vernon co., W Mo., on Little Osage R., and 15 mi/24 km NW of Nevada; 37°58′N 94°33′W.

Stotesbury (STOTS-buhr-ee), uninc. village (1990 pop. 20), Raleigh co., S W.Va., 10 mi/16 km SW of Beckley.

Stotts City, city (1990 pop. 235), Lawrence co., SW Mo., near Spring R., 21 mi/34 km E of Carthage; 37°06′N 93°57′W. Fruit, vegetables; dairying; cattle.

Stottville, village (□ 4 sq mi/10.4 sq km; 1990 pop.

1,369), Columbia co., SE N.Y., 4 mi/6.4 km NE of Hudson; 42°17′N 73°45′W.

Stoughton, city (1990 pop. 8,786), Dane co., S Wis., on both banks of Yahara R., and suburb 14 mi/23 km SSE of Madison; 42°55′N 89°13′W. In dairying and farming area; ships tobacco; mfg. (transportation equip., machinery, wood prods., electronic equip.). L. Kegonsa State Park to NW. Settled c.1847, inc. 1882.

Stoughton (STOU-tuhn), town (1991 pop. 721), SE Sask., W Canada, 40 mi/64 km E of Weyburn. RR junction; grain elevators.

Stoughton (STO-tuhn), town (1990 pop. 26,777), Norfolk co., E Mass., 14 mi/23 km S of Boston; 42°07′N 71°06′W. Largely residential town; shoe and textile industries in the 1800s. Today mfg. includes electrical and medical equip., machinery, sporting and plastic goods. Founded 1637, inc. 1726.

Stout, town (1990 pop. 192), Grundy co., central Iowa, 12 mi/19 km W of Cedar Falls; 42°31′N 92°42′W. In agr. area.

Stout, Ohio: see ROME.

Stoutland, town (1990 pop. 207), Camden co., central Mo., in the Ozark Mts., 13 mi/21 km NE of Lebanon; 37°48′N 92°30′W.

Stoutsville, town (1990 pop. 26), Monroe co., NE central Mo., near Salt R., 9 mi/14.5 km NE of Paris; 39°32′N 91°50′W.

Stovall (STO-vahl), village (1990 pop. 409), Granville co., N N.C., 10 mi/16 km N of Oxford; 36°27′N 78°34′W. Tobacco, grain; poultry, livestock; dairying.

Stovepipe Wells, Calif.: see DEATH VALLEY NATIONAL MONUMENT.

Stover, city (1990 pop. 964), Morgan co., central Mo., 9 mi/14.5 km W of Versailles; 38°26′N 92°59′W. Corn, wheat; cattle, poultry; light mfg.

Stow (STO), city (1990 pop. 27,702), Summit co., NE Ohio, a suburb of Akron; 41°10′N 81°26′W. Chiefly residential; some light industry. Settled 1802, inc. as a city 1960.

Stow 1 (STO), town (1990 pop. 283), Oxford co., W Maine, 24 mi/39 km W of South Paris, partly in White Mt. Natl. Forest. **2** town (1990 pop. 5,328), Middlesex co., E central Mass., 22 mi/35 km ENE of Boston; 42°26′N 71°31′W. Dairying; apples. Rapidly suburbanizing area. Settled 1681, inc. 1683.

Stow, resort village (1990 pop. 300), Chautauqua co., extreme W N.Y., on W shore of Chautauqua L., 10 mi/ 16 km NW of Jamestown; 42°10′N 79°24′W.

Stow Creek (STO), c.20 mi/32 km long, SW N.J.; rises NW of Bridgeton; flows SW and S, forming part of border bet. Cumberland and Salem cos., to Delaware Bay above mouth of Cohansey Creek.

Stowe 1 uninc. town (1990 pop. 3,598), West Pottsgrove township, Montgomery co., SE Pa., on Schuylkill R., 2 mi/3.2 km W of Pottstown; 40°15′N 75°40′W. Mfg. (fabricated metal prods., machinery, apparel). Pottstown Municipal Airport to NE. French Creek State Park to SW. **2** resort town (1990 pop. 3,433), Lamoille co., N central Vt., 15 mi/24 km N of Montpelier; 44°29′N 72°43′W. It is surrounded by mts., including Mt. Mansfield, Vt.'s highest. One of New England's largest ski resort areas (Mt. Mansfield, Stowe, Bolton Valley, Smuggler's Notch). In addition to tourism and a thriving trade in antiques, dairying and farming are practiced here; wood prods., electronic equip., canoes, and maple sugar are made. The area has many scenic attractions, and several state forests and a state park are nearby. Site of the ski lodge owned by the Von Trapp Family Singers, of Rogers and Hammerstein's musical *The Sound of Music*. Settled 1794, inc. 1896.

Stowe (STO), township (1990 pop. 7,681), Allegheny co., SW Pa., residential suburb 4 mi/6.4 km NW of downtown Pittsburgh, on Ohio R.; 40°28′N 80°04′W. Pittsburgh State Correctional Inst. to SE.

Stowell, town (1990 pop. 1,419), Chambers co., SE Texas, 27 mi/43 km SW of Beaumont; 29°47′N 94°22′W. Agr. area (rice, soybeans; cattle). Mfg. (floodwater gates). McFadden (to SE) and Anahuac (to SW) natl. wildlife refuges nearby.

Stoy, village (1990 pop. 135), Crawford co., SE Ill., 5 mi/ 8 km W of Robinson; 39°00′N 87°49′W. In oil, natural-gas, and agr. area.

Stoystown, borough (1990 pop. 389), Somerset co., SW Pa., 9 mi/14.5 km NE of Somerset, near Stonycreek R.; 40°06′N 78°57′W. Agr. (corn, oats, hay; livestock; dairying). Mfg. (lumber, fabricated metal prods.); surface bituminous coal. Quemahoning Reservoir to N.

Strabane (STRAH-bain), uninc. town (1990 pop. 1,200), North Strabane township, Washington co., SW Pa., residential suburb 15 mi/24 km SSW of downtown Pittsburgh, and 7 mi/11.3 km NE of Washington; 40°15′N 80°11′W.

Strafford, county (□ 383 sq mi/992 sq km; 1990 pop. 104,233), SE N.H., on Maine (E) border (Salmon Falls and Piscataqua rivers); ⊙ Dover; 43°17′N 71°01′W. Bordered SSE by Great Bay. Agr. (apples, vegetables, corn, hay, nursery crops; cattle; dairying); timber; sand and gravel. Univ. of N.H. at Durham in SE. Drained by Cocheco, Bellamy, Isinglass, Lamprey, Oyster, and Berry's rivers. Northeast and Milton ponds (Salmon Falls R.) on border in NE; Merrymeeting L. and Powder Mill Fish Hatchery in NW; Bow L. in SW; Blue Hills Range, including Blue Job Mt. (1,356 ft/413 m) in W. Formed 1769.

Strafford 1 (STRA-fuhrd), town (1990 pop. 2,965), Strafford co., SE N.H., 15 mi/24 km WNW of Dover; 43°16′N 71°09′W. Drained by Big, Mohawk, and Isinglass rivers. Mfg. (machining, tool and die); nursery crops, apples; cattle; dairying). Part of Blue Hills Range in center and NE. Blue Job Mt. (1,356 ft/413 m) on NE border; Bow L. in SW. **2** uninc. town (1990 pop. 4,480), Chester co., SE Pa., residential suburb 13 mi/ 21 km NW of Philadelphia; 40°03′N 75°24′W. Mfg. includes computer software, clothing. **3** town (1990 pop. 902), Orange co., E Vt., 7 mi/11.3 km S of Chelsea; 43°51′N 72°21′W. Copper mines (now closed) opened 1793. Senator Justin Morrill b. here.

Straight River 1 c.50 mi/80 km long, SE Minn.; rises in N Freeborn co. at Geneva (original source at Geneva L. has been diverted); flows N, past Owatonna and Medford, to Cannon R. at Faribault; 43°49′N 93°15′W. **2** c.20 mi/32 km long, NW central Minn.; rises in NE Becker co., 13 mi/21 km NW of Park Rapids at 47°00′N 95°18′W; flows SW through Straight L. (3 mi/4.8 km long, ½ mi/⅕ km wide) to Shell R. 5 mi/8 km SSE of Park Rapids. Fish Hook R. is tributary. Fishing resort is on lake.

Strandburg, village (1990 pop. 74), Grant co., NE S.Dak., 13 mi/21 km NNE of Milbank; 45°02′N 96°45′W.

Strandquist (STRAND-kwist), village (1990 pop. 98), Marshall co., NW Minn., 29 mi/47 km NNW of Thief R.; 48°29′N 96°27′W. Falls. Potatoes, wheat, sugar beets, sunflowers, beans; cattle, sheep. Twin Lakes Wildlife Area to N; Old Mill State Park to SW.

Strang 1 village (1990 pop. 42), Fillmore co., SE Nebr., 7 mi/11.3 km S of Geneva; 40°25′N 97°35′W. RR junction. **2** village (1990 pop. 141), Mayes co., NE Okla., 12 mi/19 km NE of Pryor, near Neosho R.; 36°24′N 95°07′W.

Strasbourg (STRAS-buhrg), town (1991 pop. 802), S central Sask., W Canada, 45 mi/72 km NNW of Regina, at foot of Last Mt. Grain elevators; lumbering.

Strasburg 1 (STRAS-buhrg), town (1990 pop. 124), Cass co., W Mo., 12 mi/19 km NE of Harrisonville; 38°45′N 94°09′W. **2** town (1990 pop. 3,762), Shenandoah co., NW Va., 17 mi/27 km SSW of Winchester, on North Fork of Shenandoah R.; 38°59′N 78°21′W. Shipping, processing center; mfg. (plastic prods., clothing, chemicals, furniture, consumer goods; limestone production, printing and publishing). Agr. (grain, apples; poultry, livestock; dairying); timber; limestone. Hupp's Fort (c.1755) and Harmony Hall or Fort Bowman (c.1755) are nearby. Union victory in Civil War engagement (Sept. 22, 1864) at Fishers Hill (c.2 mi/3.2 km S); Belle Grove Plantation on Cedar Creek Battlefield to NE; Crystal Caverns to N. Founded c.1761.

Strasburg 1 (STRAS-buhrg), village, Arapahoe co., N central Colo., 35 mi/56 km E of Denver. Elev. 5,386 ft/ 1,642 m. Grain, beans, sunflowers, sugar beets; cattle.

Nearby, in 1870, the Kansas Pacific RR lay the last track to connect the Atlantic and Pacific coasts. **2** village (1990 pop. 473), Shelby co., central Ill., 10 mi/16 km ESE of Shelbyville; 39°21′N 88°37′W. In agr. area. **3** village (1990 pop. 553), Emmons co., S N.Dak., 10 mi/16 km S of Linton; 46°07′N 100°09′W. Cheese prods. Lawrence Welk Home Historic Site. **4** village (1990 pop. 1,995), Tuscarawas co., E Ohio, 8 mi/13 km NNW of New Philadelphia, and on small Sugar Creek; 40°36′N 81°31′W. Settled 1810.

Strasburg (STRAS-buhrg), borough (1990 pop. 2,568), Lancaster co., SE Pa., 7 mi/11.3 km SE of Lancaster; 39°58′N 76°11′W. Agr. area (grain, soybeans; poultry, livestock; dairying); limestone; mfg. (food prods.). RR Mus. Covered bridges to W, on Pequea Creek. Settled c.1733, inc. 1816.

Stratford, city (1991 pop. 27,666), S Ont., central Canada, on the Avon R., SW of Toronto; 43°22′N 80°57′W. Industrial center, with plants mfg. textiles, furniture, transportation equip., and rubber and leather prods. Food prods. from the surrounding farm area are processed here. Home of the noted Stratford Shakespearean Festival (started 1953).

Stratford 1 town (1990 pop. 49,389), Fairfield co., SW Conn., at the mouth of the Housatonic R., on L.I. Sound; 41°12′N 73°07′W. Transportation equip., helicopters, machinery, hardware items, electrical goods, foods, chemicals, consumer goods, plastics, paper prods., rubber goods, and tools are among its many manufactures. The Amer. Shakespeare Festival Theater and Acad. opened here in 1955. The David Judson house (1723) has been restored; it has a mus. Other pre-Revolutionary houses still stand. Inc. 1639. **2** town (1990 pop. 715), on border bet. Hamilton and Webster cos., central Iowa, near Des Moines R., 14 mi/23 km N of Boone; 42°16′N 93°55′W. Livestock; grain. **3** town (1990 pop. 927), Coos co., NW N.H., 10 mi/16 km N of Lancaster, on Vt. (W) state line (Connecticut R.); 44°44′N 71°31′W. Mfg. (contract stitching, book publishing; lumber). Agr. (nursery crops, vegetables; cattle, poultry; dairying); timber. Spruce Mt. (3,080 ft/939 m) in N; Sugarloaf Mt. (3,701 ft/1,128 m) in NE; part of Nash Stream State Forest in E. Includes North Stratford village in NW. Settled 1772. **4** town (1990 pop. 1,404), Garvin co., S central Okla., 16 mi/26 km W of Ada; 34°47′N 96°57′W. In strawberry-producing area; light mfg.; oil wells. **5** town (1990 pop. 85), Brown co., NE S.Dak., 13 mi/21 km SE of Aberdeen, near James R.; 45°19′N 98°17′W. **6** town (1990 pop. 1,781), ⊙ Sherman co., extreme N Texas, in high plains of the Panhandle, 32 mi/51 km NE of Dalhart; 36°20′N 102°04′W. Elev. 3,695 ft/1,126 m. RR junction ships grain, cattle; mfg. (meat processing; feeds). Est. May 1901. **7** town (1990 pop. 1,515), Marathon co., central Wis., 10 mi/16 km NNE of Marshfield; 44°47′N 90°04′W. Dairy prods.; mfg. (machinery, modular homes).

Stratford, borough (1990 pop. 7,614), Camden co., SW N.J., 10 mi/16 km SE of Camden; 39°49′N 75°01′W. Largely residential. Founded 1890, inc. 1925.

Stratford Hall, uninc. village, Westmoreland co., E Va., 36 mi/58 km ESE of Fredericksburg. "Stratford Hall" in Arlington, N Va., is also the name of the birthplace of Robert E. Lee, overlooking Potomac R. to N. Natl. shrine since 1935. Site purchased in 1716 by Thomas Lee, who built mansion 1729–1730.

Stratham (STRA-duhm), town (1990 pop. 4,955), Rockingham co., SE N.H., 8 mi/12.9 km WSW of Portsmouth; 43°01′N 70°54′W. Bounded W by Squamscott R. Nursery crops; cattle, poultry; dairying. Mfg. (chocolates, shoes, apparel). N.H. Technical Col. (Stratham campus) is here.

Strathclair (strath-KLER), village, SW Man., central Canada, 45 mi/72 km NW of Brandon; 50°24′N 100°24′W. Grain; livestock.

Strathcona (strath-KO-nuh), village (1990 pop. 40), Roseau co., NW Minn., c.30 mi/48 km N of Thief River Falls; 48°32′N 96°10′W. Grain, potatoes, sunflowers.

Strathcona Provincial Park (strath-KO-nuh) (□ 828 sq mi/2,145 sq km), SW B.C., W Canada, on central Vancouver Isl., 20 mi/32 km W of Courtenay; 40 mi/64 km long, 11 mi/18 km–36 mi/58 km wide. Heavily forested, mountainous area, with many streams. Game sanctuary; stream and lake fishing. Contains Golden Hinde mt. (7,219 ft/2,200 m) and other peaks over 5,000 ft/1,524 m. Includes S part of Buttle L.

Strathmoor Gardens, village (1990 pop. 300), Jefferson co., N Ky., suburb 4 mi/6.4 km ESE of downtown Louisville; 38°13′N 85°40′W.

Strathmoor Manor, village (1990 pop. 391), Jefferson co., N Ky., suburb 4 mi/6.4 km ESE of downtown Louisville; 38°13′N 85°40′W.

Strathmoor Village, village (1990 pop. 361), Jefferson co., N Ky., suburb 4 mi/6.4 km ESE of downtown Louisville; 38°13′N 85°40′W. Bowman Field Airport to NE.

Strathmore (STRATH-mor), town (1991 pop. 4,185), S Alta., W Canada, 30 mi/48 km E of Calgary. RR town, center of Can. Pacific RR irrigation system, and site of its supply farm.

Strathmore, uninc. town (1990 pop. 2,353), Tulare co., S central Calif., 18 mi/29 km SE of Visalin at E side of San Joaquin Valley; 36°08′N 119°04′W. Packs citrus fruit, olives, peaches, plums, nectarines; cattle, poultry.

Strathroy (strath-ROI), town (1991 pop. 10,566), S Ont., central Canada, on Sydenham R., and 20 mi/32 km W of London; 42°57′N 81°38′W. Fruit processing, woodworking, dairying, mfg. (containers, mobile homes, camper trailers, frozen fruits and vegetables).

Strattanville (STRA-tuhn-vil), borough (1990 pop. 490), Clarion co., W central Pa., 3 mi/4.8 km E of Clarion; 41°12′N 79°19′W. Agr. (corn, hay, potatoes; livestock; dairying); mfg. (modular homes, concrete prods.).

Stratton, town (1990 pop. 121), Windham co., SE Vt., in Green Mt. Natl. Forest, 23 mi/37 km NW of Brattleboro; 43°04′N 72°55′W. Stratton Mt. (3,859 ft/1,176 m), with ski area, is here.

Stratton 1 village (1990 pop. 649), Kit Carson co., E Colo., 18 mi/29 km W of Burlington; 39°17′N 102°35′W. Elev. 4,414 ft/1,345 m. Cattle; wheat, oats, sunflowers, beans, corn, sorghum. **2** village, Newton co., E central Miss., 4 mi/6.4 km NNW of Decatur. **3** village (1990 pop. 427), Hitchcock co., S Nebr., 12 mi/19 km WSW of Trenton, on Republican R., and near Kansas state line; 40°08′N 101°13′W. Dairy and poultry prods.; grain. Swanson Reservoir to SE. **4** village (1990 pop. 278), Jefferson co., E Ohio, on Ohio R., and 11 mi/18 km N of Steubenville; 40°31′N 80°38′W.

Stratton, Maine: see EUSTIS.

Straughn, town (1990 pop. 318), Henry co., E Ind., 10 mi/16 km SSE of New Castle; 39°49′N 85°17′W. In agr. area.

Strausstown (STROUS-toun), borough (1990 pop. 353), Berks co., E central Pa., 17 mi/27 km NW of Reading; 40°29′N 76°10′W. Agr. (grain, soybeans; livestock; dairying); mfg. (feeds).

Strawberry Island, islet, SE Alaska, in Glacier Bay, 12 mi/19 km NW of Gustavus; 58°31′N 136°00′W. Fishing.

Strawberry Mountain (9,038 ft/2,755 m), Grant co., E central Oregon, 10 mi/16 km S of Prairie City, in Strawberry Mt. Wilderness Area of Malheur Natl. Forest; 44°18′N 118°42′W.

Strawberry Plains, village, Jefferson co., E Tenn., on Holston R., and 14 mi/23 km ENE of Knoxville; 36°04′N 83°41′W. In agr., zinc-mining region; limestone quarry.

Strawberry Point 1 uninc. town (1990 pop. 4,377), Marin co., W Calif., residential suburb 10 mi/16 km NNW of downtown San Francisco, on small peninsula of same name in Richardson Bay (arm of San Francisco Bay). Mt. Tamalpais Game Refuge in bay, to E. Mt. Tamalpais State Park and Muir Woods Natl. Monument to W. **2** town (1990 pop. 1,357), Clayton co., NE Iowa, 14 mi/23 km SSW of Elkader; 42°40′N 91°32′W. Mfg. (concrete prods., consumer goods). To S is Backbone State Park (□ 3 sq mi/7.8 sq km), largest in the state, with a trout hatchery on Maquoketa R. Inc. 1887.

Strawberry Reservoir (□ 27 sq mi/70 sq km), Wasatch co., central Utah, on Strawberry R., in Uintah and Ouray Indian Reservation and Uinta Natl. Forest, 35 mi/56 km E of Provo; 40°08′N 111°06′W. Max. capacity 1,127,610 acre-ft. Formed by Soldier Creek Dam (272 ft/83 m high), built (1973) by the Bureau of Reclamation for irrigation; also used for water supply, power generation, recreation, flood control, and as a fish and wildlife pond.

Strawberry River 1 c.90 mi/145 km long, in N Ark.; rises near Salem in Fulton co.; flows SE to Black R. 10 mi/16 km N of Tuckerman. **2** c.70 mi/113 km long, in NE Utah; rises in Wasatch co., Wasatch Range, 15 mi/24 km SE of Heber City; flows SE into Strawberry Reservoir, then E along edge of Uintah and Ouray Indian Reservation through Starvation Reservoir just before joining the Duchesne R. at Duchesne. Strawberry Dam (77 ft/23 m high, 488 ft/149 m long; completed 1913) is near source of river, 25 mi/40 km E of Provo. Water from Strawberry Reservoir is diverted to Spanish Fork and used in irrigation of 50,000 acres/20,235 ha in Utah co.

Strawberry Valley Project, Wasatch and Duchesne cos., N central Utah. Developed by the U.S. Bureau of Reclamation for irrigating lands S of Utah L.; constructed 1906–1913. The water of Strawberry R. and its tributaries is carried by a tunnel through the Wasatch Range to a tributary of the Spanish Fork and is used for lands in the vicinity of Salem, Spanish Fork, Springville, Payson, and Santaquin. The project is supplemented by the Central Utah project.

Strawn 1 village (1990 pop. 132), Livingston co., E central Ill., 19 mi/31 km SE of Pontiac; 40°38′N 88°24′W. In agr. area. **2** village (1990 pop. 709), Palo Pinto co., N central Texas, 22 mi/35 km SW of Mineral Wells; 32°32′N 98°30′W. In coal, oil, natural-gas, agr., ranching region (cattle; peanuts, wheat). Mfg. (machinery, ordnance, bldg. materials).

Streamwood, village (1990 pop. 30,987), Cook co., NE Ill., suburb 30 mi/48 km WNW of downtown Chicago, 6 mi/9.7 km ESE of Elgin; 42°01′N 88°10′W. Mfg. (plastic prods., chemicals, consumer goods; aluminum anodizing, printing).

Streator (STREE-tuhr), city (1990 pop. 14,121), La Salle and Livingston cos., N central Ill., on the Vermillion R., 17 mi/27 km S of Ottawa; 41°07′N 88°49′W. Industrial center with diverse mfg. Coal, discovered in the early 1860s, was the principal source of livelihood until the deposits were exhausted (c.1900). Several state parks are in the area. Inc. 1874.

Street Mountain (4,216 ft/1,285 m), Essex co., NE N.Y., in the High Peaks sect. of the Adirondack Mts., 8 mi/12.9 km NW of Mt. Marcy, and 6 mi/9.7 km SSW of Lake Placid; 44°11′N 74°02′W.

Streeter, village (1990 pop. 161), Stutsman co., S central N.Dak., 36 mi/58 km SW of Jamestown; 46°39′N 99°21′W. Alkali L. to W; L. George Natl. Wildlife Refuge and Streeter Memorial State Park to NW.

Streetman, village (1990 pop. 260), on border bet. Freestone and Navarro cos., E central Texas, 17 mi/27 km SE of Corsicana; 31°52′N 96°19′W. In cotton, vegetable area; mfg. (natural-gas processing; expanded shale and clay). Richland Chambers Reservoir to N (Richland co.).

Streetsville, town, S Ont., central Canada, 16 mi/26 km WSW of Toronto; 43°35′N 79°42′W. Part of expanded city of Mississauga. Mfg.; warehousing, distribution center. Suburban community.

Stringtown, village (1990 pop. 366), Atoka co., SE Okla., 7 mi/11.3 km NNE of Atoka; 34°28′N 96°02′W. In farm area; crushed stone (1st quarry in Okla.); recreation. Atoka Reservoir immediately to W.

Stroh, village (1990 pop. 450), Lagrange co., NE Ind., 12 mi/19 km ESE of Lagrange. Agr. area. Glacial lakes. Mfg. (feed mixing and grain grinding).

Strome, village (1991 pop. 290), S central Alta., W Canada, 35 mi/56 km SE of Camrose. Mixed farming (wheat).

Stromsburg, town (1990 pop. 1,241), Polk co., E central Nebr., 17 mi/27 km N of York, and on Big Blue R., near Platte R.; 41°07′N 97°35′W. Farm trade center in prairie region; grain; livestock. Mfg. (concrete prods.). Inc. 1883.

Cross references are shown in SMALL CAPITALS. The pronunciation key is on page xv. The dates of population figures are on page xii.

Strong, town (1990 pop. 1,217), Franklin co., W Maine, 10 mi/16 km N of Farmington, and on Sandy R.; 44°47′N 70°12′W. Wood prods. Maine's Republican party organized here in 1854. Settled 1784; inc. 1801.

Strong, village (1990 pop. 624), Union co., S Ark., 19 mi/ 31 km ESE of El Dorado, near La. state line; 33°06′N 92°21′W. Lumber. Felsenthal Natl. Refuge to E.

Strong City 1 village (1990 pop. 617), Chase co., E central Kansas, on Cottonwood R., and 19 mi/31 km and 2 mi/ 3.2 km N of Cottonwood Falls, W of Emporia; 38°23′N 96°32′W. Livestock; grain. **2** village (1990 pop. 49), Roger Mills co., W Okla., 5 mi/8 km NE of Cheyenne, and on Washita R.; 35°40′N 99°35′W. In agr. area. In Black Kettle Natl. Grassland.

Strong River, c.75 mi/121 km long, central Miss.; rises in S Scott co.; flows SW past Mendenhall Pearl R. 2 mi/ 3.2 km SE of Georgetown.

Stronghurst, village (1990 pop. 799), Henderson co., W Ill., 13 mi/21 km SSE of Oquawka; 40°45′N 90°54′W. Corn, soybeans; livestock.

Strongs, village, Chippewa co., E Upper Peninsula, Mich., 31 mi/50 km WSW of Sault Ste. Marie, in Hiawatha Natl. Forest; 46°21′N 84°58′W. Lumbering. L. Superior shore 8 mi/12.9 km to N; Tahquamenon Falls State Park to NNW.

Strongsville, city (1990 pop. 35,308), Cuyahoga co., NE Ohio, residential suburb of Cleveland; 41°19′N 81°50′W. Textbook publishing company and various light mfg. The growing city's pop. doubled bet. 1970 and 1990. Settled 1816; inc. 1927.

Stroud 1 town, Chambers co., E Ala., 12 mi/19 km NNE of Lafayette. **2** town (1990 pop. 2,666), Lincoln co., central Okla., 18 mi/29 km SW of Bristow; 35°46′N 96°39′W. In agr. and oil-producing area; mfg. (fabricated metal prods., apparel). Inc. 1898.

Stroudsburg (STROUDZ-buhrg), borough (1990 pop. 5,312), ⊙ Monroe co., E Pa., 21 mi/34 km NE of Easton, in Pocono Mts. region, on Brodhead Creek, 2 mi/ 3.2 km W of its mouth on Delaware R.; 40°58′N 75°12′W. Agr. (hay; livestock; dairying). Mfg. (textiles, food prods., plastic prods., fabricated metal prods.; printing and publishing). Stroudsburg-Pocono Airport to NE. Pocono Internatl. Raceway to NW; Cherry Valley Winery to SW. Center for recreation and tourism. Appalachian Trail passes to S; Big Pocono State Park to NW; Delaware Water Gap Natl. Recreation Area and Middle Delaware Natl. Scenic R. to E. Shawnee Mt. and Fernwood ski areas to NE. Settled 1738, inc. 1815.

Stroudwater River (STROUD-waw-tuhr), 12 mi/19 km long, SW Maine; rises in N York co.; flows generally NE to Fore R. above Portland.

Struble, town (1990 pop. 67), Plymouth co., NW Iowa, 7 mi/11.3 km N of Le Mars; 42°53′N 96°11′W.

Strum, town (1990 pop. 949), Trempealeau co., W Wis., on Buffalo R., and 18 mi/29 km SSE of Eau Claire; 44°32′N 91°23′W. In dairy, poultry, and grain area; cheese; light mfg. On Buffalo R. State Trail; Viking Skyline Ski Area to E.

Struthers (STRUH-thuhrz), city (1990 pop. 12,284), Mahoning co., NE Ohio, an industrial suburb of Youngstown, on the Mahoning R.; 41°03′N 80°35′W. Although principal steel industry has declined, metal mfg. continues. Founded 1800, inc. 1922.

Stryker, village (1990 pop. 1,468), Williams co., extreme NW Ohio, on Tiffin R., and 7 mi/11 km ENE of Bryan; 41°30′N 84°25′W. Grain, wheat, hay; mfg. of ceramics.

Stuart, city (1990 pop. 1,522), on border bet. Adair and Guthrie cos., SW Iowa, 15 mi/24 km SE of Guthrie Center; 41°30′N 94°19′W. Grain; livestock (annual livestock show in Aug.). Founded 1869, inc. 1877.

Stuart 1 town (□ 6 sq mi/15.5 sq km; 1990 pop. 11,936), ⊙ Martin co., E central Fla., 18 mi/29 km SSE of Fort Pierce, and on St. Lucie R. (bridged here), near E terminus of St. Lucie Canal; 27°11′N 80°14′W. Resort; seafood-processing center. **2** town (1990 pop. 965), ⊙ Patrick co., SW Va., in foothills of Blue Ridge, 22 mi/35 km W of Martinsville, on Mayo R.; 36°38′N 80°16′W. Mfg. (fabrics, furniture, lumber); agr. (apples, peaches, grain; cattle; dairying); timber.

Stuart 1 village (1990 pop. 650), Holt co., N Nebr.,

27 mi/43 km WNW of O'Neill, and on Elkhorn R.; 42°36′N 99°08′W. Dairying; grain; livestock, poultry. **2** village (1990 pop. 228), Hughes co., central Okla., 19 mi/31 km W of McAlester; 34°53′N 96°05′W.

Stuart Lake (□ 138 sq mi/357 sq km), central B.C., W Canada, 70 mi/113 km NW of Prince George; 48 mi/ 77 km long, 1 mi/2 km–6 mi/10 km wide. Drained E by Stuart and Nechako rivers into Fraser R. At E extremity of lake is Fort St. James.

Stuarts Draft, uninc. town, Augusta co., NW Va., 10 mi/ 16 km S of Staunton, 10 mi/16 km WSW of Waynesboro, near South R.; 38°01′N 79°01′W. Mfg. (bldg. materials, medical prods., foods, fabricated metal prods.; feeds); agr. area (grain, soybeans, apples; livestock; dairying). George Washington Natl. Forest to S.

Studio City, suburban section of Los Angeles, Los Angeles co., S Calif., residential suburb 11 mi/18 km NW of downtown Los Angeles, in San Fernando Valley; drained by Los Angeles R. Light mfg. Santa Monica Mts. to S. CBS Television Studio is here.

Stump Lake, L-shaped lake in Nelson co., E central N.Dak.; 10 mi/16 km long, 2.5 mi/4 km wide; 47°54′N 98°23′W.

Sturbridge (STUHR-brij), town (1990 pop. 7,775), Worcester co., S Mass., 17 mi/27 km SW of Worcester; 42°07′N 72°05′W. Tourism is its major industry because of Old Sturbridge Village, a model of an early New England village complete with shops, a general store, and a meeting house, drawing year-round visitors. Sturbridge Auto Mus. Includes village of Fiskdale (1990 pop. 2,189). Inc. 1738.

Sturgeon 1 (STUHR-juhn), town (1990 pop. 838), Boone co., central Mo., 18 mi/29 km N of Columbia; 39°13′N 92°16′W. Corn, soybeans; cattle. Amish community to N. **2** uninc. town (1990 est. pop. 1,000), North Fayette township, Allegheny co., W Pa., suburb 12 mi/19 km WSW of downtown Pittsburgh, on Robinson Run; 40°23′N 80°12′W.

Sturgeon Bay, city (1990 pop. 9,176), NE Wis., 37 mi/ 60 km NE of city of Green Bay, on Door Peninsula; 44°49′N 87°22′W. Port at head of Sturgeon Bay (small inlet of Green Bay), at W end of ship canal cutting across the peninsula and connecting Green Bay with L. Michigan. Cherry-growing and resort center. Shipyards; mfg. (electronic equip., fabricated metal prods.). An agr. research station is to NE; Potawatomi State Park is to W and Whitefish Dunes State Park to NE; N terminus of Ahnapoe State Trail to S. Inc. 1883.

Sturgeon Falls, town (1991 pop. 5,837), E central Ont., central Canada, on Sturgeon R. (near its mouth on L. Nipissing), and 22 mi/35 km W of North Bay; 46°22′N 79°56′W. Pulp- and lumber-milling center; garnet grinding; woodworking.

Sturgeon Falls, waterfalls (46 ft/14 m high), NE Ont., central Canada, on Mattagami R., and 25 mi/40 km NNW of Timmins. Hydroelectric power.

Sturgeon Lake, village (1990 pop. 230), Pine co., E Minn., 43 mi/69 km NW of Duluth, near Moose R.; 46°22′N 92°49′W. Oats, alfalfa; cattle; poultry; dairying; mfg. (chemicals). Sturgeon L. to E, other small lakes in area; General Andrews State Forest to S.

Sturgeon Lake 1 (□ 110 sq mi/285 sq km), NW Ont., central Canada, 50 mi/80 km E of Sioux Lookout; 38 mi/61 km long, 5 mi/8 km wide. **2** (□ 18 sq mi/ 47 sq km), S Ont., central Canada, in Kawartha lake region, 4 mi/6 km N of Lindsay; 12 mi/19 km long, 2 mi/3 km wide. Drained E by Trent Canal.

Sturgeon Point, village (1991 pop. 110), S Ont., central Canada, on Sturgeon L., 8 mi/13 km N of Lindsay. Resort.

Sturgeon River, 110 mi/177 km long, SE central Ont., central Canada; rises NE of Sudbury; flows SE, past Sturgeon Falls, to L. Nipissing 4 mi/6 km SW of Sturgeon Falls.

Sturgeon River 1 (STUHR-jin), c.75 mi/121 km long, NW Upper Peninsula, NW Mich.; rises in SE Baraga co.; flows WNW into Houghton co., then N to Portage L. c.7 mi/11.3 km SE of Houghton; 46°35′N 88°16′W. **2** c.30 mi/48 km long, N Mich.; rises NE of Gaylord

in Otsego co.; flows N, past Wolverine, and through Burt L. State Park, near Indian River; 45°01′N 84°38′W.

Sturgis (STUHR-jis), town (1991 pop. 701), E Sask., W Canada, on Assiniboine R., and 50 mi/80 km N of Yorkton; 51°51′N 102°32′W. Mixed farming.

Sturgis 1 (STUHR-jis), town (1990 pop. 2,184), Union co., W Ky., 30 mi/48 km SW of Henderson, on Tradewater R.; 37°32′N 87°59′W. Mining center in bituminous-coal and agr. (livestock; grain) area; mfg. (fabricated metal prods., food, apparel, electronic equip.). Sturgis Airport to E. **2** town (1990 pop. 10,130), St. Joseph co., SW Mich., 35 mi/56 km SSE of Kalamazoo, near Ind. state line; 41°47′N 85°25′W. Mfg. (food, fabricated metal prods., plastic prods.; printing and publishing). Settled 1827; inc. as village 1855, as city 1895. **3** town (1990 pop.), ⊙ Meade co., W S.Dak., 25 mi/ 40 km NNW of Rapid City, and on branch of Belle Fourche R., at NE edge of Black Hills and Black Hills Natl. Forest; 44°24′N 103°30′W. Business center for mining and farming region; timber; flour, dairy prods.; livestock; grain; mfg. (printing and publishing; food). Sturgis Motorcycle Rally, Bear Butte (4,426 ft/1,349 m) and Box Butte State Park to NE. Black Hills Natl. Cemetery to S. Laid out near Fort Meade, an army post; est. 1878.

Sturgis (STUHR-jis), village (1990 pop. 198), Oktibbeha co., E Miss., 16 mi/26 km WSW of Starkville; 33°20′N 89°02′W. Agr. (cotton, corn; cattle); timber; mfg. (lumber). Part of Tombigbee Natl. Forest to S; Noxubee Natl. Wildlife Refuge to E.

Sturt Point, SE Victoria Isl., S Franklin dist., N.W.T., N Canada, on Queen Maud Gulf; 68°51′N 103°06′W.

Sturtevant, town (1990 pop. 3,803), Racine co., SE Wis., suburb 5 mi/8 km W of Racine; 42°42′N 87°54′W. In vegetable-farming region; RR-shipping point; some mfg.

Stutsman (STUHTS-muhn), county (□ 2,269 sq mi/ 5,877 sq km; 1990 pop. 22,241), central N.Dak.; ⊙ Jamestown.; 46°58′N 98°57′W. Agr. area drained by James R. and Pipestem and Beaver creeks. Sunflowers, rye, hay, flax, wheat; dairying; cattle, hogs, sheep. Food prods., machinery, transportation equip. Arrowwood Natl. Wildlife Refuge in NE; Chase L. Natl. Wildlife Refuge in W; Fort Seward Historic Site in E, near Jamestown; Jamestown Reservoir (Jim L.), Arrowwood, Mud, and Pipestem lakes in E; Chase L. in W. Formed 1873.

Stuttgart (STUHT-gahrt), city (1990 pop. 10,420), ⊙ Arkansas co. (along with DeWitt), E central Ark., near Bayou Meto; 34°29′N 91°32′W. RR junction. Trade and processing center of a rice-growing area. Mfg. (machinery, food; printing and publishing). Peckerwood L. Reservoir to N; Bayou Meto Wildlife Management Area to SW. Inc. 1889.

Stuyvesant (STEI-vuh-suhnt), village (1990 pop. 350), Columbia co., SE N.Y., on E bank of the Hudson R., and 9 mi/14.5 km N of Hudson; 42°24′N 73°45′W.

Stuyvesant Town (STEI-vuh-suhnt), section of borough of Manhattan, N.Y. city, SE N.Y., immediately S of Peter Cooper Village, located bet. 1st Ave. (W), the East R. (E), East 14th St. (S), and East 20th St. (N). This was one of the many housing projects planned and built bet. the end of World War II and the mid-1950s which provided apartments for low- and middle-income residents of N.Y. city. This project, composed of a series of 15-story redbrick bldgs. set amidst nicely landscaped, well-maintained grounds and playgrounds, was built by the Metropolitan Life Insurance Company, which was also responsible for Peter Cooper Village, a concurrent project, and the Parkchester project in the Bronx.

Suaqui Grande (soo-AH-kee GRAHN-dai), town (1990 pop. 1,172), Sonora, NW Mexico, on affluent of Yaqui R., and 80 mi/129 km SE of Hermosillo; 29°12′N 109°41′W. Livestock, cereals.

Subiaco (soo-bee-AK-o), village (1990 pop. 538), Logan co., W Ark., 27 mi/43 km W of Russellville; 35°17′N 93°38′W. In farm area. Light mfg. Seat of Subiaco Col. and Abbey (Benedictine).

Sublette (suhb-LET), county (☐ 4,935 sq mi/12,782 sq km; 1990 pop. 4,843), W Wyo.; ⊙ Pinedale; 42°45′N 109°55′W. Agr. region; watered by Green R. (headwaters of Fontenelle Reservoir in S); livestock, hay. Large part of Bridger-Teton Natl. Forest in W, N and NE margins of co., including part of Wind R. Mts. in NE; also including Gannett Peak (13,804 ft/4,207 m), highest point in Wyo., in N, has small glaciers. Several small reservoirs located in N center; Big Sandy Reservoir and State Recreation Area on S boundary. Bridger Wilderness Area in NE. Formed 1921.

Sublette (suhb-LET), town (1990 pop. 1,378), SW Kansas, 29 mi/47 km N of Liberal; ⊙ Haskell co.; 37°28′N 100°50′W. In agr. region (grain and alfalfa).

Sublette (SUB-LET), village (1990 pop. 394), Lee co., N Ill., 18 mi/29 km SE of Dixon; 41°38′N 89°13′W. In rich agr. area.

Sublimity, town (1990 pop. 1,491), Marion co., NW Oregon, 13 mi/21 km SE of Salem; 44°49′N 122°47′W. Agr. (fruit, berries, vegetables, nuts; poultry, hogs, sheep, cattle; dairying. Winery. Silver Falls State Park to E.

Sublimity City, uninc. town (1990 pop. 900), Laurel co., SE Ky., residential suburb 2 mi/3.2 km S of London. London-Corbin Airport to S; Levi Jackson Wilderness Road State Park to SE.

Succasunna (suh-kuh-SUH-nuh), village, Morris co., N N.J., 9 mi/14.5 km NW of Morristown. In rapidly suburbanizing area.

Success, town, Coos co., NE N.H., 4 mi/6.4 km E of Berlin, on Maine (E) state line. Drained by Stearns Brook and Chickwomepy Stream (forms Success Pond in NE). Wilderness area. Timber. Mahoosuc Range in S.

Success, village (1990 pop. 170), Clay co., extreme NE Ark., 19 mi/31 km NE of Pocahontas, near Mo. state line, on Little Black R.; 36°27′N 90°43′W.

Success Reservoir, Calif.: see TULE RIVER.

Success Village, village, NW Trinidad, Trinidad and Tobago, E of Port of Spain. Lime and coconut oil factories. New residential development.

Suchiapa (soo-chee-AH-pah), town (1990 pop. 9,270), Chiapas, S Mexico, in Chiapas Valley, 9 mi/14.5 km S of Tuxtla Gutiérez; 16°39′N 93°06′W. Agr. center (cereals, tobacco, coffee, sugarcane, fruit; livestock).

Suchiate, Mexico: see CIUDAD HIDALGO.

Suchiate River (soo-chee-AH-tai), c.100 mi/161 km long, on Mexico-Guatemala border; rises in Sierra Madre just S of Ixchiguán (Guatemala); flows SW, past Ciudad Tecúm Umán (Guatemala) and Ciudad Hidalgo (Mexico), to the Pacific Ocean 3 mi/4.8 km NW of Ocós (Guatemala); the stream forms the Mexico-Guatemala border from Unión Juárez (Mexico) to the Pacific Coast.

Súchil (SOO-cheel), town (1990 pop. 4,319), Durango, N Mexico, on interior plateau, near the Zacatecas border, on RR, 55 mi/89 km SE of Durango; 23°38′N 103°55′W. Agr. center (grain, tobacco, sugarcane, cotton, vegetables, fruit).

Sucilá (soo-see-WAH), town (1990 pop. 3,137), Yucátan, SE Mexico, 11 mi/18 km W of Tizimín; 18°39′N 95°47′W. Henequen. Corn, tropical fruit; livestock.

Suckling, Cape, S Alaska, on Gulf of Alaska, 75 mi/121 km SE of Cordova; 59°59′N 143°54′W. E extremity of Chugach Natl. Forest.

Sud (SYOOD), department (1982 pop. 502,624), SW Haiti, SW part of Jacmel Peninsula; ⊙ Les Cayes; 18°15′N 73°40′W. Agr. (tobacco, cotton, sugarcane); cattle; lignite, manganese, and chrome deposits.

Sudan, town (1990 pop. 983), Lamb co., NW Texas, on the Llano Estacado, 50 mi/80 km NW of Lubbock; 34°04′N 102°31′W. In agr. area (cattle, sheep; grain, cotton); oil and gas. Muleshoe Natl. Wildlife Refuge to SW. Inc. 1925.

Sudbury, district (☐ 18,058 sq mi/46,770 sq km; 1991 pop. 26,178), SE central Ont., central Canada, on L. Huron; ⊙ Sudbury; 47°15′N 82°00′W.

Sudbury, city (1991 pop. 92,884), central Ont., central Canada; 46°30′N 80°58′W. Center of Canada's largest mining region, which produces much of the world's nickel and large quantities of copper, platinum, gold, silver, cobalt, and sulfur. Seat of Laurentian Univ. (1960).

Sudbury 1 (SUHD-buhr-ee), town (1990 pop. 14,358), Middlesex co., E Mass., suburb 17 mi/27 km W of Boston; 42°23′N 71°25′W. Electrical and electronic equip. is manufactured. The tavern (built 1686; restored) that was the scene of Henry Wadsworth Longfellow's *Tales of a Wayside Inn* is here. Restored and working grist mill. Includes village of South Sudbury. Inc. 1639. **2** town (1990 pop. 516), Rutland co., W Vt., 17 mi/27 km NW of Rutland, in resort region; 43°46′N 73°10′W.

Sudbury Reservoir, Middlesex co., E central Mass., unit in Boston's emergency water-supply system, just SE of Marlboro; c.3 mi/4.8 km long.

Sudbury River, c.30 mi/48 km long, E Mass.; rises in ponds in E Worcester co.; flows E and N, past Framingham, joining Assabet R. to form Concord R. in Concord. Supplies reservoirs of Boston's emergency water system. Problems with mercury contamination in mid-1990s.

Sud-Est (SYOO-DEST), department (1982 pop. 367,911), SE Haiti, bounded on Caribbean Sea (S) and Dominican Republic (E) border; ⊙ Jacmel; 18°18′N 72°24′W. Bordered by Ouest (N) and Sud (W) depts. Produces cocoa, cotton, tobacco. Bauxite, manganese deposits.

Sudlersville (SUD-luhrz-vil), town (1990 pop. 428), Queen Annes co., E Md., 18 mi/29 km W of Dover (Del.); 39°11′N 75°52′W. Named for the Sudler family, the name was changed when the RR built a station here in the 1860s. Soybean-processing plant.

Sudley, uninc. town, Prince William co., NE Va., residential suburb 4 mi/6.4 km NNW of Manassas; 38°47′N 77°30′W. Manassas Natl. Battlefield Park to N.

Sudzal (sood-ZAHL), town (1990 pop. 1,037), Yucátan, SE Mexico, 4 mi/6.4 km SSE of Izamal; 20°52′N 88°59′W. Corn, citrus fruit; livestock.

Sue Peaks, Texas: see CARMEN, SIERRA DEL.

Suffern, suburban residential village (☐ 2 sq mi/5.2 sq km; 1990 pop. 11,055), Rockland co., SE N.Y., on Ramapo R., in the Ramapos, at N.J. state line, c.27 mi/43 km NW of Manhattan; 41°06′N 74°08′W. Trade center; light mfg. (cosmetics, toiletries, and pharmaceuticals); offices; in diversified-farming area. Inc. 1896.

Suffield, town (1990 pop. 11,427), Hartford co., N Conn., on the Connecticut R., near Mass. state line, 16 mi/26 km N of Hartford; 42°00′N 72°40′W. Grows and packs tobacco. Cigar making began in 1810. Agr.; mfg. of ice cream, gas, and small tools; warehousing. Suffield Acad. here. Settled c.1670.

Suffolk 1 county (☐ 120 sq mi/311 sq km; 1990 pop. 663,906), E Mass., on Massachusetts Bay and Boston Bay; ⊙ Boston; 42°22′N 70°59′W. Comprises cities of Boston, Chelsea, Revere, Winthrop, and several small isls. in Boston Harbor and the bay. Formed 1643. **2** county (☐ 2,372 sq mi/6,143 sq km; 1990 pop. 1,321,864), SE N.Y.; ⊙ Riverhead; 40°56′N 72°40′W. On central and E L.I., bounded W by Nassau co., S by the Atlantic Ocean, E by Block Isl. Sound, N by L.I. Sound. Traversed E-W by 2 parallel highways: along N shore to Orient Point, and along S shore to Montauk Point, the easternmost point of L.I. and N.Y. Served by lines of L.I. RR. Off S shore, barrier isls. shelter Great South, Moriches, Mecox, and Shinnecock bays from the Atlantic; bet. E peninsulas "flukes" of L.I. are Great Peconic, Little Peconic, and Gardiners bays, with many inlets; on N shore are Huntington and Smithtown bays and Port Jefferson Harbor. Vehicle/pedestrian ferries travel bet. Port Jefferson and Bridgeport, Conn.; and bet. Orient Point and New London, Conn. Residential and summer-resort region, with areas of large estates (notably Southampton), picturesque villages (many among oldest in state). Principal centers are Patchogue, Babylon, Amityville, Riverhead, Southampton. Duck-raising industry (though reduced substantially) is still along S shore; offshore and surf sport fishing (especially at Montauk Point); yachting. Potato farming and dairying supply N.Y. city metropolitan area (W). There has been a rapid increase in the number and acreage of vineyards and associated wineries in E Suffolk co., esp. along the North Fork from the Mattituck Hills E. Some mfg. Includes Shinnecock Indian Reservation, many state parks (Montauk Point, Hither Hills, Orient Beach, Wildwood, Sunken Meadow, Belmont L., Heckscher). Formed 1683 as one of original N.Y. cos.

Suffolk, independent city (☐ 429 sq mi/1,111 sq km; 1990 pop. 52,141), SE Va., 20 mi/32 km SW of Norfolk, includes former Nansemond co. ; 36°42′N 76°38′W. Bounded N by Hampton Roads (James R. estuary), E by Portsmouth and Chesapeake cities, S by N.C. state line, SW by Blackwater R.; drained by Nansemond R. (head of navigation). RR junction; important peanut market; mfg. (pet food, chemicals, concrete block, food processing equip., asphalt, lumber, yachts, coffee production, printing and publishing, meat prods., paper prods., bldg. materials, fertilizer; cotton ginning); agr. (barley, corn, hay, peanuts, soybeans, wheat; cattle, hogs). Paul D. Camp Community Col. (Suffolk campus); Tidewater Community Col. (Portsmouth campus) in N. Suffolk Municipal Airport in center. Burned by British in 1779, occupied (1862) by Union troops in Civil War and besieged by Longstreet in April 1863. Western Branch Reservoir in NW; Cohoon, Meade, and Kilby reservoirs in W central. Nansemond Natl. Wildlife Refuge in N; part of Great Dismal Swamp Natl. Wildlife Refuge in SE. Settled 1720; inc. as town 1808, as city 1910.

Sugar City, town (1990 pop. 1,275), Madison co., E Idaho, 4 mi/6.4 km NNE of Rexburg; 43°52′N 111°45′W. Elev. 4,892 ft/1,491 m. Sugar beets, cattle, sheep; dairying; barley. Near lower reach of Teton R.; area was flooded June 5, 1976, when Teton Dam, 13 mi/21 km E, collapsed.

Sugar City, village (1990 pop. 252), Crowley co., SE central Colo., on Bob Creek at NE end of L. Meredith reservoir, 5 mi/8 km E of Ordway; 38°13′N 103°39′W. Elev. 4,308 ft/1,313 m. Trade center for cattle and sugar beets, wheat, sorghum, vegetables. L. Henry Reservoir to NW.

Sugar Creek, city (1990 pop. 3,982), Jackson co., W Mo., on Missouri R.; suburb 8 mi/12.9 km ENE of Kansas City; 39°08′N 94°24′W. Oil refinery, cement plant; mfg. (cement, asphalt). Inc. 1920.

Sugar Creek 1 85 mi/137 km long, central and W Ind.; rises in S Clinton co., flows SW, past Crawfordsville, to join the Wabash 4 mi/6.4 km N of Montezuma. Stream is actively down-cutting rapids. Canoeing is a popular summer activity on the stream. Covered bridges in the area. **2** c.65 mi/105 km long, central Ind.; rises in W Henry co., flows W and SSW to join the Big Blue R.; from there, it forms the Driftwood R., 1 mi/1.6 km W of Edinburg.

Sugar Grove 1 village (1990 pop. 2,005), Kane co., NE Ill., suburb 9 mi/14.5 km W of Aurora; 41°46′N 88°27′W. In agr. area (grain; dairying). Mfg. Waubonsee Community Col. to NW. Aurora Municipal Airport to W. **2** village (1990 pop. 465), Fairfield co., central Ohio, 6 mi/10 km SSE of Lancaster, on Hocking R.; 39°37′N 82°32′W. In agr. area.

Sugar Grove, borough (1990 pop. 604), Warren co., NW Pa., 16 mi/26 km ENE of Corry, 8 mi/12.9 km SW of Jamestown (N.Y.), on Stillwater Creek, near N.Y. state line; 41°58′N 79°20′W. Agr. area (grain, potatoes; livestock; dairying); mfg. (food prods., lumber).

Sugar Hill, town (1990 pop. 4,557), Gwinnett co., N central Ga., just W of Buford; 34°06′N 84°02′W. Mfg. of plumbing equip., bldg. materials.

Sugar Island, E Upper Peninsula, Mich., in St. Mary's R., 2 mi/3.2 km E of Sault Ste. Marie, bet. lakes Nicolet (W) and George (E), 16 mi/26 km long, 2 mi/3.2 km–9 mi/14.5 km wide; 46°28′N 84°13′W. Mich.-Ont. boundary passes to N and E. Resort; some farming. Car ferry from Sault Ste. Marie. E unit of Bay Mills Indian Reservation on isl.

Sugar Land, city (1990 pop. 24,529), Fort Bend co., SE Texas, near Brazos R., suburb 21 mi/34 km WSW of Houston; 29°37′N 95°37′W. Drained by Oyster Creek. Agr. to S and SW. Oil and gas wells; mfg. (electronic equip., canvas prods., cables).

Cross references are shown in SMALL CAPITALS. The pronunciation key is on page xv. The dates of population figures are on page xii.

Sugar Loaf Dam, Colo.: see TURQUOISE LAKE.

Sugar Loaf Mountain (c.1,280 ft/390 m), Frederick co., N Md., in a park just E of Lilypons; 39°15′N 77°23′W. A prominent feature in the region. Used by the Union army as an observation post during the Civil War. Now a public site.

Sugar Mountain, village (1990 pop. 132), Avery co., NW N.C., 12 mi/19 km WSW of Boone, in Pisgah Natl. Forest; 36°07′N 81°51′W. Ski-resort area in Blue Ridge Mts. Blue Ridge Parkway passes to SE.

Sugar Notch, borough (1990 pop. 1,044), Luzerne co., NE central Pa., suburb 5 mi/8 km SW of Wilkes-Barre; 41°11′N 75°55′W. Mfg. (apparel). Wilkes-Barre Mt. to SE. Inc. 1867.

Sugar River, c.25 mi/40 km long, Sullivan co., SW N.H.; rises in Sunapee L., flows W, past Newport and Claremont (water power), to the Connecticut.

Sugar Valley, town, Gordon co., NW Ga., 5 mi/8 km NW of Calhoun; 34°33′N 85°00′W. Rug mfg.

Sugarbush Hill (1,939 ft/591 m), SE Forest co., NE Wis., SE of Crandon. 2d-highest point in state.

Sugarcreek, village (1990 pop. 2,062), Tuscarawas co., E Ohio, 10 mi/16 km W of New Philadelphia and on small Sugar Creek; 40°30′N 81°20′W.

Sugarcreek, borough (1990 pop. 5,532), Venango co., NW Pa., 3 mi/4.8 km NW of Franklin on French Creek; 41°26′N 79°48′W. Agr. includes dairying. Formerly a township, largely rural and including the community of Rocky Grove.

Sugarland Run, uninc. town, Loudoun co., N Va., residential suburb 21 mi/34 km NW of Washington, D.C., 11 mi/18 km ESE of Leesburg, near Potomac R.; 39°02′N 77°22′W. Dulles Internatl. Airport to SW.

Sugarloaf Mountain (4,237 ft/1,291 m), Franklin co., W Maine, 26 mi/42 km NW of Farmington; 45°01′N 70°18′W.

Sugden (SUHG-duhn), village (1990 pop. 65), Jefferson co., S Okla., 5 mi/8 km S of Waurika, and on Beaver Creek; 34°04′N 97°58′W.

Sugluk (SUG-luhk), village, N Que., Canada, on Sugluk Inlet (15 mi/24 km long) of Hudson Strait; 64°14′N 75°31′W; Hudson's Bay Company trading post.

Suisun Bay, extreme E arm of San Francisco Bay, W Calif., Solano co. (N) and Contra Costa co. (S), connected with San Pablo Bay (W) by Carquinez Strait. Receives from E the Sacramento and San Joaquin rivers. Port Chicago and Martinez are on S shore; at Martinez, drawbridge crosses bay to point near Benicia. Grizzly Bay is N extension, large marshy area on N.

Suisun City, city (1990 pop. 22,686), Solano co., W central Calif., suburb 1 mi/1.6 km S of Fairfield and on Suisun Slough (navigable connection with Suisun Bay); Grizzly Bay, N arm of Suisun Bay, 6 mi/9.7 km to S; 38°15′N 122°01′W. RR junction. Mfg. (paper prods., fertilizers); fruit, almonds, sugar beets, safflower, sunflowers, grain; cattle, lambs; packing houses. Solano Community Col. here. Travis Air Force Base to NE.

Suitland (SOOT-luhnd), uninc. city (1990 pop. 35,111), Prince Georges co., central Md., suburb of Washington, D.C.; 38°51′N 76°55′W. The name comes from Samuel Tyler Suit, who had a distillery here in the 1880s and owned property here. The Federal Bldg. Complex here, on 360 acres/146 ha of land, includes the U.S. Census Office, U.S. Hydrographic Office, the U.S. Navy Photographic Interpretation Center, and the U.S. Weather Bureau. Nearby are Washington Natl., Cedar Hill, and Memorial cemeteries.

Sulligent, town (1990 pop. 1,886), Lamar co., NW Ala., near Miss. state line, 10 mi/16 km N of Vernon. Mfg. (clothing, furniture, concrete). Settled 1887, inc. 1888.

Sullivan 1 county (□ 454 sq mi/1,176 sq km; 1990 pop. 18,993), SW Ind.; ⊙ Sullivan; 39°05′N 87°25′W. Bounded W by Wabash R., here forming Ill. state line; drained by small Busseron, Turman, and Maria creeks. Agr. (corn, wheat, soybeans, fruit, melons; livestock); bituminous-coal mines, sand and gravel; oil and natural-gas wells; timber. Mfg. at Sullivan and Farmersburg. Part of Greene-Sullivan State Forest in SE; part of Shakamak State Park in NE. Formed 1816. **2** county (□ 654 sq mi/1,694 sq km; 1990 pop. 6,326), N Mo.; ⊙ Milan, 40°13′N 93°07′W. Corn, soybeans, hay; sheep, cattle, hogs. Agr. processing at Milan. Formed 1845. **3** county (□ 551 sq mi/1,427 sq km; 1990 pop. 38,592), SW N.H.; ⊙ Newport; 43°22′N 72°14′W. Bounded W by Connecticut R. (Vt. state line). Mfg. at Newport and Claremont; agr. (apples, corn, hay, nursery crops, maple trees; cattle, poultry); timber. Resorts in Sunapee L. area on E boundary. Drained by Sugar, Little Sugar, and Cold rivers. Several covered bridges in co. Saint-Gaudens Natl. Historic Site in NW; Hubbard Hill State Forest in SW; Gile State Forest in NE; part of Honey Brook State Forest on S boundary; Pillsbury State Park in SE. Formed 1827. **4** county (□ 996 sq mi/2,580 sq km; 1990 pop. 69,277), SE N.Y., ⊙ Monticello, 41°43′N 74°45′W. Bounded W and SW by Delaware R. (here forming Pa. border); includes parts of the Catskills and the Shawangunk range. Drained by Neversink R., Shawangunk and Beaver Kills, and small Willowemoc Creek. Vacation region, with many mt. and lake resorts. Despite its proximity to N.Y. city and good infrastructure, farming has declined markedly due to changing farm economics and land values. Poultry raising is still relatively important; as is dairying. Some timber. Mfg. at Monticello. As with other Catskill cos., e.g., Delaware, Greene, Schoharie and Ulster, there has been a marked, post-1950 decline in the famous resort hotels that, for a cent. characterized the region. It remains a favorite vacation region, however, particularly for downstate New Yorkers. Formed 1809. **5** county (□ 452 sq mi/1,171 sq km; 1990 pop. 6,104), NE Pa.; ⊙ Laporte; 41°27′N 76°30′W. Scenic mt. resort area. Drained by Loyalsock and Muncy creeks. Agr. (corn, oats, hay, alfalfa; cattle; dairying); anthracite. Worlds End State Park in W center; part of Wyoming State Forest in W; includes Kettle Creek Gorge natural area in SW. Formed 1847. **6** county (□ 428 sq mi/1,109 sq km; 1990 pop. 143,596), NE Tenn.; ⊙ Blountville, 36°31′N 82°18′W. Bounded N by Va.; in Great Appalachian Valley, here traversed by mt. ridges. Drained by South Fork of Holston R., site of TVA's South Holston Dam. Includes part of Cherokee Natl. Forest. Agr. (tobacco, corn, fruit, hay); dairying; livestock raising; lumbering; limestone, clay, iron-ore deposits. Industry at Kingsport and Bristol (partly in Va.). Formed 1779.

Sullivan 1 city (1990 pop. 4,354), ⊙ Moultrie co., central Ill., 25 mi/40 km SE of Decatur; 39°36′N 88°36′W. In agr. area (corn, soybeans; livestock); mfg. (wood prods., dairy prods.). Inc. 1869. **2** city (1990 pop. 4,663), ⊙ Sullivan co., SW Ind., near small Busseron Creek, 25 mi/40 km S of Terre Haute; 39°06′N 87°25′W. RR junction. Agr. area; fruit, melons, corn, wheat, soybeans; cattle; mfg. (packaging materials, wood prods., latex prods.); bituminous-coal mines, oil and gas wells; sawmills. William H. Hays was b. here. Platted 1842. **3** city (1990 pop. 5,661), Franklin and Crawford cos., E central Mo., in Ozarks, near Meramec R., 55 mi/89 km SW of St. Louis; 38°12′N 91°09′W. Tourist and farm trade; mfg. (shoes, wire, aircraft parts, lumber prods.). Pea Ridge Iron Mine 10 mi/16 km SE in Washington co. Meramec State Park and Caverns nearby. Laid out c.1860.

Sullivan 1 town (1990 pop. 1,118), Hancock co., S Maine, on Frenchman Bay, 10 mi/16 km E of Ellsworth; 44°32′N 68°09′W. Fishing; resorts. **2** town (1990 pop. 706), Cheshire co., SW N.H., 7 mi/11.3 km NNE of Keene; 43°01′N 72°12′W. Drained by Otter Brook. Agr. (vegetables, nursery crops, apples; cattle, sheep, poultry; dairying).

Sullivan, village (1990 pop. 432), Jefferson co., SE Wis., 11 mi/18 km E of Jefferson; 43°00′N 88°35′W. In dairying region; mfg. (machinery).

Sullivan City, town (1990 pop. 2,371), Hidalgo co., S Texas, 20 mi/32 km WNW of McAllen, near Rio Grande (Mex. border); 26°16′N 98°33′W. Rich irrigated agr. area (citrus, vegetables, cotton, sugarcane). Sand, gravel. Hand-operated toll ferry, 2 mi/3.2 km S at Los Ebanos.

Sullivan Lake (□ 62 sq mi/161 sq km), SE central Alta., Canada, 40 mi/64 km NE of Drumheller; 20 mi/32 km long, 7 mi/11 km wide. Drains S into Red Deer R.

Sullivan Lake, in Morrison co., central Minn., 22 mi/35 km NE of Little Falls; 2.5 mi/4 km long, 1.5 mi/2.4 km wide; 46°08′N 93°56′W. Platte L. is just N. Fed from N and drained NW by Platte R. Resort area.

Sullivans Island, Charleston co., SE S.C., at N side of entrance to Charleston Harbor; 3.5 mi/5.6 km long; 32°46′N 79°50′W. Site of Fort Moultrie and Sullivans Isl. (1990 pop. 1,623), a resort town formerly called Moultrieville. Fort Sumter Natl. Monument to E, at entrance to harbor.

Sully, county (□ 1,070 sq mi/2,771 sq km; 1990 pop. 1,589), central S.Dak.; ⊙ Onida; 44°42′N 100°07′W. Agr. region bounded W by Missouri R. (L. Oahe reservoir). Cattle raising in W; corn, wheat in E. Drained by Okobojo and Medicine Knoll creeks. Stone L. in NW corner. Formed 1877.

Sully, town (1990 pop. 841), Jasper co., central Iowa, 12 mi/19 km SE of Newton; 41°34′N 92°50′W.

Sulphur, city (1990 pop. 20,125), Calcasieu parish, SW La., 10 mi/16 km WNW of Lake Charles city; 30°14′N 93°22′W. Trade center for an area producing natural gas, oil, and timber. Industry centers chiefly around petroleum prods., chemicals, and related enterprises. In agr. area (sorghum, soybeans; cattle; crawfish); mfg. (engines, concrete prods., machinery, lumber), printing and publishing, machining. The city was named for a now-abandoned sulfur dome. In 1924 oil was discovered nearby. An annual state high-school championship rodeo is held here. Inc. 1914. Brimstone Mus. demonstrates Frasch process of sulfur mining.

Sulphur, town (1990 pop. 4,824), ⊙ Murray co., S Okla., 24 mi/39 km SW of Ada; 34°30′N 96°58′W. Elev. 950 ft/290 m. Resort, with mineral springs (ships mineral water). Light mfg.; industrial sand. Has a state school for the deaf and a state veterans' hosp. Chicksaw Natl. Recreation Area is adjacent; Arbuckle Reservoir to S; Arbuckle Mts. (recreation area) to SW. Settled 1898.

Sulphur River, c.110 mi/177 km long, NE Texas and SW Ark.; formed in Delta co., Texas, by junction of North and South forks; flows generally E to Red R. in Miller co., Ark., c.25 mi/40 km SE of Texarkana;. Wright Patman L. reservoir (capacity c.2,000,000 acre-ft.; for conservation, flood control) is 8 mi/12.9 km SW of Texarkana. Cooper L. reservoir on South Fork, S of Cooper.

Sulphur Rock, village (1990 pop. 356), Independence co., NE central Ark., 8 mi/12.9 km E of Batesville; 35°45′N 91°30′W.

Sulphur Springs, city (1990 pop. 14,062), ⊙ Hopkins co., NE Texas, 70 mi/113 km ENE of Dallas; 33°08′N 95°36′W. RR junction; state's 2d-largest milk-producing region, many farmers of Du. origin. Agr. (vegetables, wheat, rice, corn; cattle; dairy); clay; timber; mfg. (firebrick, food processing, dairy prods., cranberry juice). Cooper L. reservoir to NW; L. Rock Reservoir to S. The city became the co. seat in 1871. Inc. 1859.

Sulphur Springs, town (1990 pop. 257), Henry co., E central Ind., 7 mi/11.3 km NW of New Castle; 40°01′N 85°26′W. In agr. area. Laid out 1853.

Sulphur Springs, village (1990 pop. 523), Benton co., extreme NW Ark., 20 mi/32 km NW of Rogers, in the Ozarks, at Mo. state line; Okla. to W boundary; 36°28′N 94°27′W. Mfg. (flour and grain). Tourism.

Sultan, town (1990 pop. 2,236), Snohomish co., NW Wash., 20 mi/32 km ESE of Everett and on Skykomish R., at mouth of Sultan R. (Henry M. Jackson Dam, forms Spada L., to NE); 47°52′N 121°48′W. Berries, vegetables; salmon. Chaplain L. to N; parts of Mt. Baker–Snoqualmie Natl. Forest to N and E; Wallace Falls State Park to E.

Sultan Mountain, peak (13,368 ft/4,075 m) in San Juan Mts., San Juan co., SW Colo., 3 mi/4.8 km SW of Silverton; 37°47′N 107°42′W. E arm of mt. called Grand Turk.

Sultepec de Pedro Ascencio Alquisiras (SOOL-te-pek dai PAI-dro ah-SEN-see-o ahl-kee-SEE-rahs), town (1990 pop. 2,597), Mexico state, central Mexico, on central plateau, 36 mi/58 km SW of Toluca de Leedo; 18°50′N 99°53′W. Elev. 7,664 ft/2,336 m. Silver, gold, lead, copper, and zinc mining; fruit growing.

Area in square miles is shown by the symbol □ capital city or county seat by ⊙

Sulzer, Mount (SUHL-tsuhr) (10,926 ft/3,330 m), S Alaska, in St. Elias Mts., 160 mi/257 km ENE of Cordova; 61°27′N 141°37′W.

Suma (SOO-mah), town (1990 pop. 1,956), Yucatan, SE Mexico, 32 mi/51 km ENE of Mérida; 21°05′N 89°09′W. Henequen.

Sumas (SOO-mahs), town (1990 pop. 744), Whatcom co., NW Wash., 20 mi/32 km NE of Bellingham, on Sumas R., port of entry near Canada (B.C.) border, opposite Huntington, B.C.; Abbotsford 3 mi/4.8 km N; 49°00′N 122°16′W. RR junction. Berries; dairying; cattle, poultry; limestone quarry.

Sumiton (SOO-mi-tuhn), village (1990 pop. 2,604), Walker co., N central Ala., 15 mi/24 km ESE of Jasper. Coal mines.

Summer Lake, Lake co., S Oregon, semi-dry body of water, 9 mi/14.5 km long, 4.5 mi/7.2 km wide. Basin (☐ c.60 sq mi/155 sq km) is 15 mi/24 km long, 5 mi/8 km wide. Fed by short Ana R. from N. No outlet. Summer L. Hot Springs SE. Winter Ridge, in Fremont Natl. Forest, to W.

Summer Shade, uninc. village (1990 pop. 400), Metcalfe co., S Ky., 13 mi/21 km SE of Glasgow, near source of Marrowbone Creek. Burley tobacco, grain, livestock; dairying; timber. Mfg. (charcoal, lumber, apparel).

Summerdale 1 town (1990 pop. 559), Baldwin co., SW Ala., 30 mi/48 km S of Bay Minette. Agr. commodities, fertilizer, oil. **2** uninc. town (1990 pop. 800), Cumberland co., S Pa., residential suburb 3 mi/4.8 km NNW of Harrisburg, on Susquehanna R.; 40°18′N 75°55′W. Blue Ridge Mts. to N.

Summerfield 1 town, Marion co., N central Fla., 14 mi/23 km SE of Ocala. Mfg. includes restaurant furniture, steel fencing. **2** uninc. town (1990 pop. 2,051), Guilford co., N central N.C., suburb 10 mi/16 km N of Greensboro, near Haw R.; 36°12′N 79°53′W. Agr. area (tobacco, grain, soybeans; livestock; dairying). Mfg. (bldg. materials, steel).

Summerfield 1 village (1990 pop. 509), St. Clair co., SW Ill., 20 mi/32 km E of East St. Louis; 38°36′N 89°45′W. In agr. area (dairying; soybeans, wheat, sorghum; hogs). **2** village (1990 pop. 169), Marshall co., NE Kansas, at Nebr. state line, 19 mi/31 km NE of Marysville; 40°00′N 96°20′W. In grain area. **3** village (1990 pop. 295), Noble co., E Ohio, 8 mi/13 km NE of Caldwell; 39°48′N 81°20′W.

Summerhill, borough (1990 pop. 614), Cambria co., W central Pa., 9 mi/14.5 km ENE of Johnstown, on Little Conemaugh R.; 40°22′N 78°45′W. Agr. (corn, hay, potatoes; dairying); timber; mfg. (lumber, wood prods.).

Summerland, town (1991 pop. 9,253), S B.C., Canada, on SW shore of Okanagan L., 9 mi/14 km NW of Penticton; 49°39′N 117°33′W. Elev. 1,370 ft/418 m. Apple-growing center, also peaches, pears, apricots, cherries, grapes; winery, fruit cannery; meat packing. Agr. research station; govt. fish hatchery here.

Summerland, uninc. village, Santa Barbara co., SW Calif., on Santa Barbara Channel, 5 mi/8 km E of Santa Barbara. Offshore oil field; oil refining. Cattle; grain, fruit, avocados, vegetables. Capenteria State Beach to E; Los Padres Natl. Forest to N.

Summerland Island, islet, Jefferson co., N N.Y., largest of the Summerland group of the Thousand Isls., in the St. Lawrence R., at Ont. border, 4.5 mi/7.2 km NE of Alexandria Bay; 44°23′N 75°54′W.

Summers, county (☐ 367 sq mi/951 sq km; 1990 pop. 14,204), S W.Va.; ⊙ Hinton; 37°39′N 80°51′W. Mt. region, on Allegheny Plateau; Keeney Knob (in E) rises to 3,927 ft/1,197 m; drained by New R. and its branches, the Greenbrier and Bluestone rivers. Bluestone L. reservoir in S, in Bluestone State Park and Wildlife Management Area. Bluestone Natl. Scenic R. and part of Pipestem State Park in SW; part of New R. Gorge Natl. R. in N. Agr. (corn, oats, potatoes, alfalfa, hay, nursery crops); cattle, sheep. Timber, some natural gas. Formed 1871.

Summerside, town (1991 pop. 7,474), SW P.E.I., Canada, on Bedeque Bay, an arm of Northumberland Strait; 46°24′N 63°47′W. The isl.'s 2d-largest city, it is a tourist center and port. Potatoes, dairy prods., and oysters are produced in the region. Army base nearby, now closed.

Summerside, uninc. village (1990 pop. 4,573), Clermont co., extreme SW Ohio, an E suburb of Cincinnati; 39°07′N 84°17′W.

Summersville 1 town (1990 pop. 571), Shannon and Texas cos., S central Mo., in the Ozarks, 14 mi/23 km NNE of Mountain View; 37°10′N 91°39′W. Cattle. Mfg. (apparel). **2** town (1990 pop. 2,906), ⊙ Nicholas co., central W.Va., 40 mi/64 km E of Charleston, near Gauley R.; 38°16′N 80°50′W. Coal-mining area. RR terminus. Agr. (corn, apples); cattle, poultry. Mfg. (printed prods., concrete, coal processing; dairy prods.; winery). Carnifex Ferry Battlefield State Park is 7 mi/11.3 km SW. Gauley R. forms Summersville L. reservoir and Wildlife Management Area to E and SW; Gauley R. Natl. Recreation Area to SW; Monongahela Natl. Forest to E.

Summersville, uninc. village (1990 pop. 300), Green co., central Ky., 5 mi/8 km NNW of Greensburg, near Pitman Creek. Tobacco, grain; livestock; dairying. Mfg. (feeds).

Summersville Lake, reservoir, Nicholas co., central W.Va., on Gauley R., 6 mi/9.7 km SW of Summersville; 6 mi/9.7 km long; 80°53′N 38°12′W. Max. capacity 390,800 acre-ft. Formed by Summersville Dam (342 ft/104 m high), built (1965) by the Army Corps of Engineers for water storage. Summersville L. Wildlife Management Area surrounds lake, Gauley R. Natl. Recreation Area downstream (W).

Summerton, town (1990 pop. 975), Clarendon co., central S.C., 22 mi/35 km S of Sumter; 33°36′N 80°20′W. Mfg. of oil seals and gaskets. Agr. area for poultry, cattle, grain, tobacco, cotton, timber.

Summertown, town (1990 pop. 153), Emanuel co., E central Ga., 10 mi/16 km NNE of Swainsboro; 32°45′N 82°17′W.

Summerville, city (1990 pop. 22,519), Dorchester co., SE S.C., 21 mi/34 km NW of Charleston; 33°00′N 80°10′W. Winter resort. Mfg. includes machining, aluminum skirting, automotive transmissions, furniture frames, typewriter ribbons, saw blades, monofilaments, driveshafts, printing and publishing, bricks, lumber, gaskets and seals, nonedible food casings. Agr. includes poultry, hogs, corn soybeans, cotton. Nearby area was great plantation center in 18th and 19th cents.; has estates and homes of period. Middleton Place and Magnolia Gardens to SE. Settled c.1795, inc. 1847.

Summerville, town (1990 pop. 5,025), ⊙ Chattooga co., NW Ga., 18 mi/29 km NW of Rome, near Chattooga R.; 34°29′N 85°21′W. Mfg. of work gloves, carpets and yarns, wire harnesses. State fish hatchery nearby. Inc. 1839.

Summerville, village (1990 pop. 111), Union co., NE Oregon, 12 mi/19 km NNE of La Grande; 45°29′N 118°00′W. Umatilla Natl. Forest to NW.

Summerville, borough (1990 pop. 675), Jefferson co., W central Pa., 6 mi/9.7 km WSW of Brookville, on Red Bank Creek; 41°07′N 79°11′W. Agr. (grain, alfalfa; livestock, dairying); mfg. (mining equip., clay bricks). Settled c.1812, inc. 1887.

Summit 1 county (☐ 619 sq mi/1,603 sq km; 1990 pop. 12,881), central Colo.; ⊙ Breckenridge; 39°37′N 106°06′W. Drained by Blue R., which forms Dillon Reservoir at center, Green Mountain Reservoir in NW. Once mainly mining and sheep-grazing region; is now a major tourism and recreation area. All of co. but Blue R. margins and NW corner is in Arapaho Natl. Forest. Zinc, gold, silver. Includes part of Gore Range and Arapaho Natl. Forest. Has 5 ski resorts; Breckenridge (SW), Copper Mountain (SW), Keystone (E), Loveland (E), and Arapaho Basin (E). Formed 1861. **2** county (☐ 413 sq mi/1,070 sq km; 1990 pop. 514,990), NE Ohio; ⊙ Akron; 41°07′N 81°32′W. Drained by Cuyahoga and Tuscarawas rivers. Includes Portage Lakes (recreation). In the Glaciated Plain physiographic region. Agr. area (corn, vegetables; poultry); mfg. at Akron, Barberton, and Cuyahoga Falls (bakery prods., lumber and wood prods., coatings, plastic goods, paints, household furniture, laminated and coated paper, chemicals, boilers, composites, computers, tires, stone, clay, and glass prods., hand and edge tools and hardware, metal stampings, aircraft parts and equip., bicycles and other sporting goods, industrial machinery). Limestone, sandstone quarries; sand, gravel, clay, salt deposits. Formed 1840. **3** county (☐ 1,882 sq mi/4,874 sq km; 1990 pop. 15,518), NE Utah; ⊙ Coalville; 40°52′N 110°58′W. Mining and sheep- and cattle-grazing area bordering SW corner of Wyo. and drained in W by Weber R. Wasatch Natl. Forest and Uinta Mts. here. Nearly all of pop. in W end of co. in Weber Valley. Gold, silver, lead, coal mines. Vegetables, alfalfa in irrigated region around Coalville; dairying; timber, oil, natural gas. Formed 1854. Ski resort around Park City, in SW. Echo Reservoir and Rockport Reservoir and State Park are in W; small part of Wasatch Natl. Forest, Wasatch Range, along SW boundary; almost all of central and E parts of co. in Wasatch Natl. Forest; small part of Ashley Natl. Forest in extreme E.

Summit, city (1990 pop. 19,757), Union co., NE N.J., an upper-income residential suburb of the N.Y. city–N N.J. metropolitan area; 40°42′N 74°22′W. Commuter RR. Pharmaceuticals mfg.; several major companies have research facilities here. Situated on a ridge of Watchung Mt., it was the site of an important Amer. lookout post during the Revolutionary War. Settled c.1720, set off from Springfield and New Providence and est. 1869; inc. 1899.

Summit 1 uninc. town (1990 pop. 2,000), Boyd co., NE Ky., residential suburb 4 mi/6.4 km SW of Ashland. Tobacco, alfalfa, cattle. Bituminous coal. Mfg. (lumber). **2** town (1990 pop. 1,566), Pike co., SW Miss., 3 mi/4.8 km N of McComb; 31°16′N 90°28′W. In agr. (cotton, corn; cattle; dairying; timber) area; mfg. (lumber, tricot fabrics, plastic bags, poultry processing). Has Southwest Miss. Community Col. Founded 1857. **3** uninc. town (1990 pop. 2,700), Pierce co., W Wash., suburb 5 mi/8 km SE of downtown Tacoma and 3 mi/4.8 km SW of Puyallup.

Summit 1 village (1990 pop. 480), Marion co., N Ark., 23 mi/37 km E of Harrison and 2 mi/3.2 km N of Yellville, near Crooked Creek, in the Ozarks; 36°15′N 92°41′W. Bull Shoals L. Reservoir to N. **2** village (1990 pop. 9,971), Cook co., NE Ill., on Des Plaines R., 11 mi/18 km WSW of downtown Chicago; 41°46′N 87°49′W. Large corn-refining industry here and at adjacent Argo (just SW). Mfg. (sulfated oils, gelatins and food bases, tape). Limestone quarrying nearby. Inc. 1890. **3** village, in Coventry town, Kent co., W R.I., 17 mi/27 km WSW of Providence. **4** village (1990 pop. 242), Lexington co., W central S.C., 22 mi/35 km WSW of Columbia on N fork Edisto R.; 33°55′N 81°25′W. Mfg. of bedroom furniture. Agr. includes livestock; grain, soybeans. **5** village (1990 pop. 267), Roberts co., NE S Dak., 25 mi/40 km S of Sisseton and on Coteau des Prairies, in Lake Traverse (Sisseton) Indian Reservation; 45°17′N 97°02′W.

Summit, hamlet, Glacier co., on Flathead co. line, NW Mont., on Continental Divide at Marias Pass, 50 mi/80 km SW of Cut Bank, and on SE boundary of Glacier Natl. Park; 48°21′N 113°22′W. Elev. c.5,280 ft/1,609 m. Statue of John F. Stevens, discoverer of pass, is here.

Summit, Ga.: see TWIN CITY.

Summit Hill, borough (1990 pop. 3,332), Carbon co., E Pa., 7 mi/11.3 km WSW of Jim Thorpe; 40°49′N 75°50′W. Agr. (potatoes, dairying); mfg. (monuments). Mauch Chunk L. reservoir to E.

Summit Lake, village, N central B.C., Canada, 30 mi/48 km N of Prince George, on John Hart Highway, at E end of Summit Lake; 54°17′N 122°38′W. Service center for travelers, logging, sportsmen. Lodge.

Summit Mountain, Nev.: see MONITOR RANGE.

Summit Peak (13,300 ft/4,054 m), Archuleta co., SW Colo., on Continental Divide, in San Juan Mts., 18 mi/29 km ENE of Pagosa Springs; 37°21′N 106°41′W. San Juan Natl Forest (W); Rio Grande Natl. Forest (E).

Summitville, town (1990 pop. 1,010), Madison co., E central Ind., 16 mi/26 km N of Anderson; 40°20′N 85°38′W. In agr. area; mfg. (wooden pallets, tools). Laid out 1867.

Summitville 1 resort village (1990 pop. 700), Sullivan

co., SE N.Y., in the Shawangunk range, 12 mi/19 km ESE of Monticello; 41°37′N 74°27′W. **2** village (1990 pop. 125), Columbiana co., E Ohio, 5 mi/8 km SW of Lisbon; 40°40′N 80°53′W.

Summitville, locality, SW Colo., 15 mi/24 km NE of Summit Peak. Former center for gold-mining dist. that closed in the 1940s, reopened in 1989, using a technology that caused dangerous toxic wastes. Mining had to be abandoned and site taken over by Environmental Protection Agency (EPA).

Sumner 1 (SUHM-nuhr), county (□ 1,184 sq mi/ 3,067 sq km; 1990 pop. 25,841), S Kansas; ⊙ Wellington; 37°14′N 97°29′W. Level to gently rolling plain, bordering S on Okla.; drained in SW by Chikaskia R., in NE by Ninnescah and Arkansas rivers. Wheat, corn, sorghum, cattle, hogs. Industrial machinery. Formed 1871. **2** county (□ 552 sq mi/1,430 sq km; 1990 pop. 103,281), N Tenn.; ⊙ Gallatin, 36°28′N 86°28′W. Bounded N by Ky., S by Cumberland R.; drained by headstreams of Red R. and by Drake Creek. Livestock, dairy prods., wheat, hay, tobacco, strawberries, apples, corn. Formed 1786.

Sumner, city (1990 pop. 1,083), Lawrence co., SE Ill., 10 mi/16 km W of Lawrenceville; 38°43′N 87°51′W. In oil, natural gas, and agr. area. Inc. 1887. Red Hills State Park nearby.

Sumner 1 town (1990 pop. 2,078), Bremer co., NE Iowa, on Little Wapsipinicon R., and 20 mi/32 km ENE of Waverly; 42°51′N 92°05′W. Dairy-prods. packing; mfg. of feed, chemicals, coops. Inc. 1892. **2** town (1990 pop. 761), Oxford co., W Maine, 14 mi/23 km N of South Paris; 44°21′N 70°27′W. In lumbering, recreational area. Wood prods. Village of East Sumner is partly in Hartford town. **3** town (1990 pop. 140), Chariton co., N central Mo., near mouth of Locust Creek in Grand R., 13 mi/21 km SW of Brookfield; 39°39′N 93°14′W. Grain; corn, soybeans, livestock. RR junction. Swan Lake Natl. Wildlife Refuge to SE; Fountain Grove State Wildlife Refuge to NW; 40 ft/12 m statue of a wild goose. **4** town (1990 pop. 6,281), Pierce co., W central Wash., suburb 10 mi/16 km ESE of Tacoma, on Puyallup R., at mouth of White R.; 47°13′N 122°14′W. Berries, flower bulbs, fruit, vegetables; dairying; poultry; mfg. (concrete, cheese, plastics prods., store fixtures, yeast, wood panels, aircraft parts, paperboard mill, wood treating, organic fibers). Settled 1855 inc. 1891.

Sumner 1 village (1990 pop. 209), Worth co., S central Ga., 6 mi/9.7 km E of Sylvester; 31°31′N 83°44′W. Tire retreading, peanut processing. **2** village (1990 pop. 368), ⊙ Tallahatchie co. (seat shared with Charleston), NW central Miss., 19 mi/31 km SE of Clarksdale; 33°58′N 90°22′W. Agr. (cotton, corn, wheat, soybeans; cattle); mfg. (industrial uniforms). **3** village (1990 pop. 210), Dawson co., S central Nebr., 17 mi/27 km NE of Lexington and on Wood R; 40°57′N 99°30′W. **4** village, Noble co., N Okla., 9 mi/14.5 km ENE of Perry, on Black Bear Creek.

Sumner Strait, SE Alaska, in Alexander Archipelago, bet. Prince of Wales Isl. (S), Kupreanof Isl. (N), and Kuiu Isl. (W), extending from Iphigenia Bay on the Pacific to head of Clarence Strait.

Sumpter, village (1990 pop. 119), Baker co., NE Oregon, 18 mi/29 km W of Baker City, in Wallowa-Whitman Natl. Forest; 44°44′N 118°12′W.

Sumrall (SUHM-rahl), town (1990 pop. 903), Lamar co., SE Miss., 16 mi/26 km WNW of Hattiesburg; 31°25′N 89°32′W. In agr. (cotton, corn; poultry, cattle) and pine-timber area; mfg. (apparel).

Sumter 1 county (□ 913 sq mi/2,365 sq km; 1990 pop. 16,174), W Ala.; ⊙ Livingston. In Black Belt, on Miss. state line, bounded E by Tombigbee R. Corn, soybeans; livestock; lumber milling. Formed 1832. **2** county (□ 580 sq mi/1,502 sq km; 1990 pop. 31,577), central Fla., bounded partly W and S by Withlacoochee R.; ⊙ Bushnell; 28°42′N 82°04′W. Agr. produce area, with swamps in W and many scattered lakes, including L. Panasoffkee; also produces citrus fruit, corn, cattle, and poultry; some forestry (lumber, naval stores). Formed 1853. **3** county (□ 493 sq mi/1,277 sq km; 1990 pop. 30,228), SW central Ga.; ⊙ Americus; 32°02′N 84°12′W. Bounded E by Flint R., drained by Muckalee Creek. Mfg at Americus. Coastal plain agr. (cotton, corn, soybeans, peanuts, wheat, oats); cattle, hogs, poultry. Formed 1831. **4** county (□ 682 sq mi/1,766 sq km; 1990 pop. 102,637), central S.C.; ⊙ Sumter; 33°55′N 80°22′W. Bounded W by Wateree R., NE by Lynches R.; drained by Black R.; N part of L. Marion is in S. Includes Poinsett State Park and Forest. Mfg. of sand, gravel, clay. Agr. and lumbering area producing hogs, cattle, dairying, wheat, rye, oats, tobacco, sorghum, peanuts, hay, cotton. Formed 1785.

Sumter, city (1990 pop. 41,943), ⊙ Sumter co., central S.C., 40 mi/64 km ESE of Columbia, on Pocotalingo R; 33°56′N 80°23′W. It is the commercial, processing, and shipping center of a timber and agr. region. Chief crops are tobacco and cotton, also livestock, grain, peanuts, sorghum. Mfg. (concrete, industrial systems, textiles, hand tools, processed meats, corrugated containers, printing and publishing, chemical transfer systems, lumber, plywood, paper). Of interest are the tombs of Revolutionary War Gen. Thomas Sumter and Joel Poinsett, for whom the poinsettia is named. Swan L. Iris Gardens, with its numerous types of trees and flora, attract many visitors. Morris Col., Central Carolina Technical Col. (2-year), and a branch of the Univ. of S.C. at Sumter (2-year) are in the city. Shaw Air Force Base is 9 mi/14.5 km W; city limits extend to it. Gallery of art here. Settled c.1740, inc. 1845.

Sumter, Fort, S.C.: see FORT SUMTER.

Sun, village (1990 pop. 429), St. Tammany parish, La., 15 mi/24 km NE of Covington, near Bogue Chitto (S) and Pearl R. (E; Miss. boundary); 30°39′N 89°54′W. Bogue Chitto Natl. Wildlife Refuge to E. Agr. area. Catfish, crawfish; alligators.

Sun City 1 uninc. city (1990 pop. 38,126), Maricopa co., central Ariz., residential suburb 15 mi/24 km NW of downtown Phoenix, near New R. Mfg. (printing and publishing, rocks and gems). Large retirement community. **2** uninc. city (1990 pop. 14,930), Riverside co., S Calif., 20 mi/32 km SSE of Riverside; 33°43′N 117°12′W. Dairying; cattle, poultry; grain, alfalfa, nursery stock. Mfg. (electronic transformers, printing and publishing).

Sun City, village (1990 pop. 88), Barber co, S Kansas, on Medicine Lodge R., and 19 mi/31 km SSW of Pratt; 37°22′N 98°55′W. In cattle and wheat area; gypsum mining.

Sun City Center, town (□ 5 sq mi/13 sq km; 1990 pop. 8,326), Hillsborough co., W central Fla., 24 mi/39 km SSE of Tampa; 27°43′N 82°20′W. Mfg. includes polystyrene prods., machine parts.

Sun City West, uninc. city (1990 pop. 15,997), Maricopa co., central Ariz., residential suburb 20 mi/32 km NW of downtown Phoenix, at fringe of urbanized area. Large retirement community.

Sun Coast, local name for the gulf of Mexico of SW Fla., bet. the Tampa Bay metropolis on the N and Naples on the S. Includes the resort cities of Sarasota, Venice, and Fort Myers.

Sun Lakes, uninc. town (1990 pop. 6,578) , Maricopa co., central Ariz., residential suburb 17 mi/27 km SSE of downtown Phoenix, near Gila R. Irrigated agr. area on urban fringe (fruit, vegetables, grain, cotton, livestock). Retirement community. Gila R. Indian Reservation to S and W.

Sun Prairie, city (1990 pop. 15,333), Dane co., S Wis., near small Koshkonong Creek, suburb 11 mi/18 km NE of Madison; 43°10′N 89°13′W. In farm area; porcelain mfg.; canned foods, dairy prods., wood and laminated materials. Georgia O'Keeffe b. here. Settled c.1837, inc. 1868.

Sun River, c.130 mi/209 km long, Mont.; rising in the Rocky Mts. formed by joining of North and South forks at upper (W) end of Gibson Reservoir (Teton–Lewis and Clark co. lines), 36 mi/58 km SW of Choteau, NW Mont.; flowing generally E past Simms and Vaughn, joining the Missouri R. at Great Falls. The Sun R. project of the U.S. Bureau of Reclamation utilizes the Sun and its tributaries to irrigate c.92,000 acres/ 37,232 ha of land. Of the system of dams and reservoirs, Gibson Dam is one of the project's largest. North Fork of the Sun rises at Continental Divide, on Teton–Lewis and Clark co. line; flows S c.25 mi/40 km. Sun R. Game Preserve to W. South Fork of the Sun rises at Continental Divide, W Lewis and Clark co.; flows N c. 20 mi/ 32 km, joining North Fork to form Sun R., receives West Fork 7 mi/11.3 km SSW of its mouth. West Fork of the Sun rises at Continental Divide, W Lewis and Clark co., in Sun R. Game Preserve; flows S and E c.15 mi/24 km to South Fork. Also called Medicine R.

Sun River Terrace, village (1990 pop. 532), Kankakee co., NE Ill., residential suburb 6 mi/9.7 km E of Kankakee, on Kankakee R.; 41°07′N 87°43′W.

Sun Valley, uninc. city (1990 pop. 11,391), Washoe co., W Nev., residential suburb and mobile-home haven, 3 mi/4.8 km N of downtown Reno; 39°36′N 119°46′W. Mfg. (wood pallets).

Sun Valley, town (1990 pop. 938), Blaine co., 14 mi/ 23 km N of Hailey and 1 mi/1.6 km N of Ketchum, S central Idaho; 43°41′N 114°20′W. Elev. 5,920 ft/1,804 m. It is a popular year-round resort with both winter and summer sports, golf and year-round ice skating, including performances by renowned skaters. Mfg. (light mfg., micro-brewery). It was founded as a ski resort in 1936 by W. Averell Harriman, then board chairman of the Union Pacific RR; the RR purchased the land and built the resort to attract more passenger traffic to the West. In 1964 it was sold to a land-development corporation; in 1967, Bill Janss, a former Olympic skier, became sole owner. The Hemingway Memorial, on a bluff overlooking a swift-flowing trout stream, was dedicated in 1966. Surrounded by Sawtooth Natl. Forest. Inc. 1967.

Sun Valley, village (1990 pop. 329), Lamar co., NE Texas, 7 mi/11.3 km E of Paris; 33°40′N 95°25′W. Agr. area (cotton, peanuts, soybeans, cattle).

Sun Valley, suburban section of Los Angeles, Los Angeles co., S Calif., 13 mi/21 km NNW of downtown Los Angeles, in San Fernando Valley. Mfg. (filters, aircraft engines, broadcast equip., welding equip., store fixtures, metal plating, aluminum die castings, corrugated boxes, hand tools, musical instruments, paints, printing, concrete prods., cabinets). Verdago Mts. to E. Hollywood Burbank Airport to S.

Sunapee (SUHN-uh-pee), town (1990 pop. 2,559), Sullivan co., SW N.H., 4 mi/6.4 km ENE of Newport. Drained by Sugar R. Town center on W shore of Sunapee L. Cattle, poultry; nursery crops, corn, apples. Tourism. L. Sunapee in E.

Sunapee Lake (SUHN-uh-pee), Merrimack and Sullivan cos., W central N.H., drained W by Sugar R. Boating, fishing resort; 9 mi/14.5 km long, 3 mi/4.8 km wide. Mfg. (machining, lumber). Mt. Sunapee (2,743 ft/ 836 m) is just S; winter sports. Towns of Newbury at S end, Sunapee on W shore. Mt. Sunapee State Park and Mt. Sunapee ski area to S. Elev. 1,100 ft/335 m.

Sunbelt, S tier of the U.S., focused on Fla., Texas, Ariz., and Calif., and extending as far N as Va. The term gained wide use in the 1970s, when the economic and political impact of the nation's overall shift in pop. to the S and W became conspicuous. Areas near the Mex. border have received millions of immigrants since the 1960s. Economic growth in many Sunbelt cities since World War II has stimulated interregional migration from the NE U.S. and the Rustbelt; by 1990, Los Angeles, San Diego, Phoenix, Houston, Dallas, and San Antonio were among the 10 largest cities in the U.S. The warm climate has attracted large retirement communities, especially in Fla. and Ariz. In addition, the birth rate in the Sunbelt is about 10% greater than that in the rest of the country. Attracted by the relative lack of labor unions and the prospect of cheaper labor than was generally available in the N, manufacturers began to locate in the SE in significant numbers after World War II; aerospace firms and defense contractors were drawn to the vicinity of military bases in S Calif. and throughout the SW. Texas, La., and Okla. benefited from the oil booms of the 1970s. In addition, the enormous tourist industries of the Sunbelt (especially Fla. and S Calif.) have brought the region considerable

Area in square miles is shown by the symbol □ capital city or county seat by ⊙

wealth; high-technology and its related industries have also had a substantial impact on Calif. (Silicon Valley) and Ariz. Although overall the expansion of the Sunbelt's economy in recent decades has been dramatic, the distribution of the region's prosperity has been uneven; of the 25 metropolitan areas with the lowest per capita income in 1990, 23 were in the Sunbelt. The rapid fall of oil prices in the 1980s hurt the economies of the energy-producing areas of the Sunbelt; Houston was especially hard hit. By the 1980s, the Los Angeles area, beset by problems ranging from air pollution to a growing pop. of unskilled immigrants, came increasingly to resemble some of the troubled metropolitan areas of the N. Politically, the rise of the Sunbelt has generally been viewed as advantageous to the Republican party, especially in presidential elections. Since 1970, the Sunbelt has gained more than 25 electoral votes, mostly at the expense of the NE and Midwest.

Sunburg, village (1990 pop. 117), Kandiyohi co., S central Minn., 17 mi/27 km NW of Willmar; 45°21′N 95°14′W. Mfg. of feeds; agr. (dairying; livestock, grains). Monson Lake State Park to W; Norway L. and Sibley State Park to E.

Sunburst, village (1990 pop. 437), Toole co., N Mont., 26 mi/42 km N of Shelby; Canada (Alta.) border at Sweetgrass 8 mi/12.9 km N. Kevin-Sunburst oil field extends S; 48°53′N 111°55′W. Oil storage facilities. Wheat, barley, oats, cattle, hogs.

Sunbury, county (☐ 1,079 sq mi/2,795 sq km; 1991 pop. 23,575), S central N.B., Canada, E of Fredericton; ⊙ Burton; 45°55′N 66°20′W.

Sunbury (SUHN-buhr-ee), city (1990 pop. 11,591), ⊙ Northumberland co., E central Pa., 40 mi/64 km N of Harrisburg on the Susquehanna R. (bridged N and W), 1 mi/1.6 km S of mouth of West Branch of Susquehanna R., mouth of Shamokin Creek to S; 40°51′N 76°47′W. Agr. area (grain, apples; livestock; dairying); mfg. (food prods., fiberboard insulation, steel wire and cable, printing and publishing, apparel, textiles, wood prods.). The city was the site of a Native Amer. village in the early 18th cent. In 1742 a mission was established, and in 1756 Fort Augusta was built (parts of the fort still stand). Thomas A. Edison worked in Sunbury. Immediately S on the Susquehanna R. is Shamokin Dam, a large "fabridam" — a dam of a fabric that can be collapsed and inflated. Co. Historical Society Mus. Shikellamy State Park to NW. Laid out 1772, inc. 1921.

Sunbury, village (1990 pop. 2,046), Delaware co., central Ohio, 12 mi/19 km ESE of Delaware; 40°14′N 82°52′W. In agr. area.

Suncook, N.H.: see PEMBROKE.

Suncook River (SUN-kuk), c.35 mi/56 km long, S central N.H.; rises in ponds E of Gilmanton, SE central Belknap co.; flows S through Crystal L. and Upper and Lower Suncook lakes, then SW, past Pittsfield, receives Little Suncook R. from E at Epsom, flows to Merrimack R. at Suncook village, 6 mi/9.7 km SE of Concord.

Sundance, town (1990 pop. 1,139), ⊙ Crook co., NE Wyo., just NW of Black Hills, 60 mi/97 km NW of Rapid City, S.Dak.; 44°23′N 104°22′W. Elev. 4,750 ft/1,448 m. Trade point in livestock (cattle, sheep), grain (wheat, hay, alfalfa, oats) region; timber; coal mines, oil refinery. Devils Tower Natl. Monument to NW; parts of Black Hills Natl. Forest to N and E; Sundance Mt. (5,800 ft/1,768 m) just S.

Sunday Cove Island (☐ 10 sq mi/26 sq km), E N.F., Canada, in Notre Dame Bay, 45 mi/72 km W of Twillingate; 7 mi/11 km long, 3 mi/5 km wide; 49°33′N 55°50′W. On S coast is fishing village of Port Anson.

Sunderland 1 town (1990 pop. 3,399), Franklin co., W Mass., on Connecticut R., and 8 mi/12.9 km S of Greenfield; 42°28′N 72°34′W. Tobacco. Mt. Toby State Forest and Mt. Sugarloaf Reservation nearby. **2** town (1990 pop. 872), Bennington co., SW Vt., on Batten Kill and 18 mi/29 km N of Bennington, in Green Mts.; 43°04′N 73°04′W.

Sunderland, village, S Ont., Canada, on Beaverton R., and 18 mi/29 km WSW of Lindsay. Dairying, mixed farming.

Sundial Mountain (10,438 ft/3,182 m), SW Alta., Canada, near B.C. border, in Rocky Mts., in Jasper Natl. Park, 50 mi/80 km. SSE of Jasper; 52°13′N 117°37′W.

Sundown, town (1990 pop. 1,759), Hockley co., NW Texas, on the Llano Estacado, 30 mi/48 km ESE of Lubbock; 33°27′N 102°29′W. RR-spur terminus in oil field. Cattle; cotton; sorghum; mfg. (natural gas processing, oil field equip.). Inc. after 1940.

Sundown, resort village (1990 pop. 200), Ulster co., SE N.Y., in the Catskills, 25 mi/40 km WSW of Kingston; 41°53′N 74°28′W.

Sundridge, village (1991 pop. 937), SE central Ont., Canada, on Bernard L., 40 mi/64 km S of North Bay; 45°46′N 79°24′W. Lumbering.

Sunfield, village (1990 pop. 610), Eaton co., S central Mich., 22 mi/35 km W of Lansing; 42°45′N 84°59′W. In farm area.

Sunfish Lake, village (1990 pop. 413), Dakota co., SE Minn., residential suburb 5 mi/8 km S of downtown St. Paul; 44°52′N 93°05′W. Several small lakes in area; Sunfish L. in center.

Sunflower, county (☐ 707 sq mi/1,831 sq km; 1990 pop. 32,867), W Miss.; ⊙ Indianola; 33°36′N 90°35′W. Rich lowland cotton-growing region, drained by Sunflower and Quiver rivers. Agr. (corn, oats, rice, soybeans, wheat, pecans, hay, alfalfa; cattle; timber); catfish. Formed 1844.

Sunflower, town (1990 pop. 729), Sunflower co., W Miss., 20 mi/32 km W of Greenwood; 33°32′N 90°32′W. In agr. area (cotton, corn, soybeans, rice, pecans; cattle); catfish; mfg. (fish oils and meal).

Sunflower River or **Big Sunflower River**, 240 mi/386 km long, NW and W central Miss.; rises in Moon L., oxbow lake, 1 mi/1.6 km NE of Mississippi R., in N Coahoma co.; flows S past Clarksdale, Sunflower, and Indianola, to Yazoo R., 20 mi/32 km SW of Yazoo city. Entire river is a bayou of Mississippi R., flows entirely within Mississippi R. Flood Plain, roughly parallelling Mississippi., in one of its former channels, (up to 35 mi/56 km apart).

Sunken Meadow State Park, N.Y.: see KINGS PARK.

Sunland, suburban section of Los Angeles, Los Angeles co., S Calif., 15 mi/24 km N of downtown. Mfg. (apparel); olives, citrus fruit. Big Tujunga Canyon to NE. Angeles Natl. Forest to NE.

Sunland Park, town (1990 pop. 8,179), Dona Ana co., S N. Mex., suburb 4 mi/6.4 km WNW of downtown El Paso, Texas, on Rio Grande (begins as Texas state border here) and Mexico (Chihuahua) border (S); 31°48′N 106°34′W. Irrigated agr. area. Mfg. (bricks, wood cabinets, wood doors, concrete slabs). Sunland Park Racetrack to N.

Sunlight Peak (14,059 ft/4,285 m), La Plata co., SW Colo., in San Juan Mts., c.13 mi/21 km SSE of Silverton, NNW of Windom Peak; 37°37′N 107°35′W.

Sunman, town (1990 pop. 623), Ripley co., SE Ind., 15 mi/24 km NE of Versailles; 39°14′N 85°06′W. In agr. area; mfg. (offset printing). Laid out 1856.

Sunniland, village, Collier co., SW Fla., c.40 mi/64 km SE of Fort Myers, in Big Cypress Swamp. Contains 1st successful oil wells drilled in Fla.

Sunnside, uninc. town (1990 pop. 700), San Diego co., S Calif., residential suburb 10 mi/16 km ESE of downtown San Diego, on Sweetwater R. Sweetwater Reservoir to NE; Upper and Lower Otay reservoirs to SE.

Sunny Isles, town (☐ 1 sq mi/2.6 sq km; 1990 pop. 11,772), Dade co., SE Fla., 13 mi/21 km NE of Miami; 25°55′N 80°07′W.

Sunny Side, village (1990 pop. 215), Spalding co., W central Ga., 6 mi/9.7 km NNW of Griffin; 33°20′N 84°17′W.

Sunnymead, Calif.: see MORENO VALLEY.

Sunnyside, town (1990 pop. 11,238), Yakima co., S Wash., 30 mi/48 km SE of Yakima, bet. Sunnyside Canal (N) and Yakima R. (S), Roza Canal (farther N), 46°19′N 120°01′W. RR junction. In irrigated farm area producing fruits and vegetables, wheat, barley, oats; dairying; mfg. (fats and oils, printing and publishing, farm machinery, canned fruits and vegetables, wine, truck trailers, plastic pipe, pickled vegetables, mobile homes,

food-processing plants). Sunnyside Mus. here. Rattlesnake Hills to N; Yakima Indian Reservation to W. Inc. 1902.

Sunnyside, village (1990 pop. 339), Carbon co., E Utah, 25 mi/40 km E of Price; 39°32′N 110°24′W. Elev. 6,800 ft/2,073 m. Terminus of RR spur. Coal, coke. Coal mine opened 1906, oldest continuously operating mine W of Mississippi R.

Sunnyside, section of NW Queens borough, N.Y. city, SE N.Y.; 40°44′N 73°56′W. Large RR yards; also residential. Sunnyside Gardens, a planned workers' community of the 1920s, still remains as distinct type of Eng.-style housing.

Sunnyslope, uninc. town (1990 pop. 3,766), Riverside co., S Calif., residential suburb 5 mi/8 km NW of Riverside; 34°01′N 117°25′W. Jurupa Mt. (2,217 ft/676 m) to NW.

Sunnyvale, city (1990 pop. 117,229), Santa Clara co., W Calif., suburb 8 mi/12.9 km WNW of San Jose, 33 mi/53 km SE of San Francisco, and 5 mi/8 km S of S end of San Francisco Bay; 37°23′N 122°02′W. Mfg. (semiconductors, machinery and instruments, electric and electronic prods., communications equip., aerospace prods., medical equip., software). Sunnyvale has been marked by a continued increase in pop. since the 1970s. Moffett Field Naval Air Station (Moffett Air Force Base), which contributes to the city's economy and industrial development, is located to N. Branch of Hetch Hetchy Aqueduct runs E-W in N; Santa Cruz Mts. to SW; Stevens Creek on W side; Great America theme park to E. Settled 1849, inc. 1912.

Sunnyvale, town (1990 pop. 2,228), Dallas co., N Texas, suburb 13 mi/21 km E of downtown Dallas, near E Fork Trinity R. (forms L. Ray Hubbard to NE; part of town boundary); 32°47′N 96°33′W. Drained by Duck Creek. Agr. to E. Mfg. (metal prods.).

Sunol, uninc. village, Alameda co., W Calif., suburb 20 mi/32 km SE of Oakland on Alameda Creek, at mouth of Sinbad Creek, 4 mi/6.4 km S of Pleasanton, at S end of Sunol Ridge (2,188 ft/667 m). Cattle. Niles Canyon just W; San Antonio Reservoir to E; Calaveras Reservoir to S.

Sunray, town (1990 pop. 1,729), Moore co., extreme N Texas, in high plains of the Panhandle, 40 mi/64 km E of Dalhart; 36°01′N 101°49′W. Wheat; natural gas wells; mfg. (pinto bean processing, natural gas processing and oil refining, carbon black). Inc. after 1940.

Sunrise, city (☐ 18 sq mi/47 sq km; 1990 pop. 64,407), Broward co., SE Fla., 8 mi/12.9 km W of Fort Lauderdale; 26°08′N 80°17′W. Major office and commercial center and site of Sawgrass Mills, one of the largest factory-outlet malls in U.S. Home of Fla. Panthers natl. hockey league team.

Sunrise, village, Platte co., SE Wyo., near North Platte R., 23 mi/37 km NE of Wheatland, adjacent to (E of) Hartville. Elev. 4,900 ft/1,494 m.

Sunrise Beach, village (1990 pop. 497), Llano co., S central Texas, residential and recreational community 48 mi/77 km WNW of Austin, on W shore of L. Lyndon B. Johnson reservoir (Colorado R.); 30°35′N 98°25′W.

Sunrise Heights, village, Calhoun co., S Mich., unincorporated suburb 1 mi/1.6 km SE of Battle Creek on Kalamazoo R.; 42°17′N 85°10′W.

Sunrise Manor, uninc. city (1990 pop. 95,362), Clark co., SE Nev., suburb 5 mi/8 km NE of downtown Las Vegas, bounded on N by North Las Vegas; 36°11′N 115°02′W. Nellis Air Force Base to E. Sunrise Mt. Natural Area to SE.

Sunset 1 town (1990 pop. 2,201), St. Landry parish, S central La., 12 mi/19 km N of Lafayette; 30°25′N 92°04′W. Agr. (cotton, rice, sugarcane). Oil and natural-gas fields nearby. **2** town (1990 pop. 5,128), Davis co., N Utah, residential suburb 7 mi/11.3 km SW of Ogden and 24 mi/39 km NNW of Salt Lake City, near Great Salt L.; 41°08′N 112°01′W. Elev. 4,420 ft/1,347 m. Settled 1870s. Bounded on E by Hill Air Force Base.

Sunset, uninc. village (1990 pop. 200), Montague co., N Texas, c.50 mi/80 km NNW of Fort Worth. In farm area. L. Carter reservoir to W.

Sunset Beach, uninc. town (1990 pop.), Orange co., S Calif., on the Pacific Ocean, suburb 25 mi/40 km SSE of downtown Los Angeles and 7 mi/11.3 km SE of Long Beach, on Sunset Bay, residential marina area of Huntington Beach City, immediately to NE. Marshy area of Bolsa Bay to SE, behind beach margin. Meadowlark Airport to E; Bolton Chica State Beach to SE.

Sunset Beach, village (1990 pop. 311), Brunswick co., SE N.C., 44 mi/71 km SW of Wilmington, on Atlantic Ocean; 33°52′N 78°30′W. Intracoastal Waterway canal passes through village; Tubbs Inlet to E. Fish, crabs, oysters. Beach resort area. Mfg. (fishing nets).

Sunset Crater National Monument (□ 5 sq mi/13 sq km), Coconino co., N Ariz., 12 mi/19 km NNE of Flagstaff. Volcanic cinder cone believed to have been formed c.A.D. 1090, upper part appears as though colored by a sunset; lava floes; ice cave. Bounded on all sides by Coconino Natl. Forest. Proclaimed 1930.

Sunset Hills, town (1990 pop. 4,915), St. Louis co., E Mo., residential suburb 12 mi/19 km WSW of downtown St. Louis and 3 mi/4.8 km S of Kirkwood, on Meramec R.

Sunset Park, residential, commercial, and industrial section of W Brooklyn borough of N.Y. city, SE N.Y.; 40°38′N 74°00′W. Bush Terminal industrial complex (1890s); Brooklyn Army Terminal (1918), which handled the tremendous amount of troop traffic bet. U.S. and Europe during World War II, was converted to a light industrial park attracting apparel industry, often with illegal sweatshops. Originally, many Irish and Ital. immigrants settled here; with the decline of the port activities and an outmigration of the Irish and Italians, Hispanics began to move in; a Scandinavian community developed in the late 19th cent. From 1980s on, many Chinese have taken up residence here, creating a "Little Chinatown."

Sunset Peak, Mont.: see SNOWCREST RANGE.

Sunset Valley, village (1990 pop. 327), Travis co., S Texas, residential suburb 5 mi/8 km SW of downtown Austin, drained by Williamson Creek; 30°13′N 97°49′W. Agr. area to W and S.

Sunshine Peak (14,001 ft/4,268 m), Hinsdale co., SW Colo., in San Juan Mts., 15 mi/24 km NE of Silverton, and SSW of Redcloud Peak; 37°55′N 107°25′W.

Sunshine Skyway Bridge, S Fla., carring Interstate Highway 275 across the mouth of Tampa Bay bet. St. Petersburg in Pinellas co. and Brandenton in Manatee co.; 11 mi/18 km span. One of Fla.'s most famous landmarks, it was rebuilt in the mid-1980s following a disasterous barge collision with the bridge that killed more than 30 people when a section of the roadway collapsed.

Suntrana, village, S central Alaska, 50 mi/80 km SE of Nenana. Part of Healy.

Sunuapa (soo-noo-AH-pah), town (1990 pop. 384), Chiapas, S Mexico, in Gulf lowland, 38 mi/61 km SW of Villahermosa; 17°31′N 93°18′W. Cacao, rice. A Zoqu-Indian community.

Sunwapta Peak (suhn-WAHP-tuh) (10,875 ft/3,315 m), SW Alta., Canada, near B.C. border, in Rocky Mts., in Jasper Natl. Park, 50 mi/80 km SE of Jasper; 52°21′N 117°17′W.

Superior, city (1990 pop. 27,134), ⊙ Douglas co., NW Wis., 2 mi/3.2 km SE of Duluth, on Superior Bay of L. Superior, at the mouths of the St. Louis and the Nemadji rivers. Port of entry with many RR lines. The natural harbor, shared with Duluth (Minn.), has some of the nation's largest coal and ore docks; copper, limestone, and grain are also shipped. Superior has shipyards, flour milling, an oil refinery; mfg. lumber, machinery, hand tools, RR-track materials. Tourists are attracted to the surrounding scenic features. The area was visited by the Fr. explorers Radisson (1661) and Duluth (1679). The city grew after iron ore was discovered (1880s) in the Gogebic range. The Univ. of Wis. at Superior is here. American Falls (SE) and Pattison Falls (to S) state parks in area; Mont Du Lac Ski Area to SW. Inc. 1883.

Superior 1 town (1990 pop. 3,468), Pinal co., S central Ariz., near Pinal Mts., 55 mi/89 km E of Phoenix; 33°17′N 111°06′W. Elev. 2,820 ft/860 m. Agr. (cattle, sheep); copper, silver, and gold mines in vicinity. In Tonto Natl. Forest; Boyce Thompson State Arboretum to W. **2** town (1990 pop. 128), Dickinson co., NW Iowa, 8 mi/12.9 km E of Spirit Lake; 43°25′N 94°57′W. Livestock; grain. **3** town (1990 pop. 881), ⊙ Mineral co., W Mont., on the Clark Fork, and 48 mi/77 km WNW of Missoula; 47°11′N 114°54′W. Area surrounded by Lolo Natl. Forest. Timber, hay; mfg (sawmill, decorative bark, safety helmets). **4** town (1990 pop. 2,397), Nuckolls co., S Nebr., 40 mi/64 km SSE of Hastings and on Republican R. at Kansas state line; 40°01′N 98°04′W. RR junction. Trade center; grain; mfg. (cheese, printing). Founded 1876.

Superior 1 village (1990 pop. 255), Boulder co., rapidly growing suburb, N central Colo., just E of Front Range, 15 mi/24 km NW of downtown Denver, 7 mi/11.3 km SE of Boulder; 39°55′N 105°09′W. Elev. 5,490 ft/1,673 m. **2** uninc. village (1990 pop. 200), McDowell co., S W.Va., 3 mi/4.8 km ESE of Welch. **3** village (1990 pop. 273), Sweetwater co., SW Wyo., 18 mi/29 km NE of Rock Springs; 41°45′N 108°57′W. Elev. c.7,100 ft/2,164 m. Terminus of RR spur; coal mines. Leucite Hills to N.

Superior Bay, long narrow inlet of L. Superior, in extreme NW Wis. and NE Minn., sheltered by 2 sandspits (Minnesota Point and Wisconsin Point, separates lake from Allouez Bay, E extension of Superior Bay) and forming part of the harbor for the twin ports of Duluth (Minn.) and Superior (Wis.); c.9 mi/14.5 km long, c.1 mi/1.6 km wide. A narrow neck of land forming W shore of the bay nearly divides it from St. Louis Bay (estuary of St. Louis R.).

Superior, Lake, world's largest freshwater lake (□ 31,820 sq mi/82,414 sq km), on border of U.S. (Minn., Mich., and Wis.) and central Canada (Ont.), largest, highest, and deepest of the Great Lakes; 350 mi/563 km long, max. width 160 mi/257 km, max. depth 1,302 ft/397 m. Bordered W by NE Minn., N and E by SW Ont., and S by NW Mich. and NW Wis. Surface elev. 602 ft/183 m. Drains into L. Huron through the St. Marys R. and receives the waters of many short, swift-flowing streams including the Nipigon, Kaministikwia, St. Louis, and Pigeon rivers. The largest isls. are Isle Royale, Isle St. Ignace, and Simpson and Michipicoten isls. The shoreline is irregular (with many large bays, inlets, and peninsulas) and in places is high and rocky. The waters of L. Superior are generally purer than those of the lower lakes and are minimally polluted; a U.S.-Can. pact (1972) was established to prevent pollution and to maintain and improve the water's quality. Commercial and sport fishing are important; and tourism is popular in the lake area. L. Superior is part of the Great Lakes–St. Lawrence Seaway system, and it is reached by ocean-going and lake vessels through the Sault Ste. Marie Canals, which bypass rapids in the St. Marys R. The principal cargoes are grain, flour, and iron ore. The lake does not freeze completely, but ice impedes navigation mid-Dec.–late March at the lake's outlet and from early Dec. to the end of April in harbors on the S shore. Fog and rough water are hazards. The chief Can. cities on the lake are Michipicoten and Thunder Bay (both in Ont.). The principal cities on the U.S. shore are Marquette (Mich.), Superior, Ashland (both in Wis.), and Duluth (Minn.). Recreational facilities are found on Isle Royale (part of a U.S. natl. park), in Pukaskwa Natl. Park (Ont.), and at state and provincial parks on the lake's shores and isls.; the U.S. Apostle Isls. and Pictured Rocks natl. lakeshores are here. Étienne Brulé, the Fr. explorer, probably visited the lake in 1616; Pierre Radisson and the sieur des Groseilliers explored it 1659–1660; Father Allouez established (1665) a mission near Ashland; and the sieur Duluth visited the lake in 1678–1679.

Superior, Village of, Douglas co., NW Wis., suburb 5 mi/8 km S of city of Superior, S of city limit. Residential. Cattle. Timber area.

Superstition Mountains 1 Pinal and Maricopa cos., S central Ariz., 30 mi/48 km E of Mesa, S of Salt R.; rise to 5,057 ft/1,541 m in Superstition Mt. (site of legendary Lost Dutchman Mine); 33°24′N 111°24′W. Partly in Tonto Natl. Forest. **2** Imperial co., S Calif., low (c.700 ft/213 m) desert range along W side of Imperial Valley; 32°57′N 115°49′W. Mining. Superstitious Mt. (759 ft/231 m); SW of Salton Sea.

Supply, uninc. village, Brunswick co., SE N.C., 25 mi/40 km SW of Wilmington, on short stream flowing S to Lockwood Folly Inlet, arm of Atlantic Ocean; Green Swamp to N. Agr. area; fishing. Mfg. (trailers, signs, fishing equip.).

Suquamish (suh-KWAHM-ish), uninc. town (1990 pop. 3,105), Kitsap co., W Wash., 12 mi/19 km NW of downtown Seattle, on Port Madison bay, arm of Puget Sound; 47°44′N 122°35′W. Fishing; tourism. Old Man House state park to S; Port Madison Indian Reservation W; Bainbridge Isl. to S. Suquamish Mus. and bridge to Bainbridge Isl. to SW.

Surf City, resort borough (1990 pop. 1,375), Ocean co., E N.J., on Long Beach isl., and 25 mi/40 km NE of Atlantic City; 39°39′N 74°10′W. Settled 1690 by whalers.

Surf City, town (1990 pop. 970), Pender co., SE N.C., 24 mi/39 km SSW of Jacksonville, on Topsail Isl. on Atlantic Ocean; 34°25′N 77°33′W. Intracoastal Waterway passes to NW behind isl. Beach resort.

Surfside, resort town (1990 pop. 4,108), Dade co., SE Fla., 4 mi/6.4 km N of Miami Beach; 25°52′N 80°07′W.

Surfside Beach, town (1990 pop. 3,845), Horry co., E S.C., 7 mi/11.3 km SW of Myrtle Beach on Atlantic Ocean in Grand Strand Beach resort area; 33°36′N 78°58′W. Resorts, tourism. Mfg. includes cabinets, commercial printing. Myrtle Beach State Park to NE; Myrtle Beach civic Jet Port to NE.

Surfside Beach, village (1990 pop. 611), Brazoria co., SE Texas, residential suburb 5 mi/8 km E of Freeport, in Brazosport Area, bet. Gulf of Mexico and Intracoastal Waterway; 28°56′N 95°16′W. Recreation. Brazoria Natl. Wildlife Refuge to NE. Includes Velasco, historic port.

Surgidero de Batabanó (SUR-hee-DER-o dai bah-tuh-bah-no), town, La Habana prov., W Cuba, port for Batabanó (2.5 mi/4 km N), 30 mi/48 km S of Havana; 22°39′N 82°19′W. RR terminus and fishing center (lobster, tuna, sponges); charcoal burning, lumbering. Point of embarkation for ferry service to Isla de la Juventud.

Suring (SUHR-ing), village (1990 pop. 626), Oconto co., NE Wis., on Oconto R., and 38 mi/61 km NW of Green Bay; 45°00′N 88°22′W. In lumbering and dairying area; mfg. (lumber, furniture, wood components, pallets). Menominee Indian Reservation to W; Nicolet Natl. Forest to NW.

Surprise, town (1990 pop. 7,122), Maricopa co., central Ariz., residential suburb 20 mi/32 km NW of downtown Phoenix; 33°39′N 112°28′W. Mfg. (tortillas, printing, ornamental iron). Luke Air Force Base to S.

Surprise, village (1990 pop. 55), Butler co., E Nebr., 17 mi/27 km NW of Seward and on Big Blue R; 41°6′N 97°18′W.

Surprise Valley, Modoc co., NE Calif., along Nev. state line, and S of Oregon state line, E of Warner Mts. (in Modoc Natl. Forest); c.50 mi/80 km long N-S. Cedarville is near its center, Fort Bidwell in N. Contains the large, intermittently dry Alkali Lakes: Middle (in center), Upper (in N), and Lower (in S) lakes. Farming, stock raising; timber. Cow Hend L. (dry) in far N end.

Surrency (SUHR-en-see), town (1990 pop. 253), Appling co., SE central Ga., 8 mi/12.9 km ESE of Baxley; 31°43′N 82°12′W.

Surrey, county (1991 pop. 767,133), E Jamaica, comprising E 3d of the isl., with Kingston, includes Port Royal, St. Andrew, St. Thomas, and Portland parishes; 18°16′N 76°53′W. Set up in 1758, it is now a region without administrative functions.

Surrey, city (1991 pop. 245,173), SW B.C., Canada, residential suburb 15 mi/24 km SE of Vancouver and S of Fraser R.; 46°04′N 62°49′W. Boundary Bay to SW. Mfg. (gypsum prods., surgical supplies, transportation equip., prefabricated buildings), wire drawing, steel mill, meat packing. Includes village of Port Mann.

Surrey, village (1990 pop. 856), Ward co., central N.Dak.,

7 mi/11.3 km E of Minot; 48°14′N 101°07′W. Two branches of Burlington Northern RR join here.

Surry 1 (SUH-ree), county (☐ 537 sq mi/1,391 sq km; 1990 pop. 61,704), NW N.C.; ⊙ Dobson; 36°25′N 80°41′W. In Piedmont region; bounded N by Va. state line, S by Yadkin R. Agr. area (tobacco, corn, dairying, wheat, soybeans, hay, chickens, cattle), timber, stone and granite quarrying; mfg. at Elkin and Mt. Airy. Pilot Mt. State Park in E; Home Creek Living Historical Farm in SE corner. Blue Ridge (Natl.) Parkway closely follows W boundary (Alleghany co.). Formed 1770. **2** county (☐ 310 sq mi/803 sq km; 1990 pop. 6,145) SE Va.; ⊙ Surry; 37°07′N 76°53′W. In Tidewater region; bounded N and NE by James R., S by Blackwater R. Agr. (peanuts, corn, wheat, soybeans, melons; cattle, hogs; dairying); timber. Surry 1 and 2 Nuclear Power Plants on James R., in N. Historic bldgs. at Bacons Castle and Claremont. Chippokes Plantation State Park in NE; Hog Isl. State Wildlife Management Area in NE. Formed 1652.

Surry 1 fishing, resort town (1990 pop. 1,004), Hancock co., S Maine, on Blue Hill Bay just SW of Ellsworth; 44°29′N 68°30′W. **2** town (1990 pop. 667), Cheshire co., SW N.H., on the Ashuelot, and 7 mi/11.3 km N of Keene; 43°01′N 72°19′W. Drained by Thompson Brook, with Ashuelot R. forms Surry Mountain L. reservoir. Agr. (vegetables, nursery crops; cattle, sheep, poultry; dairying). **3** town (1990 pop. 192), ⊙ Surry co., SE Va., 33 mi/53 km ESE of Petersburg, near James R. (ferry to Jamestown to N); 37°08′N 76°50′W. Mfg. (peanut processing, meat processing); agr. (peanuts, grain, soybeans, melons; livestock). Home (c.1650) of Thomas Rofle; Bacons Castle to E; Smith's Fort to N. Chippokes Plantation State Park to E. Surry 1 and 2 Nuclear Power Plants to N, on James R.

Susan River, c.40 mi/64 km long, NE Calif.; rises in SW Lassen co., E of Lassen Volcanic Natl. Park; flows E, past Susanville, to Honey L. (dry).

Susank (SOO-sank), village (1990 pop. 61), Barton co., central Kansas, 18 mi/29 km N of Great Bend; 38°38′N 98°46′W.

Susanville, city (1990 pop. 7,279), ⊙ Lassen co., NE Calif., at E base of the Sierra Nevada, on Susan R., at head of fertile Honey L. valley; 40°25′N 120°39′W. Elev. 4,195 ft/1,279 m. Cattle; grain, potatoes, strawberries; sawmill. Annual co. stock show and rodeo held here. Seat of Lassen Col. Lassen Volcanic Natl. Park is c.40 mi/64 km W; Lassen Natl. Forest to W, Plumas Natl. Forest to S; Honey L. (dry) to SE, Eagle L. to NW. Sierra Army depot to SE. Settled 1853; inc. as town in 1900; became city in 1940.

Susitna (soo-SIT-nuh), village, S Alaska, on Susitna R., and 30 mi/48 km NW of Anchorage.

Susitna River (soo-SIT-nuh), 300 mi/483 km long, S Alaska; rises in Susitna Glacier on Mt. Hayes in Alaska Range near 63°30′N 147°15′W; flows in winding course generally SW to Curry, then S, past Talkeetna, Chulitna, and Susitna, to head of Cook Inlet 25 mi/40 km W of Anchorage. Receives Talkeetna and Yentna rivers. Navigable 85 mi/137 km to Talkeetna.

Susquehanna (SUS-kwuh-HA-nah), county (☐ 832 sq mi/2,155 sq km; 1990 pop. 40,380), NE Pa.; ⊙ Montrose; 41°49′N 75°47′W. Bounded N by N.Y. state line; drained by Susquehanna R., West Branch. Agr. (corn, oats, hay, alfalfa; hogs, cattle; dairying). Some mfg. at Montrose and Hallstead. Lackawanna R. rises in E; Salt Springs State Park in N. Formed 1810.

Susquehanna 1 and 2 Nuclear Power Plants, Pa.: see LUZERNE, CO.

Susquehanna, river, 444 mi/715 km long; rising in Otsego L., central N.Y., and winding SE and SW through E central Pa. to Chesapeake Bay near Havre de Grace, Md. The bay is the drowned lower course of the river that has resulted from a post-Pleistocene rise in sea level. The West Branch (c.160 mi/257 km), which rises in the Allegheny Mts., W Pa., and follows a circuitous course E to Sunbury, Pa., is the river's chief tributary in Pa. The Susquehanna R. traverses an anthracite coal region, which in the 19th cent. spawned the major heavy industrial coal and steel core of the U.S.; the many significant mining and industrial cities on its banks were forced to scale down production as the steel and coal industries declined in the early 1980s. These include Binghamton and Oswego, N.Y., and Pittston, Wilkes-Barre, Harrisburg, and Scranton (on the Lackawanna tributary), Pa. The shallow, swift-flowing river is unsuited for navigation. Several hydroelectric power plants are located on the Susquehanna; the Conowingo plant (Md.) is one of the largest non-Federal power stations in the nation. The Susquehanna and its tributaries have extensive flood-control works. However in June 1972, the river, swollen by the torrential rains of Hurricane Agnes, breached 40-ft/12-m dikes in places and flooded much of the basin, causing one of the greatest flood disasters in U.S. history.

Susquehanna, Pa.: see SUSQUEHANNA DEPOT.

Susquehanna Depot (SUS-kwuh-HA-nah DEE-po), borough (1990 pop. 1,760), Susquehanna co., NE Pa., 37 mi/60 km N of Scranton, on Susquehanna R., bridged to Oakland (N); 41°56′N 75°35′W. Agr. (corn, hay; livestock; dairying); mfg. (lumber, apparel, food processing). Also called Susquehanna.

Susquehanna Flats (SUS-kwuh-HA-nah), NE Md., marshlands at mouth of Susquehanna R. on Chesapeake Bay. Noted for waterfowl hunting.

Susquehanna Trails (SUS-kwuh-HA-nah), uninc. town (1990 pop. 1,419), York co., SE Pa., residential development 23 mi/37 km SE of York on Muddy Creek at mouth of Fishing Creek; 39°45′N 76°22′W.

Sussex, town (1991 pop. 4,132), S N.B., Canada, on Kennebecasis R., and 40 mi/64 km NE of St. John; 45°43′N 65°31′W. Dairying and poultry center; trout fishing. Gypsum worked in region. Noted for covered bridges (17 in Kings co.). Founded by Loyalists in 1796.

Sussex 1 county (☐ 1,195 sq mi/3,095 sq km; 1990 pop. 113,229), S Del.; ⊙ Georgetown; 38°40′N 75°20′W. Bounded S and W by Md. state line, N in part by Mispillion R., NE by Delaware Bay (N.J. state line), and E by the Atlantic Ocean; drained by Broadkill, Indian, Pocomoke, and Nanticoke rivers. Agr. area (fruit, grain; livestock; dairying); mfg. at Georgetown and Milford. Resorts on coast. Largest of Delaware's 3 cos. Cape Henlopen State Park in NE; Holts Landing, Delaware Seashore, and Fenwick Isl. state parks in SE; Trap Pond State Park in S; Robert L. Graham Wildlife Area in SW; Assawoman Wildlife Area in SE; Prime Hook Natl. Wildlife Refuge in NE; Ellendale and Redden state forests in N center; Cypress Swamp in S, on Md. border. Formed 1683. **2** county (☐ 528 sq mi/1,368 sq km; 1990 pop. 130,943), extreme NW N.J., bounded W by the Delaware, N by N.Y. state line; ⊙ Newton; 41°08′N 74°41′W. Mt. and lake recreational area, including Kittatinny Mtn. ridge, site of scenic and historic Stokes State Forest and High Point (elev. 1,803 ft/550 m; in state park), highest point in state, and Delaware Water Gap National Recreational Center. Agr. (poultry, fruit, hay, nursery prods., dairy prods., livestock); limestone deposits; mfg. (textiles, metal prods., paper, clothing, rubber and plastic prods., mineral wool, pens). Drained by Musconetcong, Wallkill, and Pequest rivers, and Paulins Kill. Formed 1753. Suburban residential pressure in E. **3** county (☐ 492 sq mi/1,274 sq km; 1990 pop. 10,248), SE Va.; ⊙ Sussex; 36°55′N 77°15′W. In Tidewater region; bounded NE in part by Blackwater R.; drained by Nottoway R. (forms part of SW boundary). Agr. (esp. peanuts; also wheat, soybeans, corn, tobacco, melons; hogs, cattle, poultry); timber. Formed 1754.

Sussex, town (1990 pop. 5,039), Waukesha co., SE Wis., on branch of Fox R., and a suburb 16 mi/26 km NW of Milwaukee, and 8 mi/12.9 km N of Waukesha; 43°08′N 88°13′W. In dairying and vegetable-farming area; mfg. (formulations to accelerate biodegradation of oil spills, concrete, packaging); stone quarrying.

Sussex, uninc village, ⊙ Sussex co., SE Va., 21 mi/34 km SSE of Petersburg; 36°54′N 77°16′W. Agr. (livestock, poultry; peanuts, tobacco, grain). Co. courthouse (1828).

Sussex, borough (1990 pop. 2,201), Sussex co., NW N.J., 13 mi/21 km NNE of Newton; 41°12′N 74°36′W. Trade center for dairying, poultry-raising area; nurseries. Settled 1734, inc. 1902.

Sustiacacán (soos-tee-ah-kah-KAHN), town (1990 pop. 1,080), Zacatecas, N central Mexico, 8 mi/12.9 km WSW of Jérezdiz García Salinas; 22°36′N 103°05′W. Elev. 6,857 ft/2,090 m. Grain, vegetables, maguey; livestock.

Susupuato de Guerrero (soo-soo-PWA-AH-to de ge-RE-ro), town (1990 pop. 935), ⊙ Susupuato municipio, Michoacán, central Mexico, 17 mi/27 km S of Zitácuaro; 19°13′N 100°24′W. Elev. 5,558 ft/1,694 m. Silver deposits. Livestock.

Sutersville (SOO-tuhrs-vil), borough (1990 pop. 755), Westmoreland co., SW Pa., 18 mi/29 km SE of Pittsburgh, on Youghiogheny R.; 40°14′N 79°47′W. Agr. (corn, hay; livestock; dairying); mfg. (cabinets, windows, and doors).

Sutherland, town, S central Sask., Canada, near South Saskatchewan R., E suburb of Saskatoon; 52°08′N 106°36′W. RR division point.

Sutherland 1 town (1990 pop. 714), O'Brien co., NW Iowa, 11 mi/18 km SE of Primghar; 42°58′N 95°30′W. **2** town (1990 pop. 1,032), Lincoln co., SW central Nebr., 19 mi/31 km W of North Platte city, and on South Platte R., bet. North and South Platte rivers; 41°9′N 101°7′W. Grain; mfg. (tarps, boat covers). Reservoir and power plant, part of Platte Valley power and irrigation project, are here; reservoir fed by water diverted through concrete conduit from Kingsley Dam. RR junction to E. Sutherland Reservoir to S (on Tri-County Supply Canal) and Sutherland State Recreation Area.

Sutherland Springs, uninc. village (1990 pop. 362), Wilson co., S Texas, 29 mi/47 km ESE of San Antonio, on Cibolo Creek. In cattle area; peanuts, vegetables. Nearby is Sutherland Springs Park, former resort, with mineral springs.

Sutherlin (SUH-thuhr-luhn), town (1990 pop. 5,020), Douglas co., SW Oregon, 13 mi/21 km N of Roseburg; 43°23′N 123°18′W. RR junction. Winery to W at Umpqua. Timber; dairy prods.; poultry, sheep, cattle.

Sutter, county (☐ 608 sq mi/1,575 sq km; 1990 pop. 64,415), N central Calif.; ⊙ Yuba City; 39°02′N 121°42′W. Low-lying region in Sacramento Valley. W border formed by Sacramento and Butte rivers, E border formed in part by Feather and Bear rivers; drained in S by Feather R. Sutter Buttes (natural gas wells here) are in N. Nursery prods.; alfalfa, safflower, beans, wheat, barley, oats, corn, rice, sugar beets, tomatoes, prunes, peaches, melons. Processing of farm prods. Waterfowl hunting in marshes; fishing. Sutter Buttes in NW; Sutter Natl. Wildlife Refuge in center. Formed 1850.

Sutter, uninc. town (1990 pop. 2,606), Sutter co., N central Calif., in Sacramento Valley, 8 mi/12.9 km WNW of Yuba City; 39°10′N 121°45′W. Agr. (walnuts, rice, wheat, beans, safflower, sugar beets, fruit); mfg. farm machinery; waterfowl hunting. Sutter Buttes are to NW; Sutter Natl. Wildlife Refuge to S; Colusa-Sacramento R. State Recreation Area to W.

Sutter Buttes, Sutter co., N central Calif., isolated group of 4 jagged volcanic peaks, in Sacramento Valley, E of Sacramento R., just N of Sutter; c.10 mi/16 km in diameter. Highest peak (South Butte) is c.2,117 ft/645 m. Natural gas wells. Also called Marysville Buttes.

Sutter Creek, town (1990 pop. 1,835), Amador co., central Calif., on Sutter Creek, and c.39 mi/63 km ESE of Sacramento, in 1849 Calif. gold rush region; 38°23′N 120°48′W. Gold mines; walnuts, grain, grapes; cattle; winery; mfg. transformers. Pardes Reservoir to S. Settled in 1850s, inc. 1874.

Sutter's Mill, Calif.: see COLOMA.

Sutton, town (1991 pop. 1,587), S Que., Canada, on Missisquoi R., and 20 mi/32 km SSE of Granby. Lumbering; dairying. Resort; skiing.

Sutton, Canada: see SUTTON WEST, village.

Sutton, county (☐ 1,454 sq mi/3,766 sq km; 1990 pop. 4,135), W Texas; ⊙ Sonora; 30°30′N 100°32′W. In broken uplands of Edwards Plateau. Elev. c.2,000 ft/610 m. Drained by Devil's R., source of North Llano R. Sheep and goat ranching; leading co. in the shipment of wool, mohair; also beef cattle; oil and natural gas. Formed 1887.

Sutton 1 agr. town (1990 pop. 6,824), Worcester co., S central Mass., 9 mi/14.5 km S of Worcester; 42°08′N 71°45′W. Includes villages of Manchaug and Wilkinsonville, on Blackstone R. and partly in Grafton town. Purgatory Chasm natural feature and state park. Settled c.1715. **2** town (1990 pop. 1,353), Clay co., S Nebr., 12 mi/19 km NE of Clay Center, and on branch of Big Blue R., on Loess Plain in prairie region; 40°36′N 97°51′W. Grain; livestock; dairy and poultry prods. Settled 1869. **3** town (1990 pop. 1,457), Merrimack co., S central N.H., 23 mi/37 km NW of Concord; 43°21′N 71°55′W. Drained by Lane R. Mfg. (optical instruments, canvas prods.); agr. (nursery crops, vegetables, apples; poultry, livestock; dairying). Resort area. Kezar L. in N center. Wadleigh State Park in center. **4** town (1990 pop. 854), Caledonia co., NE Vt., 15 mi/24 km N of St. Johnsbury; includes part of Willoughby State Forest; 44°38′N 72°01′W. **5** town (1990 pop. 939), ⊙ Braxton co., central W.Va., 53 mi/85 km NE of Charleston, on Elk R., forms Sutton L. reservoir in Elk R. Wildlife Management Area to E; 38°40′N 80°42′W. Gas and oil area. Agr. (grain, apples); livestock. Timber. Mfg. (RR ties, printing and publishing). Inc. 1826.

Sutton, village, S Alaska, on Matanuska R., and 12 mi/19 km NE of Palmer, on Glenn Highway. Former U.S. navy coal mine.

Sutton Island, Maine: see CRANBERRY ISLES.

Sutton Place, residential district of Manhattan borough of N.Y. city, SE N.Y., along East R., in vicinity of 57th St. Beekman Place dist. adjoins on S. Upper-income neighborhood.

Sutton West, village, S Ont., Canada, near L. Simcoe, 30 mi/48 km W of Lindsay. Dairying, mixed farming. Sometimes called Sutton.

Suttons Bay, village (1990 pop. 561), Leelanau co., NW Mich., 15 mi/24 km NW of Traverse City, on West Arm of Grand Traverse Bay; 44°58′N 85°39′W. In fruit growing and resort area; winery; fruit processing; mfg. (hoses).

Suwanee (suh-WAH-nee), town (1990 pop. 2,412), Gwinnett co., N central Ga., 26 mi/42 km NE of Atlanta; 34°03′N 84°04′W. Mfg. includes storage tanks, lumber, stone processing, cellular phones, metal fabrication, commercial printing. Site of training camp for Atlanta Falcons professional football team.

Suwannee (SWAH-nee), county (□ 1,790 sq mi; 1990 pop. 26,780), N central Fla.; ⊙ Live Oak; 30°11′N 82°59′W. Flatwoods area with small lakes, bounded by Suwannee (W, S) and Santa Fe (S) rivers. Farming (corn, peanuts, cotton, tobacco, vegetables), livestock raising (hogs, cattle), and some lumbering. Formed 1858.

Suwannee (suh-WAH-nee), river, c.240 mi/386 km long; rises in the Okefenokee Swamp, SE Ga.; winds generally S through N Fla. to the Gulf of Mexico; 30°59′N 82°16′W. Dredged to accommodate shallow-draft vessels for 135 mi/217 km upstream. Its name was used in Stephen Foster's famous song "Old Folks at Home" (also known as "Swanee River").

Suwarof, Alaska: see NAKNEK.

Sverdrup Channel, N Franklin dist., N.W.T., Canada, arm extending S from Arctic Ocean, bet. Axel Heiberg Isl. (E) and Meighen Isl. (W); 70 mi/113 km long, 40 mi/64 km wide; 80°00′N 97°00′W.

Swain (SWAIN), county (□ 540 sq mi/1,399 sq km; 1990 pop. 11,268), W N.C.; ⊙ Bryson City; 35°29′N 83°29′W. Bounded N by Tenn. state line, W extension of co. bounded on S by Little Tennessee R. (dammed to form Fontana and Cheoah reservoirs). Agr. (cattle, hay), lumbering; mt. resort region. Heavily forested mt. area; largely included in Great Smoky Mts. Natl. Park; contains part of Eastern Cherokee Indian Reservation (Qualla Boundary) in E, adjacent to park. Appalachian Trail follows N boundary and crosses NW and SW (c. ⅔ of co.), in Great Smoky Mts. Natl. Park (N.C.-Tenn.). S part of co. in Nantahal Natl. Forest. SW terminus of Blue Ridge Parkway (natl. park unit) in E. Formed 1871.

Swaine Island, islet, E N.F., Canada, on N side of Bonavista Bay, 45 mi/72 km ENE of Gander; 49°8′N 53°32′W. Lighthouse.

Swainsboro (SWAINZ-buhr-o), town (1990 pop. 7,361), ⊙ Emanuel co., E central Ga., c.65 mi/105 km SSW of Augusta; 32°35′N 82°20′W. Mfg. includes metal fabrication, clothing, furniture; lumber. Founded 1814; inc. 1853.

Swale Island, E N.F., Canada, in Bonavista Bay, 28 mi/45 km W of Bonavista; 5 mi/8 km long, 1 mi/2 km wide.

Swaledale, town (1990 pop. 190), Cerro Gordo co., N Iowa, 13 mi/21 km SSW of Mason City; 42°58′N 93°19′W. Limestone quarry, sand and gravel pits nearby.

Swallow Falls State Park, Garrett co., NW Md., in the Alleghenies bet. Youghiogheny R., and W.Va. state line, just NW of Oakland. Recreational area containing Swallow Falls (highest in Md., dropping c.70 ft/21 m). Garrett State Forest and Herrington Manor State Park are nearby.

Swampscott (SWAWMP-skawt), suburban town (1990 pop. 13,650), Essex co., E Mass., once a summer resort on Massachusetts Bay; 42°28′N 70°54′W. The Mary Baker Eddy house is preserved. Includes village of Beach Bluff. Settled 1629, set off from Lynn and inc. 1852.

Swan, town (1990 pop. 76), Marion co., S central Iowa, near Des Moines R., 14 mi/23 km NE of Knoxville; 41°28′N 93°18′W. In agr. area.

Swan Island, Sagadahoc co., SW Maine, in the Kennebec, 10 mi/16 km above Bath; 4 mi/6.4 km long. Formerly known as Perkins township.

Swan Lake, village, S Man., Canada, in Pembina Mts., 45 mi/72 km SW of Portage la Prairie; 49°24′N 98°48′W. Grain, livestock. Adjoining is Chippewa Indian Reserve.

Swan Lake, W Man., Canada, 30 mi/48 km NE of Swan R. Drains N into L. Winnipegosis, 20 mi/32 km long, 9 mi/14 km wide.

Swan Lake 1 Waldo co., S Maine, at Swanville, 7 mi/11.3 km N of Belfast; 3 mi/4.8 km long, 1 mi/1.6 km wide. **2** Itasca co., NE central Minn., 16 mi/26 km ENE of Grand Rapids; 4 mi/6.4 km long; 47°18′N 93°10′W. Fed and drained (SW) by Swan R. into Mississippi R. Fishing resorts. Village of Pengilly at N end of lake. **3** Sullivan co., SE N.Y., 4 mi/6.4 km W of Liberty; 4 mi/6.4 km long; 41°45′N 74°47′W. Resort village (1990 pop. 1,200) on shore. **4** Nicollet co., S Minn., 8 mi/12.9 km E of New Ulm, drains SE past small dam through Nicollet Creek to Minnesota R.; 44°18′N 94°14′W. Elev. 980 ft/299 m. Irregular shore, generally circular in shape; 5 mi/8 km wide. Courtland Bay extends 3 mi/4.8 km NW; several smaller bays. Brooks, Anderson, and Johnson Isls. comprise Swan L. Wildlife Area.

Swan Peak, Mont.: see SWAN RANGE.

Swan Quarter or **Swanquarter**, uninc. village (1990 pop. c.300), ⊙ Hyde co., E N.C., 18 mi/29 km SE of Belhaven, on Swanquarter Bay, inlet of Pamlico Sound. Agr. area (cotton, grain, soybeans; hogs); fish, crabs. Mfg. (crab meat processing). Ferry to Ocracoke village, on Ocracoke Isl., 30 mi/48 km to SE, in Outer Banks. Swanquarter Natl. Wildlife Refuge to SW, S, and E, along Pamlico Sound shore; L. Mattamuskeet Natl. Wildlife Refuge to NE.

Swan Range, range, in Rocky Mts. of NW Mont.; rises at Flathead R; extends SE to Blackfoot R.; 48°28′N 114°01′W. Bounded on E by Hungry Horse Reservoir and the South Fork of Flathead R., on W by Swan R. Swan Peak (elev. 9,255 f/ 2,821 m). Largely in Flathead Natl. Forest.

Swan River, town (1991 pop. 3,917), W Man., Canada, on Swan R., and 80 mi/129 km N of Dauphin; 52°06′N 101°16′W. Lumbering and distributing center; grain, livestock.

Swan River 1 60 mi/97 km long, in NE Minn.; rises in Swan L., Itasca co., 13 mi/21 km SW of Hibbing; 47°17′N 93°11′W. Flows SW, passes E of Trout L., then SSE past Warba, turns W before entering Mississippi R. 20 mi/32 km SE of Grand Rapids, at Jacobsen. **2-**

c.80 mi/129 km long, in NW Mont.; rises in the Mission Range near Grey Wolf L., NW Missoula co.; flows 1st NE through Lindbergh L. reservoir, then NNW, bet. Mission (W) and Swan (E) ranges, through Swan R. State Forest and Swan R. Natl.Wildlife Refuge, and through Swan L. (10 mi/16 km long, 1 mi/1.6 km max. width), then W to NE end of Flathead L. at Bigfork.

Swan Valley, village (1990 pop. 141), Bonneville co., SE Idaho, on Snake R., and 36 mi/58 km E of Idaho Falls; 43°26′N 111°19′W. Elev. 5,277 ft/1,608 m. Caribou Natl. Forest to SW, Targhee Natl. Forest to NE.

Swanee, Ga.: see SUWANNEE, river.

Swannanoa (swahn-uh-NO-uh), uninc. town (1990 pop. 3,538), Buncombe co., W N.C., suburb 9 mi/14.5 km E of Asheville, in the Blue Ridge Mts.; 35°36′N 82°23′W. Nearby is Swannanoa RR tunnel (1,800 ft/549 m long; completed 1879). Agr. area (tobacco, corn; chickens, cattle; dairying). Mfg. (explosives, textiles, machining, electronics, crushed stone and gravel, industrial connectors, antennas, cutting tools, tool and die). Seat of Warren Wilson Col. Part of Pisgah Natl. Forest to N. Blue Ridge Parkway passes to W and N.

Swans Island, town (1990 pop. 348), Hancock co., S Maine, on Swans, Marshall, and other small isls.; 6 mi/9.7 km long, 1 mi/1.6 km–4 mi/6.4 km wide; and 5 mi/8 km SW of Mt. Desert Isl. In Blue Hill Bay, just SW of Mt. Desert Isl.

Swansboro (SWAHNZ-buhr-o), town (1990 pop. 1,165), Onslow co., E N.C., 17 mi/27 km ESE of Jacksonville, on Atlantic coast, at entrance to White Oak R. estuary (bridged E to Cedar Point); 34°41′N 77°07′W. Intracoastal Waterway channel passes to SE, Bogue Inlet connects waterway and estuary to open Atlantic. Agr. area (cotton, grain, tobacco; poultry, hogs). Mfg. (concrete, cultured marble prods.). Hammocks Beach State Park to SW; Croatan Natl. Forest to NE.

Swansea (SWAHN-see), town (1990 pop. 15,411), Bristol co., SE Mass., suburb of Fall R., on an inlet of Mt. Hope Bay; 41°46′N 71°13′W. Once a vast farmland, it has become chiefly residential. Agr. is still cultivated. Many of its inhabitants were massacred in King Philip's War (1675), but the town was later rebuilt and prospered. Includes villages of North Swansea, Ocean Grove (1990 pop. 3,169), South Swansea, Touisset. Founded 1667, inc. 1785.

Swansea 1 (SWAHN-see), village (1990 pop. 8,201), St. Clair co., SW Ill., just N of Belleville and within St. Louis metropolitan area; 38°32′N 89°59′W. Inc. 1895. **2** village (1990 pop. 527), Lexington co., central S.C., 20 mi/32 km S of Columbia; 33°44′N 81°06′W. Mfg. includes meat casings, metal stampings, handguards, sportswear; agr. includes dairying, poultry, livestock, grains, soybeans, peaches.

Swanson Reservoir, Hitchcock co., SW Nebr., on Republican R., 23 mi/37 km W of McCook and W of Trenton; 6 mi/9.7 km long; 40°10′N 101°03′W. Max. capacity 361,500 acre-ft. Formed by Trenton Dam (92 ft/28 m high), built (1953) by the Bureau of Reclamation for irrigation, flood control, and recreation. Swanson Reservoir State Recreation Area on both shores.

Swanton (SWAHN-tuhn), town (1990 pop. 5,636), including Swanton village, Franklin co., NW Vt., on Missisquoi R. and L. Champlain, and 7 mi/11.3 km N of St. Albans; 44°54′N 73°07′W. Bldg. materials, winter sports equip., lime; agr. (dairy prods.). Port of entry for frequent aircraft. Jesuit mission est. here c.1700. Eng. settlement began 1765. Smugglers' hq. in early 19th cent. Town attacked by British in War of 1812.

Swanton 1 village (1990 pop. 145), Saline co., SE Nebr., 8 mi/12.9 km SW of Wilber and on branch of Big Blue R; 40°22′N 97°04′W. **2** village (1990 pop. 3,557), Fulton co., NW Ohio, 19 mi/31 km W of Toledo, on Ai Creek; 41°35′N 83°54′W. Construction materials.

Swanville, resort town (1990 pop. 1,130), Waldo co., S Maine, on Swan L., just N of Belfast; 44°31′N 69°00′W. Swan L. State Park is on NE shore of lake.

Swanville, village (1990 pop. 324), Morrison co., central Minn., 14 mi/23 km WSW of Little Falls on Swan R.; 45°55′N 94°38′W. Agr. (grain, sunflowers, potatoes; livestock; dairying); mfg. (concrete).

Swanzey (SWAHN-zee), town (1990 pop. 6,236), Cheshire co., SW N.H., 4 mi/6.4 km S of Keene; 42°52′N 72°17′W. Drained by Ashuelot R. Mfg. (baskets; additives and dyes); agr. (nursery crops, vegetables; cattle, poultry; dairying); timber. Includes villages of East Swanzey, 2 mi/3.2 km SSE of Swanzey village, and West Swanzey (1990 pop. 1,055), 3 mi/4.8 km W of Swanzey village. Inc. 1753.

Swarthmore (SWAHTH-mor), borough (1990 pop. 6,157), Delaware co., SE Pa., residential suburb 11 mi/ 18 km WSW of downtown Philadelphia, on Crum Creek; 39°53′N 75°20′W. Light mfg. Seat of Swarthmore Col. (1864). Scott Arboretum.

Swartswood (SWAHRTS-wood), village, Sussex co., NW N.J., 4 mi/6.4 km WNW of Newton, on Swartswood L. (c.2 mi/3.2 km long; drains SW into Paulins Kill). State park here. Scene of massacre by Indians (1756). State park nearby.

Swartz (SWAHRTS), uninc. village (1990 pop. 3,698), Ouachita parish, NE central La., 9 mi/14 km NE of Monroe; 32°34′N 92°00′W. In natural gas field; timber; agr. (cotton, fruit, vegetables); mfg. (wooden prods.).

Swartz Creek, town (1990 pop. 4,851), Genesee co., SE central Mich., suburb 8 mi/12.9 km SW of Flint, and on the small Swartz Creek; 42°57′N 83°49′W. In farm area; light mfg.

Swastika, village, E Ont., Canada, 5 mi/8 km SW of Kirkland L.; 48°06′N 80°06′W. RR junction; gold mining; farming.

Swatara Creek (SWAH-tah-rah), 60 mi/97 km long, E central Pa.; rises in W central Schuylkill co. 5 mi/8 km W of Minersville; 40°41′N 76°21′W. Flows SW, passes S of Trenton, flows through Swatara State Park and through gap in Blue Mt. ridge, past Hershey and Hummelstown, to Susquehanna R. at Middletown.

Swayzee, town (1990 pop. 1,059), Grant co., E central Ind., 9 mi/14.5 km WSW of Marion; 40°31′N 85°49′W. In agr. area; canned tomato prods.

Swea City, town (1990 pop. 634), Kossuth co., N Iowa, 22 mi/35 km N of Algona; 43°22′N 94°18′W. Feed milling.

Sweden, town (1990 pop. 222), Oxford co., W Maine, 16 mi/26 km WSW of South Paris; 44°07′N 70°49′W.

Sweden, village, Bamberg co., S central S.C., 3 mi/ 4.8 km N of Denmark. Named by RR company. Agr. includes cotton and soybeans.

Swedesboro, borough (1990 pop. 2,024), Gloucester co., SW N.J., on Raccoon Creek, and 17 mi/27 km SW of Camden; 39°45′N 75°18′W. Tin cans, plastics, closures; agr., poultry. Settled by Swedes 1641, inc. 1902. Partly burned by British, 1778. Trinity Church built 1784.

Swedesburg (SWEEDS-buhrg), uninc. village, Montgomery co., SE Pa., suburb 2 mi/3.2 km S of Norristown, near Schuylkill R.; 40°06′N 75°19′W.

Sweeny, town (1990 pop. 3,297), Brazoria co., S Texas, 14 mi/23 km W of Lake Jackson city; 29°03′N 95°42′W. Mfg. (chemical and oil refining). Inc. after 1940.

Sweet Briar, uninc. village, Amherst co., central Va., 11 mi/18 km NNE of Lynchburg, c.3 mi/4.8 km SW of Amherst. Sweet Briar Col. for women (1901) here.

Sweet Grass, county (☐ 1,862 sq mi/4,823 sq km; 1990 pop. 3,154), S Mont.; ⊙ Big Timber; 45°49′N 109°57′W. Agr. area drained by Yellowstone and Boulder rivers and Sweet Grass Creek. Wheat, barley, hay; cattle, sheep, hogs. Parts of Gallatin Natl. Forest in NW and S; small part of Lewis and Clark Natl. Forest in NW corner; part of Absaroka-Beartooth Wilderness Area in S; Greycliff Prairie Dog Town State Park at center of co.; part of Custer Natl. Forest and Absaroka Range in S. Formed 1895. Present boundaries est. 1920.

Sweet Home, town (1990 pop. 6,850), Linn co., W Oregon, on South Santiam R., 25 mi/40 km SE of Albany; 44°23′N 122°42′W. RR junction. Agr. (fruit, vegetables, berries). Lumber. Site of East Linn Mus. Foster Reservoir and Fish Hatchery to E; Green Peter Reservoir to NE. Cascadia State Park to E; Willamette Natl. Forest to E. Settled in 1840s; inc. 1893.

Sweet Home, village, Pulaski co., central Ark., 5 mi/ 8 km SSE of Little Rock, on Fourche Bayou, near Arkansas R. (David D. Terry Lock and Dam to E.) Mfg. (construction aggregates).

Sweet Island, Maine: see ISLE OF SPRINGS.

Sweet Springs, city (1990 pop. 1,595), Saline co., central Mo., on Blackwater R., and 16 mi/26 km SW of Marshall; 38°57′N 93°25′W. Corn, wheat, soybeans; hogs, cattle; dairying; mfg. (home appliances). Settled 1826. Former mineral-springs resort.

Sweet Springs or **Sweetsprings**, uninc. village, Monroe co., SE W.Va., 18 mi/29 km SW of Covington, Va., near Va. state line. Formerly a noted spa, whose heyday was in 1830s; large hotel here is now home for the aged.

Sweetgrass, village (1990 pop. 100), Toole co., N Mont., on Canada (Alta.) border, 37 mi/60 km N of Shelby. Port of entry opposite Coutts, Alta. In agr. region; wheat, barley, oats; cattle, hogs. Oil wells to W and S.

Sweetsburg, village, S Que., Canada, on Yamaska R., and 2 mi/3 km E of Cowansville. Dairying; pigs.

Sweetser, town (1990 pop. 924), Grant co., E central Ind., 4 mi/6.4 km W of Marion; 40°34′N 85°46′W. Vegetables, soybeans, corn; hogs. Laid out 1871.

Sweetwater, county (☐ 10,491 sq mi/27,172 sq km; 1990 pop. 38,823), SW Wyo.; ⊙ Green R.; 41°39′N 108°53′W. Mining and cattle- and sheep-raising area, bordering on Utah and Colo., both to S; watered by Green R. (forms Flaming Gorge Reservoir in S, which extends into Utah) and Sandy Creek. Coal, oil, natural gas and trona (source of soda ash) found here; sand and gravel. Mfg. at Green R. and Rock Springs; agr. (alfalfa, oats). Most of Great Divide Basin of Continental Divide dominates NE part; Big Sandy State Recreation Area on N boundary; part of Flaming Gorge Natl. Recreation Area in S; Seedskadee Natl. Wildlife Refuge in NW. Formed 1867.

Sweetwater 1 city (1990 pop. 5,066), Monroe co., SE Tenn., 14 mi/23 km NE of Athens, 35°36′N 84°28′W. In barite-mining and farming area; mfg. (trailers, hosiery, lumber prods.). Meiji Gakuin, the first fully accredited Jap. high school in the U.S., is here. Inc. 1897. **2** city (1990 pop. 11,967), ⊙ Nolan co., W Texas, c.40 mi/ 64 km W of Abilene; 32°28′N 100°24′W. Elev. 2,164 ft/ 660 m. RR junction, and trade, processing, shipping, distribution center for ranching and agr. area; ships livestock, wool, mohair, grain, cotton, feed; mfg. of gypsum prods., agr. machinery. Has annual livestock show. Nearby are L. Sweetwater (SE) and L. Trammel (SW), recreational areas. Founded c.1876, moved 1881 to site on RR; grew as cattle-shipping point.

Sweetwater, river, c.150 mi/241 km long, S central Wyo.; rises in S part of Wind R. Range at the Continental Divide; flows generally E, through mountainous cattle-raising area, to Pathfinder Reservoir on North Platte R.; lower 12 mi/19 km forms Sweetwater Arm of reservoir. Old Oregon/Mormon Trail follows most of river's course.

Sweetwater Lake, Ramsey co., E central N.Dak., NNE of Devils L.; 48°13′N 98°49′W; 5 mi/8 km long. Irregular shape.

Sweetwater, Lake, reservoir, Nolan co., W Texas, on Sweetwater Creek, 5 mi/8 km SE of Sweetwater; 2 mi/ 3.2 km long; 32°22′N 100°15′W. Capacity 16,700 acre-ft. Formed by dam. Resort.

Sweetwater Lake, Calif.: see SWEETWATER RIVER.

Sweetwater Mountains, in Calif. and Nev., a N-S range just E of the Sierra Nevada, in Lyon co., W Nev., and Mono co., E Calif. Rises to 11,664 ft/3,555 m at Wheeler Peak, 10 mi/16 km N of Bridgeport.

Sweetwater River, c.55 mi/89 km long, San Diego co., S Calif.; rises in mts. c.50 mi/80 km E of San Diego; flows SW through Loveland and Sweetwater reservoirs to San Diego Bay just S of Natl. City. Dams impound reservoirs: Sweetwater L., 3 mi/4.8 km long; L. Loveland, formed by L. Loveland Dam. Cuyamaco Rancho State Park.

Swepsonville (SWEP-suhn-vil), uninc. town (1990 pop. 1,195), Alamance co., N central N.C., on Haw R., and 6 mi/9.7 km SE of Burlington; 36°01′N 79°21′W. Tobacco, grain, sweet potatoes; chickens, hogs; dairying. Mfg.

Swift, county (☐ 752 sq mi/1,948 sq km; 1990 pop. 10,724), SW Minn.; ⊙ Benson; 45°17′N 95°40′W. In part of Lac qui Parle Wildlife Area. Bounded in SW corner by Minnesota R. (dam forms Marsh L. Reservoir). Drained by Pomme de Terre and Chippewa rivers. Agr. (wheat, corn, oats, alfalfa, hay, soybeans, sugar beets, beans; sheep, hogs, cattle, poultry; dairying). Monson L. State Park in E; small natural lakes in far W and NE. Formed 1870.

Swift Creek Reservoir (☐ 7 sq mi/18 sq km), Skamania co., SW Wash., on Lewis R., in Gifford Pinchot Natl. Forest, 40 mi/64 km E of Longview; 46°05′N 122°13′W. Max. capacity 755,500 acre-ft. Formed by Swift No. 1 Dam (412 ft/126 m high), built (1958) for power generation. Yale L. downstream; Mt. St. Helens just N.

Swift Current, city (1991 pop. 14,815), SW Sask., Canada, on Swift Current Creek. Distributing and processing center for a farm and oil region. Other industries are helium extraction, lumbering, and the mfg. of farm machinery and plastic goods. Govt. experimental farm nearby.

Swift Diamond River, c.20 mi/32 km long, Coos co., N N.H.; rises 5 mi/8 km N of Dixville Notch in Diamond Ponds; flows ESE to Magalloway R. at Maine state line, 5 mi/8 km N of Umbagog L. Dead Diamond R., c.18 mi/29 km long; rises in 3 short branches (West, Middle, East; each c. 5 mi/8 km long) in NE Coos co.; flows S to Swift Diamond R. 2 mi/3.2 km NW of its mouth, joins it 2 mi/3.2 km above mouth, N of Wentworth Location village.

Swift River 1 c.20 mi/32 km long, W Maine; rises in Franklin co. S of Mooselookmeguntic L.; flows S to the Androscoggin at Rumford. **2** c.24 mi/39 km long, E N.H.; rises in White Mt. Natl. Forest, NE Grafton co., 10 mi/16 km E of North Woodstock; flows E to Saco R. at Conway.

Swift River, Mass.: see QUABBIN RESERVOIR.

Swifton, town (1990 pop. 830), Jackson co., NE Ark., 25 mi/40 km N of Jonesboro; 35°49′N 91°07′W. In agr. area; mfg. (fish cookers).

Swinburne, Cape, S tip of Prince of Wales Isl., S Franklin dist., N.W.T., Canada, on McClintock Channel and Franklin Strait; 71°12′N 99°09′W.

Swinburne Island, small artificial isl. in Lower N.Y. Bay, just off E shore of Staten Isl., SE N.Y., part of Staten Isl. borough of N.Y. city; 40°34′N 74°03′W. Former quarantine station.

Swindle Island (☐ 120 sq mi/311 sq km), SW B.C., Canada, in Hecate Strait, 16 mi/26 km long, 2 mi/3 km–10 mi/16 km wide; 52°32′N 128°35′W. Klemtu fishing village on NE coast. Just S is Price Isl. (☐ 47 sq mi/ 122 sq km), 14 mi/23 km long, 6 mi/10 km wide.

Swink 1 village (1990 pop. 584), Otero co., SE Colo., on Arkansas R. at mouth of Timpus Creek, and 5 mi/8 km WNW of La Junta; 38°00′N 103°37′W. Elev. 4,118 ft/ 1,255 m. In irrigated sugar-beet region; cattle. **2** village, Choctaw co., SE Okla., 19 mi/31 km E of Hugo. In farm area.

Swisher, county (☐ 900 sq mi/2,331 sq km; 1990 pop. 8,133), NW Texas; ⊙ Tulia; 34°31′N 101°43′W. On the Llano Estacado; elev. 3,100 ft/945 m–3,600 ft/1,097 m. Caprock escarpment in E is broken by Tule Canyon. Drained by Tule Creek and N Tule Draw. Wheat growing, cattle ranching; grain sorghum, corn, cotton. Part of MacKenzie Reservoir (Tule Creek) on E boundary. Formed 1876.

Swisher, town (1990 pop. 645), Johnson co., E Iowa, 15 mi/24 km NNW of Iowa City; 41°50′N 91°42′W.

Swisshelm Mountain (7,185 ft/2,190 m), Cochise co., SE Ariz., 23 mi/37 km N of Douglas; 31°40′N 109°32′W.

Swissvale (SWIS-vail), borough (1990 pop. 10,637), Allegheny co., SW Pa., suburb 7 mi/11.3 km ESE of downtown Pittsburgh, near Monongahela R.; 40°25′N 79°53′W. Mfg. Settled c.1760, inc. 1898.

Switchback, uninc. village (1990 pop. 180), McDowell co., S W.Va., 12 mi/19 km ESE of Welch, in coal region.

Switz City, town (1990 pop. 257), Greene co., SW Ind., 6 mi/9.7 km W of Bloomfield; 39°02′N 87°03′W. In agr. area; mfg. (wooden pallets).

Switzer (SWITS-uhr), uninc. town (1990 pop. 1,004), Logan co., SW W.Va., 4 mi/6.4 km S of Logan; 37°47′N 81°58′W. Bituminous-coal mining.

Switzerland, county (☐ 223 sq mi/578 sq km; 1990 pop.

7,738), SE Ind.; ⊙ Vevay; 38°49′N 85°02′W. Bounded E and S by Ohio R., here forming Ky. state line. Agr. (hay, tobacco; cattle). Mfg. at Vevay and Patriot. Heavily forested. Formed 1814.

Swoyersville (SWOI-yuhrs-vil), borough (1990 pop. 5,630), Luzerne co., NE central Pa., suburb 3 mi/4.8 km N of Wilkes-Barre, on Susquehanna R.; 41°17′N 75°52′W. Mfg. (machinery, textiles, consumer goods; printing); some anthracite coal. Wilkes-Barre Wyoming Valley Airport to E. Francis Slocum State Park to N. Inc. 1888.

Swuamscott River, N.H.: see EXETER RIVER.

Sycamore, city (1990 pop. 9,708), ⊙ De Kalb co., N Ill., 20 mi/32 km W of Elgin; 41°58′N 88°42′W. Trade, industrial, and shipping center in rich agr. area. Highly diversified mfg. Founded c.1840, inc. 1859.

Sycamore 1 village, Talladega co., E central Ala., 14 mi/23 km SSW of Talladega, in part of Talladega Natl. Forest. Cotton milling. **2** (SIK-uh-mor), village (1990 pop. 417), Turner co., S central Ga., 2 mi/3.2 km SSE of Ashburn; 31°40′N 83°38′W. Mfg. of fabricated metal prods., clothing, chemicals. **3** village (1990 pop. 919), Wyandot co., N central Ohio, 8 mi/13 km NNE of Upper Sandusky, and on small Sycamore Creek; 40°57′N 83°10′W. Grain, fruit; livestock, poultry; dairy prods. **4** village (1990 pop. 208), Allendale co., SW S.C., 6 mi/9.7 km ENE of Allendale; 33°02′N 81°13′W. Agr. includes soybeans, peanuts, cotton, grain; livestock.

Sycamore Hills, village (1990 pop. 667), St. Louis co., E Mo., residential suburb 9 mi/14.5 km WNW of downtown St. Louis, E of Overland; 38°42′N 90°20′W.

Sydenham (SI-duh-nuhm, SID-nuhm), village, SE Ont., Canada, on small Sydenham L., 14 mi/23 km NNW of Kingston; 46°09′N 60°10′W. Dairying, farming.

Sydenham River, 10 mi/16 km long, S Ont., Canada; rises W of London, flows WSW, past Dresden and Wallaceburg, to L. St. Clair 14 mi/23 km WNW of Chatham.

Sydney, city (1991 pop. 26,063), Cape Breton Isl., N.S., Canada, on the NE coast at the head of the South Arm of Sydney Harbour; 46°09′N 60°10′W. A port and the commercial, trade, and industrial center of an important coal-mining area. The city has steel mills and plants mfg. wood, aluminum, food prods., and chemicals. Sydney was founded (1783) by United Empire Loyalists and was the capital (1784–1820) of Cape Breton prov. St. George's Church (1786) is one of the oldest Anglican churches in Canada.

Sydney Harbour, inlet of the Atlantic, NE Nova Scotia, Canada, in E coast of Cape Breton Isl.; 10 mi/16 km long, 3 mi/5 km wide at entrance. At North Sydney, inlet divides into West Arm (4 mi/6 km long) and South Arm (5 mi/8 km long). On inlet are Sydney, North Sydney, and Sydney Mines. Sydney Harbour freezes over in Jan. for 3 months.

Sydney Mines, town (1991 pop. 7,551), Cape Breton Isl., N.S., Canada, on Sydney Harbour; 46°14′N 60°13′W. Coal-mining center, coal having been mined in the area since 1784. Steel mills, foundries, and machine shops.

Sykeston (SEIKS-tuhn), village (1990 pop. 167), Wells co., central N.Dak., 13 mi/21 km W of Carrington; 47°28′N 99°24′W.

Sykesville, town (1990 pop. 2,303), Carroll co., N Md., near S branch of Patapasco R., 20 mi/32 km WNW of Baltimore; 39°22′N 76°59′W. In agr. area; mfg. (clothing, woolens, boxes, wormseed oil); cannery. The town is named for James Sykes, who bought 1,000 acres/400 ha here in 1825. The RR arrived in 1830 and a station remains but no trains stop. Springfield State Hosp., est. 1894, is here, and Patapasco State Forest and the Hugg-Thomas Wildlife Refuge extend along the Patapasco river shores.

Sykesville (SEIKS-vil), borough (1990 pop. 1,387), Jefferson co., W central Pa., 5 mi/8 km SW of Du Bois, on Stump Creek; 41°02′N 78°49′W. Agr. area (corn, hay; dairying); mfg. (machinery; commercial printing); bituminous coal; timber.

Sylacauga (si-luh-KAW-guh), city (1990 pop. 12,520), Talladega co., central Ala., 22 mi/35 km SSW of Talladega; 33°10′N 86°15′W. Processing center for a livestock and timber area. Built upon a solid bed of cream-white marble, it has quarries; marble has been produced since 1840. Textiles, clothing, metal goods, fertilizers, and dairy items are also made. Nearby is Flagg Mt., which was a signal relay station during the Civil War. Inc. 1839.

Sylmar, suburban section of Los Angeles city, Los Angeles co., S Calif., 23 mi/37 km NW of downtown Los Angeles and 3 mi/4.8 km NW of San Fernando. Industrial area, mfg. (electronic components and equip., navigation and communications equip., medical instruments, apparel, transportation equip., fabricated metal prods., consumer goods, glass prods., paper prods.). Los Angeles Mission Col. (2-year). San Fernando Mission to S; Van Norman Lakes in W; Angeles Natl. Forest and San Gabriel Mts. to E.

Sylva, town (1990 pop. 1,809), ⊙ Jackson co., W N.C., 40 mi/64 km SW of Asheville; 35°22′N 83°13′W. Near Tuckasegee R. In Nantahala Natl. Forest. Cattle; corn, tobacco. Diversified mfg. Blue Ridge Parkway passes 10 mi/16 km to NE. Eastern Cherokee (Qualla Boundary) Indian Reservation to N. Southwestern Community Col. Inc. 1899.

Sylvan Beach, resort village (1990 pop. 1,119), Oneida co., central N.Y., on E shore of Oneida L., 13 mi/21 km W of Rome; 43°12′N 75°43′W.

Sylvan Dam, Morrison co., central Minn., on Crow Wing R., 23 mi/37 km N of Little Falls; 22 ft/7 m high; 46°19′N 94°22′W. Built (1913) for power generation.

Sylvan Grove (sil-vuhn), village (1990 pop. 321), Lincoln co., central Kansas, on Saline R., and 13 mi/21 km W of Lincoln; 39°00′N 98°23′W. Livestock; grain.

Sylvan Lake, town (1991 pop. 4,197), S central Alta., Canada, on Sylvan L. (9 mi/14 km long, 2 mi/3 km wide), 13 mi/21 km W of Red Deer; 52°18′N 114°05′W. Mixed farming, dairying.

Sylvan Lake (SIL-van), town (1990 pop. 1,884), Oakland co., SE Mich., suburb 3 mi/4.8 km SW of Pontiac, on E side of Sylvan L.; 42°37′N 83°19′W. Light mfg. Inc. 1921 as village, 1946 as city.

Sylvan Lake, Ind.: see ROME CITY.

Sylvan Pass, Wyo.: see ABSAROKA RANGE.

Sylvan Springs, town (1990 pop. 1,440), Jefferson co., N central Ala., just W of Birmingham; 33°31′N 87°02′W.

Sylvania (sil-VAIN-yuh), city (1990 pop. 17,301), Lucas co., NW Ohio, a suburb of Toledo at the Mich. state line; 41°43′N 83°42′W. Chiefly residential. Bldg. materials, cement, light mfg. Has a junior col. Inc. 1867.

Sylvania (sil-VAIN-yuh), town (1990 pop. 2,871), ⊙ Screven co., E Ga., 21 mi/34 km NNE of Statesboro; 32°45′N 81°38′W. In farm and timber area. Mfg. includes carpet yarns, lumber, clothing, bearings; textile finishing and dyeing. Founded 1847; inc. 1854.

Sylvania (sil-VAI-nee-ah), borough (1990 pop. 203), Bradford co., N Pa., 4 mi/6.4 km WNW of Troy; 41°48′N 51°76′W. Agr. includes dairying; livestock; corn. State forest nearby.

Sylvarena (sil-vuh-REE-nuh), village (1990 pop. 110), Smith co., S central Miss., 8 mi/12.9 km E of Raleigh; 32°00′N 89°22′W. Agr. (cotton, corn; livestock).

Sylvester, town (1990 pop. 5,702), ⊙ Worth co., S central Ga., 20 mi/32 km E of Albany; 31°32′N 83°50′W. In farm and timber area. Mfg. includes foods, transportation equip., clothing; meat and peanut processing. Inc. 1898.

Sylvester 1 uninc. village (1990 pop. 79), Fisher co., NW central Texas, 20 mi/32 km NNE of Sweetwater, on Clear Fork of Brazos R. In agr. and cattle-ranching area. **2** village (1990 pop. 191), Boone co., W central W.Va., 20 mi/32 km S of Charleston, on Big Coal R.; 38°00′N 81°33′W. Mfg. (mining equip.; coal processing); bituminous coal.

Sylvia (SIL-vee-uh), village (1990 pop. 308), Reno co., S central Kansas, on North Fork of Ninnescah R., and 27 mi/43 km WSW of Hutchinson; 37°57′N 98°24′W. In wheat region.

Symerton (SIM-er-ton), village (1990 pop. 110), Will co., NE Ill., 14 mi/23 km S of Joliet; 41°19′N 88°02′W. In agr. area.

Symmes River, c.60 mi/97 km long, S Ohio; flows from Jackson L. (c.4 mi/6 km long, 5 mi/8 km wide) to the Ohio R., just S of Chesapeake, which is across the Ohio R. from Huntington, W.Va.

Symsonia (sim-SO-nee-uh), uninc. village (1990 pop. 700), Graves co., W Ky., 12 mi/19 km SSE of Paducah, near West Fork of Clarks R. Tobacco, grain; livestock; timber. Mfg. Kaler Bottom Wildlife Management Area to S.

Syosset, village (□ 4 sq mi/10.4 sq km; 1990 pop. 18,967), Nassau co., SE N.Y., on W L.I., 9 mi/14.5 km NE of Mineola; 40°49′N 73°30′W. Extensive mfg. (electronic equip., pharmaceuticals, photographic equip., bldg. materials, plastic prods.).

Syracuse, city (□ 25 sq mi/65 sq km; 1990 pop. 163,860), ⊙ Onondaga co., central N.Y., on Onondaga L. and the Barge Canal; 43°02′N 76°08′W. A port of entry, its mfg. includes air conditioners, electrical and electronic equip., motor vehicle and aircraft parts, chinaware, shoes, machinery, and pharmaceuticals. Salt springs were discovered in what is now Syracuse in 1654. Salt-making, the city's chief industry from its settlement until after the Civil War, declined due to competition. However, its favorable location on the Erie Canal (opened here in 1819) and on RR stimulated industrial development. The city is the seat of Syracuse Univ., Le Moyne Col., the State Univ. of N.Y. Upstate Medical Center, and 2 community colls. Cultural facilities include the Everson Mus. of Fine Arts. Syracuse is also the capital of the Iroquois (or, more properly, the Hondinonshonni, or People of the Longhouse) Nation, and the city continues its 18th-cent. tradition as Keeper of the Council Fire. It was here, on the E shore of Onondaga L., that the Five (later Six) Nations ended their internecine warfare and territorial disputes with the planting of the Tree of Peace and the burial of war weapons beneath it. The arrival of the French and British soon after, however, quickly pitted the tribes against one another again. Of interest are a salt mus. and reconstructed 1856 salt factory on E side of Onondaga L., as well as an Erie Canal mus. A hugely successful annual state fair has been held here since 1841. Nearby is Hancock Internatl. Airport and the Onondaga Reservation. Recreational lakes and streams are abundant in the area. Settled c.1788, inc. as a city 1848.

Syracuse 1 town (1990 pop. 2,729), Kosciusko co., N Ind., on L. Wawasee, 13 mi/21 km NNE of Warsaw; 41°25′N 85°45′W. Agr. area; resort; mfg. (mobile homes, transportation equip., boats, feeds, fabricated metal prods., rubber prods.). Laid out 1837. **2** town (1990 pop. 1,606), ⊙ Hamilton co., SW Kansas, on Arkansas R., and 45 mi/72 km W of Garden City; 37°58′N 101°45′W. Shipping point for farm produce in livestock and grain area. Hamilton State Fishing L. to NW. Inc. 1887. **3** town (1990 pop. 185), Morgan co., central Mo., near Lamine R., 5 mi/8 km W of Tipton; 38°40′N 92°52′W. **4** town (1990 pop. 1,646), Otoe co., SE Nebr., 16 mi/26 km W of Nebraska City, and on Little Nemaha R; 40°39′N 96°10′W. Livestock; grain; poultry prods.; mfg. (glass prods., feeds, pharmaceutical prods.; printing). **5** town (1990 pop. 3,702), Davis co., N central Utah, suburb 24 mi/39 km NNW of downtown Salt Lake City, and 10 mi SW of Ogden, near Great Salt L. Elev. c.4,300 ft/1,311 m. Howard Slough Waterfowl Management Area to W; causeway to Antelope Isl. State Park to W.

Syracuse, village (1990 pop. 827), Meigs co., SE Ohio, 3 mi/5 km SE of Pomeroy, and on Ohio R.; 38°59′N 81°58′W. In coal-mining and livestock area.

Sysladobsis Lake (sis-luh-DAHB-sis), reservoir, Wash., Penobscot, and Hancock cos., E Maine, at W end of West Grand L., 33 mi/53 km W of Calais; 9 mi/14.5 km long; 45°11′N 67°59′W. Pocumpus L., W arm of West Grand L., to E; Upper Sysladobsis L. to NW.

T

Tabaquite (tah-bah-KEET), village, central Trinidad, Trinidad and Tobago, on RR and 20 mi/32 km SE of Port of Spain. Oil wells.

Tabasco (tah-BAHS-ko), state (□ 9,783 sq mi/ 25,338 sq km; 1990 pop. 1,501,744), E Mexico, on the Gulf of Campeche; ⊙ Villahermosa; 17°15′N 90°59′W. Tabasco is predominantly a tropical plain, once densely forested, broken by numerous rivers, swamps, and lagoons. The climate is hot and humid, and rainfall in some areas exceeds 200 in/508 cm annually. Tropical agr. (bananas, cacao, sugarcane, hardwoods, and fruits) and cattle raising were the leading economic activities, but rich oil fields discovered along the coast have become Tabasco's economic mainstay. Petrochemical industry at Coatzacoalcos and Minatitlán. The area, 1st explored by the Spanish in 1518, was conquered in 1530 by Francisco de Montejo. During the 17th and early 18th cent., Tabasco was contested bet. Spain and England.

Tabasco (tah-BAHS-ko), town (1990 pop. 5,435), Zacatecas, N central Mexico, on Juchipila R. and 27 mi/ 43 km ENE of Tlaltenango de San (chez) Román; 21°52′N 102°55′W. Elev. 5,249 ft/1,600 m. Grain, tropical fruit; livestock. Formerly Villa del Refugio.

Taber (TAI-buhr), town (1991 pop. 6,660), S Alta., NE of Lethbridge; 49°47′N 112°09′W. The area is irrigated for crop and livestock raising. The town has a sugar beet refinery and a vegetable cannery. Coal, oil, and natural gas are found nearby.

Tabernacle (TA-buhr-na-kuhl), township (1990 pop. 7,360), Burlington co., S N.J., 20 mi/32 km ESE of Camden; 39°49′N 74°39′W. Inc. 1901.

Tabernash, village, Grand co., N Colo., 30 mi/48 km W of Boulder, on Fraser R. Elev. 8,320 ft/2,536 m. Tourism; timber; mfg. of wood cabinets. Arapaho Natl. Forest to NE and S. Winter Park Ski Area to S; Silver Creek Ski Area to NW.

Tabiona, village (1990 pop. 120), Duchesne co., NE Utah, 22 mi. NW of Duchesne and on Duchesne R.; 40°21′N 110°42′W. Elev. 6,100 ft/1,859 m. Trade center for ranchers. Cattle, sheep, alfalfa. At W edge of Uintah and Ouray Indian Reservation. Uinta Range and Ashley Natl. Forest to N.

Table Grove, village (1990 pop. 408), Fulton co., W central Ill., 15 mi/24 km WSW of Lewiston; 40°22′N 90°25′W. In agr. and bituminous-coal-mining area.

Table Mountain, Tuolumne co., central Calif., near Stanislaus R. Mass of basalt (formed by lava) with a flat top (2,200 ft/671 m high, c.30 mi/48 km long, 1,200 ft/366 m–1,500 ft/457 m wide), W of Jamestown. Rich source of gold in 1850s.

Table Rock, village (1990 pop. 308), Pawnee co., SE Nebr., 7 mi/11.3 km NNE of Pawnee City and on North Fork of Big Nemaha R; 40°10′N 96°05′W. RR junction. Grain; livestock; dairy and poultry prods.

Table Rock (3,124 ft/952 m), monadnock in the Blue Ridge Mts., Pickens co., NW S.C., c.20 mi/32 km NW of Greenville, in scenic Table Rock State Park (3,068 acres/1,242 ha); 35°03′N 82°42′W. It consists of a flat top capping vertical cliffs, resembling a table. Pinnacle Mt. (3,425 ft/1,044 m) and a peculiar formation called The Stool (2,500 ft/762 m) are nearby.

Table Rock Lake, reservoir, SW Mo. and NW Ark., on White R., mostly in Mark Twain Natl. Forest, 42 mi/ 68 km S of Springfield, Mo. and 6 mi/9.7 km SW of Branson, Mo.; c.70 mi/113 km long; 36°36′N 93°18′W. Max. capacity 3,462,000 acre-ft. Long Creek enters from S, forming 10-mi/16-km arm; James R. forms c.25-mi/40-km arm. Formed by Table Rock Dam (252 ft/77 m high), built (1959) for flood control and power generation. City of Kimberling on N shore. Table Rock State Park at dam.

Tableland, village, S central Trinidad, Trinidad and Tobago, 13 mi/21 km E of San Fernando. Cacao.

Tabletop, Canada: see JACQUES CARTIER, MOUNT.

Tabor, town (1990 pop. 957), on Fremont-Mills co. line, SW Iowa, 10 mi/16 km N of Sidney; 40°53′N 95°40′W. Animal feed.

Tabor (TAI-bor), village (1990 pop. 403), Bon Homme co., SE S.Dak., 11 mi/18 km ESE of Tyndall; 42°57′N 97°39′W. Mfg. (golf bags). Sand Creek and Tabor State Lakeside Use Areas to S on Mo. R. (Lewis and Clark L.). Founded by the Hutterische Community, an early communistic Christian group.

Tabor City (TAI-buhr), town (1990 pop. 2,330), Columbus co., SE N.C., 16 mi/26 km SSW of Whiteville, near S.C. state line; 34°08′N 78°52′W. Tobacco, peanuts, cotton, sweet potatoes; livestock. Mfg. (commercial printing, textiles and apparel, ventilation equip., lumber).

Tacajó, (tah-kah-HO), town, Holguín prov., E Cuba, 23 mi/37 km E of Holguín; 22°52′N 75°56′W. Sugarcane, fruit. The sugar mill Fernando de Dios is 1 mi/1.6 km SE.

Tacámbaro de Codallos (tah-KAHM-bah-ro de ko-DAH-yos), city (1990 pop. 16,487) and township, ⊙ Tacámbaro municipio, Michoacán, W central Mexico, on central plateau, on RR and 45 mi/72 km SSW of Morelia on Mexico Highway 41; 19°13′N 101°27′W. Elev. 5,174 ft/1,577 m. Agr. center (cereals, sugarcane, tobacco, fruit); flour milling, tanning, alcohol distilling.

Tacaná (tah-kah-MAH), volcano (13,310 ft/4,057 m), on the Mexico-Guatemala border; 15°8′N 92°6′W. The 2d-highest peak in Central Amer. Major eruptions occurred in 1855 and 1878.

Tacarigua (tah-gah-REE-gwah), village, N central Trinidad, Trinidad and Tobago, on RR and 10 mi/16 km E of Port of Spain; 10°40′N 61°23′W. Rice growing (irrigation). Has industrial school.

Tacna, uninc. town (1990 pop. 950), Yuma co., SW Ariz., 38 mi/61 km E of Yuma, near Gila R. Irrigated agr. area (cotton, citrus, dates, sugar beets, alfalfa, vegetables, grain). Barry M. Goldwater (formerly Luke) Air Force Range to S. Yuma Proving Ground (U.S. Army) to N.

Tacoma, city (1990 pop. 176,664), ⊙ Pierce co., W Wash., 26 mi/42 km SSW of Seattle, borders Puget Sound on W and NE, harbor is in Commencement Bay, separated from Kitsap Peninsula by the Narrows, bridged on W (Tacoma Narrows Bridge, suspension); 47°15′N 122°28′W. Ferry to Vashon Isl., N. It is the 3d-largest city in Wash. (Tacoma is gaining on 2d-place Spokane; margin was 35,000 in 1960, now only 500 in 1990). It is a major seaport and RR terminus and one of the chief industrial cities in the NW. Once known as the lumber capital of Amer., it is still an important center for forest-prods. industries; diversified light and heavy mfg. There are also shipyards and many docks. Points of interest include the nation's tallest totem pole, built in 1903 by Alaskan Native Americans; and Point Defiance Park in N tip of city, containing a zoo, an aquarium, a children's park, a forestry mus., Wash. State Historical Mus., Tacoma Art Mus., and a reconstruction of Fort Nisqually (1833). The city is the seat of the Univ. of Puget Sound, Pacific Lutheran Univ. (at Parkland, to S), and Tacoma and Fort Steilacoom community cols. It has an arboretum, a number of art galleries, the Tacoma Dome and the state historical society mus. A lilac festival is held annually in the city. Tacoma is the gateway to Mt. Rainier Natl. Park and many recreational areas. The Tacoma Narrows suspension bridge links the city with the Olympic Peninsula; it replaced "Galloping Gertie," which collapsed (1940) in a windstorm only 4 months after it had opened. McChord Air Force Base, Fort Lewis (a major army training center), and Camp Murray natl. guard hq. are nearby. Inc. 1884.

Tacoma Lakes (tuh-KO-muh), reservoir consisting of Baker, Sand, Woodbury, and Little Purgatory ponds, Litchfield town, Kennebec co., S Maine, on small stream, just S of L. Cobbosseecontee and 10 mi/16 km SW of Augusta; 44°12′N 69°38′W. In resort area.

Tacoma, Mount, Wash.: see MOUNT RAINIER NATIONAL PARK.

Taconic Mountains, range of the Appalachian Mts., extending c.150 mi/240 km N-S bet. the Green Mts. and the Hudson Valley along parts of New York's border with Vermont, Massachusetts, and Connecticut. Mt.

Equinox (3,816 ft/1,163 m) is the highest point. The Taconics, among the oldest mts. in North Amer., have been worn low by millions of years of erosion. The Berkshire Hills, W Mass., are part of the range. Taconic State Park along the N.Y.-Mass. and N.Y.-Conn. borders is a popular recreational area.

Taconic State Parkway, scenic N-S, multilane, controlled-access highway, E N.Y., running 144 mi/232 km from Hawthorne Circle in central Westchester co. N to the junction of the Berkshire sec. of the Gov. Thomas E. Dewey Thruway, 21 mi/34 km SE of Albany. The 1st stretch of road (then called the Eastern State Parkway) was opened July 1935; the final 16-mi/26-km stretch connecting to the Thruway opened Nov. 1963. The total cost of the project was $50 million. At S end, it connects to Saw Mill River, Spring Brook, and Cross Westchester Parkways, and traverses the magnificent rural Taconic-Berkshire Mt. range, a 150-mi/241-km extension of the Appalachians along the N.Y. state border with Conn. and Mass. It is a popular route from metropolitan N.Y. city to S New England.

Taconite (TA-kuh-neit), village (1990 pop. 310), Itasca co., N central Minn., 9 mi/14.5 km of Grand Rapids at W end of Mesabi Iron Range; 47°19′N 93°21′W. Iron mines in area; mfg. (concrete).

Taconite Harbor (TA-kuh-neit), locality, Cook co., NE Minn., 73 mi/117 km NE of Duluth, on L. Superior; 47°31′N 90°55′W. Transfer point from Erie Mining Company RR to lake freighter (lakers) from iron mining operation at Mesaba, NE of Aurora, St. Louis co., in Mesabi Iron Range, 37 mi/92 km to W. Superior Natl. Forest to N; Finland State Forest to W.

Tacony (tah-KO-nee), residential and industrial section of NE Philadelphia, Philadelphia co., SE Pa. on Delaware R.; 40°01′N 75°02′W. Tacony-Palmyra Bridge (main span 2,324 ft/708 m; opened 1929) here to Palmyra, N.J.

Taco-Taco (TAH-ko–TAH-ko), town, Pinar del Río prov., W Cuba, on RR and river of same name, 40 mi/ 64 km NE of Pinar del Río; 22°39′N 83°11′W. Tobacco, sugarcane, fruit. Sugar mill José Martí 8 mi/12.9 km NE.

Tacotalpa (tah-ko-TAHL-pah), city (1990 pop. 5,890) and township, Tabasco, SE Mexico, on Tacotalpa (affluent of Grijalva) R. and 28 mi/45 km S of Villahermosa; 17°36′N 92°49′W. Rice, beans, coffee.

Tacuba (tah-KOO-bah), NW section of Mexico city, central Mexico; 28°03′N 107°07′W. Residential and mfg. suburb (machinery, rubber). San Gabriel church is notable; during Holy Week Indians enact a passion play. Many archaeological remains nearby. Founded by Tepaneca Indians; was later admitted into Aztec confederacy. Was occupied by Spanish and was partly destroyed (1521).

Tacubaya (tah-koo-BAH-yah), W section of Mexico city, central Mexico. Fashionable residential suburb; textile, glass, clothing, dairy, and food industries. Site of Natl. Astronomical Observatory (19°24′N 99°11′W).

Tadoussac (TAD-oo-sak), village (1991 pop. 832), S Que., Canada, at the confluence of the Saguenay and the St. Lawrence rivers; 48°09′N 69°43′W. It is a summer resort in a dairying and lumbering region. The site was visited by Jacques Cartier in 1535. An attempt (1600–1601) to establish a Fr. colony here failed, but Tadoussac later became the site of the oldest Christian mission in Canada and an important Fr. fur-trading post.

Taft, city (1990 pop. 5,902), Kern co., S central Calif., in San Joaquin Valley, 28 mi/45 km WSW of Bakersfield; 35°08′N 119°27′W. Supply and refining center in productive oil region; mfg. petroleum prods. Federal prison. Cattle; grain, cotton, fruit, nuts; dairying. 2-yr col. here. Taft Heights (N), South Taft (S) are residential suburbs. Irrigation reservoir to E; Los Padres Natl. Forest to S. Inc. 1910.

Taft, town (1990 pop. 3,222), San Patricio co., S Texas, 19 mi/31 km N of Corpus Christi; 27°58′N 97°23′W. Elev. 34 ft/10 m. In agr. area (cotton, grain sorghums, cattle); mfg. (steel tanks, liquid fertilizers, garden supplies); oil, natural gas field nearby. Taft Blackland Mus. Inc. 1929.

Taft 1 uninc. village, St. Charles parish, SE La., 19 mi/31 km W of New Orleans, on W bank of Mississippi R.; 29°59′N 90°26′W. In agr. area (sugarcane, vegetables, cattle). Catfish, crawfish, alligators. Mfg. (chemicals, industrial gases, tin, antimony stabilizers). **2** village (1990 pop. 400), Muskogee co., E Okla., 10 mi/16 km W of Muskogee, on Arkansas R.; 35°45′N 95°32′W. In agr. area. **3** village, Lincoln co., W Oregon, 4 mi/6.4 km S of Lincoln City, on Pacific Ocean at narrow entrance to Siletz Bay, estuary of Siletz R. Resort.

Taft Heights, uninc. town (1990 pop. 2,050), Kern co., S central Calif., residential suburb 1 mi/1.6 km N of Taft, 28 mi/45 km WSW of Bakersfield; 35°08′N 119°28′W. Buena Vista L., irrigation reservoir, to E. Irrigated agr. area.

Taft Point, Calif.: see YOSEMITE NATIONAL PARK.

Taftville, New London co., SE Conn., 4 mi/6.4 km NNE of Norwich. A postal section of Norwich.

Taghum (TA-guhm), village, SE B.C., Canada, in Selkirk Mts., on Kootenay R. and 5 mi/8 km W of Nelson. Gold and silver mining.

Tagish Lake (TA-gish) (□ 115 sq mi/298 sq km), S Yukon and NW B.C., Canada, W of Atlin L., 40 mi/64 km SE of Whitehorse; c.70 mi/113 km long, 1 mi/2 km–3 mi/5 km wide. Several arms extend from main body of lake. Drained N by Lewes R.

Tagus (TAIG-uhs), village, Mountrail co., NW central N.Dak., 22 mi/35 km E of Stanley; 48°20′N 100°56′W.

Tahdziú (tahd-see-OO), town (1990 pop. 1,807), Yucatán, SE Mexico, 5 mi/8 km N of Peto; 20°12′N 88°57′W. Henequen, sugar, fruit.

Tahlequah (TAL-uh-kwah), city (1990 pop. 10,398), ⊙ Cherokee co., E Okla., 25 mi/40 km ENE of Muskogee; 35°54′N 94°58′W. Elev. 872 ft/266 m. Trade and commercial center for agr., fruit growing, and livestock-raising region; dairying; mfg. (contract sewing, printing, diverse light mfg., feed). Seat of Northeastern State Univ.; Cherokee Nation hq. and Heritage Center here. Murrell Home State Memorial to S; Cherokee Landing (on Tenkiller L.) State Park to S; Sequoyah State Park and Western Hills Lodge to W, on Fort Gibson L. State fish hatchery nearby. Settled by Cherokees in 1839, and made the capital of Cherokee Indian Nation.

Tahmek (tah-MEK), town (1990 pop. 3,263), Yucatán, SE Mexico, 25 mi/40 km ESE of Mérida on Mexico Highway 180; 20°53′N 89°16′W. Henequen.

Tahoe City, village, Placer co., E Calif., 30 mi/48 km SW of Reno, Nev., in the Sierra Nevada, on NW shore of L. Tahoe, in Tahoe Natl. Forest. Resort, tourism. Several ski areas, including Squaw Valley to NW, site of 1960 Winter Olympics. D.L. Bliss State Park to S.

Tahoe, Lake (□ 193 sq mi/500 sq km), on the Calif.-Nev. state line. Fed by many streams, the lake occupies a basin in the Sierra Nevada. It is drained by the Truckee R. L. Tahoe lies 6,229 ft/1,899 m above sea level, but its depth (1,645 ft/501 m) prevents it from freezing. South Lake Tahoe, Calif. at S end, largest community on lakeshore; also Tahoe City and Tahoe Vista on N end. The lake, explored in 1844 by John Frémont, is noted for its clearness. L. Tahoe is a major, year-round vacation spot, and since the 1950s, gambling resorts have been constructed along the Nevada shoreline, at Stateline, Crystal Bay, Incline Valley. Encircled by scenic highway; popularity of lake and proximity to major cities has led to traffic congestion in area. In Tahoe and Eldorado Natl. Forests (Calif.), Toiyabe Natl. Forest (Nev.) and Placer and El Dorado cos, E Calif., and Douglas and Washoe cos.; Lake Tahoe State Park on E side. Several ski resorts in area, including Squaw Valley (NW), 1960 Winter Olympics site.

Tahoe Vista, uninc. town (1990 pop. 1,144), Placer co., E Calif., 20 mi/32 km SSW of Reno, Nev., at N end of L. Tahoe, in Tahoe Natl. Forest; 39°15′N 120°03′W. Tourism. Northstar-at-Tahoe Ski Area to N.

Tahoka, town (1990 pop. 2,868), ⊙ Lynn co., NW Texas, on the Llano Estacado, 30 mi/48 km S of Lubbock; 33°09′N 101°47′W. Elev. 3,090 ft/942 m. In irrigated agr. and livestock region (cotton, grain, sorghums, wheat; cattle, sheep, hogs); mfg. (mobile sprayers). Small Tahoka L. is c.9 mi/14.5 km N. Settled 1903, inc. 1915.

Taholah (tah-HO-lah), village (1990 pop. 788), Grays Harbor co., W Wash., on Pacific coast, at mouth of Quinault R., and 32 mi/51 km NW of Hoquiam. Hq. of Quinault Indian Reservation, in SW part of reservation; 47°20′N 124°17′W. Salmon. Copalis Natl. Wildlife Refuge is offshore.

Tahquamenon River (tah-KWAH-me-nahn), c.80 mi/129 km long, N Mich.; rising in the E Upper Peninsula, in W Luce co.; flowing E, past McMillan and Newberry and NE, through Tahquamenon Falls State Park to Whitefish Bay of L. Superior; 46°28′N 85°50′W. Runs through Tahquamenon State Park. It was once a well-known logging river. It is noted for its waterfalls and is celebrated in Henry Wadsworth Longfellow's *Hiawatha.*

Tahsis, village (1986 pop. 1,445), Canada, W coast of Vancouver Isl., at end of Tahsis Inlet; 49°55′N 126°40′W. Sawmills ship directly overseas.

Tahtsa Lake, W central B.C., Canada, in Coast Mts., in Tweedsmuir Park, 180 mi/290 km W of Prince George; 53°42′N 127°26′W. Elev. 2,783 ft/848 m. Drained E into Ootsa L. by short Tahtsa R.

Taiya Inlet (TEI-yuh), SE Alaska, NNE arm (12 mi/19 km long) of Chilkoot Inlet, an arm of Lynn Canal, NNW of Juneau; 59°25′N 135°18′W. Extends from Haines to Skagway. Taiya, at head of Taiya Inlet near Skagway, is beginning point for Chilkoot Trail.

Takakkaw Falls (TA-kuh-koh), in Yoho Natl. Park, B.C., Canada, in the Rockies; drop an estimated 1,200 ft/366 m–1,600 ft/488 m in 3 leaps to Yoho R. Sometimes spelled Takkakaw Falls.

Takkakaw Falls, Canada: see TAKAKKAW FALLS.

Takla Lake (□ 98 sq mi/254 sq km), central B.C., Canada, 60 mi/97 km ENE of Smithers; 57 mi/92 km long, 2 mi/3 km wide. Near SE end the NW Arm extends 18 mi/29 km NW. Drains SE into Stuart L.

Takoma Park (tah-KO-ma), city (1990 pop. 16,700), Montgomery co., W central Md., residential suburb of Washington, D.C.; 38°59′N 77°00′W. Initially called Brightwood by the RR, the suburb was founded in 1883 by Benjamin Franklin Gilbert. The current name, presumbly an Indian word for "High Up-Near Heaven" was spelled with a "k" to distinguish it from Tacoma, Wash. A tablet to Glbert's memory was dedicated in 1939 in Gilbert Memorial Park. Water from a spring here was once sold all over the East. Since the 1890s, Takoma has been world hqs. of the Seventh Day Adventists. It is the seat of Columbia Union Col. and the Takoma Branch of Montgomery Col., est. in 1945 as the first junior col. in the nation. A tree at Maple Ave. and Sligo Creek Parkway, in which Union soldiers carved the names of all presidents of the U.S. up until then, still survives. The town once resided in both Montgomery and Prince Georges cos., but the Prince Georges portion was transferred to Montgomery on July 1,1997. The long-standing co. boundary was shifted so the city could be united.

Takotna, village (1990 pop. 38), SW central Alaska, on Takotna R., 15 mi/24 km W of McGrath; 62°56′N 156°04′W. Placer gold mining.

Takshak, village, SW central Alaska, at Devils Elbow, sharp bend in southernmost point of lower Yukon R.; 61°28′N 162°10′W.

Taku (TAI-koo), village, NW B.C., Canada, near Alaska border, on Graham Inlet of Tagish L., 7 mi/11 km NW of Atlin, 100 mi/161 km NNE of Juneau; 59°38′N 133°51′W. Former gold mining.

Taku Glacier, SE Alaska, in Coast Range, 30 mi/48 km NNE of Juneau; 30 mi/48 km wide, 30 mi/48 km long; 58°28′N 134°5′W. Drains into Taku Inlet (S) and Lynn Canal (SW).

Taku Inlet, SE Alaska, opens on Stephens Passage, 10 mi/16 km SE of Juneau; extends 25 mi/40 km N. Receives Taku R. and Taku Glacier.

Taku River (TAI-koo), 180 mi/290 km long, N B.C., Canada, and SE Alaska; rises W of Dease L.; flows generally W to Coast Mts. SE of Atlin L., then SW, crossing into Alaska 5 mi/8 km SW of Tulsequah, to Taku Inlet 25 mi/40 km NE of Juneau.

Tala (tah-lah), city (1990 pop. 24,563) and township, Jalisco, W Mexico, 23 mi/37 km W of Guadalajara; 20°39′N 103°43′W. Elev. 4,413 ft/1,345 m. Sugarcane center.

Talala (tuh-LA-luh), village (1990 pop. 206), Rogers co., NE Okla., 15 mi/24 km NNW of Claremore; 36°31′N 95°42′W. Light mfg. Oologah L. reservoir to E.

Talbot 1 county (□ 395 sq mi/1,023 sq km; 1990 pop. 6,524), W Ga.: ⊙ Talbotton; 32°43′N 84°32′W. Bounded NE by Flint R. Intersected by fall line. Agr. (peaches); cattle; sawmilling. Formed 1827. **2** county (1990 pop. 30,549), E Md.; ⊙ Easton; 38°45′N 76°11′W. A peninsula on the Eastern Shore, bounded W by Chesapeake Bay. Tidewater agr. area (vegetables, grain, dairy prods.; poultry, cattle); canneries handle much produce. Has large seafood industry (fish, oysters, crabs). Resort area (yachting, hunting, fishing). Wye Oak State Park (near Wye Mills) is in the co. as well as several Chesapeake Bay Isls. (notably Tighlman Isl.). Formed 1661.

Talbot Island, barrier island along Atlantic shore, Duval co., extreme NE Fla., separated from the mainland by salt marshes; at N end is Nassau Sound, separating it from Amelia Isl., at S end is mouth of St. Johns R.; 7.5 mi/12.1 km long, 2 mi/3.2 km wide.

Talbotton, town (1990 pop. 1,046), ⊙ Talbot co., W Ga., 28 mi/45 km ENE of Columbus; 32°41′N 84°32′W. Founded 1828.

Talco, village (1990 pop. 592), Titus co., NE Texas, Sulphur R., 33 mi/53 km SE of Paris; 33°21′N 95°05′W. Trade center for oil field (discovered 1935); agr. (cattle, dairying, poultry; watermelons); asphalt, oil refineries. Inc. 1936.

Talcottville, uninc. village (1990 pop. 120), Lewis co., N N.Y., on W side of Black R. valley, 18 mi/29 km S of Lowville and just N of Boonville; 43°32′N 75°22′W. N.J.-born writer and critic Edmund Wilson spent most of his life in Black R. valley area, which overlooks the Adirondack Mts. to E and is backed by Tug Hill Upland to W. Wilson memorialized his Talcottville home and the region's preindustrial character in his book *Upstate.*

Talent, town (1990 pop. 3,274), Jackson co., SW Oregon, 7 mi/11.3 km SE of Medford, on Bear Creek; 44°32′N 123°06′W. Agr. (fruit, wheat, oats, barley). Glass fabrication. Parts of Rogue River Natl. Forest to S and E.

Taliaferro (tal-uh-FER-o), county (□ 195 sq mi/505 sq km; 1990 pop. 1,915), NE Ga.; ⊙ Crawfordville; 33°34′N 82°53′W. Drained by Little and Ogeechee rivers. Piedmont agr. (cotton, corn, grain, fruit); cattle, hogs; sawmilling area. Formed 1825.

Talihina (tal-uh-HEE-nee), town (1990 pop. 1,297), Le Flore co., SE Okla., in the Ouachita Mts., 31 mi/50 km SW of Poteau; 34°45′N 95°02′W. In recreation area; timber. Talimena State Park to E; Ouachita Natl. Forest to E. Founded 1888, inc. 1905.

Talkeetna, village, S Alaska, on Susitna R. at mouth of Chalitna R., and 80 mi/129 km N of Anchorage, on road connecting to Parks Highway. Jump off point for mt. climbers climbing Mt. McKinley. Airport.

Talkeetna Mountains, range in S Alaska, N of Matanuska R., extending c.150 mi/241 km NE–SW along Susitna R. NE of Anchorage. Rises to c.8,000 ft/2,438 m.

Talking Rock, town (1990 pop. 62), Pickens co., N Ga., 5 mi/8 km N of Jasper; 34°31′N 84°31′W. Mfg. includes crushed stone, veneer stone.

Tallaboa (tah-yah-BO-ah), village, S P.R., on the coast, 5 mi/8 km W of Ponce.

Talladega (ta-luh-DEE-guh), county (□ 760 sq mi/1,968 sq km; 1990 pop. 74,107), E central Ala.; ⊙ Talladega; 33°26′N 86°05′W. Bounded W by Coosa R.; drained by its affluents. Parts of Talladega Mts. and of Talladega Natl. Forest in E. Soybeans, corn; poultry; iron mines. Formed 1832.

Talladega (ta-luh-DEE-guh), city (1990 pop. 18,175), ⊙ Talladega co., NE central Ala., 23 mi/37 km SW of Anniston, in the Blue Ridge foothills. There are significant marble and limestone quarries. Textiles, furniture, industrial rubber, and metal prods. are the chief mfg. In Nov. 1813, Andrew Jackson defeated a force of Creeks at this Native Amer. border town. The city is the seat of Talladega Col. and also home of the Ala. Inst. for the Deaf and Blind. Many antebellum homes remain. The Talladega Superspeedway N of town hosts 2 professional auto races each year; the Winston 500 in May and the Diehard 500 in July. Inc. 1835.

Talladega Mountains (ta-luh-DEE-guh), E central Ala., low-lying range in Clay and Talladega cos., E of Birmingham. Rise to 2,407 ft/734 m in Cheaha Mt., highest point in state. Occupies part of Talladega Natl. Forest.

Talladega Springs (ta-luh-DEE-guh), town, Talladega co., central Ala., on Coosa R. and 30 mi/48 km SW of Talladega.

Tallahala Creek (tal-uh-HAL-uh), c.95 mi/153 km long, SE Miss.; rises in N Jasper co.; flows generally S, past Laurel, to Leaf R. 3 mi/4.8 km WNW of New Augusta.

Tallahassee (tal-la-HASS-see), city (□ 64 sq mi/166 sq km; 1990 pop. 124,773), ☉ Fla. and Leon co., NW Fla.; 30°27′N 84°16′W. It is a wholesale trade and distribution center for the surrounding lumber, livestock, and agr. area. The state govt., Fla. State Univ., Fla. Agr. and Mechanical Univ., and a community col. are major sources of employment. Mfg. (lumber and wood prods., food processing). A fast-growing city, marked by a pop. increase of 53% bet. 1980 and 1990. Inc. 1825.

Tallahatchie (tal-uh-HACH-ee), county (□ 652 sq mi/1,689 sq km; 1990 pop. 15,210), NW central Miss.; ☉ Sumner and Charleston; 33°57′N 90°10′W. Drained by Tallahatchie R. (forms part of S boundary). Agr. (cotton, corn, soybeans, rice, sorghum, wheat; cattle; timber). Formed 1833.

Tallahatchie River (tal-uh-HACH-ee), 230 mi/370 km long, N Miss.; rises in S Tippah co.; flows SW and S past New Albany, through Sardis L. reservoir past Batesville and to E of Sumner, joins Yalobusha R. 2 mi/3.2 km N of Greenwood to form the Yazoo R. Receives Yocona R. from E 16 mi/26 km SW of Batesville, and Coldwater R. from N 3 mi/4.8 km W of mouth of Yocona. Sometimes called Little Tallahatchie R. above Yocona R.

Tallapoosa (tah-luh-POO-suh), county (□ 766 sq mi/1,984 sq km; 1990 pop. 38,826), E Ala.; ☉ Dadeville. Piedmont region drained by Tallapoosa R. and Martin L. Cotton; livestock; timber; textiles. Formed 1832.

Tallapoosa, town (1990 pop. 2,805), Haralson co., NW Ga., 17 mi/27 km NW of Carrollton, near Ala. state line; 33°45′N 85°17′W. Mfg. of rubber prods., clothing, wooden furniture. Settled c.1856; inc. 1860.

Tallapoosa (tal-uh-POO-suh), river, 268 mi/431 km long, Ga. and Ala.; rises in NW Ga.; flows SW through E Ala., joining the Coosa R. near Montgomery, Ala., to form the Alabama R.; 33°46′N 84°57′W. Martin, Thurlow, and Yates dams provide hydroelectric power, flood control, and recreation. Martin Dam impounds L. Martin, with an area of 63 sq mi/163 sq km.

Tallapoosa City (tah-luh-POO-suh), uninc. area, Tallapoosa co., E Ala.

Tallassee, city (1990 pop. 5,112), Elmore and Tallapoosa cos., E central Ala., on Tallapoosa R. (dammed for power here by Thurlow Dam), and 25 mi/40 km SSW of Dadeville. Mfg. (clothes, cotton yarn and fabrics, water meters, boxes, aerospace parts). Site of Tukabatchee (Creek Indian town) is just S; site of only Confederate Armory to survive the Civil War.

Tallaweka (ta-luh-WEE-kuh), uninc. town, Elmore co., E central Ala.

Talleyville, uninc. town (1990 est. pop. 6,346), New Castle co., N Del., 6 mi/9.7 km N of downtown Wilimington; 39°48′N 75°33′W. Suburb of Wilimington. Site of Brandywine Col. and Widener Univ. School of Law.

Tallgrass Prairie Preserve, refuge (□ 58 sq mi/150 sq km), Osage co., N Okla. Hqs. bldg. is c.10 mi/16 km N of Pawhuska. Owned by Nature Conservancy and open to the public via county roads. Goal is for the 37,000-acre/14,974-ha preserve to become a functioning prairie ecosystem. Over 500 species of plants present. A herd of Bison roams the preserve. Controlled burns are conducted to mimic presettlement prairie fires.

Tallmadge, city (1990 pop. 14,870), Summit co., NE Ohio, an industrial suburb E of Akron; 41°06′N 81°25′W. Settled 1807, inc. 1950. Its historic architecture includes a 19th-century Congregational church near the city's center.

Tallman Mountain State Park (□ c.1 sq mi/2.6 sq km), Rockland co., SE N.Y., on bluff above W bank of the Hudson R., SE of Piermont; 41°02′N 73°55′W. Recreational area (swimming, sports, picnicking); part of Palisades Interstate Park.

Tallula (ta-LUE-lah), village (1990 pop. 598), Menard co., central Ill., 17 mi/27 km WNW of Springfield; 39°57′N 89°56′W. In agr. area.

Tallulah (tuh-LOO-luh), city (1990 pop. 8,526), ☉ Madison parish, NE La., 19 mi/31 km WNW of Vicksburg (Miss.); RR junction; 32°25′N 91°11′W. In rich lowland cotton-producing area; corn, rice, soybeans, crawfish; mfg. (food prods., uniforms). Has U.S. agr. experiment station. Oxbow lakes (fishing, camping), formed by the Mississippi, are nearby. Mississippi R. port facilities, 5 mi/8 km NE. Tensas River Natl. Wildlife Refuge to SW.

Tallulah Falls (tuh-LOO-luh), town (1990 pop. 147), Rabun and Habersham cos., extreme NE Ga., at falls of Tallulah R., and 9 mi/14.5 km S of Clayton; 34°43′N 83°23′W. The 3-mi/4.8-km-long Tallulah Gorge provided a setting for tourism development from the 1930s to the 1950s.

Tallulah Park (tuh-LOO-luh), town, Habersham co., NE Ga., on Tallulah R. 11 mi/18 km S of Clayton; 34°42′N 83°23′W.

Tallulah River (tuh-LOO-luh), c.40 mi/64 km long, extreme NE Ga.; rises on Wine Spring Bald just across N.C. state line; flows S and E through a deep gorge to join Chattooga R. at S.C. state line, 3 mi/4.8 km SE of Tallulah Falls, forming Tugaloo R.; 35°02′N 83°02′W. Contains 6 power dams forming reservoirs, including lakes Burton and Rabun.

Talmage 1 (TAL-mij), village, Dickinson co., central Kansas, 8 mi/12.9 km NNW of Abilene. Agr. area (wheat, cattle); mfg. (transformers). **2** (TAL-mej), village (1990 pop. 246), Otoe co., SE Nebr., 13 mi/21 km SW of Nebraska City and on Little Nemaha R; 40°31′N 96°1′W.

Talmage (TAL-mij), township, Washington co., E Maine, 30 mi/48 km NW of Calais. Sometimes spelled Talmadge.

Talmo (TAL-mo), village (1990 pop. 189), Jackson co., NE central Ga., 10 mi/16 km SE of Gainesville; 34°11′N 83°43′W. Mfg. (tools) and poultry processing.

Taloga (tuh-LO-guh), village (1990 pop. 415), ☉ Dewey co., W Okla., on Canadian R. and 37 mi/60 km SE of Woodward; 36°02′N 98°57′W. Elev. 1,709 ft/521 m. In livestock-raising and agr. area. Oil and natural gas deposits.

Talpa, uninc. village (1990 pop. 127), Coleman co., central Texas, 17 mi/27 km W of Coleman. In agr. area. Hords Creek L. to NE.

Talpa de Allende (TAHL-pah de ai-EN-de), town (1990 pop. 6,117), Jalisco, central Mexico, in coastal ranges, 50 mi/80 km WSW of Ameca; 20°22′N 104°58′W. Banana-growing center; sugarcane, cotton, rice, tobacco. Gold, silver, lead, copper, and zinc mining.

Talquin, Lake, reservoir (□ 25 sq mi/65 sq km), Gadsden and Leon cos., NW Fla., in the panhandle, on Ochlockonee R., 25 mi/40 km W of Tallahassee; 30°23′N 84°39′W. Max. capacity 150,000 acre-ft. Formed by Jackson Bluff Dam (22 ft/7 m high), built (1928) for power generation. Appalachicola Natl. Forest just S; Lake Talquin Recreational Area near dam.

Taltson River (TOL-suhn), abandoned trading post, S Mackenzie dist., N.W.T., Canada, on S shore of Great Slave L., at mouth of small Taltson R., 35 mi/56 km ENE of Fort Resolution; 61°23′N 112°45′W.

Tama, county (□ 722 sq mi/1,870 sq km; 1990 pop. 17,419), central Iowa; ☉ Toledo; 42°04′N 92°31′W. Prairie agr. area (hogs, cattle, poultry, corn, oats, soybeans) drained by Iowa R. and Wolf Creek. State parks. Mesquakie Indian Settlement W of Tama. Formed 1843.

Tama, city (1990 pop. 2,697), Tama co., central Iowa, on Iowa R. and 2 mi/3.2 km S of Toledo; 41°57′N 92°34′W. RR junction (spur to Toledo). Mfg. (paperboard and packaging materials; meat processing). Mesquakie Indian Settlement to W. Plotted 1862, inc. 1869.

Tamaha (TAH-mah-hah), village (1990 pop. 188), Haskell co., E Okla., on Robert S. Kerr Reservoir (Arkansas

R.), 33 mi/53 km SE of Muskogee; 35°24′N 95°00′W. Sequoyah Natl. Wildlife Refuge to N, on L. Kerr. Recreation.

Tamalín (tah-mah-LEEN), town (1990 pop. 4,180), Veracruz, E Mexico, in Sierra Madre Oriental foothills, 39 mi/63 km NW of Túxpan de Rodríguez Cano; 21°21′N 97°48′W. Cereals, sugarcane, coffee, tobacco, fruit.

Tamalpais, Mount, peak (2,572 ft/784 m), Marin co., W Calif., 12 mi/19 km NNW of downtown San Francisco, across the Golden Gate from San Francisco. The mt. is a game preserve and a resort. The city of Mill Valley and Muir Woods Natl. Monument, a redwood grove, lie at its base.

Tamalpais Valley, uninc. town (1990 pop. 5,761), Marin co., W Calif., residential suburb 8 mi/12.9 km NNW of downtown San Francisco. Tamalpais Game Refuge, in Richardson Bay, to E; Muir Woods Natl. Monument and Mt. Tamalpais State Park to NW. Statistically reported as Tamalpais Valley–Homestead Valley; Homestead Valley 2 mi/3.2 km to N.

Tamaqua (tah-MAH-kwah), borough (1990 pop. 7,943), Schuylkill co., E Pa., on Little Schuylkill R., 15 mi/24 km NE of Pottsville; 40°48′N 75°55′W. Agr. (dairying); mfg. (industrial gases and chemicals, powdered metals, food prods., explosives, asphalt, thermal wear, aluminum compounds; anthracite coal). Tamaqua L. and State Park to NW. Settled 1799, laid out 1829, inc. 1832.

Tamarac, city (□ 11 sq mi/28 sq km; 1990 pop. 44,822), Broward co., SE Fla., 15 mi/24 km NW of Fort Lauderdale; 26°11′N 80°15′W. Mfg. includes commercial printing, apparel, landscape equip., trailers, optical glass.

Tamarac River (TA-muh-rak), c.45 mi/72 km long, NW Minn.; rises in N Marshall co., c.30 mi/48 km NNW of Thief River Falls; flows generally W to Red R., 22 mi/35 km SSW of Hallock; 48°30′N 96°27′W.

Tamarack (TA-muh-rak), village (1990 pop. 53), Aitkin co., E Minn., c.45 mi/72 km W of Duluth near Sandy R., in lake resort region; 46°38′N 93°07′W. Numerous lakes in regions. Savanna State Forest to N.

Tamarindo (tah-mah-REEN-do), town (1990 pop. 138), ☉ Carrillo Puerto Minicipio, Veracruz, Mexico, 6 mi/10 km SW of Adalberto Tejeda. Elev. 325 ft/100 m. Rolling terrain at foot of the Sierra Madre, water available from the Río Blanco. Hot climate. Agr. (corn, beans, sugarcane, sesame, rice, fruits); wood, and cattle. Poor roads. Also called El Tamarindo.

Tamaroa (tam-ah-ROW-ah), village (1990 pop. 780), Perry co., SW Ill., 9 mi/14.5 km ENE of Pickneyville; 38°08′N 89°13′W. In bituminous-coal-mining and agr. area.

Tamasopo (tah-mah-SO-po), town (1990 pop. 3,403), San Luis Potosí, N central Mexico, 38 mi/61 km E of Río Verde; 21°55′N 99°24′W. Grain, cotton, fruit; stock.

Tamaulipas (tah-mah-oo-LEE-pahs), state (□ 30,734 sq mi/79,601 sq km; 1990 pop. 2,249,581), NE Mexico, on the Gulf of Mexico; ☉ Ciudad Victoria; 22°13′N 97°08′W. The central and W parts of the state are in the mts. of the Sierra Madre Oriental. In the N and S are arable plains, particularly in the long panhandle beginning at Nuevo Laredo and following the Rio Grande opposite Texas to Matamoros. The coast is low, sandy, fringed with lagoons, and (except for Matamoros and Tampico) lightly populated, mainly by fishermen and resorts. The extreme SW mining area borders on the vast semiarid basins of central Mexico. Except in the elevated interior, the climate is hot and humid. The state's greatest source of wealth is petroleum and its by-products, but agr. and cattle raising are also important. Tamaulipas is a leading natl. producer of sugarcane and cotton; cereals, tobacco, and corn are other major crops. Maquiladoras, foreign-owned mfg. plants that finish goods for U.S. export, have rapidly grown throughout the state. The Spanish 1st explored the territory in 1519, and after conquering the Tamaulipans, they abandoned the area. Eur. colonization began in 1747; independence was won from Spain in 1821. Franciscan missions flourished in the 18th cent.

Tamayo (tah-MAH-yo), town (1993 pop. 10,890), Bahoruco prov., SW Dominican Republic, on Yaque del

Sur R. (Barahona prov. line), 14 mi/23 km NW of Barahona.

Tamazula, Mexico: see TAMAZULA DE VICTORIA.

Tamazula de Gordiano (tah-mah-SOO-lah de gor-dee-AH-no), city (1990 pop. 16,239) and township, Jalisco, central Mexico, on interior plateau, 16 mi/26 km ESE of Ciudad Guzmán on Mexico Highway 110; 19°38′N 103°12′W. Agr. center (corn, chickpeas, alfalfa, fruit, sugarcane, tobacco, livestock).

Tamazula de Victoria (tah-mah-SOO-lah de veek-to-REE-ah), town (1990 pop. 1,012), ⊙ Tamazula municipio (1990 pop. 21,842), Durango, N Mexico, at W foot of Sierra Madre Occidental, near Sinaloa border, on affluent of Culiacán R. and 30 mi/48 km ENE of Culiacán Rosales; 24°55′N 106°58′W. Silver, gold, copper mining.

Tamazulapam del Espíritu Santo (tah-mah-ZOO-lah-pahm del es-PEE-ree-too SAHN-to), town (1990 pop. 1,784), in E central Oaxaca, Mexico, 26 mi/42 km ENE of San Pablo Villa de Mitla. Elev. 6,168 ft/1,880 m. A Mixe-speaking community. Mountainous region with temperate climate. Agr. (corn, beans, wheat, fruits), woods, mezcal processing and livestock. Tapestry textiles.

Tamazulapan del Progreso, Mexico: see VILLA DE TAMAZULAPAN DEL PROGRESO.

Tamazunchale (tah-mah-zoon-CHAH-le), city (1990 pop. 19,223) and township, San Luis Potosí, E Mexico, in fertile Gulf plain on Moctezuma R., on Inter-Amer. Highway 85 and 70 mi/113 km SW of Pánuco; 21°18′N 98°46′W. Agr. center (tobacco, sugarcane, coffee, cereals, fruit; livestock). Poxtara resort is 2 mi/3.2 km from town.

Tamboril (TAHM-bo-reel), town (1993 pop. 14,551), 7 mi/11km NE of Santiago de los Caballeros, Santiago Prov., N Dominican Republic; 19°29′N 70°36′W. Town in Cibao valley, a rich agr. area (coffee, rice, bananas, tabacco). Sometimes called Peña.

Tamesí River (tah-me-SEE), c.250 mi/402 km long, in Tamaulipas, NE Mexico; rises in Sierra Madre Oriental W of Ciudad Victoria; flows SE and E, past Xicoténcatl and along Tamaulipas-Veracruz border, to Gulf lagoons (linked with Pánuco R.) NW of Tampico. Called Guayalejo R. in upper course.

Tamiahua (rahm-ee-AH-wah), town (1990 pop. 5,914), Veracruz, E Mexico, at S end of Tamiahua Lagoon, 23 mi/37 km N of Túxpam de Rodríguez Cano; 21°16′N 97°26′W. Agr. center (corn, sugarcane, fruit).

Tamiahua Lagoon (tahm-ee-AH-wah), on Gulf coast of Veracruz, E Mexico, extends 65 mi/105 km SSE from SE of Tampico to Tamiahua, where narrow channel opens on ocean; c.12 mi/19 km wide. Contains number of large isls. Navigable for small craft.

Tamiami Trail (tammy-AMMY), name given in the 1920s to the 250 mi/402 km segment of U.S. 41 that connects Tampa on the W central coast of Fla. to Miami at the state's SE corner. Was the 1st E-W highway to cross Big Cypress Natl. Reserve and the Everglades directly from the Gulf of Mexico coast to the Atlantic Ocean. Today the name mainly refers to the 2-lane, trans-Everglades section of U.S. 41 that runs 85 mi/137 km across this wilderness from just E of Naples to metropolitan Maimi's W edge. A scenic route that attracts millions of tourists annually, it also provides the only access to the Shark Valley portion of Everglades Natl. Park.

Tamms, village (1990 pop. 748), Alexander co., extreme S Ill., 16 mi/26 km NNW of Cairo; 37°14′N 89°16′W. In agr. area.

Tamora, village (1990 pop. 51), Seward co., SE Nebr., 7 mi/11.3 km W of Seward; 40°53′N 97°13′W.

Tampa (TAM-puh), city (□ 167 sq mi/433 sq km; 1990 pop. 280,015), ⊙ Hillsborough co., W central Fla.; 27°57′N 82°28′W. A port of entry with a major harbor on Tampa Bay. The 3d-largest city in the state, Tampa has long been a shipping and mfg. hub on the Gulf Coast. It has a thriving cigar industry, breweries, and seafood and citrus-packing houses. Ybor City, a historic area, once known as "Cigar City," had the world's largest cigar factory. Area now has nighclubs, restaurants, the Ybor City State Mus., and a few remaining cigar factories. Its port is one of the largest in the U.S.,

with phosphate docks and elevators. A new wave of suburban growth after 1970 has left Tampa at the center of the burgeoning metropolitan region that encompasses St. Petersburg and Clearwater. The city extends down a peninsula, with Old Tampa Bay on the W, Tampa Bay to the S, and Hillsborough Bay on the E. MacDill Air Force Base is situated at the tip of the peninsula. Tampa is linked by 3 long bridges to Clearwater and St. Petersburg, on the Pinellas peninsula. The city is the seat of the Univ. of Tampa (a magnificent example of Moorish architecture, originally built as a huge hotel), the Univ. of Southern Fla., and a junior col. It has an internatl. airport known nationally for its efficiency. Inc. 1855.

Tampa (TAMP-uh), village (1990 pop. 113), Marion co., central Kansas, 15 mi/24 km NNW of Marion; 38°32′N 97°09′W. In grain, livestock, and oil-producing area.

Tampa Bay (TAM-puh), inlet of the Gulf of Mexico, W central Fla., separated from the Gulf by numerous small isls.; 25 mi/40 km long and 7 mi/11.3 km–12 mi/19 km wide. It receives the Hillsborough R. St. Petersburg is on the W neck, Old Tampa Bay, and Tampa is on Hillsborough Bay, the E neck. Has dredged shipping channels; spanned at its mouth by the Sunshine Skyway Bridge, which was reopened in 1987 aftar being destroyed by a barge several years earlier.

Tampacán (tahm-pah-KAHN), town (1990 pop. 1,173), San Luis Potosí, E Mexico, in fertile Gulf plain, 45 mi/72 km SSE of Ciudad Valles; 21°25′N 98°44′W. Tobacco, coffee, sugarcane; livestock.

Tampamolón Corona (tahm-po-mo-LON ko-RO-nah), city (1990 pop. 1,941) and township, San Luis Potosí, E Mexico, 33 mi/53 km SSE of Ciudad Valles. Sugarcane, tobacco, coffee, fruit; stock.

Tampico (tahm-PEE-ko), city (1990 pop. 272,690) and township, Tamaulipas state, E Mexico, on the Pánuco R., a few miles inland from the Gulf of Mexico, on Mexico Highways 70, 81, and 180; 22°13′N 97°51′W. Rivaling Veracruz as Mexico's most important seaport, Tampico is used primarily for Mexico's petroleum industry and fishing. It possesses excellent modern facilities and also serves as an export center for Tamaulipas state's other goods, including cattle, hides, sugar, and additional agr. prods. In pre-Columbian times, the Tampico area was the site of the Huastec kingdom, which later became a tributary of the Aztec Empire. Span. settlement dates back to the founding of a Franciscan mission there in the 1530s. Tampico was occupied by a U.S. force during the Mex. War and by Fr. troops in 1862, during the Fr. intervention. With the discovery of oil (c.1900) by Eng. and Amer. geologists, rapid development of petroleum industries began; before Mexico expropriated foreign-owned property, about ⅓ of Tampico's landowners were Americans. The city boomed while much of the rest of Mexico was in revolutionary turmoil. Tampico is the seat of a state univ. and an active cultural center.

Tampico (TAM-pi-coh), village (1990 pop. 833), Whiteside co., NW Ill., 17 mi/27 km SSE of Morrison; 41°37′N 89°47′W. In agr. area; ships grain. Birthplace of Ronald Reagan.

Tampico Alto (tahm-PEE-ko AHL-to) or **Tampico el Alto**, town (1990 pop. 1,955), Veracruz, E Mexico, in Gulf lowland, 8 mi/12.9 km SSE of Tampico; 22°07′N 97°48′W. Cereals, sugarcane, cattle.

Tampico Lagoon (tahm-pee-KO) (□ 200 sq mi/518 sq km), on Gulf coast of northernmost Veracruz, E Mexico, just S of Pánuco R. mouth; 22°16′N 97°50′W. Also called Puerto Viejo Lagoon for Puerto Viejo (Villa Cuauhtémoc), on NE shore.

Tams (TAMZ), uninc. village (1990 pop. 100), Raleigh co., S W.Va., 10 mi/16 km SW of Beckley. Coal-mining area.

Tamuín (tah-moo-EEN), town (1990 pop. 14,003), SE San Luis Potosí, Mexico, 16 mi/26 km E of Ciudad Valles, on Mexico Highway 70; 20°18′N 98°46′W. Hot climate. Agr. (beans, oranges), forestry, cattle. Formerly known as Guerrero and Villa de Guerrero. Here the 1st oil well for commercial production in Mexico was drilled.

Tamworth (TAM-wuhrth), town (1990 pop. 2,165), Carroll co., E N.H., at S edge of White Mts., 25 mi/40 km

NE of Laconia; 43°51′N 71°16′W. Drained by Bearcamp, Chocorua, and Wonalancet rivers. Mfg. (filtration systems for electroplating, machining); agr. (vegetables, apples, nursery crops; cattle, hogs, poultry; dairying); timber. Resort area. Includes villages of South Tamworth, mfg. (wood fuel chips, fire logs), and CHOCORUA in E. Hemenway State Forest in N; White Lake State Park in SE.

Tamworth, village, SE Ont., Canada, on Salmon R. and 30 mi/48 km NW of Kingston; 44°28′N 76°59′W. Dairying, mixed farming.

Tanacross, village (1990 pop. 106), E Alaska, on upper Tanana R. and 130 mi/209 km WSW of Dawson, on Alaska Highway; 63°24′N 143°20′W. Sometimes called Tanana Crossing.

Tanaga Island, Andreanof Isls., Aleutian Isls., SW Alaska, 5 mi/8 km W of Kanaga Isl.; 25 mi/40 km long, 3 mi/4.8 km–20 mi/32 km wide; 51°48′N 177°57′W. Rises to 6,975 ft/2,126 m on Tanaga Volcano (NW), reportedly dormant. World War II airstrip on SW shore.

Tánamo (TAH-nuh-mo), sugar-mill village, Holguín prov., E Cuba, on SW Sagua de Tánamo Bay, 20 mi/32 km E of Mayarí; 20°38′N 75°22′W. Sugar mill Frank País 6 mi/9.7 km E.

Tánamo Bay (TAH-nuh-mo), sheltered Atlantic inlet, Holguín prov., E Cuba, 20 mi/32 km E of Mayarí; 6 mi/9.7 km long, 4 mi/6.4 km wide; 20°39′N 75°20′W. Linked with ocean by narrow channel called Boca de Tánamo.

Tanana, village (1990 pop. 345), central Alaska, on N side of Yukon R., opposite mouth of Tanana R. and 135 mi/217 km WNW of Fairbanks; 65°10′N 152°05′W. Airfield. Historic meeting place for interior natives named Nuklukayet. Formerly site of Fort Gibbon, U.S. Army post.

Tanana (TAN-uh-no), river, 600 mi/966 km long, Canada; rising in W Yukon Territory near the Alaskan border; flowing NW across Alaska to the Yukon R.; navigable for small boats to Fairbanks, the largest city on the river. The Tanana valley, near Fairbanks, is central Alaska's chief farming area; grains, potatoes, and other vegetables are grown. The Tanana, explored by Rus. traders c.1860, became an important route to the Yukon goldfields in 1898. A sect. of the Alaska Highway runs parallel to the river.

Tanana Crossing, Alaska: see TANACROSS.

Tancanhuitz de Santos (tahn-kahn-WEETZ de SAHN-tos) or **Ciudad Santos**, city, San Luis Potosí, E Mexico, in E foothills of Sierra Madre Oriental, 28 mi/45 km S of Ciudad Valles. Agr. center (cotton, sugarcane, tobacco, fruit; livestock). Formerly Ciudad Santos. Also known as General Pedro Antonio Santos. Some Huastrec-speaking pop. in Municipio

Tancítaro (tahn-see-tah-ro), town (1990 pop. 3,653), Michoacán, W central Mexico, at S foot of Tancítaro volcano, 23 mi/37 km SW of Uruapan; 19°20′N 102°22′W. Sugarcane, coffee, fruit.

Tancítaro (tahn-SEE-tah-ro), volcano (12,615 ft/3,845 m), Michoacán, W Mexico, at S end of Sierra de los Tarascos, 22 mi/35 km WSW of Uruapan; 19°26′N 102°18′W. Highest peak in state. Often snowcapped. Parícutin volcano is just N.

Tancoco (tahn-KO-ko), town (1990 pop. 1,860), Veracruz, E Mexico, in Sierra Madre Oriental foothills, 33 mi/53 km NW of Túxpam de Rodríguez Cano; 21°17′N 97°47′W. Cereals, sugar, coffee, fruit. Some Huastec-speaking pop.

Tancook Island or **Great Tancook Island**, largest isl. in Mahone Bay, S N.S., Canada, 7 mi/11 km SE of Chester; 3 mi/5 km long, 1 mi/2 km wide.

Tanetze de Zaragoza (tahn-NET-zai dai zah-rah-GO-zah), town (1990 pop. 1,328), NE central Oaxaca, Mexico, 13 mi/21 km ENE of Ixtlan de Juárez; 17°40′N 96°20′W. Elev. 5,951 ft/1,814 m. Mountainous terrain. Temperate climate. Agr., cattle, and forestry.

Taney, county (□ 656 sq mi/1,699 sq km; 1990 pop. 25,561), SW Mo.; ⊙ Forsyth; 36°38′N 93°02′W. In the Ozarks; drained by White R., Ark. to S. Popular, growing resort and recreation area. Retirement communities. Livestock; cedar, pine, oak timber. Tourism. Bull Shoals, Taneycomo, and Table Rock lakes, on the White

R. Table Rock State Park and Dam SW of Hollister. Part of Mark Twain Natl. Forest in NE. Branson, long a destination for vacationers from St. Louis and Kansas City, has gained natl. recognition as a major entertainment center, rivaling Nashville, Tenn., for its country-music halls. Silver Dollar City theme park W of Branson. Formed 1837.

Taneycomo, Lake, reservoir, S Mo., in Taney co. near Forsyth, impounding the White River by Osage Beach Dam (1912). Bet. Bull Shoals reservoir to E and Table Rock L. to W. Hydroelectric power. Maximum storage capacity of 9,175 acre-ft and surface area of 2,100 acres/850 ha.

Taneytown (TAW-nee-town), city (1990 pop. 3,695), Carroll co., N Md., 22 mi/35 km NE of Frederick; 39°40′N 77°10′W. In agr. area; mfg. (clothing, rubber rainwear); cannery. Nearby are co. fairgrounds, amusement park, and the birthplace of Francis Scott Key. The town was laid out by Frederick Taney in 1740, whose descendant, Roger B. Taney, as chief justice of the Supreme Court (1836–1864) wrote the Dred Scott decision denying Negro slaves legal rights. The Taneytown grandfather clocks, made here in the late 1700s and early 1800s, are now collectors' items. Gen. George C. Meade had his hq. 1 mi/1.6 km N of town during the battle of Gettysburg, and the Lutheran Church steeple was used for signalling with flags and flares. Inc. as city 1931.

Taneyville, town (1990 pop. 279), Taney co., S Mo., in the Ozarks, near White R., 5 mi/8 km NE of Forsyth; 36°44′N 93°01′W.

Tangamandapio, Mexico: see SANTIAGO TANGAMANDAPIO.

Tangancícuaro de Arista (tahn-gahn-SEE-kwah-ro de ah-REES-tah), town (1990 pop. 16,091), ⊙ Tangancícuaro municipio, Michoacán, central Mexico, on central plateau, 10 mi/16 km SE of Zamora on Mexico Highway 15; 19°54′N 102°08′W. Agr. center (cereals, sugarcane, tobacco, fruit; livestock).

Tangelo Park (TAN-jeh-lo), town (1990 pop. 2,663), Orange co., central Fla., 6 mi/9.7 km SW of Orlando; 28°27′N 81°27′W.

Tangent (TAN-jent), village (1990 pop. 556), Linn co., W Oregon, 5 mi/8 km S of Albany, near Calapooia R. Dairying, poultry, livestock, fruit, berries, vegetables, grain.

Tangier, town (1990 pop. 659), Accomack co., E Va., on Tangier Isl. (c.5 mi/8 km long, 1.5 mi/2.4 km wide) in Chesapeake Bay, 14 mi/23 km SW of Crisfield, Md. (ferry connections to Onancock and Fleeton, Va., and Crisfield, Md.); 37°49′N 75°59′W. Fish, crabs, oysters; tourism. Airfield.

Tangier (tan-JEER), village, S N.S., Canada, at head of Tangier Harbour of the Atlantic, 50 mi/80 km ENE of Halifax; 44°48′N 62°42′W. Lumbering, fishing port; in gold-mining region.

Tangier, island, Accomack co., E Va., in S Chesapeake Bay, 20 mi/32 km WNW of Accomac. Village of Tangier on narrow neck near center of isl. Capt. John Smith 1st visited in 1608, settlers arrived from Cornwall, England (1620). Isolated from the mainland, the people of Tangier developed a distinct culture. Fishing industry threatened by overfishing and pollution of bay. Intracoastal Waterway passes through center of bay to W.

Tangier Sound, protected passage of Chesapeake Bay, off the E shore of Md. and Va.; c.30 mi/48 km long, 3 mi/4.8 km–7 mi/11.3 km wide, it extends from Watts Isl. (S) to Fishing Bay (N), and is connected (NW) with the bay by Hooper Strait. On W, marsh isls. (among them Tangier, Smith, South Marsh, Bloodsworth) border it. In SE, it is separated from Pocomoke Sound (partly in Va.) by marsh isls. and shoals.

Tangipahoa (TAN-ji-puh-HO-uh), parish (□ 803 sq mi/2,080 sq km; 1990 pop. 85,709), SE La.; ⊙ Amite; 30°44′N, 90°31′W. Bounded E partly by Tchefuncte R., S by L. Maurepas, Pass Manchac, and L. Pontchartrain, N by Miss. state line, W partly by Natalbany R.; drained by Tangipahoa R. Agr. (strawberries, peppers, home gardens, nursery crops, sweet potatoes, vegetables, cattle, poultry, horses, rabbits; dairying), catfish, shrimp, alligators. Logging; clay. Resorts; hunting, fishing. Named from Indian word meaning ear of corn. Formed 1869. One of the Florida Parishes of SE La., former Br. colony of W Florida. North Pass roughly parallels Pass Manchac, N of it. Joyce State Wildlife Area in S; Sandy Hollow State Wildlife Area in N. Zemurray Gardens.

Tangipahoa (TAN-ji-puh-HO-uh), village (1990 pop. 569), Tangipahoa parish, SE La., on Tangipahoa R. and 38 mi/61 km N of Ponchatoula; 30°53′N 90°31′W. In agr. area (vegetables, sweet potatoes; dairying), catfish. Sandy Hollow State Wildlife Area to SE.

Tangipahoa River (tan-juh-puh-HO-uh), c.110 mi/177 km long, in Miss. and La.; rises NW of McComb in SW Miss.; flows generally S, through Percy Quin Reservoir, W of McComb, past Osyka, Miss., into SE La., past Tangipahoa and Amite, to L. Pontchartrain.

Tanglewood, Mass.: see LENOX.

Tanhuato de Guerrero (tah-WAH-to de ge-RE-ro), town (1990 pop. 6,420), ⊙ Tanhuato municipio, Michoacán, central Mexico, on central plateau, 19 mi/31 km WSW of La Piedad de Cabados on Mexico Highway 110; 20°17′N 102°20′W. Agr. center (cereals, vegetables, livestock).

Taniche (tah-NEE-che), town (1990 pop. 1,063), S Oaxaca, Mexico, in Ejutla judicial dist., 1.2 mi/2 km W of Ejutla de Crespo in Valle Grande arm of Oaxaca valley; 16°32′N 96°45′W. Elev. 4,593 ft/1,400 m. Small farming.

Taninul, Mexico: see CIUDAD VALLES.

Tanlajás (tahn-lah-HAHS), town (1990 pop. 958), San Luis Potosí, E Mexico, 24 mi/39 km SSE of Ciudad Valles; 21°40′N 98°52′W. Cotton, sugarcane, coffee, fruit; livestock. Some Huastrec-speaking pop.

Tannersville, resort village (□ 1 sq mi/2.6 sq km; 1990 pop. 465), Greene co., SE N.Y., in the Catskills, 14 mi/23 km W of Catskill; 42°11′N 74°07′W.

Tanque Verde (TAN-cuh ver-DEE), uninc. town (1990 pop. 850), Pinal co., S central Ariz., suburb 12 mi/19 km ENE of downtown Tucson, on Tanque Verde Creek. Agr. (sheep, cattle, poultry). Part of Suguaro Natl. Monument to SE; part of Coronado Natl. Forest to E. Spencer Canyon Ski Area to N, at Mt. Lemmon.

Tanquián de Escobedo (tahn-kee-AHN de es-ko-BE-do), town (1990 pop. 8,303), San Luis Potosí, E Mexico, in fertile Gulf plain, on Moctezuma R. and 45 mi/72 km SW of Pánuco; 21°38′N 98°40′W. Coffee, tobacco, sugarcane, fruit; livestock.

Tantalus, Mount, hill (2,013 ft/614 m), S Oahu isl., Honolulu co, Hawaii, 3 mi/4.8 km NE of Honolulu; 21°20′N 157°49′W. Steep, scenic drive to summit; in Honolulu Forest Reserve.

Tantima (tahn-TEE-mah), town (1990 pop. 1,070), Veracruz, E Mexico, in Sierra Madre Oriental foothills, 38 mi/61 km NW of Túxpam de Rodríguez Cano; 21°20′N 97°50′W. Cereals, fruit. Some Huastrec-speaking pop.

Tantoyuca (tahn-to-YOO-kah), city (1990 pop. 22,567) and township, Veracruz, E Mexico, in E foothills of Sierra Madre Oriental, 60 mi/97 km NW of Túxpam de Rodríguez Cano; 21°21′N 98°12′W. Agr. center (cereals, coffee, sugarcane, tobacco, fruit). Some Huastec-speaking pop.

Tununak, Inuit village (1990 pop. 316), W Alaska, on W Nelson Isl., on Bering Sea; 60°34′N 165°20′W. Also spelled Tununak.

Taopi (tai-YO-pee), village (1990 pop. 83), Mower co., SE Minn., near Iowa state line, 19 mi/31 km ESE of Austin; 43°33′N 92°38′W. Agr. (corn, oats, livestock, dairying, and poultry).

Taos (TOUS), county (□ 2,204 sq mi/5,708 sq km; 1990 pop. 23,118), N N.Mex.; ⊙ Taos; 36°34′N 105°37′W. Grain; cattle- and sheep-grazing area; watered by Rio Grande; borders on Colo. (N) Sangre de Cristo Mts. extend N-S, rising to 13,161 ft/4,011 m in Wheeler Peak (13,161 ft/4,011 m) in E, highest point in N.Mex. Parts of Carson Natl. Forest in ESE and W; Pueblo Indian areas at Taos and in S. Formed 1852. San Lorenzo Pueblo (Picuris) in S; Pueblo de Taos Indian Reservation in E center, includes town of Taos and Taos Pueblo; Kit Carson State Park in S center near Taos; Orilla Verde Natl. Recreation Area in SW; Wild Rivers Natl. Recreation Area and Rio Grande Gorge on Rio Grande, in center; ski areas in NE.

Taos (TOUS), town (1990 pop. 4,065); ⊙ Taos co., N N.Mex., 70 mi/113 km NNe of Santa Fe, in Pueblo de Taos Indian Reservation, bet. the Rio Grande and the Sangre de Cristo Mts.; 36°23′N 105°34′W. Elev. 7,000 ft/2,134 m. Founded c.1615, inc. 1934. Mfg. (sheepskin clothing, Indian drums, moccasins, printing and publishing, auto parts). In an area of pueblos, adobes, and scenic mt. beauty, Taos developed as an art colony (principally after 1898) and attracted many painters and writers, notably John Marin and D. H. Lawrence. Artist organizations and galleries include the Harwood Foundation (gallery, studios, and school; owned by the Univ. of N.Mex.). The town was founded in the early 17th cent. by Spaniards. For many years, Taos was an important Native Amer. and Span. trading point. It was the center of the Pueblo revolt (1680) and of a Native Amer. uprising (1847). Kit Carson's grave and preserved house (1825) are there. The city is also the hq. for Carson Natl. Forest. Nearby are recreational facilities and regularly held Native Amer. festivals. Vietnam Veterans' Chapel 14 mi/23 km E at Palo Flechado Pass (9,101 ft/2,774 m); Rio Grande Gorge and Wild Rivers Natl. Recreation Area to NW; parts of Carson Natl. Forest to N and SE; Taos Ski Valley to NE; Taos Pueblo to NE.

Taos (TOUS), pueblo (□ 15 sq mi/39 sq km; 1990 pop. 1,187), Taos co., N N.Mex., 2 mi/3.2 km NE of Taos, in Pueblo de Taos Indian Reservation (1990 pop. 4,065); 36°28′N 105°33′W. The inhabitants, Pueblo of the Tanoan linguistic family, grow grain and raise livestock. In the early 17th cent., Taos became the seat of the Span. mission of San Geronimo; in the Pueblo revolt of 1680, led by Popé, the mission was destroyed. A 2d revolt occurred in 1847. The anc. Pueblo communal dwellings in Taos are considered architectural masterpieces.

Tapachula (tah-pah-CHOO-lah), city (1990 pop. 138,858) and township, Chiapas state, SE Mexico, at the foot of the Chiapas highlands and near the Guatemala border on Mexico Highway 200; 14°54′N 92°15′W. It is the commercial center of a coffee-growing region and an important transportation link bet. Mexico and Central Amer. Ceramics and leather goods are produced by local artisans.

Tapalapa (tah-pah-LAH-pah), town (1990 pop. 1,285), Chiapas, S Mexico, in spur of Sierra Madre, 29 mi/47 km N of Tuxtla Gutiérrez; 17°10′N 93°06′W. Corn, fruit. In Zoque-speaking area.

Tapalpa (tah-PAHL-pah), town (1990 pop. 4,471), Jalisco, W Mexico, 25 mi/40 km NW of Ciudad Guzmán; 20°15′N 103°50′W. Grain, alfalfa, fruit, vegetables.

Tapaste (tah-PAH-stai), town, La Habana prov., W Cuba, at S foot of Escaleras de Jaruco hills, near Natl. Highway and 15 mi/24 km ESE of Havana; 23°03′N 82°09′W. Sugarcane; livestock. Outside the town are the spectacular El Cura Caverns.

Tapilula (tah-pee-LOO-lah), town (1990 pop. 5,129), Chiapas, S Mexico, in spur of Sierra Madre, 33 mi/53 km NNE of Tuxtla Gutiérrez on Mexico Highway 195; 17°14′N 93°02′W. Corn, sugarcane, tobacco, fruit. In Zoque-speaking area.

Tapoco (TAP-uh-ko), uninc. village, Graham co., W N.C., 11 mi/18 km NW of Robbinsville and 37 mi/60 km S of Knoxville, Tenn., near Tenn. state line, on Little Tennessee R. at mouth of Cheoah R. Cheoah Dam (hydroelectric plant) is just E; Santertlah Dam and Lake to SE. Great Smoky Mts. Natl. Park to NE; Nantahala Natl. Forest to SW and S, including Joyce Kilmer Memorial Forest, to S; Cherokee Natl. Forest (Tenn.) to W.

Tappahannock (tap-uh-HAN-uk), town (1990 pop. 1,550), ⊙ Essex co., E Va., 40 mi/64 km NE of Richmond, on Rappahannock R. (bridged); 37°55′N 76°52′W. Mfg. (lumber, concrete, brake shoes, laser printer parts, fabrics, cannery); agr. (grain, soybeans; cattle). Municipal Airport to W. Founded 1680 as a port; inc. 1914.

Tappan, suburban village (□ 2 sq mi/5.2 sq km; 1990 pop. 6,867), Rockland co., SE N.Y., at N.J. border, 6 mi/9.7 km SSW of Nyack; 41°01′N 73°57′W. De Wint Mansion was Washington's hq. in 1780 and 1783. John André, Br. spy in the Amer. Revolution, was tried and hanged here. Pop. figure includes Sparkill.

Tappan Lake, reservoir (☐ 4 sq mi/10.4 sq km), Harrison co., E central Ohio, on Little Stillwater Creek, 15 mi/24 km SE of New Philadelphia; 40°22′N 81°14′W. Max. capacity 61,660 acre-ft. Formed by Tappan Dam (52 ft/16 m high), built (1936) by Army Corps of Engineers for flood control; also used for recreation and as a fish and wildlife pond.

Tappan Zee, section of the Hudson R., c.10 mi/16 km long, SE N.Y.; widening of r. bet. Irvington (S) and Croton Point (N); 2 mi/3.2 km–3 mi/4.8 km wide bet. Nyack and Tarrytown, spanned by Tappan Zee Bridge.

Tappen, village (1990 pop. 239), Kidder co., central N.Dak., 14 mi/23 km E of Steele; 46°52′N 99°37′W. L. George Natl. Wildlife Refuge and Streeter Memorial State Park to S; Camp Grassick and Slade Natl. Wildlife Refuge to SW; several lakes in area.

Tar Heel, village (1990 pop. 115), Bladen co., SE N.C., 15 mi/24 km NE of Lumberton, on Cape Fear R.; 34°43′N 78°47′W. Tobacco, peanuts, cotton, grain; livestock.

Tar River, 217 mi/349 km long, NE N.C.; rises in E Person co. E of Roxboro, 7 mi/11.3 km E of Roxboro; flows generally SE, past Louisburg, Rocky Mount, Tarboro, Greenville (head of navigation), and Washington to Pamlico R. estuary, arm of Pamlico Sound.

Tara Hills, uninc. town (1990 pop. 4,998), Contra Cost co., W Calif., residential suburb 12 mi/19 km N of downtown Oakland and 4 mi/6.4 km N of Richmond, on San Pablo Bay; 38°00′N 122°19′W.

Tarandacuao (tah-rahn-dah-KWAH-o), city (1990 pop. 6,921) and township, Guanajuato, central Mexico, on Lerma R. and 15 mi/24 km E of Acámbaro; 20°03′N 100°04′W. Cereals, sugarcane, vegetables; livestock.

Tarará (tah-rah-RUH), town, Ciudad de la Habana province, NW Cuba; 23°12′N 82°12′W. Prerevolutionary fishing town and 2d-home beach community, currently a suburban town in metropolitan Havana. Seaside camp for volunteer youth groups such as Havana. Cubaños *pioneros* and a medical camp for children seeking care from Chernobyl nuclear accident in former Soviet Union.

Tarascos, Sierra de los (tah-RAHS-kos, see-E-rah dai los), mountain range in W Michoacán, W Mexico, W and NW of Uruapan. Forms part of E-W volcanic belt of central Mexico; c.25 mi/40 km long NE-SW. Volcano PARICUTÍN is in S.

Tarboro, city (1990 pop. 11,037), ⊙ Edgecombe co., E central N.C., 15 mi/24 km E of Rocky Mount, on Tar R.; 35°54′N 77°33′W. Agr. area (livestock; tobacco, cotton, peanuts). Mfg. (telecommunications cable, cordless power tools, printing and publishing, children's vehicles, lumber prods., furniture, apparel and industrial textiles, fertilizers, food prods.). Edgecombe Community Col. Tarboro Historic Dist. Natl. Recreation Trail. Hobson Pittman Memorial Art Gal. Laid out 1760; inc. 1775.

Tarentum (TER-en-tuhm), borough (1990 pop. 5,674), Allegheny co., W central Pa., industrial suburb, 17 mi/27 km NE of Pittsburgh, on Allegheny R. (bridged); 40°36′N 79°45′W. Mfg. (fabricated metal prods., concrete, furniture, printing); bituminous coal. Penn Airport to W. Deer L. Regional Park to NW. On site of Indian village, laid out 1829, inc. 1842.

Taretan (tah-RE-tahn), town (1990 pop. 6,134) Michoacán, central Mexico, 11 mi/18 km SE of Uruapan on RR; 19°20′N 101°55′W. Sugarcane, coffee.

Targhee Pass (TAHR-gee) (7,072 ft/2,156 m), on Continental Divide, SW Mont. and E Idaho, 8 mi/12.9 km W of West Yellowstone, Mont. just S of Hebgen L. and W of Yellowstone Natl. Park. Used (1877) by Chief Joseph and Nez Percé Indians in retreat from U.S. troops. U.S. Highway 20 passes through.

Tariffville, Conn.: see SIMSBURY.

Tarímbaro (tah-REEM-bah-ro), town (1990 pop. 4,556), Michoacán, central Mexico, 6 mi/9.7 km N of Morelia; 19°47′N 101°08′W. Elev. 5,249 ft/1,600 m. Cereals, fruit, livestock.

Tarimoro (tah-ree-MO-ro), city (1990 pop. 11,856) and township, Guanajuato, central Mexico, on central plateau, 30 mi/48 km SW of Querétaro. Agr. center (grain, alfalfa, sugarcane, fruit, vegetables; livestock).

Tarkio, city (1990 pop. 2,243), Atchison co., extreme NW Mo., on Tarkio R., 55 mi/89 km NW of St. Joseph; 40°26′N 95°22′W. Corn, wheat; cattle, hogs. Laid out 1880.

Tarkio River, c.130 mi/209 km long, in SW Iowa and NW Mo.; rises in Montgomery co., Iowa; flows generally S to the Missouri 33 mi/53 km NW of St. Joseph. Flooding occurred in 1993.

Tarlton, village (1990 pop. 315), Pickaway co., S central Ohio, 9 mi/14 km ESE of Circleville; 39°33′N 82°46′W. Tarlton Cross Mound nearby.

Tarnov, village (1990 pop. 61), Platte co., E central Nebr., 14 mi/23 km NNW of Columbus, on branch of Platte R.; 41°36′N 97°30′W.

Tarpaulin Cove, small bight, SE Mass., in S shore of Naushon Isl., c.6 mi/9.7 km SW of Woods Hole; c.½ mi/⅘ km across. Lighthouse. Was a pirates' haven; reputedly last port of call for Captain Kidd.

Tarpon Springs (TARP-puhn), city (☐ 16 sq mi/41 sq km; 1990 pop. 17,906), Pinellas co., W central Fla., port on Anclote R. (bridged here) near its mouth on the Gulf, 23 mi/37 km NW of Tampa; 28°08′N 82°46′W. A major sponge-fishing center and market. Sponge industry founded by Gr. divers in 1905. City has colorful Gr. religious festivals that draw many visitors.

Tarpum Bay, town, central Bahama Isls., on W shore of S central Eleuthera Isl., 13 mi/21 km S of Governor's Harbour, 70 mi/113 km E of Nassau; 25°N 76°13′W. Pineapple growing.

Tarrant, county (☐ 897 sq mi/2,323 sq km; 1990 pop. 1,170,103), N Texas; ⊙ Fort Worth; 32°46′N 97°17′W. Commercial, industrial center of wide region. Highly urbanized in center and E parts and with Fort Worth at its center, this co. is the smaller partner in the Dallas–Fort Worth urbanized region. While Dallas's growth has radiated in all directions and has extended beyond Dallas co.'s boundaries, Fort Worth's growth has been mainly confined to Tarrant co., primarily to E and NE. The co.'s development owes as much to Dallas's growth as to Fort Worth's. Besides Fort Worth, other major cities include Arlington, Mansfield, Haltom City, Hurst, and part of Grand Prairie (partly in Dallas co.). Drained by West and Clear forks of Trinity R., and here joining numerous creeks; includes Worth and Eagle Mt. lakes in NW (recreation, water supply). Agr. (dairying; grains, cotton, pecans, sorghum, vegetables, nursery crops; livestock, including cattle, poultry, horses, emus, ostriches, and rheas) is still important in the S, W, and NW margins of the co. Natural gas; sand and gravel, stone. Oil refining, meat packing, grain milling and shipping, diversified mfg. at Fort Worth. Dallas–Fort Worth Internatl. Airport, a major factor in attracting industry, straddles the Tarrant and Dallas cos. line in NE. Grapevine Recreation Area is in NE corner, N of the airport; Fort Worth Nature Center and Refuge is in NW. Benbrook L. in SW, L. Arlington in E center, part of Grapevine L. (NE) and L. Joe Pool (SE). Formed 1849.

Tarrant City (TER-ruhnt), city (1990 pop. 8,046), Jefferson co., N central Ala.; N suburb of Birmingham. Mfg. (fabricated cast-iron prods.). Also known as Tarrant.

Tarryall Creek, 50 mi/80 km long, central Colo.; rises at Continental Divide, in Front Range, NW Park co.; flows SE, through Tarryall Reservoir, past Tarryall Mts. (to NE), turns NNE 5 mi/8 km above entering the South Platte R. 10 mi/16 km NNW of Florissant.

Tarryall Mountains, in Front Range, Park and Jefferson cos., central Colo., just W of South Platte R. and N of Tarryall Creek. Chief peaks include South Tarryall Peak (11,206 ft/3,416 m), North Tarryall Peak (11,902 ft/3,628 m), Buffalo Peak (11,589 ft/3,532 m), and Bison Peak (12,431 ft/3,789 m). Buffalo Peak was formerly known as Freeman or Freemans Peak.

Tarrytown 1 village (1990 pop. 130), Montgomery co., E central Ga., 11 mi/18 km NW of Vidalia; 32°19′N 82°34′W. **2** village (☐ 5 sq mi/13 sq km; 1990 pop. 10,739), Westchester co., SE N.Y., residential suburb of N.Y. city, on the E bank of the Hudson R. opposite Nyack; 41°03′N 73°52′W. Hq. of several companies. Mfg. includes motor vehicle assembly, laboratory instruments, food processing, and heating equip. It is the E terminus of the Tappan Zee Bridge and the seat of Marymount Col. Fordham Univ. of N.Y. city maintains a branch campus here. Of interest are Sunnyside, the home of Washington Irving; Sleepy Hollow cemetery, where Irving is buried; Philipsburg Manor, an estate; and Lyndhurst (1838), a Gothic Revival mansion. Philipsburg Manor, an early trading center complex NW of village center, includes a Du. farmhouse (c.1683) and a restored operating gristmill. Settled in the 17th cent. by Dutch, inc. 1870.

Tarzana, suburban residential section of Los Angeles, Los Angeles co., S Calif., 7 mi/11.3 km NW of downtown, in San Fernando Valley. Mfg. (metal processing, machinery). Santa Monica Mts. Natl. Recreation Area to S; Los Encinos State Historical Park to E; Encino Reservoir to SE, Los Angeles R. to N, Sepulveda Dam Flood Control Area to NE.

Taschereau (tah-shuh-RO), village (1991 pop. 684), W Que., Canada, bet. small L. Taschereau (N) and Robertson L. (S), 30 mi/48 km NNE of Rouyn; 48°40′N 78°42′W. RR junction; lumbering; dairying.

Tascosa, uninc. village (1990 pop. 25), Oldham co., extreme N Texas, in the Panhandle, on Canadian R., 30 mi/48 km NW of Amarillo. Elev. 3,176 ft/968 m. Founded as sheep camp in 1870s, became a booming cow town in the 1880s. Tascosa remained active until 1930s, but now it is virtually deserted. Former co. seat; former co. courthouse is now Julian Bivins Mus. (named for rancher who donated his land for Boys' Ranch, a home for underprivileged youths established here in 1939). Boot Hill Cemetery also here.

Taseko, Mount (tuh-SEH-ko) (10,057 ft/3,065 m), SW B.C., Canada, in Coast Mts., 140 mi/225 km N of Vancouver.

Tasiujaq, village (1991 pop. 152), N Que., Canada, W shore of Ungava Bay, W side of base of Ungava Peninsula. Inuit community. Hunting, fishing, trapping.

Tasley, village, Accomack co., E Va., in Eastern Shore area, 1 mi/1.6 km SW of Accomac; 37°42′N 75°42′W. RR shipping point for Onancock (to W) and Accomac. Mfg. (printing and publishing); agr. (vegetables, grain; livestock).

Tasquillo (tahs-KEE-yo), town (1990 pop. 2,242), Hidalgo, central Mexico, on Tula R., 45 mi/72 km NW of Pachuca de Soto, on the Inter-Amer. Highway (85); 20°33′N 99°18′W. Elev. 5,643 ft/1,720 m. Cereals, maguey, beans, fruit; livestock. Thermal springs nearby.

Tataltepec de Valdés (tah-TAHL-te-pek de vahl-DES), town (1990 pop. 1,468), SW Oaxaca, Mexico, 20 mi/32 km E of Santiago Jamiltepec. Mountainous terrain in the Verde R. basin; 16°19′N 97°33′W. Hot climate. Agr. (corn, beans, coffee, sugarcane, tropical fruits); woods; cattle and poultry. Pop. speaks Mixteco.

Tatamagouche (ta-tuh-muh-GOOSH), village, N N.S., Canada, at head of Tatamagouche Bay of Nothumberland Strait, 32 mi/51 km WNW of New Glasgow; 45°43′N 63°17′W. Dairying center.

Tatamy (TA-tah-mee), borough (1990 pop. 873), Northampton co., E Pa., 4 mi/6.4 km NNW of Easton, on Bushkill Creek; 40°44′N 75°15′W. Mfg. (metal prods., apparel); agr. (grain, soybeans, apples; livestock; dairying). Jacobsburg State Park to NW; Eastern Airport is here, to E.

Tatatila (tah-tah-TEE-lah), town (1990 pop. 872), Veracruz, E Mexico, 17 mi/27 km NW of Xalapa Enriquez; 19°42′N 97°06′W. Elev. 5,804 ft/1,769 m. Corn, coffee. In Totonac-Indian area.

Tate, county (☐ 410 sq mi/1,062 sq km; 1990 pop. 21,432), NW Miss.; ⊙ Senatobia; 34°38′N 89°56′W. Bounded W and NW by Coldwater R., forms Arkabutla Reservoir in NW. Agr. (cotton, corn, wheat, soybeans, hay; cattle; timber; dairying). Formed 1873.

Tate, village, Pickens co., N Ga., 13 mi/21 km NNE of Canton; 34°25′N 84°22′W. Marble-quarrying center.

Tate Springs, resort village, Grainger co., E Tenn., 40 mi/64 km NE of Knoxville, on Cherokee L. Mineral springs.

Tatitlek, native village (1990 pop. 119), S Alaska, on Prince William Sound, 40 mi/64 km NW of Cordova; 60°52′N 146°40′W. Fishing.

Tatla Lake, village, W central B.C., Canada, near midpoint of Route 20, c.200 mi/322 km W of Bella Coola and 200 mi/322 km E of Williams Lake, at SW end of Tatla L. Service center for logging industry, sportsmen. Lodge.

Tatlow, Mount (10,050 ft/3,063 m), SW B.C., Canada, in Coast Mts., 150 mi/241 km NNW of Vancouver; 51°23′N 123°52′W.

Tatnam, Cape, NE Man., Canada, on Hudson Bay, 50 mi/80 km ENE of York Factory; 57°15′N 91°05′W.

Tatoosh Island, Wash.: see FLATTERY, CAPE.

Tattnall (TAT-nuhl), county (□ 488 sq mi/1,264 sq km; 1990 pop. 17,722), E central Ga.; ⊙ Reidsville; 32°02′N 82°04′W. Bounded SW by Altamaha R.; drained by Ohoopee R. Coastal plain agr. (corn, soybeans, wheat, cotton, tobacco, peanuts); cattle, hogs, poultry; sawmilling area. Formed 1801.

Tatum, town (1990 pop. 1,289), on border bet. Panola and Rusk cos., E Texas, 17 mi/27 km SSW of Marshall; 32°18′N 94°31′W. In oil, agr. area (dairying; cattle; vegetables, watermelons); mfg. (gypsum wallboard). Martin Creek L. State Park to S.

Tatum 1 (TAI-tuhm), village (1990 pop. 768), Lea co., SE N.Mex., near Texas state line, 22 mi/35 km N of Lovington; 33°15′N 103°19′W. Wheat, alfalfa, cotton; livestock region; mfg. Oil deposits in vicinity. Mescalero Sands to W. **2** (TAIT-uhm), village (1990 pop. 49), Marlboro co., NE S.C., 5 mi/8 km ENE of Bennettsville; 34°38′N 79°35′W. Mfg. of paper and paperboard; agr. includes timber and cotton.

Tatums (TAIT-uhms), village (1990 pop. 176), Carter co., S Okla., 25 mi/40 km NW of Ardmore; 34°28′N 97°28′W. Oil-producing area; agr. (cattle; grain).

Taughannock Falls State Park (tuh-GAHN-ik), W central N.Y., on W shore of Cayuga L., c.8 mi/12.9 km NNW of Ithaca; 42°33′N 76°36′W. In deep gorge of small creek entering lake here is spectacular Taughannock Falls (215 ft/66 m high). Sports facilities; swimming.

Taum Sauk Mountain (TAHM-SAWK) (1,772 ft/540 m), SE Mo., SW of Ironton; 37°34′N 90°43′W. Highest peak of St. Francois Mts. and highest point in state.

Taunton (TAWN-tuhn), city (1990 pop. 49,832), ⊙ Bristol co., SE Mass., on the Taunton R.; 41°54′N 71°05′W. Has been a center of the silverware industry since 1824; other mfg. includes rubber, textiles, clothing, leather, gold and silver prods., and plastics. The city was an ironworking center from 1656 to 1876. Nearby are 3 state parks. Settled 1638, inc. as a city 1864.

Taunton (TAWN-tuhn), village (1990 pop. 175), Lyon co., SW Minn., 17 mi/27 km NW of Marshall; 44°35′N 96°03′W. Agr. (alfalfa; dairying; livestock); mfg. (feeds). On North Branch of Yellow Medicine R.

Taunton River (TAWN-tuhn), 44 mi/71 km long, SE Mass.; rises in S Norfolk co.; flows generally SW and S, past Taunton (head of navigation), to head of Mt. Hope Bay at Fall River city, where its mouth is part of harbor.

Tavani (TA-vuh-nee), abandoned trading post, SE Keewatin dist., N.W.T., Canada, on Mistake Bay of Hudson Bay; 62°04′N 93°07′W.

Tavaputs Plateau (TA-vah-poots), E Utah; name sometimes applied to EAST TAVAPUTS PLATEAU and WEST TAVAPUTS PLATEAU.

Tavares (tuh-VER-reez), town (□ 4 sq mi/10.4 sq km; 1990 pop. 7,383), ⊙ Lake co., central Fla., 28 mi/45 km NW of Orlando, bet. lakes Eustis and Dora, in citrus-fruit and resort area; 28°48′N 81°44′W.

Taviche, Mexico: see SAN JERÓNIMO TAVICHE.

Tavistock, village, S Ont., Canada, 8 mi/13 km ESE of Stratford. Milling, agr. implement mfg.; dairying.

Tavistock, residential borough (1990 pop. 35), Camden co., SW N.J., 6 mi/9.7 km SE of Camden; 39°52′N 75°01′W. Started as golf course.

Tawakoni, Lake, reservoir (□ 56 sq mi/145 sq km), where Van Zandt, Rains, and Hunt cos. meet, NE central Texas, on Sabine R. near its source, 50 mi/80 km E of Dallas; c.20 mi/32 km long; 32°49′N 95°54′W. Max. capacity 1,267,221 acre-ft. Formed by Iron Bridge Dam (67 ft/20 m high), built (1960) by the Sabine R. Authority for irrigation and water supply; also used for recreation. L. Tawakoni State Park on SW shore.

Tawas City (TAH-WAHS), town (1990 pop. 2,009), ⊙ Iosco co., NE Mich., 48 mi/77 km NNE of Bay City, on Tawas Bay (an inlet of Saginaw Bay); 44°16′N 83°31′W. Sheltered on E by Tawas Point State Park. Resort, in region of lakes, streams, and farms; tourism. Lumber milling; RR shops, gypsum mines; mfg. (motor vehicle parts). 10 mi/16 km NW Lumbermen's Monument; part of Huron Natl. Forest to N. Settled c.1853; inc. as village 1885, as city 1895.

Tawas Lake (TAH-WAHS), Iosco co., NE Mich., just N of Tawas City, near L. Huron, c.3 mi/4.8 km long, 1.5 mi/2.4 km wide; 44°18′N 83°29′W. Resort.

Taxco de Alarcón (TAHS-ko de ah-lahr-KON), city (1990 pop. 41,836) and township, Guerrero state, S Mexico; 18°32′N 99°36′W. Founded in 1529 as a silver-mining community, Taxco was also an important stop bet. Mexico city and Acapulco in Span. colonial trade with the Philippines. It achieved real prominence as a mining center under José de la Borda, who after 1717 constructed roads and built the superb colonial church. Clinging to the side of a mt., Taxco is a splendid example of the Span. colonial town, with steep, cobbled streets, overhanging grilled balconies, red-tile roofs, and glazed tiles set in white or pastel adobe walls. Modern bldgs. are prohibited, and colonial monuments are protected by the Mex. govt. A famous center of silversmithing, Taxco attracts artists, writers, and tourists.

Taximaroa, Mexico: see CIUDAD HIDALGO.

Taylor 1 county (□ 1,232 sq mi/3,191 sq km; 1990 pop. 17,111), N central Fla., on Gulf of Mexico (S) and bounded W by Aucilla R.; ⊙ Perry; 30°01′N 83°37′W. Flatwoods area, with large swamps and many small lakes. Forestry (lumber, naval stores), cattle raising, farming (corn, peanuts), and fishing. Limestone deposits. Formed 1856. **2** county (□ 380 sq mi/984 sq km; 1990 pop. 7,642), W central Ga.; ⊙ Butler; 32°33′N 84°15′W. Bounded N and E by Flint R. Intersected by the fall line. Agr. (cotton, corn, peanuts, soybeans, wheat); cattle, hogs, poultry; sawmilling. Formed 1852. **3** county (□ 534 sq mi/1,383 sq km; 1990 pop. 7,114), SW Iowa, on Mo. state line (S); ⊙ Bedford; 40°43′N 94°41′W. Prairie agr. area (corn, hogs, hay; cattle, poultry) drained by One Hundred and Two, Little Platte, and East Nodaway rivers. L. of Three Fires State Park atcenter, N of Bedford. **4** county (□ 277 sq mi/717 sq km; 1990 pop. 21,146), central Ky.; ⊙ Campbellsville; 37°22′N 85°19′W. Drained by Green R. (forms Green R. L. reservoir in S), Big Pitman and Robinson creeks. Rolling agr. area (burley tobacco, corn, oats, hay, wheat, alfalfa, soybeans; hogs, poultry, cattle; dairying); timber; limestone quarries. Mfg. (including wood prods.) at Campbellsville. Green R. L. State Park in S. Formed 1848. **5** county (□ 919 sq mi/2,380 sq km; 1990 pop. 119,655), W central Texas; ⊙ Abilene; 32°18′N 99°52′W. Elev. c.1,700 ft/518 m–2,400 ft/732 m. Drained to N by Elm Creek and other tributaries of Brazos R., to S by Colorado R. tributaries. Diversified agr. (cotton, grain sorghum, wheat, hay; cattle). Oil, natural gas wells; stone; clay, caliche; sand and gravel. Recreation on L. Abilene and Abilene State Park near center of co. Mfg., processing at Abilene. Formed 1858. **6** county (□ 175 sq mi/453 sq km; 1990 pop. 15,144), N W.Va.; ⊙ Grafton; 39°20′N 80°02′W. On Allegheny Plateau; drained by Tygart R. Includes part of Tygart L. reservoir and State Park in S; part of Valley Falls State Park in N; Pleasant Creek Wildlife Management Area on S border. Agr. (alfalfa, hay); cattle. Timber, natural-gas field. Mfg. at Grafton. Formed 1844. **7** county (□ 984 sq mi/2,549 sq km; 1990 pop. 18,901), N central Wis.; ⊙ Medford; 45°12′N 90°30′W. Drained by Black, Yellow, Jump, and Rib rivers. Dairying; farming barley, hay; livestock raising; sawmilling. Includes large Miller Dam Flowage (reservoir) in southernmost unit of Chequamegon Natl. Forest in N center; several small resort lakes. Formed 1875.

Taylor 1 city (1990 pop. 70,811), Wayne co., SE Mich., suburb 11 mi/18 km SW of Detroit, SSW of Dearborn; 42°13′N 83°16′W. A small rural village until World War II, it grew from a pop. of c.5,000 to its present size. Its growth has been commercial as well as residential, and its mfg. includes adhesives, bldg. materials, furniture, sheet metal, motor vehicle parts, motorcycles, metal stampings. Founded 1847 as a township, inc. as a city 1968. **2** city (1990 pop. 11,472), Williamson co., central Texas, 29 mi/47 km NE of Austin; 30°34′N 97°24′W. Trade, shipping, processing center for rich agr. area (cotton, corn, wheat; cattle); ships agr. produce; mfg. (furniture, consumer goods). Plotted 1876, inc. 1877.

Taylor 1 town (1990 pop. 1,352), Houston co., SW Ala., 5 mi/8 km SW of Dothan; 31°10′N 85°28′W. **2** town (1990 pop. 2,418), Navajo co., E central Ariz., 28 mi/45 km S of Holbrook, on Silver Creek; 34°27′N 110°06′W. Cattle, sheep; timber. Apache-Sitgreaves Natl. Forest to S. Fish hatchery to SE at White Mt. Lake.

Taylor 1 village, NW Alaska, on Seward Peninsula, 80 mi/129 km N of Nome; 65°41′N 164°47′W. Placer gold mining. Airfield. At end of highway connecting Nome to the areas of the N. **2** village (1990 pop. 621), Columbia co., SW Ark., 18 mi/29 km SW of Magnolia, near La. state line; 33°06′N 93°27′W. L. Erling Reservoir (Bodcaw Bayou) to W. **3** village (1990 pop. 288), Lafayette co., N Miss. 8 mi/12.9 km SSW of Oxford; 34°16′N 89°34′W. In agr. (cotton, corn; cattle) and timber area. **4** village (1990 pop. 186), ⊙ Loup co., central Nebr., 25 mi/40 km NW of Ord, on North Loup R.; 41°46′N 99°22′W. Livestock; grain. Nearby scenic spot is Cheesebrough Canyon. **5** village (1990 pop. 163), Stark co., W N.Dak., 17 mi/27 km E of Dickinson; 46°53′N 102°25′W. **6** village (1990 pop. 419) Jackson co., W central Wis., 38 mi/61 km SSE of Eau Claire; 44°19′N 91°07′W. In dairying region.

Taylor, borough (1990 pop. 6,941), Lackawanna co., NE Pa., suburb 3 mi/4.8 km SW of Scranton, on Lackawanna R.; 41°23′N 75°42′W. Mfg. (printing, modular homes, apparel). Anthracite Mus. to N. Settled c.1800.

Taylor, S.C.: see TAYLORS.

Taylor Creek, town (□ 4 sq mi/10.4 sq km; 1990 pop. 4,081), Okeechobee co., central Fla., 3 mi/4.8 km SSE of the town of Okeechobee on the N shore of L. Okeechobee; 27°13′N 80°47′W.

Taylor Highway, highway, E central Alaska, near Yukon Territories (Canada) border. Designated Alaska Route 5, the gravel road begins in S at Tetlin Junction on Alaska Highway. It runs NNE across Sitz Mts. through village of Chicken to village of Eagle, on the Yukon R., its N terminus. The Top of the World Highway branches E from Jack Wade Junction 65 mi/105 km S of Eagle to Dawson and Whitehorse, Yukon Territories. Access to Fortymile Natl. Wild and Scenic Riverway (Bureau of Land Management) at Chicken. Fortymile Mining Dist. was one of the richest gold-producing areas during the 1890s; continues to be actively mined.

Taylor Lake Village, town (1990 pop. 3,394), Harris co., SE Texas, in area referred to as Clear Lake City, residential suburb 23 mi/37 km SE of Houston; 29°34′N 95°02′W. Bounds Taylor L. (Taylor Bayou) on E, Mud L. (Armand Bayou) on W; near Clear L., S. NASA Johnson Space Center to W.

Taylor Mill, town (1990 pop. 5,530), Kenton co., N Ky., residential suburb 6 mi/9.7 km S of Cincinnati (Ohio), 4 mi/6.4 km S of Covington, near Licking R.; 39°00′N 84°30′W. Urban fringe area; agr. (dairying; poultry, cattle; burley tobacco).

Taylor, Mount (11,301 ft/3,445 m), NW N.Mex., volcanic cone and highest point in San Mateo Mts., 20 mi/32 km ENE of Grants. In section of Cibola Natl. Forest.

Taylor Park, reservoir (□ 3 sq mi/7.8 sq km), Gunnison co., W central Colo., on Taylor R., in Gunnison Natl. Forest, 24 mi/38 km NE of Gunnison and 11 mi/18 km W of Cottonwood Pass (12,126ft/3,696 m) on Continental Divide; 38°49′N 106°36′W. Max. capacity 111,260 acre-ft. Formed by Taylor Park Dam (206 ft/63 m high), built (1937) by the Bureau of Reclamation for irrigation.

Taylor River, c.50 mi/80 km long, W central Colo.; rises near Castle Peak in Elk Mts., NE Gunnison co., near Continental Divide; flows SE through Taylor Park Reservoir, then SW, joining Slate R. at Almont to form Gunnison R. Taylor Park Dam (206 ft/63 m high, 675 ft/206 m long) is 16 mi/26 km NE of Almont; completed 1937 as unit in Uncompahgre reclamation project; forms Taylor Park Reservoir (capacity 106,200 acre-ft). In Gunnison Natl. Forest.

Cross references are shown in SMALL CAPITALS. The pronunciation key is on page xv. The dates of population figures are on page xii.

Taylor Springs, village (1990 pop. 670), Montgomery co., S central Ill., just S of Hillsboro; 39°07′N 89°30′W. In agr. and bituminous coal–mining area.

Taylors, uninc. city (1990 pop. 19,619), Greenville co., NW S.C., on Enoree R. and residential suburb 8 mi/12.9 km NE of Greenville; 34°55′N 82°18′W. Mfg. (textiles, clothing, iron foundry, paperboard, consumer goods, printing and publishing). Agr. includes livestock; grain, tomatoes, soybeans, peaches. Developed on site of Chick Springs as a former summer resort.

Taylors Falls, village (1990 pop. 694), Chicago co., E Minn., 38 mi/61 km NE of St. Paul, opposite (W of) St. Croix Falls, Wis.; 45°24′N 92°39′W. Agr. (grain; cattle, poultry; dairying); mfg. (meat processing, printing). St. Croix Wild R. State Park to NW; Interstate State Park to S (mutually established parks in both Wis. and Minn.); Lower St. Croix Natl. Scenic Riverway to S; St. Croix Natl. Scenic Riverway to N; Wild Mt. Ski Area to NW.

Taylors Island, low, marshy island, Dorchester co., E Md., in Chesapeake Bay, 14 mi/23 km WSW of Cambridge, separated from mainland (E) by narrow creeks (bridged); c.8 mi/12.9 km long, 4 mi/6.4 km wide. Center of Eastern Shore's muskrat-trapping industry; summer resort (fishing, duck hunting). The only village is also called Taylors Isl. (vegetables, seafood canneries). Settled in 1659 by Thomas Taylor, an effort was made in the early 18th cent. to established a silk industry by planting mulberry trees to nourish silk worms in an area known as Mulberry Grove. A 12-ft/4-m-by-12-ft/4-m early log schoolhouse has been relocated from a plantation to the churchyard of Grace Church. A wildlife management refuge is on the isl.

Taylorsville 1 town (1990 pop. 774), ⊙ Spencer co., N central Ky., 28 mi/45 km SE of Louisville, on Salt R., at mouth of Brashears Creek; 38°01′N 85°20′W. In Bluegrass agr. area (grain, burley tobacco; livestock; dairying). Taylorsville L. reservoir and State Park to SE. Est. 1799. **2** town (1990 pop. 1,412), Smith co., S central Miss., 20 mi/32 km WNW of Laurel, near Leaf R.; 31°49′N 89°25′W. RR terminus. Agr. (cotton, corn; cattle, poultry, hogs); mfg. (sausage processing, plywood and particleboard). **3** town (1990 pop. 1,566), ⊙ Alexander co., W central N.C., 18 mi/29 km NW of Statesville; 35°55′N 81°10′W. RR terminus. Tobacco, grain, soybeans, poultry, cattle; dairying. Mfg. (textiles, lumber, wire prods., furniture, meat processing, apparel, paper prods.). L. Hickory and Lookout Shoals L., reservoirs on Catawba R. to S. Inc. 1887.

Taylorsville 1 village (1990 pop. 269), Bartow and Polk cos., NW Ga., 12 mi/19 km WSW of Cartersville; 34°05′N 84°59′W. Mfg. includes food handling equip. **2** village (1990 pop. 1,044), Bartholomew co., S central Ind., 5 mi/8 km N of Columbus, bet. Flatrock and Driftwood rivers; 39°18′N 85°57′W. Agr. area. Service center for Camp Atterbury military reserve to W. Laid out 1849.

Taylorsville Lake, reservoir (□ 5 sq mi/13 sq km), Nelson, Spencer, and Anderson cos., N central Ky., on Salt R., 17 mi/27 km NE of Bardstown; 38°00′N 85°19′W. Max. capacity 291,670 acre-ft. N arm also fed by Beech R. Formed by Taylorville L. Dam (143 ft/44 m high), built (1983) by Army Corps of Engineers for flood control; also used for recreation. Taylorsville L. State Park near dam on N shore.

Taylortown, village (1990 pop. 543), Moore co., central N.C., residential suburb 6 mi/9.7 km WNW of Southern Pines; 35°13′N 79°29′W. Tobacco, grain; livestock.

Taylorville, city (1990 pop. 11,133), ⊙ Christian co., central Ill., c.24 mi/39 km SE of Springfield; 39°31′N 89°15′W. In a farm, coal, and oil area; inc. 1881. Agr. (wheat, corn, soybeans, sorghum); mfg. (soybean processing, metal prods., meatpacking). L. Taylorville is SE.

Tayoltita (tah-yo-TEE-tah), mining town (1990 pop. 3,643) and township, ⊙ San Dimas township, Durango, N Mexico, on W slope of Sierra Madre Occidental, 80 mi/129 km W of Victoria de Durango; 24°05′N 105°56′W. Silver, gold, lead, copper mining.

Tazewell 1 (TAZ-wel), county (□ 657 sq mi/1,702 sq km; 1990 pop. 123,692), central Ill.; ⊙ Pekin; 40°30′N 89°30′W. Bounded NW by Illinois R.; drained by Mackinaw R. Several communities have grown as result of close proximity to Peoria: East Peoria, Pekin, Morton, Creve Coeur, Washington. Agr. (corn, hay, soybeans, barley; cattle, hogs, poultry; dairying). Sand and gravel deposits. Diversified mfg.: machinery, food prods. Includes Spring L. Conservation Area. Formed 1827. **2** county (□ 519 sq mi/1,344 sq km; 1990 pop. 45,960), SW Va.; ⊙ Tazewell; 37°07′N 81°33′W. In Allegheny Mts.; bounded N by W.Va. state line; includes parts of Jefferson Natl. Forest in S and E. Drained by Clinch R. Some mfg.; agr. (corn, tobacco, hay, alfalfa; cattle, sheep, hogs; dairying); timber; limestone quarrying; bituminous coal mining. Appalachian Trail follows SE boundary. Formed 1799.

Tazewell 1 (TAZ-wuhl), town (1990 pop. 2,150), ⊙ Claiborne co., NE Tenn., 38 mi/61 km NNE of Knoxville, 36°27′N 83°34′W. In mt.-timber, coal-mining, and agr. area; woodworking. **2** (TAZ-wel), town (1990 pop. 4,176), ⊙ Tazewell co., SW Va., in Allegheny Mts., 20 mi/32 km SW of Bluefield; 37°07′N 81°31′W. Commercial center; mfg. (mining equip., bldg. materials, printed circuit boards); agr. (livestock; corn, wheat, potatoes; dairying); bituminous coal mining; limestone quarrying. Crab Orchard Mus. Settled 1769; inc. 1866.

Tazlina Glacier, S Alaska; rises in Chugach Mts. at 61°30′N 146°35′W; flows 20 mi/32 km N to Tazlina L.

Tazlina Lake, S Alaska, 50 mi/80 km NNE of Valdez, 18 mi/29 km long, 1 mi/1.6 km–4 mi/6.4 km wide; 61°50′N 146°29′W. Fed by Tazlina and Nelchina glaciers; drained NE by Tazlina R.

Tchefuncte River (chuh-FUNK-tuh), c.40 mi/64 km long, SE La.; rises near Miss. state line E of Kentwood (on boundary bet. Tangipahoa and Washington parishes), flows S into St. Tammany parish, to L. Pontchartrain at N end. Fairview Riverside State Park near river's mouth. Also called Chefuncte R.

Tchula (CHOO-lah), town (1990 pop. 2,186), Holmes co., central Miss., 22 mi/35 km S of Greenwood, on Tchula L. slough; 33°10′N 90°13′W. Agr. (cotton, corn, soybeans; cattle; timber). Morgan Brake Natl. Wildlife Refuge to N, Hillside Natl. Wildlife Refuge to S.

Tea, village (1990 pop. 786), Lincoln co., SE S.Dak., 7 mi/11.3 km SW of Sioux Falls; 43°27′N 96°50′W. Mfg. (motor vehicle parts).

Teabo (te-AH-bo), town (1990 pop. 3,932), Yucátan, SE Mexico, 19 mi/31 km E of Ticul; 20°24′N 89°17′W. Henequen, sugarcane, fruit, timber.

Teachey (TEE-chee), village (1990 pop. 244), Duplin co., E N.C., 38 mi/61 km N of Wilmington; 34°46′N 78°00′W. Tobacco, cotton, grain; livestock. Mfg. (feeds).

Teague, town (1990 pop. 3,268), Freestone co., E central Texas, c.50 mi/80 km E of Waco; 31°37′N 96°16′W. Agr. (melons, vegetables, peaches; cattle, horses; pecans). RR mus.; L. Limestone reservoir to SW. Founded 1906.

Teaneck (TEE-nek), residential suburban township (1990 pop. 37,825), Bergen co., NE N.J., near the Hackensack R.; 40°53′N 74°00′W. Mfg. includes jewelry, electrical equip., food seasonings. Teaneck developed rapidly after the construction of the George Washington Bridge (1931), which connects N.J. with N.Y. city. Fairleigh Dickinson Univ. has a campus here. The city has several 18th-cent. homes. Settled in the early 1600s, inc. 1895.

Teapa (te-AH-pah), city (1990 pop. 19,703) and township, Tabasco, SE Mexico, on navigable affluent of Grijalva R., near Chiapas border, 30 mi/48 km S of Villahermosa, on Mexico Highway 195; 18°35′N 92°56′W. Rice, beans, coffee, cacao, fruit; livestock; timber. In Zoque-Indian area.

Teapot Dome, NE Natrona co., central Wyo., 30 mi/48 km NNE of Casper, teapot-shaped rock formation, which rises above oil-bearing plain, set aside in 1915 by President Wilson as naval oil reserve. Certain aspects of the way in which Albert B. Fall, U.S. Secretary of the Interior in Harding's administration, leased (1922) the govt. oil fields to Harry F. Sinclair led to an investigation (1923), great notoriety, and criminal prosecutions resulting in Fall's conviction (1929).

Tear of the Clouds, Lake, small tarn (lake of glacial origin), Essex co., NE N.Y., on NW slope of Mt. Marcy, near source of Opalescent R. (fed by Feldspar Creek; headstream of Hudson R.); 44°07′N 73°39′W.

Teaticket, Mass.: see FALMOUTH.

Teayo, Mexico: see CASTILLO DE TEAYO.

Teays Valley (TAIZ), uninc. town (1990 pop. 8,436), Putnam co., W central W.Va., 18 mi/29 km WNW of Charleston, 4 mi/6.4 km E of Hurricane; 38°27′N 81°55′W. Agr. (corn, tobacco); cattle, poultry.

Tecali de Herrera (te-KAH-lee de RE-rah), town (1990 pop. 3,257), Puebla, central Mexico, on central plateau, 18 mi/29 km ESE of Puebla; 18°54′N 97°58′W. Cereals, vegetables. Marble and onyx deposits nearby.

Tecalitlán (te-kah-kee-TLAHN), town (1990 pop. 13,265), Jalisco, central Mexico, 33 mi/53 km NE of Colima, on Mexico Highway 110; 19°28′N 103°18′W. Elev. 3,399 ft/1,036 m. Sugar-growing center.

Tecámac, Mexico: see TECÁMAC DE FELIPE VILLANUEVA.

Tecámac de Felipe Villanueva (te-KAH-mahn de fe-LEE-pe vee-yah-noo-E-vahn), town (1990 pop. 10,776), ⊙ Tecámac municipio, Mexico state, central Mexico, 23 mi/37 km NE of Mexico city on the Inter-Amer. Highway (85), within the Zona Metropolitana de la Ciudad de México; 19°42′N 98°58′W. Maguey, cereals.

Tecamachalco (te-kah-mah-CHAHL-ko), city (1990 pop. 17,490) and township, Puebla, central Mexico, on central plateau, on RR, 33 mi/53 km ESE of Puebla on Mexico Highway 150; 18°52′N 97°43′W. Agr. center (corn, wheat, maguey). Has colonial churches.

Tecate (te-KAH-te), city (1990 pop. 40,240) and township, Baja California, NW Mexico, on U.S. border, 25 mi/40 km E of Tijuna on Mexico Highway 2 and at terminus of Mexico Highway 3; 32°33′N 116°38′W. Agr. center in irrigated area (cotton, fruit, vegetables); brewery, maquiladora plants. On U.S. side is village of Tecate, a port of entry.

Techaluta de Montenegro (te-chah-LOO-stah de mon-te-NE-gro), town (1990 pop. 2,149), Jalisco, W Mexico, on L. Sayula, on RR, 45 mi/72 km SE of Ameca, on Mexico Highway 54; 20°04′N 103°33′W. Elev. 4,715 ft/1,437 m. Alfalfa, fruit, vegetables; livestock.

Teche, Bayou (tesh, BEI-yoo), stream, 125 mi/201 km long, S La.; formed by tributary bayous and flowing SE to the Atchafalaya R. near Morgan City; 29°43′N 91°17′W. Navigable for more than 100 mi/161 km, it flows through a fertile sugarcane area. Bayou Teche was the setting for Henry Wadsworth Longfellow's *Evangeline.* Longfellow Evangeline State Commemorative Area on W side of bayou, N of St. Martinville.

Tecoanapa (te-ko-ah-NAH-pah), town (1990 pop. 3,146), Guerrero, SW Mexico, in Pacific lowland, 82 mi/132 km ESE of Acapulco de Juárez; 16°30′N 98°42′W. Sugarcane, fruit; livestock.

Tecoh (te-KO), town (1990 pop. 6,763), Yucátan, SE Mexico, 18 mi/29 km SSE of Mérida; 20°42′N 89°30′W. Henequen, sugar, corn, tropical fruit.

Tecolotlán (te-ko-lo-TLAHN), town (1990 pop. 7,031), Jalisco, W Mexico, 23 mi/37 km S of Ameca near Mexico Highway 80; 20°10′N 104°07′W. Elev. 4,199 ft/1,280 m. Agr. center (grain, sugarcane, cotton, fruit; livestock).

Tecolutla (tee-ko-LOO-tlah), town (1990 pop. 3,098), Veracruz, E Mexico, minor port at mouth of Tecolutla R., in Gulf lowland, 21 mi/34 km E of Papantla de Olarte; 20°30′N 97°00′E.

Tecom, Mexico: see TEKOM.

Tecomán (te-ko-MAHN), city (1990 pop. 60,938) and township, Colima, W Mexico, on Armería R., on Pacific coastal plain, 25 mi/40 km SSW of Colima, on Mexico Highway 200 and RR; 18°54′N 103°52′W. Agr. center (rice, corn, sugarcane, tobacco, coffee, cacao, fruit).

Tecomatlán (te-ko-mah-TLAHN), town (1990 pop. 1,721), Puebla, central Mexico, on Mixteco R., 37 mi/60 km SSE of Izúcar de Matamoros; 18°06′N 98°18′W. Cereals, sugarcane, fruit; livestock.

Tecopa, uninc. village, Inyo co., E Calif., 72 mi/116 km NE of Barstow, in Mojave Desert. Cattle. Tecopa Hot Springs to N. Nopah Range to NE. Death Valley Natl. Monument to W.

Tecozautla (te-ko-SOU-tlah), city (1990 pop. 4,906) and township, Hidalgo, central Mexico, 12 mi/19 km N of Huichapan; 20°32′N 99°38′W. Elev. 5,577 ft/1,700 m. Corn, beans, potatoes, fruit; livestock.

Tecpan de Galeana (TEK-pahn de gah-le-AH-nah), city (1990 pop. 17,884) and township, Guerrero, SW Mexico, in Pacific lowland, 55 mi/89 km WNW of Acapulco de Juárez, on Mexico Highway 200; 17°11′N 100°38′W. Agr. center (rice, sugarcane, fruit; livestock); pearl fisheries on coast. Anc. unexcavated pyramids nearby.

Tecpatán (tek-pah-TAHN), town (1990 pop. 3,163), Chiapas, S Mexico, 29 mi/47 km NNW of Tuxtla Gutiérrez; 17°08′N 93°18′W. Corn, sugarcane, tobacco, fruit. A Zoque-Indian town.

Tecuala (te-koo-AH-lah), town (1990 pop 15,388), Nayarit, W Mexico, on Pacific coastal plain, on Acaponeta R., 70 mi/113 km NNW of Tepic; 22°24′N 105°30′W. Agr. center (corn, cotton, tobacco, sugarcane, bananas, tomatoes; livestock); tobacco processing.

Tecuanipan, Mexico: see SAN JERÓNIMO TECUANIPAN.

Tecumseh (ti-KUHM-see), residential town (1991 pop. 10,495), S Ont., Canada, on L. St. Clair, 6 mi/10 km E of Windsor; 42°19′N 82°54′W.

Tecumseh 1 (te-KUHM-see), town (1990 pop. 7,462), Lenawee co., SE Mich., 9 mi/14.5 km NE of Adrian, on Raisin R.; 42°00′N 83°56′W. Ships sand, gravel; mfg. (machinery, motor vehicle parts, paper prods., metal prods.). Has Native-Amer. village sites and earthworks. Settled 1824, inc. 1837. **2** (tuh-KUHM-suh), town (1990 pop. 1,702), Johnson co., SE Nebr., 40 mi/64 km SE of Lincoln, on North Fork of Big Nemaha R.; 40°22′N 96°11′W. Grain, fruit; livestock; mfg. (poultry processing). Founded 1859. **3** town (1990 pop. 5,750), Pottawatomie co., central Okla., suburb 5 mi/8 km S of Shawnee; 35°15′N 96°55′W. In grain, livestock, and produce area; mfg. (motor vehicles).

Tecumseh (tuh-KUHM-suh), village, Shawnee co., NE Kansas, suburb 5 mi/8 km E of Topeka, on Kansas R. Mfg. (plastic prods.).

Tecumseh, Mount (te-KUHM-se), peak (4,004 ft/1,220 m) of White Mts., SE Grafton co., N.H., near Waterville Valley; 43°58′N 71°33′W. Site of Waterville Valley ski area.

Tee Harbor, village, SE Alaska, on E shore of Lynn Canal, 16 mi/26 km NW of Juneau, on Glacier Highway.

Teeswater (TEEZ-woh-tuhr), village (1991 pop. 1,066), S Ont., Canada, 12 mi/19 km SW of Walkerton; 43°59′N 81°17′W. Dairying; lumber, flour mills.

Tega Cay (TEE-guh), town (1990 pop 3,016), York co., N S.C., residential and retirement community 6 mi/9.7 km N of Rock Hill, 18 mi/29 km SSW of Charlotte (N.C.), on E shore of L. Wylie reservoir, 1 mi/1.6 km NW of Catawba Dam near N.C.-S.C. state line; 35°01′N 81°01′W.

Tehachapi, city (1990 pop. 5,791), Kern co., S central Calif., 35 mi/56 km SE of Bakersfield, in valley of Tehachapi Mts., near Tehachapi Creek; 35°08′N 118°27′W. Elev. 3,950 ft/1,204 m. Has state prison for women. Agr., including fruit growing, nuts, grain, cotton, and cattle; mfg. turbines. Just E is Tehachapi Pass. Settled near by in 1854, moved here to RR in 1876. Inc. 1909.

Tehachapi Mountains, transverse range (c.4,000 ft/1,220 m–8,000 ft/2,440 m), S Kern co., S central Calif., linking S end of the Sierra Nevada (E) with the Coast Ranges (W), and at S end of San Joaquin Valley; crossed by Tejon (SW) and Tehachapi (NE) passes; 35°02′N 118°29′W. Pacific Crest Scenic Trail follows length of ridge. Los Angeles Aqueduct passes to SE.

Tehachapi Pass (c.3,793 ft/1,156 m), SE Kern co., S central Calif., across Tehachapi Mts., c.45 mi/72 km ESE of Bakersfield, near S end of the Sierra Nevada. State Highway 58 passes through. Major windpower site along with Altamont and San Gorgono passes.

Tehama, county (□ 2,951 sq mi/7,643 sq km; 1990 pop. 49,625), N Calif.; ⊙ Red Bluff; 40°08′N 122°14′W. Lies across N part of Central Valley (here drained by Sacramento R. and South Fork of Cottonwood R.); extensions of Klamath Mts. and the Coast Ranges are in W; in E is the Sierra Nevada. N boundary formed in part by Middle Cottonwood, Cottonwood, and Battle rivers. Part of Lassen Volcanic Natl. Park is in NE. Parts of Lassen (E), Mendocino (SW), and Shasta-Trinity (W) natl. forests. Cattle; honey; alfalfa, wheat, barley, oats, rice, corn, beans, almonds, walnuts, olives. Lumbering (pine, fir, cedar); sand and gravel quarrying. Has processing industries (notably olives and olive oil at Corning), fruit drying. Black Butte L. reservoir on S boundary; Woodson Bridge State Recreation Area in S; William B. Ide State Historical Park in center. Formed 1856.

Tehama, city (1990 pop. 401), Tehama co., N Calif., 12 mi/19 km S of Red Bluff, on Sacramento R.; 40°01′N 122°07′W. RR junction. Grain, walnuts, prunes; dairying; cattle, poultry.

Tehuacán (te-wah-KAHN), city (1990 pop. 139,450) and township, Puebla, central Mexico, 65 mi/105 km SE of Puebla, on Mexico Highways 125 and 150; 18°27′N 97°23′W. RR junction; health resort; processing and agr. center (corn, sugarcane, rice, alfalfa, fruit; livestock); flour milling, tanning, wine and liquor distilling; mfg. of straw hats, yarns and fabrics, chemicals. Called "Carlsbad of Mexico" because of famed mineral springs. Has old colonial churches.

Tehuacana, village (1990 pop. 322), Limestone co., E central Texas, 38 mi/61 km ENE of Waco; 31°44′N 96°32′W. Dairying; cotton; vegetables, peaches. L. Mexia to S; Confederate Ruin Grounds State Historic Site to NE. Was seat of Trinity Univ., 1869–1902.

Tehuantepec, Mexico: see SANTO DOMINGO TEHUANTEPEC.

Tehuantepec, Gulf of (te-WAHN-te-pek), large inlet of the Pacific, on coast of Oaxaca and Chiapas, S Mexico; extends 300 mi/483 km WNW-ESE from Puerto Angel to Barra Suchiate (near Guatemala border). Salina Cruz is main port. Receives Tehuantepec R. Several large lagoons indent shore, including Mar Muerto Superior, Mar Muerto Inferior, Mar Muerto.

Tehuantepec, Isthmus of (te-WAHN-te-pek), c.125 mi/201 km wide at its narrowest, S Mexico, bet. the Bay of Campeche and the Gulf of Tehuantepec. It is mostly a rolling, tropical lowland with the lowest pass elev. at 750 ft/229 m above sea level. Building of an inter-oceanic canal here was long considered, but estimated costs proved prohibitive. A transisthmian RR bet. Coatzacoalcos and Salina Cruz was opened in 1907. Oil pipelines and Trans-Isthmian Highway (Mexico Highway 185) cross the isthmus. Major oil production at Reforma in N, important petroleum shipping port at Salina Cruz in S. Mex. govt. plans for major transportation and electric power development for region.

Tehuantepec River (te-WAHN-te-pek), c.150 mi/241 km long, Oaxaca, S Mexico; rises in Sierra Madre SE of Miahuatlán de Porfirio Díaz; flows SE in large curve, past Santo Domingo Tehuantepec, to Gulf of Tehuantepec 3 mi/4.8 km E of Salina Cruz; 16°10′N 95°07′W.

Tehuipango (te-wee-PAHN-go), town (1990 pop. 1,061), Veracruz, E Mexico, in Sierra Madre Oriental, 23 mi/37 km S of Orizaba; 18°31′N 97°08′W. Elev. 7,815 ft/2,382 m. Agr. center (corn, coffee, sugarcane, fruit).

Tehuitzingo (te-weet-SEEN-go), town (1990 pop. 4,869), Puebla, central Mexico, 20 mi/32 km SE of Izúcar de Matamoros on the Inter-Amer. Highway (180); 18°20′N 98°16′W. Agr. center (sugarcane, fruit, corn; livestock).

Teidemann, Mount, Canada: see TIEDEMANN, MOUNT.

Tejon Pass (tai-hon), passage (c.4,183 ft/1,275 m) through Tehachapi Mts., on line bet. Los Angeles and Kern cos., SW Calif. Old Fort Tejon (est. 1854) State Park is to N.

Tejupilco de Hidalgo (te-hoo-PEEL-ko de ee-DAHL-go), city (1990 pop. 15,474), ⊙ Tejupilco municipio, Mexico state, central Mexico, 40 mi/64 km SW of Toluca de lerdo on Mexico Highway 130; 18°55′N 100°10′W. Coffee, sugarcane, fruit; livestock.

Tekal de Venegas (te-KAHL de ve-NE-gahs), town (1990 pop. 2,159), Yucatán, SE Mexico, 6 mi/9.7 km NE of Izamal; 21°01′N 88°57′W. Henequen. Corn, tropical fruit.

Tekamah (tuh-KUH-muh), town (1990 pop. 1,852), ⊙ Burt co., E Nebr., 35 mi/56 km N of Omaha, near Missouri R; 41°46′N 96°13′W. Farm trading center; dairy prods., grain. Mfg. (ovens, printing). Pelican Point State Recreation Area on Missouri R. to NE. Inc. 1855.

Tekantó (te-kahn-TO), town (1990 pop. 3,376), Yucatán, SE Mexico, 33 mi/53 km E of Mérida; 21°01′N 89°06′W. Henequen, sugar, corn.

Tekax, Mexico: see TEKAX DE ALVARO OBREGÓN.

Tekax de Álvaro Obregón (te-KASH de AHL-vah-ro o-bre-GON), city (1990 pop. 18,527) and township, ⊙ Tekax municipio, Yucatan, SE Mexico, at foot of Puuc hills, on RR, 55 mi/89 km SSE of Mérida; 20°12′N 89°17′W. Agr. center (henequen, sugarcane, tobacco, corn, tropical fruit; timber). Has beautiful colonial church. Grottoes and Maya ruins nearby.

Tekit (te-KEET), town (1990 pop. 6,566), Yucatán, SE Mexico, 33 mi/53 km SE of Mérida; 20°32′N 89°20′W. Henequen, sugarcane, corn, fruit, timber.

Tekoa (TEE-ko), town (1990 pop. 1,292), Whitman co., SE Wash., near Idaho state line, 25 mi/40 km NE of Colfax, on Hangman Creek. RR junction. Wheat, barley, oats, peas, lentils; lumber. Coeur d'Alene Indian Reservation (Idaho) to E.

Tekom (te-KOM), town (1990 pop. 1,803), Yucatán, SE Mexico, 5 mi/8 km SSW of Valladolid on Mexico Highway 295; 20°34′N 88°14′W. Henequen, fruit; timber. Sometimes spelled Tecom.

Tekonsha (te-KAHN-shuh), village (1990 pop. 722), Calhoun co., S Mich., 18 mi/29 km SE of Battle Creek and on St. Joseph R.; 42°05′N 84°59′W. In farm area; food processing; mfg. motor vehicle parts.

Telchac (tel-CHAK), town (1990 pop. 3,358), ⊙ Telchac Pueblo municipio, Yucatán, SE Mexico, 28 mi/45 km NW of Mérida on Mexico Highway 172; 21°12′N 89°16′W. In henequen-growing region.

Telchac Pueblo, Mexico: see TELCHAC.

Telchac Puerto (tel-CHAK poo-ER-to), town (1990 pop. 1,113), Yucatán, SE Mexico, on bar offshore, 25 mi/40 km E of Progreso at terminus of Mexico Highway 172; 21°21′N 89°20′E. Henequen.

Telegraph Creek, village, NW B.C., Canada, on Stikine R., 120 mi/193 km ESE of Juneau; 57°54′N 131°09′W. Gold mining, commercial fishing; tourism. Former telegraph terminal.

Telephone, uninc. village (1990 pop. 210), Fannin co., NE Texas, 15 mi/24 km NE of Bonham, near Red R. Agr. area (cattle; peanuts, wheat, soybeans). Mfg. (food). Caddo Natl. Grassland to SE.

Telescope Peak (11,049 ft/3,368 m), Inyo co., E Calif., in Panamint Range, in W part of Death Valley Natl. Monument; rises steeply above Death Valley 17 mi/27 km W of its lowest point (282 ft/86 m below sea level); 36°10′N 117°05′W.

Telfair (TEL-fer), county (□ 444 sq mi/1,150 sq km; 1990 pop. 11,000), S central Ga.; ⊙ McRae; 31°56′N 82°56′W. Bounded S by Ocmulgee R., NE by Little Ocmulgee R. Coastal plain agr. (wheat, oats, cotton, corn, peanuts, tobacco, pecans); cattle, hogs; timber. Formed 1807.

Telford (TEL-fuhrd), borough (1990 pop. 4,238), Montgomery and Bucks cos., SE Pa., suburb 25 mi/40 km NNW of Philadelphia; 40°19′N 75°19′W. Mfg. (machinery, electronic equip., crushed stone, plastic prods., steel prods., glass prods.). Agr. (grain, soybeans; livestock; dairying). Settled 1860; Bucks co. part inc. 1886, Montgomery co. part inc. 1897. West Telford inc. with Telford 1935.

Telkwa (TEHL-kwuh), village (1991 pop. 959), W central B.C., Canada, on Bulkley R., at mouth of Telkwa R., 8 mi/13 km SE of Smithers. Elev. 1,693 ft/516 m. Coal mining; mfg. leather goods; creamery; cattle.

Tell City, city (1990 pop. 8,088), ⊙ Perry co., S Ind., on Ohio R., 45 mi/72 km E of Evansville; 37°57′N 86°46′W. Trade center in agr. and bituminous-coal area. Mfg. (electric motors, furniture, wood prods.). Settled 1857 by Swiss.

Teller, county (□ 558 sq mi/1,445 sq km; 1990 pop. 12,468), central Colo.; ⊙ Cripple Creek; 38°52′N 105°09′W. Drained by Trout and Rule creeks. Mining, ranching, and livestock-grazing area; gold, silver. Includes part of Front Range and Pike Natl. Forest in N and E. Cripple Creek dist., famous gold-producing region, is in S. Summit of Pikes Peak (14,110 ft/4,301 m) just E of co. line. Florissant Fossil Beds Natl. Monument in W; Mueller State Park in S center. Formed 1899.

Teller, village (1990 pop. 151), W Alaska, W Seward Peninsula, on Port Clarence, bay of Bering Sea, 60 mi/97 km NNW of Nome; 65°15′N 166°21′W. Supply center for gold-placer area; tin, graphite, and copper in vicinity. Airfield. Amundsen and Ellsworth landed here (1926) after North Pole flight of dirigible *Norge*. Original base for introduction of reindeer into Alaska.

Tellico Lake, reservoir (□ 22 sq mi/57 sq km), mostly in Loudon co., E Tenn., on Little Tennessee R., bet. Cherokee Natl. Forest and Tennessee R., 45 mi/72 km SW of Knoxville; 35°47′N 84°16′W. Max. capacity 467,600 acre-ft. Extends N-S. Formed by Tellico Dam (129 ft/39 m high), built (1979) by TVA for navigation; also used for flood control, power generation, water storage, and recreation. Fort Loudon State Historical Area at S end of reservoir

Tellico Plains, town (1990 pop. 657), Monroe co., SE Tenn., on Tellico R. (tributary of Little Tennessee R.), 45 mi/72 km SW of Knoxville, 35°22′N 84°18′W. In scenic Cherokee Natl. Forest, in area of agr., lumbering, barite mining. State fish hatchery nearby.

Telluride (TEL-yoo-reid), town (1990 pop. 1,309), ⊙ San Miguel co., SW Colo., in San Juan Mts., 90 mi/145 km SSE of Grand Junction; 37°56′N 107°48′W. Elev. 8,745 ft/2,665 m. Trade and tourist center in sheep, dairying, mining region. Mfg. (printing and publishing). Tourism. Gold, silver, lead mines. Pop. exceeded 5,000 at peak of gold production (c.1890). Telluride Ski Area is here. Bridal Veil Falls nearby. Wilson Peak 12 mi/19 km SW; Mt. Sneffels 5 mi/8 km N. Inc. 1887.

Teloloapan (te-lo-lo-AH-pahn), city (1990 pop. 17,763) and township, Guerrero, SW Mexico, on S slopes of central plateau, 25 mi/40 km W of Iguala de la Independencia; 18°21′N 99°51′W. Elev. 5,315 ft/1,620 m. Agr. center (cereals, tobacco, coffee, fruit, resin, vanilla); mfg. (vegetable oils, soap).

Temagami, Canada: see TIMAGAMI.

Temamatla (te-mah-MAHT-lah), town (1990 pop. 2,902), Mexico state, central Mexico, 25 mi/40 km SE of Mexico city, and in the Zona Metropolitana de la Ciudad de Mexico; 19°12′N 98°53′W. Sugarcane, cereals; livestock.

Temascal, Mexico: see NUEVO SOYALTEPEC.

Temascal Lake Natural Park, Mexico: see NUEVO SOYALTEPEC.

Temascalapa (te-mahs-kah-LAH-pah), town (1990 pop. 3,703), Mexico state, central Mexico, 32 mi/51 km NNE of Mexico city, and part of the Zona Metropolitana de la Ciudad de Mexico; 19°50′N 98°54′W. Cereals, maguey; livestock.

Temascalcingo (te-mahs-kahl-SEEN-go), town (1990 pop. 7,327), Mexico state, central Mexico, 15 mi/24 km NE of El Oro; 19°55′N 100°00′W. Cereals, fruit; livestock. Formerly called Temascalcingo de José María Velasco.

Temascaltepec de González (te-mahs-KAHL-te-pahk), town (1990 pop. 1,987), ⊙ Temascaltepec municipio, Mexico state, central Mexico, 30 mi/48 km SW of Toluca de Lerdo, on Mexico Highway 130; 19°02′N 100°03′W. Elev. 5,807 ft/1,770 m.

Temax (te-MASH), town (1990 pop. 6,000), Yucatán, SE Mexico, on RR, 45 mi/72 km ENE of Mérida, on Mexico Highway 176; 21°10′N 88°53′W. Henequen center.

Temblor Range (c.2,000 ft/610 m–4,300 ft/1,311 m), S central Calif.; meets SE end of Diablo Range along line bet. Kern and San Luis Obispo cos. and extends c.50 mi/80 km SE, bordering San Joaquin Valley (NE) and Carrizo Plain (SW), to meet San Emigdio Mts. near S end of the valley. Oil fields at E base. McKittrick Summit (4,331 ft/1,320 m), 35 mi/56 km W of Bakersfield, in center of range.

Temecula, city (1990 pop. 27,099), Riverside co., S Calif., 25 mi/40 km NE of Oceanside, c.75 mi/121 km SE of Los Angeles and 53 mi/85 km N of San Diego, in Temecula Valley, on Marrieta Creek, at its mouth of Temecula R.; 33°30′N 117°08′W. Grain, nursery stock, avocados; poultry, cattle; dairying; mfg. (electronic equip., industrial and medical instruments, aluminum prods., machinery, lighting equip.). Area has experienced rapid growth since 1980 (when the pop. was 4,289) due to an influx of people from Los Angeles and San Diego areas. San Diego Aqueduct runs N-S to E; parts of Cleveland Natl. Forest to NW and SE; Vail L. reservoir to E; Pechanga Indian Reservation to SE; Murrieta and Temecula hot springs to N.

Temelec, uninc. town (1990 pop. 1,594), Sonoma co., W Calif., residential suburb 11 mi/18 km S of Santa Rosa, near Petaluma R.; 38°16′N 122°30′W. Dairying; poultry; grain, some fruit.

Temiscaming, Timiskaming (both: ti-MIS-kuh-ming) or**Témiscamingue** (tai-mis-kah-MAHG), town (1991 pop. 2,944), SW Que., Canada, at the S end of L. Timiscaming, NE of North Bay; 46°43′N 79°05′W. A paper mill is the town's most important industry. Gold, silver, cobalt, and arsenic are mined in the region.

Temiscaming, Lake, Fr. *Témiscamingue*, expansion (□ 121 sq mi/313 sq km) of the Ottawa R., SW Que., Canada, extending 62 mi/100 km SE from New Liskeard to Temiscaming. The surrounding area is rich in minerals.

Temiscamingue or **Témiscamingue** (both: tuh-MI-skuh-ming), county (□ 8,977 sq mi/23,250 sq km; 1991 pop. 17,381), SW Que., Canada, on Ont. border; ⊙ Ville Marie.

Témiscamingue, Canada: see TEMISCAMING.

Temiscouata or **Témiscouata** (both: teh-mis-KWA-tuh), county (□ 1,151 sq mi/2,981 sq km; 1991 pop. 23,348), SE Que., Canada, on Maine and N.B. borders; ⊙ Notre Dame du Lac; 47°40′N 68°50′W.

Témiscouata, Lake, SE Que., Canada, 30 mi/48 km E of Rivière du Loup; 28 mi/45 km long, 3 mi/5 km wide; 47°40′N 68°50′W. Drained by Madawaska R.

Temixco (te-MESH-ko), town (1990 pop. 65,058), Morelos, central Mexico, 5 mi/8 km S of Cuernavaca on Mexico Highway 95; 18°51′N 99°14′W. Elev. 4,081 ft/1,244 m. Sugarcane, rice, wheat, coffee, fruit; livestock.

Temoac (te-mo-AHK), town (1990 pop. 4,211), Morelos, central Mexico, 12 mi/19 km ESE of Cuautla; 18°46′N 98°47′W. Sugarcane, corn, fruit; livestock.

Temoaya (te-mo-AH-yah), town (1990 pop. 2,130), central Mexico state, Mexico, 14 mi/22 km NNE of Toluca de Lerdo; 19°28′N 99°35′W. Agr. resources are corn, wool, and livestock.

Témoris (te-mo-rees), town (1990 pop. 808), ⊙ Guazapares township, Chihuahua, N Mexico, in Sierra Madre Occidental on Chihuahua-Pacific RR, 160 mi/257 km SW of Chihuahua. Silver, gold, copper deposits.

Temósachi (te-MO-sah-chee), town (1990 pop. 2,232), Chihuahua, N Mexico, in Sierra Madre Occidental, on headstream of Yaqui R., 77 mi/124 km NW of Cuahtemoc, on RR; 28°58′N 107°50′W. Elev. 6,234 ft/1,900 m. Corn, wheat, beans; cattle. A major viewpoint on Copper Canyon RR. In Takahumara-Indian area. Formerly spelled Temósachic.

Temozón (te-mo-SON), town (1990 pop. 3,873), Yucatán, SE Mexico, 12 mi/19 km N of Valladolid. Henequen, corn, sugarcane.

Tempe (tem-PEE), city (1990 pop. 141,865), Maricopa co., S Ariz., on Salt R., 7 mi/11.3 km ESE of Phoenix; 33°23′N 111°55′W. It has been one of the fastest-growing U.S. cities; its pop. more than doubled bet. 1970 and 1990. City is now surrounded by other municipalities: Scottsdale (N), Mesa (E), Chandler (S), Phoenix (W). Tempe is a health resort and an agr. center, with lands irrigated by the Salt R. project (Western Canal crosses city in S); mfg. (machinery, electrical equip., glass, rubber, paper and plastic prods., apparel, chemicals, communications equip., tools). The city is also the seat of Arizona State Univ., which has expanded rapidly to become a principal economic factor in Tempe's growth. The univ.'s auditorium was designed by Frank Lloyd Wright. Tempe is home to a Natl. Football League team, the Ariz. Cardinals, at Ariz. State Univ.'s Sun Devil Stadium; training camp of Calif. Angels baseball team. Native Amer. ruins are nearby. To N, across the Salt R. is Papago City Park (Phoenix) including Phoenix Zoo; Phoenix South Mt. Park to W. Inc. 1894.

Temperance, village (1990 pop. 6,542), Monroe co., SE Mich., 13 mi/21 km SW of Monroe; 41°46′N 83°34′W. Mfg. (furniture, metal fabrication).

Temperanceville, uninc. village, Accomack co., E Va., 14 mi/23 km NNE of Accomac, on Delmarva (Eastern Shore) peninsula, bet. Atlantic Ocean (E) and Chesapeake Bay (W); 37°53′N 75°32′W. Mfg. (poultry processing); agr. (livestock; fruit, vegetables, grain). NASA Wallops Flight Center to E.

Temple, city (1990 pop. 46,109), Bell co., central Texas, 60 mi/97 km NNE of Austin; 31°06′N 97°21′W. Bounded by Leon R. on SW. Its twin city of Killeen is 21 mi/34 km W, the gateway to large Fort Hood Military Reservation. In a rich blackland region, Temple has grain and textile mills, RR shops, and plants that make computer printers and terminals, furniture, and school and office supplies. Draughton Miller Airport to NW. Several state and federal agencies have agr. research centers here. Temple also has 3 private hosps., which remain an economic factor in the the city's growth and development. Texas A (?is)& M School of Medicine, Temple Jr. Col. Belton L. reservoir to W, Stillhouse Hollow L. reservoir to SW. Est. 1880; inc. 1882.

Temple 1 town (1990 pop. 1,870), Carroll co., W Ga., 11 mi/18 km NNE of Carrollton; 33°44′N 85°02′W. Mfg. of egg- and poultry-processing equip., clothing, furniture. **2** town (1990 pop. 560), Franklin co., W central Maine, just NW of Farmington; 44°42′N 70°17′W. **3** town (1990 pop. 1,194), Hillsborough co., S N.H., 21 mi/34 km WNW of Nashua; 42°49′N 71°50′W. Mfg. (machining); agr. (pumpkins, fruit, vegetables; livestock; dairying). Part of Miller State Park in NW; Pack Monadnock Mt. (2,280 ft/695 m) in NW; Temple Mt. (2,081 ft/634 m) and Temple Mt. Ski Area in NW. **4** town (1990 pop. 1,223), Cotton co., S Okla., 22 mi/35 km SE of Lawton, near Red R.; 34°16′N 98°13′W. In agr. area (cotton, wheat; livestock); cotton ginning; mfg. (steel prods.). Wawika L. reservoir to E. Settled 1902.

Temple, borough (1990 pop. 1,491), Berks co., SE central Pa., suburb 5 mi/8 km N of Reading; 40°24′N 75°55′W. RR junction. Mfg. (motor parts, food processing, apparel, fabricated metal prods.); limestone quarries. L. Ontelaunee reservoir to N. Founded 1857.

Temple City, city (1990 pop. 31,100), Los Angeles co., S Calif. residential suburb 11 mi/18 km ENE of Los Angeles; 34°06′N 118°04′W. The city has light mfg. (special trade machinery) and service businesses. El Monte Airport to SE. Settled 1827, inc. 1960.

Temple, Mount (11,636 ft/3,547 m), SW Alta., Canada, near B.C. border, in Rocky Mts., in Banff Natl. Park, 30 mi/48 km WNW of Banff; 51°21′N 116°12′W.

Temple Terrace, city (□ 4 sq mi/10.4 sq km; 1990 pop. 16,444), Hillsborough co., W central Fla., suburb 6 mi/9.7 km NE of Tampa, on Hillsboro R.; 28°02′N 82°22′W.

Templeton, Canada: see SAINTE ROSE DE LIMA.

Templeton 1 uninc. town, San Luis Obispo co., SW Calif., 18 mi/29 km N of San Luis Obispo, on Salinas R.; 35°33′N 120°43′W. Santa Lucia Range to SW; part of Los Padres Natl. Forest to S. Cattle; grain, nursery prods., flowers, vegetables, avocados, apples. **2** town (1990 pop. 321), Carroll co., W central Iowa, 11 mi/18 km SSW of Carroll; 41°55′N 94°56′W. In agr. area. **3** town (1990 pop. 6,438), Worcester co., N central Mass., 13 mi/21 km W of Fitchburg; 42°34′N 72°04′W. Furniture, paper and chemical prods. Includes villages of Baldwinsville, seat of institution for handicapped children, and East Templeton. Templeton State Forest nearby. Settled 1751, inc. 1762. **4** uninc. town (1990 pop. 800), Boggs township, Armstrong co., W Pa., 8 mi/12.9 km N of Kittanning, on the Allegheny R. (RR bridge), 1 mi/1.6 km S of mouth of Mahoning Creek; 40°55′N 79°27′W. Hay; dairying.

Templeville, town (1990 pop. 66), Caroline and Queen Anne cos., E Md., near Del. state line, 13 mi/21 km W of Dover (Del.); 39°08′N 75°46′W. The N side is in Del. and the S in Md., and it was named for the Temple family, one of whom was a governor of Delaware.

Tempoal de Sánchez (tem-po-AHL de SAHN-chez), city (1990 pop. 12,218) and township, Veracruz, E Mexico, on affluent of Moctezuma R., 16 mi/26 km NW of Tantoyuca on Mexico Highway 105; 21°32′N 98°23′W. Cereals, coffee, sugarcane, fruit; livestock.

Ten Mile Lake (□ 18 sq mi/47 sq km), N N.F., Canada, 12 mi/19 km E of Ferolle Point; 15 mi/24 km long, 2 mi/3 km wide; 51°5′N 56°40′W. Drains into Gulf of St. Lawrence. Round L. just NE.

Ten Mile Lake, Cass co., central Minn., near Leech L., 7 mi/11.3 km S of Walker; 5 mi/8 km long, 2.5 mi/4 km wide. Resort area. Source of Boy R., which flows from NE end of lake to Birch L.; S part in Foothills State Forest; N part in Chippewa Natl. Forest.

Ten Mile Peak (c.12,375 ft/3,772 m), central Colo., in Rocky Mts., 3 mi/4.8 km SSW of Frisco. Overlooks town.

Ten Pound Island, islet in harbor of Gloucester, E Mass. Lighthouse.

Ten Sleep, village (1990 pop. 311), Washakie co., N central Wyo., on Nowood Creek, at mouth of Ten Sleep Creek, just W of Bighorn Mts., 25 mi/40 km E of Worland; 44°01′N 107°27′W. Elev. 4,206 ft/1,282 m. Supply point in sheep and cattle region; agr. (alfalfa, barley); lumber. Powder R. Pass. is ENE. Bighorn Natl. Forest to NE; Meadlowlark Ski Area to NE.

Ten Thousand Islands, group of small isls. in the Gulf of Mexico, off SW Fla., covered with mangrove forests and surrounded by clam beds. Most of the isls. are in Everglades Natl. Park.

Ten Thousand Smokes, Valley of, Alaska: see KATMAI NATIONAL MONUMENT AND PRESERVE.

Tenabo (ten-AH-bo), city (1990 pop. 5,154) and township, Campeche, SE Mexico, on NW Yucatán Peninsula, 10 mi/16 km SW of Hecelchakán on Mexico Highway 180; 20°02′N 90°12′E. Sugarcane, tobacco, henequen, fruit; livestock.

Tenabo, Mount, Nev.: see CORTEZ MOUNTAINS.

Tenafly (TE-nuh-flei), residential suburban borough (1990 pop. 13,326), Bergen co., NE N.J.; 40°55′N 73°57′W. It is located along the Palisades and the E edge of the Hudson R. Inc. 1894.

Tenaha, town (1990 pop. 1,072), Shelby co., E Texas, c.45 mi/72 km SSE of Marshall; 31°56′N 94°14′W. RR junction; agr. (vegetables, watermelons; cattle, poultry); timber; mfg. (lumber, poultry processing, wood shavings); oil, gas wells.

Tenakee, village (1990 pop. 94), SE Alaska, on E shore of Chichagof Isl., 45 mi/72 km SW of Juneau, NW of Angoon; 57°46′N 135°08′W. Fishing and canning. Also called Tenakee Springs.

Tenamaxtlán (ten-ah-mash-TLAHN), town (1990 pop. 3,793), Jalisco, W Mexico, 21 mi/34 km SSW of Ameca; 20°13′N 104°11′W. Agr. center (oranges, cotton, sugarcane, rice, tobacco).

Tenampa (te-NAHM-pah), town (1990 pop. 1,730), Veracruz, E Mexico, in Sierra Madre Oriental, 19 mi/31 km S of Xalapa Enriquez; 19°15′N 96°53′W. Elev. 3,707 ft/1,130 m. Corn, fruit.

Tenampulco (te-nahm-POOL-ko), town (1990 pop. 1,171), Puebla, E Mexico, in Gulf lowland, 20 mi/32 km SSW of Papantla de Olarte; 20°15′N 97°27′W. Sugarcane, coffee, tobacco, fruit. In Totonac-Indian area.

Tenancingo (te-nahn-SEEN-go), city (1990 pop. 24,774) and township, Mexico state, central Mexico, on central plateau, 26 mi/42 km SSE of Toluca de Lerdo on Mexico Highway 55; 18°57′N 99°35′W. Elev. 6,634 ft/2,022 m. Agr. center (grain, sugarcane, fruit, vegetables; livestock); textile milling. Formerly called Tenancingo de Degollado.

Tenancingo (te-nahn-SEEN-go), town (1990 pop. 9,749), Tlaxcala, central Mexico, 7 mi/11.3 km N of Puebla; 19°09′N 98°11′W. Cereals, alfalfa, beans; livestock.

Tenango de Arista (te-NAHN-go de ah-REES-tah), town (1990 pop. 14,148), ⊙ Tenango del Valle municipio, Mexico state, central Mexico, in Toluca Valley, on RR, 35 mi/56 km SW of Mexico city on Mexico Highway 55; 19°10′N 99°34′W. Agr. center (cereals, vegetables; livestock); dairying.

Tenango de Doria (te-NAHN-go de DO-ree-ah), town (1990 pop. 1,628), Hidalgo, central Mexico, 37 mi/60 km NE of Pachuca de Soto; 20°21′N 98°13′W. Corn, wheat, sugarcane, fruit; livestock.

Tenango de Río Blanco (te-NAHN-go de REE-o-BLAHN-ko), town (1990 pop. 37,632), ⊙ Río Blanco municipio, Veracruz, E Mexico, in Sierra Madre Oriental, at SE foot of Pico de Orizaba, on RR, 3 mi/4.8 km W of Orizaba on Mexico Highway 150; 18°49′N 97°14′W. Cotton-milling center (yarn and cloth); brewery, mfg. of printing presses. Dam and hydroelectric station on Río Blanco nearby.

Tenango de Tepopula (te-NAHN-go de TE-po-POO-lah), town (1990 pop. 3,503), ⊙ Tenango del Aire municipio, Mexico state, central Mexico, 27 mi/43 km SE of Mexico city, within the Zona Metropolitana de la Ciudad de Mexico; 19°10′N 98°51′W. Cereals, vegetables; stock.

Tenango del Aire, Mexico: see TENANGO DE TEPOPULA.

Tenango del Valle, Mexico: see TENANGO DE ARISTA.

Tenants Harbor, Maine: see SAINT GEORGE.

Tenares (te-NAH-res) or **Villa Tenares**, town (1993 pop. 6,308), Espaillat prov., N Dominican Republic, 12 mi/19 km E of Moca. Agr. (cacao, coffee, bananas, fruit).

Tenayuca, Mexico: see TLALNEPANTLA DE BAZ.

Tenejapa (te-ne-HAH-pah), town (1990 pop. 1,292), Chiapas, S Mexico, in Sierra de Hueytepec, 9 mi/14.5 km NE of San Cristóbal de las Casas; 16°49′N 92°31′W. Elev. 6,463 ft/1,970 m. Wheat, fruit. In Tzeltal-Maya speaking area.

Tenino (ten-EIN-o), town (1990 pop. 1,292), Thurston co., W Wash., 13 mi/21 km S of Olympia; 46°52′N 122°51′W. Vegetables; poultry; mfg. (machining); logging, sandstone quarry. Wolf Haven (wolf sanctuary) here. Millersylvania State Park to NW.

Tenkiller Lake, reservoir, Cherokee and Sequoyah cos., E Okla., on Illinois R., 20 mi/32 km SE of Tulsa; c.25 mi/40 km long; 35°34′N 95°02′W. Formed by Tenkiller Dam. Cherokee Landing and Tenkiller state parks on SE shore.

Tenleytown, residential and commercial section of NW Washington, D.C., centered at Wisconsin and Nebraska Aves.; 38°57′N 77°05′W. It developed after 1900 as a working-class community. The highest point of land in D.C. (410 ft/125 m) is here, and Amer. Univ. is just SW.

Tennant, town (1990 pop. 78), Shelby co., W Iowa, 8 mi/12.9 km SW of Harlan; 41°36′N 95°26′W. In agr. area.

Tennessee, state (□ 42,146 sq mi/109,158 sq km; 1995 est. pop. 5,256,051), S central U.S., admitted in 1796 as the 16th state; 35°50′N 86°25′W. ⊙ NASHVILLE, which is the state's 2d-largest city. The largest city is MEMPHIS. The state is bounded on the N by Ky. and Va.; on the E by N.C.; on the S by Ga., Ala., and Miss.; and on the W by the Mississippi R., which separates it from Mo. and Ark. Although Tenn. is now primarily industrial, with most of its pop. in urban areas, many Tennesseans still derive their livelihood from the land of the state's 3 sharply defined regions or grand divisions: E Tenn., Middle Tenn., and W Tenn. In E Tenn. the Great Smoky Mts., Cumberland Plateau, and the narrow river valleys and heavily forested foothills generally restrict farming to tobacco, hay, and livestock raising, but this region has extensive coal mines as well as 2 of Tenn.'s most industrialized cities, CHATTANOOGA (4th-largest in the state) and KNOXVILLE (3d-largest). Middle Tenn. is hemmed in by the Tennessee R., which flows SW through E Tenn. into N Ala., looping back up into W Tenn. in its circuitous route to the Ohio R. Gently rolling, fertile, bluegrass country, it is ideal for livestock raising and dairy farming, along with corn, wheat, soybeans, tobacco, fruit, and vegetables. Middle Tenn. is still noted for its fine horses and mules, e.g., the Tenn. walking horse. W Tenn., with its rich river-bottom lands, on which most of the state's cotton and soybeans are grown, lies bet. the Tennessee and the Mississippi rivers. The average rainfall ranges from 40 in/102 cm to 50 in/127 cm, and the climate ranges from humid continental in the N of the state to humid subtropical in S Tenn.; the rigors of winter usually affect only the most mountainous parts of E Tenn. The state's major crops are soybeans, hay, tobacco, and cotton; cattle, dairy prods., and hogs are also principal farm commodities. Tenn.'s leading mineral, in dollar value, is stone; zinc ranks 2d (Tenn. leads the nation in its production), followed by cement. Industry is diversified; the state's leading mfg. includes chemicals and related prods., foods, electrical machinery, primary metals, automobiles, textiles and apparel, and stone, clay, and glass items. Aluminum production has been important since World War I. Tenn. has long been a major tourist destination, due largely to its beautiful scenery and such popular attractions as Graceland, home of Elvis Presley, and the Grand Ole Opry, now based at OPRYLAND USA, a 120-acre/49-ha theme park. Many lakes, some of them publicly owned, have been built by the TVA and the U.S. Army Corps of Engineers. The TVA has also developed the LAND BETWEEN THE LAKES, an enormous Ky.-Tenn. recreation area. More than 50 state parks, covering more than 160,000 acres/64,752 ha, and parts of the Great Smoky Mts. Natl. Park, Cherokee Natl. Forest, Cumberland Gap Natl. Historical Park, Big South Fork Natl. R. and Recreation Area, and the Appalachian Trail are in Tenn. Sportsmen and visitors are attracted to Reelfoot L., originally formed by an earthquake; cypress stumps and other remains of a formerly dense forest, together with the lotus bed covering the shallow waters, give the lake an eerie beauty. Tenn. has long been known as a natl. music center, from the country music capital of Nashville to the blues and jazz of Memphis. It also has many sites of historic interest, including the Hermitage, home of Andrew Jackson; the Andrew Johnson Natl. Historic Site; the Fort Donelson and Shiloh natl. military parks; and Stones R. Natl. Battlefield. Part of the Chickamauga and Chattanooga Natl. Military Park is also in Tenn. The Natchez Trace Natl. Parkway generally follows the old Natchez Trace, and W Tenn. abounds in artifacts of the Mound Builders. Cherokee, Chickasaw, Shawnee, and Creek were in the region when it was 1st visited by a Eur. expedition under De Soto in 1540. Fr. explorers came down the Mississippi R., claiming both sides for France, and c.1682 La Salle built Fort Prudhomme, possibly on the site of present-day Memphis. The French established additional trading posts in the area, but they suffered continual harassment from the Chickasaw. Meanwhile, Eng. fur traders and long hunters (frontiersmen who spent long periods hunting in this area) came over the mts. from the Carolinas and Va., prevailed over the Cherokee, and made ineffectual the Fr. claims to the area, which in any event the French lost (1763) as a result of the Fr. and Indian Wars. The 1st permanent settlement was made (1769) in the Watauga R. valley of E Tenn. by Virginians; they were soon joined by North Carolinians, including perhaps a few refugees of the Regulator movement. In 1772 these hardy settlers living beyond the frontier formed the Watauga Assn., the 1st attempt at govt. in Tenn., and in 1777, at their request, N.C. organized those settlements into Washington co.; Jonesboro (now spelled Jonesborough), the co. seat and oldest town in Tenn., was founded 2 years later. In the Amer. Revolution, John Sevier was among the notable Tennesseans who served with distinction. When, after the war, N.C. ceded its W lands to the federal govt., the E Tenn. settlers, incensed at being transferred without their consent, formed a short-lived independent state (1784–1788) under John Sevier called FRANKLIN. The cession was repealed in 1789, and in 1790 the federal govt. created the Territory of the U.S. S of the Ohio R. (Southwest Territory), with William Blount as governor. This act disposed of various schemes to place the area under the control of Span. La., and, in 1796, Tenn., with substantially its present boundaries, was admitted to the Union, with its capital at Knoxville. It was the 1st state to be carved out of natl. territory. Armed with land grants awarded for service in the Amer. Revolution, veterans and speculators swarmed in from the Carolinas, Va., Pa., and even from New England via such overland routes as the Wilderness Road and Cumberland Gap. Others poled keelboats from the Ohio up the Cumberland and Tennessee rivers. By the time Andrew Jackson became president (1829), the state was prospering. The 1st steamboat had reached Nashville in 1819, the year in which Memphis, soon to become the metropolis of a fast-growing cotton kingdom, was platted. Internal improvements—canals and then RRs—were pushed, and a new, smaller wave of immigrants (predominantly Irish and Ger.) arrived after the Cherokee and the Chickasaw were banished W in the late 1830s. Insatiable land hunger, the spirit of adventure, and personal considerations carried many white Tennesseans beyond the state; among them were Gov. Samuel Houston and David Crockett, both of whom had been conspicuous in the fight for Texan independence. A decade later the response of Tenn. for volunteers in the Mex.-Amer. War was so overwhelming that it earned the nickname of the "Volunteer State." Tennessee's James K. Polk, a Jackson protégé, was president of the U.S. during that war. Although slaves were numerous in W Tenn., and to a lesser extent in Middle Tenn., and free blacks were subjected to a series of discriminatory regulations, the state was initially pro-Union. Secession was rejected in a popular referendum on Feb. 9, 1861. However, after the firing on Fort Sumter and Lincoln's call for troops, the pro-Confederate element, led by Gov. Isham G. Harris, canvassed the state, and on June 8, 1861, another referendum approved secession by a ⅔ majority. In the Civil War, Tenn. was, after Va., the biggest and bloodiest battleground. The rivers served as Union invasion routes. Nashville was occupied by Gen. D. C. Buell in Feb. 1862, after the victories of Gen. Ulysses S. Grant on the lower Tennessee and Cumberland rivers at FORT HENRY and FORT DONELSON. In April one of the bloodiest battles of the war took place near the Miss. state line (see SHILOH NATIONAL MILITARY PARK), and Memphis fell to a Union fleet in June. Confederate general Braxton Bragg, defeated at Perryville, Ky., in Oct. 1862, retreated further in Jan. 1863, after the battle of Murfreesboro, and Grant completely routed him (Nov. 1863) in the Chattanooga campaign. The Confederates did manage to hold onto Knoxville until Sept. 1863, and their cavalry, particularly the forces of Gen. N. B. Forrest and Gen. J. H. Morgan, remained active. An army under Gen. J. B. Hood made a last desperate attempt to regain the state late in 1864 but was defeated at the city of FRANKLIN (Nov. 30) and annihilated at Nashville (Dec. 15–16) by Federals under G. H. Thomas. The Union military govt. which had been set up under Andrew Johnson in 1862 was succeeded in April 1865, by a civil govt. headed by Brownlow. An amendment to the state constitution of 1834 freed the slaves. Tenn. was the 1st Southern state to be readmitted to the Union (March 1866). Economically, the farm-tenancy system, which had replaced the plantation system, brought much misery; industry, however, made advances after the war. The iron and steelworks of E Tenn. were unable to meet the competition of Birmingham, Ala., but coal mining continued and textile production increased. The use of convict labor in the mines precipitated the state's 1st major labor disturbance (1891–1892), but not until 1936 was the convict-leasing system abolished. A statewide Prohibition bill was passed over a governor's veto in 1909 (and wasn't repealed until 1939), and the affair so divided the Democratic party that in 1910 a Republican was elected governor for the 1st time since 1880. In World War I the thousands of Tennessean volunteers in the U.S. armed forces included Sergeant Alvin C. York, who became one of the nation's most highly publicized heroes. In 1925 the state attracted internatl. attention with the famous Scopes trial at Dayton, and the fact that the state law banning the teaching of evolution was not repealed until 1967 indicates the strong hold that Protestant fundamentalism had on the people; in 1973 a bill prohibiting the teaching of evolution as a fact was passed. One of the most important events in Tenn. since the Civil War was the establishment of the TVA. Although opposed by private power companies, the TVA succeeded in providing hydroelectric power cheaply and in abundance, bringing modern comforts to thousands. Over the years it has expanded and been supplemented by other projects for water-resources development. Most important, the TVA was chiefly responsible for the basic change in the state's economy from agr. to industry and for the significant growth and diversification of industry, especially during and after World War II. The TVA has also come to be associated with atomic energy, for it provides the power for Oak Ridge, one of the sources of production of the constituents for the 1st atomic bombs. In addition to growth in the service, trade, and finance sectors of the state economy, Tenn. has been very aggressive in attracting new industry since the late 1970s. Many of the firms who have been setting up new factories and distribution centers in Tenn. come from Northern industrial states and Japan. Tenn. has had 3 constitutions: the 1st was drafted in 1796, the 2d in 1834, and the present constitution dates from 1870. Tennessee's executive branch is headed by a governor, elected for a 4-year term. The state's bicameral legislature has a senate, with 33 members elected for 4-year terms, and a house, with 99 members elected for 2-year terms. The state elects 2 senators and 9 representatives to the U.S. Congress and has 11 electoral votes. Among the state's many institutions of higher learning are the Univ. of Tenn., with its main campus at Knoxville; E Tenn. State Univ., at Johnson City; Fisk Univ. and Vanderbilt Univ., at Nashville; The Univ. of Memphis, at Memphis; Tenn. Technological Univ., at Cookeville; and the Univ. of the South, at Sewanee. Tenn. has 95 cos.: ANDERSON, BEDFORD, BENTON, BLEDSOE, BLOUNT, BRADLEY, CAMPBELL, CANNON, CARROLL, CARTER, CHEATHAM, CHESTER, CLAIBORNE, CLAY, COCKE, COFFEE, CROCKETT, CUMBERLAND, DAVIDSON, DECATUR, DE KALB, DICKSON, DYER, FAYETTE, FENTRESS, FRANKLIN, GIBSON, GILES, GRAINGER, GREENE, GRUNDY, HAMBLEN, HAMILTON, HANCOCK, HARDEMAN, HARDIN, HAWKINS, HAYWOOD, HENDERSON, HENRY, HICKMAN, HOUSTON, HUMPHREYS, JACKSON, JEFFERSON, JOHNSON, KNOX, LAKE, LAUDERDALE, LAWRENCE, LEWIS, LINCOLN, LOUDON, MCMINN, MCNAIRY, MACON, MADISON, MARION, MARSHALL, MAURY, MEIGS, MONROE, MONTGOMERY, MOORE, MORGAN, OBION, OVERTON, PERRY, PICKETT, POLK, PUTNAM, RHEA, ROANE, ROBERTSON, RUTHERFORD, SCOTT, SEQUATCHIE, SEVIER, SHELBY, SMITH, STEWART, SULLIVAN, SUMNER, TIPTON, TROUSDALE, UNICOI, UNION, VAN BUREN, WARREN, WASHINGTON, WAYNE, WEAKLEY, WHITE, WILLIAMSON, WILSON.

Tennessee, village (1990 pop. 127), McDonough co., W Ill., 9 mi/14.5 km WSW of Macomb; 40°24′N 90°50′W. In agr. area.

Tennessee Pass (10,424 ft/3,177 m), central Colo., in Park Range, crosses Continental Divide N-S, 8 mi/12.9 km N of Leadville. Crossed by RR and U.S. Highway 24.

Tennessee River, the principal tributary of the Ohio R.; c.650 mi/1,046 km long; formed by the confluence of the Holston and French Broad rivers near Knoxville, Tenn., and follows a U-shaped course to enter the Ohio R. at Paducah, Ky. Its drainage basin covers c.41,000 sq mi/106,190 sq km and includes parts of 7 states. Navigation was long impeded by variations in channel depths and by rapids, such as Muscle Shoals. However, the TVA (est. 1933) converted the river into a chain of lakes held back by 9 major dams (Kentucky, Pickwick Landing, Wilson, Wheeler, Guntersville, Nickajack, Chickamauga, Watts Bar, and Fort Loudoun). As a result of these improvements, river traffic has increased, flooding has been controlled, a water-oriented recreation industry has been established, and hydroelectric power generated at the dams has attracted new industries to the region. A canal, completed in the 1980s, links the Tennessee R. with the Gulf of Mexico by way of the Tombigee R. During the Civil War, the Tennessee R. was a prime approach for a Union invasion of the South.

Tennessee-Tombigbee Waterway, c.234 mi/377 km long, Ala. and Miss.; constructed by the U.S. Army Corps of Engineers, 1972–1984, connecting the Tennessee and Tombigbee rivers; flows from NE Miss., running S from the Tennessee R. and crossing into Ala. at Aliceville L., then SSE toward Demopolis, Ala. Increased commerce by shortening the distance of waterborne shipping from many states to the Gulf of Mexico.

Tenney, village (1990 pop. 4), Wilkin co., W Minn., 17 mi/27 km SSE of Breckenridge; 46°02′N 96°27′W. Grain.

Tennille (ten-EEL), town (1990 pop. 1,552), Washington co., E central Ga., 3 mi/4.8 km S of Sandersville; 32°56′N 82°49′W. Mfg. of lumber and clothing. Inc. 1875.

Tennyson, town (1990 pop. 267), Warrick co., SW Ind., 9 mi/14.5 km NE of Boonville; 38°05′N 87°07′W. Agr. area.

Tennyson, village (1990 pop. 378), Grant co., SW Wis., 10 mi/16 km WSW of Platteville; 42°41′N 90°41′W.

Tenochtitlán (te-noch-teet-lahn), anc. city in the central valley of Mexico. The capital of the Aztec people, it was founded (c.1325) on a marshy isl. in L. Texcoco. It was a flourishing city (with an est. pop. of bet. 200,000 and 300,000), connected with the mainland by 3 great causeways. These ran along massive dike constructions erected to prevent the salty floodwaters of the E lake from mingling with the fresh water surrounding the isl. city. The dikes thereby protected the unique system of lake agr. known as chinampas. Canals served to convey traffic throughout the city, including to and from the bustling, highly organized market at Tlatelolco. The ceremonial precinct contained many structures, including a great pyramid sacred to the Aztec war god Huitzilopochtli. It was to Tenochtitlán and the court of Montezuma that Hernán Cortés came, and it was from Tenochtitlán that the Spanish fled on the night of June 30, 1520, under heavy Aztec attack—the so-called *noche triste.* Cortés returned in 1521, took the city after a 3-month siege, razed it, and captured the ruler, Cuauhtémoc. The Spaniard founded present-day Mexico city on the ruins.

Tenochtitlán, congregación (1990 pop. 2,006) and township, Veracruz, E Mexico, in Sierra Madre Oriental, 18 mi/29 km N of Xalapa; 19°44′N 96°58′W. Elev. 4,921 ft/1,500 m. Coffee, fruit.

Tenosique, Mexico: see TENOSIQUE DE PINO SUÁREZ.

Tenosique de Pino Suárez (te-no-SEE-ke de PEE-no SWAH-res), city (1990 pop. 23,562) and township, ⊙ Tenosique municipio, Tabasco, SE Mexico, on Usumacinta R., 115 mi/185 km ESE of Villahermosa; 17°28′N 91°25′W. Rubber, fruit, tobacco, rice, timber.

Tensas (TEN-suhs), parish (□ 623 sq mi/1,614 sq km; 1990 pop. 7,103), E La.; ⊙ St. Joseph; 31°55′N 91°14′W. Bounded E and SE by Mississippi R., W in part by Tensas R., drained in NW by Tensas R.; part of lowland region called Tensas Basin. Agr. (cotton, corn, sorghum, peanuts, rice, soybeans, wheat; cattle, hogs). Logging, mfg. (apparel). Includes lakes St. Joseph and Bruin (fish hatchery) in E; fishing. Part of Big L. State Wildlife Area and part of Tensas R. Natl. Wildlife Refuge in NW. Formed 1843.

Tensas River (TEN-suhs), c.175 mi/282 km long, E La.; rises in East Carroll parish as Tensas Bayou, meanders S into Madison parish, then SSW as Tensas R., through Tensas R. Natl. Wildlife Refuge, joining the Ouachita R. at Jonesville; 31°37′N 91°48′W. Drains Tensas Basin, a portion (c.100 mi/161 km long N-S) of the Mississippi R. lowland.

Tensaw River, 35 mi/56 km long, E bayou of Mobile R., SW Ala.; flowing S from Mobile R. near Mt. Vernon, through Baldwin co., to Mobile Bay E of Mobile.

Tensed, village (1990 pop. 90), Benewah co., N Idaho, 30 mi/48 km N of Moscow; 47°10′N 116°55′W. In the Coeur d'Alene Indian Reservation.

Tenstrike, resort village (1990 pop. 184), Beltrami co., N Minn., 16 mi/26 km NE of Bemidji, at end of Gull R.; 47°39′N 94°40′W. Grain; timber; mfg. (treated lumber). Chippewa Natl. Forest to E.

Teocalli Mountain, peak (13,208 ft/4,026 m) in Rocky Mts., Gunnison co., W central Colo., 8 mi/12.9 km NE of Crested Butte; 38°57′N 106°53′W.

Teocaltiche (te-o-kahl-TEE-che), city (1990 pop. 19,627) and township, Jalisco, central Mexico, on interior plateau, near Zacatecas border, 40 mi/64 km SW of Aguascalientes on Mexico Highway 25; 21°26′N 102°34′W. Elev. 5,653 ft/1,723 m. Agr. center (grain, alfalfa, beans, chickpeas, fruit; livestock).

Teocelo (te-o-SEE-lo), city (1990 pop. 7,581) and township, Veracruz, E Mexico, in Sierra Madre Oriental, 10 mi/16 km S of Xalapa Enríquez; 19°23′N 96°57′W. Agr. center (corn, coffee, oranges).

Teococuilco de Marcos Pérez (te-o-ko-KWEEL-ko dai MAHR-kos PE-rez), town (1990 pop. 1,598), N central Oaxaca, Mexico, 12 mi/20 km W of Ixtlán de Juárez; 17°21′N 96°37′W. Elev. 6,280 ft/1,914 m. Mountainous terrain. Temperate climate. Agr. (cereals, mezcal, fruits).

Teocuitatlán de Corona (te-o-kwee-taht-LAHN), town (1990 pop. 4,080), Jalisco, central Mexico, 40 mi/64 km S of Guadalajara; 20°07′N 103°24′W. Agr. center (grain, alfalfa, beans, fruit, tobacco; livestock).

Teojomulco, Mexico: see SANTO DOMINGO TEOJOMULCO.

Teolocholco (te-o-lo-CHO-ko) or **San Luis Teolocholco**, town (1990 pop. 11,670), Tlaxcala, central Mexico, 15 mi/24 km N of Puebla; 19°15′N 98°11′W. Corn, wheat, barley, alfalfa.

Teoloyucan (te-o-lo-YOO-kahn), town (1990 pop. 31,685), Mexico state, central Mexico, on RR, 23 mi/37 km N of Mexico city, in the Zona Metropolitana de la Ciudad de Mexico; 19°49′N 99°10′W. Elev. c.7,415 ft/2,260 m. Grain; livestock.

Teopantlán (te-o-pahn-TLAHN), town (1990 pop. 2,281), Puebla, central Mexico, 23 mi/37 km SSW of Puebla; 18°43′N 98°16′W. Elev. 5,020 ft/1,530 m. Cereals, sugar, fruit; livestock. Also called Santiago Teopantlán.

Teopanzolco (te-o-ahn-ZOL-ko), historic site, NE Morelos, Mexico, 11 mi/17 km E of Cuernavaca, off of Mexico Highway 95. This pyramid was discovered during the Mex. Revolution, when the site was used as a position for cannons attacking Cuernavaca. The concussions of the cannons displaced the surface dirt, revealing the pyramid. The Tlahuica Indians built Teopanzolco in 1000 and had their capital in Cuernavaca. Later the Aztecs conquered the area and built another pyramid on top of the 1st one. There is a central plaza, a large pyramid, a smaller pyramid, rectangular platforms, and one circular platform at this site. Many of the bldgs. here are believed to have been constructed bet. 1200 and 1500.

Teopisca (te-o-PEES-kah), town (1990 pop. 8,482), Chiapas, S Mexico, in Sierra de Hueytepec, 18 mi/29 km SE of San Cristóbal de las Casas, on Inter-Amer. Highway (190); 16°31′N 92°29′W. Elev. 5,741 ft/1,750 m. Corn, fruit; timber. Some Tzotzil-Maya people live here.

Teotepec, Cerro (te-O-te-pek), highest mountain (12,139 ft/3,700 m) in Guerrero, SW Mexico, in Sierra Madre del Sur, 40 mi/64 km WSW of Chilpancingo de los Bravo; 17°30′N 100°12′W.

Teotihuacán (te-o-tee-wah-KAHN), anc. commercial and religious center (□ c.7 sq mi/18.1 sq km) in the central valley of Mexico, c.30 mi/48 km NE of Mexico city; 19°42′N 98°51′W. Teotihuacán is the largest and most impressive urban site of anc. Amer. The Pyramid of the Sun, the tallest in Mexico, is 216 ft/66 m high and covers approximately 10 acres/4 ha at the base. Occupied from about 200 B.C. to 650, this is an important archeological site and a popular tourist attraction.

Teotihuacán de Arista (te-o-tee-wah-KAHN dai ah-REES-tah), town (1990 pop. 13,763), ⊙ Teotihuacán municipio, central Mexico, 19 mi/30 km NE of Mexico city and adjacent to Teotihuacán archaeological site; included within the Zona Metropolitana de la Ciudad de México. Elev. 7,382 ft/2,250 m. Agr., tourism. Sometimes called San Juan Teotihuacán.

Teotitlán de Flores Magón (te-o-tee-TLAHN de FLOres mah-GON), town (1990 pop. 5,439), Oaxaca, S Mexico, 15 mi/24 km W of Huautla; 18°10′N 97°08′W. Agr. center (cereals, beans, sugarcane, coffee, cotton, fruit; livestock). Formerly called Teotitlán del Camino.

Teotitlán del Camino, Mexico: see TEOTITLÁN DE FLORES MAGÓN.

Teotitlán del Valle (te-o-tee-TLAHN del VAH-ye), town (1990 pop. 4,430), Oaxaca, S Mexico, 17 mi/27 km ESE of Oaxaca; 17°02′N 96°30′W. Weaving center, known for bright serapes with idol design. Was capital of the Zapotec during 11th and 12th cents. Temple and pyramid in honor of Quetzalcoatl are on hill nearby.

Teotlalco (te-o-TLAHL-ko), town (1990 pop. 1,283),

Puebla, central Mexico, 22 mi/35 km SW of Izúcar de Matamoros; 18°28′N 98°46′W. Cereals, fruit; livestock.

Teotongo (te-o-TON-go), town (1990 pop. 762), NW Oaxaca, Mexico, 19 mi/31 km ESE of Huajuapam de León. Elev 6,752 ft/2,058 m. Mountainous terrain. Temperate climate. Agr. (cereals, fruits, mezcal), woods. Also called Santiago Teotongo.

Tepache (te-PAH-che), town (1990 pop. 2,213), Sonora, NW Mexico, 90 mi/145 km ENE of Hermosillo; 29°28′N 109°26′W. Cereals; livestock.

Tepakán, town (1990 pop. 2,321), Yucatán, SE Mexico, 37 mi/60 km E of Mérida; 21°03′N 89°03′W. Henequen. Tropical fruit, corn; livestock.

Tepalcatepec (te-pahl-KAH-te-pek), town (1990 pop. 14,827), Michoacán, W central Mexico, on Tepalcatepec R., 33 mi/53 km NNW of Aratzingán de la Constitución; 19°11′N 102°50′W. Rice, sugar, fruit.

Tepalcingo (te-pahl-seen-go), town (1990 pop 9,358.), Morelos, central Mexico, 33 mi/53 km SE of Cuernavaca, on Mexico Highway 115; 18°38′N 98°51′W. Agr. center (rice, sugarcane, fruit, vegetables). Also called Tepalcingo de Hidalgo.

Tepanco de López (te-PAHN-ko de LO-pez), town (1990 pop. 2,014), Puebla, central Mexico, 13 mi/21 km NW of Tehuacán on Mexico Highway 150; 18°33′N 97°33′W. Elev. 5,906 ft/1,800 m. Corn, sugarcane, fruit; livestock. In Popoluca Indian area.

Tepango de Rodríguez (te-PAHN-go de rod-REE-gez), town (1990 pop. 3,096), Puebla, central Mexico, in Sierra Madre Oriental, 10 mi/16 km NE of Zacatlán; 20°00′N 97°49′W. Elev. 4,987 ft/1,520 m. Coffee, tobacco, corn, sugarcane, fruit.

Tepatepec (te-PAH-te-pek), town (1990 pop. 8,864), ⊙ Francisco I. Madero municipio, Hidalgo, central Mexico, 25 mi/40 km WNW of Pachuca de Soto; 20°14′N 99°05′W. Corn, beans, potatoes, maguey; livestock.

Tepatitlán de Morelos (te-pah-teet-LAHN de mo-RElos), city (1990 pop. 34,036), NW Jalisco, Mexico, 40 mi/64 km NNW of Guadalajara, on Mexico Highway 80; 20°48′N 102°45′W. Elev. 6,102 ft/1,860 m. Main agr. (corn, beans, dairy prods.) area with cattle raising. Main center of important commercial and industrial region of Los Altos.

Tepatlán, Mexico: see SAN FELIPE TEPATLÁN.

Tepatlaxco (te-paht-LASH-ko), town (1990 pop. 1,291), Veracruz, E Mexico, in Sierra Madre Oriental, 13 mi/21 km NNE of Córdoba; 19°04′N 96°50′W. Fruit.

Tepatlaxco de Hidalgo (te-paht-LASH-ko de ee-DAHL-go), town (1990 pop. 12,083), Puebla, central Mexico, on central plateau, 16 mi/26 km E of Puebla, on Mexico Highway 129, on RR; 19°04′N 97°58′W. Agr. center (grain, maguey; livestock).

Tepeaca (te-pe-AH-kah), city (1990 pop. 16,967) and township, Puebla, central Mexico, on central plateau, on RR, 21 mi/34 km ESE of Puebla, on Mexico Highway 150; 18°57′N 97°54′W. Maguey-growing and -processing (pulque) center; fruit (pears, apples, nuts), cereals, vegetables. Marble and onyx deposits nearby. Has picturesque old churches, ruins of early colonial fortified convent.

Tepeapulco (te-pe-ah-POOL-ko), town (1990 pop. 13,226), Hidalgo, central Mexico, 28 mi/45 km SE of Pachuca de Soto; 19°45′N 98°31′W. Maguey.

Tepechitlán (te-pe-chee-TLAHN), (1990 pop. 3,696), Zacatecas, N central Mexico, 8 mi/12 km S of Tlaltenango de Sanchez Román; 21°40′N 103°20′W. Grain, fruit, sugarcane, vegetables; livestock.

Tepecoacuilco de Trujano (te-pe-ko-ah-KWEEL-ko de troo-HAH-no), town (1990 pop. 6,639), Guerrero, SW Mexico, 6 mi/9.7 km SE of Iguala de la Independencia; 18°17′N 99°27′W. Cereals, sugarcane, fruit, forest prods. (rubber, resin, vanilla).

Tepehuacán de Guerrero (te-pe-wah-KAHN de ge-REro), town (1990 pop. 728), Hidalgo, central Mexico, in foothills of Sierra Madre Oriental, 23 mi/37 km E of Jacala; 20°59′N 98°49′W. Elev. 6,047 ft/1,843 m. Corn, tobacco, sugarcane, fruit.

Tepehuanes (te-pe-WAH-nes), town (1990 pop. 4,280), ⊙ Tepehuanes municipio, Durango, N Mexico, in Sierra Madre Occidental, 28 mi/45 km NW of Santiago

Papasquiaro; 25°22′N 105°41′W. Elev. 5,863 ft/1,787 m. RR terminus; mining (silver, gold, lead, copper).

Tepeji, Mexico: see TEPEXI DE RODRÍGUEZ.

Tepeji de Ocampo (te-pe-HEE de o-KAHM-po), town (1990 pop. 25,185), ⊙ Tepeji del Río de Ocampo municipio, Hidalgo, central Mexico, 40 mi/64 km WSW of Pachuca de Soto; 19°54′N 99°20′W. Agr. center (cereals, cotton, fruit, vegetables); cotton, flour mills. Also called Tepeji del Río de Ocampo.

Tepeji del Río de Ocampo, Mexico: see TEPEJI DE OCAMPO.

Tepelmeme de Morelos, Mexico: see TEPELMEME VILLA DE MORELOS.

Tepelmeme Villa de Morelos (te-pel-ME-me VEE-yah dai mo-RE-los), town (1990 pop. 639), NW Oaxaca, Mexico, 34 mi/55 km ENE of Huajuapam de Leónon, on unpaved road; 17°51′N 97°21′W. Elev. 6,864 ft/2,092 m. Steep terrain. Cold climate. Agr. (cereals, fruits, mezcal), wood.

Tepemaxalco, Mexico: see SAN FELIPE TEPEMAXALCO.

Tepeojuma (te-pe-o-HOO-mah), town (1990 pop. 4,645), Puebla, central Mexico, on RR, 13 mi/21 km S of Atlixco, 6 mi/9.7 km off Inter-Amer. Highway (190); 18°42′N 98°28′W. Elev. 5,118 ft/1,560 m. Cereals, sugarcane; livestock. Also called San Cristóbal Tepeojuma.

Tepetitla (te-pe-TEE-tlah), town (1990 pop. 6,227), ⊙ Tepetitla de Lardizábal municipio, Tlaxcala, central Mexico, on Puebla border, 15 mi/24 km NW of Puebla; 19°15′N 98°23′W. Elev. 7,218 ft/2,200 m. Cereals, maguey, alfalfa; livestock. Also known as San Mateo Tepetitla.

Tepetitla de Lardizábal, Mexico: see TEPETITLA.

Tepetitlán (te-pe-tee-TLAHN), town (1990 pop. 657), Hidalgo, central Mexico, 45 mi/72 km W of Pachuca Desoto; 20°11′N 99°53′W. Corn, maguey; livestock.

Tepetlán (te-pet-LAHN), town (1990 pop. 1,585), Veracruz, E Mexico, in Sierra Madre Oriental, 13 mi/21 km NE of Xalapa Enríquez; 19°41′N 96°47′W. Coffee.

Tepetlaoxtoc (te-pe-tlah-OSH-to), town (1990 pop. 3,571), Mexico state, central Mexico, 23 mi/37 km ENE of Mexico city; and in the Zona Metropolitana de la Ciudad de México; 19°35′N 98°49′W. Cereals; livestock. Formerly called Tepetlaoxtoc de Hidalgo.

Tepetlixpa (te-pe-TLISH-pah), town (1990 pop. 9,380), Mexico state, central Mexico, 35 mi/56 km SE of Mexico city on Mexico Highway 115; on RR; included within the Zona Metropolitana de la Ciudad d México; 19°02′N 98°49′W. Agr. center (cereals, fruit; livestock).

Tepetongo (te-pe-TON-go), town (1990 pop. 1,678), Zacatecas, N central Mexico, 45 mi/72 km SW of Zacatecas; 22°28′N 103°09′W. Elev. 7,251 ft/2,210 m. Cereals, vegetables; livestock.

Tepetzintla 1 (te-pet-ZEEN-tlah), town (1990 pop. 1,045), Puebla, central Mexico, 9 mi/14.5 km ENE of Zacatlán; 19°58′N 97°50′W. Cereals, fruit. Also called Santa Mariá Tepetzintla. **2** town (1990 pop. 4,311), Veracruz, S Mexico, in Sierra Madre Oriental foothills, 32 mi/51 km NW of Túxpam de Rodríguez Cano, on Mexico Highway 127; 21°11′N 97°51′E. Corn, sugarcane, coffee, fruit. Petroleum production.

Tepexco (te-PESH-ko), town (1990 pop. 1,503), Puebla, central Mexico, 15 mi/24 km WNW of Zvúcar de Matamoros, on Mexico Highway 160; 18°38′N 98°41′W. Corn, sugarcane, fruit.

Tepexi de Rodríguez (te-PE-hee de rod-REE-ges), town (1990 pop. 3,331), Puebla, central Mexico, on central plateau, 37 mi/60 km SE of Puebla; 18°36′N 97°58′W. Elev. 5,728 ft/1,746 m. Sugarcane, livestock. In the Popo Loca Indian area. Sometimes called Tepeji.

Tepexpan, Mexico: see SANTA CRUZ TEPEXPAN.

Tepeyahualco (te-pe-yah-WAHL-ko), town (1990 pop. 1,485), Puebla, central Mexico, on RR, 38 mi/61 km W of Xalapa Enríquez; 19°29′N 97°29′W. Elev. 5,958 ft/1,816 m. Corn, maguey.

Tepeyahualco Cuauhtémoc (te-pe-yah-WAHL-ko kwo-TE-mok), town (1990 pop. 1,767), ⊙ Tepeyahualco de Cuauhtémoc municipio, Puebla, central Mexico, 27 mi/43 km SE of Puebla; 18°48′N 97°52′W. Cereals, beans.

Tepeyanco, Mexico: see SAN FRANCISCO TEPEYANCO.

Tepezalá (te-pe-sah-LAH), town (1990 pop. 3,098), ⊙ Tepezalá municipio, Aguascalientes, N central Mexico, 25 mi/40 km NNE of Aguascalientes; 22°13′N 102°10′W. Elev. 6,942 ft/2,116 m. Some silver and copper mining; livestock raising.

Tepic (te-PEEK), city (1990 pop. 206,967) and township, ⊙ Tepic municipio and Nayarit state, W Mexico, on the Tepic R., on Mexico Highway 15; 21°30′N 104°53′W. Elev. 3,002 ft/915 m. A commercial center, Tepic lies in a prosperous maize, sugarcane, and cattle-raising area. The city has sugar mills and textile factories. Wild mt. scenery surrounds Tepic, which, despite modernization, retains some of its colonial charm.

Tepopa, Cape (te-PO-pah), rocky headland on Gulf of California, Sonora, NW Mexico, opposite (N of) Tiburón Isl., 90 mi/145 km WNW of Hermosillo; 30°16′N 112°53′W. Overlooked by Tepoca Peak (299 ft/91 m).

Teposcolula, Mexico: see SAN JUAN TEPOSCOLULA.

Tepotzotlán (te-po-so-TLAHN), town (1990 pop. 24,100), Mexico state, central Mexico, on central plateau, 20 mi/32 km NNW of Mexico city, and in the Zona Metopolitana de la Ciudad de México; 19°43′N 99°13′W. Grain, maguey; livestock. Old church and monastery, founded 1584 by Jesuits, now is a natl. monument; decorated with pictures by famous Mex. artists. Location for Oscar Levis' *Life of a Mexican Village*. Recently the area has been developed as weekend retreat for local Mexicans, with country club, golf course, and residential and commercial bldgs. Surrounded by natl. forest.

Tepoztlán, town (1990 pop. 12,279), Morelos, central Mexico, on RR, 12 mi/19 km NE of Cuernavaca; 18°59′N 99°06′W. Sugarcane, fruit, vegetables. Picturesque Hahuatl village; has 16th-cent. monastery. Tepozteco pyramid is nearby.

Tequesquitengo, Lake (te-ke-kee-TEN-go) (□ 48 sq mi/124 sq km), Morelos, central Mexico, 4 mi/6.4 km N of Jojutla de Juárez; 18°37′N 99°16′W. Popular fishing and hunting resort.

Tequesta (te-KESS-tuh), town (□ 2 sq mi/5.2 sq km; 1990 pop. 4,499), Palm Beach co., SE Fla., 18 mi/29 km N of West Palm Beach; 26°57′N 80°05′W. Light mfg.

Tequexquitla (te-kesh-KEE-tlah), town (1990 pop. 9,186), ⊙ El Carmen Tequexquitla municipio, Tlaxcala, central Mexico, 40 mi/64 km NE of Puebla; 19°18′N 97°39′W. Cereals, alfalfa, beans; livestock.

Tequila (te-KEE-lah), city (1990 pop. 17,609) and township, Jalisco, W Mexico, on RR, 35 mi/56 km WNW of Guadalajara, on Mexico Highway 15; 20°53′N 103°48′W. Elev. 3,996 ft/1,218 m. Maguey- and banana-growing center; tequila mfg. Also called Santiago de Tequila.

Tequila (te-KEE-lah), town (1990 pop. 2,381), Veracruz, E Mexico, in Sierra Madre Oriental, 9 mi/14.5 km S of Orizaba Elev. 5,394 ft/1,644 m. Coffee, sugarcane, fruit. Formerly called Roa Bárcena.

Tequisquiapan (te-kees-kee-AH-pahn), town (1990 pop. 19,231), Querétaro, central Mexico, on affluent of Moctezuma R., 33 mi/53 km E of Querétaro, on Mexico Highway 120 and near El Centenario dam; 20°31′N 99°53′W. Elev. 5,633 ft/1,717 m. Grain, alfalfa, beans; livestock. Hydroelectric plant nearby.

Tequixquiac, Mexico: see SANTIAGO TEQUIXQUIAC.

Terlingua, uninc. village (1990 pop. 25), Brewster co., extreme W Texas, in the Big Bend area, c.70 mi/113 km S of Alpine. Elev. 2,720 ft/829 m. Mercury mines active in late 19th cent. For most of 20th cent. it has been a ghost town. Revived now as tourism center for Rio Grande and Big Bend Natl. Park. S is scenic Santa Elena Canyon on the Rio Grande (Mex. border) in Big Bend Natl. Park. Site of annual Chili Cookoff since 1967.

Terlton (TUHRL-tuhn), village (1990 pop. 121), Pawnee co., N Okla., 28 mi/45 km W of Tulsa; 36°11′N 96°29′W. In agr. area. Keystone L. reservoir to E.

Terminal Island, Los Angeles co., S Calif., artificial island in Los Angeles Harbor (W) and Long Beach Harbor (E); c.6 mi/9.7 km long. Connected N by Terminal Isl. Freeway across Cerritos Channel to Wilmington, W by Vincent Thomas Bridge across Main Channel, E by short bridge to Long Beach proper, across Entrance Channel, linking Cerritos Channel with Long Beach Harbor to San Pedro. Here are Fish Harbor (1,200 fishing vessels), fish canneries (tuna, sardines, mackerel) and by-products plants; mfg. (food processing, petroleum refining); shipyards; a federal prison; meteorological station; and a navy seaplane base. U.S. Naval Shipyard in SE, mainly in Long Beach. San Pedro Bay, Pacific Ocean, to S.

Términos, Laguna de (TER-mee-nos, lah-GOO-nah dai), lagoon, inlet of the Gulf of Campeche, in Campeche, SE Mexico, on SW Yucatán Peninsula; 45 mi/72 km long, 12 mi/19 km–15 mi/24 km wide. Carmen Isl. is across its entrance. Receives Palizada and Candelaria rivers.

Terminus Dam, Calif.: see KAWEAH, LAKE.

Terra Alta, town (1990 pop. 1,713), Preston co., N W.Va., near Md. state line, 24 mi/39 km SE of Morgantown; 39°26′N 79°32′W. Agr. (grain, apples); livestock; dairying; poultry. Mfg. (clothing, commercial printing). Alpine L. Ski Resort to W. Briery Mt. Wildlife Management Area to SW. Inc. 1890.

Terra Bella, uninc. town (1990 pop. 2,740), Tulare co., S central Calif., 30 mi/48 km SE of Visalia; 35°58′N 119°02′W. Fruit (apples, peaches, plums), olives, nuts, grain; nursery prods.; cattle, poultry; paper mill.

Terra Nova, Lake (TEH-ruh NO-vuh) (□ 10 sq mi/26 sq km), SE N.F., Canada, on Terra Nova R., 35 mi/56 km SSE of Gander; 8 mi/13 km long, up to 3 mi/5 km wide. At E end is settlement of Terra Nova.

Terra Nova National Park (□ 153 sq mi/396 sq km), E N.F., Canada, on Bonavista Bay. Est. 1957. It is a rugged, deeply indented coastal area with forests and bogs.

Terra Nova River, 70 mi/113 km long, SE N.F., Canada; flows NE, through several lakes, including L. St. John and Terra Nova L., to Bonavista Bay 30 mi/48 km SE of Gander.

Terrace, city (1991 pop. 11,433), W B.C., Canada, on Skeena R., 70 mi/113 km ENE of Prince Rupert; 54°30′N 128°35′W. Lumbering, brick making, furniture mfg., mixed farming.

Terrace Park, village (1990 pop. 2,133), Hamilton co., extreme SW Ohio, on Little Miami R., 12 mi/19 km E of Cincinnati; 39°09′N 84°19′W. Residential. Settled 1791, inc. 1893.

Terral (TER-uhl), village (1990 pop. 469), Jefferson co., S Okla., 20 mi/32 km SSE of Waurika, on Red R. (Texas line); 33°53′N 97°56′W.

Terre Haute, city (1990 pop. 57,483), ⊙ Vigo co., W Ind., on the Wabash R.; 39°28′N 87°23′W. The commercial and trade center of a farm and coal-mining region, its diverse mfg. includes food prods., beverages, paper goods, aluminum prods., and farm and communications equip. Other mfg. (aluminum prods., meat processing, chemicals, printing and publishing, pharmaceuticals, RR ties, corrugated paper prods., concrete, food, paints, plastics, consumer goods, machinery). Founded (1811) as Fort Harrison, it grew as a river town. Terre Haute was on the Wabash and Erie Canal and is an important RR junction. Eugene Debs and Theodore Dreiser were born here, and a park is dedicated to the memory of the songwriter Paul Dreiser (Dreiser's brother). Points of interest include the Debs home, the Early Wheels Mus., an art gallery, and a historical mus. Terre Haute is the seat of Indiana State Univ. Rose-Hulman Inst. of Technology, and a branch of Indiana Vocational Technical Col. (Ivy Tech). Nearby are St. Mary-of-the-Woods Col. and the Terre Haute Federal Penitentiary. A Fr. settlement from 1720–1763, the city was laid out and inc. 1816.

Terre Hill (TER HIL), borough (1990 pop. 1,282), Lancaster co., SE Pa., 15 mi/24 km SSW of Reading; 40°09′N 76°02′W. Mfg. (apparel and concrete prods.). Agr. area (grain, apples; livestock; dairying).

Terre, Massif de (TER, mah-SEEF duh), mountains, NW Artibonite dept., Haiti, N of Gonaïves. Rise to 3,573 ft/1,089 m. Contain rich deposits of copper, bauxite, manganese.

Terre Noire Creek (tuhr NAWR), c.45 mi/72 km long, Clark co., SW Ark.; rises W of Arkadelphia; flows SE to Little Missouri R., 2 mi/3.2 km above (W of) its junction with Ouachita R.

Terrebonne (ter-BON), county (□ 782 sq mi/2,025 sq km), S Que., Canada, on Mille Îles R., NW of Montreal; ⊙ St. Jérôme; 46°00′N 74°10′W.

Terrebonne (TER-ruh-BON) [Fr. = good land], parish (□ 1,391 sq mi/3,603 sq km; 1990 pop. 96,982), SE La.; ⊙ Houma; 29°35′N 90°43′W. On Gulf of Mexico (S) and bounded partly E by small Bayou Pointe au Chien, W by Atchafalaya R.; swampy coast is indented by Atchafalaya, Caillou, and Terrebonne bays. Intersected by Bayou Terrebonne and numerous smaller bayous. Crossed by Intracoastal Waterway; Houma Navigation Canal connects waterway and Houma with Gulf; drained by Grand Caillou, Du Large, Terrebonne, and Black bayous; includes several lakes, including Boudreaux, de Cade, Mechant, and Caillou lakes. Canning and shipping of seafood, vegetables; oil and natural gas deposits; mfg. (iron and steel fabrication, machinery; shipbuilding); sugar milling; agr. (sugarcane, vegetables; cattle), crawfish, oysters, shrimp, crabs, finfish, alligators. Fur trapping, hunting, fishing. Formed 1822. Antebellum houses include Ducross, Magnolia, and Southdown. Part of Pointe au Chien State Wildlife Area in SE; Atchafalaya Delta State Wildlife Area off SW coast.

Terrebonne, suburban town (1991 pop. 39,678), S Que., Canada, on Mille Îles R., 12 mi/19 km NNW of Montreal; 45°42′N 73°37′W. Tobacco processing, woodworking, mfg.

Terrebonne Bay (TEH-ruh-BON), shallow inlet of the Gulf of Mexico, Terrebonne parish, SE La., c.60 mi/97 km SSW of New Orleans; c.12 mi/19 km long N-S; 29°08′N, 90°33′W. Receives Bayou Terrebonne and Houma Navigation Canal, branch of Intracoastal Waterway. Oil, gas wells in SE part. Adjoins Timbalier Bay (E), L. Pelto (W). Oyster beds, crabs; shrimping, fishing. Oil and natural gas deposits. Also called Cat Isl. Bay.

Terrebonne, Bayou (TER-ruh-BON, BEI-yoo), c.55 mi/89 km long, SE La.; rises in Lafourche parish; flows S through Terrebonne parish for most of its course, past Houma (head of shallow-draft navigation), to head of Terrebonne Bay; lower course partly canalized; intersects Intracoastal Waterway at Houma. Houma Navigation Canal parallels bayou about 12 mi/19 km to W.

Terre-de-Bas (ter–duh–BAH), islet (□ 3.65 sq mi/9.6 sq km), Les Saintes isls., Guadeloupe dept., Fr. West Indies, just W of Terre-de-Haut, 11 mi/18 km SSE of Basse-Terre; 15°52′N 61°38′W. Fishing, livestock raising; mfg. of charcoal. Sometimes called Terre-d'en-Bas or Terre-du-Bas. A smaller islet of that name is in the Petite Terre group, 27 mi/43 km ESE of Pointe-à-Pitre, Guadeloupe.

Terre-de-Haut (ter–duh–O), islet (□ 1.75 sq mi/4.7 sq km), Les Saintes isls., Guadeloupe dept., Fr. West Indies, just E of Terre-de-Bas, 12 mi/19 km SE of BasseTerre; 15°52′N 61°35′W. Fishing, livestock raising; mfg. of charcoal. Sometimes called Terre-d'en-Haut or Terre-du-Haut. A smaller islet of that name is in the Petite Terre group, 27 mi/43 km ESE of Pointe-á-Pitre, Guadeloupe.

Terrell 1 (TER-uhl), county (□ 338 sq mi/875 sq km; 1990 pop. 10,653), SW Ga.; ⊙ Dawson; 31°47′N 84°26′W. Bounded NE by Kinchafoonee R., and SW by Ichawaynochaway Creek. Coastal plain agr. (cotton, corn, peanuts, wheat, soybeans); cattle, hogs. Formed 1856. **2** county (□ 2,357 sq mi/6,105 sq km; 1990 pop. 1,410), extreme W Texas; ⊙ Sanderson; 30°13′N 102°04′W. Broken high plateau area (elev. 1,700 ft/518 m–2,800 ft/853 m), bounded S by the Rio Grande (Mex. border), partly on E by Pecos R. Ranching (sheep, goats; some cattle; alfalfa); hunting; natural gas and oil; limestone. Part of Rio Grande Wild and Scenic R. (Natl. Park System) in S. Formed 1905.

Terrell, city (1990 pop. 12,490), Kaufman co., N Texas, 30 mi/48 km E of Dallas; 32°43′N 96°17′W. Agr. (cattle, horses; nurseries; peaches; cotton; wheat); mfg. (motor vehicle parts, chemicals, air filtration prods., apparel, lead and lead alloys). A state hosp., Trinity Valley Jr. Col. and Southwest Christian Col. are in Terrell. L. Tawakoni State Park to NE; L. Ray Hubbard reservoir to NW. Inc. 1883.

Terrell Hills, city (1990 pop. 4,592), Bexar co., S central Texas, residential suburb 4 mi/6.4 km NE of San Antonio, near San Antonio R.; 29°28′N 98°27′W. Fort Sam Houston and Natl. Cemetery to SE. Inc. 1939.

Terrell, Mount (11,530 ft/3,514 m), in Fish L. Plateau, Sevier co., S central Utah, 24 mi/39 km E of Richfield, in Fishlake Natl. Forest.

Terrenate (te-te-NAH-te) or **San Nicolás Terrenate**, town (1990 pop. 3,100), Tlaxcala, central Mexico, 23 mi/37 km NE of Tlaxcala; 19°29′N 97°55′W. Elev. 8,990 ft/2,740 m. Maguey center.

Terre-Neuve (ter-NUHV), town (1982 pop. 592), Artibonite dept., NW Haiti, in the small Terre-Neuve range, 13 mi/21 km NNW of Gonaïves; 19°36′N 72°47′W. Copper mines in cotton-, tobacco-, and fruit-growing region. Also iron, gold, lead, zinc, silver deposits.

Terrier-Rouge (te-ryai–ROOZH), town, Nord dept., N Haiti, on Plaine du Nord, 17 mi/27 km ESE of Cap-Haïtien; 19°38′N 71°57′W. Sisal, fruit.

Terril, town (1990 pop. 383), Dickinson co., NW Iowa, 11 mi/18 km SSE of Spirit Lake; 43°18′N 94°58′W. In livestock and grain area.

Terry, county (□ 890 sq mi/2,305 sq km; 1990 pop. 13,218), NW Texas; ⊙ Brownfield; 33°10′N 102°20′W. Elev. 3,200 ft/975 m–3,600 ft/1,097 m. On Llano Estacado, here crossed by intermittent Sulphur Springs Draw and Sulphur Draw. Agr., esp. grain sorghum; also wheat, peanuts, cotton, vegetables; livestock (cattle). Oil, natural gas wells; sodium sulfate. Formed 1876.

Terry 1 village (1990 pop. 613), Hinds co., W Miss., 15 mi/24 km SSW of Jackson, near Pearl R.; 32°06′N 90°17′W Agr. (cotton, corn; poultry, cattle); light mfg. **2** village (1990 pop. 659), ⊙ Prairie co., E Mont., on Yellowstone R., 40 mi/64 km NE of Miles City; 46°48′N 105°19′W. Shipping point for corn, wheat, barley, beans, hay, sheep, cattle, coal. Center of sheep ranching. Mouth of Powder R. 6 mi/9.7 km to SW. Terry Badlands to NW. Cherry Creek roughly forms the N border of the Badlands. Founded 1882, inc. 1912.

Terry Fox, Mount (8,694 ft/2,650 m), E central B.C., Canada, adjacent to W end of Mt. Robson Provincial Park; not accessible by road. Viewpoint on Highway 61 (Yellowhead Highway), 4 mi/7 km W of Mt. Robeson; W gate, 15 mi/24 km N of Valemount. Named in 1981 for cancer victim who attempted to run across Canada E-W; he got as far as Thunder Bay, Ont., raising $25 million for cancer research. Mt. Terry Fox Provincial Park (□ 4,769 acres/1,930 ha) has picnic facilities.

Terry Peak (7,070 ft/2,155 m), Pennington co., W S.Dak., 4 mi/6.4 km W of Lead, in Black Hills; 44°19′N 103°50′W. Terry Peak Ski Area.

Terrytown, uninc. city (1990 pop. 23,787), Jefferson parish, SE La., residential suburb 4 mi/6 km SE of New Orleans; 29°54′N 90°02′W. New Orleans Naval Air Station to S.

Terrytown, village (1990 pop. 656) , Scotts Bluff co., W Nebr., on S side of Platte R.; 41°51′N 103°40′W. Residential suburb of twin cities of Scottsbluff, to N across river, and Gering, in S; Oregon Trail passes through town.

Terryville, Conn.: see PLYMOUTH.

Tescott, village (1990 pop. 317), Ottawa co., central Kansas, on Saline R., 12 mi/19 km SW of Minneapolis; 39°00′N 97°52′W. Livestock; grain.

Teslin (TEZ-lin), Indian village (1991 pop. 181), S Yukon, Canada, near B.C. border, on Teslin L., 90 mi/145 km ESE of Whitehorse and on Alaska Highway; 60°10′N 132°44′W. Fur-trading post; services, Royal Can. Mounted Police post.

Teslin Lake (TEHS-lin), narrow lake, 80 mi/129 km long, NW B.C. and S Yukon Territory, Canada, SE of Whitehorse. It receives the Nisutlin R. and is drained by the Teslin R., one of the headwaters of the Yukon R.

Tessville, Ill.: see LINCOLNWOOD.

Tesuque (tuh-SOO-ke), pueblo (□ 26 sq mi/67 sq km; 1990 pop. 697), Santa Fe co., N central N.Mex., 10 mi/16 km NNW of Santa FE, in Sangre de Cristo Mts.; 35°47′N 105°58′W. Elev. 6,370 ft/1,942 m. Crafts are pottery making and painting. Feast day occurs Nov. 12. Village discovered 1540 by Coronado expedition, settled at present site c.1700. Village (pueblo) now center of land grant.

Tesuque (tuh-SOO-kai), uninc. town (1990 pop. 1,490), Santa Fe co., N central N.Mex., suburb 4 mi/6.4 km N of Santa Fe; 35°46′N 105°55′W. Mfg. (bronze castings). Adjoins Tesuque Pueblo land grant to N; parts of Santa Fe Natl. Forest to E and W. Santa Fe Opera is here.

Tetachuck Lake (TEH-tuh-chuk), W central B.C., Canada, in Coast Mts., in Tweedsmuir Park, 120 mi/193 km WSW of Prince George, E of Eutsuk L., 18 mi/29 km long, 1 mi/2 km–2 mi/3 km wide; 53°20′N 125°50′W. Drains E into Nechako R.

Tetecala (te-tah-KAH-lah) or **Tetacala**, city (1990 pop. 4,520), Morelos, central Mexico, 17 mi/27 km SSW of Cuernavaca, on Mexico Highway 55; 18°43′N 99°24′W. Elev. 3,280 ft/1,000 m. Coconut growing. Gold resources, but not developed. Anc. Indian town. Xochicalco pyramid and ruins of old fortified city are nearby. Also called Tetecala de la Reforma.

Tetela de Ocampo (te-TE-lah), town (1990 pop. 2,485), ⊙ Tetala de Ocampo, Puebla, central Mexico, 13 mi/21 km SE of Zacatlán; 19°49′N 97°48′W. Elev. 2,382 ft/726 m. Corn, sugarcane, fruit.

Tetela del Volcán (te-TE-lah del rol-KAHN), town (1990 pop. 6,414), Morelos, central Mexico, at SW foot of Popocatépetl, on RR, 20 mi/32 km W of Atlixco; 18°52′N 98°43′W. Corn, sugarcane, fruit; livestock.

Teteles de Avila Castillo (te-TE-les dai AH-ver-lah kas-TEE-yo), town (1990 pop. 3,258), Puebla, central Mexico, 6 mi/9.7 km WNW of Teziutlán, on Mexico Highway 129; 19°52′N 97°26′W. Elev. 7,382 ft/2,250 m. Coffee, fruit, sugarcane.

Tetepango (te-te-PAHN-go), town (1990 pop. 5,402), Hidalgo, central Mexico, on RR, 28 mi/45 km W of Pachuca de Soto; 20°04′N 99°09′W. Cereals, fruit, vegetables; livestock.

Teterboro, borough (1990 pop. 22), Bergen co., NE N.J., 5 mi/8 km E of Passaic; 40°51′N 74°03′W. Makes aircraft parts and general aviation equip.; large freight airport here is administered by Port of N.Y. Authority. Named Bendix 1937, renamed Teterboro 1943.

Tetipac (te-TEE-pahk), city (1990 pop. 1,517), Guerrero, SW Mexico, on S slope of central plateau, 7 mi/11.3 km NNW of Taxco de Alarcón; 18°39′N 99°40′W. Cereals, sugarcane, fruit.

Tetiz (te-TEES), town (1990 pop. 2,887), ⊙ Tetiz municipio, Yucatán, SE Mexico, 20 mi/32 km W of Mérida, on Mexico Highway 25; 20°58′N 89°56′W. Henequen growing.

Tetla (tet-lah) or **Santiago Tetla**, town (1990 pop. 7,934), Tlaxcala, central Mexico, 3 mi/4.8 km NE of Apizaco; 19°28′N 98°10′W. Elev. 8,366 ft/2,550 m. Corn, wheat, barley, alfalfa, beans, maguey; livestock. Also known as Atipac.

Tetlatlahuca (te-tlah-thal-WAH-kah) or **Santa Isabel Tetlatlahuca**, town (1990 pop. 7,570), Tlaxcala, central Mexico, 15 mi/24 km NNW of Puebla; 19°14′N 98°17′W. Elev. 7,339 ft/2,237 m. Cereals; livestock. Also known as Santa Isabel Tetlahuaca.

Tetlin, native village (1990 pop. 87), E Alaska, near upper Tanana R., 30 mi/48 km SE of Tanacross; 63°09′N 142°31′W. Within Tetlin Indian Reservation.

Tetlin Junction, village, SE Alaska, at junction of Alaska Highway, 11 mi/18 km ESE of Tanacross. Junction Alaska and Taylor highways.

Teton 1 (TEE-tuhn), county (□ 450 sq mi/1,166 sq km; 1990 pop. 3,439), E Idaho; ⊙ Driggs; 43°45′N 111°13′W. Plateau area bordering on Wyo. (E), bounded on N by Bitch Creek and in part by Teton R., and including irrigated valley of Teton R. (source in S of co.). Foothills of Teton Range on E boundary. Dairying, agr. (potatoes, dry beans, alfalfa, barley; cattle). Part of Targhee Natl. Forest in SW. Formed 1915. Parts of Targhee Natl. Forest in NE and SW. **2** county (□ 2,292 sq mi/5,936 sq km; 1990 pop. 6,271), N central Mont.; ⊙ Choteau; 47°51′N 112°14′W. Irrigated agr. region drained by Teton R. Sun R. forms S boundary, North Fork of Sun R. and Continental Divide form W boundary. Wheat, barley, oats, alfalfa, hay; cattle, sheep, hogs. Part of Lewis and Clark Natl. Forest in W, includes part of Bob Marshall Wilderness Area; Freezeout L. reservoir in S; Pishkun Reservoir and Wildlife Management Area in SW. Formed 1893. Present boundaries est. 1921. **3** county (□ 4,221 sq mi/10,932 sq km; 1990 pop. 11,172), NW Wyo.; ⊙ Jackson; 43°55′N 110°34′W. Grain, livestock area, bordering Montana and Idaho on W; watered by Snake R. and Jackson L.; alfalfa, barley. Jackson Hole Valley is at center of co. The Natl. Elk Refuge is SE of Grand Teton Natl. Park; Gros Ventre Range in SE; part of Bridger-Teton Natl. Forest in NE and SE. Grand Teton Natl. Park is at center. Part of Targhee Natl. Forest in W; Teton Range also in W. Continental Divide runs through N part of co.; John D. Rockefeller Natl. Parkway in N center; S part of Yellowstone Natl. Park is also in N (park was formerly independent of any co.), park includes Yellowstone, Shoshone and Lewis lakes. Formed 1921.

Teton, village (1990 pop. 570), Fremont co., E Idaho, 5 mi/8 km S of St. Anthony and on Teton R.; 43°54′N 111°40′W. Elev. 5,004 ft/1,525 m. Peas, potatoes, wheat. This area was flooded June 5, 1976, with collapse of Teton dam 8 mi/12.9 km ENE.

Teton (TEE-tahn), river, c.60 mi/97 km long; rising in W Wyoming, in forks (including Teton, Darby, and Fox creeks) in Wyo. and Idaho, and Trail Creek, Idaho, which all unite in SE Idaho. The Teton flows N receiving Bitch Creek from Wyo. (E), and W past Rexburg to Henrys Fork of Snake R., 5 mi/8 km W of Rexburg, Idaho. In its early course it runs through Teton Basin, formerly Pierre's Hole; a battle with the Gros Ventres Native Americans was fought (1832) here. Collapse of Teton Dam June 5, 1976 flooded valley below, killing 11.

Teton Pass, Wyo.: see TETON RANGE.

Teton Range (TEE-tahn), part of the Rocky Mts.,Teton co., NW Wyo., and Teton co., SE Idaho, just S of Yellowstone Natl. Park. The highest peaks are along the E front of the range, which drops dramatically within Grand Teton Natl. Park, with Grand Teton (13,772 ft/4,198 m) the highest. Only the W base of the range lies within Idaho. Teton Pass (8,431 ft/2,570 m) is 8 mi/12.9 km W of Jackson. The W part, or "back range," lies mostly in Targhee Natl. Forest, and is the source of the Teton R. which flows W to the Snake R. The 1st recorded person to see (c.1807) the range is Amer. fur trapper John Colter, a member of the Lewis and Clark expedition. Fur trappers and traders, known as "mountain men," followed suit to frequent the range in the 1st ½ of the 19th cent.

Teton River (TEE-tuhn), c.150 mi/241 km long, Mont.; rises in the Rocky Mts. NW Teton co. at Continental Divide; flows E, then SE past Choteau, then E passing near Fort Benton before joining Marias R., 1 mi/1.6 km W of its confluence with Missouri R. 6 mi/9.7 km upstream from its mouth. Teton R. comes within ½ mi/⅘ km of Missouri R.

Tetonia, village (1990 pop. 132), Teton co., E Idaho, 6 mi/9.7 km N of Driggs, near Teton R.; 43°49′N 111°10′W. Mfg. (furniture). Targhee Natl. Forest to E (Wyo.), SW and N.

Tetragona, Mount (teh-truh-GO-nuh) (4,511 ft/1,375 m), NE Lab., Canada, near head of Seven Isls. Bay; 59°18′N 63°55′W.

Teuchitlán (te-oo-chee-TLAHN), town (1990 pop. 3,272), Jalisco, W Mexico, 32 mi/51 km W of Guadalajara and at N end of L. la Vega; 20°41′N 103°52′W. Elev. 3,996 ft/1,218 m. Corn, wheat, sugarcane, fruit, vegetables. Guachimonton archeological site nearby.

Téul de González Ortega (TE-ool dai gon-SAH-les or-TE-gah), town (1990 pop. 3,095), Zacatecas, N central Mexico, on interior plateau, 23 mi/37 km SSW of Tlaltenango de Sanchez Román; 21°30′N 103°28′W. Elev. 4,222 ft/1,287 m. Agr. center (grain, sugarcane, fruit, livestock).

Teulon (TOO-lahn), village (1991 pop. 1,016), SE Man., Canada, 35 mi/56 km N of Winnipeg; 50°23′N 97°16′W. Dairying; grain.

Teutopolis (too-TOP-uh-lis), village (1990 pop. 1,417), Effingham co., SE central Ill., 3 mi/4.8 km E of Effingham; 39°07′N 88°28′W. In agr. area. Seat of St. Joseph's Seminary.

Tewksbury (TOOKS-be-ree), town (1990 pop. 27,266), Middlesex co., NE Mass.; 42°37′N 71°14′W. It was once the site of a Native Amer. colony. Primarily residential, the town has some light industry and mfg (pharmaceuticals, animal feedstocks, fats, computer equip.). A

Cross references are shown in SMALL CAPITALS. The pronunciation key is on page xv. The dates of population figures are on page xii.

state hosp. is here. Settled 1637, set off from Billerica and inc. 1734.

Texada Island (tek-SAI-duh) (□ 118 sq mi/306 sq km), in Strait of Georgia, SW B.C., Canada, 50 mi/80 km NW of Vancouver; separated from mainland by Malaspina Strait; 31 mi/50 km long, 4 mi/6 km wide; 49°40'N 124°24'W. Rises to 2,892 ft/881 m. Limestone; crabs, herring, shrimp, salmon; timber. Vanada and Blubber Bay are main settlements. Ferry from Powell River to Blubber Bay.

Texana, Lake, reservoir (□ 19 sq mi/49 sq km), Jackson co., S Texas, on Navidad R., 30 mi/48 km ENE of Victoria; 28°54'N 95°36'W. Max. capacity 199,028 acre-ft. Formed by Palmetto Bend Dam (93 ft/28 m high), built (1980) by the Bureau of Reclamation for water supply; also used for power generation and recreation. L. Texana State Park on NW shore.

Texarkana, city (1990 pop. 31,656), Bowie co., Texas, on the Texas-Ark. state line, near Red R.; 33°26'N 94°04'W. Physically one city, Texarkana is actually 2 separate municipalities. The state line runs through the center of the post office; the 2 city halls are 2 blocks to either side of the post office. Texarkana is a major RR junction and center of transportation and trade for a large agr. and pine forest area. Its many industries include cotton processing, lumbering and woodworking, and the mfg. of tires, ammunition, pulp and paperboard, medical equip., RR ties, and cooking oil. Huge Red R. Army Depot—a fighting vehicle maintenance and military supply depot. Seat of East Texas State Univ. at Texarkana and Texarkana Col. Wright Patman L., large reservoir to the SW, serves as a resort area. Inc. 1880.

Texarkana Dam, Texas: see WRIGHT PATMAN LAKE.

Texas, state (□ 268,600 sq mi/695,677 sq km; 1995 est. pop. 18,723,991), S central U.S., admitted to the Union in 1845 as the 28th state; 31° 11'N 99°20'W; ⊙ AUSTIN. HOUSTON, DALLAS, and SAN ANTONIO are the largest cities. The 2d-largest state in the Union, Texas is roughly spade-shaped. Its Panhandle projects N into Okla., bounded on N and E by it, and with N.Mex. on the W. Below the Panhandle, Texas continues its W border with N.Mex. then extends W with N.Mex. (N) and Mex. (SW). The Rio Grande marks the entire S and SW internatl. boundary of Texas with Mexico. On the SE Texas is bounded by the Gulf of Mexico, and on the E by La. (the Sabine R. forms much of the line). Texas' extreme NE corner is bounded E and N (Red R.) by Arkansas; the Red R. also marks the boundary with Okla. W to the Panhandle. The vast expanse of Texas contains great regional differences (the distance from Beaumont to El Paso is greater than that from N.Y. city to Chicago). E Texas—the land bet. the Sabine and Trinity rivers—is Southern in character, part of it is similar to its E neighbor La., with pine-covered hills, cypress swamps, bayous, and remnants of the great cotton plantations founded before the Civil War. Cotton farming has been supplemented by diversified agr., including rice cultivation; almost all of the state's huge rice crop comes from E Texas, and the industrial cities of BEAUMONT and PORT ARTHUR are surrounded by rice fields. The inland pines still supply a timber industry (including, lumber, pulpwood, cedar oil, by-prods.); HUNTSVILLE, LUFKIN, and NACOGDOCHES are important lumber towns. The real wealth of E Texas, however, comes from the immense, rich oil fields. LONGVIEW is an oil center, and TYLER is the center of the E Texas Oil Field. Oil is also the principal economic support of Beaumont and Port Arthur and the basis for much of the heavy industry that crowds the Gulf Coast. The industrial heart of the coastal area is Houston, the largest city in the South and the Southwest and the 4th-largest in the nation. Houston's rapid development has been primarily oil-based supplemented by the digging (1912–1914) of a ship canal to the Gulf of Mexico, making it the nation's 3d-largest port in tonnage handled. Other Texas Gulf ports are Port Arthur, TEXAS CITY, Brazosport Arm (includes FREEPORT), PORT LAVACA, CORPUS CHRISTI, and BROWNSVILLE. The S Gulf Coast is a popular tourist area, and some of the ports, such as Texas City and Corpus Christi, have economies dependent on both heavy industry and tourism. The Intracoastal Waterway follows the length of Texas' Gulf Coast, most of it using deepened channels in existing barrier lagoons, such as Laguna Madre and Matagorda Bay, and man-made channels in the swampy coastal plain 1 mi/1.6 km inland. Allows barge shipping and direct access to river systems in states to E. Brownsville, the southernmost Texas city and the terminus of the Intracoastal Waterway, is also the shipping center for the intensively farmed and irrigated sect. along the lower Rio Grande, where citrus fruits, watermelons, and vegetables are grown. The long stretch of plain along the Rio Grande valley is largely given over to cattle ranching. Texas has 1,000 mi/1,609 km of border with Mex., and many S and W Texas towns have a strong Mex. influence. Influx of immigrants from Lat. Amer. in 1980s and 1990s has swelled Texas' Hispanic pop., so that much of the state now speaks both Eng. and Span. LAREDO is the most important gateway to Mex., with highway and RR access to Mexico city and other Mex. cities. The 1st region to be farmed when Americans came to Texas in the 1820s was the bottoms of the lower Brazos and the Colorado rivers, but not until settlers moved into the rolling blackland prairies of central and N central Texas was the agr. wealth of the area realized. The heart of this region is the trading and shipping center of WACO; at the SW extremity is San Antonio, the commercial center of a wide cotton, grain, and cattle country. To the N, the area surrounding Dallas and its neighboring city of FORT WORTH has become one of the most rapidly developing sects. of the U.S. Their traditional industries of oil refining, grain milling, and cotton and food processing were greatly supplemented in World War II by huge aircraft mfg., which continues today, and now includes the high-technology computer and electronics industries. The Balcones Escarpment marks the W margin of the Gulf Coastal Plain; in central Texas the line is visible in a series of rapids, springs, and rough, tree-covered hills. To the W lie the S central plains and the Edwards Plateau; they are essentially extensions of the Great Plains but are sharply divided from the high, windswept, and canyon-cut Llano Estacado [Span. = staked plains] in the W Panhandle by the erosive div. of the Caprock Escarpment. No traces of the subtropical lushness of the Gulf Coastal Plain are found in these regions; the climate is semiarid, with occasional blizzards blowing across the flat land in winter. The Red R. area in N, including the farming center of WICHITA FALLS, can be extremely cold in winter, though without the severity that is intermittently experienced in the commercial center of the Panhandle, AMARILLO, or in the dry-farming area around LUBBOCK. NE Texas (esp. Dallas–Fort Worth), other than being on the S margin of winter snows, is known for its frequent and severe ice storms. Cattle ranching, which began in the late 1870s, still continues, and huge ranches vie with extensive wheat and cotton farms for domination of the treeless land. Oil and grain, however, revolutionized the economy of this sect. of the state. The entire area of Texas W of 100°W is semiarid to arid. S of the Panhandle lie the rolling plains around ABILENE, a region cultivated in cotton, sorghum, and wheat, and the site of newer oil fields discovered in the 1940s. The dry fields of W Texas are still given over to ranching, except for small irrigated areas that can be farmed. SAN ANGELO serves as the commercial center of this area. The Midland-Odessa oil patch (one of the world's premier oil fields) lies NE of the Pecos R. and is part of the Permian (W Texas) Basin, which extends into SE N.Mex. The land beyond the Pecos R., rising to the mts. with high, sweeping plains and rough uplands, offers the finest scenery of Texas. In the far W are several isolated mt. ranges, extensions of the Rocky Mt. System, including the Davis Mts. and Guadalupe Mts. Guadalupe Peak, near the N.Mex. boundary, is the highest point in the state (8,751 ft/2,667 m). Most of these ranges are surrounded by the N part of the Chihuahuan Desert, noted for its sparse scrubby vegetation and salt pans. The wilderness of the Big Bend of the Rio Grande is typical of the barrenness of most of this area, where water and people are almost equally scarce. El Paso, a thriving city of diverse industries and an important center of trade with Mex., is a pop. oasis in that desolate region. In the state as a whole, mineral resources compete with industry for primary economic importance. Texas is the wealthiest mineral producer in the nation; its chief minerals are oil, natural gas, and natural gas liquids. Texas is the nation's 2d leading petroleum state, and ranks 1st in the production of natural gas and natural gas liquids. The state is also a major producer of helium, salt, sulfur, sodium sulfate, clays, gypsum, cement, limestone, and talc. Texas produces an enormous variety of prods., including chemicals, petroleum, food prods., transportation equip., machinery, and primary and fabricated metals. The mfg. and research and development of high-technology electronic equip., such as computers, has become one of the state's leading industries. Agriculturally, Texas is one of the most important states in the country. Largely because of its size, it easily leads the rest of the country in the production of cattle, cotton, and cottonseed, and it ranks 2d in the growing of vegetables, watermelons, and strawberries. Texas has more farms, farmland, sheep, and lambs than any other state. Other livestock includes Angora goats, hogs, and poultry (esp. in NE); ratite raising (ostriches, emus, rheas) has become popular in many E cos. Other agr. includes sorghum grain, citrus fruits, wheat, pecans, peanuts, oats, barley, hay, corn, rice, peaches, apples, and dairy prods. Wool and mohair are also important. Texas also has an important commercial fishing industry. Principal catches are shrimp, oysters, crabs, and menhaden. Crawfish, catfish, and alligators are aquafarmed in SE. The 1st Span. settlement in the region that is now Texas was made (1682) at Ysleta on the site of El Paso. Several missions were established in the area; but the Comanche, the Apache, and other Native Amer. tribes resented their encroachment, and the settlements did not flourish. The 1st mission, founded in 1690 near the Neches, was named Francisco de los Tejas after the so-called *tejas* [= friends] Native Americans. This is also the origin of the state's name. By the early 19th cent. Americans were covetously eyeing Texas, esp. after the Louisiana Purchase (1803). Stephen F. Austin (nicknamed "the father of Texas"), in Dec. 1821, led 300 families across the Sabine to the region bet. the Brazos and Colorado rivers, where they established the 1st Amer. settlement in Texas. The newly independent govt. of Mexico, pleased with Austin's prospering colony, readily offered grants to other Amer. entrepreneurs and even huge land tracts to individual settlers. Americans from all over the Union, but particularly from the South, poured into Texas, and within a decade considerable settlements had been established at Brazoria, Washington-on-the-Brazos, San Felipe de Austin, Anahuac, and Gonzales. After the Texas Revolution, at a convention called at Washington-on-the-Brazos (March 2, 1836), Texas declared its independence from Mexico. A constitution was adopted and David Burnet was named interim president. The arrival of Santa Anna with a large army resulted in the famous defense of the ALAMO and the massacre of several hundred Texans captured at GOLIAD. Santa Anna then divided his huge force to cover as much territory as possible. The small Texas army, commanded by Samuel Houston, protected their rear flank, retreating strategically until Houston finally maneuvered Santa Anna into a cul-de-sac formed by heavy rains and flooding bayous, near the site of present-day Houston. In the Battle of SAN JACINTO (April 21, 1836), Houston surprised the larger Mex. force and scored a resounding victory. Santa Anna was captured and compelled to recognize the independence of Texas. Texans sought annexation to the U.S., but antislavery forces in the U.S. vehemently opposed the admission of another slave state, and Texas remained an independent republic for almost 10 years. President Tyler narrowly pushed the admission of Texas through Congress shortly before the expiration of his term; Texas formally accepted annexation in July 1845. This act was the immediate cause of the Mex.-Amer. War. In the decades following the war the Western element in Texas was strengthened as stock raising became dominant. This was the era of the buffalo hunter and of the last of the

Native Amer. uprisings. From the open range and then from great fenced ranches, Texas cowboys drove herds of longhorn cattle to the railheads in Kansas, and even farther to the grasslands of Mont. The traditional symbols of Texas—the "10-gallon" hat, the cattle brand, and spurs and saddles—are also the traditional symbols of the Old West. As RRs advanced across the state during the 1870s, farmlands were increasingly settled. Many Eur. immigrants—esp. Germans and Bohemians (Czechs)—came to live in the plains (and this influx continued into the 20th cent., when it was augmented by the arrival of many Mexicans). Oil was discovered in nearly every part of the state beginning in the 19th cent., and the industry developed rapidly during the 1st years of the 20th cent. However, in the meantime conditions worsened for the tenant farmers, who by 1910 made up the majority of cultivators. The significance of the petrochemical and natural gas industries increased during World War II, when the aircraft industry also became prominent and military bases were established throughout Texas. The postwar years brought continued prosperity and industrial expansion, although in the 1950s the state experienced the worst drought in its history and had its share of destructive hurricanes and flooding. Many projects for increased flood control, improved irrigation, and power supply have been undertaken in Texas; notable among these are Denison Dam, forming L. Texoma (shared bet. Texas and Okla.); Lewisville Dam and its reservoir, supplying Fort Worth and Dallas; L. Texarkana on the Sulphur R.; and Falcon Dam and its reservoir on the Rio Grande. The Amistad Dam on the Rio Grande, serving both the U.S. and Mexico, was completed in 1969. In the 1960s, Texas began to develop its technology industry as oil became less easy to exploit. This development continued even after soaring oil prices in the 1970s caused the Texas economy to boom. Since then, Texas has become a preferred location for the hq. of many large corporations from airlines and retail chains to telecommunications and chemicals. High-technology industries boomed in the 1980s, esp. in the Dallas–Fort Worth metroplex, the vast Houston metropolitan area, and the Austin area. The state's economy proved it was still vulnerable to the fluctuations of the energy industry in the mid-1980s, when falling oil prices resulted in massive layoffs. In addition, several military bases in the state have been closed or downsized as a result of cutbacks in the Dept. of Defense in the mid- to late 1990s. Texas has continued to grow; its pop. increased over 19% bet. 1980 and 1990 and its economy slowly began a period of recovery in the 1990s. The location of large numbers of U.S. and other foreign-owned factories (maquiladoras) in Mexico along the Rio Grande has sparked a great deal of trade on both sides of the border; NAFTA went into effect Jan. 1, 1994, with the expectation of trade to increase. This increase was short-lived, however, due to 1995 drastic devaluation of Mex. peso. Texas politics have contributed such outstanding natl. figures as Sam Rayburn, longtime Speaker of the U.S. House of Representatives, and Lyndon B. Johnson, who became president after the assassination of John F. Kennedy in Dallas (1963) and was reelected to the presidency in 1964. The state's executive branch is headed by a governor elected for a 4-year term. The state's bicameral legislature has a senate with 31 members elected for 4-year terms and a house with 150 representatives elected for 2 years. The state elects 2 senators and 30 representatives to the U.S. Congress and has 32 electoral votes. Near Waco, over 100 Branch Davidian cult members were engaged in a shoot-out with Federal agents on Feb. 28, 1993, killing 4 agents; the stand-off that followed ended April 19, when agents stormed the cult compound; 72 cult members died in the shoot-out and fire that followed. Among the many institutions of higher learning in Texas are the Univ. of Texas, mainly at Austin, but with large branches at Arlington, San Antonio, El Paso, and the Dallas suburb of Richardson; Baylor Univ., at Waco; E Texas State Univ., at Commerce; Univ. of N Texas at Denton; Rice Univ., at Houston; Southern Methodist Univ., at Dallas; Texas

Arts and Industries Univ., at Kingsville; Texas Agr. and Mechanical Univ., at College Station (with branches at Kingsville, Canyon, Corpus Christi and Laredo); Texas Christian Univ., at Fort Worth; and Texas Southern Univ. and the Univ. of Houston, both at Houston. The Lyndon B. Johnson Space Center is also in the Houston area. Other places of interest in the state include Big Bend Natl. Park, Guadalupe Mts. Natl. Park, Amistad Natl. Recreation Area, Padre Island Natl. Seashore, Alibates Flint Quarries Natl. Monument, San Jose Mission Natl. Historic Site and Arkansas Natl. Wildlife Refuge, winter home of the whooping crane. Texas has 254 COS.: ANDERSON, ANDREWS, ANGELINA, ARANSAS, ARCHER, ARMSTRONG, ATASCOSA, AUSTIN, BAILEY, BANDERA, BASTROP, BAYLOR, BEE, BELL, BEXAR, BLANCO, BORDEN, BOSQUE, BOWIE, BRAZORIA, BRAZOS, BREWSTER, BRISCOE, BROOKS, BROWN, BURLESON, BURNET, CALDWELL, CALHOUN, CALLAHAN, CAMERON, CAMP, CARSON, CASS, CASTRO, CHAMBERS, CHEROKEE, CHILDRESS, CLAY, COCHRAN, COKE, COLEMAN, COLLIN, COLLINSWORTH, COLORADO, COMAL, COMANCHE, CONCHO, COOKE, CORYELL, COTTLE, CRANE, CROCKETT, CROSBY, CULBERSON, DALLAM, DALLAS, DAWSON, DEAF SMITH, DELTA, DENTON, DE WITT, DICKENS, DIMMIT, DONLEY, DUVAL, EASTLAND, ECTOR, EDWARDS, ELLIS, EL PASO, ERATH, FALLS, FANNIN, FAYETTE, FISHER, FLOYD, FOARD, FORT BEND, FRANKLIN, FREESTONE, FRIO, GAINES, GALVESTON, GARZA, GILLESPIE, GLASSCOCK, GOLIAD, GONZALES, GRAY, GRAYSON, GREGG, GRIMES, GUADALUPE, HALE, HALL, HAMILTON, HANSFORD, HARDEMAN, HARDIN, HARRIS, HARRISON, HARTLEY, HASKELL, HAYS, HEMPHILL, HENDERSON, HIDALGO, HILL, HOCKLEY, HOOD, HOPKINS, HOUSTON, HOWARD, HUDSPETH, HUNT, HUTCHINSON, IRION, JACK, JACKSON, JASPER, JEFF DAVIS, JEFFERSON, JIM HOGG, JIM WELLS, JOHNSON, JONES, KARNES, KAUFMAN, KENDALL, KENEDY, KENT, KERR, KIMBLE, KING, KINNEY, KLEBERG, KNOX, LAMAR, LAMB, LAMPASAS, LA SALLE, LAVACA, LEE, LEON, LIBERTY, LIMESTONE, LIPSCOMB, LIVE OAK, LLANO, LOVING, LUBBOCK, LYNN, MCCULLOCH, MCLENNAN, MCMULLEN, MADISON, MARION, MARTIN, MASON, MATAGORDA, MAVERICK, MEDINA, MENARD, MIDLAND, MILAM, MILLS, MITCHELL, MONTAGUE, MONTGOMERY, MOORE, MORRIS, MOTLEY, NACOGDOCHES, NAVARRO, NEWTON, NOLAN, NUECES, OCHILTREE, OLDHAM, ORANGE, PALO PINTO, PANOLA, PARKER, PARMER, PECOS, POLK, POTTER, PRESIDIO, RAINS, RANDALL, REAGAN, REAL, RED RIVER, REEVES, REFUGIO, ROBERTS, ROBERTSON, ROCKWALL, RUNNELS, RUSK, SABINE, SAN AUGUSTINE, SAN JACINTO, SAN PATRICIO, SAN SABA, SCHLEICHER, SCURRY, SHACKELFORD, SHELBY, SHERMAN, SMITH, SOMERVELL, STARR, STEPHENS, STERLING, STONEWALL, SUTTON, SWISHER, TARRANT, TAYLOR, TERRELL, TERRY, THROCKMORTON, TITUS, TOM GREEN, TRAVIS, TRINITY, TYLER, UPSHUR, UPTON, UVALDE, VAL VERDE, VAN ZANDT, VICTORIA, WALKER, WALLER, WARD, WASHINGTON, WEBB, WHARTON, WHEELER, WICHITA, WILBARGER, WILLACY, WILLIAMSON, WILSON, WINKLER, WISE, WOOD, YOAKUM, YOUNG, ZAPATA, ZAVALA.

Texas 1 county (□ 1,183 sq mi/3,064 sq km; 1990 pop. 21,476), S central Mo.; ⊙ Houston; 37°19′N 91°57′W. In the Ozarks. Livestock (cattle) region, corn, wheat, hay; pine, oak, cedar timber. Mfg. at Cabool, Houston, Summersville, and Licking. Recreation (canoeing, fishing, floating). Part of Mark Twain Natl. Forest in NW. Formed 1845. **2** county (□ 2,048 sq mi/5,304 sq km; 1990 pop. 16,419), central Okla. Panhandle; ⊙ Guymon; 36°45′N 101°28′W. In high plains, the middle of 3 cos. in Panhandle; bounded N by Kansas, S by Texas; intersected by North Canadian (Beaver) R. and small Coldwater, Goff, and Palo Dura creeks. Agr. (wheat, barley, grain, sorghum; cattle). Some mfg. at Guymon. Oil and gas wells. Optima Natl. Wildlife Refuge surrounds Optima L. (North Canadian R.) in E. Formed 1907.

Texas City, city (1990 pop. 40,822), Galveston co., S Texas, on Galveston Bay, 8 mi/12.9 km NW of Galveston, 34 mi/55 km SE of Houston. Twin city to Galveston, connected to Galveston Isl. by bridge across entrance to West Bay. It is a RR terminus and an industrial city and port with huge oil refineries, chemical processing, petrochemical plants, a large copper

smelter, and factories making plastics and pipes. In April 1947, a nitrate-laden ship exploded, causing a series of blasts and fires in the city; over 500 people were killed. 5-mi/8-km Texas City Dike extends into bay, storm surge barrier. Col. of the Mainland is in Texas City, also has an art gallery. Gulf Greyhound Park racetrack. Inc. 1911.

Texcaltitlán (tesh-kahl-tee-TLAHN) or **Santiago Texcaltitlán**, town (1990 pop. 1,516), Mexico state, central Mexico, 31 mi/50 km SW of Toluca de Lerdo; 18°54′N 99°55′W. Sugarcane, cereals; coffee; livestock.

Texcalyacac, Mexico: see SAN MATEO TEXCALYACAC.

Texcatepec (tesh-KAH-te-pek), town (1990 pop. 986), Veracruz, E Mexico, 103 mi/166 km NE of Pachuca de Soto; 20°34′N 98°37′W. Elev. 6,890 ft/2,100 m. Corn, fruit.

Texcoco de Mora (teks-KO-ko dai MO-rah), city (1990 pop. 74,194) and township, Mexico state, central Mexico, on central plateau, near L. Texcoco, on RR, 18 mi/29 km E of Mexico city, a part of the Zona Metropolitana de la Ciudad de Mexico; 19°30′N 98°57′W. Elev. 7,474 ft/2,278 m. Mfg. (textiles and yarn, glassware) and agr. center (maguey; cereals; livestock); caustic soda and potash plant. Anc. capital of an Aztec kingdom, it was then the 2d-most important town of Mexico, a member of the Triple Alliance (with Tendchtitlan and Tlacolpán) and long a cultural center. Many archaeological sites (pyramids, temples). Has a 16th-cent. church. Summer palace of King Netzahualcóyotl was situated on Texcotzingo Hill, 5 mi/8 km E. Site of the famous Chapingo agr. school and the Internatl. Center for Improvement of Corn and Wheat. Texcotzingo ruins are 7 mi/11.3 km E. Also spelled Tezcuco de Mora.

Texcoco, Lake, Mexico: see MEXICO, city, and TENOCHTITLÁN.

Texcotzingo, Mexico; see TEXCOCO DE MORA.

Texhoma (teks-HO-muh), town (1990 pop. 746), Texas co., central Okla. Panhandle, and Sherman co., extreme N Texas, 20 mi/32 km SW of Guymon, 80 mi/129 km N of Amarillo, on state line; 36°30′N 101°47′W. Shipping point in grain, cattle area.

Texhoma, village (1990 pop. 291), Sherman co., extreme N Texas, 90 mi/145 km N of Amarillo, on Okla. boundary; 36°30′N 101°47′W. Agr. area (wheat, corn; cattle). Oil and natural gas. Twin town of Texhoma, Okla., 1 mi/1.6 km NE.

Texhuacán (te-wah-KAHN), town (1990 pop. 1,391), Veracruz, E Mexico, in Sierra Madre Oriental, 20 mi/32 km SSW of Córdoba, in the Sierra Zongolica; 18°37′N 97°02′W. Elev. 4,921 ft/1,500 m. Coffee, fruit.

Texico, town (1990 pop. 966), Curry co., E N.Mex., on Texas state line, 7 mi/11.3 km E of Clovis, opposite Farwell and Texico (Texas); 34°23′N 103°02′W. On boundary bet. Central and Mountain time zones. Trade center for ranching region.

Texistepec (te-HEES-te-pek), town (1990 pop. 8,956), Veracruz, SE Mexico, on Isthmus of Tehuantepec, 20 mi/32 km WSW of Minatitlán; 17°53′N 94°47′W. Sugarcane, coffee, fruit. A Popoluca-Indian community.

Texline, village (1990 pop. 425), Dallam co., extreme N Texas, on high plains of the Panhandle, 35 mi/56 km NW of Dalhart, at N.Mex. state line, Okla. boundary 5 mi/8 km NNE; 36°22′N 103°01′W. In wheat and cattle region; feeds.

Texola (teks-HO-luh), village (1990 pop. 45), Beckham co., W Okla., at Texas state line, 19 mi/31 km WSW of Sayre; 35°13′N 99°59′W. Cotton.

Texoma, Lake, reservoir, on border bet. S Okla. and NE Texas, on Red R., 18 mi/29 km NNE of Sherman (Texas); c.50 mi/80 km long; 33°48′N 96°34′W. Max. capacity 5,382,000 acre-ft. Fed by Wildhorse R. Has N (Washita R.; c.30 mi/48 km long) and S (12 mi/19 km long) arms. Formed by Denison Dam (135 ft/41 m high), built (1944) by the Army Corps of Engineers for flood control, water supply and power generation. Partly in Tishomingo Natl. Wildlife Refuge; L. Texoma State Resort Park on W shore and Fort Washita on E shore of the Wildhorse (Okla.) sect. of reservoir. Part of Texas sect. in Hagerman Natl. Wildlife Refuge; Dwight D. Eisenhower State Park on S bank.

Cross references are shown in SMALL CAPITALS. The pronunciation key is on page xv. The dates of population figures are on page xii.

Texon, uninc. village, Reagan co., W Texas, 75 mi/121 km WSW of San Angelo. Hq. for oil field.

Teya (TE-yah), town (1990 pop. 359), Yucatán, SE Mexico, 38 mi/61 km E of Mérida; 21°05′N 89°06′W. Henequen. Citrus fruit, corn, beans; livestock.

Teyahalee Bald, N.C.: see SNOWBIRD MOUNTAINS.

Tezcuco de Mora, Mexico: see TEXCOCO DE MORA.

Teziutlán (te-see-oo-TLAHN), city (1990 pop. 43,867) and township, Puebla, central Mexico, on plateau, near Veracruz border, on RR terminus; and 75 mi/121 km NE of Puebla on Mexico Highway 129; 19°49′N 97°22′W. Elev. 6,575 mi/10,581 km. Trade, agr. (coffee, tobacco, sugarcane, corn, apples, pears, plums, oranges), and mfg. (cigars, ceramics, leather goods) center. Copper mines nearby. Picturesque colonial town.

Tezoatlán de Segura y Luna (te-zo-aht-LAHN dai se-GOO-nah ee LOO-nah), town (1990 pop. 2,182), NW Oaxaca, Mexico, 9 mi/15 km S of Huajuapam de León; 17°42′N 97°49′W. Mountainous terrain irrigated by the Mixteco R. Temperate climate. Agr. (corn, beans, wheat, potatoes, fruits, chile, mezcal), woods, cattle and dairy prods., and handmade textiles.

Tezonapa (te-zon-AH-pah), town (1990 pop. 5,378), central Veracruz, Mexico, 7 mi/39 km NW of Tierra Blanca; 18°36′N 96°43′W. Humid tropical climate in foothills of Sierra Zongolica. On RR, on paved road. Rugged terrain near the Tonto R.

Tezontepec (te-SON-te-pek), town (1990 pop. 4,430), ⊙ Villa de Tezontepec municipio, Hidalgo, central Mexico, on RR, 20 mi/32 km SSW of Pachuca de Soto; 19°52′N 98°49′W. Elev. 7,631 ft/2,326 m. Grain, maguey; livestock. Also called Villa Tezontepec.

Tezontepec de Aldama (te-SON-te-pek dai ahl-DAH-mah), town (1990 pop. 20,373), Hidalgo, central Mexico, on Tula R., 36 mi/58 km W of Pachuca de Soto, on Tula R.; 20°11′N 99°16′W. Elev. 6,562 ft/2,000 m. Agr. center (corn, wheat, maguey, beans, fruit; livestock).

Tezopaco, Mexico: see ROSARIO.

Tezoyuca (te-so-YOO-kah), town (1990 pop. 6,022), Mexico state, central Mexico, 20 mi/32 km NE of Mexico City, in the Zona Metropolitana de la Ciudad de México; 19°36′N 98°54′W. Maguey, cereals; livestock.

Tezzeron Lake (TEH-zuh-rahn) (□ 24 sq mi/62 sq km), central B.C., Canada, 10 mi/16 km NE of Stuart L., 50 mi/80 km NNW of Vanderhoof; 14 mi/23 km long, 2 mi/3 km–4 mi/6 km wide. Drains into Stuart L.

Thacher Island, NE Mass., just off E side of Cape Ann; ½ mi/⁸⁄₁₀ km long; 42°38′N 70°35′W. Cape Ann and one other lighthouse here. The isl. is a Natl. Wildlife Refuge.

Thackerville, village (1990 pop. 290), Love co., S Okla., 10 mi/16 km S of Marietta, within bend of Red R.; 33°47′N 97°08′W. Mfg. (leather prods.). L. Texoma is E.

Thaddeus Kosciuszko National Memorial (TAH-dai-uhs kuh-SHOO-sko), city of Philadelphia, Philadelphia co., SE Pa., at 301 Pine St., downtown. Commemorates the life and work of Thaddeus Kosciuszko. Authorized 1972.

Thames (tehmz), river, c.160 mi/260 km long, S Ont., Canada; rises NW of Woodstock; flows SW past London and Chatham to L. St. Clair. It is navigable to Chatham, near which was fought (1813) the battle of the Thames in the War of 1812.

Thames (THAIMZ), river, c.15 mi/24 km long; formed by the confluence of the Yantic and Shetucket rivers at Norwich, E Conn.; flows S to L.I. Sound at New London. Primarily a tidal estuary, it is New London's harbor and the site of the U.S. Coast Guard Acad. and a U.S. Navy submarine base. Since 1878 it has been the scene of Yale-Harvard rowing contest.

Thamesford (TEMZ-fuhrd), village, S Ont., Canada, on Middle Thames R., and 12 mi/19 km ENE of London. Dairying, farming.

Thamesville (TEMZ-vil), village (1991 pop. 1,046), S Ont., Canada, on Thames R. and 16 mi/26 km NE of Chatham; 42°33′N 81°58′W. Dairying; lumbering; brick and tile mfg.

Thamesville, village, New London co., SE Conn., on Thames R. and 2 mi/3.2 km S of Norwich.

Thane, fishing village, SE Alaska, on Gastineau Channel 5 mi/8 km SE of Juneau at end of Thane Road; 58°16′N 134°20′W.

Thatch Cay (KEE), islet (□ c.1 sq mi/2.6 sq km), U.S. Virgin Isls., off NE shore of St. Thomas Isl., at N entrance of Pillsbury Sound, 5 mi/8 km E of Charlotte Amalie; 18°22′N 64°51′W. Elev. 482 ft/147 m.

Thatcher, town (1990 pop. 3,763), Graham co., E Ariz., on Gila R., and 3 mi/4.8 km WNW of Safford; 32°50′N 109°45′W. In irrigated agr. area. Gila Mts. are N, Pinaleno Mts. S. Founded 1881 by Mormons.

Thatcher, village (1990 pop. c. 150), Las Animas co., S Colo., 35 mi/56 km NE of Trinidad. Elev. c.5,420 ft/1,652 m. Helium deposits here. Coal mining. Pinon Canyon Military Reserve to E; parts of Comanche Natl. Grassland to NE.

Thawville, village (1990 pop. 241), Iroquois co., E Ill., 22 mi/35 km WSW of Watseka; 40°40′N 88°06′W. In rich agr. area.

Thaxton (THAKS-tuhn), village (1990 pop. 431), Pontotoc co., N Miss., 10 mi/16 km WNW of Pontotoc; 34°18′N 89°10′W. Timber; cotton, corn; cattle; dairying. Mfg. (furniture). Holly Springs Natl. Forest to NW.

Thayer (THAI-uhr), county (□ 575 sq mi/1,489 sq km; 1990 pop. 6,635), SE Nebr., ⊙ Hebron; 40°10′N 97°35′W. Agr. area bounded S by Kansas; drained by Little Blue R. Farm machinery, irrigation systems, brooms and mops; corn, wheat, sorghum, alfalfa, cattle, hogs; dairying. Old Oregon Trail co. E-W on N side of Little Blue R. Formed 1871.

Thayer, city (1990 pop. 1,996), Oregon co., S Mo., on Spring R. on Ark. state line, and 23 mi/37 km SE of West Plains; 36°31′N 91°32′W. Mfg. (curtains, wood prods.); cattle; ships lumber. Inc. 1890. Grand Gulf St. Park to W.

Thayer, town (1990 pop. 79), Union co., S Iowa, 16 mi/26 km E of Creston; 41°01′N 94°02′W. Livestock, grain.

Thayer 1 (THAI-uhr), village (1990 pop. 730), Sangamon co., central Ill., 18 mi/29 km SSW of Springfield; 39°32′N 89°45′W. In agr. and bituminous coal area. **2** village (1990 pop. 435), Neosho co., SE Kansas, 13 mi/21 km S of Chanute; 37°29′N 95°28′W. In diversified farming area. Gas and oil wells nearby. **3** village (1990 pop. 64), York co., SE central Nebr., 10 mi/16 km NNE of York and on branch of Big Blue R.; 40°58′N 97°29′W.

Thayne (THAIN), village (1990 pop. 267), Lincoln co., W Wyo., on Salt R., near Idaho state line, and 14 mi/23 km N of Afton, in Star Valley; 42°55′N 111°00′W. Elev. 5,790 ft/1,765 m. Mfg. (cheese, butter); agr. (barley, alfalfa; sheep, cattle). Bridger-Teton Natl. Forest to E.

The Battery, N.Y.: see BATTERY, THE.

The Bight, town, central Bahama Isls., on central Cat Isl., 135 mi/217 km ESE of Nassau; 24°19′N 75°23′W. Produces sisal, corn, potatoes, fruit.

The Colony, city (1990 pop. 22,113), Denton co., N Texas, residential suburb 20 mi/32 km NNW of downtown Dallas, on E arm of Lewisville L. reservoir; 33°05′N 96°53′W. Agr. area on N fringe of Dallas–Fort Worth Metroplex. Lewisville State Park to NW.

The Dalles (DALZ), city (1990 pop. 11,060), ⊙ Wasco co., N Oregon, on the Columbia R. 73 mi/117 km E of Portland. Elev. 98 ft/30 m. The site grew up as a settlement, c.1852, around a fort (now a mus.). Busy inland port; ships passing through the locks at Bonneville Dam (c.50 mi/80 km downstream) can tie up at The Dalles and proceed upstream through the locks of The Dalles Dam, 3 mi/4.8 km upstream (E). A processing and shipping point. Agr. (cherries, apples, wheat, oats, barley; hogs, cattle). Mfg. (canned cherries, lumber, millwork, plastic prods., aluminum prods.; printing and publishing). Recreation. It is the sole entry to the Columbia R. Gorge, the only low-level pass route through the Cascade and Sierra Mts. between S Calif. and Canada. The site became the terminus of the OREGON TRAIL. A gorge and rapids once rendered the river unnavigable at The Dalles, but they were bypassed by a canal with several locks built (1908–1915). In 1957, the gorge, rapids, and canal were inundated by L. Celilo Reservoir, formed by The Dalles Dam c. 3 mi/4.8 km above the city. Highway bridge below the dam. Deschutes R. State Recreation Area to E; Mayer and Memaloose State Parks to NW; Horsethief L. State Park

(Wash.) to NE; Mt. Hood Natl. Forest to SW. Inc. 1857. Also known as City of the Dalles.

The Dalles Dam oregon: see CELILO, LAKE.

The Dells, Wis.: see DELLS OF THE WISCONSIN.

The Forks, plantation (1990 pop. 30), Somerset co., W central Maine, at confluence of Dead and Kennebec rivers, c.45 mi/72 km NNW of Skowhegan; 45°16′N 69°55′W. Hunting, fishing area.

The Glen, N.Y.: see GLEN, THE.

The Hummocks, village, Newport co., SE R.I., on N point of Rhode Isl.

The Narrows, Allegany co., W Md., a narrow defile where Wills Creek flows between Haystack Mt. and Wills Mt. in the Alleghenies. Known as "The Gateway to the West," because the Natl. Road cuts through the Appalachain plateau here from Cumberland 6 mi/9.7 km NW.

The Narrows, N.Y.: see NEW YORK BAY.

The Pas, town (1991 pop. 6,166), W Man., Canada, on the Saskatchewan R.; 53°49′N 101°14′W. Founded as a fur-trading post, it became in 1920 the starting point and hq. of the Hudson Bay RR to Churchill and an outfitting point for prospecting and mining expeditions into the N mineral belt of Man. and Sask. In 1967 the provincial govt. began the development of a forest prods. industry in the area.

The Plains, town (1990 pop. 219), Fauquier co., N Va., 10 mi/16 km N of Warrenton, near Little R.; 38°51′N 77°46′W. Agr. (grain, soybeans, apples; dairying).

The Plains, uninc. village (1990 pop. 2,644), Athens co., SE Ohio, on Hocking R., just N of Athens; 39°22′N 82°08′W.

The Rock, town (1990 pop. 88), Upson co., W central Ga., 7 mi/11.3 km NE of Thomaston; 32°58′N 84°14′W.

The Village, city (1990 pop. 10,353), Oklahoma co., central Okla., residential suburb 7 mi/11.3 km NNW of downtown Oklahoma City; 35°34′N 97°33′W. Mfg. (printing). L. Hefner reservoir to W.

The Woodlands, city (1990 pop. 29,205), Montgomery co., SE Texas, suburb 30 mi/48 km N of downtown Houston, near Spring Creek, in N fringe of Houston urbanized area; 30°09′N 95°29′W. Agr. and timber. Mfg. (machinery, oil well drilling bits, printing, medical prods.).

Thealka (THAL-kuh), uninc. village (1990 pop. 800), Johnson co., E Ky., 1 mi/1.6 km E of Paintsville, on Levisa Fork. Bituminous coal.

Theater District, N.Y.: see CLINTON.

Thebes (THEBZ), village (1990 pop. 461), Alexander co., extreme S Ill., on the Mississippi, and 21 mi/34 km NW of Cairo; 37°12′N 89°27′W.

Thedford (THED-fuhrd), village (1991 pop. 791), S Ont., Canada, 30 mi/48 km ENE of Sarnia; 43°10′N 81°51′W. Milling. Limestone quarried nearby.

Thedford, village (1990 pop. 243), ⊙ Thomas co., central Nebr., 60 mi/97 km N of North Platte, and on Middle Loup R.; 41°58′N 100°34′W. Livestock; mfg. (livestock handling equip.). Halsey Unit of Nebr. Natl. Forest to E.

Thelon Game Sanctuary (□ 15,000 sq mi/38,850 sq km), E Mackenzie and W Keewatin dists., N.W.T., Canada, on upper Thelon R., bet. Aberdeen L. (E) and Artillery L., 50 mi/80 km NE of Fort Reliance. Largest musk-ox herd on N. Amer. mainland.

Thelon River, c.550 mi/885 km long, N.W.T., Canada; rises in E Mackenzie dist., E of Great Slave L.; flows generally NE through Thelon Game Sanctuary to Keewatin Dist. boundary, then E through Aberdeen and Schultz lakes to Baker L. (opening on Chesterfield Inlet). Receives Dubawnt R.

Theodore, agr. village (1991 pop. 473), SE central Sask., Canada, near Whitesand R., 25 mi/40 km NW of Yorkton; 51°26′N 102°55′W.

Theodore, village (1990 pop. 6,509), Mobile co., SW Ala., 12 mi/19 km S of Mobile, near Mobile Bay; 30°33′N 88°10′W. Lumber, millwork, cement, chemicals, and natural gas processing. Bellingrath Gardens nearby.

Theodore Roosevelt Birthplace, historic site, Manhattan, SE N.Y. Birthplace and boyhood home of President Theodore Roosevelt. Authorized 1962.

Theodore Roosevelt Inaugural Historic Site, on Delaware Ave., Buffalo, W N.Y., Ansley Wilcox House, where Theodore Roosevelt took the oath of office (1901) as 26th U.S. president. Authorized 1966.

Theodore Roosevelt Island National Park, Washington, D.C., wilderness preserve in the Potomac River; a tribute to the "conservationist President." Authorized 1932.

Theodore Roosevelt Lake, reservoir (□ 27 sq mi/ 70 sq km), Gila and Maricopa cos., central Ariz., on Salt R., in Tonto Natl. Forest, 60 mi/97 km ENE of Phoenix; 33°40′N 111°10′W. Max. capacity 1,555,140 acre-ft. Fed by Tonto R. Formed by Theodore Roosevelt Dam (284 ft/87 m high), built (1911) by Bureau of Reclamation, Dept. of the Interior for irrigation, power generation, and recreation. Tonto Natl. Monument S of dam. Sierra Ancha to N of reservoir.

Theodore Roosevelt National Park, W N.Dak., in the N.Dak. Badlands; 47°14′N 103°37′W. Covers 110 sq mi/ 285 sq km; wilderness 47 sq mi/122 sq km. There are three units—the North Unit, the Elkhorn Ranch Unit (both in Billings co.), and the South Unit (McKenzie co.)—all three units are on the Little Missouri R. Roosevelt first came to the area in 1883 to hunt bison and other big game. In 1884 he established the Elkhorn Ranch, and for several years after that he returned to the ranch for short periods. The ranch house and other bldgs. have been accurately reconstructed. The landscape of the park is marked by tablelands, buttes, canyons, and rugged hills; animal life is diverse. Among the attractions are petrified forests. Authorized 1947 as the Theodore Roosevelt Natl. Memorial Park; redesignated 1978.

Theresa, town (1990 pop. 771), Dodge co., E Wis., on Rock R., and 18 mi/29 km S of Fond du Lac; 43°31′N 88°27′W. Cheese. Hunting. Horicon Marsh State Wildlife Area to W.

Theresa (thuh-REE-sah), village (□ 1 sq mi/2.6 sq km; 1990 pop. 889), Jefferson co., N N.Y., on Indian R., and 18 mi/29 km NNE of Watertown; 44°12′N 75°47′W. Lakes (resorts) nearby.

Therma, N.Mex.: see EAGLE NEST.

Thermal, uninc. village, Riverside co., S Calif., in Coachella Valley, 23 mi/37 km SE of Palm Springs, and 2 mi/ 3.2 km SE of Coachella. Irrigated agr. area (dates, citrus, cotton, grain; nursery stock); date processing. Coachella Canal to NE; Salton Sea and Salton Sea State Recreation Area 10 mi/16 km to SE; Torrez Martinez Indian Reservation to S.

Thermalito, uninc. town (1990 pop. 5,646), Butte co., N central Calif., residential suburb 1 mi/1.6 km W of Oroville, on Feather R.; 39°30′N 121°37′W. Walnuts, almonds, olives, kiwi fruit, plums; grain, cattle. L. Oroville reservoir (Feather R.) to E. Thermolito Afterbay; irrigation reservoir, to W.

Thermopolis (thuhr-MAHP-uh-lis), town (1990 pop. 3,247), ⊙ Hot Springs co., N central Wyo., on Bighorn R., and 110 mi/177 km NW of Casper; 43°38′N 108°12′W. Elev. 4,326 ft/1,319 m. Resort and trade center in livestock, sugar beet and grain region. Mfg. (hand guns); oil fields, coal. Mineral hot springs at Hot Springs State Park to W; Wyo. State Buffalo Herd roams in hills near park. Large Wind R. Indian Reservation to SW. Founded 1897.

Thessalon (THE-suh-lahn), town (1991 pop. 1,543), S central Ont., Canada on L. Huron 40 mi/64 km ESE of Sault Ste. Marie, opposite Drummond Isl.; 46°15′N 83°33′W. In farming, dairying, fishing, lumbering area.

Thetford (THET-foord), town (1990 pop. 2,438), Orange co., E Vt., on the Connecticut R., and 16 mi/26 km SE of Chelsea, in agr. area; 43°49′N 72°15′W. Mfg. (furniture, wood prods.). Settled 1764. Includes villages of Thetford Hill, East Thetford, Union Village, North Thetford, Post Mills, and Thetford center.

Thetford Mines, city (1991 pop. 17,273), S Que., Canada, NE of Sherbrooke and S of Quebec; 46°05′N 71°18′W. The city, developed after the discovery (1876) of large asbestos deposits, is located in 1 of the world's largest asbestos-producing regions. Chromium and feldspar are also mined. Mfg. (printing presses, trailers and campers, baked goods); steel foundry.

Thibodaux (TIB-uh-do), city (1990 pop. 14,035), elev. 14 ft/5 m, ⊙ Lafourche parish, SE La., 42 mi/68 km WSW of New Orleans, on Bayou Lafourche; RR junction to SE; 29°48′N 90°49′W. Commercial center of an oil, gas, sugarcane, and farm area in the bayou country. Crawfish, alligators, shrimp, crabs, catfish, quail, pheasants; dairying; mfg. (dairy prods., raw sugar, tractors and loaders, sugarcane harvesters, marsh buggies, candy, lumber); printing and publishing. Among the many antebellum plantation houses in the area is one (built 1790) for Chief Justice Edward Douglass White. Nicholls State Univ. is here. Annual Mardi Gras celebrations attract visitors. Inc. 1838.

Thief River, 37 mi/60 km long, NW Minn.; rises in Thief L. (□ 11 sq mi/28 sq km; 5 mi/8 km long, 3 mi/4.8 km wide), Thief L. Wildlife Area, 48°29′N 95°56′W; flows SSW, through marshy area and through Mud L. (Agassiz Natl. Wildlife Refuge), to Red Lake R. at town of Thief River Falls. Elev. 1,160 ft/354 m.

Thief River Falls, town (1990 pop. 8,010), ⊙ Pennington co., NW Minn., c.40 mi/64 km ENE of Fargo, N.Dak. on Red Lake R., at mouth of Thief R.; 48°06′N 96°10′W. Elev. 1,136 ft/346 m. RR junction. Commercial center and shipping point for agr. area (grain, sunflowers; dairying; poultry, sheep); mfg. (fiberglass components, cold weather outerwear, dairy prods., satellite communication prods., granular separation machinery, turkey processing, crates, meat processing, linens).

Thielson, Mount (THEEL-suhn), (9,182 ft/2,799 m), on Douglas-Klamath co. line, SW central Oregon, peak in Mt. Thielson Wilderness Area of the Cascade Range, c.15 mi/24 km N of Crater L.

Thiensville (THEENS-vil), town (1990 pop. 3,301), Ozaukee co., E Wis., on Milwaukee R., and suburb 13 mi/21 km N of downtown Milwaukee; 43°14′N 87°58′W. Once dairy and farm area, is now in urban growth area. Light mfg. Surrounded by city of Mequon.

Thimble Islands, S Conn., group of many small isls. in L.I. Sound, SE of Branford and 9 mi/14.5 km SE of New Haven. Hotels, summer homes.

Thiotte (tee-OT), town (1982 pop. 1,930), Sud-Est dept., Haiti, 38 mi/61 km SE of Port-au-Prince; 18°15′N 71°51′W. Coffee growing; bauxite deposits.

Third Connecticut Lake, N.H.: see CONNECTICUT LAKES.

Third Lake, village (1990 pop. 1,248), Lake co., NE Ill., residential suburb 41 mi/66 km NW of downtown Chicago, 3 mi/4.8 km E of Round L. Beach; 42°22′N 88°00′W.

Thistle, Md.: see ILCHESTER.

Thomas 1 county (□ 552 sq mi/1,430 sq km; 1990 pop. 38,986), S Ga.; ⊙ Thomasville; 30°52′N 83°55′W. Bounded S by Fla. state line; drained by Ochlockonee and Aucilla rivers. Coastal plain agr. (cotton, tobacco, corn, soybeans, wheat, peanuts); cattle, hogs; timber. Formed 1825. **2** county (□ 1,074 sq mi/2,782 sq km; 1990 pop. 8,258), NW Kansas; ⊙ Colby; 39°21′N 101°02′W. Rolling plain, drained by Saline R. (S) and headstreams of Solomon R. and Sappa Creek. Wheat, barley, sorghum, cattle, sheep, hogs. Mountain-Central time zone boundary on W co-boundary (co. is in central time zone). Formed 1885. **3** county (□ 713 sq mi/ 1,847 sq km; 1990 pop. 851), central Nebr.; ⊙ Thedford, located in Sand Hills region; 41°55′N 100°34′W. Ranching area drained by Middle Loup and Dismal rivers. Cattle, hogs, grain. Central and Mountain time zone border follows W boundary. Part of Halsey Unit, Nebr. Natl. Forest (planted) in E. Formed 1825.

Thomas, town (1990 pop. 1,246), Custer co., W Okla., 14 mi/23 km N of Weatherford; 35°45′N 98°45′W. RR junction. In agr. area (wheat, cotton). Plotted 1902.

Thomas, village (1990 pop. 573), Tucker co., NE W.Va., 10 mi/16 km ENE of Parsons, near Md. state line; 39°8′N 79°30′W. Coal-mining and agr. region. Blackwater Falls State Park is to S. Monongahela Natl. Forest to W and S; Fairfax Stone State Monument to N. Founded 1884.

Thomas A. Edison Lake, reservoir, Fresno co., S Calif., on Mono Creek, 40 mi/64 km SE of Yosemite Village, in Sierra Natl. Forest; 5 mi/8 km long; 37°20′N 119°01′W. Elev. 7,612 ft/2,320 m. Max. capacity 125,000 acre-ft. Formed by Vermilion Valley Dam (151 ft/46 m high), built by the Southern Calif. Edison Co. for water supply and power generation.

Thomas, Fort, Ky.: see FORT THOMAS.

Thomas Hill Reservoir (□ 7 sq mi/18.1 sq km), Randolph co., N central Mo., 60 mi/96 km NNW of Columbia; 39°33′N 92°38′W. Formed by dam (70 ft/21 m high), built (1966) for flood control; also used for recreation.

Thomas Jefferson Memorial, Washington, D.C., authorized 1934. Classical structure with a statue of Jefferson. The Memorial overlooks the Tidal Basin and the well-known cherry trees which surround it.

Thomas Stone Historic Site, S Md. Authorized 1978, Georgian style home, Habre de Venture (c.1742), of Thomas Stone, a signer of the Declaration of Independence. The original paneling of the drawing room is now in the Baltimore Mus. of Art.

Thomasboro, village (1990 pop. 1,250), Champaign co., E Ill., 8 mi/12.9 km N of Urbana; 40°14′N 88°11′W. In agr. area.

Thomassique (to-mah-SEEK), town (1982 pop. 3,260), Centre dept., Haiti, 12 mi/19 km SE of Hinche; 19°05′N 71°50′W. Agr. (cotton, sugarcane, citrus fruit growing); cattle raising, bee-keeping; cotton processing.

Thomaston 1 town (1990 pop. 497), Marengo co., W Ala., c.20 mi/32 km SE of Demopolis. Lumber. **2** town (1990 pop. 6,947), Litchfield co., W Conn., on Naugatuck R., and 8 mi/12.9 km N of Waterbury; 41°40′N 73°04′W. Clock-making center since early 19th cent; glass prods., injection molding, wire, metal pressed sheets and rods, metal shears, electronic equip. and other metal fabrication, machinery; agr. (dairy prods., vegetables, fruit). Settled 1728, set off from Plymouth 1875. **3** town (1990 pop. 9,127), ⊙ Upson co., W central Ga., near the Flint R.; 32°53′N 84°20′W. Mfg. (plastics, metal fabrication, treated lumber, textiles and yarns, printing, apparel, tire cord, pianos, speakers). It is a textile center with textile mills (the first was est. 1833) and plants making textile prods. Of interest are an old covered bridge and a number of historic homes. The Thomaston-Upson Arts Council (TUAC) operates a downtown gallery and community theater. Inc 1857. **4** (TAHM-uh-stuhn), town (1990 pop. 3,306), including Thomaston village, Knox co., S Maine, with small port at head of St. George R. inlet, just SW of Rockland; 44°05′N 69°10′W. Cement plant. State prison. "Montpelier," home of Henry Knox, is restored. Trading post c.1630; fort 1719; inc. 1777.

Thomasville 1 city (1990 pop. 17,457), ⊙ Thomas co., SW Ga., near the Fla. state line; 30°50′N 83°59′W. It is a agr. trade center, with a large fresh-vegetable market. Mfg. (lumber, clothing and textiles, plastics, jet engine blades, PVC pipe, sawmill machinery, pumps, food and beverages, mobile homes, printing and publishing, furniture); meat-packing, tourism. The city has a mild climate and is a winter resort. More than 25,000 rose bushes line the city streets, and an annual rose festival is held here. Inc. 1831. **2** city (1990 pop. 15,915), Davidson co., central N.C., in the Piedmont region, 17 mi/ 27 km SE of Winston-Salem, and 21 mi/34 km SW of Greensboro; 35°53′N 80°04′W. RR junction. Tobacco, grain, barley; poultry, livestock; dairying. Mfg. (textiles and apparel, labels, furniture, steel rails, furniture, plastic prods., crushed stone, metal prods., plywood, structural steel fabricating; printing and publishing). N.C. Vietnam Veterans Memorial. The Big Chair, 18 ft/5 m symbol of town's furniture industry. Inc. 1854.

Thomasville, town (1990 pop. 4,301), Clarke co., SW Ala., 15 mi/24 km N of Grove Hill. Lumber milling; apparel mfg. Ala. Southern Community Col. here. Founded 1887.

Thomazeau (to-mah-ZO), town (1982 pop. 1,914), Ouest dept., S Haiti, on Cul-de-Sac plain, 18 mi/29 km ENE of Port-au-Prince; 18°39′N 72°05′W. Agr. (coffee, sugarcane, cotton, fruits).

Thomonde (to-MONGD), village (1982 pop. 2,481), Centre dept., E central Haiti, 9 mi/14.5 km SSE of Hinche; 19°01′N 71°58′W. Sugarcane, fruit, tobacco.

Thompson, city (1991 pop. 14,977), central Man., Canada, on the Burntwood R.; 55°45′N 97°52′W. A mining town, it developed after large nickel deposits were discovered in the area in 1956.

Thompson 1 textile town (1990 pop. 8,668), Windham

co., extreme NE Conn., on R.I. and Mass. state lines, on Quinebaug R., and 4 mi/6.4 km NE of Putnam; 41°58′N 71°52′W. Agr., plastics, and candy. Includes former mill villages of Mechanicsville, Wilsonville, Grosvenor Dale, and North Grosvenor Dale (1990 pop. 1,705). Thompson village has early 19th-cent. houses. Quaddick Reservoir here. Settled 1707, set off from Killingly 1785. **2** town (1990 pop. 498), Winnebago co., N Iowa, 10 mi/16 km NW of Forest City; 43°22′N 93°46′W. **3** town (1990 pop. 930), Grand Forks co., E N.Dak., 11 mi/18 km S of Grand Forks; 47°46′N 97°06′W. Potato growing area.

Thompson, uninc. village (1990 pop. 291), Fayette co., SW Pa., 10 mi/16 km NW of Uniontown, and 1 mi/ 1.6 km W of Republic; 41°51′N 75°30′W.

Thompson, borough (1990 pop. 291), Susquehanna co., NE Pa., 7 mi/11.3 km SE of Susquehanna; 41°51′N 75°30′W. Hay, corn; dairying. Numerous small lakes in area.

Thompson, river, 304 mi /489 km long, S B.C., Canada; formed by the junction of the North Thompson and the South Thompson rivers at Kamloops; flows W and S to the Fraser R. at Lytton. The North Thompson is usually considered part of the main stream. The river was explored (1808) by Simon Fraser and named by him for David Thompson, a fellow explorer.

Thompson and Meserves Purchase, land purchase, Coos co., N central N.H., 10 mi/16 km SSW of Berlin, in White Mt. Natl. Forest. Wilderness area includes mts. Madison, Adams, Clay, and Washington, in Mt. Washington State Park, on S boundary. Appalachian Trail passes through S.

Thompson Cone, N.Mex.: see MIMBRES MOUNTAINS.

Thompson Falls (TAHM-suhn), town (1990 pop. 1,319), ⊙ Sanders co., NW Mont., on the Clark Fork R., and 67 mi/108 km SW of Kalispell; 47°36′N 115°20′W. Lead, silver, antimony, sandstone quarries; hay, barley, timber; mfg. (log homes, lumber). Area surrounded by Lolo Natl. Forest; Thompson Falls State Park to NW. Sanders Co. Historical Society. Near the site of the North-West Co.'s Saleesh House (est. 1809). Formerly called Thompson.

Thompson Island, E Mass., in Dorchester Bay section of Boston Harbor, SSE of downtown Boston; c.1 mi/ 1.6 km long. Site of Summer Outward Bound Education Center.

Thompson Lake, village, S Mackenzie dist., N.W.T., Canada, on small Thompson L., 30 mi/48 km ENE of Yellowknife; 62°37′N 113°28′W. Gold mining.

Thompson Lake (TAHMP-suhn), SW Maine, 9 mi/ 14.5 km W of Auburn; c.9 mi/14.5 km long; drains N, past Oxford, into Little Androscoggin R. Resorts.

Thompson, Lake, lake, Kingsbury co., E S.Dak., SE of De Smet; 3 mi/4.8 km long, 2 mi/3.2 km wide; 44°17′N 97°28′W. Largest natural lake in S.Dak.

Thompson Peak, in Santa Fe co., N central N.Mex., in Sangre de Cristo Mts., 8 mi/12.9 km E of Santa Fe; 35°40′N 105°48′W. Elev. 10,554 ft/3,217 m. In Santa Fe Natl. Forest.

Thompson Peak, Calif.: see TRINITY CO.

Thompson River 1 c.175 mi/282 km long, S Iowa and N Mo.; rises near Greenfield, Iowa; flows SE and S to Grand R. near Chillicothe, Mo. **2** c.50 mi/80 km long, NW Mont.; rises in Thompson Lakes (small chain c.10 mi/16 km long, ½ mi/⁹⁄₁₀ km wide), in SE corner of Lincoln co.; flows S, past Cabinet Mts., to the Clark Fork 5 mi/8 km E of Thompson Falls town.

Thompsons Creek, c.50 mi/80 km long, SE Miss.; rises in N Wayne co.; flows generally S to Leaf R. c.8 mi/ 12.9 km E of New Augusta, NE of Beaumont. Also called Thompson Creek.

Thompsontown, borough (1990 pop. 582), Juniata co., central Pa., 17 mi/27 km E of Lewistown, on Juniata R.; 40°34′N 77°14′W. Mfg. (wooden cabinets and vanities, fertilizer). Agr. area (corn, hay; poultry, livestock; dairying). Part of Tuscarora State Forest, on Tuscarora Mt. ridge, to S.

Thompsonville, uninc. town (1990 pop. 3,560), Washington co., SW Pa., residential suburb 13 mi/21 km SSW of Pittsburgh near Chartiers Creek in urban fringe; 40°16′N 80°07′W.

Thompsonville 1 village (1990 pop. 602), Franklin co., S Ill., 11 mi/18 km SE of Benton; 37°54′N 88°45′W. In bituminous coal, agr. area. **2** village (1990 pop. 416), Benzie co., NW Mich., on Betsie R., and 10 mi/16 km SE of Beulah; 44°31′N 85°56′W. Crystal Mt. Ski Area to W.

Thompsonville, Conn.: see ENFIELD, village.

Thomson, town (1990 pop. 6,862), ⊙ McDuffie co., E Ga., 28 mi/45 km W of Augusta; 33°28′N 82°30′W. Mfg. includes floorings, particle board, carpets, apparel, industrial castings, crushed stone; meat processing. Inc. 1854.

Thomson 1 village (1990 pop. 538), Carroll co., NW Ill., near the Mississippi, 9 mi/14.5 km NNE of Clinton (Iowa); 41°57′N 90°05′W. In rich agr. area (corn, soybeans; cattle, hogs; dairying). **2** village (1990 pop. 132), Carlton co., E Minn., 16 mi/26 km SW of Duluth, and 1 mi/1.6 km SE of Carlton, on St. Louis R., 5 mi/8 km W of Wis. state line; 46°39′N 92°23′W. Agr. (dairying; poultry; oats, alfalfa,). Jay Cook State Park is to E.

Thonotosassa (tho-no-to-SASS-uh), town, Hillsborough co., W central Fla., 12 mi/19 km ENE of Tampa, on small L. Thonotosassa. Peat mining nearby.

Thor, town (1990 pop. 205), Humboldt co., N central Iowa, 7 mi/11.3 km E of Dakota City; 42°41′N 94°02′W.

Thor, Mount (9,673 ft/2,948 m), SE B.C., Canada, in Monashee Mts., 28 mi/45 km S of Revelstoke; 50°36′N 118°05′W.

Thorburn, village, N N.S., Canada, 6 mi/10 km ESE of New Glasgow. Coal mining.

Thoreau (thuh-RO), uninc. town (1990 pop. 1,099), McKinley co., NW N.Mex., 30 mi/48 km ESE of Gallup, on Rio San Jose, near its source. Timber. Cattle, sheep, alfalfa. Part of Cibola Natl. Forest to S; Bluewater L. State Park to SE; Casamero Pueblo Ruins to NE; Continental Divide to W in Zuni Mts.

Thorhild, village (1991 pop. 449), central Alta., Canada, 45 mi/72 km NNE of Edmonton; 54°09′N 113°07′W. Coal mining; oil and gas; wheat, barley; dairying.

Thorn Hill, village (1990 pop. 146), Franklin co., N central Ky., residential suburb N of Frankfort.

Thornapple River, c.80 mi/129 km long, S central and SW Mich.; rises SW of Lansing in Eaton co.; flows NW, past Vermontville, Nashville, Hastings, and Middleville, to Grand R. 9 mi/14.5 km E of Grand Rapids; 42°35′N 84°42′W.

Thornbrough Channel, SW B.C., Canada, W entrance of Howe Sound from Strait of Georgia, separates Gambier Isl. (E) and W shore of Howe Sound; 17 mi/27 km long, 1 mi/2 km–3 mi/5 km wide. Port Mellon, Gibsons Landing, and Hopkins Landing are on W shore.

Thornburg, town (1991 pop. 91), Keokuk co., SE Iowa, 11 mi/18 km NW of Sigourney; 41°27′N 92°19′W. Livestock, grain.

Thornburg (THORN-buhrg), borough (1990 pop. 461), Allegheny co., SW Pa., residential suburb 4 mi/6.4 km W of downtown Pittsburgh, Chartiers Creek; 40°25′N 80°04′W.

Thornbury, town (1991 pop. 1,646), S Ont., Canada, on Nottawasaga Bay, inlet of Georgian Bay, 24 mi/39 km E of Owen Sound; 44°34′N 80°26′W. Apple packing, flour milling, brick and tile mfg.

Thorndale 1 (THORN-dail), uninc. town (1990 pop. 3,518), Chester co., SE Pa., residential suburb 3 mi/ 4.8 km E of Coatsville; 40°00′N 75°45′W. Light mfg.; agr. includes dairying, livestock; grain, apples. Shannon Memorial Airport to S. **2** town (1990 pop. 1,092), Milam co., central Texas, 23 mi/37 km NE of Austin, on Brushly Creek; 30°36′N 97°12′W. Agr. (cotton, corn, wheat; poultry, cattle); feeds. Settled 1880, inc. 1929.

Thorndike, town (1990 pop. 702), Waldo co., S Maine, 15 mi/24 km NW of Belfast; 44°36′N 69°13′W. In agr., recreational area.

Thorndike, Mass.: see PALMER.

Thorne, village, Rolette co., N N.Dak., 17 mi/27 km SW of Rolla, near Wolf Creek; 48°44′N 99°55′W. Turtle Mt. Indian Reservation to NE.

Thorne Bay, village (1990 pop. 569), Prince of Wales Isl., SE Alaska, 40 mi/64 km NW of Ketchikan, on Thorne Bay, Clarence Strait; 55°39′N 132°31′W. Connected by road to other communities on isl. Inc. 1982, one of the newest communities in Alaska. Logging, fishing. Pulp mill.

Thorne Centre, village, SW Que., Canada, 40 mi/64 km NW of Ottawa. Mica mining.

Thornhill, city, S Ont., Canada, 12 mi/19 km N of Toronto; 43°48′N 79°25′W. Suburban community; part of Richmond Hill (city). Mfg. (cereals; kitchen cabinets, scales).

Thornloe (THORN-lo), village (1991 pop. 132), E Ont., Canada, 16 mi/26 km NNW of Haileybury; 42°19′N 79°41′W. In lumbering and mining region (gold, silver, cobalt).

Thornton, city (1990 pop. 55,031), Adams co., NE Colo., a residential and industrial suburb 8 mi/12.9 km N of downtown Denver, near South Platte R.; 39°53′N 104°57′W. Elev. 5,268 ft/1,606 m. Mfg. (computer graphics systems, plywood, coffee and tea, bldg. components, infant furniture, architectural woodwork, automobile accessories, sheet metal fabricating, air distribution equip., instrumentation recorders, pneumatic equip., oil and gas developement, space systems). Thornton has grown tremendously along with the Denver metropolitan area; the pop. increased more than 4-fold bet. 1970 and 1990. State Fish Hatchery to E. Inc. 1956.

Thornton 1 uninc. town (1990 pop. 850), San Joaquin co., central Calif., 10 mi/16 km NW of Lodi, on Mokelumne R. Tomatoes, vegetables, melons, fruit; dairying; poultry. Mfg. (tomato prods.). **2** town (1990 pop. 431), Cerro Gordo co., N Iowa, 17 mi/27 km SSW of Mason City; 42°56′N 93°23′W. In agr. area. **3** town (1990 pop. 1,505), Grafton co., central N.H., 9 mi/ 14.5 km N of Plymouth; 43°55′N 71°37′W. Drained by Pemigewasset R. Agr. (vegetables, fruit, nursery crops; poultry, cattle; dairying); timber. Parts of White Mt. Natl. Forest in E and W.

Thornton 1 village (1990 pop. 502), Calhoun co., S Ark., 24 mi/39 km NE of Camden; 33°46′N 92°29′W. In agr. and timber area, on Champagnolle Creek. **2** village (1990 pop. 2,778), Cook co., NE Ill., suburb 22 mi/ 35 km S of downtown Chicago; 41°34′N 87°37′W. Mfg. (furniture, packing materials, asphalt paving mixtures, crushed stone). Inc. 1900.

Thornton, R.I.: see JOHNSTON, village.

Thornton, village (1990 pop. 540), Limestone co., E central Texas, 33 mi/53 km ESE of Waco; 31°24′N 96°34′W. Trade point in cotton, cattle area. L. Limestone to E.

Thornton River, c.40 mi/64 km long, N Va.; rises in Blue Ridge in Rappahannock co.; flows generally SE to Rappahannock R. 9 mi/14.5 km NE of Culpeper; 38°39′N 78°19′W.

Thorntown, town (1990 pop. 1,506), Boone co., central Ind., near Sugar Creek, and 9 mi/14.5 km NW of Lebanon; 40°08′N 86°37′W. In livestock and grain area; mfg. (machinery, metal prods.). Laid out 1831.

Thornville, village (1990 pop. 758), Perry co., central Ohio, 20 mi/32 km NW of New Lexington; 39°54′N 82°25′W. In agr. area.

Thornwood, residential village (☐ 5 sq mi/13 sq km; 1990 pop. 7,025), Westchester co., SE N.Y., just S of Pleasantville; 41°06′N 73°45′W. Pop. also includes part of Valhalla.

Thorofare, town, Gloucester Co., SW N.J. 8 mi/12.9 km SW of Camden. Mfg. includes business forms, bearings, electrical connectors, and baked goods.

Thorold (THOR-old), city (1991 pop. 17,542), S Ont., Canada, part of Niagara Regional Municipality, on the Welland Ship Canal; 43°07′N 79°12′W. Suburb of St. Catharines; mfg. (abrasives).

Thorp, town (1990 pop. 1,657), Clark co., central Wis., 36 mi/58 km ENE of Eau Claire; 44°57′N 90°47′W. In dairying region; cheese mfg.; other mfg. (work benches, platform trucks, furniture). Inc. as village in 1893, as city in 1948.

Thorpe, locality, McDowell co., S W.Va., 1 mi/1.6 km E of Gary; part of Gary, separate Post Office. Bituminous-coal area. Mfg. (generators, plastic bottles, wooden cabinets).

Thorsby, town (1990 pop. 1,465), Chilton co., central Ala., 6 mi/9.7 km NW of Clanton. In fruit and cotton area; lumber; mfg. apparel, veneer. Seat of Thorsby Inst.

Thorsby (THORZ-bee), village (1991 pop. 708), central Alta., Canada, near North Saskatchewan R., 32 mi/51 km SW of Edmonton. Coal mining; oil and gas; wheat, oats, barley, hogs.

Thousand Island Park, N.Y.: see WELLESLEY ISLAND.

Thousand Islands, a group of more than 1,800 isls. and 3,000 shoals in the St. Lawrence R., E of L. Ontario, N N.Y. and S Ont., Canada; stretching c.50 mi/80 km along the U.S.-Can. line. Most of the isls. are in Canada; Wolfe Isl., Ont. (48 sq mi/124 sq km), is the largest. The isls. are part of a belt of metamorphic rock connecting the Adirondack Mts. and the Can. Shield; they were formed at the end of the Ice Age, when the St. Lawrence R. became the chief outlet of the Great Lakes. The forested region is a popular summer resort; many of the isls. are privately owned. Numerous parks, including Canada's St. Lawrence Isls. Natl. Park. The 5-span Thousand Isls. Bridge and Highway (6 mi/10 km long; opened 1938) bet. the N.Y. and Ont. mainlands crosses several isls. and channels.

Thousand Islands International Bridge, links U.S. and Canada, spanning the St. Lawrence bet. Collins Landing, N.Y., and vicinity of Gananoque, Ont., Canada; c.6 mi/10 km long; 44°20′N 75°58′W. Consists of 2 main suspension structures, 3 smaller bridges, and roadways across Wellesley and Hill isls. Completed 1938.

Thousand Oaks, city (1990 pop. 104,352), Ventura co., S Calif., 34 mi/55 km WNW of downtown Los Angeles, 20 mi/32 km E of Oxnard, and Pacific Ocean 9 mi/14.5 km to S; 34°11′N 118°52′W. In a farm area (avocados, citrus, vegetables, strawberries; nursery prods.). It has light industry and mfg. (petroleum production, pharmaceuticals, motor vehicles, toy dolls, computer peripherals; printing and publishing). In the expanding and developing S Calif. area, Thousand Oaks is one of the fastest-growing U.S. cities, marked by a pop. increase of more than 35% bet. 1980 and 1990. Once known generally as the Conejo Valley, it became a stagecoach stop in 1874. Calif. Lutheran Univ. is there. Santa Monica Mts. Natl. Recreation Area to S. Inc. 1964.

Thousand Palms, uninc. town (1990 pop. 4,122), Riverside co., S Calif., 8 mi/12.9 km E of Palm Springs, in Coachella Valley; 33°49′N 116°23′W. Resort area; mfg. golf equip. Agua Caliente Indian Reservation to W; Joshua Tree Natl. Monument to NE.

Thrall, village (1990 pop. 550), Williamson co., central Texas, 34 mi/55 km NE of Austin; 30°35′N 97°17′W. In farm area (cattle; cotton; wheat, corn); some oil; mfg. (tillage equip.). Oil booms (1925, 1930).

Three Forks, village, S B.C., Canada, in Selkirk Mts., near Slocan L., 35 mi/56 km N of Nelson. Silver, lead, zinc mining (declining).

Three Forks, town (1990 pop. 1,203), Gallatin co., SW Mont. 30 mi/48 km NW of Bozeman, SW of point at which Gallatin, Jefferson, and Madison rivers join to form Missouri R., town straddles point bet. Jefferson and Madison rivers; 45°54′N 111°33′W. Wheat, hay, cattle; mfg. (pine boards, cement, talc prods.). Missouri Headwaters State Park NE of town; Lewis and Clark Caverns State Park to SW; Madison Buffalo Jump State Park to SE. Site of town was visited by Lewis and Clark Expedition (1804), which named the rivers.

Three Hills, town (1991 pop. 2,884), S Alta., Canada, 30 mi/48 km NW of Drumheller; 51°42′N 113°16′W. Coal mining; grain elevators; wheat, oats, cattle.

Three Lakes, village, Oneida co., N Wis., 15 mi/24 km NE of Rhinelander, in lake region. Lumbering, farming. Winery; mfg. (cutting and stripping blades). Nicolet Natl. Forest to E, Amer. Legion State Forest to W, Sheltered Valley Ski Area here.

Three Mile Island, Dauphin co., S central Pa., in Susquehanna R. (York Haven Dam at lower (S) end of isl. forms Frederic L. in river), 10 mi/16 km SE of Harrisburg, Pa., site of Three Mile Isl. Nuclear Power Plant; 40°09′N 76°43′W. On Mar. 28, 1979, failure of the cooling system of the No. 2 Nuclear reactor led to overheating and partial melting of its uranium core and production of hydrogen gas, which raised fears of an explosion and dispersal of radioactivity. Thousands living near the plant, including people in the towns of Middletown 3 mi/4.8 km to N, Elizabethtown 6 mi/9.7 km to E, and Bainbridge 4 mi/6.4 km to SE, left the area before the 12-day crisis ended, during which time some radioactive water and gases were released. A federal investigation, assigning blame to human, mechanical, and design errors, recommended changes in reactor licensing and personnel training, as well as in the structure and function of the Nuclear Regulatory Commission. The accident also increased public concern and scrutiny over the dangers of nuclear power and the construction and maintenance of nuclear power plants.

Three Oaks, town (1990 pop. 1,786), Berrien co., extreme SW Mich., 17 mi/27 km W of Niles; 41°47′N 86°36′W. In area growing fruit, corn, grains, wheat, tomatoes; hogs; mfg. (plastic moldings, hardware packaging). Has mus. containing Native Amer. and historic relics. Warren Dunes State Park to N. Settled 1850, inc. 1867.

Three Rivers, Canada: see TROIS RIVIÈRES.

Three Rivers 1 town (1990 pop. 7,413), St. Joseph co., SW Mich., 25 mi/40 km S of Kalamazoo, and on St. Joseph R. near influx of short Portage and Rocky rivers; 41°56′N 85°37′W. Trade and industrial center for farm area; mfg. (machinery, paper and plastic prods., transportation equip., home furnishings); nursery. Has remains of Native Amer. village sites and garden beds. A Fr. trading post and Jesuit mission were located here in 17th cent. Swiss Valley Ski Area to W. Settled 1829; inc. as village 1855, as city 1895. **2** town (1990 pop. 1,889), Live Oak co., S Texas, 28 mi/45 km W of Beeville and on Frio R. just below influx of Atascosa R., and just above mouth of the Frio on the Nueces R.; 28°28′N 98°10′W. Elev. 145 ft/44 m. A trade center in agr., cattle, hogs, oil and gas producing area; mfg. (gasoline and diesel fuel). Tips State Recreation Park to S; Choke Canyon L. reservoir to NW; Choke Canyon State Park to W. Est. 1913, inc. 1927.

Three Rivers 1 uninc. village, Tulare co., central Calif., on Kaweah R., and 22 mi/35 km ENE of Visalia, in Sierra Nevada foothills. In Sequoia Natl. Forest. Hq. for Kings Canyon and Sequoia natl. parks, Sequoia Natl. Park to E and NE, Kings Canyon Natl. Park c.20 mi/32 km NE. L. Kaweah reservoir to SW; Lookout Point Ranger Station to E. **2** village, Otero co., S central N.Mex., just W of Sierra Blanca, 30 mi/48 km NNW of Alamogordo. Elev. 4,568 ft/1,392 m. In livestock region. Mescalero Apache Indian Reservation is E; Three Rivers Natl. Recreaction Site to E; in NE end of Tularosa Valley; part of Lincoln Natl. Forest to NE.

Three Rivers, Mass.: see PALMER.

Three Saints Bay, small inlet, SE Kodiak Isl., S Alaska, on Gulf of Alaska, W of Sitkalidak Isl., 60 mi/97 km SW of Kodiak; 57°08′N 153°30′W. Site of Rus. settlement in Alaska, est. 1784 by Grigorii Shelekhov (Gregory Shelekov) and named after one of his ships; moved to Kodiak, 1792. Now site of Old Harbor village.

Three Sisters, on Lane-Deschutes co. line, 3 peaks in Three Sisters Wilderness Area of Cascade Range, central Oregon, W of Bend; 44°08′N 121°46′W. Peaks include North Sister (10,085 ft/3,074 m), Middle Sister (10,047 ft/3,062 m), and South Sister (10,358 ft/3,157 m). Each Sister has large glaciers.

Three Sisters, The, mountain (9,744 ft/2,970 m), SW Alta., Canada, near B.C. border, in Rocky Mts., on SE edge of Banff Natl. Park, 15 mi/24 km SE of Banff.

Three Springs, borough (1990 pop. 422), Huntingdon co., S central Pa., 14 mi/23 km SSW of Mount Union, on Three Springs Creek; 40°12′N 77°58′W. Light mfg.; agr. (alfalfa; poultry, livestock); timber. Memmi Airport to S.

Throckmorton, county (□ 915 sq mi/2,370 sq km; 1990 pop. 1,880), N Texas; ⊙ Throckmorton; 33°10′N 99°12′W. Drained by Brazos R. and its Clear Fork. Agr. (wheat, cotton, grain sorghums, oats, mesquite); livestock (mainly cattle; some sheep, horses). Oil and gas wells. Formed 1858.

Throckmorton, town (1990 pop. 1,036), ⊙ Throckmorton co., N Texas, c.60 mi/97 km SW of Wichita Falls; 33°10′N 99°10′W. In oil and gas area; cattle, sheep, horse, agr. (wheat; cotton); mfg. (machinery). Settled before 1880, inc. 1917.

Throgs Neck, peninsula in the Bronx borough of N.Y. city, SE N.Y., marking N side of mouth of East R. on L.I. Sound. Lighthouse at its tip (40°48′N 73°47′W). Here is U.S. Fort Schuyler, seat of N.Y. State Maritime Col. N terminus for Throgs Neck Bridge from Queens.

Throgs Neck Bridge, suspension bridge connecting boroughs of Queens and Bronx, N.Y. city, SE N.Y., spans East R. at W end of L.I. Sound; viewed as the dividing line between the 2 bodies of water; 40°48′N 73°48′W. The 1,800-ft/549-m span was designed by world-renowned engineer O. H. Ammann in 1961. A vital link at a critical junction of expressways, the bridge was built to relieve congestion crossing the Whitestone Bridge 1 mi/1.6 km W. On the Bronx side the bridge feeds into the Bruckner–Cross Bronx Expressway (I-95), Hutchinson River Parkway, and New England Thruway, and leads to N.J., Westchester co., upstate N.Y., and New England. On the Queens side, it has links to the Cross Isl. Expressway, the L.I. Expressway, and the Grand Central Parkway, and leads to Manhattan, L.I., Brooklyn, and points W. Name derived from Throg's Neck, a long peninsula of land jutting into L.I. sound and settled by John Throgmorton in 1643. Near the bridge on the Bronx side are the residential communities of Throgs Neck and Locust Point and the State Univ. of N.Y., Maritime Col. at Fort Schuyler. On the Queens side are the residential communities of Beechhurst, Bayside, and Little Bay Park, as well as historic Fort Totten (which was closed as an active fort in 1995).

Throop, borough (1990 pop. 4,070), Lackawanna co., NE Pa., suburb 4 mi/6.4 km NE of downtown Scranton, on Lackawanna R.; 41°26′N 75°35′W. Mfg. (machinery, bulk gas, septic tanks). Formerly an anthracite coal-mining center. Moosic Mts. to SE.

Thunder Bay, city (1991 pop. 113,946), SW Ont., Canada, on Thunder Bay inlet of L. Superior; 48°24′N 89°14′W. The city was created in 1970 by the amalgamation of the twin cities of Fort William and Port Arthur and 2 adjoining townships. It is one of Canada's major ports, shipping wheat, lumber, coal, and iron ore. The city has shipyards, grain elevators, lumber and pulp and paper mills, breweries, and an oil refinery. Mfg. includes structural steel, buses, trucks, aircraft, paper, and chemical prods. Port Arthur, originally a military post, was founded in the late 19th cent. Fort William was built by the North West Company in 1801 to serve as its W hq. It was the site of a fur-trading post built in 1679 and of Fort Kaministikwia, built by the French in 1717 and later abandoned. Kakabeka Falls, nearby, is a source of water power. Lakehead Univ.

Thunder Bay, inlet on NW shore of L. Superior, W Ont., Canada; 32 mi/51 km long, 13 mi/21 km wide at mouth. On W shore are Port Arthur and Fort William. Receives Kaministikwia R.

Thunder Bay River, c.60 mi/97 km, NE Mich.; rises near Atlanta in Montmorency co. (44°57′N 84°14′W); flows generally E through forest and farm area, past Hillman, to Thunder Bay (an inlet of L. Huron) at Alpena. Furnishes power. Chief tributaries are North Branch (c.40 mi/64 km long), Lower South Branch (flows out of large Hubbard L. reservoir; c.20 mi/32 km long), and Upper South Branch (flows through large Fletcher Pond reservoir; c.30 mi/48 km long).

Thunder Lake, Cass co., N central Minn., 27 mi/43 km SW of Grand Rapids; 3 mi/4.8 km long, 1 mi/1.6 km wide; 46°58′N 93°52′W. Resorts area. S part in Land O'Lakes State Forest. Drains NE to Big Rice L. through Pug Hole L.

Thunderbolt, town (1990 pop. 2,786), Chatham co., E Ga., just E of Savannah, along Intracoastal Waterway (drawbridge) near the Atlantic; 32°02′N 81°03′W. Light mfg. and fishing, and boat repair and storage facilities; seafood restaurants face coastal marshes.

Thurlow Dam, E Ala., in Tallapoosa R., at Tallassee. Privately built power dam (62 ft/19 m high, 1,846 ft/563 m long) completed 1931. Formerly known as Lower Tallassee Dam.

Thurlow Islands (THUHR-lo) (□ 72 sq mi/186 sq km), SW B.C., Canada, group of 2 isls. at N end of Discovery Passage, bet. Strait of Georgia and Queen Charlotte

Strait NW of Sonora Isl.; 12 mi/19 km long, 3 mi/5 km wide. At E end is Blind Channel fishing village. East Thurlow Isl. is 11 mi/18 km long, 4 mi/6 km–6 mi/10 km wide; N end is Thurlow or Shoal Bay.

Thurman, town (1990 pop. 239), Fremont co., extreme SW Iowa, 37 mi/60 km NW of Sidney; 40°49′N 95°45′W. Limestone quarries. Forney L. State Preserve to N.

Thurmond, village (1990 pop. 39), Fayette co., S central W.Va., 7 mi/11.3 km S of Fayetteville, near New R; 37°57′N 81°04′W. Coal-mining and agr. region. New R. Gorge Natl. R. to N, W, and S.

Thurmont, town (1990 pop. 3,398), Frederick co., N Md., at E base of the Blue Ridge, and 15 mi/24 km N of Frederick; 39°37′N 77°25′W. In agr. area. Mfg. of shoes; also goldfish raising. Settled in 1751 by Jabob Weller and his family. The town was called Mechanicsville orginally, but when the Western Maryland RR was completed in 1872, the name was changed to Thurmont, meaning "gateway to the mountains." The closest community to Camp David, it has played host to Winston Churchill, Nikita Khrushchev, and various Kennedys. Catoctin Recreational Demonstration Area as well as Catochin Natl. Park are nearby.

Thurso (THUHR-so), town (1991 pop. 2,478), SW Que., Canada, on Ottawa R., and 24 mi/39 km ENE of Ottawa; 45°35′N 75°14′W. Lumbering; dairying; livestock raising.

Thurston 1 county (□ 396 sq mi/1,026 sq km; 1990 pop. 6,936), NE Nebr.; ⊙ Pender; 42°9′N 96°32′W. Farm area bounded E by Missouri R. and Iowa; drained by Logan Creek. Entire co. with Indian reservations, but most land is neither tribal nor owned by Indians: Winnebago Indian Reservation (small part in Dixon co.) in N ½, Omaha Indian Reservation (partly in neighboring Burt and Cuming cos.) in S. Mfg. (machinery); agr. (cattle, hogs, corn; dairying). Formed 1889. **2** county (□ 773 sq mi/2,002 sq km; 1990 pop. 161,238), W Wash.; ⊙ OLYMPIA (also the state ⊙); 46°56′N 122°50′W. Bounded NE by Nisqually R. (forms Alder L. reservoir in SE corner), N by Puget Sound; drained by Skookumchuck, Deschutes, and Black rivers. Lumber, coal; oysters, livestock, blueberries, carrots, hay, nuts, dairy prods., poultry. Includes Nisqually Indian Reservation and small part of Mt. Baker–Snoqualmie Natl. Forest in SE corner. Indented by Eld, Budd, and Henderson inlets in N. Part of Chehalis Indian Reservation in SW; Nisqually Indian Reservation in E; part of Fort Lewis Military Reservation in E. Nisqually Natl. Wildlife Refuge, and Tolmie State Park in W center. Skookumchuck Reservoir in S. Formed 1852.

Thurston 1 village (1990 pop. 98), Thurston co., NE Nebr., 5 mi/8 km N of Pender and on Logan Creek; 42°10′N 96°42′W. Mfg. (fertilizer injection equip., agr. equip., fertilizer). Located in SW part of Winnebego Indian Reservation **2** village (1990 pop. 539), Fairfield co., central Ohio, 10 mi/16 km N of Lancaster; 39°51′N 82°32′W. In livestock raising and farming area.

Thwart Island (□ 11 sq mi/28 sq km), E N.F., in the Bay of Exploits, inlet of Notre Dame Bay, 30 mi/48 km SW of Twillingate; 6 mi/10 km long, 3 mi/5 km wide; 49°19′N 55°12′W.

Tianguismanalco (tee-ahn-gwees-mahn-AHL-ko), town (1990 pop. 4,528), Puebla, central Mexico, 18 mi/29 km WSW of Puebla; 18°57′N 98°26′W. Elev. 7,185 ft/2,190 m. Corn, wheat, sugarcane, fruit. Also called San Juan Tianguismanalco.

Tianguistenco de Galeana (tee-ahn-gwees-TEN-ko dai gah-le-AH-nah), town (1990 pop. 12,299), ⊙ Tianguistenco municipio, Mexico state, central Mexico, 13 mi/21 km SE of Toluca de Lerdo; 19°11′N 99°27′W. Cereals, livestock; dairying.

Tianguistengo (tee-ahn-gwees-TEN-go), town (1990 pop.1,452), Hidalgo, central Mexico, 42 mi/68 km N of Pachuca de Soto; 20°46′N 98°39′W. Corn, beans, fruit, cotton, vegetables.

Tiber Reservoir, Mont.: see ELWELL, LAKE.

Tiblemont (tee-bluh-MO), village, W Que., Canada, 26 mi/42 km NE of Val d'Or. Gold mining.

Tiburon, city (1990 pop. 7,532), Marin co., W Calif., at tip of Tiburon Peninsula (c.4 mi/6.4 km long) on W San Francisco Bay, residential suburb 7 mi/11.3 km N of downtown San Francisco; 37°54′N 122°28′W. RR terminus. Bathing, boating, fishing. Passenger ferry to Angel Isl. (state park) to SE; Richmond–San Rafael Bridge to N. Mt. Tamalpais Game Refuge to NW in Richardson Bay.

Tiburon (tee-byoo-RON), town (1982 pop. 2,224), Sud dept., SW Haiti, at SW extremity of Jacmel Peninsula, 45 mi/72 km WNW of Les Cayes; 18°20′N 74°24′W. Cacao; lumbering, coffee processing. Fishing port.

Tiburón Island (tee-boo-RON) (□ 458 sq mi/1,186 sq km), Sonora, NW Mexico, in Gulf of California, just off W coast of Sonora, Mexico, 75 mi/121 km W of Hermosillo; c.30 mi/48 km long, c.18 mi/29 km wide; 29°N 112°30′W. Rises to 3,996 ft/1,218 m. Separated from mainland by Canal del Infierrillo strait. Bahan Kino to SE; Punta las Animas on SW end; Entire isl. is in Isla Tiburón Biosphere reserve.

Tiburon Peninsula, Haiti: see JACMEL PENINSULA.

Ticaboo, uninc. village, Garfield co., S Utah, 73 mi/117 km WSW of Monticello. Cattle. Bullfrog Basin Marina, est. 1963, 10 mi/16 km S on Powell reservoir (Colorado R.) in Glen Canyon Natl. Recreation Area, toll ferry to Halls Crossing Marina carries State Highway 276 traffic across lake. Tourism.

Tice (TYS), town (□ 1 sq mi/2.6 sq km; 1990 pop. 3,971), Lee co., SW Fla., 4 mi/6.4 km NE of Fort Myers; 26°40′N 81°49′W.

Tickfaw (TIK-faw), village (1990 pop. 565), Tangipahoa parish, SE La., 9 mi/14 km N of Ponchatoula; 30°35′N 90°30′W. Timber and agr. area (vegetables, strawberries; dairying; cattle, horses). Mfg. (timber processing, pumps).

Tickfaw River (TIK-faw), c.105 mi/169 km long, in Miss. and La.; rises in E Amite co., SW Miss.; flows S, into La., past Easleyville and Holden, then SE to Natabulny R., 2 mi/3.2 km NW of its mouth on L. Maurepas.

Ticonderoga, resort village (□ 1 sq mi/2.6 sq km; 1990 pop. 2,770), Essex co., NE N.Y., on a neck of land bet. Lakes George and Champlain; 43°51′N 73°25′W. At Ticonderoga and nearby Crown Point, several battles in the Fr. and Indian War took place. Fort Carillon, built there by the French in 1755, was successfully defended by Montcalm against James Abercromby in 1758, but it fell to Jeffrey Amherst in 1759, when it was renamed Fort Ticonderoga. It was captured (May 10, 1775) by a detachment of Green Mountain Boys under Ethan Allen and troops commanded by Benedict Arnold. In the Saratoga campaign it was abandoned (1777) without a fight by Arthur St. Clair to John Burgoyne. The British gave up the fort after the campaign but reoccupied it for a short time in 1780. The fort was restored as a mus. in 1909. The hq. of the N.Y. State Historical Assn. is at Ticonderoga; the bldg. is a reproduction of John Hancock's house and contains collections of historical material and paintings. A ferry crosses L. Champlain to Shoreham, Vt. Settled in the 17th cent., inc. 1889.

Ticul (tee-KOOL), city (1990 pop. 22,866) and township, Yucatán, SE Mexico, 40 mi/64 km S of Mérida, on Mexico Highway 184; 20°22′N 89°31′W. On RR; agr. center (henequen, sugarcane, corn, tropical fruit; timber). Has fine colonial bldgs. Famous Uxmal Maya ruins are 12 mi/19 km W.

Tidioute (TI-dee-oot), borough (1990 pop. 791), Warren co., NW Pa., 17 mi/27 km SW of Warren, on Allegheny R.; 41°40′N 79°24′W. Oil and gas field to W and SW.

Tie Siding, village, Albany co., SE Wyo., just W of Laramie Mts., 16 mi/26 km SSE of Laramie. Elev. c.7,753 ft/2,363 m. RR junction. Supply point in ranching region. Part of Medicine Bow Natl. Forest to NE.

Tiedemann, Mount (TEED-muhn) (12,000 ft/3,658 m), SW B.C., Canada, in Coast Mts., 170 mi/274 km NW of Vancouver, just N of Mt. Waddington. Also spelled Mount Teidemann.

Tierra Amarilla (tee-ER-uh ah-muh-REE-uh), uninc. village (1990 pop. 800), ⊙ Rio Arriba co., N N.Mex., on Rio Brazos, near its confluence with Rio Chama, San Juan Mts. to E, 74 mi/119 km NNW of Santa Fe. Elev. 7,524 ft/2,293 m. Cattle, sheep, poultry; chiles. Coal mines in vicinity. El Vado Dam and Reservoir (El Vado L. State Park) are 13 mi/21 km SW, Carson Natl. Forest E; fish hatchery to W; Brazos Peak (11,403 ft/3,476 m) to NE; Jicarilla Apache Indian Reservation to W; Heron L. Reservoir and State Park to W; Continental Divide to W.

Tierra Blanca (tee-E-rah BLAHN-kah), city (1990 pop. 39,473) and township, Veracruz, E Mexico, in Gulf lowland, 55 mi/89 km SSW of Veracruz, on Mexico Highway 145; 18°28′N 96°21′W. RR junction; agr. center situated amid rich tropical forest vegetation; coffee, sugarcane, bananas, palms (coyol).

Tierra Blanca Creek, c.90 mi/145 km long, E N.Mex. and extreme N Texas; rises as intermittent stream in E Curry co., N.Mex., near Grady; flows generally E into Deaf Smith co., Texas, past Hereford to join Palo Duro Creek E of Canyon to form Prairie Dog Town Fork of Red R. Dam near Canyon forms Buffalo L. (34°55′N 102°06′W), a recreation center, Buffalo L. Natl. Wildlife Refuge surrounds it.

Tierra Buena, uninc. town (1990 pop. 2,878), Sutter co., N central Calif., suburb 3 mi/4.8 km WNW of Yuba City; 39°10′N 121°40′W. Grain, vegetables, sugar beets, alfalfa, safflower; dairying, poultry. RR junction.

Tierra Colorada (tee-E-rah ko-lo-RAH-dah), town (1990 pop. 10,090), ⊙ Juan A. Escudero Municipio, in S central Guerrero, Mexico 38 mi/61 km S of Chilpancingo de los Bravo, on Mexico Highway 95; 17°10′N 99°30′W. Elev 984 ft/300 m. Agr. produces corn, beans, plantains, mango; cattle. Wood prods.

Tierra Vieja Mountains, Texas: see SIERRA VIEJA.

Tierrablanca (tee-E-rah BLAHN-kah), city (1990 pop. 1,241), in NE part of Guanajuato, Mexico, in the region of Sierra Gorda, 40 mi/64 km ESE of San Miguel de Allende; 21°06′N 100°10′W. Agr. (corn, beans, and wheat). Unpaved road connects the city with San José Iturbide.

Tierranueva (tee-E-rah-noo-E-vah), town (1990 pop. 4,499), San Luis Potosí, N central Mexico, 45 mi/72 km SE of San Luis Potosí; 21°41′N 100°34′W. Elev. 7,260 ft/2,213 m. Corn, cotton, beans, fruit; livestock.

Tieton (TEI-tuhn), village (1990 pop. 693), Yakima co., S Wash., in the Cascades near Tieton R., 15 mi/24 km NW of Yakima; 46°42′N 120°45′W. Wheat, barley, hops, fruit, vegetables; dairying; cattle, sheep. Timber. Rimrock L., formed by Tieton Dam, to W. Mt. Baker–Snoqualmie Natl. Forest and William O. Douglas Wilderness Area to W.

Tieton Dam, Wash.: see RIMROCK LAKE.

Tiffin, city (1990 pop. 18,604), ⊙ Seneca co., N central Ohio, on the scenic Sandusky R. in a farm area; 41°07′N 83°10′W. China, glassware, machinery, wire and cable, and electrical equip. are made in the city. Heidelberg Col., Tiffin Univ. (a business school), and a state hosp. are here. Inc. 1835.

Tiffin, town (1990 pop. 460), Johnson co., E Iowa, 8 mi/12.9 km WNW of Iowa City; 41°42′N 91°40′W. In agr. area; feeds.

Tiffin River, c.75 mi/121 km long, in Mich. and Ohio; rises in SE Mich.; flows S, into NW Ohio, through Fulton, Williams, and Defiance cos., to the Maumee R. just W of Defiance (city); 41°16′N 84°23′W.

Tift, county (□ 269 sq mi/697 sq km; 1990 pop. 34,998), S central Ga., ⊙ Tifton; 31°28′N 83°32′W. Agr. includes peanuts, corn, wheat, soybeans, cotton, tobacco; cattle, hogs. Mfg. at Tifton. Intersected by Little R. Formed 1905.

Tifton (TIF-tuhn), city (1990 pop. 14,215), ⊙ Tift co., S central Ga.; 31°28′N 83°31′W. Location on Interstate 75 has led to city becoming an important truck-based distribution center. Mfg. includes siding and roofing, yarns, agr. chemicals and equip., feeds, meat packing, apparel, textiles, aluminum prods.; machining. Agr. crops are tobacco, cotton, and vegetable crops. Abraham Baldwin Agr. col., a 2-year unit of the univ. system of Ga., and a state agr.-experiment station are in Tifton. The Ga. agr. Agriama Center provides a permanent display of the agr. heritage of the area. Inc. 1890.

Tigard (TEI-guhrd), city (1990 pop. 29,344), Washington and Clackamas cos., NW Oregon, suburb 10 mi/16 km

SW of downtown Portland, near Tualatin R.; 45°25′N 122°46′W. RR junction. Agr. (fruit, vegetables, nuts; poultry, cattle); dairy prods. Mfg. (yogurt, candy, millwork, printing, publishing, plastics, iron castings, sheet metal work, motors). Oswego L. Reservoir to E.

Tiger, village (1990 pop. 301), Rabun co., extreme NE Ga., in Blue Ridge Mts.,3 mi/4.8 km SSW of Clayton; 34°51′N 83°26′W. Mfg. includes bed frames and metal stampings.

Tiger River, S.C.: see TYGER RIVER.

Tigerton, town (1990 pop. 815), Shawano co., E central Wis., 32 mi/51 km SE of Wausau; 44°44′N 89°03′W. Sawmilling; lumber.

Tigerville, uninc. village, Greenville co., NW S.C., in foothills of the Blue Ridge Mts., 14 mi/23 km N of Greenville. Mfg. includes printing, vermiculite. Seat of North Greenville Col.

Tightwad, village (1990 pop. 50), Henry co., W central Mo., 10 mi/16 km WNW of Warsaw; 38°18′N 93°32′W. Surrounded except on W by Truman L., on W margin of Ozarks Region. Of interest is the Bank of Tightwad.

Tignall (TIG-nuhl), town (1990 pop. 711), Wilkes co., NE Ga., 9 mi/14.5 km N of Washington; 33°52′N 82°44′W. Mfg. of textiles and apparel.

Tignish (tig-NISH), village (1991 pop. 893), NW P.E.I., Canada, on the Gulf of St. Lawrence, 40 mi/64 km NNW of Summerside, and at N terminus of the isl.; 46°57′N 64°02′W. RR; fishing center and tourist resort.

Tiguabos (tee-GWAH-bos), town, Guantánamo prov., E Cuba, on RR, and 11 mi/18 km NW of Guantánamo; 20°14′N 75°22′W. In sugar-growing region.

Tigvariak Island (tig-VAH-ree-yak), NE Alaska, in Arctic Ocean, 51 mi/82 km ESE of Beechey Point; 2 mi/3.2 km long, 1 mi/1.6 km wide; 70°13′N 147°10′W.

Tihuatlán (tee-wah-TLAHN), town (1990 pop. 10,335), Veracruz, E Mexico, in Sierra Madre Oriental foothills, 19 mi/31 km SSW of Túxpam de Rodríguez Cano on Mexico Highway 130; 20°43′N 97°32′W. Corn, sugarcane, coffee, fruit.

Tijeras (ti-HER-uhs), uninc. village (1990 pop. 340), Bernalillo co., N central N.Mex., suburb 24 mi/39 km E of Albuquerque, in section of Cibola Natl. Forest; 35°05′N 106°22′W. Mfg. (cement). Sandia Mts. lie between town and city of Albuquerque; Manzano Mts. to S. Sandia Peak Ski Area and Sandia Crest Recreation Area to N.

Tijuana (tee-HWAH-nah), city (1990 pop. 698,752) and township, Baja California state, NW Mexico, just S of the U.S. border, and at terminus of Mexico Highways 1 and 2; 32°29′N 117°10′W. Once a gaudy border city, noted for its racetracks (Agua Caliente) and bullfights, it is now a large industrial city. An irrigated agr. area surrounds the city. During the prohibition era Tijuana gained fame as a wide-open town. It expanded considerably in the wake of a booming tourist trade after World War II, and again in recent years as the border area has become increasingly industrialized. Hundreds of maquiladoras — low-cost foreign-owned mfg. plants, including apparel and televisions, that finish goods for U.S. export — have opened in the region around Tijuana. One of the fastest growing cities in Mexico. General Abelardo L Rodriguez Internatl. airport to SE. Major gateway for illegal Mex. immigration to US.

Tijuana River (tee-HWAH-nah), c.120 mi/193 km long, intermittent stream in Baja California Norte, NW Mexico and S Calif., U.S., SE of San Diego. Rises c.45 mi/ 72 km ENE of Ensenada in Sierra de Juárez; flows WNW past Tijuana, crosses U.S.-Mexico border 5 mi/ 8 km E of Pacific Ocean, continues W through San Ysidro sect. of San Diego city, to Pacific Ocean, 10 mi/ 16 km S of downtown San Diego and 2 mi/3.2 km S of Imperial Beach. Abelardo L. Rodríguez Dam is on river SE of Tijuana, for municipial use and irrigation.

Tikikluk, village, N Alaska, c. 80 mi/129 km S of Barrow; 70°30′N 157°W. Sometimes spelled Tikigiluk.

Tila (TEE-lah), town (1990 pop. 4,527), Chiapas, S Mexico, 45 mi/72 km ENE of San Cristóbal de las Casas; 17°24′N 92°29′W. Elev. 3,806 ft/1,160 m. Cereals, fruit.

Tilapa (tee-lah-pah), town (1990 pop. 2,453), Puebla, central Mexico, 5 mi/8 km W of Izúcar de Matamoros;

18°10′N 97°06′W. Elev. 4,101 ft/1,250 m. Corn, sugarcane, fruit.

Tilbury (TIL-be-ree), town (1991 pop. 4,362), S Ont., Canada, 16 mi/26 km SW of Chatham; 42°15′N 82°26′W. Mfg. of motor vehicle bodies, bricks, tiles.

Tilden 1 village (1990 pop. 919), Randolph co., SW Ill., 22 mi/35 km NNE of Chester; 38°12′N 89°40′W. In agr. and bituminous coal-mining area. **2** village (1990 pop. 895), Antelope and Madison cos., NE central Nebr., 22 mi/35 km W of Norfolk and on Elkhorn R.; 42°02′N 97°49′W. Livestock, grain; dairy prods. **3** uninc. village (1990 pop. 500), ⊙ McMullen co., S Texas, on Frio R. and c.40 mi/64 km E of Cotulla. Elev. 270 ft/82 m. Cattle; mfg. (gas processing, sulphur processing). Choke Canyon L. reservoir to E.

Tilden, Fort, N.Y.: see ROCKAWAY PENINSULA.

Tilghman Island (TIL-man), low, sandy isl. (c.4 mi/ 6.4 km long, 1.5 mi/2.4 km wide), Talbot co., E Md., in Chesapeake Bay on N side of mouth of Choptank R.; separated from mainland by narrow channel (bridged). Center of large fishing, oystering and crabbing industry, resort for anglers and duck hunters. Villages include Tilghman and Avalon at N end, Fairbank at S end.

Tillamook (TIL-uh-muk), county (☐ 1,333 sq mi/ 3,452 sq km; 1990 pop. 21,570), NW Oregon; ⊙ Tillamook; 45°28′N 123°46′W. Bounded W by Pacific Ocean. Drained by Nehalem R., Tillamook R., Trask R. and Nestucca R. Dairy prods. Logging; fisheries; wineries. Large part of Tillamook State Forest dominates co. in N, E, and center. Part of Siuslaw Natl. Forest in S. There are 9 state parks in Tillamook co., all coastal, including Oswald West and Nehalem Bay State Parks in NW and Cape Meares and Cape Lookout State Parks in W. Coastline indicated by several bays; largest of which is Tillamook Bay, 5 mi/8 km long, 2 mi/3.2 km wide, with narrow entrance at Garibaldi. Formed 1853.

Tillamook (TIL-uh-muk), town (1990 pop. 21,570), ⊙ Tillamook co., NW Oregon, on Tillamook R. at mouth of Trask R., near head of Tillamook Bay, 4 mi/6.4 km E of Pacific Ocean, 55 mi/89 km W of Portland; 45°27′N 123°50′W. Dairy center (cheese). Fisheries. Wineries. Mfg. (meat prods., lumber, asphalt; printing and publishing, helium purification). Recreation. Fish hatchery to SE. Tillamook State Forest to E; Siuslaw Natl. Forest to S; Cape Meares State Park and Lighthouse to W. Site of Tillamook County Historical Mus. Originally known as Lincoln, then Hoquarton, and finally (1885) Tillamook. Inc. 1891.

Tillamook Head (TIL-uh-muk), Clatsop co., NW Oregon, high promontory (c. 1,200 ft/366 m) in Ecola State Park, 18 mi/29 km SW of Astoria.

Tillar (TIL-uhr), village (1990 pop. 221), Drew and Desha cos., SE Ark., 7 mi/11.3 km NW of McGehee, near Bayou Bartholomew; 33°42′N 91°27′W.

Tillatoba (til-uh-TO-buh), village (1990 pop. 124), Yalobusha co., N central Miss., 15 mi/24 km NNW of Grenada; 33°58′N 89°54′W. Agr. (cotton, corn; poultry, cattle; timber). Sect. of Holly Springs Natl. Forest to E.

Tillery, Lake, reservoir, Stanley and Montgomery cos., W central N.C., backed up in Yadkin (Pee Dee) R., 10 mi/16 km SE of Albemarle; c.15 mi/24 km long; 35°12′N 80°03′W. Bodin Dam at N tip. Uwharrie R. enters from N. Formed by Tillery Dam, built for power generation. Morrow Mt. State Park on W shore, Uwharrie Natl. Forest on E shore.

Tilley, village (1991 pop. 322), SE Alta., Canada, 50 mi/ 80 km NW of Medicine Hat. Wheat, flax; cattle.

Tillman, county (☐ 879 sq mi/2,277 sq km; 1990 pop. 10,384), SW Okla.; ⊙ Frederick; 34°22′N 98°55′W. Bounded S by Red R. (here forming Texas line), and W by its North Fork; also drained by the Deep Red Run (L. Frederick reservoir in N). Agr. area (cotton, sorghum, vegetables, peanuts; cattle). Mfg. at Frederick and Grandfield. Formed 1907.

Tillman, village, Jasper co., S S.C., 8 mi/12.9 km W of Ridgeland. Named for Benjamin R. Tillman (known as "Pitchfork Ben"), governor (1890–1894) and U.S. senator (1894–1918). Agr. includes cotton, soybeans, corn, watermelons.

Tillman's Corner, village (1990 pop. 17,988), Mobile co., SW Ala., 9 mi/14.5 km SW of Mobile; 30°35′N 88°11′W. Residential community near 2 major highway intersections.

Tillsonburg, town (1991 pop. 12,019), S Ont., Canada, 24 mi/39 km ENE of St. Thomas; 42°52′N 80°44′W. Mfg. of machinery, agr. implements; tobacco processing. Tobacco and fruit region.

Tilton 1 town, Whitfield co., NW Ga., 8 mi/12.9 km SSE of Dalton, and on Conasauga R.; 34°39′N 84°56′W. **2** town (1990 pop. 3,240), Belknap co., central N.H., 2 mi/3.2 km E of Franklin; 43°28′N 71°34′W. Bounded S by Winnipesaukee R. (opposite Northfield), on E by Silver L. and Tilton L. (connected by Winnipesaukee R.). Mfg. (machining, electrical equip., printing and publishing, construction materials, rubber and plastic prods.); agr. (nursery crops, vegetables, apples; cattle, poultry; dairying). Known as Sanbornton Bridge until separated from Sanbornton in 1869.

Tilton, village (1990 pop. 2,729), Vermilion co., E central Ill., suburb 3 mi/4.8 km S of downtown Danville, near Salt Fork of Vermilion R.; 40°05′N 87°38′W. RR junction. Mfg. (metal stampings, prefabricated garages, aluminum castings and patterns). Inc. 1884.

Tiltonsville or **Tiltonville**, village (1990 pop. 1,517), Jefferson co., E Ohio, on Ohio R., and 14 mi/23 km SSW of Steubenville; 40°10′N 80°42′W. Concrete blocks, lumber. Called Grover until 1890.

Tiltonville, Ohio: see TILTONSVILLE.

Timagami or **Temagami**, village, E central Ont., Canada, at E end of L. Timagami, 27 mi/43 km SSW of Haileybury; 47°04′N 79°47′W. Gold and iron mining; lumbering.

Timagami, Lake (☐ 90 sq mi/233 sq km), E central Ont., Canada, 30 mi/48 km SW of Haileybury. Irregular in shape, deeply indented by several bays, it is 30 mi/ 48 km long, 20 mi/32 km wide; contains numerous isls. Drains E into Montreal R.

Timbalier Bay (tim-buhl-YAI), SE La., shallow inlet of the Gulf of Mexico, c.55 mi/89 km SSW of New Orleans; c.14 mi/23 km long. Oil and gas wells; oyster beds; fishing. Adjoins Terrebonne Bay (W), L. Raccourci (N); Timbalier and East Timbalier isls. are bet. bay and gulf.

Timbalier Island (tim-buhl-YAI), Terrebonne parish, SE La., bet. Timbalier Bay (N) and the Gulf of Mexico (S), c.65 mi/105 km SSW of New Orleans; c.7 mi/11 km long. Timbalier lighthouse (29°03′N 90°22′W) is offshore. East Timbalier Isl. (c.2 mi/3 km long), a bird refuge, is 8 mi/13 km E in Lafourche parish; 29°03′N 90°28′W.

Timber Creek Reservoir, Cowley co., S Kansas, on Winfield Creek, 10 mi/16 km NE of Winfield; 3 mi/ 4.8 km long; 37°21′N 96°52′W. Max. capacity of 52,317 acre-ft. Formed by dam (75 ft/23 m high), built (1970) by the city of Winfield for flood control and water supply.

Timber Lake, village (1990 pop. 517), ⊙ Dewey co., N central S.Dak., 30 mi/48 km WSW of Mobridge; 45°25′N 101°04′W. In agr. area. Mfg. (cheese). Little Moreau State Recreational Area to S. Service center for N part of Cheyenne River Indian Reservation, which takes in all of Dewey and Ziebach cos.

Timber Lake, Colo.: see HORSE CREEK RESERVOIR.

Timber Mountain, Nev.: see GRANT RANGE.

Timberlake, uninc. city, Campbell co., central Va., residential suburb 7 mi/11.3 km SSW of Lynchburg; 37°19′N 79°15′W. Lynchburg Municipal Airport to E.

Timberlake 1 uninc. village, Person co., N N.C., 23 mi/ 37 km N of Durham, on Flat R. Grain, tobacco, soybeans, livestock; timber. Mfg. (textiles, transportation equip.). **2** village (1990 pop. 833), Lake co., NE Ohio, on L. Erie, 22 mi/35 km NE of Cleveland; 41°40′N 81°26′W.

Timberville, town (1990 pop. 1,596), Rockingham co., NW Va., in Shenandoah Valley, 14 mi/23 km NNE of Harrisonburg; 38°38′N 78°46′W. Mfg. (poultry processing); agr. area (dairying; livestock, poultry; grain, soybeans, apples, peaches); timber. On North Fork Shenandoah R.

Timblin (TIM-blin), borough (1990 pop. 165), Jefferson co., W central Pa., 12 mi/19 km W of Punxsutawney, on Pine Run Creek; 40°58′N 79°12′W. Hay; dairying.

Time, village (1990 pop. 36), Pike co., W Ill., 28 mi/45 km WSW of Jacksonville; 39°33′N 90°43′W. In agr. area (corn, wheat, sorghum, soybeans; cattle, hogs).

Times Square, in N.Y. city, SE N.Y., formed by the intersection of Broadway, 7th Ave., and 42d St.; 40°46′N 73°58′W. This famous square was named for the bldg. here occupied by the *New York Times*. The bldg., located in the center of the square, is still well-known for its band of electric lights that transmits continually updated news items. Times Square and the adjacent area form one of the most concentrated entertainment dists. in the nation, featuring legitimate theaters, movie houses, shops, newsstands, bars, and restaurants. It became notorious for its many pornographic theaters and general tawdriness, and the city began a major clean-up effort in the 1990s. The stretch of Broadway at Times Square, jammed with noisy traffic and illuminated at night by a profusion of enormous electric signs, is known as the "Great White Way." On New Year's Eve close to a million people congregate here to celebrate the arrival of the new year and to see the ball drop from the One Times Square bldg.

Timewell, Ill.: see MOUND STATION

Timilpan (ti-MIL-pahn), town (1990 pop. 446), in N central Mexico state, Mexico, 41 mi/66 km N of Touca de Lerdo, near Huapango Resevoir. Elev. 8,793 ft/2,680 m. Also called San Andrés Timigpan.

Timiskaming (tuh-MI-skuh-ming), district (□ 5,896 sq mi/15,271 sq km; 1991 pop. 38,983), E central Ont., Canada, on L. Timiskaming and on Que. border; ⊙ Haileybury; 47°50′N 80°30′W.

Timiskaming, Canada: see TEMISCAMING.

Timiskaming, Lake (□ 110 sq mi/285 sq km), SW Que. and E Ont., Canada, expansion of Ottawa R., extending 62 mi/100 km bet. Timiskaming (SSE) and New Liskeard (NNW); 1 mi/2 km–10 mi/16 km wide. Elev. 589 ft/180 m. In N part are several isls.; on NW shore is Haileybury, with adjoining mining region.

Timken, village (1990 pop. 87), Rush co., central Kansas, on Walnut Creek, and 8 mi/12.9 km ESE of La Crosse; 38°28′N 99°10′W. Wheat, cattle.

Timmins, town (1991 pop. 47,461), central Ont., Canada, on the Mattagami R.; 48°28′N 81°20′W. Timmins is the commercial center of the rich Porcupine gold-mining dist., where gold was 1st discovered in 1909. Silver, copper, lead, and zinc are also mined here. Breweries and pulp, paper, and lumber mills.

Timmonsville, town (1990 pop. 2,182), Florence co., E central S.C., 11 mi/18 km SW of Florence; 34°07′N 79°56′W. Mfg. includes business forms, textiles, aparel; agr includes tobacco, cotton, grain, vegetables; timber; hogs, chickens.

Timnath, village (1990 pop. 190), Larimer co., N Colo., on Cache la Poudre R., and 6 mi/9.7 km SE of Fort Collins; 40°31′N 104°58′W. Elev. 4,877 ft/1,487 m. Oil and gas; mfg. (cabinets).

Timonium (ti-MO-nee-uhm), village (1990 pop. 16,442), Baltimore co., N Md., c.10 mi/16 km N of downtown Baltimore. Pop. figure includes Lutherville.

Timothy Lake, reservoir, Clackamas co., NW Oregon, on Oak Grove Fork of Clackamas R., in Mt. Hood Natl. Forest, 20 mi/32 km SSW of Mt. Hood; 4 mi/6.4 km long, 2 mi/3.2 km wide; 45°06′N 121°47′W. Elev. 3,218 ft/981 m; max. capacity 81,000 acre-ft. Formed by Timothy L. Dam (100 ft/30 m high), built (1956) by Portland General Electric for power generation.

Timpanogos Cave (TIM-puh-NO-guhs), national monument, NE Utah co., N Utah, 13 mi/21 km N of Provo, on American Fork R., bounded on all sides by Wasatch Natl. Forest. Covers 250 acres/101 ha; authorized 1922. Limestone cavern NW of Mt. Timpanogos; known for helictites (crystalline formations).

Timpanogos, Mount (tim-puh-NO-guhs), highest peak (11,750 ft/3,581 m) in Wasatch Range, E Utah co., N central Utah, 10 mi/16 km N of Provo; 40°23′N 111°38′W. Timpanogos Cave Natl. Monument is on NW slope.

Timpas Creek, 54 mi/87 km long, SE Colo.; rises in SW corner Otero co.; flows NE through Comanche Natl. Grassland, to Arkansas R. at Swink, 5 mi/8 km WNW of La Junta. Intermittent in upper course.

Timpson, town (1990 pop. 1,029), Shelby co., E Texas, near Attoyac Bayou, c.45 mi/72 km S of Marshall; 31°54′N 94°24′W. Agr. (cattle, poultry; vegetables, watermelons); timber; mfg. (lumber). Natural gas and oil, lignite nearby. L. Murvaul reservoir to N.

Tims Ford Lake, reservoir (□ 12 sq mi/31 sq km), mainly in Franklin co., S central Tenn., on Elk R.; 35°12′N 86°16′W. Has 3 main branches. Formed by Tims Ford Dam (175 ft/53 m high), built (1970) by TVA for flood control; also used for power generation, water storage, and recreation. Town of Winchester on SE end of reservoir. Tims Ford State Rustic Park on peninsula formed bet. NW and SW branches

Tims Ford Lake, Tenn.: see ELK RIVER.

Timucuy (tee-MOO-koo-ee), town (1990 pop. 2,684), Yucatán, SE Mexico, 12 mi/19 km SSE of Mérida; 20°45′N 89°35′W. Henequen, tropical fruit, corn, beans; livestock.

Tin City, village, W Alaska, W Seward Peninsula, on Bering Strait, 6 mi/9.7 km SE of Wales, 100 mi/161 km NW of Nome. Tin mining.

Tina (TEI-nuh), town (1990 pop. 199), Carroll co., NW central Mo., 11 mi/18 km N of Carrollton; 39°32′N 93°26′W.

Tina, Monte (TEE-nah, MON-tai), peak, S central Dominican Republic, in the Cordillera Central, 55 mi/89 km WNW of Santo Domingo; 18°45′N 70°42′W. Long considered highest peak (10,301 ft/3,140 m) in the West Indies, it is sometimes said to be only 9,281 ft/2,829 m, 2d to Pico Duarte, to NW. Also known as Loma Tina or Alto Bandera.

Tinajas Altas Mountains (tee-NAH-hahs), in extreme SW corner of Ariz., Yuma co., E of Yuma Desert, SE of Yuma. Extends into Sonora Mexico. Coyote Wash to NE.

Tindall, town (1990 pop. 46), Grundy co., N Mo., on Weldon R., and 6 mi/9.7 km N of Trenton; 40°09′N 93°36′W.

Tingambato (teen-gahm-BAH-to), town (1990 pop. 5,413), Michoacán, central Mexico, 9 mi/14.5 km ENE of Uruapan, on Mexico Highway 120; 19°30′N 101°52′W. Sugarcane, coffee, cereals, fruit.

Tingley, town (1990 pop. 179), Ringgold co., S Iowa, 10 mi/16 km N of Mount Ayr, and 16 mi/26 km SSE of Creston; 40°51′N 94°12′W. In agr. area.

Tingréla (tin-GRAI-lah), town, N Côte d'Ivoire, 65 mi/105 km N of Boundiali; 10°29′N 06°24′W. Manioc, yams, sorghum, millet, maize, beans, peanuts, tobacco, cotton; cattle. Also spelled Tengréla.

Tingüindín (teen-gween-DEEN), town (1990 pop. 5,647), Michoacán, central Mexico, 20 mi/32 km SW of Zamora; 19°45′N 102°29′W. Sugarcane, tobacco, fruit; livestock.

Tingwick (TING-wik), village, S Que., Canada, 8 mi/13 km N of Asbestos. Asbestos mining.

Tinicum (TIN-i-kuhm), township (1990 pop. 4,440), Delaware co., SE Pa., residential suburb 9 mi/14.5 km SW of Philadelphia on Tinicum Isl.; 39°51′N 75°16′W. Includes the communities of Essington and Lester. Philadelphia Internatl. Airport in E; Valley Forge State Forest to S on Little Tinicum Isl.

Tinicum Island (TIN-i-kuhm), Delaware and Philadelphia cos., SE Pa., in the Delaware R., SW of Philadelphia, formerly separated from the mainland by creeks and marshes; 39°51′N 75°17′W. Tinicum township, Delaware co., in W; part of city of Philadelphia in E. John Heinz Natl. Wildlife Refuge in N; Philadelphia Internatl. Airport is here; Darby Creek in NW; Governor Printz Landing Site (1643) in SW end. Site of the 1st Eur. settlement in Pa.; capital of NEW SWEDEN colony from 1643 to 1655.

Tinker Air Force Base, Okla.: see OKLAHOMA CITY.

Tinley Park, village (1990 pop. 37,121), Cook and Will cos., NE Ill., residential suburb 26 mi/42 km SW of downtown Chicago; 41°34′N 87°47′W. A growing suburb, its pop. more than tripled bet. 1970 and 1990. Mfg. (brushes and brooms, electronics); surrounded by remnant agr. (corn, cattle; dairying). Inc. 1892.

Tinmouth (TIN-muhth), town (1990 pop. 455), Rutland co., W Vt., on Clarendon R., and 12 mi/19 km S of Rutland; 43°27′N 73°03′W. Dairy prods.

Tinsman (TINZ-muhn), village (1990 pop. 69), Calhoun co., S Ark., near Mono Bayou, 28 mi/45 km ENE of Camden; 33°37′N 92°20′W.

Tintah (TIN-tah), village (1990 pop. 74), Traverse co., W Minn., 17 mi/27 km NE of Wheaton, near South Fork Rabbit R.; 46°00′N 96°19′W. Grain, sunflowers; livestock; light mfg.

Tinton Falls (TIN-tuhn), borough (1990 pop. 12,361), Monmouth co., E central N.J., 8 mi/12.9 km W of Asbury Park; 40°16′N 74°05′W. Mfg. (telecommunications and tungsten prods., inks). Inc. 1950.

Tinum (tee-NOOM), town (1990 pop. 1,723), Yucatán, SE Mexico, 12 mi/19 km NW of Valladolid; 20°46′N 88°23′W. Henequen, sugarcane, corn; timber. Maya ruins are nearby. Sometimes spelled Tinún.

Tioga 1 (tei-O-gah), county (□ 522 sq mi/1,352 sq km; 1990 pop. 52,337), S N.Y., bounded S by Pa. state line; ⊙ Owego; 42°10′N 76°17′W. Dairying area, with diversified mfg. esp. at Owego; also poultry raising, grain growing. Intersected by Susquehanna R., and drained by Cayuta, Catatonk, and Owego creeks. Formed 1791. **2** (TEE-o-gah), county (□ 1,137 sq mi/2,945 sq km; 1990 pop. 41,126), N Pa.; ⊙ Wellsboro; 41°46′N 77°15′W. Bounded N by N.Y. state line; SE corner by Lycoming Creek; drained E by Tioga R., NW by Cowanesque R., W by Pine Creek. Agr. and timber area. Mfg. at Wellsboro; bituminous coal, natural gas. Agr. (corn, oats, hay, alfalfa; hogs, cattle; dairying). Recreation. Cowanesque L. reservoir in N; Hammond and Tioga reservoirs in N center; Leonard Harrison State Park in SW center; Wills Creek State Park in center; parts of Tioga State Forest in W, SW, S center, and SE. Formed 1804.

Tioga (tei-O-guh), town (1990 pop. 1,278), Williams co., NW N.Dak., 36 mi/58 km NE of Williston; 48°23′N 102°56′W. Propane, sulphur and natural gas.

Tioga 1 (tei-O-guh), uninc. village (1990 pop. 2,158), Rapides parish, central La., 5 mi/8 km N of Alexandria; 31°23′N 92°25′W. RR junction. In agr. and timber region; mfg. (fabricated steel for substations, wood prods., lumber, industrial valves). U.S. veterans hosp. to S. **2** village (1990 pop. 625), Grayson co., N Texas, 22 mi/35 km SW of Sherman, on E arm of L. Ray Roberts reservoir; 33°28′N 96°55′W. Cattle; cotton; recreation. L. Kiowa to NW.

Tioga (TEE-o-gah), borough (1990 pop. 638), Tioga co., N Pa., 7 mi/11.3 km NNW of Mansfield, on Tioga R., at mouth of Crooked Creek; 41°53′N 77°08′W. Mfg. (lumber, corrugated boxes); agr. (corn, hay; dairying). Tioga L. reservoir (Tioga R.) to S, Hammond L. reservoir (Crooked Creek) to SW, 2 connected by channel.

Tioga Center, resort village (1990 pop. 600), Tioga co., S N.Y., on the Susquehanna R., and 23 mi/37 km E of Elmira; 42°03′N 76°21′W.

Tioga Pass (elev. 9,944 ft/3,031 m), Tuolumne-Mono co. line, E Calif., across the Sierra Nevada, just W of Mono L. E gateway to Yosemite Natl. Park. Ranger station. State Highway 120 passes through.

Tioga River (TEE-o-gah), 55 mi/89 km long, in Pa. and N.Y.; rises in W Bradford co., N Pa.; 41°45′N 76°51′W. It flows first SW, through Tioga State Forest, then NW, past Blossburg and Mansfield, through Tioga L. reservoir (joined by channel to Hammond L. reservoir, on Crooked Creek, to W), into N.Y., where it joins Cohocton R. to form the Chemung at Corning.

Tionesta, uninc. village, Modoc co., NE Calif., c.40 mi/64 km WNW of Alturas, in Modoc Natl. Forest. Timber; cattle, sheep. Lava Beds Natl. Monument to NW.

Tionesta (TEE-o-NES-tah), borough (1990 pop. 634), ⊙ Forest co., NW Pa., 14 mi/23 km ENE of Oil City, on Allegheny R., at mouth of Tionesta Creek (c.60 mi/97 km long), which forms Tionetta L. reservoir to SE; 41°30′N 79°27′W. Mfg. (printing and publishing, sand and gravel processing); oil field to N. Agr. (grain; livestock; dairying). Allegheny Natl. Forest to E; Cornplanter State Forest to N.

Tioughnioga River (tei-uhf-nee-O-guh), c.70 mi/113 km long, central N.Y.; rises in SW Madison co.; flows SW past Cortland, then generally SSE to Chenango R. at

Chenango Forks. At Cortland, main stream (sometimes called East Branch above this point) receives West Branch (c.15 mi/24 km long).

Tipp City, city (1990 pop. 6,027), Miami co., W Ohio, 8 mi/13 km S of Troy and on Great Miami R.; 39°58′N 84°11′W. Pulp and paper prods., furniture, transportation equip., metal prods. Formerly called Tippecanoe City.

Tippah (TIP-uh), county (□ 460 sq mi/1,191 sq km; 1990 pop. 19,523), N Miss., bordering N on Tenn. state line; ⊙ Ripley; 34°46′N 88°54′W. Drained by Hatchie and Tallahatchie rivers, and Tippah Creek. Agr. (cotton, corn, soybeans; cattle; dairying); pine timber. Part of Holly Springs Natl. Forest in NW; Tippah County L. state lake in center. Formed 1836.

Tippecanoe, county (□ 503 sq mi/1,303 sq km; 1990 pop. 130,598), W central Ind.; ⊙ Lafayette; 40°23′N 86°53′W. Intersected by the Wabash R., Tippecanoe R., and Wildcat Creek. RR junction. Rich agr. area; wheat, corn, soybeans; hogs, cattle. Mfg. plants at Lafayette and West Lafayette. Sand and gravel. Tippecanoe Battlefield State Memorial in N. Formed 1826.

Tippecanoe, village (1990 pop. 320), Marshall co., N central Ind., 14 mi/23 km SE of Plymouth, on Tippecanoe R. Agr. (soybeans, corn; cattle; dairying); mfg. (steel roofing, fabricated structural metal). Laid out 1882.

Tippecanoe City, Ohio: see TIPP CITY.

Tippecanoe River, c.170 mi/274 km long, Ind.; rises in the lake dist. of NE Ind.; flows SW to join the Wabash R., near Lafayette. U.S. Gen. William Henry Harrison fought the Shawnees in the Battle of Tippecanoe, Nov. 7, 1811, on the site of Battle Ground, Ind. The Native Americans, encouraged by their chief, Tecumseh, and by the British, became threatened by the continued U.S. advance into their territory. At the time of Harrison's expedition, Tecumseh was away and his brother, the Prophet, led the group. They attacked U.S. forces at dawn but were repelled; their village was subsequently razed by Harrison's forces. Claimed as a U.S. victory, the battle was at best indecisive; the power of the Shawnees was broken, however, despite the subsequent Amer. retreat.

Tipton 1 county (□ 260 sq mi/673 sq km; 1990 pop. 16,119), central Ind.; ⊙ Tipton; 40°19′N 86°03′W. Agr. area (corn, soybeans, wheat; hogs, cattle). Mfg. at capital. Drained by Cicero Creek, Turkey Creek, and South Fork of Wildcat Creek. Flattest co. in Ind. Formed 1844. **2** county (□ 458 sq mi/1,186 sq km; 1990 pop. 37,568), W Tenn.; ⊙ Covington; 35°30′N 89°46′W. Bounded W by the Mississippi, N by Hatchie R. Predominantly cotton-growing, fruit-growing, and livestock-raising area; cotton processing and some mfg. at Covington. Formed 1823.

Tipton 1 city (1990 pop. 4,751), ⊙ Tipton co., central Ind., on Cicero Creek, and 15 mi/24 km SSE of Kokomo; 40°17′N 86°02′W. In agr. area (grain; livestock); mfg. (sheet metal fabricating, hybrid corn and soybean seeds, fiberglass boats, packaged meats, motor vehicle stampings. Laid out 1839. **2** city (1990 pop. 2,998), ⊙ Cedar co., E Iowa, 22 mi/35 km ENE of Iowa City; 41°46′N 91°07′W. Mfg. (feed; electronics; fiberglass tanks; beverages; wood prods.); limestone quarries. Inc. 1857. **3** city (1990 pop. 2,026), Moniteau co., central Mo., 12 mi/19 km W of California; 38°38′N 92°46′W. Corn, wheat, soybeans; cattle, hogs. Mfg. (motors, luggage, shoes). Laid out 1858.

Tipton 1 uninc. town (1990 pop. 1,383), Tulare co., S central Calif., 18 mi/29 km S of Visalia; 36°04′N 119°19′W. Cotton, sugar beets, grains, fruit, nuts, grapes; cattle, hogs, poultry. Mfg. (canned citrus prods.). Pixley Natl. Wildlife Refuge to S. **2** town (1990 pop. 1,043), Tillman co., SW Okla., near North Fork of Red R., 10 mi/16 km NW of Frederick; 34°30′N 99°08′W. In agr. area (cotton, alfalfa, corn, grain, peanuts; dairy prods.). Organized 1910. **3** uninc. town (1990 pop. 1,194), Blair co., central Pa., 10 mi/16 km NNE of Altoona on Tipton Run near its mouth on Juniata R.; 40°38′N 78°17′W. Mfg. includes electronic equip., machinery. Agr. includes dairying; livestock; hay.

Tipton, village (1990 pop. 267), Mitchell co., N central Kansas, 21 mi/34 km SW of Beloit; 39°20′N 98°28′W. Grain; livestock.

Tipton, Mount (7,364 ft/2,245 m), Mohave co., W Ariz., c.25 mi/40 km N of Kingman; 35°32′N 114°11′W. Highest peak in Cerbat Mts.

Tiptonville, town (1990 pop. 2,149), ⊙ Lake co., NW Tenn., on Reelfoot L., 22 mi/35 km NNW of Dyersburg, 36°23′N 89°29′W. Center of recreation area (hunting, fishing, bathing). Agr.; lumbering.

Tiquicheo (tee-kee-CHEE-o), town (1990 pop. 4,394), ⊙ Tiquicheo de Nicolás Romero municipio, Michoacán, central Mexico, 14 mi/23 km NE of Huetamo, on Mexico Highway 51; 18°53′N 100°44′W. Rice, sugarcane, fruit.

Tiro (TEI-ro), village (1990 pop. 246), Crawford co., N central Ohio, 15 mi/24 km NE of Bucyrus; 40°54′N 82°46′W. In agr. and timber area.

Tisbury (TIZ-be-ree), town (1990 pop. 3,120), Dukes co., SE Mass., on N Martha's Vineyard, 20 mi/32 km SE of New Bedford; 41°27′N 70°37′W. Main ferry service port in Vineyard Haven to Woods Hole. Resort; fishing. Includes Vineyard Haven village and West Chop village, on headland (with lighthouse) at W side of entrance to harbor of Vineyard Haven. Settled 1660, inc. 1671.

Tisdale (TIZ-dail), town (1991 pop. 3,045), central Sask., Canada, 75 mi/121 km ESE of Prince Albert. Grain elevators, flour and lumber mills.

Tishomingo (tish-uh-MING-o), county (□ 444 sq mi/1,150 sq km; 1990 pop. 17,683), extreme NE Miss.; ⊙ Iuka; 34°44′N 88°14′W. Borders E and NE on Ala. state line, N on Tenn. state line; on NE is Pickwick L. Reservoir, impounded by Pickwick Dam (Tenn.). Tennessee R. forms part of Ala. state line. Hilly, rising to 806 ft/246 m in Woodall Mt. (highest point in state), in N center and drained by tributaries of Tennessee and Tombigbee rivers. Agr. area (soybeans, wheat, corn, sweet potatoes; hogs); timber. Mfg. of clay and wood prods. Clay, sandstone, limestone, phosphorus, and bauxite deposits. John Bell Williams Wildlife Management Area (Divide Sect.) in W; Tishomingo State Park in SE, J.P. Coleman State Park in NE, on Pickwick L.; Natchez Trace (Natl.) Parkway passes through co. SW corner to E. Tennessee-Tombigbee Waterway passes through co., SW corner to N, passes through Bay Springs L. reservoir, on W co. line, joins Pickwick L. in N; large Bear R. Arm on E boundary. Formed 1836.

Tishomingo (tish-uh-MING-o), town (1990 pop. 3,116), ⊙ Johnston co., S Okla., 24 mi/39 km NW of Durant, on L. Texoma, 34°14′N 96°40′W. Elev. 670 ft/204 m. Trade center for agr. and recreation area; mfg.; industrial sand and gravel. Murray State Col. here. Tishomingo Natl. Wildlife Refuge, on Washita arm of L. Texoma, to SE; Devils Den Park to N. Settled 1850; was capital of the Chickasaw Nation after c.1855.

Tishomingo (tish-uh-MING-o), village (1990 pop. 332), Tishomingo co., extreme NE Miss., 12 mi/19 km S of Iuka; 34°38′N 88°13′W. Agr. (soybeans, grain; hogs); mfg. (apparel, motor vehicle bodies). Clay, sandstone, phosphorus rock, and bauxite deposits nearby. Tishomingo State Park and Natchez Trace (Natl.) Parkway to SE. Bay Springs L. reservoir on Tennessee-Tombigbee Waterway to W.

Tiskilwa, village (1990 pop. 830), Bureau co., N Ill., on Bureau Creek, 6 mi/9.7 km SSW of Princeton; 41°17′N 89°30′W. In agr. area; mfg. (dairy prods.).

Titchfield, small hamlet of Port Antonio, Portland parish, in NE Jamaica, 27 mi/43 km NE of Kingston; 18°10′N 76°27′W. Residential sect. of Port Antonio on promontory. Includes Titchfield Trust Lands. Titchfield High School is more than 100 years old.

Titonka, town (1990 pop. 612), Kossuth co., N Iowa, 14 mi/23 km NE of Algona; 43°14′N 94°02′W. Feed milling.

Tittabawassee River (ti-TAB-ah-WAH-see), c.75 mi/121 km long, E central Mich.; rises in SW Ogemaw co.; flows S and E, past Midland, to join the Shiawassee to form the Saginaw R. just SW of Saginaw. Flows through Wixom L. reservoir above Edenville and Sanford L. reservoir, above Sanford. Short West and East branches join main stream near its head.

Tittmann, Mount (11,565 ft/3,525 m), S Alaska, in St. Elias Mts., 120 mi/193 km NW of Yakutat; 61°08′N 141°14′W.

Titus, county (□ 425 sq mi/1,101 sq km; 1990 pop. 24,009), NE Texas; ⊙ Mount Pleasant; 33°13′N 94°58′W. Bounded N by Sulphur R., S by Big Cypress Creek; drained by White Oak Bayou. Forested area (pine, oak; timber), with agr. (grain sorghum, peanuts, corn, watermelons; hay; dairying; cattle, poultry. Large oil production; also natural gas, lignite. Mfg., oil refining, farm prods. processing at Mt. Pleasant. L. Monticello in SW, arm of larger Bob Sandler, on S boundary, L. Bob Sandler State Park on N shore. Formed 1846.

Titusville 1 (TEI-duss-vil), city (□ 24 sq mi/62 sq km; 1990 pop. 39,394), seat of Brevard co., E central Fla., on Indian R. (a lagoon); 28°35′N 80°49′W. It is a growing regional trade center. The construction in the 1950s of the space center on nearby Cape Canaveral brought tourism and commercial enterprises to the area and caused the city's pop. to increase tenfold in less than a decade. Inc. 1886. **2** (TEI-tuhs-vil), city (1990 pop. 6,434), Crawford co., NW Pa., on Oil Creek, 40 mi/64 km SE of Erie; 41°37′N 79°40′W. Mfg. (consumer goods, fabricated metal prods., plastic prods., lumber, food prods., printing and publishing). Agr. area (potatoes, soybeans, corn, hay; dairying). Drake Well Memorial Park and Mus. marks site of 1st successful oil well (1859) in U.S.; city grew in oil boom of 1860s; its last oil refinery closed in 1950. Shriver Airport to S; Oil Creek State Park to S. Settled 1796, laid out 1809, inc. as borough 1847, as city 1866.

Tiverton, town (1990 pop. 14,312), Newport co., SE R.I., bet. the Sakonnet R. and the Mass. state line; 41°39′N 71°12′W. Tiverton is a summer resort center in a farm area, and there are fisheries. Tiverton Four Corners is an isolated and picturesque village on Sakonnet R. A bridge completed in 1956 connects the town to Portsmouth. The Revolutionary era Fort Barton was near Tiverton village. Settled 1680, included in Mass. until 1746, inc. 1747.

Tiverton (TI-vuhr-tuhn), village (1991 pop. 814), S Ont., Canada, near L. Huron, 8 mi/13 km NNE of Kincardine; 44°23′N 66°13′W. Dairying.

Tivoli, village (□ 1 sq mi/2.6 sq km; 1990 pop. 1,035), Dutchess co., SE N.Y., just SE of Saugerties, across the Hudson R.; 42°03′N 73°54′W.

Tixcacalcupul (teesh-kah-kal-koo-POOL), town (1990 pop. 1,891), Yucatán, SSW Mexico, 11 mi/18 km SSE of Valladolid, on Mexico Highway 295; 20°32′N 88°16′W. Henequen; tropical woods; fruit.

Tixkokob (teesh-ko-KOB), town (1990 pop. 8,459), ⊙ Tixkokob municipio, Yucatan, SE Mexico, 14 mi/23 km E of Mérida, on Mexico Highway 80; 21°00′N 89°25′W. RR junction in henequen-growing region. Mayan ruins of Aké in area.

Tixméhuac (teesh-ME-wahk), town (1990 pop. 2,059), ⊙ Tixméhuac municipio, Yucatán, SE Mexico, 11 mi/18 km E of Tekax; 20°10′N 89°07′W. Henequen, sugarcane, fruit, timber. Formerly spelled Tixméuac.

Tixméuac, Mexico: see TIXMÉHUAC.

Tixpéhual (tesh-PE-wahl), town (1990 pop. 2,807), Yucatán, SE Mexico, on RR, Mexico Highway 80; 11 mi/18 km E of Mérida; 20°59′N 89°31′W. Henequen. Formerly spelled Tixpéual.

Tixpéual, Mexico: see TIXPÉHUAL.

Tixtla de Guerrero (TEESH-tlah dai ge-RE-ro), city (1990 pop. 17,079) and township, Guerrero, SW Mexico, in Sierra Madre del Sur, 5 mi/8 km NE of Chilpancingo de los Bravo; 17°35′N 99°22′W. Elev. 4,741 ft/1,445 m. Agr. center (cereals, sugarcane, tobacco, coffee, fruit); lumbering. Former capital of Guerrero. Birthplace of revolutionary leader Vicente Guerrero. Mex. patriot Morelos y Pavón won victory here over Span. royalists (1811).

Tizapán el Alto (tee-sah-PAHN el AHL-to), town (1990 pop. 13,398), Jalisco, central Mexico, on S shore of L. Chapala, 40 mi/64 km SE of Guadalajara, on Mexico Highway 15; 20°11′N 103°02′W. Cereals, vegetables, fruit; livestock.

Tizayuca (tee-sah-TOO-kah), town (1990 pop. 22,419), Hidalgo, central Mexico, on RR, on Inter-Amer. Highway (85), 27 mi/43 km SW of Pachuca de Soto; 19°51′N

99°00′W. Agr. center (cereals, beans, maguey; stock). The only municipality outside the Federal dist. and the state of Méxicoto be included inthe Zona Metropolitana de la Ciudad de México.

Tizimín (tee-see-MEEN), city (1990 pop. 34,174) and township, Yucatán, SE Mexico, 95 mi/153 km E of Mérida; 21°10′N 88°09′W. RR terminus; agr. center (henequen, chicle, corn, fruit); tropical wood.

Tlachichilco (tlah-chee-CHEEL-ko), town (1990 pop. 932), Veracruz, E Mexico, in Sierra Madre Oriental, 56 mi/90 km WSW of Túxpam de Rodríguez Cano; 20°39′N 98°13′W. Elev. 2,625 ft/800 m.

Tlachichuca (tlahn-chee-CHOO-kah), town (1990 pop. 5,809), Puebla, central Mexico, at NW foot of Pico de Orizaba, on RR, 9 mi/14.5 km NNE of Ciudad Serdán; 19°06′N 92°25′W. Elev. 8,497 ft/2,590 m. Cereals, maguey; livestock.

Tlacoachistlahuaca (tlah-ko-ah-chees-tlah-WAH-kah), town (1990 pop. 3,009), Guerrero, SW Mexico, on S slope of Sierra Madre del Sur, 13 mi/21 km NE of Ometepec; 16°49′N 98°18′W. Fruit.

Tlacoapa (tlah-ko-AH-pah), town (1990 pop. 1,608), SE Guerrero, Mexico 43 mi/70 km SE of Chilpancingo de los Bravo; 17°16′N 98°45′W. In Sierra Madize del Sur. Agr. (corn, beans, chile, plaintains, pineapple, mango, citrus, avocados); marble quarry, cotton and wool textiles.

Tlacochahuaya de Morelos, Mexico: see SAN JERÓNIMO TLACOCHAHUAYA.

Tlacojalpan (tlah-ko-MAHL-pahn), town (1990 pop. 3,769), Veracruz, SE Mexico, on Papaloapan R., 15 mi/24 km SW of Cosamaloapan; 18°14′N 95°57′W. Sugarcane, bananas.

Tlacolula de Matamoros (tlah-kah-LOO-lah dai mah-tah-MO-ros), city (1990 pop. 9,731) and township, ⊙ Tlacolula de Matamoros municipio, Oaxaca de Juárez, S Mexico, in Sierra Madre del Sur, 18 mi/29 km SE of Oaxaca; 16°57′N 96°28′W. Elev. 5,413 ft/1,650 m. RR terminus; mining (gold, silver, lead) and agr. (cereals, sugarcane, coffee, tobacco, fruit; livestock) center. Nationally famous for making tequila and Mezcal. Market center, known for colorful display. Has 16th-cent. parish church, and 19,800-ft/6,035-m aqueduct, finished 1846. Indian town dates from 1250; settled 1560 by Spanish.

Tlacolulan (tlah-ko-LOO-lahn), town (1990 pop. 1,058), ⊙ Tlacolulan municipio, Veracruz, E Mexico, in Sierra Madre Oriental, 11 mi/18 km NNW of Xalapa Enríquez; 19°40′N 96°59′W. Elev. 5,682 ft/1,732 m. Corn, coffee, fruit. In Totonac Indian area.

Tlacotalpan (tlah-ko-TAHL-pahn), city (1990 pop. 9,025), Veracruz, SE Mexico, in Sotavento lowlands, on Papaloápan R., 32 mi/51 km WNW of San Andrés Tuxtla, on Mexico Highway 175; 18°36′N 95°43′W. Agr. center (coconuts, sugarcane, coffee, bananas; cattle). Anc. Indian post. Site of U.S. defeat (1847) in Mex.-Amer. War.

Tlacotepec (tlah-ko-te-pek), town (1990 pop. 6,263), ⊙ General Heliodoro Castillo municipio, Guerrero, SW Mexico, in isolated area of Sierra Madre del Sur, on unpaved road, 33 mi/53 km WNW of Chilpancingo de los Bravo; 17°47′N 99°58′W. Elev. 5,052 ft/1,540 m. Sugarcane, coffee, tobacco, fruit.

Tlacotepec, Cerro (tlah-KO-te-pek, SEH-ro), mountain (11,467 ft/3,495 m), Guerrero, SW Mexico, in Sierra Madre del Sur, just SE of Cerro Teotepec, 38 mi/61 km NNW of Acapulco de Juárez, 25 mi/40 km SSW of Tlacotepec; 17°23′N 100°05′W.

Tlacotepec de Benito Juárez (tlah-KO-te-pek), town (1990 pop. 6,660), Puebla, central Mexico, 23 mi/37 km NW of Tehuacán, on Mexico Highway 150; 18°39′N 97°47′W. Corn, sugarcane, palms; livestock. In Popoloca Indian area.

Tlacotepec de Díaz (tlah-KO-te-pek dai DEE-ahs), town (1990 pop. 1,250), SE Puebla, Mexico, 35 mi/56 km ESE of Tehuacan; 18°24′N 96°51′W. Rugged terrain in the Papaloapan R. basin. Hot climate. Agr. (sugarcane, rice, cereals, fruits), wood. No road access.

Tlacotepec de Mejía (tlah-KO-te-pek dai me-HEE-ah), town (1990 pop. 2,165), Veracruz, E Mexico, in Sierra Madre Oriental, 8 mi/12.9 km ENE of Huatusco; 19°11′N 96°50′W. Corn, coffee, fruit.

Tlacotepec Plumas (tlah-KO-te-pek PLOO-mahs), town (1990 pop. 570), NW Oaxaca, Mexico, 24 mi/39 km E of Huajuapam de Léon; 17°40′N 97°27′W. Elev. 6,339 ft/1,932 m. Partly mountainous terrain. Temperate to cold climate. Agr.

Tlacuilotepec (tlah-kweel-O-te-pek), town (1990 pop. 1,483), Puebla, central Mexico, 10 mi/16 km N of Huauchinango; 20°19′N 98°03′W. Elev. 4,144 ft/1,263 m. Coffee, sugarcane, fruit.

Tláhuac (TLAH-wahk), delegación (1990 pop. 206,700) and township, Federal dist., central Mexico, suburb 15 mi/24 km SE of Mexico city; 19°16′N 99°01′W.

Tlahualilo, Mexico: see TLAHUALILO DE ZARAGOZA.

Tlahualilo de Zaragoza (tlah-wah-LEE-lo dai sah-rah-GO-sah), city (1990 pop. 11,422) and township, ⊙ Tlahualilo municipio, Durango, N Mexico, in irrigated area, 40 mi/64 km N of Torreón; 26°06′N 103°25′W. Elev. 3,714 ft/1,132 m. RR terminus. Agr. center (cotton, grain, fruit, vegetables, sugarcane). Sometimes called Zaragoza.

Tlahuapan, Mexico: see SANTA RITA TLAHUAPAN.

Tlahuelilpan (tlah-we-LEEL-pahn), town (1990 pop. 6,459), Hidalgo, central Mexico, 33 mi/53 km W of Pachuca de Soto, at junction of Mexico Highway 19 with Inter-Amer. Highway (85); 20°08′N 99°14′W. Elev. 6,234 ft/1,900 m. Cereals, beans, cotton, fruit; livestock.

Tlahuiltepa (tlah-wheel-TE-pah), town (1990 pop. 320), in NE part of Hidalgo, Mexico, 57 mi/92 km NNW of Pachuca de Soto; 20°51′N 98°55′W. Elev. 7,054 mi/11,352 km. Very mountainous region. Agr. and forestry.

Tlajomulco, Mexico: see TLAJOMULCO DE ZÚÑIGA.

Tlajomulco de Zúñiga (tlah-ho-MMOL-ko dai SOO-nyee-gah), town (1990 pop. 11,567), Jalisco, W Mexico, on RR, 15 mi/24 km SSW of Guadalajara; 20°28′N 103°27′W. Wheat-growing center; corn, chickpeas, beans, fruit; livestock. Formerly called Tlajomulco.

Tlalchapa (tlahl-CHAH-pah), town (1990 pop. 4,934), Guerrero, SW Mexico, in Río Balsas valley, 15 mi/24 km ENE of Ciudad Altamirano; 18°24′N 100°28′W. Cereals, sugar, cotton, fruit.

Tlalixcoyan (tlah-leesh-KO-yahn), town (1990 pop. 2,306), Veracruz, E Mexico, 28 mi/45 km S of Veracruz; 18°48′N 96°05′W. Coffee, fruit; livestock.

Tlalixtac de Cabrera (tlah-LEEKS-tak dai kah-BRE-rah), town (1990 pop. 4,924), central Oaxaca, Mexico, 5 mi/8 km E of Oaxaca de Juárez in the Oaxaca valley; 17°04′N 96°39′W. Elev. 5,085 ft/1,550 m. Temperate climate. Resources are agr., cattle, pottery, and handmade arts and crafts sold in Oaxaca de Juárez.

Tlalixtaquilla (tlah-leesh-tah-KEE-yah), town (1990 pop. 2,082), ⊙ Tlalixtaquilla de Maldonado municipio, Guerrero, SW Mexico, in Sierra Madre del Sur, near Oaxaca border, 14 mi/23 km E of Tlapa de Comonfort; 17°31′N 98°28′W. Cereals, fruit; livestock.

Tlalmanalco (tlahl-mah-MAHL-ko), town (1990 pop. 9,892), Mexico state, central Mexico, on RR, 28 mi/45 km SE of Mexico city in the Zona Metropolitana de la Ciudad de México; 19°13′N 98°48′W. Cereals, vegetables; livestock; paper mfg. Has old Franciscan convent with frescoes. Formerly was Tlalmanalco de Velázquez municipio.

Tlalnelhuayocan (tlahl-nel-wahYO-kahn), town (1990 pop. 756), Veracruz, E Mexico, 4 mi/6.4 km NW of Xalapa Enréiquez; 19°34′N 96°58′W. Elev. 6,299 ft/1,920 m. Coffee.

Tlalnepantla (tlahl-ne-PAHN-tlah), city (1990 pop. 2,827) and township, Morelos, central Mexico, 17 mi/27 km. ENE of Cuernavaca; 19°00′N 98°59′W. Peach-growing center; sugarcane, vegetables; livestock.

Tlalnepantla de Baz (tlahl-ne-PAHN-tlah dai bahs), city (1990 pop. 702,270) and township, ⊙ Tlalnepantla municipio, Mexico state, S central Mexico, on the Tlalnepantla R.; 19°32′N 99°11′W. Elev. 7,474 ft/2,278 m. Within the Zona Metropolitana de la Ciudad de México. It is a communications and industrial center that owes its importance largely to its proximity to Mexico city. Smelting, metalworking, machinery, and chemical mfg. are among the chief industries. Tenayuca, well-preserved Aztec pyramid, is here. Airport.

Tlalpan (tlahl-pahn), city (1990 pop. 484,866), ⊙ Tlalpan delegation, Federal dist., central Mexico, 10 mi/16 km S of Mexico city; 19°17′N 99°09′W. Elev. 7,526 ft/2,294 m. Resort and residential suburb on NW slopes of extinct Cerro Ajusco volcano, with orchards, picturesque fountains. Textile- and paper-milling center. Has church of San Agustín de las Cuevas (1532). Anc. Aztec city. Famous Cuicuilco pyramid, 1.5 mi/2.4 km W. Sometimes spelled Tlalpam.

Tlalpujahua de Rayón (tlahl-poo-HAH-wah dai rah-YON), town (1990 pop. 2,842), ⊙ Tlalpujahua de Rayón municipio, Michoacán, central Mexico, on central plateau, 3 mi/4.8 km W of El Oro; 19°50′N 100°10′W. Silver, gold mining. Mineral zones most important of state. Mineral resources exploited since before conquest by indigenous people. Metallurgical plant here now processes gold, silver, lead, copper. Products exported through El Oro.

Tlaltenango (tlahl-te-NAHN-go), town (1990 pop. 4,338), Puebla, central Mexico, 13 mi/21 km NW of Puebla; 19°10′N 98°20′W. Grain, maguey, fruit.

Tlaltenango de Sánchez Román (tlahl-te-NAHN-go dai SAHN-ches ro-MAHN), town (1990 pop. 12,213), Zacatecas, N central Mexico, on Tlaltehango R., 80 mi/129 km SW of Zacatecas; 21°47′N 103°18′W. Elev. 5,656 ft/1,724 m. Agr. center (grain, fruit, tobacco, sugarcane; livestock).

Tlaltetela (tlahl-te-TE-lah), town (1990 pop. 3,602), Veracruz, E Mexico, in Sierra Madre Oriental, 22 mi/35 km S of Xalapa Enríquez; 19°12′N 96°58′W. Coffee, fruit. Formerly called Axocuapan.

Tlaltizapán (tlahl-tee-sah-PAHN), town (1990 pop. 8,835), Morelos, central Mexico, on RR, 17 mi/27 km SSE of Cuernavaca; 18°41′N 99°07′W. Rice, wheat, sugarcane, coffee, fruit; stock.

Tlanalapa (tlah-nah-LAH-pah), town (1990 pop. 6,474), Hidalgo, central Mexico, 25 mi/40 km SE of Pachuca de Soto; 19°49′N 98°36′W. Cereals, maguey; livestock.

Tlanchinol (tlahn- CHEE-no), town (1990 pop. 3,193), Hidalgo, central Mexico, 19 mi/31 km SW of Huejutla, on Mexico Highway 105; 20°59′N 98°39′W. Cereals, sugarcane, tobacco, fruit.

Tlanepantla (tlah-ne-PAHN-tlah), town (1990 pop. 3,149), Puebla, central Mexico, 25 mi/40 km ESE of Puebla; 18°51′N 97°54′W. Cereals, vegetables.

Tlaola (tlah-O-lahn), town (1990 pop. 1,217), Puebla, central Mexico, 8 mi/12.9 km ESE of Huauchinango; 20°09′N 97°57′W. Corn, sugarcane, fruit.

Tlapa de Comonfort (TLAH-pah dai ko-mo-FORT), city (1990 pop. 20,863) and township, Guerrero, SW Mexico, in Sierra Madre del Sur, 60 mi/97 km E of Chilpancingo de los Bravo; 17°32′N 98°34′W. Elev. 3,543 ft/1,080 m. Cereals, sugarcane, fruit, forest prods. (resin, rubber, vanilla).

Tlapacoya (tlah-pah-KO-yah), town (1990 pop. 1,006), Puebla, central Mexico, 12 mi/19 km ESE of Huauchinango; 20°06′N 97°53′W. Sugarcane, coffee, fruit.

Tlapacoyan (tlah-pah-KO-yahn), city (1990 pop. 26,064) and township, Veracruz, E Mexico, in Sierra Madre Oriental, 37 mi/60 km NW of Xalapa Enríquez, on Mexico Highway 131; 19°58′N 97°12′W. Agr. center (corn, sugarcane, coffee, tobacco, fruit).

Tlapanalá (tlah-pah-nah-LAH), town (1990 pop. 3,030), Puebla, central Mexico, 8 mi/12.9 km NW of Izúcar de Matamoros; 18°41′N 98°32′W. Cereals, sugarcane; livestock.

Tlapehuala (tlah-pe-WAH-lah), town (1990 pop. 9,266), Guerrero, SW of Mexico, on Río Balsas, 11 mi/18 km SE of Ciudad Altamirano; 18°13′N 100°31′W. Sugarcane, tobacco, coffee, cotton, fruit, cereals, forest prods. (resin, rubber, vanilla).

Tlaquepaque (tlah-ke-PAH-ke), town (1990 pop. 328,031) and township, Jalisco state, SW Mexico, in the Guadalajara metropolitan area; 20°39′N 103°15′W. Essentially a suburb of Guadalajara. Its folklore and local artisanry, as well as its proximity to Guadalajara, make Tlaquepaque a popular tourist spot. It underwent commercial renovation in the 1970s to increase tourism. Occasionally called San Pedro.

Tlaquilpa (tlah-KEEl-pah), town (1990 pop. 1,195), ⊙ Tlaquilpan municipio, Veracruz, E Mexico, in Sierra Zongolica, 17 mi/27 km S of Orizaba; 18°37′N 97°07′W. Elev. 5,906 ft/1,800 m. Coffee, corn, fruit. Sometimes spelled Tlaquilpan.

Area in square miles is shown by the symbol □ capital city or county seat by ⊙

Tlaquilpan, Mexico: see TLAQUILPA.

Tlaquiltenango (tlah-keel-te-NAHN-go), town (1990 pop. 16,327), Morelos, central Mexico, on RR, 20 mi/32 km SSE of Cuernavaca; 18°38′N 99°10′W. Rice, sugar, fruit, vegetables.

Tlatlauquitepec (tlaht-la-oo-KEE-te-pek), town (1990 pop. 6,946), Puebla, central Mexico, 9 mi/14.5 km WNW of Teziutlán; 19°49′N 97°30′W. Elev. 7,415 ft/2,260 m. Corn, coffee, sugarcane, fruit, vegetables.

Tlatlaya (tlaht-LAH-yahr), town (1990 pop. 530), Mexico state, central Mexico, 26 mi/42 km SW of Sultepec; 18°37′N 100°11′W. Elev. 7,415 ft/2,260 m. Sugarcane, fruit; silver and gold deposits.

Tlaxcala (tlahks-KAH-lah), state (□ 1,555 sq mi/4,027 sq km; 1990 pop. 761,277), E central Mexico; ⊙ Tlaxcala; 19°06′N 97°37′W. It is the smallest and one of the most densely populated Mex. states. The W part lies within Mexico's central plateau; the remainder, however, is extremely mountainous, with a temperate to cold climate. Maguey, cereals, and subsistence crops are grown in the valleys. Light mfg. has developed on a significant scale. Textiles and bulls bred for bullfighting are traditional and still important prods. of the state. In the mts. are the sources of the Río Balsas. Defeated by Hernán Cortés after fierce resistance, the Tlaxcaltecs later became valuable Span. allies against the Aztecs.

Tlaxcala, Mexico: see TLAXCALA DE XICHOHTÉNCATL.

Tlaxcala de Xicontónoatl (tlahks-KAH-lah dai heekon-TEN-kahtl), city (1990 pop. 50,486) and township, ⊙ Tlaxcala municipio and state, E central Mexico; 19°20′N 98°12′W. It is the site of the oldest Christian church in Mexico, founded (1521) by the Span. explorer Hernán Cortés. Nearby is a famous Mex. shrine, the Santuario y Colegiata de Ocotlán. Usually spelled Tlaxcala.

Tlaxco (TLAHKS-ko), city (1990 pop. 8,141) and township, Tlaxcala, central Mexico, on central plateau, 21 mi/34 km NNE of Tlaxcala on Mexico Highway 119; 19°38′N 98°06′W. Elev. 8,018 ft/2,444 m. RR terminus; maguey-growing and -processing center. Also called Tlaxco de Morelos.

Tlaxco (TLAHKS-ko), town (1990 pop. 1,407), Puebla, central Mexico, 18 mi/29 km N of Huauchinango; 20°26′N 98°01′W. Coffee, sugarcane, tobacco, fruit. In Totonac Indian area.

Tlaxco de Morelos, Mexico: see TLAXCO, city.

Tlaxcoapan (tlahks-ko-AH-pahn), town (1990 pop. 10,237), Hidalgo, central Mexico, on RR, 32 mi/51 km W of Pachuca de Soto on Mexico Highway 19; 20°05′N 99°13′W. Elev. 6,890 ft/2,100 m. Cereals, cotton, fruit, tobacco; livestock; flour mills.

Tlaxiaca, Mexico: see SAN AGUSTÍN TLAXIACA.

Tlaxiaco, Mexico: see HEROICA CIUDAD DE TLAXIACO.

Tlayacapan (tlah-yah-KAH-pahn), town (1990 pop. 5,532), Morelos, central Mexico, 17 mi/27 km E of Cuernavaca; 18°56′N 98°59′W. Sugarcane, fruit, vegetables; livestock.

Tlazazalca (tlah-sah-SAHL-kah), town (1990 pop. 3,925), Michoacán, central Mexico, 15 mi/24 km E of Zamora, on Mexico Highway 37; 19°58′N 102°04′W. Cereals, fruit; livestock.

Tlell (tuh-LEL), village, W B.C., Canada, on E Graham Isl., on Hecate Strait, at mouth of Tlell R., 30 mi/48 km SSE of Massett; 53°35′N 131°56′W. Lumbering; livestock raising.

Tlilapan (tlee-LAHpahn), town (1990 pop. 1,543), Veracruz, E Mexico, 3 mi/4.8 km S of Orizaba. Coffee, fruit. Sometimes spelled Tulapan.

Toa Alta (TO-ah AHL-tah), town (1990 pop. 44,101), N P.R., 10 mi/16 km SW of San Juan. Industrial and commercial area; mfg. (chemical and electric prods.), textiles, pharmaceuticals); agr. (vegetables; livestock). Residential suburban developments.

Toa Baja (TO-ah BAH-hah), town (1990 pop. 89,454), N P.R., on La Plata R., 9 mi/14.5 km W of San Juan. Industrial and commercial area; light mfg.; agr. (fruit, sugarcane; cattle). Many residents commute to work in other cities. Founded 1511. Has one of oldest churches (1775) in P.R. A candied-fruit factory is nearby.

Toa, Cuchillas de (TO-ah, koo-CHEE-yuhz dai), range,

Guantánamo prov., E Cuba, 20 mi/32 km W of Baracoa; extends 30 mi/48 km NW bet. Toa to Sagua de Tánamo rivers; rises to over 2,200 ft/671 m bet. Guaso Meseta and Plurial Mt. range. Yields timber and cocoa.

Toa River (TO-uh), 73 mi/118 km long, Guantánamo prov., E Cuba; rises at S foot of the Cuchillas de Toa, flows E to coast 4 mi/6.4 km NNW of Baracoa. Drains 407 sq mi/1,053 sq km of Toa and Moa highlands and empties into Atlantic Ocean just NW of Baracoa.

Toano, uninc. town, James City co., SE Va., 8 mi/12.9 km NNW of Williamsburg; 37°22′N 76°48′W. Mfg. (glass and wood prods.); agr. (tobacco, grain, soybeans; cattle; dairying). York R. State Park to NE.

Toano Mountains (tuh-WAH-no) (6,000 ft/1,830 m– 9,000 ft/2,740 m), NE Nev., in E Elko co., near Utah line. Union Pacific RR and Interstate 80 cut the range at Silver Zone Pass (5,940 ft/1,811 m), 75 mi/121 km E of Elko. N extension of Goshute Mts. Bonneville Salt Flats to E. Sometimes spelled Toana.

Toast, uninc. town (1990 pop. 2,125), Surry co., NW N.C., residential suburb 2 mi/3.2 km W of Mt. Airy; 36°30′N 80°37′W. In agr. area (dairying; livestock; grain, tobacco).

Tobacco River 1 c.40 mi/64 km long, E central Mich.; rises near Farwell in Clare co.; flows generally E, past Clare and Beaverton, to Tittabawassee R. in N Midland co. **2** c.17 mi/27 km long, NW Mont.; rises in Lincoln co. 11 mi/18 km SE of Eureka; flows NW past Eureka, to L. Koocanusa reservoir (Kootenai R.) at Rexford, 6 mi/9.7 km S of U.S./Canada (B.C.) border.

Tobacco Root Mountains, range of Rocky Mts., Madison co., SW Mont., rise N of Virginia City, extend N to Jefferson R. Highest points are Granite Peak (10,590 ft/3,228 m), Mt. Bradley (10,482 ft/3,195 m), and Ward Peak (10,267 ft/3,129 m). Part of Deerlodge Natl. Forest in N; part of Beaverhead Natl. Forest in S. Numerous small lakes of glacial origin, especially along crest of range. Silver, lead, and gold mines here.

Tobago (to-BAI-go), island (□ 116 sq mi/300 sq km; 1990 pop. 18,600), the smaller of 2 isls. comprising the Republic of Trinidad and Tobago, Lesser Antilles, West Indies, 21 mi/34 km NE of Trinidad, ⊙ Scarborough; 11°15′N 60°40′W. Crown Point Airport on SW tip of isl. in center of resort area. Central mt. range, 18 mi/29 km long, rises to 1,890 ft/576 m; fertile valleys. Sighted by Columbus in 1498; taken by Britain in 1628 for cocoa and sugar growing; became ward of Trinidad in 1889 when sugar growing was abandoned. Achieved independence in 1962, with Trinidad, after pulling out of the West Indies Federation and becoming independent member of the Br. Commonwealth. Beaches and tourist activities in S; fishing villages, mountainous rain forest and ecotourism in N. Tourism is being encouraged with the building of a new cruise ship complex and harbor redevelopment at Scarborough and a number of new hotels.

Tobago Forest Reserve (to-BAI-go), nature preserve, Tobago, Trinidad and Tobago, on S coast near Hillsborough Dam. Est. 1765; oldest protected forest in the Caribbean. Rain forest, bird sanctuary.

Tobias (tuh-BEI-uhs), village (1990 pop. 127), Saline co., SE Nebr., 20 mi/32 km WSW of Wilber; 40°25′N 97°20′W. RR junction. Livestock; grain, poultry prods.

Tobin, Mount, Nev.: see TOBIN RANGE.

Tobin Range (TO-bin), E Pershing co., N Nev., c.35 mi/56 km SE of Winnemucca; 40 mi/64 km long SSW-NNE; 40°22′N 117°31′W. Mt. Tobin (9,775 ft/2,979 m), near center; Spring Creek to W, flows S into Humboldt Salt Marsh.

Tobique River (to-BEEK), c.100 mi/161 km long, NE N.B., Canada; rises at foot of Mt. Carleton, flows SW to St. John R. at Andover.

Toby, Mount (10,537 ft/3,212 m), SE B.C., Canada, in Selkirk Mts., 60 mi/97 km NE of Nelson; 50°13′N 116°33′W.

Tocatlán (to-kaht-LAHN), town (1990 pop. 3,711), E Tlaxcala, Mexico, 10 mi/16 km NW of Huamantla; 19°23′N 98°01′W. Steep, rugged terrain. Temperate climate. Agr. (cereals, fruits), woods; cattle and poultry raising. Mostly Otomi Indian pop.

Toccoa (tuh-KO-uh), town (1990 pop. 8,266), ⊙ Stephens co., NE Ga., c.40 mi/64 km N of Athens, near

S.C. state line; 34°35′N 83°19′W. Industrial center; mfg. (aircraft parts, furniture, clothing, thread, crushed stone, printing and publishing, concrete prods., wire prods., fabrics). Toccoa Falls (186 ft/57 m high) nearby. Inc. 1875.

Toccoa, Lake, Ga.: see BLUE RIDGE LAKE.

Toccoa River (tuh-KO-uh), c.30 mi/48 km long, N Ga.; rises in Union co.; flows NW meandering greatly until it reaches Blue Ridge L. in Fannin co.; 34°40′N 84°05′W.

Toccopola (tahk-uh-PO-luh), town (1990 pop. 154), Pontotoc co., N Miss., 13 mi/21 km W of Pontotoc; 34°15′N 89°13′W. In agr., dairying, and timber area.

Tochimilco (to-chee-MEEl-ko), town (1990 pop. 2,873), Puebla, central Mexico, on RR, 26 mi/42 km WSW of Puebla, on SW slopes of Popocatepetl; 18°54′N 98°34′W. Cereals, sugarcane, vegetables.

Tochimiltzingo (to-chee-meelt-ZEEN-go), town (1990 pop. 606), SW Puebla, Mexico, 3.1 mi/5 km SE of Atlixco; 18°48′N 98°19′W. Elev. 6,070 ft/1,850 m. Mild climate. On a gravel road. In Rio Grande drainage. Mainly subsistence farming.

Tochtepec (toch-te-pek), town (1990 pop. 4,233), Puebla, central Mexico, 30 mi/48 km ESE of Puebla; 18°50′N 97°49′W. Elev. 6,562 ft/2,000 m. Cereals, vegetables.

Toco (TO-ko), village, NE Trinidad, Trinidad and Tobago, 2 mi/3.2 km W of Galera Point, 40 mi/64 km ENE of Port of Spain; 10°47′N 61°03′W. In coconut-growing region. Fishing; fine beaches. The community was studied by Melville J Herskovits, and he wrote about his findings in *Trinidad Village* (1947).

Tocumbo (to-KOOM-bo), town (1990 pop. 2,427), Michoacán, central Mexico, on small lake, 25 mi/40 km SW of Zamora; 19°42′N 102°32′W. Elev. 4,265 ft/1,300 m. Corn, sugarcane, fruit; livestock.

Todd 1 county (□ 377 sq mi/976 sq km; 1990 pop. 10,940), S Ky.; ⊙ Elkton; 36°50′N 87°10′W. Bounded S by Tenn.; drained by Pond R., Elk and West forks of Red R. Rolling agr. area (dark tobacco, hay, alfalfa, soybeans, wheat, barley, corn, fruit; hogs, cattle, poultry; dairying); timber, stone quarries. Jefferson Davis State Historical Site in W. Part of L. Malone reservoir in NE corner. Formed 1819. **2** county (□ 979 sq mi/2,536 sq km; 1990 pop. 23,363), W central Minn.; ⊙ Long Prairie; 46°04′N 94°54′E. Watered by Long Prairie R.; Sauk and Big Birch lakes are in S boundary. Agr. (brans, potatoes, hay, alfalfa, oats, barley; sheep, hogs, cattle, poultry; dairying); deposits of marl and peat. Numerous small lakes, especially in S and E. Formed 1855. **3** county (□ 1,391 sq mi/3,603 sq km; 1990 pop. 8,352), S S.Dak., borders Nebr. on S; 43°10′N 100°43′W. Administratively attached to Tripp co. to E. Entire co. is coterminus with Rosebud Indian Reservation; drained by Little White and Keya Paha rivers. Grain; cattle. In Mountain time zone. Boundary bet. Mountain and Central time zones follows E co. boundary and E ½ of S boundary. Formed 1909.

Todd, uninc. village, Ashe and Watauga cos., NW N.C., 8 mi/12.9 km NNE of Boone, on South Fork of New R.

Todd Island, islet, S Franklin dist., N.W.T., Canada, in Simpson Strait, off Booth Point, S King William Isl.; 68°27′N 96°27′W. Graves and other relics of Franklin expedition (1847–1848) were found here by Hall (1861–1865).

Toddville, fishing village, Dorchester co., E Md., near Fishing Bay, 19 mi/31 km S of Cambridge.

Todos Santos, village, Baja California Sur, Lower Baja California, NW Mexico, on Pacific coast, 50 mi/80 km S of La Paz, on Mexico Highway 1; 23°27′N 110°13′W. Sugarcane, fruit. Cerro el Picacho (7,100 ft/2,164 m) to NE.

Todos Santos Islands, 2 barren rocks (□ 0.5 sq mi/1.3 sq km) on Pacific coast of NW Baja California Norte, NW Mexico, at entrance to Todos Santos Bay, 10 mi/16 km SW of Ensenada, 5 mi/8 km NW of Cabo Punta Banda; 31°48′N 116°48′W. Lighthouse. Guano deposits.

Todt Hill, N.Y.: see STATEN ISLAND.

Tofield (TO-feeld), town (1991 pop. 1,620), central Alta.,

Canada, near Beaverhill L., 25 mi/40 km NNE of Camrose; 53°22′N 112°40′W. Oil and natural gas; coal mining, mixed farming; wheat, barley; hogs.

Tofino (tuh-FEE-no), village, SW B.C., Canada, on W central Vancouver Isl., on Clayoquot Sound, 50 mi/80 km W of Port Alberni; 49°08′N 125°55′W. Sawmilling, gold mining. Artists' colony, ecotourism center. Opposite are Vargas and Meares isls.

Tofty, locality, N central Alaska, 15 mi/24 km W of Manley Hot Springs. Former gold-mining town, renowned for its high yields. Mining continues in area. Fishing, hunting. Est. 1908.

Togiak (TO-gee-yak), Eskimo village (1990 pop. 613), SW Alaska, at head of Togiak Bay inlet (12 mi/19 km long, 18 mi/29 km wide at mouth) of Bristol Bay, 70 mi/113 km W of Dillingham; 58°56′N 160°34′W. Fishing.

Togo (TO-go), village (1991 pop. 165), SE Sask., Canada, on Man. border, 40 mi/64 km ENE of Yorkton. Mixed farming.

Togus, Maine: see CHELSEA.

Togus Pond (TO-guhs), reservoir, Kennebec co., S Maine, source of Togus R., 4 mi/6.4 km E of Augusta; 1.5 mi/2.4 km long; 44°18′N 69°43′W. The Togus flows 7 mi/11.3 km SW to the Kennebec R.

Tohak Lake, central Keewatin dist., N.W.T., Canada, N of Baker L.; 50 mi/80 km long, 3 mi/5 km–12 mi/19 km wide; 65°13′N 96°15′W. Drains SE into Chesterfield Inlet.

Tohakum Peak, Nev.: see LAKE RANGE.

Tohopekaliga Lake (toh-hoh-peh-kuh-LYE-guh), Osceola co., central Fla., 18 mi/29 km S of Orlando; c.11 mi/18 km long, 2 mi/3.2 km–5 mi/8 km wide. Kissimmee is at N end. The lake is joined by Kissimmee R. (rising here) to Hatcheha L. (S), and connected by canal with East Tohopekaliga L. (c.5 mi/8 km in diameter), just NE.

Toiyabe Range (toi-YAH-bee), in Nye and Lander cos., central Nev., extends N-S bet. Reese R. (W) and Big Smokey Valley (E); 38°47′N 117°15′W. Mt. Callahan (10,187 ft/3,105 m) in N; Bunker Hill (11,474 ft/3,497 m) in center; Arc Dome (11,773 ft/3,588 m) in S. All but far N is in Toiyabe Natl. Forest. Austin is mining and ranching center in NW foothills.

Tok, town (1990 pop. 935), E central Alaska, 200 mi/322 km SE of Fairbanks and 140 mi/225 km SW of Dawson, Yukon Territory, Canada, near Tanana R.; 63°17′N 143°02′W. Located on Alaska Highway at junction of Glenn Highway (NE terminus). Airstrip. Highway-services center. Also called Tok Junction.

Tok Cut-Off, highway in E Alaska, extends 136 mi/219 km SW from Alaska Highway at Tok Junction, 11 mi/18 km ESE of Tanacross, to Richardson Highway just N of Gulkana. Provides short-cut to Valdez, connects with Glenn Highway (to Anchorage) S of Gulkana. Serves Slana, Chistochina, Gakona. Crosses Mentasta Pass.

Tokeland, uninc. village (1990 pop. 450), Pacific co., SW Wash., 9 mi/14.5 km WNW of South Bend, on Toke Point, at N end of Willapa Bay. Mfg. (fresh and frozen seafood, especially crabs). Part of Willapa Natl. Wildlife Refuge to W; Shoalwater Indian Reservation to NW; Grayland Beach State Park to NW.

Tokewanna Peak, Utah: see UINTA MOUNTAINS.

Toklat, village, central Alaska, on Kantishna R., and 40 mi/64 km W of Nenana.

Tolar, village (1990 pop. 523), Hood co., N central Texas, c.40 mi/64 km SW of Fort Worth; 32°23′N 97°55′W. In agr. area (cattle; peanuts, pecans). Squaw Creek L. reservoir to SE.

Tolcayuca (to-kah-YOO-kah), town (1990 pop. 4,621), Hidalgo, central Mexico, 19 mi/31 km SW of Pachuca de Soto; 19°57′N 98°55′W. Elev. 8,107 ft/2,471 m. Grain, beans, maguey; livestock.

Tolchester Beach (TAWL-chess-ter), summer resort village, Kent co., E Md., on the Eastern Shore, 21 mi/34 km E of Baltimore, across Chesapeake Bay. Once a highly popular resort, the entire property is now a private marina.

Toledo (tuh-LEE-do), city (1990 pop. 332,943), ⊙ Lucas co., NW Ohio, on the Maumee R. at its junction with L. Erie; 41°40′N 83°35′W. With a natural harbor, RRs,

and highways, it is a port of entry and one of the chief shipping centers on the Great Lakes. Oil, coal, farm prods., and numerous manufactures (primarily motor vehicle parts) are exported; iron ore is the principal import. Toledo is also an industrial and commercial center, with large oil refineries, a glassmaking industry, shipyards, and plants that manufacture vehicles, powertrain assemblies, machinery, and chemicals. The health-care industry is also significant. Gen. Anthony Wayne built Fort Industry here in 1794 after the Battle of Fallen Timbers. The city was settled (1817) as Port Lawrence on that site and in 1833 was consolidated with nearby Vistula as Toledo. In 1835–1836 the "Toledo War" occurred, a boundary dispute that was settled by Congress in favor of Ohio when Mich. became a state. Steps in the development of the city included the opening of the canals in the 1840s, the arrival of numerous RR lines, the development of the Ohio coalfields, the tapping of gas and oil deposits in the late 19th cent., and the establishment of the Libbey glassworks in 1888. Seat of the Univ. of Toledo, the Medical Col. of Ohio at Toledo, and a junior business col. Points of interest include the Toledo Mus. of Art, a large zoo, and the Anthony Wayne suspension bridge (1931). The site of the Battle of Fallen Timbers, a natl. historic landmark, is in a nearby state park. Inc. 1837.

Toledo 1 (tuh-LEE-do), town (1990 pop. 2,380), ⊙ Tama co., central Iowa, near Iowa R., 17 mi/27 km ESE of Marshalltown; 41°59′N 92°34′W. Terminus of RR spur from Tama. Mfg. (lumber prods.; fertilizers; seed corn processing). Iowa Juvenile Home here. Mesquakie Indian Settlement to SW. Inc. 1866. **2** town (1990 pop. 3,174), ⊙ Lincoln co., W Oregon, 30 mi/48 km W of Corvallis, on Yaquina R. 3 mi/4.8 km NE of its entrance to Yaquina Bay; 44°37′N 123°55′W. Lumber, paper mills. Dairy prods.; poultry, sheep, cattle. Part of Siuslaw Natl. Forest to S. Founded c. 1868, inc. 1905.

Toledo 1 (tuh-LEE-do), village (1990 pop. 1,199), ⊙ Cumberland co., SE central Ill., 15 mi/24 km SSE of Mattoon; 39°16′N 88°14′W. In agr. area. **2** village (1990 pop. 586), Lewis co., SW Wash., 16 mi/26 km SSE of Chehalis, and on Cowlitz R.; 46°26′N 122°51′W. Logging, dairying, lumber prods. Trout and salmon hatcheries to N on Cowlitz R. Toledo Winlock Airport to NE. Lewis and Clark State Park to W.

Toledo Bend Reservoir (tuh-LEE-do), W La. and E Texas, on Sabine R., at River Bend (Texas), 19 mi/31 km W of Leesville (La.); c.70 mi/113 km long, max. 7 mi/11.3 km wide; 31°10′N 93°34′W. Max. capacity 5,100,000 acre-ft. Largest reservoir in La. Formed by Toledo Bend Dam (earth construction; 95 ft/29 m high), built (1968) for irrigation, power generation, and flood control. Unit of Sabine Natl. Forest (Texas) covers most of W shore; N. Toledo Bend State Park (La.) on E shore.

Tolimán (to-lee-MAHN), city (1990 pop. 2,136), and township, Querétaro, central Mexico, on central plateau, 35 mi/56 km NE of Querétaro; 20°55′N 99°56′W. Elev. 5,649 ft/1,722 m. Known for opal mines. Agr. center (grain, sugarcane, cotton, tobacco, fruit; livestock).

Tolimán (to-lee-MAHN), town (1990 pop. 1,440), Jalisco, W Mexico, near Colima Volcano, 30 mi/48 km SE of Autlán de Navarro; 19°35′N 103°50′W. Elev. 2,543 ft/775 m. Agr. center (grain, vegetables, sugarcane, cotton, fruit).

Tolland, county (□ 417 sq mi/1,080 sq km; 1990 pop. 128,699), NE Conn., on Mass. border; ⊙ Rockville; 41°51′N 72°20′W. Mfg. (textiles, lumber, thread, wood prods., buttons, paper goods), agr. (dairy prods.; poultry; vegetables, potatoes, tobacco, fruit). Resorts on lakes. Has several state forests. Drained by Willimantic, Hockanum, Scantic, and Hop rivers. Constituted 1785.

Tolland 1 (TAW-luhnd), town (1990 pop. 11,001), Tolland co., NE Conn. on Willimantic R., and 18 mi/29 km NE of Hartford; 41°52′N 72°22′W. In hilly agr. area; dairying. Shenipsit L. is W. Settled and inc. 1715. **2** agr. town (1990 pop. 289), Hampden co., SW Mass., 23 mi/37 km W of Springfield; 42°05′N 73°01′W. State forest here.

Tollesboro (TOLZ-buhr-o), uninc. town (1990 pop.

808), Lewis co., NE Ky., 11 mi/18 km ESE of Maysville. Tobacco, soybeans, grain; cattle; dairying. Timber.

Tolleson, town (1990 pop. 4,434), Maricopa co., S central Ariz., suburb 10 mi/16 km W of Phoenix, in irrigated Salt R. valley; 33°27′N 112°15′W. Diverse mfg. On Roosevelt District Canal. Settled 1911, inc. 1929.

Tolley (TAHL-ee), village (1990 pop. 79), Renville co., N.Dak., 15 mi/24 km W of Mohall, near Souris R.; 48°43′N 101°49′W. Upper Souris Natl. Wildlife Refuge to E.

Tolna (TAHL-nuh), village (1990 pop. 230), Nelson co., E central N.Dak., 16 mi/26 km SSW of Lakota; 47°49′N 98°26′W. RR terminus. Devils Lake Sioux Indian Reservation to W; Stump L. to N.

Tolono (tah-LONE-uh), village (1990 pop. 2,605), Champaign co., E Ill., 9 mi/14.5 km S of Urbana; 39°59′N 88°15′W. In agr. area. Marker on site where Lincoln last spoke (1861) to the people of Ill., on his way to Washington.

Tolovana, village, central Alaska, on Tanana R., and 30 mi/48 km NW of Nenana. Placer gold mining.

Tolstoy, village (1990 pop. 69), Potter co., N central S.Dak., 22 mi/35 km NE of Gettysburg; 45°12′N 99°36′W.

Toluca (tah-LOO-kah), city (1990 pop. 1,315), Marshall co., N central Ill., 15 mi/24 km ESE of Lacon; 41°00′N 89°07′W. In agr. area. Inc. 1894.

Toluca de Lerdo (to-LOO-kah dai LER-fo), city (1990 pop. 327,865) and township, ⊙ Toluca municipio (1990 pop. 487,630) and Mexico state, central Mexico, on Mexico Highways 13, 55, and 130; 19°17′N 99°39′W; Elev. 8,793 ft/2,680 m. Located on the central plateau, Toluca has a cool climate year-round. It was established as a Span. settlement in 1530 by Hernán Cortés, who had received the Valle de Toluca as a grant from Emperor Charles V. The surrounding plain is fertile, producing grain, fruits, and vegetables. Cattle raising is important. The city has become increasingly industrialized, and has food processing and beverage plants, as well as flour, cotton, and woolen mills. Motor vehicle mfg. The city is still known for its traditional handicrafts. Two small rivers run through the city, and nearby is an inactive volcano, the Nevado de Toluca, called also Xinantecatl and Cinantécatl. Airport.

Toluca Lake, suburban section of Los Angeles, Los Angeles co., S Calif., 10 mi/16 km NW of downtown, in San Fernando Valley, bet. Burbank (NE) and Universal City (S). Alameda Avenue (N) and Los Angeles R. (S). Small Toluca L. here.

Toluca, Nevado de (to-LOO-kah, ne-VAH-do dai), Aztec *Cinantécatl* or *Zinantécatl*, extinct volcano (14,954 ft/4,558 m), Mexico state, Mexico, 13 mi/21 km SSW of Toluca de Lerdo; 19°06′N 99°46′W. Has deep crater lakes.

Toluca Valley, Mexico state, central Mexico, basin of the large central plateau, W of Valley of Mexico, with Toluca de Lerdo at its center. Elev. over 8,793 ft/2,680 m. Densely populated area; carries on intensive dairy farming. Gold mining at El Oro.

Tom Bean, town (1990 pop. 827), Grayson co., N Texas, 11 mi/18 km SE of Sherman; 33°31′N 96°28′W. In agr. area (cattle; cotton); mfg. (machining).

Tom Green, county (□ 1,540 sq mi/3,989 sq km; 1990 pop. 98,458), W Texas; ⊙ San Angelo; 31°24′N 100°27′W. On N Edwards Plateau; elev. c.1,700 ft/518 m–2,600 ft/792 m. Drained by North, Middle, and South Concho rivers, here joining to form Concho R. Mainly ranching region (sheep, goats, cattle); irrigated agr. (cotton, oats, wheat, sesame, grain sorghum, hay). Oil and gas wells; limestone; freshwater pearls. Hunting, fishing; tourist trade. O.C. Fisher L. (N Concho), Twin Buttes Reservoir and L. Nasworthy (both at confluence of Middle and South Concho rivers). Formed 1874.

Tom Miller Dam, Texas: see AUSTIN LAKE.

Tom, Mount (1,202 ft/366 m), W central Mass., just N of Holyoke; 42°14′N 72°38′W. Highest point of Mt. Tom Range, which lies mostly within Mt. Tom state reservation (3 sq mi/7.8 sq km). Hiking and ski trails, campgrounds. Mount Tom village is just N, in Easthampton.

Toma, La, Dominican Republic: see LA TOMA.

Tomah, town (1990 pop. 7,570), Monroe co., W central Wis., on branch of Lemonweir R., and 38 mi/61 km ENE of La Crosse; 43°59′N 90°30′W. In dairy and livestock region; processes lumber, dairy prods.; mfg. (tempered glass, ice fishing equip., bedding, apparel). RR junction to W at Tunnel City. On Tonah lake. Fort McCoy Military Reservation to W. Inc. 1883.

Tomahawk, town (1990 pop. 3,328), Lincoln co., N Wis., on Wisconsin R. (Mohawskin L.), and 36 mi/58 km N of Wausau, in wooded lake-resort region; 45°28′N 89°43′W. Mfg. (metal fabrication, stainless steel vessels and tanks). Plotted 1887, inc. 1891.

Tomales Bay, narrow inlet of Pacific Ocean, NW of San Francisco, extending into NW Marin co., W Calif.; c.14 mi/23 km long, 1 mi/1.6 km wide. Tomales village is c.2 mi/3.2 km inland, near mouth of bay; bay is a continuation of San Andreas fault. Dairying; resort. Point Reyes Natl. Seashore is on peninsula at W side of bay.

Tomasaki, Mount, Utah: see LA SAL MOUNTAINS.

Tomatlán 1 (to-mah-TLAHN), town (1990 pop. 6,849), Jalisco, W Mexico, in lowland near Pacific coast, on Tomatlán R., 60 mi/97 km WNW of Autlán de Navarro; 19°56′N 105°15′W. Sugarcane, cotton, rice, bananas. **2** town (1990 pop. 3,404), ⊙ Tomatlán municipio, Veracruz, E Mexico, at E foot of Pico de Orizaba, and 12 mi/19 km NNW of Córdoba; 19°01′N 97°00′W. Elev. 4,452 ft/1,357 m. Coffee, sugarcane, fruit.

Tomatlán, Mexico: see BUENAVISTA TOMATLÁN.

Tomball, town (1990 pop. 6,370), Harris co., S Texas, suburb 28 mi/45 km NW of Houston, near Spring Creek; 30°06′N 95°37′W. Growing suburban area in oil, timber, agr. region; mfg. (meat processing, concrete, oil field equip., sheet metal fabrication. Tomball Col. (2-year). Inc. 1935.

Tombigbee, river, c.400 mi/644 km long, in Miss. and Ala.; formed by joining of East Fork of Tombigbee R. (rises in Prentiss co., NE Miss., flows S past Fulton c.70 mi/113 km) and Oldtown Creek in N Monroe co., NE Miss.; flows S through Aberdeen L. and Columbus L. reservoirs, past Columbus, Miss. through Aliceville L. reservoir on Miss.-Ala. border, past Gainesville and Demopolis, Ala. Here it receives Black Warrior R. from NE above Demopolis Dam, and continues S through Coffeeville Dam, past Jackson, joining Alabama R. 30 mi/48 km N of Mobile to form Mobile R. The Tombigbee is an important artery for manufactured goods. Dams and locks improve navigation on the river. The TENNESSEE-TOMBIGBEE WATERWAY was completed in 1985 to add an additional link bet. the Mississippi R. System and the Gulf coast for barge traffic. The Waterway replaces river's original channel in its midcourse, parallels channel to E in its upper course, above Aberdeen L.

Tombstone, city (1990 pop. 1,220), Cochise co., SE Ariz., 60 mi/97 km SE of Wilcox and 17 mi/27 km NE of Sierra Vista; 31°43′N 110°03′W. Elev. 4,539 ft/1,383 m. A tourist attraction, the city became a natl. historic landmark in 1962. Silver was discovered here in 1877 by Ed Schieffelin, a prospector, who 2 years later laid out and named the city. Tombstone quickly became one of the richest and most lawless mining towns in the Southwest. Its newspaper, *Epitaph*, was first published in 1880. The city was county seat from 1881 to 1929. Large-scale mining ended by 1890. Landmarks include Boot Hill Graveyard, where many desperados are buried; Bird Cage Theater, now a mus.; and O.K. Corral, scene of a climactic gun battle bet. the Clanton gang and Wyatt Earp, his brother Virgil, and Doc Holliday. Tombstone Courthouse State Historic Park. The city's violent past is reenacted each year at the 3-day Helldorado celebrations. San Pedro Riparian Natl. Conservation Area to W, on San Pedro R.; sect. of Coronado Natl. Forest to NE, including Cochise Stronghold Memorial Park, in Dragoon Mts. Inc. 1881.

Tome, uninc. town (1990 pop. 1,695), Valencia co., central N.Mex., 25 mi/40 km S of Albuquerque, on Rio Grande; 34°43′N 106°43′W. Dairying; cattle, sheep; grain, corn, alfalfa. Part of Cibola Natl. Forest to E.

Tomhannock Reservoir, Rensselaer co., E N.Y., 11 mi/18 km NNE of Troy; c.6 mi/9.7 km long; 42°52′N 73°34′W.

Tomkins Cove, village (1990 pop. 850), Rockland co., SE N.Y., 4 mi/6.4 km SW of Peekskill, across the Hudson R.; 41°15′N 73°59′W. Bear Mt. sect. of Palisades Interstate Park is just N.

Tomlinson Run State Park, W.Va.: see CHESTER.

Tompkins, county (□ 491 sq mi/1,272 sq km; 1990 pop. 94,097), W central N.Y.; ⊙ Ithaca; 42°27′N 76°28′W. Includes S end of Cayuga L. (resorts) and Taughannock Falls State Park. Dairying and farming area (grain, fruit; poultry). Mfg. at Ithaca. Formed 1817.

Tompkins, village (1991 pop. 227), SW Sask., Canada, in the Cypress Hills, 32 mi/51 km ENE of Maple Creek. Wheat; livestock.

Tompkinsville, town (1990 pop. 2,861), ⊙ Monroe co., S Ky., 24 mi/39 km SSE of Glasgow; 36°42′N 85°41′W. Corn, wheat, burley tobacco, watermelons; livestock. Lumber, industrial machinery, apparel, coaxial cable. In nearby Old Mulkey Meeting House State Historical Site (to SW) is oldest (1804) log church in Ky. Dale Hollow Reservoir 15 mi/24 km SE. Cumberland River Ferry to E.

Tompkinsville, port and industrial sect. of Staten Isl. borough of N.Y. city, SE N.Y., on NE Staten Isl., just S of St. George; 40°38′N 74°04′W.

Toms Brook, town (1990 pop. 227), Shenandoah co., NW Va., near North Fork of Shenandoah R., 4 mi/6.4 km SW of Strasburg; 38°57′N 78°26′W. Dairying; livestock; grain, apples. Limestone.

Toms River, village (1990 pop. 7,524), ⊙ Ocean co., E N.J., on Toms R., near Barnegat Bay, and 20 mi/32 km SSE of Freehold; 39°57′N 74°10′W. Formerly a whaling, fishing, and shipping center. Shellfishing, tourism, boatbuilding; clay, timber; fruit; poultry. Co. mus. and several 18th-cent. bldgs., large retirement community, and Ocean County Col. here. A Revolutionary privateering port, burned (1782) by Loyalists and British.

Toms River, 19 mi/31 km long, in N Ocean co., N.J.; flows SE and E past Toms River village (head of navigation), to Barnegat Bay; broadens into tidal inlet in lower 5 mi/8 km. Resorts, fishing villages around mouth.

Tonalá (to-nah-LAH), city (1990 pop. 26,919) and township, Chiapas, S Mexico, in Pacific lowland, on RR, 60 mi/97 km SW of Tuxtla Gutiérrez, on Mexico Highway 200; 16°08′N 93°41′W. Processing and agr. center (rice, sugarcane, cacao, tobacco, coffee; fruit; livestock). Tanning; salt mining; forest industry.

Tonalá (to-nah-LAH), town (1990 pop. 151,190), Jalisco, central Mexico, 8 mi/12.9 km ESE of Guadalajara, off highway; 22°34′N 103°44′W. Agr. center (grain, sugarcane, tobacco, vegetables; fruit); pottery.

Tonalá River (to-nah-LAH), c.100 mi/161 km long, in SE Mexico; rises in N foothills of Sierra Madre on Isthmus of Tehuantepec; flows in its entire length NW along Veracruz-Tabasco border to Gulf of Campeche 20 mi/32 km ENE of Coatzacoalcos; 16°53′N 99°08′W. Called Pedregal R. in upper course.

Tonalea, uninc. village, Coconino co., N Ariz., in Navajo and Hopi Indian reservations (joint use area), 85 mi/137 km NNE of Flagstaff. Sheep, cattle; crafts. Navajo Natl. Monument is N. White Mesa Natural Bridge to N.

Tonasket (tuh-NAS-kit), town (1990 pop. 847), Okanogan co., N Wash., 24 mi/39 km NNE of Okanogan, and on Okanogan R. at mouth of Bonaparte Creek; 48°42′N 119°26′W. Apples; cattle; logging. Parts of Okanogan Natl. Forest to E and W.

Tonatico (to-nah-TEE-jo), town (1990 pop. 6,313), Mexico state, central Mexico, 35 mi/56 km S of Toluca de Lardo, on Mexico Highway 55; 18°47′N 99°41′W. Sugarcane, fruit, coffee; livestock.

Tonawanda, city (□ 4 sq mi/10.4 sq km; 1990 pop. 17,284), Erie co., NW N.Y., on the Niagara R. at the terminus of the N.Y. State Barge Canal; 43°00′N 78°52′W. An industrial suburb of Buffalo and a lake port, it is a commercial center and transshipment point. Mfg. (steel, office equip., chemicals, paint, plastics). Inc. as village 1854, as city 1903.

Tonawanda Creek, c.90 mi/145 km long, N.Y.; rises in W Wyoming co., flows N, NW, and W past Batavia and through Tonawanda Indian Reservation to Niagara R. at Tonawanda. Partly canalized as a sect. of N.Y. State Barge Canal.

Tonaya (to-NAH-yah), town (1990 pop. 3,181), Jalisco, W Mexico, near the Sierra Tapalpa, 23 mi/37 km E of Autlán de Navarro; 19°47′N 103°58′W. Elev. 4,331 ft/1,320 m. Grain, sugarcane, tobacco, fruit.

Tonayán (to-nah-YAHN), town (1990 pop. 1,164), Veracruz, E Mexico, in Sierra Madre Oriental, 11 mi/18 km N of Xalapa Enríquez; 19°41′N 96°55′W. Elev. 4,987 ft/1,520 m. Corn, fruit. In Totonac Indian area.

Tonganoxie (tahn-guh-NAHK-see), town (1990 pop. 2,347), Leavenworth co., NE Kansas, 17 mi/27 km SW of Leavenworth and 12 mi/19 km NE of Lawrence. Corn, sorghum; hogs, cattle. Leavenworth State Fishing L. to W.

Tongass National Forest (□ 25,860 sq mi/66,977 sq km), S Alaska, bet. S slope of St. Elias Mts. and the Pacific coast bet. Yakutat Bay and Dry Bay. Wildlife, fishing; tourism. Logging is restricted. Est. 1907.

Tongue of the Ocean, deep Atlantic channel, central Bahama Isls., on E edge of the Great Bahama Bank; extends c.100 mi/161 km S from New Providence Isl. along E coast of Andros Isl.

Tongue River 1 60 mi/97 km long, in E Cavalier co., N.Dak.; flows E and ENE past Cavalier to Pembina R. near Pembina 4 mi/6.4 km S of Can. border; 48°45′N 98°14′W. **2** 265 mi/426 km long, in N Wyo. and SE Mont.; rises in Bighorn Mts. 40 mi/64 km W of Sheridan co., Wyo.; flows NE past Dayton, Wyo., into Mont. through Tongue R. Reservoir; forms E boundary of North Cheyenne Indian Reservation, and joins Yellowstone R. at Miles City, Mont.

Tonica (TUH-ni-kuh), village (1990 pop. 715), La Salle co., N Ill., 8 mi/12.9 km S of La Salle; 41°12′N 89°04′W. Dairy prods.; cattle, hogs; corn, soybeans, wheat; charcoal briquettes.

Tonila (to-NEE-lah), town (1990 pop. 3,307), Jalisco, W Mexico, at SE foot of Colima volcano, 22 mi/35 km SSW of Ciudad Guzmán, on Mexico Highway 54; 19°24′N 103°31′W. Agr. center (corn, sugarcane, tobacco, fruit).

Tonka Bay (TAWN-kuh), town (1990 pop. 1,472), Hennepin co., E Minn., 17 mi/27 km WSW of Minneapolis, on neck of land bet. Upper L. (W) and Lower L. (E) of L. Minnetonka; 44°55′N 93°35′W. Mfg. (plastic prototypes). Gideon Bay to SE.

Tonkawa (TAHN-kuh-wah), town (1990 pop. 3,127), Kay co., N Okla., 13 mi/21 km W of Ponca City, and on Salt Fork of Arkansas R.; 36°40′N 97°18′W. Nonferrous castings, steel storage tanks. Oil and natural gas wells. Seat of Northern Okla. Jr. Col. Settled 1893; inc. 1894.

Tonopah 1 (TOH-noh-pah), uninc. town (1990 pop. 54), Maricopa co., W central Ariz., 50 mi/80 km W of Phoenix, S of Hayden-Rhodes Aqueduct, on Interstate Highway 10. Elev. 1,490 ft/454 m. Cattle, sheep; grain, hay. Hummingbird Springs and Big Horn Mts. Wilderness Areas to NW. **2** (to-nuh-PUH), town (1990 pop. 3,616), ⊙ Nye co., at Esmeralda co. border, S central Nev., 80 mi/129 km ESE of Hawthorne; 38°06′N 117°15′W. Elev. 6,030 ft/1,838 m. Supply point in mining (gold, silver); cattle, sheep, and barley area. Central Nev. Mus. here. Toiyabe Natl. Forest to NE; Natl. Wildhorse Management Area to ESE. Large Nellis Air Force Bombing and Gunnery Range to SE. Settled 1900, with discovery of rich silver deposits.

Tontitown (TAHN-tee-toun), village (1990 pop. 460), Washington co., NW Ark., 8 mi/12.9 km NNW of Fayetteville, in the Ozarks; 36°10′N 94°14′W. Wine-grape growing; mfg. (metal roofing and siding). Small unit of Ozark Natl. Forest to SW.

Tonto Basin, depression S of the Mogollon Rim, NE Gila co., central Ariz., 65 mi/105 km NNE of Phoenix. Town of Payson in N part. Tonto Creek flows c.45 mi/72 km S from the basin to enter Theodore Roosevelt L. reservoir behind Theodore Roosevelt Dam. In Tonto Natl. Forest.

Tonto National Monument (□ 2 sq mi/5.2 sq km), Gila co., central Ariz., 55 mi/89 km ENE of Phoenix, near S shore of Theodore Roosevelt L. reservoir. Well-preserved 13th–14th-cent. cliff dwellings built by Salado Native Americans in the Salt R. valley. Proclaimed 1907.

Tontogany (tahn-TAH-guh-nee), village (1990 pop. 364), Wood co., NW Ohio, 5 mi/8 km WNW of Bowling Green; 41°25′N 83°45′W.

Tony, village (1990 pop. 114), Rusk co., N Wis., 5 mi/8 km ENE of Ladysmith; 45°28′N 91°00′W. Dairying, cheese. Big Falls Flowage reservoir to N.

Tooele (tuh-WIL-uh), county (□ 7,287 sq mi/18,873 sq km; 1990 pop. 26,601), NW Utah; ⊙ Tooele; 40°27′N 113°10′W. Mining and grazing area bordering W on Nev. Includes Stansbury Mts. and parts of Wasatch Natl. Forest (incl. Deseret Peak Wilderness Area) in E center and SE, part of Great Salt L. in NE (incl. Stansburg and Carrington isls.), and much of Great Salt L. Desert in W. Cattle, poultry; alfalfa, wheat, barley. Copper, lead, zinc, gold, silver, salt, magnesium. Skull Valley Indian Reservation in E center; Timpie Springs Waterfowl Management Area in NE. Bonneville Speedway Automobile Testing Site in NW, near Wendover. Military installations include Dugway Proving Grounds, Deseret Test Center, and Wendover Air Force Firing Range, all large tracts entirely within W part of co.; part of Hill Air Force Base Firing Range in NW; Tooele Army Depot, storing chemical weapons, in E at Tooele. Formed 1850.

Tooele (tuh-WIL-uh), city (□ 12 sq mi/31 sq km; 1990 pop. 13,887), ⊙ Tooele co., N central Utah, 28 mi/45 km SW of Salt Lake City, 10 mi/16 km S of Great Salt L.; 40°32′N 112°17′W. Elev. 5,100 ft/1,554 m. Rapidly growing suburb of Salt Lake City, in farm area. RR junction. A major employer is the U.S. Tooele Army Depot, which stores nearly ½ of the country's chemical weapons arsenal. A chemical agent disposal facility was built here in 1996. Lead ore-smelting industry. The Elton Tunnel (4 mi/6 km long; built 1937–1942) in the Oquirrh Mts. (E) leads to the source of the ores in Bingham Canyon. Of interest are the remains of stops on the Pony Express (S). Unit of Wasatch Natl. Forest, incl. Deseret Peak Wilderness Area, to W. Settled 1849 by Mormons on a California wagon route. Inc. 1853.

Tool, town (1990 pop. 1,712), Henderson co., Texas, 50 mi/80 km SE of Dallas; 32°16′N 96°10′W. Oil and natural gas. Agr. area (cattle; vegetables, melons). Clear Creek Reservoir to E.

Toole (TOOL), county (□ 1,945 sq mi/5,038 sq km; 1990 pop. 5,046), N Mont.; ⊙ Shelby; 48°39′N 111°42′W. Agr. region bordering Canada (Alta.) on N; drained S by Marias R. and Willow Creek in E. Marias R. forms part of SW boundary. L. Elwell (Tiber Reservoir) in SE. Wheat, barley, hay; cattle, sheep, hogs; petroleum, natural gas. Formed 1914.

Toombs (TOOMZ), county (□ 369 sq mi/956 sq km; 1990 pop. 24,072), E central Ga.; ⊙ Lyons; 32°07′N 82°20′W. Bounded S by Altamaha R., NE by Ohoopee R. Coastal plain agr. area (wheat, soybeans, cotton, corn, peanuts, tobacco); cattle, hogs. Mfg. at Vidalia and Lyons. Formed 1905.

Toomsboro (TOOMZ-buhr-o), town (1990 pop. 617), Wilkinson co., central Ga., 32 mi/51 km E of Macon; 32°49′N 83°05′W. Lumber.

Toone, town (1990 pop. 279), Hardeman co., SW Tenn., 20 mi/32 km S of Jackson; 35°21′N 88°57′W. In timber, agr. area.

Topanga, village, Los Angeles co., S Calif., in Santa Monica Mts., 8 mi/12.9 km NW of Santa Monica, 21 mi/34 km NW of Los Angeles, and 4 mi/6.4 km N of Pacific Ocean coast. Intermittent Topanga Creek flows c.8 mi/12.9 km S through Topanga Canyon to the Pacific at Topanga Beach. In Santa Monica Mts. Natl. Recreation Area. Los Tunas State Beach to W of Topanga Beach.

Topaz Lake, Douglas co., W Nev. and Mono co., E Calif. Artificial body of water on West Walker R. Irrigation; recreation. Bounded by part of Toiyabe Natl. Forest to N and E.

Topeka (tuh-PEE-kuh), city (1990 pop. 119,883), ⊙ state and of Shawnee co., NE Kansas, 65 mi/105 km W of Kansas City, Kansas, on the Kansas R.; 39°02′N 95°41′W. In a rich agr. region, it is an important shipping point for cattle and wheat and a wholesaling, marketing, and processing center for farm prods. Insurance businesses, printing and publishing firms, grain mills, meatpacking houses, large RR repair shops, and plants that make tires and rubber prods., shoes, and cellophane. The world famous Menninger Foundation is a treatment center for mental illness. A ferry was est. here in 1842 on the Oregon Trail. The city was laid out in 1854 by Free State settlers from Lawrence and New England and was founded as the center for C. K. Holliday's projected RR (the Atchison, Topeka, and Santa Fe). A short-lived Free State constitution was framed in the city in 1855. Topeka was selected state capital when Kansas was admitted to the Union in 1861. It is the seat of Washburn Univ. of Topeka. A city of broad, tree-shaded streets, it has the mus. and lib. of the state historical society, the Mulvane Art Mus., the state lib., a notable Episcopal cathedral, and a park system that includes a beautiful rose garden. The capitol is modeled after the one in Washington, D.C. Inc. 1857.

Topeka, town (1990 pop. 912), Lagrange co., NE Ind., 10 mi/16 km SW of Lagrange; 41°32′N 85°32′W. Agr. area (hay; poultry; dairying); mfg. (boats, carbide-tipped tools, modular homes, trailers). Laid out 1843.

Topeka (to-PEE-ka), village (1990 pop. 93), Mason co., central Ill., 8 mi/12.9 km ENE of Havanna; 40°19′N 89°55′W. In agr. area (corn, wheat, soybeans); popcorn processing.

Topia (to-PEE-ah), mining settlement (1990 pop. 1,869) and township, ⊙ Topia municipio, Durango, N Mexico, on W slopes of Sierra Madre Occidental, 55 mi/89 km NE of Culiacán Rosares; 25°12′N 106°34′W. Elev. 6,401 ft/1,951 m. Silver, gold, copper mining. Wheat.

Topinabee (TAHP-nah-BEE), village, Cheboygan co., N Mich., 13 mi/21 km SSW of Cheboygan, on SW shore of Mullett L.; 45°29′N 84°35′W. Resort area.

Topo Chico (TO-po CHEE-ko), village, Nuevo León, N Mexico, in foothills of Sierra Madre Oriental, 4 mi/6.4 km NW of Monterrey; 25°43′N 100°19′W. Thermal springs; bathing resort.

Topock (to-pahk), uninc. village, Mohave co., W Ariz., on L. Havasu reservoir (Colorado R., Calif. border), 38 mi/61 km SW of Kingman and 10 mi/16 km SSE of Needles, Calif. Agr. inspection station. Toppock Bridge carried U.S. Highway 66 (popular Route 66). Highway I-40 and RR bridges to Calif. Havasu Natl. Wildlife Refuge protects Ariz. side of lake here; Warm Springs Wilderness Area to E; Fort Mojave Indian Reservation to N; Chemehuevi Valley Indian Reservation (Calif.) to S.

Topolobampo (to-po-lo-BAHM-po) or **Tobobampo**, town (1990 pop. 716), Sinaloa municipio, NW Mexico, port on inlet of Gulf of California, 8 mi/12.9 km S of Los Mochis; 25°36′N 109°04′W. RR terminus in Río Fuerte irrigation area producing corn, sugarcane, chickpeas, fruit, vegetables; fishing. Terminus of ferry route to Baja California.

Toppenish (TAHP-uh-nish), town (1990 pop. 7,419), Yakima co., S Wash., 18 mi/29 km SSE of Yakima, in NE part of Yakima Indian Reservation; 46°23′N 120°19′W. Potatoes, hay, fruit, hops; cattle; food processing, printing and publishing. Yakima Nation Mus. here. Toppenish Creek to S; Toppenish Ridge and Toppenish Natl. Wildlife Refuge to SW; Fort Simcoe State Park 25 mi/40 km W. Inc. 1907.

Topsail, village, SE N.F., Canada, on SE side of Conception Bay, NE Avalon Peninsula, 10 mi/16 km WSW of St. John's; 47°33′N 55°34′W. Fishing port, seaside resort. Hydroelectric plant.

Topsail Beach (TAHP-suhl), village (1990 pop. 346), near SW end of Topsail Isl., Pender co., SE N.C., 21 mi/34 km NE of Wilmington, on Atlantic Ocean; 34°22′N 77°37′W. Beach resort area.

Topsail Island (TAHP-suhl), Pender and Onslow cos., SE N.C., sand barrier island on Atlantic; Intracoastal Waterway passes to NW (bridged in two places); 23 mi/37 km long, 1 mi/1.6 km wide. New River Inlet (former end of isl.) 5 mi/8 km SW of end of island. Includes resort villages of Topsail Beach, Surf City, and North Topsail Beach.

Topsfield, town (1990 pop. 5,754), Essex co., NE Mass., 8 mi/12.9 km NNW of Salem; 42°38′N 70°57′W. Chalk, sand, and gravel deposits. Has Parson-Capen House, 17th-cent. Bradley-Palmer State Park, Ipswich River Wildlife Sanctuary. Settled c.1635; inc. 1648.

Topsfield, village (1990 pop. 235), Washington co., E Maine, 50 mi/80 km NNW of Machias; 45°27′N 67°47′W. In hunting, fishing area.

Topsham 1 (TAHPS-uhm), town (1990 pop. 8,746), including Topsham village, Sagadahoc co., SW Maine, on the Androscoggin R. (water power), opposite Brunswick; 43°57′N 69°57′W. Also includes village of Pejepscot. Settled c.1730; inc. 1764. **2** (TAHP-suhm), town (1990 pop. 944), Orange co., E Vt., on Waits R., and 14 mi/23 km ESE of Barre; 44°07′N 72°15′W.

Topton, borough (1990 pop. 1,987), Berks co., E central Pa., 16 mi/26 km NE of Reading; 40°30′N 75°42′W. RR junction. Mfg. (fabricated metal prods.); agr. (apples, grain; poultry, livestock; dairying). Doe Mt. Ski Area to E. Founded 1859; inc. 1875.

Toquema Range, Nev.: see TOQUIMA RANGE.

Toquerville (TO-ker-vil), village (1990 pop. 488), Washington co., SW Utah, 20 mi/32 km NE of St. George, on Ash Creek; 37°14′N 113°17′W. Cattle, barley, alfalfa, fruit. Landmark old winery (1865). Zion Natl. Park to E; Dixie Natl. Forest to NW. Settled 1858.

Toquima Range (tuh-KWEE-muh), central Nev., largely in Nye co., extends N into Lander co.; runs N-S bet. Toiyabe Range to W (separated by Big Smokey Valley), and Monitor Range to E (separated by Monitor Valley), in part of Toiyabe Natl. Forest. Highest point is Mt. Jefferson (11,807 ft/3,599 m), 54 mi/87 km NNE of Tonopah. Bald Mt. (9,274 ft/2,827 m) in S, Wildcat Peak (10,507 ft/3,203 m) in N. Sometimes spelled Toquema.

Tor Bay, inlet of the Atlantic, E N.S., Canada, 12 mi/19 km SE of Guysborough; 5 mi/8 km long, 10 mi/16 km wide at entrance.

Torbay (TOHR-bai), town (1991 pop. 4,707), SE N.F., Canada, on NE coast of Avalon Peninsula, 7 mi/11 km NNW of St. John's; 47°40′N 52°45′W. Fishing (shellfish, herring, squid); cod fishing suspended in mid-1990s. Site of a Can. air base in World War II.

Torbeck (tor-BEK), agr. town (1982 pop. 1,397), Sud dept., SW Haiti, on SW coast of Jacmel Peninsula, 5 mi/8 km SW of Les Cayes; 18°10′N 73°49′W. Citrus fruit.

Torch Lake 1 Antrim co., NW Mich., c.17 mi/27 km NE of Traverse City, separated from Grand Traverse Bay and Elk L. (W) by narrow neck of land; c.17 mi/27 km long, 2 mi/3.2 km wide; 45°59′N 85°18′W. Resorts, parks on shores. Joined by short river to L. Skegemog (S). **2** Houghton co., NW Upper Peninsula, Mich., on Keweenaw Peninsula, 5 mi/8 km ENE of Houghton; c.6 mi/9.7 km long, 1.5 mi/2.4 km wide; 47°09′N 88°25′W. Lake Linden village on N shore. Channel leads S from lake into Keweenaw Waterway. Torch L., its neighbors, Elk L. and the East and West arms of nearby Traverse Bay, were all formed by south-moving glacial lobes, unlike most lakes on L. Michigan's E shore, which are formed in back of sand dunes.

Tormentine, Cape (TOR-muhn-tein), easternmost point of N.B., Canada, on Northumberland Strait opposite Prince Edward Isl., 50 mi/80 km E of Moncton; 46°06′N 63°46′W. Lobster fishing port and RR terminal. Herring, lobster, and scallop beds in strait. RR and automobile ferry to Port Borden, P.E.I. Bridge linking the cape to P.E.I. across Northumberland Strait was built in 1997.

Tornado, uninc. town (1990 pop. 1,006), Kanawha co., W central W.Va., 13 mi/21 km WNW of Charleston, on Big Coal R.; 38°19′N 81°51′W. Corn, tobacco; cattle, poultry.

Tornado Mountain (10,169 ft/3,100 m), on border bet. Alta. and B.C., Canada, in Rocky Mts., 40 mi/64 km NE of Fernie.

Torngat Mountains, N Lab., Canada, northernmost range of the Laurentian Plateau, bet. the Atlantic coast and the Que. border, extends c.120 mi/190 km N-S, rising to 5,160 ft/1,573 m in Cirque Mt.

Toro, Lake (TOH-ro), S Que., Canada, in the Laurentians, 90 mi/145 km N of Montreal; 18 mi/29 km long, 15 mi/24 km wide. Elev. 1,178 ft/359 m. Drains into St. Maurice R.

Toro Negro River (TO-ro NAI-gro), c.25 mi/40 km long, in central P.R., rises in the Cordillera Central NW of Villalba, flows N to the Manatí R. There is a hydroelectric plant along its lower course. Toro Negro Forest Reserve nearby includes tallest peak on isl., Cerro de Punta (4,389 ft/1,338 m).

Toro Peak, Calif.: see SANTA ROSA MOUNTAINS.

Toronto (tuh-RAHN-to), city (1991 pop. 635,395) officially the Toronto Metropolitan Municipality (1991 pop. 2,275,771; includes boroughs of Etobicoke, York, North York, East York, and Scarborough), S Ont., Canada, on L. Ontario; ⊙ Ont.; 43°39′N 79°23′W. It is the largest metropolitan area in Canada; a port of entry; and an important commercial, financial, and industrial center; also the country's banking and stock-exchange center and its chief wholesale-distribution point. Its importance as a port and transshipment point has increased since the opening (1959) of the St. Lawrence Seaway. The influx of many Eur. and Asian migrants has dramatically diversified the city's ethnic composition, along with rapid suburbanization and extensive redevelopment of the downtown and waterfront areas. Ont.'s wealth of raw materials and hydroelectric power make the city an industrial powerhouse. The city and its surrounding area produce more than ½ of Canada's mfg. goods. Slaughtering and meatpacking, printing and publishing, and the mfg. of aircraft, farm implements, electrical machinery, and metal prods. The city has the country's leading service sector and attracts a growing amount of high-technology businesses. It is also a major tourist center. The site was an early fur-trading post. The French built (1749) Fort Rouille here to counteract Brit. influence in the Niagara country, but the post was destroyed (1759) to prevent its occupation by the British. The British purchased the site from the Native Americans in 1787 and it became the home of many Amer. Loyalists. It was chosen by Sir John Simcoe in 1793 to be the capital of Upper Canada and was named York. In the War of 1812 the city was raided twice by the Americans, and many bldgs. were destroyed. In 1834 it was inc. as Toronto. The city was the scene of the insurrection led by William Lyon Mackenzie in 1873. Toronto has many bldgs. of historical interest and numerous parks. Exhibition Park is the site of the annual Can. Natl. Exhibition. The city hall is a modernistic structure completed in 1965. The 1,821 ft/554 m CN Tower (1976), a telecommunications spire, is the tallest freestanding structure in the world. The Skydome, a baseball stadium for the Toronto Blue Jays, was completed in 1989. The Univ. of Toronto was chartered in 1827 and opened in 1843 as King's Col. It was renamed in 1850 and is Canada's largest univ. and most important graduate research center. York Univ. and Ryerson Polytechnical Instit. are also in Toronto. Other notable institutions are the Pontifical Instit. of Medieval Studies; the Osgoode Hall law school; the Ontario Science Centre; and the Royal Ontario Mus., housing an important collection of Chin. art. Toronto has Anglican and R.C. bishoprics and is the hq. of the United Church of Canada.

Toronto, city (1990 pop. 6,127), Jefferson co., E Ohio, 7 mi/11 km N of Steubenville, and on Ohio R.; 40°27′N 80°36′W. Steel prods., clay prods., glass, machinery. Laid out 1818.

Toronto, town (1990 pop. 132), Clinton co., E Iowa, on Wapsipinicon R., and 29 mi/47 km NNW of Davenport; 41°53′N 90°51′W.

Toronto 1 (tuh-RAHN-to), village (1990 pop. 317), Woodson co., SE Kansas, on Verdigris R., and 28 mi/45 km WSW of Iola; 37°47′N 95°57′W. In livestock, grain, and oil area. Toronto Reservoir and State Park to S, for flood control and water conservation on the Verdigris. **2** village (1990 pop. 201), Deuel co., E S.Dak., 13 mi/21 km S of Clear L.; 44°34′N 96°38′W.

Toronto Islands (tuh-RAHN-to), group of isls., S Ont., Canada, in L. Ontario, just S of Toronto, separated from mainland by strip channels, within narrow spit of land (Centre Isl.) that forms Toronto harbor. Residential. Filtration plant. City park, beaches, amusement park. Ferry from downtown; airport.

Toronto, Lago, Mexico: seePRESA LA BOQUILLA.

Torquay (TOR-kwai), village (1991 pop. 285), SE Sask., Canada, 23 mi/37 km W of Estevan; 49°08′N 103°29′W. Mixed farming.

Torrance (TOR-uhns), county (□ 3,346 sq mi/8,666 sq km; 1990 pop. 10,285), central N.Mex.; ⊙ Estancia; 34°38′N 105°50′W. Agr. (corn, hay, alfalfa, beans, wheat, rye, oats, barley, pumpkins, apples); cattle area, watered by Laguna del Perro. Parts of Cibola Natl. Forest in W and S; part of Manzano Mts. in W; part of Isleta Indian Reservation in NW; Manzano State Park in W; Abo Pueblo Ruins and Quarai Pueblo Ruins units of Salinas Pueblo Missions Natl. Monument in W. Formed 1903.

Torrance, city (1990 pop. 133,107), Los Angeles co., SW Calif., suburb 15 mi/24 km SW of Los Angeles; 33°50′N 118°20′W. Borders on Pacific on SW. Aircraft, electronics, aluminum prods., steel, communications equip., food processing, construction machinery. Torrance Municipal Airport in S, Redondo State Beach to W; South Coast Botanical Gardens to S; Palos Verdes peninsula to S. Founded in 1911; developed as a planned industrial city. Inc. 1921.

Torreón (to-re-ON), city (1990 pop. 439,436) and township, Coahuila state, N Mexico, on the Nazas R., and on Mexico Highways 30 and 40; 25°34′N 103°25′W. It is the metropolis of the Laguna District. Cotton and wheat are the principal crops, and cattle raising is important. Industries include rubber mfg., iron and steel production, cotton and flour milling, and a brewery. The city is also one of the leading commercial and RR centers of N Mexico. Founded 1893.

Torreon (tor-ee-ON), uninc. village, Torrance co., central N.Mex., 32 mi/51 km SE of Albuquerque. Elev. 6,700 ft/2,042 m. In ranching, farming area. Pueblo ruins here. Part of Cibola Natl. Forest and Manzano Mts. to W; Mosca Peak 8 mi/12.9 km NW.

Torrey, village (1990 pop. 122), Wayne co., S central Utah, 15 mi/24 km ESE of Loa, and on Fremont R.; 38°17′N 111°25′W. Elev. 6,800 ft/2,073 m. Alfalfa; cattle; logging. Capitol Reef Natl. Park to E; Fishlake Natl. Forest to N; Dixie Natl. Forest to S.

Torrey Mountain, Mont.: see PIONEER MOUNTAINS.

Torreys Peak (14,267 ft/4,349 m), on border bet. Summit and Clear Creek cos., central Colo., on Continental Divide, in Front Range, c.45 mi/72 km W of Denver and SE of Loveland Pass; 39°38′N 105°49′W. Arapaho Natl. Forest (W); Pike Natl. Forest (E).

Torrington, city (1990 pop. 33,687), Litchfield co., NW Conn., on the Naugatuck R.; 41°49′N 73°07′W. It is the industrial and commercial hub of NW Conn. and is known for its metal (esp. brass) and machinery mfg. The 1st machine-made brass goods in the country were produced in Torrington in 1834. The city was also the site of the world's 1st condensed-milk plant; the process of homogenization was invented in Torrington. The abolitionist John Brown was born there; his birthplace burned in 1918, and the spot is marked by a plaque. Of interest are a wildlife sanctuary and conservation area, noted for its mt. laurel; and a mus. with early Amer. glass exhibits and a John Brown room. A branch of the Univ. of Conn. is in Torrington. Inc. 1740.

Torrington, town (1990 pop. 5,651), ⊙ Goshen co., SE Wyo., on North Platte R., near Nebr. state line, 75 mi/121 km NNE of Cheyenne; 42°04′N 104°10′W. Elev. 4,104 ft/1,251 m. Trade center for mining and irrigated agr. region; sugar beets, grain, beans, potatoes; livestock; mfg. (feeds, sugar-beet processing, printing and publishing, chemicals, fertilizer, concrete prods.). Oregon, Mormon, and Texas cattle trails converge here. Oil wells, coal mines in vicinity. Fossil beds nearby. Eastern Wyo. Community Col. here. Hawk Springs Reservoir and State Recreation Area to S.

Tortola, island (1991 pop. 13,232), B.V.I., about 1 mi/2.5 km NE of St. John (U.S.V.I.), ⊙ Road Town. Ferries connect port at West End with St. Thomas (U.S.V.I.). Highest point is Mt. Sage (1,800 ft/550 m). Produces sweet potatoes, avocados, bananas, sugarcane. Marine-yachting center at Nanny Cay.

Tortue, Île de la, Haiti: see TORTUGA.

Tortuga (TAWR-too-guh), village, W central Trinidad, Trinidad and Tobago, 8 mi/12.9 km NE of San Fernando. In cacao-growing region. Its Notre Dame de Montserrat has shrine of Black Virgin.

Tortuga (tor-TOO-gah) [Span. = turtle], island (□ c.70 sq mi/181 sq km), off N Haiti; 20°04′N 72°49′W. It was a notorious rendezvous of pirates in the 17th cent. It is called Île de la Tortue by the Haitians.

Tortuga Island (□ 2.5 sq mi/6.5 sq km), in Gulf of California, off E coast of Baja California peninsula, Baja California Sur, NW Mexico, 25 mi/40 km NE of Santa Rosalía; 3 mi/4.8 km long, 2 mi/3.2 km wide. Rocky, uninhabited; rises to 1,016 ft/310 m.

Tortugas (tor-TOO-guhs), uninc. village, Doña Ana co., S N.Mex. Community founded by Native Americans from Isleta del Sur near Juarez, Chihuahua, 2 mi/3.2 km SSE of Las Cruces, near Rio Grande. N.Mex. State Univ. to E; Tortugas Mt. (4,931 ft/1,503 m) to E.

Tortugas, Fla.: see DRY TORTUGAS.

Tortuguero Canal (tohr-too-GAI-ro), bet. Moín and Barra del Colorado, Costa Rica, on NE coast. Constructed to connect Moín (Limón) with Barra del Colorado and provide access to small coastal communities along the NE coast, such as Tortuguero and Parismina.

Tortuguero Lagoon (tor-too-GWAI-ro), N P.R., near the ocean, c.3 mi/4.8 km long. Freshwater lagoon fed by underground water. NE of Manatí. Former army training camp nearby.

Toston (TAHS-tuhn), village (1990 pop.100), Broadwater co., W central Mont., on Missouri R., and 41 mi/66 km SE of Helena. In irrigated grain and livestock region. Parts of Helena Natl. Forest to E and NW.

Totatiche (to-tah-TEE-che), town (1990 pop. 2,030), Jalisco, W Mexico, near Zacatecas border, 18 mi/29 km SW of Colotlán; 21°56′N 103°27′W. Elev. 5,807 ft/1,770 m. Grain, alfalfa; livestock.

Totolac (to-to-LAHK), town (1990 pop. 7,235), Tlaxcala, central Mexico, 2 mi/3.2 km W of Tlaxcala; 19°19′N 98°15′W. Elev. 7,244 ft/2,208 m. Grain, maguey, alfalfa; livestock. Also San Juan Totolac.

Totolapa (to-to-LAH-pah), town (1990 pop. 3,206), Chiapas, S Mexico, at S foot of Sierra de Hueytepec, 10 mi/16 km SSW of San Cristóbal de las Casas; 16°36′N 92°41′W. Cereals, fruit; livestock. Atzotzic-Maya community.

Totolapan (to-to-LAH-pahn), town (1990 pop. 3,797), Morelos, central Mexico, 22 mi/35 km ENE of Cuernavaca; 18°58′N 98°55′W. Elev. 6,260 ft/1,908 m. Sugarcane, fruit; livestock.

Totoltepec de Guerrero (to-TOL-te-pek), town (1990 pop. 900), Puebla, central Mexico, 13 mi/21 km ENE of Acatlán; 18°14′N 97°51′W. Elev. 4,347 ft/1,325 m. Cereals, sugarcane, livestock.

Totontepec Villa de Morelos (te-TON-te-pek VEE-yah de mo-RE-los), town (1990 pop. 1,745), E Oaxaca, Mexico, 37 mi/60 km NE of Tlacolula de Matamoros; 17°13′N 96°03′W. Elev. 6,070 ft/1,850 m. Mountainous terrain. Temperate climate. Agr. (corn, beans, mezcal, wheat, chile, fruits; cattle), woods. A Mixe-speaking town. Formerly known as Santa María Totontepec, Villa de Zertuche.

Tototlán (to-to-TLAHN), town (1990 pop. 9,207), Jalisco, central Mexico, 37 mi/60 km ESE of Guadalajara, on Mexico Highway 90; 20°33′N 102°48′W. Elev. 6,562 ft/2,000 m. Wheat-growing center.

Totowa (TO-tuh-wuh), borough (1990 pop. 10,177), Passaic co., NE N.J., a suburb just W of Paterson on the Passaic R.; 40°53′N 74°13′W. Diverse mfg. Inc. 1898.

Tottenham, village, S Ont., Canada, 30 mi/48 km NW of Toronto; 44°01′N 79°48′W. Dairying, grain.

Tottenville, a residential section of Staten Isl. borough of N.Y. city, SE N.Y., on S tip of Staten Isl., across Arthur Kill (bridged) from Perth Amboy, N.J.; 40°31′N 74°15′W. S terminus of Staten Isl. RR. Mfg. (telecommunications and navigational equip.). Billiou House (built 1680s), also known as Conference House, was the scene of an unsuccessful attempt to negotiate an end to the Revolutionary War.

Totutla (to-TOO-lahn), town (1990 pop. 2,843), Veracruz, E Mexico, in Sierra Madre Oriental, 4 mi/6.4 km N of Huatusco, on Mexico Highway 125; 19°13′N 96°56′W. Elev. 4,364 ft/1,330 m. Fruit.

Touchet (too-SHAI), uninc. village (1990 pop. 410), Walla Walla co., SE Wash., 16 mi/26 km W of Walla Walla, and 3 mi/4.8 km N of Oregon state line, near Walla Walla R. and mouth of Touchet R. Wheat, barley, oats, rye, grapes; hogs.

Touchet River, c.85 mi/137 km long, SE Wash.; rises in Umatilla Natl. Forest; flows NW, W, and S, past Dayton, Waitsburg, and Prescott, to Walla Walla R. at Touchet. Main stream c.65 mi/105 km long; North Fork c.25 mi/40 km long; South Fork c.20 mi/32 km long; both rise in Umatilla Natl. Forest, S Columbia co., and merge 2 mi/3.2 km S of Dayton.

Tougaloo (TOO-guh-loo), village, Hinds co., W Miss., 7 mi/11.3 km NNE of Jackson. Seat of Tougaloo Col. (founded 1867). Now part of city of Jackson (N part).

Toughkenamon (TUF-ke-NAH-muhn), uninc. town (1990 pop. 1,273), Chester co., SE Pa., 3 mi/4.8 km WSW of Kennett Square; 39°49′N 75°45′W. Mfg. (machinery); food processing. Agr. (dairying, livestock, poultry; soybeans, grain, mushrooms). New Garden Airport to W.

Touisset (too-ISS-et), resort village, in Bristol town, Bristol co., R.I., on Mount Hope Bay, 13 mi/21 km SE of Providence. Beach, sailing.

Touisset, Mass.: see SWANSEA.

Toulon (TWO-lahn), city (1990 pop. 1,328), ⊙ Stark co., N central Ill., 10 mi/16 km SSE of Kewanee; 41°05′N 89°51′W. In agr. (corn, soybeans, wheat; livestock, poultry) and bituminous-coal area. Rock Island State Trail nearby. Inc. 1859.

Toutle River (TOOT-uhl), c.60 mi/97 km long, Cowlitz co., SW Wash.; rises as North Fork (c.25 mi/40 km long) in Columbia Natl. Forest, formerly rose in Spirit L. until May 18, 1980, eruption of Mt. Saint Helens when debris on N slope buried upper stream bed; flows W to Cowlitz R. 3 mi/4.8 km N of Castle Rock. Receives South Fork (c.30 mi/48 km long), which rises on Mt. St. Helens, at Toutle village. During Mt. Saint Helens eruption, mud flows surged down both streams, especially North Fork, and debris remains in riverbed.

Tovey, village (1990 pp. 533), Christian co., central Ill., 9 mi/14.5 km WNW of Taylorville, on W arm of Sangchris L. reservoir; 39°35′N 89°27′W. Sangchris L. State Park to N. Also known as Humphrey.

Tow, uninc. village (1990 pop. 305), Llano co., S central Texas, 17 mi/27 km NE of Llano, on Colorado R., at head of L. Buchanan reservoir. Agr. and recreation area; winery.

Towanda (tuh-WAHN-duh), town (1990 pop. 1,289), Butler co., S Kansas, 8 mi/12.9 km W of El Dorado; 37°47′N 97°00′W. In cattle and grain region. Oil wells nearby.

Towanda (tah-WAN-dah), village (1990 pop. 856), McLean co., central Ill., 6 mi/9.7 km NE of Bloomington; 40°33′N 88°54′W. In rich agr. area.

Towanda (TO-wan-dah), borough (1990 pop. 3,242), ⊙ Bradford co., NE Pa., 29 mi/47 km SE of Elmira, N.Y., on Susquehanna R.; 41°46′N 76°27′W. Mfg. (chemicals and metals, crushed stone, printing and publishing); limestone; timber. Agr. (dairying). Sect. of Tioga State Forest to S; Mt. Pisgah State Park to W. Settled 1794, laid out 1812 as Meansville, inc. and renamed 1828.

Towaoc, village, Montezuma co., SW Colo., 13 mi/21 km SW of Cortez; 37°12′N 108°43′W. Agr. (sheep; wheat, hay). Mfg. (pottery). Residential and service center on Ute Mt. Indian Reservation. Mesa Verde Natl. Park to E.

Tower, village (1990 pop. 502), St. Louis co., NE Minn., 24 mi/39 km NNE of Virginia, on S shore of Vermilion L., at W end of Vermilion Iron Range; 47°48′N 92°17′W. In resort and iron-mining region. Light mfg. The 1st iron mines at Vermilion L. opened here 1884 (including Soudan Underground Mine, now in state park to N). Vermilion L. Indian Reservation to NW; Bear Head L. State Park to E; parts of Superior Natl. Forest to N and

SW; parts of Kabetogama State Forest to NW and SE; Pike R. enters Vermilion L. to W.

Tower City, village (1990 pop. 233), Cass co., E N.Dak., 22 mi/35 km W of Casselton; 46°55′N 97°40′W.

Tower City, borough (1990 pop. 1,518), Schuylkill co., E central Pa., 19 mi/31 km WSW of Pottsville, near Wiconisco Creek; 40°35′N 76°32′W. Mfg. (electronic equip., apparel). Agr. (grain; poultry, livestock, dairying). Laid out 1868; inc. 1892.

Tower Hill, village (1990 pop. 601), Shelby co., central Ill., 9 mi/14.5 km W of Shelbyville; 39°23′N 88°57′W. In farm area; grain milling.

Tower Lakes, village (1990 pop. 1,333), Lake co., NE Ill., residential suburb 37 mi/60 km NW of downtown Chicago, 4 mi/6.4 km NW of Lake Zürich; 42°13′N 88°09′W. Tower L. at center of community.

Towers Mountain, (7,628 ft/2,325 m), in Bradshaw Mts., central Ariz., 22 mi/35 km SSE of Prescott, in Prescott Natl. Forest; 34°14′N 112°22′W.

Town and Country, city (1990 pop. 9,519), St. Louis co., E Mo., suburb, mostly residential, 15 mi/24 km W of downtown St. Louis; 38°37′N 90°28′W. Site of Mo. Baptist Col.

Town Creek, town (1990 pop. 1,379), Lawrence co., NW Ala., near L. Wilson (in Tennessee R.), 16 mi/26 km NW of Moulton. Mfg. (wood prods., apparel); cotton ginning.

Town of Pines, town (1990 pop. 789), Porter co., NW Ind., suburb 3 mi/4.8 km WSW of Michigan City, 2 mi/3.2 km S of L. Michigan; 41°41′N 86°57′W. Indiana Dunes Natl. Lakeshore to N.

Towner, county (□ 1,042 sq mi/2,699 sq km; 1990 pop. 3,627), N N.Dak., borders on Manitoba, Canada, on N; ⊙ Cando; 48°41′N 99°15′W. Prairie, watered by creeks and streams. Agr. (wheat, barley, cattle). Formed 1883. Rock L. in N; Hurricane L. in extreme SW corner.

Towner, village (1990 pop. 669), ⊙ McHenry co., N central N.Dak., 41 mi/66 km E of Minot, on Souris R. (Mouse R.); 48°21′N 100°24′W. RR junction. Diversified agr. (hay, dairy prods., poultry, sunflowers, grain), cattle shipping.

Towns, county (□ 172 sq mi/445 sq km; 1990 pop. 6,754), NE Ga., on N.C. state line; ⊙ Hiawassee; 34°55′N 83°44′W. In Chattahoochee Natl. Forest and the Blue Ridge, rising to 4,784 ft/1,458 m at Brasstown Bald; drained by Hiwassee R., forming Chatuge L. (N). Mfg. (textiles, apparel). Agr. (corn, hay, potatoes, fruit); cattle, hogs; lumber. Resort area. The Appalachian Trail traverses E side of co. Formed 1856.

Towns, town, Telfair co., S central Ga., 9 mi/14.5 km ESE of McRae, and on Little Ocmulgee R.; 32°00′N 82°45′W.

Townsend (TOUN-zuhnd), resort city (1990 pop. 329), Blount co., E Tenn., on Little R., and 23 mi/37 km SSE of Knoxville; 35°41′N 83°45′W. Great Smoky Mts. Natl. Park is nearby.

Townsend 1 (TOUN-suhn), town (1990 pop. 8,496), Middlesex co., N Mass., 9 mi/14.5 km NE of Fitchburg, near N.H. state line; 42°40′N 71°43′W. Granite. Mfg. (plastic and needlecraft prods.). Includes village of Townsend Harbor. State forest. Settled 1676, inc. 1732. **2** town (1990 pop. 1,635), ⊙ Broadwater co., W central Mont., at upper (S) end of Canyon Ferry L. Reservoir, on Missouri R., and 30 mi/48 km SE of Helena; 46°19′N 111°31′W. Gold and silver mines. Agr. (dairying; wheat, barley, hay; cattle, hogs, sheep), timber. Mfg. (quick lime). Parts of Helena Natl. Forest to E and W. Broadwater County Mus. Founded 1883, inc. 1895.

Townsend, village (1990 pop. 322), New Castle co., N central Del., 3 mi/4.8 km S of Middletown; 39°23′N 75°41′W. Agr. area (grain, vegetables, fruit; livestock, poultry; dairying).

Townsend Harbor, Mass.: see TOWNSEND.

Townsends Inlet, SE N.J., navigable passage (bridged) entering Intracoastal Waterway and Townsends Sound from the Atlantic 2.5 mi/4 km S of Sea Isle City. Townsends Inlet village (resort), on S Ludlam Beach, is just N of inlet; to NW, sheltered from ocean by barrier beaches, is Townsends Sound (c.2.5 mi/4 km long), with Intracoastal Waterway passing along E edge.

Townshend (TOUNZ-end), town (1990 pop. 1,019), including Townshend village, Windham co., SE Vt., on

West R., and just N of Newfane; 43°04′N 72°39′W. Mfg. (wood prods., printing). Townshend State Forest here. Flood control dam on West R.

Townsville, uninc. village, Vance co., N N.C., 12 mi/19 km N of Henderson, near Va. state line. Kerr reservoir and its arms to N and E. Kerr L. State Recreation Area to SE.

Townville, borough (1990 pop. 358), Crawford co., NW Pa., 11 mi/23 km E of Meadville; 41°40′N 79°52′W. Mfg. (fabricated metal prods.). Agr. (corn, hay; livestock; dairying).

Towson, uninc. city (1990 pop. 49,445), ⊙ Baltimore co., N Md., a residential and industrial suburb of Baltimore; 39°24′N 76°37′W. Named for Colonial inn that was located here. Towson became the seat of Baltimore co. in 1850, and accommodates govt. and Blue Cross–Blue Shield offices as well as being the site of Goucher Col. and Towson State Univ. Settled c.1750.

Toxaway (TAHKS-uh-wai), uninc. village, Anderson co., NW S.C., residential area S of Anderson.

Toxey, town (1990 pop. 211), Choctaw co., SW Ala., 14 mi/23 km S of Butler; 31°54′N 88°18′W.

Toyah, village (1990 pop. 115), Reeves co., extreme W Texas, 19 mi/31 km SW of Pecos; 31°18′N 103°47′W. In ranching area (cattle, sheep).

Trabuco Highlands, uninc. town (1990 pop. 3,191), Orange co., S Calif., residential suburb 6 mi/9.7 km E of Mission Viejo, in Santa Ana Mts.; 33°37′N 117°34′W. Cleveland Natl. Forest to N and E.

Tracadie 1 (TRA-kuh-dee), village, NE N.S., Canada, on George Bay, 16 mi/26 km E of Antigonish. Fishing port. Acadian Fr. settlement. Has Trappist monastery (1825). **2** fishing village, N central P.E.I., Canada, on Tracadie Bay, 12 mi/19 km NE of Charlottetown.

Tracy, city (1990 pop. 33,558), San Joaquin co., central Calif., 15 mi/24 km SW of Stockton, in the San Joaquin valley, near Delta-Mendota Canal; 37°45′N 121°26′W. RR junction. Agr. (cattle, dairying; grapes, sugar beets, tomatoes, grain, fruit, nuts, vegetables; nursery prods.). Mfg. (furniture, chemicals, concrete prods., liquor, electronic equip., printing and publishing, paper prods.); food processing. A pumping plant in Tracy is part of the Central Valley project. Hetch Hetchy Aqueduct passes to S. Inc. 1910.

Tracy 1 town (1990 pop. 2,059), Lyon co., SW Minn., 17 mi/27 km SSE of Marshall; 44°14′N 95°37′W. Agr. trading center (soybeans, alfalfa, grain; livestock, dairying, poultry). Mfg. (construction materials, feeds, magnetic components, concrete). L. Shetek to S. Settled 1872; inc. as city 1893. **2** town (1990 pop. 287), Platte co., W Mo., Platte R. opposite Platte City; 39°22′N 94°47′W.

Tracy City, resort town (1990 pop. 1,556), Grundy co., SE central Tenn., in the Cumberlands, 30 mi/48 km WNW of Chattanooga; 35°15′N 85°45′W. In timber and coal region. Inc. since 1940.

Tradewater River, c.110 mi/177 km long, W Ky.; rises in N central Christian co.; flows generally NW, past Pennyville Forest State Resort Park and Lake Beshear reservoir (on tributary), past Dawson Springs, to Ohio R. 5 mi/8 km SW of Sturgis.

Trading Bay, S Alaska, on W shore of Cook Inlet, 60 mi/97 km WSW of Anchorage; 10 mi/16 km long, 30 mi/48 km wide; 60°55′N 151°33′W. Receives Chakachatna R.

Traer, town (1990 pop. 1,552), Tama co., central Iowa, near Wolf Creek, 23 mi/37 km SSW of Waterloo; 42°11′N 92°27′W. Mfg. (food, transportation equip., fabricated metal prods., concrete). State park nearby. Inc. 1875.

Trafalgar, town (1990 pop. 531), Johnson co., central Ind., 7 mi/11.3 km SW of Franklin; 39°25′N 86°09′W. In agr. area. Mfg. (wood prods.). Laid out 1850.

Trafford, town (1990 pop. 739), Jefferson co., N central Ala., 20 mi/32 km N of Birmingham; 33°49′N 86°45′W. Coal mining.

Trafford (TRA-fuhrd), borough (1990 pop. 3,345), Westmoreland and Allegheny cos., SW Pa., suburb 13 mi/21 km ESE of downtown Pittsburgh; 40°22′N 79°45′W. Mfg. (chemicals, machinery, electrical equip., printing). Agr. (corn, hay; dairying). Inc. 1904.

Trail, city (1991 pop. 7,919), SE B.C., Canada, on the Columbia R., just N of the Wash. border; 49°06′N 117°43′W. Mining area (lead, zinc, silver, gold); smelting center. Mfg. (chemicals).

Trail Creek, town (1990 pop. 2,463), La Porte co., NW Ind., S suburb of Michigan City, 9 mi/14.5 km NW of La Porte; 41°42′N 86°52′W.

Trail of Tears National Affiliated Area, N.C., Tenn., Ga., Ala., Okla., Ark. Commemorates the routes of forced migration of more than 15,000 Cherokee from their ancestral homes to Indian territory (now Okla. 1828–1845), also Choctaw, Creek, Chickasaw, and Seminole from other states. Authorized 1987.

Trail of the Lonesome Pine, SW Va. and SE Ky., name sometimes applied to scenic route (mainly following Ky. Highway 15 and U.S. Highway 23) across Cumberland Mts. (part of Appalachians Mts.) through region described in John Fox's novel *The Trail of the Lonesome Pine*, 36°56′N 82°24′W. Route extends SE from Wolfe co., E central Ky., crosses Pine Mt. ridge at Pound Gap, on Ky./Va. state line, then S and SW into Lee co., SW Va.

Traill, county (□ 862 sq mi/2,233 sq km; 1990 pop. 8,752), E N.Dak.; ⊙ Hillsboro; 47°27′N 97°10′W. Agr. area bounded E by Red R. of the North (Minn. state line); drained by Goose and Elm rivers. Agr. (wheat, corn, barley, soybeans, flax, beans; cattle, hogs) beet-sugar refining. Formed 1875.

Trainor (TRAI-nuhr), borough (1990 pop. 2,271), Delaware co., SE Pa., suburb 14 mi/23 km SW of downtown Philadelphia, 1 mi/1.6 km SW of Chester, on Delaware R.; 39°49′N 75°24′W. Mfg. (machinery, petroleum prods.).

Trammel, Lake, Nolen co., W Texas, impounded by dam in small Sweetwater Creek (a S tributary of Clear Fork of Brazos R.), c.40 mi/64 km W of Abilene; c.1 mi/1.6 km long.

Tramping Lake, village (1991 pop. 143), W Sask., Canada, 50 mi/80 km SW of North Battleford; 52°08′N 108°57′W. Wheat.

Trans-Canada Highway, c.4,800 mi/7,700 km long, S Canada; dedicated 1962; completed 1970. The world's longest natl. highway, it traverses N. Amer. from St. John's, N.F., to Victoria, B.C. Ferry routes form vital links at the E (to N.F.) and W (Vancouver Isl.) ends of the highway. Spur to P.E.I. via ferry; major spur serves N Ont.

Transcona (tran-SKO-nuh), city, SE Man., Canada; suburb of Winnipeg; 49°53′N 97°00′W.

Transquaking River (tarnz-KWAY-king), c.25 mi/40 km long, Dorchester co., E Md., on the Eastern Shore; rises just S of Secretary; flows through muskrat-trapping marshes to head of Fishing Bay.

Transylvania (tran-suhl-VAIN-yuh), county (□ 380 sq mi/984 sq km; 1990 pop. 25,520), W N.C.; ⊙ Brevard; 35°12′N 82°47′W. In Blue Ridge Mts.; bounded S by S.C. state line; large part of co. in Pisgah Natl. Forest in W and SW, includes Cradle of Forestry in Amer. Historic Site in N; drained by French Broad R. Limited agr. (vegetables, hay, corn, cattle); timber (oak, poplar, chestnut, hemlock). Resort region. Mfg. at Brevard and Pisgah Forest. Sassafras Mt. (3,560 ft/1,085 m) on S boundary, highest point in neighboring S.C. Looking Glass Falls in N (85 ft/26 m); Toxaway (123 ft/37 m), High (125 ft/38 m), and Rainbow (200 ft/61 m) falls in SW. Whitewater Falls (upper cascade 441 ft/134 m) in SW corner, highest falls in E U.S. Formed 1861.

Trappe, town (1990 pop. 974), Talbot co., E Md., 6 mi/9.7 km NNE of Cambridge; 38°40′N 76°04′W. Vegetable canneries. Some believe the name came from a Trappist monastery whose remains are believed to be in a farmhouse S of town. Others attribute it to an old tavern, "The Partridge Trap." Historic homes in the vicinity include Wilderness (c.1810), built by Daniel Martin, twice governor of Maryland (1829–1931) and Hampden, very early 18th cent. The site of Crosidare was the birthplace of John Dickinson, author of *Letters from a Pennsylvania Farmer*, an attack on Br. tax policies written in 1767. Dickinson served both as president of Delaware (1781) and president of Pennsylvania from 1782 to 1786. The house was destroyed in 1976.

Trappe (TRAP), borough (1990 pop. 2,115), Montgomery co., SE Pa., residential suburb 9 mi/14.5 km NW of Norristown; 40°11′N 75°28′W. Mfg. (electrical equip., computers). Agr. area (apples, grain; livestock; dairying). Oldest Lutheran church (1743) in Amer. here.

Trapper Creek, town (1990 est. pop. 700), S central Alaska, near Susitna R., 5 mi/8 km W of Talkeetna and Alaska RR. Located on George Parks Highway (Route 3), at junction of Petersville Road. Tourism. Mt. McKinley and Denali Natl. Park and Preserve 55 mi/89 km to NNW. General area has attracted new settlement since the highway's opening in 1971.

Trapper Peak, Mont.: see BITTERROOT RANGE.

Trappist, Ky.: see GETHSEMANE.

Traskwood, village (1990 pop. 488), Saline co., central Ark., 9 mi/14.5 km SSW of Benton; 34°27′N 92°40′W.

Travelers Rest, town (1990 pop. 3,069), Greenville co., NW S.C., suburb 8 mi/12.9 km N of Greenville, in foothills of the Blue Ridge Mts.; 34°58′N 82°26′W. Mfg. (chemicals, fabricated metal prods., paper prods.). Agr. (livestock, poultry; grain, tomatoes, soybeans, peaches).

Traverse (TRA-vuhrs), county (□ 585 sq mi/1,515 sq km; 1990 pop. 4,463), W Minn.; ⊙ Wheaton; 45°46′N 96°28′E. Area bounded on W by S.Dak. and N.Dak.; boundary formed by Traverse and Mud L. reservoirs (S.Dak. on Bois de Sioux R.) and by Bois de Sioux R. (S.Dak. and N.Dak). Watered by Mustinka R. and its West Branch. Agr. (alfalfa, wheat, corn, oats, barley, soybeans, sugar beets, beans, sunflowers; hogs, sheep). Formed 1862.

Traverse, Cape, on S coast of P.E.I., Canada, at narrowest point of Northumberland Strait, 3 mi/5 km SE of Port Borden, and 9 mi/14 km NE of Cape Tormentine, N.B.; 46°13′N 63°40′W.

Traverse City, city (1990 pop. 15,155), ⊙ Grand Traverse co., N Mich., 110 mi/177 km N of Grand Rapids, at the head of the West Arm of Grand Traverse Bay; 44°45′N 85°35′W. In a resort and cherry-growing region (esp. Old Mission Peninsula to N), with annual cherry festival. Tourism and food processing are major industries; mfg. (transportation equip., consumer goods, sand and gravel, fabricated metal prods.). Protestant missionaries came to the area in 1839. The production of lumber was the major economic activity until c.1915, when the supply was depleted and farming began. Northwestern Michigan Col. (2-year); Interlochen State Park and Center for the Arts to SW; Traverse City State Park and Holiday Ski Area to E; Sleeping Bear Dunes Natl. Lakeshore to NW on Leelanau Peninsula. Inc. 1881.

Traverse, Lake (TRA-vuhrs), on the Minn.-S.Dak. state line; c.30 mi/48 km long. Drained to the NE into Mud L. by the Bois de Sioux R., impounded by White Rock Dam (1948). Lake is fed by Mustinka R. from NE at its NE end, 1 mi/1.6 km E of its outflow, also by small streams from NW and SE.

Travis, county (□ 1,022 sq mi/2,647 sq km; 1990 pop. 576,407), S central Texas; ⊙ Austin; 30°19′N 97°46′W. Crossed SW-NE by Balcones Escarpment; drained by Colorado R. (power, flood-control dams). Agr. (cotton, grain sorghum, pecans) in E and SE; dairying; ranching (hogs, horses, cattle) in hilly W and NW; mohair, wool marketed. Lime, sand and gravel, stone; oil and gas. Mfg., processing at Austin. Seat of Univ. of Texas, and commercial center. Austin L. and L. Travis in W; recreational areas among lakes, hills of W. Formed 1840.

Travis, a residential sect. of Staten Isl. borough of N.Y. city, SE N.Y., on W Staten Isl., near Arthur Kill; 40°36′N 74°10′W.

Travis Air Force Base, Calif.: see FAIRFIELD.

Travis, Lake, reservoir (□ 45 sq mi/117 sq km), at Marshall Ford, Travis and Burnet cos., S central Texas, on Colorado R., 12 mi/19 km NW of Austin; c.50 mi/80 km long; 30°24′N 97°53′W. Pedernales R. forms 5-mi/8-km S arm. Marble Falls Dam at NW tip. Max. capacity 3,223,000 acre-ft. Formed by Mansfield (formerly Marshall Ford) Dam, built (1942) for flood control, power generation, water supply, and irrigation.

Treadwell, village, SE Alaska, on Douglas Isl., just SE of Douglas. Mining settlement, largely abandoned. The gold mines here, once among the richest in Alaska, operated from 1881 to 1917, when a cave-in halted operations.

Treasure, county (□ 984 sq mi/2,549 sq km; 1990 pop. 874), S central Mont.; ⊙ Hysham; 46°12′N 107°16′W. Bighorn R. forms part of W boundary. Agr. area drained by Yellowstone R. (wheat, barley, corn, sugar beets, beans, hay; cattle, sheep). Formed 1919.

Treasure Coast, local name for the lower middle Atlantic coast of Fla. bet. Jupiter on the S and Melbourne on the N. Includes resort cities of Vero Beach, Fort Pierce, Jensen Beach, and Juno Beach.

Treasure Island, town (□ 5 sq mi/13 sq km; 1990 pop. 7,266), Pinellas co., W central Fla., 7 mi/11.3 km W of St. Petersburg, on Gulf of Mexico; 27°46′N 82°46′W.

Treasure Island, artificial island in San Francisco Bay, San Francisco co., W Calif., 4 mi/6.4 km NE of downtown San Francisco, 6 mi/9.7 km WNW of downtown Oakland, part of San Francisco city, just N of Yerba Buena Isl. (land bridge); 400 acres/162 ha. Constructed as site of Golden Gate Internatl. Exposition (1939–1940). Both isls. became Treasure Island Naval Air Station in 1941, scheduled by Pentagon to be closed. Street accessible to both sides of bay via Bay Bridge.

Treasure Lake, uninc. town (1990 pop. 2,185), Clearfield co., central Pa., residential suburb 4 mi/6.4 km NE of DuBois; 41°10′N 78°43′W.

Treasure Mountain, peak (13,528 ft/4,123 m) in Rocky Mts., N Gunnison co., W central Colo., 14 mi/23 km NW of Crested Butte; 39°01′N 107°07′W.

Treat's Island, Maine: see LUBEC.

Tred Avon River (tred AY-von), c.12 mi/19 km long, E Md.; irregular estuary entering Choptank R. in central Talbot co., on the Eastern Shore. Navigable to just below Easton. The name is presumably a corruption of Third Haven.

Treece (TREES), village (1990 pop. 172), Cherokee co., extreme SE Kansas, at Okla. state line, 11 mi/18 km S of Columbus; 37°00′N 94°50′W.

Trego (TREE-go), county (□ 899 sq mi/2,328 sq km; 1990 pop. 3,694), W central Kansas; ⊙ Wakeeney; 38°55′N 99°51′W. Located in Smoky Hills region, drained in N by Saline R., in S by Smoky Hill R. Agr. (wheat, sorghum, corn, cattle). Cedar Bluff Reservoir and State Park in S. Formed 1879.

Treherne (truh-HUHRN), village (1991 pop. 661), S Man., Canada, 30 mi/48 km SW of Portage la Prairie, at N end of Pembina Mts.; 49°38′N 98°42′W. Oil and gas wells, flour mills.

Trelawny, parish (1991 pop. 70,463), Cornwall co., W central and N Jamaica; ⊙ Falmouth; 18°30′N–18°15′N 77°46′W–77°27′W. A semi-arid region with limestone hills and plateaus, bounded W by St. James, S by the Cockpit Country with Manchester and Elizabeth parishes, E by St. Ann parish. Watered by Martha Brae R. Along the coast were, in colonial times, large sugar estates; with their decline the parish lost much of its importance. Agr (sugarcane, coffee, bananas, ginger, pimento, honey, rum, dyewood; mules).

Tremblant, Mount (TREHM-bluhnt), **Mont Tremblant** (mo trah-BLAH), or **Trembling Mountain**, peak (3,150 ft/960 m), SW Que., Canada, in the Laurentians, 70 mi/113 km NW of Montreal in Montagne Tremblante Park, a popular ski resort. At its foot is Trembling L. or L. de la Montagne Tremblante (7 mi/11 km long).

Trembleur Lake (□ 45 sq mi/117 sq km), central B.C., Canada, N of Stewart L., 75 mi/121 km E of Smithers; 20 mi/32 km long, 2 mi/3 km–3 mi/5 km wide. Drains SE into Stuart L.

Tremont (TREM-ahnt), resort town (1990 pop. 1,324), Hancock co., S Maine, on S Mt. Desert Isl.; 44°16′N 68°25′W. Fishing. Inc. 1848.

Tremont 1 (TREE-mont), village (1990 pop. 2,088), Tazewell co., central Ill., 13 mi/21 km SSE of Peoria; 40°31′N 89°29′W. In agr. area. **2** village (1990 pop. 342), Itawamba co., NE Miss., 8 mi/12.9 km ESE of Fulton, near Ala. state line; 34°13′N 88°15′W. Agr. area (cotton, corn, soybeans; poultry, cattle); timber. Mfg. (machinery, apparel); sand and gravel processing.

Tremont (TREE-mahnt), borough (1990 pop. 1,814),

Schuylkill co., E central Pa., 10 mi/16 km WSW of Pottsville, on Good Spring Creek; 40°37′N 76°23′W. Mfg. (concrete prods.); anthracite coal. Swatara State Park to SW. Laid out 1844, inc. 1866.

Tremont City, village (1990 pop. 493), Clark co., W central Ohio, 6 mi/10 km N of Springfield, near Mad R.; 40°01′N 83°50′W.

Tremonton (TREE-mahn-tuhn), town (1990 pop. 4,264), Box Elder co., N Utah, near Bear R., and 16 mi/26 km NNW of Brigham City; 41°43′N 112°10′W. Elev. 4,322 ft/1,317 m. Processing point in sugar-beet and wheat, barley, alfalfa area; cattle, sheep; dairying. Hq. of La-Z-Boy Chair Company Salt Creek Waterfowl Management Area to SW; Wasatch Range and Wasatch Natl. Forest to E. Settled 1888; inc. 1906.

Trempealeau (TREM-pah-lo), county (□ 742 sq mi/1,922 sq km; 1990 pop. 25,263), W Wis.; ⊙ Whitehall; 44°17′N 91°20′W. Bounded partly on W by Trempealeau R., SW by the Mississippi R. (Minn. state line), SE by Black R.; drained by Buffalo, Black, and Trempealeau rivers. Agr. (dairying; barley, oats, corn, soybeans, alfalfa, hay, tobacco; cattle, hogs, sheep, poultry); timber. Processing of farm prods. Includes Perrot State Park and Great River State Trail in S, on Mississippi R, Buffalo R. State Trail in N; Viking Skyline Ski Area in N. Formed 1854.

Trempealeau (TREM-pah-lo), town (1990 pop. 1,039), Trempealeau co., W Wis., on the Mississippi at Lock and Dam No. 6, and 16 mi/26 km NNW of La Crosse, in hilly area; 44°00′N 91°26′W. Mfg. (machinery). On Great River State Trail. Trempealeau Bluffs, Perrot State Park to NW, Native Amer. mounds, and site of old Fr. fort are nearby. Upper Mississippi Natl. Wildlife and Fish Refuge.

Trempealeau River (TREM-pah-lo), c.70 mi/113 km long, W Wis.; rises in Jackson co.; flows W, past Whitehall, then SW, past Arcadia, to the Mississippi just E of Winona, Minn.

Trenche River (trash), 75 mi/121 km long, central Que., Canada; rises in Laurentian Plateau 50 mi/80 km W of L. St. John; flows S to the Saint Maurice 22 mi/35 km N of La Tuque. Hydroelectric plant (completed 1950) at Trenche near junction with the Saint Maurice.

Trent 1 village (1990 pop. 211), Moody co., E S.Dak., 10 mi/16 km S of Flandreau, and on Big Sioux R.; 43°54′N 96°39′W. **2** village (1990 pop. 319), Taylor co., W central Texas, 22 mi/35 km W of Abilene; 32°29′N 100°07′W. In cotton, cattle area.

Trent Canal, waterway system, 240 mi/386 km long, S Ont., Canada, connecting L. Ontario, from the Bay of Quinte, with L. Huron at Georgian Bay; built 1833–1848. It utilizes the Trent R. to Rice L., the Otonabee R. through Peterborough, the Kawartha Lakes and artificial channels to L. Simcoe and L. Couchiching, and the Severn R. to Georgian Bay. The system, with numerous dams and locks, has only 20 mi/32 km of artificial channels. It was designed primarily to shorten the shipping route bet. lakes Ontario and Huron, but has proved more valuable as a source of water power. Used mainly by pleasure craft, it is open to navigation from May to Oct.

Trent River, 150 mi/241 km long, SE Ont., Canada; issues from Rice L.; flows in a winding course E and S, past Campbellford, to Bay of Quinte at Trenton. Forms part of Trent Canal system, which links Georgian Bay and L. Ontario.

Trent River, c.80 mi/129 km long, E N.C.; rises at Duplin-Lenoir co. line; flows generally E past Trenton and Pollocksville, to Neuse R. at New Bern.

Trent Woods, town (1990 pop. 2,366), Craven co., E N.C., residential suburb 4 mi/6.4 km WSW of New Bern, on Trent R.; 35°04′N 77°05′W. Croatan Natl. Forest to S. Agr. area (tobacco, cotton, peanuts, grain; poultry, livestock).

Trenton 1 town (1991 pop. 2,957), N N.S., Canada, on East R. just N of New Glasgow. Mfg. (transportation equip., fabricated metal prods.). **2** town (1991 pop. 16,908), SE Ont., Canada, on the Bay of Quinte at the mouth of the Trent R., and at the S end of the Trent Canal. Mfg. (textiles, electronic equip., paper prods., metal prods.). A Royal Can. Air Force base is to the E.

Trenton 1 city (1990 pop. 2,481), Clinton co., SW Ill., 18 mi/29 km W of Carlyle; 38°36′N 89°40′W. In agr. region (corn, wheat; livestock, poultry). Inc. 1865. **2** city (1990 pop. 20,586), Wayne co., SE Mich., suburb 14 mi/23 km SSW of downtown Detroit, on the Trenton Channel of Detroit R. opposite Grosse Ile.; 42°08′N 83°11′W. In a farm area. An early river port. Mfg. (fabricated metal prods., chemicals, transportation equip.). Grosse Ile Municipal Airport to SE. Settled 1816, inc. as a city 1957. **3** city (1990 pop. 6,129), ⊙ Grundy co., N Mo., on Thompson R., and 20 mi/32 km N of Chillicothe; 40°04′N 93°35′W. Agr. (corn, wheat; cattle, sheep). Mfg. (fabricated metal prods., food, concrete). Grain and livestock market. Regional shopping and service center. North Central Col. Crowder State Park to NW. Ruskin Col. (a socialist experiment) here 1897–1905. Laid out 1841. **4** city (1990 pop. 88,675), ⊙ N.J. (since 1790) and of Mercer co. (since 1719), W N.J., at the head of navigation on the Delaware R.; 40°13′N 74°45′W. Situated bet. Philadelphia and N.Y. city, it is an important transportation hub. Its pottery industry dates from Colonial times. Other leading mfg. (fabricated metal prods., rubber goods, textiles, plastics). Trenton's pop. as well as industrial production have steadily declined since 1970; however, suburban development occurred in the 1980s, especially to the city's NE, and there had been some downtown redevelopment. The settlement was 1st called the Falls, then Stacy's Mills, and finally Trenton. In the Amer. Revolution, Trenton was the scene of a battle when Washington crossed (Dec. 25, 1776) the ice-clogged Delaware and surprised and captured (Dec. 26) 918 Hessians. The Americans, avoiding a Br. relief force led by Cornwallis, then struck at Princeton. A 155-ft/47-m granite monument topped by a statue of Washington commemorates the battle, and the place where the Americans crossed the Delaware is marked in a state park N of the city. Trenton grew as a commercial center and became the site of many industries; the famous Roebling Works, where wire rope is mfg., was est. in 1848. The city's noteworthy bldgs. include the golden-domed capitol (1792), much remodeled and enlarged; the capitol annex (1931); the state cultural center, with a mus., planetarium, and state lib.; the World War I memorial bldg. (1932); the old barracks, built in 1758 and restored as a mus.; and the William Trent House (1719), the city's oldest standing bldg., also a mus. The explorer Zebulon Pike was born in Lamberton, now part of Trenton. In the city are various state institutions. Six Flags Great Adventure and Safari Park in nearby Jackson to E. Settled by Friends 1679, inc. as a city 1792. **5** city (1990 pop. 6,189), Butler co., SW Ohio, 10 mi/16 km NE of Hamilton; 39°28′N 84°28′W. **6** city (1990 pop. 4,836), ⊙ Gibson co., NW Tenn., on North Fork of Forked Deer R., and 25 mi/40 km E of Dyersburg, 35°59′N 88°56′W. In cotton-, strawberry-, and cabbage-growing area, Mfg. (textiles, motors), lumber milling.

Trenton 1 town (□ 1 sq mi/2.6 sq km; 1990 pop. 1,287), ⊙ Gilchrist co., N central Fla., 30 mi/48 km W of Gainesville; 29°36′N 82°49′W. Lumbering, farming. **2** town (1990 pop. 1,994), ⊙ Dade co., extreme NW Ga., 16 mi/26 km SW of Chattanooga, Tenn., at foot of Lookout Mt.; 34°52′N 85°31′W. Mfg. (textiles, fabricated metal prods., lumber). **3** town (1990 pop. 1,060), Hancock co., S Maine, at mouth of Union R., just SSE of Ellsworth; 44°25′N 68°24′W. In fishing, resort area.

Trenton 1 village (1990 pop. 378), Todd co., S Ky., near Tenn. state line, 16 mi/26 km SE of Hopkinsville; 36°43′N 87°15′W. In agr. area (grain, tobacco; livestock, poultry; dairying). Mfg. (machinery, grain elevators). **2** village (1990 pop. 656), ⊙ Hitchcock co., S Nebr., 22 mi/35 km W of McCook, and on Republican R; 40°10′N 101°00′W. Agr. (grain, livestock; dairy and poultry prods.). Massacre Canyon Monument to NE; Swanson Reservoir and State Recreation Area to W. **3** village (1990 pop. 248), ⊙ Jones co., SE N.C., 15 mi/24 km SE of Kinston, on Trent R.; 35°03′N 77°20′W. Agr. (tobacco, cotton, peanuts, grain; livestock). Mfg. (apparel). Croatan Natl. Forest to E. Hoffmann Forest to S. **4** village (1990 pop. 303), Edgefield co., W S.C., 7 mi/11.3 km ESE of Edgefield; 33°44′N 81°50′W. Mfg. (plastic prods., textiles). Agr. (poultry, livestock; dairying; grain, peaches). **5** village (1990 pop. 655), Fannin co., NE Texas, 13 mi/21 km SW of Bonham; 33°25′N 96°20′W. Shipping point in agr. area (cotton, peanuts; cattle). Mfg. (plastic prods., fixtures). **6** village (1990 pop. 464), Cache co., N Utah, 16 mi/26 km NNW of Logan; 41°54′N 111°56′W. Elev. 4,461 ft/1,360 m. Wheat, barley; cattle; dairying.

Trenton Dam, Nebr.: see SWANSON RESERVOIR.

Trenton Falls, N.Y.: see WEST CANADA CREEK.

Trentwood, uninc. town (1990 pop. 4,060), Spokane co., E Wash., residential suburb 10 mi/16 km ENE of downtown Spokane, on Spokane R.; 47°42′N 117°13′W. RR junction. Vegetables, wheat, alfalfa; cattle, sheep. Mfg. (aluminum).

Trepassey Bay (truh-PA-see), inlet of the Atlantic, SE N.F., Canada, on S coast of Avalon Peninsula, 65 mi/105 km SSW of St. John's; 10 mi/16 km long, 15 mi/24 km wide at entrance; 46°40′N 53°22′W. At head is fishing town of Trepassey (1991 pop. 1,198).

Tres Cruces, Cerro, peak (10,308 ft/3,142 m) in Chiapas, S Mexico, in main range of Sierra Madre, 15 mi/24 km NW of Motozintla de Mendoza; 17°38′N 96°48′W.

Tres Hermanas Mountains (trais er-MAWN-uhs), (max.5,805 ft/1,769 m), in Luna co., SW N.Mex., near Mex. border. Gold, silver, copper, and onyx mines.

Tres Marías, Las (tres mah-REE-ahs, lahs), archipelago, in the Pacific Ocean, c.60 mi/97 km W of Nayarit state, Mexico; 19°04′N 99°13′W. Elev. 2,018 ft/615 m. Of the 4 isls., 2 (María Madre, which is the largest (c.56 sq mi/145 sq km) and is also a federal penal colony, and María Magdalena) produce maguey, salt, and lumber. María Cleófahs and San Juanito complete the group.

Tres Piedras (trais pee-E-druhs), village, Taos co., N N.Mex., 28 mi/45 km NW of Taos, in S foothills of San Juan Mts. Elev. 8,081 ft/2,463. Agr. (cattle, sheep; grain, potatoes). San Juan Mts. run N-S to W; San Antonio Peak (10,908 ft/3,325 m) to N; at E edge of sect. of Carson Natl. Forest.

Tres Valles (tres VAH-yes), village/congregación (1990 pop. 15,635) and township, ⊙ Tres Valles municipio, Veracruz, SE Mexico, Gulf lowland, 19 mi/31 km SE of Tierra Blanca; 18°18′N 96°09′W. RR junction; banana and mango growing.

Tres Zapotes (tres sah-PO-tes), village (1990 est. pop. 854), SE Veracruz, E Mexico, 15 mi/24 km W of San Andrés Tuxtla, near Cerro de las Mesas on N edge of Tuxtlas Mts. (in former Olmec heartland); 18°30′N 95°30′W. Pre-Maya monument dating from 381 B.C.–31 B.C. was found here (1939) near a colossal Olmec stone head. Evidence here of early writing.

Tresckow (TRES-ko), uninc. town (1990 pop. 1,033), Banks township, Carbon co., E central Pa., 3 mi/4.8 km S of Hazleton; 40°55′N 75°58′W. In former anthracite coal-mining region.

Treutlen (TROOT-len), county (□ 202 sq mi/523 sq km; 1990 pop. 5,994), E central Ga.; ⊙ Soperton; 32°24′N 82°34′W. Bounded SW by Oconee R. Mfg. (apparel, textiles). Coastal plain agr. (tobacco, corn, peanuts, wheat, cotton, soybeans; cattle, hogs). Formed 1917.

Trevilians (truh-VIL-yenz), uninc. village, Louisa co., central Va., 22 mi/35 km E of Charlottesville, 5 mi/8 km NW of Louisa; 38°03′N 78°04′W. Agr. (dairying; cattle; grain, tobacco). Site of Civil War Battle of Trevilians, Confederate victory (June 1864).

Trevor, village, Kenosha co., SE Wis., 15 mi/24 km WSW of Kenosha, on Ill. state line. Located in small lakes area. Recreation. Mfg. (cork and rubber prods.).

Trevorton (TRE-vuhr-tuhn), village (1990 pop. 2,058), Zerbe township, Northumberland co., E central Pa., 5 mi/8 km W of Shamokin, on Zerbe Run; 40°46′N 76°40′W. Anthracite-coal region. Mfg. (apparel).

Treynor, town (1990 pop. 897), Pottawattamie co., SW Iowa, 14 mi/23 km ESE of Council Bluffs; 41°13′N 95°36′W.

Trezevant (TREH-zi-vuhnt), town (1990 pop. 874), Carroll co., NW Tenn., 11 mi/18 km W of Huntingdon, 36°01′N 88°37′W. In farm area.

Tri Lakes, village (1990 pop. 3,299), Whitley co., NE Ind., 7 mi/11.3 km NNE of Columbia City; 41°13′N 85°29′W.

Agr. (soybeans, corn, hay; cattle; dairying). Several small lakes in area. Recreation.

Triadelphia (trei-uh-DEL-fee-uh), town (1990 pop. 835), Ohio co., W.Va., 5 mi/8 km E of Wheeling; 40°02′N 80°37′W. Agr. (grain); livestock; dairying. Bear Rocks Lakes Wildlife Management Area to E.

Triangle, uninc. town (1990 pop. 4,740), Prince William co., NE Va., 18 mi/29 km SSE of Manassas, near Potomac R.; 38°32′N 77°18′W. Quantico Marine Corps Base, Quantico Natl. Veterans Cemetery to S. Marine Corps Mus. to SE. Leesylvania State Park to NE; Prince William Forest Park to NW.

Triangles, The, reef (c.12 mi/19 km long) of several islets in Gulf of Mexico, 115 mi/185 km W of Celestún, Yucátan; 20°58′N 92°19′W. Coral formed from nearby coast of Campeche. Lighthouse at 20°58′N 92°20′W.

Tribbey (TRIB-ee), village (1990 pop. 288), Pottawatomie co., central Okla., 17 mi/27 km SSW of Shawnee; 35°05′N 97°05′W. Agr. area.

Tribeca, section of borough of Manhattan, N.Y. city, SE N.Y., bounded on N by Canal St., Broadway on E, Vesey St. on S, and West St. on W; 40°43′N 74°00′W. This is one of Lower Manhattan's oldest and most distinctive dists.; name derives from "Triangle Below Canal St." An early-19th-cent. residential area, it soon became N.Y. city's prime wholesaling market for textiles and foods; stores, warehouses, lofts, and factories were constructed to meet the demands of business. By early 20th cent., however, it had become a forgotten, neglected backwater as the city continued growing in a N direction. The Washington Market Urban Renewal Project (1960s) displaced many businesses, and many industrial architectural treasures were demolished, esp. in the SW part. In 1970s artists began moving into large loft spaces in the remaining bldgs., attracted by low rents. The city, hoping both to retain light mfg. and to avoid the construction of high-rise bldgs. in this neighborhood, required artists who lived here to be certified by the Dept. of Cultural Affairs. Despite the upscale shops that have crept in with the gentrification of the dist., the gritty industrial-commercial character is evident. There is a 90-block Historical Dist., which has the most spectacular concentration of commercial architecture in America. Marble-fronted bldgs. (built c.1800–1930), many with intricate cast-iron structures and facades, exhibit a rich, eclectic collection of Federal, Art Deco, Italianate, Romanesque Revival, and neo-Grecian styles.

Tribes Hill, village (□ 2 sq mi/5.2 sq km; 1990 pop. 1,060), Montgomery co., E central N.Y., on Mohawk R., and 5 mi/8 km W of Amsterdam; 42°57′N 74°17′W.

Triborough Bridge, a 3.5-mi/5.6-km complex of fixed, lift, and suspension bridges and viaducts connecting the boroughs of Manhattan, Queens, and Brooklyn, N.Y. city, SE N.Y., crosses Wards and Randalls isls., as well as the Harlem R. and stretches of the East R. known as the Bronx Kills; 40°47′N 73°56′W. Designed by Aymar Embury II and engineered by one of the world's foremost bridge engineers, O. H. Ammann (who also engineered the George Washington, Bronx-Whitestone, and Verrazano-Narrows bridges). The Triborough Bridge was begun in 1929, but because of the Great Depression was not completed until 1936; the total cost was $44.2 million. The Triborough Bridge was envisioned by N.Y. city park commissioner Robert Moses as a vital link in the highway system to connect the East Side Drive extension along Manhattan's E side waterfront to the Major Deegan Expressway heading N in the Bronx.

Tribune (TRIB-yoon), town (1990 pop. 918), ⊙ Greeley co., W Kansas, 55 mi/89 km NW of Garden City; 38°28′N 101°45′W. Elev. 3,543 ft/1,080 m. Grain, wheat, sorghum; cattle.

Tricorner Knob (5,960 ft/1,817 m), W N.C., peak of Great Smoky Mts., 15 mi/24 km E of Gatlinburg, Tenn.; 35°41′N 83°15′W.

Trident (TREI-dent), village (1990 pop. 35), Gallatin co., SW Mont., 28 mi/45 km NW of Bozeman, on Missouri R. Its name derives from confluence of Gallatin, Jefferson, and Madison rivers nearby. Missouri Headwaters State Park to SW. Agr. (wheat, hay, cattle). Mfg. (cement).

Trident Park (10,141 ft/3,091 m), SE B.C., Canada, in Selkirk Mts., on W edge of Hamber Provincial Park, 60 mi/97 km N of Revelstoke; 51°53′N 118°08′W.

Trigg, county (□ 481 sq mi/1,246 sq km; 1990 pop. 10,361), SW Ky.; ⊙ Cadiz; 36°48′N 87°52′W. Bounded S by state of Tenn., W by Tennessee R. (Kentucky L. Reservoir); drained by Cumberland (L. Barkley reservoir), and Little and Muddy Fork Little rivers. Gently rolling agr. area (tobacco, wheat, corn, hay, alfalfa, soybeans; hogs, cattle); limestone quarries; timber. Part of Land Between the Lakes Recreational Area in W (TVA); part of Fort Campbell Military Reservation in SE (extends into Tenn.); L. Barkley State Resort Park in W center. Formed 1820.

Trigo Mountains (2,767 ft/843 m), La Paz co., SW Ariz., near Colorado R. (Calif. state line). N extension is Dome Rock Range.

Trimble, county (□ 156 sq mi/404 sq km; 1990 pop. 6,090), N Ky.; ⊙ Bedford; 38°36′N 85°20′W. Bounded W and N by Ohio R. (Ind. state line); drained by Little Kentucky R. Gently rolling upland agr. area (burley tobacco, hay, alfalfa, soybeans, wheat, corn; cattle, poultry; dairying), in N part of Bluegrass region. Timber; stone quarries; sand and gravel. Formed 1837.

Trimble 1 town (1990 pop. 405), Clinton co., NW Mo., 10 mi/16 km SW of Plattsburg; 39°28′N 94°33′W. Smithville Lake to E. **2** town (1990 pop. 694), on Dyer-Obion co. line, NW Tenn., 16 mi/26 km NE of Dyersburg, 36°12′N 89°11′W. In farm area.

Trimble, village (1990 pop. 441), Athens co., SE Ohio, 10 mi/16 km N of Athens, and on small Sunday Creek; 39°29′N 82°04′W.

Trimont (TREI-mawnt), village (1990 pop. 745), Martin co., S Minn., 15 mi/24 km NW of Fairmont; 43°45′N 94°43′E. Near Cedar Creek, forms Cedar L. to W; Little Twin and Big Twin lakes to SW. In grain, livestock, and poultry area. Soybeans; mfg. (meat processing fertilizers, bin level indicator switches, mugs, and specialties). Formed by merger of Monterey and Triumph in late 1950s.

Trimountain, village, Houghton co., NW upper peninsula, Mich., 7 mi/11.3 km SW of Houghton, on Keweenaw Peninsula; 47°03′N 88°39′W.

Trimuph, Minn.: see TRIMONT.

Trinchera, village, Las Animas co., S Colo., 27 mi/43 km ESE of Trinidad, on Trinchera Creek, near N.Mex. state line. Elev. 5,800 ft/1,768 m. Livestock-shipping point. Coal and oil extraction area.

Trinchera Creek, c.50 mi/80 km long, Corrilla co., S Colo.; rises in Sangre de Cristo Mts.; flows W, past Fort Garland, to the Rio Grande 12 mi/19 km SSE of Alamosa. Small reservoirs, Mountain Home Reservoir to SE at Fort Garland, and Smith Reservoir to SW. There is also a Trinchera Creek (c.18 mi/29 km) to E in Las Animas co., Colo.; rises at Colo.-N.Mex. boundary; flows NNE past village of Trinchera to Purgatoire R.

Trincheras (treen-CHE-rahs), town (1990 pop. 1,241), N Sonora state, Mexico, 43 mi/69 km ESE of Caborca, on RR; 30°23′N 111°33′W. Flat terrain with gradual elevs. of 1,969 ft/600 m, on the Magdalena R. Dry desert climate with summer rains.

Tring Jonction (zhohk-SYOH), village (1991 pop. 1,370), S Que., Canada, 33 mi/53 km SSE of Quebec; 46°16′N 71°00′W. Dairying; pig raising.

Trinidad, city (1994 est. pop. 38,000), Sancti Spíritus prov., central Cuba; 21°48′N 79°59′W. Second-largest city in prov. Tobacco processing is the chief industry, although other agr. processing has been developed. Original settlement of Diego Velázquez's seven towns (villas) in 1514, Trinidad flourished as a port and was attacked several times by the British during the colonial era. Declared a UNESCO World Heritage Site, the town is a living relic of the colonial period, along with adjacent Iznaga Valley to E. Growing as a tourist destination with a seaside resort; internatl. airport at Cienfuegos, 1 hour away by road. Historic preservation efforts seek to preserve 18th- and 19th-cent. bldgs. and position the city as a prime tourist center in S central Cuba for sightseeing, caving, swimming, and related recreation.

Trinidad, city (1990 pop. 362), Humboldt co., NW Calif., on the coast, 17 mi/27 km N of Eureka; 41°04′N 124°08′W. Timber; cattle, sheep; redwood mill. Nearby is Trinidad Head, a promontory 400 ft/122 m high, with lighthouse. Redwood Natl. Park to N; site of Trinidad State Beach; Patrick's Point State Park to N.

Trinidad 1 town (1990 pop. 8,580), ⊙ Las Animas co., S Colo., on Purgatoire R., just E of Sangre de Cristo Mts., and 75 mi/121 km S of Pueblo, near N.Mex. state line; 37°10′N 104°30′W. Elev. 6,025 ft/1,836 m. RR, shipping, and industrial center for coal-mining and cattle region; wheat, sorghum, hay; mfg. (printing and publishing). City grew with development of coal mines, which supply smelters in Pueblo. Natl. Historic Dist. downtown. Trinidad State Jr. Col., Kit Carson Mus. and statue, Mitchell Mus. of Western Art here. Annual rodeo. Part of San Isabel Natl. Forest to NW; Trinidad L. Reservoir and State Park to W. Pinon Canyon Military Reserve to NE. Settled 1859 on Santa Fe Trail near Raton Pass; inc. 1876. **2** town (1990 pop. 1,056), Henderson co., E Texas, on the Trinity, and 22 mi/35 km ENE of Corsicana, on Trinity R.; 32°08′N 96°05′W. Agr. area; lignite mines; oil and gas; mfg. (liquid hydrocarbon). Cedar Creek Reservoir to N.

Trinidad, island (□ 1,864 sq mi/4,827 sq km; average length 50 mi/80 km N-S, average width 37 mi/60 km), Trinidad and Tobago, in the Atlantic Ocean, 10 mi/16 km off Venezuela coast; ⊙ Port of Spain. Lies just N of the Orinoco delta; borders W on the Gulf of Paria; separated from Venezuela by narrow channels: Dragon's Mouth (NW) and Serpent's Mouth (S); situated 350 mi/563 km E of Caracas and 600 mi/966 km SE of San Juan, P.R. Southernmost and largest of the Lesser Antilles, of roughly square shape with 2 peninsulas (NW and SW) jutting into the Gulf of Paria, it extends bet. 10°02′N–10°50′N and 60°55′W–61°56′W. Has humid, tropical climate, in path of NE trade winds. Mean annual temp. 76°F/24°C.; main rainy period June–Dec., rainfall varying bet. 50 in/127 cm and 120 in/305 cm. The isl. is free from hurricanes. Trinidad belongs geologically to the South Amer. continent. Generally low and level, crossed E-W by 3 ranges of hills rising in Mt. Aripo (N) to 3,085 ft/940 m. Watered by numerous unnavigable rivers, among them the Caroni and Ortoire. Swamps adjoin most of isl.'s indented coastline, which has many fine beaches (bathing, fishing) and provides good anchorage on the Gulf of Paria. Still covered largely by virgin forests. Its best known landmark is the Pitch L. near La Brea (SW), a vast seepage of natural asphalt now covering c.114 acres/46 ha. In the same W region (Pointe-à-Pierre), and in S and center, are large petroleum deposits, the chief source of income. Among the agr. prods. yielded by the fertile soil are cacao, coconuts, copra, sugarcane, coffee, citrus fruits, and tonka beans, which are exported, as are rum, bitters, lime oil, timber. Fishing along the coast (tarpon, cavalla, kingfish, mackerel, snappers, groupers). Deer, ducks, wild hogs, armadillos abound. Largest city, leading commercial center, and a major Caribbean port is Port of Spain; the Piarco Internl. Airport is 12 mi/19 km ESE of it. Petroleum is shipped through the oil-refining centers of San Fernando and Pointe-à-Pierre. Trinidad ranks high as a winter resort, noted for its fine beaches and equable climate. The isl., called by aboriginal Indians *Iere* [Land of the Humming Bird], was discovered by Columbus on July 31, 1498. The Spanish made only feeble attempts at colonization. Sir Walter Raleigh destroyed the anc. capital, San José de Oruña (now St. Joseph), in 1595. Trinidad was raided by the Dutch (1640) and the French (1677 and 1690). Spain opened the isl. to foreign R.C. settlers in 1783; this led to a large influx of Fr. refugees from Haiti. Trinidad was surrendered to Great Britain in 1797, which was confirmed by a treaty of 1802. After 1845, East Indian immigrants were introduced. Several naval and army air bases (total □ 56 sq mi/145 sq km) were leased in 1940 to the U.S. for 99 years, though they were not est. until 1941; largest in NW and N. The colony was granted universal suffrage in 1945. The white pop. is chiefly composed of English, Portuguese, French, and Spanish. About ⅓ are of East Indian descent, and there are several thousand Chinese, but the

Afr. element predominates. English is generally spoken. Trinidad is divided into 8 cos. and 3 municipalities (Port of Spain, San Fernando, and Arima).

Trinidad and Tobago (to-BAI-go), republic (□ 1,980 sq mi/5,128 sq km; 1990 pop. 1,234,388), West Indies; ⊙ PORT OF SPAIN; 11°00'N 61°00'W. The country consists of 2 isls.: Trinidad (□ 1,864 sq mi/4,827 sq km) and Tobago (□ 116 sq mi/300 sq km). Lying just N of the Orinoco R. delta in Venezuela, Trinidad is largely flat plain or undulating except for a range of low mts. (the highest point is Mt. Aripo, 3,085 ft/940 m) in the N and volcanic hills in S. Pitch L., in the SW, is the world's largest (114 acres/46 ha) basin of natural asphalt. Divided into 8 cos. (St. David, St. George, St. Andrew, Caroni, Nariva, Mayaro, Victoria, and St. Patrick). Tobago, just NE of Trinidad, is the exposed top of a mt. ridge (max. ht. 1,800 ft/549 m) that runs from NE to SW of isl. and is densely forested with large reserves of hardwoods. The climate of both isls. is warm and humid, and rainfall (from June to Dec.) is abundant, particularly where the trade winds sweep in over the eastern coasts. The pop. of the isls. is predominantly of black Afr. and East Indian descent, and the remainder are of Eur., Middle Eastern, and Chin. origin. English is the official language, but a Fr. patois is widely spoken. The main exports are petroleum, petroleum prods., and chemicals. Trinidad possesses sizable petroleum reserves, and its prosperity is linked directly to the production of petroleum and related prods. The decline in worldwide petroleum prices in the 1980s caused economic problems from which Trinidad is still recovering. Nonetheless, the isl. continues to enjoy one of the highest standards of living in the Caribbean. The isls. have a large tourist industry. Trinidad was visited by Christopher Columbus in 1498 but was not colonized because of the lack of precious metals. It was raided by the Dutch (1640) and the French (1677, 1690) and by Br. sailors. Britain captured it in 1797 and received formal title in 1802. Tobago had been settled by the English in 1616, but the settlers were driven out by the indigenous Caribs. The isl. was held by the Dutch and the French before being acquired by the British in 1803. The isls. were joined politically in 1888. Before becoming an independent nation in 1962, the isls. were part of the short-lived West Indies Federation (see WEST INDIES) from 1958 to 1962. In 1976 Trinidad and Tobago gained full independence as a republic. The country has a parliamentary form of govt.

Trinidad de Zaachila, Mexico: see TRINIDAD ZAACHILA.

Trinidad García de la Cadena, Mexico: see GARCÍA DE LA CADENA.

Trinidad Head, Calif.: see TRINIDAD.

Trinidad Sánchez, Mexico: see ZITLALTEPEC.

Trinidad, Sierra de, mountain range (rises in the Pico de Potrerillo to 3,054 ft/931 m), Sancti Spíritus, Villa Clara and Cienfuegos provs., central Cuba, just N of Trinidad. On its slopes fruits and sugarcane are grown. Has sand quarries. The Sierra de San Juan adjoins W. Along with Escambray Mts., these ranges are collectively called Cumanayagua.

Trinidad Zaachila (tree-nee-DAHD zah-CHEE-lah), town (1990 pop. 912), central Oaxaca, Mexico, 7 mi/12 km S of Oaxaca de Juárez, and 2 mi/3.2 km S of Villa de Zarchila; 16°55'N 96°46'W. Elev. 5,322 ft/1,622 m. Agr. (fruits, mezcal); handmade textiles. Temperate climate.

Trinitaria, La, Mexico: see VILLA LA TRINITARIA.

Trinité (tree-nee-TAI), town, E Martinique, minor port 11 mi/18 km NE of Fort-de-France. Trades in agr. produce (sugarcane, pineapples); sugar milling; rum distilling. Adjacent to Parc Naturel, protected area. Sometimes La Trinité.

Trinity 1 county (□ 3,179 sq mi/8,234 sq km; 1990 pop. 13,063), N Calif.; ⊙ Weaverville. Mt. area, mostly within Klamath Mts., with Coast Ranges in SW; rises to 9,038 ft/2,755 m at Mt. Eddy on NE boundary, 9,002 ft/2,744 m at Thompson Peak on N border. Drained by Trinity, Eel, and Mad rivers. Gold mining (since gold rush days); also sand and gravel; hay; nursery prods.; timber. Mt. scenery, camping, hiking attract vacationers. Pacific Crest Scenic Trail follows NE boundary. Trinity Unit of Whiskeytown-Shasta-Trinity Natl. Recreation Area in NE, including Clair Engle L. reservoir (Trinity R.); in NW is Salmon-Trinity Alps Wilderness Area; in S is a reserve of wilderness lands; part of Six Rivers Natl. Forest in SW, part of Mendocino Natl. Forest in SE corner, parts of Trinity Natl. Forest throughout center and N, part of Shasta Natl. Forest to NE; Weaverville Joss House State Historical Park in center. Formed 1850. **2** county (□ 714 sq mi/1,849 sq km; 1990 pop. 11,445), E Texas; ⊙ Groveton; 40°40'N 123°07'W. Bounded SW by Trinity R., NE by Neches R. Includes part of Davy Crockett Natl. Forest in most of NE ½ of co. Wooded area (timber is chief industry); also livestock (cattle, hogs, poultry), some agr. (hay, vegetables, peaches, pecans). Some oil and natural gas, lignite; sand and gravel, clay. L. Livingston reservoir. Formed 1850.

Trinity 1 town (1990 pop. 1,380), Morgan co., N Ala., near Wheeler Reservoir (in Tennessee R.), 5 mi/8 km W of Decatur. Stone quarry. **2** town (1990 pop. 5,469), Randolph co., central N.C., suburb 4 mi/6.4 km S of High Point, near source of Uwharrie R.; 35°53'N 80°00'W. Agr. area (tobacco, grain, soybeans; dairying; poultry, livestock); mfg. (furniture, lumber). **3** town (1990 pop. 2,648), Trinity co., E Texas, near the Trinity R., 18 mi/29 km NE of Huntsville; 30°56'N 95°22'W. Oil and gas; pine timber; vegetables, peaches, pecans; lumber milling; mfg. (steel prods.). Sam Houston Natl. Forest to S; Davy Crocket Natl. Forest to NE; L. Livingston to S and SE of town. Settled c.1873; inc. 1903.

Trinity, village, SE N.F., Canada, on NW side of Trinity Bay, on RR, and 40 mi/64 km NNW of Carbonear. Fishing port.

Trinity Bay, inlet of the Atlantic Ocean, 80 mi/129 km long, SE N.F., Canada, bet. the Avalon Peninsula and the mainland; 48°00'N 53°40'W. With its small fishing settlements, it preserves the flavor of 19th-cent. N.F. Hearts Content, a small port on the E shore, was the W terminal of the 1st permanent transatlantic cable laid (1866) by Cyrus West Field; stayed in use until mid-1960s.

Trinity Bay, Texas: see GALVESTON BAY.

Trinity Cape, SE central Que., Canada, on the Saguenay, 30 mi/48 km above its mouth, and 36 mi/58 km ESE of Chicoutimi; 1,500 ft/457 m high. Just ESE is Eternity Cape.

Trinity Dam, Calif., see CLAIR ENGLE LAKE.

Trinity Islands, group of 2 small isls. (Sitkinak Isl., Tugidak Isl.), S Alaska, in Gulf of Alaska, S of Kodiak Isl.; 56°32'N 154°25'W.

Trinity Pond, lake E N.F., Canada, 20 mi/32 km SW of Bonavista; 48°24'N 53°25'W; 6 mi/10 km long, 1 mi/2 km wide. Drains into Trinity Bay.

Trinity Range, NW Nev., largely in Pershing co., extends SW into Churchill co., W of Lovelock and Humboldt R.; 40°13'N 118°44'W. Highest point is Trinity Peak (7,332 ft/2,235 m).

Trinity River 1 130 mi/209 km long, in NW Calif.; rises in NE Trinity co.; flows 1st S through Clair Engle L. (Trinity Dam) and Lewiston L. reservoirs both in sect. of Whiskeytown-Shasta-Trinity Natl. Recreation Area, then NW, S of Weaverville through Trinity Natl. Forest, and Hoopa Indian Reservation. Principal tributary is 50 mi/80 km long South Fork, which rises in SE Trinity co.and flows NW. Since gold rush days, placer and hydraulic gold mining. **2** river, c.510 mi/821 km long; rises in NE Texas in 3 forks: the Clear Fork runs into the West Fork at Fort Worth, and the Elm Fork joins the West Fork to form the main stream at Dallas. The Trinity then flows SE to Trinity Bay, an arm of Galveston Bay of Gulf of Mexico. West Fork of the Trinity rises in S Archer Co., N Texas; flows generally SE c.140 mi/225 km through Fort Worth to its confluence with Elm Fork in Dallas. Reservoirs are L. Bridgeport, 15 mi/24 km W of Decatur, and Eagle Mt. L. and L. Worth, both NW of Fort Worth. Clear Fork of the Trinity rises in N Parker co., N Texas; flows c.50 mi/80 km, first SE through L. Weatherford, then NE through L. Benbrook, joining W Fork in downtown Fort Worth. Elm Fork of the Trinity rises in E Montague co., N Texas; flows E past Gainesville, then S through L. Ray Roberts and Lewisville L., merging with W Fork, W of downtown Dallas to form main Trinity R. East Fork of the Trinity rises in S Grayson co., NE Texas; flows S through lakes Lavon and Ray Hubbard; joins Trinity R. 25 mi/40 km SE of downtown Dallas. Despite numerous reservoirs on its upper forks and lower tributaries, the main Trinity R. itself has only one impoundment, the large L. Livingston reservoir, 60 mi/97 km NNE of Houston. Massive flooding of the river occurred in the winter of 1991, recorded as among the nation's worst floods in the 20th cent.

Trinity Ville or **Trinityville**, town (1991 pop. 2,614), St. Thomas parish, SE Jamaica, at S foot of Blue Mts., 18 mi/29 km E of Kingston; 17°57'N 76°32'W. In fruit-growing region (coconuts, bananas, sugarcane, coffee).

Trion (TREI-uhn), town (1990 pop. 1,661), Chattooga co., NW Ga., 22 mi/35 km NNW of Rome, and on Chattooga R.; 34°33'N 85°19'W. Mfg. includes textiles, farm equip., vending machines; food packaging center. Settled 1847; inc. 1863.

Triplett, town (1990 pop. 58), Chariton co., N central Mo., near Grand R., 6 mi/9.7 km NNW of Brunswick; 39°30'N 93°11'W. Corn, soybeans.

Tripoli (trip-OEW-lah), town (1990 pop. 1,188), Bremer co., NE Iowa, near Wapsipinicon R., 12 mi/19 km ENE of Waverly; 42°48'N 92°15'W. Food cannery. Sand and gravel pits nearby. Settled 1850; inc. 1894.

Tripp, county (□ 1,617 sq mi/4,188 sq km; 1990 pop. 6,924), S S.Dak., borders Nebr. on S; ⊙ Winner; 43°20'N 99°52'W. Agr. area bounded N by White R. and watered by Dog Ear and Old Lodge creeks and artificial lakes. Corn, wheat, sorghum, hay; dairy prods.; cattle, hogs, sheep, poultry. Mountain/Central Time Zone boundary follows W co. boundary (co. is in Central). Formed 1893.

Tripp, town (1990 pop. 664), Hutchinson co., SE S.Dak., 33 mi/53 km S of Mitchell; 43°13'N 97°58'W. Grain; dairy prods.; livestock, poultry; honey. Co. fair takes place here annually.

Tripp Pond, reservoir, c.2.5 mi/4 km long, Androscoggin co., SW Maine, c.8 mi/12.9 km W of Auburn and W of Poland; 44°04'N 70°25'W. Resort lake. Thompson L. to W.

Tritle, Mount (7,782 ft/2,372 m), Yavapai co., central Ariz., N of Bradshaw Mts., 8 mi/12.9 km S of Prescott, in Prescott Natl. Forest; 34°25'N 112°26'W.

Triton Island (TREI-tuhn) (□ 8 sq mi/21 sq km), E N.F., Canada, in Notre Dame Bay, 40 mi/64 km WSW of Twillingate; 7 mi/11 km long, 2 mi/3 km wide; 49°31'N 55°40'W. Fishing.

Triumph, village (1990 pop. with Buras 3,072), Plaquemines parish, extreme SE La., on W bank (levee) of the Mississippi R., and 55 mi/89 km SE of New Orleans; 29°20'N 89°28'W. Elev. 10 ft/3 m. In the delta; citrus-fruit growing (oranges), vegetables, tomatoes. Nearby are old Fort Jackson (1815) and Fort St. Philip (1795), which figured in Confederate defense of New Orleans (1862).

Triunfo, Mexico: see EL TRIUNFO.

Triunfo, El, Mexico: see EL TRIUNFO.

Trochu (TRO-shoo), town (1991 pop. 907), S central Alta., Canada, 55 mi/89 km NE of Calgary; 51°50'N 113°14'W. Coal mining; oil and gas; grain elevators; wheat, oats, barley.

Trois Pistoles (trwah pee-STOHL), town (1991 pop. 3,886), SE Que., Canada, on the St. Lawrence, and 27 mi/43 km NE of Rivière du Loup; 48°07'N 69°10'W. Lumbering, pulp milling; in dairying region. Fr. language immersion training institute here.

Trois Rivières (trwah reev-YEHR) or **Three Rivers**, city (1991 pop. 49,426), S Que., Canada, at the confluence of the St. Lawrence and St. Maurice rivers; 46°21'N 72°33'W. Port and industrial center. The city was founded (1634) by Champlain and took its name from the 3 channels through which the St. Maurice enters the St. Lawrence. It became a major Fr. trading post and fortified port and was the starting point of many explorers and missionaries. In 1737 the 1st iron forges in Que. were built in Trois Rivières. During the 19th cent. lumbering was the major industry, but with the utilization of water power after 1900 the pulp and paper industry became dominant. Mfg. also includes textiles, foodstuffs, and electrical appliances. A branch of the Que. Univ. is here.

Trois Rivières, Les (trwah ree-VYER, lai), river, c.65 mi/105 km long, N Haiti; rises in the Massif du Nord SE of Plaisance; flows NW to the Atlantic at Port-de-Paix. Not navigable.

Trois-Ilets (twah–zee-LE), town, SW Martinique, on Fort-de-France Bay, opposite Fort-de-France (5 mi/8 km SSE). Coffee and sugar growing; limekiln; sugar milling, rum distilling. Tourist center, water sports, hotels, casinos. Empress Josephine b. here (June 23, 1763).

Trois-Rivières (twah–ree-VYER), town, S Basse-Terre isl., Guadeloupe, minor port 4 mi/6.4 km ESE of Basse-Terre city. Agr. (coffee, cacao, vanilla).

Trojan Nuclear Power Plant oregon: see COLUMBIA, co., and PRESCOTT.

Trommald (TRUH-mawld), village (1990 pop. 80), Crow Wing co., central Minn., near Mississippi R., 14 mi/23 km NE of Brainerd; 46°30′N 94°01′E. In Cuyuna Iron Range, iron mining district, and in Crow Wing State Forest, and 3 mi/4.8 km NW of Crosby.

Trona, uninc. village, San Bernardino co., S Calif., in Mojave Desert, 65 mi/105 km NNW of Barstow. Processing plant extracts potash from Searles L., to SE, a large playa. Separate units of China L. Naval Weapons Center to W and SE; Death Valley Natl. Monument to NE; Panamint Valley to N.

Trooper, uninc. town (1990 pop. 5,137), Montgomery co., SE Pa., residential suburb 17 mi/27 km NW of Philadelphia on the Schuylkill R.; 40°08′N 75°24′W.

Trophy Mountain (9,000 ft/2,743 m), S B.C., Canada, in Cariboo Mts., 80 mi/129 km NNE of Kamloops; 51°47′N 119°48′W.

Tropic, village (1990 pop. 374), Garfield co., S Utah, 22 mi/35 km SE of Panguitch; 37°37′N 112°05′W. Elev. 6,300 ft/1,920 m. Cattle; alfalfa, barley. Bryce Canyon Natl. Park just W; Dixie Natl. Forest to N and W; Kodachrome Basin State Park to SE.

Trosky (TRAW-skee), village (1990 pop. 120), Pipestone co., SW Minn., near S.Dak. state line, 8 mi/12.9 km SSE of Pipestone, on Poplar Creek; 43°53′N 96°15′E. Agr. (corn, soybeans; livestock). Split Rock Creek State Park to W.

Trotter, uninc. village, Dunbar township, Fayette co., SW Pa., 10 mi/16 km NE of Uniontown, and 2 mi/3.2 km W of Connellsville; 40°00′N 79°37′W.

Trotwood, city (1990 pop. 8,816), Montgomery co., W Ohio, 5 mi/8 km WNW of Dayton; 39°48′N 84°18′W.

Trou (TROO), town, Nord dept., N Haiti, 16 mi/26 km ESE of Cap-Haïtien; 19°38′N 72°01′W. In agr. region (tobacco, sugarcane, sisal, fruits). Sometimes called Le Trou or Trou-du-Nord.

Trouin (troo-ANG), village, Ouest dept., S Haiti, 23 mi/37 km WSW of Port-au-Prince; 18°22′N 72°39′W. Coffee growing.

Troup (TROOP), county (□ 446 sq mi/1,155 sq km; 1990 pop. 55,536), W Ga.; ⊙ La Grange; 33°02′N 85°02′W. Bounded W by Ala. state line; drained by Chattahoochee R. Mfg. centers at La Grange, Hogansville, and West Point. Agr. prods. include fruits; cattle; timber.

Troup, city (1990 pop. 1,659), on Cherokee-Smith co. line, E Texas, 16 mi/26 km SE of Tyler; 32°08′N 95°07′W.

Trousdale (TROUZ-dail), county (□ 116 sq mi/300 sq km; 1990 pop. 5,920), N Tenn.; ⊙ Hartsville; 36°23′N 86°10′W. Bounded S by Cumberland R. Livestock; tobacco, corn, grain, hay. Formed 1870.

Trousers Lake (□ 3 sq mi/8 sq km; 4 mi/6 km long, 2 mi/3 km wide), N central N.B., Canada, 35 mi/56 km E of Grand Falls; 47°00′N 66°56′W.

Trout Creek, town (1991 pop. 662), SE central Ont., Canada, 24 mi/39 km S of North Bay; 45°59′N 79°22′W. Lumbering.

Trout Creek Pass (9,487 ft/2,892 m), at S end of Park Range, Chaffe-Park co. line, central Colo., 10 mi/16 km ENE of Buena Vista, crossed by U.S. Highway 24/285.

Trout Hall, town, Clarendon parish, central Jamaica, on Minho R., on May Pen–Frankfield RR, and 15 mi/24 km NW of May Pen; 18°08′N 77°20′W. Fruit-growing region (citrus).

Trout Lake, village, Chippewa co., E Upper Peninsula, Mich., 27 mi/43 km NW of St. Ignace; 46°11′N 85°01′W. In Hiawatha Natl. Forest. Trade center for resort area; logging. Carp L. (3 mi/4.8 km long), Frenchman L. and Johnson L. to S.

Trout Lake (□ 156 sq mi/404 sq km), NW Ont., Canada, in Patricia dist., 90 mi/145 km NW of Sioux Lookout; 17 mi/27 km long, 14 mi/23 km wide. Drains S into English R.

Trout Lake 1 , Itasca co., N central Minn., at W end of Mesabi Iron Range, 6 mi/9.7 km ENE of Grand Rapids; 4.5 mi/7.2 km long, 1 mi/1.6 km wide; 47°27′N 93°33′E. Large ore-processing plant is on lake. Iron-mining towns of Bovey and Coleraine are at N end. Trout Creek (1 mi/1.6 km long) drains from E side of lake into Swan R. **2** Vilas co., N Wis., 20 mi/32 km NW of Eagle R. city, in wooded resort area; 5 mi/8 km long, 2 mi/3.2 km wide. Musky, walleye, bass. In N. Highland State Forest.

Trout Peak, Wyo.: see ABSAROKA RANGE.

Trout River, village, S Que., Canada, frontier point on N.Y. border, 10 mi/16 km SE of Huntingdon; 49°29′N 58°07′W. Dairying.

Trout Run, village, Lycoming co., N central Pa., 11 mi/18 km NNW of Williamsport, on Lycoming Creek; 41°23′N 77°03′W. Hunting, fishing, lumbering area. Mfg. (roof and floor trusses). Rose Valley L. reservoir to E.

Trout Run Reservoir, Berks co., SE Pa. The dam creating this reservoir is 104 ft/32 m high and is on Trout Run; 40°20′N 75°42′W. Built in 1974 by the borough of Boyertown for water supply purposes. The reservoir is quite small with a max. water storage capacity of only 1,000 acre-ft.

Troutdale 1 town (1990 pop. 7,892), Multnomah co., NW Oregon, suburb 13 mi/21 km E of downtown Portland, on Sandy R., 2 mi/3.2 km S of its confluence with the Columbia R.; 45°32′N 122°23′W. On RR. Mfg. (prefabricated buildings, diagnostic packing, concrete, aluminum, barges, tugboats). Lewis and Clark State Park to E; Dabney State Park to SE. Portland Troutdale Airport to N. **2** town (1990 pop. 196), Grayson co., SW Va., in Blue Ridge, 9 mi/14.5 km SSE of Marion, in Mt. Rogers Natl. Recreation Area (part of Jefferson Natl. Forest); 36°42′N 81°26′W. Mfg. (clothing); agr. (dairying; livestock; corn, tobacco). Mt. Rogers, highest point in Va. (5,724 ft/1,745 m), 6 mi/9.7 km W; Grayson Highlands State Park to S.

Troutman (TROUT-muhn) or **Troutmans**, town (1990 pop. 1,493), Iredell co., W central N.C., 5 mi/8 km S of Statesville; 35°42′N 80°53′W. Agr. area (tobacco, grain, soybeans; poultry, livestock; dairying). Mfg. (polymer concrete drains, structural automobile components, furniture, stainless steel tubing). Duke Power State Park, on L. Norman reservoir (Catawba R.), to SW.

Troutville, town (1990 pop. 455), Botetourt co., W central Va., 6 mi/9.7 km S of Fincastle; 37°24′N 79°52′W. Mfg. (pipe fabrications, steel fence posts); agr. (dairying; livestock; grain, apples).

Troutville (TROUT-vil), borough (1990 pop. 226), Clearfield co., W central Pa., 7 mi/11.3 km SSW of Du Bois, near Stump Creek; 41°01′N 78°47′W. Corn, hay, grain; livestock.

Troy 1 city (1990 pop. 13,051), ⊙ Pike co., SE Ala., on the Conecuh R.; 31°48′N 85°58′W. Lumber and wood prods.; mfg. of textiles, truck bodies, feed, plastic containers, and food prods.; agr. (pecans). Troy State Univ. and the co. mus. are here. Inc. 1843. **2** city (1990 pop. 6,046), Madison co., SW Ill., 16 mi/26 km ENE of East St. Louis, suburb of St. Louis; 38°43′N 89°53′W. Highway junction. In bituminous coal and agr. area (corn, wheat, soybeans, vegetables); mfg. (cable trays, prosthetics, concrete, dairy prods.). Settled as Columbia 1814; renamed Troy 1819; inc. as city 1892. **3** city (1990 pop. 72,884), Oakland co., SE Mich., a growing suburb 16 mi/26 km NNW of downtown Detroit; 42°34′N 83°08′W. Drained by R. Rouge. Major suburban development and residential growth occurred in the city after 1975, as urban migration from Detroit became extensive. Its varied manufactures include automobiles and parts, electronics, chemicals, door systems, video and compact discs. Troy contains many historic buildings and is the site of Walsh Col. of Accountancy and Business Administration. Oakland Troy Airport in S. Settled 1821; inc. 1955. **4** city (1990 pop. 3,811), ⊙ Lincoln co., E Mo., near Cuivre R., 30 mi/48 km NW of St. Charles; 38°58′N 90°58′W. Corn, soybeans; cattle, poultry; mfg. (auto parts, shop lasts). Cuivre R. State Park to NE. Laid out c.1819. **5** city (□ 10 sq mi/26 sq km; 1990 pop. 54,269), ⊙ Rensselaer co., E N.Y., on the E bank of the Hudson R.; 42°43′N 73°40′W. Once known esp. for its mfg. of collars and shirts it now produces other important prods.: motor vehicle parts, rototillers, instruments, and RR supplies. Henry Hudson explored (1609) the area near Troy, and the site was included in the patroonship given to Kiliaen Van Rensselaer by the chartered Du. West India Company. From 1812 to 1920 it was industrially prosperous, and many inventions were made here. During the past 50 years, Troy has suffered from the urban blight of many river towns and has lost a large number of its industries. It is the seat of Rensselaer Polytechnic Inst., Russell Sage Col., Hudson Valley Community Col., and the Emma Willard School, the oldest private girls' school in the country. Samuel Wilson of Troy, who was concerned with army beef supply in the War of 1812, is said to have been the original "Uncle Sam." Many bldgs. of architectural and historic interest are preserved. The town was laid out in 1786; inc. 1816. **6** city (1990 pop. 19,478), ⊙ Miami co., W central Ohio, on the Great Miami R.; 40°02′N 84°13′W. In a farm area. Welding machinery, food processing machinery, motor generators, paper prods., and tools are manufactured. Growth and industrialization came with the arrival of the Miami and Erie Canal in 1837. A disastrous flood in 1913 resulted in the creation of the first flood protection district in the U.S. Inc. 1814.

Troy 1 town (1990 pop. 465), Perry co., S Ind., on the Ohio R. at mouth of small Anderson R., and 4 mi/6.4 km NW of Tell City; 38°00′N 86°48′W. In agr. area; mfg. (oil refining, heat exchangers). Laid out 1815. **2** town (1990 pop. 1,073), ⊙ Doniphan co., extreme NE Kansas, 13 mi/21 km W of St. Joseph, Mo.; 39°47′N 95°05′W. Elev. 950 ft/290 m. Shipping center for apple-growing region. Apple Blossom Festival takes place here annually in Aug. Indian mounds have been excavated nearby. RR junction to W. Founded 1855; inc. 1860. **3** town (1990 pop. 802), Waldo co., S Maine, 19 mi/31 km NW of Belfast; 44°40′N 69°15′W. In agr., recreational area. **4** town (1990 pop. 953), Lincoln co., NW Mont., 17 mi/27 km W of Libby, and on Kootenai R., near Idaho line; 48°28′N 115°54′W. Timber, hay; silver; mfg. (house logs). Lowest elev. in Mont. (1,820 ft/555 m) at point where Kootenai R. crosses into Idaho, 12 mi/19 km NNW of Troy. Cabinet Mts. to SW and SE. Purcell Mts. to N. Bull L. to S. Cabinet Mts. Wilderness Area to SE; area surrounded by Kootenai Natl. Forest. Ross Creek Cedar Grove to S (500-year old Western Red cedars avg. 175 ft/53 m in ht.). Troy Mus. and Visitor's Center. **5** town (1990 pop. 2,097), Cheshire co., SW N.H., 9 mi/14.5 km SSE of Keene; 42°49′N 72°11′W. Drained by South Branch Ashuelot R. Mfg. (automotive fabrics, lumber, women's accessories, contract packaging); agr. (vegetables, nursery crops; cattle, poultry; dairying). Monadnock Mt. to NE, in Jaffrey town. Settled 1762; inc. 1815. **6** town (1990 pop. 3,404), ⊙ Montgomery co., central N.C., 40 mi/64 km S of High Point; 35°21′N 79°53′W. Agr. trade (cotton, peaches, tobacco, grain; poultry, cattle, hogs); mfg. (knitting machinery, rugs, printing and publishing, textiles and apparel, lumber). Uwharrie Natl. Forest to W and S. Inc. 1879. **7** town (1990 pop. 1,047), Obion co., NW Tenn., 8 mi/13 km SW of Union City, 36°20′N 89°10′W. In agr. and livestock area. **8** town (1990 pop. 1,395), Bell co., central Texas, 23 mi/37 km SSW of Waco, and 6 mi/9.7 km NNE of Temple; 31°11′N 97°18′W. Agr. area (cattle; cotton, wheat, corn); timber. Mfg. (fiberglass paint, farm equip. assembly). **9** town (1990 pop. 1,609), Orleans co., N Vt., on Missisquoi R., and 12 mi/19 km WSW of Newport, on Que. (Canada) line; 44°55′N 72°23′W. Dairying; wood prods. Includes North Troy village, a port of entry. Granted 1792; organized 1802. Fortified against smugglers in War of 1812. **10** uninc. town (1990 pop. 125), Gilmer co., central

W.Va., on the Little Kanawha R., 7 mi/11.3 km NNE of Glenville. Mfg. (lumber).

Troy 1 village (1990 pop. 699), Latah co., N Idaho, 10 mi/16 km E of Moscow; 46°45′N 116°46′W. Timber; cattle, sheep; alfalfa, oats, barley; mfg. (wood fencing). **2** village (1990 pop. 140), Greenwood co., W S.C., 16 mi/26 km SSW of Greenwood, in Sumter Natl. Forest; 33°59′N 82°17′W. Mfg. includes lumber, machining; agr. includes timber.

Troy (TROI), borough (1990 pop. 1,262), Bradford co., N Pa., 21 mi/34 km S of Elmira, N.Y., on Sugar Creek; 41°46′N 76°47′W. Mfg. (lumber, stationery, meat processing, valves, printing and publishing); agr. (apples, corn, hay; dairying). Farm Mus. Tioga State Forest, on Armenia Mt., to SW. Settled 1793; inc. c.1844.

Troy Grove, village (1990 pop. 259), La Salle co., N Ill., on Little Vermilion R., and 14 mi/23 km NW of Ottawa; 41°28′N 89°04′W. Dairying; mfg. coated sand, glass. Has state monument to James Butler "Wild Bill" Hickok, b. here.

Troy Peak, Nev.: see GRANT RANGE.

Truchas (TROO-chuhs), uninc. village (1990 pop. 275), Rio Arriba co., N N.Mex., in Sangre de Cristo Mts., 9 mi/14.5 km NNE of Santa Fe. Elev. 7,622 ft/2,323 m. Sheep, cattle; wheat, alfalfa. Trading point in grain and livestock area. Santa Fe Natl. Forest to N, E, and S. North Truchas Peak (13,024 ft/3,970 m) 11 mi/18 km ESE.

Truchas Peak (TROO-chuhs), mountain (13,102 ft/3,993 m), Rio Arriba–Mora co. line, N N.Mex., in Sangre de Cristo Mts., c.25 mi/40 km NE of Santa Fe; 35°57′N 105°38′W. In Santa Fe Natl. Forest.

Truckee, city (1990 pop. 3,484), Nevada co., E Calif., on Truckee R., in the Sierra Nevada, at E end of Donner Pass, 25 mi/40 km SW of Reno, Nev.; 39°20′N 120°12′W. Elev. 5,820 ft/1,774 m. Winter sports. Sand and gravel. Surrounded by Tahoe Natl. Forest, N, W, and S; L. Tahoe is 10 mi/16 km SE; Donner L. is just W; Northstar-at-Tahoe Ski Area to S; Sugarbowl and Tahoe Donner ski areas to S.

Truckee, river, c.100 mi/161 km long; rises in L. Tahoe, Placer co., E Calif., at Tahoe City; flows N past Truckee, then NE receives Little Truckee R. from NW before entering Nev.; flows past Reno and Sparks, turns N at Wadsworth and enters S end of Pyramid L. (brackish lake in Great Basin); has no outlet; in Pyramid L. Indian Reservation. L. Tahoe Dam of the Newlands project is on the Truckee; Boca is on Little Truckee.

Truckee Pass, (elev. c.5,800 ft/1,768 m), E Calif., in the Sierra Nevada near Truckee (Nevada co.), on historic Emigrant Trail.

Truesdale 1 town (1990 pop. 132), Buena Vista co., NW Iowa, 6 mi/9.7 km N of Storm L.; 42°43′N 95°10′W. **2** town (1990 pop. 285), Warren co., E central Mo.; 38°48′N 91°07′W. Residential community adjacent to Warrenton. Sometimes spelled Truesdail.

Trujillo, Dominican Republic: see SANTO DOMINGO, city.

Trujillo Alto (troo-HEE-yo AHL-to), town (1990 pop. 61,120), E P.R., on Loíza R., and 11 mi/18 km SE of San Juan. Industrial and commercial center; mfg. (clothing, wood prods., steel, cement, chemical prods.). Settled in early 19th cent. by settlers from Canary Isls. Residential suburban developments.

Trujillo Valdes, Dominican Republic: see PERAVIA.

Truman, town (1990 pop. 1,292), Martin co., S Minn., 12 mi/19 km N of Fairmont; 43°49′N 94°26′E. Agr. (soybeans, grain; livestock); mfg. (concrete, lumber). Near Perch Creek, forms Perch L. to SW.

Trumann, town (1990 pop. 6,304), Poinsett co., NE Ark., 15 mi/24 km SE of Jonesboro; 35°40′N 90°31′W. In agr. (cotton, rice, wheat, soybeans) and timber area; woodworking plant. Mfg. (lighting fixtures, pianos [Baldwin], doors, plywood, furniture, air-conditioner parts, conveyors). St. Francis Sunken Lands Wildlife Management Area to E.

Trumansburg, village (□ 1 sq mi/2.6 sq km; 1990 pop. 1,611), Tompkins co., W central N.Y., in Finger Lakes region, 10 mi/16 km NW of Ithaca, near Cayuga L.; 42°32′N 76°39′W. Agr. (poultry; fruits, grain). Settled 1792; inc. 1865.

Trumbauersville (TRUN-bau-uhrs-vil), borough (1990 pop. 894), Bucks co., SE Pa., 3 mi/4.8 km SW of Quakertown; 40°24′N 75°22′W. Mfg. (glass, plastic prods.); agr. (grain; poultry, livestock; dairying). Quakertown Airport to N.

Trumbull (TRUM-buhl), county (□ 630 sq mi/1,632 sq km; 1990 pop. 227,813), NE Ohio; ⊙ Warren; 41°19′N 80°46′W. Bounded E by Pa. line; drained by Mahoning and Grand rivers and Mosquito and Pymatuning creeks. Includes Mosquito Creek Reservoir. In the Glaciated Plain physiographic region. Agr. area (cattle; dairying; corn, soybeans); mfg. (dairy prods., home furnishings and furniture, motor vehicle parts, aircraft engines and parts, pressed and blown glass, electric lamps) at Warren, Niles, and Girard, industrial suburbs of Youngstown. Sand and gravel pits; oil and gas extraction. Formed 1800.

Trumbull, town (1990 pop. 32,016), Fairfield co., SW Conn.; 41°15′N 73°12′W. Largely residential, the town has some light industry. Settled in the 1660s, inc. 1797.

Trumbull, village (1990 pop. 225), Clay co., S Nebr., 9 mi/14.5 km NE of Hastings; 40°40′N 98°16′W.

Trumbull, Mount (8,028 ft/2,447 m), NE Mohave co., NW Ariz., c.70 mi/113 km SW of Kanab, Utah, N of Colorado R.; 36°24′N 113°08′W.

Truro (TROOR-o), town (1991 pop. 11,683), central N.S., Canada, near the head of Cobequid Bay, an arm of the Bay of Fundy; 45°22′N 63°18′W. It is a RR and industrial center, with lumber mills, printing plants, and other factories. The Nova Scotia Agr. Col. here is the hq. of the provincial agr. extension service. An early Acadian settlement called Cobequid, the town was destroyed (1755) when the Acadians were expelled. After 1759 it received settlers from New England and Northern Ireland, who named the town for Truro, England.

Truro 1 (TROO-ro), town (1990 pop. 391), Madison co., S central Iowa, near South R., 12 mi/19 km SE of Winterset; 41°12′N 93°50′W. In agr. area. **2** town (1990 pop. 1,573), Barnstable co., SE Mass., near N tip of Cape Cod, 8 mi/12.9 km SE of Provincetown; 42°01′N 70°04′W. Formerly thriving port and fishing center. Includes North Truro village; site of Cape Cod or Highland Light (1st installed 1797), 1 of most powerful on Atlantic coast; also has naval radio and Coast Guard stations. Summer resort; artist colony. South Truro village is resort. Includes part of Cape Cod Natl. Seashore. Settled 1700; inc. 1709.

Truscott, uninc. village (1990 pop. 187), Knox co., N Texas, near North Fork of Wichita R., c.75 mi/121 km W of Wichita Falls. In cattle ranching, cotton, vegetable, wheat, and sorghum region.

Trussville, city (1990 pop. 8,266), Jefferson co., N central Ala., 15 mi/24 km NE of Birmingham. Mfg. (fire extinguishers, road signs; poultry processing). Cahaba Village, a federal subsistence homestead, is here. Ala. Boys Industrial School nearby. Inc. 1940.

Truth or Consequences, town (1990 pop. 6,221), ⊙ Sierra co., SW N.Mex., 77 mi/124 km NNW of Las Cruces, on Rio Grande (bet. Caballo Reservoir, S and Elephant Butte Reservoir, NE), E of Black Range; 33°08′N 107°15′W. Elev. 4,242 ft/1,293 m. Health resort with hot mineral springs; trade center in cattle, sheep; dairying; agr. (alfalfa, vegetables, chilis, jalapeños); mfg. (concrete block). Sierra Caballo to SE; San Mateo Mts. to N; part of Cibola Natl. Forest to N; part of Gila Natl. Forest to W; Elephant Butte L. State Park to NE; Caballo L. and Percha Dam State Parks to S. Formerly called Hot Springs; people voted to rename it in 1950, after radio and television game show hosted by Ralph Edwards. Sometimes still referred to as Hot Springs.

Truxton, village (1990 pop. 500), Cortland co., central N.Y., on Tioughnioga R., and 11 mi/18 km NE of Cortland; 42°42′N 76°01′W.

Tryon (TREI-uhn), town (1990 pop. 1,680), Polk co., W N.C., at S.C. state line, 15 mi/24 km SE of Hendersonville, near Pacolet R., in the Blue Ridge foothills; 35°12′N 82°14′W. Corn; cattle. Mfg. (synthetic fiber waste processing, cotton, yarn, printing and publishing). L. Lanier reservoir to S (in S.C.). Inc. 1885.

Tryon 1 (TREI-uhn), uninc. village, ⊙ McPherson co., W central Nebr., 28 mi/45 km NNW of North Platte. Grain, alfalfa; livestock. **2** village (1990 pop. 514), Lincoln co., central Okla., 17 mi/27 km SSE of Stillwater; 35°52′N 96°57′W.

Tsaile (sai-lee), uninc. town (1990 pop. 1,043), Apache co., NE Ariz., 110 mi/177 km NNE of Holbrook, in Navajo Indian Reservation. Near Tsaile Creek (forms Tsalie L. to S), which flows intermittently SW into Canyon de Chelly Natl. Monument. Cattle, sheep. Crafts. Navajo Community Col. is here. Dinosaur Tracks site to W.

Tsala Apopka Lake (SAH-luh uh-POP-kuh), c.16 mi/26 km long, E Citrus co., central Fla., c.55 mi/89 km NNE of Tampa. Shallow and largely overgrown with water lilies, it has many isls. and very irregular shore; has outlets into swamplands (E), which are drained by Withlacoochee R.

Tsar, Mount (11,232 ft/3,424 m), SE B.C., Canada, near Alta. border, in Rocky Mts., in Hamber Provincial Park, 55 mi/89 km SSE of Jasper; 52°06′N 117°48′W.

Tschida, Lake, reservoir, c.7 mi/11.3 km long, Grant co., SW N.Dak., on Heart R., 50 mi/80 km WNW of Bismarck; 46°37′N 101°50′W. Max. capacity 430,000 acre-ft. Formed by Heart Butte Dam (118 ft/36 m); built by the Bureau of Reclamation for irrigation and flood control.

Tsimshian Peninsula (simp-SHEE-AN), W B.C., Canada, in Prince Rupert region, extends 36 mi/58 km NW into Chatham Sound from mouth of Skeena R. to mouth of Portland Inlet, separated from mainland by Work Channel (30 mi/48 km long, 1 mi/2 km wide); 12 mi/19 km wide at base; rises to 3,350 ft/1,021 m. Off W coast are Digby, Kaien (on which is Prince Rupert), and Smith isls. Port Simpson village is in N. Sometimes spelled Tsimpsean Peninsula.

Tualatin (too-WAHL-uh-tin), city (1990 pop. 15,013), Washington and Clackamas cos., NW Oregon, suburb 10 mi/16 km SW of Portland, on Tualatin R.; 45°22′N 122°46′W. Agr. (fruits, nuts, vegetables; poultry, cattle); mfg. (dairy prods., soft drinks, building materials, furniture, printing and publishing, bacteriological media, plastics, pottery, incineration equip., tools, electrical connectors).

Tualatin River (too-WAHL-uh-tin), c.60 mi/97 km long, SW Wash. co., NW Oregon; rises W of Portland; flows N, then E past Forest Grove and Hillsboro, then SE past Tualatin to Willamette R., at West Linn above (SW) Oregon City.

Tuba City, uninc. town, Coconino co., N Ariz., 65 mi/105 km NNE of Flagstaff; elev. 4,940 ft/1,506 m. Sheep, cattle; crafts; administration and trading point in W part of Navajo Indian Reservation; Hopi Indian Reservation, surrounded by Navajo Reservation, to E.

Tubac, Ariz.: see NOGALES.

Túbano, Dominican Republic: see PADRE LAS CASAS.

Tubutama (too-boo-TAH-mah), town (1990 pop. 390), Sonora state, NW Mexico, on Altar (affluent of Magdalena) R., and 45 mi/72 km SW of Nogales; 30°52′N 111°29′W. Wheat, corn, beans, cotton, sugarcane.

Tucannon River (too-KAN-uhn), c.70 mi/113 km long, SE Wash.; rises in Umatilla Natl. Forest, E Columbia co.; flows generally NW to Snake R. 2 mi/3.2 km NW of Starbuck. Mouth of Palouse R. (on Snake R.) 5 mi/8 km downstream (NW).

Tuckahoe, uninc. city, Henrico co., E central Va., residential suburb 7 mi/11.3 km WNW of downtown Richmond, on James R. (bridged); 37°35′N 77°35′W. Univ. of Richmond to E.

Tuckahoe 1 (TUH-kuh-ho), village, Cape May co., S N.J., on Tuckahoe R., and 15 mi/24 km NNE of Cape May Court House. Agr. area. Settled by Quakers before 1700. **2** residential village (1990 pop. 6,302), town of Eastchester, Westchester co., SE N.Y., just E of Yonkers and N of Bronxville, in N.Y. city metropolitan area; 40°57′N 73°49′W. Mfg. (connectors, cable and cable assemblies, bulk pharmaceuticals, grinding machines, tools for electronics assemblies). Settled 1684; inc. 1903.

Tuckahoe Creek (tuk-uh-HO), c.45 mi/72 km long, E Md., on the Eastern Shore; rises just SW of Templemore; flows generally SSW, forming Queen Annes–

Caroline and Talbot-Caroline co. lines, to Choptank R. 6 mi/9.7 km SW of Denton.

Tuckahoe River (TUH-kuh-ho), c.25 mi/40 km long, S N.J.; rises in SW Atlantic co.; flows S and E, past Tuckahoe (head of navigation), through Great Cedar Swamp, to Great Egg Harbor Bay S of Great Egg Harbor R. mouth.

Tuckasegee River (tuh-kuh-SEE-jee), 50 mi/80 km long, W N.C.; rises in the Blue Ridge Mts. c.10 mi/16 km W of Brevard, in E Jackson co.; flows NW past Cullowhee, Whittier, and Bryson City, to Little Tennessee R. 9 mi/14.5 km W of Bryson City, where it forms an E arm of Fontana L. reservoir (5 mi/8 km long, 1 mi/1.6 km wide; also known as Glenville L.), on S boundary of Great Smoky Mts. Natl. Park, on small West Fork of Tuckasegee R. (c.25 mi/40 km long), 22 mi/35 km SW of Bryson City.

Tucker, county (□ 421 sq mi/1,090 sq km; 1990 pop. 7,728), NE W.Va., at base of Eastern Panhandle; ⊙ Parsons; 39°06′N 79°34′W. On Allegheny Plateau, with Laurel Ridge along W border; drained by Cheat, Laurel Fork, Shavers Fork, and Blackwater rivers. Most of co., except NW and NE, is in Monongahela Natl. Forest, includes Fernow Experimental Forest in SW. Blackwater Falls State Park in E center. Coal-mining, limestone quarrying; timber. Agr. (corn, oats, potatoes, alfalfa, hay; cattle, poultry). Mfg. at Parsons. Fairfax Stone State Monument on N border; Canaan Valley State Park in SE. Formed 1856.

Tucker, suburb of Atlanta, DeKalb co., NW central Ga., 12 mi/19 km ENE of Atlanta; 33°51′N 84°13′W. Mfg. (plastic prods., computer components and equip., printing and publishing, furniture, construction materials, industrial chemicals); steel fabrication, meat processing; office and distribution center.

Tucker Island, SE N.J., sandy barrier isl. (c.2 mi/3.2 km long) bet. Great Bay and the Atlantic Ocean, and bet. Beach Haven Inlet (N) and Little Egg Inlet (S); seaward side is called Tucker Beach.

Tuckerman, town (1990 pop. 2,020), Jackson co., NE Ark., 30 mi/48 km WSW of Jonesboro; 35°43′N 91°12′W. In agr. area (soybeans, rice).

Tuckerman Ravine, N.H.: see PRESIDENTIAL RANGE.

Tuckernuck Island (TUH-kuhr-nuhk), c.5 mi/8 km long, Nantucket co., SE Mass., in the Atlantic Ocean just W of Nantucket Isl.; separated from Martha's Vineyard (NW) by Muskeget Channel.

Tucker's Town, Bermuda, part of SE Bermuda Isl., in St. George's parish.

Tuckerton, resort borough (1990 pop. 3,048), Ocean co., SE N.J., near Little Egg Harbor, 16 mi/26 km N of Atlantic City, at head of navigation of short Tuckerton Creek; 39°36′N 74°19′W. Boatyards; fishing. Settled c.1700; inc. 1901. Important 18th-cent. port; raided by British, 1778.

Tuckertown Lake, reservoir (□ 4 sq mi/10.4 sq km), Davidson and Rowan cos., central N.C., on Yadkin R., 23 mi/37 km W of Kannapolis; 35°29′N 80°11′W. Max. capacity 6,897 acre-ft. Formed by Tuckertown Dam (66 ft/20 m high), built (1962) for power generation.

Tucson (TOO-sawn), city (1990 pop. 405,390), ⊙ Pima co., SE Ariz.; 32°12′N 110°53′W. The 2d-largest city in the state, it is situated in a desert plain surrounded by mts., on Santa Cruz R. near mouth of Rillito R. (both intermittent). An important and rapidly developing transportation and tourist center; its dry, sunny, and hot climate attracts vacationers and health seekers. Tucson Internatl. Airport to S. The city also has large electronic, optic, and biotechnology research industries and serves as the processing and distributing center for the cotton and livestock raised in the area and for the many mining (chiefly copper) operations. Mfg. (machinery, electronic equip., communications equip., textiles, and metal, plastic, concrete, paper, rubber, and food prods.). Tucson is one of the fastest-growing U.S. cities, marked by a pop. increase of more than 52% bet. 1970 and 1990. The 1st Span. settlers arrived in the late 17th cent., and in 1700, Father Eusebio Kino founded Mission San Xavier del Bac 9 mi/14.5 km S of the Native American village of Tucson. The city was est. 1776 as a walled presidio. Tucson became a military border post of New Spain, of Mexico, and, after its transfer under the Gadsden Purchase, of the U.S. It served as territorial capital from 1867 to 1877. In 1873, Fort Lowell was built 2 mi/3.2 km N of the city. The Southern Pacific RR arrived in 1880, and the city is now a RR junction. Among the city's many points of interest are the "Old Adobe" (1868); Colossal Cave; Fort Lowell (reconstructed, now a mus.); the beautiful San Xavier Del Bac Mission, in San Xavier Indian Reservation, to S (present bldg. erected 1783–1797); "Old Tucson," a movie-set replica to the W of the city in Tucson Mt. Park, incl. Ariz.-Sonora Desert Mus.; and the adjacent Saguaro Natl. Monument. A fiesta and rodeo is held each Feb. Tucson is the seat of the Univ. of Arizona, Pima Community Col. (3 campuses), and state schools for the handicapped and for deaf and blind. It is the training camp of Colorado Rockies baseball team; has the Ariz. Opera Company, Ballet Ariz., Tucson Symphony Orchestra. Mus. include Old Pueblo Mus. to N, University of Ariz. Mus. of Art, Ariz. Historical Society Mus., Pima Air Mus., and Internatl. Wildlife Mus. to W. Other area attractions are Univ. of Ariz. Experimental Farm to N; U.S. Coast and Geodetic Survey Magnetic Observatory NE of city; Flandrum Planetarium; Catalina State Park to N; Rillito Downs Racetrack to N; Pima co. Rodeo Grounds in S part of city; Spencer Canyon Ski Area; Tucson Mt. Unit of Saguaro Natl. Monument to NW, Rincon Mt. Unit to E; Coronado Natl. Forest to NE, including Pusch Ridge Wilderness Area and Sabino Canyon Visitor Center; Biosphere 2 environmental experimental site 35 mi/56 km to NE at Mt. Lemmon. Nearby military installation is Davis-Monthan Air Force Base, in SE part of the city, a large Strategic Air Command base that includes the Aerospace Maintenance and Recreation Center (AMARE), a storage center for the country's largest concentration of military aircraft. Inc. 1877.

Tucson Mountains, W of Tucson, Pima co., SE Ariz.; Amole Peak (4,450 ft/1,356 m) is a landmark. Tucson Mt. Unit of Saguaro Natl. Monument in N; Tucson Mt. Park in S.

Tucuche, El (to-KOOCH, el), peak (3,072 ft/936 m), N Trinidad, Trinidad and Tobago, 9 mi/14.5 km NE of Port of Spain.

Tucumcari (TOO-kuhm-ker-ee), town (1990 pop. 6,831), ⊙ Quay co., E N.Mex., S of Canadian R., 173 mi/278 km E of Albuquerque, and 100 mi/161 km W of Amarillo, Texas; 35°10′N 103°43′W. RR junction, with repair shops; trade and cattle and sheep shipping center in irrigated grain region; cotton, grain, alfalfa, corn; mfg. (bricks, meatpacking). Hq. of Tucumcari irrigation project here. Conchas L. and Conchas L. State Park (both on the Canadian R.) are 30 mi/48 km WNW; Ute Reservoir (also on Canadian R.) and Ute L. State Park to NE; Tucumari Creek to NE. Inc. 1908. Growth followed arrival (1901) of RR.

Tuftonboro (TUF-tuhn-buh-ro), town (1990 pop. 1,842), Carroll co., E N.H., 17 mi/27 km NE of Laconia; 43°40′N 71°16′W. Bounded SW by L. Winnipesaukee, W by Moultonborough Bay, drained by Melvin and Beech rivers. Dan Hole Pond in N. Mt. Shaw (2,975 ft/907 m) on NW boundary. Vegetables, nursery crops; cattle, hogs, poultry; dairying. Includes village of Mirror Lake in S, Melvin Village in SW.

Tug Fork, river, 154 mi/248 km long, S W.Va., E Ky., and SW Va.; rises in E McDowell co., S W.Va.; flows generally NW, past Welch; forms Va.-W.Va. state line for c.4 mi/6.4 km, continues as Ky.-W.Va. state line, flowing past Williamson, W.Va.; joins Louisa Fork at Louisa, Ky., to form Big Sandy R.

Tugaloo, dam, on NE Ga. (Rabun co.) and W S.C. (Oconee co.) border, on Tugaloo R., 38 mi/61 km WNW of Anderson (S.C.); 170 ft/52 m high; 34°43′N 83°21′W. Built (1923) for power generation.

Tugaloo River 1 (TUHG-uh-loo), 45 mi/72 km long, NE Ga. and NW S.C.; formed SE of Tallulah Falls, Ga., by junction of Chattooga and Tallulah rivers; flows SE, along Ga.-S.C. state line, joining Seneca R. 13 mi/21 km WSW of Anderson, S.C., to form Savannah R.; 34°42′N 83°21′W. Has 2 dams in upper course. **2** NW S.C.; formed by the confluence of the Chatooga R. and Tallulah R.; defines portion of NW boundary of S.C. with Ga.; joins with Seneca R. to form Savannah R.

Tugaske (tuh-GA-skee), village (1991 pop. 157), S Sask., Canada, 50 mi/80 km NW of Moose Jaw. Grain elevators.

Tujunga, suburban sect. of Los Angeles (city), Los Angeles co., S Calif., 14 mi/23 km N of downtown Los Angeles, in San Fernando Valley, at base of San Gabriel Mts. Residential. Mfg. (printing and publishing; medical instruments). Annexed 1932 by the city of Los Angeles. Tujunga (or Big Tujunga) Canyon, a recreational area, is N; Angeles Natl. Forest to N.

Tujunga Creek or **Big Tujunga Creek**, S Calif., intermittent stream, tributary of Los Angeles R.; rises in San Gabriel Mts.; flows W and SW, through Tujunga (Big Tujunga) Canyon (recreational area), through Hansen Flood Control Basin, and across San Fernando Valley, to Los Angeles R., 4 mi/6.4 km SW of Burbank. Wide gravel bed of lower course, generally dry, is called Tujunga Wash. Flood-control works include Big Tujunga No. 1 Dam (251 ft/77 m high, 800 ft/244 m long; completed 1931), on upper course; Hansen Dam (122 ft/37 m high, 10,509 ft/3,203 m long; completed 1940), on lower course.

Tuklung, village, SW Alaska, c. 70 mi/113 km NW of Dillingham.

Tuktoyaktuk or **Tuk**, village (1991 pop. 918), NW Mackenzie dist., N.W.T., Canada, on Refuge Cove, bay of the Beaufort Sea, 20 mi/32 km ENE of mouth of E channel of Mackenzie R. delta, 80 mi/129 km NNE of Inuvik; 69°27′N 133°02′W. Settled in 1934 with transfer of Hudson's Bay Co. post from Herschel Isl., Yukon Territory; transshipment point from river boats to seagoing ships; transport base for High Arctic and Beaufort Sea oil production and exploration. Trapping, whaling, sealing. Radio and Television stations. In Reindeer Grazing Reserve. Annual reindeer harvest (herd of 10,000). Located in area noted for its pingos, ice-covered hills, created by permafrost heaving, that rise above the flat delta. N terminus of winter road from Inuvik. Scheduled air service. Formerly Port Brabant.

Tukwila (tuhk-WI-luh), city (1990 pop. 11,874), King co., W central Wash., suburb 10 mi/16 km S of downtown Seattle, and 15 mi/24 km NNE of Tacoma, W of Renton; 47°29′N 122°16′W. RR junction. Mfg. (aerospace parts, paints, computers, plastic bags, synthetic rubber, dental equip.; plastic bottles, soft drinks, printing, inks, office machines). L. Washington to N; Seattle–Tacoma (Sea Tac) Internatl. Airport to SW. Site of Southcenter Mall, one of the largest shopping centers in U.S.

Tula (TOO-luh), village, Lafayette co., N Miss., 13 mi/21 km SE of Oxford. In agr. area (cotton, corn; cattle); timber.

Tula, anc. city in the present state of Hidalgo, central Mexico; 23°00′N 99°41′W. It was one of the chief urban centers of the Toltec. The city is believed to be Tollán, the legendary Toltec capital mentioned in a number of postconquest sources, including Bernardino de Sahagún's *Historia General de las Cosas de Nueva Espana* (Span. = *General History of the Things of New Spain*) as well as in documents in indigenous hieroglyphics known as *códices*. Archaeological investigations in the ceremonial precinct have revealed impressive architectural remains including pyramidal structures and ball courts. One of the former was surmounted by a temple to the Toltec hero-god Quetzalcoatl and had unusual sculptured columns in the form of warriors. These columns have been restored. Architectural and stylistic correspondences bet. Tula and several Mayan centers on the N Yucatán peninsula, primarily at the site of Chichén Itzá, indicate that Toltec influence pervaded the area. Work at Tula indicates a beginning Toltec state may have existed 75 mi/121 km from Teotihuacan. Kukulkan (Mayan name for Quetzalcoatl) arrived in Yucatán, est. Toltec center at Chichén Itzá.

Tula (TOO-lah), a national park, in E Hidalgo, Mexico, 43 mi/69 km E of Mexico city, Mexico.

Tula de Allende (TOO-lah de ah-YEN-de), town (1990 pop. 24,171), in SW Hidalgo, Mexico, on the left bank of the Tula R., 55.6 mi/89.5 km W of the city of Puchuca de Soto; 20°03′N 99°20′W. Elev. 6,778 ft/2,066 m. On RR, good communication with Mexico city. On Tula R. Agr. (wheat, alfalfa,) and cattle raising. Archeological ruins of ancient Tula (famous in Mex. history) are nearby.

Tula River (too-lah), c.100 mi/161 km long, central Mexico; rises NW of Mexico city; flows N and NW, past Tula, Mixquiahuala, and Ixmiquilpan, to Moctezuma R. at Querétaro border, 9 mi/14.5 km SW of Zimapán; 20°40′N 99°30′W.

Tulainyo Lake, E Calif., tiny lake (c.12,020 ft/3,664 m) just N of Mt. Whitney, in the Sierra Nevada. One of highest in U.S.

Tulalip (tuh-LAH-lip), village (1990 pop. 300), Skagit co., NW Wash., on Puget Sound, 6 mi/9.7 km NW of Everett, in Tulalip Indian Reservation (1990 pop. 7,103). Native Amer. Agency hq. for Tulalip, and other nearby Indian reservations.

Tulameen (tuh-luh-MEEN), ghost town, S B.C., Canada, in Cascade Mts., on Tulameen R., at mouth of Otter Creek, and 55 mi/89 km W of Penticton; 49°33′N 120°45′W. Cattle, timber; tourism, skiing.

Tulancingo (too-lahn-SEEN-go), city (1990 pop. 75,477) and township, ⊙ Tulancingo de Bravo municipio, Hidalgo, central Mexico, on central plateau, 24 mi/39 km E of Pachuca de Soto on RR, on Mexico Highway 130; 20°06′N 99°20′W. Agr. center (corn, wheat, vegetables, maguey, livestock); dairying, flour- and textile milling.

Tulare, county (□ 4,824 sq mi/12,494 sq km; 1990 pop. 311,921), central Calif.; ⊙ Visalia; 36°14′N 118°48′W. Extends E from San Joaquin Valley to crest of the Sierra Nevada; Mt. Whitney (14,495 ft/4,418 m), highest point in U.S., is on E boundary. Drained by Kaweah, St. Johns, Tule, and Kern rivers. Sugar beets, beans, wheat, oats, corn, citrus fruit, nuts, olives, berries, grapes, apples; nursery prods.; cotton; turkeys, cattle, hogs. Logging (pine, fir); sand and gravel, tungsten; clay deposits; marble and granite quarries. Farm-produce packing, processing, and shipping (at Visalia, Tulare, Porterville, Lindsay, Exeter, Woodlake, Dinuba); lumber milling. Pacific Crest Scenic Trail runs N-S near E boundary; includes SEQUOIA NATIONAL PARK, and parts of Kings Canyon Natl. Park in NE; Inyo and Sequoia natl. forests in E; Tule R. Indian Reservation is at S center; Pixley Natl. Wildlife Refuge and Colonel Allensworth State Historical Park in SW. Formed 1852.

Tulare, city (1990 pop. 33,249), Tulare co., S central Calif., 10 mi/16 km SSW of Visalia, near Kaweah R., in the San Joaquin valley; 36°12′N 119°20′W. RR junction. Farm produce, processing, shipping (grapes, fruit, nuts, grain, sugar beets); cotton, and dairying region; winery; dairy prods. Mfg. (concrete, sheet metal work, plumbing fixtures, lumber, measuring devices, pumps). Inc. 1888.

Tulare, (too-LER) village, Spink co., E central S.Dak., 10 mi/16 km S of Redfield; 44°44′N 98°30′W.

Tulare Lake, dry lake, Kings co., S central Calif., in Central Valley, 30 mi/48 km WSW of Visalia; c.50 mi/80 km long, c.35 mi/56 km wide. Remnants of the Kings, Kaweah, and Tule rivers flow into the lake bed, most of their waters having been diverted for irrigation. Crossed by network of roads and irrigation channels; most agr. seasons, Tulare L. is almost without water. Visited by the Spanish in 1772.

Tularosa (TOO-luh-ro-suh), town (1990 pop. 2,615), Otero co., S N.Mex., just W of Sacramento Mts., 13 mi/21 km NNW of Alamogordo; 33°04′N 106°01′W. Elev. 4,514 ft/1,376 m. Trade and livestock (cattle, sheep) shipping point; timber. Plotted 1862. Mescalero Apache Indian Reservation to E; part of Lincoln Natl. Forest to SE; Three Rivers Petroglyph Natl. Recreation Site to NE, near Sierra Blanca. On E side of Tularosa Valley; White Sands Missile Range to W.

Tularosa Basin (TOO-luh-ro-suh), desert basin in S N.Mex. and W Texas; from the Rio Grande near El Paso extends N-S c.130 mi/209 km, 20 mi/32 km–40 mi/64 km wide. Sierra Oscura, San Andres, and Organ mts. to W; Sacramento and Jicarilla mts. to E; the Malpais, volcanic lava field, in N; large gypsum sand dunes of White Sands Natl. Monument in center.

Tularosa Mountains (TOO-luh-ro-suh), W N.Mex., in Catron co., just E of Tularosa R., near Ariz. border, W of Continental Divide within Gila Natl. Forest; 33°54′N 108°31′W. Highest point, Eagle Peak (9,802 ft/2,988 m).

Tularosa River (TOO-luh-ro-suh), W N.Mex.; rises in several forks in Catron co.; flows c.40 mi/64 km SW, past Aragon, to San Francisco R., just S of Reserve. Drains part of Apache Natl. Forest. Tularosa Mts. to SE.

Tulcingo de Valle (tool-SEEN-go dai LAH-le), town (1990 pop. 3,765), Puebla, central Mexico, 40 mi/64 km S of Izúcar de Matamoros; 18°03′N 98°26′W. Elev. 3,681 ft/1,122 m. Corn, sugarcane, fruit; livestock.

Tule, Mexico: see SANTA MARÍA DEL TULE.

Tule Creek (TOO-lee), NW Texas, formed on Llano Estacado W of Tulia by intermittent headstreams; flows c.45 mi/72 km E and NE to Prairie Dog Town Fork of Red R.; lower course of c.15 mi/24 km is through scenic Tule Canyon, gorge cut in Caprock escarpment by stream's descent from high plains. North Tule Draw, intermittent, enters from NW, 10 mi/16 km E of Tulin.

Tule, El, Mexico: see EL TULE.

Tule Lake, NE Siskiyou co., N Calif., near Oregon state border. Has variable area. Receives Lost R. (N). Used for storage of irrigation water for surrounding region. In Tule Natl. Wildlife Refuge. Tulelake city is just N, Lava Beds Natl. Monument just S.

Tule River, S central Calif., formed in the Sierra Nevada E of Porterville in S central Tulare co., by its North and Middle forks; flows c.50 mi/80 km SW and W past Porterville, into Tulare L. through network of irrigation canals. North Fork flows through Success Reservoir, Middle Fork rises in Tule River Indian Reservation.

Tulelake, city (1990 pop. 1,010), Siskiyou co., N Calif., 25 mi/40 km SE of Klamath Falls, Oregon, near Lost R.; 41°57′N 121°28′W. Grain, potatoes, onions, horseradish; cattle, sheep, lambs. Mfg. (pumice- and horseradish-processing). In World War II, a relocation camp for evacuated Japanese and Jap.-Americans was nearby. Lava Beds Natl. Monument and Tule L. (Natl. Wildlife Refuge) are S; Modoc Natl. Forest to E; Lower Klamath Natl. Wildlife Refuge to W, Clear L. Natl. Wildlife Refuge to SE. Inc. 1937.

Tulia, town (1990 pop. 4,699), ⊙ Swisher co., NW Texas, on Llano Estacado, 25 mi/40 km N of Plainview; 34°32′N 101°46W. Elev. 3,501 ft/ 1,067 m. Processing and shipping center for wheat, milo, corn, sorghum, cotton; cattle region. Mfg. (manifold valves, farm equip.). MacKenzie Reservoir to E; Tule Canyon is nearby. Settled 1890, inc. 1909.

Tullahassee (tuhl-uh-HAS-ee), village (1990 pop. 92), Wagoner co., E Okla., 7 mi/11.3 km NW of Muskogee, near Arkansas R. (S) and Verdigris R. (NE); 35°50′N 95°26′W.

Tullahoma, (tuh-luh-HO-mah), city (1990 pop. 16,761), Coffee and Franklin cos., central Tenn., near Tims Ford Reservoir (Elk R.), 55 mi/89 km NW of Chattanooga; 35°22′N 86°13′W. An industrial center in a highland timber and farm area. Mfg. (aircraft equip., clothing, sporting goods, and stationery prods.). Tullahoma's industrial growth was spurred during World War II by the est. nearby of Camp Forrest, an infantry training center. After the war, the Camp Forrest reservation became the site of the huge Arnold Engineering Development Center and Arnold Air Force Base, a permanent aeronautical research and testing installation serving NASA and the U.S. armed forces. The Univ. of Tenn. Space Inst. and a community col. are in the city. Settled c.1850 as a RR labor camp, inc. 1903.

Tulloch Dam, Calif.: see STANISLAUS RIVER.

Tulloch Point (TUH-luhk), S extremity of King William Isl., S Franklin dist., N.W.T., Canada, on Simpson Strait, opposite Adelaide Peninsula; 68°27′N 97°5′W.

Tullos (TUH-luhs), village (1990 pop. 427), La Salle parish central La., 36 mi/58 km N of Alexandria, near Castor Creek; 31°49′N 92°20′W. In agr. area (soybeans, cotton); timber. Oil fields nearby.

Tully, village (1990 pop. 911), Onondaga co., central N.Y., in Tully Valley, 14 mi/23 km S of Syracuse; 42°47′N 76°06′W. One of many former Finger Lake valleys, with rich agr. soils. Mfg. (swimming pool chemicals). Agr. (poultry; potatoes, cabbage, hay). Tully L., a complex of shallow natural lakes, 2 mi/3.2 km W of village.

Tully Lake, Worcester co., N central Mass., on East Branch Tully R., 4 mi/6 km N of Athol; 42°38′N 72°14′W. Max. capacity 35,800 acre-ft. Formed by Tully Dam (54 ft/138 m high), built (1949) by Army Corps of Engineers for flood control. Tully Lake Recreation Area on E Side.

Tullytown (TUHL-lee-toun), borough (1990 pop. 2,339), Bucks co., SE Pa., residential suburb, 6 mi/9.7 km SSW of Trenton, and 21 mi/34 km NE of downtown Philadelphia, on Delaware R.; 40°08′N 74°48′W. Mfg. (corrugated boxes, concrete prods., hospital pads, compressors). Steel plant to E, see FAIRLESS HILLS. "Pennsbury Manor," restored home of William Penn, in Pennsbury Manor State Park, to E; Van Scriver L. (backwater lake of Delaware R.) to NE.

Tulsa, county (□ 587 sq mi/1,520 sq km; 1990 pop. 503,341), NE Okla.; ⊙ Tulsa; 36°07′N 95°56′W. Intersected by Arkansas R. (S) and Bird Creek (N). Grain, soybeans; cattle, horses, sheep. Important oil and gas production, oil refining; agricultural chemical production. A long co. N-S; highly urbanized in middle, agr. N and far S. Formed 1907.

Tulsa, city (1990 pop. 367,302), ⊙ Tulsa and Osage cos., NE Okla., 85 mi/137 km NE of Oklahoma City, on the Arkansas R. E of its junction with the Cimarron R.; 36°07′N 95°55′W. It became an inland port with the opening (1971) of the McClellan–Kerr Waterway, a 440-mi/708-km system linking it with the Gulf of Mexico; includes part of Catoosa on Verdigris R. to NE. Tulsa is the focal point of a major metropolitan area marked by a growing economy and pop. since 1975. It is an important center of the nation's petroleum industry with large refineries and plants that produce petroleum prods. and related equip. However, the refining functions have been declining in recent years. Some major oil concerns have their business offices and research laboratories here. Other mfg. includes printing and publishing, air conditioners, bricks, asphalt, oil-field equip., molded rubber prods., metal castings, agricultural chemicals, plumbing equip.; glass prods., power tools, polyethylene film, communications equip., aircraft parts, aerostructures. Tulsa grew as a cattle-shipping village after the coming of the RR in 1882 and boomed with the discovery of oil nearby in 1901. An extensive park system (which includes Mohawk and Turkey Mt. parks) and well-planned communities characterize the residential aspect of the city. Tulsa is also a cultural and educational center with an opera and orchestra; a large theater; art and history museums (Philbrook Art Center, Thomas Gilcrease Mus.), the Univ. of Tulsa, Oral Roberts Univ., and an inst. of Amer. art and history. Tulsa Internatl. Airport in NE part of city; Jones Airport in SW. Tulsa State Fairgrounds. Inc. 1898.

Tultepec, Mexico: see SANTA MARÍA TULTEPEC.

Tultitlán de Mariano Escobedo (tool-teet-LAHN dai mah-ree-AH-no es-ko-BE-do), town (1990 pop. 16,266), ⊙ Tultitlán municipio, Mexico state, central Mexico, 15 mi/24 km N of Mexico city, and in the Zona Metropolitana de la Ciudad de México; 19°39′N 09°09′W. Grain, maguey; livestock.

Tuluksak, Inuit village (1990 pop. 358), W Alaska, on lower Kuskokwim R., and 35 mi/56 km NE of Bethel; 61°07′N 160°56′W.

Tulum (too-LOOM), a national park, on E Quintana Roo, Mexico, 19 mi/30 km N of Felipe Carillo (port), on the coast, and a highly popular tourist attraction. Built bet. 564–593 as a planned city with 50 structures, it was later enclosed by walls 16.4 ft/5 m thick with one unwalled side facing the Caribbean Sea. Tulum was the main port of trade for most Maya centers on the Yucatán peninsula.

Tumacacori National Historical Park (too-muh-KAH-ko-ree) Santa Cruz co., S Ariz. at Tumacacori,

17 mi/27 km NNW of Nogales near Santa Cruz R. Mission rebuilt by Franciscans on site visited by Father Eusebio F. Kino in 1691. Covers 17 acres/7 ha. Authorized 1908.

Tumbalá (toom-bah-LAH), town (1990 pop. 1,622), Chiapas, S Mexico, in spur of Sierra Madre, 45 mi/72 km NNE of San Cristóbal de las Casas; 17°18′N 92°19′W. Cereals, fruit.

Tumbiascatío de Ruíz (toom-bee-ahs-kah-TEE-o de roo-EES), town (1990 pop. 3,632), in S central Michoacán, Mexico. In a W extension of the Sierra Madre del Sur, 16 mi/25 km NW of Arteaga; 18°31′N 102°21′W. Access by horse trails only.

Tumbler Ridge, town (1991 pop. 4,650), NW B.C., Canada, 60 mi/97 km SW of Dawson Creek, on E bank of Murray R. Est. late 1980s with open-pit mines. S terminus of Route 29 from Chetwynd. New RR line crosses Hart Range from Prince George.

Tumwater, city (1990 pop. 9,976), Thurston co., W Wash., suburb 2 mi/3.2 km S of Olympia, and on Deschutes R.; 47°00′N 122°55′W. Founded 1845 as 1st Amer. settlement in Puget Sound area. Mfg. (rubber hose and belting, clothing, welding equip.; soft drinks, beer; trusses, lumber); logging. Black Hills to SW; Millersylvania State Park to S. Olympic Municipal Airport to S. Sometimes considered the end of the Oregon Trail.

Tunapuna (TOO-na-POO-na), town, NW Trinidad, Trinidad and Tobago, on RR, and 9 mi/14.5 km E of Port of Spain. Sugar center. Its inhabitants are predominantly Indian.

Tunas de Zaza (TOO-nuhs dai ZAH-zuh), village, Sancti Spíritus prov., central Cuba; 21°38′N 79°33′W. Caribbean port for Sancti Spíritus (20 mi/32 km N; linked by RR, though the prov.'s sugar is exported through Cienfuegos and Caibarién), with fine harbor at mouth of Zaza R. Ships chiefly sugarcane and lumber; also tobacco, honey, and beeswax. Sometimes called Zaza.

Tunbridge, town (1990 pop. 1,154), Orange co., E Vt., on First Branch of White R., and just S of Chelsea; 43°53′N 72°29′W. Woodworking, dairy prods. Annual Union Agr. Fair known as "World's Fair" is here.

Tungsten, village, Boulder co., N central Colo., on middle of Boulder Creek, in Front Range, 2 mi/3.2 km ENE of Nederland, and 30 mi/48 km WNW of Denver. Elev. c.7,800 ft/2,377 m. Tungsten deposits. Surrounded by Roosevelt Natl. Forest; Barker Reservoir to W.

Tunica (TOO-nik-uh), county (□ 480 sq mi/1,243 sq km; 1990 pop. 8,164), NW Miss.; ⊙ Tunica; 34°39′N 90°22′W. Bounded NW and W by Mississippi R., (Ark. state border), Tunixca L., 12 mi/19 km long oxbow lake of Mississippi R., forms part of W boundary; and drained in SE and bounded E in part by Coldwater R. Rich agr. area (cotton, corn, sorghum, soybeans, wheat, rice; cattle; timber); catfish. Formed 1836. Formerly impoverished, it is now a major gambling center, with many casinos and hotels.

Tunica (TOO-nik-uh), town (1990 pop. 1,175), ⊙ Tunica co., NW Miss., near Mississippi R., 35 mi/56 km SSW of Memphis, Tenn.; 34°41′N 90°22′W. Trade center for agr. area (cotton, corn, rice; cattle); catfish. Mfg. (agr. chemicals, catfish processing, bedding). Tunica L. to W, former channel of Mississippi R.

Tunica (TOO-ni-kuh), uninc. village (1990 pop. 29), West Feliciana parish, SE La., 38 mi/61 km NW of Baton Rouge, on E bank of Mississippi R.; 30°55′N 91°33′W. Tunica Swamp nearby. Angola State Penitentiary is 1 mi/1.6 km to W. Tunica Hills State Wildlife Area with rare flora and fauna to E.

Tunis Mills (TOO-nis), village, Talbot co., E Md., on the Eastern Shore 18 mi/29 km NNW of Cambridge and on inlet of Miles R. Fayette Gibson, the last of his family to live in what is now the site of Marengo, is credited locally with being the inventor of the first reaper exhibited at the Easton Fairgrounds in 1833. The Anchorage was built in the mid-18th cent. by Richard Bruff. The wings were added in the mid-19th cent. by Lt. Charles Lowndes and his wife, Sarah, whose sister, Ann Catherine, was the wife of Adm. Franklin Buchanan (1800–1874), the first superintendent of the Naval Academy. Buchanan commanded the Confederate ironclad Virginia (Merrimac), and was wounded in the battle with the Union's Monitor. He was also in command of the Confederate forces when Adm. David Farragut defeated them at the Battle of Mobile Bay on August 5, 1864.

Tunkás (toon-kahs), town (1990 pop. 3,012), Yucatán, SE Mexico, on RR., 18 mi/29 km E of Izamal; 20°54′N 88°42′W. Henequen, sugarcane, corn.

Tunkhannock (tuhn-KAH-nuk), borough (1990 pop. 2,251), ⊙ Wyoming co., NE Pa., 17 mi/27 km WNW of Scranton, on Susquehanna R., at mouth of Tunkhannock Creek; 41°32′N 75°57′W. Mfg. (furniture grade lumber, machinery, printing and publishing). Agr. area (grain; livestock, dairying); timber. L. Carey reservoir to N. Settled 1775, inc. 1841.

Tunnel Hill, town (1990 pop. 970), Whitfield co., NW Ga., 6 mi/9.7 km NW of Dalton; 34°51′N 85°02′W. Mfg. (feeds, textiles, carpets).

Tunnelhill (TUH-nuhl-hil), borough (1990 pop. 365), Cambria co., W central Pa., 1 mi/1.6 km SE of Gallitzin; 40°28′N 78°32′W. Also spelled Tunnel Hill.

Tunnelton 1 village, Lawrence co., S Ind., 10 mi/16 km SE of Bedford. Agr. area. Near Devil's Backbone and Big Tunnel, Indiana's longest RR tunnel. Laid out 1859. **2** village (1990 pop. 331), Preston co., N W.Va., 8 mi/12.9 km SSW of Kingwood; 39°′23N 79°′45W. RR junction. W.Va. N RR, excursion train to Kingwood.

Tununak, Alaska: see TANUNAK.

Tunungayualuk Island, just off E Lab., Canada; 12 mi/19 km long, 11 mi/18 km wide; 56°4′N 61°4′W.

Tuolumne, county (□ 2,236 sq mi/5,791 sq km; 1990 pop. 48,456), central and E Calif.; ⊙ Sonora; 38°01′N 119°57′W. In the Sierra Nevada, here crossed by Sonora Pass. Bounded on NW by Stanislaus R. and its North Fork. Drained by Middle and South forks Stanislaus R., and by Tuolumne R. (hydroelectric, irrigation, water supply projects). W portion is in 1849 Calif. Gold Rush region. Hay, apples; cattle; timber. Lumbering (pine, fir, cedar); gold; marble, limestone, sand and gravel quarrying. Many campgrounds, lakes and streams (trout fishing), hiking trails, winter sports facilities. Cattle grazing, some farming (fruit, hay), poultry raising. N half of Yosemite Natl. Park is in E; large part of Stanislaus Natl. Forest in center and NE, Emigrant Basin Wilderness Area (NE); part of Calaveras Big Trees State Park on NW boundary; Cherry L. reservoir in center, New Don Pedro Reservoir in S, Hetch Hetchy Reservoir, on North Fork Tuolumne R., in Yosemite Natl. Park in E; Hetch Hetchy Aqueduct, which runs across S part of co., delivers water to San Francisco Bay Area. Sonora, Jamestown, and Columbia were once gold camps. Formed 1850.

Tuolumne, uninc. town (1990 pop. 1,686), Tuolumne co., central Calif., in the Sierra Nevada, 6 mi/9.7 km E of Sonora, in 1849 Calif. Gold Rush region; 37°58′N 120°14′W. Timber; cattle; hay; apples. Tuolumne Indian Rancheria (reservation) to N; Stanislaus Natl. Forest to E.

Tuolumne River, c.110 mi/177 km long, central Calif.; rises in YOSEMITE NATIONAL PARK in SE Tuolumne co., (Lyell Fork); flows W to San Joaquin R., 10 mi/16 km W of Modesto. In Yosemite Park are rivers; Grand Canyon of the Tuolumne; Hetch Hetchy Valley, and Reservoir (formed by O'Shaughessy Dam). W of Yosemite Park, Hetch Hetchy Aqueduct diverts from river and parallels it to S; crosses river at Don Pedro Reservoir, then roughly parallels river to N, lower course paralleled to N by Modesto Main Canal (irrigation). In SW Tuolumne co. is Don Pedro Dam (284 ft/87 m high, 1,040 ft/317 m long; completed 1923 for irrigation and power), impounding Don Pedro Reservoir (c.10 mi/16 km long). Farther downstream are offstream Modesto and Turlock reservoirs, both fed by the Tuolumne, used for irrigation.

Tupelo (TOO-puh-lo), city (1990 pop. 30,685), ⊙ Lee co., NE Miss., on the Natchez Trace. RR junction. It is the trade, processing, and shipping center for a cotton, grain, dairying, and livestock area. Once important for timber, the city is named after the Tupelo, or black gum tree. Mfg. (dairy prods., furniture, lighting fixtures, corrugated partitions, concrete and foam prods.; tires, wood- and metalworking machinery; mirrors, plastic bags, apparel; snack foods, chicken processing). Private John Allen Fish Hatchery is here. Union troops repulsed an attack by Gen. N. B. Forrest (July 14, 1864) but nevertheless retreated. Nearby is the scene of a victory of Chickasaw and Br. forces over the Choctaw and French (May 26, 1736). Tupelo Natl. Battlefield is here, on W Main street. Brice's Cross Roads Natl. Battlefield Site to N. Tupelo Mus., Tupelo Artist Guild Gallery. The 2-room house where Elvis Presley was born (1935) and mus. are here. Tombigbee State Park to E, Trace State Park to W; Natchez Trace (Natl.) Parkway passes city to NW. Founded 1859, inc. 1870.

Tupelo 1 (TOO-puh-lo), village (1990 pop. 208), Jackson co., NE Ark., 15 mi/24 km S of Newport; 35°23′N 91°13′W. **2** village (1990 pop. 323), Coal co., S central Okla., 20 mi/32 km SE of Ada; 34°36′N 96°25′W.

Tupelo (TOO-puh-lo), National Battlefield, Lee co., NE Miss., on W Main Street in Tupelo. Civil War battle July 13–14, 1864, at this site. Covers 1 acre/0.4 ha. Authorized 1929.

Tupper or **Tupper Creek**, village, E B.C., Canada, on Alta. border, 19 mi/31 km SSE of Dawson Creek; lumbering, grain; livestock.

Tupper Lake, resort village (□ 1 sq mi/2.6 sq km; 1990 pop. 4,087), Franklin co., N N.Y., in the Adirondacks, 17 mi/27 km SE of Saranac L. village; 44°13′N 74°28′W. Near Tupper L. (□ c.6 sq mi/15.5 sq km; 8 mi/12.9 km long; sometimes called Big Tupper L.). Woodworking. Little Tupper L. (□ c.4 sq mi/10.4 sq km; c.5 mi/8 km long) is 12 mi/19 km SSW. Settled 1890, inc. 1902.

Tuque, La (TOOK, lah), town (1991 pop. 10,003), S Que., Canada, on St. Maurice R., and 80 mi/129 km N of Trois Rivières; pulp milling center, mfg. Hydroelectric station.

Turbeville (TUHR-bee-vil), village (1990 pop. 698), Clarendon co., E central S.C., 19 mi/31 km E of Sumter; 33°53′N 80°01′W. Mfg. includes clothing; agr. area known for tobacco growing. Also produces grain, cotton; cattle, poultry.

Turbio, Río (toor-BEE-on), river, c.100 mi/161 km long, Guanajuato, central Mexico; rises N of León in Sierra Madre Occidental; flows S, past San Francisco del Rincón and Manuel Doblado, to Lerma R. 12 mi/19 km SE of Pénjamo.

Turbotville (TUHR-buht-vil), borough (1990 pop. 675), Northumberland co., E central Pa., 16 mi/26 km N of Sunbury; 41°06′N 76°46′W. Agr. (grain; poultry, livestock; dairying).

Turicato (too-ree-KAH-to), town (1990 pop. 1,743), Michoacán, central Mexico, 13 mi/21 km SSE of Tacámbaro; 19°02′N 101°26′W. Cereals, fruit, sugarcane.

Turiguanó Island (toor-ee-gwah-NO), off Ciego de Ávila prov., E Cuba, 9 mi/14.5 km N of Morón; 15 mi/24 km long, 6 mi/9.7 km wide; 22°17′N 78°43′W. Bounded by Leche Lagoon (S), and Perro's Bay (N), it is linked with main isl. by a road cutting through tidal marshes.

Turin 1 (TUHR-in), town (1990 pop. 189), Coweta co., W Ga., 10 mi/16 km ESE of Newnan; 33°20′N 84°38′W. Mfg. of concrete and masonery. **2** town (1990 pop. 95), Monona co., W Iowa, 6 mi/9.7 km E of Onawa; 42°01′N 95°58′W. In agr. area.

Turin, village (□ 1 sq mi/2.6 sq km; 1990 pop. 295), Lewis co., N central N.Y., on Black R. and 12 mi/19 km SSE of Lowville; 43°37′N 75°24′W. In timber area. Winter recreation (downhill skiing and snowmobiling) center.

Turkey, town (1990 pop. 507), Hall co., NW Texas, just below Caprock escarpment, c.40 mi/64 km W of Childress; 34°23′N 100°54′W. Elev. 2,348 ft/716 m. In agr. area (cotton; peanuts; cattle, hogs); feeds.

Turkey, village (1990 pop. 234), Sampson co., S central N.C., 8 mi/12.9 km E of Clinton; 34°59′N 78°11′W. Tobacco, cotton, peanuts, grain; poultry, livestock. Mfg. (machining).

Turkey Creek, village (1990 pop. 283), Evangeline parish, S central La., 25 mi/40 km S of Alexandria; 30°52′N 92°25′W. In agr. area (cotton, rice, sweet potatoes; cattle). Chicot State Park to SE; Crooked Creek State Recreation Area to SW.

Turkey Creek, c.65 mi/105 km long, rises in Alfalfa co., N Okla., flows SSE past Enid and Hennessey to Cimarron R. c.8 mi/12.9 km N of Kingfisher.

Turkey Point, Md.: see ELK NECK.

Turkey River, 135 mi/217 km long, Iowa; rises in Howard co., NE Iowa; flows SE past Elkader to Mississippi R. 6 mi/9.7 km SSE of Guttenberg. Receives Volga R. at Garber.

Turkey Run State Park, Parke co., W Ind., 9 mi/14.5 km NNE of Rockville. One of Ind.'s most popular state parks, especially in summer and fall. Canoeing. In covered bridge area.

Turks and Caicos Islands, crown colony of Great Britain (□ 166 sq mi/430 sq km; 1990 pop. 11,465), West Indies; 21°44′N 71°35′W. There are more than 30 cays and isls., of which only 6 are inhabited. The ⊙ is on Grand Turk. The isls. are geographically a southeastern continuation of the Bahamas. Lobster and conch are primary exports; the economic mainstays are tourism and offshore banking. Scuba diving is especially important. The pop. is largely of black Afr. descent. The isls. were first visited by Europeans in 1512 when Ponce de León landed there.

Turks Island Passage, c.20–mi/32–km-wide channel in the Caribbean, separating Caicos Isls. (W) from Turks Isls. (E), at about 21°40′N 71°W.

Turks Islands, E group of TURKS AND CAICOS Isls., crown colony of Great Britain, West Indies, 135 mi/217 km NNW of Cap-Haïtien (Haiti), separated from Caicos Isls. by Turks Island Passage (also called Christopher Columbus Passage); bet. 21°10′–21°31′N and 71°5′–71°15′W. Isls. consist of Grand Turk and Salt Cay and some smaller islets. On Grand Turk is the capital of the dependency. Tourism is major industry, especially noted for scuba diving and sport fishing.

Turley (TUHR-lee), uninc. town (1990 pop. 2,930), Tulsa co., NE Okla., residential suburb 6 mi/9.7 km N of Tulsa; 36°15′N 95°58′W. Oil refining.

Turlock, city (1990 pop. 42,198), Stanislaus co., central Calif., 12 mi/19 km SSE of Modesto; 37°30′N 120°51′W. Marked by rapid growth since the 1970s, it is the center of the Turlock irrigation dist., which uses the waters of the Tuolumne R. in this fertile farm area (dairying; poultry; vegetables, fruit, nuts, melons, grapes). The city has poultry-processing plants and mfg. of food, machinery, fabricated metal prods., plastic prods. California State Univ., Stanislaus is located here. Inc. 1908.

Turnagain Arm (TUHR-nuh-gin), NE arm of Cook Inlet, S Alaska, on N side of Kenai Peninsula, 15 mi/24 km S of Anchorage; 50 mi/80 km long, 2 mi/3.2 km–13 mi/21 km wide. Named 1778 by Capt. James Cook. Has among highest tides in the world.

Turner 1 county (□ 290 sq mi/751 sq km; 1990 pop. 8,703), S central Ga.; ⊙ Ashburn; 31°43′N 83°38′W. Drained by Little and Alapaha rivers. Coastal plain agr. (peanuts, cotton, corn, tobacco, soybeans, wheat; cattle, hogs). Formed 1905. **2** county (□ 617 sq mi/1,598 sq km; 1990 pop. 8,576), SE S.Dak.; ⊙ Parker; 43°18′N 97°09′W. Rich agr. area drained by Vermillion R. and its E & W forks, which converge E of Parker. Corn, soybeans; cattle, hogs, sheep; dairy prods.; honey. Formed 1871.

Turner 1 town (1990 pop. 4,315), Androscoggin co., SW Maine, on the Androscoggin and 20 mi/32 km N of Auburn; 44°16′N 70°15′W. Agr. (apples, eggs); lumber mills. Includes Turner Center village, long known for dairying. Settled c.1773, inc. 1786. **2** town (1990 pop. 1,281), Marion co., NW Oregon, 7 mi/11.3 km SE of Salem; 44°51′N 122°57′W. Agr. (fruit, vegetables, berries, nuts; poultry; dairying). Ankeny Natl. Wildlife Refuge to SW.

Turner 1 village, Wyandotte co., NE Kansas, on inside bend of Kansas R.; 3 mi/4.8 km WSW of downtown Kansas City, Kansas. Now part of city. **2** village (1990 pop. 158), Arenac co., E Mich., 14 mi/23 km NE of Standish, near Au Gres R.; 44°08′N 83°47′W. In farm area; gypsum refining. **3** village (1990 pop. 175), Blaine co., N Mont.; 42 mi/68 km NNW of Malta. Wheat; cattle, sheep. Port of entry on Canada (Sask.) border, 11 mi/18 km N. Black Coulee Natl. Wildlife Refuge to S.

Turner Center, Maine: see TURNER.

Turner Valley, town (1991 pop. 1,352), SW Alta., Canada, at foot of Rocky Mts., on Sheep R. and 27 mi/43 km SSW of Calgary; 50°41′N 114°16′W. Center of major oil and natural gas area, extending c.10 mi/16 km N and S from village. Oil refineries; gas pipe lines to Calgary, Lethbridge, and other S Alta. towns. Production began 1914.

Turners Falls, Mass.: see MONTAGUE.

Turners Station, village, Henry co., N Ky., 22 mi/35 km SW of Warsaw, in Bluegrass region.

Turney, town (1990 pop. 155), Clinton co., NW Mo., 4 mi/6.4 km N of Lathrop; 39°38′N 94°19′W.

Turon (TUHR-on), village (1990 pop. 393), Reno co., S central Kansas, 30 mi/48 km WSW of Hutchinson; 37°48′N 98°25′W. RR junction. In wheat area.

Turpin Hills, uninc. village (1990 pop. 4,927), Hamilton co., extreme SW Ohio, SE of the city of Cincinnati and on Kentucky line; 39°06′N 84°22′W.

Turquino (toor-KEE-no), Span. *Pico Turquino*, peak (6,749 ft/1,975 m), Santiago de Cuba prov., SE Cuba, in the Sierra Maestra range; 19°59′N 76°55′W. It is the highest point on the isl. Scene of intense guerrilla activity during the rebel insurgency led by Fidel Castro in the late 1950s.

Turquoise Lake, reservoir, Lake co., central Colo., on Lake Fork Arkansas R., 4 mi/6.4 km W of Leadville; 4 mi/6.4 km long, 39°15′N 106°21′W. Max. capacity of 135,500 acre-ft. Formed by Sugar Loaf Dam (129 ft/39 m high), built (1968) by the Bureau of Reclamation for irrigation. W end and N shore in San Isabel Natl. Forest.

Turrell (tuhr-EL), town (1990 pop. 988), Crittenden co., E Ark., 21 mi/34 km NW of Memphis (Tenn.), Mississippi R. to E; 35°22′N 90°15′W. RR junction. In cotton and rice growing area. Wapanocca Natl. Wildlife Refuge to SE.

Turtle Bay, a dist. of E Manhattan borough of N.Y. city, SE N.Y., along East R. N of 42d St.; 40°45′N 73°57′W. Site of the hq. of the UN.

Turtle Creek (TUHR-tuhl KREEK), borough (1990 pop. 6,566), Allegheny co., SW Pa., suburb 10 mi/16 km ESE of downtown Pittsburgh, near Turtle Creek; 40°24′N 79°49′W. Mfg. (fabricated metal prods., galvanized steel, transportation equip.); bituminous coal. Trading post near here c.1750. Settled c.1765, inc. 1892.

Turtle Creek, c.35 mi/56 km long, S Wis.; rises in L. Delevan SE of town of Delavan in Walworth co.; flows W past Delavan, then SW to Rock R. at Beloit.

Turtle Lake 1 village (1990 pop. 681), McLean co., central N.Dak., 17 mi/27 km NNE of Washburn on McClusky Canal; 47°31′N 100°53′W. RR terminus; some mfg.; cattle; coal; grain; dairy prods. Turtle L. to W; Audubon Natl. Wildlife Refuge to NW; several small lakes to E **2** village (1990 pop. 817), Barron co., NW Wis., 21 mi/34 km WSW of Rice L. Wooded lake-resort area; 45°23′N 92°08′W. Some mfg. Casino. St. Croix Indian Reservation to NW; several small lakes in area.

Turtle Lake, Itasca co., N central Minn., 26 mi/42 km NNW of Grand Rapids in Chippewa Natl. Forest; 4.5 mi/7.2 km long, 2 mi/3.2 km wide; 47°37′N 93°42′E. Resort area. Drains S through Turtle R. to Bowstring R.

Turtle Mountain, in N N.Dak. and S Manitoba, plateau 2,000 ft/610 m above sea level, 300 ft/91 m–400 ft/122 m above surrounding country; extends 20 mi/32 km N-S, 40 mi/64 km E-W; 48°55′N 100°34′W. It has timber, numerous lakes, and small deposits of low-grade manganese. Turtle Mt. Indian Reservation is in valley on SE border of plateau.

Turtle River, village (1990 pop. 62), Beltrami co., N Minn., 10 mi/16 km NNE of Bemidji; 47°35′N 94°45′E. Turtle River L. to E; L. Bemidji to S.

Turtleford, town (1991 pop. 459), W Sask., Canada, 50 mi/80 km NW of North Battleford; 53°23′N 108°58′W. Wheat, oats.

Turton, village (1990 pop. 76), Spink co., NE central S.Dak., 24 mi/39 km ENE of Redfield; 45°02′N 98°05′W.

Tuscaloosa, county (□ 1,352 sq mi/3,502 sq km; 1990 pop. 150,522), W central Ala.; ⊙ Tuscaloosa. Coastal plain drained by Black Warrior, Sipsey, and North rivers. Cotton, corn, soybeans; poultry; timber; coal, iron. Mfg. at Tuscaloosa. Formed 1818.

Tuscaloosa, city (1990 pop. 77,759), W central Ala., on the Black Warrior R., c.45 mi/72 km SW of Birmingham. Transportation and mfg. center, with industries centered on the region's coal, iron, and timber. Mfg. of food, steel, chemicals, paper. Agr. also remains important. The city is the seat of the Univ. of Ala. and Stillman Col., also Shelton State Community Col. Tuscaloosa was settled (1816) on the site of a Native Amer. village after the Creek revolt of 1813. It was the capital of Ala. from 1826 to 1846. In the Civil War, Tuscaloosa was partly burned. Points of interest include the Old Tavern (1827) and the huge antebellum homes, such as the President's Mansion. Inc. 1819.

Tuscaloosa Lake, Reservoir, Tuscaloosa co., W Ala., on the North R., 5 mi/8 km NNE of Tuscaloosa; c.15 mi/24 km long; 33°15′N 87°30′E. Max. capacity of 325,000 acre-ft. Formed by Lake Tuscaloosa Dam (132 ft/40 m high) built (1971) by the city of Tuscaloosa for water supply, flood control, and recreation.

Tuscarawas (tus-kuh-RO-wuhs), county (□ 571 sq mi/1,479 sq km; 1990 pop. 84,090), E Ohio; ⊙ New Philadelphia; 40°27′N 81°28′W. Intersected by Tuscarawas R., Stillwater Creek, and small Sugar, Sandy, and Conotton creeks. Includes part of Atwood Reservoir. In the Glaciated Plain physiographic region. Agr. (poultry, cattle, corn); mfg. at New Philadelphia, Dover, and Newcomerstown (paper prods., chemicals, plastics, construction materials, fabricated metal prods.); coal mines, clay pits. Formed 1808.

Tuscarawas, village (1990 pop. 826), Tuscarawas co., E Ohio, 7 mi/11 km SSE of New Philadelphia; 40°23′N 81°24′W.

Tuscarawas River, c.125 mi/201 km long, E and central Ohio; rises in Summit co. in NE Ohio; flows generally S through Stark and Tuscarawas cos., then W to unite with the Walhonding at Coshocton to form the Muskingum; 40°16′N 81°52′W. Flood control reservoir at Dover, on main stream; Tappan, Piedmont, Clendening, Leesville, Atwood reservoirs are on tributaries. Ohio and Erie Canal was alongside the river for its full length.

Tuscarora (TUHS-ka-ROR-ah), uninc. town (1990 pop. 1,073), Schuylkill township, Schuylkill co., E central Pa., 4 mi/6.4 km SW of Tamaqua, near source of Schuylkill R.; 40°45′N 76°03′W. Anthracite coal region. Tuscarora State Park to N; Locust L. State Park to NW.

Tuscarora (tuhs-kuh-RO-ruh), village (1990 pop. 24), Elko co., NE Nev., near South Fork Owyhee R., bet. Tuscarora Mts. (W), Independence Mts. (E), 40 mi/64 km NNW of Elko. In 1870s and 1880s, was chief camp of rich silver and gold dist. Had pop. of 4,000 in late 1800s; now again a gold-mining community.

Tuscarora Mountain, S Pa., NE-SW ridge (1,500 ft/457 m–1,900 ft/579 m) of the Appalachian Mts.; 40°14′N 77°44′W–39°57′N 77°56′W. Runs from N end of Cove Mtn. near Md. border NE c.70 mi/113 km, to Juniata R., opposite Millerstown, forms E or SE boundaries of Fulton, Huntingdon, and Juniata cos., W boundary of Franklin co., and NW boundary of Percy co.

Tuscola (tuh-SKO-lah), county (□ 913 sq mi/2,365 sq km; 1990 pop. 55,498), E Mich., bounded NW by Saginaw Bay; ⊙ Caro; 43°29′N 83°26′W. Drained by Cass R. and its affluents. Agr. (sugar beets, beans, corn, wheat, oats, soybeans, barley, potatoes, fruit; livestock, poultry; dairy prods.); fisheries. State game refuge in co. Organized 1850.

Tuscola, city (1990 pop. 4,155), E central Ill., 21 mi/34 km S of Urbana; ⊙ Douglas co.; 39°47′N 88°16′W. Agr. (corn, wheat; dairy prods.; livestock, poultry). Platted 1857, inc. 1861.

Tuscola, village (1990 pop. 620), Taylor co., W central Texas, 16 mi/26 km S of Abilene; 32°12′N 99°47′W. In cotton, cattle area. L. Abilene recreation area and Abilene State Park; fishing resort is c.5 mi/8 km W.

Tuscumbia (tuhs-KUHM-bee-uh), city (1990 pop. 8,413), NW Ala., on left bank of Tennessee R. 5 mi/8 km S of Florence; ⊙ Colbert co. Tires and rubber prods., lumber, plastics, apparel, furniture. Helen Keller b. here. Industries stimulated by construction of Wilson Dam (5 mi/8 km NE) and development of TVA. Site of Ala. Music Hall of Fame. Settled c.1815.

Tuscumbia, town (1990 pop. 148), on Osage R. and 11 mi/18 km SE of Eldon, central Mo.; ⊙ Miller co.; 38°14′N 92°27′W. Cattle, turkeys; mfg. (wood prods.); sand and gravel. Platted 1837.

Tuscumbia River (tuh-SKUHM-bee-uh), c.50 mi/80 km long, in Miss. and Tenn.; rises near Boonesville in Prentiss co., NE Miss.; flows N and NW into SW Tenn., to Hatchie R. 6 mi/9.7 km E of Middleton; largely chanelized.

Tushar Mountains, Piute and Beaver cos., SW central Utah, mostly in Fishlake Natl. Forest; extend S from Pavant Mts. along W bank of Sevier R. Chief peaks: Circleville Mt. (11,440 ft/3,487 m), Mt. Belknap (12,137 ft/3,699 m), and Delano Peak (12,173 ft/3,710 m).

Tushka (TUHSH-kuh), village (1990 pop. 256), Atoka co., SE Okla., 5 mi/8 km SW of Atoka; 34°19′N 96°10′W. Agr. area.

Tuskegee (tuhs-KEE-gee), city (1990 pop. 12,257), SE Ala., midway bet. Montgomery, Ala. and Columbus, Ga.; ⊙ Macon co. In a cotton, corn, and dairy region. It has gristmills and plants that make cottonseed oil and fertilizer. In 1960 a Supreme Court decision voided a 1957 Ala. law that had excluded Afr.-Amer. residents from the city's pop. by altering Tuskegee's city limits. A number of antebellum houses remain, and nearby is a natl. forest. Tuskegee is best known as the seat of Tuskegee Inst., now a natl. historic site, est. 1881 by Booker T. Washington as a normal and industrial school for Afr.-Americans. The institute grew into one of the most respected predominantly Afr.-Amer. cols. in the nation. Settled before 1763, inc. 1843.

Tuskegee Institute Historic Site (tuhs-KEE-gee), S Ala., 1st institution of higher learning for the vocational training of Afr.-Americans; founded in 1881 by Booker T. Washington. Authorized 1974.

Tussey Mountain (TUS-see MOUN-ten), ridge, S and central Pa., runs NE-SW (1,900 ft/579 m–2,200 ft/671 m) part of Appalachian Mt. system; 40°11′N 78°20′W– 40°46′N 77°43′W. It runs c.95 mi/153 km NE from point in S Bedford co. at Pa.-Md. state line to S part of Centre co., forming part of boundary bet. Blair and Huntingdon cos.; sandstone. Raystown Branch Juniata R. runs through gap W of Everett; Little Juniata R. gap 10 mi/16 km SE of Tyrone.

Tustin, city (1990 pop. 50,689), Orange co., S Calif., suburb 33 mi/53 km SE of downtown Los Angeles and 20 mi/32 km ESE of Long Beach; 33°44′N 117°49′W. Plastics, furniture, computers, electronic equip. Tustin's pop. increased almost tenfold bet. 1960 and 1970, and it more than doubled bet. 1970 and 1990. Santa Ana Marine Corps Air Base to S, El Toro Marine Corps Air Station to SE. Both scheduled by Pentagon to be closed. Santa Ana Mts. to E. Founded 1868, inc. 1927.

Tustin, village (1990 pop. 236), Osceola co., central Mich., 10 mi/16 km SSW of Cadillac and on small South Branch of Manistee R.; 44°06′N 85°27′W. Manistee Natl. Forest to NW.

Tustin Foothills, uninc. city (1990 pop. 24,358), Orange co., S Calif., residential suburb 3 mi/4.8 km NE of Tustin, 5 mi/8 km E of Santa Ana; 33°46′N 117°48′W. Citrus, avacodos; dairying, nursery livestock.

Tustumena Lake (23 mi/37 km long, 2 mi/3.2 km–7 mi/11.3 km wide), S Alaska, on W Kenai Peninsula, 40 mi/64 km W of Seward. Game hunting, fishing.

Tutotepec, Mexico: see SAN BARTOLO TUTOTEPEC.

Tuttle, town (1990 pop. 2,807), Grady co., central Okla., 21 mi/34 km SW of Oklahoma City; 35°17′N 97°45′W. In agr. area (cotton, wheat, alfalfa; livestock); mfg. (concrete, furniture).

Tuttle (TUHT-uhl), village (1990 pop. 160), Kidder co., central N.Dak., 20 mi/32 km NNE of Steele; 47°08′N 99°59′W.

Tuttle Creek Lake, c.30 mi/48 km long, Marshall co. and on Riley-Pottawatomie co. border, NE Kansas, on Big Blue R., 5 mi/8 km N of Manhattan; 39°12′N 96°32′W. Max. storage capacity 2,346,000 acre-ft. Receives Black Vermillion R. at N end. Formed by Tuttle Creek Dam (150 ft/46 m high), built (1962) for flood control, irrigation, and water supply. Tuttle Creek State Park on shore.

Tutwiler (TUHT-wei-luhr), town (1990 pop. 1,391), Tallahatchie co., NW central Miss., 15 mi/24 km SSE of Clarksdale; 34°00′N 90°25′W. Agr. area (cotton, corn, wheat, soybeans; cattle).

Tuxcacuesco (toosh-kah-kwes-ko), town (1990 pop. 1,065), Jalisco, W Mexico, 21 mi/34 km ESE of Autlán de Navarro; 19°41′N 103°58′W. Grain, sugarcane, fruit, tobacco.

Tuxcueca (toosh-kwe-kah), town (1990 pop. 1,308), Jalisco, central Mexico, on S shore of L. Chapala, 36 mi/58 km SSE of Guadalajara, on Mexico Highway 15; 20°10′N 103°12′W. Grain, beans, fruit; livestock.

Tuxedo Lake, N.Y.: see TUXEDO PARK.

Tuxedo Park, upper-income residential village (□ 3 sq mi/7.8 sq km; 1990 pop. 706), Orange co., SE N.Y., on Ramapo R. and Tuxedo L. (c. 1.5 mi/2.4 km long), in the Ramapo Mts., 6 mi/9.7 km NW of Suffern; 41°12′N 74°12′W. Tuxedo Park colony here, a private residential development begun (1886) by Pierre Lorillard, became known for its sports and social functions. King's Col. relocated here from Briarcliff Manor.

Túxpam, Mexico: see TÚXPAM DE RODRÍGUEZ CANO.

Túxpam de Rodríguez Cano (TOOSH-pahm de rod-REE-gez KAH-no), city (1990 pop. 69,224), ⊙ Túxpam municipio, Veracruz, E Mexico, on Tuxpan R. (7 mi/11.3 km from its mouth on the Gulf) and 100 mi/161 km NNW of Xalapa Enríquez; 20°57′N 97°23′W. Oil-pumping and -loading station, with petroleum wells. Exports timber, chicle, rubber, vanilla, dyewood, hides. Tanning, lumbering, liquor distilling. Tropical agr. dist.; produces bananas, plant fibers. Formerly Túxpan.

Tuxpan (TOOSH-pahn), city (1990 pop. 25,895), and township, Jalisco, W Mexico, on interior plateau, on RR and 11 mi/18 km SE of Ciudad Guzmán, near Mexico Highway 54; ⊙ Tuxpan municipio; 19°31′N 103°20′E. Elev. 4,131 ft/1,259 m. Agr. center (corn, sugarcane, fruit, livestock). Largely populated by Nahuatl-speaking Indians.

Tuxpan 1 (TOOSH-pahn), town (1990 pop. 6,819), Michoacán, central Mexico, 11 mi/18 km SSE of Ciudad Hidalgo, on mexico Highway 15; ⊙ Tuxpan municipio; 19°34′N 100°28′W. Elev. 5,741 ft/1,750 m. Corn, sugarcane, beans, fruit; livestock. **2** town (1990 pop. 24,454), Nayarit, W Mexico, on Pacific coastal plain, on San Pedro R. (sometimes called Tuxpan R.), and 40 mi/64 km NW of Tepic; 21°58′N 105°20′W. Processing and agr. center (corn, cotton, sugarcane, tobacco, beans, tomatoes, bananas).

Tuxpan River 1 (TOOSH-pahn), c.110 mi/177 km long, W Mexico; rises in Sierra Madre Occidental in Jalisco NE of Ciudad Guzmán; flows SW and S, past Tuxpan, and along Colima-Michoacán border, to the Pacific 6 mi/9.7 km NNW of San Juan de Lima Point. Also known as Coahuayana River. **2** c.100 mi/161 km long, Veracruz, E Mexico; rises in Sierra Madre Oriental near Hidalgo-Veracruz border N of Huauchinango; flows NE and E to Gulf of Mexico at Túxpam de Rodríguez Cano; 19°20′N 100°33′W. Navigable for smaller ships c.35 mi/56 km upstream. Called Pantepec R. in upper course. Sometimes spelled Túxpam River.

Tuxpan River, W Mexico: see MEZQUITAL RIVER.

Tuxtepec, Mexico: see SAN JUAN BAUTISTA TUXTEPEC.

Tuxtilla (toosh-TEE-yaj), town (1990 pop. 2,178), Veracruz, SE Mexico, on Papaloapan R. and 11 mi/18 km SW of Cosamaloapan; 18°14′N 95°54′W. Sugarcane, bananas.

Tuxtla Chico (TOOSH-tlah CHEE-ko), town (1990 pop. 6,093), Chiapas, S Mexico, in Pacific lowland, on Mexico Highway 200, near Guatemala border, 7 mi/11.3 km ENE of Tapachula; 14°58′N 92°11′W. Coffee, cacao, sugarcane, fruit; livestock.

Tuxtla Gutiérrez (TOOSH-tlah goo-tee-E-res), city (1990 pop. 289,626) and township, SE Mexico, in the fertile Grijalva valley and at the foot of the Chiapas highlands, on Inter-American Highway (190); ⊙ Chiapas state; 16°45′N 93°09′W. Agr. and cattle raising are the chief occupations, and there is trade in timber. The city's excellent communications facilities have made it the focal distribution point for the region's prods.

Tuxtla Volcano (TOSH-tlah) (5,085 ft/1,550 m), Veracruz, SE Mexico, 8 mi/12.9 km N of San Andrés Tuxtla. Last erupted 1793; fairly dormant since then, although it emits smoke. Also known as San Martín Tuxtla Volcano.

Tuxtlas, Los, Mexico: see SAN ANDRÉS TUXTLA.

Tuzamapan de Galeana (too-sah-MAH-pahn dai gahle-AH-nah), town (1990 pop. 1,775), Puebla, central Mexico, 32 mi/51 km ESE of Huauchinango; 20°05′N 97°34′W. Coffee, sugarcane, tobacco, fruit. In Totomal-Indian area.

Tuzantán (too-sahn-TAHN), town (1990 pop. 2,041), Chiapas, S Mexico, in Pacific lowland, 3 mi/4.8 km E of Huixtla; 15°09′N 92°25′W. Coffee, sugarcane, lemons; livestock. Sometimes Tuzantán de Morelos.

Tuzantla (too-SAHN-tlah), town (1990 pop. 3,862), Michoacán, central Mexico, 30 mi/48 km SSW of Zitácuaro, on Mexico Highway 51; 19°12′N 100°34′W. Cereals, sugarcane, fruit.

Tuzigoot National Monument (801 acres/324 ha), Yavapai co., central Ariz., 34 mi/55 km SW of Flagstaff and 3 mi/4.8 km NNE of Cottonwood. Excavated ruins dating 1100–1450 A.D. of a large Sinagua pueblo. Surrounded by Prescott Natl. Forest. Authorized 1939.

Twain Harte, uninc. town (1990 pop. 2,170), Tuolumne co., central Calif., in the Sierra Nevada, 10 mi/16 km ENE of Sonora; 38°02′N 120°14′W. Winter sports. 1849 Calif. Gold Rush region. Stanislaus Natl. Forest to E. Named for authors Mark Twain and Bret Harte who lived, wrote, and traveled in Nev. and Calif. during rush years.

Tweed, village (1991 pop. 1,626), SE Ont., Canada, on Stoco L., 22 mi/35 km N of Belleville; 44°28′N 77°18′W. Some mfg.

Tweed Island, W N.F., Canada, on N side of the Bay of Islands, 27 mi/43 km NW of Corner Brook; 2 mi/3 km long, 1 mi/2 km wide; 49°14′N 58°22′W.

Tweedsmuir Park (□ 5,400 sq mi/13,986 sq km), W central B.C., Canada, 120 mi/193 km WSW of Prince George, on E slope of Coast Mts. Has several peaks over 7,000 ft/2,134 m high and numerous lakes, the largest of which are Eutsuk, Whitesail, Tahtsa, and Tetachuck. Ootsa L. is on N boundary of park.

Twelvepole Creek, 29 mi/47 km long, W W.Va., formed at Wayne by junction of East Fork (c.45 mi/72 km long) and West Fork (c.50 mi/80 km long); both rise in Mingo co. and flow generally NW; flows N and NW to Ohio R. just E of Ceredo.

Twentynine Palms, city (1990 pop. 11,821), San Bernardino co., S Calif., 73 mi/117 km E of San Bernardino, in S part of Mojave Desert; 34°08′N 116°04′W. Desert resort area; cattle. Hq. for Joshua Tree Natl. Monument (just S); Twentynine Palms Marine Corps Base to N; Twentynine Palms Indian Reservation to S, at edge of natl. monument.

Twiggs, county (□ 363 sq mi/940 sq km; 1990 pop. 9,806), central Ga.; ⊙ Jeffersonville; 32°40′N 83°26′W. Bounded W by Ocmulgee R. Coastal plain agr. (cotton, corn, peanuts; cattle, hogs); timber; kaolin clay mining. Formed 1809.

Twila (TWEI-luh), uninc. village, Harlan co., SE Ky., 6 mi/9.7 km SSW of Harlan, in the Cumberland Mts. Bituminous coal.

Twilight (TWEI-leit), borough (1990 pop. 252), Washington co., SW Pa., 2 mi/3.2 km SSE of Charleroi; 40°06′N 79°53′W. Corn; livestock; dairying.

Twillingate, town (1991 pop. 1,397), on NE coast of Twillingate Isl., E N.F., Canada, 170 mi/274 km NW of St. John's; 49°40′N 54°46′W. Fishing port. Has govt. services. Lumbering nearby.

Twillingate Island (□ 12 sq mi/31 sq km), E N.F., Canada, in Notre Dame Bay, 40 mi/64 km ESE of Cape St. John; 7 mi/11 km long, up to 4 mi/6 km wide; 49°40′N 54°46′W. Twillingate, chief settlement, is on NE coast. Fishing and lumbering are chief occupations.

Twin Bridges, village (1990 pop. 374), Madison co., SW Mont., 33 mi/53 km SSE of Butte; 45°32′N 112°20′W. Beaverhead and Ruby rivers converge just S of town to form Jefferson R., Big Hole R. enters N of town. Hay; cattle, horses; mining dist. Beaverhead Rock State Park to SW; part of Beaverhead Nalt. Forest to SE; parts of

Deerlodge Natl. Forest to NW and E. Originally called The Bridges.

Twin Brooks, village (1990 pop. 54), Grant co., NE S.Dak., 7 mi/11.3 km W of Milbank; 45°12′N 96°47′W.

Twin Buttes, a double-coned peak (5,685 ft/1,733 m), Navajo co., E Ariz., 14 mi/23 km E of Holbrook; 35°23′N 109°54′W.

Twin Buttes Reservoir, Tom Green co., W central Texas, on Middle Concho and South Concho rivers (continuous dam impounds both rivers 4 mi/6.4 km above their confluence forming 2 reservoirs linked by channel), 8 mi/12.9 km SW of San Angelo; 31°21′N 100°29′W. Max. capacity 1,088,000 acre-ft. Middle Arm 10 mi/16 km long, S Arm 5 mi/8 km long. Formed by Twin Buttes Dam (128 ft/39 m high), built (1962) by the Bureau of Reclamation for irrigation, flood control, and water supply.

Twin City, town (1990 pop. 1,466), Emanuel co., E central Ga., 11 mi/18 km E of Swainsboro; 32°35′N 82°10′W. Mfg. of structural steel and apparel. Inc. 1924 as a consolidation of Graymont and Summit.

Twin Falls, county (□ 1,928 sq mi/4,994 sq km; 1990 pop. 53,580), S Idaho; ⊙ Twin Falls; 42°21′N 114°40′W. Livestock and dairying area bordering on Nev. (S) and bounded N by Snake R. Irrigated regions are in N, along Snake R., and in SW, along Salmon Falls Creek. Potatoes, dry beans, sugar beets, onions; apples, peaches, cherries; sheep, cattle; commercial fish hatchery in NE. Includes part of Snake R. Plain in N, mt. region in S. Salmon Creek and Cedar Creek reservoirs in SW; Hagerman Fossil Beds Natl. Monument in NW; Balanced Rock in NW; Magic Mt. Ski Area and part of Sawtooth Natl. Forest in SE. Formed 1907.

Twin Falls, city (1990 pop. 27,591), S Idaho, 110 mi/177 km SE of Boise, at mouth of Rock Creek, on the Snake R.; ⊙ Twin Falls co.; 42°34′N 114°28′W. The city began as a center of a private irrigation project, which is supplemented by the Minidoka project of the U.S. Bureau of Reclamation. One of the falls of Twin Falls in the nearby gorge is harnessed for hydroelectric power. Sugar beets, potatoes, corn, beans, and grains are processed, as well as livestock, trout, and dairy prods. Commercial fish hatcheries in area. Scenic attractions include the deep Snake R. canyon and Shoshone Falls (212 ft/65 m high). Col. of Southern Idaho (2 year), Herrett Mus. of Indian History, Twin Falls Historical Mus. Twin Falls City-County Airport. Sun Valley to N, Magic Mt. Ski Area to S; Sawtooth Natl. Forest to SSE. Inc. 1905.

Twin Islands, SE Keewatin dist., N.W.T., Canada, group (□ 55 sq mi/142 sq km) of 2 small isls. in James Bay, NE of Akimiski Isl.; 53°10′N 80°10′W. Game sanctuary.

Twin Lakes 1 uninc. town (1990 pop. 5,379), Santa Cruz co., W Calif., on Monterey Bay, a suburb 2 mi/3.2 km SE of Santa Cruz, on Pacific Ocean; 36°58′N 122°00′W. New Brighton State Beach is here. **2** town (1990 pop. 3,989), Kenosha co., extreme SE Wis., 10 mi/16 km ESE of L. Geneva, near Ill. boundary; 42°31′N 88°15′W. Farm and recreation area; light mfg. Small lakes in area.

Twin Lakes 1 village, Lake co., central Colo., in Sawatch Mts., 12 mi/19 km SSW of Leadville, just W of Twin Lakes Reservoir. Elev. 9,220 ft/2,810 m. Fishing resort. Gold and silver deposits. Nearby is Twin Lakes Tunnel 9 mi/14.5 km to W, extending c.4 mi/6.4 km through Sawatch Mts., in Continental Divide, and conducting water from Roaring Fork R. through reservoir to North Fork Lake Creek branch of Arkansas R. Mt. Elbert, highest point in Colo. (14,433 ft/4,399 m) is 4 mi/6.4 km NW of village. Surrounded by San Isabel Natl. Forest. **2** village, Lowndes co., S Ga., 10 mi/16 km SSE of Valdosta; 30°41′N 83°12′W. On 2 small lakes.

Twin Lakes, two linked lakes; in Penobscot co., central Maine, 6 mi/9.7 km W of Millinocket (each c.4 mi/6.4 km long). Receive West Branch of Penobscot R. from Pemadumcook L. (N).

Twin Lakes 1 Conn.: see SALISBURY. **2** Mich.: see LEWISTON.

Twin Mountain, village, N.H.: see CARROLL, town.

Twin Mountain, peak (8,920 ft/2,719 m), NW Baker co., 10 mi/16 km W of Haines, Oregon; 44°55′N 118°09′W. See ELKHORN RIDGE.

Twin Oaks, town (1990 pop. 506), St. Louis co., E Mo., near the Meramec R., residential suburb 15 mi/24 km W of downtown St. Louis; 38°34′N 90°30′W.

Twin Peak (8,878 ft/2,706 m), Placer co., E Calif., in the Sierra Nevada, 6 mi/9.7 km W of Tahoe City, W of L. Tahoe; 39°06′N 120°13′W.

Twin Peaks (10,341 ft/3,152 m), central Idaho, on Custer/Lemhi co. line, 13 mi/21 km WNW of Challis in SALMON RIVER MTS.; 44°36′N 114°28′W.

Twin Valley, town (1990 pop. 821), Norman co., NW Minn., on Wild Rice R. and 12 mi/19 km ESE of Ada; 47°15′N 96°15′E. Agr. (wheat, sunflowers, potatoes, sugar beets, alfalfa); mfg. (chemicals, food prods.). White Earth Indian Reservation to E.

Twining, village (1990 pop. 169), Arenac co., E Mich., 12 mi/19 km NE of Standish; 44°06′N 83°48′W. In farm area.

Twins, The, mountain (12,085 ft/3,684 m), SW Alta., Canada, near B.C. border, in Rocky Mts., on S edge of Jasper Natl. Park, 50 mi/80 km SE of Jasper.

Twinsburg, city (1990 pop. 9,606), Summit co., NE Ohio, 15 mi/24 km NNE of Akron, on State Highway junctions of 91 and 82, and just off I-480; 41°19′N 81°37′W. Auto stamping plant; electronics; chain drug store hq. Internatl. convention for twins called Twins Day Festival held in Chamberlin Park in August. More than 2,000 sets of twins attend each year.

Twisp, town (1990 pop. 872), Okanogan co., N Wash., 25 mi/40 km W of Okanogan and on Methow R. at mouth of Twisp R.; 48°22′N 120°08′W. Apples; timber. Recreational area. Twisp Pass (6,066 ft/1,849 m) to W in Cascade Range (local trail crosses through). Loup Loup Pass (4,020 ft/1,225 m) to E.

Twitchell Reservoir, San Luis Obispo co., SW Calif., on Cuyama R., 7 mi ENE of Santa Maria; 9 mi/14.5 km long; 34°58′N 120°18′W. Max. capacity 398,000 acre-ft. Formed by Twitchell Dam (211 ft/64 m high), built (1958) by the Bureau of Reclamation for flood control, irrigation, and water supply. Generally dry.

Two Buttes, village (1990 pop. 63), Baca co., SE Colo., 16 mi/26 km NE of Springfield near Horse Creek; 37°33′N 102°24′W. Elev. 4,125 ft/1,257 m. Two Buttes Reservoir and State Fishing Lake to NW.

Two Buttes Reservoir, Baca co., extreme SE Colo., on Two Butte Creek, 16 mi/26 km NNE of Springfield; 2 mi/3.2 km long; 37°37′N 102°44′W. Max. capacity of 58,934 acre-ft. Formed by Two Butte Dam (106 ft/32 m high), built (1966) by the Colo. Div. of Wildlife for irrigation and recreation.

Two Harbors, town (1990 pop. 3,651), NE Minn., 25 mi/40 km NE of Duluth on L. Superior (N shore); ⊙ Lake co.; 47°01′N 91°40′E. Resort; timber; tourism; dairying; shipping center for iron ore from Mesabi and Vermilion iron ranges to NW; RR repair shops; terminus of RR from iron mines and other points. Grew as lumber- and ore-shipping point. U.S. coast guard base is here. Huge docks are prominent feature of city. Superior Natl. Forest to N; Gooseberry Falls and Split Rock Lighthouse state parks to NE; Flood Bay State Park to E; Cloquet Valley State Forest to NE. Muncipal Airport to W. Settled 1882, inc. as village 1888, as city 1907.

Two Hills, town (1991 pop. 1,075), E Alta., Canada, on the small Vermilion Lakes, near North Saskatchewan R., 45 mi/72 km NW of Vermilion; 53°43′N 111°45′W. Cereal food mfg., mixed farming; grain; livestock.

Two Islets, group of 2 islets off E N.F., Canada, 35 mi/56 km E of Fogo Isl.; 49°45′N 53°14′W. Together with Funk Isl., just E, they were the last breeding grounds of the now extinct great auk.

Two Mountains, Lake of the (□ 63 sq mi/163 sq km), S Que., Canada, expansion of the Ottawa R., extends 24 mi/39 km bet. Rigaud and Jesus Isl.; 1 mi/2 km–6 mi/10 km wide. Contains Île Bizard. Drains NE into the St. Lawrence by Mille Îles and Prairies rivers.

Two Rivers, city (1990 pop. 13,030), Manitowoc co., E Wis., on L. Michigan at the mouth of the Twin R.; 44°09′N 87°34′W. Two Rivers is closely associated with its twin city, Manitowoc (6 mi/9.7 km SW), both of which are highly industrialized. Mfg. (furniture, wood prods., electrical equip., fixtures). Fishing. A U.S. coast guard station (est. 1872) is in Two Rivers. Nuclear plant. Point Beach State Forest on L Michigan to NE. Inc. 1878.

Two Rivers, c.85 mi/137 km long, stream in Kittson co., NW Minn.; formed by confluence of North Branch and South Branch, 8 mi/12.9 km WNW of Hallock; 48°46′N 96°55′E; flows 5 mi/8 km WNW to Red R. of the North (N.Dak. state line). North Branch Two Rivers rises in NE Kittson co.; flows WSW c.40 mi/64 km past Lancaster to join South Branch. South Branch Two Rivers rises in central Roseau co., 9 mi/14.5 km SW of Roseau, flows WSW past Badger and Greenbush, then WNW, through L. Bronson (L. Bronson State Park) and past Hallock, where it receives Middle Branch from E, then joins North Branch; much of upper course is channelized. Middle Branch Two Rivers, source is ill-defined among swamps and draining ditches of E Kittson co., flows c.25 mi/40 km W to Hallock.

Twodot, village (1990 pop. 40), Wheatland co., central Mont., on Musselshell R. at mouth of Big Elk Creek and 11 mi/18 km W of Harlowton. Hay; cattle, sheep. Martinsdale Reservoir to W. Also known as Two Dot.

Ty Ty (TEI tei), town (1990 pop. 579), Tift co., S central Ga., 8 mi/12.9 km W of Tifton; 31°28′N 83°39′W.

Tybee Island (TEI-bee), town, on Tybee Island (1990 pop. 2,842), Chatham co., Ga., 15 mi/24 km SE of Savannah; 32°01′N 80°52′W. Residential and beach area. Small resort and residential with public beaches. The abandoned Fort Sreven site, now being converted to residential use and the Tybee lighthouse, first built in 1791, are the most famous landmarks. It guides shipping through Tybee Roads in the approach to the Savannah R. Both the lighthouse and adjacent Tybee Mus. are open to the public.

Tybee Island (TEI-bee), one of the Sea Isls., in Chatham co., SE Ga., just off the coast, 15 mi/24 km ESE of Savannah, at mouth of Savannah R.; connected to mainland by causeway; c.4 mi/6.4 km long, 3 mi/4.8 km wide); 31°58′N 80°53′W. Lighthouse (32°01′N 80°51′W) and Fort Screven at N end; Tybee Beach (formerly called Savannah Beach). Little Tybee Isl. is just S.

Tye, town (1990 pop. 1,088), Taylor co., W central Texas, residential suburb 7 mi/11.3 km W of downtown Abilene, adjoins Abilene W city limits; 32°27′N 99°52′W. Agr. area (cattle; cotton). Dyess Air Force Base 1 mi/1.6 km S.

Tyee (tei-YEE), village, SE Alaska, on S tip of Admiralty Isl., 22 mi/35 km W of Kake across Frederick Sound. Fishing; cannery.

Tyee, Wash.: see BEAVER.

Tygart (TEI-guhrt), river, c.160 mi/257 km long, E W.Va.; source at Randolph-Pocahontas co. line; flows N past Elkins, then NNW past Belington and Philippi, through Tygart L. reservoir (State Park), past Grafton, and through Valley Falls State Park; joins the W. Fork R. at Fairmont to form the Monongahela R. Locally referred to as Tygart Valley R.

Tygart Valley River, W.Va.: see TYGART.

Tygarts Creek (TIG-uhrts), c.90 mi/145 km long, NE Ky.; rises in SW Carter co.; flows generally NNE, past Olive Hill, to Ohio R. at South Shore, opposite Portsmouth, Ohio.

Tyger River (TEI-guhr), c.45 mi/72 km long, NW S.C.; formed S of Spartanburg by the joining of North and Middle branches 12 mi/19 km S of Spartanburg in the Blue Ridge; flows SE through section of Sumter Natl. Forest and part of Whitmire to Broad R. at Shelton. North Fork is c.25 mi/40 km long and Middle Fork is c.35 mi/56 km long. Also spelled Tiger R.

Tyler 1 county (□ 935 sq mi/2,422 sq km; 1990 pop. 16,646), E Texas; ⊙ Woodville; 30°46′N 94°22′W. Bounded N and E by Neches R. Timber (pine, hardwoods) is important; Christmas trees; livestock (cattle, hogs); agr. (vegetables); catfish. Some oil and natural gas produced. Hunting, fishing. B.A. Steinhagen L. in NE; all or part of 4 units of Big Thicket Natl. Preserve along Neches R. (E) and in S and E parts of co. Formed 1846. **2** county (□ 261 sq mi/676 sq km; 1990 pop. 9,796), NW W.Va.; ⊙ Middlebourne; 39°28′N 80°52′W.

Bounded NW by Ohio R. (Ohio state line); drained by Middle Island and McElroy Creeks. Oil and natural-gas wells. Corn, alfalfa, hay, nursery crops; cattle, sheep; dairying. Some mfg. (including petroleum processing) at Sistersville. Jug and Conaway Run Wildlife Management Areas in center. Formed 1814.

Tyler, city (1990 pop. 75,450), ⊙ Smith co., E Texas, 90 mi/145 km ESE of Dallas; 32°19′N 95°17′W. In the heart of the rich East Texas oil field, it has refineries and other oil-based industries. The growing city is a RR junction and the location of the administrative hq. of various oil companies. Heavy and light mfg. The city's rose-growing and horticultural crops industries are among the nation's largest. There is a huge municipal rose garden and an annual fall rose festival. Mus. of art and planetarium. Texas Col., Univ. of Texas at Tyler, and Tyler Jr. Col. Pounds Field aiport to W. Nearby are a number of small lakes as well as Tyler State Park. Inc. 1847.

Tyler, town (1990 pop. 1,257), Lincoln co., SW Minn., 21 mi/34 km NE of Pipestone; 44°16′N 96°08′W. RR junction to E. Agr. trading point for livestock, poultry; grain, soybeans, alfalfa; dairying; mfg. (concrete). Lake Benton to W. Settled 1879.

Tyler, Ky.: see OAKDALE.

Tyler Park, uninc. town, Fairfax co., NE Va., residential suburb 9 mi/14.5 km W of Washington, D.C.; 38°52′N 77°11′W. Natl. Memorial Park Cemetery to NW.

Tyler Run–Queen Gate, uninc. town (1990 pop. 2,739), York co., SE Pa., residential suburb 3 mi/4.8 km SSE of York; 39°55′N 76°42′W.

Tylertown, town (1990 pop. 1,938), ⊙ Walthall co., S Miss., 20 mi/32 km ESE of McComb, on McGee Creek near La. state line; 31°07′N 90°08′W. In agr. (cotton, corn; cattle; dairying) and timber area; mfg. (apparel, lumber, meat processing, saw blades, sawmill equip.). L. Walthall State Lake to S.

Tylertown, Md.: see SMITH ISLAND.

Tyndall, village, SE Man., central Canada, 24 mi/39 km NE of Winnipeg; 50°05′N 96°40′W. Dairying; grain.

Tyndall, town (1990 pop. 1,201), ⊙ Bon Homme co., SE S.Dak., 70 mi/113 km SW of Sioux Falls; 42°59′N 97°51′W. Mfg. (plastics, consumer goods). Municipal power plant is here. Springfield State Recreation Area on Missouri R. (Lewis and Clark L.). Founded 1879.

Tyndall, Mount (14,018 ft/4,273 m), on border bet. Tulare and Inyo cos., E Calif., in the Sierra Nevada, 6 mi/9.7 km NNW of Mt. Whitney, and on E border of Sequoia Natl. Park; 36°39′N 118°20′W.

Tyngsboro (TINGZ-buh-ro) or **Tyngsborough**, town (1990 pop. 8,642), Middlesex co., NE Mass., on Merrimack R., and 6 mi/9.7 km WNW of Lowell; 42°40′N 71°26′W. Electronic components, fibre optics. State Forest nearby. Settled 1660, inc. 1809.

Tyonek (tei-YO-nik), village (1990 pop. 154), S Alaska, on NW shore of Cook Inlet, 45 mi/72 km WSW of Anchorage; 61°04′N 151°13′W. Fishing; area contains massive coal deposits. In Tyonek Indian Reservation.

Tyringham (TEER-ing-ham), town (1990 pop. 369), Berkshire co., SW Mass., in the Berkshires, 14 mi/23 km S of Pittsfield; 42°14′N 73°12′W. Appalachian Trail through town. Mt. Wilcox (2,112 ft/644 m) and Beartown State Forest nearby.

Tyro (TIR-o), village (1990 pop. 243), Montgomery co., SE Kansas, near Okla. state line, 14 mi/23 km SSW of Independence; 37°02′N 95°49′W. In livestock-raising and agr. region. Oil and gas fields here.

Tyrone 1 (tei-RON), town (1990 pop. 2,724), Fayette co., W central Ga., 13 mi/21 km ENE of Newnan; 33°28′N 84°36′W. Mfg. (asphalt, crushed granite, concrete). **2** town (1990 pop. 800), Texas co., central Okla. Panhandle, near Kansas state line, 30 mi/48 km NE of Guymon; 36°57′N 101°04′W. Grain; cattle.

Tyrone (tei-RON), uninc. village, Grant co., SW N.Mex., 9 mi/14.5 km SW of Silver City. Elev. 5,780 ft/1,762 m. Health resort. Burro Mts. (including Burro Peak) are SW; parts of Gila Natl. Forest are to SW and N, in major copper mining dist. Continental Divide passes to W.

Tyrone (TEI-ron), borough (1990 pop. 5,743), Blair co., central Pa., 15 mi/24 km NE of Altoona, on Little Juniata R.; 40°40′N 78°15′W. Shipping center. Mfg. (printing and publishing, machinery, tungsten carbide, food, construction materials, pharmaceuticals, paper prods.). Agr. (apples, grain; livestock, dairying). Rothrock State Forest to E. Laid out c.1850, inc. 1857.

Tyronza (tuhr-AHN-zuh), town (1990 pop. 858), Poinsett co., NE Ark., 29 mi/47 km SE of Jonesboro; 35°29′N 90°21′W. In agr. area.

Tyrrell (tuhr-EL), county (□ 600 sq mi/1,554 sq km; 1990 pop. 3,856), NE N.C., ⊙ Columbia; 35°52′N 76°10′W. Bounded N by Albemarle Sound, E and part of S by Alligator R. estuary. Forested and swampy tidewater area. Agr. area (wheat, oats, hay, peanuts, potatoes, cotton, soybeans; hogs, corn), fishing. Phelps L. and Pettigrew State Park on W boundary. Intracoastal Waterway passes through Alligator R. Formed 1729.

Tyrrell, Mount (9,610 ft/2,929 m), SE B.C., Canada, in Selkirk Mts., 50 mi/80 km NNE of Nelson; 50°02′N 116°45′W.

Tyson, Vt.: see PLYMOUTH.

Tysons Corner, uninc. city (1990 pop. 13,124), Fairfax co., N Va., residential suburb 10 mi/16 km W of Washington, D.C., 6 mi/9.7 km NE of Fairfax; 38°55′N 77°13′W. Wolf Trap Farm Park for the Performing Arts (unit of Natl. Park Service) to NW. Tysons Corner Shopping Center. Virginia's largest business district (electronic equip.); hq. of several natl. corporations; one of best-developed "edge cities" in the U.S.

Tzarácua Falls (dzah-RAH-kwah), Michoacán, central Mexico, on affluent of Tepalcatepec R., 4 mi/6.4 km SW of Uruapan.

Tzicatlacoyan (tzee-kaht-lah-KOI-yahn), town (1990 pop. 657), central Puebla, Mexico, 9 mi/14 km SE of Los Reyes de Juárez; 18°50′N 98°02′W. Elev. 6,562 ft/2,000 m. Temperate climate. Resources are agr. (fruits), marble, wood, cattle. The Manuel Avila Camacho Dam makes the land very fertile.

Tzimol (tzee-MOL), town (1990 pop. 3,399), Chiapas, S Mexico, 6 mi/9.7 km SSW of Comitán de Domínguez; 16°16′N 92°16′W. Fruit, cotton, sugar, corn.

Tzintzuntzan (tzeen-TZOON-tzahn), city (1990 pop. 2,644) and township, Michoacán, central Mexico, on E shore of L. Pátzcuaro, 26 mi/42 km WSW of Morelia; 19°37′N 101°35′W. Anc. capital of Tarascan empire, with many ruins and stone idols in vicinity. Sometimes Zintzuntzan.

Tzitzio (tzeet-ZEE-o), town (1990 pop. 912), Michoacàn, central Mexico, 15 mi/24 km SE of Morelia; 19°34′N 100°55′W. Agr. (corn, beans; livestock). Sometimes Zitzio.

Tzompantepec (tzom-PAHN-te-pek), town (1990 pop. 1,335), Tlaxcala, central Mexico, 10 mi/16 km NE of Tlaxcala; 19°23′N 98°06′W. Elev. 8,166 ft/2,489 m. Agr. (cereals, maguey; livestock). Also known as San Salvador.

Tzucacab (tzoo-KAH-kahb), town (1990 pop. 8,024), Yucatán, SE Mexico, 19 mi/31 km SE of Tekax, on Mexico Highway 184; 20°04′N 89°03′W. Henequen, fruit; timber.

U

Uayma (oo-AI-mah), town (1990 pop. 2,053), Yucatán, SE Mexico, 8 mi/12.9 km WNW of Valladolid; 20°42′N 88°20′W. Corn, henequen, sugarcane, tropical fruit.

Ubehebe Crater, Calif.: see DEATH VALLEY NATIONAL MONUMENT.

Ubly (UHB-lee), village (1990 pop. 821), Huron co., E Mich., 7 mi/11.3 km SSE of Bad Axe, and on North Branch of Cass R.; 43°42′N 82°55′W. In farm area (grain, potatoes, beans; livestock); meat processing.

Uchi Lake, village, NW Ont., central Canada, in Patricia dist., on Uchi L. (4 mi/6 km long), 75 mi/121 km NNW of Sioux Lookout. Gold mining.

Ucluelet (yook-LOO-lit), village (1991 pop. 1,595), SW B.C., W Canada, on SW Vancouver Isl., on Ucluelet Inlet (5 mi/8 km long) of Barkley Sound, 22 mi/35 km SE of Tofino; 48°56′N 125°31′W. Fishing (salmon, herring, shrimp, crabs), farming; timber. Port of entry. Pacific Rim Natl. Park and Long Beach are popular tourist destinations.

Ucon, town (1990 pop. 895), Bonneville co., SE Idaho, suburb 8 mi/12.9 km NNE of Idaho Falls, on Willow Creek, near Snake R.; 43°35′N 111°58′W. Elev. 4,801 ft/ 1,463 m. Junction of RR spur to E. Irrigated agr. area (potatoes, grain; dairying; cattle, sheep; mfg. (machinery). Ririe Reservoir to E.

Ucú (oo-KOO), town (1990 pop. 1,694), ☉ Ucú municipio, Yucatán, SE Mexico, 9 mi/14.5 km NW of Mérida; 20°21′N 89°45′W. Henequen; corn, tropical fruit.

Udall (YOO-dahl), village (1990 pop. 824), Cowley co., SE Kansas, 23 mi/37 km SSE of Wichita; 37°23′N 97°07′W. In grain and cattle area. Oil fields nearby.

Udell, town (1990 pop. 76), Appanoose co., S Iowa, near source of Fox R., 8 mi/12.9 km ENE of Centerville; 40°46′N 92°44′W.

Uehling (YOO-ling), village (1990 pop. 273), Dodge co., E Nebr., 20 mi/32 km N of Fremont, and on Logan Creek; 41°43′N 96°30′W.

Ugashik (OO-guh-shik), village (1990 pop. 7), SW Alaska, on Alaska Peninsula, on Ugashik R. and lower Ugashik L., and 6 mi/9.7 km E of Pilot Point; 57°34′N 157°16′W. Fishing; fish cannery.

Uharie River, N.C.: see UWHARRIE RIVER.

Uhrichsville (YUHR-riks-vil), city (1990 pop. 5,604), Tuscarawas co., E Ohio, 8 mi/13 km SE of New Philadelphia, and on Stillwater Creek; 40°24′N 81°21′W. Coal- and oil-related industries. Settled 1804; plotted 1833; inc. 1921 as city.

Uinkaret Plateau, Mohave co., NW Ariz., extends c.50 mi/80 km N from Colorado R. bet. Kanab (SE) and Shivwits (W) plateaus. Mounts Trumbull (8,029 ft/ 2,447 m) and Emma (7,702 ft/2,348 m) are in S.

Uinta (yoo-IN-tuh), county (☐ 2,087 sq mi/5,405 sq km; 1990 pop. 18,705), SW Wyo., on Utah (S and W) border; ☉ Evanston; 41°17′N 110°32′W. Livestock (sheep); grain (hay, alfalfa) region; watered by Blacks Fork of Green R. and Bear R. Coal, oil, and natural gas found here. Foothills of Uinta Mts. in S; small part of Wasatch Natl. Forest extends into S part of co. from Utah. Bear R. Divide range in NW; Bear R. State Park in W. Fort Bridger State Historic Site in E center. Formed 1869.

Uinta Mountains (yoo-IN-tuh), range of the Rocky Mts. extending c.120 mi/190 km E-W in NE Utah, parallel to Wyo. state line to N. Rises to Kings Peak (13,498 ft/ 4,123 m), the highest point in Utah. Also Hayden Peak (12,479 ft/3,804 m), Mt. Lovenia (13,219 ft/4,029 m), Tokewanna Peak (13,165 ft/4,013 m). The Uinta Mts. are almost totally part of natl. forests. Phosphates are mined here. The mts. are a series of anticlines.

Uinta River (yoo-IN-tuh), c.50 mi/80 km long, E Utah; rises near Kings Peak (highest point in Utah; 13,528 ft/ 4,123 m) in Uinta Mts.; flows generally SE through Uintah and Ouray Indian Reservation, to Duchesne R.

20 mi/32 km SW of Vernal. In High Uintas Wilderness Area of Wasatch Natl. Forest on small glacial lakes.

Uintah (yoo-IN-tah), county (☐ 4,499 sq mi/ 11,652 sq km; 1990 pop. 22,211), NE Utah; ☉ Vernal; 40°07′N 109°31′W. Mt. and plateau area crossed NE-SW by Green R. (forms part of W border in S), bordering on Colo. on E. Cattle, sheep; oil, natural gas, asphalt; gilsonite mining. Ouray Natl. Wildlife Reserve in center; Red Fleet Reservoir and State Park and Steinaker Reservoir and State Park in N center; part of Uintah and Ouray Indian Reservation in W, and part of its large Hill Creek Extension unit in SW; part of Dinosaur Natl. Monument in NE (extends into Colo.); part of Ashley Natl. Forest in NW. Formed 1850.

Uintah (yoo-IN-tah), town (1990 pop. 760), Weber co., N Utah, residential suburb 5 mi/8 km SE of Ogden, and 25 mi/40 km N of Salt Lake City, on Weber R.; 41°08′N 111°55′W. Cattle; fruit; dairying. Terminus of Union Pacific RR; moved to Ogden 1869. Wasatch Range and Natl. Forest to E. Hill Air Force Base to SW. Settled 1850.

Ukasiksalik Island, E Lab., E Canada, at entrance of Davis Inlet; 6 mi/10 km long, up to 9 mi/14 km wide; 55°53′N 60°53′W.

Ukiah (yoo-KEI-yah), city (1990 pop. 14,599), Mendocino co., NW Calif., 55 mi/89 km NW of Santa Rosa, on Russian R.; 39°09′N 123°13′W. Fruit, grapes, hops, nursery stock; cattle; dairying; timber. Mfg. (textiles, foods; winery). Monticello L. reservoir to NE. One of the world's few internatl. latitude observatories is located here. Seat of Mendocino Col (2-year). Inc. 1876.

Ukiah (yoo-KEI-uh), village (1990 pop. 250), Umatilla co., NE Oregon, 35 mi/56 km SSW of Pendleton, on Camas Creek; 45°07′N 118°55′W. Timber; wheat. Ukiah-Dale (S) and Battle Mt. (N) state parks in area; parts of Umatilla Natl. Forest to E and W.

Ukivok, Alaska: see KING ISLAND.

Ulen, town (1990 pop. 50), Boone co., central Ind., just N of Lebanon; 40°04′N 86°28′W. Agr. area.

Ulen (YOO-len), village (1990 pop. 547), Clay co., W Minn., on South Branch of Wild Rice R., and 28 mi/ 45 km NE of Fargo (N.Dak.); 47°04′N 96°15′E. Terminus of RR spur. Agr. (wheat, potatoes, sugar beets, sunflowers; livestock, poultry; dairying). White Earth Indian Reservation.

Ullin (UH-lin), village (1990 pop. 402), Pulaski co., extreme S Ill., 19 mi/31 km N of Cairo, on Cache R.; 37°16′N 89°10′W. In agr. area.

Ulm 1 (UHLM), village (1990 pop. 193), Prairie co., E central Ark., 8 mi/12.9 km NE of Stuttgart; 34°34′N 91°27′W. Peckerwood L. Reservoir to NW. **2** village (1990 pop. 325), Cascade co., W central Mont., on Missouri R. near mouth of Smith R., and 11 mi/18 km SW of Great Falls. Wheat, barley, hay; cattle, sheep. Ulm Pishkun State Park to N, place where bison were driven over cliff by Native Americans. Founded 1883.

Ulmer (OL-muhr), village (1990 pop. 90), Allendale co., SW S.C., 35 mi/56 km SSW of Orangeburg, near Salkehatchie R.; 33°06′N 81°12′W. Mfg. of textiles; agr. includes cotton and livestock.

Ulster, county (☐ 1,160 sq mi/3,004 sq km; 1990 pop. 165,304), SE N.Y., on Hudson R. (E); ☉ Kingston; 41°53′N 74°15′W. Mainly in the Catskill Mts.; also includes N part of the Shawangunk range and part of the highlands of the Hudson R. Drained by Wallkill R., and by Rondout, Esopus, and other creeks. Ashokan Reservoir is on co. Summer-resort area; has several lakes (including Mohonk, Minnewaska). Dairying, farming (fruit, potatoes); poultry raising. Mfg. at Kingston and Marlboro. Formed 1683.

Ulster Heights, resort village (1990 pop. 150), Ulster co., SE N.Y., in the Catskill Mts., 6 mi/9.7 km NW of Ellenville; 41°46′N 74°29′W. Lakes nearby.

Ulster Spring, town (1991 pop. 1,391), Trelawny parish, W central Jamaica, 30 mi/48 km NW of May Pen; 18°19′N 77°31′W. Tropical fruit, spices; livestock.

Ulupalakua (OO-loo-PAH-lah-KOO-ah), village (1990 pop. 200), SW corner of Maui isl., Maui co., Hawaii, 16 mi/26 km SSE of Kahului, inland 3 mi/4.8 km from S and SW coasts, to which there is no road access. S terminus of Kula

Highway from N; W terminus of Piilani Highway to isolated SE coast. Eucalyptus forest area. Cattle; timber; winery. Kula and Kahikinui forest reserves to NE; Polipoli Springs State Recreational Area to NE.

Ulysses (yoo-LI-seez), town (1990 pop. 5,474), ☉ Grant co., SW Kansas, on North Fork Cimarron R., and 35 mi/56 km SW of Garden City; 37°34′N 101°21′W. In wheat area; natural-gas fields. Mfg. (petrol refining, natural-gas distribution; chemicals, concrete, machinery, feeds). Inc. 1921.

Ulysses 1 (yoo-LI-seez), village (1990 pop. 385), Lawrence co., NE Ky., 12 mi/19 km NE of Paintsville, near Levisa Fork river. Burley tobacco, corn; cattle. Bituminous coal. **2** village (1990 pop. 256), Butler co., E Nebr., 13 mi/21 km NNW of Seward, and on Big Blue R.; 41°04′N 97°12′W. Grain.

Ulysses (YOO-li-sees), borough (1990 pop. 653), Potter co., N Pa., 15 mi/24 km NE of Coudersport; 41°53′N 77°45′W. Mfg. of lumber and wood prods.; agr. includes dairying; livestock; corn, alfalfa, potatoes; timber. Denton Hill State Park and Ski Area to S. Pa. Lumber Mus. to S.

Umaknak Island, Alaska: see AMAKNAK ISLAND.

Umán (oo-MAHN), town (1990 pop. 21,781), ☉ Umán municipio, Yucatán, SE Mexico, 10 mi/16 km SW of Mérida, at junction of Mexico Highways 180 and 261, on RR; 20°53′N 89°45′W. Elev. 29.5 ft/9 m. Henequen, corn, tropical fruit.

Umatilla (yoo-muh-TIL-uh), county (☐ 3,231 sq mi/ 8,368 sq km; 1990 pop. 59,249), NE Oregon; ☉ Pendleton; 45°35′N 118°43′W. Columbia R. forms part of Wash. state line in NW. Drained by Umatilla R. Part of Blue Mts. in E and S. Agr. (wheat, oats, barley, corn, beans, pears, onions, potatoes, apples, grapes, plums, peaches; hogs, sheep, cattle); wineries. Parts of Umatilla Natl. Forest in E and S, including part of Umatilla Wilderness Area in E. Umatilla Indian Reservation in center, E of Pendleton. Cold Springs Reservoir and Natl. Wildlife Refuge and Hat Rock State Park in NW. McKay Creek Natl. Wildlife Refuge at center, S of Pendleton. Emigrant Springs State Park in SE; Ukiah-Dale and Battle Mt. state parks in S. Part of Umatilla Ordnance Depot on Wash. state line in NW.

Umatilla 1 (yoo-muh-TIL-luh), town (☐ 2 sq mi/ 5.2 sq km; 1990 pop. 2,350), Lake co., central Fla., 31 mi/ 50 km NNW of Orlando; 28°55′N 81°40′W. Ships citrus fruit. **2** town (1990 pop. 3,046), Umatilla co., N Oregon, 30 mi/48 km NW of Pendleton, on Umatilla R. where it joins the Columbia R. (bridged; I-82), opposite Plymouth (Wash.); 45°54′N 119°19′W. Agr. (apples, plums, peaches, vegetables); mfg. PVC pipe. Umatilla Ordnance Depot to SW. McNary Dam, on Columbia R., to E. Umatilla Natl. Wildlife Refuge to W, on Columbia R.; Hat Rock State Park and Cold Springs Natl. Wildlife Refuge to E.

Umatilla, Lake (yoo-muh-TIL-uh), reservoir (☐ 86 sq mi/223 sq km), on border bet. N central Oregon and S central Wash., on Columbia R., 25 mi/40 km ENE of The Dalles (Oregon); c.85 mi/137 km long; 45°43′N 120°40′W. Elev. 266 ft/81 m. Max. capacity 2,530,000 acre-ft. Formed by John Day Lock and Dam (219 ft/67 m high, 5,640 ft/1,719 m long), built (1959–1968) by the U.S. Army Corps of Engineers on the state line for power generation; also used for flood control, navigation, and recreation.

Umatilla River (yoo-muh-TIL-uh), c.85 mi/137 km long, Oregon; rises in E Umatilla co., NE Oregon, in the Blue Mts; flows W through Umatilla Indian Reservation, past Pendleton, then NW to the Columbia R. at the town of Umatilla. This river is central to an irrigated region producing fruit, vegetables, and grain.

Umbagog, reservoir (☐ 4 sq mi/10.4 sq km), Coos co., N N.H., on Androscoggin R., 20 mi/32 km N of Berlin; 44°47′N 71°07′W. Max. capacity 119,250 acre-ft. Formed by Errol Dam (25 ft/8 m high), built (1887) for power generation.

Umbazooksus Lake (uhm-buh-ZOOK-suhs), Piscataquis co., N central Maine, 50 mi/80 km NNE of Greenville, in wilderness recreational area; 3.5 mi/5.6 km long, 1 mi/1.6 km wide. Joined by stream to Chesuncook L.

Umiat (OO-mee-yat), emergency airport, N Alaska, on Colville R., and 170 mi/274 km SE of Barrow; 69°23′N 152°10′W. Periodic base for petroleum exploration.

Umiujaq, village (1991 pop. 284), NW Que., E Canada, on E shore of Hudson Bay, W side of Ungava Peninsula, 250 mi/402 km NE of Chisasibi. Populated by Inuit and Cree peoples. James Bay Hydro Project to E. Hunting, fishing, trapping. Scheduled air service.

Umnak (OOM-nak), island, off SW Alaska, one of the largest of the Aleutian Isls.; c.83 mi/134 km long. Has a volcanic peak, Mt. Vsevidof (7,236 ft/2,206 m).

Umpire, village, Howard co., SW Ark., 26 mi/42 km NNW of Nashville, near Saline R. Ouachita Natl. Forest to N; Howard Co. Wildlife Management Area to SW.

Umpqua River (UHMP-kwah), 111 mi/179 km long, W Oregon; formed 6 mi/9.7 km NNW of Roseberg, E Douglas co., at confluence of North Umpqua (100 mi/161 km long) and South Umpqua (95 mi/153 km long) rivers, which rise in Cascade Range, in Umpqua Natl. Forest; flows N and W through Coast Range to the Pacific Ocean Range Bay at Reedsport. Parts of Wallowa-Whitman Natl. Forest to E and W.

Umsaskis Lake (uhm-SAS-kis), Aroostook co., N Maine, 65 mi/105 km W of Presque Isle; joined by Allagash R. to Churchill and Long lakes; 5 mi/8 km long.

Unadilla (yoo-nuh-DIL-uh), town (1990 pop. 1,620), Dooly co., central Ga., 39 mi/63 km S of Macon; 32°16′N 83°44′W. Machining.

Unadilla 1 (YOO-nuh-dil-uh), village (1990 pop. 294), Otoe co., SE Nebr., 23 mi/37 km ESE of Lincoln, and on Little Nemaha R.; 40°40′N 96°16′W. Little Nemaha State Wayside Area to E. **2** (uh-nah-DIL-lah), village (1990 pop. 1,265), Otsego co., central N.Y., on Susquehanna R. at mouth of Unadilla R., and 35 mi/56 km NE of Binghamton; 42°19′N 75°19′W. Mfg. (machinery, furniture); in farming and dairying area. Settled 1790, inc. 1827.

Unadilla River (u-nah-DIL-lah), c.60 mi/97 km long, central N.Y.; rises in S Herkimer co.; flows SW and S, past West Winfield, to Susquehanna R. at Unadilla.

Unaka Mountains, SE U.S., name often applied to a SW div. (2,000 ft/610 m–6,000 ft/1,829 m) of the Appalachian Mts. running NE-SW along Tenn.-N.C. state line and extending into Va. and Ga., bet. Great Appalachian Valley (NW) and the Blue Ridge escarpment (SE). Reach highest elevations in Great Smoky Mts.; also include Iron Mts. and Unicoi, Chilhowee, Stone, Bald, and Holston ranges. Natl. forests (chiefly Cherokee, Pisgah, and Nantahala) cover most of range. Name sometimes restricted to mts. in Unicoi and Carter cos. of Tenn. and Avery and Mitchell cos. of N.C., bet. Nolichucky and Doc rivers; rise to 5,258 ft/1,603 m in Unaka Mt., c.5 mi/8 km E of Erwin (Tenn.) on N.C. state line.

Unalakleet, village (1990 pop. 714), W Alaska, on E shore of Norton Sound, at mouth of Unalakleet R., 150 mi/241 km ESE of Nome; 63°52′N 160°47′W. Fishing, reindeer herding. Airfield.

Unalaska (oo-nuh-LAS-kah), village (1990 pop. 3,089), on N shore of Unalaska Isl., Aleutian Isls., SW Alaska, 3 mi/4.8 km S of Dutch Harbor (with which it is now unified); 53°55′N 166°30′W. Major internatl. fishing port and supply center; fish canning; supply point for fishermen. Home base of Coast Guard in Bering Sea area. Has oldest surviving Rus. Orthodox church in Alaska.

Unalaska (oo-nuh-LAS-kah), rugged island, off SW Alaska, one of the largest Aleutian Isls.; 30 mi/48 km long. Visited (c.1759) by Rus. explorers, the isl. was a center of Rus. fur trade until it was superseded by Kodiak. Spruces planted here by the Russians remain among the few trees in the Aleutians. The main towns on the isl. are Unalaska and Dutch Harbor.

Uncanoonuc Mountains (uhn-kuh-NOO-nuhk), Hillsborough co., S N.H., twin peaks near Goffstown, 5 mi/8 km W of Manchester; 42°59′N 71°35′W. Elev. of N peak, 1,320 ft/402 m; S peak, 1,321 ft/403 m.

Uncertain, village (1990 pop. 194), Harrison co., NE Texas, 16 mi/26 km NE of Marshall, on shore of Caddo L.; 32°42′N 94°07′W. Elev. 195 ft/59 m. Resort area; tourism. Named by steamboat captains who had difficulty mooring here. Home of Uncertain Club Society, early 1900s. Caddo L. State Park to W. Inc. 1961.

Uncompahgre, river, c.75 mi/121 km long, SW Colo.; rises in the San Juan Mts., N San Juan co.; flows NW past Montrose to the Gunnison R. at Delta. Its waters are used for irrigation. Gunnison Tunnel diverts water from the Gunnison R. to the Uncompahgre valley.

Uncompahgre Peak (14,309 ft/4,361 m), NW Hinsdale co., SW Colo., in the San Juan Mts., NE of Ouray, and 8 mi/12.9 km WNW of Lake City; 38°04′N 107°27′W. In Uncompaghre Natl. Forest.

Uncompahgre Plateau, SW Colo., high tableland extending c.60 mi/97 km NW-SE, mainly in Mesa and Montrose cos., extends into Ouray and San Miguel cos., bet. San Miguel and Gunnison rivers; rises to 10,338 ft/3,151 m in SE end. Lies within part of Uncompahgre Natl. Forest. Bisects Montrose co., isolating SW part of co.

Underhill, town (1990 pop. 2,799), Chittenden co., NW Vt., in Green Mts., 15 mi/24 km E of Burlington; 44°31′N 72°52′W. Resorts. Includes part of Mt. Mansfield State Forest.

Underwood 1 town (1990 pop. 515), Pottawattamie co., SW Iowa, on Mosquito Creek, and 12 mi/19 km NE of Council Bluffs; 41°23′N 95°40′W. **2** town (1990 pop. 976), McLean co., central N.Dak., 48 mi/77 km NNW of Bismarck; 47°27′N 101°08′W. Coal mines; diversified farming. Fort Mandan Historic Site to S; Audubon Natl. Wildlifge Refuge in L. Audubon (E extension of L. Sakakawea Reservoir) to N; Garrison Dam and Fish Hatchery to W.

Underwood 1 village (1990 pop. 550), on border bet. Clark and Scott cos., S Ind., 5 mi/8 km S of Scottsburg. Clark State Forest to SW; Pigeon Roost State Memorial to NE. Cattle; hay, corn. **2** village (1990 pop. 284), Otter Tail co., W Minn., SW of North Turtle L., 10 mi/16 km E of Fergus Falls; 46°17′N 95°52′W. Livestock, poultry; grain; dairying; light mfg. South Turtle L. to E.

Unga (OON-guh), village, on SE Unga Isl., Shumagin Isls., SW Alaska; 55°11′N 160°30′W. Cod-fishing center. It was an otter-fishing station under Russians. Scene of extensive gold-mining activity c.1900.

Unga Island (OON-guh), largest of Shumagin Isls., SW Alaska, off SW Alaska Peninsula; 20 mi/32 km long, 11 mi/18 km–14 mi/23 km wide; 55°16′N 160°41′W. Rises to 2,270 ft/692 m. Cod fishing and canning. Unga village on SE.

Ungava (uhn-GAH-vuh), **New Quebec**, or **Nouveau Québec**, district (□ 239,780 sq mi/621,030 sq km) of N Que., NE Canada, extending S from Ungava Bay; 60°00′N 74°00′W. It formerly included the whole Labrador-Ungava peninsula and was originally under the Hudson's Bay Company; made part of the N.W.T. in 1869, it became a separate dist. in 1895, bordered E by the strip of Lab. belonging to N.F. In 1912 it was added to Que. prov. and in 1927 its border with Lab. was established. Drained by Caniapiscau, Koksoak, Whale, and Larch rivers. Comprises a high plateau which forms watershed bet. the St. Lawrence R. and Hudson Bay. Region contains immense iron deposits at Schefferville, on Que.-Lab. border, and Labrador City in Lab., in S part of dist. Plans for development include hydroelectric power project on upper Caniapiscau R. (reservoir is part of James Bay Hydro Project), and RR to Sept Îles. Dist. includes settlement of Kuujjuaq (Fort Chimo) and Crystal I air base.

Ungava Bay (uhng-GAH-vuh), inlet of the Atlantic Ocean, N Que., E Canada, extending c.200 mi/320 km S from Hudson Strait bet. the N Que. mainland and the N tip of the Lab. peninsula; 160 mi/257 km wide at its mouth; 59°30′N 67°30′W.

Unicoi (YOO-ni-koi), county (□ 185 sq mi/479 sq km; 1990 pop. 13,694), NE Tenn.; ⊙ Erwin; 36°06′N 82°26′W. Mt. region, with Bald Mts. partly along N.C. state line (SW, S); drained by Nolichucky R. Includes part of Cherokee Natl. Forest. Lumbering; agr. (tobacco, fruit, hay), livestock raising; some industry at Erwin. Natl. fish hatchery nearby. Formed 1875.

Unicoi (YOO-ni-koi), village, Unicoi co., NE Tenn., 9 mi/14 km S of Johnson City, near N.C. state line, 36°12′N 82°21′W. In scenic mt. region.

Unicoi Mountains (YOO-ni-koi), range of the Appalachians along Tenn.-N.C. state line, SW of Great Smoky Mts. Natl. Park, bet. Little Tennessee and Hiwassee rivers. Includes Hooper Bald (5,600 ft/1,707 m), 10 mi/16 km W of Robbinsville (N.C.), and Haw Knob (5,472 ft/1,668 m), 2 mi/3 km farther W, on state line; Snowbird Mts. are an E extension. Situated in Cherokee and Nantahala natl. forests; sometimes considered a range of Unaka Mts. Includes Citico Creek, Joyce Kilmer–Slickrock, and Bald R. Gorge wildernesses.

Unimak (YOO-nee-mak), village, on SW Unimak Isl., Aleutian Isls., SW Alaska, 80 mi/129 km ENE of Dutch Harbor; 54°35′N 164°07′W. Fishing.

Unimak (YOO-nee-mak), volcanic island, off W Alaska; 70 mi/113 km long (largest of the Aleutian Isls.). Nearest of the chain to the Alaska Peninsula. Continually inhabited for c.10,000 years. Shishaldin volcano (9,372 ft/2,857 m) is located here.

Unimak Pass (YOO-nee-mak), sea passage in NE Aleutian Isls., bet. Unimak (NE) and Krenitzin (SW) isls., SW Alaska, bet. N Pacific Ocean and Bering Sea; 20 mi/32 km–30 mi/48 km wide; 54°20′N 164°50′W. Easternmost and most important navigation channel through Aleutian Isls. from N Pacific to Bering Sea.

Union 1 county (□ 1,055 sq mi/2,732 sq km; 1990 pop. 46,719), S Ark., on La. (S) state line; ⊙ El Dorado; 33°09′N 92°39′W. Bordered NE and E by Ouachita R., Felsenthal Lock and Dam (impounds L. Jack Lee) on E border, H. K. Thatcher Lock and Dam on N border, both dams on Ouachita R. Oil center of state; natural gas (drilling, refining, mfg. of petroleum prods.). Agr. (cattle, hogs, chicken; vegetables). Parts of Felsenthal Natl. Wildlife Refuge and Lower Ouachita Wildlife Management Area in E. Formed 1829. **2** county (□ 249 sq mi/645 sq km; 1990 pop. 10,252), N central Fla.; ⊙ Lake Butler; 30°02′N 82°22′W. Flatwoods area with several small lakes. Farming (corn, vegetables, peanuts); cattle raising; forestry (lumber, naval stores). Formed 1921. **3** county (□ 329 sq mi/852 sq km; 1990 pop. 11,993), N Ga., on N.C. (N) state line; ⊙ Blairsville; 34°50′N 83°59′W. In the Blue Ridge, largely in Chattahoochee Natl. Forest; drained by Nottely R. (dam and reservoir in N). Brasstown Bald (4,784 ft/1,458 m) in E. Agr. (corn); cattle, hogs; stone quarrying. Formed 1832. **4** county (□ 422 sq mi/1,093 sq km; 1990 pop. 17,619), S Ill., on Mo. (W; Mississippi R.) state line; ⊙ Jonesboro; 37°27′N 89°15′W. Bounded at extreme NW corner by Big Muddy R.; drained by Cache R. Agr. area (grain, fruit, vegetables, sorghum; cattle; dairy prods.), with some mfg. Limestone, granite, marble quarries. Includes part of Shawnee Natl. Forest. Hilly area (Ill. Ozarks) includes Bald Knob. Trail of Tears State Forest, part of Giant City State Park; Pine Hills Recreational Area; Union Co. Conservation area in W and N. One of 17 Ill. cos. to retain Southern-style commission form of co. govt. Formed 1818. **5** county (□ 165 sq mi/427 sq km; 1990 pop. 6,976), E Ind., on Ohio (E) state line; ⊙ Liberty; 39°37′N 84°55′W. Drained by East Fork of Whitewater R. Agr. (soybeans, hay, corn; cattle, hogs); dairying. Some mfg. at Liberty. N ½ of Brookville Reservoir in SW, with Quakertown State Recreation Area on W shore and Whitewater State Park near E shore. Formed 1821. **6** county (□ 425 sq mi/1,101 sq km; 1990 pop. 12,750), S Iowa; ⊙ Creston; 41°02′N 94°15′W. Rolling prairie agr. area (hogs, cattle, poultry; corn, oats) drained by Little Platte, Grand, and Thompson rivers; bituminous-coal deposits. Summit L. reservation and Green Valley State Park in NW. General flooding in area in 1993. Formed 1851. **7** county (□ 363 sq mi/940 sq km; 1990 pop. 16,557), W Ky., on Ill. (W; Ohio R.) and Ind. (N; Ohio R.) state lines; ⊙ Morganfield; 37°39′N 87°57′W. Bounded S by Tradewater R. Rolling upland agr. area (corn, wheat, hay, alfalfa, soybeans; hogs, cattle). Bituminous coal, sand and gravel. Some mfg. at Sturgis and Morganfield. Uniontown Lock and Dam on Ohio R. is N, 2 mi/3.2 km E of confluence of

Wabash R. (from N). Higgins-Henry Wildlife Management Area in E. Formed 1811. **8** county (□ 416 sq mi/1,077 sq km; 1990 pop. 22,085), N Miss.; ⊙ New Albany; 34°29′N 89°00′W. Drained by Tallahatchie and Hatchie rivers and Oldtown Creek. Includes part of Holly Springs Natl. Forest in W. Agr. (cotton, corn, soybeans; cattle; dairying; timber). Mfg. at New Albany and Sherman. Formed 1870. **9** county (□ 105 sq mi/272 sq km; 1990 pop. 493,819), NE N.J., on Passaic R. (NW) and Newark Bay and Arthur Kill (both E); ⊙ Elizabeth; 40°39′N 74°18′W. Industrial, residential area, with many bedroom communities; mfg. (chemicals, clothing, machinery, motor vehicles, consumer goods, electronic goods, transportation equip., tools, concrete and stone prods., chemicals, plastics, rubber goods, paper prods.); container seaport. Drained by Rahway R. Formed 1857. **10** county (□ 3,831 sq mi/9,922 sq km; 1990 pop. 4,124), extreme NE N.Mex., on Colo. (N), Texas, and Okla. (both E) state lines; ⊙ Clayton; 36°28′N 103°28′W. Cattle, sheep; triticale, sorghum, hay, alfalfa, wheat, oats, corn, barley, millet. Watered N by Cimarron R. and Carrizo and Ute creeks; source of Cimarron (larger of 2 Cimarron rivers in region) in NW corner. Most of co. is high plateau (5,000 ft/1,524 m–6,000 ft/1,829 m) of Great Plains. Capulin Volcano Natl. Monument in NW; sect. of Kiowa Natl. Grassland in E; Clayton L. State Park in E center. Formed 1893. **11** county (□ 639 sq mi/1,655 sq km; 1990 pop. 84,211), S N.C., on S.C. (S and SW) state line; ⊙ Monroe; 34°59′N 80°31′W. Bordered NE by Rocky R. in Piedmont region. Agr. area (wheat, oats, soybeans, barley, cotton, corn, hay; chickens, turkeys, cattle, hogs; dairying) and timber area; mfg. at Monroe. Source of Lynches R. in S. Formed 1842. **12** county (□ 434 sq mi/1,124 sq km; 1990 pop. 31,969), central Ohio; ⊙ Marysville; 40°18′N 83°23′W. Drained by Darby Creek, and small Mill and Rush creeks. In the Till Plains physiographic region. Agr. area (hogs, cattle, poultry; dairy prods.; corn, soybeans); mfg. at Marysville (chemicals, transportation equip.); limestone quarries, sand and gravel pits. Formed 1820. **13** county (□ 2,038 sq mi/5,278 sq km; 1990 pop. 23,598), NE Oregon; ⊙ La Grande; 45°19′N 118°00′W. Mt. area crossed by Grande Ronde R. Powder and North Powder rivers and Anthony Creek form part of S border. Blue Mts. in W and N. Wallowa Mts. in E. Agr. (apples, cherries, potatoes, wheat, oats, barley; hogs, sheep, cattle); timber. Parts of Wallowa-Whitman Natl. Forest in E and W, including parts of Eagle Cap Wilderness Area in E; part of Umatilla Natl. Forest in N; Catherine Creek State Park in S; Hilgard Junction and Red Bridge state parks in W. Formed 1864. **14** county (□ 317 sq mi/821 sq km; 1990 pop. 36,176), central Pa.; ⊙ Lewisburg; 40°57′N 77°03′W. Bounded E by West Branch of Susquehanna R.; forested recreation area in W part. Agr. area (corn, wheat, oats, hay, alfalfa; poultry; dairying). Mfg. at Lewisburg and Mifflinburg; limestone. Lewisburg Federal Penintentiary in E, N of Lewisburg; part of Allenwood Federal Prison Camp in NE. Part of Tiadaghton State Forest in N; part of Bald Eagle State Forest in SW; part of Shikellamy State Park in SE corner. Formed 1813. **15** county (□ 515 sq mi/1,334 sq km; 1990 pop. 30,337), N S.C.; ⊙ Union; 34°42′N 81°38′W. Bounded by Pacolet (N), Enoree (S), and Broad (E) rivers; drained by Tyger R. Includes part of Sumter Natl. Forest that encompasses S ½ of co. Mfg. includes sand, timber, vermiculite, textiles, ropes, fabricated metal prods., plastics, medical equip.; printing and publishing. Mainly agr., producing hay, grain, soybeans, peaches; cattle. Formed 1785. **16** county (□ 467 sq mi/1,210 sq km; 1990 pop. 10,189), SE S.Dak., on Iowa (E; Big Sioux R.) and Nebr. (SW; Missouri R.) state lines; ⊙ Elk Point; 42°51′N 96°40′W. Agr. area (dairy prods.; hay, corn, soybeans; honey; cattle, hogs). Union Co. State Park in NW. Formed 1862. **17** county (□ 212 sq mi/549 sq km; 1990 pop. 13,694), NE Tenn.; ⊙ Maynardville; 36°17′N 83°51′W. Bounded NW by Powell R.; crossed by Clinch R., here forming part of Norris Reservoir. Partly mountainous; traversed by ridges of the Appalachians. Agr. (tobacco; livestock). Formed 1850.

Union, parish (□ 906 sq mi/2,347 sq km; 1990 pop. 20,690), N La., on Ark. (N) state line; ⊙ Farmerville; 32°46′N, 92°24′W. Bounded E by Ouachita R.; drained by Bayou de L'Outre, Corney Bayou, and Bayou D'Arbonne. Contains large natural-gas field. Agr. (home gardens; vegetables, watermelons; cattle, horses, poultry, hogs; dairying), catfish. Logging; wood prods., chemicals. Bayou D'Arbonne L. reservoir and State Park at S center of parish. Upper Ouachita Natl. Wildlife Refuge in NE; part of D'Arbonne Natl. Wildlife Refuge in SE; Union State Wildlife Area in N center. Formed 1839.

Union 1 city (1990 pop. 5,909), ⊙ Franklin co., E central Mo., near Missouri R., 42 mi/68 km W of St. Louis; 38°27′N 91°00′W. Corn, wheat; dairying; cattle. Trade and service center; mfg. (flour, shoes, paper prods., plastic prods., electrical goods, apparel). East Central Col. here. Laid out 1826. **2** city (1990 pop. 5,501), Montgomery co., W Ohio, 11 mi/18 km NW of Dayton, and on Stillwater R. **3** city (1990 pop. 9,836), ⊙ Union co., N S.C., 25 mi/40 km SE of Spartanburg; 34°43′N 81°37′W. Mfg. includes cotton, plastic, and metal prods.; medical devices; printing and publishing. In agr. area for grain, peaches, apples; poultry, livestock; timber. Fine old houses in vicinity. Settled 1791.

Union 1 town (1990 pop. 612), Tolland co., NE Conn., on Mass. state line, 8 mi/12.9 km SW of Southbridge (Mass.); 41°59′N 72°09′W. Includes Mashapaug village, Mashapaug Pond (□ c.1 sq mi/2.6 sq km; resort); state forests. **2** town (1990 pop. 8,375), Fulton co., NW central Ga., 16 mi/26 km SW of Atlanta; 33°35′N 84°32′W. Mfg. includes crushed stone, millwork, lumber, textiles. Located in rapidly growing suburban area S of the city of Atlanta. **3** town (1990 pop. 448), Hardin co., central Iowa, near Iowa R., 8 mi/12.9 km S of Eldora; 42°14′N93°03′W. Rendering works. **4** town (1990 pop. 1,001), Boone co., N Ky., 15 mi/24 km SW of Cincinnati (Ohio) and 13 mi/21 km SW of Covington; 38°57′N 84°40′W. Tobacco; livestock, poultry; dairying. Big Bone Lick State Park to SW. **5** town (1990 pop. 1,989), Knox co., S Maine, on St. George R., 10 mi/16 km NW of Rockland; 44°13′N 69°17′W. Settled 1774, inc. 1786. **6** town (1990 pop. 1,875), Neshoba and Newton cos., E central Miss., 29 mi/47 km WNW of Meridian; 32°34′N 89°07′W. In agr. (cotton, corn; cattle, poultry), timber, and dairying area; mfg. (plastic prods., transportation equip., apparel, wood prods., furniture). **7** or **Union City**, town (1990 pop. 1,000), Canadian co., central Okla., 23 mi/37 km WSW of Oklahoma City, near Canadian R. Wheat; cattle; dairying; mfg. (bldg. materials). **8** town (1990 pop. 1,847), Union co., NE Oregon, on Catherine Creek, 14 mi/23 km SE of La Grande, W of Wallowa Mts.; 45°12′N 117°52′W. Elev. 2,789 ft/850 m. Trade center for cherries, apples, potatoes, grain, and timber. Catherine Creek State Park to SE. Cove Hot Springs to N. Inc. 1878.

Union 1 village (1990 pop. 542), McHenry co., NE Ill., on Kishwaukee R., and 8 mi/12.9 km SW of Woodstock; 42°13′N 88°32′W. In agr. area (corn; dairying); mfg. (consumer goods, transportation equip., fabricated metal prods.). Ill. RR Mus. here. **2** village (1990 pop. 299), Cass co., SE Nebr., 8 mi/12.9 km NNW of Nebraska City, near Missouri R.; 40°48′N 95°55′W. RR junction. **3** uninc. village, Hertford co., NE N.C., 3 mi/4.8 km NNW of Ahoskie. Cotton, tobacco, peanuts, grain; livestock, poultry. **4** village (1990 pop. 566), ⊙ Monroe co., SE W.Va., 18 mi/29 km ESE of Hinton; 37°35′N 80°32′W. Agr. (grain); livestock, poultry; dairying; timber. Mfg. (lumber; transportation equip.). Moncove L. State Park and Wildlife Management Area to E; Jefferson Natl. Forest (Va., W.Va.) to SE.

Union, industrial township (1990 pop. 50,024), Union co., NE N.J. Steel and metal prods., paint mfg. Site of a Revolutionary battle in 1780. Seat of Kean Univ. of N.J. Settled 1749 by colonists from Conn., set off from Elizabethtown 1808.

Union, N.H.: see WAKEFIELD.

Union Bay, village, SW B.C., W Canada, on E Vancouver Isl., on Strait of Georgia, opposite Denman Isl., 10 mi/16 km SE of Courtenay; 49°36′N 124°53′W. Lumbering port; mixed farming.

Union Beach, borough (1990 pop. 6,156), Monmouth co., E N.J., on Raritan Bay, and 7 mi/11.3 km SE of Perth Amboy; 40°27′N 74°10′W. Chiefly residential. Inc. 1925.

Union Bridge, town (1990 pop. 910), Carroll co., N Md., 17 mi/27 km NE of Frederick, on Little Pipe R.; 39°34′N 77°11′W. In agr. area; RR shops, clothing factories, cement works. First called Buttersburg because it was a dairy center, then Pipe Creek Settlement because of its location on Little Pipe R., it became Union Bridge when the 1st bridge was built over the river. The RR arrived in 1868, and the station is preserved as the hq. and mus. of the Western Md. RR Historical Society. Has Pipe Creek Quaker Meeting House (1768; rebuilt after a fire in 1935). The town is believed to be the site of the 1st nail factory, and another prototype of the 1st modern reaper was made here by John B. Thomas. The scissors action in this invention is used in modern reapers and combine harvesters. The cement works here has been operating continuously since 1910.

Union, Cape, NE Ellesmere Isl., NE Franklin dist., N.W.T., N Canada, on the Lincoln Sea of the Arctic Ocean, at entrance of Robeson Channel; 82°13′N 61°07′W.

Union Center, village (1990 pop. 197), Juneau co., central Wis., on Baraboo R., and 30 mi/48 km NW of Baraboo; 43°40′N 90°15′W. In dairying region; mfg. of machinery.

Union City 1 city (1990 pop. 53,762), Alameda co., W Calif., suburb 20 mi/32 km SE of downtown Oakland, on Alameda Creek, E of San Francisco Bay; 37°36′N 122°01′W. In an agr. region. Mfg. (metal and plastic prods., wool, paper prods., food prods., tool and die, consumer goods, labels; iron foundry). A rapidly growing city, its pop. more than tripled bet. 1970 and 1990. Coyote Hills Regional Park to W, at mouth of Alameda Creek. Inc. 1959, with the merger of Decoto and Alvarado dists. **2** city (1990 pop. 3,612), Randolph co., E Ind. and W Ohio, 30 mi/48 km E of Muncie; 40°12′N 84°49′W. Ships agr. prods. and livestock; mfg. (sugar processing; wood prods., transportation equip., lumber, textiles); sawmill. Ind. and Ohio sects. are separate corporations. Laid out 1849. **3** city (1990 pop. 58,012), Hudson co., NE N.J., on the Palisades overlooking the Hudson R., directly opposite N.Y. city; 40°46′N 74°01′W. This densely populated city has many small firms, most of them in the embroidery field. Other mfg. includes fabricated metal prods., consumer goods, machinery, apparel, transportation equip., electrical goods, and dairy prods. Inc. 1925. **4** city (1990 pop. 10,513), ⊙ Obion co., W Tenn., near Ky. (N) state line, c.110 mi/177 km NNE of Obion; 36°26′N 89°03′W. A trade, processing, and shipping center in a livestock, grain, cotton, and fruit-growing region. Mfg. includes transportation equip., fabricated metal prods., and fireplaces. A Civil War cemetery, a monument to unknown Confederate dead, and an eternal-flame memorial are here. Inc. 1867.

Union City, town (1990 pop. 1,767), Branch and Calhoun cos., S Mich., 17 mi/27 km S of Battle Creek, at confluence of Coldwater and St. Joseph rivers; 42°04′N 85°08′W. In agr. (corn, soybeans; hogs) and dairying area; mfg. of electrical prods., machinery. Native Amer. mounds in vicinity. Union L. to W. Settled 1830, inc. 1866.

Union City, borough (1990 pop. 3,537), Erie co., NW Pa., 19 mi/31 km SE of Erie, on South Branch French Creek; 41°53′N 79°50′W. Mfg. (lumber, plastic prods., wood prods., furniture, fabricated metal prods.; printing and publishing; sand, gravel, and stone processing); agr. (potatoes, grain; livestock; dairying). Growth stimulated by oil boom of 1860s. Union City Amer. Historical Mus. Canadohta L. reservoir (residential development) to S; Union City L. reservoir, on French Creek, to NW. State fish hatchery is here. Settled c.1785, inc. 1863.

Union City, Okla.: see UNION.

Union Dale, borough (1990 pop. 303), Susquehanna co., NE Pa., 10 mi/16 km N of Carbondale, on West Branch Lackawanna R. (forms Stillwater L. reservoir to S);

41°42'N 75°28'W. Corn, hay; dairying; logging. Elk Mt. Ski Area to W.

Unión de Reyes (oo-nee-ON dai RAI-yaiz), town, Matanzas prov., W Cuba, RR junction 17 mi/27 km S of Matanzas; 22°48'N 81°34'W. In agr. region (sugarcane; livestock); foundries. Sugar mills Juan Avila 5 mi/8 km NE and Puerto Rico Libre 5 mi/8 km S.

Unión de San Antonio (oo-nee-ON dai sahn ahn-to-NEE-o), city (1990 pop. 4,760), Jalisco, central Mexico, 20 mi/32 km W of León; 21°06'N 101°58'W. Corn, wheat, beans; livestock.

Unión de Tula (oo-nee-ON dai TOO-lah), town (1990 pop. 8,418), Jalisco, W Mexico, 40 mi/64 km SSW of Ameca, on Mexico Highway 80; 19°57'N 104°16'W. Agr. center (grain, sugarcane, cotton, tobacco, fruit).

Union, Fort, Mont.: see FORT UNION TRADING POST NATIONAL HISTORIC SITE.

Union Gap, town (1990 pop. 3,120), Yakima co., S Wash., suburb 3 mi/4.8 km S of Yakima, on Yakima R.; 46°34'N 120°29'W. In irrigated agr. region; fruits and vegetables, hops, peppermint; dairying; cattle, sheep, poultry. Mfg. (furniture, millwork, coffee, wood prods., paper prods.; printing and publishing, meatpacking). Agr. mus. here. Yakima Indian Reservation to S.

Union Grove, town (1990 pop. 3,669), Racine co., SE Wis., 12 mi/19 km WSW of Racine; 42°40'N 88°02'W. In farm area; mfg. (rubber prods., fabricated metal prods.). Dragway. Bong State Recreation Area to SW.

Union Grove 1 uninc. village, Iredell co., W central N.C., 17 mi/27 km N of Statesville. Tobacco, grain, cotton; poultry, livestock; timber. Mfg. (machinery, lumber, wood prods., feeds). **2** village (1990 pop. 271), Upshur co., NE Texas, 10 mi/16 km NW of Longview; 32°34'N 94°54'W. Oil and natural gas. Agr. (dairying; cattle, poultry; vegetables); timber. L. Gladewater reservoir to W.

Unión Hidalgo (oon-YON hee-DAHL-go), town (1990 pop. 11,949), SE Oaxaca, Mexico, 12 mi/20 km E of Juchitán de Zaragoza; 16°28'N 94°49'W. In the S part of Isthmus of Tehuantepec. RR connects with Juchitán. Very hot climate. Prosperous cattle industry. Agr. (corn, sesame); fishing.

Union Hill, village (1990 pop. 37), Kankakee co., NE Ill., 15 mi/24 km W of Kankakee; 41°06'N 88°99'W. Agr. (corn, soybeans; dairying); lumber processing.

Union Island, St. Vincent and the Grenadines, West Indies, S of St. Vincent, SW of Mayreau, 40 mi/64 km SSW of Kingstown; 12°35'N 61°25'W. Center of S Grenadines. Clifton Harbor is safe anchorage on E coast, where tours depart for Tobago Cays. Clifton and Ashton are the 2 villages. Cotton growing.

Unión Juárez (oo-nee-ON HWAH-res), town (1990 pop. 2,466), Chiapas, S Mexico, at SE foot of Tacaná volcano, on Guatemala border, 17 mi/27 km NNE of Tapachula; 15°04'N 92°05'W. Elev. 4,154 ft/1,266 m. Coffee.

Union, Lake, King co., W Wash., in Seattle, 2 mi/3.2 km N of downtown, linked to Puget Sound (W) and L. Washington (E) by ship canal. Viewing of pleasure craft, other boats, through locks is popular attraction.

Union Lake, N.J.: see MAURICE RIVER.

Union Mills 1 village (1990 pop. 650), LaPorte co., NW Ind., 9 mi/14.5 km SSW of LaPorte. Agr. area. Settled 1832, laid out 1849. **2** village, Carroll co., N Md., 35 mi/56 km NW of Baltimore. The Shriver Homestead here, begun by Andrew and David Shriver in 1797, is a 23-room house in which the furnishings of 6 generations of the family are on display in their original settings. The house, with its adjacent grist- and sawmills, contains one of the most complete collections of Americana in any private bldg.

Union, Mount, peak (7,979 ft/2,432 m), Yavapai co., central Ariz., 10 mi/16 km SSE of Prescott, in Prescott Natl. Forest; 34°24'N 112°24'W.

Union Park, town (□ 3 sq mi/7.8 sq km; 1990 pop. 6,890), Orange co., central Fla., 10 mi/16 km ENE of Orlando; 28°33'N 81°14'W.

Union Point, town (1990 pop. 1,753), Greene co., NE central Ga., 6 mi/9.7 km ENE of Greensboro; 33°37'N 83°05'W. Mfg. includes textile production and clothing.

Union River, c.30 mi/48 km long, S Maine; rises in N Hancock co.; flows S through Graham L., past Ellsworth (falls here), to mouth at Union R. Bay, 8-mi/12.9-km inlet of Blue Hill Bay.

Union Springs, city (1990 pop. 3,975), ⊙ Bullock co., SE Ala., 38 mi/61 km SE of Montgomery, in the Black Belt. Lumber; textiles, fertilizer. Settled 1836.

Union Springs, village (□ 1 sq mi/2.6 sq km; 1990 pop. 1,142), Cayuga co., W central N.Y., on E shore of Cayuga L., 8 mi/12.9 km SW of Auburn; 42°51'N 76°41'W. Summer resort; some mfg. (transportation equip., plastic prods.); dairy prods.; farming.

Union Star, town (1990 pop. 432), De Kalb co., NW Mo., 14 mi/23 km NW of Maysville; 39°58'N 94°35'W. Corn, wheat; cattle.

Union Valley Reservoir, El Dorado co., E central Calif., on Silver Creek, 26 mi/42 km WSW of South Lake Tahoe, in Eldorado Natl. Forest; 4 mi/6.4 km long; 38°51'N 120°25'W. Max. capacity 271,000 acre-ft. Formed by Union Valley Dam (425 ft/130 m high), built (1963) by the city of Sacramento for water supply and power generation.

Unión, Villa, Mexico: see VILLA UNIÓN.

Union Village, neighborhood, North Smithfield, Providence co., R.I., 13 mi/21 km NNW of Providence.

Uniondale, uninc. residential city (□ 2 sq mi/5.2 sq km; 1990 pop. 20,328), Nassau co., SE N.Y., on L.I.; 40°42'N 73°35'W. Downtown suburban growth since the 1970s in Uniondale is marked by the construction of a large arena, new hotels, and office and retail sites.

Uniondale, town (1990 pop. 289), Wells co., E Ind., 7 mi/11.3 km NNE of Bluffton; 40°50'N 85°14'W. In agr. area; mfg. (feed mixing). Laid out 1883.

Uniontown, city (1990 pop. 12,034), ⊙ Fayette co., SW Pa., 40 mi/64 km SSE of Pittsburgh, on Redstone Creek; 39°53'N 79°43'W. RR junction. Farm trade center and an industrial city. Formerly noted for its production of coal and coke, the city now has industries with diversified mfg. (machinery, medical supplies, clothing, food prods., lumber, transportation equip.; printing and publishing). Agr. (apples, alfalfa; livestock; dairying). Fayette campus of Pa. State Univ. is here. Gen. George C. Marshall b. here. Nearby is Fort Necessity, built by George Washington; Fort Necessity Natl. Battlefield to SE; Searight Tollhouse Mus. to NW; Connellsville Airport to NE; Chestnut Ridge to SE; Forbes State Forest to S, including Laurel Caverns; Ohiopyle State Park to E. Settled c.1767, inc. as city 1916.

Uniontown 1 town (1990 pop. 1,730), Perry co., W central Ala., 17 mi/27 km SW of Marion. Cord, textiles. Settled early 19th cent. **2** town (1990 pop. 1,008), Union co., W Ky., 19 mi/31 km W of Henderson, on Ohio R.; 37°46'N 87°55'W. In agr. and bituminous-coal area; grain, soybeans; livestock; mfg. (apparel). Settled c.1810; inc. 1840. **3** uninc. town (1990 pop. 800), Coal township, Northumberland co., E central Pa., 1 mi/1.6 km NW of Shamokin, on Shamokin Creek; 40°48'N 76°34'W. Shamokin State Hosp. is here.

Uniontown 1 village (1990 pop. 290), Bourbon co., SE Kansas, 15 mi/24 km W of Fort Scott; 37°51'N 94°58'W. In dairying and general farming region. **2** village (1990 pop. 277), Whitman co., SE Wash., near Idaho state line, 10 mi/16 km NNW of Lewiston (Idaho), on Union Flat Creek; 46°32'N 117°05'W. Wheat, barley, oats; sheep, hogs.

Unionville, village, in city of Markham, S Ont., central Canada, 16 mi/26 km NNE of Toronto; 43°52'N 79°18'W. Suburban community.

Unionville, city (1990 pop. 1,989), ⊙ Putnam co., N Mo., 29 mi/47 km NW of Kirksville; 40°28'N 93°00'W. Corn, wheat, soybeans; cattle, sheep; coal mining to E. Mfg. of labels and decals. Inc. c.1855.

Unionville, town (1990 pop. 133), Appanoose co., S Iowa, 11 mi/18 km NE of Centerville; 40°49'N 92°42'W. In agr. area. Several small units of Stephens State Forest to NE.

Unionville 1 village (1990 pop. 2,710), Tift co., S Ga., near Tifton; 31°26'N 83°30'W. **2** village (1990 pop. 590), Tuscola co., E Mich., 21 mi/34 km ENE of Bay City, near Saginaw Bay; 43°38'N 83°28'W. In farm area; grain elevators; fishing tackle. **3** village (1990 pop. 548), Orange co., SE N.Y., near N.J. state line, 9 mi/14.5 km SE of Port Jervis; 41°17'N 74°33'W. Mfg. (textiles, rubber goods). Summer resort. **4** uninc. village, Union co., S N.C., 10 mi/16 km NNE of Monroe. Cotton, grain; poultry, livestock.

Unionville, borough (1990 pop. 284), Centre co., central Pa., 5 mi/8 km W of Bellefonte, on Bald Eagle Creek; 40°54'N 77°52'W. Agr. (corn, hay; livestock; dairying). Bald Eagle Mt. ridge to SE.

Unionville Center, village (1990 pop. 238), Union co., central Ohio, 5 mi/8 km SSE of Marysville; 40°08'N 83°20'W.

Uniopolis (yoo-nee-AH-puh-lis), village (1990 pop. 261), Auglaize co., W Ohio, 10 mi/16 km S of Lima; 40°36'N 84°05'W. In agr. area.

United Nations Headquarters, in midtown Manhattan, N.Y. city, SE N.Y., on East R., bounded by 42d St. (S), 48th St. (N), Roosevelt Drive (E), and 1st Ave. (W); 40°45'N 73°57'W. Hq. of the UN, an organization of sovereign states founded in 1945 which promotes internatl. peace and cooperation. Strictly speaking, the site is not part of the city, the state, or even the U.S. Built on an 18-acre/7-ha site known as Turtle Bay (which, ironically, was the site of abattoirs until 1946). The land was purchased by the Rockefeller family, which then donated it to the city for the UN site. The dominant feature is the 39-story Secretariat Bldg., but other bldgs. include the General Assembly and Conference and Lib. bldgs. Flags of all member nations fly outside hq. Staffed by c.23,000 employees, representing over 150 countries; issues its own stamps.

United States, republic (□ 3,787,425 sq mi/9,809,431 sq km; 1995 est. pop. 262,755,270), N. Amer., consisting of 50 states and a Federal dist.; ⊙ WASHINGTON, D.C.. The full name is the United States of Amer. The outlying territories and areas of the U.S. include: in the Caribbean Basin, PUERTO RICO (since 1952 a commonwealth associated with the U.S.) and the U.S. VIRGIN ISLANDS (purchased from Denmark in 1917); in the Pacific Ocean, GUAM (ceded by Spain after the Span.-Amer. War), AMERICAN SAMOA, WAKE ISLAND, the Republic of PALAU, and several other isls. The U.S. also has Compacts of Free Assn. with the Republic of the MARSHALL ISLANDS and the Federated States of MICRONESIA. The NORTHERN MARIANA ISLANDS are a self-governing commonwealth in union with the U.S. Excluding ALASKA and HAWAII, the conterminous U.S. stretches across central N. Amer. from the Atlantic (E) to the Pacific (W) oceans, and from Canada on the N to Mexico and the Gulf of Mexico on the S. The state of Alaska is located in extreme NW N. Amer. bet. the Arctic and Pacific oceans and is bordered by Canada on the E. The state of Hawaii, an isl. chain, is situated in the E central Pacific Ocean c.2,100 mi/3,400 km SW of San Francisco. The continental U.S. may be divided into several regions: the New England states (MAINE, NEW HAMPSHIRE, VERMONT, MASSACHUSETTS, RHODE ISLAND, and CONNECTICUT), the Middle Atlantic states (NEW YORK, NEW JERSEY, PENNSYLVANIA, DELAWARE, MARYLAND, VIRGINIA, and WEST VIRGINIA), the Southeastern states (NORTH CAROLINA, SOUTH CAROLINA, GEORGIA, FLORIDA, ALABAMA, MISSISSIPPI, LOUISIANA, ARKANSAS, TENNESSEE, and KENTUCKY), the states of the Midwest (OHIO, INDIANA, ILLINOIS, MICHIGAN, WISCONSIN, MINNESOTA, IOWA, and MISSOURI), the Great Plains states (NORTH DAKOTA, SOUTH DAKOTA, NEBRASKA, and KANSAS), the Mountain states (MONTANA, IDAHO, WYOMING, COLORADO, and UTAH), the Southwestern states (OKLAHOMA, TEXAS, NEW MEXICO, and ARIZONA), and the states of the Far West (WASHINGTON, OREGON, CALIFORNIA, and NEVADA). Alaska is the largest state in area (□ 656,424 sq mi/1,700,578 sq km) and R.I. is the smallest (□ 1,545 sq mi/4,003 sq km). Calif. has the largest pop. (1990 pop. 29,760,021), while Wyo. has the fewest people (1990 pop. 453,588). The largest U.S. cities are NEW YORK, LOS ANGELES, CHICAGO, HOUSTON, and PHILADELPHIA; among the other major cities are BOSTON, BALTIMORE, Washington, D.C., ATLANTA, MIAMI, PITTSBURGH,

CLEVELAND, DETROIT, COLUMBUS, TAMPA, INDIANAPOLIS, MILWAUKEE, MINNEAPOLIS, SAINT LOUIS, MEMPHIS, NEW ORLEANS, KANSAS CITY, DALLAS, SAN ANTONIO, DENVER, SALT LAKE CITY, PHOENIX, SAN FRANCISCO, PORTLAND, SAN JOSE, SEATTLE, SAN DIEGO, and HONOLULU. The conterminous U.S. is divided into 7 broad physiographic divs.: from E to W, the Atlantic–Gulf Coastal Plain; the Appalachian Highlands; the Interior Plains; the Interior Highlands; the Rocky Mt. System; the Intermontane Region; and the Pacific Mt. System. An 8th div., the Laurentian Uplands, a part of the CANADIAN SHIELD, dips into the U.S. from Canada in the Great Lakes region. It is an area of little local relief, with an irregular drainage system and many lakes, as well as some of the oldest exposed rocks in the U.S. The Atlantic–Gulf Coastal Plain extends along the E and SE coasts of the U.S. from E L.I. to the Rio Grande; Cape Cod and the isls. off SE Mass. are also part of this region. Although narrow in the N, the Atlantic Coastal Plain widens in the S, merging with the Gulf Coastal Plain in Fla. The Atlantic and Gulf coasts are essentially coastlines of submergence, with numerous estuaries, embayments, isls., sandspits, and barrier beaches backed by lagoons. The NE coast has many fine natural harbors, such as those of NEW YORK BAY and CHESAPEAKE BAY, but S of the great capes of the N.C. coast (Fear, Lookout, and Hatteras) there are few large bays. A principal feature of the lagoon-lined Gulf Coast is the great delta of the MISSISSIPPI R. The Atlantic Coastal Plain rises in the W to the rolling Piedmont (the falls along which were an early source of waterpower), a hilly, transitional zone leading to the APPALACHIAN MOUNTAINS. These anc. mts., a once-towering system now worn low by erosion, extend SW from SE Canada to the Gulf Coastal Plain in Ala. In E New England, the Appalachians extend to the Atlantic Ocean, forming a rocky, irregular coastline. The Appalachians and the ADIRONDACK MOUNTAINS of N.Y. (which are geologically related to the Can. Shield) include all the chief highlands of the E U.S.; Mt. MITCHELL (6,684 ft/2,037 m high), in the Black Mts. of N.C., is the highest point of E N. Amer. Extending over 1,000 mi/1,610 km from the Appalachians to the Rocky Mts. and lying bet. the Great Lakes (N) and the Gulf Coastal Plain (S) are the undulating Interior Plains. Once covered by a great inland sea, the Interior Plains are underlain by sedimentary rock. Almost all of the region is drained by one of the world's greatest river systems — the Mississippi-Missouri. The Interior Plains may be divided into 2 sects.: the fertile central lowlands, the agr. heartland of the U.S.; and the GREAT PLAINS, a treeless plateau that gently rises from the central lowlands to the foothills of the Rocky Mts. The BLACK HILLS of S.Dak. form the region's only upland area. The Interior Highlands are located just W of the Mississippi R. bet. the Interior Plains and the Gulf Coastal Plain. This region consists of the rolling Ozark Plateau (see OZARKS) to the N and the OUACHITA MOUNTAINS, which are similar in structure to the ridge and valley sect. of the Appalachians, to the E. W of the Great Plains are the lofty ROCKY MOUNTAINS. This geologically young and complex system extends into the NW U.S. from Canada and runs S into N.Mex. There are numerous high peaks in the Rockies; the highest is Mt. ELBERT (14,433 ft/4,399 m). The Rocky Mts. are divided into 4 sects. — the Northern Rockies, the Middle Rockies, the Wyo. (Great Divide) Basin, and the Southern Rockies. Along the crest of the Rockies is the CONTINENTAL DIVIDE, separating Atlantic-bound drainage from that heading for the Pacific Ocean. Bet. the Rocky Mts. and the ranges to the W is the Intermontane Region, an arid expanse of plateaus, basins, and ranges. The COLUMBIA PLATEAU, in the N of the region, was formed by volcanic lava and is drained by the COLUMBIA and its tributary the SNAKE R., both of which have cut deep canyons into the plateau. The enormous COLORADO PLATEAU, an area of sedimentary rock, is drained by the COLORADO R. and its tributaries; there the Colorado R. has entrenched itself to form the GRAND CANYON, one of the world's most impressive scenic wonders. W of the plateaus is the Basin and Range prov., an area of extensive semidesert. The lowest point in N. Amer., in DEATH VALLEY NATIONAL MONUMENT (282 ft/86 m below sea level), is there. The largest basin in the region is the GREAT BASIN, an area of interior drainage (the HUMBOLDT R. is the largest stream) and of numerous salt lakes, including the GREAT SALT LAKE. Bet. the Intermontane Region and the Pacific Ocean is the Pacific Mt. System, a series of ranges generally paralleling the coast, formed by faulting and volcanism. The CASCADE RANGE, with its numerous volcanic peaks, extends S from SW Canada into N Calif., and from there is continued S by the SIERRA NEVADA, a great fault block. Mt. WHITNEY (14,495 ft/4,418 m), in the Sierra Nevada, is the highest peak in the conterminous U.S. W of the Cascades and the Sierra Nevada and separated from them by a structural trough are the COAST RANGES, which extend along the length of the U.S. Pacific coast. The Central Valley in Calif., the Willamette Valley in Oregon, and the Puget Sound lowlands in Wash. are part of the trough. The San Andreas Fault, a fracture in the earth's crust, parallels the trend of the Coast Ranges from San Francisco Bay SE to NW Mexico; earthquakes are common along its entire length. The Pacific Coastal Plain is narrow, and in many cases the mts. plunge directly into the sea. A coastline of emergence, it has few isls., except for the Channel Isls. (see SANTA BARBARA ISLANDS) and those in Puget Sound; there are few good harbors besides PUGET SOUND, SAN FRANCISCO BAY, and SAN DIEGO BAY. Alaska may be divided into 4 physiographic regions; they are, from N to S, the Arctic Lowlands, the coastal plain of the Arctic Ocean; the Rocky Mt. System, of which the BROOKS RANGE is the northernmost sect.; the Central Basins and Highlands Region, which is dominated by the YUKON R. basin; and the Pacific Mt. System, which parallels Alaska's S coast and which rises to Mt. MCKINLEY (20,320 ft/6,194 m), the highest peak of N. Amer. The isls. of SE Alaska and those of the ALEUTIAN ISLANDS chain are partially submerged portions of the Pacific Mt. System and are frequently subjected to volcanic activity and earthquakes. These isls. are the tops of volcanoes that rise from the floor of the Pacific Ocean; MAUNA KEA and MAUNA LOA are active volcanoes. The terrain of the N U.S. was formed by the great continental ice sheets that covered N N. Amer. during the late Cenozoic Era. The S edge of the ice sheet is roughly traced by a line of terminal moraines extending W from E L.I. and then along the course of the OHIO and Missouri rivers to the Rocky Mts.; land N of this line is covered by glacial material. Alaska and the mts. of the NW U.S. had extensive mt. glaciers and were heavily eroded. Large glacial lakes (see BONNEVILLE, LAKE; LAHONTAN, LAKE) occupied sects. of the Basin and Range prov.; the Great Salt L. and the other lakes of this region are remnants of the glacial lakes. The U.S. has an extensive inland waterway system, much of which has been improved for navigation and flood control and developed to produce hydroelectricity and irrigation water by such agencies as the U.S. Bureau of Reclamation, the U.S. Army Corps of Engineers, and the TVA. Some of the world's larger dams, man-made lakes, and hydroelectric power plants are on U.S. rivers. The Mississippi-Missouri river system (c.3,890 mi/6,300 km long), is the longest in the U.S. and the 2d-longest in the world. With its hundreds of tributaries, chief among which are the RED RIVER, the Ohio, and the ARKANSAS, the Mississippi basin drains over ½ of the nation. The Yukon, Columbia, Colorado, and RIO GRANDE also have huge drainage basins. Other notable river systems include the CONNECTICUT, HUDSON, DELAWARE, SUSQUEHANNA, POTOMAC, JAMES, ALABAMA, TRINITY, SAN JOAQUIN, , and SACRAMENTO. The Great Salt L. and ILIAMNA are the largest U.S. lakes outside of the GREAT LAKES and LAKE OF THE WOODS, which are shared with Canada. The ILLINOIS WATERWAY connects the Great Lakes with the Mississippi R., and the NEW YORK STATE BARGE CANAL links them with the Hudson. The INTRACOASTAL WATERWAY provides sheltered passage for shallow draft vessels along the Atlantic and Gulf coasts. The U.S. has a broad range of climates, varying from the tropical rain forest of Hawaii and the tropical savanna of S Fla. (where the EVERGLADES are found) to the subarctic and tundra climates of Alaska. E of the 100th meridian (the general dividing line bet. the dry and humid climates) are the humid subtropical climate of the SE U.S. and the humid continental climate of the NE U.S. Extensive forests are found in both these regions. W of the 100th meridian are the steppe climate and the grasslands of the Great Plains; trees are found along the water courses. In the SW U.S. are the deserts of the basin and range prov., with the hottest and driest spots in the U.S. Along the Pacific coast are the Mediterranean-type climate of S Calif. and, extending N into SE Alaska, the marine West Coast climate. The Pacific Northwest is one of the wettest parts of the U.S. and is densely forested. The Rocky Mts., Cascades, and Sierra Nevada have typical highland climates and are also heavily forested. In addition to the Grand Canyon in Ariz. and Great Salt L. in Utah, widely publicized geographic marvels of the U.S. include NIAGARA FALLS, on the border bet. N.Y. and Canada (Ont.); the pink cliffs of BRYCE CANYON NATIONAL PARK, in Utah; and the geysers of YELLOWSTONE NATIONAL PARK, primarily in Wyo. Its mineral and agr. resources are tremendous. Although it was virtually self-sufficient in the past, increasing consumption, esp. of energy, continues to make it dependent on certain imports. It is, nevertheless, the world's largest producer of both electrical and nuclear energy. It leads all nations in the production of natural gas, lead, aluminum, sulfur, and salt. It is also a leading producer of copper, coal, steel, crude oil, iron ore, silver, uranium, and zinc. The U.S. produces 48% of the world's mica, 45% of its molybdenum, and 42% of its magnesium. Although its output has declined, the U.S. is among the world leaders in the production of pig iron and ferroalloys, motor vehicles, and synthetic rubber. Agriculturally, the U.S. is 1st in the production of meat, cheese, corn, soybeans, and tobacco. The U.S. is also one of the largest producers of cattle, hogs, cow's milk, butter, cotton, oats, wheat, barley, and sugar. (For more detailed accounts of agr. and industrial prods., see separate articles on the states, cities, towns, and villages.). Major U.S. exports are motor vehicles, food, iron and steel-mill prods., chemicals, computers and computer software, civilian aircraft, armaments, and consumer goods. The Northeast has seen a shift over several decades from a traditional mfg. center to financial services and high-tech businesses. The same period also saw a relocation of many U.S. industries to the mid-South, South, and far West as well as its revival in the Midwest. The leading imports include ores and metal scraps, petroleum and petroleum prods., machinery, transportation equip. (esp. motor vehicles), paper and paper prods. Major trading partners are Canada, Japan, Mexico, Germany, and the U.K. The volume of trade has been steadily increasing. The GDP has continued to rise, and in 1990 it was easily the largest in the world at c.$5.4 trillion, and in 1996 had increased to an estimated $6.4 trillion. The development of the economy has been spurred by the growth of a complex network of communications not only by RR, highways, inland waterways, and air but also by telephone, radio, television, computer, and facsimile machine. Over 70% of the pop. is urban, and the great majority of the inhabitants are of Eur. descent. About 12% of the total pop. is of Afr. or Afr.-Caribbean origin. The Asian pop. in 1990 totaled 7,273,662 (almost 3% of the nation's total pop.), comprised predominantly of people of Chin., Filipino, Indian, Jap., Korean, and Vietnamese origin. The Hispanic pop., which includes people of Mex., Puerto Rican, Cuban, Dominican, and Lat. Amer. descent, accounted in 1990 for 9% of the total U.S. pop. Hispanics are the fastest-growing ethnic group in the U.S. and are expected to become the nation's largest minority early in the 21st cent. In 1990, the Native Amer. pop. of the U.S. was 1,878,285, which included Natives of Alaska such as Eskimos and Aleuts. Roughly 38% of Native Americans live on reservations, trust lands, territories, or other lands under Native Amer. jurisdiction. In addition to the original group of Br. settlers in the colonies of the Atlantic coast, numerous other natl. groups were introduced by immigration. Large numbers of Afr. slaves were imported chiefly to work on the plantations of the South (though slavery was also very common in urban areas of the Mid-Atlantic colonies during the 17th and 18th cents.). When the U.S. was developing rapidly with the settlement of the West (where some earlier groups of Fr. and Span. settlers were absorbed), immigrants from Europe poured into the land. An important early group was the Scotch-Irish. Just before the middle of the 19th cent., Irish and Ger. immigrants were predominant. A little later the Scandinavian nations supplied many settlers. After the Civil War, the immigrants came mainly from the nations of S and E Europe: from Italy, Greece, Russia, Rus. Poland, and from Austria-Hungary and the Balkans. During this period, there were also large numbers of immigrants from China and Japan. During the peak years of immigration bet. 1890 and 1924 over 15 million immigrants arrived here. The immigration law of 1924 heavily restricted immigration until the mid-1960s. Since the 1980s, the largest numbers of immigrants have come from Mexico and E Asia. The govt. of the U.S. is that of a federal republic set up by the Constitution of the U.S., adopted by the Constitutional Convention of 1787. There is a div. of powers bet. the Federal and the state govts. The Federal govt. consists of 3 branches: the executive, the legislative, and the judicial. The executive power is vested in the President and, in the event of his incapacity, the Vice President. The executive conducts the administrative business of the nation with the aid of a cabinet composed of the Attorney General and the Secretaries of the Depts. of State; Treasury; Defense; Interior; Agr.; Commerce; Labor; Health and Human Services; Education; Housing and Urban Development; Transportation; Energy; and Veterans' Affairs. The Congress of the U.S., the legislative branch, is bicameral and consists of the Senate and the House of Representatives. The judicial branch is formed by the Federal courts and headed by the U.S. Supreme Court. The members of the Congress are elected by universal suffrage as are the members of the Electoral Col., which formally chooses the President and the Vice President. There is complete religious freedom in the U.S., and the overwhelming majority of Americans are Christians. In turn, the majority of Christians are Protestants, with varieties of self-identified evangelicals and fundamentalists forming most of this group; the 2d-largest Christian group embraces the R.C. Church; the Orthodox Eastern Church is also represented. In addition, roughly 2.5% of Americans adhere to Judaism and almost 2% are members of the Islamic faith. Education in the U.S. is administered chiefly by the states. Each of the 50 states has a free and public primary and secondary school system. There are also in the U.S. over 3,500 institutions of higher learning, both privately supported and state supported. Numerous and diverse Native Amer. peoples inhabited the entire continent for millennia, having originally crossed the Bering Strait and gradually migrated S and E. Now-vanished cultures of particular interest included the Anasazi (SW) and the Mound Builders (Midwest). Eur. exploration was spurred after Christopher Columbus, sailing for the Span. monarchy, made his voyage to the Caribbean Sea in 1492. John Cabot explored the N. Amer. coast for England in 1498. Various explorers charted the Southeast and Southwest (mainly for Spain) and the Midwest (mostly for France). England, Spain, and France were the chief nations to establish colonies here, although the Neth. (for whom Henry Hudson explored what is now N.Y.) and Sweden (on the lower Delaware R.) also founded settlements during the 17th cent. The 1st permanent Eur. settlement was SAINT AUGUSTINE (Fla.), founded in 1565 by the Spaniard Pedro Menéndez de Avilés. Span. control came to be exercised over Fla., West Florida (now Miss., Ala., S Ga.), Texas, and a large part of the Southwest, including Calif. For the purposes of finding precious metals and of converting heathens to Catholicism, the Span. colonies here were relatively unfruitful and thus were never fully developed. The French established strongholds on the St. Lawrence R. (Quebec and Montreal) and spread their influence over the Great Lakes country and along the Mississippi; the colony of Louisiana was a flourishing Fr. settlement. The Fr. govt., like the Span., tolerated only the R.C. faith, and it implanted the rigid and feudalistic seignorial system of France in its N. Amer. possessions. Partly for these reasons, the Fr. settlements attracted few colonists. The Eng. settlements, which were on the Atlantic seaboard, developed in patterns more suitable to the New World, with greater religious freedom (though not everywhere) and economic opportunity. The 1st permanent Eng. settlement was made at JAMESTOWN (Va.) in 1607. Early Va. settlements were managed by a chartered commercial company, the Va. Company; economic motives were paramount to the company. The Va. colony early passed to control by the crown and became a characteristic type of Eng. colony—the royal colony. The corporate colony—controlled by its own resident corporation—was initiated by the settlement of the Pilgrims at Plymouth Colony in 1620 and by the establishment of the more important Mass. Bay colony by the Puritans in 1630; religion was the main inspiration for the founding of both. The corporate status of the Plymouth Colony, evinced in the Mayflower Compact, was est. 1626 by the purchase of company and charter from the holders in England. Conn. and R.I., offshoots of Mass., received royal charters, granted in the 1660s. A 3d type of colony was the proprietary, founded by lords proprietors under quasi-feudal grants from the king; prime examples are Md. (under the Calvert family) and Pa. (under William Penn). The religious and political turmoil of the Puritan Revolution in England, as well as the repression of the Huguenots in France, helped to stimulate emigration to the Eng. colonies. Hopes of economic betterment brought thousands from England as well as a number from Germany and other continental countries. To obtain passage across the Atlantic, the poor often indentured themselves to masters in the colonies for a specified number of years. The colonial pop. was also swelled by criminals transported from England as a means of punishment. Once established as freedmen, former bondsmen and transportees were frequently allotted land with which to make their way in the New World. Africans were kidnapped and brought here along the brutal Middle Passage, the 1st shipment arriving in Du. New Amsterdam (now N.Y. city) in 1619. The colonies were subject to Eng. mercantilism in the form of Navigation Acts, which benefited them at 1st, establishing a monopoly of the Eng. market for certain colonial prods. Distinct colonial economies emerged, reflecting the regional differences of climate and topography. Agr. was of primary importance in all the regions. In New England many crops were grown, maize being the closest to a staple, and agr. holdings were usually of moderate size. The fur trade's initial importance in the area faded after the NEW ENGLAND CONFEDERATION defeated Philip in King Philip's War and the Native Americans were dispersed. Fishing and commerce gained in importance, and the economic expansion of Mass. encouraged the founding of other New England colonies (N.H., Vt., and what would become Maine). In the middle colonies small farms abounded, interspersed with occasional great estates, and diverse crops were grown, wheat being most important. Land there was almost universally held through some form of feudal grant, as it was also in the South. Commerce grew quickly in the middle colonies, and large towns flourished, notably Philadelphia and N.Y. By the late 17th cent. small farms in the coastal areas of the South were beginning to give way to large plantations; these were developed with the slave labor of Africans, imported in ever-increasing numbers. Plantations were almost exclusively devoted to cultivation of the great Southern staples—tobacco, rice, and, later, indigo. Fur trade and lumbering were long important. Although some towns developed, the Southern economy remained the least diversified and the most rural in colonial Amer. In religion, too, the colonies developed in varied patterns, ranging from complete toleration (R.I., N.J., S.C.), to havens for Catholics (Md.) and Quakers (Pa.) that became increasingly Anglican, to the religious theocracy of a Puritan oligarchy (Mass.). Anglicans were also much in evidence further S, as were Presbyterians, most of them Scotch-Irish. Politically, the colonies developed representative institutions, the most important being the vigorous colonial assemblies. Popular participation was somewhat limited by property qualifications. In the proprietary colonies, particularly, the settlers came into conflict with the executive authority. Important points of difference arose over the granting of large estates to a few, over the great power of the proprietors, over the failure of the proprietors (who generally lived in England) to cope with problems of defense, and over religious grievances, frequently stemming from a struggle for dominance bet. Anglicans and other groups. In corporate Mass. religious grievances were created by the zealous Puritan demands for conformity. These conflicts, together with England's desire to coordinate empire defenses against France and to gain closer control of the colonies' thriving economic life, stimulated England to convert corporate and proprietary colonies into royal ones. In general, royal control brought more orderly govt. and greater religious toleration, but it also focused the colonists' grievances on the mother country. The policies of the governors, who were the chief instruments of Eng. will in the colonies, frequently met serious opposition. The colonial assemblies clashed with the governors esp. over matters of taxation. The assemblies successfully resisted royal demands for permanent income to support royal policies and used their powers over finance to expand their own jurisdiction. As the 18th cent. progressed, colonial grievances were exacerbated. The Br. mercantile regulations, beneficial to agr., impeded the colonies' commercial and industrial development. However, economic and social growth continued, and by the mid-18th cent. there had been created a greater sense of a separate, thriving, and distinctly Amer.—albeit varied—civilization. In New England, Puritan values were modified by the impact of commerce and by the influence of the Enlightenment, while in the South the planter aristocracy developed a lavish and gentlemanly mode of life. Enlightenment ideals also gained influential adherents in the South. Higher education flourished in such institutions as Harvard (Mass.), William and Mary (Va.), and King's Col. (now Columbia Univ., N.Y.). The varied accomplishments of Benjamin Franklin epitomized colonial common sense at its most enlightened and productive level. A religious movement of importance emerged in the revivals of the Great Awakening, stimulated by Jonathan Edwards; the movement ultimately led to a strengthening of Methodism. Also inherent in this movement was egalitarian sentiment, which progressed but was not to triumph in the colonial era. One manifestation of egalitarianism was the long-continued conflict bet. the men of the frontiers and the wealthy Eastern oligarchs who dominated the assemblies, a conflict exemplified in the Regulator Movement. Colonial particularism, still stronger than natl. feeling, caused the failure of the Albany Congress to achieve permanent union. However, internal strife and disunity remained a less urgent issue than the controversy with Great Britain. After the Br. and colonial forces had combined to drive the French from Canada and the Great Lakes region in the Fr. and Indian War (1754–1763), the colonists felt less need of Br. protection; but at this very time the British began colonial reorganization in an effort to impose on the colonists the costs of their own defense. Thus was set off the complex chain of events that united colonial sentiment against Great Britain and culminated in the Amer. Revolution (1775–1783). Significant battles included Lexington, Concord (Mass., the 1st ones), Bennington (Va.), Saratoga (N.Y.), Brandywine (Pa.), Trenton (N.J.), and Yorktown (Va., scene of the Br. surrender). The newly independent Thirteen Colonies were Mass., N.H., Conn., R.I., N.Y., N.J., Pa., Del., Md., Va., N.C., S.C., and Ga.; their territories were recognized as extending N to Canada and W to the Mississippi R. The Revolution also broadened representation in govt., advanced the movement for separation of church and state in Amer., increased opportunities for westward expansion, and brought the abolition of the remnants of feudal land tenure. The view that the Revolution had been fought for local liberty against strong central control reinforced the particularism of the states and was reflected in the weak union established under the Articles of Confederation. Before ratification of the Articles (1781), conflicting claims of states to Western territories had been settled by the cession of Western land rights to the Federal govt.; the Ordinance of 1787 established a form of govt. for territories and a method of admitting them as states to the Union. But the natl. govt. floundered. It could not obtain commercial treaties or enforce its will in internatl. relations, and, largely because it could not raise adequate revenue and had no executive authority, it was weak domestically. Local economic depressions bred discontent that erupted in such episodes as Shays' Rebellion. Advocates of strong central govt. bitterly attacked the Articles; supported particularly by professional and propertied groups, they had a profound influence on the Constitution drawn up by the Constitutional Convention of 1787. The Constitution created a natl. govt. with ample powers for effective rule, which were limited by "checks and balances" to forestall tyranny or radicalism. Its concept of a strong, orderly Union was popularized by the *Federalist Papers* of Alexander Hamilton, James Madison, and John Jay, which played an important part in winning ratification of the Constitution by the separate states. The 1st man to be elected President was the hero of the Revolution, George Washington, who introduced many govt. practices and institutions, including the cabinet. Jay's Treaty (1794) allayed friction with Great Britain. Hamilton, as Washington's Secretary of the Treasury, promulgated a strong state and attempted to advance economic development by a neomercantilist program; this included the establishment of a protective tariff, a mint, and the 1st Bank of the U.S. as well as assumption of state and private Revolutionary debts. The controversy raised by these policies bred divs. along factional and, ultimately, party lines. Hamilton and his followers, who eventually formed the Federalist party, favored wide activity by the Federal govt. under a broad interpretation of the Constitution. Their opponents, who adhered to principles laid down by Thomas Jefferson and who became the Democratic Republican (or Democratic) party, favored narrow construction — limited Federal jurisdiction and activities. To an extent these divs. were supported by economic differences, as the Democrats largely spoke for the agrarian point of view and the Federalists represented propertied and mercantile interests. Men like John Adams had mixed views on the good sense of the masses, and many more conservative thinkers associated the "people" with vulgarity and ineptitude. The Federalists generally represented a pessimistic and the Democrats an optimistic view of man's inherent capacity to govern and develop himself; in practice, however, the values held by these 2 groups were often mixed. The Federalists were victorious in electing John Adams to the presidency in 1796. Federalist conservatism and anti-Fr. sentiment were given vent in the Alien and Sedition Acts of 1798 and in other acts. Deteriorating relations with France were seen in the XYZ Affair and the "half war" (1798–1800), in which U.S. warships engaged Fr. vessels in the Caribbean. The so-called Revolution of 1800 swept the Federalists from power and brought Jefferson to the presidency. Jefferson did bring a plainer and more republican style to govt., and under him the Alien and Sedition Acts and other Federalist laws were allowed to lapse or were repealed. He moved toward stronger use of Federal powers, however, in negotiating the Louisiana Purchase (1803). In foreign policy Jefferson steered an officially neutral course bet. Great Britain and France, resisting the war sentiment roused by Br. impressment of Amer. seamen and by both Br. and Fr. violations of Amer. shipping. He fostered the drastic Embargo Act of 1807 in an attempt to gain recognition of Amer. rights through economic pressure, but the embargo struck hardest against the Amer. economy, esp. in New England. Under Jefferson's successor, Madison, the continued depredations of Amer. shipping, combined with the clamor of Amer. "war hawks" who coveted Canada and Fla., led to the War of 1812, which was, however, opposed in New England. The Treaty of Ghent settled no specific issues of the war, but did confirm the independent standing of the young republic. Politically, the period that followed was the so-called "era of good feeling." The Federalists had disintegrated under the impact of the country's westward expansion and its new interests and ideals. Democrats of all sects. had by now adopted a Federalist approach to natl. development and were temporarily in agreement on a nationalist, expansionist economic policy. This policy was implemented in 1816 by the introduction of internal improvements, a protective tariff, and the 2d Bank of the U.S. The same policies were continued under James Monroe, whose Monroe Doctrine (1823), which proclaimed U.S. opposition to Eur. intervention or colonization in the Amer. hemisphere, introduced the long-continuing U.S. concern for foreign involvement in the Americas. Domestically, the strength of the Federal govt. was increased by the judicial decisions of John Marshall, who had already helped establish the power of the U.S. Supreme Court. By 1820, however, sectional differences were arousing political discord. The sects. of the country had long been developing along independent lines. In the North, merchants, manufacturers, inventors, farmers, and factory hands were busy with commerce, agr. improvements, and the beginnings of the Industrial Revolution. In the South, Eli Whitney's cotton gin had brought in its wake a new staple: cotton was king, and the new states of Ala., La., and Miss. were the center of the cotton kingdom. The accession of Fla. (1819) further swelled the domain of the South. The Amer. West was expanding as the frontier rapidly advanced. Around the turn of the cent. settlement of territory W of the Appalachians had given rise to the new states of Ky., Tenn., and Ohio. Settlers continued to move farther W, and the frontier remained a molding force in Amer. life. The Missouri Compromise (1820) temporarily resolved the issue of slavery in new states, but under the presidency of John Quincy Adams sectional differences were aggravated. Particular friction, leading to the nullification movement, was created by the tariff of 1828, which was highly favorable to Northern mfg. but a "Tariff of Abominations" to the agrarian South. In the 1820s and 1830s the advance of democracy brought manhood suffrage to many states and virtual direct election of the President, and party-nominating conventions replaced the caucus. Separation of church and state became virtually complete. An era of political vigor was begun with the election (1828) of Andrew Jackson to the presidency. If Jackson was not, as sometimes represented, the incarnation of frontier democracy, he nonetheless symbolized the advent of the common man to political power. He provided powerful executive leadership, attuned to popular support, committing himself to a strong foreign policy and to internal improvements for the West. His stand for economic individualism and his attacks on such bastions of the moneyed interests as the Bank of the U.S. won the approval of the growing middle class. Jackson acted firmly for the Union in the nullification controversy. But the South became increasingly dissident, and John C. Calhoun emerged as its chief spokesman with his "states' rights" doctrine. Opponents of Jackson's policies, including both Northern and Southern conservative propertied interests, amalgamated to form the Whig party, in which Henry Clay and Daniel Webster were long the dominant figures. The Panic of 1837 was the 1st of many such periodic economic upheavals. The West was winning greater attention in Amer. life, and in the 1840s expansion to the Pacific was fervently proclaimed as the "manifest destiny" of the U.S. Annexation of the republic of Texas (which had won its own independence from Mexico), long delayed primarily by controversy over its slave-holding status, precipitated the Mex. War; by the Treaty of Guadalupe Hidalgo the U.S. acquired ⅖ of the territory then belonging to Mexico, including Calif. and the present Amer. Southwest. In 1853 these territories were rounded out by the Gadsden Purchase. The dispute with the U.K. over the Oregon Country (the Northwest) was resolved peacefully. "Manifest destiny" was virtually fulfilled. In Calif. the discovery of gold in 1848 brought the rush of forty-niners, swelling the pop. and making statehood for Calif. a pressing question. The westward movement was also stimulated by many other factors. The great profits from open-range cattle ranching brought a stream of ranchers to the area (this influx was to reach fever pitch after the Civil War). The Amer. farmer, with his abundant land, was often profligate in its cultivation, and as the soil depleted he continued to move farther W, settling the virgin or Indian-occupied territory. Soil exhaustion was particularly rapid in the South, where a 1-crop economy prevailed, but because cotton profits were frequently high the plantation system quickly spread as far W as Texas. Occupation of the West was also sped by Eur. immigrants hungry for land, including Mormons seeking a permanent home (they eventually settled Utah). By the mid-19th cent. the territorial gains and westward movement of the U.S. were focusing legislative argument on the extension of slavery to the new territories and breaking down the Missouri Compromise. The Wilmot Proviso illustrated Northern antislavery demands, while Southerners, too, became increasingly intransigent. Only with great effort was the Compromise of 1850 achieved, and it was to be the last such natl. agreement. The new Western states, linked in outlook to the North, had long since caused the South to lose hold of the House of Representatives, and Southern parity in the Senate was threatened by the prospective addition of more free states than slaveholding ones. The South obtained stronger enforcement of Fugitive Slave Laws. The passage of the Kansas-Nebr. Bill (1854), which repealed the Missouri Compromise, led to violence bet. factions in "bleeding Kansas" and spurred the founding of the new Republican Party. It became increasingly difficult to take a middle stand on the slavery issue, and extremists came to the fore on both sides. Southerners, unable to accept the end of slavery, upon which their entire system of life was based, and fearful of slave insurrection (esp. after the revolt led by Nat Turner in 1831), felt threatened by the Abolitionists, who regarded themselves as leaders in a moral crusade. Southerners attempted to uphold slavery as universally beneficial and biblically sanctioned, while Northerners were increasingly unable to countenance the institution. Vigorous antislavery groups like the Free-Soil Party had already arisen, and as the conflict became more embittered it rent the older parties, such as the Whigs, whose Northern wing was largely absorbed in the new antislavery Republican Party. The Democrats were also torn, and the compromise policies of Stephen A. Douglas were of dwindling satisfaction to a divided nation. Moderation could not withstand the impact of the decision in the Dred Scott case, which denied the right of Congress to prohibit slavery in the territories, or the provocation of John Brown's raid on Harpers Ferry, W.Va. (1859). The climax came in 1860 when the Republican Abraham Lincoln defeated 3 opponents to win the presidency. Southern leaders, feeling there was no possibility of fair treatment under a Republican administration, resorted to secession from the Union and formed the Confederate States of Amer. The northernmost slaveholding states (Del., Md., Ky., and Mo.) — known as "Border States" — did not secede but remained deeply divided; part of Va. split off from Confederate Va. in 1861 to form the state of W.Va. The attempts of the seceding states to take over Federal property within their borders (notably Fort Sumter in

Area in square miles is shown by the symbol □ capital city or county seat by ⊙

Charleston, S.C.) precipitated the Civil War (1861–1865). The main theaters of the war were N Va. (scene of the battles of Bull Run, Manassas, Chancellorsville), the Mississippi valley (Vicksburg), and E Tenn. and N Ga. (Shiloh, Chickamauga). Although Southern forces invaded the North on 2 occasions (defeated at Antietam, Md., and then at Gettysburg, Pa.), the bulk of the fighting was confined to the South, which was utterly devastated in 1865, when Confederate Gen. Robert E. Lee surrendered to Ulysses S. Grant at Appomattox, Va. Slavery had already been abolished in the seceding states by Lincoln's Emancipation Proclamation (1863). The ensuing problems of Reconstruction in the South were complicated by bitter struggles, including the impeachment of President Andrew Johnson in 1868. Military rule in parts of the South continued through the administrations of Ulysses S. Grant, which were also notable for their outrageous corruption. The era of Reconstruction ended when the South reentered natl. politics after the disputed election of 1876. Thus ended a period of political gains by Afr.-Americans in the South, who were reduced, as dependent sharecropping farmers and as brutalized freedmen, to disenfranchised 2d-class citizens, a condition formalized by "Jim Crow Laws" by the turn of the cent. and upheld by Supreme Court "separate but equal" decisions. The remainder of the 19th cent. was marked by RR bldg. (assisted by generous Federal land grants), the disappearance of the Amer. frontier, the discovery and exploitation of great mineral wealth, and industrialization based on important technological innovations. Textile mills using water power had been in place in New England since the turn of the cent. but the Civil War saw a tremendous expansion in mfg., with the growth of an economy based on steel, oil, RRs, and machines. By 1900, the U.S. economy ranked foremost in the world. Mammoth corporations such as the Standard Oil trust were formed, and "captains of industry" like John D. Rockefeller and financiers like J. P. Morgan controlled huge resources. The latter part of the 19th cent. also saw the rise of the modern Amer. city. Rapid industrialization attracted huge numbers of people to cities from abroad as well as rural Amer. The widespread use of steel and electricity allowed innovations which transformed the urban landscape. Electricity was also used to power streetcars, elevated RRs, and subways, as well as lighting and such innovations as elevators and telephones. The growth of mass transit allowed people to live further away from work, and was therefore largely responsible for the demise of the "walking city." With the advent of skyscrapers, which utilized steel construction technology, cities were able to grow vertically as well as horizontally. Into the "land of promise" poured new waves of immigrants; some acquired dazzling riches, but many others suffered in a competitive and unregulated economic age. Behind the facade of the "Gilded Age," with its aura of peace and general prosperity, a whole range of new problems was created, demanding new solutions. In the 1870s the expanding Granger Movement attempted to combat RR and marketing abuses and to achieve an element of agrarian cooperation; this movement stimulated some regulation of utilities on the state level. Labor, too, began to challenge grueling factory conditions, but the opposition of business to unions was frequently overpowering, and the bulk of labor remained unorganized. Some strike successes were won by the Knights of Labor, but this union, discredited by the Haymarket Square Riot, was succeeded in prominence by the less divisive Amer. Federation of Labor. Mass. led the way (1874) with the 1st effective state legislation for an 8-hr. day, but similar state and natl. legislation was sparse, and the Federal govt. descended harshly on labor in the bloody strike at Pullman (Ill.) and in other disputes. Belief in laissez faire and the influence of big business in both natl. parties, esp. in the Republican Party, delayed any widespread reform. Civil service reforms, including a civil service act, replaced the vast, troublesome presidential patronage system with a regular, efficient administration. In 1884 a reform group, led by Carl Schurz, bolted from the Republicans and helped elect Grover Cleveland, the 1st Democratic President since before the Civil War. The Sherman Antitrust Act was passed in 1890. The attempt of the Greenback Party to combine sponsorship of free coinage of silver and other aids to the debtor class with planks favorable to labor had failed, but reform forces were gathering strength, as witnessed by the rise of the Populist Party. The reform movement was spurred by the economic panic of 1893, and in 1896 the Democrats nominated for President William Jennings Bryan, who had adopted the Populist platform. He orated eloquently for free silver, but was defeated by William McKinley, who gained ardent support from big business. By the 1890s a new wave of expansionist sentiment was affecting U.S. foreign policy. With the purchase of Alaska (1867) and the rapid settlement of the last Western territory, Oklahoma, Amer. capital and attention were directed toward the Pacific and the Caribbean. The U.S. established commercial and then political hegemony in the Hawaiian Isls. and annexed them in 1898. In that year expansionist energy found release in the Span.-Amer. War, which resulted in U.S. acquisition of P.R., the Philippines Isls., and Guam, and in a U.S. quasi-protectorate over Cuba. Amer. ownership of the Philippines involved military subjugation of the people, who rose in revolt when they realized that they would not be granted their independence; the Philippine Insurrection (1899–1901) cost more Amer. lives and dollars than the Span.-Amer. War. Widening its horizons, the U.S. formulated the Open Door Policy (1900), which expressed its interest in China. Established as a world power with interests in 2 oceans, the U.S. intervened in the Panama revolution to facilitate construction of the Panama Canal; this was but one of its many involvements in Lat. Amer. affairs under Theodore Roosevelt (1901–1909) and later presidents. By now, the progressive reform movement had taken definite shape. Progressivism was partly a mode of thought, as witnessed by the progressive education program of John Dewey; as such it was a pragmatic attempt to mold modern institutions for the benefit of all. Progressives, too, were the muckrakers, who attacked abuse and waste in industry and in society. In its politics as shaped by R. M. la Follette and others, progressivism adopted many Populist planks but promoted them from a more urban and forward-looking viewpoint. Progressivism was dramatized by the magnetic Roosevelt, who denounced "malefactors of great wealth" and demanded a "square deal" for labor; however, in practice he was a rather cautious reformer. He did make some attacks on trusts, and he promoted regulation of interstate commerce as well as passage of the Pure Food and Drug Act (1906) and legislation for the conservation of natural resources. Roosevelt later split with the Republicans in 1912 and ran for the presidency on the Progressive Party ticket, but lost to Democratic reform candidate, Woodrow Wilson. Wilson's "New Freedom" brought many progressive ideas to legislative fruition. The Federal Reserve System and the Federal Trade Commission (FTC) were established, and the Adamson and Clayton Antitrust acts were passed. Perhaps more than on the natl. level, progressivism triumphed in the states in legislation beneficial to labor, in the furthering of education, and in the democratization of electoral procedures. Wilson did not radically alter the aggressive Caribbean policy of his predecessors; U.S. marines were sent to Nicaragua, and difficulties with Mexico were capped by the landing of U.S. forces at Veracruz and by the campaign against Francisco (Pancho) Villa. The nation's interest in world peace had already been expressed through participation in the Hague Conferences, and when World War I burst upon Europe, Wilson made efforts to keep the U.S. neutral; in 1916 he was reelected on a peace platform. However, Amer. sympathies and interests were actively with the Allies (esp. with the U.K. and France), and although Britain and Germany both violated Amer. neutral rights on the seas, Ger. submarine attacks constituted the more dramatic provocation. On April 6, 1917, the U.S. entered the war on the side of the Allies and provided crucial manpower and supplies for the Allied victory. Wilson's Fourteen Points to insure peace and democracy captured the popular imagination of Europe and were a factor in Germany's decision to seek an armistice; however, at the Paris Peace Conference after the war, Wilson was thwarted from fully implementing his program. In the U.S., isolationist sentiment against participation in the League of Nations, an integral part of the Treaty of Versailles, was led by Senator William E. Borah and other "irreconcilables." The majority of Republican senators, led by Henry Cabot Lodge, insisted upon amendments that would preserve U.S. sovereignty, and although Wilson fought for his original proposals, they were rejected. Isolationist sentiment prevailed during the 1920s, and while the U.S. played a major role in the naval conferences for disarmament and in the engineering of the Kellogg-Briand Pact, which outlawed war, its general lack of interest in internatl. concerns was seen in its highly nationalistic economic policies, notably its insistence (later modified) on collecting the war debts of foreign countries and the passage of the Hawley-Smoot Tariff Act. The country voted for a return to "normalcy" when it elected Warren G. Harding president in 1920, but the ensuing period was a time of rapid change, and the old normalcy was not to be regained. The Republican govts. of the decade, although basically committed to laissez faire, actively encouraged corporate mergers and subsidized aviation and the merchant marine. Harding's administration, marred by the Teapot Dome scandal, gave way on his death to the presidency of Calvin Coolidge, and the nation embarked on a spectacular industrial and financial boom. In the 1920s the nation became increasingly urban, and everyday life was transformed as the "consumer revolution" brought the spreading use of automobiles, telephones, radios, and other appliances. The pace of living quickened, and mores became less restrained, while fortunes were rapidly accumulated on the skyrocketing stock market, in real estate speculation, and elsewhere. To some it seemed a golden age. But agr. was not prosperous, and industry and finance became dangerously overextended. In 1929 there began the Great Depression, which reached worldwide proportions. In 1931, President Herbert Hoover proposed a moratorium on foreign debts, but this and other measures failed to prevent economic collapse. In the 1932 election Hoover was overwhelmingly defeated by the Democrat Franklin D. Roosevelt. The new president immediately instituted his New Deal with vigorous measures. To meet the critical financial emergency he instituted a "bank holiday." Congress, called into special session, enacted a succession of laws, some of them to meet the economic crisis with relief measures, others to put into operation long-range social and economic reforms. Some of the most important agencies created were the Natl. Recovery, Agr. Adjustment, and Public Works administrations, the Civilian Conservation Corps, and the TVA. This program was further broadened in later sessions with other agencies, notably the Securities and Exchange Commission (SEC) and the Works Progress (later, Projects) Administration. Laws also created a social security program. The program was dynamic and, in many areas, unprecedented. It created a vast machinery by which the state could promote economic recovery and social welfare. Opponents of these measures argued that they violated individual rights, besides being extravagant and wasteful. Adverse decisions on several of the measures by the U.S. Supreme Court tended to slow the pace of reform and caused Roosevelt to attempt unsuccessfully to revise the court. Although interest centered chiefly on domestic affairs during the 1930s, Roosevelt continued and expanded the policy of friendship toward the Lat. Amer. nations which Hoover had initiated; this full-blown "good-neighbor" policy proved generally fruitful for the U.S. Roosevelt was reelected by an overwhelming majority in 1936 and won easily in 1940, being the 1st president to be elected to a 3d term. The ominous situation abroad was chiefly responsible for Roosevelt's remaining at the natl. helm.

Cross references are shown in SMALL CAPITALS. The pronunciation key is on page xv. The dates of population figures are on page xii.

By the late 1930s the Axis nations (Germany and Italy) in Europe as well as Japan in East Asia had already disrupted world peace. As wars began in China, Ethiopia, and Spain, the U.S. sought at 1st to bulwark its insular security by the Neutrality Act. As Axis aggression led to the outbreak of the Eur. war in Sept. 1939, the U.S. persisted in its neutrality, despite increasing sympathy for the Allies. But after the fall of France in June 1940, the support for beleaguered Britain became more overt. In March 1941, Lend-Lease aid was extended to the British and, in Nov., to the Russians. The threat of war had already caused the adoption of Selective Service to build the armed strength of the nation. Hemisphere defense was enlarged, and the U.S. drew closer to the U.K. with the issuance of the Atlantic Charter. In Asian affairs the Roosevelt govt. had vigorously protested Japan's career of conquest and its establishment of the "Greater East Asia Co-Prosperity Sphere." After the Jap. takeover of Fr. Indochina (July 1941), with its inherent threat to the Philippines, the U.S. govt. froze all Jap. assets here. Diplomatic relations grew taut, but U.S.-Jap. discussions were still underway when, on Dec. 7, 1941, Jap. bombs fell on Pearl Harbor (Hawaii). The U.S. promptly declared war, and 4 days later Germany and Italy declared war on the U.S. The Philippines were lost to Japan, which also occupied 3 Aleutian isls. The country mobilized its resources, transforming factories to war plants and sending troops to Europe, Afr., and the Pacific. War-related activities revitalized the natl. economy, helping it rebound from the Great Depression. Many govt. agencies were created to control and coordinate materials, transportation, and manpower. Since many Jap. immigrants lived in the W U.S., fears that they would act as spies for Tokyo led to their imprisonment in internment camps, mostly in the West. Because no battles took place on Amer. soil, the U.S. was the only major power to emerge from the war with its infrastructure intact. The war provided the opportunity for the U.S. to demonstrate the strength of its resources and its prestige and power in world affairs. Roosevelt (and, later, Truman), Winston Churchill, and Joseph Stalin met at several conferences to plan strategy and the postwar settlement. Roosevelt was also a key figure in the plans for the UN. After his sudden death in April 1945, Harry S. Truman became president. A month later the Eur. war ended when Germany surrendered on May 7, 1945; war continued with Japan, against whom the U.S. used a fateful and revolutionary weapon, the atomic bomb. The Jap. surrender, announced Aug. 14, 1945, and signed Sept. 2, brought the war to a close. Peacetime readjustment was successfully effected and included such programs as the "G.I. Bill." The economy boomed in fulfilling the demands for long-unobtainable consumer goods. The shortening of the postwar factory work week and the proportionate reduction of wages precipitated strikes, causing the govt. to pass the Taft-Hartley Labor Act (1947). Some inflation occurred by 1947 as wartime economic controls were abandoned. Congress passed a host of Truman's measures relating to min. wages, public housing, farm surpluses, and credit regulation; thus was instituted acceptance of comprehensive govt. intervention in times of prosperity. The most striking postwar development was America's new peacetime involvement in internatl. affairs. Relations with the Soviet Union worsened during the late 1940s. The Truman Doctrine attempted to thwart Soviet expansion in Europe; massive loans, culminating in the Marshall Plan, were vital in reviving Eur. economies. As the Cold War intensified, the U.S. took steps (1948) to nullify the Soviet blockade of Berlin and played the leading role in forming a new alliance of Western nations, the NATO. Entering the Korean War, the U.S. cast off its traditional peacetime isolationism and accepted its position as a prime mover in world affairs. Internatl. policy had significant repercussions at home, where the fear of domestic Communism and subversion became a natl. obsession, culminating in such sensational events as the Alger Hiss case, the McCarthy hearings, and the trial and execution of Julius and Ethel Rosenberg. Security measures and loyalty checks in the govt. and elsewhere were tightened and alleged Communists were prosecuted under the Smith Act of 1940. In 1952, Dwight D. Eisenhower was swept into office. By the mid-1950s, Amer. was in the midst of a great industrial boom, and stock prices were skyrocketing. In foreign affairs the Eisenhower administration was internationalist in outlook, although it sternly opposed Communist power. Some antagonism came from the neutral nations of Asia and Afr., partly because of the U.S. association with former colonial powers and partly because U.S. foreign aid more often than not had the effect of strengthening ruling oligarchies abroad. In the race for technological superiority the U.S. exploded (1952) the 1st hydrogen bomb, but was 2d to the USSR in launching (Jan. 31, 1958) an artificial satellite and in testing an intercontinental guided missile. However, spurred by Soviet advances, the U.S. made rapid progress in space exploration and missile research. In the crucial domestic issue of racial integration, the U.S. Supreme Court in a series of decisions supported the efforts of Afr.-Amer. citizens to achieve full civil rights. In 1959, Alaska and Hawaii became the 49th and 50th states of the Union. Despite hopes for "peaceful coexistence," negotiations with the USSR for nuclear disarmament failed to achieve accord and tensions grew (e.g., Berlin). In 1961, the older Eisenhower gave way to the youngest President ever elected, John F. Kennedy, who defeated the Republican candidate, Richard M. Nixon. President Kennedy called for "new frontiers" of Amer. endeavor. Kennedy's foreign policy combined such humanitarian innovations as the Peace Corps and the Alliance for Progress with the traditional opposition to Communist aggrandizement. After breaking relations with Fidel Castro's Cuba, the U.S. supported (1961) an ill-fated anti-Castro invasion of Cuba. In 1962, in reaction to the presence of Soviet missiles in Cuba, the U.S. blockaded Soviet military shipments to Cuba and demanded the dismantling of Soviet bases there. The 2 great powers seemed on the brink of war, but within a week the USSR acceded to U.S. demands. In the meantime the U.S. achieved an important gain in space exploration with the orbital flight around the earth in a manned satellite by Col. John H. Glenn. The tensions of the cold war eased when, in 1963, the U.S. and the Soviet Union reached an accord on a limited ban of nuclear testing. On Nov. 22, 1963, President Kennedy was assassinated; he was succeeded by Lyndon B. Johnson, who was able to bring many Kennedy measures to legislative fruition. Significant progress toward racial equality was achieved with a momentous Civil Rights Act (1964), a Voting Rights Act (1965), and the 24th Amendment to the Constitution, which abolished the poll tax. Other legislation, reflecting Johnson's declaration of a "war on poverty" and his stated aim of creating a "Great Society," included a comprehensive Economic Opportunity Act (1964) and bills providing for tax reduction, medical care for the aged, an increased min. wage, urban rehabilitation, and aid to education. Ironically, internatl. problems dominated Johnson's 2d term, and Johnson himself pursued an aggressive course, dispatching (April 1965) troops to the Dominican Republic during disorders there and escalating Amer. participation in the Vietnam War. Authorization for the latter was claimed by Johnson to have been given (Aug. 1964) by Congress in the Tonkin Gulf Resolution. The Federal military budget soared, and inflation became a pressing problem. The Vietnam War provoked increasing opposition at home, manifested in marches and demonstrations in which casualties were sometimes incurred and thousands of people were arrested. An impression of general lawlessness and domestic disintegration was heightened by serious race riots that erupted in cities across the nation, most devastatingly in the Watts dist. of Los Angeles (1965) and in Detroit and Newark (1967), and by various racial and political assassinations, notably those of Martin Luther King, Jr., Senator Robert F. Kennedy (1968), and Malcolm X. Other manifestations of social upheaval were the increase of drug use, esp. among the young, and the rising rate of crime, most noticeable in the cities. Opposition to Amer. involvement in the Vietnam War so eroded Johnson's popularity that he chose not to run again for President in 1968. Violence broke out during the Democratic natl. convention in Chicago when police and natl. guardsmen battled some 3,000 demonstrators in what a natl. investigating committee later characterized as "a police riot." Nixon, the Republican candidate, ran on a platform promising an end to the Vietnam War and stressing the need for domestic "law and order"; he won a narrow victory. Gov. George C. Wallace of Ala. carried 5 Southern states. The Congress remained Democratic. Pronouncing the "Nixon doctrine"—that thenceforth other countries would have to carry more of the burden of fighting Communist domination, albeit with substantial Amer. economic aid—Nixon began a slow withdrawal of Amer. troops from Vietnam. When Nixon in the spring of 1970 ordered U.S. troops into neutral Cambodia to destroy Communist bases and supply routes there, a wave of demonstrations, some of them violent, swept Amer. campuses. Students were killed by natl. guardsmen at Kent State Univ. (Ohio) and at Jackson State Col. (Miss.), and 448 cols. and univs. temporarily closed down. Antiwar activity declined, however, when Amer. troops were removed from Cambodia after 60 days. The institution of draft reform, the continued withdrawal of U.S. soldiers from Vietnam, and a sharp decrease in U.S. casualties all contributed toward dampening antiwar sentiment and lessening the war as an issue of public debate. Open racial flare-ups abated after the tumult of the 1960s (although the issue of the busing of children to achieve integration continued to arouse controversy). The growing movement of women demanding social, economic, and political equality with men also reflected the changing times. A dramatic milestone in the country's space program was reached in July 1969, with the landing of 2 men on the moon, the 1st of several such manned flights. Significant unmanned probes of several of the planets followed, and in 1973 the 1st space station was orbited. In domestic policy Nixon appeared to favor an end to the many reforms of the 1960s. He was accused by civil rights proponents of wooing Southern support by seeking delays in the implementation of school integration. Such actions by his administration were overruled by the Supreme Court. Nixon twice attempted to appoint conservative Southern judges to the U.S. Supreme Court and was twice frustrated by the Senate, which rejected both nominations. In an attempt to control the spiraling inflation inherited from the previous administration, Nixon concentrated on reducing Federal spending. Federal budget cuts contributed to a general economic slowdown but failed to halt inflation, so that the country experienced the unprecedented misfortune of both rising prices and rising unemployment; the steady drain of gold reserves after almost 3 decades of enormous foreign aid programs, a new balance-of-trade deficit, and the instability of the dollar in the internatl. market also affected the economy. In Aug. 1971, Nixon resorted to the freezing of prices, wages, and rents; these controls were continued under an ensuing, more flexible but comprehensive program known as Phase II. Another significant move was the devaluation of the dollar in Dec. 1971; it was further devalued in 1973 and again in 1974. In keeping with his announced intention of moving the U.S. from an era of confrontation to one of negotiation, Nixon made a dramatic visit to the People's Republic of China in Feb. 1972, opening the way for a normalization of relations. A trip to Moscow followed in the spring, culminating in the signing of numerous agreements with the Soviet Union, the most important being 2 strategic arms limitations accords (SALT). Meanwhile, although U.S. ground troops were being steadily withdrawn from Vietnam, U.S. bombing activity was increasing. Finally Congress halted the bombing and limited Nixon's power to commit troops. A cease-fire in Vietnam was not achieved until Jan. 1973. Nixon was reelected (Nov.

Area in square miles is shown by the symbol ☐   capital city or county seat by ⊙

1972) in a landslide, losing only Mass. and D.C. But his 2d term was marred, and finally destroyed, by the Watergate affair. Nixon resigned on Aug. 9, the 1st president in the history of the republic to be driven from office under the threat of impeachment. His successor, Vice President Gerald R. Ford promised to continue Nixon's foreign policy, particularly the improvement of relations with China and the USSR. In domestic affairs, the U.S. was hurt by skyrocketing fuel prices due to an Arab oil embargo. Ford attempted to formulate new policies to stem the ever-increasing inflation rate, which by late 1974 had reached the most severe levels since the period following World War II. He was also confronted with mounting unemployment and with the threat of a devastating world food crisis. The Democratic contender in the 1976 presidential election, former Ga. governor James E. "Jimmy" Carter, ran a brilliant and tireless campaign based on populist appeals to honesty and morality. In domestic affairs, Carter focused a great deal of attention on energy issues, creating the Dept. of Energy in 1977 and insisting on the necessity of nuclear energy as an alternative to fossil fuel consumption. However, nuclear energy in the U.S. suffered a severe setback in 1979 when an accident at the Three Mile Isl. power facility near Harrisburg (Pa.) resulted in the partial meltdown of the reactor core. States with large energy industries such as Texas, La., Wyo., and Colo. all benefited from extremely high energy prices throughout the 1970s. Alaska's economy also boomed as the Alaska pipeline began transporting oil in 1977. Soaring oil prices as well as increased foreign competition dealt a severe blow to Amer. industry, esp. heavy industries such as automobile and steel mfg. located in America's Rustbelt. Central cities in the U.S. experienced great hardship in the 1960s and 1970s. Rising crime rates and racial unrest during the 1960s accelerated the outmigration of people and businesses to the suburbs. By the late 1970s, many large cities had lost their middle class core pops. and suffered severe budgetary problems. Inflation continued to rise dramatically as it had during Ford's administration and eventually reached a 30-year high in 1979. Efforts to control inflation such as raising interest rates plunged the economy into recession. In 1977 Carter signed the Panama Canal Treaty and a year later Congress voted to turn over the canal to Panama in 1999. Carter's greatest achievement in foreign policy came in 1978 when he mediated unprecedented negotiations bet. Egypt and Israel at Camp David (Md.); the 2 countries later signed a peace treaty. Also in that year the U.S. resumed official diplomatic relations with China and Carter entered into a 2d round of SALT talks with the USSR. Carter's pledge to stand against nations that abused human rights resulted in a grain and high-technology embargo of the Soviet Union in response to the Soviet invasion of Afghanistan. Carter also organized a boycott of the 1980 Moscow Olympics. His decision in 1979 to allow Muhammad Reza Shah Pahlevi, the deposed leader of Iran, to receive medical treatment in the U.S. inflamed the already passionate anti-Amer. sentiment in that nation. On Nov. 4, 1979, a group of militants seized the U.S. embassy in Iran, taking 66 hostages., destroying Carter's credibility as a leader. With the hostage crisis omnipresent in the media and the nation's economy sliding deeper into recession, Carter lost the 1980 election to Ronald Reagan, the oldest man elected president (at 70). On Jan. 20, 1981, the day of Reagan's inauguration, Iran released all of the Amer. hostages. Reagan's coattails proved to be long as the Republicans made large gains in the House of Representatives and won control of the Senate for the 1st time since 1954, ushering in a new wave of conservatism. His program of "supply-side economics" sought to increase economic growth through reduced taxes which would in turn create even greater tax revenue. Critics argued that his tax cuts only benefited corporations and wealthy individuals. Reagan drastically cut spending on social programs as part of his vow to balance the federal budget. In labor disputes, he was decidedly anti-union, firing 13,000 striking air traffic controllers. The U.S. economy continued to worsen; in 1983 the unemployment rate reached its highest point since the Great Depression at almost 11%. By the end of that year, however, oil prices began to drop which slowed the inflation rate and the economy began to recover. Reagan's deregulaton of the banking, airline, and many other industries spurred enormous amounts of economic activity. In 1984 the unemployment rate fell and the dollar was strong in foreign markets. With the economy recovering, Reagan was favored in the 1984 presidential election. Democratic nominee Walter F. Mondale chose U. S. Representative Geraldine Ferraro as his running mate; she was the 1st woman to gain a major party's vice presidential nomination. Reagan scored an overwhelming victory, carrying 49 states and winning a record 525 electoral votes. Economic recovery did not last, however; while Reagan was cutting govt. funding for social programs the defense budget skyrocketed to levels not seen since World War II. The Federal budget deficit also soared and in 1987, Reagan submitted the 1st trillion-dollar budget to Congress. In addition, the deregulated economy proved extremely volatile; financial scandals were prevalent and the trade imbalance grew. Finally in 1987 the stock market crashed, falling a record 508 points in 1 day. Reagan's foreign policy was aggressively anti-Communist as he discarded the policy of détente employed by his predecessors. He revived Cold War rhetoric, referring to the Soviet Union as the "evil empire" and used increased defense spending to enlarge the U.S. nuclear arsenal and fund the Strategic Defense Initiative. In 1981, Reagan imposed sanctions against Poland after the establishment of a military govt. there. He also sought aid for the Contras—counterrevolutionaries seeking to overthrow the Marxist govt. in Nicaragua. At the same time the U.S. was secretly mining Nicaraguan harbors. In 1983 Reagan ordered the invasion of the tiny Caribbean nation of Grenada; the action was roundly criticized by the world community but succeeded in toppling the pro-Cuban regime. In 1986 the space shuttle *Challenger* exploded shortly after liftoff, killing the entire 7-person crew. Reagan's aggressive policies in the Middle East worsened already bad relations with Arab nations; he ordered (1986) air strikes against Libya in retaliation for Libyan-sponsored terrorist attacks. Although he had vowed never to negotiate with terrorists, members of the Reagan administration did just that in the Iran-Contra affair. Against the wishes of the Secretary of State and the Secretary of Defense, Reagan officials arranged the illegal sale of arms to Iran in exchange for the release of Amer. hostages in the Middle East. The profits from the sales were then diverted to the Contra rebels in Nicaragua. Reagan improved his image before he left office, however, by agreeing to a series of arms reduction talks initiated by Soviet president Mikhail Gorbachev. Reagan was also able leave a powerful legacy by appointing 3 conservative Supreme Court justices, including Sandra Day O'Connor, the 1st woman to serve on the high court. George Bush succeeded him, who vowed a continuation of Reagan's policies and in foreign affairs was equally aggressive. In 1989, after a U.S.-backed coup failed to oust Panamanian President Manuel Noriega, Bush ordered the invasion of Panama by U.S. troops. Bush's major military action, however, was the Pers. Gulf War, launched to drive Iraqi troops from Kuwait. Challenged by the savings and loan industry, which had collapsed after deregulation during the Reagan administration, Bush lost popularity. The U.S. went through a transitional period during the 1980s and early 1990s, when the severe decline of traditional mfg. (begun in the 1970s) forced a large-scale shift of the economy to services and other sectors. States with large service, trade, and high-technology industries (such as many Sunbelt states) grew in pop. and thrived economically. Meanwhile, states heavily dependent on mfg., including much of the Midwest, suffered severe unemployment and outmigration. Midwestern states grew less than 5% during the 1980s while Sunbelt states grew bet. 15% and 50%. In addition, the end of the Cold War, precipitated by the dissolution of the Warsaw Pact and the collapse of Soviet Communism, resulted in a reduction of the U.S. armed forces as well as the opening of new markets in an increasingly global economy. In April 1992, one of the worst race riots in U.S. history erupted in Los Angeles, killing 58, injuring thousands, and causing more than $1 billion in damage. NAFTA (1992) was designed to make the U.S., Mexico, and Canada more competitive in the world marketplace, though there are fears that the agreement will result in even greater exportation of U.S. jobs to Mexico where labor is less expensive. After the Pers. Gulf War the nation turned its attention to the domestic problems of recession and high unemployment. Bush's inability to institute a program for economic recovery made him vulnerable in the 1992 presidential election to the Democratic nominee, Ark. governor Bill Clinton. Clinton, a political moderate, was particularly successful in appealing to voters (esp. in the Midwest and West) who had previously abandoned the Democratic Party to vote for Reagan. Clinton was reelected in 1996, defeating former Senate majority leader Bob Dole. In Jan. 1998, reports surfaced of an affair bet. Clinton and a White House intern, leading to a year-long investigation of the president's conduct, and culminating in his impeachment on Dec. 19, 1998 by the House of Representatives on charges of perjury and obstruction of justice. After a trial in the Senate, Clinton was acquitted of the charges in Feb. 1999.

United States Naval Observatory, a Federal astronomical observatory, Wash., D. C. It evolved from the Navy's oldest scientific institution, the Depot of Charts and Instruments, founded in 1830; the observatory was completed in 1844 and moved to its present site in 1893. It was formerly administered through the Bureau of Navigation and is now under the jurisdiction of the chief of naval operations. The principal instrument at the Washington hq. is an Alvan Clark 26-in/66-cm refracting telescope, which has been in almost continuous operation since its installation in 1873, when it was the largest of its kind in the world. The original mounting and drive were replaced during the 1893 move. Other equip. includes a number of ordinary refracting and reflecting telescopes and special telescopes (photographic zenith tubes) used in the precise determination of time. The observatory's Flagstaff Station in Ariz. has 61-in/155-cm and 40-in/102-cm reflecting telescopes; in 1978, J. Christy discovered Pluto's moon Charon with the former. The main programs of the Naval Observatory involve continual observations of the positions and motions of celestial bodies for astronomical and navigational purposes and for the derivation and broadcasting of accurate time signals. Atomic, cesium, and mercury ion clocks, and hydrogen maser frequency standards, are all used for the observatory's time system, which is accurate to within a few billionths of a second per day. Since 1894 the U. S. Naval Observatory has included the Nautical Almanac Office, which publishes the *Amer. Ephemeris and Nautical Almanac*. The observatory also has an extensive lib.

United States Range, N Ellesmere Isl., NE Franklin dist., N.W.T., N Canada; extends c.250 mi/400 km WSW-ENE across N part of isl. (the region called Grant Land), from Nansen Sound to the Lincoln Sea of the Arctic Ocean, in lat. 82°00′N. Rises to over 11,000 ft/3,350 m.

Unity, town (1991 pop. 2,227), W Sask., W Canada, 45 mi/72 km SW of North Battleford; 52°26′N 109°10′W. Natural-gas and salt production; dairying, flour milling; grain; livestock.

Unity 1 resort town (1990 pop. 1,817), Waldo co., S Maine, on Unity Pond, and 18 mi/29 km NW of Belfast; 44°35′N 69°19′W. Seat of Unity Col. **2** town (1990 pop. 1,341), Sullivan co., SW N.H., 7 mi/11.3 km SE of Claremont; 43°17′N 72°16′W. Drained by Little Sugar R. Nursery crops, corn, apples; cattle, poultry; timber.

Unity 1 village (1990 pop. 87), Baker co., NE Oregon, 27 mi/43 km SW of Baker City, on small branch of Burnt R.; 44°26′N 118°11′W. Livestock; grain; timber.

Unity Reservoir and Unity L. State Park to N; Wallowa-Whitman Natl. Forest to N, W, and S, including Monument Rock Wilderness Area to S. **2** village (1990 pop. 452), on border bet. Clark and Marathon cos., central Wis., 14 mi/23 km NNW of Marshfield; 44°51′N 90°18′W. In dairying and farming area.

Unity Pond, Waldo co., S Maine, near Unity, 20 mi/32 km NW of Belfast; 4 mi/6.4 km long, 1.5 mi/2.4 km wide. Noted for fishing.

Universal, town (1990 pop. 392), Vermillion co., W Ind., 12 mi/19 km NNW of Terre Haute; 39°37′N 87°27′W. In agr. and bituminous-coal area (surface mines). Laid out 1911.

University City 1 city (1990 pop. 40,087), St. Louis co., E Mo.; 38°40′N 90°19′W. Mainly residential suburb 7 mi/11.3 km W of downtown St. Louis. Mfg. (textiles, metal fabrication and fabricated metal parts). Washington Univ. bet. University City and Clayton. Inc. 1906. **2** city (1990 pop. 13,057), Bexar co., S central Texas, suburb 15 mi/24 km NE of downtown San Antonio, on Cibolo Creek; 29°33′N 98°18′W. Agr. area; light mfg. Randolph Air Force Base to S.

Universal City, uninc. suburb surrounded by Los Angeles, Los Angeles co., S Calif., in Hollywood area, just SW of Burbank. Universal motion picture studios here; petroleum refining. Burbank to NE, Hollywood to S.

University Heights, city (1990 pop. 14,790), Cuyahoga co., NE Ohio; 41°29′N 81°32′W. A residential suburb E of Cleveland. Seat of John Carroll Univ. Inc. 1925.

University Heights 1 town (1990 pop. 1,042), Johnson co., E Iowa, residential suburb 1 mi/1.6 km W of downtown Iowa City (surrounded by Iowa City); 41°38′N 91°33′W. **2** uninc. town, Albemarle co., N central Va., residential suburb 5 mi/8 km W of Charlottesville; 38°02′N 78°31′W. Inst. of Textile Technology.

University Heights, a residential section of W Bronx borough of N.Y. city, SE N.Y., opposite N Manhattan; 40°52′N 73°55′W. Edgar Allen Poe resided in a cottage here. Pop. predominantly Hispanic (esp. Dominican) and Afr.-Amer, with some Vietnamese and Cambodians. Called University Heights when N.Y. Univ. moved most of its operations here from Lower Manhattan in 1894, but N.Y. Univ. sold campus in 1974 to the City Univ. of N.Y. for Bronx Community Col. Hall of Fame for Great Americans, est. 1901 to honor contributors to Amer. society, occupies a curving 650-ft/198-m colonnade around the campus' Grand Memorial Lib. Added to Natl. Register of Historic Places in 1966; renovated in 1985 at a cost of $3 million.

University Park 1 city (1990 pop. 6,204), Will co., NE Ill., suburb 30 mi/48 km SSW of downtown Chicago; 41°26′N 87°42′W. Mfg. (electronic equip., plastic prods., food prods., machinery, paper prods.). Seat of Governors State Univ. **2** city (1990 pop. 22,259), Dallas co., N Texas, a residential suburb, 5 mi/8 km N of downtown Dallas; 32°51′N 96°47′W. It and neighboring Highland Park (S) surrounded by Dallas. Seat of Southern Methodist Univ. Dallas Love Field Airport to W. Inc. 1924.

University Park 1 town (1990 pop. 604), Mahaska co., S central Iowa, adjacent to Oskaloosa; 41°17′N 92°37′W. Seat of Kletzing Col. **2** town (1990 pop. 2,243), Prince Georges co., central Md., NE of Washington, D.C.; 38°58′N 76°56′W. This suburban community, adjoining the S side of College Park, was inc. 1936, 9 years prior to College Park. **3** uninc. town (1990 pop. 4,520), Dona Ana co., S N.Mex., residential suburb 2 mi/3.2 km SSE of downtown Las Cruces, near Rio Grande; 32°16′N 106°45′W. Tortugas Mt. (4,914 ft/1,498 m) to E. Campus of N.Mex. State Univ. is here.

Unwin, Mount (10,723 ft/3,268 m), W Alta., W Canada, near B.C. border, in Rocky Mts., in Jasper Natl. Park, 30 mi/48 km SE of Jasper, overlooking Maligne L.

Upham (UHP-uhm), village (1990 pop. 205), McHenry co., N N.Dak., 22 mi/35 km NW of Towner, near Souris R. (Mouse R.); 48°34′N 100°43′W. J. Clark Salyer Natl. Wildlife refuge to N.

Upland, city (1990 pop. 63,374), San Bernardino co., S Calif., suburb 35 mi/56 km E of downtown Los Angeles, and 3 mi/4.8 km N of Ontario, at the foot of the San Gabriel Mts.; 34°07′N 117°40′W. Mfg. (foods, electronic and electric prods., bldg. materials, textiles, fabricated metal prods., tool and die, machinery, consumer goods). Upland has gradually become more urbanized, and its pop. has grown rapidly since the 1970s. Cable Airport in W. San Gabriel Mts. and San Bernardino Natl. Forest to N; Angeles Natl. Forest to NW; Mt. Baldy Ski Area to N. Inc. 1906.

Upland, town (1990 pop. 3,295), Grant co., E central Ind., 11 mi/18 km SE of Marion; 40°28′N 85°31′W. Agr. area; mfg. (machinery). Seat of Taylor Univ. and Miller Purdue Experimental Farm. Laid out 1867.

Upland, village (1990 pop. 169), Franklin co., S Nebr., 26 mi/42 km SSE of Kearney; 40°19′N 98°54′W.

Upland, borough (1990 pop. 3,334), Delaware co., SE Pa., residential suburb 13 mi/21 km SW of downtown Philadelphia, and 1 mi/1.6 km NW of Chester, on Chester Creek; 39°51′N 75°22′W. Mfg. (consumer goods; machining). Inc. 1869.

Uplands Park, town (1990 pop. 499), St. Louis co., E Mo., residential suburb 7 mi/11.3 km NW of downtown St. Louis; 38°41′N 90°16′W.

Upolu Point (oo-PO-loo), Hawaii isl., Hawaii co., Hawaii, N extremity of isl., on Kohala Peninsula, 62 mi/100 km NW of Hilo, on Alenuihaha Channel of Pacific Ocean; 20°16′N 155°51′W.

Upper Ammonoosuc River (a-muh-NOO-suhk), c.15 mi/24 km long, N N.H.; rises 9 mi/14.5 km SW of Berlin, in S central Coos co.; flows N then W past Groveton to Connecticut R. at Northumberland.

Upper Arlington, city (1990 pop. 34,128), Franklin co., central Ohio; 40°01′N 83°04′W. Residential suburb of Columbus. Inc. 1918.

Upper Baker Dam, Wash.: see BAKER LAKE.

Upper Bay, N.Y. and N.J.: see NEW YORK BAY.

Upper Bear Creek Reservoir (□ 2 sq mi/5.2 sq km), NW Ala., on Bear Creek, 13 mi/21 km SE of Russellville; 34°16′N 87°42′W. Max. capacity 35,500 acre-ft. U-shaped; both arms extend NE. Formed by Upper Bear Creek Dam (85 ft/26 m high), built (1978) by TVA for flood control, recreation, and water storage.

Upper Bingham, Utah: see BINGHAM CANYON.

Upper Brookville, residential village (□ 4 sq mi/10.4 sq km; 1990 pop. 1,453), Nassau co., SE N.Y., on NW L.I., 3 mi/4.8 km ESE of Glen Cove; 40°50′N 73°33′W.

Upper Canada: see ONTARIO.

Upper Chateaugay Lake (sha-to-GAI), reservoir, Clinton and Franklin cos., NE N.Y., on Chateaugay R., in Adirondack Mts. and Adirondack Park, 25 mi/40 km W of Plattsburg. Consists of Upper Chateaugay L. (4 mi/6.4 km long, 2 mi/3.2 km wide; 44°45′N 73°58′W) and, 5 mi/8 km downstream, Lower Chateaugay L. (3 mi/4.8 km long; 44°49′N 74°02′W).

Upper Cormorant Lake, Minn.: see CORMORANT LAKE.

Upper Crystal Spring, reservoir, San Mateo co., central Calif., along San Andreas Rift Zone, in San Francisco State Fish Hatchery, 6 mi/9.7 km W of Redwood City; 37°29′N 122°19′W. Terminus of Hetch Hetchy Aqueduct (providing water supply to San Francisco); Pulgas Water Temple located at SE end.

Upper Darby, township (1990 pop. 81,177), Delaware co., SE Pa., residential suburb 6 mi/9.7 km SW of downtown Philadelphia and immediately W of the city (across Cobbs Creek); 39°55′N 75°16′W. In 2 sects., separated by Lansdowne borough. Includes villages of Upper Darby, Highland Park, Bywood, and part of Drexel Hill (partly in Haverford township). Mainly residential, with some mfg. Inc. 1907.

Upper Deerfield, township (1990 pop. 6,927), Cumberland co., S N.J., 6 mi/9.7 km N of Bridgeton; 39°29′N 75°13′W. Inc. 1922.

Upper Delaware National Wild and Scenic River and Riverway, NE Pa., SE N.Y. (□ 117 sq mi/303 sq km). Equally divided bet. the 2 states. Fishing and Boating. Comprises 73 mi/117 km of the Upper Delaware R. The Upper Delaware was an important transportation route for both Native Americans and Eur. settlers. Authorized 1978.

Upper Des Lacs Lake, reservoir (□ 7 sq mi/18.1 sq km), Mountrail and Burke cos., N central N.Dak., on Des Lacs R., in Des Lacs Natl. Wildlife Refuge, 55 mi/88 km NW of Minot; 48°42′N 102°06′W. Max. capacity 64,000 acre-ft. Extends N to Can. (Sask.) border. Formed by Dam #2 (12 ft/4 m high), built (1935) as a fish and wildlife pond.

Upper East Side, section of borough of Manhattan, N.Y. city, SE N.Y., on NE side of Manhattan, bet. 5th Ave. and Central Park (W), East R. (E), East 59th St.–Queensboro Bridge (S), and East Harlem and East 96th St. (N); 40°47′N 73°56′W. The Mt. Sinai Hospital complex on the N is also part of the dist. This is the sect. of town (esp. along 5th, Madison, and Park aves.) that perhaps most characterizes the posh lifestyle and wealth of N.Y. city to outsiders. Assortment of high-rise apartment bldgs., clubs and other businesses, consulates, private schools, and corporate hq. This stretch of 5th Ave. is known as "Mus. Mile," with such institutions as the Metropolitan Mus. of Art, the Solomon R. Guggenheim Mus., the Cooper-Hewitt Mus., the Jewish Mus., the Goethe Inst., the Inst. for Contemporary Photography, the Mus. of the City of N.Y., Museo del Barrio, and the Whitney Mus. Marymount and Hunter cols. are here, as is an enormous medical complex which includes Cornell Medical Center. Home to Gracie Mansion, the mayor's official residence. The Yorkville neighborhood (around 86th St.) was once one of the city's main concentrations of Ger. immigrants.

Upper Fairmount, village (1990 pop. 500), Somerset co., SE Md., near Big Annemessex R., 21 mi/34 km SSW of Salisbury.

Upper Gull Lake, Minn.: see GULL LAKE.

Upper Holter Lake, Mont.: see HOLTER LAKE.

Upper Iowa River, 160 mi/257 km long, Minn. and Iowa; rises in Mower co., SE Minn., 16 mi/26 km ESE of Austin; flows ESE past LeRoy (Minn.), into NE Iowa, at Chester (43°37′N 93°37′W), then generally E, past Decorah, to Mississippi R. 5 mi/8 km N of Lansing.

Upper Jay, resort village (1990 pop. 500), Essex co., NE N.Y., in the Adirondack Mts., 12 mi/19 km ENE of Lake Placid; 44°20′N 73°48′W.

Upper Klamath Lake (KLAM-uhth), natural large freshwater lake, Klamath co., S Oregon, extends N from city of Klamath Falls; 20 mi/32 km long, 8 mi/12.9 km wide. Borders Winema Natl. Forest on W and NE. Receives Williamson R. in N, drains S through Link R. and L. Ewauna into Klamath R. Upper Klamath Natl. Wildlife Refuge, main unit, at NW end. Hanks Marsh Unit in SE. Used for irrigation. Short channel connects lakes to Agency L. to N.

Upper Marlboro, town (1990 pop. 745), ⊙ Prince Georges co., central Md., 15 mi/24 km ESE of Washington, D.C.; 38°49′N 76°46′W. Most co. offices have been relocated in Hyattsville, closer to the centers of pop. The exception is the courthouse (1880; massively enlarged many times since). The town has been a tobacco-marketing center (tobacco auctions) for 3 cents. An agr. substation of Univ. of Md. is here. Laid out in 1706, it is named after the first Duke of Marlborough, an ancestor of Winston Churchill. Co. seat since 1721.

Upper Mesa Falls, Fremont co., E Idaho, cascade (114 ft/35 m high), Henry's Fork R., branch of Snake R., 8 mi/12.9 km NE of Ashton. Lower Mesa Falls (65 ft/20 m), 2 mi/3.2 km downstream (SSE).

Upper Montclair, N.J.: see MONTCLAIR.

Upper Narrows Dam, Calif.: see YUBA RIVER.

Upper Nyack (NEI-yak), suburban village (□ 4 sq mi/10.4 sq km; 1990 pop. 2,084), Rockland co., SE N.Y., on W bank of the Hudson R., just N of Nyack; 41°06′N 73°54′W.

Upper Peninsula, region (□ 16,450 sq mi/42,606 sq km; 1990 pop. 313,915), on peninsula, N Mich., across St. Mary's R. from Canada (E; Ont.), on Wis. (SW) state line, and on lakes Superior (N), Michigan (SW), and Huron (SE). Comprises 16 cos. Straits of Mackinac to S. Includes offshore isls., notably Drummond Isl. (L. Huron) and Isle Royale (L. Superior). Generally referred to as the U.P., its residents refer to themselves as Yoopers. An extension of the Can. Shield, the U.P. is characterized by pine and broad-leaf forests. Meager topsoil and long cold winters limit agr. to some dairying, forage crops, potatoes, rutabagas (the latter used in a local meat pie dish called pasties). Once a major copper- and iron-ore-mining dist., 80% of world's copper was produced here in 1920s, all but 2 iron mines have closed. Economy sustained by tourism; extensive snowmobile trails provide winter recreation. K. I. Sawyer Air Foce Base, 15 mi/24 km S of Marquette. Isle Royale Natl. Park and Keweenaw Peninsula, which protrudes into L. Superior, is noted for its heavy lake-effect snows. Connected to Lower Mich. (Lower Peninsula) by Mackinac Bridge. Sometimes called Upper Mich.

Upper Pohatcong Mountain, N.J.: see POHATCONG MOUNTAIN.

Upper Providence 1 township (1990 pop. 9,727), Delaware co., SE Pa., residential suburb 12 mi/19 km W of Philadelphia; 39°56′N 75°24′W. Dairying, cattle; nursery prods. to the W. Tyler Aboretum to W. State parks nearby. **2** township (1990 pop. 9,682), Montgomery co., SE Pa., 8 mi/12.9 km WNW of Norristown; 39°57′N 75°25′W. Agr. includes dairying; livestock; grain, soybeans, apples.

Upper Red Lake, Minn.: see RED LAKE.

Upper Red Rock Lake, Mont.: see RED ROCK LAKES.

Upper Rice Lake, Clearwater co., NW central Minn., 20 mi/32 km WSW of Bemidji; 47°23′N 95°17′W. Elev. 1,500 ft/457 m. Circular in shape, 2 mi/3.2 km wide. Short streams drain W to Wild Rice R., near its source. Lower Rice L. 7 mi/11.3 km to WSW.

Upper Saddle River, residential borough (1990 pop. 7,198), Bergen co., NE N.J., on small Saddle R., and 12 mi/19 km NNW of Hackensack; 41°03′N 74°05′W.

Upper Saint Clair, township (1990 pop. 19,692), Allegheny co., W Pa., residential suburb 9 mi/14.5 km SSW of Pittsburgh; 40°20′N 80°04′W. Urban fringe area with some agr. Mayview State Hosp. to W.

Upper Saint Regis Lake, N.Y.: see SAINT REGIS RIVER.

Upper Sandusky (san-DUH-skee), city (1990 pop. 5,906), ⊙ Wyandot co., N central Ohio, 17 mi/27 km NNW of Marion, and on Sandusky R.; 40°50′N 83°17′W. In agr. area; creameries, poultry hatcheries, greenhouses. Machinery, metal and clay prods., brick, transportation equip. Limestone quarries. Wyandot Natl. Mus. of Native Amer. and pioneer relics is here. Laid out 1843.

Upper Saranac Lake, N.Y.: see SARANAC LAKES.

Upper Spavinaw Lake, Okla.: see SPAVINAW LAKE.

Upper Tallassee Dam, Ala.: see YATES DAM.

Upper Township, township (1990 pop. 10,681), Cape May co., S N.J., 3 mi/4.8 km W of Ocean City; 39°15′N 74°43′W. Inc. 1798.

Upper West Side, section of borough of Manhattan, N.Y. city, SE N.Y., bet. Central Park (E), Hudson R. (W), Lincoln Center (beginning at West 60th St.; S), and West 96th St. (N); 40°48′N 73°58′W. The N border is fluid, sometimes extending up to West 110th or 125th streets. Broadway is the main commercial artery. Network studios, the construction of new luxury apartments, and the remodelling of older bldgs. have made this the city's new boomtown, but this growth has created some problems with increased traffic and congestion, the transformation of Broadway into a dark canyon, and the displacement of lower-income residents. The Amer. Mus. of Natural History, Lincoln Center, the Julliard School of Music, the Children's Mus. of Manhattan, and Fordham Univ.'s Lincoln Center Campus are among the attractions here. Also, just N of Lincoln Center, is the ambitious Special Lincoln Square Dist., a privately funded project involved in community improvement. Riverside Park stretches 2.5 mi/4 km along the E shore of Hudson R. from 72nd to 125th sts.

Upsala (UHP-suh-luh), village (1990 pop. 371), Morrison co., central Minn., 15 mi/24 km SW of Little Falls, on North Branch Two Rivers; 45°48′N 94°34′W. Agr. (grain, potatoes); dairying; livestock, poultry.

Upshur 1 (UHP-shuhr), county (□ 592 sq mi/1,533 sq km; 1990 pop. 31,370), NE Texas; ⊙ Gilmer; 32°43′N 94°56′W. Bounded SW by Sabine R., in NE by Big Cypress Creek; source of Little Cypress Bayou; drained by Big Sandy Creek. Partly wooded (mainly pine; extensive lumbering); large oil production (in East Texas field); also natural gas, sand and gravel. Agr. (hay; vegetables, peaches, sweet potatoes); livestock (cattle, poultry); dairying. L. O' the Pines reservoir in NE, L. Gladewater in S. Formed 1846. **2** county (□ 355 sq mi/919 sq km; 1990 pop. 22,867), central W.Va.; ⊙ Buckhannon; 38°53′N 80°13′W. On Allegheny Plateau; drained by Buckhannon R. Agr. (potatoes, alfalfa, hay, apples, nursery crops); cattle, poultry. Bituminous-coal mines, natural-gas wells; timber. Mfg. at Buckhannon. Includes part of Audra State Park in NE. W.Va. State Wildlife Center in W; part of Stonecoal L. Wildlife Management Area on W border. Formed 1851.

Upson (UHP-suhn), county (□ 328 sq mi/850 sq km; 1990 pop. 26,300), W central Ga.; ⊙ Thomaston; 32°53′N 84°18′W. Bounded W and S by Flint R. Textile mfg. at Thomaston and Silvertown. Piedmont peach-raising area; cotton; cattle, hogs, poultry; timber. Formed 1824.

Upton, village (1991 pop. 934), S Que., E Canada, 12 mi/19 km E of St. Hyacinthe. Dairying; livestock raising.

Upton, county (□ 1,241 sq mi/3,214 sq km; 1990 pop. 4,447), W Texas; ⊙ Rankin; 31°21′N 102°02′W. Elev. 2,500 ft/762 m–3,200 ft/975 m. High prairies in N and E; Castle and King mts. in SW. Ranching region (chiefly sheep; some goats, cattle); agr. (cotton, pecans); oil, natural-gas wells. Formed 1887.

Upton 1 town (1990 pop. 70), Oxford co., W Maine, on Umbagog L., and 40 mi/64 km NW of South Paris. In hunting, fishing area. **2** town (1990 pop. 4,677), Worcester co., S central Mass., 13 mi/21 km SE of Worcester; 42°11′N 71°36′W. Dairying; vegetables; lumber. Includes village of West Upton. State Forest. Settled 1728, inc. 1735. **3** town (1990 pop. 980), Weston co., NE Wyo., near source of Beaver Creek, just W of Black Hills, 27 mi/43 km NW of Newcastle; 44°06′N 104°37′W. Elev. c.4,234 ft/1,291 m. Shipping point for bentonite, livestock, grain, and lumber. Located in Thunder Basin Natl. Grassland.

Upton, village (1990 pop. 719), Hardin and Larue cos., central Ky., 15 mi/24 km S of Elizabethtown; 37°27′N 85°54′W. Agr. (tobacco, grain; cattle, hogs; dairying). Mfg. (crushed stone, lime); limestone-quarrying area.

Urania (yoo-RAI-nee-uh), town (1990 pop. 782), La Salle parish, central La., 40 mi/64 km N of Alexandria, near Castor Creek; 31°52′N 92°17′W. In timber- and oil-producing area; millwork, wood prods. Home of Henry Hardtner, father of reforestation in the South. A Yale Univ. forestry camp is here.

Uranium City, town, NW Sask., W Canada, on L. Athabasca, near the N.W.T. border; 59°34′N 108°37′W. A large uranium-mining area from the 1950s, the closure of its mines in 1982 led to economic collapse.

Uravan, village, Montrose co., W Colo., on San Miguel R., and c.45 mi/72 km WSW of Montrose. Elev. 4,992 ft/1,522 m. Named for local uranium and vanadium deposits. Uncompahgre (to NE) and Marti La Sal (to W) natl. forests nearby.

Urbana 1 (uhr-BA-nuh), city (1990 pop. 36,344), ⊙ Champaign co., E central Ill., adjoining CHAMPAIGN; 40°06′N 88°12′W. With Champaign, its twin city, Urbana is a trade, medical, and educational center in a fertile farm area. Agr. (corn, wheat, soybeans; dairying); mfg. (bituminous concrete, fabricated metal parts, transportation equip.). Best known as a seat of the Univ. of Ill. at Urbana-Champaign. A tablet in the co. courthouse commemorates a speech made by Abraham Lincoln in 1854. Co. fairgrounds here. Inc. 1833. **2** city (1990 pop. 11,353), ⊙ Champaign co., W central Ohio; 40°06′N 83°45′W. In a farm and livestock area. Hatcheries and plants make a variety of manufactures. During the War of 1812 the city was an outfitting point for the Great Lakes area. Urbana Col. is here. Nearby are the Ohio Caverns. Inc. 1814.

Urbana 1 (uhr-BA-nuh), town (1990 pop. 595), Benton co., E central Iowa, near Cedar R., 20 mi/32 kmNNW of Cedar Rapids; 42°13′N 91°52′W. Wood prods. **2** town (1990 pop. 350), Dallas co., SW central Mo., 14 mi/23 km NNW of Buffalo; 37°50′N 93°10′W.

Urbana, village (1990 pop. 400), Wabash co., N central Ind., 7 mi/11.3 km NNE of Wabash. Mfg. (tanks and hoppers, sheet metal fabricating). Soybeans, corn; livestock. Laid out 1854.

Urbancrest, village (1990 pop. 862), Franklin co., central Ohio, a SW suburb of Columbus; 39°54′N 83°05′W.

Urbandale, city (1990 pop. 23,500), Polk co., central Iowa, a residential suburb 5 mi/8 km NW of Des Moines; 41°38′N 93°44′W. The growing city has light industry and warehousing; mfg. (bottling; machinery, bldg. materials, paper prods., vitamins and health prods.). Living History Farm is here. Inc. 1917.

Urbank (UHR-baink), village (1990 pop. 73), Ottertail co., W Minn., 30 mi/48 km SE of Fergus Falls; 46°07′N 95°30′W. Agr. (grain; livestock). Inspiration Peak (1,750 ft/533 m) State Park to NW.

Urbanna (uhr-BA-nuh), town (1990 pop. 529), Middlesex co., E Va., 14 mi/23 km ENE of West Point, on Rappahannock R. at mouth of Urbanna Creek; 37°38′N 76°34′W. Oysters. Resort area.

Urbano Noris (oor-BAH-no NO-rees), town, (1994 pop. 21,000), Holguín prov., E Cuba, on central RR, and 20 mi/32 km SSE of Holguín, at E edge of Cauto R. valley; 20°32′N 76°08′W. Sugar-milling center. Airstrip to SE. Formerly San Germń.

Ures (OO-res), city (1990 pop. 4,146) and township, Sonora, NW Mexico, on Sonora R., and 40 mi/64 km NE of Hermosillo; 29°26′N 110°24′W. Agr. center (wheat, corn, beans; livestock).

Uriah (yuh-REI-uh), village, Monroe co., SW Ala., 20 mi/32 km SW of Monroeville.

Uriangato (oo-ree-ahn-GAH-to), city (1990 pop. 37,845) and township, Guanajuato, central Mexico, 37 mi/60 km SW of Celaya, on Mexico Highway 43; 20°09′N 101°11′W. Agr. center (corn, wheat, sugarcane, vegetables, fruit; livestock).

Urich (YOO-rik), city (1990 pop. 498), Henry co., W central Mo., near South Grand R., 14 mi/23 km WNW of Clinton; 38°27′N 94°00′W. Soybeans, corn, wheat; cattle; meat processing.

Uripitijuata, Cerro, peak (11,155 ft/3,400 m), Michoacán, N central Mexico, 18 mi/29 km SSW of Zamora; 19°45′N 102°20′W. Volcanic cone. Also Cerro Patamsan.

Urique (oo-REE-ke), town (1990 pop. 692), ⊙ Urique municipio, Chihuahua, N Mexico, in Sierra Madre Occidental, on Urique R. (affluent of the Río Verde), and 150 mi/241 km SW of Chihuahua; 27°13′N 107°50′W. Elev. 1,965 ft/599 m.

Urique River (oo-REE-kai), c.120 mi/193 km long, Chihuahua, NW Mexico; rises in Sierra Madre Occidental; flows NW and S, past Urique, joining the Río Verde near Sinaloa border to form the Río Fuerte.

Ursa, village (1990 pop. 506), Adams co., W central Ill., 9 mi/14.5 km N of Quincy; 40°04′N 91°22′W. Grain, soybeans; livestock; dairying. Mfg. of plastic prods., feeds.

Ursina (UHR-sei-nah), borough (1990 pop. 327), Somerset co., SW Pa., 18 mi/29 km SW of Somerset, on Casselman R., opposite (E of) borough of Confluence, near its mouth on Youghiogheny R.; 39°49′N 79°19′W. Agr. (corn, oats; livestock; dairying). Ohiopyle State Park to W; Youghiogheny R. L. reservoir to SW.

Úrsulo Galván (oor-soo-lo gahl-VAHN), town (1990 pop. 5,109), Veracruz, E Mexico, in Gulf lowland, 22 mi/35 km NW of Veracruz; 19°24′N 96°21′W. Corn, fruit; livestock.

Uruáchi (oo-roo-AH-chee), mining settlement (1990 pop. 480) and township, ⊙ Uruáchi municipio (1990 pop. 7,314), Chihuahua, N Mexico, in Sierra Madre Occidental, 88 mi/142 km ENE of Ciudad Obregón; 27°51′N 108°14′W. Elev. 4,308 ft/1,313 m. Gold, silver mining. Formerly Uruáchic.

Uruapan (oo-roo-AH-pahn), city (1990 pop. 187,623) and township, ⊙ Uruapan municipio, Michoacán state, W Mexico, 61 mi/98 km WSW of Morrelia; 19°24′N 102°03′W. Elev. 5,361 ft/1,634 m. An attractive city with gardens and parks, it is in a semitropical, mountainous agr. region. The city, founded in 1540, is the center of the mfg. of gourd lacquerware by the Native Tarascan people. Local craftsmen also produce glassware, woodwork, and embroideries. Not far from

Cross references are shown in SMALL CAPITALS. The pronunciation key is on page xv. The dates of population figures are on page xii.

Uruapan is the volcano Parícutin. Formerly Uruapan del Progreso.

U.S. Holocaust Memorial Museum, 14th St. and Wallenberg Place S.W., Washington, D.C. Dedicated in 1993 as a memorial to the 11 million people (6 million Jews, as well as 5 million gypsies, homosexuals, intellectuals, dissidents, and others) killed by the Nazis 1933–1945. The bldg. is a natl. memorial that was funded with both Federal monies and private donations. Designed by architect James Ingo Freed. The mus. includes a research lib.

Useful, uninc. rural community, Osage co., central Mo., 9 mi/14.5 km E of Linn. Of interest are the Useful Antique Store, Useful Cemetery, and Useful churches.

Usibelli (EE-yoo-si-BE-lee), village, central Alaska, c.30 mi/48 km SE of Nenana.

Usk (UHSK), uninc. village (1990 pop. 210), Pend Oreille co., NE Wash., 13 mi/21 km NW of Newport, on Pend Oreille R. (bridge). Timber; mfg. (pulp mill, sawmill). Parts of Kaniksu Natl. Forest to E and W; Kalispell L. to W.

Usquepaug (OOS-kwe-pawg), village, Richmond and South Kingstown towns, Washington co., S central R.I., on Queen R., and 24 mi/39 km SSW of Providence. In agr. area.

Usquepaug River, R.I.: see QUEEN RIVER.

USS Arizona Memorial, S Oahu isl., Honolulu co., Hawaii, in Pearl Harbor, E of Ford Isl. Authorized 1980, a memorial shrine to Amer. World War II losses here, built astride submerged battleship, sunk on Dec. 7, 1941, in surprise attack by Japanese. Accessible by passenger ferry from NE.

Usumacinta (oo-soo-mah-SEEN-tah), river, c.600 mi/966 km long, extreme S Mexico; formed by the Chixoy and Pasión rivers; flows NE through Tabasco state to the Bay of Campeche; 18°24′N 92°38′W. Demarcates the Guatemalan-Mex. border for c.70 mi/113 km. Navigable for c.300 mi/483 km upstream by small boats and is used to move logs and chicle downstream. Near its mouth some of the channels of the Usumacinta merge with the Grijalva R.

Utah (YOO-tah), state (□ 84,904 sq mi/219,902 sq km, including 2,577 sq mi/6,674 sq km of inland water surface; 1995 est. pop. 1,951,408), W U.S. One of the Rocky Mt. states; admitted 1896 as the 45th state of the Union; 39°22′N 111°34′W. ⊙ and largest city SALT LAKE CITY; it is also the hq. of the Church of Jesus Christ of Latter-Day Saints (Mormons), which founded the state and to a large extent still dominates it. Other important cities are OGDEN and PROVO. Bordered N by Idaho, NE by Wyo., E by Colo., S by Ariz., and W by Nev.; the SE corner touches the NW corner of N.Mex. (only point in U.S. common to 4 states). The state has 2 dissimilar regions abruptly separated by the Wasatch Range (part of the Rocky Mts.), which runs generally S from the Idaho state line. To the E of the Wasatch rise high mts. and irregular plateaus; along its W foothills lie the major cities of Utah, while further W is the Great Salt L. Desert and its S extensions. In the NE the snow-capped Uinta Mts., which run E-W, reach the state's highest elev. in Kings Peak (13,528 ft/4,123 m). The dissected Colorado Plateau stretches S, rugged and largely uninhabited except in isolated river valleys. Deep, tortuous canyons cut by the Colorado R., the Green R. (its main tributary), and its other tributaries impede travel but create vistas of remarkable grandeur. W Utah, part of the Great Salt L. Desert, was once submerged beneath an extensive Pleistocene lake, L. Bonneville. During many thousands of years the amount of water in the lake fluctuated, then subsided, leaving behind a salt-strewn desert, wide expanses of arid but nonalkaline soil, and a series of lakes. GREAT SALT LAKE, the largest of these, has through evaporation reached a concentration of mineral salts several times that of the ocean. Gull, pelican, and blue heron are found around the lake and have rookeries on its isls. Much of the lakeshore is bordered by mud and salt flats. Other Utah remnants of L. Bonneville are Utah L., S of Salt Lake City, and Sevier L. (intermittent) in W Utah. The Oquirrh Mts., rising S of the lake, dip to form pleasant beaches at the water's edge, then emerge as isls. within the lake and rise again in the Promontory Mts. on the N lakeshore. Utah L., to the S, is the largest natural body of fresh water in the state and drains into Great Salt L. through the Jordan R. Bet. Great Salt L. and the Wasatch Range and curving SW toward the Ariz. state line is a river-crossed strip, an agr. oasis, and the center of the life of Utah. On terraces left by the anc. L. Bonneville are situated the major cities. Irrigation of the rich but arid land has long been the challenge of Utah's agr. development. Major reclamation projects, such as the Weber R., Weber R. Basin, Moon L., and Strawberry Valley projects, assist numerous private enterprises in storing water for distribution and in aiding flood control. Construction on the $325 million Central Utah Project began in 1967; it consists of a vast complex of dams, canals, and aqueducts which carry water across the Wasatch Range to the Salt L. valley. L. Powell, reservoir of Glen Canyon Dam (on Colorado R.) just S of the Ariz. state line, and Flaming Gorge Dam (NE; on Green R.) are important parts of the Colorado R. storage project in Utah. Yet the arduous task of converting deserts to productive soil has confined the tilled land, including isolated farms in river valleys and a considerable amount of dry-farming land, to a small percentage of the state's total area. Major crops are alfalfa, barley, and wheat, but the bulk of income from agr. is based on livestock and livestock prods., including sheep, cattle, some hogs, and an expanding poultry industry. Abundant sunshine provides some compensation for inadequate rainfall, and the climate is moderate, except in the high elevs. Agrarian life was well suited to the principles of the Mormons when they came to found their Zion here; the difficulties of agr. in the dry land were an advantage since the Mormons offered little inducement to outsiders. The development of resources other than agr. ones was more or less frowned upon by the Mormon Church and, in general, was initiated by non-Mormons (called "Gentiles" by the Mormons). However, a wealth of minerals made mineral exploitation almost inevitable and, in turn, stimulated the construction of RRs. Today much of the pop. is directly or indirectly engaged in mining. Copper is the chief metal, followed in economic importance by gold and magnesium. Other important mineral prods. include molybdenum, beryllium (the 1st major discovery was in 1960), asphalt, silver, lead, tin, and fluorspar, mercury, vanadium, potassium salts, manganiferous ore, and uranium. For many years high freight rates and the long distances from markets, together with a Mormon distrust of industrialization, tended to discourage extensive mfg. However, the establishment of defense plants and U.S. armed forces installations in the state during World War II spurred a phenomenal industrial growth. The proximity of high-grade iron, coal, limestone, salt, and gravel have made Provo an important steel-mill center. Industrial plants now extend from Provo to Brigham City, with the largest concentration in the Salt Lake City area. Utah is the 2d-most productive center in the U.S. for computer hardware and software. It is also a center for aerospace research and the production of all kinds of missiles, spacecraft, electronic systems, and related items. Other major mfg. includes processed foods, machinery, fabricated metalware, and petroleum prods. Tourism has become so important to the state's economy that it outranks mining, ranching, and farming combined. Thousands of visitors come annually to view the many natural wonders, most notably Great Salt L. (N) and the spectacular Bryce Canyon and Zion natl. parks (S). Ski resorts, particularly in the Wasatch Range, have become popular tourist destinations. Other attractions are Canyonlands and Arches natl. parks (SE); Natural Bridges, Cedar Breaks, Dinosaur, Hovenweep, Rainbow Bridge, and Timpanogos Cave natl. monuments; Glen Canyon Natl. Recreation Area; and Golden Spike Natl. Historic Site. The Bonneville Salt Flats in Great Salt L. Desert in the W are famous as an automotive speedway. There are many natl. forests and a number of Native Amer. reservations. Capitol Reef Natl. Park (S) contains anc. cliff dwellings, caves with interesting glyphs, and numerous artifacts of prehistoric man. Recent anthropological studies have produced evidence that the Utah area was inhabited as early as c.9,000 B.C. Although some of Coronado's men under García López de Cárdenas may have entered S Utah in 1540, the 1st definite penetration by Europeans did not occur until 1776, when the Span. missionaries Silvestre Vélez de Escalante and Francisco Atanasio Domínguez opened the route for the Old Span. Trail bet. Santa Fe and Utah L. By the Treaty of 1819 bet. the U.S. and Spain, the large area of which Utah was a part was officially recognized as a Span. possession (it passed to the U.S. in 1848 with the Treaty of Guadalupe Hidalgo after the Mex.-Amer. War). In the 1820s the mt. men, in search of rich beaver streams, made their way over the difficult terrain, thoroughly exploring the region. The Amer. discovery of Great Salt L. is generally credited to James Bridger, but Étienne Provot, Jedediah S. Smith, and others also have claims. The Can. fur trader Peter Skene Ogden led 4 Snake R. expeditions into the area and is commemorated in the name of one of Utah's leading cities. Bet. 1824 and 1830 the riches in furs were exhausted, and a decade was to pass before the arrival of the next transients—W-bound emigrants. In 1841 the 1st Calif.-bound emigrant train, usually called the Bidwell party, left the Oregon Trail and made its way across the Great Salt L. Desert. Several years later Miles Goodyear became Utah's 1st non–Native Amer. settler when he set up a trading post at the site of present-day Ogden, naming it Fort Buenaventura. The ill-fated Donner party broke trail over the difficult mts. E of Great Salt L. in 1846 and proceeded in their tragic journey W across the desert. Permanent settlement began in 1847 with the arrival of the 1st of the hosts of persecuted Mormons, seeking a "gathering place for Israel" in some undesired and isolated spot. It is said that when Brigham Young, their leader, surmounted the Wasatch Range and looked out over the green valley of Great Salt L., he knew that the place had been found. On July 24, 1847, now celebrated as Pioneer Day, he entered the valley. Young was to prove himself one of the greatest administrators and leaders in 19th-cent. Amer. Under his direction and in communal fashion the ground was plowed and planted, the Temple foundation was laid, and Salt Lake City was plotted directly on compass lines. Gradually the Latter-Day Saints assembled, their ranks swelled by streams of emigrants from the U.S. and abroad (particularly the U.K. and Scandinavia). More and more of the arid land yielded to their pioneering irrigation. In the next 50 years they not only had to learn the techniques of wresting a living from the desert and of combating frequent invasions of grasshoppers, but they also had to face opposition from the Federal govt. In 1850 a large area, of which the present state was a part, was constituted Utah Territory and Young was appointed governor. The name Deseret [=honeybee], chosen by the Mormons, was discarded, but the beehive remains a ubiquitous symbol of Mormon activity throughout Utah. The Native Americans, dispossessed of their lands and foreseeing further encroachment, became embittered, and the Mormons were threatened by the powerful Ute, eventually leading to the Walker (1853–1854) and the Black Hawk (1865–1868) wars. There were also conflicts bet. the Mormons and the Calif.-bound immigrants, but greater trouble came with the gradual disintegration of relations bet. the Mormons and the Federal govt. Numerous petitions for statehood were denied because of the practice of polygamy, publicly avowed by the Mormons in 1852. Friction was increased by the assigning to Utah of non-Mormon, and often incompetent, Federal judges, and clashes bet. church and Federal interpretation of the law were frequent. Stories of Mormon violence toward non-Mormon settlers circulated in the East, and antagonism, much of it based on misunderstanding, grew out of proportion. In 1857 a "state of substantial rebellion" was declared by the Federal govt.; Young was removed from his post, and President James Buchanan directed U.S. army troops to proceed against the Mormons. The Mormons prepared for warfare, calling in outlying settlers, and guerrilla bands harrassed the W-bound troop supply trains of Albert S. Johnston. The affair, known as the "Utah War" or the "Mormon campaign," was finally settled peacefully, but great ill feeling had developed, particularly after the massacre at MOUNTAIN MEADOWS. Some settlers who during the disturbances had made an exodus to land S of the Utah Valley remained to spread colonization there. This turbulent episode was succeeded by several difficult decades. Congressional acts forbidding polygamy were passed in 1862, 1882, and 1887. In the attempt to enforce them, civil liberties were infringed upon and some Mormon church properties were expropriated. In 1890 a church edict advising members to abstain from the practice of polygamy was ratified, and civil rights and church properties were restored. Long before Utah became a state in 1896, its area had been reduced to its present size by the creation of the territories of Nev. and Colo. in 1861 and Wyo. Territory in 1868. The influx of settlers included many non-Mormon groups, and cultural and economic isolation had been broken by the development of mining as well as by the completion of the Union Pacific RR, which in 1869 joined the Central Pacific RR (NW of Ogden), completing the nation's 1st transcontinental RR. Agr. was hampered by a court interpretation of water rights in 1880 that favored a concept of water as private property. Not until the Reclamation Act of 1902 was the principle designating water as public property restored, buttressed by the state act of 1903 that vested the ownership of water in the state. Urbanization has proceeded rapidly. World War II spurred industrial growth, and the development of hydroelectric power during the 1950s attracted new industries. The Federal govt. has become the state's largest employer and owns over 60% of Utah's land. Computer software and other high-technology firms have located here, giving the state a diversified and robust economy. Utah still operates under its 1st constitution, adopted in 1895 and effective with statehood in 1896. The state's executive branch is headed by a governor elected for a 4-year term. Utah's bicameral legislature has a senate with 30 members elected for 4-year terms and a house of representatives with 75 members elected for 2 years. The state sends 2 senators and 3 representatives to the U.S. Congress and has 5 electoral votes. The state's leading institutions of higher learning include Brigham Young Univ., at Provo; the Univ. of Utah, at Salt Lake City; and Utah State Univ., at Logan. Utah has 29 cos.: BEAVER, BOX ELDER, CACHE, CARBON, DAGGETT, DAVIS, DUCHESNE, EMERY, GARFIELD, GRAND, IRON, JUAB, KANE, MILLARD, MORGAN, PIUTE, RICH, SALT LAKE, SAN JUAN, SANPETE, SEVIER, SUMMIT, TOOELE, UINTAH, UTAH, WASATCH, WASHINGTON, WAYNE, and WEBER.

Utah, county (□ 2,141 sq mi/5,545 sq km; 1990 pop. 263,590), N central Utah; ⊙ Provo; 40°07'N 111°40'W. Irrigated agr. area drained by Utah L. and tributaries, Provo, American Fork, and Spanish Fork rivers. Large Utah L. drained by Jordan R., in W center of co. Part of Wasatch Range is in E, including Mt. Timpanogos and Timpanogos Cave Natl. Monument. Agr. (cattle, sheep; hay, alfalfa, wheat, barley, apples, cherries, sugar beets, vegetables); mining (iron, copper, silver, lead, zinc, limestone, clay, calcite). Mfg. at Provo. Sundance Ski Area in NE. Timpanogos Cave Natl. Monument in NE; part of Fort Williams Military Reservation in NW; Stage Coach and Camp Floyd state historical parks in W; Utah L. State Park on E shore of Utah L. at Provo; part of Uinta Natl. Forest in NE and S; part of Manti–La Sal Natl. Forest in SE; small part of Ashley Natl. Forest in extreme SE. Formed 1850.

Utah Lake (□ c.150 sq mi/389 sq km), Utah co., N central Utah. Natural lake; largest freshwater lake and 2d-largest natural lake in the state. City of Provo on E shore, city of Orem near lake just N of Provo, town of Lehi at N end. Located in the Great Basin. It drains through the Jordan R. to the Great Salt L. Utah L., with Great Salt L. and several intermittent lakes in W Utah, are what remains of the prehistoric L. Bonneville. The Provo R. project and the Strawberry Valley Project irrigate the region. Bird and waterfowl preserves are here, as is Utah L. State Park (on E shore of Provo).

Ute, town (1990 pop. 395), Monona co., W Iowa, 20 mi/32 km E of Onawa; 42°02'N 95°42'W. In livestock and grain area.

Ute Pass (9,165 ft/2,793 m), Teller co., central Colo., in Front Range, 10 mi/16 km NW of Pikes Peak. Used in latter ½ of 19th cent. by miners en route to goldfields of Cripple Creek and Leadville. Now crossed by U.S Highway 24.

Ute Pass, Colo.: see WILLIAMS RIVER MOUNTAINS.

Ute Peak (YOOT) (10,093 ft/3,076 m) of Sangre de Cristo Mts., Taos co., N N.Mex., near Colo. state line, 8 mi/12.9 km WSW of Costilla, and E of Rio Grande; 36°56'N 105°41'W.

Utica 1 (YOO-ti-kuh), city (1990 pop. 5,081), Macomb co., SE Mich., suburb 21 mi/34 km N of downtown Detroit, and on Clinton R.; 42°37'N 83°01'W. Surrounded by Sterling Heights and Shelby Township. In dairy and vegetable (rhubarb) area; flour mill. Mfg. (transportation equip., wire and steel prods., hardware). Rochester-Utica State Recreation Area to NW; state park nearby. Settled 1817; inc. as village 1838, as city 1931. **2** city (□ 16 sq mi/41 sq km; 1990 pop. 68,637), ⊙ Oneida co., central N.Y., on the Mohawk R. and the Barge Canal; 43°06'N 75°13'W. Mfg. includes electric and electronic goods, transportation equip., machinery, consumer goods, leather and canvas prods., paper goods, textiles, medical equip., tools, and metal prods. Like the string of industrial towns and cities from S New England through upstate N.Y. and into the Midwest, Utica has experienced a major reduction in mfg. activity in the past several decades, and is in serious financial straits; many public services have been curtailed to save money. In a large dairy region; crushed stone and stone prods. Settled in 1773 on the site of old Fort Schuyler (1758), it was destroyed (1776) in a Native Amer. and Tory attack and resettled after the Revolution. Its location on the Erie and other canals and on the RRs stimulated its industrial development. Utica has an extensive park system, with winter and summer sports facilities. Seat of Utica Col. (a branch of Syracuse Univ.), the State Univ. of N.Y. Col. of Technology, Mohawk Valley Community Col., Utica School of Commerce, and a state psychiatric center. Inc. 1862.

Utica 1 (YOO-ti-kuh), town (1990 pop. 411), Clark co., SE Ind., 7 mi/11.3 km NE of Jeffersonville, on Ohio R.; 38°20'N 85°39'W. Agr. area; mfg. (boats, barges, dry docks). Laid out 1816. **2** town (1990 pop. 1,033), Hinds co., W Miss., 29 mi/47 km WSW of Jackson; 32°06'N 90°37'W. Agr. (cotton, corn, soybeans; cattle, poultry; timber); mfg. (apparel, rope, furniture parts). Mus. of the Southern Jewish Experience, to NE. Natchez Trace (Natl.) Parkway passes to NW. **3** uninc. town (1990 pop. 1,478), Oconee co., NW S.C., residential suburb 2 mi/3.2 km E of Seneca; 34°40'N 82°55'W.

Utica 1 (YOO-ti-kuh), village (1990 pop. 208), Ness co., W central Kansas, 20 mi/32 km NW of Ness City; 38°38'N 100°10'W. In grain and livestock region. **2** village (1990 pop. 220), Winona co., SE Minn., 17 mi/27 km W of Winona; 43°58'N 91°57'W. Agr. (dairying; livestock, poultry; grain). Mfg. (medical prods.). Richard J. Drorer Memorial State Forest to SE and NE. Whitewater Wildlife Area to N. **3** village (1990 pop. 45), Judith Basin co., central Mont., on Judith R., and 32 mi/51 km WSW of Lewistown. Silver, lead, gold, sapphires, and zinc are mined to SW at Sapphire Village at edge of Little Belt Mts. Wheat, barley, hay; cattle. Ackley L. State Park to E; Lewis and Clark Natl. Forest to W. Utica Mus. Founded 1879. **4** village (1990 pop. 718), Seward co., SE Nebr., 13 mi/21 km W of Seward; 40°53'N 97°20'W. Grain; mfg. (bookbinding; feeds, trailers). **5** village (1990 pop. 1,997), Licking co., central Ohio, 12 mi/19 km N of Newark, and on North Fork of Licking R.; 40°14'N 82°26'W. In rich agr. area (fruit). **6** village (1990 pop. 115), Yankton co., SE S.Dak., 10 mi/16 km NNW of Yankton; 42°58'N 97°30'W.

Utica (YOO-ti-kah), borough (1990 pop. 242), Venango co., NW Pa., 7 mi/11.3 km WNW of Franklin, on French Creek; 41°26'N 79°57'W. Agr. (corn; dairying); logging.

Utik Lake, NE central Man., central Canada; 24 mi/39 km long, 5 mi/8 km wide; 55°17'N 95°55'W. Drains NE into Hayes R.

Utopia, Lake (□ 5 sq mi/13 sq km), SW N.B., E Canada, 3 mi/5 km NE of St. George; 5 mi/8 km long, 2 mi/3 km wide. Drains into Magaguadavic R.

Utowana Lake, Hamilton co., NE central N.Y., in the Adirondacks, 3 mi/4.8 km SW of Blue Mountain L. village; c.2.5 mi/4 km long; 43°50'N 74°33'W. Joined by streams to Raquette L. (W), and to small Eagle L. and thence to Blue Mountain L. (E).

Utuado (oo-too-AH-do), town (1990 pop. 34,980), W central P.R., on N slopes of the Cordillera Central, 14 mi/23 km S of Arecibo. Second-largest coffee producer in P.R.; agr. center (citrus fruits, plantains, bananas; livestock). Mfg. (clothing, plastic prods., paper prods., chemicals). Adjoining E is the large Toro Negro unit of the Caribbean Natl. Forest. Numerous caves with ethnological and paleontological remains nearby. Center of "jibaro" culture (mixture of Taino and Span. descendants). Caguana Indian Ceremonial Park nearby (small mus.).

Utukok River (YOO-duh-kok), c.200 mi/322 km long, NW Alaska; rises in Brooks Range near 68°33'N 161°07'W; flows generally N to Arctic Ocean at 70°08'N 162°13'W. Utukok settlement at mouth.

Uvalda (yoo-VAHL-duh), village (1990 pop. 561), Montgomery co., E central Ga., 14 mi/23 km SSW of Vidalia; 32°02'N 82°31'W. Mfg. includes clothing and food prods.

Uvalde (OO-val-dee), county (□ 1,558 sq mi/4,035 sq km; 1990 pop. 23,340), SW Texas; ⊙ Uvalde; 29°21'N 99°45'W. Crossed E-W by Balcones Escarpment, dividing hilly N (part of Edwards Plateau) from S plains; drained by Nueces, West Nueces, Frio, Leona, and Sabinal rivers. Ranching (esp. hogs, goats, sheep; also cattle); mohair, wool shipped; extensive beekeeping, some irrigated agr. (vegetables, wheat, corn, oats, sorghum, cotton, fruit). Asphalt mines; sand and gravel, stone. Hills, canyons, spring-fed streams attract tourists; hunting. Garner State Park in N. Formed 1850.

Uvalde (OO-val-dee), city (1990 pop. 14,729), ⊙ Uvalde co., SW Texas, 70 mi/113 km ESE of Del Rio, on Leona R.; 29°13'N 99°46'W. Elev. 913 ft/278 m. RR junction in agr. (cattle, sheep, goats, hogs; vegetables, cotton, wheat) area. Wool, mohair, and vegetable- and frozen-food-processing facilities. Minerals (asphalt compounds, lime, sand, gravel) are also mined in the area. Southwest Texas Jr. Col. is here, as is the home of Vice President John Nance Garner (now a mus.). Founded c.1854, inc. as a city 1921.

Uwharrie River (yoo-WAHR-ee), c.60 mi/97 km long, central N.C.; rises in NE Randolph co., S of High Point; flows S to Yadkin (Pee Dee) R. in L. Tillery reservoir 8 mi/12.9 km E of Albermarle; lower course flows through Uwharrie Natl. Forest. Also spelled Uharie R.

Uxbridge (UHKS-brij), suburban town (1991 pop. 14,092), S Ont., central Canada, 35 mi/56 km NNE of Toronto; 44°06'N 79°07'W. Located in Durham Regional Municipality. Milling; dairying.

Uxbridge, town (1990 pop. 10,415), Worcester co., S Mass., on Blackstone R., and 16 mi/26 km SE of Worcester; 42°04'N 71°38'W. Dairying; vegetables. Settled 1662, inc. 1727.

Uxmal (oosh-MAHL), anc. city, N Yucatán peninsula, S Mexico, in the Puuc hills; 20°21'N 89°46'W. A Late Classic-period Maya center which flourished bet. A.D. 600 and A.D. 900. It is one of the finest expressions of Maya architecture known as the Puuc style. There is a mus. at the site, much of which is reconstructed.

Uyak Bay (OO-yak), S Alaska, W Kodiak Isl., inlet of Shelikof Strait, 60 mi/97 km WSW of Kodiak; 35 mi/56 km long, 1 mi/1.6 km–5 mi/8 km wide .

Uzinki, Alaska: see OUZINKIE.

V

Vacaville, city (1990 pop. 71,479), Solano co., central Calif. 30 mi/48 km WSW of Sacramento; 38°22′N 121°58′W. In a farm and orchard area (fruit, almonds, grain, sugar beets, sunflowers, safflower, beans, tomatoes; nursery prods.; cattle, lambs). Food prods. are made in the city, and fruits and vegetables are canned; mfg. (industrial machinery, pipe shields, aluminum prods., mattresses and metal plate work). Vacaville has grown tremendously in size as the central Calif. area has boomed; its pop. growing almost 4-fold bet. 1970 and 1990. A state prison medical facility; Travis Air Force Base and Hosp. to S; Mt. Vaca (2,819 ft/859 m). Inc. 1892.

Vache, île à (VAHSH, ee lah), Caribbean island (□ 20 sq mi/52 sq km), off SW Haiti, 7 mi/11.3 km SSE of Les Cayes; 8 mi/12.9 km long, c.2 mi/3.2 km wide. Agr. (cotton, citrus fruit); cattle. Fishing. Chromite deposits. Also spelled Île à Vaches.

Vader (VAI-duhr), village (1990 pop. 414), Lewis co., SW Wash., 25 mi/40 km S of Chehalis, on Olequa Creek, at mouth of Stillwater Creek, Cowlitz R. 1 mi/1.6 km to E; 46°24′N 122°58′W. Seaquest State Park on Silver L. reservoir, to E.

Vadnais Heights (VAD-nuhs), city (1990 pop. 11,041), Ramsey co., E Minn., residential suburb 7 mi/11.3 km N of downtown St. Paul and 10 mi/16 km NE of downtown Minneapolis; 45°03′N 93°04′W. Mfg. (printed circuit boards, labels and nameplates, plastic molds, hearing aids). White Bear L. to E; L. Vadnais in SW corner.

Vado (VAH-do), uninc. village (1990 pop. 325), Dona Ana co. S N.Mex., 15 mi/24 km SSE of Las Cruces, and 24 mi/39 km NNW of El Paso, Texas, on Rio Grande. In irrigated agr. area. Mfg. (fresh and dried chile prods.).

Vaiden (VAI-duhn), town (1990 pop. 789), ☉ Carroll co. (seat shared with Carrollton), central Miss., 27 mi/ 43 km ESE of Greenwood, near Big Black R.; 33°19′N 89°45′W. Agr. (cotton, soybeans; cattle; timber).

Vail 1 town (1990 pop. 3,569), Eagle co., W central Colo., 70 mi/113 km W of Denver, on Gore Creek, in Gore Range of Rocky Mts.; 39°38′N 106°21′W. Surrounded by White R. Natl. Forest. Light mfg.; printing and publishing. Nation's largest ski resort and summer recreation area. Majority of homes are 2d homes. Colo. Ski Mus. and Ski Hall of Fame here. **2** town (1990 pop. 388), Crawford co., W Iowa, 9 mi/14.5 km ENE of Denison; 42°03′N 95°12′W. In agr. area.

Vail Pass, Colo.: see GORE RANGE.

Val Barette (vahl bah-RET), village (1991 pop. 551), SW Que., E Canada, on small L. Gauvin, in the Laurentians, 8 mi/13 km ESE of Mont Laurier; 46°31′N 75°21′W. Dairying.

Val Brillant (vahl bree-LAH), village (1991 pop. 1,024), SE Que., E Canada, on L. Matapedia, 22 mi/35 km SSW of Matane; 48°32′N 67°34′W. Dairying, lumbering.

Val David (vahl dah-VEED), village (1991 pop. 2,976), S Que., E Canada, in the Laurentians, on North R., and 4 mi/6 km ESE of Ste. Agathe-des-Monts; 46°02′N 74°12′W. Dairying; ski resort.

Val d'Or (vahl dor), town (1991 pop. 23,842), SW Que., E Canada, SE of Rouyn-Noranda; 48°07′N 77°46′W. Mining center. Gold was discovered in the region in 1909; copper, zinc, lead, and molybdenum are also mined.

Val Jalbert (vahl zhahl-BER), village, S central Que., E Canada, on S shore of L. St. John, at mouth of Ouiatchouan R., 5 mi/8 km SE of Roberval. Lumbering. Nearby are 236-ft/72-m waterfalls.

Val Marie (vahl mah-REE), village (1991 pop. 219), S Sask., W Canada, near Mont. border, 70 mi/113 km S of Swift Current; 49°14′N 107°44′W. Wheat; livestock.

Val Morin (vahl mo-RE), village (1991 pop. 1,366), S Que.,

E Canada, in the Laurentians, on North R., and 5 mi/ 8 km SW of Ste. Agathe-des-Monts. Dairying; ski resort.

Val Saint Michel (vahl se mee-SHEL), town, S Que., E Canada, 10 mi/16 km W of Quebec; 46°52′N 71°26′W. Dairying; vegetables, poultry.

Val Verde, county (□ 3,232 sq mi/8,371 sq km; 1990 pop. 38,721), SW Texas; ☉ Del Rio; 29°53′N 101°09′W. Partly on Edwards Plateau; bounded SW and S by the Rio Grande (Mex. border), SE by Sycamore Canyon; drained by Pecos R. and Devil's R. A leading Texas sheep-raising co.; goat ranches also important; cattle and horse breeding. Some irrigated agr. in Rio Grande valley: grapes. Devil's R. State Park (no road access) near center of co., Seminole Canyon State Park in S. Rio Grande forms large Internatl. Amistad Reservoir on S border, large Devil's R. Arm extends NE; surrounded by Amistad Natl. Recreation Area, including Mex. counterpart. Formed 1885.

Val Verde, uninc. town (1990 pop. 1,689), Los Angeles co., S Calif., residential suburb 33 mi/53 km NW of Los Angeles, in Sierra Madre, near Santa Clara R.; 34°27′N 118°40′W. Castaic L. reservoir (State Recreation Area) to N; L. Piru reservoir to W.

Valatie (vuh-LAH-shah), village (□ 1 sq mi/2.6 sq km; 1990 pop. 1,487), Columbia co., SE N.Y., on Kinderhook Creek, and 13 mi/21 km NNE of Hudson; 42°24′N 73°40′W. In dairying, poultry-raising, and apple-growing region. Inc. 1856.

Valcartier or **Valcartier Village** (vahl-kahr-TYAI), village, S Que., E Canada, 15 mi/24 km WNW of Quebec. Dairying. Nearby is Can. Forces base.

Valcour Island, in L. Champlain, Clinton co., NE N.Y., 5 mi/8 km SSE of Plattsburgh; c.2 mi/3.2 km long; 44°37′N 73°25′W. Valcour village is nearby, on N.Y. shore. One of 1st naval engagements in the Amer. Revolution was fought here (1776) bet. Br. fleet and Amer. ships under Benedict Arnold.

Valcourt (vahl-KOOR), town (1991 pop. 2,284), S Que., E Canada, 20 mi/32 km ENE of Granby; 45°29′N 72°19′W. Dairying center; lumbering.

Valders (VAHL-duhrs), town (1990 pop. 905), Manitowoc co., E Wis., 11 mi/18 km W of Manitowoc; 44°04′N 87°53′W. Dairy prods.; meat processing; marble and stone.

Valdes Island (VAHL-des), (□ 9 sq mi/23 sq km), SW B.C., W Canada, Gulf Isls., in Strait of Georgia bet. Gabriola Isl. (NW) and Galiano Isl. (SE), 25 mi/40 km SW of Vancouver; 10 mi/16 km long, 1 mi/2 km wide; 49°04′N 123°38′W. Farming, lumbering. Mainly private cabins; no scheduled ferries.

Valdese (val-DEEZ), town (1990 pop. 3,914), Burke co., W central N.C., 6 mi/9.7 km E of Morganton; 35°45′N 81°33′W. Grain, soybeans; chickens. Mfg. (textiles, apparel, lithium batteries, bakery prods.). Farm colony started here in 1893 by Waldensians from Cottian Alps, N Italy. L. Rhodhiss reservoir (Catawba R.) to N. Inc. 1921.

Valdez (val-DEEZ), city (1990 pop. 4,068), Valdez-Cordova census div., S Alaska, at the head of Valdez Arm inside PRINCE WILLIAM SOUND; 61°07′N 146°16′W. It has tourist and fishing industries, as well as salmon spawning grounds. The city's excellent landlocked, ice-free harbor was explored and named by the Spaniards in 1790. Valdez was est. 1898 as a debarkation point for those seeking a route to the Yukon goldfields that would obviate the necessity of paying duty to Canada. Connected to Fairbanks and Anchorage over Thompson pass via Richardson and Glenn highways. The city was devastated by the 1964 earthquake; the resulting tidal wave swept over the wharf and destroyed downtown Valdez. It was rebuilt at a location 5 mi/8 km W of the old site. Valdez is the S terminus of the trans-Alaskan (Alyeska) oil pipeline, built in the 1970s (begun 1974, completed 1977), that originates in Prudhoe Bay. Its port facilities were greatly enlarged in the mid-1970s. On Mar. 24, 1989, the oil tanker *Exxon Valdez* hit a reef near Valdez and spilled approximately 11 million gals/ 41 million liters of oil into Prince William Sound. Clean-up efforts ensued, but much wildlife was killed

or endangered as a result of the environmental disaster. Inc. 1901.

Valdez, village, Las Animas co., S Colo., on Purgatoire R., and 11 mi/18 km WSW of Trinidad. Elev. 6,470 ft/ 1,972 m. Coal mining.

Valdez Arm (val-DEEZ), S Alaska, deep-water inlet (28 mi/45 km long, 3 mi/4.8 km wide) of Prince William Sound; 60°58′N 146°49′W. Extends NE to Valdez; upper part called Port Valdez.

Valdosta (val-DAHS-tuh), city (1990 pop. 39,806), ☉ Lowndes co., S Ga., near the Fla. state line, in lake region, on I-75; 30°51′N 83°17′W. Airport. Large naval stores market and a processing, distributing, and commercial center for a tobacco, cotton, pecan, watermelon, and livestock area. Mfg. includes potting soil, food and beverages, paper and textile bags, agr. chemicals, printing and publishing, industrial batteries, concrete, polyethylene film, boats, resins; lumber; soybean processing. Valdosta State Univ., a unit of the Univ. System of Ga., is here. Major factory-direct outlet store. Moody Air Force Base is to the N. Inc. 1860.

Vale, town (1990 pop. 1,491), ☉ Malheur co., E Oregon, on Malheur R. between mouths of Willow Creek and Bully Creek; 43°58′N 117°14′W. Elev. 2,400 ft/732 m. Trade center for sugar beet, livestock, and potato area. Vale Irrigation Project (est. 1928; includes 32,000 acres/ 12,950 ha in vicinity of Vale) uses water from Malheur R. and its North Fork. Owyhee Dam is 24 mi/39 km S. Bully Creek Reservoir to W. RR terminus to NW. Settled 1864, inc. 1889.

Vale, uninc. village, Lincoln co., W central N.C., 12 mi/ 19 km S of Hickory. Cotton, grain; poultry, livestock. Mfg. (machinery, furniture, textiles, metal fabrication, lumber, leather goods).

Valen, Isle (VA-lin), island (□ 4 sq mi/10 sq km), SE N.F., E Canada, in Placentia Bay, 22 mi/35 km NW of Argentia; 3 mi/5 km long, 2 mi/3 km wide; 47°30′W 54°23′W. Fishing.

Valencia (vuh-LEN-see-uh), county (□ 1,068 sq mi/ 2,766 sq km; 1990 pop. 45,235), W N.Mex.; ☉ Los Lunas; 34°43′N 106°47′W. Cattle, sheep; dairying; corn, hay, alfalfa, oats, barley, grapes, apples; Christmas trees. Watered by Rio Grande and Rio Puerco. Small part of Cibola Natl. Forest in E; part of Isleta Indian Reservation along N border. Cibola co. created out of large part of W Valencia corner. Formed 1852.

Valencia 1 (vuh-LEN-see-uh), uninc. town, Los Angeles co., S Calif., industrial suburb 32 mi/51 km NW of downtown Los Angeles, on Santa Clara R. Mfg. (hardware, transportation equip., machinery, electrical apparatus, communications equip., lab instruments, tool and die, medical equip., computers, printing and publishing, chemicals). Six Flags Magic Mt. and Six Flags Hurricane Harbor. Calif. Inst. of the Arts is here. Castaic L. State Recreation Area to N; parts of Angeles Natl. Forest to N and E. RR junction to N. **2** town (1990 pop. 3,917), Valencia co., central N.Mex., 21 mi/34 km S of Albuquerque, 2 mi/3.2 km ESE of Los Lunas; 34°47′N 106°41′W. Cattle, sheep; dairying; grain, corn, alfalfa. Isleta Indian Reservation to N; part of Cibola Natl. Forest to E.

Valencia (vah-LEN-see-ah), village, N Trinidad, Trinidad and Tobago, 20 mi/32 km E of Port of Spain; 10°41′N 61°10′W. Sawmilling.

Valencia (vah-LEN-see-ah), borough (1990 pop. 364), Butler co., W Pa., 16 mi/26 km N of Pittsburgh, on Breakneck Creek; 40°40′N 79°59′W.

Valencia Heights (vah-LEN-see-uh), uninc. town (1990 pop. 4,122), Richland co., central S.C., 2 mi/3.2 km SE of downtown Columbia; 33°58′N 80°59′W.

Valenciana (vah-len-see-AH-nah) or **La Valenciana**, former silver-mining hamlet and mine; 21°02′N 101°15′W. Guanajuato municipio, Guanajuato, central Mexico, just N of Guanajuato. From 1781 to 1800, Mexico supplied more than 60% of world's silver from here. Wells are now flooded and mines inactive. Mining machinery still here.

Valentine, town (1990 pop. 2,826), ☉ Cherry co., N Nebr., located in Sand Hills region, 120 mi/193 km E of Chadron, and on Niobrara R., near S. Dak. state line; 42°52′N 100°32′W. Elev. 2,579 ft/786 m. Tourism important, aided by canoeing on Niobrara R. and location near Midpoint on Cowboy Trail (longest trail on abandoned RR right of way). Livestock, grain, dairy and poultry prods. Mfg. (printing, agr. equip.). Sand Hills Mus. here. Nearby are state fish hatchery (to NE). Snake R. Falls, site of Fort Niobrara, and Fort Niobrara Natl. Wildlife Refuge to E. Settled 1882.

Valentine 1 uninc. village, Mohave co., NW Ariz., near Grand Wash Cliffs, 26 mi/42 km NE of Kingman, in small sect. of Hualapai Indian Reservation. **2** village (1990 pop. 217), Jeff Davis co., extreme W Texas, 33 mi/53 km NW of Marfa; 30°35′N 104°30′W. Elev. 4,431 ft/1,351 m. In livestock region.

Valeria, town (1990 pop. 69), Jasper co., central Iowa, 14 mi/23 km E of Newton; 41°43′N 93°19′W.

Valerio Trujano (vah-LE-ree-o troo-HAH-no), town (1990 pop. 961), N Oaxaca, Mexico, 4.3 mi/7 kms SW of San Juan Bautista Cuicatlán; 17°47′N 96°59′W. Elev. 3,281 ft/1,000 m.

Valier 1 (va-LIR), village (1990 pop. 708), Franklin co., S Ill., 8 mi/12.9 km WNW of Benton; 38°01′N 89°02′W. In bituminous-coal-mining, oil, and agr. area. **2** (VAL-yuhr), village (1990 pop. 519), Pondera co., N Mont., on N shore of L. Frances, and 17 mi/27 km NW of Conrad; 48°17′N 112°15′W. Terminus of RR spur from Conrad. In irrigated region; cattle, hogs, sheep; wheat, barley, oats, and hay. Oil and natural-gas field to N. Blackfeet Indian Reservation to NW.

Valinda, uninc. city (1990 pop. 18,735), Los Angeles co., S Calif., residential suburb 16 mi/26 km E of downtown Los Angeles, and 3 mi/4.8 km SW of West Covina; 34°02′N 117°56′W. San Jose Hills to E.

Valladolid (vah-yah-DO-leed), city (1990 pop. 29,279) and township, Yucatán, SE Mexico, 90 mi/145 km ESE of Mérida; 20°40′N 88°11′W. RR terminus; agr. center (henequen, corn, beans, cotton, sugarcane, coffee, fruit; timber). Historic colonial town with fine bldgs. Site of bloody uprising (1847).

Valladolid, Mexico: see MORELIA.

Valle Crucis (val-ee KROO-sis), uninc. village, Watauga co., NW N.C., 7 mi/11.3 km W of Boone, on Watauga R., at NE edge of Pisgah Natl. Forest. Est. 1842 as Episcopal Mission. Mast General Store, est. 1883. Mt. resort area.

Valle de Allende (VAH-ye-de ah-YEN-de), town (1990 pop. 3,680), ⊙ Allende municipio, Chihuahua, N Mexico, 16 mi/26 km E of Hidalgo del Parral; 26°58′N 105°30′W. Elev. 5,092 ft/1,552 m. Former silver- and gold-mining center.

Valle de Banderas (VAH-ye dai bahn-DE-rahs), town (1990 pop. 4,376), ⊙ Bahía de Banderas municipio, Nayarit, W Mexico, near Banderas Bay, 55 mi/89 km SSW of Tepic; 20°50′N 105°18′W. Corn, cotton, sugarcane, rice, tobacco, tomatoes, bananas.

Valle de Bravo (VAh ye dai BRAH-vo), city (1990 pop. 15,472) and township, Mexico state, central Mexico, 32 mi/51 km W of Toluca de Lerdo; 19°12′N 100°10′W. Cereals, fruit; livestock; dairying. Site of East Molino hydroelectric plant on Valle de Bravo Reservoir. El Molino and several other hydroelectric plants in the area provide electric power for Toluca de Lerdo and Mexico city.

Valle de Guadalupe (VAH-lai dai gwah-dah-LOO-pai), town (1990 pop. 3,650), Jalisco, central Mexico, 24 mi/39 km SW of San Juan de los Lagos, on Mexico Highway 80; 21°00′N 102°37′W. Elev. 5,873 ft/1,790 m. Grain, beans; livestock.

Valle de Juárez (VAH-yai dai HWAH-res), town (1990 pop. 3,266), Jalisco, central Mexico, 45 mi/72 km E of Sayula; 19°56′N 102°56′W. Elev. 5,741 ft/1,750 m. Corn, wheat, beans, fruit; livestock. Sometimes called El Valle.

Valle de Santiago (VAh-yai dai sahn-tee-AH-go), city (1990 pop. 56,009) and township, Guanajuato, central Mexico, on central plateau, in Lerma R. basin, 26 mi/42 km S of Guanajuato, on Mexico Highway 43; 20°25′N 101°15′W. Elev. 5,623 ft/1,714 m. Agr. center (wheat, sweet potatoes, fruit; livestock); shoe mfg., lumber milling.

Valle de Tehuacán Ecological Reserve (VAH-yai dai te-hwah-KAHN), a biological reserve, in SW Puebla, Mexico, 17 mi/27 km SW of Tehuacán on Zapotitlan R. Wild corn dated 20,000 B.C. was found in caves in the Valley of Tehuacán. Large deposits of fossilized sea life dated 120 million years ago have also been discovered in this valley. Some of these artifacts are on display in the Mus. of the Valley of Tehuacán (Museo del Valle de Tehuacán), which is housed in the 16th-cent. El Carmen Convent, on Reforma Ave., in the town of Tehuacán.

Valle de Zaragoza (vah-yai dai sah-rah-GO-sah), town (1990 pop. 289), Jimenez municipio, Chihuahua, N Mexico, on Conchos R., near L. Toronto, and 37 mi/60 km NNW of Hidalgo del Parral; 27°29′N 105°48′W. Corn, cotton, tobacco, sugarcane; livestock; lumbering. Also known as Conchos.

Valle del Rosario (VAH-yai del ro-SAH-ree-o), town (1990 pop. 367), ⊙ Rosario municipio, in S Chihuahua, Mexico, 47 mi/76 km NW of Hidalgo del Parral; 27°20′N 06°19′W. On Balleza R. in outliers of Sierra Madre Occidental. Agr. and cattle raising; mining. Roads undeveloped.

Valle, El 1 Mexico: see VALLE DE JUÁREZ. **2** Mexico: see BUENAVENTURA.

Valle Grande Mountains (VEI-yuh GRAHN-dai) or **Jemez Mountains**, N N.Mex., NW of Santa Fe, mainly in NE Sandoval co., extend N into Rio Arriba co., and E into Los Alamos co., W of the Rio Grande; extend N-S from Jemez Creek to Rio Chama; 36°26′N 106°10′W. Elev. 9,000 ft/2,743 m. Range surrounds Valle Grande, enormous caldera (covers c.180 acres/73 ha). Prominent points include Cerro Pelado (10,109 ft/3,081 m) and Redondo Peak (11,254 ft/3,430 m). Los Alamos is just SE.

Valle Hermoso (VAH-yai er-MO-sah), city (1990 pop. 33,904), NW Tamaulipas, Mexico, 6 mi/10 km SW of Heroica Matamoros, Tamaulipas, Mexico, 23°39′N 99°46′W. Established by Mex. citizens repatriated from U.S. during 1930s. Irrigated farming.

Valle Nacional, Mexico: see SAN JUAN BAUTISTA VALLE NACIONAL.

Valle Nuevo Scientific Reserve (VAH-YAI noo-AI-vo), nature preserve, La Vega prov., Dominican Republic. One of several preserves designated in 1983, it extends from Valle Nuevo Military Post to the Pyramids (boundary marker about 24 mi/39 km S Constanza). It is one of the most natural examples of woodland in the Dominican Republic and features species otherwise found only in Canada and the U.S., propagated by migrating birds.

Valle Vista, uninc. town, Riverside co., S Calif., suburb 30 mi/48 km SE of Riverside, on San Jacinto R., in San Jacinto Valley; 33°45′N 116°54′W. Sobaba Indian Reservation to SE. San Bernardino Natl. Forest to E.

Vallecillo (vah-ye-SEE-yo), town, Nuevo León, N Mexico, on Inter-Amer. Highway (85), and 70 mi/113 km NNE of Monterrey; 26°40′N 99°58′W. Sugarcane, cotton, cactus fibers.

Vallecito Dam, Colo.: see LOS PINOS RIVER.

Vallecito Reservoir (□ 4 sq mi/10.4 sq km), La Plata co., SW Colo., on Los Pinos R., in San Juan Natl. Forest, 18 mi/29 km ENE of Durango; 37°23′N 107°35′W. Max. capacity 136,200 acre-ft. Formed by Vallecito Dam (162 ft/49 m high), built (1941) by the Bureau of Reclamation for irrigation; also used for flood control and recreation.

Vallée de Jacmel, La (vah-LAI duh ZHAK-MEL), village, Sud-Est dept., Haiti, 7 mi/11.3 km NW of Jacmel. Citrus fruits; bauxite deposite nearby.

Vallée Jonction (vah-LAI zhohk-SYO), **L'Enfant Jésus**, or **Valley Junction**, village (1991 pop. 1,906), S Que., E Canada, on Chaudiére R., and 35 mi/56 km SSE of Que. city; 46°22′N 70°55′W. RR center; mfg.; dairying.

Vallejo, city (1990 pop. 109,199), Solano co., W Calif., on San Pablo Bay at the mouth of the Napa R.; 38°07′N 122°16′W. Port; trade and processing center for farm prods.; flour milling and meatpacking are significant industries. Its main source of employment is the U.S. naval shipyard on Mare Isl., just W of the city. Vallejo is among the fastest-growing U.S. cities, marked by a pop. increase of 36% bet. 1980 and 1990. Founded by Admiral David Farragut in 1854, the city covers 1,500 acres/607 ha and has 4 drydocks and 8 shipbuilding ways. Submarines and destroyers are built and repaired here. Vallejo was created to be the state capital, but became the nominal capital (1852–1853). The Calif. Maritime Acad. is in Vallejo. Nearby are Travis Air Force Base and a state park. Inc. 1866.

Valles, Mexico: see CIUDAD VALLES.

Valley 1 county (□ 3,733 sq mi/9,668 sq km; 1990 pop. 6,109), central Idaho; ⊙ Cascade; 44°45′N 115°34′W. Mt. and plateau area bounded E by Middle Fork of Salmon R., and drained by North Fork of Payette R. Livestock raising; lumbering; oats; cattle. Mercury, gold, silver, lead. All but North Fork Payette valley in W covered by natl. forests, Payette Natl. Forest in N, Boise Natl. Forest in SE and SW; part of Frank Church R. of No Return Wilderness Area in E; several small lakes and reservoirs in W ½ of co. Formed 1917. **2** county (□ 5,062 sq mi/13,111 sq km; 1990 pop. 8,239), NE Mont.; ⊙ Glasgow; 48°22′N 106°40′W. Irrigated agr. area bordering Canada (Sask.) on N. Border forms Central-Mountain time zone boundary, Mont. is in Mountain time zone. Bounded S by Missouri R., forms Fort Peck Reservoir in SW. Drained by Milk and West Fork Poplar rivers, and Porcupine Creek. Wheat, barley, oats, hay; cattle, sheep, hogs; bentonite. Glasgow Air Force Base in N center, is now St. Marie and a site for aircraft testing. Part of Charles M. Russell Natl. Wildlife Refuge in SW, surrounds Fort Peck Reservoir. Porcupine Creek forms W border of Fort Peck Indian Reservation in E. Formed 1893. Present boundaries est. 1920. **3** county (□ 570 sq mi/1,476 sq km; 1990 pop. 5,169), central Nebr.; ⊙ Ord; 41°34′N 98°58′W. Agr. region drained by North Loup and Middle Loup rivers. Cattle, hogs; dairying; corn, dairy prods. Fort Hartsuff State Historical Park in NW. Formed 1873.

Valley, city (1990 pop. 8,173), Chambers co., East Ala., 3 mi/4.8 km SE of Lanett, near Ga. state line, on Chattahoochee R. bet. West Point L. and L. Harding; 32°48′N 85°10′W. Fabric, towel mfg. A branch of Southern Union State Community Col. here. Inc. 1980, combining the villages of Fairfax, Langdale, River View, and Shawmut.

Valley, town (1990 pop. 1,775), Douglas co., E Nebr., 23 mi/37 km W of downtown Omaha, and on Platte R.; 41°18′N 96°20′W. RR junction. Mfg. (center pivot and other irrigation systems, industrial respiratory masks, concrete prods., radio receivers, fabricated pipe fittings). Satellite community of Omaha.

Valley Brook, village (1990 pop. 744), Oklahoma co., central Okla., suburb 5 mi/8 km SSE of downtown Oklahoma City; 35°23′N 97°28′W. Commercial area.

Valley Center 1 uninc. town (1990 pop. 1,711), San Diego co., S Calif., suburb 38 mi/61 km NNE of downtown San Diego; 33°13′N 117°01′W. Cattle; grain, fruit. Oil and natural gas. San Pasqual Indian Reservation to E; Rincon and La Jolla Indian Reservations to NE. Palomar State Park (Mt. Palomar Observatory) to NE. **2** town (1990 pop. 3,624), Sedgwick co., S central Kansas, on Little Arkansas R., and suburb 10 mi/16 km N of Wichita; 37°50′N 97°22′W. RR junction. In wheat region; grain storage. Mfg. (plastics, wood prods., aircraft parts). Oil and gas wells nearby.

Valley City, town (1990 pop. 7,163), ⊙ Barnes co., SE N.Dak., 60 mi/97 km W of Fargo, and on Sheyenne R.; 46°55′N 98°00′W. RR junction; mfg. (fertilizer, transportation equip., plastic bottles, electronic controls, medical equip.; printing and publishing); flour milling; dairy prods., grain. Valley City State Col. Settled 1872, inc. 1883. Fish hatcheries to NW at Bald Hill Dam (L. Ashtabula).

Valley Falls 1 town (1990 pop. 1,253), Jefferson co., NE Kansas, on Delaware R., and 24 mi/39 km NNE of Topeka; 39°20′N 95°27′W. Dairying. Perry L. Reservoir to S. Laid out 1855; inc. as village 1869; as city 1871. **2** uninc. town (1990 pop. 3,504), Spartanburg co., NW S.C., residential suburb 5 mi/8 km NW of downtown Spartanburg; 35°00′N 81°58′W.

Valley Falls 1 village (1990 pop. 527), Rensselaer co.,

E.N.Y., on Hoosic R., and 13 mi/21 km NNE of Troy; 42°53′N 73°33′W. In dairying and grain-growing area. **2** industrial village (1990 pop. 11,175), administrative center of Cumberland town, Providence co., NE R.I., on Blackstone R., and 5 mi/8 km N of Providence; 41°55′N 71°23′W.

Valley Forge, uninc. town (1990 pop. 1,500), Chester co., SE Pa., suburb 18 mi/29 km NW of Philadelphia; 40°05′N 75°28′W. Mfg. includes fertilizers, steel pipe fittings, printing inks and coatings, explosive devices, surgical appliances; printing and publishing. Valley Forge Natl. Historical Park to NE. Pickens Creek Reservoir to NW.

Valley Forge National Historical Park, Montgomery and Chester cos., SE Pa., 17 mi/27 km NW of Philadelphia, on the Schuylkill R.; 40°06′N 75°26′W. Here, during the Amer. Revolution, the main camp of the Continental Army was established (Dec. 1777–June 1778) under the command of Gen. George Washington. The winter was severe, food and clothing were inadequate, and illness and suffering pervaded the camp. The number of ragged and half-starved troops dwindled through desertion; the remaining men, about 11,000, talked of mutiny but were held together by their loyalty to Washington and to the patriotic cause. Two distinguished foreigners, Fr. Gen. Lafayette and Prussian Gen. Steuben, shared the misery of the troops; Steuben drilled and organized the men, transforming the loose-jointed army into an integrated force. Center for tourism. Earthworks, bldg. re-creations, monument. Authorized 1976 (3,468 acres/1,403 ha).

Valley Green, uninc. town (1990 pop. 3,017), York co., SE Pa., residential community 9 mi/14.5 km SSE of Harrisburg, and 2 mi/3.2 km W of Goldsboro, on Fishing Creek; 40°09′N 76°47′W.

Valley Grove, village (1990 pop. 569), Ohio co., N W.Va., in Northern Panhandle, 8 mi/12.9 km ENE of Wheeling, near Pa. state line; 40°05′N 80°34′W. Mfg. (computer parts). Bear Rocks Lakes Wildlife Management Area to E.

Valley Head, town (1990 pop. 577), De Kalb co., NE Ala., 10 mi/16 km NE of Fort Payne, and 45 mi/72 km NNE of Gadsden, near Ga. state line. Shipping point for farm produce; lumber; mfg. (textiles).

Valley Hi (VAL-lee HEI), borough (1990 pop. 19), Fulton co., S Pa., 9 mi/14.5 km ENE of Everett, on Oregon Creek, in Buchanan State Forest; 40°01′N 78°11′W.

Valley Hill, uninc. town (1990 pop. 1,802), Henderson co., SW N.C., residential suburb 2 mi/3.2 km SW of Hendersonville, in Blue Ridge Mts.; 35°17′N 82°29′W. Homes Educational State Forest to SW.

Valley Junction, Canada: see VALLÉE JONCTION.

Valley Junction, Iowa: see WEST DES MOINES.

Valley Mills, town (1990 pop. 1,085), Bosque co., central Texas, on Bosque R., and 21 mi/34 km WNW of Waco; 31°39′N 97°28′W. In farm area (dairying; cattle; wheat, sorghum, corn); mfg. (tool and die).

Valley of the Ten Thousand Smokes, Alaska: see KATMAI NATIONAL MONUMENT AND PRESERVE.

Valley Park, city (1990 pop. 4,165), St. Louis co., E Mo., on Meramec R., suburb 15 mi/24 km WSW of downtown St. Louis; 38°32′N 90°28′W. Mfg. (cotton prods.; aluminum forging; resins, cement; metal heat treating). Castlewood State Park to W; 1993 flooding heavily damaged the city.

Valley Springs, town (1990 pop. 739), Minnehaha co., SE S.Dak., 13 mi/21 km E of Sioux Falls, near Minn. state line, and near Pipestone Creek; 43°34′N 96°27′W. Palisades State Park to N.

Valley Springs, uninc. village, Calaveras co., central Calif., in Sierra Nevada foothills, 30 mi/48 km NE of Stockton. Walnuts, olives; honey; cattle. New Hogan L. to SE (Calaveras R.) and Pardee Reservoir to N, Comanche Reservoir to NW, both of Mokelumne R.

Valley Station, uninc. city (1990 pop. 22,840), Jefferson co., N Ky., residential suburb 11 mi/18 km SSW of downtown Louisville, near Ohio R.; 38°06′N 85°51′W.

Valley Stream, village (□ 3 sq mi/7.8 sq km; 1990 pop. 33,946), Nassau co., SE N.Y., on L.I., a residential suburb of N.Y. city; 40°39′N 73°42′W. Valley Stream State Park is here. JFK Internatl. Airport is to the W. Site of Green Acres Mall, one of the largest shopping centers in U.S. Inc. 1925.

Valley, The, city, ⊙ Anguilla, B.W.I. located in approximately the center of the isl.; 18°03′N 63°04′W. Anguilla Arts and Crafts Center, Devonish Cotton Gin Gall., and Old Factory Plaza are among the attractions located here. Served by Wall Black Airport.

Valley View 1 uninc. town (1990 pop. 2,112), Kane co., NE Ill., residential suburb 3 mi/4.8 km N of St. Charles, near Fox R.; 41°57′N 88°17′W. **2** uninc. town (1990 pop. 1,749), Schuylkill co., E central Pa., 18 mi/29 km N of Pottsville, bet. Deep Creek (N) and Pine Creek (S); 40°38′N 76°32′W. Mfg. (printing and publishing); agr. (corn, hay; poultry, livestock; dairying). **3** uninc. town (1990 pop. 2,911), York co., S Pa., residential suburb 2 mi/3.2 km W of York; 39°57′N 76°42′W.

Valley View 1 village (1990 pop. 2,137), Cuyahoga co., N Ohio, a SE suburb of Cleveland, on Cuyahoga R.; 41°23′N 81°36′W. **2** village (1990 pop. 640), Cooke co., N Texas, 9 mi/14.5 km S of Gainesville, near Elm Fork of Trinity R.; 33°29′N 97°09′W. In agr. area; feeds. L. Ray Roberts to SE.

Valley Village, town (1990 pop. 3,540), Jefferson co., N Ky., residential suburb 14 mi/23 km SSW of downtown Louisville, on Ohio R. Agr. area (tobacco, grain; livestock).

Valleyfield, city (1991 pop. 27,598), S Que., E Canada, on the Beauharnois Canal, at the NE end of L. St. Francis, SW of Montreal. A port of entry and industrial center, it has cotton and synthetic textile mills, a zinc refinery, and plants making chemicals, clothing, and rubber goods.

Valleyview or **Valley View**, village (1990 pop. 604), Franklin co., central Ohio, a W suburb of Columbus; 39°58′N 83°04′W.

Valliant, town (1990 pop. 873), McCurtain co., extreme SE Okla., 17 mi/27 km WNW of Idabel; 34°00′N 95°05′W. RR junction. In agr. and lumbering area; mfg. (bag paper). Pine Creek L. reservoir to N.

Vallière (vah-LYER), town, Nord-Est dept., NE Haiti, at source of the Grande Rivière du Nord, 28 mi/45 km SE of Cap-Haïtien; 19°26′N 71°55′W. Agr. (rice, coffee, citrus fruit); gold deposits. Also spelled Vallières.

Vallonia, village (1990 pop. 500), Jackson co., S central Ind., 12 mi/19 km SW of Seymour, on East Fork White R. Corn; cattle. Driftwood State Fish Hatchery and Starve Hollow State Beach to S. Part of Jackson-Washington State Forest to SE. Founded 1810.

Valmead (VAL-meed), uninc. village, Caldwell co., W central N.C., suburb 2 mi/3.2 km N of Lenoir. Pisgah Natl. Forest to NW.

Valmeyer (VAL-mei-er), town (1990 pop. 897), Monroe co., SW Ill., 8 mi/12.9 km WSW of Waterloo; 38°17′N 90°18′W. In agr. area (wheat, barley, sorghum; dairying); mfg. (wood prods., commercial printing). Town established by Swiss farmers at the end of the 19th cent. on rich Miss. bottom land. Town flooded twice in Sept. and Oct. of 1993, with 90% of the homes beyond repair. A new town was constructed 2 mi/3 km E of the old Valmeyer on 500 acres/200 ha of former dairy lands at an elev. of 400 ft/122 m.

Valmy (VAHL-mee), uninc. village (1990 pop. 200), Humboldt co., N Nev., 14 mi/23 km NW of Battle Mountain town, near Humboldt R. Service center on Interstate Highway 80. Sheep, cattle.

Valona (vuh-LO-nuh), town, McIntosh co., SE Ga., 10 mi/16 km NE of Darien; 31°28′N 81°20′W. Crabmeat processing.

Valparaiso (val-puh-RAI-zo), city (1990 pop. 24,414), ⊙ Porter co., NW Ind.; 41°29′N 87°03′W. Mfg. (metal prods., liquid fertilizer, popcorn, storage tanks, ferrite powder, paving materials, firefighting equip., tool and die, magnets, electronics, food-processing equip., plastic pails, fabric screen printing). The city is the seat of Valparaiso Univ. and a branch of Ind. Vocational Technical Col. (Ivy Tech). Nearby recreational sites include lakes and ski areas. Commonly referred to as Valpo. Laid out 1836, inc. 1850.

Valparaíso (vahl-pah-rah-EE-so), town (1990 pop. 9,688), ⊙ Valparaíso municipio, Zacatecas, N central Mexico, on interior plateau, 70 mi/113 km E of Zacatecas; 22°46′N 103°34′W. Elev. 16,677 ft/5,083 m. Agr. center (corn, wheat, chickpeas, alfalfa, chilies; livestock).

Valparaiso (val-puh-REI-zo), town (□ 12 sq mi/31 sq km; 1990 pop. 4,672), Okaloosa co., NW Fla., on Choctawhatchee Bay, c.45 mi/72 km ENE of Pensacola; 30°29′N 86°30′W. Eglin Air Force Base is just SW.

Valparaiso (val-puh-REI-zo), village (1990 pop. 481), Saunders co., E Nebr., 20 mi/32 km NNW of Lincoln; 41°04′N 96°49′W. Grain; livestock.

Valsayn (VAHL-sain), govt. livestock farm, NW Trinidad, Trinidad and Tobago, just S of St. Joseph. Here last Span. governor signed treaty of capitulation (1797). New residential developments.

Valverde (vahl-VER-dai), province (□ 220 sq mi/570 sq km; 1993 pop. 146,087), NW Dominican Republic; 19°37′N 71°00′W. N border follows Cordillera Septrional; otherwise in fertile Cibao Valley, drained by Río Yaque del Norte. Agr. (sugarcane, rice; rice processing). Also gold washing and lumbering.

Valverde, Dominican Republic: see MAO.

Van, town (1990 pop. 1,854), Van Zandt co., NE Texas, 23 mi/37 km NW of Tyler, near source of Neches R.; 32°31′N 95°38′W. Oil field and natural-gas center. Mfg. (gas processing).

Van, uninc. village, Boone co., W central W.Va., 8 mi/12.9 km SE of Madison. RR junction. Mfg. (coal processing); bituminous-coal mining.

Van Alstyne, town (1990 pop. 2,090), Grayson co., N Texas, 15 mi/24 km S of Sherman; 33°25′N 96°34′W. Elev. 632 ft/193 m. In cattle and cotton area. Mfg. (armored vehicles, patio-door and window screens, horse pads and grooming prods.); oil and gas. Est. 1853.

Van Buren 1 (van BYUHR-uhn), county (□ 724 sq mi/1,875 sq km; 1990 pop. 14,008), N central Ark.; ⊙ Clinton; 35°34′N 92°29′W. Drained by Middle Archeys and South forks of Little Red R. Agr. (cattle, hogs, poultry); timber. Part of Ozark Natl. Forest in SW; Gulf Mt. Wildlife Management Area in W center; part of large Greers Ferry L. Reservoir in E. Formed 1833. **2** county (□ 490 sq mi/1,269 sq km; 1990 pop. 7,676), SE Iowa, on Mo. state line; ⊙ Keosauqua; 40°45′N 91°58′W. Prairie agr. area (hogs, cattle, sheep, poultry; corn, soybeans, hay) drained by Des Moines and Fox rivers. Bituminous-coal mines, limestone quarries. Lacey Keosauqua State Park in S; unit of Shimek State Forest SW of Keosauqua; and partial unit in SE corner of co. Rivers flooded here in 1993. Formed 1836. **3** county (□ 1,090 sq mi/2,823 sq km; 1990 pop. 70,060), SW Mich.; ⊙ Paw Paw; 42°15′N 86°02′W. Bounded W by L. Michigan; drained by Paw Paw and Black rivers. Fruit-growing region (esp. apples, cherries, peaches, plums; also strawberries, grapes); carrots, green beans, asparagus; livestock, poultry; dairy prods.; wineries, vineyards. Mfg. at South Haven and Paw Paw. Resorts; fisheries, nurseries. Van Buren State Park in NW on L. Michigan; Timber Ridge Ski Area in NE corner; small lakes distributed throughout co. Palisades nuclear power plant (initial criticality May 24, 1971) is 5 mi/8 km S of South Haven; uses cooling water from L. Michigan, and has a max. dependable capacity of 730 MWe. Organized 1837. **4** (van BYOO-ruhn), county (□ 255 sq mi/660 sq km; 1990 pop. 4,846), central Tenn.; ⊙ Spencer; 35°42′N 85°28′W. Bounded N by Caney Fork of Cumberland R.; hilly region in the Cumberlands. Coal mines; livestock; some farming, lumbering. Includes Fall Creek Falls State Park. Formed 1840.

Van Buren (van BYUHR-uhn), city (1990 pop. 14,979), ⊙ Crawford co., NW Ark., on Arkansas R., and suburb 5 mi/8 km NE of downtown Fort Smith; 35°27′N 94°20′W. James W. Trimble Lock and Dam (Arkansas R.) to SE. Mfg. (canned vegetables, wire prods., oak furniture, steel belts for tires; poultry prods., handblown glass; doors); RR shops. Hardwood timber, natural-gas wells in region. Settled 1818, inc. 1843.

Van Buren 1 (van BYUHR-uhn), town (1990 pop. 934), Grant co., E central Ind., 11 mi/18 km ENE of Marion; 40°37′N 85°31′W. Agr. area; popcorn. **2** town (1990 pop.

3,045), Aroostook co., NE Maine, on St. John R., and 33 mi/53 km N of Presque Isle; 47°10′N 68°00′W. In lumbering and potato-growing area. Port of entry; trade center. Includes Keegan and Van Buren villages. Inc. 1881. **3** town (1990 pop. 893), ⊙ Carter co., S Mo., in the Ozarks, on Current R., and 38 mi/61 km NW of Poplar Bluff; 37°00′N 91°00′W. Mfg. (caps, lumber prods.). Along Current R. is the Ozark Natl. Scenic Riverways, including Big Spring (former state park) to S. Mark Twain Natl. Forest to SW. Tourism; outfitting center for canoeing and fishing.

Van Buren or **Vanburen**, village (1990 pop. 337), Hancock co., NW Ohio, 7 mi/11 km N of Findlay; 41°08′N 83°39′W. Van Buren State Park is nearby.

Van Deusenville, Mass.: see GREAT BARRINGTON.

Van Ettan Lake, Mich.: see PINE RIVER.

Van Etten, village (1990 pop. 552), Chemung co., S N.Y., near Cayuta Creek, 15 mi/24 km NE of Elmira; 42°12′N 76°32′W. In agr. area.

Van Horn, town (1990 pop. 2,930), ⊙ Culberson co., extreme W Texas, in mt. region, c.110 mi/177 km SE of El Paso; 31°02′N 104°49′W. Elev. 4,010 ft/1,222 m. In scenic cattle- and sheep-ranching region; vegetables, pecans, melons; cotton. Mfg. (ceramic tile, talc, crushed stone); tourist trade. Inc. after 1940.

Van Horn Mountains, extreme W Texas, range extending c.25 mi/40 km S from region S of Van Horn.

Van Horne, town (1990 pop. 695), Benton co., E central Iowa, 10 mi/16 km SSW of Vinton; 42°00′N 92°05′W. In agr. area.

Van Houten (van HOO-tuhn), village, Colfax co., NE N.Mex., 11 mi/18 km SW of Raton. Elev. 6,750 ft/2,057 m. A ghost town.

Van Lear, town (1990 pop. 2,035), Johnson co., E Ky., near Levisa Fork, 4 mi/6.4 km SE of Paintsville; 37°46′N 82°45′W. In agr. (tobacco; livestock), coal-mining, and oil-producing region of the Cumberland Mts. Butcher Hollow, home of Loretta Lynn, country singer, is here. Jenny Wiley State Resort Park on Dewey L. reservoir to SE.

Van Meter, town (1990 pop. 751), Dallas co., central Iowa, on Raccoon R., near mouth of South Raccoon R., and 6 mi/9.7 km SSE of Adel; 41°31′N 93°57′W. In agr. area.

Van Norden, Lake, Calif.: see YUBA RIVER.

Van Nuys, suburban section in Los Angeles co., S Calif., (part of Los Angeles since 1915), in San Fernando Valley, 15 mi/24 km NW of downtown Los Angeles (city). Municipal govt. branch offices for the valley are here. Mfg. (aerospace parts, paper, plastics, rubber, and metal prods.; aluminum sporting goods, electronic components, baked goods, measuring devices, and navigation systems). Van Nuys Airport and Bush Gardens theme park to NW. Los Angeles Valley Col. (2-year).

Van Tassell (van TAS-uhl), village (1990 pop. 8), Niobrara co., E Wyo., on Niobrara R., near Nebr. state line, and 20 mi/32 km ESE of Lusk; 42°39′N 104°05′W. Elev. 4,736 ft/1,444 m. RR junction to NW.

Van Vleck, town (1990 pop. 1,534), Matagorda co., S Texas, 5 mi/8 km ENE of Bay City; 29°02′N 95°52′W. Agr. area (rice, cotton, grains; cattle). Oil and natural gas. Mfg. (fertilizer).

Van Wert (van WUHRT), county (□ 409 sq mi/1,059 sq km; 1990 pop. 30,464), W Ohio; ⊙ Van Wert; 40°52′N 84°35′W. Bounded W by Ind. state line; drained by Little Auglaize R. and headwaters of Auglaize R. In the Till Plains and Lake Plains physiographic regions. Diversified farming (corn, wheat, soybeans; livestock, poultry). Mfg. (soybean oils, paper boxes, gaskets, packing and sealing devices, metal stampings, vehicle parts and accessories); limestone quarries, clay pits; nurseries. Formed 1837.

Van Wert (van wuhrt), city (1990 pop. 10,891), ⊙ Van Wert co., NW Ohio, near the Ind. state line; 40°52′N 84°35′W. In a rich grain-farming area. Fabricated metal prods., electronic equip., machinery, and cheeses are made here. The city is known for its peonies, which blossom all over town in early June. Inc. 1848.

Van Wert 1 (van WUHRT), town, Polk co., NW Ga., 14 mi/23 km E of Cedartown; 33°59′N 85°02′W. **2** town (1990 pop. 249), Decatur co., S Iowa, 10 mi/16 km N of Leon; 40°52′N 93°47′W. In livestock area.

Van Wyck, uninc. village, Lancaster co., N S.C., 10 mi/16 km ESE of Rock Hill near Catawba R., and near N.C. state line. Andrew Jackson State Park to E. Mfg. (bricks and explosives). Agr. (poultry, livestock; soybeans, cotton, grain).

Van Zandt, county (□ 859 sq mi/2,225 sq km; 1990 pop. 37,944), NE Texas; ⊙ Canton; 32°33′N 95°50′W. Bounded NE by Sabine R., partly E by Neches R. (source in SE). Rich diversified agr., livestock area, with large oil, salt, natural-gas production; also iron, ore, clay. Cotton, vegetables, sweet potatoes, hay, grains; nurseries (esp. roses); extensive dairying and livestock raising (cattle, hogs). Sabine R. forms L. Tawakoni in NW corner of co. L. Tawakoni State Park on co. border. Formed 1848.

Vanadium (vun-NAI-dee-uhm), village, Grant co., SW N.Mex., in foothills of Pinos Altos Mts., 1.5 mi/2.4 km E of Bayard. Elev. 6,003 ft/1,830 m. Silver, lead, copper, zinc mined here. Santa Rita Open Pit Copper Mine to SE; Gila Natl. Forest to N.

Vananda (vuh-NAN-duh), village, SW B.C., W Canada, on N Texada Isl., port on Malaspina Strait, 20 mi/32 km ENE of Courtenay across Strait of Georgia; 49°45′N 124°33′W. Limestone quarrying, fishing; timber.

Vananda (vuh-NAN-duh), village, Rosebud co., E central Mont., on Horse Creek, and 18 mi/29 km NW of Forsyth. Hay; cattle, sheep.

Vance, county (□ 269 sq mi/697 sq km; 1990 pop. 38,892), N N.C.; ⊙ Henderson; 36°21′N 78°24′W. Bounded N by Va. state line, S by Tar R. Piedmont tobacco and timber area; tungsten deposits (mined near Henderson); timber. Agr. area (corn, wheat, soybeans, hay, tobacco; cattle). Mfg. at Henderson. Kerr L. State Recreation Area in N, on large S arm of Kerr Reservoir, which extends out of Va. Formed 1881.

Vance, town (1990 pop. 248), Tuscaloosa co., W central Ala., 20 mi/32 km E of Tuscaloosa; 33°17′N 87°14′W. Lumbering. In pine forest area. In 1993, Vance was selected as the site of a new sport utility motor vehicle plant, with production scheduled to begin in 1997.

Vance, village (1990 pop. 214), Orangeburg co., S central S.C., 25 mi/40 km E of Orangeburg, near L. Marion; 33°26′N 80°25′W. Santee R. to NE. Agr. (livestock, poultry; grain, watermelons; cotton, tobacco, peanuts).

Vance Air Force Base, Okla.: see ENID.

Vanceboro 1 (VANS-buhr-o), town (1990 pop. 201), Washington co., E Maine, on Spednik L. and St. Croix R., 60 mi/97 km N of Machias; 45°34′N 67°28′W. Port of entry; hunting, fishing, lumbering. **2** town (1990 pop. 946), Craven co., E N.C., 15 mi/24 km NNW of New Bern; 35°17′N 77°09′W. Grain, cotton, tobacco, peanuts; poultry, livestock. Mfg. (water treatment compounds, women's clothing, windshield wipers).

Vanceboro Reservoir (VANS-buhr-o), (□ 29 sq mi/75 sq km), on U.S. (Maine)–Can. (N.B.) border, on St. Croix R., near Vanceboro (Maine); 45°34′N 67°26′W. Max. capacity 214,470 acre-ft. Formed by Vanceboro Dam (16 ft/5 m high), built (1967) for power generation.

Vanceburg, town (1990 pop. 1,713), ⊙ Lewis co., NE Ky., 18 mi/29 km SW of Portsmouth, Ohio, on Ohio R.; 38°35′N 83°19′W. In agr. area (grain, tobacco; livestock; dairying). Mfg. (lumber, shoes, concrete). Cabin Creek Covered Bridge to NW. Settled c.1796; inc. 1827.

Vancleave (van-KLEEV), uninc. town (1990 pop. 3,214), Jackson co., SE Miss., 14 mi/23 km NW of Pascagoula; 30°32′N 88°40′W. Agr. area (cotton, corn, pecans, honey); timber; catfish. Ward Bayou Wildlife Managment Area to E; Mississippi Sandhill Crane Natl. Wildlife Refuge to S.

Vancouver, city (1991 pop. 471,844), SW B.C., W Canada, on Burrard Inlet of the Strait of Georgia, opposite Vancouver Isl., and just N of the Wash. border; 49°15′N 123°08′W. It is the 3d-largest city in Canada, the largest city in W Canada, and the chief Can. Pacific port, with an excellent year-round harbor. It is also the major W terminus of trans-Can. RRs, highways, and airways. Its location on hills with views of the harbor and the mts. of the Coast Range as well as its mild winter climate make it a year-round tourist center. As Canada's main connection to other Pacific Rim countries, Vancouver has become increasingly ethnically diverse as large numbers of Chin., Jap., and E Indian migrants have settled in the city. Vancouver's Chinatown is 2d only to San Francisco's. The city's industries include lumbering, ship construction, fish processing; sugar- and oil refining; banking and financial services. Tourism. It has textile and knitting mills; plants making metal, wood, paper, and mineral prods. Vancouver is the W terminus of a pipeline bringing oil to the W coast from Edmonton, Alta. At Point Grey in metropolitan Vancouver is the Univ. of B.C. Also, Simon Fraser Univ., and the B.C. Inst. of Technology are in the city. Stanley Park (900 acres/364 ha), one of the city's many parks, has a zoo and famous gardens and specimens of native trees. An internatl. exposition devoted to transportation, Expo '86, brought internatl. recognition and 20 million visitors to the city. The city was settled before 1875 and called Granville; it was inc. 1886, after a RR link was built, and named in honor of Capt. George Vancouver.

Vancouver, city (1990 pop. 46,380), ⊙ Clark co., SW Wash., on the Columbia R. opposite Portland, Oregon, 7 mi/11.3 km N of downtown Portland, with which it is connected by bridges (2 highway, 1 RR); 45°38′N 122°38′W. Rapidly growing suburb of Portland. An important deepwater port, it has an extensive shipping industry, many lumber mills, and an enormous grain elevator. Power from the nearby Bonneville Dam supplies its industries. Mfg. (adhesives, wire drawing, sheet metal, industrial gases, audiovisual equip.; metal prods., wood trusses, printing and publishing, paper, electrical housewares, mining machinery, transportation equip., ship construction; truck trailers, cabinets, diapers, plastics, furniture, pallets, clothing, industrial valves). It was founded by the Hudson's Bay Company as Fort Vancouver in 1825–1826. After the area was ceded to the U.S. in 1846, the U.S. army established (1849) a fort here, which remains in operation. Clark Col. (2-year), art gallery, and sports stadium here. It is also the hq. for Gifford Pinchot Natl. Forest. Historic attractions include Fort Vancouver Natl. Historic Site in center of city; Covington House (1845), one of the oldest houses in the state; and the Ulysses S. Grant house and mus. Ridgefield Natl. Wildlife Refuge to NW; Battle Ground L. State Park to NE. Inc. 1857.

Vancouver, Cape, W Alaska, on Bering Sea, at N end of Etolin Strait, W extremity of Nelson Isl., opposite Nunivak Isl.; 60°37′N 165°14′W.

Vancouver Island (□ 12,408 sq mi/32,137 sq km; 1986 est. pop. 485,000), SW B.C., W Canada, in the Pacific Ocean; largest isl. off W N. Amer.; c.285 mi/460 km long and c.30 mi/50 km–80 mi/130 km wide; separated from the mainland by Queen Charlotte, Georgia, and Juan de Fuca straits. The rugged isl., a partially submerged portion of the Coast Mts., rises to 7,219 ft/2,200 m at Golden Hinde Mt. Level plains extend inland from the E coastline. The Pacific coastline is deeply indented by numerous fjords and inlets. The isl. has a mild humid climate; W Vancouver Isl. receives the greatest amount of precipitation in N. Amer. There are many lakes and streams but no navigable rivers. The isl. is heavily forested; lumbering and wood processing are major industries. Vancouver Isl. is underlaid by a mineral-rich batholith, from which iron, copper, and gold are mined. Coal is extracted from a depression at the edge of the batholith; the mines at Nanaimo provide most of the coal for B.C. Fishing, agr., and tourism are other important economic activities. Pacific Rim Natl. Park, Fort Rodd Hill Natl. Historic Park, and Strathcona Provincial Park are here. Pop. is concentrated along the E coast; VICTORIA (the provincial capital), Nanaimo, Port Alberni, and Esquimalt (site of a large naval base) are the largest cities. There are many small ports and fishing settlements. Both Spain and Britain claimed the isl.; it was sighted (1774) by Juan Pérez, the Span. explorer, and Capt. James Cook was the 1st (1778) to land here. In 1788, John Meares, an Eng. trader, built a fort on NOOTKA SOUND, which was later occupied by Span. forces. In 1792, the isl. was circumnavigated and chartered by Capt. George Vancouver. Br. sovereignty over Vancouver was confirmed (1846) when the U.S.–Can. border was drawn through Juan de Fuca Strait by the Oregon Treaty. Vancouver Isl. was made a crown colony in 1849, and in 1866 became part of B.C.

Vancouver, Mount (15,700 ft/4,785 m), on Yukon-Alaska border, in St. Elias Mts., 160 mi/257 km W of Whitehorse, on SE edge of Seward Glacier; 60°20′N 139°41′W.

Vandalia 1 (van-DAIL-yah), city (1990 pop. 6,114), Fayette co., S central Ill., on Kaskaskia R., and 29 mi/47 km N of Centralia; 38°58′N 89°05′W. In agr. and oil-producing area; corn, wheat, sorghum, soybeans; poultry; cattle; dairy prods. Mfg. (telephone booths; rubber and plastics prods.). Was 2d capital of Ill. (1820–1839). Lincoln and Douglas served in legislature here. Points of interest include old capitol (Vandalia State House State Historic Site; 1836), preserved as state memorial; old Presbyterian church; Lincoln collection in lib. State penal farm is nearby. W terminus of historic Natl. Road. Inc. 1821. **2** city (1990 pop. 2,683), Audrain co., NE central Mo., 23 mi/37 km ENE of Mexico; 39°18′N 91°29′W. Corn, soybeans, wheat; cattle, hogs; mfg. (refractory or fire bricks; plastic bricks; apparel, aluminum windows and doors; dresses); coal. Inc. 1874. **3** (van-DAI-lyuh), city (1990 pop. 13,882), Montgomery co., W central Ohio, a suburb of Dayton; 39°52′N 84°11′W. Motor vehicle parts are among the city's manufactures (chassis systems). Natl. skeet-shooting competitions. Inc. 1848.

Vandalia (van-DAI-lee-uh), village (1990 pop. 357), Cass co., SW Mich., 5 mi/8 km E of Cassopolis, on N side of Donnell L.; 41°55′N 85°54′W. In farm area. Swiss Valley Ski Area to E.

Vandemere (VAN-duh-mir), village (1990 pop. 299), Pamlico co., E N.C., 22 mi/35 km ENE of New Bern, on Bay R. inlet of Pamlico Sound; 35°11′N 76°39′W. Fish, crabs, shrimp.

Vandenberg Air Force Base, U.S. military installation, (□ 5.4 sq mi/14 sq km; 1990 pop. 9,846), Santa Barbara co., SW Calif., NW of Lompoc, and near Pacific Ocean coast; 34°45′N 120°31′W. Chief Pacific coast launch site for military satellites. It has an Intercontinental Ballistic Missile (ICBM) range.

Vandenberg Village, uninc. town (1990 pop. 5,971), Santa Barbara co., SW Calif., residential community 4 mi/6.4 km N of Lompoc; 34°43′N 120°28′W. Grain, fruit, nuts; dairying; cattle. Vandenberg Air Force Base to W.

Vander (VAN-duhr), uninc. town (1990 pop. 1,179), Cumberland co., S central N.C., residential suburb, 6 mi/9.7 km E of downtown Fayetteville; 35°02′N 78°47′W.

Vanderbilt, village (1990 pop. 605), Otsego co., N Mich., 21 mi/34 km SE of Petoskey; 45°08′N 84°39′W. In recreation area. Mfg. (motor vehicle parts, metal tubing).

Vanderbilt (VAN-duhr-bilt), borough (1990 pop. 545), Fayette co., SW Pa., 4 mi/6.4 km WNW of Connellsburg, near Youghiogheny R.; 40°01′N 79°39′W. Agr. (corn, hay; livestock; dairying).

Vanderbilt, uninc. village (1990 pop. 667), Jackson co., S Texas, 21 mi/34 km E of Victoria, near confluence of Lavaca and Navidad rivers. Oil and natural gas. Cattle; rice, cotton. Mfg. (oil and gas processing). Lavaca Bay, arm of Gulf of Mexico, to S. L. Texana to NE.

Vanderbilt Mansion, historic site, Dutchess co., E N.Y., on E shore of Hudson R., 8 mi/12.9 km NNW of Poughkeepsie; 41°48′N 73°56′W. A neglected 600-acre/243-ha estate known as Hyde Park when it was bought in 1895 by Frederick Vanderbilt, the publicity-shy grandson of Cornelius Vanderbilt and son of William Vanderbilt (both the richest men in Amer. during their lifetimes). Frederick and his wife Louise were drawn here by the beauty of the Hudson Valley, with views of the Shawangunk and Catskill Mts. to the W and ready access to N.Y. city on the Vanderbilts' own N.Y. Central RR. Like many of their wealthy neighbors, the Vanderbilts spent only a few weeks a year here. After Louise Vanderbilt died in 1926, Frederick lived here until his death in 1938. His niece Margaret Van Alen donated 211 acres/85 ha (including the Victorian-style mansion) as a natl. monument in 1940. Site is representative of both the lifestyle of the wealthiest Amer. *nouveau riche* and of the glamorous era that went along with it.

Vanderburgh, county (□ 235 sq mi/609 sq km; 1990 pop. 165,058), SW Ind.; ⊙ EVANSVILLE; 38°01′N 87°35′W. Bounded S by Ohio R., here forming Ky. state line; drained by small Pigeon Creek. Agr. (wheat, soybeans, corn); bituminous-coal mining. Extensive mfg. at Evansville; shipping and industrial center for SW Ind. Angel Mounds State Memorial in SE corner. Formed 1818.

Vandercook Lake, village (1990 pop. 4,642), Jackson co., S Mich., suburb 4 mi/6.4 km S of Jackson, on Kalamazoo R.; 42°11′N 84°23′W. Jackson Community Col. and Mich. Space Center to S.

Vandergrift (VAN-duhr-grift), borough (1990 pop. 5,904), Westmoreland co., W central Pa., 24 mi/39 km NE of Pittsburgh, on Kiskiminetas R.; 40°36′N 79°34′W. Mfg. (stainless steel; machinery; printing and publishing, food prods.); bituminous coal. Agr. (soybeans, grain; livestock; dairying). Laid out 1895, inc. 1897.

Vanderhoof, village (1991 pop. 4,023), central B.C., W Canada, on Nechako R., and 50 mi/80 km W of Prince George; 54°01′N 124°00′W. Cattle-shipping center; distributing point for the Nechako valley mixed-farming area; dairying.

Vandiver (van-DEI-vuhr), village, Shelby co., central Ala., 17 mi/27 km E of Birmingham.

Vandling, borough (1990 pop. 660), Lackawanna co., NE Pa., 19 mi/31 km NNE of Scranton, and 1 mi/1.6 km S of Forest City, on the Lackawanna R.; 41°37′N 75°28′W. Former anthracite-coal area.

Vanduser (VAN-doo-zuhr), town (1990 pop. 187), Scott co., SE Mo., in Mississippi alluvial plain, 15 mi/24 km SSW of Benton; 36°59′N 89°41′W.

Vanegas (VAHN-e-gahs), town (1990 pop. 2,688), San Luis Potosí, N central Mexico, on interior plateau, 25 mi/40 km NW of Matehuala; 23°54′N 100°58′W. RR junction; cereals, maguey. Silver, gold, and copper deposits nearby.

Vanguard, village (1991 pop. 249), S Sask., W Canada, on Noteken Creek, and 35 mi/56 km SE of Swift Current; 49°54′N 107°18′W. Wheat; livestock.

Vanier 1 or **Ville-de-Vanier**, city (1991 pop. 10,833), S central Que., E Canada, suburb 2 mi/3 km W of Quebec city, on St. Charles R. Mfg. (shoes, prepared meats, flat glass, electrical instruments). **2** city (1991 pop. 18,150), SE Ont., central Canada, at the confluence of the Rideau and Ottawa rivers. It is an industrial suburb of Ottawa.

Vankleek Hill (van-KLEEK), town (1991 pop. 2,062), SE Ont., central Canada, 50 mi/80 km E of Ottawa; 45°31′N 74°39′W. Lumbering, pump mfg.; dairying.

Vanleer, town (1990 pop. 369), Dickson co., N central Tenn., 40 mi/64 km W of Nashville; 36°14′N 87°27′W. In timber and farm area.

Vanlue (VAN-loo), village (1990 pop. 373), Hancock co., NW Ohio, 9 mi/14 km ESE of Findlay; 40°58′N 83°29′W. In agr. region.

Vanna (VAN-uh), town, Hart co., NE Ga., 11 mi/18 km NE of Hartwell; 34°14′N 83°04′W.

Vanport, township (1990 pop. 1,700), Beaver co., W Pa., residential suburb, 2 mi/3.2 km WSW of Beaver on Ohio R.; 40°41′N 80°19′W. Agr. (dairying; livestock). Includes village of Vanport.

Vanport City, village, NW Oregon, just N of Portland, on the Columbia R. opposite Vancouver, Wash. Built 1942–1943 to house shipyard workers (pop. of 42,000 during World War II); after 1945, it became a low-cost housing project. On May 30, 1948, the town was submerged when floodwaters breached the Columbia R. embankment, causing some loss of life and great destruction. Now part of Portland and referred to as North Portland.

Vansant, uninc. town, Buchanan co., SW Va., 35 mi/56 km NE of Norton, on Levisa Fork R.; 37°13′N 82°05′W. Mfg. (coal processing). Agr. (tobacco, potatoes; cattle); bituminous coal.

Vansittart Island (van-SI-tuhrt), SE Franklin dist., N.W.T., Canada, in Foxe Channel, just off S Melville Peninsula; 47 mi/76 km long, 6 mi/10 km–16 mi/26 km wide; 65°55′N 84°05′W.

Varadero (vahr-uh-DER-o), town, Matanzas prov., W Cuba, near base of Hicacos Peninsula, 22 mi/35 km ENE of Matanzas; 23°10′N 81°15′W. Popular seaside resort, has fine large beaches (Playa Varadero, Playa Azul) along peninsula. Fishing, boating; tourism. Juan Gualberto Gómez Internatl. Airport nearby SE of Varadero, just 6 mi/9.7 km E of Matanzas. Recent investment by Span. hotels. In 1995 had 8,000 hotel rooms, or 4 out of every 5 in Cuba. Labor supply drawn from nearby Cárdenas. Tollbooth added in 1996 just outside town.

Vardaman (VAHR-duh-muhn), town (1990 pop. 920), Calhoun co., N central Miss., 36 mi/58 km E of Grenada, near Yalobusha R.; 33°52′N 89°10′W. Agr. (cotton, corn, soybeans, sorghum; cattle; timber); mfg. (furniture).

Varennes (vah-REN), town (1991 pop. 14,758), S Que., E Canada, on the St. Lawrence, 14 mi/23 km NNE of Montreal; 45°41′N 73°26′W. Agr.; dairying; mineral springs.

Vargas Island (VAHR-guhs) (□ 11 sq mi/28 sq km), SW B.C., W Canada, in Clayoquot Sound off W Vancouver Isl., 50 mi/80 km W of Port Alberni, 5 mi/8 km long, 2 mi/3 km–5 mi/8 km wide. Yarksis Indian village is in E.

Varina 1 (vuh-REIN-uh), town (1990 pop. 102), Pocahontas co., N central Iowa, 12 mi/19 km SSW of Pocahontas; 42°39′N 94°54′W. **2** uninc. town, Henrico co., E central Va., suburb 6 mi/9.7 km SSE of Richmond, near James R. (Varina-Enon Bridge to S). Richmond Natl. Battlefield Park and Cemetery to SW, Presquile Natl. Wildlife Refuge to SE.

Varna (VAHR-nuh), village (1990 pop. 405), Marshall co., N central Ill., 10 mi/16 km E of Lacon; 41°02′N 89°13′W. In agr. area (corn, soybeans; cattle).

Varnado (VAHR-nuh-do), village (1990 pop. 236), Washington parish, SE La., 7 mi/11 km N of Bogalusa, near Pearl R.; 30°54′N 89°50′W. In timber and agr. area.

Varnamtown (VAHR-nuhm-toun), village (1990 pop. 404), Brunswick co., SE N.C., 28 mi/45 km SW of Wilmington, on Lockwood Folly Inlet, arm of Atlantic Ocean; 33°56′N 78°14′W. Intracoastal Waterway canal passes to S and crosses inlet entrance. Fishing.

Varnell (vahr-NEL), town (1990 pop. 358), Whitfield co., N Ga., 10 mi/16 km N of Dalton; 34°54′N 84°58′W. Mfg. of carpeting.

Varner, village, Lincoln co., SE Ark., 25 mi/40 km ESE of Pine Bluff near Arkansas R. In agr. area. Cummins Correctional Unit to NE.

Varnville, town (1990 pop. 1,970), Hampton co., SW S.C., just SE of Hampton; 32°51′N 81°04′W. Mfg. includes lumber, machining, plastic production; agr. includes livestock; grain, soybeans, peanuts, cotton, watermelons, peaches.

Vascus Point (VAS-kuhs), headland, S St. Croix Isl., U.S.V.I., 3 mi/4.8 km S of Christiansted; 17°42′N 64°43′W.

Vashon (VA-shahn), uninc. town (1990 pop. 1,000), King co., W Wash., in NE center of Vashon Isl., 11 mi/18 km SSW of Seattle, 13 mi/21 km N of Tacoma. Puget Sound 1 mi/1.6 km E.

Vashon Island (VA-shahn), King co., W Wash., in Puget Sound, just N of Tacoma; 13 mi/21 km long. Bounded E by Puget Sound and Quartermaster Harbor, on W by Colvos Passage, on S by Dalco Passage. Connected by narrow isthmus to Maury Isl., to SE. Includes villages of Burton and Vashon. Fresh flowers and vegetables, berries; poultry; dairying; light mfg. at Vashon village. Point Vashon at N end. Vashon Isl. Airport in N. Ferries from N to Seattle and Southworth, ferry from S to Tacoma.

Vasquez Mountains, Grand co., N central Colo., in Front Range; extend N-S bet. Williams and Fraser rivers; include part of Continental Divide; 39°47′N 105°51′W. Chief peaks are Byers Peak (12,804 ft/3,903 m) and Vasquez Peak (12,947 ft/3,946 m), c.45 mi/72 km W of Denver. Covered in part by Arapaho Natl. Forest.

Area in square miles is shown by the symbol □   capital city or county seat by ⊙

Vass (VAS), village (1990 pop. 670), Moore co., central N.C., 8 mi/12.9 km NE of Southern Pines, near source of Little R.; 35°15′N 79°16′W. Tobacco, grain; livestock. Mfg. (wood prods., apparel, meat prods.).

Vassalboro (VAS-uhl-buhr-o), town (1990 pop. 3,679), Kennebec co., SW Maine, on the Kennebec, 10 mi/16 km NNE of Augusta; 44°25′N 69°39′W. Settled c.1760, inc. 1771. Sometimes spelled Vassalborough.

Vassan (vah-SAHN), village (1991 pop. 1,013), W Que., E Canada, near L. la Motte, 11 mi/18 km NW of Val d'Or. Gold, molybdenum, bismuth mining.

Vassar, town (1990 pop. 2,559), Tuscola co., E Mich., 18 mi/29 km ESE of Saginaw, on Cass R.; 43°22′N 83°34′W. Major RR junction. Mfg. of iron castings; lumber; agr. (potatoes, sugar beets, grain, beans; poultry). Settled 1849, inc. 1871 as village, as city 1945.

Vauclin (vo-KLANG), town, SE Martinique, on the Atlantic, at E foot of Vauclin volcano, 15 mi/24 km ESE of Fort-de-France. In coffee and sugar region; fishing port and market town. Sometimes called Le Vauclin.

Vaucluse (vou-KLOOS), uninc. village, Aiken co., SW S.C., 6 mi/9.7 km NW of Aiken. Agr. includes cotton, grain; livestock. Early textile center.

Vaudreuil (vo-DROOL), county (□ 201 sq mi/521 sq km), S Que., E Canada, on Ont. border, and on Ottawa R.; ⊙ Vaudreuil; 45°25′N 74°10′W.

Vaudreuil, town (1991 pop. 11,187), ⊙ Vaudreuil co., S Que., E Canada, on S side of L. of the Two Mountains, 24 mi/39 km SW of Montreal; 45°24′N 74°02′W. Agr.; resort.

Vaughan (VAWN), uninc. village, Warren co., N N.C., 9 mi/14.5 km E of Warrenton. Timber; tobacco; livestock. Mfg. (lumber). L. Gaston reservoir to N.

Vaughn (VAWN), town (1990 est. pop. 2,000), Cascade co., W central Mont., 11 mi/18 km WNW of Great Falls, on Muddy Creek near its confluence with Sun R. Cattle, sheep; dairying; wheat, barley, oats, potatoes, hay. Ulm Pishkun State Park to S.

Vaughn (VAHN), village (1990 pop. 633), Guadalupe co., central N.Mex.; 34°36′N 105°12′W. Shipping point for sheep, cattle. RR junction. Settled 1905, inc. 1916.

Vaux, Mount (vo) (10,891 ft/3,320 m), SE B.C., W Canada, in Rocky Mts., in Yoho Natl. Park, 40 mi/64 km W of Banff.

Vauxhall (VAHKS-hol), town (1991 pop. 977), S Alta., W Canada, 40 mi/64 km NE of Lethbridge; 50°04′N 112°06′W. Wheat.

V. C. Bird, airport, Antigua, Antigua and Barbuda, West Indies, 5 mi/8 km E of St. John's on N coast of isl.; 17°08′N 61°41′W. Serviced by several internatl. and regional airlines.

V. C. Summer Nuclear Station, power plant, N central S.C., near Jenkinsville, and 20 mi/32 km NW of Columbia on Broad R. Went on-line 1983; capacity of 600,000 kw.

Veazie (VEE-zee), town (1990 pop. 1,633), Penobscot co., S Maine, on the Penobscot just above Bangor; 44°50′N 68°43′W. Maine's 1st RR built here, 1836.

Veblen, village (1990 pop. 321), Marshall co., NE S.Dak., 23 mi/37 km ENE of Britton; 45°51′N 97°17′W. Located in L. Traverse (Sisseton Wahpeton) Indian Reservation. Mfg. of cheese. Sica Hollow State Park to SE.

Vedder Crossing, village, SW B.C., W Canada, near Wash. border, 5 mi/8 km SSW of Chilliwack. Dairying; livestock; fruit, vegetables.

Veedersburg, town (1990 pop. 2,192), Fountain co., W Ind., on Coal Creek, 7 mi/11.3 km ESE of Covington; 40°07′N 87°16′W. Agr. (livestock; grain); mfg. (concrete, iron prods., motor vehicle parts); bituminous-coal area. Laid out 1872.

Vega, town (1990 pop. 840), ⊙ Oldham co., extreme N Texas, in plains of the Panhandle, 35 mi/56 km W of Amarillo; 35°15′N 102°25′W. Elev. 3,040 ft/927 m. In cattle and wheat and sorghum region. Oil and gas.

Vega Alta (VAI-gah AHL-tah), town (1990 pop. 34,559), N P.R., 14 mi/23 km WSW of San Juan. Mfg. and commercial industries. Mfg. (plastic and electric prods.; motor vehicle parts, pharmaceuticals). Stores, malls in area. Livestock. Vega Alta Forest Reserve nearby (W).

Vega Baja (VAI-gah BAH-hah), town (1990 pop. 55,997), N P.R., 17 mi/27 km W of San Juan. Industrial, commercial, tourism area. Industrial parks, stores, malls, residential area. Mfg. (electric parts, carpets, and furniture) nearby. Airport 3 mi/4.8 km NW. Popular beaches are nearby on the coast, tourism. Agr. (sugarcane, pineapple).

Vega de Alatorre (VAI-gah dai ah-lah-TO-re), town (1990 pop. 6,176), Veracruz, E Mexico, in Gulf lowland, 14 mi/23 km E of Misantla, on Mexico Highway 180; 20°02′N 96°40′W. Corn, coffee, tobacco.

Vega Real, La, Dominican Republic: see LA VEGA REAL.

Vegas, town, La Habana prov., W Cuba, on RR, near Natl. Highway, 37 mi/60 km SE of Havana; 22°48′N 81°49′W. Sugarcane, vegetables; cattle. Also called Las Vegas.

Vegreville (VEH-gruh-vil), town (1991 pop. 5,138), central Alta., W Canada, on Vermilion R., 60 mi/97 km E of Edmonton; 53°30′N 112°03′W. Distributing center for rich farming region; grain; dairying; mixed farming; livestock.

Veguitas (vai-GEE-tuhz), town, Granma prov., E Cuba, on Central Highway, and RR, 13 mi/21 km E of Manzanillo; 20°21′N 76°54′W. Vegetables, sugarcane, tobacco; fruit; cattle. Sugar mill Ranulfo Leyva 3 mi/4.8 km E.

Velarde (vuh-LAHR-dee), uninc. village (1990 pop. 950), Rio Arriba co., N N.Mex., on Rio Grande, just W of Sangre de Cristo Mts., 33 mi/53 km N of Santa Fe. Elev. 5,600 ft/1,707 m. Trading point for agr. area; fruit, chilies, alfalfa; cattle; mfg. (meat prods., minerals). Part of Santa Fe Natl. Forest to E and W, Carson Natl. Forest to N.

Velardeña (ve-lahr-DE-nyah), mining settlement (1990 pop. 2,978), Cuencame municipio, Durango, N Mexico, on RR, 40 mi/64 km SSW of Torreón; 20°54′N 103°44′W. Silver, gold, lead, copper mining.

Velasco, city, Brazoria co., S Texas, opposite Freeport at mouth of Brazos R. Now part of village of Surfside Beach. Settled in early 1820s; scene of battle (1832) bet. Texans and Mexicans, and signing (1836) of treaty ending Texas Revolution. Grew (esp. after 1940) in Freeport boom. Inc. after 1940.

Velasco, Cuba: see VELAZCO.

Velazco (vai-LAHZ-ko), town, Holguín prov., E Cuba, on RR, 14 mi/23 km NW of Holguín; 20°21′N 76°54′W. Sugarcane, tobacco, fruit; cattle. Also spelled Velasco.

Velda Village, town (1990 pop. 1,597), St. Louis co., E Mo., residential suburb 7 mi/11.3 km W of St. Louis; 38°41′N 90°17′W.

Velda Village Hills, village (1990 pop. 1,315), St. Louis co., E Mo., residential suburb 7 mi/11.3 km W of St. Louis; 38°41′N 90°17′W. Inc. since 1940.

Velma, village (1990 pop. 661), Stephens co., S Okla., 16 mi/26 km E of Duncan, near Wildhorse Creek; 34°27′N 97°40′W. Wheat; cattle; oil field.

Velva (VEL-vuh), town (1990 pop. 968), McHenry co., central N.Dak., 21 mi/34 km SE of Minot, and on Souris R. (Mouse R.); 48°03′N 100°55′W. Mfg. (food processing); lignite mines; diversified farming; grain; livestock. Laid out 1886, inc. 1905.

Venado (ve-NAH-do), town (1990 pop. 3,902), San Luis Potosí, N central Mexico, on interior plateau, 55 mi/89 km N of San Luis Potosí; 22°56′N 101°05′W. Agr. center (wheat, corn, beans, cotton). Agr. experiment station.

Venango (vuh-NANG-go), county (□ 683 sq mi/1,769 sq km; 1990 pop. 59,381), NW Pa.; ⊙ Franklin; 41°23′N 79°45′W. Oil-producing region drained by Allegheny R. Mfg. at Franklin and Oil City; sandstone, natural gas. Agr. (corn, hay, alfalfa; hogs, cattle; dairying). Oil City is its industrial center. Drake Well Memorial Park SE of Titusville (in N edge of co.) marks site of 1st successful oil well, 1859. Oil Creek State Park in NE; Clear Creek State Forest (Allegheny R. Tract) in SW. Formed 1800.

Venango, village (1990 pop. 192), Perkins co., S Nebr., 18 mi/29 km WSW of Grant, at Colo. state line; 40°45′N 102°02′W. Dried beans.

Venango (vuh-NANG-go), borough (1990 pop. 289), Crawford co., NW Pa., 10 mi/16 km N of Meadville, on French Creek; 41°46′N 80°06′W. Agr. (corn, hay; livestock; dairying).

Venedocia (ve-nuh-DO-shuh), village (1990 pop. 158), Van Wert co., W Ohio, 8 mi/13 km SE of Van Wert, near Little Auglaize R.; 40°47′N 84°27′W.

Venedy (VEN-e-dee), village (1990 pop. 158), Washington co., SW Ill., 16 mi/26 km WNW of Nashville; 38°23′N 89°39′W. In agr. area (wheat, corn, soybeans, sorghum; hogs, poultry; dairying).

Veneta (vuh-NEET-uh), town (1990 pop. 2,519), Lane co., W Oregon, 13 mi/21 km W of Eugene, on Long Tom R., at head of Fern Ridge Reservoir; 44°02′N 123°20′W. Timber; dairying; livestock; grain, fruit, berries. Sawmill. Siuslaw Natl. Forest to W.

Venetian Village, uninc. town (1990 pop. 3,133), Lake co., NE Ill., residential suburb 43 mi/69 km NW of Chicago, 1 mi/1.6 km SW of Lindenhurst, on N side of Fourth L.; 42°23′N 88°02′W.

Venetie (VEE-ni-tei), village (1990 pop. 182), N central Alaska, on Chandalar R. at mouth of East Chandalar R., 60 mi/97 km NW of Fort Yukon; 67°00′N 146°24′W. In Venetie Indian Reservation.

Venezuela, sugar-mill village, Camagüey prov., E Cuba, 7 mi/11.3 km S of Ciego de Ávila; 21°44′N 78°48′W. Formerly called Stewart.

Veniaminof Crater (ve-NEE-ya-mi-nof), active volcano (7,075 ft/2,156 m), SW Alaska, on Alaska Peninsula, 40 mi/64 km WSW of Chignik; 56°12′N 159°22′W. Glaciers cover upper slopes.

Venice 1 resort city (□ 7 sq mi/18.1 sq km; 1990 pop. 16,922), Sarasota co., W central Fla., 18 mi/29 km S of Sarasota, on Gulf coast; 27°06′N 82°25′W. RR terminus; ships cucumbers. 2 city (1990 pop. 3,571), Madison co., SW Ill., on the Mississippi (bridged to St. Louis), suburb of St. Louis, N of East St. Louis; 38°40′N 90°10′W. Settled 1804, plotted 1841; inc. as village in 1873, as city in 1897.

Venice, village (1990 pop. 458), Plaquemines parish, extreme SE La., 65 mi/105 km SE of New Orleans; 29°16′N 89°21′W. In the delta; levees protecting W bank of the Mississippi end near here. Fur trapping; hunting; fishing. Ship repair. Oil and natural-gas fields. Terminus of State Highway 3, short road continues to Tidewater, 5 mi/8 km SSW. Embarkation point for visits to Breton Natl. Wildlife Refuge in Chandeleur Isls., to NE, and Delta Natl. Wildlife Refuge to SE. Pointe a Loutre State Wildlife Area also to SE. Also called Jump.

Venice, suburban section of Los Angeles, Los Angeles co., S Calif., 12 mi/19 km WSW of downtown, along Santa Monica Bay, just S of Santa Monica and W of Culver City. Residential and beach-resort area. Oil field (1930); oil refinery; mfg. (consumer goods, meat prods.). Venice City Beach (State Beach) and Marina del Rey boat harbor are here. Santa Monica State Beach adjacent to area. Annexed 1925 by Los Angeles.

Venta, La, Mexico: see LA VENTA.

Ventnor or **Ventnor City** (VENT-nuhr), resort city, Atlantic co., SE N.J., on Absecon Beach just SW of Atlantic City. It is a popular seaside resort adjacent to Atlantic City. Located on a 10-mi/16-km sandbar known as Absecon Beach, Ventnor City is residential and noted for its elaborate homes. Inc. 1903.

Ventura, county (□ 1,846 sq mi/4,781 sq km; 1990 pop. 669,016), S Calif.; ⊙ Ventura; 34°22′N 119°57′W. Bounded by Pacific Ocean on S. Mainly mountainous; chief agr. land is wide delta of Santa Clara R., here entering the Pacific Ocean. Also drained by Ventura and Santa Clara rivers. Agr. (avocados, broccoli, celery, lettuce, spinach, strawberries, citrus fruits, barley; flowers, nursery prods., apiary prods.; dairying). Oil and natural-gas fields, refineries; stone quarrying. Santa Paula, Ventura (San Buenaventura mission here), Oxnard, Fillmore are agr. processing, packing, and shipping centers. Includes Santa Barbara Isl. in Channel Islands c.30 mi/48 km S of coast, part of Channel Islands Natl. Park; Mt. Pinos (in N) is 8,831 ft/2,692 m and Pine Mt. (7,510 ft/2,289 m) in center; part of Los Padres Natl. Forest covers over half of N part of co., part of Leo Carillo State Beach in S, Emma Wood and McGrath state beaches in S, Point Mugu State Park in

S; part of Santa Monica Natl. Recreation Area in SE. Formed 1873.

Ventura, city (1990 pop. 92,575), ⊙ Ventura co., SW Calif., 57 mi/92 km WNW of downtown Los Angeles, and 7 mi/11.3 km NW of Oxnard, on the Pacific coast, near mouth of Santa Clara R. RR junction in a farm (citrus fruits, avocados, vegetables; flowers, nursery prods.; dairying) and oil region. Fruit and vegetable packing, petroleum production, sporting goods, and oil field services are the major industries. Tourism also contributes to the economy. Ventura has grown rapidly along with the southern California area, and its population almost doubled bet. 1970 and 1990. A mission called San Buenaventura (still the official name of the city) to W, founded by Junípero Serra in 1782, has been restored. The Ventura city hall is on the Natl. Register of Historic Places. In the city is Ventura Col. (2-year). Emma Wood State Beach is here; L. Casitas reservoir to NW. Inc. 1866.

Ventura, resort village (1990 pop. 590), Cerro Gordo co., N Iowa, near Clear L., and 13 mi/21 km W of Mason City; 43°07′N 93°27′W.

Venturia (ven-TUHR-ee-uh), village (1990 pop. 30), McIntosh co., S N.Dak., 9 mi/14.5 km WSW of Ashley, near S.Dak. state line; 46°00′N 99°32′W.

Venú, Dominican Republic: see VERAGUA.

Venus, town (1990 pop. 977), Johnson co., N central Texas, 25 mi/40 km SSE of Fort Worth; 32°25′N 97°05′W. In agr. area; mfg. (restaurant equip.).

Venustiano Carranza (ve-noos-tee-AH-no kah-RAHN-zah), city (1990 pop. 11,553) and township, Chiapas state, S Mexico, in Sierra Madre, 45 mi/72 km SE of Tuxtla Gutiérrez; 16°19′N 92°33′W. Cereals, sugarcane, tobacco, fruits; livestock. Tzotzil Maya–speaking pop. in rural areas. Until 1934, called San Bartolomé.

Venustiano Carranza 1 (ve-noos-tee-AH-no kah-RAHN-zah), town (1990 pop. 11,342), Michoacán state, central Mexico, S of L. Chapala on Mexico Highway 15; 19°43′N 103°41′W. Agr. center (cereals, vegetables, fruits; livestock). Formerly called San Pedro Caro. **2** town (1990 pop. 5,245), N Puebla state, Mexico, 14 mi/23 km W of Poza Rica, on the E slope of Sierra Madre Oriental in the San Marcos Cazones R. basin; 20°30′N 97°41′W. Hot, humid climate. Agr. (corn, beans, plantains, sugarcane, coffee, oranges, vanilla, chilis); cattle raising. In Totonac-Indian area.

Venustiano Carranza (ve-noos-tee-AH-no kah-RAHN-zah), delegación (1990 pop. 519,628), in the NE region of Distrito Federal, Mexico; 19°43′N 103°41′W.

Vera, village (1990 pop. 167), Washington co., NE Okla., 20 mi/32 km NNE of Tulsa, near Caney R.; 36°27′N 95°52′W. Trading point for farming and livestock-raising area.

Vera Cruz, town (1990 pop. 83), Wells co., E Ind., on the Wabash R., and 6 mi/9.7 km SE of Bluffton; 40°42′N 85°05′W. In agr. area. Ouabache State Park nearby to NW. Laid out 1848.

Veracruz (ve-RAH KROOZ), city (1990 pop. 303,152) and township, ⊙ Veracruz municipio, Veracruz state, E central Mexico, on the Gulf of Mexico, on Mexico Highways 140 and 180; 19°12′N 96°06′W. Commercial and industrial center of an important oil region, as well as a major tourist resort. Sulfur and potassium and rich oil and gas resources on Continental Shelf. Naval construction, iron and steel industry, food shipping, electric energy. Coastal trading. The city stands on a low, sandy plain surrounded by dunes and swamps, some of which have been reclaimed and are very fertile. In 1519 the Span. explorer Hernán Cortés landed near the site later chosen (1599) for the present city. The harbor is guarded by the fortress of San Juan de Ulúa. In 1847, U.S. troops under Gen. Winfield Scott landed at Veracruz to begin the major campaign of the Mexican War. In 1914 an incident involving U.S. sailors in Tampico led President Woodrow Wilson to land troops in Veracruz, where they remained for 6 months. Mexico later responded by severing diplomatic relations.

Veracruz-Llave (ve-rah-KROOZ–YAH-ve) [Span. = true cross], state (□ 27,759 sq mi/71,896 sq km; 1990 pop.

6,228,239), E central Mexico; 17°08′N 93°37′W; ⊙ XALAPA ENRÍQUEZ. Stretching c.430 mi/692 km along the Gulf of Mexico and reaching from 30 mi/48 km to 100 mi/161 km inland, Veracruz rises from a tropical coastal plain into the temperate valleys and highlands of the Sierra Madre Oriental. The state shares with neighboring PUEBLA the highest peak in Mexico, CITLALTÉPETL, or Orizaba. Most of central Veracruz is mountainous. The few navigable rivers are the Coatzacoalcos, Papaloapan, Pánuco, and Tamesí. The state is a leading natl. producer of coffee, sugarcane, corn, and rice, and produces a wide variety of other crops. Cattle raising is practiced in the semitropical and temperate zones. From the tropical forests come dyewoods and hardwoods, chicle, and rubber, and in the colder regions maguey, various cacti, and coniferous forests are found. The state's principal natural resource and dominant industry is oil. The mountains contain relatively unexploited deposits of gold, silver, iron, and coal. Veracruz ranks high in the production of foods and beverages, as well as chemical mfg. and metalworking. In anc. times the area was a hub of pre-Columbian civilizations, including the Olmecs, the Huastecs, and the Remojadas. Some groups were tributary to the Aztecs by the time Juan de Grijalva explored the coast in 1518. Veracruz became a state in 1824. Major cities include VERACRUZ, CÓRDOBA, COATZACOALCOS, and Xalapa Enríquez.

Veradale, uninc. town (1990 pop. 7,836), Spokane co., E Wash., suburb 9 mi/14.5 km E of downtown Spokane, on Spokane R.; 47°39′N 117°13′W. Mfg. (pesticides, light mfg.). Walk in the Wild Zoo to NW.

Veragua (ver-AH-gwah), village, Espaillat prov., N Dominican Republic, near coast, 27 mi/43 km ENE of Santiago. Agr. (cacao, rice, coffee). Formerly called Venú.

Verchères (ver-SHER), county (□ 199 sq mi/515 sq km), S Que., E Canada, on the St. Lawrence R., and on Richelieu R.; ⊙ Verchères; 45°45′N 73°15′W.

Verchères, village (1991 pop. 4,781), ⊙ Verchères co., S Que., E Canada, on the St. Lawrence R., and 20 mi/ 32 km NNE of Montreal; 45°46′N 73°21′W. Food processing, boatbuilding; resort. Opposite, in the St. Lawrence, is Verchères Isl. Fort Verchères was defended (1692) by Madeleine de Verchères against the Iroquois.

Verchères Island (8 mi/13 km long, 1 mi/2 km wide), S Que., E Canada, in the St. Lawrence R., 20 mi/32 km NE of Montreal.

Verda (VUHR-duh), town (1990 pop. 1,133), Harlan co., SE Ky., in the Cumberland Mts., 5 mi/8 km E of Harlan, on Clover Fork of Cumberland R. Bituminous coal; timber.

Verde (vuhr-DEE), river, c.190 mi/306 km long; rises in Yavapai co., central Ariz. NW of Prescott; flows N as intermittent stream, then E and S, past Cottonwood, Camp Verde, through Horseshoe L. and Bartlett reservoirs, joins Salt R. 23 mi/37 km ENE of Phoenix. The valley supported early Native Amer. civilizations and is dotted with ruins, such as those at Tuzigoot Natl. Monument. Bartlett and Horseshoe dams are on the Verde R. Receives East Verde R. 22 mi/35 km SSE of Camp Verde.

Verde, Río (VER-dai REE-o), c.175 mi/282 km long, Chihuahua state, NW Mexico; rises in Sierra Madre Occidental at Durango border; flows NW, joining Urique R. near Sinaloa border to form the Río Fuerte.

Verde, Río, c.120 mi/193 km long, San Luis Potosí state, N central and NE Mexico; 15°59′N 97°50′W; rises in Sierra Madre Oriental NE of San Luis Potosí; flows SE, past San Nicolás Tolentino and Río Verde city, to Santa María R. (headstream of the Pánuco) 15 mi/24 km E of Aquismón.

Verde, Río, 124 mi/200 km long, E central Mexico; rises E of San Luis Potosí in Sierra Alvarez; flows ESE past Ríoverde, through El Potosí National Park to join Santa María R. in Sierra Madre Oriental. Called Río San Nicolás in upper course.

Verde, Río, Mexico: see ATOYAC RIVER, Oaxaca state.

Verdel, village (1990 pop. 59), Knox co., NE Nebr., 30 mi/ 48 km NW of Creighton, and on Ponca Creek, near Missouri R.; 42°48′N 98°11′W.

Verden, village (1990 pop. 546), Grady co., central Okla., 8 mi/12.9 km WNW of Chickasha, and on Washita R.; 35°04′N 98°05′W. In agr. area; feeds.

Verdi (VER-dee), uninc. town (1990 pop. 1,140), Washoe co., W Nev., 8 mi/12.9 km W of Reno, at Calif. state line, in Sierra Nevada range. Mfg. (aerospace metal forgings). Toiyabe Natl. Forest to S; Tahoe Natl. Forest (Calif.) to W.

Verdigre (VER-di-gree), village (1990 pop. 607), Knox co., NE Nebr., 12 mi/19 km NW of Creighton, near Missouri R.; 42°36′N 98°02′W. Dairy and poultry prods.; livestock; grain.

Verdigris River, 351 mi/565 km long, in SE Kansas and NE Okla.; rises in E Chase co. in E central Kansas SW of Emporia; flows SSE, past Madison, through Toronto, and past Altoona, then S, past Neodesha, Independence, and Coffeyville, entering Okla. in Nowata co.; then through the large Oologah L. reservoir and joining Arkansas R. 5 mi/8 km NE of Muskogee. Drains farming and livestock-raising area. Gas and oil wells, and deposits of limestone, clay, and shale in river basin. Chief tributaries: Caney, Fall, and Elk rivers. Lower 20 mi/32 km are part of Arkansas river transportation system; barge port facilities W of Waggoner.

Verdon 1 village (1990 pop. 242), Richardson co., SE Nebr., 8 mi/12.9 km NW of Falls City, near Missouri R.; 40°08′N 95°42′W. Verdon L. State Recreation Area to W. **2** village (1990 pop. 7), Brown co., NE S.Dak., 25 mi/40 km SE of Aberdeen; 45°14′N 98°05′W.

Verdugo City, suburban sect. of Glendale city, Los Angeles co., S Calif., in foothills of San Gabriel Mts., c.10 mi/16 km N of downtown Los Angeles. Centered around Verdugo Park, Canada Blvd.

Verdun, (vuhr-DUHN), city (1991 pop. 61,307), S Que., E Canada, on the S shore of Montreal island, on the St. Lawrence R.; 45°27′N 73°34′W. Residential suburb of Montreal.

Verdun, W.Va.: see VERDUNVILLE.

Verdunville (VUHR-duhn-vil), uninc. town (1990 pop. 900), Logan co., SW W.Va., suburb 3 mi/4.8 km W of Logan. Bituminous coal. Chief Logan State Park to NE.

Vere Plain, S lowland region of Clarendon parish, S Jamaica, along mouth of Minho R., E continuation of St. Dorothy Plains; 17°50′N 77°17′W. In the irrigated area, sugarcane is largely cultivated. Formerly a parish with Alley as its capital.

Vereda Nueva (vai-RAI-duh noo-AI-vah), town, La Habana prov., W Cuba, 22 mi/35 km SW of Havana; 22°53′N 82°32′W. In agr. region (tobacco, sugarcane, vegetables).

Veregin, Canada: see VERIGIN.

Vergas (VUHR-guhs), village (1990 pop. 287), Otter Tail co., W Minn., 30 mi/48 km NNE of Fergus Falls, at N end of Long L.; 46°39′N 95°47′W. Agr. (dairying; poultry; grain, sugar beets). Mfg. (cellulose insulation). Numerous small lakes in area.

Vergennes (VUHR-ginz), city (1990 pop. 2,578), Addison co., W Vt., on Otter Creek, near L. Champlain, and 21 mi/34 km S of Burlington; 44°10′N 73°15′W. Trade center for dairying; resort region; mfg. (electronic equip.). Region disputed by claimants of N.H. and N.Y. grants before Amer. Revolution. Macdonough's fleet built here in War of 1812. Anc. Indian implements excavated here. Settled 1766; set off 1788; city inc. 1794.

Vergennes (VER-jens), village (1990 pop. 314), Jackson co., SW Ill., 9 mi/14.5 km N of Murphysboro; 37°53′N 89°20′W. In agr. region (wheat, soybeans, sorghum, corn).

Verigin or **Veregin** (VE-ruh-jin), agr. village (1991 pop. 126), E Sask., central Canada, 8 mi/13 km W of Kamsack.

Vermejo River (vuhr-MEE-ho), 60 mi/97 km long, NE N.Mex.; rises NW Colfax co. in Sangre de Cristo Mts. at Colo. state line; flows SE, past Dawson, to Canadian R., c.30 mi/48 km SSW of Raton.

Vermilion, county (□ 902 sq mi/2,336 sq km; 1990 pop. 88,257), E Ill., on Ind. state line (E); ⊙ Danville; 40°10′N 87°44′W. Drained by Vermilion and Little Vermilion rivers; include L. Vermilion and Kickapoo State

Park. Rich agr. area (corn, soybeans; dairy prods.; cattle, poultry); bituminous coal mining; food prods. Formed 1826.

Vermilion (VUHR-mil-yuhn), parish (□ 1,224 sq mi/3,170 sq km; 1990 pop. 50,055), S La.; ⊙ Abbeville; 29°58′N 92°07′W. On the Gulf of Mexico (S), and bounded partly N by Bayou Queue de Tortue, Mermentau R. and L. Arthur form extreme NW boundary, and bounded on SE by Vermilion Bay; drained by Vermilion R. Crossed at center (E-W) by Intracoastal Waterway. Southwest Pass separates SE corner from Marsh Isl. (Iberia parish). Large portion of parish composed of marsh. Agr. (home gardens, nursery crops, rice, sugarcane, soybeans, vegetables, cattle, horses, hogs, exotic fowl), crawfish, shrimp, crabs, alligators. Logging, rice milling, cotton ginning; mfg. apparel. Oil and gas wells. Contains White L., in swampy coastal area in SW; also a bird sanctuary. Part of Rockefeller State Refuge in SW corner; Paul J. Rainey State Refuge in SE corner. Formed 1844.

Vermilion, resort city (1990 pop. 11,127), Erie co., N Ohio, 10 mi/16 km WSW of Lorain, near mouth of Vermilion R. on L. Erie; 41°25′N 82°19′W. Makes lighting fixtures, food prods.; fisheries. Settled c.1808.

Vermilion (vuhr-MIL-yuhn), town (1991 pop. 3,891), E Alta., W Canada, near Sask. border, on Vermilion R., and 100 mi/161 km E of Edmonton; 53°21′N 110°51′W. Oil production and refining; dairying, logging; oats, wheat, rye, cattle.

Vermilion, village (1990 pop. 283), Edgar co., E Ill., 6 mi/9.7 km ESE of Paris; 39°34′N 87°35′W. In agr. area. Formerly Vermillion.

Vermilion Bay, village, NW Ont., central Canada, at N end of Eagle L., 25 mi/40 km W of Dryden; 49°51′N 93°23′W. Gold mining, lumbering. Airfield.

Vermilion Bay (VUHR-mil-yuhn), arm of the Gulf of Mexico in S La., 11 mi/18 km S of New Iberia, and at mouth of Vermilion R. (entering at NW); c.22 mi/35 km long NE-SW, 10 mi/16 km wide; 29°43′N, 91°58′W. Bounded on NE, NW, and SW by mainland, on SE by Marsh Isl. Southwest Passage connects it to Gulf in S. Partly cut off from Gulf by Marsh Isl.; separated from West Cote Blanche Bay (E) by Cypremort Point (State Park). Oil and natural gas fields.

Vermilion Iron Range (vuhr-MIL-yuhn), iron-mining district in St. Louis co., NE Minn., extends c. 20 mi/32 km W to E, from S shore of Vermilion L. to Ely, Mesabi Iron Range c. 10 mi/16 km to S, parallels Vermilion Range. Ore discovered (1865) by Eames brothers. The 1st shipment took place 1884, following gold rush that collapsed when assays failed to confirmed promised values. Iron ore is shipped to Two Harbors, on L. Superior. Chief mining points are Ely, Tower, and Soudan.

Vermilion Lake (vuhr-MIL-yuhn) (□ 59 sq mi/153 sq km), St. Louis co., NE Minn., c.15 mi/24 km W of Ely, at W end of Vermilion Iron Range, N and NW extremities of lake in Superior Natl. Forest; c.35 mi/56 km long, 8 mi/12.9 km wide. Elev. 1,359 ft/414 m. Fed from S by Pike R. Large Trout Lake to N, drains S into lake through short stream. Resort area. Has N outlet in Vermilion R; numerous isls., including large Pine Isl. in N (6 mi/9.7 km long, 2 mi/3.2 km wide), Ely Isl. in SE, and extremely irregular shoreline. Chippewa Indian Reservation and iron mines (Tower and Soudan) are on S shore. Lake includes 10-mi/16-km NW extension, including Wakemup Bay, connected by Oak Narrows and Wakemup Narrows in W. Soudan Underground Mine State Park on S shore. Vermilion L. Indian Reservation on peninsula (Echo Point) in S.

Vermilion, Lake, reservoir, Vermilion co., E Ill., in NE part of Danville city, on North Fork of Vermilion R.; 4 mi/6.4 km long; 40°09′N 87°39′W. Recreational area; residential development on S shore.

Vermilion Pass (5,376 ft/1,639 m), in Rocky Mts., on Alta.-B.C. border, W Canada, 22 mi/35 km W of Banff; 51°09′N 116°07′W. It was 1st crossed 1858 by Dr. Hector of the Palliser expedition.

Vermilion River 1 175 mi/282 km long, E Alta., W Canada; rises S of Vegreville; winds N and E, past Vegreville, through small Vermilion Lakes, to North Saskatchewan R. 30 mi/48 km NE of Vermilion. **2** 100 mi/161 km long, S central Que., E Canada; rises NNE of L. Toro; flows NE to St. Maurice R. 22 mi/35 km NW of La Tuque.

Vermilion River 1 (VUHR-mil-yuhn), c.75 mi/121 km long, E Ill.; formed by North and South branches in Livingston co.; flows generally NW, past Pontiac and Streator, to Illinois R. at Oglesby, opposite La Salle. **2** 30 mi/48 km long, E Ill. and W Ind., formed by Middle Fork and North Fork at Danville; flows E and SE, across Ind. state line, to the Wabash N of Cayuga. Middle Fork, c.85 mi/137 km long; rises in Ford co.; flows SE. North Fork, c.50 mi/80 km long; rises in Benton co., Ind.; flows SW into Ill., then S. Dam impounds L. Vermilion (4 mi/6.4 km long; resort) just N of Danville. South (or Salt) Fork, c.70 mi/113 km long; rises in Champaign co.; flows S, then ENE, to Middle Fork W of Danville. Middle Fork especially scenic. **3** c.72 mi/116 km long, S La.; formed by small streams S of Opelousas (St. Landry parish); flows S, past Lafayette and Abbeville, to Vermilion Bay. Navigable (shallow draft) for 49 mi/79 km above mouth; crossed by Intracoastal Waterway 1 mi/2 km N of its mouth. Shallow draft port 6 mi/10 km above mouth at Esther; 29°45′N, 92°09′W. Named after the red color of the river bluffs. **4** 45 mi/72 km long, in St. Louis co., NE Minn.; rises in Vermilion L., exits through Vermilion Dam from NW part of lake, 26 mi/42 km W of Ely; flows NNW, forming boundary of Kabetogama State Forest (W) and Superior Natl. Forest (E), turns to NNE into Superior Natl. Forest and enters Crane L. near Can. (Ont.) border. **5** c.30 mi/48 km long, N Ohio; rises near Greenwich; flows N, past Wakeman, to L. Erie near Vermilion. **6** c.40 mi/64 km long, SE Minn.; rises in SE Scott co., 28 mi/45 km SSW of Minneapolis; flows ENE past Farmington, Vermillion, and Hastings, 1st enters Mississippi R. through 2 mi/3.2 km long channel E of Hastings and 1 mi/1.6 km W of mouth of St. Croix R., then continues SE as a parallel stream (to SW of) Mississippi R., entering Mississippi through several channels in a complex system of lakes, isls., sloughs, and marshes; 47°57′N 92°28′W. Prairie Isl. Indian Reservation in area.

Vermilion Valley Dam, Calif.: see THOMAS A. EDISON LAKE.

Vermilion-on-the-Lake, village, Lorain co., N Ohio, on L. Erie, near Vermilion.

Vermillion, county (□ 259 sq mi/671 sq km; 1990 pop. 16,773), W Ind.; ⊙ Newport; 39°51′N 87°28′W. Bounded W by Ill. state line, E by Wabash R. Drained by Vermilion R. Bituminous-coal mining; soybeans, corn; cattle; timber. Some mfg. at Clinton and Cayuga. Ernie Pyle State Memorial at Dana. Wabash R. Ordnance Depot SW of Newport. Formed 1824.

Vermillion, city (1990 pop. 10,034), ⊙ Clay co., SE S.Dak., 50 mi/80 km SSW of Sioux Falls, near Missouri R., and on Vermillion R.; 42°46′N 96°55′W. Mfg. (high pressure washers, printing, brushes). Univ. of S.Dak. is here. Ft. Vermillion, a fur trading post, was built nearby in 1835. Clay County State Rec. Area to W. W.H. Over Mus.; Yankton Federal Prison Camp City was settled 1859, inc. 1873.

Vermillion 1 (vuhr-MIL-yuhn), village (1990 pop. 113), Marshall co., NE Kansas, 22 mi/35 km ESE of Marysville; 39°43′N 96°15′W. In grain area. **2** village (1990 pop. 510), Dakota co., SE Minn., 7 mi/11.3 km SW of Hastings, and 20 mi/32 km SSE of St. Paul on small affluent of Mississippi R.; 44°40′N 92°57′W. Agr. (grain; livestock, poultry).

Vermillion River, 45 mi/72 km long, E S.Dak.; East Fork, 55 mi/89 km long; rises in L. Whitewood, Kingsbury co., flows S; West Fork, 50 mi/80 km long; rises in Miner co.; flows S and E; 43°23′N 97°04′W. They join E of Parker. Vermillion R. flows S to Mo. R., S of Vermillion.

Vermont, [Fr. = green mountain], state (□ 9,615 sq mi/24,908 sq km land; 1995 est. pop. 584,771), NE U.S., in New England, admitted to the Union in 1791 as the 14th state; ⊙ MONTPELIER; 44°16′N 72°37′W. Vt. is bounded on the N by the Can. prov. of Que., on the E by N.H. (the Connecticut R. forms the state line), on the S by Mass., and on the W by N.Y. (L. Champlain constitutes more than ½ of this border). BURLINGTON is the largest city. The forested Green Mts. constitute the dominant physiographic feature of the state. There are 5 distinct regions in the state. Largest and most important are the Green Mts. proper, which extend down the center of the state from the Can. border to the Mass. state line, rising to Vt.'s highest peak in Mt. Mansfield (4,393 ft/1,339 m). The Taconic Mts., occupying the SW portion of the state, contain Vt.'s important marble deposits. The Champlain Lowland adjoins L. Champlain, and E of the Green Mts. and extending from the Can. border to somewhat below the middle of the state is the Vermont Piedmont, so called because of the hilly topography. The 5th region is the granite Northeast Highlands, which are isolated peaks or monadnocks not connected with the principal range. The rivers of Vt. (the only completely inland state of New England) flow either into the Connecticut R. or into L. Champlain. The Winooski rises E of the Green Mts. and cuts directly through them to L. Champlain. Grand Isle co., comprising several isls. and a peninsula jutting down into L. Champlain from Canada, is connected to Vt. proper by causeways. Vt. has a short summer and a humid, continental climate, with abundant rainfall and a growing season that varies from 120 days in the Connecticut valley to 150 in the L. Champlain region. Winter brings heavy snows, which usually cover the ground for at least 3 full months. With its rugged terrain, much of it still heavily wooded, Vt. has limited areas of arable land, but the state is well suited to grazing (the Justin Morgan breed of horses was developed here). Dairy farming traditionally has been dominant in agr., but its importance economically has diminished. Hay is the state's chief crop, and Vt. is famous for its maple syrup. The state's most valuable mineral resources are stone, sand and gravel, and talc. In RUTLAND and Proctor, industry was formerly based on the quarrying and finishing of marble, and at BARRE, the famous Vt. granite is quarried and processed. Machine and machine-tool mfg. is a major industry and computer electronics has become important. The textile industry, once important in Burlington, has generally declined, but the mfg. of computer components, food prods., pulp and paper, and plastics has helped to compensate for this loss. Cottage industries have long thrived in Vt., making a variety of prods. from knitwear to ice cream. Tourism is vitally important to the state economy. Every summer thousands of vacationers are drawn by the scenic mts. and the picturesque New England villages, while climbers attack the many accessible peaks and hikers take on the Long Trail that runs the length of the state along the Green Mt. ridge. In the winter thousands of skiers flock to the slopes at Mad River Glen, Bromley, Stowe, and elsewhere. The 1st European known to have entered the area that is now Vt. was Samuel de Champlain, who, after beginning the colonization of Que., journeyed S with a Huron war party in 1609 to the beautiful lake to which he gave his name. The French did not attempt any permanent settlement until 1666, when they built a fort and a shrine to Ste. Anne on the ISLE LA MOTTE in L. Champlain. However, this and later Fr. settlements were abandoned, and until well into the 18th cent. the region was something of a no-man's land. Fort Dummer, built (1724) by the English near the site of BRATTLEBORO, is considered the 1st permanent Eur. settlement in what is now Vt. However, Vt.'s history may be said to have begun in 1741, when Benning Wentworth became royal governor of N.H. According to his commission, N.H. extended W across the Merrimack R. until it met "with our [i.e., the king's] other Governments." Since the Eng. crown had never publicly proclaimed the E limits of the colony of N.Y., this vague description bred considerable confusion. Wentworth, assuming that N.Y.'s modified boundary with Conn. and Mass. (20 mi/32 km E of the Hudson R.) would be extended even farther N, made (1749) the 1st of the N.H. Grants — the township called Bennington — to a group that included his relatives and friends. However, N.Y. claimed that its boundary extended as far E as the Connecticut R., and Gov. George Clinton of N.Y. (father of Sir Henry Clinton) promptly informed Governor Wentworth that he had no authority to make such a grant. Wentworth thereupon suggested that the dispute bet. N.Y. and N.H. over control of Vt. be referred to the crown. The outbreak of the last of the Fr. and Indian Wars in 1754 briefly suspended interest in the area, but after the British captured Ticonderoga and Crown Point in 1759, Wentworth resumed granting land in the area of present Vt. In 1764 the Br. authorities upheld N.Y.'s territorial claim to Vt. N.Y. immediately tried to assert its jurisdiction—Wentworth's grants were declared void, and new grants (for the same lands) were issued by the N.Y. authorities. Those who held their lands from N.H. resisted, and a controversy, long in the making, now exploded. N.Y. and N.H. land speculators had most at stake, with the N.H. grantees, 1st on the scene, having the advantage. Regional pride among the New England settlers played a large part in creating resistance to N.Y. authority. Chief among the leaders of this resistance was Ethan Allen, who organized the Green Mountain Boys. N.Y. courts were forcibly broken up, and armed violence was directed against New Yorkers until the outbreak of the Amer. Revolution in 1775, when the British became the major threat. At the beginning of the Revolution, Ethan Allen and the Green Mountain Boys captured TICONDEROGA, and Seth Warner took CROWN POINT. In Jan. 1777, Vt. (as its citizens were soon calling the region) proclaimed itself an independent state at WESTMINSTER. Chiefly because of the opposition of N.Y., the Continental Congress refused to recognize Vt. as the 14th colony or state. The convention that met at WINDSOR in July reaffirmed Vt.'s independent status and adopted a constitution, notable chiefly because it was the 1st in the U.S. to provide for universal manhood suffrage. Thomas Chittenden was elected the 1st governor. The Green Mountain Boys under Seth Warner and John Stark made an important contribution to the Amer. cause with their victory at Bennington in Aug. 1777. Later, Ethan Allen and his brother Ira Allen, acting on their own, entered into devious negotiations with Br. agents, possibly with the intent of annexing Vt. to Canada. The talks were inconclusive and ended when the Americans finally triumphed at Yorktown in 1781. For 10 years Vt. remained an independent state, performing all the offices of a sovereign govt. (such as coining money, setting up post offices, naturalizing new citizens, and appointing ambassadors) and gradually becoming more and more independent. Not until 1791, after many delays and misunderstandings—and, most important, after the dispute with N.Y. was finally adjusted (1790) by payment of $30,000—did Vt. enter the Union. It was the 1st state to be admitted after the adoption of the Constitution by the 13 original states. In the next 2 decades Vt. had the greatest pop. increase in its history, from 85,425 in 1790 to 217,895 in 1810. As in the earliest days, most of the settlers migrated from S New England, and since the more desirable lands in the river valleys were soon taken up, many of them settled in the less hospitable hills. Although the Embargo Act of 1807 aided the development of many small mfg. establishments, it was bitterly opposed by Vt. for its disruption of the profitable trade with Canada. The War of 1812 was unpopular in Vt. as in the rest of New England, and during the war extensive smuggling across the Can. border occurred. Vt. was threatened by Br. invasion from Canada until the Americans, under Thomas Macdonough, won (1814) the battle of L. Champlain. Lacking an aristocracy of wealth, Vt. was the most democratic state in New England. Jeffersonian Democrats held control for most of the early 19th cent. Beginning in the 1820s political and social life in Vt. was considerably affected by the activities of those opposed to Freemasonry, and in the presidential election of 1832 Vt. was the only state carried by William Wirt, candidate of the Anti-Masonic Party. Anti-Masonry agitation was soon succeeded by even more vigorous efforts in behalf of another cause—the one against slavery. In the Mex.-Amer. War, which it viewed as an undertaking solely to increase slave territory, Vt. was apathetic, but no Northern state was more energetic in support of the Union cause in the Civil War, and Vermonters strongly favored Lincoln over Vt.-born Stephen Douglas. One of the most bizarre incidents of the war was the Confederate raid (1864) on SAINT ALBANS, a town which, after the war, also figured in the equally bizarre attempt of the Fenians to invade Canada in the cause of Irish independence. The economy of the state, meanwhile, was in the midst of a series of sharp dislocations. The rise of woolen mfg. in towns and villages during the early 19th cent. had created a demand for foodstuffs for the nonfarming pop. Consequently, commercial farming began to crowd out the subsistence farming that had predominated since the mid-18th cent. Grain and beef cattle became the chief market produce, but when the rapidly expanding W began to supply these commodities more cheaply and when wool textile mills began to spring up in S New England, Vt. turned to sheep raising. After the Civil War, however, the sheep industry, unable to withstand the competition of Western, Australian, and S. Amer. wool, began to diminish. The rural pop. declined as many farmers migrated westward or turned to the easier life of the cities; abandoned farms became a common sight. The transition to dairy farming in the 20 years following the war staved off a permanent decline in Vt.'s agr. Since the 1960s, Vt.'s economy has grown significantly as the tourist industry has boomed and with the attraction of high-technology computer facilities to the Burlington area. Vt.'s economic prosperity has conflicted in recent years with its concern for environmental issues. The state has tried to preserve its natural beauty, enacting strict laws regarding industrial pollution and the conservation of natural resources. Vt. is governed under a constitution adopted in 1793. The state legislature, called the general assembly, consists of a senate with 30 members and a house of representatives with 150 members, all elected to serve 2-year terms. The governor is elected for a 2-year term. Vt. sends 2 senators and 1 representative to the U.S. Congress, and has 3 electoral votes. Among Vt's institutions of higher education are Bennington Col., Middlebury Col., and the Univ. of Vt., at Burlington. Vt. has 14 cos.: ADDISON, BENNINGTON, CALEDONIA, CHITTENDEN, ESSEX, FRANKLIN, GRAND ISLE, LAMOILLE, ORANGE, ORLEANS, RUTLAND, WASHINGTON, WINDHAM, and WINDSOR.

Vermont, village (1990 pop. 806), Fulton co., W central Ill., 17 mi/27 km SW of Lewiston; 40°17'N 90°25'W. In agr. and bituminous-coal area. RR junction.

Vermont Yankee Nuclear Power Plant, Vt.: see WINDHAM, CO.

Vermontville, village (1990 pop. 776), Eaton co., S central Mich., 10 mi/16 km WNW of Charlotte, and on Thornapple R.; 42°37'N 85°01'W. In farm area. Mfg. (magnetic recording labels).

Vernal (VUHR-nul), town (1990 pop. 6,644), ⊙ Uintah co., NE Utah, on Ashley Creek, branch of Green R. 12 mi/19 km to SE, and 125 mi/201 km E of Salt Lake City; 40°27'N 109°32'W. Elev. 5,322 ft/1,622 m. Trade and processing center for ranching and agr. area; lumber; mfg. (oil drills, diamonds). Coal mines and petroleum nearby. Whiterocks State Fish Hatchery to W; Jones Hole Federal Fish Hatchery to NE. Dinosaur Natl. History Mus. here. Ashley Natl. Forest is N, in Uinta Mts.; Dinosaur Natl. Monument is 12 mi/19 km E; Ouray Natl. Wildlife Reserve to S; Red Fleet Reservoir and State Park to NE; Steinaker Reservoir and State Park to N; Flaming Gorge Dam Reservoir and Natl. Recreation Area 35 mi/56 km N; large Uintah and Ouray Indian Reservations to W and S. Settled 1878; inc. 1879. Known as Ashley Center until 1893.

Vernal Falls, Calif.: see YOSEMITE NATIONAL PARK.

Vernalis, uninc. village, San Joaquin co., central Calif., 10 mi/16 km SE of Tracy, near San Joaquin R. Fruit, avocados, vegetables, grain; dairying; cattle, poultry. Mfg. (metal cans, feeds). Durham Ferry State Recreation Area to N.

Verndale, village (1990 pop. 560), Wadena co., W central Minn., 7 mi/11.3 km SSE of Wadena, near Wing R.; 46°23'N 95°00'W. Agr. (dairying; poultry; oats, barley, rye). Mfg. (prefabricated homes). Lyons State Forest to NE.

Vernon, city (1991 pop. 23,514), S B.C., W Canada, near the N end of Okanagan L.; 50°16'N 119°16'W. The center of a fruit-growing and dairying area, it has packing and dehydrating plants. Lumber mills, sawmills, and food processing plants.

Vernon (VUHR-nuhn), parish (□ 1,360 sq mi/3,522 sq km; 1990 pop. 61,961), W La.; ⊙ Leesville; 31°08'N, 93°16'W. Bounded W by Sabine R., here forming Texas state line and Bayou Toro; drained by Calcasieu R. and Bayou Anacoco (part of S boundary). Includes part of Kisatchie Natl. Forest. Agr. (home gardens, sweet potatoes, watermelons; cattle, poultry, hogs; dairying). Logging. Lumber, apparel; sand and gravel. Named after George Washington's home, Mount Vernon. Fort Polk, U.S. Army base, is SE at center of parish. Part of Peason Ridge State Wildlife Area in N; Boise-Vernon State Wildlife Area and Anacoco Prairie State Game and Fish Preserve in W; large unit of Kisatchie Natl. Forest in SE. Formed 1871.

Vernon 1 county (□ 838 sq mi/2,170 sq km; 1990 pop. 19,041), W Mo.; ⊙ Nevada; 37°51'N 94°20'W. On Osage R. (N); drained by Little Osage and Marmaton rivers. Corn, wheat, soybeans, sorghum, hay, pecans; cattle, poultry; strip coal mines, oil wells. Mfg. at Nevada; Schell-Osage Conservation Area in NE corner. Formed 1851. **2** county (□ 816 sq mi/2,113 sq km; 1990 pop. 25,617), ⊙ Viroqua, SW Wis., bounded W by the Mississippi (here forming Iowa and Minn. state lines); 43°35'N 90°49'W. Drained by Kickapoo, Bad Axe, and Baraboo rivers. Dairying; barley, corn, alfalfa, hay; cattle, hogs, sheep, poultry; tobacco growing and processing. Wildcat Mt. State Park in NE; Upper Mississippi Wildlife and Fish Area and Blackhawk Recreation Area (Army Corps of Engineering) in SW; Lock and Dam No. 8 on Mississippi R. in W, at Genoa. Formed 1851.

Vernon, city (1990 pop. 12,001), ⊙ Wilbarger co., N Texas, on Pease R., near the Okla. state line (Red R.); 34°08'N 99°17'W. Elev. 1,205 ft/367 m. Agr. (cotton, wheat, alfalfa, cattle, hogs); mfg. (helicopters, oil soluble drilling muds, meat processing). Oil and gas. Vernon is hq. for the 500,000-acre/202,350-ha W. T. Waggoner Ranch. The city was founded in 1880 on the cattle trail to Dodge City; it has since become a highway center. Vernon Regional Jr. Col. is here. Inc. 1890. Town originally named Eagle Flats.

Vernon 1 town (1990 pop. 2,247), ⊙ Lamar co., W Ala., 48 mi/77 km NW of Tuscaloosa. Cotton ginning; mfg. (clothing, furniture, electric heating elements, waste-handling and recycling equip.). **2** town (1990 pop. 29,841), Tolland co., N Conn.; 41°50'N 72°27'W. Mfg. includes electronic components and silk screens. Vernon merged with Rockville in 1965 and is closely associated with the nearby towns of Ellington and Tolland in the greater Hartford area. Rockville General Hospital is largest employer. Settled c.1726, inc. 1808. **3** town (1990 pop. 370), ⊙ Jennings co., SE Ind., on small Vernon Fork, and 20 mi/32 km NW of Madison; 38°59'N 85°37'W. Agr. area. Crosley State Fish and Wildlife Area nearby to S. Laid out 1815. **4** town (1990 pop. 1,850), Windham co., extreme SE Vt., on the Connecticut R., just below Brattleboro; 42°45'N 72°31'W. Power dam and a state fish hatchery are here. Nuclear power plant.

Vernon 1 village (1990 pop. 152), Los Angeles co., S Calif., industrial suburb 2 mi/3.2 km S of downtown Los Angeles; 34°00'N 118°13'W. Meat packing (Union Stockyards). **2** village (1990 pop. 207), Marion co., S central Ill., 16 mi/26 km NNW of Salem; 38°47'N 89°05'W. In agr. area; ships pears, peaches. **3** village (1990 pop. 913), Shiawassee co., S central Mich., 8 mi/12.9 km SE of Owosso; 42°56'N 84°01'W. In farm area. **4** village (1990 pop. 1,274), Oneida co., central N.Y., 11 mi/18 km SSW of Rome; 43°04′N 75°32′W. Some mfg. **5** village (1990 pop. 181), Tooele co., W central Utah, 20 mi/32 km NW of Eureka; 40°05′N 112°27′W. Elev. 5,511 ft/1,680 m. Agr. (cattle; alfalfa, barley, wheat). Settled 1863. Onaqui Mts. to W; part of Wasatch Natl. Forest to S. Dugway Proving Grounds to W. Benmore Soil Conservation Project in area.

Vernon, township (1990 pop. 21,211), Sussex co., NW N.J., 5 mi/8 km E of Sussex; 41°12′N 74°28′W. Mfg. metal and machine parts. Vernon Valley–Great Gorge and Theme Park here. Inc. 1798.

Vernon Center, village (1990 pop. 339), Blue Earth co., S Minn., on Blue Earth R., and 16 mi/26 km SSW of Mankato; 43°57′N 94°10′W. In grain and livestock area. Mfg. (fertilizer).

Vernon Hills, village (1990 pop. 15,319), Lake co., NE Ill., suburb 30 mi/48 km NW of downtown Chicago, 7 mi/11.3 km W of Lake Forest, near Des Plaines R.; 42°14′N 87°57′W. RR junction; mfg. (tool and die, transmissions, bar-coding machines).

Vernonburg, town (1990 pop. 74), Chatham co., Ga., 5 mi/8 km S of Savannah; 31°58′N 81°07′W.

Vernonia (vuhr-O-nee-uh), town (1990 pop. 1,808), Columbia co., NW Oregon, on Nehalem R., at mouth of Rock Creek; 45°51′N 123°11′W. Dairy prods. Timber. Poultry. Tourism. Parts of Clatsop State Forest to W and NE; Tillamook State Forest to SW. Inc. 1891.

Vero Beach (VIR-ro), city (□ 12 sq mi/31 sq km; 1990 pop. 17,350), seat of Indian R. co., E central Fla., on Indian R. (a lagoon and part of the Intracoastal Waterway); 27°38′N 80°23′W. A fruit-producing center and a fishing resort, it also has diversified light mfg. Significant urban growth occurred in Vero Beach throughout the 1970s and 1980s. Main highway junction at intersection of Florida Turnpike and I-95. Founded c.1888, inc. 1919.

Verona 1 (vuh-RO-nuh), town (1990 pop. 515), Hancock co., S Maine, on Verona Isl. (□ c.6 sq mi/15.5 sq km), at mouth of Penobscot R., near Bucksport, and 16 mi/26 km W of Ellsworth; 44°31′N 68°46′W. **2** town (1990 pop. 2,893), Lee co., NE Miss., suburb 5 mi/8 km S of Tupelo; 34°11′N 88°43′W. In agr. area (cotton, corn, wheat, soybeans; poultry, cattle; dairying); mfg. (lawn mowers, office partitions, mattresses, polyurethane and polyester, bathroom fixtures, cordage, apparel, furniture). Natchez Trace (Natl.) Parkway passes to W. **3** town (1990 pop. 546), Lawrence co., SW Mo., in the Ozarks, and 5 mi/8 km W of Aurora; 36°57′N 93°47′W. Fruit, vegetables; dairying; mfg. (mold inhibitors for bakery prods.). **4** uninc. town, Augusta co., NW Va., suburb 5 mi/8 km NNE of Staunton, near Middle R.; 38°12′N 79°00′W. Mfg. (air-conditioning and heating units, razor blades); agr. (dairying; livestock; grain, apples, peaches). **5** town (1990 pop. 5,374), Dane co., S Wis., a suburb 10 mi/16 km SW of Madison; 42°59′N 89°32′W. In dairying region; mfg. (diffusers, registers; post frame bldgs., molded plastic parts, printing). Agr. research station to N; E terminus of Military Ridge State Trail.

Verona 1 village (1990 pop. 242), Grundy co., NE Ill., 12 mi/19 km SSW of Morris; 41°13′N 88°30′W. In agr. area. **2** village (1990 pop. 600), Oneida co., central N.Y., 16 mi/26 km W of Utica; 43°08′N 75°37′W. Agr. (dairy farming, field corn, hay and vegetables); site of Oneida Nation's Turning Stone Casino (□ 68,000 sq ft/6,317 sq m; opened in 1990), 1st legal gambling casino in N.Y. state in over a cent. Costing $10 million, it is one of the largest table game operations in the U.S., with 168 gaming tables. The casino is Oneida co.'s 2nd-largest employer; next door is a luxury hotel. Owned and operated by the Oneida, one of 70 tribes across the U.S. who are allowed to offer gambling under the Indian Gaming Act of 1988, which was designed to generate wealth on impoverished reservations. **3** village (1990 pop. 103), La Moure co., SE N.Dak., 11 mi/18 km E of La Moure; 46°22′N 98°04′W. **4** village (1990 pop. 472), on Preble-Montgomery co. line, W Ohio, 20 mi/32 km WNW of Dayton; 39°54′N 84°29′W. In agr. area.

Verona 1 borough (1990 pop. 13,597), Essex co., NE N.J., 7 mi/11.3 km NNW of Newark; 40°49′N 74°14′W. It is primarily residential. Inc. 1907. **2** borough (1990 pop. 3,260), Allegheny co., SW Pa., suburb 10 mi/16 km ENE of downtown Pittsburgh, on Allegheny R.; 40°30′N 79°50′W. Mfg. (machinery, heat exchange cleaning equip., pharmaceuticals, electrical conduits). Inc. 1871.

Verona Park, uninc. village, Calhoun co., S Mich., suburb 1 mi/1.6 km N of Battle Creek.

Verplanck, residential village (1990 pop. 1,650), Westchester co., SE N.Y., on E bank of the Hudson R., and 3 mi/4.8 km SW of Peekskill; 41°15′N 73°57′W. Brickyards once provided product for Old Croton Aqueduct.

Verrazano-Narrows Bridge, vehicular suspension bridge, N.Y. city, across the Narrows at the entrance to N.Y. Harbor, linking the boroughs of Brooklyn and Staten Isl.; 40°36′N 74°02′W. Designed by O. H. Ammann, the bridge was completed in 1964. It is the longest suspension bridge in the U.S., with a main span of 4,260 ft/1,298 m. There are 2 levels, each holding 6 traffic lanes.

Verret, Lake (vuh-REHT), W Assumption parish, SE La., 7 mi/11 km W of Napoleonville, in the Atachafalaya R. basin; c.10 mi/16 km long; 29°53′N 91°10′W. Fishing. Roughly parallels Belle R. to W. Channel connects it in S to Grassy L. and L. Palourde.

Verrettes (ve-RET), agr. town (1982 pop. 3,670), Artibonite dept., central Haiti, on Artibonite R., and 16 mi/26 km ESE of Saint-Marc; 19°03′N 72°28′W. Citrus fruit, coffee, rice; cattle.

Versailles (vuhr-SAILZ), city (1990 pop. 2,365), ⊙ Morgan co., central Mo., near L. of the Ozarks, 30 mi/48 km SE of Sedalia; 38°25′N 92°50′W. Wheat, corn, dairying; cattle, poultry; mfg. (lead pencils, hose couplings, satin apparel); timber; farm trade. Founded c.1835.

Versailles 1 (vuhr-SAILZ), town (1990 pop. 1,791), ⊙ Ripley co., SE Ind., 22 mi/35 km SE of Greensburg; 39°04′N 85°16′W. In agr. area; mfg. (industrial fasteners); limestone quarries. Versailles State Park nearby to E. Laid out 1819. **2** town (1990 pop. 7,269), ⊙ Woodford co., central Ky., 13 mi/21 km W of Lexington, and 12 mi/19 km SE of Frankfort; 38°02′N 84°43′W. RR terminus. In Bluegrass agr. region (burley tobacco, bluegrass seed, grain; livestock, esp. horses); mfg. (plastic tubing, steel frame cutting, power distribution transformers, fluorescent lamps, book printing, signs, electronics, auto windshields, air conditioner hoses). Nearby are Pisgah Presbyterian Church (est. 1784) and "Woodburn" and other noted Bluegrass horse farms. Nostalgia Station Toy and Train Mus. Buckley Wildlife Sanctuary to NW. Bluegrass Scenic RR and Mus. County Historical Society Mus. Founded 1792.

Versailles 1 village (1990 pop. 480), Brown co., W Ill., near Illinois R., 9 mi/14.5 km SE of Mt. Sterling; 39°52′N 90°39′W. In agr. area. **2** village (1990 pop. 2,351), Darke co., W Ohio, 11 mi/18 km NE of Greenville; 40°13′N 84°29′W. In agr. area (poultry; grain, fruit, tobacco, vegetables). Settled 1819, inc. 1855.

Versailles, borough (1990 pop. 1,821), Allegheny co., SW Pa., residential suburb 12 mi/19 km SE of downtown Pittsburgh, and 2 mi/3.2 km S of McKeesport, on Youghiogheny R.; 40°19′N 79°49′W. Inc. 1892.

Versailles, Conn.: see SPRAGUE.

Versalles (ver-SEI-yais), N residential section of Matanzas, in SW corner of Matanzas Bay, Matanzas prov., W Cuba; 23°05′N 81°33′W.

Vershire (VUHR-shir), town (1990 pop. 560), Orange co., E Vt., on Ompompanoosuc R., and 7 mi/11.3 km W of Chelsea; 43°57′N 72°19′W. Abandoned copper mines here produced heavily in late 19th cent.

Verte, Île (VERT, eel) or **Green Island**, in the St. Lawrence, SE Que., E Canada, 12 mi/19 km NNE of Rivière du Loup; 8 mi/13 km long, 1 mi/2 km wide; 48°02′N 69°26′W.

Vertientes (ver-tee-AIN-taiz), site of sugar-mill Panamá, Camagüey prov., E Cuba, 18 mi/29 km WSW of Camagüey; 21°15′N 78°10′W.

Vesta, village (1990 pop. 302), Redwood co., SW Minn., on Redwood R., and 15 mi/24 km W of Redwood Falls; 44°30′N 95°24′W. Agr. (grain, soybeans; livestock, poultry; dairying). Mfg. (Western tack, feeds).

Vestaburg (VES-tah-buhrg), uninc. town (1990 pop. 1,200), East Bethlehem township, Washington co., SW Pa., 17 mi/27 km SE of Washington on Monongahela R.; 40°00′N 79°59′W. Agr. (apples, corn; livestock; dairying).

Vestal, village (1990 pop. 5,000), Broome co., S N.Y., on the Susquehanna R., opposite Endicott, and 7 mi/11.3 km W of Binghamton; 42°02′N 76°01′W. Prominent retailing here and E to Johnson City–Binghamton area.

Vestavia Hills (ves-TAI-vee-uh), suburb (1990 pop. 19,749), Jefferson co., N central Ala., suburb S of Birmingham; 33°26′N 86°47′W.

Vetagrande (ve-tah-GRAHN-dai), town (1990 pop. 976), ⊙ Vetagrande municipio, Zacatecas, N central Mexico, on interior plateau, 5 mi/8 km N of Zacatecas; 22°50′N 102°33′W. Elev. 8,386 ft/2,556 m. Silver mining; lead and copper deposits; maguey, cereals, livestock.

Veteran, village (1991 pop. 297), SE Alta., W Canada, 60 mi/97 km S of Wainwright; 52°01′N 111°07′W. Grain, mixed farming, dairying.

Vevay (VEE-vee), town (1990 pop. 1,393), ⊙ Switzerland co., SE Ind., on the Ohio, and 17 mi/27 km E of Madison; 38°44′N 85°04′W. Agr. (cattle; hay, tobacco; dairy prods.); mfg. (footwear, painting of motor vehicle and appliance trim). Historic community (architecture). Edward Eggleston was b. here. Settled 1802 by Swiss; laid out 1813.

Vian (vei-AN), town (1990 pop. 1,414), Sequoyah co., E Okla., 12 mi/19 km WNW of Sallisaw; 35°30′N 94°58′W. In agr. and recreation area (corn, soybeans). Tenkiller Reservoir and State Park is NW and Robert S. Kerr L. (Arkansas R.) is just S; Sequoyah Natl. Wildlife Refuge to S on L. Kerr. Cherokee Court House to W.

Vibank (VI bangk), village (1991 pop. 375), S Sask., W Canada, 30 mi/48 km ESE of Regina. Wheat.

Vibbard (VIB-buhrd), uninc. rural community, Ray co., NW Mo., 11 mi/18 km NW of Richmond.

Viborg, town (1990 pop. 763), Turner co., SE S.Dak., 16 mi/26 km S of Parker; 43°10′N 97°04′W.

Viburnum, town, Iron co., Mo., 60 mi/97 km SW of St. Louis in a unit of the Mark Twain Natl. Forest. Located in the "New Lead Belt," discovered in 1955; 90% of U.S. lead mined here.

Vicco (VEI-ko), village (1990 pop. 244), Perry co., SE Ky., in Cumberland foothills, 8 mi/12.9 km ESE of Hazard, on Carr Fork of Kentucky R.; 37°13′N 83°03′W. Tobacco; bituminous coal. Carr Fork L. reservoir to E.

Vicente Guerrero (vee-sen-tai ge-RE-ro), city (1990 pop. 13,346) and township, Durango, N Mexico, on RR, and 50 mi/80 km SE of Victoria de Durango and off Mexico Highway 45; 23°43′N 104°00′W. Elev. 6,299 ft/1,920 m. Agr. center (corn, wheat, sugarcane, cotton, tobacco, vegetables, fruit). Elev. 6,398 ft/1,950 m. Formerly Muleros. Sometimes Villa Vicente Guerrero.

Vicente Noble (vee-SEN-tai NO blai) or **Noble**, town (1996 pop. 9,896), Barahona prov., SW Dominican Republic, near the Yaque del Sur, 12 mi/19 km N of Barahona; 18°23′N 71°05′W. Agr. (sugarcane, coffee, hardwood). Until 1943, Alpargatal.

Vicente, Point, Los Angeles co., S Calif., promontory, on Palos Verdes peninsula, 11 mi/18 km W of Long Beach at Rancho Palos Verdes, on Pacific Ocean. Lighthouse.

Viceroy, village (1991 pop. 64), S Sask., W Canada, near Willowbunch L., 30 mi/48 km ESE of Assiniboia, in coal-mining region. Wheat.

Vici (VEI-sei), town (1990 pop. 751), Dewey co., W Okla., 21 mi/34 km SSE of Woodward; 36°08′N 99°17′W. In agr. and cattle-raising area; oil and natural-gas fields; mfg. (inorganic chemicals).

Vicksburg, city (1990 pop. 20,908), ⊙ Warren co., W Miss., 40 mi/64 km WNW of Jackson, much of it on a bluff overlooking the Mississippi R. (bridged to La.) at the mouth of the Yazoo R.; 32°19′N 90°52′W. Downtown faces Yazoo R., formerly the main channel of Mississippi R. RR junction. An important port, it is the commercial, processing, and shipping center for a cotton, timber, and livestock area. Diversified mfg. (asphalt and lumber prods., fuels, apparel, mobile homes, concrete and metal prods., petroleum refining, lime and gravel processing, plastic bottles, heating equip., poultry and paper processing, rubber powders, tubing and pipes, fertilizers). There was a Fr. fort near here in the early 18th cent., and the Spanish established Fort Nogales in 1791. The area came into U.S. possession in 1798. Vicksburg became a busy river port, and in the Civil War it was a major objective in Grant's Vicksburg Campaign. The city fell July 4, 1863, after 14 months of naval shelling, 7 months of land assault, and 47 days of total siege. River traffic, which fell off greatly in the late 19th and early 20th cent., has been aided by the U.S. Mississippi R. Commission, whose hq. are at Vicksburg. To SE is the U.S. Waterways Experiment Station. Antebellum homes are in the city and the surrounding area. Sections of the city were flooded in April 1973. In Vicksburg Natl. Military Park N and E of downtown are Confederate and Union trenches and fortifications of the Civil War siege and battles; also Vicksburg Natl. Cemetery. N of the city is a natl. cemetery containing Civil War dead, including c.13,000 unknown Union soldiers brought from temporary burial places all over the South. Gray and Blue Naval Mus., Toys and Soldiers Mus., Coca-Cola Mus., Coca-Cola 1st bottled here in 1894, USS *Cairo* Mus., Union gunboat raised after 100 years under water, on display at Vicksburg Natl. Military Park. Inc. 1825.

Vicksburg, town (1990 pop. 2,216), Kalamazoo co., SW Mich., 12 mi/19 km SSE of Kalamazoo, near Portage R.; 42°07'N 85°31'W. In farm area (livestock; soybeans, fruit, grain, peppermint; dairy prods.); mfg. of paper prods. and plastic molding. Known for Egyptian lotuses grown nearby. Annual Vicksburg Old Car Festival. Several lakes in area. Inc. 1871.

Vicksburg (□ 3 sq mi/7.8 sq km), National Military Park, Warren co., W Miss., 2 mi/3.2 km N and E of downtown Vicksburg. Site of Civil War battle and siege of Vicksburg includes Vicksburg Natl. Cemetery. Reconstructed trenches and forts; commemorates 47-day siege by Union forces that led to surrender of city by Confederates July 4, 1863. Drive through park includes Union Drive in N, Confederate Drive in SE. Authorized 1899.

Victor, town (1990 pop. 966), on Iowa-Poweshiek co. line, E central Iowa, 11 mi/18 km SSW of Marengo; 41°43'N 92°17'W. Mfg. (auto parts; plastic molding); livestock; grain.

Victor 1 village (1990 pop. 258), Teller co., central Colo., in Front Range, Pikes Peak 10 mi/16 km to NE, 20 mi/32 km WSW of Colorado Springs; 38°42'N 105°08'W. Elev. 9,693 ft/2,954 m. Gold-mining point in the historic Cripple Creek dist. Many of the over 300 19th-cent. bldgs. that still stand are empty. Nearby Gold Coin, Independence, and Portland mines are famous producers of gold. S terminus of narrow gauge RR to Cripple Creek. Pike Natl. Forest to E, 5 mi/8 km SE of Cripple Creek. **2** village (1990 pop. 292), Teton co., SE Idaho, near Wyo. state line, 10 mi/16 km S of Driggs, near source of Teton R.; 43°36'N 111°07'W. Elev. 6,207 ft/1,892 m. Cattle; potatoes, beans; alfalfa, barley. In W foothills of Teton Range; Grand Teton Natl. Park, Wyo., to E. Targhee Natl. Forest to E, S, and W. **3** village (1990 pop. 500), Ravalli co., W Mont., 33 mi/53 km S of Missoula, and on Bitterroot R., at mouth of Sweathouse Creek. Timber, cattle, hay, mfg. (prefabricated log structures, cabinets). Bitterroot Range and Idaho state line to W; Sapphire Mts. and parts of Bitterroot Natl. Forest to E and W; Selway-Bitterroot Wilderness Area to W. Victor Heritage Mus. Founded 1881. **4** village (□ 1 sq mi/2.6 sq km; 1990 pop. 2,308), Ontario co., W central N.Y., 15 mi/24 km SE of Rochester; 42°58'N 77°24'W. Mfg. (bearings, materials handling equip., fiberglass materials, packaging, insulators); agr. (grain, beans, sweet corn, peas). Inc. 1879.

Victor Mills, village, Spartanburg co., NW S.C., 12 mi/19 km W of Spartanburg.

Victor Rosales (VEEK-tor ro-SAH-les), town (1990 pop. 16,051), ⊙ Calera municipio, Zacatecas, N central Mexico, on RR, and 15 mi/24 km NNW of Zacatecas, on Mexico Highways 45–49; 22°57'N 102°42'W. Elev. 7,336 ft/2,236 m. Agr. center (grain, alfalfa, vegetables; livestock).

Victoria 1 county (□ 2,074 sq mi/5,372 sq km; 1991 pop. 20,786), NW N.B., E Canada, on Maine border; ⊙ Grand Falls. Drained by St. John R. **2** county (□ 1,105 sq mi/2,862 sq km; 1991 pop. 8,708), NE N.S., E Canada, in Cape Breton Isl.; ⊙ Baddeck. **3** county (□ 1,348 sq mi/3,491 sq km; 1991 pop. 63,332), S Ont., central Canada, on Burnt R.; ⊙ Lindsay.

Victoria, city (1991 pop. 71,228), ⊙ B.C., SW Canada, on Vancouver Isl. and Juan de Fuca Strait; 48°26'N 123°21'W. It is the largest city on the isl. and its major port and business center. In addition to its importance as the seat of provincial govt., Victoria is noted as a residential city because of its mild climate, beautiful scenery, many parks (including Beacon Hill Park) and drives. It is also a popular center for Amer. and Can. tourists. It has sawmills and woodworking plants, fish-processing factories, grain elevators, and cold-storage plants. The city is the base of a deep-sea fishing fleet; a large naval installation is nearby. Founded (1843) as Fort Camosun, a Hudson's Bay Company post, the city was later called Fort Victoria. When Vancouver Isl. became a crown colony, a town was laid out on the site (1851–1852), named Victoria, and made the capital of the colony. With the discovery (1858) of gold on the B.C. mainland, Victoria became the port, supply base, and outfitting center for miners on their way to the Cariboo gold fields. In 1866, when the isl. was administratively united with the mainland, Victoria remained the capital of the colony and became the provincial capital in 1871. It is the seat of the Dominion Astrophysical Observatory and the Univ. of Victoria.

Victoria, town (1991 pop. 1,831), SE N.F., E Canada, on Avalon Peninsula on W shore of Conception Bay, just N of Carbonear. Hydroelectric station.

Victoria, county (□ 313.5 sq mi/812 sq km; 1990 pop. 213,286), SW Trinidad, Trinidad and Tobago, bordering on the Gulf of Paria; 10°15'N 61°20'W.

Victoria (veek-TO-ree-ah), city (1990 pop. 1,961) and township, Guanajuato, central Mexico, 21 mi/34 km ESE of San Luis de la Paz; 21°23'N 100°12'W. Elev. 7,093 ft/2,162 m. Barley.

Victoria, town, NW Grenada, West Indies, on St. Mark Bay 9 mi/14.5 km NNE of St. George's; 12°11'N 61°42'W. Cacao, coconuts. Formerly called Grand Pauvre.

Victoria, county (□ 888 sq mi/2,300 sq km; 1990 pop. 74,361), S Texas; ⊙ Victoria, bounded NE by Arenosa Creek, bounded S by San Antonio R.; 28°48'N 96°58'W. Drained by Guadalupe R. and Coleto Creek (forms part of W border of co.); touches Lavaca Bay in E. Cattle-ranching area; also dairying, agr. (corn, cotton, rice, soybeans). Oil, natural gas wells; sand and gravel deposits. Formed 1836. Coleto Creek reservoir on W boundary.

Victoria, city (1990 pop. 55,076), ⊙ Victoria co., S Texas, on the Guadalupe R., 100 mi/161 km SE of San Antonio; 28°49'N 96°58'W. Elev. 93 ft/28 m. RR junction. In a prosperous farm, cattle, and oil area. The Victoria Barge Canal (completed in 1962) connects the growing city with the Intracoastal Waterway. Mfg. (printing and publishing, storage tanks, plastics, steel fabricating, high-density polyethylene, oil drilling and rig equip., concrete beams, pressure vessels). It is the seat of Victoria Col. (2-year) and the Univ. of Houston at Victoria. A zoo and mus. of history and fine arts are also in the city. Coleto Creek reservoir to W.

Victoria 1 town (1990 pop. 1,157), Ellis co., central Kansas, 9 mi/14.5 km E of Hays; 38°51'N 99°09'W. In agr. region. Small oil fields in vicinity. Cathedral of the Plains in town. **2** town (1990 pop. 1,830), Lunenburg co., S Va., 23 mi/37 km SSE of Farmville; 36°59'N 78°13'W. Mfg. (shoes, furniture); agr. area (tobacco, grain, soybeans; cattle); timber. Lunenburg Co. Airport to SE. Settled 1909; inc. 1916.

Victoria 1 village (1990 pop. 2,354), Carver co., SE central Minn., suburb 22 mi/35 km WSW of downtown Minneapolis; 44°52'N 93°39'W. Mfg. (candy, electronic components, cabinets, boathouses). Carver Park Reserve in NW. L. Minnetonka to N (bay extends into Victoria); other small lakes in area. **2** village (1990 pop. 299), Knox co., NW central Ill., 14 mi/23 km ENE of Galesburg; 41°01'N 90°05'W. In agr. area; bituminous-coal area.

Victoria, Mexico see: CIUDAD VICTORIA.

Victoria Dam, Mich.: see ONTONAGON RIVER.

Victoria de Durango (veek-TO-ree-ah dai doo-RAHN-do) city (1990 pop. 348,036) and township, ⊙ Durango municipio and Durango state, N central Mexico, on Mexico Highways 40 and 45; 24°01'N 104°40'W. Minerals are the chief prod., but the city is also an agr., commercial, and tourist center. Founded as a mining town in 1563, Durango served as capital of the region of Nueva Viscaya. Nearby is the Cerro del Mercado (640 ft/195 m), a hill of rich iron ore. Durango's cathedral is a massive example of early 18th-cent. architecture. Also called Durango.

Victoria Harbour, village (1991 pop. 1,553), S Ont., central Canada, on Georgian Bay, 20 mi/32 km NW of Orilla; 44°45'N 79°46'W. Lumbering.

Victoria Lake (□ 14 sq mi/36 sq km), SW N.F., E Canada, on Victoria R., 50 mi/80 km SE of Corner Brook, at foot of Annieopsquotch Mts.; 17 mi/27 km long, 2 mi/3 km wide.

Victoria Mines, village, NE N.S., E Canada, on Cape Breton Isl., on Sydney Harbour, 7 mi/11 km N Sydney. Coal mining. Nearby is Low Point cape.

Victoria Peak (7,095 ft/2,163 m), SW B.C., W Canada, central Vancouver Isl., 55 mi/89 km NW of Courtenay.

Victoria River, 85 mi/137 km long, headstream of Exploits R., SW N.F., E Canada; rises W of the Long Range Mts.; flows ENE, through Victoria L., to Red Indian L.

Victoria Strait, S Franklin dist., N.W.T., N Canada, arm of the Arctic Ocean, near 69°30'N 100°00'W, bet Victoria Isl. (W) and King William Isl. (E), connecting Queen Maud Gulf (S) with McClintock Channel (NW) and Franklin Strait (NE); 100 mi/161 km long, 50 mi/80 km–80 mi/129 km wide. At S entrance are Jenny Lind Isl. and the Royal Geographical Society Isls.

Victoria, Villa, Mexico: see VILLA VICTORIA.

Victoriaville, town (1991 pop. 21,495), S Que., E Canada, at the confluence of the Nicolet and Bulstrode rivers, SE of Trois-Rivières; 46°03'N 71°58'W. An industrial center, it has factories that make furniture, clothing, sheet metal, bricks, and farm equip.

Victorville, city (1990 pop. 40,674), San Bernardino co., S Calif., 29 mi/47 km N of San Bernardino, on Mojave R.; 34°31'N 117°20'W. In irrigated agr. (cattle, poultry; apples, pears, plums, peaches, alfalfa, grain); mfg. (flat glass, paint, concrete, cement); printing and publishing, and limestone quarrying area of Mojave Desert. Gold, granite. George Air Force Base to NW. Victor Valley Col. (2-year). Dude and cattle ranches nearby.

Victory, town (1990 pop. 50), Essex co., NE Vt., on Moose R., and 11 mi/18 km NE of St. Johnsbury; hunting, fishing; 44°32'N 71°49'W.

Victory Mills, village, Saratoga co., E N.Y., near the Hudson R., 9 mi/14.5 km E of Saratoga Springs; 43°05'N 73°36'W. In dairying area. Mfg. (packaging and folding cartons). Also called Victory.

Vidalia (vi-DAIL-yuh), city (1990 pop. 11,078), Toombs co., E central Ga., c.75 mi/121 km W of Savannah; 32°13'N 82°24'W. Mfg. includes clothing, computer parts, plastic prods., concrete pipe, air-conditioning equip. Best known for sweet Vidalia onions. Excellent genealogical library and art and history mus. Historic homes.

Vidalia (vi-DAIL-yuh), town (1990 pop. 4,953), ⊙ Concordia parish, E central La., on Mississippi R., 2 mi/3 km NW of Natchez (Miss.); 31°34'N 91°27'W. In agr. area (rice, soybeans, vegetables, cattle), catfish; mfg. (activated alumina). Settled c.1786 by the Spanish who built a military post opposite Natchez. Town was moved back from river after bldg. of new levees for flood control in 1939.

Vidette (vid-ET), village, Burke co., E Ga., 14 mi/23 km WSW of Waynesboro; 33°02'N 82°14'W.

Vidor (VEI-dor), city (1990 pop. 10,935), Orange co., SE Texas, suburb 7 mi/11.3 km NE of Beaumont, and

15 mi/24 km E of Orange; 30°07′N 94°00′W. Cattle, rice; metal fabricating.

Vieja Mountains, Texas: see SIERRA VIEJA.

Vienna, village (1991 pop. 481), S Ont., central Canada, near L. Erie, 22 mi/35 km ESE of St. Thomas. Dairying, mixed farming, fruit growing.

Vienna 1 (vei-EN-uh), city (1990 pop. 1,446), ⊙ Johnson co., S Ill., 33 mi/53 km NNE of Cairo; 37°24′N 88°53′W. In fruitgrowing region; wheat, corn; livestock; dairy prods. Inc. 1837. **2** (vee-EN-uh), city (1990 pop. 10,862), Wood co., NW W.Va., suburb 4 mi/6.4 km N of Parkersburg, on Ohio R.; 39°19′N 81°32′W. Mfg. (construction material, gas and oil processing, computer equip., consumer goods). Agr. (grain, tobacco, soybeans); livestock; poultry. Ohio Valley Col. to W. Laid out 1774.

Vienna 1 (vei-EN-uh), town (1990 pop. 2,708), ⊙ Dooly co., central Ga., 8 mi/12.9 km N of Cordele; 32°05′N 83°47′W. Trade and processing center for farm and timber area; vegetable canning, pecan shelling, sawmilling; mfg. of particle board, pumps, resins, overalls, air conditioners. Inc. 1841. **2** (vee-EN-uh), town (1990 pop. 417), Kennebec co., S Maine, 18 mi/29 km NW of Augusta; 44°32′N 70°00′W. In agr., resort, lumbering region. **3** town (1990 pop. 264), Dorchester co., E Md., 15 mi/24 km ESE of Cambridge, and on Nanticoke R. (bridged); 38°29′N 75°50′W. Name believed to have been derived from Vinnacokasimmon, Emperor of the Nanticokes. Neighboring land was set aside as a reservation for Nanticoke Indians when the town was laid out in 1706. Originally known as Emperors' Landing, it became a port of entry with its own customs officials in 1768, and the boatyards were considered worthy of attack by the British in 1782. Ferries provided transportation until a bridge was built in 1931. Today, Route 50 traffic thunders over the bridge headed for the Atlantic beaches and further S. The small frame customs house built in 1791 and used until 1866 is still on Water St. **4** town (1990 pop. 611), ⊙ Maries co., central Mo., near Gasconade R., 23 mi/37 km NW of Rolla; 38°11′N 91°57′W. Agr. (corn, hay, hogs; cattle; timber; hats). **5** town (1990 pop. 14,852), Fairfax co., N Va., urbanized area 11 mi/18 km W of Washington, D.C., 4 mi/6.4 km NNE of Fairfax; 38°53′N 77°15′W. Some computer software research industry in area. Originally called Springfield, Vienna became the site of Fairfax co.'s 1st courthouse (1742). Wolf Trap Farm Park for the Performing Arts is in N. Area has grown rapidly since 1970s. Tysons Corner to NE. Dulles Internatl. Airport to W. Inc. 1890.

Vienna 1 village (1990 pop. 404), Lincoln parish, N La., 4 mi/6 km N of Ruston; 32°37′N 92°39′W. Timber and agr. area (peaches, cattle, poultry). **2** village (1990 pop. 93), Clark co., E central S.Dak., 17 mi/27 km SE of Clark; 44°42′N 97°30′W. In agr. area.

Vienna, Ohio: see SOUTH VIENNA.

Vieques (vee-AI-kais), island (□ 51 sq mi/132 sq km; 1990 pop. 8,602), off E P.R., c.6 mi/9.7 km E of Fajardo. It is hilly, with a dry, warm climate. The town of Vieques, commonly called Isabel Segunda, was founded in 1843 and is the main pop. center. Highest point (983 ft/ 300 m) is Pico Pirata. The isl. has gained popularity as a holiday resort. Fishing, tourism, camping and picnicking. Has phosphorescent bay (Mosquito Bay; E). The major portion of Vieques is used as a training area for the U.S. Navy. Lighthouse on N side. Conde de Mirasol Fort on N side. Mus. of archaeology and natural history. Accessible by planes from San Juan and Fajardo, ferries from Fajardo.

Viesca (vee-ES-kah), city (1990 pop. 3,463) and township, Coahuila, N Mexico, in irrigated Laguna dist., 40 mi/64 km ESE of Torreón; 25°20′N 102°48′W. Elev. 3,586 ft/1,093 m. Near RR; agr. center (cotton, wheat, corn, wine, vegetables, fruit); silver, lead, copper deposits.

Viesca, Laguna de (vee-ES-kah, lah-GOO-nah dai), depression in Laguna dist. of Coahuila, N Mexico, 5 mi/ 8 km N of Viesca; c.12 mi/19 km in diameter. Has water only during rainy period, when Aguanaval R. reaches it.

Vietnam Veterans Memorial, monument, Constitution Avenue and 21st St., NW Washington, D.C. On July 1, 1980, Congress designated 2 acres/0.8 ha in the W ½ of Constitution Gardens as a site for a memorial to those who died in the Vietnam War. The architect was 21-year-old Maya Ying Lin, whose design called for 2 polished black granite walls to be set at a 125° angle and inscribed with the names of the 58,000 killed or missing in action from 1956–1975. The memorial was dedicated in 1983.

Vieux Desert, Lac, Wis. and Mich.: see LAC VIEUX DESERT.

Vieux Fort (vyaw FAWR), town (1991 pop. 4,051), S St. Lucia, 19 mi/31 km S of Castries. On fertile plain (bananas, coconuts); 13°44′N 60°58′W. Commercial port; light industry. In vicinity was started (1939) the Barbados Land Settlement. Just NE of town is Hewanorra Internatl. Airport, a converted World War II U.S. Air Force base, which handles most of St. Lucia's commercial air traffic.

Vieux-Bourg-d'Acquin (vyuh–BOOR–dah-KANG), village (1982 pop. 1,079), Sud dept., Haiti, 37 mi/60 km N of Aquin; 18°18′N 73°21′W. Sisal growing.

Vieux-Fort (vyuh–FAWR), town, S Basse-Terre isl., Guadeloupe, 3 mi/4.8 km S of Basse-Terre city. Agr. (coffee, cacao, vanilla).

Vieux-Habitants (vyuh–zah-bee-TAHNG), town, SW Basse-Terre isl., Guadeloupe, 5 mi/8 km NNW of Basse-Terre city. Coffee, cacao; mfg. of soap.

View Cove, village, SE Alaska, on E shore of Dall Isl., Alexander Archipelago, 30 mi/48 km S of Craig. Limestone quarrying.

View Park–Windsor Hills, uninc. city (1990 pop. 11,769), Los Angeles co., S Calif., residential suburb 6 mi/9.7 km WSW of downtown Los Angeles, 1 mi/1.6 km E of Culver City; 34°00′N 118°21′W.

Vigas, Las, Mexico: see LAS VIGAS DE RAMÍREZ.

Vigía, Punta de la (vee-HEE-uh, POON-tuh dai luh), cape on S central coast of Cuba, Cienfuegos prov., at W gate of Cienfuegos Bay, 7 mi/11.3 km S of Cienfuegos; 22°02′N 80°28′W.

Vigie Beach, St. Lucia: see CASTRIES.

Vigie Peninsula (vee-JEE), W St. Lucia, on N side of Castries Bay. Popular beach resort, lighthouse, ruined fortifications, duty-free mall at Pointe Seraphine. Regional airport for charter and some U.S. flights.

Vigo (VEE-go), county (□ 410 sq mi/1,062 sq km; 1990 pop. 106,107), W Ind.; ⊙ Terre Haute; 39°26′N 87°23′W. Bounded W by Ill. state line; intersected by the Wabash; drained by small Honey, Otter, and Prairie creeks. Agr. (corn, soybeans, wheat; hogs; cattle; timber); bituminous-coal mines. Extensive mfg. at Terre Haute, which is a commercial, banking, and industrial center for large surrounding area. Formed 1818.

Viking, town (1991 pop. 1,109), E Alta., W Canada, 65 mi/ 105 km ESE of Edmonton; 53°05′N 111°47′W. Natural-gas production; dairying, mixed farming, grain.

Viking, village (1990 pop. 103), Marshall co., NW Minn., and 13 mi/21 km NW of Thief R. Falls; 48°13′N 96°24′W. Grain area; sunflowers, flax, alfalfa; cattle, sheep.

Vilano Beach (vuh-LAH-no), town (□ 1 sq mi/ 2.6 sq km; 1990 pop. 1,867), St. Johns co., NE Fla., 5 mi/ 8 km NNE of St. Augustine; 29°56′N 81°17′W.

Vilas (VEI-lahs), county (□ 1,017 sq mi/2,634 sq km; 1990 pop. 17,707), N Wis., bounded N by Mich. (boundary bet. Central and Eastern time zones); ⊙ Eagle R.; 46°02′N 89°30′W. Drained by Wisconsin and Manitowish rivers. Mostly a resort area with woods and numerous lakes (including Lac Vieux Desert and Trout L.); lumbering. Contains most of Northern Highland State Forest, part of Amer. Legion State Forest, part of Nicolet Natl. Forest in E, small part of Chequamegon Natl. Forest in extreme SW; Gateway and Chanticlear Ski Areas in E; part of Lac du Flambeau Indian Reservation in SW. Formed 1893.

Vilas 1 village (1990 pop. 105), Baca co., SE Colo., 10 mi/ 16 km E of Springfield; 37°22′N 102°27′W. Elev. 4,158 ft/ 1,267 m. Cattle, wheat. Comanche Natl. Grassland to SW. **2** village (1990 pop. 28), Miner co., SE central S.Dak., 4 mi/6.4 km W of Howard; 44°00′N 97°35′W.

Villa, [Span. = town], Mexico: for towns whose name begins thus but are not so listed, see under the following name.

Villa Adalberto Tejeda (VEE-yah ah-dahl-BER-to te-HE-dah), town (1990 pop. 1,876), ⊙ Camerón de Tejeda municipio, Veracruz, E Mexico, in foothills of Sierra Madre Oriental, on RR, and 33 mi/53 km WSW of Veracruz; 19°02′N 96°39′W. Coffee, sugarcane, fruit. Formerly Camarón.

Villa Ahumada, Mexico: see AHUMADA.

Villa Aldama (VEE-yah ahl-DAH-mah), town (1990 pop. 2,056), Veracruz, E Mexico, in Sierra Madre Oriental, 20 mi/32 km WNW of Xalapa Enríquez; 28°51′N 105°54′W. Coffee, corn, fruit, sugar; wood.

Villa Altagracia (VEE-yah ahl-tah-GRAH-see-ah), town (1993 pop. 27,462), San Cristóbal prov., S central Dominican Republic, in foothills of the Cordillera Central, 23 mi/37 km NW of Santo Domingo; 18°38′N 70°15′W. Agr. (rice, coffee, fruit).

Villa Alvarez, Mexico: see ZIMATLÁN DE ÁLVAREZ.

Villa Álvaro Obregón, Mexico: see ÁLVARO OBREGÓN.

Villa Azueta (VEE-yah ah-soo-AI-tah), town (1990 pop. 6,532), ⊙ José Azueta municipio, Veracruz, SE Mexico, in Gulf lowland, 38 mi/61 km SW of San Andrés Tuxtla, on RR; 18°04′N 95°42′W. Agr. center (sugarcane, bananas; livestock).

Villa Chalcatongo, Mexico: see CHALCATONGO DE HIDALGO.

Villa Clara (VEE-yuh KLAH-ruh), province (□ 3,067 sq mi/7,944 sq km; 1994 est. pop. 880,000); ⊙ Santa Clara. The core of the former, larger Las Villas prov., which was divided (1975) into 3 new provs.: Cienfuegos (SW), Sancti Spíritus (E), and Matanzas (W), along with the present (smaller) Villa Clara. Covering 7.2% of Cuban territory, it includes the central plain, hills ranging bet. 900 ft/274 m and 1,200 ft/366 m, and the N part of Escambray mts., with a max. elev. of 3,740 ft/1,140 m. Villa Clara has a key reservoir system, including Alarcanes, Minerva, and Habanilla reservoirs for electricity generation. Pressures for more hydroelectrical energy to replace cheap Soviet oil in the 1990s has had a detrimental effect on fish pop. About ¼ of the land (500,000 acres/202,350 ha) is used for sugarcane production. Has 28 sugar mills. Also corn, fruit, cereals, and vegetables. Excellent pastures. Gold, copper, zinc, manganese, asphalt, and zeolite deposits. Leading ports are Caibarién (sponge-fishing hq.) and Isabela de Sagua. Other important centers include Sagua la Grande, Placetas, and Manicaragua. Traversed by the Central and Natl. highways and both Northern and Southern RRs. Formerly called Las Villas prov., then (larger) Villa Clara prov. Major cities are Santa Clara, Sagua la Grande, Placetas, Caibarien, and Manicaragua.

Villa Comaltitlán (VEE-yah ko-mahl-teet-LAHN), town (1990 pop. 6,021), Chiapas, S Mexico, in Pacific lowland, 9 mi/14.5 km NW of Huixtla, on Mexico Highway 200; 15°14′N 92°34′W. Cacao, sugarcane, coffee, fruit; livestock.

Villa Corona (VEE-yah ko-RO-nah), town (1990 pop. 5,829), Jalisco, W Mexico, on L. Atotonilco, 27 mi/ 43 km SW of Guadalajara, on Mexico Highway 80; 20°25′N 103°41′W. Agr. center (grain, beans, alfalfa, sugarcane, fruit; livestock).

Villa Coronado, Mexico: see CORONADO.

Villa Corregidora, Mexico: see EL PUEBLITO.

Villa Corzo (VEE-yah KOR-so), city (1990 pop. 6,327), ⊙ Villa Corzo township, Chiapas, S Mexico, in Sierra Madre, 30 mi/48 km SSW of Venustiano Carranza; 16°12′N 93°15′W. Farming. Formerly Angel Albino Corzo.

Villa Cuauhtémoc (VEE-yah kwou-TAI-mok), town (1990 pop. 11,306), ⊙ Otzolotepec municipio, Mexico state, central Mexico, 28 mi/45 km W of Mexico city. Cereals; livestock.

Villa de Allende (VEE-yah dai ah-YEN-de), town (1990 pop. 856), Mexico state, central Mexico, 14 km W of Toluca de Lerdo; 19°23′N 100°08′W. Elev. 6,890 ft/ 2,100 m. Cereals; livestock. Also known as Allende. Formerly San José Allende.

Villa de Álvarez (VEE-yah dai AHL-vah-re), town (1990 pop. 35,877), Colima, W Mexico, in W foothills of Sierra Madre Occidental, 2 mi/3.2 km NW of Colima, and essentially a part of the larger city; 19°18′N 103°41′W. Elev. 1,839 ft/561 m.

Villa de Arista (VEE-yah dai ah-REES-tah), town (1990 pop. 4,788), San Luis Potosí, N central Mexico, 35 mi/56 km NNE of San Luis Potosí. Wheat, corn, beans, cotton, maguey.

Villa de Arriaga (VEE-yah dai ah-ree-AH-gahn), town (1990 pop. 3,796), San Luis Potosí, N central Mexico, on interior plateau, 32 mi/51 km SW of San Luis Potosí, on Mexico Highway 70-80; 22°53′N 101°25′W. Grain, beans, fruit; livestock.

Villa de Cecilia, Mexico: see CIUDAD MADERO.

Villa de Cos (VEE-yah dai kos), town (1990 pop. 3,164), ⊙ Villa de Cos municipio, Zacatecas, N central Mexico, 38 mi/61 km NNE of Zacatecas; 23°20′N 102°20′W. Elev. 6,725 ft/2,050 m. Agr. (beans, rice, wheat; livestock).

Villa de Etla (VEE-yah dai ET-lah), town (1990 pop. 5,220), N central Oaxaca, Mexico, 16 mi/25 km NW of Oaxaca de Juárez, on RR, and on Inter-Amer. Highway (190); 17°12′N 96°48′W. Good roads and RR connections. Agr. (corn, beans, wheat, potatoes, fruits, mezcal); woods; cattle, and dairy prods. Formerly San Pedro y San Pablo Etla.

Villa de García (VEE-yah dai gahr-SEE-ah), town (1990 pop. 9,845), ⊙ García municipio, Nuevo León, N Mexico, in foothills of Sierra Madre Oriental, on RR, and 20 mi/32 km WNW of Monterrey; 25°49′N 100°35′W. Elev. 2,287 ft/697 m. Agr. center (tomatoes, barley; livestock). Also García.

Villa de Guadalupe (VEE-yah dai gwah-dah-loo-pai), town (1990 pop. 1,091), San Luis Potosí, N central Mexico, 21 mi/34 km SSW of Matehuala; 19°34′N 99°07′W. Elev. 6,693 ft/2,040 m. Maguey, corn; livestock. Magdalenas thermal springs 6 mi/9.7 km NW.

Villa de Guadalupe, Mexico: see ARROYO SECO.

Villa de la Paz (VEE-yah dai lah PAHS), town (1990 pop. 3,871), ⊙ La Paz municipio, San Luis Potosí, N central Mexico, at E foot of Sierra Catorce, 5 mi/8 km W of Matehuala; 24°10′N 110°17′W. Elev. 5,906 ft/1,800 m. RR terminus; mining center (silver, gold, copper, zinc).

Villa de Ramos (vee-yah dai RAH-mos), town (1990 pop. 2,011), Villa de Ramos municipio, San Luis Potosí, N central Mexico, in interior basin, 20 mi/32 km NW of Salinas de Hidalgo; 25°30′N 105°08′W. Elev. 7,251 ft/2,210 m. Corn, wheat, beans; livestock.

Villa de Reyes (VEE-yah dai RAI-es), town (1990 pop. 6,701), San Luis Potosí, N central Mexico, in interior basin, near Guanajuato state border, 25 mi/40 km S of San Luis Potosí; 21°48′N 100°56′W. Elev. 5,968 ft/1,819 m. Agr. center (grain, fruit, beans; livestock). Sometimes Reyes.

Villa de San Sebastián, Mexico: see CONCORDIA.

Villa de Tamazulapam del Progreso (VEE-yah dai tah-mah-zoo-lah-PAHM del pro-GRAI-so), town (1990 pop. 4,582), Oaxaca, S Mexico, on Inter-Amer. Highway (190), and 17 mi/27 km SE of Huajuapam de León de Nochixtlán; 17°41′N 97°33′W. Cereals, sugarcane, fruit; livestock. Formerly Tamazulapan del Progreso.

Villa de Tezontepec, Mexico: see TEZONTEPEC.

Villa de Zaachila (VEE-yah dai SAH-ah-CHEE-lah), town (1990 pop. 10,716), Oaxaca, S Mexico, in Sierra Madre del Sur, on RR, and 7 mi/11.3 km S of Oaxaca; 16°57′N 96°45′W. Cereals, sugarcane, tobacco, fruit. Pre-Columbian ruins are nearby. Once capital of powerful Zapotec people. Formerly Zaachila, also Santa María Zaachila.

Villa de Zaragoza (VEE-yah dai sah-rah-GO-sah), town (1990 pop. 5,947), ⊙ Zaragoza municipio, San Luis Potosí, N central Mexico, in Sierra Madre Oriental, 18 mi/29 km SE of San Luis Potosí; 22°02′N 100°43′W. Elev. 6,316 ft/1,925 m. Corn, cotton, fruit; livestock.

Villa del Carbón (VEE-yah del kahr-BON), town (1990 pop. 5,420), Mexico state, central Mexico, 26 mi/42 km NW of Mexico city, on Mexico Highway 13; 19°44′N 99°28′W. Elev. 7,218 ft/2,200 m. Grain, fruit; livestock.

Villa del Pueblito, Mexico: see EL PUEBLITO.

Villa del Refugio, Mexico: see TABASCO.

Villa Díaz Ordaz (VEE-yah DEE-ahz or-DAHZ), town (1990 pop. 2,949), central Oaxaca, Mexico, 4.3 mi/6.9 km NE of Tlacolula de Matamoros; 16°58′N 96°27′W. Elev. 5,479 ft/1,670 m. Road connects with Mexico Highway 190 at Tlacoluca de Matamoros. Agr. (corn, beans, wheat, mezcal); cattle; dairy prods.; poultry raising. Fabrics. Also Santa Domingo del Valle.

Villa Escalante, Mexico: see SANTA CLARA DEL COBRE.

Villa Escobedo (VEE-yah es-ko-BAI-do), village (1990 pop. 102), Hidalgo de Parral municipio, Chihuahua, N Mexico, 5 mi/8 km NW of Hidalgo del Parral; 27°00′N 105°44′W. Old mining center.

Villa Escobedo, Mexico: see ESCOBEDO.

Villa Frontera, Mexico: see FRONTERA.

Villa García (VEE-yah gahr-SEE-ah), town (1990 pop. 4,562), ⊙ Villa García municipio, Zacatecas, N central Mexico, 55 mi/89 km SE of Zacatecas; 22°10′N 101°57′W. Elev. 7,874 ft/2,400 m. Agr. (beans, corn, wheat, onions, fruits; livestock).

Villa Gonzáles Ortega (VEE-yah gon-SAH-les or-TAI-gah), town (1990 pop. 4,761), Zacatecas, N central Mexico, 45 mi/72 km ESE of Zacatecas; 22°30′N 101°55′W. Grain, maguey, beans; livestock. Formerly El Carro.

Villa Grove, city (1990 pop. 2,734), Douglas co., E Ill., on Embarras R., and 8 mi/12.9 km ENE of Tuscola; 39°51′N 88°09′W. In agr. area; RR shops. Ships grain, fruit. Inc. 1904.

Villa Grove, village, Saguache co., S central Colo., on Kerber Creek near its confluence with San Luis Creek, bet. foothills of Sawatch (W) and Sangre de Cristo (E) mts., and 15 mi/24 km NE of Saguache. Elev. c.7,980 ft/2,432 m. Ranching.

Villa Guerrero 1 (VEE-yah gai-RAI-ro), town (1990 pop. 3,747), Jalisco, W Mexico, 16 mi/42 km NNW of Colotlán; 21°59′N 103°36′W. Elev. 5,856 ft/1,785 m. Corn, wheat; livestock. **2** town (1990 pop. 6,841), Mexico state, central Mexico, 27 mi/43 km S of Toluca de Lerdo. Cereals, sugarcane, fruit; livestock.

Villa Gustavo A. Madero, Mexico: see GUSTAVO A. MADERO.

Villa Heights, uninc. town, Henry co., S Va., residential suburb 2 mi/3.2 km NW of Martinsville, near Smith R.; 36°42′N 79°54′W.

Villa Hidalgo 1 (VEE-yah ee-DAHL-go), town (1990 pop. 836), ⊙ Hidalgo municipio, Durango, N Mexico, 65 mi/105 km SE of Hidalgo del Parral. Corn, candelilla; livestock. **2** town (1990 pop. 8,583), Jalisco, central Mexico, 32 mi/51 km SW of Aguascalientes; 26°16′N 104°54′W. Elev. 5,945 ft/1,812 m. Corn, wheat, beans, alfalfa; livestock. Formerly Paso de Sotos. **3** town (1990 pop. 1,935), in E central Oaxaca, Mexico, 28 mi/45 km E of Oaxaca de Juárez; 17°11′N 96°10′W. Located on the right bank of the Cajones R., which runs between the sierras of Ixtlán and Villa Alta. Elev. 3,852 ft/1,174 m. An isolated Native Zapotec community without all-weather roads. Temperate climate. Agr. (corn, beans, chilies, sugarcane). Formerly Hidalgo Yalang. **4** town (1990 pop. 2,020), San Luis Potosí, N central Mexico, 29 mi/47 km NE of San Luis Potosí, on Mexico Highway 57; 22°27′N 100°42′W. Corn, wheat, cotton, maguey. Formerly Iturbide. **5** town (1990 pop. 1,762), NE Sonora, Mexico, 82 mi/132 km S of Agua Prieta, on the Bavispe R.; 30°03′N 109°09′W. Elev. 1,919 ft/585 m. Hot climate. Paved roads. Was populated by Native Ípatas people. **6** town (1990 pop. 3,248), ⊙ Villa Hidalgo municipio, Zacatecas, WNW central Mexico, on interior plateau, 50 mi/80 km SW of San Luis Potosí; 22°21′N 101°42′W. Elev. 7,405 ft/2,257 m. Silver mining. Formerly Santa Rita.

Villa Hidalgo, Mexico: see HIDALGO.

Villa Hills (VIL-uh), town (1990 pop. 7,739), Kenton co., N Ky., residential suburb 6 mi/9.7 km WSW of Cincinnati (Ohio), and 5 mi/8 km W of Covington, near Ohio R.; 39°03′N 84°35′W. Anderson Ferry, on Ohio R., to NE. Cincinnati–Northern Ky. Internatl. Airport to SW.

Villa Jara, Mexico: see PASO DEL MACHO.

Villa Jaragua (VEE-yah hah-RAH-gwah), town (1993 pop. 7,718), Bahoruco prov., SW Dominican Republic, 30 mi/50 km NW of Barahona; 18°29′N 71°30′W. Agr. (coffee, cereals, fruit); timber. Formerly called José Trujillo Valdez, or Trujillo Valdez.

Villa Jiménez (VEE-yah hee-MAI-nes), town (1990 pop. 5,068), ⊙ Jiménez municipio, Michoacán, central Mexico, 40 mi/64 km WNW of Morelia; 19°55′N 101°35′W. Agr. center (corn, sugarcane, fruit; livestock).

Villa Juárez (VEE-yah HWAH-res), town (1990 pop. 4,124), San Luis Potosí, N central Mexico, on interior plateau, 45 mi/72 km ENE of San Luis Potosí; 22°20′N 100°17′W. Agr. center (corn, wheat, beans, cotton, maguey). Formerly Carbonera.

Villa Juárez, Mexico: see CIUDAD MANTE.

Villa la Trinitaria (VEE-yah lah tree-nee-TAH-ree-yah), town (1990 pop. 5,503), ⊙ La Trinitaria municipio, Chiapas, S Mexico, in Sierra Madre, 10 mi/16 km SSE of Comitán de Domínguez on Inter-Amer. Highway (190). Elev. 5,262 ft/1,604 m. Cereals, sugarcane, tobacco, fruit; livestock. Customhouse. Zapaluta until 1934. Tojolabal Maya-speakers occupy rural areas of municipio.

Villa López, Mexico: see LÓPEZ.

Villa Madero (VEE-yah mah-DAI-ro), town (1990 pop. 4,009), ⊙ Madero municipio, Michoacán, central Mexico, 26 mi/42 km S of Morelia. Cereals, fruit; livestock.

Villa Mainero (VEE-yah mah-ee-NAI-ro), town (1990 pop. 534), ⊙ Mainero municipio, Tamaulipas, NE Mexico, at E foot of Sierra Madre Oriental, 65 mi/105 km NW of Ciudad Victoria, and 4 mi/6.4 km W of Mexico Highway 85 (at Magueyes); 24°35′N 99°36′W. Cereals, sugarcane; livestock.

Villa Mariano Matamoros (VEE-yah mah-ree-AH-no mah-tah-MO-ros), town (1990 pop. 4,385), ⊙ Ixtacuixtla de Mariano Matamoros municipio, central Mexico, 9 mi/14.5 km W of Tlaxcala. Elev. 7,192 ft/2,192 m. Maguey-growing center. Thermal springs nearby. Also known as Ixtacuixtla or San Felipe Ixtacuixtla.

Villa Matamoros, Mexico: see MATAMOROS.

Villa Morelos (VEE-yah mo-RAI-los), town (1990 pop. 3,073), ⊙ Morelos municipio, Michoacán, central Mexico, 30 mi/48 km NW of Morelia; 20°00′N 101°25′W. Cereals, fruit, vegetables; livestock.

Villa Nicolás Romero (VEE-yah nee-ko-LAHS ro-MAI-ro), town (1990 pop. 146,342), ⊙ Nicolás Romero municipio, Mexico state, central Mexico, 18 mi/29 km NW of Mexico city, and in the Zona Metropolitana de la Ciudad de México; 19°37′N 99°18′W. RR terminus and industrial center; agr. (grain, fruit; livestock).

Villa Obregón, Mexico: see CAÑADAS DE OBREGÓN.

Villa Ocampo (VEE-yah o-KAHM-po), town (1990 pop. 1,444), ⊙ Ocampo municipio, Durango, N Mexico, on upper Florido R., near Chihuahua border, and 35 mi/56 km SSE of Hidalgo del Parral, 1.2 mi/1.9 km off Mexico Highway 15, on unpaved road; 26°29′N 105°30′W. Cereals, cotton; livestock.

Villa Ocampo, Mexico: see OCAMPO.

Villa Park, city (1990 pop. 6,299), Orange co., S Calif., residential suburb 27 mi/43 km SE of downtown Los Angeles, and 5 mi/8 km E of Anaheim, surrounded by city of Orange; 33°49′N 117°49′W. Chino Hills State park to NE. Citrus-growing region being displaced by rapid urbanization.

Villa Park, village (1990 pop. 22,253), Du Page co., NE Ill.; 41°53′N 87°58′W. It is a residential suburb W of Chicago. Inc. 1914.

Villa Pesqueira, town (1990 pop. 723), Sonora, NW Mexico, on RR, and 23 mi/37 km N of Hermosillo; 29°26′N 110°24′W. Elev. 1,417 ft/432 m. Sugarcane, corn, wheat, fruit. Also known as Pesqueira or Matapa.

Villa Purificación (VEE-yah poo-ree-fee-kah-see-ON), town (1990 pop. 4,297), Jalisco, W Mexico, in Sierra Cacoma, 19 mi/31 km WSW of Autlán de Navarro. Corn, sugarcane, cotton, rice, tobacco, bananas. Also known as Purificación.

Villa Rica (VIL-uh RIK-uh), town (1990 pop. 6,542), Carroll and Douglas cos., W Ga., 31 mi/50 km W of Atlanta; 33°44′N 84°55′W. Mfg. includes machinery, rubber prods., apparel, textiles, fabricated metal prods., plastic prods., furniture, crushed aggregate. Suburb of Atlanta. One of the oldest towns in W Ga. Settled after discovery of gold here 1826; inc. 1830.

Villa Rivas (VEE-yah REE-vahs), **Villa Riva,** or **Riva,** town (1993 pop. 3,934), Duarte prov., E central Dominican Republic, in fertile La Vega Real valley, on Yuna R., on RR, and 24 mi/39 km ESE of San Francisco de Macorís; 19°10′N 69°50′W. Agr. (cacao, rice).

Villa Sola de Vega, Mexico: see SAN MIGUEL SOLA DE VEGA.

Villa Tejupam de la Unión (VEE-yah TAI-hoo-pahm dai lah oon-YON), town (1990 pop. 995), NW Oaxaca, Mexico, 19 mi/30 km SE of Huajuapam de León, and 1 mi/1.6 km off the Inter-Amer. Highway (190); 17°39′N 97°29′W. Elev. 6,860 ft/2,091 m. Mountainous terrain with temperate climate. Activities are growing cereals, processing mezcal, and forestry. Formerly Santiango Tejupam.

Villa Tenares, Dominican Republic: see TENARES.

Villa Unión 1 (VEE-yah oon-YON), town (1990 pop. 4,504), Coahuila, N Mexico, 32 mi/51 km SSW of Piedras Negras (on U.S. [Texas] border); 28°14′N 100°44′W. Cereals, isttle fibers, candelilla wax; cattle. Also known as Rosales. **2** town (1990 pop. 9,651), ⊙ Poanas municipio, Durango, N Mexico, 40 mi/64 km ESE of Victoria de Durango; 23°59′N 104°01′W. Agr. center (corn, wheat, cotton, sugarcane, vegetables; livestock). Also known as San Esteban.

Villa Vasquez (VEE-yah VAHS-kez), town (1993 pop. 10,429), 15 mi/23 km SE of Monte Cristi, Monte Cristi prov., NW Dominican Republic; 19°45′N 71°27′W. In rice-growing area.

Villa Vicente Guerrero (VEE-yah SEN-te ge RE-ro) town, ⊙ San Pablo del Monte municipio (1990 pop. 36,865), Tlaxcala, central Mexico, on central plateau, 5 mi/8 km N of Puebla. Elev. 7,415 ft/2,260 m. Built on SW side of volcano La Malinche. Agr. center (corn, wheat, barley, maguey, alfalfa, beans;, livestock); flour milling, pulque distilling. Called San Pablo del Monte until 1940.

Villa Vicente Guerrero, Mexico: see VICENTE GUERRERO.

Villa Victoria 1 (VEE-yah veek-TO-ree-ah), town (1990 pop. 2,404), Mexico state, central Mexico, 25 mi/40 km NW of Toluca de Lerdo; 19°26′N 99°59′W. Cereals; livestock. Near Villa Victoria Dam. **2** town (1990 pop. 756), ⊙ Chinicuila municipio, Michoacán, W Mexico, 40 mi/64 km SE of Colima; 18°47′N 103°24′W. Rice, sugarcane, fruit.

Villaflores (VEE-yah-FLO-res), city (1990 pop. 24,670), ⊙ Villaflores municipio, Chiapas, S Mexico, 38 mi/61 km SSW of Tuxtla Gutierrez; 16°14′N 93°16′W. Elev. 2,001 ft/610 m. Agr. center (corn, beans, sugarcane, tropical fruit).

Village Green, uninc. town (1990 pop. c.5,000), Delaware co., SE Pa., residential suburb 14 mi/23 km SW of Philadelphia, and 3 mi/4.8 km NW of Chester; 39°52′N 75°25′W. Tank farms in area.

Village Mills, uninc. village (1990 pop. 300), Hardin co., SE Texas, 35 mi/56 km NW of Beaumont. Timber. Cattle, hogs; egg production. Mfg. (machinery, medical instruments). Units of Big Thicket Natl. Preserve to NW and E; visitor station to SE.

Village of the Branch, village (1990 pop. 1,669), Suffolk co., SE N.Y., on central L.I., 9 mi/14.5 km SW of Port Jefferson; 40°51′N 73°01′W.

Village Park, town (1990 pop. 7,407), central Oahu isl., Honolulu co., Hawaii, 11 mi/18 km NW of Honolulu, near Waikele Stream; 21°23′N 158°01′W. Wheeler Air Force Base to N. Residential suburb.

Village Shires (SHEI-uhrs), uninc. town (1990 pop. 4,364), Bucks co., SE Pa., residential suburb 18 mi/29 km NE of Philadelphia, and 11 mi/18 km W of Trenton (N.J.) on Mill Creek; 40°12′N 74°58′W. Springfield L. Reservoir to N.

Villagrán (vee-yah-GRAHN), city (1990 pop. 18,114) and township, Guanajuato, central Mexico, on Lerma R., and 12 mi/19 km W of Celaya, on Mexico Highway 45, on RR; 20°31′N 100°59′W. Agr. center (grain, alfalfa,

sugarcane, vegetables, fruit; livestock). Formerly El Guaje.

Villagrán (vee-yah-GRAHN), town (1990 pop. 1,292), Tamaulipas, NE Mexico, at E foot of Sierra Madre Oriental, near Inter-Amer. Highway (85), and 27 mi/43 km SSE of Linares; 24°29′N 99°30′W. Sugarcane, cereals; livestock.

Villahermosa (vee-yah-er-MO-sahn), city (1990 pop. 261,231) and township, ⊙ Centro municipio and of Tabasco state, SE Mexico, on the Grijalva R.; 18°00′N 92°53′W. The city, which has good communications facilities (on Mexico Highways 180, 186, and 195), is the commercial and distribution center for the surrounding region. Oil is the economic mainstay. Founded in the 16th cent. The city possesses a large collection of Olmec and Mayan artifacts, which are exhibited in the Regional Anthropological Mus. and the La Venta Park Mus.

Villalba (vee-YAHL-bah), town (1990 pop. 23,559), central P.R., in the Cordillera Central, 10 mi/16 km NE of Ponce. Primary bean-growing center of P.R. Coffee also grown. Mfg. (food prods., fabricated metal prods., machinery, electric equip.). Adjoining N is the Toro Negro hydroelectric plant.

Villaldama (vee-ahl-DAH-mah), city (1990 pop. 2,728) and township, ⊙ Villaldama municipio, Nuevo León, N Mexico, in N valley of Sierra Madre Oriental, on RR, and 55 mi/89 km NNW of Monterrey; 26°29′N 100°25′W. Elev. 1,539 ft/469 m. Agr. center (beans, corn, fruit, wheat).

Villamar (vee-yah-MAHR), town (1990 pop. 3,325), ⊙ municipio, Michoacán, central Mexico, 9 mi/14.5 km ESE of Sahuayo de Morelos, on Mexico Highway 15; 20°01′N 102°36′W. Cereals, beans, sugarcane, fruit; livestock. Formerly Guarachita.

Villanova (VI-lah-NO-vah), uninc. village, Radnor township, Delaware co., SE Pa., suburb 11 mi/18 km NW of downtown Philadelphia; 40°02′N 75°20′W. Light mfg. Seat of Villanova Univ.

Villanueva (vee-yah-NWAI-vah), city (1990 pop. 1,752) and township, Zacatecas, N central Mexico, on interior plateau, on Juchipila R., and 35 mi/56 km SW of Zacatecas; 22°21′N 102°53′W. Elev. 6,414 ft/1,955 m. Agr. center (grain, sugarcane, tobacco, vegetables; livestock). Anc. Aztec ruins are at Quemada nearby.

Villard (vi-LAHRD), village (1990 pop. 247), Pope co., W Minn., 7 mi/11.3 km NE of Glenwood; 45°42′N 95°16′W. Livestock and poultry area; dairy prods.; grain, soybeans, beans; mfg. (machinery). E side of short chain of lakes; on E shore of Villard L. Leven L. to NW; Amelia L. to SW.

Villas, Las, Cuba: see VILLA CLARA.

Ville Lasalle, Canada: see LASALLE.

Ville Marie (VEEL mah-REE), village (1991 pop. 2,581), ⊙ Timiskaming co., W Que., E Canada, on L. Timiskaming, 70 mi/113 km N of North Bay; 47°20′N 79°26′W. Dairying; cattle market; in gold-, silver-, and copper-mining region.

Ville Marie du Montréal, Canada: see MONTREAL.

Ville Platte (VIL PLAT), city (1990 pop. 9,037), ⊙ Evangeline parish, S central La., 33 mi/53 km NNW of Lafayette; 30°42′N 92°17′W. Trade center for vegetables, rice, cotton, soybeans, sugarcane, and cattle; lumber area. Mfg. (apparel, machinery, carbon black, transportation equip.; food processing, printing and publishing). Settled in early 19th cent. Also called Flat Town. Chicot State Park and La. State Arboretum to N.

Villemontel (veel-mon-TEL), village, W Que., E Canada, 12 mi/19 km WNW of Amos; 48°37′N 78°22′W. Dairying; cattle; grain, potatoes.

Villisca (vi-LIS-kah), city (1990 pop. 1,332), Montgomery co., SW Iowa, on Middle Nodaway R. near confluence of West Nodaway R., and 15 mi/24 km ESE of Red Oak; 40°55′N 94°58′W. Ships hogs, cattle. Bituminous-coal mines nearby. Viking L. State Park to NW. Inc. 1869.

Vilna (VIL-nuh), village (1991 pop. 314), E central Alta., W Canada, 65 mi/105 km NE of Edmonton; 54°07′N 111°55′W. Farming, lumbering.

Vilonia (vi-LO-nee-uh), town (1990 pop. 1,133), Faulkner

co., central Ark., 25 mi/40 km N of Little Rock; 35°04′N 92°12′W. Mfg. (fabricated metal prods.).

Vina (VEE-nuh), town (1990 pop. 356), Franklin co., NW Ala., 22 mi/35 km SW of Russellville, near Miss. state line. Lumber; motor homes.

Viñales (veen-YAHL-ais), town, Pinar del Río prov., W Cuba, 13 mi/21 km N of Pinar del Río; 22°43′N 83°43′W. Mfg. of cigars; lumbering. Oil, coal, and copper deposits nearby. Sulphurous waters at San Vicente (5 mi/8 km N). In vicinity (N) is the picturesque Viñales Valley, a renowned landscape and tourist site noted for its calcareous formations and fine panoramas.

Vinalhaven (VEI-nuhl-hai-vuhn), town (1990 pop. 1,072), Knox co., S Maine, 15 mi/24 km ESE of Rockland; 44°01′N 68°54′W. Resort, fishing center on Vinalhaven Isl. (irregular; 8 mi/12.9 km long) in Penobscot Bay.

Vincennes, city (1990 pop. 19,859), ⊙ Knox co., SW Ind., on the Wabash R.; 38°41′N 87°31′W. Center of an extensive farm area. Mfg. (printing; magnetic wire, transportation equip., glass, chemicals, paper prods., food prods., machinery, asphalt, fabricated steel, wood prods.). Vincennes is the oldest continually inhabited settlement in Ind. Although 1702 is a traditional date for its founding, Fr. fur traders had almost certainly come long before then. By 1732 it had been fortified by the younger sieur de Vincennes and was an important Fr. settlement. Occupied by the British in 1763, the town, in the Amer. Revolution, was a main object of the expedition of George Rogers Clark. Aided by Francis Vigo, Francis Busseron, and Father Gibault, Clark triumphantly took the Br. Fort Sackville in Feb. 1779. Vincennes was capital of Ind. Territory 1800–1813, and a treaty with the Native Americans was signed here in 1805. A magnificent memorial (dedicated 1936) to George Rogers Clark is included in George Rogers Clark Natl. Memorial located on site of Fort Sackville; captured from British by Clark in 1779. "Grouseland," (built 1803–1804) the home of William H. Harrison, 9th U.S. president, is a natl. historic landmark. Ind. Territory State Memorial is in the N part of the city. Vincennes Univ. dates from 1801. Inc. 1814.

Vincent, uninc. city (1990 pop. 13,713), Los Angeles co., S Calif., residential suburb 31 mi/50 km NNE of downtown Los Angeles, in N foothills of San Gabriel Mts.; 34°06′N 117°55′W. Soledad Pass to W. Part of Aneles Natl. Forest to S.

Vincent 1 town (1990 pop. 1,767), Shelby co., central Ala., 20 mi/32 km NE of Columbiana, near Coosa R. Clothing. Deposits of coal, iron, and limestone in vicinity. **2** town (1990 pop. 185), Webster co., central Iowa, 10 mi/16 km NE of Fort Dodge; 42°35′N 94°01′W. In agr. area; soybean processing.

Vincent, village, Washington co., SE Ohio, 15 mi/24 km SW of Marietta.

Vincentown, village, Burlington co., W N.J., 4 mi/6.4 km SSE of Mount Holly.

Vinco (VIN-ko), uninc. town (1990 pop. 1,586), Cambria co., W central Pa., 6 mi/9.7 km NNE of Johnstown, on Hinckston Run Creek; 40°24′N 78°50′W. Agr. includes dairying; livestock. Saltlick Reservoir to SE.

Vine Grove, town (1990 pop. 3,586), Hardin co., N central Ky., 11 mi/18 km NW of Elizabethtown; 37°48′N 85°58′W. In agr. area (grain, burley tobacco; livestock; dairying); mfg. (hunting knives). Fort Knox Military Reservation, including U.S. Gold Bullion Depository, to NE.

Vine Hill, uninc. town (1990 pop. 3,214), Contra Costa co., W Calif., residential suburb 12 mi/19 km NNE of downtown Oakland, and 1 mi/1.6 km SE of Martinez, near Suisun Bay; 38°01′N 122°05′W. John Muir Natl. Historic site to W.

Vineland, village, S Ont., central Canada, on L. Ontario, 8 mi/13 km W of St. Catharines. Apples, stone fruit, grapes, berries.

Vineland, city (1990 pop. 54,780), Cumberland co., S N.J.; 39°27′N 75°00′W. In a poultry and fruit area. The growing city has cooperative markets, large glassworks (with offices designed by William Lescaze), and food-processing and clothing industries. Cumberland Co.

Col. is here. Settled 1861 as a planned agr. community concentrating on viticulture until vineyards were destroyed by disease in late 19th cent.; inc. 1952 when combined with Landis township. In 1882, just 3 mi/4.8 km S of Vineland in Salem co., the 1st of N.J.'s immigrant Jewish farm colonies was established; agr. economy supplemented by garment mfg.

Vineyard, village (1990 pop. 151), Utah co., N central Utah, suburb 2 mi/3.2 km W of Orem, and 6 mi/9.7 km NW of Provo, on Utah L.; 40°18'N 111°45'W. Steel Mill to S.

Vineyard Haven, village (1990 pop. 1,762) in Tisbury town, Dukes co., SE Mass., on N Martha's Vineyard, 12 mi/19 km SE of New Bedford; 41°28'N 70°37'W. Summer resort. Passenger ferry connections with Woods Hole. Formerly a whaling, fishing, and salt-making center; has good harbor on Vineyard Sound. Raided by British in 1778.

Vineyard Sound, SE Mass., separates Martha's Vineyard from Elizabeth Isls. and SW tip of Cape Cod; c.20 mi/32 km long, 3 mi/4.8 km–7 mi/11.3 km wide.

Vining, town (1990 pop. 78), Tama co., central Iowa, 10 mi/16 km E of Toledo; 41°59'N 92°23'W. In agr. area.

Vining 1 (VEI-ning), village (1990 pop. 55), on border bet. Clay and Washington cos., N Kansas, on Republican R., and 17 mi/27 km E of Concordia; 39°34'N 97°17'W. Grain; livestock. **2** village (1990 pop. 84), Otter Tail co., W Minn., S of East Battle L., 26 mi/42 km E of Fergus Falls; 46°15'N 95°31'W. Dairying; grain. Inspiration Park State Park to S.

Vinita (vi-NEE-tuh), town (1990 pop. 5,804), ⊙ Craig co., NE Okla., 52 mi/84 km NE of Tulsa; 36°38'N 95°09'W. Elev. 700 ft/213 m. RR junction. In agr., cattle-raising, and recreation area; mfg. (electronic and electrical prods. and equip., foods, textiles); coal mining. Pensacola Dam is 12 mi/19 km SE. L. O' the Cherokees nearby. Founded c.1870.

Vinita Park (vi-NEE-tuh), town (1990 pop. 2,001), St. Louis co., E Mo., residential and industrial suburb 9 mi/14.5 km NW of downtown St. Louis; 38°41'N 90°20'W. Mfg. (food prods.; printing). Inc. since 1940.

Vinita Terrace (vi-NEE-tuh), town (1990 pop. 338), St. Louis co., E Mo., residential suburb 9 mi/14.5 km NW of downtown St. Louis; 38°40'N 90°19'W.

Vinton, county (□ 411 sq mi/1,064 sq km; 1990 pop. 11,098), S Ohio; ⊙ McArthur; 39°15'N 82°28'W. Drained by Raccoon Creek, and small Salt and Little Raccoon creeks. Includes Zaleski State Forest. In the Unglaciated Plain physiographic region. Agr. area (cattle; corn, fruit). Mfg. at McArthur (lumber and wood prods., ordnance); coal mines, limestone quarries. Formed 1850.

Vinton, city (1990 pop. 5,103), ⊙ Benton co., E central Iowa, on Cedar R., and 22 mi/35 km NW of Cedar Rapids; 42°09'N 92°01'W. RR junction. Agr. trade center; poultry packing. Mfg. (lumber; machinery, limestone prods., fertilizer, feeds; printing). Limestone quarries nearby. Has Iowa Braille and Sight Saving School. Settled 1839, inc. 1869.

Vinton 1 (VIN-tuhn), town (1990 pop. 3,154), Calcasieu parish, extreme SW La., near Sabine R. and Texas state line, 22 mi/35 km W of Lake Charles city; 30°12'N 93°35'W. Oil. Shallow draft port to S on branch of Intracoastal Waterway. Delta Downs Racetrack, thoroughbred and quarterhorse racing, to W. Sabine Isl. State Wildlife Area and Nibletts Bluff Park to W. Settled c.1880. **2** town (1990 pop. 7,665), Roanoke co., SW Va., residential suburb 2 mi/3.2 km E of Roanoke, near Roanoke R.; 37°16'N 79°53'W. Blue Ridge Parkway passes to E and S. Settled 1797; inc. 1884.

Vinton 1 village (1990 pop. 293), Gallia co., S Ohio, 13 mi/21 km NW of Gallipolis, and on Raccoon Creek. In agr. area. **2** village (1990 pop. 605), El Paso co., extreme W Texas, suburb 14 mi/23 km NNW of downtown El Paso, on new channel of Rio Grande; 31°57'N 106°35'W. Old channel to W (N.Mex. state line).

Vintondale (VIN-tuhn-dail), borough (1990 pop. 582), Cambria co., W central Pa., 10 mi/16 km N of Johnstown, on Blacklick Creek; 40°28'N 78°54'W. Agr. (hay; dairying); timber.

Viola (vei-O-luh), town (1990 pop. 123), Warren co., central Tenn., 11 mi/18 km SSW of McMinnville, 35°32'N 85°52'W.

Viola 1 (vei-O-luh), village (1990 pop. 320), Fulton co., N Ark., 9 mi/14.5 km WNW of Salem; 36°23'N 91°58'W. **2** village (1990 pop. 153), Kent co., central Del., 8 mi/12.9 km SSW of Dover; 39°02'N 75°34'W. In agr. area. N. G. Wilder Wildlife Area to W. **3** village (1990 pop. 964), Mercer co., NW Ill., 8 mi/12.9 km E of Aledo; 41°12'N 90°35'W. Agr. **4** village (1990 pop. 185), Sedgwick co., S Kansas, 23 mi/37 km SW of Wichita; 37°28'N 97°38'W. In wheat region. Mfg. (machinery). **5** village (1990 pop. 644), on border bet. Vernon and Richland cos., SW Wis., on Kickapoo R., and 36 mi/58 km SE of La Crosse; 43°30'N 90°40'W. In dairying and livestock-raising area; mfg. wood prods.

Violet, uninc. city (1990 pop. 8,574), St. Bernard parish, extreme SE La., 10 mi/16 km ESE of New Orleans, and on E bank of the Mississippi R., in Mississippi Delta; 29°54'N 89°54'W. Mfg. (transportation equip.; shrimp processing). Here is W terminus (lock) of L. Borgne Canal (Violet Canal), connecting river with L. Borgne (E).

Virden, city (1990 pop. 3,635), Macoupin co., SW central Ill., 21 mi/34 km SSW of Springfield; 39°30'N 89°46'W. In agr. and bituminous-coal-mining area. Corn, wheat, soybeans. Mfg. (bldg. materials, tile). Inc. 1861.

Virden (VUHR-duhn), town (1991 pop. 2,894), SW Man., central Canada, near Assiniboine R., 45 mi/72 km W of Brandon; 49°51'N 100°56'W. Mixed farming, dairying.

Virden (VUHR-duhn), village (1990 pop. 108), Hidalgo co., SW N.Mex., on Gila R., near Ariz. state line, and 29 mi/47 km NW of Lordsburg; 32°41'N 109°00'W. Cattle; grain, alfalfa, cotton, chilies.

Vírgenes, Las Tres, Mexico: see LAS TRES VÍRGENES.

Virgie (VUHR-jee), uninc. town (1990 pop. 600), Pike co., E Ky., in the Cumberland Mts., 10 mi/16 km SSW of Pikeville. Mfg. (machining; lumber); bituminous coal.

Virgil 1 village (1990 pop. 249), Kane co., NE Ill., 13 mi/21 km NW of Geneva; 41°57'N 88°32'W. Grain; dairying; mfg. fiberglass prods. **2** village (1990 pop. 91), Greenwood co., SE Kansas, on Verdigris R., and 18 mi/29 km NE of Eureka; 37°58'N 96°00'W. Livestock; grain. **3** village (1990 pop. 33), Beadle co., E central S.Dak., on Cain Creek, and 10 mi/16 km SW of Huron; 44°17'N 98°25'W.

Virgilina (vuhr-ji-LEI-nuh), town (1990 pop. 161), Halifax co., S Va., at N.C. state line, 18 mi/29 km SSE of Halifax, opposite Virgilina (N.C.); 36°32'N 78°46'W. Agr. (grain, soybeans, tobacco; cattle).

Virgin, village (1990 pop. 229), Washington co., SW Utah, 20 mi/32 km ENE of St. George, and on Virgin R.; 37°12'N 113°12'W. Cattle; orchards. Zion Natl. Park to NE.

Virgin Gorda, B.W.I.: see VIRGIN ISLANDS.

Virgin Islands, group of about 100 small islands, West Indies, E of P.R., divided politically bet. the U.S. and the U.K.; 18°00'N 64°40'W. Although constituting the westernmost part of the Lesser Antilles, the V.I. form a geological unit with P.R. and the Greater Antilles; they are of volcanic origin overlaid with limestone. Subject to occasional hurricanes bet. Aug. and Oct. and prone to light earthquakes. The water supply is almost completely dependent on rainfall and is preserved in cisterns; some also comes from desalinization plants. The tropical climate, with its cooling NE trade winds, and the picturesque quality of the isls., enhanced by their Old World architecture, have encouraged a large tourist trade. But the predominantly Afro-Caribbean pop. remains poor. The isls. were 1st visited by Europeans when Columbus landed on St. Croix in 1493. The U.S.V.I. (□ 133 sq mi/344 sq km; 1990 pop. 101,809) were purchased from Denmark in 1917 for $25 million because of their strategic position alongside the approach to the Panama Canal. Under a law passed in 1954, the isls. are administered by the U.S. Dept. of the Interior; a governor and senate are locally elected. The ⊙ CHARLOTTE AMALIE is on St. Thomas; other cities are Christiansted and Frederiksted, both on St. Croix. Although 68 isls. comprise the group, only the 3 largest are of importance—St. Croix (□ 80 sq mi/207 sq km), St. Thomas (□ 32 sq mi/83 sq km), and St. John (□ 20 sq mi/52 sq km). St. Thomas is mountainous and encloses many snug harbors and bays. Charlotte Amalie is noted for one of the finest harbors in the Caribbean. St. Croix, with less mountainous terrain, has an economy that is dependent upon mfg., tourism, and agr. Food crops are raised; sugarcane is no longer grown but rum is still distilled. Cattle are raised on all 3 isls. Widescale reconstruction is currently underway as a result of considerable damage sustained during 1995 hurricane season. The VIRGIN ISLANDS NATIONAL PARK covers most of St. John. Settlement of St. Thomas was begun by the Dan. West India Company in 1672; St. John was claimed by Denmark in 1683, and St. Croix was purchased from France in 1733. The isls. became a Dan. royal colony in 1754. In 1801, and again 1807–1815, the isls. were in Br. hands. Immediately to the NE are the Br. V.I., Br. crown colony (□ 59 sq mi/153 sq km; 1990 pop. 16,115); ⊙ Road Town, on Tortola. They are ruled by a governor (appointed by the crown) and an executive and a legislative council. There are over 30 isls.; 16 are inhabited. The principal ones are Tortola, Anegada, and Virgin Gorda. Tourism and offshore banking are the most important economic activities. Virgin Gorda has airport. Unlike the U.S.V.I., the Br. V.I. sustained only minimal damage during the 1995 hurricane season. Britain acquired the isls. from the Dutch in 1666.

Virgin Islands National Park (□ 23 sq mi/60 sq km), St. John isl., U.S.V.I. The park, with beaches, coves, and headlands, is rich in tropical-plant, animal, and marine life. Bordeaux Mt. (1,277 ft/389 m) is the highest point on the isl. Remains of prehistoric settlements and of Dan. colonial sugar plantations are here. Est. 1956.

Virgin Mountains (8,000 ft/2,438 m), SE Nev. (Clark co.) and NW Ariz. (Mohave co.), E of Virgin R. and L. Mead, N of Colorado R., and SE of Mesquite (Nev.); 36°45'N 114°13'W.

Virgin Passage, Caribbean strait, bet. Culebra Isl. of P.R. (W) and St. Thomas Isl. of U.S.V.I. (E); 13 mi/21 km wide. Dotted by many rocks and cays.

Virgin River, 200 mi/322 km long, SW U.S.; formed by confluence of East Fork Virgin and North Fork Virgin rivers just S of Zion Natl. Park at Springdale, SW Utah; flows generally SW, part of St. George, across NW corner of Ariz., past Littlefield and Mesquite (Nev.), to L. Mead (Colorado R. reservoir) in SE Nev., 40 mi/64 km E of Las Vegas. Used for irrigation; figs, cotton, and pomegranates grown in valley. Lower 30 mi/48 km forms large N arm of L. Mead.

Virginia, state (□ 42,776 sq mi/110,771 sq km; 1995 est. pop. 6,618,358), E U.S., northernmost of the Southern states, oldest of the 13 Colonies; ⊙ RICHMOND; 37°34'N 78°31'W. Officially a commonwealth. VIRGINIA BEACH is the largest city; other important cities include ALEXANDRIA and ARLINGTON (suburbs of Wash., D.C.) and NORFOLK, NEWPORT NEWS, CHESAPEAKE, HAMPTON, PORTSMOUTH, and Suffolk (all in the Hampton Roads area in the SE) and Lynchburg, ROANOKE. Charlottesville, Bristol, and Danville. Va. is roughly triangular in shape, bounded S by N.C. and Tenn., E by Atlantic Ocean, NE by Md. (border formed by Potomac R.), NW by W.Va., and extreme W by Ky. A small sect. of Va. (2 cos.) in E occupies the S end of the Delmarva peninsula (includes parts of Md. and Del.), bet. Chesapeake Bay and the Atlantic Ocean, locally referred to as the Eastern Shore. Chesapeake Bay Bridge-Tunnel (18 mi/29 km long) crosses entrance of the bay, joining the 2 parts of the state. The coastal plain or Tidewater region extends along the W shore of Chesapeake Bay; it is generally flat and swampy and is cut by 4 great tidal rivers (estuaries)—the Potomac (forming most of Md. state line), the Rappahannock, the York, and the James—all arms of the bay. This region has vast forests of pine and hardwood, highlighted in early spring by flowering redbud and dogwood. W of the Tidewater is a fall line that rises to c.300 ft/90 m (passing through Richmond) with the Piedmont region beyond it—a rolling, generally fertile country that broadens gradually as it extends S to the N.C. state line. Farther W is the Blue Ridge range, front range of the Appalachian Mt. system, which rises abruptly from the Piedmont, carpeted with bluegrass and ablaze in spring with rhododendron and mountain laurel; just beyond the Blue Ridge, in the SW, is the state's highest peak, Mt. Rogers (5,729 ft/1,743 m). Bet. the Blue Ridge and Va.'s W border are several ridges that run generally SW-NE, separated by paralleling valleys, the most prominent being the Valley of Va., or Shenandoah Valley, in the N. Dotting the Va. landscape are the classic, Gr. revival homes and historic public bldgs. with their characteristic stately porticos. Like many SUNBELT states, Virginia's economy is highly diversified. Agr., once the mainstay of the state's economy, has been surpassed in importance by other sectors of the economy. Tobacco, Virginia's traditional main crop, is still produced in substantial quantities, and hay, corn, soybeans, peanuts, potatoes, and apples (esp. in the Shenandoah Valley) are important. Wine producing has become more significant to the economy. Cattle, hogs, poultry and dairying are still important and N Va. is noted for its horse farms. The Atlantic and Chesapeake waters yield clams, oysters, crabs, and fish, though overfishing and pollution have threatened the industry. Coal is Virginia's chief mineral; stone, cement, sand, and gravel are also important. Roanoke is a center for the RR transport-equip. industry, and large shipyards are located on the shores of Hampton Roads, esp. Newport News. Norfolk serves as a major U.S. naval base, and Portsmouth as a U.S. naval shipyard; Hampton is an important center for aeronautical research. Other leading industries include tourism and the mfg. of chemicals, electrical equip., along with food, textile, and paper prods. Va. (named for Elizabeth I, the Virgin Queen) originally designated the whole vast area of N. Amer. not held by the Spanish or French. The colony on ROANOKE ISLAND, organized by Sir Walter Raleigh, failed, but the English soon made another attempt slightly farther N. In 1606, James I granted a charter to the London Company (later better known as the Va. Company), a group of merchants lured by the thought of easy profits in mining and trade. The company sent 3 ships and 144 men under captains Christopher Newport, Bartholomew Gosnold, and John Ratcliffe to establish a base, and the tiny force entered Chesapeake Bay in April 1607. On a peninsula in the James R. they founded (May 13, 1607) the 1st permanent Eng. settlement in Amer., which they called JAMESTOWN. It soon became clear that the company's original plans were unrealistic, and the Jamestown settlers began a long and unexpected struggle to live off the land. By 1608, despite the firm and resourceful leadership of John Smith, hunger and disease had reduced their numbers to 38. The company responded by sending supplies and men and new leadership in Sir Thomas Gates, who was to take charge as deputy governor under the authority of a new charter (1609). Gates arrived in 1610 to find that only a handful of settlers had survived the terrible winter (the "starving time") of 1609–1610. He decided to take them back to England, but he had just set sail in June 1610, when his superior, Gov. Thomas West, Baron De la Warr, ordered them to reoccupy Jamestown. Although sickness and starvation continued to take a heavy toll, the settlement at last began to make headway under the harsh regimes of Sir Thomas Dale, De la Warr's successor in 1611, and later under that of Sir Samuel Argall. Tobacco, 1st cultivated by John Rolfe in 1612, gave the company new hope of a profitable return on its investment. To encourage settlement and improve agr. productivity it granted colonists (still technically employees and shareholders) the right to own private gardens, then, at the urging of Sir Edwin Sandys, promised to give 100 acres/40 ha of its land to purchasers of stock and 50 acres/20 ha to any settler who brought over other settlers at his own expense (the "head-right" system). The company also set up smaller joint-stock companies to settle vast tracts known as "colonies" or "hundreds." As additional incentives to immigration the company instructed Gov. George Yeardley in 1619 to form a House of Burgesses—the 1st representative assembly in the New World—and in 1620 began to import women. But although these various expedients did succeed in attracting new settlers and strengthening the colony, the company itself failed to prosper. Rolfe's marriage (1614) to Pocahontas, daughter of chief Powhatan, had secured good relations with the Native Americans for a time, but in 1622 Powhatan's son Opechancanough led the Powhatan Confederacy in a surprise attack on the colony, killing 350 settlers (about ⅓ of the total community). Eng. retaliation effectively ended Native Amer. resistance, except for a final uprising of the Confederacy in 1644. However, the 1622 attack had delivered a fatal blow to the company, and in 1624, beset by internal dissension, it surrendered its charter to the crown. After almost 2 decades as a private enterprise, Va. became a royal colony, the 1st in Eng. history. Partly because the Eng. kings were occupied with affairs at home, the Va. House of Burgesses was able to continue its functions, and it won formal recognition in the late 1630s; thus representative govt. under royal domain was assured. By 1641, when Sir William Berkeley became governor, the colony was well established and extended on both sides of the James R. up to its falls. Three-quarters of the settlers (c.7,500 in 1641) had come as indentured servants or apprentices, but many of them became freemen and small farmers. In 1641 there were also about 250 Africans (the 1st had arrived in 1619 on a Du. ship), most of whom were indentured servants rather than slaves. The freeholders, together with the merchant class (from which were descended most of the "First Families of Va."), controlled the govt. Only whites were enfranchised, and property qualifications for voting continued during and after the colonial period. Most of the settlers were Anglicans, and during the civil war in England, many well-to-do Englishmen (mainly Anglicans and supporters of Charles I, if not actually Cavaliers) came here. The colony was understandably loyal to the crown until 1652, when an expedition sent by Oliver Cromwell forced it to adhere to the Puritan Commonwealth. With the Commonwealth busy at home, Va. was practically independent until 1660, engaging in free trade with foreigners, esp. the Dutch, and enjoying the profits of the expanding tobacco and fur trade. This prosperous era came to an end with the Restoration in 1660. The Navigation Acts forced the tobacco trade to use only Eng. ships and Eng. ports, which were at 1st insufficient to handle it; tobacco piled up in Va. and in England, and prices plummeted. The wealthy planters weathered this depression, but the small farmers faced ruin. Serious discontent spread and was aggravated by Gov. Berkeley's high-handed policies, by his favoritism for the wealthy Tidewater planters, and by his refusal to sanction a campaign against the Native Americans attacking the frontier; these grievances brought the eruption of Bacon's Rebellion in 1676. The death of Nathaniel Bacon left the yeomen leaderless, and they were put down so ruthlessly that Berkeley was recalled to England. Expansion of the plantation system was made possible only with the use of slave labor (1st recognized in law in 1662), and tens of thousands of Africans were being imported every year by the end of the cent. Small, independent cultivators, unable to compete with the plantation-slave system, formed the nucleus of a poor, white class that drifted S or pioneered to the West. Also contributing to westward settlement were the Fr. Huguenots, who arrived by the end of the 17th cent. and began to settle the Piedmont. Westward movement was stimulated under Gov. Alexander Spotswood, who himself discovered (1716) the Swift Run Gap in the Blue Ridge Mts., leading into the Shenandoah Valley. Spotswood also imported (1714–1717) Germans to work his iron furnaces in the Piedmont area, and numerous Germans followed their countrymen. They helped settle the Shenandoah Valley (beginning c.1730) as did many newcomers from Pa.—Ger. Lutherans, Eng. Quakers, Scotch-Irish Presbyterians, and a lesser number of Welsh Baptists. Soil exhaustion from continuous tobacco cultivation speeded the westward march, as did the settlement activities of land speculators like Spotswood and William Byrd (d. 1744). Many land speculators were indebted E planters who hoped to salvage their fortunes. The Ohio Company grant (1749) furthered exploration beyond the Allegheny Mts. and brought conflict with the French. The activities and interests of the new frontier settlements contrasted sharply with the plantation life of the Tidewater region, where the lavish material life of the planter aristocracy was complemented by high cultural accomplishments and by the spread of the ideas of the Enlightenment. The last of the Fr. and Indian Wars, in which Virginians—notably Col. George Washington—were prominent, ended the Fr. obstacle to westward migration. After the war many indebted planters were disturbed by Br. limitations on westward settlement. With Mass., Va. was a leader in the movement that culminated in the Amer. Revolution, although Va. was never as politically discontented or as radical as Mass., despite the burning oratory of Patrick Henry and the enlightened political writings of Thomas Jefferson and other spokesmen. In 1773 the Burgesses at Williamsburg (the capital since 1699), led by Richard Henry Lee, formed an Intercolonial Committee of Correspondence. The Va. leaders proposed (May 1774) a congress of all the colonies; delegates were chosen at the First Va. Convention (Aug.) and in Sept., Va.'s Peyton Randolph was elected president of the First Continental Congress. The next year, in June, George Washington was made commander in chief of the Continental Army. After the patriots forced the royal governor, John Murray, Earl of Dunmore, to flee, the Fifth Va. Convention (May 6–June 29, 1776) declared the colony's independence, instructed the Va. delegates to the Continental Congress to propose general colonial independence (resulting in the Declaration of Independence written by Thomas Jefferson), and adopted a declaration of rights and the 1st constitution of a free Amer. state, both drawn up by George Mason. Patrick Henry was elected the 1st governor. Although the British had burned Norfolk in Jan. 1776, they did not invade the state in full force until 1779, when they took Portsmouth and Suffolk. Continentals under Lafayette came to Va. in 1780, and the Br. cause was lost as Amer. land forces and a Fr. fleet combined to bring about Cornwallis' surrender (Oct. 19, 1781) in the Yorktown Campaign. Meanwhile, George Rogers Clark and his Virginians had wrested (1779) from the British the Northwest Territory, and in 1784 Va. yielded its claim to this area to the Federal govt. During the Revolution a degree of religious freedom had been instituted in Va. under the lead of Jefferson. Other reforms had removed entail and primogeniture from land tenure, liberalized the legal code, and abolished further importation of slaves. A liberal law for formal emancipation of slaves was passed in 1782 and remained in force for over 20 years. In 1786 a statute for religious freedom, championed by James Madison, completed the disestablishment of the Anglican Church and established complete religious equality for all Virginians. In replacing the unsatisfactory Articles of Confederation with the Constitution of the U.S., Virginians, esp. James Madison, again played leading roles. Other leaders such as Patrick Henry, Edmund Pendleton, and Edmund Randolph at various times opposed the document, but the state ratified it (June 26, 1788) with Tidewater and W Va. support, and another Virginian, Chief Justice John Marshall, later gave it much of its strength. The Old Dominion ceded (1789) a portion of its Potomac lands to the U.S. for the creation of the D.C., which was retroceded to Virginia in 1847. In 1792, Ky., a Va. co. since 1776, was admitted to the Union as a separate state. After Madison and Jefferson raised an opposition to the financial program of Treasury Secretary Alexander Hamilton, Va. supported the emerging Democratic-Republican Party's struggle against the Federalist U.S. and became a hotbed of states' rights sentiment. Of the 1st 12 presidents of the U.S., 7 were Virginians—Washington, Jefferson, Madison, James Monroe (these 4 comprising

---

Cross references are shown in SMALL CAPITALS. The pronunciation key is on page xv. The dates of population figures are on page xii.

the "Va. Dynasty"), William Henry Harrison, John Tyler, and Zachary Taylor. These presidents sometimes expanded natl. power and natl. development to an extent which many states' rights Virginians deemed unconstitutional. However, Va. itself, stimulated by W Va. complaints, embarked on a vigorous policy of internal improvements in the 2d and 3d decades of the 19th cent. The Tidewater majority made few concessions to W demands for manhood suffrage and other reforms in the constitution of 1830. Economically, however, the whole state benefited from transportation improvements, from the growth of scientific agr. and the spread of wheat cultivation, and from the growth of such industries as tobacco processing and iron mfg. As the cotton economy grew in the newer Southern states the Tidewater became a breeding ground for the slaves they needed. Elsewhere in the state, especially in the W, antislavery sentiment was strong in the early 19th cent., and following the slave insurrection (1831) of Nat Turner the House of Delegates voted down a bill to abolish slavery by the narrow margin of 7 votes. The insurrection did result in harsher laws and more conservative policies regarding blacks. The constitution of 1851, granted suffrage to "every white male citizen," and effected reapportionment of representation. For the most part Virginians labored to avert conflict bet. N and S. But "fire-eaters" such as Edmund Ruffin and abolitionists such as John Brown of HARPERS FERRY fame, shaped the course that led to the Civil War. Secession came (April 17, 1861) only after all attempts to keep peace had failed. Va. joined the Confederacy, and Richmond became the Confederate capital. Robert E. Lee entered the military service of the new Southern govt., but not a few Virginians such as Winfield Scott, George H. Thomas, and David G. Farragut remained loyal to the Union. Most Virginians W of the Appalachians also opposed secession, and on June 20, 1863, this sect. was admitted to the Union as the new state of W.Va. Va. was the chief battleground of the Civil War. In the beginning the Union armies were repeatedly set back—at the 1st Battle of BULL RUN (July 21, 1861), in the 7 Days battles of the Peninsular Campaign (April-July 1862) after the *Monitor* and *Merrimack* had clashed in Hampton Roads, and in lesser but related campaigns such as the triumph of Thomas J. (Stonewall) Jackson in the Shenandoah Valley. The 2d Battle of Bull Run (Aug. 1862) was a smashing victory for Lee, but in the Antietam Campaign (Sept. 1862) he fared no better than Union Gen. George B. McClellan in invading enemy country. However, in the battles of Fredericksburg (Dec. 13, 1862) and Chancellorsville (May 2–4, 1863), the Federals under Gen. Ambrose E. Burnside and then under Gen. Joseph Hooker were again repulsed. Thus encouraged, Lee and his lieutenants—James Longstreet, R. S. Ewell, A. P. Hill, and J. E. B. Stuart—undertook another invasion of the N but failed against George G. Meade in the Gettysburg Campaign (June–July 1863). That marked the beginning of the end for the Confederacy, although it took considerable bloody pounding by Gen. U. S. Grant in the Wilderness Campaign (May–June 1864) and the siege of PETERSBURG (1864–1865) before Lee surrendered the remnants of his Army of N Va. at Appomattox Courthouse on April 9, 1865. President Jefferson Davis had already fled Richmond, and the Confederacy soon collapsed. The war left its marks on the land and the people. The Shenandoah Valley was particularly desolate after the campaigns of Confederate Gen. Jubal A. Early and Union Gen. Philip H. Sheridan in 1864. But poverty-stricken as it was from the war, the state, under Gov. Francis H. Pierpont, had the consolation of escaping the worst aspects of Reconstruction. Radical Republicans were but briefly in power. On the recommendation (1869) of President Ulysses Grant, Congress allowed Va. to vote without coercion, and the state passed the essential clauses of a constitution that the Radicals had drafted (1868), providing for free public schools and heavy taxes on land. More important, Va. was enabled to elect to office its own moderate party, the "white Republicans," led by Gen. William Mahone. Radical sway was ended. In 1870, after the Va. assembly had ratified the 14th and 15th amendments to the Constitution, the state was readmitted to the Union. The end of slavery and the hard agr. times of postwar decades also ended the plantation system in Va. and brought some increase in farm tenancy, but the economy benefited from diversification as fruit farming and the cigarette industry became important. To offset declines in demand for dark Va. tobacco, bright-leaf tobacco was increasingly grown. In 1902 a new state constitution invoked rigorous literacy tests for voting, completing the long process of reducing the black electorate. During the years preceding World War I, Va.'s prosperity grew as dairy farming in particular gained importance, and during the war agr. boomed, as did industry, especially the important shipbuilding works at Hampton Roads. The name of Woodrow Wilson lengthened the list of Virginian Presidents. In the mid-1920s, Harry Flood Byrd assumed direction of the state's powerful Democratic organization, formerly headed by U.S. Senator Thomas S. Martin and Methodist Episcopal Bishop James Cannon, Jr. Byrd, governor from 1926 to 1930 and U.S. Senator from 1933 until 1965, became the most influential figure in the state. As chief executive he put through a sound reorganization of the state govt., brought about the passage of the 1st antilynching law of any state, and improved the highway system. However, the organization's chief boast was that the state was entirely free of debt due to a rigid "pay-as-you-go" policy. Liberals criticized this financial policy for scrimping on public education and welfare. In the Great Depression of the 1930s the state fared better than many states. Its industries had not been overexpanded, and, more important, the state's economy was built around consumer goods—foods, textiles, and tobacco—that remained in relatively high demand. Farmers benefited from the Agr. Adjustment Administration, but conservative Virginians resisted some of the economic policies of the New Deal. In World War II, Va. was the scene of much military training, and the shipyards at Hampton Roads and other industries again aided the war effort. In the prosperous postwar period the conservative Byrd organization maintained its power. After the 1954 Supreme Court decision on integration, attempts at desegregating Virginia's schools proceeded slowly. After Va. courts and Federal courts ruled illegal the order by Gov. J. Lindsay Almond, Jr., to close public schools in 9 cos., a lame compromise of "local option" was adopted. With the exception of Prince Edward co., where schools remained closed from 1959 until 1964, all parts of Va. had accepted token integration by the mid-1960s. Va. benefited from increased military expenditures in the 1980s as the state's shipbuilding industry thrived. The greatest growth however, has come in the private sector; N Va. suburbs of Washington, D.C., such as Vienna and Reston, have flourished. The Va. constitution was revised extensively in the late 1960s. The legislature (called the General Assembly) consists of a House of Delegates of 100 members, elected to 2-year terms, and a Senate with 40 members, elected to 4-year terms. The governor serves a 4-year term and is ineligible for reelection. In 1989 Douglas Wilder, a Democrat, became the first Afr.-Amer. elected governor in the U.S. Va. sends 10 Representatives and 3 Senators to the U.S. Congress and has 13 electoral votes. Virginia's shores, mts., mineral springs, natural wonders, and numerous historic sites draw thousands of visitors annually. Major tourist attractions are Shenandoah Natl. Park in N, Colonial Natl. Historical Park at Williamsburg in SE, and Arlington House Natl. Memorial in N. Other historic points of interest include Appomattox Court House Natl. Historical Park; Manassas Nat. Battlefield Park in NE; Richmond Natl. Battlefield Park in E center; Booker T. Washington Natl. Monument in E; and George Washington Birthplace Natl. Monument in S; Jamestown Natl. Historic Site in E; Natl. Capital Parks (shared with Washington, D.C., and Md.) in NE; and several natl. cemeteries and military parks (see NATIONAL PARKS AND MONUMENTS, table). Among Va.'s institutes of higher learning are the Univ. of Va., main campus at Charlottesville, with Mary Washington Col. at Fredericksburg; George Mason Univ., at Fairfax; Arlington and Prince William; the Col. of William and Mary in Va., mainly at Williamsburg; Hampton University, at Hampton; Randolph-Macon Col., at Ashland; Randolph-Macon Woman's Col., at Lynchburg; Sweet Briar Col., at Sweet Briar; Va. Military Inst. and Washington and Lee Univ., at Lexington; Va. Polytechnic Inst. and State Univ., at Blacksburg; and Va. State University, at Petersburg. Va. has 95 cos.: ACCOMACK, ALBEMARLE, ALLEGHANY, AMELIA, AMHERST, APPOMATTOX, ARLINGTON, AUGUSTA, BATH, BEDFORD, BLAND, BOTETOURT, BRUNSWICK, BUCHANAN, BUCKINGHAM, CAMPBELL, CAROLINE, CARROLL, CHARLES CITY, CHARLOTTE, CHESTERFIELD, CLARKE, CRAIG, CULPEPER, CUMBERLAND, DICKENSON, DINWIDDIE, ESSEX, FAIRFAX, FAUQUIER, FLOYD, FLUVANNA, FRANKLIN, FREDERICK, GILES, GLOUCESTER, GOOCHLAND, GRAYSON, GREENE, GREENSVILLE, HALIFAX, HANOVER, HENRICO, HENRY, HIGHLAND, ISLE OF WIGHT, JAMES CITY, KING AND QUEEN, KING GEORGE, KING WILLIAM, LANCASTER, LEE, LOUDOUN, LOUISA, LUNENBURG, MADISON, MATHEWS, MECKLENBURG, MIDDLESEX, MONTGOMERY, NELSON, NEW KENT, NORTHAMPTON, NORTHUMBERLAND, NOTTOWAY, ORANGE, PAGE, PATRICK, PITTSYLVANIA, POWHATAN, PRINCE EDWARD, PRINCE GEORGE, PRINCE WILLIAM, PULASKI, RAPPAHANNOCK, RICHMOND, ROANOKE, ROCKBRIDGE, ROCKINGHAM, RUSSELL, SCOTT, SHENANDOAH, SMYTH, SOUTHAMPTON, SPOTSYLVANIA, STAFFORD, SURRY, SUSSEX, TAZEWELL, WARREN, WASHINGTON, WESTMORELAND, WISE, WYTHE, YORK; there are also 40 independent cities, which are separate from their adjoining cos., a rarity among other states: ALEXANDRIA, BEDFORD, BRISTOL, BUENA VISTA, CHARLOTTESVILLE, CHESAPEAKE, CLIFTON FORGE, COLONIAL HEIGHTS, COVINGTON, DANVILLE, EMPORIA, FAIRFAX, FALLS CHURCH, FRANKLIN, FREDERICKSBURG, GALAX, HAMPTON, HARRISONBURG, HOPEWELL, LEXINGTON, LYNCHBURG, MANASSAS, MANASSAS PARK, MARTINSVILLE, NEWPORT NEWS, NORFOLK, NORTON, PETERSBURG, POQUSON, PORTSMOUTH, RADFORD, RICHMOND, ROANOKE, SALEM, STAUNTON, SUFFOLK, VIRGINIA BEACH, WAYNESBORO, WILLIAMSBURG, and WINCHESTER.

Virginia, city (1990 pop. 1,767), ⊙ Cass co., W central Ill., 30 mi/48 km WNW of Springfield; 39°57′N 90°12′W. In agr. area (corn, sorghum, soybeans; cattle, hogs). Mfg. fertilizer tanks. Inc. as village in 1842, as city in 1872.

Virginia, town (1990 pop. 9,410), St. Louis co., NE Minn., 55 mi/89 km NNW of Duluth, in the Mesabi Iron Range; 47°31′N 92°30′W. Has iron mines, foundries and mfg. (mining services, printing and publishing; dairy prods., rubber prods., taconite filter bags, beverages, plastic prods.; foundry). Agr. (dairying; poultry; oats, alfalfa); timber. Tourism is economically important, and many recreational and ski areas are nearby. Giant Ridge Ski Area to E; Suprise Natl. Forest to N. Virginia-Eveleth Airport 6 mi/9.7 km to S. Inc. 1892.

Virginia, village (1990 pop. 94), Gage co., SE Nebr., 13 mi/21 km E of Beatrice; 40°15′N 96°30′W.

Virginia Beach, independent city (□ 306 sq mi/793 sq km; 1990 pop. 393,069), SE Va., city center 18 mi/29 km E of Norfolk, includes former Princess Anne co., on Atlantic coast at entrance to Chesapeake Bay; 36°44′N 76°02′W. Bounded in S by N.C. state line, E by Atlantic Ocean, N by Chesapeake Bay, W by Norfolk and Chesapeake. RR terminus; mfg. (rubber prods., electrical and electronic equip., signs, asphalt, machinery, hardware, plastic prods., foods, glass prods., chemicals, bldg. materials, textiles, transportation equip., consumer goods, foods., concrete prods., wood prods.; fish processing, printing and publishing, contract embroidery). Agr. (barley, wheat, corn, soybeans; livestock; dairy prods.); tourism. Oceana Naval Air Station in center; Camp Pendleton Military Reservation in E; U.S. Navy Amphibious Training Center in NW; Ft. Story Military Reservation in NE, at Cape Henry. Virginia Beach, Va.'s largest city, is among the fastest-growing U.S. cities, with a pop. increase of nearly 50% bet.

1980 and 1990. Long a popular resort, with beaches, a boardwalk, sportfishing; known for seafood. Seat of Atlantic Univ.; Regent Univ.; Tidewater Community Col. (Virginia Beach campus); Va. Wesleyan Col. on Norfolk border. Chesapeake Bay Bridge-Tunnel (opened 1964) links Virginia Beach with Cape Charles, on Delmarva Peninsula, to N. Cape Henry memorial cross, site of landing of 1st Eng. colonists (1607); Cape Henry lighthouse (1791; restored); oldest brick residence in U.S. (1636; restored); Alan B. Shepard civic center, geodesic aluminum-domed structure. Seashore State Park in NE, near Cape Henry; False Cape State Park in SE; Back Bay Natl. Wildlife Refuge, part of Mackay Isl. Natl. Wildlife Refuge in SE, on Back Bay, arm of Currituck Sound. Inc. 1906.

Virginia City 1 village (1990 pop. 142), ⊙ Madison co., SW Mont., on Alder Creek, and 51 mi/82 km SW of Bozeman; 45°18′N 111°57′W. Elev. 4,930 ft/1,503 m. In agr. region; timber; gold mining. Browns Gulch Mining dist. to SW. Parts of Beaverhead Natl. Forest to N and S. First town inc. in Mont. (1864), it was founded in 1863, when gold was discovered here in Alder and Browns gulches, and served as territorial capital (1865–1875). Mus. contain relics of gold-rush period. Virginia City/Madison Co. Historic Mus. and Thompson-Hickman Memorial Mus. **2** uninc. village (1990 pop. 920), ⊙ Storey co., W Nev., E of Virginia Range, 17 mi/27 km SE of Reno, and 12 mi/19 km NE of Carson City. Elev. 6,500 ft/1,981 m. Tourist center in former mining boom town (gold, silver); precious metals mining; mfg. (environmental prods.); dairying; poultry, cattle; hay. Settled 1859, when discovery (1857) of Comstock Lode (chiefly silver) in nearby Mt. Davidson was made known. Grew with increase in mining operations and had pop. of c.11,000 in 1880. The *Territorial Enterprise* (early newspaper on which Mark Twain worked as reporter) was published here after 1861. His 1st assignment as a writer, after working a mining claim at Unionville, Nev. Several mus., including The Red Light Mus., Mark Twain Mus. of Memories, and Nev. Gambling Mus.

Virginia Falls, SW Mackenzie dist., N.W.T., N Canada, in Mackenzie Mts., on South Nahanni R.; c.61°25′N 125°35′W. Drops 316 ft/96 m.

Virginia Hills, uninc. town, Fairfax co., N Va., residential suburb 3 mi/4.8 km WSW of Alexandria, 9 mi/14.5 km SSW of Washington, D.C.; 38°46′N 77°05′W.

Virginia Mountains, W Nev., roughly triangular range E of Reno, bet. Carson R. valley (S) and Pyramid L. (NE). Truckee R. divides range W-E, separating it into Pyramid (N) and Virginia (S; more commonly known as Washoe) ranges. Latter rises to 7,864 ft/2,397 m in Mt. Davidson (site of Comstock Lode), just W of Virginia City.

Virginia Peak (13,088 ft/3,989 m), Chaffee co., central Colo. 13 mi/21 km WSW of Granite, bet. North and South Forks of Clear co., in San Isabel Natl. Forest, to E of Continental Divide; 38°57′N 106°28′W.

Virginia Range, Nev.: see VIRGINIA MOUNTAINS.

Viroqua (vuhr-O-kwah), town (1990 pop. 3,922), ⊙ Vernon co., SW Wis., 26 mi/42 km SE of La Crosse; 43°33′N 90°53′W. In dairying and tobacco-growing area; mfg. (printing, light mfg.). Settled 1851, inc. 1885.

Visalia, city (1990 pop. 75,636), ⊙ Tulare co., S central Calif., 34 mi/55 km SE of Fresno, in the San Joaquin Valley; 36°20′N 119°19′W. RR junction. Its economy is centered around agr. (cotton, grapes, olives, citrus, tree fruit; nursery prods.) and livestock (cattle, hogs, poultry). Mfg. includes electronic prods., metal prods., transportation equip., and paper goods; also printing

and publishing. Visalia has been marked by rapid growth along with the central Calif. area; its pop. nearly tripled bet. 1970 and 1990. The Col. of the Sequoias (2-year) is located here. Nearby are various recreational areas, and Sequoia and Kings Canyon natl. parks lie to NE; Sequoia Natl. Forest to E. Founded 1852, inc. 1874.

Visalia (vi-SAIL-yuh), village (1990 pop. 190), Kenton co., N Ky., on Licking R., and 12 mi/19 km S of Covington; 38°55′N 84°27′W. Tobacco; cattle; dairying.

Vista, city (1990 pop. 71,872), San Diego co., SW Calif., suburb 35 mi/56 km N of downtown San Diego, 6 mi/9.7 km E of Pacific Ocean; 33°11′N 117°14′W. In an agr. and resort area. Mfg. (metal and plastics prods., electronic equip. and prods., food prods., consumer goods, fabricated metal prods., computer supplies). Vista has grown tremendously along with the San Diego metropolitan area; its pop. nearly tripled bet. 1970 and 1990. Palomar Col. (2-year) is in nearby San Marcos, to SE. Camp Pendelton Marine Corps Base to NW. Inc. 1963.

Vista Hermosa de Negrete (VEES-tah er-MO-sah dai nai-GRAI-tai), town (1990 pop. 9,219), ⊙ Vista Hermosa municipio, Michoacán, central Mexico, near Lerma R., and 20 mi/32 km E of Ocotlán; 20°16′N 102°29′W. Agr. center (cereals, fruit, vegetables; livestock). Sometimes called El Molino.

Vivian, town (1990 pop. 4,156), Caddo parish, extreme NW La., 28 mi/45 km NW of Shreveport, near Texas state line; 32°52′N 94°00′W. Center of oil-producing area; mfg. (fabricated metal prods., timber, fiberglass boats and truck trailers); lumber; agr. Inc. 1904. Recreation area. Black Bayou L. to NE, Caddo L. to S.

Vivian 1 village, Lyman co., S central S.Dak., on Medicine Creek, and 30 mi/48 km S of Pierre; 43°55′N 100°17′W. Fort Pierre Natl. Grassland to N. **2** uninc. village (1990 pop. 100), McDowell co., S W.Va., 5 mi/8 km E of Welch.

Vogtle 1 and 2 Nuclear Power Plants, Ga. see BURKE.

Volant (VO-lahnt), borough (1990 pop. 152), Lawrence co., W Pa., 8 mi/12.9 km NNE of New Castle, on Neshannock Creek; 41°06′N 80°15′W. Mfg. (transportation equip.; sand and gravel processing; bituminous coal; agr. (corn, hay; dairying). Covered bridges to SW.

Volcan de San Martín (vol-KAHN dai sahn mahr-TEEN), volcano (5,988 ft/1,825 m), in NE Veracruz, Mexico, 25 mi/40 km NW of Catemaco, and N of San Andrés Tuxtla.

Volcano, town (1990 pop. 1,516), E Hawaii isl., Hawaii co., Hawaii, 20 mi/32 km SSW of Hilo, on Hawaii Belt Road, 13 mi/21 km inland from SE coast, at E entrance to Hawaii Volcanoes Natl. Park. Tourism. The large Kilauea Caldera and its Halemaumau Crater are to W; Chain of Craters extends to SSE from here; active lava flows, Hawaii's most active volcanic zone, to SE. Kilauea State Recreational Area to NW; Olaa Forest Reserve to N. Mauna Loa volcano to W.

Volcano, uninc. village (1990 pop. 1,516), Amador co., central Calif., on Sutter Creek. Old gold rush camp in Sierra Nevada foothills, c.45 mi/72 km E of Sacramento. In 1849 Calif. gold rush region. Eldorado Natl. Forest to E.

Volga 1 town (1990 pop. 306), Clayton co., NE Iowa, on Volga R., and 8 mi/12.9 km SSW of Elkader; 42°47′N 91°32′W. In agr. and dairying region; feeds. Also called Volga City. **2** town (1990 pop. 1,263), Brookings co., E S.Dak., 7 mi/11.3 km W of Brookings, near Big Sioux R.; 44°19′N 96°55′W. Mfg. (dairy prods.). Oakwood Lakes State Park to N; RR junction to E.

Volga River, c.60 mi/97 km long, NE Iowa; rises in Fayette co.; flows ESE to Turkey R. at Garber. Flooded in 1993.

Volin, village (1990 pop. 175), Yankton co., SE S.Dak., 12 mi/19 km ENE of Yankton; 42°57′N 97°10′W.

Voltaire (vol-TER), village (1990 pop. 63), McHenry co., central N.Dak., 5 mi/8 km SE of Velva; 48°01′N 100°50′W.

Voluntown, town (1990 pop. 2,113), New London co., SE Conn., on R.I. (E) state line, 12 mi/19 km ENE of Norwich; 41°34′N 71°49′W. In recreational area; state forests here.

Volusia (vuh-LOO-shuh), county (□ 1,432 sq mi/3,709 sq km; 1990 pop. 370,712), E central Fla., on the St. Johns R. (W, partly S border) and the Atlantic Ocean (E); ⊙ De Land; 29°04′N 81°08′W. Lowland area, hilly in W, with many lakes and scattered swamps; contains several lagoons in E, including Halifax and Hillsborough rivers, and Mosquito Lagoon. Agr. (citrus fruit, vegetables; dairy prods.; poultry), forestry (lumber, naval stores), fishing. Tourist resorts along coast. Formed 1854.

Vona, village (1990 pop. 104), Kit Carson co., E Colo., 25 mi/40 km W of Burlington, on Spring Creek; 39°17′N 102°44′W. Elev. c.4,504 ft/1,373 m. Farm trade in agr. area (cattle; wheat, sunflowers, corn).

Vonda (VAHN-duh), town (1991 pop. 125), S central Sask., W Canada, 28 mi/45 km NE of Saskatoon; 52°19′N 106°06′W. In agr. area; grain elevators, foundry.

Voorhees (VOO-reez), town (1990 pop. 24,559), Camden co., SW N.J., surburban, residential area with extensive shopping center; 39°51′N 74°57′W. Camden Co. Lib. is here.

Voorheesville (VAW-reez-vil), suburban village (□ 3 sq mi/7.8 sq km; 1990 pop. 3,225), Albany co., E N.Y., 8 mi/12.9 km W of Albany; 42°38′N 73°55′W. Mfg. of machinery.

Voyageurs National Park (voi-yuh-ZHUHRZ) (□ 341 sq mi/883 sq km), N Minn., mainly in St. Louis co., extends W into Koochiching co., borders N on Canada (Ont.), 20 mi/32 km E of Internatl. Falls; 84°30′N 92°50′W. Fishing, boating, snowmobiling, cross-country skiing, canoeing. Scenic N lakes region; interesting glacial features and history. Routes of Fr.-Can. voyageurs. Bounded SE by Superior Natl. Forest; S by Kabetogama State Forest; includes SE part of Rainy L. and S part of Namakan L.(both on internatl. border), also large Kabetogama L. reservoir. Road access from S. Authorized 1971.

Vredenburgh (VRE-den-burg), town (1990 pop. 313), Monroe and Wilcox cos., SW Ala., 14 mi/23 km S of Camden. Lumber.

Vsevidof, Mount (vuh-SHAI-vi-dof), (7,236 ft/2,206 m), SW Alaska, on W Umnak Isl., Aleutian Isls., 15 mi/24 km NNE of Nikolski; 53°08′N 168°42′W. Snow-covered volcano.

Vuelta Abajo (VWAIL-tuh uh-BAH-ho), district, Pinar del Río prov., W Cuba, along the S piedmont of the Órganos Mts. c.90 mi/145 km long, c.10 mi/16 km wide. Famous for the fine quality of its tobacco, which is some of the world's best, Vuelta Abajo supplies a large proportion of the total Cuban crop.

Vulcan, town (1991 pop. 1,466), S Alta., W Canada, 50 mi/80 km SE of Calgary; 50°24′N 113°15′W. Oil production; grain elevators, flour mills.

Vulcan, village, Dickinson co., SW Upper Peninsula, Mich., 10 mi/16 km ESE of Iron Mt.; 45°46′N 87°51′W. Vulcan U.S.A. Ski Area here; Iron Mt. Iron Mine to W (tourist attraction).

Vulture Mountains, Maricopa co., W central Ariz., SW of Wickenburg, W of Hassayampa R.; rise to c.3,000 ft/914 m; 33°52′N 112°47′W. A once-important gold-mining area.

W

W. Kerr Scott Dam, N.C.: see WILKESBORO RESERVOIR.
Waas, Mount, Utah: see LA SAL MOUNTAINS.
Wabamun (WAH-buh-muhn), village (1991 pop. 600), central Alta., W Canada, on Wabamun L. (12 mi/19 km long, 6 mi/10 km wide), 40 mi/64 km W of Edmonton. Mixed farming, lumbering.
Waban, Mass.: see NEWTON.
Wabana, town (1986 pop. 4,057), N end Bell Isl., Conception Bay, N.F., E Canada; 47°39′N 52°56′W. Fish plant, service center.
Wabana, Lake (WAW-buh-naw), Itasca co., N central Minn., 12 mi/19 km N of Grand Rapids; 4 mi/6.4 km long, 3 mi/4.8 km wide; 47°25′N 93°31′W. Resorts. Drains SE through Wabana and Clearwater creeks to Prairie R. Wakeman Bay extends 2 mi/3.2 km SW; Little Wabana L. beyond SE end flows into Wabana L. Chippewa Natl. Forest to N.
Wabash 1 (WAH-bash), county (□ 227 sq mi/588 sq km; 1990 pop. 13,111), SE Ill.; ⊙ Mount Carmel; 38°26′N 87°50′W. Bounded E and S by Wabash R.; drained by Bonpas Creek. Agr. area (corn, soybeans); some mfg. Petroleum, natural gas, coal. Formed 1824. **2** county (□ 421 sq mi/1,090 sq km; 1990 pop. 35,069), NE central Ind.; ⊙ Wabash; 40°51′N 85°47′W. Agr. area (cattle, hogs; dairying; soybeans, wheat, corn); 40°51′N 85°47′W. Mfg. at Wabash. Drained by Wabash, Eel, Salamonie, and Mississinewa rivers. Formed 1834.
Wabash, city (1990 pop. 12,127), ⊙ Wabash co., N central Ind., on the Wabash R., and 17 mi/27 km SW of Huntington; 40°48′N 85°50′W. It is an agr. trade center for grain (wheat, corn, soybeans), vegetables, and fruit. Diverse mfg. It was the world's 1st electrically lighted city; one of the original street lamps is on exhibition in the co. courthouse. Nearby Salamonie (to E) and Mississinewa (to SW) dams (completed 1966 and 1967) provide flood protection and water recreation. Laid out 1834, inc. 1849.
Wabash River, c.475 mi/764 km long, Ind., Ill., and Ohio; rises in Grand L., W Ohio; flows NW into Ind., then generally SW through Ind., becoming the Ind.-Ill. border before emptying into the Ohio R.; largest northern tributary of the Ohio; 37°47′N 88°01′W. The Wabash's major tributaries are the Tippecanoe and White rivers. Dams on the Wabash control floods, produce hydroelectricity, and regulate navigation; sand and gravel barges constitute the chief traffic on the river. In the fertile Wabash basin corn and livestock are raised. Vincennes, Terre Haute, and Lafayette, Ind., and Danville, Ill., are on the Wabash.
Wabasha (WAW-buh-shaw), county (□ 549 sq mi/1,422 sq km; 1990 pop. 19,744), SE Minn.; ⊙ Wabasha; 44°16′N 92°14′W. Bounded E by Mississippi R. (Wis. border). Drained by Zumbro R. Agr. area (hay, alfalfa, corn, oats, barley, soybeans, peas, apples; sheep, hogs, cattle, poultry; dairying). Lock and Dam No. 4 in E, on Mississippi R., below L. Pepin; Carley State Park on S border; part of Whitewater Wildlife Area in SE; part of Richard J. Dorer Memorial Hardwood State Forest across S ½ of co. Formed 1849.
Wabasha (WAW-buh-shaw), town (1990 pop. 2,384), ⊙ Wabasha co., SE Minn., 30 mi/48 km NW of Winona on Mississippi R. (bridged), SE of L. Pepin (natural lake on Mississippi R.); 44°22′N 92°02′W. Resort. Trade and shipping center for grain, soybeans, apples; dairying; poultry, livestock. Mfg. (flour processing, electrical panels, printing and publishing, concrete). Lock and Dam No. 4 to SE; Upper Mississippi R. Natl. Wildlife Refuge along river margins; Coffee Mill Ski Area to W. Plotted 1843, inc. 1858.
Wabasso (wuh-BASSO), town (□ 2 sq mi/5.2 sq km; 1990 pop. 1,145), Indian River co., E central Fla., 10 mi/16 km N of Vero Beach; 27°45′N 80°26′W. Citrus fruit processing.

Wabasso (wuh-BA-so), village (1990 pop. 684), Redwood co., SW Minn., 11 mi/18 km SW of Redwood Falls; 44°23′N 95°15′W. Agr. (grain, soybeans, alfalfa; livestock, poultry; dairying); mfg. of wood prods.
Wabatongushi Lake (wah-buh-TOHNG-guh-shee), central Ont., Canada, 120 mi/193 km N of Sault Ste. Marie; 20 mi/32 km long, 3 mi/5 km wide. Elev. 1,147 ft/ 350 m. Drained into L. Superior by Michipicoten R.
Wabaunsee (wah-BUHN-see), county (□ 799 sq mi/ 2,069 sq km; 1990 pop. 6,603), E central Kansas; ⊙ Alma; 38°57′N 96°12′W. Dissected plain, bounded N by Kansas R. Drained by Mill and Dragoon creeks. Poultry, cattle, hogs; wheat, sorghum, hay, soybeans; meat processing. Formed 1859.
Wabbaseka (wah-buh-SEK-uh), village (1990 pop. 332), Jefferson co., central Ark., 15 mi/24 km NE of Pine Bluff, and on Wabbaseka R.; 34°21′N 91°47′W. Bayou Meto Wildlife Management Area to E.
Wabek, village, Mountrail co., NW central N.Dak., 31 mi/50 km SE of Stanley, and 6 mi/9.7 km E of Parshall, in Fort Berthold Indian Reservation; 47°58′N 101°57′W.
Wabeno (wah-BEE-no), village, Forest co., NE Wis., on Oconto R., and 39 mi/63 km ESE of Rhinelander. RR terminus. Sawmilling; lumber; sport fishing, hunting. In Nicolet Natl. Forest. Several small units of Potawatoni Indian Reservation in area.
Wabigoon Lake (WAH-bi-goon), NW Ont., central Canada, 75 mi/121 km E of Kenora; 16 mi/26 km long, 7 mi/11 km wide. Dryden on NW shore. Drains WNW into English R. On shore are gold mines, soapstone quarries.
Wabush, town (1991 pop. 2,331), W Lab., E Canada, 4 mi/ 6 km SSE of Labrador City; 52°55′N 66°52′W. Iron-mining center developed in the 1960s.
Wabuska (wuh-BUHS-kuh), uninc. village (1990 pop. 150), Lyon co., W Nev., 10 mi/16 km N of Yerington. Elev. 4,290 ft/1,308 m. Cattle, sheep; hay, vegetables; dairying. Mfg. (plastic prods.). Paiute Indian Reservation to S; Mason Valley Wildlife Management Area to SE.
Waccamaw River (WAH-kuh-maw), 140 mi/225 km long, SE N.C. and E S.C.; rises in small lake in SE Bladen co., SE N.C.; flows S through L. Waccamaw 15 mi/24 km NE of Whiteville, then SW into E S.C., roughly paralleling Atlantic coast (to SE) past Conway, to Winyah Bay near Georgetown. Tidal in lower 92 mi/ 148 km; 12 ft/4 m navigation channel to Conway, 44 mi/71 km above mouth. Intracoastal Waterway follows for c.30 mi/48 km from Winyah Bay to border bet. S.C. and N.C.
Wachapreague (waw-cha-PREEG), town (1990 pop. 291), Accomack co., E Va., 7 mi/11.3 km S of Accomac, on small bay joined to the Atlantic by Wachapreague Inlet; 37°36′N 75°41′W. Sportfishing resort.
Wachusett Mountain (wah-CHOO-set) (2,006 ft/ 611 m), solitary peak in N central Mass., c.8 mi/12.9 km SW of Fitchburg, in state reservation (□ 2 sq mi/ 5.2 sq km); 42°29′N 71°53′W. Road to summit; campgrounds, ski trails and lodge. Observation point.
Wachusett Reservoir (wah-CHOO-set), Worcester co., central Mass., on South Branch Nashua R., central Mass., 8 mi/13 km NNE of Worcester; 42°24′N 71°41′W. Max. capacity 229,000 acre-ft. Impounded by Wachusett Dam (114 ft/35 m high), built (1906) for water supply; also used for power generation. Receives some of its water from Quabbin Reservoir and supplies the Boston area on main aqueduct for Mass. Water Resource Authority system.
Waco 1 (WAIK-o), city (1990 pop. 461), Haralson co., NW Ga., 11 mi/18 km NNW of Carrollton; 33°42′N 85°11′W. **2** (WAI-ko), city (1990 pop. 103,590), ⊙ McLennan co., E central Texas, on the Brazos R. just below the mouth of the Bosque R. (forms L. Waco on W side of city), 87 mi/140 km SSW of Dallas; 31°34′N 97°10′W. RR junction and a trading, shipping, and industrial center in an agr. area. Diversified mfg. The Huecos (Wacos) had villages here, and the site attracted other settlers years before the city was laid out in 1849. Rich blacklands supported cotton plantations

and cattle ranches before the Civil War, but the city suffered a severe decline after the war. Prosperity returned when its suspension bridge (still a tourist attraction) was built across the Brazos (1870) and the RR arrived (1881). In 1993, the Branch Davidian cult compound was destroyed, with a loss of 72 lives, in a raid by federal agents. Cameron Park in downtown and Speegleville Park, on W side of L. Waco, provide recreation. Waco is the seat of Baylor Univ., Paul Quinn Col., a branch of Texas State Technical Col. (to N, in Northcrest), and McLennan Community Col. Points of interest include several historic homes, a reconstructed Texas Ranger fort (built 1837), and Texas Central Zoo. "Home of Dr. Pepper," flavor blended here in 1885, site of Dr. Pepper Mus. and Free Enterprise Inst., on Natl. Register of Historic Places. Inc. 1856.
Waco (WAI-ko), town (1990 pop. 86), Jasper co., SW Mo., near Spring R., and 12 mi/19 km NNW of Joplin; 37°15′N 94°35′W.
Waco 1 (WAI-ko), village (1990 pop. 211), York co., SE central Nebr., 7 mi/11.3 km E of York; 40°53′N 97°27′W. Woodburning stoves. **2** (WAIK-o), uninc. village (1990 pop. 320), Cleveland co., SW N.C., 8 mi/12.9 km NE of Shelby; 35°21′N 81°25′W. Cotton, grain; poultry, livestock; mfg. (commercial printing, fertilizer).
Waco, Lake, Texas: see BOSQUE RIVER.
Waconia (wuh-KO-nyuh), town (1990 pop. 3,498), Carver co., S central Minn., 12 mi/19 km NW of Chaska; and 27 mi/43 km WSW of Minneapolis, on S shore of Waconia L.; 44°51′N 93°47′W. In poultry, livestock; grain area. Dairy prods., hard disk drives, valves, kitchen cabinets, printed circuit boards, printing, fertilizer. Inc. 1921.
Waddell Dam, Ariz., see PLEASANT LAKE,
Waddington, town (1990 pop. 3,803), Union co., S N.C., residential suburb 14 mi/23 km S of Charlotte, near S.C. state line. In agr. area (cotton, grain; poultry, livestock).
Waddington, village (□ 2 sq mi/5.2 sq km; 1990 pop. 944), St. Lawrence co., N N.Y., port of entry on the St. Lawrence R., and 17 mi/27 km NE of Ogdensburg; 44°51′N 75°12′W. Paper milling. Summer resort; sports fishing. Ferry nearby to Morrisburg, Ont.
Waddington, Mount (13,260 ft/4,042 m), SW B.C., W Canada, in Coast Mts., 170 mi/274 km NW of Vancouver; 51°22′N 125°15′W.
Wade, township (1990 pop. 243), Aroostook co., NE Maine, on the Aroostook R., and 13 mi/21 km NW of Presque Isle; 46°47′N 68°15′W.
Wade, village (1990 pop. 238), Cumberland co., central N.C., 10 mi/16 km NE of Fayetteville, on Cape Fear R.; 35°09′N 78°44′W. Timber; livestock, poultry; grain, tobacco; lumber prods.
Wade Hampton, uninc. city (1990 pop. 20,014), Greenville co., NW S.C., residential suburb 6 mi/9.7 km NE of Greenville; 34°52′N 82°19′W. Paris Mt. State Park to NW.
Wadena (waw-DEE-nuh), county (□ 543 sq mi/ 1,406 sq km; 1990 pop. 13,154), W central Minn.; ⊙ Wadena; 46°34′N 94°57′W. Drained by Crow Wing, Leaf, and Wing rivers. Hay, alfalfa, oats, barley, rye, beans; sheep, cattle, poultry; dairying; peat deposits. Several small lakes, especially in N; Lyons State Forest in E; Huntsville State Forest in NE. Formed 1858.
Wadena (wah-DEE-nuh), town (1991 pop. 1,599), SE central Sask., W Canada, 75 mi/121 km NW of Yorkton; 51°57′N 103°48′W. Woodworking; lumber, flour, and grain milling; dairying.
Wadena 1 (wah-DEE-nah), town (1990 pop. 236), Fayette co., NE Iowa, on Volga R., and 17 mi/27 km NE of Oelwein; 42°50′N 91°39′W. Limestone quarries nearby. **2** (waw-DEE-nuh), town (1990 pop. 4,131), ⊙ Wadena co., W central Minn., on Leaf R., and 42 mi/68 km WNW of Brainerd; 46°26′N 95°07′W. Elev. 1,350 ft/ 411 m. Trading point in grain; livestock, poultry; and dairying area; light mfg. Lyons State Forest to NE. Municipal airport to E. Settled 1871, inc. 1881.
Wadesboro, town (1990 pop. 3,645), ⊙ Anson co., S N.C., 45 mi/72 km SE of Charlotte, near S.C. state line; 34°58′N 80°04′W. RR junction. Cotton, tobacco, grain;

poultry, livestock. Mfg. (apparel, feeds, orthopedic prods.). Blewett Falls L. reservoir to E. Settled c.1785.

Wading River, resort village (□ 9 sq mi/23.3 sq km; 1990 pop. including Wildwood 5,317), Suffolk co., SE N.Y., near N shore of L.I., 11 mi/18 km E of Port Jefferson; 40°57′N 72°49′W. Just E is Wildwood State Park (covers 395 acres/160 ha).

Wading River (WAI-ding), SE N.J., formed in S Burlington co. by junction of West and East branches; flows c.12 mi/19 km SE to Mullica R. c.8 mi/12.9 km above its mouth.

Wadley 1 (WAHD-lee), town (1990 pop. 517), Randolph co., E Ala., on Tallapoosa R., and 15 mi/24 km SSW of Wedowee. Lumber; mfg. of clothing. Southern Union State Community Col. here. **2** town (1990 pop. 2,473), Jefferson co., E Ga., 18 mi/29 km NNW of Swainsboro, near Ogeechee R.; 32°52′N 82°24′W. Mfg. includes lumber, sawmill machinery, clothing.

Wadmalaw Island (WAHD-muh-law), Charleston co., SE S.C., one of Sea Isls., 11 mi/18 km SW of Charleston, bet. Edisto and Johns isls.; 11 mi/18 km long, 2 mi/3.2 km–11 mi/18 km wide. Bounded by Stono R. to NW, North Edisto R. to SW, narrow channel to S. Connected by short highway bridge to Johns Isl. (NE) Rockville village is on S shore. Agr. includes tomatoes.

Wadsworth, city (1990 pop. 15,718), Medina co., NE Ohio, an industrial suburb of Akron; 41°01′N 81°44′W. Matches, iron and steel valves, and rubber prods. are manufactured in the city. Settled c.1816, inc. 1866.

Wadsworth 1 village (1990 pop. 1,826), Lake co., NE Ill., suburb 41 mi/66 km NNW of downtown Chicago, 6 mi/9.7 km NW of Waukegan, near Wis. state line, on Des Plaines R.; 42°26′N 87°55′W. Mfg. (transformer cores). **2** uninc. village (1990 pop. 640), Washoe co., W Nev., 29 mi/47 km ENE of Reno, on Truckee R., in S end of Pyramid L. Indian Reservation; 39°37′N 119°17′W. Cattle, poultry, hay; dairying. Fernley Wildlife Management Area to E; Virginia Mts. to W. Originally a RR community.

Wadsworth, Fort, N.Y.: see STATEN ISLAND.

Waelder (WEL-duhr), town (1990 pop. 745), Gonzales co., S central Texas, 21 mi/34 km E of Luling; 29°41′N 97°17′W. Trade, shipping point in cattle, poultry, peanuts area; meat processing.

Wag Water River, c.25 mi/40 km long, St. Mary parish, E central and N Jamaica; rises in foothills of Blue Mts. 9 mi/14.5 km N of Kingston; flows N to the Caribbean just W of Annotto Bay; 18°15′N 76°49′W. Not navigable. Dammed near its source, providing water for Kingston.

Wagener (WAG-nuhr), town (1990 pop. 731), Aiken co., SW S.C., c. 20 mi/32 km ENE of Aiken; 33°38′N 81°21′W. Mfg. includes men's outerwear and feeds. Agr. includes livestock, poultry; grain, cotton, peanuts, peaches.

Wager Bay, trading post, N central Keewatin dist., N.W.T., N Canada, at head of Wager Bay, an inlet (110 mi/177 km long) of Roes Welcome Sound; 65°55′N 90°49′W.

Waggaman (WAB-uh-muhn), uninc. town (1990 pop. 9,405), Jefferson parish, SE La., suburb 6 mi/10 km W of downtown New Orleans, on Mississippi R.; 29°57′N 90°14′W. Port area. Mfg. (steel casings, barge repair).

Wagner, town (1990 pop. 1,462), Charles Mix co., SE S.Dak., 23 mi/37 km WNW of Tyndall; 43°04′N 98°17′W. On Choteau Creek in Yankton Indian Reservation (headquarters to SW at Marty).

Wagner, Mount, Wyo.: see SALT RIVER RANGE.

Wagon Mound, village (1990 pop. 319), Mora co., NE N.Mex., in SE foothills of Sangre de Cristo Mts., 45 mi/72 km NE of Las Vegas; 36°00′N 104°42′W. Elev. 6,195 ft/1,888 m. Trade center; cattle, some sheep; grain alfalfa, fruit, nuts. Turkey Mts. to W; Charette Lakes to NW; section of Kiowa Natl. Grasslands, including Canadian R. Canyon to E.

Wagon Wheel Gap, village, Mineral co., SW Colo., on Rio Grande, in San Juan Mts., and 8 mi/12.9 km SE of Creede. Elev. c.8,390 ft/2,557 m. Fishing resort with mineral springs; kayaking. Surrounded by Rio Grande Natl. Forest.

Wagoner, county (□ 591 sq mi/1,531 sq km; 1990 pop. 47,883), E Okla.; ⊙ Wagoner; 35°57′N 95°31′W. Bounded S by Arkansas R.; bordered on E by Neosho R.; drained by Neosho and Verdigris rivers. Agr. (wheat, corn, soybeans; livestock; dairying); mfg. at Wagoner and Coweta. Oil, natural-gas wells. Urban growth from Tulsa in far NW corner of co., including part of city of Broken Arrow. Fort Gibson L. reservoir on E boundary (Neosho R.), including Bay State Park. Formed 1907.

Wagoner, town (1990 pop. 6,894), ⊙ Wagoner co., E Okla., 14 mi/23 km N of Muskogee, suburb of Tulsa, bet. Verdigris R. (SW), and Neosho R. (E; Ft. Gibson L.); 35°57′N 95°22′W. Elev. 586 ft/179 m. Trade center for agr. area (corn, soybeans, wheat); lumber; mfg. (steel pipe, PVC fill, shopping carts). Oil and natural-gas wells. Bay State Park to SE; Sequoyah State Park to E. Founded c.1887.

Wagram (WAI-gruhm), village (1990 pop. 480), Scotland co., S N.C., 9 mi/14.5 km NE of Laurinburg, on Drowning Creek; 34°53′N 79°22′W. Agr. area (cotton, tobacco, grain; chickens, hogs); mfg. (bath towels).

Wahiawa (WAH-hee-ah-WAH), city (1990 pop. 17,386), Honolulu co., Hawaii, on central Oahu, 17 mi/27 km NW of Honolulu on Kaukonahua Stream; bet. Waianae Range (W) and Koolau Range (E); 21°30′N 158°01′W. Mfg. (pottery). In an area that produces pineapple, it is a commercial and trucking center for the pineapple industry. Schofield Barracks Military Reservation to W, Schofield Barracks East Range to E; Wheeler Army Airfield to S.

Wahiawa (WAH-hee-ah-WAH), village, S Kauai co., Hawaii.

Wahkiakum (waw-KEI-uh-kuhm), county (□ 286 sq mi/741 sq km; 1990 pop. 3,327), SW Wash.; ⊙ Cathlamet; 46°17′N 123°26′W. Bounded S by Columbia R. (Oregon state line). Cattle; salmon, fish; timber; dairying; hay, potatoes. Co. includes Puget Isl., in Columbia R., bridge to isl.; Puget Isl. Ferry to Oregon. Columbian White-Tailed Deer Natl. Wildlife Refuge in S. Formed 1854.

Wahkon (WAW-kuhn), village (1990 pop. 197), Mille Lacs co., E Minn., 34 mi/55 km SE of Brainerd on Mille Lacs L., on Wahkon Bay; 46°07′N 93°31′W. Agr. (grain; livestock, poultry; dairying); mfg. (gears, log homes). Father Hennepin State Park to NE; Mille Lacs Wildlife Area to S. Source of Knife R. to S.

Wahneta (wah-NETAH), town (□ 2 sq mi/5.2 sq km; 1990 pop. 4,024), Polk co., central Fla., 5 mi/8 km S of Winter Haven; 27°57′N 81°43′W. Mfg. includes fiberglass boats and tanks.

Wahoo, town (1990 pop. 3,681), ⊙ Saunders co., E Nebr., 27 mi/43 km N of Lincoln, 35 mi/56 km NW of Omaha, and on branch of Platte R.; 41°13′N 96°37′W. Dairy and poultry prods.; grain. Mfg. (rendering plant, envelopes, corrugated steel pipe, vegetable processing, concrete, printing, plastic injection molding). Pioneer State Wayside Area to S. City founded 1865.

Wahpeton 1 (WAH-pe-ton), town (1990 pop. 484), Dickinson co., NW Iowa, just SW of Spirit L., on W shore of West Okoboji L.; 43°22′N 95°10′W. Recreation area; state parks nearby. **2** (WAH-puh-tuhn), town (1990 pop. 8,751), ⊙ Richland co., SE N.Dak., 45 mi/72 km S of Fargo, and on Red R.; 46°16′N 96°36′W. Bois des Sioux R. (Minn.-N. Dak. state line) flows N to form Red R. here. Located in a rich agr. area. RR junction. Metal stampings; mfg. (magnetic media prods., production machinery, printing and publishing, barley storage, transportation equip., food prods.). Site of N.Dak. State Col. of Science and the Wahpeton Indian school. Inc. 1884.

Waiakoa (WEI-o-KO-ah), village, central Maui, Maui co., Hawaii, 12 mi/19 km SE of Kahului. Kula Botanical Gardens to SE; Kula Forest Reserve to SE; Polopoli Springs State Recreational Area to S; Haleakala Natl. Park to E; serpentine Haleakala Crater Road from Waiakoa provides access to park, to Haleakala Tracking Station (includes astronomical observatories), and to Puu Ulaula (10,023 ft/3,055 m; highest point on Maui).

Waialeale (WEI-AH-lai-AH-lai), peak (5,148 ft/1,569 m), Kauai isl., Kauai co., Hawaii, 11 mi/18 km NW of Lihue. Second highest point on Kauai; reputed to be rainiest locality on earth.

Waialua (WEI-ah-LOO-ah), town (1990 pop. 3,943), Oahu, Honolulu co., Hawaii, on N coast, near Waialua Bay, 23 mi/37 km NW of Honolulu; 21°34′N 158°07′W. Mfg. (kukui nuts); Hawaii Kukui Nut Factory. Makua Military Reservation and Dillingham Field (Air Force) to W; Waianae Range to SW. Mokuleia Beach Co. Park to W.

Waianae (WEI-ah-NAH-ai), town (1990 pop. 8,758), W Oahu, Honolulu co., Hawaii, 23 mi/37 km NW of Honolulu on coast, near mouth of Kawiwi Stream; 21°26′N 158°10′W. Waianae Range to E; Lualualei U.S. Naval Reservation nearby. Lualualei Beach Co. Park to S.

Waianae Range (WEI-ah-NAH-ai), volcanic range, along W side of Oahu isl., Honolulu co., Hawaii. Of volcanic origin. Large Lualualei Naval Reservation in S center; remainder of range covered by 10 forest reserves. It rises to Mt. Kaala (4,046 ft/1,233 m) in N, the highest point on the isl. Traversed at center by Kolekole Road.

Waiehu (WEI-AI-hoo), town (1990 pop. 3,200), Maui isl., Maui co., Hawaii, suburb 2 mi/3.2 km NW of Kahului, and 2 mi/3.2 km NNE of Wailuku, at mouth of Waiehu Stream. Halekii-Pihana Heiaus (temples) State Monument to S. Waiehu Beach Park here.

Waikane (WEI-KAH-nai), village (1990 pop. 717), Oahu isl., Honolulu co., Hawaii, 13 mi/21 km N of Honolulu on NE coast; 21°30′N 157°52′W. On Kamehameha Highway. Fruits, vegetables; fish. Kualoa Regional Park to NE; Mokolii Isl. (Chinaman's Hat) to NE; Waiahole Forest Reserve, in Koolau Range, to W.

Waikapu (WEI-kah-POO), village (1990 pop. 729), W central Maui isl., Maui co., Hawaii, at center of isthmus connecting W and E Maui, 2 mi/3.2 km S of Wailuku; 20°50′N 156°31′W. Maui Plantation is here. West Maui Forest Reserve to W.

Waikiki (WEI-KEE-KEE), district, famous beach and resort center 4 mi/6.4 km SE of downtown Honolulu on SE Oahu isl., Honolulu co., Hawaii. Tourism is the economic mainstay; Waikiki is known the world over for its beach and recreational facilities, esp. surfing. Lined with luxury hotels, Waikiki has the Honolulu zoo, an aquarium, shopping malls, Internatl. Market Place; partly residential. Fort DeRussy is located here. Extinct DIAMOND HEAD volcano is to SE.

Waikoloa Village (WEI-ko-LO-ah), town (1990 pop. 2,248), N Hawaii isl., Hawaii co., Hawaii, 45 mi/72 km WNW of Hilo, 10 mi/16 km SW of Waimea, and 5 mi/8 km inland from W coast; 19°55′N 155°49′W. Residential community in heart of major cattle-ranching area. Large Parker Ranch to NE. Polo Grounds to E.

Wailea (WEI-LAI-ah), town (1990 pop. 3,400), Maui isl., Maui co., Hawaii, 13 mi/21 km S of Kahului, on Maui's SW coast; 20°40′N 156°25′W. Tourism. Several beach parks, large Waimea Golf Course in area. Whale watching late spring and summer.

Wailua (WEI-LOO-ah), city (1990 pop. 3,870), E Maui isl., Maui co., Hawaii, 20 mi/32 km E of Kahului, on Wailua Bay, NE coast. Called Wailua Homestead by Bureau of Census to distinguish it from Wailua 13 mi/21 km to SE. Pineapples, fruit; fish. Pauwalu Point Lighthouse to N; Keanue Arboretum and Kaumahina State Wayside to NW. Area bounded on W, S, and SE by Koolau Forest Reserve. Puaa Kaa State Wayside to SE.

Wailua 1 (WEI-LOO-ah), village, E Maui isl., Maui co., Hawaii, 29 mi/47 km SE of Kahului, on Waiaama Bay, SE coast, at mouth of Honolewa Stream (Wailua Falls to N); 22°03′N 159°20′W. Fish. Hana Forest Reserve to N; coastal extension of Haleakala Natl. Park to SW. **2** village, Kauai isl., Kauai co., Hawaii, 16 mi/26 km NNE of Lihue, on Wailua Bay, E coast, at mouth of Wailua R.; 22°04′N 159°22′W. Sugarcane; fish. Tourism. Wailua River State Park, incl. Opaekaa Falls, to W; Nounou Forest Reserve to NW; Kalepa Forest Reserve to SW, Lydgate State Park to S. Univ. of Hawaii Experimental Station 4 mi/6.4 km W.

Wailuku (WEI-LOO-koo), city (1990 pop. 10,688), ⊙ Maui co., N Maui, Hawaii, "twin" city to the larger Kahului 2 mi/3.2 km to E, 90 mi/145 km ESE of Honolulu; Kahului Bay 1 mi/1.6 km to NE of downtown; 20°53′N 156°30′W. Tourist center. Mfg. (printing and publishing, ice cream). Maui Correctional Center to S. Maui Community Col. to E at Kahului. Maui Historical Society Mus. Halekii-Pihana Heiaus State Monument to NE. Maui Jinsha Shinto Shrine to NE, near coast. Maui Zoological and Botanical Gardens to E. Kepaniwai Heritage Gardens to W. Waiehu Beach Park and Waihee Beach Park to N; Iao State Park, including Iao Needle rock formation, to W; West Maui Forest Reserve to N.

Waimanalo (WEI-MAH-NAH-lo), village (1990 pop. 3,508), SE Oahu, Honolulu co., Hawaii, 10 mi/16 km ENE of Honolulu; 21°21′N 157°43′W. Mfg. (food preparations). Bellows Air Force Base is here, to NE. Waimanalo Beach State Recreational Area to SE, on coast; Koolau Range to SE.

Waimanalo Beach (WEI-MAH-NAH-lo), town (1990 pop. 4,185), SE Oahu isl., Honolulu co., Hawaii, on Waimanalo Bay, E coast; 21°19′N 157°41′W. Tourism. Fish, prawns. Bellows Air Force Base (inactive) to NW; Waimanalo Beach Park to S; Waimanalo Forest Reserve to SW.

Waimanalo Pali (WAI-WAH-NAH-lo PAH-lee), a pass through Koolau Range, leads down from Makapuu Point to E seaboard, Hawaii.

Waimea 1 (WEI-MAI-ah), town (1990 pop. 5,972), N Hawaii isl., Hawaii co., Hawaii, 42 mi/68 km NW of Hilo isl., 8 mi/12.9 km from NE coast, and 9 mi/14.5 km from W coast; 20°01′N 155°38′W. On Mamalahoa Highway (Hawaii Belt Road). Kohala Forest Reserve to N; Mauna Kea (13,796 ft/4,205 m), highest point in Hawaii, to SE, in Mauna Kea Forest Reserve. On huge (210,000 acres/84,987 ha) Parker cattle ranch; Parker Ranch Visitor Center and Mus.; Parker Ranch Race Track to S. Waimea-Kohala Airport to S; Polo Grounds 7 mi/11.3 km to S; Hawaii Preparatory Acad. and Kamuela Mus. to W. With post office name of Kamuela. **2** town (1990 pop. 1,840), Kauai isl., Kauai co., Hawaii, 19 mi/31 km W of Lihue, on S coast, at mouth of Waimea R., on Kaumualii Highway, at terminus of Waimea Canyon Drive; the "Grand Canyon of the Pacific." Waimea Canyon State Park 6 mi/9.7 km to N. Tourism. Sugarcane, tropical fruit; fish. Menehune Ditch, ancient stone irrigation channel, to N; Lucy Wright Beach Park is here; Rus. Fort Elizabeth State Park to SE. Captain Cook Landing site to W.

Waimea (WEI-MAI-ah), village, N Oahu isl., Honolulu co., Hawaii, 25 mi/40 km NNW of Honolulu, on N coast. Waimea Bay to SW, receives Waimea R. Sugarcane, cattle, fish. Comsat Tracking Station to NE. Pupukea Beach Park is here. Puuomahuka Heiau State Monument to S.

Waimea Canyon (WEI-MAI-ah), W central Kauai isl., Kauai co., Hawaii, 20 mi/32 km WNW of Lihue; referred to as "Grand Canyon of the Pacific"; c.10 mi/16 km long, 1 mi/1.6 km wide. Waimea R. flows S through canyon. Puu Ka Pele on W edge. Mostly in Puu Ka Pele Forest Reserve; Waimea Canyon State Park and scenic drive on W rim; Kokee State Park is N.

Wainscott, village (1990 pop. 1,350), Suffolk co., SE N.Y., on Long Island, 3 mi/4.8 km E of Bridgehampton; 40°56′N 72°14′W. In summer-resort area.

Wainwright, town (1991 pop. 4,732), E Alta., W Canada, SE of Edmonton, and near the Sask. border; 52°50′N 110°52′W. Trade center and RR division point for an oil and natural-gas area. It has oil refineries, grain elevators, and flour mills. Nearby is a military base.

Wainwright 1 village (1990 pop. 492), NW Alaska, on Chukchi Sea, at mouth of Kuk R., 90 mi/145 km WSW of Barrow; 70°39′N 159°46′W. Fishing. Oil and coal deposits nearby. **2** village (1990 pop. 223), Muskogee co., E Okla., 15 mi/24 km SW of Muskogee; 35°36′N 95°34′W. Agr. area.

Waipahu (WEI-PAH-hoo), city (1990 pop. 31,435), S Oahu, Honolulu co., Hawaii, 11 mi/18 km NW of Honolulu; on W Loch, near Pearl Harbor, at mouth of Waikele Stream; 21°23′N 158°00′W. Mfg. (soaps, steel mill, baked goods, vehicle parts, apparel, prepared meats, house furnishings). Pearl Harbor U.S. Naval Base to S.

Waite (WAIT), town (1990 pop. 119), Washington co., E Maine, c.45 mi/72 km NNW of Machias; 45°21′N 67°37′W. In hunting, fishing area.

Waite Hill, village (1990 pop. 454), Lake co., NE Ohio, c.15 mi/24 km ENE of Cleveland; 41°36′N 81°23′W.

Waite Park, town (1990 pop. 5,020), Stearns co., central Minn., suburb 4 mi/6.4 km SW of St. Cloud, bounded NW by Sauk R.; 45°32′N 94°13′W. RR junction. Agr. (grain; livestock; poultry); Mfg. (restaurant fixtures, steel shapes, machining; printing and publishing, stone layout plates, aircraft overhead cranes).

Waits River (WAITZ), c.20 mi/32 km long, E Vt.; rises E of Barre; flows SE to the Connecticut R. at Bradford.

Waitsburg, town (1990 pop. 990), Walla Walla co., SE Wash., 18 mi/29 km NE of Walla Walla; and on Touchet R., at mouth of Coppei Creek; 46°16′N 118°09′W. RR junction. Potatoes, wheat, fruit, barley, alfalfa; hogs. Lewis and Clark Trail State Park to E.

Waitsfield (WAITZ-feeld), town (1990 pop. 1,422), Washington co., W central Vt., on Mad R., and 15 mi/24 km WSW of Montpelier; 44°10′N 72°47′W. Dairy prods. Skiing nearby (Mad R. Glen).

Wajay (wuh-HEI), town, suburb (satellite town) in Ciudad de la Habana prov., W Cuba, 9 mi/14.5 km SSW of Havana; 23°00′N 82°24′W. Tobacco, vegetables, fruit. Formerly spelled Guajay.

Wakarusa, town (1990 pop. 1,667), Elkhart co., N Ind., 10 mi/16 km N of Goshen; 41°32′N 86°01′W. In agr. area (dairy prods.; grain); mfg. (transportation equip., cookers and roasters). Laid out 1852.

Wakarusa River (wah-kuh-ROO-suh), c.50 mi/80 km long, E Kansas; rises in E Wabaunsee co. SW of Topeka; flows E past S side of Lawrence to Kansas R. at Eudora, 8 mi/12.9 km E of Lawrence.

Wakaw (WAH-ko), town (1991 pop. 965), central Sask., W Canada, on Wakaw L. (12 mi/19 km long), 40 mi/64 km S of Prince Albert; 52°39′N 105°44′W. Mixed farming; dairying.

Wake, county (□ 857 sq mi/2,220 sq km; 1990 pop. 423,380), central N.C.; ⊙ RALEIGH; 35°47′N 78°39′W. In Piedmont region; agr. area (tobacco, cotton, corn, wheat, oats, barley, soybeans, sorghum, hay; chickens, cattle, hogs); drained by Neuse R., forms Falls L. reservoir in N. Mfg. at Raleigh, also at Zebulon, Garner, and Cary. Granite quarrying. Harris Nuclear Power Plant, (initial criticality January 3, 1987) is 20 mi/32 km SW of Raleigh, uses cooling water from the Makeup Reservoir, and has a max. dependable capacity of 860 MWe. Part of Harris L. reservoir in SW; Falls L. State Recreation Park in N; William B. Umstead State Park in NW; part of Research Triangle Park in NW; smaller Wheeler and Benson reservoirs in S center. City of Raleigh and its suburbs at center of co., with development occurring mainly NW, toward Durham (Durham co.). Formed 1770.

Wake Forest, town (1990 pop. 5,769), Wake co., central N.C., 15 mi/24 km NNE of Raleigh; 35°58′N 78°31′W. Agr. area (cotton, tobacco, grain, soybeans; poultry, livestock). Mfg. (street sweepers, textile dyeing and finishing, pneumatic valves; printing and publishing). Falls L. Reservoir and State Recreation Area to W. Southeastern Baptist Seminary (1833).

Wake Island, atoll (□ 3 sq mi/7.8 sq km), central Pacific, bet. Hawaii and Guam, c.2,300 mi/3,701 km W of Honolulu, Hawaii; 4.5 mi/7.2 km long, 1.5 mi/2.4 km wide; 166°35′E, 19°18′N. Includes horseshoe shaped Wake Isl. and 2 islets (Wilkes, with Kuku Point, W, and Peale, with Toki Point, NW). Isl. is isolated, not part of any isl. group. Peacock Point at SE end of Wake, Heel Point at NE end. Administered by U.S. Air Force, it is a U.S. commercial and military base under the jurisdiction of the FAA. There is no indigenous pop. Wake Isl. was discovered by the Spanish in 1568, visited by the British in 1796 and named after Capt. William Wake, and annexed by the U.S. (1898). The isl. became (1935) a commercial air base on route to the Orient and later served as a U.S. military base. In Dec. 1941, Wake Isl. was seized by the Japanese. U.S. forces bombed the isl. from 1942 until Japan's surrender in 1945. Wake Airport and small settlement in E, on main isl. Used as refueling stop; no industries.

Wake Village, town (1990 pop. 4,757), Bowie co., NE Texas, a residential suburb 5 mi/8 km W of downtown Texarkana; 33°25′N 94°06′W. Drained by S Wagner Creek. Inc. 1944. Also called Wake.

Wakeeney (WAH-kee-nee), town (1990 pop. 2,161), ⊙ Trego co., W central Kansas, 32 mi/51 km WNW of Hays, bet. Saline and Smoky Hill rivers; 39°01′N 99°52′W. Elev. 2,450 ft/747 m. In grain and livestock region; dairying. Prehistoric fossils have been found in vicinity; mus. here. Cedar Bluff Reservoir and State Park to S. Sometimes spelled WaKeeney. Inc. 1880.

Wakefield, village, SW Que., E Canada, on Gatineau R., and 17 mi/27 km NE of Hull; 45°39′N 75°58′W. Magnesia, lime mfg. Tourism, ski resort area; covered bridge.

Wakefield, town (1991 pop. 2,724), Trelawny parish, NW Jamaica, 12 mi/19 km SE of Montego Bay; 18°25′N 77°43′W. Road junction.

Wakefield 1 town (1990 pop. 24,825), Middlesex co., NE Mass., a suburb N of Boston; 42°30′N 71°04′W. Chiefly residential, the town has some light industry. Mfg. (plastics, heat sinks, burning systems, telecommunications). Includes village of Greenwood. Settled 1639, inc. 1812. **2** town (1990 pop. 2,318), Gogebic co., W Upper Peninsula, Mich., 12 mi/19 km ENE of Ironside; 46°28′N 89°55′W. Cattle; forage crops; sawmilling; mfg. (wood prods.); resort. Settled 1866; inc. as village 1887, as city 1919. **3** town (1990 pop. 1,082), Dixon and Wayne cos., NE Nebr., 12 mi/19.2 km ENE of Wayne, and on Logan Creek; 42°16′N 96°52′W. Grain; egg processing. **4** town (1990 pop. 3,057), Carroll co., SE N.H., 17 mi/27 km N of Rochester; 43°35′N 71°00′W. Bounded by Maine state line (formed in SE by Salmon Falls R., which drains Great East L. and Horn Pond, on state line); Province L. in NE corner, Pine River Pond in center, Lovell L. in S. Drained by Pine R. and Branch R. Includes villages of Union, mfg. (foam packaging), and Sanbornville. Nursery crops, vegetables, apples; poultry, cattle; dairying. Mfg. (plastic parts). **5** town (1990 pop. 1,070), Sussex co., SE Va., 28 mi/45 km SE of Petersburg; 36°58′N 76°59′W. Mfg. (lumber); in agr. area (peanuts, tobacco, melons, grain, soybeans; poultry, livestock). Municipal Airport to NW.

Wakefield 1 village (1990 pop. 900), Clay co., N central Kansas, on W shore of Milford L. reservoir (Republican R.), and 16 mi/26 km NW of Junction City; 39°13′N 97°01′W. Shipping point in cattle and grain region. Landscape Arboretum here. **2** village, administrative center of South Kingstown town, Washington co., S R.I., 27 mi/43 km SSW of Providence. Birthplace of Oliver Hazard Perry is mus.

Wakeman, village (1990 pop. 948), Huron co., N Ohio, 11 mi/18 km E of Norwalk, and on Vermilion R.; 41°15′N 82°24′W.

Wakemup Bay, Minn.: see VERMILION LAKE.

Wakenda (waw-ken-DAW), town (1990 pop. 89), Carroll co., NW central Mo., near Missouri R., 7 mi/11.3 km ESE of Carrollton; 39°19′N 93°22′W.

Wakita (wah-KEET-uh), village (1990 pop. 453), Grant co., N Okla., 12 mi/19 km WNW of Medford; 36°52′N 97°55′W. In agr. area (grain; cattle).

Wakonda (wuh-KON-duh), village (1990 pop. 329), Clay co., SE S.Dak., 17 mi/27 km NNW of Vermillion; 43°00′N 97°06′W.

Wakonda Lake, at Glen Elder, N Kansas, on Solomon Creek, 11 mi/18 km W of Beloit; 12 mi/19 km long; 39°29′N 98°17′W. Max. capacity 1,129,000 acre-ft. North Solomon and South Solomon rivers join here. Formed by dam (40 ft/12 m high), built (1969) by the Bureau of Reclamation for flood control. Cawker City on N shore. Glen Elder State Park at dam.

Area in square miles is shown by the symbol □   capital city or county seat by ⊙

Wakulla (wuh-KUL-luh), county (□ 735 sq mi/ 1,904 sq km; 1990 pop. 14,202), NW Fla., bounded S by Apalachee Bay (Gulf of Mexico), and W by Ochlockonee R.; ⊙ Crawfordville; 30°08′N 84°22′W. Lowland area drained by St. Marks and Wakulla rivers. Coast is a natl. wildlife refuge; W interior is part of Apalachicola Natl. Forest. Agr. (cattle, hogs; corn, peanuts, vegetables), forestry (lumber, naval stores), and fishing. Formed 1843.

Wakulla (wuh-KUL-luh), village, Wakulla co., NW Fla., 15 mi/24 km SSW of Tallahassee. Wakulla Springs, a resort, is 4 mi/6.4 km W; its large, deep spring is source of Wakulla R., which flows c.10 mi/16 km SE to St. Marks R. at St. Marks.

Walbridge, village (1990 pop. 2,736), Wood co., NW Ohio, 5 mi/8 km SE of Toledo; 41°35′N 83°29′W.

Walburg, uninc. village (1990 pop. 250), Williamson co., central Texas, 30 mi/48 km NNE of Austin. Agr. and timber area. Mfg. (oak furniture).

Walcott, town (1990 pop. 1,356), Scott co., E Iowa, 11 mi/ 18 km WNW of Davenport; 41°35′N 90°46′W. Mfg. (lubricants; wheels and rims; fertilizer).

Walcott, village, Greene co., NE Ark., 11 mi/18 km W of Paragould. Crowley's Ridge State Park is nearby; Lake Frierson State park to S.

Walcott, Lake, reservoir, S Idaho, at joining of Minidoka, Blaine, and Cassia cos., on Snake R., in Minidoka Natl. Wildlife Refuge, 10 mi/16 km ENE of Rupert; c.10 mi/16 km long; 42°39′N 113°28′W. Max. capacity 107,240 acre-ft. Formed by earth-fill Minidoka Dam (86 ft/26 m high, 650 ft/198 m long), completed 1913 for irrigation and power generation. Power plant.

Walden 1 town (1990 pop. 890), ⊙ Jackson co., N Colo., on headstream of North Platte R., bet. Park Range and Medicine Bow Mts., and 55 mi/89 km SW of Laramie, Wyo., near Wyo. state line; 40°43′N 106°16′W. Elev. 8,099 ft/2,469 m. Supply point in sheep, hay, and grain region; coal mines. **2** town (1990 pop. 703), Caledonia co., NE Vt., 10 mi/16 km W of St. Johnsbury; 44°28′N 72°15′W. Agr.

Walden, village (□ 2 sq mi/5.2 sq km; 1990 pop. 5,836), Orange co., SE N.Y., on Wallkill R., and 10 mi/16 km WNW of Newburgh; 41°33′N 74°11′W. Former factory town, now residential village with a few small industries; in dairying and resort area. Inc. 1855.

Walden Pond, Mass.: see CONCORD.

Walden Ridge, SE Tenn., a ridge-like portion of Cumberland Plateau, in Appalachian system; from Tennessee R. W of Chattanooga extends c.60 mi/97 km NNE, paralleling Sequatchie R. (W), bet. Sand Mt. (S) and Crab Orchard Mts. (N). Averages 2,000 ft/610 m, rising to c.3,000 ft/914 m at N end. Signal Mtn., just NW of Chattanooga, is a spur; 35°31′N 86°12′W; 35°41′N 84°57′W.

Waldheim (WOLD-heim), town (1991 pop. 812), S central Sask., W Canada, 35 mi/56 km N of Saskatoon; 52°37′N 106°39′W. Mixed farming; dairying. First settled by Mennonites.

Waldo (WAWL-do), county (□ 852 sq mi/2,207 sq km; 1990 pop. 33,018), S Maine, on Penobscot Bay; ⊙ Belfast; 44°28′N 69°07′W. Drained by Penobscot, Sebasticook, and Sheepscot rivers. Agr.; fishing; resort region. Agr. in inland lake region (apples, potatoes, garden vegetables); dairying. Also tourism. Formed 1827.

Waldo 1 (WAHL-do), town (1990 pop. 1,495), Columbia co., SW Ark., 7 mi/11.3 km NNW of Magnolia; 33°21′N 93°17′W. Livestock raising and timber area; woodworking; mfg. (lumber polyurethanes). Founded in 1830s. Logoly State Park to E. **2** town (□ 1 sq mi/2.6 sq km; 1990 pop. 1,017), Alachua co., N central Fla., 13 mi/ 21 km NE of Gainesville; 29°47′N 82°10′W. In agr. area. **3** town (1990 pop. 626), Waldo co., S Maine, just NW of Belfast.

Waldo 1 village (1990 pop. 57), Russell co., N central Kansas, 16 mi/26 km N of Russell; 39°07′N 98°47′W. Livestock, grain. **2** village (1990 pop. 340), Marion co., central Ohio, 9 mi/14 km SSE of Marion, and on Olentangy R.; 40°28′N 83°05′W. **3** village (1990 pop. 442),

Sheboygan co., E Wis., on small Onion R., and 12 mi/ 19 km WSW of Sheboygan; 43°40′N 87°57′W. In dairy and farm area.

Waldoboro (WAWL-do-buhr-o), fishing, resort town (1990 pop. 4,601), Lincoln co., SW Maine, 15 mi/24 km ENE of Wiscasset, at head of Medomak R. inlet; 44°06′N 69°22′W. Light mfg. Settled 1748 by Germans, inc. 1773.

Waldorf 1 village (1990 pop. 15,058), Charles co., S Md., 20 mi/32 km SSE of Washington, D.C.; 38°38′N 76°54′W. The name means "Village in the Woods," but that hasn't been appropriate for decades. Bet. 1948–1968, it was a gambling mecca when that pastime was legal in the 3 S counties of Maryland. It is now part of the "Million Dollar Motel Row," that stretches along U.S. 301 to the Potomac R. Bridge 20 mi/32 km S. Cedarville State Forest is nearby. **2** village (1990 pop. 243), Waseca co., S Minn., 14 mi/23 km SW of Waseca, on Little Cobb R.; 43°55′N 93°42′W. Dairying; poultry, livestock; grain, soybeans.

Waldport, town (1990 pop. 1,595), Lincoln co., W Oregon, near Pacific Ocean at entrance to Alsea Bay, estuary of Alsea R., 40 mi/64 km WSW of Corvallis; 44°25′N 124°03′W. Timber. Crabs, shrimp, clams. Poultry, sheep, cattle. Siuslaw Natl. Forest to E and S; several coastal state parks and state waysides to N and S; Nelson State Wayside to E.

Waldron (WAWL-druhn), town (1990 pop. 3,024), ⊙ Scott co., W Ark., 38 mi/61 km SSE of Fort Smith near Poteau R.; 34°53′N 94°05′W. RR terminus. In timber and farm area; poultry processing. Mfg. (lumber, monitoring systems for paper industry, poultry processing). Town and vicinity surrounded by Ouachita Natl. Forest; L. Hinkle reservoir to W.

Waldron 1 village (1990 pop. 800), Shelby co., central Ind., 6 mi/9.7 km SE of Shelbyville. Corn, wheat; hogs. Laid out 1854. **2** village (1990 pop. 19), Harper co., S Kansas, at Okla. state line, 13 mi/21 km SW of Anthony; 37°00′N 98°10′W. In wheat area. **3** village (1990 pop. 581), Hillsdale co., S Mich., 18 mi/29 km SE of Hillsdale, near Ohio state line; 41°43′N 84°25′W. In livestock and grain region. Sheet metal fabricating.

Waldwick (WAWL-dwik), borough (1990 pop. 9,757), Bergen co., NE N.J., 9 mi/14.5 km NNW of Hackensack; 41°00′N 74°07′W. Residential community NW of N.Y. city. Inc. 1919.

Wales 1 town (1990 pop. 1,566), Hampden co., S Mass., 18 mi/29 km E of Springfield; 42°04′N 72°14′W. State forest and state park nearby. **2** town (1990 pop. 2,471), Waukesha co., SE Wis., 23 mi/37 km W of Milwaukee, and 7 mi/11.3 km W of Waukesha; 43°00′N 88°22′W. In dairying and farming area; mfg. (carbide cutters, bimetallic cylinders). On Glacial Drumlin State Trail.

Wales 1 village (1990 pop. 161), at W extremity of Seward Peninsula, W Alaska, on Bering Strait, 110 mi/177 km NW of Nome; 65°36′N 168°04′W. **2** village (1990 pop. 48), Cavalier co., NE N.Dak., 15 mi/24 km NW of Langdon; 48°53′N 98°35′W. **3** village, Giles co., S Tenn., 4 mi/6 km NNW of Pulaski. Mines phosphate rock. **4** village (1990 pop. 189), Sanpete co., central Utah, in irrigated Sanpete Valley, 15 mi/24 km N of Manti; 39°29′N 111°38′W. Coal. Part of Uinta Natl. Forest to W.

Wales Corner, town, Androscoggin co., SW Maine, 9 mi/14.5 km NE of Lewiston.

Walesboro, village, Bartholomew co., S central Ind., 5 mi/8 km S of Columbus. In agr. area. Mfg. (diesel engines).

Waleska (wah-LES-kuh), town (1990 pop. 700), Cherokee co., NW Ga., 7 mi/11.3 km NW of Canton; 34°19′N 84°33′W.

Walhalla 1 (wahl-HAHL-uh), town (1990 pop. 1,131), Pembina co., NE N.Dak., near Can. border, 80 mi/ 129 km NNW of Grand Forks, and on Pembina R.; 48°55′N 97°55′W. Resort; port of entry; RR terminus; potato-shipping center; livestock; grain. Founded as trading post and mission 1848. Walhalla Historical Site to the SW; Frostfire Mt. Ski Area to W; Gingras State

Historic Site to N. Plotted 1877, inc. 1885. **2** (wawl-HAH-luh), town (1990 pop. 3,755), ⊙ Oconee co., NW S.C., 38 mi/61 km W of Greenville, near the Blue Ridge; 34°46′N 83°03′W. Mfg. includes cotton textiles, clothing, and bearings; agr. includes corn, wheat, timber, soybeans; livestock, poultry. Summer resort. Oconee State Park (1,165 acres/471 ha; recreational facilities) is c.5 mi/8 km NW. Founded c.1850.

Walhonding River (wahl-HAHN-ding), c.20 mi/32 km long, central Ohio; formed by junction of Mohican and Kokosing rivers 16 mi/26 km NW of Coshocton; flows E, uniting with the Tuscarawas at Coshocton to form the Muskingum; 40°16′N 81°52′W. Near Nellie, Mohawk Dam (2,330 ft/710 m long, 111 ft/34 m high above streambed; completed 1937; for flood control) impounds Mohawk Reservoir (capacity 285,000 acre-ft.).

Walk, Lake, Texas: see DEVIL'S RIVER.

Walker 1 county (□ 805 sq mi/2,085 sq km; 1990 pop. 67,670), NW central Ala.; ⊙ Jasper. Hilly area crossed by Mulberry Fork. Coal mining; hay, corn; livestock, poultry; timber; natural-gas production. The co., along with Jefferson co., once accounted for 60% of Ala.'s coal production, but now the industry is declining. Formed 1832. **2** county (□ 447 sq mi/1,158 sq km; 1990 pop. 58,340), NW Ga.; ⊙ LaFayette; 34°44′N 85°18′W. Bounded SW by Ala. state line. Agr. (corn, soybeans, wheat); cattle, hogs; limestone. Includes parts of Chickamauga and Chattanooga Natl. Military Park and Chattahoochee Natl. Forest. Formed 1833. **3** county (□ 801 sq mi/2,075 sq km; 1990 pop. 50,917), E central Texas; ⊙ Huntsville; 30°44′N 95°34′W. Processing, shipping center. Bounded NE by Trinity R. and L. Livingston reservoir, NW by Bedins Creek; drained by tributaries of the Trinity and the West Fork San Jacinto rivers. Includes part of Sam Houston Natl. Forest across much of S part of co. Rolling wooded area (pine, hardwood timber chief industry); sand and gravel, clay mining; some gas and oil wells. Livestock (cattle, some horses); agr. (cotton, grain sorghum, hay). Hunting, fishing. Huntsville State Park in S center. Part of L. Conroe on S boundary. Formed 1846.

Walker, city (1990 pop. 17,279), Kent co., SW Mich., suburb 3 mi/4.8 km W and N of downtown Grand Rapids; 42°58′N 85°45′W. Mfg. (metal stampings, iron castings, theater and auditorium seating, assembly tracks). Grand R. borders on S and E.

Walker 1 town, Linn co., E Iowa, 21 mi/34 km NNW of Cedar Rapids. Feed milling; livestock supplements; fertilizer. **2** town (1990 pop. 3,727), Livingston parish, SE La., 19 mi/31 km E of Baton Rouge; 30°29′N 90°52′W. Mfg. (flow control systems, pipe fabrications); In agr. area (peppers, cucumbers, cattle, poultry, exotic fowl; dairying); timber. **3** town (1990 pop. 950), ⊙ Cass co., N central Minn., 28 mi/45 km SSE of Bemidji at SW end of Leech L., in Chippewa Natl. Forest; 47°05′N 94°34′W. Elev. 1,320 ft/402 m. Dairying; poultry, cattle, sheep; oats, alfalfa; timber; light mfg. Leech L. Indian Reservation is to N and E; Paul Bunyan State Forest to W; Welsh L. State Forest to N. Walker Mus. of Natural History and Indian Life is here. **4** town (1990 pop. 283), Vernon co., W Mo., 8 mi/12.9 km NE of Nevada; 37°53′N 94°13′W.

Walker Air Force Base, Roswell, N.Mex. opened in 1942, served as a strategic air command base until closing in 1967. Now the Roswell Industrial Air Center.

Walker Lake, uninc. village (1990 pop. 700), Mineral co., W Nev., 10 mi/16 km NW of Hawthorne, on W shore of Walker L. Walker L. State Recreation Area to N; Hawthorne Naval Ammunition Dump to S; Wassuk Range to W.

Walker Lake, salt lake (□ c.105 sq mi/272 sq km), Mineral co., W Nev., on Walker R., 75 mi/121 km SE of Reno, and 5 mi/8 km N of Carson City; 18 mi/29 km long, 7 mi/11.3 km wide; 38°35′N 118°42′W. River enters from N. Remnant of prehistoric Lake Lahontan and has no outlet. Walker Lake State Recreation Area on W shore. Hawthorne Naval Ammunition Plant on S shore.

Walker Mountain, ridge, SW Va., in Allegheny Mts.; from point W of Bristol, extends c.110 mi/177 km NE to New R. N of Radford. Elev. 2,000 ft/610 m–3,000 ft/914 m. NE part in Jefferson Natl. Forest.

Walker Pass, NE Kern co., S central Calif., pass across in Kiavah Mts. of the S Sierra Nevada, 53 mi/85 km ENE of Bakersfield, 10 mi/16 km WNW of Ridgecrest. State Highway 178 passes through. Elev. c.5,250 ft/1,600 m.

Walker River, 50 mi/80 km long, W Nev.; formed in S central Lyon co. at confluence of East Walker and West Walker rivers 7 mi/11.3 km S of Yerington; flows N past Yerington, then SE through Walker R. Indian Reservation, and small reservoir (on Indian reservation), to N end of Walker L. Gillis Range to E; Wassuk Range to W. East Walker R. (c.75 mi/121 km long) rises in Sierra Nevada range, NW Mono co., E Calif., at NE boundary of Yosemite Natl. Park, flows NE past Bridgeport, through Bridgeport Reservoir, and into Nev., then N.

Walkersville, town (1990 pop. 4,145), Federick co., N Md., 6 mi/9.7 km NNE of Frederick; 39°29′N 77°21′W. Trade point in agr. area; also mfg., apparel. The name was bestowed by the RR in honor of George Walker, the owner of the land on which the station was built. Nearby is Glade Valley Farm for thoroughbreds. The RR line from here to Taneytown was abandoned in 1972, but re-opened in the 1980s by an interest group and called the Maryland Midland RR.

Walkerton, town (1991 pop. 4,939), ⊙ Bruce co., S Ont., central Canada, on South Saugeen R., and 30 mi/48 km SSW of Owen Sound; 44°08′N 81°09′W. Metalworking; milling; dairying; mfg. of dies and castings.

Walkerton, town (1990 pop. 2,061), St. Joseph co., N Ind., 19 mi/31 km SW of South Bend; 41°28′N 86°29′W. Ships mint, onions, grain; mfg. (rollers, textiles, trailers, wire harnesses, doors, fiberglass rods). Laid out 1856.

Walkertown, town (1990 pop. 1,200), Forsyth co., N central N.C., suburb 8 mi/12.9 km NE of downtown Winston-Salem; 36°10′N 80°09′W. Belews L. reservoir to NE. Agr. area (tobacco, grain; cattle). Mfg. (tool and die, fabric cutting and sewing).

Walkerville, E suburb of Windsor, S Ont., central Canada, on Detroit R., opposite Detroit. Mfg. of automobiles, automobile accessories, steel prods. Distillery. Merged 1935 with Windsor.

Walkerville 1 village (1990 pop. 262), Oceana co., W Mich., 34 mi/55 km NNE of Muskegon; 43°42′N 86°07′W. In orchard and farm area. In Manistee Natl. Forest. **2** village (1990 pop. 605), Silver Bow co., SW Mont., suburb 2 mi/3.2 km N of downtown Butte (generally considered a dist. of Butte); 46°02′N 112°32′W. Elev. 6,360 ft/1,939 m. Copper mines. Deerlodge Natl. Forest to N. Settled c.1878 (by miners from Cornwall, England). Inc. 1891.

Wall, village (1990 pop. 834), Pennington co., SW central S.Dak., 50 mi/80 km E of Rapid City, near Badlands Natl. Monument; 43°59′N 102°14′W. Home of the Wall Drugstore, profusely advertised along I-90; takes up nearly a city block, a city within a city, a self-made tourist attraction. Natl. Grasslands Visitor Center serves area's natl. grassland. N entrance to Badlands Natl. Park to S. Buffalo Gap Natl. Grasslands to S.

Wall, borough (1990 pop. 853), Allegheny co., SW Pa., residential suburb 12 mi/19 km ESE of downtown Pittsburgh, near Turtle Creek; 40°23′N 79°47′W. White Oak Regional Park to S. Inc. 1904.

Wall, township (1990 pop. 20,244), Monmouth co., NE N.J., 5 mi/8 km SW of Asbury Park; 40°10′N 74°05′W. Residential area. Inc. 1851.

Wall Lake, town (1990 pop. 875), Sac co., W Iowa, 18 mi/29 km NW of Carroll; 42°16′N 95°05′W. Mfg. (food prods., fertilizer); livestock; grain. Black Hawk L. State Park to NE.

Wall Street, narrow street in the lower part of Manhattan, N.Y. city, extending E from Broadway to the East R. It is the center of one of the greatest financial dists. in the world, and by extension the term "Wall St." has come to signify U.S. financial interests. In the dist., which extends several blocks N and S of Wall St., are the N.Y. and the Amer. Stock Exchanges as well as commodity exchanges and the homes of numerous commercial and investment banks and law firms. Facing Wall St., on the W side of Broadway, is Trinity Church (founded 1696). Federal Hall Natl. Memorial, 1 block E, was erected on the site of the former Federal Hall, where George Washington was inaugurated in 1789 and where the 1st Congress met. Wall St. received its name from a stockade, or wall, built in 1653 by Du. colonists to protect the settled area S of it from assault by the English and the native pop.

Walla Walla, county (□ 1,299 sq mi/3,364 sq km; 1990 pop. 48,439), SE Wash., bounded by Oregon on S; ⊙ Walla Walla; 46°14′N 118°29′W. RR junction. Agr. (wheat, fruit, vegetable, peas, asparagus, potatoes, hay, alfalfa, corn; hogs; timber); food processing. Bounded by Snake R. on N and NW, forms L. Sacajawea (Ice Harbor Dam) and L. Herbert C. West (Lower Monumental Dam), Columbia R. on W (forms L. Wallala, McNary Dam); drained by Touchet and Walla Walla rivers. Whitman Mission Natl. Historical Site is near Walla Walla city; McNary Natl. Wildlife Refuge in W, at confluence of Columbia and Snake rivers; small part of Umatilla Natl. Forest in SE corner. Formed 1854.

Walla Walla, city (1990 pop. 26,478), ⊙ Walla Walla co., SE Wash., c.115 mi/185 km SSW of Spokane, and 33 mi/53 km NE of Pendleton (Oregon), on Mill Creek, 5 mi/8 km E of its junction with Walla Walla R., 4 mi/6.4 km N of the Oregon state line; 46°04′N 118°20′W. RR junction. It is a trade, processing, and distributing center for a fertile farm and lumber area. Fruits and vegetables (esp. green peas) are canned and frozen in numerous plants there, grain is processed for animal feeds, and cans are manufactured; mfg. (pesticides, printing and publishing, packaging machinery, archery equip., irrigation equip., plumbing fixtures, wine, wood prods.). The city also has a pulp and paper mill; logging. Umatilla Natl. Forest (Wash. and Oregon state line) to SE. The old fur-trading Fort Walla Walla was established near that site in 1818; the mission of Marcus Whitman was also built (1836) nearby. Wagon trains began bringing settlers in the 1840s, and Steptoeville (later Walla Walla) grew around the U.S. military Fort Walla Walla (est. 1856). The name was changed when the settlement became co. seat in 1859. Walla Walla is a dist. hq. of the U.S. Army Corps of Engineers. It is also the seat of Whitman Col., Walla Walla Col. (to SW, in College Place), and Walla Walla Community Col., and Wash. State Penitentiary to NW of city. Whitman Mission Natl. Historical Site to W. Walla Walla City-Co. Airport to NE. Inc. 1862.

Walla Walla River, c. 60 mi/97 km long, at Umatilla-Wallowa co. line, NE Oregon-SW Wash.; rises in Blue Mts. in Oregon; flows NW near Walla Walla, past Touchet, Wash., to Columbia R. at Wallula, 10 mi/16 km SSE of Pasco. Its valley is irrigated and dry-farm agr. area.

Wallabout Bay, NW Brooklyn borough, N.Y. city, SE N.Y., bay on Brooklyn shoreline of East R., bet. Williamsburg and Manhattan bridges; 40°42′N 73°58′W. Site of Brooklyn Navy Yard, a former U.S. Naval shipyard. During Revolutionary War tens of thousands of Continental Army soldiers were imprisoned aboard rotting hulks of Royal Navy prison ships in deplorable conditions; 11,000 of them perished from cold, diseases, and starvation. A 149-ft/45-m Doric column bearing bronze braziers and lit by an eternal flame, erected in 1908, stands as a memorial to the Prison Ship martyrs.

Wallace, village, W N.S., E Canada, on Wallace Harbour, small inlet of Northumberland Strait, 30 mi/48 km NNW of Truro. Resort.

Wallace, county (□ 914 sq mi/2,367 sq km; 1990 pop. 1,821), W Kansas; ⊙ Sharon Springs; 38°54′N 101°45′W. Gently sloping to rolling plains region, bordering W on Colo.; drained by N and S Forks of Smoky Hill R. and Ladder Creek. Cattle, sheep; barley, wheat, sorghum, corn. Highest point (4,039 ft/1,231 m) in Kansas, Mt. Sunflower, is in W, on Colo. state line. One of 4 Kansas cos. in Mountain time zone; Mountain and Central time zone follows E co. boundary. Formed 1888.

Wallace 1 town (1990 pop. 1,010), ⊙ Shoshone co., N Idaho, 45 mi/72 km ESE of Coeur d'Alene; 47°28′N 115°55′W. Elev. 2,728 ft/831 m. Junction of RR spurs to Burke and Mullen. Trading center for mining, lumbering region in Coeur d'Alene Mts.; mfg. (plastic pipe, copper and silver concentrates, hand-held rock drill parts). Lead, silver, zinc mines nearby in Coeur d'Alene mining dist. Historic Wallace Depot, Sierra Silver Mine tours, Wallace Dist. Mining Mus. Bordello Mus.; complete town on register of historic places. Coeur d'Alene Natl. Forest to N, St. Joe Natl. Forest to S. Founded 1884 as Placer Center; inc. 1888 as Wallace. **2** town (1990 pop. 89), Fountain co., W Ind., 14 mi/23 km WSW of Crawfordsville; 39°59′N 87°09′W. Agr. area. Shades State Park nearby to SE. Laid out 1832. **3** town (1990 pop. 2,939), Duplin co., SE N.C., 36 mi/58 km N of Wilmington; 34°44′N 78°00′W. Agr. area (tobacco, cotton, grain, sweet potatoes; poultry, livestock); mfg. (yarn, concrete, blazers and suits, cotton dyeing and finishing, turkey processing, printing and publishing).

Wallace 1 village (1990 pop. 75), Wallace co., W Kansas, on Smoky Hill R., and 8 mi/12.9 km E of Sharon Springs; 38°54′N 101°35′W. Fort Wallace Cemetery and Mus. **2** village (1990 pop. 308), Lincoln co., SW central Nebr., 30 mi/48 km SW of North Platte, and on Red Willow R. Grain; livestock; dairy prods. **3** uninc. village, Marlboro co., NE S.C., 3 mi/4.8 km NE of Cheraw near Great Pee Dee R. Mfg. includes textiles, bricks; agr. includes cotton, grain; hogs. **4** village (1990 pop. 83), Codington co., NE S.Dak., 22 mi/35 km NW of Watertown, in small lakes area; 45°05′N 97°28′W.

Wallace Dam, Ga.: see SINCLAIR, LAKE.

Wallace Lake, reservoir, on Caddo and De Soto parish border, NW La., on Bayou Pierre, 12 mi/19 km SSE of Shreveport; 8 mi/12.9 km long; 32°21′N 93°39′W. Max. capacity 96,200 acre-ft. Formed by dam; built (1943) for flood control.

Wallaceburg, town (1991 pop. 11,846), SE Ont., Canada, on the Sydenham R. near L. St. Clair; 42°35′N 82°22′W. Port of entry with light industry.

Wallaceton (WAWL-uhs-toun), borough (1990 pop. 319), Clearfield co., central Pa., 9 mi/14.5 km SE of Clearfield; 40°58′N 78°17′W. Mfg. (veneer logs); agr. (corn; livestock; dairying).

Wallagrass (WAHL-uh-gras), plantation (1990 pop. 582), Aroostook co., N Maine, 9 mi/14.5 km S of Fort Kent, and on Fish R.; 47°08′N 68°37′W. In forest area. Settled 1820 by Acadians; inc. 1859.

Walland (WAH-luhnd), resort village, Blount co., E Tenn., on Little R., and 18 mi/29 km SSE of Knoxville, in a gap of Chilhowee Mts.; 35°44′N 83°49′W. Mineral spring.

Walled Lake, village (1990 pop. 6,278), Oakland co., SE Mich., suburb 11 mi/18 km SW of Pontiac, 25 mi/40 km WNW of downtown Detroit, and N of Novi, at N end of Walled L.; 42°31′N 83°28′W. Mfg. (plastic toys, hardware, glass table tops, motor vehicle parts, jet engines).

Wallen, village (1990 pop. 1,000), Allen co., NE Ind., suburb 6 mi/9.7 km NNW of downtown Ft. Wayne. Smith Airport to SE. Laid out 1870.

Wallenpaupack, Lake (WAWL-uhn-paw-pak), reservoir, NE Pa., on Wayne/Pike co. line in Pa.; c.11 mi/18 km long, 1 mi/1.6 km wide; 41°27′N 75°11′W. Formed 1926 by hydroelectric dam on Wallenpaupack Creek near Hawley at NE end of lake; creek flows NE into Lackawaxen R. Resort area, residential developments on both shores.

Waller, county (□ 518 sq mi/1,342 sq km; 1990 pop. 23,390), SE Texas; ⊙ Hempstead; 30°00′N 95°58′W. Bounded W by Brazos R., E in part by Spring Creek; also drained by tributaries of San Jacinto R. Irrigated area; agr. (corn, rice, hay), livestock (cattle, hogs, sheep, goats); timber. Natural gas, oil wells; sand and gravel. Formed 1873.

Waller, town (1990 pop. 1,493), Waller co., SE Texas, 40 mi/64 km NW of Houston; 30°03′N 95°55′W. In rich agr. area (cattle, rice, corn, hay); mfg. (machinery).

Wallface Mountain (3,860 ft/1,177 m), Essex co., NE N.Y., in the High Peaks sect. of the Adirondacks, just W of Mt. MacIntyre across Indian Pass, and c.7 mi/11.3 km WNW of Mt. Marcy; 44°08′N 74°02′W. Its E face is 1,300-ft/396-m precipice rising above the pass.

Wallingford 1 town (1990 pop. 40,822), New Haven co., S Conn.; 41°27′N 72°47′W. Its silverware industry dates from c.1835. Fruit growing and mfg. plastics, steel, precision instruments, and hardware are among the town's other industries. Choate preparatory school for boys is here, now coordinated with Rosemary Hall, a girls' preparatory school formerly located at Greenwich, Conn. A branch of the Oneida Community was founded in the town in 1851. Lyman Hall was b. here. Inc. 1670. **2** town (1990 pop. 196), Emmet co., NW Iowa, 6 mi/9.7 km SSE of Estherville; 43°19′N 94°47′W. Sand pits. **3** town (1990 pop. 2,184), Rutland co., W central Vt., on Otter Creek, and 10 mi/16 km S of Rutland; 43°27′N 72°55′W. Dairy prods.; ice caves nearby. Includes East Wallingford village. Chartered 1761, settled 1773.

Wallington, borough (1990 pop. 10,828), Bergen co., NE N.J., on the Passaic R. opposite Passaic; 40°51′N 74°06′W. Mfg. includes paint, pens, medical equip., dairy prods., and plastics. Inc. 1895.

Wallins Creek, village (1990 pop. 261), Harlan co., SE Ky., 4 mi/6.4 km WSW of Harlan, in the Cumberlands, on Cumberland R.; 36°49′N 83°24′W. In bituminous-coal and timber region; mfg. (mining equip.). Part of Daniel Boone Natl. Forest to N.

Wallis, town (1990 pop. 1,001), Austin co., S Texas, near San Bernard R. (SW) and Brazos R. (NE), c.45 mi/72 km WSW of Houston; 29°37′N 96°03′W. RR junction; agr. (cotton, corn, peanuts; poultry, cattle, sheep, hogs); mfg. (cabinets and stove fixtures, concrete prods.).

Wallkill, village (□ 3 sq mi/7.8 sq km; 1990 pop. 2,125), Ulster co., SE N.Y., on Wallkill R., and 10 mi/16 km NW of Newburgh; 41°36′N 74°09′W. Mfg. (transformers, ferrites, electronics components); summer resort.

Wallkill River, c.90 mi/145 km long, NW N.J. and SE N.Y.; rises S of Sparta, N.J. (dammed here to form L. Mohawk); flows N and NE to Rondout Creek SW of Kingston, N.Y., shortly above creek's mouth on the Hudson; has power dams. The Wallkill valley, flanked by ridges of the Appalachians, is part of Great Appalachian Valley, and links the Kittatinny valley (N.J.) with the Hudson R. valley.

Walloomsac, village (1990 pop. 150), Rensselaer co., E N.Y., on Hoosic R., and 2 mi/3.2 km NE of Hoosick Falls; 43°04′N 73°10′W. Nearby is Bennington Battlefield State Park.

Walloomsac River (WAWL-oom-sik), c.30 mi/48 km long, SW Vt. and E N.Y.; rises E of Pownal, Vt., in Green Mts.; flows N and W, past Bennington, to Hoosic R. below Hoosick Falls, N.Y.

Walloon Lake, NW Mich., 5 mi/8 km SW of Petoskey, 9 mi/14.5 km long, 1 mi/1.6 km wide; 45°16′N 85°00′W. Fishing, boating, swimming. N half forms boundary bet. Charlevoix and Emmett cos. Village of Walloon L. at SE end.

Wallowa (wah-LOU-uh), county (□ 3,151 sq mi/8,161 sq km; 1990 pop. 6,911), extreme NE Oregon; ⊙ Enterprise; 45°34′N 117°10′W. Livestock grazing and logging area bordering on Wash. (N) and Snake R., Idaho (E), drained by Wallowa, Imnaha and Grande Ronde rivers. Wallowa Mts. are in S and E. Hells Canyon of the Snake R. extends N-S along E boundary. Agr. (potatoes, wheat, oats, barley; hogs, sheep, cattle); timber. Silver, gold. Snake and Imnaha R. junction scene of 1887 massacre of 31 Chin. gold miners. Large part of Hells Canyon Natl. Recreation Area to E. Hells Canyon Dam in SE. Parts of Wallowa-Whitman Natl. Forest in SW, S, SE, and N center. Part of Umatilla Natl. Forest in NW; Minam State Recreation Area in W; Wallowa L. State Park in S. Formed 1887.

Wallowa (wah-LOU-uh), town (1990 pop. 748), Wallowa co., NE Oregon, 15 mi/24 km NW of Enterprise, on Wallowa R. at mouth of Bear Creek; 45°34′N 117°31′W. Lumber. Eagle Cap Wilderness Area to S; parts of Wallowa-Whitman Natl. Forest to S and NE; parts of Umatilla Natl. Forest to NW; Minam State Recreation Area to W. Inc. 1899.

Wallowa Lake (wah-LOU-uh), reservoir, Wallowa co., NE Oregon, on Wallowa R., at foot of Wallowa Mts., 7 mi/11.3 km SSE of Enterprise; 4 mi/6.4 km long;

45°19′N 117°12′W. Formed by dam, built for irrigation. Wallowa State Park at S end; Old Joseph Monument at dam.

Walls, uninc. village, De Soto co., NW Miss., suburb 13 mi/21 km SSW of downtown Memphis, Tenn. Cotton, corn, soybeans; cattle. Mfg. (upholstered furniture, modular bank bldgs.). Horn L. to W, Oxbow L. in former channel of Mississippi R.

Wallsburg, village (1990 pop. 252), Wasatch co., N central Utah, 10 mi/16 km S of Heber City, on Deer Creek; 40°23′N 111°25′W. Uinta Natl. Forest to W, S, and E; Deer Creek Reservoir to NW; Deer Creek State Park to W.

Wallula (wah-LOO-la), uninc. village (1990 pop. 150), Walla Walla co., SE Wash., on Columbia R. (L. Wallula reservoir), N of confluence of Walla Walla R., 28 mi/45 km W of Walla Walla. RR junctions to N and S. Wheat, barley, rye; cattle, sheep; mfg. (corrugated boxes, meatpacking). Early boom town, built near site of old Fort Walla Walla (1817); terminus of one of state's 1st RRs, completed 1875, removed 1 mi/1.6 km from its original site with completion of McNary Dam. Wallula Gap, narrowing of Columbia R., to SW.

Wallula, Lake (wah-LAH-luh), reservoir, N Oregon and S Wash., on Columbia R., 3 mi/4.8 km E of Umatilla, Oregon; c.45 mi/72 km long; 45°56′N 119°17′W. Elev. 341 ft/104 m. Formed by McNary Lock and Dam (183 ft/56 m high), built (1947–1956) by the U.S. Army Corps of Engineers on the Oregon-Wash. border for power generation, irrigation, and navigation.

Wallum Lake, reservoir, in Burrillville, extreme NW R.I. and Douglas, S Mass., on Clear Creek, 18 mi/29 km NW of Providence, R.I.; 2 mi/3.2 km long; 42°00′N 71°45′W. Douglas State Forest (Mass.) on NW shore; Buck Hill Management Area (R.I.) on SW shore.

Walnut, city (1990 pop. 29,105), Los Angeles co., S Calif., suburb 20 mi/32 km E of downtown Los Angeles, and 5 mi/8 km SW of Pomona, on San Juan Creek; 34°02′N 117°52′W. Mfg. (fabricated metal prods., electronic equip., tool and die, machinery, transportation equip., computer terminals). Puente Hills to S, San Jose Hills to N. Seat of Mt. San Antonio Col (2-yr.).

Walnut, town (1990 pop. 857), Pottawattamie co., SW Iowa, 13 mi/21 km NW of Atlantic, near source of Walnut Creek; 41°28′N 95°13′W. Mfg. (fertilizers).

Walnut 1 village (1990 pop. 1,463), Bureau co., N Ill., 14 mi/23 km NNW of Princeton; 41°33′N 89°35′W. Dairy prods., grain. **2** village (1990 pop. 214), Crawford co., extreme SE Kansas, 21 mi/34 km NW of Pittsburg; 37°36′N 95°04′W. In diversified agr. area; feed milling. **3** village (1990 pop. 523), Tippah co., N Miss., 22 mi/35 km W of Corinth, near Tenn. state line; 34°57′N 88°54′W. Timber; mfg. (elevator controls, wooden pallets, apparel). Holly Springs Natl. Forest to SW.

Walnut Bayou, stream, Madison parish, La. Abandoned section of Mississippi R. source at 32°16′N 91°06′W. A road on its levee used by Gen. U. S. Grant in Vicksburg campaign to move soldiers and supplies to Hard Times (an abandoned plantation) on the banks of the Mississippi R.

Walnut Canyon National Monument, Coconino co., N Ariz., 8 mi/12.9 km E of downtown Flagstaff. Covers 2,250 acres/911 ha. Sinagua cliff dwellings (12th-cent.) built into shallow caves and ledges. Created by Presidential Proclamation (1915). Bounded by Coconino Natl. Forest N, E and S, by city of Flagstaff W.

Walnut Cove, town (1990 pop. 1,088), Stokes co., N N.C., 15 mi/24 km NNE of Winston-Salem; 36°17′N 80°08′W. RR junction. Tobacco, grain, soybeans; poultry, livestock; mfg. (machining, feeds, stainless steel prods.).

Walnut Creek, city (1990 pop. 60,569), Contra Costa co., W Calif., suburb 10 mi/16 km ENE of downtown Oakland, in the San Francisco Bay area; 37°54′N 122°02′W. It is the trade and shipping center of an extensive agr. area (being displaced by rapid urban growth) where walnuts, apples, vegetables, and nursey stock are among the major prods. Mfg. (dehydrated fruits and vegetables, machinery, industrial glass, chemicals, medical instruments, electronic equip.). Business

growth has developed greatly in the city and its environs since 1975, and industry has become increasingly important to the economy. Mokelumne Aqueduct passes NW of city. Diablo State Park to E, Mt. Diablo (3,849 ft/1,173 m). Inc. 1914.

Walnut Creek, village (1990 pop. 623), Wayne co., E central N.C., 10 mi/16 km ESE of Goldsboro; 35°18′N 77°52′W. Agr. area (tobacco, peanuts, cotton, grain, soybeans; poultry, livestock).

Walnut Creek 1 creek, c.70 mi/113 km long, in SW Iowa; rises in extreme S Shelby co.; flows S and SE to West Nishnabotna R. 11 mi/18 km W of Shenandoah. Used for hydroelectric power. Flooded in 1993. **2** 139 mi/224 km long, in W central Kansas; N and S branches rise in Lane co.; both flow c.30 mi/48 km to S of Ness City; flows E, past Bazine and Albert, to Arkansas R. 5 mi/8 km E of Great Bend.

Walnut Grove 1 town (1990 pop. 717), Etowah co., NE Ala., 17 mi/27 km WNW of Gadsden. **2** town (1990 pop. 549), Greene co., SW Mo., in the Ozarks, near Sac R., 20 mi/32 km NW of Springfield; 37°24′N 93°32′W.

Walnut Grove 1 uninc. village, Sacramento co., central Calif., on Sacramento R., and 23 mi/37 km S of Sacramento. Corn, grains, tomatoes, citrus, pears, sugar beets, beans; dairying. **2** village (1990 pop. 458), Walton co., N central Ga., 9 mi/14.5 km SW of Monroe; 33°45′N 83°51′W. **3** village (1990 pop. 625), Redwood co., SW Minn., 28 mi/45 km SW of Redwood Falls, 22 mi/35 km SE of Marshall, on Plum Creek; 44°13′N 95°28′W. In grain, livestock, and poultry area; dairy prods.; soybeans, alfalfa; mfg. (mining equip.). **4** village (1990 pop. 389), Leake co., central Miss., 10 mi/16 km SSE of Carthage; 32°36′N 89°27′W. Agr. (cotton, corn, soybeans; cattle, poultry; dairying); mfg. (apparel, industrial gloves). Golden Memorial State Park to SE.

Walnut Hill 1 village (1990 pop. 133), Marion co., S Ill., 12 mi/19 km SSW of Salem; 38°28′N 89°02′W. Agr. and oil area. **2** village (1990 pop. 3,332), Sullivan co., extreme NE Tenn., 4 mi/6 km W of Bristol, near Va. state line.

Walnut Log, village, Obion co., NW Tenn., on Reelfoot L., 15 mi/24 km W of Union City.

Walnut Park, uninc. city (1990 pop. 14,722), Los Angeles co., S Calif., residential suburb 5 mi/8 km S of downtown Los Angeles; 33°58′N 118°13′W.

Walnut Ridge, town (1990 pop. 4,388), ⊙ Lawrence co., NE Ark., 21 mi/34 km NW of Jonesboro; 36°04′N 90°57′W. In agr. area (sorghum, wheat, rice). Mfg. (metal culverts, consumer goods, apparel, luggage, golf bags, power tools, wood tool handles). Inc. 1880. Williams Baptist Col. at College City, to N.

Walnut River, 121 mi/195 km long, S Kansas; formed by confluence of several headstreams in NE corner of Butler co.; flows SW, through El Dorado L. reservoir, past El Dorado, then S, past Augusta and Winfield, to Arkansas R. at Arkansas City.

Walnut Springs, village (1990 pop. 716), Bosque co., central Texas, c.50 mi/80 km NW of Waco; 32°03′N 97°45′W. In farm area.

Walnutport, borough (1990 pop. 2,055), Northampton co., E Pa., 12 mi/19 km NNW of Allentown, on Lehigh R., opposite Slatington; 40°45′N 75°35′W. Mfg. (electroplating and polishing, apparel). Agr. includes apples, soybeans, grain; livestock, dairying. Appalachian Trail passes to N, on Blue Mt. ridge. Inc. 1909.

Walpi (wal-PEE) [Hopi = place of the gap], pueblo, Coconino co., NE Ariz., on a mesa NE of Flagstaff. Its inhabitants are Pueblo who speak the Hopi language (Uto-Aztecan linguistic family). It was founded as a refuge in anticipation of Span. retaliation for the Pueblo revolt (1680). Founded c.1700.

Walpole 1 industrial and residential town (1990 pop. 20,212), Norfolk co., E Mass., 12 mi/19 km SW of Boston; 42°09′N 71°15′W. Mfg. (machinery, trailers, fences, roofing). Walpole is the site of a state prison. Includes village of East Walpole. Settled 1659, inc. 1724. **2** town (1990 pop. 3,210), Cheshire co., SW N.H., 12 mi/19 km NW of Keene; 43°04′N 72°24′W. Bounded W by Connecticut R. (Vt. state line), drained by Cold R. Includes village of North Walpole. Nursery crops, vegetables;

cattle, sheep, poultry; dairying. Mfg. (asphalt, platform tennis courts, furniture, machine parts, printing and publishing, anodizing). Settled 1749, inc. 1752.

Walpole, Maine: see SOUTH BRISTOL, village.

Walpole Island, S Ont., central Canada, in delta of St. Clair R., on NE shore of L. St. Clair; 10 mi/16 km long, 4 mi/6 km wide. Consists of marshland and is chiefly inhabited by Indians. Tecumseh's grave is on the reservation here.

Walsenburg, town (1990 pop. 3,300), ⊙ Huerfano co., S Colo., on Cucharas R., just E of Sangre de Cristo Mts., and 45 mi/72 km S of Pueblo; 37°37′N 104°46′W. Elev. 6,182 ft/1,884 m. RR junction. Trade center for livestock, poultry, and grain region; mfg. (jewelry, apparel). Grew with development of coal deposits in vicinity. Parts of San Isabel Natl. Forest to NW and SW; Martin L. and Lathrop State Park to W; Concharas Reservoir to NE; Orlando Reservoir to N. Laid out and inc. 1873.

Walsh, county (□ 1,285 sq mi/3,328 sq km; 1990 pop. 13,840), NE N.Dak.; ⊙ Grafton; 48°22′N 97°43′W. Rich agr. area drained by Forest and Park rivers; bounded E by Red R. of the North (Minn. state line). Cattle, hogs, wheat, rye, barley, sugar beets, potatoes; beet-sugar refining, industrial machinery. Formed 1881. L. Ardoch in SE; Homme Reservoir in center.

Walsh, village (1990 pop. 692), Baca co., SE Colo., 18 mi/29 km E of Springfield, on Bear Creek; 37°23′N 102°16′W. Elev. 3,955 ft/1,205 m. Cattle, wheat, barley, corn, sorghum.

Walsh, Mount (14,780 ft/4,505 m), SW Yukon, N Canada, near Alaska border, in St. Elias Mts., 170 mi/274 km W of Whitehorse; 61°01′N 139°59′W.

Walshville, village (1990 pop. 44), Montgomery co., SW central Ill., 11 mi/18 km SW of Hillsboro; 39°04′N 89°37′W. In agr. and coal area.

Walsingham, Cape (WAHL-sing-uhm), SE Baffin Isl., SE Franklin dist., N.W.T., N Canada, at tip of Cumberland Peninsula, on Davis Strait; 66°02′N 61°56′W. Discovered by Davis, 1585.

Walstonburg (WAHL-stuhn-buhrg), village (1990 pop. 188), Greene co., E central N.C., 16 mi/26 km SE of Wilson; 35°35′N 77°42′W. Tobacco, grain, cotton, poultry, hogs. Mfg. (apparel, grain processing).

Walter Bouldin Dam (WAHL-tuhr BUL-din), Elmore co., central Ala., on new channel of the Coosa R., 15 mi/24 km N of Montgomery; 32°37′N 86°17′W. Elev. 52 ft/16 m. Gravity and earth construction, built (1967) by the Ala. Power Co. for hydroelectric generation. Forms a reservoir that joins directly into L. Jordan reservoir; max. capacity of 230,000 acre-ft.

Walter F. George Reservoir or **Lake Eufaula**, SE Ala. and SW Ga., on the Chattahoochee R., 33 mi/53 km NNE of Dothan, Ala.; 31°38′N 85°04′W. Max. capacity of 934,400 acre-ft. Formed by Walter F. George Dam (101 ft/31 m high), built (1962) by the Army Corps of Engineers for navigation, power, and flood control. Lakepont Resort and George T. Bagby state parks and Eufaula Natl. Wildlife Refuge on its shores.

Walterboro, city (1990 pop. 5,492), ⊙ Colleton co., S S.C., 45 mi/72 km W of Charleston; 32°53′N 80°40′W. Mfg. includes sand and clay, modular bldgs., lumber, fiberglass fabrics, motor vehicle belts; agr. includes livestock, poultry; grain, tobacco, watermelons; logging. Army Corps of Engineers Basin Natl. Wildlife Reserve to S. Colleton State Park to N. Hunting and fishing nearby.

Walters, town (1990 pop. 2,519), ⊙ Cotton co., S Okla., 17 mi/27 km SSE of Lawton, near Cache Creek; 34°21′N 98°18′W. NW RR terminus, spur from Waurika. In grain, cotton, and livestock area; light mfg. Waurika L. reservoir to SE.

Walters, village (1990 pop. 86), Faribault co., S Minn., 16 mi/26 km WSW of Albert Lea, near Iowa state line; 43°36′N 93°40′W. Agr. area (grain, soybeans; livestock); mfg. (agr. equip.).

Walthall (WAWL-thawl), county (□ 404 sq mi/1,046 sq km; 1990 pop. 14,352), S Miss.; ⊙ Tylertown; 31°08′N 90°05′W. Bordered S by La.; drained by the Bogue Chitto R. and McGee Creek. Agr. (cotton, corn;

cattle; dairying; timber). L. Walthall State Lake in S. Formed 1910.

Walthall (WAWL-thawl), village (1990 pop. 167), ⊙ Webster co., central Miss., 28 mi/45 km WNW of Starkville; 33°36′N 89°16′W. Agr. (cotton, corn; cattle).

Waltham (WAWL-tham), city (1990 pop. 57,878), Middlesex co., E Mass., a suburb of Boston, on the Charles R.; 42°23′N 71°14′W. Important high-technology and computer center. Electronic equip. and parts, precision instruments, medical diagnostic testing equip., cameras, machinery, and fabricated metals are among its varied manufactures. It was known as the seat of the Waltham Watch Company, which produced the first machine-made watches in the U.S. in 1854, and whose red-brick bldgs. along the Charles R. housed the world's largest watch and clock company. The operation closed in 1950. Brandeis Univ. and Bentley Col. are in the city. Of note are the many colonial structures. Birthplace of Mass. textile industry and site of Charles R. Mus. of Industry; Gore Place Mansion and Lyman Estates. New England hq. for U.S. Army Corps of Engineers. Settled c.1634; set off from Watertown 1738; inc. as a city 1884.

Waltham 1 (WAHL-tham), town (1990 pop. 276), Hancock co., S Maine, on Graham L., and 13 mi/21 km NNE of Ellsworth; 44°41′N 68°20′W. **2** (WAWL-tham), town (1990 pop. 454), Addison co., W Vt., on Otter Creek, and 24 mi/39 km S of Burlington; 44°07′N 73°13′W.

Waltham (WAWL-thuhm), village (1990 pop. 170), Mower co., SE Minn., 11 mi/18 km NNE of Austin; 43°49′N 92°52′W. Dairying; livestock; corn, soybeans.

Walthill (WAWL-thil), village (1990 pop. 747), Thurston co., NE Nebr., 12 mi/19 km E of Pender, near Missouri R.; 42°08′N 96°29′W. Dairy prods.; livestock, grain. Located near center of Omaha Indian Reservation; Winnebago Indian Reservation to N.

Walthourville (WAHL-thuhr-vil), town (1990 pop. 2,024), Liberty co., SE Ga., 5 mi/8 km N of Hinesville; 31°47′N 81°38′W. Mfg. of asphalt compounds, yarns, and fabrics.

Walton 1 county (□ 1,046 sq mi/2,709 sq km; 1990 pop. 27,760), NW Fla., bounded E (partly) by Choctawhatchee R., N by Ala. state line, and S by Gulf of Mexico; ⊙ De Funiak Springs. Rolling terrain in N rising to 345 ft/105 m (highest point in state); coastal plain in S along Choctawhatchee Bay and the Gulf; co. is drained by Shoal R. Agr. (corn, peanuts, cotton; poultry, cattle, hogs). Has part of Choctawhatchee Natl. Forest in SW. Formed 1824. **2** county (□ 330 sq mi/855 sq km; 1990 pop. 38,586), N central Ga.; ⊙ Monroe; 33°47′N 83°44′W. Bounded NE by Apalachee R.; drained by Alcovy R. Piedmont agr. (soybeans, peaches); cattle, poultry. Mfg. at Monroe. Rapidly growing rural co. bet. Atlanta and Athens. Formed 1818.

Walton 1 town (1990 pop. 1,053), Cass co., N central Ind., 9 mi/14.5 km SE of Logansport; 40°40′N 86°14′W. Agr. area; mfg. (houseplant and lawn fertilizers, wire springs; grain mixing). Laid out 1852. **2** town (1990 pop. 2,034), Boone co., N Ky., 16 mi/26 km SSW of Covington, in N part of Bluegrass region; 38°52′N 84°37′W. Agr. area (corn, burley tobacco; livestock, poultry; dairying); mfg. (concrete, gaskets, transportation equip., roof trusses, patient gowns, vertical lifts, linerboard). Bullock Pen L. reservoir to S; Big Bone Lick State Park to W.

Walton 1 village (1990 pop. 226), Harvey co., S central Kansas, 7 mi/11.3 km NE of Newton; 38°07′N 97°15′W. In wheat area; mfg. snack foods. **2** village (□ 1 sq mi/2.6 sq km; 1990 pop. 3,326), Delaware co., S N.Y., in the Catskills, on West Branch of Delaware R., and 40 mi/64 km ENE of Binghamton; 42°10′N 75°07′W. Summer resort.; mfg. (aerosol lab and test equip., transportation equip., dairy prods., engraving machines, metal castings). Bluestone quarries. Site of the Delaware Co. Fair, one of the Catskill region's most popular summer attractions. Inc. 1851.

Waltonville, village (1990 pop. 396), Jefferson co., S Ill., 9 mi/14.5 km SW of Mount Vernon; 38°12′N 89°02′W. In agr. area. Rend Lake Game Management Area to E.

Walworth 1 county (□ 744 sq mi/1,927 sq km; 1990 pop. 6,087), N central S.Dak.; ⊙ Selby; 45°25′N 100°01′W. Agr. area bounded W by Missouri R. (L. Oahe reservoir); drained by Swan Creek in S. Wheat, other grains; dairy prods., cattle, hogs. L. Hiddenwood State Park in N. Formed 1873. **2** county (□ 576 sq mi/1,492 sq km; 1990 pop. 75,000), SE Wis., bounded S by Ill. state line; ⊙ Elkhorn; 42°40′N 88°32′W. Drained by Turtle Creek and several other small streams. Surrounded by metropolitan areas. Resort and recreation area with several lakes, notably L. Geneva, popular area for retirement and seasonal homes. Comprises extensive dairying region; also farming (wheat, corn, soybeans, peas, potatoes; cattle, hogs, sheep, poultry), and some mfg. Big Fort Beach State Park, on L. Geneva, in SE; S part of Kettle Moraine State Forest (S unit) in NW. Formed 1836.

Walworth, town (1990 pop. 1,614), Walworth co., SE Wis., 23 mi/37 km ESE of Janesville; 42°31′N 88°35′W. In agr. area (dairy prods.; poultry, grain); mfg. (soy sauce, pillow forms, ceiling tiles, wooden store fixtures, steel shearing). L. Geneva is 2 mi/3.2 km E.

Wamac (WAH-mak), city (1990 pop. 1,501), in Marion, Washington, and Clinton cos., S Ill., suburb 1 mi/1.6 km S of Centralia, 14 mi/23 km SW of Salem; 38°30′N 89°09′W. RR junction. Inc. 1916.

Wamego (wah-MEE-go), town (1990 pop. 3,706), Pottawatomie co., NE Kansas, on Kansas R., and 14 mi/23 km E of Manhattan; 39°12′N 96°18′W. In livestock and grain region. Mfg. (construction machinery, feeds). Inc. 1869.

Wamplers Lake, in Jackson and Lenawee cos., SE Mich., 14 mi/23 km NNW of Adrian; c.2 mi/3.2 km long, 1 mi/1.6 km wide; 42°04′N 84°09′W. Resort. W. J. Hayes State Park and Mich. Internatl. Speedway on S side.

Wampsville, village (□ 1 sq mi/2.6 sq km; 1990 pop. 501), ⊙ Madison co., central N.Y., 24 mi/39 km E of Syracuse; 43°04′N 75°42′W. In dairying area.

Wampum (WAHM-puhm), borough (1990 pop. 666), Lawrence co., W Pa., 8 mi/12.9 km S of New Castle, on Beaver R.; 40°53′N 80°20′W. Mfg. (concrete prods.); bituminous coal; limestone; agr. (grain, soybeans; livestock; dairying). Settled 1796, inc. 1876.

Wamsutter (WAHM-suht-uhr), village (1990 pop. 240), Sweetwater co., S Wyo., 65 mi/105 km E of Rock Springs, in Great Divide Basin; 41°40′N 107°58′W. Elev. c.6,709 ft/2,045 m. Sheep, cattle.

Wanakena (wah-nah-KEE-nuh), resort village (1990 pop. 250), St. Lawrence co., N N.Y., 35 mi/56 km ENE of Carthage, in the Adirondacks, at influx of Oswegatchie R. into Cranberry L.; 44°08′N 74°55′W.

Wanamassa (wuh-nuh-MAH-suh), village (1990 pop. 4,530), Monmouth co., E N.J., near the coast, 12 mi/19 km E of Freehold; 40°14′N 74°01′W. Largely residential.

Wanamie (wah-NAH-mee), uninc. village, Newport township, Luzerne co., E central Pa., 10 mi/16 km SW of Wilkes-Barre; 41°10′N 76°02′W. State correctional institution and hosp. to NW.

Wanamingo (waw-nuh-MEENG-go), town (1990 pop. 847), Goodhue co., SE Minn., 25 mi/40 km NW of Rochester, on North Branch Zumbro R., at mouth of Shingle Creek; 44°18′N 92°47′W. Agr. (grains, soybeans, peas; livestock, poultry; dairying); mfg. (feeds and fertilizers, cabinets).

Wananish (wah-nah-NEESH), uninc. village, Columbus co., S N.C., 9 mi/14.5 km E of Whiteville, NE of L. Waccamaw.

Wanapitei Lake (wah-nuh-PI-tee), SE central Ont., central Canada, 16 mi/26 km NE of Sudbury; 10 mi/16 km long, 10 mi/16 km wide. Drained S by Wanapitei R. (75 mi/121 km long) into Georgian Bay.

Wanapum Lake, reservoir (□ 23 sq mi/60 sq km), Grant co., central Wash., on Columbia R., 28 mi/45 km ESE of Ellensburg; 46°08′N 120°01′W. Max. capacity 796,000 acre-ft. Extends N to Rock Isl. Dam. Formed by Wanapum Dam (103 ft/31 m high), built (1963) for power generation; also used for flood control. Priest Rapids L. downstream; Gingko Petrified Forest State Park on W bank.

Wanaque (WUH-nuh-kee), borough (1990 pop. 9,711), Passaic co., NE N.J., in the Ramapos, on Wanaque R., and 10 mi/16 km NW of Paterson; 41°02′N 74°17′W. Includes mfg. of candles, metal prods., and precision ceramics in villages of HASKELL and MIDVALE. Inc. 1918. Nearby is Wanaque Reservoir (c.6 mi/9.7 km long, 1 mi/1.6 km wide; largest in N.J.), formed by dam in Wanaque River, which drains Greenwood L. on N.Y.-N.J. state line; flows c.18 mi/29 km SE and S to Pequannock R. just N of Pompton Plains.

Wanaque Reservoir (□ 4 sq mi/10.4 sq km), Passaic co., N N.J., on Wanaque R., just N of Pompton Lakes; 74°18′N 41°00′W. Formed by Furnace Road and Green Swamp dams, built (1928) for water supply.

Wanatah, town (1990 pop. 852), LaPorte co., NW Ind., 8 mi/12.9 km ESE of Valparaiso; 41°26′N 86°53′W. Mfg. (aluminum roll foil). Dairying; fruit, vegetables. Laid out 1865.

Wanchese (WAHN-cheez), uninc. town (1990 pop. 1,380), Dare co., E N.C., 6 mi/9.7 km SSE of Manteo, on SW end of Roanoke Isl.; 35°50′N 75°38′W. Roanoke Sound to E (Outer Banks opposite), Croatan Sound to W (mainland opposite), Pamlico Sound to S; Atlantic Ocean 5 mi/8 km to E. Mfg. (boatbuilding, machining).

Wanda, village (1990 pop. 103), Redwood co., SW Minn., 15 mi/24 km SSW of Red Wood Falls; 44°19′N 95°12′W. Agr. (oats; livestock; dairying). Near Sleepy Eye Creek.

Wando (wahn-DO), uninc. village, Berkeley co., SE S.C., 12 mi/19 km NE of Charleston, on Cooper R. at S edge of Francis Marion Natl. Forest. Mfg. includes telepathalic acid, ship repair.

Waneta Lake, in Finger Lakes region, W central N.Y., just E of Keuka L.; c.3 mi/4.8 km long, ½ mi/⁹⁄₁₀ km wide; 42°27′N 77°06′W. Connected by streams to Lamoka L. (S) and to Keuka L. Formerly called Little L.

Wanette (wah-NET), village (1990 pop. 346), Pottawatomie co., central Okla., 25 mi/40 km SSW of Shawnee, near Canadian R.; 34°57′N 97°01′W. In agr. area.

Wann, village (1990 pop. 126), Nowata co., NE Okla., 12 mi/19 km NE of Bartlesville, near Kansas state line; 36°54′N 95°47′W.

Wantage (WUH-tij), township (1990 pop. 9,487), Sussex co., NW N.J., 1 mi/1.6 km NW of Sussex; 41°14′N 74°31′W. Inc. 1798.

Wantagh, uninc. residential city (□ 4 sq mi/10.4 sq km; 1990 pop. 18,567), Nassau co., SE N.Y., on the S shore of L.I.; 40°40′N 73°30′W. A causeway leads to Jones Beach State Park.

Wapakoneta (wah-puh-kuh-NE-tuh), city (1990 pop. 9,214), ☉ Auglaize co., W Ohio, 13 mi/21 km SSW of Lima, and on Auglaize R.; 40°34′N 84°11′W. Founded 1833. Neil Armstrong Air and Space Mus. is here.

Wapanucka (wah-puh-NUHK-uh), village (1990 pop. 402), Johnston co., S Okla., 17 mi/27 km ENE of Tishomingo; 34°22′N 96°25′W. In farm area; mfg. (wood trusses). Boggy Depot State Park to E. One of 1st schools of Chickasaw Nation was opened here in 1852.

Wapato (WAH-pah-to), town (1990 pop. 3,795), Yakima co., S Wash., 11 mi/19 km S of Yakima, near Yakima R. in NE part of Yakima Indian Reservation; 46°27′N 120°25′W. Hay, potatoes, tomatoes, wheat, fruit, vegetables, peppermint, hops; mfg. (furniture, fiber drums and cans, wine; printing and publishing). Inc. 1908.

Wapawekka Lake (wo-puh-WE-kuh), central Sask., W Canada, at foot of the Wapawekka Hill, 140 mi/225 km NE of Prince Albert; 30 mi/48 km long, 8 mi/13 km wide. Drains E into Churchill R. through Deschambault L.

Wapella (wuh-PE-luh), town (1991 pop. 429), SE Sask., W Canada, 16 mi/26 km WNW of Moosomin; 50°15′N 101°58′W. Grain elevators.

Wapella (wah-PEL-ah), village (1990 pop. 608), De Witt co., central Ill., 5 mi/8 km N of Clinton; 40°13′N 88°57′W. In agr. area (corn, soybeans).

Wapello, county (□ 436 sq mi/1,129 sq km; 1990 pop. 35,687), SE Iowa; ☉ Ottumwa; 41°01′N 92°24′W. Prairie agr. area (hogs, sheep, cattle, poultry; corn, soybeans, wheat) drained by Des Moines R. and Cedar Creek; bituminous-coal mines. Mfg. at Ottumwa. Air Power

Mus. 8 mi/12.9 km SW of Ottumwa. Grave of Chief Wapello at Agency. River flooding occurred in 1993. Formed 1843.

Wapello (WAH-pel-o), city (1990 pop. 2,013), ☉ Louisa co., SE Iowa, on Iowa R., and 25 mi/40 km N of Burlington; 41°10′N 91°11′W. Mfg. (plastic prods.; lumber; envelopes); livestock; grain. Mark Twain Natl. Wildlife Refuge to E. Settled 1837, inc. 1856.

Wappapello Lake (wah-puh-PEL-lo), reservoir (□ 36 sq mi/93 sq km), Wayne and Butler cos., SE Mo., on St. Francis R., 14 mi/23 km NNE of Poplar Bluff; c.20 mi/32 km long; 36°55′N 90°16′W. Max. capacity 613,000 acre-ft. Formed by Wappapello Dam (earthfill; 109 ft/33 m high, 2,700 ft/823 m long), built (1941) for flood control, power generation, and recreation. Partly in Mark Twain Natl. Forest.

Wappinger Creek, c.35 mi/56 km long, SE N.Y.; rises in N Dutchess co.; flows SSW, past Wappingers Falls (water power), to the Hudson R. 8 mi/12.9 km S of Poughkeepsie.

Wappingers Falls, village (□ 1 sq mi/2.6 sq km; 1990 pop. 4,605), Dutchess co., SE N.Y., in the Hudson highlands, on Wappinger Creek (water power) near its mouth on the Hudson R., and 7 mi/11.3 km S of Poughkeepsie; 41°36′N 73°55′W. Mfg. (lighting equip., commercial woodworking, cabinets). Society of the Cincinnati founded here in 1783. Inc. 1871.

Wapsipinicon River, c.225 mi/362 km long, NE and E Iowa; rises on Minn. state line NNW of McIntire; flows SE, past Independence and Anamosa, to Mississippi R. 20 mi/32 km NE of Davenport. Receives Little Wapsipinicon R. (c.40 mi/64 km long) and Buffalo Creek. Flooding occurred, causing widespread crop and property damage, in 1993. Sometimes known as Wapsis.

Waquoit (Mass.: see FALMOUTH.

War, town (1990 pop. 1,081), McDowell co., S W.Va., on Dry Fork R., 11 mi/18 km SSW of Welch; 37°17′N 81°40′W. Semibituminous-coal-mining and agr. region. Berwind L. Wildlife Management Area to S. Inc. 1920.

Waramaug, Lake (wahr-e-MAHG), reservoir, in Warren and Washington towns, Litchfield co., W Conn., on East Aspetuck R., 13 mi/21 km SW of Torrington; 3 mi/4.8 km long; 41°40′N 73°20′W. New Preston village at S end. L. Waramaug State Park at NW end; Mt. Bushnell State Park Reserve at S end.

Warba (WOR-buh), village (1990 pop. 137), Itasca co., NE central Minn., 14 mi/23 km SE of Grand Rapids, on Swan R.; 47°08′N 93°16′W. Agr. (alfalfa; cattle). Shallow L. to W.

Ward 1 county (□ 2,044 sq mi/5,294 sq km; 1990 pop. 57,921), N central N.Dak.; ☉ Minot; 48°13′N 101°32′W. Agr. area drained by Souris and Des Lacs rivers. Lignite mines; oil and gas extraction; sand and gravel deposits; food prods., beverages, millwork; mfg. in Minot; diversified farming (dairy prods., cattle, wheat, sunflowers, barley, oats, rye, hay; nurseries); marble. Small part of Fort Berthold Indian Reservation in SW corner; part of Des Lacs Natl. Wildlife Refuge in far NW (Upper and Lower Des Lacs lakes); part of Upper Souris Natl. Wildlife Refuge in N; Minot Air Force Base in N. Formed 1885. **2** county (□ 835 sq mi/2,163 sq km; 1990 pop. 13,115), extreme W Texas; ☉ Monahans; 31°30′N 103°05′W. In Pecos valley; Pecos R. is W and S border. Elev. c.2,500 ft/762 m. Oil and natural-gas fields, sand and gravel; ranching (cattle, horses, hogs, goats), agr. (cotton, alfalfa, grain sorghums, pecans, hay). Formed 1887.

Ward, town (1990 pop. 1,269), Lonoke co., central Ark., 28 mi/45 km NE of Little Rock, on Cypress Bayou; 35°01′N 91°57′W. In agr. area; mfg. (home satellite antennas).

Ward 1 village (1990 pop. 159), Boulder co., N central Colo., on Front Range, 13 mi/21 km WNW of Boulder, near S St. Vrain Creek; 40°04′N 105°30′W. Elev. c.9,258 ft/2,822 m. Gold mining. Surrounded by Roosevelt Natl. Forest. Rocky Mt. Natl. Park to NW. **2** village (1990 pop. 132), Saluda co., W central S.C., 20 mi/32 km W of Aiken; 33°51′N 81°43′W. Agr. includes poultry, livestock; grain, cotton. **3** village (1990

pop. 35), Moody co., E S.Dak., 10 mi/16 km NE of Flandreau, near Minn. state line; 44°09′N 96°27′W.

Ward, locality, Kanawha co., W central W.Va., 15 mi/24 km SE of Charleston, in coal and oil area.

Ward Hunt Island, NE Franklin dist., N.W.T., N Canada, in the Arctic Ocean, just off N Ellesmere Isl.; 9 mi/14.5 km long, 3 mi/4.8 km wide; 83°05′N 75°W.

Wardell (wahr-DEL), town (1990 pop. 325), Pemiscot co., in the bootheel of extreme SE Mo., near the Mississippi, and 14 mi/23 km NNW of Caruthersville; 36°21′N 89°49′W.

Warden, town (1990 pop. 1,639), Grant co., E central Wash., 14 mi/23 km SE of Moses Lake; 46°58′N 119°03′W. RR junction. In Columbia basin agr. region; vegetables, mint, sugar beets, wheat, alfalfa, potatoes, beans. Potholes Reservoir (O'Sullivan Dam) and State Park to W; Columbia Natl. Wildlife Refuge to SW.

Wardensville, village (1990 pop. 140), Hardy co., NE W.Va., in Eastern Panhandle, on Capacon R., 20 mi/32 km E of Moorefield; 39°04′N 78°35′W. Mfg. (wooden furniture). Lost R. (underground river) to W; George Washington Natl. Forest to S, E, and NE.

Wardle, Mount (9,218 ft/2,810 m), SE B.C., W Canada, near Alta. border, in Rocky Mts., in Kootenay Natl. Park, 25 mi/40 km SW of Banff; 50°57′N 116°01′W.

Wardner, village (1990 pop. 246), Shoshone co., N Idaho, 1 mi/1.6 km S of Kellogg; 47°31′N 116°08′W. In mining (zinc, lead) dist. At N edge of St. Joe Natl. Forest.

Wards Island, N.Y. city, SE N.Y., in East R. bet. Roosevelt Isl. (S), Randalls Isl. (N); 40°47′N 73°56′W. Covers 255 acres/103 ha, crossed by roadway of Triborough Bridge, it is connected with Manhattan by a pedestrian drawbridge (1951) giving access to recreational facilities here.

Wardsboro, town (1990 pop. 654), Windham co., SE Vt., 17 mi/27 km NW of Brattleboro; 43°01′N 72°49′W. Wood prods. Partly in Green Mtn. Natl. Forest.

Wardsville, village (1991 pop. 447), S Ont., central Canada, on Thames R., and 24 mi/39 km NE of Chatham. Fruit.

Wardsville, village (1990 pop. 513), Cole co., central Mo., residential and farming suburb 4 mi/6.4 km S of Jefferson City, near Osage R.; 38°29′N 92°10′W. Cattle; hay.

Ware (WER), county (□ 907 sq mi/2,349 sq km; 1990 pop. 35,471), SE Ga.; ☉ Waycross; 31°03′N 82°25′W. Bounded S by Fla. state line; drained by Satilla R. Coastal plain agr. (tobacco, corn, wheat, cotton, soybeans); cattle, hogs, poultry; timber. Okefenokee Swamp occupies S part. Founded 1824.

Ware, town (1990 pop. 9,808), including Ware village, Hampshire co., central Mass., on Ware R., and 22 mi/35 km W of Worcester; 42°17′N 72°17′W. Textiles, shoes, apparel. Settled c.1717, inc. 1761.

Ware River, c.45 mi/72 km long, central Mass.; rises in N Worcester co.; flows generally SW, joining Quaboag R. to form Chicopee R. in Palmer town.

Ware Shoals, village (1990 pop. 2,497), Greenwood co., NW S.C., on Saluda R., and 15 mi/24 km SW of Laurens; 34°23′N 82°14′W.

Wareham (WER-uhm), town (1990 pop. 19,232), Plymouth co., SE Mass., on an inlet of Buzzards Bay; 41°46′N 70°42′W. It is a resort as well as a shipping point for cranberries and shellfish. Includes villages of East Wareham, Onset (resort 1990 pop. 1,461), South Wareham, West Wareham (1990 pop. 2,059). Settled 1678, inc. 1739.

Warfield, village (1990 pop. 364), Martin co., E Ky., in Cumberland Mts., on Tug Fork R. (bridged), opposite Kermit, W.Va., and 15 mi/24 km NW of Williamson, W.Va.; 37°50′N 82°25′W.

Warkworth, village, SE Ont., Canada, on Mill Creek, and 26 mi/42 km W of Belleville. Dairying, mixed farming.

Warm Mineral Springs, town (□ 2 sq mi/5.2 sq km; 1990 pop. 4,041), Sarasota co., W central Fla., 10 mi/16 km E of Venice; 27°03′N 82°16′W.

Warm Springs 1 town (1990 pop. 407), Meriwether co., Ga., 18 mi/29 km E of Thomaston, and 65 mi/105 km SW of Atlanta; 32°53′N 84°41′W. Mfg. of plywood and pine furniture. Active tourist community. Nearby are many attractions, including Roosevelt's Little White

House, Roosevelt State Park, and Calloway Gardens. The entire area, including the Little White House and Warm Springs resort, is designated a Natl. Historic landmark. Formerly called Bullochville; inc. as Warm Springs (1924). **2** uninc. town (1990 pop. 2,287), Jefferson co., N central Oregon, on Shitike Creek, near Deschutes R., 11 mi/18 km NW of Madras; 44°46′N 121°17′W. Hq. of Warm Springs Indian Reservation. Potatoes, grain; poultry, sheep, cattle.

Warm Springs, uninc. village, ⊙ Bath co., W Va., in Allegheny Mts., 25 mi/40 km NW of Lexington, in George Washington Natl. Forest; 38°02′N 79°47′W. Elev. 2,950 ft/899 m. Mfg. (lumber); agr. (cattle); timber. Resort area; mineral springs. Douthat State Park to S; Hidden Valley and Blowing Springs recreation areas to W; L. Moomaw reservoir and Recreation Area to SW.

Warm Springs, locality, Deer Lodge co., SW Mont., on the Clark Fork. Silver Bow Creek becomes Clark Fork R. here. Hay; livestock. Deerlodge Nalt. Forest to E and W and 8 mi/12.9 km ENE of Anaconda, now part of city of Anaconda. Mont. State Hosp., Women's Correctional Center, mineral springs here. Also known as Warmsprings.

Warm Springs, resort, Meriwether co., W Ga., 18 mi/29 km W of Thomaston, and 65 mi/105 km SW of Atlanta; 32°53′N 84°40′W. The salutary properties of the water springing from Pine Mt. were known to Native Americans, and settlers learned of them in the late 18th cent. By the 1830s, a resort was built. Destroyed by fire in 1865, it was soon rebuilt and became fashionable by the end of the 19th cent. President Franklin D. Roosevelt, who found the water beneficial after his attack of poliomyelitis, est. (1927) the Georgia Warm Springs Foundation to help other victims of the disease, and he gave the foundation his 2,600-acre/1,052-ha farm here; facilities restored again in 1990s. Roosevelt retained the cottage known as the Little White House (now a natl. landmark), in which he died in 1945. Nearby is the town, inc. in 1924 as Warm Springs, formerly named Bullochville.

Warm Springs Tailing Pond, Deerlodge co., W Mont. This dam and 2 others were built by the Anaconda Company between 1960–1963. These dams are earth construction and form tailings ponds for the mining company. Warm Springs, Mont., is located just NE of Anaconda and the dams are 2 mi/3.2 km, 4 mi/6.4 km, and 5 mi/8 km upstream.

Warminster (WAHR-min-stuhr), uninc. city (1990 pop. 28,522), Bucks co., SE Pa., suburb 18 mi/29 km N of Philadelphia; 40°12′N 75°06′W. Mfg. includes centrifugal machinery, assembly and packaging, electronics, tool and die, plastic prods., printing, asphalt, gutters, wire assemblies. Military establishments in area scheduled for closing in late 1990s.

Warminster Heights (WAHR-min-stuhr HEITS), uninc. town (1990 pop. 4,310), Bucks co., SE Pa., residential suburb 17 mi/27 km N of Philadelphia, and 2 mi/3.2 km SE of Warminster; 40°11′N 75°04′W. U.S. Naval Development Center to NE, scheduled for closing in late 1990s.

Warner, village (1991 pop. 412), S Alta., W Canada, near Mont. border, 40 mi/64 km SE of Lethbridge; 49°17′N 112°12′W. Farming, ranching.

Warner 1 town (1990 pop. 2,250), Merrimack co., S central N.H., 16 mi/26 km NW of Concord; 43°16′N 71°49′W. Drained by Lane R. Nursery crops, vegetables, apples; poultry, livestock; dairying. Mfg. (electrical equip., light mfg.). Two covered bridges. Rollins State Park in N; part of Winslow State Park in extreme N, which includes Mt. Kearsarge (2,931 ft/893 m). Settled c.1740, inc. 1774. **2** town (1990 pop. 1,479), Muskogee co., E Okla., 18 mi/29 km S of Muskogee; 35°29′N 95°18′W. Connors State Col. is here.

Warner, Mount (9,296 ft/2,833 m), SW B.C., W Canada, in Coast Mts., 130 mi/209 km N of Vancouver; 51°04′N 123°12′W.

Warner Mountains, in extreme NE Calif. mainly E Modoc co., extends S into Lassen co. and N into Lake co., S Oregon. Rises c.5,000 ft/1,525 m–10,000 ft/3,050 m (Eagle Peak near S end); a N-S range c.85 mi/137 km long. Hunting, fishing; logging. Surprise Valley is E. Alakli lakes to E, Goose L. to NW (Orly, Calif.); Fort Bidwell Indian Reservation (Calif.) N, Cedar Pass (6,305 ft/1,922 m) in center; occupies part of Modoc Natl. Forest, Calif., and Fremont Natl. Forest, Oregon.

Warner River, c.25 mi/40 km long, S central N.H.; rises W of Bradford; flows E, past Warner, to Contoocook R. 9 mi/14.5 km WNW of Concord.

Warner Robins, city (1990 pop. 43,726), Houston co., central Ga., near Macon; 32°36′N 83°38′W. In an agr. region (peanuts, grain, fruit; livestock); mfg. (commercial printing, cabinets, avionics equip., lumber, plastics, roof trusses). The city grew with the construction of the adjacent Robins Air Force Base (one of the largest air force installations in the South and hq. of the Continental Air Command) and its economy relies on the base. Before World War II, a small country hamlet called Wellston existed on that site. After the air force base and a major air force supply depot were established, a city boomed. The city and base were named for Gen. Warner Robins (1882–1940), considered the originator of the air force's systems of supply and maintenance. Also located here is the Warner Robins Air Logistics Center. A mus. of aviation on the perimeter of the base has become a major tourist attraction. Inc. 1943.

Warner Springs, uninc. village, San Diego co., S Calif., 21 mi/34 km NE of Ramona. Cattle. Mfg. (electronic transformers). Los Coyotes Indian Reservation to E. Part of Cleveland Natl. Forest to N. Cañada Agua Caliente (canyon) to NE. Pacific Crest Natl. Scenic Trail passes to W.

Warr Acres (WOR), city (1990 pop. 9,288), Oklahoma co., central Okla., residential suburb near Oklahoma City; 35°31′N 97°37′W. Wiley Post Airport to W. L. Hefner reservoir to NE.

Warren, village, E central Ont., Canada, on Veuve R., and 40 mi/64 km W of North Bay; 46°26′N 80°18′W. Dairying, lumbering, mixed farming.

Warren 1 county (□ 287 sq mi/741 sq km; 1990 pop. 6,078), E Ga.; ⊙ Warrenton; 33°25′N 82°41′W. Bounded W by Ogeechee R. Intersected by the fall line. Mfg. (apparel, textiles, wood prods.); agr. (cotton); cattle, hogs; timber; granite and stone quarrying. Formed 1793. **2** county (□ 543 sq mi/1,406 sq km; 1990 pop. 19,181), W Ill.; ⊙ Monmouth; 40°51′N 90°37′W. Agr. (corn, soybeans; livestock, poultry, cattle, hogs). Mfg. (agr. machinery, pottery, sheet metal prods., furnaces). Drained by Henderson Creek and small Swan Creek. Formed 1825. **3** county (□ 366 sq mi/948 sq km; 1990 pop. 8,176), W Ind.; ⊙ Williamsport; 40°21′N 87°22′W. Bounded W by Ill. state line, SE by Wabash R. Wheat, corn, oats, soybeans; hogs, cattle. Mfg. at Williamsport. Formed 1827. **4** county (□ 573 sq mi/1,484 sq km), S central Iowa; ⊙ Indianola, 41°20′N 93°33′W. Prairie agr. area (cattle, hogs, poultry; corn, oats) drained by North, South, and Middle rivers; bituminous-coal deposits. Lake Ahquabi State Park to S. Formed 1846. **5** county (□ 547 sq mi/1,417 sq km; 1990 pop. 76,673), S Ky.; ⊙ Bowling Green; 36°59′N 86°24′W. Bounded N by Green R.; drained by Barren R., Gasper and Drake creeks, Trammel and West forks of Drake Creek. Rolling agr. area (burley tobacco, corn, hay, alfalfa, soybeans, wheat; poultry, hogs, cattle; dairying). Limestone quarries, oil and gas wells. Diversified mfg. at Bowling Green. Formed 1796. **6** county (□ 618 sq mi/1,601 sq km; 1990 pop. 47,880), W Miss.; ⊙ VICKSBURG; 32°21′N 90°50′W. Bounded W by the Mississippi R. (La. state line), E and S by Big Black R.; intersected by Yazoo R. (forms parts of NW state line). Agr. (cotton, corn, soybeans; cattle; timber); limestone. Mfg. at Vicksburg. Large sect. of Miss. (10 mi/16 km long, 5 mi/8 km wide) lies W of Mississippi R., extends to Palymer L., isolated by new river channel. Vicksburg Natl. Military Park in W, N of downtown Vicksburg. Formed 1809. **7** county (□ 428 sq mi/1,109 sq km; 1990 pop. 19,534), E central Mo.; ⊙ Warrenton, 38°46′N 91°10′W. Bounded S by Missouri R. Wheat, corn, soybeans, apples, grapes; livestock; mfg. at Warrenton. Reifsnider State Forest SE of Warrenton; Daniel Boone Memorial Forest in W. Daniel and Rebecca Boone Grave and Monument E of Marthasville. Large area of bottomland was flooded in 1993, damaging Marthasville and other towns. Formed 1833. **8** county (□ 361 sq mi/935 sq km), NW N.J., in hilly region bounded W by Delaware R., SE and E by Musconetcong R.; ⊙ Belvidere; 40°50′N 74°57′W. Mfg. (textiles, candy, paper, chemicals, plastics prods., iron foundries, industrial machinery, electronic equip.); agr. (dairy prods., vegetable, poultry, fruit, grain). In NW is part of Kittatinny Mt. ridge (cut by Delaware R. W of Blairstown to form Delaware Water Gap). Includes state forests, Jenny Jump Mt., and part of Stephens State Park. Drained by Pohatcong and Pequest rivers and Paulins Kill. Formed 1824. **9** county (□ 931 sq mi/2,411 sq km; 1990 pop. 59,209), E N.Y.; ⊙ L. George, 43°33′N 73°50′W. Situated in the S Adirondacks; bounded E by L. George; drained by the Hudson and Schroon rivers. Year-round resort region, with many lakes (Schroon, Brant, Loon, Friends, Luzerne), state parks, hiking and skiing trails. Dairying; poultry and livestock raising; some farming (hay, clover), lumbering. Some mfg. at Glens Falls. Formed 1813. **10** county (□ 443 sq mi/1,147 sq km; 1990 pop. 17,265), N N.C., ⊙ Warrenton; 36°23′N 78°05′W. In Piedmont region, bounded N by Va. state line. Agr. area (corn, wheat, oats, soybeans, sorghum, hay, tobacco; chickens, dairying, cattle, hogs) and timber area; drained by Roanoke R. Part of L. Gaston reservoir in NE and arm of Kerr Reservoir in NW, both on Roanoke R. Formed 1779. **11** county (□ 408 sq mi/1,057 sq km; 1990 pop. 113,909), SW Ohio; ⊙ Lebanon; 39°26′N 84°10′W. Intersected by Little Miami R.; also drained by small Todd, Caesar, and Turtle creeks. Includes Fort Anc. State Memorial Park. In the Till Plains physiographic region. Agr. area (sheep, corn, soybeans, fruit, tobacco); mfg. at Franklin, Lebanon, Waynesville (textile goods, folding paperboard boxes and other paper prods.); sand and gravel pits. Formed 1803. **12** county (□ 897 sq mi/2,323 sq km; 1990 pop. 45,050), NW Pa.; ⊙ Warren; 41°48′N 79°16′W. Bounded N by N.Y. state line. Plateau area drained by Allegheny R., which forms large Allegheny Reservoir in NE (extends into N.Y.) behind Kinzua Dam; also drained by Conewango and Brokenstraw creeks. Mfg. at Warren. Oil wells and refineries. Agr. (corn, oats, hay, alfalfa, potatoes; sheep, hogs, cattle; dairying). Had lumber boom in mid-19th cent. followed by oil boom. Chapman State Park in S center. Part of Allegheny Natl. Forest in E and SE. Formed 1800. **13** county (□ 443 sq mi/1,147 sq km; 1990 pop. 32,992), central Tenn.; ⊙ McMinnville, 35°41′N 85°47′W. East portion in the Cumberlands; drained by affluents of Caney Fork of Cumberland R. Center Hill Reservoir and Great Falls Dam and Reservoir are NE of McMinnville. To the E is Cumberland Caverns, a registered natl. landmark and the second largest cave in the U.S. Livestock raising, general farming, peaches, apples; some mfg. (chiefly at McMinnville). Marble and granite quarries. Tree nurseries. Formed 1807. **14** county (□ 216 sq mi/559 sq km; 1990 pop. 26,142), N Va.; ⊙ Front Royal; 38°54′N 78°12′W. In Shenandoah Valley; Blue Ridge is in E, part of Massanutten Mtn. in W; includes part of Shenandoah Natl. Park in S (includes N part of Skyline Drive). North and South forks of Shenandoah R. join in N to form Shenandoah R. Mfg. at Front Royal; agr. (livestock; dairying; apples, peaches, corn, wheat, hay, alfalfa); limestone quarrying; tourism. Appalachian Trail follows E boundary. Formed 1836.

Warren 1 city (□ 34 sq mi/88 sq km; 1990 pop. 144,864), Macomb co., SE Mich., a suburb 11 mi/18 km N of downtown Detroit; 42°29′N 83°01′W. Important metalworking center where steel is processed; mfg. includes tools and dies, and transportation equip., although the auto industry has suffered significantly since the late 1970s. A large General Motors technical center and Macomb Community Col. are in Warren. U.S. Army Mobility Command Arsenal here. Detroit Arsenal (mfg. of transportation equip.) closed in 1996. Est. 1837; inc. as a city 1957. **2** city (1990 pop. 50,793), ⊙ Trumbull co.,

NE Ohio; 41°14′N 80°49′W. In the fertile Mahoning valley. An early coal center, Warren's industries have greatly diversified. Steel, metal-forming machinery, electrical equip., lamps, wiring harnesses for vehicles, and automobile and truck parts are the principal manufactures. The Trumbull Branch of Kent State Univ. is in the city. Settled 1799, inc. as a city 1905.

Warren 1 town (1990 pop. 6,455), ⊙ Bradley co., S Ark., c.45 mi/72 km S of Pine Bluff; 33°36′N 92°04′W. Lumber-milling and woodworking town. Produces tomatoes. Mfg. (women's apparel, lumber, oak flooring). **2** town (1990 pop. 1,226), Litchfield co., W Conn., in Litchfield Hills, 12 mi/19 km WSW of Torrington township; 41°44′N 73°20′W. Agr. resorts. Includes 2 state parks, parts of L. Waramaug (SW) and Shepaug Reservoir (E). **3** town (1990 pop. 1,185), Huntington co., NE central Ind., on Salamonie R., and 14 mi/23 km SSE of Huntington; 40°41′N 85°25′W. In agr. area (poultry, livestock; soybeans, grain); mfg. (corrugated containers, poultry processing, feed grinding). Laid out 1836. **4** town (1990 pop. 3,192), Knox co., S Maine, just W of Rockland, and on St. George R. Agr., lumber; 44°07′N 69°15′W. Settled 1736, inc. 1776. **5** town (1990 pop. 4,437), including Warren village, Worcester co., S central Mass., on Quaboag R., and 20 mi/32 km WSW of Worcester; 42°12′N 72°12′W. Electric switchboards, power presses, textile printing, pumps, and knit goods. Settled 1664, inc. as Western 1742, renamed Warren 1834. Includes West Warren village. **6** town (1990 pop. 1,813), ⊙ Marshall co., NW Minn., on Snake R., and 23 mi/37 km NE of Grand Forks, N.Dak., in Red R. valley; 48°12′N 96°46′W. Elev. 853 ft/260 m. Agr. (wheat, sunflowers, flax, potatoes, beans, sugar beets; cattle, sheep, poultry); mfg. (fertilizer). Old Mill State Park to NE. Settled 1878, inc. 1891. **7** town (1990 pop. 820), Grafton co., W central N.H., on Baker R., and 16 mi/26 km SSE of Woodsville; 43°57′N 71°53′W. Wood prods., mica and granite quarries; winter sports. N.H. state sanitarium near Glencliff village (N). **8** town (1990 pop. 11,385), Bristol co., E central R.I., on the Kickemuit and Warren rivers at the mouth of Narragansett Bay; est. as an Eng. trading post 1632 and inc. as a town 1747; 41°43′N 71°16′W. Badly damaged by the British in May 1778 during the Revolutionary War, it recovered to become, successively, a major shipbuilding, whaling and, in the 19th cent., textile center. Today an industrial and resort town, its manufactures include auto equip., clothing, plastics, and luggage. Many fine old houses and several 19th cent. churches survive, including St. Mark's Episcopal (1829). **9** town (1990 pop. 1,172), Washington co., W central Vt., on Mad R., and 19 mi/31 km SW of Montpelier; 44°07′N 72°51′W. Partly in Green Mtn. Natl. Forest. Sugarbush Valley ski area is here.

Warren 1 village, Cochise co., SE Ariz., in Mule Mts., near Mex. border, 4 mi/6.4 km SE of Bisbee. Elev. 5,250 ft/1,600 m. Copper, silver, zinc, and gold mines nearby. Tourist attractions; site of Lavender Pit–Copper Queen Mine. **2** village (1990 pop. 1,550), Jo Daviess co., NW Ill., near Wis. state line, 24 mi/39 km NW of Freeport; 42°29′N 89°59′W. In agr. area (dairying; cattle, hogs, oats, barley); mfg. (electric motors, switches). Tri-county fair held here annually. Apple R. Canyon State Park is nearby. Settled 1843; inc. 1859. **3** village (1990 pop. 250), Tyler co., E Texas, 38 mi/61 km NNW of Beaumont; 32°32′N 94°54′W. Agr. and timber. Oil and natural gas. Units of Big Thicket Natl. Preserve to W, S, and E.

Warren (WAHR-uhn), borough (1990 pop. 11,122), ⊙ Warren co., NW Pa., 18 mi/29 km SSE of Jamestown, N.Y., and 105 mi/169 km NNE of Pittsburgh, on the Allegheny R. (which forms large Allegheny Reservoir behind Kinzua Dam 7 mi/11.3 km to E); 41°50′N 79°08′W. Mfg. (fabricated metal prods., transportation equip., machinery, plastic prods., electronic equip., food prods.; printing and publishing). Agr. area (grain; livestock; dairying). An early logging center, Warren is located in wooded country near oil and natural-gas reserves. The hq. of Allegheny Natl. Forest is here; the forest is to S and E; Warren State Hosp. complex to N; Chapman State Park to S. Laid out c.1795, inc. 1832.

Warren, township (1990 pop. 10,830), Somerset co., N N.J., 5 mi/8 km W of Plainfield; 40°38′N 74°31′W. Residential with some light industry. Inc. 1806.

Warren, Fort, partially restored fort, E Mass. Civil War fort and prisoner of war camp, also used in Span.-Amer. War, World War I, and World War II. Abandoned after World War II. Used as hq. and visitor center of the Boston Harbor Isls. State Park. Ferry service from downtown Boston.

Warren River, c.9 mi/14.5 km long, Mass. and R.I.; formed in SE Mass. near state line by junction of Palmer R. and small stream; flows S into R.I., widening in lower course to form harbor at Warren, to Narragansett Bay at mouth of Providence R.

Warren South, Pa.: see SOUTH WARREN.

Warrendale (WAHR-uhn-dail), uninc. village, Allegheny co., W Pa., industrial suburb 15 mi/24 km N of Pittsburgh in urban fringe; 40°39′N 80°04′W. Mfg. includes mining equip., hand tools, machinery, plastic prods., circuit breakers, ceramic filters, waste water treatment equip., scientific instrumentation.

Warrens, village (1990 pop. 343), Monroe co., W central Wis., 38 mi/61 km WSW of Wisconsin Rapids; 44°07′N 90°30′W. Central Wis. Conservation. Area to East Black R. State Forest to NW. Dairying, alfalfa, corn. Mfg. (cranberry equip.).

Warrensburg, city (1990 pop. 15,244), ⊙ Johnson co., W Mo.; 38°45′N 93°43′W. Inc. as a city 1855. The city is situated in a livestock and farm region that principally raises wheat, corn, sorghum, and cattle. Mfg. (circuit boards, can openers, aluminum castings, mowers, uniforms, clothing, chemicals, and electronic components). Statue of dog (Old Drum) on courthouse lawn, a tribute to canine who saved his master's life. Central Mo. State Univ. is in Warrensburg; airport to W; Whiteman Air Force Base to E; Knob Noster State Park to E.

Warrensburg 1 village (1990 pop. 1,274), Macon co., central Ill., 7 mi/11.3 km NW of Decatur; 39°55′N 89°03′W. Agr. (corn, wheat, soybeans; livestock); mfg. aerosol cans. **2** village (□ 9 sq mi/23.3 sq km; 1990 pop. 3,204), Warren co., E N.Y., in the Adirondacks, on Schroon R. near its mouth on the Hudson R., and 14 mi/23 km NNW of Glens Falls; 43°30′N 73°46′W. Trade center in farm and resort area; lumber, paper milling.

Warrensville, uninc. village, Ashe co., NW N.C., 20 mi/32 km NNE of Boone, on North Fork New R.

Warrensville Heights, city (1990 pop. 15,745), Cuyahoga co., NE Ohio, a suburb of Cleveland; 41°26′N 81°31′W. Although chiefly residential, it has plants that manufacture machinery, automobile equip., and cardboard containers. The home of a summer stock musical theater-in the-round. Inc. 1927.

Warrenton 1 city (1990 pop. 2,056), ⊙ Warren co., E Ga., 38 mi/61 km W of Augusta; 33°25′N 82°40′W. Mfg. includes lumber, apparel, metal office furniture, crushed stone; in agr. and timber area. Inc. as town 1810, as city 1908. **2** city (1990 pop. 3,596), ⊙ Warren co., E central Mo., 35 mi/56 km W of St. Charles; 38°49′N 91°08′W. Corn, soybeans; cattle; mfg. (textiles, transportation equip., insulated glass, soft drinks, copper ingots, sheet metal). Founded c. 1835.

Warrenton 1 town (1990 pop. 949), ⊙ Warren co., N N.C., 32 mi/51 km NNW of Rocky Mount; 36°23′N 78°09′W. Agr. area (grain, tobacco, soybeans, chickens; livestock; dairying); mfg. (modern tobacco hogsheads, furniture, wooden pallets, shirts, textiles, buttons). Founded 1779. **2** town (1990 pop. 2,681), Clatsop co., extreme NW Oregon, 3 mi/4.8 km WSW of Astoria on S side of Columbia R. estuary, 2 mi/3.2 km E of the Pacific Ocean; 46°10′N 123°55′W. Columbia Beach, at entrance to Youngs Bay, and at mouth of Skiparon R., 1.5 mi/2.4 km channel on the river gives ships access to town. RR spur to Hammond. Mfg. (fish hatcheries, fish foods, crab and salmon processing, lumber, farm equipment, fur farms). Poultry. Point Adams Coast Guard Station nearby. Camp Rilea Military Reservation to SW. Fort Clatsop Natl. Memorial 2 mi/3.2 km SE. Fort Stevens State Park to NW; Del Rey Beach State Wayside to S. Inc. 1899. **3** town (1990 pop. 4,830), ⊙ Fauquier co., N Va., at foot of Blue Ridge, 17 mi/27 km WSW of Manassas; 38°43′N 77°47′W. Light mfg.; in rich agr. area (grain, soybeans, apples, peaches; livestock); horse breeding, racing. Vint Hill Farm Military Reservation to E. Settled 18th cent.; inc. 1810.

Warrenville, city (1990 pop. 11,333), Du Page co., NE Ill., suburb 30 mi/48 km W of downtown Chicago, 10 mi/16 km NE of Aurora; 41°49′N 88°11′W. Agr. (corn; dairying); mfg. (wood prods., metal castings). Fermi Natl. Accelerator Lab (W).

Warrenville, uninc. town, Aiken co., SW S.C., 5 mi/8 km WSW of Aiken. Mfg. includes machining; agr. includes cotton, peanuts, grains, peaches; livestock, poultry.

Warrenville, Conn.: see ASHFORD, village.

Warrick, county (□ 390 sq mi/1,010 sq km; 1990 pop. 44,920), SW Ind.; ⊙ Boonville; 38°06′N 87°16′W. Bounded S by Ohio R., here forming Ky. state line; drained by small Pigeon and Little Pigeon creeks. Corn, hay, soybeans; cattle. One of Ind.'s leading coal-producing cos. (surface mines); bituminous coal; diversified mfg. Formed 1813.

Warrington, uninc. city (□ 9 sq mi/23.3 sq km; 1990 pop. 16,040), Escambia co., extreme NW Fla., a suburb 8 mi/12.9 km SW of Pensacola, on Pensacola Bay; 30°22′N 87°17′W. Although chiefly residential, it has shipyards and waterfront industries.

Warrington (WAHR-eeng-tuhn), uninc. town (1990 pop. 6,980), Bucks co., SE Pa., suburb 20 mi/32 km N of Philadelphia; 40°14′N 75°08′W. Mfg. includes machinery, protective clothing, fabricated metal prods., chemicals, measuring instruments.

Warrior, town (1990 pop. 3,280), Jefferson co., N central Ala., c.20 mi/32 km N of Birmingham. Coal mines; mfg. furniture.

Warrior Run (WAHR-ee-yuhr), borough (1990 pop. 656), Luzerne co., NE central Pa., residential suburb 5 mi/8 km SW of Wilkes-Barre; 41°11′N 75°57′W. Wilkes-Barre Mt. to SE. Inc. 1895.

Warroad (WOR-rod), town (1990 pop. 1,679), Roseau co., NW Minn., 21 mi/34 km ENE of Roseau on Muskeg Bay, SW end of L. of the Woods, at mouth of Warroad R.; 48°54′N 95°19′W. Elev. 1,065 ft/325 m. Port of entry; RR terminus. Agr. (dairying; poultry, cattle, sheep; grain, flax); mfg. (apparel, lumber, concrete). Parts of Beltrami Isl. State Forest to NW and S; Hayes L. State Park to SW; parts of Red L. Indian Reservation to S and NE (in NW angle); Warroad Internatl. Seaplane Base on L. of the Woods. Settled 1890, inc. 1901.

Warsaw 1 city (1990 pop. 1,882), Hancock co., W Ill., on the Mississippi, and 3 mi/4.8 km SSW of Keokuk; 40°21′N 91°25′W. In agr. area (corn, wheat, soybeans; cattle, hogs; dairy prods.); mfg. Limestone quarries. Laid out 1834, inc. 1837. Two forts were est. here in 1814. **2** city (1990 pop. 10,968), ⊙ Kosciusko co., N Ind., on Tippecanoe R., and 40 mi/64 km, WNW of Fort Wayne; 41°14′N 85°51′W. Located in Indiana's lake region; RR junction. Agr. region (corn; dairying; cattle, poultry); mfg. (concrete, ink, machinery, food processing, projection screens, transportation equip., medical equip., chemicals, furniture, fabricated metal prods.); lumber milling. Laid out 1836, inc. 1854. **3** city (1990 pop. 1,696), ⊙ Benton co., central Mo., on Osage R., at W end or "headwaters" of L. of the Ozarks, and 33 mi/53 km S of Sedalia; 38°14′N 93°22′W. Corn, wheat; cattle, hogs; fishing; mfg. (walnut gunstocks, apparel). Hydroelectricity; water-recreation activities; tourism. Harry S. Truman Dam and Truman L., also on the Osage, are on the N side of Warsaw, and empty into the L. of the Ozarks.

Warsaw 1 town (1990 pop. 1,202), ⊙ Gallatin co., N Ky., 30 mi/48 km SW of Covington on Ohio R.; Markland Locks and Dam to W (1963); 38°47′N 84°53′W. Trade center in outer Bluegrass agr. region (burley tobacco, grain, soybeans; cattle, horses; dairying); nurseries; mfg. (meat processing, concrete prods., wooden furniture frames). Gallatin Co. Historical Society. **2** town (1990 pop. 2,859), Duplin co., SE N.C., 27 mi/43 km

SSW of Goldsboro; 35°00′N 78°05′W. RR junction. Cucumbers, sweet potatoes, peppers, grain, tobacco, cotton; poultry, livestock. Mfg. (machinery, textiles, lumber, concrete blocks). **3** town (1990 pop. 961), ⊙ Richmond co., E Va., 45 mi/72 km SE of Fredericksburg; 37°57′N 76°45′W. Mfg. (clothing, lumber; printing and publishing); agr. (grain, soybeans; cattle); timber. Rappahannock Community Col. (Warsaw campus).

Warsaw 1 village (□ 4 sq mi/10.4 sq km; 1990 pop. 3,830), ⊙ Wyoming co., W N.Y., 17 mi/27 km S of Batavia; 42°44′N 78°08′W. Agr. (grain, hay, vegetables). Service center for region's dynamic dairy and grain-growing farms. Settled 1803, inc. 1843. **2** village (1990 pop. 699), Coshocton co., central Ohio, on Walhonding R., and 8 mi/13 km WNW of Coshocton; 40°20′N 82°00′W. Molding sand, leather goods, food prods.

Warson Woods, town (1990 pop. 2,049), St. Louis co., E Mo.; residential suburb 9 mi/14.5 km W of downtown St. Louis; 38°36′N 90°23′W.

Wartburg (WORT-buhrg), city (1990 pop. 932), ⊙ Morgan co., NE central Tenn., 22 mi/35 km WNW of Oak Ridge, in the Cumberlands, 36°06′N 84°36′W. In coal-mining and lumbering area; mfg. apparel.

Wartrace (WOR-trais), town (1990 pop. 494), Bedford co., central Tenn., 9 mi/14 km E of Shelbyville, 35°32′N 86°20′W.

Warwick, parish (1991 pop. 7,900), SW Bermuda, on Bermuda Isl.; 32°15′N 64°48′W.

Warwick (WOR-wik), town (1991 pop. 2,836), S Que., E Canada, 40 mi/64 km N of Sherbrooke; 45°57′N 71°59′W. Woolen milling, woodworking; mfg. of machinery, plastics, lumber, paperboard, cheese, needles and pins.

Warwick, former county (□ 71 sq mi/184 sq km), SE Va., now part of Newport News independent city.

Warwick, city (1990 pop. 85,427), Kent co., central R.I., at the head of Narragansett Bay; 41°42′N 71°25′W. Its now closed textile industry dated from 1794. Other manufactures include machinery, metals, pipes and tubing, and silverware. The town includes the neighborhoods of Apponaug, on Greenwich Bay; Hillsgrove, site of the T. F. Green state airport; Warwick; and former resort villages. Warwick village was nearly destroyed (1676) in King Philip's War. Gaspee Point, S of Pawtuxet, was the scene of the burning of the Br. revenue cutter Gaspee in 1772; annual "Gaspee Days" commemorate the event. Warwick has the Community Col. of R.I. and a very large music arena. Rocky Point is one of the NE's oldest amusement parks. Nathanael Greene was b. here. Settled by Samuel Gorton 1642, inc. as a city 1931.

Warwick 1 (WOR-wik), town (1990 pop. 501), Worth co., S central Ga., 12 mi/19 km SW of Cordele; 31°50′N 83°55′W. Power dam, 2 mi/3.2 km NW, in Flint R. forms L. Blackshear (□ c.12.5 sq mi/32.4 sq km; c.10 mi/16 km long). **2** town (1990 pop. 740), Franklin co., N Mass., 15 mi/24 km NE of Greenfield; 42°41′N 72°20′W. State forest here.

Warwick 1 (WOR-wik), village (□ 2 sq mi/5.2 sq km; 1990 pop. 5,984), Orange co., SE N.Y., near N.J. border, 19 mi/31 km ESE of Port Jervis; 41°15′N 74°21′W. Mfg. (stop watches, chronographs, rubber gaskets, and rubber goods); in fruit-growing area. State Training School for Boys here. Warwick Village Historic Dist. Settled c.1746, inc. 1867. **2** village (1990 pop. 80), Benson co., E central N.Dak., 20 mi/32 km SSE of Devils L., in Devils Lake Sioux Indian Reservation; 47°51′N 98°42′W. **3** (WOR-ik), village (1990 pop. 160), Lincoln co., central Okla., 7 mi/11.3 km WSW of Chandler; 35°41′N 97°00′W. Agr. and oil-producing area.

Warwick Neck, central R.I., peninsula bet. Greenwich Bay (W) and Narragansett Bay (E). Residential, resort area. Warwick Point, with lighthouse, is at S end.

Wasatch (WAH-sach), county (□ 1,209 sq mi/3,131 sq km; 1990 pop. 10,089), N central Utah; ⊙ Heber City; 40°19′N 111°09′W. Strawberry R. and Strawberry Reservoir in S and Provo R. in NW (forms Jordanelle and Deer Creek reservoirs) are used for irrigation; barley, oats, alfalfa, sugar beets, vegetables, fruit; dairying; cattle, sheep; sand and gravel. Lead, silver, and zinc mines are in vicinity of Heber. Jordaneele Reservoir and State Park in NW; Deer Creek Reservoir and State Park and Wasatch Mt. State Park in NW; parts of Uinta Natl. Forest in NW, N-S through center and in SE; small parts of Ashley and Wasatch natl. forests in NE corner; Strawberry Reservoir in Uinta Natl. Forest in S. Co. formed 1862.

Wasatch Plateau (WAH-sach), central Utah, high tableland at S extension of Wasatch Range, largely in Sanpete and Emery cos. Rises to 10,986 ft/3,349 m in Musinia Peak, and to 11,300 ft/3,444 m in South Tent. Lies within Manti-La Sal Natl. Forest. Part of Fishlake Natl. Forest in S. Is penetrated by irrigation tunnels conducting water from headstream of San Rafael R., on E, to Sanpete Valley, on W.

Wasatch Range, part of the Rocky Mts., extending c.250 mi/402 km S from SE Idaho to central Utah. Mt. Timpanogos, the highest peak (11,750 ft/3,581 m), in S Timpanogos Cave Natl. Monument. Many streams on the W flank of the Wasatch carry water into the oasis of the Jordan Valley and Great Salt L. E shore, which stretches along the W foothills; where Utah's principal cities and most of the state's pop. are found. Emigrant Canyon, just E of Salt Lake City, a site of early Mormon migration and influence is now a major winter-resort area. Skiing is an important industry throughout range. Much of the range is covered by Wasatch Natl. Forest, (Utah); Cache Natl. Forest (Idaho). The waters of the range, except for extreme SE, are within the Great Basin drainage system.

Wasco (WAS-ko), county (□ 2,395 sq mi/6,203 sq km; 1990 pop. 21,683), N Oregon; ⊙ The Dalles; 45°09′N 121°09′W. Bounded N by the Columbia R., forms Wash. state line. Drained by Deschutes R., which forms part of the E boundary. Bounded in SE by John Day R. Columbia R. forms Bonneville Reservoir in NW, L. Celilo Reservoir (The Dalles Dam) in NE. Agr. (apples, grapes, cherries, oats, barley, wheat; hogs, cattle); timber. Part of Deschutes R. State Recreation area in NE; Mayer and Memaloose State Parks in NW; part of Warm Springs Indian Reservation in SW; part of Mt. Hood Natl. Forest and part of Cascade Range in W. Formed 1854.

Wasco, city (1990 pop. 12,412), Kern co., S central Calif., in San Joaquin Valley, 24 mi/39 km NW of Bakersfield; 35°36′N 119°20′W. Agr. (cotton, fruit, beans, tomatoes, vegetables, sugar beets, potatoes, grain); cattle; dairying. Gypsum production; oil wells nearby. Colonel Allensworth State Historical Park to N; Kern Natl. Wildlife Refuge to NW. Inc. 1945.

Wasco (WAS-ko), village (1990 pop. 374), Sherman co., N Oregon, 23 mi/37 km E of The Dalles; 45°35′N 120°42′W. Agr. (wheat, barley, oats; poultry, cattle). Deschutes R. State Recreation Area to W; J. S. Burres State Park to SE; John Day State Scenic Waterway to E and SE. Wasco State Airport to E.

Waseca (waw-SEE-kuh), county (□ 432 sq mi/1,119 sq km; 1990 pop. 18,079), S Minn.; ⊙ Waseca; 44°01′N 93°35′W. Agr. (soybeans, alfalfa, corn, oats; sheep, hogs, cattle, poultry; dairying). Drained by Le Sueur and Little Cobb rivers. L. Elysian in NW. Formed 1857.

Waseca (waw-SEE-kuh), town (1990 pop. 8,385), ⊙ Waseca co., S Minn., 26 mi/42 km ESE of Mankato, bet. Clear L. (E) and Loon L. (W); 44°04′N 93°30′W. Elev. 1,159 ft/353 m; RR junction. Resort; trade center for agr. area (grain, soybeans, peas; livestock, poultry); mfg. (printing and publishing, archery supplies, frozen peas and corn, transportation equip., grain for livestock and poultry, printing ink, machinery). Municipal airport to W. Settled before 1870.

Washago (wuh-SHAH-go), village, S Ont., central Canada, on Severn R., at N end of L. Couchiching, 11 mi/18 km NE of Orillia; 44°45′N 79°20′W. Resort; dairying.

Washakie (WAH-shuh-kee), county (□ 2,242 sq mi/5,807 sq km; 1990 pop. 8,388), N central Wyo.; ⊙ Worland; 43°54′N 107°40′W. Irrigated agr. and oil and natural-gas area; watered by Bighorn R. and Nowood Creek. Agr. (barley, sugar beets, hay, alfalfa, beans; sheep). Part of Bighorn Mts. in E; small part of Bighorn Natl. Forest in NE corner, including Meadowlark Ski Area. Formed 1911.

Washakie Needles, Wyo.: see ABSAROKA RANGE.

Washakie Pass, Wyo.: see WIND RIVER RANGE.

Washburn, county (□ 853 sq mi/2,209 sq km; 1990 pop. 13,772), NW Wis.; ⊙ Shell L.; 45°53′N 91°47′W. Drained by Namekagon and Yellow rivers. Wooded terrain with many lakes. Beans; cattle, sheep; summer resort area. St. Croix Natl. Scenic Riverway (Namekagon R.) crosses center of co. E-W; Nest of Eagles Ski Area near co. center. Formed 1883.

Washburn 1 town (1990 pop. 1,880), Aroostook co., NE Maine, on the Aroostook R., and 10 mi/16 km NW of Presque Isle; 46°47′N 68°06′W. In farming, lumbering region. Settled c.1829, inc. 1861. **2** town (1990 pop. 1,506), ⊙ McLean co., central N.Dak., 36 mi/58 km N of Bismarck, and on Missouri R.; 47°17′N 101°01′W. Lignite mines; livestock, dairy prods., wheat, rye, flax. Cross Ranch State Park to S; Fort Mandan Historic Site to W. **3** town (1990 pop. 2,285), ⊙ Bayfield co., extreme N Wis., on W shore of Chequamegon Bay of L. Superior, 7 mi/11.3 km N of Ashland; 46°40′N 90°53′W. Commercial center for dairying, lumbering, and fruit-growing area; mfg. iron castings. A ranger station; Bayfish State Fish Hatchery to NE; agr. research station 8 mi/12.9 km S; Chaquamegon Natl. Forest to W. Founded 1884, inc. 1904.

Washburn, village (1990 pop. 1,075), in Woodford co., central Ill., 22 mi/35 km NE of Peoria; 40°55′N 89°17′W. In agr. area (corn, soybeans; cattle).

Washburn Range, U-shaped ridge in Rocky Mts. of Yellowstone Natl. Park, NW Wyo., W of Yellowstone R., in N ½ of park; 44°47′N 110°26′W. Highest point, Mt. Washburn (10,243 ft/3,122 m). Dunraven Pass (8,859 ft/2,700 m) crossed by highway.

Washington, state (□ 71,301 sq mi/184,675 sq km; 1995 est. pop. 5,430,940), extreme NW conterminous U.S., in the Pacific NW, admitted 1889 as the 42d state; ⊙ OLYMPIA; 47°07′N 120°41′W. SEATTLE, SPOKANE, and TACOMA are the largest cities. Wash. is bounded on the N by the Can. prov. of B.C., on the E by Idaho, on the S by Oregon (with the Columbia R. marking much of the border), and on the W by the Pacific Ocean, with Puget Sound in the NW and 2 inlets, Grays Harbor and Willapa Bay, farther S. The deep S indentation of Puget Sound and its SW arm, Hood Canal, create the Olympic Peninsula to W—a wet region with dense temperate rain forests of spruce, fir, cedar, and hemlock—much of it included in Olympic Natl. Park, where the Olympic Mts. rise 7,965 ft/2,428 m in Mt. Olympus and Kitsap Peninsula, arrowhead-shaped land extension bet. Hood Canal and Puget Sound. Puget Sound, the focal point of the state's economic development, is entered from the Pacific by the Strait of Juan de Fuca, bet. Olympic Peninsula and Vancouver Isl. (Canada), or the Strait of Georgia, which separates Vancouver Isl. from mainland Canada. It is navigable and has many beautiful bays and inlets, locally known as "harbors," on which are situated such important commercial and industrial cities as Seattle, Tacoma, and Everett. More than 300 isls. dot Puget Sound and waters N of its entrance; they include the picturesque and historic San Juan Archipelago which lies bet. straits of Georgia (N) and Juan de Fuca (S), and Whidbey Isl., NE of sound's main entrance (Admiralty Inlet). The boldest physiographic feature is the Cascade Range, which runs N and S, E of Puget Sound, and divides the state into W and E sects. of contrasting physical (and corresponding economic) characteristics. While most of the range rises to mts. of the 5,000 ft/1,524 m–7,000 ft/2,134 m category, several peaks, all extinct snowcapped volcanoes, rise to 10,000 ft/3,048 m or more; Mt. Rainier is the highest (14,410 ft/4,392 m) in the state. The Cascades block the E movement of cool, moist ocean air of the Alaska Current, creating a rainy coastal climate to the W and a semiarid continental climate regime to the E. Thus, the coastal region, esp. on W side of Olympic Peninsula, ranks among the wettest areas in the Western Hemisphere, averaging in higher elevs. as much as 150 in/381 cm of rainfall per year and containing some of the heaviest stands of timber in the world. In contrast, the dry E sect. is nearly treeless, except in mountainous areas of the NE and extreme SE, with just sufficient rainfall for the dry farming of wheat and hay in the Palouse Hills. Much of E Wash. is too arid to grow crops without irrigation, from the Columbia R. basin and its main tributaries, the Snake, Yakima, and Spokane rivers. Additional water is provided to inland areas by streams descending E out of the Cascades. It is in this margin that most of Wash.'s famous fruit-growing industry has been established, most noted for its apples. Cattle and sheep graze in arid drylands of E Wash. Spokane is the commercial and transportation hub of the entire region bet. the Cascades and the Rockies, known as the "Inland Empire," an area extending into B.C., Idaho, Mont., and Oregon. However, irrigation has converted many of the river valleys E of the Cascades (esp. the Yakima and Wenatchee) into garden areas. Wash. leads the country in the production of apples with 50% of U.S. total and is also a major wheat-producing state. Most production occurs in the hilly Palouse area in the E portion of the state. Miles of apple, pear, peach, and cherry orchards in the irrigated area just E of the Cascades create the landscape of spring beauty for which the state is famous. Wash. is a major producer of sweet cherries, as well as of asparagus and green peas. Other major crops include hay and potatoes; also grapes for a rapidly expanding wine industry. Cattle, dairy goods, and poultry are also economically important, esp. in W. Areas along Puget Sound noted for strawberries, blueberries, and raspberries, also for tulip and daffodil bulbs. Areas around Yakima grow hops, spearmint, and peppermint. Washington's great water resources provide not only irrigation but enormous hydroelectric power. The Columbia R. is important to the life and economy of the state; originally used as a means of transport and a salmon-fishing field for many Native Amer. tribes. Because of the rapid drop from its origin to its mouth, the Columbia is one of the greatest sources of hydroelectric power in the world. It begins in B.C. in the NE, is joined by its greatest tributary, the Snake, and continues W as the Wash.-Oregon state line, cutting its way through the Cascades and the lower Pacific Coast Range in magnificent gorges to reach the Pacific. Grand Coulee Dam (1942), one of the world's largest concrete dams and greatest potential power-producing structures, and Bonneville Dam have been supplemented, on the river's upper course, by Chief Joseph and Rocky Reach dams (completed 1961), Priest Rapids Dam (1962), and Wanapum Dam (1963), also Rock Isl. and Wells dams, and, on its lower course, by The Dalles Dam (1957), John Day Dam (1968), and McNary Dam (1953), all shared with Oregon. The dams on the lower course were designed as power, flood-control, and navigation projects, whereas the dams on the upper course are integral to the Columbia basin project (with the Grand Coulee as the key unit), providing power, flood control, and extensive irrigation to the Columbia Plateau. Dams on the Skagit R. and others in W (including Ross and Diablo) supply power to Seattle and the surrounding area. Seattle, a great shipping point for Asia and a natural gateway to Alaska (Puget Sound is at S end of the protected Inside Passage, which continues N through Strait of Georgia) is one of the major cities in the U.S. and a center for the state's leading industry: the manufacture of jet airplanes, missiles, and spacecraft. The state's 2d-largest industry is food processing; this is based on the state's diversified irrigated farming and dairying as well as on its abundant fishing resources. Salmon is the biggest catch, but halibut, herring, oysters, prawns, and crabs are also caught in significant numbers. Despite the vast acreage of semiarid land E of the Cascades, more than ½ of the state's area is forested, and the old lumber and wood-prods. industry, so important in the early development of the state, is today its third largest industry. Many of Wash.'s cities (Tacoma, Bellingham, Everett, Anacortes) began as sawmill centers, and lumber, pulp, paper, and related items are still their major prods.; other important mfg. include chemicals and primary metals, esp. aluminum. The abundant water produced at federal dams and marketed on a long-run basis to the aluminum industry has made the state the nation's leading aluminum producer. Chief minerals found here include sand and gravel, cement, stone, and diatomite; gold, silver, lead, and zinc are also found in the Okanogan Highlands. High-technology mfg. is important in the Seattle metropolitan area, Vancouver, and Spokane. Research and advanced services are also of growing importance, including software giant Microsoft. Tourism is an increasingly important industry. Thousands of visitors are annually attracted to Mt. Rainier Natl. Park, Olympic Natl. Park, North Cascades Natl. Park (created 1968), Fort Vancouver and Whitman Mission natl. historic sites, and Coulee Dam Natl. Recreation Area. Mt. SAINT HELENS, a volcanic peak in the Cascades, erupted in 1980, killing 60 people and causing billions of dollars in damage. It was established as Mt. Saint Helens Natl. Volcanic Monument in 1982 and has become a popular tourist attraction and important scientific research site. Among Wash.'s natl. forests are Olympic, Mt. Baker, Snoqualmie, Gifford Pinchot in W; Wenatchee and Okanogan in center; Colville and part of Kaniksu in NE; and part of Umatilla in SE. Indian reservations include Yakima in S center, Colville in N center, Spokane in NE, and several smaller residentials, esp. in W. Rugged mt. slopes and the simple grandeur of the scenery draw many climbers during the summer months, and in winter excellent snowfields near Seattle and Tacoma attract crowds of skiers. Wash.'s early history is shared with that of the whole Oregon Territory. The perennial search for the NORTHWEST PASSAGE aroused initial interest in the area. Of the early explorers along the Pacific coast, Span. expeditions under Juan Pérez (1774) and Bruno Heceta (1775) are the first known to have definitely skirted the coast of what is now Wash. Capt. James Cook's Eng. expedition (1778) first opened up the area to the maritime fur trade with China, and Br. fur companies were soon exploring the West and encountering Russians pushing S from posts in Alaska. In 1787, Charles William Barkley found the inland channel, later named the Juan de Fuca Strait. In 1792, the Br. explorer George Vancouver and the Amer. fur trader Robert Gray crossed paths along the Wash. coast. Vancouver sailed into Puget Sound and mapped the area, and Gray, convinced of the existence of a great river that the other explorers rejected, found the entrance, and sailed up the Columbia, establishing U.S. claim to the areas that it drained. Although, the Lewis and Clark expedition, which reached the area in 1805, and early settlements helped to further the Amer. claims to the region, Br. counterclaims meant rights to the territory remained in question bet. the British and Americans. Diplomatic efforts eventually set the boundary at lat. 49°N in 1846. Fort Vancouver, on the site of present-day Vancouver, sheltered Amer. overland traders—particularly Jedediah Smith, Benjamin Bonneville, and Nathaniel Wyeth—and later the Amer. missionaries, who settled in the area N of the Columbia. Partly as a protective measure against conflict with Native Americans, the Oregon Territory, embracing the Wash. area, was created in 1847; but in 1853 the region was divided, and Wash. Territory (containing a part of what is now Idaho) was set up. Meanwhile, some of the pioneers on the Oregon Trail began to turn N and settled New Market, or Tumwater (near present Olympia). Lumber and fishing industries arose in the Puget Sound country to supply the demand to the S (particularly lumber and food for Calif. gold seekers), and other towns, including Seattle, were founded. Meanwhile Gov. Isaac Stevens, who also served as superintendent of Indian affairs, set about persuading the Native Americans to sell much of their lands and settle on reservations. Treaties with the coast tribes were quickly concluded, but the inland tribes revolted, and hostilities with the Cayuse, the Yakima, and the Nez Percé tribes continued for many years. (The Native Amer. pop. of Wash. was 81,483 in 1990.) Gold was 1st discovered in Wash. in 1852 by a Hudson's Bay Company agent at Fort Colville, but the Yakima War was then in progress and hindered extensive mining activity. In 1860 the Orofino Creek and Clearwater R. deposits were uncovered, bringing a rush of prospectors to the Walla Walla area. The great influx of settlers was delayed, however, until the 1880s, when transport by RR became possible (the first of 3 transcontinental RRs linked to Wash. was completed in 1883). The pop. almost quadrupled bet. 1880 and 1890; although the majority of the new settlers were from the East and Midwest, the territory also absorbed large numbers of foreign immigrants. Chin. laborers had been brought in during the 1860s to aid in placer mining; after 1870 they were followed by substantial groups of Scan., Ger., Rus., Du., and Jap. immigrants. By the time Wash. became a state in 1889, the wide sagebrush plains and grasslands of E Wash. had been given over to cattle and sheep, agr. was flourishing in the fertile valleys, and the lumber industry had been founded. Although some agrarian and labor dissatisfaction with the RRs and other big corporations existed, giving rise to the Granger movement and the Populist party, the discovery of gold in Alaska in 1897 brought renewed prosperity. Seattle, the primary departure point for the Klondike, became a boom town. Labor and election reform laws were enacted, and the primary, the initiative, the referendum, and the recall were adopted. At the same time came labor clashes that gave Wash. a reputation as a radical state. The extreme policies of the Industrial Workers of the World (IWW; also known as the "Wobblies") proved appealing to the shipyard and dock workers and to the loggers, and in 1917 the War Dept. was forced to intervene in a lumber dispute. A general strike after World War I had a crippling effect on the state's economy; antilabor feeling increased, and the famous incident at Centralia resulted in bloody strife bet. the IWW and the Amer. Legion. The alarmed and brutal reaction of management to radical labor policies produced a confrontation situation that hindered the institution of remedial measures until the onset of the lean days of the 1930s and the emergence of the New Deal. Wash. was an important center of the defense industry during World War II, particularly with the immense aircraft industry in Seattle and the Atomic Energy Commission's Hanford Works N of Richland. Decades later it was discovered that the Hanford Works had leaked large amounts of radioactive waste in the 1940s and 1950s, and it is now a major fuel waste dump site under the Dept. of Energy (formerly the Atomic Energy Commission). To the W of Hanford is Yakima Military Training site. The large Jap.-Amer. pop. in the state (more than 15,000 persons) was moved E, suffering great physical and emotional hardship. In the postwar period the climate of public affairs began to change, owing in part to the political power of Dave Beck and organized labor, and also to the continuing widespread prosperity brought by booming aircraft production, expanding aluminum-processing industries, and a growing sea and air trade with the Far East. Since the 1970s, Wash. has developed a significant high-technology sector, nurtured by research centers such as the Univ. of Wash. and the Fred Hutchinson Cancer Research Center. Wash. has also attracted a large number of firms from Calif., including computer software manufacturers and biotechnology companies. Wash., like neighboring Oregon, is vitally concerned with protecting its environment and movements to slow economic growth have gained momentum. Wash. still operates under its first constitution, adopted in 1889. Its executive branch is headed by a governor elected for a 4-year term. The bicameral legislature has a senate with 49 members elected for 4-year terms and a house of representatives with 98 members elected for 2-year terms. The state sends 2 Senators and 9 Representatives to the U.S. Congress and has 11 electoral votes. Among the state's institutions of higher learning are the Univ. of Wash. and Seattle Univ., at Seattle; Wash. State Univ., at Pullman; Gonzaga Univ. and Whitworth Col., at

Spokane; Pacific Lutheran Univ., at Tacoma; and Whitman Col., at Walla Walla. Wash. has 39 cos.: ADAMS, ASOTIN, BENTON, CHELAN, CLALLAM, CLARK, COLUMBIA, COWLITZ, DOUGLAS, FERRY, FRANKLIN, GARFIELD, GRANT, GRAYS HARBOR, ISLAND, JEFFERSON, KING, KITSAP, KITTITAS, KLICKITAT, LEWIS, LINCOLN, MASON, OKANOGAN, PACIFIC, PEND OREILLE, PIERCE, SAN JUAN, SKAGIT, SKAMANIA, SNOHOMISH, SPOKANE, STEVENS, THURSTON, WAHKIAKUM, WALLA WALLA, WHATCOM, WHITMAN, and YAKIMA.

Washington 1 county (□ 1,088 sq mi/2,818 sq km; 1990 pop. 16,694), SW Ala.; ⊙ Chatom, 31°24′N 88°10′W. Coastal plain on Miss. state line, bounded E by Tombigbee R.; drained by Escatawapa R. Soybeans, corn; poultry; timber; natural-gas production. Formed 1800. **2** county (□ 956 sq mi/2,476 sq km; 1990 pop. 113,409), NW Ark.; ⊙ Fayetteville; 35°58′N 94°14′W. Bounded W by Okla. state line; drained by Illinois and White rivers; situated in Ozark region. Livestock and poultry raising (cattle, hogs, chickens, turkeys); dairy prods. Mfg. at Fayetteville and Springdale. Timber; coal. Urbanized in N center, pop. has since swelled by retirees and seasonal residents. Devils Den State Park is in S; parts of Ozark Natl. Forest in NW, S, and SE; part of Beaver L. Reservoir (White R.) in NE; Prairie Grove Battlefield State Park near center. Formed 1828. **3** county (□ 2,524 sq mi/6,537 sq km; 1990 pop. 4,812), NE Colo.; ⊙ Akron; 39°58′N 103°12′W. Drained in NW corner by S Platte R., in SE by Arikaree R. and Gordon Creek, in SW by Beaver and Sand creeks. Agr. area (wheat, hay, sunflowers, beans, oats, corn, sugar beets); cattle. Prewitt Reservoir, on small tributary of S Platte R., is in NW. Formed 1887. **4** county (□ 597 sq mi/1,546 sq km; 1990 pop. 16,919), NW Fla., bounded W by Choctawatchee R.; ⊙ Chipley; 30°36′N 85°40′W. Rolling agr. area (corn, peanuts, cotton, vegetables; livestock) with many small lakes; drained by Holmes Creek. Has forest industries (lumber milling, naval-stores mfg.). Formed 1843. **5** county (□ 684 sq mi/1,772 sq km; 1990 pop. 19,112), E central Ga.; ⊙ Sandersville; 32°58′N 82°47′W. Bounded E by Ogeechee R. and W by Oconee R. Coastal plain agr. (cotton, corn, wheat, oats, peanuts); cattle, hogs; kaolin-clay-mining area. Formed 1784. **6** county (□ 1,473 sq mi/3,815 sq km; 1990 pop. 8,550), W Idaho; ⊙ Weiser; 44°27′N 116°47′W. Mt. area bounded W by Snake R. and state of Oregon and cut (N-S) by irrigated valley of Weiser R. Agr. (cattle; sheep; dairying; potatoes, sugar beets; hay, alfalfa, wheat, apples, plums); iron and mercury deposits, silver and lead. Includes parts of Payette Natl. Forest in N; Brownlee Dam and Reservoir in NW corner. Middle sect. of W boundary marks the border of the Pacific and Mountain time zones; co. is in Mountain time zone. Formed 1879. **7** county (□ 564 sq mi/1,461 sq km; 1990 pop. 14,965), SW Ill.; ⊙ Nashville; 38°21′N 89°26′W. Bounded N by Kaskaskia R.; drained by Little Muddy R. and Beaucoup Creek. Agr. area (wheat, soybeans, corn, sorghum; hogs, poultry; dairy prods.), with some mfg. (machinery, flour); also bituminous-coal mining, oil. Washington Co. Conservation Area in S. Formed 1818. **8** county (□ 516 sq mi/1,336 sq km; 1990 pop. 23,717), S Ind.; ⊙ Salem; 38°36′N 86°07′W. Bounded N by Muscatatuck R. and East Fork of White R.; drained by Blue R., Lost R., small Twin Creek. Corn, hay; cattle; dairying; limestone quarrying; timber. Mfg. at Salem. Elk Creek State Fishing Area and S unit of Jackson-Washington State Forest in NE. Part of Clark Natl. Forest in extreme E; Karst topography in SW. Formed 1813. **9** county (□ 570 sq mi/1,476 sq km; 1990 pop. 19,612), SE Iowa; ⊙ Washington; 41°20′N 91°43′W. Iowa R. forms NE border. Prairie agr. area (hogs, cattle, poultry; corn, oats) drained by Skunk and English rivers. Lake Darling State Park in SW corner. Formed 1838. **10** county (□ 898 sq mi/2,326 sq km; 1990 pop. 7,073), N Kansas; ⊙ Washington; 39°48′N 97°06′W. Gently rolling plain, bordering N on Nebr.; drained in E by Little Blue R., W drained by branches of Republican R. Corn, hogs, cattle, poultry; wheat, sorghum, soybeans, alfalfa; dairying. Wash. State Fishing L. in N. Formed 1860. **11** county (□ 301 sq mi/780 sq km; 1990 pop. 10,441), central Ky.; ⊙ Springfield; 37°46′N 85°11′W. Bounded NW by Beech Fork and Chaplin rivers (both cross co.); SW by Hardins Creek. Includes Lincoln Homestead State Park, in center near Springfield. Rolling upland agr. area (burley tobacco, hay, alfalfa, soybeans, sorghum, wheat, corn; poultry, hogs, cattle; dairying). In Bluegrass region. Some timber. Formed 1792. **12** county (□ 3,255 sq mi/8,430 sq km; 1990 pop. 35,308), most easterly in Maine and U.S., on N.B. line (Canada); ⊙ Machias; 45°00′N 67°30′W. Agr., blueberry-gathering and processing, lumbering, pulp and paper milling, resorts, hunting, fishing, sardine-packing. Drained by St. Croix (on N.B. border), Machias, East Machias, and Dennys rivers. Formed 1789. **13** county (□ 468 sq mi/1,212 sq km; 1990 pop. 121,393), W Md.; ⊙ Hagerstown; 39°36′N 77°49′W. Bounded N by Pa. state line, S and SW by Potomac R., here separating Md. from W.Va. and Va.; drained by Antietam, Conococheague, Beaver, and several other creeks. Cumberland Valley (locally Hagerstown Valley) is bordered E by the Blue Ridge (locally called South Mt. and Elk Ridge), W by Bear Pond Mts. and Sideling Hill. Agr. (wheat, corn, peaches, apples, berries, agr.; poultry, dairy prods.); ornamental fish, aquatic plants are raised. Limestone quarries, sand pits. Diversified mfg., esp. at Hagerstown; RR shops, canneries, grain mills. Excellent hunting and fishing in NW and NE. Includes Antietam Natl. Battlefield Site and Antietam Natl. Cemetery (near Sharpsburg); Fort Frederick State Park (W); U.S. Camp Ritchie (active in World War II); and parts of Gathland State Park (SE) and Washington Monument (E) state parks. Formed and named for George Washington in 1776, it was originally settled by Swiss and French as well as Eng. and Scottish colonists. **14** county (□ 423 sq mi/1,096 sq km; 1990 pop. 145,896), E Minn.; ⊙ Stillwater; 45°02′N 92°55′W. Bounded S by Mississippi R. (Lock and Dam No. 2 forms Spring L.); E by St. Croix R. (forms L. St. Croix and Wis. state line). Agr. area (hay, corn, soybeans, oats, alfalfa; cattle, sheep); food processing and mfg. at Stillwater. Lower St. Croix Natl. Scenic Riverway on St. Croix R.; Afton State Park in SE; William O'Brien State Park in NE. Numerous small lakes, glacial in origin, distributed in center and N parts of co. Forest L. is in NW; White Bear L. of W on W boundary. Formed 1849. **15** county (□ 761 sq mi/1,971 sq km; 1990 pop. 67,935), W Miss.; ⊙ Greenville, 33°17′N 90°57′W. Bounded W by the Mississippi R. (Ark. state line), E in part by Sunflower R., SW corner touches NE corner of La.; intersected by several creeks and bayous. Agr. (cotton, alfalfa, corn, wheat, soybeans, rice, sorghum; cattle; timber); catfish. L. Lee in W and L. Ferguson in NW, both oxbow lakes, form part of Ark.-Miss. state line, L. Washington, oxbow lake of Mississippi R. in SW; Yazoo Natl. Wildlife Refuge in S, Stoneyville Natl. Wildlife Refuge in N; Leroy Percy State Park in S center, Winterville Mounds State Park and Mus. in NW. Formed 1827. **16** county (□ 760 sq mi/1,968 sq km; 1990 pop. 20,380), SE central Mo.; ⊙ Potosi, 37°58′N 90°53′W. In the Ozarks; drained by Big. R. Agr., esp. corn, hay, livestock; mining region (barite, iron). Mfg. at Potosi. Large Pea Ridge Iron Mine in NW corner; part of largest lead dist. in world but lead, which was mined here beginning in the 1720s, is no longer mined in the co. Much of the land surface is scarified from past mining activity. Part of Meramec State Park in NW corner; Washington State Park in NE. Mo. State Correctional Center (max. security) at Potosi. Part of Mark Twain Natl. Forest in SW. Settled by French in 18th century. Creole Fr. is still spoken at Old Mines. Formed 1813. **17** county (□ 393 sq mi/1,018 sq km; 1990 pop. 16,607), E Nebr.; ⊙ Blair; 41°33′N 96°16′W. Agr. area bounded E by Missouri R. and Iowa. Metal prods.; cattle, dairying, hogs, corn, alfalfa. Limestone. Fort Calhoun nuclear power plant, initial criticality August 6, 1973, is 19 mi/31 km N of Omaha, uses cooling water from the Missouri R., and has a max. dependable capacity of 492 MWe. Fort Atkinson State Historical Park in SE. De Soto Bend Natl. Wildlife Area in E, in former river bend on Iowa side of Missouri R. belonging to Nebr. Formed 1854. **18** county (□ 845 sq mi/2,189 sq km; 1990 pop. 59,330), E N.Y.; ⊙ Hudson Falls, 43°19′N 73°25′W. Bounded NW by L. George, E by Vt. border, W by the Hudson R. Part of L. Champlain is in N. Drained by Batten Kill, and Poultney, Mettawee, and Hoosic rivers; traversed by Champlain division of the N.Y. State Barge Canal. Resorts on small lakes. Farming (potatoes, fruit, corn, oats; poultry); dairying. Timber; slate, limestone quarries. Mfg. at Cambridge, Granville, Greenwich, Hudson Falls, Whitehall. Formed 1772. **19** county (□ 424 sq mi/1,098 sq km; 1990 pop. 13,997), E N.C.; ⊙ Plymouth; 35°50′N 76°33′W. Bounded N by Albemarle Sound, NW by Roanoke R.; (pine, gum) tidewater area. Agr. area (peanuts, tobacco, corn, wheat, oats, soybeans, sorghum, potatoes, cotton; chickens, hogs, cattle), timber, fishing. Mfg. at Plymouth. Part of Phelps L. in SE; Pungo L. on S boundary. Somerset Place State Historic Site and Pettigrew State Park, on Phelps L. in E. Formed 1799. **20** county (□ 637 sq mi/1,650 sq km; 1990 pop. 62,254), SE Ohio; ⊙ Marietta; 39°30′N 81°25′W. Bounded SE by Ohio R., here forming W. Va. state line; intersected by Muskingum and Little Muskingum rivers and small Duck Creek. In the Unglaciated Plain physiographic region. Agr. (livestock; dairy prods.; fruit, corn); mfg. at Marietta (office furniture, synthetic rubber, plastics, laboratory apparatus and furniture); oil and gas extraction; limestone quarries. Formed 1788. **21** county (□ 424 sq mi/1,098 sq km; 1990 pop. 48,066), NE Okla.; ⊙ Bartlesville; 36°43′N 95°54′W. Bounded N by Kansas state line; drained by Caney R. Agr. (fruit, wheat, soybeans; cattle; dairying); mfg. (metal industries, transportation equip., business forms). Oil and natural-gas fields, and refining; mfg. at Bartlesville and Dewey. Copan L. in N. Formed 1907. **22** county (□ 726 sq mi/1,880 sq km; 1990 pop. 311,554), NW Oregon; ⊙ Hillsboro; 45°33′N 123°05′W. Mt. area in Coast Range. Drained by Tualatin R. Agr. (apples, cherries, pears, plums, peaches, grapes, nuts, berries, corn, brans, onions, potatoes; poultry, hogs, sheep, cattle); dairy prods.; nurseries, wineries; mfg. (electronics, high technology); logging. Bald Peak State Park on SW border; part of large Tillamook State Forest in W. Formed 1843. **23** county (□ 860 sq mi/2,227 sq km; 1990 pop. 204,584), SW Pa.; ⊙ Washington; 40°11′N 80°15′W. Bounded W by W.Va. state line, E by Monongahela R. Coal-mining and mfg. area. Mfg. at Washington, Canonsburg, McMurray, and Charleroi; bituminous coal; oil, gas, limestone. Agr. area (corn, wheat, oats, barley, hay, alfalfa, apples; sheep, hogs, cattle, dairying). Urbanization from Pittsburgh area (Allegheny co.) in NE margin of co. In dispute bet. Va. and Pa. until 1784. Indian chief Logan driven from area 1774 by Lord Dunmore, governor of Va. George Washington owned land here. Hillman State Park in NW; Cross Creek Reservoir and Co. Park in W center; co. has numerous covered bridges, esp. in S. Formed 1781. **24** county (□ 367 sq mi/951 sq km; 1990 pop. 110,006), SW R.I., on Conn. state line and Block Isl. Sound; ⊙ South Kingstown; 41°23′N 71°37′W. Commonly known as South co. Resorts; mfg. (textiles, furniture, wood prods., food prods.), printing; agr. (turf grass, nursery, potatoes; poultry). Once famous for granite quarries. Resorts on Block Isl. Sound and Narragansett Bay. State airport at Westerly, Narragansett Indian Reservation at Charlestown, and Univ. of R.I. at Kingston are here. Includes state parks and several lakes. Drained by Wood, Hunt, Queen, and Pawcatuck rivers. Inc. 1729. **25** county (□ 327 sq mi/847 sq km; 1990 pop. 92,315), NE Tenn.; ⊙ Jonesborough, oldest town in state, 36°17′N 82°30′W. In Great Appalachian Valley; mtn. ridges in S and SE; bounded NE by Watauga R.; drained by Nolichucky R. Includes part of Cherokee Natl. Forest. Agr. (fruit, tobacco, corn, hay), dairying, livestock raising. Iron ore, lead, zinc, manganese, clay deposits; limestone quarries; hardwood timber. Industry at JOHNSON CITY. Formed 1777 as first co. in Tenn. at request of Watauga Assn. of settlers. **26** county (□ 621 sq mi/1,608 sq km; 1990 pop. 26,154), S central Texas; ⊙ Brenham; 30°12′N 96°24′W. Bounded E by Brazos R., N by Yegua Creek, W by Cummins Creek.

Rich agr. area; cotton, corn, grains, nursery plants; also beef cattle, hogs, horses, poultry; dairying. Oil, natural-gas wells, stone. Mfg., processing at Brenham. Yegua Creek forms Somerville L. in NW. Formed 1836. **27** county (□ 2,430 sq mi/6,294 sq km; 1990 pop. 48,560), SW Utah; ⊙ St. George; 37°16′N 113°31′W. Mt. area bordering on Nev. (W) and Ariz. (S) and drained by Virgin R. Lowest point in Utah at Beaver Dam Wash in SW (c.2,000 ft/610 m). Livestock grazing (cattle); alfalfa, barley, potatoes, cotton; timber. Shivwits Indian Reservation is in SW; main portion of Zion Natl. Park in NE; part of Dixie Natl. Forest in N and NW, includes Pine Valley Mt. Wilderness Area in N; part of Beaver Dam Wilderness Area on S boundary; Joshua Tree Natl. Area in SW; Gunlock State Park in W center; Snow Canyon State Park and Quail Creek State Park near center of co. Formed 1852. **28** county (□ 695 sq mi/1,800 sq km; 1990 pop. 54,928), central Vt.; ⊙ Montpelier; 44°16′N 72°37′W. Granite-quarrying center of state; marble, talc; dairy prods., textiles, wood prods., machinery, maple sugar; winter sports. Includes part of Green Mtn. Natl. Forest and Camels Hump, one of highest peaks of Green Mts. Drained by Winooski and Mad rivers. Organized 1810. **29** county (□ 567 sq mi/1,469 sq km; 1990 pop. 45,887), SW Va.; ⊙ Abingdon; 36°43′N 81°57′W. In Great Appalachian Valley; bounded S by Tenn. state line; includes parts of Clinch Mtn. (NW), Walker Mtn. (N center), Iron Mts. (SE); drained by North, Middle, and South forks of Holston R.; part of South Holston Reservoir in S. Diversified mfg. at Abingdon and Bristol, an independent city separate from co. (adjacent to Bristol, Tenn.); processing of agr. prods.; agr. (cattle, sheep, poultry; dairying; tobacco, hay, alfalfa, corn); limestone; gypsum mining. Includes part of Jefferson Natl. Forest in N and a sect. of Appalachian Trail in Mt. Rogers Natl. Recreation Area, in SE (part of Jefferson Natl. Forest). Mtn. resorts. Formed 1776. **30** county (□ 435 sq mi/1,127 sq km; 1990 pop. 95,328), E Wis.; ⊙ West Bend; 43°22′N 88°14′W. Drained by Milwaukee and Menomonee rivers and small Rubicon R. Hilly dairying and farming area (barley, oats, wheat, corn, soybeans, peas; hogs, sheep, poultry); processing of dairy prods., canning of fruit and vegetables; other industry at West Bend. Resort lakes; winter sports. Kettle Moraine State Forest (N unit) in N part; Sunburst Ski Area in N; Pike Lake State Park in SW. The city of Germantown in SE part of co. is part of Milwaukee urban mass. Formed 1836.

Washington, parish (□ 665 sq mi/1,722 sq km; 1990 pop. 43,185), SE La.; ⊙ Franklinton; 30°51′N, 90°08′W. Bounded N and E by Miss. state line (E by Pearl R.), W in part by Tchefuncte R.; drained by the Bogue Chitto. Has extensive forests, esp. long-leaf yellow pine. Agr. (hay, home gardens, nursery crops, sweet potatoes, vegetables, watermelons, cattle, exotic fowl; dairying). Logging, lumber milling and paper prods.; other mfg. at Bogalusa. Oil and natural-gas deposits. One of Florida Parishes of SE La., former Br. colony of Western Florida. Ben's Creek State Wildlife Area in E. Formed 1819.

Washington 1 city (1990 pop. 10,099), Tazewell co., central Ill., suburb 10 mi/16 km E of Peoria; 40°42′N 89°26′W. Trade center in agr. area (corn, hay, barley, soybeans; dairying); mfg. (RR wheels, transportation equip., machining, transformers). Inc. 1857. **2** city (1990 pop. 10,838), ⊙ Daviess co., SW Ind.; 38°40′N 87°10′W. Turkey processing and farming are the chief economic activities. Mfg. (carbon steel prods., magnetic ferrite powder, concrete, asphalt, computers). Glendale State Fish and Wildlife Area to SE. Settled 1805, laid out 1815, inc. as a city 1871. **3** city (1990 pop. 7,074), ⊙ Washington co., SE Iowa, 27 mi/43 km SSW of Iowa City; 41°17′N 91°41′W. RR junction. Agr. trade center; mfg. (consumer goods, fabricated metal prods., feeds, farm equip., heat transfer prods.). Lake Darling State Park to SW. Inc. 1864. **4** city (1990 pop. 10,704), Franklin co., E central Mo., on Missouri R., and 40 mi/64 km W of St. Louis; 38°32′N 91°00′W. Dairying; cattle, corn, soybeans, wheat; mfg. (apparel, corncob pipes, motors,

transformers, transportation equip., restaurant equip., business prods., titanium processing); tourism. Very strong Ger. heritage. River port; landing field. Mo. R. bridge. Settled before 1818, inc. 1841. **5** city (1990 pop. 15,864), ⊙ Washington co., SW Pa., 23 mi/37 km SSW of Pittsburgh, on Chartiers Creek; 40°10′N 80°15′W. RR junction. Bituminous-coal region, including U.S. Steel Corp. coal-mining operations. Mfg. (fabricated metal prods., valves, soft drinks, titanium rods, slip cast refractories, corrugated boxes, plastics prods., machinery, printing and publishing, iron molds for glass industry, wire and cable, tool and die, concrete); coal mining; limestone quarries. Agr. area (apples, alfalfa, grain; livestock, dairying). David Bradford House, erected in 1788, was a meeting place in the Whiskey Rebellion (1794). Le Moyne House (1812) was the home of Dr. Francis Le Moyne, an abolitionist leader. Washington and Jefferson Col. (1781; oldest col. W of the Alleghenies) is here. Washington Co. Airport to SW; Arden Trolley Mus. to N. Settled 1769, laid out 1781, inc. as a city 1924.

Washington 1 town (1990 pop. 3,905), Litchfield co., W Conn., on Shepaug R., and 16 mi/26 km WNW of Waterbury; 41°38′N 73°19′W. Township is in hilly agr. and resort region. Includes villages of New Preston (resort on L. Waramaug; 1990 pop. 1,217), Washington Depot, and Washington. Gunnery and Rumsey Hall schools here. Settled 1734, inc. 1779. **2** town (1990 pop. 4,279), ⊙ Wilkes co., NE Ga., c.45 mi/72 km WNW of Augusta, 33°44′N 82°44′W. Mfg. of textile, plastics, medical prods., concrete, fabricated metal prods.; in agr., dairying, and timber region. Many old classic-revival houses, including the Robert Toombs house (built 1794–1801; remodeled 1837 by Toombs). Settled 1773; laid out 1780. **3** town (1990 pop. 1,304), ⊙ Washington co., NE Kansas, c.50 mi/80 km NNW of Manhattan; 39°49′N 97°02′W. RR junction. Trading and shipping center for grain and livestock region; dairy prods. Wash. State Fishing L. to NW. Inc. 1875. **4** town (1990 pop. 795), Mason co., NE Ky., 3 mi/4.8 km SW of Maysville; 38°37′N 83°48′W. Agr. (burley tobacco, soybeans, grain; livestock; dairying). Laid out on Simon Kenton's land; chartered 1786 by Va. legislature. An early trade center, town was for a time a chief settlement of Ky.; the *Mirror*, 3d newspaper in Ky. was est. here 1797. **5** town (1990 pop. 1,253), St. Landry parish, S central La., 5 mi/8 km N of Opelousas, on Bayou Teche; 30°37′N 92°04′W. In agr. area (cotton, rice, sugarcane; cattle). Once the largest steamboat port between New Orleans and St. Louis. Antebellum houses in area. Thistlethwaite State Wildlife Area to NE. Settled before 1820, inc. 1836. **6** town (1990 pop. 1,185), Knox co., S Maine, 14 mi/23 km NW of Rockland, and on Washington Pond; 44°16′N 69°23′W. Nearby lake is 3 mi/4.8 km long. **7** town (1990 pop. 615), Berkshire co., W Mass., 8 mi/12.9 km SE of Pittsfield; 42°22′N 73°10′W. State forest here. **8** town, Macomb co., SE Mich., 12 mi/19 km NW of Mt. Clemens; 42°43′N 83°02′W. Satellite community of Detroit. Mfg. (iron grinding, transportation equip.). Stony Creek Metropark to W. **9** town (1990 pop. 628), Sullivan co., SW N.H., 12 mi/19 km S of Newport; 43°10′N 72°05′W. Nursery crops, corn; cattle, poultry. Part of Highland L. in S; Ashuelot Pond in SE. Pillsbury State park in N. **10** town (1990 pop. 9,075), ⊙ Beaufort co., E N.C., 50 mi/80 km SE of Rocky Mount, at head of Pamlico R. estuary, at mouth of Tar R. (bridged); 35°33′N 77°02′W. RR junction. Shipping center for farming, fishing, and timber area; agr. area (peanuts, tobacco, cotton, grain, potatoes; hogs). Mfg. (fabricated metal prods., plastic prods., machinery, consumer goods, transportation equip., fertilizer, lumber, apparel). Beaufort Co. Community Col. Goose Creek State Park to E. First town in U.S. named for George Washington. Founded before 1776. **11** town (1990 pop. 4,198), Washington co., SW Utah, 5 mi/8 km E of St. George, near Virgin R.; 37°07′N 113°29′W. Cattle; Dixie Natl. Forest to N; Quail Creek Reservoir State Park to NE. **12** town (1990 pop. 937), Orange co., E central Vt., just SE of Barre; 44°04′N

72°25′W. Dairy prods. **13** town (1990 pop. 198), ⊙ Rappahannock co., N Va., in E foothills of Blue Ridge, 19 mi/31 km W of Warrenton; 38°42′N 78°09′W. Mfg. (lumber; printing and publishing); agr. (cattle; apples, alfalfa); timber. Plotted 1749 by George Washington. **14** uninc. town (1990 pop. 1,030), Wood co., NW W.Va., 6 mi/9.7 km W of Parkersburg, near Ohio R.; 39°14′N 81°40′W. Mfg. (industrial gases, industrial insulation, plastic prods., steel pipe, thermoplastic compounds). Blennerhassett Isl. Historic State Park, in Ohio R., to NE.

Washington 1 village (1990 pop. 148), Hempstead co., SW Ark., 9 mi/14.5 km NW of Hope; 33°46′N 93°40′W. One of oldest towns in Ark., settled c.1824; was state capital from 1863 to 1865 and, until 1938, co. seat. Old Washington Historical State Park in town. Hope Wildlife Management Area to E. **2** village, Adams co., SW Miss., 6 mi/9.7 km E of Natchez. Agr. (cotton, corn, soybeans). Home to the historic Jefferson Military Col., founded 1802. It was the first chartered educational institution in the state. Natchez Airport to NE; Natchez State Park to NE. **3** village (1990 pop. 125), Washington co., E Nebr., 10 mi/16 km SW of Blair and on branch of Missouri R.; 41°23′N 96°12′W.

Washington, Ohio: see WASHINGTON COURT HOUSE.

Washington 1 village (1990 pop. 279), McClain co., central Okla., 28 mi/45 km S of Oklahoma City; 35°03′N 97°28′W. Oil field nearby; mfg. (oil field valves). **2** industrial village of Coventry town, Kent co., central R.I., on South Branch of Pawtuxet R., and 12 mi/19 km SSW of Providence. **3** uninc. village (1990 pop. 265), Washington co., S central Texas, on the Brazos R. Elev. 200 ft/61 m. Originally named Washington-on-the-Brazos, it was the scene of the Texas declaration of independence from Mexico on March 2, 1836; 1842–1846 it was the seat of the Republic of Texas's govt. Washington-on-the-Brazos State Historical Park occupies part of original town site. Settled 1821, est. 1834. Also called Old Washington.

Washington, borough (1990 pop. 6,474), Warren co., NW N.J., 11 mi/18 km NE of Phillipsburg; 40°45′N 74°58′W. Mfg. (wire and cable, apparel, porcelain and brass prods.); agr. (corn, oats, hay); nursery and dairy prods. Settled 1741; inc. 1868.

Washington Boro, uninc. village, Manor township, Lancaster co., SE Pa., 3 mi/4.8 km SE of Columbia, on the Susquehanna R. (L. Clarke reservoir, formed by Safe Harbor Dam, 6 mi/9.7 km SSE); 39°59′N 76°28′W. Agr. grain; livestock; dairying. Formerly a borough.

Washington Court House, city (1990 pop. 12,983), ⊙ Fayette co., SW Ohio, on Paint Creek, in a farm, dairy, and poultry area; laid out and founded c.1810, inc. 1831. Mfg. includes shoes, gloves, dairy prods., and automobile and aircraft parts.

Washington Crossing 1 village, Mercer co., W N.J., on Delaware R., opposite Washington Crossing, Pa., and 8 mi/12.9 km NW of Trenton; 40°59′N 74°04′W. State park commemorates George Washington's crossing of the Delaware (Christmas night, 1776) to capture Trenton. **2** uninc. village (1990 pop. 800), Bucks co., SE Pa., 9 mi/14.5 km NW of Trenton, N.J., on Delaware R., opposite Washington Crossing, N.J.; 40°17′N 74°52′W. Mfg. (printing and publishing). One of 2 sites where George Washington and 2,400 troops crossed to N.J. Christmas night, Dec. 25, 1776, to capture Trenton from the Hessians. Washington Crossing State Historic Site is here; Washington Crossing State Park 4 mi/6.4 km to NW.

Washington, D.C., (□ c.68 sq mi/177 sq km; 1990 pop. 606,900), ⊙ U.S.; coextensive (since 1878, when GEORGETOWN became a part of Washington) with the DISTRICT OF COLUMBIA, on the Potomac R.; 38°54′N 77°01′W. Inc. 1802. It is the center of a metropolitan area (1990 pop. 4,222,880) extending into Md., Va., and W.Va. It is the legislative, administrative, and judicial center of the U.S. It has little industry; its business is govt., and hundreds of thousands of govt. employees work in the metropolitan area. Washington is also a major tourist attraction, drawing millions of visitors every year. In 1790 the rivalry of Northern and

Southern states for the capital's location ended when Jefferson's followers supported Hamilton's program for Federal assumption of state debts in return for an agreement to situate the natl. capital on the banks of the Potomac R. George Washington selected the exact spot. The "Federal City" was designed by Pierre L'Enfant and laid out by Andrew Ellicott. Construction began on the White House in 1792 and on the Capitol the following year. John Adams was the 1st President to occupy the White House. Congress held its 1st session in Washington in 1800, moving from Philadelphia, and Thomas Jefferson was the first President to be inaugurated in the new capitol. In the War of 1812 the British captured and sacked (1814) Washington, burning most of the public bldgs., including the Capitol and the White House. The city grew slowly. Even after 1850 it was still "a sea of mud," and not until the 20th cent. did it cease to be an unkempt, rural city and assume its present urban aspect. Though strongly manned during the Civil War, it was several times threatened by the Confederates, notably by Gen. Jubal A. Early in 1864. After 1901, Washington was developed on the basis of the resurrected L'Enfant plan — a gridiron arrangement of streets cut by diagonal avenues radiating from the Capitol and White House, with an elaborate system of parks. The city spreads out with broad tree-shaded thoroughfares and open vistas at frequent intervals, with 8 sq mi/20.7 sq km of water surface. The numerous impressive govt. bldgs. near the city's center are built of white or gray stone in the classical style, and there are also many fine homes. Among other attractive bldgs. are the embassies and legations of many foreign countries, many of them lining "Embassy Row" on Massachusetts Ave. The larger of the city's fine parks are W Potomac Park, which extends S from the Lincoln Memorial and includes the Tidal Basin, flanked by the famous Jap. cherry trees; E Potomac Park, an area of reclaimed land jutting S from the Jefferson Memorial; ROCK CREEK PARK, with almost 1,800 acres/728 ha of natural woodlands and extensive recreation facilities, and the adjoining Natl. Zoological Park; and Anacostia Park, adjacent to the Natl. Arboretum. Besides the Capitol and the White House, some other important govt. bldgs. and places of historic interest are the Blair House for visiting heads of state, the Senate office bldgs. and the House of Representatives office bldgs., the Supreme Court Bldg., the Pentagon (in Va.), the Federal Bureau of Investigation bldg., the Library of Congress, the Natl. Archives Bldg., and Constitution Hall. Ford's Theatre, where Lincoln was shot, has been restored. Best known of the city's many statues and monuments are the Washington Monument, at the W end of the long grass Mall; the Lincoln Memorial, with its pool reflecting the marble shaft of the Washington Monument; the Vietnam Veterans Memorial, a V-shaped monument in polished black granite near the Lincoln Memorial; the Holocaust Memorial; and the Thomas Jefferson Memorial, overlooking the Tidal Basin. The ARLINGTON MEMORIAL BRIDGE across the Potomac connects the capital with ARLINGTON NATIONAL CEMETERY. Also in Arlington is the U.S. Marine Corps War Memorial, one of the largest statues ever cast in bronze. In the Potomac itself lies Theodore Roosevelt Island, a thickly wooded islet with many foot trails. Among Washington's famous churches are the Washington Natl. Cathedral (Protestant Episcopal) on Mt. St. Alban, which was completed in 1990 and contains the tomb of Woodrow Wilson; and the Natl. Shrine of the Immaculate Conception, the largest R.C. church in the U.S. The city's many institutions of higher education include Amer. Univ., the Natl. Defense Univ., the Catholic Univ. of Amer., Georgetown Univ., George Washington Univ., Howard Univ., Univ. of D.C. and Trinity Col. Among the many cultural attractions of the capital are the Natl. Gall. of Art, the Freer Gall. of Art, and the other centers under the auspices of the Smithsonian Inst.; the John F. Kennedy Center for the Performing Arts; the Corcoran Gall. of Art; the Phillips Collection and the Phillips Gall. of Art; the Hiskhorn Mus. and Sculpture Garden; and the Folger Shakespeare Library. Site of Robert Francis Kennedy Stadium. The city's newest attraction is the Downtown Sports Arena, built in 1997. The U.S. Naval Observatory, the U.S. Naval Research Laboratory, the Smithsonian Inst., the Brookings Inst., the Natl. Institutes of Health, Natl. Acad. of Science, Pan-Amer. Univ., the Natl. Georaphic Society and Explorer's Hall, the Natl. Air and Space Mus., and the Carnegie Inst. of Washington are among the institutions dedicated to scientific research and education. Also in Washington are Walter Reed Army Medical Center, including the Army Medical School and Walter Reed Army Hosp., and the U.S. Soldiers Home (1851), the oldest in the country. Military installations in the area include Fort McNair, Fort Myer, ANDREWS AIR FORCE BASE, and Bolling Air Force Base. Of historic interest nearby in Md. is Fort Washington (built 1809, destroyed 1814, rebuilt by 1824). In the 1970s work was begun on the construction of a 103-mi/166-km subway system. The system was virtually complete by the mid-1990s. The capital's main transport hubs are Union Station and Washington Natl. and Dulles Internatl. airports (both in Va.). In 1974 the Admiral's House on the grounds of the U.S. Naval Observatory was designated the temporary official residence of the Vice President. Through the years the city has been a focus for natl. political activity. In the 1960s and early 1970s over 200,000 demonstrated for civil rights and roughly 100,000 demonstrated against the war in Vietnam. Massive rallies in the 1980s and 1990s, some numbering up to 500,000 people, have been held concerning such issues as gay rights and abortion. Washington has long been a gateway for blacks emigrating from the South, and today its pop. is almost ⅔ Afr.-Amer. Many of these citizens live in poverty and, as in other urban areas, there are problems of homelessness, drug addiction, violent crime, failing schools, and limited law enforcement resources. Yet Washington is a city of contrasts — extensive areas of dilapidated row houses and apartments are only a short distance from beautifully refurbished town houses on CAPITOL HILL. The city's problems have been exacerbated by the transient nature of its workforce. Washington's pop. has declined 19% since 1970; much of the outmigration has been to the outlying, affluent suburbs in Va. and Md. In April 1968, the assassination of Martin Luther King, Jr., touched off 6 days of violence, looting, and burning in Washington. Army troops were called in to quell the disorders and to protect important govt. bldgs. In 1871, Washington lost its charter as a city and a territorial govt. was inaugurated to govern the entire D.C. Congress took direct control of the dist.'s govt. in 1874, providing for a mayor appointed by the President and a commission chosen by Congress; the residents were disfranchised. The 23rd Amendment (1961) to the Constitution gave inhabitants the right to vote in presidential elections; the D.C. was accorded 3 electoral votes. In 1970 legislation was enacted authorizing election of a nonvoting delegate to the House of Representatives. The present system of govt., approved in a referendum in 1974, provides for an elected mayor and a 13-member city council but reserves for Congress the right to review the budget and legislation passed by the council and to retain direct control over an enclave containing most of the Federal bldgs. and monuments. The 1st elections were held in Nov. 1974. There have been numerous attempts by the D.C. to gain statehood and achieve full representation in Congress, but all of these have failed. The city ran enormous budget deficits throughout the late 1980s and 1990s, in part because of its lack of tax-paying industry, flight of middle-class residents to the suburbs, and poor fiscal management.

Washington Grove, town (1990 pop. 434), Montgomery co., central Md., 19 mi/31 km NNW of Washington, D.C.; 39°08'N 77°10'W. A camp meeting ground of the Methodist Church originally, the original atmosphere has been retained by narrow paths in front of the old houses. Automobile roads have been built in back of them.

Washington Heights, residential district (□ 1 sq mi/2.6 sq km; 1990 pop. 1,159) of N Manhattan borough of N.Y. city, SE N.Y., lying along the Hudson R. N of 135th St.; 41°28'N 74°25'W. Terminus (E) of George Washington Bridge to Fort Lee, N.J. Includes site of Fort Washington, captured by the British (Nov. 1776) in the Amer. Revolution. Morris-Jumel Mansion (1765) was Washington's hq. in 1776. Largely populated by Ger. Jewish refugees in the 1930s and 1940s, but with large outmigration by Jews, Greeks, and Germans in the 1960s. Neighborhood is now mostly pop. by recent immigrants, largely from Lat. Amer. and the Caribbean; the neighborhood has one of the largest concentrations of Dominicans in the U.S. Seat of Yeshiva Univ. Also site of Audubon Ballroom, where Malcolm X was shot in 1965; it is now part of the Columbia Presbyterian Medical Center.

Washington Irving Island, NE Franklin dist., N.W.T., N Canada, on W side of Kane Basin, off E Ellesmere Isl.; 3 mi/5 km long; 79°34'N 73°15'W.

Washington Island (□ c.20 sq mi/52 sq km), NE Door co., NE Wis., in NW L. Michigan, just off the N tip of the Door Peninsula. Green Bay to W; village of Washington on N side. The isl. was visited by the Fr. explorers Pierre Radisson (1657) and Robert La Salle (1679). It has a large Icelandic settlement and is a resort area; tourism. Airport. Ferry access to Rock Isl. State Park to NE, passenger ferry to Gells Rock, car ferry to Northport, both on N tip of Door Peninsula.

Washington Lake, in Washington co., W Miss., oxbow lake (c.7 mi/11.3 km long) formed by shift to W of main channel of Mississippi R., 20 mi/32 km S of Greenville (predates establishment of Ark.-Miss. state line). Fishing, duck hunting.

Washington, Lake, King co., W Wash., large freshwater lake forming E boundary of Seattle; connected to L. Union and Puget Sound by L. Washington Ship Canal (8 mi/12.9 km long; large locks), S end fed by Cedar R., N end fed by Sammamish R.; c.20 mi/32 km long. It serves as docking, shipbuilding, and repair area. Residential Mercer Isl. (5 mi/8 km long; in S) is connected to E (1 mi/1.6 km) and W (2 mi/3.2 km) shores by L. Washington (Morrow) Bridge (6.5 mi/10.5 km long; includes 3.5 mi/5.6 km on isl.), part of which is supported by pontoons. Seattle and Bellevue connected by Evergreen Point Bridge. St. Edward State Park on NE shore; Campus of Univ. of Wash. on W shore. Other cities on lake: Renton (S end), Bellevue (E shore), Kirkland (E. shore), Kenmore (N end), and Mercer Isl. on Mercer Isl.

Washington Monument, hollow shaft, located on a 106 acres/43 ha site at the W end of the Mall, Washington, D.C.; 555 ft, 5⅛ in/169.3 m high. Dedicated 1885. In 1783, Congress passed a resolution approving an equestrian statue of George Washington, and in 1791 architect Pierre L'Enfant included a site for the statue near the present location of the monument in his plans for the Federal city. However, Washington objected to the idea. After Washington's death in 1799, plans for a memorial were discussed but none were adopted until 1832, when the private Wash. Natl. Monument Society was formed. Its activity brought gifts of money, as well as blocks of stone from each state, some foreign governments, and private individuals. These "tribute blocks" carry inscriptions on the inside walls of the monument. Architect Robert Mills's elaborate Gr. temple design was accepted for the monument, and on July 4, 1848, the cornerstone was laid. Work on the project was interrupted by political quarreling in the 1850s; by the Civil War, funds became scarce. It was not until 1876 that Congress took over the project and appropriated money for the monument. The base, entirely different from Mills's design, was completed in 1880; the aluminum top was positioned in 1884; and the monument was opened to the public in 1888. The top may be reached by stairs or elevator.

Washington, Mount, mountain (6,288 ft/1,917 m) in PRESIDENTIAL RANGE, N N.H., in White Mt. Natl. Forest; 44°16'N 71°18'W. Highest peak in N.H. and in NE U.S. Meterological station at summit. Mt. Washington is known for its extreme climate. Winds of 231 mph/372 km per hour have been clocked here and with annual average temp. of 27°F and annual snowfall of 185 in/470 cm, it has a reputation of having the most treacherous climate in the world. Auto road to summit. Has 3 mi/4.8 km long cog RR, completed to summit in 1869, first of its kind in the world.

Washington Nuclear 2 Nuclear Power Plant, Wash.: see BENTON, CO.

Washington Park, town (□ 1 sq mi/2.6 sq km; 1990 pop. 6,930), Glades co., central Fla., 12 mi/19 km NW of Clewiston on the W shore of L. Okeechobee adjacent to Moore Haven; 26°07'N 80°10'W.

Washington Park 1 village (1990 pop. 7,431), St. Clair co., SW Ill., E of East St. Louis and suburb of St. Louis within St. Louis metropolitan area; 38°37'N 90°05'W. Some agr. to E (wheat, soybeans; cattle); mfg. (gas heating stoves, barbecue grills). Inc. 1917. **2** village (1990 pop. 403), Beaufort co., E N.C., 3 mi/4.8 km E of Washington, near Pamlico R. estuary; 35°31'N 77°01'W. Tobacco, grain, cotton, peanuts; livestock.

Washingtons Birthplace, Va.: see GEORGE WASHINGTON BIRTHPLACE.

Washingtonville 1 village (□ 2 sq mi/5.2 sq km; 1990 pop. 4,906), Orange co., SE N.Y., 9 mi/14.5 km SW of Newburgh; 41°25'N 74°09'W. Mfg. of distilled beverages, including wines and brandy spirits; in dairying and resort area. **2** village (1990 pop. 894), on Columbiana-Mahoning co. line, E Ohio, 4 mi/6 km E of Salem; 40°54'N 80°46'W.

Washingtonville, borough (1990 pop. 228), Montour co., central Pa., 7 mi/11.3 km NNW of Danville, on Chillisquaque Creek; 41°02'N 76°40'W. Mfg. (fertilizer). Agr. area (grain; poultry; livestock; dairying). L. Chillisquaque reservoir, in Montour Preserve, to N.

Washinton Terrace, city (1990 pop. 8,189), Weber co., N Utah, residential suburb 5 mi/8 km S of Ogden, 25 mi/40 km N of Salt Lake City. Elev. 4,550 ft/1,387 m. Hill Air Force Base to SW. Est. 1942 as temporary World War II housing project.

Washita (WAHSH-uh-tuh), county (□ 1,009 sq mi/2,613 sq km; 1990 pop. 11,441), W Okla.; ⊙ Cordell; 35°17'N 98°59'W. Intersected by Washita R. and Elk Creek. Agr. (wheat, cotton, sorghum, hay, peanuts; cattle, sheep); mfg. at Cordell and Sentinel; oil and natural gas. Crowder L. State Park. Formed 1891.

Washita (WASH-i-taw) river, c.450 mi/724 km long; rising in Hemphill co., E of Miami, in the Texas Panhandle; flows E into Okla. and through Black Kettle Natl. Grassland (Texas, Okla.), then SE through Foss L. reservoir, past Clinton, Chickasha, Paul's Valley, entering large arm of L. Texoma (Red R.) and Tichomingo. It is a variation spelling of Ouachita. The battle of the Washita (1868), in which General Custer defeated the Cheyenne, took place on the river, near the town of Cheyenne, Okla.

Washoe (wuh-SHO), county (□ 6,551 sq mi/16,967 sq km; 1990 pop. 254,667), NW Nev.; ⊙ Reno; 40°37'N 119°40'W. Mt. area bordering on Calif. (W) and Oregon (N), drained in S by Truckee R., which flows into S end of Pyramid L. and forms part of Co. boundary on S (W Storey co.). Pyramid L., Pyramid Range, and Pyramid L. Indian Reservation are in S center; NE part of L. Tahoe is in SW corner (gambling, recreation, ski resorts). Smoke Creek Desert and Granite Range are near Gerlach. Cattle; sand and gravel, gold, silver gypsum at Empire; mfg. at Reno and Sparks. Reno is 2d in state to Las Vegas as a gambling and entertainment center. Formed 1861. Part of Sheldon Natl. Wildlife Refuge in N; part of Toiyabe Natl. Forest and part of L. Tahoe Nevada State Park in SW corner.

Washoe (wuh-SHO), village, Carbon co., S Mont., 3 mi/4.8 km ESE of Red Lodge, near Bear Creek, in NE foothills of Beartooth Range. Formerly source of coal for the Anaconda smelters.

Washoe City, uninc. village, Washoe co., W Nev. 10 mi/16 km NNW of Carson City, near N end of Washoe L. New Washoe City 3 mi/4.8 km to SE. Toiyabe Natl. Forest to W. Historic Bowers Mansion (1864) is here, built for first millionaires of Comstock Lode.

Washoe Lake (wuh-SHO), salt lake, Washoe co., W Nev., at S end of Virginia Range, 16 mi/26 km S of

Reno, and 5 mi/8 km N of Carson City; 3.5 mi/5.6 km long, 2 mi/3.2 km wide; 39°15'N 119°48'W. New Washoe City to E. Washoe L. State Park on E shore.

Washoe Range, Nev.: see VIRGINIA MOUNTAINS.

Washougal (wahsh-OO-guhl), town (1990 pop. 4,764), Clark co., SW Wash., 15 mi/24 km E of Vancouver, and on Columbia R., at mouth of Washougal R. (c.35 mi/56 km long); 45°35'N 122°20'W. Vegetables, berries; dairying; timber; mfg. (plastic pipe, wood treating, paints, lumber, electronic components). Bonneville Dam 18 mi/29 km ENE. Settled 1860, inc. 1908.

Washta, town (1990 pop. 284), Cherokee co., NW Iowa, on Little Sioux R., and 14 mi/23 km SW of Cherokee; 42°34'N 43°95'W. Sand and gravel pits.

Washtenaw (WAWSH-te-naw), county (□ 722 sq mi/1,870 sq km; 1990 pop. 282,937), SE Mich.; 42°15'N 83°50'W. ⊙ Ann Arbor. Drained by Huron and Raisin rivers. Agr.; cattle, sheep, hogs, poultry; wheat, oats, corn, soybeans, apples; dairy prods. Mfg. at Ann Arbor, Ypsilanti, and Willow Run. Co. has several small lakes (resorts) in N and NW. Co. is being encroached upon from NE by urban development from metropolitan Detroit; Ann Arbor and Ypsilanti are satellite communities to urban area. Pinckney State Recreation Area in N; Waterloo State Recreation Area on W boundary. Organized 1826.

Washtucna (wahsh-TUHK-nuh), village (1990 pop. 231), Adams co., SE Wash., 47 mi/76 km N of Walla Walla; 46°45'N 118°19'W. In Columbia basin agr. region; wheat, barley, oats, cattle. Palouse Falls and Lyons Ferry state parks, both on Palouse R., to SE.

Washunga, town, Kay co., N Okla., 15 mi/24 km ENE of Ponca City. Submerged by Kaw L. reservoir.

Wasilla, village (1990 pop. 4,028), S Alaska, 30 mi/48 km NNE of Anchorage, on Alaska RR, and on branch of Glenn Highway; 61°34'N 149°27'W. Agr.; tourism. Developing suburb of Anchorage. Iditarod Mus.

Waskada (wuhs-KAW-duh), village (1991 pop. 289), SW Man., central Canada, 65 mi/105 km SW of Brandon; near N.Dak. and Sask. (Canada) borders; 49°06'N 100°48'W. Grain; livestock.

Waskatenau (wahs-KAH-tuh-no), village (1991 pop. 257), central Alta., W Canada, near North Saskatchewan R., 50 mi/80 km NE of Edmonton; 54°05'N 112°47'W. Wheat; livestock.

Waskesiu Lake (wahs-kuh-SOO), central Sask., W Canada, in Prince Albert Natl. Park, 50 mi/80 km NNW of Prince Albert; 15 mi/24 km long, 2 mi/3 km–6 mi/10 km wide. Drains E into Montreal L. and Churchill R.

Waskom, town (1990 pop. 1,812), Harrison co., E Texas, 16 mi/26 km E of Marshall, and 19 mi/31 km W of Shreveport, La., near La. state line; 32°28'N 94°03'W. Elev. 371 ft/113 m. Oilfield trade point; cattle; timber; mfg. industrial hydrocarbon, hot dip galvanizing. Caddo L. reservoir and State Park to N. Est. 1850 as Powellton, changed to Waskom Station 1872.

Wasque Point (WAIS-kwee), southernmost point and beach on Chappaquiddick Isl., Martha's Vineyard, Mass.

Wassaic, residential village (1990 pop. 700), E Dutchess co.; E N.Y., near Conn. state line, 26 mi/42 km NE of Poughkeepsie; 41°48'N 73°34'W.

Wassuk Range, W Nev., E spur of Sierra Nevada, in Mineral co., just W of Walker L. Rises to 10,520 ft/3,206 m at Corey Peak and 11,245 ft/3,427 m at Mt. Grant (highest point), 10 mi/16 km WNW of Hawthorne. On tract of Hawthorne U.S. Naval Ammunition Dump; S part in Toiyabe Natl. Forest.

Wasta, village (1990 pop. 82), Pennington co., SW central S.Dak., 40 mi/64 km E of Rapid City; 44°04'N 102°27'W. In cattle area. Buffalo Gap Natl. Grassland & Badlands Natl. Park to S.

Waswanipi River, Canada.: see NOTTAWAY RIVER.

Wataga (wah-TAI-guh), village (1990 pop. 879), Knox co., NW central Ill., 6 mi/9.7 km NE of Galesburg; 41°01'N 90°16'W. In agr. area (corn, soybeans; cattle; hogs; dairying).

Watauga (wah-TAW-guh), county (□ 312 sq mi/808 sq km; 1990 pop. 36,952), NW N.C.; ⊙ Boone;

36°13'N 81°42'W. Bounded in NW by Tenn. state line. In Blue Ridge Mts.; drained by Watauga, Yadkin, South Fork and New rivers. Agr. area (tobacco, vegetables, corn, hay; cattle); timber and mfg. resort region including ski areas. Blue Ridge (Natl.) Parkway crosses co. in S. Part of Pisgah Natl. Forest in W and SW; Cone Memorial Park, former estate, in S. Formed 1849.

Watauga, city (1990 pop. 20,009), Tarrant co., N Texas, residential suburb 8 mi/12.9 km NNE of downtown Fort Worth; 32°52'N 97°15'W. Mfg. (porcelain dolls).

Watauga River (wah-TAW-guh), 60 mi/97 km long; rises in central Watauga co., in the Blue Ridge Mts., NW N.C., W of Boone; flows NW into NE Tenn., through Watauga L. reservoir where it receives Roan R. from NE, past Elizabethton, joins South Fork Holston R. in Boone L. reservoir 10 mi/16 km N of Johnson City.

Watch Hill, resort village in Westerly town, Washington co., SW R.I., on Watch Hill Point (extreme SW point of state), on sandy peninsula bet. the Atlantic and Little Narragansett Bay. Fishing, yachting; fine beach extends along sandbar to Napatree Point (W). Lighthouse, coast guard station near village.

Watchung (WAH-chuhng), borough (1990 pop. 5,110), Somerset co., N central N.J., in Watchung Mts., 16 mi/26 km SW of Newark; 40°38'N 74°26'W. In rapidly suburbanizing area. Inc. 1926.

Watchung Mountains (WAH-chuhng), 2 long low ridges of volcanic origin, from 400 ft/122 m to 500 ft/152 m high, N central N.J. They curve c.40 mi/64 km bet. Paterson and Somerville. Basalt is quarried here. The Watchungs have been the scene of extensive suburban development since the 1970s.

Water Island, islet (□ c.1 sq km/2.6 sq km), off S St. Thomas Isl., U.S.V.I., outside St. Thomas Harbor, 1 mi/1.6 km SW of Charlotte Amalie. On it is Fort Segarra, with installations of U.S. Army Chemical Service moved here 1948 from Panama.

Water Mill, resort village (1990 pop. 1,893), Suffolk co., SE N.Y., on SE L.I., 2 mi/3.2 km NE of Southampton; 40°55'N 72°21'W.

Water Valley, town (1990 pop. 3,610), a ⊙ Yalobusha co. (seat shared with Coffeeville), N central Miss., 28 mi/45 km NNE of Grenada; 34°09'N 89°37'W. Agr. (cotton, corn, watermelons; cattle, hogs, poultry; timber); mfg. (textiles, chicken processing, tool and die, fuel injection systems). Sect. of Holly Springs Natl. Forest to SW; Enid L. reservoir to W; George Payne Cossak State Park on S shore. Inc. 1858.

Water Valley, village (1990 pop. 321), Graves co., SW Ky., on Bayou de Chien, 18 mi/29 km SW of Mayfield; 36°34'N 88°48'W. Agr. (tobacco, grain; livestock, poultry; dairying); clay.

Waterboro, town (1990 pop. 4,510), York co., SW Maine, just N of Alfred; 43°35'N 44°70'W. Leather goods, boxes. Waterboro Center is resort area. Settled 1768, inc. 1787.

Waterbury, industrial city (1990 pop. 108,961), New Haven co., W Conn., on the Naugatuck R.; 41°33'N 73°02'W. It is a financial and commercial center of W Conn. Once famous as the brass center of U.S. Clocks and watches, tools, instruments, plastics, chemicals, and electronic parts are among the many other manufactures of Waterbury. The city's historical society has notable collections. Waterbury is the site of a branch of the Univ. of Conn., Post Col., Mattatuck Community Col., and a state technical col. Settled 1674; inc. as a city 1853.

Waterbury, town (1990 pop. 4,589), including Waterbury village, Washington co., central Vt., on Winooski R., and 11 mi/18 km NW of Montpelier. Wood prods., machine tools, electronic equip., ice cream, and maple prods.; 44°23'N 72°45'W. Vt. State Hosp. for mentally ill is here. Site of Little R. Dam, built after 1927 flood. Chartered 1763, settled 1783.

Waterbury, village (1990 pop. 95), Dixon co., NE Nebr., 18 mi/29 km W of Sioux City, Iowa, near Missouri R.; 42°27'N 96°44'W.

Waterdown, village, S Ont., central Canada, 6 mi/10 km N of Hamilton; 43°20'N 79°53'W. Food processing;

woodworking; refractory; mixed farming, fruit; dairying. Suburban community, part of new city of Flamborough.

Wateree, village, Richland co., central S.C., on Wateree R. (bridged), and 25 mi/40 km SE of Columbia. Poinsett State park and Manchester State Forest to E. Congaree Swamp Natl. Monument to W. Agr. includes poultry, livestock; grain.

Wateree (WAW-tuh-ree), river, S.C., c.75 mi/121 km long; continuation of the Catawba R. changes names at L. Wateree reservoir c.30 mi/48 km NNE of Columbia, S.C., on Fairfax-Lancaster co. line, N central S.C.; flows SE past Camden, and joins Congaree R. c.35 mi/56 km SE of Columbia to form Santee R.

Waterford, village, S Ont., central Canada, on Lynn R., and 7 mi/11 km N of Simcoe; 42°56′N 80°17′W. Dairying; fruit, vegetables.

Waterford, city (1990 pop. 4,771), Stanislaus co., central Calif., in San Joaquin Valley, 12 mi/19 km E of Modesto, on Tuolumne R.; 37°39′N 120°46′W. Irrigated farming, fruit growing, grain, vegetables, melons; dairying; poultry, cattle. Modesto Main Canal to N; Modesto and Turlock reservoirs to E; Turlock L. State Recreation Area to E.

Waterford 1 town (1990 pop. 17,930), New London co., SE Conn., on L.I. Sound; 41°21′N 72°09′W. Mainly residential, it has some publishing, a recording and film studio, a major retail center for SE Conn., and other light industry; commercial and sport fishing also are prevalent; high-technology military acoustics. Millstone Point Nuclear Power Stations, 1, 2, 3, (1st operational in 1969), serves Waterford's electric needs as well as a larger New England area. An annual conference for playwrights is held in the town. **2** town (1990 pop. 1,299), Oxford co., W Maine, 10 mi/16 km WSW of South Paris; 44°11′N 70°43′W. Wood prods. Birth and burial place of Artemus Ward. **3** town (1990 pop. 1,190), Caledonia co., NE Vt., on the Connecticut R., resort area just E of St. Johnsbury; 44°22′N 71°56′W. Includes village of Lower Waterford. Moore Dam here. Settled c.1653, inc. as a separate town from New London, 1801.

Waterford 1 village (1990 pop. 2,370), Saratoga co., E N.Y., on W bank of the Hudson R. at influx of Mohawk R. (bridged), and on the N.Y. State Barge Canal, just N of Cohoes; 42°47′N 73°40′W. Mfg. (chemicals, nonwoven needle-punched prods., transportation equip., computer chips). Inc. 1794. **2** uninc. village, Loudoun co., N Va., 5 mi/8 km NW of Leesburg; 39°11′N 77°36′W. **3** village (1990 pop. 2,431), Racine co., SE Wis., on Fox R. (Tichigan L. to N), and 25 mi/40 km SW of Milwaukee; 42°45′N 88°13′W. In agr. area; mfg. (plastic moldings, consumer goods, machining); summer resort.

Waterford, borough (1990 pop. 1,492), Erie co., NW Pa., 13 mi/21 km SSE of Erie, near LeBoeuf Creek (which forms LeBoeuf L. reservoir on S); 41°57′N 79°59′W. Mfg. (potato prods., fabricated metal prods., cabinets); agr. (potatoes, soybeans, grain; livestock; dairying). Resort. Union City L. reservoir to E. Ruins of Fort Le Boeuf, built 1753 by French, here.

Waterford, township (1990 pop. 10,940), Camden co., S N.J., 15 mi/24 km SE of Medford; 39°43′N 74°49′W. Inc. 1798.

Waterford Nuclear Power Plant, La.: see SAINT CHARLES.

Waterford Township, city, Oakland co., SE Mich., suburb 7 mi/11.3 km NW of Pontiac; 42°42′N 83°24′W. In agr. area. Summer camps. Mfg. (steel fabrication, ski equip., interior lighting; publishing). Oakland-Pontiac Airport in W. Site of Summit Place,one of the largest shopping centers in the U.S. Numerous lakes. Pontiac L. State Recreation Area to W; Dodge Brothers No. 3 State Park site in city, Dodge Brothers No. 4 State Park to S.

Waterford Works or **Waterford**, village, Camden co., SW N.J., 20 mi/32 km SE of Camden, in orchard and vineyard area. Had 18th-cent. bog-iron mines, 19th-cent. glassworks. Wharton State Forest to E.

Watergate Building, NW Washington, D.C., on Virginia Ave. NW, near Rock Creek Parkway. Hotel, apartment, and office complex that was the site of 1972 break-in at Democratic Party offices by operatives hired by President Richard Nixon's re-election campaign. The break-in sparked investigations that uncovered far-reaching scandal in the Nixon administration and ultimately led to Nixon's resignation in Aug. 1974.

Waterloo (wah-tuhr-LOO), county (□ 516 sq mi/1,336 sq km), S Ont., central Canada, on Grand R.; ⊙ Kitchener; 43°30′N 80°35′W.

Waterloo (WAH-tuhr-loo), city (1991 pop. 71,181), SE Ont, central Canada; 43°28′N 80°32′W. It is a suburb of Kitchener. Several large insurance companies have their main offices here; industries include distilleries and plants making furniture, farm machinery, and metal prods. The dist. was settled (1800–1805) by Mennonites from Pa. The Univ. of Waterloo and Wilfrid Laurier Univ. are here.

Waterloo (WAH-tuhr-loo), town (1991 pop. 3,964), S Que., E Canada, SE of Montreal; 45°21′N 72°31′W. It is the center of a farming region known for its mushrooms. Mfg. includes plastics, wire goods, and baby carriages.

Waterloo 1 city (1990 pop. 5,072), ⊙ Monroe co., SW Ill., 18 mi/29 km S of East St. Louis, in St. Louis metropolitan area; 38°19′N 90°09′W. In agr. area (grain; dairy prods.; poultry); light mfg. Plotted 1818; inc. 1849. **2** city (1990 pop. 66,467), ⊙ Black Hawk co., NE Iowa, on the Cedar R.; 42°29′N 92°20′W. Originally a center for sawmills and flour mills, Waterloo is a trade and industrial center in a farm and livestock area. The city's chief industries include meatpacking and the mfg. of farm machinery, plastics, bakery prods., fabricated metal prods., rebuilt RR cars, transportation equip., tool boxes, lubricants, soybean processing, printing, beverages, apparel, concrete prods. The Natl. Dairy Cattle Congress is held here each September. A 10-acre/4-ha replica of the isl. where the protagonist of Daniel Defoe's *Robinson Crusoe* was shipwrecked has been built in the Cedar R. at Waterloo. Hawkeye Inst. of Technology (commmunity col.; 1967) and the Waterloo Greyhound Park race track are here. George Wyth State Park is in NW part of city, on boundary with Cedar Falls. Inc. 1868.

Waterloo 1 town (1990 pop. 250), Lauderdale co., extreme NW Ala., on Pickwick Landing Reservoir (on Tennessee R.), 24 mi/39 km NW of Florence. **2** town (1990 pop. 2,040), DeKalb co., NE Ind., on small Cedar Creek, and 5 mi/8 km NNE of Auburn; 41°26′N 85°02′W. Livestock; hay, soybeans; dairy prods.; mfg. (screw machine prods., prefabricated steel bldgs., pallets, aluminum castings, molded rubber prods.). Laid out 1856. **3** town (1990 pop. 2,712), Jefferson co., S Wis., on small Waterloo Creek, and 21 mi/34 km NE of Madison; 43°10′N 88°59′W. In dairying region; mfg. (printing and publishing; wooden pallets, bicycles, pickles). Inc. 1859.

Waterloo 1 village (1990 pop. 479), Douglas co., E Nebr., 18 mi/29 km W of downtown Omaha, and on Elkhorn R., near Platte R.; 41°17′N 96°17′W. Grain; printing. Satellite community of Omaha. **2** village (□ 2 sq mi/5.2 sq km; 1990 pop. 5,116), ⊙ Seneca co., W central N.Y., in Finger Lakes region, on Seneca R., bet. Seneca and Cayuga lakes, and 7 mi/11.3 km ENE of Geneva; 42°53′N 76°51′W. Summer recreation. Official birthplace of the Memorial Day celebaration, May 5, 1866 (celebrated on May 30). Inc. 1824. **3** village (1990 pop. 191), Linn co., W Oregon, 17 mi/27 km SE of Albany, on South Santiam R.; 44°30′N 122°49′W. Fruit, vegetables; dairying; timber. **4** village (1990 pop. 122), Laurens co., NW central S.C., 13 mi/21 km NNE of Greenwood; 34°21′N 82°03′W. Agr. includes poultry, livestock; grain; dairying. L. Greenwood Reservoir on Saluda R. to S.

Waterman, village (1990 pop. 1,074), De Kalb co., N Ill., 17 mi/27 km SSW of Sycamore; 41°46′N 88°46′W. In rich agr. area (dairy prods.; corn, soybeans; sheep, poultry); mfg. food prods. Shabonna L. State Park to SW.

Waterproof, town (1990 pop. 1,080), Tensas parish, NE La., 50 mi/80 km SW of Vicksburg (Miss.), and near Mississippi R.; 31°49′N 91°23′W. In agr. area (cotton, rice, soybeans, peanuts; cattle, hogs); mfg. L. St. John to SW. Original town was flooded so it was moved to what was referred to as a waterproof knoll.

Watersmeet, village, Gogebic co., W Upper Peninsula, Mich., 29 mi/47 km NW of Iron R., and 45 mi/72 km ESE of Ironwood on Middle Branch of Ontonagon R.; 46°16′N 89°10′W. In Ottawa Natl. Forest. Trade center for farm and resort area; sawmill. Watersmeett Housing Project (Indian reservation). Numerous lakes in area.

Waterton Lakes National Park, (□ 203 sq mi/526 sq km), SW Alta., W Canada, SW of Lethbridge and at the U.S. border, adjoining Glacier Natl. Park. Est. 1895. It is the Can. sect. of Waterton-Glacier Internatl. Peace Park, created (1932) by acts of the Can. Parliament and the U.S. Congress. The area is mountainous, rising to c.9,600 ft/2,930 m at Mt. Blakiston, and contains the Waterton Lakes, the largest of which extends across the border into Mont.

Waterton-Glacier International Peace Park, Canada: see GLACIER NATIONAL PARKWATERTON LAKES NATL. PARK.

Watertown 1 city (□ 8 sq mi/20.7 sq km; 1990 pop. 29,429), ⊙ Jefferson co., N N.Y., on the Black R.; 43°58′N 75°54′W. Mfg. includes papermaking machinery, foundry and die castings, irrigation equip., electric motors, RR equip., and high-pressure aircraft hydraulic systems; dairy region. The falls on the river (more than 100 ft/30 m high) provided power for the city's many small industries. Watertown also attracts shoppers as a result of its proximity to Canada, the Adirondacks, and the Thousand Isls. resort area. Jefferson Community Col. and Public Square Historic Dist. are in the city. The Fort Drum military reservation (hq. of U.S. Army 10th Mt. Light Infantry Div. and Natl. Guard Training Facility) are nearby. Settled c.1800, inc. as a city 1869. **2** city (1990 pop. 17,592), ⊙ Codington co., NE S.Dak., on the Big Sioux R.; 44°54′N 97°10′W. It is the distributing, shipping, and trading center for an extensive agr. area. Light industries and tourism add to Watertown's economy. Two large lakes adjoining the city provide recreation. Mfg. (transportation equip., polyurethane foam prods., turkey processing, signs, bldg. systems, fiberglass prods., agr. machinery and prods.). Sandy Shore State Recreation Area to W, Pelican State Recreation Area to SW. Lake Anna Vocational Technical Inst. Near S tip of triangular Lake Traverse (Sisseton Wahpeton) Indian Reservation; Terry Redlin Mus., World Wildlife Mus.; Bramble Park & Zoo. RR junction. Inc. 1885. **3** city (1990 pop. 1,250), Wilson co., N central Tenn., 12 mi/19 km SE of Lebanon; 36°06′N 86°08′W. **4** city (1990 pop. 19,142), Dodge and Jefferson cos., SE Wis., 40 mi/64 km WNW of Milwaukee, 33 mi/53 km ENE of Madison, at the falls of the Rock R.; 43°11′N 88°43′W. Major RR junction. Mfg. is diverse (electronics, furnaces, metal recycling, fiberglass, plastics, carbonated beverage bottling, hardware); cheese, and its agr. market is economically important. Carl Schurz lived here. His wife, Margarethe, est. 1856 the 1st U.S. kindergarten here; it has been restored and moved to the grounds of the Octagon House (c.1849), the city's historical mus. Inc. 1854.

Watertown 1 town (1990 pop. 20,456), Litchfield co., W Conn.; 41°37′N 73°07′W. Mfg. includes textiles, plastics, chemicals, mattresses, and brass goods. A method for processing silk thread developed here (1849) and led to the foundation of a major silk industry in the 19th cent. Portions of a state park and a state forest are in Watertown. Taft, a preparatory school, is here. Set off from Waterbury and inc. 1780. **2** town (□ 3 sq mi/7.8 sq km; 1990 pop. 3,340), Columbia co., N central Fla., 9 mi/14.5 km SSW of Lake City; 30°11′N 82°35′W. In lumbering area. **3** town (1990 pop. 33,284), Middlesex co., E Mass., on the Charles R.; 42°22′N 71°11′W. An industrial suburb of Boston, its mfg. includes machinery, electronic equip., precision instruments, clothing, plastic, rubber, and food prods. A Federal arsenal, built in 1816, was greatly enlarged during both World Wars;

most of it is owned by the town, for town, and arsenal mall and businesses, but the U.S. govt. has retained a sect. for research. The Perkins School for the Blind (est. 1829 in Boston) moved to Watertown in 1912. Settled 1630, inc. 1785. **4** town (1990 pop. 2,408), Carver co., S central Minn., on South Fork Crow R., 29 mi/47 km W of Minneapolis, and 15 mi/24 km NW of Chaska; 44°57'N 93°50'W. Agr. (livestock, poultry; dairying; grain, soybeans, alfalfa); mfg. (printing and publishing, light mfg). Small natural lakes in area.

Waterville, town (1991 pop. 1,337), S Que., E Canada, on Coaticook R., and 8 mi/13 km S of Sherbrooke; 45°17'N 71°53'W. Dairying; livestock raising.

Waterville, city (1990 pop. 17,173), Kennebec co., S Maine, at the falls of the Kennebec R., opposite Winslow; 44°32'N 69°39'W. It is the trade distribution and medical center of a lake resort area. Mfg. (paper and wood prods.). During the early 1900s, Waterville had 5 shipyards that built many ocean and river vessels. Colby Col. (1813) and Thomas Col. (1894) are here. Home of Hathaway Shirts, oldest shirt-making company in U.S. (est.1837). Settled 1754, inc. as a city 1888.

Waterville 1 town (1990 pop. 140), Allamakee co., extreme NE Iowa, 10 mi/16 km ESE of Waukon; 43°12'N 91°17'W. In dairy region. Limestone quarries nearby. **2** town (1990 pop. 1,771), Le Sueur co., S Minn., 15 mi/24 km WSW of Faribault; 44°13'N 93°34'W. Resort area; agr. trade center (grain, soybeans, peas; livestock, poultry; dairying); mfg. (communications equip., plastic bags). Town is on Tetonka L. reservoir (NW) and Sakatah L. (NE), connected by short stream; Waterville Creek enters Sakatah L. from South Sakatah L. State Park to E. Inc. as village 1878, as city 1898. **3** town (1990 pop. 532), Lamoille co., N central Vt., on North Branch Lamoille R., and 18 mi/29 km SE of St. Albans, in Green Mts.; 44°42'N 72°45'W. **4** town (1990 pop. 995), ⊙ Douglas co., central Wash., 18 mi/29 km NE of Wenatchee; 47°39'N 120°04'W. In Columbia basin agr. region; wheat, barley, oats, rye; cattle, sheep. Columbia R. (L. Entiat reservoir) to W and N. Founded 1886.

Waterville 1 village (1990 pop. 601), Marshall co., NE Kansas, on Little Blue R., and 11 mi/18 km SSW of Marysville; 39°41'N 96°45'W. In grain region; poultry packing. Mfg. (farm machinery, meat prods.). **2** village (□ 1 sq mi/2.6 sq km; 1990 pop. 1,664), Oneida co., central N.Y., 14 mi/23 km SSW of Utica; 42°55'N 75°22'W. Mfg. (plastic injection molding); in dairying and farming area (corn, hay). George Eastman b. here. Inc. 1871. **3** village (1990 pop. 4,517), Lucas co., NW Ohio, 14 mi/23 km SW of downtown Toledo, and on Maumee R.; 41°29'N 83°44'W. In agr. area; limestone quarries, oil and gas wells; nurseries. Glass, metal, rubber prods.; food prods.

Waterville, Mass.: see WINCHENDON.

Waterville Lake, reservoir, Haywood co., W N.C., near Tenn. state line, on Pigeon R., 15 mi/24 km N of Waynesville, in Pisgah Natl. Forest, just E of Great Smoky Mts. Natl. Park; 35°41'N 83°01'W.

Waterville Valley, town (1990 pop. 151), Grafton co., central N.H., 16 mi/26 km NE of Plymouth; 43°54'N 71°27'W. Drained by Mad R., in White Mt. Natl. Forest. Timber. Mt. Osceola (4,326 ft/1,319 m) on N border; Waterville Natl. Forest Campground and Waterville Valley ski resort in center.

Watervliet, industrial city (□ 1 sq mi/2.6 sq km; 1990 pop. 11,061), Albany co., E N.Y., on the Hudson R., opposite Troy, near the terminus of the N.Y. State Barge Canal; 42°43'N 73°42'W. The U.S. Watervliet Arsenal here, which specializes in the production of heavy ordnance, was est. 1813. Steel prods. and water and pressure-sensitive tapes are also made. In 1776, Ann Lee founded the 1st Amer. community of Shakers (United Society of Believers) in Watervliet. Founded by the Dutch 1735, inc. as a city 1896.

Watervliet (WAW-tuhr-vuh-LEET), town (1990 pop. 1,867), Berrien co., extreme SW Mich., 13 mi/21 km NE of St. Joseph, and on Paw Paw R.; 42°11'N 86°15'W. In orchard and farm area; poultry; Paw Paw L. (resort) is just N. Mfg. (paper prods., brushes). Settled in 1830s; inc. as village 1891, as city 1925.

Watford, village (1991 pop. 1,524), S Ont., central Canada, 26 mi/42 km E of Sarnia; 42°57'N 81°53'W. Lumber and flour milling, wire mfg.

Watford City, town (1990 pop. 1,784), ⊙ McKenzie co., W N.Dak., 29 mi/47 km SE of Williston, on Cherry Creek; 47°47'N 103°16'W. Trade center; lignite mines; oil and gas fields; wheat; livestock; dairy. Inc. 1934; became the capital in 1941. North Unit of Theodore Roosevelt Natl. Park to S; Fort Berthold Indian Reservation 25 mi/40 km E.

Watford Island, W Bermuda, bet. Somerset and Boaz isls.; 1,000 ft/305 m long, 600 ft/183 m wide; 32°18'N 64°51'W. Connected by road with adjacent isls.

Watha (WAI-thuh), village (1990 pop. 99), Pender co., SE N.C., 7 mi/11.3 km NNW of Burgaw, near Northeast Cape Fear R.; 34°38'N 77°57'W. Grain, tobacco, peanuts; livestock, poultry. Mfg. (wind chimes).

Wathena (wah-THEE-nuh), town (1990 pop. 1,160), Doniphan co., extreme NE Kansas, on Missouri R., and 6 mi/9.7 km W of St. Joseph, Mo.; 39°45'N 94°57'W. Shipping point for fruit (chiefly apples) and general agr. region. Mfg. (plastics prods., snack foods, fertilizers; steel fabrication). Severe flooding occurred in area 1993.

Watkins, town (1990 pop. 849), Meeker co., S central Minn., 20 mi/32 km SW of St. Cloud; 45°18'N 94°24'W. Agr. (grain, soybeans, peas; livestock, poultry; dairying); light mfg. Clear L. to SW.

Watkins Glen, resort village (□ 1 sq mi/2.6 sq km; 1990 pop. 2,207), ⊙ Schuyler co., W central N.Y., in the Finger Lakes region, at the S end of Seneca L.; 42°22'N 76°52'W. It is in a grape and wine area and has salt mine just N. Its setting of cliffs, waterfalls, and unusual rock formations made by an interwinding stream attracts many visitors. The resort hotel here is famed for its mineral spring water. An internatl. Grand Prix sports-car race was held here annually until 1981. Watkins Glen State Park adjoins the village. Inc. 1842.

Watkinsville, town (1990 pop. 1,600), ⊙ Oconee co., NE central Ga., 7 mi/11.3 km SSW of Athens; 33°52'N 83°25'W. Mfg includes industrial equip., electrical wire and cable, motor vehicle seats, materials handling equip., concrete.

Watoga State Park (wah-TO-guh), Pocahontas co., E W.Va., 7 mi/11.3 km S of Marlinton, E of Greenbrier R., in the Allegheny Mts., bounded N and E by Monongahela Natl. Forest; S by Calvin Price State Forest. Covers c.10,000 acres/4,047 ha; Greenbrier R. State Trail passes through W. Forested game refuge and recreational area.

Watonga (wah-TAHNG-uh), town (1990 pop. 3,408), ⊙ Blaine co., W central Okla., 30 mi/48 km NW of El Reno, near North Canadian R.; 35°51'N 98°24'W. Elev. 1,515 ft/462 m. In agr. area; grain elevators; mfg. of cheese and gypsum prods. Roman Nose State Park to N. Settled 1892.

Watonwan (WAW-tuhn-wan), county (□ 439 sq mi/1,137 sq km; 1990 pop. 11,682), S Minn.; ⊙ St. James; 43°58'N 94°36'W. Drained by Watonwan R. and its South Fork. Agr. area (soybeans, alfalfa, corn, oats; hogs, cattle, sheep, poultry). Formed 1860.

Watonwan River (WAW-tuhn-wan), c.65 mi/105 km long, SW Minn.; rises in central Cottonwood co., 9 mi/14.5 km NNW of Windom (44°01'N 95°13'W); flows c.90 mi/145 km E, past Madelia, to Blue Earth R., 8 mi/12.9 km SW of Mankato. South Fork Watonwan R. rises in Fish L., on Cottonwood-Jackson co. border. Flows E, then NE; passes SE of St. James, and joins Watonwan R. 2 mi/3.2 km W of St. James.

Watrous (WAH-truhs), town (1991 pop. 1,872), S central Sask., W Canada, near Little Manitou L., 60 mi/97 km ESE of Saskatoon; 51°40'N 105°28'W. Grain elevators; mixed farming.

Watrous (wuh-TROOS), uninc. village (1990 pop. 175), Mora co., N central N.Mex., on Mora R., at mouth of Sapello Creek (Sangre de Cristo Mts to W.), and 20 mi/32 km NE of Las Vegas. Elev. 6,413 ft/126 m. Lumber shipping point. Ruins of Fort Union (1851–1891), in Fort Union Natl. Monument to N; Turkey Mts. to N.

Watseka (wat-SEE-kah), city (1990 pop. 5,424), ⊙ Iroquois co., E Ill., on Iroquois R. at mouth of small Sugar Creek, and 25 mi/40 km SSE of Kankakee; 40°46'N 87°43'W. RR junction. In rich agr. area (corn, soybeans; cattle; poultry); mfg. (steel tape, surveying equip., food prods., circuit devices, metal stampings, business forms). Plotted as Middleport on site of an early trading post; renamed 1865; inc. 1867. Henry Bacon b. here.

Watson, town (1991 pop. 884), S central Sask., W Canada, 26 mi/42 km E of Humboldt. RR junction; grain elevators.

Watson, town (1990 pop. 137), Atchison co., NW Mo., 12 mi/19 km W of Tarkio, near new mouth of Nishnabotna R. on Missouri R.; 40°28'N 95°37'W.

Watson 1 village (1990 pop. 282), Desha co., SE Ark., 20 mi/32 km NNE of McGehee; 33°53'N 91°15'W. In agr. area. **2** village (1990 pop. 646), Effingham co., SE central Ill., 7 mi/11.3 km S of Effingham; 39°01'N 88°34'W. In agr. area (wheat, soybeans; cattle, hogs). **3** village (1990 pop. 211), Chippewa co., SW Minn., 5 mi/8 km NW of Montevideo on Chippewa R.; 45°00'N 95°47'W. Agr. area (grain, soybeans, sugar beets; hogs, sheep). Minnesota R. (in Lac qui Parle Wildlife Area) to SW; Lac qui Parle State Park and Lac qui Parle L. on Minn. R., to NW.

Watson Lake, town (1991 pop. 912), SE Yukon Territory, Canada, near the Liard R., and the B.C. border; 60°07'N 128°48'W. Elev. 2,265 ft/690 m. It is a Royal Can. Mounted Police Post, with an airfield and a radio station, located on the Alaska Highway, opened 1942. Inc. 1984. Called Fish L. in 1800s.

Watsontown (WAT-suhn-toun), borough (1990 pop. 2,310), Northumberland co., E central Pa., 16 mi/26 km NNW of Sunbury, on West Branch of Susquehanna R.; 41°04'N 76°51'W. Mfg. (textiles, bricks, iron castings); shale quarries. Agr. (potatoes, grain; poultry, livestock; dairying). Allenwood Prison Camp (U.S. Penitentiary) to NW; Bald Eagle and Tidaghton state forests to W. Laid out 1794, inc. 1867.

Watsonville, city (1990 pop. 31,099), Santa Cruz co., W Calif., 27 mi/43 km S of San Jose, 15 mi/24 km ESE of Santa Cruz, and 4 mi/6.4 km E of Pacific Ocean (Monterey Bay), on the Pajaro R. near Monterey Bay; 36°55'N 121°46'W. It is a growing trade and processing center for vegetables, fruits, berries, and flowers; mfg. (petroleum refining; frozen food specialties, canned fruits and vegetables). Granite is quarried in area, and bricks and aluminum parts are among the city's mfg. Watsonville's pop. more than doubled bet. 1970 and 1990. Nearby are beach and mt. resorts; Sunset State Beach to W; Moss Landing State Historical Park to S; Forest of Nisene Marks State Park to NW; Santa Cruz Mts. to NE, including Mt. Madonna (6,224 ft/1,897 m). Founded 1852, inc. 1868.

Watterson Park, town (1990 pop. 1,542), Jefferson co., N Ky., residential suburb 5 mi/8 km SSE of downtown Louisville; 38°11'N 85°41'W.

Watts, village (1990 pop. 303), Adair co., E Okla., near Illinois R. (L. Frances to E), near Ark. state line, 5 mi/8 km SSW on Springs, Ark., and 22 mi/35 km NE of Tahlequah; 36°06'N 94°34'W. Small L. Francis (fishing) is formed here by dam on Illinois R.

Watts, suburban section of Los Angeles, Los Angeles co., S Calif., 6 mi/9.7 km S of downtown Los Angeles. Named after C. H. Watts, a Pasadena realtor, the sect. became part of Los Angeles in 1926. Artist Simon Rodia's celebrated Watts Towers are here. Historically an impoverished black ghetto, Watts was the site of 6 days of race riots in 1965 that claimed 34 lives and caused over $200 million in property damage. Race riots again erupted in 1992 after the acquittal of white police officers who beat a black motorist; 58 people died and approximately $1 billion in property was destroyed. The Afr.-Amer. pop. has declined in recent decades while the area's Hispanic pop. has grown significantly. In 1990, almost 40% of Watts's residents were living below the poverty line. Pepperdine Univ. to W has relocated to Malibu.

Watts Bar Lake, reservoir, on Meigs and Rhea co. border and in Roane and Loudoun cos., E Tenn., on Tennessee R., 15 mi/24 km NE of Dayton; 72 mi/116 km long; 35°37′N 84°46′W. Max. capacity 1,132,000 acre-ft. Clinch R. forms c.20 mi/32 km NE arm. Formed by Watts Bar Dam (concrete construction, earth-fill wing; 112 ft/34 m high), built (1942) by TVA for flood control and power supply. Watts Bar Nuclear Power Plant is here.

Watts Island, Accomack co., E Va., in Chesapeake Bay bet. Tangier Isl. (W) and Eastern Shore (Delmarva Peninsula; E), 11 mi/18 km NW of Onancock; c.2 mi/3.2 km long; 37°48′N 75°53′W. Watts Isl. lighthouse is on Little Watts Isl., just S.

Watts Mills, uninc. town (1990 pop. 1,535), Laurens co., NW central S.C., residential suburb 2 mi/3.2 km NE of Laurens; 34°31′N 81°59′W. Formerly known as Wattsville.

Wattsburg (WATS-buhrg), borough (1990 pop. 486), Erie co., NW Pa., 15 mi/24 km SE of Erie, on French Creek at confluence of its West Branch; 42°00′N 79°48′W. Mfg. (lumber, machinery); agr. (corn; livestock; dairying); timber. Union City L. reservoir (French co.) to SW. Ida M. Tarbell b. near here.

Watuppa Ponds (waw-TUH-puh), reservoirs consisting of 2 ponds, in E part of Fall River city, Bristol co., SE Mass.; 7.5 mi/12.1 km long; 41°42′N 71°06′W. Land bridge (crossed by Interstate Highway 195) at center separates North Watuppa Pond (4 mi/6.4 km long) from South Watuppa Pond (3.5 mi/5.6 km long). Supplies water for Fall R.

Waubaushene (wo-buh-SHEEN), village, S Ont., central Canada, on Georgian Bay, 18 mi/29 km NW of Orillia; 44°45′N 79°42′W. Dairying; grain.

Waubay, town (1990 pop. 642), Day co., NE S.Dak., 10 mi/16 km E of Webster, between Blue Dog and Bitter lakes; 45°19′N 97°18′W. Large Waubay L. to NW; Waubay Natl. Wildlife Refuge to N. Blue Dog Fish Hatchery. Lake Traverse (Sisseton Wahpeton) Indian Reservation to E. Resort.

Waubay Lake, Day co., NE S.Dak.; 9 mi/14.5 km long, 5 mi/8 km wide at widest point; 45°19′N 97°18′W. Resort; Cormorant Isl. is in it.

Waubeek, village, Linn co., E Iowa, on Wapsipinicon R., and 17 mi/27 km NE of Cedar Rapids. Limestone quarries nearby.

Waubesa, Lake (wau-BE-sah), one of the Four Lakes, Dane co., S Wis., 4 mi/6.4 km in SE Madison; connected with L. Monona (N) and L. Kegonsa (SE) by Yahara R.; c.3 mi/4.8 km long, 1.5 mi/2.4 km wide. City of Monona on N end, McFarland on E shore.

Waubun (WAW-buhn), village (1990 pop. 330), Mahnomen co., NW Minn., 10 mi/16 km S of Mahnomen, in W part of White Earth Indian Reservation; 47°10′N 95°56′W. Resort area; agr. (grain, sunflowers, alfalfa, wild rice). White Earth State Forest to E.

Wauchula (waw-CHOO-luh), town (□ 2 sq mi/ 5.2 sq km; 1990 pop. 3,253), ⊙ Hardee co., central Fla., c.25 mi/40 km S of Bartow, near Peace R.; 27°33′N 81°48′W. Ships agr. produce (esp. strawberries); has citrus-fruit canneries; mfg. (boxes).

Waucoba Mountain, Calif.: see INYO MOUNTAINS.

Waucoma, town (1990 pop. 277), Fayette co., NE Iowa, on Little Turkey R., and 11 mi/19 km NW of West Union; 43°03′N 92°01′W. Fertilizer, feed. Limestone quarries, sand and gravel pits nearby.

Wauconda (wah-KON-dah), village (1990 pop. 6,294), Lake co., NE Ill., on small Bangs L., suburb 38 mi/61 km NW of downtown Chicago, and 16 mi/26 km WSW of Waukegan; 42°16′N 88°08′W. Agr. (grain; dairying); diverse light mfg. (construction equip., marking equip., food prods., sheet metal prods.).

Waugoshance Point (wah-GO-shanz), Emmet co., NW Mich., a narrow and irregular peninsula extending c.4 mi/6.4 km W into L. Michigan, and 10 mi/16 km WSW of Mackinaw City; 45°45′N 85°00′W. Included in Wilderness State Park. Small Waugoshance Isl. is ½ mi/⁸⁄₁₀ km beyond point (W).

Waukee, town (1990 pop. 2,512), Dallas co., central Iowa, 14 mi/23 km W of Des Moines, satellite community of Des Moines; 41°36′N 93°51′W. Mfg. (nurseries; printing and publishing; bldg. fixtures).

Waukegan, city (1990 pop. 69,392), ⊙ Lake co., NE Ill.,

on L. Michigan, suburb 39 mi/63 km NNW of downtown Chicago; 42°22′N 87°52′W. It has a good harbor and is the 1st port of call in Ill. on the St. Lawrence Seaway route. Its industries are closely allied with those of Chicago and Milwaukee. Mfg. (fluorescent fixtures, electrical wire, transportation equip., keyboards, leather prods., paper prods., asphalt roofing materials; printing). Waukegan was settled (1835) as Little Fort near an old Fr. stockade on the site of a Native Amer. village; Ill. Beach State Park to N; Great Lakes Naval Training station to S. Inc. 1852.

Waukesha (WAW-ke-shaw), county (□ 580 sq mi/ 1,502 sq km; 1990 pop. 304,751), SE Wis.; ⊙ Waukesha; 43°01′N 88°18′W. Hilly dairying and farming area, with many resort lakes. Drained by Fox and Bark rivers. Urbanized in E, extension of Milwaukee metropolitan area. Mfg. at Waukesha, Oconomowoc, Menomonec Falls, Brookfield, New Berlin, and other communities; processing of dairy prods. is important throughout co.; wheat, corn, soybeans, potatoes; hogs, sheep; stone quarries. NE part of S unit of Kettle Moraine State Forest in SW, E part of Glacial Drumlin State Trail crosses co. E-W, terminating here. Formed 1846.

Waukesha (WAW-ke-shaw), city (1990 pop. 56,958), ⊙ Waukesha co., SE Wis., on the Fox R.; 43°00′N 88°14′W. It is an industrial center in a dairy area. Waukesha was a stop on the Underground RR; after the Civil War it became a health resort. Its bottled waters are shipped widely. Mfg. includes dairy and food processing equip., marine hardware, engines, bearings, castings, rubber prods., printing and publishing, and electronic equip. Carroll Col., Waukesha Co. Area Technical Col. to N at Pewaukee, and the Univ. of Wis., Waukesha Campus are here. Native Amer. mounds are preserved in the city's Cutler Park. Terminus (E) of Glacial Drumlin State Trail; Pewaukee L. to NW. Inc. 1896.

Waukewan, Lake (WAW-kee-wawn), Belknap co., central N.H., resort lake just W of Meredith, drains into L. Winnipesaukee to E through short stream, 9 mi/ 14.5 km NNW of Laconia; 2 mi/3.2 km long.

Waukomis (waw-KO-mis), town (1990 pop. 1,322), Garfield co., N Okla., 8 mi/12.9 km S of Enid; 36°16′N 97°54′W. Wheat; cattle; dairying.

Waukon, city (1990 pop. 4,019), ⊙ Allamakee co., extreme NE Iowa, 16 mi/26 km E of Decorah; 43°16′N 91°28′W. Mfg. (concrete, lime and rock prods.; feeds); livestock shipping. Limestone quarries nearby. Has annual corn festival. Settled 1849, inc. 1883.

Waunakee, town (1990 pop. 5,897), Dane co., S Wis., on tributary of Yahara R., and a suburb 8 mi/12.9 km NNW of Madison; 43°11′N 89°27′W. In farming and dairying area; dairy prods.; mfg. (dairy equip., gear reducers, pharmaceutical prods.; printing). Governor Nelson State Park to S in L. Mendota.

Wauneta (WAW-nai-tuh), village (1990 pop. 675), Chase co., S Nebr., 15 mi/24 km SE of Imperial, and on Frenchman Creek; 40°25′N 101°22′W. Grain, flour, feed. Power plant is here.

Waupaca (wah-PAK-uh), county (□ 765 sq mi/ 1,981 sq km; 1990 pop. 46,104), central Wis.; ⊙ Waupaca; 44°28′N 88°58′W. Drained by Wolf and Embarrass rivers. Dairying and general farming area (wheat, corn, soybeans, peas, beans, potatoes, hay; cattle, hogs, sheep, poultry); some mfg. Includes chain of lakes; Hartman Creek State Park in SW. Formed 1851.

Waupaca (wah-PAK-uh), town (1990 pop. 4,957), ⊙ Waupaca co., central Wis., on Waupaca R. (tributary of Wolf R.), and 34 mi/55 km W of Appleton; 44°21′N 89°04′W. In timber and farm area (potatoes; livestock; dairy prods.); mfg. (printing, sand and gravel, filters, garage doors). Center of lake-resort region. Wis. Veterans Home here. Hartman Creek State Park to W. Inc. 1875.

Waupun (WAH-puhn), town (1990 pop. 8,207), on Fond du Lac–Dodge co. line, E central Wis., on Rock R., and 17 mi/27 km SW of Fond du Lac; 43°37′N 88°44′W. In farm and dairy region; mfg. (cheese, dairy prods.; power cords and cables, fasteners, chemicals). The state prison and a state hosp. are here. On route of 1st U.S.

auto race. Horicon Natl. Wildlife Refuge. Settled 1838, inc. 1878.

Wauregan (war-e-GIN), village (1990 pop. 1,079), Windham co., E Conn., 16 mi/26 km ENE of Willimantic, on S end of Wauregan Pond; 41°45′N 71°54′W. A postal sect. of Plainfield.

Waurika (waw-REE-kuh), town (1990 pop. 2,088), ⊙ Jefferson co., S Okla., 23 mi/37 km S of Duncan, and on Beaver Creek; 34°11′N 98°01′W. Elev. 882 ft/269 m. RR junction. Trade center for agr. area (grain, cotton, corn; cattle, sheep); mfg. (belts, leather goods); oil. Chisolm Trail historical mus. here. Waurika L. reservoir (Beaver Creek) to N. Settled c.1890, inc. 1903.

Waurika Lake, reservoir (□ 16 sq mi/41 sq km), Jefferson co., S central Okla., on Beaver Creek, 35 mi/56 km SE of Lawton; 34°14′N 98°04′W. Max. capacity 908,400 acre-ft. Formed by Waurika L. Dam (106 ft/ 32 m high), built (1977) by Army Corps of Engineers for flood control; also used for irrigation, water supply, and recreation. Chisholm Trail Mus. just S.

Wausa (WAW-suh), village (1990 pop. 598), Knox co., NE Nebr., 7 mi/11.3 km SE of Bloomfield; 42°30′N 97°32′W. Dairying; grain; livestock, poultry.

Wausau (WAH-saw), city (1990 pop. 37,060), ⊙ Marathon co., central Wis., on the Wisconsin R., above mouths of Big Rib R. (from W), and Eau Clair R. (from E); 44°57′N 89°38′W. It is an industrial, commercial, and agr. city in the heart of the state's dairy region. Its many manufactures include wood prods., electric motors, knives, machinery, plastics; steel fabrication. Well known for its Wausau Insurance Company. Wausau is also the hq. of a state project that stores and then sells river water for local industrial use. A technical institute is in the city. Rib Mt. State Park, to SE; tourism. Settled 1839, inc. 1872.

Wausaukee (wah-SAW-kee), village (1990 pop. 656), Marinette co., NE Wis., on small Wausaukee R., and 25 mi/40 km NW of Marinette, in lake region; 45°22′N 87°57′W. Mfg. (fabricated metal prods. and fiberglass structures).

Wauseon (WO-see-ahn), city (1990 pop. 6,322), ⊙ Fulton co., NW Ohio, 32 mi/51 km WSW of Toledo; 41°33′N 84°08′W. In farming and dairying area; mfg. (electrical equip., food prods., furniture, transportation equip., machinery, construction materials). Settled 1835, inc. 1852.

Waushara (wah-SHAH-rah), county (□ 637 sq mi/ 1,650 sq km; 1990 pop. 19,385), central Wis.; ⊙ Wautoma; 44°06′N 89°14′W. Dairying and farming area (corn, soybeans, peas, beans, potatoes; sheep); timber. Many small lakes (resorts) at W end of L. Poygan (extension of Wolf R. to E) in co. Drained by small White and Pine rivers and Willow Creek. Wild Rose State Fish Hatchery in N. Formed 1851.

Wautoma (waw-TO-muh), town (1990 pop. 1,784), ⊙ Waushara co., central Wis., near small White R., 37 mi/ 60 km W of Oshkosh; 44°04′N 89°17′W. In farm and timber area; dairy prods.; mfg. (vitamins, health food). Summer resort. Nordic Mt. Ski Area to NE. Inc. as village in 1901, as city in 1940.

Wauwatosa (waw-wuh-TO-suh), city (1990 pop. 49,366), Milwaukee co., SE Wis., a suburb 4 mi/6.4 km W of downtown Milwaukee, on the Menomonee R.; 43°03′N 88°01′W. Mfg. (transportation equip., printing adhesives, electroplating). Mt. Mary Col. to N in Milwaukee, Lutheran Col. on S border. Milwaukee co. institutions located here, including co. zoo. Settled 1835, inc. as a city 1897.

Wauzeka (wah-ZEE-kah), village (1990 pop. 595), Crawford co., SW Wis., near confluence of Wisconsin and Kickapoo rivers, 13 mi/21 km ENE of Prairie du Chien; 43°03′N 90°54′W. Wood prods. State wildlife area; Kickapoo Indian Caverns here.

Waveland 1 town (1990 pop. 474), Montgomery co., W Ind., near small Little Raccoon Creek, 14 mi/23 km SSW of Crawfordsville; 39°53′N 87°03′W. Agr. area (grain; livestock). Shades State Park nearby to N. Laid out 1835. **2** town (1990 pop. 5,369), Hancock co., SE Miss., 18 mi/29 km WSW of Gulfport, 3 mi/4.8 km SW of Bay St. Louis, on Mississippi Sound; 30°17′N

89°22′W. Beach resort area. Light mfg. Buccaneer State Park in SW.

Waverley, Mass.: see BELMONT.

Waverly 1 city (1990 pop. 1,402), Morgan co., central Ill., 21 mi/34 km SW of Springfield; 39°35′N 89°57′W. In agr. area (corn, wheat, soybeans; cattle, hogs). Inc. 1867. **2** city (1990 pop. 8,539), ⊙ Bremer co., NE Iowa, on Cedar R., and 17 mi/27 km NNW of Waterloo; 42°43′N 92°28′W. RR junction. Processes poultry, dairy prods.; canneries; mfg. of malt syrup, pharmaceuticals, feed, farm tools, caskets, cement blocks, gauges, industrial machinery, draperies and bedspreads, backhoes, cranes, instant dehydrated food mixes, kitchen cutlery. Seat of Wartburg Col. (coeducational; 1868) with Waverly Mus. (1894); and of a Lutheran orphan's home. Ski Villa Ski Area is N. Inc. 1859. **3** city (1990 pop. 4,477), ⊙ Pike co., S Ohio, 14 mi/23 km S of Chillicothe, and on Scioto R. Market center for agr. area; lumber, wood prods., concrete prods. L. White State Park (resort) is nearby. Founded 1829. **4** city (1990 pop. 3,925), ⊙ Humphreys co., central Tenn., 55 mi/89 km W of Nashville, near Kentucky Reservoir, 36°05′N 87°48′W. In timber, livestock-raising region; makes boots, wood prods. Indian mounds nearby. Laid out 1836.

Waverly 1 town (1990 pop. 152), Lee and Chambers cos., E Ala., 12 mi/19 km NW of Opelika. Lumber. **2** town (□ 4 sq mi/10.4 sq km; 1990 pop. 2,071), Polk co., central Fla., 9 mi/14.5 km S of Haines City; 27°58′N 81°37′W. Mfg. of fertilizer, insecticides; citrus-fruit packing. **3** town (1990 pop. 837), Lafayette co., W central Mo., on Missouri R., and 19 mi/31 km E of Lexington; 39°12′N 93°31′W. Grain, apples; livestock. Missouri R. bridge. **4** town (1990 pop. 1,869), Lancaster co., SE Nebr., 12 mi/19 km NE of Lincoln, near Salt Creek of Platte R.; 40°54′N 96°31′W. Mfg. (structural steel fabrication, steel tubing, plastic injection moldings, hydraulic cranes). Satellite community of Lincoln. **5** town (1990 pop. 2,223), Sussex co., SE Va., 21 mi/34 km SE of Petersburg, near Blackwater R.; 37°01′N 77°05′W. Trade center in agr. area (peanuts, tobacco, melons, soybeans; poultry, livestock); mfg. (particleboard, adhesives); timber. Inc. 1892.

Waverly 1 village (1990 pop. 618), Coffey co., E Kansas, 15 mi/24 km NE of Burlington; 38°23′N 95°35′W. In livestock and grain area. **2** (WAIV-uhr-lee), village (1990 pop. 345), Union co., W Ky., 16 mi/26 km WSW of Henderson; 37°42′N 87°49′W. Agr. (livestock; grain, alfalfa); mfg. (septic tanks); bituminous coal. **3** village (1990 pop. 600), Wright co., S central Minn., 8 mi/12.9 km SW of Buffalo, at S end of Waverly L.; 45°04′N 93°58′W. In grain and livestock area; (soybeans; dairying; poultry); mfg. (machining). **4** village (□ 2 sq mi/5.2 sq km; 1990 pop. 4,787), Tioga co., S N.Y., near Pa. state line, on Chemung R., and 16 mi/26 km ESE of Elmira; 42°00′N 76°32′W. Mfg. (feed, commercial beeswax, beekeeping supplies, livestock feed supplements, electric insulating varnishes); agr. (dairy prods.; poultry; bees and honey). Specialized medical facility with neighboring community of Sayre, Pa., separated politically by state line but integrated economically. Inc. 1853. **5** village (1990 pop. 37), Spokane co., E Wash., 22 mi/35 km SSE of Spokane, on Hangman Creek; 47°20′N 117°14′W. In wheat-growing region.

Waverly Hall (WAIV-uhr-lee), town (1990 pop. 769), Harris co., W Ga., 21 mi/34 km NE of Columbus; 32°41′N 84°44′W.

Wawa (WAH-wuh), village, central Ont., central Canada, near Wawa L. (5 mi/8 km long), 100 mi/161 km NNW of Sault Ste. Marie; 48°00′N 84°47′W. Iron mining.

Wawa (WAH-wah), uninc. town, Delaware co., SE Pa. suburb 16 mi/26 km WSW of Philadelphia on Chester Creek; 39°54′N 75°27′W. Mfg. of dairy prods. Agr. includes dairying, cattle; nursery stock. Urban fringe area.

Wawaitin Falls (wuh-WEI-tin), waterfalls (126 ft/38 m high), NE Ont., central Canada, on Mattagami R., at N end of Kenogamissi L., 11 mi/18 km SW of Timmins.

Wawaka, village, Noble co., NE Ind., 11 mi/18 km W of

Kendallville. Agr. area. Mfg. (fertilizer and grain blending, custom metal fabricating). Glacially formed lakes nearby. Laid out 1857.

Wawanesa (wah-wuh-NEE-suh), village (1991 pop. 482), SW Man., central Canada, on Souris R., and 21 mi/34 km SE of Brandon; 49°31′N 99°41′W. In livestock, mixed farming area.

Wawarsing, resort village (1990 pop. 800), Ulster co., SE N.Y., just W of the Shawangunk range, on Rondout Creek, and 3 mi/4.8 km NE of Ellenville; 41°45′N 74°25′W.

Wawasee, Lake, N Ind., at Syracuse; c.4 mi/6.4 km long. Largest natural lake in Ind. (glacially formed). Resort center area nearby to S. Tri-Co. State Fish and Wildlife.

Wawota (wuh-WO-tuh), town (1991 pop. 654), SE Sask., W Canada, near Man. border, on Little Pipestone Creek, and 23 mi/37 km SW of Moosomin; 49°54′N 102°01′W. Mixed farming.

Waxahachie (WAHK-sah-hach-ee), city (1990 pop. 18,168), ⊙ Ellis co., N Texas, 17 mi/27 km S of Dallas; 32°24′N 96°50′W. Elev. 585 ft/178 m; RR junction. A market center (esp. for cattle) in the rich blackland prairie. Mfg. (coated reinforcing steel, apparel, bathtubs, honey, wooden prods.; glass bottles, fiberglass, paper, and steel prods., windows and skylights, fabricated metal prods.). Southwestern Junior Col. of the Assemblies of God is here. Bardwell L. to SE. Inc. 1861.

Waxell Ridge (WAK-suhl), S Alaska, uneven expanse of peaks and glaciers in E portion of Chugach Mts., N of Bering Glacier; 60°40′N 143°00′W.

Waxhaw (WAKS-haw), town (1990 pop. 1,294), Union co., S N.C., 12 mi/19 km SW of Monroe, near S.C. state line; 34°55′N 80°44′W. Agr. area (cotton, grain, soybeans; poultry, livestock). Mfg. (textile machinery, sheet metal fabricating, business forms).

Wayah Bald, N.C.: see NANTAHALA MOUNTAINS.

Waycross, city (1990 pop. 16,410), ⊙ Ware co., SE Ga.; 31°13′N 82°22′W. Mfg. includes utility poles and pilings, apparel, printing and publishing, fiberglass boats, plywood processing, beef processing, paper boxes, burial vaults. Waycross is a RR and highway center in a pine lumber, livestock, tobacco, and pecan area. It has a tobacco auction market. Waycross State Forest, Okefenokee Swamp Park, and a natl. wildlife refuge are all located nearby. Settled 1818, inc. 1874.

Wayland 1 town (1990 pop. 838), Henry co., SE Iowa, 14 mi/23 km NNW of Mount Pleasant; 41°08′N 91°39′W. In livestock and grain area; metal prods. Amish-Mennonite colony here. **2** town (1990 pop. 11,874), Middlesex co., E Mass., suburb W of Boston; 42°22′N 71°22′W. Electronic and chemical research is carried on here. Includes village of Cochituate (1990 pop. 6,046). L. Cochituate State Park nearby. Settled c.1638, inc. 1835. **3** town (1990 pop. 2,751), Allegan co., SW Mich., 20 mi/32 km S of Grand Rapids; 42°40′N 85°38′W. In farm area (cucumbers, apples, corn, hay; poultry); mfg. (auto test equip., tool and die). Yankee Springs State Recreation Area to SE (Barry co.). Settled 1836, inc. 1858. **4** town (1990 pop. 391), Clark co., extreme NE Mo., near Mississippi and Des Moines rivers, 8 mi/12.9 km E of Kahoka; 40°23′N 91°34′W.

Wayland 1 village (1990 pop. 359), Floyd co., E Ky., in Cumberland foothills, 16 mi/26 km W of Pikeville; 37°27′N 82°47′W. Bituminous coal; timber, oil, and gas in area. **2** village (□ 1 sq mi/2.6 sq km; 1990 pop. 1,976), Steuben co., W central N.Y., 40 mi/64 km S of Rochester; 42°34′N 77°35′W. Mfg. of office furniture; agr. (dairy prods.; grain, onions, potatoes). Inc. 1877.

Waymart (WAI-mahrt), borough (1990 pop. 1,337), Wayne co., NE Pa., 5 mi/8 km E of Carbondale; 41°35′N 75°24′W. Mfg. (children's shirts, feeds); agr. (alfalfa, corn; livestock; dairying). Fairview State Hosp. to W; Moosic Mt. to W; numerous lakes and ponds in area; L. Ladore reservoir to S. Inc. 1851.

Wayne 1 (WAIN), county (□ 648 sq mi/1,678 sq km; 1990 pop. 22,356), SE Ga.; ⊙ Jesup; 31°33′N 81°55′W. Bounded NE by Altamaha R., SW by Little Satilla R. Coastal plain agr. (tobacco, honey, peanuts, soybeans, cotton, corn); cattle, hogs; timber; textile mfg. at Jesup.

RR hub for SE Ga. Okefenokee Heritage Center and forest mus. Okefenokee Natl. Wildlife Refuge. Entrance to Okefenokee Swamp Park nearby as well as Laura S. Parker State Park. Formed 1803. **2** county (□ 715 sq mi/1,852 sq km; 1990 pop. 17,241), SE Ill.; ⊙ Fairfield; 38°26′N 88°25′W. Agr. area (livestock (cattle); sorghum, wheat, hay, soybeans, corn; dairying). Oil wells. Mfg. (auto parts). Drained by Little Wabash R. and small Elm Creek. Formed 1819. Sam Dale L. Conservation Area in NW. **3** county (□ 404 sq mi/1,046 sq km; 1990 pop. 71,951), E Ind.; ⊙ Richmond; 39°52′N 85°01′W. Bounded E by Ohio state line; drained by Greens, E and W forks of Whitewater R. Agr. (corn, wheat, soybeans; cattle, hogs, poultry; dairy prods.; flower growing); mfg. at Richmond; timber. Highest point in Ind. (1,257 ft/383 m) 3 mi/4.8 km NE of Fountain City (NE part of co.). Formed 1810. **4** county (□ 527 sq mi/1,365 sq km; 1990 pop. 7,067), S Iowa, on Mo. state line (S); ⊙ Corydon; 40°45′N 93°18′W. Prairie agr. area (hogs, sheep, cattle, poultry; corn, soybeans, oats), with bituminous-coal deposits mined in E and S; drained by a branch of Chariton R. Bob White State Park in W. Field flooding occurred in 1993. Formed 1846. **5** (WAIN), county (□ 484 sq mi/1,254 sq km; 1990 pop. 17,468), S Ky.; ⊙ Monticello; 36°48′N 84°49′W. In Cumberland foothills; bounded S by Tenn.; crossed by Cumberland R. (forms large L. Cumberland reservoir in NW, including 2 large arms; also forms part of N and NW co. border); drained by Beaver Creek. Hilly agr. area (burley tobacco, hay, alfalfa, soybeans, wheat, corn; hogs, cattle, poultry; dairying); bituminous-coal mines, oil wells, rock quarries; timber. Includes small part of Daniel Boone Natl. Forest in SE corner. Formed 1800. **6** county (□ 672 sq mi/1,740 sq km; 1990 pop. 2,111,687), SE Mich.; ⊙ Detroit; 42°15′N 83°17′W. Bounded E by Detroit R. (forms internatl. border with Canada and prov. of Ont.) and L. St. Clair; SE corner touches L. Erie; drained by Huron R. and the system of parkways and "metroparks," R. Rouge and its branches. Detroit and the mfg. cities of its metropolitan area produce most of U.S. motor vehicles and auto parts. Co. has many residential suburbs of Detroit; nurseries; remnant agr. in SW and extreme NW corner (soybeans, corn; hogs, poultry). Fishing; salt mining. Lake and ocean-going shipping facilities along Detroit R. City of Detroit occupies most of NE ¼ of co. Suburb communities are located generally to W and S, with additional urban growth occurring N into Macomb and Oakland cos. Other major cities include Dearborn, Romulus, Taylor, Southgate, Trenton, and Livonia. Detroit and its S suburbs are highly industrialized, esp. with motor vehicle plants and related industries. Detroit Metropolitan Wayne Co. Airport at Romulus, Willow Run Airport on W border. Maybury State Park in NW corner. Formed 1796. **7** county (□ 813 sq mi/2,106 sq km; 1990 pop. 19,517), SE Miss.; ⊙ Waynesboro; 31°39′N 88°42′W. Bordered E by Ala.; drained by Chickasawhay R. and Bucatunna and Thompsons creeks. Includes part of De Soto Natl. Forest in SW. Agr. (cotton, corn); poultry, cattle; timber. Lakeland Park State L. in E. Formed 1809. **8** county (□ 777 sq mi/2,012 sq km; 1990 pop. 11,543), SE Mo.; ⊙ Greenville; 37°08′N 90°29′W. In Ozark region; drained by St. Francis and Black rivers. Corn, hay; livestock; oak, pine, hickory timber; granite. Mfg. at Piedmont; stream, lake and forest recreation. Mingo Natl. Wildlife Refuge in SE; Sam A. Baker State Park and Coldwater State Forest in N. Parts of Mark Twain Natl. Forest to S; Wappapello Dam and L. in SE. Formed 1818. **9** county (□ 443 sq mi/1,147 sq km; 1990 pop. 9,364), NE Nebr.; ⊙ Wayne; 42°12′N 97°09′W. Farm area drained by Logan Creek. Wayne State Col. Mfg. (modular homes, refrigerated semi-truck trailers, fabricated metal, pillows and mattresses, kiosks and signs, printing, feed). Transportation equip.; cattle, hogs, poultry; corn, alfalfa; dairy and poultry prods. Formed 1870. **10** county (□ 1,384 sq mi/3,585 sq km; 1990 pop. 89,123), W N.Y.; ⊙ Lyons; 43°16′N 77°02′W. Bounded N by L. Ontario (resorts on lake); drained by Canandaigua Outlet, Clyde R., and small Mud Creek; crossed by N.Y. State Barge Canal.

Rich fruit- and nut-growing region, apple-growing center of state; diversified mfg. at Lyons, Newark, and Sodus. Also dairy farming. Ginna nuclear power plant is 20 mi/32 km NE of Rochester; uses cooling water from L. Ontario, and has a generating capacity of 470 MW. Named in honor of Amer. Revolutionary Gen. "Mad" Anthony Wayne. Formed 1823. **11** county (□ 556 sq mi/1,440 sq km; 1990 pop. 104,666), E central N.C.; ⊙ Goldsboro; 35°21′N 78°00′W. Coastal plain area, intersected by Neuse R., source of Northeast Cape Fear R. in SE. Agr. area (wheat, oats, soybeans, hay, sweet potatoes, chickens, turkeys; some dairying; cattle, hogs; tobacco, cotton, corn); mfg. at Goldsboro. Cliffs of the Nuese State Park in SE; Waynesborough State Park in center, at Goldsboro; Charles B. Aycock State Historic Site in N. Formed 1779. **12** county (□ 561 sq mi/1,453 sq km; 1990 pop. 101,461), N central Ohio; ⊙ Wooster; 40°50′N 81°53′W. Intersected by Killbuck Creek, small Chippewa and Sugar creeks, and L. Fork of Mohican R. In the Glaciated Plain physiographic region. Agr. (livestock, poultry; corn, fruit; dairy prods.); mfg. at Wooster and Orrville (food prods.; paper, metal, and plastic prods.; electronics; iron foundries; motor vehicle parts and accessories; consumer goods). Sand and gravel pits; oil and gas wells; salt production. Agr. research station is near Wooster. Formed 1812. **13** county (□ 750 sq mi/1,943 sq km; 1990 pop. 39,944), NE Pa.; ⊙ Honesdale; 41°38′N 75°18′W. Lake region drained by Lackawaxen R.; bounded N and NE by N.Y. state line (NE border formed by Delaware R.), part of SE border formed by Wallenpaupack Creek (forms L. Wallenpaupack reservoir). Source of Lehigh R. in SW corner (forms part of SW border). Agr. (corn, oats, hay, alfalfa, apples; sheep, hogs, cattle; dairying). Recreation. Several rural, residential developments in Pocono Mts. in S; part of Moosic Mts. in W; part of Pocono Mts. in S. Formed 1798. **14** county (□ 741 sq mi/1,919 sq km; 1990 pop. 13,935), S Tenn.; ⊙ Waynesboro; 35°14′N 87°48′W. Bounded S by Ala.; drained by Buffalo R. and tributaries of Tennessee R. Timber, limestone, and iron-ore deposits; lumbering; mfg. of wood prods.; diversified agr. (corn, cotton, soybeans; livestock). Formed 1819. **15** county (□ 2,466 sq mi/6,387 sq km; 1990 pop. 2,177), S central Utah; ⊙ Loa; 38°20′N 110°53′W. Mt. and plateau area drained by Fremont, Muddy, and Dirty Devil rivers and bounded on E by Green and Colorado rivers. Main part of Capital Reef Natl. Park is E of Torrey in W center of co.; parts of Dixie and Fishlake natl. forests in W; parts of Glen Canyon Natl. Recreation Area and Canyonlands Natl. Park in E; Bicknell Bottoms Waterfowl Managment Area and Fish Hatchery and Loa Fish Hatchery in W. Agr. (alfalfa, barley; cattle). Formed 1892. **16** county (□ 512 sq mi/1,326 sq km; 1990 pop. 41,636), W W.Va.; ⊙ Wayne; 38°08′N 82°25′W. On Allegheny Plateau; bounded W by Tug Fork and Big Sandy rivers (Ky. state line), N by Ohio R. (Ohio state line); drained by Twelvepole Creek. Agr. (corn, tobacco, alfalfa, hay, nursery crops); cattle. Bituminous-coal mines, oil and natural-gas wells; sand and gravel pits; timber. Mfg. at Wayne and Ceredo. Beech Fork State Park and Beech Fork L. (reservoir) Wildlife Management Area in NE; East Lynn L. (reservoir) Wildlife Management Area in E; Cabwaylingo State Forest in S. Formed 1842.

Wayne 1 city, ⊙ Wayne co., NE Nebr., 37 mi/60 km SW of Sioux City, Iowa, and on branch of Logan Creek. Wheat, corn; dairy and poultry prods.; mfg. (beverages) Wayne State Col. is here. Plotted 1881. **2** city (1990 pop. 19,899), Wayne co., SE Mich., a suburb 16 mi/26 km WSW of downtown Detroit, on the Lower R. Rouge; 42°16′N 83°23′W. Mfg. (ring forgings, metal framing, trucks, printing). Parkway along river. Inc. as a village 1869, and with surrounding areas as a city 1960.

Wayne 1 (WAIN), town (1990 pop. 1,029), Kennebec co., S Maine, on Androscoggin L., and 16 mi/26 km W of Augusta; 44°20′N 70°04′W. Wood prods., toys. **2** uninc. town (1990 pop. 8,900), Radnor township, Delaware co., SE Pa., suburb 13 mi/21 km NW of downtown Philadelphia; 40°02′N 75°23′W. Mfg. (commercial printing, electroplating printing and publishing, emission control catalytics); crushed stone. **3** town (1990 pop. 1,128), ⊙ Wayne co., W W.Va., 14 mi/23 km S of Huntington, on Twelvepole Creek (forms East Lynn L. reservoir to SE); 38°13′N 82°26′W. Bituminous-coal region. Mfg. (food processing, printing and publishing, lumber). East Lynn Wildlife Management Area to SE; Beech Fork State Park and Beech Fork L. (reservoir) Wildlife Management Area to NE.

Wayne 1 village (1990 pop. 1,541), Du Page and Kane cos., NE Ill., residential suburb 37 mi/60 km WNW of downtown Chicago, 3 mi/4.8 km NE of St. Charles, near Fox R.; 41°57′N 88°15′W. RR junction. **2** village (1990 pop. 803), Wood co., NW Ohio, 11 mi/18 km ESE of Bowling Green; 41°18′N 83°28′W. Eggs, dairy prods., grain; oil wells. Until 1931, called Freeport. **3** village (1990 pop. 519), McClain co., central Okla., near Canadian R., 7 mi/11.3 km SSE of Purcell; 34°55′N 97°19′W. Mfg. (pickled beets, rugs).

Wayne, township (1990 pop. 47,025), Passaic co., NE N.J., 5 mi/8 km W of Paterson; 40°57′N 74°15′W. Industrial township with paper bags, sheet metal, munitions, lubricants, scales, household prods., electrical parts, plastic laminates, navigation equip., pharmaceuticals, and security systems among its leading prods. Willowbrook, one of the largest shopping centers in the U.S., is here. Inc. 1847.

Wayne City, village (1990 pop. 1,099), Wayne co., SE Ill., 13 mi/21 km WSW of Fairfield; 38°21′N 88°35′W. In agr. area.

Wayne, Fort, Mich.: see DETROIT.

Wayne Heights (WAIN), uninc. town (1990 pop. 1,683), Franklin co., S Pa., residential suburb 2 mi/3.2 km ESE of Waynesboro; 39°45′N 77°32′W. Agr. includes dairying; livestock, poultry; grain, apples. Appalachian Trail passes to E on South Mt.

Waynesboro 1 (WAINZ-buhr-o), city (1990 pop. 5,701), ⊙ Burke co., E Ga., 26 mi/42 km S of Augusta; 33°05′N 82°01′W. Mfg. includes safes, printing and publishing, food service equip., lumber, industrial transformers, textiles. Laid out 1783; inc. 1812. Alima Vogtle I and II nuclear power plants nearby. **2** city (1990 pop. 1,824), ⊙ Wayne co., S Tenn., 25 mi/40 km WNW of Lawrenceburg, 35°19′N 87°46′W. In timber and diversified agr. region; lumbering; wood prods., boots. **3** independent city (□ 14 sq mi/36 sq km; 1990 pop. 18,549), NW Va., separate from surrounding Augusta co., in Shenandoah Valley, 28 mi/45 km W of Charlottesville, on South R.; 38°04′N 78°54′W. RR junction; mfg. (concrete, textiles, furniture, printing, wooden prods., metal fabrication, iron and aluminum castings); agr. area (grain, soybeans, apples; poultry, livestock; dairying); tourism. Site of Union victory in Battle of Waynesboro (March 1865). Waynesboro Airport to W. George Washington Natl. Forest (including Sherando Recreational Area and Wintergreen Resort) to S and Shenandoah Natl. Park to NE. Skyline Drive, Appalachian Trail pass to SE. Settled c.1736, inc. as a city 1948.

Waynesboro, town (1990 pop. 5,143), ⊙ Wayne co., SE Miss., 29 mi/47 km E of Laurel, near Chickasawhay R.; 31°40′N 88°38′W. Trade center for agr. (cotton, corn; cattle, poultry; timber) area; mfg. (lumber, printing and publishing, industrial chemicals, electric blankets, poultry feed). Lakeland Park State L. to NE.

Waynesboro (WAINS-buhr-o), borough (1990 pop. 9,578), Franklin co., S Pa., 10 mi/16 km NE of Hagerstown, Md., bet. East and West branches Antietam Creek, near Md. state line; 39°45′N 77°34′W. Mfg. (machinery, printing and publishing, valves, compressors, prefabricated homes, machine tools); limestone. Agr. (apples, grain; poultry, livestock; dairying). Resort center. Occupied 1863 by Confederates. Appalachian Trail passes to E; Mont Alto State Park to N; Michaux State Forest to NE; Fort Richie Military Reserve (Md.) to SE. Settled 1798, inc. 1818.

Waynesburg 1 (WAINZ-buhrg), uninc. village (1990 pop. 500), Lincoln co., central Ky., 10 mi/16 km NW of Mt. Vernon, near Dix R. Timber. Burley tobacco, grain; livestock; dairying. Mfg. (wooden pallets, roof trusses). **2** village (1990 pop. 1,068), Stark co., E central Ohio, 11 mi/18 km SE of Canton; 40°40′N 81°15′W. Makes tile, brick, refractories.

Waynesburg (WAINS-buhrg), borough (1990 pop. 4,270), ⊙ Greene co., SW Pa., 18 mi/29 km S of Washington, on South Fork Tenmile Creek; 39°53′N 80°11′W. Mfg. of mining machinery, fabricated metal prods., plastic prods., printing and publishing; subsurface bituminous-coal mining; agr. includes hay, dairying; timber. Waynesburg Col. here; Greene Co. Airport to E; state park 14 mi/23 km to W. Laid out 1796, inc. 1816.

Waynesfield, village (1990 pop. 831), Auglaize co., W Ohio, 11 mi/18 km SSE of Lima; 40°36′N 83°58′W. In agr. area.

Waynesville 1 town (1990 pop. 3,207), ⊙ Pulaski co., S central Mo., in Ozarks, on Gasconade R., 26 mi/42 km WSW of Rolla; 37°49′N 92°13′W. Fruit; cattle; tourism. Service center for Fort Leonard Wood, army training base. **2** town (1990 pop. 6,758), ⊙ Haywood co., W N.C., 25 mi/40 km WSW of Asheville, SE of Great Smoky Mts. Natl. Park; 35°28′N 83°00′W. Mfg. (automotive hose, chemicals, furniture, medical equip.). Blue Ridge (Natl.) Parkway passes to SW. N.C. Internatl. folk festival (Folkmost). Parts of Pisgah Natl. Forest to N, SW, and SE. Settled before 1800; inc. 1871.

Waynesville 1 village (1990 pop. 440), De Witt co., central Ill., 18 mi/29 km SSW of Bloomington; 40°14′N 89°07′W. In agr. area. **2** village (1990 pop. 1,949), Warren co., SW Ohio, 6 mi/10 km NNE of Lebanon, and on Little Miami R.; 39°32′N 84°05′W. Food prods. Laid out 1796.

Waynetown, town (1990 pop. 911), Montgomery co., W Ind., 10 mi/16 km WNW of Crawfordsville; 40°05′N 87°04′W. Agr. area; mfg. (livestock feed); timber. Laid out 1830.

Waynewood, uninc. town, Fairfax co., NE Va., residential suburb 6 mi/9.7 km S of Alexandria, 12 mi/19 km S of Washington, D.C., on Potomac R.; 38°43′N 77°02′W. Light mfg.

Waynoka (wai-NO-kuh), town (1990 pop. 947), Woods co., NW Okla., 19 mi/31 km SW of Alva, near Cimarron R.; 36°35′N 98°52′W. RR center. Mfg. (utility boxes). Little Sahara State Park to S. Settled c.1893, inc. 1910.

Wayzata (wei-ZE-duh), town (1990 pop. 3,806), Hennepin co., E Minn., suburb 12 mi/19 km W of downtown Minneapolis, on Browns, Wayzata, and Gray's bays of L. Minnetonka; 44°58′N 93°30′W. RR junction. Mfg. (sheet lead and lead prods., bolts and nuts, dairy prods., wire harnesses, magnetic tape head, pay phones, nuclear shielding prods., transformers, printing and publishing, bakery prods.).

Weakley (WEEK-lee), county (□ 576 sq mi/1,492 sq km; 1990 pop. 31,972), NW Tenn.; ⊙ Dresden; 36°17′N 88°43′W. Bounded N by Ky.; drained by headstreams of Obion R. Tobacco, corn, cotton; livestock (leading hog grower); fruit; timber; clay pits. Some mfg. at Dresden. Formed 1823.

Weare (WER), town (1990 pop. 6,193), Hillsborough co., S N.H., 12 mi/19 km SW of Concord; 43°04′N 71°43′W. Drained by Piscataquog R., forms Everett L. in NE and L. Horace in NW. Mfg. (sand and gravel processing, printed circuit boards, lumber); agr. (apples, vegetables; poultry, livestock; dairying); timber. Clough State Park in NE. Inc. 1764.

Weatherby, town (1990 pop. 91), De Kalb co., NW Mo., 6 mi/9.7 km E of Maysville; 39°54′N 94°14′W.

Weatherby Lake, town (1990 pop. 1,613), Platte co., E Mo., residential suburb 14 mi/23 km NW of downtown Kansas City; 39°14′N 94°42′W. Kansas City Internatl. Airport to N.

Weatherford 1 city (1990 pop. 10,124), Custer co., W Okla., 14 mi/23 km ESE of Arapaho, near Deer Creek; 35°32′N 98°41′W. Trade center in agr. area (wheat, cotton); mfg. (office supplies, construction materials, publishing and printing, gypsum prods.). Seat of Southwestern State Univ. Crowder L. State Park to S. Founded 1893. **2** city (1990 pop. 14,804), ⊙ Parker co., N central Texas, 27 mi/43 km W of downtown Fort Worth; 32°45′N 97°46′W. Elev. 1,052 ft/321 m. Satellite of Dallas–Fort Worth area. RR spur junction. It is in a fertile region that yields horticultural crops, peanuts, pecans, and peaches; cattle, horses. Mfg. (oil field equip. and tools, silicone rubber prods., metal prods., diverse light mfg.), meat processing. Weatherford Col. (2-year) is here. Fort Wolters, a major helicopter center, is nearby. L. Weatherford to E; L. Mineral Wells State Park to W. Inc. 1856.

Weatherly (WE-thuhr-lee), borough (1990 pop. 2,640), Carbon co., E central Pa., 7 mi/11.3 km E of Hazleton, on Hazle Creek; 40°56′N 75°49′W. Mfg. (wooden prods., aircraft power supplies). Agr. area (potatoes, corn, hay; dairying). Lehigh Creek State Park to NE. Inc. 1863.

Weathersby, village, Simpson co., S central Miss., 3 mi/4.8 km ESE of Mendenhall.

Weathersfield, town (1990 pop. 2,674), Windsor co., SE Vt., resort area on the Connecticut R., just below Windsor; 43°23′N 72°28′W. Includes villages of Ascutney (near Mt. Ascutney; ski area), and Perkinsville. Ascutney Mt. and Wilgus state parks are here. Soapstone and talc quarries. Settled c.1775–1780.

Weaubleau (WAH-blo), town (1990 pop. 436), Hickory co., central Mo., 12 mi/19 km SW of Hermitage; 37°53′N 93°32′W. Hay, wheat; cattle.

Weaver, city (1990 pop. 2,715), Calhoun co., E Ala., 7 mi/11.3 km N of Anniston.

Weaver Mountains, Yavapai co., W central Ariz., 15 mi/24 km SW of Prescott; 34°09′N 112°41′W. Rises to 4,135 ft/1,260 m. Peeples Valley to E. Important gold strikes in the 1860s–1870s.

Weaverville 1 uninc. town (☐ 35 sq mi/91 sq km; 1990 pop. 3,370), ⊙ Trinity co., N Calif., in Klamath Mts., near Trinity R., 30 mi/48 km NW of Redding; 40°46′N 122°57′W. Gold; hay, nursery prods.; timber. Many bldgs., including Joss House, a Chin. temple restored to its 1873 splendor, date from gold rush days; Weaverville Joss House State Historic Park to W; units of Whiskeytown-Shasta-Trinity Natl. Recreation Area to NE and E; Trinity Natl. Forest to N and W. **2** town (1990 pop. 2,107), Buncombe co., W N.C., 7 mi/11.3 km N of Asheville; 35°42′N 82°33′W. Has mineral springs. Agr. area (tobacco, corn; dairying; cattle); mfg. (apparel, construction materials, lubrication equip., machinery, audio equip., consumer goods).

Webb, county (☐ 3,375 sq mi/8,741 sq km; 1990 pop. 133,239), S Texas; ⊙ Laredo; 27°46′N 99°19′W. Important U.S.-Mex. border city on the Rio Grande, which forms W and SW boundary of co. Irrigated agr. area in valley of Rio Grande, produces vegetables, melons; also some cotton, grain sorghums. Cattle ranching in uplands. Oil, natural-gas wells; caliche, stone, sand and gravel, uranium, coal deposits. L. Casa Blanca State Park in SW, near Laredo (Casa Blanca L. formed by Chacon Creek). Formed 1848.

Webb 1 town (1990 pop. 1,039), Houston co., SE Ala., 7 mi/11.3 km ENE of Dothan. Structural steel fabrication. **2** town (1990 pop. 167), Clay co., NW Iowa, 15 mi/24 km SSE of Spencer; 42°57′N 95°00′W. In livestock and grain area.

Webb, village (1990 pop. 605), Tallahatchie co., NW central Miss., 31 mi/50 km NNW of Greenwood; 33°57′N 90°20′W. RR junction to SE. Agr. (cotton, corn, soybeans; cattle).

Webb City, city (1990 pop. 7,449), Jasper co., SW Mo., near Spring R., suburb 5 mi/8 km NE of downtown Joplin; 37°08′N 94°28′W. Mfg. (shoes, clothing, industrial scales, wood furniture, explosives, dairy prods.); gravel pits. Plotted 1875.

Webb City, village (1990 pop. 99), Osage co., N Okla., 26 mi/42 km WNW of Pawhuska; 36°48′N 96°42′W. In agr. area. Kaw L. reservoir to W.

Webb, Lake, Franklin co., W central Maine, near Weld; 4 mi/6.4 km long. Drains through Webb R. c.15 mi/24 km S to the Androscoggin.

Webber, village (1990 pop. 39), Jewell co., N Kansas, 12 mi/19 km NE of Mankato, near Nebr. state line; 39°55′N 98°02′W. In grain and livestock region. Lovewell Reservoir and State Park to S.

Webbers Falls, village (1990 pop. 722), Muskogee co., E Okla., 21 mi/34 km SE of Muskogee, and on Arkansas R., opposite Gore; 35°30′N 95°09′W. Site of a flood-control reservoir on the Arkansas is nearby, headwaters of Robert S. Kerr L. reservoir.

Webbers Falls Reservoir, Muskogee co., E Okla., on Arkansas R., 19 mi/31 km SE of Muskogee; c.35 mi/56 km long; 35°33′N 95°10′W. Max. capacity 165,200 acre-ft. Verdigris R. enters upper reach from NW, forming c.35-mi/56-km-long arm. Formed by Webbers Falls Lock and Dam (54 ft/16 m high), built (1970) by the Army Corps of Engineers for navigation and power generation. City and Port of Muskogee on upper part of lake. Greenleaf State Park on E shore.

Webberville, village (1990 pop. 1,698), Ingham co., S central Mich., 20 mi/32 km ESE of Lansing; 42°40′N 84°10′W. In farm area.

Webbwood, town (1991 pop. 588), SE central Ont., central Canada, on Spanish R., and 45 mi/72 km WSW of Sudbury; 46°16′N 81°53′W. Nickel, copper, gold mining; lumbering.

Weber (WEE-buhr), county (☐ 659 sq mi/1,707 sq km; 1990 pop. 158,330), N Utah; ⊙ Ogden; 41°17′N 111°55′W. Agr. area drained by Weber and Ogden rivers. N and S borders converge at a point at center in Great Salt L. in W, incl. Fremont Isl. Cattle, sheep; alfalfa, barley, wheat, sugar beets, fruit, and vegetables are raised in irrigated area in vicinity of Ogden (important mfg. and shipping center). Fort Buenaventura State Historical Park at center; Ogden Bay Waterfowl Management Area in SW; part of Wasatch Range in E center; Wasatch Natl. Forest covers most of E ½ of co., includes ski resorts. Co. formed 1850.

Weber City, town (1990 pop. 1,377), Scott co., SW Va., residential suburb 5 mi/8 km N of Kingsport, Tenn., 2 mi/3.2 km SE of Gate City, just N of Tenn. state line, near North Fork Holston R.; 36°37′N 82°33′W.

Weber River (WEE-buhr), c.125 mi/200 km long, Utah; rises in small glacial lakes in the Uinta Mts., N central Utah; flows NW past Oakley, through Rockport L. reservoir, past Coalville, through Echo Reservoir, past Morgan and Ogden, where it receives the Ogden R. from the NE, then W to Ogden Bay, Great Salt L., in Weber co. The combined stream flows to the Great Salt L. The Weber has long been used for irrigation and is part of the U.S. Bureau of Reclamation's Weber basin project. Among the dams on the Weber are Wanship Dam (completed 1957) and Echo Dam (completed 1931).

Webster 1 county (☐ 210 sq mi/544 sq km; 1990 pop. 2,263), W Ga.; ⊙ Preston; 32°03′N 84°33′W. Coastal plain area intersected by Kinchafoonee R. Agr. (corn, cotton, wheat, peanuts); cattle, hogs; sawmilling. Formed 1853. **2** county (☐ 718 sq mi/1,860 sq km; 1990 pop. 40,342), central Iowa; ⊙ Fort Dodge; 42°25′N 94°10′W. Prairie agr. area (cattle, hogs, poultry; corn, soybeans, hay) drained by Des Moines R. Contains valuable gypsum bed (mined at Fort Dodge); also coal deposits, clay, sand and gravel. Dolliver Memorial and Brushy Creek state parks and Woodman Hollow State Preserve are all in SE ¼ of co. The co. experienced widespread flooding in 1993. Formed 1851. **3** county (☐ 335 sq mi/868 sq km; 1990 pop. 13,955), W Ky.; ⊙ Dixon; 37°31′N 87°40′W. Bounded NE by Green R., SW by Tradewater R. Rolling agr. area (burley and dark tobacco, sorghum, alfalfa, soybeans, wheat, corn; hogs, cattle); bituminous-coal mines, gas wells; timber. Mfg. at Providence. Formed 1860. **4** county (☐ 423 sq mi/1,096 sq km; 1990 pop. 10,222), central Miss.; ⊙ Walthall; 33°36′N 89°16′W. Drained by Big Black R. (forms most of S border). Agr. (cotton, corn, soybeans; cattle; timber). Natchez Trace (Natl.) Parkway passes N-S through E end of co. Formed 1874. **5** county (☐ 590 sq mi/1,528 sq km; 1990 pop. 23,753), S central Mo.; ⊙ Marshfield; 37°16′N 92°52′W. In the Ozarks; drained by James R. and Niangua R. Corn, wheat, fruit, tomatoes, apples; cattle; dairying; oak timber. Mfg. at Marshfield and Seymour; Amish community near Seymour. Formed 1855. **6** county (☐ 575 sq mi/1,489 sq km; 1990 pop. 4,279), S Nebr.; ⊙ Red Cloud; 40°10′N 98°30′W. Agr. area bounded S by Kansas; drained by Republican R. and Little Bear R. Cattle; dairying; hogs; corn, wheat, soybeans, sorghum, alfalfa. Limestone. Superior-Courtland Diversion Dam and Republican Valley State Wayside Area in SE. Formed 1871. **7** county (☐ 556 sq mi/1,440 sq km; 1990 pop. 10,729), central W. Va.; ⊙ Addison; 38°29′N 80°25′W. On Allegheny Plateau; drained by Elk, Gauley, Williams, and Cranberry rivers. Part of Monongahela Natl. Forest in S. Bituminous-coal mining; timber. Agr. (potatoes, alfalfa, hay); cattle. Hunting, fishing. Includes Holly R. State Park in N. Big Ditch Wildlife Management Area in SW. Formed 1860.

Webster, parish (☐ 626 sq mi/1,621 sq km; 1990 pop. 41,989), NW La.; ⊙ Minden; 32°37′N, 93°17′W. On Ark. state line (N) and partly bounded E by Black L. Bayou, and partly by Bodcau Bayou on W. Agr. (cotton, hay, sweet potatoes, vegetables, watermelons; cattle, horses, poultry; dairying). Oil and natural-gas wells and refineries; sand, gravel pits. Logging. Lumber and paper milling. Drained by Bayou Dorcheat (navigable). Named after Daniel Webster. Webster parish fair held annually. Includes part of Kisatchie Natl. Forest in E center; part of Bodcau State Wildlife Area on W border; L. Bistineau State Park in S. Formed 1871.

Webster 1 town (1990 pop. 103), Keokuk co., SE Iowa, 7 mi/11.3 km N of Sigourney; 41°26′N 92°10′W. Grain; livestock. **2** town (1990 pop. 16,196), Worcester co., S Mass., near the Conn. state line; 42°03′N 71°51′W. Mfg. (clothing, lenses, fabrics, textiles). The town was named for Daniel Webster and became a textile center in the early 19th cent. through the efforts of Samuel Slater, a pioneer in the U.S. textile industry. Includes village of East Village. Settled c.1713, set off from Dudley and Oxford and inc. 1832. **3** town (1990 pop. 1,405), Merrimack co., S central N.H., 12 mi/19 km NW of Concord; 43°18′N 71°43′W. Bounded E in part by Beaverdam Brook, drained by Blackwater R., part of Blackwater Reservoir in NW. Mfg. (x-ray chemicals and chemical mixers); agr. (nursery crops, vegetables, apples; livestock, poultry; dairying). L. Winnipocket in NW. **4** (WEB-stuhr), uninc. town (1990 pop. 1,000), Westmoreland co., SW Pa., 19 mi/31 km S of Pittsburgh, on Monongahela R. (bridged to Donora, to W); 40°11′N 79°50′W. Mfg. of nuclear machine parts; agr. includes corn; livestock; dairying. **5** town (1990 pop. 2,107), ⊙ Day co., NE S.Dak., 48 mi/77 km E of Aberdeen, in lake region (to E); 45°20′N 97°31′W. Resort; shipping point for livestock and poultry prods.; wheat, hogs; dairy prods.; mfg. (pillows, concrete, iron and aluminum foundry). Co. fairgrounds are here. Plotted 1880. **6** town (1990 pop. 4,678), Harris co., SE Texas, suburb 21 mi/34 km SE of downtown Houston, on Clear Creek; 29°31′N 95°07′W. Mfg. (medical equip., aircraft subassemblies, oil field equip.). NASA Johnson Space Center to NE. Houston Metro Airlines airfield to NW.

Webster 1 suburban village (☐ 35 sq mi/91 sq km; 1990 pop. 5,464), Monroe co., W N.Y., near L. Ontario, 10 mi/16 km ENE of Rochester; 43°12′N 77°25′W. Mfg.; in fruit-growing area. Inc. 1905. **2** village (1990 pop. 410), Jackson co., W N.C., on Tuckasegee R., 2 mi/3.2 km S of Sylva; 35°21′N 83°12′W. Cattle; corn, tobacco. **3** village (1990 pop. 623), Burnett co., NW Wis., in lake region, 23 mi/37 km WNW of Spooner; 45°52′N 92°21′W. Dairy prods., woodworking; mfg. (brakes and clutches, concrete). Governor Knowles State Forest and St. Croix Natl. Scenic Riverway to W and NW; St. Croix Indian Reservation to SE on Big Sand L.; numerous lakes in area.

Webster, Maine: see SABATTUS.

Webster City, city (1990 pop. 7,894), ⊙ Hamilton co., central Iowa, on Boone R., and 17 mi/27 km E of Fort Dodge; 42°27′N 93°49′W. RR junction; mfg. and trade center (farm machinery and equip., food prods., concrete, printing, lumber). Sand and gravel pits nearby. Has Iowa Central junior col. and a pioneer mus. Brushy Creek State Park to SW. Settled 1851, inc. 1874.

Webster Groves, city (1990 pop. 22,987), St. Louis co., E Mo., a residential suburb 10 mi/16 km SW of downtown St. Louis; 38°35′N 90°20′W. Mfg. (optical instruments; diversified light mfg.). It is the seat of Webster Univ. and Eden Theological Seminary. Inc. 1896.

Webster Lake, N.H.: see FRANKLIN.

Webster, Mount, N.H.: see PRESIDENTIAL RANGE.

Webster Reservoir (□ 18 sq mi/47 sq km), Rooks co., on South Fork Solomon R., 37 mi/60 km NNE of Hayes; 39°25′N 99°25′W. Max. capacity 401,650 acre-ft. Formed by Webster Dam (154 ft/47 m high), built (1956) by the Bureau of Reclamation for flood control; also used for irrigation. Webster State Park on N shore.

Webster Springs, town (1990 pop. 674), ⊙ Webster co., central W.Va., 67 mi/108 km ENE of Charleston, on Elk R. Resort area, with mineral springs. Hunting, fishing nearby. Agr. (potatoes); cattle. Mfg. (lumber; coal processing). Holly R. State Park to N. Inc. 1892 as Addison, still its official name.

Weches (WEE-siz), uninc. village (1990 pop. 26), Houston co., E Texas, 20 mi/32 km NE of Crockett, in Davy Crockett Natl. Forest, near Neches R. Nearby, in Tejas Mission State Historical Park, is replica of Mission San Francisco de los Tejas (1690), 1st Span. mission in E Texas. Community settled by 1847.

Wedgeport, town, SW N.S., E Canada, on the Atlantic, 10 mi/16 km SE of Yarmouth; 43°44′N 65°58′W. Fishing (noted for its tuna), lumbering. Irish moss center. Until 1909 called Tusket Wedge.

Wedowee (wee-DAU-wee), town (1990 pop. 796), ⊙ Randolph co., E Ala., near confluence of Little Tallapoosa and Tallapoosa rivers, 37 mi/60 km ESE of Talladega. Clothing mfg. Racial tensions flared in early 1994 when the high school principal threatened to cancel the school's prom if interracial couples attended. The high school was burned in Aug. 1994 in a fire set by an arsonist.

Weed, city (□ 3 sq mi/7.8 sq km; 1990 pop. 3,062), Siskiyou co., N Calif., at W base of Mt. Shasta, 25 mi/40 km SW of Yreka; 41°25′N 122°23′W. Cattle, sheep, lambs; grain, potatoes, onions; timber. RR junction to SE. Parts of Shasta Natl. Forest to E and W; Ski Shasta Ski Area to NE; Mt. Shasta to E. Col of Siskiyous 2-year).

Weed Heights, uninc. village (1990 pop. 230), Lyon co., W Nev., residential suburb 1 mi/1.6 km W of Yerington, near Walker R.

Weed Patch, uninc. town (1990 pop. 1,892), Kern co., S central Calif., 10 mi/16 km SSE of Bakersfield. Cotton, melons, vegetables, fruits, nuts, grain, potatoes; dairying.

Weedon, village (1991 pop. 653), S Que., E Canada, on St. Francis R., and 30 mi/48 km NE of Sherbrooke. Lumbering; dairying.

Weedsport, village (1990 pop. 1,996), Cayuga co., W central N.Y., on the N.Y. State Barge Canal, and 20 mi/32 km W of Syracuse; 43°02′N 76°33′W. Mfg. of feed, flour, furniture; lumber milling; agr. (dairy prods.; poultry; fruit). Inc. 1831.

Weehawken (wee-HAW-kuhn), township (1990 pop. 12,385), Hudson co., NE N.J., on the Hudson R. opposite Manhattan (N.Y. city; connected by the Lincoln Tunnel); 40°46′N 74°01′W. It is mostly residential. "Highwood," the James Gore King estate, was the scene in 1804 of the duel bet. Aaron Burr and Alexander Hamilton. A bronze bust commemorates Hamilton, who was fatally wounded. Inc. 1859.

Weekapaug (WEE-ka-pawg), coast village in Westerly town, Washington co., SW R.I., 5 mi/8 km SE of Westerly village. Beach resort.

Weeki Wachee (WEE-kee WACH-ee), village (□ 1 sq mi/2.6 sq km; 1990 pop. 53), Hernando co., W central Fla., 12 mi/19 km SW of Brooksville; 28°31′N 82°34′W.

Weeks, village, Iberia parish, S La., on Weeks Isl. (one of the Five Isls.), a salt dome in sea marshes just inland from E shore of Weeks Bay NE extension of Vermilion Bay, Gulf of Mexico, 13 mi/21 km S of New Iberia; 29°48′N 91°48′W. Elev. c.200 ft/61 m. RR terminus. Intracoastal Waterway runs bet. village and bay. Mfg. (infrared optical materials). Oil and natural-gas field. Salt mine nearby. Cypremort Point State Park to SW.

Weeksbury, town (1990 pop. 850), Floyd co., SE Ky., in Cumberland foothills, 16 mi/26 km SW of Pikeville, on Beaver Creek. Bituminous coal.

Weeksville, uninc. village, Pasquotank co., NE N.C., 6 mi/9.7 km SSE of Elizabeth City, on Pasquotank R. estuary, near Albermarle Sound. In agr. area. U.S. Coast Guard Air Station to N.

Weems, uninc. village, Lancaster co., E Va., 16 mi/26 km NNE of Gloucester, on Rappahannock R. estuary (Robert Norris Bridge to SE), at entrance to Corrotoman R. estuary; 37°39′N 76°26′W. Fish, oysters, crabs.

Weenusk (WEE-nuhsk), village, N Ont., central Canada, on Hudson Bay, at mouth of Winisk R.; 55°15′N 85°13′W. Hudson's Bay Company trading post.

Weeping Water, town (1990 pop. 1,008), Cass co., SE Nebr., 17 mi/27 km SW of Plattsmouth, and on Weeping Water Creek, near Missouri R.; 40°52′N 96°08′W. RR junction. Mfg. (phosphates, calcium carbonate, crushed limestone); grain; livestock; fruit. City inc. 1857.

Weeping Water Creek, c.40 mi/64 km long, SE Nebr.; rises E of Lincoln; flows E, past Weeping Water, to Missouri R. near Nebraska City.

Weggs, Cape, N Ungava Peninsula, NW Que., E Canada, on Hudson Strait; 62°28′N 73°43′W.

Weidman (WEED-man), village (1990 pop. 696), Isabella co., central Mich., 11 mi/18 km NW of Mount Pleasant; 43°41′N 84°58′W. In agr. area; mfg. (refrigerators and freezers); sawmill. Isabella Indian Reservation to N.

Weigelstown (WEI-guhls-toun), uninc. town (1990 pop. 8,665), York co., S Pa., residential suburb 5 mi/8 km NW of York on Conewago Creek; 39°59′N 76°49′W. Agr. includes dairying; livestock; poultry; grain, soybeans, apples.

Weimar (WEI-mahr), town (1990 pop. 2,052), Colorado co., S Texas, c.85 mi/137 km W of Houston; 29°41′N 96°46′W. Elev. 408 ft/124 m. In agr. area (rice, cotton, soybeans, sorghum, peanuts). Feed and egg processing, mfg. oil field packing and gaskets. Oil and natural gas. Laid out 1873.

Weiner (WEEN-uhr), village (1990 pop. 655), Poinsett co., NE Ark., 19 mi/31 km NNW of Jonesboro; 35°37′N 90°54′W. In agr. area; light mfg. (rice prods.). Earl Bliss Bayou DeView Wildlife Management Area to W.

Weinert, village (1990 pop. 235), Haskell co., NW central Texas, 60 mi/97 km N of Abilene; 33°19′N 99°40′W. In cotton, peanuts, grain; cattle; irrigation area.

Weippe (WE-eip-pe), village (1990 pop. 532), Clearwater co., N Idaho, 14 mi/23 km ESE of Orofino; 46°23′N 115°57′W. Cattle; barley, wheat, alfalfa; timber. Mfg. (lumber, cedar posts). Clearwater Natl. Forest to E; Nez Perce Indian Reservation to SW.

Weir 1 (WIR), village (1990 pop. 730), Cherokee co., extreme SE Kansas, 8 mi/12.9 km S of Pittsburg, near Mo. state line; 37°18′N 94°46′W. In diversified agr. region; mfg. of bricks and tiles. Clay pits in vicinity. **2** (WER), village (1990 pop. 525), Choctaw co., central Miss., 7 mi/11.3 km WSW of Ackerman, on Yockanookany R.; 33°15′N 89°17′W. Agr. (cotton, corn; cattle). **3** (WIR), village (1990 pop. 230), Williamson co., central Texas, near San Gabriel R.; 30°40′N 97°35′W. Agr. area (cotton, wheat, corn; cattle). Limestone.

Weir Farm (WIR), historic site, Fairfield co., SW Conn., c.8 mi/12.8 km N of Norwalk. Authorized 1990. Home and studio of the Amer. impressionist painter J. Alden Weir.

Weirgate (WIR-gait), uninc. village (1990 pop. 461), Newton co., E Texas, near Sabine R., 62 mi/100 km ESE of Lufkin. Timber; lumber processing. Sabine Natl. Forest to N.

Weirs Beach (WERZ), village, in Laconia, Belknap co., central N.H., suburb 5 mi/8 km N of Laconia, on SW shore of L. Winnipesaukee, at entrance to Paugus Bay. On site of anc. Native Amer. village and fish weirs. Tourist attractions include Weirs Beach Water Slide, Funspot Amusement Park, Surf Coaster; excursion boat tours of lake. Winnipesaukee Scenic RR passes through village, from Laconia to Meredith.

Weirton (WIR-tun), city (1990 pop. 22,124), Brooke and Hancock cos., N W.Va., in Northern Panhandle, 23 mi/37 km NNE of Wheeling, and 30 mi/48 km W of Pittsburgh, Pa., on the Ohio R. (Ohio state line, bridged to Steubenville, Ohio, 3 mi/4.8 km to SW), near mouth of Harmon Creek; 40°23′N 80°33′W. Coal mining. Mfg. (steel, chemicals, cans, hard chrome, slag cement, pet food, bakery prods., printing). Agr. (grain, apples, nursery crops); cattle; dairying. Mountaineer Racetrack, thoroughbred racing, to N; Raccoon Creek State Park (Pa.) to NE. Tomlinson Run State Park and Hillcrest Wildlife Management Area to N. Peter Tarr Iron Furnace (c.1790), made cannonballs for War of 1812. City limits extend 5 mi/8 km from Ohio state line (W) to Pa. state line (E). Settled 1790s, inc. 1947.

Weiser (WEE-zuhr), town (1990 pop. 4,571), ⊙ Washington co., W Idaho, on Snake R. (here forming Oregon state line), at mouth of Weiser R., and 60 mi/97 km NW of Boise; 44°15′N 116°58′W. Elev. 2,123 ft/647 m. RR junction in trade and fruit-shipping center for irrigated agr. area (fruit, alfalfa, potatoes, sugar beets; livestock); dairying; timber; metalworking; mfg. (homes, mobile homes, cabinet doors and shelving). Hq. Payette Natl. Forest. Intermountain Inst. is here. Mann Creek Reservoir to N, Paddock Valley and Crane Creek reservoirs to E. Hitt Mt. Ski Area to N. Laid out 1877, moved 1 mi/1.6 km W when fire destroyed original city (1890).

Weiser River, 90 mi/14 km long, Idaho; rises in Seven Devils Mts., N Adams co., W Idaho; flows SSW, past Council and Cambridge, turning W before entering Snake R. at Weiser. Receives Little Weiser R. just S of Cambridge. Used for irrigation.

Weiss Lake, Cherokee co., NE Ala., on manmade spillway bypassing the Coosa R., 14 mi/23 km NE of Gadsden; c.45 mi/72 km long; 34°10′N 85°44′W. Extends E into Floyd co., Ga. Little R. enters N. Max. capacity of 1,433,300 acre-ft. Formed by Weiss Dam (64 ft/20 m high), built (1961) by the Ala. Power Company for power generation and flood control.

Weissport (WEIS-port), borough (1990 pop. 472), Carbon co., E Pa., residential suburb 1 mi/1.6 km SE of Lehighton, across Lehigh R.; 40°49′N 75°42′W.

Wekusko Lake (wi-KOO-sko), W Man., central Canada, 65 mi/105 km NW of L. Winnipeg; 16 mi/26 km long, 8 mi/13 km wide. Drains NE into Nelson R. On E shore is Herb Lake village.

Welborn, village, Wyandotte co., NE Kansas, former suburb 5 mi/8 km NW of downtown Kansas City, Kansas. Part of city.

Welch, city (1990 pop. 3,028), ⊙ McDowell co., S W.Va., on Tug Fork R. 24 mi/39 km NW of Bluefield; 37°25′N 81°34′W. Semibituminous-coal-mining center, in Pocahontas coalfield. Timber. Mfg. (coal processing, printing and publishing). Agr. (apples). Berwind L. Wildlife Management Area to SW. State hosp. here. Settled 1885; inc. 1894.

Welch, village (1990 pop. 499), Craig co., NE Okla., 10 mi/16 km W of Miami; 36°52′N 95°05′W. In farm area; mfg. (saddle trees). Lead, coal mines.

Welchpool, Canada: see CAMPOBELLO ISLAND.

Welcome 1 town (1990 pop. 790), Martin co., S Minn., 8 mi/12.9 km W of Fairmont, on Lily Creek, near Iowa state line; 43°40′N 94°37′W. RR junction. Agr. (grain, soybeans; livestock); mfg. (air conditioners). Fox L. to W. **2** uninc. town (1990 pop. 3,377), Davidson co., central N.C., 12 mi/19 km S of Winston-Salem; 35°54′N 80°15′W. Agr. area (tobacco, grain, sweet potatoes, soybeans; poultry, livestock; dairying). Mfg. (metal fabricating, machining, alarm boxes, flour). **3** uninc. town (1990 pop. 6,560), Greenville co., NW S.C., residential suburb 3 mi/4.8 km WSW of downtown Greenville, near Saluda R.; 34°49′N 82°27′W. Co. fairgrounds here.

Weld, county (□ 4,021 sq mi/10,414 sq km; 1990 pop. 131,821), NE Colo.; ⊙ Greeley; 40°32′N 104°24′W. It is the 2d-largest co. in Colo. Coal-mining and irrigated agr. area, bordering on Wyo. and Nebr.; watered by South Platte R., Cache la Poudre R., Big and Little Thompson rivers. State's richest agr. co. Cattle, poultry, eggs; wheat, hay, corn, sunflowers, beans, sorghum, oats, barley, sugar beets, fruit, vegetables. Oil and natural gas. Barbour Ponds State Park in SW; all of Pawnee Natl. Grassland in N and NE; Lower Latham and Milton reservoirs in S; Empire and Riverside reservoirs in SE. Formed 1861.

Weld, town (1990 pop. 430), Franklin co., W central Maine, on L. Webb, and 14 mi/23 km WNW of Farmington; 44°42′N 70°27′W. Includes part of Mt. Blue State Park.

Weldon 1 town (1990 pop. 151), Decatur co., S Iowa, 9 mi/14.5 km S of Osceola, near sources of Weldon and Chariton rivers; 40°53′N 93°44′W. In livestock area. **2** town (1990 pop. 1,392), Halifax co., NE N.C., suburb 4 mi/6.4 km ESE of Roanoke Rapids, on Roanoke R.; 36°25′N 77°36′W. RR junction. Agr. area (cotton, tobacco, grain, potatoes; chickens, hogs; sweet potatoes). Mfg. (lumber, apparel, tungsten carbide inserts, plywood, stainless steel furniture, steel fabricating). Halifax Community Col.

Weldon, village (1990 pop. 361), De Witt co., central Ill., 12 mi/19 km ESE of Clinton; 40°07′N 88°45′W. Corn, soybeans.

Weldon River, c.70 mi/113 km long, S Iowa and N Mo.; rises near Weldon, Iowa; flows S to Thompson R. near Trenton, Mo. Partly canalized.

Weleetka (wuh-LEET-uh), town (1990 pop. 1,112), Okfuskee co., E central Okla., 10 mi/16 km SW of Henryetta, and on North Canadian R.; 35°20′N 96°08′W. Trade center for agr. area (melons, corn, grain, peanuts).

Welfare Island, N.Y.: see ROOSEVELT ISLAND.

Welland (WEL-uhnd), city (1991 pop. 47,914), SE Ont., central Canada, on the Welland Ship Canal; 42°59′N 79°15′W. It is a canal port and an industrial center. Cotton, iron, steel, and many other goods are made in Welland. The city is also a distributing center for a fruit-growing area.

Welland River, S Ont., central Canada; rises S of Hamilton; forms part of Welland Ship Canal, enters Niagara R. at Chippawa. Lower course also called Chippawa.

Welland Ship Canal, 27.6 mi/44.4 km long, SE Ont., central Canada, connecting L. Ontario with L. Erie and bypassing Niagara Falls. Built bet. 1914 and 1932 by Canada to replace a canal opened in 1829, it can accommodate (min. depth 27 ft/8 m) the largest lake ships. Its 8 locks overcome a 326-ft/99-m difference in level bet. the lakes. The L. Ontario entrance is near Port Dalhousie; the L. Erie entrance is at Port Colborne. It is part of the St. Lawrence Seaway system.

Wellersburg (WEL-luhrs-buhrg), borough (1990 pop. 213), Somerset co., SW Pa., 7 mi/11.3 km NW of Cumberland, Md., at Md. state line, on North Branch Jennings Run; 39°43′N 78°50′W.

Wellesley (WELZ-lee), town (1990 pop. 26,615), Norfolk co., E Mass., a residential suburb SW of Boston; 42°18′N 71°17′W. Its many educational institutions include several private preparatory schools, Babson Col. (map and globe mus. here), Wellesley Col. (art mus. here), and Mass. Bay Community Col. Environmental research done here. Settled 1660, inc. 1881.

Wellesley (WELZ-lee), village, S Ont., central Canada, on Nith R., and 14 mi/23 km W of Kitchener. Dairying, mixed farming, fruit growing.

Wellesley Island, one of largest of the Thousand Isls., Jefferson co., N N.Y., in the St. Lawrence R., at Ont. border, just W of Alexandria Bay; c.7.5 mi/12.1 km long, 1 mi/1.6 km–3 mi/4.8 km wide; 44°19′N 76°00′W. Thousand Isl. Park village (resort), and Watterson Point and Dewolf Point state parks (camping, bathing, fishing) are here. Isl. is crossed by roadway of Thousand Isls. Internatl. Bridge, whose spans link it to N.Y. shore and to Hill Isl., Ont. (N). Small Mary Isl. (state park here) is just off NE tip. Formerly Wells Isl.

Wellfleet (WEL-fleet), town (1990 pop. 2,493), Barnstable co., SE Mass., near N end of Cape Cod, 12 mi/19 km SSE of Provincetown; 41°55′N 70°02′W. Summer resort; fishing village. Formerly oystering, whaling, and fishing center. Includes South Wellfleet village, with remains of 1st U.S. transatlantic wireless station (1901). Part of Cape Cod Natl. Seashore. Settled c.1720, set off from Eastham 1763.

Wellfleet, village (1990 pop. 63), Lincoln co., S central Nebr., 25 mi/40 km S of North Platte, and on Medicine Creek, branch of Republican R.; 40°45′N 100°43′W.

Wellford, town (1990 pop. 2,511), Spartanburg co., NW S.C., 9 mi/14.5 km W of Spartanburg; 34°57′N 82°05′W. Mfg. includes nylon and polyester material, fabric, textile waste processing, polyethylene pipes, corrugated boxes. Agr. includes dairying, poultry; grains; hogs; peaches.

Wellington, county (□ 1,019 sq mi/2,639 sq km; 1991 pop. 159,609), S Ont., central Canada, on Grand R.; ⊙ Guelph; 43°48′N 80°30′W.

Wellington 1 village, SW B.C., W Canada, on SE Vancouver Isl., 4 mi/6 km NW of Nanaimo. Coal mining; mixed farming; timber. **2** village (1991 pop. 1,426), SE Ont., central Canada, on Wellington Bay of L. Ontario, 13 mi/21 km S of Belleville. Resort; dairying; fruit, vegetables.

Wellington, city (1990 pop. 779), Lafayette co., W central Mo., on Missouri R., and 7 mi/11.3 km WSW of Lexington; 39°08′N 93°59′W. Corn, wheat; cattle; mfg. (food processing equip.).

Wellington 1 town (1990 pop. 1,340), Larimer co., N Colo., 10 mi/16 km NNE of Fort Collins, on Boulder Creek; 40°42′N 105°00′W. Elev. c.5,201 ft/1,585 m. Supply point; sugar beets, grain, beans and vegetables. Mfg. (dry beans and vegetable processing). Lakes nearby, fishing, wildlife area. **2** town (1990 pop. 8,411), ⊙ Sumner co., S Kansas, on small affluent of Arkansas R., and 27 mi/43 km S of Wichita; 37°16′N 97°24′W. Trade and RR center, in wheat region. Mfg. (flour milling, aircraft parts wood prods., aerospace components). Called "wheat capital of the world." Grew as trading point on Chisholm Trail. Further growth followed development (in early 1930s) of oil fields in vicinity. Chisholm Trail marker. Laid out 1871, inc. 1872. **3** lumbering town (1990 pop. 270), Piscataquis co., central Maine, 20 mi/32 km SW of Dover-Foxcroft; 45°04′N 69°34′W. **4** uninc. town, Lyon co., W Nev., 18 mi/29 km SW of Yerington, on Walker R. Cattle, sheep; hay. Artesia L. to N; Topaz L. to SW. Toiyabe Natl. Forest to S and E. Fish hatchery to N. **5** town (1990 pop. 2,456), ⊙ Collingsworth co., extreme N Texas, on rolling prairie of the E Panhandle, 30 mi/48 km N of Childress, near Salt Fork of Red R.; 34°51′N 100°12′W. Elev. 2,078 ft/633 m. RR spur terminus; in cotton, wheat, peanuts, and cattle region. Light mfg. Oil and gas. Inc. 1909. **6** town (1990 pop. 1,632), Carbon co., E central Utah, 5 mi/8 km SE of Price, on Price R.; 39°32′N 110°44′W. Elev. 5,400 ft/1,646 m. Cattle; coal mining, carbon-dioxide gas. Settled 1880. Junction of RR spur to Sunnyside, to SE. **7** uninc. town, Fairfax co., NE Va., residential suburb, 4 mi/6.4 km S of Alexandria, 11 mi/18 km S of Washington, D.C., on Potomac R.; 38°17′N 77°03′W.

Wellington 1 village (1990 pop. 294), Iroquois co., E Ill., 17 mi/27 km S of Watseka; 40°32′N 87°40′W. In rich agr. area. **2** village (1990 pop. 593), Jefferson co., N Ky., a suburb 5 mi/8 km ESE of downtown Louisville; 38°13′N 85°40′W. Farmington Historical Home (1810) is here. **3** village (1990 pop. 593), Menifee co., E central Ky., 36 mi/58 km E of Winchester. Burley tobacco; cattle. Timber. Daniel Boone Natl. Forest to NW. **4** village (1990 pop. 4,140), Lorain co., N Ohio, 14 mi/23 km S of Elyria; 41°10′N 82°13′W. In dairying and grain area; makes castings, trucks, steel prods., glass cloth, livestock medicines.

Wellington Channel, central Franklin dist., N.W.T., N Canada, arm of the Arctic Ocean, bet. Cornwallis Isl. (W) and Devon Isl. (E); 120 mi/193 km long, 25 mi/40 km–40 mi/64 km wide; 75°30′N 93°30′W. Extends N from Barrow Strait; opens WNW on Queens Channel and Penny Strait (total length 80 mi/129 km).

Wellman, town (1990 pop. 1,085), Washington co., SE Iowa, 15 mi/24 km NE of Washington; 41°28′N 91°50′W. Processed turkeys, feed, concrete. Settled 1879, inc. 1880.

Wells, village, S central B.C., W Canada, in Cariboo Mts., 75 mi/121 km SE of Prince George. Elev. 4,063 ft/1,238 m. Gold and silver mining (declining). Gold-mining boom town in 1930s. Tourism, skiing. Barkerville Historical Park 5 mi/8 km E.

Wells 1 county (□ 370 sq mi/958 sq km; 1990 pop. 25,948), E Ind.; ⊙ Bluffton; 40°44′N 85°13′W. Agr. area (livestock; dairy prods.; soybeans, wheat, corn); mfg., including farm-prods. processing; limestone quarrying. Drained by Wabash and Salamonie rivers. Ouabache State Park E of Bluffton. Formed 1835. **2** county (□ 1,298 sq mi/3,362 sq km; 1990 pop. 5,864), formerly known as Gingras co., central N.Dak.; ⊙ Fessenden, in Drift Prairie; 47°34′N 99°40′W. Agr. area drained by Sheyenne and James rivers, connected by New Rockford Canal SE of Harvey. Dairy prods.; wheat, barley, flax, rye, hay, sunflowers; poultry, livestock (cattle). Formed 1873.

Wells 1 town (1990 pop. 7,778), York co., SW Maine, on the coast, and 13 mi/21 km SE of Alfred; 43°19′N 70°37′W. Includes summer resorts of Wells Beach and Ogunquit. Was a center of attack in Indian wars. Settled c.1640, inc. 1653. **2** town, Delta co., S Upper Peninsula, Mich., 2 mi/3.2 km N of Escanaba, on Little Bay De Noc. RR junction; 45°46′N 87°04′W. Hiawatha Natl. Forest to E. **3** town (1990 pop. 2,465), Faribault co., S Minn., 20 mi/32 km WNW of Albert Lea, near Maple Creek; 43°44′N 93°43′W. RR junction. Agr. trade center (corn, oats, peas, soybeans: livestock, poultry); mfg. (feeds, machining, canned peas and corn, chicken and turkey prods., prestressed concrete). Walnut L. Wildlife Area to SW; Freeborn L. to E. Settled before 1870. **4** town (1990 pop. 1,256), Elko co., NE Nev., 45 mi/72 km NE of Elko; 41°06′N 114°57′W. Elev. 5,630 ft/1,716 m. RR junction; cattle, sheep; hay. Est. 1869, consisted of Wells Fargo offices, saloon, and RR office in a boxcar; inc. 1927. East Humboldt Range is SW; Snow Water L. to S. **5** town (1990 pop. 761), Cherokee co., E Texas, 15 mi/24 km NW of Lufkin; 31°29′N 94°57′W. In agr. area; timber; mfg. lumber mill sorter slings. Davey Crockett Natl. Forest to SW. **6** town (1990 pop. 902), Rutland co., W Vt., on L. St. Catharine and N.Y. state line, 17 mi/27 km SW of Rutland; 43°25′N 73°12′W. Slate quarries.

Wells, village (1990 pop. 600), Hamilton co., E central N.Y., in the Adirondacks, on East Branch of Sacandaga R., and 32 mi/51 km N of Amsterdam; 43°27′N 74°16′W. Logging.

Wells Beach, Maine: see WELLS.

Wells Gray Provincial Park (□ 1,820 sq mi/4,714 sq km), E B.C., W Canada, in Cariboo Mts., 90 mi/145 km N of Kamloops. It rises to over 9,000 ft/2,743 m; 52°20′N 120°00′W. Has Hobson, Clearwater, Azure, and Murtle lakes. Hunting, fishing.

Wells Island, N.Y.: see WELLESLEY ISLAND.

Wells, Port, S Alaska, bay on NE shore of Kenai Peninsula, 60 mi/97 km ESE of Anchorage, opens into Prince William Sound; 60°54′N 148°12′W.

Wells River, village (1990 pop. 424), in Newbury town, Orange co., E Vt., 25 mi/40 km NE of Chelsea; c.15 mi/24 km long ; 44°08′N 72°04′W. Dairy prods. Wells R., rising in Groton State Forest, enters the Connecticut here.

Wellsboro (WELS-buhr-o), borough (1990 pop. 3,430), ⊙ Tioga co., N Pa., 37 mi/60 km NNW of Williamsport; 41°45′N 77°17′W. RR junction to N. Mfg. (machinery, food prods., lumber, printing and publishing, apparel); coal, natural gas in area. Agr. area (corn, hay; livestock; dairying). Parts of Tioga State Forest to N, W, and SE; Colton Point State Park to SW; Hills Creek State Park to NE. Settled c.1800, laid out 1806, inc. 1830.

Wellsburg 1 town (1990 pop. 682), Grundy co., central Iowa, 10 mi/16 km NW of Grundy Center; 42°25′N 92°55′W. In agr. area. **2** town (1990 pop. 3,385), ⊙ Brooke co., N W.Va., in Northern Panhandle, on the Ohio R. (Ohio state line), 15 mi/24 km NNE of Wheeling; 40°16′N 80°36′W. Mfg. (paper bags, corrugated boxes, glassware, storage cabinets). Coal mining; timber. Agr. (grain, apples); cattle; dairying. Brooks Glass Company (1879). Plotted 1790; chartered 1797.

Wellsburg, village (1990 pop. 617), Chemung co., S N.Y., on Chemung R., and 7 mi/11.3 km SE of Elmira, near Pa. state line; 42°00′N 76°43′W.

Wellsford, village, Kiowa co., S Kansas, 16 mi/26 km W of Pratt. In grain and livestock region.

Wellston, city (1990 pop. 6,049), Jackson co., S Ohio, 7 mi/11 km NE of Jackson; 39°07′N 82°32′W. Mfg. (machinery, clothing, store fixtures, tools); coal mines; vegetable gardens. Plotted 1874.

Wellston 1 town (1990 pop. 3,612), St. Louis co., E Mo., industrial and residential suburb 6 mi/9.7 km NW of downtown St. Louis; 38°40′N 90°17′W. Industrial base declined significantly in the 1970s. Mfg. (sheet metal fabrication, printing). Inc. since 1940. **2** town (1990 pop. 912), Lincoln co., central Okla., 28 mi/45 km ENE of Oklahoma City, and on the Deep Fork, Canadian R.; 35°41′N 97°03′W. In agr. and oil-producing area; mfg. (marble prods.).

Wellsville, city (1990 pop. 1,430), Montgomery co., E central Mo., 7 mi/11.3 km NNW of Montgomery City; 39°04′N 91°34′W. Corn, soybeans; hogs, cattle; mfg. (bricks, cement). Laid out 1856.

Wellsville 1 town (1990 pop. 1,563), Franklin co., E Kansas, 18 mi/29 km SW of Olathe; 38°43′N 95°04′W. In livestock and grain region. Mfg. (converted paper prods., windows). Oil wells nearby. Douglas State Fishing L. to NW. **2** town (1990 pop. 2,206), Cache co., N Utah, on Little Bear R., and 8 mi/12.9 km SW of Logan, 9 mi/14.5 km NE of Brigham City; 41°37′N 111°55′W. Elev. 4,495 ft/1,370 m. Trade and processing center for dairying and irrigated agr. area (vegetables, wheat, barley; cattle); cheese processing. Settled 1856 by Mormons, inc. 1866. Hyrum Reservoir and State Park is 3 mi/4.8 km E. Part of Wasatch Natl. Forest, including Wellsville Mt. Wilderness Area to W. Mts. to W rise 5,000 ft/1,524 m directly out of valley, one of sharpest elev. changes in world. **Wellsville 1** village (□ 2 sq mi/5.2 sq km; 1990 pop. 5,241), Allegany co., W N.Y., on Genesee R., and 21 mi/34 km SW of Hornell; 42°07′N 77°57′W. Mfg. of oilwell supplies, turbines, advanced technology industrial systems, industrial heat exchangers, wooden furniture and wood items; in farming and dairying area. Site of David A. Howe Lib. (1937), with mus. and theater. Special mus. (Mather Homestead) for visually impaired. Settled c.1795, inc. 1871. **2** village (1990 pop. 4,532), Columbiana co., E Ohio, on Ohio R., and 14 mi/23 km SE of Lisbon; 40°36′N 80°39′W. Pottery, chinaware, firebrick. Founded in late 18th cent.

Wellsville (WELS-vil), borough (1990 pop. 304), York co., S Pa., 12 mi/19 km WNW of York; 40°02′N 76°56′W. Mfg. (sheet metal fabricating, machinery, aluminum extensions and billets); agr. (grain; livestock; dairying). Ski Roundtree ski area to N; Gifford Pinchot State Park to NE.

Wellton, town (1990 pop. 1,066), Yuma co., SW Ariz., 28 mi/45 km E of Yuma, near Gila R.; 32°40′N 114°08′W. Elev. 250 ft/76 m. Irrigated agr. area (cotton, citrus, melons, vegetables, grain, dates; livestock). Barry M. Goldwater (formerly Luke) Air Force Range to S; Yuma Proving Ground (U.S. Army) to N.

Wellwood, village, SW Man., central Canada, 30 mi/48 km ENE of Brandon. Livestock; grain.

Welsh, town (1990 pop. 3,299), Jefferson Davis parish, SW La., 24 mi/39 km E of Lake Charles city; 30°14′N 92°49′W. In rice-producing area; sweet potatoes; cattle; crawfish, catfish; mfg. (irrigation pumps). Oil field nearby. Settled 1880; inc. 1889.

Welton, town (1990 pop. 177), Clinton co., E Iowa, 21 mi/34 km W of Clinton; 41°54′N 90°35′W. In agr. area.

Welwyn (WEL-win), agr. village (1991 pop. 161), SE Sask., W Canada, 14 mi/23 km NNE of Moosomin, near Man. border.

Wembley, town (1991 pop. 1,347), W Alta., W Canada, near B.C. border and near Wapiti R., 14 mi/23 km W of Grande Prairie; 55°09′N 119°09′W. Lumbering, mixed farming.

Wenatchee (wen-ACH-ee), city (1990 pop. 21,756), ⊙ Chelan co., central Wash., 93 mi/150 km ESE of Seattle, on the Columbia R., near mouth of Wenatchee R. (Rock Isl. Reservoir), in the E foothills of the Cascade Range; 47°26′N 120°19′W. RR junction to N. "Apple Capital of the World." It is a resort and a commercial center in a fertile fruit-growing valley famous for its apples, pears, grain; livestock. Wenatchee's major industries are food processing and the production of aluminum (at Malaga, to SE); mfg. (food prods., plastics, consumer goods, sportswear, dehydrated fruits, conveyors, printing and publishing). In the city are Wenatchee Valley Col., a horticulture experiment station, and North Central Wash. Mus. containing Native Amer. artifacts. Nearby Rock Isl. Dam, 13 mi/21 km ESE (downstream on Columbia R.), supplies Wenatchee with power. Wenatchee Natl. Forest to W and NW; Wenatchee Confluence State Park N of city; Lincoln Rock State Park and Rocky Reach Dam (Columbia R.) to N. Leavenworth Ski Area to NW; Badger Mt. Ski Area to NE; Mission Ridge Ski Area and Squilchuck State Park to S. Inc. 1892.

Wenatchee Mountains, Wash.: see CASCADE RANGE.

Wendell 1 town (1990 pop. 1,963), Gooding co., S Idaho, 20 mi/32 km NW of Twin Falls; 42°47′N 114°42′W. Mfg. (dried cranberries, bean soup mix; meatpacking). Malad Gorge State Park to NW; Thousand Springs outlet of Lord R., to SW. **2** (WEN-del), town (1990 pop. 899), Franklin co., N Mass., 12 mi/19 km E of Greenfield; 42°34′N 72°25′W. State forest here. **3** (WEND-uhl), town (1990 pop. 2,822), Wake co., central N.C., 14 mi/23 km E of Raleigh; 35°46′N 78°22′W. Agr. area (cotton, tobacco, soybeans, grain; poultry; livestock). Mfg. Settled c.1890; inc. 1903.

Wendell (WEN-duhl), village (1990 pop. 159), Grant co., W Minn., 7 mi/11.3 km WNW of Elbow Lake town, near Mustinka R. (forms Lightning L. to N); 46°02′N 96°05′W. Grain; dairying; poultry.

Wendover, town (1990 pop. 1,127), Tooele co., W Utah, 115 mi/185 km W of Salt Lake City, at Nev. state line; 40°44′N 114°02′W. Elev. 4,232 ft/1,290 m. Potash processing. To SE is Wendover Air Force Firing Range. Bonneville Salt Flats, in Great Salt L. Desert, are c.10 mi/16 km E. Silver Isl. Mts. to NE; Goshute Mts. to SW (Nev.). Bonneville Speedway 15 mi/24 km ENE.

Wendy Hills, town (1990 pop. 2,452), Jefferson co., N Ky., residential suburb 6 mi/9.7 km E of downtown Louisville.

Wenham (WEN-uhm), residential town (1990 pop. 4,212), Essex co., NE Mass., 5 mi/8 km N of Salem, on small lake; 42°36′N 70°53′W. Has old houses. Settled 1635, set off from Salem 1643.

Wenona (win-NO-nah), city (1990 pop. 950), Marshall co., N central Ill., 18 mi/29 km E of Lacon; 41°02′N 89°02′W. In agr. area; ships grain, soybeans. Inc. 1867.

Wenona, Md.: see DEAL ISLAND.

Wenonah (win-NO-nah), village (1990 pop. 40), Montgomery co., S central Ill., 17 mi/27 km NNE of Hillsboro; 39°19′N 89°17′W. In agr. and bituminous-coal area.

Wenonah (wi-NO-nuh), borough (1990 pop. 2,331), Gloucester co., SW N.J., on Mantua Creek, and 11 mi/18 km S of Camden; 39°47′N 75°09′W. Inc. 1883. In suburban area.

Wentworth, county (□ 458 sq mi/1,186 sq km), S Ont., central Canada, at head of L. Ontario; ⊙ Hamilton; 43°15′N 80°00′W.

Wentworth 1 town (1990 pop. 138), Newton co., SW Mo., 8 mi/12.9 km NW of Monett; 36°59′N 94°04′W. **2** town (1990 pop. 630), Grafton co., W N.H., 12 mi/19 km WNW of Plymouth; 43°51′N 71°55′W. Drained by Baker R. and its South Branch. Nursery crops; cattle, poultry; dairying; timber. Plummer Ledge Natual Area on N boundary; part of White Mt. Natl. Forest in NE.

Wentworth 1 uninc. village, ⊙ Rockingham co., N N.C., 7 mi/11.3 km NW of Reidsville. Tobacco; grain; livestock. Rockingham Community Col. **2** village (1990 pop. 181), Lake co., E S.Dak., 8 mi/12.9 km E of Madison; 44°00′N 96°57′W. In agr. area. L. Madison to E.

Wentworth, Lake, Carroll co., E N.H., resort lake in town of Wolfeboro, drains into L. Winnipesaukee, 2 mi/3.2 km to SW; 4 mi/6.4 km long, 2 mi/3.2 km wide. Wentworth State Park on N shore.

Wentworths Location, town, Coos co., NE N.H., 26 mi/42 km NNE of Berlin, bounded E by Maine state line, drained by Magalloway R. Mfg. (lumber, software); livestock; timber. Greenough Ponds in W. Big Isl. State Forest in E. Sometimes called Wentworth.

Wentzville, city (1990 pop. 5,088), St Charles co., E Mo., 20 mi/32 km W of St. Charles; 38°48′N 90°51′W. Corn, soybeans; mfg. (motor vehicles). Tobacco-mfg. center in 1870s. Plotted 1855.

Wepawaug River (wep-e-WAHG), c.20 mi./32 km long, SW Conn.; rises near Woodbridge; flows SSW to L.I. Sound at Milford.

Werner, village, Dunn co., W central N. Dak., 36 mi/58 km NNE of Dickinson, and on Spring Creek; 47°21′N 102°27′W. Little Missouri Bay of L. Sakakawea Reservoir to N.

Wernersville (WER-nuhrs-vil), borough (1990 pop. 1,934), Berks co., SE central Pa., 8 mi/12.9 km W of Reading; 40°19′N 76°04′W. Agr. (apples, grain; poultry, livestock; dairying); limestone. Resort. State Hosp. to W; Blue Marsh L. reservoir (State Recreation Area) to N. Founded c.1855.

Wescosville (WES-kos-vil), uninc. town (1990 pop. 1,200), Lehigh co., E Pa., residential suburb 5 mi/8 km SW of Allentown; 40°34′N 75°33′W. Trach Cellar Winery to W; Bieber Farmhouse dating back to the 1700s to the E.

Weskeag River (WES-keg), Knox co., S Maine, 4-mi/6.4-km inlet forming harbor of South Thomaston, just SW of Rockland.

Weslaco, city (1990 pop. 21,877), Hidalgo co., extreme S Texas, 14 mi/23 km W of McAllen; 26°09′N 97°58′W. Elev. 70 ft/21 m. Rio Grande (Mex. border) 8 mi/12.9 km S. In the irrigated region of the lower Rio Grande valley. Agr. (cotton, vegetables); mfg. (sheet metal, tortillas, concrete, corrugated containers, metal cans, work pants). The city's name was derived from the initials of the W. E. Stewart Land Company, which promoted the townsite in 1917; inc. 1921. Weslaco is linked to Mex. by an internatl. bridge (10 mi/16 km SSE at Progreso). Area is home to some 6,000 "Winter Texans."

Wesley 1 town, Emanual co., E central Ga., 7 mi/11.3 km S of Swainsboro; 32°29′N 82°19′W. **2** town (1990 pop. 444), Kossuth co., N Iowa, 12 mi/19 km E of Algona; 43°05′N 93°59′W. In livestock and grain area. **3** town (1990 pop. 146), Washington co., E Maine, 20 mi/32 km NW of Machias; 44°55′N 67°39′W. In blueberry-growing region.

Wesley, village (1991 pop. 1,917), NE Dominica, B.W.I., 20 mi/32 km NNE of Roseau; 15°34′N 61°19′E. Coconuts, limes.

Wesley Hills, village (□ 3 sq mi/7.8 sq km; 1990 pop. 4,305), Rockland co., SE N.Y., 2 mi/3.2 km NW of Viola, 10 mi/16 km NW of Nyack; 41°09′N 74°04′W.

Wesleyville, town (1991 pop. 1,126), E N.F., E Canada, on N side of Bonavista Bay, 40 mi/64 km NW of Cape Bonavista; 49°09′N 119°09′W. Fishing port; lumbering.

Wesleyville (WES-lee-vil), borough (1990 pop. 3,650), Erie co., NW Pa., residential suburb 3 mi/4.8 km E of downtown Erie; 42°08′N 80°00′W. Drained by Fourmile Creek. L. Erie 1 mi/1.6 km to NW. RR shops. Pa. State Univ., Behrend Campus, to SE. Settled 1797, laid out 1828, inc. 1912.

Wesserunsett Lake (wes-uh-RUHN-set), in Somerset co., central Maine, resort lake 4 mi/6.4 km NW of Skowhegan; 3.5 mi/5.6 km long.

Wessington, town (1990 pop. 265), Beadle and Hand cos., E central S.Dak., 25 mi/40 km WNW of Huron, and on Cain Creek; 44°27′N 98°42′W. Mfg. (gates and animal stalls).

Wessington Springs, town (1990 pop. 1,083), ⊙ Jerauld co., SE central S.Dak., 25 mi/40 km SW of Huron; 44°04′N 98°34′W. In agr. area. City founded 1880.

Wesson (WES-uhn), town (1990 pop. 1,510), Copiah co., SW Miss., 41 mi/66 km SSW of Jackson; 31°41′N 90°24′W. Agr. (cotton, corn; cattle; dairying; timber); mfg. (jeans, power distribution equip.). Seat of Copiah-Lincoln Col. (2-year).

Wesson (WES-uhn), village, Union co., S Ark., 9 mi/14.5 km SW of El Dorado, near La. state line.

West, town (1990 pop. 2,515), McLennan co., E central Texas, 17 mi/27 km N of Waco; 31°48′N 97°05′W. Agr. (cotton, grain; cattle, hogs); dairying; feed processing, pork processing, printing. Settled 1878, inc. 1894.

West, village (1990 pop. 184), Holmes co., central Miss., 32 mi/51 km SE of Greenwood, and on Big Black R. Agr. (cotton, corn; cattle).

West Acton, Mass.: see ACTON.

West Albany, suburb, Albany co., E N.Y., just NW of downtown Albany; 42°41′N 73°47′W.

West Alexander, borough (1990 pop. 301), Washington co., SW Pa., 15 mi/24 km WSW of Washington, near W.Va. state line; 40°06′N 80°30′W. Mfg. (metal and plastic prods.); agr. (corn, hay; livestock; dairying). Dutch Fork L. reservoir to NE; several covered bridges in area, esp. to S.

West Alexandria, village (1990 pop. 1,460), Preble co., W Ohio, 5 mi/8 km E of Eaton; 39°45′N 84°32′W. In agr. area.

West Allis, city (1990 pop. 63,221), Milwaukee co., SE Wis., a residential and industrial suburb 4 mi/6.4 km WSW of downtown Milwaukee; 43°00′N 88°01′W. A banking and mfg. (motor vehicles, food prods., tools, machines) city. State fairgrounds. Inc. 1902.

West Aspetuck River, c.15 mi/24 km long, W Conn.; rises in W Litchfield co. E of Kent; flows generally S, joining East Aspetuck R. just above junction with the Housatonic near New Milford. Aspetuck R. is S, in Fairfield co.

West Athens, uninc. town (1990 pop. 8,859), Los Angeles co., S Calif., residential suburb 11 mi/18 km SSW of downtown Los Angeles, and 4 mi/6.4 km N of Gardena; 33°55′N 118°18′W.

West Auburn, Mass.: see AUBURN.

West Baden Springs or **West Baden**, town (1990 pop. 675), Orange co., S Ind., on Lost R., and 8 mi/12.9 km W of Paoli; 38°34′N 86°37′W. Mineral springs. Hoosier Natl. Forest nearby. Old resort area. Settled 1851.

West Bainbridge (DAIN-brij), village, Decatur co., SW Ga., near Bainbridge; 30°55′N 84°35′W.

West Baldwin, hamlet of Baldwin township, Cumberland co., SW Maine, on Saco R., c.25 mi/40 km WNW of Portland; 43°49′N 70°46′W.

West Baraboo (BER-ruh-boo), town (1990 pop. 1,021), Sauk co., S central Wis., suburb 1 mi/1.6 km W of Baraboo; 43°28′N 89°46′W. Mirror L. State Park to NW; Devils L. State Park to SE. Dairying. Tourism.

West Barnet, Vt.: see BARNET.

West Barnstable, Mass.: see BARNSTABLE.

West Barrington, neighborhood, in Barrington town, Bristol co., R.I., on Narragansett Bay, 7 mi/11.3 km S of Providence.

West Baton Rouge (BA-tuhn ROOZH), parish (□ 201 sq mi/521 sq km; 1990 pop. 19,419), SE central La.; ☉ Port Allen; 30°27′N, 91°13′W. Bounded E by the Mississippi. Agr. (corn, hay, soybeans, sugarcane; cattle, horses, exotic fowl), crawfish; logging, mfg. (food prods., chemicals, petroleum and coal prods., metal prods., lumber); clay deposits. Has many Indian mounds. Smallest parish in La. Formed 1807.

West Battle Lake, Minn.: see BATTLE LAKE.

West Bay, town (1989 pop. 5,632), in Cayman Isls., crown colony of Great Britain, West Indies, on W coast of Grand Cayman isl.; 19°22′N 81°25′W. Turtle Farm is a tourist attraction and conservation center.

West Bay, Texas: see GALVESTON BAY.

West Belmar, village (1990 pop. 2,498), Monmouth co., E N.J., near Belmar, and 13 mi/21 km ESE of Freehold; 40°10′N 74°02′W. Chiefly residential.

West Bend, city (1990 pop. 23,916), ☉ Washington co., E Wis., on the West Branch of Milwaukee R.; 43°25′N 88°10′W. Farm implements, dairy items, electronic components, and leather prods. are made here. Lizard Mound State Park to NE, Sunburst Ski Area to NW; S end of Kettle Morraine State Forest (N unit) to N; Silver, Little Cedar, and Big Cedar lakes to SW. Inc. 1885, consolidated with Barton in 1961.

West Bend, town (1990 pop. 862), Palo Alto and Kossuth cos., NW Iowa, 16 mi/26 km SE of Emmetsburg; 42°57′N 94°27′W. Feed milling; soybean prods. Grotto of the Redemption to N.

West Bishop, uninc. town (1990 pop. 2,908), Inyo co., SE Calif., residential suburb 2 mi/3.2 km WSW of Bishop, near Bishop Creek; 37°22′N 118°27′W. Bishop Indian Reservation to NE. Cattle.

West Blocton, town (1990 pop. 1,468), Bibb co., W central Ala., 12 mi/19 km N of Centreville. Coal mines; clothing mfg.

West Bloomfield Township, city (1990 pop. 54,843), Oakland co., SE Mich., suburb 20 mi/32 km NW of downtown Detroit and 6 mi/9.7 km SW of Pontiac; 42°34′N 83°22′W. Mfg. of wood prods. and furniture. Source of R. Rouge. Numerous small lakes in N part of city and to N, W, and E. Proud L. State Recreation Area to W; Bloomer State Park No. 1 in W part of city, Dodge Bros. State Park. No. 3 in N part.

West Bountiful, town (1990 pop. 4,477), Davis co., N Utah, suburb 8 mi/12.9 km N of downtown Salt Lake City, W of Bountiful, near Great Salt L., drained by Holbrook Creek; 40°53′N 111°54′W. Wasatch Range and Natl. Forest to E; Farmington Bay Waterfowl Management Area to NW. Inc. 1948.

West Boylston (BOILS-tuhn), residential town (1990 pop. 6,611), Worcester co., central Mass., on Wachusett Reservoir, and 6 mi/9.7 km N of Worcester; 42°22′N 71°47′W. Settled 1642, inc. 1808. Includes village of Oakdale.

West Branch 1 town (1990 pop. 1,908), Cedar co., E Iowa, 9 mi/14.5 km E of Iowa City ; 41°40′N 91°20′W. In agr. area. Mfg. (urethane foam prods.; printing; feeds). Herbert Hoover was b. here in 1874. Herbert Hoover Natl. Hist. Site with 187 acres/76 ha, including birthplace, Friends Meetinghouse, mus., and gravesite of President Hoover and his wife. **2** town (1990 pop. 1,914), ☉ Ogemaw co., NE central Mich., 47 mi/76 km NNW of Bay City, and on small West Branch of Rifle R.; 44°16′N 84°14′W. In recreation and agr. area (cattle; grain); mfg. (wood and lumber prods., automotive parts, garage doors, cutting tools) Annual trout festival held here. Airport to SE. Inc. as village 1885, as city 1905.

West Brewster, Mass.: see BREWSTER.

West Bridgewater, residential town (1990 pop. 6,389), Plymouth co., E Mass., 24 mi/39 km S of Boston, just S of Brockton; 42°01′N 71°02′W. Agr. (produce; dairying; poultry). Massasoit's deed to settlers is in historical mus. here. Ames-Nowell State Park nearby. Settled 1651, set off from Bridgewater 1822. Includes village of West Bridgewater.

West Brookfield, agr. town (1990 pop. 3,532), Worcester co., central Mass., on Quaboag R., and 17 mi/27 km W of Worcester; 42°15′N 72°10′W. Settled 1664, inc. 1848. Includes village of West Brookfield.

West Brooklyn, village (1990 pop. 164), Lee co., N Ill., 19 mi/31 km ESE of Dixon; 41°41′N 89°09′W. In agr. area.

West Brownsville, borough (1990 pop. 1,170), Washington co., SW Pa., on Monongahela R. opposite (1 mi/1.6 km NW of) Brownsville; 40°01′N 79°53′W. Mfg. (fiberglass prods.); agr. (apples, corn, hay; livestock; dairying); bituminous coal in area. James G. Blaine b. here, 1830. Maxwell Lock and Dam 4 mi/6.4 km WSW, on Monongahela R. Laid out 1831, inc. c.1852.

West Buechel (BYOO-chuhl), town (1990 pop. 1,587), Jefferson co., N Ky., residential suburb 6 mi/9.7 km SE of downtown Louisville; 38°12′N 85°40′W.

West Burke, Vt.: see BURKE.

West Burlington, town (1990 pop. 3,083), Des Moines co., SE Iowa, adjoins Burlington on W; 40°49′N 91°10′W. RR shops; mfg. (electronic prods. and equip., textiles; precast concrete prods.). Has Southeastern Community Col. and Catholic grotto. Founded 1883.

West Cache Creek, Okla.: see CACHE CREEK.

West Caicos, uninhabited island (□ 10.4 sq mi/26.9 sq km), Turks and Caicos Isls., crown colony of Great Britain, West Indies, SSW of Blue Hills isl., on Caicos Passage; 8 mi/12.9 km long, 2 mi/3.2 km wide; 21°40′N 72°30′W. Site of many shipwrecks, which attract divers and treasure hunters. Beaches, reefs, and small airstrip.

West Caldwell (KAWLD-wuhl), borough (1990 pop. 10,422), Essex co., NE N.J., a residential suburb of Newark and N.Y. city, 9 mi/14.5 km NNW of Newark; 40°51′N 74°17′W. Light mfg. Inc. 1904.

West Camp, village (1990 pop. 400), Ulster co., SE N.Y., on W bank of the Hudson R., and 15 mi/24 km N of Kingston; 42°07′N 73°56′W. In summer-resort and agr. area.

West Canada Creek, c.75 mi/121 km long, N.Y.; rises in lakes of the Adirondacks in central Hamilton co.; flows generally SW to Prospect, then SE, past Middleville, to Mohawk R. at Herkimer Dam, 2 mi/3.2 km E of Prospect. Impounds Hinckley Reservoir (□ c.5 sq mi/13 sq km; c.7 mi/11.3 km long). At Trenton Falls (c.12 mi/19 km N of Utica) is a scenic gorge, with several falls supplying power to Utica.

West Canton (KAN-tuhn), uninc. town (1990 pop. 1,119), Haywood co., W N. C., suburb 3 mi/4.8 km W of Canton, near Pigeon R.; 35°32′N 82°52′W.

West Cape May, borough (1990 pop. 1,026), Cape May co., extreme S N.J., just W of Cape May city; 38°56′N 74°56′W.

West Caroga Lake, N.Y.: see CAROGA LAKE.

West Carroll, parish (□ 356 sq mi/922 sq km; 1990 pop. 12,093), NE La., ☉ Oak Grove; 32°52′N, 91°23′W. Bounded E by Bayou Macon, W by Boeuf R., N by Ark. state line. Agr. (cotton, peaches, corn, sorghum, wheat, rice, soybeans, sweet potatoes, vegetables; cattle, hogs; dairying). Mfg. (leather gloves and mittens, prefabricated metal bldgs.); logging. Oil and natural-gas wells. Formed 1877. Includes Poverty Point State Commemorative Area in SE.

West Carrollton City, city (1990 pop. 14,403), Montgomery co., W Ohio, near Great Miami R., and 7 mi/11 km SSW of downtown Dayton; 39°40′N 84°15′W. Paper prods. Sand and gravel pits nearby.

West Carson, uninc. city (1990 pop. 20,143), Los Angeles co., S Calif., residential suburb 13 mi/21 km SSW of downtown Los Angeles, 2 mi/3.2 km W of Carson; 33°49′N 118°17′W. Bounded by Los Angeles on W, Harbor Freeway on E.

West Carthage, village (□ 1 sq mi/2.6 sq km; 1990 pop. 2,166), Jefferson co., N N.Y., on Black R., opposite Carthage, and 15 mi/24 km E of Watertown; 43°58′N 75°37′W. Inc. 1888.

West Chatham, Mass.: see CHATHAM.

West Chester, town (1990 pop. 178), Washington co., SE Iowa, 7 mi/11.3 km WNW of Washington; 41°20′N 91°49′W.

West Chester, borough (1990 pop. 18,041), ☉ Chester co., SE Pa., suburb 28 mi/45 km W of downtown Philadelphia; 39°57′N 75°36′W. West Chester is a trade and processing center. Diversified mfg.; esp. high-technology mfg. Agr. (apples, mushrooms, vegetables, soybeans, grain; poultry, livestock; dairying). Seat of West Chester Univ. of Pa.; Brandywine State Historical Park to S on Brandywine Creek, on the site of the battle of Brandywine (1777); West Chester Airport to NE; Cheyney Univ. of Pa., 4 mi/6.4 km to SE; the Turk's Head Inn (1747), an early stagecoach stop, still stands. Inc. 1799.

West Chicago, city (1990 pop. 14,796), Du Page co., NE Ill., 3 mi/4.8 km W of Wheaton; 41°53′N 88°13′W. Inc. 1873. Mostly residential, the city produces map prods.

West Chop, Mass.: see TISBURY.

West City, village (1990 pop. 747), Franklin co., S Ill., just W of Benton; 38°00′N 88°57′W. In bituminous-coal-mining, oil, and agr. area. Inc. 1911.

West Claremont, N.H.: see CLAREMONT.

West College Corner, town (1990 pop. 686), Union co., E Ind., on Ohio state line, adjacent to Col. Corner (Ohio), and 6 mi/9.7 km SE of Liberty; 39°34′N 84°49′W.

West Columbia, city (1990 pop. 10,588), Lexington co., central S.C., residential suburb on Congaree R., formed by the junction of Broad and Saluda rivers upstream; 33°59′N 81°04′W. Diverse mfg. Riverbanks Zoological and Botanical Gardens to W. Renamed 1938 from Brookland or New Brookland.

West Columbia, town (1990 pop. 4,372), Brazoria co., S Texas, c.45 mi/72 km SSW of Houston, 12 mi/19 km W of Angleton, in Brazosport area, near Brazos R.; 29°08′N 95°39′W. Elev. 40 ft/12 m. Oil center in agr. area (sorghum, rice; cattle); mfg. (concrete, tortillas). Founded 1826; with neighboring East Columbia (1990 uninc. pop. 95) on Brazos, was important in Austin's colony, and briefly (1836) the capital of Texas Republic. Revived after 20th-cent. oil development; inc. 1938. Varner-Hogg State Historical Park here.

West Compton, uninc. town (1990 pop. 5,451), Los Angeles co., S Calif., residential suburb 9 mi/14.5 km S of downtown Los Angeles and 3 mi/4.8 km WNW of Compton; 33°54′N 118°16′W. Bounded by Los Angeles on W and N.

West Concord, town (1990 pop. 871), Dodge co., SE Minn., 24 mi/39 km WNW of Rochester; 44°08′N 92°54′W. Agr. (grains, soybeans, peas; livestock, poultry; dairying); mfg. (feeds).

West Conshohocken (CAHN-shuh-HAH-ken), borough (1990 pop. 1,294), Montgomery co., SE Pa., suburb 11 mi/18 km NW of downtown Philadelphia, on Schuylkill R. opposite Conshohocken (1 mi/1.6 km to E); 40°04′N 75°19′W. Mfg. (commercial printing, creosote, solder paste, medical prods.). Appleford-Parsons Bank Arboretum to S. Settled 1850, inc. 1874.

West Cote Blanche Bay (KOT BLAHNSH), arm of the Gulf of Mexico, in St. Mary parish, S La., c.20 mi/32 km S of New Iberia, betw. Marsh Isl. (SW) and marshy mainland coast (N); c.15 mi/24 km long E-W, 11 mi/18 km wide; 29°40′N, 91°44′W. Opens into Vermilion Bay (W), East Cote Blanche Bay (SE). Swimming and fishing on NW shore. Cypremort Point State Park on W side.

West Covina, city (□ 16 sq mi/41 sq km; 1990 pop. 96,086), Los Angeles co., S Calif., suburb 18 mi/29 km E of downtown Los Angeles, in the San Gabriel valley; 34°03′N 117°55′W. Mfg. (power transformers, printing and publishing). Drained by Walnut Creek. Before World War II, West Covina was a small rural community where walnuts, wheat, and livestock were raised. Urban and economic growth occurred after 1945, as the Los Angeles metropolitan area began intense development. Primarily residential, the city increased in pop. by more than 40% bet. 1970 and 1990. San Jose Hills in S. Settled 1905, inc. 1923.

West Crossett (KRAWS-et), village (1990 pop. 2,019), Ashley co., SE Ark.,1 mi/1.6 km W of Crossett; 33°08′N 92°01′W.

West Danville, village, Boyle co., central Ky., just W of Danville, in outer Bluegrass agr. region.

West Danville, Vt.: see DANVILLE.

West De Pere, Wis.: see DE PERE.

West Decatur, Pa.: see BLUE BALL.

West Dennis, Mass.: see DENNIS.

West Deptford, township (1990 pop. 19,380), Gloucester co., S N.J., 5 mi/8 km S of Gloucester city; 39°50′N 75°11′W. Inc. 1871.

West Des Moines, city (1990 pop. 31,702), Polk co., S central Iowa, a growing suburb 5 mi/8 km W of Des Moines; 41°34′N 93°45′W. Diversified mfg.; hybrid seed corn and sorghum. Walnut Woods State Park to S. Inc. 1893 as Valley Junction, renamed 1938.

West Des Moines River, Minn. and Iowa: see DES MOINES R.

West Dundee (duhn-DEE), village (1990 pop. 3,728), Kane co., NE Ill., on Fox R. (bridged here), just N of Elgin, satellite community c.36 mi/58 km WNW of Chicago; 42°06′N 88°17′W. In agr. area (dairy prods.; livestock). Settled in 1830s; inc. 1887. With East Dundee, across river, it composes community known as Dundee.

West Easton, borough (1990 pop. 1,163), Northampton co., E Pa., on Lehigh R., residential suburb 2 mi/3.2 km W of Easton, on Lehigh R.; 40°40′N 75°14′W. Inc. 1890.

West Eaton, resort village (1990 pop. 500), Madison co., central N.Y., 29 mi/47 km SE of Syracuse; 42°51′N 75°39′W. Lakes nearby.

West Edmonton Mall, shopping mall, Edmonton, Alta., W Canada, located W side of 170 St., 5 mi/8 km W of downtown. Dubbed "the world's largest mall" with 800 stores, 100 restaurants, ice arena, water and amusement park, aviary, aquarium, hotel. Constructed in phases 1981–1988.

West Elizabeth, borough (1990 pop. 634), Allegheny co., SW Pa., suburb 13 mi/21 km SSE of downtown Pittsburgh, on Monongahela R. (bridged to Elizabeth to E); 40°16′N 79°53′W. Mfg. (asphalt, hydrocarbon resin). Laid out 1833, inc. 1848.

West Elk Mountains, Colo.: see ELK MOUNTAINS.

West Elkton, village (1990 pop. 208), Preble co., W Ohio, 10 mi/16 km WNW of Middletown; 39°35′N 84°33′W. In agr. area.

West Elmira (el-MEI-ruh), village (□ 3 sq mi/7.8 sq km; 1990 pop. 5,218), Chemung co., S N.Y., just W of Elmira; 42°05′N 76°50′W.

West End, town, Grand Bahama Isl., NW Bahama Isls., port at W tip of the isl., 60 mi/97 km E of West Palm Beach, Fla., and 155 mi/249 km NW of Nassau; 26°11′N 78°58′W.

West End 1 village (□ 3 sq mi/7.8 sq km; 1990 pop. 1,825), Otsego co., central N.Y., W extension of Oneonta; 42°28′N 75°05′W. **2** uninc. village, Moore co., central N.C., 11 mi/18 km WNW of Southern Pines. Timber; tobacco; livestock. Mfg. (woodworking, machinery, commercial printing, wooden furniture, roof and floor trusses).

West End Anniston, suburb of Anniston, Calhoun co., E Ala., bet. Anniston and the Anniston Army Depot.

West Fairlee, town (1990 pop. 633), Orange co., E Vt., on Ompompanoosuc R., and 12 mi/19 km SE of Chelsea; 43°56′N 72°13′W. L. Fairlee is SE, in agr. and resort region.

West Fairview, borough (1990 pop. 1,403), Cumberland co., S central Pa., residential suburb 2 mi/3.2 km NW of downtown Harrisburg, on Susquehanna R. opposite Harrisburg, at mouth of Conodoguinet Creek; 40°16′N 76°55′W. Laid out 1815.

West Falmouth, Mass.: see FALMOUTH.

West Fargo, city (1990 pop. 12,287), Cass co., E N.Dak. suburb, 5 mi/8 km W of Fargo on Sheyenne R.; 46°52′N 96°54′W. RR junction; mfg. (farm equip. parts, sugar beet prods., steel prods.); meatpacking, agr. distributing.

West Farmington, village (1990 pop. 542), Trumbull co., NE Ohio, 13 mi/21 km NW of Warren, and on Grand R.; 41°23′N 80°58′W. In agr. area.

West Feliciana (fuh-LEE-shee-an-uh), parish (□ 410 sq mi/1,062 sq km; 1990 pop. 12,915), SE central La.; ⊙ St. Francisville; 30°47′N, 91°23′W. Bounded W by Mississippi R., N by Miss. state line. Agr. (cotton, corn, soybeans, sweet potatoes; cattle; dairying). Logging. Sand, gravel. Paper mills. Formed 1824. Area known for antebellum houses including Rosedown, the Cottage, Catalpa, and the Myrtles. State penitentiary in NW of county at Angola. River Bend Nuclear Power Plant, initial criticality Oct. 31, 1985, is 24 mi/39 km NNW of Baton Rouge, uses cooling water from the Mississippi R., and has a max. dependable capacity of 936 MWe. One of Florida Parishes of SE La., former Br. colony of W Florida. Annual Audubon Pilgrimage held here. Small L. Rosemound in N; Tunica Hills State Wildlife Area in NW; Locust Group and Audubon State Commemorative Areas in SE.

West Fork, town (1990 pop. 1,607), Washington co., NW Ark., 9 mi/14.5 km SSW of Fayetteville, in the Ozarks, and on small West Fork of White R.; 35°55′N 94°10′W. Mfg. Devil's Den State Park to S.

West Fork, river, c.80 mi/129 km long, central W.Va.; rises in S Upshur co.; flows N through Stonewall Jackson L. reservoir (State Park and Wildlife Management Area), past Weston and Clarksburg, and joins Tygart R. at Fairmont to form Monongahela R.

West Forks, plantation (1990 pop. 63), Somerset co., W central Maine, on the Kennebec, at mouth of Dead R., and 40 mi/64 km NNW of Skowhegan; 45°23′N 70°01′W. Hunting, fishing.

West Frankfort (FRANK-fort), city (1990 pop. 8,526), Franklin co., S Ill., 7 mi/11.3 km S of Benton; 37°53′N 88°55′W. Trade center in bituminous-coal (large shaft mine), oil, and agr. (livestock; produce; poultry; fruit) area. Inc. 1901; annexed Frankfort Heights in 1923.

West Franklin, village, Merrimack co., S central N.H., within city of Franklin, 1 mi/1.6 km W of city center, on Pemijewasset R. Mfg. (industrial staples, aluminum extrusions, non-ferrous castings).

West Freehold, uninc. area (1990 pop. 11,166), Monmouth co., central N.J., 3 mi/4.8 km SW of Freehold.

West Gardiner (GAHRD-nuhr), township (1990 pop. 2,531), Kennebec co., S Maine, just W of Gardiner; 44°13′N 69°52′W. Set off from Gardiner, 1850.

West Gate, uninc. town, Prince William co., NE Va., residential suburb 27 mi/43 km WSW of Washington, D.C., 3 mi/4.8 km NNW of Manassas, near Bull Run creek; 38°46′N 77°30′W. Manassas Natl. Battlefield Park to NW. Northern Va. Community Col. (Manassas Campus) is here.

West Glacier (GLAI-shuhr), village (1990 pop. 300), Flathead co., NW Mont., near SW end of L. McDonald, on Middle Fork Flathead R., and 27 mi/43 km. NE of Kalispell. W entrance to Glacier Natl. Park. Area bounded by Glacier Natl. Park on N, by Flathead Natl. Forest on S, includes Great Bear Wilderness Area to SE. Flathead Natl. Wild and Scenic R. extends NW and SE from here on North and Middle Forks of Flathead R. Formerly Belton.

West Glens Falls, village (□ 4 sq mi/10.4 sq km; 1990 pop. 5,964), Warren co., E N.Y.; 43°17′N 73°41′W.

West Gloucester, Mass.: see GLOUCESTER.

West Glover, Vt.: see GLOVER.

West Goshen (GO-shuhn), uninc. town (1990 pop. 8,948), Chester co., SE Pa., residential suburb 2 mi/3.2 km E of West Chester; 39°58′N 75°34′W.

West Grand Lake, in W Washington co., E Maine, 21 mi/34 km WNW of Calais; 8 mi/12.9 km long.

West Greenland Current, cold ocean current in Lab. Sea of North Atlantic Ocean, flowing N along SW coast of Greenland. Formed by merger of East Greenland Current and North Atlantic water of Cape Farewell. One terminal branch flows N through Davis Strait; the other turns W to join the Lab. Current. Carries icebergs.

West Greenville, former town, Greenville co., NW S.C., annexed 1948 by Greenville.

West Greenwich, rural town (1990 pop. 3,492), Kent co., W central R.I., 20 mi/32 km SW of Providence; 41°38′N 71°40′W. Agr.; lumbering; recreation area. Includes villages of Escoheag, Nooseneck (administrative center), Nooseneck Hill, and West Greenwich Center. State forests and Arcadia State Management Area. Set off from East Greenwich 1741.

West Grove, borough (1990 pop. 2,128), Chester co., SE Pa., 16 mi/26 km NW of Wilmington, Del.; 39°49′N 75°49′W. Mfg. (mushroom processing; immunochemicals, wooden furniture). Agr. area (soybeans, mushrooms, roses, grain; poultry; dairying). White Clay Creek State Park (Pa.-Del.) to SE; Star Rose Gardens to W; New London Airport to SW.

West Gulfport, village, Harrison co., SE Miss. Part of city of Gulfport.

West Hamlin, village (1990 pop. 423), Lincoln co., W W.Va., on Guyandotte R., 5 mi/8 km W of Hamlin; 38°16′N 82°12′W. Agr. (corn, tobacco); cattle.

West Harrison, town (1990 pop. 318), Dearborn co., SE Ind., on Whitewater R., and 12 mi/19 km N of Lawrenceburg, at Ohio state line, contiguous to Harrison, Ohio; 39°16′N 84°49′W.

West Hartford, town (1990 pop. 60,110), Hartford co., central Conn., a suburb of Hartford; 41°46′N 72°45′W. Industrial production, which comprises a geographically small part of West Hartford, includes machinery, motor vehicle equip., chemical prods., and plastics. An affluent residential town, there are numerous commercial and professional offices. Site of major retail malls. St. Joseph Col., the Univ. of Hartford, a branch of the Univ. of Conn., and the Amer. School for the Deaf (1817). Of interest is Noah Webster's birthplace and the home of Samuel Clemens (Mark Twain). Settled c.1679, inc. 1854.

West Hartsville, village, Darlington co., NE S.C., just W of Hartsville.

West Harwich, Mass.: see HARWICH.

West Hattiesburg (HAT-eez-buhrg), uninc. town (1990 pop. 5,450), Lamar co., SE Miss., residential suburb 5 mi/8 km W of downtown Hattiesburg; 31°19′N 89°22′W. Agr. area (cotton, corn; cattle).

West Haven 1 town (1990 pop. 54,021), New Haven co., S Conn.; 41°16′N 72°58′W. A suburb across the West R. from New Haven. Although mainly residential, there are diversified mfg. industries. The production of buckles dates from the 1850s. Other industries include durable and nondurable goods, chemicals, pharmaceuticals, artificial stone prods. In the Amer. Revolution, the town was pillaged (1779) by the British. The Univ. of New Haven is here. Of interest are colonial houses. Settled 1638, inc. as a separate borough 1873. **2** town (1990 pop. 273), Rutland co., W Vt., on L. Champlain, and 18 mi/29 km W of Rutland; 43°38′N 73°21′W. Dairy prods., lumber.

West Haverstraw, village (☐ 1 sq mi/2.6 sq km; 1990 pop. 9,183), Rockland co., SE N.Y., near W bank of the Hudson R., just NW of Haverstraw; 41°12′N 73°59′W. Mfg. of synthetic cold-metal solders. State home for crippled children here. Includes Garnerville. Inc. 1883.

West Hazleton (HAI-suhl-tuhn), borough (1990 pop. 4,136), Luzerne co., E central Pa., suburb 1 mi/1.6 km W of Hazleton, near Black Creek; 40°58′N 76°00′W. Mfg. (zinc die castings, steel file cabinets, plastic prods., textiles, apparel, food prods., metal jar caps). Inc. 1889.

West Helena (HEL-uh-nuh), city (1990 pop. 9,695), Phillips co., E Ark., 3 mi/4.8 km WNW of Helena, near Mississippi R.; 34°32′N 90°39′W. RR center. Mfg. (chemicals, lumber, apparel, swimming pool filters, peroxides, farm equip.). Founded 1909, inc. 1917. Phillips Co. Community Col. to E in Helena.

West Hempstead, uninc. city (☐ 2 sq mi/5.2 sq km; 1990 pop. 17,689), Nassau co., SE N.Y., on L.I.; 40°42′N 73°39′W. It is chiefly residential. Pop. figure includes Lakeview.

West Hickory, N.C.: see HICKORY.

West Hill Reservoir, Worcester co., central Mass., on West R., 12 mi/19 km SE of Worcester; 42°07′N 71°37′W. Max. capacity 29,500 acre-ft. Formed by West Hill Dam (43 ft/13 m high), built (1961) by Army Corps of Engineers for flood control; also used for recreation. Also known as Dry Reservoir.

West Hills, uninc. town (1990 pop. 1,240), Armstrong co., W Pa., residential suburb 1 mi/1.6 km W of Kittaning, near Allegheny R.; 40°49′N 79°32′W.

West Hillsboro, uninc. village, Orange co., N central N.C., near Hillsboro.

West Hollywood, city (1990 pop. 36,118), Los Angeles co., S Calif., suburb 8 mi/12.9 km W of downtown Los Angeles, W of Hollywood dist., and E of Beverly Hills; 34°05′N 118°22′W. Residential area bounded N, E, and S by city of Los Angeles. Warner Studios are here.

West Homestead, borough (1990 pop. 2,495), Allegheny co., SW Pa., residential suburb 5 mi/8 km SE of downtown Pittsburgh, on Monongahela R. (bridged); 40°23′N 79°55′W. Mfg. (consumer goods). Inc. 1900.

West Huntsville, uninc. village, Madison co., N Ala., just SW of Huntsville.

West Hurley, village (☐ 4 sq mi/10.4 sq km; 1990 pop. 2,252), Ulster co., SE N.Y., at E end of Ashokan Reservoir, 6 mi/9.7 km NW of Kingston; 42°00′N 74°06′W. In summer-resort and agr. area.

West Indian Island, E N.F., E Canada, in the Atlantic Ocean E of Notre Dame Bay, just S of Fogo Isl.; 5 mi/8 km long, 1 mi/2 km wide; 49°32′N 54°20′W. East Indian Isl. to E.

West Indies, archipelago, bet. N. and S. Amer., curving c.2,500 mi/4,020 km from Fla. to the coast of Venezuela and separating the Caribbean Sea and the Gulf of Mexico from the Atlantic Ocean; 20°00′N 70°00′W. The archipelago, sometimes called the Antilles, is divided into 3 groups, the BAHAMAS, the Greater Antilles (CUBA, JAMAICA, HAITI, the DOMINICAN REPUBLIC, and PUERTO RICO), and the Lesser Antilles (LEEWARD ISLANDS, WINDWARD ISLANDS, TRINIDAD AND TOBAGO, BARBADOS, and the isls. off the N coast of Venezuela). The Br. dependent territories are the CAYMAN ISLANDS, the TURKS AND CAICOS ISLANDS, ANGUILLA, MONTSERRAT, and the Br. VIRGIN ISLANDS. The Du. possessions are Aruba and the Neth. Antilles (CURAÇAO, BONAIRE, SAINT EUSTATIUS, SABA, and part of SAINT MARTIN). The Fr. isls. (sometimes called the Fr. West Indies) are GUADELOUPE and its dependencies and MARTINIQUE. The U.S. possessions are the U.S.V.I. and P.R. SANTA MARGARITA belongs to Venezuela. Many of the isls. are mountainous, and some have partly active volcanoes. Hurricanes occur frequently, but the warm climate (tempered by NE trade winds) and the clear tropical seas have made the West Indies a very popular tourism area. Some 34 million people live on the isls., and the majority of inhabitants are of black Afr. descent. Before Eur. settlement, the isls. were inhabited by 3 different peoples: the Arawaks, the Caribs, and the Ciboney. These indigenous tribes were effectively wiped out by Eur. colonists. Christopher Columbus was the 1st European to visit several of the isls. (in 1492). In 1496 the 1st permanent Eur. settlement was made by the Spanish on HISPANIOLA. By the mid-1600s the English, French, and Dutch had established settlements in the area, and in the following cent. there was constant warfare among the Eur. colonial powers for control of the isls. Some isls. flourished as trade centers and became targets for pirates. Large numbers of Africans were imported to provide slave labor for the sugarcane plantations that developed here in the 1600s. The political status of the isls. varies: Antigua and Barbuda, Barbados, Cuba, Haiti, Dominica, the Dominican Republic, Grenada, Jamaica, the Bahama Isls., St. Kitts and Nevis, Saint Lucia, St. Vincent and the Grenadines, and Trinidad and Tobago are independent. The Neth. Antilles and Aruba officially have equal status with Holland in the Kingdom of the Neth. Guadeloupe and Martinique are overseas depts. and administrative regions of France, P.R. is a commonwealth in association with the U.S., and the U.S.V.I. have territorial status. In 1958, 10 Br. territories (until then known as B.W.I.) joined to form the West Indies Federation. Trinidad and Tobago, Jamaica, and Barbados were the principal members, but the federation included most of the Leeward and Windward isls., then under Br. control. The seat of govt. was Port-of-Spain (Trinidad). Slated for independence in 1962, the federation did not survive its troubled infancy. Jamaica, the most populous and prosperous member, voted (1961) to leave the federation, fearing that it would have to shoulder the burdens of the economically underdeveloped members; Trinidad and Tobago followed suit and the federation was dissolved in May 1962. Jamaica became an independent member of the Commonwealth of Nations in 1962, as did Barbados in 1966 and the Bahama Isls. in 1973. In 1967 the West Indies Associated States were created, made up of Antigua, St. Kitts and Nevis, Dominica, Grenada, St. Lucia, and St. Vincent. Each of the states was voluntarily associated with the U.K. and fully self-governing in its internal affairs. Over the next 2 decades, all of those states gained full independence, the last being St. Kitts and Nevis in 1983.

West Jefferson, town (1990 pop. 1,002), Ashe co., extreme NW N.C., 18 mi/29 km NE of Boone, in the Blue Ridge Mts.; 36°23′N 81°29′W. Tobacco, corn; cattle; dairying; timber. Mfg. (motor vehicles, foods, consumer goods, lumber, bldg. materials, electric goods, furniture). Mt. Jefferson and New R. state parks to E.

West Jefferson, village, Madison co., central Ohio, 10 mi/16 km ENE of London. In grain-growing area; corn cannery.

West Jordan, city (1990 pop. 42,892), Salt Lake co., N central Utah, on Jordan R., and suburb 12 mi/19 km S of downtown Salt Lake City; 40°36′N 111°59′W. Elev. 4,200 ft/1,280 m. Sugar beets, wheat, barley; cattle, sheep; dairying. Mfg. (machinery, bldg. materials, apparel, fabricated metal prods., computer prods., plastics, rubber prods., electronic goods., ordnance, transportation equip., furniture). Settled 1849; inc. after 1940. Salt Lake City municipal airport No. 2. Kennecott Bingham open-cut copper mine (largest in world), to SW.

West Kittanning (KI-tah-ning), borough (1990 pop. 1,253), Armstrong co., W Pa., suburb 1 mi/1.6 km SW of Kittaning, on Allegheny R. (bridged), opposite Kittanning, and 35 mi/56 km NE of Pittsburgh; 40°48′N 79°31′W. Agr. (hay, corn; dairying). Lock and Dam No. 7 here.

West Lafayette, city (1990 pop. 25,907), Tippecanoe co., W Ind., a suburb of Lafayette, on the Wabash R.; 40°26′N 86°55′W. A primarily residential city, it is the seat of Purdue Univ. Nearby is the Tippecanoe battlesite, where William Henry Harrison fought (1811) the Native Amer. chief Tecumseh. Corn, wheat, soybeans, rye, oats; hogs, cattle. Mfg. (machinery, electronics goods, chemicals, consumer goods, traffic barricades). Founded 1845, inc. 1924.

West Lafayette, village (1990 pop. 2,129), Coshocton co., central Ohio, 5 mi/8 km E of Coshocton; 40°16′N 81°45′W. Metal prods., novelties.

West Lake Hills, town (1990 pop. 2,542), Travis co., S Texas, residential suburb 4 mi/6.4 km W of downtown Austin, near Colorado R.; 30°17′N 97°48′W. Tom Miller Dam (Austin L.) to E.

West Lancaster, uninc. town (1990 pop. 750), Lancaster co., SE Pa., residential suburb 2 mi/3.2 km W of Lancaster, on Little Conestoga Creek; 40°02′N 76°21′W. Wheatland, home of President James Buchanan, to N.

West Lawn, borough (1990 pop. 1,606), Berks co., SE central Pa., residential suburb 3 mi/4.8 km W of Reading; 44°19′N 75°59′W. Mfg. (apparel, machinery components). Inc. 1920.

West Lebanon, town (1990 pop. 760), Warren co., WSW Ind., 5 mi/8 km W of Williamsport; 40°16′N 87°23′W. Grain; mfg. (fabricated metal prods., prefabricated bldgs.; seed). Laid out 1830.

West Lebanon (LE-bah-nahn), uninc. village, North Lebanon township, Lebanon co., SE central Pa., residential suburb 2 mi/3.2 km W of Lebanon; 40°20′N 76°26′W.

West Lebanon, N.H.: see LEBANON.

West Leechburg, borough (1990 pop. 1,359), Westmoreland co., W central Pa., 23 mi/37 km NE of Pittsburgh, and 1 mi/1.6 km W of Leechburg, on Kiskiminetas R.; 40°37′N 79°37′W. Agr. (corn, hay; livestock; dairying). Crooked Creek L. reservoir and park to NE. Inc. 1928.

West Leipsic (LIP-sik), village (1990 pop. 244), Putnam co., NW Ohio, adjacent to Leipsic, and 6 mi/10 km NNE of Ottawa; 41°03′N 84°00′W.

West Liberty 1 town (1990 pop. 2,935), Muscatine co., SE Iowa, 14 mi/23 km NW of Muscatine; 41°34′N 91°15′W. In farming and livestock-raising area. Mfg. (poultry and feather processing; feed and supplements). Inc. 1867. **2** town (1990 pop. 1,887), ⊙ Morgan co., E Ky., on Licking R., and 40 mi/64 km ESE of Mount Sterling city; 37°54′N 83°16′W. Trade center for agr. (burley tobacco, corn, sorghum; cattle) area. Mfg. (lumber, apparel, concrete; printing and publishing); coal, oil, gas, and timber area. West Liberty Airport to S. Daniel Boone Natl. Forest to NW; Cave Run L. reservoir to NW. Est. 1823. **3** town (1990 pop. 1,434), Ohio co., N W.Va., in Northern Panhandle, 9 mi/14.5 km NE of Wheeling; 40°10′N 80°35′W . Agr. (grain); livestock; dairying. Mfg. (coal processing). West Liberty State Col. Castleman Run Wildlife Management Area to E.

West Liberty, village (1990 pop. 1,613), Logan co., W central Ohio, 7 mi/11 km S of Bellefontaine, and on Mad R.; 40°15′N 83°45′W. In grain, livestock, and dairy area; condensed milk, grain prods. Ohio Caverns are nearby.

West Liberty, borough (1990 pop. 282), Butler co., W Pa., 13 mi/21 km NW of Butler, near Slippery Rock Creek; 41°00′N 80°03′W. Agr. (corn, hay; livestock; dairying). Moraine State Park to S.

West Line, town (1990 pop. 98), Cass co., W Mo., near South Grand R., on Kansas state line, 14 mi/23 km W of Harrisonville; 38°37′N 94°35′W.

West Linn, city (1990 pop. 16,367), Clackamas co., NW Oregon, residential suburb 10 mi/16 km S of downtown Portland, on Willamette R. bet. confluences of Clackamas and Tualatin rivers, opposite Oregon City; 45°22′N 122°38′W. Fruit, nuts; poultry; dairy prods.; nurseries. Marylhurst Col. to N. Mary S. Young State Park in N part of city. Settled in 1840s, inc. 1913.

West Logan, village (1990 pop. 524), Logan co., SW W.Va., a suburb 2 mi/3.2 km NNW of Logan, on Guyandotte R.; 37°52′N 81°59′W. Chief Logan State Park to NW.

West Long Branch, borough (1990 pop. 7,690), Monmouth co., E N.J., 13 mi/21 km ENE of Freehold; 40°17′N 74°01′W. "Shadow Lawn," here, was President Wilson's summer White House, which now is the main bldg. of Monmouth Col. Settled 1711, inc. 1908.

West Lorne, village (1991 pop. 1,477), S Ont., central Canada, 25 mi/40 km WSW of St. Thomas; 42°36′N 81°36′W. Dairying, mixed farming, fruit growing.

West Los Angeles, suburban sect. of W Los Angeles, S Calif., 12 mi/19 km W of downtown Los Angeles, NE of Santa Monica. Site of U.S. veterans' home and hosp. West Coast Univ. is here. Sometimes called Sawtelle.

West Manayunk (MA-nah-yuhnk), uninc. village, in Lower Merion township, Montgomery co., SE Pa., residential suburb 7 mi/11.3 km NW of downtown Philadelphia, on Schuylkill R. opposite Manayunk sect. of Philadelphia; 40°01′N 75°14′W.

West Manchester, village (1990 pop. 464), Preble co., W Ohio, 6 mi/10 km N of Eaton; 39°54′N 84°37′W. In agr. area.

West Manchester, Mass.: see MANCHESTER.

West Mancos River, Colo.: see MANCOS RIVER.

West Mansfield, village (1990 pop. 830), Logan co., W central Ohio, 11 mi/18 km E of Bellefontaine; 40°23′N 83°32′W. In agr. area.

West Marion, uninc. village (1990 pop. 1,291), McDowell co., W N.C., residential suburb 2 mi/3.2 km W of Marion; 35°38′N 82°01′W.

West Mayfield, borough (1990 pop. 1,312), Beaver co., W Pa., residential suburb 2 mi/3.2 km N of Beaver Falls, on Beaver R.; 40°46′N 80°20′W.

West Medway, Mass.: see MEDWAY.

West Melbourne (MEL-buhrn), town (□ 5 sq mi/ 13 sq km; 1990 pop. 8,399), Brevard co., E central Fla., 3 mi/4.8 km W of Melbourne; 28°04′N 80°40′W. Mfg. includes electrical and electronic prods. and equip.

West Memphis, city (1990 pop. 28,259), Crittenden co., NE Ark., suburb 7 mi/11.3 km W of downtown Memphis (Tenn), on the Mississippi R. (2 interstate highway bridges, 1 RR bridge to Memphis, Tenn.); 35°08′N 90°10′W. RR junction. It is a timber and cotton center with diverse industries. Mfg. (machinery, chemicals, petroleum prods., consumer goods, beverages, paper prods., fabricated metal goods, bldg. materials). A greyhound-racing park is here. Founded c.1910 as Bragg's Spur, inc. as a city under its present name 1927.

West Menlo Park (MEN-lo), uninc. town (1990 pop. 3,959), San Mateo co., W Calif., residential suburb 27 mi/43 km SSE of downtown San Francisco, and 1 mi/1.6 km W of Menlo Park; 37°26′N 122°12′W. Santa Cruz Mts. to SW.

West Middlesex, borough (1990 pop. 982), Mercer co., W Pa., 4 mi/6.4 km SE of Sharon, on Shenango R.; 41°10′N 80°27′W. Mfg. (printing and publishing, steel fabricating; fiberglass prods., food prods., fabricated metal prods.). Agr. area (potatoes, corn, hay; dairying). Settled 1821, laid out 1836, inc. 1864.

West Middletown, borough (1990 pop. 166), Washington co., SW Pa., 10 mi/16 km NW of Washington; 40°15′N 80°25′W. Agr. (corn; livestock; dairying). Cross Creek Co. Park adjoins borough on NE, including Cross Creek L. reservoir.

West Mifflin, borough (1990 pop. 23,644), Allegheny co., SW Pa., a suburb 8 mi/12.9 km SE of downtown Pittsburgh, N and SW of Monongahela R.; 40°21′N 79°54′W. Mfg. (bldg. materials, transportation equip., fabricated metal prods., asphalt). Allegheny Co. Airport to W; Community Col. of Allegheny Co., South Campus, to SW.

West Milan, N.H.: see MILAN.

West Milford, township (1990 pop. 25,430), Passaic co., NE N.J., 20 mi/32 km NW of Paterson, in Bearfort Mts.; 41°06′N 74°24′W. Inc. 1834.

West Milford 1 village (1990 pop. 25,430), Passaic co., N N.J., on Pinecliff L. (c.1.5 mi/2.4 km long), 16 mi/26 km NW of Paterson; 41°06′N 74°24′W. Bldg. supplies. In suburban area. **2** village (1990 pop. 519), Harrison co., N W.Va., on the West Fork R., 6 mi/9.7 km SW of Clarksburg; 39°12′N 80°24′W. Agr. (corn); cattle, poultry. Watters Smith Memorial State Park to S.

West Millbury, Mass.: see MILLBURY.

West Millgrove, village (1990 pop. 171), Wood co., NW Ohio, 11 mi/18 km SE of Bowling Green; 41°14′N 83°29′W. Limestone quarry.

West Milton, uninc. town (1990 pop. 850), Union co., central Pa., residential suburb 1 mi/1.6 km W of Milton, on West Branch Susquehanna R.; 41°01′N 76°52′W. Agr. includes dairying; livestock; grain. Milton State Park on isl. in river, to E.

West Milton 1 village (1990 pop. 350), Saratoga co., E N.Y., 5 mi/8 km WNW of Ballston Spa; 43°02′N 73°56′W. Site of 2 nuclear reactors operated by the U.S. Dept. of Energy, training sailors to operate nuclear submarines and other nuclear-powered marine vessels. Two other reactors have been deactivated. **2** village (1990 pop. 4,348), Miami co., W Ohio, 7 mi/11 km SW of Troy, and on Stillwater R.; 39°57′N 84°19′W. In agr. area; mfg. Settled 1807, inc. 1835.

West Milwaukee (mil-WAW-kee), village (□ 2 sq mi/ 5.2 sq km; 1990 pop. 3,973), Milwaukee co., SE Wis., a suburb 2 mi/3.2 km WSW of downtown Milwaukee; 43°00′N 87°58′W. Has heaviest concentration of industry in Milwaukee area. Industries include mfg. air and hydraulic cylinders, machinery. Eighty percent of the land is zoned for industrial and mercantile establishments. This village employs twice the number who live here. Inc. 1906.

West Mineral, village (1990 pop. 226), Cherokee co., extreme SE Kansas, 15 mi/24 km SW of Pittsburg; 37°16′N 94°55′W. In diversified agr. region.

West Monroe, city (1990 pop. 14,096), Ouachita parish, N La., on the Ouachita R., suburb 1 mi/1.6 km W of Monroe; 32°31′N 92°09′W. In timber area. Mfg. (timber, lumber, paper and paper goods, fabricated metal prods., plastic prods., machinery, cottonseed oil); printing and publishing. Inc. 1851. Cheniere Brake State Fish Preserve and lake to SW.

West Musquash Lake, Maine: see EAST MUSQUASH LAKE.

West Mystic, Conn.: see GROTON.

West Nanticoke (NAN-ti-kok), uninc. town (1990 pop. 1,230), Plymouth township, Luzerne co., NE central Pa., 2 mi/3.2 km NNW of Nanticoke, and 6 mi/9.7 km WSW of Wilkes-Barre, on Susquehanna R.; 41°13′N 76°00′W. Part of Lackawanna State Forest to N.

West New Boston, Mass.: see SANDISFIELD.

West New Brighton, a residential sect. of Staten Isl. borough of N.Y. city, SE N.Y., on N Staten Isl., on Kill Van Kull; 40°38′N 74°06′W. Mfg.

West New York, town (1990 pop. 38,125), Hudson co., NE N.J., 5 mi/8 km N of Jersey City, atop the Palisades, across the Hudson R. from N.Y. city; 40°47′N 74°00′W. Residential town with some light industry (textiles, clothing; also a leading U.S. embroidery center). The waterfront, 1 mi/1.6 km long, can accommodate oceangoing vessels. Settled 1790, inc. 1898.

West Newbury, town (1990 pop. 3,421), Essex co., NE Mass., on Merrimack R., and 11 mi/18 km NE of Lawrence; 42°48′N 70°58′W. Settled 1635, inc. 1820.

West Newton, borough (1990 pop. 3,152), Westmoreland co., SW Pa., 20 mi/32 km SE of Pittsburgh, on Youghiogheny R.; 40°12′N 79°46′W. Mfg. (fabricated metal prods., machinery, electrical prods.; printing). Agr. area (grain, apples, soybeans; livestock; dairying). Coyle Airport to NE. Site Native Amer. massacre of settlers, 1763. Laid out 1796, inc. 1842.

West Newton, Mass.: see NEWTON.

West Nishnabotna River, Iowa: see NISHNABOTNA RIVER.

West Nodaway River, Iowa: see NODAWAY RIVER.

West Norriton, township (1990 pop. 15,209), Montgomery co., SE Pa., residential suburb 16 mi/26 km NW of Philadelphia, and 2 mi/3.2 km W of Norristown, on Schuylkill R.; 40°07′N 75°22′W. Agr. includes dairying; livestock; grain. Valley Forge Natl. Historical Park to SW. Includes the community of Jeffersonville.

West Okoboji (o-ko-BO-jee), town (1990 pop. 263), Dickinson co., NW Iowa, summer resort on West Okoboji L. (c.6 mi/9.7 km long, 1 mi/1.6 km–2 mi/3.2 km wide), just SW of Spirit L.; 43°21′N 95°10′W. Several state parks nearby.

West Orange 1 town (1990 pop. 39,103), Essex co., NE N.J., a residential suburb 4 mi/6.4 km NW of Newark; 40°47′N 74°15′W. "Glenmont," Thomas Edison's home in Llewellyn Park, and his laboratory (now a mus.) are included in the Edison Natl. Historic Site. Set off from Orange 1862, inc. 1900. **2** town (1990 pop. 4,187), Orange co., SE Texas, suburb 2 mi/3.2 km W of Orange, on Adams Bayou, near Sabine R.; 30°04′N 93°45′W.

West Ossipee, N.H.: see OSSIPEE.

West Outlet Dam, Maine: see MOOSEHEAD LAKE.

West Paducah (puh-DOO-kuh), uninc. village, McCracken co., W Ky., suburb 7 mi/11.3 km W of Paducah. In agr. area. Mfg. (meat processing; machinery, burial vaults).

West Palm Beach, city (□ 52 sq mi/135 sq km; 1990 pop. 67,643), ⊙ Palm Beach co., SE Fla., on L. Worth (a lagoon) opposite Palm Beach (linked by bridges); 26°45′N 80°07′W. Has experienced significant urbanization since 1970. It has commercial fishing and is a center for the research and production of aeronautical and electronic equip. Tourism is also important. In the city are the Univ. of Palm Beach, a business col., a community col., the Norton Gal. and School of Art, and a science mus. and planetarium. Nearby transportation facilities include Palm Beach Internatl. Airport and Port Palm Beach, one of Fla.'s busiest ports. Inc. 1894.

West Park, village (1990 pop. 850), Ulster co., SE N.Y., on W bank of the Hudson R., and 6 mi/9.7 km N of Poughkeepsie; 41°48′N 73°58′W. In grape-growing and resort area. Restored home of John Burroughs is here.

West Paterson, borough (1990 pop. 10,982), Passaic co., NE N.J., a suburb of Paterson; 40°53′N 74°12′W. Electric, electronic, and photographic prods. Inc. 1914.

West Pearl River, La.: see PEARL RIVER.

West Pelzer, town (1990 pop 989), Anderson co., NW S.C., 15 mi/24 km SSW of Greenville, 1 mi/1.6 km W of Pelzer, near Saluda R.; 34°38′N 82°28′W. Agr. includes dairying; poultry, livestock; grain, soybeans, sorghum.

West Pensacola (pen-suh-KO-luh), city (□ 7 sq mi/ 18.1 sq km; 1990 pop. 22,107) adjacent to Pensacola (W), Escambia co., extreme NW Fla., 3 mi/4.8 km W of city center; 30°25′N 87°16′W.

West Peoria (pee-YOR-ree-uh), city (1990 pop. 5,314), Peoria co., central Ill., suburb 2 mi/3.2 km W of downtown Peoria; 40°42′N 89°37′W. Bradley Univ. to E.

West Pittsburg, uninc. city (1990 pop. 17,453), Contra Costa co., W Calif., residential suburb 20 mi/32 km NE of downtown Oakland, W of Pittsburg, near Suisun Bay, at mouth of Sacramento–San Joaquin estuary; 38°02′N 121°58′W.

West Pittsburg, uninc. town (1990 pop. 1,133), Lawrence co., W Pa., 5 mi/8 km S of New Castle, on Beaver R.; 40°55′N 80°21′W. Mfg. includes sand and gravel processing; bldg. materials, fabricated metal prods. Agr. includes dairying; livestock; hay.

West Pittsfield, Mass.: see PITTSFIELD.

West Pittston (PITS-tuhn), borough (1990 pop. 5,590), Luzerne co., NE Pa., suburb 6 mi/9.7 km NE of Wilkes-Barre, on Susquehanna R. opposite (NW of) Pittston; 41°19′N 75°47′W. Mfg. (apparel, wood prods.); anthracite coal. Frances Slocum State Park to NW. Inc. 1857.

West Plains, city (1990 pop. 8,913), ⊙ Howell co., S Mo., in the Ozark Mts., 90 mi/145 km ESE of Springfield; 36°44′N 91°51′W. Shopping and service center for a large area of the central Ozarks. Agr. shipping center; livestock market; dairy, grain, lumber prods. Mfg. (furniture, wood prods., electric goods; printing); timber; tourism. Has a campus of Southwest Mo. State Univ. Was totally destroyed during Civil War. Laid out c.1858.

West Point 1 town (1990 pop. 3,571), Troup co., W Ga., 14 mi/23 km SW of La Grange, at Ala. state line (formed here by Chattahoochee R.); 32°53′N 85°10′W. Textile center; mfg. of carpet, textile machining, commercial printing. Inc. 1831. **2** town, Lee co., SE Iowa, 9 mi/14.5 km NW of Fort Madison. In livestock area. Mfg. (soybean seed; ice cubes and blocks). **3** town

(1990 pop. 1,216), Hardin co., N central Ky., 20 mi/ 32 km SSW of Louisville, on the Ohio R., at mouth of Salt R.; 37°59′N 85°57′W. RR junction. Agr. area. Former river port (1800s). At N edge of Fort Knox Military Reservation; Bridges to the Past, 3 stone bridges, to S; Fort Dunfield, Union fort in Civil War, to S. Est. 1796. **4** town (1990 pop. 8,489), ⊙ Clay co., E Miss., 15 mi/ 24 km WNW of Columbus; 33°36′N 88°38′W. RR junction. Agr. (cotton, corn, wheat; cattle, hogs, poultry; dairying). Mfg. (fabricated metal prods., consumer goods, furniture, lumber, chemicals, wood prods.; meat processing, machining, printing and publishing). Waverly Mansion (c.1852). Columbus Air Force Base to E. Columbus L. reservoir to SE, Tenessee-Tombigbee Waterway to E. Inc. 1858. **5** town (1990 pop. 3,250), ⊙ Cuming co., E Nebr., 29 mi/47 km NW of Fremont, and on Elkhorn R.; 41°50′N 96°42′W. Farm trade center. Mfg. (alfalfa prods., machinery, foods, fabricated metal prods., feeds; meat processing). Dead Timber State Recreation Area to S (Dodge co.). Co. mus. and park here. Inc. 1858. **6** town (1990 pop. 4,258), Davis co., N Utah, suburb 10 mi/16 km SW of Ogden, and 22 mi/35 km NW of Salt Lake City, just E of Great Salt L.; 41°07′N 112°05′W. Elev. 4,300 ft/1,311 m. Settled 1885, originally named Muskrat Springs. Causeway to Antelope Isl. State Park (Great Salt L.) to SW. Howard Slough Waterfowl Management Area to W. **7** town (1990 pop. 2,938), King William co., E Va., 19 mi/31 km N of Williamsburg, at confluence of Mattaponi and Pamunkey rivers (which form York R. estuary); 37°32′N 76°47′W. RR terminus; mfg. (sheet metal fabricating; chemicals, paper, foods; agr. area (grain, soybeans; cattle; dairying); timber; fish, crabs, oysters. Mattaponi (to NW) and Pamunkey (to W) Indian reservations nearby. Settled 17th cent.; inc. 1870.

West Point 1 village (1990 pop. 146), White co., central Ark., 7 mi/11.3 km ESE of Searcy, on Little Red R.; 35°12′N 91°36′W. **2** village (1990 pop. 1,079), Hancock co., W Ill., 14 mi/23 km SE of Keokuk; 40°43′N 91°27′W. In agr. and bituminous-coal area. **3** uninc. village, Montgomery co., SE Pa., suburb 17 mi/27 km NNW of Philadelphia, on Wissahickon Creek; 40°12′N 75°17′W. Mfg. includes chemicals.

West Point, U.S. military post (☐ 25 sq mi/65 sq km; 1990 pop. 8,024), seat of the U.S. Military Acad., on the high W bank of the Hudson R., SE N.Y. state, N of N.Y. city; 41°21′N 74°01′W. Site of Amer. Revolutionary forts guarding the Hudson R. Constitution Isl., in the river, is also in the reservation. The plan of Benedict Arnold to surrender (1780) West Point to the British was discovered with the capture of Major John André.

West Point, cape at W extremity of Anticosti Isl., E Que., E Canada, on the St. Lawrence R.; 49°52′N 64°31′W. Lighthouse, radio beacon.

West Point, peninsula, SW Maine, on E shore of Casco Bay, near Phippsburg.

West Point Lake, reservoir, W Ga. and E Ala., on Chattahoochee R., 3 mi/4.8 km NNE of Lanett, Ala.; c.30 mi/48 km long; 32°54′N 85°11′W. Max. capacity 711,000 acre-ft. Formed by West Point Dam (near Ala.-Ga. state line; 106 ft/32 m high), built (1974) by the Army Corps of Engineers for flood control and power generation.

West Points, cape at W extremity of P.E.I., E Canada, on Northumberland Strait, on N side of Egmont Bay, 30 mi/48 km NW of Summerside; 46°37′N 64°23′W. Lighthouse.

West Poland, Maine: see POLAND.

West Portsmouth, uninc. village (1990 pop. 3,551), Scioto co., S Ohio, just NW of Portsmouth; 38°46′N 83°02′W.

West Puente Valley (PWEN-tai), uninc. city (1990 pop. 20,254), Los Angeles co., S Calif., residential suburb 14 mi/23 km E of downtown Los Angeles, 2 mi/3.2 km W of La Puente; 34°03′N 117°58′W.

West Quoddy Head (KWAW-dee), promontory extending into the Atlantic Ocean, SE Maine, SE of Lubec; the easternmost point in the continental U.S. A lighthouse is here.

West Reading (RE-ding), borough (1990 pop. 4,142),

Berks co., SE central Pa., on Schuylkill R. opposite (1 mi/1.6 km W of) Reading; 40°19′N 75°57′W. Mfg. (textiles; commercial printing). Founded 1873, inc. 1907.

West Richland, town (1990 pop. 3,962), Benton co., S Wash., 4 mi/6.4 km NW of Richland, on Yakima R.; 46°19′N 119°24′W. Irrigated agr. area (vegetables, potatoes, beans, alfalfa, wheat; cattle). U.S. Dept. of Energy Hanford Site to N.

West River, c.50 mi/80 km long, SE Vt.; rises in Green Mts., near Weston; flows S and SE, past Newfane, to the Connecticut R. at Brattleboro. Several flood control dams.

West Riverside, village (1990 pop. 530), Missoula co., W Mont., 5 mi/8 km E of Missoula, on Clark Fork river, at mouth of Blackfoot R., opposite Milltown. Residential community for largest lumber mill in Mont. (at Milltown).

West Road River, B.C., Canada: see BLACKWATER RIVER.

West Rockingham, uninc. village, Richmond co., S N.C., 3 mi/4.8 km W of Rockingham.

West Roxbury, Mass.: see BOSTON.

West Rushville, village (1990 pop. 134), Fairfield co., central Ohio, just W of Rushville, and 9 mi/14 km ENE of Lancaster; 39°46′N 82°26′W.

West Rutland, town (1990 pop. 2,448), Rutland co., SW central Vt., just W of Rutland; 43°36′N 73°03′W. Marble quarries; limestone; dairy prods. Set off from Rutland in 1886.

West Sacramento, city (☐ 22 sq mi/57 sq km; 1990 pop. 28,898), Yolo co., central Calif., suburb opposite (1 mi/ 1.6 km W of) downtown Sacramento, on Sacramento R., at junction of Sacramento Deep Water Canal, from Suisun Bay; 38°34′N 121°33′W. Port facilities; mfg. (fabricated metal prods., bldg. materials, medical instruments, foods and beverages, computer prods., ink, paper goods, electronic equip., elevators, millwork, transportation equip., fertilizers, asphalt); agr. (rice, wheat, sugar beets, tree fruits, vegetables, melons, beans, tomatoes).

West Saint Paul, city (1990 pop. 19,248), Dakota co., SE Minn., a suburb 3 mi/4.8 km S of downtown St. Paul, adjoining St. Paul, W, SE, and S of Mississippi R.; 44°53′N 93°05′W. Mfg. (inks, apparel, paper goods, chemicals, ice, medical supplies). Inc. 1889.

West Salem, town (1990 pop. 3,611), La Crosse co., W Wis., near La Crosse R., 9 mi/14.5 km SE of La Crosse; 43°53′N 91°04′W. In timber and farm area; dairy prods.; lumber; mfg. (microfilm and microfiche readers). On La Crosse State Trail. House of Pulitzer Prize winner Hamlin Garland is here. Inc. 1893.

West Salem 1 village (1990 pop. 1,042), Edwards co., SE Ill., 12 mi/19 km NNE of Albion; 38°31′N 88°00′W. Livestock, poultry; grain. **2** village (1990 pop. 1,534), Wayne co., N central Ohio, 13 mi/21 km NE of Ashland; 40°58′N 82°06′W. Dairy prods.; poultry; textiles.

West Salem, urban area, Polk co., NW Oregon, on Willamette R., opposite Salem.

West Sand Lake, village (☐ 4 sq mi/10.4 sq km; 1990 pop. 2,251), Rensselaer co., E N.Y., 7 mi/11.3 km SE of Troy; 42°38′N 73°36′W. In fruit-growing area.

West Sayville, village (☐ 1 sq mi/2.6 sq km; 1990 pop. 4,680), Suffolk co., SE N.Y., on S shore of L.I. and Great South Bay, just W of Sayville; 40°43′N 73°06′W. Mfg. of electronic prods., foods. In summer resort and recreation area.

West Seneca (SE-ne-kuh), town (1990 pop. 47,866), Erie co., W N.Y., 7.5 mi/12.1 km SE of downtown Buffalo; 42°50′N 78°45′W. Pop. figure includes Ebenezer, Gardenville, and Winchester.

West Shefford, village, S Que., E Canada, on Centre Yamaska R., and 7 mi/11 km SSE of Granby. Dairying; lumbering.

West Shore, large business complex at the W central edge of Tampa adjacent to Tampa Internatl. Airport, SW Fla. Completed only in the late 1980s, this complex has already become one of the state's largest concentrations of commercial office space.

West Siloam Springs (SAH-lohm), village (1990 pop.

539), Delaware co., NE Okla., residential suburb 3 mi/ 4.8 km W of Siloam Springs (Ark.), in Ozark Mts., near Illinois R.; 36°10′N 94°94′W.

West Slope, uninc. town (1990 pop. 7,959), Washington co., NW Oregon, residential suburb 5 mi/8 km WSW of downtown Portland, and 2 mi/3.2 km ENE of Beaverton; 45°30′N 122°46′W.

West Smithfield, uninc. town (1990 pop. 2,411), Johnston co., central N.C., residential suburb 3 mi/4.8 km W of Smithfield, near source of Neuse R.; 35°31′N 78°21′W.

West Spanish Peak, Colo.: see SPANISH PEAKS.

West Springfield, uninc. city, Fairfax co., NE Va., residential suburb 9 mi/14.5 km WSW of Alexandria, 12 mi/19 km SW of Washington, D.C., on Accotink Creek; 38°47′N 77°13′W. Light mfg. L. Accotink Park to N; Fort Belvoir Proving Grounds to S.

West Springfield, town (1990 pop. 27,537), Hampden co., SW Mass., on the Connecticut R. opposite Springfield; 42°07′N 72°39′W. Light mfg. includes paper, plastics prods., chemicals, and ignition systems. Storrowton, a reconstructed colonial village, is on the grounds of the annually held Eastern States Exposition. Settled 1654; set off from Springfield and inc. 1774.

West Stafford, Conn.: see STAFFORD.

West Stewartstown, N.H.: see STEWARTSTOWN.

West Stockbridge, resort town (1990 pop. 1,483), Berkshire co., W Mass., 10 mi/16 km SW of Pittsfield, near N.Y. state line; 42°19′N 73°23′W. Agr.; lime kilns. Settled 1766; set off from Stockbridge 1774. Includes village of State Line.

West Sunbury (SUHN-buh-ree), borough (1990 pop. 177), Butler co., W Pa., 10 mi/16 km N of Butler; 40°00′N 79°54′W. Agr. (corn, hay; livestock; dairying). Mfg. (flour; machining). Moraine State Park to SW.

West Swanzey, N.H.: see SWANZEY.

West Tavaputs Plateau (TA-vah-poots), E Utah, high tableland in Carbon and Duchesne cos.; extends W to Wasatch Plateau; Grera R. to E separates it from East Tavaputs Plateau. Rises to 10,047 ft/3,062 m in Mt. Bartles and to 10,285 ft/3,135 m in Bruin Peak.

West Telford, Pa.: see TELFORD.

West Terre Haute, town (1990 pop. 2,495), Vigo co., W Ind., near Wabash R., 2 mi/3.2 km W of Terre Haute; 39°28′N 87°27′W. Scrap-iron processing. St. Mary-of-the-Woods Col. to N. Laid out 1836, inc. 1933.

West Thompson Lake, reservoir, Windham co., extreme NE Conn., on Quinebaug R., 3 mi/5 km N of Putnam; 41°57′N 71°54′W. Covers 211 acres/85 ha. Max. capacity 47,800 acre-ft. Extends N almost to Mass. state line. Formed by West Thompson L. Dam (70 ft/21 m high), built (1965) by Army Corps of Engineers for flood control; also used for recreation.

West Tisbury (TIZ-buh-ree), town (1990 pop. 1,704), Dukes co., SE Mass., on central Martha's Vineyard, 21 mi/34 km SE of New Bedford; 41°25′N 70°40′W. Agr.; fishing; tourist trade. Dukes Co. Airport. State Forest. Includes North Tisbury village. Settled 1669, inc. 1861.

West Torrington, village, W of Torrington, Goshen co., SE Wyo., on North Platte R.

West Union, city (1990 pop. 2,490), ⊙ Fayette co., NE Iowa, 24 mi/39 km S of Decorah; 42°57′N 91°48′W. Mfg. (bldg. materials, dairy prods., foods, feed, transportation equip., consumer goods); limestone quarries. Echo Valley State Park to SE. Inc. 1857.

West Union, town (1990 pop. 830), ⊙ Doddridge co., N W.Va., on Middle Isl. Creek, 24 mi/39 km W of Clarksburg; 39°17′N 80°46′W. Agr. region (potatoes, alfalfa, apples); cattle, poultry. Mfg. (lumber, apparel). Gas and oil wells. North Bend State Trail passes E-W through town. Inc. 1850.

West Union 1 village (1990 pop. 54), Todd co., W central Minn., near Sauk R., 15 mi/24 km SE of Alexandria; 45°47′N 95°04′W. Dairying; poultry; grain. **2** village (1990 pop. 3,096), ⊙ Adams co., S Ohio, 30 mi/48 km W of Portsmouth; 38°48′N 83°32′W. In tobacco and grain area. Laid out 1804. **3** village (1990 pop. 260), Oconee co., NW S.C., 37 mi/60 km WSW of Greenville, and 1 mi/1.6 km E of Walhalla; 34°45′N 83°02′W. Mfg.

includes electronic goods and equip., wood prods. and lumber, plastic prods. Agr. includes livestock, poultry; corn, wheat.

West Unity, village (1990 pop. 1,677), Williams co., extreme NW Ohio, 9 mi/14 km NE of Bryan; 41°35′N 84°26′W. Electrical apparatus, furniture.

West University Place, city (1990 pop. 12,920), Harris co., SE Texas, residential suburb 5 mi/8 km SW of downtown Houston, near Brays Bayou; 29°43′N 95°25′W. Completely surrounded by the city of Houston. Rice Univ. to E; Astrodome to SE. Inc. 1925.

West Upton, Mass.: see UPTON.

West Valley, village (1990 pop. 500), Cattaraugus co., W N.Y., 35 mi/56 km S of Buffalo; 42°24′N 78°37′W. In 1966, a private company opened a plant here to recover uranium and plutonium for re-use, the idea being that the proliferation of nuclear power plants in the U.S. would deplete Amer. supply of these materials if they were not conserved and recycled. This notion turned out to be wrong, and by 1972 the plant had closed. In 1980 President Jimmy Carter approved legislation for an 8-year, $400-million cleanup of the plant. The cleanup, relying solely on robotic labor to handle the radioactive waste, is still continuing, and the cost has already reached $1.1 billion; currently, the final cost is estimated at $1.5 billion.

West Valley City, city (1990 pop. 86,976), Salt Lake co., N central Utah, suburb 7 mi/11.3 km SW of downtown Salt Lake City, on Jordan R.; 40°41′N 112°00′W. Mfg. (flour, beverages). Area settled 1848. City formed in 1980 from combination of Brighton, Granger, Hunter, and Pleasant Green suburbs. Pop. in 1990 edged past that of Provo, making it Utah's 2d-largest city.

West Van Lear, uninc. town (1990 pop. 850), Johnson co., E Ky., 3 mi/4.8 km SE of Paintsville, and 1 mi/1.6 km NNW of Van Lear, on Levisa Fork river. Bituminous coal. Tobacco; livestock. Mfg. (machining).

West Vancouver, city (1991 pop. 38,783), SW B.C., W Canada, residential suburb 4 mi/6 km NW of downtown Vancouver, at base of Coast Mts. on Strait of Georgia, at entrance to Burrard Inlet, bet. mouth of Capilano R. (E) and Howe Sound (W). Includes community of Horseshoe Bay, port for ferries to Nanaimo, Langdale, and Bowen Isl. Skiing at Hollyburn Mt. in Cypress Provincial Park. Pulp mill; tourism. Lighthouse at Lighthouse Park; scenic Marine Drive.

West View, uninc. town, Spartanburg co., NW S.C., residential suburb 4 mi/6.4 km WSW of downtown Spartanburg. Spartanburg Regional Airport to E.

West View, borough (1990 pop. 7,734), Allegheny co., SW Pa., residential suburb 5 mi/8 km NNW of downtown Pittsburgh; 40°31′N 80°01′W. Inc. 1905.

West Virginia, state (□ 24,231 sq mi/62,759 sq km; 1995 est. pop. 1,828,140), E central U.S., admitted (1863) as the 35th state of the Union; ⊙ CHARLESTON, which is also the largest city; HUNTINGTON is the 2d-largest city. WHEELING and PARKERSBURG are also important urban centers. Extremely irregular in both outline and terrain, W.Va. has 2 narrow projections—the NORTHERN PANHANDLE, which extends N bet. Ohio and Pa., and the EASTERN PANHANDLE, which extends NE bet. Md. (with the Potomac R. forming the state line) and Va. The jagged Va.-W.Va. state line continues SW from the Eastern Panhandle, roughly following the E escarpment of the Allegheny Plateau (known as the Allegheny Front) to shape W.Va.'s E border. The state is bounded E and S by Va., SW by Ky. (border formed by Big Sandy R. and its Tug Fork), NW by Ohio (border formed by the Ohio R.), and N by Pa. and Md. Nicknamed the "Mountain State," W.Va. is very hilly and rugged, with the highest mean elev. (1,500 ft/457 m) of any state E of the Mississippi R. Nearly all of W.Va. is on the Allegheny Plateau, which descends W from the Allegheny mt. country in a series of parallel NE-SW ridges. Characteristic of the plateau are narrow valleys and—in the E and center—many gorges, water and wind gaps, falls, and rapids. The Eastern Panhandle, a part of the Appalachian ridge and valley country, contains the state's lowest point (240 ft/73 m) near Harpers Ferry where the Shenandoah R. joins the Potomac, as well as its highest point, SPRUCE KNOB (4,860 ft/1,481 m). W.Va. is well drained; its important rivers include the Tug Fork, the NEW RIVER, LITTLE KANAWHA RIVER, CHEAT RIVER, and MONONGAHELA and KANAWHA rivers, all of which flow to the Ohio R. The New and Kanawha rivers combine to form the most important waterway entirely within the state. In the river valleys are most of the town sites, all of the major roads and RRs, and almost all of the level land for farms. The Ohio, Kanawha, and Monongahela rivers also carry large amounts of barge traffic. Although natural lakes are lacking, there are numerous mineral springs throughout the state, notably at the resorts of BERKELEY SPRINGS and WHITE SULPHUR SPRINGS. W.Va.'s climate is generally of the humid continental type, with hot summers (except in the highest areas) and cool to cold winters. The annual precipitation ranges generally W-E c.30 in/c.76 m–c.60 in/c.152 m and averages 45 in/114 m. Farming is not extensive and is confined to the river-bottom lands, a few small plateaus, and the N end of the rolling, fertile Valley of Virginia in the Eastern Panhandle. Hay, apples, corn, and tobacco are the principal crops, while cattle, hogs, poultry, and dairying lead in market receipts. The pop. is nevertheless predominately rural, with bituminous-coal mining being one of the state's most widespread economic activities. It is among the nation's leading producers of bituminous coal, although coal production has declined. Natural gas, limestone, cement, salt, and oil are also important; natural-gas and oil fields begin in the Northern Panhandle and extend S across the state. Utilizing these mineral resources the state has major steel, glass, chemical (including synthetic textile), and high-technology industries; they are concentrated in the highly industrialized Ohio and Kanawha river valleys, which tie the state economically to Pa., Ohio, and other industrial states. Charleston is a leading industrial center; Huntington, Parkersburg, Wheeling, and WEIRTON are also important. Other mfg. includes primary and fabricated metals and machinery. Steel mills extend W from Pittsburgh into the Northern Panhandle; Wheeling is a mfg. hub in that area. Timber has long been an important resource in the state, and c.⅔ of the land is still forested, most of it in valuable hardwoods; important species include walnut, chestnut, oak, yellow poplar, and ash. Softwoods are also present. W.Va.'s natural beauty is spectacular, and the excellent hunting, fishing, hiking, camping, white-water rafting, and skiing offered here attract a growing tourist industry. The state has numerous state parks, public hunting areas, and state forests; Monongahela Natl. Forest is in E, and a portion of George Washington Natl. Forest (extends from Va.) is on extreme E border; a small part of Jefferson Natl. Forest (also from Va.) is in SE; New R. Gorge Natl. R. and Bluestone Natl. R. are in center; Gauley R. Natl. Recreation Area is in center. Other tourist attractions include the main part of HARPERS FERRY Natl. Historical Park in the extreme NE corner, and various prehistoric mounds built by Native Americans, most notably Grave Creek Mound in MOUNDSVILLE, one of the nation's largest. The Mound Builders were the earliest known inhabitants. When the 1st Europeans arrived, however, the region was for the most part unpopulated, serving as a common hunting ground (and therefore a battleground) for the settlers and Native Americans. This part of Va., which later became W.Va., was penetrated by explorers and fur traders as early as the 1670s. It was cut off from the E regions by rugged mts. and remained uninhabited for over a cent. after Va. had thriving colonies. What is now the Eastern Panhandle attracted the 1st Eur. settlers. They were Germans and Scotch-Irish, and they came not over the Blue Ridge mts. from Va. but rather down the valleys from Pa. The 1st settlement, est. c.1730 by Ger. families and named Mecklenburg (now called Shepherdstown), is the oldest town in the state. Homes sprang up along the rivers, and settlers began laboriously making their way over the mts., eventually coming into conflict with the French; this conflict was the direct cause of the last Fr. and Indian War (1754–1763). An influx of settlers after 1763 brought increasingly violent confrontation with the Native Amer. people, and during the Amer. Revolution the area was invaded 3 times by Br.-led Native Amer. forces. W Virginians overwhelmingly supported ratification of the U.S. Constitution; they wanted a strong Federal govt. that would quell further conflict with the Native Americans and that would enrich commerce along the Ohio, a river of central importance to their economic life. Pop. growth and prosperity were spurred by the opening of the Mississippi with the Louisiana Purchase in 1803, by the resulting expansion and improvement of river-borne commerce, and by the completion (1818) of the Natl. Road at Wheeling. Va. was politically dominated by the wealthy tidewater planters, who were overrepresented in the state legislature because slaves were counted in apportioning representation and slavery was considerably rarer in W Va. As a result, the W Virginians suffered from inequitable taxation, and their demands for internal improvements and public education were not met. The 2 sects. were being pulled further apart by economic differences—W Va. was becoming an industrialized coal and steel center—and by the increasing prominence of the slavery issue. At the outset of the Civil War, the NW cos. of Va. overwhelmingly opposed the state's ordinance of secession (April 17, 1861). Unable to halt Va.'s secession from the Union, westerners in the state were quick to take advantage of a long-awaited opportunity for their own separation from Va. Protected by Federal troops, delegates representing most of Va.'s W cos. met at Wheeling on June 11, 1861, and nullified the Va. ordinance of secession, declared the offices of the state govt. at Richmond to be vacated, and formed the "restored govt." of Va. Creation of a new state was overwhelmingly approved in the referendum of Oct. 24, and in Nov. another convention at Wheeling began to draft the state constitution that was approved in April 1862. President Lincoln proclaimed (April 20, 1863) admission of a new state, W.Va., to be effective 60 days thence, on June 20, 1863. The Confederates failed to hold on to the region militarily; several battles resulting in Union victories were fought at Philippi (June 3, 1861), Rich Mt. (July 11), Corrick's Ford (July 13), and Carnifax Ferry (Sept. 10). Gen. Robert E. Lee's attempt to rally the Confederate forces ended in defeat at Cheat Mt. (Sept. 12–13). The strategically important Eastern Panhandle was the scene of continual fighting; not originally a part of W.Va., it had been quickly annexed (1863) because it contained the Baltimore and Ohio RR. (W.Va.'s possession of this area was confirmed by the U.S. Supreme Court in 1871.) In 1885 the capital, which had been shuttled back and forth bet. Wheeling and Charleston, became fixed at Charleston. Three years earlier, along the border region bet. W.Va. and Ky., there had begun the now famous Hatfield-McCoy feud, which was to encompass many killings and embroil the governors of the 2 states in lengthy and heated controversy. Of great significance to W.Va. was the state's industrial expansion in the late 19th cent. Based on rich resources and supported by the in-migration of Southern Afr.-Americans and Northern and immigrant laborers, industrialization marked a change from the largely self-sufficient economy of local communities to one of dependence on industry's profits and labor's wages. W.Va.'s great chemical industry was founded during World War I when Ger. chemicals could no longer be imported, and it was greatly expanded during World War II. Both wars also brought unprecedented boom periods to the mines and the steel mills. The state's rapid industrialization, however, was long accompanied by serious labor problems. This was esp. true in the coal mines, where wages were low and working conditions dangerous. Unionization was bitterly resisted by mine owners, and strikes throughout the latter part of the 19th cent. and the 1st ⅓ of the 20th cent. were often marked by serious and extended violence. Reform measures in the 1930s under the New Deal finally assured the miners their right to organize; membership in the United Mine Workers of Amer.

(UMWA) soared, and by 1937 labor leaders enjoyed tremendous political power in the state. During the 1950s, economic weakness in the coal industry, combined with the mechanization and automation that enabled mines to operate at top efficiency with far fewer employees, helped bring about the highest unemployment rate in the country and a major exodus of pop. — down 7.2% from 1950 to 1960 and another 6.2% from 1960 to 1970. Economic conditions improved during the 1960s, as Federal aid poured into the state and massive efforts were made to attract new industry. More recently, the ravages of surface, or strip, mining have become a major political issue; in March 1971, the state legislature took initial steps toward control. W.Va.'s coal-based economy recovered in the 1970s as energy prices rose dramatically; it also was the only decade since 1950 in which the pop. grew. In the 1980s energy prices fell and employment in the mines rapidly declined as W.Va. suffered through one of the worst economic periods in the state's history. By 1983, W.Va.'s unemployment rate had risen to 21% as the state's mfg. base crumbled. W.Va.'s pop. declined 8% from 1980 to 1990. By the end of the 1980s, however, the state was attempting a modest recovery through large amounts of foreign investment and further development of the tourist industry. W.Va.'s 1st constitution was ratified in 1862; it was amended in 1863 to provide for the gradual abolition of slavery, as required by Congress before the granting of statehood. The present constitution dates from 1872. W.Va.'s executive branch is headed by a governor elected for a 4-year term. The state's bicameral legislature has a senate with 34 members elected for 4-year terms and a house of delegates with 100 members elected for 2-year terms. The state sends 2 Senators and 3 Representatives to the U.S. Congress and has 5 electoral votes. Democrats have played the dominant role in W.Va. politics since the Great Depression of the 1930s. The state's leading institution of higher learning is W.Va. Univ., which has 2 main campuses at Morgantown. W.Va. has 55 cos.: BARBOUR, BERKELEY, BOONE, BRAXTON, BROOKE, CABELL, CALHOUN, CLAY, DODDRIDGE, FAYETTE, GILMER, GRANT, GREENBRIER, HAMPSHIRE, HANCOCK, HARDY, HARRISON, JACKSON, JEFFERSON, KANAWHA, LEWIS, LINCOLN, LOGAN, MC-DOWELL, MARION, MARSHALL, MASON, MERCER, MINERAL, MINGO, MONONGALIA, MONROE, MORGAN, NICHOLAS, OHIO, PENDLETON, PLEASANTS, POCAHONTAS, PRESTON, PUTNAM, RALEIGH, RANDOLPH, RITCHIE, ROANE, SUMMERS, TAYLOR, TUCKER, TYLER, UPSHUR, WAYNE, WEBSTER, WETZEL, WIRT, WOOD, and WYOMING.

West Walker River, c.75 mi/121 km long, in E Calif. and W Nev.; rises in the Sierra Nevada range NW of Mono L., Mono co., E Calif., at N border of Yosemite Natl. Park; flows generally NE past Coleville (Calif.), then into Nev., joining East Walker R. in Lyon co. 7 mi/11.3 km S of Yerington to form Walker R. Part of flow in upper course is diverted into artificial Topaz L., on state line, and used for irrigation.

West Wareham, Mass.: see WAREHAM.

West Warren, Mass.: see WARREN.

West Warwick, town (1990 pop. 29,268), Kent co., central R.I., on the Pawtuxet R.; 41°42'N 71°31'W. Once important for textile mfg., it still has fine mill architecture, which has survived the industry's decline. West Warwick includes the village of River Point and several other former textile mill villages. Set off from Warwick and inc. 1913.

West Wendover (wen-DO-vuhr) or **Wendover**, uninc. town (1990 pop. 2,007), Elko co., NE Nev., on Utah state line, 50 mi/80 km ESE of Wells, and adjacent to Wendover (Utah; E); 40°46'N 114°07'W. Goshute Mts. to SW. Wendover Air Force Auxiliary Field to S. Bonneville Speedway and Salt Flats (Utah) to E. Developed in 1980s as gambling resort for travelers on Interstate Highway 80.

West Wildwood, borough (1990 pop. 453), Cape May co., S N.J., on barrier isl., 6 mi/9.7 km S of Cape May Court House, in resort area; 39°00'N 74°49'W.

West Willington, Conn.: see WILLINGTON.

West Windsor, township (1990 pop. 16,021), Mercer co., N.J., 8 mi/12.9 km E of Trenton; 40°17'N 74°37'W. Residential with rapid pop. growth in recent decades. Inc. 1798.

West Windsor, town (1990 pop. 923), Windsor co., E Vt., just W of Windsor; 43°29'N 72°29'W. Cabinet-making; talc. Includes village of Brownsville.

West Winfield, village (1990 pop. 871), Herkimer co., central N.Y., 15 mi/24 km S of Utica, and on Unadilla R.; 42°52'N 75°11'W. In agr. area; summer resort.

West Wyoming, borough (1990 pop. 3,117), Luzerne co., NE central Pa., suburb 5 mi/8 km NE of Wilkes-Barre, and 1 mi/1.6 km NW of Wyoming; 41°19'N 75°50'W. Mfg. includes transportation equip., textiles, bldg. materials, lumber. Wilkes-Barre Wyoming Valley Airport to S. Inc. 1898.

West Wyomissing (wei-YO-mi-sing), uninc. town (1990 pop. 3,097), Berks co., SE central Pa., residential suburb 4 mi/6.4 km W of Reading; 40°19'N 75°59'W.

West Yarmouth, Mass.: see YARMOUTH.

West Yellowstone, town (1990 pop. 913), Gallatin co., SW Mont., near Madison R. (which forms Hebgen L. reservoir to NW), near Idaho (SW; Continental Divide) and Wyo. (E) state lines; 44°40'N 111°07'W. Surrounded, except on E, by Gallatin Natl. Forest; Targhee Natl. Forest (Idaho) to W and S. W entrance to Yellowstone Natl. Park. Tourism. Federation of Flyfishers, Grizzly Discovery Center, Yellowstone IMAX Theater, Mus. of the Yellowstone. Originally called Riverside, then, later, Yellowstone.

West York, borough (1990 pop. 4,283), York co., S Pa., residential suburb 2 mi/3.2 km W of York; 39°57'N 76°45'W. RR junction. Inc. 1905.

Westampton, township (1990 pop. 6,004), Burlington co., N.J., 1 mi/1.6 km N of Mount Holly; 40°01'N 74°49'W. Inc. 1850.

Westboro, town (1990 pop. 182), Atchison co., NW Mo., 7 mi/11.3 km NNE of Tarkio; 40°32'N 95°19'W.

Westborough, town (1990 pop. 14,133), Worcester co., E central Mass., on the Assabet R.; 42°16'N 71°37'W. The town, which is largely residential, produces electronic components, tools, pharmaceuticals, dyes, computer software and network systems, and other prods. The birthplace of Eli Whitney, the inventor of the cotton gin, is preserved. Inc. 1717.

Westbourne, village, S Man., central Canada, on Whitemud R., and 16 mi/26 km NW of Portage la Prairie; 50°08'N 98°34'W. Livestock; grain.

Westbourne (WEST-buhrn), village, Campbell co., NE Tenn., 10 mi/16 km NE of La Follette. Norris Reservoir is S.

Westbrook, city (1990 pop. 16,121), Cumberland co., SW Maine, an industrial suburb W of Portland; 43°41'N 70°20'W. Mfg. includes paper, machinery, and wood prods. An industrial park is here. Founded 1657, inc. as a city 1891.

Westbrook 1 town (1990 pop. 5,414), Middlesex co., S Conn., on L.I. Sound, and 25 mi./40 km E of New Haven; 41°17'N 72°27'W. Recreational and commercial fishing, and resort activities. Settled c.1664, inc. 1840. **2** town (1990 pop. 852), Cottonwood co., SW Minn., 20 mi/32 km NW of Windom; 44°02'N 95°25'W. Diversified-farming area (grain, soybeans, alfalfa; livestock). Talcot L. Wildlife Area to S; small lakes in area.

Westbrook, village (1990 pop. 237), Mitchell co., W Texas, 9 mi/14.5 km WSW of Colorado City; 32°21'N 101°00'W. In cattle-ranching and agr. (cotton) region. L. Colorado City State Park to E.

Westbrookville, village (1990 pop. 500), Sullivan co., SE N.Y., at foot of the Shawangunk range, 11 mi/18 km NE of Port Jervis; 41°30'N 74°34'W.

Westbury, residential village (□ 2 sq mi/5.2 sq km; 1990 pop. 13,060), Nassau co., SE N.Y., on L.I.; 40°45'N 73°35'W. Harness races are held at Roosevelt Raceway here. Settled 1650, inc. 1932.

Westby, town (1990 pop. 1,866), Vernon co., SW Wis., 22 mi/35 km SE of La Crosse; 43°38'N 90°51'W. In agr. area (tobacco; livestock; dairy prods.); tobacco warehouses; wood millwork. Inc. 1920.

Westby (WEST-bee), village (1990 pop. 253), Sheridan

co., extreme NE Mont., on N.Dak. state line, 25 mi/40 km ENE of Plentywood, 50 mi/80 km NNW of Williston (N.Dak.), and 8 mi/12.9 km S of Can. (Sask.) border; 48°52'N 104°04'W. Wheat, barley, oats, sugar beets; hay; hogs, sheep, cattle. Numerous lakes in area.

Westchester, county (□ 500 sq mi/1,295 sq km; 1990 pop. 874,866), SE N.Y.; ⊙ White Plains; 41°08'N 73°45'W. Bounded W by the Hudson R. (here widening into Tappan Zee), S by N.Y. city (of whose metropolitan area it is a part), SE by L.I. Sound and Conn., E by Conn., N by Putnam co. Chiefly an affluent suburban residential region, with industrial and residential cities (e.g., White Plains, Yonkers, Mount Vernon, Peekskill, New Rochelle, Rye). Known for its country estates, hilly woodlands, and lakes (including Kensico Reservoir in Bronx R., reservoirs of Croton R. water-supply system, and Mohegan and Peach lakes). Drained by small Byram, Mianus, and Rippowam rivers. Many corporate hq. and office complexes; some light industry. Traversed by chief highways connecting N.Y. city with upstate and New England communities: landscaped parkways (Bronx R., Taconic State, Hutchinson R., Saw Mill R., and Cross Co. parkways), and historic Albany and Boston post roads. Served by N.Y., New Haven, and Hartford RR and 3 divs. of N.Y. Central RR, all of which are now part of Metro-North RR and Amtrak. Its shore communities are known for yachting. Many recreational areas and parks throughout co. Indian Point 2 and Indian Point 3 nuclear power plants are 24 mi/39 km N of N.Y. city. Formed 1683.

Westchester, city (□ 4 sq mi/10.4 sq km; 1990 pop. 29,883), Dade co., SE Fla., 7 mi/11.3 km W of Miami; 25°45'N 80°20'W.

Westchester, village (1990 pop. 17,301), Cook co., NE Ill., W suburb of Chicago; 41°51'N 87°53'W.

Westchester, Conn.: see COLCHESTER.

Westchester Heights, residential and industrial section of E central Bronx borough of N.Y. city, SE N.Y. RR yards.

Westcliffe, village (1990 pop. 312), ⊙ Custer co., S central Colo., on Grape Creek, bet. Sangre de Cristo and Wet mts., 45 mi/72 km WSW of Pueblo; 38°07'N 105°28'W. Elev. 7,888 ft/2,404 m. Sheep, cattle; dairy prods. Tourism. Silver, lead mines in vicinity. Parts of San Isabel Natl. Forest to SW and E; De Weese Reservoir to N.

Westend, suburb of High Point, Guilford co., N central N.C. There is also a hamlet called West End in Moore co.

Westerlo (WES-tuhr-loo), resort village (1990 pop. 680), Albany co., E N.Y., in the Catskill Mts., 17 mi/27 km SW of Albany; 42°28'N 74°02'W. Lakes nearby.

Westerly (WES-tuhr-lee), town (1990 pop. 21,605), Washington co., extreme SW R.I., bet. the Pawcatuck R. and Block Isl. Sound; 41°20'N 71°48'W. Textiles and granite quarrying were important c.1850. Now mfg. includes musical instruments; substantial trade market; also, a bedroom and resort town. Embraces 11 villages. A bridge (1932) connects the village of Westerly with Conn. F. L. Olmstead's architectural firm designed the fine Wilcox Park (1898) in the town center. A state airport is here. Inc. 1669.

Western, village (1990 pop. 264), Saline co., SE Nebr., 13 mi/21 km WSW of Wilber; 40°23'N 97°12'W. Grain; livestock; dairy and poultry prods.

Western Duck Island, S central Ont., central Canada, one of the Manitoulin Isls., in L. Huron, 4 mi/6 km S of Manitoulin Isl.; 2 mi/3 km long, 2 mi/3 km wide. Inner Duck Isl. (1 mi/2 km long) is 2 mi/3 km E.

Western Grove, village (1990 pop. 415), Newton co., NW Ark., 10 mi/16 km SE of Harrison; 36°06'N 92°57'W. Buffalo Natl. R. to S. Firewood.

Western Head, cape, SW N.S., E Canada, on W shore of Liverpool Bay, 4 mi/6 km SSE of Liverpool; 43°59'N 64°40'W.

Western Island, NE N.F., E Canada, one of the St. Barbe Isls., at entrance of White Bay, 22 mi/35 km NW of Cape St. John; 3 mi/5 km long; 50°12'N 55°51'W.

Western Reserve, tract of land in NE Ohio, on the S shore of L. Erie, retained by Conn. in 1786 when it ceded its claims to its W lands of the Old Northwest Territory. In 1792, Conn. gave 500,000 acres/202,350 ha, called "firelands," to citizens whose property was burned during the Amer. Revolution. The Conn. Land Company bought (1795) the remaining land, and Cleveland was est. 1796 as the 1st permanent settlement in the reserve. In 1880 the reserve gained govt. when it was included in the Northwest Territory as Trumbull co.; later this region was divided into 10 cos. and parts of 4 others. The chief cities are Cleveland, Akron, Youngstown, Ashtabula, Lorain, and Sandusky.

Western Springs, village (1990 pop. 11,984), Cook co., NE Ill., residential suburb 15 mi/24 km WSW of downtown Chicago; 41°47′N 87°54′W. Ships seeds, nursery plants. Inc. 1886.

Westernport, town (1990 pop. 2,454). Allegany co., W Md., on North Branch of the Potomac R. (bridged to Piedmont, W.Va.) in the Alleghenies, and 19 mi/31 km SW of Cumberland; 39°29′N 79°02′W. Once a stopping point for traders and others headed W along Native Amer. trails to the Ohio R. Bituminous coal was boomed out on rafts during flood seasons in the 19th cent. as were logs. Paper pulp has replaced coal as the principal industry. Settled c.1790.

Westerville, city (1990 pop. 30,269), Delaware and Franklin cos., central Ohio; 40°07′N 82°55′W. Seed and grain cleaners, fabricated steel, and dairy prods. are made. Seat of Otterbein Col. Hoover Reservoir is to the E. Inc. 1858.

Westfall, village, Malheur co., E Oregon, 23 mi/37 km W of Vale on Bully Creek. Elev. 3,002 ft/915 m.

Westfield, city (1990 pop. 38,372), Hampden co., SW Mass., residential and industrial suburb of Springfield, on the Westfield R.; 42°08′N 72°46′W. Bicycles, electronics, machinery, and paper and metal prods. are made. Westfield State Col. is here. Stanley Park nearby. Settled c.1660, inc. as a city 1920.

Westfield 1 town (1990 pop. 3,304), Hamilton co., central Ind., 5 mi/8 km N of Carmel; 40°03′N 86°08′W. In agr. area; mfg. (textiles, chemicals, machinery, transportation equip., fabricated metal prods., plastic prods., feed; steel cutting). Laid out 1834. **2** town (1990 pop. 160), Plymouth co., NW Iowa, near Big Sioux R., 23 mi/37 km W of Le Mars; 42°45′N 96°36′W. **3** town (1990 pop. 589), Aroostook co., NE Maine, on Presque Isle Stream, 8 mi/12.9 km SE of Presque Isle; 46°32′N 67°58′W. **4** town (1990 pop. 28,870), Union co., NE N.J.; 40°38′N 74°20′W. Almost entirely residential. A Revolutionary War cemetery is here. Settled late 17th cent. as part of Elizabethtown. Inc. 1903. **5** town (1990 pop. 422), Orleans co., N Vt., on Missisquoi R., and 11 mi/18 km WSW of Newport; 44°52′N 72°28′W. In agr. area; wood prods. **6** town (1990 pop. 1,125), Marquette co., central Wis., on branch of Montello R. (tributary of Fox R.), and 24 mi/39 km N of Portage; 43°52′N 89°29′W. In agr. area (potatoes, rye, corn); poultry prods., cheese. Westfield State Fish Hatchery to W; wildlife area. Hunting.

Westfield 1 village (1990 pop. 676), Clark co., E Ill., 17 mi/27 km WNW of Marshall; 39°27′N 88°00′W. Agr. (corn, wheat, soybeans, sorghum; cattle, hogs, poultry). **2** village (□ 3 sq mi/7.8 sq km; 1990 pop. 3,451), Chautauqua co., extreme W N.Y., near L. Erie, 17 mi/27 km SW of Dunkirk; 42°19′N 79°34′W. Mfg. of paper goods; large grape-juice and grape-concentrate industry (since 1896); in grape-growing area. In 1873 Thomas and Charles Bradwell Welch, ardent Prohibitionists, devised method of pressing Concord grapes into unfermented wine. Settled 1800, inc. 1833.

Westfield, borough (1990 pop. 1,119), Tioga co., N Pa., 16 mi/26 km NW of Wellsboro; 41°55′N 77°32′W. Mfg. (printing and publishing); agr. (hay; livestock; dairying). Inc. 1867.

Westfield River, c.60 mi/97 km long, W Mass.; rises in Hoosac Range in N Berkshire co.; flows generally SE, through Westfield, to the Connecticut R. opposite Springfield. Furnishes water power to mfg. towns. Lower course once known as Agawam R. West Branch

(c.25 mi/40 km long) and Middle Branch (c.20 mi/32 km long) enter from W in Huntington, below dam impounding Knightville Reservoir (c.3.5 mi/5.6 km long).

Westfir (WEST-fuhr), village (1990 pop. 278), Lane co., W Oregon, 2 mi/3.2 km NW of Oakridge, on Middle Fork Willamette R. (forms Lookout Point Reservoir to NW), at mouth of North Fork Willamette R.; 43°45′N 122°30′W. Area surrounded by Willamette Natl. Forest. Timber; tourism.

Westford 1 town (□ 31 sq mi/80 sq km; 1990 pop. 16,392), Middlesex co., NE Mass., suburb of Boston; 42°35′N 71°26′W. Although chiefly residential, there are apple orchards, granite quarries (which have long been in operation), and a book lithography firm. Mfg. also of textile machinery and electronics. Of interest are 2 saltbox houses (17th cent.) and the Old Fletcher Tavern (1713). Includes villages of Forge Village, Graniteville (site of former granite quarries). Nashoba Valley Ski Area. Settled 1653, set off from Chelmsford and inc. 1729. **2** town (1990 pop. 1,740), Chittenden co., NW Vt., on Browns R., and 14 mi/23 km NE of Burlington; 44°36′N 73°00′W. Maple sugar.

Westgard Pass, Calif.: see INYO MOUNTAINS.

Westgate, town (1990 pop. 207), Fayette co., NE Iowa, 8 mi/12.9 km NNW of Oelwein; 42°46′N 92°00′W. In agr. area.

Westgate Hills, uninc. town (1990 pop. 1,060), Northampton co., E Pa., residential suburb 2 mi/3.2 km NNW of Bethlehem; 40°38′N 75°24′W. Lehigh Vallley Internatl. Airport to W.

Westhampton (wes-TAM-tuhn), town (1990 pop. 1,327), Hampshire co., W central Mass., 8 mi/12.9 km W of Northampton; 42°18′N 72°47′W.

Westhampton, resort village (□ 14 sq mi/36 sq km; 1990 pop. 2,129), Suffolk co., SE N.Y., on S shore of L.I., on an inlet of Moriches Bay, 6 mi/9.7 km S of Riverhead; 40°50′N 72°39′W. Just S is Westhampton Beach, shore resort. Much like most of S L.I. shore zone, suffering from significant beach erosion due to a succession of mid-1990s Atlantic hurricanes. Within the greater Westhampton region of L.I.'s S fork; part of the original Quogue Purchase of 1666. Westhampton's 1st summer house built by Gen. John A. Dix in 1879; then a 3-day journey by stage from Brooklyn until L.I. RR extended to Sag Harbor in 1870. By 1920s Westhampton and "The Hamptons" were the summering place for the rich and famous. Inc. 1928.

Westhampton Beach, N.Y.: see WESTHAMPTON.

Westhaven-Moonstone, uninc. town (1990 pop. 1,109), Humboldt co., NW Calif., 16 mi/26 km N of Eureka, on Pacific Ocean; 41°02′N 124°06′W. Timber; cattle. Trinidad State Beach to NW; Redwood Natl. Park to N.

Westhoff, uninc. village (1990 pop. 410), De Witt co., S Texas, 39 mi/63 km NW of Victoria. Oil and natural gas. Agr. area (cattle, hogs; wheat, sorghum, grains). Mfg. (machinery).

Westhope, village (1990 pop. 578), Bottineau co., N N.Dak., 28 mi/45 km W of Bottineau, near Souris R. (Mouse R.); 48°54′N 101°01′W. RR terminus. Grain; livestock; dairy prods. U.S. customs station here (Can. border 7 mi/11.3 km N). J. Clark Salyer Natl. Wildlife Refuge to E.

Westlake 1 city (1990 pop. 5,007), Calcasieu parish, SW La., on Calcasieu R., and suburb 3 mi/5 km W of Lake Charles; 30°15′N 93°16′W. RR junction. Oil refining, mfg. (chemicals, bldg. materials). Town shares part of L. Charles. Inc. since 1940. Oil-producing region to W. Sam Houston Jones State Park to N. **2** city (1990 pop. 27,018), Cuyahoga co., NE Ohio, suburb of Cleveland; 41°27′N 81°55′W. A growing city; mfg. includes ink and plastics and chemicals. Inc. as a city 1956.

Westlake, village (1990 pop. 185), Tarrant and Denton cos., N Texas, residential suburb 17 mi/27 km NNE of Fort Worth; 32°59′N 97°12′W. Agr. to N; growing urban fringe area. Grapevine L. reservoir to E.

Westlake Village, city (1990 pop. 7,455), Los Angeles

and Ventura cos., S Calif., industrial suburb 34 mi/55 km WNW of downtown Los Angeles, and 2 mi/3.2 km SE of Thousand Oaks; 34°08′N 118°49′W. Mfg. (electrical and electronic equip., shoes, foods and food prods., computers and computer equip., cosmetics, machinery; printing and publishing). Santa Monica Mts. Natl Recreation Area to S.

Westland, city (1990 pop. 84,724), Wayne co., SE Mich., suburb 20 mi/32 km W of downtown Detroit; 42°19′N 83°22′W. Drained in N by Middle R. Rouge, in S by Lower R. Rouge; parkways on both rivers. Mfg. (fabricated metal prods., transportation equip., plastic prods., electrical equip.). Nankin Mills Nature Center on N border.

Westlock, town (1991 pop. 4,719), central Alta., W Canada, 45 mi/72 km NNW of Edmonton; 54°09′N 113°52′W. Grain elevators, flour mills; dairying, mixed farming.

Westmanland, plantation (1990 pop. 72), Aroostook co., NE Maine, on Little Madawaska R., and 22 mi/35 km NW of Presque Isle; 46°58′N 68°14′W.

Westminster, town (1991 pop. 6,826), SW Ont., central Canada, suburb 6 mi/10 km. S of London, an amalgamation of communities of Scottsville, Lambeth, Glanworth. MacDonald-Cartier Freeway (Highway 401) runs NE-SW; intersection of Highway 402 Freeway to Sarnia. Mostly rural. Mixed farming; dairying; fruit, tobacco, peanuts.

Westminster 1 city (□ 10 sq mi/26 sq km; 1990 pop. 78,118), Orange co., S Calif., suburb 31 mi/40 km SE of downtown Los Angeles, and 10 mi/16 km E of Long Beach; 33°45′N 118°00′W. Mfg. (metal heat treating, printing and publishing; machinery, hardware, fabricated metal prods.). Seal Beach U.S. Naval Weapons Station to W and Los Alamitos Naval Air Base to NW. Westminster has been marked by urban growth during 1970s along with most of S Calif. Pacific Ocean coast 5 mi/8 km to SW. Very high concentration of Vietnamese-Americans — "Little Saigon." Founded 1870 as a temperance colony for Presbyterians, inc. 1957. **2** city (1990 pop. 74,625), Adams and Jefferson cos., N central Colo., residential suburb 7 mi/11.3 km NW of downtown Denver, near Clear Creek; 39°52′N 105°02′W. Elev. 5,280 ft/1,609 m. Mfg. (electronic equip., leather goods, aerial lifts). Westminster has been marked by tremendous residential growth, along with the entire Denver metropolitan area; its pop. nearly quadrupled bet. 1970 and 1990. Front Range Community Col. here. Jefferson County Airport and Standley L. reservoir to W. Inc. 1911. **3** city (1990 pop. 13,068), ⊙ Carroll co., N Md., 29 mi/47 km NW of Baltimore; 39°35′N 77°01′W. In agr. area; mfg. (clothes, shoes, tools, whiskey); canneries, meatpacking plants. Laid out as 5 separate villages (accounting for its 2-mi/3.2-km main street) in 1764, it was called Winchester until 1768 when the name was changed to avoid confusion with Winchester, Va. Western Maryland Col., founded by the Methodist Church in 1867, is said to be the 1st co-educational col. started below the Mason-Dixon Line. The Carroll County Mus. contains early Amer. flags, 19th-cent. dolls and a glass collection that belonged to Mrs. H. L. Mencken, wife of the Baltimore writer. A postal mus. in the bldg. commemorates the 1st R.F.D. service, which was tried out here. The courthouse was built in 1837, and the Carroll County Farm Mus. contains an 1850 period farmhouse, barn, and outbuildings along with draft horses and early farm machinery.

Westminster 1 town (1990 pop. 6,191), Worcester co., N Mass., 6 mi/9.7 km SW of Fitchburg; 42°33′N 71°55′W. Mfg. (foods, wood prods., electronic equip.); dairying. Has state park, state forests. Settled 1737, inc. 1759. **2** town (1990 pop. 3,120), Oconee co., NW S.C., 45 mi/72 km WSW of Greenville; 34°40′N 83°05′W. Mfg. includes textiles, consumer goods, tools, wood prods., furniture, fabricated metal prods. Agr. includes dairying; poultry; apples, corn, wheat, timber, soybeans. Tourist trade for nearby Blue Ridge Mts. **3** town (1990 pop. 3,026), Windham co., SE Vt., on the Connecticut R., and 10 mi/16 km ENE of Newfane; 43°04′N

72°30′W. Scene of violence (1775) over conflicting N.Y. and N.H. jurisdiction. Vt. declared independent state of New Connecticut at convention here (1777). *Vermont Gazette* or *Green Mountain Post Boy*, state's 1st newspaper, issued here (1781). Granted 1735 or 1736, regranted 1752, chartered 1772. Includes villages of Westminster and North Westminster.

Westminster, village (1990 pop. 388), Collin co., N Texas, 20 mi/32 km SSE of Sherman; 33°21′N 96°27′W. In agr. area.

Westmont, uninc. city (1990 pop. 31,044), Los Angeles co., S Calif., 7 mi/11.3 km WSW of downtown Los Angeles; 33°57′N 118°18′W. Baldwin Hills and Inglewood Oil Field to W. Kenneth Hahn St. Recreation Area to NW.

Westmont 1 village (1990 pop. 21,228), Du Page co., NE Ill., residential suburb 20 mi/32 km W of downtown Chicago, and 17 mi/27 km E of Aurora; 41°47′N 87°58′W. Remnant agr.; mfg. (fabricated metal prods., computer equip., machinery, paper goods, electrical goods, dental equip.). Inc. 1921. **2** village, Camden co., SW N.J. in suburban area, 5 mi/8 km SE of Camden.

Westmont, borough (1990 pop. 5,789), Cambria co., W central Pa., residential suburb 2 mi/3.2 km W of Johnstown; 40°19′N 78°57′W. Gallitzin State Forest to NW.

Westmore, resort town (1990 pop. 305), Orleans co., N Vt., on Willoughby L., and 13 mi/21 km SE of Newport; 44°45′N 72°01′W. Agr. Includes part of Willoughby State Forest.

Westmoreland, county (□ 1,430 sq mi/3,704 sq km; 1991 pop. 114,745), SE N.B., E Canada, on Northumberland Strait, at N.S. border; ⊙ Dorchester.

Westmoreland, parish (1991 pop. 126,136), Cornwall co., SW Jamaica; ⊙ Savanna-la-Mar; 18°21′N–18°04′W 78°22′N–77°53′W. Bounded by Hanover (N), St. James (E), and St. Elizabeth (SE) parishes. Occupies, with South Negril Point, westernmost part of the isl.; watered by Cabaritta R. Has fertile plains, producing principally rice, sugarcane, breadfruit; cattle, horses, mules; coffee, cacao, ginger, annatto, pimento, and logwood. Savanna-la-Mar is its leading port and trading center. Negril has expanded the parish as a prime tourism attraction area.

Westmoreland 1 county (□ 1,036 sq mi/2,683 sq km; 1990 pop. 370,321), SW Pa.; ⊙ Greensburg; 40°18′N 79°28′W. Bounded NE by Kiskiminetas and Conemaugh rivers, SW by Monongahela R., NW by Allegheny R.; drained by Youghiogheny R. (forms part of W border) and Loyalhanna Creek. Laurel Hill ridge along SE border. Mining (bituminous coal; limestone, sand and gravel, oil, natural gas) and mfg. region. Mfg. at New Kensington, Murrysville, Jeanette, Greensburg, Scottdale, and Latrobe. Agr. area (corn, wheat, oats, hay, alfalfa, apples; sheep, hogs, cattle; eggs; dairying). Urban growth has occurred in W and central parts of co., from Pittsburgh metropolitan area to W. Native Amer. chief Pontiac defeated here 1763; Revolutionary Rattlesnake Flag originated here 1775. Hannastown was subject of dispute bet. Pa. and Va. Chestnut Ridge crosses co. N-S in E center; Beaver Run Reservoir in NW; Linn Run State Park in SE; Keystone State Park in N; part of Forbes State Forest in SE; Laurel Mt. State Park in SE; part of Laurel Ridge State Park in E and NE. Formed 1773. **2** county (□ 252 sq mi/653 sq km; 1990 pop. 15,480), E Va.; ⊙ Montross; 38°06′N 76°47′W. In N part of Northern Neck peninsula; bounded NE by Potomac R. estuary, SW in part by Rappahannock R. Seafood canning; agr. (barley, wheat, corn, soybeans, tomatoes, tobacco, hay; cattle, poultry); fish, oysters, crabs. "Wakefield," birthplace of George Washington (George Washington Birthplace Natl. Monument), and STRATFORD HALL, Robert E. Lee's birthplace, both N, on Potomac R. Resorts (notably Colonial Beach); Westmoreland State Park in N, also on Potomac R. Formed 1653.

Westmoreland 1 town (1990 pop. 541), ⊙ Pottawatomie co., NE Kansas, 45 mi/72 km NW of Topeka; 39°23′N 96°24′W. Elev. 1,270 ft/387 m. In cattle and grain region. Pottawatomie State Fishing L. No. 1 to N. **2**- (WEST-muhr-luhnd), town (1990 pop. 1,596), Cheshire co., SW N.H., 8 mi/12.9 km WNW of Keene, and on Connecticut R. (W; Vt. state line); 42°57′N 72°26′W. Hyland Hill (1,510 ft/460 m) on E border. Timber; dairying; poultry, cattle, sheep; nursery crops, vegetables, apples. Mfg. (wood prods.). **3** (WEST-MOR-luhnd), town (1990 pop. 1,726), Summer co., N Tenn., near Ky. state line, 16 mi/26 km NE of Gallatin; 36°34′N 86°15′W. In strawberry-growing region.

Westmoreland City, uninc. town (1990 pop. 1,500), North Huntingdon township, Westmoreland co., SW Pa., 10 mi/16 km E of McKeesport, on Brush Creek; 40°19′N 79°40′W. Mfg. (machining; lab equip.); agr. (grain, soybeans; livestock; dairying).

Westmorland, city (1990 pop. 1,380), Imperial co., S Calif., in Imperial Valley, 15 mi/24 km N of El Centro, 6 mi/9.7 km S of Salton Sea; 33°02′N 115°37′W. Inc. 1932. Sometimes spelled Westmoreland. Natl. Parachute Test Range to SW.

Westmount, city (1991 pop. 20,239), S Que., E Canada, on Montreal isl.; 45°29′N 73°36′W. A primarily Eng.-speaking W residential suburb of Montreal, it became a city in 1908.

Weston, county (□ 2,400 sq mi/6,216 sq km; 1990 pop. 6,518), NE Wyo., on S.Dak. (E) state line; ⊙ Newcastle; 43°50′N 104°33′W. Drained by South Fork Cheyenne R. and Beaver Creek. Oats; cattle; timber. Oil, natural gas and clay found here. Large part of Thunder Basin Natl. Grassland in N to S and in SW. Part of Black Hills and Black Hills Natl. Forest in NE. Formed 1890.

Weston 1 planned city (1997 est. pop. 15,000), Broward co., SE Fla., 15 mi/24 km W of Fort Lauderdale. Upscale planned town and business complex that surrounds major freeway intersection. One of Fla.'s largest retail concentrations was built just NE in the 1990s, focusing on Sawgrass Mills (among the nation's largest outlet malls). **2** city (1990 pop. 1,528), Platte co., W Mo., on Missouri R., and 30 mi/48 km NW of Kansas City; 39°24′N 94°54′W. Wheat, corn; only tobacco market W of Mississippi R. Flour milling; winery; distillery (McCormick whiskey, 1 of 2 in Mo.). Antiques, crafts, artists' colony. Weston Bend State Park. Area flooded 1993. Founded 1837. Early rivertown rival of Kansas City and St. Joseph.

Weston 1 residential town (1990 pop. 8,648), Fairfield co., SW Conn., near Saugatuck R., 6 mi/9.7 km N of Norwalk; 41°13′N 73°22′W. Settled c.1670, inc. 1787. **2** town (1990 pop. 42), Webster co., W Ga., 23 mi/37 km WSW of Americus; 31°59′N 84°37′W. **3** town (1990 pop. 207), Aroostook co., E Maine, on Grand L., and 28 mi/45 km S of Houlton; 45°43′N 67°51′W. **4** town (1990 pop. 10,200), Middlesex co., E Mass., affluent suburb W of Boston; 42°22′N 71°18′W. The town is mainly residential. Regis Col., the Weston-Boston Col. Geophysical Observatory, and many 18th-cent. bldgs. are here. Includes village of Kendall Green. Settled c.1642, set off from Watertown and inc. 1713. **5** town (1990 pop. 488), Windsor co., S central Vt., on West R., and c.30 mi/48 km SW of Woodstock; 43°19′N 72°47′W. Partly in Green Mt. Natl. Forest. **6** town (1990 pop. 4,994), ⊙ Lewis co., central W. Va., 18 mi/29 km SSW of Clarksburg, on the West Fork R. (forms Stonewall Jackson L. reservoir, a State Park and Wildlife Management Area, to S); 39°02′N 80°28′W. Agr. (corn, potatoes); livestock. Oil, gas, and timber region. Mfg. (glass, fabricated metal prods., shoes, clothing labels). Ancestral home of Stonewall Jackson. Walkerville Covered Bridge to S. Jackson's Mill Historic Site and State 4-H Camp to N. Stonecoal L. reservoir (Wildlife Management Area) to SE. Founded 1818.

Weston 1 village, Las Animas co., S Colo., junction of North and South forks of Purgatoire R., in E foothills of Sangre de Cristo Mts., 20 mi/32 km W of Trinidad. Elev. c.6,976 ft/2,126 m. Lumbering; agr. Culebra Peak (14,069 ft/4,288 m) is 17 mi/27 km W. San Isabel Natl. Forest to NW. **2** village (1990 pop. 390), Franklin co., SE Idaho, near Utah state line, 5 mi/8 km SW of Preston; 42°02′N 111°59′W. Elev. 4,743 ft/1,446 m. Wheat, barley; sugar beets; sheep, cattle; dairying. Weston Canyon and Caribou Natl. Forest to NW. **3** village (1990 pop. 299), Saunders co., E Nebr., 7 mi/11.3 km W of Wahoo, and on branch of Platte R.; 41°11′N 96°44′W. **4** village (1990 pop. 1,716), Wood co., NW Ohio, 8 mi/13 km WSW of Bowling Green; 41°20′N 83°48′W. Corn, wheat; hogs; food processing. **5** village (1990 pop. 606), Umatilla co., NE Oregon, 20 mi/32 km NE of Pendleton, 17 mi/27 km S of Walla Walla (Wash.), on Pine Creek; 45°49′N 118°25′W. Agr. (vegetables, apples, potatoes, plums, beans). Mfg. (frozen foods). Umatilla Indian Reservation to S; Umatilla Natl. Forest, including Umatilla Wilderness Area, to SE. **6** village (1990 pop. 362), Collin co., N Texas, 41 mi/66 km NNE of Dallas, and 20 mi/32 km SSW of Sherman; 33°19′N 96°38′W. Agr. area (cotton, wheat, sorghum; cattle).

Westover, town (1990 pop. 4,201), Monongalia co., N W.Va., suburb 1 mi/1.6 km W of Morgantown, on Monongahela R. (bridged), opposite Morgantown; 39°38′N 79°58′W. Coal region. Agr. (grain); livestock, poultry. Mfg. (commercial printing; machinery). Inc. 1911.

Westover, village, Somerset co., SE Md., 18 mi/29 km SSW of Salisbury. Site of the co.'s largest freshwater spring.

Westover (WES-to-vuhr), borough (1990 pop. 446), Clearfield co., central Pa., 8 mi/12.9 km NE of Barnesboro, on Chest Creek; 40°45′N 78°40′W. Surface bituminous coal. Agr. (corn, hay; livestock; dairying).

Westover, suburb (1990 pop. 600) of Binghamton, Broome co., S N.Y., 3 mi/4.8 km W of city center; 42°07′N 75°59′W.

Westover Air Force Base, Mass.: see SPRINGFIELD.

Westover Hills, uninc. town (1990 pop. 790), New Castle co., N Del., residential suburb 2 mi/3.2 km WNW of downtown Wilmington; 39°46′N 75°35′W. Hagley Mus. to N; Mus. of Natural History to NW. Univ. of Del. (Wilmington campus) to E.

Westover Hills, village (1990 pop. 672), Tarrant co., N Texas, residential suburb 5 mi/8 km W of downtown Fort Worth, surrounded by Fort Worth.

Westphalia 1 (west-FAI-lee-uh), town (1990 pop. 144), Shelby co., W Iowa, near sources of Keg and Silver creeks, 6 mi/9.7 km NW of Harlan; 41°43′N 95°23′W. **2** town (1990 pop. 287), Osage co., central Mo., near Osage R., 7 mi/11.3 km SW of Linn; 38°26′N 92°00′W. Mfg. (transportation equip.); cattle; corn, wheat; wine region. Center of region settled by Ger. immigrants beginning in 1835.

Westphalia 1 (west-FAI-lee-uh), village (1990 pop. 152), Anderson co., E Kansas, 15 mi/24 km WSW of Garnett; 38°10′N 95°29′W. In livestock, grain, and dairy region. **2** village (1990 pop. 780), Clinton co., S central Mich., 18 mi/29 km NW of Lansing; 42°55′N 84°47′W. In farm area.

Westport, village (1991 pop. 664), SE Ont., central Canada, on Upper Rideau L., 30 mi/48 km NNE of Kingston. Woodworking, dairying, boatbuilding; furniture.

Westport 1 residential town (1990 pop. 24,410), Fairfield co., SW Conn., on L.I. Sound at the mouth of the Saugatuck R.; 41°07′N 73°20′W. Retailing and office center for Fairfield co. It serves as a popular residence for affluent N.Y. city commuters. Westport has a summer theater. William Tryon landed at Compo Beach before his raid on Danbury in 1777. A number of 18th-cent. houses remain. Settled 1645–1650, inc. 1835. **2** town (1990 pop. 1,478), Decatur co., SE central Ind., 12 mi/19 km SSW of Greensburg; 39°11′N 85°35′W. In agr. area; mfg. (plastic prods., glass prods.). Laid out 1836. **3** fishing town (1990 pop. 663), Lincoln co., S Maine, 8 mi/12.9 km S of Wiscasset, and on isl. in Sheepscot R.; 43°54′N 69°42′W. **4** resort town (1990 pop. 13,852), Bristol co., SE Mass., 7 mi/11.3 km SE of Fall River, and on short Westport R., near R.I. state line; 41°34′N 71°05′W. Includes villages of Acoaxet, Central Village, Horseneck Beach (Mass. state park and state beach), Westport Mills (industrial), South Westport, North Westport (1990 pop. 4,697), and Westport Point (on sheltered S inlet). Vineyard and winery. Settled 1670, set off from Dartmouth 1787. **5** uninc. town (1990 pop. 1,280), Lincoln co., W central N.C., 10 mi/16 km SW of Mooresville, on W shore of L. Norman reservoir (Catawba R.); 35°30′N 80°58′W. **6** town (1990 pop. 1,892), Grays Harbor co., W Wash., at S side of entrance to Grays Harbor, 15 mi/24 km WSW of Aberdeen; 46°54′N 124°07′W. Summer resort; mfg. (fresh and frozen seafood; shipbuilding). Westhaven State Park to W, on Pacific coast; Westport Light State Park, on Pacific Ocean; Two Harbors State Park to S. Passenger ferry to Ocean Shores, on N side of harbor entrance. Maritime mus.

Westport 1 village (1990 pop. 47), Pope co., W Minn., 12 mi/19 km ENE of Glenwood, on Ashley Creek, forms Westport L. to SW; 45°42′N 95°10′W. In grain area; mfg. (fabricated metal prods.). **2** resort village (1990 pop. 500), Essex co., NE N.Y., on L. Champlain, 24 mi/39 km N of Ticonderoga; 44°10′N 73°26′W. Lumber. Annual co. fair and a summer regatta held here. **3** village (1990 pop. 326), Pawnee co., N Okla., 19 mi/31 km W of Tulsa, on Keystone L. reservoir (Arkansas R.); 36°11′N 96°20′W. Recreation area. Feyodi Creek State Park to NW.

Westport Annex, village, Johnson co., S suburb of Kansas City, E Kansas.

Westport Mills, Mass.: see WESTPORT.

Westport Point, Mass.: see WESTPORT.

Westside, town (1990 pop. 348), Crawford co., W Iowa, 14 mi/23 km ENE of Denison; 42°04′N 95°05′W. Processed soybeans, feed.

Westview, town, SW B.C., W Canada, on the Strait of Georgia, 3 mi/5 km SSE of Powell R.; 49°51′N 124°32′W. Lumbering center.

Westview, village, Cuyahoga co., N Ohio, 14 mi/23 km SW of downtown Cleveland.

Westville, town (1991 pop. 4,228), N N.S., E Canada, 5 mi/8 km SW of New Glasgow; 45°33′N 62°43′W. Coal-mining center.

Westville 1 town (1990 pop. 5,255), La Porte co., NW Ind., 10 mi/16 km WSW of La Porte; 41°32′N 86°55′W. In agr. area; mfg. (feed and fertilizer blending). Settled 1836, laid out 1851. **2** town (1990 pop. 1,374), Adair co., E Okla., 20 mi/32 km E of Tahlequah, near Ark. state line; 35°59′N 94°34′W. Mfg. (electric motors). **3** uninc. town (1990 pop. 2,200), Greenville co., NW S.C., residential suburb 3 mi/4.8 km W of downtown Greenville.

Westville, village (1990 pop. 3,387), Vermilion co., E Ill., 4 mi/6.4 km S of Danville; 40°02′N 87°38′W. RR junction. Bituminous-coal mines; agr. (corn, soybeans; cattle; dairy prods.). Plotted 1873, inc. 1896.

Westville, residential borough (1990 pop. 4,573), Gloucester co., SW N.J., on Delaware R., at mouth of Big Timber Creek, and 5 mi/8 km S of Camden; 39°52′N 75°07′W. Oil refining, mfg. (clothing, chemicals, glass, fabricated metal prods.). Inc. 1924.

Westville Dam, Mass.: see QUINEBAUG RIVER.

Westville Lake, reservoir, Worcester co., S central Mass., on Quinebaug R., 1 mi/2 km W of Southbridge; 42°05′N 72°04′W. Max. capacity 24,000 acre-ft. Formed by Westville Dam (67 ft/20 m high), built (1962) by Army Corps of Engineers for flood control; also used for recreation. Old Sturbridge Village on W bank of reservoir.

Westwego (west-WEE-go), city (1990 pop. 11,218), Jefferson parish, SE La., on W bank (levee) of the Mississippi R., opposite New Orleans; 29°54′N 90°08′W. River and seaport and seafood-processing center; shipbuilding; mfg. (chemicals, boats, dairy prods., fiberglass prods., bldg. materials, machinery). Offshore oil fields nearby. Salvador State Wildlife Area to SW; Bayou Segnette State Park to SE.

Westwood 1 uninc. town (□ 5 sq mi/13 sq km; 1990 pop. 2,017), Lassen co., NE Calif., 20 mi/32 km NW of Susanville, near North Fork of Feather R.; 40°18′N 121°00′W. Mt. Meadows Reservoir to SE; L. Almanor Reservoir to SW; parts of Lassen Natl. Forest to N and S; Coppervale Ski Area and Freedonyer Peak (5,771 ft/ 1,759 m) to E. **2** uninc. town (1990 pop. 734), Boyd co., NE Ky., a residential suburb 2 mi/3.2 km NW of Ashland, near the Ohio R.; 38°16′N 85°35′W. **3** affluent residential town (1990 pop. 12,557), Norfolk co., E Mass.,

in the Greater Boston area; 42°13′N 71°13′W. Mfg. (clothing). It has several early 18th-cent. bldgs. Includes village of Islington. Settled 1640, inc. 1897.

Westwood 1 village (1990 pop. 104), Henry co., SE Iowa, 5 mi/8 km WNW of Mt. Pleasant, on Skunk R.; 40°57′N 91°37′W. Corn, soybeans; cattle, hogs. **2** village (1990 pop. 1,772), Johnson co., E Kansas, suburb of Kansas City, Kansas, 3 mi/4.8 km S of downtown, and on Mo. (E) state line; 39°02′N 94°37′W. Hq. of Sprint Corp. Inc. after 1940.

Westwood, residential borough (1990 pop. 10,446), Bergen co., NE N.J., suburb in the N.Y.-N.J. metropolitan area; 40°59′N 74°01′W. Some light mfg. Inc. 1894.

Westwood Hills, village (1990 pop. 383), Johnson co., E Kansas, suburb 3 mi/4.8 km S of downtown Kansas City, Kansas, and on Mo. (E) state line; 39°02′N 94°36′W.

Westwood Hills. W residential section of Los Angeles, Los Angeles co., S Calif., 10 mi/16 km W of downtown Los Angeles, W of Beverly Hills. Univ. of Calif. at Los Angeles (UCLA) is here.

Westworth Village, town (1990 pop. 2,350), Tarrant co., N Texas, residential suburb 5 mi/8 km W of downtown Fort Worth, on West Fork of Trinity R.; 32°45′N 97°25′W. Surrounded by city of Fort Worth. Carswell Air Force Base (now closed) and L. Worth reservoir to NW.

Wet Mountains, S central Colo., range of Rocky Mts. in Custer, Fremont, Huerfano, and Pueblo cos.; extend SSE from Arkansas R. to Huerfano R. Highest point is Greenhorn Mt. (12,347 ft/3,763 m) in S tip. Include part of San Isabel Natl. Forest.

Wetaskiwin (we-TA-skuh-win), city (1991 pop. 10,634), central Alta., W Canada, 40 mi/64 km S of Edmonton; 52°58′N 113°23′W. RR junction. Coal mining, oil and natural-gas production; grain elevators, flour mills, dairying; cattle, poultry.

Wethersfield, town (1990 pop. 25,651), Hartford co., central Conn., on the Connecticut R., adjoining Hartford on the N; 41°42′N 72°40′W. Wethersfield, which is largely residential, relies on the motel-gas-restaurant trade, and marine terminals for gasoline and fuel oils. Mfg. includes tools, machinery, frozen foods, dies, fabricated metal and metal prods., chemicals; printing, warehousing. Hq. of Conn. Light and Power Company Computer Center and Northeast Utilities Service Company; Dept. of Transportation, Labor Dept., and State Motor Vehicles Dept. The oldest permanent Eng. settlement in Conn., Wethersfield has preserved many colonial bldgs. They include the Joseph Webb House, where Gen. George Washington and the Comte de Rochambeau met secretly in 1781 to coordinate the efforts of Fr. forces with the Amer. army in the Amer. Revolution. Settled 1634 by colonists from Watertown, Mass.; inc. 1637.

Wetmore, village (1990 pop. 284), Nemaha co., NE Kansas, 12 mi/19 km NNW of Holton; 39°37′N 95°48′W. Livestock; grain.

Wetonka, village (1990 pop. 12), McPherson co., N S.Dak., 18 mi/29 km NW of Aberdeen; 45°37′N 98°46′W.

Wetterman Peak (14,017 ft/4,272 m), in San Juan Mts., Ouray and Hinsdale cos., SW Colo., 8 mi/12.9 km ENE of Ouray, in Uncompahgre Natl. Forest. Uncompahgre Peak 2 mi/3.2 km to ENE.

Wetumka (wuh-TUHM-kuh), town (1990 pop. 1,427), Hughes co., central Okla., 13 mi/21 km NE of Holdenville, near North Canadian R.; 35°14′N 96°14′W. In agr. area (peanuts, melons, corn). Natural-gas deposits. Settled by Creek people.

Wetumpka (wuh-TUHM-kuh), city (1990 pop. 4,670), ⊙ Elmore co., E central Ala., on Coosa R., and 12 mi/ 19 km NNE of Montgomery. Agr. trade center in cotton and corn region. Woodworking; mfg. (textiles, chalkboards). Wildlife mus. Native Amer. mounds and site of Fort Toulouse are nearby. Jordan Dam in Coosa R., 5 mi/8 km NNW, is unit in hydroelectric development.

Wetzel (WET-zuhl), county (□ 361 sq mi/935 sq km; 1990 pop. 19,258), N W.Va., on Ohio (W; Ohio R.) and Pa. (N) state lines; ⊙ New Martinsville. Drained by

small Fish and Fishing creeks. Oil and natural-gas wells; sand and gravel pits. Agr. (corn, potatoes, hay); cattle, poultry, sheep. Mfg. at New Martinsville. Lewis Wetzel Wildlife Management Area in S. Hannibal Lock and Dam, and Lock and Dam No. 15 in W, on Ohio R. Formed 1846.

Wewahitchka (wee-wuh-HICH-kuh), town (□ 6 sq mi/ 15.5 sq km; 1990 pop. 1,779), ⊙ Gulf co., NW Fla., 28 mi/45 km E of Panama City, on Dead L.; 30°06′N 85°12′W. Ships tupelo honey. Inc. 1925.

Weweantic River (wee-wee-AN-tik), c.20 mi/32 km long, Plymouth co., SE Mass.; rises in Carver; flows generally S, through Wareham, to Buzzards Bay.

Wewoka (wee-WO-kuh), town (1990 pop. 4,050), ⊙ Seminole co., central Okla., 10 mi/16 km SE of Seminole; 35°08′N 96°30′W. Elev. 809 ft/247 m. Distribution and shipping point for oil-producing and agr. region (corn, wheat; livestock). Mfg. (brick, tile, wood prods.). Seminole Nation Hq. and Mus. here. L. Wewoka (recreation) is nearby. Was the capital of the Sowinde Nation, founded 1866; inc. as town 1907, as city 1925.

Wexford, county (□ 575 sq mi/1,489 sq km; 1990 pop. 26,360), NW Mich.; ⊙ Cadillac; 44°20′N 85°34′W. Intersected by Manistee R., and drained by Clam R. Agr.; cattle; mixed grains, green beans; dairy prods. Mfg. at Cadillac. Resorts (summer and winter). Part of Manistee Natl. Forest in SW ⅓, a state fish hatchery at Harrieta, Lost Pines Lodge Ski Area near co. center, Caberfae Ski Area in SW, and a state park are here. Includes lakes Mitchell and Cadillac, William Mitchell State Park in SE, bet. lakes. Organized 1869.

Wexford, uninc. town (1990 pop. 1,100), Allegheny co., W Pa., suburb 11 mi/18 km N of Pittsburgh; 40°37′N 80°03′W. Mfg. includes machinery, wood prods., fabricated metal and metal prods. Agr. includes dairying; livestock, poultry; corn. North Park L. reservoir to SE.

Weyauwega (wei-uh-WEE-guh), town (1990 pop. 1,665), Waupaca co., central Wis., on Waupaca R. (tributary of Wolf R.), and 25 mi/40 km W of Appleton; 44°19′N 88°55′W. Trade center in dairying, and grain-and potato-growing area; dairy prods. (cheese). Mfg. (fabricated metal prods.). Settled c.1850, inc. 1939.

Weybridge (WAI-brij), town (1990 pop. 749), Addison co., W Vt., on Otter Creek, just NW of Middlebury; 44°02′N 73°13′W. Univ. of Vt. Morgan Horse Farm is here.

Weyburn (WAI-buhrn), city (1991 pop. 9,673), SE Sask., W Canada, SE of Regina; 49°40′N 103°51′W. A trade center for a wheat-growing and oil-producing region, it has grain elevators and a feed mill. Power-line and transmission cables, and steel, plastic, and glass prods. are mfg.

Weyerhauser (WEI-uhr-hou-suhr), village (1990 pop. 283), Rusk co., N Wis., 7 mi/11.3 km WSW of Ladysmith; 45°25′N 91°24′W. In farm area; wood prods. Hardscrabble Ski Area to NW. Was important lumber town in late 1800s (lumber company named after it).

Weyers Cave (WEI-uhs), uninc. village, Augusta co., NW Va., 12 mi/19 km NNE of Staunton; 38°17′N 78°54′W. Mfg. (chemicals). Shenandoah Natl. Park to SE: Grand Cavern Regional Park to SE. Shenandoah Valley Airport. Blue Ridge Community Col.

Weymouth (WAI-muhth), town (1990 pop. 54,063), Norfolk co., E Mass., suburb of Boston on Hingham Bay; 42°13′N 70°57′W. The state's 2d-oldest settlement (settled 1622), it is chiefly residential. Electronic components, fertilizer, and chemicals are made. Shoe industry dates back to the 1850s. Abigail Adams b. here. The U.S. naval air station in nearby South Weymouth is scheduled to close. Includes villages of East Weymouth, North Weymouth, South Weymouth. Inc. 1635.

Weymouth (WAI-muhth), village, W N.S., E Canada, on St. Mary Bay, 18 mi/29 km SW of Digby; 44°25′N 65°59′W. Fishing; lumbering.

Weymouth Fore River (WAI-muhth), inlet of Hingham Bay (arm of Boston Bay), E Mass., bet. Braintree and Quincy (W and NW) and Weymouth (S and E). Used for shipping. USS *Salem*, state historic site, at the Fore R. Shipyard.

Whalan (HWAI-luhn), village (1990 pop. 94), Fillmore

co., SE Minn., 9 mi/14.5 km ENE of Preston, on Root R.; 43°43′N 91°55′W. Agr. (corn, soybeans; livestock, poultry). Surrounded by Richard J. Dorer Memorial Hardwood State Forest.

Whale Island, Canada: see AVIGALIK ISLAND.

Whale Peak (13,078 ft/3,986 m), in Front Range, bet. Park and Summit cos., central Colo.; 39°29′N 105°51′W.

Whale River, 300 mi/483 km long, N Que., E Canada; rises N of Michikamau L., near Lab. border; flows N, through several lakes, to Ungava Bay 30 mi/48 km NE of Fort Chimo. There are numerous rapids. Formerly important salmon stream.

Whaleback, small island, Rockingham co., SE N.H., off entrance to Portsmouth harbor. Lighthouse.

Whaley Lake, resort lake, Dutchess co., SE N.Y., 16 mi/26 km SE of Poughkeepsie; c.1.5 mi/2.4 km long; 41°34′N 73°40′W.

Wharton, county (□ 1,094 sq mi/2,833 sq km; 1990 pop. 39,955), S Texas; ⊙ Wharton; 29°16′N 96°13′W. On Gulf coastal plains, bounded NE by San Bernard R.; drained by Colorado R. RR junction. A leading sulphur-producing area of U.S.; also oil, natural gas. Agr. (rice, cotton, corn, sorghum); cattle ranching; irrigated area. Hunting, fishing. Formed 1846.

Wharton, town (1990 pop. 9,011), ⊙ Wharton co., S Texas, on Colorado R., and c.55 mi/89 km SW of Houston; 29°19′N 96°05′W. In oil- and gas- and sulphur-producing, cattle-raising, and agr. area (rice, cotton, corn). Mfg. (plastic prods.), machining. Seat of Wharton Co. Jr. Col. Founded 1847, inc. 1902.

Wharton 1 village (1990 pop. 378), Wyandot co., N central Ohio, 9 mi/14 km W of Upper Sandusky; 40°52′N 83°28′W. Cannery. **2** uninc. village (1990 pop. 350), Boone co., W central W.Va., 13 mi/21 km SE of Madison. Mfg. (coal processing).

Wharton, residential borough (1990 pop. 5,405), Morris co., N central N.J., on old Morris Canal, and 8 mi/12.9 km NNW of Morristown; 40°53′N 74°34′W. Chemicals. Inc. 1895.

What Cheer, town (1990 pop. 762), Keokuk co., SE Iowa, 9 mi/14.5 km NW of Sigourney; 41°23′N 92°20′W. Mfg. (brick, tile, pottery, feed). Clay pits nearby. Founded 1865, inc. 1880.

Whatcom (WAHT-kuhm), county (□ 2,503 sq mi/6,483 sq km; 1990 pop. 127,780), NW Wash., on Can. (B.C.) border and Puget Sound; ⊙ Bellingham (seaport); 48°50′N 121°54′W. Includes Mts. Baker and Shuksan, in Mt. Baker Natl. Forest, and Lummi Indian Reservation; drained by Baker, Nooksack, and Skagit rivers. Rich agr. region in W (berries, tulips, grain, vegetables; cattle, poultry); salmon, oysters, crabs, clams; lumber; minerals (gold, silver, coal). Includes Lummi Isl. and Point Roberts in W; snowcapped Mt. Baker (10,775 ft/3,284 m) at center of co. Mt. Baker Natl. Recreation Area on S slopes. Baker L., formed by Upper Baker Dam, in S center. Birch Bay State Park in W; Peace Arch State Park in NW; Larrabee State Park in SW; parts of North Cascades Natl. Park in E center and SE; Diablo Dam and L. and Ross Dam and L., both in Ross Natl. Recreation Area, in E. Formed 1854.

Whately (WAIT-lee), town (1990 pop. 1,375), Franklin co., W central Mass., near the Connecticut R., 8 mi/12.9 km N of Northampton; 42°26′N 72°39′W. Tobacco, onions.

Whatley, village, Clarke co., SW Ala., 5 mi/8 km SE of Grove Hill. Farming, lumbering.

Wheat Ridge, city (1990 pop. 29,419), Jefferson co., N central Colo., a suburb 7 mi/11.3 km WNW of downtown Denver, drained by Clear Creek; 39°46′N 105°05′W. Elev. 5,445 ft/1,660 m. Chiefly residential, Wheat Ridge is the site of an annual carnation festival. Front Range of Rocky Mts. to W. Colo. RR Mus. to W. Inc. 1969.

Wheatcroft, village (1990 pop. 206), Webster co., W Ky., 23 mi/37 km WNW of Madisonville; 37°29′N 87°51′W. Agr. (tobacco, grain; livestock; timber); mfg. (rebuilt pumps, machining); coal mining.

Wheatfield, town (1990 pop. 621), Jasper co., NW Ind., 18 mi/29 km N of Rensselaer. Agr. area; marble prods. Jasper-Pulaski State Fish and Wildlife Area and Nursery nearby to SE.

Wheatland (WEET-luhnd), county (□ 1,428 sq mi/3,699 sq km; 1990 pop. 2,246), central Mont.; ⊙ Harlowton; 46°28′N 109°51′W. Agr. region drained by Musselshell R. Wheat, barley, oats, hay; cattle, hogs, sheep. Little Belt Mts. in NW, forms part of N border. Martinsdale Reservoir on W border; parts of Lewis and Clark Natl. Forest in SW corner and NW; Deadman's Basin Reservoir and State Park in SE. Formed 1917.

Wheatland 1 town (1990 pop. 1,631), Yuba co., N central Calif., 12 mi/19 km SE of Marysville, on Bear R.; 39°01′N 121°26′W. Peaches, prunes kiwi fruit, walnuts, wheat; dairying; cattle. Camp for West Reservoir (Bear R.) to E; Beale Air Force Base to NE. **2** town (1990 pop. 439), Knox co., SW Ind., 12 mi/19 km ESE of Vincennes; 38°40′N 87°19′W. Agr. area (wheat, melons, fruit, corn, soybeans). Laid out 1858. **3** town (1990 pop. 723), Clinton co., E Iowa, near Wapsipinicon R., 34 mi/55 km W of Clinton; 41°49′N 90°50′W. **4** town (1990 pop. 363), Hickory co., central Mo., in the Ozark Mts., 5 mi/8 km W of Hermitage; 37°56′N 93°24′W. **5** town (1990 pop. 3,271), ⊙ Platte co., SE Wyo., near Laramie R., 65 mi/105 km N of Cheyenne, near Chugwater Creek; 42°02′N 104°57′W. Elev. 4,733 ft/1,443 m. In irrigated sugar-beet and cattle region; wheat. Mfg. (marble prods., stone, fabricated metal prods., consumer goods); logging. Mica quarries in vicinity. Annual rodeo. Nearby is Eagle Nest Gap, pass on Oregon Trail. Grayrocks Reservoir to NE. Laramie Mts. and part of Medicine Bow Natl. Forest to W. Settled c.1885.

Wheatland (WEET-luhnd), borough (1990 pop. 760), Mercer co., W Pa., suburb 3 mi/4.8 km S of Sharon, on Shenango R.; 41°12′N 80°30′W. RR yards to NW. Mfg. (fabricated metal prods.). West Middlesex Airport to S. Settled 1812, inc. 1872.

Wheatley (HWEET-lee), village (1991 pop. 1,574), S Ont., central Canada, near L. Erie, 8 mi/13 km ENE of Leamington; 42°06′N 82°27′W. Tobacco, fruit, vegetables.

Wheatley, village (1990 pop. 413), St. Francis co., E Ark., 20 mi/32 km WSW of Forrest City; 34°55′N 91°06′W. Lumber.

Wheaton 1 city (1990 pop. 51,464), ⊙ Du Page co., NE Ill., residential suburb W of Chicago; 41°51′N 88°06′W. Religious center and the hq. of the Theosophical Society of Amer. Many evangelical organizations are also based here. Wheaton Col. is here, and 2 mus. are nearby. Inc. 1859. **2** uninc. city (1990 pop. 58,300), Montgomery co., central Md., residential suburb of Washington, D.C. It grew around a tavern established here and was originally called Mitchell's Crossroads. After the Civil War, George Plyer, a former Union soldier, became the postmaster and named it for his commander, Union Gen. Frank Wheaton, in the defense of nearby Fort Stevens. Horticultural displays can be seen at Brookside Gardens. **3** city (1990 pop. 637), Barry co., SW Mo., in the Ozark Mts., 13 mi/21 km SW of Monett; 36°45′N 94°03′W. Fruit, vegetables; dairying; cattle; poultry processing.

Wheaton, town (1990 pop. 1,615), ⊙ Traverse co., W Minn., 38 mi/61 km SW of Fergus Falls, on Mustinka R. 6 mi/9.7 km NE of its entrance to NE end of L. Traverse (1 mi/1.6 km E of lake's outflow in Bois de Sioux R.); 45°48′N 96°30′W. Elev. 1,019 ft/311 m. Agr. (grain, sunflowers, sugar beets, soybeans, beans; livestock, poultry; dairying); mfg. (printing and publishing). Mud L. to W (on Bois de Sioux R.). Settled 1884, inc. 1887.

Wheaton (WEET-uhn), village (1990 pop. 106), Pottawatomie co., NE Kansas, 8 mi/12.9 km NE of Westmoreland; 39°30′N 96°19′W. Livestock; grain.

Wheeler 1 county (□ 300 sq mi/777 sq km; 1990 pop. 4,903), SE central Ga.; ⊙ Alamo; 32°07′N 82°43′W. Bounded E and N by Oconee R., S by Ocmulgee R., SW by Little Ocmulgee R. Textile and apparel mfg. Coastal plain agr. (corn, wheat, soybeans, cotton, tobacco, peanuts); cattle, hogs. Formed 1912. **2** county (□ 575 sq mi/1,489 sq km; 1990 pop. 948), NE central Nebr. at edge of Sand Hills; ⊙ Bartlett; 41°55′N 98°31′W. Largely grazing area drained by Cedar R. Cattle, hogs; dairying; corn. Pibel L. State Recreation Area in S. Formed 1877. **3** county (□ 1,715 sq mi/4,442 sq km; 1990 pop. 1,396), N central Oregon; ⊙ Fossil; 44°43′N 120°01′W. Mt. area crossed by John Day R. (forms NW border). Timber. Sheep, cattle. Part of Umatilla Natl. Forest in NE; John Day Fossil Beds Natl. Monument, Clarno Unit, in NW; Painted Hills Unit in SW center; Shelton State Park in N center; Clarno State Park in NW; part of Ochoco Natl. Forest in S, including Bridge Creek Wilderness area in SW; part of Black Canyon Wilderness Area in SE. Formed 1899. **4** county (□ 915 sq mi/2,370 sq km; 1990 pop. 5,879), extreme N Texas, in Eastern Panhandle, on Okla. (E) state line; ⊙ Wheeler; 35°23′N 100°16′W. Elev. 2,000 ft/610 m–2,800 ft/853 m. Drained by North Fork of Red R. Underlaid by E part of huge Panhandle natural-gas and oil field; oil and gas wells; clay, caliche, silica, gypsum deposits; agr. (grain, including sorghum and wheat; cotton; cattle, horses, hogs, ostriches). Formed 1876.

Wheeler, town (1990 pop. 1,393), ⊙ Wheeler co., extreme N Texas, in the Panhandle, c.40 mi/64 km ESE of Pampa; 35°26′N 100°16′W. Elev. 2,520 ft/768 m. Oil and natural gas; cotton, wheat; cattle, horses, ostriches.

Wheeler 1 village (1990 pop. 161), Jasper co., SE Ill., 10 mi/16 km WNW of Newton; 39°02′N 88°19′W. In agr. area (grain; cattle); mfg. wood prods. **2** village (1990 pop. 500), Porter co., NW Ind., 7 mi/11.3 km NW of Valparaiso. In urban growth fringe area. Dairying. Laid out 1858. **3** village, Valley co., NE Mont., 14 mi/23 km SE of Glasgow, and near Fort Peck Reservoir. Fort Peck Dam to E (Missouri R.), in extensively irrigated region. Charles M. Russell Natl. Wildlife Refuge to S, surrounds reservoir. **4** village (1990 pop. 335), Tillamook co., NW Oregon, 35 mi/56 km S of Astoria, near the mouth of the Nehalem R.; 45°41′N 123°52′W. Timber. Dairy prods.; cattle. Tourism. Fish hatchery to E. Manhattan Beach State Wayside to S; Nehalem Bay State Park to W; Tillamook State Forest to E. **5** village (1990 pop. 348), Dunn co., W Wis., 11 mi/18 km N of Menomonie; 45°02′N 91°54′W. In dairying area. Deepwood Ski Area to E; Tainter L. to SE.

Wheeler Field, U.S. Army airfield (1990 pop. 2,600), central Oahu isl., Honolulu co., Hawaii, 15 mi/24 km NW of Honolulu; 21°28′N 158°02′W. Schofield Barracks Military Reservation to NW. Est. 1922. Along with Pearl Harbor, it was bombed by Japanese on Dec. 7, 1941. City of Wahiawa to N; Waikele Stream passes through S.

Wheeler Lake, NW Ala., on Tennessee R., 17 mi/27 km E of Florence, c.15 mi/24 km upstream from (E of) Wilson Dam; 74 mi/119 km long, 1 mi/1.6 km–3 mi/4.8 km wide; 34°47′N 87°22′W. Max. capacity 1,150,400 acre-ft. Extends into 6 cos. Receives Elk, Flint, Paint Rock rivers. Formed by concrete Wheeler Dam (72 ft/22 m high, 6,342 ft/1,933 m long), a major TVA project completed in 1936 for navigation, flood control, and power generation. Decatur on S shore. Wheeler Natl. Wildlife Refuge is just E of Decatur, on both shores of reservoir.

Wheeler Peak 1 (13,063 ft/3,982 m) in White Pine co., E Nev., in Snake Range, 36 mi/58 km SE of Ely; 38°59′N 114°18′W. In Great Basin Natl. Park. Highest point in range, 2d-highest point in state. Lehman Caves, former natl. monument, to E of peak, within park. **2** peak (13,161 ft/4,011 m) in N N.Mex., Taos co., in Sangre de Cristo Mts., 14 mi/23 km NE of Taos; 36°33′N 105°24′W. Highest point in N.Mex.

Wheeler Peak, Calif.: see SWEETWATER MOUNTAINS.

Wheelersburg, uninc. village (1990 pop. 5,113), Scioto co., S Ohio, on the Ohio R., 6 mi/10 km E of Portsmouth; 38°44′N 82°51′W.

Wheeling, city (1990 pop. 34,882), ⊙ Ohio co., N W.Va., 135 mi/217 km NNE of Charleston, in the Northern Panhandle, on the Ohio R. (bridged) opposite Martins Ferry (Ohio); 40°04′N 80°42′W. Mfg. and commercial center in an area rich in coal and natural gas. Mfg. (fabricated metals and metal prods., chemicals, ceramics, glass, plastics, textiles, bldg. materials, tools, tobacco, paper goods; machining, scrap-metal recycling,

Cross references are shown in SMALL CAPITALS. The pronunciation key is on page xv. The dates of population figures are on page xii.

vegetable processing, printing). Fort Fincastle, renamed Fort Henry, built in 1774; town became the W terminus of the Natl. Road in 1818, a port of entry in 1831, and a railhead in 1852. A center of pro-Unionist activity during the Civil War, the city was the site of the Wheeling Conventions (1861–1862), which provided a means of forming a new state out of the N and W cos. of Va. Was 1st capital of W.Va. in 1863. Wheeling Jesuit Col., and W.Va. Northern Community Col. are here. Points of interest include the site of Fort Henry; St. Joseph's Cathedral; the Point Overlook Mus.; Civic Arena (hockey); Stifel Fine Arts Center; Jamboree USA, in Capitol Music Hall; Wheeling Downs Racetrack (thoroughbred racing) on Wheeling Isl., Ohio R., in downtown; Oglebay Park to NE, includes Mansion Mus., Good Zoo, Oglebay Ski Area and resort lodge. Wheeling Suspension Bridge (1849) collapsed 1854, cables reused in recent restoration. Settled 1769, inc. as a city 1836.

Wheeling, village (1990 pop. 29,911), Cook co., NE Ill., suburb 25 mi/40 km NW of downtown Chicago; 42°07'N 87°55'W. Mfg. (machinery, computer supplies, fabricated metal prods., paper prods., security devices, insulation, chemicals; food processing). Founded c.1830, inc. 1894. Forest Inst. of Professional Psychology here.

Wheelock, town (1990 pop. 481), Caledonia co., NE Vt., 12 mi/19 km NW of St. Johnsbury; 44°34'N 72°08'W.

Wheelock (WEE-lahk), village (1990 pop. 23), Williams co., NW N.Dak., 20 mi/32 km NE of Williston; 48°17'N 103°15'W.

Wheelwright, town (1990 pop. 721), Floyd co., SE Ky., in Cumberland foothills, 15 mi/24 km SW of Pikeville, near Beaver Creek; 37°20'N 82°43'W. Bituminous coal.

Wheelwright, Mass.: see HARDWICK.

Whelen Springs (WAI-len), village (1990 pop. 116), Clark co., S central Ark., 21 mi/34 km SSW of Arkadelphia, near Little Missouri R.; 33°49'N 93°07'W.

Whetstone Mountains, Cochise co., SE Ariz., N of Fort Huachuca, in part of Coronado Natl. Forest. Apache Peak (7,711 ft/217 m) is highest point; 31°48'N 110°25'W.

Whetstone River, c.35 mi/56 km long, NE S.Dak.; formed near Wilmot, S Roberts co.; flows SE and E to Minnesota R. just S of Ortonville (Minn.); 45°16'N 96°34'W. Small dike near mouth diverts part of flow into S end of Big Stone L.

Whidbey Island (WID-bee), Island co., NW Wash., one of largest (c.40 mi/64 km long) isls. in U.S., in Puget Sound NW of Everett. Includes towns of Oak Harbor, Coupeville, and Langley. At N end is Deception Pass, a swift tidal strait, bridge (1935) to Fidalgo Isl., which is connected by bridges to mainland. Whidbey Isl. Naval Air Station in N; Ebey's Landing Natl. Historic Reserve at Coupeville, E center. State parks include Deception Pass and Joseph Whidbey (N), Fort Ebey and Fort Casey (W), South Whidbey (S). Ferry connections to Port Townsend (W), on Olympic Peninsula, and to Mukitiro (SE), on mainland. Largest of 2 main isls. (with Camano Isl.) that comprise co., no connections (bridge or ferry). Separated from Camano on E by Saratoga Passage, bounded W by Strait of Juan de Fuca and Admiralty Inlet (Puget Sound), SE by Possession Sound.

Whigham (WIG-uhm), village (1990 pop. 605), Grady co., SW Ga., 7 mi/11.3 km W of Cairo; 30°53'N 84°19'W. In farm area. Mfg. of trusses, clothing.

Whippany (HWI-puh-nee), industrial village, Morris co., NE N.J., on Whippany R., and 4 mi/6.4 km NE of Morristown. Mfg. (paper prods.); dairy prods.

Whippany River (HWI-puh-nee), c.20 mi/32 km long, N N.J.; rises W of Morristown; flows generally ENE, past Morristown and Whippany, to Rockaway R. just above its junction with Passaic R.

Whiskeytown Lake, reservoir, Shasta Co., N Calif., on Clear Creek, 8 mi/12.9 km W of Redding; 6 mi/9.7 km long; 40°35'N 122°31'W. Elev. 369 ft/112 m. Max. capacity 276,000 acre-ft. Formed by Whiskeytown Dam (263 ft/80 m high), built (1963) by the Bureau of Reclamation for irrigation, power generation, and flood control. In Whiskeytown Unit of Whiskeytown-Shasta-Trinity Natl. Recreation Area.

Whiskeytown-Shasta-Trinity National Recreation Area (□ 66 sq mi/171 sq km), Shasta and Trinity cos., N Calif. Reservoirs and forestland; the Natl. Park Service runs the Whiskeytown unit, and the Forest Service administers the Shasta and Trinity units. Consists of 3 sects.: Trinity R. Unit has Clair Engle and Lewiston reservoirs on Trinity R., bounded by Trinity Natl. Forest, Ormsby co. c.25 mi/40 km NW of Redding; Whiskeytown Unit has Keswick Reservoir on Clear Creek c.10 mi/16 km W of Shasta co.; Shasta Unit has larger Shasta L. reservoir, formed by Sacramento R. and its tributaries, Pit and McCloud rivers, c.15 mi/24 km N of Redding, bounded by Shasta Natl. Forest, including L. Shasta Caverns W, N, and E. Authorized 1965.

Whispering Pines, town (1990 pop. 1,243), Moore co., central N.C., residential suburb 7 mi/11.3 km N of Southern Pines; 35°15'N 79°22'W.

Whistler, town (1990 est. pop. 4,459), SW B.C., W Canada, 60 mi/97 km N of Vancouver, on W side of Cheakamus R., and on Squamish Highway; 49°58'N 123°09'W. Planned resort community opened in 1980. Entrance to Garibaldi Provincial Park. Popular ski resorts; chairlift to Mt. Blackombe (7,493 ft/2,284 m).

Whistler, uninc. village, Mobile co., SW Ala., 5 mi/8 km NW of Mobile. Cedar Creek State Park is nearby.

Whistler Mountain (7,159 ft/2,182 m), SW B.C., W Canada, in Coast Range, 55 mi/89 km N of Vancouver, SE of Whistler. One of the most popular ski slopes in the world, has led to rapid development of Whistler Village resort area and towns along Squamish Highway. Chairlift. Formerly London Mt.

Whitaker (WI-tuh-kuhr), borough (1990 pop. 1,416), Allegheny co., SW Pa., residential suburb 7 mi/11.3 km SE of downtown Pittsburgh, on Monongahela R. (bridged); 40°23'N 79°53'W. Inc. 1906.

Whitakers, town (1990 pop. 860), Nash and Edgecombe cos., NE central N.C., 12 mi/19 km NNE of Rocky Mount; 36°06'N 77°42'W. In agr. area (tobacco, cotton, peanuts, grain, sweet potatoes; chickens, cattle, hogs); mfg. (engines, clothing).

Whitby, town (1991 pop. 61,281), SE Ont., central Canada, NE of Toronto, on L. Ontario; 43°52'N 78°56'W. It has a good harbor. Mfg. includes transportation and electronic equip.

White 1 county (□ 1,042 sq mi/2,699 sq km; 1990 pop. 54,676), central Ark.; ⊙ Searcy; 35°15'N 91°44'W. Bordered E by White R., Cypress Bayou forms most of S border; drained by the Bayou Des Arc and Departee Creek and intersected by Little Red R. Leads Ark. in strawberry production; also produces cotton, potatoes, vegetables, pecans, rice, wheat, soybeans; cattle, hogs. Mfg. at Searcy, Judsonia, and Bald Knob. Timber; mineral springs. Formed 1835. Henry Gray–Hurricane L. Wildlife Management Area in E. **2** county (□ 242 sq mi/627 sq km; 1990 pop. 13,006), NE Ga.; ⊙ Cleveland; 34°39'N 83°45'W. Drained by Chattahoochee R. Agr. (corn); poultry, cattle, hogs; timber. Resort area. Chattahoochee Natl. Forest occupies N part. Formed 1857. **3** county (□ 501 sq mi/1,298 sq km; 1990 pop. 16,522), SE Ill.; ⊙ Carmi; 38°05'N 88°10'W. Bounded E by Wabash R.; drained by Little Wabash R. Agr. (wheat, corn, soybeans, sorghum; cattle, poultry). Mfg. of clothing, wood prods., dairy prods.; food processing. Coal, oil, and natural-gas wells. Formed 1815. **4** county (□ 508 sq mi/1,316 sq km; 1990 pop. 23,265), NW central Ind.; ⊙ Monticello; 40°45'N 86°52'W. Partly bounded E by Tippecanoe R.; drained by Tippecanoe R., Big Monon Creek, and small Little Monon Creek. Agr. area (corn, oats, rye; cattle, hogs). Mfg. at Monticello and Monon; quarries. Resorts and recreation areas on lakes Shafer (N) and Freeman (S). Formed 1834. **5** county (□ 385 sq mi/997 sq km; 1990 pop. 20,090), central Tenn.; ⊙ Sparta, 35°56'N 85°27'W. In the Cumberlands; bounded (S, W) by Caney Fork. Great Falls and Center Hill reservoirs in SW. Coal mining, limestone quarrying; lumbering; livestock raising, dairying; agr. (esp. tobacco; also corn, hay, vegetables). Formed 1806.

White 1 village (1990 pop. 542), Bartow co., NW Ga., 9 mi/14.5 km NNE of Cartersville; 34°17'N 84°45'W. Mfg. includes metal fabrication and machining and textile mfg. **2** village, (1990 pop. 536), Brookings co., E S.Dak., 12 mi/19 km NE of Brookings, and on branch of Big Sioux R.; 44°26'N 96°38'W.

White Bay, inlet of the Atlantic Ocean, NE N.F., E Canada; 60 mi/97 km long, 20 mi/32 km wide at entrance. At entrance of bay are St. Barbe, or Horse, Isls. Several fishing settlements on shore of bay.

White Bear Lake, city (1990 pop. 24,704), Ramsey co., with small extension into Washington co., SE Minn., suburb 9 mi/14.5 km NE of downtown St. Paul, on White Bear L.; 45°04'N 93°00'W. Mfg. (chemicals, medical supplies, electrical prods., foods, consumer goods; machining, printing and publishing, steel fabricating, wood treating). Seat of Lakewood Community Col. Bald Eagle L. to N. Inc. 1922.

White Bear Lake, in Washington and Ramsey cos., E Minn., 10 mi/16 km NNE of St. Paul; 3 mi/4.8 km long, 2 mi/3.2 km wide; 45°04'N 92°58'W. City of White Bear Lake on W shore; Dellwood on NE; Mahtomedi on E and SE; Birchwood Village on S.

White Bird, village (1990 pop. 108), Idaho co., N Idaho, 13 mi/21 km SW of Grangeville, on Salmon R.; 45°46'N 116°18'W. Elev. 1,593 ft/486 m. Parts of Nez Perce Natl. Forest to E and SW. Pittsburg Landing, downstream terminus of Hells Canyon. Snake R. (rafting trips) 12 mi/19 km to SW, opposite Oregon state line. Neck of land bet. Salmon and Snake rivers lies within Mountain time zone; all areas to W, N and E, including White Bird village, are in Pacific time zone. White Bird Summit (pass; 4,245 ft/1,294 m) to N.

White Bluff, town (1990 pop. 1,988), Dickson co., N central Tenn., 29 mi/47 km W of Nashville; 36°06'N 87°13'W. In timber and farm area. Montgomery Bell recreation area is nearby.

White Butte (3,506 ft/1,069 m), Slope co., SW N.Dak., 15 mi/24 km NNE of Bowman; 46°23'N 103°18'W. Highest point in state.

White Castle, town (1990 pop. 2,102), Iberville parish, SE central La., on the Mississippi R., and 19 mi/31 km S of Baton Rouge; 30°10'N 91°10'W. In sugarcane area; mfg. (raw sugar). Toll ferry from Carville. Nottoway Plantation nearby. Hansen's Disease Center across river.

White Center, uninc. city (1990 pop. 15,700), King co., W Wash., residential suburb 6 mi/9.7 km S of downtown Seattle, near Puget Sound. Seattle-Tacoma (SeaTac) Internatl. Airport to SE.

White City, village (1990 pop. 229), Macoupin co., SW Ill., 17 mi/27 km SSE of Carlinville; 39°04'N 89°45'W. In agr. (cattle, hogs; corn, wheat, soybeans, sorghum) and bituminous-coal area.

White City 1 town (□ 7 sq mi/18.1 sq km; 1990 pop. 4,645), St. Lucie co., E central Fla., 2 mi/3.2 km S of Fort Pierce, on Indian R.; 27°22'N 80°20'W. **2** uninc. town (1990 pop. 5,891), Jackson co., SW Oregon, suburb 8 mi/12.9 km N of Medford, near Rogue R.; 42°25'N 122°49'W. Planned community; RR junction. Major timber center. Mfg. (lumber and wood prods., millwork, chemicals; printing). Veterans facilities. TouVelle State Park to W. Burrill Airport in W part of town.

White City, village (1990 pop. 533), Morris co., E central Kansas, 17 mi/27 km SSE of Junction City; 38°47'N 96°43'W. In grazing and agr. region.

White Cloud, town (1990 pop. 1,147), ⊙ Newaygo co., W central Mich., on White R., and 34 mi/55 km NE of Muskegon; 43°32'N 85°46'W. In farm area; mfg. (lumber, refractory prods., fabricated metal prods.). In Manistee Natl. Forest; White Cloud State Park to S, Newaygo State Park to SE.

White Cloud, village (1990 pop. 255), Doniphan co., extreme NE Kansas, on Missouri R., near Nebr. state line, and 17 mi/27 km NW of Troy; 39°58'N 95°17'W. Apple growing, general agr. The burial mounds and ruins of Native Amer. villages have been found nearby. Sac and Fox Indian Reservations to NW (Kansas and Nebr.).

White Deer, town (1990 pop. 1,125), Carson co., extreme N Texas, in high plains of the Panhandle, 40 mi/64 km

ENE of Amarillo; 35°25′N 101°10′W. RR spur junction; natural-gas and helium and oil wells; hay, wheat, corn; cattle. Natural-gas processing, mfg. machinery.

White Earth 1 village (1990 pop. 319), Becker co., W Minn., 19 mi/31 km N of Detroit Lakes, in SW part of White Earth Indian reservation; 47°06′N 95°51′W. White Earth L. 4 mi/6.4 km to NE; Mission L. to S. Hosp. and mission school are here. Tamarac Natl. Wildlife Refuge to SE. Numerous small lakes in area. **2** village (1990 pop. 73), Mountrail co., NW N.Dak., 18 mi/29 km W of Stanley, and on White Earth R.; 48°22′N 102°46′W. Small ranches, farms.

White Earth Lake, Becker co., W Minn., in White Earth Indian Reservation, 20 mi/32 km NNE of Detroit Lakes; 3 mi/4.8 km long, 1 mi/1.6 km wide; 47°07′N 95°45′W. Fed from NE by Gull Creek. Source of White Earth R. (drains NW), which flows 25 mi/40 km NNW to Mahnomen.

White Earth River, 50 mi/80 km long, NW N.Dak.; rises in SE Davids co.; flows E and S largely in Mountrail co., to Missouri R. (L. Sakakawea reservoir); 48°37′N 102°39′W.

White Fox, village (1991 pop. 442), E central Sask., W Canada, 7 mi/11 km NW of Nipawin; 53°27′N 104°05′W. Dairying; grain.

White Hall, city (1990 pop. 2,814), Greene co., W central Ill., 10 mi/16 km N of Carrollton; 39°26′N 90°24′W. Agr. (corn, wheat, soybeans, sorghum; cattle, hogs; dairy prods.). Mfg. (medical supplies, consumer goods). Here is memorial, designed by Lorado Taft, to Annie Louise Keller, teacher killed saving pupils during tornado in 1927. Founded 1820, inc. 1837.

White Haven, borough (1990 pop. 1,132), Luzerne co., E central Pa., 14 mi/23 km SSE of Wilkes-Barre, on Lehigh R.; 41°03′N 75°46′W. Mfg. (electronic equip.). Hickory Run State Park to SE. Inc. c.1853.

White Horse Beach, Mass.: see PLYMOUTH.

White House, minor port (1991 pop. 3,157), Westmoreland parish, SW Jamaica, 15 mi/24 km SE of Savanna-la-Mar; 18°05′N 77°58′W. Ships logwood.

White House, city (1990 pop. 2,987), Sumner and Robertson cos., central Tenn., 23 mi/37 km NNE of Nashville; 36°28′N 86°39′W. In tobacco-growing area. Inc. 1971.

White House, Washington, D.C., at 1600 Pennsylvania Ave., NW. Authorized 1943. Official residence of the U.S. president. Cornerstone laid in 1792.

White House Station, village, Hunterdon co., W N.J., 9 mi/14.5 km NW of Somerville. Poultry; grain, fruit; dairy. Pharmaceuticals.

White Iron Lake, Lake and St. Louis cos., NE Minn, 4 mi/6.4 km SE of Ely, in Superior Natl. Forest; 6 mi/9.7 km long, 1.5 mi/2.4 km wide; 47°52′N 91°48′W. Resort area. Fed (from Birch L. to S) and drained (NE to Farm L.) by South Fork Kawishiwi R., which splits to E and returns to itself in Farm L.

White Island, E Keewatin dist., N.W.T., N Canada, in Frozen Strait, off S Melville Peninsula (N), just NW of Southampton Isl.; 38 mi/61 km long, 6 mi/10 km–10 mi/16 km wide; 65°47′N 84°45′W.

White Island, N.H.: see ISLES OF SHOALS.

White Lake 1 village, Oakland co., SE Mich., suburb 14 mi/23 km NW of Pontiac; 42°41′N 83°33′W. Light mfg. Alpine Valley Ski Area and Pontiac L. State Recreation Area to E. **2** resort village, Muskegon co., SW Mich.; 45°09′N 88°46′W. **3** village (1990 pop. 390), Bladen co., SE N.C., 7 mi/11.3 km ESE of Elizabethtown, at N end of White L. in center of Bladen Lakes State Forest, W of Colly Creek; 34°38′N 78°30′W. Timber; recreation. **4** village (1990 pop. 419), Aurora co., S S.Dak., 11 mi/18 km W of Plankinton; 43°43′N 98°42′W. White L. (dry) to N. **5** village, Langlade co., NE Wis., 45 mi/72 km ENE of Wausau, on White L. Sawmilling; mfg. (machinery, wood prods.). Langlade Fish Hatchery to N. Menominee Indian Reservation to S in Menominee co. Nicolet Natl. Forest to E.

White Lake 1 Vermilion parish, S La., 33 mi/53 km SW of Lafayette, and 8 mi/13 km N of Gulf of Mexico coast, in marshy region; c.13 mi/21 km long (E-W), c.6 mi/10 km wide (N-S); 29°44′N 92°30′W. Joined by navigable waterways to Callican and Grand lakes (NW), Intracoastal Waterway (passing to E-W to N), and Freshwater Bayou Canal (E; connects with Intracoastal Waterway). Abundant coastal and marsh birds, reptiles, and mammals. Pecan Isl., a low ridge in the marsh to S. **2** Sullivan co., SE N.Y., 8 mi/12.9 km W of Monticello; c.1.3 mi/2.1 km long; 41°42′N 74°50′W. White Lake (1990 pop. 140) and Kauneonga Lake (1990 pop. 1,200), resort villages are here.

White Marsh, uninc. village, Gloucester co., E Va., 5 mi/8 km S of Gloucester; 37°20′N 76°31′W. Light mfg.; agr. (grain, soybeans; cattle). "Belroi," birthplace of Walter Reed, and Abingdon Church (1754–1755) are nearby.

White Mountain, village (1990 pop. 180), W Alaska, on S Seward Peninsula, 60 mi/97 km E of Nome; 64°40′N 163°25′W.

White Mountains 1 in E Ariz., on NE border of Fort Apache Indian Reservation,W of Eager and Springerville. Apache-Sitgreaves Natl. Forest to NE. Highest points are Greens (10,133 ft/3,089 m) and Baldy (11,403 ft/3,476 m) peaks. Part of a large volcanic mass. Sunrise Ski Area on W slopes. **2** range in Inyo and Mono cos., E Calif. and Esmeralda co., SW Nev.; extending c.55 mi/89 km S from Montgomery Pass (Nev.; 7,132 ft/2,174 m) to N end of Inyo Mts. 13 mi/21 km SE of Bishop (Calif.); 37°38′N 118°15′W. Mts. partly bound Owens Valley on E. White Mt. peak (14,246 ft/4,342 m), 20 mi/32 km NNE of Bishop, is highest point. Boundary Peak (13,140 ft/4,005 m), in N, is highest point in Nev.; just S, in Calif., is Montgomery Peak (13,441 ft/4,097 m). **3** part of the Appalachian system, N central N.H. and SW Maine, rising to 6,288 ft/1,917 m at Mt. Washington in the Presidential Range and to 5,249 ft/1,600 m at Mt. Lafayette in the Franconia Mts., N.H. Crawford Notch separates these 2 main groups. Formed in the latter part of the Paleozoic era, the White Mts. are remnants of a much higher granite mt. mass, significantly worn by glaciation, which carved Franconia and Crawford notches, as well as the ravines on Mt. Washington. Much of the mt. area (c.1,200 sq mi/3,108 sq km) is included in White Mt. Natl. Forest (N.H., Maine). Nationally noted for their varied and beautiful scenery, the White Mts. have long been one of the most popular year-round resort areas in the country.

White Oak, town (1990 pop. 5,136), Gregg co., E Texas, suburb 5 mi/8 km W of Longview; 32°31′N 94°51′W. Cattle, horses. Timber. Oil and natural gas. Mfg. (steel fabricating, machining; motor vehicles, plastic prods.).

White Oak, borough (1990 pop. 8,761), Allegheny co., W Pa., residential suburb 12 mi/19 km SE of downtown Pittsburgh, and 2 mi/3.2 km SE of McKeesport; 40°20′N 79°47′W. Light mfg. Airport to E; White Oak Park to E. Inc. 1948.

White Oak, uninc. community (1990 pop. 18,671), Montgomery and Prince Georges cos., central Md., suburb of Washington, D.C.

White Oak Creek, c.75 mi/121 km long, NE Texas; rises W of Sulphur Springs, Hopkins co.; flows generally E to Sulphur R. c.20 mi/32 km ENE of Mount Pleasant.

White Otter Lake, W Ont., central Canada, 120 mi/193 km WNW of Thunder Bay; 22 mi/35 km long, 5 mi/8 km wide. Elev. 1,392 ft/424 m. Drains S into Seine R.

White Pass, village, NW B.C., W Canada, on U.S. (Alaska) border, on Skagway R., and 14 mi/23 km NNE of Skagway (Alaska), on White Pass and Yukon RR, and on White Pass Highway connecting Skagaway with Whitehorse (Yukon Territory).

White Pass (2,888 ft/880 m), in the Coast Mts., on the U.S. (Alaska)-Canada (B.C.) border, NE of Skagway (Alaska). A hazardous trail through the pass was made (1897) by prospectors going to the Klondike, as an alternate route to the Chilkoot Pass. Bet. 1898 and 1900 the White Pass and Yukon RR was built from Skagway to White Horse (Yukon), to provide transportation from the Pacific tidewater to the Yukon valley. The RR suspended service in 1982, though it still operates tourist trains in summer to L. Bennett. Crossed by White Pass Highway.

White Pigeon, town (1990 pop. 1,458), St. Joseph co., SW Mich., 35 mi/56 km S of Kalamazoo, near Ind. state line; 41°47′N 85°38′W. RR junction; mfg. (paper prods., mobile homes, transportation equip., bldg. prods.); poultry; dairying; soybeans. Settled c.1827, inc. 1837.

White Pine, county (□ 8,897 sq mi/23,043 sq km; 1990 pop. 9,264), E Nev., on Utah (E) border; ⊙ Ely; 39°26′N 114°54′W. Mt. region in Pacific time zone (border of Mountain time zone to E). The country's 16th-largest co. Snake and Schell Creek ranges are in E; Egan Range in center and White Pine Mts. are in SW. Parts of Humboldt Natl. Forest are in SE, center, SW, and NW. Great Basin Natl. Park in SE, former Lehman Caves Natl. Monument in park. Mining (gold, silver, sand and gravel); cattle, sheep. Formed 1869. Part of Ruby L. Natl. Wildlife Refuge in NW; part of Goshute Indian Reservation in NE, extends into Utah; Ward Charcoal Ovens State Historical Monument and Cave L. State Recreational Area in S center.

White Pine, town (1990 pop. 1,771), Jefferson co., E Tenn., near Douglas Reservoir, 37 mi/60 km ENE of Knoxville; 36°06′N 83°17′W. In timber and farm region; wood prods., textiles.

White Pine Mine, Mich.: see PORCUPINE MOUNTAINS.

White Pine Mountains, E Nev., in White Pine co., extends S into Nye co., N of Grant Range, in sect. of Humboldt Natl. Forest. Rise to 10,745 ft/3,275 m in Mt. Hamilton and 11,513 ft/3,509 m in Currant Mt., 37 mi/60 km SW of Ely, on co. line.

White Plains 1 city (1990 pop. 286), Greene co., NE central Ga., 11 mi/18 km SE of Greensboro; 33°28′N 83°02′W. **2** city (□ 9 sq mi/23.3 sq km; 1990 pop. 48,718), ⊙ Westchester co., SE N.Y., N of N.Y. city; 41°01′N 73°45′W. The primary employment center for the co., the city has some very large shopping malls, some light industries, and serves as the hq. for several corporations and laboratories. Several corporate parks ring the city, and the central business dist. (rebuilt in 1964) offers retail stores. Site of a cultural co. center, a branch of Pace Univ., and the N.Y. School for the Deaf. Combined corporate hq. of several major Texaco Co. divs. are here. Settled by Puritans from Conn. in 1683. The state convention that ratified the Declaration of Independence met (1776) here. The battle of White Plains (1776), a principal engagement of the Amer. Revolution, followed Gen. George Washington's retreat from N.Y. city. Washington briefly made his hq. here at the Elijah Miller House, which still stands. Other bldgs. from the Amer. Revolutionary period are also preserved. Inc. as a village 1866 (originally named Quarrapas by Siwanoy people), as a city 1916.

White Plains, uninc. town (1990 pop. 1,027), Surry co., NW N.C., residential suburb 5 mi/8 km S of Mount Airy; 36°27′N 80°38′W. In agr. area (tobacco, soybeans, grain; poultry, livestock; dairying).

White Plains, village (1990 pop. 598), Hopkins co., W Ky., 12 mi/19 km SSE of Madisonville; 37°11′N 87°23′W. Coal mining; agr. (burley tobacco, grain; livestock; timber).

White River, village, central Ont., central Canada, on White R., and 150 mi/241 km NNW of Sault Ste. Marie; 48°35′N 85°17′W. Elev. 1,223 ft/373 m. Lumbering.

White River, village (1990 pop. 595), ⊙ Mellette co., S S.Dak., 60 mi/97 km SSW of Pierre, and on Little Fork White R. (former South Fork); 43°34′N 100°44′W. In farming and cattle area. Hydroelectric plant is here.

White River, c.200 mi/322 km long, Alaska and SW Yukon; rises in Alaska in St. Elias Mts. at foot of Mt. Sulzer; flows E, crossing into Yukon, and turns NNE, past Snag, to Yukon R. 60 mi/97 km S of Dawson. Glacially fed river, former trail connecting Copper and Chitina rivers to Yukon R.

White River, c.20 mi/32 km long, on border bet. St. Mary and St. Ann parishes, N Jamaica; flows NNW to the coast 3 mi/4.8 km E of Ocho Rios; 17°52′N–18°25′N 76°16′W–77°04′W. Dam and hydroelectric station.

White River 1 c.30 mi/48 km long, E Ariz.; formed in SW Apache co., W of White Mts., in NE part of Fort Apache Indian Reservation; flows SW to Black R., forming Salt R. in Gila co., c.40 mi/64 km NE of Globe. **2** in W Mich., formed by South Branch (45 mi/72 km long; rises in Newaygo co.; flows SE, past White Cloud and Hesperia; 43°40′N 44°85′W) and North Branch (15 mi/24 km long; rises in NW Newaygo co.; flows W then S); widens just below Montague into White L. (c.5 mi/8 km long, 1 mi/1.6 km wide; resort), which drains from W end into L. Michigan through short outlet. **3** 507 mi/816 km long, in Nebr. and S.Dak.; rises in Sioux co., NW Nebr. at c.4,800 ft/1,463 m; flows NE, through Badlands of S.Dak., to Missouri R. near Chamberlain. Drainage basin (□ 10,200 sq mi/ 26,418 sq km) has deposits of manganese. Passes through Badlands Natl. Park in S and E extensions of park. Pine Ridge to S and SE in Nebr. and part of S.Dak. **4** c.100 mi/161 km long, in NW Texas; formed by small headstreams (esp. Running Water Draw) in Hale co.; flows SE to Salt Fork of Brazos R. 25 mi/40 km E of Post; partly intermittent. White River L. reservoir is 42 mi/68 km ESE of Abilene. **5** c.50 mi/80 km long, in E Vt.; rises near Granville in Green Mts.; flows SE, receiving First, Second, and Third branches, to the Connecticut R. at White River Junction. **6** c.75 mi/ 121 km long, in W Wash.; rises on NE slopes of Mt. Rainier; flows N and NW, past Buckley, then S, joining Puyallup R. at Sumner. E of Buckley is Mud Mt. Dam (425 ft/130 m high, 700 ft/213 m long; completed 1948) for flood control. West Fork rises on N slopes of Mt. Rainier; flows c.25 mi/40 km N, joining mainstream 20 mi/32 km ESE of Buckley. **7** c.12 mi/19 km long, SE Wis.; rises in L. Geneva in Walworth co.; flows NE, past city of Lake Geneva, to Fox R. at Burlington. Generates power for both cities. **8** c.690 mi/1,110 km long, Ark. and Mo.; rises in the Boston Mts., NW Ark.; flows N into SW Mo., then generally SE through NE Ark. to the Mississippi R. Its chief tributaries are the Black and Little Red rivers. Near its mouth, the White is joined to the Arkansas R. by a cutoff on canal (for barge traffic from Arkansas to Mississippi rivers). The White is navigable for shallow-draft vessels c.300 mi/483 km upstream. Bull Shoals, Table Rock, and Beaver dams are major projects on the river. Bull Shoals L. (□ 111 sq mi/ 288 sq km), on the Ark.-Mo. state line, is the largest reservoir. Narrow lake connects Table Rock and Bull Shoals reservoirs in Mo. **9** 307 mi/494 km long, Ind.; rises in Randolph co., E Ind.; flows W and SW through Muncie and Indianapolis to join the Wabash R. near the East Fork of White R. (282 mi/454 km long), its chief tributary, the White drains much of central East Mt. Carmel and S Ind.

White River Junction, industrial, commercial, and RR center (1990 pop. 2,521) in town of Hartford, Windsor co., E Vt., on Connecticut R., at mouth of White R., and 10 mi/16 km E of Woodstock. Wood prods., dairy prods., textiles. Gateway to Green Mt. resorts.

White Rock, city (1991 pop. 16,314), SE B.C., W Canada, on Georgia Strait, and on the U.S. (Wash.) border; 49°02′N 122°49′W. Customs port and resort center with a residential area.

White Rock, uninc. town (1990 pop. 6,192), Los Alamos and Santa Fe cos., N central N.Mex., 17 mi/27 km NW of Santa Fe, on Rio Grande; 35°47′N 106°12′W. Grain, corn, alfalfa; cattle, sheep. Mfg. (office supplies). Bandelier Natl. Monument to S.

White Rock 1 village, in town of Westerly, Washington co., SE R.I., on Pawcatuck R. **2** uninc. village, Richland co., central S.C., 18 mi/29 km NW of Columbia. Mfg. of apparel and consumer goods. L. Murray reservoir to S. **3** village (1990 pop. 7), Roberts co., extreme NE corner of S.Dak., 30 mi/48 km NE of Sisseton, on Bois de Sioux R. (Minn. state line), and S of N.Dak. border; 45°55′N 96°34′W.

White Rock Lake, reservoir (□ c.2 sq mi/5.2 sq km), N Texas, on White Rock Creek (N tributary of Trinity R.), in White Rock L. Park, 6 mi/9.7 km NE of downtown Dallas; 3 mi/4.8 km long; 32°49′N 96°43′W. Impounded by dam. Recreation. Dallas Arboretum and Botanical Garden on E shore.

White Rock Mountain, peak (c.13,532 ft/4,125 m) in Rocky Mts., Gunnison co., W central Colo., 8 mi/ 12.9 km NNE of Crested Butte; 38°58′N 106°55′W.

White Salmon, town (1990 pop. 1,861), Klickitat co., S Wash., 2 mi/3.2 km NNE of Hood River (Oregon),

57 mi/92 km ENE of Vancouver (Wash.), and on Columbia R. (Bonneville Reservoir), at mouth of White Salmon R. (bridge); 45°44′N 121°29′W. Wheat, vegetables, alfalfa, potatoes; logging; salmon. Winery to N. Yakima Indian Reservation and Conboy L. Natl. Wildlife Refuge to NE; Gifford Pinchot Natl. Forest to NW, including Indian Heaven Wilderness Area. Spring Creek, Willard, and Little White Salmon natl. fish hatcheries to W.

White Salmon River, c.50 mi/80 km long, S Wash.; rises in Cascade Range at Mt. Adams in NE Skamania co., in Gifford Pinchot Natl. Forest; flows S to Columbia R. near town of White Salmon.

White Sands, desert, S central N.Mex., in Tularosa Basin. It is near the center of (and lends its name to) U.S. White Sands Missile Range, a center for military weapons research and testing. The desert includes White Sands Natl. Monument in S; San Andres Natl. Wildlife Refuge is to W; Holloman Air Force Base to E.

White Sands National Monument (□ 224 sq mi/ 580 sq km), Otero and Doña Ana cos., S central N.Mex., c.15 mi/24 km WSW of Alamogordo. In S part of White Sands Desert. Tularosa Basin, largest gypsum dunes field in world; some dunes are 60 ft/18 m high. Region has flora and fauna adapted to conditions and characteristics, such as sand coloration, of the environment. Bounded N, W, and S by White Sands Missile Range. Holloman Air Force Base to E. Authorized 1933.

White Sands Missile Range (□ 2 sq mi/5.2 sq km; 1990 pop. 2,616), S central N.Mex.: extends through 5 cos. (mainly in Tularosa Basin), generally W of Alamogordo and NE of Las Cruces R.; c.120 mi/193 km long N-S, c.40 mi/64 km wide; 32°22′N 106°29′W. White Sands desert in E center; San Andres Mts. in W; part of Sierra Oscura to N. Tract is crossed in S by U.S. Highway 70/ 82, where main entrance and facilities are located. Tract surrounds San Andres Natl. Wildlife Refuge and White Sands Natl. Monument in S center. Holloman Air Force Base is E of tract, near Alamogordo. White Sands Space Harbor, landing site for space shuttle missions, at center. Trinity Site, site of 1st atomic explosion (July 16, 1945), is in N, W of Sierra Oscura, at edge of Jornada del Muerto plain.

White Settlement, city (1990 pop. 15,472), Tarrant co., N Texas, residential suburb 8 mi/12.9 km W of downtown Fort Worth, surrounded by Fort Worth; 32°45′N 97°27′W. Drained by Farmers Branch of West Fork of Trinity R. Mfg. apparel. Formerly called Liberator Village or Liberator. Carswell Air Force Base to NE. L. Worth reservoir to N. Inc. after 1940.

White Stone, town (1990 pop. 372), Lancaster co., E Va., 18 mi/29 km NNE of Gloucester, near Rappahannock R. estuary (bridged to SW), Chesapeake Bay to E; 37°38′N 76°23′W. Light mfg. Windmill Point to E. White Stone Beach (resort) is nearby; Tides Inn and Lodge resort to W.

White Sulphur Springs 1 town, Meriwether co., W Ga., 15 mi/24 km SE of La Grange. **2** town (1990 pop. 963), ⊙ Meagher co., central Mont., on North Fork Smith R., 4 mi/6.4 km NE of the confluence with South Fork (forming Smith R.), and 55 mi/89 km E of Helena; 46°33′N 110°54′W. Gold, silver, and lead mines. Cattle; timber; grain, hay, mfg. (wood prods.). Hot Sulphur Springs (2 posts) in town used for therapeutic and recreational purposes. Smith R. State Park to NW; Little Belt Mts. to N, Big Belt Mts. to SW, Castle Mts. to SE; Helena Natl. Forest to SW, part of Lewis and Clark Natl. Forest to N and SE. Meagher Co. Historical Assn., Inc. Originally called Brewer Springs. **3** town (1990 pop. 2,779), Greenbrier co., SE W.Va., 8 mi/12.9 km E of Lewisburg, in the Allegheny Mts.; 37°47′N 80°17′W. Elev. 1,917 ft/584 m. Mfg. (concrete). Natl. fish hatchery. Has 1830s spring house. Well-known resort area, with mineral springs, since early 1800s. Historic Greenbrier Resort has 2-story bunker beneath hotel designed to house 1,150 members of Congress during a nuclear war (built 1958; decommissioned 1995). Monongahela Natl. Forest to N; George Washington Natl. Forest to E; Greenbrier State Forest to S. Settled c.1750.

White Tank Mountains, range in N central Maricopa

co., central Ariz., W of Phoenix, N of Gila R. Rises to 4,200 ft/1,280 m. Hayden-Rhodes Aqueduct passes to N.

White Top Mountain (5,520 ft/1,682 m), on border bet. Smyth and Grayson cos., SW Va., in Iron Mts., spur of Appalachian Mts., near N.C. and Tenn. state lines, 15 mi/24 km SSW of Marion, 3 mi/4.8 km WSW of Mt. Rogers, in Mt. Rogers Natl. Recreation Area (Jefferson Natl. Forest); 36°38′N 81°36′W.

White Water, uninc. village, Riverside co., S Calif., suburb 7 mi/11.3 km NNW of Palm Springs. Stone quarrying. San Bernardino Mts. to NW; San Jacinto Mts. to SW. San Jacinto Wilderness Area to S.

Whiteash, village (1990 pop. 249), Williamson co., S Ill., 3 mi/4.8 km N of Marion; 37°47′N 88°55′W. In bituminous-coal-mining and agr. (grain; dairying) area.

Whitebreast Creek, c.80 mi/129 km long, S Iowa; rises in Clarke co.; flows E and NE to Des Moines R. 6 mi/ 9.7 km NE of Knoxville.

Whitechurch-Stouffville (STO-vil), city (1991 pop. 18,357), S Ont., central Canada, 24 mi/39 km NNE of Toronto; 43°58′N 79°15′W. Dairying, mixed farming; mfg. (fabricated metal prods.). Suburban community. Includes village of same name.

Whitecourt, town (1986 pop. 5,737), 110 mi/177 km NW of Edmonton, Alta., W Canada. at confluence of McLeod and Athabasca rivers; 54°08′N 115°41′W. Lumbering; oil and gas; pulp and fiberboard mills.

Whiteface, village (1990 pop. 512), Cochran co., NW Texas, 43 mi/69 km W of Lubbock; 33°36′N 102°36′W. Oil and gas; cotton, wheat; cattle.

Whiteface Mountain (4,872 ft/1,485 m), Essex co., NE N.Y., in the High Peaks sect. of the Adirondack Mts., 7 mi/11.3 km NNE of Lake Placid; 44°22′N 73°55′W. State-developed skiing center here. Highway ascends peak almost to summit, whose meteorological station (est. 1937) is reached by elevator.

Whiteface River, 70 mi/113 km long, St. Louis co., NE Minn.; formed by confluence of North and South branches in White Face Reservoir, 35 mi/56 km N of Duluth, at edge of Superior Natl. Forest (47°16′N 92°11′W); flows SW, to E of Meadowlands, joining St. Louis R. 6 mi/9.7 km NE of Floodwood. North Branch Whiteface R., c.30 mi/48 km long; rises in Mud L., E St. Louis co., 47 mi/76 km NNE of Duluth; flows SW. South Branch Whiteface R., c.20 mi/32 km long; rises in E St. Louis co., 37 mi/60 km N of Duluth, near West Branch Cloquet R.; flows SW, then NW to E arm of Whiteface Reservoir. Both branches are in Superior Natl. Forest.

Whitefield 1 town (1990 pop. 1,931), Lincoln co., S Maine, on Sheepscot R., and 12 mi/19 km N of Wiscasset; 44°12′N 69°37′W. Settled c.1770, inc. 1809. **2** town (1990 pop. 1,909), Coos co., NW N.H., in White Mts., 9 mi/14.5 km ENE of Littleton; 44°22′N 71°35′W. Drained by Johns R. and Bog Brook. Timber; dairying; poultry, livestock; nursery crops, vegetables. Mfg. (furniture, lumber, wood prods.). Granted 1774, inc. 1804.

Whitefish, town (1990 pop. 4,368), Flathead co., NW Mont., 15 mi/24 km N of Kalispell, on Whitefish R., at S end of Whitefish L.; 48°25′N 114°20′W. Lake resort. In lumbering region; sawmills (timber). Barley, potatoes; cattle, hogs. Mfg. (electrical equip., coffee). Stumptown Historical Society Mus. Whitefish Range to N; Whitefish L. State Park to W; Salish Mts. to SW; Flathead Natl. Forest to N and W; Big Mt. Ski Area to N; Stillwater State Forest to NW, beyond N end of lake; Blanchard L. to S. Founded in 1903, inc. 1911.

Whitefish Bay, city (1990 pop. 14,272), Milwaukee co., SE Wis., residential suburb 5 mi/8 km NNE of downtown Milwaukee, on L. Michigan; 43°06′N 87°54′W. Inc. 1892.

Whitefish Bay, W Ont., central Canada, E inlet of L. of the Woods, bounded S by Aulneau Peninsula; 34 mi/ 55 km long, 1 mi/2 km–10 mi/16 km wide. Contains numerous islets.

Whitefish Bay, in Mich. and Ont., SE arm of L. Superior; c.30 mi/48 km long NW-SE, 15 mi/24 km–34 mi/ 55 km wide; 46°28′N 84°48′W. Traversed by Can. border. Peninsula terminating at Whitefish Point is at W side of entrance; here are Whitefish Point village (Mich.), a lighthouse. St. Marys R. flows out of L. Superior in SE to connect with L. Huron. Butchawana and Goulais bays on E (Ont.) side, Tahquamenon Bay of Mich side, in SW. Île Parisienne (Ont.), isl. 5 mi/8 km long (N–S), 1 mi/1.6 km wide, E of center.

Whitefish Lake 1 (☐ 11 sq mi/28 sq km), in Crow Wing co., central Minn., 23 mi/37 km N of Brainerd; 7.5 mi/12.1 km long, 4 mi/6.4 km wide; 46°41′N 94°10′W. Elev. 1,231 ft/375 m. Fed (from W) and drained (SE through Rush and Cross lakes, continuations of Whitefish L.) by Pine R. Has fishing, boating, swimming resorts. Village of Manhattan Beach at NE end, on Big Trout L. (bay). Divided into Upper (W) and Lower (E) Whitefish lakes by 1-mi/1.6-km-wide passage; several bays, connected to lakes by narrow passages, are named as lakes: Lower Hay, Bertha, and Clamshell lakes (SW), Pig and Rush lakes (SE), Island L. (E), Big Trout L. (NE), Arrowhead L. (N). Crow Wing State Forest to SE. **2** in Flathead co., NW Mont., 15 mi/24 km N of Kalispell, just S of Whitefish Range; 6 mi/9.7 km. long, 1 mi/1.6 km wide; fed at N end by Swift, West Fork, and Lazy creeks, drained at S end by Whitefish R. Used for recreation. Town of Whitefish and Whitefish L. State Park at S end.

Whitefish Point, Mich.: see WHITEFISH BAY.

Whitefish Range, in Rocky Mts. of NW Mont., rises just N of U.S.-Canada (B.C.) border in B.C. and W of North Fork Flathead R.; extends SE to Whitefish (Mont.); continues further into B.C. as MacDonald Range; bounded on E by Glacier Natl. Park; 48°45′N 114°35′W. Elevs. of 6,000 ft/1,829 m–8,100 ft/2,469 m. Lies partly within Flathead Natl. Forest.

Whitefish River, c.45 mi/72 km long, S Upper Peninsula, N Mich.; rises in E Marquette co.; flows SE into Delta co., then SW to N end of Little Bay De Noc; 46°03′N 86°52′W.

Whitehall, city (1990 pop. 20,572), Franklin co., central Ohio, suburb of Columbus; 39°58′N 82°53′W. Mfg. includes water coolers and packaged meats. A large Federal defense construction supply center is here. Inc. 1948.

Whitehall 1 town, Clarke co., NE central Ga., 4 mi/6.4 km SSE of Athens; 33°54′N 83°21′W. **2** town (1990 pop. 3,027), Muskegon co., SW Mich., 12 mi/19 km NNW of Muskegon opposite Montague, on White L.; 43°23′N 86°20′W. In fruit-growing area near L. Michigan. Mfg. (fabricated metal prods., electronic equip., machinery). Resort. Swed. midsummer festival held here. White R. Station Mus.; Duck L. State Park to S; Manistee Natl. Forest to NE. Inc. 1867 as village, as city 1943. **3** town (1990 pop. 1,067), Jefferson co., SW Mont., on Jefferson R. at mouth of Whitehall Creek, and 32 mi/51 km ESE of Butte; 45°52′N 112°06′W. Gold, silver mines. Hay, wheat, oats. Livestock; formerly a dairying center. Parts of Deerlodge Natl. Forest to N and S; Lewis and Clark Caverns State Park to E. Jefferson Valley Mus. here. **4** town (1990 pop. 1,494), ⊙ Trempealeau co., W Wis., on Trempealeau R., and 32 mi/51 km SSE of Eau Claire; 44°22′N 91°18′W. In dairy, poultry, and grain area; trade and shipping center; mfg. (lumber, furniture components). Settled 1855; inc. as village in 1887, as city in 1941.

Whitehall, village (☐ 4 sq mi/10.4 sq km; 1990 pop. 3,071), Washington co., E N.Y., at S end of L. Champlain, on Champlain R. to N.Y. State Barge Canal, and 21 mi/34 km NNE of Glens Falls; 43°33′N 73°25′W. Summer resort. Some mfg. Settled 1759, inc. 1806.

Whitehall 1 borough (1990 pop. 14,451), Allegheny co., SW Pa., suburb 6 mi/9.7 km S of downtown Pittsburgh; 40°21′N 79°59′W. Mfg. (fabricated metal prods., dairy prods., bldg. materials). Inc. 1948. **2** borough (1990 pop. 14,451), Lehigh co., E Pa., residential suburb 2 mi/3.2 km NW of downtown Allentown, on Jordan Creek; 40°21′N 79°59′W.

Whitehaven 1 fishing village, Wicomico co., SE Md., 13 mi/21 km SW of Salisbury, and on Wicomico R. Vegetable cannery. Named after the hometown in England of George Gale, who settled here in the early 18th cent. A 3-car ferry still provides transportation across

the river. Nearby is Green Hill Protestant Episcopal Church (c.1733). **2** former village, Shelby co., SW Tenn., just N of Miss. state line. Inc. 1969 into Memphis.

Whitehead Island, Knox co., S Maine, 3.5 mi/5.6 km NE of Tenants Harbor. Lighthouse.

Whitehorn Mountain (11,101 ft/3,384 m), E B.C., W Canada, near Alta. border, in Rocky Mts., in Mt. Robson Provincial Park, 55 mi/89 km WNW of Jasper.

Whitehorse, city (1991 pop. 17,925), ⊙ Yukon Territory, NW Canada, in S Yukon, on the Yukon R.; 60°43′N 135°03′W. Elev. 2,305 ft./703 m. River port. On the Alaska Highway; was terminus of the White Pass and Yukon RR from Skagway (Alaska; suspended service in 1982). The city is the center of a gold-mining, hunting, and fur-trapping region that attracts growing numbers of tourists. After an economic lull in the mid-1980s, the discovery of the world's largest tungsten reserve at Mae Pass revitalized the city. Territorial capital since 1952. It is hq. of the Royal Can. Mounted Police for S Yukon and has an airport, radio and TV stations, a weather station, and Yukon Col. It was an important supply and stage center during the Klondike gold rush (1897–1898). During World War II it was the center of the Canol oil project (closed in 1945). SS *Klondike* Natl. Historic Site has retired riverboats.

Whitehouse, town (1990 pop. 4,032), Smith co., E Texas, 10 mi/16 km SSE of Tyler; 32°13′N 95°13′W. Lakes Tyler (Angelina R.) and Tyler East both to E. Oil and natural gas. Agr. area (horticultural crops, rose bushes, fruits, vegetables, cattle). Mfg. (machinery, fabricated metal prods.).

Whitehouse, village (1990 pop. 2,528), Lucas co., NW Ohio, 16 mi/26 km WSW of downtown Toledo; 41°31′N 83°48′W. Dairy prods., fruit; mfg. of automotive parts, glass.

Whiteland, town (1990 pop. 2,446), Johnson co., central Ind., 5 mi/8 km N of Franklin; 39°33′N 86°05′W. In agr. area. Mfg. (foam prods., wood prods.). Laid out 1863.

Whitelaw, village, W Alta., W Canada, 32 mi/51 km WSW of Peace R.; 56°06′N 118°05′W. Lumbering; mixed farming (wheat).

Whitelaw, town (1990 pop. 700), Manitowoc co., E Wis., 8 mi/12.9 km WNW of Manitowoc; 44°08′N 87°49′W. Dairying; livestock; grain, vegetables, fruit. Mfg. (wire rope, foods).

Whitelick Creek, c.40 mi/64 km long, central Ind.; rises in S Boone co.; flows generally S, past Plainfield, Mooresville, and Brooklyn, to West Fork of White R. 5 mi/8 km NNE of Martinsville.

Whiteman Air Force Base, Johnson co., W Mo., 17 mi/27 km W of Sedalia, 3 mi/4.8 km S of Knob Noster. Knob Noster State Park to NW. Minuteman missile site, deactivated in 1990s. Base's role has increased with closing of Richards Grebaur Air Force Base in Kansas City.

Whitemouth, village, SE Man., central Canada, on Whitemouth R., and 50 mi/80 km E of Winnipeg; 49°57′N 95°58′W. Dairying; grain.

Whitemud River, 150 mi/241 km long, SW and S Man., central Canada; rises S of Riding Mt. Natl. Park; flows E, past Neepawa, Gladstone, and Westbourne, to S end of L. Manitoba 23 mi/37 km NW of Portage la Prairie.

Whiteoak, uninc. rural community, Dunklin co., in the bootheel of extreme SE Mo., near St. Francis R., 7 mi/11.3 km N of Kennett.

Whiteriver, uninc. town, Navajo co., E Ariz., on White R., in Fort Apache Indian Reservation, and c.55 mi/89 km NE of Globe. Elev. c.5,224 ft/1,592 m. Trading point and hq. for Indian reservation; logging; cattle, sheep, hogs; corn, alfalfa; crafts. White Mts. nearby.

Whitesail Lake, W central B.C., W Canada, in Coast Mts., in Tweedsmuir Park, 170 mi/274 km WSW of Prince George, just NW of Eutsuk L.; 28 mi/45 km long, 1 mi/2 km–3 mi/5 km wide. Drains N into Ootsa L.

Whitesand River, 120 mi/193 km long, SE Sask., W Canada; issues from small Whitesand L. 50 mi/80 km NW of Yorkton; flows in an arc SE and NE to Assiniboine R. at Kamsack.

Whitesboro, town (1990 pop. 3,209), Grayson co., N Texas, 13 mi/21 km W of Sherman; 33°39′N 96°54′W. RR junction; cattle; peanuts, wheat; light mfg. L. Kiowa reservoir to SW; Hagerman Natl. Wildlife Refuge to NE.

Whitesboro, village (☐ 1 sq mi/2.6 sq km; 1990 pop. 4,195), Oneida co., central N.Y., on Mohawk R. and the N.Y. State Barge Canal, and 4 mi/6.4 km WNW of Utica; 43°07′N 75°17′W. Mfg. of transportation equip., electronics, caskets. Settled 1784, inc. 1813.

Whitesburg, town (1990 pop. 1,636), ⊙ Letcher co., SE Ky., 22 mi/35 km SSE of Hazard, in the Cumberland Mts., on North Fork Kentucky R.; 37°07′N 82°49′W. Bituminous coal; mfg. (machinery, wood prods. and lumber; printing). Formerly a lumbering town. Clay, sand and gravel, timber, some agr. in region. Southeast Community Col.–Whitesburg Campus. Pine Mt. Wildlife Management Area and Bad Branch State Nature Preserve to S; Pine Mt. Ridge and Jefferson Natl. Forest to SE. Settled 1840, inc. 1872.

Whitesburg, village (1990 pop. 643), Carroll co., W Ga., 11 mi/18 km SE of Carrollton, near Chattahoochee R.; 33°29′N 84°55′W. Mfg. of rope, fabricated metal prods.

Whiteshed, Alaska: see POINT WHITESHED.

Whiteshed, Point, Alaska: see POINT WHITESHED.

Whiteside, county (☐ 697 sq mi/1,805 sq km; 1990 pop. 60,186), NW Ill.; ⊙ Morrison; 41°45′N 89°54′W. Bounded NW by the Mississippi R.; drained by Rock R. and Rock and Elkhorn creeks. Agr. (cattle, hogs, poultry; corn, soybeans, hay). Limestone quarries. Processing of farm and dairy prods.; mfg. at Morrison and Sterling-Rock Falls. Formed 1836. Prophetstown and Rockwood state parks; Big Bend Conservation Area.

Whiteside, town (1990 pop. 79), Lincoln co., E Mo., near North Fork of Cuivre R., 14 mi/23 km N of Troy; 39°10′N 91°01′W.

Whitestone, residential section of N Queens borough of N.Y. city, SE N.Y., on the East R. opposite the Bronx, bet. Powell's Cove and Little Bay, N of Flushing and E of College Park; 40°48′N 73°49′W. Some mfg. Bronx-Whitestone and Throgs Neck bridges cross East R. here.

Whitestown, town (1990 pop. 476), Boone co., central Ind., 7 mi/11.3 km SE of Lebanon; 40°00′N 86°21′W. In agr. area; mfg. (machinery, vinyl signs). Laid out 1851.

Whitesville, town (1990 pop. 486), Boone co., W central W.Va., on Big Coal R., 17 mi/27 km ESE of Madison; 37°58′N 81°32′W. Agr.; bituminous-coal area; lumber milling.

Whitesville 1 village (1990 pop. 682), Daviess co., NW Ky., 15 mi/24 km ESE of Owensboro, near source of Panther Creek; 37°40′N 86°52′W. Agr. (tobacco, grain; livestock, poultry; dairying); mfg. (printing). **2** village (1990 pop. 800), Allegany co., W N.Y., 10 mi/16 km SE of Wellsville, near Pa. state line; 42°02′N 77°46′W. Mfg. (dairy prods., wood prods.); timber.

Whitetail, village (1990 pop. 100), Daniels co., NE Mont., 13 mi/21 km NE of Scobey. Whitetail Port of Entry on Canada (Sask.) border, 7 mi/11.3 km N, on Whitetail Creek. Whitetail Reservoir to S. Wheat, barley, hay; cattle, sheep, hogs. RR terminus (from E).

Whiteville 1 town (1990 pop. 5,078), ⊙ Columbus co., S N.C., 36 mi/58 km SE of Lumberton; 34°19′N 78°42′W. RR terminus. Tobacco market and trade center; mfg. (textiles and apparel, transportation equip., fabricated metal prods., paper prods., wood prods.; printing and publishing). Southeastern Community Col. L. Waccamaw State Park to SE. Founded 1810. **2** town (1990 pop. 1,050), Hardeman co., SW Tenn., 27 mi/43 km SW of Jackson; 35°20′N 89°09′W. In agr. area.

Whitewater, city (1990 pop. 12,636), Jefferson and Walworth cos., SE Wis., 17 mi/27 km NE of Janesville; 42°49′N 88°44′W. In a dairy and farm area. Foundry; various light mfg. (machinery and machinery parts). Seat of the Univ. of Wis. at Whitewater. Kettle Moraine State Forest to SE. Inc. 1885.

Whitewater 1 town (1990 pop. 111), Wayne co., E Ind., near East Fork of Whitewater R., and 9 mi/14.5 km NNE of Richmond, near Ohio state line; 39°56′N

84°48′W. **2** town (1990 pop. 103), Cape Girardeau co., SE Mo., on Whitewater R., and 10 mi/16 km S of Jackson; 37°14′N 89°47′W.

Whitewater 1 village, Mesa co., W Colo., on Gunnison R., at mouth of Whitewater Creek, and 8 mi/12.9 km SE of Grand Junction. Elev. c.4,660 ft/1,420 m. Cattle, sheep-shipping point in irrigated agr. area. **2** village (1990 pop. 683), Butler co., S central Kansas, 21 mi/34 km NNE of Wichita; 37°57′N 97°09′W. RR junction. In grain and livestock area. **3** village (1990 pop. 125), Phillips co., N Mont., 30 mi/48 km NNE of Malta, on Whitewater Creek. Wheat, barley, oats; livestock. Whitewater Reservoir (separate from river) to N. Port of Morgan on Canada (Sask.) border 18 mi/29 km NW.

Whitewater, locality, Marion co., N Ark., at junction of White R. and Crooked Creek, 20 mi/32 km SW of Mountain Home, in the Ozark Mts.; 36°10′N 92°28′W. Started as a recreational retirement development in the late 1970s, plans called for 180 acres/73 ha to be subdivided. The lots were sold off in 1985 to reduce the debt on the mortgage by its owners (who included then-Gov. Bill Clinton). Whitewater became the focus of Congressional inquiry in the mid-1990s, based upon allegations that a fraudulent loan had been made to permit the owners to initiate the development.

Whitewater Baldy, peak (10,892 ft/3,320 m) in Mogollon Mts., S Catron co., SW N.Mex., c.45 mi/72 km NNW of Silver City; 33°19′N 108°38′W. In Gila Natl. Forest; source of West Peak Gila R. to S.

Whitewater Bay, shallow mangrove-lined inlet of the Gulf of Mexico, in Everglades Natl. Park, extreme S Fla., enclosed S and partly W by Cape Sable; c.15 mi/24 km long, 4 mi/6.4 km–8 mi/12.9 km wide. Contains many small isls.

Whitewater River 1 c.70 mi/113 km long, in Ind. and Ohio; formed by headstreams S of Winchester, E Ind., with West Fork flowing generally S and SE, past Brookville (at influx of East Fork, c.55 mi/89 km long), to Great Miami R. in Hamilton co. (Ohio), 15 mi/24 km W of Cincinnati. **2** c.50 mi/80 km long, SE Mo.; rises in St. Francois co.; flows SE and S through the E Ozark Mts., and is diverted into the Headwaters Diversion Channel to the Mississippi R. S of Cape Girardeau. Formerly flowed into the Little R. and swamps of SE Mo.

Whitewood, town (1991 pop. 1,064), SE Sask., W Canada, 30 mi/48 km WNW of Moosomin; 50°20′N 102°15′W. Grain elevators; lumbering.

Whitewood, town (1990 pop., 891), Lawrence co., W S.Dak., 7 mi/11.3 km NNE of Deadwood, at N edge of Black Hills; 44°27′N 103°38′W. Black Hills Natl. Forest to S. Mfg. (logging; timber and wood prods., feed supplements).

Whitewood, Lake, Kingsbury co., E S.Dak., near L. Preston; 7 mi/11.3 km long, 1 mi/1.6 km wide; 44°20′N 97°17′W.

Whitewright, town (1990 pop. 1,713), Grayson co., N Texas, 15 mi/24 km SE of Sherman; 33°30′N 96°23′W. Peanuts; cattle, poultry; meat processing, feed mfg. Oil and gas. Settled 1877, inc. 1888.

Whitfield, county (☐ 291 sq mi/754 sq km; 1990 pop. 72,462), NW Ga., on Tenn. (N) state line; ⊙ Dalton; 34°48′N 84°58′W. Bordered E by Conasauga R. Agr. (corn); cattle, hogs, poultry; timber; marble; mfg. at Dalton. Part of Chattahoochee Natl. Forest in S. Formed 1851.

Whitfield, uninc. town (1990 pop. 2,585), Berks co., SE central Pa., residential suburb 5 mi/8 km W of Reading; 40°20′N 76°00′W. Blue Marsh L. reservoir to NW.

Whiting, city (1990 pop. 5,155), Lake co., extreme NW Ind., on L. Michigan, near Ill. state line, adjacent to SE Chicago; 41°41′N 87°29′W. In the Calumet industrial region, mfg. (chemicals; petroleum refining, asphalt roofing, machining). Settled 1885, laid out 1889, inc. 1903.

Whiting 1 town (1990 pop. 683), Monona co., W Iowa, 7 mi/11.3 km NNW of Onawa; 42°07′N 96°09′W. Mfg. (grain elevators). **2** town (1990 pop. 407), Washington co., E Maine, 15 mi/24 km ENE of Machias; 44°45′N 67°15′W. **3** town (1990 pop. 407), Addison co., W Vt.,

on Otter Creek, and 10 mi/16 km S of Middlebury; 43°51′N 73°12′W. Dairying. **4** town (1990 pop. 1,838), Portage co., central Wis., suburb 2 mi/3.2 km SE of Stevens Point, on Wisconsin R.; 44°29′N 89°33′W.

Whiting, village (1990 pop. 213), Jackson co., NE Kansas, 10 mi/16 km NE of Holton; 39°35′N 95°36′W. RR junction. In livestock and grain region.

Whiting River, 50 mi/80 km long, W Canada (NW B.C.) and SE Alaska; rises in B.C. near 58°20′N 132°58′W; flows SW to Stephens Passage 30 mi/48 km SE of Juneau.

Whitingham (WEI-ting-ham), town (1990 pop. 1,177), Windham co., SE Vt., 17 mi/27 km WSW of Brattleboro, partly in Green Mt. Natl. Forest; 42°46′N 72°52′W. Wood prods., maple prods. Includes Jacksonville village, L. Whitingham here, is formed by Harriman Dam in Deerfield R. (water power). Brigham Young b. here (monument).

Whitinsville, Mass.: see NORTHBRIDGE.

Whitlash (WIT-lash), village (1990 pop. 10), Liberty co., N Mont., 43 mi/69 km NE of Shelby, on Breed Creek. Sweet Grass Hills to SW. Wheat, barley, hay; livestock; gas and oil. Whitlash Port of Entry at Canada (Alta.) border, 6 mi/9.7 km N.

Whitley 1 (WIT-lee), county (☐ 337 sq mi/873 sq km; 1990 pop. 27,651), NE Ind.; ⊙ Columbia City; 41°08′N 85°30′W. Agr. area (livestock, poultry; corn, wheat, soybeans; dairy prods.). Some mfg. at Columbia City and South Whitley. Drained by Eel R. Many small glacial lakes in N part. Formed 1835. **2** county (☐ 445 sq mi/1,153 sq km; 1990 pop. 33,326), SE Ky., on Tenn. (S) state line; ⊙ Williamsburg; 36°45′N 84°09′W. In the Cumberlands; bordered NW by Cumberland R. (crosses co. E-W) and N by Laurel R. (forms Laurel R. reservoir). Agr. (burley tobacco, hay, corn; cattle); bituminous-coal mining; gas wells; hardwood timber. Part of Daniel Boone Natl. Forest in W ½ of co.; part of Cumberland Falls State Resort Park, on W border. Formed 1818.

Whitley City (WIT-lee), town (1990 pop. 1,133), ⊙ McCreary co., SE Ky., in the Cumberland Mts., 26 mi/42 km SSE of Somerset; 36°43′N 84°28′W. Bituminous-coal mining; timber, some agr.; mfg. (wood prods., concrete; printing and publishing). McCreany Co. Airport to SE. Surrounded by Daniel Boone Natl. Forest; Cumberland Falls State Park to NE; Big South Fork Natl. River and Recreation Area (Ky. and Tenn.) to SW.

Whitley Home State Park, Ky.: see CRAB ORCHARD.

Whitman, county (☐ 2,177 sq mi/5,638 sq km; 1990 pop. 38,775), SE Wash., on Idaho (E) state line, bounded on S by Snake R. (forms L. Herbert G. West in SW, Little Goose Reservoir in S, Lower Granite L. reservoir in SE); 46°54′N 117°31′W. Drained by Palouse R. (forms part of W border) and Pine, Rock, and Union Flat creeks. Broad plateau and low hills underlain by volcanic basalt, punctuated by buttes over 3,000 ft/914 m high. Irrigated agr. area (peas, lentils, wheat, barley, oats, alfalfa, hay; cattle, sheep, hogs). Region referred to as the Palouse Country. Steptoe Memorial Battlefield (N), Steptoe Butte (NE), and part of Palouse Falls (SW) state parks.

Whitman, town (1990 pop. 13,240), Plymouth co., SE Mass., S of Boston; 42°05′N 70°57′W. It is an industrial town mfg. plastics and foundry prods. Settled c.1670, set off from Abington and inc. 1875. The Toll House (1709) is restored.

Whitman, village (1990 pop. 100), Grant co., Nebr., 72 mi/116 km E of Alliance. Gudmundson Sand Hills Laboratory of Univ. of Nebr. (research center on livestock and ecological problems) nearby.

Whitman Knob, W.Va.: see RICH MOUNTAIN.

Whitman Mission National Historic Site, Walla Walla co., SE Wash., 6 mi/9.7 km WSW of Walla Walla, on Walla Walla R. Covers 98 acres/40 ha. Site of the mission of Dr. Marcus and Narcissa Whitman, who preached among local Native Americans; the pair was killed in 1847; was landmark on Oregon Trail. Authorized 1936.

Whitmire (WIT-meir), town (1990 pop. 1,702), Newberry co., NW central S.C., on Enoree R., and 22 mi/35 km E of Laurens, in Sumter Natl. Forest; 34°30′N

81°37′W. Mfg. of textiles. Agr. includes poultry, livestock; dairying; grain; lumber.

Whitmore Lake, uninc. village, Washtenaw co., SE Mich., 9 mi/14.5 km N of Ann Arbor, on S end of small Whitmore L.; 42°26′N 83°44′W. Resort.

Whitmore Village, town (1990 pop. 3,373), N central Oahu isl., Honolulu co., Hawaii, 16 mi/26 km NNW of Honolulu, 2 mi/3.2 km NE of Wahiawa; 21°30′N 158°01′W. Residential community. Helemano Military Reservation immediately NE. Ewa Forest Reserve to E.

Whitnel (WIT-nuhl), uninc. village, Caldwell co., W central N.C., suburb 2 mi/3.2 km SE of Lenoir.

Whitney 1 uninc. town, Spartanburg co., NW S.C., residential suburb 2 mi/3.2 km N of Spartanburg. **2** town (1990 pop. 1,626), Hill co., N central Texas, 30 mi/48 km NNW of Waco; 31°56′N 97°19′W. Cotton, grain; cattle; dairying; light mfg. Tourist center. Est. 1879. About 5 mi/8 km SW is Whitney Dam (L. Whitney State Park) in Brazos R. Aquilla L. reservoir to E.

Whitney 1 village (1990 pop. 38), Dawes co., NW Nebr., 13 mi/21 km WSW of Chadron, and on White R.; 42°46′N 103°15′W. Nearby Whitney L. reservoir, an artificial lake used for fishing and irrigation, is to W. **2** uninc. village, Baker co., NE Oregon, 23 mi/37 km SW of Baker City, on North Fork Burnt R., in Wallowa-Whitman Natl. Forest.

Whitney, Lake, reservoir, on border bet. Bosque and Hill cos., central Texas, on Brazos R. 25 mi/40 km N of Waco; c.35 mi/56 km long; 31°51′N 97°22′W. Max. capacity 2,017,000 acre-ft. Formed by Whitney Dam (163 ft/50 m high), built (1946) for power generation and flood control. L. Whitney State Park on E shore.

Whitney, Mount, peak (14,494 ft/4,418 m), on border bet. Tulare and Inyo cos., E Calif., in the Sierra Nevada, at the E border of Sequoia Natl. Park; 36°34′N 118°17′W. The peak is named for geologist Josiah D. Whitney, who surveyed it in 1864. Was highest point in U.S. until Alaska became a state (Jan. 3, 1959); only c.75 mi/121 km WNW of Death Valley, lowest point (-282 ft/-86 m) in U.S. (and in Western Hemisphere).

Whitney Point, village (☐ 1 sq mi/2.6 sq km; 1990 pop. 1,054), Broome co., S N.Y., on Tioughnioga R. at mouth of Otselic R., and 16 mi/26 km N of Binghamton; 42°19′N 75°58′W. In farming and dairying area. Whitney Point flood-control reservoir (3.5 mi/5.6 km long) for Binghamton located here.

Whitney State Park, Lake, Texas: see WHITNEY, LAKE.

Whitneyville, town (1990 pop. 241), Washington co., E Maine, on Machias R., and just W of Machias; 44°43′N 67°31′W.

Whitsett (WIT-set), uninc. village, Guilford co., N central N.C., 15 mi/24 km W of Burlington. Agr. area (tobacco, grain; poultry, livestock; dairying). Mfg. (electronic equip., tobacco prods., paper prods.).

Whitshed, Point, Alaska: see POINT WHITESHED.

Whittemore, town (1990 pop. 535), Kossuth co., N Iowa, 10 mi/16 km W of Algona; 43°03′N 94°25′W.

Whittemore, village (1990 pop. 463), Iosco co., NE Mich., 14 mi/23 km WSW of Tawas City; 44°13′N 83°47′W. In farm area; mfg tool and die.

Whitten, town (1990 pop. 137), Hardin co., central Iowa, near Iowa R., 8 mi/12.9 km SSE of Eldora; 42°15′N 93°00′W.

Whittier (WI-tee-yuhr), city (☐ 12 sq mi/31 sq km; 1990 pop. 77,671), Los Angeles co., S Calif., suburb 12 mi/19 km ESE of downtown Los Angeles; 33°58′N 118°01′W. In oil area. Mainly residential. Mfg. includes foods and food prods., transportation equip., machinery, clay and steel prods., elevators, paper prods., consumer goods, electronic and electromedical equip., furniture, fabricated metal prods., rubber prods., filters; printing and publishing. Several companies have their administrative hq. here. Founded by Quakers in 1887, it was the hometown of former President Richard M. Nixon. Seat of Whittier Col. and Rio Hondo Col. (2-year). Pio Pica State Historic Park in NW in Whittier contains the mansion of the last Mex. governor of California, Pio Pica. Inc. 1898.

Whittier 1 village (1990 pop. 243), S Alaska, on SE Kenai Peninsula, at head of Port Wells, arm of Prince William

Sound, 50 mi/80 km SE of Anchorage; 60°46′N 148°45′W. Ice-free seaport, terminus of Alaska RR branch; fishing and logging center. Connected by tunnel to portage. Built by U.S. military during World War II. **2** (WI-tee-yuhr), uninc. village, Swain co., W N.C., 5 mi/8 km E of Bryson City, and on Tuckasegee R. Timber; corn, oats, tobacco; cattle, hogs. Mfg. (textiles, furniture). SE entrance to Great Smoky Mts. Natl. Park and SW terminus of Blue Ridge (Natl.) Parkway 7 mi/11.3 km to NE. Parts of Eastern Cherokee Indian Reservation to N and S; Nantahala Natl. Forest to S; Great Smoky Mts. Natl. Park to N.

Whitwell, city (1990 pop. 1,622), Marion co., SE Tenn., 16 mi/26 km NW of Chattanooga, in Sequatchie Valley, 35°12′N 85°31′W.

Wholdaia Lake, expansion of Dubawnt R., SE Mackenzie dist., N.W.T., N Canada, near Keewatin dist., border; 45 mi/72 km long, 5 mi/8 km–20 mi/32 km wide; 60°45′N 104°20′W.

Whonock (HWAH-nuhk), village, SW B.C., W Canada, on Fraser R., and 28 mi/45 km E of Vancouver. Lumbering; dairying; fruit, vegetables.

Whycocomagh (hwei-KO-muh), village, NE N.S., E Canada, central Cape Breton Isl., at head of St. Patrick Channel of Great Bras d'Or, 50 mi/80 km WSW of Sydney; 45°58′N 61°07′W. Popular resort. Nearby is Native Amer. reservation.

Wianno, Mass.: see BARNSTABLE.

Wiarton (WEI-uhr-tuhn), town (1991 pop. 2,313), S Ont., central Canada, on Saugeen Peninsula, on Colpay Bay (inlet of Georgian Bay), 16 mi/26 km NW of Owen Sound; 44°44′N 81°08′W. Port; milling, dairying, boatbuilding, furniture mfg. Site of govt. fish hatchery.

Wibaux (wee-BO), county (□ 890 sq mi/2,305 sq km; 1990 pop. 1,191), E Mont.; ⊙ Wibaux; 46°58′N 104°15′W. Agr. region bordering on N.Dak. (E); Yellowstone R. is far NW corner border. Drained by Beaver Creek. Wheat, barley, hay; cattle, sheep; oil. Lamesteer Natl. Wildlife Refuge in S. Formed 1914. Present borders est. 1919.

Wibaux (wee-BO), village (1990 pop. 628), ⊙ Wibaux co., E Mont., 26 mi/42 km ESE of Glendive, and on Beaver Creek, near N.Dak. state line; 47°00′N 104°11′W. Wheat, barley, oats, hay; cattle, sheep. Lamesteer Natl. Wildlife Refuge to S. Wilbaux Co. Mus. Originally called Keith, later Mingusville.

Wichita 1 (WI-chuh-taw), county (□ 718 sq mi/1,860 sq km; 1990 pop. 2,758), W Kansas; ⊙ Leoti; 38°28′N 101°20′W. Drained by White Woman Creek in center and Ladder Creek in N. Rolling plain area. Wheat, sorghum, corn; cattle. In Central time zone; border with Mountain time zone follows W co. line. Formed 1886. **2** county (□ 633 sq mi/1,639 sq km; 1990 pop. 122,378), N Texas, on Okla. (N; Red R.) state line; ⊙ Wichita Falls; 33°59′N 98°42′W. Commercial, shipping, industrial center of wide region. Drained by Wichita R., small creeks. Includes L. Wichita (irrigation, water supply; fishing) on S border. A leading Texas petroleum-producing co.; Wichita Falls, Electra, Burkburnett are oil centers; also stone, sand and gravel. Agr. (wheat, cotton; extensive irrigation); livestock (cattle, horses). Formed 1858.

Wichita (WI-chuh-taw), city (1990 pop. 304,011), ⊙ Sedgwick co., S central Kansas, at the confluence of the Arkansas and the Little Arkansas rivers; 37°41′N 97°20′W. It is the chief commercial and industrial center of S Kansas and the largest city in the state. It has RR shops, flour mills, meatpacking plants, grain elevators, oil refineries, and a huge aircraft industry. Other mfg. includes machinery, electrical prods., computer equip. Located on the site of a village (1863–1865) inhabited by Wichita Native Americans who had been driven out of Okla. and Texas for their Union sympathies during the Civil War. A trading post was est. here in 1864 and the city was founded in 1868 by settlers serving the Chisholm Trail. In 1872 the RR was extended here and the city boomed as a cow town. After 1880 it became the trade center of an agr. and livestock region. Oil was discovered just E in 1915. The city has many civic and cultural facilities, including an art mus., a symphony orchestra, a modernistic convention and cultural complex (Century II), and a large speech-and-hearing rehabilitation center. It has fine parks, a zoo, a "cow-town" restoration, and 2 large stadiums. Seat of Wichita State Univ., Friends Univ., Kansas Newman Col., and Berean Christian Col. Nearby is McConnell Air Force Base. Inc. 1870.

Wichita Falls, city (1990 pop. 96,259), ⊙ Wichita co., N Texas, on the Wichita R., 105 mi/169 km NW of Fort Worth; 33°53′N 98°31′W. Elev. 946 ft/288 m. The hq. of numerous oil companies are here, and oil-field machinery is a leading prod. Also transportation equip., machinery, electronic and electrical equip., wood prods., fabricated metal and metal prods., plastic, rubber prods., concrete, consumer goods, foam prods.; printing. Agr. and ranching still remain important to the city's economy. Named for Native Amer. Wichitas and for the falls that have since been reduced to an area of rapidly flowing water in the Wichita R. The area was probably settled by Americans in the 1870s, but the town did not grow until the coming of the RR in 1882. Formerly a shipping point for wheat and cattle from nearby ranches, the city achieved tremendous prosperity with the oil booms of 1919 and 1937 in the vicinity. Seat of Midwestern State Univ. To N is Sheppard Air Force Base and Wichita Falls Municipal Airport. L. Wichita (on Holiday Reservoir) on S border (city limits and co. line). L. Arrowhead reservoir and State Park to SE. Inc. 1889.

Wichita, Lake, Texas: see WICHITA RIVER.

Wichita Mountains, low granite range (c.60 mi/97 km long, 25 mi/40 km wide), mainly in Comanche co., also Kiowa and Caddo cos., SW Okla., 15 mi/24 km NW of Lawton Mts. Rise to max. elev. of 2,464 ft/751 m at Mt. Scott; other peaks include Bakers Peak (2,423 ft/739 m) and Wichita Mt. (2,441 ft/744 m). Wichita Mts. Natl. Wildlife Refuge (buffalo, elk, pronghorn antelope, deer, birds), and L. Lawtonka (recreation) are here.

Wichita River, c.250 mi/402 km long, Texas; rises in intermittent streams on E Llano Estacado; flows E and NE, past Wichita Falls, to Red R. in Clay co. Main branch (called North Fork in upper course) receives from S the intermittent Middle Fork, and merges with South Fork to form main river 15 mi/24 km NW of Seymour (c.95 mi/153 km long; partly intermittent). W of Wichita Falls, dams impound L. Kemp (c.12 mi/19 km long; capacity 720,000 acre-ft.) and Diversion L. (c.7 mi/11.3 km long; capacity 97,000 acre-ft.) for water supply, irrigation. Lakes are recreational areas; fishing. Just SW of Wichita Falls is L. Wichita (92,000 acre-ft.; irrigation, water supply; fishing), formed by dam in a small S tributary, Holiday Creek. Also called Big Wichita R.

Wickenburg, town (1990 pop. 4,515), Maricopa co., W central Ariz., on Hassayampa R., and 52 mi/84 km NW of Phoenix; 33°58′N 112°45′W. Winter resort; dude ranches in vicinity; cattle, sheep. Mfg. (asphalt, consumer goods, concrete prods.,). RR junction to W. Part of Prescott Natl. Forest to NE; Hieroglyphic Mts. to E.

Wickerham Manor–Fisher, locality (1990 pop. 1,931), Washington co., SW Pa., residential suburb of Pittsburgh, 2 mi/3.2 km NW of Monesson; 40°10′N 79°54′W.

Wickes (WIKS), village (1990 pop. 570), Polk co., W Ark., 20 mi/32 km SSW of Mena; 34°17′N 94°20′W. Lumber milling. Cossatot R. State Park to NE; Gillham L. reservoir and Howard Co. Wildlife Management Area to SE; Ouachita Natl. Forest to NE.

Wickett, village (1990 pop. 560), Ward co., extreme W Texas, in the Pecos valley, 30 mi/48 km ENE of Pecos; 31°34′N 103°00′W. Livestock; cotton, alfalfa; mfg. machinery, oil and natural-gas processing.

Wickford, resort village, in North Kingstown, Washington co., S central R.I., on inlet of Narragansett Bay, and 17 mi/27 km S of Providence. Lobster fisheries. Bypassed by 19th-cent. development, it has many fine 18th-cent. bldgs., including St. Paul's Episcopal Church. State trout hatchery nearby. Settled soon after 1650.

Wickham West, village, S Que., E Canada, 9 mi/14 km S of Drummondville. Dairying; livestock raising.

Wickiup Reservoir (WI-kee-uhp) (□ 18 sq mi/47 sq km), Deschutes co., central Oregon, on Deschutes R., in Deschutes Natl. Forest, 30 mi/48 km SW of Bend; 43°01′N 121°42′W. Max. capacity 20,217 acre-ft. Formed by Wickiup Dam (100 ft/30 m high), built (1949) by the Bureau of Reclamation for irrigation; also used for recreation and as a fish and wildlife pond. Three Sisters Wilderness Area nearby.

Wickliffe (WIK-lif), city (1990 pop. 14,558), Lake co., NE Ohio; 41°36′N 81°28′W. Mfg. (chemicals, machinery, meters). Borromeo Col. of Ohio and the Rabbinical Col. of Telshe are here. Inc. 1916.

Wickliffe (WIK-lif), town (1990 pop. 851), ⊙ Ballard co., W Ky., 9 mi/14.5 km SE of Cairo, Ill., on the Mississippi R., 5 mi/8 km S of mouth of the Ohio R.; 36°58′N 89°04′W. Agr. (dark and burley tobacco, corn, soybeans; cattle, hogs; dairying); clay pits, timber;. Mfg. (fabricated metal prods., rough lumber, paper pulp). Hunting, fishing nearby. Swan L. (NW) and Peal (N) wildlife management areas nearby; Wickliffe Mounds Mus. and Archaeological Site to N, overlooking river confluence; Bridges to Ill. and Mo. to NW.

Wicomico (wei-KO-mi-ko), county (□ 399 sq mi/1,033 sq km; 1990 pop. 74,339), SE Md., on Del. (N) state line; ⊙ Salisbury; 38°22′N 75°38′W. On the Eastern Shore (Delmarva Peninsula); bordered E by Pocomoke R. (fringed by great swamp), SW by Wicomico R., W and NW by Nanticoke R. Tidewater agr. area (fruit, esp. strawberries; vegetables, sweet potatoes; dairy prods.) with some timber, but primarily one of the largest chicken-raising areas in the country. Clothing factories, vegetable and fruit factories, lumber mills (esp. at Salisbury). Fishing, muskrat trapping. Formed in 1867, its name is Native Amer., supposedly refering to a town on the banks of the Wicomico R. and meaning "a pleasant place to live."

Wicomico River 1 c.37 mi/60 km long, in S Md.; rises near border bet. Charles and Prince Georges cos.; flows generally S through swamps to the Potomac R. just below Rock Point. Its estuary (c.2 mi/3.2 km wide at mouth) is navigable for c.14 mi/23 km. **2** c.33 mi/53 km long, on the Eastern Shore, Md.; rises in North Wicomico co. near Del. state line; flows generally SW, past Salisbury (head of navigation), to Monie Bay (a N arm of Tangier Bay).

Wiconisco (WI-kah-nis-ko), township (1990 pop. 1,372), Dauphin co., E central Pa., 1 mi/1.6 km NE of Lykens, on Wiconisco Creek; 40°34′N 76°41′W. Includes town of Wiconisco.

Widen (WEI-duhn), uninc. village (1990 pop. 200), Clay co., central W.Va., 12 mi/19 km E of Clay. Coal-mining area. Agr. (alfalfa); cattle. RR terminus.

Widener (WEI-duh-nuhr), village (1990 pop. 381), St. Francis co., E Ark., 6 mi/9.7 km E of Forrest City, and on St. Francis R. bet. new (dredged) channel to W and old (natural) channel to E; 35°01′N 90°40′W.

Wiggins, town (1990 pop. 3,185), ⊙ Stone co., SE Miss., 32 mi/51 km N of Gulfport; 30°51′N 89°08′W. Agr. (cotton, corn, pecans, honey; poultry; timber). Mfg. (paper prods., fabricated metal prods., lumber prods.). Part of De Soto Natl. Forest to N and E, also further to S; Flint Creek Reservoir to N.

Wiggins, village (1990 pop. 499), Morgan co., NE Colo., on Kiowa Creek, 15 mi/24 km W of Fort Morgan; 40°13′N 104°04′W. Elev. 4,540 ft/1,384 m. Supply point in cattle, sugar-beet, wheat, and sunflower region. Oil-producing region. Empire Reservoir to NW; Jackson Reservoir and Jackson State Park to N.

Wilbarger, county (□ 978 sq mi/2,533 sq km; 1990 pop. 15,121), N Texas, on Okla. (N, Red R.) state line; ⊙ Vernon; 34°04′N 99°14′W. Drained by Pease R. and Beaver Creek (forms Santa Rosa L. in S). Rich agr. area in N (cotton, wheat, alfalfa); large-scale cattle ranching in S; some hogs, horses. Large oil production and natural gas. Clay mining. Formed 1858.

Wilber, town (1990 pop. 1,527), ⊙ Saline co., SE Nebr., 18 mi/29 km NW of Beatrice, and on Big Blue R.; 40°28′N 96°57′W. Nebr. Czech. Festival here 1st weekend of Aug. since 1961. Wilber Czech Mus. Flour; grain;

livestock; dairy and poultry prods. Mfg. (fabricated metal prods., feeds). Inc. 1879.

Wilberforce, uninc. village (1990 pop. 2,639), Greene co., S central Ohio, 3 mi/5 km NE of Xenia; 39°43′N 83°53′W. Seat of Wilberforce and Central State univs.

Wilborn (WIL-buhrn), village, Lewis and Clark co., W central Mont., 25 mi/40 km. NW of Helena, on Canyon Creek, at mouth of Virginia Creek. Supply point; silver, gold, and lead mines; sawmill; livestock.

Wilbraham (WIL-bruh-ham), town (1990 pop. 12,635), Hampden co., S central Mass., 12 mi/19 km ENE of Springfield; 42°08′N 72°26′W. It is mainly residential. Wilbraham Acad. (1817) is here. Includes village of North Wilbraham. Settled 1730, inc. 1763.

Wilbur, town (1990 pop. 863), Lincoln co., E Wash., 48 mi/77 km NNE of Moses Lake; 47°46′N 118°42′W. Agr.; ships wheat, barley, oats, alfalfa, potatoes; logging. Grand Coulee Dam 17 mi/27 km NW, forms Franklin D. Roosevelt L. Coulee Dam Natl. Recreation Area to N, on lake. Keller Ferry (free) crosses lake, 12 mi/19 km to N. Settled 1884.

Wilbur Cross Parkway, Conn.: see MERRITT PARKWAY.

Wilbur D. Mills Lock and Dam (58 ft/18 m high), bet. Desha and Arkansas cos., SE Ark., on Arkansas R., near Mississippi R., 40 mi/64 km SE of Pine Bluff; 34°00′N 91°19′W. Built (1967) by Army Corps of Engineers for flood control, recreation, navigation, and as a fish and wildlife pond. Also known as Lock and Dam No. 2.

Wilbur Park, town (1990 pop. 522), St. Louis co., E Mo., residential suburb 8 mi/12.9 km SSW of downtown St. Louis; 38°32′N 90°18′W.

Wilburton (WIL-buhr-tuhn), town (1990 pop. 3,092), ⊙ Latimer co., SE Okla., 26 mi/42 km E of McAlester, in the Ouachita Mts. (S), near Fourche Malin Creek; 34°55′N 95°17′W. Mfg. (contract sewing; electrical equip.); ranching, coal mining; gas wells. Seat of Eastern Okla. State Col. Sardis L. reservoir to S; Robbers Cave State Park to N. Settled 1890, inc. 1902.

Wilcox, village (1991 pop. 230), S Sask., W Canada, 26 mi/42 km S of Regina. Wheat.

Wilcox 1 county (□ 907 sq mi/2,349 sq km; 1990 pop. 13,568), SW central Ala.; ⊙ Camden. In the Black Belt; drained by Alabama R. Corn; cattle; lumber milling. Formed 1819. **2** county (□ 383 sq mi/992 sq km; 1990 pop. 7,008), S central Ga.; ⊙ Abbeville; 31°58′N 83°26′W. Bounded E by Ocmulgee R.; drained by Alapaha R. Coastal plain agr. (cotton, corn, peanuts); lumber. Formed 1857.

Wilcox, uninc. town (1990 pop. 900), Elk co., N Pa., 5 mi/8 km N of Johnsonburg, on West Branch of Clarion R.; 41°34′N 78°41′W. Mfg. (fabricated metal prods., tool and die); natural gas; agr. (hay; livestock; dairying). Bendigo State Park to SE; Elk State Park and Elk State Forest to E.

Wilcox, village (1990 pop. 349), Kearney co., S Nebr., 12 mi/19 km ESE of Holdrege; 40°21′N 99°10′W. Livestock; grain.

Wild Ammonoosuc River, N.H.: see AMMONOOSUC RIVER.

Wild Horse Reservoir, Elko co., NE Nev., on East Fork Owyhee R., at SE edge of the Humboldt Natl. Forest, 55 mi/89 km N of Elko; 6 mi/9.7 km long; 41°41′N 115°49′W. Max. capacity 94,000 acre-ft. Formed by Wild Horse Dam (90 ft/27 m high), built (1969) by the Bureau of Reclamation for irrigation and recreation. Wild Horse State Recreation Area at SE end.

Wild Rice River 1 160 mi/257 km long, in Minn.; rises in Mud L. in Clearwater co., NW Minn., 17 mi/27 km W of Bemidji; flows generally W, through Lower Rice L. and through White Earth Indian Reservation, past Mahnomen, Twin Valley, and to S of Ada (where Marsh R. comes within 1/10 mi/ km of creating NW outlet to Red R.), to Red R. of the North, on N.Dak. state line, 2 mi/3.2 km S of Halstad and 15 mi/24 km W of Ada; 47°23′N 95°18′W. Receives Upper Rice L. (5 mi/8 km long, 1 mi/1.6 km wide; ½ dry) through 2-mi/3.2-km sidestream near its source. **2** c.100 mi/161 km long, N.Dak.; rises in Sargent co. near S.Dak. state line; meanders E, through L. Tewaukon and Sisseton Wahpeton Indian Reservation, and N to W of Wahpeton,

from where it roughly parallels Red R. until it enters Red R. of the North 8 mi/12.9 km S of Fargo; 47°00′N 97°47′W.

Wild Rose, village (1990 pop. 676), Waushara co., central Wis., on small Pine R., and 36 mi/58 km WNW of Oshkosh; 44°10′N 89°15′W. In agr. area; mfg. (fabricated metal prods., timber). Wild Rose State Fish Hatchery.

Wildcat, village, Okmulgee co., E central Okla., 7 mi/11.3 km NE of Henryetta, W of Grayson, near Deer Fork of Canadian R. In agr. area. Known for a time as Grayson.

Wildcat Creek, 81 mi/130 km long, Ind.; rises in Tipton co.; flows E, NE, and W to Kokomo, then W to join the Wabash creek 4 mi/6.4 km N of Lafayette. Receives South Fork (c.40 mi/64 km long) near its mouth.

Wildcat Mountain, peak (4,415 ft/1,346 m) of White Mts., SE Coos co., near Carroll co. border, E N.H., SE of Mt. Washington, and 14 mi/23 km S of Berlin, in White Mt. Natl. Forest; 44°15′N 71°12′W. Appalachian Trail passes to N. Site of Wildcat Mt. ski area and gondola lift.

Wildcat Peak, Nev.: see TOQUIMA RANGE.

Wilder, town (1990 pop. 1,232), Canyon co., SW Idaho, 11 mi/18 km W of Caldwell, near Oregon state line, bet. Boise (NE) and Snake (SW) rivers; 43°41′N 116°55′W. RR terminus of RR spur from Caldwell. Potatoes, corn, dry beans; fruit; mfg. (fertilizers).

Wilder 1 (WEIL-duhr), village (1990 pop. 691), Campbell co., N Ky., a suburb 3 mi/4.8 km S of downtown Cincinnati (Ohio), near Licking R.; 39°02′N 84°28′W. Mfg. (metal fabrication, die cutting; consumer goods, tile, ice, wood prods.). **2** village (1990 pop. 83), Jackson co., SW Minn., 18 mi/29 km NW of Jackson; 43°49′N 95°12′W. Grain; livestock area.

Wilder, Vt.: see HARTFORD.

Wilder Dam, W N.H. and E Vt., on Connecticut R., 2 mi/3.2 km N of White River Junction; 43°40′N 72°18′W. Max. capacity 104,000 acre-ft. Built in 1950 by the New England Power Company for power generation.

Wilderness, uninc. village, Spotsylvania and Orange cos., NE Va., 13 mi/21 km W of Fredericksburg, near Rapidan R.; 38°18′N 77°45′W. Agr. area (dairying; livestock; grain, soybeans). Scene of indecisive Civil War Battle of the Wilderness (May 5–6, 1864). Prelude to unsuccessful Union attacks on Spotsylvania and, later, Cold Harbor. Battle sites here and to E, at Chancellorsville, included in Fredericksburg and Spotsylvania County Battlefields Memorial Natl. Military Park. Germana Community Col. to NW. L. of the Woods reservoir to W.

Wilderness Road, principal avenue of W migration for U.S. pioneers c.1790–1840, blazed in 1775 by the Amer. frontiersman Daniel Boone and an advance party of the Transylvania Company Feeders from the E (Richmond, Va.) and the N (Harpers Ferry, W.Va.), who converged at Fort Chiswell in the Shenandoah valley. Boone's road ran SW from there through the valley, then W across the Appalachian Mts. and through Cumberland Gap into the Ky. bluegrass region and to the Ohio R. The road followed old buffalo traces and Native Amer. paths, but much of it had to be cut through the wilderness. In the early years, Native Americans killed many travelers who passed through their lands on the road. After Ky. became a state in 1792, the road was widened to accommodate wagons. Private contractors, authorized to keep up sects. of the road, charged tolls for its use. With the bldg. of the Natl. Road, the Wilderness Road was neglected and finally abandoned in the 1840s. Since 1926 the Wilderness Road has been a sect. of U.S. Route 25, the Dixie Highway.

Wildhorse Creek, c.55 mi/89 km long, S Okla.; rises near Marlow in Stephens co.; flows E to Washita R., Garvin co., just NW of Davis.

Wildomar, uninc. city (1990 pop. 10,411), Riverside co., S Calif., residential suburb 26 mi/42 km S of Riverside; 33°37′N 117°15′W. Cleveland Natl. Forest and Elsinore Mts. to W.

Wildrose, village (1990 pop. 193), Williams co., NW N.Dak., 40 mi/64 km NNE of Williston; 48°37′N 103°10′W.

Wildwood, village, central Alta., W Canada, on Chip L. (12 mi/19 km long, 5 mi/8 km wide), 70 mi/113 km W of Edmonton; 53°37′N 115°15′W. Mixed farming, lumbering.

Wildwood 1 city (1990 pop. 16,742), St. Louis co., E Mo., suburb 24 mi/39 km W of downtown St. Louis, on Missouri R. (N). Sparsely populated wooded area inc. 1995 to prevent overdevelopment of area. Babler State Park is here. **2** city (1990 pop. 4,484), Cape May co., SE N.J., on an isl. off Cape May; 38°59′N 74°49′W. Large commercial fisheries; popular summer seaside resort. Settled 1882, inc. as a city 1911.

Wildwood 1 town (1990 pop. 3,421), Sumter co., central Fla., 22 mi/35 km S of Ocala. Adjacent to one of Fla.'s most important expressway junctions where N terminus of Fla. Turnpike intersects I-75, the state's leading N-S artery on the W side of the Fla. peninsula. **2** uninc. town (1990 pop. 2,034), Lake co., NE Ill., residential suburb 37 mi/60 km NW of downtown Chicago, 8 mi/12.9 km W of Waukegan, near Gages L., E of Grayslake; 42°20′N 87°59′W.

Wildwood, uninc. village (1990 pop. 499), Hardin co., SE Texas, 37 mi/60 km NW of Beaumont. Cattle; egg production. Oil and natural gas. Units of Big Thicket Natl. Preserve to N and E.

Wildwood Crest, resort borough (1990 pop. 3,631), Cape May co., S N.J., on barrier isl. off Cape May Peninsula, just S of Wildwood; 38°58′N 74°50′W.

Wildwood State Park, N.Y.: see WADING RIVER.

Wiley, village (1990 pop. 406), Prowers co., SE Colo., near Arkansas R., 6 mi/9.7 km NW of Lamar; 38°09′N 102°43′W. Terminus of RR spur from Lamar. Sugar beets; wheat; cattle. L. Harty State Park to SW. Cluster of reservoirs to N includes Thruston, King, Nee, Shah, Nee Noshe, Nee So Pah, and Nee Grande (the Nee Reservoirs) reservoirs.

Wilhelm Lake, reservoir (□ 3 sq mi/7.8 sq km), Mercer co., NW Pa., on Sandy Creek, in Maurice K. Goddard State Park, 15 mi/24 km W of Franklin; 42°22′N 80°05′W. Max. capacity 66,400 acre-ft. Formed by L. Wilhelm Dam (50 ft/15 m high), built (1969) by U.S. Dept. of Agr., Natural Resource Conservation Service for flood control; also used for recreation.

Wilkes 1 county (□ 474 sq mi/1,228 sq km; pop. 10,597), NE Ga.; ⊙ Washington; 33°47′N 82°44′W. Piedmont agr. (hay, sweet potatoes, peaches); cattle, hogs, poultry; timber; mfg. at Washington. Formed 1777. **2** county (□ 759 sq mi/1,966 sq km; 1990 pop. 59,393), NW N.C.; ⊙ Wilkesboro; 36°12′N 81°10′W. Mostly in the Blue Ridge Mts.; drained by Yadkin R., which forms W border. Agr. (chickens, cattle; dairying; wheat, soybeans, hay, honey, tobacco, cotton, corn). Mfg. at Wilkesboro and North Wilkesboro. Stone quarrying. Mt. resorts. Blue Ridge (Natl.) Parkway follows NW border. Rendezvous Mt. Educational State Forest in W center; Stone Mt. State Park on N border; Scott Kerr (Wilkesboro) Reservoir in SW center. Formed 1777.

Wilkes-Barre (WILKS–BAHR), city (1990 pop. 47,523), ⊙ Luzerne co., E Pa., 100 mi/161 km NNW of Philadelphia, and 16 mi/26 km SW of Scranton (its larger twin city), on the SE bank of the Susquehanna R., opposite Kingston; 41°15′N 75°52′W. Once a major anthracite-coal center, Wilkes-Barre has factories (machinery, consumer goods, fabricated metal prods., electrical goods, footwear, chemicals, vinyl prods., transportation equip., apparel, wire prods., textiles, food prods., plastic prods.; printing and publishing). Named for John Wilkes and Isaac Barré, defenders of the colonies before Parliament. The settlement was burned in 1778 by the British and Native Americans, just after the Wyoming Valley massacre; it was again burned in 1784. In Wilkes-Barre are Wilkes Univ., including Sordoni Art Gall., King's Col., Col. Misericordia, and Pa. State Univ., Nesbitt Campus (to NW at Kingston). The Swetland Homestead (early 1800s) is of historical interest. Much of Wilkes-Barre was severely damaged by the flooding of the Susquehanna in 1972.

Area in square miles is shown by the symbol □   capital city or county seat by ⊙

Wilkes-Barre Scranton Internatl. Airport 11 mi/18 km to NE; Wilkes-Barre Wyoming Valley Airport to N; Pocono Downs Race Track (horse racing) to NE; Kirby Center for the Performing Arts; Lackawanna State Forest to E; Frances Slocum State Park to N. Settled 1769, inc. as a city 1871.

Wilkesboro, town (1990 pop. 2,964), ⊙ Wilkes co., NW N.C., 50 mi/80 km W of Winston-Salem, on Yadkin R. (bridged to North Wilkesboro); 36°08'N 81°09'W. Mfg. (apparel, glass, lumber, fabricated metal prods., dairy prods., textiles; poultry processing). Wilkes Community Col. Rendezvous Mt. Educational State Forest to NW; W. Scott Kerr (Wilkesboro) Reservoir to W; North Wilkesboro Speedway to N; Stone Mt. State Park to N. Founded c.1777; inc. 1889.

Wilkesboro Reservoir, Wilkes co., NW N.C., on Yadkin R., 3 mi/4.8 km W of Wilkesboro; 8 mi/12.9 km long; 36°08'N 81°11'W. Max. capacity 153,000 acre-ft. Formed by W. Kerr Scott Dam (137 ft/42 m high), built (1963) by the Army Corps of Engineers for flood control.

Wilkeson, village (1990 pop. 366), Pierce co., W central Wash., 22 mi/35 km ESE of Tacoma; 47°06'N 122°03'W.

Wilkesville, village (1990 pop. 151), Vinton co., S Ohio, near Raccoon Creek, 21 mi/34 km SW of Athens; 39°04'N 82°19'W.

Wilkie, town (1991 pop. 1,401), W Sask., W Canada, 30 mi/48 km SW of North Battleford; 52°25'N 108°42'W. RR divisional point; grain elevators. Lumbering; livestock raising.

Wilkin, county (□ 751 sq mi/1,945 sq km; 1990 pop. 7,516), W Minn.; ⊙ Breckenridge; 46°21'N 96°28'W. Drained by Otter Tail and Rabbit rivers; bounded W by Bois de Sioux R. and Red R. of the North (both form N.Dak. state line). Agr. area (wheat, alfalfa, soybeans, corn, oats, barley, sugar beets, beans, sunflowers; hogs). Rothsay Wildlife Area in NE.

Wilkins, township (1990 pop. 7,585), Allegheny co., W Pa., residential suburb 8 mi/12.9 km E of Pittsburgh, near the Monongahela R.; 40°25'N 79°49'W.

Wilkinsburg, borough (1990 pop. 21,080), Allegheny co., SW Pa., residential suburb 6 mi/9.7 km E of downtown Pittsburgh; 40°26'N 79°52'W. Mfg. includes book publishing and printing. Settled c.1800, inc. 1887.

Wilkinson 1 county (□ 452 sq mi/1,171 sq km; 1990 pop. 10,228), central Ga.; ⊙ Irwinton; 32°48'N 83°10'W. Bounded NE by Oconee R. Coastal plain agr. (cotton, peanuts); kaolin clay mining; timber. Formed 1803. **2** county (□ 687 sq mi/1,779 sq km; 1990 pop. 9,678), extreme SW Miss., on La. (S and W) state line; ⊙ Woodville; 31°09'N 91°19'W. Mississippi R. forms W border, bordered N by Homochitto R.; drained by Buffalo R. Agr. (cotton, corn; cattle; timber). Includes part of Homochitto Natl. Forest in NE. Old River L., oxbow lake of Mississippi R., in E, on NW border (shifting river channel predates establishment of La.-Miss. state line). Clark Creek Nature Area in SW. Formed 1802.

Wilkinson, town (1990 pop. 446), Hancock co., central Ind., 10 mi/16 km NE of Greenfield; 39°53'N 85°37'W. In agr. area; mfg. (agr. equip.). Laid out 1883.

Wilkinson Heights, uninc. town (1990 pop. 3,394), Orangeburg co., S central S.C., residential suburb 3 mi/4.8 km W of Orangeburg; 33°29'N 80°49'W. Edisto Gardens to NE.

Wilkinsonville, Mass.: see SUTTON.

Will, county (□ 849 sq mi/2,199 sq km; 1990 pop. 357,313), NE Ill., on Ind. (E) state line; ⊙ Joliet; 41°26'N 87°58'W. Chicago urban growth has spread S and SW into Will co., esp. around Joliet and along I-55. Agr. (corn, soybeans; poultry; dairy prods.). Limestone deposits. Diversified mfg. in industrial region of NE, adjoining Chicago metropolitan area. Crossed by Chicago Sanitary and Ship Canal; drained by Des Plaines, Du Page, and Kankakee rivers. Nuclear power plants Braidwood 1 (initial criticality May 29, 1987) and Braidwood 2 (initial criticality March 8,1988) are 24 mi/39 km SSW of Joliet; both use cooling water from the Kankakee R. and each has a max. dependable capacity of 1,120 MWe. Formed 1836.

Willacoochee (wi-luh-KOO-chee), town (1990 pop. 1,205), Atkinson co., S Ga., 17 mi/27 km SW of Douglas; 31°20'N 83°03'W. Mfg. includes textiles and apparel.

Willacy, county (□ 784 sq mi/2,031 sq km; 1990 pop. 17,705), extreme S Texas, on Gulf of Mexico (E); ⊙ Raymondville; 26°29'N 97°35'W. Laguna Madre separates Padre Isl. (sand barrier) from mainland; Gulf Intracoastal Waterway passes through Laguna Madre and Arroyo Colorado forms part of the laguna's S border. In rich irrigated agr. region of lower Rio Grande valley (cotton, sorghum, sugarcane, corn, vegetables); also ranching (beef and dairy cattle, horses, hogs, poultry). Oil wells and natural gas. Fishing; warm winter climate attract tourists. N edge of co. in large King Ranch. Small part of Padre Isl. Natl. Seashore in NE. Port Mansfield Channel (1962), man-made break in Padre Isl., allows ship access to Laguna Madre and Port Mansfield. Formed 1911, reorganized 1921.

Willamette (wuh-LAM-et), river, 240 mi/386 km long, Oregon; rises in several headstreams in the Cascade Range, W Oregon, with main stream formed 4 mi/6.4 km SE of Eugene at confluence of Middle and Coast forks; flows N past Eugene, Corvallis, Albany, Salem, Oregon City, and through Portland to the Columbia R. 12 mi/19 km NW of Portland. The Middle Fork, c.75 mi/121 km long; rises in SE Linn co.; flows NW through Hills Creek Reservoir, past Oakridge, and through Lookout Point Reservoir. The Coast Fork, c.55 mi/89 km long; rises in N Douglas co.; flows N through Cottage Grove Reservoir, past Cottage Grove and Creswell. The river is navigable for most of its course. Its wide, fertile valley is a major fruit-growing and dairying region. There is also diversified agr., mfg., and an important lumber industry. A Federal project begun in 1938 harnesses the forks and tributaries for flood control, water supply, and power production with numerous dams and reservoirs. First settled in the 1830s, the Willamette Valley was the goal of many pioneers traveling W on the Oregon Trail. The region quickly became the chief source of food on the West Coast, esp. during the Calif. gold rush in the mid-1800s. Rapidly settled after 1846, the Willamette R. valley has long been the most densely populated part of Oregon. The valley corridor from Portland and Beavertown to Eugene has become known as "Silicon Forest," as economy has shifted from forestry to computer chips and other components.

Willamette Pass (wuh-LAM-et) (5,128 ft/1,563 m), on border bet. Lane and Klamath cos., E central Oregon, in Cascade Range, 58 mi/93 km SE of Eugene. Odell L. to SE. State Highway 58 and RR pass through. Also called Salt Creek Pass.

Willamina (wil-uh-MEE-nuh), town (1990 pop. 1,717), Yamhill and Polk cos., NW Oregon, 25 mi/40 km WNW of Salem, on South Yamhill R.; 45°04'N 123°28'W. Timber; fruits, vegetables; poultry, sheep, cattle; dairy prods. Part of Siuslaw Natl. Forest to W; Van Duzer Forest Corridor Wayside State Park to W.

Willapa (WI-luh-pah), village (1990 pop. 350), Pacific co., SW Wash., on Willapa R., 3 mi/4.8 km SE of Raymond. Agr.; logging. Willapa Bay is a large, sheltered harbor (c.25 mi/40 km long) separated from Pacific Ocean by North Beach Peninsula; 20 mi/32 km long (from S), 1 mi/1.6 km wide, N of mouth of the Columbia R., and S of Grays Harbor. Receives Willapa R., c.50 mi/80 km long; rises in SE Pacific co.; flows generally NW, past Raymond, to N end of Willapa Bay.

Willard, city (1990 pop. 6,210), Huron co., N Ohio, 17 mi/27 km SSW of Norwalk; 41°03'N 82°43'W. In fruit, vegetable, and grain area; makes rubber goods, food and dairy prods., lumber, burial vaults.

Willard 1 town (1990 pop. 2,177), Greene co., SW Mo., 14 mi/23 km NW of Springfield, near Little Sac R. Stockton L. reservoir and State Park to NW. Dairying; cattle, poultry, hogs; strawberries, hay. Mfg. (wood prods., cut stone, limestone). **2** town (1990 pop. 1,298), Box Elder co., N Utah, 7 mi/11.3 km S of Brigham City, near Great Salt L.; 41°24'N 112°02'W. Elev. 4,360 ft/1,329 m. Sugar beets, peaches, cherries, barley, alfalfa; cattle; dairying. Wasatch Range and Natl. Forest to E; Willard Bay State Park and Harold S. Crane Waterfowl Management Area both on Great Salt L. to W. Willard Reservoir, formed by dikes extending from Great Salt L.'s E shore, provides fresh water to area. Settled 1851 as Willow Creek.

Willard 1 (WIL-uhrd), village (1990 pop. 110), Shawnee co., NE Kansas, on Kansas R., and 14 mi/23 km W of Topeka; 39°05'N 95°56'W. **2** uninc. village, Carter co., NE Ky., 9 mi/14.5 km SSE of Grayson. Agr. (tobacco, alfalfa; cattle); mfg. (dog food). **3** village (1990 pop. 183), Torrance co., central N.Mex., 11 mi/18 km S of Estancia, just NE of Chupadero Mesa; 34°35'N 106°01'W. Elev. 6,091 ft/1,857 m. Trade center in cattle region; grain, alfalfa, beans, corn. Laguna del Perro is to E. Parts of Cibola Natl. Forest to W and S. **4** village (1990 pop. 600), Seneca co., W central N.Y., on E shore of Seneca L., 25 mi/40 km NW of Ithaca; 42°41'N 76°53'W. Willard Psychiatric Center and Willard Correctional Facility located here.

Willards, town (1990 pop. 708), Wicomico co., SE Md., near Pocomoke R., 14 mi/23 km E of Salisbury; 38°23'N 75°21'W. Named for Willards Thompson, an executive of the Baltimore and Ohio RR.

Willcox, town (1990 pop. 3,122), Cochise co., SE Ariz., 65 mi/105 km E of Tucson; 32°15'N 109°50'W. Elev. 4,163 ft/1,269 m. Ships cattle; dude ranches. Mfg. (printing and publishing, meatpacking; machinery, concrete). Fort Bowie Natl. Historic Site and Chiracahua Natl. Monument to SE; Dos Cabezas Mts. to SE; Willcox Playa, dry lake bed, to S; parts of Coronado Natl. Forest to N, NW, and SW. SW sect. has Mt. Glen (7,512 ft/2,290 m) and Cochise Stronghold Memorial Park.

Willemstad (VI-luhm-staht), city (1981 pop. 31,883), Curaçao isl., ⊙ Neth. Antilles. The commercial and industrial center of the Neth. Antilles as well as a free port and tourist center. It is important as a transshipment point and refining center for petroleum sent across the Gulf of Venezuela from Maracaibo (Venezuela); however, the petroleum demand declined in the mid-1980s. Willemstad has a distinctive Du. character with streets lined by narrow, gabled houses.

Willernie (WI-luhr-nee), village (1990 pop. 584), Washington co., E Minn., residential suburb 9 mi/14.5 km NE of downtown St. Paul, near SE end of White Bear L.; 45°02'N 92°57'W. Mfg. (medical supplies).

Willey, town (1990 pop.78), Carroll co., W central Iowa, 6 mi/9.7 km SSE of Carroll; 41°58'N 94°49'W.

Willey, Mount (WI-lee) (4,302 ft/1,311 m), NE Grafton co., N central N.H., in White Mts., W of Crawford Notch, and SW of Presidential Range; 44°11'N 71°25'W.

William "Bill" Dannelly Reservoir, Wilcox and Dallas cos., SW Ala., on the Alabama R., 31 mi/50 km SW of Selma; c.80 mi/129 km long; 32°02'N 87°23'W. Extends NE to Robert F. Henry Dam. Max. capacity of 331,800 acre-ft. Formed by Millers Ferry Dam (55 ft/17 m) built (1970) by the Army Corps of Engineers for navigation and power generation. Roland Cooper State Park on S shore.

William H. Harsha Lake, reservoir (□ 3 sq mi/7.8 sq km), Clermont co., SW Ohio, on East Fork of Little Miami R., 19 mi/31 km E of Cincinnati; 38°57'N 84°05'W. Max. capacity 294,800 acre-ft. Formed by William H. Harsha L. Dam (205 ft/ 62 m high), built (1973) by Army Corps of Engineers for flood control; also used for water supply and recreation. Also known as East Fork L. East Fork State Park at E end of reservoir.

William Henry, Fort, N.Y.: see FORT WILLIAM HENRY.

William Howard Taft Historic Site, SW Ohio. Birthplace and early home of President William Howard Taft. Authorized 1969.

Williamburg, town, Iowa co., E central Iowa, on Old Mans Creek, and 29 mi/47 km SW of Cedar Rapids. Inc. 1884.

Williams 1 county (□ 2,064 sq mi/5,346 sq km 1990 pop. 21,129), NW N.Dak., on Mont. (W) state line; ⊙ Williston; 48°21'N 103°28'W. Agr. area bounded S by Missouri R. (L. Sakakawea). Coal mines, oil wells (developed 1951), natural-gas fields; wheat, barley, mustard, hay; cattle; dairy prods. Lewis and Clark State Park in

S; Fort Union Trading Post and Fort Buford state historic sites in SW corner; L. Zahl Natl. Wildlife Refuge in N. W border follows border bet. Mountain (Mont.) and Central (N.Dak.) time zones. Formed 1891. **2** county (□ 421 sq mi/1,090 sq km; 1990 pop. 36,956), extreme NW Ohio, on Mich. (N) and Ind. (W) state lines; ⊙ Bryan; 41°33′N 84°35′W. Intersected by St. Joseph and Tiffin rivers. In the Till Plains physiographic region. Livestock, poultry; corn, soybeans, wheat; diversified mfg., esp. at Bryan and Montpelier (furniture, transportation equip., plastic prods., fabricated metal prods., machinery, electronic prods., consumer goods). Sand, gravel pits. Formed 1824.

Williams, city (□ 4 sq mi/10.4 sq km; 1990 pop. 2,297), Colusa co., N central Calif., 8 mi/12.9 km SW of Colusa; 39°09′N 122°08′W. Fruit, rice, tomatoes, walnuts, almonds, wheat, sugar beets, grapes; cattle. Colusa (E) and Delevan (N) natl. wildlife refuges nearby; Colusa R. to E.

Williams 1 town (1990 pop. 2,532), Coconino co., N central Ariz., in Kaibab Natl. Forest, 30 mi/48 km W of Flagstaff; 35°15′N 112°10′W. Elev. 6,770 ft/2,063 m. Junction of RR spur N to Grand Canyon Village; tourist point; agr. (cattle, sheep; timber). Mfg. (sawmill; printing and publishing; electrical goods). Settled 1876–1878. Bill Williams Mt. (9,264 ft/2,824 m), including Williams Ski Area is to S. Grand Canyon Natl. Park to N. **2** town (1990 pop. 368), Hamilton co., central Iowa, 15 mi/24 km E of Webster City; 42°29′N 93°32′W. In agr. area.

Williams 1 village (1990 pop. 212), Lake of the Woods co., NW Minn., 17 mi/27 km WNW of Baudette; 48°46′N 94°57′W. Agr. (potatoes, oats, barley, alfalfa, flax, wheat); light mfg. Zippel Bay State Park, on L. of the Woods to NE; Beltrami Isl. State Forest and parts of Red L. Indian Reservation to SW and S. **2** village (1990 pop. 188), Colleton co., S S.C., 15 mi/24 km NW of Walterboro; 33°01′N 80°50′W. Mfg. of lumber; agr. includes livestock, poultry; timber; grain.

Williams Bay, town (1990 pop. 2,108), Walworth co., SE Wis., on small arm of L. Geneva, 6 mi/9.7 km WSW of Lake Geneva; 42°34′N 88°32′W. Mfg. of textiles, consumer goods. Yerkes Observatory of Univ. of Chicago is here.

Williams Fork, river, c.30 mi/48 km long, in N central Colo.; formed in S Grand co., at Continental Divide, in Arapaho Natl. Forest; flows NNW, bet. Vasquez and Williams R. Mts., through Williams Fork Reservoir, to Colorado R. 5 mi/8 km W of Hot Sulphur Springs.

Williams Fork Reservoir, Grand co., N Colo., on Williams Fork R. 2 mi/3.2 km SW of its junction with the Colorado R., 6 mi/9.7 km WSW of Hot Sulphur Springs; 3 mi/4.8 km long; 40°01′N 106°12′W. Max. capacity of 109,075 acre-ft. Formed by Williams Fork Dam (190 ft/58 m high), built (1956) by the Denver Water Board for water supply.

Williams, Fort, Maine: see COTTAGE, CAPE.

Williams Lake, village, S central B.C., W Canada, at foot of Cariboo Mts., on Williams L. (5 mi/8 km long), near Fraser R., 130 mi/209 km S of Prince George; 52°07′N 122°09′W. Center of Chilcotin cattle-raising dist.; lumbering.

Williams, Mount, in Chugach Mts., S Alaska, 40 mi/64 km NNW of Katalla; 60°44′N 144°55′W.

Williams Peak, Colo.: see WILLIAMS RIVER MOUNTAINS.

Williams River, c.25 mi/40 km long, in E Vt.; rises near Andover; flows E and SE to the Connecticut R. near Rockingham.

Williams River, Ariz.: see BILL WILLIAMS RIVER.

Williams River Mountains, N central Colo., in Front Range; extend N-S bet. Blue and Williams rivers. Highest point is Williams Peak (11,619 ft/3,541 m). Ute Pass (9,524 ft/2,903 m), on border bet. Summit and Grand cos., in Arapaho Natl. Forest. Colo. has 2 other passes so named.

Williams Town, town, central Bahama Isl., the Bahamas, on Little Exuma Isl., just S of the Tropic of Cancer, 14 mi/23 km ESE of George-Town (Great Exuma Isl.); 23°25′N 75°34′W.

Williamsbridge, residential section of central Bronx borough of N.Y. city, SE N.Y.; 40°53′N 73°52′W. Named for a 1673 bridge across the Bronx R. here, where an old village developed.

Williamsburg, county (□ 936 sq mi/2,424 sq km; 1990 pop. 36,815), E central S.C.; ⊙ Kingstree; 33°37′N 79°43′W. Bounded S by Santee R.: drained by Black R. Agr. includes dairying; livestock; grains, soybeans, cotton, tobacco, sorghum; timber. Hunting and fishing attract tourists. Formed 1785.

Williamsburg, independent city (1990 pop. 11,530), ⊙ James City co., SE Va., on a peninsula bet. James and York rivers, separate from adjacent James City (W) and York (E) cos.; 37°16′N 76°42′W. Mfg. (beverages, electrical goods, fabricated metal prods., paper prods., plastic prods., consumer goods; printing and publishing). Popular tourist attraction. Seat (since 1693) of Col. of William and Mary. Eastern State Hosp. (1773). Temporary Va. capital after burning of Jamestown (1676) during Bacon's Rebellion, permanent capital 1699–1779. Scene of important conventions during Amer. independence movement, but declined after capital moved to Richmond (1779). Scene of skirmishes during Peninsular Campaign of Civil War (May 5, 1862). Financial support of John D. Rockefeller, Jr., initiated large-scale restoration of the city, which has become a major tourist center; 700 bldgs. removed, 83 renovated, 413 rebuilt on original sites. Williamsburg retains its colonial appearance, with green formal gardens and many craft shops where revived trades are practiced. Colonial capitol bldg. (reconstructed); Raleigh Tavern (reconstructed), rendezvous of Revolutionary patriots; courthouse of 1770; Bruton Parish Church (1710–1715); governor's palace (reconstructed); public gaol; magazine. Abby Aldrich Rockefeller mus. houses noted folk art collection. The Colonial Parkway passes through Williamsburg, connecting it with the Jamestown (to SW) and Yorktown (to E) sects. of Colonial Natl. Historical Park; parkway is included in park. Camp Peary Military Reservation to N; U.S. Naval Weapons Station and Supply Center to E. Busch Gardens "Old Country" theme park to SE; Waller Mill Reservoir to N. Settled 1632 as Middle Plantation, laid out and renamed 1699, inc. 1722.

Williamsburg 1 town (1990 pop. 5,493), ⊙ Whitley co., SE Ky., in the Cumberland Mts., on Cumberland R., and 27 mi/43 km WNW of Middlesboro; 36°44′N 84°10′W. Coal mining, gas; hardwood timber; agr. (corn, tobacco; cattle). Mfg. (lumber, rubber prods., textiles, apparel, electrical prods., concrete, plastic prods.; meat processing, printing and publishing). Seat of Cumberland Col. Many Native Amer. artifacts have been found in this area. Cumberland Mus. Cumberland Falls State Resort Park to SW; Daniel Boone Natl. Forest to W. Est. 1817. **2** town (1990 pop. 2,515), Hampshire co., W central Mass., on Mill R., in the Berkshires, and 8 mi/12.9 km NW of Northampton; 42°24′N 72°44′W. Ornamental hardware. Settled 1735, set off from Hatfield 1771. Includes village of Haydenville.

Williamsburg 1 village (1990 pop. 253), Fremont co., S central Colo., near Arkansas R., 30 mi/48 km WNW of Pueblo, 5 mi/8 km SE of Canon City; 38°22′N 105°10′W. Elev. c.5,380 ft/1,640 m. Coal mining. Sheep. San Isabel Natl. Forest to SW. **2** village (1990 pop. 261), Franklin co., E Kansas, 14 mi/23 km SW of Ottawa; 38°28′N 95°28′W. Livestock; grain, apples. **3** village, Dorchester co., E Md., near Marshyhope Creek, 15 mi/24 km ENE of Cambridge. The 1st house was built here in 1804, but the town didn't receive its present name until 1840. Legend has it the earlier name was Bunker Hill because so many fights took place here. **4** village (1990 pop. 456), Sierra co., SW N.Mex., 3 mi/4.8 km W of Truth or Consequences, near N end of Caballo Reservoir (Rio Grande); 33°07′N 107°17′W. Irrigated agr. area. Mfg. (machine tools, windmill towers). **5** village (1990 pop. 2,322), Clermont co., SW Ohio, 5 mi/8 km ESE of Batavia, and on East Fork of Little Miami R.; 39°03′N 84°03′W. Agr. (corn, wheat, tobacco); mfg. of chairs. Inc. 1800.

Williamsburg, borough (1990 pop. 1,456), Blair co., central Pa., on Frankstown Branch of Juniata R., 11 mi/18 km ESE of Altoona; 40°27′N 78°12′W. Mfg. (paper prods.); agr. (corn, hay; livestock; dairying). Canoe L. reservoir and Canoe Creek State Park to W; Cove Valley Airport to SW. Settled 1790, laid out 1795, inc. 1827.

Williamsburg, residential and industrial section of NW Brooklyn borough of N.Y. city, SE N.Y., on East R. (W) opposite Manhattan's Lower East Side (linked by Williamsburg Bridge), S of Greenpoint, W of Bushwick, and N of Bedford-Stuyvesant; 40°43′N 73°57′W. A cent. ago, a major N.Y. city industrial center (distilleries, shipyards, potteries); mfg. has now declined greatly, but many workshops remain, esp. for metal- and woodworking, foods, and Brooklyn Beer. In the 19th cent., community was mostly Irish and Ger.; in early 20th cent., East Eur. Jewish immigrants began to arrive. By the 1920s, this area was the city's most densely populated neighborhood. Today, the neighborhood is mostly Hispanic (esp. from P.R. and Central Amer.), but it is also home to many Hasidic Jewish sects, including the Satmar (South Williamsburg). Includes an old Ital. enclave. Burgeoning artist community in what is known as the Northside. Setting for Betty Smith's novel *A Tree Grows in Brooklyn*. Laid out in 1810, became part of Brooklyn in 1855.

Williamsburg Bridge, 1,600-ft/488-m suspension span, N.Y. city, SE N.Y., across East R. bet. lower Manhattan (Lower East Side) and NW Brooklyn (Williamsburg); 40°43′N 73°58′W. With vehicular road, RRs; built 1903.

Williamsfield, town (1991 pop. 2,800), Manchester parish, W central Jamaica, on Jamaica RR, and 2.5 mi/4 km NE of Mandeville (for which it is the RR station); 18°04′N 77°29′W. Popular mt. resort (elev. c.2,000 ft/610 m).

Williamsfield, village (1990 pop. 571), Knox co., W central Ill., near Spoon R., 18 mi/29 km E of Galesburg; 40°55′N 90°01′W. Agr. (corn, soybeans; cattle, hogs; dairying).

Williamson 1 county (□ 444 sq mi/1,150 sq km; 1990 pop. 57,733), S Ill.; ⊙ Marion; 37°44′N 88°56′W. Bituminous-coal-mining and agr. area (corn, wheat, fruit; livestock; dairy prods.). Textiles. Drained by Big Muddy R., South Fork of Saline R., and Crab Orchard Creek (dammed to form Crab Orchard L.; resorts) one of largest in state. One of 17 cos. to retain Southern-style commission form of co. govt. Formed 1839. **2** county (□ 594 sq mi/1,538 sq km; 1990 pop. 81,021), central Tenn.; ⊙ Franklin, 35°54′N 86°54′W. Drained by Harpeth R. Agr. (livestock; tobacco, hay, apples; dairy prods.); phosphate mining. Mfg. at Franklin and Brentwood. Formed 1799. **3** county (□ 1,136 sq mi/2,942 sq km; 1990 pop. 139,551), central Texas; ⊙ Georgetown; 30°38′N 97°35′W. Drained by San Gabriel R. and its North and South forks and Brushy Creek. Ranching (cattle) in hilly W; agr. (cotton, corn, wheat) in rich blackland prairies of E. Timber (mainly cedar and oak); limestone quarries, sand and gravel; some oil. Mfg. at Georgetown,Taylor. N fringe of Austin urbanized area, and extension of Austin corporate limits, in S central part of co. Hunting, fishing in W. L. Georgetown in W center; Granger L. in NE. Formed 1848.

Williamson, city (1990 pop. 4,154), ⊙ Mingo co., SW W.Va., on Tug Fork R., at Ky. state line, 60 mi/97 km SW of Charleston, opposite (N of) South Williamson (Ky.); 37°40′N 82°16′W. Trade and distribution center for bituminous-coal field (W.Va. and Ky.). Mfg. (printing and publishing, light mfg.). Natural-gas and oil wells. Timber nearby. Laurel Creek Wildlife Management Area to N. Inc. 1892.

Williamson 1 town (1990 pop. 295), Pike co., W central Ga., 7 mi/11.3 km SW of Griffin; 33°11′N 84°22′W. Mfg. includes stone processing; bldg. materials. **2** town (1990 pop. 166), Lucas co., S Iowa, 5 mi/8 km NNE of Chariton; 41°05′N 93°15′W. In livestock-raising area. State park nearby.

Williamson, village (1990 pop. 1,850), Wayne co., W N.Y., 21 mi/34 km ENE of Rochester; 43°15′N 77°11′W. Some mfg; in fruit-growing region.

Williamson, Mount (14,375 ft/4,382 m), Inyo co., E Calif., in the Sierra Nevada, 6 mi/9.7 km N of Mt. Whitney, and 2 mi/3.2 km E of Sequoia Natl. Park; 36°39′N 118°18′W. In Inyo Natl. Forest.

Williamson River, c. 75 mi/121 km long, E central Klamath co., Oregon; rises in Winema Natl. Forest at Furgo Mt. (6,810 ft/2,076 m), S Oregon; flows 25 mi/40 km N, then 50 mi/80 km SSW through marshland of Klamath Forest Natl. Wildlife Refuge, past Chiloquin, to Upper Klamath L., 20 mi/32 km NNW of Klamath Falls. Flow is underground for a short distance in the lower course. Receives Sprague R., a tributary, from E at Chiloquin.

Williamsport, city (1990 pop. 31,933), ⊙ Lycoming co., central Pa., 68 mi/109 km N of Harrisburg, on the Susquehanna R., at mouth of Lycoming Creek; 41°14′N 77°02′W. It is a tourist center, a mfg. city, and the trade and distribution point for an agr. area. Mfg. (plastic prods., lumber, fabricated metal and metal prods., apparel, furniture, paper prods., food prods., machinery, wood prods., fiberglass prods., leather prods., transportation equip.; printing). Agr. (apples, corn, potatoes, hay; livestock; dairying). Grew with the development of the lumber industry in the 19th cent. Home of Little League baseball; the Little League world series is held here each year and the Peter J. McGovern Little League Mus. is in South Williamsport. Williamsport–Lycoming County Airport to E; Allenwood Federal Prison Camp to SE; Lycoming Col.; Pa. Col. of Technology; sects. of Tiadaghton State Forest to N and S; Susquehanna State Park in SW part of city. Settled 1772, inc. as a borough 1806, as a city 1866.

Williamsport 1 town (1990 pop. 1,798), ⊙ Warren co., W Ind., on the Wabash R., and 24 mi/39 km WSW of Lafayette; 40°17′N 87°17′W. In grain-growing area; sand and gravel; mfg. (machinery; soybean and wheat seed processing, beef processing). Laid out 1828. **2** town (1990 pop. 2,103), Washington co., W Md., on the Potomac R., at mouth of Concocheague Creek, and 7 mi/11.3 km SW of Hagerstown; 39°36′N 77°49′W. Laid out on the high ground under the sponsorship of Gen. Otho Holland Williams in 1787, Williamsport petitioned Congress to become the site of the new Federal city. After an inspection by Gen. Washington, the petition was denied because the proximity of Great Falls limited access. Became the W terminus of the Western Maryland RR and a port for boats coming up the Chesapeake and Ohio Canal. A long-established tannery as well as brick kilns and limestone quarrying enterprises provide the community's economic base.

Williamsport, village (1990 pop. 851), Pickaway co., S central Ohio, 9 mi/14 km W of Circleville, and on Deer Creek; 39°04′N 82°19′W. In agr. area (grain, soybeans).

Williamston 1 town (1990 pop. 2,922), Ingham co., S central Mich., 14 mi/23 km ESE of Lansing, and on Red Cedar R.; 42°41′N 84°16′W. In farm area. Mfg. (plastics, machinery). Settled c.1835, inc. 1871 as village, as city 1945. **2** town (1990 pop. 5,503), ⊙ Martin co., E N.C., 40 mi/64 km E of Rocky Mount, and on navigable Roanoke R.; 35°51′N 77°03′W. Agr. area (cotton, tobacco, peanuts, grain, soybeans, sorghum; chickens, cattle, hogs); timber. Mfg. (grain milling, commercial printing, meat and peanut processing; lumber, machinery, textiles, apparel). Fort Branch Battlefield State Historical Site to NW at Hamilton. Inc. 1779. **3** town (1990 pop. 3,876), Anderson co., NW S.C., on Saluda R., and 17 mi/27 km S of Greenville; 34°37′N 82°28′W. Mfg. includes textile mill, clothing plant; printing and publishing. Agr. includes dairying; poultry, livestock; grain, soybeans, sorghum.

Williamstown, village, SE Ont., central Canada, on North Raisin R., and 12 mi/19 km NE of Cornwall. Dairying, mixed farming.

Williamstown 1 town (1990 pop. 3,023), ⊙ Grant co., N Ky., 31 mi/50 km S of Covington; 38°38′N 84°33′W. Trade and shipping center for Bluegrass agr. area (burley tobacco, corn, hay; livestock, poultry; dairying); mfg. (bldg. materials, plastic prods., fabricated metal prods.). Mullins Wildlife Management Area to N; Williamstown L. reservoir to NE. Area settled c.1790; est. 1825. **2** town (1990 pop. 8,220), Berkshire co., extreme NW Mass., in the Berkshire Mts., on Hoosic R., and 6 mi/9.7 km W of North Adams; 42°42′N 73°14′W. Mfg. (wire, photographic supplies, beverages); dairying; poultry. Seat of Williams Col. Has 2 art mus. Mt. Greylock is just S. Includes Williamstown village. Settled 1749, inc. 1765. **3** town (1990 pop. 2,839), Orange co., central Vt., 10 mi/16 km NNW of Chelsea; 44°06′N 72°32′W. Chartered 1781, settled 1784. **4** town (1990 pop. 2,774), Wood co., NW W.Va., 10 mi/16 km NNE of Parkersburg, on the Ohio R. (bridged), opposite (S of) Marietta (Ohio); 39°23′N 81°27′W. Agr. region (grain, tobacco, soybeans); livestock, poultry. Mfg. (glassware, machinery). Wood Co. Airport to S. Lock and Dam No. 17 to SE on Ohio R. Settled 1787.

Williamstown 1 village (1990 pop. 10,981), Gloucester co., SW N.J., 6 mi/9.7 km E of Glassboro; 39°41′N 74°58′W. Mfg. (clothing, canned goods), agr. (poultry; vegetables, fruit). Settled before 1800. **2** village (1990 pop. 600), Oswego co., central N.Y., 31 mi/50 km E of Oswego; 43°27′N 75°54′W. Lumber and wood prods.

Williamstown, borough (1990 pop. 1,509), Dauphin co., E central Pa., 25 mi/40 km NE of Harrisburg; 40°34′N 76°37′W. Mfg. (metal fabrication, apparel, electrical goods); agr. (corn, hay; poultry, livestock; dairying). Part of Weiser State Forest to S. Laid out 1869.

Williamsville, city (1990 pop. 391), Wayne co., SE Mo., in Ozark region, on Black R., and 17 mi/27 km NNW of Poplar Bluff; 36°58′N 90°32′W. Mfg. (plastic prods.); timber. Recreation. Surrounded by Mark Twain Natl. Forest.

Williamsville, village, W Trinidad, Trinidad and Tobago, on RR, and 6 mi/9.7 km ENE of San Fernando. Sugar growing. Has housing development.

Williamsville 1 village (1990 pop. 1,140), Sangamon co., central Ill., 10 mi/16 km NNE of Springfield; 39°57′N 89°33′W. Grain; dairy prods.; livestock. **2** residential village (□ 1 sq mi/2.6 sq km; 1990 pop. 5,583), Erie co., W N.Y., suburb 4 mi/6.4 km NE of Buffalo; 42°57′N 78°44′W. Mfg. (machinery). Erie Co. Community Col. North Campus here. Settled c.1800, inc. 1869.

Willie (WIL-ee), town, Liberty co., SE Ga., 34 mi/55 km W of Savannah; 32°00′N 81°40′W.

Williford (WIL-uh-fuhrd), village (1990 pop. 69), Sharp co., N Ark., 37 mi/60 km NNE of Batesville, and on Spring R.; 36°15′N 91°21′W. Harold E. Alexander Wildlife Management Area to W.

Willimansett, Mass.: see CHICOPEE.

Willimantic (wi-li-MAN-tik), city (1990 pop. 14,746), now uninc., in town of Windham, ⊙ Windham co., E central Conn., 24 mi/39 km ESE of Hartford, at junction of Willimantic and Natchaug rivers (which form Shetucket R.); 41°43′N 72°13′W. Once known as the Thread City (cotton spinning since 1822); mfg. (textiles, metal prods., tools, machinery, hardware, transportation equip., optical goods). Inc. 1893.

Willimantic (wil-uh-MAN-tik), resort town (1990 pop. 170), Piscataquis co., central Maine, on Sebec L., and 10 mi/16 km NW of Dover-Foxcroft; 45°18′N 69°22′W. Includes Sebec Lake village.

Willimantic River, c.35 mi/56 km long, NE Conn.; formed by several branches near Stafford Springs; flows S, joining Natchaug R. to form Shetucket R. at Willimantic. Near South Coventry is site of flood-control dam.

Willingboro, township (1990 pop. 36,291), Burlington Co. W N.J., near Delaware R., on Rancocas Creek; 40°01′N 74°53′W. The original name of Willingboro was temporarily changed to Levittown after World War II. Residential and commercial town.

Willingdon, village (1991 pop. 355), central Alta., W Canada, 23 mi/37 km N of Vegreville; 53°50′N 112°07′W. RR junction. Tanning; mixed farming, dairying.

Willingdon, Mount (11,044 ft/3,366 m), SW Alta., W Canada, near B.C. border, in Rocky Mts., in Banff Natl. Park, 50 mi/80 km NW of Banff; 51°45′N 116°15′W.

Willington, town (1990 pop. 5,979), Tolland co., NE Conn., on Willimantic R., and 23 mi/37 km ENE of Hartford; 41°53′N 72°15′W. Farming; sawmills; machined parts, and electroplating. Includes mfg. villages of South Willington and West Willington. Inc. 1727.

Willis, town (1990 pop. 2,764), Montgomery co., E Texas, 20 mi/32 km S of Huntsville; 30°25′N 95°28′W. In timber area; mfg. (lumber, electrical goods, plastic prods., fabricated metal prods.). L. Conroe to W; Sam Houston Natl. Forest to NW, N, and E. Inc. 1937.

Willis, village (1990 pop. 86), Brown co., NE Kansas, 9 mi/14.5 km S of Hiawatha; 39°43′N 95°30′W. In corn, livestock, and dairying region. Kickapoo Indian Reservation to W.

Willis Island, E N.F., E Canada, in Bonavista Bay, 30 mi/48 km WNW of Cape Bonavista; 3 mi/5 km long, 2 mi/3 km wide; 48°47′N 53°44′W.

Williston, city (1990 pop. 13,131), ⊙ Williams co., NW N.Dak., on the Missouri R. (L. Sakakawea, at entrance to Little Muddy Creek Arm), c.110 mi/177 km W of Minot; 48°09′N 103°37′W. Elev. 1,880 ft/573 m. An early riverboating town, its importance increased with the arrival of the Great Northern RR (1887) and later by the discovery (1951) of rich oil reserves in the Williston Basin. It is the trade, processing, and shipping center of a spring-wheat and livestock region, with an oil refinery, stockyards, grain elevators, and dairy-processing plants. Huge reserves of lignite, as well as natural gas and salt are in the area. Of interest are Fort Union Trading Post Natl. Historic Site and Fort Buford State Historic Site to SW. Univ. of N.Dak. Williston Campus; Lewis and Clark State Park to E. Inc. 1904

Williston 1 town (□ 5 sq mi/13 sq km; 1990 pop. 2,179), Levy co., N central Fla., 34 mi/55 km WNW of Ocala; 29°22′N 82°27′W. Lumbering; limestone quarrying. **2** town (1990 pop. 3,099), Barnwell co., W S.C., 33 mi/53 km WSW of Orangeburg; 33°23′N 81°25′W. Mfg. includes textiles, machinery, consumer goods, clothing, electrical goods. Agr. includes watermelons, cotton, peanuts, grain; livestock, poultry. **3** town (1990 pop. 4,887), Chittenden co., NW Vt., on the Winooski R., and 7 mi/11.3 km SE of Burlington; 44°26′N 73°04′W. Wood prods., consumer goods, plastics, and metal prods. Large shopping malls. Chartered 1763, settled 1774, inc. 1786.

Williston Park, residential village (1990 pop. 7,516), Nassau co., SE N.Y., on W L.I., just N of Mineola; 40°45′N 73°39′W. Inc. 1926.

Willisville, village (1990 pop. 577), Perry co., SW Ill., 13 mi/21 km WSW of Pickneyville; 37°58′N 89°35′W. In agr. and bituminous-coal-mining area.

Willits, city (1990 pop. 5,027), Mendocino co., NW Calif., in a valley of the Coast Ranges, 18 mi/29 km N of Ukiah; 39°25′N 123°21′W. Cattle; hay; dairying; fruit, beans; timber. Mfg. (sheet metal work; fabricated metal prods., machinery). Mendocino Natl. Forest to E; Jackson State Forest to W. Founded c.1865, inc. 1888.

Willmar (WIL-muhr), city (1990 pop. 17,531), ⊙ Kandiyohi co., central Minn. 52 mi/84 km SW of St. Cloud, on Hawk Creek; 45°07′N 95°02′W. Hawk Creek forms Willmar and Foot lakes in city. Elev. 1,131 ft/345 m. RR junction and div. point. Shipping center for grain and livestock; mfg. (consumer goods, beverages, fabricated metal prods., bldg. materials, machinery, wood prods.; turkey processing, printing and publishing). Willmar Vocational and Community Col. is here. Sibley State Park to N; numerous lakes in area. Municipal airport to W. Settled 1856; inc. as a city 1901.

Willoughby, city (1990 pop. 20,510), Lake co., NE Ohio, on the Chagrin R., near L. Erie; 41°39′N 81°24′W. Mfg. includes rubber prods., electronic prods., and clothing. Nearby is Kirtland Temple (1833–1836), a Mormon church, built by Joseph Smith and his followers. Settled c.1800, inc. as a city 1951.

Willoughby, Lake, in town of Westmore, Orleans co., N Vt., on Willoughby Brook, 20 mi/32 km N of St. Johnsbury, and 15 mi/24 km S of Can. (Que.) border; c.5 mi/8 km long; 44°44′N 72°03′W. Drains NW; brook flows c.10 mi/16 km NW to Barton R., at Orleans. Scenic resort lake.

Willoughby Spit, Norfolk city, SE Va., sandbar bet. Willoughby Bay of Hampton Roads harbor (SW) and Chesapeake Bay (NE), at S end of entrance to Hampton Roads harbor (James R. estuary); 36°50′N 76°16′W. Hampton Roads Bridge-Tunnel extends from Willoughby Spit to just W of Old Point Comfort (city of Hampton), opposite. Norfolk Naval Base to SW.

Willow 1 village, S Alaska, near Susitna R., 40 mi/64 km N of Anchorage, on Parks Highway. Supply point for gold-mining region and for sportsmen (trout fishing); tourism. Airfield. Formerly sometimes called Willow Station. **2** village (1990 pop. 142), Greer co., SW Okla., 12 mi/19 km N of Mangum; 35°02′N 99°30′W.

Willow Bunch, town (1991 pop. 476), S Sask., W Canada, near Willowbunch L., 24 mi/39 km SE of Assiniboia; 49°24′N 105°38′W. Coal.

Willow City, village (1990 pop. 281), Bottineau co., N N.Dak., 17 mi/27 km SSE of Bottineau; 48°36′N 100°17′W. Grain (wheat, rye, oats). Ox and Willow creeks are nearby.

Willow Creek, uninc. town (1990 pop. 1,576), Humboldt co., NW Calif., 30 mi/48 km ENE of Eureka, on Trinity R.; 40°53′N 123°40′W. Timber; cattle. Area surrounded by Six Rivers Natl Forest.

Willow Creek, village, W central Alaska, 160 mi/257 km NE of Bethel, on Iditarod R. Air access only. Short road connects villages of Flat and Iditarod to NE. Kuskokwim Mts. to E.

Willow Creek, 70 mi/113 km long, SE Morrow co., N Oregon; rises in Blue Mts. c. 20 mi/32 km SE of Heppner; flows generally NW through Willow Creek Reservoir, then past Heppner to the Columbia R. 10 mi/16 km NE of Arlington. Used for irrigation.

Willow Grove, uninc. city (1990 pop. 16,325), Montgomery co., SE Pa., suburb 13 mi/21 km N of downtown Philadelphia, in Abington, Upper Dublin, and Hatsboro townships; 40°08′N 75°07′W. Mfg. (electrical equip., textiles, hardware, machinery; printing). U.S. Naval Air Station to N.

Willow Hill, village (1990 pop. 268), Jasper co., SE Ill., 7 mi/11.3 km E of Newton, near Embarras R.; 38°59′N 88°01′W. Sam Parr State Park to W. Grain; livestock; oil.

Willow Lake, village (1990 pop. 317), Clark co., E central S.Dak., 18 mi/29 km SSE of Clark; 44°37′N 97°38′W. In agr. and livestock area.

Willow Park, town (1990 pop. 2,328), Parker co., N central Texas, 18 mi/29 km W of Fort Worth, on Clear Fork Trinity R., at SE end of L. Weatherford, on fringe of Dallas–Fort Worth area; 32°45′N 97°39′W. Agr. (cattle, horses; peanuts, peaches, pecans; horticulture).

Willow River, village (1990 pop. 284), Pine co., E Minn., 46 mi/74 km SW of Duluth, 35 mi/56 km N of Pine City, on Kettle R., at mouth of Willow R.; 46°19′N 92°50′W. Dairying; poultry, livestock; alfalfa, oats; timber; mfg. (lumber). General C. C. Andrews State Forest to N.

Willow Run, residential and industrial suburb and uninc. area, Washtenaw co., SE Mich., 4 mi/6.4 km ENE of Ypsilanti; 42°15′N 83°34′W. Motor vehicles and farm machinery are made here in huge Willow Run plant, which produced bombers in World War II. Willow Run Airport to SE (mainly in Wayne co.). Univ of Mich. has aeronautical research center at airport here.

Willow Springs, city (1990 pop. 2,038), Howell co., S Mo., in the Ozark Mts., on the drainage divide separating several rivers, 75 mi/121 km SE of Springfield; 36°59′N 91°58′W. Cattle and poultry market; mfg. (transportation equip.); timber; recreation. Mark Twain Natl. Forest to W.

Willow Springs, village (1990 pop. 4,509), Cook co., NE Ill., suburb 16 mi/26 km WSW of downtown Chicago; 41°43′N 87°52′W. Mfg. (fabricated metal prods., electrical goods, chemicals); remnant agr. On Sanitary and Ship Canal.

Willow Station, Alaska: see WILLOW.

Willow Street, uninc. town (1990 pop. 5,817), Lancaster co., SE Pa., suburb 5 mi/8 km S of Lancaster; 39°58′N 76°16′W. Mfg. includes beverages, fabricated metals, boats. Agr. includes dairying; livestock, poultry; grain, soybeans. Lancaster Co. Winery to S. Covered bridges in area.

Willowbrook, uninc. city (1990 pop. 32,772), Los Angeles co., S Calif., suburb 9 mi/14.5 km S of downtown Los Angeles; 33°55′N 118°15′W. In mfg. dist. bet. Compton (S) and Watts (N).

Willowbrook, village (1990 pop. 8,598), Du Page co., NE Ill., suburb 24 mi/39 km WSW of downtown Chicago; 41°45′N 87°57′W. Residential and commercial area. Mfg. (insulation, consumer goods, plastics, chemicals), printing.

Willowbunch Lake, S Sask., W Canada, 17 mi/27 km SE of Assiniboia; 22 mi/35 km long, 1 mi/2 km wide.

Willowick, city (1990 pop. 15,269), Lake co., NE Ohio, a suburb of Cleveland on L. Erie; 41°38′N 81°28′W. It is chiefly residential. Inc. 1924.

Willows, city (1990 pop. 5,988), ⊙ Glenn co., N central Calif., in Sacramento Valley, 22 mi/35 km SW of Chico; 39°31′N 122°12′W. In agr. area irrigated from Sacramento R. Rice and other grain, fruit, nuts, olives, sugar beets; cattle, sheep, poultry; dairying; nursery prods. Stony Gorge Reservoir to W; Mendocino Natl. Forest to W; Sacramento Natl. Wildlife Refuge to S; Tehama Colusa Canal passes to W. Inc. as town in 1886, as city in 1935.

Wills Creek, c.65 mi/105 km long, in E and central Ohio; formed by junction of small forks near Pleasant City; flows NW and W, past Cambridge, Kimbolton, and Plainfield, to Muskingum R. 8 mi/13 km S of Coshocton; 40°09′N 81°54′W. Flood control reservoir (capacity 196,000 acre-ft.) is impounded by dam on lower course.

Wills Mountain, in NW Md. and S Pa., ridge (1,600 ft/488 m–2,400 ft/732 m) of the Appalachian mt. system, running c.35 mi/56 km NE from just N of Cresaptown (Md.) to Raystown Branch of Juniata R. just W of Bedford (Pa.); 39°43′N 78°44′W. Just NW of Cumberland (Md.), Wills Creek cuts through Cumberland Narrows, a beautiful gorge 1,000 ft/305 m deep, which was discovered in 1755 by Braddock's army. A natural E-W gateway across the Appalachians, it was traversed by Old Cumberland (or Natl.) road, and is now followed by U.S. Route 40. The mt. is named for a Native American known as Will, who befriended early settlers and is supposed to be buried atop Will's Knob.

Wills Point, town (1990 pop. 2,986), Van Zandt co., NE Texas, 16 mi/26 km E of Terrell. Elev. 518 ft/158 m. Trade, shipping center in cattle, cotton area; grains, vegetables; nurseries; dairying. Mfg. (printing; concrete). L. Tawakoni reservoir and State Park to N. Est. 1873.

Willsboro, resort village (1990 pop. 950), Essex co., NE N.Y., near mouth of Bouquet R., on L. Champlain, 23 mi/37 km S of Plattsburgh; 44°23′N 73°23′W. Mfg. of consumer goods, chemicals, plastic prods., textiles. NW are Long Pond (c. 1.5 mi/2.4 km long) and Highlands Forge L. (1.5 mi/2.4 km long).

Willshire (WIL-shuhr), village (1990 pop. 541), Van Wert co., W Ohio, on St Marys R., at Ind. state line, and 14 mi/23 km SW of Van Wert; 40°45′N 84°48′W. Sawmills.

Wilmar (WIL-mahr), village (1990 pop. 637), Drew co., SE Ark., 8 mi/12.9 km W of Monticello; 33°37′N 91°55′W. In agr. area.

Wilmer, town (1990 pop. 2,479), Dallas co., N Texas, suburb 13 mi/21 km SE of downtown Dallas, near Trinity R. ; 32°36′N 96°40′W. Agr. area in urban fringe (cotton, vegetables; cattle; dairying). Mfg. (lumber, moldings, machine parts). Lancaster Municipal Airport to SW.

Wilmerding (WIL-muhr-ding), borough (1990 pop. 2,222), Allegheny co., SW Pa., suburb 11 mi/18 km ESE of downtown Pittsburgh, on Turtle Creek; 40°23′N 79°48′W. Mfg. (machinery). Inc. 1890.

Wilmette (wil-MET), village (1990 pop. 26,690), Cook co., NE Ill., residential suburb 15 mi/24 km NNW of downtown Chicago, on L. Michigan; 42°04′N 87°43′W. Commercial printing. Mallinkrodt Col. of the North Shore, Natl. Louis Univ. of Evanston, Wall Center (house of worship) of the Bahai Faith, and a U.S. coast guard station are nearby. Inc. 1872.

Wilmington 1 city (1990 pop. 71,529), ⊙ New Castle co., NE Del., on the Delaware R., at mouth of Christina R. and Brandywine Creek; 39°44′N 75°31′W. The largest city in the state, it is a port of entry handling considerable domestic and foreign shipping. It has large shipyards and RR shops and is a major chemical center with mfg. plants. Hq. of the huge Du Pont Corp. and its research and experimental laboratories. Mfg. (machinery, electronic prods., plastics prods., chemicals, hardware, leather goods, foods, feeds, fabricated metal prods., medical prods., transportation equip., furniture, ordnance, beverages, photographic equip., gypsum prods., glass prods., apparel, computer equip., fabricated textile prods., consumer goods; petroleum refining, printing and publishing; steel foundry and mill). In 1682, William Penn came into possession of the region. Shipping and mfg. grew early, and industry was well developed when E. I. Du Pont established a powder mill on the Brandywine here in 1802. In the late 20th cent., as residents and businesses moved to the suburbs, the city became a pioneer in neighborhood revitalization using an urban homesteading program. Univ. of Del. at Wilmington and Goldey-Beacom Col. (7 mi/11.3 km to N) are here. Widener Univ. School of Law to N. Del. Technical and Community Col. at Stanton (5 mi/8 km to SW). Fort Christina Monument at confluence of Christina R. and Brandywine Creek. Wilmington's many historic bldgs. include Old Swedes Church (1698). Other points of interest are Rodney Square (civic center), the Del. Acad. of Medicine, the Del. Art Center, and several mus. New Castle Co. Airport is 6 mi/9.7 km to SW; Del. Memorial Bridge 3 mi/4.8 km to SSE (to N.J.); Mus. of Natural History to NW; Winterthur Mus. and Gardens to NW (former Du Pont estate); Del. Park Horse Race Track to SW; Brandywine Creek State Park to N; Bellevue and Fox Point state parks to NE. Highest point in Del. (442 ft/135 m; unnamed) is 6 mi/9.7 km to N, on Pa. state line. Settled 1638, inc. as a city 1832. **2** city (1990 pop. 4,743), Will co., NE Ill., on Kankakee R. (bridged here), and 15 mi/24 km SSW of Joliet; 41°17′N 88°09′W. Trade center in agr. and bituminous-coal-mining area. Mfg. (consumer goods, electrical equip.; copper and nickel etching). Agr. (corn, soybeans; dairy prods.; poultry). Island Park in river is resort. Abandoned Joliet Army Ammunition Plant to N, Des Plaines Conservation Area to NW. Settled c.1839, inc. 1875. **3** city (1990 pop. 55,530), ⊙ New Hanover co., SE N.C., 120 mi/193 km SSE of Raleigh; 34°12′N 77°54′W. A port of entry on the Cape Fear R. estuary, 30 mi/48 km N of its entrance on Atlantic Ocean W of Cape Fear; Atlantic Ocean (Wrightsville Beach) 8 mi/12.9 km ESE. It has an excellent harbor and is the state's largest port. Mfg. (chemicals and plastics, machinery, rubber prods., yachts, bldg. materials, apparel, paper prods., fabricated metal and metal prods., fiber optics, foods, tools, fertilizers, vitamins; printing and publishing). The Br. Gen. Cornwallis held the town in 1781. During the Civil War, Wilmington was the last Confederate port to close; Confederate blockade runners used it until the fall of Fort Fisher on Jan. 15, 1865. Many large cargo ships were built in the shipyards during World War II. The Univ. of N.C. at Wilmington (to E). The USS *North Carolina* is moored across river to W. Cape Fear Community Col. Carolina Beach State Park and Ebert Fisher State Recreation Area to S, on Pleasure Isl.; Airlie Gardens to E. Cape Fear Mus., Wilmington RR Mus., Mus. of design Arts, St. John's Mus. of Art, Hughes Gall.; Thalian Hall opera house. One of 2 N.C. state ports (other is Morehead City). Chandlers Wharf, Cotton Exchange. Settled 1732, inc. as a city 1866. **4** city (1990 pop. 11,199), ⊙ Clinton co., SW Ohio; 39°26′N 83°50′W. In a farm (chiefly corn and hogs) area. Tools, machinery, fabricated metal prods., and transportation equip. are made. Seat of Wilmington Col. State park is nearby. Settled 1810, inc. 1828.

Wilmington 1 town (1990 pop. 17,651), Middlesex co., NE Mass., suburb of Boston, on the Ipswich R.; 42°34′N 71°10′W. Important high-tech town. Economic enterprises include space research and the mfg. of plastics, machinery, medical equip., and electronics. Settled 1639, inc. 1730. **2** town (1990 pop. 1,968), Windham co., S Vt., on Deerfield R., and 15 mi/24 km W of Brattleboro, in Green Mts.; 42°52′N 72°51′W. Wood prods.; winter sports (Haystack Mt. Ski Area). Includes Wilmington village. Chartered 1751, settled c.1770.

Wilmington, resort village (1990 pop. 700), Essex co., NE

N.Y., in the Adirondack Mts., 11 mi/18 km NE of Lake Placid; 44°22′N 73°50′W. Road to Whiteface Mt. (4,867-ft/1,483-m summit; accessible by road) ski center, starts here. Wilmington Mt. (3,458 ft/1,054 m) is NW.

Wilmington, port and industrial section of Los Angeles, Los Angeles co., S Calif., on man-made Los Angeles Harbor, 18 mi/29 km S of city center, NE of San Pedro. Has freight terminals, industrial container port and landing for Santa Catalina Isl. ferries. Oil wells; oil refining and shipping; mfg. (petroleum production and refining, food [esp. seafood] processing, fabricated metal prods., bldg. materials, wood prods.). Laid out 1857 as port of New San Pedro, renamed 1863; was military post and supply depot in Civil War. RR's coming to harbor dist. (1869) and construction of small jetty (1871) stimulated its growth, as well as San Pedro's; the 2 cities were consolidated (1909) with Los Angeles and modern harbor development followed. Los Angeles Harbor Col. (2-year). Includes Long Beach Naval Shipyard, on Terminal Isl.

Wilmington Island, one of the Sea Isls, in Chatham co., SE Ga., just off the Atlantic coast, 10 mi/16 km ESE of Savannah, bet. 2 distributaries of Savannah R.; c.7 mi/11.3 km long, 4 mi/6.4 km wide; 32°00′N 80°57′W. Marshy; connected with mainland by causeway.

Wilmington Manor, uninc. town (1990 est. pop 8,568), New Castle co., central Del., 5 mi/8 km SW of downtown Wilmington, and 1 mi/1.6 km N of New Castle; 39°41′N 75°35′W. Suburb of Wilmington. Shopping centers. Site of Wilmington Col.

Wilmington Mountain, N.Y.: see WILMINGTON.

Wilmont (WIL-mawnt), village (1990 pop. 351), Nobles co., SW Minn., 16 mi/26 km NW of Worthington, near source of Jack Creek; 43°45′N 95°49′W. Grain; livestock, poultry; dairying.

Wilmore, town (1990 pop. 4,215), Jessamine co., central Ky., 17 mi/27 km SW of Lexington, near Kentucky R., in Bluegrass region; 37°52′N 84°39′W. Agr. area (burley tobacco, corn, wheat; dairying). Mfg. (concrete, beverages; printing); limestone quarry. Seat of Asbury Col., Asbury Theological Seminary. Herrington L. reservoir on Dix R., to S; Palisades of the Kentucky R. to SW (cliff formations); High Bridge, RR bridge (1877) over Kentucky R., to SW.

Wilmore, village (1990 pop. 78), Comanche co., S Kansas, 8 mi/12.9 km NE of Coldwater; 37°20′N 99°12′W. Shipping point for livestock and grain area.

Wilmore (WIL-mor), borough (1990 pop. 277), Cambria co., W central Pa., 11 mi/18 km ENE of Johnstown, on Little Conemaugh R.; 40°23′N 78°43′W. Agr. (hay; livestock; dairying).

Wilmot 1 (WIL-maht), town (1990 pop. 1,047), Ashley co., SE Ark., 33 mi/53 km S of Dermott, on Bayou Bartholomew, near La. state line; 33°03′N 91°34′W. In cotton and rice area. Overflow Natl. Wildlife Refuge to W. **2** (WIL-mawt), town (1990 pop. 935), Merrimack co., S central N.H., 26 mi/42 km NW of Concord; 43°27′N 71°55′W. Drained by Blackwater R. and Kimpton Brook. Mfg. (wood prods.); agr. (apples, nursery crops, vegetables; poultry, livestock; dairying); timber; garnet deposits. Small part of Gile State Forest on NW border. Winslow State Park with Mt. Kearsarge (2,931 ft/893 m) on SE border.

Wilmot 1 village (1990 pop. 566), Roberts co., NE S.Dak., 20 mi/32 km SSE of Sisseton, on North Fork Whetstone Creek; 45°24′N 96°51′W. Resort; diversified farming in area. Hartford Beach State Park to E (on Big Stone L., Minnesota R.). **2** village (1990 pop. 261), Stark co., E central Ohio, 16 mi/26 km SW of Canton; 40°39′N 81°38′W. Makes cheese. State Wilderness Center with interpretive center, hiking trails, picnic area, primeval woods, natural habitats.

Wilsall (WIL-suhl), village (1990 pop. 225) Park co., S Mont., near Shields R. and mouth of Muddy Creek, and 23 mi/37 km N of Livingston. Cattle; barley, oats, hay, vegetables. Cottonwood Reservoir to N. Parts of Gallatin Natl. Forest to E and W.

Wilsey, village (1990 pop. 149), Morris co., E central Kansas, 11 mi/18 km W of Council Grove; 38°38′N 96°40′W. Grazing, agr.

Wilson 1 county (□ 575 sq mi/1,489 sq km; 1990 pop. 10,289), SE Kansas; ⊙ Fredonia; 37°34′N 95°44′W. Dissected plain, drained by Verdigris and Fall rivers. Cattle, hogs; wheat, sorghum, soybeans, hay, strawberries. Mfg. at Fredonia and Neodesha. Wilson State Fishing L. in NE. Toronto L. Dam above NW border. Formed 1865. **2** county (□ 374 sq mi/969 sq km; 1990 pop. 66,061), E central N.C.; ⊙ Wilson; 35°42′N 77°55′W. Drained by small Contentnea Creek. Coastal plain; area producing corn, wheat, hay, sweet potatoes, tobacco, cotton; chickens, hogs; dairying; timber. Mfg. at Wilson. Formed 1855. **3** county (□ 580 sq mi/1,502 sq km; 1990 pop. 67,675), N central Tenn.; ⊙ Lebanon; 36°10′N 86°18′W. Bounded N by Old Hickory Reservoir (Cumberland R.). Livestock; timber; agr. (corn, tobacco, hay); dairying. Mfg. at Lebanon. Extensive cedar glades at Cedars of Lebanon State Park and Forest. Formed 1799. **4** county (□ 808 sq mi/2,093 sq km; 1990 pop. 22,650), S Texas; ⊙ Floresville; 29°10′N 98°05′W. Drained by San Antonio R. and Cibolo Creek. Agr., esp. peanuts, watermelons, grain sorghums; also corn, sunflowers, fruit. Livestock (cattle, hogs, poultry). Some oil and gas. Clay mining. Formed 1860.

Wilson, city (1990 pop. 36,930), ⊙ Wilson co., E N.C.; 35°43′N 77°55′W. RR junction. In a rich agr. region (tobacco, peanuts, cotton, grain, sweet potatoes; chickens, hogs; dairying). It is a commercial and industrial center with a large tobacco market. Mfg. (tobacco processing; printing and publishing; food processing; metal, paper, and plastic fabricating; glass prods., livestock beds, bldg. materials, foods, fiberglass prods., electrical prods., chemicals, apparel). Seat of Barton Col. (formerly Atlantic Christian Col.) and Wilson Tech. Community Col. Inc. 1849.

Wilson 1 town (1990 pop. 1,068), Mississippi co., NE Ark., 25 mi/40 km SSW of Blytheville, near Mississippi R.; 35°34′N 90°02′W. Agr. (cotton, alfalfa, rice, soybeans); mfg. (machinery, foods). Hampson Mus. State Park is here. **2** town (1990 pop. 707), East Feleciana parish, La., 7 mi/11.3 km NW of Clinton; 30°55′N 91°06′W. In timber and small farm area. **3** town (1990 pop. 1,639), Carter co., S Okla., 17 mi/27 km W of Ardmore; 34°09′N 97°25′W. In oil and natural-gas and agr. area (livestock; vegetables, peanuts, corn, grain).

Wilson 1 village (1990 pop. 834), Ellsworth co., central Kansas, 14 mi/23 km WNW of Ellsworth, near Smoky Hill R.; 38°49′N 98°28′W. In wheat and livestock region. Known as the "Czech Capital." Wilson State Park and Wilson L. reservoir to NW. Founded 1871, inc. 1883. **2** village (1990 pop. 1,307), Niagara co., W N.Y., on L. Ontario, 30 mi/48 km N of Buffalo; 43°18′N 78°49′W. Summer resort; some mfg. (foods). Inc. 1858. **3** village (1990 pop. 568), Lynn co., NW Texas, 20 mi/32 km SSE of Lubbock; 33°19′N 101°43′W. Oil and natural gas. Ranching area (cattle, sheep; wheat, cotton). **4** village (1990 pop. 163), St. Croix co., W Wis., 29 mi/47 km E of Hudson; 44°57′N 92°10′W. In dairying region. Eau Galle Dam Recreation Area (Army Corps of Engineering) to S.

Wilson, borough (1990 pop. 7,830), Northampton co., E Pa., residential suburb 2 mi/3.2 km W of Easton, near Lehigh R.; 40°41′N 75°14′W. Inc. 1920.

Wilson Creek, village (1990 pop. 148), Grant co., E central Wash., 22 mi/35 km ENE of Ephrata, on Crab Creek, at mouth of Wilson Creek; 47°25′N 119°08′W. In Columbia basin agr. area; wheat, alfalfa; cattle. Billy Clapp L. (Pinto Dam) reservoir to W.

Wilson Lake, NW Ala., on the Tennessee R., 2 mi/3.2 km E of Florence; 34°47′N 87°37′W. Extends 14 mi/23 km E to Wheeler Dam. Receives Town Creek. Max. storage capacity of 641,000 acre-ft. Formed by Wilson Dam (116 ft/35 m high), built by the TVA for navigational, flood control, and hydroelectric purposes.

Wilson Lake, reservoir (□ 14 sq mi/36 sq km), Russell co., N central Kansas, on Saline R., 50 mi/80 km WNW of Salina; 38°58′N 98°30′W. Max. capacity 736,000 acre-ft. Formed by Wilson Dam (130 ft/40 m high), built (1964) by Army Corps of Engineers for flood control; also used for irrigation and recreation. Wilson State Park near dam.

Wilson Mills, uninc. village, Johnston co., central N.C., 5 mi/8 km N of Smithfield, near Neuse R.

Wilson, Mount 1 peak (5,710 ft/1,740 m high), S Calif., in the San Gabriel Mts., in Angeles Natl. Forest, 5 mi/8 km NE of Pasadena, and 17 mi/27 km NE of downtown Los Angeles. Site of Mt. Wilson Observatory (est. 1904), one of the Hale Observatories; houses a 100-in/254-cm telescope. **2** peak (5,445 ft/1,660 m) in NW Ariz., 13 mi/21 km E of Boulder City (Nev.), S of L. Mead; 34°55′N 111°45′W. Highest peak in Black Mts. L. Mead Natl. Recreation Area to W, N, and E. **3** (14,246 ft/4,342 m), highest point in San Miguel Mts., on border bet. San Miguel and Dolores cos., SW Colo., 12 mi/19 km SW of Telluride, and 1 mi/1.6 km S of Wilson Peak; 37°50′N 107°59′W. Also on border of Uncompahgre and San Juan natl. forests. Known unofficially as Mt. Franklin Roosevelt.

Wilson Peak (14,017 ft/4,272 m), San Miguel co., SW Colo., in Rocky Mts., 11 mi/18 km SW of Telluride, and 1 mi/1.6 km N of Mt. Wilson, in Uncompahgre Natl. Forest; 37°51′N 107°59′W.

Wilson Pond, resort lake in Wilton, Franklin co., W central Maine; 2.25 mi/3.7 km long. Source of Wilson Stream, which flows c.15 mi/24 km E to Sandy R.

Wilson's Creek National Battlefield (□ 2 sq mi/5.2 sq km), Mo., 10 mi/16 km SW of Springfield. This site was the location of the 1st major Civil War battle (Aug. 10, 1861) fought W of the Mississippi R. Outnumbered and beaten Union troops were allowed to retreat and regroup to win later engagements; kept Mo. from seceding. Authorized 1960.

Wilsonville 1 town (1990 pop. 1,185) Shelby co., central Ala., on Coosa R., and c.9 mi/14.5 km NE of Columbiana. Coal refining. **2** town (1990 pop. 7,106), Clackamas co., NW Oregon, suburb 16 mi/26 km SSW of downtown Portland, on Willamette R.; 45°18′N 122°46′W. Nurseries; dairying; poultry; fruit, berries, nuts. Mfg. (millwork, printing; fabricated metal prods., greenhouse equip., computers). Campoeg (SW) and Molalla R. (SE) state parks.

Wilsonville 1 village (1990 pop. 609), Macoupin co., SW Ill., 21 mi/34 km ENE of Alton; 39°04′N 89°51′W. **2** village (1990 pop. 136), Furnas co., S Nebr., 16 mi/26 km W of Beaver City, and on Beaver Creek; 40°06′N 100°06′W. Livestock; grain.

Wilsonville, Conn.: see THOMPSON.

Wilton 1 town (1990 pop. 602), Shelby co., central Ala., 19 mi/31 km SW of Columbiana. **2** uninc. town (1990 pop. 3,858), Sacramento co., central Calif., 15 mi/24 km SE of Sacramento, on Cosumnes R.; 38°25′N 121°13′W. Citrus, grain, tomatoes; dairying; poultry. **3** town (1990 pop. 15,989), Fairfield co., SW Conn.; 41°12′N 73°26′W. It is a residential and agr. town with electronic research development as an industry. Includes village of Cannondale (bicycle mfg.). Settled c.1701, inc. 1802. **4** town (1990 pop. 2,577), Muscatine co., SE Iowa, 11 mi/18 km N of Muscatine; 41°35′N 91°01′W. Mfg. (plastic pipe; abrasives); steel mills. Formerly called Wilton Junction. Inc. 1863. **5** town (1990 pop. 4,242), Franklin co., W central Maine, 7 mi/11.3 km SW of Farmington, on Wilson Pond (resort); 44°37′N 70°14′W. Canned foods. Includes Wilton village. Settled 1789 as Tyngtown, inc. 1803 as Wilton. **6** town (1990 pop. 3,122), Hillsborough co., S N.H., 17 mi/27 km SW of Manchester; 42°49′N 71°46′W. Drained by Souhegan R. and Stony and Blood brooks. Mfg. (fabricated metal prods., computer equip., plastics, perfumes, bottled water, paper prods., machinery); agr. (fruit, vegetables, corn, nursery crops; livestock; dairying). Inc. 1762.

Wilton 1 village (1990 pop. 449), Little River co., extreme SW Ark., 20 mi/32 km NNW of Texarkana; 33°44′N 94°09′W. Millwood L. reservoir to E. **2** village (1990 pop. 171), Beltrami co., NW central Minn., 6 mi/9.7 km W of Bemidji, at E edge of Mississippi Headwaters State Forest; 47°30′N 94°59′W. RR junction. Livestock; dairying; timber. **3** village (1990 pop. 728), McLean and Burleigh cos., central N.Dak., 25 mi/40 km N of Bismarck, near Missouri R.; 47°09′N 100°46′W. RR junction; lignite mines; dairy prods.; livestock; wheat, corn, flax. **4** village (1990 pop. 478), Monroe co., W central Wis., on Kickapoo R., 35 mi/56 km E of La Crosse, on La Crosse State Trail; 43°48′N 90°31′W. In dairy and livestock area.

Wilton Woods, uninc. town, Fairfax co., NE Va., residential suburb 2 mi/3.2 km WSW of Alexandria, 9 mi/14.5 km SSW of Washington, D.C., near Cameron Run creek; 38°47′N 77°05′W.

Wimauma (wi-MAW-muh), town (□ 3 sq mi/7.8 sq km; 1990 pop. 2,932), Hillsborough co., W central Fla., 20 mi/32 km SSE of Tampa; 27°42′N 82°18′W.

Wimberley, town (1990 pop. 2,403), Hays co., S central Texas, 11 mi/18 km NW of San Marcos, and on Blanco R.; 29°59′N 98°05′W. In livestock area; agr. (cotton, wheat, fruits, vegetables); light mfg.; tourism.

Wimbledon, village (1990 pop. 275), Barnes co., E central N.Dak., 28 mi/45 km NW of Valley City; 47°10′N 98°27′W.

Wimico, Lake (WI-mi-ko), reservoir, Gulf co., at Franklin co. border, NW Fla., 7 mi/11.3 km NW of Apalachicola, and 5 mi/8 km N of St. Vincent Sound; c.5 mi/8 km long, 1 mi/1.6 km wide; 29°46′N 85°05′W. Forms part of Intracoastal Waterway bet. Apalachicola R. and St. Andrews Bay.

Winamac, town (1990 pop. 2,262), ⊙ Pulaski co., NW Ind., on Tippecanoe R., c.45 mi/72 km NNE of Lafayette; 41°03′N 86°36′W. Trade center in agr. area (livestock; grain, soybeans); mfg. (machinery, steel prods.). Settled 1837, laid out 1839, inc. 1868.

Winborn, village, Benton co., N Miss., 14 mi/23 km SE of Holly Springs, in Holly Springs Natl. Forest. Timber.

Winburne (WIN-buhrn), uninc. town (1990 pop. 800), Cooper township, Clearfield co., central Pa., 15 mi/24 km ESE of Clearfield; 40°57′N 78°08′W. Agr. (grain; livestock; dairying).

Winchendon (WIN-chen-duhn), town (1990 pop. 8,805), Worcester co., N Mass., 15 mi/24 km NW of Fitchburg, in wooded country, near N.H. state line; 42°40′N 72°04′W. Furniture, paper and plastic prods.; poultry; dairying. State park and state forest nearby. Includes villages of Waterville and Winchendon. Settled 1753, inc. 1764.

Winchester, village (1991 pop. 2,432), SE Ont., central Canada, 28 mi/45 km SE of Ottawa; 45°06′N 75°21′W. Milling, furniture mfg., dairying.

Winchester 1 (WIHN-ches-ter), city, ⊙ Scott co., W central Ill., 14 mi/23 km SW of Jacksonville; 39°37′N 90°27′W. In agr. area (corn, wheat, soybeans; poultry). Has statue of Stephen A. Douglas, who here taught school. Here, too, Lincoln made his 1st speech on the Kansas-Nebr. issue. Platted 1830, inc. 1843. **2** city (1990 pop. 5,095), ⊙ Randolph co., E Ind., on West Fork of White R., 20 mi/32 km E of Muncie; 40°10′N 84°59′W. Shipping center for livestock; grain; dairy prods.; mfg. (glass prods., steel stampings, machinery, iron prods., food). Anc. Indian earthworks are NW. Settled 1812. **3** city (1990 pop. 15,799), ⊙ Clark co., central Ky.; 38°00′N 84°11′W. RR junction. The center of a burley tobacco-growing, dairying, and livestock-raising area in the Bluegrass region; mfg. (crushed limestone, steel fabrication, soft drinks, pharmaceuticals, mining equip., furniture, paper prods., apparel, dairy prods., feeds, machining, printing and publishing). Henry Clay made his last speech in Ky. in the old courthouse here. Clark Mansion (1813); Pioneer Telephone Mus. here. Fort Boonesborough and Boones Station state parks to SW. Winchester is the hq. of Daniel Boone Natl. Forest. Inc. 1793. **4** uninc. city (1990 pop. 23,365), Clark co., S Nev., residential suburb 3 mi/4.8 km SSW of Las Vegas, generally SE of Sahara Avenue and W of Interstate Highway 15; 36°08′N 115°07′W. Part of uninc. S ½ of city of Las Vegas. RR junction. Internatl. airport to SE. **5** (WIN-CHES-tuhr), city (1990 pop. 6,305), ⊙ Franklin co., S Tenn., on Tims Ford Reservoir (Elk R.), 45 mi/72 km WNW of Chattanooga; 35°11′N 86°07′W; in livestock, dairying area; mfg. of clothing, rubber, metal, and plastic prods. Nearby is Hundred Oaks Castle. Town founded c.1814. **6** independent city (□ 9 sq mi/23.3 sq km; 1990 pop. 21,947), ⊙ Frederick co., N Va., separate from surrounding Frederick co., in Shenandoah valley, 67 mi/108 km WNW of Washington, D.C.; 39°10′N 78°10′W. RR junction; mfg. (motor vehicle parts, furniture, plastics prods., machining, bldg. materials, foods and beverages, lumber, flour, crushed limestone, printing and publishing, clothing); trade, processing, and shipping center for an orchard dist. noted for its apples; agr. (apples, grain; livestock; dairying). George Washington began his career as a surveyor here (1748). Center during Fr. and Indian Wars for defense against Native Amer. raids, hq. of Washington, commander of Va. troops. Home and burial place (in Mt. Hebron Cemetery) of Gen. Daniel Morgan. During the Civil War the city suffered severely, changing hands many times. Hq. of Stonewall Jackson (winter of 1861–1862) and of Gen. Philip Sheridan (winter of 1864–1865). Old Presbyterian Church (1790); annual apple festival. Shenandoah Univ., originally a music conservatory (1875). Birthplace of Willa Cather, Richard E. Byrd. Winchester Regional Airport to SE. Settled 1732 near a Native Amer. village in Lord Fairfax's domain, inc. as a city 1874.

Winchester 1 uninc. town (1990 pop. 1,689), Riverside co., S Calif., 21 mi/34 km SE of Riverside; 33°43′N 117°05′W. Dairying; cattle, poultry; grain, alfalfa, nursery prods. San Diego Aqueduct to SE. **2** town (1990 pop. 11,524), Litchfield co., NW Conn., in the Litchfield Hills; 41°55′N 73°05′W. It includes Winsted (1990 pop. 8,254), an industrial center where ball bearings, paper prods., bldg. materials, electrical equip., screw machine prods., metal products, and pet supplies are manufactured. A community col. is in Winsted, as are many early 18th-cent. mansions. Of interest are a little red schoolhouse (1815) and the Winchester Historical Society, located in the Rockwell House (1813). Winchester lies at the gateway to the Berkshire Hills, in a region of lakes and mountain laurel. Settled 1732, inc. 1771. **3** town (1990 pop. 20,267), Middlesex co., E Mass., suburb of Boston; 42°27′N 71°09′W. It is chiefly residential. Industry includes bookbinding, wire belts, electronic components. Settled 1640, inc. 1850. **4** town (1990 pop. 1,678), St. Louis co., E Mo., residential suburb 18 mi/29 km W of St. Louis, just E of Ballwin; 38°35′N 90°31′W. **5** town (1990 pop. 4,038), Cheshire co., SW N.H., bounded S by Mass. state line, 12 mi/19 km SSW of Keene; 42°47′N 72°24′W. Drained by Ashuelot R. and Roaring Brook. SW corner less than 1 mi/1.6 km from Connecticut R. Mfg. (lumber, paper, printing and publishing); agr. (vegetables, nursery crops; cattle, poultry; dairying); timber. Includes part of Pisgah State Park in NW, including Pisgah Reservoir and Kilburne Pond. Includes village of Ashuelot near center. There are 2 covered bridges. Settled 1732, inc. 1753.

Winchester 1 village (1990 pop. 239), Drew co., SE Ark., 11 mi/18 km NNW of McGehee, near Bayou Bartholomew (W) and Boeuf R. (E); 33°46′N 91°28′W. Fish farms nearby. **2** village (1990 pop. 262), Lewis co., W Idaho, 19 mi/31 km W of Nezperce; 46°14′N 116°37′W. Cattle; alfalfa, grain. In Nez Perce Indian Reservation. Soldier Meadow Reservoir and Winchester State Park to SW. **3** village (1990 pop. 613), Jefferson co., NE Kansas, 8 mi/12.9 km NNE of Oskaloosa; 39°19′N 95°16′W. In grain-growing, stock-raising, and farming region. **4** residential village, Erie co., W N.Y., just SE of and part of the older industrial fringe of Buffalo; 42°52′N 78°47′W. **5** village (1990 pop. 978), Adams co., S Ohio, 11 mi/18 km NNW of West Union; 38°57′N 83°39′W. In agr. area. **6** village (1990 pop. 301), Okmulgee co., E central Okla., 22 mi/35 km S of Tulsa; 35°47′N 95°59′W. Grain, peanuts; cattle.

Wind Cave National Park (□ 44 sq mi/114 sq km), Custer co., SW S.Dak., 30 mi/48 km SSW of Rapid City, in the Black Hills, SW S.Dak. Est. 1903. Wind Cave, discovered in 1881, was named for the strong air currents that blow in and out of it. The limestone cave has unusual calcite-crystal and boxwork formations. The park's surface is a game preserve characterized by rolling grasslands and pine-covered ridges where bison, elk, deer, and pronghorn antelope can be found; several prairie dog towns are in the park. Visitors' Center. Large Custer State Park adjoins on N. Drained by Beaver Creek.

Wind Gap (WIND GAP), borough (1990 pop. 2,741), Northampton co., E Pa., 14 mi/23 km NNE of Bethlehem; 40°51′N 75°17′W. Mfg. (bldg. equip., clothing); agr. (apples, potatoes, hay; dairying). Slate quarries in area. Cherry Valley Winery to N; Appalachian Trail passes to N on Blue Mt. ridge and NE on Kittantinny Mt. Inc. 1893.

Wind Lake, town (1990 pop. 3,748), Racine co., SE Wis., on Wind L., 17 mi/27 km SW of Milwaukee Recreation Area; 42°49′N 88°09′W.

Wind Mountain (10,190 ft/3,106 m), SW Alta., W Canada, near B.C. border, in Rocky Mts., near Banff Natl. Park, 20 mi/32 km SE of Banff; 50°58′N 115°16′W.

Wind Point, village (1990 pop. 1,941), Racine co., SE Wis., residential suburb 4 mi/6.4 km NNE of Racine; 42°46′N 87°46′W. Located at Wind Point, on L. Michigan.

Wind River, c.110 mi/177 km long, Fremont co., W central Wyo.; rises at Continental Divide in NW Fremont co., N part of Wind River Range in Shoshone Natl. Forest, flows SE entering Wind River Indian Reservation, past Dubois, joining Popo Agie R. at Riverton to form Bighorn R. Flows through Wind River Indian Reservation for most of its length. Wind R. diversion dam, 35 mi/56 km NW of Riverton, is part of Riverton power and reclamation project; irrigated valley produces grain, beans, sugar beets.

Wind River Range, part of the Rocky Mts., W Wyo., running SE c.120 mi/190 km; the Continental Divide follows most of its central ridge; 42°42′N 109°07′W. Generally, W of Continental Divide is in Bridger-Teton Natl. Forest (Sublette co.); E of Continental Divide is in Shoshone Natl. Forest (Fremont co.). Gannett Peak (13,804 ft/4,207 m) is the highest point in Wyo. A number of historic passes cross these mts. South Pass (elev. 7,412 ft/2,301 m), at the S end of the range, was the most important pass on the Oregon Trail through the Rocky Mts.

Windber (WIND-buhr), borough (1990 pop. 4,756), Somerset co., SW central Pa., 6 mi/9.7 km SSE of Johnstown, on Paint Creek; 40°13′N 78°49′W. Mfg. (clothing, dairy prods., motor vehicle bodies); surface bituminous coal; agr. (grain; livestock; dairying). Gallitzin State Forest to E. Laid out 1897, inc. 1900.

Windcrest, town (1990 pop. 5,331), Bexar co., S central Texas, residential suburb 8 mi/12.9 km NE of San Antonio; 29°31′N 98°22′W.

Windemere (WIND-uh-mir), uninc. town (1990 pop. 4,604), New Hanover co., SE N.C., residential suburb 5 mi/8 km E of Wilmington; 34°14′N 77°50′W.

Winder (WEIN-duhr), town (1990 pop. 7,373), ⊙ Barrow co., NE central Ga., 19 mi/31 km W of Athens; 33°59′N 83°43′W. Mfg. (clothing, metal fabrication, poultry packaging, printing and publishing). Inc. 1893. Russell, home of former U.S. senator Richard B. Russell, Jr., located nearby.

Windermere (WIN-duhr-mir), village, S Ont., central Canada, in Muskoka lake region, on Rosseau L., 15 mi/24 km NW of Bracebridge; 50°28′N 115°58′W. Resort.

Windermere (WIN-duh-mir), town (1990 pop. 1,371), Orange co., central Fla., 10 mi/16 km WSW of Orlando; 28°30′N 81°31′W.

Windermere Lake, expansion of Columbia R., SE B.C., W Canada, on slope of Rocky Mts., 50 mi/80 km SSW of Banff, 9 mi/14 km long, 1 mi/2 km–2 mi/3 km wide. Elev. 2,624 ft/800 m. Noted for its scenic beauty; here are resorts of Invermere and Athalmer.

Windfall or **Windfall City**, town (1990 pop. 779), Tipton co., central Ind., 7 mi/11.3 km NE of Tipton; 40°22′N 85°58′W. In agr. area; mfg. (wire prods., seed soybeans). Laid out 1853.

Windham 1 (WIND-uhm), county (□ 521 sq mi/1,349 sq km; 1990 pop. 102,525), NE Conn., on Mass. and R.I. state lines; ⊙ Putnam and Willimantic; 41°49′N 71°59′W. Agr. area (dairy prods.; vegetables; poultry) and mfg. centers producing machinery, cutlery, metal prods., clothing, paper and rubber goods, shoes, chemicals, furniture, optical goods, wood prods.

Has several state parks and forests; resorts on small lakes. Drained by Quinebaug, Natchaug, Shetucket, Little, Moosup, and French rivers. Constituted 1726. **2** county (⊙ 798 sq mi/2,067 sq km; 1990 pop. 41,588), SE Vt., bounded E by the Connecticut R. and rising to Green Mts. in W; ⊙ Newfane; 42°59′N 72°43′W. Dairying; mfg. (wood prods., textiles, paper, machinery, shoes, sports equip.); resorts. Drained by West and Deerfield rivers; includes part of Green Mt. Natl. Forest. Organized 1779. Vermont Yankee nuclear power plant, initial criticality March 24, 1972, is 5 mi/8 km S of Brattleboro, in Vernon, uses cooling water from the Connecticut R. and has a max. dependable capacity of 540 MWe.

Windham 1 (WIND-uhm), town (1990 pop. 22,039), Windham co., E Conn., 2 mi/3.2 km SE of Willimantic; 41°42′N 72°10′W. The township includes the industrial city of Willimantic. Industry includes the mfg. of rubber, radio and electric parts, machinery, steel, and insulation prods. At Windham Center (settled c.1688) are several old bldgs. Includes village of South Windham (1990 pop. 1,644). Inc. 1692. **2** residential and resort town (1990 pop. 13,020), Cumberland co., SW Maine, on Presumpscot R., 8 mi/12.9 km NW of Portland; 43°47′N 70°24′W. Includes part of South Windham village. Settled 1737, inc. 1762. **3** town (1990 pop. 9,000), Rockingham co., SE N.H., 8 mi/12.9 km ENE of Nashua, 5 mi/8 km W of Salem; 42°48′N 71°17′W. Drained by Beaver and Golden brooks. Mfg. (electronic equipment, consumer goods); agr. (nursery crops, apples, vegetables, beans; poultry, cattle; dairying). Canobie L. on E boundary. Cobbetts L. in E. **4** resort town (1990 pop. 251), Windham co., SE Vt., 15 mi/24 km N of Newfane, in Green Mts.; 43°10′N 72°43′W. Elev. c.2,000 ft/610 m. Talc mines. Includes village of South Windham.

Windham 1 (WIN-duhm), village, SE Alaska, on bay of Stephens Passage, opposite Admiralty Isl., 60 mi/97 km SE of Juneau. **2** village (1990 pop. 40), Judith Basin co., central Mont., on Sage Creek, 35 mi/56 km W of Lewistown. Cattle, sheep; hay, grain. Lewis and Clark Natl. Forest to SW; Ackley Lake State Park to SE. Sod Buster Mus. **3** resort village (1990 pop. 450), Greene co., SE N.Y., in the Catskills, 21 mi/34 km WNW of Catskill; 42°19′N 74°12′W. **4** village (1990 pop. 2,943), Portage co., NE Ohio, 10 mi/16 km NE of Ravenna; 41°14′N 81°02′W. In agr. area.

Windmill Point, Mass.: see NANTASKET BEACH.

Windom, city (1990 pop. 4,283), ⊙ Cottonwood co., SW Minn., 61 mi/98 km WSW of Mankato, on Des Moines R.; 43°52′N 95°07′W. Elev. 1,360 ft/415 m. Trade center for agr. area (grain, soybeans, alfalfa; livestock); mfg. (meat processing, printing and publishing, furniture, feeds, concrete, fertilizer). Heron L. is 10 mi/16 km SW. Kilen Woods State Park to S; Talcot L. Wildlife Area to W; small lakes in area. Plotted 1870, inc. as village 1875, as city 1920.

Windom 1 village (1990 pop. 136), McPherson co., central Kansas, 22 mi/35 km N of Hutchinson; 38°22′N 97°54′W. In wheat region. **2** village (1990 pop. 269), Fannin co., NE Texas, 11 mi/18 km E of Bonham; 33°33′N 96°00′W. In agr. area.

Windom Peak (14,082 ft/4,292 m), La Plata co., SW Colo., in San Juan Mts., 13 mi/21 km SSE of Silverton, in San Juan Natl. Forest; 37°37′N 107°35′W. Continental Divide 5 mi/8 km to NE.

Window Rock, uninc. town, Apache co., NE Ariz., at N.Mex. state line, 19 mi/31 km WNW of Gallup, N.Mex. Elev. 6,850 ft/2,088 m. Central agency hq. and location of Navajo Indian Capitol (bldg.), for huge Navajo Indian Reservation, in SE edge of reservation. Canyon de Chelly Natl. Monument to NW; natural bridge to N; Franciscan Mission at St. Michaels 2 mi/3.2 km W.

Windsor, city (1991 pop. 191,435), S Ont., central Canada, on the Detroit R. opposite Detroit (Mich.); 42°20′N 83°02′W. It is Canada's leading port of entry from the U.S. and is in a rich agr. region. Its mfg. includes automobiles, industrial machinery, food and beverages, salt, and chemicals. The city was settled by the French in 1749. After the Amer. Revolution many Loyalists settled in the area. In the early 20th cent., when Ford, General Motors, Chrysler, and other automobile companies built plants in the area, Windsor was known as the "Auto Capital of the British Empire." The city is the seat of Windsor Univ.

Windsor 1 town (1991 pop. 3,625), central N.S., E Canada, at the mouth of the Avon R. on an arm of Minas Basin. It is the center of a gypsum and limestone-quarrying area. Mfg. includes fertilizers, bldg. materials, and lumber prods. Windsor was settled by Acadians (1703) and called Pisiquid. After their expulsion it was settled by New Englanders and renamed in 1764. It is the site of Fort Edward, built (1750) by the British. King's Col., the 1st Eng. university in Canada, was founded in Windsor in 1789 but moved in 1923 to Halifax as part of Dalhousie Univ. **2** town (1991 pop. 4,813), S Que., E Canada, on St. Francis R., 14 mi/23 km NNW of Sherbrooke. Paper milling; lumbering; dairying; hydroelectric plant. Inc. 1899.

Windsor, county (□ 976 sq mi/2,528 sq km; 1990 pop. 54,055), E Vt., bounded E by the Connecticut R.; ⊙ Woodstock; 43°34′N 72°34′W. Mfg. (machinery, tools, textiles, wood and metal prods., sports equip.); lumber, dairying, maple sugar. Summer and winter resorts. Includes Mt. Ascutney, Okemo Mt., and Suicide Six ski areas. Drained by Ottauquechee, White, Black, and Williams rivers. Organized 1781.

Windsor 1 city (1990 pop. 13,371), Sonoma co., W Calif., 9 mi/14.5 km NNW of Santa Rosa, near Russian R.; 38°33′N 122°48′W. Grapes, apples, grain, vegetables, nursery stock; dairying; poultry, sheep. Sonoma County Airport to S. **2** city (1990 pop. 774), Shelby co., central Ill., 11 mi/18 km E of Shelbyville; 41°12′N 90°26′W. In agr. area; dairy prods.; corn, soybeans. Inc. 1869. **3** city (1990 pop. 3,044), Henry co., W central Mo., 20 mi/32 km SW of Sedalia; 38°31′N 93°31′W. Corn, wheat, soybeans; cattle; mfg. (metal fabrication). Settled 1855, inc. 1873.

Windsor 1 town (1990 pop. 5,062), Weld co., N Colo., on Cache la Poudre R., 10 mi/16 km WNW of Greeley; 40°29′N 104°54′W. Elev. c.4,800 ft/1,463 m. In sugar-beet and grain region, fruit. Mfg. (paper prods., photographic film, lumber). Oil and gas production. Inc. 1890. **2** town (1990 pop. 27,817), Hartford co., N Conn., at the confluence of the Farmington and Connecticut rivers, just N of Hartford; 41°52′N 72°40′W. Settled by Plymouth Colony in 1633, Windsor was the 1st Eng. settlement in Conn. and is the state's oldest town. Although primarily residential, the town has a variety of light industries; it was once renowned for its tobacco production and still grows some wrapper-shade-grown tobacco. Other industry includes the mfg. of iron prods., paper prods., computer components, tools, machinery, electronics; insurance. The Amer. statesman Oliver Ellsworth b. here; his home is a mus. Colonial bldgs. in Windsor include Fyler House (1640) and the Joseph Loomis House. **3** town (1990 pop. 1,895), Kennebec co., S Maine, just E of Augusta; 44°19′N 69°34′W. **4** town (1990 pop. 770), Berkshire co., W Mass., in the Berkshires, 11 mi/18 km ENE of Pittsfield; 42°31′N 73°02′W. State forest; Wahconah Falls State Park nearby. **5** town (1990 pop. 107), Hillsborough co., S N.H., 24 mi/39 km W of Concord; 43°06′N 72°01′W. Apples, vegetables; livestock; dairying. Black and White ponds in center. **6** town (1990 pop. 2,056), ⊙ Bertie co., NE N.C., 45 mi/72 km W of Rocky Mount, and on Cashie R. (head of navigation); 36°00′N 76°56′W. Fishing. Albermarle Sound 15 mi/24 km to E. Agr. area (peanuts, tobacco, cotton, grain, soybeans; chickens, hogs). Mfg. (furniture laminating, plywood, crabmeat processing, lumber, apparel). Settled 1721; inc. 1776. **7** town (1990 pop. 3,714), Windsor co., E Vt., on the Connecticut R., 12 mi/19 km S of Woodstock; 43°28′N 72°25′W. Mfg. (machinery, metal, and wood prods., lumber); agr. (dairy prods., maple sugar); winter sports (Ascutney Ski Resort). Town chartered 1761 by N.H., 1772 by N.Y.; settled 1764. State's constitutional convention (1777) and 1st legislature (1778) met here; Old Constitution House, now a mus., is memorial. Includes Windsor village. **8** town (1990 pop. 1,025), Isle of Wight co., SE Va., 11 mi/18 km NW of Suffolk; 36°48′N 76°44′W. Light mfg; agr. area (grain, soybeans, cotton, peanuts, melons; livestock).

Windsor 1 village (□ 1 sq mi/2.6 sq km; 1990 pop. 1,051), Broome co., S N.Y., on the Susquehanna R., 14 mi/23 km ESE of Binghamton; 42°04′N 75°38′W. In dairying area; summer resort. **2** village (1990 pop. 124), Aiken co., SW S.C., 12 mi/19 km ESE of Aiken; 33°28′N 81°31′W. Aiken State Park to N. Savannah R. Nuclear Site to SW.

Windsor, borough (1990 pop. 1,355), York co., S Pa., 9 mi/14.5 km ESE of York; 39°55′N 76°34′W. Mfg. (food prods., wood prods.). Agr. area (apples, soybeans, grain; livestock; dairying). Inc. 1905.

Windsor Dam, Mass.: see QUABBIN RESERVOIR.

Windsor Heights, town (1990 pop. 5,190), Polk co., central Iowa, residential suburb 5 mi/8 km WNW of Des Moines; 41°36′N 93°42′W.

Windsor Lake (□ 4 sq mi/10 sq km), SE N.F., E Canada, on NE Avalon Peninsula, 4 mi/6 km NW of St. John's; 3 mi/5 km long, 1 mi/2 km wide; 47°35′N 52°47′W. Near E shore is St. John's Airport.

Windsor Locks, town (1990 pop. 12,358), Hartford co., N Conn., on the Connecticut R.; 41°55′N 72°39′W. Once a tobacco-farming center (and still home to a specialty cigar–tobacco industry), it has aircraft, aerospace, and paper industries, as well as food processing, electronics, and machines. The town developed industrially after a canal, with locks, was built (1829) around the rapids here. Bradley Internatl. Airport is here, as are a number of mus. Settled 1663, set off from Windsor and inc. 1854.

Windsor Reservoir, Weld co., N Colo., on canalized side stream of Cache la Poudre R., 10 mi/16 km ESE of Fort Collins, 3 mi/4.8 km N of Windsor, 4 mi/6.4 km long; 40°29′N 104°52′W. Max. capacity of 20,404 acre-ft. Formed by Windsor Dam (43 ft/13 m high), built (1975) by the Windsor Reservoir and Canal Company for irrigation. Windsor L. reservoir is 3 mi/4.8 km S.

Windthorst, village (1990 pop. 367), Archer co., N Texas, 20 mi/32 km S of Witchita Falls; 33°34′N 98°26′W. Agr. area (wheat; cattle; dairying). L. Arrowhead reservoir to N.

Windward Passage, strait, bet. Cuba and Haiti, connecting the Atlantic Ocean and Caribbean Sea, c.50 mi/80 km wide; 20°00′N 74°00′W. It provides a direct route from the E U.S. to the Panama Canal. Known as the Paso de los Vientos.

Windy Hill Beach, uninc. village, Horry co., E S.C., 10 mi/16 km NE of Myrtle Beach on Atlantic Ocean, resort on Grand Strand beach.

Windy Lake, trading post, S Keewatin dist., N.W.T., N Canada, W of Nueltin L.; 60°35′N 99°50′W.

Wine Islands, N Ohio; name sometimes given to isls. in L. Erie N and NW of Sandusky; best known are Bass Isls. and Kelleys Isl.

Wine Spring Bald, N.C.: see NANTAHALA MOUNTAINS.

Winesburg, village, Holmes co., central Ohio, 7 mi/11 km NE of Millersburg. In agr. area.

Winfall, village (1990 pop. 501), Perquimans co., NE N.C., 2 mi/3.2 km N of Hertford on Perquimans R.; 36°12′N 76°27′W. Peanuts, cotton, grain, potatoes; chickens, livestock. Mfg. (fertilizers).

Winfield, village, S central Alta., W Canada, 50 mi/80 km SW of Edmonton; 52°58′N 114°26′W. Farming; dairying.

Winfield, city (1990 pop. 11,931), ⊙ Cowley co., S central Kansas, on the Walnut R., 34 mi/55 km SSE of Wichita; 37°16′N 96°58′W. Elev. 1,150 ft/351 m. RR junction. The economy is based on agr. and oil and gas wells. Mfg. (plastics prods., concrete, machinery, metal prods., heating equip.). Southwestern Col. is here. Inc. 1873.

Winfield 1 town (1990 pop. 672), Lincoln co., E Mo., near Mississippi R., 13 mi/21 km E of Troy; 39°00′N 90°44′W. Mfg. (apparel, furniture). Lock and Dam No. 25 (Winfield Dam). **2** town (1990 pop. 3,689), Marion co., NW Ala., 18 mi/29 km SE of Hamilton. Cotton milling; lumber. Coal mines in vicinity. **3** town, Lake co., NW Ind., 3 mi/4.8 km E of Crown Point. **4** town

(1990 pop. 1,051), Henry co., SE Iowa, 12 mi/19 km NNW of Mt. Pleasant; 41°07′N 91°26′W. Mfg. **5** town (1990 pop. 1,164), ⊙ Putnam co., W central W.Va., on the Kanawha R., 19 mi/31 km NW of Charleston; 38°31′N 81°52′W. Agr. (corn, tobacco); livestock, poultry. Coal-mining area. Mfg. (concrete, light mfg.).

Winfield 1 village (1990 pop. 7,096), Du Page co., NE Ill., just W of Wheaton, suburb 30 mi/48 km W of Chicago; 41°52′N 88°09′W. Agr. (corn, soybeans; dairying); mfg. **2** uninc. village, Union co., central Pa., 4 mi/6.4 km SSE of Lewisburg on West Branch of Susquehanna R.; 40°54′N 76°51′W. Mfg. of feeds, food, textiles; agr. includes dairying; livestock; corn. **3** village (1990 pop. 345), Titus co., NE Texas, 8 mi/12.9 km W of Mt. Pleasant; 33°10′N 95°06′W. Watermelons; poultry; dairying. Lakes Monticello and Bob Sandlin (State Park) to S.

Winfred, village (1990 pop. 54), Lake co., E S.Dak., 12 mi/19 km W of Madison; 44°00′N 97°21′W.

Wing, village (1990 pop. 208), Burleigh co., central N.Dak., 33 mi/53 km NE of Bismarck; 47°08′N 100°16′W.

Wingate 1 town (1990 pop. 275), Montgomery co., W Ind., 13 mi/21 km NW of Crawfordsville; 40°10′N 87°04′W. In agr. area. **2** town (1990 pop. 2,821), Union co., S N.C., 5 mi/8 km E of Monroe; 34°58′N 80°27′W. Cotton, grain; livestock; dairying; mfg. (wood prods., consumer goods). Seat of Wingate Col.

Wingate, fishing village, Dorchester co, E Md., 19 mi/31 km S of Cambridge, on Honga R.

Wingdale, village (1990 pop. 650), in town of Dover, Dutchess co., SE N.Y., near Conn. state line, 20 mi/32 km ESE of Poughkeepsie; 41°39′N 73°34′W. Magnesium plant. Seat of N.Y. State Harlem Valley Psychiatric Center and Harlem Valley Secure Center (youth community facility).

Winger, village (1990 pop. 167), Polk co., NW Minn., 33 mi/53 km SE of Crookston, near Sand Hill R.; 47°32′N 95°59′W. Agr. (grain, sunflowers, potatoes; poultry; dairying). White Earth Indian Reservation to S.

Wingham, town (1991 pop. 3,018), S Ont., central Canada, on Maitland R., 22 mi/35 km ENE of Goderich; 43°53′N 81°18′W. Mfg. (woodworking, milling).

Wingo, village (1990 pop. 568), Graves co., W Ky., 9 mi/14.5 km SW of Mayfield; 36°38′N 88°44′W. Clay-mining and agr. area (tobacco, grain; livestock; dairying); mfg. (apparel) .

Winhall, town (1990 pop. 482), Bennington co., SW Vt., on small Winhall R., 24 mi/39 km WSW of Springfield, in Green Mts.; 43°10′N 72°55′W. Strattom Mt. ski area. Includes Bondville village.

Winifred (WI-nuh-fruhd), village (1990 pop. 150), Fergus co., central Mont., on Dog Creek (intermittent), 35 mi/56 km N of Lewistown; 47°34′N 109°23′W. McClelland Ferry, 10 mi/16 km N crosses Missouri R. Cattle; grain; natural gas. Charles M. Russell Natl. Wildlife Refuge to E; Upper Missouri Natl. Wild and Scenic R. to N.

Winisk River (WI-nisk), 300 mi/483 km long, N Ont., central Canada; issues from Winisk L., in Patricia dist.; flows N and NE to Hudson Bay at Weenusk.

Wink, town (1990 pop. 1,189), Winkler co., W Texas, 30 mi/48 km NE of Pecos; 31°45′N 103°09′W. Supply center for oil, natural-gas fields; salt; cattle, horses. Inc. 1928.

Winkelman, village (1990 pop. 676), Gila co., SE central Ariz., 52 mi/84 km NNE of Tucson on Gila R., at mouth of San Pedro R.; 32°59′N 110°46′W. Elev. 1,972 ft/601 m. Trade center for copper. Limestone and gypsum mining and agr. area (cattle, sheep). San Carlos Indian Reservation to E.

Winkler, county (□ 841 sq mi/2,178 sq km; 1990 pop. 8,626), W Texas; ⊙ Kermit; 31°51′N 103°02′W. High plains, bounded N by N.Mex. state line (NW sect. of co. indented by SE corner of N.Mex.). Elev. c.2,700 ft/823 m–3,000 ft/914 m. W-facing Caprock escarpment is in E. Oil, natural-gas fields, large-scale cattle ranching, horses. Formed 1887.

Winkler, town (1991 pop. 6,397), S Man., central Canada, 60 mi/97 km SW of Winnipeg; 49°11′N 97°56′W. Grain; mixed farming.

Winlaw, village, S B.C., W Canada, on Slocan R., 16 mi/26 km NW of Nelson, in lumbering and mining (gold, silver, tungsten) region.

Winlock, town (1990 pop. 1,027), Lewis co., SW Wash., 12 mi/19 km S of Chehalis, on Olequa Creek; 46°29′N 122°57′W. Vegetables; poultry; mfg. (bldg. materials, sawmill, veneer); timber. Toledo Winlock Airport to E. Lewis and Clark State Park to E.

Winn, parish (□ 950 sq mi/2,461 sq km; 1990 pop. 16,269), N central La.; ⊙ Winnfield; 31°55′N 92°39′W. Bounded W by Saline R., SE by Castor Creek; intersected by Dugdemona R. Agr. (blueberries, hay, vegetables; cattle, poultry). Logging, gypsum quarrying. Some mfg. (millwork, chemicals, lumber). Earl K. and Huey P. Long born in Winnfield. Includes part of Kisatchie Natl. Forest in W and S; part of Catahoula Natl. Preserve in S; Saline L., part of NW La. State Wildlife Area, on W border. Formed 1852.

Winn, town (1990 pop. 479), Penobscot co., E central Maine, on the Penobscot, 50 mi/80 km NNE of Bangor; 45°27′N 68°20′W. Hunting, fishing area.

Winnapaug Pond (WIN-na-pawg), SW R.I., salt pond c.2.5 mi/4 km long, separated from Block Isl. Sound by sandbar, with inlet just W of Weekapaug.

Winnebago 1 county (□ 519 sq mi/1,344 sq km; 1990 pop. 252,913), N Ill., bordered by Wis. (N); ⊙ Rockford; 42°19′N 89°09′W. Drained by Rock, Pecatonica, and Kishwaukee rivers. Agr. (dairying, corn, oats, soybeans; cattle, hogs, sheep); mfg. Site of Rock Cut State Park. Formed 1836. **2** county (□ 401 sq mi/1,039 sq km; 1990 pop. 12,122), N Iowa, on Minn. state line; ⊙ Forest City; 43°22′N 93°43′W. Prairie agr. area (hogs, poultry; corn, oats) drained by Lime Creek; sand and gravel pits. L. Harmon in N; Rice L. and Rice L. State Park on E co. line; Pilot Knob State Park on S co. line. Formed 1851. **3** county (□ 578 sq mi/1,497 sq km; 1990 pop. 140,320), E central Wis.; ⊙ Oshkosh; 44°03′N 88°38′W. Bounded E by L. Winnebago; drained by Wolf and Fox rivers. Primarily a dairying and farming area (barley, oats, wheat, corn, soybeans, peas; hogs, sheep, poultry) with extensive mfg. (esp. paper and other wood prods.) at Oshkosh, Menasha, and Neenah. Contains Poygan, Wenneconne, and Butte des Morts lakes (on Wolf R.) and Rush L., in SW. Formed 1840.

Winnebago 1 village (1990 pop. 1,840), Winnebago co., N Ill., 8 mi/12.9 km W of Rockford; 42°16′N 89°14′W. In agr. area. **2** village (1990 pop. 1,565), Faribault co., S Minn., 10 mi/16 km N of Blue Earth, near Blue Earth R. and its confluence with Elm Creek, from W; 43°46′N 94°10′W. Agr. (grain, soybeans; livestock); mfg. (concrete, fertilizer, bldg. materials). Rice L. to NE. Settled before 1865. **3** village (1990 pop. 705), Thurston co., NE Nebr., 19 mi/31 km S of Sioux City, Iowa, near Missouri R.; 42°14′N 96°28′W. Located in E part of Winnebago Indian Reservation. Winnebago tribal agency here; tribal powwow held in late July. Tribal pop. on reservation c.1,100. Omaha Indian Reservation to S.

Winnebago, Lake (□ 215 sq mi/557 sq km), E Wis.; largest lake in state. Fed and drained by the Fox R., the lake is part of an all-water route bet. the Great Lakes and the Mississippi R. Cities on lake are Fond du Lac (S end), Oshkosh (on W side at entrance of Wolf R.), Neenah and Menasha (N end, at exit of Fox R.). Major recreation area.

Winneconne, town (1990 pop. 2,059), Winnebago co., E central Wis., on Wolf R. at its exit from L. Winneconne, 10 mi/16 km NW of Oshkosh; 44°06′N 88°42′W. Dairying; mfg. (farm machinery).

Winneconne, Lake, Wis.: see POYGAN, LAKE.

Winnecook, Maine: see BURNHAM.

Winnemucca (win-uh-MUH-kuh), town (1990 pop. 6,134), ⊙ Humboldt co., N Nev., on Humboldt R., 5 mi/8 km SW of mouth of Little Humboldt R., at N end of Sonoma Range, 150 mi/241 km NE of Reno; 40°58′N 117°43′W. Elev. 4,320 ft/1,317 m. Trade center and livestock-shipping point; cattle, sheep; potatoes, hay; mfg. (food processing, printing and publishing, electrical equip.). Gold, silver, copper, tungsten mines nearby. Humboldt Mus., Buckaroo Hall of Fame here. Advertises itself as "city of paved streets." Chimney Dam Reservoir to NE; part of Humboldt Natl. Forest, in Santa Rosa Range, to N; Rye Patch Reservoir on Humboldt R., to SW. Settled 1850 as trading post (French Ford), renamed 1868, inc. 1917.

Winnemucca Lake (win-uh-MUH-kuh), W Nev., on line bet. Washoe and Pershing cos., E of Pyramid L. and Lake Range; c.25 mi/40 km long, 5 mi/8 km wide. Intermittent lake. Includes E edge of Pyramid L. Indian Reservation.

Winner, town (1990 pop. 3,354), ⊙ Tripp co., S S.Dak., 70 mi/113 km SSE of Pierre; near Dog Ear Creek; 43°22′N 99°51′W. Trading center for farming and cattle-raising region, shipping point for turkeys and other poultry prods.; grain, dairy prods.; honey. Founded after 1908.

Winneshiek, county (□ 689 sq mi/1,785 sq km; 1990 pop. 20,487), NE Iowa, on Minn. state line; ⊙ Decorah; 43°17′N 91°50′W. Prairie agr. area (hogs, cattle, poultry; corn, oats, hay; dairying) drained by Upper Iowa and Turkey rivers; many limestone quarries. World's Smallest Church at Festina in S; Fort Atkinson State Preserve in SW; Nor Ski Runs Ski Area NW of Decorah. Formed 1847.

Winnetka, village (1990 pop. 12,174), Cook co., NE Ill., residential suburb N of Chicago, on L. Michigan; 42°06′N 87°44′W. It is renowned for its public school system, various educational institutions, and its maverick teaching methods under the Winnetka Plan. Inc. 1869.

Winnetoon, village (1990 pop. 59), Knox co., NE Nebr., 4 mi/6.4 km NW of Creighton; 42°30′N 97°57′W.

Winnett (WI-nuht), town (1990 pop. 188), ⊙ Petroleum co., central Mont., on McDonald Creek, 50 mi/80 km E of Lewistown; 47°00′N 108°21′W. Oil wells to E; wheat, barley, hay; sheep, cattle. Petrolia L. on Flatwillow Creek, at confluence of Elk Creek, to SE. Units of War Horse Natl. Wildlife Refuge to NW and SW.

Winnfield, city (1990 pop. 6,138), ⊙ Winn parish, N central La., c.45 mi/72 km NNW of Alexandria, near Dugdemona R.; 31°55′N 92°39′W. RR junction. In pine woods region; gypsum mining, lumbering; mfg. (lumber, concrete prods., resins, crushed gypsum, printing and publishing). In agr. area (blueberries, vegetables; cattle, poultry). Birthplace of Earl K. and Huey P. Long, 2 mi/3 km E. Separate units of Kisatchie Natl. Forest to W and SE; Catahoula Natl. Preserve to SE. Inc. 1855.

Winnibigoshish, Lake (wi-ni-bi-GO-shish), reservoir (□ 179 sq mi/464 sq km), on line bet. Itasca and Cass cos., N central Minn., on Mississippi R., in Chippewa Natl. Forest and Leech L. Indian Reservation, 30 mi/48 km E of Bemidji, and 30 mi/48 km NW of Grand Rapids; 47°26′N 94°03′W. Elev. 1,300 ft/396 m. Natural lake with water level raised by Winnibigoshish Dam (23 ft/7 m high), built (1884) by Army Corps of Engineers for flood control; also used for water supply and recreation. River enters lake from W (from Cass L. 10 mi/16 km to W), exits from E end, flowing SE; Waboose Bay, N end of Leech L., 3 mi/4.8 km to SW. Also fed from N by Third R. Many state parks.

Winnie, town (1990 pop. 2,238), Chambers co., SE Texas, 26 mi/42 km SW of Beaumont; 29°49′N 94°22′W. McFadden Natl. Wildlife Refuge to SE; Anahuac Natl. Wildlife Refuge to SW. Agr. (rice, soybeans; cattle). Mfg. (fertilizer).

Winnipeg (WIN-i-pehg), city (1991 pop. 616,790), ⊙ Man., SE Man., central Canada, at the confluence of the Red and Assiniboine rivers; 49°53′N 97°10′W. It is the prov.'s largest city and one of the world's largest wheat markets. A RR, commercial, industrial, and distribution center, it has an intl. airport, RR shops, grain elevators, stockyards, meatpacking and motor vehicle plants, flour and textile mills, and breweries. The city's history reflects the history of early Fr. and Br. explorers and fur traders. In 1738, the sieur de la Vérendrye built the 1st post on the site, Fort Rouge, but it was later abandoned. Other posts were built in the Red R. region, which was fiercely contested by the North West Company and the Hudson's Bay Company. The conflict reached its height in the struggle over the Red River Settlement. The 2 companies were merged in 1821. Fort Gibraltar, a post of the North West Company on the site of present-day Winnipeg, was renamed Fort Garry and became the leading post in the region. In 1835 its name was changed to Winnipeg. Settlement was spurred by the construction of a RR line in 1881. Much of the city had to be rebuilt after the Red R. flood (1950). Throughout the 1970s and 1980s many new developments (a new city hall, hotels, a convention center, office bldgs.) have been constructed. In the city are the Royal Winnipeg Ballet, the Man. Theater Group, and a symphony orchestra. An annual festival, the Folklorama, is dedicated to celebrating the city's increasingly cosmopolitan character. The Univ. of Man. and the Univ. of Winnipeg are also here.

Winnipeg, river, c.200 mi/320 km long, Man., central Canada; issuing from the N end of L. of the Woods, SW Ont., and flowing in a winding course generally NW to the SE end of L. Winnipeg, SE Man. There are 6 hydroelectric stations on its course, supplying most of S Man. with electricity; the largest station is at Seven Sisters Falls. The river was 1st traveled by the sons of Can. explorer Vérendrye and was much used by explorers and fur traders.

Winnipeg Beach, town (1991 pop. 641), SE Man., central Canada, on L. Winnipeg, 45 mi/72 km N of Winnipeg. Resort.

Winnipeg, Lake (□ 9,465 sq mi/24,514 sq km), S central Man., central Canada, N of Winnipeg, 264 mi/425 km long and 25 mi/40 km–68 mi/109 km wide. The 3rd-largest lake in the country, it is a remnant of the glacial L. Agassiz. It receives the Red, Winnipeg, and Saskatchewan rivers and many lesser streams and is drained NE by the Nelson R. to Hudson Bay. It is surrounded by valuable timberland; there are several summer resorts on its shores. The lake has extensive fishing resources. It was explored (1733) by the Vérendrye expedition and was an important route of early explorers and fur traders.

Winnipegosis (win-ni-pehg-O-sis), village (1991 pop. 771), W Man., central Canada, on L. Winnipegosis, at mouth of Mossy R., 35 mi/56 km NNE of Dauphin; 51°39′N 99°55′W, Pike-fishing center; lumber and flour milling.

Winnipegosis, Lake (win-i-pehg-O-sis) (□ 2,086 sq mi/5,403 sq km), W Man., central Canada, 125 mi/201 km long and 25 mi/40 km wide. Remnant of glacial L. Agassiz. It drains SE into L. Manitoba and then into L. Winnipeg. Important pike fisheries.

Winnipesaukee, Lake (WI-ni-puh-SAW-kee) (□ 78 sq mi/202 sq km), on line bet. Carroll and Belknap cos., E central N.H. Largest lake in the state. Irregular in shape, with many arms of significance, Moultonborough Bay (NE), 10 mi/16 km long; Paugus Bay and Opeche Bay (SW), and Alton Bay (SE). It has 283 mi/455 km of shoreline and many small isls. Winnipesaukee R., central N.H., exits from Opeche Bay of L. Winnipesaukee at Laconia, Belknap co., flows 1 mi/1.6 km SW into Winnisquam L., continues SW through Tilton L. and Silver L., past Tilton, joins Pemigewasset R. at Franklin to form Merrimack R. (15 mi/24 km long). Resort area.

Winnisquam Lake (WI-nis-kwawm), Belknap co., central N.H., with city of Laconia on E shore, 7.5 mi/12.1 km long. Resort area. Winnipesaukee R. drains into SE side of lake from Opeche Bay of L. Winnipesaukee, at Laconia, exits lake in SW to Tilton L. Winnisquam village is on S shore.

Winnsboro 1 (WINZ-buh-ruh), town (1990 pop. 5,755), ⊙ Franklin parish, NE La., 33 mi/53 km SE of Monroe, on small Turkey Creek; 32°10′N 91°43′W. Trade center for rich agr. region (cotton, hay, rice, sorghum, corn, sweet potatoes; cattle); mfg. (dairy equip., fishing boats), printing, soft drink bottling. Founded c.1844, inc. 1902. **2** town (1990 pop. 3,475) ⊙ Fairfield co., N central S.C., 26 mi/42 km N of Columbia; 34°22′N 81°05′W. Mfg. includes clothing, motor vehicles, automotive trim, crushed stone, granite, plywood. Agr.

includes cattle; corn, hay, timber. State parks and reservoirs surround the area. Settled mid-18th cent., inc. 1785. **3** town (1990 pop. 2,904), Wood and Franklin cos., NE Texas, c.50 mi/80 km ESE of Greenville; 32°57′N 95°17′W. In cattle, dairying (butter and powdered milk) area. Timber; vegetables. Mfg. (electronic equip., wooden and metal prods.). Oil wells nearby. L. Winnsboro reservoir to SW; L. Cypress Springs reservoir to NE. Est. 1854.

Winnsboro Mills, uninc. town (1990 pop. 2,275), Fairchild co., N central S.C., residential suburb 2 mi/3.2 km SSE of Winnsboro; 34°21′N 81°04′W.

Winona (win-O-nuh), village, S Ont., central Canada, on L. Ontario, 11 mi/18 km ESE of Hamilton; 43°13′N 79°36′W. Fruit; winery, fruit canning. Suburban community in Hamilton-Wentworth Regional Municipality.

Winona (wi-NO-nuh), county (□ 641 sq mi/1,660 sq km; 1990 pop. 47,828), SE Minn.; ⊙ Winona; 43°58′N 91°46′W. Agr. area (hay, soybeans, corn, oats, barley, alfalfa; sheep, hogs, cattle, poultry; dairying); food processing and mfg. at Winona. Bounded E and NE by Mississippi R. (forms Wis. state line). Upper Mississippi R. Natl Wildlife Refuge along river in NE; parts of Richard J. Dorer Memorial Hardwood State Forest throughout co.; John A. Latsch State Park in N; O. L. Kipp State Park in E; parts of Whitewater State Park and Whitewater Wildlife Area in NW. Locks and dams Nos. 5, 5A, 6, and 7 on Mississippi R. (successively, heading downstream). Formed 1854.

Winona 1 (wi-NO-nuh), city (1990 pop. 25,399), ⊙ Winona co., SE Minn., 38 mi/61 km E of Rochester on the Mississippi R. (Lock and Dam No. 5A is here; No. 6 to E); 44°02′N 91°39′W. RR junction and center. Mfg. (food processing, construction equip., fabricated metal prods., candy, soft drinks, bldg. materials, printing and publishing, textiles, spices and extracts, apparel, light fixtures). Winona grew as river traffic increased, and the city developed as a mfg. and commercial center. Highway bridge and RR bridges cross river. St. Mary's Col., St. Teresa Col., and Winona State Univ. are here. Historical mus. here. Upper Mississippi R. Natl. Wildlife Refuge on river margins (hq. is here); Richard J. Dorer Memorial Hardwood State Forest to W, S, and E; L. Winona, on Gilmore Creek, S of downtown. Max Conrad Field Airport to NE. The sculptor James Earle Fraser was b. here. Inc. 1857. **2** (wei-NO-nuh), city (1990 pop. 1,081), Shannon co., S Mo., in the Ozarks, 35 mi/56 km NE of West Plains; 37°00′N 91°19′W. Fruit; livestock; lumber; mfg. (headware; wood prods.); recreation. Surrounded by Mark Twain Natl. Forest.

Winona (wuh-NO-nuh), town (1990 pop. 5,705), ⊙ Montgomery co., central Miss., 26 mi/42 km E of Greenwood; 33°29′N 89°43′W. RR junction. In agr. (cotton, corn, soybeans; cattle) area; timber region; mfg. (steel fabrication, apparel, lumber prods., motor vehicle parts, furniture, plastics).

Winona 1 (win-O-nuh), uninc. village, Coconino co., N central Ariz., 13 mi/21 km E of Flagstaff, in Coconino Natl. Forest. Archaeological excavations have been made at Indian ruins in area. Walnut Canyon Natl. Monument to SW. **2** village (1990 pop. 194), Logan co., W Kansas, 22 mi/35 km WSW of Oakley; 39°03′N 101°14′W. In grain and cattle region. **3** village (1990 pop. 457), Smith co., E Texas, 12 mi/19 km NE of Tyler, near the Sabine; 32°29′N 95°10′W. In agr. area; natural-gas processing. Oil and gas. Tyler State Park to W. **4** uninc. village (1990 pop. 200), Fayette co., S central W.Va., near New R., 6 mi/9.7 km E of Fayetteville. In agr. and coal-mining area. Babcock State Park to S; New R. Gorge Natl. R. to SW.

Winona Lake, town (1990 pop. 4,053), Kosciusko co., N Ind., on Winona L. (c.1 mi/1.6 km long), just SE of Warsaw; 41°13′N 85°49′W. Mfg. (medical equip., publishing). Seat of Grace Theological Seminary.

Winona, Lake (win-O-nuh), Saline co., central Ark., on Alum Fork Creek, 33 mi/53 km W of Little Rock, in Ouachita Natl. Forest; c.4 mi/6.4 km long; 34°47′N 92°51′W. Max. capacity of 63,264 acre-ft. Formed by L.

Winona Dam (98 ft/30 m high), built by Little Rock to supply water to the city.

Winooski, city (1990 pop. 6,649), Chittenden co., NW Vt., on Winooski R., just E of Burlington; 44°30′N 73°11′W. Wood and paper prods., furniture, weighing instruments, tools. St. Michael's Col. here. Native Amer. name means "land of onions." Mills built here just after Amer. Revolution. City set off from Colchester and inc. 1922.

Winooski, river, 90 mi/145 km long, Vt.; rising in NE of the state; flowing SW, then NW, passing Montpelier and Waterbury and entering L. Champlain near Burlington and Winooski. There are flood control and hydroelectric power projects on the river.

Winside, village (1990 pop. 434), Wayne co., NE Nebr., 8 mi/12.9 km WSW of Wayne, on branch of Logan Creek; 42°10′N 97°10′W. Grain; dehydrated alfalfa.

Winslow 1 town (1990 pop. 8,190), Navajo co., E central Ariz., 53 mi/85 km from Flagstaff, near Little Colorado R. Elev. 4,850 ft/1,478 m. Agr. (cattle, sheep; corn, alfalfa; timber); mfg. (lumber, apparel). Navajo and Hopi Indian reservations to N; Painted Desert to N; Apache-Sitgreaves Natl. Forest to S; Homolovi Ruins State Park to NE; Meteor Crater to W. **2** town (1990 pop. 875), Pike co., SW Ind., on Patoka R., 8 mi/12.9 km SSE of Petersburg; 38°23′N 87°13′W. In agr. area; mfg. (treated RR ties); bituminous-coal mines; clay pits; timber. Surface-mined land. Pike State Forest nearby to E. Laid out 1837. **3** town (1990 pop. 7,997), Kennebec co., S Maine, on the Kennebec R. opposite Waterville, at influx of the Sebasticook, 17 mi/27 km NNE of Augusta; 44°31′N 69°34′W. Paper, pulp mills; dairy, agr. area. Site of former Fort Halifax (1754). Town inc. 1771. Includes Winslow village.

Winslow 1 village (1990 pop. 342), Washington co., NW Ark., 18 mi/29 km S of Fayetteville, in the Ozarks; 35°47′N 94°07′W. Mfg. (canned vegetables and fruits). Separate units of Ozark Natl. Forest to E and SW; Devil's Den State Park (recreational area) is SW. **2** village (1990 pop. 317), Stephenson co., N Ill., on Pecatonica R. (bridged here), near Wis. state line, 16 mi/26 km NNW of Freeport; 42°29′N 89°47′W. In agr. area (corn, barley, oats, cattle, hogs; dairying); mfg. (stereo equip.). L. Le-Aqua-Na State Park to SW. **3** village (1990 pop. 140), Dodge co., E Nebr., 12 mi/19 km N of Fremont, on Elkhorn R.; 41°36′N 96°30′W. RR junction.

Winslow (WINZ-lo), township (1990 pop. 30,087), Camden co., S N.J., 18 mi/29 km SE of Camden; 39°42′N 74°54′W. Inc. 1845.

Winsted, city (1990 pop. 8,254) in Winchester town, ⊙ Litchfield co., NW Conn., on Still R., 8 mi/12.9 km N of Torrington; 41°55′N 73°04′W. Mfg. (consumer goods, apparel, cutlery, fishing tackle, electrical equip., tools, thread, wood and paper prods.); agr. (vegetables; dairy prods.; poultry). Major flood damage in 1955. Resorts on Highland L. Clockmaking here since 1807. Inc. 1917.

Winsted, town (1990 pop. 1,581), McLeod co., S central Minn., 40 mi/64 km W of Minneapolis, on W side of Winsted L.; 44°58′N 94°02′W. Agr. (grain, soybeans; livestock; dairying); mfg. (lumber, dairy processing equip., fabricated stainless steel). Several small lakes in area.

Winston 1 county (□ 631 sq mi/1,634 sq km; 1990 pop. 22,053), NW Ala.; ⊙ Double Springs. Drained by branches of Sipsey Fork. Corn, hay, melons; poultry; lumber milling. William. B. Bankhead Natl. Forest throughout. Formed 1850. **2** county (□ 610 sq mi/1,580 sq km; 1990 pop. 19,433), E central Miss.; ⊙ Louisville; 33°05′N 89°02′W. Drained by Noxubee R. and Lobutcha Creek; source of Pearl R. Agr. (cotton, corn; poultry, cattle; dairying; timber). Legion State Park in center; part of Nanih Waiya Historic Site, sacred Choctaw mounds (c.100 B.C.), in SE; part of Tombigbee Natl. Forest in N; part of Noxubee Natl. Wildlife Refuge in NE. Formed 1833.

Winston 1 town (□ 5 sq mi/13 sq km; 1990 pop. 9,118), Polk co., central Fla., 5 mi/8 km W of Lakeland; 28°02′N 82°00′W. **2** town, Douglas co., NW central

Ga., 26 mi/42 km W of Atlanta; 33°43′N 84°49′W. Mfg. of furniture. **3** town (1990 pop. 251), Daviess co., NW Mo., 9 mi/14.5 km WSW of Gallatin; 39°52′N 94°08′W. **4** town (1990 pop. 3,773), Douglas co., SW Oregon, 5 mi/8 km SSW of Roseburg, on South Umpqua R., at mouth of Looking-glass Creek; 43°07′N 123°24′W. Plums, apples, pears, peaches; sheep, cattle; timber. Mfg. (millwork). Wild animal park nearby.

Winston, village (1990 pop. 50), Broadwater co., W central Mont., near Beaver Creek, 21 mi/34 km ESE of Helena. In mining and agr. region, silver, lead, gold, uranium, thorium. Canyon Ferry L. reservoir and State Park to E (Missouri R.); Elkhorn Mts. and part of Helena Natl. Forest to SW.

Winston Park, village, Kenton co., N Ky., near Licking R., residential suburb 5 mi/8 km S of Cincinnati (Ohio), 3 mi/4.8 km S of Covington.

Winston-Salem, city (1990 pop. 143,485), ⊙ Forsyth co., central N.C., 25 mi/40 km W of Greensboro; 36°06′N 80°15′W. Yadkin R. to W; in the Piedmont region. The 3d largest city in N.C. in 1990. One of N.C.'s foremost industrial centers, Winston-Salem is a major tobacco manufacturer. Large amounts of tobacco are stored and auctioned in numerous warehouses here. Mfg. (electrical equip., printing and publishing, concrete, bldg. materials, aluminum prods., lumber, food and beverages, steel fabricating, machining, furniture, corn milling, automotive equip., textiles and apparel, asphalt, paper prods., crushed stone). The village of Bethabara, the 1st Moravian settlement in N.C., was est. nearby in 1753. In 1766 the Moravians built their central town, Salem, a few miles away, and most of the industries and residents of Bethabara moved here. Winston was est. in 1849 as the co. seat. The 2 communities were united in 1913. Moravian culture has been sustained in the city through long-range efforts to restore the 18th-cent. village of Old Salem (some 40 bldgs. erected bet. 1767 and 1811 are extant). Historic Bethabara Park in NW, also Old Salem S of downtown. Winston-Salem is the seat of Wake Forest Univ. (including Mus. of Anthropology), Winston-Salem State Univ., Salem Col., N.C. School of the Arts, Forsyth Tech. Community Col., a Bible col., and Salem Acad. (est. 1772). Site of Hanes Mall, one of the largest shopping centers in U.S. Belews L. reservoir to NE. Tanglewood Park to SW. Mus. of Early Southern Decorative Arts. Dixie Classic Fairgrounds. Piedmont Craftsmen, Inc., crafters outlet. Inc. 1913.

Winstonville, village (1990 pop. 277), Bolivar co., NW Miss., 22 mi/35 km SSW of Clarksdale; 33°54′N 90°45′W. Agr. (cotton, corn, soybeans; cattle).

Winter, village (1990 pop. 383), Sawyer co., N Wis., 43 mi/69 km E of Spooner; 45°49′N 91°00′W. L. Chippewa to NW. Chequamegon Natl. Forest to N, Flambeau R. State Forest to E; on Tuscobia State Tribal Forested area.

Winter Garden, irrigated year-round agr. region, SW Texas, SW of San Antonio, extending E from valley of the Rio Grande. Includes parts of Maverick, Zavala, Frio, La Salle, Dimmit cos.; principal shipping, processing centers are Eagle Pass, Crystal City. Irrigation from the Rio Grande and artesian wells. Known for winter vegetables (esp. spinach), citrus, melons, corn, peanuts.

Winter Garden, town (☐ 4 sq mi/10.4 sq km; 1990 pop. 9,745), Orange co., central Fla., 12 mi/19 km W of Orlando, on L. Apopka; 28°33′N 81°34′W. Packing and shipping center (citrus fruit, vegetables).

Winter Harbor, resort town (1990 pop. 1,157), Hancock co., S Maine, on peninsula at entrance to Frenchman Bay, opposite Mt. Desert Isl., 20 mi/32 km SE of Ellsworth; 44°20′N 68°04′W.

Winter Harbour, small inlet of Viscount Melville Sound, SE Melville Isl., W Franklin dist., N.W.T., N Canada; 74°46′N 110°45′W.

Winter Haven, city (☐ 19 sq mi/49 sq km; 1990 pop. 24,725), Polk co., central Fla.; 28°02′N 81°43′W. It is a marketing, processing, and shipping center for one of the state's chief citrus-fruit regions, with fruit-canning

plants and packing houses. Tourism is also economically important. Settled 1883.

Winter Park, city (☐ 8 sq mi/20.7 sq km; 1990 pop. 22,242), Orange co., central Fla., 5 mi/8 km NE of Orlando in a heavily suburbanized area; 28°36′N 81°20′W. It is the seat of Rollins Col. Within the city are 12 lakes, some of which are connected by navigable canals. The city is known for its large oak trees and parks, and a sinkhole that is a popular tourist attraction. Settled in the 1850s, inc. 1887.

Winter Park, village (1990 pop. 528), Grand co., N Colo., 28 mi/45 km WSW of Boulder, on Fraser R., N of Berthoud Pass and W of Rollins Pass; 39°53′N 105°46′W. Elev. 9,110 ft/2,777 m. Continental Divide to E and S; surrounded by Arapaho Natl. Forest. Popular ski resort; tourism.

Winter Springs, town (☐ 13 sq mi/34 sq km; 1990 pop. 22,151), Seminole co., central Fla., 12 mi/19 km N of Orlando; 28°40′N 81°16′W. Mfg. includes meat prods.

Winterhaven, uninc. village, Imperial co., S Calif., in Yuma Indian Reservation, on Colorado R., 1 mi/1.6 km N of Yuma (Ariz.). Picacho State Recreation Area to N.

Winterport, town (1990 pop. 3,175), Waldo co., S Maine, on the Penobscot, 16 mi/26 km NNE of Belfast; 44°40′N 68°54′W. Wood prods. Inc. 1860.

Winters, city (1990 pop. 4,639), Yolo co., central Calif., 25 mi/40 km W of Sacramento, on Puntah Creek; 38°32′N 121°59′W. Agr. (peaches, prunes, apricots, pears, melons, walnuts, almonds, wheat, rice); mfg. (food processing, motor vehicles). Berryessa Peak to NW (3,057 ft/932 m); L. Berryessa to W. Inc. 1898.

Winters, town (1990 pop. 2,905), Runnels co., W central Texas, 35 mi/56 km SSW of Abilene; 31°58′N 99°55′W. Elev. 1,860 ft/567 m. RR terminus; in agr. area (cotton, sorghum, wheat; cattle, sheep). Mfg. (feeds, storage tanks, machinery). Oil and gas. Settled 1880, inc. 1909.

Winterset, city (1990 pop. 4,196), ⊙ Madison co., S central Iowa, near Middle R., 28 mi/45 km SW of Des Moines; 41°20′N 94°01′W. Ships fruit, grain; livestock; produces hybrid seed corn, feed, concrete, metal prods.; limestone quarries nearby, tourism. Covered bridge; annual covered bridge festival. John Wayne b. here. Site of novel and film, *Bridges of Madison County*. State park is SW. The original Delicious apple tree was discovered near here in 1872. Founded 1846, inc. 1876.

Winterstown (WIN-tuhrs-toun), borough (1990 pop. 581), York co., S Pa., 10 mi/16 km SSE of York; 39°50′N 76°36′W. Agr. (apples, grain; livestock; dairying).

Wintersville, village (1990 pop. 4,102), Jefferson co., E Ohio, 3 mi/5 km W of Steubenville; 40°22′N 80°42′W. Land office here for 1st land sales in Northwest Territory. Inc. 1947.

Winterthur, historic site, New Castle co., N Del., 6 mi/9.7 km NW of Wilmington; 39°48′N 75°36′W. This du Pont estate is now a mus. housing the country's largest collection of 1640–1860 Amer.-made arts, furntiture, and collectibles.

Winterville, plantation (1990 pop. 217), Aroostook co., NE Maine, on St. Froid L., and 20 mi/32 km S of Fort Kent; 46°58′N 68°37′W. In hunting, fishing area.

Winterville 1 town (1990 pop. 876), Clarke co., NE central Ga., 6 mi/9.7 km E of Athens; 33°58′N 83°17′W. **2** town (1990 pop. 3,069), Pitt co., E N.C., 5 mi/8 km S of Greenville, on Swift Creek; 35°31′N 77°24′W. Agr. area (tobacco, cotton, peanuts, grain, sweet potatoes; chickens, cattle, hogs). Mfg. (steel fabricating, computer hardware, machining, food processing).

Winthrop 1 town (1990 pop. 742), Buchanan co., E Iowa, near Buffalo Creek, 8 mi/12.9 km E of Independence; 42°28′N 91°43′W. Dairy prods. **2** town (1990 pop. 5,968), Kennebec co., SW Maine, 10 mi/16 km W of Augusta; 44°19′N 69°57′W. In lake region of resorts and farms; textile mfg. Includes Winthrop village. Settled 1765, inc. 1771. **3** residential town (1990 pop. 18,127), Suffolk co., E Mass., on a peninsula extending into Boston Bay at Point Shirley; 42°23′N 70°58′W. Point Shirley used to overlook a channel called Shirley Gut, but it was filled in in 1932 to create a causeway to Deer Isl. Several houses of historical interest (17th–18th cent.)

remain, including Governor Winthrop's house. Settled 1635, set off from North Chelsea and inc. 1852. **4** town (1990 pop. 1,279), Sibley co., S Minn., 7 mi/11.3 km W of Gaylord; 44°32′N 94°21′W. Agr. trading point (grain; livestock; dairy prods.); mfg. (dairy prods., hardwood). Indian L. to NE; Sand L. to S. Settled 1881, inc. as village 1884, as city 1910.

Winthrop 1 village (1990 pop. 227), Little River co., extreme SW Ark., 14 mi/23 km S of DeQueen; 33°49′N 94°20′W. Charcoal. **2** village (1990 pop. 302), Okanogan co., N Wash., 25 mi/40 km WNW of Okanogan, on Methow R., at mouth of Chewach R.; 48°28′N 120°11′W. In recreational region; timber; mfg. (lumber). Winthrop Natl. Fish Hatchery here. North Cascades Natl. Park to NW; Pearrygin L. State Park to NE; Okanogan Natl. Forest to E, N, and W, including L. Chelan–Sawtooth Wilderness Area to W.

Winthrop Harbor, village (1990 pop. 6,240), Lake co., extreme NE Ill., at Wis. state line and L. Michigan, suburb 44 mi/71 km N of Chicago, 9 mi/14.5 km N of Waukegan, 8 mi/12.9 km S of Kenosha (Wis.); 42°28′N 87°49′W. Northernmost community on Ill. shore of L. Michigan. Ill. Beach State Park here.

Winton 1 uninc. town (1990 pop. 7,559), Merced co., central Calif., 12 mi/19 km NW of Merced, near Merced R.; 37°23′N 120°37′W. Dairying; poultry; sweet potatoes, beans, tomatoes, grain, almonds, melons. **2** town (1990 pop. 796), ⊙ Hertford co., NE N.C., 43 mi/69 km E of Roanoke Rapids, on Chowan R., 4 mi/6.4 km SSE of mouth of Meherin R.; 36°23′N 76°56′W. RR terminus to E. Timber; tobacco, cotton, peanuts, grain, potatoes, sweet potatoes; chickens, hogs. Mfg. (aluminum prods.). Richard J. Gatling b. here.

Winton 1 village (1990 pop. 169), St. Louis co., NE Minn., 4 mi/6.4 km NE of Ely, on W end of Fall L., in Superior Natl. Forest; 47°55′N 91°47′W. Light mfg. Boundary Waters Canoe Area to N and E; outfitting point for canoe trips. **2** uninc. village, Lackawanna co., NE Pa., suburb 7 mi/11.3 km NE of Scranton, on Lackawanna R.; 41°28′N 75°32′W. Part of Jessup borough. Settled 1849, inc. 1877. **3** village, Sweetwater co., SW Wyo., 12 mi/19 km NNE of Rock Springs. Elev. 6,945 ft/2,117 m. Coal mines.

Winyah Bay (WIN-yaw), estuary, Georgetown co., S.C., c.50 mi/80 km NE of Charleston, 14 mi/23 km long; receives Waccamaw, Great Pee Dee, and Black rivers (all navigable); traversed by Intracoastal Waterway. Georgetown is at head of bay. North Isl. (c.8 mi/12.9 km long) extends almost across its mouth; lighthouse at 33°13′N 79°11′W. South and Cat isls. combine (c.9 mi/14.5 km long) at S side of bay entrance.

Wiota, town (1990 pop. 160), Cass co., SW Iowa, 7 mi/11.3 km E of Atlantic; 41°23′N 94°53′W. In agr. area.

Wirt (WUHRT), county (☐ 234 sq mi/606 sq km; 1990 pop. 5,192), NW W.Va., ⊙ Elizabeth; 39°01′N 81°22′W. Drained by the Little Kanawha and Hughes rivers. Agr. (corn, tobacco, potatoes, alfalfa, hay, nursery crops); cattle, poultry; some dairying. Palestine State Fish Hatchery in center. Hughes R. Wildlife Management Area in NE. Formed 1848.

Wirt (WUHRT), village, Carter co., S Okla., 24 mi/39 km WNW of Ardmore. In oil-producing area.

Wiscasset (wis-KAS-uht), town (1990 pop. 3,339), ⊙ Lincoln co., S Maine, on Sheepscot R., 10 mi/16 km NE of Bath; 44°00′N 69°41′W. Resort and small port; flourishing place in sailing-ship days. Has colonial homes; courthouse (1824) still in use. Nuclear power plant nearby is scheduled to be closed in the future. Settled 1663, inc. 1802.

Wiscoal (WIS-kuhl), village, Knott co., E Ky., in Cumberland foothills, 7 mi/11.3 km E of Hazard, 1 mi/1.6 km N of Vicco. Bituminous coal.

Wisconsin, state (☐ 65,500 sq mi/169,645 sq km; 1995 est. pop. 5,122,871), N central U.S., admitted as the 30th state of the Union in 1848; ⊙ MADISON; 44°28′N 89°30′W. MILWAUKEE is the largest city (Madison is 2d); GREEN BAY, KENOSHA, and RACINE are other major cities. Water forms most of the state's borders; to the E lies L. Michigan and to far N, L. Superior; in the NE, Wis. borders the Upper Peninsula of Mich., and the

Menominee, Brule, and Montreal rivers. The St. Croix and the Mississippi rivers mark most of the W border with Minn. and all of the W border with Iowa, and the St. Louis R. forms part of Minn. border in extreme NW. Lat. 42°30′N separates Wis. from Ill. on S. The most notable physiographic feature of the state is its many lakes (over 8,500), esp. in the wooded N, ranging in size from LAKE WINNEBAGO (□ 215 sq mi/557 sq km) to relatively tiny glacial lakes. The Wisconsin R., with its extensive dam system, runs generally S through the middle of the state until it turns W (just NW of Madison) to flow into the Mississippi R. To the E the Menominee, the Peshtigo, the Wolf, and the Fox rivers flow E and NE into L. Michigan, while to the NW the Chippewa, the Flambeau, and the Black rivers make their way to the Mississippi. The rough isolation of the N country is cut by part of the Penotee range, from which considerable iron ore was extracted before 1965. Iron mining was resumed briefly in 1969, but has since stopped altogether; large deposits remain. Sand and gravel, stone, and lime are other valuable mineral resources; zinc mines (as well as lead) are found in the DRIFTLESS AREA in the SW, including Baraboo Range (mts.), an area bypassed by pleistocene glaciation. The N and E parts of Wis. are dominated by glacial land fractures, including drumlins, eskers, kettles, moraines, and the aforementioned glacial lakes. Kettle Moraine, which runs SW-NE about 80 mi/129 km to W and N of Milwaukee, is a significant feature. Important copper deposits were discovered in the N in the 1970s. The state's greatest natural resource since its earliest days has been lumber. Giant forests (white pines in the N, hardwoods elsewhere) once covered all except the S prairie. While reckless exploitation in the late 19th cent. drastically reduced the magnificent stands, extensive conservation and reforestation measures have saved the valuable lumber industry, and today the N ⅓ of Wis.'s land area is forested, including Chequamegon and Nicolet Natl. Forest and several state forests. Much of S ⅔ is devoted to dairying. One of the nation's largest dairy herds grazes here, and Wis. is a U.S. leader in the production of milk and cheese. The industry owes its existence to the state's large percentage of immigrants from Germany and N Europe and to glacially deposited soils mainly suitable for pasture. After dairy prods. and cattle, its most valuable farm commodities are hogs and corn. Other important crops are hay, oats, potatoes, alfalfa, and a great variety of vegetables and fruits, including cranberries. Food processing, predictably, is one of the state's foremost industries, surpassed only by the mfg. of machinery, which is centered in Milwaukee, Madison, OSHKOSH, and Racine. Milwaukee, LA CROSSE, and other cities have been traditionally known for their brewing industry, which has dwindled as a result of consolidation of the industry but remains important. The pulp, paper, and paper prods. industrial complex in Green Bay and APPLETON is one of the largest in the nation. Other important mfg. includes transportation equip., metal prods., farm implements, and lumber. Most of Wis.'s major industries are to be found within metropolitan Milwaukee. Smaller cities, such as Appleton and JANESVILLE, have greatly increased their industrial base. Wis. has numerous ports on the Great Lakes (including Milwaukee and Green Bay on L. Michigan) capable of accommodating ocean and lake vessels. The superb harbor at SUPERIOR (shared with Duluth, Minn.), on L. Superior, has sizeable shipyards and among the nation's largest coal and ore docks. Wis.'s lakes, streams, and woodlands have made it a haven for hunters, fishers, and water- and winter-sports enthusiasts. Tourism is a burgeoning industry as well, particularly the quaint villages on the relatively undeveloped Door peninsula in Door co. Apostle Isls. Natl. Lakeshore is in far N, on L. Superior. The Great Lakes offered an easy access from Canada to the region that is now Wis., and the Frenchman Jean Nicolet arrived at the site of Green Bay in 1634 in search of fur pelts and the NW Passage. He was followed by other traders and missionaries, among them Radisson and Groseilliers; Marquette and Joliet, who discovered the upper Mississippi; and Aco and Hennepin, from the party of La Salle. Meanwhile the spread of settlers in the East was bringing the Ottawa, the Huron, and other Native Amer. tribes into Wis., where they in turn displaced the Winnebago, the Kickapoo, and others. Similarly, the Ojibwa drove their kinsmen the Sioux W from Wis. Only the Menominee remained relatively settled. Nicolas Perrot helped (1667) establish Green Bay as the center of the Wis. fur trade, and in 1686 he formally claimed all the region for France. The fur trade flourished despite the 50-year war bet. the Fox and the French, and the historic Fox-Wis. portage was used by generations of traders from Green Bay and PRAIRIE DU CHIEN in their search for beaver and other furs. Like all of New France, Wis. fell to the British with the end of the Fr. and Indian Wars (1763). Br. traders mingled with the French and eventually gained the bulk of the fur trade. The British hold continued even after the end of the Amer. Revolution, when the Old Northwest formally passed (1783) to the U.S. and was made (1787) a part of the Northwest Territory. After Jay's Treaty (1794), NW strongholds were turned over to the Americans, but the British continued to dominate the fur trade from the Can. border. In the War of 1812, Wis. again fell into Br. hands. It was only with the Treaty of Ghent that effective U.S. territorial control began and that the Amer. Fur Co. gained control of much of the fur trade. Present-day Wis. was transferred from Ill. Territory to Mich. Territory in 1818. By then the fur trade was diminishing, but the lead mines in SW Wis. had long been known, and booming lead prices in the 1820s brought the 1st large rush of settlers. The region's great agr. potential was also apparent, and after 1825 a considerable number of Easterners began arriving via the newly built Erie Canal and the Great Lakes. They settled in the Milwaukee area and along the waterways. The U.S. army preserved order from key forts est. at Green Bay (1816), Prairie du Chien (1816), and Portage (1828) and built bridges, trails, and roads throughout the region. The Native Americans were hostile to the incursions of aggressive settlers, culminating in the Black Hawk War (1832); this revolt, brutally crushed, was the last Native Amer. resistance of serious consequence in the area. In 1836, Wis. was made a territory, and the legislators chose a compromise site for the capital, midway bet. the Milwaukee and W centers of pop.; thus the city of Madison was founded. By 1840 pop. in the territory had risen above 130,000, but the people, fearing higher taxes and stronger govt., rejected propositions for statehood 4 times. In addition politicians were initially unwilling to yield Wis. claims to a strip of land around Chicago and to what is now the Upper Peninsula of Mich. However, hopes that statehood would bring improved communications and prosperity became dominant; the claims were yielded, and Wis. achieved statehood in 1848. The state constitution provided protection for indebted farmers, limited the establishment of banks, and granted liberal suffrage (in fact, in 1869 Wis. was the 1st state to give women the vote). These measures and the state's rich soil attracted immigrants from Europe. The influx of Germans was esp. heavy, and some parts of Wis. assumed the tidy semi-Ger. look that has persisted, along with an astonishing survival of the Ger. language. Contributions were also made, then and later, by Irish, Scandinavians, Russians, and Poles. Public education developed slowly. Similarly, the Univ. of Wis. (chartered 1848) was slow to assume importance. The Panic of 1857 had distressing effects when the state's RRs went bankrupt. Steadily antislavery, state citizens were active in the formation of the Republican party. In the Civil War, Wis. rallied to the Union side, though some Ger. immigrants, opposed to compulsory military service back in Germany, were against even voluntary war service. However, the boom times brought by the war mitigated discontent, and economic and social growth was rapid during the 1860s and after. RRs and other means of communication linked Wis. closely to the East. The meatpacking and brewing industries of Milwaukee began to assume importance in the 1860s. Wheat briefly was dominant, esp. in S Wis., but was superseded in the 1870s as states further W became wheat producers and Wis. shifted to more diversified farming. Its great dairy industry developed, spurred by an influx of skilled dairy farmers from N.Y. and Scandinavia and by the efforts of the Wis. Dairymen's Association (est. 1872). In these years the great pine forests of N Wis. began to be greatly exploited, and in the 1870s lumbering became the state's most important industry. Oshkosh and La Crosse flourished. With lumbering came large paper and wood-prod. industries, and the opening of iron mines in Minn. and Mich. promoted the N Great Lakes ports and increased industrial opportunities. Although hard hit in the panics of 1873 and 1898, Wis. was generally prosperous in the late 19th cent. A trend toward liberal political views developed, including Socialism (in Milwaukee) and esp. Progressivism. Reform sentiment blossomed in the Progressive movement, led by Robert M. La Follette. Its efforts to achieve good effective govt. for all resulted in a direct primary law (1903), in legislation to regulate RRs and industry, in pure food laws, in high civil service standards, and in efforts toward cooperative nonpartisan action to solve labor problems. Progressivism was helped a great deal by its relationship with the facilities and brainpower of the Univ. of Wis., which brought such diverse benefits as the spread of scientific agr. methods and labor reforms. Wis. was generally prosperous in the 1920s; industrialization made rapid strides, reforestation of the once-great but now-exhausted timberland was stimulated by state legislation, and the dairying industry continued to grow. Wis. was alone in voting for its native son, La Follette, when he ran for president on the Progressive party ticket in 1924. Wis.'s pioneer old-age pension act (1925) and its unemployment compensation act (1931) served as models for natl. Social Security a few years later. The Great Depression of the 1930s struck industrialized Milwaukee particularly hard, but some relief was provided by the New Deal, and in addition Gov. Philip La Follette attempted, in his "Little New Deal," to improve agr. marketing, promote electrification, and enforce fair labor practices. During World War II, Wis.'s shipbuilding industry flourished. In the prosperous post-war era, urbanization and industrial growth continued. A controversial Wis. politician on the natl. scene was Sen. Joseph McCarthy, but his methods and approach were balanced by other political strains in the state; Milwaukee, in the same period, again elected a Socialist mayor. The Democratic party, long no match for Republican or progressive forces in state elections, gained strength in the late 1950s and 1960s. In the late 1980s, Wis.'s mfg. sector proved viable in the face of a nationwide decline. The state's mfg. base remains strong despite the attraction to Southern states in the late 20th cent. Urbanization has greatly expanded in the SE corner, along L. Michigan. The Milwaukee and Chicago (Ill.) metropolitan areas have physically merged. Wis. still operates under its 1st constitution, adopted in 1848. Its executive branch is headed by a governor elected for a 4-year term. Wis.'s bicameral legislature has a senate with 33 members elected for 4-year terms and an assembly with 99 members elected for 2 years. The state elects 2 senators and 9 representatives to the U.S. Congress and has 11 electoral votes. The extensive Univ. of Wis. has campuses at Madison (the main campus), Milwaukee, Eau Claire, Green Bay, La Crosse, Oshkosh, Kenosha, Platteville, River Falls, Stevens Point, Menomonie, Superior, and Whitewater. Other notable institutions of higher learning are Beloit Col., at Beloit; Lawrence Univ., at Appleton; and Marquette Univ., at Milwaukee. Wis. has 72 COS.: ADAMS, ASHLAND, BARRON, BAYFIELD, BROWN, BUFFALO, BURNETT, CALUMET, CHIPPEWA, CLARK, COLUMBIA, CRAWFORD, DANE, DODGE, DOOR, DOUGLAS, DUNN, EAU CLAIRE, FLORENCE, FOND DU LAC, FOREST, GRANT, GREEN, GREEN LAKE, IOWA, IRON, JACKSON, JEFFERSON, JUNEAU, KENOSHA, KEWAUNEE, LA CROSSE, LAFAYETTE, LANGLADE, LINCOLN, MANITOWOC, MARATHON, MARINETTE, MARQUETTE, MENOMINEE, MILWAUKEE, MONROE, OCONTO, ONEIDA,

OUTAGAMIE, OZAUKEE, PEPIN, PIERCE, POLK, PORTAGE, PRICE, RACINE, RICHLAND, ROCK, RUSK, SAINT CROIX, SAUK, SAWYER, SHAWANO, SHEBOYGAN, TAYLOR, TREMPEALEAU, VERNON, VILAS, WALWORTH, WASHBURN, WASHINGTON, WAUKESHA, WAUPACA, WAUSHARA, WINNEBAGO, and WOOD.

Wisconsin, river, c.430 mi/692 km long, Wis.; rising in the Lake Dist., in Lac Vieux Desert on Wis.-Mich. state line, 15 mi/24 km NNE of Eagle River, NE Wis., and flowing generally S across central Wis. to the Mississippi R. near Prairie du Chien. Flows past Rhinelander, Wausau, Stevens Point, and Portage. At Portage it is connected by a short canal with the Fox R., and thus with L. Michigan. There are many hydroelectric power facilities on the river. The scenic Dells of the Wisconsin (famous gorge area) are 15 mi/24 km NW of Portage. Major reservoirs include Petenwell and Castle Rock lakes, S of Wisconsin Rapids, and L. Wisconsin, SW of Portage.

Wisconsin Dells, town (1990 pop. 2,393), Columbia co., S central Wis., on Wisconsin R. (water power), 14 mi/23 km WNW of Portage; 43°37′N 89°46′W. In agr. area (dairy prods.; grain, potatoes); mfg. (motor vehicles, candy); summer resort. Gateway to the Wisconsin Dells. Rocky Arbor State Parks to NW. Settled c.1850, inc. 1925. Until 1931, called Kilbourn.

Wisconsin, Lake, in S central Wis., 7 mi/11.3 km NE of Prairie du Sac, 10 mi/16 km SW of Portage. Artificial lake formed by power dam on Wisconsin R.; c.5 mi/8 km long, c.3 mi/4.8 km wide. Crossed by ferry at Merrimac.

Wisconsin Rapids, city (1990 pop. 18,245), ⊙ Wood co., central Wis., 70 mi/113 km WNW of Appleton on the Wisconsin R.; 44°23′N 89°49′W. Paper, heating equip., concrete, steel castings are produced. Dairy farms, agr., and a large cranberry industry also contribute to the area's economy. Alexander Field airport here. State Nursery to S. Powers Bluff Ski Area to NW. Grand Rapids (E bank) and Centralia (W bank), located on the river here, were consolidated in 1900, and the name was changed in 1920 to Wisconsin Rapids. Inc. 1869.

Wisdom, village (1990 pop. 135), Beaverhead co., SW Mont., 42 mi/68 km SSW of Anaconda, on Big Hole R. Sheep, cattle; hay, potatoes. Mfg. (hats). Timber. Beaverhead Natl. Forest to E and W; Anaconda-Pintler Wilderness Area to N; Big Hole Natl. Battlefield and Nez Percé Natl. Historic Trail. to W. Originally called Crossings.

Wise 1 county (□ 922 sq mi/2,388 sq km; 1990 pop. 34,679), N Texas; ⊙ Decatur; 33°13′N 97°39′W. Drained by West Fork of Trinity R., dammed to form L. Bridgeport (water supply for Fort Worth; recreation area) in W, drained also by Big Sandy and Denton creeks; also includes headwaters of Eagle Mt. L. in SE. Diversified agr., wheat, oats, peanuts, hay; cattle, horses, sheep, hogs, poultry; extensive dairying. Clay mining, limestone quarrying; sand and gravel. Gas and oil. Processing, mfg. at Decatur. Formed 1856. Wise Co. State Park on E shore of L. Bridgeport. **2** county (□ 404 sq mi/1,046 sq km; 1990 pop. 39,573), SW Va.; ⊙ Wise; 36°58′N 82°37′W. In Cumberland Mts. bounded NW by Ky. state line; drained by Powell and North Fork Pound rivers; SE corner drained by Clinch R. Co. does not include independent city of Norton. Agr. (hay, tobacco; cattle); timber; limestone; bituminous-coal fields, iron mines. Most of co. in Jefferson Natl. Forest, especially W, N, and S. Mt. resorts. High Knob Recreation Area in S, North Fork of Pound L. Recreation Area in N. Formed 1856.

Wise, town (1990 pop. 3,193), ⊙ Wise co., SW Va., in Cumberland Mts., near Ky. state line, 4 mi/6.4 km NE of Norton, on Yellow Glade Creek; 36°58′N 82°34′W. Trade center for agr. area (cattle; tobacco; hay); bituminous coal; limestone. Clinch Valley Col (Univ. of Va.). Damaged by Union troops in Civil War. Lonesome Pine Airport to NE. Settled as Big Glades; later named Gladville; renamed Wise in 1924.

Wiseman, village (1990 pop. 33), N central Alaska, on upper Koyukuk R., 55 mi/89 km NE of Bettles; 67°25′N 150°07′W. Supply center for rich placer gold region.

Wishek, town (1990 pop. 1,171), McIntosh co., S N.Dak., 18 mi/29 km NNW of Ashley; 46°15′N 99°33′W. RR junction; mfg. (agr. equip.); dairy prods.; livestock; wheat. Green L. and Doyle Memorial State Park to SE; Beaver L. State Park to N.

Wishkah River (WISH-kuh), c.40 mi/64 km long, Grays Harbor co., SW Wash.; rises in Olympic Natl. Forest; flows S to Chehalis R. at Aberdeen, E of its entrance to Grays Harbor.

Wishon Reservoir, Fresno co., S Calif., on North Fork of Kings R., 48 mi/77 km ENE of Redding, in Sierra Natl. Forest; 4 mi/6.4 km long; 37°00′N 118°59′W. Elev. 6,549 ft/1,996 m. Max. capacity of 128,000 acre-ft. Formed by Wishon Dam (250 ft/76 m high), built by Pacific Gas and Electric Company for power generation.

Wisner 1 (WEIZ-nuhr), town (1990 pop. 1,153), Franklin parish, NE La., 45 mi/72 km SE of Monroe, near Deer Creek; 31°59′N 91°40′W. In agr. area (cotton, corn, soybeans); logging; mfg. (catfish, concrete). Turkey Creek L. reservoir to W. **2** (WIZ-nuhr), town (1990 pop. 1,253), Cuming co., NE Nebr., 14 mi/23 km NW of West Point, on Elkhorn R.; 41°59′N 96°54′W. Livestock center, shipping point in rich agr. region; dairy and poultry prods., grain. Mfg. (fertilizers; lumber). Plotted 1871.

Wissahickon Creek (WI-sah-HI-kuhn), c.40 mi/64 km long, SE Pa.; rises E of Lansdale in Montgomery co., flows S past Ambler and through W part of Philadelphia, to Schuylkill R., 5 mi/8 km NNW of downtown; 40°01′N 75°12′W. Most of its length is located within park land, including Fort Washington State Park, S of Ambler.

Wissota, Lake, Chippewa co., W central Wis., just E of Chippewa Falls. Formed from Chippewa R. by backwater from power dam at Chippewa Falls; 4 mi/6.4 km long, 2 mi/3.2 km wide. Receives Yellow R. from E. L. Wissota State Park on NE shore.

Wister (WIS-tuhr), town (1990 pop. 956), Le Flore co., SE Okla., 8 mi/12.9 km SW of Poteau; 34°58′N 94°43′W. In agr. area. Wister Dam and Reservoir is just S, on Poteau R. Kerr Mus.; RR junction to E.

Wister Lake (WIS-tuhr), reservoir, at Wister, Le Flore co., E Okla., on Poteau R., in Wister State Park, 9 mi/14.5 km SW of Poteau; 8 mi/12.9 km long; 94°42′N 34°56′W. Max. capacity 430,000 acre-ft. Formed by Wister L. Dam (75 ft/23 m high), built (1949) by the Army Corps of Engineers for flood control.

Withee, village (1990 pop. 503), Clark co., central Wis., 45 mi/72 km ENE of Eau Claire; 44°57′N 90°35′W. In dairying and livestock-raising area; mfg. (sawmilling, animal feed).

Witherbee, village (1990 pop. 750), Essex co., NE N.Y., in the Adirondacks, near L. Champlain, 18 mi/29 km NNW of Ticonderoga; 44°05′N 73°32′W. In former iron-mining region.

Witherspoon, Mount (12,012 ft/3,661 m), S Alaska, in Chugach Mts., 40 mi/64 km WNW of Valdez; 61°24′N 147°12′W.

Withlacoochee River 1 (with-luh-KOO-chee), c.160 mi/257 km long, central Fla.; rises in Polk co. in swampy area E of Polk City; flows W and N to Dunnellon, then W to Gulf of Mexico near Yankeetown. Receives outlet of L. Panasoffkee. Channel dredged for 85 mi/137 km above mouth. **2** c.115 mi/185 km long, in Ga. and Fla.; rises in Tift co., S central Ga.; flows SSE, into Fla., to Suwannee R., 14 mi/23 km SE of Madison, Fla.; 31°19′N 83°17′W. Receives Little R. (c.80 mi/129 km long) just NW of Valdosta, Ga.

Witt, city (1990 pop. 866), Montgomery co., central Ill., 10 mi/16 km NE of Hillsboro; 39°15′N 89°20′W. Grain; cattle; dairying.

Witten, town (1990 pop. 87), Tripp co., S S.Dak., 12 mi/19 km NW of Winner, on Cottonwood Creek. Inc. 1938.

Wittenberg 1 uninc. town, Perry co., E Mo., on Mississippi R., just NW of Grand Tower (Ill.); 18 mi/29 km ESE of Perryville. Landing point for Ger. immigrants, 1830s–1840s. Settled c. 1800. **2** town (1990 pop. 1,145), N Shawano co., E central Wis.; 44°49′N 89°10′W. Transition area from dairying and farming to forest. Mfg. (metal fabrication).

Wittenberg, Mount, Ulster co., SE N.Y., 29 mi/47 km SW of Catskill; 42°01′N 74°21′W. Elev. 3,802 ft/1,159 m.

Wittmann, uninc. village (1990 pop. 600), Maricopa co., W central Ariz., 32 mi/51 km NW of Phoenix, N of Hayden-Rhodes Aqueduct. Cattle, sheep; grain. Chrysler Corp. Ariz. Proving Grounds, automobile test site.

Wixom (WIKS-uhm), city (1990 pop. 8,550), Oakland co., SE Mich., 28 mi/45 km WNW of Detroit, 15 mi/24 km SW of Pontiac; 42°31′N 83°32′W. Mfg. (machinery, cleaning compounds, tools, consumer goods, fabricated metal prods.). Proud L. State Recreation Area to N, Island L. State Recreation Area to W, and Kensington Metropark to W. Oakland Southwest Airport to W. Small lakes in N.

Wixon Valley, village (1990 pop. 186), Brazos co., E central Texas, residential suburb 6 mi/9.7 km N of Bryan; 30°45′N 96°19′W. Agr. area.

Woburn (WOO-buhrn), city (1990 pop. 35,943), Middlesex co., NE Mass.; 42°29′N 71°10′W. It has electrical, pharmaceutical, chemical, and leather industries, as well as greenhouses. Formerly a major center for tanneries. The scientist Benjamin Thompson (Count Rumford) b. here; his house is now a mus. Environmental Protection Agency superfund site here. Settled 1640, inc. as a city 1888.

Woburn (WO-buhrn), village, Burke co., NW N.Dak., 8 mi/12.9 km W of Bowbells; 48°49′N 102°25′W.

Woden, town (1990 pop. 259), Hancock co., N Iowa, 18 mi/29 km NW of Garner; 43°13′N 93°54′W. Livestock; grain.

Wofford Heights, uninc. town (1990 pop. 2,270), Kern co., S central Calif., 37 mi/60 km NE of Bakersfield, on N arm of Isabella L. reservoir (Kern R.) in S part of Sierra Nevada; 35°43′N 118°28′W. Timber; cattle. Parts of Sequoia Natl. Forest surround area. Resort community. Shirley Meadows Ski Area is here.

Wohoa Bay (WAH-ho), inlet at mouth of Chandler R., Washington co., E Maine; bounded by Jonesport on W, Roque Isl. on E; 7 mi/11.3 km long, 2 mi/3.2 km wide. Formerly called Chandler Bay.

Woking (WO-king), village, W Alta., W Canada, near B.C. border, on Saddle R., 30 mi/48 km N of Grande Prairie; 55°36′N 118°46′W. Lumbering, farming; wheat.

Wolbach (WAWL-bash), village (1990 pop. 280), Greeley co., E central Nebr., 12 mi/19 km SE of Greeley; 41°23′N 98°23′W. Dairy prods.; grain.

Wolcott 1 town (1990 pop. 13,700), New Haven co., central Conn.; 41°36′N 72°58′W. There is some light mfg. of tools and novelties in the area. Bronson (Amos) Alcott was born nearby. Inc. 1796. **2** town (1990 pop. 886), White co., NW central Ind., 14 mi/23 km W of Monticello; 40°46′N 87°02′W. In agr. area; mfg. (consumer goods, fertilizer). Laid out 1861. **3** town (1990 pop. 1,229), Lamoille co., N central Vt., on Lamoille R., 23 mi/37 km N of Barre; 44°34′N 72°26′W. Trade center for agr.

Wolcott, village (□ 1 sq mi/2.6 sq km; 1990 pop. 1,544), Wayne co., W N.Y., 22 mi/35 km NNW of Auburn; 43°13′N 76°48′W. Some mfg.; agr.-shipping point (fruit, dairy prods.). Summer resort. Inc. 1873.

Wolcottville, town (1990 pop. 879), on Noble-Lagrange co. line, NE Ind., 8 mi/12.9 km SSE of Lagrange; 41°32′N 85°22′W. In lake-resort and agr. area; mfg. (wire prods., fiberglass, feed mixing, grain mixing and blending). Settled 1837, laid out 1849.

Wolf Creek 1 c.60 mi/97 km, E central Iowa; rises in Grundy co.; flows S, E, and ENE to Cedar R. near La Porte City. **2** c.110 mi/177 km long, Texas and Okla.; rises in Ochiltree co. in N Texas; flows E into Okla., then NE, past Gage, to North Canadian R. at Fort Supply. Fort Supply L. reservoir is near its mouth.

Wolf Creek Dam, Ky.: see CUMBERLAND, LAKE.

Wolf Creek Nuclear Power Plant, Kansas: see COFFEY.

Wolf Creek Pass, S Mineral co., SW Colo., on Continental Divide, in San Juan Mts. Elev. 10,850 ft/3,307 m. U.S. Highway 160 passes through. Rio Grande Natl. Forest (N), San Juan Natl. Forest (S).

Wolf Lake 1 village (1990 pop. 4,110), Lake co., W Mich., 7 mi/11.3 km N of Baldwin, on E side of Wolf L.; 43°15′N 86°06′W. Resort area. Manistee Natl. Forest immediately W. **2** village (1990 pop. 35), Becker co., W Minn., 23 mi/37 km E of Detroit Lakes, at SE end of Wolf L., at exit of Blueberry R.; 46°47′N 95°21′W. Agr. (dairying; grain). Smoke Hills State Forest to N.

Wolf Lake, in NE Ill. and NW Ind., on state line, and partly within SE Chicago; c.3 mi/4.8 km long.

Wolf Neck, peninsula, SW Maine; extending 3 mi/4.8 km into Casco Bay, near Freeport. Resort area.

Wolf Point, town (1990 pop. 2,880), ⊙ Roosevelt co., NE Mont., on Missouri R. (bridge 5 mi/8 km to E) at mouth of Wolf Creek, 45 mi/72 km ESE of Glasgow; 48°05′N 105°38′W. Located in S part of Fort Peak Indian Reservation. Wheat-shipping point. Wolf Point Area Historical Society Mus.; John Deere Tractor Collection and Mus. here. Fort Peck Dam and Reservoir 36 mi/58 km W surrounded by Charles M. Russell Natl. Wildlife Refuge; Wolf Point Internatl. Airport to E; racetrack to E. Settled 1878, inc. 1915.

Wolf River 1 c.60 mi/97 km long, S Miss.; rises in SW Lamar co.; flows SSE, passes E of Poplarville, turns WSW before entering St. Louis Bay of Mississippi Sound. **2** c.45 mi/72 km long, SW Tenn.; formed by joining of North and South forks at Moscow, Fayette co.; flows WNW past Germantown and Bartlett in E suburban Memphis, continues through N part of Memphis, turns SSE before joining Mississippi R. in downtown Memphis. South Fork, c.30 mi/48 km long, rises in NE Benton co., N Miss., flows NW to Moscow, Tenn. North Fork, c.20 mi/32 km long, rises in W Hardeman co., SE Tenn.; flows generally SW. **3** c.240 mi/386 km long, NE Wis.; rises in W Forest co.; flows generally S, past Shawano and New London, widens into L. Poygan, part Winneconne enters Butte des Morts L. 10 mi/16 km NW of Oshkosh. Receives Embarrass R. at New London. Formerly important for log driving. Whitewater canoeing through Menominee Indian Reservation.

Wolf Trap, uninc. city, Fairfax co., NE Va., residential suburb 11 mi/18 km WNW of Washington, D.C.; 38°56′N 77°17′W. Wolf Trap Farm Park for the Performing Arts is here.

Wolf Trap Farm Park for the Performing Arts, Fairfax co., NE Va., 11 mi/18 km WNW of Washington, D.C., N of Vienna; on an area of 130 acres/53 ha. Set in a rolling, wooded landscaped area to provide artistic enjoyment and recreation; 1st natl. park for the performing arts. Stagehouse is 10 stories high. Authorized 1966.

Wolfdale (WULF-dail), uninc. town (1990 pop. 2,906), Washington co., SW Pa., residential suburb 3 mi/4.8 km NW of Washington; 40°12′N 80°17′W. Agr. includes dairying; livestock; corn. Cross Creek reservoir and co. park to NW.

Wolfe, county (□ 680 sq mi/1,761 sq km; pop.), S Que., E Canada, on St. Francis and Nicolet rivers; ⊙ Ham Sud; 45°45′N 71°30′W.

Wolfe, county (□ 222 sq mi/575 sq km; 1990 pop. 6,503), E central Ky.; ⊙ Campton; 37°44′N 83°29′W. In Cumberland Mts.; drained by Red R. Mt. agr. area (burley tobacco, hay, corn; cattle). Includes part of Natural Bridge State Resort Park on W border and part of Daniel Boone Natl. Forest; part of Red R. Natl. Geological Area in N. Formed 1860.

Wolfe City, town (1990 pop. 1,505), Hunt co., NE Texas, 16 mi/26 km N of Greenville; 33°22′N 96°04′W. In cotton, grain, cattle area; mfg. (bldg. materials, paper prods., publishing and printing). Inc. 1873.

Wolfe Island (□ 48 sq mi/124 sq km), SE Ont., central Canada, at head of L. Ontario, at entrance to the St. Lawrence, opposite Kingston, 18 mi/29 km long, 1 mi/2 km wide; 44°12′N 76°26′W. Largest of the Thousand Isls. Heavily wooded until end of 19th cent., now intensively cultivated; popular resort. Just S is U.S. border. Village of Marysville on NW shore. Ferry from Kingston.

Wolfeboro, town (1990 pop. 4,807), Carroll co., E N.H., 13 mi/21 km E of Laconia; 43°37′N 71°10′W. Bounded by L. Winnipesaukee in SW. Mfg. (printing and publishing, pewter accessories, plastic molding, electronic components); agr. (apples, nursery crops, vegetables; cattle, hogs, poultry; dairying); timber. Summer resort, trade center, lake port; winter sports. Seat of Brewster Acad. L. Wentworth in S, Wentworth State Park on N shore; Perry Hollow and Nordic Skier ski areas in S; Libby Mus.; General John Wentworth State Historic Site is here. Includes village of Wolfeboro Falls, 1 mi/1.6 km N of town center, near W outlet of L. Wentworth, with mfg. (apparel, printing and publishing). Settled c.1760.

Wolfforth, town (1990 pop. 1,941), Lubbock co., NW Texas, 7 mi/11.3 km SW of Lubbock; 33°30′N 102°00′W. Diverse agr. area (cattle, sheep, hogs; cotton, wheat, sunflowers, eggs). Oil and natural gas. Mfg. (metal fabrication).

Wolford (WOL-fuhrd), village (1990 pop. 56), Pierce co., N central N.Dak., 16 mi/26 km NE of Rugby; 48°30′N 99°42′W. Terminus of RR spur from York. Grassy and Spring lakes to N.

Wolfville, town (1991 pop. 3,475), W central N.S., E Canada, on the SW shore of Minas Basin; 45°05′N 64°22′W. It is a market center for a dairy and fruit-growing area. Acadia Univ. (1839) is the town's main employer and its cultural center.

Wollaston, Mass.: see QUINCY.

Wollaston, Cape (WU-luhs-tuhn), SW Victoria Isl., SW Franklin dist., N.W.T., Canada, on Amundsen Gulf, on S side of entrance of Minto Inlet; 71°04′N 118°08′W.

Wollaston Lake (□ 796 sq mi/2,062 sq km), NE Sask., W Canada, NW of Reindeer L. It drains into both the Churchill and the Mackenzie river systems.

Wollaston Peninsula, SW part of Victoria Isl., SW Franklin dist., N.W.T., Canada, extending W into Amundsen Gulf bet. Prince Albert Sound (N) and Dolphin and Union Strait (S), 140 mi/225 km long, 60 mi/97 km–70 mi/113 km wide. Cape Baring (70°01′N 116°58′W) is its W extremity. Named Wollaston Land (1821) by Sir John Franklin; name was changed to Wollaston Peninsula by Geographic Board of Canada.

Wolseley, town (1991 pop. 853), SE Sask., W Canada, 60 mi/97 km E of Regina. Grain elevators.

Wolsey, village (1990 pop. 442), Beadle co., E central S.Dak., 12 mi/19 km W of Huron, on branch of James R.; 44°24′N 98°28′W. RR junction.

Wolstenholme (WO-stuhn-home) or **Eric Cove**, trading post, NW Ungava Peninsula, NW Que., E Canada, on Eric Cove (small inlet of Hudson Strait); 62°32′N 77°24′W. Radio station. Cape Wolstenholme, NW extremity of Ungava Peninsula, is 5 mi/8 km NW; 62°34′N 77°30′W.

Wolstenholme, Cape (1,260 ft/384 m), headland, W limit of Hudson Strait, Canada. Summer nesting for murres.

Wolverine, village (1990 pop. 283), Cheboygan co., N Mich., 19 mi/31 km SE of Petoskey, on Sturgeon R.; 45°16′N 84°36′W. In resort and farm area.

Wolverine Lake, town (1990 pop. 4,727), Oakland co., SE Mich., 10 mi/16 km SW of Pontiac, 28 mi/45 km WNW of Detroit; 42°33′N 83°28′W. Proud L. State Recreation Area to W and N (2 units).

Wolverton, village (1990 pop. 158), Wilkin co., W Minn., 22 mi/35 km S of Fargo (N.Dak.), 22 mi/35 km N of Breckenridge, on Red R.; 46°33′N 96°44′W. Agr. (wheat, sugar beets, potatoes); mfg. (fertilizer).

Wolves, The, group of 5 islets in the Bay of Fundy, SW N.B., E Canada, off Maine coast, 12 mi/19 km NE of Eastport, 10 mi/16 km NNE of Grand Manan; 44°57′N 66°41′W.

Woman Lake, Cass co., N central Minn., 18 mi/29 km SE of Walker, S of Leech L.; 4 mi/6.4 km long, 3 mi/4.8 km wide; 46°57′N 94°16′W. Resort area. Leech L. Indian Reservation to N. Woman L. drains NE from Broadwater Bay through narrow passage to Girl L., which drains SE through Boy R., which ultimately flows to Leech L. Man and Baby lakes are NW of Woman L.; Child and Kid lakes are to W; Little Boy L. is to E.

Womelsdorf (WO-muhls-dorf), borough (1990 pop. 2,270), Berks co., SE central Pa., 14 mi/23 km W of Reading, on Tulpehocken Creek; 40°22′N 76°11′W. Mfg. (footwear, chocolate, graphite). Agr. (soybeans, nursery prods., grain; livestock; dairying). Conrad Weisel Homestead to W. Settled 1723, laid out 1762, inc. 1833.

Womelsdorf, W.Va.: see COALTON.

Womens Bay, Coast Guard base on NE Kodiak Isl., S Alaska, on Womens Bay, inlet of Chiniak Bay of Gulf of Alaska, 10 mi/16 km SW of Kodiak; 57°42′N 152°31′W. Major naval base during World War II.

Women's Rights Historical Park, Seneca Falls, W N.Y.; 42°55′N 76°48′W. Authorized 1980. The Declaration of Sentiments, calling for women to be granted the vote, was drafted here. Includes Wesleyan Methodist Chapel, site of July 18–19, 1848, Women's Rights Convention (held 72 years before passage of the 19th Amendment) and the homes and offices of Elizabeth Cady Stanton, Lucretia Mott, Amelia Jenks Bloomer (who popularized baggy "bloomers") and other notable early women's rights activists. Women's Rights Natl. Convention Days in July and Women's Equality Day in late Aug.

Wonder Lake, village (1990 pop. 1,024), McHenry co., NE Ill., residential satellite community of Chicago, 8 mi/12.9 km NNE of Woodstock, on N sides of Wonder L.; 42°22′N 88°22′W. Agr. area. Galt Wonder Lake Airport to N.

Wonewoc (WAHN-e-wahk), village (1990 pop. 793), Juneau co., S central Wis., on Baraboo R., 28 mi/45 km NW of Baraboo; 43°38′N 90°13′W. In agr. area (poultry, fruit); mfg. (batteries, wood prods.).

Wononskopomuc, Lake (we-nahn-ske-PAH-muhk), reservoir, in Salisbury town, Litchfield co., NW Conn., on branch of Housatonic R., 21 mi/34 km NW of Torrington, 3 mi/4.8 km E of N.Y. state line; 1 mi/1.6 km long; 41°57′N 73°26′W. Lakeville village to N.

Wood 1 county (□ 618 sq mi/1,601 sq km; 1990 pop. 113,269), NW Ohio; ⊙ Bowling Green; 41°22′N 83°37′W. Bounded NW by Maumee R., and intersected by Portage R. In the Lake Plains physiographic region. Diversified farming (corn, soybeans, wheat; livestock; fruit). Mfg. at Bowling Green, North Baltimore, Perrysburg, Rossford (canned fruits and vegetables, paper prods., oils and greases, rubber goods, flat glass, lime, metal stampings, motor vehicle parts and accessories, surgical and medical instruments). Limestone quarries. Formed 1820. **2** county (□ 695 sq mi/1,800 sq km; 1990 pop. 29,380), NE Texas; ⊙ Quitman; 32°46′N 95°22′W. Bounded SW and S by Sabine R., drained by its tributaries, including Lake Fork and Big Sandy creeks. Agr. (vegetables, grain, corn, hay); extensive dairying, poultry raising; also cattle, hogs, horses. Extensive timber, Christmas trees; large oil production; also natural gas, sand and gravel, clay. Hunting, fishing. Formed 1850. Governor Hogg Shrine State Historical Site in W center. Several reservoirs: large Lake Fork Reservoir (NW), Quitman and Winnsboro (N), Holbrook (SW), Hawkins (SE). **3** county (□ 376 sq mi/974 sq km; 1990 pop. 86,915), NW W.Va.; ⊙ Parkersburg; 39°12′N 81°30′W. Bounded W by Ohio R. (Ohio state line); drained by Little Kanawha R. Oil and natural-gas wells, bituminous coal; clay. Agr. (corn, wheat, tobacco, soybeans, alfalfa, hay, nursery crops); cattle, hogs, poultry, sheep. Extensive mfg. at Parkersburg and Vienna. Blennerhassett Isl. Historic State Park (Ohio R.) in W; W part of North Bend State Trail in E. Lock and Dam No. 17 (Ohio R.) in NE. Formed 1798. **4** county (□ 809 sq mi/2,095 sq km; 1990 pop. 73,605), central Wis.; ⊙ Wisconsin Rapids; 44°27′N 90°02′W. Drained by Wisconsin and Yellow rivers. Dairying and general farming area (barley, corn, soybeans, beans, potatoes, hay; cattle, sheep; cranberries); mfg. at Marshfield and Wisconsin Rapids. State Nursery in SE. Powers Bluff Ski Area at center. Formed 1856.

Wood 1 uninc. village, Franklin co., N central N.C., 15 mi/24 km NE of Louisburg, near Fishing Creek. **2** village (1990 pop. 73), Mellette co., S S.Dak., 14 mi/23 km ESE of White R.; 43°30′N 100°28′W.

Wood Buffalo National Park (□ 17,300 sq mi/44,807 sq km), NE Alta., W Canada, extending into the Fort Smith region of the N.W.T.; est. 1922 to protect the only remaining herd of buffalo. It lies bet. L. Athabasca and Great Slave L. and is crossed by the Peace R. A vast, unfenced region of forests, plains, and lakes, it is the largest game preserve in N. Amer., containing buffalo, bear, beaver, caribou, moose, and varied waterfowl, including whooping cranes.

Wood Dale, city (1990 pop. 12,425), Du Page co., NE Ill., suburb 16 mi/26 km W of Chicago, and 17 mi/27 km ESE of Elgin; 41°58′N 87°58′W. Mfg. (marble prods., bookbinding, inks); some agr. (corn, oats, vegetables).

Wood, Fort Leonard, Mo.: see FORT LEONARD WOOD.

Wood Island, village, SE P.E.I., E Canada, near coast, 25 mi/40 km SE of Charlottetown. Nearby is terminal of car ferry to Pictou, N.S.

Wood Island, village, NE Kodiak Isl., SW Alaska, 4 mi/6.4 km W of Kodiak, on Chiniak Bay. Sometimes called Woody Isl.; village is sometimes confused with Woody Isl., 7 mi/11.3 km E in Chiniak Bay. Connected to Kodiak by bridge. Has small boat harbor.

Wood Island, SW Maine, at mouth of Saco R. Lighthouse.

Wood Lake 1 village (1990 pop. 406), Yellow Medicine co., SW Minn., 10 mi/16 km S of Granite Falls; 44°38′N 95°31′W. Agr. (grain, soybeans, alfalfa: livestock); mfg. (furniture, feed milling). Wood L. to N, Curtis L. to SE. **2** village (1990 pop. 59), Cherry co., N Nebr., 23 mi/37 km SE of Valentine; 42°38′N 100°14′W. Trade center for ranch region.

Wood, Mount (15,880 ft/4,840 m), SW Yukon, N Canada, near Alaska border, 200 mi/322 km WNW of Whitehorse; 61°15′N 140°33′W.

Wood, Mount, Mont.: see BEARTOOTH RANGE.

Wood River, city (1990 pop. 11,490), Madison co., SW Ill., on the Mississippi R. 2 mi/3.2 km above its junction with the Missouri, 7 mi/11.3 km WNW of Edwardsville, industrial suburb of St. Louis; 38°51′N 90°04′W. It has oil refinery and pipeline terminals. Mfg. (petroleum additives, concrete prods.). Inc. 1923.

Wood River, town (1990 pop. 1,156), Hall co., S Nebr., 15 mi/24 km SW of Grand Isl., on Wood R.; 40°49′N 98°35′W. Grain; livestock. Cheyenne State Wayside to S.

Wood River 1 c.22 mi/35 km long, in Conn. and R.I.; rises in branches in W R.I. and in Windham co., E Conn.; flows SE and S, through R.I., to Pawcatuck R. NNE of Bradford. **2** 110 mi/177 km long, S central Nebr.; rises in S Custer co.; flows SE to near Kearney, then ENE paralleling Platte R., ENE, past Shelton, Wood R., and Grand Isl., to Platte R. SW of Central City.

Wood River Junction, village, in Richmond town, Washington co., R.I., 30 mi/48 km SW of Providence.

Wood Village, town (1990 pop. 2,814), Multnomah co., NW Oregon, residential suburb 12 mi/19 km E of Portland, 2 mi/3.2 km S of Columbia R.; 45°31′N 122°25′W. Aluminum smelter at Troutdale, which adjoins it to E. Portland Troutdale Airport to NE. Multnomah Greyhound Race Track is here.

Woodacres, uninc. town (1990 pop. 1,478), Marin co., W Calif., residential suburb 20 mi/32 km NW of San Francisco, 6 mi/9.7 km WNW of San Rafael; 38°01′N 122°38′W. Cattle, poultry; nuts, fruits. Point Reyes Natl. Seashore to W.

Woodall Mountain (806 ft/246 m), Tishomingo co., extreme NE Miss., 3 mi/4.8 km W of Iuka; 34°47′N 88°14′W. Highest point in the state.

Woodbine 1 town (1990 pop. 1,212), ⊙ Camden co., extreme SE Ga., 18 mi/29 km SW of Brunswick, on Satilla R.; 30°57′N 81°43′W. Mfg. of agr. prods., cabinets. **2** town (1990 pop. 1,500), Harrison co., W Iowa, on Boyer R., 9 mi/14.5 km NE of Logan; 41°44′N 95°42′W. In agr. area (apples, grain; livestock). Inc. 1877.

Woodbine 1 village (1990 pop. 186), Dickinson co., central Kansas, 16 mi/26 km SE of Abilene; 38°47′N 96°57′W. Grain; livestock. **2** uninc. village (1990 pop. 900), Whitley co., SE Ky., in the Cumberland Mts., 3 mi/4.8 km S of Corbin. In bituminous-coal–mining area; agr. (tobacco, corn; cattle). Daniel Boone Natl. Forest to W. **3** village, Carroll co., N central Md., on South Branch of Patapsco R., 25 mi/40 km W of Baltimore. **4** village, Davidson co., central Tenn., SE suburb of Nashville.

Woodbine, borough (1990 pop. 2,678), Cape May co., SE N.J., 23 mi/37 km SW of Atlantic City; 39°13′N 74°48′W.

Agr. area. Belleplain State Forest is W. In 1880s it was developed as a Jewish agr. community supported by Baron de Hirsch. Inc. 1903.

Woodbourne, uninc. town (1990 pop. 2,953), Bucks co., SE Pa., residential suburb 6 mi/9.7 km W of Trenton (N.J.), 22 mi/35 km NE of Philadelphia; 40°12′N 74°53′W.

Woodbourne, village, Montgomery co., SW Ohio, S of Dayton; 39°40′N 84°10′W.

Woodbridge, city, S Ont., central Canada, on Humber R., 12 mi/19 km NW of Toronto; 43°47′N 79°36′W. Dairying, mixed farming; mfg. (apparel, rubber prods., motor vehicles, hardware, pasta, fruit processing, plastic prods., soft drinks). Suburban community included in new city of Vaughan.

Woodbridge, uninc. city, Prince William co., NE Va., suburb 22 mi/35 km SSW of Washington, D.C., on Potomac R., at mouth of Occoquan R.; 38°38′N 77°15′W. Mfg. (concrete prods., printing and publishing, fabricated metal prods., furniture).

Woodbridge 1 uninc. town (1990 pop. 3,456), San Joaquin co., central Calif., residential suburb 3 mi/4.8 km NW of Lodi, on Mokelumne R.; 38°10′N 121°19′W. Avocados, fruit, grapes, vegetables. **2** residential town (1990 pop. 7,924), New Haven co., S Conn., just NW of New Haven; 41°21′N 73°00′W. Dairy prods., fruit, poultry. Settled before 1660, inc. 1784.

Woodbridge, township (1990 pop. 93,086), Middlesex co., NE N.J., 9 mi/14.5 km NE of New Brunswick; 40°33′N 74°17′W. Mfg. (chemicals, furniture, food); boat yards; also commercial and retail center. Settled 1665 by colonists from Mass., led by John Woodbridge. Had sawmill in 1682, printing press in 1751. Includes villages of Fords, Sewaren, Port Reading, Hopelawn, and Keasbey. Site of Woodbridge Center, one of the largest shopping centers in the U.S. Inc. 1669.

Woodburn 1 city (1990 pop. 1,321), Allen co., NE Ind., 19 mi/31 km ENE of Fort Wayne, near Ohio state line; 41°08′N 84°51′W. In agr. area (corn, soybeans). Mfg. (grain processing, metal fabrication, tires). Indiana's least populated city. Laid out 1865. Until 1936, called Shirley City. **2** city (1990 pop. 13,404), Marion co., NW Oregon, 17 mi/27 km NE of Salem, near the Pudding R.; 45°08′N 122°51′W. RR junction. Agr. (hops, vegetables, fruit; poultry); dairy prods. Mfg. (fruit, veneer, motor vehicles, machinery, stainless steel). Retirement center. Champoeg State Park to N. Inc. 1889.

Woodburn, town (1990 pop. 240), Clarke co., S Iowa, 9 mi/14.5 km E of Osceola; 41°00′N 93°35′W. In agr. area.

Woodburn, village (1990 pop. 343), Warren co., S Ky., 12 mi/19 km SSW of Bowling Green; 36°50′N 86°31′W. In agr. area (tobacco, grain; livestock; dairying); mfg. (crushed stone, signs, machining).

Woodburn Hills, uninc. village, Spartanburg co., NW S.C., residential suburb 3 mi/4.8 km E of Spartanburg.

Woodbury, county (□ 877 sq mi/2,271 sq km; 1990 pop. 98,276), W Iowa; ⊙ Sioux City; 42°23′N 96°02′W. Bounded on W by Big Sioux R. (forms S.Dak. statae line here) and Missouri R. (forms Nebr. state line here). Prairie agr. area (hogs, cattle; corn, oats, barley) drained by Little Sioux R. and its West Fork. Stone State Park in NW corner; Browns L. State Park in SW. Mfg. at Sioux City. Some flooding occurred here in 1993. Formed 1851.

Woodbury 1 city (1990 pop. 20,075), Washington co., E Minn., residential suburb 8 mi/12.9 km ESE of St. Paul, bet. Mississippi R. (W) and St. Croix R. (E); 44°54′N 92°55′W. Several small lakes within city, esp. in N. Mfg. (electronic equip., abrasives, printing and publishing, medical prods.). **2** residential city (1990 pop. 10,904), ⊙ Gloucester co., SW N.J., in the Philadelphia-Camden metropolitan area; 39°50′N 75°09′W. Trade and service center, with petrochemical cos. nearby. Originally a Quaker settlement, Woodbury tried to remain neutral during the Amer. Revolution; however, the armies of both sides occupied the town, and many battles were fought in the vicinity. The city's 18th-cent. bldgs. include the Cooper House, where Cornwallis stopped in 1777, and a Friends' meetinghouse. The co. historical

society has collections in the John Lawrence House (1765). Settled 1683, inc. as a city 1871.

Woodbury 1 town (1990 pop. 8,131), Litchfield co., W Conn., on Pomperaug R., 8 mi/12.9 km W of Waterbury; 41°33′N 73°12′W. Dairy prods., machine shops, tool shops, welding and woodworking shops. Fine 18th-cent. houses, several old churches. Settled 1672, chartered 1674. **2** town (1990 pop. 1,429), Meriwether co., W Ga., 17 mi/27 km WNW of Thomaston; 32°59′N 84°35′W. Mfg. of sporting equip., polyurethane foam, paper prods. **3** town (1990 pop. 2,287), ⊙ Cannon co., central Tenn., on East Fork of Stones R., 19 mi/31 km E of Murfreesboro; 35°49′N 86°04′W. **4** town (1990 pop. 766), Washington co., N central Vt., 15 mi/24 km NNE of Montpelier; 44°26′N 72°24′W. Granite.

Woodbury, village (1990 pop. 117), Butler co., W central Ky., 16 mi/26 km NW of Bowling Green, on Green R., at mouth of Barren R.; 37°10′N 86°38′W.

Woodbury, borough (1990 pop. 239), Bedford co., S Pa., 18 mi/29 km SSE of Altoona, on Yellow Creek, in Morrison Cove valley; 40°13′N 78°22′W. Agr. (apples, corn, oats; livestock; dairying).

Woodbury Heights, borough (1990 pop. 3,392), Gloucester co., SW N.J., S of Woodbury, 39°49′N 75°09′W. Mfg. (clothing, concrete blocks). Settled c.1770, inc. 1915.

Woodcliff Lake, borough (1990 pop. 5,303), Bergen co., NE N.J., on Woodcliff L. (c.1 mi/1.6 km long), near N.Y. state line, 10 mi/16 km NNE of Paterson; 41°01′N 74°03′W. Largely residential. Inc. 1910.

Woodcock, borough (1990 pop. 148), Crawford co., NW Pa., 8 mi/12.9 km N of Meadville, on Gravel Run; 41°45′N 80°04′W. Agr. (dairying; livestock; corn). Woodcock Creek L. reservoir to S.

Woodcrest, uninc. town (1990 pop. 7,746), Riverside co., S Calif., residential suburb 5 mi/8 km S of Riverside; 33°54′N 117°22′W. Mockingbird Canyon and Reservoir to W; L. Mathews to SW; March Air Force Base to E. Val Verde Tunnel (Colorado R. Aqueduct) passes to S.

Wooden Ball Island, Maine: see MATINICUS ISLE.

Woodfibre, village, SW B.C., W Canada, on W shore of Howe Sound, 30 mi/48 km N of Vancouver, 8 mi/13 km SW of Squamish by ferry. Pulp milling.

Woodfield, uninc. town (1990 pop. 8,862), Richland co., central S.C., residential suburb 7 mi/11.3 km NE of Columbia on N border of Fort Jackson Military Reservation; 34°03′N 80°55′W. Sesquicentennial State Park to NE.

Woodfin, town (1990 pop. 2,736), Buncombe co., W N.C., residential suburb 5 mi/8 km N of Asheville, on French Broad R.; 35°38′N 82°35′W.

Woodford 1 county (□ 542 sq mi/1,404 sq km; 1990 pop. 32,653), central Ill.; ⊙ Eureka; 40°47′N 89°12′W. Bounded W by L. Peoria, a widening of Illinois R.; drained by Mackinaw R. and Panther Creek. Some urban growth from Peoria in extreme W (Germantown Hills). Agr. (corn, oats, soybeans; cattle, hogs, poultry; dairying). Mfg. (tile, concrete blocks, dairy and food prods., feed). Metamora Courthouse State Historic Site at Metamora. Formed 1841. **2** county (□ 191 sq mi/495 sq km; 1990 pop. 19,955), central Ky.; ⊙ Versailles; 38°02′N 84°44′W. In Bluegrass region; bounded W, SW, and S by Kentucky R., N and NE by Elkhorn Creek. Gently rolling upland agr. area (burley tobacco, hay, alfalfa, soybeans, wheat, corn; cattle, horses). Mfg. at Versailles. Formed 1788.

Woodford, town (1990 pop. 331), Bennington co., SW Vt., just E of Bennington, in Green Mts.; 42°52′N 73°04′W. Woodford village (elev. 2,215 ft/675 m) is one of state's highest, and has the highest church in Vt.

Woodford, village (1990 pop. 200), Orangeburg co., central S.C., 18 mi/29 km NW of Orangeburg; 33°40′N 81°06′W.

Woodhaven, city (1990 pop. 11,631), Wayne co., SE Mich., residential suburb 15 mi/24 km SSW of Detroit; 42°07′N 83°14′W. Drained by Marsh and Brownstown creeks. Mfg. (wood prods., metal fabrication).

Woodhaven, residential section of SW Queens borough of N.Y. city, SE N.Y., S of Forest Park, E of E N.Y. (Brooklyn); 40°41′N 73°52′W. Some mfg.

Woodhull 1 village (1990 pop. 808), Henry co., NW Ill., 12 mi/19 km SSW of Cambridge; 41°10′N 90°19′W. In agr. area; ships grain. Site of commercial seed-processing plant. **2** village (1990 pop. 350), Steuben co., S N.Y., 19 mi/31 km WSW of Corning; 42°03′N 77°23′W. Cheese and other dairy prods.; poultry; grain.

Woodinville, village (1995 pop. 9,615), King co., W Wash., suburb 12 mi/19 km NE of Seattle, on Sammamish R. RR junction. Area is partially agr. (dairying; poultry; vegetables, berries). Mfg. (machinery, dental equip., wire prods., furniture, wineries, plastic prods., aluminum prods., printing and publishing, communications equip., fabricated rubber goods, flat glass, aircraft parts, wood prods.).

Woodlake, city (1990 pop. 5,678), Tulare co., S central Calif., in Sierra Nevada foothills, 12 mi/19 km NE of Visalia L. Kaweah reservoir to E, formed by Terminus Dam; 36°25′N 119°06′W. Fruit, nuts, grapes; cattle, poultry; dairying. Settled 1914, inc. 1939.

Woodland, city (1990 pop. 39,802), ⊙ Yolo co., N central Calif., 15 mi/24 km NW of Sacramento, near Cache Creek; 38°41′N 121°46′W. In a fertile farm area yielding tomatoes, wheat, rice, beans, vegetables, walnuts, almonds, melons, safflower, and sugar beets. It is a growing mfg. center with numerous plants and related warehousing operations (canned vegetables, rice milling, beet-sugar refining). Wine is made in the area. Woodland has many historic homes and is the site of a state historical farm. Inc. 1871.

Woodland 1 town (1990 pop. 552), Talbot co., W Ga., 16 mi/26 km WSW of Thomaston; 32°47′N 84°34′W. **2** town (1990 pop. 760), Northampton co., NE N.C., 35 mi/56 km NNE of Tarboro; 36°19′N 77°12′W. Tobacco, peanuts, cotton, grain; livestock. Mfg. (apparel, consumer goods, bldg. materials). **3** uninc. town (1990 pop. 800), Bradford township, Clearfield co., central Pa., 5 mi/8 km ESE of Clearfield; 40°59′N 78°20′W. Mfg. (lumber); surface and underground bituminous coal. **4** town (1990 pop. 2,500), Cowlitz co., SW Wash., 20 mi/32 km NNW of Vancouver, on Lewis R., 4 mi/6.4 km NE of its confluence with Columbia R.; 45°55′N 122°45′W. Trade center for agr. area; vegetables; dairying; poultry; mfg. (wood prods., motor vehicles, sawmill machinery); timber, limestone. Hulda Kluger Lilac Gardens; Paradise Point State Park to SE. Woodland State Airport here. L. Merwin reservoir and Cedar Creek Grist Mill to E. Settled 1842; inc. 1906.

Woodland 1 village (1990 pop. 313), Iroquois co., E Ill., 4 mi/6.4 km S of Watseka; 40°42′N 87°43′W. In rich agr. area. **2** village, in Baileyville township, Washington co., E Maine. Paper mill. Hydroelectric power. **3** village (1990 pop. 466), Barry co., SW Mich., 9 mi/14.5 km NW of Hastings; 42°43′N 85°07′W. In farm area. **4** village, Jackson co., S Mich., uninc. suburb 3 mi/4.8 km S of Jackson. **5** village (1990 pop. 496), Hennepin co., E Minn., residential suburb 12 mi/19 km W of Minneapolis, at E end of L. Minnetonka; 44°57′N 93°30′W. Wayzata Bay on N. **6** village (1990 pop. 182), Chickasaw co., NE central Miss., 40 mi/64 km SSW of Tupelo; 33°46′N 89°02′W. Mfg. (apparel, furniture). **7** resort village (1990 pop. 125), Ulster co., SE N.Y., in the Catskills, 20 mi/32 km WNW of Kingston; 42°03′N 74°20′W. State campsite here.

Woodland, township (1990 pop. 1,402), Aroostook co., NE Maine, just W of Caribou; 46°52′N 68°06′W. Inc. 1880.

Woodland Beach 1 resort village, Anne Arundel co., central Md., on South R., 5 mi/8 km SW of Annapolis. A crossroads pub helps retain old rural atmosphere. **2** village (1990 pop. 2,309), Monroe co., SE Mich., 5 mi/8 km ENE of Monroe; 41°56′N 83°18′W.

Woodland Beach, Del.: see BOMBAY HOOK ISLAND.

Woodland Heights, uninc. town (1990 pop. 1,471), Venango co., NW Pa., residential suburb 1 mi/1.6 km S of Oil City; 41°24′N 79°42′W.

Woodland Hills, village (1990 pop. 301), Utah co., N central Utah, 14 mi/23 km S of Provo, 3 mi/4.8 km SE of Payson; 40°00′N 111°39′W. Cattle, sheep. Uinta Natl. Forest to S.

Woodland Hills, suburban section of Los Angeles, Los Angeles co., S Calif., in W San Fernando Valley, 21 mi/34 km WNW of downtown. Los Angeles Pierce Col.; Chatsworth Reservoir to N; Motion Picture Country House and Hosp. to W; Santa Monica Mts. Natl. Recreation Area to S. Until 1941 called Girard.

Woodland Park 1 town (1990 pop. 4,610), Teller co., central Colo., in Front Range, 15 mi/24 km NW of Colorado Springs, on Trout Creek, 10 mi/16 km N of Pikes Peak; 39°00′N 105°02′W. Elev. 8,465 ft/2,580 m. Oil, gas, and metal mining. Trout fishing. Pikes Peak Mus., Ute Pass Historical Mus. here. Ute Pass (9,165 ft/2,793 m) to W, surrounded except on SW by Pike Natl. Forest. **2** uninc. town (1990 pop. 950), Lycoming co., N central Pa., residential suburb 4 mi/6.4 km NW of Williamsport, on Lycoming Creek; 41°17′N 77°03′W. Agr. includes dairying; corn, hay, potatoes.

Woodland Park, village, S Alaska, near Anchorage.

Woodlawn 1 uninc. town (1990 pop. 32,907), Baltimore co., N Md., residential suburb of Baltimore; 39°19′N 76°45′W. Called Powhattan in 1856 after the company name for a local mill, the site was renamed when Woodlawn Cemetery Company bought up the site when the mill burned in 1902. The Social Security Administration has its hqs. here and the complex is the 5th-largest federal bldg. in the country, covering 2 million sq ft/185,800 sq m of office space. Pop. includes Woodmoor. **2** uninc. town (1990 pop. 1,810), Lehigh co., E Pa., residential suburb 3 mi/4.8 km W of Allentown; 40°36′N 75°31′W.

Woodlawn 1 village (1990 pop. 582), Jefferson co., S Ill., 8 mi/12.9 km W of Mt. Vernon; 38°19′N 89°02′W. In agr. area. **2** village (1990 pop. 308), Campbell co., N Ky., suburb 2 mi/3.2 km ESE of Cincinnati (Ohio), 1 mi/1.6 km E of Newport; 39°05′N 84°28′W. **3** village (1990 pop. 2,674), Hamilton co., extreme SW Ohio, suburb 10 mi/16 km N of Cincinnati; 39°15′N 84°28′W. Inc. 1941.

Woodlawn, residential section of N Bronx borough of N.Y. city, SE N.Y., S of Yonkers; 40°54′N 73°53′W. To S is Woodlawn Cemetery, a 400-acre/162-ha burial ground with the graves of many celebrities and politicians, including Miles Davis, Duke Ellington, Jay Gould, Fiorello LaGuardia, Herman Melville, and F. W. Woolworth.

Woodlawn Heights, town (1990 pop. 109), Madison co., E central Ind., just NW of Anderson; 40°07′N 85°42′W.

Woodlawn Orchards, village, Jackson co., S Mich., uninc. suburb 4 mi/6.4 km E of Jackson, near Grand R.

Woodlawn Park, town (1990 pop. 1,099), Jefferson co., N Ky., residential suburb 6 mi/9.7 km E of Louisville; 38°15′N 85°37′W.

Woodlawn Park, village (1990 pop. 170), Oklahoma co., central Okla., residential suburb 8 mi/12.9 km WNW of Oklahoma City; 35°30′N 97°39′W. L. Overholser (North Canadian R.) to W.

Woodlyn (WUD-lin), uninc. city (1990 pop. 10,151), Ridley township, Delaware co., SE Pa., residential suburb 10 mi/16 km SW of Philadelphia, on Crum Creek; 39°52′N 75°20′W. Taylor Memorial Arboretum to W.

Woodlynne, residential borough (1990 pop. 2,547), Camden co., SW N.J., S suburb of Camden; 39°55′N 75°05′W. Laid out 1892, inc. 1901.

Woodman, village (1990 pop. 120), Grant co., extreme SW Wis., on Wisconsin R., 17 mi/27 km E of Prairie du Chien; 43°05′N 90°47′W. In farm area. Bull Run Ski Area to NE.

Woodmere, uninc. town (□ 2 sq mi/5.2 sq km; 1990 pop. 15,578), one of the "Five Towns of," Nassau co., SE N.Y., on L.I.; 40°38′N 73°43′W. It is chiefly residential.

Woodmere, village (1990 pop. 834), Cuyahoga co., N Ohio, suburb 11 mi/18 km ESE of Cleveland; 41°27′N 81°28′W.

Woodridge 1 village (1990 pop. 26,256), Du Page co., NE Ill., suburb 23 mi/37 km WSW of Chicago; 41°44′N 88°02′W. It is a growing residential community W of Chicago, in a wooded and agr. area. Mfg. (scales). Inc. 1959. **2** resort village (□ 1 sq mi/2.6 sq km; 1990 pop. 783), Sullivan co., SE N.Y., 7 mi/11.3 km NE of Monticello; 41°42′N 74°34′W.

Wood-Ridge, borough (1990 pop. 7,506), Bergen co., NE N.J., just E of Passaic; 40°51′N 74°05′W. Mfg. (ceramics, electric lamps); printing. Settled before the Revolution, inc. 1894.

Woodruff, county (□ 594 sq mi/1,538 sq km; 1990 pop. 9,520), E central Ark.; ⊙ Augusta; 35°11′N 91°14′W. Bounded W by White R.; drained by Cache R., Cache Bayou, and Bayou DeView. Agr. (cotton, rice, wheat, soybeans, sorghum). Mfg. at Augusta, Cotton Plant, and McCrory. Commercial fishing, mussel-shell gathering; timber. Rex Hancock–Black Swamp Wildlife Management Area at center. Formed 1862.

Woodruff 1 town (1990 pop. 4,365), Spartanburg co., NW S.C., 16 mi/26 km S of Spartanburg; 34°44′N 82°01′W. Mfg. includes vermiculite, food-service equip., coal processing, textiles, hardwood pallets; agr. includes dairying; poultry, cattle; soybeans, peaches, apples, grains. Inc. 1876. **2** town, Oneida co., N Wis., 22 mi/35 km NW of Rhinelander. Mfg. (lumber and flooring). Extensive lake region, near Amer. Legion State Forest (E), Northern Highlands State Forest to N; N terminus of Bearskin State Trail to S at Minocqua; Lac du Flambeau Indian Reservation to NW. Agr. research station to SE.

Woodruff, village (1990 pop. 135), Rich co., N Utah, 10 mi/16 km S of Randolph, on Woodruff Creek, near Bear R. and Wyo. state line; 41°31′N 111°09′W. Elev. 6,344 ft/1,934 m. Agr. (alfalfa, barley, wheat; cattle). Settled winter 1870–1871. Woodruff Narrows Reservoir to E; Neponset Reservoir to S; Wasatch Natl. Forest to W.

Woodruff Place, neighborhood, Marion co., central Ind., within the boundaries of Indianapolis. Located E of Indianapolis and now part of the city. Historic area, noteworthy architecture. Laid out 1872, inc. 1876.

Woods, county (□ 1,290 sq mi/3,341 sq km; 1990 pop. 9,103), NW Okla.; ⊙ Alva; 36°46′N 98°51′W. Bounded N by Kansas state line, W and S borders formed by Cimarron R.; drained by Salt Fork of Arkansas R. and Eagle Chief Creek. Agr. (wheat, sorghum; cattle) area. Sand and gravel pits, salt and gypsum deposits. Northwestern State Univ. at Alva. Little Sahara State Park in S, on Cimarron R. Formed 1893.

Woods Cross, town (1990 pop. 5,384), Davis co., N Utah, suburb 8 mi/12.9 km N of Salt Lake City, on Mill Creek; 40°52′N 111°54′W. Elev. 4,292 ft/1,308 m. Fruits, vegetables; dairying; oil refining. Great Salt L. is just W. Wasatch Range and Natl. Forest to E. Inc. 1935.

Woods Heights, village (1990 pop. 708), Ray co., W Mo., 3 mi/4.8 km E of Excelsior Springs; 39°20′N 94°09′W. Residential, agr. area.

Woods Hole, uninc. village (1990 pop. 1,080) and seaport in the town of Falmouth, Barnstable co., SE Mass., at the SW extremity of Cape Cod. It is the departure point for nearby isl. resorts (Martha's Vineyard, Nantucket). Woods Hole is the site of an important marine biology laboratory and of the Oceanographic Institution and Exhibit Center, which maintains the research ship *Atlantis* and submarine *Alvin* that discovered the *Titanic* and *Bismarck*. A fish hatchery and aquarium and a U.S. Coast Guard station are also here.

Woods Island (□ 3 sq mi/8 sq km), W N.F., E Canada, on S side of the Bay of Isls., 15 mi/24 km NW of Corner Brook; 3 mi/5 km long, 2 mi/3 km wide; 49°06′N 58°13′W. Fishing.

Woodsboro 1 town (1990 pop. 513), Frederick co., N Md., 10 mi/16 km NNE of Frederick; 39°32′N 77°19′W. The Rosebud Perfume Company was founded here in 1891 and still maintains offices here although the salve is now made in Baltimore and the perfume in N.Y. city. Laid out by Joseph Wood, a Revolutionary War officer who built a house here before 1776, it was Woods Town, then Woodsberry, then Woodsborough before becoming Woodsboro in 1922. **2** town (1990 pop. 1,731), Refugio co., S Texas, 38 mi/61 km N of Corpus Christi; 28°14′N 97°19′W. Trade center in farm, cattle, petroleum and natural-gas area; oil and gas processing. Inc. 1928.

Woodsburgh, village (1990 pop. 1,190), Nassau co., SE N.Y., on SW L.I., just E of Cedarhurst; 40°37′N 73°42′W. In summer-resort area.

Woodsfield, village (1990 pop. 2,832), ⊙ Monroe co., E

Ohio, 29 mi/47 km NE of Marietta; 39°46′N 81°07′W. In agr. area; coal mines, oil and gas wells; hardwood timber. Mfg. tools. Settled 1815, inc. 1834.

Woodside 1 town (1990 pop. 5,035), San Mateo co., W Calif., suburb 25 mi/40 km S of San Francisco, 5 mi/8 km W of Palo Alto; 37°25′N 122°16′W. Small Searsville L. reservoir to S on Sausal Creek. San Francisco State Fish and Game Refuge to NW. Hetch Hetchy Aqueduct passes to N. **2** uninc. town (1990 pop. 1,360), Foster township, Luzerne co., E central Pa., residential suburb 1 mi/1.6 km S of Freeland; 41°00′N 75°54′W. **3** uninc. town (1990 pop. 2,947), Bucks co., SE Pa., residential suburb 6 mi/9.7 km W of Trenton (N.J.), 24 mi/39 km NE of Philadelphia; 40°13′N 74°51′W.

Woodside 1 village (1990 pop. 140), Kent co., central Del., 7 mi/11.3 km SSW of Dover; 39°04′N 75°34′W. Shipping point in agr. area (grain. fruit, vegetables; poultry; dairying). Parts of N.G. Wilder Wildlife Area to W and SW. **2** village, Greenville co., NW S.C., residential suburb W of Greenville on Long Creek.

Woodside, residential section of W Queens borough of N.Y. city, SE N.Y.; 40°45′N 73°55′W. Some mfg. Once heavily Irish, now the neighborhood has a diverse mix of residents, including mainland and Hong Kong Chinese, Koreans, Dominicans, Colombians, Asian Indians, Filipinos, Guyanese, Peruvians, and Irish.

Woodside East, uninc. town (1990 est. pop. 1,655), Kent co., central Del., 5 mi/8 km S of Dover; 39°04′N 75°32′W. Surburban community near Dover.

Woodson, county (☐ 505 sq mi/1,308 sq km; 1990 pop. 4,116), SE Kansas; ⊙ Yates Center; 37°53′N 95°44′W. Dissected plain, crossed in NE by Neosho R., in SW by Verdigris R. Cattle, hogs, corn, wheat, soybeans, hay; textiles. There are scattered oil fields. Toronto L. reservoir and Toronto State Park in SW corner; Woodson State Fishing L. in SW. Formed 1855.

Woodson 1 village (1990 pop. 472), Morgan co., W central Ill., 6 mi/9.7 km S of Jacksonville; 39°37′N 90°13′W. In agr. area (corn, wheat, soybeans; cattle, hogs). **2** village (1990 pop. 262), Throckmorton co., N Texas, 14 mi/23 km SE of Throckmorton; 33°00′N 99°02′W. In agr. area; mfg. trailers.

Woodson Terrace, city (1990 pop. 4,362), St. Louis co., E Mo.; residential suburb 12 mi/19 km NW of St. Louis; 38°43′N 90°21′W. Adjacent to Lambert–St. Louis Airport. Publishing.

Woodstock, city (1991 pop. 30,075), S Ont., central Canada, SW of Hamilton; 43°08′N 80°45′W. It is an industrial center with diversified mfg. such as electrical equip., motor vehicles, musical instruments, dental equip., textiles, fertilizer, and cheese. The surrounding country has mixed farming, dairying, and livestock raising.

Woodstock, town (1991 pop. 4,631), ⊙ Carleton co., W N.B., E Canada, on St. John R., 45 mi/72 km WNW of Fredericton, near Maine border. In mining (zinc, copper, lead), dairying, and fruit-growing (apples, plums) region; lumbering; mfg. of furniture, agr. machinery, dairy prods. Has agr. col. Former iron-mining center.

Woodstock, city (1990 pop. 14,353), ⊙ McHenry co., NE Ill., 36 mi/58 km E of Rockford, 53 mi/85 km NW of Chicago; 42°18′N 88°26′W. Grain, dairying; mfg. (paper prods., medical equip., food prods., machinery, chemicals). McHenry County Community Col. to SE.

Woodstock 1 town (1990 pop. 6,008), Windham co., NE Conn., on Mass. state line, 6 mi/9.7 km NW of Putnam; 41°58′N 72°01′W. Agr.; mfg. of electrical equip., aircraft components, plastics, toiletries, foods, and fiberglass components. Has 18th- and 19th-cent. houses. Settled 1686, inc. 1690. **2** town (1990 pop. 1,167), Grafton co., W central N.H., 14 mi/23 km N of Plymouth; 43°58′N 71°44′W. Drained by Pemigewasset R. Agr. (nursery crops; cattle, poultry; dairying). North Woodstock village is commercial center of town, including Clark's trading post. Russell Pond State Campground in E; parts of White Mt. Natl. Forest in E and W; Loon Mt. Ski Area to NE in Lincoln; Hobo Scenic RR; Appalachian Trail crosses NW corner; Mt. Moosilauke (4,810 ft/1,466 m) to W in Benton. **3** resort town (1990 pop. 3,212), ⊙ Windsor co., E Vt., on Ottauquechee R., and 23 mi/37 km E of Rutland; 43°36′N 72°32′W. Includes Woodstock village. Summer and winter resorts (Suicide Six ski area); mfg. (ski lifts, furniture, pottery, bldg. materials); agr. (dairy prods., maple sugar). Noted for fine old houses, restored inn, and village green. Hiram Powers, George P. Marsh, John Cotton Dana b. here. Billings Fram mus. here. Chartered and settled c.1761. **4** town (1990 pop. 3,182), ⊙ Shenandoah co., NW Va., 28 mi/45 km SW of Winchester, near North Fork of Shenandoah R.; 38°52′N 78°31′W. Mfg. (printing and publishing, fruit- and vegetable-packing equip.); trade center in agr. area (apples, grain, soybeans; livestock; dairying); timber. Site of Woodstock Military Acad. On crest of Massanutten Mt. (SE) is observation tower overlooking Shenandoah Valley. Settled 1752; inc. 1872.

Woodstock 1 village, Howard co., N Md., on Patapsco R., 14 mi/23 km W of Baltimore. Seat of Woodstock Col. and Seminary (R.C.), founded by the Jesuits in 1869 and for many years the only Jesuit seminary in the U.S. The Jesuits moved out in 1970, and part of the premises is now used by the Jobs Corps. Patapsco State Park nearby. **2** village (1990 pop. 159), Pipestone co., SW Minn., 12 mi/19 km E of Pipestone; 44°00′N 96°05′W. Agr. (corn, oats, soybeans; livestock; dairying); mfg. (feeds). **3** village (1990 pop. 1,870), Ulster co., SE N.Y., in E foothills of the Catskill Mts.; 42°02′N 74°07′W. Best known for its association with the famous 3-day music festival in 1969 that featured such musicians and bands as The Who, the Grateful Dead, Joan Baez, Jimi Hendrix, and the Jefferson Airplane. (Though the festival was named for Woodstock, it wasn't actually held here; because village officials would not approve the event, it was held on a 600-acre/243-ha dairy farm near Bethel, 60 mi/97 km SW.) But Woodstock had a reputation as an artists' colony and progressive retreat long before the 1960s. A tannery center in the 19th cent., it became an art colony in 1902, when wealthy Englishman Ralph Radcliffe Whitehead, a student of Ruskin, established Byrdcliffe, a working community of artists and craftspeople, on the side of Overlook Mt. Included were workshops, studios, a theater, and a lib. Subsequently weavers, painters, potters, musicians, and actors began to flock here. In 1906 the Manhattan-based Arts Student League opened a summer school here, and the adjacent Maverick colony, which had broken away from the Byrdcliffe group, drew social reformers, artists, and performers. The 1st Woodstock festivals (probably sedate tea parties with folk music and dancing) took place at Byrdcliffe from 1915 to 1931. In 1921 several factions of the Communist party convened at Overlook Mt. Hotel here and formed the Communist Party of Amer. In the early 1960s, Woodstock attracted many young social protesters, casual drug users, folk musicians, and other members of the hippie movement; the Woodstock Festival in 1969, attended by 400,000–600,000 people and immortalized in the 1970 documentary *Woodstock*, solidified the village's reputation as a counterculture country retreat. To this day, much of its pop. consists of aging hippies, and the village remains a magnet for tourists, artists, and drifters. The 25th anniversary of Woodstock was observed in 1994 with another music festival, this time held at Saugerties (10 mi/16 km E). **4** village (1990 pop. 296), Champaign co., W central Ohio, 13 mi/21 km ENE of Urbana; 40°10′N 83°31′W. In agr. area.

Woodstock, suburb (1990 pop. 4,361) of Atlanta, Cherokee co., NW Ga., 24 mi/39 km NNW of city center; 34°06′N 84°31′W. Mfg. includes aircraft assemblies, beverages, concrete, and wood and marble prods.

Woodstock, township (1990 pop. 1,194), Oxford co., W Maine, 12 mi/19 km S of Rumford; 44°23′N 70°35′W. Wood prods. Includes Bryant Pond, resort on small lake draining S into Little Androscoggin R.

Woodston, village (1990 pop. 121), Rooks co., N Kansas, on South Fork of Solomon R., 9 mi/14.5 km E of Stockton; 39°27′N 99°05′W. Wheat; livestock.

Woodstown, borough (1990 pop. 3,154), Salem co., SW N.J., on Salem R., 8 mi/12.9 km NE of Salem; 39°38′N 75°19′W. In agr. region; mfg. (bricks, clothing). Has 18th-cent. Friends' meetinghouse. Quaker center since settlement before 1725; inc. 1882.

Woodsville, village (1990 pop. 1,122), ⊙ Grafton co., W N.H., in NW part of Haverhill, 17 mi/27 km SW of Littleton on Connecticut R., opposite Wells River (Vt.), at mouth of Ammonoosuc R.; 44°08′N 72°01′W., Both rivers are bridged here. Former RR center. Mfg. (bldg. materials, printing and publishing, lumber); agr. (vegetables, apples, nursery crops; cattle; dairying); timber.

Woodville, village (1991 pop. 680), S Ont., central Canada, 13 mi/21 km W of Lindsay. Dairying; farming; fruit.

Woodville 1 town, Jackson co., NE Ala., 20 mi/32 km SE of Huntsville, near Paint Rock R. **2** uninc. town (1990 pop. 1,559), Tulare co., S central Calif., 15 mi/24 km S of Visalia; 36°05′N 119°12′W. Fruit, grapes, nuts, grain, cotton, sugar beets; cattle, hogs, poultry. **3** town (1990 pop. 415), Greene co., NE central Ga., 8 mi/12.9 km NE of Greensboro; 33°40′N 83°07′W. Lumber and wood prods. **4** town (1990 pop. 1,393), ⊙ Wilkinson co., extreme SW Miss., 32 mi/51 km S of Natchez, near La. state line; 31°06′N 91°17′W. Agr. (cotton, corn; cattle; timber); mfg. (wood chips, apparel, lumber). Rosemont Plantation to E; Old Pond Store (1880) 13 mi/21 km WSW. Clark Creek Nature Area to W, near Mississippi R.; Homochitto Natl. Forest to NE. Inc. 1811. **5** town (1990 pop. 2,636), ⊙ Tyler co., E Texas, c.50 mi/80 km NNW of Beaumont; 30°46′N 94°25′W. Lumber milling, mfg. (wood chips, aluminum prods., jewelry displays); Christmas trees; cattle; vegetables; catfish. Oil and gas. Alabama and Coushatta Indian Reservation to W. Several units of Big Thicket Natl. Preserve to SW, S, and E. B.A. Steinhagen L. (Neches R.) State Park 16 mi/26 km E. Settled c.1847, inc. 1929. **6** town (1990 pop. 942), St. Croix co., W Wis., 23 mi/37 km E of Hudson; 44°57′N 92°17′W. Trade center for dairying, farming, and livestock-raising area; mfg. (wire assemblies, metal stampings). (Army Corps of Engineering) Eau Galle Dam Recreation Area to S.

Woodville 1 village, Jackson co., S Mich., uninc. suburb 3 mi/4.8 km W of Jackson; 42°15′N 84°29′W. **2** village (1990 pop. 1,953), Sandusky co., N Ohio, 16 mi/26 km SE of Toledo, on Portage R.; 41°27′N 83°22′W. In grain and livestock area; limestone quarrying and processing. Founded c.1836. **3** village (1990 pop. 31), Marshall co., S Okla., on peninsula extending into L. Texoma, 14 mi/23 km W of Durant (at New Woodville, 2 mi/3.2 km N of original townsite flooded by L. Texoma, 1944); 33°58′N 96°39′W. L. Texoma State Park; recreation.

Woodville, township (1990 pop. 215), Penobscot co., central Maine, on the Penobscot, 18 mi/29 km SE of Millinocket; 45°31′N 68°25′W. In lumbering area.

Woodward, county (☐ 1,246 sq mi/3,227 sq km; 1990 pop. 18,976), NW Okla.; ⊙ Woodward; 36°25′N 99°15′W. Intersected by North Canadian (Beaver) R., and Wolf Creek; Cimarron R. forms NE border. Wolf Creek is impounded here by Fort Supply Dam in W. Agr. (wheat, alfalfa, oats), cattle raising. Mfg. at Woodward. Oil and natural-gas deposits. Alabaster Caverns State Park in N; Boiling Springs State Park near co. center. Formed 1893.

Woodward, city (1990 pop. 12,340), ⊙ Woodward co., NW Okla., on North Canadian R., c.85 mi/137 km W of Enid; 36°25′N 99°24′W. Elev. 1,906 ft/581 m. Market and processing center for wheat and cattle and oil and natural-gas area, also producing hay, poultry; mfg. (oil field equip., apparel, crude iodine, printing and publishing). Oil and natural gas. Includes Southern Plains Range Research Station, U.S. agr. experiment station. Mus. of Pioneer History and Plains Indians here. Boiling Springs State Park to E. Settled 1893.

Woodward, town (1990 pop. 1,197), Dallas co., central Iowa, 24 mi/39 km NW of Des Moines; 41°51′N 93°55′W. Food processing (corn, oats). Coal mines nearby. Woodward State Hosp. and School are here. N end of Saylorville Reservoir to E.

Woodward, uninc. village, Jefferson co., N central Ala., just SW of Birmingham. Pig iron, industrial chemicals, tar, coke-oven gas, granulated slag.

Woodway 1 town (1990 pop. 8,695), McLennan co., E central Texas, residential suburb 7 mi/11.3 km SW of Waco, near L. Waco reservoir (Bosque R.); 31°30′N 97°13′W. **2** town (1990 pop. 914), Snohomish co., on King co. line, NW Wash., residential suburb 13 mi/21 km N of Seattle, 1 mi/1.6 km S of Edmonds, on Puget Sound; 47°48′N 122°25′W.

Woodworth 1 village (1990 pop. 754), Rapides parish, central La., 12 mi/19 km S of Alexandria; 31°09′N 92°30′W. Mfg. (asphalt, concrete, concrete prods.). Alexander State Forest and Indian Creek Recreation Area to E; Kisatchie Natl. Forest and Claiborne Range Military Reservation to W. **2** village (1990 pop. 102), Stutsman co., central N.Dak., 33 mi/53 km WNW of Jamestown; 47°08′N 99°17′W. Chase L. Natl. Wildlife Refuge to SW. **3** village, Kenosha co., extreme SE Wis., near Des Plaines R., 8 mi/12.9 km W of Kenosha.

Woody Island, Alaska: see WOOD ISLAND.

Wool Market or **Woodmarket**, uninc. town (1990 pop. 1,166), Harrison co., SE Miss., residential community 8 mi/12.9 km NW of Biloxi, 8 mi/12.9 km NE of Gulfport near Biloxi R.; 30°28′N 89°00′W. Agr. area (cotton, corn, pecans, citrus); timber. De Soto Natl. Forest to N.

Wooldridge, town (1990 pop. 54), Cooper co., central Mo., on Missouri R., 13 mi/21 km ESE of Boonville; 38°54′N 92°31′W. Corn, soybeans, cattle. Severely damaged by flood of 1993.

Wooldridge, mining village, Campbell co., NE Tenn., near Ky. state line, 45 mi/72 km NNW of Knoxville, in Cumberland foothills; in coal region.

Woolsey, town (1990 pop. 120), Fayette co., W central Ga., 11 mi/18 km NW of Griffin; 33°22′N 84°25′W.

Woolstock, town (1990 pop. 212), Wright co., N central Iowa, 7 mi/11.3 km N of Webster City; 42°34′N 93°50′W. In agr. area.

Woolwich (WUL-wich), town (1990 pop. 2,570), Sagadahoc co., S Maine, on the Kennebec opposite Bath; 43°58′N 69°46′W. Boatbuilding, agr. Includes Nequasset village on small Nequasset L. Settled 1638, destroyed in Indian wars, resettled 1734, inc. 1759.

Woonasquatucket River (woo-NOS-qua-tuck-et), c.16 mi/26 km long, N R.I.; rises SW of Woonsocket; flows generally SE, through Smithfield town, past mill villages (water power), and through Providence, joining Moshassuck R. just before entering Providence R. Woonasquatucket Reservoir (Stillwater Reservoir; c. 2.5 mi/4 km long) and others are formed by dams.

Woonsocket, city (1990 pop. 43,877), Providence co., N R.I., on both sides of the Blackstone R.; 42°00′N 71°30′W. The demise of the textile industry, which long shaped the city, hurt its economy, but it remains a leading mfg. center. Worsted woolen weaving and package dyeing are still carried on; more contemporary mfg. is electronic equip., plastics, and sporting goods. Of interest are the river falls in the center of the city and the unusual potholes worn by swirling stones in the riverbed. Also in Woonsocket is one of the state's 1st public libraries, in which Abraham Lincoln spoke (1860); the John Arnold House (1712); and the Woonsocket Company Mill (1830s), a complex of industrial bldgs. and worker housing. Settled c.1666, set off from Cumberland 1867, inc. as a city 1888.

Woonsocket, town (1990 pop. 766), ⊙ Sanborn co., SE central S.Dak., 85 mi/137 km WSW of Sioux Falls; 44°02′N 98°16′W. In agr. area; mfg. (taxidermy supplies). Twin Lakes State Lakeside Use Area to S. Settled 1883, inc. 1888.

Wooster (WUHS-tuhr), city (1990 pop. 22,191), ⊙ Wayne co., N central Ohio; 40°49′N 81°56′W. In a farm area. Paper, plastics, brass, food, and plastic prods. A state agr. research and development station is nearby. The city is the seat of the Col. of Wooster, which was chartered in 1866 and opened in 1870. Inc. 1817.

Worcester 1 (WUH-stuhr), county (1990 pop. 35,028), SE Md.; 38°14′N 75°17′W. On the Eastern Shore (Delmarva Peninsula); bounded S by Va. state line, SW and NW by Pocomoke R. (flows across co.), N by Del. state line. It is the only Md. co. that is bordered by the ocean. Off its Atlantic shore, a N-S chain of bays forms inland waterway bet. mainland and barrier isls. Tidewater agr. area (potatoes, fruit, dairy prods.; poultry); large timber stands (mainly softwoods) E of Pocomoke R.; lumber mills, vegetable canneries, clothing factories. Shores have small fishing towns and resorts, best know of which are Ocean City (noted for deep-sea fishing). Great cypress swamps, including part of Pocomoke State Forest lie along Pocomoke R. Formed 1742, it was named for the Earl of Worcester. **2** county (□ 1,579 sq mi/4,090 sq km; 1990 pop. 709,705), ⊙ Worcester and Fitchburg, central Mass.; 42°21′N 71°55′W. Bordering on N.H., R.I., and Conn.; drained by Blackstone, Nashua, Assabet, Millers, and Ware rivers; give water power to such industrial centers as Worcester, Fitchburg, Leominster, Milford, Webster. Agr. (vegetables; dairying). Wachusett Mt. and Reservoir are in co. Includes state forests, resort lakes. Formed 1731.

Worcester (WUH-stuhr), industrial city (1990 pop. 169,759), ⊙ Worcester co., central Mass., on the Blackstone R.; 42°16′N 71°49′W. The 2d largest city in Mass. and New England. The canalization (1828) of the Blackstone R. marked the beginning of Worcester's rapid industrial development. A port of entry, its mfg. includes machinery, metal goods, chemicals, plastics, paper prods., pharmaceuticals, glass, electrical equip., textiles, clothing, and shoes. There is also a printing and publishing industry, and state hosps. add to the city's economy. Settled in 1673, Worcester suffered Native Amer. attacks in 1675 and 1683. In Shays's Rebellion the courthouse was besieged (1786) by insurgents. The 1st women's suffrage natl. convention was held (1850) in Worcester. Edward Everett Hale was pastor there from 1842 to 1856. Worcester is the seat of 13 cols. and univs., incl. Clark Univ., Worcester Polytechnic Inst., Worcester State Col., Col. of the Holy Cross, Assumption Col., Univ. of Mass. Medical School and Medical Center, and several junior cols. It has a number of notable mus., 2 zoos, and an annual music festival (dating from 1858). Also of interest is a huge 3-level factory outlet with a Plexiglas dome. There is also an art mus., science center, Goodard Rocket Mus., Higgins Armory Mus., and the Amer. Antiquerian Society. L. Quinsigamond and 2 state parks are in the vicinity. The Worcester Centrum hosts contemporary music concerts and sporting events. Inc. 1722.

Worcester 1 (WUH-stuhr), uninc. town (1990 pop. 900), Montgomery co., SE Pa., suburb 17 mi/27 km NNW of Philadelphia, on Zacharias Creek; 40°12′N 75°20′W. Mfg. includes computers, asphalt, epoxy compounds. **2** (WORS-tuhr), town (1990 pop. 906), Washington co., N central Vt., on North Branch of Winooski R., 7 mi/11.3 km N of Montpelier; 44°25′N 72°34′W.

Worcester (WOO-stuhr), village (1990 pop. 900), Otsego co., central N.Y., 12 mi/19 km SE of Cooperstown, in the Catskills; 42°35′N 74°43′W. Small lakes nearby. Some mfg.

Worden 1 village (1990 pop. 896), Madison co., SW Ill., 27 mi/43 km NE of East St. Louis; 38°55′N 89°50′W. RR junction. In agr. (wheat, corn, sorghum, cattle) and oil area. Inc. 1877. **2** village (1990 pop. 380), Yellowstone co., S Mont., near Yellowstone R., 20 mi/32 km NE of Billings. In irrigated agr. region. Beans, potataoes, sugar beets. Agr. research center to SW, Pompey's Pillar Natl. Historic Landmark to E. Sandstone butte with William Clark's name inscribed on it, only evidence of Lewis and Clark Expedition (1806).

Worden, Fort, Wash.: see PORT TOWNSEND.

Worden Pond, in South Kingstown, Washington co., S R.I., in the Great Swamp, 4 mi/6.4 km W of Wakefield; c.2 mi/3.2 km wide; 41°26′N 71°34′W. Largest natural lake in state. Source of Pawcatuck R., drains W; receives Chipuxet R. from N. Great Swamp Management Area on N shore.

Worland (WOR-luhnd), town (1990 pop. 5,742), ⊙ Washakie co., N central Wyo., on Bighorn R., 115 mi/185 km NW of Casper; 44°00′N 107°57′W. Elev. 4,061 ft/1,238 m. Trade center for irrigated sugar-beet and sheep region. Mfg. (meat processing; dairy prods.; soft drinks; printing and publishing; aluminum prods.); agr. (beans, grain); timber. Founded 1903.

Worland (WOR-luhnd), uninc. rural community, Bates co., W Mo., near Marais des Cygnes R., 15 mi/24 km WSW of Butler. On Kansas state line.

World Financial Center, office complex and entertainment center, SW Manhattan, N.Y. city, SE N.Y., bordered on W by Hudson R., on E by West Side Highway, on N by Vesey St., and on S by the Battery City Park complex. The complex consists of 4 reflective glass and granite office bldgs. (34–51 stories, 6 million sq ft/557,400 sq m of office space, 300,000 sq ft/27,870 sq m of retail space); a Winter Garden with a 125-ft-/38-m-high glass-vaulted atrium; an enclosed, skylit courtyard; a landscaped public plaza (3.5 acres/1.4 ha); and 2 octagonal wings on either side of Liberty St. designed as a gateway from the city to the Hudson R.

World Trade Center, office complex, SW Manhattan, N.Y. city, SE N.Y., on Lower West Side, bounded on S by Liberty St., on N by Vesey St., on W by West St., and on E by Church St. Owned by the Port Authority of N.Y. and N.J., it was created in 1962 as the world center of commerce. The 110-story "Twin Towers" of the complex, overlooking adjacent Battery Park City, are the city's tallest bldgs. (1,160 ft/354 m). There are 4 additional low-rise bldgs. occupying the 16-acre/6-ha site. The amount of office space (10 million sq ft/929,000 sq m) here is 7 times that of the Empire State Bldg.The high design and construction costs were controversial issues at the time. On Feb. 26, 1993, a powerful bomb exploded in an underground garage; 4 terrorists were later found guilty of the incident.

Worley, village (1990 pop. 182), Kootenai co., N Idaho, 20 mi/32 km SSW of Coeur d'Alene, near Wash. state line; 47°24′N 116°55′W. Cattle; alfalfa, oats. On Coeur d'Alene Indian Reservation. Heyburn State Park to E; Coeur d'Alene L. to NE.

Wormleysburg (WURM-lees-buhrg), borough (1990 pop. 2,847), Cumberland co., S central Pa., residential suburb 2 mi/3.2 km W of Harrisburg, on Susquehanna R. (bridged) opposite Harrisburg, at mouth of Conodoguinet Creek; 40°15′N 76°54′W. Laid out 1815.

Woronoco, Mass.: see RUSSELL.

Worth 1 county (□ 574 sq mi/1,487 sq km; 1990 pop. 19,745), S central Ga.; ⊙ Sylvester; 31°33′N 83°51′W. Mfg. of wood prods., apparel, and textiles. Coastal plain agr. (peanuts, cotton, tobacco, corn, wheat, soy beans); cattle, hogs, poultry; timber. Formed 1853. **2** county (□ 401 sq mi/1,039 sq km; 1990 pop. 7,991), N Iowa, on Minn. state line; ⊙ Northwood; 43°22′N 93°16′W. Prairie agr. area (hogs, cattle, poultry; corn, oats, soybeans; dairying) drained by Shell Rock R. Silver L. in NW; Rice L. on W border. Formed 1851. **3** county (□ 267 sq mi/692 sq km; 1990 pop. 2,440), NW Mo.; ⊙ Grant City; 40°28′N 94°25′W. Borders Iowa on N; drained by Grand R. Wheat, corn; cattle; some mfg. at Grant City. Smallest co. in Mo. in land area and pop. Formed 1861.

Worth 1 town, Turner co., S central Ga., 15 mi/24 km SSE of Cordele; 31°45′N 83°40′W. **2** town (1990 pop. 103), Worth co., NW Mo., on Middle Fork of Grand R., 7 mi/11.3 km S of Grant City; 40°24′N 94°27′W.

Worth, village (1990 pop. 11,208), Cook co., NE Ill., suburb 15 mi/24 km SW of Chicago; 41°41′N 87°47′W. Mfg. (conveyors, steel processing, packaging materials, furniture). On Calumet Sag Channel.

Worth, Lake, reservoir, Tarrant co., N Texas, on West Fork of Trinity R., 5 mi/8 km WNW of Fort Worth, within Fort Worth city limits, bet. Lakeside (W) and Lake Worth (E); c.10 mi/16 km long; 32°46′N 97°24′W. Eagle Mt. Dam at NW tip. Recreational area. Carswell Air Force Base on S shore, near dam; Fort Worth Nature Center and Refuge on NW shore.

Wortham, town (1990 pop. 1,020), Freestone co., E central Texas, 22 mi/35 km S of Corsicana; 31°47′N 96°27′W. In agr. (cattle, peaches, pecans, vegetables) and oil-producing area; timber; mfg. valves, steel fabricating. Confederate Reunion Grounds State Historical Site to SW. Inc. 1910.

Worthing, village (1990 pop. 371), Lincoln co., SE S.Dak.,

13 mi/21 km S of Sioux Falls; 43°19′N 96°45′W. Mfg. (indoor aviaries).

Worthing, SE residential suburb and seaside resort of Bridgetown, SW Barbados, B.W.I.

Worthington 1 city (1990 pop. 9,977), ⊙ Nobles co., SW Minn., on Okabena L., near Iowa state line, c.90 mi/145 km SW of Mankato; 43°37′N 95°35′W. Elev. 1,593 ft/486 m. Resort; agr. trade center (soybeans, corn, oats, alfalfa; cattle, sheep, hogs, poultry; dairying); mfg. (machinery, poultry processing, printing and publishing, feeds, mobile homes, hog processing). RR junction to SW. In area of small natural lakes of glacial origin; at NE end of Okabena L. where Okabena Creek exits lake. Municipal Airport to N. Settled 1871. **2** city (1990 pop. 14,869), Franklin co., central Ohio, suburb of Columbus; 40°05′N 83°01′W. Mainly residential, it has some light industry. Worthington Col. is here. Of note are the Orange Johnson House (1816) and the Ohio RR Mus. Superabrasives mfg. Settled 1803, inc. 1835.

Worthington 1 town (1990 pop. 1,473), Greene co., SW Ind., on West Fork of White R., at influx of Eel R., 6 mi/9.7 km NNW of Bloomfield; 39°07′N 86°59′W. In agr. area (grain; livestock). Mfg. (pork slaughtering and processing). Bituminous-coal mines nearby. Laid out 1849. **2** town (1990 pop. 439), Dubuque co., E Iowa, 23 mi/37 km WSW of Dubuque; 42°23′N 91°07′W. **3** town (1990 pop. 1,751), Greenup co., NE Ky., residential suburb 7 mi/11.3 km NW of Ashland, on Ohio R.; 38°32′N 82°44′W. **4** town (1990 pop. 1,156), Hampshire co., W central Mass., 17 mi/27 km ESE of Pittsfield; 42°24′N 72°57′W. Dairying. **5** town (1990 pop. 86), Putnam co., N Mo., on Chariton R., 16 mi/26 km ESE of Unionville; 40°24′N 92°41′W.

Worthington, village (1990 pop. 233), Marion co., N W.Va., 7 mi/11.3 km WSW of Fairmont, on West Fork R.; 39°27′N 80°15′W. Agr. (corn, apples; livestock). Mfg. (mining equip., machinery).

Worthington, borough (1990 pop. 713), Armstrong co., W central Pa., 6 mi/9.7 km WNW of Kittanning, near Patterson Creek; 40°50′N 79°37′W. RR junction to NW. Agr. (grain; livestock; dairying); mfg. (cooling systems, limestone processing).

Worthville, village (1990 pop. 191), Carroll co., N Ky., 9 mi/14.5 km SE of Carollton, on Eagle Creek, near its confluence with Kentucky R. (to W), in N part of Bluegrass region; 38°36′N 85°04′W. Agr. (tobacco; livestock).

Worthville, borough (1990 pop. 65), Jefferson co., W central Pa., 14 mi/23 km NW of Punxsutawney, on Sandy Creek; 41°01′N 79°08′W. Agr. (corn, hay; livestock; dairying).

Wotton (WAH-tuhn), village (1991 pop. 919), S Que., E Canada, 8 mi/13 km ESE of Asbestos. Asbestos mining.

Wounded Knee, village (1990 pop. 18), Shannon co., SW S.Dak.; 12 mi/19 km NE of Pine Ridge Indian Reservation. Site of the last major battle of the Indian Wars and the Wounded Knee Massacre. After the murder of Sitting Bull, a band of Sioux, led by Big Foot, fled to Pine Ridge, but were captured by the 7th Cavalry on Dec. 28, 1890, and brought to the creek (29 soldiers were killed in the battle). The next day, unarmed Indian men, women, and children were shot by U.S. troops.

Wrangell Island, off SE Alaska in the Alexander Archipelago, S of the mouth of the Stikine R., 30 mi/48 km long and 5 mi/8 km to 14 mi/23 km wide. It was occupied in 1834 by Russians, who named it for the Rus. explorer and Governor General of Alaska Baron Ferdinand von Wrangel. The city of Wrangell, on the N coast, grew around a fort built to prevent encroachment by the Hudson's Bay Company traders. From 1867 to 1877 it was a U.S. military post; later it became an outfitting point for hunters and explorers as well as for miners using the Stikine R. route to the Yukon. Fishing and mining are pursued in the area. Lumber mill closed in 1990s.

Wrangell Mountains, volcanic mts., S Alaska, extending c.100 mi/160 km SE from the Copper R. to the Can. border, where they meet the St. Elias Mts.; 56°32′N 132°19′W. Mt. Blackburn (16,390 ft/4,996 m) is the highest peak. There is a cosmic radiation observatory on Mt. Wrangell (14,163 ft/4,317 m). Minerals such as gold, copper, and zinc are found in the area. Named for the Rus. explorer Baron Ferdinand von Wrangel, the mts. comprise a portion of the Wrangell–St. Elias Natl. Park and Preserve.

Wrangell Narrows, narrow and shallow channel, SE Alaska, bet. Mitkof and Kupreanof Isls., Alexander Archipelago, S of Petersburg, part of the Inside Passage. Extraordinary navigation lights.

Wrangell–Saint Elias National Park and Preserve, (□ 13,018 sq mi/33,717 sq km), preserve (□ 7,589 sq mi/19,656 sq km), and wilderness (□ 19,768 sq mi/51,199 sq km), SW Alaska; 62°00′N 143°00′W. Proclaimed natl. monument 1978, est. as natl. park 1980. No facilities. Largest unit in the Natl. Park System; numerous peaks over 16,000 ft/4,877 m; abundant wildlife; N. Amer.'s largest glaciated area. Lies adjacent to Yukon's Kluane Natl. Park. Includes Mt. St. Elias (18,008 ft/5,489 m).

Wray, town (1990 pop. 1,998), ⊙ Yuma co., NE Colo., on North Fork of Republican R., in the Sand Hills, near Nebr. state line, 150 mi/241 km ENE of Denver; 40°04′N 102°13′W. Elev. 3,516 ft/1,072 m. Wheat; dairy prods.; cattle. Mfg. (health foods). Fish hatchery to SW. Beecher Isl. Battleground site to S, commemorating battle (1868) bet. Indians and incoming settlers. Inc. 1906.

Wreck Island, Northampton co., E Va., off Atlantic coast, 12 mi/19 km E of Cape Charles city, c.3 mi/4.8 km long; 37°16′N 75°47′W. Cobb Isl. and Sand Shoal Inlet to N; Ship Shoal Isl. to S. Cobb Isl. Bay to NW, South Bay to SW.

Wren, village (1990 pop. 190), Van Wert co., W Ohio, 11 mi/18 km WSW of Van Wert, near Ind. state line; 40°48′N 84°46′W. In agr. area.

Wrens (RENS), town (1990 pop. 2,414), Jefferson co., E Ga., 28 mi/45 km SW of Augusta; 33°13′N 82°23′W. Agr. trade center; mfg.(air-conditioning equip. and controls, pecan and clay processing, food processing); sawmilling. Founded 1884.

Wrenshall (REN-shawl), village (1990 pop. 296), Carlton co., E Minn., near St. Louis R., 4 mi/6.4 km W of Wis. state line, 17 mi/27 km SW of Duluth; 46°37′N 92°22′W. Agr. (dairying; poultry; oats, alfalfa); mfg. (liquid gasses). Jay Cooke State Park to NE.

Wrentham (REN-thuhm), town (1990 pop. 9,006), Norfolk co., SE Mass., 18 mi/29 km NNE of Providence, R.I.; 42°03′N 71°22′W. Summer resort; mfg. (metal prods., valves, machinery). State school for mentally handicapped children here. State Forest. Settled 1669, inc. 1673; includes Wrentham village.

Wright 1 county (□ 582 sq mi/1,507 sq km; 1990 pop. 14,269), N central Iowa; ⊙ Clarion; 42°43′N 93°43′W. Rolling prairie agr. area (livestock; corn, oats, soybeans, grain) drained by Iowa and Boone rivers. Contains Morse, Cornelia, Elm, and Wall lakes (natural), running N-S through center of co. Bituminous-coal deposits (S), sand and gravel pits. Widespread flooding occurred here in 1993 (N central Iowa was corner of flood zone). Formed 1851. **2** county (□ 714 sq mi/1,849 sq km; 1990 pop. 68,710), S central Minn.; ⊙ Buffalo; 45°10′N 93°58′W. Agr. area (alfalfa, hay, corn, oats, barley, soybeans; sheep, hogs, cattle, poultry; dairying). Bounded N by Mississippi R., on NW by Clearwater R. (forms Clearwater L.); drained by Crow R. (forms SE border). Numerous small natural lakes scattered throughout co., including Pelican L. in NE; L. Maria State Park in N. Monticello nuclear power plant, initial criticality Dec. 10, 1970; is 30 mi/48 km NW of Minneapolis, uses cooling water from the Mississippi R., and has a max. dependable capacity of 536 MWe. Formed 1855. **3** county (□ 684 sq mi/1,772 sq km; 1990 pop. 16,758), S central Mo.; ⊙ Hartville; 37°16′N 92°27′W. In the Ozarks; drained by Gasconade R. Peaches, apples; hay, cattle; dairying; lumber. Mark Twain Natl. Forest in NE corner. Formed 1841.

Wright, town (1990 pop. 1,236), Campbell co., NE Wyo., 35 mi/56 km S of Gillette; 43°45′N 105°30′W. Cattle; grain, sugar beets, beans; mfg. of explosives. Thunder Basin Natl. Grassland to S.

Wright, village (1990 pop. 144), Carlton co., E Minn., 42 mi/68 km WSW of Duluth, on Tamarack R.; 46°40′N 93°00′W. Agr. (dairying; poultry; oats); mfg. (outdoor stoves). Tamarack L. to SE; Savanna State Forest to NW; Fond du Lac State Forest to E.

Wright Brothers National Memorial, Dare co., NE N.C., 4 mi/6.4 km SE of Kitty Hawk, at Kill Devil Hills-town, in Outer Banks; on an area of 431 acres/174 ha. Site of 1st sustained flight of a heavier-than-air craft, by Wilbur and Orville Wright, Dec. 17, 1903. Authorized 1927.

Wright City 1 town (1990 pop. 1,250), Warren co., E central Mo., 7 mi/11.3 km E of Warrenton; 38°49′N 91°01′W. Mfg. (furniture). **2** town (1990 pop. 836), McCurtain co., extreme SE Okla., 15 mi/24 km NW of Idabel, near Little R.; 34°03′N 95°00′W. In agr. area; lumber. Pioneer Creek L. reservoir to NW.

Wright Patman Lake, reservoir, on border bet. Bowie and Cass cos., extreme NE Texas, on Sulphur R., 8 mi/12.9 km SW of Texarkana; c.20 mi/32 km long; 33°17′N 94°09′W. Max. capacity 5,730,800 acre-ft. Formed by Texarkana Dam (93 ft/28 m high), built (1957) by the Army Corps of Engineers for water supply. Atlanta State Park on S shore, near dam.

Wright-Patterson Air Force Base, U.S. military installation (□ 13 sq mi/34 sq km), W Ohio, NE of Dayton; 39°48′N 84°04′W. Est. 1917. One of the largest airport installations in the world, it is the Air Force's main research and development base (esp. materials and avionics research), and the hq. of the Air Force Logistics Command (natl. center for defense activities). The Aerospace Medical Laboratory, Air Force graduate school, and the Air Force Mus. are also on the base.

Wrightson, Mount (9,453 ft/2,881 m), N Santa Cruz co., SE Ariz., 27 mi/43 km NNE of Nogales, at Pima co. line, in Coronado Natl. Forest; 31°41′N 110°50′W. Highest peak in Santa Rita Mts. Site of Smithsonian Astrophysical Observatory. Sometimes called Old Baldy.

Wrightstown, town (1990 pop. 1,262), Brown co., E Wis., on Fox R., 15 mi/24 km SSW of Green Bay, 15 mi/24 km ENE of Appleton; 44°19′N 88°10′W. In dairying region; cheese spreads.

Wrightstown, borough (1990 pop. 3,843), Burlington co., central N.J., 15 mi/24 km SE of Trenton; 40°01′N 74°37′W. Fort Dix Military Reservation and McGuire Air Force Base here; fort (formerly Camp Dix) was built in World War I, renamed and made a permanent garrison in 1939. It was the U.S. Army's largest training center in World War II; it closed in 1992. Residential and commercial services here served the base.

Wrightsville 1 town (1990 pop. 1,062), Pulaski co., central Ark., 9 mi/14.5 km SSE of Little Rock, near Arkansas R. (to E); 34°36′N 92°13′W. In farm and timber area. Mfg. **2** town (1990 pop. 2,331), ⊙ Johnson co., E central Ga.,17 mi/27 km NE of Dublin; 32°43′N 82°43′W. Mfg. includes windows, clothes, meat processing. Inc. 1866. **3** uninc. town (1990 pop. 4,752), New Hanover co., SE N.C., residential suburb 4 mi/6.4 km NNE of Wilmington. New Hanover Internatl. Airport to S.

Wrightsville, borough (1990 pop. 2,396), York co., S Pa., 12 mi/19 km W of Lancaster, 2 mi/3.2 km W of Columbia, on Susquehanna R.; 40°01′N 76°31′W. Agr. area (grain, soybeans, apples; livestock; dairying); mfg. (concrete, fabricated metal prods.); dolomite quarries. Samuel S. Lewis State Park to S. Settled 1730, laid out 1811, inc. 1834.

Wrightsville Beach, town (1990 pop. 2,937), New Hanover co., SE N.C., 8 mi/12.9 km E of Wilmington, on a narrow isl. (c.5 mi/8 km long) on the Atlantic Ocean; 34°12′N 77°47′W. Beach resort area; Intracoastal Waterway to W (bridge to mainlands). Mfg. (consumer goods, machinery). Mason Inlet to N, Masonboro Inlet to S.

Wrightwood, uninc. town (1990 pop. 3,308), San Bernardino co., S Calif., 30 mi/48 km NW of San Bernardino, 40 mi/64 km NE of Los Angeles, in San Bernardino Natl. Forest, in N edge of San Gabriel Mts.; 34°22′N 117°38′W. Holiday Hill Ski Area is here; Ski Sunrise Ski Area to W. Mojave Desert to NE.

Wrigley, village (1991 pop. 174), SW Mackenzie dist.,

N.W.T., N Canada, on Mackenzie R., port at mouth of Wrigley R.; 63°16′N 123°37′W. Trading post; airfield, radio station. Scheduled air service. Founded (1877) 24 mi/39 km upstream, Mackenzie Highway extended to Wrigley in 1904 and it was moved to present site. Sometimes called Fort Wrigley.

Wroxeter (RAHK-si-tuhr), village, S Ont., central Canada, on Maitland R., 30 mi/48 km ENE of Goderich. Dairying; mixed farming.

Wupatki National Monument (woo-PAHT-kee), (□ 54 sq mi/140 sq km), Coconino co., N central Ariz., 28 mi/45 km NNE of Flagstaff; 35,253 acres/14,267 ha. Bounded by Little Colorado R. on E and by Coconino Natl. Forest on S, San Francisco Mts. to SW. Area of pre-Columbian Native Amer. ruins, including more than 800 pueblo sites dating from c.A.D. 1065. Largest pueblo ruin is Wupatki, which accommodated 150–200 persons at max. occupancy (12th cent.), thought to be ancestors of Hopi Indians. Settlement of region followed eruption in 11th cent. of nearby Sunset Crater, which produced soil-enriching ash and made farming possible. Est. 1924.

Wurtland (WUHRT-luhnd), town (1990 pop. 1,221), Greenup co., NE Ky., suburb 8 mi/12.9 km NW of Ashland, on Ohio R.; 38°32′N 82°46′W. Agr. (tobacco, corn; cattle). Mfg. (plastic prods., chemicals), steel processing.

Wurtsboro, resort village (□ 1 sq mi/2.6 sq km; 1990 pop. 1,046), Sullivan co., SE N.Y., 10 mi/16 km NNW of Middletown, at base of the Shawangunk range; 41°34′N 74°29′W.

Wyaconda (WEI-yuh-KAHN-duh), city (1990 pop. 347), Clark co., extreme NE Mo., near Wyaconda R., 11 mi/18 km W of Kahoka; 40°23′N 91°55′W. Agr. (corn, soybeans; hogs; cattle). Mfg. (fertilizer).

Wyaconda River, c.60 mi/97 km long, S Iowa and NE Mo.; N and S forks rise in Davis co., Iowa; flow SE, meeting NE of Wyconda (Mo.), Mississippi R. at La Grange.

Wyalusing (WEI-yah-loo-sing), borough (1990 pop. 686), Bradford co., NE Pa., 12 mi/19 km SE of Towanda, on Susquehanna R.; 41°40′N 76°15′W. Agr. (corn, hay; livestock; dairying). Mfg. (fabricated metal prods., wood prods.), food processing. French Azilum Historical Site to NW.

Wyalusing State Park (wei-ah-LOO-sing) (□ 4 sq mi/10.4 sq km), Grant co., extreme SW Wis., on bluffs near confluence of Wisconsin and Mississippi (Iowa state line) rivers. Has caves, waterfalls, and curious rock formations. On Sentinel Ridge (590 ft/180 m above the Mississippi) are Native Amer. mounds.

Wyandanch, village (□ 4 sq mi/10.4 sq km; 1990 pop. 8,950), Suffolk co., SE N.Y., on central L.I., 4 mi/6.4 km E of Farmingdale; 40°45′N 73°22′W. Mfg. (electrical equip., transportation equip., fabricated metal prods., telecommunications, fiberglass prods., packaging). Belmont L. Park is S. Predominantly Afr.-Amer. community.

Wyandot (WEI-uhn-daht, WEIN-daht), county (□ 406 sq mi/1,052 sq km; 1990 pop. 22,254), N central Ohio; ⊙ Upper Sandusky; 40°51′N 83°17′W. Drained by Sandusky R. and small Broken Sword and Tymochtee creeks. In the Till Plains physiographic region. Agr. (livestock; corn, soybeans, wheat, fruit; poultry; dairy prods.). Mfg. at Upper Sandusky and Carey (plastics prods., electronic equip., transportation equip.); limestone quarries, gravel pits. Formed 1845.

Wyandotte (WEI-uhn-daht), county (□ 155 sq mi/401 sq km; 1990 pop. 161,993), NE Kansas; ⊙ Kansas City; 39°06′N 94°46′W. Rolling to hilly area, partly bounded N by Missouri R. (Mo. state line), E by Mo.; drained by Kansas R., which forms part of S border. Sand and gravel. Industries at Kansas City. Agr. (vegetables, peaches, strawberries). About 80% of land area is made up of city of Kansas City, in E, remainder made up of cities of Bonner Springs and Edwardsville in W, and small uninc. pockets in NW and extreme SW corner. Wyandotts Co. L. in N, in Kansas City. Fairfax Municipal Airport in E. Formed 1855.

Wyandotte (WAIN-DAHT), city (1990 pop. 30,938), Wayne co., SE Mich., a suburb 8 mi/12.9 km SW of downtown Detroit on the Detroit R., borders Ecorse R. on N; 42°12′N 83°09′W. Salt deposits here supply the city's extensive chemical industry. Other mfg. (concrete, pharmaceuticals, machinery). Bessemer steel was first commercially produced in the city in 1864 by W. F. Durfee. A Wyandotte village was here in the 19th cent.; of interest is a totem pole depicting Wyandotte history. Wyandotte Natl. Wildlife Refuge, on Grassy Isl., in Detroit R. (not within city). Inc. as a city 1867.

Wyandotte (WEI-uhn-daht), village (1990 pop. 366), Ottawa co., extreme NE Okla., 9 mi/14.5 km SE of Miami, and near Spring R. arm of L. of the Cherokees (Neosho R.); 36°47′N 94°43′W. Mfg. (fabricated metal prods.). Twin Bridges State Park to W.

Wyandotte Cave, one of the largest natural caverns in the U.S., Crawford co., S Ind., c.25 mi/40 km W of New Albany. There are more than 23 mi/37 km of passages and several large and beautiful chambers on 5 levels. Saltpeter was mined there until the middle of the 19th cent. Native Americans mined flint from the cave and traded it throughout the E U.S. Discovered in 1798.

Wyanet, village (1990 pop. 1,017), Bureau co., N Ill., on old Illinois and Mississippi Canal, and 6 mi/9.7 km W of Princeton; 41°21′N 89°34′W. RR junction. Agr. (corn, soybeans; cattle, hogs; dairying). Fish hatchery nearby.

Wyano (WEI-yah-no), uninc. town (1990 pop. 750), Westmoreland co., SW Pa., 10 mi/16 km SSW of Greensburg; 40°11′N 79°41′W. Mfg. (ironworks). Agr. (dairying; livestock; corn, hay).

Wyatt, town (1990 pop. 376), Mississippi co., extreme SE Mo., near Mississippi R., 7 mi/11.3 km E of Charleston; 36°54′N 89°13′W. Inc. 1954.

Wyckoff (WEI-kawf), township (1990 pop. 15,372), Bergen co., NE N.J., 8 mi/12.9 km N of Paterson; 41°00′N 74°10′W. Residential area. Mfg. (baked goods). Inc. 1798.

Wye East River, Md.: see WYE RIVER.

Wye Island, Md.: see WYE RIVER.

Wye Mills, village, Queen Annes and Talbot cos., E Md., 26 mi/42 km N of Cambridge. The state tree of Md., a 400-year-old white oak, is in Wye Oak State Park.

Wye Oak State Park, Md.: see WYE MILLS.

Wye River, c.13 mi/21 km long, on the Eastern Shore, Md.; estuary extending S from point E of Queenstown to Eastern Bay. A branch, Wye East R. (c.15 mi/24 km long), extends S and SE from near Wye Mills, along Talbot–Queen Annes co. line to Wye R. near its mouth. Wye Isl. (c.5 mi/8 km long, bridged to mainland) lies between river branches. River, isl., house, institute, mills, and plantation are all named after the Wye R. in Wales, probably by the Lloyds family who were of Welsh descent and owned much of the surrounding land.

Wyeville (WEI-vil), village (1990 pop. 154), Monroe co., W central Wis., on Lemonweir R., and 45 mi/72 km ENE of La Crosse; 44°01′N 90°23′W. RR junction in dairy and livestock area. Central Wis. Conservation Area and Necedah Natl. Wildlife Refuge to NE.

Wykoff (WEI-kawf), village (1990 pop. 493), Fillmore co., SE Minn., 22 mi/35 km SSE of Rochester; 43°42′N 92°16′W. Agr. (grain; livestock, poultry; dairying); timber. Mfg. (lumber). Surrounded by Richard J. Dorer Memorial Hardwood State Forest. Forestville–Mystery Cave State Park to SE; karst topography in area.

Wylie, town (1990 pop. 8,716), Collin co., N Texas, suburb 21 mi/34 km NE of downtown Dallas, on fringe of urban growth area; 33°02′N 96°30′W. Mfg. (machinery, electrical equip., transportation equip.). Recreation. L. Lavon is N; L. Ray Hubbard reservoir to SE.

Wylie, Lake, reservoir (□ 19 sq mi/49 sq km), York co., N central S.C., on Catawba R., 12 mi/19 km E of York; 35°01′N 81°00′W. Max. capacity 246,435 acre-ft. Formed by Lake Wylie Dam (105 ft/32 m high), built (1925) for power generation.

Wyman Lake (WEI-muhn), at Moscow, Somerset co., W Maine, on the Kennebec R., 2 mi/3.2 km NNW of Bingham village; 8 mi/12.9 km long; 45°04′N 69°54′W.

Formed by Wyman Dam (earth and rockfill; 143 ft/44 m high, Maine's highest), built (1931) for power generation and flood control.

Wymore (WEI-mor), town (1990 pop. 1,611), Gage co., SE Nebr., 10 mi/16 km SSE of Beatrice, and on Big Blue R., near Kansas state line; 40°07′N 96°40′W. Agr. (livestock; grain). Mfg. (musical instrument parts and music stands). Founded 1871.

Wynantskill (WEI-nants-kill), village (1990 pop. 3,329), Rensselaer co., E N.Y., just SE of Troy; 42°42′N 73°38′W. In dairying area.

Wyncote (WIN-kot), uninc. town (1990 pop. 2,960), in Cheltenham township, Montgomery co., SE Pa., residential suburb 10 mi/16 km N of downtown Philadelphia, on Tacony Creek; 40°05′N 75°09′W. Light mfg.

Wyndmere (WEIND-mer), village (1990 pop. 501), Richland co., SE N.Dak., 25 mi/40 km W of Wahpeton, near Wild Rice R.; 46°15′N 97°07′W. RR junction.

Wyndmoor (WIND-mor), uninc. town (1990 pop. 5,682), Montgomery co., SE Pa., residential suburb 10 mi/16 km NNW of Philadelphia; 40°04′N 75°11′W. Mfg. (telecommunications, fabricated metal prods.).

Wynne (WIN), town (1990 pop. 8,187), ⊙ Cross co., E Ark., c.45 mi/72 km W of Memphis (Tenn.), and 14 mi/23 km N of Forrest City on W slope of Crowley's Ridge; 35°13′N 90°47′W. Ships peaches, rice, lumber, cotton. Mfg. (footware, food, fabricated metal prods.). Village Creek State Park to SE. Founded 1863.

Wynnewood or **Wynne Wood** (WI-ni-wuhd), town (1990 pop. 2,451), Garvin co., S central Okla., 7 mi/11.3 km SSE of Pauls Valley, on Washita R.; 34°38′N 97°09′W. Trade and shipping point for agr. area (livestock; peanuts, alfalfa, pecans). Mfg. (concrete, gasoline refining, Christmas tree lights).

Wynnewood, uninc. village, Lower Merion township, Montgomery co., SE Pa.; 40°00′N 75°16′W. Light mfg.

Wynona (win-ON-uh), village (1990 pop. 531), Osage co., N Okla., 8 mi/12.9 km S of Pawhuska; 36°32′N 96°19′W.

Wynoochee Lake (wei-NOO-chee), reservoir, Grays Harbor co., W Wash., on Wynoochee R., in Olympic Natl. Forest, 30 mi/48 km NNE of Aberdeen; 3 mi/4.8 km long; 47°22′N 122°36′W. Max. capacity 70,000 acre-ft. Formed by Wynoochee Dam (162 ft/49 m high), built (1973) by the Army Corps of Engineers for flood control and water supply.

Wynoochee River, c.60 mi/97 km long, NE Grays Harbor co., W Wash.; rises in Olympic Natl. Forest; flows S through Wynoochee L. reservoir to Chehalis R. W of Montesano; near S boundary of Olympic Natl. Park.

Wynot (WEI-nawt), village (1990 pop. 213), Cedar co., NE Nebr., 10 mi/16 km NNE of Hartington, near Missouri R.; 42°44′N 97°10′W.

Wynyard (WIN-yuhrd), town (1991 pop. 2,022), S central Sask., W Canada, near Quill Lakes, 90 mi/145 km NNE of Regina, at foot of Touchwood Hills; 51°46′N 104°11′W. Grain elevators. Resort.

Wyocena (wei-O-se-nuh), village (1990 pop. 620), Columbia co., S central Wis., 8 mi/12.9 km SE of Portage; 43°29′N 89°18′W. In agr. area.

Wyola (wei-O-luh), village (1990 pop. 125), Big Horn co., S Mont., on Little Bighorn R., near Wyo. state line, and 43 mi/69 km SSE of Hardin, in SE part of Crow Indian Reservation. Agr. (wheat, barley, sugar beets, hay; cattle). Big Horn Natl. Forest (Wyo.) to SW.

Wyoming, village (1991 pop. 2,048), S Ont., central Canada, 15 mi/24 km E of Sarnia; 42°57′N 82°07′W. In oil-producing region; dairying, mixed farming, milling.

Wyoming, state (□ 97,818 sq mi/253,349 sq km; 1995 est. pop. 480,184), W U.S., admitted as the 44th state of the Union in 1890; ⊙ CHEYENNE, the largest city; 42°58′N 106°47′W. CASPER and LARAMIE are the 2d and 3d largest cities. The state, rectangular in shape, is bounded on the N by Mont., on the E by S.Dak. and Nebr., on the S by Colo. and Utah, and on the W by Utah, Idaho, and Mont. Wyo. is traversed (SE to NW) by the Rocky Mts., which separate into widely dispersed ranges. Bighorn Mts. (N), Laramie Mts. (SE), Medicine Bow Mts. (S), Wind River Range (W center), with largest concentration in NW (Teton, Absaroka, Gros Ventre ranges). The ranges are interrupted by broad, semi-arid basins—Bighorn (N), Shoshone (center), Laramie

(SE), Bridger and Great Divide (SW). E of the mts. is the rolling country of the Great Plains, generally a 1-mi-/1.6-km–high region covered with grasses and sage. In the NE corner, the Black Hills edge across the state line from S.Dak.; the Bear Lodge Mts. are an extension of the Hills. In the central sect. of the state is a stretch of unbroken high plain, across which the wagon trains rolled W over the Oregon, Mormon, Overland, and other trails. In the extreme NE the low, wooded Black Hills give way to eroded badlands extending W to the banks of the Powder R., which wanders through some of the most famous cattle country in the U.S. W beyond the Powder is the tall grass country that was the hunting ground of the Crow until the Sioux, following the buffalo, pushed the Crow into the mts. The Sioux fell in turn before the relentless advance of settlers, and today farms and ranches occupy this fertile and beautiful plains area. In SE Wyo. the higher tablelands are interrupted by the Laramie and Medicine Bow ranges. Across this region travelers to the Pacific coast made their way when wars with the Native Americans in the 1860s endangered treks on the regular Oregon Trail. The RR followed the wagons and coaches as the Union Pacific laid its tracks across the S part of the region. In SW central Wyo. is the natural gateway through the Rockies: the broad, grassy South Pass (7,550 ft/2,301 m). Immediately N of the pass is the Wind R. Range, with the highest elev. in the state at Gannett Peak (13,804 ft/4,207 m). Still farther N rise the Gros Ventre and Absaroka ranges, and to the W, near the Idaho state line, the glorious Tetons loom above a lake and valley country of incomparable beauty. From the mt. heights snows melt to feed a number of rivers; the Snake flows W into Idaho and on to the Columbia R., the Yellowstone N and E into Mont. to the Missouri R., and the Green R. S into Utah to join the Colorado R. The North Platte flows SE into Nebr. to form the Platte R. This wealth of surface water supplements the scant rainfall, and water is impounded for irrigation, flood control, and in some cases hydroelectric power. Dry farming—producing hay, wheat, and barley—is supplemented by the more diversified yield (esp. sugar beets and dry beans) of the irrigated fields. Most of the inhabitants of the state derive their livelihood directly or indirectly from farming or ranching. The most valuable farm commodities, in terms of cash receipts, are cattle, hay, sugar beets, and sheep. Sparse grasses over much of the region necessitate a large grazing area for each animal; sheep graze in places unfit for cattle, and both sheep and cattle range by permit in the natl. forests. Cooperative grazing tracts are on the increase. Horses, a prized essential of ranching, are carefully raised and trained. Mining comprises the largest sector of the state's economy, accounting for over ¼ of the Gross State Product. Oil wells were first drilled in the 1860s, and today petroleum is the state's 2d most important mineral behind coal. In 1988, Wyo. ranked first in the production of coal, sodium carbonate, and uranium. Considerable amounts of gold, iron, and various clays are mined. The production of petroleum and petroleum prods., centered in Casper, is the state's leading industry. Other important mfg. (processed foods, clay, glass, wood prods.). About ⅙ of Wyo. is forested land. Wyo. has several natl. forests—Shoshone, Bridger-Teton, Targhee (part) in NW, Bighorn in N, part of Black Hills in NE, Medicine Bow in SE, part of Wasatch in SW. Thunder Basin Natl. Grasslands is in NE. The state's natural beauty draws hundreds of thousands of visitors annually, making tourism a major source of revenue. Wyo. has 2 spectacular natl. parks: Grand Teton, which embraces the most stunning portion of the Teton Range, and Yellowstone, which occupies the NW corner of the state and extends into Mont. and Idaho. Yellowstone is the oldest natl. park in the world and until the 1970s was the largest of all U.S. natl. parks. Until 1970s, Yellowstone was independent of neighboring cos., now split bet. Park and Teton cos. Its geysers, hot springs, waterfalls, and canyons are world famous. Wyo. is also prime hunting and fishing country. The nation's largest herds of elk and antelope are there; deer, moose, and bear are plentiful, and the rivers, lakes, and streams teem with fish. Also in the state are Devils Tower (NE) and Fossil Butte (SW) natl. monuments and 2 natl. recreational areas, Bighorn Canyon (N; extends into Mont.) and Flaming Gorge (SW; extends into Utah). In addition, the multitude of rodeos, rendezvous roundups, frontier celebrations, and dude ranches draw a large number of vacationers every year. Portions of present Wyo. were at one time claimed by Spain, France, and England; the acquisition of the territory by the U.S. was completed through 5 major annexations—the Louisiana Purchase in 1803, the Treaty of 1819 with Spain, cession by the republic of Texas in 1836 and partition from Texas after it was annexed in 1845, the Treaty of Guadalupe Hidalgo (1848) after the Mex. War, and the internatl. agreement (1846) with Great Britain concerning the Columbia R. country (see OREGON). The early development of Wyo. was closely linked with the fur trade and the great W migrations. Fr. trappers and explorers may have reached the area in the middle to late 18th cent., but the first authentic accounts of the region were provided by John Colter, who, trapped in the Wyo. mts. for several years, returned to St. Louis in 1810 with fantastic accounts of the steaming geysers and great canyons of the Yellowstone. Colter returned W, and other fur traders made their way into Wyo. The overland party on its way to found Astoria on the Columbia R. went through Teton Pass in 1811. The following year Robert Stuart, returning from Astoria, crossed South Pass and followed much of the route that was to be the Oregon Trail. Only the hardiest and most self-sufficient could survive the Native Amer. attacks and the rugged isolation of the country. With the expeditions of William H. Ashley, the mt. men entered the country, and some of the most famous of those early explorers—Thomas Fitzpatrick, James Bridger, and Jedediah S. Smith—crossed and recrossed the land. Attracted by the fur trade, Capt. B. L. E. de Bonneville organized a sizable expedition, and his were the first wagons to go (1832) through South Pass. The first permanent trading post was Fort William (1834), famous under its later name, Fort Laramie. In 1843, Fort Bridger (now in a state park) was built. The area also aroused the interest of John C. Frémont, who made an expedition in 1842. By the 1840s the route W through Wyo. was in steady use by caravans headed toward Oregon, and fur-trading posts became stations on the Oregon Trail. As the fur trade declined, many former trappers and mountaineers settled along the trail, furnishing horses and other supplies to the migrants and purchasing debilitated stock to be put to pasture and sold the following year. Mormons trekking to Utah (Brigham Young led the first party in 1847) and 49ers rushing to the gold fields of Calif. joined the many thousands traversing the mt. passes of Wyo. A number of Mormons settled for a time in W Wyo. The death of Mormon pioneers in a blizzard (1856) and the thousands of graves along the Oregon Trail give an indication of the toll taken by disease, starvation, attacks by Native Americans, and winter snows. Despite the hardships, telegraph stations (1861) and stagecoach and freight lines were established, and in 1860–1861 pony express riders crossed Wyo. on their route bet. St. Joseph, Mo., and Sacramento, Calif. Native Americans hostile to encroachment in the early 1860s forced the rerouting of stagecoaches to the S, along the OVERLAND TRAIL. Native Americans, displaced from their former homes in the E and W, and waging internecine warfare for control of the rich buffalo ranges, feared further encroachment by the settlers on their hunting grounds, esp. after the opening (1864) of the Bozeman Trail. Treaties were made and broken by both sides, and wars with the Sioux persisted, particularly in the Powder R. valley. Meanwhile, S Wyo. was relatively free of attacks, and a gold rush, stimulated by the discoveries at South Pass (1867), brought the first heavy influx of settlers to that region; the flow was increased by the uncovering of vast coal deposits in SW Wyo. Probably the greatest stimulus to settlement was the completion (1868) of the Wyo. sector of the Union Pacific RR. Towns, including Cheyenne, sprang up beside the tracks, and trade thrived on the demands of the road crews and the new settlers. In 1868 the region became the Territory of Wyo., with Cheyenne as its capital. Wyo. pioneered in political equality when, in 1869, the first territorial legislature granted the vote to women. The territory continued to advance economically as huge herds of cattle were driven up over the Texas or Long Trail. Native Amer. resistance had been put down by the late 1870s. The Arapaho were placed on the Wind R. Reservation with their former enemies, the Shoshone, and cattlemen safely moved their herds to grasslands throughout Wyo. Cattle rustling became so common that the authorities could not control it, and juries grew fearful of returning just verdicts against criminals. The Wyo. Stock Growers Assn. was organized in 1873 to protect cattle owners, and members frequently formed vigilante groups to administer their own justice. The struggle reached its ht. in the Johnson county cattle war of 1892. Lawlessness was also exemplified by the Hole-in-the-Wall gang, which broadened its activities to include bank and train robberies as well as cattle theft. Gradually, vast areas were fenced in and winter pastures were established. The influx of sheep in the late 1890s, however, brought new violence. Cattlemen made frantic efforts to exclude the sheep from close grazing on the precious grasslands. Homesteaders were also unwelcome, and many left when they realized that the country was unsuited for small acreage cultivation. However, pop. increase was steady, advancing from about 9,000 in 1870 to over 90,000 in 1900. With expanding pop. came development in other ways: eager frontiersmen rapidly (and somewhat chaotically) established schools, and in 1887 the Univ. of Wyo. was founded. Statehood was achieved in 1890, and in keeping with its frontier ideals, Wyo. adopted a liberal state constitution that included the secret ballot. The Carey Act of 1894, providing for the reclamation and settlement of land, stimulated further agrarian development and, in addition, pointed out the need for conservation and efficient use of water. The establishment of natl. parks protected the timberlands and extensive grazing areas, and water power was harnessed to furnish electricity for farms and industries. In politics, the progressive movement found numerous adherents in Wyo.; in 1915, after one of the most bitter fights in the state's history, progressive forces triumphed over the RR and related interests with the establishment of a state utilities commission. A workmen's compensation law was passed in 1915, and in that year also the legislature authorized the Univ. of Wyo. to accept Federal grants for agr. experiments and demonstrations. Thus were begun the state's outstanding and widespread services for agrarian improvement. In 1924, Wyo. became the first state to elect a woman governor, Nellie Taylor Ross. By then the state ranked 4th in the nation in the production of crude oil, but the valuable finds at TEAPOT DOME are probably remembered best as the symbol of corruption in the administration of President Warren Harding. Under the New Deal, Wyo. was well served by the natl. soil conservation programs, which benefited dry farmers who had extended operations into semi-arid regions and had suffered severely in the drought years beginning in the late 1920s. The cooperative movement in agr. also gained ground in this period and has since continued to grow. One of the most important events in the state since World War II was the discovery of uranium. Uranium is still mined, esp. in the Gas Hills Dist. of Fremont co., central Wyo. Trona, a natural source of soda ash, is mined in the SW around Rock Springs and Green River. New oil finds also helped to offset economic losses resulting from a disastrous 4-year-long drought in the 1950s. The decade from the early 1970s to the early 1980s was a boom period for Wyo. as high energy prices boosted the state's coal, oil, and natural-gas industries. By the mid-1980s, however, energy prices were falling and the state economy declined from its lack of diversity. Wyo. also has suffered from the environmental effects of the energy industry; pollution has become a serious problem in some mining towns. In the 1980s, the pop. of Wyo. declined over 3% and the state now ranks last in the nation. The state still operates under its first constitution, adopted in 1890. The executive branch is headed by a governor elected for a 4-year term. Wyo.'s bicameral legislature has a senate with 30 members elected for 4-year terms and a house of representatives with 64 members elected for 2 years. The state sends 2 Senators and 1 Representative to the U.S. Congress and has 3 electoral votes. Wyo. has 23 cos.: ALBANY, BIG HORN, CAMPBELL, CARBON, CONVERSE, CROOK, FREMONT, GOSHEN, HOT SPRINGS, JOHNSON, LARAMIE, LINCOLN, NATRONA, NIOBRARA, PARK, PLATTE, SHERIDAN, SUBLETTE, SWEETWATER, TETON, UINTA, WASHAKIE, and WESTON.

Wyoming 1 county (□ 596 sq mi/1,544 sq km; 1990 pop. 42,507), N.Y.; ⊙ Warsaw; 42°42′N 78°13′W. Drained by Genesee R. and Tonawanda and Cattaraugus creeks; includes part of Letchworth State Park, in valley of the Genesee. Dairying and farming area (vegetables, grain, fruit). Diversified mfg., esp. at Warsaw and Perry. Formed 1841. **2** county (□ 404 sq km/1,046 sq km; 1990 pop. 28,076), NE Pa.; ⊙ Tunkhannock; 41°31′N 76°01′W. Hilly region drained by scenic Susquehanna R. and Tunkhannock Creek. Agr. (corn, oats, hay, alfalfa; cattle; dairying); timber; sand and gravel. Some mfg. at Tunkhannock. Settled in 18th cent. by New Englanders; formed 1842. **3** county (□ 501 sq mi/ 1,298 sq km; 1990 pop. 28,990), S W.Va.; ⊙ Pineville; 37°36′N 81°32′W. On Allegheny Plateau; drained by Guyandotte R. and its Clear Fork. An important bituminous- and semibituminous-coal–producing co. Timber; natural gas. Agr. (corn, potatoes); cattle. Twin Falls State Park in E; parts of W. D. Bailey L. reservoir (Guyandotte R.) and Wildlife Management Area in W. Formed 1850.

Wyoming 1 city (1990 pop. 1,462), Stark co., N central Ill., 5 mi/8 km ESE of Toulon; 41°03′N 89°46′W. Agr. (corn, oats, wheat). On Rock Island State Trail. Inc.

1865. **2** city (1990 pop. 63,891), Kent co., W Mich., largely residential suburb 5 mi/8 km SSW of downtown Grand Rapids, on the Grand R.; 42°53′N 85°42′W. Mfg. (fabricated metal prods., transportation equip.), food processing. Native Amer. mounds in adjacent Grandville. Settled 1832, inc. 1959. **3** city (1990 pop. 8,128), Hamilton co., extreme SW Ohio, a N suburb of Cincinnati; 39°13′N 84°29′W. Settled 1865, inc. 1874.

Wyoming 1 town (1990 pop. 977), Kent co., central Del., 3 mi/4.8 km SW of Dover; 39°07′N 75°33′W. In agr. area (grain, fruit, vegetables; poultry, livestock; dairying). Wyoming L. to NW. **2** town (1990 pop. 659), Jones co., E Iowa, 15 mi/24 km E of Anamosa; 42°03′N 91°00′W. Grain; livestock. **3** town (1990 pop. 2,142), Chisago co., E Minn., on South Branch Surprise R.; 45°19′N 93°00′W. Agr. (grain; cattle, poultry; dairying). Mfg. (fabricated metal prods., machinery, fiberglass prods., transportation equip., plastic prods., fixtures).

Wyoming, village (1990 pop. 478), Wyoming co., W N.Y., 15 mi/24 km SSE of Batavia; 42°39′N 78°05′W. Mfg. (electrical prods. and equip., food packing, lumber, textiles). Agr. (corn, wheat, hay); timber.

Wyoming, borough (1990 pop. 3,255), Luzerne co., NE central Pa., 5 mi/8 km NNE of Wilkes-Barre, on Susquehanna R. (bridged); 41°18′N 75°50′W. Mfg. (machinery); some anthracite coal. Wilkes-Barre Wyoming Valley Airport to SW. Wyoming Battle Monument commemorates Wyoming Valley massacre (1778) of settlers by Torfes and Indians. Inc. 1885.

Wyoming, R.I.: see RICHMOND.

Wyoming Range, in Rocky Mts. of W Wyo., Lincoln and Sublette cos., near Idaho state line, just E of Salt R. Range and Greys R.; extends c.40 mi/64 km N-S. Highest point, Wyoming Peak (11,378 ft/3,468 m). Located mostly within Bridger-Teton Natl. Forest. Greys R. Valley to W.

Wyoming Valley, Luzerne co., NE Pa., through which flows the Susquehanna R.; c.20 mi/32 km long, 3 mi/ 4.8 km–4 mi/6.4 km wide; 41°15′N 75°54′W. Wilkes-Barre is the major city of this once-rich anthracite-coal

region, some anthracite-coal mining continues; main activity is mfg. and agr. Wilkes-Barre Mt. on SE, Shickshinny and Larksville mts. on NW. The valley was the scene of a long contest bet. Conn. and Pa. over conflicting land claims based on 17th-cent. charters, resulting in the 1st Pennamite War (1769–1771) and the 2d Pennamite War (1784).The Compromise Act of 1799 enabled the Pa. legislature to settle with the Conn. claimants.

Wyomissing (WEI-o-MIS-ing), borough (1990 pop. 7,332), Berks co., SE central Pa., 3 mi/4.8 km WSW of Reading; 40°19′N 75°58′W. Mfg. (construction materials, beverages, printing, apparel). Berks Co. Heritage Center. Founded 1896, inc. 1906.

Wyomissing Hills (WEI-o-MIS-ing), borough (1990 pop. 2,469), Berks co., SE central Pa., residential suburb 3 mi/4.8 km W of Reading. Penn. State Univ. Berks Campus; 40°19′N 75°58′W.

Wythe (WITH), county (□ 464 sq mi/1,202 sq km; 1990 pop. 25,466), SW Va.; ⊙ Wytheville; 36°55′N 81°05′W. Partly in Great Appalachian Valley, traversed by ridges, with Allegheny Mts. in N and NW, part of Iron Mts. in S; drained by New R. Mfg. at Wytheville; agr. (cabbage, corn, hay, alfalfa, potatoes; cattle, sheep, hogs; dairying); timber; lead, zinc mines; limestone. Includes part of Jefferson Natl. Forest, part of Mt. Rogers Natl. Recreation Area. Formed 1790.

Wytheville (WITH-vil), town (1990 pop. 8,038), ⊙ Wythe co., SW Va., 65 mi/105 km WSW of Roanoke, near Reed Creek; 36°57′N 81°05′W. Mfg. (rubber prods., apparel, transportation equip., printing, plastics prods.). Trade, market, processing point for agr. area (vegetables, grain, apples; livestock; dairying); rock quarrying. Wytheville Community Col. Stony Fork Recreational Area to NW. Wytheville Fish Cultural Station (hatchery) to E. Founded 1792, inc. 1839.

Wytopitlock, Maine: see REED.

Wytopitlock Lake (wit-uh-PIT-lahk), Aroostook co., E Maine, 27 mi/43 km SW of Houlton; 3 mi/4.8 km long. Source of Wytopitlock Stream, which flows 15 mi/ 24 km SE to Mattawamkeag R.

Xalapa, Mexico: see XALAPA ENRÍQUEZ.

Xalapa Enríquez (hah-LAH-pah en-REE-kes), city (1990 pop. 279,451) and township, ⊙ Veracruz state, E central Mexico, on the slopes of the Sierra Madre Oriental, on Mexico Highways 125 and 140; 19°32′N 96°56′W. In a rich agr. region of fertile valleys. Its cool climate, beautiful parks and artificial lakes, and the proximity of interesting villages and of scenic Mt. Orizaba make Xalapa a popular resort. The site of a pre-Columbian city, Xalapa was captured by Cortés in 1519. It was a commercial center during the Span. colonial era, but declined in the late 18th cent., after which it served as an important military base. Seat of the Univ. of Veracruz. Also spelled Jalapa; often called Xalapa.

Xalisco (hah-LEES-ko), town (1990 pop. 14,898), ⊙ Xalisco municipio, Nayarit, W Mexico, near Pacific coast, 4 mi/6.4 km SSW of Tepic, on Mexico Highway 15. Elev. 7,251 ft/2,210 m. Agr. center (corn, beans, sugarcane, coffee, bananas; cattle). Old Aztec town. Formerly Jalisco.

Xaloztoc (hah-LOS-tok), town (1990 pop. 12,988), Tlaxcala, central Mexico, 13 mi/21 km NE of Tlaxcala; 19°35′N 98°05′W. Elev. 8,504 ft/2,592 m. Cereals, maguey, vegetables; livestock. Also known as San Cosme.

Xalpatlahauc (hahl-pah-TLAH-wahk), town (1990 pop. 3,353), Guerrero, SW Mexico, in Sierra Madre del Sur, 7 mi/11.3 km SW of Tlapa de Comonfort; 17°15′N 98°40′W. Elev. 2,133 ft/650 m. Cereals, fruit; livestock.

Xaltocan (hahl-TO-kahn), town (1990 pop. 4,106), Tlaxcala, central Mexico, 8 mi/12.9 km NNE of Tlaxcala; 19°25′N 98°40′W. Elev. 8,176 ft/2,492 m. Cereals, maguey; livestock. Also San Martín Xaltocan.

Xaltocan, Lake (hahl-TO-kahn), central Mexico, 1 of 5 shallow, interconnected lakes that occupied the Valley of México in pre-Columbian times. Along with lakes Zumpango and Texcoco, it is saline. A system of canals and tunnels constructed at various times since the Span. colonial period has drained the original lake, the bed of which is now occupied by part of Mexico city.

Xayacatlán de Bravo (hah-yah-kaht-LAHN dai BRAH-vo), town (1990 pop. 1,088), Puebla, central Mexico, 5 mi/8 km NE of Acatlán; 18°15′N 97°58′W. Elev. 4,888 ft/1,490 m. Rice, sugarcane, fruit; livestock. San Jerónimo Xayacatlán is 3 mi/4.8 km E.

Xenia (ZEE-nee-uh), city (1990 pop. 24,664), ⊙ Greene co., SW Ohio; 39°41′N 83°57′W. Trade and industrial center in a farm area. Mfg. includes transportation equip., plastics, foods, transportation equip., machinery. The co. historical mus. is here. A tornado destroyed about ½ of the city on April 3, 1974. Inc. 1814.

Xenia (ZEEN-yah), village (1990 pop. 424), Clay co., S central Ill., 12 mi/19 km SW of Louisville; 38°38′N 88°38′W. In agr., oil, and natural-gas area.

Xicalango, Mexico: see MEDELLÍN DE BRAVO.

Xichú (hee-CHOO), city (1990 pop. 884) and township, Guanajuato, central Mexico, in the Sierra Gorda, 30 mi/48 km E of San Luis de la Paz; 21°26′N 100°05′W. Elev. 7,559 ft/2,304 m. Gold, silver, sulphur, aluminum, marble.

Xico (HEE-ko), city (1990 pop. 12,417) and township, ⊙ Xico municipio, Veracruz, E Mexico, at SE foot of Cofre de Perote, 10 mi/16 km SSW of Xalapa Enríquez; 19°25′N 97°00′W. Orange growing. Also spelled Jico; formerly called Xicochimalco.

Xicohténcatl, Papalotla de, Mexico: see PAPALOTLA.

Xicohtzingo, Mexico: see XICOTZINGO.

Xicoténcatl (hee-ko-TEN-kahtl), city (1990 pop. 8,001) and township, Tamaulipas, NE Mexico, 50 mi/80 km SSE of Ciudad Victoria; 22°59′N 98°56′W. Livestock.

Xicoténcatl National Park (hee-ko-TEN-kahtl), central Tlaxcala, Mexico, at Tizatlán, 3 mi/4.8 km NE of Tlaxcala, on Mexico Highway 117. Site of the anc. capital, Tizatlán, founded in 1348 by the Tlaxcalans. The site is noted for its anc. murals with original colors still visible, depicting the wars with the Aztecs, along with eagles, jaguars, fish, and scorpions.

Xicotepec, Mexico: see XICOTEPEC DE JUÁREZ.

Xicotepec de Juárez (hee-KO-tai-pek dai HWAH-rez), town (1990 pop. 29,901), ⊙ Xicotepec municipo, N Puebla, Mexico, 11 mi/18 km NE of Huanchinango, on Mexico Highway 130; 20°18′N 97°58′W. Elev. 2,789 ft/850 m. Hot humid climate. Produces most of the oranges in the state, as well as corn, beans, coffee, plantains, peanuts, chilies, and vanilla. There is a prosperous cattle industry. Very active commerce.

Xicotlán (hee-kot-LAHN), town (1990 pop. 694), Puebla, central Mexico, 38 mi/61 km S of Izúcar de Matamoros; 18°04′N 98°31′W. Elev. 4,731 ft/1,442 m. Corn; livestock.

Xicotzingo (hee-kot-ZEEN-go), town (1990 pop. 8,563), S Tlaxcala, Mexico, 9 mi/14.5 km N of Puebla, and near RR; 19°11′N 98°13′W. Elev. 6,562 ft/2,000 m. Agr. (corn, beans, pulque, fruits); woods; cattle and poultry raising. Also San Toribio Xicotzingo; also spelled Xicohtzingo.

Xilitla (hee-lee-tlah), town (1990 pop. 4,764), San Luis Potosí, E Mexico, at E foot of Sierra Madre Oriental, 45 mi/72 km S of Ciudad Valles, on Mexico Highway 120; 21°28′N 99°00′W. Elev. 2,133 ft/650 m. Coffee-growing center.

Xocchel (hok-CHEL), town (1990 pop. 2,680), Yucatán, SE Mexico, 30 mi/48 km ESE of Mérida on Mexico Highway 180; 20°50′N 89°11′W. Henequen, sugarcane, corn.

Xochi, Mexico: see XOCHICOATLÁN.

Xochiapulco, Mexico: see CINCO DE MAYO.

Xochiatipán (ho-chee-ah-tee-PAHN), town (1990 pop. 1,192), Hidalgo, central Mexico, 23 mi/37 km SSE of Huejutla de Reyes; 20°50′N 98°17′W. Elev. 3,937 ft/1,200 m. Corn, rice, sugarcane, tobacco; livestock.

Xochicalco, Mexico: see TETECALA.

Xochicoatlán (ho-chee-ko-TLAHN), town (1990 pop. 1,223), Hidalgo, central Mexico, 31 mi/50 km SSW of Huejutla de Reyes; 20°48′N 98°40′W. Elev. 5,577 ft/1,700 m. Corn, beans, fruit, cotton, tomatoes. Also known as Xochi.

Xochihuehuetlán (ho-chee-hwe-hwe-TLAHN), town (1990 pop. 4,134), Guerrero, SW Mexico, near Oaxaca-Puebla border, 25 mi/40 km NNE of Tlapa de Comonfort; 17°55′N 98°26′W. Elev. 3,445 ft/1,050 m.

Xochiltepec (ho-CHEEL-te-pek), town (1990 pop. 1,738), Puebla, central Mexico, 37 mi/60 km SW of Izúcar de Matanmoros; 18°11′N 98°52′W. Elev. 4,528 ft/1,380 m. Corn, sugarcane.

Xochimilco (ho-chee-MEEL-ko), town (1990 pop. 271,151) and delegación, Federal District, S central Mexico, suburb of Mexico city; 19°08′N 99°09′W. Elev. 7,461 ft/2,274 m. Mainly a commercial and tourist center, it is famous for its cypress-lined canals and flowers (*Xochimilco* is a native Amer. word meaning "plantation of flowers"). In pre-Hispanic times the Mexica (Aztecs) built garden plots (*chinampas*) in L. Xochimilco on which they grew vegetables and flowers to be shipped to Mexico city on the canals. The *chinampas* survive today in Xochimilco. Boating on the canals is popular among tourists and city residents. Colonial landmarks in the area include a 16th-cent. church.

Xochistlahuaca (ho-chees-tlah-WAH-kahm), town (1990 pop. 4,040), Guerrero, SW Mexico, on S slope of Sierra Madre del Sur, 15 mi/24 km NE of Ometepec; 16°47′N 98°15′W. Fruit; livestock.

Xochitepec (ho-CHEE-te-pek), town (1990 pop. 10,255), Morelos, central Mexico, 9 mi/14.5 km S of Cuernavaca; 18°47′N 99°14′W. Elev. 3,658 ft/1,115 m. Rice, sugarcane, coffee, fruit; livestock.

Xochitlán (ho-chee-TLAHN), town (1990 pop. 3,717), Puebla, central Mexico, 38 mi/61 km SE of Puebla; ⊙ Xochitlán Todos Santos municipio; 18°43′N 97°47′W. Elev. 6,890 ft/2,100 m. Cereals, maguey; livestock.

Xochitlán de Romero Rubio (ho-chee-TLAHN dai ro-ME-ro ROO-bee-o), town (1990 pop. 3,037), Puebla, central Mexico, in SE foothills of Sierra Madre Oriental, 22 mi/35 km ENE of Zacatlán; ⊙ Xochitlán de Vicente Suárez municipio; 19°59′N 97°36′W. Elev. 3,652 ft/1,113 m. Sugarcane, coffee, tobacco, fruit. Also known as Xochitlán.

Xochitlán de Vicente Suárez, Mexico: see XOCHITLÁN DE ROMERO RUBIO.

Xochitlán Todos Santos, Mexico: see XOCHITLÁN.

Xonacatlan, Mexico: see XONACATLÁN DE VICENCIO.

Xonacatlán de Vicencio (ho-mah-kaht-LAHN), town (1990 pop. 13,078), Mexico state, central Mexico, 11 mi/18 km NW of Toluca de Lerdo; ⊙ Xonacatlán municipio; 19°24′N 99°32′W. Grain; livestock. Also known as San Francisco Xonacatlán.

Xoxocotla (ho-ho-KO-tlah), town (1990 pop. 2,114), Veracruz, E Mexico, in Sierra Madre Oriental, on Puebla border, in Sierra Zongolica, 14 mi/23 km SSW of Orizaba; 18°41′N 99°15′W. Elev. 6,519 ft/1,987 m. Coffee, fruit.

Y

Yabucoa (yah-boo-KO-ah), town (1990 pop. 36,483), SE P.R., in hills 8 mi/12.9 km SW of Humacao. Sugar growing; livestock; fishing. Sugar mill and refinery here. Large oil refinery. Its landing, Puerto Yabucoa, is 3.5 mi/5.6 km E.

Yachats (YAH-hahts), village (1990 pop. 533), Lincoln co., W Oregon, 43 mi/69 km WSW of Corvallis, on Pacific Ocean, at mouth of Yachats R.; 44°18′N 124°05′W. Resort area. Timber; fish. Yachats State Park is SE of town; Neptune Beach State Park to S; Siuslaw Natl. Forest to E.

Yacolt (YAK-uhlt), village (1990 pop. 600), Clark co., SW Wash., 20 mi/32 km NE of Vancouver, near East Fork Lewis R.; 45°52′N 122°25′W. Oats, berries, lettuce, alfalfa. Cedar Creek Grist Mill to NW. Battle Ground L. State Park to SW; Gifford Pinchot Natl. Forest to E; Merwin L. reservoir to N and Yale L. reservoir to NE, both on Lewis River.

Yaddo, NW section (1990 pop. 25) of Saratoga Springs, Saratoga co., N N.Y., 30 mi/48 km N of Albany; 43°04′N 73°46′W. An elegant 40-acre/16-ha retreat for composers, writers, and visual artists, the opulent, stone manor was built at the turn of the cent. by Spencer and Katrina Trask as a residence. The estate was turned into an artists' colony 4 years after Katrina Trask's death in 1922. The manor plays host to as many as 25 resident artists; among the 2,500 Yaddo alumni have been Saul Bellow, Aaron Copland, Katharine Anne Porter, Virgil Thomson, Eudora Welty, Philip Roth, John Cheever, Milton Avery, Bernard Malamud, Leonard Bernstein, and Truman Capote.

Yadkin (YAD-kuhn), county (□ 337 sq mi/873 sq km; 1990 pop. 30,488), NW N.C., ☉ Yadkinville; 36°09′N 80°40′W. In the Piedmont region; bounded N and E by Yadkin R. Tobacco, corn, wheat, oats, barley, soybeans, hay; dairying; cattle. Timber (pine, oak). Formed 1850.

Yadkin, N.C.: see PEE DEE RIVER.

Yadkin College (YAD-kuhn), uninc. village, Davidson co., central N.C., 9 mi/14.5 km NW of Lexington, near Yadkin R.

Yadkinville (YAD-kuhn-vil), town (1990 pop. 2,525), NW N.C., 22 mi/35 km W of Winston-Salem; ☉ Yadkin co.; 36°07′N 80°39′W. Tobacco, grain; poultry, livestock; dairying. Mfg. (lumber, concrete prods., textiles).

Yago (ee-ah-go), village (1990 pop. 4,108), Santiago Ixcuintla municipio, Nayarit, W Mexico, on Santiago R., and 26 mi/42 km NNW of Tepic; 21°50′N 105°04′W. On RR; corn, tobacco, tomatoes, bananas. Silver and gold mines nearby. Settled by Spanish in 1531; church built in 1603.

Yaguajay (yah-gwuh-HEI), town, Sancti Spíritus prov., central Cuba, near N coast, on RR, and 20 mi/32 km SE of Caibarién; 22°20′N 79°14′W. Agr. center (sugarcane, tobacco; cattle). Nearby are the sugar mills of Obdulio Morales (NW) and Simón Bolívar (NNE). At Judas Point (8 mi/12.9 km NE) are well-known caverns.

Yaguaramas (yuh-gwuh-RAHM-uhz), town, Cienfuegos prov., central Cuba, on RR, and 18 mi/29 km WNW of Cienfuegos; 22°15′N 80°43′W. Charcoal burning.

Yaguate (yah-GWAH-tai), village (1993 pop. 3,484), San Cristóbal prov., S Dominican Republic, near the coast, 22 mi/35 km WSW of Santo Domingo; 18°20′N 70°11′W. In agr. region (rice, coffee, fruit).

Yahara River (ya-HAHR-uh), c.45 mi/72 km long, S Wis.; rises in N Dane co., and links the Four Lakes; flows S and SE, through L. Mendota, through city of Madison, then through L. Monona and city of Monona, L. Waubesa, and L. Kegonsa, past Stoughton, to Rock R. 9 mi/14.5 km NW of Janesville. Formerly Catfish R.

Yahk (YAK), village, S B.C., Canada, near Mont. and Idaho state lines, 30 mi/48 km SW of Cranbrook; 49°05′N 116°06′W. RR and highway junctions; lumbering.

Yahualica (yah-wah-LEE-kah), town (1990 pop. 1,322), Hidalgo, central Mexico, 12 mi/19 km SSE of Huejutla de Reyes; 21°08′N 102°51′W. Corn, rice, sugarcane, fruit; livestock.

Yahualica, Mexico: see YAHUALICA DE GONZÁLES GALLO.

Yahualica de González Gallo (yah-wah-LEE-kah dai gon-SAH-les GAH-yo), town (1990 pop. 13,406), Jalisco, central Mexico, 45 mi/72 km NE of Guadalajara, on Mexico Highway 25; 21°11′N 102°53′W. Agr. center (corn, wheat, vegetables, fruit; livestock). Also known as Yahualica.

Yajalón (yah-hah-LON), city (1990 pop. 9,961) and township, Chiapas, S Mexico, 25 mi/40 km NNW of Ocosingo; 17°10′N 92°20′W. Corn, sugarcane, fruit. The municipio has a large Tzeltal Maya-speaking pop.

Yakataga, Cape (YA-kuh-TA-guh), S Alaska, on Gulf of Alaska, 100 mi/161 km WNW of Yakutat; 60°01′N 142°24′W.

Yakima (YAK-uh-mah), county (□ 4,311 sq mi/ 11,165 sq km; 1990 pop. 188,823), S Wash.; ☉ Yakima; 46°28′N 120°45′W. Mountainous area in Cascade Range, divided by Yakima valley; fertile irrigated agr. region (corn, potatoes, alfalfa, hay, onions, asparagus, peppermint, spearmint, wheat, barley, oats, grapes, apples, hops; cattle, sheep, poultry; dairying); lumbering. Mfg. (plastic prods., paper, chemicals, aircraft parts, malt, wine, food and beverages, machinery, small arms, agr. equip., meat processing, construction materials, printing and publishing). Includes parts of Snoqualmie Natl. Forest, which contains parts of Norse Peak, William O. Douglas, and Goat Rocks wilderness areas; also includes Yakima Indian Reservation. L. Rimrock and Bumping L. reservoirs in NW; part of Gifford Pinchot Natl. Forest in SW, including part of Mt. Adams Wilderness Area. Co. borders Mt. Rainier Natl. Park in NW; NE corner bounded by Columbia R., Priest Rapids Dam and L. Most of large Yakima Indian Reservation in S ½ of co., extends into Klickitat co. Fort Simcoe State Park in center of co.; Toppenish Natl. Wildlife Refuge in SE center. Part of U.S. Military Reservation–Yakima Training Center and Firing Range in NE. Formed 1865.

Yakima (YAK-uh-mah), city (1990 pop. 54,827), ☉ Yakima co., S central Wash., c.110 mi/177 km SE of Seattle, on the Yakima R. just below (SE of) its confluence with the Naches; 46°35′N 120°32′W. RR junction. It is the trade and shipping center of an extensive irrigated agr. valley noted for its fruit, hops, and mint; other agr. includes grain, vegetables; dairying. It has several fruit canneries; mfg. (plastic prods., paper, chemicals, aircraft parts, malt, food and beverages, machinery, small arms, agr. equip., meat processing, construction materials, printing and publishing). Located in Yakima are a junior col., a school of nursing, a state fish hatchery SW of city, and the Central Wash. Fairgrounds. U.S. Military Reservation–Yakima Training Center and Firing Range to NE; Yakima Indian Reservation to S. Snoqualmie Natl. Forest to W. The city is also a gateway to Mt. Rainier Natl. Park. Inc. 1886.

Yakima (YAK-uh-mah), river, 203 mi/327 km long, S central Wash.; rises in NW Kittitas co., in the Cascade Range, central Wash., in Alpine Lakes Wilderness Area of Wenatchee Natl. Forest; flows SE through Keechelus Reservoir, past Cle Elum, Ellensburg, Yakima, Toppenish and Prosser, to the Columbia R. near Kennewick. Forms NE boundary of Yakima Indian Reservation. The U.S. Bureau of Reclamation's Yakima project (begun in 1906) utilizes the Yakima and its tributaries to irrigate c.460,000 acres/186,160 ha and has helped make the river valley an important farming (vegetables, grain; dairying; livestock) and fruit-growing region. A major unit of the project is the Keechelus Dam (completed 1917).

Yakobi Island (ya-KO-bee), SE Alaska, in Alexander Archipelago, W of Chichagof Isl., separated by Lisianski Strait; 17 mi/27 km long, 7 mi/11.3 km wide; 57°58′N 136°28′W. Sometimes spelled Jacobi.

Yakutat (YA-koo-tat), village (1990 pop. 534), SE Alaska, on Yakutat Bay on Gulf of Alaska, near base of Alaska Panhandle, 200 mi/322 km WNW of Juneau; 59°33′N 139°45′W. Fishing (salmon, halibut, crab); hunting; fish processing. Nearby is airfield built in World War II. Surge of Hubbard Glacier, 1986, closed off Russell Fiord N of town. Malaspina Glacier, largest in N. Amer., is across bay; major tourist attraction.

Yakutat Bay (YA-koo-tat), SE Alaska, inlet of Gulf of Alaska, near base of Alaska Panhandle, 40 mi/64 km SE of Mt. Elias, 200 mi/322 km WNW of Juneau; 75 mi/ 121 km long, 20 mi/32 km wide at mouth; 59°40′N 139°55′W. Contains Khantaak and Knight isls.; Disenchantment Bay, continued by Russell Fiord, is NE arm. Several large glaciers flow into upper bay. Yakutat village on E shore.

Yalalag, Mexico: see VILLA HIDALGO.

Yale, village, SW B.C., Canada, at head of navigation on Fraser R., and 35 mi/56 km NW of Chilliwack; 49°34′N 121°26′W. Fraser R. Canyon begins N of town; formidable obstacle to road and RR systems. Lumbering. Fort Yale, post of Hudson's Bay Company, est. here 1848.

Yale 1 town (1990 pop. 220), Guthrie co., W central Iowa, 11 mi/18 km NE of Guthrie Center; 41°46′N 94°21′W. In agr. area. **2** town (1990 pop. 1,977), St. Clair co., E Mich., 21 mi/34 km NW of Port Huron; 43°07′N 82°47′W. In grain-growing, and dairy, poultry, livestock farming area; some mfg. Settled 1859; inc. as village 1885, as city 1905. **3** town (1990 pop. 1,392), Payne co., N central Okla., near Cimarron R., 21 mi/34 km E of Stillwater; 36°06′N 96°42′W. In oil- and natural gas–producing and agr. area (grain; livestock; dairying); mfg. (fabricated metal prods.). Home of Jim Thorpe, Native Amer. Olympic athlete and football player. Inc. 1903.

Yale 1 village (1990 pop. 94), Jasper co., SE Ill., 12 mi/ 19 km NE of Newton; 39°07′N 88°01′W. In agr. area (grain; cattle). **2** village (1990 pop. 128), Beadle co., E central S.Dak., 12 mi/19 km ENE of Huron; 44°25′N 97°59′W.

Yale Dam, Wash.: see LEWIS RIVER.

Yale Lake, reservoir, Clark and Cowlitz cos., SW Wash., on Lewis R., bet. Swift Reservoir and L. Merwin, 28 mi/ 45 km ESE of Longview; 45°59′N 122°21′W. Max. capacity 402,000 acre-ft. Formed by Yale Dam (323 ft/ 98 m high), built (1953) for power generation; also used for flood control, recreation, and as a fish and wildlife pond.

Yale, Mount (14,196 ft/4,327 m), Chaffee co., central Colo., in Collegiate Range of Sawatch Mts., which also includes mounts Columbia, Harvard, Princeton, and Oxford, 9 mi/14.5 km W of Buena Vista. In San Isabel Natl. Forest, E of Continental Divide.

Yale Point (8,050 ft/2,454 m), Apache co., NE Ariz., at E end of Black Mesa, 27 mi/43 km WNW of Canyon de Chelly Natl. Monument.

Yalkabul Point (yahl-kah-BOOL), cape on bar off N coast of Yucatán, SE Mexico, 70 mi/113 km ENE of Progreso; 21°32′N 88°37′W.

Yallahs or **Yallahs Bay**, town (1991 pop. 6,902), St. Thomas parish, SE Jamaica, on coast, 17 mi/27 km ESE of Kingston; 17°52′N 76°34′W. Bananas, coconuts. Yallahs Point is 2.5 mi/4 km SE, adjoining a salt pond.

Yalobusha (yal-uh-BUSH-uh), county (□ 495 sq mi/ 1,282 sq km; 1990 pop. 12,033), N central Miss.; ☉ Coffeeville and Water Valley; 34°01′N 89°43′W. Drained by Yocona (forms Enid L. reservoir in N) and Skuna (forms N arm Grenada L. reservoir in S) rivers. Agr. (cotton, corn, watermelons, soybeans; cattle; timber. Includes sect. of Holly Springs Natl. Forest in SW; George Payne Cossar State Park in NW, on S shore Enid L. Formed 1833.

Yalobusha River (yal-uh-BUSH-uh), 165 mi/266 km long, central Miss.; rises in W Chickasaw co.; flows S, W, and SW, past Calhoun City, through Grenada L. reservoir, where it receives Skuna R. from NE (N arm of lake extends into Yalobusha co.), and past Grenada, joining Tallahatchie R. to form Yazoo R. 2 mi/3.2 km N of Greenwood.

Yamachiche (ya-muh-SHEESH), village (1991 pop.

2,784), ⊙ St. Maurice co., S Que., Canada, on Petit Yamachiche R. (near its mouth on the St. Lawrence), and 15 mi/24 km WSW of Trois Rivières; 46°17′N 72°50′W. Dairying.

Yamasá (yah-mah-SAH), town (1993 pop. 6,377), Trujillo prov., central Dominican Republic, on S slopes of the Cordillera Central, 22 mi/35 km NNW of Santo Domingo; 18°47′N 70°03′W. In agr. region (rice, coffee, cacao, tobacco, fruit; livestock).

Yamaska (yuhm-A-skuh), county (□ 365 sq mi/ 945 sq km), S Que., Canada, on the St. Lawrence, St. Francis, Nicolet, and Yamaska rivers; ⊙ St. François du Lac; 46°00′N 72°50′W.

Yamaska, village (1991 pop. 453), S Que., Canada, on Yamaska R., near its mouth on the St. Lawrence, 10 mi/ 16 km ESE of Sorel; 46°00′N 72°55′W. Dairying; pigs.

Yamaska River, 110 mi/177 km long, S Que., Canada; rises in the Sutton Mts. N of Vt. border; flows NW to Farnham, thence N, past St. Hyacinthe and Yamaska, to L. St. Peter 9 mi/14 km ENE of Sorel. Chief tributaries are Centre Yamaska and North Yamaska rivers, which it receives near Farnham.

Yamhill (YAM-hil), county (□ 718 sq mi/1,860 sq km; 1990 pop. 65,551), NW Oregon; ⊙ McMinnville; 45°13′N 123°18′W. Agr. area bounded on E by Willamette R. and on W by Coast Range. Drained by Yamhill R. and its North and South forks. Agr. (corn, brans, onions, wheat, barley, oats, berries, nuts, pears, plums, cherries, peaches, apples; poultry, sheep, cattle); nurseries, wineries; timber; dairy prods. Part of Siuslaw Natl. Forest in SW; Bald Peak State Park on NE boundary; Maud Williamson State Park in SE; Erratic Rock Wayside State Park in S.

Yamhill (YAM-hil), town (1990 pop. 867), Yamhill co., NW Oregon, 25 mi/40 km SW of Portland, on North Yamhill R.; 45°20′N 123°10′W. Dairy prods.; orchards, vineyards; poultry. Siuslaw Natl. Forest to SW; Tillamook State Forest to NW; Bald Peak State Park to NE.

Yamhill River, c. 12 mi/19 km long, NW Oregon; formed 2 mi/3.2 km E of McMinnville by North Yamhill R. (c. 25 mi/40 km long) and South Yamhill R. (c. 50 mi/80 km long); rises in Coast Range; flows E to Willamette R. 5 mi/8 km S of Newberg.

Yampa Canyon, Colo.: see DINOSAUR NATIONAL MONUMENT.

Yampa River, village (1990 pop. 317), Routt co., NW Colo., on Yampa R. (source c.15 mi/24 km SW), and 23 mi/37 km S of Steamboat Springs; 40°08′N 106°54′W. Elev. 7,890 ft/2,405 m. Transport center. Coal mining; timber; cattle, sheep; hay, wheat, barley. Units of Routt Natl. Forest to E and W. Park Range to E.

Yampa River, c.250 mi/402 km long, NE Garfield co., Routt Natl. Forest, NW Colo.; rises in Rocky Mts.; flows NE, past Steamboat Springs, then W, past Hayden and Craig, through Yampa Canyon (c.1,600 ft/ 488 m deep) in Dinosaur Natl. Monument, to Green R. 18 mi/29 km N of Dinosaur, near Utah state line. Tributary, Little Snake R., enters river 32 mi/51 km ENE of Dinosaur.

Yancey (YAN-see), county (□ 313 sq mi/811 sq km; 1990 pop. 15,419), W N.C.; ⊙ Burnsville; 35°53′N 82°18′W. Bounded NW by Tenn. state line, NE by Nolichucky R.; drained by South Toe and Cane rivers; traversed by ranges of the Blue Ridge and Black Mts., including Mt. Mitchell (6,684 ft/2,037 m), highest point E of the Rocky Mts.; Bald Mts. and Appalachian Trail are along Tenn. state line. Includes parts of Pisgah Natl. Forest (S, NW). Blue Ridge (Natl.) Parkway follows S and SE co. line. Farming (tobacco, hay; cattle; corn); livestock raising; timber; mining (mica, kaolin, feldspar); resort area, including ski resort in NW. Formed 1833.

Yancey, village, Harlan co., SE Ky., 4 mi/6.4 km S of Harlan, in the Cumberland Mts. Bituminous coal.

Yanceyville (YAN-see-vil), town (1990 pop. 1,973), ⊙ Caswell co., N N.C., 15 mi/24 km S of Danville, Va.; 36°24′N 79°20′W. Agr. area (tobacco, grain, soybeans, sorghum, potatoes; cattle; hogs); timber. Mfg. (apparel, textiles, electronic equip.). Piedmont Community Col. Hyco reservoir (Hyco R.) to NE.

Yanga (YAHN-gah), town (1990 pop. 5,255), Veracruz, E Mexico, in Sierra Madre Oriental, 9 mi/14.5 km ESE of Córdoba, on Mexico Highway 150; 18°50′N 96°48′W. Coffee, fruit. Formerly San Lorenzo.

Yankee Lake, village (1990 pop. 88), Trumbull co., NE Ohio, 10 mi/16 km E of Warren; 41°16′N 80°34′W.

Yankee Stadium, baseball park, S Bronx sect. of borough of Bronx, N.Y. city, SE N.Y., bet. Major Deegan Expressway (I-87) and Grand Concourse, S of 161st St.; 40°50′N 73°56′W. Nicknamed "The House That Ruth Built" because of the immense popularity of Yankee player Babe Ruth. Construction began May 5, 1922, and the stadium (capacity 57,545) hosted its 1st ball game April 18, 1923; Ruth hit his 1st home run here the same day. The stadium (11.6 acres/4.7-ha) includes the 3.5-acre/1.4-ha playing field and the famous Monument Park, with memorials to such Yankee greats as Gehrig, Stengel, Munson, Maris, Ruth, Barrow, DiMaggio, Mantle, Rizzuto, Howard, Ford, McCarthy, Martin, Dickey, Berra, and Reynolds. There are also monuments to popes Paul VI and John Paul II. There currently is speculation that the Yankees will abandon the stadium, but nothing has been decided yet.

Yankee-Rowe Nuclear Power Plant, Mass.: see FRANKLIN.

Yankeetown, village (□ 20 sq mi/52 sq km; 1990 pop. 635), on Levy-Citrus co. line, N central Fla., on Withlacoochee R. near its mouth on the Gulf, and c.50 mi/ 80 km SSW of Gainesville; 29°01′N 82°45′W. Sports resort.

Yankton, county (□ 532 sq mi/1,378 sq km; 1990 pop. 19,252), SE S.Dak., on Nebr. state line; ⊙ Yankton; 43°00′N 97°23′W. Farming area drained by James R. and bounded S by Missouri R. (Gavins Point Dam and Lewis and Clark L. reservoir W of Yankton) forms Nebr. state line. Mfg. at Yankton. Agr. (hay, soybeans, corn, fruit; cattle, hogs; dairy prods.); marble. Yankton and Gavins Point state recreation areas in SW. Formed 1862.

Yankton, city (1990 pop. 12,703), ⊙ Yankton co., extreme SE S.Dak., on the Missouri R. A RR and trade center in an agr. region, it has grain elevators and creameries. Mfg. (metal prods., marble prods., electrical equip., printing, consumer goods, feeds); food processing. Settled 1858 as a fur-trading post, Yankton was the Dakota territorial capital 1861–1879; the old capitol bldg. still stands. The former Yankton Col. is now the Yankton Federal Prison. Mount Marty Col. is here. To W, Lewis and Clark L., formed by Gavins Point Dam (completed 1956), is part of the Missouri R. basin project. Fish hatchery at dam. Chan Gurney Municipal Airport. Inc. 1869.

Yantic River, c.12 mi/19 km long, Bozrah, SE Conn.; formed by small streams near Bozrah; flows SE to join Shetucket R., forming the Thames at Norwich.

Yantis, village (1990 pop. 210), Wood co., NE Texas, 42 mi/68 km NNW of Tyler; 32°55′N 95°34′W. Surrounded, except on N, by large L. Fork Reservoir. Agr., timber, and recreation area.

Yaonáhuac (yah-o-NAH-wahk), town (1990 pop. 2,956), Puebla, central Mexico, 8 mi/12.9 km WNW of Teziutlán; 19°52′N 97°27′W. Corn, sugarcane, fruit. Also Santiago Yaonáhuac.

Yaphank, village (□ 13 sq mi/34 sq km; 1990 pop. 4,637), Suffolk co., SE N.Y., on E central L.I., 6 mi/9.7 km NE of Patchogue; 40°49′N 72°55′W. U.S. Camp Upton here was a U.S. army induction center in World Wars I and II.

Yaque del Norte (YAH-kai del NOR-tai), river, c.125 mi/ 201 km long, central and NW Dominican Republic; rises in the Cordillera Central SE of the Pico Trujillo; flows N, past Santiago, where it turns WNW, past Guayubín, through the fertile Cibao region, to the Atlantic 2 mi/3.2 km W of Monte Cristi. Lower course navigable for small craft in rainy season.

Yaque del Sur (YAH-kai del SOOR), river, c.80 mi/ 129 km long, W central and SW Dominican Republic; rises in the Cordillera Central SE of the Pico Duarte, flows S, past Cabral, to Neiba Bay (Caribbean) 5 mi/ 8 km N of Barahona. Partly navigable for small craft.

Yaqui River (YAH-kee), river, c.200 mi/322 km long, Sonora, NW Mexico; formed 12 mi/19 km N of Sahuaripa in W outliers of Sierra Madre Occidental by Bavispe R. and other affluents; flows S and SW, through plateaus and alluvial lowlands, past Suaqui Grande, Soyopa, Onavas, and Bácum, to Gulf of Calif. in large delta 28 mi/45 km SE of Guaymas, S of Bay of Guaymas; 27°37′N; length, with longest tributary, c.420 mi/ 676 km. Largest river in Sonora. Used for irrigation, esp. along its lower course, where wheat, corn, rice, and fruit are grown. Dammed at Buena Vista and El Novillo. Not navigable.

Yaquina River (yuh-KWEN-uh), 50 mi/80 km long, E Lincoln co., W Oregon; rises NW of Corvallis; flows generally W in a very serpentine course, past Toledo, to Yaquina Bay, estuary of Yaquina R., at Newport.

Yara (YAH-ruh), town, Granma prov., E Cuba, on Central Highway, on RR, and 11 mi/18 km ESE of Manzanillo; 20°18′N 76°56′W. Noted for its tobacco. Site of proclamation of Cuban independence (1868), which led to outbreak of the Ten Years War.

Yardley, borough (1990 pop. 2,288), Bucks co., SE Pa., residential suburb, 5 mi/8 km WNW of Trenton, N.J., and 27 mi/43 km NE of downtown Philadelphia, on Delaware R. (bridged); 40°14′N 74°50′W. Agr. (grain; poultry, livestock; dairying). Diversified light mfg. Pennsylvania Canal parallels Delaware R. Washington Crossing Historical Park, 1 of 2 places where George Washington crossed Delaware R., Dec. 25, 1776, to N. Settled 1682, inc. c.1895.

Yarmouth (YAHR-muhth), city (1991 pop. 7,781), SW N.S., Canada, on the Atlantic Ocean; 43°50′N 66°07′W. It is a port, with exports of lumber, fish, berries, and Irish moss. Mfg. (wood prods., iron prods., textiles). Yarmouth, a summer resort and tourist center, has 2 ferry connections with Maine (Portland and Bar Harbor). The region was visited (1604) by Champlain, who named it Cap Fourchu, and it became a Fr. fishing settlement. In 1759 a few settlers came to the site of the city from Yarmouth, Mass., and called it after their former home. The city was founded in 1761, when a larger group of settlers came from Sandwich, Mass. They were followed by Acadians (1767) from the Grand Pré dist. and by United Empire Loyalists (1785).

Yarmouth, resort town (1990 pop. 21,174), Barnstable co., SE Mass., on the S shore of Cape Cod. The main street of this residential town is lined with well-preserved old houses. Of special interest is the Thacher House (1680). The Yarmouth port is a historic dist. Includes villages of South Yarmouth (1990 pop. 10,358), Bass River, West Yarmouth (1990 pop. 5,409; site of Seagull Beach, and access to Great Isl. and Gammon Point). Settled and inc. 1639.

Yarnell, uninc. town (1990 pop. 800), Yavapai co., central Ariz., 25 mi/40 km SW of Prescott, in Peeples Valley. Agr. (cattle, hay). Part of Prescott Natl. Forest to E.

Yarrow Point, uninc. town (1990 pop. 962), King co., W Wash., residential suburb 6 mi/9.7 km ENE of downtown Seattle, on E shore of L. Washington; 47°39′N 122°13′W. Bridle Trails State Park to E. Evergreen Point Bridge to Seattle to SW.

Yates, village, W Alta., Canada, 5 mi/8 km NE of Edson. Pulp mill; power plant.

Yates, county (□ 371 sq mi/961 sq km; 1990 pop. 22,810), W central N.Y.; ⊙ Penn Yan; 42°38′N 77°05′W. Situated in Finger Lakes region; bounded E by Seneca L.; includes parts of Keuka and Canadaigua lakes (resorts). Drained by small Flint Creek. Grape-growing area; also other fruits, wheat, potatoes, hay, dry beans. Diversified mfg., especially at Penn Yan. Named after Joseph C. Yates, who was governor of N.Y. state at the time U.S. became a nation. In 1789, the 1st wheat crop was raised in W N.Y. (destined to be, for a period, nation's main wheat-growing region). Formed 1823.

Yates Center, town (1990 pop. 1,815), ⊙ Woodson co., SE Kansas, 18 mi/29 km W of Iola; 37°52′N 95°44′W. Shipping point for grain area (corn, wheat, oats, hay). Oil wells in vicinity. Mfg. (apparel), natural-gas distribution. RR junction to E. Woodson State Fishing L. to SW. Inc. 1884.

Yates City, village (1990 pop. 760), Knox co., W central Ill., 22 mi/35 km WNW of Peoria; 40°46′N 90°00′W. RR junction; corn, soybeans; livestock; dairying.

Yates Dam, on border of Elmore and Tallapoosa cos., E Ala., in Tallapoosa R., 27 mi/43 km ENE of Montgomery; 87 ft/27 m high, 1,261 ft/384 m long; 32°33′N 85°53′W. Privately built power dam completed 1928. Narrow reservoir extends 11 mi/18 km N to Martin Dam. Formerly known as Upper Tallassee Dam.

Yatesboro (YAITS-buhr-o), uninc. village, Cowanshannock township, Armstrong co., W central Pa., 9 mi/14.5 km E of Kittaning, on Cowanshannock Creek; 40°48′N 79°20′W. In bituminous-coal area.

Yatesville, town (1990 pop. 409), Upson co., W central Ga., 11 mi/18 km ENE of Thomaston; 32°55′N 84°08′W.

Yatesville (YAITS-vil), borough (1990 pop. 506), Luzerne co., NE central Pa., residential suburb 6 mi/9.7 km ENE of Wilkes-Barre, and 10 mi/16 km SW of Scranton, near Susquehanna R.; 41°17′N 75°46′W.

Yatesville Lake, reservoir (□ 4 sq mi/10.4 sq km), Lawrence co., E Ky., on Blaine Creek, 3 mi/4.8 km from W.Va. state line, and 20 mi/32 km SW of Huntington (W.Va.); 38°07′N 82°42′W. Max. capacity 83,300 acre-ft. Formed by Yatesville Dam (77ft/22 m high), built (1988) by Army Corps of Engineers for flood control; also used for recreation and as a fish and wildlife pond. Yatesville L. State Park at N end near dam.

Yathkyed Lake (□ 860 sq mi/2,227 sq km), S central Keewatin dist., N.W.T., Canada; 45 mi/72 km long, 5 mi/8 km–21 mi/34 km wide; 62°40′N 98°00′W. Drained N by Kazan R.

Yauco (YOU-ko), town (1990 pop. 42,058), SW P.R., on the Yauco R. It has a thriving coffee industry. A commercial, industrial, and residential area. Mfg. (food, apparel, furniture). Hosp. Large pop. of Corsican descendants.

Yauhquemehcan (yah-do-ke-ME-kahn), town (1990 pop. 4,892), Tlaxcala, central Mexico, 7 mi/11.3 km NNE of Tlaxcala; 19°25′N 98°10′W. Elev. 8,251 ft/2,515 m. Agr. (maguey, cereals, alfalfa; livestock). Also known as San Dionisio Yauhquemehcan.

Yaupon Beach (yo-PAHN), village (1990 pop. 734), Brunswick co., SE N.C., 25 mi/40 km SSW of Wilmington, on Oak Isl., on Atlantic Ocean (S); 33°54′N 78°04′W. Mouth of Cape Fear R. (lighthouse) to E; Intracoastal Waterway canal passes to N. Beach resort area.

Yautepec de Zaragoza (yah-OO-te-pek), city (1990 pop. 29,110) and township, ⊙ Yautepec municipio, Morelos, central Mexico, on RR, and 11 mi/18 km ESE of Cuernavaca, on Mexico Highway 138; 18°52′N 99°03′W. Elev. 4,206 ft/1,282 m. Agr. center (rice, wheat, sugarcane, coffee, oranges, vegetables; livestock).

Yavapai, county (□ 8,128 mi/13,080 km; 1990 pop. 107,714), W central Ariz.; ⊙ Prescott; 34°36′N 112°32′W. Plateau region with Black Hills in NE, Black Mesa in N, and Juniper Mts. in NW. Verde, Santa Maria, and Agua Fria (forms part of S boundary) rivers cross co. Includes Montezuma Castle and Tuzigoot natl. monuments in NE, parts of Prescott Natl. Forest in center and E. Jerome is former mining center. Gold, silver, copper, lead, zinc. Agr. (alfalfa, hay, wheat, corn, fruit; cattle). Bloody Basin in SE; Red Rock and Dead Horse Ranch state parks in NE; Jerome and Fort Verde state historical parks in NE; Camp Verde Indian Reservation in NE; NW corner is in Hualapai Indian Reservation; part of Tonto Natl. Forest in SE; small part of Kaibab Natl. Forest in N. Formed 1864, 21st-largest co. in U.S.

Yaxcabá (yahsh-kah-BAH), town (1990 pop. 2,261), Yucatán, SE Mexico, 15 mi/24 km E of Sotuta; 20°32′N 88°50′W. Henequen, corn.

Yaxchilán (yahsh-chee-LAHN) [=green stones], a historic site, in E Chiapas, Mexico, near Bonampak, deep in the Chiapas jungle on the Usumacinta R. This important site is reached with river transport or unimproved track. The site is not restored and lacks tourist facilities.

Yaxe (YAH-hai), town (1990 pop. 1,946), S central Oaxaca, Mexico, 14 mi/23 km ESE of Ocotlán de Morelos; 16°44′N 96°29′W. Elev. 5,164 ft/1,574 m. Agr.

Yaxkukul (yahsh-koo-KOOL), town (1990 pop. 2,117), Yucatán, SE Mexico, 17 mi/27 km NE of Mérida; 21°05′N 89°30′W. Henequen; corn, tropical fruit.

Yazoo (YAH-zoo), county (□ 934 sq mi/2,419 sq km; 1990 pop. 25,506), W central Miss.; ⊙ Yazoo City; 32°46′N 90°24′W. Bounded E and SE by Big Black R. Intersected by Yazoo R. and other streams of Yazoo system. Agr. (cotton, corn, hay, wheat, sorghum, soybeans; cattle; timber); catfish; oil fields in S. Formed 1823.

Yazoo Basin, Miss.: see YAZOO RIVER.

Yazoo City (YAH-zoo), city (1990 pop. 12,427), ⊙ Yazoo co., W central Miss., 39 mi/63 km NNW of Jackson, on the Yazoo R.; 32°51′N 90°24′W. It is a trade, processing, and industrial center in a cotton, cattle, and soybean area. Mfg. (machinery, transportation equip., lumber, chemicals, apparel, wire prods., concrete); catfish processing. In the Civil War, the ironclad ram CSS *Arkansas* was built in a Confederate navy yard here. Union troops occupied the city in May 1864 and burned many of its bldgs. Antebellum historic dist. Yazoo Historic Mus. Hillside Natl. Wildlife Refuge to NE, Panther Swamp Natl. Wildlife Refuge to W. Inc. 1830.

Yazoo River (YAH-zoo), 188 mi/303 km long, W central Miss.; formed in Leflore co. by the confluence of the Tallahatchie and Yalobusha rivers, 2 mi/3.2 km N of Greenwood; flows SSW past Greenwood, Belzoni, and Yazoo City, joins Mississippi R. at Vicksburg through former channel of Mississippi R. Major cotton-growing region. In the spring of 1973 about 2,800 sq mi/7,252 sq km of the Yazoo basin were inundated by backwaters of Mississippi R. The term *yazoo* is generally applied to any stream that has a belated confluence with the main river. Original mouth is upstream to NW.

Ybor City, Fla.: see TAMPA.

Yeadon (YAI-duhn), borough (1990 pop. 11,980), Delaware co., SE Pa., residential suburb 5 mi/8 km SW of downtown Philadelphia, on Cobbs Creek; 39°55′N 75°15′W. Light mfg. Inc. 1894.

Yeager (YAIG-uhr), village (1990 pop. 40), Hughes co., central Okla., 6 mi/9.7 km NNE of Holdenville; 35°09′N 96°20′W. In agr. area.

Yeagertown (YAI-guhr-toun), uninc. town (1990 pop. 1,150), Derry township, Mifflin co., central Pa., residential suburb 3 mi/4.8 km N of Lewistown, on Kishacoquillas Creek; 40°38′N 77°34′W. Agr. area (grain; poultry, livestock; dairying). Mfg. (printing and publishing).

Yecapixtla (ye-kah-PEESH-tlah), town (1990 pop. 10,536), Morelos, central Mexico, on RR, and 8 mi/12.9 km NE of Cuautla; 18°53′N 98°52′W. Elev. 5,259 ft/1,603 m. Sugarcane, grain, fruit; livestock.

Yécora (ye-ko-rah), town (1990 pop. 1,592), Sonora, NW Mexico, in W outliers of Sierra Madre Occidental, near Chihuahua border, 130 mi/209 km ESE of Hermosillo; ⊙ municipio; 28°19′N 108°58′W. Elev. 1,509 ft/460 m. Silver, lead, copper mining. Wood; fruit (oranges); livestock.

Yecuatla (ye-KWAH-tlah), town (1990 pop. 3,458), ⊙ Yecuatlán municipio, Veracruz, E Mexico, in Sierra Madre Oriental foothills, 27 mi/43 km NNE of Xalapa Enríquez; 19°52′N 96°45′W. Elev. 2,851 ft/869 m. Corn, sugarcane, coffee, fruit.

Yegua Creek, 40 mi/64 km long, S central Texas; rises in W Washington co.; flows generally ENE through Somerville L. to the Brazos 12 mi/19 km W of Navasota. E Yegua Creek rises in SE Milam co.; flows SE, joining main stream at Somerville L., 20 mi/32 km NW of Brenham.

Yehualtepec (ye-WAHL-te-pek), town (1990 pop. 5,568), Puebla, central Mexico, 40 mi/64 km SE of Puebla; 18°47′N 97°39′W. Cereals, maguey.

Yell, county (□ 948 sq mi/2,455 sq km; 1990 pop. 17,759), W central Ark.; ⊙ functions shared by Danville and Dardanelle; 35°00′N 93°24′W. Bounded NE by Arkansas R.; drained by Petit Jean and Fourche La Fave rivers. Agr. (cattle, hogs, chickens; wheat, soybeans). Timber; sand and gravel. Petit Jean Wildlife Management Area follows river in E. Part of Blue Mt. L. in NW. Large part in S is in Ouachita Natl. Forest; part of Ozark Natl. Forest in N; Mt. Nebo State Park (recreation) in N. Nimrod Reservoir in SE (dam is in Perry co.). Formed 1840.

Yellow Creek Lake, reservoir, Indiana co., W central Pa., on Yellow Creek, in Yellow Creek State Park, 8 mi/12.9 km ESE of Indiana; 3 mi/4.8 km long; 40°34′N 79°02′W. Max. capacity 975,000 acre-ft. Formed by Yellow Creek Dam (62 ft/19 m high), built (1972) by the Pa. Department of Forests and Water for flood control.

Yellow Grass, town (1991 pop. 535), S Sask., Canada, 18 mi/29 km NW of Weyburn; 49°49′N 104°09′W. Grain elevators; mixed farming.

Yellow Medicine, county (□ 763 sq mi/1,976 sq km; 1990 pop. 11,684), SW Minn.; ⊙ Granite Falls; 44°43′N 95°51′W. Bounded W by S.Dak. and NE by Minnesota R.; drained by Lac qui Parle and Yellow Medicine rivers. Agr. (corn, oats, wheat, soybeans, alfalfa, sugar beets; hogs, cattle, sheep); granite. Upper Sioux Agency State Park and Monument and Upper Sioux Indian Reservation in E, on Minnesota R. Formed 1871.

Yellow Medicine River, c.100 mi/161 km long, SW Minn.; rises in Lincoln co. near S.Dak. state line; flows NE through L. Shaokatan reservoir, past Ivanhoe and Hanley Falls, to Minnesota R. 8 mi/12.9 km SE of Granite Falls; 44°24′N 96°21′W. North Branch Yellow Medicine R., c.40 mi/64 km long; rises in W Lincoln co., 7 mi/11.3 km W of Ivanhoe; flows NE for most of its course, turning SE at Porter to enter Yellow Medicine R. South Branch Yellow Medicine R., c.55 mi/89 km long; rises in central Lincoln co., 7 mi/11.3 km SSW of Ivanhoe; flows generally NE in very serpentine course, to SE of Ivanhoe and past Minneota to Yellow Medicine R. 4 mi/6.4 km NE of Minneota.

Yellow Mountain, N.C.: see COWEE MOUNTAINS.

Yellow Pine, uninc. village (1990 est. pop. 50), Valley co., central Idaho, in mts., 40 mi/64 km E of McCall. Service center for mining camps, Forest Service, ranchers. One of most remote permanent settlements. Road open summer only.

Yellow River 1 c.100 mi/161 km long, in Ala. and Fla.; rises E of Dozier in S Ala.; flows SW across NW Fla. into East Bay 6 mi/9.7 km S of Milton; receives Shoal R. **2** c.45 mi/72 km long, N central Ga.; rises 3 mi/4.8 km S of Lawrenceville; flows S past Porterdale to Lake Jackson, 9 mi/14.5 km NE of Jackson; 34°01′N 83°58′W. **3** c.50 mi/80 km long, in N and NW Ind.; rises in St. Joseph co.; flows SW and W to the Kankakee R. 7 mi/11.3 km W of Knox. **4** c.30 mi/48 km long, in Barron co., NW Wis.; rises in lakes c.20 mi/32 km NW of Rice L.; flows SE past Barron to Red Cedar R. 10 mi/16 km S of town of Rice L. **5** c.60 mi/97 km long, central Wis.; rises in Clark co.; flows SSE to Wisconsin R. 9 mi/14.5 km NE of Mauston. **6** c.65 mi/105 km long, central Wis.; rises in Taylor co., in Chequamegon Natl. Forest; flows generally SW through Miller Dam Flowage, past Gilman and Cadott to Chippewa R. at L. Wissota reservoir, 5 mi/8 km E of city of Chippewa Falls. Formerly important for log driving. **7** c.55 mi/89 km long, NW Wis.; rises in central Washburn co., in Spooner L. NE of Spooner; flows generally NW, through lake region, including Yellow L., to St. Croix R. at Danbury.

Yellow Springs, village (1990 pop. 3,973), Greene co., S central Ohio, 8 mi/13 km NNE of Xenia; 39°48′N 83°54′W. In grain, vegetable, and poultry area. Seat of Antioch Col. Bronze prods., plastic goods, food processing, printing. Settled c.1820, inc. 1856.

Yellowhead Highway or **Route 16**, 1,785 mi/2,873 km long (excluding ferry), in Man., Sask., Alta., and B.C., Canada. Starts at Winnipeg, Man., on E; coincides with Trans-Canada Highway first 60 mi/97 km; turns WNW 10 mi/16 km W of Portage La Prairie, Man.; follows old Ellice Trail which led homesteaders W in late 1800s. Passes through Neepawa and Minnedosa, Man.; Yorkton, Wynyard, Saskatoon, N. Battleford, and Lloydminster, Sask.; Lloydminster, Vermilion, Vegreville, Edmonton, Edson, and Jasper, Alta.; Prince George, Vanderhoof, Terrace, and Prince Rupert, B.C. Recent extension includes ferry to Queen Charlotte Isls. and

65 mi/105 km road section on Graham Isl., terminating at Masset. Named for Iroquois guide employed by Hudson's Bay Company. Highway crosses Continental Divide on B.C.–Alta. border at Yellowhead Pass.

Yellowhead Pass (3,711 ft/1,131 m), in the Rocky Mts., on the border bet. Alta. and B.C., Canada, and W of Jasper, Alta. Used by highway and RR.

Yellowjacket Mountains, in Lemhi co., E Idaho, bet. Salmon R. (E and N) and Middle Fork Salmon R., and W of town of Salmon. N extension of Salmon R. Mts. Rise to 10,082 ft/3,073 m in Mt. McGuire. In Salmon Natl. Forest, W part is in Frank Church River of No Return Wilderness Area.

Yellowknife, city (1991 pop. 15,179), ⊙ N.W.T., Canada, Fort Smith region, on N shore of Great Slave L. at the mouth of the Yellowknife R.; 62°27′N 114°21′W. It is the largest city in the N.W.T. and a mining, supply, and transportation center, with an airport, radio and meteorological stations, a post of the Royal Can. Mounted Police, and regional offices of other federal agencies. The city has grown with increased mining and with the assumption of functions previously administered by the federal govt. The town was founded (1935) after the discovery of rich deposits of gold. Another mine was discovered in 1944 and a new townsite was established the next year. The city, named after a Native Amer. tribe, became capital of the N.W.T. in 1967.

Yellowstone, county (□ 2,649 sq mi/6,861 sq km; 1990 pop. 113,419), S Mont.; ⊙ Billings; 45°57′N 108°16′W. Agr. area drained by Yellowstone R. and Pryor Creek. Hay, wheat, barley, oats, corn, beans, sugar beets; cattle, sheep; sulfur, limestone, clay, coal. Mfg. at Billings. Bighorn R. forms part of NE boundary; Pompey's Pillar Natl. Historic Landmark in NE center; part of Crow Indian Reservation in SE; L. Elmo and Pictograph Cave State Parks at SW center of co., near Billings. Formed 1883. Present boundaries est. 1925.

Yellowstone Lake, Wyo.: see YELLOWSTONE NATIONAL PARK.

Yellowstone National Park (□ 3,468 sq mi/8,982 km), world's 1st natl. park (est. 1872), Park and Teton cos., NW Wyo., extending into Gallatin and Park cos., Montana and Fremont co., Idaho. (Formerly independent of any co., and counted as 3 co. equivalents, one for each state, by Census Bureau, park was absorbed by adjacent cos. during 1970s.) It lies mainly on a volcanically active basin in the Rocky Mts., crossed by the Continental Divide in SW, c.8,000 ft/2,438 m above sea level, surrounded by mountains from 10,000 ft/3,048 m to 14,000 ft/4,267 m high. The basin lies within center and SW parts of park; remainder is mountainous. Most of the plateau is formed from once-molten lava; volcanic activity is still evidenced by nearly 10,000 hot springs, 200 geysers, and many vents and hot-mud pots. The more prominent geysers are unequaled in size, power, and variety of action. Old Faithful, the best known although not the largest geyser, erupted at an average interval of 64.5 mins. prior to 1959 earthquake; current (1995) interval is c.74 min., 21–23 times per day; shoots c.11,000 gals/41,640 liters of water some 150 ft/46 m high. Mammoth Hot Springs, a series of 5 terraces with reflecting pools, continues to grow, as residue from the mineral-rich steaming water is deposited. The park's other natural wonders include petrified forests, lava formations, and the "black glass" Obsidian Cliff. Eagle Peak (11,358 ft/3,462 m), on park's E boundary, is the highest point in the park. Yellowstone L. (137 sq mi/355 sq km; largest natural lake in Wyo., 110 mi/177 km shoreline), the Grand Canyon of the Yellowstone, and 41 waterfalls, most notably Yellowstone Falls (lower 308 ft/94 m high, upper 109 ft/33 m high), are on the Yellowstone R., which crosses the park. A wide variety of flowers and other plant life can be found here. Bears, mountain sheep, elk, bison, moose, many smaller animals, and more than 200 kinds of birds inhabit the park, one of the world's largest wildlife sanctuaries. Until the late 1980s evergreen forests covered almost 90% of the park; however, massive fires in 1988 destroyed much of the area and its forestation.

Yellowstone River, 671 mi/1,080 km long; rises at Younts Peak (12,165 ft/3,708 m) at Continental Divide, SW Park co., in NW Wyo.; flows N then generally NE through Mont. to enter the Missouri R. in far W N.Dak. The river drains c.70,400 sq mi/182,336 sq km. It receives the Bighorn, Powder, Tongue, and many smaller rivers. The river flows through Yellowstone Natl. Park in NW Wyoming S to N. There, the river feeds and drains Yellowstone L., the largest high-alt. (elev. 7,731 ft/2,356 m) lake in N. Amer. After leaving the lake, the river drops at Yellowstone Falls, 109 ft/33 m at the Upper Falls, then 308 ft/94 m at the Lower Falls, before entering the deep and spectacular Grand Canyon of the Yellowstone (19 mi/31 km long); Tower Falls, 132 ft/40 m high, is at the N end of the canyon. The river's waters in Mont. have been used for irrigation since the late 1860s. In Mont., the river flows N, then turns ENE at Livingston, flowing past Billings, Miles City, Glendive, and Sidney, before entering W N.Dak., where it continues c.15 mi/24 km before entering the Missouri R. in the upper reach of L. Sakakawea Reservoir (Garrison Dam). The lower 20 mi/32 km of Yellowstone R. is a narrow arm of the reservoir. There are no major dams or reservoirs on the river itself. The U.S. Bureau of Reclamation operates several projects on the Yellowstone that are used for irrigation, flood control, power production, and recreation. These include the Huntley project near Billings, Mont., the Buffalo Rapids project near Glendive, Mont., and the Savage unit of the Missouri R. basin project.

Yellowtail Dam, Mont.: see BIGHORN LAKE.

Yellville, town (1990 pop. 1,181), ⊙ Marion co., N Ark., 23 mi/37 km E of Harrison, on Crooked Creek, in the Ozarks; 36°13′N 92°41′W. Light mfg. Tourism. Bull Shoals L. reservoir to N. Buffalo R. Natl. Park to S and SE (includes the former Buffalo R. State Park).

Yelm, town (1990 pop. 1,337), Thurston co., W Wash., 15 mi/24 km SE of Olympia, near Nisqually R.; 46°57′N 122°36′W. Vegetables, blueberries; dairying; mfg. (plastic prods., plumbing fixtures). Fort Lewis Military Reservation to N and W; Nisqually Indian Reservation to NW.

Yemassee (YEM-ah-see), town (1990 pop. 728), Hampton and Beaufort cos., S S.C., 20 mi/32 km NNW of Beaufort, near the Combahee R; 32°41′N 80°50′W. Good hunting in vicinity. Mfg. (plastics, timber, wooden pallets); agr. (livestock; grain, tomatoes, soybeans); logging.

Yentna River, 100 mi/161 km long, in S Alaska; rises in Mt. Dall glacier system near 62°25′N 152°00′W; flows SE to Susitna R. 2 mi/3.2 km N of Susitna. Receives Skweena R.

Yeoman, town (1990 pop. 131), Carroll co., NW central Ind., 7 mi/11.3 km NNW of Delphi, and near L. Freeman; 40°40′N 86°43′W. In agr. area. Laid out 1880.

Yerba Buena Island, San Francisco co., W Calif., in San Francisco Bay, part of city of San Francisco, 3 mi/4.8 km NE of San Francisco and 5 mi/8 km WNW of downtown Oakland; covers an area of 320 acres/130 ha. It is the midpoint of the San Francisco–Oakland Bay Bridge, which crosses the island through a tunnel. Land bridge to Treasure Isl. to N, both islands part of Treasure Isl. Naval Air Station, which has been scheduled by the Pentagon to be closed. On the isl. are several govt. installations, including a Coast Guard lighthouse service and base. Street access from bridge to isl. Formerly Goat Isl.

Yerington (YE-ring-tuhn), town (1990 pop. 2,367), ⊙ Lyon co., W Nev., on Walker R., and 35 mi/56 km ESE of Carson City; 38°59′N 119°09′W. Elev. 4,384 ft/1,336 m. Shipping point in mining (copper, gold, silver) area; cattle, sheep; hay, vegetables, and dairying. Mfg. waste compactor systems.Confluence of East and West Walker rivers to S. Fort Churchill State Historic Park to N; Walker R. Indian Reservation to E; Mason Valley Wildlife Management Area to NE; Toiyabe Natl. Forest to S. Settled 1860, inc. 1907.

Yerkes Observatory, astronomical observatory located in Williams Bay, Wis., 7 mi/11.3 km W of town of Lake Geneva, on the shore of L. Geneva. It was founded in 1892 with funds provided by C. T. Yerkes, and its first director was G. E. Hale. The observatory is administered by the Univ. of Chicago. The principal instrument is a 40-in/102-cm refracting telescope, completed in 1897, the largest of its type in the world; its size is very near the practical limit for a refractor because of distortions caused by the weight of the lens itself. Other equip. includes a 41-in/104-cm and two 24-in/61-cm reflecting telescopes and a number of specialized instruments. Principal programs include astrometry, and studies of comets, galaxies, and the interstellar medium.

Yermo, uninc. town (1990 pop. 1,092), San Bernardino co., S Calif., 10 mi/16 km E of Barstow, on Mojave R., in Mojave Desert. Cattle. Calico Ghost Town to NW.

Yesca, La, Mexico: see LA YESCA.

Yetter, town (1990 pop. 49), Calhoun co., central Iowa, 12 mi/19 km WSW of Rockwell City; 42°19′N 94°50′W.

Ymir (WEI-mir), village, SE B.C., Canada, in Selkirk Mts., on Salmo R., and 15 mi/24 km S of Nelson. Elev. 4,220 ft/1,286 m. Mining (gold, silver, lead, zinc); timber.

Yoakum, county (□ 799 sq mi/2,069 sq km; 1990 pop. 8,786), NW Texas; ⊙ Plains; 33°10′N 102°49′W. Elev. 3,400 ft/1,036 m–3,900 ft/1,189 m. On Llano Estacado, and bordering W on N.Mex. Formerly entirely a cattle-ranching area, now also produces and refines oil and natural gas, salt; agr. (grains, sorghum, peanuts, cotton). Formed 1876.

Yoakum, town (1990 pop. 5,611), De Witt and Lavaca cos., S Texas, 35 mi/56 km N of Victoria; 29°17′N 97°09′W. In livestock area (hogs, cattle; dairying); agr. (wheat, sorghum, hay); mfg. (leather goods, saddles and riding equip.; gas processing; meat processing). Oil and natural gas. Founded 1887, inc. 1891.

Yobain (yo-BAH-een), town (1990 pop. 1,809), Yucatán, SE Mexico, 37 mi/60 km NE of Mérida; 21°14′N 89°07′W. Henequen, tropical fruit, corn.

Yockanookany River (yah-kuh-NUK-uh-nee), c.65 mi/105 km long, in central Miss.; rises in Choctaw co., N of Ackerman; flows SW past Ethel and Koscinsko to Pearl R. 10 mi/16 km WSW of Carthage. Sometimes spelled Yokahockany or Yockahockany.

Yocona River (yuh-KO-nuh), 130 mi/209 km long, in N Miss.; rises in W Pontotoc co., flows generally W through Crowder to the Tallahatchie R. in E Quitman co. 3 mi/4.8 km W of Crowdee. Enid Dam impounds reservoir near Enid.

Yoder (YO-duhr), village (1990 pop. 136), Goshen co., SE Wyo., near Nebr. state line, and 12 mi/19 km SSW of Torrington; 41°55′N 104°17′W. Elev. 4,245 ft/1,294 m.

Yodocono de Pofririo Díaz, Mexico: see MAGDELENA YODOCONO DE PORTIRIO DÍAZ.

Yoe (YO), borough (1990 pop. 947), York co., S Pa., suburb 6 mi/9.7 km SE of York, on Mill Creek; 39°54′N 76°38′W.

Yogana (yo-GAH-nah), town (1990 pop. 1,677), S Oaxaca, Mexico, 8 mi/12.9 km SSW of Ejutla de Crespo, on Miahuatlán R.; 16°28′N 96°48′W. Elev. 5,709 ft/1,740 m. Agr. and cattle resources.

Yoho National Park (YO-ho) (□ 507 sq mi/1,313 sq km), SE B.C., Canada, in the Rocky Mts. at the Alta. border. It lies W of the Continental Divide, adjoining Banff and Kootenay natl. parks, and contains lakes, glaciers, waterfalls, and high mts., with a number of peaks more than 10,000 ft/3,048 m high. Park hq. are at Field, which is a center for mt. climbing. Est. 1886.

Yokahockany River, Miss.: see YOCKANOOKANY RIVER.

Yoknapatawpha, Nobel Prize author William Faulkner (1897–1967) fictionalized Oxford, his home county in N Miss., using a Chickasaw tribal term for the region ("furrowed plow") that had fallen into disuse. Several real names and locations were retained, including a RR line and the Tallahatchie R., but the county seat, Oxford, became Jefferson, and the Yocona R., the Yoknapatawpha. Most of the sites given in Faulkner's work are, in fact, fictional.

Yolo, county (□ 1,012 sq mi/2,621 sq km; 1990 pop. 141,092), central Calif.; ⊙ Woodland; 38°42′N 121°53′W.

In Sacramento Valley, co. is bounded E by Sacramento R., and rises to foothills in W. Drained by Cache and Putah creeks. Putah Creek forms part of S boundary. Year-round agr. (sugar beets, tomatoes, asparagus, wheat, rice, fruits, olives, beans, nuts); livestock raising (sheep, beef cattle); dairying. Sand, gravel, mercury; natural gas. Processing industries (beet sugar, canned and dried fruits). Has suburbs of Sacramento in E. Berryessa Peak on W boundary; Sacramento Deep Water Canal runs N-S in E part of co., joins Sacramento R. at West Sacramento. Formed 1850.

Yolyn (yo-LIN), uninc. village (1990 pop. 500), Logan co., SW W.Va., 7 mi/11.3 km ESE of Logan. Bituminous-coal area. Mfg. (coal processing).

Yonah (YO-nuh), dam, NE Ga. (Habersham co.) and W S.C. (Oconee co.), on Chatooga R., 38 mi/61 km WNW of Anderson; 90 ft/27 m high; 36°41′N 83°21′W. Built (1925) for power generation. Forms L. Yonah on Chatooga R.; max. capacity 11,700 acre-ft.

Yoncalla (YAHNK-uh-luh), town (1990 pop. 919), Douglas co., W Oregon, 33 mi/53 km SSW of Eugene; 43°36′N 123°17′W. Timber; plums; sheep, cattle. Cottage Grove Reservoir to NE.

Yonkers, city (□ 20 sq mi/52 sq km; 1990 pop. 188,082), Westchester co., SE N.Y., on the E bank of the Hudson R., in a hilly region just N of the Bronx borough of N.Y. city; 40°57′N 73°52′W. Mfg. includes chemicals, cable, wire, machinery, clothing, electronic equip., RR cars, printing and publishing. The area was included in the land grant given (1646) by the chartered Du. West India Company to the New Netherland lawyer Adriaen Van der Donck. It was a trading center in colonial days. Water power from the Nepperhan R. attracted early industries, such as the Otis elevator works, sugar refining, and the country's largest carpet mill (now all closed). Yonkers is the seat of St. Joseph's Seminary and the Boyce Thompson Inst. for Plant Research. Also in the city are Philipse Manor, built in the 17th cent. by Frederick Philipse, and the Hudson R. Mus. and Space Planetarium. It was the home of W. C. Handy, "Father of the Blues." Inc. 1855.

Yorba Linda, city (1990 pop. 52,422), Orange co., S Calif., suburb 27 mi/43 km ESE of downtown Los Angeles, 6 mi/9.7 km NE of Anaheim, near Santa Ana R.; 33°54′N 117°46′W. In a region of citrus fruits. Mfg. (coffee, food and beverage machinery, screw-machine production, semiconductors, looseleaf binders, aircraft parts, plastics prods., electromedical apparatus). The city has grown tremendously along with the S California area; its pop. increased 5-fold bet. 1970 and 1990. Yorba Linda is the birthplace of former President Richard M. Nixon. Large Chino Hills State Park to E; Yorba Linda Reservoir in S. Inc. 1967.

York, county (□ 3,545 sq mi/9,182 sq km; 1991 pop. 82,326), W central N.B., Canada, extending NE from Maine border; ⊙ Fredericton; 44°00′N 79°30′W. Drained by St. John R.

York, city (1991 pop. 140,525), borough of metropolitan Toronto, S central Ont., Canada, 5 mi/8 km NW of downtown Toronto; 48°45′N 64°35′W. Primarily residential. Weston Recreation Centre.

York 1 county (□ 1,271 sq mi/3,292 sq km; 1990 pop. 164,587), southernmost co. in Maine, bet. N.H. state line and coast; ⊙ Alfred; 43°24′N 70°40′W. Drained by Salmon Falls and Piscataqua (on N.H. state line), Saco, Mousam, and Ossippee rivers. Mfg. (textiles, wood prods., shoes, machinery) at Biddeford and Saco; agr. (market gardening; dairying); lumbering; fishing. Summer resorts on coast and lakes. Oldest co. in state; named Yorkshire 1658. Cumberland and Lincoln cos. set off 1670. **2** county (□ 576 sq mi/1,492 sq km; 1990 pop. 14,428), SE Nebr.; ⊙ York; 40°52′N 97°35′W. Agr. region on Loess Plains drained by Big Blue R. and W. Fork Big Blue R. Part of Rainwater Basin, with several state wildlife areas in depressions not already drained for crops. Mfg. (aircraft parts, mobile homes, dairy and poultry prods.); agr. (cattle, hogs; dairying; corn, soybeans, sorghum). Formed 1870. **3** county (□ 910 sq mi/2,357 sq km; 1990 pop. 339,574), S Pa.; ⊙ York. Bounded E by Susquehanna R., S by Md. state line; drained by Conewago, Muddy, and Codorus creeks; 39°55′N 76°43′W. Agr. (corn, wheat, oats, barley, hay, alfalfa, soybeans, potatoes, grapes, apples; poultry, sheep, hogs, cattle; dairying); limestone. Mfg. at York, Emigsville, Hanover, and Red Lion. Co. is urbanized around York (in N center) and in N tip (near Harrisburg). Samuel S. Lewis State Park in NE; L. Marburg reservoir in Codorus State Park in SW; Gifford Pinchot State Park in NW center. Nuclear power plants: Peach Bottom 2 (initial criticality Sept. 16, 1973; max. dependable capacity of 1,055 MWe) and Peach Bottom 3 (initial criticality Aug. 7, 1974; max. dependable capacity of 1,034 MWe) are 18 mi/29 km S of Lancaster. Use cooling water from the Susquehanna R. Formed 1749. **4** county (□ 695 sq mi/1,800 sq km; 1990 pop. 131,497), N S.C.; ⊙ York. Bounded W in part by Broad R., E in part by Catawba R., N by N.C. state line; formed by dam N of Rock Hill; 34°58′N 81°10′W. Part of Kings Mt. Natl. Military Park in NW. Mfg. includes textiles, at Clover, Fort Mill, Rock Hill, and York and in surrounding villages. Also mining of granite, sand, and gravel. Agr. includes poultry, hogs, cattle; dairying; corn, wheat, oats, soybeans, sorghum, hay, peaches. Nuclear power plants Catawba 1 (initial criticality Jan. 7, 1985) and Catawba 2 (initial criticality May 8, 1986) are 6 mi/9.7 km NNW of Rock Hill. They use cooling water from L. Wylie, and each has a max. capacity of 1,129 MWe. Formed 1785. **5** county (□ 215 sq mi/557 sq km; 1990 pop. 42,[illegible]), SE Va.; ⊙ Yorktown; 37°13′N 76°26′W. In Tidewater region, bounded on NE by York R., SW by James R., E by Chesapeake Bay. Some agr., some livestock; fishing, oystering. Yorktown is part of Colonial Natl. Historical Park, which includes Colonial Parkway to Williamsburg and Jamestown. Formed 1634.

York 1 city (1990 pop. 42,192), ⊙ York co., SE Pa., 22 mi/35 km SSE of Harrisburg, on Codorus Creek; 39°57′N 76°43′W. It is a market, trade, processing, and distribution center in the Pa. Dutch country. Agr. area (grain, soybeans, apples; poultry, livestock; dairying); large and diversified mfg. base (monorail systems, hydraulic turbines, heavy-equip. parts, programmable controls, stoneware, dinnerware, nuclear components, motorcycles, armored vehicles, food processing, swimming pools, office furniture). A meeting place (1777–1778) of the Continental Congress. During the Civil War, occupied briefly (1863) by Confederates. York Airport to W. York Univ. of Pa. and Pa. State Univ.–York (2-year) are here. Harley-Davidson Motorcycle Mus. and plant tours, Fire Mus. of York, Agr. Mus. of York, Industrial Mus. of York Co., Strand Capitol Performing Arts Center, Co. Agr. Society Fairgrounds, York Symphony Orchestra, several colonial houses remain. Samuel S. Lewis State Park to E; lakes Williams and Redman (reservoirs) to S. Laid out 1741; inc. as a city 1887. **2** city (1990 pop. 6,709), ⊙ York co., N S.C., 13 mi/21 km WNW of Rock Hill; 35°00′N 81°14′W. RR junction; processing center for agr. area; mfg. (computers, clothing, metal finishing, printing and publishing, textiles), agr. (cotton, peaches, grain, soybeans, sorghum; livestock, poultry; dairying). York Co. Historical Center here. State parks and reservoirs surround city. Settled in 1750s.

York 1 town (1990 pop. 3,160), Sumter co., W Ala., 10 mi/16 km SW of Livingston. Farm trade; clothing; lumbering. **2** town (1990 pop. 9,818), York co., SW Maine, on the coast NE of Kittery; 43°11′N 70°40′W. Its villages include York (formerly York Village) and summer resorts York Beach and York Harbor. Nearly destroyed (1692) in Indian wars. Many colonial bldgs.; stone jail (1653) is historical mus. Has pre-Revolutionary pile drawbridge, rebuilt 1933. Settled 1624 as Agamenticus; chartered 1641 as Gorgeana, 1st English city chartered in America; inc. 1652 as York. **3** town (1990 pop. 7,884), ⊙ York co., SE Nebr., 45 mi/72 km W of Lincoln, and on branch of Big Blue R; 40°52′N 97°35′W. RR junction. Trade center for farming region. Agr. (grain); mfg. (grain-handling equip., mobile homes, air filters, processed meat, pet food, ethanol, pipe, gears and shafts, printing). York Col. here. Plotted 1869; inc. 1872.

York Beach, Maine: see YORK, town.

York Factory, fur-trading post, NE Man., Canada, on Hudson Bay, at the mouth of the Hayes R., just E of the mouth of the Nelson R. The name was used for several early (late 17th-cent.) posts in the area, which changed hands during the struggle bet. England and France for control of the rich fur trade. The British gained final control after the Peace of Utrecht (1713). The present post (built 1788–1793) was a major warehouse for the Hudson's Bay Company. It was closed in 1957. In 1968 it became a Natl. Historic Site.

York Harbor, resort village (1990 pop. 2,555) of York town, York co., SW Maine, 24 mi/39 km S of Alfred, at mouth of York R.; 43°08′N 70°39′W.

York Haven, borough (1990 pop. 758), York co., S Pa., 10 mi/16 km N of York, on Susquehanna R., mouth of Conewago Creek, 1 mi/1.6 km to SE; 40°06′N 76°43′W. Agr. (grain; livestock; dairying); mfg. (lead microwave frames, bakery equip., septic tanks). York Haven Dam 1 mi/1.6 km to N, and Three Mile Isl. Nuclear Plant 2 mi/3.2 km to N, both on Susquehanna R.

York River, c.6 mi/9.7 km long, SW Maine, tidal stream; flows SE to the Atlantic Ocean at York Harbor; 43°12′N 70°46′W.

York River, 40 mi/64 km long, E Va., estuary (1 mi/1.6 km–2.5 mi/4 km wide); receives Pamunkey and Mattaponi rivers at its head at West Point; flows SE to Chesapeake Bay 17 mi/27 km N of Newport News; bridged at Yorktown 10 mi/16 km W of its mouth; 37°31′N 76°46′W. Part of Colonial Natl. Historical Park (Yorktown sect.) on SE shore. Navigable. York R. State Park; Camp Peary Military Reservation, U.S. Naval Supply Center, U.S. Naval Weapons Station, Coast Guard Reserve Training Center along S side of estuary.

York Springs, borough (1990 pop. 547), Adams co., S Pa., 23 mi/37 km SSW of Harrisburg; 40°00′N 77°07′W. Agr. (apples, grain; poultry, livestock; dairying); mfg. (clothing). York Sulphur Springs, on Bermudian Creek, to SE; L. Meade reservoir (residential development) to SE.

York Village, Maine: see YORK, town.

Yorkana (YOR-ka-nah), borough (1990 pop. 285), York co., S Pa., 8 mi/12.9 km E of York. Agr. (grain, apples; livestock; dairying); 39°58′N 76°34′W. Samuel S. Lewis State Park to E.

Yorklyn, uninc. village (1990 pop. 600), New Castle co., N Del., 8 mi/12.9 km NW of Wilmington on Red Clay Creek, at Pa. state boundary; 39°41′N 75°41′W. Mfg. (plastics); agr. (livestock, poultry; dairying).

Yorkshire 1 (YORK-shuhr), uninc. town (1990 pop. 1,700), York co., S Pa., residential suburb 3 mi/4.8 km E of York; 39°57′N 76°39′W. **2** uninc. town, Prince William co., NE Va., residential suburb 24 mi/39 km WSW of Washington, D.C., 5 mi/8 km NNE of Manassas, near Bull Run Creek; 38°47′N 77°27′W. Mfg. (petroleum refining, printing and publishing). Bull Run Natl. Battlefield Park to W.

Yorkshire, village (1990 pop. 126), Darke co., W Ohio, 17 mi/27 km NNE of Greenville; 40°19′N 84°29′W. In agr. area.

Yorkton, city (1991 pop. 15,315), SE Sask., Canada, NE of Regina; 51°13′N 102°28′W. RR center with large stockyards, warehouses, a flour mill, brick and cement plants, and a farm-implement plant.

Yorktown 1 town (1990 pop. 4,106), Delaware co., E central Ind., on White R., and 6 mi/9.7 km W of Muncie; 40°10′N 85°29′W. Agr. area; mfg. (metal castings, tool and die). Laid out 1836. **2** town (1990 pop. 100), Page co., SW Iowa, 7 mi/11.3 km W of Clarinda; 40°44′N 95°09′W. In agr. region. **3** town (1990 pop. 2,207), De Witt co., S Texas, on Coleto Creek, 33 mi/53 km WNW of Victoria; 28°58′N 97°30′W. Elev. 266 ft/81 m. In agr. (peaches, pecans; cattle, hogs, poultry) area; dairying; mfg. (oil-field tools, sausage processing). Oil and natural gas. Laid out 1848; inc. 1871.

Yorktown, uninc. village (1990 pop. 270), ⊙ York co., SE Va., 15 mi/24 km NW of Hampton, on York R. estuary (bridged), 10 mi/16 km W of its entrance on Chesapeake Bay. Part of Colonial Natl. Historical Park, which also includes Jamestown, 14 mi/23 km W. Important colonial tobacco port; reached its zenith c.1750. The

Yorktown Campaign (1781) ended Amer. Revolution; battlefield surrounds the town. Besieged (April-May 1862) by Union troops in Civil War during the Peninsular Campaign, taken May 4. Customhouse (c.1706; restored 1929); Grace Church (1697); Moore House (c.1725), site of negotiations over terms of Cornwallis's surrender; Yorktown Monument (1881), commemorating 1781 victory; Yorktown Natl. Cemetery. U.S. Coast Guard Reserve Training Center to SE; U.S. Naval Weapons Center to NW. Newport News Park and City Reservoir to SW. Settled 1631; laid out 1691.

Yorktown, township (1990 pop. 33,407), N Westchester co., SE N.Y., containing villages of Yorktown Heights and Yorktown; 41°18′N 73°49′W. Rapidly growing exurb of metropolitan N.Y. city. Nearby, at Crompound (2.5 mi/4 km E of Peekskill), is the former anarchist Mohegan colony designed by Lewis Mumford in 1923 and led by American Harry Kelly and Englishmen Joseph Cohen and Leonard Abbott. Also known as the 12 Mohegan Colony and the Modern School Movement, the colony flourished both here and in the Stetton colony in N.J.

Yorktown Heights, residential village (□ 5 sq mi/ 13 sq km; 1990 pop. 7,690), Westchester co., SE N.Y., 8 mi/12.9 km E of Peekskill; 41°16′N 73°46′W. IBM's T. J. Watson Research Center is located here. Pop. figure includes part of Amawalk.

Yorkville 1 village (1990 pop. 3,925), ⊙ Kendall co., NE Ill., on Fox R. (bridged here), and 10 mi/16 km SW of Aurora; 41°38′N 88°27′W. Dairying; mfg. (confections, toolboxes, circuit boards, seasonings). Silver Springs State Park to W. **2** village (1990 pop. 1,246), on Jefferson-Belmont co. line, E Ohio, on Ohio R., and 11 mi/ 18 km S of Steubenville; 40°09′N 80°42′W.

Yorkville, district of Upper East Side, N Manhattan borough of N.Y. city, SE N.Y., lying approximately bet. 72d and 96th streets E of 3d Ave. At one time, center of Ger. community in N.Y. city. Gracie Mansion (built 1799), residence of N.Y. city mayor since 1942, is here; also Carl Schurz Park.

Yorkville, suburb (1990 pop. 2,972) of Utica, Oneida co., central N.Y., along former industrial axis paralleling the N.Y. State Barge Canal and N.Y. Central RR (Conrail), 2 mi/3.2 km NW of city center; 43°07′N 75°17′W. Mfg. of pesticides and electric motors. Henry Inman, one of the most prominent and versatile of the 1st generation of Amer.-trained artists, was b. here in 1801.

Yosemite Lakes, uninc. town (1990 pop. 2,367), Mariposa co., central Calif., 3 mi/4.8 km SE of Mariposa; 37°11′N 119°46′W. Yosemite Natl. Forest and Sierra Natl. Forest to NE. Residential community.

Yosemite National Park (□ 1,189 sq mi/3,080 sq km), Tuolumne, Mariposa, and Madera cos., E central Calif. Located in the Sierra Nevada, it is a glacier-scoured area of great beauty; Mt. Lyell (13,114 ft/3,997 m) is the highest peak. Enclosed within the park is the famed Yosemite Valley (elev. c.4,000 ft/1,200 m), surrounded by cliffs and pinnacles; Half Dome, which reaches an elev. of c.4,800 ft/1,463 m above the valley, and El Capitan, which rises perpendicularly c.3,600 ft/1,097 m above the valley, are the highest of the surrounding peaks. The world's 3 largest monoliths of exposed granite are found in the park. There are also many beautiful lakes, rivers, streams, and waterfalls, the most noted of which is Yosemite Falls, the highest in N. Amer., with a drop of 2,425 ft/739 m in 2 segments; Ribbon Falls has a 1,612 ft/491 m drop. Three groves of sequoias are within the park's limits, which also include other types of trees and more than 1,000 varieties of flowering plants. In the scenic Hetch Hetchy Reservoir in Grand Canyon of the Tuolumne, in NW center, Hetch Hetchy Aqueduct delivers from reservoir water to San Francisco. Pacific Crest Natl. Scenic Trail, including John Muir Trail, crosses NE sect. of park; Merced Grove and Tuolumne Grove giant sequoias in W, Mariposa giant sequoias (Mariposa Grove) in S; Badger Pass Ski Area in SW; Nevada Falls, Bridalveil Falls, Illilovette Falls, Yosemite Falls are all in center of park. During 1980s and 1990s Yosemite became an example of park overcrowding, with park rangers serving the same function as city police controlling traffic and crime. Est. 1890 as a result of the efforts of conservationist John Muir.

Yost, uninc. village, Box Elder co., NW Utah, near Idaho state line, 85 mi/137 km WNW of Brigham City. Cattle, sheep. Part of Sawtooth Natl. Forest to S and E.

Youbou (YOO-bo), village, SW B.C., Canada, on S Vancouver Isl., on Cowichan L., 25 mi/40 km WNW of Duncan; 48°53′N 124°12′W. Lumbering.

Youghiogheny River (yah-kuh-GAIN-ee), c.135 mi/ 217 km long, in W.Va., Md., and Pa.; rises in extreme SE Preston co., W.Va. at Backbone Mt., near W border of Md.; flows NNW past Oakland, Md., enters Pa. in Youghiogheny R. L. reservoir; continues past Connellsville, W. Newton, and Versailles to Monongahela R. at McKeesport; navigable for c.20 mi/32 km above mouth. Youghiogheny Dam (184 ft/56 m high; 1,610 ft/ 491 m long; completed 1944 for flood control, pollution abatement) impounds Youghiogheny Reservoir above Confluence, Pa. Somerfield, Pa., where there once was a famous pioneer ford, was inundated by reservoir.

Youghiogheny River Lake, reservoir (□ 4 sq mi/ 10.4 sq km), SW Pa. (Fayette and Somerset cos.) and W Md. (Garrett co.), on Youghiogheny R., 9 mi/15 km ESE of Uniontown; 39°48′N 79°22′W. Max. capacity 300,000 acre-ft. Formed by Youghiogheny Dam (184 ft/ 56 m high), built (1944) by Army Corps of Engineers for flood control; also used for recreation.

Young, county (□ 930 sq mi/2,409 sq km; 1990 pop. 18,126), N Texas; ⊙ Graham; 33°10′N 98°42′W. Drained by Brazos R., here receiving its Clear Fork and tributary creeks; headwaters of Possum Kingdom L. reservoir (Brazos R.) in SE corner. Agr. (wheat, cotton, pecans, hay, nurseries); livestock (cattle, goats, sheep, hogs). Oil, natural-gas fields; sand and gravel; large coal deposits. Processing, mfg. at Graham, Olney, Newcastle. Formed 1856. L. Graham Reservoir in center.

Young, village (1991 pop. 352), S central Sask., Canada, 45 mi/72 km SE of Saskatoon. Grain elevators; lumbering; dairying.

Young America, town (1990 pop. 1,354), Carver co., S central Minn., 33 mi/53 km WSW of Minneapolis, and 1 mi/1.6 km NE of Norwood, on Young America and Braunworth lakes; 44°46′N 93°55′W. Agr. (grain, soybeans, corn; dairying; livestock); mfg. (irrigation systems).

Young Harris, village (1990 pop. 604), Towns co., NE Ga., 37 mi/60 km NW of Toccoa, in the Blue Ridge; 34°56′N 83°51′W. A col. town (Young Harris Col.) with many beautiful bldgs.

Young Island, islet, St. Vincent and the Grenadines, West Indies, 656 ft/200 m off S coast of St. Vincent, 2 mi/ 3.2 km SE of Kingstown; 13°08′N 61°12′W. Privately owned by resort.

Youngstown, village (1991 pop. 245), SE Alta., Canada, 30 mi/48 km ESE of Hanna; 51°32′N 111°12′W. RR junction; grain elevators, flour mills; livestock.

Youngstown, city (1990 pop. 95,732), ⊙ Mahoning co., NE Ohio, near Pa. state line; 41°05′N 80°39′W. Formerly a major U.S. iron and steel center. During the 1970s, many of the steel mills closed, and the pop. of the city fell significantly. Some steel prods. are still produced; other mfg. includes plastic goods, electric lamps, light machinery, aluminum goods, and household items. Aluminum extrusion and allied industries provide major employment. Discovery of iron ore, coal, and limestone led to the construction of the first iron furnace in 1803. The city's growth was spurred by the opening of the Pennsylvania and Ohio Canal (1839), the arrival of the RR (1853), and the establishment of steel plants in the 1890s. Youngstown is in one of Ohio's richest coal-producing areas. It is the seat of Youngstown State Univ. and Butler Art Inst. The city also has a community playhouse, a symphony center, and a notable park with extensive gardens. Founded 1797; inc. 1849.

Youngstown, town (1990 pop. 2,542), Maricopa co., central Ariz., residential suburb 16 mi/26 km NW of downtown Phoenix; 33°35′N 112°17′W. Luke Air Force Base to SW.

Youngstown, village (□ 1 sq mi/2.6 sq km; 1990 pop. 2,075), Niagara co., W N.Y., on Niagara R. near its mouth on L. Ontario, and 25 mi/40 km N of Buffalo; 43°15′N 79°02′W. Just N is Fort Niagara (which has been restored).

Youngstown (YUNGS-toun), borough (1990 pop. 370), Westmoreland co., SW Pa., 2 mi/3.2 km S of Latrobe near Loyalhanna Creek; 40°16′N 79°22′W. Mfg. includes high-temperature-materials testing. Agr. includes dairying; livestock; corn. Chestnut Ridge to SE.

Youngsville, town (1990 pop. 1,195), Lafayette parish, S La., 10 mi/16 km S of Lafayette; 30°06′N 92°00′W. In agr. area (sugarcane, rice, vegetables; cattle; dairying); mfg. (pipe cutting, fittings, steel bldgs.). Oil and natural-gas deposits in vicinity.

Youngsville 1 resort village (1990 pop. 850), Sullivan co., SE N.Y., 7 mi/11.3 km W of Liberty; 41°48′N 74°53′W. Dairying. **2** village (1990 pop. 424), Franklin co., N central N.C., 19 mi/31 km NNE of Raleigh; 36°01′N 78°28′W. Grain, soybeans, sweet potatoes; poultry, cattle, hogs. Mfg. (printed circuit boards, kitchen ventilation systems, blueprinting machines, wood prods., plating plates, pharmaceutical supplies, clothing).

Youngsville (YUNGS-vil), borough (1990 pop. 1,775), Warren co., NW Pa., 8 mi/12.9 km W of Warren, on Brokenstraw Creek, 3 mi/4.8 km W of its mouth on Allegheny R.; 41°51′N 79°19′W. Mfg. (wood prods., lumber); oil and gas. Allegheny Natl. Forest to SE. Settled 1795.

Youngwood (YUNG-wud), borough (1990 pop. 3,372), Westmoreland co., SW Pa., 25 mi/40 km SE of Pittsburgh, and 5 mi/8 km SSW of Greensburg, on Sewickley Creek; 40°14′N 79°34′W. Dairying; livestock; grain, soybeans. Mfg. (steel-mold bases, semiconductor devices). Inc. 1902.

Yountville, city (1990 pop. 3,259), Napa co., W Calif., 7 mi/11.3 km NNW of Napa; 38°23′N 122°22′W. State veterans' home and state game farm nearby.

Youth, Isle of, Cuba: see JUVENTUD, ISLA DE LA.

Ypsilanti (IP-si-LAN-tee), city (1990 pop. 24,846), Washtenaw co., SE Mich., 5 mi/8 km SE of Ann Arbor, and 30 mi/48 km WSW of downtown Detroit, on the Huron R., at head of Ford L.; 42°14′N 83°37′W. Satellite community of Detroit; a residential, commercial, and farm-trade center. Light industry (motor-vehicle parts, specialty printing). Native Amer. trails once crossed this site, and a Native Amer. village and a Fr. trading post (1809–c.1819) were here. Willow Run Airport to E. Eastern Michigan Univ. and Cleary Col. are here; Historical Mus., Depot Town, pastoral historic dist. with parks. Inc. 1832.

Ypsilon Mountain, Colo.: see MUMMY RANGE.

Yreka (why-ree-kah), city (1990 pop. 6,948), ⊙ Siskiyou co., N Calif., 78 mi/126 km N of Redding, near Shasta R., bet. Klamath Mts. (W) and Cascade Range (E), near Oregon state line; 41°44′N 122°38′W. Elev. c.2,600 ft/ 792 m. In agr. (potatoes, sugar beets, grain, onions; cattle, lambs); mfg. (veneer, printing and publishing); mining, timber, and resort area. Hq. for Klamath Natl. Forest (parts are to W and SE). Co. mus. Boomed as gold-mining town of Shasta Butte City in 1851; renamed 1852; inc. 1857.

Ysleta, SE suburb of El Paso, El Paso co., extreme W Texas. Bridge to Ciudad Juarez, Mexico.

Yuba (you-bah), county (□ 631 sq mi/1,634 sq km; 1990 pop. 58,228), N central Calif.; ⊙ Marysville; 39°16′N 121°21′W. Extends NE from Feather R. (forms W boundary) through Sacramento Valley to lower W slope of the Sierra Nevada; also drained by Yuba (forms part of E boundary) and Bear (forms S border) rivers. Gold dredging. Orchards (peaches, grapes, prunes, kiwi fruit, olives, nuts); farming (rice, wheat, oats, corn); dairying; livestock raising (cattle). Pine, fir, cedar timber. Mining of platinum and silver; quarrying of sand and gravel. Hunting, fishing. Includes parts of Plumas and Tahoe natl. forests in NE; Englebright Reservoir (Yuba R.) on E border; part of Beale Air Force Base in SE; Camp Far West Reservoir (Bear R.) in SE corner; Bullards Bar and Collins reservoirs in NE. Formed 1850.

Yuba (YOO-buh), village (1990 pop. 77), Richland co., S

central Wis., on Pine R., and 14 mi/23 km N of Richland Center; 43°32′N 90°25′W. In dairying region.

Yuba City, city (1990 pop. 27,437), ⊙ Sutter co., N central Calif., 35 mi/56 km N of Sacramento, on the Feather R., opposite (W of) Marysville (Yuba co.) and mouth of Yuba R; 39°08′N 121°37′W. Elev. 70 ft/21 m. RR junction and a growing processing center for fruits, walnuts, rice, grain, sugar beets, beans, and vegetables. Light mfg. (dehydrated fruits and vegetables, medical instruments, packaging paper, trusses, metal plate work, farm machinery) supplements the economy. Beale Air Force Base is to E; Yuba Co. Airport to SE. Sutter Natl. Wildlife Refuge to SW; Sutter Buttes 2,100 ft/640 m to NW. Founded 1849 during the gold rush. Inc. 1908.

Yuba Pass (6,700 ft/2,042 m), Sierra co., NE Calif., across the Sierra Nevada, 17 mi/27 km E of Downieville. Transected by State Highway 49.

Yuba River, c.35 mi/56 km long, N central Calif.; formed in Sierra Nevada c.30 mi/48 km NE of Marysville by junction of the North Yuba (c.55 mi/89 km long) and the Middle Yuba (c.45 mi/72 km long); flows SW through Englebright Reservoir, where it receives South Yuba R. (c.55 mi/89 km long) from E to Feather R. at Marysville. Receives South Yuba R. (c.55 mi/89 km long) in lower course. In South Yuba R. are: L. Spaulding (3 mi/4.8 km long), formed by L. Spaulding Dam (275 ft/84 m high, 800 ft/244 m long; completed 1919; for power), and L. Van Norden (1.5 mi/2.4 km long), impounded by power dam near Norden. Upper Narrows Dam on lower course is 260 ft/79 m high and 1,142 ft/348 m long; completed 1941 for debris control. North Yuba R. is site of New Bullards Bar Dam and reservoir of Central Valley project, replacing Bullards Bar Dam (completed 1924). River and headstreams yielded much gold after 1848. South Yuba R. rises 12 mi/19 km NW of Tahoe City, in NE Placer co., near Donner Pass; flows W through L. Van Norden and L. Spalding reservoirs to Engelbright Reservoir. Middle Yuba R. rises 22 mi/35 km NW of Tahoe City, in N Nev. co.; flows NW, then SW, to Yuba R. North Yuba R. rises c.14 mi/23 km E of Downieville, in E Sierra co.; flows W past Downieville, then S through Bullards Bar Reservoir to join Middle Fork Yuba to form Yuba R.

Yucaipa, city (1990 pop. 32,824), San Bernardino co., S Calif., in S foothills of San Bernardino Mts., suburb 15 mi/24 km ESE of San Bernardino; 34°02′N 117°02′W. Apples, citrus fruits, vegetables; poultry; mfg. (confections, egg and poultry processing, dental equip., cutting tools). Agr. being displaced by urban development. In San Bernardino Natl. Forest, to N and E. Crafton Hills Community Col. Morongo Indian Reservation to E; Goldmine Ski Area to NE; Heart Bar State Park to NE.

Yucatán (yoo-kah-TAHN), state (□ 14,868 sq mi/38,508 sq km; 1990 pop. 1,362,940), SE Mexico, occupying most of the northern part of the Yucatán peninsula; 19°39′N 87°31′W. It lies bet. Campeche and Quintana Roo states. By 300 B.C., and until Columbian times, Yucatán was populated by the Maya. Cortés came to Yucatán in 1519. The area became a state when Mexico won independence (1821), but it seceded from 1839 to 1843. Violent political uprisings in 1847 and 1910. Tourism; henequen (mostly exported to the U.S.). Citrus production has gained in importance in recent years. Roads and RR lines connect many of the larger towns with the capital, Mérida. Several of the most famous Mayan ruins, including Tulúm, Chichén Itzá, and Uxmal, are located here.

Yucatán (yoo-kah-TAHN), peninsula, (□ c.70,000 sq mi/ 181,300 sq km), mostly in SE Mexico, separating the Caribbean Sea from the Gulf of Mexico. It comprises the states of Yucatán, Campeche, and Quintana Roo, Mexico; Belize; and part of Petén, Guatemala. The peninsula is largely a low, flat limestone tableland rising to c.500 ft/152 m in the S. To the N and W the plain continues as the Campeche Bank, stretching under shallow water c.150 mi/241 km from the low, sandy shoreline. The E coast rises in low cliffs in the N and is indented by bays and paralleled by isls. and cays in the S; COZUMEL is the largest isl. Short ranges of hills cross the peninsula at scattered intervals. The only rivers are those flowing E and NW from Petén. In the N ½ of the tableland, rainfall is light and is absorbed by the porous limestone. Water for the inhabitants, who are predominantly the modern descendants of the Maya, and for livestock comes from underground rivers and wells (*cenotes*) from which it is often pumped by windmills, and from surface pools (*aguadas*). The land has tropical dry and rainy seasons, but generally in the N the climate is hot and dry most of the year, and in the S hot and humid. Most of the N ½, although covered with only a few inches of subsoil, is one of the most important henequen-raising regions of the world; the uncultivated area is under a dense growth of scrub, cactus, sapote wood, and mangrove thickets. Subsistence crops, tobacco, citrus fruits, tropical fruits, and (near the coast) cotton also are grown. Magnificent forests of tropical hardwoods in SW Campeche, Petén, and Belize provide the basis for a lumber industry. This area teems with tropical life, including jaguars, armadillos, iguanas, and the Yucatán turkey. Fishing is important along the Yucatán coast. Many of the peninsula's fine beaches and archaeological sites have been developed for tourism, which is a significant part of the peninsula's economy. MÉRIDA and CAMPECHE, Mexico, and BELIZE CITY, Belize, are the chief cities of Yucatán.

Yucatan Channel, strait, 135 mi/217 km wide (W-E), bet. Yucatán peninsula, Mexico, and Cuba, connecting Gulf of Mexico and Caribbean Sea; bet. Cape Catoche, Mexico, and Cape San Antonio, Cuba; 21°50′N 86°00′W.

Yucca, uninc. village (1990 pop. 250), Mohave co., NW Ariz., 22 mi/35 km S of Kingman, on Sacramento Wash. Service center on Interstate Highway 40. Warm Springs Wilderness Area to W; Wabayuma Wilderness Area to E. Yucca Flats automobile proving grounds are here.

Yucca House National Monument, Montezuma co., SW Colo., in the Montezuma valley, just NW of Mesa Verde, 5 mi/8 km SE of Cortez; 10 acres/4 ha. Remains of a prehistoric Native Amer. village, yet to be ecxavated. Not open to public. Authorized 1919.

Yucca Valley, uninc. city (1990 pop. 13,701), San Bernardino co., S Calif., 45 mi/72 km E of San Bernardino, and 20 mi/32 km NNE of Palm Springs; 34°07′N 116°26′W. Cattle. Mfg. (printing and publishing, light mfg.). San Bernardino Natl. Forest to W; Joshua Tree Natl. Monument to SE.

Yucuyácua, Cerro (yoo-koo-YAH-kwah, SE-ro), peak (11,076 ft/3,376 m), Oaxaca state, S Mexico, in Sierra Madre del Sur, 60 mi/97 km W of Oaxaca; 17°07′N 97°40′W.

Yukon, city (1990 pop. 20,935), Canadian co., central Okla., suburb 13 mi/21 km W of downtown Oklahoma City, and 10 mi/16 km E of El Reno, on North Canadian R. Mfg. (fabricated metal prods., concrete, machinery, printing).

Yukon (YU-kahn), uninc. town (1990 pop. 1,200), Westmoreland co., SW Pa., 9 mi/14.5 km SW of Greensburg, on Sewickley Creek; 40°12′N 79°40′W. Agr. (dairying, livestock; corn). Mfg. (paper prods.). Covered bridge to W.

Yukon (YOO-kahn), river, c.2,000 mi/3,220 km long, Canada and U.S.; rises in Atlin L., NW B.C., and receives numerous headwater streams; flows generally NW, past Dawson and across the Alaska border, to Fort Yukon, thence generally SW through central Alaska until, in a wide swing N, it enters Norton Sound of the Bering Sea through a delta that is 60 mi/97 km wide; one of the longest rivers of N. Amer. Its chief tributaries are the Teslin, Pelly, White, Stewart, Porcupine, Tanana, and Koyukuk rivers. The river is incised in the Yukon Plateau; marshy land borders much of its upper course. The Yukon is navigable for river boats 3 months of the year to Whitehorse, c.1,775 mi/2,860 km upstream. The Yukon basin is one of the most sparsely populated and least developed regions of N. Amer. Much of its history, exploration, and development centers on the river system. Its lower reaches were explored (1836–1837, 1843) by Russians, and in 1843 Robert Campbell of the Hudson's Bay Company. explored the upper course. During the Klondike gold rush (1897–1898) the Yukon was a major route to the gold fields. Greater development of the basin occurred in the mid-1900s due to its strategic location, and several military installations were later built. The Yukon R. is a major salmon-spawning ground, and salmon fishing is an important seasonal activity. The Yukon is used to generate hydroelectricity, but it remains one of the greatest undeveloped hydroelectric resources in N. Amer. On the river's banks are fur-trading posts, missions, native villages, and towns with modern airports serving vast areas.

Yukon Flats, NE Alaska, series of channels and lakes in Yukon R., roughly bet. Circle past Fort Yukon to Stevens Village; c.180 mi/290 km long, average c.30 mi/48 km wide; 66°20′N 147°00′W. Caribou herds, major wildlife; salmon fishing; fur trapping.

Yukon Territory (□ 207,076 sq mi/536,327 sq km; 1991 pop. 27,797), NW Canada, ⊙ and largest town WHITEHORSE; 63°00′N 136°00′W. Next in importance is DAWSON. The triangle-shaped territory is bordered on the N by the Beaufort Sea of the Arctic Ocean, on the E by the Fort Smith and Inuvik regions, N.W.T., on the S by B.C. and Alaska, and on the W by Alaska. The highest point in the Yukon is Mt. Logan, 19,850 ft/6,050 m) high, part of the Coast Ranges in the SW. Although most of the territory is a watershed for the Yukon R. and its tributaries, the N and SE regions drain into the Mackenzie R. system. Immediately S of the desolate arctic coast the country is uninhabited and generally unknown. The other parts of the territory have great natural beauty, with snow-fed lakes backed by perpetually white capped mts. and forests and streams abounding with wildlife. Winters are long and cold, with low humidity. During the short summers the longer days and surprisingly warm sun bring a profusion of wildflowers and enable the hardier grains and vegetables to mature. The few settlements are situated on the riverbanks. Transportation facilities are limited, and for many years the Yukon R. system was the main artery. The White Pass and Yukon RR from Whitehorse to Skagway, Alaska, was constructed during the Klondike gold rush of the 1890s, but was shut down in 1982. Air transportation now plays a vital role, and there is an internatl. airport at Whitehorse. The Alaska Highway and other all-weather roads have been built since World War II. There are hydroelectric facilities at Whitehorse, Aishihik, and Mayo. The leading industry by far in the territory is mining; lead, zinc, silver, gold, and copper are the principal minerals. Tourism is the 2d most-important industry, where the area's colorful history and beautiful scenery draw over 500,000 visitors per year. Mfg. is steadily increasing in importance, with prods. such as furniture, apparel, and handicrafts. Fishing is relatively unimportant. Trapping is the oldest industry but has declined in recent decades. The territory's history began with the explorations in the 1840s of Robert Campbell and John Bell, fur traders for the Hudson's Bay Co. Several trading posts were built on the Yukon R., and before long prospectors began to search for treasure. After the famous gold strikes in the Klondike R. region in the 1890s more than 30,000 people pushed across the icy barriers in search of gold. This colorful period has been recorded in the writings of Robert Service and Jack London. The Can. govt. acquired the Yukon from the Hudson's Bay Company in 1870 and administered it as part of the N.W.T. To meet the need for local govt. created by the influx of gold prospectors, the Yukon was made a separate dist. (1895) and then a separate territory (1898) with Dawson as capital. Whitehorse became the capital in 1952. The govt. consists of a federally appointed commissioner, an elected legislative assembly of 14 members, and a 5-member cabinet appointed by the majority party of the assembly. The territory sends 1 senator and 1 representative to the natl. parliament. Native land claims and the desire for provincial status are 2 issues that have dominated provincial politics in the Yukon in recent years. The land claim by the Yukon, a tribe of about

7,000 Native Americans, was approved by the federal govt. in 1991. Kluane Natl. Park (est. 1972) is in the St. Elias Mts.

Yukon-Charley Rivers National Preserve (□ 3,942 sq mi/10,210 sq km), central Alaska; 2,523,509 acres/1,021,264 ha; 65°30′N 143°00′W. Proclaimed natl. monument 1978, est. as Natl. Preserve 1980. Relics and cabins from 1898 gold rush. Archaeological evidence of prehistoric man. Charley R. (88 mi/142 km long) considered most spectacular wild river in Alaska. Peregrine falcon nesting area.

Yulee (YOO-lee), town (□ 23 sq mi/60 sq km; 1990 pop. 6,915), Nassau co., extreme NE Fla., 21 mi/34 km N of Jacksonville; 30°37′N 81°34′W. Diverse mfg.

Yuma, Dominican Republic: see SAN RAFAEL DEL YUMA.

Yuma 1 county (□ 5,519 sq mi/14,294 sq km; 1990 pop. 106,895), SW Ariz.; ⊙ Yuma; 32°45′N 113°54′W. Bounded N by La Paz co., W by Colorado R. (forms Calif. state line and part of Mex. border, Baja Calif. Norte state), S by Mexico (Sonora state); drained by Gila R. Cocopah Indian Reservation in SW, Gila Mts.in W, and Yuma Desert in SW. Yuma irrigation project along Gila R. is reclaimed sect. (108 sq mi/280 sq km) of Yuma Desert in vicinity of Yuma; receives water through irrigation canals proceeding from All-Amer. Canal. Agr. in project area (cotton, alfalfa, citrus fruits, vegetables; cattle, sheep, hogs). Boundary bet. Pacific and Mountain time zones follows Colorado R.; Ariz. is in Mountain time zone. Lowest point in Ariz. (70 ft/21 m) in SW corner on Colorado R.; Martinez L., near Colorado R., in W; part of Eagletail Mts. Wilderness Area in NW corner; Yuma Desert in SW; Yuma Territorial Prison State Historical Park in W, at Yuma; part of large Kofa Natl. Wildlife Refuge in N; part of large Cabeza Prieta Natl. Wildlife Refuge in SE; small part of Imperial Natl. Wildlife Refuge in W; part of large Yuma Proving Ground (U.S. Army) in NW; part of large Barry M. Goldwater Air Force Range (formerly Luke) in S and SE. Co. is 49th-largest co. in U.S.; had been 10th largest before creation of La Paz co. out of part of Yuma co. Yuma metropolitan area 4th-fastest gowing area in U.S. Formed 1864. **2** county (□ 2,369 sq mi/6,136 sq km; 1990 pop. 8,954), NE Colo.; ⊙ Wray; 40°00′N 102°25′W. Agr. area, bordering on Kansas and Nebr. (both on E); drained by Arikaree R., South Fork Republican (forms Bonny Reservoir in SE). Agr. (cattle, dairying, wheat, hay, sunflowers, beans,

sorghum, oats, corn). Bonny State Park in SE; Beecher Isl. Battleground site in E. Formed 1889.

Yuma, city (1990 pop. 54,923), ⊙ Yuma co., extreme SW Ariz., 160 mi/257 km WSW of Phoenix, and 140 mi/225 km ESE of San Diego, Calif., on the E bank of the Colorado R.; 32°40′N 114°37′W. Elev. 141 ft/43 m. Confluence of the Gila R. 3 mi/4.8 km E. It is a major trade center of an extensive irrigated farm area known for its cattle, citrus fruits, melons, vegetables, grains, and cotton. Mfg. (paper prods., machinery, construction materials, printing and publishing, toys, chemicals). Nearby military installations contribute to the city's economy—the sprawling Yuma Proving Grounds (U.S. Army) to NE and a U.S. Marine Corps air station. Early missions were built in the area by Father F. T. H. Garcés, who died in the Yuma Rebellion of 1751; however, settlement did not occur until after Fort Yuma was built (1850) to protect overlanders on the route to Calif. After 1858, Yuma was a river port and the center of a gold-mining boom. Points of interest in the area include Fort Yuma (to N across river), Cocopah Indian Reservation to S, Yuma Territorial Prison State Historical Park (built 1875; now a mus.) in city, St. Thomas Mission (16th cent.), 3 dams on the Colorado R., and the Calif. sand hills to W. Yuma has a 2-year col., Ariz. Western Col. Sprawling Barry M. Goldwater (formerly Luke) Air Force Range to SE; Imperial and Cibola natl. wildlife refuges to N on Colorado R.; Yuma Internatl. Airport in S; Yuma co. fairgrounds; Chocolate Mts. to N; Century House Mus.; Yuma Desert to S; Morelos Dam downstream, to W; Laguna and Imperial dams upstream, to NE. Mex. border in 2 directions from Yuma, Baja Calif. Norte 5 mi/8 km W, Sonora 18 mi/29 km S. Founded 1854, inc. as a city 1914.

Yuma, town (1990 pop. 2,719), Yuma co., NE Colo., 40 mi/64 km SE of Sterling; 40°07′N 102°43′W. Elev. 4,132 ft/1,259 m. In grain and livestock area. Light mfg. Flour, dairy, and poultry prods. Oil and gas area. Sand Hills in E, around Wray. Inc. 1887.

Yuma Desert, Yuma co., SW Ariz. Large semiarid region extending into Sonora, NW Mexico, and lying bet. Gila and Tinaja Altas mts. (E) and Colorado R. (W). Yuma irrigation project is reclaimed area in vicinity of Yuma, Ariz. Cocopah Indian Reservation in W.

Yumurí River (yoo-moo-REE), c.10 mi/16 km long, Matanzas prov., W Cuba; flows through Matanzas to Matanzas Bay. Along its course—outside the city—is a

gorge and the Yumurí Valley, celebrated for its beauty, and one of Cuba's finest sights.

Yuna River (YOO-nah), c.100 mi/161 km long, central Dominican Republic; rises in the Cordillera Central S of Bonao; flows NE and E, past Villa Rivas, to Samaná Bay, 3 mi/4.8 km SW of Sánchez. Lower course is being canalized; navigable for smaller craft. Main affluent, Camú R. Its valley forms E sect. of fertile La Vega Real valley.

Yunque de Baracoa, El, Cuba: see YUNQUE, EL.

Yunque, El (YOON-kai, AIL) or **El Yunque de Baracoa**, flat summit, (1,932 ft/589 m), Guantánamo prov., E Cuba, in hills 5 mi/8 km W of Baracoa; 20°20′N 74°36′W.

Yunque, El (YOON-kai, el), peak (3,494 ft/1,065 m), NE P.R., in the Sierra de Luquillo, 23 mi/37 km ESE of San Juan; 18°19′N 65°47′W. One of the isl.'s best-known peaks, a tourist resort with observation tower in Luquillo unit of Caribbean Natl. Forest. The La Mina recreational area is at its S foot. Has many waterfalls and swimming ponds.

Yurécuaro (yoo-RE-kwah-ro), town (1990 pop. 17,912), ⊙ Yurécuaro municipio, Michoacán, central Mexico, on Lerma R. (Jalisco border), on central plateau, and 15 mi/24 km W of La Piedad de Cabadas on Mexico Highway 110; 20°20′N 102°15′W. Elev. 5,052 ft/1,540 m. RR junction, agr. center (corn, wheat, beans, oranges; cattle, hogs); tanning, dairying.

Yuriria (yoo-REE-ree-ah), city (1990 pop. 23,725) and township, ⊙ Yuriria municipio, Guanajuato, central Mexico, on S shore of L. Yurriria, 30 mi/48 km SW of Celaya in the Bajió; 20°12′N 101°08′W. Elev. 6,175 ft/1,882 m. Grain, sugarcane, vegetables, fruit; livestock. Anc. Tarascan Indian city.

Yuriria, Lake (yoo-REE-ree-ah) (□ 44 sq mi/114 sq km), Guanajuato, central Mexico, on central plateau, in Lerma R. basin, 25 mi/40 km SW of Celaya. Elev. 5,686 ft/1,733 m. Linked with L. Cuizleo, 12 mi/19 km S. L. was artificially created (1548) by Father Diego de Chávez y Alvarado, by damming a stream.

Yutan (YOOT-uhn), village (1990 pop. 626), Saunders co., E Nebr., 23 mi/37 km W of Omaha, and on Platte R.; 41°14′N 96°24′W. RR junction. Two Rivers State Recreation Area to SE (Douglas co.).

Yutanduchi de Guerrero (yoo-tahn-DOO-chee dai ger-RE-ro), town (1990 pop. 1,266), W Oaxaca, Mexico, 40 mi/65 km W of Oaxaca de Juárez; 17°02′N 97°18′W. Mainly subsistence farming.

Z

Zaachila, Mexico: see VILLA DE ZAACHILA.

Zacapala (sah-kah-PAH-lah), town (1990 pop. 1,319), Puebla, central Mexico, on affluent of Atoyac R. and 33 mi/53 km SSE of Puebla; 17°24'N 96°32'W. Elev. 4,357 ft/1,328 m. Corn, sugarcane. In Popoloca-Indian area. Also known as San Juan Evangelista.

Zacapoaxtla (sah-kah-po-AHSH-tlah), city (1990 pop. 6,898) and township, Puebla, central Mexico, on plateau, 25 mi/40 km ESE of Zacatlán; 19°51'N 97°36'W. Agr. center (corn, coffee, fruit, vegetables).

Zacapu (sah-kah-poo), town (1990 pop. 42,884), Michoacán, central Mexico, on central plateau, 40 mi/64 km WNW of Morelia, on Mexico Highway 15; 19°49'N 101°48'W. RR junction; agr. center (cereals, vegetables, sugarcane, fruit, tobacco; livestock). Tarascán Indian ruins are nearby.

Zacatecas (sah-kah-TE-kahs), state (□ 28,125 sq mi/72,844 sq km; 1990 pop. 1,276,3239), N central Mexico; ⊙ Zacatecas; 21°04'N 100°48'W. Lying on the central plateau, Zacatecas is a state of semiarid basins and mountains. The Sierra Madre Occidental dominates the W ½, and a transverse spur (often over 10,000 ft/3,048 m high) of the same range, divides the state from W to E. Rainfall is light and vegetation sparse. The absence of large rivers limits irrigated agr. Cattle raising is a major activity, but the greatest industry is mining. With gold, silver, mercury, copper, iron, zinc, lead, bismuth, antimony, and salt, Zacatecas is one of Mexico's largest producers of mineral wealth. But low mineral prices have led to closure of many mines. The discovery of silver in 1558 caused a silver rush that led to settlement of the area. The state is known for its numerous examples of baroque architecture.

Zacatecas (sah-kah-TE-kahs), city (1990 pop. 100, 051) and township, ⊙ Zacatecas state, N central Mexico, on Mexico Highways 45, 49, and 54; 22°46'N 102°34'W. Elev. 8,189 ft/2,496 m. It is situated in a deep ravine surrounded by arid hills. The climate is temperate. The city is characterized by colonial bldgs. and narrow, winding, and steep cobbled streets, frequently broken by stone steps. Zacatecas is a distribution center for local mines as well as the commercial center for the region. Founded in 1548, the strategically located city was a key point in the Mex. wars and revolutions of the 19th and early 20th cents. Its cathedral was heavily pillaged during these struggles.

Zacatelco (sah-kah-TEL-ko) or **Santa Inés Zacatelco**, town (1990 pop 30,349), Tlaxcala, central Mexico, on central plateau, 12 mi/19 km N of Puebla; 19°16'N 98°12'W. Agr. center (corn, wheat, beans, alfalfa, maguey; stock); flour milling, pulque distilling.

Zacatepec de Hildalgo (sah-KAH-te-pek), town (1990 pop. 21,839), Morelos, central Mexico, 45 mi/72 km S of Cuernavaca; 18°42'N 99°10'W. Sugar-refining center.

Zacatlán (sah-kah-TLAHN), city (1990 pop. 22,091) and township, Puebla, central Mexico, on central plateau, 53 mi/85 km ESE of Pachuca de Soto on Mexico Highway 119; 19°56'N 97°58'W. Agr. center (corn, coffee, tobacco, sugarcane, fruit); noted for apples and cider. Iron and silver deposits. Pre-Columbian pyramids nearby.

Zacazonapan (sah-kah-so-NAH-pahn), town (1990 pop. 1,482), Mexico state, central Mexico, 40 mi/64 km SW of Toluca de Lerdo; 18°58'N 100°11'W. Coffee, sugarcane.

Zachary (ZA-kuh-ree), city (1990 pop. 9,036), East Baton Rouge parish, SE central La., suburb 14 mi/23 km N of Baton Rouge; 30°40'N 91°09'W. Agr.; mfg. (pulp and paper, lumber, machine parts). Historic Zachary has bldgs. built c.1900. Port Hudson State Commemorative Area to W.

Zacoalco de Torres (sah-lo-AHL-lo dai TO-res), town (1990 pop. 14,100), Jalisco, W Mexico, on L. Zacoalco, 35 mi/56 km SSW of Guadalajara, on RR and Mexico Highway 54; 20°14'N 103°33'W. Elev. 5,075 ft/1,547 m. Agr. center (grain, beans, alfalfa, fruit; livestock).

Zacualpan **1** (sah-KWAHL-pahn), town (1990 pop. 2,762), ⊙ Zacualpan municipio, Mexico state, central Mexico, 40 mi/64 km SSW of Toluca de Lerdo; 18°43'N 99°47'W. Elev. 6,726 ft/2,050 m. Former mining center (gold, silver, lead, and copper). **2** town (1990 pop. 500), ⊙ Zacualpan municipio, Veracruz, E Mexico, in Sierra Madre Oriental, 33 mi/53 km NE of Pachuca de Soto; 18°44'N 99°48'W. Elev. 2,270 ft/692 m. Cereals, sugarcane, tobacco, coffee. No road access.

Zacualpan de Amilpas (sah-KWAHL-pahn dai ah-MEEL-pahs), town (1990 pop. 2,888), ⊙ Zacualpan municipio, Morelos, central Mexico, 13 mi/21 km E of Cuautla; 18°44'N 99°48'W. Elev. 4,094 ft/1,248 m. Sugarcane, coffee, fruit; livestock.

Zacualtipán (sah-kwahl-tek-PAHN), city (1990 pop. 11,434) and township, ⊙ Zacualtipán de Angeles municipio, Hidalgo, central Mexico, in Sierra Madre Oriental, 40 mi/64 km N of Pachuca de Soto, on Mexico Highway 105; 20°40'N 98°40'W. Elev. 6,627 ft/2,020 m. Agr. center (corn, beans, fruit; stock); tanning, leather goods.

Zaleski (zuh-LE-skee), village (1990 pop. 294), Vinton co., S Ohio, c.6 mi/10 km NE of McArthur, and on Raccoon Creek; 39°17'N 82°23'W. In forested area.

Zalma (ZOUL-muh), town (1990 pop. 83), Bollinger co., SE Mo., on Castor R., 12 mi/19 km SW of Marble Hill; 37°08'N 90°04'W. Corn, wheat, soybeans; cattle.

Zama, Canada: see RAINBOW LAKE.

Zamora de Hidalgo (sah-MO-rah dai ee-DAHL-go), city (1990 pop. 109,751), ⊙ Zamora municipio, Michoacán, central Mexico, 30 mi/48 km SW of La Piedad de Cabadas, on Mexico Highway 15 and RR; 20°00'N 102°18'W. Industrial and agr. center (grain, sugarcane, tobacco, fruit, vegetables; livestock); dairying, flour milling, tanning, lumbering; mfg. of cigars, textile goods, sweets, forest prods. (resins). President Lázaro Cárdenas b. here.

Zanesfield (ZAINZ-feeld), village (1990 pop. 183), Logan co., W central Ohio, 5 mi/8 km ESE of Bellefontaine, on Mad R.; 40°20'N 83°40'W. In agr. area.

Zanesville, city (1990 pop. 26,778), ⊙ Muskingum co., central Ohio, on the Muskingum R. at its junction with the Licking R.; 39°57'N 82°01'W. Trade and industrial center with mfg. of metal prods., cement, machinery, ceramics, glassware, and electrical equip. The area has deposits of clay, oil, natural gas, sand, limestone, and iron ore. The site was selected by Ebenezer Zane, surveyor of Zane's Trace, the gateway to the Northwest Territory. A 2-year interval as state capital (1810–1812) and the city's location on waterways and the Natl. Road spurred its growth. The rivers here, which are spanned by a notable "Y" bridge, were connected to the Ohio during the canal era by 10 hand-operated locks and a 1-mi/2-km-long canal. An art institute and a branch of Ohio Univ. are in the city. Of interest are the Natl. Road–Zane Grey mus., several early homes of Federal design, and the nearby Ohio ceramics center. A state park is at Dillon Reservoir to the NW. Inc. 1815.

Zanesville, town (1990 pop. 550), on the Allen-Wells co. line, NE Ind., 14 mi/23 km SW of Fort Wayne. Corn, soybeans; hogs. Mfg. (meat processing). Laid out 1848.

Zap, village (1990 pop. 287), Mercer co., central N.Dak., 6 mi/9.7 km WNW of Beulah and on Spring Creek; 47°16'N 101°55'W. Nearby is lignite strip mine.

Zapaluta, Mexico: see VILLA LA TRINITARIA.

Zapata (zuh-PAH-tuh), county (□ 1,058 sq mi/2,740 sq km; 1990 pop. 9,279), extreme S Texas; ⊙ Zapata; 27°00'N 99°10'W. Bounded W by the Rio Grande (Mex. border here; forms large Internatl. Falcon Reservoir); drained by its small tributaries. Ranching area (cattle, sheep); some agr. (vegetables, cantaloupes, melons); some dairying. Oil, natural gas; exports gas by pipeline to Mexico. Falcon State Recreational Park on Falcon Reservoir in S part of co. Formed 1858.

Zapata, town (1990 pop. 7,119), ⊙ Zapata co., extreme S Texas; 45 mi/72 km SSE of Laredo, on the Rio Grande, on headwaters of Internatl. Falcon Reservoir (Mex. border); 26°53'N 99°15'W. Trade center in ranch area; agr. (cattle; vegetables, cantaloupes, melons); mfg. (concrete prods.). Settled in 18th cent. from old Mex. town across the river.

Zapata, Ciénaga de (sah-PAH-tah), swamp, W Cuba, N of Zapata Peninsula, extending c.100 mi/161 km NW-SE in S La Habana and Matanzas provs. Largest swamp in country. An unhealthful region abounding in tropical timber and wild birds. Source of dry peat. Commonly divided into Ciénga Occidental de Zapata (W) and Ciénaga Oriental de Zapata (E). Sometimes called Gran Ciénaga de Zapata.

Zapata Peninsula (sah-PAH-tah), Matanzas prov., SW Cuba, shoe-shaped extension of Ciénaga de Zapata marshland (N), 50 mi/80 km W of Cienfuegos; bounded by the Ensenada de la Broa (NW), Gulf of Batabanó (W), Jardines Bank (S), Cochinos Bay (E); 22°20'N 81°50'W. It is c.60 mi/97 km long E-W, up to 20 mi/32 km wide. An unhealthful region of swamps, largely covered by tropical forests (hardwood), and abounding in wildlife, it is one of only a few natl. parks in the country. Off its coast are numerous coral keys.

Zapopan (sah-PO-pahn), town (1990 pop. 668,323), Jalisco state, SW Mexico satellite town of Guadalajara; 20°43'N 103°24'W. Elev. 5,243 ft/1,598 m. The Basilica of Our Lady of Zapopan, who is said to have brought peace by a miraculous intervention in the Mixtón War (1539–1542), makes the city a pilgrimage point as well as a tourist destination. Est. 1541.

Zapotal, El, Mexico: see SAN LUCAS, Chiapas.

Zapotiltic (sah-po-TEEL-teek), town (1990 pop. 20,523), Jalisco, W Mexico, in W outliers of Sierra Madre Occidental, on RR, and 6 mi/9.7 km SE of Ciudad Guzmán, on Mexico Highway 53, 19°40'N 103°29'W. Elev. 5,049 ft/1,539 m. Corn-growing center; alfalfa, sugarcane, beans; livestock.

Zapotitlán de Mendez (sah-po teet-LAHN dai MEN-dez), town (1990 pop. 1,755), N Puebla, Mexico, 4.3 mi/7 km E of Tepango de Rodríguez; 20°00'N 97°45'W. Temperate to hot climate. Mostly Totonac-Indian pop. No roads. Agr. (sesame, sugarcane, coffee, beans, corn, vegetables, fruits); precious woods and construction lumber.

Zapotitlán de Vadillo (sah-po-teet-LAHN), town (1990 pop. 2,391), Jalisco, W Mexico, on W slope of Nevado de Colima volcano, 21 mi/34 km. SW of Ciudad Guzmán; 19°32'N 103°48'W. Agr. center (corn, alfalfa, sugarcane, beans, fruit; livestock).

Zapotitlán del Río (sah-po-teet-LAHN del REE-o), town (1990 pop. 412), SW Oaxaca, Mexico, 37 mi/60 km WSW of Oaxaca de Juárez, on Rio Grande; 16°53'N 97°14'W. Mountainous terrain. Temperate climate. Farming mainly for subsistence.

Zapotitlán Lagunas (sah-po-teet-LAHN lah-GOO-nahs), town (1990 pop. 1,828), W Oaxaca, Mexico, 3.1 mi/5 km E of the Guerrero state border, and 42 mi/68 km W of Huajuapam de León; 17°38'N 98°22'W. Elev. 5,755 ft/1,754 m. Mountainous terrain; temperate climate. Resources are agr., mezcal processing, and straw textiles.

Zapotitlán Palmas (sah-po-teet-LAHN PAHL-mahs), town (1990 pop. 1,544), NW Oaxaca, Mexico, on the Puebla state border, 7 mi/12 km NNE of Huajuapam de León; 17°53'N 97°49'W. Mountainous terrain in the Sierra of Oaxaca, in the Mixteca Alta region.

Zapotitlán Salinas (sah-po-teet-LAHN sah-LEE-nahs), town (1990 pop. 2,416), ⊙ Zapotitlán municipio, Puebla, central Mexico, 11 mi/18 km SW of Tehuacán, on Mexico Highway 125; 18°21'N 97°30'W. In Popiloca Indian area. Corn, sugar; livestock.

Zapotitlán Tablas (sah-po-teet-LAHN TAH-blahs), town (1990 pop. 980), Guerrero, SW Mexico, in Sierra Madre del Sur, 30 mi/48 km ESE of Chilapa de Álverez; 17°13'N 98°54'W. Cereals, sugarcane, fruit; livestock.

Zapotlán de Juárez (sah-po-TLAHN dai HWAH-res), town (1990 pop. 6,472), Hidalgo, central Mexico, 17 mi/27 km SW of Pachuca de Soto, on Mexico Highway 85; 19°58'N 98°51'W. Corn, maguey; livestock.

Zapotlán del Rey (sah-po-TLAHN dai rai), town (1990 pop. 2,747), Jalisco, central Mexico, 32 mi/51 km ESE of Guadalajara; 21°27'N 102°55'W. Elev. 5,020 ft/1,530 m. Grain, vegetables, fruit; livestock.

Zapotlán el Grande, Mexico: see CIUDAD GUZMÁN.

Zapotlanejo (sah-po-tlah-NAI-ho), town (1990 pop.

17,853), Jalisco, central Mexico, 19 mi/31 km E of Guadalajara, on Mexico Highway 80; 20°38'N 103°04'W. Elev. 5,236 ft/1,596 m. Agr. center (grain, beans, sugarcane, fruit; livestock).

Zaragoza (sah-rah-GO-sah), city (1990 pop. 8,992) and township, Coahuila, N Mexico, on RR, and 28 mi/45 km SW of Piedras Negras (Texas border); 28°31'N 100°54'W. Cereals, livestock, istle fibers; flour milling.

Zaragoza 1 (sah-rah-GO-sah), town (1990 pop. 1,494), ⊙ General Zaragoza municipio, Nuevo León, N Mexico, in Sierra Madre Oriental, 43 mi/69 km NW of Ciudad Victoria (Tamaulipas). Elev. 4,498 ft/1,371 m. Isolated community on unpaved road. **2** town (1990 pop. 7,473), ⊙ Zaragoza municipio, Puebla, central Mexico, on RR, and 13 mi/21 km WSW of Teziutlán, on Mexico Highway 129; 19°46'N 97°33'W. Sugarcane, corn, coffee, fruit. **3** town (1990 pop. 5,947), Veracruz, SE Mexico, on Isthmus of Tehuantepec, 6 mi/9.7 km WSW of Minatitlán; 17°16'N 97°05'W. Rice, fruit, coffee; livestock. Sometimes called San Isidro de Zaragoza.

Zaragoza, Mexico: see TLAHUALILO DE ZARAGOZA, town, Durango.

Zaragoza 1 Mexico: see SANTA INÉS DE ZARAGOZA. **2** Mexico: see VILLA DE ZARAGOZA.

Zarembo Island, SE Alaska, in Alexander Archipelago, 12 mi/19 km W of Wrangell; 14 mi/23 km long, 9 mi/14.5 km wide; 56°21'N 132°50'W.

Zautla, Mexico: seeSANTIAGO ZAUTLA.

Zavala, county (□ 1,301 sq mi/3,370 sq km; 1990 pop. 12,162), SW Texas; ⊙ Crystal City; 28°51'N 99°45'W. Drained by Nueces and Leona rivers. Partly in irrigated Winter Garden area (spinach, onions, peppers, tomatoes); also grain sorghums, corn, cotton, pecans; livestock (cattle, hogs, sheep, goats). Oil and gas. Formed 1858.

Zavalla, village (1990 pop. 701), Angelina co., E Texas, 22 mi/35 km SE of Lufkin, in Angelina Natl. Forest; 31°09'N 94°25'W. Elev. 228 ft/69 m. In lumbering area; mfg. (drilling prods., asphalt-paving mixtures). Recreation. Large Sam Rayburn Reservoir (Angelina R.) to NE.

Zaza, Cuba: see TUNAS DE ZAZA.

Zaza del Medio (ZAH-zuh dail MAI-dee-o), town, Sancti Spíritus prov., central Cuba, on RR, and 6 mi/9.7 km NE of Sancti-Spíritus; 22°00'N 79°22'W. Sugarcane, tobacco; livestock. Melanio Hernández sugar mill 3 mi/4.8 km W.

Zaza River (ZAH-zuh), 90 mi/145 km long, Sancti Spíritus prov., central Cuba; rises E of Placetas; flows S, past Zaza del Medio, to the Caribbean Sea near Tunas de Zaza. Second-longest river in Cuba.

Zealand, camp area, Coos co., N central N.H., in Zealand Notch recreational region of White Mt. Natl. Forest, NW of Crawford Notch, near Ammonoosuc R.

Zealandia (zee-LAN-dee-uh), town (1991 pop. 137), SE central Sask., Canada, 60 mi/97 km SW of Saskatoon; 51°37'N 107°45'W. Grain elevators.

Zearing, town (1990 pop. 614), Story co., central Iowa, 11 mi/18 km NE of Nevada; 42°09'N 93°17'W. Livestock; grain.

Zeballos (ze-BAH-luhs), village (1991 pop. 220), SW B.C., on NW Vancouver Isl., on Zeballos Arm (7 mi/11 km long) of Esperanza Inlet, at mouth of Zeballos R. (20 mi/32 km long), 40 mi/64 km S of Alert Bay; 49°59'N 126°51'W. Gold- and silver-mining center. Mines extend along Zeballos R. Timber. Ferry from Gold R.

Zebulon 1 (ZEB-yuh-luhn), town (1990 pop. 1,035), ⊙ Pike co., W central Ga., 11 mi/18 km SSW of Griffin; 33°06'N 84°20'W. Co. and city named for explorer Zebulon Pike. Mfg. includes sheet metal fabrication, wooden pallets, apparel. **2** town (1990 pop. 3,173), Wake co., central N.C., 18 mi/29 km E of Raleigh; 35°49'N 78°19'W. Lumber mills. Agr. area (cotton, tobacco, grain, soybeans; chickens, cattle, hogs). Mfg. (textiles, machinery, concrete, pharmaceuticals, plastic prods., printed circuit boards; printing and publishing).

Zebulon (ZEB-yuh-luhn), uninc. village (1990 pop. 500), Pike co., E Ky., 3 mi/4.8 km NE of Pikesville. Bituminous coal.

Zeeland, town (1990 pop. 5,417), Ottawa co., SW Mich., 20 mi/32 km SW of Grand Rapids, and 5 mi/8 km NE of Holland, near Black R.; 42°48'N 86°00'W. In farm area (livestock; fruit, grain, corn, hay; dairy prods.); major poultry area. Mfg. (meat and fish processing, infant formulas, garment hangers, metal stampings, window frames, office furniture, plastics, metal and floor clocks, chemicals, powdered metal parts). Located in Du. heritage area, Du. village to NW. Settled 1847 by Dutch; inc. as village 1875, as city 1907.

Zeeland, village (1990 pop. 197), McIntosh co., S N.Dak., 22 mi/35 km W of Ashley; 45°58'N 99°49'W.

Zeigler (ZIG-ler), city (1990 pop. 1,746), Franklin co., S Ill., 11 mi/18 km SW of Benton; 37°53'N 89°02'W. Bituminous-coal mines; oil; agr. (fruit, grain, livestock; dairy prods.)

Zelienople (ZEE-lee-ah-NO-puhl), borough (1990 pop. 4,158), Butler co., W Pa., 25 mi/40 km NNW of Pittsburgh, on Connoquenessing Creek; 40°47'N 80°08'W. RR junction to E. Agr. area (dairying; livestock; corn, hay, apples). Mfg. (machinery, insulating brick, crucibles, steel fabricating, printing, water treatment equip., plastic prods., corrugated fiberglass). L. Arthur reservoir, in Moraine State Park, to N. Zelienople Airport to W. Settled by Germans; laid out c.1802, inc. 1840.

Zemple, village (1990 pop. 63), Itasca co., N central Minn., 14 mi/23 km WNW of Grand Rapids near Mississippi R., N of White Oak L. (formed on side stream of Mississippi L.), in Chippewa Natl. Forest; 47°19'N 93°47'W. Leech L. Indian Reservation to S and W.

Zempoala (sem-po-AH-lah), town (1990 pop. 4,592), Hidalgo, central Mexico, on RR, and 17 mi/27 km SSE of Pachuca de Soto; 19°55'N 98°40'W. Elev. 8,307 ft/2,532 m. Cereals, maguey; livestock. Nearby is Zempoala Aquaduct built by Franciscan monks before 1585.

Zempoala (sem-po-AH-lah), an historic site, in central E Veracruz, Mexico, 25 mi/40 km N of the city of Veracruz, on the coast of the Gulf of Mexico, on Mexico Highway 180. Elev. 9,498 ft/2,895 m. Archeological site contains the ruins of ancient Totenac-Indian city. Zempoala was the first place where Hernán Cortés found Indian allies. The city may have housed as many as 30,000 people at the time. Partially excavated and restored. Sometimes called Cempoala.

Zempoaltépetl (sem-po-ahl-TE-petl), peak (11,142 ft/3,396 m), Oaxaca, S Mexico, 50 mi/80 km E of Oaxaca; situated at E end of Sierra Madre del Sur, where it converges with Sierra Madre Oriental; 17°11'N 95°58'W. Also called Zempoaltépec or Cempoaltépetl.

Zenda, village (1990 pop. 96), Kingman co., S Kansas, 16 mi/26 km SSW of Kingman; 37°26'N 98°16'W. In wheat region.

Zenith, uninc. town (1990 pop. 1,100), King co., W Wash., residential suburb, 14 mi/23 km S of downtown Seattle, and 11 mi/18 km NE of downtown Tacoma, S of Des Moines, on Puget Sound. Salt Water State Park to S. Highline Community Col. to E.

Zenon Park (ZE-nuhn), village (1991 pop. 254), E Sask., Canada, 20 mi/32 km NE of Tisdale. Dairying, wheat.

Zentla, Mexico: see COLONIA MANUEL GONZÁLEZ.

Zephyr, uninc. village (1990 pop. 198), Brown co., central Texas, 11 mi/18 km E of Brownwood. In farm area; mfg. explosives.

Zephyr Cove (ZE-fuhr), uninc. town (1990 pop. 1,434), Douglas co., W Nev., 14 mi/23 km SW of Carson City, on E shore of L. Tahoe; 38°59'N 119°55'W. Resort area. Largest snowmobiling center in West Coast area. Toiyabe Natl. Forest to E.

Zephyrhills (ZE-fuhr-rilz), town (□ 5 sq mi/13 sq km; 1990 pop. 8,220), Pasco co., W central Fla., 25 mi/40 km NE of Tampa; 28°14'N 82°10'W. Lumber, food prods., bottled water. Founded c.1911, inc. 1914.

Zia, pueblo (□ 189 sq mi/490 sq km; 1990 pop. 637), Sandoval co., NW central N.Mex., 27 mi/43 km NW of Bernalillo, in section of Zia Indian Reservation on Jemez R.; 35°32'N 106°46'W. Elev. 5,470 ft/1,667 m. Pueblo Indians make pottery and raise grain and chili. Mission of Nuestra Señora de la Asunción. Annual fiesta takes place in Aug. Village participated in Pueblo revolt of 1680.

Ziebach, county (□ 1,971 sq mi/5,105 sq km; 1990 pop. 2,220), NW central S.Dak.; ⊙ Dupree; 44°58'N 101°40'W. Agr. and cattle-raising area bounded S by Cheyenne R. and drained by Moreau R. and Cherry Creek. Cheyenne R. Indian Reservation comprises all of Ziebach co. and neighboring Dewey co. to E, total 4,229 sq mi/10,953 sq km. Small farms and ranches. Wheat; cattle, hogs. Formed 1911.

Zihuatanejo (zee-wah-tah-NE-ho), town, ⊙ José Azueta municipio, Guerrero, Mexico; 17°39'N 101°33'W. A trading port on Zihuatanejo Bay, 71 mi/114 km from Lázaro Cárdenas on Mexico Highway 200; 17°38'N 101°33'W. A fishing center with abundant clams, lobster, sea bass, and shark. A well-known and popular internatl. beach resort and cruise-ship port. Internatl. airport to the N.

Zihuateutla (zee-hwah-te-OOT-lah), town (1990 pop. 749), N Puebla, Mexico, 13 mi/21 km NE of Huauchinango; 20°16'N 97°53'W. In the Totonac-Indian language area. Mountainous terrain. Hot, humid climate. Agr. (coffee, sugarcane, wheat, vanilla, beans; tobacco, fruits); fine woods and construction lumber. Handmade textiles. Poor access by road.

Zillah (ZI-luh), town (1990 pop. 1,911), Yakima co., S Wash., 18 mi/29 km SE of Yakima, and near Yakima R., on Sunnyside Canal; 46°24'N 120°16'W. Vegetables, potatoes, mint, wheat, barley, oats; dairying; cattle, sheep, poultry. Food processing (tortillas, burritos); 3 wineries. Large Yakima Indian Reservation to SW.

Zilwaukee (zil-WAW-kee), town (1990 pop. 1,850), Saginaw co., E central Mich., suburb, 3 mi/4.8 km N of Saginaw, and on Saginaw R.; 43°28'N 83°55'W.

Zimapán (see-mah-PAHN), city (1990 pop. 8,733) and township, Zimapán municipio, Hidalgo, central Mexico, in Sierra Madre Occidental, 60 mi/97 km NW of Pachuca de Soto; 20°44'N 99°22'W. Elev. 5,948 ft/1,813 m. Mining center (silver, gold, copper, mercury). Picturesque old town founded in 1522.

Zimatlán de Álvarez (zee-mah-TLAHN dai AHL-vahree), town (1990 pop. 8,511), ⊙ Zimatlán de Álvarez municipio, Oaxaca de Juárez, S Mexico, in Atoyac R. valley, on RR, and 14 mi/23 km SSW of Oaxaca; 16°52'N 96°46'W. Elev. 5,279 ft/1,609 m. Agr. center (sugarcane, cereals, coffee, tobacco, fruit; livestock). Sometimes Villa Alvarez.

Zimmerman, town (1990 pop. 1,350), Sherburne co., E Minn., 10 mi/16 km W of Elk River, next to L. Fremont (NE); 45°26'N 93°35'W. Agr. (grain, soybeans, potatoes; hogs). Mfg. (Christmas wreaths and trees; diverse light mfg.). Sherburne Natl. Wildlife Refuge and Sand Dunes State Forest to W. Also known as Lake Fremont.

Zinacantán (see-nah-kahn-TAHN), town (1990 pop. 2,568), Chiapas, S Mexico, in Sierra de Hueytepec, 4 mi/6.4 km WNW of San Cristóbal de las Casas; 16°45'N 92°42'W. Elev. 7,060 ft/2,152 m. Wheat, fruit.

Zinacantepec (see-nah-KAHN-te-pek), town (1990 pop. 27,497), Mexico state, central Mexico, 5 mi/8 km W of Toluca de Lerdo; 97°17'N 99°44'W. Agr. center (cereals; livestock); dairying. Formerly San Miguel Zinacantepec.

Zinacatepec, Mexico: see SAN SEBASTIÁN ZINACATEPEC.

Zinantécatl, Mexico: see TOLUCA, NEVADO DE.

Zináparo (seen-AH-pah-ro), town (1990 pop. 1,745), Michoacán, central Mexico, 13 mi/21 km S of La Piedad de Cabadas, on Mexico Highway 37; 20°08'N 102°00'W. Elev. 5,413 ft/1,650 m. Cereals; livestock.

Zinapécuaro de Figueroa (seen-ah-PE-kwah-ro), town (1990 pop. 13,402), ⊙ Zinapécuaro municipio, Michoacán, central Mexico, 26 mi/42 km NE of Morelia, on Mexico Highway 120; 19°53'N 100°40'W. Elev. 6,299 ft/1,920 m. Agr. center (cereals, fruit; livestock).

Zinc, village (1990 pop. 91), Boone co., N Ark., 11 mi/18 km ENE of Harrison, in the Ozarks, near Crooked Creek.; 36°17'N 92°55'W.

Zintzuntzan, Mexico: see TZINTZUNTZAN.

Zion, city (1990 pop. 19,775), Lake co., extreme NE Ill., on L. Michigan, suburb 42 mi/68 km NNW of Chicago, 7 mi/11.3 km N of Waukegan; 42°27'N 87°50'W. Largely residential, there is some light industry as well as a nuclear power plant. Mfg. (commercial printing, paper prods., electronic equip.). Zion was founded in 1901 by John Alexander Dowie of the Christian Catholic Church. Until 1935 it was a communal society with a theocratic govt.; all property was owned by the church. The Christian Catholic Church remains an important force here. Of note are the huge Zion Hotel (1902), and Shiloh House (1902), the mansion built for the Dowie family. Ill. Beach State Park to N and S (2 units). Inc. 1902.

Zion (ZEI-uhn), uninc. town (1990 pop. 1,573), Centre co., central Pa., 5 mi/8 km E of Bellefonte, on Nittany Creek; 40°55′N 77°40′W. Agr. includes dairying; livestock; grain, soybeans.

Zion, uninc. village, Marion co., E S.C., 8 mi/12.9 km NE of Marion. Little Pee Dee State Park to NE.

Zion 1 and 2 Nuclear Power Plants, Ill.: see LAKE.

Zion National Park (□ 229 sq mi/593 sq km), NE Washington co., SW Utah, extends into Iron and Kane cos. The park is noted for its many scenic trails and its vividly colored cliffs, rock formations, and deep canyons. The fingerlike, box-shaped Koblob Canyons have sheer 1,500-ft/457-m walls. Zion Canyon, the park's main attraction, is a 15-mi/24-km-long, ½-mi/⅘-km-deep multicolored gorge cut into sandstone, shale, and limestone by the North and East Forks of the Virgin R. Vegetation in the park ranges from desert varieties in the canyons to forests on the mesas. Small animals thrive in the area, and mule deer are common. Main access to park, including Zion Canyon, is at S end, 35 mi/56 km ENE of St. George; Koblob Canyon entrance is 32 mi/51 km NNE of St. George; Koblob Plateau Road entrance is 30 mi/48 km NE of St. George. Est. 1919.

Zionsville, town (1990 pop. 5,281), Boone co., central Ind., on small Eagle Creek, 14 mi/23 km NNW of Indianapolis; 39°57′N 86°16′W. Satellite community of Indianapolis. Dairying and farming area; soybeans; hogs, cattle; mfg. (dental equip.; feed and grain blending). Settled c.1830, laid out 1852.

Ziracuaretiro (see-rah-kwah-re-TEE-ro), town (1990 pop. 2,545), Michoacán, central Mexico, 9 mi/14.5 km ESE of Uruapan; 19°25′N 101°55′W. Elev. 4,921 ft/1,500 m. Sugarcane, coffee, cereals, fruit.

Zirándaro (see-RAHN-dah-ro), town (1990 pop. 2,894), Guerrero, SW Mexico, on Río Balsas (Michocán border), and 10 mi/16 km SSW of Huetamo de Núñez; 18°29′N 100°58′W. Cereals, sugarcane, cotton, sesame, fruit.

Zirate, Cerro (see-RAH-te, SE-ro), peak (10,958 ft/3,340 m), Michoacán, central Mexico, N of L. Pátzcuaro, 25 mi/40 km W of Morelia; 19°44′N 101°30′W.

Zirkel, Mount (12,180 ft/3,712 m), N Colo., in Park Range, 20 mi/32 km WNW of Walden, on Continental Divide, on border bet. Routt co. and Jackson co.

Zitlala (seet-LAH-lah), town (1990 pop. 4,555), Guerrero, SW Mexico, on N slopes of Sierra Madre del Sur, 19 mi/31 km ENE of Chilpancingo de los Bravo; 17°38′N 99°05′W. Elev. 4,806 ft/1,465 m. Cereals, sugarcane, coffee, fruit, forest prods. (rubber, resin, vanilla).

Zitlaltepec (see-TLAHL-te-pek), town (1990 pop. 6,419), ⊙ Zitlaltepec de Trinidad Sánchez Santos municipio, Tlaxcala, central Mexico, on E slope of Malinche volcano, 22 mi/35 km NE of Puebla; 19°12′N 97°54′W. Agr. (corn, barley, alfalfa, maguey; livestock). Also known as Trinidad Sánchez.

Zitlaltepec de Trinidad Sánchez Santos, Mexico: see ZITLALTEPEC.

Zitzio, Mexico: see TZITZIO.

Zoar (ZO-uhr), village (1990 pop. 177), Tuscarawas co., E central Ohio, on the Tuscarawas R., and 8 mi/13 km N of New Philadelphia; 40°37′N 81°25′W. Founded by a group of Separatists from S Germany who, under the leadership of Joseph Michael Bimeler, emigrated to Amer. The Quakers received them in Philadelphia and assisted them in obtaining land in Ohio. The village of Zoar was laid out, a communistic system was adopted, and a strict moral and religious life was maintained. Flour and textile mills and other small industries were established, and the commune flourished. The Zoarites aided in the bldg. of the Ohio and Erie Canal. After Bimeler's death (1853), the society declined; in 1898 the communistic mode of life was abandoned. Many houses built before 1850 have been restored. The Zoar garden has also been restored. Founded 1817, inc. 1884.

Zócalo, Mexico: see PLAZA DE LA CONSTITUCIÓN.

Zona Metropolitana de la Ciudad de México (SO-nah me-tro-po-lee-TAH-no dai lah see-oo-DAHD dai ME-hee-ko), the zone of immediate urban influence of Mexico city, SE Mexico state, Mexico, and the most inclusive of several delimitations of the Mexico city metropolitan area for planning and administrative purposes; comprised of all 16 delegations of the Distrito Federal (Alvaro Obregón, Atzcapotzalco, Benito Juárez, Coyoacán, Cuajimalpa, Cuauhtemoc, Gustavo A. Madero, Iztacalco, Iztapalapa, Magdelena Conteras, Miguel Hidalgo, Milpa Alta, Tlahuac, Tlalpan, Venustiano Caranza, and Xochimilco) along with 50 nearby municipalties of Mexico state and one of SW Hidalgo state. Within the Zona Metropolitana is the Area Metropolitana de la Ciudad de México, which comprises the Distrito Federal and 11 adjoining or nearby municipios of Mexico state (Atizapan de Zaragoza, Chimalhuacan, Coalcalco, Cuautitlán, Ecatepec, Huixquilucan, La Paz, Naucalpan, Nezahualcóyotl, Tlanepantla, and Tultitlán). The Area Metropolitiana corresponds approximately to the built-up area of Mexico city, although within it are large areas left undeveloped because they are unsuitable for building or because they lie far from the city center.

Zongolica (son-go-LEE-kah), city (1990 pop. 4,652) and township, Veracruz, E Mexico, in Sierra Madre Oriental, 16 mi/26 km SSW of Córdoba, in the Sierra Zongolica; 18°40′N 96°59′W. Elev. 4,245 ft/1,294 m. Coffee, corn, fruit.

Zongolica, Sierra, Mexico: see OAXACA, SIERRA MADRE DE.

Zongozotla (son-go-SO-tlah), town (1990 pop. 3,377), Puebla, central Mexico, 18 mi/29 km ENE of Zacatlán; 19°09′N 97°44′W. Corn, coffee, tobacco.

Zontecomatlán de López y Fuentes (son-te-ko-mah-TLAHN dai LO-pes ee foo-EN-tes), town (1990 pop. 528), ⊙ Zontecomatlán municipio, Veracruz, E Mexico, in Sierra Madre Oriental, 51 mi/82 km NNW of Pachuca de Soto; 20°46′N 98°21′W. Corn, sugarcane, coffee.

Zoquiapan (so-kee-AH-pahn), town (1990 pop. 995), Puebla, central Mexico, 32 mi/51 km ESE of Huauchinango; 20°02′N 97°32′W. Cereals, coffee, fruit.

Zoquiapan National Park (so-kee-ah-PAHN) (□ 70 sq mi/181 sq km), in central México state, Mexico, 7 mi/11 km S of Ozumba, E of the Izta-Popo Natl. Park. Accessible by Mexico Highway 150. The village of Río Frío is closest to the park. Forested volcanic terrain with trails, roads, and picnic areas.

Zoquitlán (so-kee-TLAHN), town (1990 pop. 559), Puebla, central Mexico, in Sierra Mazateca, 28 mi/45 km ESE of Tehuacán; 18°20′N 97°01′W. Elev. 7,251 ft/2,210 m. Agr. center (corn, sugar, fruit; livestock).

Zozocolco de Hidalgo (so-so-KOL-kor dai ee-DAHL-go), town (1990 pop. 2,786), Veracruz state, E Mexico, in Sierra Madre Oriental foothills, 28 mi/45 km SW of Papantla de Olarte; 20°06′N 97°34′W. Corn, sugarcane, coffee, fruits. In the Totonac-Indian area. Formerly called Zozocolco.

Zulueta (sool-WAIT-uh), town, Villa Clara prov., central Cuba, on RR, and 22 mi/35 km E of Santa Clara; 22°22′N 79°35′W. Sugarcane, tobacco; livestock. Site of year-end firework celebrations.

Zumbro Falls (ZUHM-bro), town (1990 pop. 237), Wabasha co., SE Minn., at Zumbro R. (low falls), 18 mi/29 km N of Rochester; 44°17′N 92°25′W. Agr. (grain, soybeans; livestock, poultry; dairying); mfg. (meat processing, fencing equip.). Part of Richard J. Dore Memorial Hardwood State Forest to S.

Zumbro River (ZUHM-bro), 50 mi/80 km long, SE Minn.; formed by confluence of North Fork and South Fork, 16 mi/26 km N of Rochester (44°09′N 92°28′W); flows E past Zumbro Falls, through Richard J. Dorer Memorial Hardwood State Forest, for most of its course, to Mississippi R. SE of Wabasha. Drains rich agr. area. North Fork rises in SE Rice co., 5 mi/8 km E of Fairbault; flows E c.50 mi/80 km past Kenyon and Zombrota. South Fork rises in S Dodge co., 20 mi/32 km WSW of Rochester; flows c.50 mi/80 km E, then N through city of Rochester, and to Zumbro L. reservoir. Middle Fork rises in E Steele co.; flows c.40 mi/64 km E through Rice L., past Mantorville, to South Fork, 9 mi/14.5 km N of Rochester.

Zumbrota (zuhm-BRO-dah), village (1990 pop. 2,312), Goodhue co., SE Minn., on North Fork Zumbro R., and 20 mi/32 km NNW of Rochester; 44°17′N 92°40′W. Grain, soybeans; livestock, poultry; dairying; mfg. (cheese, spiral staircases; printing and publishing).

Zumpahuacán (soom-pah-wah-KAHN), town (1990 pop. 2,950), in SE Mexico state, Mexico, 24 mi/39 km ESE of Cuernauaca; 18°54′N 99°33′W. Poor roads. Agr. resources are livestock, pork, horses, and corn.

Zumpango, Mexico: see ZUMPANGO DE OCAMPO.

Zumpango de Ocampo (soom-PAHN-go dai o-KAHM-po), town (1990 pop. 29,354), ⊙ Zumpango municipio, Mexico state, central Mexico, and part of the Zona Metropolitana de la Ciudad de México, 25 mi/40 km N of Mexico city; 19°47′N 99°06′W. Elev. 7,408 ft/2,258 m. Cattle-raising center; cereals, maguey, fruit.

Zumpango del Río (soom-PAHN-go del REE-o), town (1990 pop 15,690), ⊙ Eduardo Neri municipio, Guerrero, SW Mexico, on affluent of Mezcala R. (Río Balsas system), and 7 mi/11.3 km N of Chilpancingo de los Bravo on Mexico Highway 95; 17°36′N 99°32′W. Cereals, sugarcane, tobacco, coffee, fruit, forest prods.

Zumpango, Lake (soom-PAHN-go), Mexico state, central Mexico, Valley of Mexico, just W of Zumpango; one of 5 interconnected lakes that once filled the lowest part of the valley; 4 mi/6.4 km long, 2 mi/3.2 km–3 mi/4.8 km wide. Drained by canal and tunnel system since Span. colonial times. Little remains of the original lake.

Zuñi (ZOO-nee), pueblo (□ 7 mi/11.3 km; 1990 pop. 5,857), McKinley co., W N.Mex., 30 mi/48 km SSW of Gallup, in the Zuni Reservation (1990 pop. 7,405); 35°04′N 108°50′W. Its inhabitants are Pueblo of the Zunian linguistic family. They are a sedentary people, who farm irrigated land and are noted for basketry, pottery, turquoise jewelry, and weaving. The original 7 Zuni villages are usually identified with the mythical Seven Cities of Cibola, which were publicized by Marcos de Niza. In 1540, Francisco Vásquez de Coronado attacked the villages, thinking that they had vast stores of gold. The villages were abandoned in the Pueblo revolt of 1680. The present pueblo was built c.1695 on the site of one of the original 7 villages.

Zuni, uninc. village, Isle of Wight co., SE Va., 16 mi/26 km NW of Suffolk, on Blackwater R.; 36°51′N 76°49′W. Mfg. (meat processing); agr. (grain, cotton, peanuts, melons; livestock).

Zuni Mountains (ZOO-nee), domed uplift, W N.Mex., in Cibola and McKinley cos., near Ariz. state line, SE of Gallup, on Colorado Plateau; c.70 mi/113 km long, 30 mi/48 km wide. Extensive lava beds S and SE. In part of Cibola Natl. Forest; Lookout Mt. in SE (9,128 ft/2,782 m); Continental Divide runs N-S through part of range.

Zuñi River (ZOO-nee), c.90 mi/145 km long, W N.Mex. and E Ariz.; rises in Cibola co. at Continental Divide; flows SW, through Zuñi Indian Reservation, and into Apache co., E. Ariz., 18 mi/29 km WNW of St. John, Ariz.

Zurich (ZOO-rik), village (1991 pop. 860), S Ont., Canada, near L. Huron, 22 mi/35 km S of Goderich. Lumbering, milling, dairying.

Zurich 1 (ZUHR-ik), village (1990 pop. 151), Rooks co., N central Kansas, 8 mi/12.9 km W of Plainville; 39°13′N 99°25′W. **2** village (1990 pop. 65), Blaine co., N Mont., on Milk R., and 10 mi/16 km E of Chinook. Sugar beets, wheat, barley, hay; cattle. Fort Belknap Indian Reservation to SE; oil field to SW; Bear Paw Mts. to S.

Zurumuato, Mexico: see PASTOR ORTIZ.

Zwingle, town (1990 pop. 94), on Dubuque-Jackson co. border, E Iowa, 14 mi/23 km S of Dubuque; 42°17′N 90°41′W. Dairying.

Zwolle (ZWAH-lee), town (1990 pop. 1,779), Sabine parish, W La., 60 mi/97 km S of Shreveport; 31°39′N 93°39′W. Oil fields (since 1928). Mfg. (pulpwood, plywood, lumber, RR car repair). Recreation. Settled 1896. Annual Tamale Festival. Arm of large Toledo Bend Reservoir (Sabine R.; Texas border) to SW. N. Toledo Bend State Park to SW; Sabine State Wildlife Area to S.